On 6 May 1990 the London 01 codes were replaced by two new codes – 071 for inner London and 081 for outer London. The new codes are listed at the back of this book.

LONGMAN PITMAN

OFFICE DICTIONARY

PLUS A-Z OFFICE GUIDE

Longman

Longman Group UK Limited,
Longman House, Burnt Mill, Harlow,
Essex CM20 2JE, England
and Associated Companies throughout the world.

First published 1990

British Library Cataloguing in Publication Data
Harrison, John, *1931–*
Longman Pitman office dictionary (and A–Z office guide)
1. Office practices 2. English Dictionaries
I. Title
423

ISBN 0 582 06623 9

A-Z Office Guide first published by Pitman as The Secretary's Desk Book

Printed in Great Britain by Richard Clay PLC, Bungay, Suffolk.

The Dictionary

Symbols used in pronunciation

respelling	*IPA*	*sound*
a	æ	b*a*d
ah	ɑ:	f*a*ther
aw	ɔ:	s*aw*
ay	eɪ	m*a*ke
e	e	b*e*d
ee	i:	sh*ee*p
eə	eə	th*ere*
i	ɪ	sh*i*p
ie	aɪ	b*i*te
ie·ə	aɪə	f*ire*
iə	ɪə	h*ere*
o	ɒ	p*o*t
oh	əʊ	n*o*te
oo	ʊ	p*u*t
ooh	u:	b*oo*t
ooə	ʊə	c*ure*
ow	aʊ	n*ow*
owə	aʊə	*our*
oy	ɔɪ	b*oy*
oyə	ɔɪə	empl*oyer*
u	ʌ	c*u*t
uh	ɜ:	b*ir*d
ə	ə	*a*noth*er*
onh	ã	restaur*ant*

respelling	*IPA*	*sound*
b	b	*b*ad
ch	tʃ	*ch*in
d	d	*d*ay
dh	ð	*th*ey
f	f	*f*ew
g	g	*g*ay
h	h	*h*ot
j	dʒ	*j*ump
k	k	*k*ing
kh	x	*l*o*ch*
l	l	*l*ed
m	m	*m*an
n	n	su*n*
ng	ŋ	su*ng*
p	p	*p*en
r	r	*r*ed
s	s	*s*oon
sh	ʃ	fi*sh*
t	t	*t*ea
th	θ	*th*ing
v	v	*v*est
w	w	*w*et
y	j	*y*et
z	z	*z*ero
zh	ʒ	plea*s*ure

Guide to the Dictionary

1 Order of entries

1.1 Main entries

All main entries appear in letter-by-letter alphabetical order. Words that share the same spelling but are different in origin, pronunciation, or grammatical function are distinguished by small numbers in front of them; see, for example, the entries at **lead**.

1.2 Undefined words

Words whose meaning can easily be guessed, because they consist of a base form plus a standard ending, are shown at the end of the definition for their base form:

charitable . . . *adj* . . . – **charitableness** *n*, **charitably** *adv*

The meaning of **charitableness** is not explicitly stated because it can be deduced from the meaning of **charitable** plus the meaning of **-ness**, which can be found at its own place in the dictionary. Sometimes the undefined word has the same form as its base, but a different part of speech; for example, the verb **chink** appears at the end of the entry for the noun **chink** (=a short sharp sound), and its meaning may readily be deduced as 'to make, or cause to make, a short sharp sound'.

Some words that begin with the negative prefixes **un-** and **in-** and have an obvious meaning (e g **unannounced**, **unchecked**) are shown in their due place in the dictionary but are not defined.

1.3 Idiomatic phrases

Idioms – fixed phrases whose meaning cannot be guessed from the meanings of the individual words from which they are made up – are shown at the end of the entry for the first meaningful word they contain. Thus **live it up** is entered at **live**, **on the ball** at **ball**, and **in spite of** at **spite**.

2 Alternative versions of words

Variant forms or different spellings of a word are shown immediately after the main entry. When the variant is preceded by a comma, it may be considered as common as the main entry in current usage (e g **judgment**, **judgement**); when preceded by *also*, it is rather less common.

Alternative spellings in *-ize*/*-ise* are shown in abbreviated form; e g **real·ize, -ise**
This means that **realize** can also be spelt **realise**.

Variant forms that are peculiar to British or American English are labelled *Br* or *NAm*:

jail, *Br also* **gaol** . . . *n*
gaol . . . *vb or n, chiefly Br* (to) jail

This means that the spelling **jail** is used throughout the English-speaking world, but British English also uses **gaol** (see **7.2)**

3 Inflections

This dictionary shows inflections only if they are irregular, or may cause difficulty. They are written out in full, unless they involve merely the doubling of a consonant or the change of **-c** to **-ck-**:

[1]**swat** . . . *vt* **-tt-**
picnic . . . *vi* **-ck-**

This means that the present participle and past of **swat** are **swatting** and **swatted**, and those of **picnic** are **picnicking** and **picnicked**.

3.1 Nouns

Regular plurals of nouns (e g **cats**, **matches**, **spies**) are not shown. All other plurals are given: when plurals are irregular, when alternative plurals are possible, when a plural may have an alternative pronunciation, and when plurals are regular but might have been expected to be irregular.

A noun, or an individual sense of a noun, that is always plural is labelled *pl.* Plural nouns that take a singular verb ('Genetics is . . .') are labelled '*n pl but sing in constr*'; those that take either a singular or plural verb ('Politics is . . .' or 'Politics are . . .') are labelled '*n pl but sing or pl in constr*'. Likewise, nouns in apparently singular form can be '*pl in constr*' ('Several police are . . .') or '*sing or pl in constr*' ('The crew is . . .' or 'The crew are . . .'). Nouns that can be used in the plural with the same meaning as the singular (e g **latitude/latitudes**) are labelled '*often pl with sing meaning*'.

3.2 Verbs

Regular verb forms (e g **halted**, **cadged**, **carrying**) are not shown. All other verb inflections (e g **ring**, **rang**, **rung**) are shown, including those for verbs ending in a vowel other than *-e*, for verbs which keep a final *-e* before inflections, and for verbs having alternative inflections.

Inflections are shown in the following order:

present: 1st, 2nd, and 3rd person singular; plural; present subjunctive; present participle; past: 1st, 2nd, and 3rd person singular; plural; past subjunctive; past participle.

Only the irregular inflections are shown. Certain forms (e g the entire past tense, or the past tense and the past participle) are combined if they are identical. Thus in

run . . . *vb* **-nn-**; **ran**; **run**

the present participle is **running**, the entire past tense is **ran**, and the past participle is **run**.

3.3 Adjectives and adverbs

Adjectives and adverbs whose comparative and superlative are formed with **more** and **most**, or by adding **-(e)r** and **-(e)st** (e g **nicer**, **fastest**, **happier**), are not shown.

All other inflections (e g **good** . . . **better** . . . **best**) are shown, including alternatives (e g **shy** . . . **shier**, **shyer**, **shiest**, **shyest**) and inflections that involve a change of pronunciation.

4 Capitalization

Some words, or meanings of words, can be used with or without a capital letter and this is shown by the notes *often cap* and *often not cap*. In the case of compound words, the note specifies which parts are capitalized:

pop art *n, often cap P&A* . . .

5 Definitions

5.1 The numbering and order of senses

The main meanings of a word are numbered: **1, 2, 3,** etc where there is more than one sense. Subdivisions of senses are distinguished by lower-case letters, and further subdivisions by bracketed numbers. Those meanings that would be understood anywhere in the English-speaking world are shown first, in their historical order: the older senses before the newer. After these come the meanings whose usage is restricted in some way (e g because they are used in only one area, or have gone out of current use).

5.2 Brackets

Round brackets are used in four main ways in definitions in this dictionary:

They enclose the object of a verb:

[2]**contract** *vt* . . . **2a** to catch (an illness)

They give extra information:

[3]**nap** *n* a hairy or downy surface (e g on a woven fabric)

They separate the parts of a combined definition that relate to different parts of speech:

cheep . . . *vi or n* (to utter) a faint shrill sound characteristic of a young bird

They enclose optional wording:

afloat . . . *adj or adv* **1a** borne (as if) on the water or air

This indicates that **afloat** means both 'borne on the water or air' and 'borne as if on the water or air'.

6 Examples

Definitions, particularly of words with several senses, may be followed by a phrase or sentence illustrating a typical use of the word in context. Many of these are taken, directly or with some adaptation, from specific written or spoken sources.

Examples are printed in italics between angle brackets (<>). The word being illustrated is usually represented by a swung dash (~). When an inflected form of the main entry is being illustrated, it is usually shown by a swung dash followed by the inflection:

[1]**dare** . . . *vt* to confront boldly; defy *<~d the anger of her family>*

The complete example is therefore 'dared the anger of her family'

7 Usage

Many words have peculiarities of usage that a dictionary must take account of. They may be restricted to a particular geographical area; they may be colloquial or slang, or felt to be 'incorrect'; they may have fallen out of use; and there may be limitations on the sort of context they can be used in.

This dictionary shows such restrictions in two different ways. Words, or meanings, that are limited to a particular period or area are identified by an italic label. When an italic label comes between the main entry and the first definition it refers to all meanings of the word; otherwise it applies to all subsenses of the number or letter it follows.

All other information on usage is given in a note at the end of a definition. When such a note applies to all or several meanings of a word, it follows the last definition, and is introduced by the word *USE*.

7.1 Words that are no longer in current use

The label *obs* for 'obsolete' means there is no evidence of use for a word or meaning since 1755.

The label *archaic* means that a word or meaning once current is found today only in special contexts, such as poetry or historical fiction. Comparatively modern terms which have become old-fashioned are treated in notes describing them as 'no longer in vogue', 'not now used technically', and the like.

7.2 Words that are not used throughout the English-speaking world

A word or sense limited in use to one or more of the countries of the English-speaking world is labelled accordingly:
[3]**crook** *adj, Austr & NZ* **1** ill, sick . . .

The label *Br* indicates that a word or meaning is used in Britain and also usually in the Commonwealth countries of Australasia. The label *NAm* indicates the use of a word or meaning in both the USA and Canada.

The label *dial* for 'dialect' indicates that a word or meaning belongs to the common local speech of several different places.

7.3 Words that suggest a particular style, attitude, or level of formality

Most English words can be generally used in both speech and writing, but some would be traditionally described as 'colloquial' or 'slang', and others, perhaps, as 'formal'. Words of this sort are identified by notes at the end of definitions.

The note '– infml', for 'informal', is used for words or senses that are characteristic of conversational speech and casual writing (e g between friends and contemporaries) rather than of official or 'serious' speech or writing.

The note '– slang' is used for words or meanings usually found in contexts of extreme informality. Such words may be, or may have been until recently, used by a particular social group such as criminals or drug users. They often refer to topics that are thought of as risqué or 'low'.

The note '– fml', for 'formal', is used for words or meanings characteristic of written rather than spoken English, and particularly of official or academic writings.

Other notes describe the attitude or tone of the user of a word, e g 'derog' (derogatory) or 'euph' (euphemistic).

7.4 Words that are not 'correct'

It is not the role of a responsible modern dictionary to dictate usage; it can only make statements, based on reference to a large stock of spoken and written data, as to how a word is being used by the community at large. Where appropriate, it can also warn the dictionary user that a use of a word is likely to arouse controversy or disapproval. The note '– nonstandard' is used for words or meanings that are quite commonly used in standard English but are considered incorrect by many speakers. Certain highly controversial words or meanings have the warning note '– disapproved of by some speakers'. The note '–substandard' is used for words or meanings that are widely used but are not part of standard English.

7.5 The context in which a word can appear

Many words or meanings can be used only in certain contexts within a sentence: some verbs are only used in the passive; some words can appear only in the negative, along with **not**, **never**, etc; others are always used with particular prepositions or adverbs, or in certain fixed phrases. Such restrictions are shown in a note following a definition:

abide . . . to bear patiently; tolerate – used negatively
agree . . . *vi* **2a** to be of one mind – often + *with* <*I ~ with you*>

Sometimes a word that is commonly used with the main entry word in a sentence is printed in italic within the definition:

allude . . . *vi* to make indirect, casual, or implicit reference *to*
[2]**altogether** *n the* nude <*posed in the ~*> – infml

This means that **allude** is almost always used in the phrase **allude to**, and that the noun **altogether** is almost always used with **the**.

8 Cross-references

Cross-references draw attention to a related word in another part of the dictionary. Any word printed in SMALL CAPITAL letters is a cross-reference.

An entire definition may take the form of a cross-reference. This happens either when the word used in the definition has more than one meaning, and it is necessary to specify which meaning is referred to:

[2]**flash** *n* . . . **6a** . . . c FLASHLIGHT 2

or when the word used in the definition is a compound that is a main entry in the dictionary:

rubella . . . *n* GERMAN MEASLES

9 Prefixes, suffixes, and combining forms

The most important of the word elements that can be used to form new words in English are entered in the main alphabetic sequence. These comprise prefixes (e g **pre-**, **un-**), suffixes (e g **-ous**, **-ly**), and combining forms (e g **Anglo-**, **-logy**).

Suffixes and combining forms added to the end of a word may alter the grammatical function as well as the meaning of the word. Where appropriate, this change of part of speech is indicated as follows:

-ful *suffix* (*n*→*adj*) full of <*event*ful>

This means that the suffix **-ful** is added to nouns to make adjectives.

Special Abbreviations used in this Dictionary

A ampere
abbr abbreviation
adj adjective
adv adverb
apprec appreciative
approx approximate(ly)
attrib attributive
Austr Australian

Br British

c century
C Celsius, centigrade
Can Canadian
cap capital(ized)
cgs centimetre-gram-second
cm centimetre
comb combining
conj conjunction
constr construction
cwt hundredweight

deriv derivative
derog derogatory
dial. dialect

E East(ern)
Eng English, England
esp especially
euph euphemistic

F Fahrenheit
fem feminine
fl oz fluid ounce
fml formal
fr from
Fr French
ft foot

g gram
gall gallon
Ger German

h hour
hp horsepower
humor humorous
Hz hertz

imper imperative
in inch
Ind Indian
indef indefinite
indic indicative
infin infinitive
infml informal
interj interjection
interrog interrogative

journ journalistic

k kilo-
kg kilogram
km kilometre

l litre
lb pound
lit. literally

m metre
masc masculine
MHz megahertz
mi mile
mil military
min minute
ml millilitre
mm millimetre
mph miles per hour

n noun
N North(ern)
NAm North American
naut nautical
neg negative

obs obsolete
orig original(ly)
oz ounce

p pence
part participle
pass passive
perf perfect
pers person
phr(s) phrase(s)
pl plural
prep preposition

pres present
prob probably
pron pronoun
pt pint

qt quart

rel relative

s second
S South(ern)
SAfr South Africa(n)
sby somebody
Sc Scots
Scot Scotland, Scottish
SI Système International d'Unités
sing. singular
specif specifically
st stone
sthg something
subj subjunctive
substand substandard

tech technical

UK United Kingdom
US United States
USA United States of America
usu usually

V volt
va verbal auxiliary
var variant
vb verb
vi verb intransitive
vt verb transitive
vulg vulgar

W watt
W West(ern)
WI West Indies
WWI World War 1
WWII World War 2

yd yard

A

[1]**a** /ay‖eɪ/ *n, pl* **a's, as** *often cap* **1** (a graphic representation of or device for reproducing) the 1st letter of the English alphabet **2** the 6th note of a C-major scale **3** one designated *a*, esp as the 1st in order or class

[2]**a** /ə‖ə; *strong* ay‖eɪ/ *indefinite article* **1** one – used before singular nouns when the referent is unspecified <~ *man stood up*> and before number collectives and some numbers <~ *great many*> **2** the same <*birds of* ~ *feather*> **3a(1)** any <~ *bicycle has 2 wheels*> **a(2)** one single <*can't see* ~ *thing*> **b** one particular <*glucose is* ~ *simple sugar*> **4** – used before a proper name to denote (1) membership of a class <I *was* ~ *Burton before my marriage* > (2) resemblance <~ *Daniel come to judgment*> (3) one named but not otherwise known <~ *Mrs Jones*> ***USE*** used before words or letter sequences with an initial consonant sound; compare [1]AN 1

[3]**a** /ə‖ə/ *prep* **1** PER 2 <*twice* ~ *week*> **2** *chiefly dial* on, in, at ***USE*** used before words or letter sequences with an initial consonant sound

[1]**a-** /ə-‖ə-/ *prefix* **1** on; in; at; to <*a*bed> <*a*jar> **2** in (such) a state or condition <*a*blaze> **3** in (such) a manner <*a*loud> **4** in the act or process of <*gone* a-*hunting*>

[2]**a-** /ay-, a-‖eɪ-, æ-/, **an-** /an-‖æn-/ *prefix* not; without <*a*sexual> <*a*moral> – *a-* usu before consonants other than *h*, *an-* before vowels and usu before *h* <*an*aesthetic> <*an*hedral>

A1 *adj* **1** *of a ship* having the highest possible classification of seaworthiness for insurance purposes **2** of the finest quality; first-rate

aardvark /ˈahd,vahk‖ˈɑːd,vɑːk/ *n* a large burrowing nocturnal African mammal with an extendable tongue that feeds on ants and termites [Afrikaans *aard* earth + *vark* pig]

ab- /ab-, əb-‖æb-, əb-/ *prefix* from; away; off <*ab*axial> <*ab*duct>

aback /əˈbak‖əˈbæk/ *adv* **1** unintentionally in a position to catch the wind on what is normally the leeward side – used with reference to a sail **2** by surprise – + *take* <*was taken* ~ *by her sharp retort*>

abacus /ˈabəkəs‖ˈæbəkəs/ *n, pl* **abaci** /-kie, -sie‖-kaɪ, -saɪ/, **abacuses 1** a slab that forms the uppermost part of the capital of a column **2** an instrument for performing calculations by sliding counters along rods or in grooves

[1]**abandon** /əˈband(ə)n‖əˈbænd(ə)n/ *vt* **1** to give up completely, esp with the intention of never resuming or reclaiming <~ed *his studies*> **2** to leave, often in the face of danger <~ *ship*> **3** to forsake or desert, esp in spite of an allegiance, duty, or responsibility **4** to give (oneself) over unrestrainedly *to* an emotion or activity – **abandonment** *n*

[2]**abandon** *n* freedom from constraint or inhibitions

aˈbandoned *adj* wholly free from restraint

abase /əˈbays‖əˈbeɪs/ *vt* to bring lower in rank, office, prestige, or esteem – **abasement** *n*

abash /əˈbash‖əˈbæʃ/ *vt* to destroy the self-possession or self-confidence of; disconcert – usu pass – **abashment** *n*

abate /əˈbayt‖əˈbeɪt/ *vt* **1** to put an end to; abolish <~ *a nuisance*> **2** to reduce in amount, intensity, or degree; moderate <~ *a tax*> ~ *vi* to decrease in force or intensity – **abatement** *n*

abattoir /ˈabə,twah‖ˈæbə,twɑː/ *n* a slaughterhouse [French, fr *abattre* to beat down, slaughter, deriv of Latin *ad* to + *battuere* to beat]

abbess /ˈabes‖ˈæbes/ *n* the female superior of a convent of nuns

abbey /ˈabi‖ˈæbɪ/ *n* **1** a religious community governed by an abbot or abbess **2** the buildings, esp the church, of a (former) monastery

abbot /ˈabət‖ˈæbət/ *n* the superior of an abbey of monks

abbreviate /əˈbreeviayt‖əˈbriːvɪeɪt/ *vt* to make briefer; *esp* to reduce to a shorter form intended to stand for the whole – **abbreviator** *n*

abbreviation /ə,breeviˈaysh(ə)n‖ə,briːvɪˈeɪʃ(ə)n/ *n* a shortened form of a written word or phrase

ABC *n, pl* **ABC's, ABCs 1** the alphabet **2** the rudiments of a subject – usu pl with sing. meaning in NAm

abdicate /ˈabdikayt‖ˈæbdɪkeɪt/ *vt* to relinquish (e g sovereign power) formally ~ *vi* to renounce a throne, dignity, etc – **abdicator** *n*, **abdication** *n*

abdomen /ˈabdəmən, əbˈdohmən‖ˈæbdəmən, əbˈdəʊmən/ *n* **1** (the cavity of) the part of the body between the thorax and the pelvis that contains the liver, gut, etc **2** the rear part of the body behind the thorax in an insect or other arthropod – **abdominal** *adj*, **abdominally** *adv*

abduct /əbˈdukt‖əbˈdʌkt/ *vt* to carry off secretly or by force – **abductor** *n*, **abduction** *n*

abeam /əˈbeem‖əˈbiːm/ *adv or adj* on a line at right angles to the length of a ship or aircraft

abed /əˈbed‖əˈbed/ *adv or adj* in bed

aberrant /əˈberənt‖əˈberənt/ *adj* **1** deviating from the right or normal way **2** diverging from the usual or natural type – **aberrance** *n*, **aberrancy** *n*, **aberrantly** *adv*

aberration /,abəˈraysh(ə)n‖,æbəˈreɪʃ(ə)n/ *n* **1** being aberrant, esp with respect to a moral standard or normal state **2** the failure of a mirror, lens, etc to produce exact correspondence between an object and its image **3** (an instance of) unsoundness or disorder of the mind **4** a small periodic change of apparent position in celestial bodies due to the combined effect of the motion of light and the motion of the observer **5** SPORT 5 – **aberrational** *adj*

abet /əˈbet‖əˈbet/ *vt* **-tt-** to give active encouragement or approval to – **abetment** *n*, **abettor**, **abetter** *n*

abeyance /əˈbayəns‖əˈbeɪəns/ *n* temporary inactivity; suspension <*a rule in* ~ *since 1935*>

abhor /əbˈ(h)aw‖əbˈ(h)ɔː/ *vt* **-rr-** to loathe [Latin *abhorrere*, fr *ab* from, away + *horrēre* to shudder] – **abhorrer** *n*

abhorrent /əbˈ(h)orənt, əbˈ(h)awrənt‖əbˈ(h)ɒrənt, əbˈ(h)ɔːrənt/ *adj* **1** opposed, contrary *to* **2** causing horror; repugnant – **abhorrence** *n*, **abhorrently** *adv*

abide /əˈbied‖əˈbaɪd/ *vb* **abode** /əˈbohd‖əˈbəʊd/, **abided** *vt* to bear patiently; tolerate – used negatively <*can't* ~ *such bigots*> ~ *vi* **1** to remain stable or fixed in a state **2** *archaic* to dwell – **abider** *n* – **abide by** to remain true to; comply with <abide by *the rules*>

abiding /əˈbieding‖əˈbaɪdɪŋ/ *adj* lasting – **abidingly** *adv*

ability /əˈbiləti‖əˈbɪlətɪ/ *n* **1a** being able; *esp* physical, mental, or legal power to perform <*doubted her* ~ *to walk so far*> **b** natural or acquired competence in doing; skill <*a man of great* ~> **2** a natural talent; aptitude – usu pl

-ability *also* **-ibility** /-əˈbiləti‖-əˈbɪlətɪ/ *suffix* (*vb, adj* → *n*) capacity, suitability, or tendency to (so act or be acted on) <*read*ability>

abject /ˈabjekt‖ˈæbdʒekt/ *adj* **1** wretched, miserable <~ *poverty*> **2** despicable, degraded **3** very humble, esp to the point of servility – **abjection** *n*, **abjectly** *adv*, **abjectness** *n*

abjure /əbˈjooə‖əbˈdʒʊə/ *vt* to renounce on oath or reject formally (e g a claim, opinion, or allegiance) – **abjurer** *n*, **abjuration** *n*

ablative /ˈablətiv‖ˈæblətɪv/ *n* (a form in) a grammatical case expressing typically separation, source, cause, or instrument – **ablative** *adj*

ablaze /əˈblayz‖əˈbleɪz/ *adj or adv* **1** on fire **2** radiant with light or bright colour

able /ˈaybl‖ˈeɪbl/ *adj* **1** having sufficient power, skill, resources, or qualifications *to* <*with more money I was better* ~ *to help*> **2** marked by intelligence, knowledge, skill, or competence <*the* ~st *lawyer in London*> – **ably** *adv*

-able *also* **-ible** /-əbl‖-əbl/ *suffix* **1** (*vb* → *adj*) fit for, able to, liable to, or worthy to (so act or be acted on) <*break*able> **2** (*n* → *adj*) marked by, providing, or possessing (a specified quality or attribute) <*knowledge*able> – **-ably** *suffix* (*vb, n* → *adv*)

ˌable-ˈbodied *adj* physically strong and healthy; fit

ˌable ˈseaman, ˌable-bodied ˈseaman *n* a trained person ranking below noncommissioned officer in the British navy

ablution /əˈbloohsh(ə)n‖əˈbluːʃ(ə)n/ *n* the washing of (a part of) one's body, esp in a ritual purification – **ablutionary** *adj*

abnegation /ˌabniˈgaysh(ə)n‖ˌæbnɪˈgeɪʃ(ə)n/ *n* renunciation, self-denial

abnormal /ˌabˈnawməl, əb-‖ˌæbˈnɔːməl, əb-/ *adj* deviating from the normal or average; *esp* markedly and disturbingly irregular – **abnormally** *adv*, **abnormality** *n*

abo /ˈaboh‖ˈæbəʊ/ *n, pl* **abos** *often cap, Austr* an Australian aborigine – chiefly derog – **abo** *adj*

aboard /əˈbawd‖əˈbɔːd/ *adv or prep* **1** on, onto, or within (a ship, aircraft, train, or road vehicle) **2** alongside

abode /əˈbohd‖əˈbəʊd/ *n* a home, residence – fml

abolish /əˈbolish‖əˈbɒlɪʃ/ *vt* to do away with (e g a law or custom) wholly; annul – **abolisher** *n*, **abolishment** *n*, **abolition** *n*, **abolitionary** *adj*

ˈA-ˌbomb /ay‖eɪ/ *n* ATOM BOMB

abominable /əˈbominəbl‖əˈbɒmɪnəbl/ *adj* **1** worthy of or causing disgust or hatred; detestable **2** very disagreeable or unpleasant – esp in colloquial exaggeration <~ *weather*> – **abominably** *adv*

aˌbominable ˈsnowman *n, often cap A&S* a large manlike animal reported as existing high in the Himalayas

abominate /əˈbominayt‖əˈbɒmɪneɪt/ *vt* to hate or loathe intensely – **abominator** *n*

abomination /əˌbomiˈnaysh(ə)n‖əˌbɒmɪˈneɪʃ(ə)n/ *n* **1** sthg abominable; *esp* a detestable or shameful action **2** loathing

[1]**aboriginal** /ˌabəˈrijin(ə)l‖ˌæbəˈrɪdʒɪn(ə)l/ *adj* **1** indigenous **2** of esp Australian aborigines – **aboriginally** *adv*

[2]**aboriginal** *n* an (Australian) aborigine

aborigine /ˌabəˈrijinee‖ˌæbəˈrɪdʒɪniː/ *n* **1** an indigenous inhabitant, esp as contrasted with an invading or colonizing people; *specif, often cap* a member of the indigenous people of Australia **2** *pl* the original fauna and flora of an area [Latin *aborigines* (pl,) prob fr *ab origine* from the beginning]

[1]**abort** /əˈbawt‖əˈbɔːt/ *vi* **1** to expel a premature nonviable foetus **2** to fail to develop completely; shrink away ~ *vt* **1** to induce the abortion of (a foetus) **2a** to end prematurely <~ *a project*> **b** to stop in the early stages <~ *a disease*>

[2]**abort** *n* the premature termination of a mission or procedure involving a military aircraft or spacecraft

abortion /əˈbawsh(ə)n‖əˈbɔːʃ(ə)n/ *n* **1** the spontaneous or induced expulsion of a foetus **2** a monstrosity **3** (the result of) an arresting of development of a part, process, etc – **abortionist** *n*

abortive /əˈbawtiv‖əˈbɔːtɪv/ *adj* **1** fruitless, unsuccessful <*an* ~ *attempt*> **2** imperfectly formed or developed – **abortively** *adv*, **abortiveness** *n*

abound /əˈbownd‖əˈbaʊnd/ *vi* **1** to be present in large numbers or in great quantity **2** to be amply supplied – + *in* **3** to be crowded or infested *with*

[1]**about** /əˈbowt‖əˈbaʊt/ *adv* **1** ROUND 2, 3c **2** in succession or rotation; alternately <*turn and turn* ~> **3** approximately <*cost* ~ *£5*> **4** almost <~ *starved*> **5** in the vicinity <*there was nobody* ~>

[2]**about** *prep* **1** on every side of; surrounding <*the wall* ~ *the prison*> **2a** in the vicinity of **b** on or near the person of <*have you a match* ~ *you?*> **c** in the make-up of <*a mature wisdom* ~ *him*> **d** at the command of <*has his wits* ~ *him*> **3a** engaged in <*knows what she's* ~> **b** on the verge of – + *to* <~ *to join the army*> **4a** with regard to, concerning <*a story* ~ *rabbits*> **b** intimately concerned with <*politics is* ~ *capturing votes*> **5** over or in different parts of <*walked* ~ *the streets*> **6** *chiefly NAm* – used with the negative to express intention or determination <*is not* ~ *to quit*>

[3]**about** *adj* **1** moving from place to place; *specif* out of bed **2** in existence, evidence, or circulation <*skateboards weren't* ~ *long*>

aˌbout-ˈface *vi or n, chiefly NAm* (to) about-turn

aˌbout-ˈturn *n* **1** a 180° turn to the right, esp as a drill movement **2** *chiefly Br* a reversal of direction, policy, or opinion – **about-turn** *vi*

[1]**above** /əˈbuv‖əˈbʌv/ *adv* **1a** in the sky overhead **b** in or to heaven **2a** in or to a higher place **b** higher on the same or an earlier page **c** upstairs <*the flat* ~> **3** in or to a higher rank or number <*30 and* ~> **4** upstage

[2]**above** *prep* **1** higher than the level of <*rose* ~

the clouds> **2** OVER 3 <*values safety* ~ *excitement*> **3** beyond, transcending <~ *criticism*> **4a** superior to (e g in rank) **b** too proud or honourable to stoop to **5** upstream from – **above oneself** excessively self-satisfied

[3]**above** *n, pl* **above** **1a** sthg (written) above <*the* ~ *are the main facts*> **b** a person whose name is written above **2a** a higher authority **b** heaven

[4]**above** *adj* written higher on the same, or on a preceding, page

aˌboveˈboard /-ˈbawd‖-ˈbɔːd/ *adj* free from all traces of deceit or dishonesty – **above board** *adv*

aˈboveˌmentioned /-ˌmensh(ə)nd‖-ˌmenʃ(ə)nd/ *adj* aforementioned

abracadabra /ˌabrəkəˈdabrə‖ˌæbrəkəˈdæbrə/ *n* a magical charm or incantation – used as an exclamation to accompany conjuring tricks

abrade /əˈbrayd‖əˈbreɪd/ *vt* to roughen, irritate, or wear away, esp by friction – **abradable** *adj*, **abrader** *n*

abrasion /əˈbrayzh(ə)n‖əˈbreɪʒ(ə)n/ *n* **1** a wearing, grinding, or rubbing away by friction **2** an abraded area of the skin or mucous membrane

[1]**abrasive** /əˈbraysiv, -ziv‖əˈbreɪsɪv, -zɪv/ *adj* tending to abrade; causing irritation – **abrasively** *adv*, **abrasiveness** *n*

[2]**abrasive** *n* a substance (e g emery) that may be used for grinding away, smoothing, or polishing

abreast /əˈbrest‖əˈbrest/ *adv or adj* **1** side by side and facing in the same direction <*columns of men 5* ~> **2** up-to-date in attainment or information <*keeps* ~ *of the latest trends*>

abridge /əˈbrij‖əˈbrɪdʒ/ *vt* **1** to reduce in scope; curtail <*attempts to* ~ *the right of free speech*> **2** to shorten by omission of words without changing the sense; condense – **abridger** *n*

aˈbridgment, abridgement /-mənt‖-mənt/ *n* a shortened form of a work retaining the sense and unity of the original

abroad /əˈbrawd‖əˈbrɔːd/ *adv or adj* **1** over a wide area; widely **2** away from one's home; out of doors <*few people* ~ *at this hour*> **3** beyond the boundaries of one's country **4** in wide circulation; about <*the idea has got* ~>

abrogate /ˈabrəgayt‖ˈæbrəgeɪt/ *vt* to abolish by authority; annul, repeal – **abrogation** *n*

abrupt /əˈbrupt‖əˈbrʌpt/ *adj* **1** ending as if sharply cut off; truncated **2a** occurring without warning; unexpected **b** unceremoniously curt <*an* ~ *manner*> **c** marked by sudden changes in subject matter **3** rising or dropping sharply; steep – **abruptly** *adv*, **abruptness** *n*

abscess /ˈabses, -sis‖ˈæbses, -sɪs/ *n* a pocket of pus surrounded by inflamed tissue – **abscessed** *adj*

abscond /əbˈskond‖əbˈskɒnd/ *vi* to depart secretly, esp so as to avoid arrest or punishment – **absconder** *n*

absence /ˈabsəns‖ˈæbsəns/ *n* **1** the state of being absent **2** the period of time that one is absent **3** a lack <*an* ~ *of detail*>

ˌabsence of ˈmind *n* inattention to present surroundings or occurrences

[1]**absent** /ˈabsənt‖ˈæbsənt/ *adj* **1** not present or attending; missing **2** not existing; lacking **3** preoccupied – **absently** *adv*

[2]**absent** /əbˈsent‖əbˈsent/ *vt* to take or keep (oneself) away – usu + *from*

absentee /ˌabz(ə)nˈtee‖ˌæbz(ə)nˈtiː/ *n* one who is absent or who absents him-/herself – **absentee** *adj*

ˌabsenˈteeˌism /-ˌiz(ə)m‖-ˌɪz(ə)m/ *n* persistent and deliberate absence from work or duty

ˌabsentˈminded /-ˈmiendid‖-ˈmaɪndɪd/ *adj* lost in thought and unaware of one's surroundings or actions; forgetful – **absentmindedly** *adv*, **absentmindedness** *n*

absinthe, absinth /ˈabsinth‖ˈæbsɪnθ (*Fr* absɛ̃t) *n* **1** WORMWOOD 1 **2** a green liqueur flavoured with wormwood or a substitute, aniseed, and other aromatics

absolute /ˈabsəlooht, -bz-, -ps-‖ˈæbsəluːt, -bz-, -ps-/ *adj* **1a** perfect <~ *bliss*> **b** (relatively) pure or unmixed <~ *alcohol*> **c** outright, unmitigated <*an* ~ *lie*> **2** completely free from constitutional or other restraint <*an* ~ *monarch*> **3** standing apart from a usual syntactic relation with other words or sentence elements **4** having no restriction, exception, or qualification <~ *ownership*> **5** positive, unquestionable <~ *proof*> – **absolute** *n*, **absoluteness** *n*

ˌabsoˈlutely /-li‖-lɪ/ *adv* totally, completely – often used to express emphatic agreement

ˌabsolute ˈzero *n* the lowest temperature theoretically possible at which there is a complete absence of heat and which is equivalent to about −273.16°C or 0°K

absolution /ˌabsəˈloohsh(ə)n, -bz-, -ps-‖ˌæbsəˈluːʃ(ə)n, -bz-, -ps-/ *n* the act of absolving; *specif* a declaration of forgiveness of sins pronounced by a priest

absolutism /ˌabsəˈloohtiz(ə)m, -bz-, -ps-, ˈ---ˌ--‖ˌæbsəˈluːtɪz(ə)m, -bz-, -ps-, ˈ---ˌ--/ *n* (the theory favouring) government by an absolute ruler or authority – **absolutist** *n or adj*, **absolutistic** *adj*

absolve /əbˈzolv‖əbˈzɒlv/ *vt* **1** to set free *from* an obligation or the consequences of guilt **2** to declare (a sin) of (a person) forgiven by absolution – **absolver** *n*

absorb /əbˈzawb‖əbˈzɔːb; *also* -bs-‖-bs-/ *vt* **1** to take in and make part of an existing whole; incorporate **2a** to suck up or take up <*plant roots* ~ *water*> **b** to assimilate; TAKE IN **3** to engage or occupy wholly <~*ed in thought*> **4** to receive and transform (sound, radiant energy, etc) without reflecting or transmitting <*the earth* ~*s the sun's rays*> – **absorbable** *adj*, **absorber** *n*, **absorbability** *n*

absorbent *also* **absorbant** /əbˈzawb(ə)nt‖əbˈzɔːb(ə)nt; *also* -bs-‖-bs-/ *n or adj* (sthg) able to absorb a liquid, gas, etc – **absorbency** *n*

absorbing /əbˈzawbing‖əbˈzɔːbɪŋ; *also* -bs-‖-bs-/ *adj* engaging one's full attention; engrossing – **absorbingly** *adv*

absorption /əbˈzawpsh(ə)n‖əbˈzɔːpʃ(ə)n; *also* əbˈsawpsh(ə)n‖əbˈsɔːpʃ(ə)n/ *n* **1** absorbing or being absorbed **2** total involvement of the mind <~ *in his work*> – **absorptive** *adj*

abstain /əb'stayn‖əb'steɪn/ *vi* **1** to refrain deliberately, and often with an effort of self-denial, *from* **2** to refrain from using one's vote – **abstainer** *n*

abstemious /əb'steemi·əs‖əb'stiːmɪəs/ *adj* sparing, esp in eating or drinking [Latin *abstemius*, fr *abs-* away + *temetum* mead, strong drink] – **abstemiously** *adv*

abstention /əb'stensh(ə)n‖əb'stenʃ(ə)n/ *n* **1** abstaining – often + *from* **2** an instance of withholding a vote – **abstentious** *adj*

abstinence /'abstinəns‖'æbstɪnəns/ *also* **abstinency** /-si‖-sɪ/ *n* **1** voluntary forbearance, esp from indulgence of appetite or from eating some foods – often + *from* **2** habitual abstaining from intoxicating beverages – esp in *total abstinence* – **abstinent** *adj*, **abstinently** *adv*

[1]**abstract** /'abstrakt‖'æbstrækt/ *adj* **1** detached from any specific instance or object **2** *of a noun* naming a quality, state, or action rather than a thing; not concrete **3** theoretical rather than practical **4** having little or no element of pictorial representation – **abstractly** *adv*, **abstractness** *n*

[2]**abstract** *n* **1** a summary of points (e g of a piece of writing) **2** an abstract concept or state **3** an abstract composition or creation

[3]**abstract** /əb'strakt‖əb'strækt/ *vt* **1** to remove, separate **2** to consider in the abstract **3** to make an abstract of; summarize **4** to draw away the attention of **5** to steal, purloin – euph – **abstractor, abstracter** *n*

ab'stracted *adj* preoccupied, absentminded – **abstractedly** *adv*, **abstractedness** *n*

abstraction /əb'straksh(ə)n‖əb'strækʃ(ə)n/ *n* **1** an abstract idea or term stripped of its concrete manifestations **2** absentmindedness **3** [2]ABSTRACT 3 – **abstractionism** *n*, **abstractionist** *n*, **abstractive** *adj*

abstruse /əb'stroohs‖əb'struːs/ *adj* difficult to understand; recondite – **abstrusely** *adv*, **abstruseness** *n*

[1]**absurd** /əb'suhd, -bz-‖əb'sɜːd, -bz-/ *adj* **1** ridiculously unreasonable or incongruous; silly **2** lacking order or value; meaningless – **absurdity** *n*, **absurdly** *adv*, **absurdness** *n*

[2]**absurd** *n the* state or condition in which human beings exist in an irrational and meaningless universe, and in which their life has no meaning outside their own existence – **absurdism** *n*, **absurdist** *n or adj*

abundance /ə'bund(ə)ns‖ə'bʌnd(ə)ns/ *n* **1** an ample quantity; a profusion **2** affluence, wealth **3** the relative degree of plentifulness of a living organism, substance, etc in an area

abundant /ə'bund(ə)nt‖ə'bʌnd(ə)nt/ *adj* **1a** marked by great plenty (e g of resources) <*a fair and ~ land*> **b** amply supplied *with*; abounding *in* **2** occurring in abundance <*~ rainfall*> – **abundantly** *adv*

[1]**abuse** /ə'byoohz‖ə'bjuːz/ *vt* **1** to attack in words; revile **2** to put to a wrong or improper use <*~ a privilege*> **3** to use so as to injure or damage; maltreat <*~ a dog*> – **abuser** *n*

[2]**abuse** /ə'byoohs‖ə'bjuːs/ *n* **1** a corrupt practice or custom **2** improper use or treatment; misuse **3** vehemently expressed condemnation or disapproval **4** physical maltreatment – **abusive** *adj*, **abusively** *adv*, **abusiveness** *n*

abut /ə'but‖ə'bʌt/ *vb* **-tt-** *vi* **1** *of an area* to touch along a boundary; border – + *on* or *upon* <*land ~s on the road*> **2** *of a structure* **2a** to terminate at a point of contact; be adjacent – + *on* or *against* <*the town hall ~s on the church*> **b** to lean for support – + *on* or *upon* <*the neighbours' shed ~s on our wall*> ~ *vt* to border on; touch – **abutter** *n*

abutment /ə'butmənt‖ə'bʌtmənt/ *n* **1** the place at which abutting occurs **2** the part of a structure that directly receives thrust or pressure (e g of an arch)

abysmal /ə'bizməl‖ə'bɪzməl/ *adj* **1** deplorably great <*~ ignorance*> **2** immeasurably bad – **abysmally** *adv*

abyss /ə'bis‖ə'bɪs/ *n* **1** the infernal regions or chaos of the old cosmogonies, thought of as a bottomless pit **2a** an immeasurably deep gulf **b** moral or emotional depths <*an ~ of hopelessness*> [Late Latin *abyssus*, fr Greek *abyssos*, fr *abyssos* bottomless, fr *a-* not, without + *byssos* depth]

[1]**-ac** /-ak, -ək‖-æk, -ək/ *suffix* (→ *n*) one affected with <*mani*ac>

[2]**-ac** *suffix* (→ *adj*) of or relating to <*cardi*ac>

acacia /ə'kaysh(y)ə‖ə'keɪʃ(j)ə/ *n* **1** any of a genus of woody leguminous plants of warm regions with white or yellow flowers **2** GUM ARABIC

[1]**academic** /ˌakə'demik‖ˌækə'demɪk/ *also* **academical** /-kl‖-kl/ *adj* **1a** of an institution of higher learning **b** scholarly **c** very learned but inexperienced in practical matters **2** conventional, formal <*an ~ painting*> **3** theoretical with no practical or useful bearing <*an ~ question*> – **academically** *adv*, **academicize** *vt*

[2]**academic** *n* a member (of the teaching staff) of an institution of higher learning

academician /əˌkadə'mish(ə)n‖əˌkædə'mɪʃ(ə)n/ *n* a member of an academy for the advancement of science, art, or literature

academy /ə'kadəmi‖ə'kædəmɪ/ *n* **1** *cap* **1a** the school for advanced education founded by Plato **b** the philosophical doctrines associated with Plato's Academy **2a** a secondary school; *esp* a private high school – now only in names **b** a college in which special subjects or skills are taught <*an ~ of music*> **3** a society of learned people organized to promote the arts or sciences

accede /ək'seed‖ək'siːd/ *vi* **1** to become a party (e g to a treaty) **2** to express approval or give consent, often in response to urging **3** to enter on an office or position; *esp* to become monarch <*~ to the throne*> *USE* usu + *to*

accelerate /ək'seləravt‖ək'seləreɪt/ *vt* **1** to bring about at an earlier time **2** to increase the speed of **3** to hasten the progress, development, or growth of ~ *vi* **1** to move faster; gain speed **2** to increase more rapidly – **accelerative** *adj*

acceleration /əkˌselə'raysh(ə)n‖əkˌselə'reɪʃ(ə)n/ *n* (the rate of) change, specif increase, of velocity

accelerator /ək'selərаytə‖ək'seləreɪtə/ *n* **1** a pedal in a motor vehicle that controls the speed of the motor **2** a substance that speeds up a chemical reaction **3** an apparatus for giving high velocities to charged particles (e g electrons)

[1]**accent** /'aksənt‖'æksənt/ *n* **1** a distinctive

manner of expression; *specif* a distinctive pattern in inflection, tone, or choice of words, esp as characteristic of a regional or national area **2a** prominence given to 1 syllable over others by stress or a change in pitch **b** greater stress given to 1 musical note **c** rhythmically significant stress on the syllables of a verse **3a accent, accent mark** a mark added to a letter (e g in *à, ñ, ç*) to indicate how it should be pronounced **b** a symbol used to indicate musical stress **4** a sharply contrasting detail **5** special concern or attention; emphasis <*an ~ on youth*> – **accentless** *adj*

[2]**accent** /ək'sent‖ək'sent/ *vt* **1a** to pronounce (a vowel, syllable, or word) with accent; stress **b** to mark with a written or printed accent **2** to make more prominent; emphasize

accentuate /ək'sentyoo·ayt, -choo·ayt‖ək'sentjʊeɪt, -tʃʊeɪt/ *vt* to accent, emphasize – **accentuation** *n*

accept /ək'sept‖ək'sept/ *vt* **1a** to agree to receive <*~ a gift*>; *also* to agree to <*~ an invitation*> **b** to be able or designed to take or hold (sthg applied or inserted) <*machine ~s only pennies*> **2** to give admittance or approval to <*~ her as one of the group*> **3a** to endure without protest <*~ poor living conditions*> **b** to regard as proper, normal, or inevitable **c** to recognize as true, factual, or adequate <*refused to ~ my explanation*> **4** to undertake the responsibility of <*~ a job*> ~ *vi* to receive favourably sthg offered

acceptable /ək'septəbl‖ək'septəbl/ *adj* **1** capable or worthy of being accepted; satisfactory **2** welcome or pleasing to the receiver <*compliments are always ~*> **3** tolerable – **acceptableness** *n*, **acceptably** *adv*, **acceptability** *n*

acceptance /ək'sept(ə)ns‖ək'sept(ə)ns/ *n* **1** accepting, approval **2** acceptability **3** agreement to the act or offer of another so that the parties become legally bound

[1]**access** /'akses, -səs‖'ækses, -səs/ *n* **1** a fit *of* intense feeling; an outburst <*an ~ of rage*> **2a** freedom to approach, reach, or make use of sthg <*~ to classified information*> **b** a means (e g a doorway or channel) of access **c** the state of being readily reached or obtained <*the building is not easy of ~*>

[2]**access** *vt* to get at; gain access to

accessible /ək'sesəbl‖ək'sesəbl/ *adj* **1** capable of being reached **2** of a form that can be readily grasped intellectually **3** able to be influenced <*~ to persuasion*> – **accessibly** *adv*, **accessibility** *n*

accession /ək'sesh(ə)n‖ək'seʃ(ə)n/ *n* **1** sthg added; an acquisition; *specif* a book added to a library **2** becoming joined **3** the act by which a nation becomes party to an agreement already in force **4a** an increase due to sthg added **b** acquisition of property by addition to existing property **5** the act of entering on a high office <*his ~ to the Papacy*> **6** assent, agreement – fml – **accessional** *adj*

[1]**accessory** /ək'sesəri‖ək'sesərɪ/ *n* an inessential object or device that adds to the beauty, convenience, or effectiveness of sthg else

[2]**accessory** *adj* aiding or contributing in a secondary way; supplementary, subordinate

accidence /'aksid(ə)ns‖'æksɪd(ə)ns/ *n* the part of grammar that deals with inflections

accident /'aksid(ə)nt‖'æksɪd(ə)nt/ *n* **1a** an event occurring by chance or arising from unknown causes **b** lack of intention or necessity; chance <*met by ~ rather than by design*> **2** an unexpected happening causing loss or injury **3** a nonessential property or condition of sthg **4** an irregularity of a surface (e g of the moon)

[1]**accidental** /ˌaksi'dentl‖ˌæksɪ'dentl/ *adj* **1** arising incidentally; nonessential **2a** occurring unexpectedly or by chance **b** happening without intent or through carelessness and often with unfortunate results – **accidentally** *adv*, **accidentalness** *n*

[2]**accidental** *n* **1** ACCIDENT 3 **2** (a sign indicating) a note altered to sharp, flat, or natural and foreign to a key indicated by a key signature

'accident-ˌprone *adj* having personality traits that predispose to accidents

[1]**acclaim** /ə'klaym‖ə'kleɪm/ *vt* **1** to applaud, praise **2** to hail or proclaim by acclamation <~ed *her Queen*> – **acclaimer** *n*

[2]**acclaim** *n* acclamation

acclamation /ˌaklə'maysh(ə)n‖ˌæklə'meɪʃ(ə)n/ *n* a loud expression of praise, goodwill, or assent

acclimat·ize, -ise /ə'kliemə,tiez‖ə'klaɪməˌtaɪz/ *vb* to adapt to a new climate or situation – **acclimatizer** *n*, **acclimatization** *n*

acclivity /ə'klivəti‖ə'klɪvətɪ/ *n* an ascending slope

accolade /'akəlayd‖'ækəleɪd/ *n* **1** a ceremony marking the conferral of knighthood, in which each of the candidate's shoulders is touched with a sword **2a** a mark of acknowledgment or honour; an award **b** an expression of strong praise [French, fr *accoler* to embrace, deriv of Latin *ad* to + *collum* neck]

accommodate /ə'komədayt‖ə'kɒmədeɪt/ *vt* **1** to make fit, suitable, or congruous *to* **2** to bring into agreement or concord; reconcile **3a** to give help to; oblige *with* **b** to provide with lodgings; house **4** to have or make adequate room for **5** to give consideration to; allow for – **accommodative** *adj*, **accommodativeness** *n*

accommodating /ə'komədayting‖ə'kɒmədeɪtɪŋ/ *adj* helpful, obliging – **accommodatingly** *adv*

accommodation /əˌkomə'daysh(ə)n‖əˌkɒmə'deɪʃ(ə)n/ *n* **1a** lodging, housing – usu pl with sing. meaning in NAm **b** space, premises <*office ~*> **2a** sthg needed or desired for convenience; a facility **b** an adaptation, adjustment **c** a settlement, agreement **d** a bank loan **e** the (range of) automatic adjustment of the eye, esp by changes in the amount by which the lens bends light, for seeing at different distances – **accommodational** *adj*

accompaniment /ə'kump(ə)nimənt‖ə'kʌmp(ə)nɪmənt/ *n* **1** a subordinate instrumental or vocal part supporting or complementing a principal voice or instrument **2** an addition intended to give completeness; a complement

accompany /ə'kump(ə)ni‖ə'kʌmp(ə)nɪ/ *vt* **1** to go with as an escort or companion **2** to perform an accompaniment to or for **3a** to make an addition to; supplement *with* **b** *of a thing* to happen, exist, or be found with <*the pictures that* ~ *the text*> ~ *vi* to perform an accompaniment – **accompanist** *n*

accomplice /ə'kumplis, -'kom-‖ə'kʌmplɪs, -'kɒm-/ *n* sby who collaborates with another, esp in wrongdoing

accomplish /ə'kumplish, -'kom-‖ə'kʌmplɪʃ, -'kɒm-/ *vt* **1** to bring to a successful conclusion; achieve **2** to complete, cover (a measure of time or distance) – **accomplishable** *adj*, **accomplisher** *n*

ac'complished *adj* **1** fully effected; completed <*an* ~ *fact*> **2a** skilled, proficient <*an* ~ *dancer*> **b** having many social accomplishments

ac'complishment /-mənt‖-mənt/ *n* **1** completion, fulfilment **2** an achievement **3** an acquired ability or esp social skill

[1]**accord** /ə'kawd‖ə'kɔːd/ *vt* **1** to grant, concede <~ed *them permission*> **2** to give, award <~ed *her a warm welcome*> ~ *vi* to be consistent *with*

[2]**accord** *n* **1a** ACCORDANCE 1 **b** a formal treaty of agreement **2** balanced interrelationship (e g of colours or sounds); harmony – **of one's own accord** of one's own will; unbidden – **with one accord** with the consent or agreement of all

accordance /ə'kawd(ə)ns‖ə'kɔːd(ə)ns/ *n* **1** agreement, conformity <*in* ~ *with a rule*> **2** the act of granting

ac'cording as /ə'kawding‖ə'kɔːdɪŋ/ *conj* **1** in accordance with the way in which **2** depending on how or whether

accordingly /ə'kawdingli‖ə'kɔːdɪŋlɪ/ *adv* **1** as suggested; appropriately **2** consequently, so

ac'cording to *prep* **1** in conformity with **2** as declared by **3** depending on

accordion /ə'kawdi·ən‖ə'kɔːdɪən/ *n* a portable keyboard wind instrument in which the wind is forced past free reeds by means of a hand-operated bellows – **accordionist** *n*

accost /ə'kost‖ə'kɒst/ *vt* **1** to approach and speak to, esp boldly or challengingly **2** *of a prostitute* to solicit [Middle French *accoster*, deriv of Latin *ad* to + *costa* rib, side]

[1]**account** /ə'kownt‖ə'kaʊnt/ *n* **1** a record of debits and credits relating to a particular item, person, or concern **2** a list of items of expenditure to be balanced against income – usu pl **3** a periodically rendered calculation listing purchases and credits <*a grocery* ~> **4** a business arrangement whereby money is deposited in, and may be withdrawn from, a bank, building society, etc **5** a commission to carry out a particular business operation (e g an advertising campaign) given by one company to another **6** value, importance <*a man of no* ~> **7** profit, advantage <*turned his wit to good* ~> **8** careful thought; consideration <*left nothing out of* ~> **9a** a statement explaining one's conduct <*render an* ~> **b** a statement of facts or events; a relation <*a newspaper* ~> **10** hearsay, report – usu pl <*by all* ~s *a rich man*> **11** a version, rendering <*the pianist's sensitive* ~ *of it*> – **on account of** due to; BECAUSE OF – **on no account or not on any account** in no circumstances – **on one's own account 1** on one's own behalf **2** at one's own risk – **on somebody's account** for sby's sake

[2]**account** *vt* to think of as; consider <~s *himself lucky*> – **account for 1** to give an explanation or reason for **2** to be the sole or primary explanation for **3** to bring about the defeat, death, or destruction of <accounted for *3 of the attackers*>

accountable /ə'kowntəbl‖ə'kaʊntəbl/ *adj* **1** responsible, answerable **2** explicable – **accountableness** *n*, **accountably** *adv*, **accountability** *n*

accountancy /ə'kownt(ə)nsi‖ə'kaʊnt(ə)nsɪ/ *n* the profession or practice of accounting

accountant /əkownt(ə)nt‖əkaʊnt(ə)nt/ *n* one who practises and is usu qualified in accounting

accounting /ə'kownting‖ə'kaʊntɪŋ/ *n* the recording, analysing, and checking of business and financial transactions

accoutrement /ə'koohtrəmənt‖ə'kuːtrəmənt/, *NAm also* **accouterment** /ə'koohtəmənt‖ə'kuːtəmənt/ *n* equipment, trappings; *specif* a soldier's outfit excluding clothes and weapons – usu pl

accredit /ə'kredit‖ə'kredɪt/ *vt* **1a** to give official authorization to or approval of **b** to send (esp an envoy) with credentials **c** to recognize or vouch for as conforming to a standard **2** to credit *with*, attribute *to* – **accreditable** *adj*, **accreditation** *n*

accrete /ə'kreet‖ə'kriːt/ *vb* to (cause to) grow together or become attached by accretion

accretion /ə'kreesh(ə)n‖ə'kriːʃ(ə)n/ *n* **1a** an increase in size caused by natural growth or the external adhesion or addition of matter **b** sthg added or stuck extraneously **2** the growth of separate particles or parts (e g of a plant) into one; concretion – **accretionary** *adj*, **accretive** *adj*

accrue /ə'krooh‖ə'kruː/ *vi* **1** to come as an increase or addition to sthg; arise as a growth or result **2** to be periodically accumulated <*interest has* ~d *over the year*> ~ *vt* to collect, accumulate – **accruable** *adj*, **accruement** *n*

accumulate /ə'kyoohmyoo,layt‖ə'kjuːmjʊ,leɪt/ *vt* to collect together gradually; amass ~ *vi* to increase in quantity or number

accumulation /ə,kyoohmyoo'laysh(ə)n‖ə,kjuːmjʊ'leɪʃ(ə)n/ *n* **1** increase or growth caused by esp repeated or continuous addition; *specif* increase in capital from interest payments **2** sthg that has accumulated

accumulative /ə'kyoohmyoolətiv‖ə'kjuːmjʊlətɪv/ *adj* **1** cumulative **2** tending or given to accumulation, esp of money – **accumulatively** *adv*, **accumulativeness** *n*

accumulator /ə'kyoohmyoo,laytə‖ə'kjuːmjʊ,leɪtə/ *n* **1** a part (e g in a computer) where numbers are added or stored **2** *Br* a rechargeable secondary electric cell; *also* a connected set of these **3** *Br* a bet whereby the winnings from one of a series of events are staked on the next event

accurate /'akyoorət‖'ækjʊrət/ *adj* **1** free from error, esp as the result of care <*an* ~ *estimate*> **2** conforming precisely to truth or a measurable standard; exact <~ *instruments*> – **accurately** *adv*, **accurateness** *n*, **accuracy** *n*

accursed /ə'kuhst, ə'kuhsid‖ə'kɜːst, ə'kɜːsɪd/, **accurst** /ə'kuhst‖ə'kɜːst/ *adj* **1** under a curse; ill-fated **2** damnable, detestable – **accursedly** *adv*, **accursedness** *n*

accusation /ˌakyooˈzaysh(ə)n‖ˌækjʊˈzeɪʃ(ə)n/ *n* a charge of wrongdoing; an allegation

[1]**accusative** /əˈkyoohzətiv‖əˈkjuːzətɪv/ *adj* of or being the grammatical accusative

[2]**accusative** *n* (a form (e g *me*) in) a grammatical case expressing the direct object of a verb or of some prepositions

accuse /əˈkyoohz‖əˈkjuːz/ *vt* to charge with a fault or crime; blame < ~d *him of murder*> – **accuser** *n*, **accusingly** *adv*

acˈcused *n, pl* **accused** *the* defendant in a criminal case

accustom /əˈkust(ə)m‖əˈkʌst(ə)m/ *vt* to make used *to* through use or experience; habituate – **accustomation** *n*

acˈcustomed *adj* **1** customary, habitual **2** in the habit of; used *to* < ~ *to making decisions*> – **accustomedness** *n*

[1]**ace** /ays‖eɪs/ *n* **1** a die face, playing card, or domino marked with 1 spot or pip; *also* the single spot or pip on any of these **2** (a point scored by) a shot, esp a service in tennis, that an opponent fails to touch **3** a combat pilot who has brought down at least 5 enemy aircraft **4** an expert or leading performer – **within an ace of** on the point of; very near to <*came* within an ace of *winning*>

[2]**ace** *vt* to score an ace against (an opponent)

[3]**ace** *adj* great, excellent – infml

acerbic /əˈsuhbik‖əˈsɜːbɪk/ *adj* **1** bitter or sour in taste **2** sharp or vitriolic in speech, temper, or manner – **acerbically** *adv*, **acerbity** *n*

acetate /ˈasitayt‖ˈæsɪteɪt/ *n* **1** a salt or ester of acetic acid **2** (a textile fibre or gramophone record made from) cellulose acetate

acetic /əˈseetik, -ˈset-‖əˈsiːtɪk, -ˈset-/ *adj* of or producing acetic acid or vinegar

aˌcetic ˈacid *n* a pungent liquid acid that is the major acid in vinegar

acetylene /əˈsetileen, -lin‖əˈsetɪliːn, -lɪn/ *n* a colourless unsaturated hydrocarbon gas used esp as a fuel (e g in oxyacetylene torches) – **acetylenic** *adj*

[1]**ache** /ayk‖eɪk/ *vi* **1a** to suffer a usu dull persistent pain **b** to feel anguish or distress <*heart* ~d *for her*> **2** to yearn, long <aching *to see you*> – **achingly** *adv*

[2]**ache** *n* a usu dull persistent pain

achieve /əˈcheev‖əˈtʃiːv/ *vt* **1** to carry out successfully; accomplish **2** to obtain by effort; win – **achievable** *adj*, **achiever** *n*

aˈchievement /-mənt‖-mənt/ *n* **1** successful completion; accomplishment **2** sthg accomplished, esp by resolve, persistence, or courage; a feat **3** performance in a test or academic course **4** a coat of arms with its formal accompaniments (e g helm, crest, and supporters)

Aˌchilles' ˈheel /əˈkileez, -liz‖əˈkɪliːz, -lɪz/ *n* a person's only vulnerable point [*Achilles*, legendary Greek warrior, reputedly vulnerable only in the heel]

Aˌchilles ˈtendon *n* the strong tendon joining the muscles in the calf to the heelbone

[1]**acid** /ˈasid‖ˈæsɪd/ *adj* **1a** sour or sharp to the taste **b** sharp, biting, or sour in speech, manner, or disposition; caustic **2** of, like, containing, or being an acid < ~ *soil*>; *specif* having a pH of less than 7 – **acidly** *adv*, **acidness** *n*, **acidity** *n*

[2]**acid** *n* **1** a sour substance; *specif* any of various typically water-soluble and sour compounds having a pH of less than 7 that are capable of giving up a hydrogen ion to or accepting an unshared pair of electrons from a base to form a salt **2** LSD – infml

acidic /əˈsidik‖əˈsɪdɪk/ *adj* **1** acid-forming **2** acid

acidify /əˈsidifie‖əˈsɪdɪfaɪ/ *vt* to make or convert into (an) acid – **acidifier** *n*, **acidification** *n*

ˈacid ˌrain *n* rain containing high levels of acid substances (e g sulphuric and nitric acid), caused by the release of effluent into the atmosphere

ˌacid ˈtest *n* a severe or crucial test (e g of value or suitability) [fr the use of nitric acid to test for gold]

ack-ack /ˈakˌak‖ˈækˌæk/ *adj* antiaircraft [signallers' terms for *AA*, short for *a*nti*a*ircraft]

acknowledge /əkˈnolij‖əkˈnɒlɪdʒ/ *vt* **1** to admit knowledge of; concede to be true or valid **2** to recognize the status or claims of **3a** to express gratitude or obligation for **b** to show recognition of (e g by smiling or nodding) **c** to confirm receipt of – **acknowledgeable** *adj*

acˈknowledgment *also* **acknowledgement** /-mənt‖-mənt/ *n* **1** recognition or favourable reception of an act or achievement **2** a thing done or given in recognition of sthg received **3** a declaration or avowal of a fact **4** an author's list of people to whom he/she is indebted, usu appearing at the front of a book – usu pl with sing. meaning

acme /ˈakmi‖ˈækmɪ/ *n* the highest point or stage; *esp* a perfect representative of a specified class or thing <*was the* ~ *of courtesy*>

acne /ˈakni‖ˈæknɪ/ *n* a skin disorder found esp among adolescents, characterized by inflammation of the skin glands and hair follicles and causing red pustules, esp on the face and neck – **acned** *adj*

acolyte /ˈakəliet‖ˈækəlaɪt/ *n* **1** an assistant performing minor duties in a liturgical service **2** one who attends or assists; a follower

aconite /ˈakəniet‖ˈækənaɪt/ *n* (a drug obtained from) monkshood – **aconitic** *adj*

acorn /ˈayˌkawn‖ˈeɪˌkɔːn/ *n* the nut of the oak, usu seated in a hard woody cup

[1]**acoustic** /əˈkoohstik‖əˈkuːstɪk/ *also* **acoustical** /-kl‖-kl/ *adj* **1** of sound, the sense of hearing, or acoustics **2** of or being a musical instrument whose sound is not electronically modified – **acoustically** *adv*

[2]**acoustic** *n* **1** *pl but sing in constr* the science of sound **2** the properties of a room, hall, etc that govern the quality of sound heard – usu pl with sing. meaning – **acoustician** *n*

acquaint /əˈkwaynt‖əˈkweɪnt/ *vt* to cause to know; make familiar *with* sthg

acquaintance /əˈkwaynt(ə)ns‖əˈkweɪnt(ə)ns/ *n* **1** personal knowledge; familiarity **2a** *sing or pl in constr* the people with whom one is acquainted **b** a person whom one knows but who is not a particularly close friend – **acquaintanceship** *n* – **make the acquaintance of** to come to know; meet

acquiesce /ˌakweeˈes‖ˌækwiːˈes/ *vi* to submit or comply tacitly or passively – often + *in* –

acquiescence *n*, **acquiescent** *adj*, **acquiescently** *adv*
acquire /ə'kwie·ə‖ə'kwaɪə/ *vt* **1a** to gain or come into possession of, often by unspecified means; *also* to steal – euph **b** to gain as a new characteristic or ability, esp as a result of skill or hard work **2** to locate and hold (an object) in a detector < ~ *a target by radar*> – **acquirable** *adj*, **acquirement** *n*
acquisition /ˌakwi'zish(ə)n‖ˌækwɪ'zɪʃ(ə)n/ *n* **1** acquiring, gaining **2** sby or sthg acquired or gained, esp to one's advantage – **acquisitional** *adj*, **acquisitor** *n*
acquisitive /ə'kwizətiv‖ə'kwɪzətɪv/ *adj* keen or tending to acquire and possess – **acquisitively** *adv*, **acquisitiveness** *n*
acquit /ə'kwit‖ə'kwɪt/ *vt* **-tt- 1** to free from responsibility or obligation; *specif* to declare not guilty <*the court* ~ted *him of the charge*> **2** to conduct (oneself) in a specified, usu favourable, manner – **acquitter** *n*
acquittal /ə'kwitl‖ə'kwɪtl/ *n* a judicial release from a criminal charge
acre /'aykə‖'eɪkə/ *n* **1** *pl* lands, fields **2** a unit of area equal to 4840yd^2 (4046.86m^2) **3** *pl* great quantities – infml
acreage /'ayk(ə)rij‖'eɪk(ə)rɪdʒ/ *n* area in acres
acrid /'akrid‖'ækrɪd/ *adj* **1** unpleasantly pungent in taste or smell **2** violently bitter in manner or language; acrimonious – **acridly** *adv*, **acridness** *n*, **acridity** *n*
acrimony /'akrimәni‖'ækrɪmənɪ/ *n* caustic sharpness of manner or language resulting from anger or ill nature – **acrimonious** *adj*, **acrimoniously** *adv*, **acrimoniousness** *n*
acrobat /'akrəbat‖'ækrəbæt/ *n* **1** one who performs gymnastic feats requiring skilful control of the body **2** one who nimbly and often too readily changes his position or viewpoint <*a political* ~> [Greek *akrobatēs*, fr *akrobatos* walking on tiptoe, fr *akros* topmost, extreme + *bainein* to go] – **acrobatic** *adj*, **acrobatically** *adv*
ˌacroˈbatics *n pl* **1** *sing or pl in constr* the art, performance, or activity of an acrobat **2** a spectacular performance involving great agility <*contralto's vocal* ~>
acronym /'akrənim‖'ækrənɪm/ *n* a word (e g *radar*) formed from the initial letters of other words – **acronymic** *adj*, **acronymically** *adv*
[1]**across** /ə'kros‖ə'krɒs/ *adv* **1** from one side to the other crosswise **2** to or on the opposite side **3** so as to be understandable, acceptable, or successful
[2]**across** *prep* **1a** from one side to the other of <*walk* ~ *the lawn*> **b** on the opposite side of <*lives* ~ *the street*> **2** so as to intersect at an angle <*sawed* ~ *the grain of the wood*> **3** into transitory contact with
acrostic /ə'krostik‖ə'krɒstɪk/ *n* a composition, usu in verse, in which sets of letters (e g the first of each line) form a word or phrase – **acrostic** *also* **acrostical** *adj*, **acrostically** *adv*
aˌcrylic ˈfibre /əkrilik‖əkrɪlɪk/ *n* a synthetic textile fibre made by polymerization of the liquid acrylonitrile usu with other polymers
[1]**act** /akt‖ækt/ *n* **1** a thing done; a deed **2** STATUTE 1; *also* a decree, edict **3** the process of doing <*caught in the very* ~> **4** *often cap* a formal record of sthg done or transacted **5a** any of the principal divisions of a play or opera **b** any of the successive parts or performances in an entertainment (e g a circus) **6** a display of affected behaviour; a pretence – **be/get in on the act** to be or deliberately become involved in a situation or undertaking, esp for one's own advantage
[2]**act** *vt* **1** to represent by action, esp on the stage **2** to feign, simulate **3** to play the part of (as if) in a play < ~ *the fool*> **4** to behave in a manner suitable to < ~ *your age*> ~ *vi* **1a** to perform on the stage; engage in acting **b** to behave insincerely **2** to function or behave in a specified manner < ~ed *generously*> **3** to perform a specified function; serve *as* **4** to be a substitute or representative *for* **5** to produce an effect <*wait for the medicine to* ~> – **actable** *adj*, **actability** *n*
[1]**acting** /'akting‖'æktɪŋ/ *adj* holding a temporary rank or position < ~ *president*>
[2]**acting** *n* the art or practice of representing a character in a dramatic production
[1]**action** /'aksh(ə)n‖'ækʃ(ə)n/ *n* **1** a civil legal proceeding **2** the process of acting or working, esp to produce alteration by force or through a natural agency **3a** the mode of movement of the body **b** a function of (a part of) the body **4** a voluntary act; a deed <*know him by his* ~s> **5a** the state of functioning actively <*machine is out of* ~> **b** practical, often militant, activity, often directed towards a political end <*an* ~ *group*> **c** energetic activity; enterprise <*a man of* ~> **6a(1)** an engagement between troops or ships **a(2)** [2]COMBAT 3 **b** (the unfolding of) the events in a play or work of fiction **7** an operating mechanism (e g of a gun or piano); *also* the manner in which it operates **8** (*the* most) lively or productive activity <*go where the* ~ *is*> – infml
[2]**action** *vt* to take action on; implement
ˈactionable /-əbl‖-əbl/ *adj* giving grounds for an action at law – **actionably** *adv*
ˈaction ˌpainting *n* abstract art in which spontaneous techniques (e g dribbling or smearing) are used to apply paint
activate /'aktivayt‖'æktɪveɪt/ *vt* **1** to make (more) active or reactive, esp in chemical or physical properties: e g **1a** to make (a substance) radioactive **b** to aerate (sewage) so as to favour the growth of organisms that decompose organic matter **2** *NAm* to equip or put (troops) on active duty – **activator** *n*, **activation** *n*
[1]**active** /'aktiv‖'æktɪv/ *adj* **1** characterized by practical action rather than by contemplation or speculation <*take an* ~ *interest in*> **2** quick in physical movement; lively **3a** marked by or requiring vigorous activity < ~ *sports*> **b** full of activity; busy <*an* ~ *life*> **4** having practical operation or results; effective <*an* ~ *law*> **5** *of a volcano* liable to erupt; not extinct **6** *of a verb form or voice* having as the subject the person or thing doing the action **7** of, in, or being full-time service, esp in the armed forces <*on* ~ *duty*> **8** capable of acting or reacting; activated < ~ *nitrogen*> **9** *of an electronic device* containing and sometimes directing a power source – **actively** *adv*, **activeness** *n*
[2]**active** *n* **1** an active verb form **2** the active voice of a language

activism /'aktiviz(ə)m‖'æktıvız(ə)m/ *n* a doctrine or practice that emphasizes vigorous action (e g the use of mass demonstrations) in controversial, esp political, matters – **activist** *n or adj*, **activistic** *adj*

activity /ak'tivəti‖æk'tıvətı/ *n* **1** the quality or state of being active **2** vigorous or energetic action; liveliness **3** a pursuit in which a person is active – usu pl <*social* activities>

ˌ**act of 'God** *n* a sudden event, esp a catastrophe, brought about by uncontrollable natural forces

actor /'aktə‖'æktə/, *fem* **actress** /'aktris‖'æktrıs/ *n* one who represents a character in a dramatic production; *esp* one whose profession is acting – **actorish** *adj*

act out *vt* **1a** to represent in action <*children* act out *what they read*> **b** to translate into action <*unwilling to* act out *what they believe*> **2** to express (repressed or unconscious impulses) unwittingly in overt behaviour

actual /'aktyoo(ə)l, -choo(ə)l‖'æktjʊ(ə)l, -tʃʊ(ə)l/ *adj* **1** existing in fact or reality; real **2** existing or occurring at the time; current – **actualize** *vt*, **actualization** *n*

actuality /ˌaktyoo'aləti, ˌakchoo-‖ˌæktjʊ'ælətı, ˌæktʃʊ-/ *n* an existing circumstance; a real fact – often pl

'**actually** /-li‖-lı/ *adv* **1** really; IN FACT <*nominally but not* ~ *independent*> **2** at the present moment <*the party* ~ *in power*> **3** strange as it may seem; even <*she* ~ *spoke Latin*>

actuary /'aktyoo(ə)ri, 'akchoo-‖'æktjʊ(ə)rı, 'æktʃʊ-/ *n* a statistician who calculates insurance risks and premiums – **actuarial** *adj*, **actuarially** *adv*

actuate /'aktyooayt, -choo-‖'æktjʊeıt, -tʃʊ-/ *vt* **1** to put into action or motion **2** to incite to action <~d *by greed*> – **actuation** *n*, **actuator** *n*

act up *vi* **1** to behave in an unruly manner; PLAY UP **2** to give pain or trouble <*this typewriter is* acting up *again*> ***USE*** infml

acuity /ə'kyooh·əti‖ə'kju:ətı/ *n* keenness of mental or physical perception – fml

acumen /'akyoomən‖'ækjʊmən/ *n* keenness and depth of discernment or discrimination, esp in practical matters

acupuncture /'ak(y)ooˌpungkchə‖'æk(j)ʊˌpʌŋktʃə/ *n* an orig Chinese practice of puncturing the body at particular points with needles to cure disease, relieve pain, produce anaesthesia, etc [Latin *acus* needle + English *puncture*] – **acupuncturist** *n*

acute /ə'kyooht‖ə'kju:t/ *adj* **1a** *of an angle* measuring less than 90° **b** composed of acute angles <~ *triangle*> **2a** marked by keen discernment or intellectual perception, esp of subtle distinctions <*an* ~ *thinker*> **b** responsive to slight impressions or stimuli <~ *eyesight*> **3** intensely felt or perceived <~ *pain*> **4** *esp of an illness* having a sudden severe onset and short course – contrasted with *chronic* **5** demanding urgent attention; severe <*an* ~ *housing shortage*> **6** marked with, having the pronunciation indicated by, or being an accent mark written ´ – **acutely** *adv*, **acuteness** *n*

ad /ad‖æd/ *n* an advertisement – infml

ad-, **ac-**, **af-**, **ag-**, **al-**, **ap-**, **as-**, **at-** *prefix* **1** to; towards – usu *ac-* before *c, k,* or *q* <*acculturation*>, *af-* before *f*, *ag-* before *g* <*aggrade*>, *al-* before *l* <*alliteration*>, *ap-* before *p* <*approximate*>, *as-* before *s* <*assuage*>, *at-* before *t* <*attune*>, and *ad-* before other sounds **2** near; adjacent to – in this sense always in the form *ad-* <*adrenal*>

adage /'adij‖'ædıdʒ/ *n* a maxim or proverb that embodies a commonly accepted observation

[1]**adagio** /ə'dahjioh‖ə'dɑ:dʒıəʊ/ *adv or adj* in an easy slow graceful manner – used in music [Italian, fr *ad* at, to + *agio* ease]

[2]**adagio** *n, pl* **adagios** **1** a musical composition or movement in adagio tempo **2** ballet dancing, esp a pas de deux, involving difficult feats of balance

[1]**adamant** /'adəmənt‖'ædəmənt/ *n* a stone formerly believed to be of impenetrable hardness and sometimes identified with the diamond; *broadly* any very hard unbreakable substance

[2]**adamant** *adj* unshakable in determination; unyielding – **adamancy** *n*, **adamantly** *adv*

ˌ**Adam's 'apple** /adəmz‖ædəmz/ *n* the projection in the front of the neck formed by the largest cartilage of the larynx

adapt /ə'dapt‖ə'dæpt/ *vb* to make or become fit, often by modification – **adaptable** *adj*, **adaptability** *n*, **adaptedness** *n*

adaptation /ˌadap'taysh(ə)n‖ˌædæp'teıʃ(ə)n/ *n* **1** adjustment to prevailing or changing conditions: e g **1a** adjustment of a sense organ to the intensity or quality of stimulation **b** modification of (the parts of) an organism fitting it better for existence and successful breeding **2** a composition rewritten in a new form or for a different medium – **adaptational** *adj*, **adaptationally** *adv*

adapter *also* **adaptor** /ə'daptə‖ə'dæptə/ *n* **1** a writer who adapts sthg **2** a device **2a** for connecting 2 pieces of apparatus not orig intended to be joined **b** for converting a tool or piece of apparatus to some new use **c** for connecting several pieces of electrical apparatus to a single power point, or connecting a plug of one type to a socket of a different type

add /ad‖æd/ *vt* **1** to join so as to bring about an increase or improvement <*wine* ~s *a creative touch to cooking*> **2** to say or write further **3** to combine (numbers) into a single number – often + *up* ~ *vi* **1a** to perform addition **b** to come together or unite by addition **2** to make or serve as an addition *to*

addendum /ə'dendəm‖ə'dendəm/ *n, pl* **addenda** /-də‖-də/ a supplement to a book – often pl with sing. meaning but sing. in constr

[1]**adder** /'adə‖'ædə/ *n* the common European venomous viper or other ground-living viper

[2]**adder** *n* a device (e g in a computer) that performs addition

[1]**addict** /ə'dikt‖ə'dıkt/ *vt* **1** to devote or surrender (oneself) to sthg habitually or obsessively – usu pass **2** to cause (an animal or human) to become physiologically dependent upon a habit-forming drug – **addictive** *adj*, **addiction** *n*

[2]**addict** /'adikt‖'ædıkt/ *n* **1** one who is addicted to a drug **2** DEVOTEE 2

addition /ə'dish(ə)n‖ə'dıʃ(ə)n/ *n* **1** sthg or sby

added, esp as an improvement **2** the act or process of adding, esp adding numbers **3** direct chemical combination of substances to form a single product – **in addition** also, furthermore

additional /ə'dish(ə)nl‖ə'dɪʃ(ə)nl/ *adj* existing by way of addition; supplementary – **additionally** *adv*

[1]**additive** /'adətiv‖'ædətɪv/ *adj* of or characterized by addition – **additively** *adv*, **additivity** *n*

[2]**additive** *n* a substance added to another in relatively small amounts to impart desirable properties or suppress undesirable ones

addle /'adl‖'ædl/ *vt* to throw into confusion ~ *vi* **1** *of an egg* to become rotten **2** to become confused or muddled

'**add-on** *n* an extension; *esp* a computer peripheral – **add-on** *adj*

[1]**address** /ə'dres‖ə'dres/ *vt* **1** to direct the efforts or attention of (oneself) < ~ *himself to the problem*> **2a** to communicate directly < ~es *his thanks to his host*> **b** to speak or write directly to; *esp* to deliver a formal speech to **3** to mark directions for delivery on < ~ *a letter*> **4** to greet by a prescribed form < ~ed *him as 'My Lord'* > – **addresser** *n*, **addressee** *n*

[2]**address** /ə'dres‖ə'dres/ *n* **1** dutiful and courteous attention, esp in courtship – usu pl <*paid his* ~es *to her*> **2** readiness and capability for dealing (e g with a person or problem) skilfully and smoothly; adroitness **3** a formal communication; *esp* a prepared speech delivered to an audience **4** a place of residence (where a person or organization may be communicated with); *also* a detailed description of its location (e g on an envelope) **5** a location (e g in the memory of a computer) where particular information is stored; *also* the digits that identify such a location

adduce /ə'dyoohs‖ə'dju:s/ *vt* to offer as example, reason, or proof in discussion or analysis – fml – **adducer** *n*, **adduction** *n*

add up *vi* **1** to amount *to* in total or substance <*the play* adds up *to a lot of laughs*> **2** to come to the expected total <*the bill doesn't* add up> **3** to be internally consistent; make sense ~ *vt* SIZE UP

-ade /-ayd‖-eɪd/ *suffix* (→*n*) **1a** act or action of <*block*ade> **b** individual or group of people involved in (a specified action) <*renega*de> **2** product; *esp* sweet drink made from (a specified fruit) <*lime*ade>

adenoid /'adənoyd‖'ædənɔɪd/ *adj or n* (of) an enlarged mass of lymphoid tissue at the back of the pharynx, often obstructing breathing – usu pl with sing. meaning

adenoidal /ˌadə'noydl‖ˌædə'nɔɪdl/ *adj* of (sby with enlarged) adenoids – **adenoidally** *adv*

adept /'adept, ə'dept‖'ædept, ə'dept/ *adj or n* (being) a highly skilled expert *at* – **adeptly** *adv*, **adeptness** *n*

adequate /'adikwət‖'ædɪkwət/ *adj* sufficient for a specific requirement; *esp* barely sufficient or satisfactory – **adequacy** *n*, **adequately** *adv*, **adequateness** *n*

adhere /əd'(h)iə‖əd'(h)ɪə/ *vi* **1** to give continued support, observance, or loyalty < ~ *to the treaty*> **2** to hold or stick fast (as if) by gluing, suction, grasping, or fusing ~ *vt* to cause to stick fast – **adherent** *adj*, **adherence** *n*

adherent /əd'(h)iərənt‖əd'(h)ɪərənt/ *n* a supporter of a leader, faction, etc

adhesion /əd'(h)eezh(ə)n, ad'hee-‖əd'(h)i:ʒ(ə)n, æd'hi:-/ *n* **1** the action or state of adhering **2** (the tissues united by) an abnormal union of tissues that are usu separated in the body – **adhesional** *adj*

[1]**adhesive** /əd'(h)eeziv, -siv‖əd'(h)i:zɪv, -sɪv/ *adj* causing or prepared for sticking; sticky – **adhesively** *adv*, **adhesiveness** *n*

[2]**adhesive** *n* an adhesive substance (e g glue or cement)

ad hoc /ˌad 'hok‖ˌæd 'hɒk/ *adj or adv* with respect to the particular purpose at hand and without consideration of wider application [Latin, for this]

adieu /ə'dyooh, ə'dyuh ‖ə'dju:, ə'djɜ: (*Fr* adjø/)/ *n, pl* **adieus, adieux** /ə'dyooh(z), ə'dyuh(z)‖ə'dju:(z), ə'djɜ:(z) (*Fr* ~)/ a farewell – often used interjectionally; usu poetic [Middle French, fr *a* to (fr Latin *ad*) + *Dieu* God (fr Latin *Deus*)]

ad infinitum /ˌad infi'nietəm‖ˌæd ɪnfɪ'naɪtəm/ *adv or adj* without end or limit [Latin, to an infinite extent]

adipose /'adipohs, -pohz‖'ædɪpəʊs, -pəʊz/ *adj* of animal fat; fatty – **adiposity** *n*

adjacent /ə'jays(ə)nt‖ə'dʒeɪs(ə)nt/ *adj* having a common border; *broadly* neighbouring, nearby – **adjacency** *n*, **adjacently** *adv*

adjective /'ajiktiv‖'ædʒɪktɪv/ *n* a word that modifies a noun or pronoun by describing a particular characteristic of it – **adjectival** *adj*, **adjectivally** *adv*

adjoin /ə'joyn‖ə'dʒɔɪn/ *vb* to be next to or in contact with (one another) – **adjoining** *adj*

adjourn /ə'juhn‖ə'dʒɜ:n/ *vb* to suspend (a session) until a later stated time – **adjournment** *n*

adjudge /ə'juj‖ə'dʒʌdʒ/ *vt* **1a** to adjudicate **b** to pronounce formally < ~ *him guilty*> **2** to pronounce to be; deem < ~ *the book a success*>

adjudicate /ə'joohdikayt‖ə'dʒu:dɪkeɪt/ *vt* to make a judicial decision on ~ *vi* to act as judge (e g in a competition) – **adjudicative** *adj*, **adjudicator** *n*

adjunct /'ajungkt‖'ædʒʌŋkt/ *n* **1** sthg joined to another thing as an incidental accompaniment but not essentially a part of it **2** a word or phrase (e g an adverb or prepositional phrase) that can be left out and still leave the sentence grammatically complete **3** a person, usu in a subordinate or temporary capacity, assisting another to perform some duty or service – **adjunct** *adj*, **adjunctly** *adv*, **adjunctive** *adj*, **adjunctively** *adv*

adjure /ə'jooə‖ə'dʒʊə/ *vt* **1** to charge or command solemnly (as if) under oath or penalty of a curse **2** to entreat or advise earnestly *USE* fml – **adjuration** *n*, **adjuratory** *adj*

adjust /ə'just‖ə'dʒʌst/ *vt* **1** to bring to a more satisfactory or conformable state by minor change or adaptation; regulate, correct, or modify **2** to determine the amount to be paid under an insurance policy in settlement of (a loss) ~ *vi* to adapt or conform oneself (e g to climate) – **adjustable** *adj*, **adjustive** *adj*, **adjustability** *n*

ad'justment /-mənt‖-mənt/ *n* **1** a correction

or modification to reflect actual conditions **2** a means (e g a mechanism) by which things are adjusted one to another **3** a settlement of a disputed claim or debt

adjutant /'ajoot(ə)nt‖'ædʒʊt(ə)nt/ *n* an officer who assists the commanding officer and is responsible for correspondence and for ensuring that his orders are carried out – **adjutancy** *n*

[1]**ad-lib** /ˌad 'lib‖ˌæd 'lɪb/ *adj* spoken, composed, or performed without preparation – infml

[2]**ad-lib** *vb* **-bb-** to say (e g lines or a speech) spontaneously and without preparation; improvise – **ad-lib** *n*

ad lib *adv* without restraint or limit [Modern Latin *ad libitum* in accordance with desire]

adman /'adˌman‖'ædˌmæn/ *n* a member of the advertising profession – infml

administer /əd'ministə‖əd'mɪnɪstə/ *vt* **1** to manage, supervise **2a** to mete out; dispense < ~ *punishment*> **b** to give or perform ritually < ~ *the last rites*> **c** to give remedially ~ *vi* to perform the office of administrator; manage affairs – **administrable** *adj*, **administrant** *n*

administration /ədˌmini'straysh(ə)n‖ədˌmɪnɪ'streɪʃ(ə)n/ *n* **1** the act or process of administering **2** performance of executive duties; management **3** the execution of public affairs as distinguished from the making of policy **4a** a body of people who administer **b** *cap* GOVERNMENT 5 – **administrate** *vb*, **administrational** *adj*, **administrationist** *n*

administrative /əd'ministrətiv‖əd'mɪnɪstrətɪv/ *adj* of (an) administration – **administratively** *adv*

administrator /əd'miniˌstraytə‖əd'mɪnɪˌstreɪtə/ *n* sby who administers esp business, school, or governmental affairs

admirable /'admərəbl‖'ædmərəbl/ *adj* deserving the highest respect; excellent – **admirableness** *n*, **admirably** *adv*, **admirability** *n*

admiral /'admərəl‖'ædmərəl/ *n* the commander in chief of a navy [Middle French *amiral* & Medieval Latin *admirallus*, fr Arabic *amīr-al-(baḥr)* commander of the (sea)]

'**admiralty** /-ti‖-tɪ/ *n* **1** *sing or pl in constr, cap* the executive department formerly having authority over naval affairs **2** the court having jurisdiction over maritime questions

admiration /ˌadmə'raysh(ə)n‖ˌædmə'reɪʃ(ə)n/ *n* **1** a feeling of delighted or astonished approval **2** the object of admiring respect

admire /əd'mie·ə‖əd'maɪə/ *vt* to think highly of; express admiration for – **admirer** *n*, **admiringly** *adv*

admissible /əd'misəbl‖əd'mɪsəbl/ *adj, esp of legal evidence* capable of being allowed or conceded; permissible – **admissibility** *n*

admission /əd'mish(ə)n‖əd'mɪʃ(ə)n/ *n* **1** acknowledgment that a fact or allegation is true **2a** allowing or being allowed to enter sthg (e g a secret society) **b** a fee paid at or for admission – **admissive** *adj*

admit /əd'mit‖əd'mɪt/ *vb* **-tt-** *vt* **1a** to allow scope for; permit **b** to concede as true or valid **2** to allow to enter sthg (e g a place or fellowship) ~ *vi* **1** to give entrance or access **2a** to allow, permit – often + *of* **b** to make acknowledgment – + *to*

admittance /əd'mit(ə)ns‖əd'mɪt(ə)ns/ *n* **1** permission to enter a place **2** access, entrance

admittedly /əd'mitidli‖əd'mɪtɪdlɪ/ *adv* as must reluctantly be admitted

admixture /əd'mikschə, 'admikschə‖əd'mɪkstʃə, 'ædmɪkstʃə/ *n* **1** mixing or being mixed **2** an ingredient added by mixing, or the resulting mixture – **admix** *vt*

admonish /əd'monish‖əd'mɒnɪʃ/ *vt* **1a** to indicate duties to **b** to warn about remissness or error, esp gently **2** to give friendly earnest advice or encouragement to – **admonisher** *n*, **admonishingly** *adv*, **admonishment** *n*

admonition /ˌadmə'nish(ə)n‖ˌædmə'nɪʃ(ə)n/ *n* (a) gentle friendly reproof, counsel, or warning

admonitory /əd'monit(ə)ri‖əd'mɒnɪt(ə)rɪ/ *adj* expressing admonition; warning – **admonitorily** *adv*

ad nauseam /ˌad 'nawzi·əm, -si·əm‖ˌæd 'nɔːzɪəm, -sɪəm/ *adv* in an extremely tedious manner; enough to make one sick [Latin, to sickness]

ado /ə'dooh‖ə'duː/ *n* fussy bustling excitement, esp over trivia; to-do

adobe /ə'dohbi‖ə'dəʊbɪ/ *n* **1** a building brick of sun-dried earth and straw **2** a heavy clay used in making adobe bricks – **adobe** *adj*

adolescent /ˌadə'les(ə)nt‖ˌædə'les(ə)nt/ *n* sby in the period of life between puberty and maturity [French, fr Latin *adolescere* to grow up – see ADULT] – **adolescent** *adj*, **adolescence** *n*

adopt /ə'dopt‖ə'dɒpt/ *vt* **1** to take by choice into a new relationship; *specif* to bring up voluntarily (a child of other parents) as one's own child **2** to take up and practise; take to oneself **3** to vote to accept < ~ *a constitutional amendment*> **4** *of a constituency* to nominate as a Parliamentary candidate – **adopter** *n*, **adoptable** *adj*, **adoptability** *n*, **adoption** *n*, **adoptee** *n*

adoptive /ə'doptiv‖ə'dɒptɪv/ *adj* made or acquired by adoption

adorable /ə'dawrəbl‖ə'dɔːrəbl/ *adj* sweetly lovable; charming – **adorableness** *n*, **adorably** *adv*, **adorability** *n*

adore /ə'daw‖ə'dɔː/ *vt* **1** to worship or honour as a deity **2** to regard with reverent admiration and devotion **3** to like very much – infml – **adorer** *n*, **adoration** *n*

adorn /ə'dawn‖ə'dɔːn/ *vt* **1** to decorate, esp with ornaments **2** to add to the pleasantness or attractiveness of – **adornment** *n*

a'drenal ˌgland /ə'dreenl‖ə'driːnl/ *n* an endocrine gland near the front of each kidney with an outer part that secretes steroid hormones and an inner part that secretes adrenalin

adrenalin, adrenaline /ə'drenəlin‖ə'drenəlɪn/ *n* a hormone produced by the adrenal gland that occurs as a neurotransmitter in the sympathetic nervous system and that stimulates the heart and causes constriction of blood vessels and relaxation of smooth muscle

adrift /ə'drift‖ə'drɪft/ *adv or adj* **1** afloat without motive power or mooring and at the mercy of winds and currents **2** in or into a state of being unstuck or unfastened; loose – esp in *come adrift* **3** astray – infml <*his reasoning's gone completely* ~>

adroit /ə'droyt‖ə'drɔɪt/ *adj* **1** dexterous, nimble **2** shrewd or resourceful in coping with difficulty or danger – **adroitly** *adv*, **adroitness** *n*

adulate /'adyoolayt‖'ædjʊleɪt/ *vt* to flatter or admire excessively or slavishly – **adulator** *n*, **adulation** *n*, **adulatory** *adj*

[1]**adult** /'adult, ə'dult‖'ædʌlt, ə'dʌlt/ *adj* **1** fully developed and mature; grown-up **2** of or befitting adults <*an* ~ *approach to a problem*> **3** suitable only for adults; *broadly* salacious, pornographic <~ *magazines*> [Latin *adultus*, past participle of *adolescere* to grow up, fr *ad* to + *alescere* to grow] – **adulthood** *n*

[2]**adult** *n* a grown-up person or creature; *esp* a human being after an age specified by law (in Britain, 18)

[1]**adulterate** /ə'dultərayt‖ə'dʌltəreɪt/*vt* to corrupt or make impure by the addition of a foreign or inferior substance – **adulterant** *n or adj*, **adulterator** *n*, **adulteration** *n*

[2]**adulterate** /ə'dultərət‖ə'dʌltərət/ *adj* being adulterated, debased, or impure

adulterer /ə'dultərə‖ə'dʌltərə/, *fem* **adulteress** /-ris‖-rɪs/ *n* sby who commits adultery

adultery /ə'dultəri‖ə'dʌltərɪ/ *n* (an act of) voluntary sexual intercourse between a married person and sby other than his/her spouse – **adulterous** *adj*, **adulterously** *adv*

adumbrate /'adəmbrayt‖'ædəmbreɪt/ *vt* **1** to foreshadow (a future event) vaguely **2** to outline broadly without details ***USE*** fml – **adumbration** *n*, **adumbrative** *adj*, **adumbratively** *adv*

[1]**advance** /əd'vahns‖əd'vɑːns/ *vt* **1** to bring or move forwards in position or time <~ *the date of the meeting*> **2** to accelerate the growth or progress of; further **3** to raise in rank; promote **4** to supply (money or goods) ahead of time or as a loan **5** to bring (an opinion or argument) forward for notice; propose ~ *vi* **1** to go forwards; proceed **2** to make progress **3** to rise in rank, position, or importance – **advancer** *n*

[2]**advance** *n* **1a** a moving forward **b** (a signal for) forward movement (of troops) **2a** progress in development; an improvement <*an* ~ *in medical technique*> **b** ADVANCEMENT 1a **3** a friendly or esp an amorous approach – usu pl <*her attitude discouraged all* ~s> **4** (a provision of) money or goods supplied before a return is received – **in advance** beforehand

[3]**advance** *adj* **1** made, sent, or provided ahead of time **2** going or situated ahead of others <*an* ~ *party of soldiers*>

advanced *adj* **1** far on in time or course <*a man* ~ *in years*> **2** beyond the elementary; more developed <~ *chemistry*>

Ad'vanced ˌlevel *n*, *often cap L* an examination that is the second of the 3 levels of the British General Certificate of Education and is a partial qualification for university entrance

ad'vancement /-mənt‖-mənt/ *n* **1a** (a) promotion or elevation to a higher rank or position **b** furtherance towards perfection or completeness <*the* ~ *of knowledge*> **2** an advance of money or value

advantage /əd'vahntij‖əd'vɑːntɪdʒ/ *n* **1** superiority of position or condition <*higher ground gave the enemy the* ~> – often + *of* or *over* **2** a benefit, gain; *esp* one resulting from some course of action <*a mistake which turned out to his* ~> **3** (the score of) the first point won in tennis after deuce – **to advantage** so as to produce a favourable impression or effect

advantageous /ˌadv(ə)n'tayjəs‖ˌædv(ə)n-'teɪdʒəs/ *adj* giving an advantage; favourable – **advantageously** *adv*

Advent /'advent, -vənt‖'ædvent, -vənt/ *n* **1** the 4-week period before Christmas, observed by some Christians as a season of prayer and fasting **2** the coming of Christ to earth as a human being **3** *not cap* a coming into being; an arrival <*the* ~ *of spring*>

adventitious /ˌadvən'tishəs, -ven-‖ˌædvən-'tɪʃəs, -ven-/ *adj* **1** coming accidentally or casually from another source; extraneous **2** occurring sporadically or in an unusual place <~ *buds on a plant*> – **adventitiously** *adv*, **adventitiousness** *n*

[1]**adventure** /əd'venchə‖əd'ventʃə/ *n* **1** an undertaking involving danger, risks, and uncertainty of outcome; *broadly* (an) exciting or remarkable experience **2** an enterprise involving financial risk – **adventuresome** *adj*, **adventurous** *adj*, **adventurously** *adv*, **adventurousness** *n*

[2]**adventure** *vt* to venture, risk ~ *vi* **1** to hazard oneself; dare to go or enter **2** to take a risk

adventurer /əd'venchərə‖əd'ventʃərə/, *fem* **adventuress** /-ris‖-rɪs/ *n* **1** sby who takes part in an adventure; *esp* SOLDIER OF FORTUNE **2** sby who seeks wealth or position by unscrupulous means

adverb /'advuhb‖'ædvɜːb/ *n* a word that modifies a verb, an adjective, another adverb, a preposition, a phrase, a clause, or a sentence, and that answers such questions as how?, when?, where?, etc – **adverbial** *adj*, **adverbially** *adv*

adversary /'advəs(ə)ri‖'ædvəs(ə)rɪ/ *n* an enemy, opponent, or opposing faction

adverse /'advuhs, əd'vuhs‖'ædvɜːs, əd'vɜːs/ *adj* **1** acting against or in a contrary direction <*hindered by* ~ *winds*> **2** unfavourable <~ *criticism*> – **adversely** *adv*, **adverseness** *n*

adversity /əd'vuhsəti‖əd'vɜːsətɪ/ *n* a condition of suffering, affliction, or hardship

[1]**advert** /əd'vuht‖əd'vɜːt/ *vi* to make a (glancing) reference or refer casually *to* – fml

[2]**advert** /'advuht‖'ædvɜːt/ *n*, *chiefly Br* an advertisement

advertise /'advətiez‖'ædvətaɪz/ *vt* **1** to make publicly and generally known <~d *her presence by sneezing*> **2** to announce (e g an article for sale or a vacancy) publicly, esp in the press **3** to encourage sales or patronage of, esp by emphasizing desirable qualities ~ *vi* **1** to encourage sales or patronage, esp by description in the mass media **2** to seek *for* by means of advertising – **advertiser** *n*

advertisement /əd'vuhtismənt, -tiz-, 'advə-ˌtiezmənt‖əd'vɜːtɪsmənt, -tɪz-, 'ædvəˌtaɪzmənt/ *n* a public notice; *esp* one published, broadcast, or displayed publicly to advertise a product, service, etc

advertising /'advəˌtiezing‖'ædvəˌtaɪzɪŋ/ *n* **1** the action of calling sthg to the attention of the public, esp by paid announcements **2** advertisements **3** the profession of preparing advertisements for publication or broadcast

advice /əd'vies‖əd'vaɪs/ *n* **1** recommendation

regarding a decision or course of conduct <*my ~ to you is: don't do it*> **2** communication, esp from a distance; intelligence – usu pl **3** an official notice concerning a business transaction <*a remittance ~*>

advisable /əd'viezəbl‖əd'vaɪzəbl/ *adj* fitting to be advised or done; prudent – **advisability** *n*, **advisably** *adv*

advise /əd'viez‖əd'vaɪz/ *vt* **1a** to give advice to <*~ her to try a drier climate*> **b** to caution, warn <*~ him against going*> **2** to give information or notice to; inform <*~ his friends of his intentions*> ~ *vi* to give advice – **adviser, advisor** *n*

ad'vised *adj* **1** thought out; considered – chiefly in *ill-advised, well-advised* **2** informed – in *keep someone advised* – **advisedly** *adv*

advisory /əd'viez(ə)ri‖əd'vaɪz(ə)rɪ/ *adj* **1** having or exercising power to advise **2** containing or giving advice

advocacy /'advəkəsi‖'ædvəkəsɪ/ *n* **1** active support or pleading <*her ~ of reform*> **2** the function of an advocate

[1]**advocate** /'advəkət‖'ædvəkət/ *n* **1** a professional pleader before a tribunal or court **2** one who defends or supports a cause or proposal

[2]**advocate** /'advəkayt‖'ædvəkeɪt/ *vt* to plead in favour of – **advocator** *n*, **advocatory** *adj*

adze, *NAm chiefly* **adz** /adz‖ædz/ *n* a tool that has the blade at right angles to the handle for cutting or shaping wood

aegis /'eejis‖'iːdʒɪs/ *n* auspices, sponsorship <*under the ~ of the education department*>

aeon, **eon** /'ee·ən, 'ee,on‖'iːən, 'iː,ɒn/ *n* **1** an immeasurably or indefinitely long period of time **2** a unit of geological time equal to 1000 million years

aer- /eər-‖eər-/, **aero-** *comb form* **1** air; atmosphere <aer*ate*> **2** gas <aero*sol*> **3** aircraft <aero*drome*>

aerate /'eərayt, -'-‖'eəreɪt, -'-/ *vt* **1** to combine, supply, charge, or impregnate with a gas, esp air, oxygen, or carbon dioxide **2** to make effervescent – **aerator** *n*, **aeration** *n*

[1]**aerial** /'eəri·əl‖'eərɪəl/ *adj* **1a** of or occurring in the air or atmosphere **b** consisting of air <*~ particles*> **c** growing in the air rather than in the ground or water <*~ roots*> **d** operating overhead on elevated cables or rails <*an ~ railway*> **2** lacking substance; thin **3a** of aircraft <*~ navigation*> **b** by or from an aircraft <*~ photo*> – **aerially** *adv*

[2]**aerial** *n* a conductor (e g a wire) or arrangement of conductors designed to radiate or receive radio waves

aerie /'eəri, 'iəri‖'eərɪ, 'ɪərɪ/ *n* an eyrie

aero /'eəroh‖'eərəʊ/ *adj* of aircraft or aeronautics <*an ~ engine*>

aerobatics /,eərə'batiks‖,eərə'bætɪks/ *n pl but sing or pl in constr* the performance of feats (e g rolls) in an aircraft – **aerobatic** *adj*

aerobics /eə'rohbiks‖eə'rəʊbɪks/ *n pl but sing or pl in constr* a system of physical exercises designed to improve respiration and circulation, usu executed to music and resembling a dance routine

aerodrome /'eərə,drohm‖'eərə,drəʊm/ *n, chiefly Br* an airfield

aerodynamics /,eərohdie'namiks, -di-‖,eərəʊdaɪ'næmɪks, -dɪ-/ *n pl but sing or pl in constr* the dynamics of the motion of (solid bodies moving through) gases (e g air) – **aerodynamic** *adj*, **aerodynamically** *adv*, **aerodynamicist** *n*

aerofoil /'eərə,foyl, -roh-‖'eərə,fɔɪl, -rəʊ-/ *n, chiefly Br* a body (e g an aircraft wing) designed to provide an aerodynamic reaction

aeronautics /,eərə'nawtiks‖,eərə'nɔːtɪks/ *n pl but sing in constr* the art or science of flight – **aeronautical** *adj*, **aeronautically** *adv*

aeroplane /'eərəplayn‖'eərəpleɪn/ *n, chiefly Br* an aircraft that is heavier than air, has nonrotating wings from which it derives its lift, and is mechanically propelled (e g by a propeller or jet engine)

aerosol /'eərəsol‖'eərəsɒl/ *n* **1** a suspension of fine solid or liquid particles in gas (e g fog or smoke) **2** a substance dispersed from a pressurized container as an aerosol **3** AEROSOL CONTAINER

'aerosol con,tainer *n* a metal container for substances in aerosol form

[1]**aerospace** /'eəroh,spays‖'eərəʊ,speɪs/ *n* **1** (a branch of physical science dealing with) the earth's atmosphere and the space beyond **2** the aerospace industry

[2]**aerospace** *adj* of or relating to aerospace, to vehicles used in aerospace or the manufacture of such vehicles, or to travel in aerospace

Aertex /'eə,teks‖'eə,teks/ *trademark* – used for a cellular cotton fabric

aesthete, *NAm also* **esthete** /'ees,theet‖'iːs–,θiːt/ *n* **1** one who has or professes a developed sensitivity to the beautiful in art or nature **2** one who affects concern for the arts and indifference to practical affairs

aesthetic /ees'thetik, es-, əs-‖iːs'θetɪk, es-, əs-/ *also* **aesthetical** /-kl‖-kl/, *NAm also* **esthetic** *also* **esthetical** *adj* **1a** of or dealing with aesthetics or the appreciation of the beautiful **b** artistic <*a work of ~ value*> **2** having a developed sense of beauty – **aesthetically** *adv*

aesthetics /ees'thetiks‖iːs'θetɪks/, *NAm also* **esthetics** /ees-, es-‖iːs-, es-/ *n pl but sing or pl in constr* a branch of philosophy dealing with the nature of the beautiful, with judgments concerning beauty and taste, and with theories of criticism in the arts – **aesthetician** *n*

aether /'eethə‖'iːθə/ *n* ETHER 1, 2

aetiology, *chiefly NAm* **etiology** /,eeti'oləji‖,iːtɪ'ɒlədʒɪ/ *n* (the study of) the causes or origin, specif of a disease or abnormal condition – **aetiologic, aetiological** *adj*, **aetiologically** *adv*

afar /ə'fah‖ə'fɑː/ *adv or n* (from, to, or at) a great distance <*saw her ~ off*> <*saw him from ~*>

affable /'afəbl‖'æfəbl/ *adj* **1** being pleasant and relaxed in talking to others **2** characterized by ease and friendliness; benign – **affably** *adv*, **affability** *n*

affair /ə'feə‖ə'feə/ *n* **1a** *pl* commercial, professional, or public business or matters <*world ~s*> **b** a particular or personal concern <*that's my ~, not yours*> **2a** a procedure, action, or occasion only vaguely specified **b** a social event; a party **3** *also* **affaire, affaire de coeur** a romantic or passionate attachment between 2 people who are not married to each other, often of considerable but limited duration **4** a matter causing public anxiety, controversy, or scandal **5** an object or collection of objects only vaguely specified – used with a descriptive or qualifying term; infml *<the house was a 2-storey ~>*

[1]**affect** /ə'fekt‖ə'fekt/ *vt* **1** to be given to *<~ flashy clothes>* **2** to put on a pretence of (being); feign *<~ indifference>*

[2]**affect** *vt* **1** to have a material effect on or produce an alteration in *<paralysis ~ed his limbs>* **2** to act on (e g a person or his/her mind or feelings) so as to effect a response *<was deeply ~ed by the news>*

affectation /ˌafek'taysh(ə)n‖ˌæfek'teɪʃ(ə)n/ *n* **1** an insincere display (e g of a quality not really possessed) *<the ~ of righteous indignation>* **2** a deliberately assumed peculiarity of speech or conduct; an artificiality

affected /ə'fektid‖ə'fektɪd/ *adj* **1** inclined, disposed *towards* – chiefly in *well-affected, ill-affected* **2a** given to affectation **b** assumed artificially or falsely; pretended *<an ~ interest in art>* – **affectedly** *adv*, **affectedness** *n*

affecting /ə'fekting‖ə'fektɪŋ/ *adj* evoking a strong emotional response; moving – **affectingly** *adv*

[1]**affection** /ə'feksh(ə)n‖ə'fekʃ(ə)n/ *n* **1** emotion as compared with reason – often pl with sing. meaning **2** tender and lasting attachment; fondness – **affectional** *adj*, **affectionally** *adv*

[2]**affection** *n* a disease, malady, or other bodily condition

affectionate /ə'feksh(ə)nət‖ə'fekʃ(ə)nət/ *adj* showing affection or warm regard; loving – **affectionately** *adv*

affiance /ə'fie·əns‖ə'faɪəns/ *vt* to promise (oneself or another) solemnly in marriage; betroth

affidavit /ˌafi'dayvit‖ˌæfɪ'deɪvɪt/ *n* a sworn written statement for use as judicial proof [Medieval Latin, he has made an oath, fr *affidare* to pledge, deriv of Latin *ad* to + *fides* faith]

[1]**affiliate** /ə'filiayt‖ə'fɪlɪeɪt/ *vt* to attach as a member or branch – + *to* or *with* *<the union is ~d to the TUC>* ~ *vi* to connect or associate oneself *with* another, often in a dependent or subordinate position; combine – **affiliation** *n*

[2]**affiliate** /ə'filiayt, -ət‖ə'fɪlɪeɪt, -ət/ *n* an affiliated person or organization

afˌfili'ation ˌorder /əˌfili'aysh(ə)n‖əˌfɪlɪ'eɪʃ(ə)n/ *n* a legal order that the father of an illegitimate child must pay towards its maintenance

affinity /ə'finəti‖ə'fɪnətɪ/ *n* **1** SYMPATHY 2a *<this mysterious ~ between us>* **2** an attraction, esp between substances, causing them to combine chemically **3** resemblance based on relationship or causal connection

affirm /ə'fuhm‖ə'fɜːm/ *vt* **1a** to validate, confirm **b** to state positively **2** to assert (e g a judgment of a lower court) as valid; ratify ~ *vi* **1** to testify by affirmation **2** to uphold a judgment or decree of a lower court

affirmation /ˌafə'maysh(ə)n‖ˌæfə'meɪʃ(ə)n/ *n* **1** sthg affirmed; a positive assertion **2** a solemn declaration made by sby who conscientiously declines taking an oath

[1]**affirmative** /ə'fuhmətiv‖ə'fɜːmətɪv/ *adj* **1** asserting or answering that the fact is so *<gave an ~ nod>* **2** favouring or supporting a proposition or motion *<an ~ vote>* **3** *chiefly NAm* positive *<an ~ responsibility>* – **affirmatively** *adv*

[2]**affirmative** *n* **1** an expression (e g the word *yes*) of agreement or assent **2** an affirmative proposition

[1]**affix** /ə'fiks‖ə'fɪks/ *vt* **1** to attach (physically) *<~ a stamp to a letter>*; *esp* to add in writing *<~ a signature>* **2** to impress *<~ed his seal>* – **affixable** *adj*, **affixment, affixation, affixture** *n*

[2]**affix** /'afiks‖'æfɪks/ *n* **1** an addition to the beginning or end of or an insertion in a word or root to produce a derivative word or inflectional form **2** an appendage – **affixal, affixial** *adj*

afflict /ə'flikt‖ə'flɪkt/ *vt* **1** to distress so severely as to cause persistent suffering **2** to trouble *<~ed with shyness>*

affliction /ə'fliksh(ə)n‖ə'flɪkʃ(ə)n/ *n* **1** great suffering **2** a cause of persistent pain or distress

affluent /'afloo·ənt‖'æflʊənt/ *adj* **1** flowing in abundance **2** having a generously sufficient supply of material possessions; wealthy – **affluence, affluency** *n*, **affluently** *adv*

afford /ə'fawd‖ə'fɔːd/ *vt* **1a** to be able to do or to bear without serious harm – esp + *can* *<you can't ~ to neglect your health>* **b** to be able to bear the cost of *<~ a new coat>* **2** to provide, supply *<her letters ~ no clue to her intentions>* – **affordable** *adj*

afforest /a'forist‖æ'fɒrɪst/ *vt* to establish or plant forest cover on – **afforestation** *n*

affray /ə'fray‖ə'freɪ/ *n* a (public) brawl

affront /ə'frunt‖ə'frʌnt/ *vt* to insult by openly insolent or disrespectful behaviour or language; give offence to – **affront** *n*

Afghan /'afgan‖'æfgæn/ *n* **1** a native or inhabitant of Afghanistan **2** the language of the Pathan people of Afghanistan **3** *not cap* a blanket or shawl of coloured wool knitted or crocheted in strips or squares **4 Afghan, Afghan hound** a tall hunting dog with a coat of silky thick hair – **Afghan** *adj*

aficionado /əˌfishyə'nahdoh‖əˌfɪʃjə'nɑːdəʊ/, *fem* **aficionada** /-'nahdə‖-'nɑːdə/ *n, pl* **aficionados,** *fem* **aficionadas** a devotee, fan *<~s of the bullfight>* [Spanish, fr *afición* affection, fr Latin *affectio*]

afield /ə'feeld‖ə'fiːld/ *adv* **1** to, in, or on the field **2** (far) away from home; abroad **3** out of the way; astray *<irrelevant remarks that carried us far ~>*

afire /ə'fie·ə‖ə'faɪə/ *adj or adv* on fire *<~ with enthusiasm>*

aflame /ə'flaym‖ə'fleɪm/ *adj or adv* afire

afloat /ə'floht‖ə'fləʊt/ *adj or adv* **1a** borne (as if) on the water or air **b** at sea or on ship **2** free of debt **3** circulating about; rumoured *<nasty stories were ~>* **4** flooded with or submerged under water

afoot /ə'foot‖ə'fʊt/ *adv or adj* **1** on foot **2** (in the process of) happening; astir *<there's trouble ~>*

aforementioned /ə'fawˌmenshənd‖ə'fɔːˌmenʃənd/ *adj* mentioned previously

aforesaid /əˈfawˌsed‖əˈfɔːˌsed/ *adj* aforementioned

aforethought /əˈfawˌthawt‖əˈfɔːˌθɔːt/ *adj* premeditated, deliberate – fml; esp in *with malice aforethought*

a fortiori /ˌay fawtiˈawri‖ˌeɪ fɔːtɪˈɔːrɪ/ *adv* with still greater reason or certainty – used in drawing a conclusion that is inferred to be even more certain than another <*if he can afford a house,* ~, *he can afford a tent*>

afraid /əˈfrayd‖əˈfreɪd/ *adj* **1** filled with fear or apprehension <~ *of machines*> <~ *for his job*> **2** regretfully of the opinion – in apology for an utterance <*I'm* ~ *I won't be able to go*>

afresh /əˈfresh‖əˈfreʃ/ *adv* anew, again

African /ˈafrikən‖ˈæfrɪkən/ *n or adj* (a native or inhabitant) of Africa – **Africanness** *n*

Afrikaans /ˌafriˈkahnz‖ˌæfrɪˈkɑːnz/ *n* a language of S Africa developed from 17th-c Dutch

Afrikaner /ˌafriˈkahnə‖ˌæfrɪˈkɑːnə/ *n* an Afrikaans-speaking S African of European, esp Dutch, descent

Afro /ˈafroh‖ˈæfrəʊ/ *n or adj, pl* **Afros** (a hairstyle) shaped into a round curly bushy mass

Afro- /afroh-‖æfrəʊ-/, **Afr-** *comb form* African <Afro-*American*>; African and <Afro-*Asiatic*>

[1]aft /ahft‖ɑːft/ *adv* near, towards, or in the stern of a ship or the tail of an aircraft

[2]aft *adj* rearward; [4]AFTER 2 <*the* ~ *decks*>

[1]after /ˈahftə‖ˈɑːftə/ *adv* **1** BEHIND 1b **2** afterwards

[2]after *prep* **1** behind in place or order <*shut the door* ~ *you*> – used in yielding precedence <~ *you!*> or in asking for the next turn <~ *you with the pencil*> **2a** following in time; later than <~ *breakfast*> **b** continuously succeeding <*saw play* ~ *play*> **c** in view or in spite of (sthg preceding) <~ *all our advice*> **3** – used to indicate the goal or purpose of an action <*go* ~ *gold*> **4** so as to resemble: e g **4a** in accordance with **b** in allusion to the name of **c** in the characteristic manner of **d** in imitation of **5** about, concerning <*ask* ~ *his health*>

[3]after *conj* later than the time when

[4]after *adj* **1** later, subsequent <*in* ~ *years*> **2** located towards the rear or stern of a ship, aircraft, etc

ˌafter ˈall *adv* **1** in spite of everything **2** it must be remembered <*he can't swim but,* ~, *he's only 2*>

ˈafterˌbirth /-ˌbuhth‖-ˌbɜːθ/ *n* the placenta and foetal membranes expelled after delivery of a baby, young animal, etc

ˈafterˌcare /-ˌkeə‖-ˌkeə/ *n* the care, treatment, etc given to people discharged from a hospital or other institution

ˈafterefˌfect /-iˌfekt‖-ɪˌfekt/ *n* an effect that follows its cause after an interval of time

ˈafterˌglow /-ˌgloh‖-ˌgləʊ/ *n* **1** a glow remaining (e g in the sky) where a light source has disappeared **2** a vestige of past splendour, success, or happy emotion

ˈafterˌlife /-ˌlief‖-ˌlaɪf/ *n* **1** an existence after death **2** a later period in one's life

ˈafterˌmath /-ˌmahth, -ˌmath‖-ˌmɑːθ, -ˌmæθ/ *n* **1** a second growth of forage after the harvest of an earlier crop **2** a consequence, result **3** the period immediately following a usu ruinous event

ˌafterˈnoon /-ˈnoohn‖-ˈnuːn/ *n* the time between noon and sunset – **afternoon** *adj*

ˌafterˈnoons *adv, chiefly NAm* in the afternoon repeatedly; on any afternoon

afters /ˈahftəz‖ˈɑːftəz/ *n pl, Br* a dessert – infml

ˈafter-ˌshave *n* (a) usu scented lotion for use on the face after shaving

ˈafterˌtaste /-ˌtayst‖-ˌteɪst/ *n* persistence of a flavour or impression <*the bitter* ~ *of a quarrel*>

ˈafterˌthought /-ˌthawt‖-ˌθɔːt/ *n* **1** an idea occurring later **2** sthg added later

ˈafterwards /-woodz‖-wʊdz/ *adv* after that; subsequently, thereafter <*for years* ~>

again /əˈgayn, əˈgen‖əˈgeɪn, əˈgen/ *adv* **1** so as to be as before <*put it back* ~> **2** another time; once more **3** on the other hand <*he might go, and* ~ *he might not*> **4** further; IN ADDITION <*could eat as much* ~>

[1]against /əˈgaynst, əˈgenst‖əˈgeɪnst, əˈgenst/ *prep* **1a** in opposition or hostility to <*the rule* ~ *smoking*> **b** unfavourable to <*his appearance is* ~ *him*> **c** as a defence or protection from <*warned them* ~ *opening the box*> **2** compared or contrasted with <*cost only £2, as* ~ *£3 at home*> **3a** in preparation or provision for <*saving* ~ *his retirement*> **b** with respect to; towards **4** (in the direction of and) in contact with <*rain beat* ~ *the windows*> **5** in a direction opposite to the motion or course of; counter to <*swam* ~ *the tide*> **6** in exchange for

[2]against *adj* **1** opposed to a motion or measure **2** unfavourable to a specified degree; *esp* unfavourable to a win <*the odds are 2 to 1* ~>

[1]agape /əˈgayp‖əˈgeɪp/ *adj* **1** wide open; gaping **2** in a state of wonder <~ *with expectation*>

[2]agape /əˈgahpay, ˈahgəˌpay‖əˈgɑːpeɪ, ˈɑːgəˌpeɪ/ *n* LOVE FEAST – **agapeic** *adj*

agar-agar /ˌaygahr ˈaygah‖ˌeɪgɑːr ˈeɪgɑː/ *n* a gelatinous extract from any of various red algae used esp in culture media or as a gelling agent in foods

agate /ˈagət, ˈagayt‖ˈægət, ˈægeɪt/ *n* a mineral used as a gem composed of quartz of various colours, often arranged in bands

agave /əˈgayvi‖əˈgeɪvɪ/ *n* any of a N or S American genus of plants of the daffodil family with spiny leaves

[1]age /ayj‖eɪdʒ/ *n* **1a** the length of time a person has lived or a thing existed <*a boy 10 years of* ~> **b** the time of life at which some particular qualification, power, or capacity arises <*the voting* ~ *is 18*> **c** a stage of life <*the 7* ~s *of man*> **2** a generation <*the* ~s *to come*> **3** a period of time dominated by a central figure or prominent feature <*the* ~ *of Pericles*>: e g **3a** a period in history <*the steam* ~> **b** a cultural period marked by the prominence of a specified item <*the atomic* ~> **c** a division of geological time, usu shorter than an epoch **4** an individual's development in terms of the years required by an average individual for similar development <*a mental* ~ *of 6*> **5** a long time – usu pl with sing. meaning; infml <*haven't seen* *him for* ~s> – **of age** of legal adult status

[2]**age** *vb* **aging, ageing** /ˈayjing‖ˈeɪdʒɪŋ/ *vi* **1** to become old; show the effects of increasing age **2** to become mellow or mature; ripen ~ *vt* **1** to cause to seem old, esp prematurely <*illness has* ~d *him*> **2** to bring to a state fit for use or to maturity

-age /-ij‖-ɪdʒ/ *suffix* (→ *n*) **1** aggregate or collection of <*acre*age> **2a** action or process of <*haul*age> **b** cumulative result of <*break*age> **c** rate or amount of <*dos*age> **3** house or place of <*orphan*age> **4** condition or rank of <*peer*age> **5** fee or charge for <*post*age>

aged /ˈayjid‖ˈeɪdʒɪd; *sense 1b* ayjd‖eɪdʒd/ *adj* **1** grown old: e g **1a** of an advanced age **b** having attained a specified age <*a man* ~ *40 years*> **2** typical of old age <*his* ~ *steps*> – **agedness** *n*

ageism /ˈay,jiz(ə)m‖ˈeɪ,dʒɪz(ə)m/ *n* discrimination against a person on the grounds of his/her age –**ageist** *adj*

ageless /ˈayjlis‖ˈeɪdʒlɪs/ *adj* **1** never growing old or showing the effects of age **2** timeless, eternal <~ *truths*> – **agelessly** *adv*, **agelessness** *n*

agency /ˈayjənsi‖ˈeɪdʒənsɪ/ *n* **1** a power or force through which a result is achieved; instrumentality <*communicated through the* ~ *of his ambassador*> **2** the function or place of business of an agent or representative **3** an establishment that does business for another <*an advertising* ~>

agenda /əˈjendə‖əˈdʒendə/ *n* **1** a list of items to be discussed or business to be transacted (e g at a meeting) **2** a plan of procedure; a programme [Latin, pl of *agendum* a thing to be done, fr *agere* to drive, do]

agent /ˈayjənt‖ˈeɪdʒənt/ *n* **1a** sthg or sby that produces an effect or that acts or exerts power **b** a chemically, physically, or biologically active substance **2** a person who acts for or in the place of another by authority from him/her: e g **2a** a business representative **b** one employed by or controlling an agency <*my literary* ~> **3a** a representative of a government **b** a spy

agent provocateur /,ahzhonh provokəˈtuh, ,ayjənt ‖,ɑːʒɑ̃ prɒvɒkəˈtɜː, ,eɪdʒənt (*Fr* ajɑ̃ provokatœːr)/ *n, pl* **agents provocateurs** /~/ a person employed to incite suspected people to some open action that will make them liable to punishment

,age of conˈsent *n* the age at which one is legally competent to give consent; *specif* that at which a person, esp a female, may consent to sexual intercourse

[1]**agglomerate** /əˈglomərayt‖əˈglɒməreɪt/ *vb* to (cause to) gather into a cluster or disorderly mass

[2]**agˈglomerate** /-rət‖-rət/ *adj* gathered into a ball, mass, or cluster

[3]**agˈglomerate** /-rət‖-rət/ *n* **1** a disorderly mass or collection **2** a rock composed of irregular volcanic fragments

agglutinate /əˈgloohti,nayt‖əˈgluːtɪ,neɪt/ *vt* **1** to cause to stick; fasten together (as if) with glue **2** to combine into a compound; attach to a base as an affix **3** to cause to undergo agglutination ~ *vi* to form words by agglutination – **agglutinability** *n*

agglutination /ə,gloohtiˈnaysh(ə)n‖ə,gluːtɪˈneɪʃ(ə)n/ *n* **1** the formation of compound words by combining (parts of) other words which already have a single definite meaning **2** the collection of red blood cells or other minute suspended particles into clumps, esp as a response to a specific antibody – **agglutinative** *adj*

aggrand·ize, -ise /əˈgrandiez, ˈagrən-‖əˈgrændaɪz, ˈægrən-/ *vt* **1** to give a false air of greatness to; praise highly **2** to enhance the power, wealth, position, or reputation of – **aggrandizement** *n*

aggravate /ˈagrəvayt‖ˈægrəveɪt/ *vt* **1** to make worse or more severe **2** to annoy, irritate – disapproved of by some speakers [Latin *aggravare* to make heavier, fr *ad* to + *gravare* to burden – see GRIEVE] – **aggravation** *n*

[1]**aggregate** /ˈagrigət‖ˈægrɪgət/ *adj* formed by the collection of units or particles into a body, mass, or amount: e g **a** *of a flower* clustered in a dense mass or head **b** *of a fruit* formed from the several ovaries of a single flower **c** taking all units as a whole; total <~ *earnings*> – **aggregately** *adv*, **aggregateness** *n*

[2]**aggregate** /ˈagri,gayt‖ˈægrɪ,geɪt/ *vt* **1** to bring together into a mass or whole **2** to amount to (a specified total) – **aggregative** *adj*, **aggregation** *n*, **aggregational** *adj*

[3]**aggregate** /ˈagrigət‖ˈægrɪgət/ *n* **1** a mass of loosely associated parts; an assemblage **2** the whole amount; the sum total **3a** a rock composed of closely packed mineral crystals **b** sand, gravel, etc for mixing with cement to make concrete **c** a clustered mass of individual particles of various shapes and sizes that is considered to be the basic structural unit of soil

aggression /əˈgreshən‖əˈgreʃən/ *n* **1** a hostile attack; *esp* one made without just cause **2** attack, encroachment; *esp* unprovoked violation by one country of the territory of another **3** hostile, injurious, or destructive behaviour or outlook – **aggressor** *n*

aggressive /əˈgresiv‖əˈgresɪv/ *adj* **1a** tending towards or practising aggression <*an* ~ *foreign policy*> **b** ready to attack <*an* ~ *fighter*> **2** forceful, dynamic <*an* ~ *salesman*> – **aggressively** *adv*, **aggressiveness** *n*

agˈgrieved /əˈgreevd‖əˈgriːvd/ *adj* showing or expressing resentment; hurt – **aggrievedly** *adv*

aggro /ˈagroh‖ˈægrəʊ/ *n, chiefly Br* **1** provocation, hostility **2** deliberate aggression or violence ***USE*** infml

aghast /əˈgahst‖əˈgɑːst/ *adj* suddenly struck with terror or amazement; shocked

agile /ˈajiel‖ˈædʒaɪl/ *adj* **1** quick, easy, and graceful in movement **2** mentally quick and resourceful – **agilely** *adv*, **agility** *n*

agitate /ˈajitayt‖ˈædʒɪteɪt/ *vt* **1** to move, shake **2** to excite and often trouble the mind or feelings of; disturb ~ *vi* to work to arouse public feeling for or against a cause <~d *for better schools*> – **agitatedly** *adv*, **agitation** *n*, **agitational** *adj*

agitator /ˈajitaytə‖ˈædʒɪteɪtə/ *n* **1** sby who stirs up public feeling on controversial issues **2** a device or apparatus for stirring or shaking

aglow /ə'gloh‖ə'gləʊ/ *adj* radiant with warmth or excitement

[1]**agnostic** /ag'nostik, əg-‖æg'nɒstɪk, əg-/ *n* sby who holds the view that any ultimate reality is unknown and prob unknowable; *also* one who doubts the existence of God [Greek *agnōstos* unknown, unknowable, fr *a-* not + *gnōstos* known, fr *gignōskein* to know] – **agnosticism** *n*

[2]**agnostic** *adj* of or being an agnostic or the beliefs of agnostics

Agnus Dei /ˌagnəs 'day·ee‖ˌægnəs 'deɪiː/ *n* a liturgical prayer addressed to Christ as Saviour, often set to music

ago /ə'goh‖ə'gəʊ/ *adj or adv* earlier than now <*10 years* ~>

agog /ə'gog‖ə'gɒg/ *adj* full of intense anticipation or excitement; eager

agon·ize, -ise /'agəniez‖'ægənaɪz/ *vt* to cause to suffer agony ~ *vi* **1** to suffer agony or anguish **2** to make a great effort

'**agon·ized, -ised** *adj* characterized by, suffering, or expressing agony

agonizing, -ising /'agəniezing‖'ægənaɪzɪŋ/ *adj* causing agony; painful – **agonizingly** *adv*

agony /'agəni‖'ægənɪ/ *n* **1** intense and often prolonged pain or suffering of mind or body; anguish **2** the struggle that precedes death <*his last* ~>

agoraphobia /ˌagrə'fohbi·ə‖ˌægrə'fəʊbɪə/ *n* abnormal dread of being in open spaces – **agoraphobic** *n or adj*, **agoraphobe** *n*

agrarian /ə'greəri·ən‖ə'greərɪən/ *adj* **1** of or relating to (the tenure of) fields **2** (characteristic) of farmers or agricultural life or interests

agree /ə'gree‖ə'griː/ *vt* **1** to admit, concede – usu + a clause <*I* ~ *that you're right*> **2** to bring into harmony **3** *chiefly Br* to come to terms on, usu after discussion; accept by mutual consent ~ *vi* **1** to give assent; accede – often + *to* <~ *to your proposal*> **2a** to be of one mind – often + *with* <*I* ~ *with you*> **b** to get along together **3a** to correspond **b** to be consistent **4** to suit the health – + *with* <*onions don't* ~ *with me*> **5** to correspond in grammatical gender, number, case, or person

agreeable /ə'gree·əbl‖ə'griːəbl/ *adj* **1** to one's liking; pleasing **2** willing to agree or consent – **agreeableness** *n*, **agreeably** *adv*

a'greement /-mənt‖-mənt/ *n* **1a** harmony of opinion or feeling **b** correspondence <~ *between the copy and the original*> **2a** an arrangement laying down terms, conditions, etc **b** a treaty **3** (the language or document embodying) a legally binding contract

agriculture /'agriˌkulchə‖'ægrɪˌkʌltʃə/ *n* the theory and practice of cultivating and producing crops from the soil and of raising livestock [French, fr Latin *agricultura*, fr *agr-, ager* field + *cultura* cultivation] – **agricultural** *adj*, **agriculturally** *adv*, **agriculturist, agriculturalist** *n*

agronomy /ə'gronəmi‖ə'grɒnəmɪ/ *n* a branch of agriculture dealing with field-crop production and soil management – **agronomic** *adj*, **agronomically** *adv*, **agronomist** *n*

aground /ə'grownd‖ə'graʊnd/ *adv or adj* on or onto the shore or the bottom of a body of water <*the ship ran* ~>

ague /'aygyooh‖'eɪgjuː/ *n* a (malarial) fever with regularly recurring attacks of chills and sweating – **aguish** *adj*

ah /ah‖ɑː/ *interj* – used to express delight, relief, regret, or contempt

aha /ah'hah‖ɑː'hɑː/ *interj* – used to express surprise, triumph, derision, or amused discovery

ahead /ə'hed‖ə'hed/ *adv or adj* **1a** in a forward direction **b** in front <*the road* ~> **2** in, into, or for the future <*plan* ~> **3** in or towards a better position <*get* ~ *of the rest*>

ahem /ə'hoom‖ə'hʊm/ *interj* – used esp to attract attention or express mild disapproval

ahoy /ə'hoy‖ə'hɔɪ/ *interj* – used chiefly by seamen as a greeting or warning <*land* ~>

[1]**aid** /ayd‖eɪd/ *vt* **1** to give assistance to; help **2** to bring about the accomplishment of; facilitate <~ *his recovery*> – **aider** *n*

[2]**aid** *n* **1** help; assistance; *specif* tangible means of assistance (e g money or supplies) **2a** a helper **b** sthg that helps or supports <*a visual* ~>; *specif* a hearing aid **3** a tribute paid by a vassal to his lord – **in aid of 1** in order to aid; for the use of <*sold her jewels* in aid of *charity*> **2** *Br* for the purpose of <*what's this* in aid of*?*> – infml

aide /ayd, ed‖eɪd, ed/ *n* **1** an aide-de-camp **2** *chiefly NAm* an assistant

ˌ**aide-de-'camp** /də 'kamp‖də 'kæmp/ *n, pl* **aides-de-camp** /~/ an officer in the armed forces acting as a personal assistant to a senior officer [French *aide de camp*, lit., camp assistant]

AIDS /aydz‖eɪdz/ *n* an acute infectious disease caused by a virus attacking cells that normally stimulate the production of antibodies to fight infection [*a*cquired *i*mmune *d*eficiency *s*yndrome]

ail /ayl‖eɪl/ *vt* to give pain, discomfort, or trouble to ~ *vi* to be unwell

aileron /'aylәron, -rən‖'eɪlərɒn, -rən/ *n* a movable control surface of an aircraft wing or a movable aerofoil external to the wing at the trailing edge for giving a rolling motion and providing lateral control

ailment /'aylmənt‖'eɪlmənt/ *n* a bodily disorder or chronic disease

[1]**aim** /aym‖eɪm/ *vi* **1** to direct a course; *specif* to point a weapon at an object **2** to channel one's efforts; aspire **3** to have the intention; mean <~s *to marry a duke*> ~ *vt* **1** to direct or point (e g a weapon) at a target **2** to direct at or towards a specified goal; intend <*books* ~ed *at children*>

[2]**aim** *n* **1a** the pointing of a weapon at a mark **b** the ability to hit a target **c** a weapon's accuracy or effectiveness **2** a clear intention or purpose – **aimless** *adj*, **aimlessly** *adv*, **aimlessness** *n*

ain't /aynt‖eɪnt/ **1** are not **2** is not **3** am not **4** have not **5** has not *USE* chiefly nonstandard or humor in Br but acceptable in *ain't I* meaning "am I not" in NAm

[1]**air** /eə‖eə/ *n* **1a** the mixture of invisible odourless tasteless gases, containing esp nitrogen and oxygen, that surrounds the earth **b** a light breeze **2a** empty unconfined space **b** nothingness <*vanished into thin* ~> **3a(1)** aircraft <*go by* ~> **a(2)** aviation <~ *safety*> **b** the supposed medium of transmission of radio waves; *also* radio, television <*went on the* ~> **4a** the appearance or bearing of a person; demeanour <*an* ~ *of dignity*> **b** *pl* an artificial or

affected manner; haughtiness <*to put on* ~s> **c** outward appearance of a thing <*an* ~ *of luxury*> **d** a surrounding or pervading influence; an atmosphere <*an* ~ *of mystery*> **5** a tune, melody – **in the air 1** not yet settled; uncertain **2** being generally spread round or hinted at <*rumours* in the air *that he will be promoted*>

²air *vt* **1** to expose to the air for drying, freshening, etc; ventilate **2** to expose to public view or bring to public notice **3** *chiefly Br* to expose to heat so as to warm or finish drying <~ *the sheets round the fire*> ~ *vi* to become exposed to the open air

'air ,bed *n, chiefly Br* an inflatable mattress

'air,borne /-,bawn‖-,bɔːn/ *adj* supported or transported by air

'air ,brake *n* **1** a brake operated by compressed air **2** a movable surface projected into the air for slowing an aircraft

'air ,brick *n* a building brick or brick-sized metal box perforated to allow ventilation

'air,bus /-,bus‖-,bʌs/ *n* a subsonic jet passenger aeroplane designed for short intercity flights

air chief marshal *n* an officer holding the second highest rank in the Royal Air Force

air commodore *n* an officer in the Royal Air Force ranking below air vice-marshal

'air-con,dition *vt* to equip (e g a building) with an apparatus for cleaning air and controlling its humidity and temperature; *also* to subject (air) to these processes – **air conditioner** *n*, **air conditioning** *n*

'air-,cool *vt* to cool the cylinders of (an internal-combustion engine) directly by air

'air,craft /-,krahft‖-,krɑːft/ *n, pl* **aircraft** a weight-carrying structure that can travel through the air and is supported either by its own buoyancy or by the dynamic action of the air against its surfaces

'aircraft ,carrier *n* a warship designed so that aircraft can be operated from it

'air,craftman /-mən‖-mən/ *n* a person holding the lowest rank in the Royal Air Force

'air,drop /-,drop‖-,drɒp/ *n* a delivery of cargo or personnel by parachute from an aircraft – **air-drop** *vt*

Airedale /'eə,dayl‖'eə,deɪl/, **,Airedale 'terrier** *n* any of a breed of large terriers with a hard wiry coat that is dark on the back and sides and tan elsewhere [*Airedale*, district in West Yorkshire, England]

'air,field /-,feeld‖-,fiːld/ *n* an area of land maintained for the landing and takeoff of aircraft

'air,flow /-,floh‖-,fləʊ/ *n* the motion of air round a moving or stationary object (e g in wind)

'air ,force *n* the branch of a country's armed forces for air warfare

'air ,gun *n* **1** a gun from which a projectile is propelled by compressed air **2** any of various hand tools that work by compressed air

'air ,hole *n* a hole to admit or discharge air

'air ho,stess *n* a stewardess on an airliner

airily /'eərəli‖'eərəlɪ/ *adv* in an airy manner; jauntily, lightly

'airing ,cupboard *n* a heated cupboard in which esp household linen is aired and kept dry

'air ,lane *n* a path customarily followed by aeroplanes

'airless /-lis‖-lɪs/ *adj* **1** still, windless **2** lacking fresh air; stuffy – **airlessness** *n*

'air ,letter *n* **1** an airmail letter **2** a sheet of airmail stationery that can be folded and sealed with the message inside and the address outside

'air,lift /-,lift‖-,lɪft/ *n* the transport of cargo or passengers by air, usu to an otherwise inaccessible area – **airlift** *vt*

'air,line /-,lien‖-,laɪn/ *n* an organization that provides regular public air transport

'air ,line *n, chiefly NAm* a beeline

'air,liner /-,lienə‖-,laɪnə/ *n* a passenger aircraft operated by an airline

'air ,lock *n* **1** an airtight intermediate chamber (e g in a spacecraft or submerged caisson) which allows movement between 2 areas of different pressures or atmospheres **2** a stoppage of flow caused by air being in a part where liquid ought to circulate

'air,mail /-,mayl‖-,meɪl/ *n* (the postal system using) mail transported by aircraft – **airmail** *vt*

'airman /-mən‖-mən/ *n, pl* **airmen** a civilian or military pilot, aircraft crew member, etc

air marshal *n* an officer in the Royal Air Force ranking below air chief marshal

'air,plane /-,playn‖-,pleɪn/ *n, chiefly NAm* an aeroplane

'air ,pocket *n* a region of down-flowing or rarefied air that causes an aircraft to drop suddenly

airport /'eə,pawt‖'eə,pɔːt/ *n* a fully-equipped airfield that is used as a base for the transport of passengers and cargo by air

'air ,raid *n* an attack by armed aircraft on a surface target

'air,ship /-,ship‖-,ʃɪp/ *n* a gas-filled lighter-than-air self-propelled aircraft that has a steering system

'air,sick /-,sik‖-,sɪk/ *adj* suffering from the motion sickness associated with flying – **airsickness** *n*

'air,space /-,spays‖-,speɪs/ *n* the space lying above the earth or a certain area of land or water; *esp* the space lying above a nation and coming under its jurisdiction

'air,speed /-,speed‖-,spiːd/ *n* the speed (e g of an aircraft) relative to the air

'air,strip /-,strip‖-,strɪp/ *n* LANDING STRIP

'air,tight /-,tiet‖-,taɪt/ *adj* **1** impermeable to air **2** unassailable – **airtightness** *n*

,air-to-'air *adj* (launched) from one aircraft in flight at another

air vice-marshal *n* an officer in the Royal Air Force ranking below air marshal

'air,way /-,way‖-,weɪ/ *n* **1** a passage for air in a mine **2** a designated route along which aircraft fly

'air,worthy /-,wuhdhi‖-,wɜːðɪ/ *adj* fit for operation in the air – **airworthiness** *n*

airy /'eəri‖'eərɪ/ *adj* **1a** not having solid foundation; illusory <~ *promises*> **b** showing lack of concern; flippant **2** being light and graceful in movement or manner **3** delicately thin in texture **4** open to the free circulation of air; breezy **5** high in the air; lofty – poetic – **airiness** *n*

aisle /iel‖aɪl/ *n* **1** the side division of a church separated from the nave by columns or piers **2** *chiefly NAm* a gangway [Middle French *ele, aile* wing, fr Latin *ala*]

aitch /aych‖eɪtʃ/ *n* the letter *h*

ˈaitchˌbone /-ˌbohn‖-ˌbəʊn/ *n* (the cut of beef containing) the hipbone, esp of cattle

ajar /əˈjah‖əˈdʒɑː/ *adj or adv, esp of a door* slightly open

akimbo /əˈkimboh‖əˈkɪmbəʊ/ *adj or adv* having the hands on the hips and the elbows turned outwards

akin /əˈkin‖əˈkɪn/ *adj* **1** descended from a common ancestor **2** essentially similar, related, or compatible *USE* often + *to*

al- – see AD-

[1]**-al** /-(ə)l‖-(ə)l/, **-ial** /-i·əl‖-ɪəl/ *suffix* (*n* → *adj*) (having the character) of <*fictional*>

[2]**-al** *suffix* (*vb* → *n*) action or process of <*withdrawal*>

à la /ˈah lah ‖ˈɑː lɑː (*Fr* a la)/ *prep* **1** in the manner of **2** prepared, flavoured, or served with <*spinach* ~ *crème*>

alabaster /ˈaləbastə, -bah-‖ˈæləbæstə, -bɑː-/ *n* a fine-textured usu white and translucent chalky stone often carved into ornaments – **alabaster, alabastrine** *adj*

à la carte /ˌah lah ˈkaht‖ˌɑː lɑː ˈkɑːt/ *adv or adj* according to a menu that prices each item separately [French, by the bill of fare]

alack /əˈlak‖əˈlæk/ *interj, archaic* – used to express sorrow or regret

alacrity /əˈlakrəti‖əˈlækrətɪ/ *n* promptness or cheerful readiness – fml

[1]**alarm** /əˈlahm‖əˈlɑːm/ *n* **1** a signal (e g a loud noise or flashing light) that warns or alerts; *also* an automatic device that alerts or rouses **2** the fear resulting from the sudden sensing of danger [Middle French *alarme* call to arms, fr Italian *all'arme*, lit., to the weapon]

[2]**alarm** *vt* **1** to give warning to **2** to strike with fear – **alarmingly** *adv*

aˈlarm ˌclock *n* a clock that can be set to sound an alarm at a desired time

alarmism /əˈlahˌmiz(ə)m‖əˈlɑːˌmɪz(ə)m/ *n* the often unwarranted or excessive arousing of fears; scaremongering – **alarmist** *n or adj*

alas /əˈlas, əˈlahs‖əˈlæs, əˈlɑːs/ *interj* – used to express unhappiness, pity, or disappointment

Albanian /ˌalˈbayni·ən‖ˌælˈbeɪnɪən/ *n or adj* (a native or inhabitant or the Indo-European language) of Albania

albatross /ˈalbətros‖ˈælbətrɒs/ *n* any of various large web-footed seabirds related to the petrels

albeit /awlˈbee·it‖ɔːlˈbiːɪt/ *conj* even though – fml

albino /alˈbeenoh‖ælˈbiːnəʊ/ *n, pl* **albinos** an organism with (congenitally) deficient pigmentation; *esp* a human being or other animal with a (congenital) lack of pigment resulting in a white or translucent skin, white or colourless hair, and eyes with a pink pupil – **albinic** *adj*, **albinism** *n*

album /ˈalbəm‖ˈælbəm/ *n* **1** a book with blank pages used for making a collection (e g of stamps or photographs) **2** a recording or collection of recordings issued on 1 or more long-playing gramophone records or cassettes [Latin, a white tablet, fr *albus* white]

albumen /ˈalbyoomin, alˈbyoohmin‖ˈælbjʊmɪn, ælˈbjuːmɪn/ *n* **1** the white of an egg **2** albumin

albumin /ˈalbyoomin, alˈbyoohmin‖ˈælbjʊmɪn, ælˈbjuːmɪn/ *n* any of numerous proteins that occur in large quantities in blood plasma, milk, egg white, plant fluids, etc and are coagulated by heat

alchemy /ˈalkəmi‖ˈælkəmɪ/ *n* **1** a medieval chemical science and philosophical doctrine aiming to achieve the transmutation of the base metals into gold, a cure for disease, and immortality **2** the transformation of sthg common into sthg precious – **alchemist** *n*, **alchemic, alchemical** *adj*

alcohol /ˈalkəhol‖ˈælkəhɒl/ *n* **1** a colourless volatile inflammable liquid that is the intoxicating agent in fermented and distilled drinks and is used also as a solvent **2** any of various organic compounds, specif derived from hydrocarbons, containing the hydroxyl group **3** intoxicating drink containing alcohol; *esp* spirits

[1]**alcoholic** /ˌalkəˈholik‖ˌælkəˈhɒlɪk/ *adj* **1** of, containing, or caused by alcohol **2** affected with alcoholism – **alcoholically** *adv*

[2]**alcoholic** *n* sby affected with alcoholism

alcoholism /ˈalkəhoˌliz(ə)m‖ˈælkəhɒˌlɪz(ə)m/ *n* (a complex chronic psychological and nutritional disorder associated with) excessive and usu compulsive use of alcoholic drinks

alcove /ˈalkohv‖ˈælkəʊv/ *n* **1** a nook or recess off a larger room **2** a niche or arched opening (e g in a wall or hedge) [French *alcôve*, fr Spanish *alcoba*, fr Arabic *al-qubbah* the arch]

alder /ˈawldə‖ˈɔːldə/ *n* any of a genus of trees or shrubs of the birch family that grow in moist ground

alderman /ˈawldəmən‖ˈɔːldəmən/ *n, pl* **aldermen** /-mən‖-mən/ **1** a person governing a kingdom, district, or shire as viceroy for an Anglo-Saxon king **2** a senior member of a county or borough council elected by the other councillors – not used officially in Britain after 1974 – **aldermanic** *adj*

ale /ayl‖eɪl/ *n* **1** beer **2** a malted and hopped alcoholic drink that is usually more bitter, stronger, and heavier than beer

[1]**alert** /əˈluht‖əˈlɜːt/ *adj* **1** watchful, aware **2** active, brisk – **alertly** *adv*, **alertness** *n*

[2]**alert** *n* **1** an alarm or other signal that warns of danger (e g from hostile aircraft) **2** the danger period during which an alert is in effect – **on the alert** on the lookout, esp for danger or opportunity

[3]**alert** *vt* **1** to call to a state of readiness; warn **2** to cause to be aware (e g of a need or responsibility)

ˈA ˌlevel /ay‖eɪ/ *n* ADVANCED LEVEL

alexandrine /ˌaligˈzahndrien‖ˌælɪgˈzɑːndraɪn/ *n* a line of verse consisting of 6 iambic feet – **alexandrine** *adj*

alfalfa /alˈfalfə‖ælˈfælfə/ *n, NAm* lucerne

alfresco *also* **al fresco** /alˈfreskoh‖ælˈfreskəʊ/ *adj or adv* taking place in the open air

alga /ˈalgə‖ˈælgə/ *n, pl* **algae** /ˈalji, -gi‖ˈældʒɪ, -gɪ/ *also* **algas** any of a group of chiefly aquatic nonvascular plants (e g seaweeds and pond scums) – **algal** *adj*, **algoid** *adj*

algebra /ˈaljibrə‖ˈældʒɪbrə/ *n* a branch of

mathematics in which letters, symbols, etc representing various entities are combined according to special rules of operation – **algebraist** *n*, **algebraic** *adj*

-algia /-ˈaljə‖-ˈældʒə/ *comb form* (→ *n*) pain <*neur*algia>

algorithm /ˈalgəˌridhəm‖ˈælgəˌrɪðəm/ *n* a systematic procedure for solving a mathematical problem in a finite number of steps; *broadly* a step-by-step procedure for solving a problem or accomplishing some end – **algorithmic** *adj*

[1]**alias** /ˈayli·əs‖ˈeɪlɪəs/ *adv* otherwise called or known as <*Hancock* ~ *Jones*> [Latin, otherwise, fr *alius* other]

[2]**alias** *n* an assumed name

alibi /ˈaləbie‖ˈæləbaɪ/ *n* **1** (evidence supporting) the plea of having been elsewhere when a crime was committed **2** a plausible excuse, usu intended to avert blame or punishment [Latin, elsewhere, fr *alius* other]

[1]**alien** /ˈayli·ən‖ˈeɪlɪən/ *adj* **1a** of or belonging to another person, place, or thing; strange **b** foreign <~ *property*> **2** differing in nature or character, esp to the extent of being opposed – + *to* <*ideas quite* ~ *to ours*>

[2]**alien** *n* **1** a person from another family, race, or nation; *also* an extraterrestrial being **2** a foreign-born resident who has not been naturalized; *broadly* a foreign-born citizen – **alienage** *n*, **alienism** *n*

alienate /ˈayli·əˌnayt, ˈaylyə-‖ˈeɪlɪəˌneɪt, ˈeɪljə-/ *vt* **1** to convey or transfer (e g property or a right) to another, usu by a specific act **2** to make hostile or indifferent, esp in cases where attachment formerly existed <~d *from their mothers*> **3** to cause to be withdrawn or diverted – **alienator** *n*

alienation /ˌayli·əˈnaysh(ə)n, ˌaylyə-‖ˌeɪlɪəˈneɪʃ(ə)n, ˌeɪljə-/ *n* **1** a conveyance of property to another **2** (a feeling of) withdrawal from or apathy towards one's former attachments or whole social existence

[1]**alight** /əˈliet‖əˈlaɪt/ *vi* **alighted** *also* **alit** /əˈlit‖əˈlɪt/ **1** to come down from sthg: e g **1a** to dismount **b** to disembark **2** to descend from the air and settle; land – **alightment** *n*

[2]**alight** *adj* **1** animated, alive <~ *with merriment*> **2** *chiefly Br* on fire; ignited <*paper caught* ~>

align *also* **aline** /əˈlien‖əˈlaɪn/ *vt* **1** to bring into proper relative position or state of adjustment; *specif* to place (3 or more points) in a straight line **2** to array or position on the side of or against a party or cause <*nations* ~ed *against fascism*> ~ *vi* **1** to join with others in a common cause **2** to be in or come into alignment – **alignment** *n*

[1]**alike** /əˈliek‖əˈlaɪk/ *adj* showing close resemblance without being identical

[2]**alike** *adv* in the same manner, form, or degree; equally <*peasants and nobility* ~>

alimentary /ˌaliˈment(ə)ri‖ˌælɪˈment(ə)rɪ/ *adj* of nourishment or nutrition

aliˌmentary caˈnal *n* the tubular passage that extends from the mouth to the anus and functions in the digestion and absorption of food

alimony /ˈaliməni‖ˈælɪmənɪ/ *n* **1** means of living; maintenance **2** *chiefly NAm* MAINTENANCE 3

alive /əˈliev‖əˈlaɪv/ *adj* **1** having life **2a** still in existence, force, or operation; active **b** LIVE 3b **3** realizing the existence of sthg; aware of sthg <~ *to the danger*> **4** marked by alertness **5** showing much activity or animation; swarming <*sea was* ~ *with large whales* – Herman Melville> **6** of all those living – used as an intensive following the noun <*the proudest mother* ~>

alkali /ˈalkəlie‖ˈælkəlaɪ/ *n, pl* **alkalies, alkalis** any of various chemical bases, esp a hydroxide or carbonate of an alkali metal

alkali metal *n* any of the metals lithium, sodium, potassium, rubidium, caesium, and francium that comprise group 1A of the periodic table

alkaline /ˈalkəlien‖ˈælkəlaɪn/ *adj* (having the properties) of an alkali; *specif* having a pH of more than 7 – **alkalinity** *n*

ˌ**alkaline ˈearth** *n* **1** an oxide of any of the metals calcium, strontium, and barium and sometimes also magnesium, radium, or beryllium of group IIA of the periodic table **2** any of the metals whose oxides are alkaline earths

alkaloid /ˈalkəloyd‖ˈælkəlɔɪd/ *n* any of numerous nitrogen-containing organic compounds (e g morphine) that are usu chemical bases, occur esp in flowering plants, and are extensively used as drugs – **alkaloidal** *adj*

alkane /ˈalkayn‖ˈælkeɪn/ *n* any of a series of saturated open-chain hydrocarbons (e g methane, ethane, propane, or butane)

[1]**all** /awl‖ɔːl/ *adj* **1a** the whole amount or quantity of <*sat up* ~ *night*> **b** as much as possible <*spoke in* ~ *seriousness*> **2** every one of (more than 2) **3** the whole number or sum of <~ *dogs love aniseed*> **4** every <~ *manner of hardship*> **5** any whatever <*beyond* ~ *doubt*> **6a** given to or displaying only <*was* ~ *attention*> **b** having or seeming to have (some physical feature) conspicuously or excessively <~ *ears*> – **all there** not mentally subnormal; *esp* shrewd – infml – **all very well** – used in rejection of advice or sympathy <*it's* all very well *for you to talk*>

[2]**all** *adv* **1** wholly, altogether <*sat* ~ *alone*> **2** to a supreme degree – usu in combination <all-*powerful*> **3** for each side <*the score is 2* ~>

[3]**all** *pron, pl* **all** **1** the whole number, quantity, or amount <*it was* ~ *I could do not to cry*> **2** everybody, everything <*sacrificed* ~ *for love*> – **all in all 1** generally; ON THE WHOLE 1 **2** supremely important <*she was* all in all *to him*> – **all of** fully; AT LEAST – **all the same** JUST THE SAME

[4]**all** *n* one's total resources <*gave his* ~ *for the cause*> – **in all** ALL TOLD

Allah /ˈalah, ˈalə‖ˈælɑː, ˈælə/ *n* GOD 1 – used by Muslims or in reference to the Islamic religion

allay /əˈlay‖əˈleɪ/ *vt* **1** to reduce the severity of; alleviate **2** to make quiet; pacify

ˌ**all ˈclear** *n* a signal that a danger has passed or that it is safe to proceed

allegation /ˌaliˈgaysh(ə)n‖ˌælɪˈgeɪʃ(ə)n/ *n* a statement of what one undertakes to prove

allege /əˈlej‖əˈledʒ/ *vt* to assert without proof or before proving – **alleged** *adj*

allegedly /ə'lejidli‖ə'ledʒɪdlɪ/ *adv* according to allegation – used in reporting statements that have not been verified

allegiance /ə'leejəns‖ə'liːdʒəns/ *n* **1** the obligation of a subject or citizen to his/her sovereign or government **2** dedication to or dutiful support of a person, group, or cause

allegorical /ˌali'gorikl‖ˌælɪ'gɒrɪkl/, **allegoric** /-'gorik‖-'gɒrɪk/ *adj* **1** (having the characteristics) of allegory **2** having hidden spiritual meaning that transcends the literal sense of a sacred text – **allegorically** *adv*, **allegoricalness** *n*

allegory /'alig(ə)ri‖'ælɪg(ə)rɪ/ *n* **1a** the expression by means of symbolic figures and actions of truths or generalizations about human existence **b** an instance (e g Spenser's *Faery Queene*) of such expression **2** a symbolic representation; an emblem

allegretto /ˌali'gretoh‖ˌælɪ'gretəʊ/ *adv or adj* faster than andante but not so fast as allegro – used in music

allegro /ə'legroh‖ə'legrəʊ/ *n, adv, or adj, pl* **allegros** (a musical composition or movement to be played) in a brisk lively manner [Italian, merry, deriv of Latin *alacer* lively, eager]

allele /ə'leel‖ə'liːl/ *n* any of (the alternative hereditary characters determined by) 2 or more genes that occur as alternatives at a given place on a chromosome – **allelic** *adj*, **allelism** *n*

alleluia /ˌali'looh·yə‖ˌælɪ'luːjə/ *interj* hallelujah

allergic /ə'luhjik‖ə'lɜːdʒɪk/ *adj* **1** of or inducing allergy **2** averse, antipathetic *to* – infml

allergy /'aləji‖'ælədʒɪ/ *n* **1** altered bodily reactivity to an antigen in response to a first exposure **2** exaggerated reaction by sneezing, itching, skin rashes, etc to substances that have no such effect on the average individual **3** a feeling of antipathy or aversion – infml [German *allergie*, fr Greek *allos* other + *ergon* work]

alleviate /ə'leeviˌayt‖ə'liːvɪˌeɪt/ *vt* to relieve (a troublesome situation, state of mind, etc) – **alleviative, alleviatory** *adj*, **alleviation** *n*

[1]**alley** /'ali‖'ælɪ/ *n* **1** a garden walk bordered by trees or a hedge **2** a bowling alley **3** a narrow back street or passageway between buildings – **up/down one's alley** *chiefly NAm* UP ONE'S STREET

[2]**alley** *n* a playing marble (of superior quality)

'alleyˌway /-ˌway‖-ˌweɪ/ *n* ALLEY 3

ˌall 'fours *n pl* **1** all 4 legs of a quadruped **2** hands and knees <*crawling on* ~>

alliance /ə'lie·əns‖ə'laɪəns/ *n* **1** a union of families by marriage **2** a confederation of nations by formal treaty **3** a tie, connection <*a closer* ~ *between government and industry*>

allied /'alied, ə'lied‖'ælaɪd, ə'laɪd/ *adj* **1** in close association; united **2** joined in alliance by agreement or treaty **3a** related by resemblance or common properties; associated <*heraldry and* ~ *subjects*> **b** related genetically

alligator /'aliˌgaytə‖'ælɪˌgeɪtə/ *n* either of 2 crocodilians with broad heads that do not taper towards the snout [Spanish *el lagarto* the lizard, fr *el* the + *lagarto* lizard, fr Latin *lacertus, lacerta*]

ˌall-'in *adj* **1** *chiefly Br* all-inclusive; *esp* including all costs <*an* ~ *holiday in Greece*> **2** *Br, of wrestling* having almost no holds barred

all in *adj* tired out; exhausted – infml

alliteration /əˌlitə'raysh(ə)n‖əˌlɪtə'reɪʃ(ə)n/ *n* the repetition of usu initial consonant sounds in neighbouring words or syllables (e g *thr*eatening *thr*ongs of *thr*eshers) – **alliterative** *adj*, **alliteratively** *adv*

allocate /'aləkayt‖'æləkeɪt/ *vt* **1a** to apportion and distribute (e g money or responsibility) in shares **b** to assign (sthg limited in supply) to as a share <*we've been* ~d *the top flat*> **2** to earmark, designate <~ *a section of the building for research purposes*> – **allocatable** *adj*, **allocator** *n*, **allocation** *n*

allot /ə'lot‖ə'lɒt/ *vt* **-tt-** to allocate – **allotter** *n*

allotment /ə'lotmənt‖ə'lɒtmənt/ *n, Br* a small plot of land let out to an individual (e g by a town council) for cultivation

ˌall-'out *adj* using maximum effort and resources <*an* ~ *effort to win the contest*>

ˌall 'out *adv* with maximum determination and effort; FLAT OUT – chiefly in *go all out*

ˌall'over /-'ohvə‖-'əʊvə/ *adj* covering the whole extent or surface <*a sweater with an* ~ *pattern*>

ˌall 'over *adv* **1** over the whole extent or surface <*decorated* ~ *with a flower pattern*> **2** in every respect <*that's Paul* ~>

allow /ə'low‖ə'laʊ/ *vt* **1a(1)** to assign as a share or suitable amount (e g of time or money) <~ *an hour for lunch*> **a(2)** to grant as an allowance <~ed *him £500 a year*> **b** to reckon as a deduction or an addition <~ *a gallon for leakage*> **2a** to admit as true or valid; acknowledge **b** to admit the possibility of <*the facts* ~ *only one explanation*> **3** to permit: e g **3a** to make it possible for; enable <*the gift will* ~ *me to buy a car*> **b** to fail to prevent; let <~ *herself to get fat*> ~ *vi* **1** to admit the possibility *of* <*evidence that* ~s *of only one conclusion*> **2** to make allowance *for* <~ *for expansion*>

allowable /ə'lowəbl‖ə'laʊəbl/ *adj* **1** permissible **2** assigned as an allowance <*expenses* ~ *against tax*>

[1]**allowance** /ə'lowəns‖ə'laʊəns/ *n* **1a** a (limited) share or portion allotted or granted; a ration **b** a sum granted as a reimbursement or bounty or for expenses **c** a reduction from a list price or stated price **2** a handicap (e g in a race) **3a** permission, sanction **b** acknowledgment <~ *of your claim*> **4** the taking into account of mitigating circumstances – often pl with sing. meaning <*make* ~s *for his youth*>

[2]**allowance** *vt* **1** to put on a fixed allowance **2** to provide in a limited quantity

[1]**alloy** /'aloy‖'ælɔɪ/ *n* **1** a solid substance composed of a mixture of metals or a metal and a nonmetal thoroughly intermixed **2** a metal mixed with a more valuable metal **3** an addition that impairs or debases

[2]**alloy** /ə'loy‖ə'lɔɪ/ *vt* **1** to reduce the purity or value of by adding sthg **2** to mix so as to form an alloy **3a** to impair or debase by addition **b** to temper, moderate

ˌall-'powerful *adj* having complete or sole power; omnipotent

ˌall-'purpose *adj* suited for many purposes or uses

[1]**ˌall 'right** *adv* **1** well enough <*does* ~ *in*

school> **2** beyond doubt; certainly <*he has pneumonia* ~>

2**ˌall ˈright** *adj* **1** satisfactory, acceptable <*the film is* ~ *for children*> **2** safe, well <*he was ill but he's* ~ *now*> **3** agreeable, pleasing – used as a generalized term of approval

3**ˌall ˈright** *interj* **1** – used for giving assent <~, *let's go*> **2** – used in indignant or menacing response <~*! Just you wait*>

ˌall-ˈround *adj* **1** competent in many fields <*an* ~ *athlete*> **2** having general utility **3** encompassing all aspects; comprehensive <*an* ~ *reduction in price*>

ˌall ˈround *adv* **1** by, for, or to everyone present <*ordered drinks* ~> **2** in every respect

ˌall-ˈrounder *n* one who is competent in many fields; *specif* a cricketer who both bats and bowls to a high standard

ˈallˌspice /-ˌspies‖-ˌspaɪs/ *n* (a mildly pungent spice prepared from) the berry of a W Indian tree

ˌall-ˈstar *adj* composed wholly or chiefly of star performers

ˈall-ˌtime *adj* exceeding all others yet known <*an* ~ *bestseller*>

ˌall ˈtold *adv* with everything taken into account

allude /əˈl(y)oohd‖əˈl(j)uːd/ *vi* to make indirect, casual, or implicit reference *to*

1**allure** /əˈl(y)ooə‖əˈl(j)ʊə/ *vt* to entice by charm or attraction – **allurement** *n*

2**allure** *n* power of attraction or fascination; charm

allusion /əˈlyooh·zh(ə)n, -ˈlooh-‖əˈljuːʒ(ə)n, -ˈluː-/ *n* **1** alluding or hinting **2** (the use of) implied or indirect reference, esp in literature – **allusive** *adj*, **allusively** *adv*, **allusiveness** *n*

alˈluvium /-vi·əm‖-vɪəm/ *n, pl* **alluviums, alluvia** /-vi·ə‖-vɪə/ clay, silt, or similar detrital material deposited by running water – **alluvial** *adj*

1**ally** /ˈalie‖ˈælaɪ; *also* əˈlie‖əˈlaɪ/ *vt* **1** to join, unite *with/to* <allied *himself with a wealthy family by marriage*> **2** to relate *to* by resemblance or common properties <*its beak* allies *it to the finches*> ~ *vi* to form or enter into an alliance *with*

2**ally** /ˈalie‖ˈælaɪ/ *n* **1** a sovereign or state associated with another by treaty or league **2** a helper, auxiliary

-ally /-(ə)li‖-(ə)lɪ/ *suffix* (*adj* → *adv*) 2-LY <*terrific*ally>

alma mater /ˌalmə ˈmahtə, ˈmaytə‖ˌælmə ˈmɑːtə, ˈmeɪtə/ *n* a school, college, or university which one has attended [Latin, fostering mother]

almanac, almanack /ˈawlmənak‖ˈɔːlmənæk/ *n* **1** a usu annual publication containing statistical, tabular, and general information **2** *chiefly Br* a publication containing astronomical and meteorological data arranged according to the days, weeks, and months of a given year

1**almighty** /awlˈmieti‖ɔːlˈmaɪtɪ/ *adj* **1** *often cap* having absolute power over all <Almighty *God*> **2** having relatively unlimited power <*the* ~ *dollar*> **3** great in extent, seriousness, force, etc <*an* ~ *crash*> – infml – **almightiness** *n, often cap*, **almightiest** *adj*

2**almighty** *adv* to a great degree; mighty – infml

Almighty *n* GOD 1 – + *the*

almond /ˈahmənd‖ˈɑːmənd; *also* ˈawl-‖ˈɔːl-; *NAm* al-‖æl-/ *n* (the edible oval nut of) a small tree of the rose family

ˌalmond-ˈeyed *adj* having narrow slanting almond-shaped eyes

almoner /ˈahmənə, ˈal-‖ˈɑːmənə, ˈæl-/ *n* **1** one who distributes alms **2** a social worker attached to a British hospital – not now used technically

almost /ˈawlmohst‖ˈɔːlməʊst/ *adv* very nearly but not exactly or entirely

alms /ˈahmz‖ˈɑːmz/ *n sing or pl in constr* money, food, etc given to help the poor – **almsgiver** *n*, **almsgiving** *n*

ˈalmsˌhouse /-ˌhows‖-ˌhaʊs/ *n, Br* a privately endowed house in which a poor person can live

aloe /ˈaloh‖ˈæləʊ/ *n* **1** any of a large genus of succulent plants of the lily family with tall spikes of flowers **2** the dried juice of the leaves of various aloes used esp as a purgative – usu pl but sing. in constr

aloft /əˈloft‖əˈlɒft/ *adv* **1** at or to a great height **2** at, on, or to the masthead or the upper rigging of a ship

alone /əˈlohn‖əˈləʊn/ *adj or adv* **1** considered without reference to any other; *esp* unassisted <*the children* ~ *would eat that much*> **2** separated from others; isolated <*stands* ~> **3** exclusive of other factors <*time* ~ *will show*> **4** free from interference <*leave my bag* ~> – **aloneness** *n*

1**along** /əˈlong‖əˈlɒŋ/ *prep* **1** in a line parallel with the length or direction of **2** in the course of (a route or journey) **3** in accordance with <*something* ~ *these lines*>

2**along** *adv* **1** forward, on <*move* ~> **2** as a necessary or pleasant addition; with one <*take your flute* ~> **3** in company and simultaneously *with* <~ *with all the other village boys*> **4** also; IN ADDITION <*a bill came* ~ *with the parcel*> **5** on hand, there <*I'll be* ~ *in 5 minutes*> – **all along** all the time <*knew the truth* all along>

1**aˌlongˈside** /-ˈsied‖-ˈsaɪd/ *adv* along or at the side

2**alongside, alongside of** *prep* **1** side by side with; *specif* parallel to **2** concurrently with

1**aloof** /əˈloohf‖əˈluːf/ *adv* at a distance; out of involvement

2**aloof** *adj* distant in interest or feeling; reserved, unsympathetic – **aloofly** *adv*, **aloofness** *n*

aloud /əˈlowd‖əˈlaʊd/ *adv* with the speaking voice

alpaca /alˈpakə‖ælˈpækə/ *n* **1** (the fine long woolly hair of) a type of domesticated llama found in Peru **2** a thin cloth made of or containing this wool

alpenhorn /ˈalpənˌhawn‖ˈælpənˌhɔːn/ *n* a long straight wooden horn used, esp formerly, by Swiss herdsmen to call sheep and cattle

ˈalpenˌstock /-ˌstok‖-ˌstɒk/ *n* a long iron-pointed staff, now superseded by the ice axe, for use in mountain climbing

alpha /ˈalfə‖ˈælfə/ *n* **1** the 1st letter of the Greek alphabet **2** sthg that is first; a beginning

ˌalpha and ˈomega *n* the beginning and ending

alphabet /ˈalfəbet‖ˈælfəbet/ *n* a set of characters, esp letters, used to represent 1 or more languages, esp when arranged in a conventional order; *also* a system of signs and signals that can be used in place of letters [LateLatin *alphabetum*, fr Greek *alphabētos*, fr *alpha* + *bēta*, the first 2 letters of the Greek alphabet]

alphabetical /ˌalfəˈbetikl‖ˌælfəˈbetɪkl/, **alphabetic** /-ˈbetik‖-ˈbetɪk/ *adj* **1** of or employing an alphabet **2** in the order of the letters of the alphabet – **alphabetically** *adv*

alpha particle *n* a positively charged nuclear particle identical with the nucleus of a helium atom ejected at high speed by some radioactive substances

alpine /ˈalpien‖ˈælpaɪn/ *n* an (ornamental) plant native to alpine or northern parts of the northern hemisphere

Alpine *adj* **1** *often not cap* of, growing in, or resembling the Alps; *broadly* of or resembling any mountains **2** *often not cap* of or growing in the elevated slopes above the tree line **3** of or being competitive ski events comprising slalom and downhill racing

already /awlˈredi‖ɔːlˈredɪ/ *adv* **1** no later than now or then; even by this or that time <*he had ~ left*> **2** before, previously <*had seen the film ~*>

alright /awlˈriet‖ɔːlˈraɪt/ *adv, adj, or interj* ALL RIGHT – nonstandard

Alsatian /alˈsaysh(ə)n‖ælˈseɪʃ(ə)n/ *n* (any of) a breed of large intelligent dogs often used as guard dogs [*Alsatia* Latin name of Alsace, region of France (formerly of Germany)]

also /ˈawlsoh‖ˈɔːlsəʊ/ *adv* as an additional circumstance; besides

ˈalso-ˌran *n* **1** an entrant, esp a horse, that finishes outside the first 3 places in a race **2** a person of little importance

altar /ˈawltə‖ˈɔːltə/ *n* **1** a usu raised structure or place on which sacrifices are offered or incense is burnt in worship **2** a table on which the bread and wine used at communion are consecrated or which serves as a centre of worship or ritual

ˈaltarˌpiece /-ˌpees‖-ˌpiːs/ *n* a work of art that decorates the space above and behind an altar

alter /ˈawltə‖ˈɔːltə/ *vt* **1** to make different without changing into sthg else **2** *chiefly NAm* to castrate, spay – euph ~ *vi* to become different – **alterer** *n*, **alterable** *adj*, **alterably** *adv*, **alteration** *n*, **alterability** *n*

altercation /ˌawltəkaysh(ə)n‖ˌɔːltəkeɪʃ(ə)n/ *n* a heated quarrel; *also* quarrelling

ˌalter ˈego /ˈaltə‖ˈæltə/ *n* a second self; *esp* a trusted friend [Latin, lit., another I]

[1]**alternate** /awlˈtuhnət‖ɔːlˈtɜːnət/ *adj* **1** occurring or succeeding each other by turns <*a day of ~ sunshine and rain*> **2a** *of plant parts* arranged singly first on one side and then on the other of an axis **b** arranged one above or alongside the other **3** every other; every second <*he works on ~ days*> **4** *of an angle* being either of a pair on opposite sides of a transverse line at its intersection with 2 other lines **5** *NAm* [1]ALTERNATIVE 2 – **alternately** *adv*

[2]**alternate** /ˈawltəˌnayt‖ˈɔːltəˌneɪt/ *vt* to interchange with sthg else in turn <~ *work with sleep*> ~ *vi* **1** *of 2 things* to occur or succeed each other by turns <*work and sleep* ~> **2** to undergo or consist of repeated change from one thing to another <*he* ~s *between work and sleep*> – **alternation** *n*

alternating current *n* an electric current that reverses its direction at regularly recurring intervals

[1]**alternative** /awlˈtuhnətiv‖ɔːlˈtɜːnətɪv/ *adj* **1** affording a choice, esp between 2 mutually exclusive options **2** constituting an alternative – **alternatively** *adv*

[2]**alternative** *n* **1** an opportunity or need for deciding between 2 or more possibilities **2** either of 2 possibilities between which a choice is to be made; *also* any of more than 2 such possibilities

alternator /ˈawltəˌnaytə‖ˈɔːltəˌneɪtə/ *n* an electric generator for producing alternating current

although *also* **altho** /awlˈdhoh‖ɔːlˈðəʊ/ *conj* in spite of the fact or possibility that; though

altimeter /ˈaltiˌmeetə‖ˈæltɪˌmiːtə/ *n* an instrument for measuring altitude – **altimetry** *n*

altitude /ˈaltityoohd‖ˈæltɪtjuːd/ *n* **1** the angular elevation of a celestial object above the horizon **2** the height of an object (e g an aircraft), esp above sea level **3** the perpendicular distance from the base of a geometrical figure to the vertex or the side parallel to the base – **altitudinal** *adj*

alto /ˈaltoh‖ˈæltəʊ/ *n, pl* **altos** **1a** a countertenor **b** a contralto **2** the second highest part in 4-part harmony **3** a member of a family of instruments having a range between the treble or soprano and the tenor – **alto** *adj*

[1]**altogether** /ˌawltəˈgedhə‖ˌɔːltəˈgeðə/ *adv* **1** wholly, thoroughly <*an ~ different problem*> **2** ALL TOLD **3** in the main; ON THE WHOLE **4** in every way <*more complicated ~*>

[2]**altogether** *n the* nude <*posed in the ~*> – infml

altruism /ˈaltroohˌiz(ə)m‖ˈæltruːˌɪz(ə)m/ *n* unselfish regard for or devotion to the welfare of others – **altruist** *n*, **altruistic** *adj*, **altruistically** *adv*

alum /ˈaləm‖ˈæləm/ *n* (any of various double salts with a similar crystal structure to) a sulphate of aluminium with potassium or ammonium, used esp as an emetic and astringent

alumina /əˈl(y)oohminə‖əˈl(j)uːmɪnə/ *n* aluminium oxide that occurs naturally as corundum

aluminium /ˌalyoohˈmini·əm, -yoo-‖ˌæljuːˈmɪnɪəm, -jʊ-/ *n* a bluish silver-white malleable light metallic element with good electrical and thermal conductivity and resistance to oxidation

alumnus /əˈlumnəs‖əˈlʌmnəs/, *fem* **alumna** /-nə‖-nə/ *n, pl* **alumni** /-nie‖-naɪ/, *fem* **alumnae** /-ni‖-nɪ/ *chiefly NAm* a former student of a particular school, college, or university; *broadly* a former member of any organization

alveolus /ˌalviˈohləs, alˈvee·ələs‖ˌælvɪˈəʊləs, ælˈviːələs/ *n, pl* **alveoli** /-lie‖-laɪ/ a small cavity or pit: e g **a** a socket for a tooth **b** an air cell of the lungs **c** a cell or compartment of a honeycomb – **alveolar** *adj*

always /ˈawlwayz, -wiz‖ˈɔːlweɪz, -wɪz/ *adv* **1a** at all times <*have ~ lived here*> **b** in all cases <*they ~ have long tails*> **2** on every occasion; repeatedly <*he's ~ complaining*> **3** forever, perpetually <*will ~ love you*> **4** as a last resort; at any rate <*they could ~ eat cake*>

alyssum /ˈalisəm‖ˈælɪsəm/ *n* **1** any of a genus of Old World yellow-flowered plants of the mustard family **2** an annual or perennial European plant of the mustard family that has clusters of small fragrant usu white flowers

am /əm, m‖əm, m; *strong* am‖æm/ *pres 1 sing of* BE

AM /ˌay ˈem‖ˌeɪ ˈem/ *adj* of or being a broadcasting or receiving system using amplitude modulation

amalgam /əˈmalgəm‖əˈmælgəm/ *n* **1** an alloy of mercury with another metal (e g used in making dental fillings) **2** a mixture of different elements

amalgamate /əˈmalgəmayt‖əˈmælgəmeɪt/ *vt* to unite (as if) in an amalgam; *esp* to combine into a single body

amanuensis /əˌmanyoohˈensis‖əˌmænjuːˈensɪs/ *n, pl* **amanuenses** /-seez‖-siːz/ sby employed to write from dictation or to copy manuscript

amass /əˈmas‖əˈmæs/ *vt* **1** to collect for oneself; accumulate <*~ a great fortune*> **2** to bring together into a mass; gather

amateur /ˈamətə, -chə‖ˈæmətə, -tʃə/ *n* **1** one who engages in a pursuit as a pastime rather than as a profession; *esp* a sportsman who has never competed for money **2** one who practises an art or science unskilfully; a dabbler – **amateur** *adj*, **amateurish** *adj*, **amateurishly** *adv*, **amateurishness** *n*, **amateurism** *n*

amatory /ˈamət(ə)ri‖ˈæmət(ə)rɪ/ *adj* of or expressing sexual love

amaze /əˈmayz‖əˈmeɪz/ *vt* to fill with wonder; astound – **amazement** *n*

amazing /əˈmayzing‖əˈmeɪzɪŋ/ *adj* – used as a generalized term of approval

amazon /ˈaməz(ə)n‖ˈæməz(ə)n/ *n, often cap* a tall strong athletic woman

ambassador /amˈbasədə‖æmˈbæsədə/ *n* **1** an official envoy: e g **1a** a top-ranking diplomat accredited to a foreign government or sovereign as a resident representative **b** one similarly appointed for a special and often temporary diplomatic assignment **2** a representative, messenger – **ambassadorship** *n*, **ambassadorial** *adj*

amber /ˈambə‖ˈæmbə/ *n* **1** a hard yellowish to brownish translucent fossil resin used chiefly for ornaments and jewellery **2** the colour of amber **3** a yellow traffic light meaning 'caution' – **amber** *adj*

ˈamberˌgris /-ˌgrees, -ˌgris‖-ˌgriːs, -ˌgrɪs/ *n* a waxy substance found floating in tropical waters, believed to originate in the intestines of the sperm whale, and used in perfumery as a fixative

ambi- /ambi-‖æmbɪ-/ *prefix* both; two <ambi*valent*>

ambidextrous /ˌambiˈdekstrəs‖ˌæmbɪˈdekstrəs/ *adj* **1** able to use either hand with equal ease **2** unusually skilful; versatile **3** characterized by deceitfulness and double-dealing – **ambidextrously** *adv*, **ambidexterity** *n*

ambience, ambiance /ˈambi·əns‖ˈæmbɪəns (*Fr* ɑ̃biɑ̃s) *n* a surrounding or pervading atmosphere; an environment, milieu

[1]ambient /ˈambi·ənt‖ˈæmbɪənt/ *adj* surrounding on all sides; encompassing – fml

[2]ambient *n* ambience – fml

ambiguity /ˌambiˈgyooh·əti‖ˌæmbɪˈgjuːətɪ/ *n* **1** (a word or expression with) the quality of being ambiguous or imprecise in meaning **2** uncertainty of meaning or relative position <*the basic ~ of her political stance*>

ambiguous /amˈbigyoo·əs‖æmˈbɪgjʊəs/ *adj* **1** vague, indistinct, or difficult to classify **2** capable of 2 or more interpretations [Latin *ambiguus*, fr *ambigere* to wander about, fr *ambi-* around + *agere* to lead, drive] – **ambiguously** *adv*, **ambiguousness** *n*

ambit /ˈambit‖ˈæmbɪt/ *n* **1** a limiting circumference **2** the bounds or limits of a place; the precincts **3** a sphere of influence; a scope

ambition /amˈbish(ə)n‖æmˈbɪʃ(ə)n/ *n* **1a** a strong desire for status, wealth, or power **b** a desire to achieve a particular end **2** an object of ambition – **ambitionless** *adj*

ambitious /amˈbishəs‖æmˈbɪʃəs/ *adj* **1a** having or controlled by ambition **b** desirous *of*, aspiring **2** resulting from or showing ambition <*an ~ attempt*> **3** elaborate <*cooked nothing more ~ than boiled eggs*> – **ambitiously** *adv*, **ambitiousness** *n*

ambivalence /amˈbivələns‖æmˈbɪvələns/ *n* the state of having 2 opposing and contradictory attitudes or feelings towards an object, person, etc – **ambivalent** *adj*, **ambivalently** *adv*

[1]amble /ˈambl‖ˈæmbl/ *vi* to move at an amble

[2]amble *n* **1** an easy gait of a horse in which the legs on the same side of the body move together **2** an easy gait **3** a leisurely stroll

ambrosia /amˈbrohzi·ə, -zh(y)ə‖æmˈbrəʊzɪə, -ʒ(j)ə/ *n* **1** the food of the Greek and Roman gods **2** sthg extremely pleasing to the taste or smell – **ambrosial** *adj*

ambulance /ˈambyooləns‖ˈæmbjʊləns/ *n* a vehicle equipped to transport the injured or ill

[1]ambush /ˈamboosh‖ˈæmbʊʃ/ *vt* to attack from an ambush; waylay ~ *vi* to lie in wait; lurk – **ambushment** *n*

[2]ambush *n* **1** the concealment of soldiers, police, etc in order to carry out a surprise attack from a hidden position **2** people stationed in ambush; *also* their concealed position

ameba /əˈmeebə‖əˈmiːbə/ *n, chiefly NAm* an amoeba – **amebic** *also* **ameban** *adj*, **ameboid** *adj*

ameliorate /əˈmeelyərayt‖əˈmiːljəreɪt/ *vb* to make or become better or more tolerable – **ameliorative** *adj*, **amelioration** *n*

amen /ˌahˈmen, ˌay-, ˈ-ˌ-‖ˌɑːˈmen, ˌeɪ-, ˈ-ˌ-/ *interj* – used to express solemn ratification (e g of an expression of faith) or hearty approval (e g of an assertion)

amenable /əˈmeenəbl‖əˈmiːnəbl/ *adj* **1** liable to be brought to account; answerable **2a** capable of submission (e g to judgment or test) **b** readily persuaded to yield or agree; tractable – **amenably** *adv*, **amenability** *n*

amend /ə'mend‖ə'mend/ *vt* **1** to put right; *specif* to make emendations in (e g a text) **2a** to change or modify for the better; improve **b** to alter (e g a document) formally <~ *the constitution*>

a'mendment /-mənt‖-mənt/ *n* **1** the act of amending, esp for the better **2** an alteration proposed or effected by amending

a'mends *n pl but sing or pl in constr* compensation for a loss or injury; recompense

amenity /ə'menəti, ə'mee-‖ə'menətɪ, ə'miː-/ *n* **1** sthg (e g a public facility) conducive to material comfort – often pl **2** sthg (e g a conventional social gesture) conducive to ease of social intercourse – usu pl **3** pleasantness, esp of environment – fml

[1]**American** /ə'merikən‖ə'merɪkən/ *n* **1** a N or S American Indian **2** a native or inhabitant of N or S America **3** a citizen of the USA **4** English as typically spoken and written in the USA

[2]**American** *adj* **1** (characteristic) of N or S America **2** (characteristic) of the USA **3** of the N and S American Indians

American Indian *n* a member of any of the indigenous peoples of N, S, or central America excluding the Eskimos

Americanism /ə'merikəniz(ə)m‖ə-'merɪkənɪz(ə)m/ *n* **1** a characteristic feature (e g a custom or belief) of Americans or American culture **2a** adherence or attachment to America and its culture **b** the promotion of American policies

american·ize, **-ise** /ə'merikəniez‖ə-'merɪkənaɪz/ *vb, often cap* to (cause to) have or acquire American customs, characteristics, etc – **americanization** *n, often cap*

amethyst /a'məthist‖æ'məθɪst/ *n* a semiprecious gemstone of clear purple or violet quartz [Latin *amethystus*, fr Greek *amethystos*, lit., remedy against drunkenness, fr *a-* not, without + *methyein* to be drunk, fr *methy* wine] – **amethystine** *adj*

amiable /'aymi·əbl‖'eɪmɪəbl/ *adj* **1** (seeming) agreeable and well-intentioned; inoffensive **2** friendly, congenial – **amiableness** *n*, **amiably** *adv*, **amiability** *n*

amicable /'amikəbl‖'æmɪkəbl/ *adj* characterized by friendly goodwill; peaceable – **amicableness** *n*, **amicably** *adv*, **amicability** *n*

amid /ə'mid‖ə'mɪd/ *prep* in or to the middle of – poetic

amidships /ə'mid,ships‖ə'mɪd,ʃɪps/ *adv* in or towards the middle part (of a ship)

amine /'ameen, ə'meen‖'æmiːn, ə'miːn/ *n* any of various usu organic compounds that are chemical bases and contain 1 or more amino groups – **aminic** *adj*

amino /ə'meenoh‖ə'miːnəʊ/ *adj* of, being, or containing (a derivative of) the chemical group NH_2^N united to a radical derived from a compound that is not an acid

a,mino 'acid *n* any of various organic acids containing an amino group and occurring esp in linear chains as the chief components of proteins

amir /ə'miə‖ə'mɪə/ *n* an emir

amiss /ə'mis‖ə'mɪs/ *adv or adj* **1** astray **2** out of order; at fault **3** out of place in given circumstances – usu + a negative <*a few pertinent remarks may not come ~ here*>

amity /'amiti‖'æmɪtɪ/ *n* friendship

ammeter /'ameetə‖'æmiːtə/ *n* an instrument for measuring electric current in amperes

ammo /'amoh‖'æməʊ/ *n* ammunition – infml

ammonia /ə'mohnyə, -ni·ə‖ə'məʊnjə, -nɪə/ *n* a pungent colourless gas that is a compound of nitrogen and hydrogen and is very soluble in water, forming an alkaline solution [Latin *sal ammoniacus* ammonium chloride, lit., salt of Ammon, fr *Ammon*, an Egyptian god near one of whose temples it was prepared]

ammonite /'amənict‖'æmənaɪt/ *n* a flat spiral fossil shell of a mollusc abundant esp in the Mesozoic age – **ammonitic** *adj*

ammonium /ə'mohnyəm, -ni·əm‖ə-'məʊnjəm, -nɪəm/ *n* an ion or radical derived from ammonia by combination with a hydrogen ion or atom

ammunition /,amyoo'nish(ə)n‖,æmjʊ'nɪʃ-(ə)n/ *n* **1** the projectiles, together with their propelling charges, used in the firing of guns; *also* bombs, grenades, etc containing explosives **2** material used to defend or attack a point of view

amnesia /am'neezyə, -zh(y)ə‖æm'niːzjə, -ʒ(j)ə/ *n* a (pathological) loss of memory – **amnesiac, amnesic** *adj or n*, **amnestic** *adj*

amnesty /'amnəsti‖'æmnəstɪ/ *n* the act of pardoning a large group of individuals, esp for political offences [Greek *amnēstia* forgetfulness, fr *amnēstos* forgotten, fr *a-* not + *mnasthai* to remember] – **amnesty** *vt*

amoeba, *chiefly NAm* **ameba** /ə'meebə‖ə-'miːbə/ *n, pl* **amoebas, amoebae** /-bi‖-bɪ/ any of various protozoans with lobed pseudopodia and without permanent organelles that are widely distributed in water and wet places – **amoebic** *also* **amoeban** *adj*

amok, **amuck** /ə'muk‖ə'mʌk/ *adv* **1** in a murderous frenzy; raging violently **2** OUT OF HAND 2 *USE* chiefly in *run amok* [Malay *amok*]

among /ə'mung‖ə'mʌŋ/ *prep* **1** in or through the midst of; surrounded by <*living ~ artists*> **2** by or through the whole group of <*discontent ~ the poor*> **3** in the number or class of <~ *other things he was head boy*> **4** between – used for more than 2 <*quarrel ~ themselves*> **5** through the joint action of <*made a fortune ~ themselves*>

amoral /a(y)'morəl, ə-‖æ'mɒrəl, eɪ-,ə-/ *adj* **1** being neither moral nor immoral; *specif* lying outside the sphere of ethical judgments **2** having no understanding of, or unconcerned with, morals – **amoralism** *n*, **amorally** *adv*, **amorality** *n*

amorous /'amərəs‖'æmərəs/ *adj* **1** of or relating to love **2** moved by or inclined to love or desire – **amorously** *adv*, **amorousness** *n*

amorphous /ə'mawfəs‖ə'mɔːfəs/ *adj* **1a** having no definite form; shapeless **b** without definite character; unclassifiable **2** not crystalline – **amorphously** *adv*, **amorphousness** *n*

amort·ize, **-ise** /ə'mawtiez‖ə'mɔːtaɪz/ *vt* to provide for the gradual extinguishment of (e g a mortgage), usu by periodic contributions to a sinking fund – **amortizable** *adj*, **amortization** *n*

[1]**amount** /ə'mownt‖ə'maʊnt/ *vi* to be equal in

number, quantity, or significance *to*

[2]**amount** *n* **1** the total quantity **2** the quantity at hand or under consideration <*has an enormous* ~ *of energy*>

amour /ə'maw, ə'mooə ‖ə'mɔː, ə'mʊə (*Fr* amur)/ *n* a love affair, esp when illicit

amp /amp‖æmp/ *n* **1** an ampere **2** an amplifier *USE* infml

amperage /'amp(ə)rij‖'æmp(ə)rɪdʒ/ *n* the strength of a current of electricity expressed in amperes

ampere /'ampeə‖'æmpeə/ *n* the basic SI unit of electric current [André M *Ampère* (1775-1836), French physicist]

ampersand /'ampə,sand‖'æmpə,sænd/ *n* a sign, typically &, standing for the word *and*

amphetamine /am'fetəmeen, -min‖æm'fetəmiːn, -mɪn/ *n* (any of several derivatives of) a synthetic stimulant of the brain which is a common drug of abuse

amphibian /am'fibi·ən‖æm'fɪbɪən/ *n, pl* **amphibians,** (*1*) **amphibians,** *esp collectively* **amphibia** /-bi·ə‖-bɪə/ **1** an amphibious organism; *esp* a frog, toad, newt, or other member of a class of cold-blooded vertebrates intermediate in many characteristics between fishes and reptiles **2** an aeroplane, tank, etc adapted to operate on or from both land and water – **amphibian** *adj*

amphibious /am'fibi·əs‖æm'fɪbɪəs/ *adj* **1** able to live both on land and in water **2a** relating to or adapted for both land and water <~ *vehicles*> **b** involving or trained for coordinated action of land, sea, and air forces organized for invasion **3** combining 2 positions or qualities [Greek *amphibios*, lit., living a double life, fr *amphi-* on both sides + *bios* mode of life] – **amphibiously** *adv*, **amphibiousness** *n*

amphitheatre /'amfi,thiətə‖'æmfɪ,θɪətə/ *n* **1** an oval or circular building with rising tiers of seats ranged about an open space **2a** a semicircular gallery in a theatre **b** a flat or gently sloping area surrounded by abrupt slopes **3** a place of public games or contests

amphora /'amfərə‖'æmfərə/ *n, pl* **amphorae** /-ri,-rie‖-rɪ,-raɪ/, **amphoras** a 2-handled oval jar or vase with a narrow neck and base, orig used by the ancient Greeks and Romans for holding oil or wine

ample /'ampl‖'æmpl/ *adj* **1** generous in size, scope, or capacity **2** abundant, plentiful <*they had* ~ *money for the trip*> **3** buxom, portly – chiefly euph – **ampleness** *n*, **amply** *adv*

amplifier /'ampli,fie·ə‖'æmplɪ,faɪə/ *n* a device usu employing valves or transistors to obtain amplification of voltage, current, or power

amplify /'ampli,fie‖'æmplɪ,faɪ/ *vt* **1** to expand (e g a statement) by the use of detail, illustration, etc **2** to make larger or greater; increase **3** to increase the magnitude of (a signal or other input of power) ~ *vi* to expand *on* one's remarks or ideas – **amplification** *n*

amplitude /'amplityoohd, -choohd‖'æmplɪtjuːd, -tʃuːd/ *n* **1** largeness of **1a** dimensions **b** scope; abundance **2** the extent of a vibration or oscillation measured from the mean to a maximum

amplitude modulation *n* a modulation of the strength of a wave, esp a radio carrier wave, by the characteristics of the signal carried

ampoule, *chiefly NAm* **ampul, ampule** /'ampoohl‖'æmpuːl/ *n* a hermetically sealed small bulbous glass vessel used esp to hold a sterile solution for hypodermic injection

amputate /'ampyootayt‖'æmpjʊteɪt/ *vt* to cut or lop off; *esp* to cut (e g a damaged or diseased limb) from the body – **amputator** *n*, **amputation** *n*

amputee /,ampyoo'tee‖,æmpjʊ'tiː/ *n* sby who has had a limb amputated

amuck /ə'muk‖ə'mʌk/ *adv* amok

amulet /'amyoolit‖'æmjʊlɪt/ *n* a small object worn as a charm against evil

amuse /ə'myoohz‖ə'mjuːz/ *vt* **1** to entertain or occupy in a light or pleasant manner <~ *the child with a story*> **2** to appeal to the sense of humour of <*the joke doesn't* ~ *me*> – **amuser** *n*, **amusing** *adj*, **amusingly** *adv*, **amusingness** *n*, **amusedly** *adv*

a'musement /-mənt‖-mənt/ *n* a means of entertaining or occupying; a pleasurable diversion

[1]**an** /(ə)n‖(ə)n; *strong* an‖æn/ *indefinite article* [2]A – used (1) before words with an initial vowel sound <~ *oak*> <~ *honour*> (2) frequently, esp formerly or in the USA, before words whose initial /h/ sound is often lost before the *an* <~ *hotel*> (3) sometimes, esp formerly in British writing, before words like *union* or *European* whose initial sound is /y/

[2]**an, an'** *conj* **1** and – infml **2** *archaic* if

[3]**an** *prep* [3]A – used under the same conditions as [1]AN

an- – see [2]A-

[1]**-an** /-ən‖-ən/, **-ian** *also* **-ean** *suffix* (→ *n*) **1** one who is of or belonging to <*republic*an> **2** one skilled in or specializing in <*phonetic*ian>

[2]**-an, -ian** *also* **-ean** *suffix* (→ *adj*) **1** of or belonging to <*Americ*an> **2** characteristic of; resembling <*Mozart*ean>

Anabaptist /,anə'baptist‖,ænə'bæptɪst/ *n or adj* (a member of) a Protestant sect advocating the baptism or rebaptism of adult believers – **Anabaptism** *n*

anachronism /ə'nakrə,niz(ə)m‖ə'nækrə,nɪz(ə)m/ *n* **1** an error in chronology; *esp* a chronological misplacing of people, events, objects, or customs **2** sby who or sthg that seems chronologically out of place – **anachronistic, anachronous** *adj*, **anachronistically** *also* **anachronously** *adv*

anaconda /,anə'kondə‖,ænə'kɒndə/ *n* a large semiaquatic S American snake of the boa family that crushes its prey in its coils

anaemia, *chiefly NAm* **anemia** /ə'neemyə, -mi·ə‖ə'niːmjə, -mɪə/ *n* **1a** a condition in which the blood is deficient in red blood cells, haemoglobin, or total volume **b** ischaemia **2** lack of vitality [Greek *anaimia* bloodlessness, fr *an-* not, without + *haima* blood] – **anaemic** *adj*, **anaemically** *adv*

anaesthesia, *chiefly NAm* **anesthesia** /,anəs'theezh(y)ə, -zyə‖,ænəs'θiːʒ(j)ə, -zjə/ *n* loss of sensation, esp loss of sensation of pain, resulting either from injury or a disorder of the nerves or from the action of drugs

anaesthetic, *chiefly NAm* **anesthetic** /,anəs'thetik‖,ænəs'θetɪk/ *n* a substance that produces anaesthesia, e g so that surgery can be carried out painlessly – **anaesthetic** *adj*,

anaesthetically *adv*

anaesthet·ize, -ise, *chiefly NAm* **anesthetize** /ə'neesthə,tiez‖ə'ni:sθə,taɪz/ *vt* to subject to anaesthesia, esp for purposes of surgery – **anaesthetist** *n*

anagram /'anə,gram‖'ænə,græm/ *n* a word or phrase made by rearranging the letters of another – **anagrammatic, anagrammatical** *adj*, **anagrammatically** *adv*, **anagrammatize** *vt*

anal /'aynl‖'eɪnl/ *adj* **1** of or situated near the anus **2** of or characterized by (parsimony, meticulousness, or other personality traits typical of) the stage of sexual development during which the child is concerned esp with faeces – **anally** *adv*, **anality** *n*

analgesia /,anl'jeezh(y)ə, -zyə‖,ænl'dʒi:ʒ(j)ə, -zjə/ *n* insensibility to pain without loss of consciousness – **analgesic** *adj or n*, **analgetic** *adj or n*

analog·ize, -ise /ə'naləjiez‖ə'nælədʒaɪz/ *vb* to compare by or use analogy

analogous /ə'naləgəs‖ə'næləgəs/ *adj* **1** corresponding by analogy **2** being or related to as an analogue – **analogously** *adv*, **analogousness** *n*

[1]**analogue**, *NAm chiefly* **analog** /'anəlog‖'ænəlɒg/ *n* sthg analogous or parallel to sthg else

[2]**analogue**, *NAm chiefly* **analog** *adj* of an analogue computer

analogue computer *n* a computer that operates with numbers represented by directly measurable quantities (e g voltages or mechanical rotations)

analogy /ə'naləji‖ə'nælədʒɪ/ *n* **1** inference from a parallel case **2** resemblance in some particulars; similarity **3** the tendency for new words or linguistic forms to be created in imitation of existing patterns **4** correspondence in function between anatomical parts of different structure and origin – **analogic, analogical** *adj*, **analogically** *adv*

analyse, *NAm chiefly* **analyze** /'anəliez‖'ænəlaɪz/ *vt* **1** to subject to analysis **2** to determine by analysis the constitution or structure of **3** to psychoanalyse – **analysable** *adj*

analysis /ə'naləsis‖ə'næləsɪs/ *n, pl* **analyses** /-seez‖-si:z/ **1a** examination and identification of the components of a whole **b** a statement of such an analysis **2** the use of function words instead of inflectional forms as a characteristic device of a language **3** psychoanalysis

analyst /'anəlist‖'ænəlɪst/ *n* **1** a person who analyses or is skilled in analysis **2** a psychoanalyst

analytic /,anə'litik‖,ænə'lɪtɪk/, **analytical** /-kl‖-kl/ *adj* **1** of analysis **2** skilled in or using analysis, esp in reasoning **3** characterized by analysis rather than inflection <*~ languages*> **4** psychoanalytic – **analytically** *adv*, **analyticity** *n*

anapaest, *NAm chiefly* **anapest** /'anə,pest, -,peest‖'ænə,pest, -,pi:st/ *n* a metrical foot consisting of 2 short syllables followed by 1 long – **anapaestic** *adj or n*

anarchism /'anə,kiz(ə)m‖'ænə,kɪz(ə)m/ *n* **1** a political theory holding all forms of governmental authority to be undesirable **2** the attacking of the established social order or laws; rebellion

anarchist /'anəkist‖'ænəkɪst/ *n* **1** one who attacks the established social order or laws; a rebel **2** a believer in or (violent) promoter of anarchism or anarchy – **anarchist, anarchistic** *adj*

anarchy /'anəki‖'ænəkɪ/ *n* **1a** absence of government **b** lawlessness; (political) disorder **c** a utopian society with complete freedom and no government **2** anarchism [Greek *anarchia*, fr *anarchos* having no ruler, fr *an-* not, without + *archos* ruler] – **anarchic** *adj*, **anarchically** *adv*

anathema /ə'nathəmə‖ə'næθəmə/ *n* **1a** (the object of) a ban or curse solemnly pronounced by ecclesiastical authority and accompanied by excommunication **b** a vigorous denunciation; a curse **2** sby or sthg despised <*his opinions are ~ to me*> **anathematize** *vt*

anatomist /ə'natəmist‖ə'nætəmɪst/ *n* **1** a student of anatomy (skilled in dissection) **2** one who analyses minutely and critically <*an ~ of urban society*>

anatomy /ə'natəmi‖ə'nætəmɪ/ *n* **1** (a treatise on) the biology of the structure of organisms **2** dissection **3** structural make-up, esp of (a part of) an organism **4** an analysis **5** the human body – **anatomic, anatomical** *adj*, **anatomically** *adv*

-ance /-əns‖-əns/ *suffix* (→ *n*) **1** action or process of <*further*ance>; *also* instance of (a specified action or process) <*perform*ance> **2** quality or state of <*brilli*ance>; *also* instance of (a specified quality or state) <*protuber*ance> **3** amount or degree of <*conduct*ance>

ancestor /'ansestə, -səs-‖'ænsestə, -səs-/, *fem* **ancestress** /-tris‖-trɪs/ *n* **1a** one from whom a person is descended, usu more distant than a grandparent **b** FOREFATHER 2 **2** a progenitor of a more recent (species of) organism – **ancestral** *adj*, **ancestrally** *adv*

ancestry /'ansestri, -səs-‖'ænsestrɪ, -səs-/ *n* a line of esp noble descent; a lineage

[1]**anchor** /'angkə‖'æŋkə/ *n* **1** a usu metal device dropped to the bottom from a ship or boat to hold it in a particular place **2** sby or sthg providing support and security; a mainstay **3** sthg that serves to hold an object firmly

[2]**anchor** *vt* **1** to hold in place in the water by an anchor **2** to secure firmly; fix ~ *vi* **1** to cast anchor **2** to become fixed; settle

anchorage /'angkərij‖'æŋkərɪdʒ/ *n* **1** a place (suitable) for vessels to anchor **2** a source of reassurance **3** sthg that provides a secure hold or attachment

anchorite /'angkə,riet‖'æŋkə,raɪt/, *fem* **anchoress** /'angk(ə)ris‖'æŋk(ə)rɪs/, **anchress** /'angkris‖'æŋkrɪs/ *n* one who lives in seclusion, usu for religious reasons – **anchoritic** *adj*

anchovy /'anchəvi‖'æntʃəvɪ/ *n*, a common small Mediterranean fish resembling a herring and used esp in appetizers and as a garnish; *also* any of various small fish related to this

[1]**ancient** /'aynsh(ə)nt, -chənt‖'eɪnʃ(ə)nt, -tʃənt/ *adj* **1** having existed for many years **2** of (those living in) a remote period, specif that from the earliest known civilizations to the fall of the western Roman Empire in AD 476 **3** old-fashioned, antique

[2]**ancient** *n* **1a** sby who lived in ancient times **b** *pl the* members of a civilized, esp a classical, nation of antiquity **2** *archaic* an aged person

[1]**ancillary** /an'siləri‖æn'sɪlərɪ; *NAm usu* 'ansə ˌleri‖'ænsəˌlerɪ/ *adj* **1** subordinate, subsidiary **2** auxiliary, supplementary

[2]**ancillary** *n, Br* one who assists; a helper

-ancy /-ənsi‖-ənsɪ/ *suffix* (→ *n*) quality or state of <*expect*ancy>

and /(ə)n, (ə)nd‖(ə)n, (ə)nd; *strong* and‖ænd/ *conj* **1** – used to join coordinate sentence elements of the same class or function expressing addition or combination <*cold* ~ *hungry*> <*John* ~ *I*> **2** – used, esp in Br speech, before the numbers 1-99 after the number 100 <*three hundred* ~ *seventeen*>; used also orig between tens and units <*five* ~ *twenty blackbirds*> **3** plus <*three* ~ *three make six*> **4** – used to introduce a second clause expressing temporal sequence <*came to tea* ~ *stayed to dinner*>, consequence <*water the seeds* ~ *they will grow*>, contrast <*he's old* ~ *I'm young*>, or supplementary explanation <*she's ill* ~ *can't travel*> **5** – used to join repeated words expressing continuation or progression <*ran* ~ *ran*> <*waited hours* ~ *hours*> <*came nearer* ~ *nearer*> **6** – used to join words expressing contract of type or quality <*there are aunts* ~ *aunts*> **7** – used instead of *to* to introduce an infinitive after *come, go, run, try, stop* <*come* ~ *look*> – **and all that, and all** AND SO FORTH – **and how** – used to emphasize the preceding idea; infml – **and so forth, and so on 1** and others or more of the same kind **2** and further in the same manner **3** and the rest **4** and other things – **and that** *chiefly Br* AND SO FORTH – nonstandard

andante /an'danti‖æn'dæntɪ/ *n, adv, or adj* (a musical composition or movement to be played) moderately slow

andiron /'andie·ən‖'ændaɪən/ *n* either of a pair of metal stands used on a hearth to support burning wood

androgynous /an'drojənəs‖æn'drɒdʒənəs/ *adj* having characteristics of both the male and female forms [Latin *androgynus* hermaphrodite, fr Greek *androgynos*, fr *andr-*, *anēr* man + *gynē* woman] – **androgyny** *n*

anecdote /'anikˌdoht‖'ænɪkˌdəʊt/ *n* a usu short narrative about an interesting or amusing person or incident – **anecdotist, anecdotalist** *n*, **anecdotal** *adj*

anemia /ə'neemyə, -mi·ə‖ə'ni:mjə, -mɪə/ *n*, *chiefly NAm* anaemia – **anemic** *adj*, **anemically** *adv*

anemometer /ˌani'momitə‖ˌænɪ'mɒmɪtə/ *n* an instrument for measuring the force or speed of the wind – **anemometry** *n*, **anemometric** *also* **anemometrical** *adj*

anemone /ə'neməni‖ə'nemənɪ/ *n* **1** any of a large genus of plants of the buttercup family with lobed or divided leaves and showy flowers **2** SEA ANEMONE

aneroid /'anəroyd‖'ænərɔɪd/ *adj* containing no liquid or operated without the use of liquid <*an* ~ *barometer*>

anesthesia /ˌanəs'theezyə, -zh(y)ə‖ˌænəs'θi:zjə, -ʒ(j)ə/ *n, chiefly NAm* anaesthesia – **anesthetic** *n or adj*, **anesthetist** *n*, **anesthetize** *vt*

anew /ə'nyooh‖ə'nju:/ *adv* **1** again, afresh **2** in a new form or way

angel /'aynj(ə)l‖'eɪndʒ(ə)l/ *n* **1** a spiritual being, usu depicted as being winged, serving as God's intermediary or acting as a heavenly worshipper **2** an attendant spirit or guardian **3** a messenger, harbinger <~ *of death*> **4** a very kind or loving person, esp a woman or girl **5** a financial backer of a theatrical venture or other enterprise – chiefly infml [Old French *angele*, fr Late Latin *angelus*, fr Greek *angelos*, lit., messenger] – **angelic, angelical** *adj*, **angelically** *adv*

angelica /an'jelikə‖æn'dʒelɪkə/ *n* (the candied stalks used esp as a decoration on cakes and desserts, of) a biennial plant of the carrot family

Angelus /'anjələs‖'ændʒələs/ *n* (a bell rung to mark) a devotion of the Western church said at morning, noon and evening to commemorate the incarnation

[1]**anger** /'ang·gə‖'æŋgə/ *n* a strong feeling of displeasure and usu antagonism

[2]**anger** *vb* to make or become angry

angina pectoris /an'jienə 'pektəris, pek'tawris‖æn'dʒaɪnə 'pektərɪs, pek'tɔ:rɪs/ *n* brief attacks of intense chest pain, esp on exertion, precipitated by deficient oxygenation of the heart muscles

[1]**angle** /'ang·gl‖'æŋgl/ *n* **1** a corner **2a** the figure formed by 2 lines extending from the same point or by 2 surfaces diverging from the same line **b** a measure of the amount of turning necessary to bring one line of an angle to coincide with the other at all points **3a** a precise viewpoint; an aspect **b** a special approach or technique for accomplishing an objective **4** a divergent course or position; a slant – esp in *at an angle* – **angled** *adj*

[2]**angle** *vt* **1** to place, move, or direct obliquely **2** to present (e g a news story) from a particular or prejudiced point of view; slant ~ *vi* to turn or proceed at an angle

[3]**angle** *vi* **1** to fish with a hook and line **2** to use artful means to attain an objective <~d *for an invitation*> – **angler** *n*

Angle *n* a member of a Germanic people who invaded England along with the Saxons and Jutes in the 5th c AD – **Anglian** *n or adj*

'angle ˌbracket *n* either of a pair of punctuation marks < > used to enclose matter

Anglican /'ang·glikən‖'æŋglɪkən/ *adj* of the body of churches including the established episcopal Church of England and churches of similar faith in communion with it – **Anglican** *n*, **Anglicanism** *n*

anglicism /'ang·gliˌsiz(ə)m‖'æŋglɪˌsɪz(ə)m/ *n, often cap* **1** a characteristic feature of English occurring in another language **2** adherence or attachment to England, English culture, etc

anglic·ize, -ise /'ang·gliˌsiez‖'æŋglɪˌsaɪz/ *vt, often cap* **1** to make English in tastes or characteristics **2** to adapt (a foreign word or phrase) to English usage – **anglicization** *n, often cap*

angling /'ang·gling‖'æŋglɪŋ/ *n* (the sport of) fishing with a hook and line – **angler** *n*

Anglo- /ˌang·gloh-‖ˌæŋgləʊ-/ *comb form* English nation, people, or culture <Anglo*phobia*>; English and <Anglo-*Japanese*>

ˌAnglo-A'merican *n or adj* (a) N American, esp of the USA, of English origin or descent

ˌAnglo-'Catholic *adj* of a High Church

movement in Anglicanism fostering Catholic dogmatic and liturgical traditions – **Anglo-Catholic** *n*, **Anglo-Catholicism** *n*

ˌAnglo-ˈFrench *n* the French language used in medieval England

ˌAnglo-ˈIndian *n* **1** a British person domiciled for a long time in India **2** a Eurasian of mixed British and Indian birth or descent – **Anglo-Indian** *adj*

anglophile /ˈang·gləfiel, -fil‖ˈæŋgləfaɪl, -fɪl/ *also* **anglophil** /-fil‖-fɪl/ *n, often cap* a foreigner who is greatly interested in and admires England and things English – **anglophilia** *n, often cap* **anglophilic** *adj, often cap,* **anglophilism** *n, often cap,* **anglophily** *n*

anglophobe /ˈang·gləˌfohb‖ˈæŋgləˌfəʊb/ *n, often cap* a foreigner who is averse to England and things English – **anglophobia** *n, often cap,* **anglophobic** *adj, often cap*

ˌAnglo-ˈSaxon *n* **1** a member of the Germanic peoples who conquered England in the 5th c AD and formed the ruling group until the Norman conquest **2** sby of English, esp Anglo-Saxon descent **3** OLD ENGLISH – **Anglo-Saxon** *adj*

angora /angˈgawrə‖æŋˈgɔːrə/ *n* **1** *cap* a domestic cat, goat, or rabbit with long silky hair **2** the hair of the Angora rabbit or goat **3** a fabric or yarn made (in part) of Angora rabbit hair, used esp for knitting [*Angora* (now Ankara), capital city of Turkey]

angostura bark /ˌang·gəˈstooərə‖ˌæŋgəˈstʊərə/ *n* the aromatic bitter bark of a S American tree used as a bitter and formerly as a tonic [*Angostura* (now Ciudad Bolivar), town in Venezuela]

angry /ˈang·gri‖ˈæŋgrɪ/ *adj* **1** feeling or showing anger **2** painfully inflamed <*an ~ rash*> – **angrily** *adv*, **angriness** *n*

angst /angst‖æŋst/ *n* anxiety and anguish, caused esp by considering the state of the world and the human condition

anguish /ˈang·gwish‖ˈæŋgwɪʃ/ *n* extreme physical pain or mental distress – **anguished** *adj*

angular /ˈang·gyoolə‖ˈæŋgjʊlə/ *adj* **1a** having 1 or more angles **b** forming an angle; sharp-cornered **2** measured by an angle < ~ *distance*> **3a** stiff in character or manner; awkward **b** lean, bony – **angularly** *adv*, **angularity** *n*

aniline /ˈanilin, -leen‖ˈænɪlɪn, -liːn/ *n* a liquid amine used chiefly in organic chemical synthesis (e g of dyes)

animadversion /ˌanimadˈvuhsh(ə)n‖ˌænɪmædˈvɜːʃ(ə)n/ *n* **1** a critical and usu censorious remark **2** hostile criticism *USE* fml

animadvert /ˌanimadˈvuht‖ˌænɪmædˈvɜːt/ *vi* to comment critically or adversely *on* – fml

[1]**animal** /ˈaniməl‖ˈænɪməl/ *n* **1** any of a kingdom of living things typically differing from plants in their capacity for spontaneous movement, esp in response to stimulation **2a** any of the lower animals as distinguished from human beings **b** a mammal – not in technical use **3** a person considered as a purely physical being; a creature

[2]**animal** *adj* **1** of or derived from animals **2** of the body as opposed to the mind or spirit – chiefly derog – **animally** *adv*

animalcule /ˌaniˈmalkyoohl‖ˌænɪˈmælkjuːl/ *n* a minute usu microscopic organism – **animalcular** *adj*

animalism /ˈaniməˌliz(ə)m‖ˈænɪməˌlɪz(ə)m/ *n* **1a** that state of having qualities typical of animals; lack of spiritual feeling **b** preoccupation with the satisfaction of physical drives; sensuality **2** a theory that human beings are nothing more than animals – **animalist** *n*, **animalistic** *adj*

animal kingdom *n* that one of the 3 basic groups of natural objects that includes all living and extinct animals

[1]**animate** /ˈanimət‖ˈænɪmət/ *adj* **1** possessing life; alive **2** of animal life **3** lively – **animately** *adv*, **animateness** *n*

[2]**animate** /ˈanimayt‖ˈænɪmeɪt/ *vt* **1** to give spirit and support to; encourage **2** to give life or vigour to **3** to produce in the form of an animated cartoon – **animatedly** *adv*

ˌanimated carˈtoon *n* a film that creates the illusion of movement by photographing successive positional changes (e g of drawings)

animation /ˌaniˈmaysh(ə)n‖ˌænɪˈmeɪʃ(ə)n/ *n* **1** vigorous liveliness **2** (the preparation of) an animated cartoon

animism /ˈanimiz(ə)m‖ˈænɪmɪz(ə)m/ *n* attribution of conscious life, spirits, or souls to nature or natural objects or phenomena – **animist** *n*, **animistic** *adj*

animosity /ˌaniˈmosəti‖ˌænɪˈmɒsətɪ/ *n* powerful often active ill will or resentment

animus /ˈaniməs‖ˈænɪməs/ *n* **1** a pervading attitude or spirit **2** ill will, animosity

anise /ˈanis‖ˈænɪs/ *n* a plant of the carrot family with aromatic seeds of a liquorice-like flavour; *also* aniseed

aniseed /ˈanəseed‖ˈænəsiːd/ *n* the seed of anise used esp as a flavouring (e g in liqueurs)

ankle /ˈangkl‖ˈæŋkl/ *n* **1** the (region of the) joint between the foot and the leg; the tarsus **2** the joint between the cannon bone and pastern of a horse or related animal

anklet /ˈangklit‖ˈæŋklɪt/ *n* an ornamental band or chain worn round the ankle

annals /ˈanlz‖ˈænlz/ *n pl* **1** a record of events, activities, etc, arranged in yearly sequence **2** historical records; chronicles

anneal /əˈneel‖əˈniːl/ *vt* **1** to toughen or relieve internal stresses in (steel, glass, etc) by heating and usu gradually cooling **2** to temper, toughen

[1]**annex** /əˈneks‖əˈneks/ *vt* **1** to subjoin, append **2** to take possession of; *esp* to incorporate (a country or other territory) within the domain of a state – **annexation** *n*, **annexational** *adj*, **annexationist** *n*

[2]**annex**, *chiefly Br* **annexe** /ˈaneks‖ˈæneks/ *n* **1** sthg, esp an addition to a document, annexed or appended **2** a separate or attached extra structure; *esp* a building providing extra accommodation

annihilate /əˈnie·əˌlayt‖əˈnaɪəˌleɪt/ *vt* **1** to destroy (almost) entirely **2** to defeat conclusively; rout – **annihilator** *n*, **annihilative** *adj*, **annihilatory** *adj*, **annihilation** *n*

anniversary /ˌaniˈvuhs(ə)ri‖ˌænɪˈvɜːs(ə)rɪ/ *n* (the celebration of) a day marking the annual recurrence of the date of a notable event [deriv of

Latin *anniversarius* returning annually, fr *annus* year + *vers-, vertere* to turn]

anno Domini /ˌanoh ˈdominie‖ˌænəʊ ˈdɒmɪnaɪ/ *adv, often cap A* – used to indicate that a year or century comes within the Christian era

annotate /ˈanətayt, ˈanoh-‖ˈænəteɪt, ˈænəʊ-/ *vt* to provide (e g a literary work) with notes – **annotative** *adj*, **annotator** *n*, **annotation** *n*

announce /əˈnowns‖əˈnaʊns/ *vt* **1** to make known publicly; proclaim **2a** to give notice of the arrival, presence, or readiness of **b** to indicate in advance; foretell **3** to give evidence of; indicate by action or appearance – **announcement** *n*

announcer /əˈnownsə‖əˈnaʊnsə/ *n* one who introduces television or radio programmes, makes commercial announcements, reads news summaries, or gives station identification

annoy /əˈnoy‖əˈnɔɪ/ *vt* **1** to disturb or irritate, esp by repeated acts; vex – often pass + *with* or *at* **2** to harass ~ *vi* to be a source of annoyance – **annoyance** *n*, **annoyer** *n*, **annoying** *adj*, **annoyingly** *adv*

[1]**annual** /ˈanyoo(ə)l‖ˈænjʊ(ə)l/ *adj* **1** covering or lasting for the period of a year **2** occurring or performed once a year; yearly **3** *of a plant* completing the life cycle in 1 growing season – **annually** *adv*

[2]**annual** *n* **1** a publication appearing yearly **2** sthg lasting 1 year or season; *specif* an annual plant

ˌannual ˈring *n* the layer of wood produced by a single year's growth of a woody plant

annuity /əˈnyooh·əti‖əˈnjuːətɪ/ *n* **1** an amount payable at a regular (e g yearly) interval **2** (a contract embodying) the right to receive or the obligation to pay an annuity

annul /əˈnul‖əˈnʌl/ *vt* **-ll- 1** to reduce to nothing; obliterate, cancel **2** to declare (e g a marriage) legally invalid – **annulment** *n*

annular /ˈanyoolə‖ˈænjʊlə/ *adj* of or forming a ring – **annularly** *adv*, **annularity** *n*

Annunciation /əˌnunsiˈaysh(ə)n‖əˌnʌnsɪˈeɪʃ(ə)n/ *n* (March 25 observed as a church festival commemorating) the announcement of the Incarnation to the Virgin Mary related in Luke 1:26–28

anode /ˈanohd‖ˈænəʊd/ *n* **1** the electrode by which electrons leave a device and enter an external circuit; *specif* the negative terminal of a primary or secondary cell that is delivering current **2** a positive electrode used to accelerate electrons in an electron gun [Greek *anodos* way up, fr *ana* up + *hodos* way] – **anodal** *adj*, **anodally** *adv*, **anodic** *adj*, **anodically** *adv*

[1]**anodyne** /ˈanədien‖ˈænədaɪn/ *adj* **1** easing pain **2** mentally or emotionally soothing

[2]**anodyne** *n* **1** an drug that eases pain **2** sthg that soothes or calms – **anodynic** *adj*

anoint /əˈnoynt‖əˈnɔɪnt/ *vt* **1** to smear or rub with oil or a similar substance **2a** to apply oil to as a sacred rite, esp for consecration **b** to designate (as if) through the rite of anointment; consecrate – **anointer** *n*, **anointment** *n*

anomalous /əˈnomələs‖əˈnɒmələs/ *adj* **1** deviating from a general rule or standard; irregular, abnormal **2** incongruous – **anomalously** *adv*, **anomalousness** *n*

anomaly /əˈnoməli‖əˈnɒməlɪ/ *n* **1** the angular distance of **1a** a planet from its last perihelion **b** a satellite from its last perigee **2** deviation from the common rule; an irregularity, incongruity **3** sthg anomalous – **anomalistic** *adj*

anon /əˈnon‖əˈnɒn/ *adv, archaic* **1** soon, presently **2** at another time

anonymous /əˈnonəməs‖əˈnɒnəməs/ *adj* **1** having or giving no name **2** of unknown or unnamed origin or authorship **3** nondescript – **anonymously** *adv*, **anonymousness** *n*, **anonymity** *n*

anopheles /əˈnofileez‖əˈnɒfɪliːz/ *n* any of the genus of mosquitoes that includes all those which transmit malaria to human beings – **anopheline** *adj or n*

anorak /ˈanərak‖ˈænəræk/ *n, chiefly Br* a short weatherproof coat with a hood

anorexia /ˌanəˈreksi·ə‖ˌænəˈreksɪə/ *n* (prolonged) loss of appetite; *specif* ANOREXIA NERVOSA – **anorectic** *adj or n*, **anorexigenic** *adj*

anoˌrexia nerˈvosa / nuhˈvohzə‖nɜːˈvəʊzə/ *n* pathological aversion to food induced by emotional disturbance and typically accompanied by emaciation

[1]**another** /əˈnudhə‖əˈnʌðə/ *adj* **1** being a different or distinct one <*the same scene viewed from ~ angle*> **2** some other <*do it ~ time*> **3** being one additional <*have ~ piece of pie*> **4** patterned after <*~ Napoleon*>

[2]**another** *pron, pl* **others 1** an additional one; one more **2** a different one <*he loved ~*>

[1]**answer** /ˈahnsə‖ˈɑːnsə/ *n* **1** a reply to a question, remark, etc **2** an esp correct solution to a problem **3** a response or reaction **4** sby or sthg intended to be a close equivalent or rival of another

[2]**answer** *vi* **1** to speak, write, or act in reply **2a** to be responsible or accountable *for* **b** to make amends; atone *for* **3** to correspond *to* **4** to be adequate or usable ~ *vt* **1a** to speak or write in reply to **b** to reply to in justification or explanation <*~ a charge*> **2a** to correspond to **b** to be adequate or usable for **3** to act in response to (a sound or other signal) <*~ the telephone*> **4** to offer a solution for; *esp* to solve – **answerer** *n*

answerable /ˈahns(ə)rəbl‖ˈɑːns(ə)rəbl/ *adj* **1** responsible **2** capable of being answered or refuted – **answerability** *n*

answer back *vb, esp of a child* to reply rudely (to)

ant /ant‖ænt/ *n* any of a family of insects that live in large social groups having a complex organization and hierarchy

ant- /ant-‖ænt-/ – see ANTI-

[1]**-ant** /-(ə)nt‖-(ə)nt/ *suffix* (→ *n*) **1** sby or sthg that performs (a specified action) <*claim*ant> **2** thing that causes (a specified action or process) <*expector*ant> **3** thing that is used or acted upon (in a specified manner) <*inhal*ant>

[2]**-ant** *suffix* (→ *adj*) **1** performing (a specified action) or being (in a specified condition) <*repent*ant> **2** causing (a specified action or process) <*expector*ant>

antacid /antˈasid‖æntˈæsɪd/ *adj* that corrects excessive acidity, esp in the stomach – **antacid** *n*

antagonism /anˈtagəniz(ə)m‖ænˈtægənɪz-

(ə)m/ *n* **1** hostility or antipathy, esp when actively expressed **2** opposition in physiological or biochemical action – **antagonistic** *adj*; **antagonistically** *adv*

antagonist /an'tagənist‖æn'tægənɪst/ *n* **1** an opponent, adversary **2** a drug that opposes the action of another or of a substance (e g a neurotransmitter) that occurs naturally in the body

antagon·ize, **-ise** /an'tagəniez‖æn'tægənaɪz/ *vt* **1** to oppose or counteract **2** to provoke the hostility of

antarctic /an'tahktik‖æn'tɑːktɪk/ *adj, often cap* of the South Pole or surrounding region

anˌtarctic 'circle *n, often cap A&C* the parallel of latitude approx 66$^1/_2$° south of the equator that circumscribes the south polar region

[1]**ante** /'anti‖'æntɪ/ *n* **1** a poker stake usu put up before the deal **2** an amount paid <*these improvements would raise the* ~> – infml

[2]**ante** *vt* **anteing** to put up (an ante)

ante- *prefix* **1a** prior; before <ante*date*> **b** prior to; earlier than <ante*diluvian*> **2** anterior; situated before <ante*room*>

'antˌeater /-ˌeetə‖-ˌiːtə/ *n* any of several mammals that feed (chiefly) on ants and termites

[1]**antecedent** /ˌanti'seed(ə)nt‖ˌæntɪ'siːd(ə)nt/ *n* **1** a word,phrase, or clause functioning as a noun and referred to by a pronoun **2** the premise of a conditional proposition (e g *if A* in 'if A, then B') **3** the first term of a mathematical ratio **4** a preceding thing, event, or circumstance **5a** a model or stimulus for later developments <*the boneshaker was the* ~ *of the modern bicycle*> **b** *pl* family origins; parentage

[2]**antecedent** *adj* **1** prior in time or order **2** causally or logically prior – **antecedently** *adv*

antechamber /'antiˌchaymbə‖'æntɪˌtʃeɪmbə/ *n* an anteroom

'anteˌdate /-ˌdayt‖-ˌdeɪt/ *vt* **1** to attach or assign a date earlier than the true one to (e g a document), esp with intent to deceive **2** to precede in time

ˌantedi'luvian /-di'loohvi·ən‖-dɪ'luːvɪən/ *adj* **1** of the period before the flood described in the Bible **2** completely out-of-date; antiquated – **antediluvian** *n*

antelope /'antilohp‖'æntɪləʊp/ *n*, any of various Old World ruminant mammals that are lighter and more graceful than the true oxen

ante meridiem /ˌanti mə'ridi·əm‖ˌæntɪ mə'rɪdɪəm/ *adj* being before noon – abbr *am*

ˌante'natal /-'naytl‖-'neɪtl/ *adj* of or concerned with an unborn child, pregnancy, or a pregnant woman; prenatal

antenna /an'tenə‖æn'tenə/ *n, pl* **antennae** /-ni‖-nɪ/, **antennas** **1** a movable segmented sense organ on the head of insects, myriapods, and crustaceans **2** an aerial – chiefly used in Br with reference to complex aerials – **antennal** *adj*

anterior /an'tiəri·ə‖æn'tɪərɪə/ *adj* **1** before in time **2** situated before or towards the front: e g **2a** *of an animal part* near the head; cephalic **b** *of the human body or its parts* ventral **3** *of a plant part* (on the side) facing away from the stem or axis; *also* INFERIOR 4a – **anteriorly** *adv*

anteroom /'antiˌroohm, -room‖'æntɪˌruːm, -rʊm/ *n* an outer room that leads to another usu more important one, often used as a waiting room

ante up /'anti‖'æntɪ/ *vb, chiefly NAm* PAY UP

anthem /'anthəm‖'ænθəm/ *n* **1a** an antiphon **b** a piece of church music for voices usu set to a biblical text **2** a song or hymn of praise or gladness

anther /'anthə‖'ænθə/ *n* the part of a stamen that contains and releases pollen – **antheral** *adj*

'antˌhill /-ˌhil‖-ˌhɪl/ *n* **1** a mound thrown up by ants or termites in digging their nest **2** a place (e g a city) that is overcrowded and constantly busy

anthology /an'tholəji‖æn'θɒlədʒɪ/ *n* **1** a collection of selected literary pieces or passages **2** a collection of selected non-literary works <*a fine* ~ *of Byzantine icons*> [deriv of Greek *anthologia* flower gathering, fr *anthos* flower + *legein* to gather] – **anthologist** *n*

anthracite /'anthrəˌsiet‖'ænθrəˌsaɪt/ *n* a hard slow-burning coal containing little volatile matter – **anthracitic** *adj*

anthrax /'anthraks‖'ænθræks/ *n* an often fatal infectious disease of warm-blooded animals (e g cattle, sheep, or human beings) caused by a spore-forming bacterium

anthropocentric /ˌanthrəpə'sentrik, -poh-‖ˌænθrəpə'sentrɪk, -pəʊ-/ *adj* considering human beings to be the most significant entities of the universe – **anthropocentrically** *adv*, **anthropocentricity** *n*

anthropoid /'anthrəˌpoyd‖'ænθrəˌpɔɪd/ *adj* resembling human beings or the anthropoid apes (e g in form or behaviour); apelike

ˌanthropoid 'ape *n* APE 1

anthropology /ˌanthrə'poləji‖ˌænθrə'pɒlədʒɪ/ *n* the scientific study of human beings, esp in relation to physical characteristics, social relations and culture, and the origin and distribution of races [deriv of Greek *anthrōpos* human being + *logos* speech, reason] – **anthropologist** *n*, **anthropological** *adj*, **anthropologically** *adv*

anthropomorphic /ˌanthrəpə'mawfik‖ˌænθrəpə'mɔːfɪk/, **anthropomorphous** /-fəs‖-fəs/ *adj* **1** having a human form or human attributes <~ *deities*> **2** ascribing human characteristics to nonhuman things – **anthropomorphically** *adv*, **anthropomorphously** *adv*

anthropomorphism /ˌanthrəpə'mawfiz(ə)m‖ˌænθrəpə'mɔːfɪz(ə)m/ *n* the ascribing of human behaviour, form, etc to what is not human (e g a god or animal) – **anthropomorphist** *n*, **anthropomorphize** *vt*

anthropophagous /ˌanthrə'pofəgəs‖ˌænθrə'pɒfəgəs/ *adj* feeding on human flesh – **anthropophagy** *n*

[1]**anti** /'anti‖'æntɪ/ *n, pl* **antis** an opponent of a practice or policy

[2]**anti** *prep* opposed or antagonistic to

anti-, **ant-**, **anth-** *prefix* **1a** of the same kind but situated opposite; in the opposite direction to <anti*clockwise*> **b** opposite in kind to <anti*climax*> **2a** opposing or hostile to in opinion, sympathy, or practice <anti-*Semite*> **b** opposing in effect or activity; preventing <anti*septic*>

antibiotic /ˌantibie'otik‖ˌæntɪbaɪ'ɒtɪk/ *n* a substance produced by a microorganism and able in dilute solution to inhibit the growth of or kill another microorganism – **antibiotic** *adj*, **antibiotically** *adv*

ˈantiˌbody /-ˌbodi‖-ˌbɒdɪ/ *n* a protein (e g an immunoglobulin) that is produced by the body in response to a specific antigen and that counteracts its effects (e g by neutralizing toxins or grouping bacteria into clumps)

antic /ˈantik‖ˈæntɪk/ *n* a ludicrous act or action; a caper – usu pl

anticipate /anˈtisipayt‖ænˈtɪsɪpeɪt/ *vt* **1** to give advance thought, discussion, or treatment to **2** to foresee and deal with in advance; forestall **3** to use, expend, or act on before the right or natural time **4** to act before (another) often so as to thwart **5** to look forward to as certain; expect – disapproved of by some speakers ~*vi* to speak or write in knowledge or expectation of sthg due to happen – **anticipator** *n*, **anticipatable** *adj*, **anticipative** *adj*, **anticipatively** *adv*, **anticipatory** *adj*

anticipation /anˌtisiˈpaysh(ə)n‖ænˌtɪsɪˈpeɪʃ-(ə)n/ *n* an act of looking forward; *specif* pleasurable expectation

ˌantiˈclerical /-ˈklerikl‖-ˈklerɪkl/ *adj* opposed to the influence of the clergy or church in secular affairs – **anticlerical** *n*, **anticlericalism** *n*, **anticlericalist** *n*

ˌantiˈclimax /-ˈkliemaks‖-ˈklaɪmæks/ *n* **1** (an instance of) the usu sudden and ludicrous descent in writing or speaking from a significant to a trivial idea **2** an event (e g at the end of a series) that is strikingly less important or exciting than expected – **anticlimactic, anticlimactical** *adj*, **anticlimactically** *adv*

ˌantiˈclockwise /-ˈklokwiez‖-ˈklɒkwaɪz/ *adj or adv* in a direction opposite to that in which the hands of a clock rotate when viewed from the front

ˌantiˈcyclone /-ˈsieklohn‖-ˈsaɪkləʊn/ *n* **1** a system of winds that rotates about a centre of high atmospheric pressure **2** [3]HIGH 1 – **anticyclonic** *adj*

antidote /ˈantiˌdoht‖ˈæntɪˌdəʊt/ *n* **1** a remedy that counteracts the effects of poison **2** sthg that relieves or counteracts <*an ~ to the mechanization of our society*> – **antidotal** *adj*

ˈantiˌfreeze /-ˌfreez‖-ˌfriːz/ *n* a substance added to a liquid (e g the water in a car radiator) to lower its freezing point

antigen /ˈantijən‖ˈæntɪdʒən/ *n* a protein, carbohydrate, etc that stimulates the production of an antibody when introduced into the body – **antigenic** *adj*, **antigenically** *adv*, **antigenicity** *n*

ˈanti-ˌhero, *fem* **ˈanti-ˌheroine** *n* a protagonist who lacks traditional heroic qualities (e g courage) – **anti-heroic** *adj*

ˌantiˈhistamine /-ˈhistəmin‖-ˈhɪstəmɪn/ *n* any of various compounds that oppose the actions of histamine and are used esp for treating allergies and motion sickness – **antihistaminic** *adj or n*

ˌantiˈknock /-ˈnok‖-ˈnɒk/ *n* a substance added to fuel to prevent knocking in an internal-combustion engine

ˌantiˈlogarithm /-ˈlogəˌridhəm‖-ˈlɒgəˌrɪðəm/ *n* the number corresponding to a given logarithm

ˌantimaˈcassar /-məˈkasə‖-məˈkæsə/ *n* a usu protective cover put over the backs or arms of upholstered seats

ˈantiˌmatter /-ˌmatə‖-ˌmætə/ *n* matter composed of antiparticles (e g antiprotons instead of protons, positrons instead of electrons, and antineutrons instead of neutrons)

antimony /ˈantiməni‖ˈæntɪmənɪ; *NAm* ˈantiˌmohni‖ˈæntɪˌməʊnɪ/ *n* a brittle usu metallic metalloid element used esp as a constituent of alloys – **antimonial** *adj*, **antimonious** *adj*

antinomy /anˈtinəmi‖ænˈtɪnəmɪ/ *n* a contradiction or conflict between 2 apparently valid principles

ˌantiˈparticle /-ˈpahtikl‖-ˈpɑːtɪkl/ *n* an elementary particle identical to another in mass but opposite to it in electric and magnetic properties

ˌantipaˈthetic /-pəˈthetik‖-pəˈθetɪk/ *adj* **1** feeling or causing aversion or opposition **2** opposed in nature or character *to* – **antipathetically** *adv*

antipathy /anˈtipəthi‖ænˈtɪpəθɪ/ *n* a fixed aversion or dislike; a distaste

ˌantipersonˈnel /-puhsəˈnel‖-pɜːsəˈnel/ *adj, of a weapon* (designed) for use against people

antiphon /ˈantifən, -fon‖ˈæntɪfən, -fɒn/ *n* a verse, usu from Scripture, said or sung usu before and after a canticle, psalm, or psalm verse as part of the liturgy – **antiphonal** *adj*

antipodal /anˈtipədl‖ænˈtɪpədl/ *adj* **1** of the antipodes; *specif* situated at the opposite side of the earth or moon <*an ~ meridian*> **2** diametrically opposite <*an ~ point on a sphere*>

antipodes /anˈtipəˌdeez‖ænˈtɪpəˌdiːz/ *n pl the* region of the earth diametrically opposite; *specif, often cap* Australasia – **antipodean** *adj*

[1]**antiquarian** /ˌantiˈkweəri·ən‖ˌæntɪˈkweərɪən/ *n* one who collects or studies antiquities

[2]**antiquarian** *adj* **1** of antiquarians or antiquities **2** *of books or prints* old (and rare) – **antiquarianism** *n*

antiquary /ˈantikwəri‖ˈæntɪkwərɪ/ *n* an antiquarian

antiquated /ˈantiˌkwaytid‖ˈæntɪˌkweɪtɪd/ *adj* **1** outmoded or discredited by reason of age; out-of-date **2** advanced in age

[1]**antique** /anˈteek‖ænˈtiːk/ *adj* **1** belonging to or surviving from earlier, esp classical, times; ancient **2** old-fashioned **3** made in an earlier period and therefore valuable; *also* suggesting the style of an earlier period

[2]**antique** *n* **1** *the* ancient Greek or Roman style in art **2** a relic or object of ancient times **3** a work of art, piece of furniture, or decorative object made at an earlier period and sought by collectors

antiquity /anˈtikwəti‖ænˈtɪkwətɪ/ *n* **1** ancient times; *esp* the period before the Middle Ages **2** the quality of being ancient **3** *pl* relics or monuments of ancient times

antirrhinum /ˌantiˈrienəm‖ˌæntɪˈraɪnəm/ *n* any of a large genus of plants (e g the snapdragon or a related plant) with bright-coloured 2-lipped flowers

ˌanti-ˈSemitism *n* hostility towards Jews – **anti-Semitic** *adj*, **anti-Semite** *n*

[1]**ˌantiˈseptic** /-ˈseptik‖-ˈseptɪk/ *adj* **1a** opposing sepsis (in living tissue), specif by arresting the growth of microorganisms, esp bacteria **b** of,

acting or protecting like, or using an antiseptic **2a** scrupulously clean; aseptic **b** extremely neat or orderly, esp to the point of being bare or uninteresting **3** impersonal, detached – **antiseptically** *adv*

[2]**antiseptic** *n* an antiseptic substance; *also* a germicide

ˌantiˈsocial /-ˈsohsh(ə)l‖-ˈsəʊʃ(ə)l/ *adj* **1** hostile or harmful to organized society **2a** averse to the society of others; unsociable **b** *Br* UNSOCIAL 2

antiterror /ˌantiˈterə‖ˌæntɪˈterə/ *adj* intended to combat terrorism – **antiterrorism** *n*, **antiterrorist** *adj*

antithesis /anˈtithəsis‖ænˈtɪθəsɪs/ *n, pl* **antitheses** /-seez‖-siːz/ **1a** a contrast of ideas expressed by a parallel arrangement of words (e g in 'action, not words') **b** opposition, contrast **c** the direct opposite <*his ideas are the ~ of mine*> **2** the second stage of a reasoned argument, in contrast to the thesis

antithetical /ˌantiˈthetikl‖ˌæntɪˈθetɪkl/, **antithetic** *adj* **1** constituting or marked by antithesis **2** directly opposed – **antithetically** *adv*

ˌantiˈtoxin /-ˈtoksin‖-ˈtɒksɪn/ *n* (a serum containing) an antibody capable of neutralizing the specific toxin that stimulated its production in the body – **antitoxic** *adj*

antler /ˈantlə‖ˈæntlə/ *n* (a branch of) the solid periodically shed (much branched) horn of an animal of the deer family – **antlered** *adj*

antonym /ˈantənim‖ˈæntənɪm/ *n* a word having the opposite meaning – **antonymous** *adj*, **antonymy** *n*

anus /ˈaynəs‖ˈeɪnəs/ *n* the rear excretory opening of the alimentary canal

anvil /ˈanvil‖ˈænvɪl/ *n* **1** a heavy, usu steel-faced, iron block on which metal is shaped **2** a towering anvil-shaped cloud **3** the incus

anxiety /angˈzie·əti‖æŋˈzaɪətɪ/ *n* **1a** apprehensive uneasiness of mind, usu over an impending or anticipated ill **b** an ardent or earnest wish <*~ to please*> **c** a cause of anxiety **2** an abnormal overwhelming sense of apprehension and fear, often with doubt about one's capacity to cope with the threat

anxious /ˈang(k)shəs‖ˈæŋ(k)ʃəs/ *adj* **1** troubled, worried **2** causing anxiety; worrying **3** ardently or earnestly wishing *to* – **anxiously** *adv*, **anxiousness** *n*

[1]**any** /ˈeni‖ˈenɪ/ *adj* **1** one or some indiscriminately; whichever is chosen <*~ plan is better than none*> **2** one, some, or all; whatever: e g **2a** of whatever number or quantity; being even the smallest number or quantity of <*have you ~ money?*> **b** no matter how great <*at ~ cost*> **c** no matter how ordinary or inadequate <*wear just ~ old thing*> **3** being an appreciable number, part, or amount of – not in positive statements <*not for ~ length of time*>

[2]**any** *pron, pl* **any** **1** any person; anybody <*~ of us*> **2a** any thing **b** any part, quantity, or number <*hardly ~ of it*>

[3]**any** *adv* to any extent or degree; AT ALL <*not feeling ~ better*>

anybody /ˈeniˌbodi, -bədi‖ˈenɪˌbɒdɪ, -bədɪ/ *pron* any person

ˈanyˌhow /-ˌhow‖-ˌhaʊ/ *adv* **1** in a haphazard manner <*thrown down all ~*> **2** anyway

ˈanyone /-wun, -wən‖-wʌn, -wən/ *pron* anybody

ˈanyˌplace /-ˌplays‖-ˌpleɪs/ *adv, NAm* anywhere

ˈanyˌroad /-ˌrohd‖-ˌrəʊd/ *adv, Br* anyway – nonstandard

[1]**ˈanyˌthing** /-ˌthing‖-ˌθɪŋ/ *pron* any thing whatever <*do ~ for a quiet life*> – **anything but** not at all; far from

[2]**anything** *adv* in any degree; AT ALL <*isn't ~ like so cold*>

ˈanyˌway /-ˌway‖-ˌweɪ/ *adv* **1** in any case, inevitably <*going to be hanged ~*> **2** – used when resuming a narrative <*well, ~, I rang the bell . . .*>

[1]**ˈanyˌwhere** /-ˌweə‖-ˌweə/ *adv* **1** in, at, or to any place <*too late to go ~*> **2** to any extent; AT ALL <*isn't ~ near ready*> **3** – used to indicate limits of variation <*~ from 40 to 60*>

[2]**anywhere** *n* any place

aorta /ayˈawtə‖eɪˈɔːtə/ *n, pl* **aortas, aortae** /-ti‖-tɪ/ the great artery that carries blood from the left side of the heart to be distributed by branch arteries throughout the body – **aortal** *adj*, **aortic** *adj*

apace /əˈpays‖əˈpeɪs/ *adv* at a quick pace; swiftly

apart /əˈpaht‖əˈpɑːt/ *adv* **1a** at a distance (from one another in space or time) <*towns 20 miles ~*> **b** at a distance in character or opinions <*their ideas are worlds ~*> **2** so as to separate one from another <*can't tell the twins ~*> **3** excluded from consideration <*joking ~, what shall we do?*> **4** in or into 2 or more parts <*had to take the engine ~*>

aˈpart from *prep* **1** in addition to; besides <*haven't time, quite ~ the cost*> **2** EXCEPT FOR <*excellent ~ a few blemishes*>

apartheid /əˈpaht·(h)ayt, -(h)iet‖əˈpɑːt(h)eɪt, -(h)aɪt/ *n* racial segregation; *specif* a policy of segregation and discrimination against non-Europeans in the Republic of S Africa [Afrikaans, lit., separateness]

apartment /əˈpahtmənt‖əˈpɑːtmənt/ *n* **1** a single room in a building **2** a suite of rooms used for living quarters **3** *chiefly NAm* a flat – **apartmental** *adj*

aˈpartment ˌhouse *n, NAm* a block of flats

apathetic /ˌapəˈthetik‖ˌæpəˈθetɪk/ *adj* **1** having or showing little or no feeling; spiritless **2** lacking interest or concern; indifferent – **apathetically** *adv*

apathy /ˈapəthi‖ˈæpəθɪ/ *n* **1** lack of feeling or emotion; impassiveness **2** lack of interest or concern; indifference [Greek *apatheia*, fr *apathēs* without feeling, fr *a-* not, without + *pathos* emotion, fr *paschein* to suffer]

[1]**ape** /ayp‖eɪp/ *n* **1** a (large semierect tailless or short-tailed Old World) monkey: **1a** a chimpanzee **b** a gorilla **c** any similar primate **2a** a mimic **b** a large uncouth person – **apelike** *adj*

[2]**ape** *vt* to imitate closely but often clumsily and ineptly – **aper** *n*

aperient /əˈpiəri·ənt‖əˈpɪərɪənt/ *n or adj* (a) laxative

aperitif /əˌperəˈteef, -ˈ---‖əˌperəˈtiːf, -ˈ---/ *n* an

alcoholic drink taken before a meal to stimulate the appetite

aperture /'apəchə‖'æpətʃə/ *n* **1** an open space; a hole, gap **2a** (the diameter of) the opening in an optical (photographic) system through which the light passes **b** the diameter of the objective lens or mirror of a telescope

apex /'aypeks‖'eɪpeks/ *n, pl* **apexes, apices** /'aypə,seez‖'eɪpə,siːz/ **1a** the uppermost peak; the vertex <*the ~ of a mountain*> **b** the narrowed or pointed end; the tip <*the ~ of the tongue*> **2** the highest or culminating point <*the ~ of his career*>

aphid /'ayfid‖'eɪfɪd/ *n* a greenfly or related small sluggish insect that sucks the juices of plants

aphorism /'afəriz(ə)m‖'æfərɪz(ə)m/ *n* a concise pithy formulation of a truth; an adage – **aphorize** *vi*, **aphorist** *n*, **aphoristic** *adj*, **aphoristically** *adv*

aphrodisiac /,afrə'diziak‖,æfrə'dɪzɪæk/ *n or adj* (a substance) that stimulates sexual desire [Greek *aphrodisiakos* sexual, fr *aphrodisios* of Aphrodite, fr *Aphroditē*, goddess of love] – **aphrodisiacal** *adj*

apiarist /'aypi·ərist‖'eɪpɪərɪst/ *n* a beekeeper

apiary /'aypi·əri‖'eɪpɪərɪ/ *n* a place where (hives or colonies of) bees are kept, esp for their honey

apices /'aypə,seez‖'eɪpə,siːz/ *pl of* APEX

apiculture /'aypi,kulchə‖'eɪpɪ,kʌltʃə/ *n* the keeping of bees, esp on a large scale – **apicultural** *adj*, **apiculturist** *n*

apiece /ə'pees‖ə'piːs/ *adv* for each one; individually

apish /'aypish‖'eɪpɪʃ/ *adj* resembling an ape: e g **a** slavishly imitative **b** extremely silly or affected – **apishly** *adv*, **apishness** *n*

aplomb /ə'plum, ə'plom‖ə'plʌm, ə'plɒm/ *n* complete composure or self-assurance; poise

apocalypse /ə'pokəlips‖ə'pɒkəlɪps/ *n* **1a** any of a number of early Jewish and Christian works, characterized by symbolic imagery, which describe the establishment of God's kingdom **b** *cap* REVELATION 2 – usu + *the* **2** sthg viewed as a prophetic revelation [Greek *apokalypsis* revelation, fr *apokalyptein* to uncover, fr *apo* off + *kalyptein* to cover]

apocalyptic /ə,pokə'liptik‖ə,pɒkə'lɪptɪk/ *also* **apocalyptical** /-kl‖-kl/ *adj* **1** of or resembling an apocalypse **2** forecasting the ultimate destiny of the world; prophetic **3** foreboding imminent disaster; terrible – **apocalyptically** *adv*

apocrypha /ə'pokrifə‖ə'pɒkrɪfə/ *n* **1** (a collection of) writings or statements of dubious authenticity **2** *sing or pl in constr, cap* books included in the Septuagint and Vulgate but excluded from the Jewish and Protestant canons of the Old Testament – usu + *the*

apocryphal /ə'pokrif(ə)l‖ə'pɒkrɪf(ə)l/ *adj* **1** *often cap* of or resembling the Apocrypha **2** of doubtful authenticity – **apocryphally** *adv*, **apocryphalness** *n*

apogee /'apəjee‖'æpədʒiː/ *n* **1** the point farthest from a planet or other celestial body reached by any object orbiting it **2** the farthest or highest point; the culmination <*Aegean civilization reached its ~ in Crete*> – **apogean** *adj*

apologetic /ə,polə'jetik‖ə,pɒlə'dʒetɪk/ *adj* **1a** offered in defence or vindication **b** offered by way of excuse or apology <*an ~ smile*> **2** regretfully acknowledging fault or failure; contrite – **apologetically** *adv*

a,polo'getics *n pl but sing or pl in constr* **1** systematic reasoned argument in defence (e g of a doctrine) **2** a branch of theology devoted to the rational defence of Christianity

apologia /,apə'lohjyə‖,æpə'ləʊdʒjə/ *n* a reasoned defence in speech or writing, esp of a faith, cause, or institution

apologist /ə'poləjist‖ə'pɒlədʒɪst/ *n* the author of an apologia

apolog·ize, -ise /ə'poləjiez‖ə'pɒlədʒaɪz/ *vi* to make an apology

apology /ə'poləji‖ə'pɒlədʒɪ/ *n* **1a** an apologia **b** EXCUSE 1 **2** an admission of error or discourtesy accompanied by an expression of regret **3** a poor substitute *for*

apophthegm /'apə,them‖'æpə,θem/ *n* a short, pithy, and instructive saying – **apophthegmatic, apophthegmatical** *adj*, **apophthegmatically** *adv*

apoplectic /,apə'plektik‖,æpə'plektɪk/ *adj* **1** of, causing, affected with, or showing symptoms of apoplexy **2** violently excited (e g from rage) – **apoplectically** *adv*

apoplexy /'apə,pleksi‖'æpə,pleksɪ/ *n* [2]STROKE 5

apostasy /ə'postəsi‖ə'pɒstəsɪ/ *n* **1** renunciation of a religious faith **2** abandonment of a previous loyalty; defection

apostate /ə'postayt‖ə'pɒsteɪt/ *n* one who commits apostasy – **apostate** *adj*

apostat·ize, -ise /ə'postətiez‖ə'pɒstətaɪz/ *vi* to commit apostasy

a posteriori /,ay po,stiəri'awri‖,eɪ pɒ,stɪərɪ'ɔːrɪ/ *adj* **1** inductive **2** relating to or derived by reasoning from observed facts [Latin, from the latter] – **a posteriori** *adv*

apostle /ə'pos(ə)l‖ə'pɒs(ə)l/ *n* **1** one sent on a mission; *esp* any of an authoritative New Testament group sent out to preach the gospel and made up esp of Jesus's original 12 disciples and Paul **2a** one who first advocates an important belief or system **b** an ardent supporter; an adherent <*an ~ of liberal tolerance*> [Late Latin *apostolus*, fr Greek *apostolos*, lit., sby sent away, fr *apo* off, away + *stellein* to send] – **apostleship** *n*

apostolic /,apə'stolik‖,æpə'stɒlɪk/ *adj* **1** of an apostle or the New Testament apostles **2a** of the divine authority vested in the apostles held (e g by Roman Catholics, Anglicans, and Eastern Orthodox) to be handed down through the successive ordinations of bishops **b** of the pope as the successor to the apostolic authority vested in St Peter – **apostolicity** *n*

[1]**apostrophe** /ə'postrəfi‖ə'pɒstrəfɪ/ *n* the addressing, rhetorically, of a usu absent person or a usu personified thing – **apostrophize** *vb*, **apostrophic** *adj*

[2]**apostrophe** *n* a mark ' used to indicate the omission of letters or figures, the possessive case, or the plural of letters or figures – **apostrophic** *adj*

a,pothecaries' 'weight /ə'pothək(ə)riz‖ə-

ˈpɒθək(ə)rɪz/ *n* the series of units of weight used formerly by pharmacists and based on the ounce of 8 drachms and the drachm of 3 scruples or 60 grains

apothecary /əˈpothək(ə)ri‖əˈpɒθək(ə)rɪ/ *n, archaic or NAm* **1** a pharmacist **2** PHARMACY 2

apothegm /ˈapəthem‖ˈæpəθem/ *n, NAm* an apophthegm

apotheosis /ə,pothiˈohsis‖ə,pɒθɪˈəʊsɪs/ *n, pl* **apotheoses** /-seez‖-siːz/ **1** deification **2** *the* perfect example <*she is the ~ of womanhood*> – **apotheosize** *vt*

appal, *NAm chiefly* **appall** /əˈpawl‖əˈpɔːl/ *vt* **-ll-** to overcome with consternation, horror, or dismay – **appalling** *adj*, **appallingly** *adv*

apparatchik /,apəˈrachik‖,æpəˈrætʃɪk/ *n* a member of the administrative bureaucracy of a Communist party; *broadly* a bureaucrat

apparatus /ˈapəraytəs, --ˈ--‖ˈæpəreɪtəs, --ˈ--; *NAm also* -ˈratəs‖-ˈrætəs/ *n, pl* **apparatuses, apparatus** **1a** (a piece of) equipment designed for a particular use, esp for a scientific operation **b** a group of organs having a common function **2** the administrative bureaucracy of an organization, esp a political party

[1]**apparel** /əˈparəl‖əˈpærəl/ *vt* **-ll-** (*NAm* **-l-**, **-ll-**) **1** to put clothes on; dress – chiefly fml **2** to adorn, embellish – chiefly poetic

[2]**apparel** *n* **1** garments, clothing – chiefly fml **2** sthg that clothes or adorns <*the bright ~ of spring*> – chiefly poetic

apparent /əˈparənt‖əˈpærənt/ *adj* **1** easily seen or understood; plain, evident **2** seemingly real but not necessarily so **3** having an absolute right to succeed to a title or estate <*the heir ~*> – **apparently** *adv*

apparition /,apəˈrish(ə)n‖,æpəˈrɪʃ(ə)n/ *n* **1a** an unusual or unexpected sight; a phenomenon **b** a ghostly figure **2** the act of becoming visible; appearance – **apparitional** *adj*

[1]**appeal** /əˈpeel‖əˈpiːl/ *n* **1** a legal proceeding by which a case is brought to a higher court for review **2a(1)** an application (e g to a recognized authority) for corroboration, vindication, or decision **a(2)** a call by members of the fielding side in cricket, esp by the bowler, for the umpire to decide whether a batsman is out **b** an earnest plea for aid or mercy; an entreaty **3** the power of arousing a sympathetic response; attraction <*the theatre has lost its ~ for him*>

[2]**appeal** *vt* to take (a case) to a higher court ~ *vi* **1** to take a case to a higher court **2a** to call on another for corroboration, vindication, or decision **b** to make an appeal in cricket **3** to make an earnest plea or request **4** to arouse a sympathetic response *USE* often + *to* – **appealer** *n*, **appealable** *adj*, **appealability** *n*

appealing /əˈpeeling‖əˈpiːlɪŋ/ *adj* **1** having appeal; pleasing **2** marked by earnest entreaty; imploring – **appealingly** *adv*

appear /əˈpiə‖əˈpɪə/ *vi* **1a** to be or become visible **b** to arrive <*~s promptly at 8 each day*> **2** to come formally before an authoritative body **3** to give the impression of being; seem **4** to come into public view

appearance /əˈpiərəns‖əˈpɪərəns/ *n* **1** the coming into court of a party in an action or his/her lawyer **2** a visit or attendance that is seen or noticed by others <*put in an ~ at the party*> **3a** an outward aspect; a look **b** an external show; a semblance **c** *pl* an outward or superficial indication that hides the real situation <*would do anything to keep up ~s*>

appease /əˈpeez‖əˈpiːz/ *vt* **1** to pacify, calm **2** to cause to subside; allay <*~ his hunger*> **3** to conciliate (esp an aggressor) by concessions – **appeasable** *adj*, **appeasement** *n*, **appeaser** *n*

[1]**appellant** /əˈpelənt‖əˈpelənt/ *adj* appellate

[2]**appellant** *n* one who appeals against a judicial decision

appellate /əˈpelət‖əˈpelət/ *adj* of or recognizing appeals <*an ~ court*>

appellation /,apəˈlaysh(ə)n‖,æpəˈleɪʃ(ə)n/ *n* an identifying name or title

append /əˈpend‖əˈpend/ *vt* to attach or add, esp as a supplement or appendix

appendage /əˈpendij‖əˈpendɪdʒ/ *n* **1** sthg appended to sthg larger or more important **2** a limb, seta, or other subordinate or derivative body part

appendicectomy /ə,pendiˈsektəmi‖ə,pendɪˈsektəmɪ/, *chiefly NAm* **appendectomy** /apənˈdektəmi‖æpənˈdektəmɪ/ *n* surgical removal of the appendix

appendicitis /ə,pendiˈsietəs‖ə,pendɪˈsaɪtəs/ *n* inflammation of the vermiform appendix

appendix /əˈpendiks‖əˈpendɪks/ *n, pl* **appendixes, appendices** /-di,seez‖-dɪ,siːz/ **1** a supplement (e g containing explanatory or statistical material), usu attached at the end of a piece of writing **2** the vermiform appendix or similar bodily outgrowth

appertain /,apəˈtayn‖,æpəˈteɪn/ *vi* to belong or be connected as a rightful or customary part, possession, or attribute; pertain – usu + *to*

appetite /ˈapətiet‖ˈæpətaɪt/ *n* **1** a desire to satisfy an internal bodily need; *esp* an (eager) desire to eat **2** a strong desire demanding satisfaction; an inclination – **appetitive** *adj*

appet·izer, **-iser** /ˈapətiezə‖ˈæpətaɪzə/ *n* a food or drink that stimulates the appetite and is usu served before a meal

appet·izing, **-ising** /ˈapətiezing‖ˈæpətaɪzɪŋ/ *adj* appealing to the appetite, esp in appearance or aroma – **appetizingly** *adv*

applaud /əˈplawd‖əˈplɔːd/ *vb* to express approval (of), esp by clapping the hands – **applaudable** *adj*, **applauder** *n*

applause /əˈplawz‖əˈplɔːz/ *n* **1** approval publicly expressed (e g by clapping the hands) **2** praise

apple /ˈapl‖ˈæpl/ *n* **1** (the fleshy, edible, usu rounded, red, yellow, or green fruit of) a tree of the rose family **2** a fruit or other plant structure resembling an apple – **apple of someone's eye** sby or sthg greatly cherished

apple-pie order *n* perfect order

appliance /əˈplie·əns‖əˈplaɪəns/ *n* **1** an instrument or device designed for a particular use; *esp* a domestic machine or device powered by gas or electricity (e g a food mixer, vacuum cleaner, or cooker) **2** BRACE 4e

applicable /əˈplikəbl‖əˈplɪkəbl/ *adj* appropriate – **applicability** *n*

applicant /ˈaplikənt‖ˈæplɪkənt/ *n* one who applies

application /ˌapli'kaysh(ə)n‖ˌæplɪ'keɪʃ(ə)n/ *n* **1a** an act of applying **b** a use to which sthg is put **c** close attention; diligence **2** a request, petition **3** a lotion **4** capacity for practical use; relevance – **applicative** *adj*, **applicatory** *adj*

applied /ə'plied‖ə'plaɪd/ *adj* put to practical use; *esp* applying general principles to solve definite problems < ~ *sciences*>

[1]**appliqué** /ə'pleekay, ˌaplee'kay‖ə'pliːkeɪ, ˌæpliː'keɪ/ *n* a cutout decoration fastened (e g by sewing) to a larger piece of material; *also* the decorative work formed in this manner

[2]**appliqué** *vt* **appliquéing** /-kaying‖-keɪɪŋ/ to apply (e g a decoration or ornament) to a larger surface

apply /ə'plie‖ə'plaɪ/ *vt* **1a** to bring to bear; put to use, esp for some practical purpose < ~ *pressure*> **b** to lay or spread on < ~ *varnish to a table*> **2** to devote (e g oneself) with close attention or diligence – usu + *to* <*should* ~ *himself to his work*> ~ *vi* **1** to have relevance – usu + *to* <*this rule* applies *to new members only*> **2** to make a request, esp in writing < ~ *for a job*> – **applier** *n*

appoint /ə'poynt‖ə'pɔɪnt/ *vt* **1** to fix or name officially **2** to select for an office or position **3** to declare the disposition of (an estate) to sby

ap'pointed *adj* equipped, furnished

ap'pointment /-mənt‖-mənt/ *n* **1** an act of appointing; a designation <*fill a vacancy by* ~> **2** an office or position held by sby who has been appointed to it rather than voted into it **3** an arrangement for a meeting **4** *pl* equipment, furnishings

apportion /ə'pawsh(ə)n‖ə'pɔːʃ(ə)n/ *vt* to divide and share out in just proportion or according to a plan; allot – **apportionment** *n*

apposite /'apəzit‖'æpəzɪt/ *adj* highly pertinent or appropriate; apt – **appositely** *adv*, **appositeness** *n*

apposition /ˌapə'zish(ə)n‖ˌæpə'zɪʃ(ə)n/ *n* a grammatical construction in which 2 usu adjacent nouns or noun phrases have the same referent and stand in the same syntactic relation to the rest of a sentence (e g *the poet* and *Burns* in 'a biography of the poet Burns') – **appositional** *adj*, **appositionally** *adv*

appraisal /ə'prayz(ə)l‖ə'preɪz(ə)l/ *n* an act or instance of appraising; *specif* a valuation of property by an authorized person

appraise /ə'prayz‖ə'preɪz/ *vt* to evaluate the worth, significance, or status of; *esp* to give an expert judgment of the value or merit of – **appraisement** *n*, **appraiser** *n*, **appraising** *adj*, **appraisingly** *adv*

appreciable /ə'preesh(y)əbl‖ə'priːʃ(j)əbl/ *adj* **1** capable of being perceived or measured **2** fairly large <*an* ~ *distance*> – **appreciably** *adv*

appreciate /ə'preeshiayt, -siayt‖ə'priːʃɪeɪt, -sɪeɪt/ *vt* **1a** to understand the nature, worth, quality, or significance of **b** to recognize with gratitude; value or admire highly **2** to increase the value of ~*vi* to increase in value – **appreciative** *adj*, **appreciatively** *adv*, **appreciator** *n*, **appreciatory** *adj*

appreciation /əˌpreeshi'aysh(ə)n, -si-‖əˌpriːʃɪ'eɪʃ(ə)n, -sɪ-/ *n* **1a** sensitive awareness; *esp* recognition of aesthetic values **b** a judgment, evaluation; *esp* a favourable critical estimate **c** an expression of admiration, approval, or gratitude **2** an increase in value

apprehend /ˌapri'hend‖ˌæprɪ'hend/ *vt* **1** to arrest, seize **2** to understand, perceive ~*vi* to understand

apprehension /ˌapri'hensh(ə)n‖ˌæprɪ'henʃ(ə)n/ *n* **1** the act or power of comprehending <*a man of dull* ~> **2** arrest, seizure – used technically in Scottish law **3** anxiety or fear, esp of future evil; foreboding

apprehensive /ˌapri'hensiv, -ziv‖ˌæprɪ'hensɪv, -zɪv/ *adj* viewing the future with anxiety, unease, or fear – often + *for* or *of* – **apprehensively** *adv*, **apprehensiveness** *n*

[1]**apprentice** /ə'prentis‖ə'prentɪs/ *n* **1** one who is learning an art or trade **1a** from an employer to whom he/she is bound by indenture **b** by practical experience under skilled workers **2** an inexperienced person; a novice – **apprenticeship** *n*

[2]**apprentice** *vt* to set at work as an apprentice

apprise /ə'priez‖ə'praɪz/ *vt* to give notice to; tell – usu + *of*; fml

[1]**approach** /ə'prohch‖ə'prəʊtʃ/ *vt* **1a** to draw closer to **b** to come very near to in quality, character, etc **2a** to make advances to, esp in order to create a desired result <*was* ~ed *by several film producers*> **b** to begin to consider or deal with < ~ *the subject with an open mind*> ~*vi* to draw nearer

[2]**approach** *n* **1a** an act or instance of approaching **b** an approximation **2** a manner or method of doing sthg, esp for the first time <*a highly individual* ~ *to language*> **3** a means of access <*the* ~es *to the city*> **4a** a golf shot from the fairway towards the green **b** (the steps taken on) the part of a tenpin bowling alley from which a bowler must deliver the ball **5** the final part of an aircraft flight before landing **6** an advance made to establish personal or business relations – usu pl

approachable /ə'prohchəbl‖ə'prəʊtʃəbl/ *adj* easy to meet or deal with – **approachability** *n*

approbation /ˌaprə'baysh(ə)n‖ˌæprə'beɪʃ(ə)n/ *n* formal or official approval; sanction – **approbatory** *adj*

[1]**appropriate** /ə'prohpriˌayt‖ə'prəʊprɪˌeɪt/ *vt* **1** to take exclusive possession of **2** to set apart (specif money) for a particular purpose or use **3** to take or make use of without authority or right – **appropriable** *adj*, **appropriator** *n*

[2]**appropriate** /ə'prohpri·ət‖ə'prəʊprɪət/ *adj* especially suitable or compatible; fitting – **appropriately** *adv*, **appropriateness** *n*

appropriation /əˌprohpri'aysh(ə)n‖əˌprəʊprɪ'eɪʃ(ə)n/ *n* sthg appropriated; *specif* money set aside by formal action for a particular use – **appropriative** *adj*

approval /ə'proohvl‖ə'pruːvl/ *n* **1** a favourable opinion or judgment **2** formal or official permission – **on approval** *of goods supplied commercially* to be returned without payment if found unsatisfactory

approve /ə'proohv‖ə'pruːv/ *vt* **1** to have or express a favourable opinion of **2a** to accept as satisfactory **b** to give formal or official sanction to; ratify <*Parliament* ~d *the proposed policy*>

~*vi* to take a favourable view – often + *of* <*doesn't* ~ *of fighting*> – **approvingly** *adv*

[1]**approximate** /ə'proksimət‖ə'prɒksɪmət/ *adj* nearly correct or exact – **approximately** *adv*

[2]**approximate** /ə'proksimayt‖ə'prɒksɪmeɪt/ *vt* **1** to bring near or close – often + *to* **2** to come near to; approach, esp in quality or number ~*vi* to come close – usu + *to*

approximation /ə,proksi'maysh(ə)n‖ə,prɒksɪ'meɪʃ(ə)n/ *n* sthg that is approximate; *esp* a mathematical quantity that is close in value but not equal to a desired quantity – **approximative** *adj*, **approximatively** *adv*

appurtenance /ə'puhtinəns‖ə'pɜːtɪnəns/ *n* an accessory – **appurtenant** *adj or n*

apricot /'ayprikot‖'eɪprɪkɒt/ *n* **1** (the oval orange-coloured fruit of) a temperate-zone tree of the rose family closely related to the peach and plum **2** an orange pink colour

April /'ayprəl‖'eɪprəl/ *n* the 4th month of the Gregorian calendar [Latin *Aprilis*, perhaps deriv of Greek *Aphro*, short for *Aphrodite*, goddess of love]

,**April 'fool** *n* the victim of a joke or trick played on April Fools' Day

,**April 'Fools' ,Day** *n* April 1, characteristically marked by the playing of practical jokes

a priori /ay pree'awri, ah, -rie‖eɪ priː'ɔːrɪ, ɑː, -raɪ/ *adj* **1a** relating to or derived by reasoning from self-evident propositions; deductive **b** of or relating to sthg that can be known by reason alone **c** true or false by definition or convention alone <~ *statements*> **2** without examination or analysis; presumptive [Latin, from the former] – **a priori** *adv*, **apriority** *n*

apron /'ayprən‖'eɪprən/ *n* **1** a garment usu tied round the waist and used to protect clothing **2** sthg that suggests or resembles an apron in shape, position, or use: e g **2a** the part of a stage that projects in front of the curtain **b** the extensive paved area by an airport terminal or in front of aircraft hangars

'**apron ,strings** *n pl* dominance, esp of a man by his mother or wife <*still tied to his mother's* ~>

[1]**apropos** /,aprə'poh‖,æprə'pəʊ/ *adv* **1** at an opportune time **2** BY THE WAY [French *à propos*, lit., to the purpose]

[2]**apropos** *adj* both relevant and opportune

[3]**apropos** *prep* APROPOS OF

,**apro'pos of** *prep* concerning; WITH REGARD TO

apse /aps‖æps/ *n* **1** a projecting part of a building (e g a church) that is usu semicircular or polygonal and vaulted **2** APSIS 1

apsis /'apsis‖'æpsɪs/ *n, pl* **apsides** /'apsideez‖'æpsɪdiːz/ **1** the point in an astronomical orbit at which the distance of the body from the centre of attraction is either greatest or least **2** APSE 1

apt /apt‖æpt/ *adj* **1** ordinarily disposed; likely – usu + *to* **2** suited to a purpose; relevant **3** keenly intelligent and responsive <*an* ~ *pupil*> – **aptly** *adv*, **aptness** *n*

aptitude /'aptityoohd, -choohd‖'æptɪtjuːd, -tʃuːd/ *n* **1** a natural ability; a talent, esp for learning **2** general fitness or suitability – usu + *for* – **aptitudinal** *adj*, **aptitudinally** *adv*

aqualung /'akwə,lung‖'ækwə,lʌŋ/ *n* cylinders of compressed air, oxygen, etc carried on the back and connected to a face mask for breathing underwater

aquamarine /,akwəmə'reen‖,ækwəmə'riːn/ *n* **1** a transparent blue to green beryl used as a gemstone **2** a pale blue to light greenish blue colour

[1]**aquaplane** /'akwə,playn‖'ækwə,pleɪn/ *n* a board towed behind a fast motorboat and ridden by sby standing on it

[2]**aquaplane** *vi* **1** to ride on an aquaplane **2** *of a car* to go out of control by sliding on water lying on the surface of a wet road – **aquaplaner** *n*

aquarium /ə'kweəri·əm‖ə'kweərɪəm/ *n, pl* **aquariums, aquaria** /-ri·ə‖-rɪə/ **1** a glass tank, artificial pond, etc in which living aquatic animals or plants are kept **2** an establishment where collections of living aquatic organisms are exhibited

Aquarius /ə'kweəri·əs‖ə'kweərɪəs/ *n* (sby born under) the 11th sign of the zodiac in astrology, which is pictured as a man pouring water – **Aquarian** *adj or n*

[1]**aquatic** /ə'kwotik, -kwa-‖ə'kwɒtɪk, -kwæ-/ *adj* **1** growing,living in, or frequenting water **2** taking place in or on water <~ *sports*> – **aquatically** *adv*

[2]**aquatic** *n* **1** an aquatic animal or plant **2** *pl but sing or pl in constr* water sports

aquatint /'akwətint‖'ækwətɪnt/ *n* (a print made by) a method of etching a printing plate that enables tones similar to watercolour washes to be reproduced – **aquatint** *vt*, **aquatinter** *n*, **aquatintist** *n*

,**aqua 'vitae** /'veetie, 'vie-‖'viːtaɪ, 'vaɪ-/ *n* **1** ALCOHOL 1 **2** a strong spirit (e g brandy or whisky)

aqueduct /'akwə,dukt‖'ækwə,dʌkt/ *n* a conduit, esp an arched structure over a valley, for carrying water

aqueous /'akwi·əs, 'ay-‖'ækwɪəs, 'eɪ-/ *adj* of, resembling, or made from, with, or by water – **aqueously** *adv*

aquiline /'akwilien‖'ækwɪlaɪn/ *adj* **1** of or like an eagle **2** *of the human nose* hooked – **aquilinity** *n*

[1]**-ar** /-ə‖-ə *also* -ah‖-ɑː/ *suffix* (*n* → *adj*) of, relating to, or being <*molecul*ar>; resembling <*oracul*ar>

[2]**-ar** *suffix* (→ *n*) [2]-ER <*begg*ar> <*schol*ar>

Arab /'arəb‖'ærəb/ *n* **1a** a member of a Semitic people orig of the Arabian peninsula and now widespread throughout the Middle East and N Africa **b** a member of an Arabic-speaking people **2** *not cap* **2a** a homeless vagabond; *esp* an outcast boy or girl **b** a mischievous or annoying child **3** a typically intelligent, graceful, and swift horse of an Arabian stock – **Arab** *adj*

[1]**arabesque** /,arə'besk‖,ærə'besk/ *adj* (in the style) of arabesque

[2]**arabesque** *n* **1** a decorative design or style that combines natural motifs (e g flowers or foliage) to produce an intricate pattern **2** a posture in ballet in which the dancer is supported on one leg with one arm extended forwards and the other arm and leg backwards

Arabian /ə'raybi·ən‖ə'reɪbɪən/ *n* **1** a native or inhabitant of Arabia **2** ARAB 3 – **Arabian** *adj*

[1]**Arabic** /'arəbik‖'ærəbɪk/ *adj* **1** (characteristic) of Arabia, Arabians, or the Arabs **2** of or being Arabic

[2]**Arabic** *n* a Semitic language, now the prevailing speech of Arabia, Jordan, Lebanon, Syria, Iraq, Egypt, and parts of N Africa

ˌ**Arabic** 'numeral** *n, often not cap A* any of the number symbols 0, 1, 2, 3, 4, 5, 6, 7, 8, 9

arable /'arəbl‖'ærəbl/ *n or adj* (land) being or fit to be farmed for crops – **arability** *n*

arachnid /ə'raknid‖ə'ræknɪd/ *n* any of a class (e g spiders, mites, ticks, and scorpions) of arthropods whose bodies have 2 segments of which the front bears 4 pairs of legs – **arachnid** *adj*

arbiter /'ahbitə‖'ɑ:bɪtə/ *n* a person or agency with absolute power of judging and determining

arbitrary /'ahbitrəri‖'ɑ:bɪtrərɪ/ *adj* **1** depending on choice or discretion **2a** arising from unrestrained exercise of the will **b** selected at random and without reason **3** despotic, tyrannical – **arbitrarily** *adv*, **arbitrariness** *n*

arbitrate /'ahbitrayt‖'ɑ:bɪtreɪt/ *vi* to act as arbitrator ~ *vt* **1** to act as arbiter upon **2** to submit for decision to an arbitrator – **arbitrative** *adj*

arbitration /ˌahbi'traysh(ə)n‖ˌɑ:bɪ'treɪʃ(ə)n/ *n* the settlement of a disputed issue by an arbitrator – **arbitrational** *adj*

arbitrator /'ahbiˌtraytə‖'ɑ:bɪˌtreɪtə/ *n* **1** sby chosen to settle differences between 2 parties in dispute **2** an arbiter

arboreal /ˌah'bawri·əl‖ˌɑ:'bɔ:rɪəl/ *adj* of, resembling, inhabiting, or frequenting a tree or trees – **arboreally** *adv*

arboretum /ˌahbə'reetəm‖ˌɑ:bə'ri:təm/ *n, pl* **arboretums, arboreta** /-tə‖-tə/ a place where trees and shrubs are cultivated for study and display

arbour, *NAm chiefly* **arbor** /'ahbə‖'ɑ:bə/ *n* a bower of (latticework covered with) shrubs, vines, or branches

[1]**arc** /ahk‖ɑ:k/ *n* **1** the apparent path described by a celestial body **2** sthg arched or curved **3** a sustained luminous discharge of electricity across a gap in a circuit or between electrodes; *also* ARC LAMP **4** a continuous portion of a curve (e g of a circle or ellipse)

[2]**arc** *vi* to form an electric arc

[3]**arc** *adj* INVERSE 2 – used with the trigonometric and hyperbolic functions

arcade /ah'kayd‖ɑ:'keɪd/ *n* **1** a long arched gallery or building **2** a passageway or avenue (e g between shops) – **arcaded** *adj*

Arcadia /ah'kaydi·ə‖ɑ:'keɪdɪə/ *n* a usu idealized rural region or scene of simple pleasure and quiet [*Arcadia*, pastoral region of ancient Greece] – **Arcadian** *adj*

arcane /ah'kayn‖ɑ:'keɪn/ *adj* known or knowable only to an initiate; secret

[1]**arch** /ahch‖ɑ:tʃ/ *n* **1** a typically curved structural member spanning an opening and resisting lateral or vertical pressure (e g of a wall) **2** sthg (e g the vaulted bony structure of the foot) resembling an arch in form or function **3** an archway

[2]**arch** *vt* **1** to span or provide with an arch **2** to form or bend into an arch ~*vi* to form an arch

[3]**arch** *adj* **1** principal, chief <*an* arch-*villain*> **2a** cleverly sly and alert **b** playfully saucy – **archly** *adv*, **archness** *n*

[1]**arch-** /ahch-‖ɑ:tʃ-/ *prefix* **1** chief; principal <arch*bishop*> **2** extreme; most fully embodying the qualities of (a specified usu undesirable human type) <arch*enemy*>

[2]**arch-** – see ARCHI-

-arch /-ahk‖-ɑ:k/ *comb form* (→ *n*) ruler; leader <*matri*arch>

archaeology /ˌahki'oləji‖ˌɑ:kɪ'ɒlədʒɪ/ *n* the scientific study of material remains (e g artefacts and dwellings) of past human life and activities [French *archéologie*, deriv of Greek *archaios* ancient (fr *archē* beginning) + *logos* speech, reason] – **archaeological** *adj*, **archaeologically** *adv*, **archaeologist** *n*

archaic /ah'kayik‖ɑ:'keɪɪk/ *adj* **1** (characteristic) of an earlier or more primitive time; antiquated **2** no longer used in ordinary speech or writing – **archaically** *adv*

archaism /ah'kayiz(ə)m‖ɑ:'keɪɪz(ə)m/ *n* **1** the use of archaic diction or style **2** an instance of archaic usage; *esp* an archaic word or expression **3** sthg outmoded or old-fashioned – **archaist** *n*, **archaize** *vb*, **archaistic** *adj*

archangel /ˌahk'aynjəl, '-ˌ--‖ˌɑ:k'eɪndʒəl, '-ˌ--/ *n* a chief angel – **archangelic** *adj*

archbishop /ˌahch'bishəp‖ˌɑ:tʃ'bɪʃəp/ *n* a bishop at the head of an ecclesiastical province, or one of equivalent honorary rank – **archbishopric** *n*

ˌ**arch'deacon** /-'deekən‖-'di:kən/ *n* a clergyman having the duty of assisting a diocesan bishop, esp in administrative work – **archdeaconate** *n*

ˌ**arch'diocese** /-'die·əsis‖-'daɪəsɪs/ *n* the diocese of an archbishop – **archdiocesan** *adj*

ˌ**arch'duke** /-'dyoohk‖-'dju:k/ *n* a sovereign prince – **archducal** *adj*, **archduchy** *n*, **archdukedom** *n*

archer /'ahchə‖'ɑ:tʃə/ *n* one who practises archery

archery /'ahchəri‖'ɑ:tʃərɪ/ *n* the art, practice, skill, or sport of shooting arrows from a bow

archetype /'ahkiˌtiep‖'ɑ:kɪˌtaɪp/ *n* **1** an original pattern or model; a prototype **2** IDEA 1a **3** an inherited idea or mode of thought derived from the collective unconscious – **archetypal, archetypical** *adj*, **archetypally archetypically** *adv*

archi- /ahki-‖ɑ:kɪ-/, **arch-** *prefix* **1** chief; principal <archi*trave*> **2** primitive; original; primary

archimandrite /ˌahki'mandriet‖ˌɑ:kɪ'mændraɪt/ *n* a dignitary in the Eastern church ranking below a bishop

archipelago /ˌahki'pelәgoh, ˌahchi-‖ˌɑ:kɪ'peləgəʊ, ˌɑ:tʃɪ-/ *n, pl* **archipelagoes, archipelagos** (an expanse of water with) a group of scattered islands – **archipelagic** *adj*

architect /'ahkitekt‖'ɑ:kɪtekt/ *n* **1** sby who designs buildings and superintends their construction **2** sby who devises, plans, and achieves a difficult objective [Middle French *architecte*, fr Latin *architectus*, fr Greek *architektōn* master builder, fr *archi-* chief + *tektōn* builder, carpenter]

architecture /'ahkiˌtekchə‖'ɑ:kɪˌtektʃə/ *n* **1** the art, practice, or profession of designing and erecting buildings; *also* a method or style of building **2** product or work of architecture – **architectural** *adj*, **architecturally** *adv*

architrave /'ahki,trayv‖'ɑːkɪ,treɪv/ *n* **1** the lowest part of an entablature resting immediately on the capital of the column **2** the moulded frame round a rectangular recess or opening (e g a door)

¹**archive** /'ahkiev‖'ɑːkaɪv/ *n* a place in which public records or historical documents are preserved; *also* the material preserved – often pl with sing. meaning

²**archive** *vt* to file or collect (e g records or documents) in a repository (e g an archive)

archivist /'ahkivist‖'ɑːkɪvɪst/ *n* sby in charge of archives

archway /'ahch,way‖'ɑːtʃ,weɪ/ *n* (an arch over) a way or passage that runs beneath arches

-archy /-ahki‖-ɑːkɪ/ *comb form* (→ *n*) rule; government <*mon*archy>

'**arc ,lamp** /ahk‖ɑːk/ *n* a type of electric lamp that produces light by an arc made when a current passes between two incandescent electrodes surrounded by gas

arctic /'ahktik‖'ɑːktɪk/ *adj* **1** *often cap* of the N Pole or the surrounding region **2a** extremely cold; frigid **b** cold in temper or mood

,**arctic 'circle** *n, often cap A&C* the parallel of latitude approx 66 $^1/_2$ degrees north of the equator that circumscribes the north polar region

-ard /ahd‖ɑːd/ *suffix* (→ *n*) one characterized by or associated with (a usu undesirable specified action, state, or quality) <*dull*ard>

ardent /'ahd(ə)nt‖'ɑːd(ə)nt/ *adj* characterized by warmth of feeling; eager, zealous – **ardency** *n*, **ardently** *adv*

ardour, *NAm chiefly* **ardor** /'ahdə‖'ɑːdə/ *n* **1** (transitory) warmth of feeling **2** extreme vigour or intensity; zeal

arduous /'ahdyoo·əs‖'ɑːdjʊəs/ *adj* **1** hard to accomplish or achieve; difficult, strenuous **2** hard to climb; steep – **arduously** *adv*, **arduousness** *n*

¹**are** /ə‖ə; *strong* ah‖ɑː/ *pres 2 sing or pres pl of* BE

²**are** /ah‖ɑː/ *n* a metric unit of area equal to $100m^2$

area /'eəri·ə‖'eərɪə/ *n* **1** a level piece of ground **2** a particular extent of space or surface, or one serving a special function **3** the extent, range, or scope of a concept, operation, or activity; a field – **areal** *adj*, **areally** *adv*

arena /ə'reenə‖ə'riːnə/ *n* **1** (a building containing) an enclosed area used for public entertainment **2** a sphere of interest or activity; a scene

aren't /ahnt‖ɑːnt/ **1** are not **2** am not – used in questions

arête /ə'ret, ə'rayt‖ə'ret, ə'reɪt/ *n* a sharp-crested mountain ridge

argent /'ahjənt‖'ɑːdʒənt/ *n* **1** a silver colour; *also* white – used in heraldry **2** *archaic* the metal or colour silver – **argent** *adj*

argon /'ahgon‖'ɑːgɒn/ *n* a noble gaseous element found in the air and volcanic gases and used esp as a filler for vacuum tubes and electric light bulbs [Greek *argos* idle, lazy, fr *a-* not, without + *ergon* work; so called fr its relative inertness]

argot /'ahgoh‖'ɑːgəʊ/ *n* a (more or less secret) vocabulary peculiar to a particular group

arguably /'ahgyoo·əbli‖'ɑːgjʊəblɪ/ *adv* as can be argued <~ *the best living cellist*>

argue /'ahgyooh‖'ɑːgjuː/ *vi* **1** to give reasons for or against sthg; reason **2** to contend or disagree in words ~ *vt* **1** to give evidence of; indicate **2** to consider the reasons for and against; discuss **3** to (try to) prove by giving reasons; maintain **4** to persuade by giving reasons <~d *him out of going*> **5** to give reasons or arguments in favour of <*his letter* ~s *restraint*> – **arguable** *adj*, **arguer** *n*

argument /'ahgyoomənt‖'ɑːgjʊmənt/ *n* **1** a reason given in proof or rebuttal **2a** the act or process of arguing; debate **b** a coherent series of reasons offered **c** a quarrel, disagreement **3** an abstract or summary, esp of a literary work

argumentative /,ahgyoo'mentətiv‖,ɑːgjʊ-'mentətɪv/ *adj* given to argument; disputatious – **argumentatively** *adv*

argy-bargy, **argie-bargie** /,ahji 'bahji‖,ɑːdʒɪ-'bɑːdʒɪ/ *n, chiefly Br* (a) lively discussion; (a) dispute – infml

aria /'ahri·ə‖'ɑːrɪə/ *n, pl* **arias** an accompanied melody sung (e g in an opera) by 1 voice

-arian /-'eəri·ən‖-'eərɪən/ *suffix* (→ *n*) **1** believer in <*Unit*arian>; advocate of <*veget*arian> **2** one who pursues (a specified interest or activity) <*antiqu*arian> <*libr*arian> **3** one who is (so many decades) old <*octogen*arian>

arid /'arid‖'ærɪd/ *adj* **1** excessively dry; *specif* having insufficient rainfall to support agriculture **2** lacking in interest and life – **aridity** *n*, **aridness** *n*

Aries /'eəriz, -reez‖'eərɪz, -riːz/ *n* (sby born under) the 1st sign of the zodiac in astrology, which is pictured as a ram – **Arian** *adj or n*

aright /ə'riet‖ə'raɪt/ *adv* rightly, correctly

arise /ə'riez‖ə'raɪz/ *vi* **arose** /ə'rohz‖ə'rəʊz/; **arisen** /ə'riz(ə)n‖ə'rɪz(ə)n/ **1a** to originate from a source – often + *from* **b** to come into being or to attention **2** to get up, rise – chiefly fml

aristocracy /,ari'stokrəsi‖,ærɪ'stɒkrəsɪ/ *n* **1** (a state with) a government in which power is vested in a small privileged usu hereditary noble class **2** *sing or pl in constr* a (governing) usu hereditary nobility **3** *sing or pl in constr* the whole group of those believed to be superior (e g in wealth, rank, or intellect) [Late Latin *aristocratia*, fr Greek *aristokratia*, fr *aristos* best + *kratos* strength, power]

aristocrat /'aristəkrat, ə'ri-‖'ærɪstəkræt, ə-'rɪ-/ *n* **1** a member of an aristocracy; *esp* a noble **2** one who has the bearing and viewpoint typical of the aristocracy

aristocratic /,aristə'kratik, ə,ri-‖,ærɪstə-'krætɪk, ə,rɪ-/ *adj* belonging to, having the qualities of, or favouring aristocracy – **aristocratically** *adv*

arithmetic /ə'rithmətik‖ə'rɪθmətɪk/ *n* **1** a branch of mathematics that deals with real numbers and calculations with them **2** computation, calculation – **arithmetic, arithmetical** *adj*, **arithmetically** *adv*, **arithmetician** *n*

,**arith,metic 'mean** /,arith'metik‖,ærɪθ-'metɪk/ *n* a value found by dividing the sum of a set of terms by the number of terms

,**arith,metic pro'gression** *n* a sequence (e g 3, 5, 7, 9) in which the difference between any term and its predecessor is constant

ark /ahk‖ɑːk/ *n* **1** a ship; *esp* (one like) the one built by Noah to escape the Flood **2a** the sacred chest representing to the Hebrews the presence of God among them **b** a repository for the scrolls of the Torah

[1]**arm** /ahm‖ɑːm/ *n* **1** (the part between the shoulder and the wrist of) the human upper limb **2** sthg like or corresponding to an arm: e g **2a** the forelimb of a vertebrate animal **b** a limb of an invertebrate animal **3** an inlet of water (e g from the sea) **4** might, authority <*the long ~ of the law*> **5** a support (e g on a chair) for the elbow and forearm **6** a sleeve **7** a functional division of a group or activity – **armed** *adj*, **armful** *n* – **at arm's length** far enough away to avoid intimacy

[2]**arm** *vt* **1** to supply or equip with weapons **2** to provide with sthg that strengthens or protects **3** to fortify morally **4** to equip for action or operation <~ *a bomb*> ~*vi* to prepare oneself for struggle or resistance

[3]**arm** *n* **1a** a weapon; *esp* a firearm – usu pl **b** a combat branch (e g of an army) **2** *pl* the heraldic insignia of a group or body (e g a family or government) **3** *pl* **3a** active hostilities **b** military service or profession – **up in arms** angrily rebellious and protesting strongly

armada /ahˈmahdə‖ɑːˈmɑːdə/ *n, pl* **armadas** a fleet of warships; *specif, cap* that sent against England by Spain in 1588

armadillo /ˌahməˈdiloh‖ˌɑːməˈdɪləʊ/ *n, pl* **armadillos** any of several burrowing chiefly nocturnal S American mammals with body and head encased in an armour of small bony plates [Spanish, lit., little armed one]

armament /ˈahməmənt‖ˈɑːməmənt/ *n* **1** a military or naval force **2** the military strength, esp in arms and equipment, of a ship, fort, or combat unit, nation, etc **3** the process of preparing for war

armature /ˈahməchə‖ˈɑːmətʃə/ *n* **1** an offensive or defensive structure in a plant or animal (e g teeth or thorns) **2a** the central rotating part of an electric motor or generator **b** a framework on which a modeller in clay, wax, etc builds up his/her work

[1]**armchair** /ˈahmˌcheə‖ˈɑːmˌtʃeə/ *n* a chair with armrests

[2]**armchair** *adj* **1** remote from direct dealing with practical problems <~ *strategists*> **2** sharing vicariously in another's experiences <*an ~ traveller*>

ˈ**armˌhole** /-ˌhohl‖-ˌhəʊl/ *n* an opening for the arm in a garment

armistice /ˈahmistis‖ˈɑːmɪstɪs/ *n* a temporary suspension of hostilities; a truce

armlet /ˈahmlit‖ˈɑːmlɪt/ *n* **1** a band (e g of cloth or metal) worn round the upper arm **2** a small arm (e g of the sea)

armorial /ahˈmawri·əl‖ɑːˈmɔːrɪəl/ *adj* of or bearing heraldic arms – **armorially** *adv*

armour, *NAm chiefly* **armor** /ˈahmə‖ˈɑːmə/ *n* **1a** a defensive covering for the body; *esp* a covering (e g of metal) worn in combat **b** a usu metallic protective covering (e g for a ship, fort, aircraft, or car) **2** armoured forces and vehicles (e g tanks) – **armour** *vt*, **armourless** *adj*

ˌ**armour-ˈclad** *adj* sheathed in or protected by armour

armoured /ˈahməd‖ˈɑːməd/ *adj* consisting of or equipped with vehicles protected with armour plate

armourer /ˈahmərə‖ˈɑːmərə/ *n* **1** sby who makes or looks after armour or arms **2** sby who repairs, assembles, and tests firearms

ˌ**armour ˈplate** *n* a defensive covering of hard metal plates for combat vehicles and vessels

armoury /ˈahməri‖ˈɑːmərɪ/ *n* (a collection of or place for storing) arms and military equipment

ˈ**armˌpit** /-ˌpit‖-ˌpɪt/ *n* the hollow beneath the junction of the arm and shoulder

army /ˈahmi‖ˈɑːmɪ/ *n* **1a** a large organized force for war on land **b** *often cap* the complete military organization of a nation for land warfare **2** a great multitude **3** a body of people organized to advance a cause <*the Salvation* Army>

aroma /əˈrohmə‖əˈrəʊmə/ *n, pl* **aromas 1a** a distinctive, pervasive, and usu pleasant or savoury smell **b** the bouquet of a wine **2** a distinctive quality or atmosphere

[1]**aromatic** /ˌarəˈmatik‖ˌærəˈmætɪk/ *adj* **1** of or having an aroma: **1a** fragrant **b** having a strong esp pungent or spicy smell **2** *of a chemical compound* having a molecular structure containing a ring, specif containing (a group like) a benzene ring – **aromatically** *adv*, **aromaticity** *n*, **aromaticness** *n*, **aromatize** *vt*, **aromatization** *n*

[2]**aromatic** *n* sthg aromatic

arose /əˈrohz‖əˈrəʊz/ *past of* ARISE

[1]**around** /əˈrownd‖əˈraʊnd/ *adv, chiefly NAm* **1** round **2** ABOUT (3, 5)

[2]**around** *prep, chiefly NAm* **1** round **2** ABOUT (1, 2a, 5)

[3]**around** *adj, chiefly NAm* **1** ABOUT 1 <*has been up and ~ for 2 days*> **2** in existence, evidence, or circulation <*the best singer ~*>

arouse /əˈrowz‖əˈraʊz/ *vt* **1** to awaken from sleep **2** to rouse to action; excite, esp sexually – **arousal** *n*

arpeggio /ahˈpejioh‖ɑːˈpedʒɪəʊ/ *n, pl* **arpeggios** (the sounding of) a chord whose notes are played in succession, not simultaneously [Italian, fr *arpeggiare* to play on the harp, fr *arpa* harp]

arrack, arak /ˈarak, ˈarək‖ˈæræk, ˈærək/ *n* an Asian alcoholic spirit that is a distillation of the fermented mash of rice and molasses and to which has been added the fermented sap of the coconut palm

arraign /əˈrayn‖əˈreɪn/ *vt* **1** to charge before a court **2** to accuse of wrong, inadequacy, or imperfection – **arraignment** *n*

arrange /əˈraynj‖əˈreɪndʒ/ *vt* **1** to put in order or into sequence or relationship **2** to make preparations for; plan **3** to bring about an agreement concerning; settle <~ *an exchange of prisoners of war*> **4** to adapt (a musical composition) by scoring for different voices or instruments ~*vi* to make plans <~ *to go on holiday*> – **arranger** *n*

arˈrangement /-mənt‖-mənt/ *n* **1a** a preliminary measure; a preparation <*travel* ~s> **b**

an adaptation of a musical composition for different voices or instruments **c** an informal agreement or settlement, esp on personal, social, or political matters **2** sthg made by arranging constituents or things together <*a floral* ~>

arrant /'arənt‖'ærənt/ *adj* notoriously without moderation; extreme <*an* ~ *fool*> – **arrantly** *adv*

arras /'arəs‖'ærəs/ *n, pl* **arras** a wall hanging or screen made of tapestry [*Arras*, city in France]

[1]**array** /ə'ray‖ə'reɪ/ *vt* **1** to set or place in order; marshal **2** to dress or decorate, esp in splendid or impressive clothes; adorn – **arrayer** *n*

[2]**array** *n* **1** military order <*forces in* ~> **2a** clothing, garments **b** rich or beautiful apparel; finery **3** an imposing group; a large number **4** a number of mathematical elements arranged in rows and columns **5** an arrangement of computer memory elements (e g magnetic cores) in a single plane

arrear /ə'riə‖ə'rɪə/ *n* **1** an unfinished duty **2** an unpaid and overdue debt *USE* usu pl with sing. meaning – **arrearage** *n* – **in arrears** behind in the discharge of obligations

[1]**arrest** /ə'rest‖ə'rest/ *vt* **1a** to bring to a stop <*sickness* ~ed *his activities*> **b** to make inactive **2** to seize, capture; *specif* to take or keep in custody by authority of law **3** to catch and fix or hold <~ *the attention*> – **arrester**, **arrestor** *n*, **arrestment** *n*

[2]**arrest** *n* **1a** the act of stopping **b** the condition of being stopped <*cardiac* ~> **2** the taking or detaining of sby in custody by authority of law **3** a device for arresting motion – **under arrest** in legal custody

arrival /ə'rievl‖ə'raɪvl/ *n* **1** the attainment of an end or state **2** sby or sthg that has arrived

arrive /ə'riev‖ə'raɪv/ *vi* **1** to reach a destination **2** to come <*the moment has* ~d> **3** to achieve success – **arriver** *n* – **arrive at** to reach by effort or thought <*have* arrived at *a decision*>

arrogance /'arəgəns‖'ærəgəns/ *n* aggressive conceit – **arrogant** *adj*, **arrogantly** *adv*

arrogate /'arəgayt‖'ærəgeɪt/ *vt* to claim or seize without justification, on behalf of oneself or another – **arrogation** *n*

arrow /'aroh‖'ærəʊ/ *n* **1** a projectile shot from a bow, usu having a slender shaft, a pointed head, and feathers at the end **2** sthg shaped like an arrow; *esp* a mark to indicate direction

'arrow,head /-,hed‖-,hed/ *n* **1** the pointed front part of an arrow **2** sthg shaped like an arrowhead **3** any of several related (water) plants with leaves shaped like arrowheads

'arrow,root /-,rooht‖-,ru:t/ *n* (a tropical American plant whose roots yield) a nutritive starch used esp as a thickening agent in cooking

arse /ahs‖ɑ:s/ *n* **1** the buttocks **2** the anus *USE* vulg

arsenal /'ahsənl, 'ahsnəl‖'ɑ:sənl, 'ɑ:snəl/ *n* **1** an establishment for the manufacture or storage of arms and military equipment; an armoury **2** a store, repertory

arsenic /'ahsnik‖'ɑ:snɪk/ *n* **1** a semimetallic steel-grey poisonous element **2** an extremely poisonous trioxide of arsenic, used esp as an insecticide – **arsenic** *adj*, **arsenical** *adj or n*, **arsenious** *adj*

arson /'ahsən‖'ɑ:sən/ *n* the criminal act of setting fire to property in order to cause destruction – **arsonist** *n*

[1]**art** /aht‖ɑ:t/ *archaic pres 2 sing of* BE

[2]**art** *n* **1** a skill acquired by experience, study, or observation **2** *pl* the humanities as contrasted with science **3a** the conscious use of skill and creative imagination, esp in the production of aesthetic objects; *also* works so produced **b** (any of the) fine arts or graphic arts **4** decorative or illustrative elements in printed matter

[3]**art** *adj* **1** composed, designed, or created with conscious artistry <*an* ~ *song*> **2** designed for decorative purposes <~ *pottery*>

-art – see -ARD

artefact, **artifact** /'ahtifakt‖'ɑ:tɪfækt/ *n* **1a** a usu simple object (e g a tool or ornament) produced by human workmanship **b** a product of civilization <*an* ~ *of the jet age*> **2** sthg (e g a structure seen in the microscope) unnaturally present through extraneous influences (e g from defects in the staining procedure) – **artefactual** *adj*

arterial /ah'tiəri·əl‖ɑ:'tɪərɪəl/ *adj* **1** of or (being the bright red blood) contained in an artery **2** of or being a main road – **arterially** *adv*

arteriosclerosis /ah,tiəriohsklə'rohsis‖ɑ:-,tɪərɪəʊsklə'rəʊsɪs/ *n* abnormal thickening and hardening of the arterial walls – **arteriosclerotic** *adj or n*

artery /'ahtəri‖'ɑ:tərɪ/ *n* **1** any of the branching elastic-walled blood vessels that carry blood from the heart to the lungs and through the body **2** an esp main channel (e g a river or road) of transport or communication

ar,tesian 'well /ah'teezh(ə)n, -zi·ən‖ɑ:'ti:ʒ-(ə)n, -zɪən/ *n* a well by which water reaches the surface with little or no pumping

artful /'ahtf(ə)l‖'ɑ:tf(ə)l/ *adj* adroit in attaining an end, often by deceitful or indirect means; crafty – **artfully** *adv*, **artfulness** *n*

arthritis /ah'thrietəs‖ɑ:'θraɪtəs/ *n, pl* **arthritides** /ah'thrieti,deez‖ɑ:'θraɪtɪ,di:z/ usu painful inflammation of 1 or more joints [Latin, fr Greek, fr *arthron* joint]

arthropod /'ahthrə,pod‖'ɑ:θrə,pɒd/ *n* any of a phylum of invertebrate animals (e g insects, arachnids, and crustaceans) with a jointed body and limbs and usu an outer skin made of chitin and moulted at intervals

artichoke /'ahti,chohk‖'ɑ:tɪ,tʃəʊk/ *n* **1a** a tall composite plant like a thistle **b** the partly edible flower head of the artichoke, used as a vegetable **2** JERUSALEM ARTICHOKE

[1]**article** /'ahtikl‖'ɑ:tɪkl/ *n* **1a(1)** a separate clause, item, provision, or point in a document **a(2)** *pl* a written agreement specifying conditions of apprenticeship **b** a piece of nonfictional prose, usu forming an independent part of a magazine, newspaper, etc **2** an item of business; a matter **3** a word or affix (e g *a*, *an*, and *the*) used with nouns to give indefiniteness or definiteness **4a** a particular or separate object or thing, esp viewed as a member of a class of things <*several* ~s *of clothing*> **b** a thing of a particular and distinctive kind <*the genuine* ~>

[2]**article** *vt* to bind by articles (e g of apprenticeship)

[1]**articulate** /ah'tikyoolət||ɑː'tɪkjʊlət/ *adj* **1a** divided into syllables or words meaningfully arranged **b** having the power of speech **c** expressing oneself readily, clearly, or effectively; *also* expressed in this manner **2** jointed – **articulacy** *n*, **articulately** *adv*, **articulateness** *n*

[2]**articulate** /ah'tikyoolayt||ɑː'tɪkjʊleɪt/ *vt* **1a** to utter distinctly **b** to give clear and effective utterance to < ~ *one's grievances*> **2** to unite with a joint ~ *vi* **1** to utter articulate sounds **2** to become united or connected (as if) by a joint – **articulative** *adj*, **articulator** *n*, **articulatory** *adj*

ar'ticulated *adj, chiefly Br* having 2 parts flexibly connected and intended to operate as a unit <*an* ~ *lorry*>

articulation /ah,tikyoo'laysh(ə)n, ,---'--||ɑː-,tɪkjʊ'leɪʃ(ə)n, ,---'--/ *n* **1a** the action or manner of jointing or interrelating **b** the state of being jointed or interrelated **2** a (movable) joint (between plant or animal parts) **3a** the (verbal) expression of thoughts and feelings **b** the act or manner of articulating sounds

artifact /'ahtifakt||'ɑːtɪfækt/ *n* an artefact – **artifactual** *adj*

artifice /'ahtifis||'ɑːtɪfɪs/ *n* **1** an artful device, expedient, or stratagem; a trick **2** clever or artful skill; ingenuity

artificer /ah'tifisə, 'ahtifisə||ɑː'tɪfɪsə, 'ɑːtɪfɪsə/ *n* **1** a skilled or artistic worker or craftsman **2** a military or naval mechanic

artificial /,ahti'fish(ə)l||,ɑːtɪ'fɪʃ(ə)l/ *adj* **1** made by human skill and labour, often to a natural model; man-made **2a** lacking in natural quality; affected **b** imitation, sham – **artificiality** *n*, **artificially** *adv*, **artificialness** *n*

,arti,ficial insemi'nation *n* introduction of semen into the uterus or oviduct by other than natural means

,arti,ficial respi'ration *n* the rhythmic forcing of air into and out of the lungs of sby whose breathing has stopped

artillery /ah'tiləri||ɑː'tɪlərɪ/ *n* **1** large-calibre mounted firearms (e g guns, howitzers, missile launchers, etc) **2** *sing or pl in constr* a branch of an army armed with artillery

artisan /'ahti,zan, ,--'-, 'ahtiz(ə)n||'ɑːtɪ,zæn, ,--'-, 'ɑːtɪz(ə)n/ *n* **1** a skilled manual worker (e g a carpenter, plumber, or tailor) **2** a member of the urban proletariat

artist /'ahtist||'ɑːtɪst/ *n* **1a** one who professes and practises an imaginative art **b** a person skilled in a fine art **2** a skilled performer; *specif* an artiste **3** one who is proficient in a specified and usu dubious activity; an expert – infml **4** *Austr & NAm* a fellow or character, esp of a specified sort – infml

artiste /ah'teest||ɑː'tiːst/ *n* a skilled public performer; *specif* a musical or theatrical entertainer

artistic /ah'tistik||ɑː'tɪstɪk/ *adj* **1** concerning or characteristic of art or artists **2** showing imaginative skill in arrangement or execution – **artistically** *adv*

artistry /'ahtistri||'ɑːtɪstrɪ/ *n* **1** artistic quality **2** artistic ability

'artless /-lis||-lɪs/ *adj* **1** free from artificiality; natural **2** free from deceit, guile, or craftiness – **artlessly** *adv*, **artlessness** *n*

art nouveau /,ah(t) nooh'voh||,ɑː(t) nuː'vəʊ/ *n, often cap A&N* a decorative style of late 19th-c origin, characterized esp by curved lines and plant motifs [French, lit., new art]

arty /'ahti||'ɑːtɪ/ *adj* showily or pretentiously artistic – **artily** *adv*, **artiness** *n*

arty-crafty /,ahti 'krahfti||,ɑːtɪ 'krɑːftɪ/ *adj* arty; *esp* affectedly simple or rustic in style – infml

[1]**-ary** /-(ə)ri||-(ə)rɪ/ *suffix* (→ *n*) **1** thing belonging to or connected with <*ov*ary>; *esp* place or repository of or for <*avi*ary> **2** one belonging to, connected with, or engaged in <*mission*ary>

[2]**-ary** *suffix* (→ *adj*) of or connected with <*budget*ary>

[1]**as** /əz||əz; *strong* az||æz/ *adv* **1** to the same degree or amount; equally < ~ *deaf as a post*> **2** when considered in a specified form or relation – usu used before a preposition or participle <*my opinion* ~ *distinguished from his*>

[2]**as** *conj* **1a** to the same degree that <*deaf* ~ *a post* > – usu used as a correlative after *as* or *so* to introduce a comparison <*as long ago* ~ *1930*> or as a result <*so clear* ~ *to leave no doubt*> **b** – used after *same* or *such* to introduce an example or comparison <*such trees* ~ *oak or pine*> **c** – used after *so* to introduce the idea of purpose <*he hid so* ~ *not to get caught*> **2** in the way that <*do* ~ *I say, not* ~ *I do*> – used before *so* to introduce a parallel < ~ *the French like their wine, so the British like their beer*> **3** in accordance with what <*quite good* ~ *boys go*> **4** while, when <*spilt the milk* ~ *she got up*> **5** regardless of the fact that; though <*naked* ~ *I was, I rushed out*> **6** for the reason that; seeing < ~ *it's raining, let's make toffee*> – **as it is** IN REALITY – **as it were** SO TO SPEAK

[3]**as** *pron* **1** a fact that; and this <*is ill,* ~ *you can see*> **2** which also; and so <*plays football,* ~ *do his brothers*>

[4]**as** *prep* **1** LIKE 1a, 2 **2** in the capacity, character, role, or state of <*works* ~ *an editor*>

as- – see AD-

asbestos /ə'spestos, -zb-, -sb-||ə'spestɒs, -zb-, -sb-/ *n* either of 2 minerals composed of thin flexible fibres, used to make noncombustible, nonconducting, or chemically resistant materials [deriv of Greek *asbestos* inextinguishable, fr *a-* not + *sbennynai* to quench]

ascend /ə'send||ə'send/ *vi* **1** to move or slope gradually upwards; rise **2a** to rise from a lower level or degree < ~ *to power*> **b** to go back in time or in order of genealogical succession ~ *vt* **1** to go or move up **2** to succeed to; begin to occupy – esp in *ascend the throne* – **ascendable, ascendible** *adj*, **ascending** *adj*

ascendancy *also* **ascendency** /ə'send(ə)nsi||ə'send(ə)nsɪ/ *n* controlling influence; domination

[1]**ascendant** *also* **ascendent** /ə'send(ə)nt||ə'send(ə)nt/ *n* **1** *the* degree of the zodiac that rises above the eastern horizon at any moment (e g at one's birth) **2** a state or position of dominant power or importance – esp in *in the ascendant*

[2]**ascendant** *also* **ascendent** *adj* **1** rising **2** superior, dominant – **ascendantly** *adv*

ascension /ə'sensh(ə)n||ə'senʃ(ə)n/ *n* the act or process of ascending

Aˈscension ˌDay *n* the Thursday 40 days after Easter observed in commemoration of Christ's ascension into Heaven

ascent /əˈsent‖əˈsent/ *n* **1a** the act of going, climbing, or travelling up **b** a way up; an upward slope or path **2** an advance in social status or reputation; progress

ascertain /ˌasəˈtayn‖ˌæsəˈteɪn/ *vt* to find out or learn with certainty – **ascertainable** *adj*

ascetic /əˈsetik‖əˈsetɪk/ *also* **ascetical** /-kl‖-kl/ *adj* **1** practising strict self-denial as a spiritual discipline **2** austere in appearance, manner, or attitude – **ascetic** *n*, **ascetically** *adv*, **asceticism** *n*

ascribe /əˈskrieb‖əˈskraɪb/ *vt* to refer or attribute (sthg) *to* a supposed cause or source – **ascribable** *adj*

ascription /əˈskripsh(ə)n‖əˈskrɪpʃ(ə)n/ *n* the act of ascribing; attribution

asepsis /ayˈsepsis, ə-, a-‖eɪˈsepsɪs, ə-, æ-/ *n* **1** the condition of being aseptic **2** the methods of making or keeping sthg aseptic

aseptic /ayˈseptik, ə-, a-‖eɪˈseptɪk, ə-, æ-/ *adj* **1** preventing infection **2** free or freed from disease-causing microorganisms – **aseptically** *adv*

asexual /ayˈseksyooəl, -ˈseksh(ə)l, ə-‖eɪˈseksjʊəl, -ˈsekʃ(ə)l, ə-/ *adj* **1** lacking sex (organs) **2** produced without sexual action or differentiation **3** without expression of or reference to sexual interest – **asexually** *adv*

ˈ**as for** *prep* concerning; IN REGARD TO – used esp in making a contrast <~ *the others, they'll arrive later*>

ˈ**as from** *prep* not earlier or later than <*takes effect* ~ *July 1st*>

[1]**ash** /ash‖æʃ/ *n* (the tough elastic wood of) any of a genus of tall trees of the olive family

[2]**ash** *n* **1a** the solid residue left when material is thoroughly burned or oxidized **b** fine particles of mineral matter from a volcano **2** *pl* the remains of sthg destroyed by fire **3** *pl* the remains of a dead body after cremation or disintegration

ashamed /əˈshaymd‖əˈʃeɪmd/ *adj* **1** feeling shame, guilt, or disgrace **2** restrained by fear of shame <*was* ~ *to beg*> – **ashamedly** *adv*

ˈ**ash ˌcan** *n, NAm* a dustbin

[1]**ashen** /ˈash(ə)n‖ˈæʃ(ə)n/ *adj* of or made from the wood of the ash tree

[2]**ashen** *adj* **1** consisting of or resembling ashes **2** deadly pale; blanched <*his face was* ~ *with fear*>

Ashes /ˈashiz‖ˈæʃɪz/ *n pl* a trophy played for in a series of cricket test matches between England and Australia – + *the* [so called fr a jesting reference to the ashes of the dead body of English cricket after an Australian victory in 1882]

ashore /əˈshaw‖əˈʃɔː/ *adv* on or to the shore

ˈ**ashˌtray** /-ˌtray‖-ˌtreɪ/ *n* a (small) receptacle for tobacco ash and cigar and cigarette ends

ˌ**Ash ˈWednesday** *n* the first day of Lent [so called fr the custom of sprinkling ashes on penitents' heads]

ashy /ˈashi‖ˈæʃɪ/ *adj* **1** of ashes **2** [2]ASHEN 2

Asian /ˈaysh(ə)n, ˈayzh(ə)n‖ˈeɪʃ(ə)n, ˈeɪʒ(ə)n/ *adj* (characteristic) of the continent of Asia or its people – **Asian** *n*

Asiatic /ˌayziˈatik, ˌayzhi-‖ˌeɪzɪˈætɪk, ˌeɪʒɪ-/ *adj* Asian – **Asiatic** *n*

[1]**aside** /əˈsied‖əˈsaɪd/ *adv or adj* **1** to or towards the side <*stepped* ~> **2** out of the way <*put his work* ~> **3** apart; IN RESERVE **4** APART 3

[2]**aside** *n* **1** an utterance meant to be inaudible; *esp* an actor's speech supposedly not heard by other characters on stage **2** a digression

aˈside from *prep, chiefly NAm* APART FROM

as ˈif *conj* **1** as it would be if <*it was* ~ *he had lost his best friend*> **2** as one would do if <*shook his head* ~ *to say no*> **3** that <*it's not* ~ *she's poor*> **4** – used in emphatic repudiation of a notion <~ *I cared!*>

asinine /ˈasinien‖ˈæsɪnaɪn/ *adj* stupid – **asininely** *adv*, **asininity** *n*

ask /ahsk‖ɑːsk/ *vt* **1a** to call on for an answer <*I* ~ed *him about his trip*> **b** to put a question about <*I* ~ed *his whereabouts*> **c** to put or frame (a question) <~ *a question of him*> **2a** to make a request of <*she* ~*ed her teacher for help*> **b** to make a request for <*she* ~ed *help from her teacher*> **3** to behave in such a way as to provoke (an unpleasant response) <*just* ~ing *to be given a good hiding*> **4** to set as a price <~ed *£1500 for the car*> **5** to invite <~ *him to dinner*> ~ *vi* to seek information <*he* ~ed *after the old man's health*> – **asker** *n*

askance /əˈskahns‖əˈskɑːns/ *adv* with disapproval or distrust – esp in *look askance*

askew /əˈskyooh‖əˈskjuː/ *adv or adj* awry – **askewness** *n*

ˈ**asking ˌprice** /ˈahsking‖ˈɑːskɪŋ/ *n* the price set by the seller

aslant /əˈslahnt‖əˈslɑːnt/ *prep, adv, or adj* (over or across) in a slanting direction

asleep /əˈsleep‖əˈsliːp/ *adj* **1** in a state of sleep **2** dead – euph **3** lacking sensation; numb

as ˈlong as *conj* **1** providing, while; SO LONG AS **2** *chiefly NAm* since; INASMUCH AS

ˈ**as of** *prep, chiefly NAm* AS FROM

asp /asp‖æsp/ *n* a small venomous snake of Egypt

asparagus /əˈsparəgəs‖əˈspærəgəs/ *n* (any of a genus of Old World perennial plants of the lily family including) a tall plant widely cultivated for its edible young shoots

aspect /ˈaspekt‖ˈæspekt/ *n* **1a** the position of planets or stars with respect to one another, held by astrologers to influence human affairs; *also* the apparent position (e g conjunction) of a body in the solar system with respect to the sun **b** a position facing a particular direction <*the house has a southern* ~> **2a** appearance to the eye or mind **b** a particular feature of a situation, plan, or point of view – **aspectual** *adj*

aspen /ˈaspən‖ˈæspən/ *n* any of several poplars with leaves that flutter in the lightest wind

asperity /əˈsperəti‖əˈsperətɪ/ *n* **1** rigour, hardship **2** roughness of surface; unevenness **3** roughness of manner or temper; harshness

aspersion /əˈspuhsh(ə)n‖əˈspɜːʃ(ə)n/ *n* **1** a sprinkling with water, esp in religious ceremonies **2** a calumnious or unwarranted doubt <*he cast* ~s *on her integrity*>

asphalt /ˈasfalt, -felt, ash-‖ˈæsfælt, -felt, æʃ-; *NAm* ˈasfawlt‖ˈæsfɔːlt/ *n* **1** a brown to black bituminous substance found in natural beds and also obtained as a residue in petroleum or coal tar refining **2** an asphaltic composition used for surfacing roads and footpaths – **asphaltic** *adj*

asphodel /'asfə,del‖'æsfə,del/ *n* any of various Old World plants of the lily family with long spikes of flowers

asphyxia /ə'sfiksi·ə‖ə'sfɪksɪə/ *n* a lack of oxygen in the body, usu caused by interruption of breathing, and resulting in unconsciousness or death – **asphyxiate** *vb*, **asphyxiation** *n*, **asphyxiator** *n*

aspic /'aspik‖'æspɪk/ *n* a clear savoury jelly (e g of fish or meat stock) used as a garnish or to make a meat, fish, etc mould

aspidistra /,aspi'distrə‖,æspɪ'dɪstrə/ *n* any of various Asiatic plants of the lily family with large leaves, often grown as house plants

[1]**aspirate** /'aspirət‖'æspɪrət/, **aspirated** /'aspiraytid‖'æspɪreɪtɪd/ *adj* pronounced with aspiration

[2]**aspirate** /'aspirayt‖'æspɪreɪt/ *vt* **1** to pronounce (a vowel, consonant, or word) with an *h*-sound **2** to draw or remove (e g blood) by suction

[3]**aspirate** /'aspirət‖'æspɪrət/ *n* **1** (a character, esp *h*, representing) an independent /h/ sound **2** an aspirated consonant (e g the *p* of *pit*) **3** material removed by aspiration

aspiration /,aspi'raysh(ə)n‖,æspɪ'reɪʃ(ə)n/ *n* **1** the pronunciation or addition of an aspirate **2** a drawing of sthg in, out, up, or through (as if) by suction: e g **2a** the act of breathing (sthg in) **b** the withdrawal of fluid from the body **3a** a strong desire to achieve sthg high or great **b** an object of such desire

aspire /ə'spie·ə‖ə'spaɪə/ *vi* to seek to attain or accomplish a particular goal – usu + *to* < ~d *to a career in medicine* > – **aspirant** *n or adj*, **aspirer** *n*

aspirin /'asprin‖'æsprɪn/ *n, pl* **aspirin, aspirins** (a tablet containing) a derivative of salicylic acid used for relief of pain and fever

as re'gards /ri'gahdz‖rɪ'gɑːdz/ *prep* with respect to; IN REGARD TO

[1]**ass** /as‖æs/ *n* **1** the donkey or a similar long-eared hardy gregarious mammal related to and smaller than the horse **2** a stupid, obstinate, or perverse person or thing

[2]**ass** *n, chiefly NAm* the arse

assail /ə'sayl‖ə'seɪl/ *vt* **1** to attack violently with blows or words **2** to prey on < ~ed *by doubts* > – **assailable** *adj*, **assailant** *n*

assassin /ə'sasin‖ə'sæsɪn/ *n* a murderer; *esp* one who murders a politically important person, for money or from fanatical motives [Medieval Latin *assassinus* one of an order of secret Muslim murderers, fr Arabic *ḥashshāshīn*, pl of *ḥashshāsh* one who smokes or chews hashish]

assassinate /ə'sasinayt‖ə'sæsɪneɪt/ *vt* to murder suddenly or secretly, usu for political reasons – **assassination** *n*, **assassinator** *n*

[1]**assault** /ə'sawlt‖ə'sɔːlt/ *n* **1** a violent physical or verbal attack **2a** an attempt to do or immediate threat of doing unlawful personal violence **b** rape **3** an attempt to attack a fortification by a sudden rush

[2]**assault** *vt* **1** to make an (indecent) assault on **2** to rape – **assaulter** *n*, **assaultive** *adj*

[1]**assay** /ə'say‖ə'seɪ/ *n* analysis of an ore, drug, etc to determine the presence, absence, or quantity of 1 or more components

[2]**assay** *vt* **1a** to analyse (e g an ore) for 1 or more valuable components **b** to judge the worth or quality of **2** to try, attempt – fml – **assayer** *n*

assegai, assagai /'asigie‖'æsɪgaɪ/ *n* a slender iron-tipped hardwood spear used in southern Africa

assemblage /ə'semblij‖ə'semblɪdʒ/ *n* **1** a collection of people or things; a gathering **2** a three-dimensional collage made from scraps, junk, and odds and ends (e g of cloth, wood, stone etc)

assemble /ə'sembl‖ə'sembl/ *vt* **1** to bring together (e g in a particular place or for a particular purpose) **2** to fit together the parts of ~ *vi* to gather together; convene – **assembler** *n*

assembly /ə'sembli‖ə'semblɪ/ *n* **1** a company of people gathered for deliberation and legislation, entertainment, or worship; *specif* a morning gathering of a school for prayers and/or for the giving out of notices **2** *cap* a legislative body **3a** an assemblage **b** assembling or being assembled **4** a bugle, drum, etc signal for troops to assemble or fall in **5** (a collection of parts assembled by) the fitting together of manufactured parts into a complete machine, structure, etc

as'sembly ,line *n* **1** an arrangement of machines, equipment, and usu workers in which work passes through successive operations until the product is assembled **2** a process for turning out a finished product in a mechanically efficient but often cursory manner

[1]**assent** /ə'sent‖ə'sent/ *vi* to agree to sthg – **assentor, assenter** *n*

[2]**assent** *n* acquiescence, agreement

assert /ə'suht‖ə'sɜːt/ *vt* **1** to state or declare positively and often forcefully **2** to demonstrate the existence of – **assertor** *n* – **assert oneself** to compel recognition of esp one's rights

assertion /ə'suhsh(ə)n‖ə'sɜːʃ(ə)n/ *n* a declaration, affirmation

assertive /ə'suhtiv‖ə'sɜːtɪv/ *adj* characterized by bold assertion; dogmatic – **assertively** *adv*, **assertiveness** *n*

assess /ə'ses‖ə'ses/ *vt* **1a** to determine the rate or amount of (e g a tax) **b** to impose (e g a tax) according to an established rate **2** to make an official valuation of (property) for the purposes of taxation **3** to determine the importance, size, or value of – **assessable** *adj*, **assessment** *n*

assessor /ə'sesə‖ə'sesə/ *n* **1** a specialist who advises a court **2** an official who assesses property for taxation **3** *chiefly Br* sby who investigates and values insurance claims

asset /'aset‖'æset/ *n* **1a** *pl* the total property of a person, company, or institution; *esp* that part which can be used to pay debts **b** a single item of property **2** an advantage, resource **3** *pl* the items on a balance sheet showing the book value of property owned

asseverate /ə'sevərayt‖ə'sevəreɪt/ *vt* to affirm solemnly – fml – **asseveration** *n*, **asseverative** *adj*

assiduity /,asi'dyooh·əti‖,æsɪ'djuːətɪ/ *n* **1** diligence **2** solicitous or obsequious attention to a person

assiduous /ə'sidyoo·əs‖ə'sɪdjʊəs/ *adj* marked by careful unremitting attention or persistent application; diligent – **assiduously** *adv*, **assiduousness** *n*

[1]**assign** /ə'sien‖ə'saɪn/ *vt* **1** to transfer (property) to another, esp in trust or for the benefit of creditors **2** to appoint to a post or duty **3** to fix authoritatively; specify, designate – **assignability** *n*, **assignable** *adj*, **assigner**, **assignor** *n*

[2]**assign** *n* **1** ASSIGNEE 1, 2 **2** sby to whom property or a right is legally transferred

assignation /ˌasig'naysh(ə)n‖ˌæsɪg'neɪʃ(ə)n/ *n* **1** the act of assigning; *also* the assignment made **2** a meeting, esp a secret one with a lover – **assignational** *adj*

assignee /ˌasie'nee‖ˌæsaɪ'niː/ *n* **1** a person to whom an assignment is made **2** a person appointed to act for another **3** ASSIGN 2

assignment /ə'sienmənt‖ə'saɪnmənt/ *n* **1a** a position, post, or job to which one is assigned **b** a specified task or amount of work assigned by authority **2** (a document effecting) the legal transfer of property

assimilate /ə'similayt‖ə'sɪmɪleɪt/ *vt* **1a** to take in or absorb into the system (as nourishment) **b** to absorb; *esp* to take into the mind and fully comprehend **2a** to make similar – usu + *to* or *with* **b** to absorb into a cultural tradition **3** to compare, liken – usu + *to* or *with* ~*vi* to become assimilated – **assimilable** *adj*, **assimilative** *adj*, **assimilator** *n*, **assimilatory** *adj*, **assimilation** *n*

[1]**assist** /ə'sist‖ə'sɪst/ *vi* **1** to give support or aid **2** to be present as a spectator ~*vi* to give support or aid to – **assistance** *n*, **assistant** *n*

[2]**assist** *n* the officially recorded action of a player who by throwing a ball in baseball or by passing a ball or puck in basketball, lacrosse, or ice hockey enables a teammate to put an opponent out or score a goal

assize /ə'siez‖ə'saɪz/ *n, often cap* the periodical sessions of the superior courts formerly held in every English county for trial of civil and criminal cases – usu pl with sing. meaning

[1]**associate** /ə'sohs(h)iayt‖ə'səʊsɪeɪt,-əʊʃɪ-/ *vt* **1** to join as a friend, companion, or partner in business <~ *ourselves with a larger firm*> **2** to bring together in any of various ways (e g in memory, thought, or imagination) ~ *vi* **1** to come together as partners, friends, or companions **2** to combine or join with other parts; unite *USE* often + *with* – **associatory** *adj*

[2]**associate** /ə'sohs(h)i·ət‖ə'səʊsɪət,-əʊʃɪ-/ *adj* **1** closely connected (e g in function or office) with another **2** having secondary or subordinate status <~ *membership in a society*>

[3]**associate** /ə'sohs(h)i·ət, -ayt‖ə'səʊsɪət, -eɪt, -əʊʃɪ-/ *n* **1** a fellow worker; partner, colleague **2** a companion, comrade **3** sthg closely connected with or usu accompanying another **4** one admitted to a subordinate degree of membership <*an* ~ *of the Royal Academy*> – **associateship** *n*

association /əˌsohs(h)i'aysh(ə)n‖əˌsəʊsɪ'eɪʃ(ə)n, -əʊʃɪ-/ *n* **1** an organization of people having a common interest; a society, league **2** sthg linked in memory, thought, or imagination with a thing or person; a connotation **3** the formation of mental connections between sensations, ideas, memories, etc – **associational** *adj*

asˌsociation ˈfootball *n* soccer

assonance /'asənəns‖'æsənəns/ *n* **1** resemblance of sound in words or syllables **2** repetition of esp only the vowel sounds (e g in *stony* and *holy*) or only the consonant sounds, as an alternative to rhyme – **assonant** *adj or n*

as ˈsoon as *conj* immediately at or just after the time that

assort /ə'sawt‖ə'sɔːt/ *vt* to distribute into groups of a like kind; classify ~*vi* to suit or match well or ill with sthg – **assortative** *adj*, **assorter** *n*

asˈsorted *adj* **1** consisting of various kinds **2** suited by nature, character, or design; matched <*an ill-*assorted *pair*>

asˈsortment /-mənt‖-mənt/ *n* a collection of assorted things or people

assuage /ə'swayj‖ə'sweɪdʒ/ *vt* to lessen the intensity of (pain, suffering, desire, etc); ease – **assuagement** *n*

assume /ə'syoohm‖ə'sjuːm/ *vt* **1a** to take to or upon oneself; undertake **b** to invest oneself formally with (an office or its symbols) **2** to seize, usurp **3** to pretend to have or be; feign **4** to take as granted or true; suppose – often + *that* – **assumability** *n*, **assumable** *adj*, **assumably** *adv*

assumption /ə'sum(p)sh(ə)n‖ə'sʌm(p)ʃ(ə)n/ *n* **1a** the taking up of a person into heaven **b** *cap* August 15 observed in commemoration of the assumption of the Virgin Mary **2** the act of laying claim to or taking possession of sthg **3a** the supposition that sthg is true **b** a fact or statement (e g a proposition, axiom, or postulate) taken for granted

assurance /ə'shawrəns, -'shooə-‖ə'ʃɔːrəns, -'ʃʊə-/ *n* **1a** a pledge, guarantee **b** *chiefly Br* (life) insurance **2a** the quality or state of being sure or certain; freedom from doubt **b** confidence of mind or manner; *also* excessive self-confidence; brashness **3** sthg that inspires or tends to inspire confidence

assure /ə'shaw, -'shooə‖ə'ʃɔː, -'ʃʊə/ *vt* **1** to make safe; insure (esp life or safety) **2** to give confidence to; reassure **3** to inform positively **4** to guarantee the happening or attainment of; ensure

[1]**asˈsured** *adj* **1** characterized by self-confidence **2** satisfied as to the certainty or truth of a matter; convinced – **assuredly** *adv*, **assuredness** *n*

[2]**assured** *n, pl* **assured**, **assureds** an insured person

aster /'astə‖'æstə/ *n* any of various chiefly autumn-blooming leafy-stemmed composite plants with often showy heads

[1]**asterisk** /'astərisk‖'æstərɪsk/ *n* a sign * used as a reference mark, esp to denote the omission of letters or words or to show that sthg is doubtful or absent [Greek *asteriskos*, lit., little star, fr *astēr* star]

[2]**asterisk** *vt* to mark with an asterisk; star

astern /ə'stuhn‖ə'stɜːn/ *adv or adj* **1** behind the stern; to the rear **2** at or towards the stern of a ship **3** backwards <*the captain signalled full* ~>

[1]**asteroid** /'astəroyd‖'æstərɔɪd/ *n* any of thousands of small planets mostly between Mars and Jupiter – **asteroidal** *adj*

[2]**asteroid** *adj* **1** starlike **2** of or like a starfish
asthma /'as(th)mə‖'æs(θ)mə/ *n* (an allergic condition marked by attacks of) laboured breathing with wheezing and usu coughing, gasping, and a sense of constriction in the chest – **asthmatic** *adj or n*, **asthmatically** *adv*
as 'though *conj* AS IF
astigmatic /,astig'matik‖,æstɪg'mætɪk/ *adj* affected with, relating to, or correcting astigmatism – **astigmatically** *adv*
astigmatism /a'stigmətiz(ə)m, ə-‖æ-'stɪgmətɪz(ə)m, ə-/ *n* a defect of an optical system (e g a lens or the eye) in which rays from a single point fail to meet in a focal point, resulting in a blurred image
astir /ə'stuh‖ə'stɜː/ *adj* **1** in a state of bustle or excitement **2** out of bed; up
'as to *prep* **1a** with regard or reference to; about – used esp with questions and speculations **b** AS FOR **2** by; ACCORDING TO <*graded ~ size and colour*>
astonish /ə'stonish‖ə'stɒnɪʃ/ *vt* to strike with sudden wonder or surprise – **astonishing** *adj*, **astonishingly** *adv*, **astonishment** *n*
astound /ə'stownd‖ə'staʊnd/ *vt* to fill with bewilderment and wonder – **astounding** *adj*, **astoundingly** *adv*
astr-, astro- *comb form* star; heavens; outer space <astro*physics*>
astrakhan, astrachan /,astrə'kahn, -'kan, -kən‖,æstrə'kɑːn, -'kæn, -kən/ *n, often cap* **1** fur from the curled black fleece of newborn Asiatic lambs **2** a woollen fabric with curled and looped pile [*Astrakhan*, city in USSR]
astral /'astrəl‖'æstrəl/ *adj* **1** (consisting) of stars **2** (consisting) of a spiritual substance held in theosophy to be the material of which sby's supposed second body is made up, that can be seen by specially gifted people – **astrally** *adv*
astray /ə'stray‖ə'streɪ/ *adv or adj* **1** off the right path or route **2** in error; away from a proper or desirable course or development
[1]**astride** /ə'stried‖ə'straɪd/ *adv* with the legs wide apart
[2]**astride** *prep* **1** on or above and with 1 leg on each side of **2** extending over or across; spanning
[1]**astringent** /ə'strinj(ə)nt‖ə'strɪndʒ(ə)nt/ *adj* **1** capable of making firm the soft tissues of the body; styptic **2** rigidly severe; austere – **astringency** *n*, **astringently** *adv*
[2]**astringent** *n* an astringent substance
astro- – see ASTR-
astrolabe /'astrə,layb‖'æstrə,leɪb/ *n* an instrument used, before the invention of the sextant, to observe the position of celestial bodies
astrology /ə'stroləji‖ə'strɒlədʒɪ/ *n* the art or practice of determining the supposed influences of the planets on human affairs – **astrologer** *n*, **astrological** *adj*, **astrologically** *adv*
astronaut /'astrə,nawt‖'æstrə,nɔːt/ *n* sby who travels beyond the earth's atmosphere [deriv of Greek *astron* star + *nautes* sailor]
astronautics /,astrə'nawtiks‖,æstrə'nɔːtɪks/ *n pl but sing or pl in constr* the science of the construction and operation of vehicles for travel in space – **astronautic, astronautical** *adj*, **astronautically** *adv*
astronomer /ə'stronəmə‖ə'strɒnəmə/ *n* sby who is skilled in or practises astronomy
astronomical /,astrə'nomikl‖,æstrə-'nɒmɪkl/, **astronomic** /-'nomik‖-'nɒmɪk/ *adj* **1** of astronomy **2** enormously or inconceivably large – infml – **astronomically** *adv*
astronomy /ə'stronəmi‖ə'strɒnəmɪ/ *n* a branch of science dealing with the celestial bodies
astrophysics /,astroh'fiziks‖,æstrəʊ'fɪzɪks/ *n pl but sing or pl in constr* a branch of astronomy dealing with the physical and chemical constitution of the celestial bodies – **astrophysical** *adj*, **astrophysicist** *n*
Astroturf /'astrə,tuhf‖'æstrə,tɜːf/ *trademark* – used for an artificial grass-like surface that is used for lawns and sports fields
astute /ə'styooht, ə'schooht‖ə'stjuːt, ə'stʃuːt/ *adj* shrewdly perspicacious – **astutely** *adv*, **astuteness** *n*
asunder /ə'sundə‖ə'sʌndə/ *adv or adj* **1** into parts <*torn ~*> **2** apart from each other in position <*wide ~*>
asylum /ə'sieləm‖ə'saɪləm/ *n* **1** a place of refuge for criminals, debtors, etc; a sanctuary **2** a place of retreat and security; a shelter **3a** the protection from the law or refuge afforded by an asylum **b** protection from arrest and extradition given by a nation to political refugees **4** an institution for the care of the destitute or afflicted, esp the insane
asymmetric /aysi'metrik‖eɪsɪ'metrɪk/, **asymmetrical** /-kl‖-kl/ *adj* not symmetrical
at /ət‖ət; *strong* at‖æt/ *prep* **1** – used to indicate presence or occurrence in, on, or near a place imagined as a point <*~ a hotel*> <*sick ~ heart*> **2** – used to indicate the goal or direction of an action or motion <*aim ~ the target*> **3a** – used to indicate occupation or employment <*~ the controls*> **b** when it comes to (an occupation or employment) <*an expert ~ chess*> **4** – used to indicate situation or condition <*~ liberty*> **5** in response to <*laugh ~ his jokes*> **6** – used to indicate position on a scale (e g of cost, speed, or age) <*~ 90 mph*> **7** – used to indicate position in time <*~ 3 o'clock*> **8** from a distance of <*shot him ~ 30 paces*> – **at a** as a result of only 1; by or during only 1 <*drank it* at *a gulp*> – **at it** doing it; *esp* busy <*been hard* at *it all day*> – **at that 1** at that point and no further <*let it go* at that> **2** which makes it more surprising; IN ADDITION <*she says sack him, and maybe I will* at that>
at- – see AD-
at 'all *adv* to the least extent or degree; under any circumstances <*not ~ far*> – **not at all** – used in answer to thanks or to an apology
atavism /'atəviz(ə)m‖'ætəvɪz(ə)m/ *n* (an individual or character showing) recurrence in (the parts of) an organism of a form typical of ancestors more remote than the parents – **atavist** *n*, **atavistic** *adj*, **atavistically** *adv*
ate /et, ayt‖et, eɪt/ *past of* EAT
[1]**-ate** /-ət, -ayt‖-ət, -eɪt/ *suffix* (→ *n*) **1** product of (a specified process) <*distill*ate> **2** chemical compound or complex anion derived from (a specified compound or element) <*sulph*ate>
[2]**-ate** *suffix* (→ *n*) **1** office, function, or rank of <*consul*ate> **2** individual or group of people

holding (a specified office or rank) or having (a specified function) <*electorate*> <*candidate*>

[3]**-ate, -ated** *suffix* (→ *adj*) **1** being in or brought to (a specified state) <*passionate*> **2** marked by having <*craniate*> **3** resembling; having the shape of <*foliate*>

[4]**-ate** *suffix* (→ *vb*) **1** act (in a specified way) <*pontificate*> <*remonstrate*> **2** act (in a specified way) upon <*assassinate*> **3** cause to become; cause to be modified or affected by <*activate*> **4** provide with <*aerate*>

atelier /əˈteliay, ˈatəlyay‖əˈtelɪeɪ, ˈætəljeɪ/ *n* an artist's or designer's studio or workroom

atheism /ˈaythi·iz(ə)m‖ˈeɪθɪɪz(ə)m/ *n* the belief or doctrine that there is no deity – **atheist** *n*, **atheistic, atheistical** *adj*, **atheistically** *adv*

athlete /ˈathleet‖ˈæθliːt/ *n* sby who is trained in, skilled in, or takes part in exercises, sports, etc that require physical strength, agility, or stamina [Latin *athleta*, fr Greek *athlētēs*, fr *athlein* to contend for a prize, fr *athlon* prize, contest]

ˌathlete's ˈfoot *n* ringworm of the feet

athletic /athˈletik‖æθˈletɪk/ *adj* **1** of athletes or athletics **2** characteristic of an athlete; *esp* vigorous, active – **athletically** *adv*, **athleticism** *n*

athˈletics *n pl but sing or pl in constr, Br* competitive walking, running, throwing, and jumping sports collectively

at ˈhome *n* a reception given at one's home

[1]**athwart** /əˈthwawt‖əˈθwɔːt/ *adv* **1** across, esp in an oblique direction **2** in opposition to the right or expected course

[2]**athwart** *prep* **1** across **2** in opposition to

-ation /-ˈaysh(ə)n‖-ˈeɪʃ(ə)n/ *suffix* (*vb* → *n*) **1** action or process of <*flirtation*> **2** result or product of (a specified action or process) <*alteration*> **3** state or condition of <*agitation*>

-ative /-ətiv‖-ətɪv/ *suffix* (*vb, n* → *adj*) **1** of, relating to, or connected with <*authoritative*> **2** tending to; disposed to <*talkative*>

atlas /ˈatləs‖ˈætləs/ *n* **1** *cap* one who bears a heavy burden **2** a bound collection of maps, charts, or tables **3** the first vertebra of the neck

atmosphere /ˈatməsfiə‖ˈætməsfɪə/ *n* **1** a mass of gas enveloping a celestial body (e g a planet); *esp* all the air surrounding the earth **2** the air of a locality **3** a surrounding influence or environment **4** a unit of pressure chosen to be a typical pressure of the air at sea level and equal to 101,325 newtons per square metre (about 14.7lb/in^2) **5** a dominant aesthetic or emotional effect or appeal [deriv of Greek *atmos* vapour + *sphaira* sphere] – **atmospheric** *adj*, **atmospherically** *adv*

ˌatmoˈspherics *n pl* (the electrical phenomena causing) audible disturbances produced in a radio receiver by electrical atmospheric phenomena (e g lightning)

atoll /ˈatol, əˈtol‖ˈætɒl, əˈtɒl/ *n* a coral reef surrounding a lagoon

atom /ˈatəm‖ˈætəm/ *n* **1** any of the minute indivisible particles of which according to ancient materialism the universe is composed **2** a tiny particle; a bit <*not an ~ of truth in it*> **3** the smallest particle of an element that can exist either alone or in combination, consisting of various numbers of electrons, protons, and neutrons **4** nuclear power [Latin *atomus*, fr Greek *atomos*, fr *atomos* indivisible, fr *a-* not + *temnein* to cut]

ˈatom ˌbomb *n* **1** a bomb whose violent explosive power is due to the sudden release of atomic energy derived from the splitting of the nuclei of plutonium, uranium, etc by neutrons in a very rapid chain reaction **2** HYDROGEN BOMB – **atom-bomb** *vt*

atomic /əˈtomik‖əˈtɒmɪk/ *adj* **1** of or concerned with atoms, atom bombs, or atomic energy **2** *of a chemical element* existing as separate atoms – **atomically** *adv*

atomic energy *n* energy liberated in an atom bomb, nuclear reactor, etc by changes in the nucleus of an atom

atomic number *n* the number of protons in the nucleus of an atom which is characteristic of a chemical element and determines its place in the periodic table

atomic pile *n* REACTOR 2

atomic weight *n* the ratio of the average mass of an atom of an element to the mass of an atom of the most abundantly occurring isotope of carbon

atom·ize, -ise /ˈatəmiez‖ˈætəmaɪz/ *vt* to reduce to minute particles or to a fine spray – **atomization** *n*

atonal /aˈtohnl, ay-‖æˈtəʊnl, eɪ-/ *adj* organized without reference to a musical key and using the notes of the chromatic scale impartially – **atonalism** *n*, **atonalist** *n*, **atonally** *adv*, **atonalistic** *adj*, **atonality** *n*

atone /əˈtohn‖əˈtəʊn/ *vi* to supply satisfaction *for*; make amends *for* <*the* atoning *death of Christ*> – **atonement** *n*

-ator /-aytə‖-eɪtə/ *suffix* (→ *n*) [1]-OR <*commentator*>

atrium /ˈatri·əm, ˈay-‖ˈætrɪəm, ˈeɪ-/ *n, pl* **atria** /ˈatri·ə, ˈay-‖ˈætrɪə, ˈeɪ-/ *also* **atriums** **1** an inner courtyard open to the sky (e g in a Roman house) **2** an anatomical cavity or passage; *specif* a chamber of the heart that receives blood from the veins and forces it into a ventricle or ventricles – **atrial** *adj*

atrocious /əˈtrohshəs‖əˈtrəʊʃəs/ *adj* **1** extremely wicked, brutal, or cruel; barbaric **2** of very poor quality <*~ handwriting*> – **atrociously** *adv*, **atrociousness** *n*

atrocity /əˈtrosəti‖əˈtrɒsətɪ/ *n* **1** being atrocious **2** an atrocious act, object, or situation

[1]**atrophy** /ˈatrəfi‖ˈætrəfɪ/ *n* **1** (sometimes natural) decrease in size or wasting away of a body part or tissue **2** a wasting away or progressive decline; degeneration – **atrophic** *adj*

[2]**atrophy** *vb* to (cause to) undergo atrophy

atropine /ˈatrəpeen, -pin‖ˈætrəpiːn, -pɪn/ *n* a poisonous alkaloid found in deadly nightshade and used in medicine to inhibit activities of the nervous system

attach /əˈtach‖əˈtætʃ/ *vt* **1** to seize by legal authority **2** to bring (oneself) into an association **3** to appoint to serve with an organization for special duties or for a temporary period **4** to fasten **5** to ascribe, attribute *~vi* to become attached; stick *USE* often + *to* – **attachable** *adj*

attaché /ə'tashay‖ə'tæʃeɪ/ *n* a technical expert on a diplomatic staff

at'taché ˌcase *n* a small thin case used esp for carrying papers

at'tachment /-mənt‖-mənt/ *n* **1** a seizure by legal process **2a** fidelity – often + *to* <~ *to a cause*> **b** an affectionate regard **3** a device attached to a machine or implement **4** the physical connection by which one thing is attached to another

[1]**attack** /ə'tak‖ə'tæk/ *vt* **1** to set upon forcefully in order to damage, injure, or destroy **2** to take the initiative against in a game or contest **3** to assail with unfriendly or bitter words **4** to begin to affect or to act on injuriously **5** to set to work on, esp vigorously ~*vi* to make an attack – **attacker** *n*

[2]**attack** *n* **1** the act of attacking; an assault **2** a belligerent or antagonistic action or verbal assault – often + *on* **3** the beginning of destructive action (e g by a chemical agent) **4** the setting to work on some undertaking **5** a fit of sickness or (recurrent) disease **6a** an attempt to score or to gain ground in a game **b** *sing or pl in constr* the attacking players in a team or the positions occupied by them; *specif* the bowlers in a cricket team

attain /ə'tayn‖ə'teɪn/ *vt* to reach as an end; achieve ~*vi* to come or arrive by motion, growth, or effort – + *to* – **attainable** *adj*, **attainability** *n*

attainder /ə'tayndə‖ə'teɪndə/ *n* a penalty enforced until 1870 by which sby sentenced to death or outlawry forfeited his/her property and civil rights

attainment /ə'taynmənt‖ə'teɪnmənt/ *n* sthg attained; an accomplishment

attar /'atə‖'ætə/ *n* a fragrant essential oil (e g from rose petals); *also* a fragrance [Persian *'atir* perfumed, fr Arabic, fr *'itr* perfume]

[1]**attempt** /ə'tempt‖ə'tempt/ *vt* to make an effort to do, accomplish, solve, or effect, esp without success

[2]**attempt** *n* **1** the act or an instance of attempting; *esp* an unsuccessful effort **2** an attack, assault – often + *on*

attend /ə'tend‖ə'tend/ *vt* **1** to take charge of; LOOK AFTER **2** to go or stay with as a companion, nurse, or servant **3** to be present with; accompany, escort **4** to be present at ~ *vi* **1a** to apply oneself <~ *to your work*> **b** to deal with **2** to apply the mind or pay attention; heed *USE* – often + *to* – **attender** *n*

attendance /ə'tend(ə)ns‖ə'tend(ə)ns/ *n* **1** the number of people attending **2** the number of times a person attends, usu out of a possible maximum

[1]**attendant** /ə'tend(ə)nt‖ə'tend(ə)nt/ *adj* accompanying or following as a consequence

[2]**attendant** *n* one who attends another to perform a service; *esp* an employee who waits on customers

attention /ə'tensh(ə)n‖ə'tenʃ(ə)n/ *n* **1** attending, esp through application of the mind to an object of sense or thought **2** consideration with a view to action **3a** an act of civility or courtesy, esp in courtship – usu pl **b** sympathetic consideration of the needs and wants of others **4** a formal position of readiness assumed by a soldier – usu as a command – **attentional** *adj*

attentive /ə'tentiv‖ə'tentɪv/ *adj* **1** mindful, observant **2** solicitous **3** paying attentions (as if) in the role of a suitor – **attentively** *adv*, **attentiveness** *n*

attenuate /ə'tenyooayt‖ə'tenjʊeɪt/ *vt* **1** to make thin **2** to lessen the amount, force, or value of; weaken **3** to reduce the severity, virulence, or vitality of ~*vi* to become thin or fine; diminish – **attenuation** *n*

attest /ə'test‖ə'test/ *vt* **1a** to affirm to be true **b** to authenticate esp officially **2** to be proof of; bear witness to **3** to put on oath ~*vi* to bear witness, testify – often + *to* – **attester** *n*, **attestation** *n*

attic /'atik‖'ætɪk/ *n* a room or space immediately below the roof of a building

[1]**Attic** *adj* (characteristic) of the ancient Greek state of Attica or the city of Athens

[2]**Attic** *n* a Greek dialect of ancient Attica which became the literary language of the Greek-speaking world

[1]**attire** /ə'tie·ə‖ə'taɪə/ *vt* to put garments on; dress, array; *esp* to clothe in fancy or rich garments

[2]**attire** *n* dress, clothes; *esp* splendid or decorative clothing

attitude /'atityoohd‖'ætɪtju:d/ *n* **1** the arrangement of the parts of a body or figure; a posture **2** a feeling, emotion, or mental position with regard to a fact or state **3** a manner assumed for a specific purpose **4** a ballet position in which one leg is raised at the back and bent at the knee **5** the position of an aircraft or spacecraft relative to a particular point of reference (e g the horizon) – **attitudinal** *adj*

attitudin·ize, -ise /ˌati'tyoohdiniez‖ˌætɪ'tju:dɪnaɪz/ *vi* to assume an affected mental attitude; pose

attorney /ə'tuhni‖ə'tɜ:nɪ/ *n* **1** sby with legal authority to act for another **2** *NAm* a lawyer – **attorneyship** *n*

atˌtorney 'general *n, pl* **attorneys general, attorney generals** *often cap A&G* the chief legal officer of a nation or state

attract /ə'trakt‖ə'trækt/ *vt* to cause to approach or adhere: e g **a** to pull to or towards oneself or itself <*a magnet* ~s *iron*> **b** to draw by appeal to interest, emotion, or aesthetic sense <~ *attention*> ~*vi* to possess or exercise the power of attracting sthg or or sby <*opposites* ~> – **attractable** *adj*, **attractor** *n*, **attractive** *adj*, **attractively** *adv*, **attractiveness** *n*

attraction /ə'traksh(ə)n‖ə'trækʃ(ə)n/ *n* **1** a characteristic that elicits interest or admiration – usu pl **2** the action or power of drawing forth a response (e g interest or affection); an attractive quality **3** a force between unlike electric charges, unlike magnetic poles, etc, resisting separation **4** sthg that attracts or is intended to attract people by appealing to their desires and tastes

[1]**attribute** /'atribyooht‖'ætrɪbju:t/ *n* **1** an inherent characteristic **2** an object closely associated with a usu specified person, thing, or office

[2]**attribute** /ə'tribyooht‖ə'trɪbju:t/ *vt* to reckon

as originating in an indicated fashion – usu + *to* – **attributable** *adj*, **attributer** *n*, **attribution** *n* – **attribute to 1** to explain by indicating as a cause **2** to regard as a characteristic of (a person or thing)

attributive /ə'tribyootiv‖ə'trɪbjʊtɪv/ *adj* **1** relating to or of the nature of an attribute **2** directly preceding a modified noun (e g *city* in *city streets*) – **attributive** *n*, **attributively** *adv*

attrition /ə'trish(ə)n‖ə'trɪʃ(ə)n/ *n* **1** sorrow for one's sins arising from fear of punishment **2** the act of rubbing together; friction; *also* the act of wearing or grinding down by friction **3** the act of weakening or exhausting by constant harassment or abuse <*war of* ~> – **attritional** *adj*

attune /ə'tyoohn‖ə'tju:n/ *vt* to bring into harmony; tune – **attunement** *n*

atypical /ˌay'tipikl‖ˌeɪ'tɪpɪkl/ *adj* not typical; irregular – **atypically** *adv*, **atypicality** *n*

aubergine /'ohbəzheen, -jeen‖'əʊbəʒi:n, -dʒi:n/ **1** (the edible usu smooth dark purple ovoid fruit of) the eggplant **2** a deep reddish purple colour

aubrietia /aw'breeshə‖ɔ:'bri:ʃə/ *n* any of various trailing spring-flowering rock plants of the mustard family [Claude *Aubriet* (1668-1743), French painter of flowers & animals]

auburn /'awbən‖'ɔ:bən/ *adj or n* (of) a reddish brown colour

[1]auction /'awksh(ə)n‖'ɔ:kʃ(ə)n/ *n* **1** a public sale of property to the highest bidder **2** the act or process of bidding in some card games

[2]auction *vt* to sell at an auction – often + *off* <~ed *off the silver*>

auction bridge *n* a form of bridge differing from contract bridge in that tricks made in excess of the contract are scored towards game

auctioneer /ˌawksh(ə)n'iə‖ˌɔ:kʃ(ə)n'ɪə/ *n* an agent who sells goods at an auction – **auctioneer** *vt*

audacious /aw'dayshəs‖ɔ:'deɪʃəs/ *adj* **1a** intrepidly daring; adventurous **b** recklessly bold; rash **2** insolent – **audaciously** *adv*, **audaciousness** *n*, **audacity** *n*

audible /'awdəbl‖'ɔ:dəbl/ *adj* heard or capable of being heard – **audibly** *adv*, **audibility** *n*

audience /'awdi·əns‖'ɔ:dɪəns/ *n* **1a** a formal hearing or interview <*an* ~ *with the pope*> **b** an opportunity of being heard <*the court refused him* ~> **2** *sing or pl in constr* a group of listeners or spectators

[1]audio /'awdioh‖'ɔ:dɪəʊ/ *adj* **1** of or being acoustic, mechanical, or electrical frequencies corresponding to those of audible sound waves, approx 20 to 20,000Hz **2a** of sound or its reproduction, esp high-fidelity reproduction **b** relating to or used in the transmission or reception of sound

[2]audio *n* the transmission, reception, or reproduction of sound

audio- *comb form* **1** hearing <audio*meter*> **2** sound <audio*phile*> **3** auditory and <audio*visual*>

audiometer /ˌawdi'omitə‖ˌɔ:dɪ'ɒmɪtə/ *n* an instrument for measuring the sharpness of hearing – **audiometry** *n*, **audiometric** *adj*

audiovisual /ˌawdioh'viz(h)yooəl‖ˌɔ:dɪəʊ-'vɪzjʊəl, -'vɪʒjʊəl/ *adj* of (teaching methods using) both hearing and sight

[1]audit /'awdit‖'ɔ:dɪt/ *n* (the final report on) a formal or official examination and verification of an account book

[2]audit *vt* to perform an audit on – **auditable** *adj*

[1]audition /aw'dish(ə)n‖ɔ:'dɪʃ(ə)n/ *n* **1** the power or sense of hearing **2** the act of hearing; *esp* a critical hearing **3** a trial performance to appraise an entertainer's abilities

[2]audition *vt* to test (e g for a part) in an audition ~*vi* to give a trial performance – usu + *for*

auditor /'awditə‖'ɔ:dɪtə/ *n* **1** one who hears or listens; *esp* a member of an audience **2** one authorized to perform an audit

auditorium /ˌawdi'tawri·əm‖ˌɔ:dɪ'tɔ:rɪəm/ *n*, *pl* **auditoria** /-ri·ə‖-rɪə/, **auditoriums** the part of a public building where an audience sits

auditory /'awdit(ə)ri‖'ɔ:dɪt(ə)rɪ/ *adj* of or experienced through hearing

au fait /ˌoh 'fay‖ˌəʊ 'feɪ/ *adj* **1** fully competent; capable **2** fully informed; familiar *with* [French, lit., to the point]

auger /'awgə‖'ɔ:gə/ *n* **1** a tool for boring holes in wood consisting of a shank with a central tapered screw and a pair of cutting lips with projecting spurs that cut the edge of the hole **2** any of various instruments or devices shaped like an auger

aught /awt‖ɔ:t/ *pron* **1** all <*for* ~ *I care*> **2** *archaic* anything

augment /awg'ment‖ɔ:g'ment/ *vb* to make or become greater; increase – **augmentable** *adj*, **augmenter, augmentor** *n*, **augmentation** *n*

[1]augur /'awgə‖'ɔ:gə/ *n* one held to foretell events by omens; a soothsayer; *specif* an official diviner of Ancient Rome

[2]augur *vt* **1** to foretell, esp from omens **2** to give promise of; presage ~*vi* to predict the future, esp from omens

augury /'awgyoori‖'ɔ:gjʊrɪ/ *n* **1** predicting the future from omens or portents **2** an omen, portent

august /aw'gust‖ɔ:'gʌst/ *adj* marked by majestic dignity or grandeur – **augustly** *adv*, **augustness** *n*

August /'awgəst‖'ɔ:gəst/ *n* the 8th month of the Gregorian calendar [Latin *Augustus*, fr *Augustus* Caesar (63BC – AD14), 1st Roman emperor]

auk /awk‖ɔ:k/ *n* a puffin, guillemot, razorbill, or related short-necked diving seabird of the northern hemisphere

auld lang syne /ˌawld lang 'sien‖ˌɔ:ld læŋ 'saɪn; *often* zien‖zaɪn/ *n* the good old times [Scots, lit., old long ago]

aunt /ahnt‖ɑ:nt/ *n* **1a** the sister of one's father or mother **b** the wife of one's uncle **2** – often used as a term of affection for a woman who is a close friend of a young child or its parents

ˌAunt 'Sally /'sali‖'sælɪ/ *n* **1** an effigy of a woman at which objects are thrown at a fair **2** *Br* an easy target of criticism or attack

au pair /ˌoh 'peə‖ˌəʊ 'peə/ *n* a foreign girl who does domestic work for a family in return for room and board and the opportunity to learn the language of the family [French, on even terms]

aura /'awrə‖'ɔ:rə/ *n* **1** a distinctive atmosphere

surrounding a given source **2** a luminous radiation; a nimbus **3** a sensation experienced before an attack of a brain disorder, esp epilepsy

aural /'awrəl‖'ɔːrəl/ *adj* of the ear or the sense of hearing – **aurally** *adv*

aureole /'awriohl‖'ɔːrɪəʊl/, **aureola** /aw'ree·ələ, ə-‖ɔː'riːələ, ə-/ *n* **1** a radiant light surrounding the head or body of a representation of a holy figure **2** the halo surrounding the sun, moon etc when seen through thin cloud – **aureole** *vt*

au revoir /ˌoh rə'vwah ‖ˌəʊ rə'vwɑː (*Fr* o rəvwa:r)/ *n* goodbye – often used interjectionally

auricle /'awrikl‖'ɔːrɪkl/ *n* **1a** PINNA 2 **b** an atrium of the heart – not now in technical use **2** an ear-shaped lobe

auricular /aw'rikyoolə‖ɔː'rɪkjʊlə/ *adj* **1** of or using the ear or the sense of hearing **2** told privately <*an ~ confession*> **3** understood or recognized by the sense of hearing **4** of an auricle

auriferous /aw'rifərəs‖ɔː'rɪfərəs/ *adj* gold-bearing

aurora /aw'rawrə‖ɔː'rɔːrə/ *n, pl* **auroras, aurorae** /-ri‖-rɪ/ dawn – **auroral** *adj*, **aurorean** *adj*

auˌrora au'stralis /aw'strahlis‖ɔː'strɑːlɪs/ *n* a phenomenon in the S hemisphere corresponding to the aurora borealis

auˌrora bore'alis /bawri'ahlis‖bɔːrɪ'ɑːlɪs/ *n* a luminous electrical phenomenon in the N hemisphere, esp at high latitudes, that consists of streamers or arches of light in the sky

auscultation /ˌawskəl'taysh(ə)n‖ˌɔːskəl'teɪʃ(ə)n/ *n* the act of listening to the heart, lungs, etc as a medical diagnostic aid – **auscultate** *vt*

auspice /'awspis‖'ɔːspɪs/ *n* **1** a (favourable) prophetic sign **2** *pl* kindly patronage and guidance

auspicious /aw'spish(ə)s‖ɔː'spɪʃ(ə)s/ *adj* **1** affording a favourable auspice; propitious **2** attended by good auspices; prosperous – **auspiciously** *adv*, **auspiciousness** *n*

Aussie /'ozi‖'ɒzɪ/ *n* an Australian – infml

austere /aw'stiə, o'stiə‖ɔː'stɪə, ɒ'stɪə/ *adj* **1** stern and forbidding in appearance and manner **2** rigidly abstemious; self-denying **3** unadorned, simple – **austerely** *adv*, **austereness** *n*

austerity /aw'sterəti, o-‖ɔː'sterətɪ, ɒ-/ *n* **1** an austere act, manner, or attitude **2** enforced or extreme economy

[1]Austr-, Austro- *comb form* south; southern <Austro*asiatic*>

[2]Austr-, Austro- *comb form* Austrian and <Austro-*Hungarian*>

Australasian /ˌostrə'layzh(y)ən‖ˌɒstrə'leɪʒ(j)ən; *also* ˌaw-‖ˌɔː-/ *n or adj* (a native or inhabitant) of Australasia, the islands of the S & central Pacific

Australian /o'straylyən‖ɒ'streɪljən; *also* aw-‖ɔː-/ *n* **1** a native or inhabitant of Australia **2** the speech of the aboriginal inhabitants of Australia **3** English as spoken and written in Australia – **Australian** *adj*

Austrian /'ostri·ən, 'aw-‖'ɒstrɪən, 'ɔː-/ *n or adj* (a native or inhabitant) of Austria

aut-, auto- *comb form* **1** self; same one; of or by oneself <auto*biography*> **2** automatic; self-acting; self-regulating <auto*dyne*>

autarchy /'awtahki‖'ɔːtɑːkɪ/ *n* absolute sovereignty

autarky *also* **autarchy** /'awtahki‖'ɔːtɑːkɪ/ *n* national (economic) self-sufficiency and independence – **autarkic, autarkical** *adj*

authentic /aw'thentik‖ɔː'θentɪk/ *adj* **1** worthy of belief as conforming to fact or reality; trustworthy **2** not imaginary, false, or imitation; genuine – **authentically** *adv*, **authenticity** *n*

authenticate /aw'thentikayt‖ɔː'θentɪkeɪt/ *vt* to (serve to) prove the authenticity of – **authenticator** *n*, **authentication** *n*

author /'awthə‖'ɔːθə/, *fem* **authoress** /-res, -ris‖-res, -rɪs/ *n* **1a** the writer of a literary work **b** (the books written by) sby whose profession is writing **2** sby or sthg that originates or gives existence; a source – **authorial** *adj*

authoritarian /awˌthori'teəri·ən‖ɔːˌθɒrɪ'teərɪən/ *adj* of or favouring submission to authority rather than personal freedom – **authoritarian** *n*, **authoritarianism** *n*

authoritative /aw'thoritətiv‖ɔː'θɒrɪtətɪv/ *adj* **1a** having or proceeding from authority; official **b** entitled to credit or acceptance; conclusive **2** dictatorial, peremptory – **authoritatively** *adv*, **authoritativeness** *n*

authority /aw'thorəti‖ɔː'θɒrətɪ/ *n* **1a** a book, quotation, etc referred to for justification of one's opinions or actions **b** a conclusive statement or set of statements **c** an individual cited or appealed to as an expert **2a** power to require and receive submission; the right to expect obedience **b** power to influence or command **c** a right granted by sby in authority; authorization **3a** *pl the* people in command **b** persons in command; *specif* government **c** *often cap* a governmental administrative body **4a** grounds, warrant <*had excellent ~ for his strange actions*> **b** convincing force; weight <*his strong tenor lent ~ to the performance*>

author·ize, -ise /'awthəriez‖'ɔːθəraɪz/ *vt* **1** to invest with authority or legal power; empower – often + infin **2** to establish (as if) by authority; sanction – **authorizer** *n*, **authorization** *n*

Authorized Version *n* an English version of the Bible prepared under James I, published in 1611, and widely used by Protestants

'authorship /-ship‖-ʃɪp/ *n* **1** the profession or activity of writing **2** the identity of the author of a literary work

autism /'awtiz(ə)m‖'ɔːtɪz(ə)m/ *n* a disorder of childhood development marked esp by inability to form relationships with other people – **autistic** *adj*

auto /'awtoh‖'ɔːtəʊ/ *n, pl* **autos** *chiefly NAm* MOTOR CAR

[1]auto- – see AUT-

[2]auto- *comb form* self-propelling; automotive <auto*cycle*>.

autobahn /'awtohˌbahn, 'ow-‖'ɔːtəʊˌbɑːn, 'aʊ-/ *n* a German motorway

autobiography /ˌawtəbie'ogrəfi‖ˌɔːtəbaɪ'ɒgrəfɪ/ *n* the biography of a person written by him-/herself; *also* such writing considered as a genre – **autobiographer** *n*, **autobiographic, autobiographical** *adj*

autocracy /aw'tokrəsi‖ɔː'tɒkrəsɪ/ *n* government by an autocrat

autocrat /'awtəkrat‖'ɔːtəkræt/ *n* **1** one who

rules with unlimited power **2** a dictatorial person – **autocratic** *adj*, **autocratically** *adv*

autocue /ˈɑwtoh,kyooh/ *n* a device that enables a person being televised to read a script without looking away from the camera

,autoˈerotism /-ˈeərətiz(ə)m‖-ˈeərətɪz(ə)m/ *n* sexual gratification obtained by oneself without the participation of another person – **autoerotic** *adj* **autoerotically** *adv*

¹autograph /ˈawtə,grahf, -,graf‖ˈɔːtə,grɑːf, -,græf/ *n* an identifying mark, specif a person's signature, made by the individual him-/herself [deriv of Greek *autographos* written with one's fr *autos* same, self + *graphein* to write]

²autograph *vt* to write one's signature in or on

automate /ˈawtəmayt‖ˈɔːtəmeɪt/ *vt* **1** to operate by automation **2** to convert to largely automatic operation ~*vi* to undergo automation – **automatable** *adj*

¹automatic /,awtəˈmatik‖,ɔːtəˈmætɪk/ *adj* **1a** acting or done spontaneously or unconsciously **b** resembling an automaton; mechanical **2** having a self-acting or self-regulating mechanism <*an ~ car with ~ transmission*> **3** *of a firearm* repeatedly ejecting the empty cartridge shell, introducing a new cartridge, and firing it – **automatically** *adv*, **automaticity** *n*

²automatic *n* an automatic machine or apparatus; *esp* an automatic firearm or vehicle

,auto,matic ˈpilot *n* a device for automatically steering a ship, aircraft, or spacecraft

automation /awtəˈmaysh(ə)n‖ɔːtəˈmeɪʃ(ə)n/ *n* **1** the technique of making an apparatus, process, or system operate automatically **2** automatic operation of an apparatus, process, or system by mechanical or electronic devices that take the place of human operators

automatism /awˈtomətiz(ə)m‖ɔːˈtɒmətɪz(ə)m/ *n* **1** an automatic action **2** a theory that conceives of the body as a machine, with consciousness being merely an accessory – **automatist** *n*

automaton /awˈtomət(ə)n‖ɔːˈtɒmət(ə)n; *also* ,awtəˈmayt(ə)n‖,ɔːtəˈmeɪt(ə)n/ *n, pl* **automatons, automata** /-tə‖-tə/ **1** a mechanism having its own power source; *also* a robot **2** a person who acts in a mechanical fashion

automobile /ˈawtəmə,beel‖ˈɔːtəmə,biːl/ *n, NAm* MOTOR CAR – **automobile** *vi*, **automobilist** *n*

autonomous /awˈtonəməs‖ɔːˈtɒnəməs/ *adj* self-governing, independent – **autonomously** *adv*

autonomy /awˈtonəmi‖ɔːˈtɒnəmɪ/ *n* **1** self-determined freedom and esp moral independence **2** self-government; *esp* the degree of political independence possessed by a minority group, territorial division, etc – **autonomist** *n*

autopsy /ˈawtopsi‖ˈɔːtɒpsɪ/ *n* a postmortem examination – **autopsy** *vt*

ˈauto,strada /-,strahdə‖-,strɑːdə/ *n, pl* **autostradas, autostrade** /-day‖-deɪ/ an Italian motorway

,autosugˈgestion /-səˈjeschən‖-səˈdʒestʃən/ *n* an influencing of one's attitudes, behaviour, or physical condition by mental processes other than conscious thought – **autosuggest** *vt*

autumn /ˈawtəm‖ˈɔːtəm/ *n* **1** the season between summer and winter, extending, in the northern hemisphere, from the September equinox to the December solstice **2** a period of maturity or the early stages of decline – **autumnal** *adj*, **autumnally** *adv*

auxiliary /awgˈzilyəri‖ɔːgˈzɪljərɪ/ *adj* **1** subsidiary **2** being a verb (e g *be*, *do*, or *may*) used typically to express person, number, mood, voice, or tense, usu accompanying another verb **3** supplementary

²auxiliary *n* **1** an auxiliary person, group, or device **2** an auxiliary verb **3** a member of a foreign force serving a nation at war

¹avail /əˈvayl‖əˈveɪl/ *vb* to be of use or advantage (to) – **avail oneself of** to make use of; take advantage of

²avail *n* benefit, use – chiefly after *of* or *to* and in negative contexts <*of little ~*> <*to no ~*>

available /əˈvayləbl‖əˈveɪləbl/ *adj* **1** present or ready for immediate use **2** accessible, obtainable **3** qualified or willing to do sthg or to assume a responsibility <*~ candidates*> **4** present in such chemical or physical form as to be usable (e g by a plant) <*~ nitrogen*> – **availableness** *n*, **availably** *adv*, **availability** *n*

avalanche /ˈavəlahnch‖ˈævəlɑːntʃ/ *n* **1** a large mass of snow, rock, ice, etc falling rapidly down a mountain **2** a sudden overwhelming rush or accumulation of sthg

¹avant-garde /,avong ˈgahd‖,ævɒŋ ˈgɑːd/ *n the* group of people who create or apply new ideas and techniques in any field, esp the arts; *also* such a group that is extremist, bizarre, or arty and affected – **avant-gardism** *n*, **avant-gardist** *n*

²avant-garde *adj* of the avant-garde or artistic work that is new and experimental

avarice /ˈavəris‖ˈævərɪs/ *n* excessive or insatiable desire for wealth or gain – **avaricious** *adj*, **avariciously** *adv*, **avariciousness** *n*

avatar /ˈavətah‖ˈævətɑː/ *n* **1** an earthly incarnation of a Hindu deity **2** an incarnation in human form

avenge /əˈvenj‖əˈvendʒ/ *vt* **1** to take vengeance on behalf of **2** to exact satisfaction for (a wrong) by punishing the wrongdoer – **avenger** *n*

avenue /ˈavənyooh‖ˈævənjuː/ *n* **1** a line of approach **2** a broad passageway bordered by trees **3** an often broad street or road **4** *chiefly Br* a tree-lined walk or driveway to a large country house situated off a main road

aver /əˈvuh‖əˈvɜː/ *vt* **-rr- 1** to allege, assert **2** to declare positively – fml – **averment** *n*

¹average /ˈavərij, ˈavrij‖ˈævərɪdʒ, ˈævrɪdʒ/ *n* **1** a partial loss or damage sustained by a ship or cargo; *also* a charge arising from this, usu distributed among all chargeable with it **2** a single value representative of a set of other values; *esp* ARITHMETIC MEAN **3** a level (e g of intelligence) typical of a group, class, or series **4** a ratio expressing the average performance of a sports team or sportsman as a fraction of the number of opportunities for successful performance [Middle French *avarie* damage to ship or cargo, fr Italian *avaria*, fr Arabic *'awārīyah* damaged merchandise]

²average *adj* **1** equalling an arithmetic mean **2a** about midway between extremes **b** not out of the ordinary; common – **averagely** *adv*, **averageness** *n*

[3]**average** *vi* to be or come to an average <*the gain* ~d *out to 20 per cent*> ~ *vt* **1** to do, get, or have on average or as an average sum or quantity <~s *12 hours of work a day*> **2** to find the arithmetic mean of **3** to bring towards the average **4** to have an average value of

averse /ə'vuhs‖ə'vɜːs/ *adj* having an active feeling of repugnance or distaste – + *to* or *from* – **aversely** *adv*, **averseness** *n*

aversion /ə'vuhsh(ə)n‖ə'vɜːʃ(ə)n/ *n* **1** a feeling of settled dislike for sthg; antipathy **2** *chiefly Br* an object of aversion; a cause of repugnance – **aversive** *adj*

avert /ə'vuht‖ə'vɜːt/ *vt* **1** to turn away or aside (e g the eyes) in avoidance **2** to see coming and ward off; avoid, prevent

aviary /'ayvyəri‖'eɪvjərɪ/ *n* a place for keeping birds

aviation /ˌayvi'aysh(ə)n‖ˌeɪvɪ'eɪʃ(ə)n/ *n* **1** the operation of heavier-than-air aircraft **2** aircraft manufacture, development, and design

aviator /'ayviaytə‖'eɪvɪeɪtə/, *fem* **aviatrix** /-triks‖-trɪks/ *n* the pilot of an aircraft

avid /'avid‖'ævɪd/ *adj* urgently or greedily eager; keen – **avidly** *adv*, **avidness** *n*, **avidity** *n*

avionics /ˌayvi'oniks‖ˌeɪvɪ'ɒnɪks/ *n pl but sing or pl in constr* the development and production of electrical and electronic devices for use in aviation and spaceflight

avocado /ˌavə'kahdoh‖ˌævə'kɑːdəʊ/ *n, pl* **avocados** *also* **avocadoes** (a tropical American tree bearing) a pulpy green or purple pear-shaped edible fruit [Spanish, alteration of *aguacate*, fr Nahuatl *ahuacatl*, short for *ahuacacuahuitl*, lit., testicle tree]

avocation /ˌavə'kaysh(ə)n‖ˌævə'keɪʃ(ə)n/ *n* a subordinate occupation pursued in addition to one's vocation, esp for enjoyment; a hobby – **avocational** *adj*, **avocationally** *adv*

avocet /'avəset‖'ævəset/ *n* a black and white wading bird with webbed feet and a slender upward-curving bill

avoid /ə'voyd‖ə'vɔɪd/ *vt* **1a** to keep away from; shun **b** to prevent the occurrence or effectiveness of **c** to refrain from **2** to make legally void – **avoidable** *adj*, **avoidably** *adv*, **avoidance** *n*, **avoider** *n*

avoirdupois /ˌavwahdooh'pwah, ˌavədə-'poyz‖ˌævwɑːduː'pwɑː, ˌævədə'pɔɪz/, **avoirdupois weight** *n* the series of units of weight based on the pound of 16 ounces and the ounce of 16 drams

avow /ə'vow‖ə'vaʊ/ *vt* to acknowledge openly, bluntly, and without shame – **avower** *n*, **avowal** *n*, **avowedly** *adv*

avuncular /ə'vungkyoolə‖ə'vʌŋkjʊlə/ *adj* **1** of an uncle **2** kindly, genial

await /ə'wayt‖ə'weɪt/ *vt* **1** to wait for **2** to be in store for

[1]**awake** /ə'wayk‖ə'weɪk/ *vb* **awoke** /ə'wohk‖ə-'wəʊk/ *also* **awaked; awoken** /ə'wohkən‖ə-'wəʊkən/ *vi* **1** to emerge from sleep or a sleeplike state **2** to become conscious or aware of sthg – usu + *to* <awoke *to their danger*> ~ *vt* **1** to arouse from sleep or a sleeplike state **2** to make active; stir up <awoke *old memories*>

[2]**awake** *adj* **1** roused (as if) from sleep **2** fully conscious; aware – usu + *to*

awaken /ə'waykən‖ə'weɪkən/ *vb* to awake – **awakener** *n*

[1]**award** /ə'wawd‖ə'wɔːd/ *vt* **1** to give by judicial decree **2** to confer or bestow as being deserved or needed – **awardable** *adj*, **awarder** *n*

[2]**award** *n* **1** a final decision; *esp* the decision of arbitrators in a case submitted to them **2** sthg that is conferred or bestowed, esp on the basis of merit or need

aware /ə'weə‖ə'weə/ *adj* having or showing realization, perception, or knowledge; conscious – often + *of* – **awareness** *n*

awash /ə'wosh‖ə'wɒʃ/ *adj* **1** covered with water; flooded **2** marked by an abundance

[1]**away** /ə'way‖ə'weɪ/ *adv* **1** on the way; along <*get* ~ *early*> **2** from here or there; hence, thence <*go* ~ *and leave me alone!*> **3a** in a secure place or manner <*locked* ~> **b** in another direction; aside <*looked* ~> **4** out of existence; to an end <*echoes dying* ~> **5** from one's possession <*gave* ~ *a fortune*> **6a** on, uninterruptedly <*clocks ticking* ~> **b** without hesitation or delay <*do it right* ~> **7** by a long distance or interval; far <~ *back in 1910*>

[2]**away** *adj* **1** absent from a place; gone <~ *for the weekend*> **2** distant <*a lake 10 miles* ~> **3** played on an opponent's grounds <*an* ~ *game*>

awe /aw‖ɔː/ *vt or n* (to inspire with) an emotion of dread, veneration, and wonder

awesome /'aws(ə)m‖'ɔːs(ə)m/ *adj* inspiring or expressing awe – **awesomely** *adv*, **awesomeness** *n*

'**aweˌstruck** /-ˌstruk‖-ˌstrʌk/ *also* **awestricken** /-ˌstrikən‖-ˌstrɪkən/ *adj* filled with awe

[1]**awful** /'awf(ə)l‖'ɔːf(ə)l/ *adj* **1** extremely disagreeable or objectionable **2** exceedingly great <*an* ~ *lot to do*> – used as an intensive; chiefly infml – **awfully** *adv*, **awfulness** *n*

[2]**awful** *adv* very, extremely – nonstandard

awkward /'awkwəd‖'ɔːkwəd/ *adj* **1** lacking dexterity or skill, esp in the use of hands; clumsy **2** lacking ease or grace (e g of movement or expression) **3a** lacking social grace and assurance **b** causing embarrassment <*an* ~ *moment*> **4** poorly adapted for use or handling **5** requiring caution <*an* ~ *diplomatic situation*> **6** deliberately obstructive – **awkwardly** *adv*, **awkwardness** *n*

awl /awl‖ɔːl/ *n* a pointed instrument for marking surfaces or making small holes (e g in leather)

awning /'awning‖'ɔːnɪŋ/ *n* **1** an often canvas rooflike cover, used to protect sthg (e g a shop window or a ship's deck) from sun or rain **2** a shelter resembling an awning – **awninged** *adj*

awoken /ə'wohkən‖ə'wəʊkən/ *past part of* AWAKE

AWOL /'aywol‖'eɪwɒl/ *adj, often not cap* absent without leave

awry /ə'rie‖ə'raɪ/ *adv or adj* **1** in a turned or twisted position or direction; askew **2** out of the right or hoped-for course; amiss

[1]**axe,** *NAm chiefly* **ax** /aks‖æks/ *n* **1** a tool that has a cutting edge parallel to the handle and is

used esp for felling trees and chopping and splitting wood **2** drastic reduction or removal (e g of personnel) – **axe to grind** an ulterior often selfish purpose to further

[2]**axe,** *NAm chiefly* **ax** *vt* **1a** to hew, shape, dress, or trim with an axe **b** to chop, split, or sever with an axe **2** to remove abruptly (e g from employment or from a budget)

axiom /'aksi·əm||'æksɪəm/ *n* **1** a generally recognized truth **2a** a proposition regarded as a self-evident truth **b** a postulate

axiomatic /ˌaksi·ə'matik||ˌæksɪə'mætɪk/ *adj* of or having the nature of an axiom; *esp* self-evident – **axiomatically** *adv*

axis /'aksis||'æksɪs/ *n, pl* **axes** /-seez||-siːz/ **1a** a straight line about which a body or a geometric figure rotates or may be supposed to rotate **b** a straight line with respect to which a body or figure is symmetrical **c** any of the reference lines of a coordinate system **2a** the second vertebra of the neck on which the head and first vertebra pivot **b** any of various parts that are central, fundamental, or that lie on or constitute an axis **3** a plant stem **4** any of several imaginary reference lines used in describing a crystal structure **5** a partnership or alliance (e g the one between Germany and Italy in WW II)

axle /'aksl||'æksl/ *n* **1** a shaft on or with which a wheel revolves **2** a rod connecting a pair of wheels of a vehicle; *also* an axletree

axolotl /'aksəlotl, ˌaksə'lotl||'æksəlɒtl, ˌæksə-'lɒtl/ *n* any of several salamanders of mountain lakes of Mexico

ayatollah /ˌie·ə'tolə||ˌaɪə'tɒlə/ *n* a leader of the Shiite branch of Islam in Iran [Persian *āyatollāh*, fr Arabic *āyatullāh* manifestation of God]

[1]**aye** *also* **ay** /ay||eɪ/ *adv* ever, always, continually

[2]**aye** *also* **ay** /ie||aɪ/ *adv* yes – used as the correct formal response to a naval order <~,~, *sir*>

[3]**aye** *also* **ay** /ie||aɪ/ *n* an affirmative vote or voter

azalea /ə'zaylyə||ə'zeɪljə/ *n* any of a group of rhododendrons with funnel-shaped flowers and usu deciduous leaves

azimuth /'azimәth||'æzɪməθ/ *n* **1** an arc of the horizon expressed as the clockwise angle measured between a fixed point (e g true N or true S) and the vertical circle passing through the centre of an object **2** horizontal direction – **azimuthal** *adj*, **azimuthally** *adv*

Aztec /'aztek||'æztek/ *n* a member, or the language, of the Indian people that founded the Mexican empire conquered by Cortes in 1519 – **Aztecan** *adj*

azure /'azyooə, 'ay-, -zhə||'æzjʊə, 'eɪ-, -ʒə/ *n* **1a** sky blue **b** blue – used in heraldry **2** *archaic* LAPIS LAZULI – **azure** *adj*

B

b /bee||biː/ *n, pl* **b's, bs** *often cap* **1** (a graphic representation of or device for reproducing) the 2nd letter of the English alphabet **2** the 7th note of a C-major scale **3** one designated *b*, esp as the 2nd in order or class

baa, ba /bah||bɑː/ *vi or n* (to make) the bleat of a sheep

babble /'babl||'bæbl/ *vb* **1a** to utter meaningless or unintelligible sounds **b** to talk foolishly; chatter **2** to make a continuous murmuring sound ~ *vt* **1** to utter in an incoherently or meaninglessly repetitious manner **2** to reveal by talk that is too free – **babble** *n*, **babblement** *n*, **babbler** *n*

babe /bayb||beɪb/ *n* **1** a naive inexperienced person **2a** an infant, baby – chiefly poetic **b** a girl, woman – slang; usu as a noun of address

Babel /'baybl||'beɪbl/ *n, often not cap* **1** a confusion of sounds or voices **2** a scene of noise or confusion [the Tower of *Babel*, biblical structure (Genesis 11:4–9) intended to reach heaven which incurred the wrath of God, who punished the builders by making their speech mutually unintelligible]

baboon /bə'boohn||bə'buːn/ *n* any of several large African and Asiatic primates having dog-like muzzles and usu short tails

babu /'bahˌbooh||'bɑːˌbuː/ *n* **1** a Hindu gentleman – a form of address corresponding to *Mr* **2** an Indian with some education in English – chiefly derog

[1]**baby** /'baybi||'beɪbɪ/ *n* **1a(1)** an extremely young child; *esp* an infant **a(2)** an unborn child **a(3)** an extremely young animal **b** the youngest of a group **2** an infantile person **3** a person or thing for which one feels special responsibility or pride **4** a person; *esp* a girl, woman – slang; usu as a noun of address – **babyish** *adj*, **babyhood** *n*

[2]**baby** *adj* very small

[3]**baby** *vt* to tend or indulge with often excessive or inappropriate care

'baby-ˌsit *vi* **-tt-; baby-sat** to care for a child, usu for a short period while the parents are out – **baby-sitter** *n*

'baby ˌtalk *n* the imperfect speech used by or to small children

baccalaureate /ˌbakə'lawri·ət||ˌbækə'lɔːrɪət/ *n* the academic degree of bachelor

baccarat /'bakərah, --'-||'bækərɑː, --'-/ *n* a card game in which 3 hands are dealt and players may bet on either or both hands against the dealer's

bacchanal /'bakənl||'bækənl/ *n* **1a** a devotee of Bacchus; *esp* one who celebrates the Bacchanalia **b** a reveller **2** drunken revelry or carousal; bacchanalia [Latin *bacchanalis* of Bacchus, fr *Bacchus*, Greco-Roman god of wine] – **bacchanal** *adj*

bacchanalia /ˌbakə'naylyə||ˌbækə'neɪljə/ *n, pl* **bacchanalia** **1** *pl, cap* a Roman festival of Bacchus celebrated with dancing, song, and revelry **2** a drunken feast; an orgy – **bacchanalian** *adj or n*

baccy /'baki||'bækɪ/ *n, chiefly Br* tobacco – infml

bachelor /'bachələ, 'bachlə||'bætʃələ, 'bætʃlə/ *n* **1** a recipient of what is usu the lowest degree conferred by a college or university **2** an unmarried man **3** a male animal (e g a fur seal) without a mate during breeding time – **bachelordom** *n*, **bachelorhood** *n*

'bachelor ˌgirl *n* an unmarried girl or woman who lives independently

bacillus /bə'siləs‖bə'sɪləs/ *n, pl* **bacilli** /-lie‖-laɪ/ a usu rod-shaped bacterium; *esp* one that causes disease

[1]back /bak‖bæk/ *n* **1a** the rear part of the human body, esp from the neck to the end of the spine **b** the corresponding part of a quadruped or other lower animal **2a** the side or surface behind the front or face; the rear part; *also* the farther or reverse side **b** sthg at or on the back for support <*the ~ of a chair*> **3** (the position of) a primarily defensive player in some games (e g soccer) – **backless** *adj* – **with one's back to the wall** in a situation from which one cannot retreat and must either fight or be defeated

[2]back *adv* **1a(1)** to, towards, or at the rear <*tie one's hair ~*> **a(2)** away (e g from the speaker) <*stand ~ and give him air*> **b** in or into the past or nearer the beginning; ago <*3 years ~*> **c** in or into a reclining position <*lie ~*> **d** in or into a delayed or retarded condition <*set them ~ on the schedule*> **2a** to, towards, or in a place from which sby or sthg came <*put it ~ on the shelf*> **b** to or towards a former state <*thought ~ to his childhood*> **c** in return or reply <*ring me ~*> – **back and forth** backwards and forwards repeatedly

[3]back *adj* **1a** at or in the back <*~ door*> **b** distant from a central or main area; remote <*~ roads*> **2** being in arrears <*~ pay*> **3** not current <*~ number of a magazine*>

[4]back *vt* **1a** to support by material or moral assistance – often + *up* **b** to substantiate – often + *up* <*~ up an argument with forceful illustrations*> **c(1)** to countersign, endorse **c(2)** to assume financial responsibility for <*~ an enterprise*> **2** to cause to go back or in reverse **3a** to provide with a back **b** to be at the back of **4** to place a bet on (e g a horse) ~ *vi* **1** to move backwards **2** *of the wind* to shift anticlockwise **3** to have the back in the direction of sthg <*my house ~s onto the golf course*>

'backˌache /-ˌayk‖-ˌeɪk/ *n* a (dull persistent) pain in the back

back away *vi* to move back; withdraw

ˌback 'bench *n* any of the benches in Parliament on which rank and file members sit – usu pl – **back-bencher** *n*

'backˌbite /-ˌbiet‖-ˌbaɪt/ *vb* **backbit** /-ˌbit‖-ˌbɪt/; **backbitten** /-ˌbit(ə)n‖-ˌbɪt(ə)n/ to say mean or spiteful things about (sby) – **backbiter** *n*

'backˌbone /-ˌbohn‖-ˌbəʊn/ *n* **1** SPINAL COLUMN **2a** a chief mountain ridge, range, or system **b** the foundation or most substantial part of sthg **3** a firm and resolute character

'backˌbreaking /-ˌbrayking‖-ˌbreɪkɪŋ/ *adj* physically taxing or exhausting

'backˌchat /-ˌchat‖-ˌtʃæt/ *n, chiefly Br* impudent or argumentative talk made in reply, esp by a subordinate – infml

'backˌcloth /-ˌkloth‖-ˌklɒθ/ *n, Br* **1** a painted cloth hung across the rear of a stage **2** BACKGROUND 1a, 3

'backˌcomb /-ˌkohm‖-ˌkəʊm/ *vt* to comb (the hair) against the direction of growth starting with the short underlying hairs in order to produce a bouffant effect

'backˌdate /-ˌdayt‖-ˌdeɪt/ *vt* to apply (e g a pay rise) retrospectively

back down *vi* to retreat from a commitment or position

'backˌdrop /-ˌdrop‖-ˌdrɒp/ *n* a backcloth

backer /'bakə‖'bækə/ *n* **1** one who supports, esp financially **2** *Br* one who has placed a bet

[1]'backˌfire /-ˌfie·ə‖-ˌfaɪə/ *n* a premature explosion in the cylinder or an explosion in the exhaust system of an internal-combustion engine

[2]ˌback'fire *vi* **1** to make or undergo a backfire **2** to have the reverse of the desired or expected effect

'backˌgammon /-ˌgamən‖-ˌgæmən/ *n* a board game played with dice and counters in which each player tries to move his/her counters along the board and at the same time to block or capture his/her opponent's counters

'backˌground /-ˌgrownd‖-ˌgraʊnd/ *n* **1a** the scenery or ground behind sthg **b** the part of a painting or photograph that depicts what lies behind objects in the foreground **2** an inconspicuous position <*in the ~*> **3a** the conditions that form the setting within which sthg is experienced **b** information essential to the understanding of a problem or situation **c** the total of a person's experience, knowledge, and education

[1]'backˌhand /-ˌhand‖-ˌhænd/ *n* **1** a stroke in tennis, squash, etc made with the back of the hand turned in the direction of movement; *also* the side of the body on which this is made **2** handwriting whose strokes slant downwards from left to right

[2]backhand, backhanded /ˌ-'--/ *adv* with a backhand

ˌback'handed /-'handid‖-'hændɪd/ *adj* **1** using or made with a backhand **2** *of writing* being backhand **3** indirect, devious; *esp* sarcastic <*a ~ compliment*> – **backhandedly** *adv*

'backˌhander /-ˌhandə‖-ˌhændə/ *n* **1** a backhanded blow or stroke **2** *Br* a backhanded remark **3** a bribe – infml

backing /'baking‖'bækɪŋ/ *n* **1** sthg forming a back **2a** support, aid **b** endorsement

'backˌlash /-ˌlash‖-ˌlæʃ/ *n* **1** a sudden violent backward movement or reaction **2** a strong adverse reaction – **backlasher** *n*

'backˌlog /-ˌlog‖-ˌlɒg/ *n* **1** a reserve **2** an accumulation of tasks not performed, orders unfulfilled, or materials not processed

'backˌmost /-ˌmohst‖-ˌməʊst/ *adj* farthest back

'back ˌnumber *n* sby or sthg that is out of date; *esp* an old issue of a periodical or newspaper

ˌback of be'yond *n* a remote inaccessible place <*an old house in the ~*>

back off *vi* BACK DOWN

back out *vi* to withdraw, esp from a commitment or contest

'back ˌpassage *n, chiefly Br* the rectum – euph

'backˌpedal /-ˌpedl‖-ˌpedl/ *vi* **1** to move backwards (e g in boxing) **2** to back down from or reverse a previous opinion or stand

ˌback'room /-'roohm, -'room‖-'ruːm, -'rʊm/ *adj* of or being a directing group that exercises its authority in an inconspicuous and indirect way

back seat *n* an inferior position <*won't take a ~ to anyone*>

ˌback-seat ˈdriver *n* a passenger in a motor car who offers unwanted advice to the driver

ˌbackˈside /-ˈsied‖-ˈsaɪd/ *n* the buttocks

back slang *n* slang formed by spelling a word backwards and pronouncing it accordingly (e g *yob* for 'boy')

ˈbackˌslide /-ˌslied‖-ˌslaɪd/ *vi* **-slid** /-ˌslid‖-ˌslɪd/; **-slid, -slidden** /-ˌslid(ə)n‖-ˌslɪd(ə)n/ to lapse morally or in the practice of religion – **backslider** *n*

ˈbackˌspace /-ˌspays‖-ˌspeɪs/ *vi* to press a key on a typewriter which causes the carriage to move back 1 space

1**ˌbackˈstage** /-ˈstayj‖-ˈsteɪdʒ/ *adv* **1** in or to a backstage area **2** in private, secretly

2**ˈbackˌstage** *adj* **1** of or occurring in the parts of a theatre that cannot be seen by the audience **2** of the inner working or operation (e g of an organization)

ˈbackˌstairs /-ˌsteəz‖-ˌsteəz/ *adj* **1** secret, furtive <~ *political deals*> **2** sordid, scandalous <~ *gossip*>

ˈbackˌstay /-ˌstay‖-ˌsteɪ/ *n* a stay extending aft from a masthead to the stern or side of a ship

ˈbackˌstroke /-ˌstrohk‖-ˌstrəʊk/ *n* a swimming stroke executed on the back – **backstroker** *n*

ˈbackˌtrack /-ˌtrak‖-ˌtræk/ *vi* **1** to retrace a path or course **2** to reverse a position or stand

ˈbackˌup /-ˌup‖-ˌʌp/ *n* **1** sby or sthg that serves as a substitute, auxiliary, or alternative **2** sby or sthg that gives support

back up *vt* to support (sby), esp in argument or in playing a team game ~*vi* to back up a teammate

ˈbackward /-wood‖-wʊd/ *adj* **1a** directed or turned backwards **b** done or executed backwards <*a ~ somersault*> **2** retarded in development **3** of or occupying a fielding position in cricket behind the batsman's wicket **4** *chiefly NAm* diffident, shy – **backwardly** *adv*, **backwardness** *n*

ˈbackwards, *chiefly NAm* **backward** *adv* **1** towards the back **2** with the back foremost **3** in a reverse direction; towards the beginning <*say the alphabet* ~> **4** perfectly; BY HEART <*knows it all* ~> **5** towards the past **6** towards a worse state – **bend/fall/lean over backwards** to make extreme efforts, esp in order to please or conciliate

ˈbackˌwash /-ˌwosh‖-ˌwɒʃ/ *n* **1a** a backward movement in air, water, etc produced by a propelling force (e g the motion of oars) **b** the backward movement of a receding wave **2** a usu unwelcome consequence or by-product of an event; an aftermath

ˈbackˌwater /-ˌwawtə‖-ˌwɔːtə/ *n* **1** a stagnant pool or inlet kept filled by the opposing current of a river; *broadly* a body of water turned back in its course **2** a place or condition that is isolated or backward, esp intellectually

ˈbackwoods /-woodz‖-wʊdz/ *n, pl but sing or pl in constr* a remote or culturally backward area – usu + *the* – **backwoodsman** *n*

bacon /ˈbaykən‖ˈbeɪkən/ *n* (the meat cut from) the cured and often smoked side of a pig

bacteria /bakˈtiəri·ə‖bækˈtɪərɪə/ *pl of* BACTERIUM

bacteriology /bakˌtiəriˈoləji‖bækˌtɪərɪˈɒlədʒɪ/ *n* **1** a science that deals with bacteria **2** bacterial life and phenomena <*the ~ of a water supply*> – **bacteriologist** *n*, **bacteriologic, bacteriological** *adj*, **bacteriologically** *adv*

bacterium /bakˈtiəri·əm‖bækˈtɪərɪəm/ *n, pl* **bacteria** /-ri·ə‖-rɪə/ any of a group of microscopic organisms that live in soil, water, organic matter, or the bodies of plants and animals and are important to human beings because of their chemical effects and because many of them cause diseases – **bacterial** *adj*, **bacterially** *adv*

ˌBactrian ˈcamel /ˈbaktri·ən‖ˈbæktrɪən/ *n* CAMEL 1b

1**bad** /bad‖bæd/ *adj* **worse** /wuhs‖wɜːs/; **worst** /wuhst‖wɜːst/ **1a** failing to reach an acceptable standard; poor, inadequate **b** unfavourable **c** no longer acceptable, because of decay or disrepair <~ *fish*> **2a** morally objectionable **b** mischievous, disobedient **3** unskilful, incompetent – often + *at* <~ *at crosswords*> **4** disagreeable, unpleasant <~ *news*> **5a** injurious, harmful <*smoking is ~ for your health*> **b** worse than usual; severe <*a ~ cold*> **6** incorrect, faulty <~ *grammar*> **7a** suffering pain or distress; unwell <*he felt ~ because of his cold*> **b** unhealthy, diseased <~ *teeth*> **8** sorry, unhappy <*felt ~ after slighting a friend*> **9** invalid, worthless <*a ~ cheque*> **10** *of a debt* not collectible – **bad** *adv*, **badly** *adv*, **badness** *n* – **in someone's bad books** out of favour with sby

2**bad** *n* an evil or unhappy state

ˌbad ˈblood *n* ill feeling; bitterness

bade /bad, bayd‖bæd, beɪd/ *past of* BID

badge /baj‖bædʒ/ *n* **1** a device or token, esp of membership in a society or group **2** a characteristic mark **3** an emblem awarded rfor a particular accomplishment – **badge** *vt*

1**badger** /ˈbajə‖ˈbædʒə/ *n* (the pelt or fur of) any of several sturdy burrowing nocturnal mammals widely distributed in the northern hemisphere

2**badger** *vt* to harass or annoy persistently

badinage /ˈbadiˌnahzh, -nij‖ˈbædɪˌnɑːʒ, -nɪdʒ/ *n* playful repartee; banter

ˌbadly ˈoff *adj* in an unsatisfactory condition; *esp* not having enough money

badminton /ˈbadmint(ə)n‖ˈbædmɪnt(ə)n/ *n* a court game played with light long-handled rackets and a shuttle volleyed over a net [*Badminton*, estate in Gloucestershire, where it was first played]

1**baffle** /bafl‖bæfl/ *vt* to throw into puzzled confusion; perplex – **bafflement** *n*, **baffler** *n*, **bafflingly** *adv*

2**baffle** *n* **1** a device (e g a plate, wall, or screen) to deflect, check, or regulate flow (e g of a fluid or light) **2** a structure that reduces the exchange of sound waves between the front and back of a loudspeaker

1**bag** /bag‖bæg/ *n* **1a** a usu flexible container for holding, storing, or carrying sthg **b** a handbag or shoulder bag **2** sthg resembling a bag; *esp* a sagging in cloth **3a** a quantity of game (permitted to be) taken **b** spoils, loot **4** *pl chiefly Br* lots, masses – infml <*has ~s of money*> **5** a slovenly unattractive woman <*silly old* ~> – slang – **bagful** *n* – **bag and baggage 1** with all one's belongings **2** entirely, wholesale – **in the bag** as good as achieved; already certain before the test – infml

[2]**bag** *vb* **-gg-** *vi* **1** to swell out; bulge **2** to hang loosely ~ *vt* **1** to cause to swell **2** to put into a bag **3a** to take (animals) as game **b** to get possession of, seize; *also* to steal

bagatelle /ˌbagəˈtel‖ˌbægəˈtel/ *n* **1** TRIFLE 1 **2** a game in which balls must be put into or through cups or arches at one end of an oblong table

baggage /ˈbagij‖ˈbægɪdʒ/ *n* **1** portable equipment, esp of a military force **2** superfluous or useless things, ideas, or practices **3** *NAm* luggage, esp for travel by sea or air **4** a good-for-nothing woman; a pert girl – infml

baggy /ˈbagi‖ˈbægɪ/ *adj* loose, puffed out, or hanging like a bag < ~ *trousers*> – **baggily** *adv*, **bagginess** *n*

ˈ**bagˌpipe** /-ˌpiep‖-ˌpaɪp/ *n* a wind instrument consisting of a leather bag, mouth tube, chanter, and drone pipes – often pl with sing. meaning but sing. or pl in constr – **bagpiper** *n*

bah /bah‖bɑː/ *interj* – used to express disdain

[1]**bail** /bayl‖beɪl/ *n* **1** security deposited as a guarantee that sby temporarily freed from custody will return to stand trial **2** temporary release on bail **3** one who provides bail

[2]**bail** *vt* **1** to deliver (property) in trust to another for a special purpose and for a limited period **2** to release on bail **3** to procure the release of (a person in custody) by giving bail – often + *out* – **bailable** *adj*, **bailee** *n*, **bailment** *n*, **bailor** *n*

[3]**bail** *n* **1** either of the 2 crosspieces that lie on the stumps to form the wicket in cricket **2** *chiefly Br* a device for confining or separating animals

[4]**bail,** *Br also* **bale** *n* a container used to remove water from a boat

[5]**bail,** *Br also* **bale** *vt* to clear (water) from a boat by collecting in a bail, bucket etc and throwing over the side ~*vi* to parachute from an aircraft *USE* (*vt & vi*) usu + *out* – **bailer** *n*

bailey /ˈbayli‖ˈbeɪlɪ/ *n* (the space enclosed by) the outer wall of a castle or any of several walls surrounding the keep

ˈ**Bailey** ˌ**bridge** *n* a prefabricated bridge built from interchangeable latticed steel panels [Sir Donald *Bailey* (1901-85), English engineer]

bailiff /ˈbaylif‖ˈbeɪlɪf/ *n* **1** an official employed by a sheriff to serve writs, make arrests, etc **2** *chiefly Br* one who manages an estate or farm – **bailiffship** *n*

bail out, *Br also* **bale out** *vt* to help from a predicament; release from difficulty

bairn /beən‖beən/ *n, chiefly Scot & N Eng* a child

[1]**bait** /bayt‖beɪt/ *vt* **1** to provoke, tease, or exasperate with unjust, nagging, or persistent remarks **2** to harass (e g a chained animal) with dogs, usu for sport **3** to provide with bait < ~ *a hook*> – **baiter** *n*

[2]**bait** *n* **1a** sthg used in luring, esp to a hook or trap **b** a poisonous material placed where it will be eaten by pests **2** a lure, temptation

baize /bayz‖beɪz/ *n* a woollen cloth, resembling felt, used chiefly for covering and lining sthg (e g table tops or drawers)

[1]**bake** /bayk‖beɪk/ *vt* **1** to cook (e g food) by dry heat, esp in an oven **2** to dry or harden by subjecting to heat ~ *vi* **1** to cook food (e g bread and cakes) by baking **2** to become baked **3** to become extremely hot <*I'll have to stop sunbathing, I'm* baking> – **baker** *n*

[2]**bake** *n, NAm* a social gathering at which (baked) food is served

Bakelite /ˈbaykəliet‖ˈbeɪkəlaɪt/ *trademark* – used for any of various synthetic resins and plastics

ˌ**baker's** ˈ**dozen** /ˈbaykəz‖ˈbeɪkəz/ *n* thirteen [prob fr a former practice of selling 13 loaves for 12 to guard against accusations of giving short weight]

bakery /ˈbayk(ə)ri‖ˈbeɪk(ə)rɪ/ *n* a place for baking or selling baked goods, esp bread and cakes

ˈ**baking** ˌ**powder** /ˈbayking‖ˈbeɪkɪŋ/ *n* a powder that consists of a bicarbonate and an acid substance used in place of yeast as a raising agent in making scones, cakes, etc

baksheesh /ˈbakˌsheesh, - ˈ-‖ˈbækˌʃiːʃ, - ˈ-/ *n, pl* **baksheesh** money given as a tip

balaclava /ˌbaləˈklahvə‖ˌbæləˈklɑːvə/, **balaclava helmet** *n, often cap B* a knitted pull-on hood that covers the ears, neck, and throat [*Balaclava* (now usu Balaklava), village in the Crimea, USSR, where a battle of the Crimean War was fought on 25 Oct 1854]

balalaika /ˌbaləˈliekə‖ˌbæləˈlaɪkə/ *n* a musical instrument of Russian origin, usu having 3 strings and a triangular body and played by plucking

[1]**balance** /ˈbaləns‖ˈbæləns/ *n* **1** an instrument for weighing: e g **1a** a centrally-supported beam that has 2 scalepans of equal weight suspended from its ends **b** any device that measures weight and force **2** a counterbalancing weight, force, or influence **3** stability produced by even distribution of weight on each side of a vertical axis **4a** equilibrium between contrasting, opposing, or interacting elements **b** equality between the totals of the 2 sides of an account **5** an aesthetically pleasing integration of elements **6** the ability to retain one's physical equilibrium **7** the weight or force of one side in excess of another <*the* ~ *of the evidence lay on the side of the defendant*> **8a** (a statement of) the difference between credits and debits in an account **b** sthg left over; a remainder **c** an amount in excess, esp on the credit side of an account **9** mental and emotional steadiness – **balanced** *adj* – **in the balance** in an uncertain critical position; with the fate or outcome about to be determined – **on balance** all things considered

[2]**balance** *vt* **1a(1)** to compute the difference between the debits and credits of (an account) **a(2)** to pay the amount due on **b** to arrange so that one set of elements exactly equals another < ~ *a mathematical equation*> **2a** to counterbalance, offset **b** to equal or equalize in weight, number, or proportion **3** to compare the relative importance, value, force, or weight of; ponder **4** to bring to a state or position of balance ~ *vi* **1** to become balanced or established in balance

<sat balancing *on the fence>* **2** to be an equal counterpoise – often + *with* **3** to waver, hesitate *<a mind that* ~s *and deliberates>* – **balancer** *n*

ˌ**balance of ˈpayments** *n* the difference over a period of time between a country's payments to and receipts from abroad

ˌ**balance of ˈpower** *n* an equilibrium of power sufficient to prevent one nation from imposing its will upon another

ˈ**balance ˌsheet** *n* a statement of financial condition at a given date

balcony /ˈbalkəni‖ˈbælkənɪ/ *n* **1** a platform built out from the wall of a building and enclosed by a railing or low wall **2** a gallery inside a building (e g a theatre) – **balconied** *adj*

bald /bawld‖bɔːld/ *adj* **1a** lacking a natural or usual covering (e g of hair, vegetation, or nap) **b** having little or no tread *<~ tyres>* **2** unadorned, undisguised *<the ~ truth>* **3** *of an animal* marked with white, esp on the head or face – **baldish** *adj*, **baldly** *adv*, **baldness** *n*

balderdash /ˈbawldədash‖ˈbɔːldədæʃ/ *n* nonsense – often as a generalized expression of disagreement

balding /ˈbawlding‖ˈbɔːldɪŋ/ *adj* becoming bald

baldric /ˈbawldrik‖ˈbɔːldrɪk/ *n* an often ornamented belt worn over one shoulder and across the body to support a sword, bugle, etc

[1]**bale** /bayl‖beɪl/ *n* a large bundle of goods; *specif* a large closely pressed package of merchandise bound and usu wrapped for storage or transportation – **bale** *vt*

[2]**bale** *n or vb, Br* [4/5]BAIL

baleen /bəˈleen‖bəˈliːn/ *n* whalebone

baleful /ˈbaylf(ə)l‖ˈbeɪlf(ə)l/ *adj* **1** deadly or pernicious in influence **2** gloomily threatening – **balefully** *adv*, **balefulness** *n*

bale out *vt, Br* BAIL OUT

[1]**balk,** *chiefly Br* **baulk** /bawlk, bawk‖bɔːlk, bɔːk/ *n* **1** a ridge of land left unploughed **2** a roughly squared beam of timber **3** the area behind the balk lines on a billiard table

[2]**balk,** *chiefly Br* **baulk** *vt* to check or stop (as if) by an obstacle; hinder, thwart ~ *vi* **1** to stop short and refuse to proceed **2** to refuse abruptly – often + *at* *<*~ed *at the suggestion>* – **balker** *n*

[1]**ball** /bawl‖bɔːl/ *n* **1** a round or roundish body or mass: **1a** a solid or hollow spherical or egg-shaped body used in a game or sport **b** a spherical or conical projectile; *also* projectiles used in firearms *<powder and ~>* **c** the rounded slightly raised fleshy area at the base of a thumb or big toe **2** a delivery or play of the ball in cricket, baseball, etc **3** a game in which a ball is thrown, kicked, or struck; *specif, NAm* baseball **4a** a testis – usu pl; vulg **b** *pl* nonsense – often used interjectionally; vulg – **on the ball** marked by being knowledgeable and competent; alert – infml – **start/set/keep the ball rolling** to begin/continue sthg

[2]**ball** *vb* **1** to form or gather into a ball **2** to have sexual intercourse (with) – vulg

[3]**ball** *n* **1** a large formal gathering for social dancing **2** a very pleasant experience; a good time – infml

ballad /ˈbaləd‖ˈbæləd/ *n* **1** a narrative composition in rhythmic verse suitable for singing **2** a (slow, romantic or sentimental) popular, esp narrative, song – **balladic** *adj*

ballade /bəˈlahd, ba-‖bəˈlɑːd, bæ-/ *n* a fixed verse form of usu 3 stanzas with recurrent rhymes, a short concluding verse, and an identical refrain for each part

[1]**ballast** /ˈbaləst‖ˈbæləst/ *n* **1a** heavy material carried in a ship to improve stability **b** heavy material that is carried on a balloon or airship to steady it and can be jettisoned to control the rate of descent **2** sthg that gives stability, esp in character or conduct **3** gravel or broken stone laid in a bed for railway lines or the lower layer of roads

[2]**ballast** *vt* **1** to steady or equip (as if) with ballast **2** to fill in (e g a railway bed) with ballast

ˌ**ball ˈbearing** *n* a bearing having minimal friction in which hardened steel balls roll easily in a groove between a shaft and a support; *also* any of the balls in such a bearing

ˈ**ball ˌcock** *n* an automatic valve (e g in a cistern) controlled by the rise and fall of a float at the end of a lever

ballerina /ˌbaləˈreenə‖ˌbæləˈriːnə/ *n* a female, esp principal, ballet dancer

ballet /ˈbalay‖ˈbæleɪ; *NAm also* bəˈlay‖bəˈleɪ/ *n* **1** (a group that performs) artistic dancing in which the graceful flowing movements are based on conventional positions and steps **2** a theatrical art form using ballet dancing, music, and scenery to convey a story, theme, or atmosphere – **balletic** *adj*

ballistic /bəˈlistik‖bəˈlɪstɪk/ *adj* **1** of ballistics **2** actuated by a sudden impulse (e g one due to an electric discharge) – **ballistically** *adv*

balˈlistics *n pl but sing or pl in constr* **1** the science dealing with the motion of projectiles in flight **2** (the study of) the individual characteristics of and firing processes in a firearm or cartridge

ˌ**ball ˈlightning** *n* a rare form of lightning consisting of luminous balls that may move along solid objects or float in the air

ballock /ˈbolək‖ˈbɒlək/ *n* a bollock

[1]**balloon** /bəˈloohn‖bəˈluːn/ *n* **1** an envelope filled with hot air or a gas lighter than air so as to rise and float in the atmosphere **2** an inflatable usu brightly coloured rubber bag used as a toy **3** a line enclosing words spoken or thought by a character, esp in a cartoon

[2]**balloon** *vt* to inflate, distend ~ *vi* **1** to ascend or travel in a balloon **2** to swell or puff out; expand – often + *out* **3** to increase rapidly **4** to travel in a high curving arc

ballooning /bəˈloohning‖bəˈluːnɪŋ/ *n* the act or sport of riding in a balloon – **balloonist** *n*

[1]**ballot** /ˈbalət‖ˈbælət/ *n* **1** (a sheet of paper, or orig a small ball, used in) secret voting **2** the right to vote **3** the number of votes cast [Italian *ballotta*, lit., little ball, fr *balla* ball]

[2]**ballot** *vt* to vote by ballot ~*vi* to ask for a vote from *<the union* ~ed *the members>* – **balloter** *n*

ˈ**ballˌpoint** /-ˌpoynt‖-ˌpɔɪnt/, ˌ**ballpoint ˈpen** *n* a pen having as the writing point a small rotating metal ball that inks itself by contact with an inner magazine

ˈballs-ˌup, *NAm* **ball-up** *n* a state of muddled confusion caused by a mistake – slang

balls up, *NAm* **ball up** *vb* to make or become badly muddled or confused – slang

bally /ˈbali‖ˈbælɪ/ *adj or adv, Br* [1]BLOODY 4, [3]BLOODY – euph

ballyhoo /ˌbaliˈhooh‖ˌbælɪˈhuː/ *n, pl* **ballyhoos** **1** a noisy demonstration or talk **2** flamboyant, exaggerated, or sensational advertising or propaganda – **ballyhoo** *vt*

balm /bahm‖bɑːm/ *n* **1** an aromatic and medicinal resin **2** an aromatic preparation (e g a healing ointment) **3** any of various aromatic plants of the mint family **4** sthg that soothes, relieves, or heals physically or emotionally

balmy /ˈbahmi‖ˈbɑːmɪ/ *adj* **1a** having the qualities of balm; soothing **b** mild **2** barmy – **balmily** *adv*, **balminess** *n*

baloney /bəˈlohni‖bəˈləʊnɪ/ *n* nonsense – often as a generalized expression of disagreement

balsa /ˈbawlsə, ˈbolsə‖ˈbɔːlsə, ˈbɒlsə/ *n* (the strong very light wood of) a tropical American tree

balsam /ˈbawls(ə)m, ˈbol-‖ˈbɔːls(ə)m, ˈbɒl-/ *n* **1** (a preparation containing) an oily and resinous substance flowing from various plants **2a** any of several trees yielding balsam **b** any of a widely distributed genus of watery-juiced annual plants **3** BALM 4 – **balsamic** *adj*

baluster /ˈbaləstə‖ˈbæləstə/ *n* an upright, rounded, square, or vase-shaped support (e g for the rail of a staircase balustrade)

balustrade /ˌbaləˈstrayd, ˈbaləˌstrayd‖ˌbæləˈstreɪd, ˈbæləˌstreɪd/ *n* a row of balusters topped by a rail; *also* a usu low parapet or barrier

bamboo /bamˈbooh‖bæmˈbuː/ *n, pl* **bamboos** any of various chiefly tropical giant grasses including some with strong hollow stems used for building, furniture, or utensils [Malay *bambu*] – **bamboo** *adj*

bamboozle /bamˈboohzl‖bæmˈbuːzl/ *vt* to deceive by trickery – **bamboozlement** *n*

[1]**ban** /ban‖bæn/ *vt* **-nn-** to prohibit, esp by legal means or social pressure

[2]**ban** *n* **1** an ecclesiastical curse, excommunication **2** a legal or social prohibition

banal /bəˈnahl‖bəˈnɑːl/ *adj* lacking originality, freshness, or novelty; trite, hackneyed – **banally** *adv*, **banality** *n*

banana /bəˈnahnə‖bəˈnɑːnə/ *n* (a tropical tree that bears) an elongated usu tapering fruit with soft pulpy flesh enclosed in a soft usu yellow rind that grows in bunches reminiscent of the fingers of a hand

baˈnana reˌpublic *n* a small tropical country that is politically unstable and usu economically underdeveloped – derog

[1]**band** /band‖bænd/ *n* **1** a strip or belt serving to join or hold things together **2** a ring of elastic **3** a more or less well-defined range of wavelengths, frequencies, or energies of light waves, radio waves, sound waves, etc **4** an elongated surface or section with parallel or roughly parallel sides **5** a narrow strip serving chiefly as decoration: e g **5a** a narrow strip of material applied as trimming to an article of dress **b** *pl* 2 cloth strips sometimes worn at the front of the neck as part of clerical, legal, or academic dress **6** a strip distinguishable in some way (e g by colour, texture, or composition)

[2]**band** *vt* **1** to fasten a band to or tie up with a band **2** to gather together for a purpose; unite ~ *vi* to unite for a common purpose; confederate – often + *together* – **bander** *n* *n sing or pl in constr* a group of people, animals, or things; *esp* a group of musicians organized for ensemble playing and using chiefly woodwind, brass, and percussion instruments

[1]**bandage** /ˈbandij‖ˈbændɪdʒ/ *n* a strip of fabric used esp to dress and bind up wounds

[2]**bandage** *vt* to bind, dress, or cover with a bandage – **bandager** *n*

ˈBand-ˌAid *trademark* – used for a small adhesive plaster with a gauze pad

bandanna, bandana /banˈdanə‖bænˈdænə/ *n* a large colourful patterned handkerchief [Hindi *bā̃dhnū* tie-dyeing, tie-dyed cloth, fr *bā̃dhnā* to tie, fr Sanskrit *badhnāti* he ties]

ˈbandˌbox /-ˌboks‖-ˌbɒks/ *n* a usu cylindrical box of cardboard or thin wood used esp for holding hats

bandeau /ˈbandoh‖ˈbændəʊ; *NAm* -ˈ-/ *n, pl* **bandeaux** /ˈbandoh(z)‖ˈbændəʊ(z); *NAm* banˈdoh(z)‖bænˈdəʊ(z)/ a band of material worn round the head to keep the hair in place

bandit /ˈbandit‖ˈbændɪt/ *n, pl* **bandits** *also* **banditti** /banˈdeeti‖bænˈdiːtɪ/ **1** an outlaw; *esp* a member of a band of marauders **2** a political terrorist – **banditry** *n*

ˈbandˌmaster /-ˌmahstə‖-ˌmɑːstə/ *n* a conductor of an esp military band

bandolier, bandoleer /ˌbandəˈliə‖ˌbændəˈlɪə/ *n* a belt worn over the shoulder and across the chest with pockets or loops for cartridges

ˈbandsman /-mən‖-mən/ *n* a member of a musical band

ˈbandˌstand /-ˌstand‖-ˌstænd/ *n* a usu roofed stand or platform for a band to perform on outdoors

ˈbandˌwagon /-ˌwagən‖-ˌwægən/ *n* a party, faction, or cause that attracts adherents by its timeliness, momentum, etc – **jump/climb on the bandwagon** to attach oneself to a successful cause or enterprise in the hope of personal gain

[1]**bandy** /ˈbandi‖ˈbændɪ/ *vt* **1** to exchange (words) in an argumentative, careless, or lighthearted manner **2** to use in a glib or offhand manner – often + *about*

[2]**bandy** *adj* **1** *of legs* bowed **2** bowlegged – **bandy-legged** *adj*

bane /bayn‖beɪn/ *n* **1** poison – esp in combination <*rats*bane> **2** a cause of death, ruin, or trouble – **baneful** *adj*

[1]**bang** /bang‖bæŋ/ *vt* **1** to strike sharply; bump <*fell and* ~*ed his knee*> **2** to knock, beat, or strike hard, often with a sharp noise **3** to have sexual intercourse with – vulg ~ *vi* **1** to strike with a sharp noise or thump <*the falling chair* ~*ed against the wall*> **2** to produce a sharp often explosive noise or noises

[2]**bang** *n* **1** a resounding blow; a thump **2** a sudden loud noise – often used interjectionally **3** a quick burst of energy <*start off with a* ~> **4** an act of sexual intercourse – vulg

[3]**bang** *adv* **1** right, directly **2** exactly <*arrived*

~ *on 6 o'clock*> *USE* infml

[4]**bang** *n* a short squarely-cut fringe of hair – usu pl with sing. meaning

banger /'bang·ə‖'bæŋə/ *n, Br* **1** a firework that explodes with a loud bang **2** a sausage **3** an old usu dilapidated car *USE (2&3)* infml

bangle /'bang·gl‖'bæŋgl/ *n* a rigid usu ornamental bracelet or anklet

ˌ**bang-'on** *adj or adv, Br* just what is needed; first-rate – infml

banian /'banyən‖'bænjən/ *n* a banyan

banish /'banish‖'bænɪʃ/ *vt* **1** to require by authority to leave a place, esp a country **2** to dispel – **banisher** *n*, **banishment** *n*

banister *also* **bannister** /'banistə‖'bænɪstə/ *n* a handrail with its upright supports guarding the edge of a staircase – often pl with sing. meaning

banjo /'banjoh, -'-‖'bændʒəʊ, -'-/ *n, pl* **banjos** *also* **banjoes** a stringed musical instrument with a drumlike body – **banjoist** *n*

[1]**bank** /bangk‖bæŋk/ *n* **1a** a mound, pile, or ridge (e g of earth or snow) **b** a piled up mass of cloud or fog **c** an undersea elevation rising esp from the continental shelf **2** the rising ground bordering a lake or river or forming the edge of a cut or hollow **3** the lateral inward tilt of a surface along a curve or of a vehicle when following a curved path

[2]**bank** *vt* **1** to surround with a bank **2** to keep *up* to ensure slow burning **3** to build (a road or railway) with the outer edge of a curve higher than the inner ~ *vi* **1** to rise in or form a bank – often + *up* **2a** to incline an aircraft laterally when turning **b(1)** *of an aircraft* to incline laterally **b(2)** to follow a curve or incline, specif in racing

[3]**bank** *n* **1** a bench for the rowers of a galley **2** a row of keys on an alphabetic keyboard (e g of a typewriter)

[4]**bank** *n* **1** an establishment for the custody, loan, exchange, or issue of money and for the transmission of funds **2** a person conducting a gambling house or game; *specif* the banker in a game of cards **3** a supply of sthg held in reserve: e g **3a** the money, chips, etc held by the bank or banker for use in a gambling game **b** the pool of pieces belonging to a game (e g dominoes) from which the players draw **4** a place where data, human organs, etc are held available for use when needed

[5]**bank** *vi* to deposit money or have an account in a bank ~*vi* to deposit in a bank – **bank on** to depend or rely on; COUNT ON

'**bank**ˌ**book** /-ˌbook‖-ˌbʊk/ *n* the depositor's book in which a bank enters a record of his/her account

banker /'bangkə‖'bæŋkə/ *n* **1** one who engages in the business of banking **2** the player who keeps the bank in various games

'**banker's** ˌ**card** *n, Br* CHEQUE CARD

ˌ**bank 'holiday** *n* **1** *often cap B&H* a public holiday in the British Isles on which banks and most businesses are closed by law **2** *NAm* a period when banks are closed often by government fiat

banking /'bangking‖'bæŋkɪŋ/ *n* the business of a bank or a banker

'**bank** ˌ**note** *n* a promissory note issued by a bank, payable to the bearer on demand without interest, and acceptable as money

[1]**bankrupt** /'bangkrupt‖'bæŋkrʌpt/ *n* **1a** an insolvent person whose estate is administered under the bankruptcy laws for the benefit of his/her creditors **b** one who becomes insolvent **2** one who is destitute of a usu specified quality or thing <*a moral* ~> [Italian *bancarotta* bankruptcy, fr *banca* bank + *rotta* broken]

[2]**bankrupt** *vt* **1** to reduce to bankruptcy **2** to impoverish

[3]**bankrupt** *adj* **1** reduced to a state of financial ruin; *specif* legally declared a bankrupt **2a** broken, ruined <*a* ~ *professional career*> **b** destitute – + *of* or *in*

bankruptcy /'bangkˌrupsi‖'bæŋkˌrʌpsɪ/ *n* **1** being bankrupt **2** utter failure, impoverishment, or destitution

banner /'banə‖'bænə/ *n* **1a** a usu square flag bearing heraldic arms; *broadly* [4]FLAG 1 **b** an ensign displaying a distinctive or symbolic device or legend; *esp* one presented as an award of honour or distinction **2** a headline in large type running across a newspaper page **3** a strip of cloth on which a sign is painted **4** a name, slogan, or goal associated with a particular group or ideology – often + *under*

bannock /'banək‖'bænək/ *n* a usu unleavened flat bread or biscuit made with oatmeal or barley meal

banns /banz‖bænz/ *n pl* the public announcement, esp in church, of a proposed marriage – chiefly in *publish/read the banns*

[1]**banquet** /'bangkwit‖'bæŋkwɪt/ *n* an elaborate ceremonial meal for numerous people often in honour of a person; a feast

[2]**banquet** *vb* to provide with or partake of a banquet – **banqueter** *n*

banshee /'banshee ‖'bænʃiː *also* -'-/ *n* a female spirit in Gaelic folklore whose wailing warns of approaching death in a household [Scottish Gaelic *bean-sīth*, fr or akin to Old Irish *ben sīde* woman of fairyland]

[1]**bantam** /'bant(ə)m‖'bænt(ə)m/ *n* any of numerous small domestic fowl

[2]**bantam** *adj* small, diminutive

'**bantam**ˌ**weight** /-ˌwayt‖-ˌweɪt/ *n* a boxer who weighs not more than 8st 6lb (about 53.5kg) if professional or more than 51kg (about 8st) but not more than 54kg (about 8st 7lb) if amateur

[1]**banter** /'bantə‖'bæntə/ *vi* to speak or act playfully or wittily – **banterer** *n*, **banteringly** *adv*

[2]**banter** *n* good-natured repartee; badinage

banyan /'banyan‖'bænjæn/ *n* an Indian tree of the fig family with branches that send out shoots which grow down to the soil and root to form secondary trunks

baobab /'bayohˌbab, 'bayə-, 'bowˌbab‖'beɪəʊˌbæb, 'beɪə-, 'baʊˌbæb/ *n* a broad-trunked Old World tropical tree with an edible acid fruit resembling a gourd and bark used in making paper, cloth, and rope

baptism /'baptiz(ə)m‖'bæptɪz(ə)m/ *n* **1** the ritual use of water for purification, esp in the Christian sacrament of admission to the church **2** an act, experience, or ordeal by which one is purified, sanctified, initiated, or named – **baptismal** *adj*, **baptismally** *adv*

baptist /ˈbaptist‖ˈbæptɪst/ *n* **1** one who baptizes **2** *cap* a member of a Protestant denomination which reserves baptism to full believers – **Baptist** *adj*

bapt·ize, -ise /bapˈtiez, ˈ--‖bæpˈtaɪz, ˈ--/ *vt* **1** to administer baptism to **2a** to purify or cleanse spiritually, esp by a purging experience or ordeal **b** to initiate, launch **3** to give a name to (as if) at baptism; christen ~*vi* to administer baptism – **baptizer** *n*

[1]**bar** /bah‖bɑː/ *n* **1a** a straight piece (e g of wood or metal), that is longer than it is wide and has any of various uses (e g as a lever, support, barrier, or fastening) **b** a solid piece or block of material that is usu rectangular and considerably longer than it is wide **2** sthg that obstructs or prevents passage, progress, or action: e g **2a** the extinction of a claim in law **b** an intangible or nonphysical impediment **c** a submerged or partly submerged bank (e g of sand) along a shore or in a river, often obstructing navigation **3a** [6]DOCK; *also* the railing that encloses the dock **b** *often cap* **b(1)** *sing or pl in constr* the whole body of barristers **b(2)** the profession of barrister **c** a barrier beyond which nonmembers of Parliament may not pass **4** a straight stripe, band, or line much longer than it is wide: e g **4a** any of 2 or more horizontal stripes on a heraldic shield **b** STRIPE 2 **c** a strip of metal attached to a military medal to indicate an additional award of the medal **5a(1)** a counter at which food or esp alcoholic drinks are served **a(2)** a room or establishment whose main feature is a bar for the serving of alcoholic drinks **b** a place where goods, esp a specified commodity, are sold or served across a counter <*a shoe* ~> **6** (a group of musical notes and rests that add up to a prescribed time value, bounded on each side on the staff by) a bar line

[2]**bar** *vt* **-rr- 1a** to fasten with a bar **b** to place bars across to prevent movement in, out, or through **2** to mark with stripes **3a** to shut in or out (as if) by bars **b** to set aside the possibility of; RULE OUT **4a** to interpose legal objection to **b** to prevent, forbid <*no holds* ~red>

[3]**bar** *prep* except

[4]**bar** *adv, of odds in betting* being offered for all the unnamed competitors <*20 to 1* ~>

[5]**bar** *n* a unit of pressure equal to 100,000newtons per square metre (about 14.5lb/in^2)

[1]**barb** /bahb‖bɑːb/ *n* **1a** a sharp projection extending backwards from the point of an arrow, fishhook, etc, and preventing easy extraction **b** a biting or pointedly critical remark or comment **2** any of the side branches of the shaft of a feather **3** a plant hair or bristle ending in a hook

[2]**barb** *vt* to provide (e g an arrow) with a barb

[3]**barb** *n* any of a northern African breed of horses that are noted for speed and endurance and are related to Arabs

barbarian /bahˈbeəri·ən‖bɑːˈbeərɪən/ *adj* **1** of a land, culture, or people alien and usu believed to be inferior to and more savage than one's own **2** lacking refinement, learning, or artistic or literary culture – **barbarian** *n*, **barbarianism** *n*

barbaric /bahˈbarik‖bɑːˈbærɪk/ *adj* **1** (characteristic) of barbarians; *esp* uncivilized **2** savage, barbarous – **barbarically** *adv*

barbarism /ˈbahbə,riz(ə)m‖ˈbɑːbə,rɪz(ə)m/ *n* **1** (use of) a word or action unacceptable by contemporary standards; *also* the practice or display of barbarian ideas, acts, or attitudes **2** a barbarian or barbarous social or intellectual condition; backwardness

barbarity /bahˈbarəti‖bɑːˈbærətɪ/ *n* **1** barbarism **2** (an act or instance of) barbarous cruelty; inhumanity

barbarous /ˈbahb(ə)rəs‖ˈbɑːb(ə)rəs/ *adj* **1** uncivilized **2** lacking culture or refinement **3** mercilessly harsh or cruel – **barbarously** *adv*, **barbarousness** *n*

[1]**barbecue** /ˈbahbi,kyooh‖ˈbɑːbɪ,kjuː/ *n* **1** a (portable) fireplace over which meat and fish are roasted **2** meat roasted over an open fire or barbecue pit **3** a social gathering, esp in the open air, at which barbecued food is served [American Spanish *barbacoa*, prob fr Taino (a S American Indian language)]

[2]**barbecue** *vt* to roast or grill on a rack over hot coals or on a revolving spit in front of or over a source of cooking heat, esp an open fire – **barbecuer** *n*

barbed /bahbd‖bɑːbd/ *adj* **1** having barbs **2** characterized by pointed and biting criticism – **barbedness** *n*

,barbed ˈwire *n* twisted wires armed at intervals with sharp points

[1]**barbel** /ˈbahbl‖ˈbɑːbl/ *n* a European freshwater fish with 4 barbels on its upper jaw

[2]**barbel** *n* a slender tactile projecting organ on the lips of certain fishes (e g catfish), used in locating food

barber /ˈbahbə‖ˈbɑːbə/ *n* sby whose occupation is cutting and dressing men's hair and shaving – **barber** *vb*

barber's pole *n* a red and white striped pole fixed to the front of a barber's shop

barbican /ˈbahbikən‖ˈbɑːbɪkən/ *n* an outer defensive work; *esp* a tower at a gate or bridge

barbiturate /bahˈbityoorət‖bɑːˈbɪtjʊrət/ *n* **1** a salt or ester of barbituric acid **2** any of several derivatives of barbituric acid (e g thiopentone and phenobarbitone) that are used esp in the treatment of epilepsy and were formerly much used in sleeping pills

,barbi,turic ˈacid /,bahbiˈtyooərik‖,bɑːbɪtjʊərɪk/ *n* an acid used in the manufacture of barbiturate drugs and plastics

ˈbar code *n* a code of parallel lines indicating a number (e.g. a price), that can be read and registered by a computer

[1]**bard** /bahd‖bɑːd/ *n* **1** sby, specif a Celtic poet-singer, who composed, sang, or recited verses on heroes and their deeds **2** a poet; *specif* one recognized or honoured at an eisteddfod – **bardic** *adj*

[2]**bard, barde** *n* a strip of pork fat, bacon, etc for covering lean meat before roasting – **bard** *vt*

[1]**bare** /beə‖beə/ *adj* **1** lacking a natural, usual, or appropriate covering, esp clothing **2** open to view; exposed – often in *lay bare* **3a** unfurnished, empty <*the cupboard was* ~> **b**

destitute *of* **4a** having nothing left over or added; scant, mere <*the ~ necessities*> **b** undisguised, unadorned <*the ~ facts*> – **bareness** *n*

[2]**bare** *vt* to make or lay bare; uncover, reveal

ˈ**bare**ˌ**back** /-ˌbak‖-ˌbæk/, ˈ**bare**ˌ**backed** *adv or adj* on the bare back of a horse without a saddle

ˌ**bare**ˈ**faced** /-ˈfayst‖-ˈfeɪst/ *adj* lacking scruples; shameless – **barefacedly** *adv*, **barefacedness** *n*

ˈ**bare**ˌ**foot** /-ˌfoot‖-ˌfʊt/, **barefooted** /-ˈfootid‖-ˈfʊtɪd/ *adv or adj* without shoes, socks, stockings, etc; with the feet bare

ˌ**bare**ˈ**headed** /-ˈhedid‖-ˈhedɪd/ *adv or adj* without a covering for the head – **bareheadedness** *n*

barely /ˈbeəli‖ˈbeəlɪ/ *adv* **1** scarcely, hardly **2** in a meagre manner; scantily <*a ~ furnished room*>

[1]**bargain** /ˈbahgən‖ˈbɑːgən/ *n* **1** an agreement between parties concerning the terms of a transaction between them or the course of action each pursues in respect to the other **2** an advantageous purchase – **into the bargain** also

[2]**bargain** *vi* **1** to negotiate over the terms of a purchase, agreement, or contract **2** to come to terms; agree – **bargainer** *n* – **bargain for** to be at all prepared for; EXPECT 2a

[1]**barge** /bahj‖bɑːdʒ/ *n* **1a** a flat-bottomed boat used chiefly for the transport of goods on inland waterways or between ships and the shore; *also* NARROW BOAT **b** a flat-bottomed coastal sailing vessel **2a** a large naval motorboat used by flag officers **b** an ornate carved vessel used on ceremonial occasions

[2]**barge** *vi* **1** to move in a headlong or clumsy fashion **2** to intrude *in* or *into*

bargee /bahˈjee‖bɑːˈdʒiː/ *n, Br* sby who works on a barge

baritone /ˈbaritohn‖ˈbærɪtəʊn/ *n* **1** (a person with) a male singing voice between bass and tenor **2** a member of a family of instruments having a range next below that of the tenor [deriv of Greek *barytonos* deep sounding, fr *barys* heavy + *tonos* tone] – **baritone** *adj*, **baritonal** *adj*

barium /ˈbeəri·əm‖ˈbeərɪəm/ *n* a soft metallic element of the alkaline-earth group – **baric** *adj*

barium meal *n* a solution of barium sulphate swallowed by a patient to make the stomach or intestines visible in X-ray pictures

[1]**bark** /bahk‖bɑːk/ *vi* **1** to make (a sound similar to) the short loud cry characteristic of a dog **2** to speak in a curt, loud, and usu angry tone; snap ~*vi* to utter in a curt, loud, and usu angry tone – **barker** *n* – **bark up the wrong tree** to proceed under a misapprehension

[2]**bark** *n* **1** (a sound similar to) the sound made by a barking dog **2** a short sharp peremptory utterance – **barkless** *adj*

[3]**bark** *n* the tough exterior covering of a woody root or stem – **barkless** *adj*

[4]**bark** *vt* to abrade the skin of

[5]**bark** *n* **1** *NAm* a barque **2** a boat – poetic

barley /ˈbahli‖ˈbɑːlɪ/ *n* a widely cultivated cereal grass whose seed is used to make malt and in foods (e g breakfast cereals and soups) and stock feeds

ˌ**barley** ˈ**wine** *n* a strong ale

barm /bahm‖bɑːm/ *n* yeast formed during the fermenting of beer

ˈ**barman** /-mən‖-mən/, *fem* ˈ**bar**ˌ**maid** /-ˌmayd‖-ˌmeɪd/ *n* one who serves drinks in a bar

bar mitzvah /ˌbah ˈmitsvə‖ˌbɑː ˈmɪtsvə/ *n, often cap B&M* (the initiatory ceremony of) a Jewish youth of 13 who assumes adult religious duties and responsibilities

barmy /ˈbahmi‖ˈbɑːmɪ/ *adj* **1** frothy with barm **2** slightly mad; foolish – infml

barn /bahn‖bɑːn/ *n* **1** a usu large farm building for storage, esp of feed, cereal products, etc **2** an unusually large and usu bare building – **barny** *adj*

barnacle /ˈbahnəkl‖ˈbɑːnəkl/ *n* any of numerous marine crustaceans that are free-swimming as larvae but fixed to rocks or floating objects as adults – **barnacled** *adj*

ˈ**barn** ˌ**dance** *n* a type of country dance, esp a round dance or a square dance with called instructions; *also* a social gathering for such dances

ˈ**barn**ˌ**storm** /-ˌstawm‖-ˌstɔːm/ *vb, chiefly NAm vi* **1** to tour in theatrical performances **2** to pilot an aeroplane on sightseeing flights or in exhibition stunts, esp in rural districts ~*vi* to travel across while barnstorming – **barnstormer** *n*

ˈ**barn**ˌ**yard** /-ˌyahd‖-ˌjɑːd/ *n* a farmyard

barograph /ˈbarəˌgrahf, -ˌgraf‖ˈbærəˌgrɑːf, -ˌgræf/ *n* a recording barometer – **barographic** *adj*

barometer /bəˈromitə‖bəˈrɒmɪtə/ *n* **1** an instrument for determining the pressure of the atmosphere and hence for assisting in predicting the weather or measuring the height of an ascent **2** sthg that serves to register fluctuations (e g in public opinion) [Greek *baros* weight, pressure + *metron* measure] – **barometry** *n*, **barometric, barometrical** *adj*, **barometrically** *adv*

baron /ˈbarən‖ˈbærən/ *n* **1a** a feudal tenant holding his rights and title by military or other honourable service directly from a sovereign ruler **b** a lord of the realm **2a** a member of the lowest rank of the peerage in Britain **b** a European nobleman **3** a man of great power or influence in a specified field of activity **4** a joint of meat consisting of 2 loins or sirloins joined by the backbone

baroness /ˌbarəˈnes‖ˌbærəˈnes/ *n* **1** the wife or widow of a baron **2** a woman having in her own right the rank of a baron

baronet /ˌbarəˈnet, ˈbarənit‖ˌbærəˈnet, ˈbærənɪt/ *n* the holder of a rank of honour below a baron and above a knight

baronetcy /ˈbarənətsi‖ˈbærənətsɪ/ *n* the rank of a baronet

baronial /bəˈrohni·əl‖bəˈrəʊnɪəl/ *adj* **1** of or befitting a baron or the baronage **2** stately, ample

barony /ˈbarəni‖ˈbærənɪ/ *n* the domain or rank of a baron

baroque /bəˈrok‖bəˈrɒk/ *adj* (typical) of a style of artistic expression prevalent esp in the 17th c that is marked by extravagant forms and elaborate and sometimes grotesque ornamentation – **baroquely** *adv*

barque *NAm chiefly* **bark** /bahk‖bɑːk/ *n* a sailing vessel with the rearmost of usu 3 masts fore-and-aft rigged and the others square-rigged

[1]**barrack** /ˈbarək‖ˈbærək/ *n* **1** (a set or area of)

buildings for lodging soldiers in garrison – often pl with sing. meaning but sing. or pl in constr **2** a large building characterized by extreme plainness or dreary uniformity with others – usu pl with sing. meaning but sing. or pl in constr

[2]**barrack** *vt* to lodge in barracks

[3]**barrack** *vi* **1** *chiefly Br* to jeer, scoff **2** *chiefly Austr & NZ* to root, cheer – usu + *for* ~ *vt* **1** *chiefly Br* to shout at derisively; jeer **2** *chiefly Austr & NZ* to support (e g a sports team), esp by shouting encouragement – **barracker** *n*

barracuda /ˌbarəˈkyoohdə‖ˌbærəˈkjuːdə/ *n*, any of several predatory fishes of warm seas that include excellent food fishes as well as forms regarded as poisonous

[1]**barrage** /ˈbarahzh‖ˈbærɑːʒ/ *n* an artificial dam placed in a watercourse or estuary

[2]**barrage** *n* **1** a barrier, esp of intensive artillery fire, to hinder enemy action **2** a rapid series (e g of questions) – **barrage** *vt*

[1]**barrel** /ˈbarəl‖ˈbærəl/ *n* **1** an approximately cylindrical vessel with bulging sides and flat ends constructed from wooden staves bound together with hoops; *also* any similar vessel **2** a drum or cylindrical part: e g **2a** the discharging tube of a gun **b** the part of a fountain pen or pencil containing the ink or lead **c** a cylindrical or tapering housing containing the lenses, iris diaphragm, etc of a camera or other piece of optical equipment – **barrelled,** *NAm* **barreled** *adj* – **over a barrel** at a disadvantage; in an awkward situation so that one is helpless

[2]**barrel** *vt* **-ll-** (*NAm* **-l-, -ll-**) to put or pack in a barrel

ˈ**barrel** ˌ**organ** *n* a musical instrument consisting of a revolving cylinder studded with pegs that open a series of valves to admit air from a bellows to a set of pipes

barren /ˈbarən‖ˈbærən/ *adj* **1** not reproducing: e g **1a** *of a female or mating* incapable of producing offspring **b** habitually failing to fruit **2** not productive; *esp* producing inferior or scanty vegetation **3** lacking, devoid *of* **4** lacking interest, information, or charm – **barrenly** *adv*, **barrenness** *n*

[1]**barricade** /ˈbarikayd, --ˈ-‖ˈbærɪkeɪd, --ˈ-/ *vt* **1** to block off, stop up, or defend with a barricade **2** to prevent access to by means of a barricade

[2]**barricade** *n* **1** an obstruction or rampart thrown up across a way or passage to check the advance of the enemy **2** a barrier, obstacle

barrier /ˈbari·ə‖ˈbærɪə/ *n* **1** a material object (e g a stockade, fortress, or railing) or set of objects that separates, demarcates, or serves as a barricade **2** sthg immaterial that impedes or separates <~s *of reserve*> **3** a factor that tends to restrict the free movement, mingling, or interbreeding of individuals or populations

barring /ˈbahring‖ˈbɑːrɪŋ/ *prep* excepting

barrister /ˈbaristə‖ˈbærɪstə/, ˌ**barrister-at-**ˈ**law** *n* a lawyer who has the right to plead as an advocate in an English or Welsh superior court

[1]**barrow** /ˈbaroh‖ˈbærəʊ/ *n* a large mound of earth or stones over the remains of the dead; a tumulus

[2]**barrow** *n* a male pig castrated before sexual maturity

[3]**barrow** *n* a cart with a shallow box body, 2 wheels, and shafts for pushing it

ˈ**barrow** ˌ**boy** *n* a man or boy who sells goods (e g fruit or vegetables) from a barrow

ˌ**bar** ˈ**sinister** *n* **1** an imaginary heraldic shape or representation indicating bastardy **2** the condition of being of illegitimate birth

ˈ**bar**ˌ**tender** /-ˌtendə‖-ˌtendə/ *n*, *chiefly NAm* a barman

[1]**barter** /ˈbahtə‖ˈbɑːtə/ *vi* to trade by exchanging one commodity for another without the use of money ~ *vt* **1** to exchange (as if) by bartering **2** to part with unwisely or for an unworthy return – + *away* – **barterer** *n*

[2]**barter** *n* the carrying on of trade by bartering

baryon /ˈbari·ən‖ˈbærɪən/ *n* any of a group of elementary particles (e g a hyperon) that are fermions and have a mass equal to or greater than that of the proton – **baryonic** *adj*

basal /ˈbays(ə)l‖ˈbeɪs(ə)l/ *adj* **1** of, situated at, or forming the base **2** of the foundation, base, or essence; fundamental – **basally** *adv*

basalt /ˈba(y)sawlt, bəˈsawlt‖ˈbæsɔːlt, ˈbeɪs-, bəˈsɔːlt/ *n* a dense to fine-grained dark igneous rock consisting essentially of a feldspar and usu pyroxene – **basaltic** *adj*

[1]**base** /bays‖beɪs/ *n* **1a** the bottom of sthg; a foundation **b** the lower part of a wall, pier, or column considered as a separate architectural feature **c** a side or face of a geometrical figure on which it is regarded as standing **d** that part of an organ by which it is attached to another structure nearer the centre of a living organism **2a** a main ingredient **b** a supporting or carrying ingredient **3** the fundamental part of sthg; a basis **4a** a centre from which a start is made in an activity or from which operations proceed **b** a line in a survey which serves as the origin for computations **c** the locality or installations on which a military force relies for supplies or from which it starts operations **d(1)** the number with reference to which a number system is constructed **d(2)** a number with reference to which logarithms are computed ● ROOT 6 **5a** the starting place or goal in various games **b** any of the stations at each of the 4 corners of the inner part of a baseball field to which a batter must run in turn in order to score a run **6** the middle region of a transistor that controls the current flow **7** any of various typically water-soluble and acrid or brackish tasting chemical compounds that are capable of taking up a hydrogen ion from or donating an unshared pair of electrons to an acid to form a salt – **based** *adj*, **baseless** *adj*

[2]**base** *vt* **1** to make, form, or serve as a base for **2** to use as a base or basis for; establish, found – usu + *on* or *upon*

[3]**base** *adj* constituting or serving as a base

[4]**base** *adj* **1a** *of a metal* of comparatively low value and having relatively inferior properties (e g resistance to corrosion) **b** containing a larger than usual proportion of base metals **2** lacking higher values; degrading <*a drab* ~ *way of life*> **3** of relatively little value – **basely** *adv*, **baseness** *n*

ˈ**base**ˌ**ball** /-ˌbawl‖-ˌbɔːl/ *n* (the ball used in) a game played with a bat and ball between 2 teams of 9 players each on a large field centring on 4 bases arranged in a square that mark the course a batter must run to score

ˈ**base,board** /-ˌbawd‖-ˌbɔːd/ *n, NAm* SKIRTING BOARD

ˈ**base,born** /-ˌbawn‖-ˌbɔːn/ *adj* **1** of humble or illegitimate birth **2** *archaic* mean, ignoble

ˈ**base,line** /-ˌlien‖-ˌlaɪn/ *n* the back line at each end of a court in tennis, badminton, etc

ˈ**basement** /-mənt‖-mənt/ *n* the part of a building that is wholly or partly below ground level

[1]**bash** /bash‖bæʃ/ *vt* **1** to strike violently; *also* to injure or damage by striking; smash – often + *in* or *up* **2** to make a violent attack on ***USE*** infml – **basher** *n*

[2]**bash** *n* **1** a forceful blow **2** *chiefly Br* a try, attempt <*have a ~ at it*> **3** *chiefly NAm* a festive social gathering; a party ***USE*** infml

bashful /ˈbashf(ə)l‖ˈbæʃf(ə)l/ *adj* **1** socially shy or timid **2** characterized by, showing, or resulting from extreme sensitiveness or self-consciousness – **bashfully** *adv*, **bashfulness** *n*

[1]**basic** /ˈbaysik, -zik‖ˈbeɪsɪk, -zɪk/ *adj* **1** of or forming the base or essence; fundamental **2** constituting or serving as the minimum basis or starting point **3a** of, containing, or having the character of a chemical base **b** having an alkaline reaction; being an alkali **4** *of rock* containing relatively little silica **5** of, being, or made by a steelmaking process in which the furnace is lined with material containing relatively little silica – **basically** *adv*, **basicity** *n*

[2]**basic** *n* sthg basic; a fundamental

BASIC /ˈbaysik‖ˈbeɪsɪk/ *n* a high-level computer language for programming and interacting with a computer in a wide variety of applications [*B*eginner's *A*ll-purpose *S*ymbolic *I*nstruction *C*ode]

basil /ˈbaz(ə)l‖ˈbæz(ə)l/ *n* any of several plants of the mint family

basilica /bəˈzilikə, bəˈsi-‖bəˈzɪlɪkə, bəˈsɪ-/ *n* **1** an oblong building used in ancient Rome as a place of assembly or as a lawcourt and usu ending in an apse **2** an early Christian church similar to a Roman basilica **3** a Roman Catholic church given certain ceremonial privileges – **basilican** *adj*

basilisk /ˈbasilisk, ˈbazi-‖ˈbæsɪlɪsk, ˈbæzɪ-/ *n* **1** a mythical reptile whose breath and glance were fatal **2** any of several crested tropical American lizards related to the iguanas – **basilisk** *adj*

basin /ˈbays(ə)n‖ˈbeɪs(ə)n/ *n* **1a** a round open usu metal or ceramic vessel with a greater width than depth and sides that slope or curve inwards to the base, used typically for holding water for washing **b** a bowl with a greater depth than width esp for holding, mixing, or cooking food **c** the contents of a basin **2a** a dock built in a tidal river or harbour **b** a (partly) enclosed water area, esp for ships **3a** a depression in the surface of the land or ocean floor **b** the region drained by a river and its tributaries **4** an area of the earth in which the strata dip from the sides towards the centre – **basinal** *adj*, **basined** *adj*

basis /ˈbaysis‖ˈbeɪsɪs/ *n, pl* **bases** /ˈbayseez‖ˈbeɪsiːz/ **1** a foundation **2** the principal component of sthg **3** a basic principle or way of proceeding

bask /bahsk‖bɑːsk/ *vi* **1** to lie in, or expose oneself to, a pleasant warmth or atmosphere **2** to enjoy sby's favour or approval – usu + *in*

basket /ˈbahskit‖ˈbɑːskɪt/ *n* **1a** a rigid or semirigid receptacle made of interwoven material (e g osiers, cane, wood, or metal) **b** any of various lightweight usu wood containers **c** the contents of a basket **2** sthg that resembles a basket, esp in shape or use **3** a net open at the bottom and suspended from a metal ring that constitutes the goal in basketball **4** a collection, group <*the ~ of major world currencies*>

ˈ**basket,ball** /-ˌbawl‖-ˌbɔːl/ *n* (the ball used in) an indoor court game between 2 teams of 5 players each who score by tossing a large ball through a raised basket

basketry /ˈbahskitri‖ˈbɑːskɪtrɪ/ *n* (the art or craft of making) baskets or objects woven like baskets

ˈ**basket,work** /-ˌwuhk‖-ˌwɜːk/ *n* basketry

bas-relief /ˌbas riˈleef, ˌbah, ˌbahs, ˈ- -ˌ-‖ˌbæs rɪˈliːf, ˌbɑː, ˌbɑːs, ˈ- -ˌ-/ *n* sculptural relief in which the design projects very slightly from the surrounding surface

[1]**bass** /bas‖bæs/ *n,* any of numerous edible spiny-finned fishes

[2]**bass** /bays‖beɪs/ *adj* **1** deep or grave in tone **2a** of low pitch **b** of or having the range or part of a bass

[3]**bass** /bays‖beɪs/ *n* **1** the lowest part in 4-part harmony **2a** (a person with) the lowest adult male singing voice **b** a member of a family of instruments having the lowest range; *esp* a double bass or bass guitar

[4]**bass** /bas‖bæs/ *n* a coarse tough fibre from palm trees

bass clef /bays‖beɪs/ *n* a clef placing the F below middle C on the fourth line of the staff

basset /ˈbasit‖ˈbæsɪt/, ˈ**basset ,hound** *n* (any of) a breed of short-legged hunting dogs with very long ears

bassoon /bəˈsoohn‖bəˈsuːn/ *n* a double-reed woodwind instrument with a usual range 2 octaves lower than the oboe – **bassoonist** *n*

bast /bast‖bæst/ *n* **1** phloem **2** a strong woody fibre obtained chiefly from the phloem of certain plants

[1]**bastard** /ˈbahstəd, ˈba-‖ˈbɑːstəd, ˈbæ-/ *n* **1** an illegitimate child **2** sthg spurious, irregular, inferior, or of questionable origin **3a** an offensive or disagreeable person – often + *you* as a generalized term of abuse **b** a fellow of a usu specified type <*poor old ~*> – infml – **bastardly** *adj*

[2]**bastard** *adj* **1** illegitimate **2** of an inferior or less typical type, stock, or form **3** lacking genuineness or authority; false

bastard·ize, -ise /ˈbahstədiez, ˈba-‖ˈbɑːstədaɪz, ˈbæ-/ *vt* **1** to declare illegitimate **2** to debase – **bastardization** *n*

bastardy /ˈbahstədi, ˈba-‖ˈbɑːstədɪ, ˈbæ-/ *n* the quality or state of being a bastard; illegitimacy

[1]**baste** /bayst‖beɪst/ *vt* TACK 1b – **baster** *n*

[2]**baste** *vt* to moisten (e g meat) at intervals with melted butter, dripping, etc during cooking, esp roasting – **baster** *n*

[3]**baste** *vt* to beat severely or soundly; thrash

bastinado /ˌbastiˈnaydoh‖ˌbæstɪˈneɪdəʊ/ *n, pl* **bastinadoes** **1** (a blow or beating with) a stick or cudgel **2** the punishment of beating the soles of the feet with a stick – **bastinado** *vt*

bastion /ˈbasti·ən‖ˈbæstɪən/ *n* **1** a projecting part of a fortification **2** a fortified area or position **3** sthg considered a stronghold; a bulwark – **bastioned** *adj*

[1]**bat** /bat‖bæt/ *n* **1** a stout solid stick; a club **2** a sharp blow; a stroke **3** a (wooden) implement used for hitting the ball in cricket, baseball, table tennis, etc **4a** a batsman **b** a turn at batting in cricket, baseball, etc **5** a hand-held implement shaped like a table-tennis bat for guiding aircraft when landing or taxiing – **off one's own bat** through one's own efforts, esp without being prompted

[2]**bat** *vb* **-tt-** *vt* to strike or hit (as if) with a bat ~ *vi* **1** to strike a ball with a bat **2** to take one's turn at batting, esp in cricket

[3]**bat** *n* any of an order of nocturnal flying mammals with forelimbs modified to form wings

[4]**bat** *vt* **-tt-** to blink, esp in surprise or emotion <*never* ~ted *an eyelid*>

batch /bach‖bætʃ/ *n* **1** the quantity baked at 1 time **2a** the quantity of material produced at 1 operation or for use at 1 time **b** a group of jobs to be run on a computer at 1 time with the same program **3** a group of people or things; a lot

[1]**bate** /bayt‖beɪt/ *vt, archaic* to restrain – **with bated breath** anxiously, worriedly

[2]**bate** *n* a rage, temper – slang

[1]**bath** /bahth‖bɑːθ/ *n, pl* **baths** /bahths‖bɑːθs; *sense 3 often* bahdhz‖bɑːðz/ **1** a washing or soaking (e g in water or steam) of all or part of the body **2a** water used for bathing <*run a* ~> **b** a vessel for bathing in; *esp* one that is permanently fixed in a bathroom **c** (a vat, tank, etc holding) a specified type of liquid used for a special purpose (e g to keep samples at a constant temperature) **3a** a building containing an apartment or a series of rooms designed for bathing **b** SWIMMING POOL – usu pl with sing. meaning but sing. or pl in constr **c** a spa **d** *NAm* a bathroom *USE* (*3a&3c*) usu pl with sing. meaning

[2]**bath** *vb, Br vt* to give a bath to ~*vi* to take a bath

ˈ**bath ˌchair** *n, often cap B* a usu hooded wheelchair [*Bath*, town in England]

[1]**bathe** /baydh‖beɪð/ *vt* **1** to wash or soak in a liquid (e g water) **2** to moisten **3** to apply water or a liquid medicament to **4** to suffuse, esp with light ~ *vi* **1** to take a bath **2** to swim (e g in the sea or a river) for pleasure **3** to become immersed or absorbed – **bather** *n*

[2]**bathe** *n, Br* an act of bathing, esp in the sea

ˈ**bathing ˌsuit** *n* SWIMMING COSTUME

ˈ**bath ˌmat** *n* **1** a usu washable mat, often of absorbent material, placed beside a bath **2** a mat of nonslip material, esp rubber, placed in a bath to prevent the bather from slipping

bathos /ˈbaythos‖ˈbeɪθɒs/ *n* **1** a sudden descent from the sublime to the commonplace or absurd; an anticlimax **2** exceptional commonplaceness; triteness

ˈ**bathˌrobe** /-ˌrohb‖-ˌrəʊb/ *n* a loose usu absorbent robe worn before and after having a bath

ˈ**bathroom** /-ˌroohm, -room‖-ˌruːm, -rʊm/ *n* **1** a room containing a bath or shower and usu a washbasin and toilet **2** a toilet – chiefly euph

bathysphere /ˈbathisfiə‖ˈbæθɪsfɪə/ *n* a strongly built diving sphere for deep-sea observation

batik /ˈbatik‖ˈbætɪk/ *n* (a fabric or design printed by) an Indonesian method of hand-printing by coating with wax the parts to be left undyed

batiste /bəˈteest‖bəˈtiːst/ *n* a fine soft sheer fabric of plain weave made of various fibres

batman /ˈbatmən‖ˈbætmən/ *n* a British officer's servant [archaic English *bat* pack-saddle, luggage, fr Middle French *bat*, deriv of Greek *bastazein* to carry]

baton /ˈbat(ə)n, ˈbaˌton, bəˈton ‖ˈbæt(ə)n, ˈbæˌtɒn, bəˈtɒn (*Fr* batɔ̃)/ *n* **1** a cudgel, truncheon **2** a staff borne as a symbol of office **3** a wand with which a conductor directs a band or orchestra **4** a stick or hollow cylinder passed by each member of a relay team to the succeeding runner

bats /bats‖bæts/ *adj, chiefly Br* batty <*he's gone* ~> – infml

ˈ**batsman** /-mən‖-mən/ *n* sby who bats or is batting, esp in cricket – **batsmanship** *n*

battalion /bəˈtalyən‖bəˈtæljən/ *n sing or pl in constr* **1** a large body of organized troops **2** a military unit composed of a headquarters and 2 or more companies **3** a large group

[1]**batten** /ˈbat(ə)n‖ˈbæt(ə)n/ *vi* – **batten on 1** to make oneself selfishly dependent on (sby) <battened on *his rich relatives*> **2** to seize on (an excuse, argument, etc)

[2]**batten** *n* **1** a thin narrow strip of squared timber **2a** a thin strip of wood, plastic, etc inserted into a sail to keep it flat and taut **b** a slat used to secure the tarpaulins and hatch covers of a ship **3** a strip holding a row of floodlights

[3]**batten** *vt* to provide or fasten (e g hatches) with battens – often + *down*

[1]**batter** /ˈbatə‖ˈbætə/ *vt* **1** to beat persistently or hard so as to bruise, shatter, or demolish **2** to wear or damage by hard usage or blows <*a* ~ed *old hat*> ~*vi* to strike heavily and repeatedly; beat

[2]**batter** *n* a mixture that consists essentially of flour, egg, and milk or water and is thin enough to pour or drop from a spoon; *also* batter mixture (e g that used for coating fish) when cooked

[3]**batter** *vi* to slope upwards and backwards ~*vt* to cause (e g a wall) to slope upwards and backwards

[4]**batter** *n* an upwards and backwards slope of the outer face of a structure

[5]**batter** *n* the player who is batting in baseball

ˈ**battering ˌram** /ˈbatəring‖ˈbætərɪŋ/ *n* an ancient military siege engine consisting of a large wooden beam with a head of iron used for beating down walls

battery /ˈbat(ə)ri‖ˈbæt(ə)rɪ/ *n* **1a** the act of battering **b** the unlawful application of any degree of force to a person without his/her consent **2** a grouping of similar artillery guns (e g for tactical purposes) **3** *sing or pl in constr* a tactical and administrative army artillery unit equivalent to an infantry company **4** one or more cells connected together to provide an electric current: e g **4a** STORAGE CELL **b** DRY CELL; *also* a connected group of dry cells **5a** a number of similar articles, items, or devices arranged, connected, or used together; a set, series **b(1)** a large number of small cages in which egg-laying hens are kept **b(2)** a series of cages or compartments for raising or fattening animals, esp poultry **c** an impressive or imposing group; an array **6** the position of readiness of a gun for firing

[1]**battle** /ˈbatl‖ˈbætl/ *n* **1** a general hostile encounter between armies, warships, aircraft, etc **2** a combat between 2 people **3** an extended contest, struggle, or controversy

[2]**battle** *vi* **1** to engage in battle; fight **2** to contend with full strength, craft, or resources; struggle ~ *vt* **1** to fight against **2** to force (e g one's way) by battling – **battler** *n*

ˈ**battle-ˌaxe** *n* a quarrelsome domineering woman

ˈ**battle ˌcruiser** *n* a large heavily-armed warship faster than a battleship

battlement /ˈbatlmənt‖ˈbætlmənt/ *n* a parapet with indentations that surmounts a wall and is used for defence or decoration – **battlemented** *adj*

ˌ**battle ˈroyal** *n, pl* **battles royal, battle royals** **1** a fight or contest between more than 2 opponents, esp until only the winner remains on his/her feet or in the ring **2** a violent struggle or heated dispute

ˈ**battleˌship** /-ˌship‖-ˌʃɪp/ *n* the largest and most heavily armed and armoured type of warship

batty /ˈbati‖ˈbætɪ/ *adj* mentally unstable; crazy – infml – **battiness** *n*

bauble /ˈbawbl‖ˈbɔːbl/ *n* **1** a trinket or trifle **2** a jester's staff

baulk /baw(l)k‖bɔː(l)k/ *vb or n, chiefly Br* (to) balk

bauxite /ˈbawksiet‖ˈbɔːksaɪt/ *n* a mineral that is an impure mixture of earthy hydrous aluminium oxides and hydroxides and is the principal ore of aluminium [French, fr Les *Baux*, place near Arles, France] – **bauxitic** *adj*

bawd /bawd‖bɔːd/ *n* a woman who keeps a house of prostitution; a madam

[1]**bawdy** /ˈbawdi‖ˈbɔːdɪ/ *adj* boisterously or humorously indecent – **bawdily** *adv*, **bawdiness** *n*

[2]**bawdy** *n* suggestive, coarse, or obscene language

[1]**bawl** /bawl‖bɔːl/ *vb* **1** to yell, bellow **2** to cry, wail – **bawler** *n*

[2]**bawl** *n* a loud prolonged cry

bawl out *vt, chiefly NAm* to reprimand loudly or severely – infml

[1]**bay** /bay‖beɪ/ *adj, esp of a horse* of the colour bay

[2]**bay** *n* **1** a horse with a bay-coloured body and black mane, tail, and points **2** a reddish brown colour

[3]**bay** *n* **1** any of several shrubs or trees resembling the laurel **2** an honorary garland or crown, esp of laurel, given for victory or excellence

[4]**bay** *n* **1** a division of a part of a building (e g the walls or roof) or of the whole building **2** a main division of a structure; *esp* a compartment in the fuselage of an aircraft

[5]**bay** *vi* to bark with prolonged tones

[6]**bay** *n* **1** the position of one unable to retreat and forced to face a foe or danger <*brought his quarry to* ~> **2** the position of one kept off or repelled with difficulty <*police kept the rioters at* ~>

[7]**bay** *n* (a land formation resembling) an inlet of a sea, lake, etc, usu smaller than a gulf

ˈ**bay ˌleaf** *n* the leaf of the European laurel used dried in cooking

[1]**bayonet** /ˌbayəˈnet, ˈ---‖ˌbeɪəˈnet, ˈ---/ *n* a blade attached to the muzzle of a firearm and used in hand-to-hand combat [French *baïonnette*, fr *Bayonne*, city in France]

[2]**bayonet** *vt* to stab or drive (as if) with a bayonet ~*vi* to use a bayonet

ˌ**bay ˈrum** *n* a fragrant cosmetic and medicinal liquid from the (oil of the) leaves of a W Indian tree of the myrtle family

ˌ**bay ˈwindow** *n* a window or series of windows projecting outwards from the wall

bazaar /bəˈzah‖bəˈzɑː/ *n* **1** an (Oriental) market consisting of rows of shops or stalls selling miscellaneous goods **2** a fair for the sale of miscellaneous articles, esp for charitable purposes

bazooka /bəˈzoohkə‖bəˈzuːkə/ *n* an individual infantry antitank rocket launcher

be /bi, bee‖bɪ, biː; *strong* bee‖biː/ *vb, pres 1 sing* **am** /əm, m‖əm, m; *strong* am‖æm/; *2 sing* **are** /ə‖ə; *strong* ah‖ɑː/; *3 sing* **is** /z‖z; *strong* iz‖ɪz/; *pl* **are**; *pres subjunctive* **be**; *pres part* **being**; *past 1&3 sing* **was** /wəz‖wəz; *strong* woz‖wɒz/; *2 sing* **were** /wə‖wə; *strong* **wuh**‖wɜː/; *pl* **were**; *past subjunctive* **were**; *past part* **been** /bin, been‖bɪn,biːn; *strong* been‖biːn/ *vi* **1a** to equal in meaning <*January* is *the first month*> **b** to represent, symbolize <*God* is *love*> **c** to have identity with <*it's me*> <*the difficulty* is *finding them*> **d** to belong to the class of <*the fish* is *a trout*> **e** to occupy a specified position in space <*the book* is *on the table*> **f** to take place at a specified time; occur <*the concert* was *last night*> **g** to have a specified qualification <~ *quick*>, destination <~ *off*>, origin <*she* is *from India*>, occupation <*what's he up to?*>, function or purpose <*it's for you*>, cost or value <*the book* is *£5*>, or standpoint <~ *against terrorism*> **2** to exist <*I think, therefore I* am> ~ *va* **1** – used with the past participle of transitive verbs as a passive-voice auxiliary <*the money* was *found*> **2** – used as the auxiliary of the present participle in progressive tenses expressing continuous action <*he* is *reading*> or arrangement in advance <*we* are *leaving tomorrow*> **3** – used with the past participle of some intransitive verbs as an auxiliary forming archaic perfect tenses <*my father* is *come* – Jane Austen> **4** – used with *to* and an infinitive to express destiny <*he* was *to become famous*>, arrangement in advance <*I* am *to interview him today*>, obligation or necessity <*you* are *not to smoke*>, or possibility <*it* was *nowhere to be found*>

be- /bi-‖bɪ-/ *prefix* **1** (*vb* → *vb*) on; round; all over <be*smear*> **2** (*vb* → *vb*) to a great or greater degree; thoroughly <be*fuddle*> **3** (*adj* → *adj*) wearing (a specified article of dress) <be*spectacled*> **4** (*vb* → *vb*) about; to; at; upon; against; across <be*stride*> **5** (*adj, n* → *vb*) make; cause to be; treat as <be*little*> **6** (*n* → *vb*) affect, afflict, provide, or cover with, esp excessively <be*calmed*>

[1]**beach** /beech‖biːtʃ/ *n* a (gently sloping) seashore or lakeshore usu covered by sand or pebbles; *esp* the part of this between the high and low water marks

[2]**beach** *vt* to run or drive ashore

ˈbeachˌcomber /-ˌkohmə‖-ˌkəumə/ *n* one who searches along a shore for useful or salable flotsam and jetsam – **beachcomb** *vb*

ˈbeachˌhead /-ˌhed‖-ˌhed/ *n* an area on a hostile shore occupied to secure further landing of troops and supplies

beacon /ˈbeekən‖ˈbiːkən/ *n* **1** a signal fire commonly on a hill, tower, or pole; *also, Br* a high conspicuous hill suitable for or used in the past for such a fire **2a** a signal mark used to guide shipping **b** a radio transmitter emitting signals for the guidance of aircraft **3** a source of light or inspiration

[1]**bead** /beed‖biːd/ *n* **1** a small ball (e g of wood or glass) pierced for threading on a string or wire **2** *pl* (a series of prayers and meditations made with) a rosary **3** a small ball-shaped body: e g **3a** a drop of liquid **b** a small metal knob on a firearm used as a front sight **4** a projecting rim, band, or moulding [Middle English *bede* prayer, prayer bead, fr Old English *bed, gebed* prayer]

[2]**bead** *vt* **1** to adorn or cover with beads or beading **2** to string together like beads ~*vi* to form into a bead

beading /ˈbeeding‖ˈbiːdɪŋ/ *n* **1** material adorned with or consisting of beads **2a** a narrow moulding of rounded often semicircular cross section **b** a moulding that resembles a string of beads **3** a narrow openwork insertion or trimming (e g on lingerie)

beadle /ˈbeedl‖ˈbiːdl/ *n* a minor parish official whose duties include ushering and preserving order at services

beady /ˈbeedi‖ˈbiːdɪ/ *adj, esp of eyes* small, round, and shiny with interest or greed

beagle /ˈbeegl‖ˈbiːgl/ *n* (any of) a breed of small short-legged smooth-coated hounds

beagling /ˈbeegling‖ˈbiːglɪŋ/ *n* hunting on foot with beagles – **beagler** *n*

beak /beek‖biːk/ *n* **1a** the bill of a bird; *esp* the bill of a bird of prey adapted for striking and tearing **b** any of various rigid projecting mouth structures (e g of a turtle); *also* the long sucking mouth of some insects **2** a pointed structure or formation: **2a** a metal-tipped beam projecting from the bow of an ancient galley for ramming an enemy ship **b** the pouring spout of a vessel **c** a projection suggesting the beak of a bird **3** the human nose – infml **4** *chiefly Br* **4a** a magistrate – slang **b** a schoolmaster – slang – **beaked** *adj*

beaker /ˈbeekə‖ˈbiːkə/ *n* **1** a large drinking cup with a wide mouth; a mug **2** a cylindrical flat-bottomed vessel usu with a pouring lip that is used esp by chemists and pharmacists

ˌbe-all and ˈend-all *n the* chief factor; *the* essential element – often derog

[1]**beam** /beem‖biːm/ *n* **1a** a long piece of heavy often squared timber suitable for use in construction **b** the part of a plough to which the handles, standard, and coulter are attached **c** the bar of a balance from which scales hang **d** any of the principal horizontal supporting members of a building or across a ship **e** the width of a ship at its widest part **f** an oscillating lever joining an engine piston rod to a crank, esp in one type of stationary steam engine (a ~ engine) **2a** a ray or shaft of radiation, esp light **b** a collection of nearly parallel rays (e g X rays) or of particles (e g electrons) moving in nearly parallel paths **c** (the course indicated by) a radio signal transmitted continuously in one direction as an aircraft navigation aid **3** the main stem of a deer's antler **4** the width of the buttocks <*broad in the* ~> – infml – **off (the) beam** wrong, irrelevant – **on the beam** proceeding or operating correctly

[2]**beam** *vt* **1** to emit in beams or as a beam, esp of light **2** to aim (a broadcast) by directional aerials ~*vi* to smile with joy

ˌbeam-ˈends *n pl, Br* buttocks – infml – **on her beam-ends** *of a ship* about to capsize

bean /been‖biːn/ *n* **1a** (the often edible seed of) any of various erect or climbing leguminous plants **b** a bean pod used when immature as a vegetable **c** (a plant producing) any of various seeds or fruits that resemble beans or bean pods **2a** a valueless item <*not worth a* ~> **b** the smallest possible amount of money <*gave up my job and haven't a* ~> *USE* (*2*) infml

ˈbeanˌpole /-ˌpohl‖-ˌpəul/ *n* a very tall thin person – infml

[1]**bear** /beə‖beə/ *n*, **1** any of a family of large heavy mammals that have long shaggy hair and a short tail and feed largely on fruit and insects as well as on flesh **2** a surly, uncouth, or shambling person **3** one who sells securities or commodities in expectation of a fall in price

[2]**bear** *vb* **bore** /baw‖bɔː/; **borne** *also* **born** /bawn‖bɔːn/ *vt* **1a** to carry, transport <~ *gifts*> – often in combination <*air*borne *troops*> **b** to carry or own as equipment <~ˈ*arms*> **c** to entertain mentally <~ *malice*> **d** to behave, conduct **e** to have or show as a feature <~ *scars*> **f** to give as testimony <~ *false witness*> **g** to have as an identification <bore *the name of John*> **2a** to give birth to **b** to produce as yield <~ *apples*> **c** to contain – often in combination <*oil*-bearing *shale*> **3a** to support the weight of **b** to accept the presence of; tolerate <~ *pain*> **c** to sustain, incur <~ *the cost*> **d** to admit of; allow <*it won't* ~ *repeating*> ~ *vi* **1a** to become directed <*bring guns to* ~ *on a target*> **b** to go or extend in a usu specified direction <*the road* ~s *to the right*> **2** to apply, have relevance <*facts* ~ing *on the situation*> **3** to support weight or strain **4** to produce fruit; yield – **bear fruit** to come to satisfying fruition or production – **bear in mind** to think of, esp as a warning; remember – **bear with** to show patience or indulgence towards

[1]**beard** /biəd‖bɪəd/ *n* **1** the hair that grows on the lower part of a man's face, usu excluding the moustache **2** a hairy or bristly appendage or tuft (e g on a goat's chin) – **bearded** *adj*, **beardedness** *n*, **beardless** *adj*

[2]**beard** *vt* to confront and oppose with boldness, resolution, and often effrontery; defy

bear down *vt* to overcome, overwhelm ~ *vi*

1 to exert full strength and concentrated attention **2** *of a woman in childbirth* to exert concentrated downward pressure in an effort to expel the child from the womb – **bear down on 1** to weigh heavily on **2** to come towards purposefully or threateningly

bearer /ˈbearə‖ˈbeərə/ *n* **1** a porter **2** a plant yielding fruit **3** a pallbearer **4** one holding an order for payment, esp a bank note or cheque

ˈbear ˌhug *n* a rough tight embrace

bearing /ˈbearing‖ˈbeərɪŋ/ *n* **1** the manner in which one bears or conducts oneself **2** the act, power, or time of bringing forth offspring or fruit **3a** an object, surface, or point that supports **b** a machine part in which another part turns or slides – often pl with sing. meaning **4** an emblem or figure on a heraldic shield **5a** the compass direction of one point (with respect to another) **b** a determination of position **c** *pl* comprehension of one's position, environment, or situation <*lost his* ~s> **d** a relation, connection, significance – usu + *on* <*has no* ~ *on the matter*>

bearish /ˈbearish‖ˈbeərɪʃ/ *adj* marked by, tending to cause, or fearful of falling prices (e g in a stock market) – **bearishly** *adv*, **bearishness** *n*

bear out *vt* to confirm, substantiate <*research* bore out *his theory*>

ˈbearˌskin /-ˌskin‖-ˌskɪn/ *n* an article made of the skin of a bear; *esp* a tall black military hat worn by the Brigade of Guards

bear up *vt* to support, encourage ~*vi* to summon up courage, resolution, or strength <bearing up *under the strain*>

beast /beest‖biːst/ *n* **1a** an animal as distinguished from a plant **b** a 4-legged mammal as distinguished from human beings, lower vertebrates, and invertebrates **c** an animal under human control **2** a contemptible person

[1]**beastly** /ˈbeestli‖ˈbiːstlɪ/ *adj* **1** bestial **2** abominable, disagreeable – **beastliness** *n*

[2]**beastly** *adv* very <*a* ~ *cold day*> – infml

ˌbeast of ˈburden *n* an animal employed to carry heavy material or perform other heavy work (e g pulling a plough)

[1]**beat** /beet‖biːt/ *vb* **beat; beaten** /ˈbeet(ə)n‖ˈbiːt(ə)n/, **beat** *vt* **1** to strike repeatedly: **1a** to hit repeatedly so as to inflict pain – often + *up* **b** to strike directly against (sthg) forcefully and repeatedly <*shores* ~en *by heavy waves*> **c** to flap or thrash at vigorously <*a trapped bird* ~ing *the air*> **d** to strike at or range over (as if) in order to rouse game **e** to mix (esp food) by stirring; whip **f** to strike repeatedly in order to produce music or a signal **2a** to drive or force by blows <*to* ~ *off the savage dogs*> **b** to pound into a powder, paste, or pulp **c** to make by repeated treading or driving over <~ *a path*> **d(1)** to dislodge by repeated hitting <~ *the dust from the carpet*> **d(2)** to lodge securely by repeated striking <~ *a stake into the ground*> **e** to shape by beating; *esp* to flatten thin by blows <*gold* ~en *into foil*> **f** to sound or express, esp by drumbeat <~ *a tattoo*> **3** to cause to strike or tap repeatedly <~ *his foot nervously on the ground*> **4a** to overcome, defeat; *also* to surpass **b** to prevail despite <~ *the odds*> **c** to leave dispirited, irresolute, or hopeless <*a* ~en *man*> **d** to be or to bowl a ball that is too good for (a batsman) to hit **5** to act ahead of, usu so as to forestall – chiefly in *beat someone to it* **6** to indicate by beating **7** to bewilder, baffle – infml ~ *vi* **1a** to dash, strike <*the rain was* ~ing *on the roof*> **b** to glare or strike with oppressive intensity <*the sun was* ~ing *down*> **2a** to pulsate, throb **b** to sound on being struck <*the drums were* ~ing> **3a** to strike the air; flap <*the birds wings* ~ *frantically*> **b** to strike cover or range (as if) in order to find or rouse game **4** to progress with much difficulty; *specif, of a sailing vessel* to make way at sea against the wind by a series of alternate tacks across the wind – **beat about the bush** to fail to come to the point in conversation by talking indirectly or evasively – **beat it** to hurry away; scram – infml – **beat one's brains out** to try intently to resolve sthg difficult by thinking

[2]**beat** *n* **1a** a single stroke or blow, esp in a series; *also* a pulsation, throb **b** a sound produced (as if) by beating **2** each of the pulsations of amplitude produced by the mixing of sound or radio waves having different frequencies **3a** (the rhythmic effect of) a metrical or rhythmic stress in poetry or music **b** the tempo indicated to a musical performer **4** an area or route regularly patrolled, esp by a policeman **5** TACK 3b **6** a deadbeat – infml

[3]**beat** *adj* **1** of or being beatniks **2** exhausted – infml

[4]**beat** *n* a beatnik

beaten /ˈbeet(ə)n‖ˈbiːt(ə)n/ *adj* **1** hammered into a desired shape <~ *gold*> **2** defeated

beater /ˈbeetə‖ˈbiːtə/ *n* **1a** any of various hand-held implements for whisking or beating <*a carpet* ~> **b** a rotary blade attached to an electric mixer **c** a stick for beating a gong **2** one who strikes bushes or other cover to rouse game

beatific /ˌbee·əˈtifik‖ˌbiːəˈtɪfɪk/ *adj* **1** of, possessing, or imparting beatitude **2** having a blissful or benign appearance; saintly, angelic – **beatifically** *adv*

beatify /beeˈatifie‖biːˈætɪfaɪ/ *vt* **1** to make supremely happy **2** to authorize the veneration of (a dead person) by Catholics by giving the title 'Blessed' – **beatification** *n*

beating /ˈbeeting‖ˈbiːtɪŋ/ *n* **1** injury or damage inflicted by striking with repeated blows **2** a throbbing **3** a defeat

beatitude /biˈatityoohd, -choohd‖bɪˈætɪtjuːd, -tʃuːd/ *n* **1a** a state of utmost bliss **b** – used as a title for a primate, esp of an Eastern church **2** any of a series of sayings of Jesus beginning in the Authorized version of the Bible 'Blessed are'

beatnik /ˈbeetnik‖ˈbiːtnɪk/ *n* a person, esp in the 1950s and 1960s, who rejected the moral attitudes of established society (e g by unconventional behaviour and dress)

beau /boh‖bəʊ/ *n, pl* **beaux, beaus** /bohz‖bəʊz/ **1** a lover **2** *archaic* a dandy

Beaujolais /ˈbohzhəlay‖ˈbəʊʒəleɪ/ *n* a chiefly red table wine made in southern Burgundy in France

[1]**beaut** /byooht‖bjuːt/ *n, chiefly Austr & NZ* BEAUTY 3 – infml

[2]**beaut** *adj, Austr & NZ* fine, marvellous – infml

beauteous /ˈbyoohti·əs, -tyəs‖ˈbjuːtɪəs, -tjəs/

adj, archaic beautiful – **beauteously** *adv*, **beauteousness** *n*

beautician /byooh'tish(ə)n‖bju:'tɪʃ(ə)n/ *n* sby who gives beauty treatments

beautiful /'byoohtif(ə)l‖'bju:tɪf(ə)l/ *adj* **1** having qualities of beauty; exciting aesthetic pleasure or keenly delighting the senses **2** generally pleasing; excellent – **beautifully** *adv*, **beautifulness** *n*

beautify /'byoohtifie‖'bju:tɪfaɪ/ *vt* to make beautiful; embellish – **beautifier beautification** *n*

beauty /'byoohti‖'bju:tɪ/ *n* **1** the qualities in a person or thing that give pleasure to the senses or pleasurably exalt the mind or spirit; loveliness **2** a beautiful person or thing; *esp* a beautiful woman **3** a brilliant, extreme, or conspicuous example or instance **4** a particularly advantageous or excellent quality *<the ~ of my idea is that it costs so little>*

'beauty ˌsleep *n* sleep considered as being beneficial to a person's beauty

'beauty ˌspot *n* a beautiful scenic area

[1]beaver /'beevə‖'bi:və/ *n*, **1a** a large semi-aquatic rodent that has webbed hind feet, a broad flat tail, and builds dams and underwater lodges **b** the fur or pelt of the beaver **2** a hat made of beaver fur or a fabric imitation **3** an energetic hard-working person

[2]beaver *vi* to work energetically <~ing *away at the problem*>

[3]beaver *n* **1** a piece of armour protecting the lower part of the face **2** a helmet visor

bebop /'beeˌbop‖'bi:ˌbɒp/ *n* bop – **bebopper** *n*

becalm /bi'kahm‖bɪ'kɑ:m/ *vt* to keep motionless by lack of wind – usu pass

because /bi'koz, bə-, -kəz‖bɪ'kɒz, bə-, -kəz/ *conj* **1** for the reason that; since *<he rested ~ he was tired>* **2** and the proof is that *<they must be in, ~ the light's on>*

be'cause of *prep* **1** as a result of **2** for the sake of

[1]beck /bek‖bek/ *n, NEng* a brook; *esp* a pebbly mountain stream

[2]beck *n* – **at someone's beck and call** in continual readiness to obey any command from sby

beckon /'bekən‖'bekən/ *vi* **1** to summon or signal, typically with a wave or nod **2** to appear inviting ~*vt* to beckon to – **beckon** *n*

become /bi'kum‖bɪ'kʌm/ *vb* **became** /bi'kaym‖bɪ'keɪm/; **become** *vi* **1** to come into existence **2** to come to be <~ *sick*> ~*vt* to suit or be suitable to *<her clothes ~ her>* – **become of**

becoming /bi'kuming‖bɪ'kʌmɪŋ/ *adj* suitable, fitting; *esp* attractively suitable – **becomingly** *adv*

[1]bed /bed‖bed/ *n* **1a** a piece of furniture on or in which one may lie and sleep **b** a place of sexual relations; *also* LOVEMAKING 2 **c** a place for sleeping or resting **d** sleep; *also* a time for sleeping *<took a walk before ~>* **e** the use of a bed for the night **2** a flat or level surface: e g **2a** (plants grown in) a plot of ground, esp in a garden, prepared for plants **b** the bottom of a body of water; *also* an area of sea or lake bottom supporting a heavy growth of a specified organism *<an oyster ~>* **3** a supporting surface or structure; *esp* the foundation that supports a road or railway **4** STRATUM 1a **5** a mass or heap resembling a bed *<a ~ of ashes>*; *esp* a heap on which sthg else is laid *<coleslaw on a ~ of lettuce>*

[2]bed *vb* **-dd-** *vt* **1a** to provide with a bed or bedding; settle in sleeping quarters **b** to go to bed with, usu for sexual intercourse **2a** to embed **b** to plant or arrange (garden plants, vegetable plants, etc) in beds – often + *out* **c** to base, establish **3** to lay flat or in a layer ~ *vi* **1a** to find or make sleeping accommodation **b** to go to bed **2** to form a layer **3** to lie flat or flush *USE* (*vt 1a; vi 1, 2*) often + *down*

ˌbed and 'breakfast *n, Br* a night's lodging and breakfast the following morning

'bedˌbug /-ˌbug‖-ˌbʌg/ *n* a wingless blood-sucking bug that sometimes infests beds

'bedˌclothes /-ˌklohdhz‖-ˌkləʊðz/ *n pl* the covers (e g sheets and blankets) used on a bed

[1]bedding /'beding‖'bedɪŋ/ *n* **1** bedclothes **2** a bottom layer; a foundation **3** material to provide a bed for livestock **4** a stratified rock formation

[2]bedding *adj, of a plant* appropriate or adapted for culture in open-air beds

bedeck /bi'dek‖bɪ'dek/ *vt* to clothe with finery; deck out

bedevil /bi'devl‖bɪ'devl/ *vt* **1** to possess (as if) with a devil; bewitch **2** to change for the worse; spoil, frustrate **3** to torment maliciously; harass – **bedevilment** *n*

'bedˌfellow /-ˌfeloh‖-ˌfeləʊ/ *n* **1** one who shares a bed **2** a close associate; an ally

bedlam /'bedləm‖'bedləm/ *n* a place, scene, or state of uproar and confusion [*Bedlam*, popular name for the Hospital of St Mary of Bethlehem, London, a lunatic asylum, fr Middle English *Bedlem* Bethlehem] – **bedlam** *adj*

'bed ˌlinen *n* the sheets and pillowcases used on a bed

bedouin, beduin /'bedwin, 'bedooh·in‖'bedwɪn, 'bedu:ɪn/ *n, often cap* a nomadic Arab of the Arabian, Syrian, or N African deserts [French *bédouin*, fr Arabic *badāwi, bidwān*, pl of *badawi* desert dweller]

'bedˌpan /-ˌpan‖-ˌpæn/ *n* a shallow vessel used by a person in bed for urination or defecation

'bedˌpost /-ˌpohst‖-ˌpəʊst/ *n* a usu turned or carved post of a bedstead

bedraggled /bi'dragld‖bɪ'drægld/ *adj* **1** left wet and limp (as if) by rain **2** soiled and stained (as if) by trailing in mud

'bedˌridden /-ˌrid(ə)n‖-ˌrɪd(ə)n/ *adj* confined (e g by illness) to bed

'bedˌrock /-ˌrok‖-ˌrɒk/ *n* **1** the solid rock underlying unconsolidated surface materials (e g soil) **2** the basis of sthg – **bedrock** *adj*

'bedroom /-ˌroohm, -room‖-ˌru:m, -rʊm/ *n* a room furnished with a bed and intended primarily for sleeping

'bedˌside /-ˌsied‖-ˌsaɪd/ *adj* **1** of or conducted at the bedside **2** suitable for a person in bed *<~ reading>*

ˌbedside 'manner *n* the manner with which a medical doctor deals with his/her patients

ˌbed-'sitter *n, Br* a single room serving as both bedroom and sitting room

'bedˌsore /-ˌsaw‖-ˌsɔ:/ *n* a sore caused by prolonged pressure on the tissue of a bedridden invalid

[1]**bed,spread** /-,spred||-,spred/ *n* a usu ornamental cloth cover for a bed

[1]**bed,stead** /-,sted||-,sted/ *n* the framework of a bed

bee /bee||bi:/ *n* **1** a social 4-winged insect often kept in hives for the honey that it produces; *broadly* any of numerous insects that differ from the related wasps, esp in the heavier hairier body and legs and in sometimes having a pollen basket **2** *NAm* a gathering of people for a usu specified purpose <*a sewing* ~> – **beelike** *adj* – **bee in one's bonnet** an obsession about a specified subject or idea

beech /beech||bi:tʃ/ *n, pl* **beeches, beech** (the wood of) any of a genus of hardwood deciduous trees with smooth grey bark and small edible triangular nuts – **beechen** *adj*

[1]**beef** /beef||bi:f/ *n, pl* **beefs,** (*2a*) **beeves** /beevz||bi:vz/, **beef,** *NAm chiefly* **beefs** **1** the flesh of a bullock, cow, or other adult domestic bovine animal **2a** an ox, cow, or bull in a (nearly) full-grown state; *esp* a bullock or cow fattened for food **b** a dressed carcass of a beef animal **3** muscular flesh; brawn **4** a complaint – infml

[2]**beef** *vt* to add weight, strength, or power to – usu + *up* ~*vi* to complain – infml

[1]**beef,cake** /-,kayk||-,keɪk/ *n* a photographic display of muscular male physiques – infml

[1]**beef,eater** /-,eetə||-,i:tə/ *n* YEOMAN OF THE GUARD – not used technically

beefy /'beefi||'bi:fɪ/ *adj* **1** full of beef **2** brawny, powerful

beehive /'bee,hiev||'bi:,haɪv/ *n* **1** HIVE 1 **2** a scene of crowded activity – **beehive** *adj*

[1]**bee,line** /-,lien||-,laɪn/ *n* a straight direct course

been /bin, been||bɪn, bi:n; *strong* been||bi:n/ *past part of* BE; *specif* paid a visit <*has the postman* ~*?*>

beer /biə||bɪə/ *n* **1** an alcoholic drink brewed from fermented malt flavoured with hops **2** a carbonated nonalcoholic or fermented slightly alcoholic drink flavoured with roots or other plant parts <*ginger* ~> – **beery** *adj*

beeswax /'beez,waks||'bi:z,wæks/ *n* a yellowish plastic substance secreted by bees that is used by them for constructing honeycombs and is used as a wood polish

beet /beet||bi:t/ *n* **1** any of various plants with a swollen root used as a vegetable, as a source of sugar, or for forage **2** *NAm* beetroot

[1]**beetle** /'beetl||'bi:tl/ *n* any of an order of insects that have 4 wings of which the front pair are modified into stiff coverings that protect the back pair at rest

[2]**beetle** *vi Br* to move swiftly <~d *off down the road*> – infml

[3]**beetle** *n* a heavy wooden tool for hammering or ramming

beetling /'beetling||'bi:tlɪŋ/ *adj* prominent and overhanging <~ *brows*>

beetroot /'beetrooht||'bi:tru:t/ *n, chiefly Br* a cultivated beet with a red edible root that is a common salad vegetable

befall /bi'fawl||bɪ'fɔ:l/ *vb* **befell** /bi'fel||bɪ'fel/; **befallen** /bi'fawlən||bɪ'fɔ:lən/ to happen (to), esp as if by fate

befit /bi'fit||bɪ'fɪt/ *vt* **-tt-** to be proper or becoming to

befitting /bi'fiting||bɪ'fɪtɪŋ/ *adj* suitable, appropriate – **befittingly** *adv*

[1]**before** /bi'faw||bɪ'fɔ:/ *adv* **1** so as to be in advance of others; ahead **2** earlier in time; previously

[2]**before** *prep* **1a** IN FRONT OF **b** under the jurisdiction or consideration of <*the case* ~ *the court*> **2** preceding in time; earlier than **3** in a higher or more important position than <*put quantity* ~ *quality*> **4** under the onslaught of

[3]**before** *conj* **1** earlier than the time when **2** rather than

beforehand /bi'faw,hand||bɪ'fɔ:,hænd/ *adv or adj* **1** in anticipation **2** ahead of time – **beforehandedness** *n*

befriend /bi'frend||bɪ'frend/ *vt* to become a friend of purposely; show kindness and understanding to

befuddle /bi'fudl||bɪ'fʌdl/ *vt* **1** to muddle or stupefy (as if) with drink **2** to confuse, perplex – **befuddlement** *n*

beg /beg||beg/ *vb* **-gg-** *vt* **1** to ask for as a charity <~ged *alms*> **2** to ask earnestly (for); entreat <~ *a favour*> **3a** to evade, sidestep <~ged *the real problems*> **b** to assume as established or proved without justification <~ *the question*> ~ *vi* **1** to ask for alms or charity **2a** to ask earnestly <~ged *for mercy*> **b** to ask permission – usu + an infinitive <*I* ~ *to differ*> **3** *of a dog* to sit up and hold out the forepaws

beget /bi'get||bɪ'get/ *vt* **-tt-; begot**/bi'got||bɪ'gɒt/, *archaic* **begat** /bi'gat||bɪ'gæt/; **begotten** /bi'gotn||bɪ'gɒtn/, **begot** **1** to procreate as the father; sire **2** to produce as an effect; cause – **begetter** *n*

[1]**beggar** /'begə||'begə/ *n* **1** one who lives by asking for gifts **2** a pauper **3** a person; *esp* a fellow – infml <*lucky* ~>

[2]**beggar** *vt* **1** to reduce to beggary **2** to exceed the resources or abilities of <*it* ~s *description*>

[1]**beggarly** /-li||-lɪ/ *adj* **1** marked by extreme poverty **2** contemptibly mean, petty, or paltry – **beggarliness** *n*

beggary /'begəri||'begərɪ/ *n* poverty, penury

begin /bi'gin||bɪ'gɪn/ *vb* **-nn-; began** /bi'gan||bɪ'gæn/; **begun** /bi'gun||bɪ'gʌn/ *vi* **1a** to do the first part of an action; start <*if you're all ready, we'll* ~> **b** to undergo initial steps <*work on the project* began *in May*> **2a** to come into existence; arise <*the war* began *in 1939*> **b** to have a starting point <*the alphabet* ~s *with* A> ~ *vt* **1** to set about the activity of <*the children* began *laughing*> **2** to call into being; found <~ *a dynasty*> **3** to come first in <A ~s *the alphabet*> **4** to do or succeed in, in the least degree <*can't* ~ *to describe her beauty*> – **beginner** *n*

beginning /bi'gining||bɪ'gɪnɪŋ/ *n* **1** the point at which sthg begins; the start **2** the first part **3** the origin, source **4** a rudimentary stage or early period – usu pl

beg off *vi* to ask to be released from sthg

begone /bi'gon||bɪ'gɒn/ *vi* to go away; depart – usu in the infinitive or esp the imperative

begonia /bi'gohni·ə||bɪ'gəʊnɪə/ *n* any of a

large genus of tropical plants that have asymmetrical leaves and are widely cultivated as ornamental garden and house plants [Michel *Bégon* (1638-1710), French governor of Santo Domingo]

begorra /bi'gorə‖bɪ'gɒrə/ *interj, Irish* – used as a mild oath

begrudge /bi'gruj‖bɪ'grʌdʒ/ *vt* **1** to give or concede reluctantly <*he* ~d *every minute taken from his work*> **2** to envy the pleasure or enjoyment of <*they* ~ *him his wealth*> – **begrudger** *n*, **begrudgingly** *adv*

beguile /bi'giel‖bɪ'gaɪl/ *vt* **1** to deceive, hoodwink **2** to while away, esp by some agreeable occupation **3** to please or persuade by the use of wiles; charm <*her ways* ~d *him*> ~*vi* to deceive by wiles – **beguilement** *n*, **beguiler** *n*, **beguilingly** *adv*

behalf /bi'hahf‖bɪ'hɑ:f/ *n* – **on behalf of,** *NAm* **in behalf of** in the interest of; as a representative of

behave /bi'hayv‖bɪ'heɪv/ *vb* **1** to conduct (oneself) in a specified way <*she has been* behaving *badly*> **2** to conduct (oneself) properly <*you must learn to* ~ *yourself in company*> – **behaver** *n*

behaviour, *NAm chiefly* **behavior** /bi'hayvyə‖bɪ'heɪvjə/ *n* **1a** anything that an organism does involving action and response to stimulation **b** the response of an individual, group, or species to its environment **2** the way in which sthg (e g a machine) functions – **behavioural** *adj*, **behaviourally** *adv*

behaviourism /bi'hayvyə,riz(ə)m‖bɪ'heɪvjə,rɪz(ə)m/ *n* a theory holding that the proper concern of psychology is the objective study of behaviour and that information derived from introspection is not admissible psychological evidence

behead /bi'hed‖bɪ'hed/ *vt* to cut off the head of; decapitate

behest /bi'hest‖bɪ'hest/ *n* an urgent prompting or insistent request <*returned home at the* ~ *of his friends*>

[1]behind /bi'hiend‖bɪ'haɪnd/ *adv* **1a** in the place, situation, or time that is being or has been departed from <*I've left the keys* ~> **b** in, to, or towards the back <*look* ~> **2a** in a secondary or inferior position **b** IN ARREARS <~ *in his payments*> **c** slow

[2]behind *prep* **1a(1)** at or to the back or rear of <*look* ~ *you*> **a(2)** remaining after (sby who has departed) <*left a great name* ~ *him*> **b** obscured by <*malice* ~ *the mask of friendship*> **2** – used to indicate backwardness <~ *his classmates in performance*>, delay <~ *schedule*>, or deficiency <*lagged* ~ *last year's sales*> **3a** in the background of <*the conditions* ~ *the strike*> **b** in a supporting position at the back of <*solidly* ~ *their candidate*> – **behind the times** old-fashioned, out-of-date

[3]behind *n* the buttocks – slang

behindhand /bi'hiend,hand‖bɪ'haɪnd,hænd/ *adj* **1** behind schedule; IN ARREARS **2** lagging behind the times; backward

behold /bi'hohld‖bɪ'həʊld/ *vb* **beheld** /bi'held‖bɪ'held/ *vt* to see, observe ~*vi archaic* – used in the imperative to call attention – **beholder** *n*

beholden /bi'hohldn‖bɪ'həʊldn/ *adj* under obligation for a favour or gift; indebted *to*

behove /bi'hohv‖bɪ'həʊv/ *vb* to be incumbent (on), or necessary, proper, or advantageous (for) <*it* ~s *us to fight*>

beige /bayzh, bayj‖beɪʒ, beɪdʒ/ *n* a yellowish grey colour – **beige** *adj*, **beigy** *adj*

[1]being /'bee·ing‖'bi:ɪŋ/ *n* **1a** the quality or state of having existence **b** conscious existence; life <*the mother who gave him his* ~> **2** the qualities that constitute an existent thing; the essence; *esp* personality **3** a living thing; *esp* a person

[2]being *adj* – **for the time being** for the moment

bel /bel‖bel/ *n* 10 decibels [Alexander Graham *Bell* (1847-1922), US inventor]

belabour /bi'laybə‖bɪ'leɪbə/ *vt* **1** to work on or at to absurd lengths <~ *the obvious*> **2a** to beat soundly **b** to assail, attack

belated /bi'laytid‖bɪ'leɪtɪd/ *adj* delayed beyond the usual time – **belatedly** *adv*, **belatedness** *n*

[1]belay /bi'lay‖bɪ'leɪ/ *vt* **1** to secure or make fast (e g a rope) by turns round a support or bitt **2** to stop **3a** to secure (a person) at the end of a rope **b** to secure (a rope) to a person or object ~ *vi* **1** to be belayed **2** to stop; LEAVE OFF – in the imper <~ *there*> **3** to make a rope fast

[2]belay *n* **1** a method or act of belaying a rope or person in mountain climbing **2** (sthg to which is attached) a mountain climber's belayed rope

belch /belch‖beltʃ/ *vi* **1** to expel gas suddenly from the stomach through the mouth **2** to erupt, explode, or detonate violently **3** to issue forth spasmodically; gush ~ *vt* **1** to eject or emit violently **2** to expel (gas) suddenly from the stomach through the mouth – **belch** *n*

beleaguer /bi'leegə‖bɪ'li:gə/ *vt* **1** to surround with an army so as to prevent escape; besiege **2** to beset, harass

belfry /'belfri‖'belfrɪ/ *n* (a room in which a bell is hung in) a bell tower, esp when associated with a church

Belgian /'belj(ə)n‖'beldʒ(ə)n/ *n or adj* (a native or inhabitant) of Belgium

belie /bi'lie‖bɪ'laɪ/ *vt* **belying** **1** to give a false impression of **2** to show (sthg) to be false – **belier** *n*

belief /bi'leef‖bɪ'li:f/ *n* **1** trust or confidence in sby or sthg **2** sthg believed; *specif* a tenet or body of tenets held by a group **3** conviction of the truth of some statement or the reality of some being, thing, or phenomenon, esp when based on examination of evidence

believe /bi'leev‖bɪ'li:v/ *vi* **1a** to have a firm religious faith **b** to accept sthg trustfully and on faith **2** to have a firm conviction as to the reality or goodness of sthg ~ *vt* **1** to consider to be true or honest **2** to hold as an opinion; think *USE* (*vi*) often + *in* – **believable** *adj*, **believer** *n*

Be,lisha 'beacon /bə'leeshə‖bə'li:ʃə/ *n* a flashing light in an amber globe mounted on a pole that marks a zebra crossing [Leslie Hore-*Belisha* (1893-1957), English politician]

belittle /bi'litl‖bɪ'lɪtl/ *vt* to speak slightingly of – **belittlement** *n*, **belittler** *n*

[1]bell /bel‖bel/ *n* **1** a hollow metallic device, usu cup-shaped with a flaring mouth, that vibrates and gives forth a ringing sound when struck **2**

the sound of a bell as a signal; *specif* one to mark the start of the last lap in a running or cycling race or the start or end of a round in boxing, wrestling, etc **3a** a bell rung to tell the hour **b** a half-hour subdivision of a watch on shipboard indicated by the strokes of a bell **4** sthg bell-shaped: e g **4a** the corolla of any of many flowers **b** the flared end of a wind instrument

²**bell** *vt* to provide with a bell ~*vi* to take the form of a bell; flare

³**bell** *vi, of a stag or hound* to make a resonant bellowing or baying sound

belladonna /ˌbelə'donə‖ˌbelə'dɒnə/ *n* (an atropine-containing extract of) deadly nightshade [Italian, lit., beautiful lady; fr its use as a cosmetic]

'**bell-ˌbottoms** *n pl* trousers with wide flaring bottoms – **bell-bottom** *adj*

'**bellˌboy** /-ˌboy‖-ˌbɔɪ/ *n, chiefly NAm* ¹PAGE

belle /bel‖bel/ *n* a popular and attractive girl or woman

belles lettres /ˌbel 'letrə, 'letə ‖ˌbel 'letrə, 'letə (*Fr* bɛl lɛtr)/ *n pl but sing in constr* (light, entertaining, usu sophisticated) literature that has no practical or informative function – **belletrist** *n*

'**bellˌflower** /-ˌflowə‖-ˌflaʊə/ *n* any of a genus of plants (e g the harebell) having usu showy bell-shaped flowers

bellicose /'belikohs‖'belɪkəʊs/ *adj* disposed to or fond of quarrels or wars – **bellicosely** *adv*, **bellicoseness** *n*, **bellicosity** *n*

-bellied /-belid‖-belɪd/ *comb form* (*adj* → *adj*) having (such) a belly <*a big*-bellied *man*>

belligerence /bə'lij(ə)rəns‖bə'lɪdʒ(ə)rəns/, **belligerency** /-si‖-sɪ/ *n* **1** an aggressive or truculent attitude, atmosphere, or disposition **2** the state of being at war or in conflict; *specif* the status of a legally recognized belligerent

bel'ligerent /-rənt‖-rənt/ *adj* **1** engaged in legally recognized war **2** inclined to or exhibiting assertiveness, hostility, or combativeness – **belligerent** *n*, **belligerently** *adv*

bellow /'beloh‖'beləʊ/ *vi* **1** to make the loud deep hollow sound characteristic of a bull **2** to shout in a deep voice ~*vt* to bawl – **bellow** *n*

bellows /'belohz‖'beləʊz/ *n, pl* **bellows 1** a device that by alternate expansion and contraction supplies a current of air – often pl with sing. meaning **2** a pleated expandable part in a camera

'**bell ˌpush** *n* a button that is pushed to ring a bell

¹**belly** /'beli‖'belɪ/ *n* **1a** ABDOMEN 1 **b(1)** the undersurface of an animal's body **b(2)** a cut of pork consisting of this part of the body **c** the womb, uterus **d** the stomach and associated organs **2** an internal cavity; the interior **3** a surface or object curved or rounded like a human belly

²**belly** *vb* to swell, fill <*the sails* bellied>

¹'**bellyˌache** /-ˌayk‖-ˌeɪk/ *n* colic

²**bellyache** *vi* to complain whiningly or peevishly; find fault – infml – **bellyacher** *n*

'**belly ˌbutton** *n* NAVEL 1 – infml

'**belly ˌdance** *n* a usu solo dance emphasizing movements of the belly – **belly dance** *vi*, **belly dancer** *n*

'**belly ˌflop** *n* a dive into water in which the front of the body strikes flat against the surface – **belly flop** *vi*

'**bellyful** /-f(ə)l‖-f(ə)l/ *n* an excessive amount <*a* ~ *of advice*> – infml

'**belly-ˌland** *vi* to land an aircraft on its undersurface without the use of landing gear – **belly landing** *n*

'**belly ˌlaugh** *n* a deep hearty laugh

belong /bi'long‖bɪ'lɒŋ/ *vi* **1** to be in a proper situation (e g according to ability or social qualification), position, or place **2** to be attached or bound *to* by birth, allegiance, dependency, or membership **3** to be an attribute, part, or function of a person or thing <*nuts and bolts* ~ *to a car*> **4** to be properly classified <*whales* ~ *among the mammals*> – **belong to** to be the property of

belonging /bi'long·ing‖bɪ'lɒŋɪŋ/ *n* **1** a possession – usu pl **2** close or intimate relationship <*a sense of* ~>

beloved /bi'luvid, bi'luvd‖bɪ'lʌvɪd, bɪ'lʌvd/ *n or adj, pl* **beloved** (sby) dearly loved – usu in fml or religious contexts

¹**below** /bi'loh‖bɪ'ləʊ/ *adv* **1** in, on, or to a lower place, floor, or deck; *specif* on earth or in or to Hades or hell **2** UNDER 2 **3** under the surface of the water or earth

²**below** *prep* **1** in or to a lower place than; under **2** inferior to (e g in rank) **3** not suitable to the rank of; BENEATH 2 **4** covered by; underneath **5** downstream from **6** UNDER 4 <~ *the age of 18*>

³**below** *n, pl* **below** *the* thing or matter written or discussed lower on the same page or on a following page

¹**belt** /belt‖belt/ *n* **1** a strip of material worn round the waist or hips or over the shoulder for decoration or to hold sthg (e g clothing or a weapon) **2** an endless band of tough flexible material for transmitting motion and power or conveying materials **3** an area characterized by some distinctive feature (e g of culture, geology, or life forms); *esp* one suited to a specified crop – **belted** *adj*, **beltless** *adj* – **below the belt** in an unfair way <*alluding to his past misdeeds in that way was really hitting* below the belt> – **under one's belt** as part of one's experience; having been attained

²**belt** *vt* **1a** to encircle or fasten with a belt **b** to strap on **2a** to beat (as if) with a belt; thrash **b** to strike, hit – infml **3** to sing in a forceful manner or style – usu + *out*; infml ~*vi* to move or act in a vigorous or violent manner – infml

³**belt** *n* a jarring blow; a whack – infml

belting /'belting‖'beltɪŋ/ *n* **1** belts collectively **2** material for belts

belt up *vi, Br* SHUT UP – infml

bemoan /bi'mohn‖bɪ'məʊn/ *vt* to express regret, displeasure, or deep grief over; lament

bemuse /bi'myoohz‖bɪ'mjuːz/ *vt* to make confused; bewilder – **bemusedly** *adv*, **bemusement** *n*

¹**bench** /bench‖bentʃ/ *n* **1a** a long usu backless seat (e g of wood or stone) for 2 or more people **b** a thwart in a boat **2a** *often cap* **2a(1)** a judge's seat in court **a(2)** the office of judge or magistrate <*appointed to the* ~> **b** *sing or pl*

in constr the judges or magistrates **b(1)** hearing a particular case **b(2)** collectively **3a(1)** a seat for an official (e g a judge or magistrate) **a(2)** the office or dignity of such an official **b** any of the long seats on which members sit in Parliament **4** a long worktable

[2]bench *vt* **1** to exhibit (a dog) at a show **2** *NAm* to remove from or keep out of a game

bencher /'benchə‖'bentʃə/ *n, Br* any of the chief or governing members of any of the Inns of Court

'benchˌmark /-ˌmahk‖-ˌmɑːk/ *n* **1** a point of reference (e g a mark on a permanent object indicating height above sea level) from which measurements may be made, esp in surveying **2** sthg that serves as a standard by which others may be measured

[1]bend /bend‖bend/ *n* any of various knots for fastening one rope to another or to an object

[2]bend *vb* **bent** /bent‖bent/ *vt* **1** to force into or out of a curve or angle **2** to fasten <~ *a sail to its yard*> **3** to make submissive; subdue **4a** to cause to turn from a course; deflect **b** to guide or turn towards sthg; direct <*he* bent *his steps homewards*> **5** to direct strenuously or with interest; apply <bent *themselves to the task*> **6** to alter or modify to make more acceptable, esp to oneself <~ *the rules*> ~ *vi* **1** to move or curve out of a straight line or position **2** to incline the body, esp in submission; bow **3** to yield, compromise – **bend over backwards** to make extreme efforts

[3]bend *n* **1** bending or being bent **2** a curved part, esp of a road or stream **3** *pl but sing or pl in constr* CAISSON DISEASE <*a case of the* ~s> – **round the bend** mad, crazy – infml <*thought his friends must have gone* round the bend>

[1]beneath /bi'neeth‖bɪ'niːθ/ *adv* **1** in or to a lower position; below **2** directly under; underneath

[2]beneath *prep* **1a** in or to a lower position than; below **b** directly under, esp so as to be close or touching **2** not suitable to; unworthy of <~ *contempt*> **3** under the control, pressure, or influence of

Benedictine /ˌbeni'dikteen, -tin‖ˌbenɪ'dɪktiːn, -tɪn/ *n* **1** a monk or a nun of any of the congregations following the rule of St Benedict and devoted esp to scholarship **2** *often not cap* a brandy-based liqueur made orig by French Benedictine monks – **Benedictine** *adj*

benediction /ˌbeni'diksh(ə)n‖ˌbenɪ'dɪkʃ(ə)n/ *n* **1** the invocation of a blessing; *esp* the short blessing with which public worship is concluded **2** *often cap* a Roman Catholic or Anglo-Catholic devotion including the exposition of the Host and the blessing of the people with it

benefaction /ˌbeni'faksh(ə)n‖ˌbenɪ'fækʃ(ə)n/ *n* **1** the act of doing good, esp by generous donation **2** a benefit conferred; *esp* a charitable donation [Late Latin *benefactio*, fr Latin *bene* well + *facere* to do]

benefactor /'beniˌfaktə‖'benɪˌfæktə/, *fem* **benefactress** /-tris‖-trɪs/ *n* one who gives aid; *esp* one who makes a gift or bequest to a person, institution, etc

benefice /'benifis‖'benɪfɪs/ *n* an ecclesiastical office to which an income is attached – **benefice** *vt*

beneficent /bi'nefis(ə)nt‖bɪ'nefɪs(ə)nt/ *adj* doing or producing good; *esp* performing acts of kindness and charity – **beneficently** *adv*, **beneficence** *n*

beneficial /ˌbeni'fish(ə)l‖ˌbenɪ'fɪʃ(ə)l/ *adj* **1** conferring benefits; conducive to personal or social well-being **2** receiving or entitling one to receive advantage or profit, esp from property <*the* ~ *owner of an estate*> – **beneficially** *adv*, **beneficialness** *n*

beneficiary /ˌbeni'fish(ə)ri‖ˌbenɪ'fɪʃ(ə)rɪ/ *n* **1** one who benefits from sthg **2** one who receives the income or proceeds of a trust, will, or insurance policy – **beneficiary** *adj*

[1]benefit /'benifit‖'benɪfɪt/ *n* **1a** sthg that promotes well-being; an advantage **b** good, welfare <*did it for his* ~> **2a** financial help in time of need (e g sickness, old age, or unemployment) **b** a payment or service provided for under an annuity, pension scheme, or insurance policy **3** an entertainment, game, or social event to raise funds for a person or cause

[2]benefit *vb* **-t-** (*NAm* **-t-, -tt-**) *vt* to be useful or profitable to ~*vi* to receive benefit

ˌbenefit of 'clergy *n* **1** the former clerical privilege of being tried in an ecclesiastical court **2** the ministration or sanction of the church – chiefly humor <*a couple living together without* ~>

ˌbenefit of the 'doubt *n* the assumption of innocence in the absence of complete proof of guilt

benevolent /bi'nevələnt‖bɪ'nevələnt/ *adj* **1** marked by or disposed to doing good; charitable **2** indicative of or characterized by goodwill – **benevolence** *n*, **benevolently** *adv*, **benevolentness** *n*

Bengali /ben'gawli‖ben'gɔːlɪ/ *n or adj* (a native or inhabitant or the modern Indo-European language) of Bengal

benighted /bi'nietid‖bɪ'naɪtɪd/ *adj* intellectually, morally, or socially unenlightened – **benightedly** *adv*, **benightedness** *n*

benign /bi'nien‖bɪ'naɪn/ *adj* **1** gentle, gracious **2** favourable, mild <*a* ~ *climate*> **3** *of a tumour* not malignant – **benignly** *adv*, **benignity** *n*

[1]bent /bent‖bent/ *n* **1a** a reedy grass **b** a stalk of stiff coarse grass **2** any of a genus of grasses including important pasture and lawn grasses

[2]bent *adj* **1** changed from an original straight or even condition by bending; curved **2** set *on* <*was* ~ *on winning*> **3** *Br* homosexual – slang **4** *Br* corrupt; CROOKED 2 – slang

[3]bent *n* **1** a strong inclination or interest; a bias **2** a special ability or talent

benumb /bi'num‖bɪ'nʌm/ *vt* to make inactive or numb; deaden

Benzedrine /'benzədrin, -dreen‖'benzədrɪn, -driːn/ *trademark* – used for a type of amphetamine

benzene /'benzeen‖'benziːn/ *n* an inflammable poisonous liquid hydrocarbon used in the synthesis of organic chemical compounds and as a solvent – **benzenoid** *adj*

benzine /'benzeen‖'benziːn/ *n* any of various volatile inflammable petroleum distillates used esp as solvents or motor fuels

benzoin /'benzoh·in, -'--, 'benzoyn‖'benzəʊɪn,

-ˈ--, ˈbenzɔɪn/ *n* (any of various trees found in SE Asia yielding) a hard fragrant yellowish balsamic resin used esp in medicines

bequeath /biˈkweeth, biˈkweedh‖bɪˈkwi:θ, bɪˈkwi:ð/ *vt* **1** to give or leave (sthg, esp personal property) by will **2** to transmit; HAND DOWN – **bequeathal** *n*

bequest /biˈkwest‖bɪˈkwest/ *n* **1** the act of bequeathing **2** a legacy

berate /biˈrayt‖bɪˈreɪt/ *vt* to scold or condemn vehemently

bereave /biˈreev‖bɪˈri:v/ *vt* **bereaved, bereft** /biˈreft‖bɪˈreft/ to rob or deprive *of* sby or sthg held dear, esp through death – **bereavement** *n*

beˈreaved *n or adj, pl* **bereaved** (*the* person) suffering the death of a loved one

bereft /biˈreft‖bɪˈreft/ *adj* **1** deprived or robbed *of*; completely without sthg **2** bereaved

beret /ˈberay‖ˈbereɪ/ *n* a cap with a tight headband, a soft full flat top, and no peak

beriberi /ˈberiˌberi, ˌ--ˈ--‖ˈberɪˌberɪ, ˌ--ˈ--/ *n* a deficiency disease marked by degeneration of the nerves and caused by a lack of or inability to assimilate vitamin B_1

berk /buhk‖bɜ:k/ *n, Br* a burk – slang

[1]**berry** /ˈberi‖ˈberɪ/ *n* **1a** a small, pulpy, and usu edible fruit (e g a strawberry or raspberry) **b** a simple fruit (e g a currant, grape, tomato, or banana) with a pulpy or fleshy pericarp – used technically in botany **2** an egg of a fish or lobster – **berried** *adj*

[2]**berry** *vi* **1** to bear or produce berries **2** to gather or seek berries

[1]**berserk** /bəˈzuhk, buh-‖bəˈzɜ:k, bɜ:-/ *n* any of a type of ancient Scandinavian warrior who fought in a wild frenzy [Old Norse *berserkr*, fr *björn* bear + *serkr* shirt]

[2]**berserk** *adj* frenzied, esp with anger; crazed – usu in *go berserk* – **berserk** *adv*

[1]**berth** /buhth‖bɜ:θ/ *n* **1** safe distance for manoeuvring maintained between a ship and another object **2** an allotted place for a ship when at anchor or at a wharf **3** a place for sleeping (e g a bunk), esp on a ship or train **4a** a place, position <*earned the number 2* ~> **b** a job, post – infml – **give a wide berth to** to remain at a safe distance from; avoid

[2]**berth** *vt* **1** to bring into a berth; dock **2** to allot a berth to ~*vi* to come into a berth

beryl /ˈberil‖ˈberɪl/ *n* a mineral that is a silicate of beryllium and aluminium, occurs as green, yellow, pink, or white crystals, and is used as a gemstone

beryllium /bəˈrili·əm‖bəˈrɪlɪəm/ *n* a light strong metallic element

beseech /biˈseech‖bɪˈsi:tʃ/ *vt* **besought** /-sawt‖-sɔ:t/, **beseeched** **1** to beg for urgently or anxiously **2** to request earnestly; implore – **beseechingly** *adv*

beset /biˈset‖bɪˈset/ *vt* **1** to trouble or assail constantly <~ *by fears*> **2** to surround and (prepare to) attack <~ *by the enemy*> – **besetment** *n*

besetting /biˈseting‖bɪˈsetɪŋ/ *adj* constantly causing temptation or difficulty; continuously present

beside /biˈsied‖bɪˈsaɪd/ *prep* **1a** by the side of <*walk* ~ *me*> **b** in comparison with **c** on a par with **d** unconnected with; wide of <~ *the point*> **2** besides – **beside oneself** in a state of extreme agitation or excitement

[1]**beˈsides** *adv* **1** as an additional factor or circumstance <*has a wife and 6 children* ~> **2** moreover, furthermore

[2]**besides** *prep* **1** other than; unless we are to mention <*who* ~ *John would say that?*> **2** as an additional circumstance to <~ *being old, she is losing her sight*>

besiege /biˈseej‖bɪˈsi:dʒ/ *vt* **1** to surround with armed forces **2a** to crowd round; surround closely **b** to press with questions, requests, etc; importune – **besieger** *n*

besmirch /biˈsmuhch‖bɪˈsmɜ:tʃ/ *vt* to sully, soil

besom /ˈbeez(ə)m‖ˈbi:z(ə)m/ *n* BROOM 2; *esp* one made of twigs

besotted /biˈsotid‖bɪˈsɒtɪd/ *adj* **1** made dull or foolish, esp by infatuation **2** drunk, intoxicated

bespatter /biˈspatə‖bɪˈspætə/ *vt* to spatter

bespeak /biˈspeek‖bɪˈspi:k/ *vt* **bespoke** /-ˈspohk‖-ˈspəʊk/; **bespoken** /-ˈspohkən‖-ˈspəʊkən/ **1** to hire, engage, or claim beforehand **2** to indicate, signify <*her performance* ~s *considerable practice*> ***USE*** fml

bespoke /biˈspohk‖bɪˈspəʊk/ *adj, Br* **1** made-to-measure; *broadly* made or arranged according to particular requirements **2** dealing in or producing articles that are made to measure <*a* ~ *tailor*>

[1]**best** /best‖best/ *adj, superlative of* GOOD **1** excelling all others (e g in ability, quality, integrity, or usefulness) <*the* ~ *student*> **2** most productive of good <*what is the* ~ *thing to do*> **3** most, largest <*for the* ~ *part of a week*> **4** reserved for special occasions <*got out the* ~ *sherry glasses*>

[2]**best** *adv, superlative of* WELL **1** in the best manner; to the best extent or degree <*a Wednesday would suit me* ~> **2** BETTER 2 <*we'd* ~ *go*> – **as best** in the best way <*climbed over* as best *he could*>

[3]**best** *n, pl* **best** **1** the best state or part <*never at my* ~ *before breakfast*> <*the* ~ *of life is over at 20*> **2** sby or sthg that is best <*can ride with the* ~ *of them*> **3** the greatest degree of good or excellence <*always demand the* ~ *of my pupils*> **4** one's maximum effort <*did my* ~> **5** best clothes <*Sunday* ~> **6** a winning majority <*the* ~ *of 3 games*> – **at best** even under the most favourable circumstances; seen in the best light – **make the best of** to cope with an unfavourable situation in the best and most optimistic manner possible

[4]**best** *vt* to get the better of; outdo

bestial /ˈbesti·əl‖ˈbestɪəl/ *adj* **1** of beasts **2** marked by brutal or inhuman instincts or desires; *specif* sexually depraved – **bestialize** *vt*, **bestially** *adv*

bestiality /ˌbestiˈaləti‖ˌbestɪˈæləti/ *n* bestial behaviour; *specif* sexual relations between a human being and an animal

bestiary /ˈbesti·əri‖ˈbestɪərɪ/ *n* a medieval allegorical or moralizing work about real or imaginary animals

bestir /biˈstuh‖bɪˈstɜ:/ *vt* to stir up;

rouse to action

ˌbest ˈman *n* the principal attendant of a bridegroom at a wedding

bestow /biˈstoh‖bɪˈstəʊ/ *vt* to present as a gift – usu + *on* or *upon* – **bestowal** *n*

bestrew /biˈstrooh‖bɪˈstruː/ *vt* **bestrewed; bestrewed, bestrewn** /-ˈstroohn‖-ˈstruːn/ **1** to strew **2** to lie scattered over

bestride /biˈstried‖bɪˈstraɪd/ *vt* **bestrode** / -ˈstrohd‖-ˈstrəʊd/; **bestridden** / -ˈstridən‖ -ˈstrɪdən/ **1** to ride, sit, or stand astride; straddle **2** to tower over; dominate

ˌbest-ˈseller *n* **1** sthg, esp a book, which has sold in very large numbers, usu over a given period **2** an author or performer whose works sell in very large numbers – **best-selling** *adj*

¹bet /bet‖bet/ *n* **1a** the act of risking a sum of money or other stake on the forecast outcome of a future event (e g a race or contest), esp in competition with a second party **b** a stake so risked **c** an outcome or result on which a stake is gambled **2** an opinion, belief *<my ~ is it will pour with rain>* **3** a plan of action; course *<your best ~ is to call a plumber>* – infml

²bet *vb* **bet** *also* **betted; -tt-** *vt* **1** to stake as a bet – usu + *on* or *against* **2** to make a bet with (sby) **3** to be convinced that *<I ~ they don't turn up>* – infml *~vi* to lay a bet – **bet one's bottom dollar** to be virtually certain – infml – **you bet** you may be sure; certainly – slang

beta /ˈbeetə‖ˈbiːtə; *NAm usu* ˈbaytə‖ˈbeɪtə/ *n* the 2nd letter of the Greek alphabet

betake /biˈtayk‖bɪˈteɪk/ *vt* **betook** /-ˈtook‖ -ˈtʊk/; **betaken** /-ˈtaykən‖-ˈteɪkən/ to cause (oneself) to go – fml

betel /ˈbeetl‖ˈbiːtl/ *n* a climbing pepper whose leaves are chewed together with betel nut and lime, esp by SE Asians, to stimulate the flow of saliva

ˈbetel ˌnut *n* the astringent seed of the betel palm

ˈbetel ˌpalm *n* an Asiatic palm that has an orange-coloured fruit

bête noire /ˌbet ˈnwah‖ˌbet ˈnwɑː/ *n, pl* **bêtes noires** /~/ a person or thing strongly detested [French, lit., black beast]

bethink /biˈthingk‖bɪˈθɪŋk/ *vt* **bethought** / -ˈthawt‖-ˈθɔːt/ *archaic* to cause (oneself) to be reminded or to consider – usu + *of*

betide /biˈtied‖bɪˈtaɪd/ *vt* to happen to; befall *<woe ~ them if they're late!>* *~vi* to happen, esp as if by fate *<we shall remain friends, whatever may ~>* ***USE*** fml or poetic; used only in the 3rd pers sing. pres subj and infin

betoken /biˈtohkən‖bɪˈtəʊkən/ *vt* **1** to give evidence of; show **2** to presage, portend

betray /biˈtray‖bɪˈtreɪ/ *vt* **1** to deceive, lead astray **2a** to deliver to an enemy by treachery **b** to be a traitor to *<~ed his people>* **3a** to fail or desert, esp in time of need **b** to disappoint the hopes, expectation, or confidence of **4a** to be a sign of (sthg one would like to hide) **b** to disclose, deliberately or unintentionally, in violation of confidence – **betrayal** *n*, **betrayer** *n*

betroth /biˈtrohth, -ˈtrohdh‖bɪˈtrəʊθ, -ˈtrəʊð/ *vt* **betrothed** /-dhd‖-ðd/, **betrothing** /-dhing‖-ðɪŋ/ to promise to marry or give in marriage

betrothal /biˈtrohdhəl‖bɪˈtrəʊðəl/ *n* a mutual promise or contract for a future marriage

beˈtrothed *n* the person to whom one is betrothed

¹better /ˈbetə‖ˈbetə/ *adj, comparative of* GOOD *or of* WELL **1** more than half *<for the ~ part of a month>* **2** improved in health; recovered **3** of greater quality, ability, integrity, usefulness, etc

²better *adv, comparative of* WELL **1** in a better manner; to a better extent or degree **2a** to a higher or greater degree *<he knows the story ~ than you do>* **b** more wisely or usefully *<is ~ avoided>* *<I'd ~ not go>*

³better *n, pl* **better**, (1b) **betters** **1a** sthg better **b** one's superior, esp in merit or rank – usu pl **2** *the* advantage, victory *<get the ~ of him>* – **for better or for worse** whatever the outcome

⁴better *vt* **1** to make better: e g **1a** to make more tolerable or acceptable *<trying to ~ the lot of slum dwellers>* **b** to make more complete or perfect **2** to surpass in excellence; excel *~vi* to become better

ˈbetterment /-mənt‖-mənt/ *n* an improvement

¹between /biˈtween‖bɪˈtwiːn/ *prep* **1a** through the common action of; jointly engaging *<~ them, they managed to lay the carpet>* **b** in shares to each of *<divided ~ his 4 children>* **2a** in or into the time, space, or interval that separates *<in ~ the rafters>* **b** in intermediate relation to *<a colour ~ blue and grey>* **3a** from one to the other of *<travelling ~ London and Paris>* **b** serving to connect or separate *<dividing line ~ fact and fancy>* **4** in point of comparison of *<not much to choose ~ them>* **5** taking together the total effect of; WHAT WITH *<kept very busy ~ cooking, writing, and gardening>* – **between you and me** in confidence

²between *adv* in or into an intermediate space or interval

betwixt /biˈtwikst‖bɪˈtwɪkst/ *adv or prep, archaic* between

beˌtwixt and beˈtween *adv or adj* in a midway position; neither one thing nor the other

¹bevel /ˈbevl‖ˈbevl/ *n* **1** the angle or slant that one surface or line makes with another when they are not at right angles **2** an instrument consisting of 2 rules or arms jointed together and opening to any angle for drawing angles or adjusting surfaces to be given a bevel

²bevel *vb* **-ll-** (*NAm* **-l-**, **-ll-**) *vt* to cut or shape to a bevel *~vi* to incline, slant

ˈbevel ˌgear *n* (a system of gears having) a pair of toothed wheels that work shafts inclined to each other

beverage /ˈbev(ə)rij‖ˈbev(ə)rɪdʒ/ *n* a liquid for drinking; *esp* one that is not water

bevy /ˈbevi‖ˈbevɪ/ *n* a group or collection, esp of girls

bewail /biˈwayl‖bɪˈweɪl/ *vt* to express deep sorrow for; lament

beware /biˈweə‖bɪˈweə/ *vb* to be wary (of) – usu in imperative and infinitive

bewilder /biˈwildə‖bɪˈwɪldə/ *vt* to perplex or confuse, esp by a complexity, variety, or multitude of objects or considerations – **bewilderedly** *adv*, **bewilderingly** *adv*, **bewilderment** *n*

bewitch /biˈwich‖bɪˈwɪtʃ/ *vt* **1a** to influence or affect, esp injuriously, by witchcraft **b** to cast a spell over **2** to attract as if by the power of witchcraft; enchant – **bewitchingly** *adv*, **bewitchment** *n*

[1]**beyond** /bee'(y)ond‖bi:(j)'ɒnd/ *adv* **1** on or to the farther side; farther **2** as an additional amount; besides

[2]**beyond** *prep* **1** on or to the farther side of; at a greater distance than **2a** out of the reach or sphere of <~ *repair*> **b** in a degree or amount surpassing <~ *my wildest dreams*> **c** out of the comprehension of **3** BESIDES 2 **4** later than; past

[3]**beyond** *n* **1** sthg that lies beyond **2** sthg that lies outside the scope of ordinary experience; *specif* [2]HEREAFTER

bezique /bə'zeek‖bə'zi:k/ *n* a card game for 2 people that is played with a double pack of 64 cards

bhang /bang‖bæŋ/ *n* a mild form of cannabis used esp in India

[1]**bi-** /bie-‖baɪ-/ *prefix* **1a** two <bi*lingual*> **b** appearing or occurring every 2 <bi*monthly*> **c** into two parts <bi*sect*> **2a** twice; doubly; on both sides <bi*convex*> **b** appearing or occurring twice in <bi*weekly*> – often disapproved of in this sense because of the likelihood of confusion with sense 1b; compare SEMI- **3** located between, involving, or affecting 2 (specified symmetrical parts) <bi*aural*>

[2]**bi-**, **bio-** *comb form* life <bio*graphy*>; living organisms or tissue <bio*logy*>

[1]**bias** /'bie·əs‖'baɪəs/ *n* **1** a line diagonal to the grain of a fabric, often used in the cutting of garments for smoother fit – usu + *the* <*cut on the* ~> **2a** an inclination of temperament or outlook; *esp* a personal prejudice **b** a bent, tendency **c** a tendency of an estimate to deviate in one direction from a true value (e g because of non-random sampling) **3** (the property of shape or weight causing) the tendency of a bowl used in the game of bowls to take a curved path when rolled

[2]**bias** *adj, esp of fabrics and their cut* diagonal, slanting – **bias** *adv*

[3]**bias** *vt* -s-, -ss- **1** to give a prejudiced outlook to **2** to influence unfairly

bib /bib‖bɪb/ *n* **1** a covering (e g of cloth or plastic) placed over a child's front to protect his/her clothes **2** a small rectangular section of a garment (e g an apron or dungarees) extending above the waist

bible /'biebl‖'baɪbl/ *n* **1a** *cap* the sacred book of Christians comprising the Old Testament and the New Testament **b** any book containing the sacred writings of a religion **2** *cap* a copy or an edition of the Bible **3** an authoritative book <*the fisherman's* ~> [Old French, fr Medieval Latin *biblia*, fr Greek, pl of *biblion* book, diminutive of *byblos* papyrus, book, fr *Byblos*, ancient Phoenician city from which papyrus was exported]

biblical /'biblikl‖'bɪblɪkl/ *adj* **1** of or in accord with the Bible **2** suggestive of the Bible or Bible times – **biblically** *adv*

bibliography /bibli'ogrəfi‖bɪblɪ'ɒgrəfɪ/ *n* **1** the history, identification, or description of writings and publications **2** a list of writings relating to a particular topic, written by a particular author, issued by a particular publisher, etc **3** a list of the works referred to in a text or consulted by the author in its production – **bibliographer** *n*, **bibliographic, bibliographical** *adj*, **bibliographically** *adv*

bibliophile /'bibli·ə,fiel‖'bɪblɪə,faɪl/ *n* a lover or collector of books – **bibliophilic** *adj*, **bibliophilism** *n*, **bibliophilist** *n*, **bibliophily** *n*

bibulous /'bibyooləs‖'bɪbjʊləs/ *adj* prone to over-indulgence in alcoholic drinks – **bibulously** *adv*, **bibulousness** *n*

bicameral /,bie'kam(ə)r(ə)l‖,baɪ'kæm(ə)r(ə)l/ *adj* having 2 legislative chambers – **bicameralism** *n*

bicarb /'bie,kahb‖'baɪ,kɑ:b/ *n* SODIUM BICARBONATE – infml

bicarbonate /bie'kahbənət‖baɪ'kɑ:bənət/ *n* an acid carbonate; *esp* SODIUM BICARBONATE

bicentenary /,biesen'teenəri, -'te-‖,baɪsen'ti:nərɪ, -'te-/ *n or adj* (the celebration) of a 200th anniversary

bicentennial /,biesen'teni·əl‖,baɪsen'tenɪəl/ *n or adj* (a) bicentenary

biceps /'bieseps‖'baɪseps/ *n* the large muscle at the front of the upper arm that bends the arm at the elbow when it contracts; *broadly* any muscle attached in 2 places at one end

bicker /'bikə‖'bɪkə/ *vi* to engage in petulant or petty argument – **bicker** *n*, **bickerer** *n*

bicycle /'biesikl‖'baɪsɪkl/ *vi or n* (to ride) a 2 wheeled pedal-driven vehicle with handlebars and a saddle – **bicycler** *n*, **bicyclist** *n*

[1]**bid** /bid‖bɪd/ *vb* **bade** /bad, bayd‖bæd, beɪd/, **bid**, (*3*) **bid; bidden** /'bidn‖'bɪdn/, **bid** *also* **bade; -dd-** *vt* **1a** to issue an order to; tell <*he did as he was* ~> **b** to invite to come **2** to give expression to <bade *him a tearful farewell*> **3a** to offer (a price) for payment or acceptance (e g at an auction) **b** to make a bid of or in (a suit at cards) ~ *vi* to make a bid – **bidder** *n* – **bid fair** to seem likely; show promise <*she* bids fair *to become extremely attractive*>

[2]**bid** *n* **1a** the act of one who bids **b** a statement of what one will give or take for sthg; *esp* an offer of a price **c** sthg offered as a bid **2** an opportunity to bid **3** (an announcement of) the amount of tricks to be won, suit to be played in, etc in a card game **4** an attempt to win or achieve sthg

biddable /'bidəbl‖'bɪdəbl/ *adj* **1** easily led or controlled; docile **2** capable of being reasonably bid – **biddably** *adv*, **biddability** *n*

bidding /'biding‖'bɪdɪŋ/ *n* order, command <*came at my* ~>

bide /bied‖baɪd/ *vi* **bode** /bohd‖bəʊd/, **bided** /'biedid‖'baɪdɪd/; **bided** *archaic or dial* to remain awhile; stay – **bider** *n* – **bide one's time** to wait until the appropriate time comes to initiate action or to proceed

bidet /'beeday‖'bi:deɪ/ *n* a low fixture used esp for bathing the external genitals and the anus

biennial /bie'eni·əl‖baɪ'enɪəl/ *adj* **1** occurring every 2 years **2** *of a plant* growing vegetatively during the first year and fruiting and dying during the second – **biennial** *n*, **biennially** *adv*

bier /biə‖bɪə/ *n* a stand on which a corpse or coffin is placed; *also* a coffin together with its stand

biff /bif‖bɪf/ *n* a whack, blow – infml – **biff** *vt*
bifocal /bieˈfohk(ə)l‖baɪˈfəʊk(ə)l/ *adj* **1** having 2 focal lengths **2** having 1 part that corrects for near vision and 1 for distant vision <*a ~ lens*>
biˈfocals *n pl* glasses with bifocal lenses
bifurcate /ˈbiefuhˌkayt, ˈbi-, -fə-‖ˈbaɪfɜːˌkeɪt, ˈbɪ-, -fə-/ *vi* to divide into 2 branches or parts – **bifurcate** *adj*, **bifurcation** *n*
[1]**big** /big‖bɪg/ *adj* **-gg- 1** of great force <*a ~ storm*> **2a** large in bulk or extent; *also* large in number or amount <*a ~ house*> <*a ~ fleet*> **b** conducted on a large scale <*~ business*> **c** important in influence, standing, or wealth <*the ~ 4 banks*> **3a** advanced in pregnancy <*~ with child*> **b** full to bursting; swelling <*~ with rage*> **4** *of the voice* loud and resonant **5a** elder <*my ~ sister*> **b** older, grown-up <*when I'm a ~ girl, I'm going to be a nurse*> **6a** chief, outstanding <*the ~ issue of the campaign*> **b** of great importance or significance <*a ~ decision*> **7a** pretentious, boastful <*~ talk*> **b** magnanimous, generous <*that's very ~ of you*> **8** popular <*Frank Sinatra is very ~ in Las Vegas*> – infml – **biggish** *adj*, **bigness** *n*
[2]**big** *adv* **1a** outstandingly <*made it ~ in New York*> **b** on a grand scale <*think ~!*> **2** pretentiously <*he talks ~*> *USE* infml
bigamy /ˈbigəmi‖ˈbɪgəmɪ/ *n* the crime of going through a marriage ceremony with one person while legally married to another [Medieval Latin *bigamia*, fr Latin *bi-* two + Greek *gamos* marriage] – **bigamist** *n*, **bigamous** *adj*, **bigamously** *adv*
ˌbig ˈbang ˌtheory *n* a theory in cosmology: the universe originated from the explosion of a single mass of material so that the components are still flying apart
ˌBig ˈBrother *n* (the leader of) a ruthless all-powerful government
ˌbig ˈdipper /ˈdipə‖ˈdɪpə/ *n* **1** *often cap B&D, Br* ROLLER COASTER **2** *cap B&D, NAm* URSA MAJOR
ˌbig ˈend *n* the end of an engine's connecting rod nearest the crankpin
ˌbig ˈgame *n* **1** large animals hunted or fished for sport **2** an important objective; *esp* one involving risk
ˈbigˌhead /-ˌhed‖-ˌhed/ *n* a conceited person – infml
ˈbig ˌhead *n* an exaggerated opinion of one's importance – infml – **bigheaded** *adj*
bight /biet‖baɪt/ *n* **1a** the middle part of a slack rope **b** a loop in a rope **2** (a hollow formed by) a bend of a river, coast, mountain chain, etc
ˌbig ˈname *n* a very famous or important performer or personage – **big-name** *adj*
bigot /ˈbigət‖ˈbɪgət/ *n* one who is obstinately or intolerantly devoted to his/her own religion, opinion, etc – **bigoted** *adj*, **bigotedly** *adv*, **bigotry** *n*
ˌbig ˈstick *n* (the threat of using) force – infml
ˈbig ˌtime *n* *the* highest rank, esp among entertainers – infml – **big-time** *adj*, **big-timer** *n*
ˌbig ˈtop *n* the main tent of a circus
ˌbig ˈtree *n* a very large Californian evergreen tree of the pine family
ˈbigˌwig /-ˌwig‖-ˌwɪg/ *n* an important person – infml
[1]**bijou** /ˈbeeˌzhooh‖ˈbiːˌʒuː/ *n, pl* **bijous, bijoux** /-ˌzhooh(z)‖-ˌʒuː(z)/ a small dainty usu ornamental piece of delicate workmanship; a jewel
[2]**bijou** *adj, esp of a house* desirably elegant and usu small
bike /biek‖baɪk/ *vi or n* (to ride) **1** a bicycle **2** a motorcycle
bikini /biˈkeeni‖bɪˈkiːnɪ/ *n* a woman's brief 2-piece garment resembling bra and pants worn for swimming or sunbathing [French, fr *Bikini*, atoll of the Marshall islands]
bilateral /bieˈlat(ə)rəl‖baɪˈlæt(ə)rəl/ *adj* **1** having 2 sides **2** BIPARTITE 2 – **bilateralism** *n*, **bilaterally** *adv*, **bilateralness** *n*
bilberry /ˈbilb(ə)ri‖ˈbɪlb(ə)rɪ/ *n* (the bluish edible fruit of) a dwarf bushy European shrub that grows on moorland
bile /biel‖baɪl/ *n* **1** a yellow or greenish fluid secreted by the liver into the intestines to aid the digestion of fats **2** inclination to anger
bilge /bilj‖bɪldʒ/ *n* **1** the (space inside the) lowest usu rounded part of a ship's hull between the keel and the vertical sides **2** stale or worthless remarks or ideas – infml
bilingual /bieˈling·gwəl‖baɪˈlɪŋgwəl/ *adj* **1** of, containing, or expressed in 2 languages **2** using or able to use 2 languages with the fluency of a native speaker – **bilingual** *n*, **bilingualism** *n*, **bilingually** *adv*
bilious /ˈbili·əs‖ˈbɪlɪəs/ *adj* **1** marked by or suffering from disordered liver function, esp excessive secretion of bile **2** peevish, ill-natured **3** *of colours* extremely distasteful; sickly – infml – **biliously** *adv*, **biliousness** *n*
bilk /bilk‖bɪlk/ *vt* to cheat out of what is due – **bilker** *n*
[1]**bill** /bil‖bɪl/ *n* **1** (a mouthpart resembling) the jaws of a bird together with variously shaped and coloured horny coverings and often specialized for a particular diet **2** a projection of land like a beak
[2]**bill** *vi* to caress affectionately – chiefly in *bill and coo*
[3]**bill** *n* **1** a long staff with a hook-shaped blade used as a weapon up to the 18th c **2** a billhook
[4]**bill** *n* **1** a draft of a law presented to a legislature **2** a paper carrying a statement of particulars **3a** (an itemized account of) charges due for goods or services **b** a statement of a creditor's claim **4a** a written or printed notice advertising an event of interest to the public (e g a theatrical entertainment) **b** an item (e g a film or play) in a programme entertainment **5** *chiefly NAm* [2]NOTE 3c
[5]**bill** *vt* **1** to submit a bill of charges to **2a** to advertise, esp by posters or placards **b** to arrange for the presentation of as part of a programme
ˈbillˌboard /-ˌbawd‖-ˌbɔːd/ *n, chiefly NAm* HOARDING 2
[1]**billet** /ˈbilit‖ˈbɪlɪt/ *n* **1a** an official order directing that a member of a military force be provided with board and lodging (e g in a private home) **b** quarters assigned (as if) by a billet **2** a position, job <*a lucrative ~*>

[2]**billet** *vt* to provide (e g soldiers) with a billet
[3]**billet** *n* **1** a small thick piece of wood (e g for firewood) **2** a usu small bar of iron, steel, etc
billet-doux /ˌbili 'dooh, ˌbeeyay‖ˌbılı 'du:, ˌbi:jeı/ *n, pl* **billets-doux** /~/ a love letter [French *billet doux*, lit., sweet letter]
'**bill**ˌ**fold** /-ˌfohld‖-ˌfəʊld/ *n, NAm* WALLET 1
'**bill**ˌ**hook** /-ˌhook‖-ˌhʊk/ *n* a cutting tool, used esp for pruning, that has a blade with a hooked point
billiards /'bilyədz‖'bıljədz/ *n pl but sing in constr* any of several games played on an oblong table by driving small balls against one another or into pockets with a cue; *specif* one with 3 balls in which scores are made by causing a cue ball to hit 2 object balls in succession [Middle French *billard* billiard cue, billiards, fr *bille* log] – **billiard** *adj*
billion /'bilyən‖'bıljən/ *n* **1** a thousand millions (10^9) **2** an indefinitely large number – often pl with sing. meaning **3** *Br* a million millions (10^{12}) – **billion** *adj*, **billionth** *adj or n*
ˌ**bill of ex'change** *n* an unconditional written order from one person to another to pay a specified sum of money to a designated person
ˌ**bill of 'fare** *n* a menu
ˌ**bill of 'lading** *n* a receipt signed usu by the agent or owner of a ship listing goods (to be) shipped
ˌ**bill of 'rights** *n, often cap B&R* a summary in law (e g the English Statute of 1689) of fundamental rights and privileges guaranteed by the state
ˌ**bill of 'sale** *n* a formal document for the conveyance or transfer of title to goods and personal property
[1]**billow** /'biloh‖'bıləʊ/ *n* **1** a great wave, esp in the open sea **2** a rolling swirling mass (e g of flame or smoke) – **billowy** *adj*
[2]**billow** *vb* to (cause to) rise, roll, bulge, or swell out (as if) in billows
'**bill**ˌ**poster** /-ˌpohstə‖-ˌpəʊstə/ *n* one who pastes up advertisements and public notices on hoardings – **billposting** *n*
[1]**billy** /'bili‖'bılı/, '**billy** ˌ**club** *n, NAm* TRUNCHEON 2
[2]**billy,** *chiefly Austr* '**billy**ˌ**can** *n* a can of metal or enamelware with an arched handle and a lid, used for outdoor cooking or carrying food or liquid
'**billy** ˌ**goat** *n* a male goat – infml
biltong /'biltong‖'bıltɒŋ/ *n, chiefly SAfr* strips of lean meat dried in the sun
bimetallic /ˌbiemi'talik‖ˌbaımı'tælık/ *adj* (of or being a device with a part) composed of 2 different metals, esp ones that expand by different amounts when heated – **bimetal** *adj or n*
bimonthly /ˌbie'munthli‖ˌbaı'mʌnθlı/ *adj or adv* (occurring) every 2 months or twice a month
[1]**bin** /bin‖bın/ *n* **1** a container used for storage (e g of flour, grain, bread, or coal) **2** a partitioned case or stand for storing and aging bottles of wine **3** *Br* a wastepaper basket, dustbin, or similar container for rubbish
[2]**bin** *vt* **-nn-** to put or store (esp bottled wine) in a bin
binary /'bienəri‖'baınərı/ *adj* **1** consisting of or marked by 2 things or parts **2a** of, being, or belonging to a system of numbers having 2 as its base <*the ~ digits 0 and 1*> **b** involving a choice or condition of 2 alternatives (e g on or off) <~ *logic*> **3** having 2 musical subjects or 2 complementary sections <~ *form*> – **binary** *n*
[1]**bind** /biend‖baınd/ *vb* **bound** /bownd‖baʊnd/ *vt* **1a** to make secure by tying (e g with cord) or tying together **b** to confine or restrict (as if) with bonds <*he was* bound *and thrown into prison*> **c** to put under a (legal) obligation <*we are all* bound *to keep the law*> **2** to wrap round with sthg (e g cloth) so as to enclose or cover **3** to encircle, gird **4a** to cause to stick together <*add an egg to ~ the mixture*> **b** to take up and hold (e g by chemical forces); combine with <*enzymes ~ their substrates*> **5** to constipate **6** to make binding; settle <*a deposit* ~s *the sale*> **7** to protect, strengthen, cover, or decorate with (a) binding **8** to cause to be attached (e g by gratitude or affection) ~ *vi* **1** to form a cohesive mass **2** to become hindered from free operation; jam **3** to complain – infml
[2]**bind** *n* a nuisance, bore – infml – **in a bind** *chiefly NAm* in trouble or difficulty – infml
binder /'biendə‖'baındə/ *n* **1** a person who binds books **2** a usu detachable cover (e g for holding sheets of paper) **3** sthg (e g tar or cement) that produces or promotes cohesion in loosely assembled substances
[1]**binding** /'biending‖'baındıŋ/ *n* a material or device used to bind: e g **a** a covering that fastens the leaves of a book **b** a narrow strip of fabric used to finish raw edges
[2]**binding** *adj* imposing an obligation <*a ~ promise*>
bind over *vt* to impose a specific legal obligation on <*he was* bound over *to keep the peace*>
'**bind**ˌ**weed** /-ˌweed‖-ˌwi:d/ *n* any of various twining plants with usu large showy trumpet-shaped flowers
binge /binj‖bındʒ/ *n* an unrestrained indulgence in sthg; *esp* a drunken revel – infml
[1]**bingo** /'bing·goh‖'bıŋgəʊ/ *interj* **1** – used to express the suddenness or unexpectedness of an event **2** – used as an exclamation to show that one has won a game of bingo
[2]**bingo** *n* a game of chance played with cards having numbered squares corresponding to numbers drawn at random and won by covering or marking off all or a predetermined number of such squares
binnacle /'binəkl‖'bınəkl/ *n* a case, stand, etc containing a ship's compass
binocular /bi'nokyoolə‖bı'nɒkjʊlə/ *adj* of, using, or adapted to the use of both eyes – **binocularly** *adv*
bi'noculars *n pl, pl* **binoculars** a binocular optical instrument; *esp* field glasses or opera glasses
binomial /bie'nohmyəl‖baı'nəʊmjəl/ *n or adj* (a mathematical expression) consisting of 2 terms connected by a plus sign or minus sign – **binomially** *adv*
bio- – see [2]BI-
biochemistry /ˌbie·oh'kemәstri‖ˌbaıəʊ-

'kemastrɪ/ *n* chemistry that deals with the chemical compounds and processes occurring in organisms – **biochemist** *n*, **biochemical** *adj*, **biochemically** *adv*

biodegradable /ˌbie·ohdee'graydəbl‖ˌbaɪəʊdiː'greɪdəbl/ *adj* capable of being broken down, esp into simpler harmless products, by the action of living beings (e g microorganisms) – **biodegradability** *n*, **biodegrade** *vb*, **biodegradation** *n*

ˌbiogeo'graphical /-jee·ə'grafikl‖-dʒiːə'græfɪkl/, **ˌbiogeo'graphic** *adj* of or being a geographical region viewed in terms of its plants and animals

biography /bie'ogrəfi‖baɪ'ɒgrəfɪ/ *n* **1** a usu written account of a person's life **2** biographical writing as a literary genre – **biographer** *n*, **biographical, biographic** *adj*, **biographically** *adv*

bioˌlogical 'warfare *n* warfare involving the use of (disease-causing) living organisms, or chemicals harmful to plants

biology /bie'oləji‖baɪ'ɒlədʒɪ/ *n* **1** a science that deals with the structure, function, development, distribution, and life processes of living organisms **2a** the plant and animal life of a region or environment **b** the biology of an organism or group [German *biologie*, fr Greek *bios* life + *logos* speech, reason] – **biologist** *n*, **biological** *adj*, **biologically** *adv*

bionic /bie'onik‖baɪ'ɒnɪk/ *adj* **1** involving bionics; *also* having or being a bionically designed part (e g a limb) **2** having exceptional abilities or powers – not used technically – **bionically** *adv*

bi'onics *n pl but sing or pl in constr* **1** a science concerned with the application of biological systems to engineering problems **2** the use of mechanical parts to replace or simulate damaged parts of a living thing

biorhythms /'bie·ohˌridh(ə)ms/ *n pl* regular fluctuations in the activity of underlying life processes, that are believed to influence behaviour and feelings

biosphere /'bie·əˌsfiə‖'baɪəˌsfɪə/ *n* the part of the world in which life exists

biotechnology /ˌbie·ohtek'noləji‖ˌbaɪəʊtek'nɒlədʒɪ/ *n* the use of living cells or microorganisms (e g bacteria) in industry and technology to manufacture drugs and chemicals, create energy, destroy waste matter, etc

bipartisan /ˌbie'pahtizn‖ˌbaɪ'pɑːtɪzn/ *adj* of or involving 2 parties

bipartite /ˌbie'pahtiet‖ˌbaɪ'pɑːtaɪt/ *adj* **1** being in 2 parts **2** *of a treaty, contract, etc between 2 parties* **2a** having 2 correspondent parts, one for each party **b** affecting both parties in the same way **3** cleft (almost) into 2 parts <*a* ~ *leaf*> – **bipartitely** *adv*, **bipartition** *n*

biped /'bieped‖'baɪped/ *n* a 2-footed animal – **biped, bipedal** *adj*

biplane /'bieˌplayn‖'baɪˌpleɪn/ *n* an aeroplane with 2 pairs of wings placed one above and usu slightly forward of the other

¹birch /buhch‖bɜːtʃ/ *n* **1** (the hard pale close-grained wood of) any of a genus of deciduous trees or shrubs typically having a layered outer bark that peels readily **2** a birch rod or bundle of twigs for flogging – **birch, birchen** *adj*

²birch *vt* to whip (as if) with a birch

bird /buhd‖bɜːd/ *n* **1** any of a class of warm-blooded vertebrates with the body more or less completely covered with feathers and the forelimbs modified as wings **2a** a (peculiar) fellow – chiefly infml **b** *chiefly Br* a girl – infml **3** a hissing or jeering expressive of disapproval or derision – chiefly in *give somebody the bird/get the bird*; infml **4** *Br* TIME 5b – slang – **birdlike** *adj*

'birdˌbrain /-ˌbrayn‖-ˌbreɪn/ *n* a silly or stupid person – infml – **birdbrained** *adj*

'bird ˌdog *n, NAm* a gundog trained to hunt or retrieve birds

¹birdie /'buhdi‖'bɜːdɪ/ *n* **1** a (little) bird – used esp by or to children **2** a golf score of 1 stroke less than par on a hole

²birdie *vt* **birdieing** /'buhdi·ing‖'bɜːdɪɪŋ/ to play (a hole in golf) in 1 stroke under par

'birdˌlime /-ˌliem‖-ˌlaɪm/ *n* **1** a sticky substance that is smeared on twigs to snare small birds **2** the droppings of birds

ˌbird of 'paradise *n* any of numerous brilliantly coloured plumed birds of the New Guinea area

ˌbird of 'passage *n* **1** a migratory bird **2** a person who leads a wandering or unsettled life

ˌbird of 'prey *n* a hawk, vulture, or other bird that feeds on carrion or on meat taken by hunting

ˌbird's-eye 'view *n* **1** a view from above; an aerial view **2** a brief and general summary; an overview

'bird-ˌwatching *n* the observation or identification of birds in their natural environment – **bird-watcher** *n*

biretta /bi'retə‖bɪ'retə/ *n* a square cap with 3 ridges on top worn by (Roman Catholic) clergy

Biro /'bieroh‖'baɪrəʊ/ *trademark* – used for a ballpoint pen

birth /buhth‖bɜːθ/ *n* **1a** the emergence of a new individual from the body of its parent **b** the act or process of bringing forth young from within the body **2** the fact of being born, esp at a particular time or place <*a Frenchman by* ~> **3** (noble) lineage or extraction <*marriage between equals in* ~> **4** a beginning, start <*the* ~ *of an idea*> **5** natural or inherited tendency <*an artist by* ~>

'birth conˌtrol *n* control of the number of children born, esp by preventing or lessening the frequency of conception; *broadly* contraception

birthday /'buhthday, -di‖'bɜːθdeɪ, -dɪ/ *n* **1a** the day of a person's birth **b** a day of origin **2** an anniversary of a birth <*her 21st* ~>

'birthˌmark /-ˌmahk‖-ˌmɑːk/ *n* a usu red or brown blemish on the skin at birth

'birthˌrate /-ˌrayt‖-ˌreɪt/ *n* the number of (live) births per unit of population (e g 1000 people) in a period of time (e g 1 year)

'birthˌright /-ˌriet‖-ˌraɪt/ *n* sthg (e g a privilege or possession) to which a person is entitled by birth

biscuit /'biskit‖'bɪskɪt/ *n* **1** earthenware or porcelain after the first firing and before glazing **2** a light yellowish brown colour **3** *Br* any of several variously-shaped small usu unleavened thin dry crisp bakery products that may be sweet or savoury **4** *NAm* a soft cake or bread (e g a scone) made without yeast

bisect /bie'sekt||baɪ'sekt/ *vt* to divide into 2 (equal) parts ~*vi* to cross, intersect – **bisection** *n*

bisexual /bie'seksyoo(ə)l, -sh(ə)l||baɪ'seksjʊ-(ə)l, -ʃ(ə)l/ *adj* **1a** possessing characteristics of both sexes **b** sexually attracted to both sexes **2** of or involving both sexes – **bisexual** *n*, **bisexually** *adv*, **bisexuality** *n*

bishop /'bishəp||'bɪʃəp/ *n* **1** a clergyman ranking above a priest, having authority to ordain and confirm, and typically governing a diocese **2** either of 2 chess pieces of each colour allowed to move diagonally across any number of consecutive unoccupied squares – **bishophood** *n*

bishopric /'bishəprik||'bɪʃəprɪk/ *n* **1** a diocese **2** the office of bishop

bismuth /'bizməth||'bɪzməθ/ *n* a heavy metallic element – **bismuthic** *adj*

bison /'biesn||'baɪsn/ *n, pl* **bison** **1** a large shaggy-maned European bovine mammal that is now nearly extinct **2** BUFFALO 2

[1]**bisque** /bisk||bɪsk/ *n* an advantage (e g an extra turn in croquet) allowed to an inferior player

[2]**bisque** *n* a thick cream soup (e g of shellfish or game)

[3]**bisque** *n* BISCUIT 1; *esp* a type of white unglazed ceramic ware

bistro /beestroh||bi:strəʊ/ *n, pl* **bistros** a small bar, restaurant, or tavern

[1]**bit** /bit||bɪt/ *n* **1** a bar of metal or occasionally rubber attached to the bridle and inserted in the mouth of a horse **2** the biting or cutting edge or part of a tool; *also* a replaceable drilling, boring, etc part of a compound tool **3** sthg that curbs or restrains **4** the part of a key that enters the lock and acts on the bolt and tumblers

[2]**bit** *vt* **-tt-** to put a bit in the mouth of (a horse)

[3]**bit** *n* **1a** a small piece or quantity of anything (e g food) **b(1)** a usu specified small coin <*a fivepenny* ~> **b(2)** a money unit worth $^1/_8$ of a US dollar **c** a part, section <*couldn't hear the next* ~> **2** sthg small or unimportant of its kind: e g **2a** a brief period; a while **b(1)** an indefinite usu small degree, extent, or amount <*is a* ~ *of a rascal*> **b(2)** an indefinite small fraction <*3 inches and a* ~> – infml **3** all the items, situations, or activities appropriate to a given style, role, etc <*rejected the whole love and marriage* ~> **4** a small but necessary piece of work <*doing their* ~ *for Britain by refusing a pay rise*> **5** a young woman – slang – **a bit 1** somewhat, rather <a bit *difficult*> – infml **2** the smallest or an insignificant amount or degree <*not* a bit *sorry*> – infml – **a bit much** a little more than one wants to endure – **a bit of all right** *Br* sby or sthg very pleasing; *esp* a sexually attractive person – infml – **bit by bit** little by little – **bit on the side** (a person with whom one has) occasional sexual intercourse usu outside marriage – **to bits** TO PIECES

[4]**bit** *n* (the physical representation in a computer or electronic memory of) a unit of computer information equivalent to the result of a choice between 2 alternatives (e g *on* or *off*) [*bi*nary digi*t*]

[1]**bitch** /bich||bɪtʃ/ *n* **1** the female of the dog or similar flesh-eating animals **2** a malicious, spiteful, and domineering woman **3** a complaint – infml

[2]**bitch** *vi* to complain – infml

bitchy /'bichi||'bɪtʃɪ/ *adj* characterized by malicious, spiteful, or arrogant behaviour – **bitchily** *adv*, **bitchiness** *n*

[1]**bite** /biet||baɪt/ *vb* **bit** /bit||bɪt/; **bitten** /'bit(ə)n||'bɪt(ə)n/ *also* **bit** *vt* **1a** to seize with teeth or jaws, so that they enter, grip, or wound **b** to sting with a fang or other specialized part of the body <*the midges are* biting *me*> **c** to remove or sever with the teeth **2** to cut or pierce (as if) with an edged weapon **3** to cause sharp pain or stinging discomfort to **4** to take strong hold of; grip ~ *vi* **1** to bite or have the habit of biting sthg <*does that dog* ~*?*> **2** *of a weapon or tool* to cut, pierce **3** to have a sharp penetrating effect <*the sauce really* ~s> **4** *of fish* to take a bait **5** to take or maintain a firm hold – **biter** *n* – **bite off more than one can chew** to undertake more than one can perform – **bite the dust 1** to fall dead, esp in battle **2** to be finished or defeated <*another of his schemes has* bitten the dust>

[2]**bite** *n* **1a** the amount of food taken with 1 bite; a morsel **b** a small amount of food; a snack **2** a wound made by biting **3** the hold or grip by which friction is created or purchase is obtained **4** a sharp incisive quality or effect

biting /'bieting||'baɪtɪŋ/ *adj* having the power to bite <*a* ~ *wind*>; *esp* sharp, cutting <~ *irony*> – **bitingly** *adv*

'**bit ,part** *n* a small acting part, usu with spoken lines

bitt /bit||bɪt/ *n* either of a pair of posts on a ship's deck for securing ropes

[1]**bitter** /'bitə||'bɪtə/ *adj* **1a** being or inducing an acrid, astringent, or disagreeable taste similar to that of quinine that is one of the 4 basic taste sensations **b** distressing, galling <*a* ~ *sense of shame*> **2a** intense, severe <~ *enemies*> **b** very cold <*a* ~ *winter*> **c** cynical, rancorous <~ *contempt*> **3** expressive of severe grief or regret <~ *tears*> – **bitterish** *adj*, **bitterly** *adv*, **bitterness** *n*

[2]**bitter** *adv*, *NAm* bitterly

[3]**bitter** *n* **1** *pl but sing or pl in constr* a usu alcoholic solution of bitter and often aromatic plant products used esp in preparing mixed drinks or as a mild tonic **2** *Br* a very dry beer heavily flavoured with hops

bittern /'bitən||'bɪtən/ *n* any of various small or medium-sized herons with a characteristic booming cry

[1]'**bitter,sweet** /-,sweet||-,swi:t/ *n* a rambling poisonous nightshade with purple-and-yellow flowers

[2]**bittersweet** *adj* bitter and sweet at the same time; *esp* pleasant but with elements of suffering or regret <*a* ~ *ballad*> – **bittersweetly** *adv*, **bittersweetness** *n*

bitty /'biti||'bɪtɪ/ *adj* scrappy, disjointed – **bittily** *adv*

bitumen /'bityoomin||'bɪtjʊmɪn/ *n* any of various mixtures of hydrocarbons (e g tar) that occur naturally or as residues after heating petroleum, coal, etc – **bituminoid** *adj*, **bituminize** *vt*, **bituminization** *n*

bituminous /bi'tyoohminəs||bɪ'tju:mɪnəs/ *adj* resembling, containing, or impregnated with bitumen

bivalent /bieˈvaylənt‖baɪˈveɪlənt/ *adj* **1** having a valency of 2 **2** *of chromosomes* that become associated in pairs during meiotic cell division – **bivalent** *n*

bivalve /ˈbieˌvalv‖ˈbaɪˌvælv/ *n or adj* (a mollusc) having a shell composed of 2 valves

[1]**bivouac** /ˈbivoo·ak‖ˈbɪvʊæk/ *n* a usu temporary encampment under little or no shelter [French, fr Low German *biwake*, fr *bi* at + *wake* guard]

[2]**bivouac** *vi* **-ck-** to make a bivouac; camp

biweekly /ˌbieˈweekli‖ˌbaɪˈwiːklɪ/ *n, adj, or adv* (a publication) issued or occurring **a** every 2 weeks **b** twice a week

bizarre /biˈzah‖bɪˈzɑː/ *adj* **1** odd, extravagant, eccentric **2** involving sensational contrasts or incongruities – **bizarrely** *adv*, **bizarreness** *n*

blab /blab‖blæb/ *vb* **-bb-** *vt* to reveal (a secret) ~*vi* to talk indiscreetly or thoughtlessly – **blab** *n*

blabber /ˈblabə‖ˈblæbə/ *vi* to babble ~*vt* to say indiscreetly – **blabber** *n*

ˈ**blabberˌmouth** /-ˌmowth‖-ˌmaʊθ/ *n* one who talks too much

[1]**black** /blak‖blæk/ *adj* **1a** of the colour black **b** very dark in colour <*his face was ~ with rage*> **2** *often cap* **2a** having dark pigmentation; *esp* of the Negro race <~ *Americans*> **b** of black people or culture <~ *literature*> **3** dressed in black <*the ~ Prince*> **4** dirty, soiled <*hands ~ with dirt*> **5a** having or reflecting little or no light <*a ~ night*> **b** *of coffee* served without milk or cream **6a** thoroughly sinister or evil <*a ~ deed*> **b** indicative of hostility, disapproval, or discredit <*met only with ~ looks*> **7a** very dismal or calamitous <~ *despair*> **b** marked by the occurrence of disaster <~ *Friday*> **8** showing a profit <*a ~ financial statement*> **9** characterized by grim, distorted, or grotesque humour **10** bought, sold, or operating illegally and esp in contravention of official economic regulations <*the ~ economy*> **11** *chiefly Br* subject to boycott by trade-union members – **blackish** *adj*, **blackly** *adv*, **blackness** *n*

[2]**black** *n* **1** a black pigment or dye **2** the colour of least lightness that belongs to objects that neither reflect nor transmit light **3** sthg black; *esp* black clothing <*looks good in ~*> **4** one who belongs wholly or partly to a dark-skinned race; *esp* a Negro **5** (the player playing) the dark-coloured pieces in a board game (e g chess) for 2 players **6** the condition of being financially in credit or solvent or of making a profit – usu + *in the*; compare RED 3

[3]**black** *vt* **1** to make black **2** *chiefly Br* to declare (e g a business or industry) subject to boycott by trade-union members

blackamoor /ˈblakəˌmaw, -ˌmooə‖ˈblækəˌmɔː, -ˌmʊə/ *n, archaic* BLACK 4

ˌ**black-and-ˈblue** *adj* darkly discoloured from blood that has leaked under the skin by bruising

ˌ**Black and ˈTan** *n* a member of the Royal Irish Constabulary resisting the armed movement for Irish independence in 1921

ˌ**black-and-ˈwhite** *adj* **1** reproducing visual images in tones of grey rather than in colours **2a** sharply divided into 2 groups or sides **b** evaluating things as either all good or all bad <~ *morality*>

ˌ**black and ˈwhite** *n* **1** writing, print **2** a drawing or print done in black and white or in monochrome **3** black-and-white reproduction of visual images, esp by photography or television

ˈ**blackˌball** /-ˌbawl‖-ˌbɔːl/ *vt* **1** to vote against (esp a candidate for membership of a club) **2** to ostracize – **blackball** *n*

ˈ**black ˌbelt** *n* (one who has) a rating of expert in judo, karate, etc

ˈ**blackberry** /-b(ə)ri‖-b(ə)rɪ/ *n* (the usu black seedy edible fruit of) any of various prickly shrubs of the rose family

ˈ**blackˌbird** /-ˌbuhd‖-ˌbɜːd/ *n* **1** a common Old World thrush the male of which is black with an orange beak and eye rim **2** any of several American birds

ˈ**blackˌboard** /-ˌbawd‖-ˌbɔːd/ *n* a hard smooth usu dark surface for writing or drawing on with chalk

ˌ**black ˈbox** *n* **1** a usu electronic device, esp one that can be plugged in or removed as a unit, whose internal mechanism is hidden from or mysterious to the user **2** FLIGHT RECORDER

ˈ**blackˌcap** /-ˌkap‖-ˌkæp/ *n* a small Old World warbler with a black crown

ˌ**black ˈcap** *n* a black head-covering formerly worn by a judge in Britain when passing the death sentence

blackcurrant /ˈblakˌkurənt, ˌ-ˈ--‖ˈblækˌkʌrənt, ˌ-ˈ--/ *n* (the small black edible fruit of) a widely cultivated European currant

ˌ**black ˈdeath** *n, often cap B&D* a form of plague epidemic in Europe and Asia in the 14th c

blacken /ˈblakən‖ˈblækən/ *vi* to become dark or black ~ *vt* **1** to make dark or black **2** to defame, sully – **blackener** *n*

ˌ**black ˈeye** *n* a discoloration of the skin round the eye from bruising

blackguard /ˈblagəd, -ˌgahd‖ˈblægəd, -ˌgɑːd/ *n* a coarse or unscrupulous person; a scoundrel – now often humor – **blackguardism** *n*, **blackguardly** *adj or adv*

ˈ**blackˌhead** /-ˌhed‖-ˌhed/ *n* a small usu dark-coloured oily plug blocking the duct of a sebaceous gland, esp on the face

ˌ**black ˈhole** *n* a celestial body, prob formed from a collapsed star, with a very high density and an intense gravitational field, from which no radiation can escape

ˌ**black ˈice** *n, Br* transparent slippery ice (e g on a road)

blacking /ˈblaking‖ˈblækɪŋ/ *n* **1** a paste, polish, etc applied to an object to make it black **2** a boycotting of business, industry, etc by trade-union members

[1]ˈ**blackˌjack** /-ˌjak‖-ˌdʒæk/ *n* **1** [2]PONTOON **2** *NAm* a cosh

[2]ˈ**blackˌjack** *vt, NAm* to strike with a blackjack

ˌ**black ˈlead** /led‖led/ *n* graphite

ˈ**blackˌleg** /-ˌleg‖-ˌleg/ *n, chiefly Br* a worker hostile to trade unionism or acting in opposition to union policies

ˌ**black ˈletter** *n* a heavier angular style of type or lettering used esp by early European printers

ˈblackˌlist /-ˌlist‖-ˌlɪst/ *n* a list of people or organizations who are disapproved of or are to be punished or boycotted – **blacklist** *vt*

ˌblack ˈmagic *n* magic performed with the aim of harming or killing sby or sthg

ˈblackˌmail /-ˌmayl‖-ˌmeɪl/ *n* **1** (money obtained by) extortion by threats, esp of exposure of secrets that would lead to loss of reputation, prosecution, etc **2** political, industrial, or moral pressure to do sthg that is considered undesirable [[1]*black* + archaic *mail* tribute, payment, fr Old English *mal* agreement, pay, fr Old Norse *māl* speech, agreement] – **blackmail** *vt*, **blackmailer** *n*

Black Maria /ˌblak məˈrie·ə‖ˌblæk məˈraɪə/ *n* an enclosed motor vehicle used by police to carry prisoners

ˌblack ˈmarket *n* illicit trade in commodities or currencies in violation of official regulations (e g rationing)

ˌblack markeˈteer /ˌmahkiˈtiə‖ˌmɑːkɪˈtɪə/ *n* one who trades on a black market

ˌBlack ˈMass *n* a travesty of the Christian mass ascribed to worshippers of Satan

ˌBlack ˈMuslim *n* a member of an exclusively black chiefly US Muslim sect that advocates a strictly separate black community

ˈblackˌout /-ˌowt‖-ˌaʊt/ *n* **1** a period of darkness enforced as a precaution against air raids, or caused by a failure of electrical power **2** a temporary loss or dulling of vision, consciousness, or memory **3** a holding back or suppression of sthg <*a* ~ *of news about the invasion*> **4** a usu temporary loss of radio signal (e g during the reentry of a spacecraft)

black out *vi* **1** to become enveloped in darkness **2** to undergo a temporary loss of vision, consciousness, or memory **3** to extinguish or screen all lights for protection, esp against air attack ~ *vt* **1** to cause to black out **2** to suppress, esp by censorship

ˌBlack ˈPanther *n* a member of a militant organization of US blacks

ˌblack ˈpepper *n* a pungent condiment prepared from the dried black-husked berries of an E Indian plant used either whole or ground

ˌblack ˈpower *n* the mobilization of the political and economic power of US blacks, esp to further racial equality

ˌblack ˈpudding *n, chiefly Br* a very dark sausage made from suet and a large proportion of pigs blood

ˌblack ˈsheep *n* a disreputable member of a respectable group, family, etc

ˈBlackˌshirt /-ˌshuht‖-ˌʃɜːt/ *n* a member of a fascist organization having a black shirt as part of its uniform

ˈblackˌsmith /-ˌsmith‖-ˌsmɪθ/ *n* one who works iron, esp at a forge – **blacksmithing** *n*

ˈblack ˌspot *n, Br* a stretch of road on which accidents occur frequently

ˈblackˌthorn /-ˌthawn‖-ˌθɔːn/ *n* a European spiny shrub of the rose family with hard wood and small white flowers

ˌblack-ˈtie *adj* characterized by or requiring the wearing of semiformal evening dress by men including a dinner jacket and a black bow tie

bladder /ˈbladə‖ˈblædə/ *n* **1a** a membranous sac in animals that serves as the receptacle of a liquid or contains gas; *esp* the urinary bladder **b** VESICLE 1a **2** a bag filled with a liquid or gas (e g the air-filled rubber one inside a football)

blade /blayd‖bleɪd/ *n* **1** (the flat expanded part, as distinguished from the stalk, of) a leaf, esp of a grass, cereal, etc **2a** the broad flattened part of an oar, paddle, bat, etc **b** an arm of a screw propeller, electric fan, steam turbine, etc **c** the broad flat or concave part of a machine (e g a bulldozer) that comes into contact with material to be moved **d** a broad flat body part; *specif* the scapula – used chiefly in naming cuts of meat **3a** the cutting part of a knife, razor, etc **b** a sword **c** the runner of an ice skate **4** *archaic* a dashing lively man – now usu humor

blaeberry /ˈblayb(ə)ri‖ˈbleɪb(ə)rɪ/ *n, Scot* the bilberry

blah /blah‖blɑː/ *n* silly or pretentious chatter or nonsense – infml

[1]**blame** /blaym‖bleɪm/ *vt* **1** to find fault with; censure **2a** to hold responsible for sthg reprehensible <~ *him for everything*> **b** to place responsibility for (sthg reprehensible) – + *on* <~s *it on me*> – **blamable** *adj*, **blamably** *adv*, **blamer** *n*

[2]**blame** *n* **1** an expression of disapproval or reproach **2** responsibility for sthg reprehensible <*they must share the* ~ *for the crime*> – **blameful** *adj*, **blamefully** *adv*, **blameless** *adj*, **blamelessly** *adv*, **blamelessness** *n*

ˈblameˌworthy /-ˌwuhthi‖-ˌwɜːðɪ/ *adj* deserving blame – **blameworthiness** *n*

blanch /blahnch‖blɑːntʃ/ *vt* **1** to take the colour out of: **1a** to bleach (a growing plant) by excluding light **b** to scald or parboil (e g almonds or food for freezing) in water or steam in order to remove the skin from, whiten, or stop enzymatic action **2** to make ashen or pale <*fear* ~es *the cheek*> ~*vi* to become white or pale <~ed *when he heard the news*> – **blancher** *n*

blancmange /bləˈmonj, -ˈmonzh‖bləˈmɒndʒ, -ˈmɒnʒ/ *n* a usu sweetened and flavoured dessert made from gelatinous or starchy substances (e g cornflour) and milk [Middle French *blanc manger*, lit., white food]

bland /bland‖blænd/ *adj* **1a** smooth, soothing <*a* ~ *smile*> **b** unperturbed <*a* ~ *confession of guilt*> **2a** not irritating or stimulating; mild <*a* ~ *diet*> **b** dull, insipid <~ *stories with little plot or action*> – **blandly** *adv*, **blandness** *n*

blandishment /ˈblandishmənt‖ˈblændɪʃmənt/ *n* a coaxing or flattering act or utterance – often pl – **blandish** *vb*

[1]**blank** /blangk‖blæŋk/ *adj* **1a** dazed, nonplussed <*stared in* ~ *dismay*> **b** expressionless <*a* ~ *stare*> **2a** lacking interest, variety, or change <*a* ~ *prospect*> **b** devoid of covering or content; *esp* free from writing <~ *paper*> **c** not filled in <*a* ~ *cheque*> **3** absolute, unqualified <*a* ~ *refusal*> **4** having a plain or unbroken surface where an opening is usual <*a* ~ *arch*> – **blankly** *adv*, **blankness** *n*

[2]**blank** *n* **1** an empty space **2a** a void <*my mind was a* ~ *during the test*> **b** a vacant or uneventful period <*a long* ~ *in history*> **3** a dash substituted for an omitted word **4a** a piece of material prepared to be made into sthg (e g a key or coin) by a further operation **b** a

cartridge loaded with powder but no bullet

[3]**blank** *vt* **1a** to make blank – usu + *out* **b** to block – usu + *off* <~ed off *the tunnel*> **2** *NAm* to keep (an opposing team) from scoring

ˌ**blank ˈcheque** *n* **1** a signed cheque with the amount unspecified **2** complete freedom of action or control; CARTE BLANCHE

[1]**blanket** /ˈblangkit‖ˈblæŋkɪt/ *n* **1** a large thick usu rectangular piece of fabric (e g woven from wool or acrylic yarn) used esp as a bed covering or a similar piece of fabric used as a body covering (e g for a horse) **2** a thick covering or layer <*a* ~ *of snow*> [Old French *blankete*, fr *blanc* white]

[2]**blanket** *vt* to cover (as if) with a blanket <*new grass* ~s *the slope*>

[3]**blanket** *adj* applicable in all instances or to all members of a group or class

ˌ**blank ˈverse** *n* unrhymed verse, esp in iambic pentameters

blare /bleə‖bleə/ *vi* to emit loud and harsh sound ~ *vt* **1** to sound loudly and usu harshly **2** to proclaim loudly or sensationally <*headlines* ~d *his defeat*> – **blare** *n*

blarney /ˈblahni‖ˈblɑːnɪ/ *n* **1** smooth wheedling talk; flattery **2** nonsense [*Blarney stone*, a stone in Blarney Castle, near Cork, Ireland, held to give skill in flattery to those who kiss it] – **blarney** *vb*

blasé /ˈblahzay, -ˈ-‖ˈblɑːzeɪ, -ˈ-/ *adj* indifferent to pleasure or excitement as a result of excessive indulgence or enjoyment; *also* sophisticated

blaspheme /blasˈfeem‖blæsˈfiːm/ *vb* to speak of or address (God or sthg sacred) with impiety – **blasphemer** *n*

blasphemy /ˈblasfəmi‖ˈblæsfəmɪ/ *n* (the act of showing) contempt or lack of reverence for God or sthg (considered) sacred – **blasphemous** *adj*, **blasphemously** *adv*, **blasphemousness** *n*

[1]**blast** /blahst‖blɑːst/ *n* **1** a violent gust of wind **2** the sound produced by air blown through a wind instrument or whistle **3a** a stream of air or gas forced through a hole **b** a violent outburst **c** the continuous draught forced through a blast furnace **4** a sudden pernicious influence or effect <*the* ~ *of a huge epidemic*> **5** (a violent wave of increased atmospheric pressure followed by a wave of decreased atmospheric pressure produced in the vicinity of) an explosion or violent detonation **6** speed, capacity <*going full* ~ *down the road*> **7** the utterance of the word *blast* as a curse

[2]**blast** *vi* **1** to produce loud harsh sounds **2a** to use an explosive **b** to shoot **3** to shrivel, wither ~ *vt* **1** to injure (as if) by the action of wind; blight **2** to shatter, remove, or open (as if) with an explosive <~ *a new course for the stream*> **3** to apply a forced draught to **4** to cause to blast off <*will* ~ *themselves from the moon's surface*> **5a** to denounce vigorously **b** to curse, damn **c** to hit vigorously and effectively – **blaster** *n*, **blasting** *n or adj*

[3]**blast** *interj*, *Br* – used to express annoyance; slang

blasted /ˈblahstid‖ˈblɑːstɪd/ *adj* **1a** withered **b** damaged (as if) by an explosive, lightning, or the wind **2** confounded, detestable <*this* ~ *weather*> – infml

ˈ**blast ˌfurnace** *n* a furnace, esp for converting iron ore into iron, in which combustion is forced by a current of air under pressure

blast off *vi*, *esp of rocket-propelled missiles and vehicles* TAKE OFF 3 – **blast-off** *n*

blatant /ˈblayt(ə)nt‖ˈbleɪt(ə)nt/ *adj* **1** noisy, esp in a vulgar or offensive manner **2** completely obvious, conspicuous, or obtrusive, esp in a crass or offensive manner – **blatantly** *adv*, **blatancy** *n*

blather /ˈbladhə‖ˈblæðə/ *n* foolish voluble talk – **blather** *vi*, **blatherer** *n*

[1]**blaze** /blayz‖bleɪz/ *n* **1a** an intensely burning flame or sudden fire **b** intense direct light, often accompanied by heat <*the* ~ *of noon*> **2a** a dazzling display <*a* ~ *of flowers*> **b** a sudden outburst <*a* ~ *of fury*> **c** brilliance <*the* ~ *of the jewels*> **3** *pl* HELL 2a – usu as an interjection or as a generalized term of abuse <*go to* ~s>

[2]**blaze** *vi* **1a** to burn intensely **b** to flare up **2** to be conspicuously brilliant or resplendent **3** to shoot rapidly and repeatedly <~d *away at the target*> – **blazingly** *adv*

[3]**blaze** *vt* to make public or conspicuous – chiefly in *blaze abroad*

[4]**blaze** *n* **1** a broad white mark on the face of an animal, esp a horse **2** a trail marker; *esp* a mark made on a tree by cutting off a piece of the bark

[5]**blaze** *vt* **1** to mark (e g a trail) with blazes **2** to lead or pioneer in (some direction or activity) – chiefly in *blaze the trail*

blazer /ˈblayzə‖ˈbleɪzə/ *n* a jacket, esp with patch pockets, that is for casual wear or is part of a school uniform

[1]**blazon** /ˈblayz(ə)n‖ˈbleɪz(ə)n/ *n* **1** COAT OF ARMS **2** the proper formal description of heraldic arms or charges

[2]**blazon** *vt* **1** to proclaim widely – often + *forth* **2** to describe (heraldic arms or charges) in technical terms – **blazoner** *n*, **blazoning** *n*

ˈ**blazonry** /-ri‖-rɪ/ *n* **1** blazon **2** dazzling display

[1]**bleach** /bleech‖bliːtʃ/ *vt* **1** to remove colour or stains from **2** to make whiter or lighter, esp by physical or chemical removal of colour ~*vi* to grow white or lose colour – **bleachable** *adj*

[2]**bleach** *n* **1** a preparation used in bleaching **2** the degree of whiteness obtained by bleaching

ˈ**bleaching ˌpowder** /ˈbleeching‖ˈbliːtʃɪŋ/ *n* a white powder consisting chiefly of calcium hydroxide, calcium chloride, and calcium hypochlorite used as a bleach, disinfectant, or deodorant

[1]**bleak** /bleek‖bliːk/ *adj* **1** exposed, barren, and often windswept **2** cold, raw **3a** lacking in warmth or kindness **b** not hopeful or encouraging <*a* ~ *outlook*> **c** severely simple or austere – **bleakish** *adj*, **bleakly** *adv*, **bleakness** *n*

[2]**bleak** *n* a small European river fish

bleary /ˈbliəri‖ˈblɪərɪ/ *adj* **1** *of the eyes or vision* dull or dimmed, esp from fatigue or sleep **2** poorly outlined or defined – **blearily** *adv*, **bleariness** *n*

[1]**bleat** /bleet‖bliːt/ *vi* **1** to make (a sound like) the cry characteristic of a sheep or goat **2a** to talk complainingly or with a whine **b** to blather ~*vt* to utter in a bleating manner – **bleater** *n*

[2]**bleat** *n* (a sound like) the characteristic cry of a

sheep or goat

bleed /bleed‖bli:d/ *vb* **bled** /bled‖bled/ *vi* **1** to emit or lose blood **2** to feel anguish, pain, or sympathy **3** to lose some constituent (e g sap or dye) by exuding it or by diffusion **4** to be printed so as to run off an edge of a page after trimming ~ *vt* **1** to remove or draw blood from **2** to extort money from **3** to draw sap from (a tree) **4** to extract or let out some of (a contained substance) from (a container) **5** to cause (e g a printed illustration) to bleed; *also* to trim (e g a page) so that some of the printing bleeds **6** to extract or drain the vitality or lifeblood from <*high taxes* ~ing *private enterprise*>

bleeder /'bleedə‖'bli:də/ *n* **1** a haemophiliac **2** a worthless person – slang

bleeding /'bleeding‖'bli:dɪŋ/ *adj or adv* [1]BLOODY 4, [3]BLOODY – slang

[1]bleep /bleep‖bli:p/ *n* **1** a short high-pitched sound (e g from electronic equipment) **2** a bleeper

[2]bleep *vt* **1** to call (sby) by means of a bleeper **2** to replace (recorded words) with a bleep or other sound – usu + *out* <*all the obscenities were* ~ed out> ~*vi* to emit a bleep

bleeper /'bleepə‖'bli:pə/ *n* a portable radio receiver that emits a bleep as a signal that the wearer is required

blemish /'blemish‖'blemɪʃ/ *vt or n* (to spoil the perfection of by) a noticeable imperfection

blench /blench‖blentʃ/ *vi* to draw back or flinch from lack of courage

[1]blend /blend‖blend/ *vb* **blended** *also* **blent** /blent‖blent/ *vt* **1** to mix; *esp* to combine or associate so that the separate constituents cannot be distinguished **2** to prepare by thoroughly intermingling different varieties or grades ~ *vi* **1a** to mix or intermingle thoroughly **b** to combine into an integrated whole **2** to produce a harmonious effect

[2]blend *n* **1** an act or product of blending <*our own* ~ *of tea*> **2** a word (e g *brunch*) produced by combining other words or parts of words

blender /'blendə‖'blendə/ *n* an electric appliance for grinding or mixing; *specif* a liquidizer

bless /bles‖bles/ *vt* **blessed** *also* **blest** /blest‖blest/ **1** to hallow or consecrate by religious rite, esp by making the sign of the cross **2** to invoke divine care for **3a** to praise, glorify < ~ *His holy name*> **b** to speak gratefully of < ~ed *him for his kindness*> **4** to confer prosperity or happiness on **5** – used in exclamations chiefly to express mild or good-humoured surprise < ~ *my soul, what's happened now?*> **6** *archaic* to protect, preserve

blessed /'blesid‖'blesɪd/ *adj* **1a** *often cap* holy; venerated <*the* Blessed *Sacrament*> **b** *cap* – used as a title for a beatified person <Blessed *Oliver Plunket*> **2** – used as an intensive <*no one gave us a* ~ *penny*> – **blessedly** *adv*, **blessedness** *n*

blessing /'blesing‖'blesɪŋ/ *n* **1a** the invocation of God's favour upon a person **b** approval **2** sthg conducive to happiness or welfare **3** grace said at a meal

blether /'bledhə‖'bleðə/ *vi or n* (to) blather

blew /blooh‖blu:/ *past of* BLOW

[1]blight /bliet‖blaɪt/ *n* **1** (an organism that causes) a disease or injury of plants resulting in withering, cessation of growth, and death of parts without rotting **2** sthg that impairs, frustrates, or destroys **3** a condition of disorder or decay <*urban* ~>

[2]blight *vt* **1** to affect (e g a plant) with blight **2** to impair, frustrate ~*vi* to suffer from or become affected with blight

blighter /'blietə‖'blaɪtə/ *n, chiefly Br* a fellow; *esp* one held in low esteem – infml

blimey /'bliemi‖'blaɪmɪ/ *interj, chiefly Br* – used for expressing surprise; slang [short for *gorblimey*, alteration of *God blind me*]

blimp /blimp‖blɪmp/ *n* **1** a nonrigid airship **2** *cap* COLONEL BLIMP – **blimpish** *adj*, **blimpishly** *adv*, **blimpishness** *n*

[1]blind /bliend‖blaɪnd/ *adj* **1a** unable to see; sightless **b** of or designed for sightless people **2a** unable or unwilling to discern or judge < ~ *to all arguments*> **b** not based on reason, evidence, or knowledge < ~ *faith*> **3** completely insensible <*in a* ~ *stupor*> **4** without sight or knowledge of anything that could serve for guidance beforehand **5** performed solely by the use of instruments within an aircraft <*a* ~ *landing*> **6** hidden from sight; concealed <*a* ~ *corner*> **7** having only 1 opening or outlet <*a* ~ *alley*> **8** having no opening for light or passage <*a* ~ *wall*> – **blindly** *adv*, **blindness** *n*

[2]blind *vt* **1** to make blind **2** to rob of judgment or discernment **3** to dazzle ~*vi Br* to swear <*cursing and* ~ing> – infml – **blindingly** *adv* – **blind with science** to impress or overwhelm with a display of usu technical knowledge

[3]blind *n* **1** sthg to hinder sight or keep out light: e g **1a** a window shutter **b** *chiefly Br* an awning **c** a flexible screen (e g a strip of cloth) usu mounted on a roller for covering a window **d** a curtain **e** VENETIAN BLIND **2** a cover, subterfuge **3** *NAm* [3]HIDE

[4]blind *adv* **1** to the point of insensibility < ~ *drunk*> **2** without seeing outside an aircraft <*to fly* ~> **3** – used as an intensive <*swore* ~ *he wouldn't escape*>

ˌblind 'alley *n* a fruitless or mistaken course or direction

ˌblind 'date *n* a date between people who have not previously met

blinder /'bliendə‖'blaɪndə/ *n* **1** *Br* sthg outstanding; *esp* an outstanding piece of play in cricket or football – infml **2** *NAm* BLINKER 3

'blindˌfold /-ˌfohld‖-ˌfəʊld/ *vt or n* **1** (to cover the eyes of with) a piece of material (e g a bandage) for covering the eyes to prevent sight **2** (to hinder from seeing or esp understanding with) sthg that obscures vision or mental awareness

blindman's buff /ˌbliendˌmanz 'buf‖ˌblaɪndˌmænz 'bʌf/ *n* a group game in which a blindfolded player tries to catch and identify another player

'blind ˌspot *n* **1a** the point in the retina where the optic nerve enters that is not sensitive to light **b** a part of a visual field that cannot be seen or inspected <*the car has a bad* ~> **2** an area in which one lacks knowledge, understanding, or discrimination

[1]blink /blingk‖blɪŋk/ *vi* **1** to close and open the eyes involuntarily **2** to shine intermittently **3a** to wink *at* **b** to look with surprise or dismay *at* ~ *vt* **1** to cause (one's eyes) to blink **2** to evade, shirk

[2]**blink** *n* **1** a glimmer, sparkle **2** a usu involuntary shutting and opening of the eye – **on the blink** not working properly – infml

blinker /ˈblingkə‖ˈblɪŋkə/ *n* **1** a warning or signalling light that flashes on and off **2** *pl* an obstruction to sight or discernment **3** *chiefly Br* either of two flaps, one on each side of a horse's bridle, allowing only frontal vision – **blinker** *vt*, **blinkered** *adj*

blinking /ˈblingking‖ˈblɪŋkɪŋ/ *adj or adv*, *Br* [1]BLOODY 4, [3]BLOODY – euph

blip /blip‖blɪp/ *n* **1** a bleep **2** an image on a radar screen

bliss /blis‖blɪs/ *n* **1** complete happiness **2** paradise, heaven – **blissful** *adj*, **blissfully** *adv*, **blissfulness** *n*

[1]**blister** /ˈblistə‖ˈblɪstə/ *n* **1** a raised part of the outer skin containing watery liquid **2** an enclosed raised spot (e g in paint) resembling a blister **3** a disease of plants marked by large swollen patches on the leaves **4** any of various structures that bulge out <*an aircraft's radar* ~> – **blistery** *adj*

[2]**blister** *vi* to become affected with a blister ~ *vt* **1** to raise a blister on **2** to attack harshly

blistering /ˈblistəring‖ˈblɪstərɪŋ/ *adj* **1** extremely intense or severe **2** *of speed* extremely high – **blisteringly** *adv*

blithe /bliedh‖blaɪð/ *adj* **1** lighthearted, merry, cheerful **2** casual, heedless <~ *unconcern*> – **blithely** *adv*

blithering /ˈblidhəring‖ˈblɪðərɪŋ/ *adj* talking nonsense; babbling; *broadly* utterly stupid – infml

blitz /blits‖blɪts/ *n* **1a** a blitzkrieg **b** an intensive aerial bombardment; *specif, often cap the* bombardment of British cities by the German air force in 1940 and 1941 **2** an intensive nonmilitary campaign <*a* ~ *against the unions*> – chiefly journ – **blitz** *vb*

ˈ**blitz**ˌ**krieg** /-ˌkreeg‖-ˌkri:g/ *n* a violent swift surprise campaign conducted by coordinated air and ground forces [German, fr *blitz* lightning + *krieg* war]

blizzard /ˈblizəd‖ˈblɪzəd/ *n* **1** a long severe snowstorm **2** an intensely strong cold wind filled with fine snow **3** an overwhelming rush or deluge <*the* ~ *of mail at Christmas*> – **blizzardy** *adj*

bloated /ˈblohtid‖ˈbləʊtɪd/ *adj* **1** unpleasantly swollen **2** much larger than is warranted <*a* ~ *estimate*>

bloater /ˈblohtə‖ˈbləʊtə/ *n* a large herring or mackerel lightly salted and briefly smoked

blob /blob‖blɒb/ *n* **1a** a small drop of liquid **b** a small drop or lump of sthg viscous or thick **2** sthg ill-defined or amorphous

bloc /blok‖blɒk/ *n* a (temporary) combination of individuals, parties, or nations for a common purpose

[1]**block** /blok‖blɒk/ *n* **1** a compact usu solid piece of substantial material (e g wood or stone): e g **1a** a mould or form on which articles are shaped or displayed **b** a rectangular building unit that is larger than a brick **c** a usu cubical and solid wooden or plastic building toy that is usu provided in sets **d** the metal casting that contains the cylinders of an internal-combustion engine **2** HEAD 1 – slang **3a** an obstacle **b** an obstruction of an opponent's play in sports, esp in football, hockey, etc **c** interruption of the normal physiological function (e g transmission of nerve impulses) of a tissue or organ **4** a wooden or metal case enclosing 1 or more pulleys **5** (a ballet shoe with) a solid toe on which a dancer can stand on points **6a** a quantity or number of things dealt with as a unit **b** a part of a building or set of buildings devoted to a particular use **c** *chiefly NAm* (the distance along 1 side of) a usu rectangular space (e g in a town) enclosed by streets and usu occupied by buildings **7** a piece of engraved or etched material (e g wood or metal) from which impressions are printed

[2]**block** *vt* **1** to make unsuitable for passage or progress by obstruction **2** to hinder the passage, progress, or accomplishment of (as if) by interposing an obstruction **3** to shut off from view <*trees* ~ing *the sun*> **4** to obstruct or interfere usu legitimately with (e g an opponent) in various games or sports **5** to prevent normal functioning of – **blockage** *n*, **blocker** *n*

[1]**blockade** /bləˈkayd, blo-‖bləˈkeɪd, blɒ-/ *n* **1** the surrounding or blocking of a particular enemy area to prevent passage of people or supplies **2** an obstruction

[2]**blockade** *vt* to subject to a blockade – **blockader** *n*

ˌ**block and** ˈ**tackle** *n* an arrangement of pulley blocks with associated rope or cable for hoisting or hauling

ˈ**block**ˌ**buster** /-ˌbustə‖-ˌbʌstə/ *n* **1** a huge high-explosive demolition bomb **2** sby or sthg particularly outstanding or effective *USE* infml

ˈ**block**ˌ**head** /-ˌhed‖-ˌhed/ *n* an extremely dull or stupid person

ˈ**block**ˌ**house** /-ˌhows‖-ˌhaʊs/ *n* **1** a building made of heavy timbers with loopholes for firing through, observation, etc, formerly used as a fort **2** an observation post built to withstand heat, blast, radiation, etc

block in *vt* to sketch the outlines of, in a design

ˌ**block** ˈ**letter** *n* a simple capital letter

bloke /blohk‖bləʊk/ *n*, *chiefly Br* a man – infml

[1]**blond** /blond‖blɒnd/ *adj* **1a** *of hair* of a flaxen, golden, light auburn, or pale yellowish brown colour **b** of a pale white or rosy white colour <~ *skin*> **c** being a blond <*a handsome* ~ *youth*> **2a** of a light colour **b** of the colour blond – **blondish** *adj*

[2]**blond** *n* **1** sby with blond hair and often a light complexion and blue or grey eyes **2** a light yellowish brown to dark greyish yellow colour

blonde /blond‖blɒnd/ *n or adj* (a) blond – used esp for or in relation to women

[1]**blood** /blud‖blʌd/ *n* **1a** the usu red fluid that circulates in the heart, arteries, capillaries, and veins of a vertebrate animal, carrying nourishment and oxygen to, and bringing away waste

products from, all parts of the body **b** a comparable fluid of an invertebrate animal **2a** lifeblood; *broadly* life **b** human lineage; *esp* the royal lineage **c** kinship **d** descent from parents **3** temper, passion **4** people or ideas of the specified, esp innovative, kind <*need some fresh* ~ *in the organization*> **5** *archaic* a dashing lively esp young man; a rake – now usu humor

[2]**blood** *vt* **1** to stain or wet with blood; *esp* to mark the face of (an inexperienced fox hunter) with the blood of the fox **2** to give an initiating experience to (sby new to a particular field of activity)

ˈ**bloodˌbath** /-ˌbahth‖-ˌbɑːθ/ *n* a great slaughter; a massacre

ˌ**blood** ˈ**brother** *n* either of 2 men pledged to mutual loyalty, esp by a ceremonial mingling of each other's blood – **blood brotherhood** *n*

ˈ**blood** ˌ**count** *n* (the determination of) the number of blood cells in a definite volume of blood

ˈ**bloodˌcurdling** /-ˌkuhdling‖-ˌkɜːdlɪŋ/ *adj* arousing horror – **bloodcurdlingly** *adv*

-blooded /-bludid‖-blʌdɪd/ *comb form* (→ *adj*) having (such) blood or (such) a temperament <*cold*-blooded>

ˈ**blood** ˌ**feud** *n* a murderous feud between clans or families

ˈ**blood** ˌ**group** *n* any of the classes into which human beings can be separated on the basis of the presence or absence of specific antigens in their blood

ˈ**blood** ˌ**heat** *n* a temperature approximating to that of the human body; about 37°C or 98°F

ˈ**bloodˌhound** /-ˌhownd‖-ˌhaʊnd/ *n* **1** a large powerful hound of European origin remarkable for its acuteness of smell and poor sight **2** a person (e g a detective) who is keen in pursuing or tracking sby or sthg down

ˈ**bloodless** /-lis‖-lɪs/ *adj* **1** deficient in or free from blood **2** not accompanied by the shedding of blood <*a* ~ *victory*> **3** lacking in spirit or vitality **4** lacking in human feeling <~ *statistics*> – **bloodlessly** *adv*, **bloodlessness** *n*

ˈ**bloodˌletting** /-ˌleting‖-ˌletɪŋ/ *n* **1** phlebotomy **2** bloodshed

ˈ**blood** ˌ**money** *n* **1** money obtained at the cost of another's life **2** money paid to the next of kin of a slain person

ˈ**blood** ˌ**poisoning** *n* septicaemia

ˈ**blood** ˌ**pressure** *n* pressure that is exerted by the blood on the walls of the blood vessels, esp arteries, and that varies with the age and health of the individual

ˌ**blood** ˈ**red** *adj* having the colour of blood

ˈ**blood-reˌlation** *n* a person related by consanguinity

ˈ**bloodˌshed** /-ˌshed‖-ˌʃed/ *n* **1** the shedding of blood **2** the taking of life

ˈ**bloodˌshot** /-ˌshot‖-ˌʃɒt/ *adj, of an eye* having the white part tinged with red

ˈ**blood** ˌ**sport** *n* a field sport (e g fox hunting or beagling) in which animals are killed – derog; not used technically

ˈ**bloodˌstain** /-ˌstayn‖-ˌsteɪn/ *n* a discoloration caused by blood – **bloodstained** *adj*

ˈ**bloodˌstock** /-ˌstok‖-ˌstɒk/ *n sing or pl in constr* horses of Thoroughbred breeding, esp when used for racing

ˈ**bloodˌstream** /-ˌstreem‖-ˌstriːm/ *n* the flowing blood in a circulatory system

ˈ**bloodˌsucker** /-ˌsukə‖-ˌsʌkə/ *n* **1** a leech **2** a person who extorts money from another – **bloodsucking** *adj*

ˈ**bloodˌthirsty** /-ˌthuhsti‖-ˌθɜːstɪ/ *adj* eager for bloodshed – **bloodthirstily** *adj*, **bloodthirstiness** *n*

ˈ**blood** ˌ**type** *n* BLOOD GROUP

ˈ**blood** ˌ**vessel** *n* any of the vessels through which blood circulates in an animal

[1]**bloody** /ˈbludi‖ˈblʌdɪ/ *adj* **1** smeared, stained with, or containing blood **2** accompanied by or involving bloodshed **3a** murderous, bloodthirsty **b** merciless, cruel **4** – used as an intensive; slang – **bloodily** *adv*, **bloodiness** *n*

[2]**bloody** *vt* to make bloody

[3]**bloody** *adv* – used as an intensive; slang <*not* ~ *likely!*>

ˌ**Bloody** ˈ**Mary** /ˈmeəri‖ˈmeərɪ/ *n, pl* **Bloody Marys** a cocktail consisting chiefly of vodka and tomato juice

ˌ**bloody-**ˈ**minded** *adj* deliberately obstructive or unhelpful – **bloody-mindedness** *n*

[1]**bloom** /bloohm‖bluːm/ *n* a thick bar of hammered or rolled iron or steel

[2]**bloom** *n* **1a** a flower **b** the flowering state <*the roses in* ~> **2** a time of beauty, freshness, and vigour <*the* ~ *of youth*> **3a** a delicate powdery coating on some fruits and leaves **b** cloudiness on a film of varnish or lacquer **c** a mottled surface that appears on chocolate **4** a rosy or healthy appearance – **bloomy** *adj*

[3]**bloom** *vi* **1a** to produce or yield flowers **b** to support abundant plant life <*make the desert* ~> **2a** to flourish <~ing *with health*> **b** to reach maturity; blossom <*their friendship* ~ed *over the weeks*> **3** *of a body of water* to become densely populated with microorganisms, esp plankton

bloomer /ˈbloohmə‖ˈbluːmə/ *n* a stupid blunder – infml

bloomers /ˈbloohməz‖ˈbluːməz/ *n pl* a woman's undergarment with full loose legs gathered at the knee [Amelia *Bloomer* (1818-1894), US feminist]

blooming /ˈblooming, ˈblooh-‖ˈblʊmɪŋ, ˈbluː-/ *adj, chiefly Br* – used as a generalized intensive; euph <*that* ~ *idiot*>

[1]**blossom** /ˈblosəm‖ˈblɒsəm/ *n* **1a** the flower of a plant; *esp* the flower that produces edible fruits **b** the mass of bloom on a single plant **2** a high point or stage of development – **blossomy** *adj*

[2]**blossom** *vi* **1** to bloom **2** to come into one's own; develop <*a* ~ing *talent*>

[1]**blot** /blot‖blɒt/ *n* **1** a soiling or disfiguring mark; a spot **2** a mark of reproach; a blemish

[2]**blot** *vb* **-tt-** *vt* **1** to spot, stain, or spatter with a discolouring substance **2** to dry or remove with an absorbing agent (e g blotting paper) ~ *vi* **1** to make a blot **2** to become marked with a blot – **blot one's copybook** to mar one's previously good record or standing

blotch /bloch‖blɒtʃ/ *n* **1** an imperfection, blemish **2** an irregular spot or mark (e g of colour or ink) – **blotch** *vt*, **blotchily** *adv*, **blotchy** *adj*

blot out /blot‖blɒt/ *vt* **1** to obscure, eclipse **2** to destroy; WIPE OUT

blotter /ˈblotə‖ˈblɒtə/ *n* a piece of blotting paper

ˈ**blotting** ˌ**paper** /ˈbloting‖ˈblɒtɪŋ/ *n* a spongy unsized paper used to absorb ink

blotto /ˈblotoh‖ˈblɒtəʊ/ *adj, Br* extremely drunk – slang

blouse /blowz‖blaʊz/ *n* a usu loose-fitting woman's upper garment that resembles a shirt or smock and is waist-length or longer

[1]**blow** /bloh‖bləʊ/ *vb* **blew** /blooh‖bluː/; **blown** /blohn‖bləʊn/ *vi* **1** *of air* to move with speed or force <*it's* ~ing *hard tonight*> **2** to send forth a current of gas, esp air <blew *on his cold hands*> **3** to make a sound by blowing <*the whistle* blew> **4** to boast **5a** to pant **b** *of a whale* to eject moisture-laden air from the lungs through the blowhole **6** *of an electric fuse* to melt when overloaded **7** *of a tyre* to lose the contained air through a spontaneous puncture – usu + *out* ~ *vt* **1a** to set (gas or vapour) in motion **b** to act on with a current of gas or vapour **2** to damn, disregard – infml < ~ *the expense*> **3** to produce or shape by the action of blown or injected air **4** to deposit eggs or larvae on or in – used with reference to an insect **5** to shatter, burst, or destroy by explosion **6** to cause (a fuse) to blow **7** to rupture by too much pressure <blew *a gasket*> **8** to squander (money or an advantage) – slang **9** to leave hurriedly <blew *town*> – slang – **blow hot and cold** to act changeably by alternately favouring and rebuffing – **blow off steam** to release pent-up emotions – **blow one's own trumpet** to praise oneself; boast – **blow one's top** to become furious; explode with anger – infml – **blow the gaff** *Br* to let out a usu discreditable secret – **blow someone's mind 1** to cause sby to hallucinate – slang **2** to amaze sby – infml – **blow the whistle on 1** to bring (sthg secret) into the open – slang **2** to inform against – slang

[2]**blow** *n* **1** a strong wind or windy storm **2** an act or instance of blowing **3** a walk or other outing in the fresh air – infml

[3]**blow** *vt* **blew** /blooh‖bluː/; **blown** /blohn‖bləʊn/ to cause (e g flowers or blossom) to open out, usu just before dropping

[4]**blow** *n* [2]BLOOM 1b – poetic

[5]**blow** *n* **1** a hard stroke delivered with a part of the body or with an instrument **2** *pl* a hostile or aggressive state – esp in *come to blows* **3** a forcible or sudden act or effort **4** a shock or misfortune

ˈ**blow**ˌ**back** /-ˌbak‖-ˌbæk/ *n* a recoil-operated action of a firearm in which no locking or inertia mechanism hinders the rearward motion of the bolt or breechblock; *also* an automatic firearm using such an action

ˌ**blow-by-**ˈ**blow** *adj* minutely detailed <*a* ~ *account*>

blower /ˈbloh·ə‖ˈbləʊə/ *n* **1** sby or sthg that blows or is blown **2** a device for producing a current of air or gas **3** *Br the* telephone – infml

ˈ**blow**ˌ**fly** /-ˌflie‖-ˌflaɪ/ *n* any of various 2-winged flies that deposit their eggs or maggots esp on meat or in wounds; *esp* a bluebottle

ˈ**blow**ˌ**gun** /-ˌgun‖-ˌgʌn/ *n* BLOWPIPE 2

ˈ**blow**ˌ**hole** /-ˌhohl‖-ˌhəʊl/ *n* **1** a nostril in the top of the head of a whale, porpoise, or dolphin **2** a hole in the ice to which aquatic mammals (e g seals) come to breathe

blow in *vi* to arrive casually or unexpectedly – infml

ˈ**blow**ˌ**lamp** /-ˌlamp‖-ˌlæmp/ *n* a small portable burner that produces an intense flame and has a pressurized fuel tank

blown /blohn‖bləʊn/ *adj* **1** swollen **2** flyblown

ˈ**blow**ˌ**out** /-ˌowt‖-ˌaʊt/ *n* **1** a large meal –infml **2** a bursting of a container (e g a tyre) by pressure of the contents on a weak spot **3** an uncontrolled eruption of an oil or gas well

blow out *vi* **1** to become extinguished by a gust **2** *of an oil or gas well* to erupt out of control ~*vt* to extinguish by a gust

blow over *vi* to pass away without effect

ˈ**blow**ˌ**pipe** /-ˌpiep‖-ˌpaɪp/ *n* **1** a small tube for blowing air, oxygen, etc into a flame to direct and increase the heat **2** a tube for propelling a projectile (e g a dart) by blowing **3** a long metal tube used by a glassblower

blowsy *also* **blowzy** /ˈblowzi‖ˈblaʊzɪ/ *adj* **1** having a coarse ruddy complexion **2** *esp of a woman* slovenly in appearance and usu fat

ˈ**blow**ˌ**up** /-ˌup‖-ˌʌp/ *n* **1** an explosion **2** an outburst of temper **3** a photographic enlargement

blow up *vt* **1** to shatter or destroy by explosion **2** to build up or exaggerate to an unreasonable extent **3** to fill up with a gas, esp air **4** to make a photographic enlargement of ~ *vi* **1a** to explode **b** to be disrupted or destroyed (e g by explosion) **c** to become violently angry **2a** to become filled with a gas, esp air **b** to become expanded to unreasonable proportions **3** to come into being; arise

blowy /ˈbloh·i‖ˈbləʊɪ/ *adj* windy

[1]**blubber** /ˈblubə‖ˈblʌbə/ *n* the fat of large marine mammals, esp whales – **blubbery** *adj*

[2]**blubber** *vi* to weep noisily ~*vt* to utter while weeping *USE* infml

[3]**blubber** *adj* puffed out; thick < ~ *lips*>

[1]**bludgeon** /ˈblujən‖ˈblʌdʒən/ *n* a short club used as a weapon

[2]**bludgeon** *vt* **1** to hit or beat with a bludgeon **2** to overcome by aggressive argument

[1]**blue** /blooh‖bluː/ *adj* **1** of the colour blue **2** discoloured through cold, anger, bruising, or fear **3** bluish grey <*a* ~ *cat*> **4a** low in spirits **b** depressing, dismal **5** CONSERVATIVE 1 **6a** obscene, pornographic **b** off-colour, risqué – **bluely** *adv*, **blueness** *n* – **once in a blue moon** very rarely – **until one is blue in the face** unsuccessfully for ever

[2]**blue** *n* **1** a colour whose hue is that of the clear sky and lies between green and violet in the spectrum **2a** a blue pigment or dye **b** a blue preparation used to whiten clothes in laundering **3** blue clothing **4a(1)** the sky **a(2)** the far distance **b** the sea **5** any of numerous small chiefly blue butterflies **6** *often cap, Br* a usu notional award given to sby who has played in a sporting contest between Oxford and Cambridge universities; *also* sby who has been given such an award **7** *Austr* a quarrel, row – infml – **out of the blue** without warning; unexpectedly

[3]**blue** *vb* **blueing, bluing** /ˈblooh·ing‖ˈbluːɪŋ/ to (cause to) turn blue

[4]**blue** *vt* **blueing, bluing** *Br* to spend lavishly and wastefully – infml

ˌ**blue ˈbaby** *n* a baby with a bluish tint, usu from a congenital heart defect

ˈ**blueˌbell** /-ˌbel‖-ˌbel/ *n* **1** any of various plants of the lily family bearing blue bell-shaped flowers; *esp* the wild hyacinth **2** *chiefly Scot* the harebell

ˈ**blueberry** /-b(ə)ri‖-b(ə)rɪ/ *n* (the edible blue or blackish berry of) any of several shrubs of the heath family

ˈ**blueˌbird** /-ˌbuhd‖-ˌbɜːd/ *n* any of several small N American songbirds

ˌ**blue ˈblood** *n* high or noble birth – **blue-blooded** *adj*

blue book *n* an official parliamentary report or document

ˈ**blueˌbottle** /-ˌbotl‖-ˌbɒtl/ *n* **1** CORNFLOWER 2 **2** any of several blowflies of which the abdomen or the whole body is iridescent blue, that make a loud buzzing noise in flight

ˌ**blue ˈcheese** *n* cheese marked with veins of greenish-blue mould

blue chip *n* a stock issue of high investment quality that usu pertains to a substantial well-established company and enjoys public confidence in its worth and stability – **blue-chip** *adj*

ˌ**blue-ˈcollar** *adj* of or being the class of manual wage-earning employees whose duties call for the wearing of work clothes or protective clothing

blue gum *n* any of several Australian eucalyptuses grown for their wood

ˌ**blue-ˈpencil** *vt* to edit by correcting or deleting – **blue penciller** *n*

ˌ**blue ˈpeter** /ˈpeetə‖ˈpiːtə/ *n* a blue signal flag with a white square in the centre, used to indicate that a merchant vessel is ready to sail

ˈ**blueˌprint** /-ˌprint‖-ˌprɪnt/ *n* **1** a photographic print in white on a bright blue ground, used esp for copying maps and plans **2** a detailed programme of action – **blueprint** *vt*

blue ribbon *n* a ribbon of blue fabric worn as an honour or award, esp by members of the Order of the Garter

blues /bloohz‖bluːz/ *n, pl* **blues** **1** *sing or pl in constr* low spirits; melancholy – + *the* **2** (a song in) a melancholy style of music characterized by flattened thirds or sevenths where a major interval would be expected in the melody and harmony – **bluesy** *adj*

ˈ**blueˌstocking** /-ˌstoking‖-ˌstɒkɪŋ/ *n* a woman with intellectual or literary interests – derog

[1]**bluff** /bluf‖blʌf/ *adj* **1** rising steeply with a broad, flat, or rounded front **2** good-naturedly frank and outspoken – **bluffly** *adv*, **bluffness** *n*

[2]**bluff** *n* a high steep bank; a cliff

[3]**bluff** *vt* **1** to deceive (an opponent) in cards by a bold bet on an inferior hand with the result that the opponent withdraws a winning hand **2** to deceive by pretence or an outward appearance of strength, confidence, etc ~*vi* to bluff sby – **bluffer** *n*

[4]**bluff** *n* an act or instance of bluffing

[1]**blunder** /ˈblundə‖ˈblʌndə/ *vi* **1** to move unsteadily or confusedly **2** to make a blunder – **blunderer** *n*, **blunderingly** *adv*

[2]**blunder** *n* a gross error or mistake resulting from stupidity, ignorance, or carelessness

blunderbuss /ˈblundəˌbus‖ˈblʌndəˌbʌs/ *n* an obsolete short firearm with a large bore and usu a flaring muzzle [obsolete Dutch *donderbus*, fr *donder* thunder + *bus* gun]

[1]**blunt** /blunt‖blʌnt/ *adj* **1** insensitive, dull **2** having an edge or point that is not sharp **3a** aggressively outspoken **b** direct, straightforward – **bluntly** *adv*, **bluntness** *n*

[2]**blunt** *vt* to make less sharp or definite

[1]**blur** /bluh‖blɜː/ *n* **1** a smear or stain **2** sthg vague or indistinct – **blurry** *adj*, **blurriness** *n*

[2]**blur** *vb* **-rr-** *vt* **1** to obscure or blemish by smearing **2** to make indistinct or confused ~*vi* to become vague, indistinct, or confused – **blurringly** *adv*

blurb /bluhb‖blɜːb/ *n* a short publicity notice, esp on a book cover

blurt out /bluht‖blɜːt/ *vt* to utter abruptly and impulsively

[1]**blush** /blush‖blʌʃ/ *vi* **1** to become red in the face, esp from shame, modesty, or embarrassment **2** to feel shame or embarrassment – **blushingly** *adv*

[2]**blush** *n* **1** a reddening of the face, esp from shame, confusion, or embarrassment **2** a red or rosy tint – **blushful** *adj*

[1]**bluster** /ˈblustə‖ˈblʌstə/ *vi* **1** to blow in stormy gusts **2** to talk or act in a noisily self-assertive or boastful manner – **blusterer** *n*, **blusteringly** *adv*

[2]**bluster** *n* **1** a violent blowing **2** loudly boastful or threatening talk – **blusterous** *adj*, **blustery** *adj*

BO /ˌbee ˈoh‖ˌbiː ˈəʊ/ *n* a disagreeable smell, esp of stale perspiration, given off by a person's body

boa /ˈboh·ə‖ˈbəʊə/ *n* **1** a large snake (e g the boa constrictor, anaconda, or python) that crushes its prey **2** a long fluffy scarf of fur, feathers, or delicate fabric

boar /baw‖bɔː/ *n* **1a** an uncastrated male pig **b** the male of any of several mammals (e g a guinea pig or badger) **2** the Old World wild pig from which most domestic pigs derive – **boarish** *adj*

[1]**board** /bawd‖bɔːd/ *n* **1** the distance that a sailing vessel makes on 1 tack **2a** a usu long thin narrow piece of sawn timber **b** *pl* STAGE 2a(2), (3) **3a** a table spread with a meal **b** daily meals, esp when provided in return for payment **4** *sing or pl in constr* **4a** a group of people having managerial, supervisory, or investigatory powers < ~ *of directors*> **b** an official body <*the gas* ~> **5** a flat usu rectangular piece of material designed or marked for a special purpose (e g for playing chess, ludo, backgammon, etc or for use as a blackboard or surfboard) **6a** any of various wood pulps or composition materials formed into stiff flat rectangular sheets **b** cardboard – **boardlike** *adj* – **on board** aboard

[2]**board** *vt* **1** to come up against or alongside (a ship), usu to attack **2** to go aboard (e g a ship,

train, aircraft, or bus) **3** to cover with boards – + *over* or *up* < ~ *up a window*> **4** to provide with regular meals and usu lodging for a fixed price ~*vi* to take one's meals, usu as a paying customer

boarder /ˈbawdə‖ˈbɔːdə/ *n* **1** a lodger **2** a resident pupil at a boarding school

boardinghouse /ˈbawdingˌhows‖ˈbɔːdɪŋ ˌhaʊs/ *n* a lodging house that supplies meals

ˈ**boarding ˌschool** *n* a school at which meals and lodging are provided

board out *vb* to (cause to) receive regular board and usu lodging away from home <boarded *the cat* out *while they were on holiday*>

ˈ**boardroom** /-ˌroohm, -room‖-ˌruːm, -rʊm/ *n* a room in which board meetings are held

ˈ**boardsailing** *n* wind-surfing – **board-sailor** *n*

ˈ**boardˌwalk** /-ˌwawk‖-ˌwɔːk/ *n, NAm* a walk often constructed of planking, usu beside the sea

[1]**boast** /bohst‖bəʊst/ *n* **1** an act of boasting **2** a cause for pride – **boastful** *adj*, **boastfully** *adv*, **boastfulness** *n*

[2]**boast** *vi* to praise oneself ~ *vt* **1** to speak of or assert with excessive pride **2** to have or display as notable or a source of pride – **boaster** *n*

[3]**boast** *n* a usu defensive shot in squash made from a rear corner of the court and hitting a side wall before the front wall

[1]**boat** /boht‖bəʊt/ *n* **1** a small open vessel or craft for travelling across water **2** a usu small ship **3** a boat-shaped utensil or dish <*a gravy* ~> – **in the same boat** in the same situation or predicament

[2]**boat** *vi* to use a boat, esp for recreation

boater /ˈbohtə‖ˈbəʊtə/ *n* a stiff straw hat with a shallow flat crown and a brim

ˈ**boatˌhook** /-ˌhook‖-ˌhʊk/ *n* a pole with a hook at one end, used esp for fending off or holding boats alongside

ˈ**boatˌhouse** /-ˌhows‖-ˌhaʊs/ *n* a shed for boats

ˈ**boatman** /-mən‖-mən/ *n* one who works with or hires out esp pleasure boats – **boatmanship, boatsmanship** *n*

boatswain /ˈbohz(ə)n, ˈbohs(ə)n‖ˈbəʊz(ə)n, ˈbəʊs(ə)n/ *n* a petty officer on a merchant vessel or warrant officer in the navy who supervises all work done on deck and is responsible esp for routine maintenance of the ship's structure

ˈ**boat ˌtrain** *n* an express train that takes people to or from a ship

[1]**bob** /bob‖bɒb/ *vb* **-bb- 1** to move up and down in a short quick movement **2** to perform (a respectful gesture, esp a curtsy) briefly – **bobber** *n*

[2]**bob** *n* **1** a short quick down-and-up motion **2** (a method of bell ringing using) a modification of the order in change ringing

[3]**bob** *n* **1a** *Scot* a nosegay **b** a knot or twist (e g of ribbons or hair) **c** a haircut for a woman or girl in which the hair hangs loose just above the shoulders **2** FLOAT 1a **3** a hanging ball or weight on a plumb line or kite's tail **4** *pl* a small insignificant item <*bits and* ~s>

[4]**bob** *vt* **-bb- 1** to cut shorter; crop < ~ *a horse's tail*> **2** to cut (hair) in a bob

[5]**bob** *n, pl* **bob** *Br* a shilling; *also* the sum of 5 new pence – infml

bobbin /ˈbobin‖ˈbɒbɪn/ *n* **1** a cylinder or spindle on which yarn or thread is wound (e g for use in spinning, sewing, or lacemaking) **2** a coil of insulated wire or the reel it is wound on

[1]**bobble** /ˈbobl‖ˈbɒbl/ *vi* to move jerkily down and up briefly or repeatedly

[2]**bobble** *n* **1** a bobbling movement **2** a small often fluffy ball (e g of wool) used for ornament or trimming

bobby /ˈbobi‖ˈbɒbɪ/ *n, Br* a policeman – infml [*Bobby*, nickname for *Robert*, after Sir *Robert* Peel (1788-1850), English statesman who organized the London police force]

ˈ**bobˌcat** /-ˌkat‖-ˌkæt/ *n* a common N American lynx

ˈ**bobˌsleigh** /-ˌslay‖-ˌsleɪ/ *n* **1** either of a pair of short sledges joined by a coupling **2** a large usu metal sledge for 2 or 4 people used in racing

ˈ**bobˌtail** /-ˌtayl‖-ˌteɪl/ *n* a horse or dog with a bobbed tail – **bobtail, bobtailed** *adj*

bob up *vi* to emerge, arise, or appear suddenly or unexpectedly

bod /bod‖bɒd/ *n* a person – infml

bode /bohd‖bəʊd/ *vt* to augur, presage

bodice /ˈbodis‖ˈbɒdɪs/ *n* the part of a dress that is above the waist

-bodied /-bodid‖-bɒdɪd/ *comb form* (*adj, n* → *adj*) having (such) a body <*full*-bodied>

[1]**bodily** /ˈbodəli‖ˈbɒdəlɪ/ *adj* of the body

[2]**bodily** *adv* **1** IN THE FLESH, IN PERSON **2** as a whole; altogether

bodkin /ˈbodkin‖ˈbɒdkɪn/ *n* **1a** a small sharp slender instrument for making holes in cloth **b** a long ornamental hairpin **2** a blunt thick needle with a large eye used to draw tape or ribbon through a loop or hem

body /ˈbodi‖ˈbɒdɪ/ *n* **1a(1)** the organized physical substance of a living animal or plant **a(2)** a corpse **b** a human being; a person **2a** the main part of a plant or animal body, esp as distinguished from limbs and head **b** the main, central, or principal part: e g **b(1)** the nave of a church **b(2)** the part of a vehicle on or in which the load is placed **3a** the part of a garment covering the body or trunk **b** the central part of printed or written matter **c** the sound box or pipe of a musical instrument **4a** a mass of matter distinct from other masses <*a* ~ *of water*> **b** any of the 7 planets in old astronomy **c** sthg that embodies or gives concrete reality to a thing; *specif* a material object in physical space **5** *sing or pl in constr* a group of people or things: e g **5a** a fighting unit **b** a group of individuals organized for some purpose <*a legislative* ~> **6a** compactness or firmness of texture **b** comparative richness of flavour in wine

ˈ**body ˌblow** *n* a serious setback

ˈ**bodyˌguard** /-ˌgahd‖-ˌgɑːd/ *n* an escort whose duty it is to protect a person from bodily harm

ˈ**body ˌlanguage** *n* the expression of emotion by posture and movement

ˌ**bodyline** ˈ**bowling** /ˈbodilien‖ˈbɒdɪlaɪn/ *n* intimidatory fast bowling in cricket aimed persistently at the batsman's body and directed esp towards the leg side

ˌ**body** ˈ**politic** *n* a group of people under a

single government

'**body ˌsnatcher** *n* one who formerly dug up corpses illegally for dissection

'**bodyˌwork** /-ˌwuhk‖-ˌwɜːk/ *n* the structure or form of a vehicle body

Boer /'baw·ə, 'boh·ə‖'bɔːə, 'bəʊə/ *n* a S African of Dutch descent

boffin /'bofin‖'bɒfɪn/ *n, chiefly Br* a scientific expert; *esp* one involved in technological research – infml

bog /bog‖bɒg/ *n* **1** (an area of) wet spongy poorly-drained ground **2** *Br* TOILET 2 – slang – **boggy** *adj*

bog down *vb* **-gg-** *vt* to cause to sink (as if) into a bog; impede ~*vi* to become impeded

bogey *also* **bogy, bogie** /'bohgi‖'bəʊgɪ/ *n, pl* **bogeys** *also* **bogies** **1** a spectre, ghost **2** a source of fear, perplexity, or harassment **3** a golf score of 1 stroke over par on a hole

[1]**boggle** /'bogl‖'bɒgl/ *vi* **1** to be startled or amazed <*the mind* ~s> **2** to hesitate because of doubt, fear, or scruples – **boggle** *n*

[2]**boggle** *n* a bogle

bogie *also* **bogey, bogy** /'bohgi‖'bəʊgɪ/ *n, pl* **bogies** *also* **bogeys** *chiefly Br* a swivelling framework with 1 or more pairs of wheels and springs to carry and guide 1 end of a railway vehicle

bogle /'bohgl‖'bəʊgl/ *n, dial Br* a goblin, spectre; *also* an object of fear or loathing

bogus /'bohgəs‖'bəʊgəs/ *adj* spurious, sham – **bogusness** *n*

Bohemian /boh'heemyən, -mi·ən‖bəʊ'hiːmjən, -mɪən/ *n* **1a** a native or inhabitant of Bohemia **b** the group of Czech dialects used in Bohemia **2** a person (e g a writer or artist) living an unconventional life – **bohemian** *adj, often cap*

[1]**boil** /boyl‖bɔɪl/ *n* a localized pus-filled swelling of the skin resulting from infection in a skin gland

[2]**boil** *vi* **1a** *of a fluid* to change into (bubbles of) a vapour when heated **b** to come to the boiling point (of the contents) <*the kettle's* ~ing> **2** to bubble or foam violently; churn **3** to be excited or stirred <*made his blood* ~> **4** to undergo the action of a boiling liquid (e g in cooking) ~ *vt* **1** to subject to the action of a boiling liquid (e g in cooking) <~ *eggs*> **2** to heat to the boiling point (of the contents)

[3]**boil** *n* the act or state of boiling; BOILING POINT <*keep it on the* ~>

boil down *vt* **1** to reduce in bulk by boiling **2** to condense or summarize ~*vi* to amount *to* <*her speech* boiled down *to a plea for more money*>

boiler /'boylə‖'bɔɪlə/ *n* **1** a vessel used for boiling **2** the part of a steam generator in which water is converted into steam under pressure **3** a tank in which water is heated or hot water is stored

'**boiler ˌsuit** *n, chiefly Br* a one-piece outer garment combining shirt and trousers, worn chiefly to protect clothing

'**boiling ˌpoint** *n* **1** the temperature at which a liquid boils **2** the point at which a person loses his/her self-control

boil over *vi* **1** to overflow while boiling **2** to lose one's temper

boil up *vi* to rise towards a dangerous level (e g of unrest)

boisterous /'boyst(ə)rəs‖'bɔɪst(ə)rəs/ *adj* **1** noisily and cheerfully rough **2** stormy, wild – **boisterously** *adv*, **boisterousness** *n*

[1]**bold** /bohld‖bəʊld/ *adj* **1** showing or requiring a fearless adventurous spirit **2** impudent, presumptuous **3** departing from convention or tradition **4** standing out prominently; conspicuous **5** (set) in boldface – **boldly** *adv*, **boldness** *n*

[2]**bold** *n* boldface

'**boldˌface** /-ˌfays‖-ˌfeɪs/ *n* (printing in) the thickened form of a typeface used to give prominence or emphasis

bole /bohl‖bəʊl/ *n* the trunk of a tree

bolero /bə'leəroh‖bə'leərəʊ; *sense 2* 'boləroh‖'bɒlərəʊ/ *n, pl* **boleros** **1** (music for) a type of Spanish dance **2** a loose waist-length jacket open at the front

boll /bohl‖bəʊl/ *n* the seed pod of cotton or similar plants

bollard /'bolahd, -ləd‖'bɒlɑːd, -ləd/ *n* **1** a post on a wharf round which to fasten mooring lines **2** a bitt **3** *Br* a short post (e g on a kerb or traffic island) to guide vehicles or forbid access

bollock /'bolək‖'bɒlək/ *n, Br* **1** a testicle – usu pl **2** *pl* nonsense, rubbish – often used interjectionally *USE* vulg

boll weevil /bohl‖bəʊl/ *n* a weevil that infests the cotton plant

boloney /bə'lohni‖bə'ləʊnɪ/ *n* baloney

Bolshevik /'bolshəvik‖'bɒlʃəvɪk/ *n, pl* **Bolsheviks** *also* **Bolsheviki** /ˌbolshə'veeki‖ˌbɒlʃə'viːkɪ/ **1** a member of the more radical wing of the Russian Social Democratic party that seized power in Russia in 1917 **2** COMMUNIST 1 – derog [Russian *bol'shevik*, fr *bol'she* larger; fr their forming the majority group of the party] – **Bolshevik** *adj*, **bolshevism** *n, often cap*, **bolshevize** *vt*, **Bolshevization** *n*

[1]**bolshie, bolshy** /'bolshi‖'bɒlʃɪ/ *n* a Bolshevik – infml

[2]**bolshie, bolshy** *adj, Br* obstinate and argumentative; stubbornly uncooperative – infml – **bolshiness** *n*

[1]**bolster** /'bolstə‖'bɒlstə/ *n* **1** a long pillow or cushion placed across the head of a bed, usu under other pillows **2** a structural part (e g in machinery) that eliminates friction or provides support

[2]**bolster** *vt* to give support to; reinforce <~ed *up his pride*> – **bolsterer** *n*

[1]**bolt** /bolt, bohlt‖bɒlt, bəʊlt/ *n* **1a** a short stout usu blunt-headed arrow shot from a crossbow **b** a lightning stroke; a thunderbolt **2a** a sliding bar or rod used to fasten a door **b** the part of a lock that is shot or withdrawn by the key **3** a roll of cloth or wallpaper of a standard length **4a** a metal rod or pin for fastening objects together **b** a screw-bolt with a head suitable for turning with a spanner **5** a rod or bar that closes the breech of a breech-loading firearm

[2]**bolt** *vi* **1** to move rapidly; dash <*she* ~ed *for the door*> **2a** to dart off or away; flee **b** to break away from control **3** to produce seed prematurely **4** *NAm* to break away from or oppose one's political party ~ *vt* **1** to flush, start <~ *rabbits*> **2** to secure with a bolt **3** to attach or fasten with bolts **4** to swallow (e g food) hastily

or without chewing – **bolter** *n*

[3]**bolt** *adv* in a rigidly erect position <*sat ~ upright*>

[4]**bolt** *n* a dash, run

[5]**bolt** *vt* to sift (e g flour) – **bolter** *n*

ˈ**bolt-ˌhole** *n* **1** a hole into which an animal runs for safety **2** a means of rapid escape or place of refuge

[1]**bomb** /bom‖bɒm/ *n* **1a** any of several explosive or incendiary devices typically detonated by impact or a timing mechanism and usu dropped from aircraft, thrown or placed by hand, or fired from a mortar **b** ATOM BOMB; *broadly* nuclear weapons – + *the* **2** a rounded mass of lava exploded from a volcano **3** *Br* a large sum of money <*she's made a ~*> – infml **4** *NAm* a failure, flop – infml – **a bomb** *Br* very successfully – infml <*our act goes down* a bomb>

[2]**bomb** *vt* to attack with bombs; bombard *~vi* to fail; FALL FLAT – infml

bombard /bomˈbahd, ˈ--‖bɒmˈbɑːd, ˈ--/ *vt* **1** to attack with heavy artillery or with bombers **2** to attack vigorously or persistently (e g with questions) **3** to subject to the impact of electrons, alpha rays, or other rapidly moving particles – **bombardment** *n*

bombardier /ˌbombəˈdiə‖ˌbɒmbəˈdɪə/ *n* **1** a noncommissioned officer in the British artillery **2** a US bomber-crew member who aims and releases the bombs

bombast /ˈbombast‖ˈbɒmbæst/ *n* pretentious inflated speech or writing – **bombastic** *adj*, **bombastically** *adv*

ˈ**bomb ˌbay** *n* a bomb-carrying compartment in the underside of a combat aircraft

bomber /ˈbomə‖ˈbɒmə/ *n* **1** an aircraft designed for bombing **2** sby who throws or places bombs

ˈ**bombˌshell** /-ˌshel‖-ˌʃel/ *n* **1** BOMB 1a **2** sby or sthg that has a stunning or devastating effect

ˈ**bombˌsight** /-ˌsiet‖-ˌsaɪt/ *n* a sighting device for aiming bombs

ˈ**bombˌsite** /-ˌsiet‖-ˌsaɪt/ *n* an area of ground on which buildings have been destroyed by bombing, esp from the air

bona fide /ˌbohnə ˈfiedi‖ˌbəʊnə ˈfaɪdɪ/ *adj* genuine, sincere

ˌ**bona ˈfides** /ˈfiediz‖ˈfaɪdɪz/ *n sing or pl in constr* honest intentions; sincerity [Latin, good faith]

bonanza /bəˈnanzə‖bəˈnænzə/ *n* **1** an exceptionally large and rich mass of ore in a mine **2** sthg (unexpectedly) considered valuable, profitable, or rewarding [Spanish, lit., calm, fair weather, fr Medieval Latin *bonacia*, alteration of Latin *malacia* calm at sea, fr Greek *malakia*, lit., softness, fr *malakos* soft]

bonbon /ˈbonˌbon‖ˈbɒnˌbɒn/ *n* SWEET 2b; *specif* one with a chocolate or fondant coating and fondant centre

[1]**bond** /bond‖bɒnd/ *n* **1** sthg (e g a fetter) that binds or restrains **2** a binding agreement **3a** a mechanism by means of which atoms, ions, or groups of atoms are held together in a molecule or crystal **b** an adhesive or cementing material **4** sthg that unites or binds <*the ~s of friendship*> **5a** a legally enforceable agreement to pay **b** a certificate of intention to pay the holder a specified sum, with or without other interest, on a specified date **6** the system of overlapping bricks in a wall **7** the state of imported goods retained by customs authorities until duties are paid **8** a strong durable paper, now used esp for writing and typing

[2]**bond** *vt* **1** to overlap (e g bricks) for solidity of construction **2** to put (goods) in bond until duties and taxes are paid **3a** to cause to stick firmly **b** to hold together in a molecule or crystal by chemical bonds *~vi* to cohere (as if) by means of a bond – **bondable** *adj*, **bonder** *n*

bondage /ˈbondij‖ˈbɒndɪdʒ/ *n* **1** the tenure or service of a villein, serf, or slave **2a** slavery, serfdom **b** subjugation to a controlling person or force **c** a form of sexual gratification involving the physical restraint of one partner

bonded /ˈbondid‖ˈbɒndɪd/ *adj* **1** used for or being goods in bond **2** composed of 2 or more layers of fabric held together by an adhesive

ˈ**bondˌholder** /-ˌhohldə‖-ˌhəʊldə/ *n* one who holds a government or company bond

[1]**bone** /bohn‖bəʊn/ *n* **1a** (any of the hard body structures composed of) the largely calcium-containing connective tissue of which the adult skeleton of most vertebrate animals is chiefly composed **b** (a structure made of) baleen, ivory, or another hard substance resembling bone **2** *the* essential or basic part or level; *the* core <*cut expenses to the ~*> **3** *pl* the core of one's being <*I felt in my ~s that she was lying*> **4** a subject or matter of dispute <*a ~ of contention*> **5a** *pl* thin bars of bone, ivory, or wood held in pairs between the fingers and used to produce musical rhythms **b** a strip of whalebone or steel used to stiffen a corset or dress **c** *pl* dice **d** a domino – **boned** *adj*, **boneless** *adj* – **bone to pick** a matter to argue or complain about

[2]**bone** *vt* **1** to remove the bones from **2** to stiffen (a garment) with bones – **boner** *n*

[3]**bone** *adv* absolutely, utterly – chiefly in *bone dry, bone idle*

ˌ**bone ˈchina** *n* a type of translucent and durable white hard-paste porcelain made from a mixture of bone ash and kaolin

ˈ**boneˌhead** /-ˌhed‖-ˌhed/ *n* a stupid person – infml – **boneheaded** *adj*

ˈ**bone ˌmeal** *n* fertilizer or feed made of crushed or ground bone

ˈ**boneˌsetter** /-ˌsetə‖-ˌsetə/ *n* a person, esp one who is not a licensed physician, who sets broken or dislocated bones

ˈ**bone ˌshaker** *n* an early bicycle with solid tyres

bone up *vi* to try to master necessary information in a short time, esp for a special purpose – infml

bonfire /ˈbonfie·ə‖ˈbɒnfaɪə/ *n* a large fire built in the open air [Middle English *bonefire* a fire of bones, fr *bon* bone + *fire*]

[1]**bongo** /ˈbong·goh‖ˈbɒŋgəʊ/ *n*, any of 3 large striped antelopes of tropical Africa

[2]**bongo** *n, pl* **bongos** *also* **bongoes** either of a pair of small tuned drums played with the hands – **bongoist** *n*

bonhomie /ˌbonoˈmee, boˈnomi‖ˌbɒnɒˈmiː, bɒˈnɒmɪ/ *n* good-natured friendliness [French, fr *bonhomme* good-natured man, fr *bon* good +

homme man]

bonito /bə'neetoh‖bə'ni:təʊ/ *n*, any of various medium-sized tunas

bonkers /'bongkəz‖'bɒŋkəz/ *adj, chiefly Br* mad, crazy – infml

bon mot /ˌbon 'moh ‖ˌbɒn 'məʊ (*Fr* bɔ̃ mo)/ *n, pl* **bons mots, bon mots** /ˌbon 'moh(z) ‖ˌbɒn 'məʊ(z) (*Fr* ~)/ a witticism [French, lit., good word]

bonnet /'bonit‖'bɒnɪt/ *n* **1** a cloth or straw hat tied under the chin, now worn chiefly by children **2** a soft brimless cap worn by men in Scotland **3** *Br* the hinged metal covering over the engine of a motor vehicle

bonny /'boni‖'bɒnɪ/ *adj, chiefly Br* attractive, comely – **bonnily** *adv*

bonsai /bon'sie‖bɒn'saɪ/ *n, pl* **bonsai** (the art of growing) a potted plant dwarfed by special methods of culture

bonus /'bohnəs‖'bəʊnəs/ *n* **1** sthg given in addition to what is usual or strictly due **2** money or an equivalent given in addition to an employee's usual remuneration

bon vivant /ˌbon vee'vonh‖ˌbon vi:'vɑ̃ (*Fr* bɔ̃ vivɑ̃)/ *n, pl* **bons vivants, bon vivants** /~/ a person with cultivated and refined tastes, esp in regard to food and drink [French, lit., good liver]

bony, boney /'bohni‖'bəʊnɪ/ *adj* **1** consisting of or resembling bone **2a** full of bones **b** having large or prominent bones **3** skinny, scrawny

¹boo /booh‖bu:/ *interj* – used to express contempt or disapproval or to startle or frighten

²boo *n, pl* **boos** a shout of disapproval or contempt

³boo *vb* to show scorn or disapproval (of) by uttering 'boo'

¹boob /boohb‖bu:b/ *n* **1** a stupid mistake; a blunder – infml **2** BREAST 1 – slang

²boob *vi* to make a stupid mistake – infml

¹booby /'boohbi‖'bu:bɪ/ *n* **1** an awkward foolish person **2** any of several small gannets of tropical seas **3** the poorest performer in a group

²booby *n* BREAST 1 – vulg

'booby ˌhatch *n, NAm* MADHOUSE 1

'booby ˌprize *n* an award for the poorest performance in a contest

'booby ˌtrap *n* **1** a trap for the unwary or unsuspecting **2** a harmless-looking object concealing an explosive device that is set to explode by remote control or if touched – **booby-trap** *vt*

boodle /'boohdl‖'bu:dl/ *n* money, esp when stolen or used for bribery – slang

¹book /book‖bʊk/ *n* **1a** a set of written, printed, or blank sheets bound together into a volume **b** a long written or printed literary composition **c** a major division of a treatise or literary work **d** a record of business transactions – usu pl <*their* ~s *show a profit*> **2** *cap the* Bible **3** sthg regarded as a source of enlightenment or instruction **4** a packet of (paper, cardboard, etc) commodities (e g tickets, stamps, or matches) bound together **5** the bets registered by a bookmaker **6** the number of tricks that must be won at cards before any trick can have scoring value – **bookful** *n*, **booklet** *n* – **by/according to the book** by following previously laid down instructions and not using personal initiative – **in one's book** in one's own opinion

²book *vt* **1** to reserve or make arrangements for in advance <~ *2 seats at the theatre*> **2a** to take the name of with a view to prosecution **b** to enter the name of (a player) in a book for a violation of the rules usu involving foul play – used with reference to a rugby or soccer player ~ *vi* **1** to reserve sthg in advance <~ *up through your travel agent*> **2** *chiefly Br* to register in a hotel – **booker** *n*

³book *adj* **1** derived from books; theoretical **2** shown by books of account

bookable /'bookəbl‖'bʊkəbl/ *adj, chiefly Br* **1** that may be reserved in advance **2** that makes a player liable to be booked by a referee

'bookˌbinding /-ˌbiending‖-ˌbaɪndɪŋ/ *n* the craft or trade of binding books – **bookbinder** *n*, **bookbindery** *n*

'bookˌcase /-ˌkays‖-ˌkeɪs/ *n* a piece of furniture consisting of a set of shelves to hold books

'bookˌend /-ˌend‖-ˌend/ *n* a support placed at the end of a row of books

booking /'booking‖'bʊkɪŋ/ *n* **1** an engagement or scheduled performance **2** a reservation **3** an instance of being booked by a referee

'booking ˌoffice *n, chiefly Br* an office where tickets are sold and bookings made, esp at a railway station

bookish /'bookish‖'bʊkɪʃ/ *adj* **1** relying on theoretical knowledge rather than practical experience **2** literary as opposed to colloquial – **bookishly** *adv*, **bookishness** *n*

'bookˌkeeper /-ˌkeepə‖-ˌki:pə/ *n* one who records the accounts or transactions of a business – **bookkeeping** *n*

'bookˌmaker /-ˌmaykə‖-ˌmeɪkə/ *n* sby who determines odds and receives and pays off bets – **bookmaking** *n*

'bookˌmark /-ˌmahk‖-ˌmɑ:k/, **'bookˌmarker** /-ˌmahkə‖-ˌmɑ:kə/ *n* sthg used to mark a place in a book

'bookˌplate /-ˌplayt‖-ˌpleɪt/ *n* a label that is usu placed inside the cover of a book to identify the owner

'bookˌseller /-ˌselə‖-ˌselə/ *n* sby who sells books; *specif* the owner or manager of a bookshop

'bookˌshop /-ˌshop‖-ˌʃɒp/ *n* a shop where books are the main items offered for sale

'bookˌstall /-ˌstawl‖-ˌstɔ:l/ *n* a stall where books, magazines, and newspapers are sold

'book ˌtoken *n* a gift token exchangeable for books

book up *vt* to reserve all the accommodation in or services of – usu pass

'bookˌworm /-ˌwuhm‖-ˌwɜ:m/ *n* **1** any of various insect larvae that feed on the binding and paste of books **2** a person unusually fond of reading and study

¹boom /boohm‖bu:m/ *n* **1** a spar at the foot of the mainsail in fore-and-aft rig that is attached at its fore end to the mast **2** a long movable arm used to manipulate a microphone **3** a barrier across a river or enclosing an area of water to keep logs together; *also* the enclosed logs **4** a cable or line of spars extended across a river or the mouth of a harbour as a barrier to navigation

²boom /boom, boohm‖bʊm, bu:m/ *vi* **1** to make a deep hollow sound or cry **2** to experience a rapid increase in activity or importance <*business was* ~ing> ~*vt* to cause to resound

[3]boom /boom, boohm‖bʊm, buːm/ *n* **1** a booming sound or cry **2a** rapid settlement and development (e g of a town) **b** a rapid growth or increase in a specified area <*the baby* ~> **c** a rapid widespread expansion of economic activity

boomerang /ˈboohmə͵rang‖ˈbuːmə͵ræŋ/ *n* **1** a bent piece of wood shaped so that it returns to its thrower and used by Australian aborigines as a hunting weapon **2** an act or utterance that backfires on its originator – **boomerang** *vi*

[1]boon /boohn‖buːn/ *n* **1** a benefit or favour, esp when given in answer to a request **2** a timely benefit; a blessing

[2]boon *adj* close, intimate, and convivial – esp in *boon companion*

boor /booə, baw‖bʊə, bɔː/ *n* a coarse, ill-mannered, or insensitive person – **boorish** *adj*

[1]boost /boohst‖buːst/ *vt* **1** to push or shove up from below **2** to increase, raise <*plans to* ~ *production*> **3** to encourage, promote <*extra pay to* ~ *morale*> **4** to increase the force, pressure, or amount of; *esp* to raise the voltage of or across (an electric circuit)

[2]boost *n* **1** a push upwards **2** an increase in amount **3** an act that promotes or encourages

booster /ˈboohstə‖ˈbuːstə/ *n* **1** an auxiliary engine which assists (e g at take-off) by providing a large thrust for a short time **2** a supplementary dose increasing or renewing the effectiveness of a medicament

[1]boot /booht‖buːt/ *n* – **to boot** besides

[2]boot *n* **1a** an outer covering for the human foot that extends above the ankle and has a stiff or thick sole and heel **b** a stout shoe, esp for sports **2** a blow or kick delivered (as if) by a booted foot **3** *Br* the major luggage compartment of a motor car **4** summary discharge or dismissal – slang; chiefly in *give/get the boot* – **booted** *adj* – **put/stick the boot in 1** *chiefly Br* to cause added distress to one who is already defeated – infml **2** to act with brutal decisiveness – infml

[3]boot *vt* to kick

ˈboot͵black /-͵blak‖-͵blæk/ *n* sby who cleans and shines shoes

bootee, bootie /ˈbooh͵tee, -ˈ-‖ˈbuː͵tiː, -ˈ-/ *n* **1** a short boot **2** an infant's sock worn in place of a shoe

booth /booth‖bʊθ/ *n, pl* **booths** /boohths, boohdhz‖buːθs, buːðz/ **1** a stall or stand for the sale or exhibition of goods **2** a small enclosure affording privacy (e g for telephoning, dining, etc)

ˈboot͵lace /-͵lays‖-͵leɪs/ *n, Br* a long stout shoelace

[1]ˈboot͵leg /-͵leg‖-͵leg/ *adj or n, chiefly NAm* (being) smuggled or illegally produced alcoholic drink

[2]bootleg *vb, chiefly NAm* to manufacture, sell, or transport for sale (esp alcoholic drink) contrary to law – **bootlegger** *n*

ˈbootless /-lis‖-lɪs/ *adj* useless, unprofitable – fml – **bootlessly** *adv*, **bootlessness** *n*

boot out *vt* to eject or discharge summarily <*was* booted out *of office*> – infml

boots *n, pl* **boots** *Br* a servant who polishes shoes and carries luggage, esp in a hotel

ˈboot͵straps /͵straps‖͵stræps/ *n* – **haul/pull oneself up by one's own bootstraps** to improve oneself or one's situation by one's own unaided efforts

booty /ˈboohti‖ˈbuːtɪ/ *n* **1** plunder taken (e g in war) **2** a rich gain or prize

[1]booze /boohz‖buːz/ *vi* to drink intoxicating liquor to excess – slang – **boozily** *adv*, **boozy** *adj*

[2]booze *n* **1** intoxicating drink; *esp* spirits **2** a drinking spree *USE* slang

boozer /ˈboohzə‖ˈbuːzə/ *n* a public house – slang

ˈbooze-͵up *n* **1** BOOZE 2 **2** a drunken party *USE* slang

[1]bop /bop‖bɒp/ *vt or n* **-pp-** (to strike with) a blow (e g of the fist) – infml

[2]bop *n* jazz characterized by unusual chord structures, syncopated rhythm, and harmonic complexity and innovation – **bopper** *n*

[3]bop *vi* **-pp-** to dance (e g in a disco) in a casual and unrestricted manner, esp to popular music – infml

bo͵racic ˈacid /bəˈrasik‖bəˈræsɪk/ *n* BORIC ACID

borage /ˈborij, ˈburij‖ˈbɒrɪdʒ, ˈbʌrɪdʒ/ *n* a coarse hairy blue-flowered European herb

borax /ˈbawraks‖ˈbɔːræks/ *n* natural or synthetic hydrated sodium borate used esp as a flux, cleansing agent, and water softener

Bordeaux /bawˈdoh‖bɔːˈdəʊ/ *n, pl* **Bordeaux** /bawˈdoh(z)‖bɔːˈdəʊ(z)/ a red or white wine of the Bordeaux region of France

bordello /bawˈdeloh‖bɔːˈdeləʊ/ *n, pl* **bordellos** a brothel

[1]border /ˈbawdə‖ˈbɔːdə/ *n* **1** an outer part or edge **2** a boundary, frontier **3** a narrow bed of planted ground (e g beside a path) **4** an ornamental design at the edge of sthg (e g printed matter, fabric, or a rug) – **bordered** *adj*

[2]border *vt* **1** to put a border on **2** to adjoin at the edge or boundary – **borderer** *n* – **border on 1** BORDER 2 <*the USA* borders on *Canada*> **2** to resemble closely <*his devotion* borders on *the ridiculous*>

ˈBorder ͵collie *n* (any of) a breed of rough-haired, often black-and-white, stocky dogs commonly used in Britain for herding sheep

ˈborder͵line /-͵lien‖-͵laɪn/ *adj* **1** verging on one or other place or state without being definitely assignable to either **2** not quite meeting accepted standards (e g of morality or good taste)

ˈborder ͵line *n* a line of demarcation

[1]bore /baw‖bɔː/ *vt* **1** to pierce (as if) with a rotary tool **2** to form or construct by boring ~ *vi* **1a** to make a hole by boring **b** to drill a mine or well **2** to make one's way steadily or laboriously

[2]bore *n* **1** a hole made (as if) by boring **2a** an interior cylindrical cavity <*the* ~ *of a thermometer*> **b** [1]BARREL 2a **3a** the size of a hole **b** the interior diameter of a tube **c** the diameter of an engine cylinder

[3]bore *past of* BEAR

[4]bore *n* a tidal flood that moves swiftly as a steep-fronted wave in a channel, estuary, etc

[5]bore *n* a tedious person or thing

[6]bore *vt* to weary by being dull or monotonous

– **boring** *adj*, **boringly** *adv*, **boredom** *n*

ˈboreˌhole /-ˌhohl‖-ˌhəʊl/ *n* a hole drilled in the earth to obtain water, oil, etc

ˌboric ˈacid /ˈbawrik, ˈborik‖ˈbɔːrɪk, ˈbɒrɪk/ *n* a white solid acid used esp as a weak antiseptic

born /bawn‖bɔːn/ *adj* **1a** brought into existence (as if) by birth **b** by birth; native <*British*-born> **2** having a specified character or situation from birth <*a* ~ *leader*> <*nobly* ~>

ˌborn-aˈgain *adj* having undergone a conversion, esp to evangelical Christianity

borne /bawn‖bɔːn/ *past part of* BEAR

boron /ˈbawron‖ˈbɔːrɒn/ *n* a metalloid element found in nature only in combination – **boronic** *adj*

borough /ˈburə‖ˈbʌrə/ *n* **1** a British urban constituency **2a** a municipal corporation in certain states of the USA **b** any of the 5 political divisions of New York City

borrow /ˈboroh‖ˈbɒrəʊ/ *vt* **1** to take or receive with the intention of returning <~ *a book*> **2a** to appropriate for one's own use **b** to copy or imitate **3** to take (1) from a figure of the minuend in subtraction and add it as 10 to the next lowest figure ~*vi* to borrow sthg <*English* ~s *from other languages*> – **borrower** *n*

borscht /bawsht‖bɔːʃt/ *n* a soup made primarily from beetroots and served hot or cold, often with sour cream

borstal /ˈbawstl‖ˈbɔːstl/ *n, often cap, Br* a penal institution for young offenders [*Borstal*, village in Kent, England, site of the first such institution]

borzoi /ˈbawzoy, -ˈ-‖ˈbɔːzɔɪ, -ˈ-/ *n* any of a breed of large long-haired dogs developed in Russia, esp for pursuing wolves

bosh /bosh‖bɒʃ/ *n* nonsense – infml [Turkish *boş* empty, useless]

[1]**bosom** /ˈboozəm‖ˈbʊzəm/ *n* **1** the front of the human chest; *esp* the female breasts **2a** the breast considered as the centre of secret thoughts and emotions **b** close relationship <*in the* ~ *of her family*> **3** the part of a garment covering the breast

[2]**bosom** *adj* close, intimate <~ *friends*>

bosomy /ˈboozəmi‖ˈbʊzəmɪ/ *adj* having large breasts

[1]**boss** /bos‖bɒs/ *n* **1a** a protuberant part or body <*a* ~ *on an animal's horn*> **b** a raised ornamentation **c** a carved ornament concealing the intersection of the ribs of a vault or panelled ceiling **2** the enlarged part of a shaft, esp on which a wheel is mounted

[2]**boss** *n* **1** one who exercises control or authority; *specif* one who directs or supervises workers **2** a politician who controls a party organization (e g in the USA)

[3]**boss** *vt* **1** to act as director or supervisor of **2** ORDER 2a – often + *about* or *around* *USE* infml

ˌboss-ˈeyed *adj, Br* having a squint; cross-eyed – infml

bossy /ˈbosi‖ˈbɒsɪ/ *adj* domineering, dictatorial – infml – **bossiness** *n*

bosun /ˈbohz(ə)n, ˈbohs(ə)n‖ˈbəʊz(ə)n, ˈbəʊs(ə)n/ *n* a boatswain

botan·ize, -ise /ˈbotəniez‖ˈbɒtənaɪz/ *vi* to collect plants for botanical investigation; *also* to study plants, esp on a field trip

botany /ˈbotəni‖ˈbɒtənɪ/ *n* **1** a branch of biology dealing with plant life **2a** the plant life (of a region) **b** the properties and life phenomena exhibited by a plant, plant type, or plant group [deriv of Greek *botanē* pasture, herb, fr *boskein* to feed] – **botanist** *n*, **botanic** *adj*, **botanical** *adj*, **botanically** *adv*

[1]**botch** /boch‖bɒtʃ/ *vt* **1** to repair, patch, or assemble in a makeshift or inept way **2** to foul up hopelessly; bungle *USE* infml – **botcher** *n*

[2]**botch** *n* **1** sthg botched; a mess **2** a clumsy patchwork *USE* infml – **botchy** *adj*

[1]**both** /bohth‖bəʊθ/ *adj* being the 2; affecting or involving the one as well as the other <~ *his feet*>

[2]**both** *pron pl in constr* the one as well as the other <~ *of the books*> <*we're* ~ *well*>

[3]**both** *conj* – used to indicate and stress the inclusion of each of 2 or more things specified by coordinated words or word groups <*she* ~ *speaks and writes Swahili*>

[1]**bother** /ˈbodhə‖ˈbɒðə/ *vt* **1** to cause to be troubled or perplexed **2a** to annoy or inconvenience **b** – used as a mild interjection of annoyance ~ *vi* **1** to feel mild concern or anxiety **2** to take pains; take the trouble

[2]**bother** *n* **1** (a cause of) mild discomfort, annoyance, or worry **2** unnecessary fussing **3** a minor disturbance <*there was a spot of* ~ *here today*>

botheration /ˌbodhəˈraysh(ə)n‖ˌbɒðəˈreɪʃ(ə)n/ *n* **1** bothering or being bothered **2** – used as a mild interjection of annoyance

ˈbothersome /-s(ə)m‖-s(ə)m/ *adj* causing bother; annoying

[1]**bottle** /ˈbotl‖ˈbɒtl/ *n* **1a** a rigid or semirigid container, esp for liquids, usu of glass or plastic, with a comparatively narrow neck or mouth **b** the contents of a bottle **2a** intoxicating drink – slang <*hit the* ~> **b** bottled milk used to feed infants **3** *Br* NERVE 3b – slang – **bottleful** *n*

[2]**bottle** *vt* **1** to put into a bottle **2** *Br* to preserve (e g fruit) by storage in glass jars – **bottler** *n*

ˈbottle-ˌfeed *vt* **bottle-fed** /fed‖fed/ to feed (e g an infant) by means of a bottle

bottle green *adj or n* very dark green

ˈbottleˌneck /-ˌnek‖-ˌnek/ *n* **1a** a narrow stretch of road **b** a point or situation where free movement or progress is held up **2** a style of guitar playing using an object (e g a metal bar or the neck of a bottle) pressed against the strings to produce the effect of one note sliding into another

bottle up *vt* to confine as if in a bottle; restrain <bottling up *their anger*>

[1]**bottom** /ˈbotəm‖ˈbɒtəm/ *n* **1a** the underside of sthg **b** a surface on which sthg rests **c** the buttocks, rump **2** the ground below a body of water **3** the part of a ship's hull lying below the water **4a** the lowest, deepest, or farthest part or place **b** the lowest or last place in order of precedence <*started work at the* ~> **c** the transmission gear of a motor vehicle giving lowest speed of travel **d** the lower part of a two-piece garment – often pl with sing. meaning <*pyjama* ~s> **5** low-lying land along a watercourse **6** a basis, source **7** *archaic* a ship; *esp* a merchant ship –

bottomed *adj* – **at bottom** really, basically

[2]**bottom** *vt* to provide with a bottom or foundation ~*vi* to reach the bottom – usu + *out* – **bottomer** *n*

[3]**bottom** *adj* **1** of or situated at the bottom **2** frequenting the bottom <~ *fishes*> – **bottommost**

ˌ**bottom** ˈ**drawer** *n, Br* (a drawer for storing) a young woman's collection of clothes and esp household articles, kept in anticipation of her marriage

ˈ**bottomless** /-lis‖-lɪs/ *adj* **1** extremely deep **2** boundless, unlimited – **bottomlessly** *adv*, **bottomlessness** *n*

bottom line *n* **1a** the line at the bottom of a financial report that shows the final profit or loss **b** a final result; an outcome **2** the essential point; the crux; *esp* the lowest acceptable outcome of negotiations

botulism /ˈbotyooˌliz(ə)m, -chə-‖ˈbɒtjʊˌlɪz-(ə)m, -tʃə-/ *n* acute often fatal food poisoning caused by a bacterium in (preserved) food

boudoir /ˈboohdwah‖ˈbuːdwɑː/ *n* a woman's dressing room, bedroom, or private sitting room

bouffant /ˈboohfong‖ˈbuːfɒŋ/ *adj* puffed out <*a* ~ *hairstyle*>

bougainvillaea /ˌboohgənˈvilyə‖ˌbuːgən-ˈvɪljə/ *n* any of a genus of ornamental tropical American woody climbing plants with brilliant purple or red floral bracts [Louis Antoine de *Bougainville* (1729-1811), French navigator]

bough /bow‖baʊ/ *n* a (main) branch of a tree – **boughed** *adj*

bought /bawt‖bɔːt/ *past of* BUY

bouillabaisse /ˌbooh·yəˈbes ‖ˌbuːjəˈbes (*Fr* bujabɛs)/ *n* a highly seasoned fish stew

bouillon /ˈbooh·yong ‖ˈbuːjɒŋ (*Fr* bujɔ̃)/ *n* a thin clear soup made usu from lean beef

boulder /ˈbohldə‖ˈbəʊldə/ *n* a large stone or mass of rock

boulevard /ˈboohləˌvahd, -ˌvah‖ˈbuːləˌvɑːd, -ˌvɑː/ *n* a broad avenue, usu lined by trees [French, fr Middle Dutch *bolwerc* bulwark]

[1]**bounce** /bowns‖baʊns/ *vt* **1** to cause to rebound <~ *a ball*> **2** to return (a cheque) as not good because of lack of funds in the payer's account – infml ~ *vi* **1** to rebound after striking **2** to move violently, noisily, or with a springing step <~d *into the room*> **3** to be returned by a bank as not good – infml

[2]**bounce** *n* **1a** a sudden leap or bound **b** a rebound **2** verve, liveliness

bounce back *vi* to recover quickly from a blow or defeat

bouncer /ˈbownsə‖ˈbaʊnsə/ *n* **1** a man employed in a public place to restrain or remove disorderly people **2** a fast short-pitched delivery of a cricket ball that passes or hits the batsman at above chest height after bouncing

bouncing /ˈbownsing‖ˈbaʊnsɪŋ/ *adj* enjoying good health; robust

bouncy /ˈbownsi‖ˈbaʊnsɪ/ *adj* **1** buoyant, exuberant **2** that bounces readily – **bouncily** *adv*

[1]**bound** /bownd‖baʊnd/ *adj* going or intending to go <~ *for home*>

[2]**bound** *n* **1** a limiting line; a boundary **2** sthg that limits or restrains <*beyond the* ~s *of decency*> *USE* usu pl with sing. meaning

[3]**bound** *vt* **1** to set limits to **2** to form the boundary of *USE* usu pass

[4]**bound** *adj* **1a** confined <*desk*-bound> **b** certain, sure *to* <~ *to rain soon*> **2** placed under legal or moral obligation <*I'm* ~ *to say*> **3** held in chemical or physical combination <~ *water in a molecule*>

[5]**bound** *n* **1** a leap, jump **2** a bounce

[6]**bound** *vi* **1** to move by leaping **2** to rebound, bounce

boundary /ˈbownd(ə)ri‖ˈbaʊnd(ə)rɪ/ *n* **1** sthg, esp a dividing line, that indicates or fixes a limit or extent **2a** the marked limits of a cricket field **b** (the score of 4 or 6 made by) a stroke in cricket that sends the ball over the boundary

bounden /ˈbowndən‖ˈbaʊndən/ *adj* made obligatory; binding – esp in *bounden duty*

bounder /ˈbowndə‖ˈbaʊndə/ *n* a cad – not now in vogue

ˈ**boundless** /-lis‖-lɪs/ *adj* limitless – **boundlessly** *adv*, **boundlessness** *n*

bounteous /ˈbowntyəs, -ti·əs‖ˈbaʊntjəs, -tɪəs/ *adj* giving or given freely – **bounteously** *adv*, **bounteousness** *n*

bountiful /ˈbowntif(ə)l‖ˈbaʊntɪf(ə)l/ *adj* **1** generous, liberal **2** abundant, plentiful – **bountifully** *adv*, **bountifulness** *n*

bounty /ˈbownti‖ˈbaʊntɪ/ *n* **1** generosity **2** sthg given generously **3a** a financial inducement or reward, esp when offered by a government for some act or service **b** a payment to encourage the killing of vermin or dangerous animals

bouquet /boohˈkay‖buːˈkeɪ/ *n* **1** a bunch of flowers fastened together **2** a distinctive and characteristic fragrance (e g of wine)

ˌ**bouquet** ˈ**garni** /ˈgahni‖ˈgɑːnɪ/ *n* a small bunch of herbs for use in flavouring stews and soups

bourbon /ˈbuhbən, ˈbooəbən ‖ˈbɜːbən, ˈbʊəbən (*Fr* burbɔ̃)/ *n* **1** *cap* a member of a royal dynasty who ruled in France, Spain, etc **2** a whisky distilled from a mash made up of not less than 51 per cent maize plus malt and rye **3** *often cap, chiefly NAm* an extreme political reactionary – **bourbonism** *n, often cap*

[1]**bourgeois** /ˈbooəzhwah, ˈbaw-‖ˈbʊəʒwɑː, ˈbɔː-/ *n, pl* **bourgeois** **1** a middle-class person **2** one whose behaviour and views are influenced by bourgeois values or interests **3** *pl* the bourgeoisie

[2]**bourgeois** *adj* **1** middle-class **2** marked by a narrow-minded concern for material interests and respectability **3** capitalist

bourgeoisie /ˌbooəzhwahˈzee‖ˌbʊəʒwɑːˈziː/ *n sing or pl in constr* MIDDLE CLASS

[1]**bourn, bourne** /bawn‖bɔːn/ *n* a small stream

[2]**bourn, bourne** *n, archaic* a boundary, limit

bourse /booəs, baws‖bʊəs, bɔːs/ *n* EXCHANGE 4a; *specif* a European stock exchange

bout /bowt‖baʊt/ *n* **1** a spell of activity <*a* ~ *of work*> **2** an athletic match (e g of boxing) **3** an outbreak or attack of illness, fever, etc

boutique /boohˈteek‖buːˈtiːk/ *n* a small fashionable shop selling specialized goods; *also* a small shop within a large department store

bouzouki *also* **bousouki** /booˈzoohki‖bʊ-

ˈzuːkɪ/ *n* a long-necked Greek stringed instrument that resembles a mandolin

bovine /ˈbohvien‖ˈbəʊvaɪn/ *adj* **1** of oxen or cows **2** like an ox or cow (e g in being slow, stolid, or dull)

Bovril /ˈbovril‖ˈbɒvrɪl/ *trademark* – used for a concentrated beef extract

bovver /ˈbovə‖ˈbɒvə/ *n, Br* rowdy or violent disturbance; aggro

[1]bow /bow‖baʊ/ *vi* **1** to submit, yield **2** to bend the head, body, or knee in respect, submission, or greeting ~ *vt* **1** to incline (e g the head), esp in respect, submission, or shame **2** to express by bowing – **bow and scrape** to act in an obsequious manner

[2]bow /bow‖baʊ/ *n* a bending of the head or body in respect, submission, or greeting

[3]bow /boh‖bəʊ/ *n* **1** a bend, arch **2** a strip of wood, fibreglass, or other flexible material held bent by a strong cord connecting the 2 ends and used to shoot an arrow **3** an often ornamental slipknot (e g for tying a shoelace) **4** (a stroke made with) a resilient wooden rod with horsehairs stretched from end to end, used in playing an instrument of the viol or violin family

[4]bow /boh‖bəʊ/ *vb* **1** to (cause to) bend into a curve **2** to play (a stringed instrument) with a bow

[5]bow /bow‖baʊ/ *n* **1** the forward part of a ship – often pl with sing. meaning **2** [2]BOWMAN; *specif* one who rows in the front end of a boat

bowdler·ize, -ise /ˈbowdləriez‖ˈbaʊdləraɪz/ *vt* to expurgate (e g a book) by omitting or modifying parts considered vulgar [Thomas *Bowdler* (1754-1825), English editor] – **bowdlerizer** *n*, **bowdlerization** *n*

bowel /ˈbowəl‖ˈbaʊəl/ *n* **1** (a specified division of) the intestine or gut – usu pl with sing. meaning **2** *pl* the innermost parts <~s *of the earth*> – **bowelless** *adj*

[1]bower /ˈbowə‖ˈbaʊə/ *n* **1** an attractive dwelling or retreat **2** a (garden) shelter made with tree boughs or vines twisted together **3** a boudoir – poetic – **bowery** *adj*

[2]bower *n* a ship's principal anchor carried in the bows

ˈbowie ˌknife /ˈboh·i‖ˈbəʊɪ/ *n* a stout hunting knife with a sharpened part on the back edge curved concavely to the point [James *Bowie* (1796?-1836), US soldier]

[1]bowl /bohl‖bəʊl/ *n* **1** any of various round hollow vessels used esp for holding liquids or food or for mixing food **2** the contents of a bowl **3a** the hollow of a spoon or tobacco pipe **b** the receptacle of a toilet **4a** a bowl-shaped geographical region or formation **b** *NAm* a bowl-shaped structure; *esp* a sports stadium – **bowled** *adj*, **bowlful** *n*

[2]bowl *n* **1** a ball used in bowls that is weighted or shaped to give it a bias **2** *pl but sing in constr* a game played typically outdoors on a green, in which bowls are rolled at a target jack in an attempt to bring them nearer to it than the opponent's bowls

[3]bowl *vi* **1a** to participate in a game of bowling **b** to play or roll a ball in bowls or bowling **c** to play as a bowler in cricket **2** to travel in a vehicle smoothly and rapidly – often + *along* ~ *vt* **1a** to roll (a ball) in bowling **b** to score by bowling <~s *150*> **2a** to deliver (a ball) to a batsman in cricket **b** to dismiss (a batsman in cricket) by breaking the wicket – used with reference to a bowled ball or a bowler

ˌbowˈlegged /-ˈleg(i)d‖-ˈleg(ɪ)d/ *adj* having legs that are bowed outwards at the knees – **bowlegs** *n pl*

[1]bowler /ˈbohlə‖ˈbəʊlə/ *n* the person who bowls in a team sport; *specif* a member of the fielding side who bowls (as a specialist) the ball in cricket

[2]bowler, ˌbowler ˈhat *n* a stiff felt hat with a rounded crown and a narrow brim [*Bowler*, 19th-c English family of hatters]

bowline /ˈbohˌlien‖ˈbəʊˌlaɪn/ *n* **1** a rope attached to a square sail that is used to keep the windward edge of the sail taut and at a steady angle to the wind **2** a knot used to form a non-slipping loop at the end of a rope

bowling /ˈbohling‖ˈbəʊlɪŋ/ *n* any of several games in which balls are rolled at 1 or more objects

ˈbowling ˌalley *n* (a building or room containing) a long narrow enclosure or lane with a smooth usu wooden floor for bowling or playing skittles

ˈbowling ˌgreen *n* a smooth close-cut area of turf for playing bowls

bowl over *vt* **1** to strike with a swiftly moving object **2** to overwhelm with surprise

[1]bowman /ˈbohmən‖ˈbəʊmən/ *n* an archer

[2]bowman *n* a boatman, oarsman, etc in the front of a boat

bow out /bow‖baʊ/ *vi* to retire, withdraw

bowsprit /ˈbohˌsprit‖ˈbəʊˌsprɪt/ *n* a spar projecting forwards from the bow of a ship

ˌbow ˈtie /boh‖bəʊ/ *n* a short tie fastened in a bow

ˌbow ˈwindow /boh‖bəʊ/ *n* a curved bay window

bowwow /ˈbowˌwow‖ˈbaʊˌwaʊ/ *n* **1** the bark of a dog – often used imitatively **2** a dog – used esp by or to children

[1]box /boks‖bɒks/ *n, pl* **box, boxes** any of several evergreen shrubs or small trees used esp for hedges

[2]box *n* **1a** a rigid container having 4 sides, a bottom, and a cover **b** the contents of a box **2a** a small compartment (e g for a group of spectators in a theatre) **b(1)** PENALTY AREA **b(2)** PENALTY BOX **3a** a boxlike protective case (e g for machinery) **b** a shield to protect the genitals, worn esp by batsmen and wicketkeepers in cricket **c** a structure that contains a telephone for use by members of a specified organization **4** a small simple sheltering or enclosing structure **5** *Br* a gift given to tradesmen at Christmas **6** *Br* television; *specif* a television set – + *the*; infml – **boxful** *n*, **boxy** *adj*, **boxiness** *n*

[3]box *vt* **1** to provide with a box **2** to enclose (as if) in a box – + *in* or *up* **3** to hem in (e g an opponent in soccer) – usu + *in* – **box the compass** **1** to name the 32 points of the compass in their order **2** to make a complete reversal

[4]box *n* a punch or slap, esp on the ear

[5]box *vt* **1** to slap (e g the ears) with the hand **2** to engage in boxing with ~*vi* to engage in boxing

Box and Cox /koks‖kɒks/ *adv or adj, Br* alternating; IN TURN [eponymous characters, who share a room but never meet, in play by J M Morton (1811-91), English dramatist]

[1]**boxer** /ˈboksə‖ˈbɒksə/ *n* one who engages in the sport of boxing

[2]**boxer** *n* a compact medium-sized short-haired dog of a breed originating in Germany

Boxer *n* a member of a Chinese secret society which was opposed to foreign influence in China and whose rebellion was suppressed in 1900

boxing /ˈboksing‖ˈbɒksɪŋ/ *n* the art of attack and defence with the fists practised as a sport

ˈBoxing ˌDay *n* December 26, observed as a public holiday in Britain (apart from Scotland) and elsewhere in the Commonwealth, on which service workers (e g postmen) were traditionally given Christmas boxes

ˈboxing ˌglove *n* a heavily padded leather mitten worn in boxing

ˈbox ˌkite *n* a tailless kite consisting of 2 or more open-ended connected boxes

ˈbox ˌnumber *n* the number of a box or pigeon hole at a newspaper or post office where arrangements are made for replies to advertisements or other mail to be sent

ˈbox ˌoffice *n* **1** an office (e g in a theatre) where tickets of admission are sold **2** sthg that enhances ticket sales <*the publicity is all good* ~>

ˈboxˌwood /-ˌwood‖-ˌwʊd/ *n* the very close-grained heavy tough hard wood of the box tree

[1]**boy** /boy‖bɔɪ/ *n* **1a** a male child from birth to puberty **b** a son **c** an immature male; a youth **d** a boyfriend **2** a fellow, person <*the* ~s *at the office*> **3** a male servant – sometimes taken to be offensive – **boyhood** *n*, **boyish** *adj*, **boyishly** *adv*, **boyishness** *n*

[2]**boy** *interj, chiefly NAm* – used to express esp excitement or surprise

boycott /ˈboykot‖ˈbɔɪkɒt/ *vt* to engage in a concerted refusal to have dealings with (e g a person, shop, or organization), usu to express disapproval or to force acceptance of certain conditions [C C *Boycott* (1832-97), English land agent in Ireland who was ostracized for refusing to reduce rents] – **boycott** *n*, **boycotter** *n*

ˈboyˌfriend /-ˌfrend‖-ˌfrend/ *n* **1** a frequent or regular male companion of a girl or woman **2** a male lover

ˌboy ˈscout *n* SCOUT 4 – no longer used technically

bra /brah‖brɑː/ *n, pl* **bras** a woman's closely fitting undergarment with cups for supporting the breasts

[1]**braai** /brie‖braɪ/ *n, SAfr* BARBECUE 1, 3; *also* an area (e g a patio) intended for a braai

[2]**braai** *vt, SAfr* to barbecue

braaivleis /ˈbrieˌflays‖ˈbraɪˌfleɪs/ *n, SAfr* BARBECUE 1, 3

[1]**brace** /brays‖breɪs/ *n, pl* **braces,** (*1*) **braces,** *after a determiner* **brace** **1** two of a kind; a pair **2** sthg (e g a clasp) that connects or fastens **3** a crank-shaped instrument for turning a drilling bit **4a** a diagonal piece of structural material that serves to strengthen **b** a rope attached to a yard on a ship that swings the yard horizontally to trim the sail **c** *pl* straps worn over the shoulders to hold up trousers **d** an appliance for supporting a weak leg or other body part **e** a dental fitting worn to correct irregular teeth **5a** a mark { or } used to connect words or items to be considered together **b** (this mark connecting) 2 or more musical staves the parts of which are to be performed simultaneously

[2]**brace** *vt* **1a** to prepare for use by making taut **b** to prepare, steel < ~ *yourself for the shock*> **2** to turn (a sail yard) by means of a brace **3** to provide or support with a brace

bracelet /ˈbrayslit‖ˈbreɪslɪt/ *n* **1** an ornamental band or chain worn round the wrist **2** sthg (e g handcuffs) resembling a bracelet

brace up *vb* to (cause to) have more courage, spirit, and cheerfulness

bracing /ˈbraysing‖ˈbreɪsɪŋ/ *adj* refreshing, invigorating

bracken /ˈbrakən‖ˈbrækən/ *n* (a dense growth of) a common large coarse fern of esp moorland, that is poisonous to grazing animals

[1]**bracket** /ˈbrakit‖ˈbrækɪt/ *n* **1** an overhanging projecting fixture or member that is designed to support a vertical load or strengthen an angle **2a** PARENTHESIS 1b **b** either of a pair of marks ( ) used in writing and printing to enclose matter or in mathematics and logic to show that a complex expression should be treated as a single unit **c** ANGLE BRACKET **d** BRACE 5b **3** (the distance between) a pair of shots fired usu in front of and beyond a target to aid in range-finding **4** any of a graded series of income groups <*the £20,000 income* ~>

[2]**bracket** *vt* **1** to place (as if) within brackets **2** to provide or fasten with brackets **3** to put in the same category; associate – usu + *together* **4a** to get a range by firing in front of and behind (a target) **b** to establish a margin on either side of (e g an estimation)

brackish /ˈbrakish‖ˈbrækɪʃ/ *adj* slightly salty < ~ *water*> – **brackishness** *n*

bract /brakt‖brækt/ *n* **1** a usu small leaf near a flower or floral axis **2** a leaf borne on a floral axis – **bracteal** *adj*, **bracteate** *adj*, **bracted** *adj*

bradawl /ˈbradˌawl‖ˈbrædˌɔːl/ *n* an awl; *esp* one used by a woodworker

brae /bray‖breɪ/ *n, chiefly Scot* a hillside, esp along a river

[1]**brag** /brag‖bræg/ *n* a card game resembling poker

[2]**brag** *vb* **-gg-** to talk or assert boastfully – **bragger** *n*

braggadocio /ˌbragəˈdohchioh, -ˈdohkioh‖ˌbrægəˈdəʊtʃɪəʊ, -ˈdəʊkɪəʊ/ *n* empty boasting

braggart /ˈbragət‖ˈbrægət/ *n* a loud arrogant boaster – **braggart** *adj*

Brahman /ˈbrahmən‖ˈbrɑːmən/ *n* **1a** a Hindu of the highest caste traditionally assigned to the priesthood **b** the impersonal ground of all being in Hinduism **2** any of an Indian breed of humped cattle; *also* a large vigorous animal developed in the USA by interbreeding Indian cattle – **Brahmanic** *adj*

[1]**braid** /brayd‖breɪd/ *vt* **1** *chiefly NAm* PLAIT 2 **2** to ornament, esp with ribbon or braid – **braider** *n*

[2]**braid** *n* **1** a narrow piece of fabric, esp plaited cord or ribbon, used for trimming **2** *chiefly NAm* a length of plaited hair

braille /brayl‖breɪl/ *n, often cap* a system of writing or printing for the blind that uses characters made up of raised dots [Louis *Braille* (1809-52), French teacher of the blind]

[1]**brain** /brayn‖breɪn/ *n* **1a** the portion of the vertebrate central nervous system that constitutes the organ of thought and neural coordination, is made up of neurons and supporting and nutritive structures, is enclosed within the skull, and is continuous with the spinal cord **b** a nervous centre in invertebrates comparable in position and function to the vertebrate brain **2a(1)** an intellect, mind <*has a good* ~> **a(2)** intellectual endowment; intelligence – often pl with sing. meaning <*plenty of* ~s *in that family*> **b(1)** a very intelligent or intellectual person **b(2)** the chief planner of an organization or enterprise – usu pl with sing. meaning but sing. in constr **3** an automatic device (e g a computer) that performs 1 or more of the functions of the human brain for control or computation – **on the brain** as an obsession; continually in mind <*I've got that tune* on the brain *again*>

[2]**brain** *vt* **1** to kill by smashing the skull **2** to hit hard on the head – infml

ˈbrainˌchild /-ˌchield‖-ˌtʃaɪld/ *n* a product of one's creative imagination

ˈbrain ˌdrain *n the* loss of highly qualified workers and professionals through emigration

-brained *comb form* (*adj, n* → *adj*) having (such) a brain <*feather*brained>

ˈbrainless /-lis‖-lɪs/ *adj* stupid, foolish – **brainlessly** *adv*, **brainlessness** *n*

ˈbrainˌstorm /-ˌstawm‖-ˌstɔːm/ *n* **1** a fit of insanity **2** *chiefly NAm* BRAIN WAVE 2

ˈbrainˌstorming /-ˌstawming/ *n* a problem-solving technique aimed at producing as many ideas on a subject as possible

ˈbrains ˌtrust *n sing or pl in constr, chiefly Br* a group of expert advisers, esp assembled to answer questions of immediate or current interest

ˈbrainˌwashing /-ˌwoshing‖-ˌwɒʃɪŋ/ *n* a systematic attempt to instil beliefs into sby, often in place of beliefs already held – **brainwash** *vt*, **brainwash** *n*, **brainwasher** *n*

ˈbrain ˌwave *n* **1** a rhythmic fluctuation of voltage between parts of the brain **2** a sudden bright idea

brainy /ˈbrayni‖ˈbreɪnɪ/ *adj* intelligent, clever – infml – **braininess** *n*

braise /brayz‖breɪz/ *vt* to cook (e g meat) slowly by first sautéeing in hot fat and then simmering gently in very little liquid in a closed container

[1]**brake** /brayk‖breɪk/ *n* **1** a device for arresting usu rotary motion, esp by friction **2** sthg that slows down or stops movement or activity – **brakeless** *adj*

[2]**brake** *vt* to slow or stop by a brake ~ *vi* **1** to operate, manage, or apply a brake, esp on a vehicle **2** to become slowed by a brake

[3]**brake** *n* an area of overgrown rough or marshy land – **braky** *adj*

[4]**brake** *n* ESTATE CAR

bramble /ˈbrambl‖ˈbræmbl/ *n* a rough prickly shrub, esp a blackberry – **brambly** *adj*

bran /bran‖bræn/ *n* the broken husk of cereal grain separated from the flour or meal by sifting

[1]**branch** /brahnch‖brɑːntʃ/ *n* **1** a secondary shoot or stem (e g a bough) arising from a main axis (e g of a tree) **2a** TRIBUTARY 2 **b** a side road or way **c** a slender projection (e g the tine of an antler) **3** a distinct part of a complex whole: e g **3a** a division of a family descending from a particular ancestor **b** a distinct area of knowledge <*pathology is a* ~ *of medicine*> **c** a division or separate part of an organization – **branched** *adj*, **branchless** *adj*, **branchlet** *n*, **branchy** *adj*

[2]**branch** *vi* **1** to put forth branches **2** to spring out (e g from a main stem)

branch out *vi* to extend activities <*the business is* branching out *all over the state*>

[1]**brand** /brand‖brænd/ *n* **1** a charred piece of wood **2a** a mark made by burning with a hot iron, or with a stamp or stencil, to identify manufacture or quality or to designate ownership (e g of cattle) **b(1)** a mark formerly put on criminals with a hot iron **b(2)** a mark of disgrace <*the* ~ *of poverty*> **3a** a class of goods identified by name as the product of a single firm or manufacturer **b** a characteristic or distinctive kind <*a lively* ~ *of humour*> **4** a tool used to produce a brand **5** a sword – poetic

[2]**brand** *vt* **1** to mark with a brand **2** to stigmatize **3** to impress indelibly – **brander** *n*

brandish /ˈbrandish‖ˈbrændɪʃ/ *vt* to shake or wave (e g a weapon) menacingly or ostentatiously

ˌbrand-ˈnew *adj* conspicuously new and unused

brandy /ˈbrandi‖ˈbrændɪ/ *n* a spirit distilled from wine or fermented fruit juice [short for *brandywine*, fr Dutch *brandewijn*, fr Middle Dutch *brantwijn*, fr *brant* burnt, distilled + *wijn* wine]

ˈbrandy ˌsnap *n* a very thin cylindrical ginger biscuit sometimes flavoured with brandy

[1]**brash** /brash‖bræʃ/ *n* a mass of fragments (e g of ice)

[2]**brash** *adj* **1** impetuous, rash **2** uninhibitedly energetic or demonstrative **3** aggressively self-assertive; impudent – **brashly** *adv*, **brashness** *n*

brass /brahs‖brɑːs/ *n* **1** an alloy of copper and zinc **2a** *sing or pl in constr* the brass instruments of an orchestra or band **b** a usu brass memorial tablet **c** bright metal fittings or utensils **3** brazen self-assurance **4** *sing or pl in constr* BRASS HATS **5** *chiefly N Eng* money *USE* (*3, 4, & 5*) infml – **brass** *adj*

ˌbrass ˈband *n* a band consisting (chiefly) of brass and percussion instruments

ˌbrass ˈhat *n* a high-ranking military officer – infml

brassiere /ˈbrazi·ə‖ˈbræzɪə/ *n* a bra – fml

ˌbrass ˈtacks *n pl* details of immediate practical importance – esp in *get down to brass tacks*

brassy /ˈbrahsi‖ˈbrɑːsɪ/ *adj* **1** shamelessly bold; brazen **2** resembling brass, esp in colour – **brassily** *adv*, **brassiness** *n*

brat /brat‖bræt/ *n* an (ill-mannered) child

bravado /brə'vahdoh‖brə'vɑːdəʊ/ *n, pl* **bravadoes, bravados** (a display of) blustering swaggering conduct

[1]**brave** /brayv‖breɪv/ *adj* **1** courageous, fearless **2** excellent, splendid <*a* ~ *new world*> – **bravely** *adv*

[2]**brave** *vt* to face or endure with courage

[3]**brave** *n* a N American Indian warrior

bravery /'brayv(ə)ri‖'breɪv(ə)rɪ/ *n* courage, valour

[1]**bravo** /'brahvoh‖'brɑːvəʊ/ *n, pl* **bravos, bravoes** a villain, desperado; *esp* a hired assassin

[2]**bravo** /brah'voh‖brɑː'vəʊ/ *n, pl* **bravos** a shout of approval – often used interjectionally in applauding a performance

bravura /brə'v(y)ooərə‖brə'v(j)ʊərə/ *n* **1** a flamboyant brilliant style **2** a musical passage requiring exceptional agility and technical skill in execution **3** a show of daring or brilliance

[1]**brawl** /brawl‖brɔːl/ *vi* **1** to quarrel or fight noisily **2** *of water* to make a loud confused bubbling sound – **brawler** *n*

[2]**brawl** *n* **1** a noisy quarrel or fight **2** a brawling noise

brawn /brawn‖brɔːn/ *n* **1a** strong muscles **b** muscular strength **2** pork trimmings, esp the meat from a pig's head, boiled, chopped, and pressed into a mould

brawny /'brawni‖'brɔːnɪ/ *adj* muscular, strong – **brawnily** *adv*, **brawniness** *n*

[1]**bray** /bray‖breɪ/ *vi* to utter the loud harsh cry characteristic of a donkey ~ *vt* to utter or play loudly, harshly, or discordantly – **bray** *n*

[2]**bray** *vt* to crush or grind finely

[1]**brazen** /'brayz(ə)n‖'breɪz(ə)n/ *adj* **1** resembling or made of brass **2** sounding harsh and loud like struck brass **3** contemptuously bold – **brazenly** *adv*, **brazenness** *n*

[2]**brazen** *vt* to face with defiance or impudence – esp in *brazen it out*

[1]**brazier** /'brayzi·ə, 'brayzhə‖'breɪzɪə, 'breɪʒə/ *n* one who works in brass

[2]**brazier** *n* a receptacle or stand for holding burning coals

[1]**breach** /breech‖briːtʃ/ *n* **1** infraction or violation (e g of a law, obligation, or standard) <~ *of contract*> **2** a gap (e g in a wall) made by battering **3** a break in customarily friendly relations **4** a leap, esp of a whale out of water

[2]**breach** *vt* **1** to make a breach in <~ *the city walls*> **2** to break, violate <~ *an agreement*>

ˌbreach of 'promise *n* violation of a promise, esp to marry

ˌbreach of the 'peace *n* an instance of disorderly conduct

[1]**bread** /bred‖bred/ *n* **1** a food consisting essentially of flour or meal which is baked and usu leavened, esp with yeast **2** food, sustenance <*our daily* ~> **3a** livelihood <*earns his daily* ~ *as a labourer*> **b** money – slang

[2]**bread** *vt* to cover with breadcrumbs

ˌbread-and-'butter *adj* **1a** basic, fundamental <*wages, housing, and other* ~ *issues*> **b** dependable, routine <*the* ~ *repertoire of an orchestra*> **2** sent or given as thanks for hospitality <*a* ~ *letter*>

ˌbread and 'butter *n* a means of sustenance or livelihood

'breadˌbasket /-ˌbahskit‖-ˌbɑːskɪt/ *n* the stomach – slang

[1]**'breadˌcrumb** /-ˌkrum‖-ˌkrʌm/ *n* a small fragment of bread

[2]**breadcrumb** *vt* [2]BREAD

'breadˌfruit /-ˌfrooht‖-ˌfruːt/ *n* the large starchy fruit of a tropical tree that has white flesh with a breadlike texture

'breadˌline /-ˌlien‖-ˌlaɪn/ *n* **1** *Br* the level of income required for subsistence **2** *chiefly NAm* a queue of people waiting to receive food given in charity

breadth /bret·th, bredth‖bretθ, bredθ/ *n* **1** distance from side to side **2a** sthg of full width <*a* ~ *of cloth*> **b** a wide expanse <~s *of grass*> **3a** catholicity, scope **b** liberality of views or taste

'breadthways /-ˌwayz‖-ˌweɪz/, **'breadthˌwise** /-ˌwiez‖-ˌwaɪz/ *adv or adj* in the direction of the breadth <*a course of bricks laid* ~>

'breadˌwinner /-ˌwinə‖-ˌwɪnə/ *n* one whose wages are a family's livelihood – **breadwinning** *n*

[1]**break** /brayk‖breɪk/ *vb* **broke** /brohk‖brəʊk/; **broken** /'brohkən‖'brəʊkən/ *vt* **1a** to separate into parts with suddenness or violence **b** to fracture <~ *an arm*> **c** to rupture <~ *the skin*> **2** to violate, transgress <~ *the law*> **3a** to force a way through or into <*the silence was* broken *by a dog barking*> **b** to escape by force from <*he* broke *jail*> **4** to make or effect by cutting or forcing through <~ *a trail through the woods*> **5** to disrupt the order or compactness of <~ *ranks*> **6a** to defeat utterly; destroy **b** to crush the spirit of **c(1)** to train (an animal, esp a horse) for the service of human beings **c(2)** to inure, accustom <*a horse* broken *to the saddle*> **d** to exhaust in health, strength, or capacity **7a** to ruin financially **b** to reduce in rank **8a** to reduce the force or intensity of <*the bushes will* ~ *his fall*> **b** to cause failure and discontinuance of (a strike) by measures outside bargaining processes **9** to exceed, surpass <~ *a record*> **10** to ruin the prospects of <*could make or* ~ *her career*> **11a** to stop or interrupt **b** to open and bring about suspension of operation <~ *an electric circuit*> **c** to destroy the unity or completeness of <*they must be kept together; I don't want to* ~ *the collection*> **d** to destroy the uniformity of <*the straight line of the horizon was* broken *by a rocky outcrop*> **12** to cause to discontinue a habit <*tried to* ~ *him of smoking*> **13** to make known; tell <~ *the bad news gently*> **14a** to solve (a code or cipher system); CRACK 3a **b** to demonstrate the falsity of (an alibi) **15** to split into smaller units, parts, or processes; divide <~ *a £10 note*> – often + *up* or *down* **16** to open the operating mechanism of (a gun) ~ *vi* **1** to escape with sudden forceful effort – often + *out* or *away* <~ *out of jail*> **2a** to come into being, esp suddenly <*day was* ~ing> **b** to come to pass; occur <*report news stories as they* ~> **3** to effect a penetration <~ *through enemy lines*> **4** to take a different course; depart <~ *from tradition*> **5** to make a sudden dash <~ *for cover*> **6** to separate after a clinch in boxing **7** to come apart or split into pieces; burst, shatter **8** *of a wave* to curl over and disintegrate in surf or foam

9 *of weather* to change suddenly, esp after a fine spell **10** to give way in disorderly retreat **11a** to fail in health, strength, or control <*may* ~ *under questioning*> **b** to become inoperative because of damage, wear, or strain **12** to end a relationship, agreement, etc *with* **13** *esp of a ball bowled in cricket* to change direction of forward travel on bouncing **14** *of a voice* to alter sharply in tone, pitch, or intensity; *esp* to shift abruptly from one register to another <*boys' voices* ~ *at puberty*> **15** *of a horse* to fail to keep a prescribed gait **16** to interrupt one's activity for a brief period < ~ *for lunch*> **17** to make the opening shot of a game of snooker, billiards, or pool **18a** to fold, lift, or come apart at a seam, groove, or joint **b** *of cream* to separate during churning into liquid and fat **19** *chiefly NAm* to happen, develop <*for the team to succeed, everything has to* ~ *right*> – **breakable** *adj or n* – **break cover** to emerge abruptly from a hiding place – **break even** to achieve a balance between expenditure and income; *esp* to recover precisely what one spends – **break into 1a** to begin abruptly <*the horse* breaks into *a gallop*> **b** to give voice or expression to abruptly <*she* broke into *song*> **2** to enter by force <*thieves* broke into *the house*> **3** to make entry or entrance into <*trying to* break into *show business*> **4** to interrupt <*kept* breaking into *the conversation*> – **break new ground** to make or show new discoveries; pioneer – **break service/break someone's service** to win a game against the server (e g in tennis) – **break someone's heart** to cause sby heartbreak – **break the back** to do or overcome the largest or hardest part – **break the ice** to overcome initial reserve – **break wind** to expel gas from the intestine through the anus

[2]**break** *n* **1** an act or action of breaking **2a** a condition produced (as if) by breaking; a gap **b** a rupture in previously good relations **c** a gap in an otherwise continuous electric circuit **3** the action or act of breaking in, out, or forth <*a jail* ~> **4** a dash, rush <*make a* ~ *for it*> **5** the act of separating after a clinch in boxing **6a** a change or interruption in a continuous process or trend <*it makes a* ~> **b** a change from the status quo <*a sharp* ~ *with tradition*> **c** a respite from work or duty; *specif* a daily pause for play and refreshment at school **d** a planned interruption in a radio or television programme <*a* ~ *for the commercial*> **7a** the opening shot in a game of snooker, billiards, or pool **b** change in direction of forward travel, esp of a cricket ball on bouncing because of spin imparted by the bowler **c** a slow ball bowled in cricket that deviates in a specified direction on bouncing <*an off* ~> **d** the act or an instance of breaking an opponent's service in tennis **e** failure of a horse to maintain a prescribed gait **f** (a score made by) a sequence of successful shots or strokes (e g in snooker) **8** a notable variation in pitch, intensity, or tone in the voice **9** a place, situation, or time at which a break occurs: e g **9a** the point where one musical register changes to another **b** a short ornamental passage inserted between phrases in jazz **10a** a stroke of esp good luck **b** an opportunity, chance <*give me a* ~>

breakage /ˈbraykij‖ˈbreɪkɪdʒ/ *n* **1** sthg broken – usu pl **2** allowance for things broken (e g in transit)

[1]**breakaway** /ˈbraykəˌway‖ˈbreɪkəˌweɪ/ *n* **1** sby or sthg that breaks away **2** a breaking away (e g from a group or tradition); a withdrawing

[2]**breakaway** *adj* **1** favouring independence from an affiliation; withdrawing <*a* ~ *faction formed a new party*> **2** *chiefly NAm* made to break or bend easily < ~ *road signs for highway safety*>

breakdance /ˈbraykˌdahns‖ˈbreɪkˌdɑːns/ *vi or n* (to perform) an acrobatic freestyle dance, usu to the accompaniment of rock music, featuring spins on the performer's head and shoulders – **breakdancer** *n*

ˈ**breakˌdown** /-ˌdown‖-ˌdaʊn/ *n* **1** a failure to function **2** a physical, mental, or nervous collapse **3** failure to progress or have effect <*a* ~ *of negotiations*> **4** the process of decomposing < ~ *of food during digestion*> **5** a division into categories; a classification **6** a whole analysed into parts; *specif* an account in which the transactions are recorded under various categories

break down *vt* **1a** to cause to fall or collapse by breaking or shattering **b** to make ineffective <break down *legal barriers*> **c** to put an end to; suppress <*he tried to* break down *their opposition*> **2a** to divide into parts or categories **b** to separate into simpler substances **c** to take apart, esp for storage or shipment ~ *vi* **1a** to become inoperative through breakage or wear **b** to become inapplicable or ineffective; deteriorate <*relations began to* break down> **2a** to be susceptible to analysis or subdivision <*the outline* breaks down *into 3 parts*> **b** to undergo decomposition **3** to lose one's composure completely <*he* broke down *and wept*>

[1]**breaker** /ˈbraykə‖ˈbreɪkə/ *n* **1** a wave breaking into foam **2** a user of Citizens' Band radio – slang

[2]**breaker** *n* a small water cask

ˌ**break-ˈeven** *adj or n* (of or being) the point at which profit equals loss

breakfast /ˈbrekfəst‖ˈbrekfəst/ *n* (food prepared for) the first meal of the day, esp when taken in the morning – **breakfast** *vb*, **breakfaster** *n*

break in *vi* **1** to enter a house or building by force **2a** to interrupt a conversation **b** to intrude ~ *vt* **1** to accustom to a certain activity <break in *a new reporter*> **2** to use or wear until comfortable or working properly

ˈ**breakˌneck** /-ˌnek‖-ˌnek/ *adj* extremely dangerous < ~ *speed*>

break off *vi* **1** to become detached; separate **2** to stop abruptly ~*vt* to discontinue <break off *diplomatic relations*>

ˈ**breakˌout** /-ˌowt‖-ˌaʊt/ *n* a violent or forceful breaching of a restraint (e g imprisonment or siege)

break out *vi* **1** to become affected with a skin eruption <broke out *in a rash*> **2** to develop or emerge with suddenness and force <*a riot* broke out> **3** to escape ~ *vt* **1** to take from shipboard stowage ready for use **2** to unfurl (a flag) at the mast

ˈbreakˌthrough /-ˌthrooh||-ˌθruː/ *n* **1** an act or point of breaking through an obstruction **2** an attack that penetrates enemy lines **3** a sudden advance, esp in knowledge or technique

ˈbreakˌup /-ˌup||-ˌʌp/ *n* **1** a dissolution, disruption <*the* ~ *of a marriage*> **2** a division into smaller units **3** *chiefly Can* the spring thaw

break up *vt* **1** to disrupt the continuity of <*too many footnotes can* break up *a text*> **2** to decompose <break up *a chemical*> **3** to bring to an end <*it* broke up *their marriage*> **4a** to break into pieces (e g for salvage); scrap **b** to crumble **5a** to distress <*his wife's death really* broke *him* up> – infml **b** *chiefly NAm* to cause to laugh heartily – infml ~ *vi* **1a** to come to an end <*their partnership* broke up> **b** to separate, split up <*Simon and Mary have* broken up> **2** to lose morale or composure <*he is likely to* break up *under attack*>; *also* to give way to laughter **3** *Br, of a school* to disband for the holidays

ˈbreakˌwater /-ˌwawtə||-ˌwɔːtə/ *n* an offshore structure (e g a wall) used to protect a harbour or beach from the force of waves

[1]**bream** /breem||briːm/ *n,* **1** any of various European freshwater fishes related to the carps and minnows **2** any of various freshwater sunfishes

[2]**bream** *vt* [3]GRAVE

[1]**breast** /brest||brest/ *n* **1** either of 2 protuberant milk-producing glandular organs situated on the front of the chest in the human female and some other mammals **2** the fore part of the body between the neck and the abdomen **3** sthg (e g a swelling or curve) resembling a breast **4** the seat of emotion and thought; the bosom – fml

[2]**breast** *vt* **1** to contend with resolutely; confront <~ *the rush-hour traffic*> **2a** to meet or lean against with the breast or front <*the swimmer* ~ed *the waves*> **b** to thrust the chest against <*the sprinter* ~ed *the tape*> **3** *chiefly Br* to climb, ascend

ˈbreastˌbone /-ˌbohn||-ˌbəʊn/ *n* the sternum

ˈbreast-ˌfeed *vt* to feed (a baby) with the milk from the breast rather than a bottle

ˈbreastˌplate /-ˌplayt||-ˌpleɪt/ *n* a metal plate worn as defensive armour for the chest

ˈbreastˌstroke /-ˌstrohk||-ˌstrəʊk/ *n* a swimming stroke executed on the front by thrusting the arms forwards while kicking outwards and backwards with the legs, then sweeping the arms backwards – **breaststroker** *n*

ˈbreastˌwork /-ˌwuhk||-ˌwɜːk/ *n* a temporary fortification, usu consisting of a low parapet

breath /breth||breθ/ *n* **1a** a slight fragrance or smell **b** a slight indication; a suggestion <*the faintest* ~ *of scandal*> **2a** the faculty of breathing **b** an act of breathing **c** opportunity or time to breathe; respite **3** a slight movement of air **4** air inhaled and exhaled in breathing **5** spirit, animation – **out of breath** breathing very rapidly (e g from strenuous exercise) – **under one's breath** in a whisper

breathalyse *also* **breathalyze** /ˈbrethəˌliez||ˈbreθəˌlaɪz/ *vt* to test (e g a driver) for the level of alcohol in exhaled breath

ˈbreathaˌlyser *also* **breathalyzer** /-ˌliezə||-ˌlaɪzə/ *n* a device used to test the alcohol content in the blood of a motorist

breathe /breedh||briːð/ *vi* **1** to draw air into and expel it from the lungs **2** to live **3** to pause and rest before continuing **4** *of wind* to blow softly **5** *of wine* to be exposed to the beneficial effects of air after being kept in an airtight container (e g a bottle) ~ *vt* **1a** to send *out* by exhaling <~d *garlic over him*> **b** to instil (as if) by breathing <~ *new life into the movement*> **2a** to utter, express <*don't* ~ *a word of it to anyone*> **b** to make manifest; display <*the novel* ~s *despair*> **3** to allow (e g a horse) to rest after exertion **4** to inhale – **breathe down someone's neck** to keep sby under constant or too close surveillance – **breathe easily/freely** to enjoy relief (e g from pressure or danger)

breather /ˈbreedhə||ˈbriːðə/ *n* **1** a small vent in an otherwise airtight enclosure (e g a crankcase) **2** a break in activity for rest or relief – infml

breathing /ˈbreedhing||ˈbriːðɪŋ/ *n* either of the marks ʻ and ʼ used in writing Greek to indicate aspiration or its absence

ˈbreathing ˌspace *n* a pause in a period of activity, esp for rest and recuperation

breathless /ˈbrethlis||ˈbreθlɪs/ *adj* **1** not breathing; *esp* holding one's breath due to excitement or suspense **2a** gasping; OUT OF BREATH **b** gripping, intense <~ *tension*> **3** without any breeze; stuffy – **breathlessly** *adv*, **breathlessness** *n*

ˈbreathˌtaking /-ˌtayking||-ˌteɪkɪŋ/ *adj* **1** making one breathless **2** exciting, thrilling – **breathtakingly** *adv*

breathy /ˈbrethi||ˈbreθɪ/ *adj* characterized or accompanied by the audible passage of breath – **breathily** *adv*, **breathiness** *n*

breech /breech||briːtʃ/ *n* **1** the buttocks **2** the part of a firearm at the rear of the barrel

breeches /ˈbrichiz, ˈbreechiz||ˈbrɪtʃɪz, ˈbriːtʃɪz/ *n pl* **1** knee-length trousers, usu closely fastened at the lower edges **2** jodhpurs that are baggy at the thigh and close fitting and fastened with buttons from the knee to the ankle

breeches buoy *n* a seat in the form of a pair of canvas breeches hung from a life buoy running on a rope leading to a place of safety for use in rescue at sea

ˈbreechˌloader /-ˌlohdə||-ˌləʊdə/ *n* a firearm that is loaded at the breech – **breech-loading** *adj*

[1]**breed** /breed||briːd/ *vb* **bred** /bred||bred/ *vt* **1a** to produce (offspring) by hatching or gestation **b** to rear; BRING UP 1 <*born and* bred *in Somerset*> **2** to produce, engender <*despair often* ~s *violence*> **3** to propagate (plants or animals) sexually and usu under controlled conditions **4** to inculcate by training <~ *good behaviour*> **5** to produce (a fissile element) in a nuclear chain reaction ~ *vi* **1** to produce offspring by sexual union **2** to propagate animals or plants – **breeder** *n*

[2]**breed** *n* **1** a group of animals or plants, often specially selected, visibly similar in most characteristics **2** race, lineage **3** class, kind <*a new* ~ *of radicals*>

breeding /ˈbreeding||ˈbriːdɪŋ/ *n* **1** ancestry **2** behaviour; *esp* that showing good manners **3** the sexual propagation of plants or animals

ˈbreeding ˌground *n* a place or set of circumstances favourable to the propagation of certain ideas, movements, etc

[1]**breeze** /breez‖briːz/ *n* **1** a light gentle wind; *also* a wind of between 4 and 31 mph **2** a slight disturbance or quarrel – infml **3** *chiefly NAm* sthg easily done; a cinch – infml – **breezeless** *adj*

[2]**breeze** *vi* **1** to come *in* or *into*, or move *along*, swiftly and airily <*she* ~d *in as if nothing had happened*> **2** to make progress quickly and easily <~ *through the books*> – infml

[3]**breeze** *n* ashy residue from the making of coke or charcoal

ˈ**breeze-ˌblock** *n* a rectangular building block made of breeze mixed with sand and cement

breezy /ˈbreezi‖ˈbriːzɪ/ *adj* **1** windy, fresh **2** brisk, lively **3** insouciant, airy – **breezily** *adv*, **breeziness** *n*

ˈ**Bren ˌgun** /bren‖bren/ *n* a gas-operated magazine-fed light machine gun [*Br*no, city in Czechoslovakia + *En*field, town in England]

brethren /ˈbredhrin‖ˈbreðrɪn/ *pl of* BROTHER – chiefly in fml address or in referring to the members of a profession, society, or sect

Breton /ˈbret(ə)n‖ˈbret(ə)n/ *n or adj* (a native or inhabitant or the Celtic language) of Brittany

breve /breev‖briːv/ *n* **1** a curved mark used to indicate a short vowel or a short or unstressed syllable **2** a note equal in time value to 2 semibreves or 4 minims

[1]**brevet** /ˈbrevit‖ˈbrevɪt/ *n* a commission giving a military officer higher nominal rank than that for which he receives pay

[2]**brevet** *vt* **-tt-, -t-** to confer a usu specified rank on by brevet

breviary /ˈbrevi·əri, ˈbree-, -yəri‖ˈbrevɪərɪ, ˈbriː-, -jərɪ/ *n, often cap* **1** a book containing the prayers, hymns, psalms, and readings for the canonical hours **2** DIVINE OFFICE

brevity /ˈbrevəti‖ˈbrevətɪ/ *n* **1** shortness of duration; the quality of being brief **2** expression in few words; conciseness

[1]**brew** /brooh‖bruː/ *vt* **1** to prepare (e g beer or ale) by steeping, boiling, and fermentation or by infusion and fermentation **2** to contrive, plot – often + *up* <~ *up a plan*> **3** to prepare (e g tea) by infusion in hot water ~ *vi* **1** to brew beer or ale **2** to be in the process of formation <*a storm is* ~ing *in the east*> – often + *up* **3** *chiefly Br* to undergo infusion <*left the tea to* ~> – **brewer** *n*

[2]**brew** *n* **1a** a brewed beverage **b(1)** an amount brewed at once **b(2)** the quality of what is brewed <*likes a nice strong* ~> **c** a product of brewing **2** the process of brewing

ˌ**brewer's** ˈ**droop** /ˈbrooh·əz‖ˈbruːəz/ *n, Br* an inability to achieve penile erection after drinking too much alcohol – slang

brewery /ˈbrooh·əri‖ˈbruːərɪ/ *n* an establishment in which beer or ale is brewed

brew up *vi, Br* to make tea

[1]**briar** /ˈbrie·ə‖ˈbraɪə/ *n* [1]BRIER

[2]**briar** *n* **1** [2]BRIER **2** a tobacco pipe made from the root of a brier

[1]**bribe** /brieb‖braɪb/ *vt* to induce or influence (as if) by bribery ~ *vi* to practise bribery – **bribable** *adj*, **briber** *n*

[2]**bribe** *n* sthg, esp money, given or promised to influence the judgment or conduct of a person

bribery /ˈbrieb(ə)ri‖ˈbraɪb(ə)rɪ/ *n* the act or practice of giving or taking a bribe

bric-a-brac /ˈbrik ə ˌbrak‖ˈbrɪk ə ˌbræk/ *n* miscellaneous small articles, usu of ornamental or sentimental value; curios

[1]**brick** /brik‖brɪk/ *n* **1** a usu rectangular unit for building or paving purposes, typically not exceeding 215mm x 102mm x 65mm (about 8in × $3^{3}/_{4}$in × $2^{1}/_{4}$in) and made of moist clay hardened by heat **2** a rectangular compressed mass (e g of ice cream) **3** a reliable stout hearted person; a stalwart – infml

[2]**brick** *vt* to close, face, or pave with bricks – usu + *up*

ˈ**brickˌbat** /-ˌbat‖-ˌbæt/ *n* **1** a fragment of a hard material (e g a brick); *esp* one used as a missile **2** a critical remark

ˈ**brickˌfield** /-ˌfeeld‖-ˌfiːld/ *n, Br* a place where bricks are made

ˈ**brickˌlayer** /-ˌlayə‖-ˌleɪə/ *n* a person who is employed to lay bricks – **bricklaying** *n*

ˈ**brickˌwork** /-ˌwuhk‖-ˌwɜːk/ *n* (the part of) a structure made from bricks and mortar

bridal /ˈbriedl‖ˈbraɪdl/ *adj* of or for a bride or wedding; nuptial

bride /bried‖braɪd/ *n* a woman at the time of her wedding

ˈ**brideˌgroom** /-ˌgroohm, -ˌgroom‖-ˌgruːm, -ˌgrʊm/ *n* a man at the time of his wedding

ˈ**bridesˌmaid** /-ˌmayd‖-ˌmeɪd/ *n* an unmarried girl or woman who attends a bride

[1]**bridge** /brij‖brɪdʒ/ *n* **1a** a structure spanning a depression or obstacle and supporting a roadway, railway, canal, or path **b** a time, place, or means of connection or transition **2a** the upper bony part of the nose **b** an arch serving to raise the strings of a musical instrument **c** a raised platform on a ship from which it is directed **d** the support for a billiards or snooker cue formed esp by the hand **3a** sthg (e g a partial denture permanently attached to adjacent natural teeth) that fills a gap **b** a connection (e g an atom or bond) that joins 2 different parts of a molecule (e g opposite sides of a ring)

[2]**bridge** *vt* to make a bridge over or across; *also* to cross (e g a river) by a bridge – **bridgeable** *adj*

[3]**bridge** *n* any of various card games for usu 4 players in 2 partnerships in which players bid for the right to name a trump suit, and in which the hand of the declarer's partner is exposed and played by the declarer; *specif* CONTRACT BRIDGE

ˈ**bridgeˌhead** /-ˌhed‖-ˌhed/ *n* **1a** a fortification protecting the end of a bridge nearest an enemy **b** the area round the end of a bridge **2** an advanced position, usu beyond a bridge, (to be) seized in hostile territory as a foothold for further advance

ˈ**bridgeˌwork** /-ˌwuhk‖-ˌwɜːk/ *n* a dental bridge

[1]**bridle** /ˈbriedl‖ˈbraɪdl/ *n* **1** a framework of leather straps buckled together round the head of a draught or riding animal, including the bit and reins, used to direct and control it **2** a length of secured cable, esp on a boat, to which a second cable can be attached (e g for mooring) **3** a curb, restraint <*set a* ~ *on his power*>

[2]**bridle** *vt* **1** to put a bridle on **2** to restrain or control (as if) with a bridle <~ *your tongue*>

~*vi* to show hostility or resentment (e g because of an affront), esp by drawing back the head and chin

'bridle ˌpath *n* a track or right of way suitable for horseback riding

Brie /bree‖bri:/ *n* a large round cream-coloured soft cheese ripened through bacterial action

[1]**brief** /breef‖bri:f/ *adj* **1** short in duration or extent **2** in few words; concise – **briefly** *adv*, **briefness** *n*

[2]**brief** *n* **1** a papal directive, less binding than a bull **2a** a synopsis, summary **b(1)** a statement of a client's case drawn up for the instruction of counsel **b(2)** a case, or piece of employment, given to a barrister **c** a set of instructions outlining what is required, and usu setting limits to one's powers (e g in negotiating) <*her* ~ *was to reduce British payments*> **3** *pl* short close-fitting pants – **in brief** in a few words; briefly

[3]**brief** *vt* **1** to provide with final instructions or necessary information <~ *journalists about the situation*> **2** *Br* to retain (a barrister) as legal counsel

'briefˌcase /-ˌkays‖-ˌkeɪs/ *n* a flat rectangular case for carrying papers or books

briefing /'breefing‖'bri:fɪŋ/ *n* (a meeting to give out) final instructions or necessary information

[1]**brier, briar** /'brie·ə‖'braɪə/ *n* a plant with a woody, thorny, or prickly stem – **briery** *adj*

[2]**brier, briar** *n* a heath of S Europe with a root used for making pipes

[1]**brig** /brig‖brɪg/ *n* a 2-masted square-rigged sailing vessel

[2]**brig** *n* a prison in the US Navy

[1]**brigade** /bri'gayd‖brɪ'geɪd/ *n* **1** a large section of an army usu composed of a headquarters, several fighting units (e g infantry battalions or armoured regiments), and supporting units **2** an organized or uniformed group of people (e g firemen)

[2]**brigade** *vt* to form or unite into a brigade

brigadier /ˌbrigə'diə‖ˌbrɪgə'dɪə/ *n* an officer in the British army ranking below a major general and commanding a brigade

ˌbrigadier 'general *n* an officer in the US airforce or army ranking below a major general

brigand /'brigənd‖'brɪgənd/ *n* one who lives by plunder, usu as a member of a group; a bandit – **brigandage** *n*, **brigandism** *n*

brigantine /'brigənˌteen‖'brɪgənˌti:n/ *n* a 2-masted square-rigged sailing vessel differing from a brig in not carrying a square mainsail

bright /briet‖braɪt/ *adj* **1a** radiating or reflecting light; shining **b** radiant with happiness <~ *faces*> **2** *of a colour* of high saturation or brilliance **3a** intelligent, clever **b** lively, charming <*be* ~ *and jovial among your guests* – Shak> **c** promising, talented – **bright** *adv*, **brightly** *adv*, **brightness** *n*

brighten /'brietn‖'braɪtn/ *vb* to make or become bright or brighter – often + *up* – **brightener** *n*

'Bright's diˌsease /'briets‖'braɪts/ *n* any of several kidney diseases marked by albumin in the urine

brill /bril‖brɪl/ *n, pl* **brill** (a European flatfish related to) the turbot

[1]**brilliant** /'brilyənt, -li·ənt‖'brɪljənt, -lɪənt/ *adj* **1** very bright; glittering **2a** striking, distinctive <*a* ~ *example*> **b** having great intellectual ability **3** of high quality; good – infml – **brilliance** *n*, **brilliancy** *n*, **brilliantly** *adv*

[2]**brilliant** *n* a gem, esp a diamond, cut with numerous facets for maximum brilliance

brilliantine /'brilyənˌteen‖'brɪljənˌti:n/ *n* a preparation for making hair glossy and smooth

[1]**brim** /brim‖brɪm/ *n* **1** the edge or rim of a hollow vessel, a natural depression, or a cavity **2** the projecting rim of a hat – **brimless** *adj*

[2]**brim** *vi* **-mm-** to be full to the brim

brimful /ˌbrim'fool‖ˌbrɪm'fʊl/ *adj* full to the brim; ready to overflow

-brimmed /-brimd‖-brɪmd/ *comb form* (→ *adj*) having (such) a brim <*a wide*-brimmed *hat*>

brim over *vi* to overflow a brim

brimstone /'brimˌstohn‖'brɪmˌstəʊn/ *n* SULPHUR 1

brindled /'brind(ə)ld‖'brɪnd(ə)ld/ *adj* having obscure dark streaks or flecks on a grey or tawny ground

[1]**brine** /brien‖braɪn/ *n* water (almost) saturated with common salt – **briny** *adj*, **brininess** *n*

[2]**brine** *vt* to treat with brine (e g by soaking)

bring /bring‖brɪŋ/ *vt* **brought** /brawt‖brɔ:t/ **1a** to convey (sthg) to a place or person; come with or cause to come **b(1)** to attract <*his screams* brought *the neighbours*> **b(2)** to force, compel <*cannot* ~ *myself to do it*> **b(3)** to cause to achieve a particular condition <~ *water to the boil*> **2a** to cause to occur, lead to <*winter will* ~ *snow and ice*> **b** to initiate <~ *legal action*> **c** to offer, present <~ *an argument*> **3** PREFER 3 <~ *a charge*> **4** to sell for (a price) <*the car should* ~ *£800*> – **bringer** *n* – **bring home** to make unmistakably clear to – **bring to bear 1** to put to use <bring *knowledge* to bear *on the problem*> **2** to apply, exert <bring *pressure* to bear *on the management*> – **bring to book 1** to put in a position in which one must answer for one's acts **2** to cause to be reproved – **bring to light** to disclose, reveal – **bring to mind** to cause to be recalled – **bring up the rear** to come last

bring about *vt* to cause to take place; effect

bring down *vt* **1** to cause to fall or come down **2** to kill by shooting <brought *the bear* down *with one shot*> **3** to reduce **4** to cause to be depressed – usu pass – **bring the house down** to win the enthusiastic approval of the audience

bring forth *vt* **1** to bear <brought forth *fruit*> **2** to give birth to; produce **3** to offer, present <brought forth *arguments to justify her conduct*>

bring forward *vt* **1** to produce to view; introduce **2** to carry (a total) forward (e g to the top of the next page)

bring in *vt* **1** to produce as profit or return <*this will* bring in *the money*> **2** to introduce **3** to pronounce (a verdict) in court **4** to earn <*she* brings in *a good salary*>

bring off *vt* to carry to a successful conclusion; achieve, accomplish

bring on *vt* **1** to cause to appear or occur **2** to improve, help

bring out *vt* **1** to make clear **2a** to present to the public; *specif* to publish **b** to introduce (a young woman) formally to society **3** to utter **4** to cause (sby) to be afflicted with a rash, spots, etc – usu + *in* **5** to encourage to be less reticent – esp in *bring somebody out of him-/herself* **6** *chiefly Br* to instruct or cause (workers) to go on strike

bring round *vt* **1** to cause to adopt a particular opinion or course of action; persuade **2** to restore to consciousness; revive

bring to *vt* **1** to cause (a boat) to lie to or come to a standstill **2** BRING ROUND 2

bring up *vt* **1** to educate, rear **2** to cause to stop suddenly **3** to bring to attention; introduce **4** to vomit

brink /bringk‖brɪŋk/ *n* **1** an edge; *esp* the edge at the top of a steep place **2** *the* verge, onset <*on the ~ of war*>

brinkmanship /'bringkmən,ship‖'brɪŋkmən,ʃɪp/ *n* the art of going to the very brink of conflict, danger, etc before drawing back

briquette, briquet /bri'ket‖brɪ'ket/ *n* a compacted block, usu of coal-dust

brisk /brisk‖brɪsk/ *adj* **1** keenly alert; lively **2** fresh, invigorating <~ *weather*> **3** energetic, quick <*a ~ pace*> **4** sharp in tone or manner – chiefly euph – **briskly** *adv*, **briskness** *n*

brisket /'briskit‖'brɪskɪt/ *n* a joint of beef cut from the breast; *broadly* the breast or lower chest of a 4-legged animal

[1]**bristle** /'brisl‖'brɪsl/ *n* a short stiff coarse hair or filament

[2]**bristle** *vi* **1a** to rise and stand stiffly erect <*quills* bristling *in all directions*> **b** to raise the bristles (e g in anger) **2** to take on an aggressive attitude or appearance (e g in response to a slight) **3** to be filled or thickly covered (*with* sthg suggestive of bristles) ~ *vt* **1** to provide with bristles **2** to make bristly; ruffle

bristly /'brisli‖'brɪslɪ/ *adj* **1a** consisting of or resembling bristles **b** thickly covered with bristles **2** tending to bristle easily; belligerent

bristols /'bristlz‖'brɪstlz/ *n pl, Br* breasts – vulg [rhyming slang *Bristol (City)* titty, breast]

Brit /brit‖brɪt/ *n* a British person – infml

britches /'brichiz‖'brɪtʃɪz/ *n pl* breeches

[1]**British** /'british‖'brɪtɪʃ/ *n* **1** the Celtic language of the ancient Britons **2** *pl in constr* the people of Britain **3** *chiefly NAm* English as typically spoken and written in Britain

[2]**British** *adj* of Britain, its people, or their language – **Britishness** *n*

Britisher /'britishə‖'brɪtɪʃə/ *n, chiefly NAm* BRITON 2

,British 'thermal ,unit *n* the quantity of heat required to raise the temperature of 1lb of water by 1°F under standard conditions

Briton /'brit(ə)n‖'brɪt(ə)n/ *n* **1** a member of any of the peoples inhabiting Britain before the Anglo-Saxon invasions **2** a native, inhabitant, or subject of Britain

brittle /'britl‖'brɪtl/ *adj* **1a** easily broken or cracked **b** insecure, frail <*a ~ friendship*> **2** easily hurt or offended; sensitive <*a ~ personality*> **3** sharp, tense <*a ~ sound*> **4** lacking warmth or depth of feeling <~ *gaiety*> – **brittlely** *adv*, **brittleness** *n*

[1]**broach** /brohch‖brəʊtʃ/ *n* **1** any of various pointed or tapered tools: e g **1a** a bit for boring holes **b** a tool for tapping casks **2** a spit for roasting meat

[2]**broach** *vt* **1a** to pierce (a container, esp a cask or bottle) prior to using the contents; tap **b** to open up or break into (e g a store or stock of sthg) and start to use **2** to open up (a subject) for discussion

[3]**broach** *vi, of a boat* to change direction dangerously, esp so as to lie broadside to the waves – usu + *to* ~*vt* to cause (a boat) to broach

[1]**broad** /brawd‖brɔːd/ *adj* **1a** having ample extent from side to side or between limits <~ *shoulders*> **b** in width; across <*made the path 10 feet ~*> **2** extending far and wide; spacious <*the ~ plains*> **3a** open, full – esp in *broad daylight* **b** plain, obvious <*a ~ hint*> **4** marked by lack of restraint or delicacy; coarse **5a** liberal, tolerant **b** widely applicable or applied; general **6** relating to the main points <~ *outlines*> **7** dialectal, esp in pronunciation **8** *of a vowel* open – used specif of *a* pronounced as /ah/ – **broadly** *adv*

[2]**broad** *adv* in a broad manner; fully

[3]**broad** *n* **1** the broad part <~ *of his back*> **2** *often cap, Br* a large area of fresh water formed by the broadening of a river – usu pl; used chiefly with reference to such formations found in E Anglia **3** a prostitute – slang **4** *chiefly NAm* a woman – slang

,broad 'bean *n* (the large flat edible seed of) a widely cultivated Old World leguminous plant

[1]**broadcast** /'brawd,kahst‖'brɔːd,kɑːst/ *adj* cast or scattered in all directions

[2]**broadcast** *n* **1** the act of transmitting by radio or television **2** a single radio or television programme

[3]**broadcast** *vb* **broadcast** *also* **broadcasted** *vt* **1** to scatter or sow (seed) broadcast **2** to make widely known **3** to transmit as a broadcast, esp for widespread reception ~ *vi* **1** to transmit a broadcast **2** to speak or perform on a broadcast programme – **broadcaster** *n*

[4]**broadcast** *adv* to or over a broad area

,Broad 'Church *adj* of 19th-c liberal Anglicanism

'broad,cloth /-,kloth‖-,klɒθ/ *n* a twilled napped woollen or worsted fabric with a smooth lustrous finish and dense texture

broaden /'brawdn‖'brɔːdn/ *vb* to make or become broad

'broad ,jump *n, NAm* LONG JUMP

'broad,loom /-,loohm‖-,luːm/ *n or adj* (a carpet) woven on a wide loom

,broad-'minded *adj* tolerant of varied views, unconventional behaviour, etc; liberal – **broad-mindedly** *adv*, **broad-mindedness** *n*

'broad,sheet /-,sheet‖-,ʃiːt/ *n* **1** a large sheet of paper printed on 1 side only; *also* sthg (e g an advertisement) printed on a broadsheet **2** a newspaper whose page depth is the full size of a rotary press plate

[1]**'broad,side** /-,sied‖-,saɪd/ *n* **1** the side of a ship above the waterline **2** a broadsheet **3a** (the simultaneous firing of) all the guns on 1 side of a ship **b** a forceful verbal or written attack

[2]**broadside** *adv* with the broadside or broader

side towards a given object or point
ˈbroadˌsword /-ˌsawd‖-ˌsɔːd/ *n* a sword with a broad blade for cutting rather than thrusting
brocade /brəˈkayd‖brəˈkeɪd/ *n* a rich (silk) fabric woven with raised patterns – **brocade** *vt*, **brocaded** *adj*
broccoli /ˈbrokəli‖ˈbrɒkəlɪ/ *n* **1** a large hardy cauliflower **2 broccoli, sprouting broccoli** a branching form of cauliflower whose young shoots are used for food
brochure /ˈbrohshə, brohˈshooə‖ˈbrəʊʃə, brəʊˈʃʊə/ *n* a small pamphlet
[1]brogue /brohg‖brəʊg/ *n* a stout walking shoe characterized by decorative perforations on the uppers
[2]brogue *n* a dialect or regional pronunciation; *esp* an Irish accent
broil /broyl‖brɔɪl/ *vt* to cook by direct exposure to radiant heat (e g over a fire); *specif, NAm* to grill ~*vi* to become extremely hot
broiler /ˈbroylə‖ˈbrɔɪlə/ *n* a bird suitable for grilling; *esp* a young chicken
[1]broke /brohk‖brəʊk/ *past of* BREAK
[2]broke *adj* penniless – infml
broken /ˈbrohkən‖ˈbrəʊkən/ *adj* **1** violently separated into parts; shattered **2a** having undergone or been subjected to fracture <*a ~ leg*> **b** *of a land surface* irregular, interrupted, or full of obstacles **c** not fulfilled; violated <*a ~ promise*> **d** discontinuous, interrupted **3a** made weak or infirm **b** subdued completely; crushed <*a ~ spirit*> **c** not working; defective **4a** cut off; disconnected **b** adversely affected or disrupted by marital separation or divorce <*a ~ home*> **c** imperfect <*~ English*> – **brokenly** *adv*, **brokenness** *n*
ˌbroken-ˈdown *adj* **1** in a state of disrepair; wrecked, dilapidated **2** spiritually or physically ill or exhausted
ˌbrokenˈhearted /-ˈhahtid‖-ˈhɑːtɪd/ *adj* overcome by grief or despair
ˌbroken ˈwind /wind‖wɪnd/ *n* a chronic respiratory disease of horses marked by a persistent cough and heaving of the flanks – **broken-winded** *adj*
broker /ˈbrohkə‖ˈbrəʊkə/ *n* **1** one who acts as an intermediary (e g in a business deal) **2** an agent who negotiates contracts of purchase and sale (e g of commodities or securities)
brolly /ˈbroli‖ˈbrɒlɪ/ *n, chiefly Br* an umbrella – infml
bromide /ˈbrohmied‖ˈbrəʊmaɪd/ *n* **1** a compound of bromine with another element or radical; *esp* any of various bromides formerly used as sedatives **2** a commonplace or hackneyed statement or notion
bromine /ˈbrohmeen, -min‖ˈbrəʊmiːn, -mɪn/ *n* a nonmetallic element, usu occurring as a deep red corrosive toxic liquid
bronchial /ˈbrongki·əl‖ˈbrɒŋkɪəl/ *adj* of the bronchi or their ramifications in the lungs – **bronchially** *adv*
bronchitis /brongˈkietəs‖brɒŋˈkaɪtəs/ *n* (a disease marked by) acute or chronic inflammation of the bronchial tubes accompanied by a cough and catarrh – **bronchitic** *adj*
bronchus /ˈbrongkəs‖ˈbrɒŋkəs/ *n, pl* **bronchi** /ˈbrongki,-kie‖ˈbrɒŋkɪ, -kaɪ/ either of the 2 main branches of the windpipe
bronco /ˈbrongkoh‖ˈbrɒŋkəʊ/ *n, pl* **broncos** an unbroken or imperfectly broken horse of western N America
brontosaurus /ˌbrontəˈsawrəs‖ˌbrɒntəˈsɔːrəs/ *n* any of various large 4-legged and prob plant-eating dinosaurs [deriv of Greek *brontē* thunder + *sauros* lizard]
[1]bronze /bronz‖brɒnz/ *vt* **1** to give the appearance of bronze to **2** to make brown or tanned
[2]bronze *n* **1** any of various copper-base alloys; *esp* one containing tin **2** a sculpture or artefact made of bronze **3** a yellowish-brown colour **4** BRONZE MEDAL – **bronze** *adj*, **bronzy** *adj*
ˈBronze ˌAge *n* the period of human culture characterized by the use of bronze or copper tools and weapons
ˌbronze ˈmedal *n* a medal of bronze awarded to sby who comes third in a competition – **bronze medallist** *n*
brooch /brohch‖brəʊtʃ/ *n* an ornament worn on clothing and fastened by means of a pin
[1]brood /broohd‖bruːd/ *n* **1a** young birds, insects, etc hatched or cared for at one time **b** the children in one family – humor **2** a group having a common nature or origin
[2]brood *vi* **1** *of a bird* to sit on eggs in order to hatch them **2a** to dwell gloomily *on*; worry *over* or *about* **b** to be in a state of depression – **broodingly** *adv*
[3]brood *adj* kept for breeding <*a ~ mare*>
broody /ˈbroohdi‖ˈbruːdɪ/ *adj* **1** *of fowl* being in a state of readiness to brood eggs **2** contemplative, moody **3** *of a woman* feeling a strong desire or urge to be a mother – infml – **broodiness** *n*
[1]brook /brook‖brʊk/ *vt* to tolerate; STAND FOR <*she would ~ no interference with her plans*>
[2]brook *n* a usu small freshwater stream
broom /broohm, broom‖bruːm, brʊm/ *n* **1** any of various leguminous shrubs with long slender branches, small leaves, and usu showy yellow flowers **2** a brush for sweeping composed of a bundle of firm stiff twigs, bristles, or fibres bound to or set on a long handle
ˈbroomˌstick /-ˌstik‖-ˌstɪk/ *n* the long thin handle of a broom
broth /broth‖brɒθ/ *n* **1a** the stock in which meat, fish, cereal grains, or vegetables have been cooked **b** a thin soup made from stock **2** a liquid medium for culturing esp bacteria
brothel /ˈbroth(ə)l‖ˈbrɒθ(ə)l/ *n* a house in which the services of prostitutes can be bought
brother /ˈbrudhə‖ˈbrʌðə/ *n, pl* **brothers**, (*3, 4, & 5*) **brothers** *also* **brethren** /ˈbredhrin‖ˈbreðrɪn/ **1** a male having the same parents as another person; *also* a half brother or stepbrother **2a** a kinsman **b** one, esp a male, who shares with another a common national or racial origin **3** a fellow member – used as a title in some evangelical denominations **4** one, esp a male, who is related to another by a common tie or interest **5** a member of a men's religious order who is not in holy orders
ˈbrotherhood /-hood‖-hʊd/ *n* **1** the quality or state of being brothers **2a** an association (e g a religious body) for a particular purpose **b** (an

idea of) fellowship between all human beings
ˈbrother-in-ˌlaw *n, pl* **brothers-in-law** **1** the brother of one's spouse **2** the husband of one's sister
ˈbrotherly /-li||-lɪ/ *adj* **1** of, resembling, or appropriate to brothers, esp in feeling or showing platonic affection **2** filled with fellow feeling, sympathy, or compassion <*she was overwhelmed with* ~ *love for the homeless*> – **brotherliness** *n*, **brotherly** *adv*
brought /brawt||brɔːt/ *past of* BRING
brouhaha /ˈbrooh·hahˌhah||ˈbruːhɑːˌhɑː/ *n* a hubbub, uproar
brow /brow||braʊ/ *n* **1a** an eyebrow **b** the forehead **2** the top or edge of a hill, cliff, etc
ˈbrowˌbeat /-ˌbeet||-ˌbiːt/ *vt* **browbeat; browbeaten** to intimidate, coerce, or bully by a persistently threatening or dominating manner
[1]brown /brown||braʊn/ *adj* **1** of the colour brown; *esp* of dark or tanned complexion **2** (made with ingredients that are) partially or wholly unrefined or unpolished <~ *sugar*>
[2]brown *n* any of a range of dark colours between red and yellow in hue – **brownish** *adj*, **browny** *adj*
[3]brown *vb* to make or become brown (e g by sautéing)
ˌbrowned-off *adj, chiefly Br* annoyed; FED UP – infml
brownie /ˈbrowni||ˈbraʊnɪ/ *n* **1** a good-natured goblin believed to perform household chores at night **2 brownie guide, brownie** a member of the most junior section of the (British) Guide movement for girls aged from 7 to 10 **3** *chiefly NAm* a small square or rectangle of rich chocolate cake containing nuts
ˌbrown ˈstudy *n* a state of serious absorption or abstraction; a reverie
[1]browse /browz||braʊz/ *n* **1** tender shoots, twigs, and leaves of trees and shrubs that provide food for animals (e g deer) **2** a period of time spent browsing <*had a good* ~ *in the library*>
[2]browse *vt* to feed on (browse) ~ *vi* **1** *of animals* to nibble at leaves, grass, or other vegetation **2** to read or search idly *through* a book or a mass of things (e g in a shop), in the hope of finding sthg interesting – **browser** *n*
brucellosis /ˌbroohsəˈlohsis, -siz||ˌbruːsəˈləʊsɪs, -sɪz/ *n* a serious long-lasting disease, esp of human beings and cattle, caused by a bacterium [Sir David *Bruce* (1855-1931), British bacteriologist]
[1]bruise /broohz||bruːz/ *vt* **1** to inflict a bruise on **2** to crush (e g leaves or berries) by pounding **3** to wound, injure; *esp* to inflict psychological hurt on ~*vi* to be damaged by a bruise
[2]bruise *n* **1a** an injury involving rupture of small blood vessels and discoloration without a break in the skin **b** an injury to plant tissue involving underlying damage and discoloration without a break in the skin **2** an injury, esp to the feelings
bruiser /ˈbroohzə||ˈbruːzə/ *n* a large burly man; *specif* a prizefighter
brunch /brunch||brʌntʃ/ *n* a meal, usu taken in the middle of the morning, that combines a late breakfast and an early lunch [*br*eakfast + l*unch*]
brunette, *NAm also* **brunet** /broohˈnet||bruːˈnet/ *n or adj* (sby, esp a young adult woman,) having dark hair and usu a relatively dark complexion
brunt /brunt||brʌnt/ *n* the principal force or stress (e g of an attack) – esp in *bear the brunt of*
[1]brush /brush||brʌʃ/ *n* **1** (land covered with) scrub vegetation **2** *chiefly NAm & Austr* brushwood
[2]brush *n* **1** an implement composed of filaments (e g of hair, bristle, nylon, or wire) set into a firm piece of material and used esp for grooming hair, painting, sweeping, or scrubbing **2** a bushy tail, esp of a fox **3** a conductor (e g a piece of carbon or braided copper wire) that makes electrical contact between a stationary and a moving part **4** an act of brushing **5** a quick light touch or momentary contact in passing
[3]brush *vt* **1a** to apply a brush to **b** to apply with a brush **2** to remove with sweeping strokes (e g of a brush) – usu + *away* or *off* <~ed *the dirt off her coat*> **3** to pass lightly over or across; touch gently against in passing
[4]brush *vi* to move lightly, heedlessly, or rudely – usu + *by* or *past*
[5]brush *n* a brief antagonistic encounter or skirmish
ˈbrush-ˌoff *n* a quietly curt or disdainful dismissal; a rebuff – infml
brush off *vt* to dispose of in an offhand way; dismiss
brush up *vi* to tidy one's clothes, hair, etc ~*vt* to renew one's skill in; refresh one's memory of – **brushup** *n* – **brush up on** BRUSH UP *vt*
ˈbrushˌwood /-ˌwood||-ˌwʊd/ *n* **1** twigs or small branches, esp when cut or broken **2** a thicket of shrubs and small trees
ˈbrushˌwork /-ˌwuhk||-ˌwɜːk/ *n* (a particular artist's) technique of applying paint with a brush
brusque /brusk, broosk, broohsk||brʌsk, brʊsk, bruːsk/ *adj* blunt or abrupt in manner or speech, often to the point of rudeness – **brusquely** *adv*, **brusqueness** *n*
brussels sprout /ˌbruslˈsprowt||ˌbrʌslˈspraʊt/ *n, often cap B* (any of the many edible small green buds that grow on the stem of) a plant of the mustard family
brutal /ˈbroohtl||ˈbruːtl/ *adj* **1** grossly ruthless or unfeeling <*a* ~ *slander*> **2** cruel, cold-blooded <*a* ~ *attack*> **3** harsh, severe <~ *weather*> **4** unpleasantly accurate and incisive <~ *truth*> – **brutally** *adv*, **brutality** *n*
brutal·ize, -ise /ˈbrooht(ə)lˌiez||ˈbruːt(ə)lˌaɪz/ *vt* **1** to make brutal, unfeeling, or inhuman **2** to beat brutally – **brutalization** *n*
[1]brute /brooht||bruːt/ *adj* **1** characteristic of an animal in quality, action, or instinct: e g **1a** cruel, savage **b** not working by reason; mindless **2** purely physical <~ *strength*>
[2]brute *n* **1** a beast **2** a brutal person – **brutish** *adj*, **brutishly** *adv*
[1]bubble /ˈbubl||ˈbʌbl/ *vi* **1** to form or produce bubbles **2** to make a sound like the bubbles rising in liquid **3** to be highly excited or overflowing (with a feeling) <bubbling *over with happiness*>
[2]bubble *n* **1a** a usu small body of gas within a

liquid or solid **b** a thin spherical usu transparent film of liquid inflated with air or vapour **c** a transparent dome **2** sthg that lacks firmness or reality; *specif* an unreliable or speculative scheme **3** a sound like that of bubbling

ˌbubble and ˈsqueak *n, chiefly Br* a dish consisting of usu leftover potato, cabbage, and sometimes meat, fried together

ˈbubble ˌgum *n* a chewing gum that can be blown into large bubbles

[1]**bubbly** /ˈbubli‖ˈbʌblɪ/ *adj* **1** full of bubbles **2** overflowing with good spirits or liveliness; vivacious

[2]**bubbly** *n* champagne; *broadly* any sparkling wine – infml

bubo /ˈbyoohboh‖ˈbjuːbəʊ/ *n, pl* **buboes** *pl* **buboes** an inflamed swelling of a lymph gland, esp in the groin or armpit – **bubonic** *adj*

buˌbonic ˈplague /byooˈbonik, byooh-‖bjʊˈbɒnɪk, bjuː-/ *n* plague characterized by the formation of buboes

buccaneer /ˌbukəˈniə‖ˌbʌkəˈnɪə/ *n* **1** a freebooter preying on Spanish ships and settlements, esp in the W Indies in the 17th c; *broadly* a pirate **2** an unscrupulous adventurer, esp in politics or business [French *boucanier*, fr *boucaner* to smoke meat on a grid over a fire] – **buccaneer** *vi*

[1]**buck** /buk‖bʌk/ *n,* **1a** a male animal, esp a male deer, antelope, rabbit, rat, etc **b** an antelope **2** a dashing fellow; a dandy **3** VAULTING HORSE **4** *NAm* DOLLAR 2 – slang

[2]**buck** *vi* **1** *of a horse or mule* to spring into the air with the back curved and come down with the forelegs stiff and the head lowered **2** to refuse assent; balk **3** *chiefly NAm* to move or react jerkily ~ *vt* **1** to throw (e g a rider) by bucking **2** to fail to comply with; run counter to <~ *the system*>

[3]**buck** *n* **1** an object formerly used in poker to mark the next player to deal; *broadly* sthg used as a reminder **2** *the* responsibility – esp in *pass the buck*

bucked /bukt‖bʌkt/ *adj* pleased, encouraged

[1]**bucket** /ˈbukit‖ˈbʌkɪt/ *n* **1** a large open container, usu round, with tapering sides and a semicircular handle on top, used esp for holding or carrying liquids **2** sthg resembling a bucket, esp in shape or function: e g the scoop of an excavating machine

[2]**bucket** *vt* to draw or lift in buckets ~ *vi* **1** to move about jerkily or recklessly **2** *chiefly Br* BUCKET DOWN

bucket down *vi, chiefly Br* **1** *of rain* to fall heavily **2** to rain very hard

ˈbucket ˌseat *n* a round-backed separate seat for 1 person in a motor car, aircraft, etc

bucket shop *n* a business that sells airline tickets cheaply

[1]**buckle** /ˈbukl‖ˈbʌkl/ *n* a fastening consisting of a rigid rim, usu with a hinged pin, used to join together 2 loose ends (e g of a belt or strap) or for ornament

[2]**buckle** *vt* **1** to fasten with a buckle **2** to cause to bend, give way, or crumple ~ *vi* **1** to bend, warp **2** to yield; GIVE WAY

[3]**buckle** *n* a distorted formation due to buckling

buckle down *vi* to apply oneself vigorously <*she* buckled down *to her work*>

buckler /ˈbuklə‖ˈbʌklə/ *n* a small round shield held by a handle at arm's length

ˌbuckle ˈto *vi* to brace oneself or gather up one's strength to put effort into work

buckram /ˈbukrəm‖ˈbʌkrəm/ *n* a fabric of cotton or linen, with a stiff finish, used for interlinings in garments, for stiffening in hats, and in bookbinding [Old French *boquerant*, fr Old Provençal *bocaran*, fr *Bokhara*, city in central Asia]

buckshee /ˈbukshee, -ˈ-‖ˈbʌkʃiː, -ˈ-/ *adj or adv, Br* without charge; free – slang

buckshot /ˈbukˌshot‖ˈbʌkˌʃɒt/ *n* a coarse lead shot used esp for shooting large animals

ˈbuckˌskin /-ˌskin‖-ˌskɪn/ *n* a soft pliable usu suede-finished leather – **buckskin** *adj*

ˌbuckˈtooth /-ˈtoohth‖-ˈtuːθ/ *n* a large projecting front tooth – **buck-toothed** *adj*

buck up *vi* **1** to become encouraged **2** to hurry up ~ *vt* **1** to improve, smarten **2** to raise the morale or spirits of

ˈbuckˌwheat /-ˌweet‖-ˌwiːt/ *n* **1** any of a genus of plants of the dock family that have pinkish white flowers and triangular seeds **2** the seed of a buckwheat, used as a cereal grain

bucolic /byoohˈkolik‖bjuːˈkɒlɪk/ *adj* **1** of shepherds or herdsmen; pastoral **2** (typical) of rural life – **bucolically** *adv*

[1]**bud** /bud‖bʌd/ *n* **1** a small protuberance on the stem of a plant that may develop into a flower, leaf, or shoot **2** sthg not yet mature or fully developed: e g **2a** an incompletely opened flower **b** an outgrowth of an organism that becomes a new individual

[2]**bud** *vb* **-dd-** *vi* **1** *of a plant* to put forth buds **2** to develop by way of outgrowth **3** to reproduce asexually by forming and developing buds ~ *vt* **1** to produce or develop from buds **2** to graft a bud into (a plant of another kind), usu in order to propagate a desired variety

Buddhism /ˈboodiz(ə)m‖ˈbʊdɪz(ə)m/ *n* an eastern religion growing out of the teaching of Gautama Buddha that one can be liberated from the suffering inherent in life by mental and moral self-purification – **Buddhist** *n or adj*

budding /ˈbuding‖ˈbʌdɪŋ/ *adj* being in an early and usu promising stage of development <~ *novelists*>

buddleia /ˈbudli·ə‖ˈbʌdlɪə/ *n* any of a genus of shrubs or trees mostly having long showy clusters of flowers that are attractive to butterflies [Adam *Buddle* (died 1715), English botanist]

buddy /ˈbudi‖ˈbʌdɪ/ *n, chiefly NAm* **1** a companion, partner **2** [3]MATE 1c *USE* infml

budge /buj‖bʌdʒ/ *vb* **1** to (cause to) move or shift **2** to (force or cause to) change an opinion or yield

budgerigar /ˈbuj(ə)riˌgah‖ˈbʌdʒ(ə)rɪˌgɑː/ *n* a small Australian bird that belongs to the same family as the parrots and is often kept in captivity [native name in Australia]

[1]**budget** /ˈbujit‖ˈbʌdʒɪt/ *n* **1** a statement of a financial position for a definite period of time

(e g for the following year), that is based on estimates of expenditures and proposals for financing them **2** a plan of how money will be spent or allocated **3** the amount of money available for, required for, or assigned to a particular purpose [Middle English *bowgette* pouch, wallet, fr Middle French *bougette*, fr *bouge* leather bag, fr Latin *bulga*, of Gaulish origin] – **budgetary** *adj*

[2]**budget** *vt* to plan or provide for the use of (e g money, time, or manpower) in detail ~*vi* to arrange or plan a budget

[1]**buff** /buf‖bʌf/ *n* **1** a strong supple oil-tanned leather produced chiefly from cattle hides **2** *the* bare skin – chiefly in *in the buff* **3** (a) pale yellowish brown **4** a device (e g a stick or pad) with a soft absorbent surface used for polishing sthg **5** one who has a keen interest in and wide knowledge of a specified subject; an enthusiast – **buff** *adj*

[2]**buff** *vt* **1** to polish, shine **2** to give a velvety surface like that of buff to (leather) – **buffer** *n*

buffalo /ˈbufəloh‖ˈbʌfələʊ/ *n*, **1** WATER BUFFALO **2** a large N American wild ox with short horns, heavy forequarters, and a large muscular hump; *also* any similar wild ox

[1]**buffer** /ˈbufə‖ˈbʌfə/ *n* an (ineffectual) fellow – chiefly in *old buffer*; infml

[2]**buffer** *n* **1** any of various devices for reducing the effect of an impact; *esp, Br* a spring-loaded metal disc on a railway vehicle or at the end of a railway track **2** a device that serves to protect sthg, or to cushion against shock **3** a person who shields another, esp from annoying routine matters **4** a temporary storage unit (e g in a computer); *esp* one that accepts information at one rate and delivers it at another

[3]**buffer** *vt* to lessen the shock of; cushion

buffer state *n* a small neutral state lying between 2 larger potentially rival powers

[1]**buffet** /ˈbufit‖ˈbʌfɪt/ *n* **1** a blow, esp with the hand **2** sthg that strikes with telling force

[2]**buffet** /ˈbufit‖ˈbʌfɪt/ *vt* **1** to strike sharply, esp with the hand; cuff **2** to strike repeatedly; batter <*the waves* ~ed *the shore*> **3** to use roughly; treat unpleasantly <~ed *by life*>

[3]**buffet** /ˈboofay‖ˈbʊfeɪ/ *n* **1** a sideboard or cupboard often used for the display of tableware **2** a counter for refreshments **3** a meal set out on tables or a sideboard for diners to help themselves **4** *chiefly Br* a self-service restaurant or snack bar

buffoon /bəˈfoohn‖bəˈfu:n/ *n* **1** a ludicrous figure; a clown **2** a rough and noisy fool – **buffoonery** *n*

[1]**bug** /bug‖bʌg/ *n* **1** any of several insects commonly considered obnoxious; *esp* a bedbug **2** an unexpected defect or imperfection **3** a disease-producing germ; *also* a disease caused by it – not used technically **4** a concealed listening device **5** a temporary enthusiasm; a craze – infml

[2]**bug** *vt* **-gg- 1a** to plant a concealed listening device in **b** to eavesdrop on by means of a mechanical bug **2** to bother, annoy – infml

bugaboo /ˈbugəˌbooh‖ˈbʌgəˌbu:/ *n, pl* **bugaboos** *chiefly NAm* a bugbear

bugbear /ˈbugˌbeə‖ˈbʌgˌbeə/ *n* an object or (persistent) source of fear, concern, or difficulty

[1]**bugger** /ˈbugə‖ˈbʌgə/ *n* **1** a sodomite **2a** a worthless or contemptible person, esp male **b** a creature; *esp* a man <*poor* ~> **3** *chiefly Br* a cause of annoyance or difficulty *USE* (*except 1*) vulg [Middle French *bougre* heretic, sodomite, fr Medieval Latin *Bulgarus*, lit., Bulgarian]

[2]**bugger** *vt* **1** to practise sodomy on **2a** – used interjectionally to express contempt or annoyance <~ *Tom! We'll go without him*> **b** to damage or ruin, usu because of incompetence – often + *up* **3** to exhaust; WEAR OUT **4** *Br* to be evasive with or misleading to – + *around* or *about* <*don't* ~ *me about*> ~*vi Br* to fool *around* or *about*, esp by dithering or being being indecisive *USE* (*except 1*) vulg

ˌbugger ˈoff *vi, Br* to go away – vulg

buggery /ˈbugəri‖ˈbʌgərɪ/ *n* sodomy

[1]**buggy** /ˈbugi‖ˈbʌgɪ/ *adj* infested with bugs

[2]**buggy** *n* a light one-horse carriage

[1]**bugle** /ˈbyoohgl‖ˈbju:gl/ *n* a European annual plant of the mint family that has spikes of blue flowers

[2]**bugle** *n* a valveless brass instrument that is used esp for military calls

[3]**bugle** *vi* to sound a bugle – **bugler** *n*

buhl, boulle /boohl‖bu:l/ *n* inlaid decoration of tortoiseshell or ornamental metalwork (e g brass) used in cabinetwork

[1]**build** /bild‖bɪld/ *vb* **built** /bilt‖bɪlt/ *vt* **1** to construct by putting together materials gradually into a composite whole **2** to cause to be constructed **3** to develop according to a systematic plan, by a definite process, or on a particular base **4** to increase or enlarge ~ *vi* **1** to engage in building **2a** to increase in intensity <~ *to a climax*> **b** to develop in extent <*a queue was already* ~ing>

[2]**build** *n* the physical proportions of a person or animal; *esp* a person's figure of a usu specified type <*an athletic* ~>

builder /ˈbildə‖ˈbɪldə/ *n* sby who contracts to build and supervises building operations

build in *vt* to construct or develop as an integral part

building /ˈbilding‖ˈbɪldɪŋ/ *n* **1** a permanent structure (e g a school or house) usu having walls and a roof **2** the art, business, or act of assembling materials into a structure

ˈbuilding soˌciety *n* any of various British organizations in which the public can invest money, and which advance money for house purchase

ˈbuildˌup /-ˌup‖-ˌʌp/ *n* **1** sthg produced by building up <*deal with the* ~ *of traffic*> **2** praise or publicity, esp given in advance

build up *vt* **1** to develop gradually by increments <built up *a library*> **2** to promote the esteem of; praise ~*vi* to accumulate or develop appreciably <*clouds* building up *on the horizon*>

built /bilt‖bɪlt/ *adj* proportioned or formed in a specified way <*a slightly* ~ *girl*>

ˌbuilt-ˈin *adj* **1** forming an integral part of a structure <~ *cupboards*> **2** inherent

ˌbuilt-ˈup *adj* **1** made of several sections or layers fastened together **2** well-filled or fully covered with buildings <*a* ~ *area*>

bulb /bulb‖bʌlb/ *n* **1a** a short stem base of a plant (e g the lily, onion, or hyacinth), with 1 or more buds enclosed in overlapping membranous or fleshy leaves, that is formed underground as a resting stage in the plant's development **b** a tuber, corm, or other fleshy structure resembling a bulb in appearance **c** a plant having or developing from a bulb **2** INCANDESCENT LAMP **3** a rounded or swollen anatomical structure

bulbous /ˈbulbəs‖ˈbʌlbəs/ *adj* **1** growing from or bearing bulbs **2** resembling a bulb, esp in roundness <*a* ~ *nose*> – **bulbously** *adv*

[1]**bulge** /bulj‖bʌldʒ/ *n* **1** BILGE 1 **2** a swelling or convex curve on a surface, usu caused by pressure from within or below **3** a sudden and usu temporary expansion (e g in population) – **bulgy** *adj*

[2]**bulge** *vi* to jut out; swell

[1]**bulk** /bulk‖bʌlk/ *n* **1a** spatial dimension; *esp* volume **b** roughage **2a** voluminous or ponderous mass – often used with reference to the shape or size of a corpulent person **b** a structure, esp when viewed as a mass of material <*the shrouded* ~s *of snow-covered cars*> **3** the main or greater part *of* – **in bulk** in large amounts or quantities; *esp, of goods bought and sold* in amounts or quantities much larger than as usu packaged or purchased

[2]**bulk** *vt* **1** to cause to swell or to be thicker or fuller; pad – often + *out* **2** to gather into a mass ~*vi* to appear as a factor; loom <*a consideration that* ~s *large in everyone's thinking*>

[3]**bulk** *adj* (of materials) in bulk

ˈ**bulk,head** /-ˌhed‖-ˌhed/ *n* a partition or wall separating compartments (e g in an aircraft or ship)

bulky /ˈbulki‖ˈbʌlkɪ/ *adj* **1** having too much bulk; *esp* unwieldy **2** corpulent – chiefly euph – **bulkily** *adv*, **bulkiness** *n*

[1]**bull** /bool‖bʊl/ *n* **1a** an adult male bovine animal **b** an adult male elephant, whale, or other large animal **2** one who buys securities or commodities in expectation of a price rise or who acts to effect such a rise **3** BULL'S-EYE 3a

[2]**bull** *adj* BULLISH 1

[3]**bull** *vt* to try to increase the price of (e g stocks) or in (a market)

[4]**bull** *n* **1** a papal edict on a subject of major importance **2** an edict, decree

[5]**bull** *n* **1** empty boastful talk; nonsense **2** *Br* unnecessary or irksome fatigues or discipline, esp in the armed forces *USE* slang

ˈ**bull,dog** /-ˌdog‖-ˌdɒg/ *n* **1** a thickset muscular short-haired dog of an English breed that has widely separated forelegs and a short neck **2** a proctor's attendant at Oxford or Cambridge

bulldoze /ˈbool,dohz‖ˈbʊl,dəʊz/ *vt* **1** to bully **2** to move, clear, gouge out, or level off with a bulldozer **3** to force insensitively or ruthlessly

ˈ**bull,dozer** /-ˌdohzə‖-ˌdəʊzə/ *n* a tractor-driven machine with a broad blunt horizontal blade that is used for clearing land, building roads, etc

bullet /ˈboolit‖ˈbʊlɪt/ *n* a small round or elongated missile designed to be fired from a firearm; *broadly* CARTRIDGE 1a – **bulletproof** *adj*

ˌ**bulletˈheaded** /-ˈhedid‖-ˈhedɪd/ *adj* **1** having a rounded solid-looking head **2** bullheaded

bulletin /ˈboolətin‖ˈbʊlətɪn/ *n* **1** a brief public notice; *specif* a brief news item intended for immediate publication **2** a short programme of news items on radio or television

ˈ**bull,fight** /-ˌfiet‖-ˌfaɪt/ *n* a spectacle (in an arena) in which bulls are ceremonially excited, fought with, and in Hispanic tradition killed, for public entertainment – **bullfighter** *n*

ˈ**bull,finch** /-ˌfinch‖-ˌfɪntʃ/ *n* a European finch, the male of which has a rosy red breast and throat

ˈ**bull,frog** /-ˌfrog‖-ˌfrɒg/ *n* a heavy-bodied deep-voiced frog

ˌ**bullˈheaded** /-ˈhedid‖-ˈhedɪd/ *adj* stupidly stubborn; headstrong – **bullheadedly** *adv*, **bullheadedness** *n*

bullion /ˈboolyən‖ˈbʊljən/ *n* gold or silver (in bars) that has not been minted

bullish /ˈboolish‖ˈbʊlɪʃ/ *adj* **1** suggestive of a bull (e g in brawniness) **2** marked by, tending to cause, or hopeful of rising prices (e g in a stock market)

ˌ**bull ˈneck** *n* a thick short powerful neck – **bullnecked** *adj*

bullock /ˈboolək‖ˈbʊlək/ *n* **1** a young bull **2** a castrated bull

ˈ**bull,ring** /-ˌring‖-ˌrɪŋ/ *n* an arena for bullfights

ˈ**bull's-,eye** *n* **1** a small thick disc of glass inserted (e g in a ship's deck) to let in light **2** a very hard round usu peppermint sweet **3a** (a shot that hits) the centre of a target **b** sthg that precisely attains a desired end

ˈ**bull,shit** /-ˌshit‖-ˌʃɪt/ *n* nonsense – vulg

ˌ**bull ˈterrier** *n* a short-haired terrier of a breed originated in England by crossing the bulldog with a breed of terrier

[1]**bully** /ˈbooli‖ˈbʊlɪ/ *n* **1** a browbeating person; *esp* one habitually cruel to others weaker than him-/herself **2** a hired ruffian

[2]**bully** *adj* – **bully for** – used to congratulate a specified person, sometimes ironically <*well* bully for *you!*>

[3]**bully** *vt* to treat abusively; intimidate

[4]**bully**, ˈ**bully-,off** *n* a procedure for starting play in a hockey match in which 2 opposing players face each other and alternately strike the ground and the opponent's stick 3 times before attempting to gain possession of the ball

[5]**bully** *vt* to put (a hockey ball) in play with a bully ~*vi* to start or restart a hockey match with a bully – usu + *off*

bully beef *also* **bully** *n* corned beef [prob fr French *boeuf bouilli* boiled beef]

ˈ**bully,boy** /-ˌboy‖-ˌbɔɪ/ *n* a rough man, esp a hired thug

bulrush /ˈbool,rush‖ˈbʊl,rʌʃ/ *n* **1** any of a genus of annual or perennial sedges **2** the papyrus – used in the Bible **3** *Br* either of 2 species of tall reedy marsh plants with brown furry fruiting spikes

bulwark /ˈboolək‖ˈbʊlək/ *n* **1a** a solid wall-like structure raised for defence; a rampart **b** a breakwater, seawall **2a** a strong support or protection <*education as a* ~ *of democracy*> **b** a defence <*a pay rise of 30 per cent would be a* ~ *against inflation*> **3** the side of a ship above the upper deck – usu pl with sing. meaning

[1]**bum** /bum‖bʌm/ *n, chiefly Br* the

buttocks – slang

[2]**bum** *vt* **-mm-** *Br* to have anal intercourse with – vulg

[3]**bum** *vb* **-mm-** *vi* to spend time idly and often travelling casually – usu + *around*; slang ~*vt* to obtain by begging; cadge – slang

[4]**bum** *n* **1** *NAm* an idler, loafer; *specif* a vagrant, tramp **2** *chiefly NAm* an incompetent worthless person **3** *NAm* one who devotes his/her time to a specified recreational activity <*a beach* ~> *USE* slang

[5]**bum** *adj, chiefly NAm* **1** inferior, worthless <~ *advice*> **2** disabled <*a* ~ *knee*> *USE* slang

[1]**bumble** /ˈbumbl‖ˈbʌmbl/ *vi* DRONE 1

[2]**bumble** *vi* **1** to speak in a faltering manner **2** to proceed unsteadily; stumble – often + *along* – **bumbler** *n*, **bumblingly** *adv*

ˈ**bumble,bee** /-ˌbee‖-ˌbiː/ *n* any of numerous large robust hairy bees

ˈ**bum,boat** /-ˌboht‖-ˌbəʊt/ *n* a boat that brings commodities for sale to larger ships

bumf, bumph /bumf‖bʌmf/ *n, Br* (undesirable or superfluous) paperwork – infml [British slang *bumf* toilet paper, short for *bumfodder*, fr [1]*bum* + *fodder*]

[1]**bummer** /ˈbumə‖ˈbʌmə/ *n, chiefly NAm* [4]BUM 1

[2]**bummer** *n* an unpleasant experience (e g a bad reaction to a hallucinogenic drug) – infml

[1]**bump** /bump‖bʌmp/ *vt* **1** to strike or knock with force **2** to collide with **3** to dislodge with a jolt ~ *vi* **1** to knock against sthg with a forceful jolt – often + *into* **2** to proceed in a series of bumps – **bump into** to encounter, esp by chance

[2]**bump** *n* **1** a sudden forceful blow or jolt **2** a rounded projection from a surface: e g **2a** a swelling of tissue **b** a natural protuberance of the skull **3** a thrusting of the hips forwards in an erotic manner

[1]**bumper** /ˈbumpə‖ˈbʌmpə/ *n* **1** a brimming cup or glass **2** sthg unusually large

[2]**bumper** *adj* unusually large <*a* ~ *crop*>

[3]**bumper** *n* **1** a metal or rubber bar, usu at either end of a motor vehicle, for absorbing shock or minimizing damage in collision **2** a bouncer

bumpkin /ˈbum(p)kin‖ˈbʌm(p)kɪn/ *n* an awkward and unsophisticated rustic

bump off *vt* to murder – slang

bumptious /ˈbum(p)shəs‖ˈbʌm(p)ʃəs/ *adj* self-assertive in a presumptuous, obtuse, and often noisy manner; obtrusive – **bumptiously** *adv*, **bumptiousness** *n*

bumpy /ˈbumpi‖ˈbʌmpɪ/ *adj* **1** having or covered with bumps; uneven <*a* ~ *road*> **2** marked by jolts <*a* ~ *ride*> – **bumpily** *adv*, **bumpiness** *n*

bun /bun‖bʌn/ *n* **1** any of various usu sweet and round small bread rolls that may contain added ingredients (e g currants or spice) **2** a usu tight knot of hair worn esp on the back of the head **3** *chiefly N Eng* a small round sweet cake often made from a sponge-cake mixture

[1]**bunch** /bunch‖bʌntʃ/ *n* **1** a compact group formed by a number of things of the same kind, esp when growing or held together; a cluster **2** *sing or pl in constr* the main group (e g of cyclists) in a race **3** *pl, Br* a style in which the hair is divided into 2 lengths and tied, usu one on each side of the head **4** *sing or pl in constr* a group of people – infml – **bunchy** *adj*

[2]**bunch** *vb* to form (into) a group or cluster – often + *up*

[1]**bundle** /ˈbundl‖ˈbʌndl/ *n* **1a** a collection of things held loosely together **b** a package **c** a collection, conglomerate **2** a small band of mostly parallel nerve or other fibres **3** a great deal; mass <*he's a* ~ *of nerves*> **4** a sizable sum of money – slang

[2]**bundle** *vt* **1** to make into a bundle or package **2** to hustle or hurry unceremoniously <~d *the children off to school*> **3** to hastily deposit or stuff *into* a suitcase, box, drawer, etc

bundle up *vb* to dress warmly

[1]**bung** /bung‖bʌŋ/ *n* the stopper in the bunghole of a cask; *broadly* sthg used to plug an opening

[2]**bung** *vt* **1** to plug, block, or close (as if) with a bung – often + *up* **2** *chiefly Br* to throw, toss – infml **3** *Br* to put <~ *that record on*> *USE (except 1)* infml

bungalow /ˈbung·gəloh‖ˈbʌŋgələʊ/ *n* a single -storeyed house [Hindi *baṅglā*, lit., (house) in the Bengal style]

ˈ**bung,hole** /-ˌhohl‖-ˌhəʊl/ *n* a hole for emptying or filling a cask

bungle /ˈbung·gl‖ˈbʌŋgl/ *vt* to perform clumsily; botch – **bungler** *n*, **bungling** *adj*

bunion /ˈbunyən‖ˈbʌnjən/ *n* an inflamed swelling at the side of the foot on the first joint of the big toe

[1]**bunk** /bungk‖bʌŋk/ *n* **1** a built-in bed (e g on a ship) that is often one of a tier of berths **2** a sleeping place – infml

[2]**bunk** *vi* to sleep or bed *down*, esp in a makeshift bed

[3]**bunk** *n* – **do a bunk** *chiefly Br* to make a hurried departure, esp in order to escape – slang

[4]**bunk** *n* nonsense, humbug

bunk bed *n* either of 2 single beds usu placed one above the other

bunker /ˈbungkə‖ˈbʌŋkə/ *n* **1** a bin or compartment for storage; *esp* one on a ship for storing fuel **2a** a protective embankment or dugout; *esp* a fortified chamber mostly below ground **b** a golf course hazard that is an area of sand-covered bare ground with 1 or more embankments – **bunker** *vt*

bunkum /ˈbungkəm‖ˈbʌŋkəm/ *n* insincere or foolish talk; nonsense [*Buncombe* county, North Carolina, USA; fr the defence of a seemingly irrelevant speech made by its congressional representative in 1820, that he was speaking to Buncombe]

bunny /ˈbuni‖ˈbʌnɪ/ *n* RABBIT 1 – usu used by or to children

ˌ**Bunsen** ˈ**burner** /ˈbuns(ə)n‖ˈbʌns(ə)n/ *n* a gas burner in which air is mixed with the gas to produce an intensely hot blue flame [Robert *Bunsen* (1811-99), German chemist]

[1]**bunting** /ˈbunting‖ˈbʌntɪŋ/ *n* any of various birds that have short strong beaks and are related to the finches

[2]**bunting** *n* (flags or decorations made of) a lightweight loosely woven fabric

[1]**buoy** /boy‖bɔɪ/ *n* a distinctively shaped and

marked float moored to the bottom **a** as a navigational aid to mark a channel or hazard **b** for mooring a ship

[2]**buoy** *vt* **1** to mark (as if) by a buoy **2a** to keep afloat **b** to support, sustain **3** to raise the spirits of <*hope* ~s *him up*> *USE* (*2 & 3*) usu + *up*

buoyancy /'boyənsi||'bɔɪənsɪ/ *n* **1a** the tendency of a body to float or to rise when submerged in a fluid **b** the power of a fluid to exert an upward force on a body placed in it **2** resilience, vivacity – **buoyant** *adj*, **buoyantly** *adv*

bur /buh||bɜː/ *n* [1]BURR

burble /'buhbl||'bɜːbl/ *vi* **1** to make a bubbling sound; gurgle **2** to babble, prattle – **burble** *n*

[1]**burden** /'buhd(ə)n||'bɜːd(ə)n/ *n* **1a** sthg that is carried; a load **b** a duty, responsibility **2** sthg oppressive or wearisome; an encumbrance **3** capacity for carrying cargo <*a ship of a hundred tons* ~>

[2]**burden** *vt* to load, oppress

[3]**burden** *n* **1** a chorus, refrain **2** a central topic; a theme

ˌ**burden of 'proof** *n* the duty of proving an assertion

'**burdensome** /-səm||-səm/ *adj* imposing or constituting a burden; oppressive

burdock /'buhdok||'bɜːdɒk/ *n* any of a genus of coarse composite plants bearing prickly spherical flower heads

bureau /'byooəroh||'bjʊərəʊ/ *n, pl* **bureaus** *also* **bureaux** /-rohz||-rəʊz/ **1a** a specialized administrative unit; *esp* a government department **b** an establishment for exchanging information, making contacts, or coordinating activities **2** *Br* a writing desk; *esp* one with drawers and a sloping top [French, desk, cloth covering for desks, fr Old French *burel* woollen cloth, fr Late Latin *burra* shaggy cloth]

bureaucracy /byooə'rokrəsi||bjʊə'rɒkrəsɪ/ *n* **1** government characterized by specialization of functions, adherence to fixed rules, and a hierarchy of authority; *also* the body of appointed government officials **2** a system of public administration marked by excessive officialism – **bureaucratize** *vt*, **bureaucratization** *n*, **bureaucratic** *adj*, **bureaucratically** *adv*

bureaucrat /'byooərəˌkrat||'bjʊərəˌkræt/ *n* a member of a bureaucracy; *esp* a government official who follows a rigid routine

burgeon /'buhj(ə)n||'bɜːdʒ(ə)n/ *vi* **1** to send forth new growth (e g buds or branches) **2** to grow and expand rapidly

burgess /'buhjis||'bɜːdʒɪs/ *n, archaic* a citizen of a British borough

burgh /'burə||'bʌrə/ *n* a borough; *specif* a town in Scotland that has a charter

burgher /'buhgə||'bɜːgə/ *n* an inhabitant of an esp medieval borough or a town

burglar /'buhglə||'bɜːglə/ *n* sby who commits burglary – **burglarize** *vt, chiefly NAm*

burglary /'buhgləri||'bɜːglərɪ/ *n* the offence of unlawfully entering a building with criminal intent, esp to steal

burgle /'buhgl||'bɜːgl/ *vt* to commit an act of burglary against

burgomaster /'buhgəˌmahstə||'bɜːgəˌmɑːstə/ *n* the mayor of a town in certain European countries

Burgundy /'buhgəndi||'bɜːgəndɪ/ *n* a red or white table wine from the Burgundy region of France

burial /'beri·əl||'berɪəl/ *n* the act, process, or ceremony of burying esp a dead body

burk, berk /buhk||bɜːk/ *n, Br* a foolish person – infml

burlap /'buhlap||'bɜːlæp/ *n* a coarse heavy plain-woven fabric, usu of jute or hemp, used for sacking and in furniture and linoleum manufacture

[1]**burlesque** /buh'lesk||bɜː'lesk/ *n* **1** a literary or dramatic work that uses exaggeration or imitation to ridicule **2** mockery, usu by caricature **3** a US stage show usu consisting of short turns, comic sketches, and striptease acts – **burlesque** *adj*

[2]**burlesque** *vt* to imitate in a humorous or derisive manner; mock

burly /'buhli||'bɜːlɪ/ *adj* strongly and heavily built – **burliness** *n*

[1]**burn** /buhn||bɜːn/ *n, chiefly Scot* a small stream

[2]**burn** *vb* **burnt** /buhnt||bɜːnt/, **burned** /buhnd, buhnt||bɜːnd, bɜːnt/ *vi* **1a** to consume fuel and give off heat, light, and gases **b** to undergo combustion **c** to undergo nuclear fission or nuclear fusion **d** to give off light <*a light* ~ing *in the window*> **2a** *of the ears or face* to become very red and feel uncomfortably hot **b** to produce or undergo a painfully stinging or smarting sensation <*fingers* ~ing *from the cold*> **c** to receive sunburn <*kind of skin that* ~s *easily*> **d(1)** to long passionately; [1]DIE 3 <~ing *to tell the story*> **d(2)** to be filled *with*; experience sthg strongly <~ing *with fury*> **3** to become charred, scorched, or destroyed by fire or the action of heat <*the potatoes are* ~ing> ~ *vt* **1a** to cause to undergo combustion; *esp* to destroy by fire <~ed *the rubbish*> **b** to use as fuel **2a** to transform by exposure to heat or fire <~ *clay to bricks*> **b** to produce by burning <~ *a hole in the sleeve*> **3a** to injure or damage by exposure to fire, heat, radiation, caustic chemicals, or electricity **b** to execute by burning <~ *heretics at the stake*> **c** to char or scorch by exposing to fire or heat **4** to harm, exploit – often pass – **burnable** *adj* – **burn one's bridges/boats** to cut off all means of retreat – **burn the candle at both ends** to use one's resources or energies to excess; *esp* to be active at night as well as by day – **burn the midnight oil** to work or study far into the night

[3]**burn** *n* **1a** injury or damage resulting (as if) from burning **b** a burned area <*a* ~ *on the table top*> **c** a burning sensation <*the* ~ *of iodine on a cut*> **2** a firing of a spacecraft rocket engine in flight

burner /'buhnə||'bɜːnə/ *n* the part of a fuel-burning device (e g a stove or furnace) where the flame is produced

burning /'buhning||'bɜːnɪŋ/ *adj* **1a** on fire **b** ardent, intense <~ *enthusiasm*> **2a** affecting (as if) with heat <*a* ~ *fever*> **b** resembling that produced by a burn <*a* ~ *sensation on the tongue*> **3** of fundamental importance; urgent – **burningly** *adv*

burnish /'buhnish||'bɜːnɪʃ/ *vt* to make shiny or

lustrous, esp by rubbing; polish – **burnishing** *adj or n*

burnous /ˌbuhˈnoohs‖ˌbɜːˈnuːs/ *n* a hooded cloak traditionally worn by Arabs and Moors

burn out *vt* **1** to cause to be no longer active, having completed a course of development <*the disease had* burnt *itself* out> **2** to exhaust by excessive physical or mental activity <*she was a* burnt-out *case at 30*> **3** to cause to burn out ~*vi* to cease to conduct electricity when the enclosed filament or conducting wire has melted

burn up *vt* to drive along extremely fast – infml – **burn-up** *n*

[1]**burp** /buhp‖bɜːp/ *n* a belch – infml

[2]**burp** *vb* to (cause to) belch – infml

[1]**burr, bur** /buh‖bɜː/ *n* **1** a rough or prickly covering of a fruit or seed **2** sthg that sticks or clings **3** a thin rough edge left after cutting or shaping metal, plastic, etc **4** the pronunciation of /r/ in a W country or Northumberland accent **5** a small drill; *also* a bit used in a dentist's or surgeon's burr **6** a rough whirring sound – **burred** *adj*, **burry** *adj*

[2]**burr** *vi* to make a whirring sound ~*vt* to pronounce with a burr

burro /ˈbooroh‖ˈbʊrəʊ/ *n, pl* **burros** *chiefly NAm* a small donkey (used as a pack animal)

[1]**burrow** /ˈburoh‖ˈbʌrəʊ/ *n* a hole or excavation in the ground made by a rabbit, fox, etc for shelter and habitation

[2]**burrow** *vt* **1** to construct or excavate by tunnelling <~ed *its way beneath the hill*> **2** to make a motion suggestive of burrowing with; nestle <*she* ~ed *her grubby hand into mine*> ~*vi* **1** to conceal oneself (as if) in a burrow **2a** to make a burrow **b** to progress (as if) by digging **3** to make a motion suggestive of burrowing; snuggle, nestle <~ed *against her back for warmth*> **4** to make a search as if by digging <~ed *into her pocket for a 10p piece*> – **burrower** *n*

bursa /ˈbuhsə‖ˈbɜːsə/ *n, pl* **bursas, bursae** /ˈbuhsi‖ˈbɜːsɪ/ a small sac or pouch (between a tendon and a bone) – **bursal** *adj*

bursar /ˈbuhsə‖ˈbɜːsə/ *n* **1** an officer (e g of a monastery or college) in charge of funds **2** *chiefly Scot* the holder of a bursary

bursary /ˈbuhs(ə)ri‖ˈbɜːs(ə)rɪ/ *n* **1** a bursar's office **2** a grant of money to a needy student

[1]**burst** /buhst‖bɜːst/ *vb* **burst** *vi* **1** to break open, apart, or into pieces, usu from impact or because of pressure from within **2a** to give way from an excess of emotion <*his heart will* ~ *with grief*> **b** to give vent suddenly to a repressed emotion <~ *into tears*> **3a** to emerge or spring suddenly <~ *out of a house*> **b** to launch, plunge <~ *into song*> **4** to be filled to breaking point or to the point of overflowing ~*vt* **1** to cause to break open or into pieces, usu by means of pressure from within **2** to produce (as if) by bursting – **burst at the seams** to be large or full to the point of discomfort

[2]**burst** *n* **1** a sudden usu temporary outbreak **2** an explosion, eruption **3** a sharp temporary increase (of speed, energy, etc) **4** a volley of shots

burst out *vi* to begin suddenly <*he* burst out *laughing*> ~*vt* to exclaim suddenly

bury /ˈberi‖ˈberɪ/ *vt* **1** to dispose of by depositing (as if) in the earth; *esp* to inter **2** to conceal, hide <*the report was* buried *under papers*> **3** to put completely out of mind; HAVE DONE WITH <~ing *their differences*> **4** to submerge, engross – usu + *in* <buried *herself in her books*> – **bury the hatchet** to settle a disagreement; become reconciled

[1]**bus** /bus‖bʌs/ *n, pl* **-s-**, *chiefly NAm* **-ss-** **1** a large motor-driven passenger vehicle operating usu according to a timetable along a fixed route **2** a busbar

[2]**bus** *vb* **-s-, -ss-** *vi* to travel by bus ~*vt* to transport by bus; *specif, chiefly NAm* to transport (children) by bus to a school in another district where the pupils are of a different race, in order to create integrated classes

busbar /ˈbusˌbah‖ˈbʌsˌbɑː/ *n* a conductor or an assembly of conductors connected to several similar circuits in an electrical or electronic system

busby /ˈbuzbi‖ˈbʌzbɪ/ *n* **1** a military full-dress fur hat worn esp by hussars **2** the bearskin worn by the Brigade of Guards – not used technically

[1]**bush** /boosh‖bʊʃ/ *n* **1a** a (low densely branched) shrub **b** a close thicket of shrubs **2** a large uncleared or sparsely settled area (e g in Africa or Australia), usu scrub-covered or forested **3a** a bushy tuft or mass <*a* ~ *of black hair*> **b** [2]BRUSH 2

[2]**bush** *vt* to support, protect, etc with bushes ~*vi* to extend like or resemble a bush

[3]**bush, bushing** *n* a usu removable cylindrical lining for an opening used to limit the size of the opening, resist abrasion, or serve as a guide

[4]**bush** *vt* to provide (a bearing, shaft, etc) with a bush

ˈbush ˌbaby *n* a member of either of 2 genera of small active nocturnal tree-dwelling African primates

bushed *adj* **1** perplexed, confused **2** *chiefly Austr* lost, esp in the bush **3** tired, exhausted – infml

bushel /ˈbooshl‖ˈbʊʃl/ *n* **1** any of various units of dry capacity **2** a container holding a bushel

bush telegraph *n* the rapid unofficial communication of news, rumours, etc by word of mouth

bushwhack /ˈbooshˌwak‖ˈbʊʃˌwæk/ *vi* **1** to clear a path through thick woods **2** to live or hide out in the woods **3** to fight in or attack from the bush ~*vt* to ambush – **bushwhacker** *n*, **bushwhacking** *n*

bushy /ˈbooshi‖ˈbʊʃɪ/ *adj* **1** full of or overgrown with bushes **2** growing thickly or densely – **bushily** *adv*, **bushiness** *n*

business /ˈbiznis‖ˈbɪznɪs/ *n* **1a** a role, function **b** an immediate task or objective; a mission **c** a particular field of endeavour <*the best in the* ~> **2a** a usu commercial or mercantile activity engaged in as a means of livelihood **b** one's regular employment, profession, or trade **c** a commercial or industrial enterprise **d** economic transactions or dealings **3** an affair, matter <*a strange* ~> **4** movement or action performed by an actor **5a** personal concern

<none of your ~> **b** proper motive; justifying right *<you have no ~ asking me that>* **6** serious activity *<immediately got down to ~>* – **like nobody's business** extraordinarily well

'business,like /-,liek‖-,laɪk/ *adj* **1** (briskly) efficient **2** serious, purposeful

'businessman /-mən, -,man‖-mən, -,mæn/, *fem* **'business,woman** *n* **1** sby professionally engaged in commercial transactions; *esp* a business executive **2** sby with financial flair

busk /busk‖bʌsk/ *vi, chiefly Br* to sing or play an instrument in the street in order to earn money – **busker** *n*

busman /'busmən‖'bʌsmən/ *n, chiefly Br* sby who works on a bus

,busman's 'holiday *n* a holiday spent doing one's usual work

'bus-,stop *n* a place where people may board and alight from buses

¹bust /bust‖bʌst/ *n* **1** a sculpture of the upper part of the human figure including the head, neck, and usu shoulders **2** the upper part of the human torso between neck and waist; *esp* the (size of the) breasts of a woman [French *buste*, fr Italian *busto*, fr Latin *bustum* tomb]

²bust *vb* **busted** *also* **bust** *vt* **1a** to break, smash; *also* to make inoperative **b** to bring to an end; BREAK UP 3 – often + *up* **2a** to arrest **b** to raid *<police ~ed the flat below>* ~ *vi* **1a** to burst *<laughing fit to ~>* **b** BREAK DOWN 1a **2** to lose a game or turn by exceeding a limit (e g the count of 21 in pontoon) *USE* (*vt; vi 1*) infml [alteration of *burst*] – **bust a gut** to exert oneself; make a great effort – infml

³bust *n* a police raid or arrest – infml

⁴bust *adj* **1** broken – chiefly infml **2** bankrupt – chiefly in *go bust*; infml

bustard /'bustəd‖'bʌstəd/ *n* any of a family of usu large Old World and Australian game birds

buster /'bustə‖'bʌstə/ *n* **1** sby or sthg that breaks or breaks up *<crime ~s>* **2** *chiefly NAm* PAL 2a – usu as a form of address

¹bustle /'busl‖'bʌsl/ *vi* to move briskly and often ostentatiously – **bustling** *adj*, **bustlingly** *adv*

²bustle *n* noisy and energetic activity

³bustle *n* a pad or framework worn to expand and support fullness at the back of a woman's skirt

'bust-,up *n* **1** a breaking up or apart *<the ~ of their marriage>* **2** a quarrel *USE* infml

¹busy /'bizi‖'bɪzɪ/ *adj* **1** engaged in action; occupied **2** full of activity; bustling **3** foolishly or intrusively active; meddlesome **4** full of detail *<a ~ design>* **5** *NAm, esp of a telephone* in use – **busily** *adv*, **busyness** *n*

²busy *vt* to make (esp oneself) busy; occupy

'busy,body /-,bodi‖-,bɒdɪ/ *n* an officious or inquisitive person

¹but /bət‖bət; *strong* but‖bʌt/ *conj* **1a** were it not *<would collapse ~ for your help>* **b** without the necessary accompaniment that – used after a negative *<it never rains ~ it pours>* **c** otherwise than; that . . . not *<I don't know ~ what I'll go>* **2a** on the contrary; on the other hand – used to join coordinate sentence elements of the same class or function expressing contrast *<I meant to tell you ~ you weren't here>* **b** and nevertheless; and yet *<poor ~ proud>* **c** – introducing an expression of protest or enthusiasm *<~ that's ridiculous>* or embarking on a new topic *<~ to continue>*

²but *prep* **1a** with the exception of; barring *<we're all here ~ Mary>* **b** other than *<this letter is nothing ~ an insult>* **c** not counting *<the next house ~ 2>* **2** *Scot* without, lacking

³but *adv* **1** only, merely *<he is ~ a child>* **2** to the contrary *<who knows ~ that he may succeed>* **3** – used for emphasis *<get there, ~ fast>* **4** *NE Eng & Austr* however, though *<it's pouring with rain, warm ~>*

⁴but *n* a doubt, objection *<there are no ~s about it>*

butane /'byoohtayn‖'bju:teɪn/ *n* an inflammable gaseous hydrocarbon of the alkane series used esp as a fuel (e g in cigarette lighters)

¹butch /booch‖bʊtʃ/ *n, chiefly Br* a male or female homosexual who plays the masculine role in a relationship

²butch *adj, chiefly Br* aggressively masculine in appearance – used, often disparagingly, of both women and (esp homosexual) men

¹butcher /'boochə‖'bʊtʃə/ *n* **1a** sby who slaughters animals or dresses their flesh **b** sby who deals in meat **2** sby who kills ruthlessly or brutally [Old French *bouchier*, fr *bouc* he-goat, prob of Celtic origin]

²butcher *vt* **1** to slaughter and prepare for market **2** to kill in a barbarous manner **3** to spoil, ruin

butchery /'booch(ə)ri‖'bʊtʃ(ə)rɪ/ *n* **1** the preparation of meat for sale **2** cruel and ruthless slaughter of human beings **3** the action of spoiling or ruining **4** *chiefly Br* a slaughterhouse

butler /'butlə‖'bʌtlə/ *n* **1** a manservant in charge of the wines and spirits **2** the chief male servant of a household [Old French *bouteillier* servant in charge of wine, fr *bouteille* bottle]

¹butt /but‖bʌt/ *vb* to strike or shove (sthg) with the head or horns

²butt *n* a blow or thrust, usu with the head or horns

³butt *n* **1a** a backstop for catching missiles shot at a target **b** a target **c** *pl* a range, specif for archery or rifle practice **d** a low mound, wall, etc from behind which sportsmen shoot at game birds **2** an object of abuse or ridicule; a victim

⁴butt *vi* to abut – usu + *against* or *onto* ~ *vt* **1** to place end to end or side to side without overlapping **2** to join by means of a butt joint

⁵butt *n* **1** the end of a plant or tree nearest the roots **2** the thicker or handle end of a tool or weapon **3** an unused remainder; *esp* the unsmoked remnant of a cigar or cigarette

⁶butt *n* a large cask, esp for wine, beer, or water

¹butter /'butə‖'bʌtə/ *n* **1** a pale yellow solid emulsion of fat globules, air, and water made by churning milk or cream and used as food **2a** any of various vegetable oils remaining solid or semisolid at ordinary temperatures *<cocoa ~>* **b** any of various food spreads made with or having the consistency of butter *<peanut ~>* – **butterless** *adj*

²butter *vt* to spread or cook with butter

'butter ,bean *n* **1** a (large dried) lima bean **2** SIEVA BEAN

'butter,cup /-,kup‖-,kʌp/ *n* any of many

plants with usu bright yellow flowers that commonly grow in fields and as weeds

'butter,fat /-,fat‖-,fæt/ *n* the natural fat of milk and chief constituent of butter

'butter,fingers /-,fing·gəz‖-,fɪŋgəz/ *n, pl* **butterfingers** a person apt to drop things – infml

'butter,fly /-,flie‖-,flaɪ/ *n* **1** any of numerous slender-bodied day-flying insects with large broad often brightly coloured wings **2** a person chiefly occupied with the pursuit of pleasure **3** a swimming stroke executed on the front by moving both arms together forwards out of the water and then sweeping them back through the water **4** *pl* queasiness caused esp by nervous tension – infml [Old English *buterflēoge*, fr *butere* butter + *flēoge* fly; perhaps fr former belief that butterflies steal milk and butter]

'butter,milk /-,milk‖-,mɪlk/ *n* **1** the liquid left after butter has been churned from milk or cream **2** cultured milk made by the addition of suitable bacteria to milk

'butter,scotch /-,skoch‖-,skɒtʃ/ *n* (the flavour of) a brittle toffee made from brown sugar, syrup, butter, and water

butter up *vt* to charm with lavish flattery; cajole – infml

[1]buttery /'but(ə)ri‖'bʌt(ə)rɪ/ *n* a room (e g in a college) in which food and drink are served or sold

[2]buttery *adj* similar to or containing butter

butt in *vi* **1** to meddle, intrude **2** to interrupt

buttock /'butək‖'bʌtək/ *n* the back of a hip that forms one of the 2 fleshy parts on which a person sits

[1]button /'but(ə)n‖'bʌt(ə)n/ *n* **1** a small knob or disc secured to an article (e g of clothing) and used as a fastener by passing it through a buttonhole or loop **2** an immature whole mushroom **3** a guard on the tip of a fencing foil **4** PUSH BUTTON **5** sthg of little value <*not worth a* ~> – **buttonless** *adj*

[2]button *vt* to close or fasten (as if) with buttons – often + *up* <~ *up your overcoat*> ~*vi* to have buttons for fastening <*this dress* ~s *at the back*>

'button-,down *adj, of a collar* having the ends fastened to the garment with buttons

[1]'button,hole /-,hohl‖-,həʊl/ *n* **1** a slit or loop through which a button is passed **2** *chiefly Br* a flower worn in a buttonhole or pinned to the lapel

[2]buttonhole *vt* **1** to provide with buttonholes **2** to sew with buttonhole stitch – **buttonholer** *n*

[3]buttonhole *vt* to detain in conversation

'button,hook /-,hook‖-,hʊk/ *n* a hook for drawing small buttons through buttonholes

'buttons *n, pl* **buttons** *Br* a bellboy – infml

buttress /'butris‖'bʌtrɪs/ *n* **1** a structure built against a wall or building to provide support or reinforcement **2** a projecting part of a mountain **3** sthg that supports or strengthens <*a* ~ *of the cause of peace*> – **buttress** *vt*, **buttressed** *adj*

butyric acid /byooh'tirik‖bju:'tɪrɪk/ *n* an unpleasant-smelling fatty acid found esp in rancid butter

buxom /'buks(ə)m‖'bʌks(ə)m/ *adj* attractively or healthily plump; *specif* full-bosomed – **buxomness** *n*

[1]buy /bie‖baɪ/ *vb* **bought** /bawt‖bɔ:t/ *vt* **1** to acquire possession or rights to the use of by payment, esp of money; purchase **2** to obtain, often by some sacrifice <bought *peace with their lives*> **3** to bribe, hire **4** to be the purchasing equivalent of <*the pound* ~s *less today than it used to*> **5** to believe, accept <*OK, I'll* ~ *that*> – slang ~*vi* to make a purchase – **buy time** to delay an imminent action or decision; stall

[2]buy *n* an act of buying; a purchase

buyer /'bie·ə‖'baɪə/ *n* one who selects and buys stock to be sold in an esp large shop

'buyer's ,market *n* a market in which supply exceeds demand, buyers have a wide range of choice, and prices tend to be low

buy in *vt* to obtain (a stock or supply of sthg) by purchase, esp in anticipation of need; *also* to complete an outstanding securities transaction by purchase against the account of (a delaying or defaulting speculator or dealer) – **buy-in** *n*

buy off *vt* to make a payment to in order to avoid some undesired course of action (e g prosecution)

buy out *vt* **1** to purchase the share or interest of <bought out *his partner*> **2** to free (e g from military service) by payment – usu + *of* <bought *himself* out *of the army*>

buy up *vt* **1** to purchase a controlling interest in (e g a company), esp by acquiring shares **2** to buy the entire available supply of

[1]buzz /buz‖bʌz/ *vi* **1** to make a low continuous vibratory sound like that of a bee **2** to be filled with a confused murmur <*the room* ~ed *with excitement*> **3** to make a signal with a buzzer ~ *vt* **1** to cause to buzz **2** to fly over or close to in order to threaten or warn <*the airliner was* ~ed *by fighters during its approach*> **3** to summon or signal with a buzzer

[2]buzz *n* **1** a persistent vibratory sound **2a** a confused murmur or flurry of activity **b** rumour, gossip **3** a signal conveyed by a buzzer or bell; *specif* a telephone call – infml **4** *chiefly NAm* a pleasant stimulation; a kick – infml

buzzard /'buzəd‖'bʌzəd/ *n* **1** a contemptible, greedy, or grasping person **2** *chiefly Br* a common large European hawk with soaring flight, or a similar related bird **3** *chiefly NAm* a (large) bird of prey (e g the turkey buzzard)

buzzer /'buzə‖'bʌzə/ *n* an electric signalling device that makes a buzzing sound

buzz off *vi* to go away quickly – slang

buzzword /'buz,wuhd‖'bʌz,wɜ:d/ *n* a fashionable word in the jargon of a particular activity or group, often of little meaning

[1]by /bie‖baɪ/ *prep* **1a** in proximity to; near <*standing* ~ *the window*> **b** on the person or in the possession of <*keep a spare set* ~ *me*> **2a** through (the medium of); via <*delivered* ~ *hand*> **b** 11°15′ in the direction of (another compass point up to 90° away) <*north* ~ *east*> **c** up to and then beyond; past <*went right* ~ *him*> **3a** in the circumstances of; during <*studied* ~ *night*> **b** not later than <*in bed* ~ *2 am*> **4a(1)** through the instrumentality or use of <~ *bus*> **a(2)** through the action or creation of <*a trio* ~ *Mozart*> **b(1)** sired by **b(2)** with the participation of (the other parent) <*his daughter* ~ *his first wife*> **5** with the witness or sanction of <*swear ~ Heaven*> **6a** in conformity with <*acted ~ the rules*> **b** in terms of <*paid ~ the hour*> **c** from the evidence of <*judge ~ appearances*> **d** with the action of <*began ~ scolding her*> **7** with respect to <*French ~ birth*> **8** to the amount or extent of <*better ~ far*> **9** in successive units or increments of <*day ~ day*> **10** – used in division as the inverse of *into* <*divide 70 ~ 35*>, in multiplication <*multiply 10 ~ 4*>, and in measurements <*a room 15ft ~ 20ft*> **11** *chiefly Scot* in comparison with; beside – **by oneself 1** alone, unaccompanied **2** unaided

[2]**by** *adv* **1a** close at hand; near <*when nobody was ~*> **b** at or to another's home <*stop ~ for a chat*> **2** past <*saw him go ~*> **3** aside, away; *esp* in or into reserve <*keep a few bottles ~*>

ˌ**by and ˈby** *adv* soon

ˌ**by and ˈlarge** *adv* ON THE WHOLE, IN GENERAL

[1]**bye, by** /bie‖baɪ/ *n* **1** sthg of secondary importance **2** the passage to the next round of a tournament allowed to a competitor without an opponent **3** a run scored in cricket off a ball that passes the batsman without striking the bat or body – **by the bye** BY THE WAY

[2]**bye, by** *interj* – used to express farewell

[1]**bye-bye, by-by** /ˈ- ˌ-, ˌ- ˈ-/ *interj* – used to express farewell

[2]ˈ**bye-ˌbye, ˈby-ˌby** *n* bed, sleep – usu pl with sing. meaning; usu used by or to children

ˈ**by-eˌlection** *also* ˈ**bye-eˌlection** *n* a special election to fill a vacancy

[1]**bygone** /ˈbieˌgon‖ˈbaɪˌgɒn/ *adj* earlier, past; *esp* outmoded

[2]**bygone** *n* an esp domestic artefact of an early and disused type – **let bygones be bygones** to forgive and forget past quarrels

bylaw, byelaw /ˈbieˌlaw‖ˈbaɪˌlɔː/ *n* a local or secondary law or regulation

ˈ**by-ˌline** *n* **1** a secondary line; a sideline **2** the author's name printed with a newspaper or magazine article

[1]ˈ**byˌpass** /-ˌpahs‖-ˌpɑːs/ *n* **1** a passage to one side; *esp* a road built so that through traffic can avoid a town centre **2** a channel carrying a fluid round a part and back to the main stream

[2]**bypass** *vt* **1** to avoid by means of a bypass **2** to neglect or ignore, usu intentionally

ˈ**byˌplay** /-ˌplay‖-ˌpleɪ/ *n* action engaged in on the side while the main action proceeds (e g during a dramatic production)

ˈ**by-ˌproduct** *n* sthg produced (e g in manufacturing) in addition to a principal product

byre /ˈbie·ə‖ˈbaɪə/ *n, chiefly Br* a cow shed

byroad /ˈbieˌrohd‖ˈbaɪˌrəʊd/ *n* a byway

bystander /ˈbieˌstandə‖ˈbaɪˌstændə/ *n* one present but not involved in a situation or event

byte /biet‖baɪt/ *n* a string of adjacent binary digits that is often shorter than a word and is processed by a computer as a unit; *esp* one that is 8 bits long

ˈ**byˌway** /-ˌway‖-ˌweɪ/ *n* **1** a little-used road **2** a secondary or little-known aspect

ˈ**byˌword** /-ˌwuhd‖-ˌwɜːd/ *n* **1** a proverb **2** (the name of) sby or sthg taken as representing some usu bad quality

Byzantine /biˈzantien, bie-, -teen‖bɪˈzæntaɪn, baɪ-, -tiːn/ *adj* **1** (characteristic) of the ancient city of Byzantium or its empire **2** of or in a style of architecture developed in the Byzantine Empire in the 5th and 6th c, featuring a central dome carried over a square space and much use of mosaics **3** intricately tortuous; labyrinthine – **Byzantine** *n*

c /see‖siː/ *n, pl* **c's, cs 1** (a graphic representation of or device for reproducing) the 3rd letter of the English alphabet **2** the keynote of a C-major scale **3** one designated *c*, esp as the 3rd in order or class **4a** one hundred **b** *chiefly NAm* a sum of $100 – slang

cab /kab‖kæb/ *n* **1** a taxi **2** the part of a locomotive, lorry, crane, etc that houses the driver and operating controls

cabal /kəˈbal‖kəˈbæl/ *vi or n* **-ll-** (to unite in or form) a secret or unofficial faction, esp in political intrigue – **cabalist** *n*

cabaret /ˈkabəray‖ˈkæbəreɪ/ *n* a stage show or series of acts provided at a nightclub, restaurant, etc [French, lit., tavern, prob deriv of Late Latin *camera* chamber]

cabbage /ˈkabij‖ˈkæbɪdʒ/ *n* **1** a cultivated plant that has a short stem and a dense globular head of usu green leaves used as a vegetable **2a** one who has lost control of his/her esp mental and physical faculties as the result of illness or accident **b** an inactive and apathetic person *USE* (*2*) infml

cabbala, cabala, cabbalah /kəˈbahlə, ˈkabələ‖kəˈbɑːlə, ˈkæbələ/ *n, often cap* **1** a system of esoteric Jewish mysticism **2** an esoteric or mysterious doctrine, art, or subject

cabby, cabbie /ˈkabi‖ˈkæbɪ/ *n* a taxi driver – infml

caber /ˈkaybə‖ˈkeɪbə/ *n* a roughly trimmed tree trunk that is tossed in a Scottish sport

cabin /ˈkabin‖ˈkæbɪn/ *n* **1a** a room or compartment on a ship or boat for passengers or crew **b** a compartment in an aircraft for cargo, crew, or passengers **2** a small simple usu single-storied dwelling **3** *chiefly Br* CAB 2

ˈ**cabin ˌboy** *n* a boy employed as a servant on board a ship

ˈ**cabin ˌclass** *n* a class of accommodation on a passenger ship superior to tourist class and inferior to first class

ˈ**cabin ˌcruiser** *n* a private motorboat with living accommodation

cabinet /ˈkab(i)nit‖ˈkæb(ɪ)nɪt/ *n* **1a** a case for storing or displaying articles **b** an upright case housing a radio or television set **2** *sing or pl in constr, often cap* a body of advisers of a head of state, who formulate government policy

ˈ**cabinetˌmaker** /-ˌmaykə‖-ˌmeɪkə/ *n* a craftsman who makes fine furniture in wood – **cabinetmaking** *n*

[1]**cable** /ˈkaybl‖ˈkeɪbl/ *n* **1a** a strong thick rope **b** a wire rope or metal chain of great tensile

strength **2** an assembly of electrical conductors insulated from each other and surrounded by a sheath **3** a cablegram **4 cable, cable length** a nautical unit of length equal to about **4a** *Br* 185m (202yd) **b** *NAm* 219m (240yd)

[2]**cable** *vb* **1** to fasten or provide with a cable or cables **2a** to transmit (a message) by submarine cable **b** to communicate with or inform (a person) by cablegram ~*vi* to communicate by means of cablegram

ˈ**cable ˌcar** *n* a carriage made to be moved on a cable railway or along an overhead cable

ˈ**cablegram** /-ˌgram, -grəm‖-ˌgræm, -grəm/ *n* a message sent by a submarine cable

cable railway *n* a railway along which the carriages are pulled by an endless cable operated by a stationary motor; [2]FUNICULAR

ˌ**cable teleˈvision** *n* a system by which television programmes are received in the home through a cable rather than an aerial

caboodle /kəˈboohdl‖kəˈbu:dl/ *n* a collection, lot <*sell the whole* ~> – infml

caboose /kəˈboohs‖kəˈbu:s/ *n* **1** a ship's galley **2** *NAm* a wagon attached to a goods train, usu at the rear

cabriolet /ˌkabriohˈlay‖ˌkæbrɪəʊˈleɪ/ *n* a light 2-wheeled 1-horse carriage

cacao /kəˈkah·oh, -ˈkayoh‖kəˈkɑ:əʊ, -ˈkeɪəʊ/ *n, pl* **cacaos** (a S American tree bearing) the fatty seeds which are used, partly fermented and dried, in making cocoa, chocolate, and cocoa butter

cache /kash‖kæʃ/ *n* **1** a hiding place, esp for provisions or weapons **2** sthg hidden or stored in a cache – **cache** *vt*

cachet /ˈkashay, kəˈshay‖ˈkæʃeɪ, kəˈʃeɪ/ *n* **1** [3]SEAL 1; *esp* one used as a mark of official approval **2** (a characteristic feature or quality conferring) prestige **3** sthg other than the postmark that is stamped by hand on a postal item

cachou /ˈkashooh, kəˈshooh‖ˈkæʃu:, kəˈʃu:/ *n* a pill or lozenge used to sweeten the breath

cackle /ˈkakl‖ˈkækl/ *vi* **1** to make the sharp broken noise or cry characteristic of a hen, esp after laying **2** to laugh in a way suggestive of a hen's cackle **3** [1]CHATTER 2 – **cackle** *n*, **cackler** *n*

cacophony /kəˈkofəni‖kəˈkɒfənɪ/ *n* harsh or discordant sound; dissonance – **cacophonous** *adj*

cactus /ˈkaktəs‖ˈkæktəs/ *n, pl* **cacti** /-tie‖-taɪ/, **cactuses** any of a family of plants that have fleshy stems and scaly or spiny branches instead of leaves and are found esp in dry areas

cad /kad‖kæd/ *n* an unscrupulous or dishonourable man – derog; not now in vogue – **caddish** *adj*

cadaver /kəˈdavə, -ˈdahvə, -ˈdayvə‖kəˈdævə, -ˈdɑ:və, -ˈdeɪvə/ *n* a corpse

cadaverous /kəˈdav(ə)rəs‖kəˈdæv(ə)rəs/ *adj* **1** (suggestive) of a corpse **2a** unhealthily pale; pallid, livid **b** gaunt, emaciated – **cadaverously** *adv*

caddie, caddy /ˈkadi‖ˈkædɪ/ *n* one who assists a golfer, esp by carrying clubs [French *cadet* military cadet] – **caddie, caddy** *vi*

caddy /ˈkadi‖ˈkædɪ/ *n* a small box or tin used esp for holding tea [Malay *kati*, a unit of weight]

cadence /ˈkayd(ə)ns‖ˈkeɪd(ə)ns/, ˈ**cadency** /-si‖-sɪ/ *n* **1a** the rhythm and intonations in language **b** a falling inflection of the voice **2** a concluding strain; *specif* a musical chord sequence moving to a harmonic close or point of rest and giving the sense of harmonic completion **3** the modulated and rhythmic recurrence of a sound – **cadenced** *adj*, **cadential** *adj*

cadenza /kəˈdenzə‖kəˈdenzə/ *n* a technically showy sometimes improvised solo passage in a concerto

cadet /kəˈdet‖kəˈdet/ *n* **1a** a younger brother or son **b** (a member of) a younger branch of a family **2** sby training to be an officer in the armed forces or a policeman **3** a young person receiving basic military training, esp at school [French, fr French dialect *capdet* chief, deriv of Latin *capit-, caput* head] – **cadetship** *n*

cadge /kaj‖kædʒ/ *vb* to get (sthg) by asking and usu imposing on sby's hospitality or good nature – infml – **cadger** *n*

cadi /ˈkahdi, ˈkay-‖ˈkɑ:dɪ, ˈkeɪ-/ *n* a judge in a Muslim community

cadmium /ˈkadmi·əm‖ˈkædmɪəm/ *n* a bluish-white soft toxic metallic element used esp in platings and bearing metals

cadre /ˈkahdə‖ˈkɑ:də/ *n* **1** a permanent nucleus of an esp military organization, capable of rapid expansion if necessary **2** (a member of) a group of activists working for the Communist party cause

caecum, *NAm chiefly* **cecum** /ˈseekəm‖ˈsi:kəm/ *n* a cavity open at 1 end; *esp* the pouch in which the large intestine begins and into which the ileum opens – **caecal** *adj*, **caecally** *adv*

Caerphilly /keəˈfili, kah-, kə-‖keəˈfɪlɪ, kɑ:-, kə-/ *n* a mild white moist cheese

caesarean, caeˌsarean ˈsection, caesarian, *NAm* **cesarean** /siˈzeəri·ən‖sɪˈzeərɪən/ *n* a surgical incision of the abdominal and uterine walls for the delivery of offspring [fr the belief that Julius Caesar was so born]

caesura /siˈzyooərə, -ˈzhooərə‖sɪˈzjʊərə, -ˈʒʊərə/ *n, pl* **caesuras, caesurae** /-ri‖-rɪ/ a break or pause in usu the middle of a line of verse – **caesural** *adj*

café /ˈkafay‖ˈkæfeɪ/ *n* **1** *chiefly Br* a small restaurant or coffeehouse serving light meals and nonalcoholic drinks **2** *NAm* BAR 5a(2) [French, coffee, café, fr Turkish *kahve*, fr Arabic *qahwah* coffee]

cafeteria /ˌkafəˈtiəri·ə‖ˌkæfəˈtɪərɪə/ *n* a restaurant in which the customers serve themselves or are served at a counter and take the food to tables to eat

caffeine /ˈkafeen‖ˈkæfi:n/ *n* an alkaloid found esp in tea and coffee that acts as a stimulant and diuretic – **caffeinic** *adj*

caftan, kaftan /ˈkaftan‖ˈkæftæn/ *n* a loose ankle-length garment with long sleeves, traditionally worn by Arabs

[1]**cage** /kayj‖keɪdʒ/ *n* **1** a box or enclosure of open construction for animals **2** a barred cell or fenced area for prisoners **3** a framework serving as a support <*the steel* ~ *of a skyscraper*> **4** an enclosure resembling a cage in form or purpose [Old French, fr Latin *cavea* cavity, cage, fr *cavus* hollow]

[2]**cage** *vt* to put or keep (as if) in a cage

cagey *also* **cagy** /'kayji‖'keɪdʒɪ/ *adj* **1** hesitant about committing oneself **2** wary of being trapped or deceived; shrewd *USE* infml – **cagily** *adv*, **caginess** *also* **cageyness** *n*

cagoule /ka'goohl‖kæ'gu:l/ *n* a lightweight anorak [French, hood, cowl, fr Latin *cucullus*]

cahoot /kə'hooht‖kə'hu:t/ *n* a partnership, league – usu pl with sing. meaning; infml; usu in *in cahoots*

caiman /'kaymən‖'keɪmən/ *n*, a cayman

Cainozoic /ˌkaynə'zoh·ik‖ˌkeɪnə'zəʊɪk/ *adj or n* (of or being) an era of geological history that extends from about 65 million years ago to the present

cairn /keən‖keən/ *n* a pile of stones built as a memorial or landmark

caisson /'kays(ə)n, kə'soohn‖'keɪs(ə)n, kə'su:n/ *n* **1** a chest or wagon for artillery ammunition **2a** a watertight chamber used for construction work under water or as a foundation **b** a float for raising a sunken vessel **c** a hollow floating box or a boat used as a floodgate for a dock or basin **3** COFFER 4

caisson disease *n* pain, paralysis, and often collapse caused by the release of gas bubbles in tissue on too rapid reduction of pressure (e g in deep-sea diving)

cajole /kə'johl‖kə'dʒəʊl/ *vt* to persuade or deceive with deliberate flattery, esp in the face of reluctance – **cajolement** *n*, **cajoler** *n*, **cajolery** *n*

[1]**cake** /kayk‖keɪk/ *n* **1a** a usu fried or baked often unleavened breadlike food – usu in combination <*oat*cake> **b** (a shaped mass of) any of various sweet baked foods made from a basic mixture of flour and sugar, usu with fat, eggs, and a raising agent **c** a flattened usu round mass of (baked or fried) food **2** a block of compressed or congealed matter <*a* ~ *of ice*>

[2]**cake** *vt* to encrust ~*vi* to form or harden into a mass

calabash /'kaləˌbash‖'kæləˌbæʃ/ *n* (a container or utensil made from the hard shell of) a gourd

calamine /'kaləmien‖'kæləmaɪn/ *n* a pink powder of zinc oxide or carbonate with a small amount of ferric oxide, used in soothing or cooling lotions

calamity /kə'laməti‖kə'læmətɪ/ *n* **1** a state of deep distress caused by misfortune or loss **2** an extremely grave event; a disaster – **calamitous** *adj*, **calamitously** *adv*, **calamitousness** *n*

calcify /'kalsifie‖'kælsɪfaɪ/ *vb* **1** to make or become hardened by deposition of calcium salts, esp calcium carbonate **2** to make or become inflexible or unchangeable – **calcific** *adj*, **calcification** *n*

calcine /'kalsin, -sien‖'kælsɪn, -saɪn/ *vt* to heat (e g inorganic materials) without melting usu in order to drive off volatile matter or to bring about oxidation or powdering of the material ~*vi* to be calcined – **calcination** *n*

calcium /'kalsi·əm‖'kælsɪəm/ *n* a silver-white metallic element of the alkaline-earth group occurring only in combination

calculable /'kalkyooləbl‖'kælkjʊləbl/ *adj* subject to or ascertainable by calculation – **calculably** *adv*, **calculability** *n*

calculate /'kalkyoolayt‖'kælkjʊleɪt/ *vt* **1** to determine by mathematical processes **2** to reckon by exercise of practical judgment; estimate ~ *vi* **1** to make a calculation **2** to forecast consequences **3** to count, rely – + *on* or *upon*

calculating /'kalkyoolayting‖'kælkjʊleɪtɪŋ/ *adj* **1** used for making calculations <*a* ~ *machine*> **2** marked by shrewd consideration of self-interest; scheming – **calculatingly** *adv*

calculation /ˌkalkyoo'laysh(ə)n‖ˌkælkjʊ'leɪʃ(ə)n/ *n* **1** (the result of) the process or an act of calculating **2** studied care in planning, esp to promote self-interest – **calculative** *adj*

calculator /'kalkyoolaytə‖'kælkjʊleɪtə/ *n* **1** an electronic or mechanical machine for performing mathematical operations **2** a set or book of tables used in calculating

calculus /'kalkyooləs‖'kælkjʊləs/ *n, pl* **calculi** /-lie‖-laɪ/ *also* **calculuses** **1a** an abnormal hard stony mass (e g of cholesterol) in the kidney, gall bladder, or other hollow organ **b** [1]TARTAR 2 **2a** a method of computation or calculation in a special symbolic notation **b** the mathematical methods comprising differential and integral calculus

caldron /'kawldrən‖'kɔ:ldrən/ *n* a cauldron

[1]**calendar** /'kaləndə‖'kæləndə/ *n* **1** a system for fixing the beginning, length, and divisions of the civil year and arranging days and longer divisions of time (e g weeks and months) in a definite order **2** a tabular display of the days of 1 year **3** a chronological list of events or activities

[2]**calendar** *vt* to enter in a calendar

calender /'kaləndə‖'kæləndə/ *n* a machine for pressing cloth, rubber, paper, etc between rollers or plates (e g for smoothing and glazing) – **calender** *vt*

calends, kalends /'kalindz‖'kælɪndz/ *n pl but sing or pl in constr* the first day of the ancient Roman month

[1]**calf** /kahf‖kɑ:f/ *n, pl* **calves** /kahvz‖kɑ:vz/ *also* **calfs,** (*2*) **calfs** **1a** the young of the domestic cow or a closely related mammal (e g a bison) **b** the young of some large animals (e g the elephant and whale) **2** calfskin <*the book was bound in fine* ~> **3** a small mass of ice broken off from a coastal glacier, iceberg, etc – **calflike** *adj* – **in calf** *of a cow* pregnant

[2]**calf** *n, pl* **calves** the fleshy back part of the leg below the knee

'**calf ˌlove** *n* PUPPY LOVE

'**calfˌskin** /-ˌskin‖-ˌskɪn/ *n* a high-quality leather made from the skin of a calf

calibrate /'kaliˌbrayt‖'kælɪˌbreɪt/ *vt* **1** to determine the calibre of (e g a thermometer tube) **2** to determine, adjust, or mark the graduations of (e g a thermometer) **3** to determine the correct reading of (an arbitrary or inaccurate scale or instrument) by comparison with a standard – **calibrator** *n*

calibration /ˌkali'braysh(ə)n‖ˌkælɪ'breɪʃ(ə)n/ *n* a set of graduations that indicate values or positions –usu pl with sing. meaning

calibre, *NAm chiefly* **caliber** /'kalibə‖'kælɪbə/ *n* **1** the internal or external diameter of a round body (e g a bullet or other projectile) or a hollow cylinder (e g a gun barrel) **2a** degree of mental capacity or moral quality **b** degree of excellence or importance

calico /'kalikoh||'kælıkəʊ/ *n, pl* **calicoes, calicos 1** white unprinted cotton cloth of medium weight, orig imported from India **2** *NAm* brightly printed cotton fabric [*Calicut*, city in India] – **calico** *adj*

caliper /'kalipə||'kælıpə/ *vt or n, chiefly NAm* (to) calliper

caliph, calif /'kalif, 'kay-||'kælıf, 'keı-/ *n* a secular and spiritual head of Islam claiming descent from Muhammad – **caliphal** *adj*, **caliphate** *n*

calisthenics /,kalis'theniks||,kælıs'θenıks/ *n pl but sing or pl in constr, chiefly NAm* callisthenics – **calisthenic** *adj*

calk /kawk||kɔ:k/ *vt* to caulk – **calker** *n*

[1]**call** /kawl||kɔ:l/ *vi* **1a** to speak loudly or distinctly so as to be heard at a distance; shout **b** to make a request or demand <~ *for an investigation*> **c** *of an animal* to utter a characteristic note or cry **2** to make a demand in card games (e g for a particular card or for a show of hands) **3** *of a batsman* to indicate vocally to one's batting partner whether one intends to take a run or not **4** to make a brief visit – often + *in* or *by* <~ed *in at the pub*> **5** *chiefly NAm* to (try to) get into communication by telephone – often + *up* ~ *vt* **1a** to utter or announce in a loud distinct voice – often + *out* **b** to read aloud (e g a list of names) **2a** to command or request to come or be present <~ed *to testify*> **b** to cause to come; bring <~s *to mind an old saying*> **c** to summon to a particular activity, employment, or office <*was* ~ed *to active duty*> **d** to invite or command to meet; convoke <~ *a meeting*> **3** to rouse from sleep **4** to give the order for; bring into action <~ *a strike against the company*> **5a** to make a demand in bridge for (a card or suit) **b** to require (a player) to show the hand in poker by making an equal bet **6** to attract (e g game) by imitating a characteristic cry **7a** to rule on the status of (e g a tennis serve) <*the serve was* ~ed *out by the umpire*> **b** *of a cricket umpire* to pronounce the bowling delivery to be illegal **8** to give the calls for (a square dance) **9** to suspend <*time was* ~ed> **10** to speak of or address by a specified name; give a name to <~ *her Kitty*> **11a** to regard or characterize as a certain kind; consider <*can hardly be* ~ed *generous*> **b** to consider for purposes of an estimate or for convenience <~ *it an even quid*> **12** to predict, guess <~ *the toss of a coin*> **13** *chiefly NAm* to (try to) get into communication with by telephone –often + *up* – **callable** *adj*, **caller** *n* – **call a spade a spade** to speak frankly and usu bluntly – **called to the bar** admitted as a barrister – **call for 1** to call to get; collect **2** to require as necessary or appropriate <*it* called for *all her strength*> **3** to demand, order – **call in/into question** to cast doubt upon – **call it a day** to stop whatever one has been doing at least for the present – **call it quits 1** CALL IT A DAY **2** to acknowledge that the advantage is now even – **call on/upon** to require, oblige <*may be* called on *to do several jobs*> – **call someone's bluff** to challenge and expose an empty pretence or threat – **call the shots/the tune** to be in charge or control; determine the policy or procedure – **call to account** to hold responsible; reprimand – **call to order** to order (a meeting) to observe the customary rules

[2]**call** *n* **1a** an act of calling with the voice **b** the cry of an animal (e g a bird) **2a** a request or command to come or assemble **b** a summons or signal on a drum, bugle, or pipe **3a** admission to the bar as a barrister **b** a divine vocation **c** a strong inner prompting to a course of action **d** the attraction or appeal of a particular activity or place <*the* ~ *of the wild*> **4a** a demand, request **b** need, justification <*there was no* ~ *for such rudeness*> **5** a short usu formal visit **6** the name (e g of a suit in a card game) or thing called **7** the act of calling in a card game **8** the act of telephoning **9** a direction or a succession of directions for a square dance rhythmically called to the dancers **10** a usu vocal ruling made by an official of a sports contest – **on call 1** available for use **2** ready to respond to a summons or command <*a doctor* on call> – **within call** within hearing or reach of a call or summons

'**call ,box** *n, Br* a public telephone box

'**call,boy** /-,boy||-,bɔı/ *n* **1** a person who tells actors when it is time to go on stage **2** *chiefly NAm* a hotel page

call down *vt* to invoke, request <call down *a blessing on the crops*>

'**call ,girl** *n* a prostitute who accepts appointments by telephone

calligraphy /kə'ligrəfi||kə'lıgrəfı/ *n* (beautiful or elegant) handwriting [French *calligraphie*, fr Greek *kalligraphia*, fr *kallos* beauty + *graphein* to write] – **calligrapher, calligraphist** *n*, **calligraphic** *adj*, **calligraphically** *adv*

call in *vt* **1a** to withdraw from an advanced position <call in *the outposts*> **b** to withdraw from circulation <call in *bank notes and issue new ones*> **2** to summon to one's aid or for consultation <call in *an arbitrator to settle the dispute*>

calling /'kawling||'kɔ:lıŋ/ *n* **1** a strong inner impulse towards a particular course of action, esp when accompanied by conviction of divine influence **2** a vocation, profession

[1]**calliper,** *chiefly NAm* **caliper** /'kalipə||'kælıpə/ *n* **1** a measuring instrument with 2 arms that can be adjusted to determine thickness, diameter, or distance between surfaces – usu pl with sing. meaning **2** a support for the human leg extending from the knee or thigh to the foot

[2]**calliper,** *chiefly NAm* **caliper** *vt* to measure (as if) with callipers

callisthenics, *chiefly NAm* **calisthenics** /,kalis'theniks||,kælıs'θenıks/ *n pl but sing or pl in constr* (the art or practice of) systematic rhythmic bodily exercises performed usu without apparatus [Greek *kallos* beauty + *sthenos* strength] – **callisthenic** *adj*

call off *vt* **1** to draw away; divert <call *the dogs* off!> **2** to cancel <call *the trip* off>

callous /'kaləs||'kæləs/ *adj* **1** hardened and thickened **2** unfeeling; *esp* unsympathetic – **callously** *adv*, **callousness** *n*

call out *vt* **1** to summon into action <call out *the guard*> **2** to challenge to a duel **3** to order a strike of <call out *the steelworkers*>

callow /'kaloh||'kæləʊ/ *adj* **1** *of a bird* not yet

fully fledged **2** lacking adult attitudes; immature – **callowness** *n*

'call ˌsign *n* the combination of letters or letters and numbers assigned to an operator, activity, or station for identification of a radio broadcast

'call-ˌup *n* an order to report for military service

call up *vt* **1** to bring to mind; evoke **2** to summon before an authority **3** to summon together or collect (e g for a united effort) **4** to summon for active military duty

callus /'kaləs||'kæləs/ *n* **1** a hard thickened area on skin or bark **2** a mass of connective tissue formed round a break in a bone and changed into bone during healing **3** soft tissue that forms over a cut plant surface **4** a tumour of plant tissue

[1]calm /kahm||kɑːm; *NAm* kah(l)m||kɑː(l)m/ *n* **1a** the absence of winds or rough water; stillness **b** a state in which the wind has a speed of less than 1km/h (about $^5/_8$mph) **2** a state of repose free from agitation

[2]calm *adj* **1** marked by calm; still <*a ~ sea*> **2** free from agitation or excitement <*a ~ manner*> – **calmly** *adv*, **calmness** *n*

[3]calm *vb* to make or become calm

calomel /'kaləˌmel, -məl||'kæləˌmel, -məl/ *n* an insoluble compound of mercury formerly used as a purgative

Calor gas /'kalə||'kælə/ *trademark* – used for butane gas in liquid form that is contained in portable cylinders and used as a fuel (e g for domestic heating)

calorie *also* **calory** /'kaləri||'kælərɪ/ *n* **1a** the quantity of heat required to raise the temperature of 1g of water by 1°C under standard conditions **b** a kilocalorie; *also* an equivalent unit expressing the energy-producing value of food when oxidized **2** an amount of food having an energy-producing value of 1 kilocalorie [French *calorie*, fr Latin *calor* heat, fr *calēre* to be warm]

calorific /ˌkalə'rifik||ˌkælə'rɪfɪk/ *adj* of heat production

calumet /'kalyooˌmet||'kæljʊˌmet/ *n* a long highly ornamented pipe of the N American Indians smoked esp on ceremonial occasions in token of peace

calumniate /kə'lumniayt||kə'lʌmnɪeɪt/ *vt* to slander – fml – **calumniator** *n*, **calumniation** *n*

calumny /'kaləmni||'kæləmnɪ/ *n* (the act of uttering) a false charge or misrepresentation maliciously calculated to damage another's reputation – **calumnious** *adj*, **calumniously** *adv*

calve /kahv||kɑːv/ *vb* **1** to give birth to (a calf) **2** *of an ice mass* to release (a calf)

calves *pl of* CALF

Calvinism /'kalviniz(ə)m||'kælvɪnɪz(ə)m/ *n* the theological system of Calvin and his followers, marked by emphasis on the sovereignty of God and esp by the doctrine of predestination [John *Calvin* (1509-64), French theologian] – **Calvinist** *n or adj*, **Calvinistic** *adj*, **Calvinistically** *adv*

calypso /kə'lipsoh||kə'lɪpsəʊ/ *n, pl* **calypsos** *also* **calypsoes** an improvised ballad, usu satirizing current events, in a style originating in the W Indies – **calypsonian** *n or adj*

calyx /'kaliks, 'kay-||'kælɪks, 'keɪ-/ *n, pl* **calyxes, calyces** /-liˌseez||-lɪˌsiːz/ the outer usu green or leafy part of a flower or floret, consisting of sepals

cam /kam||kæm/ *n* a mechanical device (e g a wheel attached to an axis at a point other than its centre) that transforms circular motion into intermittent or back-and-forth motion

camaraderie /ˌkamə'rahdəri, -'radəri||ˌkæmə'rɑːdərɪ, -'rædərɪ/ *n* friendly good humour amongst comrades

[1]camber /'kambə||'kæmbə/ *vb* to (cause to) curve upwards in the middle

[2]camber *n* **1** a slight convexity or arching (e g of a beam or road) **2** an arrangement of the wheels of a motor vehicle so as to be closer together at the bottom than at the top

cambium /'kambi·əm||'kæmbɪəm/ *n, pl* **cambiums, cambia** /-bi·ə||-bɪə/ a thin layer of cells between the xylem and phloem of most plants that divides to form more xylem and phloem – **cambial** *adj*

cambric /'kambrik||'kæmbrɪk/ *n* a fine thin white linen or cotton fabric

came /kaym||keɪm/ *past of* COME

camel /'kaməl||'kæməl/ *n* **1** either of 2 large ruminant mammals used as draught and saddle animals in desert regions: **1a** the 1-humped Arabian camel **b** the 2-humped Bactrian camel **2** a float used to lift submerged ships **3** a light yellowish brown colour

'camel ˌhair *n* cloth, usu of a light tan colour with a soft silky texture, made from the hair of a camel or a mixture of this and wool

camellia *also* **camelia** /kə'meelyə||kə'miːljə/ *n* an ornamental shrub with glossy evergreen leaves and roselike flowers, or a related shrub or tree of the tea family

Camembert /'kaməmbeə ||'kæməmbeə (*Fr* kamɑ̃bɛːr)/ *n* a round thin-rinded soft rich cheese [*Camembert*, town in Normandy, France]

cameo /'kamioh||'kæmɪəʊ/ *n, pl* **cameos** **1a** a gem carved in relief; *esp* a small piece of sculpture cut in relief in one layer with another contrasting layer serving as background **b** a small medallion with a profiled head in relief **2** a usu brief part in literature or film that reveals or highlights character, plot, or scene **3** a small dramatic role often played by a well-known actor – **cameo** *adj or vt*

camera /'kamrə||'kæmrə/ *n* **1** *often cap* the treasury department of the papal curia **2** a lightproof box having an aperture, and esp a lens, for recording the image of an object on a light-sensitive material: e g **2a** one containing photographic film for producing a permanent record **b** one containing a device which converts the image into an electrical signal (e g for television transmission)

'cameraman /-ˌman, -mən||-ˌmæn, -mən/ *n* one who operates a (television) camera

camiknickers /'kamiˌnikəz||'kæmɪˌnɪkəz/ *n pl in constr, pl* **camiknickers** *Br* a one-piece close-fitting undergarment worn by women, that combines a camisole and knickers – **camiknicker** *adj*

camisole /'kamiˌsohl||'kæmɪˌsəʊl/ *n* a short bodice worn as an undergarment by women

camomile, **chamomile** /ˈkaməmiel‖ˈkæməmaɪl/ *n* any of several strong-scented composite plants whose flower heads are used in herbal remedies

[1]**camouflage** /ˈkaməˌflahzh, -ˌflahj‖ˈkæməˌflɑːʒ, -ˌflɑːdʒ/ *n* **1** the disguising of esp military equipment or installations with nets, paint, etc **2a** concealment by means of disguise **b** sthg (e g a disguise) designed to deceive or conceal

[2]**camouflage** *vt* to conceal or disguise by camouflage

[1]**camp** /kamp‖kæmp/ *n* **1a** a ground on which temporary shelters (e g tents) are erected **b** a temporary shelter or group of shelters erected on such ground **c** a new settlement (e g in a lumbering or mining region) **2** *sing or pl in constr* a group of people engaged in promoting or defending a theory or position <*Liberal and Conservative* ~s> **3a** military service or life **b** a place where troops are housed or trained

[2]**camp** *vi* **1** to pitch or occupy a camp **2** to live temporarily in a camp or outdoors

[3]**camp** *adj* **1** homosexual **2** exaggeratedly effeminate **3** deliberately and outrageously artificial, affected, or inappropriate, esp to the point of tastelessness ***USE*** infml – **campily** *adv*, **campness** *n*, **campy** *adj*

[4]**camp** *vi or n* (to engage in) a camp style, manner, etc – infml –**camp it up** to act or behave in an affected or esp exaggeratedly effeminate manner – infml

[1]**campaign** /ˌkamˈpayn‖ˌkæmˈpeɪn/ *n* **1** a connected series of military operations forming a distinct phase of a war **2** active military life; [1]CAMP 3a **3** a connected series of operations designed to bring about a particular result

[2]**campaign** *vi* to go on, engage in, or conduct a campaign – **campaigner** *n*

campanile /ˌkampəˈneeli‖ˌkæmpəˈniːlɪ/ *n, pl* **campaniles, campanili** /~/ a usu freestanding bell tower

campanology /ˌkampəˈnoləji‖ˌkæmpəˈnɒlədʒɪ/ *n* the art of bell ringing – **campanologist** *n*

campanula /kəmˈpanyoolə‖kəmˈpænjʊlə/ *n* a bellflower

ˌ**camp** ˈ**bed** *n* a small collapsible bed, usu of fabric stretched over a frame

camper /ˈkampə‖ˈkæmpə/ *n* **1** a person who temporarily stays in a tent, caravan, etc **2** a motor vehicle equipped for use as temporary accommodation (e g while holidaying)

camp follower *n* **1** a civilian, esp a prostitute, who follows a military unit to attend or exploit military personnel **2** a follower who is not of the main body of adherents

camphor /ˈkamfə‖ˈkæmfə/ *n* a tough gummy volatile fragrant compound obtained esp from the wood and bark of an evergreen tree and used as a liniment, plasticizer, and insect repellent – **camphoraceous** *adj*, **camphoric** *adj*

camphorate /ˈkamfərayt‖ˈkæmfəreɪt/ *vt* to impregnate or treat with camphor

campion /ˈkampi·ən‖ˈkæmpɪən/ *n* any of several Eurasian plants of the pink family with small red or white flowers

campus /ˈkampəs‖ˈkæmpəs/ *n* the grounds and buildings of a university or college

camshaft /ˈkamˌshahft‖ˈkæmˌʃɑːft/ *n* a shaft to which a cam is fastened

[1]**can** /kən‖kən; *strong* kan‖kæn/ *verbal auxiliary, pres sing & pl* **can;** *past* **could** /kəd‖kəd; *strong* kood‖kʊd/ **1a** know how to <*he* ~ *read*> **b** be physically or mentally able to <*I* ~'t *think why*> **c** may perhaps – chiefly in questions <*what* ~ *they want?*> **d** be logically inferred or supposed to – chiefly in negatives <*he* ~ *hardly have meant that*> **e** be permitted by conscience or feeling to <~ *hardly blame him*> **f** be inherently able or designed to <*everything that money* ~ *buy*> **g** be logically able to <*2 + 2* ~ *also be written 3 + 1*> **h** be enabled by law, agreement, or custom to **2** have permission to – used interchangeably with *may* **3** will – used in questions with the force of a request <~ *you hold on a minute, please?*> **4** will have to <*if you don't like it you* ~ *lump it*>

[2]**can** /kan‖kæn/ *n* **1** a usu cylindrical receptacle: **1a** a vessel for holding liquids **b** TIN 2a; *esp* a tin containing a beverage (e g beer) **2** *NAm* TOILET 2 – infml **3** *chiefly NAm* jail – slang – **canful** *adj* – **in the can** *of a film or videotape* completed and ready for release

[3]**can** *vt* **-nn-** **1** to pack or preserve in a tin **2** *chiefly NAm* to put a stop or end to – slang – **canner** *n*

Canadian /kəˈnaydi·ən‖kəˈneɪdɪən/ *n or adj* (a native or inhabitant) of Canada

canal /kəˈnal‖kəˈnæl/ *n* **1** a channel, watercourse **2** a tubular anatomical channel **3** an artificial waterway for navigation, drainage, or irrigation

canal·ize, -ise /ˈkanəliez‖ˈkænəlaɪz/ *vt* **1** to provide with or make into a canal or channel **2** to direct into preferred channels – **canalization** *n*

canapé /ˈkanəpay, -pi‖ˈkænəpeɪ, -pɪ/ *n* an appetizer consisting of a piece of bread, biscuit, etc, topped with a savoury spread

canard /kəˈnahd, ˈkanahd‖kəˈnɑːd, ˈkænɑːd/ *n* a false or unfounded report or story; a hoax

canary /kəˈneəri‖kəˈneərɪ/ *n* a small usu green to yellow finch of the Canary islands, widely kept as a cage bird [Middle French *canarie*, fr Spanish *canario*, fr *Islas Canarias* Canary Islands]

canasta /kəˈnastə‖kəˈnæstə/ *n* **1** a form of rummy usu for 4 players using 2 full packs plus jokers **2** a combination of 7 cards of the same rank in canasta

cancan /ˈkanˌkan‖ˈkænˌkæn/ *n* a dance performed by women, characterized by high kicking usu while holding up the front of a full ruffled skirt

[1]**cancel** /ˈkansl‖ˈkænsl/ *vt* **-ll-** (*NAm* **-l-**, **-ll-**) *vt* **1a** to mark or strike out for deletion **b** to omit, delete **2a** to make void; countermand, annul <~ *a magazine subscription*> **b** to bring to nothingness; destroy **c** to match in force or effect; offset – often + *out* <*his irritability* ~led *out his natural kindness* – Osbert Sitwell> **3** to call off, usu without intending to reschedule to a later time **4a** to remove (a common divisor) from a numerator and denominator **b** to remove (equivalents) on opposite sides of an equation or account **5** to deface (a stamp), usu with a set of parallel lines, so as to invalidate reuse to

neutralize each other's strength or effect; counterbalance – usu + *out* – **cancellable** *adj*, **canceller** *n*

[2]**cancel** *n* a cancellation

cancellation, *NAm also* **cancelation** /ˌkansəˈlaysh(ə)n‖ˌkænsəˈleɪʃ(ə)n/ *n* **1** sthg cancelled, esp a seat in an aircraft, theatre performance, etc **2** a mark made to cancel sthg (e g a postage stamp)

cancer /ˈkansə‖ˈkænsə/ *n* **1** *cap* (sby born under) the 4th zodiacal constellation, pictured as a crab **2** (a condition marked by) a malignant tumour of potentially unlimited growth **3** a source of evil or anguish [Latin, lit., crab] – **cancerous** *adj*, **cancerously** *adv*

candela /kanˈdaylə, -ˈdeelə‖kænˈdeɪlə, -ˈdiːlə/ *n* the SI unit of luminous intensity

candelabrum /ˌkandlˈahbrəm‖ˌkændlˈɑːbrəm/ *n, pl* **candelabra** /-brə‖-brə/ *also* **candelabrums** a branched candlestick or lamp with several lights

candid /ˈkandid‖ˈkændɪd/ *adj* **1** indicating or suggesting complete sincerity **2** disposed to criticize severely; blunt – **candidly** *adv*, **candidness** *n*

candidate /ˈkandidayt, -dət‖ˈkændɪdeɪt, -dət/ *n* **1** one who is nominated or qualified for, or aspires to an office, membership, or award **2** one who is taking an examination **3** sthg suitable for a specified action or process [Latin *candidatus*, lit. sby clothed in white, fr *candidus* white; so called fr the white toga worn by candidates for office in ancient Rome] – **candidacy** *n*

candidature /ˈkandidəchə‖ˈkændɪdətʃə/ *n*, *chiefly Br* being a candidate; *esp* standing for election

candle /ˈkandl‖ˈkændl/ *n* **1** a usu long slender cylindrical mass of tallow or wax enclosing a wick that is burnt to give light **2** sthg resembling a candle in shape or use <*a sulphur ~ for fumigation*> **3** a candela – **not worth the candle** *chiefly Br* not worth the effort; not justified by the result

ˈ**Candlemas** /-məs‖-məs/ *n* February 2 observed as a church festival in commemoration of the presentation of Christ in the temple and the purification of the Virgin Mary

ˈ**candle,power** /-ˌpowə‖-ˌpaʊə/ *n* luminous intensity expressed in candelas

ˈ**candle,stick** /-ˌstik‖-ˌstɪk/ *n* a holder with a socket for a candle

ˈ**candle,wick** /-ˌwik‖-ˌwɪk/ *n* a very thick soft cotton yarn; *also* fabric made with this yarn usu with a raised tufted pattern, used esp for bedspreads

candour, *NAm chiefly* **candor** /ˈkandə‖ˈkændə/ *n* unreserved and candid expression; forthrightness

[1]**candy** /ˈkandi‖ˈkændɪ/ *n* **1** crystallized sugar formed by boiling down sugar syrup **2** *chiefly NAm* SWEET 2b – **candy** *adj*

[2]**candy** *vt* to encrust or glaze (e g fruit or fruit peel) with sugar

ˈ**candy ,floss** /flos‖flɒs/ *n* a light fluffy mass of spun sugar, usu wound round a stick as a sweet

ˈ**candy,tuft** /-ˌtuft‖-ˌtʌft/ *n* any of a genus of plants of the mustard family cultivated for their white, pink, or purple flowers

[1]**cane** /kayn‖keɪn/ *n* **1a** a hollow or pithy usu flexible jointed stem (e g of bamboo) **b** an elongated flowering or fruiting stem (e g of a raspberry) **c** any of various tall woody grasses or reeds; *esp* sugarcane **2a** a walking stick; *specif* one made of cane **b** (*the* use of) a cane or rod for flogging **c** a length of split rattan for use in basketry

[2]**cane** *vt* **1** to beat with a cane; *broadly* to punish **2** to weave or furnish with cane <~ *the seat of a chair*>

[1]**canine** /ˈkaynien‖ˈkeɪnaɪn/ *adj* of or resembling a dog or (members of) the family of flesh-eating mammals that includes the dogs, wolves, jackals, and foxes

[2]**canine** *n* **1** any of the 4 conical pointed teeth each of which lies between an incisor and the first premolar on each side of both the top and bottom jaws **2** DOG 1

canister *also* **cannister** /ˈkanistə‖ˈkænɪstə/ *n* **1** a small usu metal box or tin for holding a dry product (e g tea or shot) **2** encased shot for close-range antipersonnel artillery fire

[1]**canker** /ˈkangkə‖ˈkæŋkə/ *n* **1a(1)** an erosive or spreading sore **a(2)** an area of local tissue death in a plant **b** any of various inflammatory animal diseases **2** a source of corruption or debasement – **cankerous** *adj*

[2]**canker** *vt* to corrupt with a malignancy of mind or spirit ~ *vi* **1** to become infested with canker **2** to undergo corruption

cannabis /ˈkanəbis‖ˈkænəbɪs/ *n* the dried flowering spikes of the female hemp plant, sometimes smoked in cigarettes for their intoxicating effect

canned /kand‖kænd/ *adj* **1** recorded for mechanical or electronic reproduction; *esp* prerecorded for addition to a sound track or a videotape **2** drunk – slang

cannelloni /ˌkanəˈlohni‖ˌkænəˈləʊnɪ/ *n* large tubular rolls of pasta (filled with meat, cheese, etc)

cannery /ˈkanəri‖ˈkænərɪ/ *n* a factory for canning foods

cannibal /ˈkanibl‖ˈkænɪbl/ *n* **1** a human being who eats human flesh **2** an animal that eats its own kind – **cannibal** *adj*, **cannibalism** *n*, **cannibalistic** *adj*

cannibal·ize, -**ise** /ˈkaniblˌiez‖ˈkænɪblˌaɪz/ *vt* to dismantle (e g a machine) in order to provide spare parts for others – **cannibalization** *n*

[1]**cannon** /ˈkanən‖ˈkænən/ *n, pl* **cannons, cannon** **1** a usu large gun mounted on a carriage **2** an automatic shell-firing gun mounted esp in an aircraft

[2]**cannon** *n, Br* a shot in billiards in which the cue ball strikes each of 2 object balls

[3]**cannon** *vi* **1a** to collide – usu + *into* **b** to collide with and be deflected *off* sthg **2** *Br* to make a cannon in billiards

cannonade /ˌkanəˈnayd‖ˌkænəˈneɪd/ *vb or n* (to attack with) heavy continuous artillery fire

ˈ**cannon,ball** /-ˌbawl‖-ˌbɔːl/ *n* a round solid missile made for firing from an old type of cannon

ˈ**cannon ,bone** *n* the leg bone between the hock and the fetlock in hoofed mammals

ˈ**cannon ,fodder** *n* people regarded merely

as material to be used in armed conflict

cannot /'kanot, -nət, kə'not‖'kænɒt, -nət, kə'nɒt/ can not – **cannot but/cannot help but** to be bound to; must <could not but *smile at the answer*>

canny /'kani‖'kænɪ/ *adj* **1** cautious and shrewd; *specif* thrifty **2** *Scot & NE Eng* careful, steady **3** *NE Eng* agreeable, comely – **cannily** *adv*, **canniness** *n*

[1]**canoe** /kə'nooh‖kə'nu:/ *n* **1** a long light narrow boat with sharp ends and curved sides usu propelled by paddling **2** *chiefly Br* a kayak [French, fr Spanish *Canoa*, from an American Indian language]

[2]**canoe** *vi* to travel in or paddle a canoe, esp as a recreation or sport ~*vt* to transport in a canoe – **canoeist** *n*

[1]**canon** /'kanən‖'kænən/ *n* **1a** a regulation or dogma decreed by a church council **b** a provision of canon law **2** the series of prayers forming the unvarying part of the Mass **3a** an authoritative list of books accepted as Holy Scripture **b** the authentic works of a writer **4a** an accepted principle, rule, or criterion **b** a body of principles, rules, or standards **5** a musical composition for 2 or more voice parts in which the melody is repeated by the successively entering voices

[2]**canon** *n* **1** a clergyman belonging to the chapter of a cathedral or collegiate church **2** CANON REGULAR

cañon /'kanyən‖'kænjən/ *n* a canyon

canonical /kə'nonikl‖kə'nɒnɪkl/, **canonic** /kə'nonik‖kə'nɒnɪk/ *adj* **1** of an esp ecclesiastical or musical canon **2** conforming to a general rule; orthodox **3** accepted as forming the canon of scripture – **canonically** *adv*, **canonicity** *n*

ca'nonicals *n pl* the vestments prescribed by canon for an officiating clergyman

canon·ize, -ise /'kanəniez‖'kænənaɪz/ *vt* **1** to recognize officially as a saint **2** to attribute authoritative sanction or approval to – **canonization** *n*

,canon 'law *n* the usu codified law governing a church

,canon 'regular *n, pl* **canons regular** a member of any of several Roman Catholic open religious communities

canoodle /kə'noohdl‖kə'nu:dl/ *vi* to caress or cuddle (with sby) – infml

[1]**canopy** /'kanəpi‖'kænəpɪ/ *n* **1a** a cloth covering suspended over a bed **b** a cover (e g of cloth) fixed or carried above a person of high rank or a sacred object **c** an awning, marquee **d** anything which seems like a cover <*a ~ of branches*> **2** an ornamental rooflike structure **3a** the transparent enclosure over an aircraft cockpit **b** the lifting or supporting surface of a parachute [Medieval Latin *canopeum* mosquito net, fr Latin *conopeum*, fr Greek *kōnōpion*, fr *kōnōps* mosquito]

[2]**canopy** *vt* to cover (as if) with a canopy

canst /kənst‖kənst; *strong* kanst‖kænst/ *archaic pres 2 sing of* [1]CAN

[1]**cant** /kant‖kænt/ *n* **1a** a sudden thrust that produces some displacement **b** the displacement so caused **2** an oblique or slanting surface; a slope

[2]**cant** *vt* **1** to give a cant or oblique edge to; bevel **2** to set at an angle; tip or tilt up or over ~ *vi* **1** to pitch to one side; lean **2** to slope

[3]**cant** *vi* to speak in cant or jargon

[4]**cant** *n* **1** jargon; *specif* the argot of the underworld **2** a set or stock phrase **3** the insincere expression of platitudes or sentiments, esp those suggesting piety

can't /kahnt‖kɑ:nt/ can not

Cantabrigian /,kantə'briji·ən‖,kæntə'brɪdʒɪən/ *n* a student or graduate of Cambridge University

cantaloupe, cantaloup /'kantə,loohp‖'kæntə,lu:p/ *n* a muskmelon with a hard ridged rind and reddish orange flesh

cantankerous /,kan'tangkərəs‖,kæn'tæŋkərəs/ *adj* ill-natured, quarrelsome – **cantankerously** *adv*, **cantankerousness** *n*

cantata /kan'tahtə‖kæn'tɑ:tə/ *n* a usu religious choral composition comprising choruses, solos, recitatives, and interludes

canteen /kan'teen‖kæn'ti:n/ *n* **1** a shop providing supplies in a camp **2** a dining hall **3** a partitioned chest or box for holding cutlery **4** a usu cloth-covered flask carried by a soldier, traveller, etc and containing a liquid, esp drinking water

[1]**canter** /'kantə‖'kæntə/ *vi* to progress or ride at a canter ~*vt* to cause to canter [short for obs *canterbury*, fr *Canterbury*, England; fr the supposed gait of pilgrims to Canterbury]

[2]**canter** *n* **1** a 3-beat gait of a quadruped, specif a horse, resembling but smoother and slower than the gallop **2** a ride at a canter

canticle /'kantikl‖'kæntɪkl/ *n* a song; *specif* any of several liturgical songs (e g the Magnificat) taken from the Bible

cantilever /'kanti,leevə‖'kæntɪ,li:və/ *n* a projecting beam or member supported at only 1 end: e g **a** a bracket-shaped member supporting a balcony or a cornice **b** either of the 2 beams or trusses that when joined directly or by a suspended connecting member form a span of a cantilever bridge

canto /'kantoh‖'kæntəʊ/ *n, pl* **cantos** a major division of a long poem

[1]**canton** /'kanton, -'-‖'kæntɒn, -'-/ *n* **1** a small territorial division of a country (e g Switzerland or France) **2** a rectangle in the right chief corner of a heraldic shield – **cantonal** *adj*

[2]**canton** /kan'ton‖kæn'tɒn; *sense 2* kən'toohn‖kən'tu:n/ *vt* **1** to divide into cantons **2** [2]BILLET

cantonment /kən'toohnmənt‖kən'tu:nmənt/ *n* (a group of usu temporary structures for) the housing of troops

cantor /'kantaw‖'kæntɔ:/ *n* a singer who leads liturgical music (e g in a synagogue)

canvas *also* **canvass** /'kanvəs‖'kænvəs/ *n* **1** a firm closely woven cloth usu of linen, hemp, or cotton used for clothing, sails, tents etc **2** a set of sails; sail **3** a cloth surface suitable for painting on in oils; *also* the painting on such a surface **4** a coarse cloth so woven as to form regular meshes as a basis for embroidery or tapestry **5** the floor of a boxing or wrestling ring – **canvaslike** *adj* – **under canvas** living in a tent

canvass *also* **canvas** /'kanvəs‖'kænvəs/ *vt* **1** to examine in detail; *specif, NAm* to examine (votes) officially for authenticity **2** to discuss, debate **3** to visit (e g a voter) in order to solicit political support or to ascertain opinions ~*vi* to seek orders or votes; solicit – **canvass** *n*, **canvasser** *also* **canvaser** *n*

canyon, cañon /ˈkanyən‖ˈkænjən/ *n* a deep valley or gorge

[1]**cap** /kap‖kæp/ *n* **1a** a soft usu flat head covering with a peak and no brim **b** (one who has gained) a head covering awarded to a player selected for a special, specif national, sports team or who is a regular member of esp a cricket team **2** a natural cover or top: e g **2a** a usu unyielding overlying rock or soil layer **b** the pileus **c** (a patch of distinctively coloured feathers on) the top of a bird's head **3** sthg that serves as a cover or protection, esp for the end or top of an object **4** a mortarboard **5** the uppermost part; the top **6** a small container holding an explosive charge (e g for a toy pistol or for priming the charge in a firearm) **7** *Br* DUTCH CAP – **capful** *n*

[2]**cap** *vt* **-pp-** **1a** to provide or protect with a cap **b** to give a cap to as a symbol of honour or rank **2** to form a cap over; crown <*the mountains were* ~ped *with mist* – John Buchan> **3** to follow with sthg more noticeable or significant; outdo

capability /ˌkaypəˈbiləti‖ˌkeɪpəˈbɪlətɪ/ *n* **1** being capable **2** a feature or faculty capable of development; potential **3** the capacity for an indicated use or development

capable /ˈkaypəbl‖ˈkeɪpəbl/ *adj* **1** susceptible <*a remark* ~ *of being misunderstood*> **2** having the attributes or traits required to perform a specified deed or action <*he is* ~ *of murder*> **3** able <*her* ~ *fingers*> *USE* (*except 3*) + *of* – **capableness** *n*, **capably** *adv*

capacious /kəˈpayshəs‖kəˈpeɪʃəs/ *adj* able to hold a great deal – **capaciously** *adv*, **capaciousness** *n*

capacitor /kəˈpasətə‖kəˈpæsətə/ *n* a component in an electrical circuit that provides ability to store a charge of electricity and usu consists of an insulator sandwiched between 2 oppositely charged conductors

capacity /kəˈpasəti‖kəˈpæsətɪ/ *n* **1a** the ability to receive, accommodate, or deal with sthg **b** an ability to contain <*a jug with a* ~ *of 2pt*> **c** the maximum amount that can be contained or produced <*working at* ~> **2** legal competence or power **3a** ability, calibre **b** POTENTIAL 1 **4** a position or role assigned or assumed <*in his* ~ *as judge*>

ˌ**cap and ˈbells** *n, pl* **caps and bells** the traditional dress of a court jester

caparison /kəˈparis(ə)n‖kəˈpærɪs(ə)n/ *n* **1** an ornamental covering for a horse, esp a warhorse in former times **2** rich clothing; adornment – **caparison** *vt*

[1]**cape** /kayp‖keɪp/ *n* a peninsula or similar land projection jutting out into water

[2]**cape** *n* a sleeveless outer (part of a) garment that fits closely at the neck and hangs loosely from the shoulders

ˌ**Cape ˈColoured** *n* a person of mixed black and white ancestry in S Africa – **Cape Coloured** *adj*

[1]**caper** /ˈkaypə‖ˈkeɪpə/ *n* **1** any of a genus of low prickly shrubs of the Mediterranean region **2** a greenish flower bud or young berry of the caper, pickled and used as a seasoning, garnish, etc

[2]**caper** *vi* to leap about in a carefree way; prance

[3]**caper** *n* **1** a joyful leap **2** a high-spirited escapade; a prank **3** *chiefly NAm* an illegal enterprise; a crime – infml

capereaillie /ˌkapəˈkayli‖ˌkæpəˈkeɪlɪ/ *n* a large African and Eurasian grouse [Scottish Gaelic *capalcoille*, lit., horse of the woods]

capillarity /ˌkapiˈlarəti‖ˌkæpɪˈlærətɪ/ *n* the elevation or depression of the surface of a liquid in contact with a solid (e g in a fine-bore tube) that depends on the relative attraction of the molecules of the liquid for each other and for those of the solid

[1]**capillary** /kəˈpiləri‖kəˈpɪlərɪ/ *adj* **1a** resembling a hair, esp in slender elongated form **b** *of a tube, passage, etc* having a very fine bore **2** involving, held by, or resulting from surface tension **3** of capillaries or capillarity

[2]**capillary** *n* a capillary tube; *esp* any of the smallest blood vessels connecting arteries with veins and forming networks throughout the body

[1]**capital** /ˈkapitl‖ˈkæpɪtl/ *adj* **1a** punishable by death <*a* ~ *crime*> **b** involving execution <~ *punishment*> **2** *of a letter* of or conforming to the series (e g A, B, C rather than a, b, c) used to begin sentences or proper names **3a** of the greatest importance or influence **b** being the seat of government **4** excellent – not now in vogue [Latin *capitalis*, fr *capit-*, *caput* head]

[2]**capital** *n* **1a** (the value of) a stock of accumulated goods, esp at a particular time and in contrast to income received during a particular period **b** accumulated possessions calculated to bring in income **c** *sing or pl in constr* people holding capital **d** a sum of money saved **2** an esp initial capital letter **3** a city serving as a seat of government – **make capital of/out of** to turn (a situation) to one's advantage

[3]**capital** *n* the top part or piece of an architectural column

ˌ**capital ˈassets** *n pl* tangible or intangible long-term assets

ˌ**capital ˈgain** *n* the profit from the sale of a capital asset (e g a house) – usu pl with sing. meaning

capitalism /ˈkapitlˌiz(ə)m‖ˈkæpɪtlˌɪz(ə)m/ *n* an economic system characterized by private ownership and control of the means of production, distribution, and exchange and by the profit motive

[1]**capitalist** /ˈkapitl·ist‖ˈkæpɪtəlɪst/ *n* **1** a person with (invested) capital; *broadly* a very wealthy person **2** one who favours capitalism

[2]**capitalist, capitalistic** /-ˈistik‖-ˈɪstɪk/ *adj* **1** owning capital **2** practising, advocating, or marked by capitalism – **capitalistically** *adv*

capital·ize, -ise /ˈkapitlˌiez‖ˈkæpɪtlˌaɪz/ *vt* **1** to write or print in capitals or with an initial capital **2** to convert into capital **3** to convert (a periodic payment) into an equivalent capital sum <~d *annuities*> **4** to supply capital for ~*vi* to gain by turning sthg to advantage – usu + *on* – **capitalization** *n*

capitation /ˌkapiˈtaysh(ə)n‖ˌkæpɪˈteɪʃ(ə)n/ *n*

a uniform payment or charge made per person

capitol /'kapitl‖'kæpɪtl/ *n* **1** a building in which a US legislative body meets **2** *cap* the building in which Congress meets at Washington

capitulate /kə'pityoolayt, -choo-‖kə-'pɪtjʊleɪt, -tʃʊ-/ *vi* **1** to surrender, often after negotiation of terms **2** to cease resisting; acquiesce

capitulation /kə,pityoo'laysh(ə)n, -choo-‖kə-,pɪtjʊ'leɪʃ(ə)n, -tʃʊ-/ *n* **1** an agreement between governments **2** the act or agreement of sby who surrenders **3** a surrender, acquiescence

capon /'kaypən, -pon‖'keɪpən, -pɒn/ *n* a castrated male chicken – **caponize** *vt*

caprice /kə'prees‖kə'priːs/ *n* **1a** a sudden and seemingly unmotivated change of mind **b** a sudden and unpredictable change or series of changes <*the* ~s *of the weather*> **2** a disposition to change one's mind impulsively [French, fr Italian *capriccio*, lit., head with hair standing on end, shudder, fr *capo* head (fr Latin *caput*) + *riccio* hedgehog (fr Latin *ericius*)]

capricious /kə'prishəs‖kə'prɪʃəs/ *adj* governed or characterized by caprice; apt to change suddenly or unpredictably – **capriciously** *adv*, **capriciousness** *n*

Capricorn /'kaprikawn‖'kæprɪkɔːn/ *n* (sby born under) the 10th zodiacal constellation, pictured as a creature resembling a goat with the tail of a fish – **Capricornian** *adj or n*

capsicum /'kapsikəm‖'kæpsɪkəm/ *n* (the many-seeded usu fleshy-walled fruit of) any of a genus of tropical herbaceous plants and shrubs of the nightshade family

capsize /kap'siez‖kæp'saɪz/ *vb* to (cause to) overturn <~ *a canoe*>

capstan /'kapstən‖'kæpstən/ *n* **1** a mechanical device consisting of an upright drum round which a rope, hawser, etc is fastened, used for moving or raising heavy weights **2** a rotating shaft that drives tape at a constant speed in a tape recorder

capsule /'kapsyoohl, -yool‖'kæpsjuːl, -jʊl/ *n* **1** a membrane or sac **1a** enclosing a body part **b** surrounding a microorganism **2** a closed plant receptacle containing spores or seeds **3** a usu gelatin shell enclosing a drug for swallowing **4** a compact usu rounded container **5** a detachable pressurized compartment, esp in a spacecraft or aircraft, containing crew and controls; *also* a spacecraft **6** a usu metal, wax, or plastic covering that encloses the top of a bottle, esp of wine, and protects the cork – **capsular** *adj*

[1]**captain** /'kaptin‖'kæptɪn/ *n* **1a(1)** an officer in the army or US airforce ranking below major **a(2)** an officer in the navy ranking below commodore **b** an officer in charge of a ship **c** a pilot of a civil aircraft **2** a distinguished military leader **3** a leader of a team, esp a sports team **4** a dominant figure <~s *of industry*> **5** *Br* the head boy or girl at a school **6** *NAm* a fire or police officer – **captaincy** *n*, **captainship** *n*

[2]**captain** *vt* to be captain of

caption /'kapshən‖'kæpʃən/ *n* **1** a heading or title, esp of an article or document **2** a comment or description accompanying a pictorial illustration **3** a film subtitle – **caption** *vt*, **captionless** *adj*

captious /'kapshəs‖'kæpʃəs/ *adj* marked by an often ill-natured inclination to stress faults and raise objections – **captiously** *adv*, **captiousness** *n*

captivate /'kaptivayt‖'kæptɪveɪt/ *vt* to fascinate or charm irresistibly – **captivatingly** *adv*, **captivation** *n*

captive /'kaptiv‖'kæptɪv/ *adj* **1a** taken and held as prisoner, esp by an enemy in war **b** kept within bounds; confined **c** held under control **2** in a situation that makes departure or inattention difficult <*a* ~ *audience*> – **captive** *n*, **captivity** *n*

captor /'kaptə‖'kæptə/ *n* one who or that which holds another captive

[1]**capture** /'kapchə‖'kæptʃə/ *n* **1** the act of gaining control or possession **2** one who or that which has been captured **3** the acquisition by an atom, molecule, ion, or nucleus of an additional elementary particle, often with associated emission of radiation

[2]**capture** *vt* **1** to take captive; win, gain **2** to preserve in a relatively permanent form <*how well the scene was* ~d *on film*> **3** to remove (e g a chess piece) from the playing board according to the rules of a game **4** to bring about the capture of (an elementary particle)

car /kah‖kɑː/ *n* **1** a vehicle moving on wheels: **1a** a chariot of war or of triumph – chiefly poetic **b** a railway carriage **c** MOTOR CAR **2** the passenger compartment of an airship or balloon **3** *NAm* the cage of a lift

carafe /kə'rahf, -'raf, 'karəf‖kə'rɑːf, -'ræf, 'kærəf/ *n* a (glass) bottle used to hold water or wine, esp at table

caramel /'karəməl, -mel‖'kærəməl, -mel/ *n* **1** a brittle brown somewhat bitter substance obtained by heating sugar and used as a colouring and flavouring agent **2** a chewy usu quite soft caramel-flavoured toffee – **caramelize** *vb*

carapace /'karə,pays‖'kærə,peɪs/ *n* a hard case (e g of chitin) covering (part of) the back of a turtle, crab, etc

carat /'karət‖'kærət/ *n* **1** a unit of weight for precious stones equal to 200mg **2** *NAm chiefly* **karat** a unit of fineness for gold equal to $^1/_{24}$ part of pure gold in an alloy

[1]**caravan** /'karə,van‖'kærə,væn/ *n* **1a** *sing or pl in constr* a company of travellers on a journey through desert or hostile regions; *also* a train of pack animals **b** a group of vehicles travelling together **2** *Br* a covered vehicle designed to be towed by a motor car or horse and to serve as a dwelling when parked [Italian *caravana*, fr Persian *kārwān*]

[2]**caravan** *vi* **-nn-** (*NAm* **-n-**, **-nn-**) to have a holiday in a caravan

caravanserai /,karə'vansərie‖,kærə-'vænsəraɪ/, *NAm chiefly* **caravansary** /-səri‖-sərɪ/ *n, pl* **caravanserais, caravanserai** a usu large inn in Eastern countries that is built round a courtyard and used as a resting place for caravans

caraway /'karəway‖'kærəweɪ/ *n* a usu white-flowered aromatic plant with pungent seeds used as a flavouring

carbide /'kahbied‖'kɑːbaɪd/ *n* a compound of carbon with a more electropositive element

carbine /'kahbien‖'kɑːbaɪn/ *n* **1** a short light rifle or musket orig carried by cavalry **2** a short light gas-operated magazine-fed automatic rifle

carbohydrate /,kahbə'hiedrayt, -boh-‖

ˌkɑːbəˈhaɪdreɪt, -bəʊ-/ *n* any of various compounds of carbon, hydrogen, and oxygen (e g sugars, starches, and celluloses) formed by green plants and constituting a major class of energy-providing animal foods

carˌbolic ˈacid /kahˈbolik‖kɑːˈbɒlɪk/ *n* phenol

carbon /ˈkahb(ə)n‖ˈkɑːb(ə)n/ *n* **1** a nonmetallic element occurring as diamond, graphite, charcoal, coke, etc and as a constituent of coal, petroleum, carbonates (e g limestone), and organic compounds **2a** a sheet of carbon paper **b** CARBON COPY 1 **3** a piece of carbon used as an element in a voltaic cell [French *carbone*, fr Latin *carbon-, carbo* ember, charcoal] – **carbonless** *adj*

[1]**carbonate** /ˈkahbənət, -nayt‖ˈkɑːbənət, -neɪt/ *n* a salt or ester of carbonic acid

[2]**carbonate** /ˈkahbənayt‖ˈkɑːbəneɪt/ *vt* **1** to convert into a carbonate **2** to impregnate with carbon dioxide; aerate – **carbonation** *n*

ˌcarbon ˈblack *n* carbon as a colloidal black substance (e g soot)

ˌcarbon ˈcopy *n* **1** a copy made with carbon paper **2** a duplicate or exact replica

ˌcarbon ˈdating *n* the dating of ancient organic material such as wood and bones by recording the amount of carbon 14 (a radioactive isotope of carbon) remaining

ˌcarbon diˈoxide *n* a heavy colourless gas that does not support combustion, is formed esp by the combustion and decomposition of organic substances, and is absorbed from the air by plants in photosynthesis

carˌbonic ˈacid /kahˈbonik‖kɑːˈbɒnɪk/ *n* a weak acid that is a solution of carbon dioxide in water and whose salts are carbonates

carboniferous /ˌkahbəˈnif(ə)rəs‖ˌkɑːbəˈnɪf(ə)rəs/ *adj* **1** producing or containing carbon or coal **2** *cap* of or being the period of the Palaeozoic era in which coal deposits formed

carbon·ize, -ise /ˈkahb(ə)nˌiez‖ˈkɑːb(ə)nˌaɪz/ *vt* to convert into carbon or a carbon-containing residue ~*vi* to become carbonized; char – **carbonization** *n*

ˌcarbon moˈnoxide *n* a colourless odourless very toxic gas formed as a product of the incomplete combustion of carbon

ˈcarbon ˌpaper *n* (a sheet of) thin paper coated on 1 side with dark pigment, used to make copies by placing between 2 sheets of paper, so that the pigment is transferred to the lower sheet by the pressure of writing or typing on the upper

Carborundum /ˌkahbəˈroondəm‖ˌkɑːbəˈrʊndəm/ *trademark* – used for various abrasives

carboy /ˈkahˌboy‖ˈkɑːˌbɔɪ/ *n* a large usu roughly spherical glass or plastic container for liquids

carbuncle /ˈkahˌbungkl‖ˈkɑːˌbʌŋkl/ *n* **1** a red gemstone, usu a garnet, cut in a domed shape without facets **2** a painful local inflammation of the skin and deeper tissues with multiple openings for the discharge of pus – **carbuncled** *adj*, **carbuncular** *adj*

carburettor, *NAm* **carburetor** /ˌkahbyoo-ˈretə, ˌkahbəˈretə‖ˌkɑːbjʊˈretə, ˌkɑːbəˈretə/ *n* an apparatus for supplying an internal-combustion engine with vaporized fuel mixed with air in an explosive mixture

carcass, *Br also* **carcase** /ˈkahkəs‖ˈkɑːkəs/ *n* **1** a dead body; *esp* the dressed body of a meat animal **2** the decaying or worthless remains of a structure **3** a framework; *esp* the framework of a tyre as distinct from the tread

carcinogen /ˈkahsinəjən‖ˈkɑːsɪnədʒən/ *n* sthg (e g a chemical compound) that causes cancer – **carcinogenesis** *n*, **carcinogenic** *adj*, **carcinogenically** *adv*, **carcinogenicity** *n*

carcinoma /ˌkahsiˈnohmə‖ˌkɑːsɪˈnəʊmə/ *n, pl* **carcinomas, carcinomata** /-mətə‖-mətə/ a malignant tumour of epithelial origin – **carcinomatous** *adj*

[1]**card** /kahd‖kɑːd/ *vt* to cleanse and disentangle (fibres) by the use of a carding machine preparatory to spinning – **carder** *n*

[2]**card** *n* an implement or machine for carding fibres or raising a nap on cloth

[3]**card** *n* **1** PLAYING CARD **2** *pl but sing or pl in constr* a game played with cards **3** a valuable asset or right for use in negotiations **4** a flat stiff usu small and rectangular piece of paper or thin cardboard: e g **4a** a postcard **b** VISITING CARD **c** PROGRAMME 1a; *esp* one for a sporting event **d** GREETINGS CARD **5** *pl, Br* the National Insurance and other papers of an employee, held by his/her employer **6** a comical or amusing fellow **7** *Br* a person of a specified type <*a knowing* ~> *USE* (*6&7*) infml – **on the cards** quite possible; likely to occur – **get/ask for one's cards** to be dismissed/resign from employment

cardamom /ˈkahdəməm‖ˈkɑːdəməm/ *n* (an E Indian plant that bears) an aromatic capsular fruit containing seeds used as a spice or condiment

[1]**ˈcardˌboard** /-ˌbawd‖-ˌbɔːd/ *n* material of similar composition to paper but thicker and stiffer

[2]**cardboard** *adj* **1** made (as if) of cardboard **2** unreal, insubstantial <*the story has too many* ~ *characters*>

ˈcard-ˌcarrying *adj* being a fully paid-up member, esp of the Communist party

cardi- /kahdi-‖kɑːdɪ-/, **cardio-** *comb form* heart; cardiac <cardio*gram*>; cardiac and <cardio*vascular*>

[1]**cardiac** /ˈkahdiak‖ˈkɑːdɪæk/ *adj* **1** of, situated near, or acting on the heart **2** of the oesophageal end of the stomach

[2]**cardiac** *n* sby suffering from heart disease

cardigan /ˈkahdigən‖ˈkɑːdɪgən/ *n* a knitted garment for the upper body that opens down the front and is usu fastened with buttons [James Thomas Brudenell, 7th Earl of *Cardigan* (1797-1868), English soldier]

[1]**cardinal** /ˈkahdinl‖ˈkɑːdɪnl/ *adj* of primary importance; fundamental [Old French, fr Late Latin *cardinalis*, fr Latin, of a hinge, fr *cardin-, cardo* hinge] – **cardinally** *adv*

[2]**cardinal** *n* a member of a body of high officials of the Roman Catholic church whose powers include the election of a new pope – **cardinalate** *n*, **cardinalship** *n*

cardinal number *n* a number (e g 1, 2, 3) that is used in simple counting and that indicates how many elements there are in a collection

ˌcardinal ˈpoint *n* any of the 4 principal

compass points north, south, east, and west

card index *n, Br* a filing system in which each item is entered on a separate card – **card-index** *vt*

ˈcardˌsharp /-ˌshahp‖-ˌʃɑːp/, **ˈcardˌsharper** /-ˌshahpə‖-ˌʃɑːpə/ *n* one who habitually cheats at cards

[1]**care** /keə‖keə/ *n* **1** a cause for anxiety **2** close attention; effort <*took* ~ *over the drawing*> **3** change, supervision <*under the doctor's* ~>; *specif, Br* guardianship and supervision of children by a local authority **4** sby or sthg that is an object of attention, anxiety, or solicitude <*the flower garden was her special* ~>

[2]**care** *vi* **1a** to feel trouble or anxiety **b** to feel interest or concern – often + *about* **2** to give care <~ *for the sick*> **3** to have a liking or taste *for* ~ *vt* **1** to be concerned about <*nobody* ~s *what I do*> **2** to wish <*if you* ~ *to go*>

careen /kəˈreen‖kəˈriːn/ *vt* **1** to cause (a boat) to lean over on one side **2** to clean, caulk, or repair (a boat) in this position ~ *vi* **1a** to careen a boat **b** to undergo this process **2** to heel over **3** *chiefly NAm* to career

[1]**career** /kəˈriə‖kəˈrɪə/ *n* **1** the course of (a particular sphere of) a person's life <*Churchill's* ~ *as a politician*> **2** a field of employment in which one expects to remain; *esp* such a field which requires special qualifications and training

[2]**career** *vi* to move swiftly in an uncontrolled fashion

caˈreer ˌgirl *adj* a woman who puts advancement in her career or profession before marriage or motherhood

careerist /kəˈriərist‖kəˈrɪərɪst/ *n* one who is intent on advancing his/her career, often at the expense of personal integrity – **careerism** *n*

carefree /ˈkeəˌfree‖ˈkeəˌfriː/ *adj* free from anxiety or responsibility

ˈcareful /-f(ə)l‖-f(ə)l/ *adj* **1** exercising or taking care **2a** marked by attentive concern **b** cautious, prudent <*be* ~ *of the horses*> – often + *to* and an infinitive <*be* ~ *to switch off the machine*> – **carefully** *adv*, **carefulness** *n*

ˈcareless /-lis‖-lɪs/ *adj* **1** not taking care **2a** negligent, slovenly **b** unstudied, spontaneous <~ *grace*> **3a** free from care; untroubled <~ *days*> **b** indifferent, unconcerned <~ *of the consequences*> – **carelessly** *adv*, **carelessness** *n*

[1]**caress** /kəˈres‖kəˈres/ *n* **1** a kiss **2** a caressing touch or stroke

[2]**caress** *vt* **1** to touch or stroke lightly and lovingly **2** to touch or affect gently or soothingly <*music that* ~es *the ear*> – **caresser** *n*, **caressingly** *adv*

caret /ˈkarət‖ˈkærət/ *n* a mark ‸ or ∧ or > used on written or printed matter to indicate an insertion to be made

ˈcareˌtaker /-ˌtaykə‖-ˌteɪkə/ *n* **1** one who takes care of the house or land of an owner, esp during his/her absence **2** one who keeps clean a large and/or public building (e g a school or office), looks after the heating system, and carries out minor repairs **3** sby or sthg temporarily installed in office <*a* ~ *government*>

ˈcareˌworn /-ˌwawn‖-ˌwɔːn/ *adj* showing the effects of grief or anxiety <*a* ~ *face*>

cargo /ˈkahgoh‖ˈkɑːgəʊ/ *n, pl* **cargoes, cargos** the goods conveyed in a ship, aircraft, or vehicle; freight

caribou /ˈkariˌbooh‖ˈkærɪˌbuː/ *n*, any of several large N American antlered deer

[1]**caricature** /ˈkarikəchə, -chooə, -tyooə‖ˈkærɪkətʃə, -tʃʊə, -tjʊə/ *n* **1** exaggeration of features or characteristics, often to a ludicrous or grotesque degree **2** a comic or satirical representation, esp in literature or art, that has the qualities of caricature **3** a distortion so gross or inferior as to seem like a caricature – **caricatural** *adj*, **caricaturist** *n*

[2]**caricature** /ˈkarikəˌchooə, -ˌtyooə‖ˈkærɪkəˌtʃʊə, -ˌtjʊə/ *vt* to make or draw a caricature of; represent in caricature

caries /ˈkeəreez, -riz‖ˈkeəriːz, -rɪz/ *n, pl* **caries** progressive decay of a tooth or sometimes a bone, caused by microorganisms

carillon /kəˈrilyən‖kəˈrɪljən/ *n* a set of bells sounded by hammers controlled from a keyboard

carious /ˈkeəri·əs‖ˈkeərɪəs/ *adj* affected with caries

Carmelite /ˈkahməˌliet‖ˈkɑːməˌlaɪt/ *n* a member of the Roman Catholic mendicant Order of Our Lady of Mount Carmel founded in the 12th c – **Carmelite** *adj*

carmine /ˈkahmin‖ˈkɑːmɪn/ *n* **1** a rich crimson or scarlet pigment **2** a vivid red

carnage /ˈkahnij‖ˈkɑːnɪdʒ/ *n* great slaughter (e g in battle)

carnal /ˈkahnl‖ˈkɑːnl/ *adj* **1** given to or marked by physical and esp sexual pleasures and appetites **2** temporal, worldly – **carnality** *n*, **carnally** *adv*

carnation /kahˈnaysh(ə)n‖kɑːˈneɪʃ(ə)n/ *n* **1** light red or pink **2** any of numerous cultivated usu double-flowered pinks

carnelian /kahˈneelyən‖kɑːˈniːljən/ *n* (a) cornelian

carnival /ˈkahnivl‖ˈkɑːnɪvl/ *n* **1** a period of merrymaking before Lent, esp in Roman Catholic countries **2** an instance of merrymaking or feasting **3a** an exhibition or organized programme of entertainment; a festival **b** *chiefly NAm* a travelling circus or funfair [Italian *carnevale*, alteration of earlier *carnelevare*, lit., removal of meat, fr *carne* flesh + *levare* to remove]

carnivore /ˈkahniˌvaw‖ˈkɑːnɪˌvɔː/ *n* a flesh-eating animal; *esp* any of an order of flesh-eating mammals

carnivorous /kahˈniv(ə)rəs‖kɑːˈnɪv(ə)rəs/ *adj* **1** of or being a carnivore; *specif* flesh-eating **2** *of a plant* feeding on nutrients obtained from animal tissue, esp insects – **carnivorously** *adv*, **carnivorousness** *n*

carob /ˈkarəb‖ˈkærəb/ *n* (the edible pod of) a Mediterranean evergreen leguminous tree with red flowers

[1]**carol** /ˈkarəl‖ˈkærəl/ *n* a popular seasonal usu religious song or ballad; *esp* a Christmas song or hymn

[2]**carol** *vb* **-ll-** (*NAm* **-l-, -ll-**) to sing (joyfully)

carotid /kəˈrotid‖kəˈrɒtɪd/ *adj or n* (of or being) the chief artery or pair of arteries that supply the head with blood

carousal /kəˈrowzl‖kəˈraʊzl/ *n* a carouse

[1]**carouse** /kəˈrowz‖kəˈraʊz/ *n* a drunken revel

[2]**carouse** *vi* **1** to drink alcoholic beverages heavily or freely **2** to take part in a drinking bout

carousel, *NAm also* **carrousel** /ˌkarəˈsel, -ˈzel‖ˌkærəˈsel, -ˈzel/ *n* **1** a rotating stand or delivery system <*a luggage ~ at the airport*> **2** *chiefly NAm* a merry-go-round

[1]**carp** /kahp‖kɑːp/ *vi* to find fault or complain querulously and often unnecessarily – infml; usu + *at*

[2]**carp** *n*, (a fish resembling or related to) a large Old World soft-finned freshwater fish often farmed for food

ˈ**car ˌpark** *n, chiefly Br* an area or building set aside for parking motor vehicles

carpel /ˈkahpl‖ˈkɑːpl/ *n* any of the structures of a flowering plant that constitute the female (innermost) part of a flower and usu consist of an ovary, style, and stigma – **carpellary** *adj*, **carpellate** *adj*

[1]**carpenter** /ˈkahpintə‖ˈkɑːpɪntə/ *n* a woodworker; *esp* one who builds or repairs large-scale structural woodwork

[2]**carpenter** *vi* to follow the trade of a carpenter ~*vt* to put together, often in a mechanical manner

carpentry /ˈkahpintri‖ˈkɑːpɪntrɪ/ *n* **1** the art or trade of a carpenter; *specif* the art of shaping and assembling structural woodwork **2** timberwork constructed by a carpenter

[1]**carpet** /ˈkahpit‖ˈkɑːpɪt/ *n* **1** a heavy woven or felted material used as a floor covering; *also* a floor covering made of this fabric **2** a surface resembling or suggesting a carpet <*a ~ of leaves*> – **on the carpet** before an authority for censure or reprimand

[2]**carpet** *vt* **1** to cover (as if) with a carpet <*snowdrops ~ the lawn*> **2** to reprimand – infml

ˈ**carpetˌbag** /-ˌbag‖-ˌbæg/ *n* a bag made of carpet fabric, common in the 19th c

ˈ**carpetˌbagger** /-ˌbagə‖-ˌbægə/ *n* **1** a Northerner who went to the American South after the Civil War in search of personal gain **2** a nonresident who meddles in the politics of a locality

carpeting /ˈkahpiting‖ˈkɑːpɪtɪŋ/ *n* (material for) carpets

ˈ**carˌport** /-ˌpawt‖-ˌpɔːt/ *n* a usu open-sided shelter for cars

carpus /ˈkahpəs‖ˈkɑːpəs/ *n, pl* **carpi** /-pie‖-paɪ/ (the bones of) the wrist – **carpal** *adj*

carriage /ˈkarij‖ˈkærɪdʒ/ *n* **1** the act of carrying **2** the manner of bearing the body; posture **3** the price or cost of carrying <*~ paid*> **4** a wheeled vehicle; *esp* a horse-drawn passenger-carrying vehicle designed for private use **5** a movable part of a machine that supports some other part <*a typewriter ~*> **6** *Br* a railway passenger vehicle; a coach

ˈ**carriageˌway** /-ˌway‖-ˌweɪ/ *n, Br* the part of a road used by vehicular traffic; *specif* LANE 2b

carrier /ˈkari·ə‖ˈkærɪə/ *n* **1** a bearer, messenger **2** an individual or organization that contracts to transport goods, messages, etc **3a** a container for carrying **b** a device, platform, machine, etc that carries <*a luggage ~ on a bicycle*> **4** a bearer and transmitter of a causative agent of disease; *esp* one who is immune to the disease **5a** a usu inactive accessory substance; VEHICLE 1 **b** a substance (e g a catalyst) by whose agency some element or group is transferred from one compound to another **6** a radio or electrical wave of relatively high frequency that can be modulated by a signal (e g representing sound or vision information), esp in order to transmit that signal **7** a mobile hole or electron capable of carrying an electric charge in a semiconductor **8** AIRCRAFT CARRIER

carrier bag /ˈ--- ˌ-, ˌ--- ˈ-/ *n, Br* a bag of plastic or thick paper used for carrying goods, esp shopping

ˈ**carrier ˌpigeon** *n* a homing pigeon (used to carry messages)

carrion /ˈkari·ən‖ˈkærɪən/ *n* **1** dead and putrefying flesh **2** sthg corrupt or rotten

carrion crow *n* the common European black crow

carrot /ˈkarət‖ˈkærət/ *n* **1** (a biennial plant with) a usu orange spindle-shaped root eaten as a vegetable **2** a promised and often illusory reward or advantage

carroty /ˈkarəti‖ˈkærətɪ/ *adj* bright orange-red in colour

[1]**carry** /ˈkari‖ˈkærɪ/ *vt* **1** to support and move (a load); transport **2a** to convey, conduct **b** to support <*this beam* carries *the weight of the upper storeys*> **3** to lead or influence by appeal to the emotions **4** to transfer from one place to another; *esp* to transfer (a digit corresponding to a multiple of 10) to the next higher power of 10 in addition **5a** to wear or have on one's person <*I never ~ money on me*> **b** to bear on or within oneself <*is* ~ing *an unborn child*> **c** to have as a mark, attribute, or property <*~ a scar*> **6** to have as a consequence, esp in law; involve <*the crime* carried *a heavy penalty*> **7** to hold (e g one's person) in a specified manner <carries *himself well*> **8** to sing with reasonable correctness of pitch <*~ a tune*> **9a** to keep in stock for sale **b** to provide sustenance for; support <*land* ~ing *100 head of cattle*> **10** to maintain through financial support or personal effort <*he* carried *the magazine single-handedly*> **11** to extend or prolong in space, time, or degree <*~ a principle too far*> **12** to gain victory for **13a** to broadcast **b** to publish <*newspapers ~ weather reports*> **14** to perform with sufficient ability to make up for the poor performance of (e g a partner or teammate) **15** to hoist and maintain (a sail) in use ~ *vi* **1** to act as a bearer **2a** to reach or penetrate to a distance <*voices ~ well*> **b** to convey itself to a reader or audience **3** to undergo or allow carriage in a specified way – **carry a torch** to be in love, esp without reciprocation; cherish a longing or devotion – **carry the can** to bear the responsibility; accept the blame – infml – **carry the day** to win, prevail

[2]**carry** *n* **1** the range of a gun or projectile or of a struck or thrown ball **2** portage

carry away *vt* to arouse to a high and often excessive degree of emotion or enthusiasm – usu passive

ˈ**carryˌcot** /-ˌkot‖-ˌkɒt/ *n, chiefly Br* a small lightweight boxlike bed, usu with 2 handles, in which a baby can be carried

carry forward *vt* to transfer (e g a total) to the succeeding column, page, or book relating to the same account

ˌcarrying-ˈon *n, pl* **carryings-on** rowdy, excited, or improper behaviour – infml

carry off *vt* **1** to cause the death of <*the plague* carried off *thousands*> **2** to perform easily or successfully <*the leading lady* carried off *her part brilliantly*> **3** to gain possession or control of; capture <carried off *the prize*>

ˈcarryˌon /-ˌon‖-ˌɒn/ *n, NAm* a piece of luggage suitable for a passenger to carry on board an aircraft

ˈcarry-ˌon *n* an instance of rowdy, excited, or improper behaviour; a to-do – infml

carry on *vt* to conduct, manage <carry on *a business*> **1** to behave in a rowdy, excited, or improper manner <*embarrassed by the way he* carries on> **2** to continue one's course or activity, esp in spite of obstacles or discouragement **3** *Br* to flirt; *also* to have a love affair – usu + *with*

ˈcarryˌout /-ˌowt‖-ˌaʊt/ *n* **1** *chiefly Scot* food or esp alcoholic drink bought to be consumed off the premises **2** *chiefly NAm & Scot* a takeaway

carry out *vt* **1** to put into execution <carry out *a plan*> **2** to bring to a successful conclusion; complete, accomplish

carry over *vt* CARRY FORWARD ~*vi* to persist from one stage or sphere of activity to another

carry through *vt* CARRY OUT ~*vi* to survive, persist <*feelings that* carry through *to the present*>

carsick /ˈkahˌsik‖ˈkɑːˌsɪk/ *adj* suffering from the motion sickness associated with travelling by car – **carsickness** *n*

[1]**cart** /kaht‖kɑːt/ *n* **1** a heavy 2-wheeled or 4-wheeled vehicle used for transporting bulky or heavy loads (e g goods or animal feed) **2** a lightweight 2-wheeled vehicle drawn by a horse, pony, or dog **3** a small wheeled vehicle

[2]**cart** *vt* **1** to carry or convey (as if) in a cart **2** to take or drag away without ceremony or by force – infml; usu + *off* <*they* ~ed *him off to jail*> **3** to carry by hand – infml – **carter** *n*

carte blanche /ˌkaht ˈblonh·sh ‖ˌkɑːt ˈblɑ̃ʃ (*Fr* kart blɑ̃ʃ)/ *n* full discretionary power <*was given* ~ *to furnish the house*> [French, lit., blank document]

cartel /kahˈtel‖kɑːˈtel/ *n* a combination of independent commercial enterprises designed to limit competition

ˈcart ˌhorse *n* any large powerful draught horse (e g a Clydesdale)

cartilage /ˈkahtilij‖ˈkɑːtɪlɪdʒ/ *n* (a structure composed of) a translucent elastic tissue that makes up most of the skeleton of very young vertebrates and becomes mostly converted into bone in adult higher vertebrates – **cartilaginous** *adj*

cartography /kahˈtogrəfi‖kɑːˈtɒgrəfɪ/ *n* map making – **cartographer** *n*, **cartographic, cartographical** *adj*

carton /ˈkaht(ə)n‖ˈkɑːt(ə)n/ *n* a box or container made of plastic, cardboard, etc

cartoon /kahˈtoohn‖kɑːˈtuːn/ *n* **1** a preparatory design, drawing, or painting (e g for a fresco) **2a** a satirical drawing commenting on public and usu political matters **b** STRIP CARTOON **3** ANIMATED CARTOON – **cartoon** *vb*, **cartoonist** *n*

cartridge /ˈkahtrij‖ˈkɑːtrɪdʒ/ *n* **1a** a tube of metal, paper, etc containing a complete charge, a primer, and often the bullet or shot for a firearm **b** a case containing an explosive charge for blasting **2** the part of the arm of a record player holding the stylus and the mechanism that converts movements of the stylus into electrical signals **3** a case containing a reel of magnetic tape designed for insertion into a tape recorder

ˈcartridge ˌbelt *n* a belt with a series of loops for holding cartridges

ˈcartridge ˌpaper *n* a stiff rough-surfaced close-grained paper (e g for drawing)

[1]**ˈcartˌwheel** /-ˌweel‖-ˌwiːl/ *n* a sideways handspring with arms and legs extended

[2]**cartwheel** *vi* to perform cartwheels

carve /kahv‖kɑːv/ *vt* **1a** to cut so as to shape **b** to produce by cutting <~d *his initials in the soft sandstone*> **2** to make or acquire (a career, reputation, etc) through one's own efforts – often + *out* <~d *out a place for himself in the firm*> **3** to cut (food, esp meat) into pieces or slices ~ *vi* **1** to cut up and serve meat **2** to work as a sculptor or engraver

carver /ˈkahvə‖ˈkɑːvə/ **1** a long sharp knife used for carving meat **2** *pl* a knife and fork used for carving and serving meat

ˈcarve-ˌup *n* **1** a competitive event in which the result has been irregularly decided beforehand – infml **2** a division into parts; *esp* the sharing out of loot – slang

carve up *vt* **1** to divide into parts or shares **2** to wound with a knife – slang

carving /ˈkahving‖ˈkɑːvɪŋ/ *n* **1** the act or art of one who carves **2** a carved object or design

caryatid /ˈkari·əˌtid, ˌkariˈatid, kəˈrie·ətid‖ˈkærɪəˌtɪd, ˌkærɪˈætɪd, kəˈraɪətɪd/ *n, pl* **caryatids, caryatides** /ˌkariˈatideez, kəˌrie·əˈteediz‖ˌkærɪˈætɪdiːz, kəˌraɪəˈtiːdɪz/ a draped female figure used as a column to support an entablature

[1]**cascade** /kasˈkayd‖kæsˈkeɪd/ *n* **1** a steep usu small fall of water; *esp* one of a series of such falls **2a** sthg arranged in a series or in a succession of stages so that each stage derives from or acts on the product of the preceding stage <*a* ~ *amplifier*> **b** an arrangement of fabric (e g lace) that falls in a wavy line **3** sthg falling or rushing forth in profusion <*a* ~ *of flowers*>

[2]**cascade** *vi* to fall (as if) in a cascade ~*vt* to connect in a cascade arrangement

cascara /kaˈskahrə‖kæˈskɑːrə/ *n* **1 cascara, cascara buckthorn** a buckthorn of the Pacific coast of the USA **2 cascara, cascara sagrada** the dried bark of cascara buckthorn, used as a mild laxative

[1]**case** /kays‖keɪs/ *n* **1a** a set of circumstances or conditions; a situation **b** a situation or object requiring investigation or action **2** an (inflectional) form of a noun, pronoun, or adjective indicating its grammatical relation to other words **3a** a suit or action that reaches a court of law **b(1)** the evidence supporting a conclusion <*the*

~ *for bringing back hanging*> **b(2)** an argument; *esp* one that is convincing **4a** an instance of disease or injury; *also* a patient suffering from a specific illness **b** an instance that directs attention to a situation or exhibits it in action; an example **5** a peculiar person; a character – infml – **in any case** without regard to or in spite of other considerations; whatever else is done or is the case – **in case 1** as a precaution; as a precaution against the event that <*take a towel* in case *you want to swim*> **2** *chiefly NAm* if – **in case of 1** in the event of <in case of *trouble, yell*> **2** for fear of; as a precaution against <*posted sentries* in case of *attack*>

[2]**case** *n* **1** a box or receptacle for holding sthg: e g **1a** a glass-panelled box for the display of specimens (e g in a museum) **b** *chiefly Br* a suitcase **c** a box together with its contents **2** a pair – chiefly with reference to pistols **3a** an outer covering <*a pastry* ~> **b** a stiff book cover that is made apart from the book and glued onto it **4** a shallow divided tray for holding printing type

[3]**case** *vt* **1** to enclose in or cover with a case; encase **2** to inspect or study (e g a house), esp with intent to rob – slang

ˈcaseˌbook /-ˌbook‖-ˌbʊk/ *n* a book containing records of illustrative cases for reference (e g in law or medicine)

case history *n* a record of history, environment, and relevant details (e g of individual behaviour or condition), esp for use in analysis, illustration, or diagnosis

casein /ˈkaysi·in, -seen‖ˈkeɪsiɪn, -siːn/ *n* a protein in milk that is precipitated by (lactic) acid or rennet, is the chief constituent of cheese, and is used in making plastics

ˈcase ˌlaw *n* law established by previous judicial decisions

casement /ˈkaysmənt‖ˈkeɪsmənt/ *n* (a window with) a sash that opens on hinges at the side

case study *n* an analysis of a person, institution, or community based on details concerning development, environment, etc

ˈcaseˌwork /-ˌwuhk‖-ˌwɜːk/ *n* social work involving direct consideration of the problems of individual people or families – **caseworker** *n*

[1]**cash** /kash‖kæʃ/ *n* **1** ready money **2** money or its equivalent paid promptly at the time of purchase

[2]**cash** *vt* **1** to pay or obtain cash for <~ *a cheque*> **2** to lead and win a bridge trick with (the highest remaining card of a suit)

ˌcash-and-ˈcarry *adj* sold for cash and collected by the purchaser

ˈcash ˌcrop *n* a crop (e g cotton or sugar beet) produced for sale rather than for use by the grower

ˈcash ˌdesk *n* a desk (e g in a shop) where payment for purchases is taken

cashew /ˈkashooh, kəˈshooh, kaˈshooh‖ˈkæʃuː, kəˈʃuː, kæˈʃuː/ *n* (the edible kidney-shaped nut of) a tropical American tree of the sumach family

[1]**cashier** /kaˈshiə‖kæˈʃɪə/ *vt* to dismiss, usu dishonourably, esp from service in the armed forces

[2]**cashier** *n* **1** one employed to receive cash from customers, esp in a shop **2** one who collects and records payments (e g in a bank)

cash in *vt* to convert into cash <cashed in *all his bonds*> ~*vi* to exploit a financial or other advantage – usu + *on* <cashing in *on the success of recent peace initiatives*>

cashmere /ˈkashmiə, -ˈ-‖ˈkæʃmɪə, -ˈ-/ *n* (yarn or fabric made from) fine wool from the undercoat of the Kashmir goat [*Cashmere* (now usu *Kashmir*), region of the Indian subcontinent]

ˈcash ˌregister *n* a machine that has a drawer for cash and is used to record and display the amount of each purchase and the money received

casing /ˈkaysing‖ˈkeɪsɪŋ/ *n* sthg that encases; material for encasing

casino /kəˈseenoh‖kəˈsiːnəʊ/ *n, pl* **casinos** a building or room used for social amusements, specif gambling [Italian, fr *casa* house, fr Latin, cabin]

cask /kahsk‖kɑːsk/ *n* **1** a barrel-shaped container, usu for holding liquids **2** a cask and its contents; *also* the quantity contained in a cask

casket /ˈkahskit‖ˈkɑːskɪt/ *n* **1** a small usu ornamental chest or box (e g for jewels) **2** *NAm* a coffin

casque /kask‖kæsk/ *n* a helmet

cassava /kəˈsahvə‖kəˈsɑːvə/ *n* (the fleshy edible starch-yielding rootstock of) any of several tropical plants of the spurge family

[1]**casserole** /ˈkasərohl‖ˈkæsərəʊl/ *n* **1** a heatproof dish with a cover in which food may be baked and served **2** the savoury food cooked and served in a casserole

[2]**casserole** *vt* to cook (food) slowly in a casserole

cassette, casette /kəˈset‖kəˈset/ *n* **1** a lightproof container for holding film or plates that can be inserted into a camera **2** a small case containing magnetic tape that can be inserted into a tape recorder

cassock /ˈkasək‖ˈkæsək/ *n* an ankle-length garment worn by the Roman Catholic and Anglican clergy or by laymen assisting in services [Middle French *casaque*, fr Persian *kazhāghand* padded jacket, fr *kazh* raw silk + *āghand* stuffed]

cassowary /ˈkasəˌweəri‖ˈkæsəˌweərɪ/ *n* any of several large flightless Australasian birds closely related to the emu

[1]**cast** /kahst‖kɑːst/ *vb* **cast** *vt* **1a** to cause to move by throwing <~ *a fishing line*> **b** to direct <~ *a shadow*> **c(1)** to send forth; emit <*the fire* ~s *a warm glow*> **c(2)** to place as if by throwing <*was* ~ *into prison*> **d** to deposit (a vote) formally **e(1)** to throw off or away <*the horse* ~ *a shoe*> **e(2)** to shed, moult **e(3)** *of an animal* to give birth to (prematurely) **2** to calculate (a horoscope) by means of astrology **3a** to arrange into a suitable form or order **b** to assign a part for (e g a play) or to (e g an actor) **4a** to shape (e g metal or plastic) by pouring into a mould when molten **b** to form by casting ~ *vi* **1** to throw out a line and lure with a fishing rod **2** to look round; seek – + *about* or *around* <*she* ~ *around uncertainly for somewhere to sit*> **3** to veer **4** to take form in a mould – **cast anchor** to lower the anchor; to anchor – **cast**

lots DRAW LOTS

[2]**cast** *n* **1a** an act of casting **b** a throw of a (fishing) line or net **2** *sing or pl in constr* the set of performers in a dramatic production **3** the distance to which sthg can be thrown **4a** a turning of the eye in a particular direction **b** a slight squint in the eye **5a** a reproduction (e g of a statue) formed by casting **b** an impression taken from an object with a molten or plastic substance **c** [1]PLASTER 3 **6a** a modification of a colour by a trace of some added colour <*grey with a greenish* ~> **b** a tinge, suggestion **7** a shape, appearance <*the delicate* ~ *of her features*> **8** the excrement of an earthworm

castanet /ˌkastəˈnet‖ˌkæstəˈnet/ *n* either of a pair of small usu wooden or plastic shells clicked together in the hand and used esp by dancers – usu pl

castaway /ˈkahstəˌway‖ˈkɑːstəˌweɪ/ *n* a person who is cast adrift or ashore as a result of a shipwreck or as a punishment – **castaway** *adj*

cast away *vt* to cause (a person or vessel) to be shipwrecked – usu passive

caste /kahst‖kɑːst/ *n* **1** any of the hereditary social groups in Hinduism that restrict the occupations of their members and their association with members of other castes **2a** a social class **b** the prestige conferred by caste **3** the system of social division by castes **4** a specialized form of a social insect (e g a soldier or worker ant) adapted to carry out a particular function in the colony

castellated /ˈkastiˌlaytid‖ˈkæstɪˌleɪtɪd/ *adj* having battlements like a castle

caster /ˈkahstə‖ˈkɑːstə/ *n* **1** a machine that casts type **2** [2]CASTOR 1, 2

caster sugar *n* finely granulated white sugar

castigate /ˈkastigayt‖ˈkæstɪgeɪt/ *vt* to punish or reprimand severely – fml – **castigator** *n*, **castigation** *n*

casting /ˈkahsting‖ˈkɑːstɪŋ/ *n* **1** sthg cast in a mould **2** sthg cast out or off

casting vote *n* a deciding vote cast in the event of a tie

ˌcast-ˈiron *adj* **1** capable of withstanding great strain; strong, unyielding <*a* ~ *stomach*> **2** impossible to disprove or falsify <*a* ~ *alibi*>

ˌcast ˈiron *n* a hard brittle alloy of iron, carbon, and silicon cast in a mould

[1]**castle** /ˈkahsl‖ˈkɑːsl/ *n* **1** a large fortified building or set of buildings **2** a stronghold **3** [3]ROOK

[2]**castle** *vb* to move (a chess king) 2 squares towards a rook and then place the rook on the square on the other side of the king

ˈcastˌoff /-ˌof‖-ˌɒf/ *n* **1** a cast-off article (e g of clothing) – usu pl **2** an estimate of the space that will be required for a given amount of text when printed

ˌcast-ˈoff *adj* thrown away or discarded, esp because outgrown or no longer wanted

cast off *vt* **1** to unfasten or untie (a boat or line) **2** to remove (a stitch or stitches) from a knitting needle in such a way as to prevent unravelling **3** to get rid of; discard <cast off *all restraint*> **4** to measure (an amount of text) to determine the space it will take up when printed ~ *vi* **1** to unfasten or untie a boat or a line **2** to finish a knitted article by casting off all the stitches

cast on *vb* to place (a stitch or stitches) on a knitting needle for beginning or enlarging a knitted article

[1]**castor** /ˈkahstə‖ˈkɑːstə/ *n* a strong-smelling substance consisting of dried glands taken from near the anus of the beaver, used esp in making perfume

[2]**castor, caster** /ˈkahstə‖ˈkɑːstə/ *n* **1** a small wheel set in a swivel mounting on the base of a piece of furniture, machinery, etc **2** a container with a perforated top for sprinkling powdered or granulated foods, esp sugar

ˌcastor ˈoil *n* a pale viscous oil from the beans of a tropical Old World plant, used esp as a purgative

cast out *vt* to drive out; expel

castrate /kaˈstrayt‖kæˈstreɪt/ *vt* **1** to deprive of sexual organs: **1a** to remove the testes of; geld **b** to remove the ovaries of; spay **2** to deprive of vitality or vigour; emasculate – **castrate** *n*, **castration** *n*

[1]**casual** /ˈkazh(y)ooəl, kazyooəl‖ˈkæʒ(j)ʊəl, kæzjʊəl/ *adj* **1** subject to, resulting from, or occurring by chance **2a** occurring without regularity; occasional **b** employed for irregular periods <*a* ~ *labourer*> **3a** feeling or showing little concern; nonchalant **b** informal, natural; *also* designed for informal wear – **casually** *adv*, **casualness** *n*

[2]**casual** *n* a casual or migratory worker

casualty /ˈkazh(y)ooəlti, -zyooəl-‖ˈkæʒ(j)ʊəltɪ, -zjʊəl-/ *n* **1** a member of a military force killed or wounded in action **2** a person or thing injured, lost, or destroyed

casuistry /ˈkazh(y)ooˌistri, ˈkazyooistri‖ˈkæʒ(j)ʊˌɪstrɪ, ˈkæzjʊɪstrɪ/ *n* plausible but false or misleading argument or reasoning, esp about morals – **casuist** *n*, **casuistic, casuistical** *adj*

[1]**cat** /kat‖kæt/ *n* **1a** a small domesticated flesh-eating mammal kept as a pet or for catching rats and mice **b** any of a family of carnivores that includes the domestic cat, lion, tiger, leopard, jaguar, cougar, lynx, and cheetah **2** a malicious woman **3** a cat-o'-nine-tails **4** a player or devotee of jazz – slang **5** a (male) person – slang

cataclysm /ˈkatəˌkliz(ə)m‖ˈkætəˌklɪz(ə)m/ *n* **1** a flood, deluge **2** a violent geological change of the earth's surface **3** a momentous event marked by violent upheaval and destruction [French *cataclysme*, fr Latin *cataclysmos*, fr Greek *kataklysmos*, fr *kataklyzein* to flood, fr *kata-* + *klyzein* to wash] – **cataclysmal, cataclysmic** *adj*

catacomb /ˈkatəˌkoohm‖ˈkætəˌkuːm/ *n* **1** a galleried subterranean cemetery with recesses for tombs **2** an underground passageway or group of passageways; a labyrinth *USE* often pl with sing. meaning

catafalque /ˈkatəˌfalk‖ˈkætəˌfælk/ *n* an ornamental structure supporting or bearing a coffin (e g during a lying in state)

catalepsy /ˈkatəˌlepsi‖ˈkætəˌlepsɪ/ *n* a trance-like state associated with schizophrenia in which the body remains rigid and immobile for prolonged periods – **cataleptic** *adj or n*

[1]**catalogue**, *NAm chiefly* **catalog** /ˈkatəlog‖ˈkætəlɒg/ **1** (a pamphlet or book containing) a complete list of items arranged systematically with descriptive details **2** a list, series *<a ~ of disasters>*

[2]**catalogue**, *NAm chiefly* **catalog** *vt* **1** to enter in a catalogue; *esp* to classify (books or information) descriptively **2** to make a catalogue of

catalysis /kəˈtaləsis‖kəˈtæləsɪs/ *n, pl* **catalyses** /-seez‖-siːz/ a change, esp an increase, in the rate of a chemical reaction induced by a catalyst

catalyst /ˈkatəlist‖ˈkætəlɪst/ *n* **1** a chemical agent that causes catalysis **2** a substance (e g an enzyme) that changes, esp increases, the rate of a chemical reaction but itself remains chemically unchanged **3** sby or sthg whose action inspires further and usu more important events

catamaran /ˈkatəmə,ran, -rahn, ,---ˈ-‖ˈkætəmə,ræn, -rɑːn, ,---ˈ-/ *n* **1** a raft made of logs or pieces of wood lashed together **2** a boat with twin hulls side by side [Tamil *kaṭṭumaram*, fr *kaṭṭu* to tie + *maram* tree]

,cat-and-ˈmouse *adj* consisting of continuous chasing and near captures and escapes

[1]**catapult** /ˈkatəpoolt, -pult‖ˈkætəpʊlt, -pʌlt/ *n* **1** an ancient military device for hurling missiles **2** a device for launching an aeroplane at flying speed (e g from an aircraft carrier) **3** *Br* a Y-shaped stick with a piece of elastic material fixed between the 2 prongs, used for shooting small objects (e g stones)

[2]**catapult** *vb* **1** to throw or launch (a missile) by means of a catapult **2** to (cause to) move suddenly or abruptly *<was* ~ed *from rags to riches overnight>*

cataract /ˈkatərakt‖ˈkætərækt/ *n* **1** clouding of (the enclosing membrane of) the lens of the eye; *also* the clouded area **2a** a (large steeply-descending) waterfall **b** steep rapids in a river **c** a downpour, deluge

catarrh /kəˈtah‖kəˈtɑː/ *n* (the mucus resulting from) inflammation of a mucous membrane, esp in the human nose and air passages – **catarrhal** *adj*

catastrophe /kəˈtastrəfi‖kəˈtæstrəfɪ/ *n* **1** a momentous, tragic, and unexpected event of extreme gravity **2** CATACLYSM 2 [Greek *katastrophē*, fr *katastrephein* to overturn, fr *kata* down + *strephein* to turn] – **catastrophic** *adj*, **catastrophically** *adv*

catatonia /,katəˈtohnyə, -ni·ə‖,kætəˈtəʊnjə, -nɪə/ *n* (a psychological disorder, esp schizophrenia, marked by) catalepsy – **catatonic** *adj or n*

ˈcat ,burglar *n, Br* a burglar who enters buildings by climbing up walls, drainpipes, etc

ˈcat,call /-,kawl‖-,kɔːl/ *n* a loud or raucous cry expressing disapproval – **catcall** *vb*

[1]**catch** /kach‖kætʃ/ *vb* **caught** /kawt‖kɔːt/ *vt* **1a** to capture or seize, esp after pursuit **b** to take or entangle (as if) in a snare <caught *in a web of deceit*> **c** to discover unexpectedly; surprise <caught *in the act*> **d** to check suddenly or momentarily **e** to cause to become entangled, fastened, or stuck *<~ a sleeve on a nail>* **2a** to seize; *esp* to intercept and keep hold of (a moving object), esp in the hands *<~ the ball>* **b** to dismiss (a batsman in cricket) by catching the ball after it has been hit and before it has touched the ground **3a** to contract; become infected with *<~ a cold>* **b** to hit, strike *<~ the mood of the occasion>* **c** to receive the force or impact of **4** to attract, arrest *<tried to ~ his attention>* **5** to take or get momentarily or quickly *<~ a glimpse of her friend>* **6** to be in time for *<~ the bus>* *<~ the last post>* **7** to grasp with the senses or the mind ~ *vi* **1** to become caught **2** *of a fire* to start to burn **3** BURN 3 *<the sugar* caught *on the bottom of the pan>* – **catchable** *adj* – **catch a crab** to make a faulty stroke in rowing – **catch it** to incur blame, reprimand, or punishment – infml – **catch one's breath 1** to rest long enough to restore normal breathing **2** to stop breathing briefly, usu under the influence of strong emotion – **catch someone on the hop** to find sby unprepared – infml

[2]**catch** *n* **1** sthg caught; *esp* the total quantity caught at one time *<a large ~ of fish>* **2** a game in which a ball is thrown and caught **3** sthg that retains or fastens *<the safety ~ of her brooch was broken>* **4** an often humorous or coarse round for 3 or more voices **5** a concealed difficulty; a snag *<there must be a ~ in it somewhere>* **6** an eligible marriage partner – infml

ˈcatch ,crop *n* a crop planted between the rows of the main crop or grown between the harvesting of a main crop and the planting of another

catcher /ˈkachə‖ˈkætʃə/ *n* a baseball player who stands behind the batter to catch balls that the batter fails to hit

catching /ˈkaching‖ˈkætʃɪŋ/ *adj* **1** infectious, contagious **2** alluring, attractive

ˈcatchment ,area *n* **1** the area from which a lake, reservoir, etc gets its rainwater **2** a geographical area from which people are drawn to attend a particular school, hospital, etc

catch on *vi* **1** to become popular **2** to understand, learn – often + *to*; infml

catch out *vt* to expose or detect in wrongdoing or error – usu passive

catchpenny /ˈkach,peni‖ˈkætʃ,penɪ; *adj also* ˈkachpəni‖ˈkætʃpənɪ/ *n or adj* (sthg) worthless but designed to appear attractive, esp by being showy – derog

ˈcatch,phrase /-,frayz‖-,freɪz/ *n* an arresting phrase that enjoys short-lived popularity

catchup /ˈkachəp‖ˈkætʃəp/ *n, chiefly NAm* ketchup

catch up *vt* **1a** to pick up, often abruptly <caught *the child* up *in her arms*> **b** to ensnare, entangle – usu + *up*; usu passive **c** to engross, absorb – usu + *in*; usu passive **2** to act or move fast enough to draw level with *<we'll* catch *you* up *later>* ~ *vi* **1** to act or move fast enough to draw level *<we'll* catch up *with you later>* **2** to acquaint oneself or deal with sthg belatedly – + *on* or *with* *<I must* catch up *on the bookkeeping>*

ˈcatch,word /-,wuhd‖-,wɜːd/ *n* **1** a word placed so as to assist a reader when turning a page **2** a word or expression associated with some school of thought or political movement; a slogan

catchy /ˈkachi‖ˈkætʃɪ/ *adj* **1** tending to attract the interest or attention *<a ~ title>* **2** easy to remember and reproduce <*a ~ tune*>

catechism /ˈkatəˌkiz(ə)m‖ˈkætəˌkɪz(ə)m/ *n* **1** instruction by question and answer **2** a manual for catechizing; *specif* a summary of religious doctrine, often in the form of questions and answers **3** a set of formal questions put as a test – **catechismal** *adj*

catech·ize, -ise /ˈkatəˌkiez‖ˈkætəˌkaɪz/ *vt* **1** to teach systematically, esp by using question and answer; *specif* to teach the articles of faith of a religion in such a manner **2** to question systematically or searchingly – **catechist** *n*, **catechizer** *n*, **catechization** *n*

categorical /ˌkatəˈgorikl‖ˌkætəˈgɒrɪkl/ *also* **ˌcateˈgoric** /-ˈgorik‖-ˈgɒrɪk/ *adj* absolute, unqualified <*a ~ denial*> – **categorically** *adv*

categor·ize, -ise /ˈkatəgəˌriez‖ˈkætəgəˌraɪz/ *vt* to put into a category; classify – **categorization** *n*

category /ˈkatəg(ə)ri‖ˈkætəg(ə)rɪ/ *n* **1** a general or fundamental form or class of terms, things, or ideas (e g in philosophy) **2** a division within a system of classification

cater /ˈkaytə‖ˈkeɪtə/ *vi* **1** to provide and serve a supply of usu prepared food **2** to supply what is required or desired – usu + *for* or *to* <*~ed to her whims all day long*> – **caterer** *n*

caterpillar /ˈkatəˌpilə‖ˈkætəˌpɪlə/ *n* a wormlike larva, specif of a butterfly or moth [Old North French *catepelose*, lit., hairy cat]

Caterpillar *trademark* – used for a tractor designed to travel over rough or soft ground and propelled by 2 endless metal belts

caterwaul /ˈkatəˌwawl‖ˈkætəˌwɔːl/ *vi* to cry noisily – **caterwaul** *n*

ˈcatˌfish /-ˌfish‖-ˌfɪʃ/ *n* any of numerous large-headed fishes with long barbels

ˈcatˌgut /-ˌgut‖-ˌgʌt/ *n* a tough cord usu made from sheep intestines and used esp for the strings of musical instruments and tennis rackets and for surgical sutures

catharsis /kəˈthahsis‖kəˈθɑːsɪs/ *n, pl* **catharses** /-seez‖-siːz/ **1** purgation **2** purification or purgation of the emotions through drama **3** the process of bringing repressed ideas and feelings to consciousness and expressing them, esp during psychoanalysis – **cathartic** *adj*

cathedral /kəˈtheedrəl‖kəˈθiːdrəl/ *n* a church that is the official seat of a diocesan bishop

ˈcatherine ˌwheel /ˈkath(ə)rin‖ˈkæθ(ə)rɪn/ *n, often cap C* a firework in the form of a wheel that spins as it burns [St *Catherine* of Alexandria (died about 307), Christian martyr tortured on a spiked wheel]

catheter /ˈkathətə‖ˈkæθətə/ *n* a tubular device for insertion into a hollow body part (e g a blood vessel), usu to inject or draw off fluids or to keep a passage open – **catheterize** *vt*

cathode /ˈkaˌthohd‖ˈkæˌθəʊd/ *n* the electrode by which electrons leave an external circuit and enter a device; *specif* the positive terminal of a primary cell or of a storage battery that is delivering current – **cathodal** *adj*, **cathodic** *adj*

cathode-ray tube *n* a vacuum tube in which a beam of electrons is projected onto a fluorescent screen to provide a visual display (e g a television picture)

catholic /ˈkath(ə)lik‖ˈkæθ(ə)lɪk/ *adj* **1** comprehensive, universal; *esp* broad in sympathies or tastes **2** *cap* **2a** of or forming the entire body of worshippers that constitutes the Christian church **b** of or forming the ancient undivided Christian church or a church claiming historical continuity from it; *specif* ROMAN CATHOLIC – **catholicism** *n*, **catholicize** *vb*

Catholic *n* a member of a Catholic church; *specif* ROMAN CATHOLIC

catholicity /ˌkathəˈlisəti‖ˌkæθəˈlɪsətɪ/ *n* **1** liberality of sentiments or views **2** universality

catkin /ˈkatˌkin‖ˈkætˌkɪn/ *n* a hanging spike-shaped densely crowded group of flowers without petals (e g in a willow)

catmint /-ˌmint‖-mɪnt/ *n* a blue-flowered plant with a strong scent that is attractive to cats

ˈcatˌnap /-ˌnap‖-ˌnæp/ *n* a brief period of sleep, esp during the day – **catnap** *vi*

ˈcatˌnip /-ˌnip‖-ˌnɪp/ *n* catmint

ˌcat-o'-ˈnine-ˌtails *n, pl* **cat-o'-nine-tails** a whip made of usu 9 knotted cords fastened to a handle

cat's cradle *n* a game in which a string looped in a pattern on the fingers of one person's hands is transferred to the hands of another so as to form a different figure

ˈcat's-ˌeye *n, pl* **cat's-eyes** **1** any of various gems (e g a chrysoberyl or a chalcedony) that reflect a narrow band of light from within **2** a small reflector set in a road, usu in a line with others, to reflect vehicle headlights

ˈcat's-ˌpaw *n, pl* **cat's-paws** **1** a light breeze that ruffles the surface of water in irregular patches **2** sby used by another as a tool or dupe **3** a hitch in a rope onto which a tackle may be hooked

ˈcatˌsuit /-ˌs(y)ooht‖-ˌs(j)uːt/ *n* a tightly fitting 1-piece garment combining top and trousers

catsup /ˈkatsəp‖ˈkætsəp/ *n, chiefly NAm* ketchup

cattle /ˈkatl‖ˈkætl/ *n, pl* bovine animals kept on a farm, ranch, etc

ˈcattle ˌgrid *n, Br* a shallow ditch in a road covered by parallel bars spaced far enough apart to prevent livestock from crossing

catty /ˈkati‖ˈkætɪ/ *adj* slyly spiteful; malicious – **cattily** *adv*, **cattiness** *n*

ˈcatˌwalk /-ˌwawk‖-ˌwɔːk/ *n* **1** a narrow walkway (e g round a machine) **2** a narrow stage in the centre of a room on which fashion shows are held

Caucasian /kawˈkayzh(y)ən‖kɔːˈkeɪʒ(j)ən/ *adj* **1** of Caucasus or its inhabitants **2** of the white race of mankind as classified according to physical features – **Caucasian** *n*, **Caucasoid** *adj or n*

caucus /ˈkawkəs‖ˈkɔːkəs/ *n* a closed political meeting to decide on policy, select candidates, etc

caudal /ˈkawdl‖ˈkɔːdl/ *adj* **1** of or being a tail **2** situated at or directed towards the hind part of the body

caught /kawt‖kɔːt/ *past of* CATCH

caul /kawl‖kɔːl/ *n* **1** the large fatty fold of membrane covering the intestines **2** the inner foetal membrane of higher vertebrates, esp when covering the head at birth

cauldron, caldron /ˈkawldrən‖ˈkɔːldrən/ *n* **1** a large open metal pot used for cooking over an open fire **2** sthg that resembles a boiling cauldron <*a ~ of intense emotions*>

cauliflower /ˈkoli,flowə‖ˈkɒlɪ,flaʊə/ *n* (a plant closely related to the cabbage with) a compact head of usu white undeveloped flowers eaten as a vegetable

caulk, calk /kawk‖kɔːk/ *vt* to stop up and make watertight (e g the seams of a boat, cracks in wood, etc) by filling with a waterproof material – **caulker** *n*

causal /ˈkawzl‖ˈkɔːzl/ *adj* **1** expressing or indicating cause; causative **2** of or being a cause <*the ~ agent of a disease*> – **causally** *adv*

causality /kawˈzaləti‖kɔːˈzælətɪ/ *n* **1** a causal quality or agency **2** the relation between a cause and its effect

causation /kawˈzaysh(ə)n‖kɔːˈzeɪʃ(ə)n/ *n* **1** the act or process of causing **2** the act or agency by which an effect is produced

causative /ˈkawzətiv‖ˈkɔːzətɪv/ *adj* **1** effective or operating as a cause or agent **2** expressing causation – **causative** *n*, **causatively** *adv*

[1]**cause** /kawz‖kɔːz/ *n* **1a** sby or sthg that brings about an effect **b** an agent that brings sthg about **c** a reason for an action or condition; a motive **2** a ground for legal action **3** a principle or movement worth defending or supporting – **causeless** *adj*

[2]**cause** *vt* to serve as the cause or occasion of – **causer** *n*

'cause /kəz‖kəz; *strong* koz‖kɒz/ *conj* because – nonstandard

cause célèbre /,kohz sayˈleb(rə) ‖,kəʊz seɪˈleb(rə) (*Fr* koːz selɛbr)/ *n, pl* **causes célèbres** /~ ~/ **1** a legal case that excites widespread interest **2** a notorious incident or episode [French, lit., celebrated case]

causeway /ˈkawz,way‖ˈkɔːz,weɪ/ *n* a raised road or path, esp across wet ground or water

caustic /ˈkostik, ˈkaw-‖ˈkɒstɪk, ˈkɔː-/ *adj* **1** capable of destroying or eating away by chemical action; corrosive **2** incisive, biting < ~ *wit*> – **caustically** *adv*, **causticity** *n*

cauter·ize, -ise /ˈkawtə,riez‖ˈkɔːtə,raɪz/ *vt* to sear or destroy (e g a wound or body tissue) with a cautery, esp in order to rid of infection – **cauterization** *n*

[1]**caution** /ˈkawsh(ə)n‖ˈkɔːʃ(ə)n/ *n* **1** a warning, admonishment; *specif* an official warning given to sby who has committed a minor offence **2** prudent forethought intended to minimize risk; care **3** sby or sthg that causes astonishment or amusement – infml <*she's a proper* ~ > – **cautionary** *adj*

[2]**caution** *vt* **1a** to advise caution to; warn; *specif* to warn (sby under arrest) that his/her words will be recorded and may be used in evidence **b** to admonish, reprove; *specif* to give an official warning to < ~ed *for disorderly conduct*> **2** *of a soccer referee* [2]BOOK 2b ~*vi* to urge, warn < ~ed *against an excess of alcohol*>

cautious /ˈkawshəs‖ˈkɔːʃəs/ *adj* careful, prudent – **cautiously** *adv*, **cautiousness** *n*

cavalcade /ˈkavl,kayd, ,--ˈ-‖ˈkævl,keɪd, ,--ˈ-/ *n* **1** PROCESSION 1; *esp* one of riders or carriages **2** a dramatic sequence or procession; a series

[1]**cavalier** /,kavəˈliə‖,kævəˈlɪə/ *n* **1** a gentleman of former times trained in arms and horsemanship; *specif* a mounted soldier **2** a gallant gentleman of former times; *esp* one in attendance on a lady **3** *cap* an adherent of Charles I of England, esp during the Civil War

[2]**cavalier** *adj* **1** debonair **2** given to or characterized by offhand dismissal of important matters **3** *cap* of the party of Charles I of England – **cavalierly** *adv*

cavalry /ˈkavəlri‖ˈkævəlrɪ/ *n, sing or pl in constr* **1** a branch of an army consisting of mounted troops **2** a branch of a modern army consisting of armoured vehicles

[1]**cave** /kayv‖keɪv/ *n* **1** a natural chamber (e g underground or in the side of a hill or cliff) having a usu horizontal opening on the surface **2** *Br* a formal withdrawing or group of people withdrawing from a political party [Old French, fr Latin *cava*, fr *cavus* hollow]

[2]**cave** *vt* to form a cave in or under; hollow out ~*vi* to explore cave or pothole systems – **caver** *n*

[3]**cave** /kayˈvee‖keɪˈviː/ *interj, Br* – used as a warning call among schoolchildren, esp at public school; compare KEEP CAVE

caveat /ˈkavi·at, ˈkay-‖ˈkævɪæt, ˈkeɪ-/ *n* **1** a cautionary remark or statement; a warning – fml **2** an official notice to a court to suspend a proceeding until the opposition has been heard [Latin, let him beware, fr *cavēre* to beware]

,caveat ˈemptor /ˈemptaw‖ˈemptɔː/ *n* the principle in commerce which states that without a guarantee the buyer takes the risk of quality upon him-/herself

cave in *vt* to cause to fall in or collapse ~ *vi* **1** to fall in or collapse **2** to cease to resist; submit – infml

ˈcave,man /-,man‖-,mæn/ *n* **1** a cave dweller, esp of the Stone Age **2** a man who acts in a rough primitive manner, esp towards women

cavern /ˈkavən‖ˈkævən/ *n* a large usu underground chamber or cave – **cavernous** *adj*, **cavernously** *adv*

caviar, caviare /ˈkaviah‖ˈkævɪɑː/ *n* **1** the salted roe of large fish (e g sturgeon) eaten as a delicacy **2** sthg considered too delicate or lofty for mass appreciation <*will be ~ to the multitude*>

cavil /ˈkavil. -vl‖ˈkævɪl. -vl/ *vi* **-ll-** (*NAm* **-l-**, **-ll-**), to raise trivial and frivolous objections – **cavil** *n*, **caviller** *n*

cavity /ˈkavəti‖ˈkævətɪ/ *n* an empty or hollowed-out space within a mass; *specif* a decaying hollow in a tooth

cavity wall *n* a wall built in 2 thicknesses, the air space between providing insulation

cavort /kəˈvawt‖kəˈvɔːt/ *vi* **1** to prance **2** to engage in extravagant behaviour

cavy /ˈkayvi‖ˈkeɪvɪ/ *n* a guinea pig or related short-tailed S American rodent

caw /kaw‖kɔː/ *vi* to utter (a sound like) the harsh raucous cry of the crow – **caw** *n*

cay /kee, kay‖kiː, keɪ/ *n* a low island or reef of sand or coral

,cayenne ˈpepper /kayˈen‖keɪˈen/ *n* **1** a pungent red condiment consisting of the ground dried pods and seeds of hot peppers **2** a hot pepper, esp a cultivated capsicum

cayman, caiman /ˈkaymən, ˈkie-‖ˈkeɪmən,

ˈkaɪ-/ *n*, any of several Central and S American reptiles related to the alligators

[1]**cease** /sees‖siːs/ *vb* to bring or come to an end; stop

[2]**cease** *n* stopping, cessation <*without* ~>

ˌ**cease-**ˈ**fire** *n* (a military order for) a cessation of firing or of active hostilities

ˈ**ceaseless** /-lis‖-lɪs/ *adj* continuing endlessly; constant – **ceaselessly** *adv*, **ceaselessness** *n*

cedar /ˈseedə‖ˈsiːdə/ *n* (the fragrant wood of) any of a genus of usu tall evergreen coniferous trees of the pine family

cede /seed‖siːd/ *vt* to yield or surrender (e g territory), usu by treaty – **ceder** *n*

cedilla /səˈdilə‖səˈdɪlə/ *n* a mark, ¸ placed under a letter (e g ç in French) to indicate an alteration or modification of its usual phonetic value

ceiling /ˈseeling‖ˈsiːlɪŋ/ *n* **1** the overhead inside surface of a room **2** the height above the ground of the base of the lowest layer of clouds **3** a prescribed or actual maximum height at which an aircraft can fly **4** an upper usu prescribed limit <*a* ~ *on rents and wages*>

celandine /ˈselənˌdien‖ˈselənˌdaɪn/ *n* **1** *also* **greater celandine** a yellow-flowered biennial plant of the poppy family **2** *also* **lesser celandine** a common yellow-flowered European perennial plant of the buttercup family

celebrant /ˈselibrənt‖ˈselɪbrənt/ *n* the priest officiating at the Eucharist

celebrate /ˈselibrayt‖ˈselɪbreɪt/ *vt* **1** to perform (a sacrament or solemn ceremony) publicly and with appropriate rites **2a** to mark (a holy day or feast day) ceremonially **b** to mark (a special occasion) with festivities or suspension of routine activities **3** to hold up for public acclaim; extol <*his poetry* ~s *the glory of nature*> ~ *vi* **1** to officiate at a religious ceremony **2** to observe a special occasion, usu with festivities – **celebration** *n*, **celebrator** *n*, **celebratory** *adj*

ˈ**celeˌbrated** *adj* widely known and often referred to – **celebratedness** *n*

celebrity /səˈlebrəti‖səˈlebrətɪ/ *n* **1** the state of being famous **2** a well-known and widely acclaimed person

celerity /səˈlerəti‖səˈlerətɪ/ *n* rapidity of motion or action – fml

celery /ˈseləri‖ˈselərɪ/ *n* a European plant of the carrot family with leafstalks eaten as a vegetable

celestial /səˈlesti·əl‖səˈlestɪəl/ *adj* **1** of or suggesting heaven or divinity; divine **2** of or in the sky or visible heavens <*a* ~ *body*> – **celestially** *adv*

celestial sphere *n* an imaginary sphere of infinite radius against which the celestial bodies appear to be projected

celibate /ˈselibət‖ˈselɪbət/ *n* one who is unmarried and does not have sexual intercourse, esp because of a religious vow – **celibacy** *n*, **celibate** *adj*

cell /sel‖sel/ *n* **1** a 1-room dwelling occupied esp by a hermit or recluse **2a** a barely furnished room for 1 person (e g in a convent or monastery) **b** a small room in a prison for 1 or more inmates **3** a small compartment (e g in a honeycomb), receptacle, cavity (e g one containing seeds in a plant ovary), or bounded space **4** the smallest structural unit of living matter consisting of nuclear and cytoplasmic material bounded by a semipermeable membrane and capable of functioning either alone or with others in all fundamental life processes **5a** a vessel (e g a cup or jar) containing electrodes and an electrolyte either for generating electricity by chemical action or for use in electrolysis **b** a single unit in a device for producing an electrical effect as a result of exposure to radiant energy **6** the primary unit of a political, esp Communist, organization **7** a basic subdivision of a computer memory that is addressable and can hold 1 unit (e g a word) of a computer's basic operating data

[1]**cellar** /ˈselə‖ˈselə/ *n* **1** an underground room; *esp* one used for storage **2** an individual's stock of wine

[2]**cellar** *vt* to store or place (e g wine) in a cellar

cellarage /ˈselərij‖ˈselərɪdʒ/ *n* **1** cellar space, esp for storage **2** the charge made for storage in a cellar

cell division *n* the process by which 2 daughter cells are formed from a parent cell

cello /ˈcheloh‖ˈtʃeləʊ/ *n, pl* **cellos** a large stringed instrument of the violin family tuned an octave below the viola – **cellist** *n*

cellophane /ˈseləˌfayn‖ˈseləˌfeɪn/ *n* regenerated cellulose in the form of thin transparent sheets, used esp for wrapping goods

cellular /ˈselyoolə‖ˈseljʊlə/ *adj* **1** of, relating to, or consisting of cells **2** containing cavities; porous **3** having a very open weave <*a* ~ *blanket*> – **cellularly** *adv*, **cellularity** *n*

cellular radio *n* a computer-controlled communications system for users of telephones in cars

celluloid /ˈselyooˌloyd‖ˈseljʊˌlɔɪd/ *n* film for the cinema; *also* FILM 3 – **celluloid** *adj*

Celluloid *trademark* – used for a tough inflammable thermoplastic composed essentially of cellulose nitrate and camphor

cellulose /ˈselyooˌlohs‖ˈseljʊˌləʊs/ *n* **1** a polysaccharide of glucose units that constitutes the chief part of plant cell walls, occurs naturally in cotton, kapok, etc, and is the raw material of many manufactured goods (e g paper, rayon, and cellophane) **2** paint or lacquer of which the main constituent is cellulose nitrate or acetate

Celsius /ˈselsi·əs‖ˈselsɪəs/ *adj* relating to, conforming to, or being a scale of temperature on which water freezes at 0° and boils at 100° under standard conditions [Anders *Celsius* (1701-44), Swedish astronomer]

Celt, Kelt /kelt‖kelt/ *n* **1** a member of a division of the early Indo-European peoples extending at various times from the British Isles and Spain to Asia Minor **2** a modern Gael, Highland Scot, Irishman, Welshman, Cornishman, Manxman, or Breton

[1]**Celtic, Keltic** /ˈkeltik‖ˈkeltɪk/ *adj* (characteristic) of the Celts or their languages

[2]**Celtic, Keltic** *n* a branch of Indo-European languages comprising Welsh, Cornish, Breton, Irish, Scots Gaelic, and Manx, which is now confined to Brittany and parts of the British Isles – **Celticist** *n*

[1]**cement** /si'ment‖sɪ'ment/ *n* **1** a powder consisting of alumina, silica, lime, iron oxide, and magnesia pulverized together and burnt in a kiln, that is used as the binding agent in mortar and concrete **2** a substance (e g a glue or adhesive) used for sticking objects together **3** sthg serving to unite firmly **4** an adhesive preparation used for filling teeth, attaching dental crowns, etc **6** concrete – not used technically [Old French *ciment*, fr Latin *caementum* stone chips used in making mortar, fr *caedere* to cut] – **cementitious** *adj*

[2]**cement** *vt* **1** to unite or make firm (as if) by the application of cement **2** to overlay with concrete

cemetery /'semətri‖'semətrɪ/ *n* a burial ground; *esp* one not in a churchyard

cenotaph /'senə,tahf‖'senə,tɑːf/ *n* a tomb or monument erected in honour of a person or group of people whose remains are elsewhere; *specif*, *cap* that standing in Whitehall in London in memory of the dead of WWs I and II [French, *cénotaphe*, fr Latin *cenotaphium*, fr Greek *kenotaphion*, fr *kenos* empty + *taphos* tomb]

[1]**censor** /'sensə‖'sensə/ *n* **1** either of 2 magistrates of early Rome who acted as census takers, inspectors of morals, etc **2** an official who examines publications, films, letters, etc and has the power to suppress objectionable (e g obscene or libellous) matter **3** a supposed mental agency that represses certain unacceptable ideas and desires before they reach consciousness – **censorial** *adj*

[2]**censor** *vt* to subject to censorship

censorious /sen'sawri·əs‖sen'sɔːrɪəs/ *adj* severely critical; given to censure – **censoriously** *adv*, **censoriousness** *n*

censorship /'sensə,ship‖'sensə,ʃɪp/ *n* **1** the act, practice, or duties of a censor; *esp* censorial control **2** the office, power, or term of a Roman censor **3** the repression in the mind of unacceptable ideas and desires

[1]**censure** /'senshə‖'senʃə/ *n* **1** a judgment involving condemnation **2** the act of blaming or condemning sternly **3** an official reprimand

[2]**censure** *vt* to find fault with and criticize as blameworthy – **censurable** *adj*, **censurer** *n*

census /'sensəs‖'sensəs/ *n* **1** a periodic counting of the population and gathering of related statistics (e g age, sex, or social class) carried out by government **2** a usu official count or tally

cent /sent‖sent/ *n* (a coin or note representing) a unit worth $^1/_{100}$ of the basic money unit of certain countries (e g the American dollar)

centaur /'sen,taw‖'sen,tɔː/ *n* any of a race of mythological creatures having the head, arms, and upper body of a man, and the lower body and back legs of a horse

centavo /sen'tahvoh‖sen'tɑːvəʊ/ *n, pl* **centavos** (a coin or note representing) a unit worth $^1/_{100}$ of the basic money unit of certain Spanish or Portuguese-speaking countries (e g Chile, Cuba, Mexico, Portugal)

centenarian /,sentə'neəri·ən‖,sentə'neərɪən/ *n* sby who is (more than) 100 years old – **centenarian** *adj*

centenary /sen'teenəri, -'tenəri‖sen'tiːnərɪ, -'tenərɪ/ *n* (the celebration of) a 100th anniversary – **centenary** *adj*

centennial /sen'teni·əl‖sen'tenɪəl/ *n, chiefly NAm* a centenary – **centennial** *adj*, **centennially** *adv*

center /'sentə‖'sentə/ *vb or n, NAm* (to) centre

centi- /senti-‖sentɪ-/ *comb form* **1** hundred <centi*pede*> **2** one hundredth (10^{-2}) part of (a specified unit) <centi*metre*>

centigrade /'senti,grayd‖'sentɪ,greɪd/ *adj* Celsius

centigram /'senti,gram‖'sentɪ,græm/ *n* one hundredth of a gram

centime /'sonteem‖'sɒntiːm/ *n* (a note or coin representing) a unit worth $^1/_{100}$ of the basic money unit of certain French-speaking countries (e g Algeria, Belgium, France)

centimetre /'sentimeetə‖'sentɪmiːtə/ *n* one hundredth of a metre (about 0.4in)

centipede /'senti,peed‖'sentɪ,piːd/ *n* any of a class of many-segmented arthropods with each segment bearing 1 pair of legs

central /'sentrəl‖'sentrəl/ *adj* **1** containing or constituting a centre **2** of primary importance; principal <*the ~ character of the novel*> **3a** at, in, or near the centre <*the plains of ~ N America*> **b** easily accessible; convenient <*our house is very ~ for the shops*> **4** having overall power or control <*decided by the ~ committee*> **5** of, originating in, or comprising the central nervous system – **centrally** *adv*, **centrality** *n*

,central 'heating *n* a system of heating whereby heat is produced at a central source (e g a boiler) and carried by pipes to radiators or air vents throughout a building (e g a house or office block)

centralism /'sentrə,liz(ə)m‖'sentrə,lɪz(ə)m/ *n* the practice or principle of concentrating power and control in a central authority – **centralist** *n or adj*, **centralistic** *adj*

central·ize, -ise /'sentrə,liez‖'sentrə,laɪz/ *vi* to come to or gather round a centre; *specif* to gather under central control (e g of government) *~vt* to bring to a centre; consolidate; *specif* to bring (power, authority, etc) under central control – **centralizer** *n*, **centralization** *n*

,central 'nervous ,system *n* the part of the nervous system which in vertebrates consists of the brain and spinal cord and which coordinates the activity of the entire nervous system

[1]**centre,** *NAm chiefly* **center** /'sentə‖'sentə/ *n* **1** the point round which a circle or sphere is described; *broadly* the centre of symmetry **2a** a place, esp a collection of buildings, round which a usu specified activity is concentrated <*a shopping ~*> **b** sby or sthg round which interest is concentrated <*the ~ of the controversy*> **c** a source from which sthg originates <*a propaganda ~*> **d** a region of concentrated population <*an urban ~*> **3** a group of nerve cells having a common function <*respiratory ~*> **4** the middle part (e g of a stage) **5** *often cap* a group, party, etc holding moderate political views **6a** a player occupying a middle position in the forward line of a team (e g in football or hockey) **b** an instance of passing the ball from a wing to the centre of a pitch or court (e g in football)

²centre, *NAm chiefly* **center** *vi* **1** to have a centre; focus – usu + *round* or *on* **2** to come to or towards a centre or central area **3** to centre a ball, puck, etc ~ *vt* **1** to place or fix in or at a centre or central area <~ *the picture on the wall*> **2** to gather to a centre; concentrate <~s *her hopes on her son*> **3** to adjust (e g lenses) so that the axes coincide **4** to pass (e g a ball or puck) from either side towards the middle of the playing area

'centre,board /-ˌbawd‖-ˌbɔːd/ *n* a retractable keel used esp in small yachts

ˌcentre-'forward *n* (the position of) a player in hockey, soccer, etc positioned in the middle of the forward line

ˌcentre of 'gravity *n* **1** CENTRE OF MASS **2** the point at which the entire weight of a body may be considered as concentrated so that if supported at this point the body would remain in equilibrium in any position

ˌcentre of 'mass *n* the point at which the entire mass of a body or system of bodies may be considered as concentrated

'centre,piece /-ˌpees‖-ˌpiːs/ *n* **1** an ornament (e g of flowers) placed in the centre of a table **2** the most important or outstanding item

centrifugal /ˌsentri'fyoohg(ə)l, sen'trifyoog-(ə)l‖ˌsentrɪ'fjuːg(ə)l, sen'trɪfjʊg(ə)l/ *adj* **1** proceeding or acting in a direction away from a centre or axis **2** using or acting by centrifugal force <*a* ~ *pump*> **3** tending away from centralization; separatist

centrifugal force *n* the force that appears to act outwardly from the centre of rotation of an object moving along a circular path

centrifuge /'sentriˌfyoohj, -ˌfyoohzh‖'sentrɪ-ˌfjuːdʒ, -ˌfjuːʒ/ *vt or n* (to subject to centrifugal action, esp in) a machine using centrifugal force, esp for separating substances of different densities – **centrifugation** *n*

centripetal /'sentriˌpetl, sen'tripitl‖'sentrɪ-ˌpetl, sen'trɪpɪtl/ *adj* **1** proceeding or acting in a direction towards a centre or axis **2** tending towards centralization; unifying – **centripetally** *adv*

centrist /'sentrist‖'sentrɪst/ *n, often cap* a member of a moderate party; *broadly* one holding moderate political views – **centrism** *n*

centurion /sen'tyooəri·ən‖sen'tjʊərɪən/ *n* an officer commanding a Roman century

century /'senchəri‖'sentʃərɪ/ *n* **1** a subdivision of the ancient Roman legion orig consisting of 100 men **2** a group, sequence, or series of 100 like things; *specif* 100 runs made by a cricketer in 1 innings **3** a period of 100 years; *esp* any of the 100-year periods reckoned forwards or backwards from the conventional date of the birth of Christ

cephalic /si'falik‖sɪ'fælɪk/ *adj* **1** of or relating to the head **2** directed towards or situated on, in, or near the head – **cephalically** *adv*

cephalopod /'sef(ə)ləˌpod‖'sef(ə)ləˌpɒd/ *n* any of a class of tentacled molluscs that includes the squids, cuttlefishes, and octopuses – **cephalopod** *adj*, **cephalopodan** *adj or n*

¹ceramic /sə'ramik‖sə'ræmɪk/ *adj* of or being (the manufacture of) a product (e g porcelain or brick) made from a nonmetallic mineral (e g clay) by firing at high temperatures

²ceramic *n* **1** *pl but sing in constr* the art or process of making ceramic articles **2** a product of ceramic manufacture – **ceramist, ceramicist** *n*

¹cereal /'siəri·əl‖'sɪərɪəl/ *adj* of or relating to (the plants that produce) grain [French *céréale*, fr Latin *cerealis* of Ceres, of grain, fr *Ceres*, Roman goddess of agriculture]

²cereal *n* **1** (a grass or other plant yielding) grain suitable for food **2** a food made from grain and usu eaten with milk and sugar at breakfast

cerebellum /ˌserə'beləm‖ˌserə'beləm/ *n, pl* **cerebellums, cerebella** /-lə‖-lə/ a large part of the back of the brain which projects outwards and is concerned esp with coordinating muscles and maintaining equilibrium – **cerebellar** *adj*

cerebral /'serəbrəl‖'serəbrəl/ *adj* **1a** of the brain or the intellect **b** of or being the cerebrum **2a** appealing to the intellect <~ *drama*> **b** primarily intellectual in nature <*a* ~ *society*> – **cerebrally** *adv*

cerebrate /'serəbrayt‖'serəbreɪt/ *vi* to use the mind; think – fml – **cerebration** *n*

cerebrum /'seribrəm‖'serɪbrəm/ *n, pl* **cerebrums, cerebra** /-brə‖-brə/ **1** BRAIN 1a **2** the expanded front portion of the brain that in higher mammals overlies the rest of the brain and consists of the 2 cerebral hemispheres

¹ceremonial /ˌserə'mohnyəl, -ni·əl‖ˌserə-'məʊnjəl, -nɪəl/ *adj* marked by, involved in, or belonging to ceremony – **ceremonialism** *n*, **ceremonialist** *n*, **ceremonially** *adv*

²ceremonial *n* **1a** a ceremonial act or action **b** a usu prescribed system of formalities or rituals **2** (a book containing) the order of service in the Roman Catholic church

ceremonious /ˌserə'mohnyəs, -ni·əs‖ˌserə-'məʊnjəs, -nɪəs/ *adj* **1** ceremonial **2** devoted to form and ceremony; punctilious – **ceremoniously** *adv*, **ceremoniousness** *n*

ceremony /'serəməni‖'serəmənɪ/ *n* **1** a formal act or series of acts prescribed by ritual, protocol, or convention **2** (observance of) established procedures of civility or politeness

cerise /sə'rees, -'reez‖sə'riːs, -'riːz/ *n or adj* (a) light purplish red

cert /suht‖sɜːt/ *n, Br* CERTAINTY 1; *esp* a horse that is sure to win a race – infml

¹certain /'suhtn‖'sɜːtn/ *adj* **1** fixed, settled <*guaranteed a* ~ *percentage of the profit*> **2a** of a particular but unspecified character, quantity, or degree <*the house has a* ~ *charm*> **b** named but not known <*a* ~ *Bill Clarke*> **3a** established beyond doubt or question; definite <*it is* ~ *that we exist*> **b** unerring, dependable <*her discernment was* ~> **4a** inevitable <*the* ~ *advance of age and decay*> **b** incapable of failing; sure – + infinitive <*she is* ~ *to do well*> **5a** assured in mind; convinced <*I'm* ~ *she saw me*> **b** assured in action; sure <*be* ~ *you catch your train*> – **certainly** *adv* – **for certain** as a certainty; assuredly

²certain *pron, pl in constr* certain ones <~ *of the questions raised were irrelevant*>

'certainty /-ti‖-tɪ/ *n* **1** sthg certain **2** the quality or state of being certain

¹certificate /sə'tifikət‖sə'tɪfɪkət/ *n* a document containing a certified statement; *esp* one declaring the status or qualifications of the holder

[2]**certificate** /sə'tifikayt‖sə'tɪfɪkeɪt/ *vt* to testify to, authorize by, or award with a certificate – **certification** *n*, **certificatory** *adj*
certify /'suhtifie‖'sɜːtɪfaɪ/ *vt* **1a** to confirm, esp officially in writing **b** to declare officially as being true or as meeting a standard **c** to declare officially the insanity of **2** to certificate, license <*a* certified *teacher*> **3** *chiefly NAm* to guarantee the payment or value of (a cheque) by endorsing on the front – **certifiable** *adj*, **certifiably** *adv*, **certifier** *n*
certitude /'suhti,tyoohd‖'sɜːtɪ,tjuːd/ *n* the state of being or feeling certain
cerulean /si'roohli·ən‖sɪ'ruːlɪən/ *adj* deep sky blue in colour
cerumen /si'roohmən‖sɪ'ruːmən/ *n* the yellow waxy secretion from the outer ear – **ceruminous** *adj*
cervical /'suhvikl‖'sɜːvɪkl/ *adj* of a neck or cervix
cervix /'suhviks‖'sɜːvɪks/ *n, pl* **cervices** /-viseez‖-vɪsiːz/, **cervixes 1** (the back part of) the neck **2** a constricted portion of an organ or body part; *esp* the narrow outer end of the uterus
cesarean *also* **cesarian** /si'zeəri·ən‖sɪ'zeərɪən/ *n, NAm* a caesarean – **cesarean** *also* **cesarian** *adj*
cessation /si'saysh(ə)n‖sɪ'seɪʃ(ə)n/ *n* a temporary or final stop; an ending
cession /'sesh(ə)n‖'seʃ(ə)n/ *n* the act or an instance of yielding rights, property, or esp territory
cesspit /'ses,pit‖'ses,pɪt/ *n* **1** a pit for the disposal of refuse (e g sewage) **2** a corrupt or squalid place
cesspool /'ses,poohl‖'ses,puːl/ *n* an underground basin for liquid waste (e g household sewage)
cetacean /si'taysh(ə)n‖sɪ'teɪʃ(ə)n/ *n* any of an order of aquatic, mostly marine, mammals that includes the whales, dolphins, and porpoises – **cetacean** *adj*, **cetaceous** *adj*
Chablis /'shabli‖'ʃæblɪ/ *n*, a very dry white table wine produced in northern Burgundy [*Chablis*, town in France]
cha-cha /'chah ,chah‖'tʃɑː ,tʃɑː/, ,**cha-cha** -'**cha** *n* (a piece of music for performing) a fast rhythmic ballroom dance of Latin American origin – **cha-cha** *vi*
[1]**chafe** /chayf‖tʃeɪf/ *vt* **1** to irritate, vex **2** to warm (part of the body) by rubbing **3a** to rub so as to wear away **b** to make sore (as if) by rubbing ~ *vi* **1** to feel irritation or discontent; fret < ~s *at his restrictive desk job*> **2** to become sore or uncomfortable as a result of rubbing
[2]**chafe** *n* (injury or wear caused by) friction
[1]**chaff** /chaf, chahf‖tʃæf, tʃɑːf/ *n* **1** the seed coverings and other debris separated from the seed in threshing grain **2** worthless matter – esp in *separate the wheat from the chaff* **3** chopped straw, hay, etc used for animal feed **4** material (e g strips of foil) ejected into the air to reflect enemy radar waves and so prevent detection – **chaffy** *adj*
[2]**chaff** *n* light jesting talk; banter
[3]**chaff** *vt* to tease good-naturedly ~*vi* to jest, banter
chaffinch /'chafinch‖'tʃæfɪntʃ/ *n* a European finch with a reddish breast, a bluish head, and white wing bars
'**chafing** ,**dish** /'chayfing‖'tʃeɪfɪŋ/ *n* a dish for cooking or keeping food warm, esp over a spirit burner at the table
chagrin /'shagrin‖'ʃægrɪn/ *vt or n* (to subject to) mental distress caused by humiliation, disappointment, or failure
[1]**chain** /chayn‖tʃeɪn/ *n* **1a** a series of usu metal links or rings connected to or fitted into one another and used for various purposes (e g support or restraint) **b** an ornament or badge of office consisting of such a series of links **c(1)** a measuring instrument of 100 links used in surveying **c(2)** a unit of length equal to 66ft (about 20.12m) **2** sthg that confines, restrains, or secures – usu pl <*the* ~s *of ignorance*> **3a** a series of linked or connected things <*a* ~ *of events*> **b** a group of associated establishments (e g shops or hotels) under the same ownership **c** a number of atoms or chemical groups united like links in a chain
[2]**chain** *vt* to fasten, restrict, or confine (as if) with a chain – often + *up* or *down*
'**chain** ,**gang** *n, sing or pl in constr* a gang of convicts chained together, usu while doing hard labour outside prison
'**chain** ,**letter** *n* a letter containing a request that copies of it, sometimes together with money or goods, be sent to a specified number of other people who should then repeat the process
'**chain** ,**mail** *n* flexible armour of interlinked metal rings
chain reaction *n* **1** a series of events so related to each other that each one initiates the next **2** a self-sustaining chemical or nuclear reaction yielding energy or products that cause further reactions of the same kind
'**chain** ,**saw** *n* a portable power saw that has teeth linked together to form a continuous revolving chain
'**chain-**,**smoke** *vb* to smoke (esp cigarettes) continually, usu by lighting one cigarette from the previous one smoked
'**chain** ,**stitch** *n* an ornamental embroidery or crochet stitch that resembles a linked chain
'**chain** ,**store** *n* any of several usu retail shops under the same ownership and selling the same lines of goods
[1]**chair** /cheə‖tʃeə/ *n* **1** a seat for 1 person, usu having 4 legs and a back and sometimes arms **2a** an office or position of authority or dignity; *specif* a professorship **b** a chairman **3** SEDAN CHAIR
[2]**chair** *vt* **1** to install in office **2** to preside as chairman of **3** *chiefly Br* to carry shoulder-high in acclaim
'**chair** ,**lift** *n* a ski lift with seats for passengers
'**chairman** /-mən‖-mən/, *fem* '**chair**,**lady**, '**chair**,**woman** *n* **1** one who presides over or heads a meeting, committee, organization, or board of directors **2** a radio or television presenter; *esp* one who coordinates unscripted or diverse material **3** a carrier of a sedan chair – **chairmanship** *n*
'**chair**,**person** /-,puhs(ə)n‖-,pɜːs(ə)n/ *n, pl* **chairpersons** a chairman or chairwoman
chaise /shez, shayz‖ʃez, ʃeɪz/ *n* a light carriage, usu having 2 wheels and a folding top

ˌchaise ˈlongue /long·g‖lɒŋg/ *n, pl* **chaise longues** *also* **chaises longues** /~ long·g(z)‖~ lɒŋg(z)/ a low sofa with only 1 armrest, on which one may recline [French, lit., long chair]

chalcedony /kal'sidəni, -'sedəni‖kæl'sɪdənɪ, -'sedənɪ/ *n* a translucent quartz that is often pale blue or grey and is used as a gemstone – **chalcedonic** *adj*

chalet /'shalay‖'ʃæleɪ/ *n* **1** a hut used by herdsmen in the Alps **2a** a usu wooden house with a steeply sloping roof and widely overhanging eaves, common esp in Switzerland **b** a small house or hut used esp for temporary accommodation (e g at a holiday camp)

chalice /'chalis‖'tʃælɪs/ *n* **1** a drinking cup; a goblet **2** an esp gold or silver cup used to hold the wine at communion

[1]chalk /chawk‖tʃɔːk/ *n* **1** a soft white, grey, or buff limestone composed chiefly of the shells of small marine organisms **2** a short stick of chalk or chalky material used esp for writing and drawing – **chalky** *adj*

[2]chalk *vt* **1** to rub or mark with chalk **2** to write or draw with chalk **3** to set down or add up (as if) with chalk – usu + *up* <~ *up the score*>, ~*vi Br* to act as scorer for a darts match

chalk out *vt* to delineate roughly; sketch <chalk out *a plan of action*>

chalk up *vt* **1** to ascribe, credit; *specif* to charge to sby's account <chalk *it* up *to me*> **2** to attain, achieve <chalked up *a record score for the season*>

[1]challenge /'chalinj‖'tʃælɪndʒ/ *vt* **1** to order to halt and prove identity <*the sentry* ~d *the stranger at the gates*> **2** to dispute, esp as being unjust, invalid, or outmoded; impugn <*uncovered new data that* ~s *old assumptions*> **3** to question formally the legality or legal qualifications of (e g a juror) **4a** to defy boldly; dare **b** to call out to duel, combat, or competition **5** to stimulate by testing the skill of (sby or sthg) <*maths* ~s *him*> – **challenger** *n*, **challenging** *adj*, **challengingly** *adv*

[2]challenge *n* **1a** a calling to account or into question; a protest **b** a command given by a sentry, watchman, etc to halt and prove identity **c** a questioning of right or validity **2a** a summons that is threatening or provocative; *specif* a call to a duel **b** an invitation to compete **3** (sthg having) the quality of being demanding or stimulating <*the job presented a real* ~>

chamber /'chaymbə‖'tʃeɪmbə/ *n* **1** a natural or artificial enclosed space or cavity **2a(1)** a room where a judge hears private cases – usu pl with sing. meaning **a(2)** *pl* a set of rooms used by a group of barristers **b** a reception room in an official or state building **3** (a hall used by) a legislative or judicial body; *esp* either of 2 houses of a legislature **4** the part of a gun that holds the charge or cartridge **5** *archaic* a room; *esp* a bedroom [Old French *chambre*, fr Late Latin *camera*, fr Latin, arched roof, fr Greek *kamara* vault]

chamberlain /'chaymbəlin‖'tʃeɪmbəlɪn/ *n* **1** a chief officer of a royal or noble household **2** a treasurer (e g of a corporation)

ˈchamberˌmaid /-ˌmayd‖-ˌmeɪd/ *n* a maid who cleans bedrooms and makes beds (e g in a hotel)

ˈchamber ˌmusic *n* music written for a small group of instruments

ˌChamber of ˈCommerce *n* an association of businessmen to promote commercial and industrial interests in the community

ˈchamber ˌorchestra *n* a small orchestra, usu with 1 player for each instrumental part

ˈchamber ˌpot *n* a bowl-shaped receptacle for urine and faeces, used chiefly in the bedroom

chameleon /shə'meelyən, kə-‖ʃə'miːljən, kə-/ *n* **1** any of a group of Old World lizards with a long tongue, a prehensile tail, and the ability to change the colour of the skin **2** sby or sthg changeable; *specif* a fickle person [Latin *chamaeleon*, fr Greek *chamaileōn*, fr *chamai* on the ground + *leōn* lion] – **chameleonic** *adj*

chamois /'shamwah‖'ʃæmwɑː/ *n, pl* **chamois** *also* **chamoix** /'shamwah(z)‖'ʃæmwɑː(z)/ **1** a small goatlike antelope of Europe and the Caucasus **2** a soft pliant leather prepared from the skin of the chamois or sheep, used esp as a cloth for polishing

chamomile /'kaməˌmiel‖'kæməˌmaɪl/ *n* camomile

[1]champ /champ‖tʃæmp/ *vt* **1** to munch (food) noisily **2** to gnaw, bite ~ *vi* **1** to make biting or gnashing movements **2** to eat noisily **3** to show impatience or eagerness – usu in *champ at the bit*

[2]champ *n* a champion – infml

champagne /sham'payn‖ʃæm'peɪn/ *n* a white sparkling wine made in the old province of Champagne in France

[1]champion /'champi·ən‖'tʃæmpɪən/ *n* **1** a militant supporter of, or fighter for, a cause or person <*an outspoken* ~ *of civil rights*> **2** one who shows marked superiority; *specif* the winner of a competitive event

[2]champion *vt* to protect or fight for as a champion

[3]champion *adj, chiefly N Eng* superb, splendid – infml

ˈchampionˌship /-ˌship‖-ʃɪp/ *n* **1** the act of championing; defence <*his* ~ *of freedom of speech*> **2** a contest held to determine a champion

[1]chance /chahns‖tʃɑːns/ *n* **1a** an event without discernible human intention or observable cause **b** the incalculable (assumed) element in existence; that which determines unaccountable happenings <*we met by* ~> **2** a situation favouring some purpose; an opportunity **3** an opportunity of dismissing a batsman in cricket **4a** the possibility of a specified or favourable outcome in an uncertain situation <*we have almost no* ~ *of winning*> **b** *pl* the more likely indications <~s *are he's already heard the news*> **5** a risk <*took a* ~ *on it*> – **chance** *adj*, **chanceless** *adj*

[2]chance *vi* **1** to take place or come about by chance; happen <*it* ~d *that the street was empty*> **2** to come or light *on* or *upon* by chance <~d *on the idea*> ~*vt* to accept the hazard of; risk

chancel /'chahnsl‖'tʃɑːnsl/ *n* the part of a church containing the altar and seats for the clergy and choir

chancellery, **chancellory** /'chahns(ə)ləri‖'tʃɑːns(ə)lərɪ/ *n* **1** the position or department of a chancellor **2** the office or staff of an embassy or consulate

chancellor /'chahns(ə)lə‖'tʃɑ:ns(ə)lə/ *n* **1a** the secretary of a nobleman, prince, or king **b** LORD CHANCELLOR **c** a Roman Catholic priest heading a diocesan chancery **2** the titular head of a British university **3** a usu lay legal officer of an Anglican diocese **4** the chief minister of state in some European countries – **chancellorship** *n*

chancery /'chahnsəri‖'tʃɑ:nsərɪ/ *n* **1a Chancery Division, Chancery** a division of the High Court having jurisdiction over causes in equity **b** a US court of equity **2** a record office for public archives or those of ecclesiastical, legal, or diplomatic proceedings **3a** a chancellor's court or office **b** the office in which the business of a Roman Catholic diocese is transacted and recorded **c** CHANCELLERY 2

chancy /'chahnsi‖'tʃɑ:nsɪ/ *adj* uncertain in outcome or prospect; risky – **chancily** *adj*, **chanciness** *n*

chandelier /ˌshandə'liə‖ˌʃændə'lɪə/ *n* a branched often ornate lighting fixture suspended from a ceiling

chandler /'chahndlə‖'tʃɑ:ndlə/ *n* a retail dealer in supplies and equipment of a specified kind <*a ship's* ~>

[1]change /chaynj‖tʃeɪndʒ/ *vt* **1a** to make different **b** to give a different position, direction, status, or aspect to <*stop* changing *your mind*> **c** to exchange, reverse – often + *over* or *round* <*just* ~ *the speaker leads over*> **2a** to replace with another <*let's* ~ *the subject*> **b** to move from one to another <~ *sides*> **c** to exchange for an equivalent sum or comparable item **d** to undergo a loss or modification of <*foliage* changing *colour*> **e** to put fresh clothes or covering on <~ *a bed*> ~ *vi* **1** to become different **2** *of the moon* to pass from one phase to another **3** to go from one vehicle of a public transport system to another **4** *of the (male) voice* to shift to a lower register; BREAK 9a **5** to undergo transformation, transition, or conversion <*winter* ~d *to spring*> **6** to put on different clothes **7** to engage in giving sthg and receiving sthg in return – usu + *with* – **changer** *n* – **change hands** to pass from the possession of one person to that of another

[2]change *n* **1a** a (marked) alteration <*has undergone a* ~ *since he was married*> **b** a substitution <*a* ~ *of players*> **c** the passage of the moon from one phase to another; *specif* the coming of the new moon **2** an alternative set, esp of clothes **3a** money of lower denominations received in exchange for an equivalent sum of higher denominations <*have you got* ~ *for a pound?*> **b** money returned when a payment exceeds the amount due **c** coins of low denominations <*a pocketful of* ~> **4** an order in which a set of bells is struck in change ringing – **changeful** *adj*, **changefully** *adv*, **changefulness** n, **changeless** *adj*, **changelessly** *adv*, **changelessness** *n*

changeable /'chaynjəbl‖'tʃeɪndʒəbl/ *adj* **1** able or apt to vary **2** capable of being altered or exchanged **3** fickle – **changeableness** *n*, **changeably** *adv*, **changeability** *n*

changeling /'chaynjling‖'tʃeɪndʒlɪŋ/ *n* a child secretly exchanged for another in infancy; *specif* a half-witted or ugly elf-child left in place of a human child by fairies

ˌchange of 'life *n the* menopause

'change-ˌover *n* a conversion to a different system or function

'change ˌringing *n* the art or practice of ringing a set of tuned (church) bells in continually varying order

[1]channel /'chanl‖'tʃænl/ *n* **1a** the bed where a stream of water runs **b** the deeper part of a river, harbour, or strait **c** a narrow region of sea between 2 land masses **d** a path along which information passes or can be stored (e g on a recording tape) **e** a course or direction of thought, action, or communication – often pl with sing. meaning <*used official* ~s *to air his grievance*> **f(1)** a band of frequencies of sufficient width for a transmission (e g from a radio or television station) **f(2)** a television station **2** a usu tubular passage, esp for liquids **3** a long gutter, groove, or furrow

[2]channel *vt* **-ll-** (*NAm* **-l-**, **-ll-**), **1** to form or wear a channel in **2** to convey into or through a channel; direct <~ *his energy into constructive activities*>

[1]chant /chahnt‖tʃɑ:nt/ *vi* **1** to sing a chant **2** to recite in a monotonous tone ~*vt* to utter as in chanting

[2]chant *n* **1** (the music or performance of) a repetitive melody used for liturgical singing in which as many syllables are assigned to each note as required **2** a rhythmic monotonous utterance or song

chanter /'chahntə‖'tʃɑ:ntə/ *n* the reed pipe of a bagpipe with finger holes on which the melody is played

ˌchantry /'chahntri‖'tʃɑ:ntrɪ/ *n* (a chapel or altar founded under) an endowment for the chanting of masses for the founder's soul

chaos /'kayos‖'keɪɒs/ *n* **1** *often cap* the confused unorganized state of primordial matter before the creation of distinct forms **2a** a state of utter confusion **b** a confused mass – **chaotic** *adj*, **chaotically** *adv*

[1]chap /chap‖tʃæp/ *n* a man, fellow – infml

[2]chap *vb* **-pp-** to (cause to) open in slits or cracks <~ped *lips*>

[3]chap *n* a crack in the skin caused by exposure to wind or cold

[4]chap *n* **1** (the fleshy covering of) a jaw **2** the lower front part of the face *USE* usu pl with sing. meaning

[1]chapel /'chapl‖'tʃæpl/ *n* **1a** a place of worship serving a residence or institution **b** a room or bay in a church for prayer or minor religious services **2** a choir of singers belonging to a chapel **3** a chapel service or assembly **4** *sing or pl in constr* the members of a trade union, esp in a printing office **5** a place of worship used by a Christian group other than an established church

[2]chapel *adj, chiefly Br* belonging to a Nonconformist church

[1]chaperon, chaperone /'shapəˌrohn‖'ʃæpəˌrəʊn/ *n* a married or older woman who accompanies a younger woman on social occasions to ensure propriety [French *chaperon*, lit., hood, deriv of Late Latin *cappa* cape]

²chaperon, chaperone *vt* to act as chaperon to; escort – **chaperonage** *n*

chaplain /'chaplin||'tʃæplɪn/ *n* **1** a clergyman in charge of a chapel **2** a clergyman officially attached to a branch of the armed forces, an institution, or a family or court – **chaplaincy** *n*, **chaplainship** *n*

chaplet /'chaplit||'tʃæplɪt/ *n* **1** a wreath to be worn on the head **2a** a string of beads **b** a part of a rosary comprising 5 decades – **chapleted** *adj*

chapter /'chaptə||'tʃæptə/ *n* **1a** a major division of a book **b** sthg resembling a chapter in being a significant specified unit <*a ~ of accidents*> **2** (a regular meeting of) the canons of a cathedral or collegiate church, or the members of a religious house **3** a local branch of a society or fraternity

'chapter ,house *n* the building or rooms where a chapter meets

¹char, charr /chah||tʃɑː/ *n*, any of a genus of small-scaled trouts

²char *vb* **-rr-** *vt* **1** to convert to charcoal or carbon, usu by heat; burn **2** to burn slightly; scorch ~ *vi* to become charred

³char *vi* **-rr-** to work as a cleaning woman

⁴char *n*, *Br* a charwoman – infml

⁵char, cha *n*, *Br* TEA 2 – infml

charabanc /'sharə,bang||'ʃærə,bæŋ/ *n*, *Br* an (old-fashioned) motor coach used for sightseeing [French *char à bancs*, lit., wagon with benches]

character /'karəktə||'kærəktə/ *n* **1a** a distinctive mark, usu in the form of a stylized graphic device **b** a graphic symbol (e g a hieroglyph or alphabet letter) used in writing or printing **c(1)** style of writing or printing **c(2)** CIPHER 2 **2a** (any of) the mental or ethical qualities that make up and distinguish the individual **b(1)** (a group or kind distinguished by) a feature used to categorize things (e g organisms) **b(2)** an inherited characteristic **b(3)** the sum of the distinctive qualities characteristic of a breed, type, etc; the (distinctive) main or essential nature of sthg <*the unique ~ of the town*> **3a** a person, esp one marked by notable or conspicuous traits **b** any of the people portrayed in a novel, film, play, etc **4** (good) reputation <*~ assassination*> **5** moral strength; integrity <*a man of ~*> – **characterless** *adj* – **in/out of character** in/not in accord with a person's usual qualities, traits, or behaviour

¹characteristic /,karəktə'ristik||,kærəktə'rɪstɪk/ *adj* serving to reveal and distinguish the individual character; typical – **characteristically** *adv*

²characteristic *n* **1** a distinguishing trait, quality, or property **2** the integral part of a common logarithm

character·ize, -ise /'karəktə,riez||'kærəktə,raɪz/ *vt* **1** to describe the character or quality of; delineate **2** to be a characteristic of; distinguish – **characterization** *n*

charade /shə'rahd||ʃə'rɑːd; *NAm* -'rayd||-'reɪd/ *n* **1** *pl but sing or pl in constr* a game in which one team acts out each syllable of a word or phrase while the other tries to guess what is being represented **2** a ridiculous pretence

charcoal /'chah,kohl||'tʃɑː,kəʊl/ *n* **1** a dark or black porous carbon prepared by partly burning vegetable or animal substances (e g wood or bone) **2** fine charcoal used in pencil form for drawing

chard /chahd||tʃɑːd/ *n* a beet with large edible dark green leaves and succulent stalks

¹charge /chahj||tʃɑːdʒ/ *vt* **1a(1)** to place a usu powder charge in (a firearm) **a(2)** to load or fill to capacity <*~ the blast furnace with ore*> **b(1)** to restore the active materials in (a storage battery) by the passage of a direct current in the opposite direction to that of discharge **b(2)** to give an electric charge to **c** to place a heraldic charge on **d** to fill with (passionate) emotion, feeling, etc **2** to command or exhort with right or authority <*I ~ you not to leave*> **3a** to blame <*~s him as the instigator*> **b** to make an assertion against; accuse <*~s him with armed robbery*> **c** to place the blame for <*~ her failure to negligence*> **d** to assert as an accusation <*~s that he distorted the data*> **4** to rush violently at; attack; *also* to rush into (an opponent), usu illegally, in soccer, basketball, etc **5a(1)** to impose a financial obligation on <*~ his estate with debts incurred*> **a(2)** to impose as financial obligation <*~ debts to an estate*> **b(1)** to fix or ask as fee or payment **b(2)** to ask payment of (a person) <*~ a client for expenses*> **c** to record (an item) as an expense, debt, obligation, or liability <*~ it to my account*> ~ *vi* **1** to rush forwards (as if) in assault **2** to ask or set a price – **chargeable** *adj* – **charge with** to impose (a task or responsibility) on

²charge *n* **1** a shape, representation, or design depicted on a coat of arms **2a** the quantity that an apparatus is intended to receive and fitted to hold; *esp* the quantity of explosive for a gun or cannon **b** power, force <*the emotional ~ of the drama*> **c(1)** a basic property of matter that occurs in discrete natural units and is considered as negative (e g when belonging to an electron) or positive (e g when belonging to a proton) **c(2)** a definite quantity of electricity; *esp* the charge that a storage battery is capable of yielding **3a** an obligation, requirement **b** control, supervision <*I leave you in ~*> **c** sby or sthg committed to the care of another **4a** an instruction, command **b** instructions given by a judge to a jury **5** the price demanded or paid for sthg <*no admission ~*> **6** an accusation, indictment, or statement of complaint **7** a violent rush forwards (e g in attack)

charge card *n* **1** a card issued by a shop authorizing the purchase of goods to be charged to the holder's account **2** a form of credit card for which the holder pays a subscription

chargé d'affaires /,shahzhay da'feə||,ʃɑːʒeɪ dæ'feə/ *n*, *pl* **chargés d'affaires** /~ da'feə(z)||~ dæ'feə(z)/ **1** a diplomat who substitutes for an ambassador **2** a diplomatic representative inferior in rank to an ambassador

¹charger /'chahjə||'tʃɑːdʒə/ *n* a large flat meat dish

²charger *n* a horse for battle or parade

'charge ,sheet *n* a police record of charges made and people to be tried in a magistrate's court

chariot /'chari·ət||'tʃærɪət/ *n* **1** a light 4-wheeled pleasure or state carriage **2** a 2-wheeled horse-drawn vehicle of ancient times used in warfare and racing

charioteer /ˌchari·ə'tiə||ˌtʃærɪə'tɪə/ *n* the driver of a chariot

charisma /kə'rizmə||kə'rɪzmə/ *n* the special magnetic appeal, charm, or power of an individual (e g a political leader) that inspires popular loyalty and enthusiasm [Greek, favour, gift, fr *charizesthai* to favour, fr *charis* grace] – **charismatic** *adj*

charitable /'charitəbl||'tʃærɪtəbl/ *adj* **1a** liberal in giving to the poor; generous **b** of or giving charity < ~ *institutions*> **2** merciful or kind in judging others; lenient – **charitableness** *n*, **charitably** *adv*

charity /'charəti||'tʃærətɪ/ *n* **1** benevolent goodwill towards or love of humanity **2a** kindly generosity and helpfulness, esp towards the needy or suffering; *also* aid given to those in need **b** an institution engaged in relief of the poor, sick, etc **c** public provision for the relief of the needy **3a** a gift for public benevolent purposes **b** an institution (e g a hospital) funded by such a gift **4** lenient judgment of others

charlady /'chahˌlaydi||'tʃɑːˌleɪdɪ/ *n*, *Br* a charwoman

charlatan /'shahlət(ə)n||'ʃɑːlət(ə)n/ *n* **1** QUACK 1 **2** one who pretends, usu ostentatiously, to have special knowledge or ability; a fraud – **charlatanism, charlatanry** *n*

Charleston /'chahlstən||'tʃɑːlstən/ *vi or n* (to dance) a lively ballroom dance in which the heels are swung sharply outwards on each step

charlock /'chahˌlok||'tʃɑːˌlɒk/ *n* a wild mustard that is a weed of cultivated ground

[1]**charm** /chahm||tʃɑːm/ *n* **1** an incantation **2** sthg worn to ward off evil or to ensure good fortune **3a** a quality that fascinates, allures, or delights **b** *pl* physical graces or attractions, esp of a woman **4** a small ornament worn on a bracelet or chain **5** a quantum property postulated to account for unexpectedly long lifetimes of particles that have quantum numbers identical to other elementary particles – **charmless** *adj*

[2]**charm** *vt* **1a** to affect (as if) by magic; bewitch **b** to soothe or delight by compelling attraction < ~s *the women with his suave manner*> **2** to control (an animal) by the use of rituals (e g the playing of music) held to have magical powers < ~ *a snake*> ~*vi* to have the effect of a charm; fascinate

charmer /'chahmə||'tʃɑːmə/ *n* an attractive or captivating person – chiefly infml

charming /'chahming||'tʃɑːmɪŋ/ *adj* extremely pleasing or delightful; entrancing – **charmingly** *adv*

'**charnel** ˌ**house** /'chahn(ə)l||'tʃɑːn(ə)l/ *n* a building or chamber in which bodies or bones are deposited

[1]**chart** /chaht||tʃɑːt/ *n* **1a** an outline map showing the geographical distribution of sthg (e g climatic or magnetic variations) **b** a navigator's map **2a** a sheet giving information in tabular form; *esp*, *pl* *the* list of best-selling popular gramophone records (produced weekly) **b** GRAPH **c** a schematic, usu large, diagram **d** a sheet of paper ruled and graduated for use in a recording instrument (e g on an electrocardiograph)

[2]**chart** *vt* **1** to make a chart of **2** to lay out a plan for **3** to display or mark (as if) on a chart

[1]**charter** /'chahtə||'tʃɑːtə/ *n* **1** a formal written instrument or contract **2a** a document that creates and defines the rights of a city, educational institution, or company **b** CONSTITUTION 4 **3** a special privilege, immunity, or exemption **4** a total or partial lease of a ship, aeroplane, etc for a particular use or group of people <*low-cost travel on* ~ *flights*>

[2]**charter** *vt* **1a** to establish or grant by charter **b** to certify as qualified <*a* ~ed *accountant*> **2** to hire or lease for usu exclusive and temporary use < ~ed *a boat*> – **charterer** *n*

'**charter** ˌ**member** *n* an original member of a society or corporation

Chartreuse /ˌshah'truhz||ˌʃɑː'trɜːz/ *trademark* – used for an aromatic usu green or yellow liqueur

charwoman /'chahˌwoomən||'tʃɑːˌwʊmən/ *n* a cleaning woman; *esp*, *Br* one employed in a private house

chary /'cheəri||'tʃeərɪ/ *adj* **1** cautious; *esp* wary of taking risks **2** slow to grant or accept <*a man very* ~ *of compliments*> – **charily** *adv*, **chariness** *n*

[1]**chase** /chays||tʃeɪs/ *vt* **1a** to follow rapidly or persistently; pursue <*he's too old to* ~ *women*> **b** to hunt **2** to cause to depart or flee; drive < ~ *the dog out of the pantry*> **3** *chiefly Br* to investigate (a matter) or contact (a person, company, etc) in order to obtain information or (hasten) results – usu + *up* ~ *vi* **1** to chase an animal, person, or thing – usu + *after* **2** to rush, hasten < ~d *all over town looking for a place to stay*>

[2]**chase** *n* **1a** the act of chasing; pursuit **b** *the* hunting of wild animals **2** sthg pursued; a quarry **3** a tract of unenclosed land set aside for the breeding of animals for hunting and fishing **4** a steeplechase

[3]**chase** *vt* **1** to ornament (metal) by indenting with a hammer and tools that have no cutting edge **2** to make by such ornamentation < ~ *a monogram*>

[4]**chase** *n* **1** a groove cut in a surface for a pipe, wire, etc **2** the part of a cannon enclosing the barrel between the trunnions and the mouth of the muzzle

[5]**chase** *n* a rectangular steel or iron frame into which printing type or blocks are locked for printing or platemaking

chaser /'chaysə||'tʃeɪsə/ *n* **1** a glass or swallow of a mild drink (e g beer) taken after spirits; *also* a drink of spirits taken after a mild drink (e g beer) **2** a horse that is a steeplechaser

chasm /'kaz(ə)m||'kæz(ə)m/ *n* **1** a deep cleft in the earth **2** an apparently unbridgeable gap <*a political* ~ *between the 2 countries*>

chassis /'shasi||'ʃæsɪ/ *n*, *pl* **chassis** /'shasiz||'ʃæsɪz/ **1** a supporting framework for the body of a vehicle (e g a car) **2** the frame on which the electrical parts of a radio, television, etc are mounted

chaste /chayst||tʃeɪst/ *adj* **1** abstinent from

(unlawful or immoral) sexual intercourse; celibate **2** pure in thought and act; modest **3** severely simple in design or execution; austere <*he wrote in a pure ~ style*> – **chastely** *adv*, **chasteness** *n*, **chastity** *n*

chasten /ˈchays(ə)n‖ˈtʃeɪs(ə)n/ *vt* **1** to correct by punishment or suffering; discipline **2** to subdue, restrain – **chastener** *n*

chastise /chasˈtiez‖tʃæsˈtaɪz/ *vt* **1** to inflict punishment on, esp by whipping **2** to subject to severe reproof or criticism – **chastisement** *n*, **chastiser** *n*

ˈ**chastity ˌbelt** /ˈchastəti‖ˈtʃæstətɪ/ *n* a device consisting of a belt with an attachment passing between the legs, designed to prevent sexual intercourse on the part of the woman wearing it

chasuble /ˈchazyoobl‖ˈtʃæzjʊbl/ *n* a sleeveless outer vestment worn by the officiating priest at mass

[1]**chat** /chat‖tʃæt/ *vi* **-tt-** to talk in an informal or familiar manner

[2]**chat** *n* **1** (an instance of) light familiar talk; *esp* (a) conversation **2** a stonechat, whinchat, or related bird

château /ˈshatoh‖ˈʃætəʊ/ *n, pl* **châteaus, châteaux** /ˈshatohz‖ˈʃætəʊz/ **1** a feudal castle or large country house in France **2** a French vineyard estate

chatelaine /ˈshatəˌlayn‖ˈʃætəˌleɪn/ *n* the mistress of a castle or large house

chat show /ˈchat ˌshoh‖ˈtʃæt ˌʃəʊ/ *n, Br* a radio or television programme in which usu well-known people are interviewed or take part in discussions

chattel /ˈchatl‖ˈtʃætl/ *n* an item of personal property – usu in *goods and chattels*

[1]**chatter** /ˈchatə‖ˈtʃætə/ *vi* **1** to produce rapid successive inarticulate sounds suggestive of language <*squirrels* ~ed *angrily*> **2** to talk idly, incessantly, or fast; jabber **3a** *esp of teeth* to click repeatedly or uncontrollably (e g from cold) **b** *of a cutting tool (e g a drill)* to vibrate rapidly whilst cutting – **chatterer** *n*

[2]**chatter** *n* **1** the sound or (vibrating) action of chattering **2** idle talk; prattle

ˈ**chatterˌbox** /-ˌboks‖-ˌbɒks/ *n* one who engages in much idle talk – infml

chatty /ˈchati‖ˈtʃætɪ/ *adj* **1** fond of chatting; talkative **2** having the style and manner of light familiar conversation <*a ~ letter*> *USE* infml – **chattily** *adv*, **chattiness** *n*

chat up *vt, Br* to engage (sby) in friendly conversation for an ulterior motive, esp with amorous intent – infml

[1]**chauffeur** /ˌshohˈfuh, ˈshohfə‖ˌʃəʊˈfɜː, ˈʃəʊfə/ *n* a person employed to drive a private passenger-carrying motor vehicle, esp a car [French, lit., stoker, fr *chauffer* to heat]

[2]**chauffeur** *vi* to work as a chauffeur ~ *vt* to transport (a person) or drive (e g a car) as (if) a chauffeur

chauvinism /ˈshohvəˌniz(ə)m‖ˈʃəʊvəˌnɪz(ə)m/ *n* **1** excessive or blind patriotism **2** undue attachment to one's group, cause, or place <*male* ~> [French *chauvinisme*, fr Nicolas *Chauvin* (*fl* 1815), French soldier of excessive patriotism and devotion to Napoleon] – **chauvinist** *n*, **chauvinistic** *adj*, **chauvinistically** *adv*

[1]**cheap** /cheep‖tʃiːp/ *n* – **on the cheap** at minimum expense; cheaply

[2]**cheap** *adj* **1a** (relatively) low in price; *esp* purchasable below the market price or the real value **b** charging a low price <*a ~ supermarket*> **c** depreciated in value (e g by currency inflation) <*~ dollars*> **2** gained with little effort <*a ~ victory*>; *esp* gained by contemptible means <*~ laughs*> **3a** of inferior quality or worth; tawdry, sleazy **b** contemptible because of lack of any fine or redeeming qualities <*~ election gimmickry*> **4** *of money* obtainable at a low rate of interest **5** *NAm* stingy – **cheap, cheaply** *adv*, **cheapish** *adj*, **cheapness** *n*

cheapen /ˈcheep(ə)n‖ˈtʃiːp(ə)n/ *vb* to make or become **a** cheap in price or value **b** lower in esteem **c** tawdry, vulgar, or inferior

[1]ˈ**cheap-ˌjack** /jak‖dʒæk/ *n* sby, esp a pedlar, who sells cheap wares

[2]**cheap-jack** *adj* **1** inferior, cheap, or worthless **2** characterized by unscrupulous opportunism <*~ speculators*>

cheapskate /ˈcheepˌskayt‖ˈtʃiːpˌskeɪt/ *n, chiefly NAm* a miserly or stingy person

[1]**cheat** /cheet‖tʃiːt/ *n* **1** a fraudulent deception; a fraud **2** one who cheats; a pretender, deceiver

[2]**cheat** *vt* **1** to deprive of sthg valuable by deceit or fraud **2** to influence or lead by deceit or fraud **3** to defeat the purpose or blunt the effects of <*~ winter of its dreariness* – Washington Irving> ~ *vi* **1a** to practise fraud or deception **b** to violate rules dishonestly (e g at cards or in an exam) **2** to be sexually unfaithful – usu + *on* – **cheater** *n*

[1]**check** /chek‖tʃek/ *n* **1** exposure of a chess king to an attack from which it must be protected or moved to safety – often used interjectionally **2** a sudden stoppage of a forward course or progress; an arrest **3** a sudden pause or break in a progression **4** one who or that which arrests, limits, or restrains; a restraint **5a** a standard for testing and evaluation; a criterion **b** an inspection, examination, test, or verification **6a** (a square in) a pattern of squares (of alternating colours) **b** a fabric woven or printed with such a design **7** a crack or break, esp in a piece of timber **8** *NAm* a cheque **9a** *chiefly NAm* a ticket or token showing ownership or identity or indicating payment made <*a luggage* ~> **b** *NAm* a counter in various games **c** *NAm* a bill, esp for food and drink in a restaurant **10** *NAm* [2]TICK 2 – **in check** under restraint or control <*held the enemy* in check>

[2]**check** *vt* **1** to put (a chess opponent's king) in check **2a** to slow or bring to a stop; brake **b** to block the progress of (e g an ice-hockey player) **3a** to restrain or diminish the action or force of; control **b** to ease off and then secure again (e g a rope) **4a** to compare with a source, original, or authority; verify **b** to inspect for satisfactory condition, accuracy, safety, or performance – sometimes + *out* or *over* **5** to mark into squares; chequer – usu in past part **6** *chiefly NAm* to note or mark with a tick – often + *off* **7a** *NAm* CHECK IN 2 **b** *chiefly NAm* to leave or accept for safekeeping in a cloakroom or left-luggage office – often + *in* **8** *chiefly dial* to rebuke, reprimand ~ *vi* **1a** *of a dog* to stop in a chase, esp when

scent is lost **b** to halt through caution, uncertainty, or fear **2a** to investigate and make sure <~ed *on the passengers' safety*> **b** *chiefly NAm* to correspond point for point; tally <*the description* ~s *with the photograph*> – often + *out* <*his story* ~ed *out*> – **checkable** *adj*, **checker** *n* – **check into** to check in at – **check up on 1** to examine for accuracy or truth, esp in order to corroborate information <check up on *the facts*> **2** to make thorough inquiries about <*police* checked up on *her*>

[1]**checker** /'chekə‖'tʃekə/ *n* **1** *chiefly NAm* a chequer **2** *NAm* a draughtsman

[2]**checker** *vt, chiefly NAm* to chequer

checkers /'chekəz‖'tʃekəz/ *n pl but sing in constr, NAm* the game of draughts

check in *vi* to report one's presence or arrival; *esp* to arrive and register at a hotel or airport ~ *vt* **1** to return or accept the return of <check in *the equipment after use*> **2** to deposit (luggage) for transport, esp by air

checklist /'chek,list‖'tʃek,lɪst/ *n* an inventory, catalogue; *esp* a complete list of checks to be made

[1]**checkmate** /,chek'mayt‖,tʃek'meɪt/ *vt* **1** to thwart or counter completely **2** to check (a chess opponent's king) so that escape is impossible [Middle French *eschec mat*, interj used to announce checkmate, fr Arabic *shāh māt*, fr Persian, lit., the king is left helpless]

[2],**check'mate** *n* **1a** the act of checkmating **b** the situation of a checkmated king **2** complete defeat *USE* (*1*) often used interjectionally

checkout /'chek,owt‖'tʃek,aʊt/ *n* a cash desk equipped with a cash register in a self-service shop

check out *vi* to complete the formalities for leaving, esp at a hotel ~*vt* to have the removal of (sthg) recorded <check out *a library book*>

checkpoint /'chek,poynt‖'tʃek,pɔɪnt/ *n* a location where inspection (e g of travellers) may take place

checkrein /'chek,rayn‖'tʃek,reɪn/ *n* a short rein attached from the bit to the saddle to prevent a horse from lowering its head

checkup /'chek,up‖'tʃek,ʌp/ *n* a (general physical) examination

Cheddar /'chedə‖'tʃedə/ *n* a hard smooth-textured cheese with a flavour that ranges from mild to strong as the cheese matures [*Cheddar*, village in Somerset, England]

[1]**cheek** /cheek‖tʃi:k/ *n* **1** the fleshy side of the face below the eye and above and to the side of the mouth **2** either of 2 paired facing parts (e g the jaws of a vice) **3** insolent boldness; impudence **4** a buttock – infml

[2]**cheek** *vt* to speak rudely or impudently to – infml

'**cheek,bone** /-,bohn‖-,bəʊn/ *n* (the bone forming) the prominence below the eye

-cheeked *comb form* (→ *adj*) having (such) cheeks <*rosy*-cheeked>

cheeky /'cheeki‖'tʃi:kɪ/ *adj* impudent, insolent – **cheekily** *adv*, **cheekiness** *n*

cheep /cheep‖tʃi:p/ *vi or n* (to utter) a faint shrill sound characteristic of a young bird

[1]**cheer** /chiə‖tʃɪə/ *n* **1** state of mind or heart; spirit <*be of good* ~> **2** happiness, gaiety **3** sthg that gladdens **4** a shout of applause or encouragement – **cheerless** *adj*, **cheerlessly** *adv*, **cheerlessness** *n*

[2]**cheer** *vt* **1a** to instil with hope or courage; comfort **b** to make glad or happy **2** to urge *on* or encourage, esp by shouts <~ed *the team on*> **3** to applaud with shouts ~ *vi* **1** to grow or be cheerful; rejoice **2** to utter a shout of applause or triumph *USE* (*vt 1*; *vi 1*) usu + *up* – **cheerer** *n*

'**cheerful** /-f(ə)l‖-f(ə)l/ *adj* **1a** full of good spirits; merry **b** ungrudging <~ *obedience*> **2** conducive to good cheer <*a* ~ *sunny room*> – **cheerfully** *adv*, **cheerfulness** *n*

cheerio /,chiəri'oh‖,tʃɪərɪ'əʊ/ *interj, chiefly Br* – used to express farewell

'**cheer,leader** /-,leedə‖-,li:də/ *n* one, esp a female, who leads organized cheering (e g at a N American football game)

cheers /chiəz‖tʃɪəz/ *interj* – used as a toast and sometimes as an informal farewell or expression of thanks

cheery /'chiəri‖'tʃɪərɪ/ *adj* cheerful – **cheerily** *adv*, **cheeriness** *n*

[1]**cheese** /cheez‖tʃi:z/ *n* **1** (an often cylindrical cake of) a food consisting of coagulated, compressed, and usu ripened milk curds **2** a fruit preserve with the consistency of cream cheese – **cheesy** *adj*, **cheesiness** *n*

[2]**cheese** *n* an important person; a boss – slang; chiefly in *big cheese*

'**cheese,cake** /-,kayk‖-,keɪk/ *n* **1** a baked or refrigerated dessert consisting of a soft filling, usu containing cheese, in a biscuit or pastry case **2** a photographic display of shapely and scantily clothed female figures – infml

'**cheese,cloth** /-,kloth‖-,klɒθ/ *n* a very fine unsized cotton gauze

,**cheesed 'off** *adj, chiefly Br* browned-off – slang

cheeseparing /'cheez,peəring‖'tʃi:z,peərɪŋ/ *n* miserly or petty economizing; stinginess – **cheeseparing** *adj*

cheetah /'cheetə‖'tʃi:tə/ *n* a long-legged spotted swift-moving African and formerly Asiatic cat [Hindi *cītā*, fr Sanskrit *citrakāya* tiger, fr *citra* bright + *kāya* body]

chef /shef‖ʃef/ *n* a skilled cook; *esp* the chief cook in a restaurant or hotel [French, short for *chef de cuisine* head of the kitchen]

chef d'oeuvre /,shay 'duhvə ‖,ʃeɪ 'dɜ:və (*Fr* ʃɛ dœ:vr)/ *n, pl* **chefs d'oeuvre** /~/ an (artistic or literary) masterpiece

[1]**chemical** /'kemikl‖'kemɪkl/ *adj* **1** of, used in, or produced by chemistry **2** acting, operated, or produced by chemicals – **chemically** *adv*

[2]**chemical** *n* a substance (e g an element or chemical compound) obtained by a chemical process or used for producing a chemical effect

chemise /shə'meez‖ʃə'mi:z/ *n* **1** a woman's one-piece undergarment **2** a usu loose straight-hanging dress

chemist /'kemist‖'kemɪst/ *n* **1** one who is trained in chemistry **2** *Br* (a pharmacist, esp in) a retail shop where medicines and miscellaneous articles (e g cosmetics and films) are sold

chemistry /'kemistri‖'kemɪstrɪ/ *n* **1** a science that deals with the composition, structure, and properties of substances and of the transformations they undergo **2a** the composition and chemical properties of a substance **b** chemical processes and phenomena (e g of an organism) <*blood* ~>

chemotherapy /ˌkeemohˈtherəpi, ˌke-‖ˌkiːməʊˈθerəpɪ, ˌke-/ *n* the use of chemical agents in the treatment or control of disease – **chemotherapeutic** *adj*, **chemotherapist** *n*

chenille /shəˈneel‖ʃəˈniːl/ *n* a (wool, cotton, silk, or rayon) yarn with protruding pile; *also* a fabric with a pile face and a chenille yarn weft

cheque /chek‖tʃek/ *n, chiefly Br* a written order for a bank to pay money as instructed; *also* a printed form on which such an order is usually written

ˈchequeˌbook /-ˌbook‖-ˌbʊk/ *n* a book containing unwritten cheques

ˈcheque ˌcard *n* a card issued to guarantee that the holder's cheques up to a specific amount will be honoured by the issuing bank

[1]**chequer,** *chiefly NAm* **checker** /ˈchekə‖ˈtʃekə/ *n* [1]CHECK 6a

[2]**chequer,** *chiefly NAm* **checker** *vt* **1** to variegate with different colours or shades; *esp* to mark with squares of (2) alternating colours **2** to vary with contrasting elements or situations <*a* ~ed *career*> *USE* usu in past participle

cherish /ˈcherish‖ˈtʃerɪʃ/ *vt* **1a** to hold dear; feel or show affection for **b** to keep or cultivate with care and affection; nurture **2** to keep in the mind deeply and with affection <*still* ~es *that memory*> – **cherishable** *adj*

cheroot /shəˈrooht‖ʃəˈruːt/ *n* a cigar cut square at both ends [Tamil *curuṭṭu*, lit., roll]

cherry /ˈcheri‖ˈtʃerɪ/ *n* **1** (the wood or small pale yellow to deep red or blackish fruit of) any of numerous trees and shrubs of the rose family, often cultivated for their fruit or ornamental flowers **2** light red

cherub /ˈcherəb‖ˈtʃerəb/ *n, pl* **cherubs,** (*1*) **cherubim** /ˈcherəbim‖ˈtʃerəbɪm/ **1** a biblical attendant of God or of a holy place, often represented as a being with large wings, a human head, and an animal body **2a** a beautiful usu winged child in painting and sculpture **b** an innocent-looking usu chubby and pretty person – **cherubic** *adj*

chervil /ˈchuhvil‖ˈtʃɜːvɪl/ *n* an aromatic plant whose leaves are used as a herb

chess /ches‖tʃes/ *n* a game for 2 players each of whom moves his/her 16 chessmen according to fixed rules across a chessboard and tries to checkmate his/her opponent's king

ˈchessˌboard /-ˌbawd‖-ˌbɔːd/ *n* a board used in chess, draughts, etc that is divided into usu 64 equal squares of 2 alternating colours

chessman /-ˌman‖-ˌmæn/ *n, pl* **chessmen** /-mən, -ˌmen‖-mən, -ˌmen/ any of the pieces (1 king, 1 queen, 2 rooks, 2 bishops, 2 knights, and 8 pawns) used by each side in playing chess

chest /chest‖tʃest/ *n* **1a** a box with a lid used esp for the safekeeping of belongings **b** a usu small cupboard used esp for storing medicines or first-aid supplies **c** a case in which a commodity (e g tea) is shipped **2** the part of the body enclosed by the ribs and breastbone – **chestful** *n*

-chested /-chestid‖-tʃestɪd/ *comb form* (→ *adj*) having (such) a chest <*flat*-chested>

chesterfield /ˈchestəˌfeeld‖ˈtʃestəˌfiːld/ *n* a heavily padded usu leather sofa

[1]**chestnut** /ˈches(t)ˌnut‖ˈtʃes(t)ˌnʌt/ *n* **1** (the nut or wood of) a tree or shrub of the beech family; *esp* SPANISH CHESTNUT **2** reddish brown **3** HORSE CHESTNUT **4** a chestnut-coloured animal, specif a horse **5** the small callus on the inner side of a horse's leg **6** an often repeated joke or story; *broadly* anything repeated excessively

[2]**chestnut** *adj* of the colour chestnut

ˌ**chest of ˈdrawers** /drawz‖drɔːz/ *n* a piece of furniture containing a set of drawers (e g for holding clothes)

chesty /ˈchesti‖ˈtʃestɪ/ *adj* **1** of, inclined to, symptomatic of, or suffering from disease of the chest – not used technically **2** having prominent breasts – slang

chevalier /ˌshevəˈliə‖ˌʃevəˈlɪə/ *n* a member of certain orders of merit (e g the French Legion of Honour)

chevron /ˈshevrən‖ˈʃevrən/ *n* a figure, pattern, or object having the shape of an (inverted) V; *esp* a sleeve badge that usu consists of 1 or more chevron-shaped stripes and indicates the wearer's rank

[1]**chew** /chooh‖tʃuː/ *vb* to crush, grind, or gnaw (esp food) (as if) with the teeth – **chewable** *adj*, **chewer** *n*, **chewy** *adj*

[2]**chew** *n* **1** the act of chewing **2** sthg for chewing <*a* ~ *of tobacco*>

ˈ**chewing ˌgum** /ˈchooh·ing‖ˈtʃuːɪŋ/ *n* a flavoured usu sweetened insoluble material (e g chicle) for chewing

chew over *vt* to meditate on; think about reflectively – infml

chiack /ˈchie·ək‖ˈtʃaɪək/ *vb, chiefly Austr* to make derisive remarks (about) – **chiack** *n*

Chianti /kiˈanti‖kɪˈæntɪ/ *n* a dry (red) Italian table wine

chiaroscuro /kiˌahrəˈskooəroh‖kɪˌɑːrəˈskʊərəʊ/ *n, pl* **chiaroscuros** **1** pictorial representation in terms of light and shade **2** the arrangement or treatment of light and shade in a painting

chic /sheek, shik‖ʃiːk, ʃɪk/ *adj or n* (having or showing) elegance and sophistication, esp of dress or manner – **chicly** *adv*, **chicness** *n*

chicane /shiˈkayn‖ʃɪˈkeɪn/ *n* a series of tight turns in opposite directions in an otherwise straight stretch of a road-racing course

chicanery /shiˈkayn(ə)ri‖ʃɪˈkeɪn(ə)rɪ/ *n* **1** deception by the use of fallacious or irrelevant arguments **2** a piece of sharp practice or legal trickery – **chicane** *vb*

chichi /ˈsheeˌshee‖ˈʃiːˌʃiː/ *adj or n* **1** showy, frilly, or elaborate (ornamentation) **2** unnecessarily elaborate or affected (behaviour, style, etc)

chick /chik‖tʃɪk/ *n* **1** a young bird; *esp* a (newly hatched) chicken **2** a young woman – slang

[1]**chicken** /ˈchikin‖ˈtʃɪkɪn/ *n* **1** the common domestic fowl, esp when young; *also* its flesh used as food **2** a young person – chiefly in *he/she is no chicken* **3a** a contest in which the participants put themselves in danger to see who is most brave **b** a coward – slang *USE* (*2&3a*) infml

[2]**chicken** *adj* scared – infml

ˈchicken ˌfeed *n* a small and insignificant amount, esp of money – infml

ˌchickenˈhearted /-ˈhahtid‖-ˈhɑːtɪd/ *adj* timid, cowardly

chicken out *vi* to lose one's nerve – infml

ˈchicken ˌpox /poks‖pɒks/ *n* an infectious virus disease, esp of children, that is marked by mild fever and a rash of small blisters

chick-pea /ˈchik ˌpee‖ˈtʃɪk ˌpiː/ *n* (the hard edible seed of) an Asiatic leguminous plant

chickweed /ˈchikˌweed‖ˈtʃɪkˌwiːd/ *n* any of various low-growing small-leaved plants of the pink family that occur commonly as weeds

chicle /ˈchikl‖ˈtʃɪkl/ *n* a gum from the milky juice of a tropical tree, used as the chief ingredient of chewing gum

chicory /ˈchik(ə)ri‖ˈtʃɪk(ə)rɪ/ *n* a usu blue-flowered European plant widely grown for its edible thick roots and as a salad plant; *also* the ground roasted root used as a coffee additive

chide /chied‖tʃaɪd/ *vb* **chid** /chid‖tʃɪd/, **chided; chid, chidden** /ˈchid(ə)n‖ˈtʃɪd(ə)n/, **chided** to rebuke (sby) angrily; scold – **chidingly** *adv*

[1]**chief** /cheef‖tʃiːf/ *n* **1** (a broad band across) the upper part of a heraldic field **2** the head of a body of people or an organization; a leader – **chiefdom, chiefship** *n*

[2]**chief** *adj* **1** accorded highest rank or office <~ *librarian*> **2** of greatest importance or influence <*the* ~ *reasons*>

ˌchief ˈjustice *n* the presiding judge of a supreme court of justice (e g the US Supreme Court)

chiefly /ˈcheefli‖ˈtʃiːflɪ/ *adv* **1** most importantly; principally, especially **2** for the most part; mostly, mainly

ˌchief of ˈstaff *n* the senior officer of an armed forces staff that serves a commander

chieftain /ˈcheeftən‖ˈtʃiːftən/, *fem* **chieftainess** /-ˈnes‖-ˈnes/ *n* a chief, esp of a band, tribe, or clan – **chieftainship** *n*

chiffon /ˈshifon, -ˈ-‖ˈʃɪfɒn, -ˈ-/ *n* a sheer (silk) fabric

chiffonier /ˌshifəˈniə‖ˌʃɪfəˈnɪə/ *n* a high narrow chest of drawers

chignon /shiˈnyon, ˈshee-‖ʃɪˈnjɒn, ˈʃiː-/ *n* a usu large smooth knot of hair worn esp at the nape of the neck

Chihuahua /chiˈwah·wə‖tʃɪˈwɑːwə/ *n* a very small round-headed large-eared dog of Mexican origin [*Chihuahua*, state & city in Mexico]

chilblain /ˈchilˌblayn‖ˈtʃɪlˌbleɪn/ *n* an inflammatory sore, esp on the feet or hands, caused by exposure to cold

child /chield‖tʃaɪld/ *n, pl* **children** /ˈchildrən‖ˈtʃɪldrən/ **1** an unborn or recently born person **2a** a young person, esp between infancy and youth **b** a childlike or childish person **c(1)** a person not yet of (a legally specified) age **c(2)** sby under the age of 14 – used in English law **3a** a son or daughter <*left the estate to her* ~ren> **b** a descendant <*the* Children *of David*> **4** one strongly influenced by another or by a place or state of affairs <*a* ~ *of the depression*> – **childless** *adj*, **childlessness** *n* – **with child** *of a woman* PREGNANT 3

child benefit *n* a (weekly) allowance paid through the post office for each child in the family

ˈchildˌbirth /-ˌbuhth‖-ˌbɜːθ/ *n* parturition

childhood /ˈchieldˌhood‖ˈtʃaɪldˌhʊd/ *n* **1** the state or period of being a child **2** an early period in the development of sthg

childish /ˈchieldish‖ˈtʃaɪldɪʃ/ *adj* **1** of or befitting a child or childhood **2** marked by or suggestive of immaturity – **childishly** *adv*, **childishness** *n*

childlike /ˈchieldˌliek‖ˈtʃaɪldˌlaɪk/ *adj* marked by innocence and trust

childminder /ˈchieldˌmiendə‖ˈtʃaɪldˌmaɪndə/ *n, chiefly Br* sby who looks after other people's children, esp while the parents are at work

ˈchild's ˌplay *n* an extremely simple task or act

[1]**chill** /chil‖tʃɪl/ *vi* **1** to become cold **2** to catch a chill **3** *of a metal* to become surface-hardened by sudden cooling ~ *vt* **1a** to make cold or chilly **b** to make (esp food or drink) cool, esp without freezing **2** to affect as if with cold; dispirit **3** to harden the surface of (metal) by sudden cooling – **chillingly** *adv*

[2]**chill** *adj* CHILLY 1, 2 – **chillness** *n*

[3]**chill** *n* **1a** a (disagreeable) sensation of coldness **b** COMMON COLD **2** a moderate but disagreeable degree of cold **3** coldness of manner

chilli, chili /ˈchili‖ˈtʃɪlɪ/ *n, pl* **chillies, chilies** the pod of a hot pepper used either whole or ground as a pungent condiment

chilly /ˈchili‖ˈtʃɪlɪ/ *adj* **1** noticeably (unpleasantly) cold **2** lacking warmth of feeling; distant, unfriendly **3** tending to arouse fear or apprehension <~ *details*> – **chilliness** *n*

[1]**chime** /chiem‖tʃaɪm/ *n* **1a** a musically tuned set of bells **b** a set of objects (e g hanging metal bars or tubes) that sound like bells when struck **2a** the sound of a set of bells – usu pl with sing. meaning **b** a musical sound like that of bells

[2]**chime** *vi* **1** to make the sounds of a chime **2** to be or act in accord <*the music and the mood* ~d *well together*> ~ *vt* **1** to cause to chime **2** to signal or indicate by chiming <*the clock* ~d *midnight*> – **chimer** *n*

[3]**chime** /chiem‖tʃaɪm/, **chimb** /chim‖tʃɪm/ *n* the projecting rim of a barrel

chime in *vi* **1** to break into a conversation or discussion, esp in order to express an opinion **2** to combine harmoniously – often + *with*

chimera /kiˈmiərə, kie-‖kɪˈmɪərə, kaɪ-/ *n* **1a** *cap* a fire-breathing female mythological monster that had a lion's head, a goat's body, and a serpent's tail **b** an imaginary monster made up of incongruous parts **2a** an illusion or fabrication of the mind; *esp* an unrealizable dream **b** a terror that exists only in the mind **3** an individual, organ, or part consisting of tissues of diverse genetic constitution and occurring esp in plants and most frequently at a graft union – **chimeric, chimerical** *adj*, **chimerically** *adv*

chimney /ˈchimni‖ˈtʃɪmnɪ/ *n* **1** a vertical structure incorporated into a building and enclosing a flue or flues for carrying off smoke; *esp* the part of such a structure extending above a roof **2** a structure through which smoke and gases (e g from a furnace or steam engine) are discharged **3** a tube, usu of glass, placed round a flame (e g of an oil lamp) to serve as a shield **4** a

narrow cleft, vent, etc (e g in rock)
ˈchimney ˌbreast *n* the wall that encloses a chimney and projects into a room
ˈchimney ˌcorner *n* a seat by or within a large open fireplace
ˈchimneyˌpiece /-ˌpees‖-ˌpiːs/ *n* a mantelpiece
ˈchimney ˌpot *n* a usu earthenware pipe at the top of a chimney
ˈchimney ˌstack *n* **1** a masonry, brickwork, etc chimney rising above a roof and usu containing several flues **2** a tall chimney, typically of circular section, serving a factory, power station, etc
ˈchimney ˌsweep *n* one whose occupation is cleaning soot from chimney flues
chimpanzee /ˌchimpanˈzee‖ˌtʃɪmpænˈziː/ *n* a tree-dwelling anthropoid ape of equatorial Africa that is smaller and less fierce than the gorilla
chin /chin‖tʃɪn/ *n* the lower portion of the face lying below the lower lip and including the prominence of the lower jaw
china /ˈchienə‖ˈtʃaɪnə/ *n* **1** porcelain; *also* vitreous porcelain ware (e g dishes and vases) for domestic use **2** chinaware; *broadly* crockery **3** *chiefly Br* BONE CHINA [Persian *chīnī* Chinese porcelain]
ˈchina ˌclay *n* kaolin
chinaman /ˈchienəmən‖ˈtʃaɪnəmən/ *n* a ball delivered by a slow left-arm bowler in cricket that is an off-break to a right-handed batsman
ˈChinaˌtown /-ˌtown‖-ˌtaʊn/ *n* the Chinese quarter of a city
ˈchinaˌware /-ˌweə‖-ˌweə/ *n* tableware made of china
chinchilla /ˌchinˈchilə‖ˌtʃɪnˈtʃɪlə/ *n* **1** (the soft pearly-grey fur of) a S American rodent the size of a large squirrel **2** (any of) a breed of domestic rabbit with long white or greyish fur; *also* (any of) a breed of cat with similar fur
1chine /chien‖tʃaɪn/ *n, Br* a steep-sided ravine, esp in Dorset or the Isle of Wight
2chine *n* **1** (a cut of meat including the whole or part of) the backbone **2** a (mountain) ridge **3** the intersection of the bottom and sides of a boat
3chine *vt* to separate the backbone from the ribs of (a joint of meat); *also* to cut through the backbone of (a carcass)
Chinese /ˌchieˈneez‖ˌtʃaɪˈniːz/ *n, pl* **Chinese** **1** a native or inhabitant of China **2** a group of related Sino-Tibetan tone languages used by the people of China; *specif* Mandarin – **Chinese** *adj*
1chink /chingk‖tʃɪŋk/ *n* **1** a small slit or fissure **2** a means of evasion or escape; a loophole <*a ~ in the law*>
2chink *n* a short sharp sound – **chink** *vb*
Chink *n* a native of China – derog
chinless /ˈchinlis‖ˈtʃɪnlɪs/ *adj, Br* lacking firmness of purpose; ineffectual – infml
chinook /shəˈnook‖ʃəˈnʊk; *also* chiˈnoohk, -ˈnook‖tʃɪˈnuːk, -ˈnʊk/ *n* **1** a warm moist south-westerly wind of the NW coast of the USA **2** a warm dry westerly wind of the E slopes of the Rocky mountains
chintz /chints‖tʃɪnts/ *n* a (glazed) printed plain-weave fabric, usu of cotton *n* a conversation, chat – infml
1chip /chip‖tʃɪp/ *n* **1a** a small usu thin and flat piece (e g of wood or stone) cut, struck, or flaked off **b** a small thin slice or piece of fruit, chocolate, etc **2** a counter used as a token for money in gambling games **3** a flaw left after a chip is removed **4** (the small piece of semiconductor, esp silicon, on which is constructed) an integrated circuit **5** CHIP SHOT **6a** *chiefly Br* a strip of potato fried in deep fat **b** *NAm & Austr* 3CRISP – **chip off the old block** a child that resembles either of his/her parents – **chip on one's shoulder** a challenging, belligerent, or embittered attitude – **when the chips are down** when the crucial or critical point has been reached
2chip *vb* **-pp-** *vt* **1a** to cut or hew with an edged tool **b(1)** to cut or break (a small piece) from sthg **b(2)** to cut or break a fragment from **2** to kick or hit (a ball, pass, etc) in a short high arc ~ *vi* **1** to break off in small pieces **2** to play a chip shot
ˈchipˌboard /-ˌbawd‖-ˌbɔːd/ *n* an artificial board made from compressed wood chips and glue
chip in *vi* **1** to contribute <*everyone* chipped in *for the gift*> **2** to interrupt or add a comment to a conversation between other people ~*vt* to contribute <chipped in *£1 for the gift*> *USE* infml
chipmunk /ˈchipˌmungk‖ˈtʃɪpˌmʌŋk/ *n* any of numerous small striped American squirrels
chipolata /ˌchipəˈlahtə‖ˌtʃɪpəˈlɑːtə/ *n* a small thin sausage [French, fr Italian *cipollata*, fr *cipollato* with onions, deriv of Latin *cepa* onion]
Chippendale /ˈchipənˌdayl‖ˈtʃɪpənˌdeɪl/ *adj or n* (of or being) an 18th-c English furniture style characterized by graceful outline and fine ornamentation [Thomas *Chippendale* (1718?-79), English cabinet-maker & designer]
chippy /ˈchipi‖ˈtʃɪpɪ/ *n* **1** a carpenter **2** *Br* a shop selling fish and chips *USE* infml
ˈchip ˌshot *n* a short shot in golf that lofts the ball to the green and allows it to roll
chiromancy /ˈkirəˌmansi‖ˈkɪrəˌmænsɪ/ *n* palmistry – **chiromancer** *n*
chiropody /kiˈropədi, shi-‖kɪˈrɒpədɪ, ʃɪ-/ *n* the care and treatment of the human foot in health and disease [deriv of Greek *cheir* hand + *pod-, pous* foot] – **chiropodist** *n*
chiropractic /ˈkirəˌpraktik‖ˈkɪrəˌpræktɪk/ *n* a system of healing disease that employs manipulation and adjustment of body structures (e g the spinal column) – **chiropractor** *n*
chirp /chuhp‖tʃɜːp/ *vi or n* (to make or speak in a tone resembling) the characteristic short shrill sound of a small bird or insect
chirpy /ˈchuhpi‖ˈtʃɜːpɪ/ *adj* lively, cheerful – infml – **chirpily** *adv*, **chirpiness** *n*
1chisel /ˈchizl‖ˈtʃɪzl/ *n* a metal tool with a cutting edge at the end of a blade used in dressing, shaping, or working wood, stone, metal, etc
2chisel *vb* **-ll-** (*NAm* **-l-**, **-ll-**), **1** to cut or work (as if) with a chisel **2** to trick, cheat, or obtain (sthg) by cheating <*he's* ~led *me out of my prize*> – slang – **chiseller** *n*
1chit /chit‖tʃɪt/ *n* an immature often disrespectful young woman, usu of slight build
2chit *n* a small slip of paper with writing on it; *esp* an order for goods

chitchat /ˈchit,chat‖ˈtʃɪt,tʃæt/ *vi or n* **-tt-** (to make) small talk; gossip – infml

chitin /ˈkietin‖ˈkaɪtɪn/ *n* a horny substance consisting of a complex carbohydrate that forms part of the hard outer covering of esp insects and crustaceans

chivalrous /ˈshiv(ə)lrəs‖ˈʃɪv(ə)lrəs/ *adj* **1** having the characteristics (e g valour or gallantry) of a knight **2** (characteristic) of knight-errantry **3a** honourable, generous **b** graciously courteous and considerate, esp to women – **chivalrously** *adv*, **chivalrousness** *n*

chivalry /ˈshiv(ə)lri‖ˈʃɪv(ə)lrɪ/ *n* **1** the system, spirit, or customs of medieval knighthood **2** the qualities (e g courage, integrity, and consideration) of an ideal knight; chivalrous conduct

chive /chiev‖tʃaɪv/ *n* a perennial plant related to the onion and used esp to flavour and garnish food – usu pl with sing. meaning

chivvy, chivy /ˈchivi‖ˈtʃɪvɪ/ *vt* **1** to tease or annoy with persistent petty attacks; harass **2** to rouse to activity – often + *up* or *along* *USE* infml

chlor-, chloro- *comb form* **1** green <chloro*phyll*> **2** (containing) chlorine <chlor*ic*>

chloride /ˈklawried‖ˈklɔːraɪd/ *n* a compound of chlorine with another element or radical; *esp* a salt or ester of hydrochloric acid

chlorinate /ˈklawri,nayt‖ˈklɔːrɪ,neɪt/ *vt* to treat or cause to combine with (a compound of) chlorine – **chlorinator** *n*, **chlorination** n

chlorine /ˈklawreen‖ˈklɔːriːn/ *n* a halogen element that is isolated as a pungent heavy greenish yellow gas

chloroform /ˈklorə,fawm‖ˈklɒrə,fɔːm/ *vt or n* (to anaesthetize with) a colourless volatile liquid used esp as a solvent and formerly as a general anaesthetic

chlorophyll /ˈklorəfil‖ˈklɒrəfɪl/ *n* **1** the green photosynthetic colouring matter of plants found in the chloroplasts **2** a waxy green chlorophyll-containing substance extracted from green plants and used as a colouring agent or deodorant

chloroplast /ˈklawroh,plast‖ˈklɔːrəʊ,plæst/ *n* a chlorophyll-containing organelle that is the site of photosynthesis and starch formation in plant cells

choc-ice /ˈchok ,ies‖ˈtʃɒk ,aɪs/ *n*, *Br* a bar of ice cream covered in chocolate

[1]**chock** /chok‖tʃɒk/ *n* a wedge or block placed under a door, barrel, wheel, etc to prevent movement

[2]**chock** *vt* **1** to provide, stop, or make fast (as if) with chocks **2** to raise or support on blocks

[3]**chock** *adv* as closely or as completely as possible

chock-a-block /,chok ə ˈblok‖,tʃɒk ə ˈblɒk/ *adj or adv* tightly packed; in a very crowded condition

chocolate /ˈchoklət‖ˈtʃɒklət/ *n* **1** a paste, powder, or solid block of food prepared from (sweetened or flavoured) ground roasted cacao seeds **2** a beverage made by mixing chocolate with usu hot water or milk **3** a sweet made or coated with chocolate **4** dark brown [Spanish, fr Nahuatl *xocoatl*] – **chocolate** *adj*

[1]**choice** /choys‖tʃɔɪs/ *n* **1** the act of choosing; selection **2** the power of choosing; an option **3a** sby or sthg chosen **b** the best part; the elite **4** a sufficient number and variety to choose among

[2]**choice** *adj* **1** worthy of being chosen **2** selected with care; well chosen **3** of high quality – **choicely** *adv*, **choiceness** *n*

choir /kwie·ə‖kwaɪə/ *n* **1** *sing or pl in constr* an organized company of singers **2** the part of a church occupied by the singers or the clergy; *specif* the part of the chancel between the sanctuary and the nave

ˈ**choir,boy** /-,boy‖-,bɔɪ/ *n* a boy singer in a (church) choir

ˈ**choir ,school** *n* a school primarily intended for the boys of a cathedral or college choir

[1]**choke** /chohk‖tʃəʊk/ *vt* **1** to check the normal breathing of by compressing or obstructing the windpipe, or by poisoning available air **2** to stop or suppress expression of or by; silence <*a ban designed to* ~ *discussion*> – often + *back* or *down* **3a** to restrain the growth or activity of <*the flowers were* ~d *by the weeds*> **b** to obstruct by filling up or clogging <*leaves* ~d *the drain*> **c** to fill completely; jam ~ *vi* **1** to become choked in breathing **2a** to become obstructed or checked **b** to become speechless or incapacitated, esp from strong emotion – usu + *up* **3** to lose one's composure and fail to perform effectively in a critical situation

[2]**choke** *n* sthg that obstructs passage or flow: e g **a** a valve in the carburettor of a petrol engine for controlling the amount of air in a fuel air mixture **b** an inductor **c** a narrowing towards the muzzle in the bore of a gun **d** a device allowing variation of the choke of a shotgun

[3]**choke** *n* the fibrous (inedible) central part of a globe artichoke

choker /ˈchohkə‖ˈtʃəʊkə/ *n* **1** a high stiff (clerical) collar **2** a short necklace or decorative band that fits closely round the throat

chokey, choky /ˈchohki‖ˈtʃəʊkɪ/ *n*, *Br* PRISON 2 – slang [Hindi *chaukī* shed, lock-up]

choler /ˈkolə, ˈkohlə‖ˈkɒlə, ˈkəʊlə/ *n* anger, irascibility – fml

cholera /ˈkolərə‖ˈkɒlərə/ *n* (any of several diseases of human beings and domestic animals similar to) an often fatal infectious epidemic disease caused by a bacterium and marked by severe gastrointestinal disorders – **choleraic** *adj*

choleric /ˈkolərik‖ˈkɒlərɪk/ *adj* **1** easily moved to (excessive) anger; irascible **2** angry, irate *USE* fml

cholesterol /kəˈlestərol‖kəˈlestərɒl/ *n* a hydroxy steroid that is present in animal and plant cells and is a possible factor in hardening of the arteries

chomp /chomp‖tʃɒmp/ *vb* to champ

choose /choohz‖tʃuːz/ *vb* **chose** /chohz‖tʃəʊz/; **chosen** /ˈchohz(ə)n‖ˈtʃəʊz(ə)n/ *vt* **1a** to select freely and after consideration **b** to decide on; *esp* to elect <chose *her as leader*> **2a** to decide <chose *to go by train*> **b** to wish <*I* ~ *not to do it*> ~*vi* to make a selection – **chooser** *n*

choosy, choosey /ˈchoohzi‖ˈtʃuːzɪ/ *adj* fastidiously selective; particular

[1]**chop** /chop‖tʃɒp/ *vb* **-pp-** *vt* **1a** to cut into or

sever, usu by a blow or repeated blows of a sharp instrument **b** to cut into pieces – often + *up* **2** to strike (a ball) so as to impart backspin ~*vi* to make a quick stroke or repeated strokes (as if) with a sharp instrument

²**chop** *n* **1** a forceful usu slanting blow or stroke (as if) with an axe or cleaver **2** a small cut of meat often including part of a rib **3** an uneven motion of the sea, esp when wind and tide are opposed **4** abrupt removal; *esp* ¹SACK 4 – + *the*; infml

³**chop** *vi* **-pp-** *esp of the wind* to change direction – **chop and change** to keep changing one's mind, plans, etc – **chop logic** to argue with minute oversubtle distinctions

ˌ**chop-'chop** *adv or interj* without delay; quickly – infml

'**chopˌhouse** /-ˌhows‖-ˌhaʊs/ *n* a restaurant specializing in meat dishes, esp chops or steaks

chopper /'chopə‖'tʃɒpə/ *n* **1** a short-handled axe or cleaver **2** a device that interrupts an electric current or a beam of radiation (e g light) at short regular intervals **3** a helicopter – infml

choppy /'chopi‖'tʃɒpɪ/ *adj, of the sea or other expanse of water* rough with small waves

'**chopˌstick** /-ˌstik‖-ˌstɪk/ *n* either of 2 slender sticks held between thumb and fingers, used chiefly in oriental countries to lift food to the mouth

chopsuey /ˌchop'sooh·i‖ˌtʃɒp'suːɪ/ *n* a Chinese dish of shredded meat or chicken with bean sprouts and other vegetables, usu served with rice and soy sauce

choral /'kawrəl‖'kɔːrəl/ *adj* accompanied with or designed for singing (by a choir) – **chorally** *adv*

chorale *also* **choral** /ko'rahl‖kɒ'rɑːl/ *n* **1** (music composed for) a usu German traditional hymn or psalm for singing in church **2** *sing or pl in constr* a chorus, choir

¹**chord** /kawd‖kɔːd/ *n* a combination of notes sounded together

²**chord** *n* **1** CORD 3a **2** a straight line joining 2 points on a curve **3** an individual emotion or disposition <*touch the right* ~> **4** the straight line joining the leading and trailing edges of an aerofoil

chore /chaw‖tʃɔː/ *n* **1** a routine task or job **2** a difficult or disagreeable task

choreography /ˌkori'ogrəfi‖ˌkɒrɪ'ɒgrəfɪ/ *n* the composition and arrangement of a ballet or other dance for the stage [French *chorégraphie*, fr Greek *choreia* dance + *graphein* to write] – **choreographer** *n*, **choreograph** *vb*, **choreographic** *adj*, **choreographically** *adv*

chorister /'koristə‖'kɒrɪstə/ *n* a singer in a choir; *specif* a choirboy

chortle /'chawtl‖'tʃɔːtl/ *vi* to laugh or chuckle, esp in satisfaction or exultation – **chortle** *n*, **chortler** *n*

¹**chorus** /'kawrəs‖'kɔːrəs/ *n* **1** (the part of a drama sung or spoken by) a character (e g in Elizabethan drama) or group of singers and dancers (e g in Greek drama) who comment on the action **2** *sing or pl in constr* **2a** an organized company of singers who sing in concert; *specif* a body of singers who sing the choral parts of a work (e g in opera) **b** a group of dancers and singers supporting the featured players in a musical or revue **3a** a part of a song or hymn recurring at intervals **b** a composition sung by a chorus **4** sthg performed, sung, or uttered simultaneously by a number of people or animals – **in chorus** in unison

²**chorus** *vb* to sing or utter in chorus

chose /chohz‖tʃəʊz/ *past of* CHOOSE

¹**chosen** /'chohz(ə)n‖'tʃəʊz(ə)n/ *adj* selected or marked for favour or special privilege <*granted to a* ~ *few*>

²**chosen** *n pl in constr the* people who are the object of divine favour

chough /chuf‖tʃʌf/ *n* an Old World bird of the crow family that has red legs, a red beak, and glossy black plumage

ˌ**choux 'pastry** /shooh‖ʃuː/ *n* a light pastry made with an egg-enriched dough

¹**chow** /chow‖tʃaʊ/ *n* food – infml

²**chow** *also* '**chow ˌchow** *n* a heavy-coated broad-headed dog with a blue-black tongue

chowder /'chowdə‖'tʃaʊdə/ *n* a thick (clam or other seafood) soup or stew

chow mein /ˌchow 'mayn‖ˌtʃaʊ 'meɪn/ *n* a Chinese dish of fried noodles usu mixed with shredded meat or poultry and vegetables

Christ /kriest‖kraɪst/ *n* **1** the Messiah **2** Jesus – **Christlike** *adj*

christen /'kris(ə)n‖'krɪs(ə)n/ *vt* **1a** BAPTIZE 1, 3 **b** to name at baptism **2** to name or dedicate (e g a ship or bell) by a ceremony suggestive of baptism **3** to name **4** to use for the first time – infml

Christendom /'kris(ə)ndəm, 'krist-‖'krɪs(ə)ndəm, 'krɪst-/ *n* the community of people or nations professing Christianity

christening /'kris(ə)ning‖'krɪs(ə)nɪŋ/ *n* the ceremony of baptizing and naming a child

¹**Christian** /'kristi·ən‖'krɪstɪən/ *n* **1a** an adherent of Christianity **b** a member of a Christian denomination, esp by baptism **2** a good or kind person regardless of religion

²**Christian** *adj* **1** of or consistent with Christianity or Christians **2** commendably decent or generous <*has a very* ~ *concern for others*> – **Christianize** *vt*, **Christianization** *n*, **Christianly** *adv*

'**Christian ˌera** *n* the period dating from the birth of Christ

Christianity /ˌkristi'anəti‖ˌkrɪstɪ'ænətɪ/ *n* **1** the religion based on the life and teachings of Jesus Christ and the Bible **2** conformity to (a branch of) the Christian religion

'**Christian ˌname** *n* **1** a name given at christening (or confirmation) **2** a forename

ˌ**Christian 'Science** *n* a religion founded by Mary Baker Eddy in 1866 that includes a practice of spiritual healing – **Christian Scientist** *n*

Christmas /'krisməs‖'krɪsməs/ *n* **1** a festival of the western Christian churches on December 25 that commemorates the birth of Christ and is usu observed as a public holiday **2 Christmas, Christmastide** /-tied/ the festival season from Christmas Eve till the Epiphany (January 6) – **Christmassy** *adj*

ˌ**Christmas 'Eve** *n* the (evening of the) day before Christmas day

ˈChristmas ˌtree *n* an evergreen or artificial tree decorated with lights, tinsel, etc at Christmas

chromatic /kroh'matik‖krəʊ'mætɪk/ *adj* **1a** of colour sensation or (intensity of) colour **b** highly coloured **2a** of or giving all the notes of the chromatic scale **b** characterized by frequent use of intervals or notes outside the diatonic scale – **chromatically** *adv*, **chromaticism** *n*

chromatic scale *n* a musical scale consisting entirely of semitones

chrome /krohm‖krəʊm/ *n* **1** (a pigment formed from) chromium **2** (sthg with) a plating of chromium

chromium /'krohmyəm, -mi·əm‖'krəʊmjəm, -mɪəm/ *n* a blue-white metallic element found naturally only in combination and used esp in alloys and in electroplating

chromosome /'krohmə͵sohm, -͵zohm‖'krəʊmə͵səʊm, -͵zəʊm/ *n* any of the gene-carrying bodies that contain DNA and protein and are found in the cell nucleus – **chromosomal** *adj*, **chromosomally** *adv*

chronic /'kronik‖'krɒnɪk/ *adj* **1a** *esp of an illness* marked by long duration or frequent recurrence – usu contrasted with ACUTE 4 **b** suffering from a chronic disease **2a** always present or encountered; *esp* constantly troubling <~ *financial difficulties*> **b** habitual, persistent <*a* ~ *grumbler*> **3** *Br* bad, terrible – infml [French *chronique*, fr Greek *chronikos* of time, fr *chronos* time] – **chronically** *adv*, **chronicity** *n*

[1]**chronicle** /'kronikl‖'krɒnɪkl/ *n* **1** a usu continuous and detailed historical account of events arranged chronologically without analysis or interpretation **2** a narrative

[2]**chronicle** *vt* **1** to record (as if) in a chronicle **2** to list, describe – **chronicler** *n*

chronograph /'krohnə͵grahf, -͵graf‖'krəʊnə͵grɑːf, -͵græf/ *n* an instrument for accurately measuring and recording time intervals – **chronographic** *adj*, **chronography** *n*

chronological /͵kronə'lojikl, ͵kroh-‖͵krɒnə'lɒdʒɪkl, ͵krəʊ-/ *also* **chronologic** /-'lojik‖-'lɒdʒɪk/ *adj* of or arranged in or according to the order of time – **chronologically** *adv*

chronology /krə'noləji‖krə'nɒlədʒɪ/ *n* **1** (the scientific study or use of) a method for setting past events in order of occurrence **2** an arrangement in order of occurrence; *specif* such an arrangement presented in tabular or list form – **chronologer, chronologist** *n*, **chronologize** *vt*

chronometer /krə'nomitə‖krə'nɒmɪtə/ *n* an instrument for measuring time; *esp* one designed to keep time with great accuracy

chrysalis /'krisəlis‖'krɪsəlɪs/ *n, pl* **chrysalides** /kri'salə͵deez‖krɪ'sælə͵diːz/, **chrysalises** (the case enclosing) a pupa, esp of a butterfly or moth

chrysanthemum /kri'zanthimәm‖krɪ'zænθɪmәm/ *n* any of various (cultivated) composite plants with brightly coloured often double flower heads [Latin, fr Greek *chrysanthemon*, fr *chrysos* gold + *anthemon* flower]

chub /chub‖tʃʌb/ *n*, (a marine or freshwater fish similar to) a European freshwater fish of the carp family

chubby /'chubi‖'tʃʌbɪ/ *adj* of large proportions; plump – **chubbiness** *n*

[1]**chuck** /chuk‖tʃʌk/ *n* – used as a term of endearment

[2]**chuck** *vt* **1** to pat, tap <~*ed her under the chin*> **2a** to toss, throw **b** to discard – often + *out* or *away* **3** to leave; GIVE UP 2 <~*ed his job*> – often + *in* or *up* ***USE*** (*except 1*) infml

[3]**chuck** *n* **1** a pat or nudge under the chin **2** a throw – infml

[4]**chuck** *n* **1** a cut of beef that includes most of the neck and the area about the shoulder blade **2** a device for holding a workpiece (e g for turning on a lathe) or tool (e g in a drill)

chuckle /chukl‖tʃʌkl/ *vi* to laugh inwardly or quietly – **chuckle** *n*, **chucklesome** *adj*, **chucklingly** *adv*

chuck out *vt* to eject (a person) from a place or an office; dismiss – infml – **chucker-out** *n*

chug /chug‖tʃʌg/ *vi or n* **-gg-** (to move or go with) a usu repetitive dull explosive sound made (as if) by a labouring engine

chukker /'chukə‖'tʃʌkə/ *n* any of the periods of play in a polo game [Hindi *cakkar* circular course, fr Sanskrit *cakra* wheel, circle]

[1]**chum** /chum‖tʃʌm/ *n* a close friend; a mate – infml; no longer in vogue

[2]**chum** *vi* **-mm-** to form a friendship, esp a close one – usu + *(up) with*; no longer in vogue

chummy /'chumi‖'tʃʌmɪ/ *adj* friendly, intimate – infml – **chummily** *adv*, **chumminess** *n*

chump /chump‖tʃʌmp/ *n* **1** a cut of meat taken from between the loin and hindleg, esp of a lamb, mutton, or pork carcass **2** a fool, duffer – infml – **off one's chump** OFF ONE'S HEAD

chunk /chungk‖tʃʌŋk/ *n* **1** LUMP 1; *esp* one of a firm or hard material (e g wood) **2** a (large) quantity <*put a sizable* ~ *of money on the race*> – infml

chunky /'chungki‖'tʃʌŋkɪ/ *adj* **1** stocky **2** filled with chunks <~ *marmalade*> **3** *of materials, clothes, etc* thick and heavy – **chunkily** *adv*, **chunkiness** *n*

[1]**church** /chuhch‖tʃɜːtʃ/ *n* **1** a building for public (Christian) worship; *esp* a place of worship used by an established church **2** *often cap* institutionalized religion; *esp* the established Christian religion of a country **3** *cap* a body or organization of religious believers: e g **3a** the whole body of Christians **b** DENOMINATION 2 **c** CONGREGATION 2 **4** an occasion for public worship <*goes to* ~ *every Sunday*> **5** the clerical profession <*considered the* ~ *as a possible career*> – **churchly** *adj*, **churchman**, *fem* **churchwoman** *n*

[2]**church** *adj* **1** of a church **2** *chiefly Br* being a member of the established state church

churching /'chuhching‖'tʃɜːtʃɪŋ/ *n* a ceremony in which a woman after childbirth is received and blessed in church – **church** *vt*

͵Church of 'England *n* the established episcopal church of England

͵Church of 'Scotland *n* the established presbyterian church of Scotland

͵church'warden /'-wawd(ə)n‖'-wɔːd(ə)n/ *n* **1** either of 2 lay parish officers in Anglican churches with responsibility esp for parish property and alms **2** a long-stemmed (clay) tobacco pipe

'church͵yard /-͵yahd‖-͵jɑːd/ *n* an enclosed piece of ground surrounding a church; *esp* one used as a burial ground

churl /chuhl‖tʃɜːl/ *n* **1a** a rude ill-bred person **b** a mean morose person **2** *archaic* a rustic, countryman

churlish /ˈchuhlish‖ˈtʃɜːlɪʃ/ *adj* **1** lacking refinement or sensitivity **2** rudely uncooperative; surly – **churlishly** *adv*, **churlishness** *n*

[1]**churn** /chuhn‖tʃɜːn/ *n* **1** a vessel used in making butter in which milk or cream is agitated to separate the oily globules from the watery medium **2** *Br* a large metal container for transporting milk

[2]**churn** *vt* **1** to agitate (milk or cream) in a churn in order to make butter **2** to stir or agitate violently ~ *vi* **1** to work a churn **2** to produce or be in violent motion

churn out *vt* to produce prolifically and mechanically, usu without great concern for quality – chiefly infml

chute /shooht‖ʃuːt/ *n* **1** a waterfall, rapid, etc **2** an inclined plane, channel, or passage down which things may pass **3** a parachute – infml

chutney /ˈchutni‖ˈtʃʌtnɪ/ *n* a thick condiment or relish of Indian origin that contains fruits, sugar, vinegar, and spices

chutzpah *also* **chutzpa** /ˈkhootspah, ˈhootspah‖ˈxʊtspɑː, ˈhʊtspɑː/ *n* brazen audacity – infml

cicada /siˈkahdə, -ˈkaydə‖sɪˈkɑːdə, -ˈkeɪdə/ *n* any of a family of insects that have large transparent wings and whose males produce a shrill singing noise

cicatrice /ˈsikətrees‖ˈsɪkətriːs/ *n* a cicatrix

cicatrix /ˈsikəˌtriks‖ˈsɪkəˌtrɪks/ *n, pl* **cicatrices** /ˌsikəˈtrieseez, siˈkaytriˌseez‖ˌsɪkəˈtraɪsiːz, sɪˈkeɪtrɪˌsiːz/ **1** a scar resulting after a flesh wound has healed **2** a mark resembling a scar: e g a mark left on a stem after the fall of a leaf or bract – **cicatricial** *adj*

cicerone /ˌsisəˈrohni, ˌchichə-‖ˌsɪsəˈrəʊnɪ, ˌtʃɪtʃə-/ *n, pl* **ciceroni** /~/ one who acts as a guide to antiquities; *broadly* a guide, mentor

-cide /-sied‖-saɪd/ *comb form* (→ *n*) **1** killer <*insecti*cide> **2** killing <*sui*cide> – **-cidal** *comb form* (→ *adj*)

cider, *Br also* **cyder** /ˈsiedə‖ˈsaɪdə/ *n* fermented often sparkling apple juice

cigar /siˈgah‖sɪˈgɑː/ *n* a small roll of tobacco leaf for smoking

cigarette, *NAm also* **cigaret** /ˌsigəˈret‖ˌsɪgəˈret/ *n* a narrow cylinder of cut tobacco enclosed in paper for smoking; *also* a similar roll of a herbal or narcotic substance

[1]**cinch** /sinch‖sɪntʃ/ *n* **1** *NAm* GIRTH 1 **2a** a task performed with ease **b** sthg certain to happen *USE* (*2*) infml

[2]**cinch** *vt* **1** *NAm* to fasten or tighten a girth round (a horse) – often + *up* **2** to make certain of; assure – infml

cinchona /singˈkohnə‖sɪŋˈkəʊnə/ *n* (the dried quinine-containing bark of) any of a genus of S American trees and shrubs

cincture /ˈsingkchə‖ˈsɪŋktʃə/ *n* a girdle, belt; *esp* a cloth cord or sash worn round an ecclesiastical vestment or the habit of a religious order

cinder /ˈsində‖ˈsɪndə/ *n* **1** (a fragment of) slag (e g from a blast furnace or volcano) **2** a fragment of ash **3** a piece of partly burned material (e g coal) that will burn further but will not flame – **cindery** *adj*

Cinderella /ˌsindəˈrelə‖ˌsɪndəˈrelə/ *n* **1** sby or sthg that suffers undeserved neglect **2** sby or sthg that is suddenly raised from obscurity to honour or importance

cinecamera /ˈsiniˌkamrə‖ˈsɪnɪˌkæmrə/ *n* a simple hand-held camera for making usu amateur films

cinema /ˈsinimə‖ˈsɪnɪmə/ *n* **1a** films considered esp as an art form, entertainment, or industry – usu + *the* **b** the art or technique of making films; *also* the effects appropriate to film **2** *chiefly Br* a theatre where films are shown

cinematic /ˌsiniˈmatik‖ˌsɪnɪˈmætɪk/ *adj* **1** made and presented as a film <~ *fantasies*> **2** of or suitable for (the making of) films – **cinematically** *adv*

cinematograph /ˌsiniˈmatəˌgrahf, -ˌgraf‖ˌsɪnɪˈmætəˌgrɑːf, -ˌgræf/ *n, chiefly Br* a film camera or projector [French *cinématographe*, fr Greek *kinēmat-, kinēma* movement (fr *kinein* to move) + *graphein* to write]

cinematography /ˌsiniməˈtogrəfi‖ˌsɪnɪməˈtɒgrəfɪ/ *n* the art or science of cinema photography – **cinematographer** *n*, **cinematographic** *adj*, **cinematographically** *adv*

cinnamon /ˈsinəmən‖ˈsɪnəmən/ *n* **1** (any of several trees of the laurel family with) an aromatic bark used as a spice **2** light yellowish brown – **cinnamic** *adj*

cinquefoil /ˈsingkˌfoyl‖ˈsɪŋkˌfɔɪl/ *n* **1** any of a genus of plants of the rose family with 5-lobed leaves **2** a design enclosed by 5 joined arcs arranged in a circle

[1]**cipher** *also* **cypher** /ˈsiefə‖ˈsaɪfə/ *n* **1a** ZERO 1 **b** sby who or sthg that has no worth or influence; a nonentity **2a** a method of transforming a text in order to conceal its meaning **b** a message in code **3** any of the Arabic numerals **4** a combination of symbolic letters; *esp* a monogram

[2]**cipher** *also* **cypher** *vt* **1** to encipher **2** to compute arithmetically

circa /ˈsuhkə‖ˈsɜːkə/ *prep* at, in, or of approximately – used esp with dates <*born* ~ *1600*>

circadian /suhˈkaydi·ən‖sɜːˈkeɪdɪən/ *adj* being, having, characterized by, or occurring in approximately day-long periods or cycles (e g of biological activity or function) <~ *rhythms*>

[1]**circle** /ˈsuhkl‖ˈsɜːkl/ *n* **1a** a closed plane curve every point of which is equidistant from a fixed point within the curve **b** the plane surface bounded by such a curve **2** sthg in the form of (an arc of) a circle: e g **2a** a balcony or tier of seats in a theatre **b** a circle formed on the surface of a sphere (e g the earth) by the intersection of a plane **3** cycle, round <*the wheel has come full* ~> **4** *sing or pl in constr* a group of people sharing a common interest, activity, or leader <*the gossip of court* ~s>

[2]**circle** *vt* **1** to enclose (as if) in a circle **2** to move or revolve round ~ *vi* to move (as if) in a circle – **circler** *n*

circlet /ˈsuhklit‖ˈsɜːklɪt/ *n* a little circle; *esp* a circular ornament

circuit /ˈsuhkit‖ˈsɜːkɪt/ *n* **1** a closed loop encompassing an area **2a** a course round a periphery **b** a racetrack **3a** a regular tour (e g by a judge) round an assigned area or territory **b** the route travelled **c** a group of church congregations with 1 pastor (e g in the Methodist church) **4a** the complete path of an electric current, usu including the source of energy **b** an array of electrical components connected so as to allow the passage of current **c** a 2-way communication path between points (e g in a computer) **5a** an association or league of similar groups **b** a chain of theatres at which productions are presented successively – **circuital** *adj*

ˈcircuit ˌbreaker *n* a switch that automatically interrupts an electric circuit under an infrequent abnormal condition

circuitous /suhˈkyooh·itəs‖sɜːˈkjuːɪtəs/ *adj* indirect in route or method; roundabout – **circuitously** *adv*, **circuitousness, circuity** *n*

[1]**circular** /ˈsuhkyoolə‖ˈsɜːkjʊlə/ *adj* **1** having the form of a circle **2** moving in or describing a circle or spiral **3** marked by the fallacy of assuming sthg which is to be demonstrated <~ *arguments*> **4** marked by or moving in a cycle **5** intended for circulation – **circularity** *n*, **circularly** *adv*, **circularness** *n*

[2]**circular** *n* a paper (e g a leaflet or advertisement) intended for wide distribution

circular·ize, -ise /ˈsuhkyooləˌriez‖ˈsɜːkjʊləˌraɪz/ *vt* **1** to send circulars to **2** to publicize, esp by means of circulars – **circularization** *n*

ˌcircular ˈsaw *n* a power-driven saw that has its teeth set on the edge of a revolving metal disc

circulate /ˈsuhkyooˌlayt‖ˈsɜːkjʊˌleɪt/ *vi* **1** to move in a circle, circuit, or orbit; *esp* to follow a course that returns to the starting point <*blood* ~s *through the body*> **2** to pass from person to person or place to place: e g **2a** to flow without obstruction **b** to become well known or widespread <*rumours* ~d *through the town*> **c** to go from group to group at a social gathering **d** to come into the hands of readers; *specif* to become sold or distributed ~*vt* to cause to circulate – **circulatable** *adj*, **circulative** *adj*, **circulator** *n*, **circulatory** *adj*

circulation /ˌsuhkyooˈlaysh(ə)n‖ˌsɜːkjʊˈleɪʃ(ə)n/ *n* **1** a flow **2** orderly movement through a circuit; *esp* the movement of blood through the vessels of the body induced by the pumping action of the heart **3a** passage or transmission from person to person or place to place; *esp* the interchange of currency <*coins in* ~> **b** the extent of dissemination; *esp* the average number of copies of a publication sold over a given period

ˈcirculatory ˌsystem /ˈsuhkyoolətri, ˌsuhkyooˈlayt(ə)ri‖ˈsɜːkjʊlətrɪ, ˌsɜːkjʊˈleɪt(ə)rɪ/ *n* the system of blood, blood and lymphatic vessels, and heart concerned with the circulation of the blood and lymph

circum- /suhkəm-‖sɜːkəm-/ *prefix* round; about <circum*navigate*>

circumcise /ˈsuhkəmˌsiez‖ˈsɜːkəmˌsaɪz/ *vt* to cut off the foreskin of (a male) or the clitoris of (a female) – **circumcision** *n*

circumference /suhˈkumfərəns‖sɜːˈkʌmfərəns/ *n* **1** the perimeter of a circle **2** the external boundary or surface of a figure or object [Middle French, fr Latin *circumferentia*, fr *circumferre* to carry round, fr *circum* round + *ferre* to carry] – **circumferential** *adj*

circumflex /ˈsuhkəmˌfleks‖ˈsɜːkəmˌfleks/ *n* an accent mark ˆ, ˉ , or ˜ used in various languages to mark length, contraction, or a particular vowel quality

ˌcircumloˈcution /-ləˈkyoohsh(ə)n‖-ləˈkjuːʃ(ə)n/ *n* **1** the use of an unnecessarily large number of words to express an idea **2** evasive speech – **circumlocutious** *adj*, **circumlocutory** *adj*

ˌcircumˈnavigate /-ˈnavigayt‖-ˈnævɪgeɪt/ *vt* to go round; *esp* to travel completely round (the earth), esp by sea – **circumnavigator** *n*, **circumnavigation** *n*

ˈcircumˌscribe /-ˌskrieb‖-ˌskraɪb/ *vt* **1** to surround by a physical or imaginary line **2** to restrict the range or activity of definitely and clearly **3** to draw round (a geometrical figure) so as to touch at as many points as possible

ˌcircumˈscription /-ˈskripsh(ə)n‖-ˈskrɪpʃ(ə)n/ *n* (a) circumscribing or being circumscribed; *esp* (the act of imposing) a restriction

ˈcircumˌspect /-ˌspekt‖-ˌspekt/ *adj* careful to consider all circumstances and possible consequences; prudent – **circumspection** *n*, **circumspectly** *adv*

circumstance /ˈsuhkəmˌstahns, -stans, -stəns‖ˈsɜːkəmˌstɑːns, -stæns, -stəns/ *n* **1** a condition or event that accompanies, causes, or determines another; *also* the sum of such conditions or events **2a** a state of affairs; an occurrence <*open rebellion was a rare* ~> – often pl with sing. meaning <*a victim of* ~s> **b** *pl* situation with regard to material or financial welfare <*he was in easy* ~s> **3** attendant formalities and ceremony <*pomp and* ~> **4** an incident viewed as part of a narrative or course of events; a fact – **in/under the circumstances** because of the conditions; considering the situation

circumstantial /ˌsuhkəmˈstansh(ə)l, -ˈstahnsh(ə)l‖ˌsɜːkəmˈstænʃ(ə)l, -ˈstɑːnʃ(ə)l/ *adj* **1** belonging to, consisting in, or dependent on circumstances **2** pertinent but not essential; incidental – **circumstantiality** *n*, **circumstantially** *adv*

ˌcircumˈvent /-ˈvent‖-ˈvent/ *vt* to check or evade, esp by ingenuity or stratagem – **circumvention** *n*

circus /ˈsuhkəs‖ˈsɜːkəs/ *n* **1a** a large circular or oval stadium used esp for sports contests or spectacles **b** a public spectacle **2a** (the usu covered arena housing) an entertainment in which a variety of performers (e g acrobats and clowns) and performing animals are involved in a series of unrelated acts **b** an activity suggestive of a circus (e g in being a busy scene of noisy or frivolous action) **3** *Br* a road junction in a town partly surrounded by a circle of buildings – usu in proper names <*Piccadilly* Circus> – **circusy** *adj*

cirque /suhk‖sɜːk/ *n* **1** a deep steep-walled basin on a mountain **2** *archaic* CIRCUS 1a

cirrhosis /siˈrohsis‖sɪˈrəʊsɪs/ *n, pl* **cirrhoses** /-ˌseez‖-ˌsiːz/ hardening (of the liver) caused by excessive formation of connective tissue – **cirrhotic** *adj or n*

cirrus /ˈsirəs‖ˈsɪrəs/ *n, pl* **cirri** /-rie‖-raɪ/ **1** TENDRIL 1 **2** a slender usu flexible (invertebrate) animal appendage **3** a wispy white cloud formation usu of minute ice crystals formed at high altitudes

cissy, **sissy** /ˈsisi‖ˈsɪsɪ/ *n, Br* **1** an effeminate boy or man **2** a cowardly person *USE* infml – **cissy** *adj*

Cistercian /siˈstuhsh(ə)n‖sɪˈstɜːʃ(ə)n/ *n* a member of an austere Benedictine order founded in 1098 at Cîteaux in France – **Cistercian** *adj*

cistern /ˈsist(ə)n‖ˈsɪst(ə)n/ *n* an artificial reservoir for storing liquids, esp water: e g **a** a tank at the top of a house or building **b** a water reservoir for a toilet **c** *chiefly NAm* a usu underground tank for storing rainwater

citadel /ˈsitədl, -ˌdel‖ˈsɪtədl, -ˌdel/ *n* **1** a fortress; *esp* one that commands a city **2** a stronghold

citation /sieˈtaysh(ə)n‖saɪˈteɪʃ(ə)n/ *n* **1a** an act of citing or quoting **b** a quotation **2** a mention; *specif* specific reference in a military dispatch to meritorious conduct – **citational** *adj*

cite /siet‖saɪt/ *vt* **1** to call upon to appear before a court **2** to quote by way of example, authority, precedent, or proof <~ *Biblical passages*> **3** to refer to or name; *esp* to mention formally in commendation or praise – **citable** *adj*

citizen /ˈsitiz(ə)n‖ˈsɪtɪz(ə)n/ *n* **1** an inhabitant of a city or town; *esp* a freeman **2** a (native or naturalized) member of a state – **citizenly** *adj*, **citizenship** *n*

ˈcitizenry /-ri‖-rɪ/ *n sing or pl in constr* the whole body of citizens

citizens' band *n, often cap C&B* a radio frequency for private communication (e g between motorists)

ˌcitric ˈacid /ˈsitrik‖ˈsɪtrɪk/ *n* an acid occurring in lemons, limes, etc, formed as an intermediate in cell metabolism, and used as a flavouring

citron /ˈsitrən‖ˈsɪtrən/ *n* **1** a (tree that bears) fruit like the lemon but larger and with a thicker rind **2** the preserved rind of the citron, used esp in cakes and puddings

citrus /ˈsitrəs‖ˈsɪtrəs/ *n, pl* **citrus, citruses** any of several often thorny trees and shrubs grown in warm regions for their edible thick-rinded juicy fruit (e g the orange or lemon) – **citrus** *adj*

city /ˈsiti‖ˈsɪtɪ/ *n* **1a** a large town **b** an incorporated British town that has a cathedral or has had civic status conferred on it **c** a usu large chartered municipality in the USA **2** a city-state **3a** *the* financial and commercial area of London **b** *cap, sing or pl in constr the* influential financial interests of the British economy [Old French *cité* capital city, fr Latin *civitas* citizenship, state, city of Rome, fr *civis* citizen]

ˌcity ˈhall *n* the chief administrative building of a city

ˌcity-ˈstate *n* an autonomous state consisting of a city and surrounding territory

civet /ˈsivit‖ˈsɪvɪt/ *n* a thick yellowish musky-smelling substance extracted from a pouch near the sexual organs of the civet cat and used in perfumery

ˈcivet ˌcat *n* a long-bodied short-legged flesh-eating African mammal from which civet is obtained

civic /ˈsivik‖ˈsɪvɪk/ *adj* of a citizen, a city, or citizenship – **civically** *adv*

ˈcivics *n pl but sing or pl in constr* a social science dealing with the rights and duties of citizens

civies /ˈsiviz‖ˈsɪvɪz/ *n pl* civvies

civil /ˈsivl‖ˈsɪvl/ *adj* **1** of citizens <~ *liberties*> **2** adequately courteous and polite; not rude **3** relating to private rights as distinct from criminal proceedings **4** *of time* based on the sun and legally recognized for use in ordinary affairs **5** of or involving the general public as distinguished from special (e g military or religious) affairs – **civilly** *adv*

ˌcivil deˈfence *n, often cap C&D* protective measures organized by and for civilians against hostile attack, esp from the air, or natural disaster

ˌcivil ˌdisoˈbedience *n* refusal to obey governmental demands (e g payment of tax) as a means of forcing concessions

ˌcivil engiˈneer *n* an engineer whose training or occupation is in the designing and construction of large-scale public works (e g roads or bridges) – **civil engineering** *n*

civilian /siˈvilyən‖sɪˈvɪljən/ *n* one who is not in the army, navy, air force, or other uniformed public body – **civilian** *adj*, **civilianize** *vt*, **civilianization** *n*

civility /siˈviləti‖sɪˈvɪlətɪ/ *n* **1** courtesy, politeness **2** a polite act or expression – usu pl

civil·ization, **-isation** /ˌsivilieˈzaysh(ə)n, -li-‖ˌsɪvɪlaɪˈzeɪʃ(ə)n, -lɪ-/ *n* **1a** a relatively high level of cultural and technological development **b** the culture characteristic of a particular time or place **2** the process of becoming civilized **3** life in a place that offers the comforts of the modern world; *specif* life in a city – often humor

civil·ize, **-ise** /ˈsiv(ə)lˌiez‖ˈsɪv(ə)lˌaɪz/ *vt* **1** to cause to develop out of a primitive state; *specif* to bring to a technically advanced and rationally ordered stage of cultural development **2** to educate, refine – **civilizable** *adj*, **civilizer** *n*

ˌcivil ˈlaw *n, often cap C&L* **1** ROMAN LAW **2** the body of private law developed from Roman law as distinct from common law **3** the law established by a nation or state for its own jurisdiction (e g as distinct from international law) **4** the law of private rights

ˌcivil ˈliberty *n* a right or freedom of the individual citizen in relation to the state (e g freedom of speech); *also* such rights or freedoms considered collectively – **civil libertarian** *n*

ˈcivil ˌlist *n* an annual allowance by Parliament for the expenses of the monarch and royal family

ˌcivil ˈmarriage *n* a marriage involving a civil contract but no religious rite

ˌcivil ˈrights *n pl* CIVIL LIBERTIES; *esp* those of status equality between races or groups – **civil righter, civil rightist** *n*

ˌcivil ˈservant *n* a member of a civil service

ˌcivil ˈservice *n sing or pl in constr* the administrative service of a government or international agency, exclusive of the armed forces

ˌcivil ˈwar *n* a war between opposing groups of citizens of the same country

civvies, **civies** /ˈsiviz‖ˈsɪvɪz/ *n pl* civilian as distinguished from military clothes – slang

ˈ**civvy ˌstreet** /ˈsivi‖ˈsɪvɪ/ *n, often cap C&S, Br* civilian life as opposed to life in the services – slang

[1]**clack** /klak‖klæk/ *vi* **1** CHATTER 2 – infml **2** to make an abrupt striking sound or sounds ~*vt* to cause to make a clatter – **clacker** *n*

[2]**clack** *n* **1** rapid continuous talk; chatter – infml **2** a sound of clacking

clad /klad‖klæd/ *adj* being covered or clothed <*ivy*-clad *buildings*>

[1]**claim** /klaym‖kleɪm/ *vt* **1a** to ask for, esp as a right **b** to require, demand **c** to take; ACCOUNT FOR 3 <*plague* ~ed *thousands of lives*> **2** to take as the rightful owner **3** to assert in the face of possible contradiction; maintain – **claimable** *adj*, **claimer** *n*

[2]**claim** *n* **1** a demand for sthg (believed to be) due <*insurance* ~> **2a** a right or title to sthg **b** an assertion open to challenge <*a* ~ *to fame*> **3** sthg claimed; *esp* a tract of land staked out

claimant /ˈklaymənt‖ˈkleɪmənt/ *n* one who asserts a right or entitlement

clairvoyance /kleəˈvoyəns‖kleəˈvɔɪəns/ *n* **1** the power or faculty of discerning objects not apparent to the physical senses **2** the ability to perceive matters beyond the range of ordinary perception – **clairvoyant** *adj or n*

clam /klam‖klæm/ *n* **1** any of numerous edible marine molluscs (e g a scallop) living in sand or mud **2** a freshwater mussel

ˈ**clamˌbake** /-ˌbayk‖-ˌbeɪk/ *n, NAm* **1** an outdoor party; *esp* a seashore outing where food is cooked on heated rocks covered by seaweed **2** a gathering characterized by noisy sociability; *esp* a political rally

clamber /ˈklambə‖ˈklæmbə/ *vi* to climb awkwardly or with difficulty – **clamberer** *n*

clammy /ˈklami‖ˈklæmɪ/ *adj* being damp, clinging, and usu cool – **clammily** *adv*, **clamminess** *n*

clamour, *NAm chiefly* **clamor** /ˈklamə‖ˈklæmə/ *vi or n* **1** (to engage in) noisy shouting **2** (to make) a loud continuous noise **3** (to make) insistent public expression (e g of support or protest) – **clamorous** *adj*, **clamorously** *adv*, **clamourousness** *n*

[1]**clamp** /klamp‖klæmp/ *n* **1** a device that holds or compresses 2 or more parts firmly together **2** a heap of wooden sticks or bricks for burning, firing, etc

[2]**clamp** *vt* **1** to fasten (as if) with a clamp **2** to hold tightly

[3]**clamp** *n, Br* a heap of potatoes, turnips, etc covered over with straw or earth

clamp down *vi* to impose restrictions; *also* to make restrictions more stringent – **clamp-down** *n*

clam up *vi* to become silent – infml

clan /klan‖klæn/ *n* **1a** a (Highland Scots) Celtic group of households descended from a common ancestor **b** a group of people related by family **2** a usu close-knit group united by a common interest or common characteristics [Scottish Gaelic *clann* offspring, clan, fr Old Irish *cland* plant, offspring, fr Latin *planta* plant] – **clansman** *n*

clandestine /klanˈdestin, ˈklandəstin‖klænˈdestɪn, ˈklændəstɪn/ *adj* held in or conducted with secrecy; surreptitious – **clandestinely** *adv*

clang /klang‖klæŋ/ *vi* **1** to make a loud metallic ringing sound **2** *esp of a crane or goose* to utter a harsh cry ~*vt* to cause to clang – **clang** *n*

clanger /ˈklang·ə‖ˈklæŋə/ *n, Br* a blunder – infml

clangour, *NAm chiefly* **clangor** /ˈklang(g)ə‖ˈklæŋ(g)ə/ *vi or n* (to make) a resounding clang or medley of clangs – **clangorous** *adj*, **clangorously** *adv*

[1]**clank** /klangk‖klæŋk/ *vb* to (cause to) make a clank or series of clanks – **clankingly** *adv*

[2]**clank** *n* a sharp brief metallic sound

clannish /ˈklanish‖ˈklænɪʃ/ *adj* tending to associate only with a select group of similar background, status, or interests – **clannishly** *adv*, **clannishness** *n*

[1]**clap** /klap‖klæp/ *vb* **-pp-** *vt* **1** to strike (e g 2 flat hard surfaces) together so as to produce a loud sharp percussive noise **2a** to strike (the hands) together repeatedly, usu in applause **b** to applaud **3** to strike with the flat of the hand in a friendly way **4** to place, put, or set, esp energetically – infml <~ *him in irons*> ~ *vi* **1** to produce a sharp percussive noise **2** to applaud

[2]**clap** *n* **1** a loud sharp percussive noise, specif of thunder **2** a friendly slap <*a* ~ *on the shoulder*> **3** the sound of clapping hands; *esp* applause

[3]**clap** *n* VENEREAL DISEASE; *esp* gonorrhoea – slang

clapboard /ˈklabəd, ˈklapˌbawd‖ˈklæbəd, ˈklæpˌbɔːd/ *n, NAm* weatherboard – **clapboard** *vt*

ˌ**clapped** ˈ**out** *adj, chiefly Br, esp of machinery* (old and) worn-out; liable to break down irreparably – infml

clapper /ˈklapə‖ˈklæpə/ *n* the tongue of a bell – **like the clappers** *Br* as fast as possible – infml

ˈ**clapper-ˌboard** *n* a hinged board containing identifying details of the scene to be filmed that is held before the camera and banged together to mark the beginning and end of each take

claptrap /ˈklapˌtrap‖ˈklæpˌtræp/ *n* pretentious nonsense; rubbish – infml

claque /klak‖klæk/ *n sing or pl in constr* **1** a group hired to applaud at a performance **2** a group of self-interested obsequious flatterers

claret /ˈklarit‖ˈklærɪt/ *n* **1** a dry red Bordeaux **2** a dark purplish red colour [Middle French (*vin*) *claret* clear wine, fr *claret* clear, fr *cler* clear] – **claret** *adj*

clarify /ˈklariˌfie‖ˈklærɪˌfaɪ/ *vt* **1** to make (e g a liquid) clear or pure, usu by freeing from suspended matter **2** to make free from confusion **3** to make understandable ~*vi* to become clear – **clarification** *n*, **clarifier** *n*

clarinet /ˌklariˈnet‖ˌklærɪˈnet/ *n* a single-reed woodwind instrument – **clarinettist,** *NAm chiefly* **clarinetist** *n*

[1]**clarion** /ˈklari·ən‖ˈklærɪən/ *n* (the sound of) a medieval trumpet

[2]**clarion** *adj* brilliantly clear <*a* ~ *call to action*>

clarity /ˈklarəti‖ˈklærətɪ/ *n* the quality or state of being clear

[1]**clash** /klash‖klæʃ/ *vi* **1** to make a clash **2a** to

come into conflict **b** to form a displeasing combination; not match <*these colours* ~> ~*vt* to cause to clash – **clasher** *n*

[2]**clash** *n* **1** a noisy usu metallic sound of collision **2a** a hostile encounter **b** a sharp conflict

[1]**clasp** /klahsp‖klɑːsp/ *n* **1** a device for holding objects or parts of sthg together **2** a holding or enveloping (as if) with the hands or arms

[2]**clasp** *vt* **1** to fasten (as if) with a clasp **2** to enclose and hold with the arms; *specif* to embrace **3** to seize (as if) with the hand; grasp

'**clasp** ˌ**knife** *n* a large single-bladed folding knife having a catch to hold the blade open

[1]**class** /klahs‖klɑːs/ *n* **1a** *sing or pl in constr* a group sharing the same economic or social status in a society consisting of several groups with differing statuses – often pl with sing. meaning <*the labouring* ~es> **b(1)** social rank **b(2)** the system of differentiating society by classes **c** high quality; elegance **2** *sing or pl in constr* a body of students meeting regularly to study the same subject **3** a group, set, or kind sharing common attributes: e g **3a** a category in biological classification ranking above the order and below the phylum or division **b** a grammatical category **4a** a division or rating based on grade or quality **b** *Br* a level of university honours degree awarded to a student according to merit

[2]**class** *vt* to classify

'**class-**ˌ**conscious** *adj* **1** actively aware of one's common status with others in a particular class **2** taking part in class war – **class-consciousness** *n*

[1]**classic** /'klasik‖'klæsɪk/ *adj* **1a** of recognized value or merit; serving as a standard of excellence **b** both traditional and enduring <*a* ~ *heritage*> **c** characterized by simple tailored and elegant lines that remain in fashion year after year <*a* ~ *suit*> **2** CLASSICAL 2 **3a** authoritative, definitive **b** being an example that shows clearly the characteristics of some group of things or occurrences; archetypal

[2]**classic** *n* **1a** a literary work of ancient Greece or Rome **b** *pl* Greek and Latin literature, history, and philosophy considered as an academic subject **2a** (the author of) a work of lasting excellence **b** an authoritative source **3** a classic example; archetype **4** an important long-established sporting event; *specif, Br* any of 5 flat races for horses (e g the Epsom Derby)

classical /'klasikl‖'klæsɪkl/ *adj* **1** standard, classic **2** of the (literature, art, architecture, or ideals of the) ancient Greek and Roman world **3a** of or being (a composer of) music of the late 18th c and early 19th c characterized by an emphasis on simplicity, objectivity, and proportion **b** of or being music in the educated European tradition that includes such forms as chamber music, opera, and symphony as distinguished from folk, popular music, or jazz **4a** both authoritative and traditional **b(1)** of or being systems or methods that constitute an accepted although not necessarily modern approach to a subject <~ *Mendelian genetics*> **b(2)** not involving relativity, wave mechanics, or quantum theory <~ *physics*> **5** concerned with instruction in the classics

classicism /'klasiˌsiz(ə)m‖'klæsɪˌsɪz(ə)m/, **classicalism** /'klasiklˌiz(ə)m‖'klæsɪklˌɪz(ə)m/ *n* **1a** the principles or style embodied in classical literature, art, or architecture **b** a classical idiom or expression **2** adherence to traditional standards (e g of simplicity, restraint, and proportion) that are considered to have universal and lasting worth – **classicalist, classicist** *n*, **classicistic** *adj*

classification /ˌklasifi'kaysh(ə)n‖ˌklæsɪfɪ'keɪʃ(ə)n/ *n* **1** classifying **2a** systematic arrangement in groups according to established criteria; *specif* taxonomy **b** a class, category – **classificatorily** *adv*, **classificatory** *adj*

classified /'klasiˌfied‖'klæsɪˌfaɪd/ *adj* withheld from general circulation for reasons of national security

classify /'klasiˌfie‖'klæsɪˌfaɪ/ *vt* **1** to arrange in classes **2** to assign to a category – **classifiable** *adj*, **classifier** *n*

classless /'klahslis‖'klɑːslɪs/ *adj* **1** free from class distinction **2** belonging to no particular social class – **classlessness** *n*

'**class**ˌ**mate** /-ˌmayt‖-ˌmeɪt/ *n* a member of the same class in a school or college

'**classroom** /-room, -ˌroohm‖-rʊm, -ˌruːm/ *n* a room where classes meet

'**class** ˌ**war** *n* the struggle for power between workers and property owners assumed by Marxist theory to develop in a capitalist society

classy /'klahsi‖'klɑːsɪ/ *adj* elegant, stylish – infml – **classiness** *n*

[1]**clatter** /'klatə‖'klætə/ *vi* **1** to make a clatter **2** to move or go with a clatter <~ed *down the stairs*> **3** to prattle ~*vt* to cause to clatter – **clatterer** *n*, **clatteringly** *adv*

[2]**clatter** *n* **1** a rattling sound (e g of hard bodies striking together) <*the* ~ *of pots and pans*> **2** a commotion <*the midday* ~ *of the business district*> – **clattery** *adj*

clause /klawz‖klɔːz/ *n* **1** a distinct article or condition in a formal document **2** a phrase containing a subject and predicate and functioning either in isolation or as a member of a complex or compound sentence – **clausal** *adj*

claustrophobia /ˌklostrə'fohbi·ə, ˌklaw-‖ˌklɒstrə'fəʊbɪə, ˌklɔː-/ *n* abnormal dread of being in closed or confined spaces [deriv of Latin *claustrum* bar, bolt + Greek *phobos* fear] – **claustrophobic** *adj*

clavichord /'klaviˌkawd‖'klævɪˌkɔːd/ *n* an early usu rectangular keyboard instrument – **clavichordist** *n*

clavicle /'klavikl‖'klævɪkl/ *n* a bone of the vertebrate shoulder typically linking the shoulder blade and breastbone; the collarbone – **clavicular** *adj*

[1]**claw** /klaw‖klɔː/ *n* **1** (a part resembling or limb having) a sharp usu slender curved nail on an animal's toe **2** any of the pincerlike organs on the end of some limbs of a lobster, scorpion, or similar arthropod **3** sthg (e g the forked end of a claw hammer) resembling a claw – **clawed** *adj*

[2]**claw** *vt* to rake, seize, dig, or make (as if) with claws ~*vi* to scrape, scratch, dig, or pull (as if) with claws

'**claw** ˌ**hammer** *n* a hammer with one end of the head forked for pulling out nails

clay /klay||kleɪ/ *n* **1a** (soil composed chiefly of) an earthy material that is soft when moist but hard when fired, is composed mainly of fine particles of aluminium silicates, and is used for making brick, tile, and pottery **b** thick and clinging earth or mud **2a** a substance that resembles clay and is used for modelling **b** the human body as distinguished from the spirit – **clayey** *adj*, **clayish** *adj*

claymore /ˈklay,maw||ˈkleɪ,mɔː/ *n* a large single-edged broadsword formerly used by Scottish Highlanders [Scottish Gaelic *claidheamh mōr*, lit., great sword]

ˌclay ˈpigeon *n* a saucer-shaped object usu made of baked clay and hurled into the air as a target for shooting at with a shotgun

[1]**clean** /kleen||kliːn/ *adj* **1a** (relatively) free from dirt or pollution **b** free from contamination or disease **c** relatively free from radioactive fallout **2** unadulterated, pure **3a** free from illegal, immoral, or disreputable activities **b** free from the use of obscenity **c** observing the rules; fair <*a ~ fight*> **4** thorough, complete <*a ~ break with the past*> **5** relatively free from error or blemish; clear; *specif* legible <*~ copy*> **6a** characterized by clarity, precision, or deftness <*architecture with ~ almost austere lines*> **b** not jagged; smooth <*a ~ edge*> **c** *of a ship or aircraft* well streamlined – **cleanly** *adv*, **cleanness** *n*

[2]**clean** *adv* **1a** so as to leave clean <*a new broom sweeps ~*> **b** in a clean manner <*fight ~*> **2** all the way; completely <*the bullet went ~ through his arm*>

[3]**clean** *vt* **1** to make clean – often + *up* **2a** to strip, empty **b** to deprive of money or possessions – often + *out* <*they ~*ed *him out completely*>; infml *~vi* to undergo cleaning – **cleanable** *adj*

[4]**clean** *n* an act of cleaning away dirt

ˌclean-ˈcut *adj* **1** cut so that the surface or edge is smooth and even **2** sharply defined **3** of wholesome appearance

cleaner /ˈkleenə||ˈkliːnə/ *n* **1** sby whose occupation is cleaning rooms or clothes **2** a substance, implement, or machine for cleaning – **to the cleaners** to or through the experience of being deprived of all one's money – infml

cleanliness /ˈklenlinis||ˈklenlɪnɪs/ *n* fastidiousness in keeping things or one's person clean – **cleanly** *adj*

cleanse /klenz||klenz/ *vb* to clean

cleanser /ˈklenzə||ˈklenzə/ *n* a preparation (e g a scouring powder or skin cream) used for cleaning

ˌclean-ˈshaven *adj* with the hair, specif of the beard and moustache, shaved off

clean up *vi* to make a large esp sweeping gain (e g in business or gambling) *~vt* to remove by cleaning – **cleanup** *n*

[1]**clear** /kliə||klɪə/ *adj* **1a** bright, luminous **b** free from cloud, mist, haze, or dust <*a ~ day*> **c** untroubled, serene <*a ~ gaze*> **2** clean, pure: e g **2a** free from blemishes **b** easily seen through; transparent **3a** easily heard **b** easily visible; plain **c** free from obscurity or ambiguity; easily understood **4a** capable of sharp discernment; keen <*this problem needs a ~ mind*> **b** free from doubt; sure <*we are not ~ what to do*> **5** free from guilt <*a ~ conscience*> **6a** net <*a ~ profit*> **b** unqualified, absolute <*a ~ victory*> **c** free from obstruction or entanglement **d** full <*6 ~ days*> – **clearly** *adv*, **clearness** *n*

[2]**clear** *adv* **1** clearly <*to cry loud and ~*> **2** *chiefly NAm* all the way <*can see ~ to the mountains today*>

[3]**clear** *vt* **1a** to make transparent or translucent **b** to free from unwanted material – often + *out* <*~ out that cupboard*> **2a** to free from accusation or blame; vindicate **b** to certify as trustworthy <*~ a man for top secret military work*> **3a** to rid (the throat) of phlegm; *also* to make a rasping noise in (the throat) **b** to erase accumulated totals or stored data from (e g a calculator or computer memory) **4** to authorize or cause to be authorized **5a** to free from financial obligation **b(1)** to settle, discharge <*~ an account*> **b(2)** to deal with until finished or settled <*~ the backlog of work*> **c** to gain without deduction <*~ a profit*> **d** to put through a clearinghouse **6a** to get rid of; remove <*~ the plates from the table*> – often + *off, up*, or *away* <*~ away the rubbish*> **b** to kick or pass (the ball) away from the goal as a defensive measure in soccer **7** to go over without touching <*the horse ~*ed *the jump*> *~ vi* **1a** to become clear – often + *up* <*it ~*ed *up quickly after the rain*> **b** to go away; vanish <*the symptoms ~*ed *gradually*> – sometimes + *off, out* <*told him to ~ out*>, or *away* <*after the mist ~*ed *away*> **c** to sell **2** to pass through a clearinghouse – **clearable** *adj*, **clearer** *n* – **clear the air** to remove elements of hostility, tension, confusion, or uncertainty from the mood or temper of the time – **clear the decks** to get things ready for action

[4]**clear** *n* – **in the clear 1** free from guilt or suspicion **2** in plaintext; not in code or cipher

clearance /ˈkliərəns||ˈklɪərəns/ *n* **1a** an authorization **b** a sale to clear out stock **c** the removal of buildings, people, etc from the space they previously occupied <*slum ~*> **d** a clearing of the ball in soccer **2** the distance by which one object clears another, or the clear space between them

ˌclear-ˈcut *adj* **1** sharply outlined; distinct **2** free from ambiguity or uncertainty

ˌclearˈheaded /-ˈhedid||-ˈhedɪd/ *adj* **1** not confused; sensible, rational **2** having no illusions about a state of affairs; realistic – **clearheadedly** *adv*, **clearheadedness** *n*

clearing /ˈkliəring||ˈklɪərɪŋ/ *n* an area of land cleared of wood and brush

ˈclearing ˌbank *n* a bank that is a member of a clearinghouse

ˈclearingˌhouse /-ˌhows||-ˌhaʊs/ *n* an establishment maintained by banks for settling mutual claims and accounts

ˌclear-ˈsighted *adj* CLEARHEADED 2; *esp* having perceptive insight – **clear-sightedly** *adv*, **clear-sightedness** *n*

clear up *vt* **1** to tidy up **2** to explain <clear up *the mystery*>

ˈclearˌway /-ˌway||-ˌweɪ/ *n*, *Br* a road on which vehicles may stop only in an emergency

cleat /kleet||kliːt/ *n* **1a** a wedge-shaped piece

fastened to sthg and serving as a support or check **b** a wooden or metal fitting, usu with 2 projecting horns, round which a rope may be made fast **2a** a projecting piece (e g on the bottom of a shoe) that provides a grip **b** *pl* shoes equipped with cleats

cleavage /'kleevij||'kli:vɪdʒ/ *n* **1** the property of a crystal or rock (e g slate) of splitting along definite planes **2** (a) division **3** CELL DIVISION **4** the splitting of a molecule into simpler molecules **5** (the space between) a woman's breasts, esp when exposed by a low-cut garment

[1]**cleave** /kleev||kli:v/ *vi* **cleaved, clove** /klohv||kləʊv/ to stick firmly and closely or loyally and steadfastly – usu + *to*

[2]**cleave** *vb* **cleaved** *also* **cleft** /kleft||kleft/, **clove** /klohv||kləʊv/; **cleaved** *also* **cleft, cloven** /'klohv(ə)n||'kləʊv(ə)n/ *vt* to divide or pass through (as if) by a cutting blow; split ~ *vi* to split, esp along the grain – **cleavable** *adj*

cleaver /'kleevə||'kli:və/ *n* a butcher's implement for cutting animal carcasses into joints or pieces

clef /klef||klef/ *n* a sign placed on a musical staff to indicate the pitch represented by the notes following it

cleft /kleft||kleft/ *n* **1** a space or opening made by splitting; a fissure **2** a usu V-shaped indented formation; a hollow between ridges or protuberances

ˌcleft 'palate *n* a congenital fissure of the roof of the mouth

clematis /klə'maytəs, 'klemətis||klə'meɪtəs, 'klemətɪs/ *n* a usu climbing or scrambling plant with usu white, pink, or purple flowers

clemency /'klemənsi||'klemənsɪ/ *n* disposition to be merciful, esp to moderate the severity of punishment due

clement /'klemənt||'klemənt/ *adj* **1** inclined to be merciful; lenient **2** *of weather* pleasantly mild – **clemently** *adv*

clench /klench||klentʃ/ *vt* **1** CLINCH 1, 2 **2** to hold fast; clutch **3** to set or close tightly < ~ed *his teeth*>

clerestory, clearstory /'kliəˌstawri||'klɪəˌstɔ:rɪ/ *n* the part of an outside wall of a room or building that rises above an adjoining roof

clergy /'kluhji||'klɜ:dʒɪ/ *n sing or pl in constr* a group ordained to perform pastoral or sacerdotal functions in an organized religion, esp a Christian church

'clergyman /-mən||-mən/ *n* an ordained minister

cleric /'klerik||'klerɪk/ *n* a member of the clergy; *specif* one in orders below the grade of priest

[1]**clerical** /'klerikl||'klerɪkl/ *adj* **1** (characteristic) of the clergy, a clergyman, or a cleric **2** of a clerk or office worker – **clerically** *adv*

[2]**clerical** *n* **1** a clergyman **2** an adherent of clericalism **3** *pl* clerical clothes

ˌclerical 'collar *n* a narrow stiff upright white collar fastening at the back and worn by clergymen

clerihew /'kleriˌhyooh||'klerɪˌhju:/ *n* a witty pseudo-biographical 4-line verse [Edmund *Clerihew* Bentley (1875-1956), English writer]

[1]**clerk** /klahk||klɑ:k; *NAm* kluhk||klɜ:k/ *n* **1** a cleric **2a** sby whose occupation is keeping records or accounts or doing general office work **b** *NAm* SHOP ASSISTANT – **clerkly** *adj*, **clerkship** *n*

[2]**clerk** *vi* to act or work as a clerk

ˌclerk of the 'works *n* the person in charge of building works in a particular place

clever /'klevə||'klevə/ *adj* **1a** skilful or adroit *with* the hands or body; nimble **b** mentally quick and resourceful; intelligent **2** marked by wit or ingenuity; *also* thus marked but lacking depth or soundness – **cleverish** *adj*, **cleverly** *adv*, **cleverness** *n*

ˌclever-'dick /dik||dɪk/ *n*, *Br* SMART ALEC – infml

[1]**clew** /klooh||klu:/ *n* **1** CLUE 1 **2** *also* **clue** (a metal loop attached to) the lower or after corner of a sail

[2]**clew** *vt* **1** CLUE 2 **2** *also* **clue** to haul (a sail) by ropes through the clews

cliché /'kleeˌshay||'kli:ˌʃeɪ/ *n* **1** a hackneyed phrase or expression; *also* the idea expressed by it **2** a hackneyed theme or situation – **cliché** *adj*, **clichéd** *adj*

[1]**click** /klik||klɪk/ *n* **1** a slight sharp sound **2** a sharp speech sound in some languages made by the sudden inrush of air at the release of an occlusion in the mouth

[2]**click** *vt* to strike, move, or produce with a click < ~ed *his heels together*> ~ *vi* **1** to operate with or make a click **2a** to strike up an immediately warm friendship, esp with sby of the opposite sex **b** to succeed <*a film that* ~s> **c** *Br* to cause sudden insight or recognition <*the name* ~ed> *USE* (*2*) infml

client /'klie·ənt||'klaɪənt/ *n* **1** a vassal, state, etc under the protection of another **2a** sby who engages or receives the advice or services of a professional person or organization **b** a customer – **clientage** *n*, **cliental** *adj*

clientele /ˌklee·on'tel||ˌkli:ɒn'tel/ *n sing or pl in constr* a body of clients

cliff /klif||klɪf/ *n* a very steep high face of rock, earth, ice, etc – **cliffy** *adj*

'cliff-ˌhanger *n* **1** an adventure serial or melodrama, usu presented in instalments each ending in suspense **2** a contest or situation whose outcome is in doubt to the very end

[1]**climacteric** /ˌklie'maktərik, ˌkliemək'terik||ˌklaɪ'mæktərɪk, ˌklaɪmək'terɪk/ *adj* of or being a critical period (e g of life)

[2]**climacteric** *n* **1** a major turning point or critical stage; *specif* one supposed to occur at intervals of 7 years **2** the menopause; *also* a corresponding period in the male during which sexual activity and competence are reduced

climactic /klie'maktik||klaɪ'mæktɪk/ *adj* of or being a climax – **climactically** *adv*

climate /'kliemət||'klaɪmət/ *n* **1** (a region of the earth having a specified) average course or condition of the weather over a period of years as shown by temperature, wind, rain, etc **2** the prevailing state of affairs or feelings of a group or period; a milieu <*a* ~ *of fear*> – **climatic** *adj*, **climatically** *adv*

climatology /ˌkliemə'toləji||ˌklaɪmə'tɒlədʒɪ/ *n* a branch of meteorology dealing with climates – **climatological** *adj*, **climatologically** *adv*, **climatologist** *n*

[1]**climax** /'klie,maks||'klaɪ,mæks/ *n* **1a** the highest point; a culmination **b** the point of highest dramatic tension or a major turning point in some action (e g of a play) **c** an orgasm **2** a relatively stable final stage reached by a (plant) community in its ecological development [Latin, fr Greek *klimax* ladder, fr *klinein* to lean]

[2]**climax** *vi* to come to a climax

climb /kliem||klaɪm/ *vi* **1a** to go gradually upwards; rise <*watching the smoke* ~> **b** to slope upwards <*the road* ~s *steadily*> **2a** to go *up, down*, etc on a more or less vertical surface using the hands to grasp or give support **b** *of a plant* to ascend in growth (e g by twining) **3** to get *into* or *out of* clothing, usu with some haste or effort ~ *vt* **1** to go upwards on or along, to the top of, or over <~ *a hill*> **2** to draw or pull oneself up, over, or to the top of, by using hands and feet <~ *a tree*> **3** to grow up or over – **climb** *n*, **climbable** *adj*, **climber** *n*

climb down *vi* BACK DOWN – **climb-down** *n*

'**climbing ,iron** *n* a crampon

clime /kliem||klaɪm/ *n* CLIMATE 1 – usu pl with sing. meaning; chiefly poetic

[1]**clinch** /klinch||klɪntʃ/ *vt* **1** to turn over or flatten the protruding pointed end of (e g a driven nail) **2** to fasten in this way ~*vi* to hold an opponent (e g in boxing) at close quarters

[2]**clinch** *n* **1** a fastening by means of a clinched nail, rivet, or bolt **2** an act or instance of clinching in boxing

clincher /'klinchə||'klɪntʃə/ *n* a decisive fact, argument, act, or remark

cling /kling||klɪŋ/ *vi* **clung** /klung||klʌŋ/ **1a** to stick as if glued firmly **b** to hold (on) tightly or tenaciously **2a** to have a strong emotional attachment or dependence **b** *esp of a smell* to linger – **clingy** *adj*

clinic /'klinik||'klɪnɪk/ *n* **1** a class of medical instruction in which patients are examined and discussed **2** a meeting held by an expert or person in authority, to which people bring problems for discussion and resolution **3a** a facility (e g of a hospital) for the diagnosis and treatment of outpatients **b** a usu private hospital

clinical /'klinikl||'klɪnɪkl/ *adj* **1** involving, based on, or noticeable from direct observation of the patient **2** analytic, detached – **clinically** *adv*

[1]**clink** /klingk||klɪŋk/ *vb* to (cause to) give out a slight sharp short metallic sound – **clink** *n*

[2]**clink** *n* PRISON 2 – slang [the *Clink*, former prison in Southwark, London]

clinker /'klingkə||'klɪŋkə/ *n* stony matter fused by fire

'**clinker-,built** *adj* having the lower edge of each external plank or plate overlapping the upper edge of the one below it <*a* ~ *boat*>

[1]**clip** /klip||klɪp/ *vt* **-pp-** to clasp or fasten with a clip

[2]**clip** *n* **1** any of various devices that grip, clasp, or hold **2** (a device to hold cartridges for charging) a magazine from which ammunition is fed into the chamber of a firearm **3** a piece of jewellery held in position by a spring clip

[3]**clip** *vb* **-pp-** *vt* **1a** to cut (off) (as if) with shears **b** to cut off the end or outer part of **c** [3]EXCISE **2** to abbreviate in speech or writing **3** to hit with a glancing blow; *also* to hit smartly – infml ~*vi* to clip sthg

[4]**clip** *n* **1a** the product of (a single) shearing (e g of sheep) **b** a section of filmed material **2a** an act of clipping **b** the manner in which sthg is clipped **3** a sharp blow **4** a rapid rate of motion *USE* (*3&4*) infml

'**clip,board** /-,bawd||-,bɔːd/ *n* a small writing board with a spring clip for holding papers

'**clip ,joint** *n* a place of public entertainment (e g a nightclub) that defrauds, overcharges, etc *USE* slang

'**clip-,on** *adj* of or being sthg that clips on

clip on *vi* to be capable of being fastened by an attached clip

clipper /'klipə||'klɪpə/ *n* **1** an implement for cutting or trimming hair or nails – usu pl with sing. meaning **2** a fast sailing ship

clippie /'klipi||'klɪpɪ/ *n, Br* a female bus conductor – infml

clipping /'kliping||'klɪpɪŋ/ *n, chiefly NAm* CUTTING 2

clique /kleek||kliːk/ *n sing or pl in constr* a highly exclusive and often aloof group of people held together by common interests, views, etc – **cliquey, cliquy** *adj*, **cliquish** *adj*, **cliquishly** *adv*, **cliquishness** *n*

clitoris /'klitəris, 'klie-||'klɪtərɪs, 'klaɪ-/ *n* a small erectile organ at the front or top part of the vulva that is a centre of sexual sensation in females – **clitoral, clitoric** *adj*

cloaca /kloh'aykə||kləʊ'eɪkə/ *n, pl* **cloacae** /-kee, -see||-kiː, -siː/ **1** a conduit for sewage **2** the chamber into which the intestinal, urinary, and generative canals discharge, esp in birds, reptiles, amphibians, and many fishes – **cloacal** *adj*

[1]**cloak** /klohk||kləʊk/ *n* **1** a sleeveless outer garment that usu fastens at the neck and hangs loosely from the shoulders **2** sthg that conceals; a pretence, disguise

[2]**cloak** *vt* to cover or hide (as if) with a cloak

,**cloak-and-'dagger** *adj* dealing in or suggestive of melodramatic intrigue and action usu involving espionage

'**cloakroom** /-room, -,roohm||-rʊm, -,ruːm/ *n* **1** a room in which outdoor clothing or luggage may be left during one's stay **2** *chiefly Br* a room with a toilet – euph

[1]**clobber** /'klobə||'klɒbə/ *n, Br* gear, paraphernalia; *esp* clothes worn for a usu specified purpose or function – infml

[2]**clobber** *vt* **1** to hit with force **2** to defeat overwhelmingly *USE* infml

cloche /klosh||klɒʃ/ *n* **1** a translucent cover used for protecting outdoor plants **2** a woman's close-fitting hat with a deeply rounded crown and narrow brim

[1]**clock** /klok||klɒk/ *n* **1** a device other than a watch for indicating or measuring time **2** a recording or metering device with a dial and indicator attached to a mechanism: e g **2a** a speedometer **b** *Br* a milometer **3** *Br* a face – slang – **clocklike** *adj* – **round the clock 1** continuously for 24 hours; day and night without cessation **2** without relaxation and heedless of time

[2]**clock** *vt* **1** to time with a stopwatch or electric timing device – used chiefly in sports **2a** to register on a mechanical recording device **b** *Br* to

attain a time, speed, etc, of – often + *up*; infml **3** to hit <~ed *him on the jaw*> – infml – **clocker** *n*

[3]**clock** *n* an ornamental pattern on the outside ankle or side of a stocking or sock

clock in *vi* to record the time of one's arrival or commencement of work by punching a card in a time clock

clock out *vi* to record the time of one's departure or stopping of work by punching a card in a time clock

ˈclock-ˌwatcher /ˌwochə‖ˌwɒtʃə/ *n* a person (e g a worker) who keeps close watch on the passage of time in order not to work a single moment longer than he/she has to – **clock-watching** *n*

ˈclockˌwise /-ˌwiez‖-ˌwaɪz/ *adv* in the direction in which the hands of a clock rotate as viewed from in front – **clockwise** *adj*

ˈclockˌwork /-ˌwuhk‖-ˌwɜːk/ *n* machinery that operates in a manner similar to that of a mechanical clock; *specif* machinery powered by a coiled spring <*a ~ toy*> – **like clockwork** smoothly and with no hitches

clod /klod‖klɒd/ *n* **1** a lump or mass, esp of earth or clay **2** an oaf, dolt **3** a gristly cut of beef taken from the neck – **cloddish** *adj*, **cloddishness** *n*, **cloddy** *adj*

clodhopper /ˈklodˌhopə‖ˈklɒdˌhɒpə/ *n* **1** a boorish or clumsy person – infml **2** a large heavy shoe – chiefly humor

[1]**clog** /klog‖klɒg/ *n* **1** a weight attached, esp to an animal, to hinder motion **2** a shoe, sandal, or overshoe with a thick typically wooden sole

[2]**clog** *vb* **-gg-** *vt* **1** to halt or retard the progress, operation, or growth of **2a** to obstruct so as to hinder motion in or through **b** to block <*the drain is* ~ged *up*> ~ *vi* to become blocked *up*

cloister /ˈkloystə‖ˈklɔɪstə/ *n* **1a** a monastic establishment **b** *the* monastic life **2** a covered passage on the side of an open court, usu having one side walled and the other an open arcade or colonnade

[1]**clone** /klohn‖kləʊn/ *n* **1** an individual that is asexually produced and is therefore identical to its parent **2** all such progeny of a single parent – used technically [Greek *klōn* twig, slip] – **clonal** *adj*, **clonally** *adv*

[2]**clone** *vt* to cause to grow (as if) as a clone

clop /klop‖klɒp/ *n* a sound made (as if) by a hoof or shoe against a hard surface – **clop** *vi*

[1]**close** /klohz‖kləʊz/ *vt* **1a** to move so as to bar passage <~ *the gate*> **b** to deny access to <~ *the park*> **c** to suspend or stop the operations of; *also* to discontinue or dispose of (a business) permanently – often + *down* **2a** to bring to an end <~ *an account*> **b** to conclude discussion or negotiation about <*the question is* ~d>; *also* to bring to agreement or settlement <~ *a deal*> **3** to bring or bind together the parts or edges of <*a* ~d *fist*> ~ *vi* **1a** to contract, swing, or slide so as to leave no opening <*the door* ~d *quietly*> **b** to cease operation <*the shops ~ at 9 pm*>; *specif, Br* to stop broadcasting – usu + *down* **2** to draw near, esp in order to fight – usu + *with* **3** to come to an end – **closable, closeable** *adj*, **closer** *n* – **close one's doors 1** to refuse admission <*the nation* closed *its doors to immigrants*> **2** to go out of business – **close one's eyes to** to ignore deliberately – **close ranks** to unite in a concerted stand, esp to meet a challenge

[2]**close** /klohz‖kləʊz/ *n* a conclusion or end in time or existence <*the decade drew to a* ~>

[3]**close** /klohs‖kləʊs; *sense 2 also* klohz‖kləʊz/ *n* **1** a road closed at one end **2** *Br* the precinct of a cathedral

[4]**close** /klohs‖kləʊs/ *adj* **1** having no openings; closed **2** confined, cramped <~ *quarters*> **3** restricted, closed <*the ~ season*> **4** secretive, reticent <*she was very ~ about her past*> **5** strict, rigorous <*keep ~ watch*> **6** hot and stuffy **7** having little space between items or units; compact, dense <~ *texture*> **8** very short or near to the surface <*the barber gave him a ~ shave*> **9** near; *esp* adjacent <*he and I are ~ relations*> **10** intimate, familiar <~ *collaboration*> **11a** searching, minute <*a ~ study*> **b** faithful to an original <*a ~ copy*> **12** evenly contested or having a (nearly) even score <*a ~ game*> – **closely** *adv*, **closeness** *n*

[5]**close** /klohs‖kləʊs/ *adv* in or into a close position or manner; near <*come ~ to ruining us*> – **close on** almost <close on *500 people*>

ˌclose ˈcall /klohs‖kləʊs/ *n* a narrow escape

ˌclose-ˈcropped /klohs‖kləʊs/ *adj* clipped short <~ *hair*>

closed /klohzd‖kləʊzd/ *adj* **1a** not open **b** enclosed <*a ~ porch*> **2a** forming a self-contained unit allowing no additions <~ *system*> **b(1)** traced by a moving point that returns to its starting point without retracing its path <*a ~ curve*>; *also* so formed that every plane section is a closed curve <*a ~ surface*> **b(2)** characterized by mathematical elements that when subjected to an operation produce only elements of the same set **b(3)** containing all the limit points of every subset <*a ~ set*> **3a** confined to a few <~ *membership*> **b** rigidly excluding outside influence <*a ~ mind*>

ˌclosed ˈcircuit *n* **1** a television installation in which the signal is transmitted by wire to a limited number of receivers, usu in 1 location **2** a connected array of electrical components that will allow the passage of current – **closed-circuit** *adj*

closedown /ˈklohzˌdown‖ˈkləʊzˌdaʊn/ *n* the act or result of closing down; *esp* the end of a period of broadcasting

ˌclosed ˈshop *n* an establishment which employs only union members

closefisted /ˌklohsˈfistid‖ˌkləʊsˈfɪstɪd/ *adj* tightfisted

ˌclose-ˈhauled /klohs‖kləʊs/ *adj or adv* with the sails set for sailing as near directly into the wind as possible

close in /klohz‖kləʊz/ *vi* **1** to gather in close all round with an oppressing effect <*despair* closed in *on her*> **2** to approach from various directions to close quarters, esp for an attack or arrest <*at dawn the police* closed in>

ˌclose-ˈknit /klohs‖kləʊs/ *adj* bound together by close ties

ˈclose ˌseason /klohs‖kləʊs/ *n, Br* a period during which it is illegal to kill or catch certain game or fish

[1]**closet** /ˈklozit‖ˈklɒzɪt/ *n* **1** a small or private room **2** WATER CLOSET **3** *chiefly NAm* a cupboard

[2]**closet** *vt* **1** to shut (oneself) up (as if) in a closet **2** to take into a closet for a secret interview

[3]**closet** *adj* being privately but not overtly as specified; secret <*a ~ socialist*>

ˈ**close-ˌup** /klohs‖kləʊs/ *n* **1** a photograph or film shot taken at close range **2** a view or examination of sthg from a small distance away

[1]**closure** /ˈklohzhə‖ˈkləʊʒə/ *n* **1** closing or being closed **2** the ending of a side's innings in cricket by declaration **3** the closing of debate in a legislative body, esp by calling for a vote

[2]**closure** *vt* to close (a debate) by closure

[1]**clot** /klot‖klɒt/ *n* **1a** a roundish viscous lump formed by coagulation of a portion of liquid (e g cream) **b** a coagulated mass produced by clotting of blood **2** *Br* a stupid person – infml

[2]**clot** *vb* **-tt-** *vi* **1** to become a clot; form clots **2** *of blood* to undergo a sequence of complex chemical and physical reactions that results in conversion from liquid form into a coagulated mass *~vt* to cause to clot

cloth /kloth‖klɒθ/ *n, pl* **cloths** /klodhz, kloths‖klɒðz, klɒθs/ **1** a pliable material made usu by weaving, felting, or knitting natural or synthetic fibres and filaments **2** a piece of cloth adapted for a particular purpose: e g **2a** a tablecloth **b** a dishcloth **c** a duster **3** (the distinctive dress of) a profession or calling distinguished by its dress; *specif the* clergy

clothe /klohdh‖kləʊð/ *vt* **clothed, clad** /klad‖klæd/ **1a** to cover (as if) with clothing; dress **b** to provide with clothes **2** to express or enhance by suitably significant language

clothes /klohdhz‖kləʊðz/ *n pl* **1** articles of material (e g cloth) worn to cover the body, for warmth, protection, or decoration **2** bedclothes

ˈ**clothes ˌbasket** *n* a basket used for storing clothes that are to be washed

ˈ**clothesˌhorse** /-ˌhaws‖-ˌhɔːs/ *n* **1** a frame on which to hang clothes, esp for drying or airing indoors **2** *chiefly NAm* a conspicuously dressy person – derog

ˈ**clothesˌline** /-ˌlien‖-ˌlaɪn/ *n* a line (e g of cord or nylon) on which clothes may be hung to dry, esp outdoors

ˈ**clothes ˌmoth** *n* any of several small yellowish moths whose larvae eat wool, fur, hair, etc

ˈ**clothes ˌpeg** *n* a wooden or plastic clip or forked device used for holding clothes or washing on a line

clothier /ˈklohdhiə‖ˈkləʊðɪə/ *n* sby who makes or sells cloth or clothing

clothing /ˈklohdhing‖ˈkləʊðɪŋ/ *n* clothes

cloture /ˈklohchə‖ˈkləʊtʃə/ *n, NAm* CLOSURE 3 – **cloture** *vt*

[1]**cloud** /klowd‖klaʊd/ *n* **1a** a visible mass of particles of water or ice at a usu great height in the air **b** a light filmy, puffy, or billowy mass seeming to float in the air **2** any of many masses of opaque matter in interstellar space **3** a great crowd or multitude; a swarm, esp of insects **4** sthg that obscures or blemishes <*their reputation is under a ~*> – **cloudless** *adj*, **cloudlet** *n*

[2]**cloud** *vi* **1** to grow cloudy – usu + *over* or *up* **2a** *of facial features* to become troubled, apprehensive, etc **b** to become blurred, dubious, or ominous *~ vt* **1a** to envelop or obscure (as if) with a cloud **b** to make opaque or murky by condensation, smoke, etc **2** to make unclear or confused **3** to taint, sully <*a ~*ed *reputation*> **4** to cast gloom over

ˈ**cloudˌburst** /-ˌbuhst‖-ˌbɜːst/ *n* a sudden very heavy fall of rain

ˈ**cloud ˌchamber** *n* a vessel containing saturated water vapour whose sudden expansion reveals the passage of an ionizing particle (e g an alpha particle) by a trail of visible droplets

ˌ**cloud ˈnine** *n* a feeling of extreme well-being or elation – usu + *on*; infml

cloudy /ˈklowdi‖ˈklaʊdɪ/ *adj* **1** (having a sky) overcast with clouds **2** not clear or transparent <*~ beer*> – **cloudily** *adv*, **cloudiness** *n*

[1]**clout** /klowt‖klaʊt/ *n* **1** *dial chiefly N Eng & Scot* CLOTH 2; *specif* a piece of cloth or rag used for household tasks (e g polishing or cleaning) – often in combination <*dish*clout> **2** a blow or lusty hit with the hand, cricket bat, etc **3** influence; *esp* effective political power ***USE*** *(2&3)* infml

[2]**clout** *vt* to hit forcefully – infml

[1]**clove** /klohv‖kləʊv/ *n* any of the small bulbs (e g in garlic) developed as parts of a larger bulb

[2]**clove** *past of* CLEAVE

[3]**clove** *n* (a tree of the myrtle family that bears) a flower bud that is used dried as a spice

ˈ**clove ˌhitch** *n* a knot used to secure a rope temporarily to a spar or another rope

cloven /ˈklohv(ə)n‖ˈkləʊv(ə)n/ *past part of* [2]CLEAVE

ˌ**cloven ˈfoot** *n* a foot (e g of a sheep) divided into 2 parts at the end farthest from the body – **cloven-footed** *adj*

ˌ**cloven ˈhoof** *n* CLOVEN FOOT – **cloven-hoofed** *adj*

clover /ˈklohvə‖ˈkləʊvə/ *n* any of a genus of leguminous plants having leaves with 3 leaflets and flowers in dense heads – **in clover** in prosperity or in pleasant circumstances

ˈ**cloverˌleaf** /-ˌleef‖-ˌliːf/ *n, pl* **cloverleafs, cloverleaves** /-ˌleevz‖-ˌliːvz/ a road junction whose plan resembles the arrangement of leaves in a 4-leaved clover and that connects 2 major roads at different levels

clown /klown‖klaʊn/ *n* **1** a jester in an entertainment (e g a play); *specif* a grotesquely dressed comedy performer in a circus **2** one who habitually plays the buffoon; a joker – **clown** *vi*, **clownery** *n*, **clownish** *adj*, **clownishly** *adv*, **clownishness** *n*

cloy /kloy‖klɔɪ/ *vt* to surfeit with an excess, usu of sthg orig pleasing *~vi* to cause surfeit – **cloyingly** *adv*

[1]**club** /klub‖klʌb/ *n* **1a** a heavy stick thicker at one end than the other and used as a hand weapon **b** a stick or bat used to hit a ball in golf and other games **c** a light spar **2a** a playing card marked with 1 or more black figures in the shape of a cloverleaf **b** *pl but sing or pl in constr* the suit comprising cards identified by this figure **3a** *sing or pl in constr* **3a(1)** an association of

people for a specified object, usu jointly supported and meeting periodically **a(2)** an often exclusive association of people that has premises available as a congenial place of retreat or temporary residence or for dining at **b** the meeting place or premises of a club **c** a group of people who agree to make regular payments or purchases in order to secure some advantage <*book* ~> **d** a nightclub – **in the club** *of a woman* pregnant – infml

[2]**club** *vb* **-bb-** *vt* to beat or strike (as if) with a club ~*vi* to combine to share a common expense or object – usu + *together*

clubbable, clubable /ˈklubəbl‖ˈklʌbəbl/ *adj* sociable

ˌ**clubˈfoot** /-ˈfoot‖-ˈfʊt/ *n* a misshapen foot twisted out of position from birth – **clubfooted** *adj*

[1]**cluck** /kluk‖klʌk/ *vi* **1** to make a cluck **2** to express fussy interest or concern – usu + *over*; infml ~*vt* to call with a cluck

[2]**cluck** *n* the characteristic guttural sound made by a hen

[1]**clue** /klooh‖kluː/ *n* **1** *also* **clew** sthg that guides via intricate procedure to the solution of a problem **2** CLEW 2

[2]**clue** *vt* **clueing, cluing 1** CLEW 2 **2** *also* **clew** to inform – usu + *in* or *up*; infml <~ *me in on how it happened*>

ˈ**clueless** /-lis‖-lɪs/ *adj, Br* hopelessly ignorant or lacking in sense – infml

[1]**clump** /klump‖klʌmp/ *n* **1** a compact group of things of the same kind, esp trees or bushes; a cluster **2** a compact mass **3** a heavy tramping sound – **clumpy** *adj*

[2]**clump** *vi* **1** to tread clumsily and noisily **2** to form clumps ~*vt* to arrange in or cause to form clumps

clumsy /ˈklumzi‖ˈklʌmzɪ/ *adj* **1a** awkward and ungraceful in movement or action **b** lacking tact or subtlety <*a* ~ *joke*> **2** awkwardly or poorly made; unwieldy – **clumsily** *adv*, **clumsiness** *n*

clung /klung‖klʌŋ/ *past of* CLING

[1]**cluster** /ˈklustə‖ˈklʌstə/ *n* a compact group formed by a number of similar things or people; a bunch: e g **a** a group of faint stars or galaxies that appear close together and have common properties (e g distance and motion) **b** the group of 4 cups that connect the teats of a cow to a milking machine – **clustery** *adj*

[2]**cluster** *vt* to collect into a cluster ~*vi* to grow or assemble in a cluster

[1]**clutch** /kluch‖klʌtʃ/ *vt* to grasp or hold (as if) with the hand or claws, esp tightly or suddenly ~ *vi* **1** to seek to grasp and hold – often + *at* **2** to operate the clutch on a motor vehicle

[2]**clutch** *n* **1** (the claws or a hand in) the act of grasping or seizing firmly **2** (a lever or pedal operating) a coupling used to connect and disconnect a driving and a driven part of a mechanism

[3]**clutch** *n* a nest of eggs or a brood of chicks; *broadly* a group, bunch

[1]**clutter** /ˈklutə‖ˈklʌtə/ *vt* to fill or cover with scattered or disordered things – often + *up*

[2]**clutter** *n* **1a** a crowded or confused mass or collection **b** scattered or disordered material **2** interfering echoes visible on a radar screen caused by reflection from objects other than the target

co- /koh-‖kəʊ-/ *prefix* **1** with; together; joint <co*exist*> **2** in or to the same degree <co*extensive*> **3a** associate; fellow <co*author*> <co-*star*> **b** deputy; assistant <co*pilot*>

[1]**coach** /kohch‖kəʊtʃ/ *n* **1a** a large usu closed four-wheeled carriage **b** a railway carriage **c** a usu single-deck bus used esp for long-distance or charter work **2a** a private tutor **b** sby who instructs or trains a performer, sportsman, etc [Middle French *coche*, fr German *kutsche*, prob fr Hungarian *kocsi (szekér)* wagon from Kocs, fr *Kocs*, village in Hungary]

[2]**coach** *vt* **1** to train intensively by instruction, demonstration, and practice **2** to act as coach to ~ *vi* **1** to go in a coach **2** to instruct, direct, or prompt as a coach – **coacher** *n*

ˈ**coachman** /-mən‖-mən/ *n* a man who drives or whose business is to drive a coach or carriage

ˈ**coachˌwork** /-ˌwuhk‖-ˌwɜːk/ *n* the bodywork of a road or rail vehicle

coagulant /kohˈagyoolənt‖kəʊˈægjʊlənt/ *n* sthg that produces coagulation

coagulate /kohˈagyoolayt‖kəʊˈægjʊleɪt/ *vb* to (cause to) become viscous or thickened into a coherent mass; curdle, clot – **coagulable** *adj*, **coagulability** *n*, **coagulation** *n*

coal /kohl‖kəʊl/ *n* **1** a piece of glowing, burning, or burnt carbonized material (e g partly burnt wood) **2** a (small piece or broken up quantity of) black or blackish solid combustible mineral consisting chiefly of carbonized vegetable matter and widely used as a natural fuel

coalesce /ˌkoh·əˈles‖ˌkəʊəˈles/ *vi* to unite into a whole; fuse – **coalescence** *n*, **coalescent** *adj*

ˈ**coalˌfield** /-ˌfeeld‖-ˌfiːld/ *n* a region in which deposits of coal occur

ˈ**coal ˌgas** *n* gas made from burning coal; *esp* gas made by carbonizing bituminous coal and used for heating and lighting

ˈ**coalˌhole** /-ˌhohl‖-ˌhəʊl/ *n* **1** a hole or chute for receiving coal **2** *Br* a compartment for storing coal

coalition /ˌkoh·əˈlish(ə)n‖ˌkəʊəˈlɪʃ(ə)n/ *n* **1a** an act of coalescing; a union **b** a body formed by the union of orig distinct elements **2** *sing or pl in constr* a temporary alliance (e g of political parties) for joint action (e g to form a government) – **coalitionist** *n*

ˌ**coal ˈtar** *n* tar obtained by the distilling of bituminous coal and used esp in making dyes and drugs

coarse /kaws‖kɔːs/ *adj* **1** of ordinary or inferior quality or value; common **2a(1)** composed of relatively large particles <~ *sand*> **a(2)** rough in texture or tone <~ *cloth*> **b** adjusted or designed for heavy, fast, or less delicate work <*a* ~ *saw with large teeth*> **c** not precise or detailed with respect to adjustment or discrimination **3** crude or unrefined in taste, manners, or language – **coarsely** *adv*, **coarseness** *n*

ˈ**coarse ˌfish** *n, chiefly Br* any freshwater fish not belonging to the salmon family – **coarse fishing** *n*

coarsen /ˈkaws(ə)n‖ˈkɔːs(ə)n/ *vb* to make or

become coarse

[1]**coast** /kohst‖kəʊst/ *n* the land near a shore; the seashore [Middle French *coste*, fr Latin *costa* rib, side] – **coastal** *adj*, **coastally** *adv*, **coastwards** *adv*

[2]**coast** *vt* to sail along the shore of ~ *vi* **1** to sail along the shore **2a** to slide, glide, etc downhill by the force of gravity **b** to move along (as if) without further application of propulsive power **c** to proceed easily without special application of effort or concern

coaster /ˈkohstə‖ˈkəʊstə/ *n* **1** a small vessel trading from port to port along a coast **2a** a tray or stand, esp of silver, for a decanter **b** a small mat used, esp under a drinks glass, to protect a surface

ˈcoast,guard /-ˌgahd‖-ˌgɑːd/ *n* (a member of) a force responsible for maintaining lookout posts round the coast of the UK for mounting rescues at sea, preventing smuggling, etc

ˈcoast,line /-ˌlien‖-ˌlaɪn/ *n* the outline or shape of a coast

[1]**coat** /koht‖kəʊt/ *n* **1** an outer garment that has sleeves and usu opens the full length of the centre front **2** the external covering of an animal **3** a protective layer; a coating – **coated** *adj*

[2]**coat** *vt* to cover or spread with a protective or enclosing layer – **coater** *n*

coat ˌhanger *n* [2]HANGER

coating /ˈkohting‖ˈkəʊtɪŋ/ *n* a layer of one substance covering another

ˌcoat of ˈarms *n, pl* **coats of arms** (a tabard or surcoat embroidered with) a set of distinctive heraldic shapes or representations, usu depicted on a shield, that is the central part of a heraldic achievement

ˈcoat ˌtails *n pl* two long tapering skirts at the back of a man's coat

coax /kohks‖kəʊks/ *vt* **1** to influence or gently urge by caresses or flattery; wheedle **2** to draw or gain by means of gentle urging or flattery <~ed *an answer out of her*> **3** to manipulate with great perseverance and skill towards a desired condition

cob /kob‖kɒb/ *n* **1** a male swan **2** CORNCOB 1 **3** (any of) a breed of short-legged stocky horses **4** *Br* a small rounded usu crusty loaf – **cobby** *adj*

cobalt /ˈkoh,bawlt‖ˈkəʊ,bɔːlt/ *n* a tough silver-white magnetic metallic element – **cobaltic** *adj*, **cobaltous** *adj*

cobber /ˈkobə‖ˈkɒbə/ *n, Austr* a man's male friend; a mate – infml

[1]**cobble** /ˈkobl‖ˈkɒbl/ *vt* **1** to repair (esp shoes); *also* to make (esp shoes) **2** to make or assemble roughly or hastily – usu + *together*

[2]**cobble** *n* a naturally rounded stone of a size suitable for paving a street

[3]**cobble** *vt* to pave with cobblestones

cobbler /ˈkoblə‖ˈkɒblə/ *n* **1** a mender or maker of leather goods, esp shoes **2** *pl, Br* nonsense, rubbish – often used interjectionally; infml

ˈcobble,stone /-ˌstohn‖-ˌstəʊn/ *n* a cobble – **cobblestoned** *adj*

cobra /ˈkobrə, ˈkohbrə‖ˈkɒbrə, ˈkəʊbrə/ *n* any of several venomous Asiatic and African snakes that have grooved fangs and when excited expand the skin of the neck into a hood [Portuguese *cobra* (*de capello*), lit., (hooded) snake, fr Latin *colubra* snake]

cobweb /ˈkob,web‖ˈkɒb,web/ *n* **1** (a) spider's web **2** a single thread spun by a spider [Middle English *coppeweb*, fr *coppe* spider (fr Old English *ātorcoppe*) + *web*] – **cobwebbed** *adj*, **cobwebby** *adj*

coca /ˈkohkə‖ˈkəʊkə/ *n* (the dried cocaine-containing leaves of) a S American shrub

cocaine /ˌkohˈkayn, kə-‖ˌkəʊˈkeɪn, kə-/ *n* an alkaloid that is obtained from coca leaves, has been used as a local anaesthetic, and is a common drug of abuse that can result in psychological dependence – **cocainism** *n*

coccyx /ˈkoksiks‖ˈkɒksɪks/ *n, pl* **coccyges** /-siˌjeez‖-sɪˌdʒiːz/ *also* **coccyxes** the end of the spinal column below the sacrum in human beings and the tailless apes – **coccygeal** *adj*

cochineal /ˌkochiˈneel‖ˌkɒtʃɪˈniːl/ *n* a red dyestuff consisting of the dried bodies of female cochineal insects, used esp as a colouring agent for food

cochlea /ˈkokli·ə‖ˈkɒklɪə/ *n, pl* **cochleas, cochleae** /-li,ee‖-lɪ,iː/ a coiled part of the inner ear of higher vertebrates that is filled with liquid through which sound waves are transmitted to the auditory nerve – **cochlear** *adj*

[1]**cock** /kok‖kɒk/ *n* **1a** the (adult) male of various birds, specif the domestic fowl **b** the male of fish, crabs, lobsters, and other aquatic animals **2** a device (e g a tap or valve) for regulating the flow of a liquid **3** the hammer of a firearm or its position when cocked ready for firing **4** *Br* – used as a term of infml address to a man **5** the penis – vulg **6** *Br* nonsense, rubbish – slang

[2]**cock** *vi* to set the hammer of a firearm ready for firing ~ *vt* **1a** to draw back and set the hammer of (a firearm) for firing **b** to draw or bend back in preparation for throwing or hitting **2a** to set erect <*the dog* ~ed *its ears*> **b** to turn, tip, or tilt, usu to one side <~ed *his head inquiringly*> **3** to turn up (e g the brim of a hat) – **cock a snook** to react with disdain or defiance <cock a snook *at authority*>

[3]**cock** *n* a small pile (e g of hay)

[4]**cock** *vt* to put (e g hay) into cocks

cockade /koˈkayd‖kɒˈkeɪd/ *n* an ornament (e g a rosette or knot of ribbon) worn on the hat as a badge – **cockaded** *adj*

cock-a-hoop /ˌkok ə ˈhoohp‖ˌkɒk ə ˈhuːp/ *adj* triumphantly boastful; exulting – infml

ˌcock-a-ˈleekie /ə ˈleeki‖ə ˈliːkɪ/ *n* a chicken and leek soup

cockatoo /ˌkokəˈtooh‖ˌkɒkəˈtuː/ *n, pl* **cockatoos** any of numerous large noisy usu showy and crested chiefly Australasian parrots

cockchafer /ˈkok,chayfə‖ˈkɒk,tʃeɪfə/ *n* a large European beetle destructive to vegetation

ˈcock,crow /-ˌkroh‖-ˌkrəʊ/ *n* dawn

ˌcocked ˈhat *n* a hat with brim turned up at 3 places to give a 3-cornered shape

cockerel /ˈkok(ə)rəl‖ˈkɒk(ə)rəl/ *n* a young male domestic fowl

ˌcocker ˈspaniel /ˈkokə‖ˈkɒkə/ *n* a small spaniel with long ears and silky coat

ˌcockˈeyed /-ˈied‖-ˈaɪd/ *adj* **1** having a

squint **2a** askew, awry **b** somewhat foolish or mad <*a ~ scheme*> *USE* infml – **cockeyedly** *adv*, **cockeyedness** *n*

[1]**cockle** /'kokl‖'kɒkl/ *n* CORN COCKLE

[2]**cockle** *n* (the ribbed shell of) a (common edible) bivalve mollusc

[3]**cockle** *n* a pucker or wrinkle – **cockle** *vb*

'cockle,shell /-,shel‖-,ʃel/ *n* **1** the shell of a cockle, scallop, or similar mollusc **2** a light flimsy boat

cockney /'kokni‖'kɒknɪ/ *n* **1** a native of London and now esp of the E End of London **2** the dialect of (the E End of) London [Middle English *cokeney* pampered child, (effeminate) townsman, lit., cocks' egg, fr *coken* (genitive pl of *cok* cock) + *ey* egg] – **cockney** *adj*, **cockneyfy** *vt*, **cockneyish** *adj*, **cockneyism** *n*

'cock,pit /-,pit‖-,pɪt/ *n* **1a** a pit or enclosure for cockfights **b** a place noted for bloody, violent, or prolonged conflict **2a** the rear part of the lowest deck of a sailing warship used as officers' quarters and for treating the wounded **b** a recess below deck level from which a small vessel (e g a yacht) is steered **c** a space in the fuselage of an aeroplane for the pilot (and crew) **d** the driver's compartment in a racing or sports car

'cock,roach /-,rohch‖-,rəʊtʃ/ *n* any of numerous omnivorous usu dark brown chiefly nocturnal insects that include some that are domestic pests

,cock'sure /-'shooə, -'shaw‖-'ʃʊə, -'ʃɔː/ *adj* cocky – infml – **cocksurely** *adv*, **cocksureness** *n*

cocktail /'kok,tayl‖'kɒk,teɪl/ *n* **1a** a drink of mixed spirits or of spirits mixed with flavourings **b** sthg resembling or suggesting such a drink; *esp* a mixture of diverse elements **2a** an appetizer of tomato juice, shellfish, etc **b** a dish of finely chopped mixed fruits

cock up *vt, chiefly Br* to spoil or render a failure by bungling or incompetence – slang – **cock-up** *n*

[1]**cocky** /'koki‖'kɒkɪ/ *adj* marked by overconfidence or presumptuousness – infml – **cockily** *adv*, **cockiness** *n*

[2]**cocky** *n, Austr & NZ* one who owns a small farm

coco /'koh,koh‖'kəʊ,kəʊ/ *n, pl* **cocos** COCONUT PALM

cocoa /'koh,koh‖'kəʊ,kəʊ/ *n* **1** the cacao tree **2a** powdered ground roasted cacao seeds from which some fat has been removed **b** a beverage made by mixing cocoa with usu hot milk [Spanish *cacao*,fr Nahuatl *cacahuatl* cacao beans]

coconut *also* **cocoanut** /'kohkə,nut‖'kəʊkə,nʌt/ *n* the large oval fruit of the coconut palm whose outer fibrous husk yields coir and whose nut contains thick edible meat and a thick sweet milk; *also* COCONUT PALM

'coconut ,palm *n* a tall (American) tropical palm

'coconut ,shy *n* a stall at a funfair where one throws balls at coconuts on stands

[1]**cocoon** /kə'koohn‖kə'kuːn/ *n* **1** (an animal's protective covering similar to) a (silk) envelope which an insect larva forms about itself and in which it passes the pupa stage **2** a (protective) covering like a cocoon (e g for an aeroplane in storage) **3** a sheltered or insulated state of existence

[2]**cocoon** *vt* to wrap or envelop, esp tightly, (as if) in a cocoon

[1]**cod** /kod‖kɒd/, **'cod,fish** *n, pl* **cod** (the flesh of) a soft-finned N Atlantic food fish or related Pacific fish

[2]**cod** *n, Br* nonsense – slang

coda /'kohdə‖'kəʊdə/ *n* **1** a concluding musical section that is formally distinct from the main structure **2** sthg that serves to round out or conclude sthg, esp a literary or dramatic work, and that has an interest of its own

coddle /'kodl‖'kɒdl/ *vt* **1** to cook (esp eggs) slowly in a liquid just below the boiling point **2** to treat with extreme care; pamper – **coddler** *n*

[1]**code** /kohd‖kəʊd/ *n* **1** a systematic body of laws, esp with statutory force **2** a system of principles or maxims <*moral ~*> **3a** a system of signals for communication **b** a system of symbols used to represent assigned and often secret meanings

[2]**code** *vt* **1** to put into the form or symbols of a code **2** to specify (an amino acid, protein, etc) in terms of the genetic code *~vi* to be or contain the genetic code *for* an amino acid, protein, etc – **codable** *adj*, **coder** *n*

codeine /'koh,deen‖'kəʊ,diːn/ *n* a derivative of morphine that is weaker in action than morphine and is given orally to relieve pain and coughing

codex /'koh,deks‖'kəʊ,deks/ *n, pl* **codices** /-di,seez‖-dɪ,siːz/ a manuscript book, esp of biblical or classical texts

codger /'kojə‖'kɒdʒə/ *n* an old and mildly eccentric man – esp in *old codger*; infml

codicil /'kohdisil‖'kəʊdɪsɪl/ *n* **1** a modifying clause added to a will **2** an appendix, supplement – **codicillary** *adj*

codify /'kohdi,fie‖'kəʊdɪ,faɪ/ *vt* **1** to reduce to a code **2** to express in a systematic form – **codifiable** *adj*, **codifiability** *n*, **codification** *n*

[1]**codling** /'kodling‖'kɒdlɪŋ/ *n* a young cod

[2]**codling** *n* any of several elongated greenish cooking apples

,cod-liver 'oil *n* an oil obtained from the liver of the cod and closely related fishes and used as a source of vitamins A and D

'cod,piece /-,pees‖-,piːs/ *n* a flap or bag concealing an opening in the front of men's breeches, esp in the 15th and 16th c

codswallop /'kodz,woləp‖'kɒdz,wɒləp/ *n, chiefly Br* nonsense – slang

coed /,koh'ed‖,kəʊ'ed/ **1** a coeducational school **2** *NAm* a female student in a coeducational institution *USE* infml – **coed** *adj*

coeducation /,koh·edyoo'kaysh(ə)n, -ejoo-‖,kəʊedjʊ'keɪʃ(ə)n, -edʒʊ-/ *n* the education of students of both sexes at the same institution – **coeducational** *adj*, **coeducationally** *adv*

coefficient /,koh·i'fish(ə)nt‖,kəʊɪ'fɪʃ(ə)nt/ *n* **1** any of the factors, esp variable quantities, that are multiplied together in a mathematical product considered in relation to a usu specified factor <*in the expression* 5xy *the ~ of* xy *is* 5> **2** a number that serves as a measure of some property or characteristic (e g of a device or process) <*~ of expansion of a metal*>

coelacanth /'seelə,kanth‖'siːlə,kænθ/ *n* any

of a family of mostly extinct fishes

coelenterate /see'lentərayt, -rət‖si:'lentəreɪt, -rət/ *n* any of a phylum of invertebrate animals including the corals, sea anemones, and jellyfishes – **coelenterate** *adj*

coenzyme /ˌkoh'enziem‖ˌkəʊ'enzaɪm/ *n* a nonprotein compound that combines with a protein to form an active enzyme and whose activity cannot be destroyed by heat

coerce /koh'uhs‖kəʊ'ɜ:s/ *vt* **1** to restrain or dominate by authority or force **2** to compel to an act or choice – often + *into* **3** to enforce or bring about by force or threat – **coercible** *adj*, **coercive** *adj*, **coercion** *n*

coeval /koh'eevl‖kəʊ'i:vl/ *adj* of the same or equal age, antiquity, or duration – **coeval** *n*, **coevality** *n*

coexist /ˌkoh·ig'zist‖ˌkəʊɪg'zɪst/ *vi* **1** to exist together or at the same time **2** to live in peace with each other – **coexistence** *n*, **coexistent** *adj*

coextensive /ˌkoh·ik'stensiv‖ˌkəʊɪk'stensɪv/ *adj* having the same scope or boundaries in space or time – **coextensively** *adv*

coffee /'kofi‖'kɒfɪ/ *n* **1a** a beverage made by percolation, infusion, or decoction from the roasted seeds of a coffee tree; *also* these seeds either green or roasted **b** COFFEE TREE **2** a cup of coffee

'coffee,house /-ˌhows‖-ˌhaʊs/ *n* an establishment that sells refreshments and commonly serves as an informal club

'coffee-,table *adj, of a publication* being outsize and lavishly produced (e g with extensive use of full-colour illustrations) as if for display on a coffee table

coffee table *n* a low table usu placed in a living room

'coffee ,tree *n* a large African evergreen shrub or small tree, widely cultivated in warm regions for its seeds

coffer /'kofə‖'kɒfə/ *n* **1** a chest, box; *esp* a strongbox **2** a treasury, exchequer; *broadly* a store of wealth – usu pl with sing. meaning **3a** a caisson **b** a cofferdam **4** a recessed decorative panel in a vault, ceiling, etc

cofferdam /'kofəˌdam‖'kɒfəˌdæm/ *n* a watertight enclosure from which water is pumped to allow construction or repair (e g of a pier or ship's hull)

coffin /'kofin‖'kɒfɪn/ *n* **1** a box or chest for the burial of a corpse **2** the horny body forming the hoof of a horse's foot – **coffin** *vt*

cog /kog‖kɒg/ *n* **1** a tooth on the rim of a wheel or gear **2** a subordinate person or part – **cogged** *adj*

cogent /'kohj(ə)nt‖'kəʊdʒ(ə)nt/ *adj* appealing forcibly to the mind or reason; convincing – **cogency** *n*, **cogently** *adv*

cogitate /'kojitayt‖'kɒdʒɪteɪt/ *vi* to ponder, usu intently and objectively; meditate ~*vt* to cogitate on ***USE*** fml – **cogitation** *n*, **cogitative** *adj*

cognac /'konyak‖'kɒnjæk/ *n* a French brandy, specif one from the departments of Charente and Charente-Maritime distilled from white wine [*Cognac*, town in France]

¹cognate /'kogˌnayt‖'kɒgˌneɪt/ *adj* **1** related by blood, esp on the mother's side **2a** related by derivation or borrowing or by descent from the same ancestral language **b** *of a noun* related in form and meaning to the verb of which it is the object **3** of the same or similar nature – **cognately** *adv*, **cognateness, cognation** *n*

²cognate *n* sthg (e g a word) cognate with another

cognition /kog'nish(ə)n‖kɒg'nɪʃ(ə)n/ *n* (a product of) the act or process of knowing that involves the processing of sensory information and includes perception, awareness, and judgment – **cognitional** *adj*, **cognitive** *adj*

cogn·izance, -isance /'kogniz(ə)ns‖'kɒgnɪz(ə)ns/ *n* **1** jurisdiction, control **2** the ability to perceive or understand **3** notice, heed <*take ~ of a fault*> ***USE*** fml or technical

cogn·izant, -isant /'kogniz(ə)nt‖'kɒgnɪz(ə)nt/ *adj* having special or certain knowledge, often from firsthand sources – fml or technical

cognomen /kog'nohmin‖kɒg'nəʊmɪn/ *n, pl* **cognomens, cognomina** /-'nominə, -'noh-‖-'nɒmɪnə, -'nəʊ-/ **1** a surname; *esp* the family (and usu 3rd) name of sby named in the ancient Roman fashion **2** a name; *esp* a descriptive nickname – fml or humor – **cognominal** *adj*

cognoscente /ˌkonyoh'shenti, ˌkognə-‖ˌkɒnjəʊ'ʃentɪ, ˌkɒgnə-/ *n, pl* **cognoscenti** /~/ a person having or claiming expert knowledge; a connoisseur

'cog,wheel /-ˌweel‖-ˌwi:l/ *n* a wheel with cogs or teeth

cohabit /koh'habit‖kəʊ'hæbɪt/ *vi* to live or exist together, specif as husband and wife – **cohabitant** *n*, **cohabitation** *n*

cohere /koh'hiə‖kəʊ'hɪə/ *vi* **1** to hold together firmly as parts of the same mass; *broadly* to stick, adhere **2a** to become united in ideas or interests **b** to be logically or aesthetically consistent

coherent /koh'hiərənt‖kəʊ'hɪərənt/ *adj* **1** having the quality of cohering **2a** logically consistent <*a ~ argument*> **b** showing a unity of thought or purpose **3** relating to, composed of, or producing (electromagnetic) waves in phase with each other <*~ light*> – **coherence, coherency** *n*, **coherently** *adv*

cohesion /koh'heezh(ə)n‖kəʊ'hi:ʒ(ə)n/ *n* the act or process of cohering – **cohesionless** *adj*, **cohesive** *adj*, **cohesively** *adv*, **cohesiveness** *n*

cohort /'kohˌhawt‖'kəʊˌhɔ:t/ *n* **1a** a group of soldiers; *esp, sing or pl in constr* a division of a Roman legion **b** a band, group **c** a group of individuals having age, class membership, or other statistical factors in common in a study of the population **2** *chiefly NAm* a companion, accomplice

¹coif /koyf‖kɔɪf/ *n* a close-fitting cap: e g **a** a hoodlike bonnet worn by nuns under a veil **b** a protective usu metal skullcap formerly worn under a hood of mail

²coif *vt* **-ff-** **1** to cover or dress (as if) with a coif **2** to arrange (hair) by brushing, combing, or curling

coiffeur /kwah'fuh ‖kwɑ:'fɜ: (*Fr* kwafœ:r)/ *n* a hairdresser

coiffure /kwah'f(y)ooə ‖kwɑ:'f(j)ʊə (*Fr* kwafy:r)/ *n* a hairstyle – **coiffured** *adj*

¹coil /koyl‖kɔɪl/ *vt* to wind into rings or spirals ~ *vi* **1** to move in a circular, spiral, or winding course **2** to form or lie in a coil – **coilability** *n*

[2]**coil** *n* **1a** (a length of rope, cable, etc gathered into) a series of loops; a spiral **b** a single loop of a coil **2** a number of turns of wire, esp in spiral form, usu for electromagnetic effect or for providing electrical resistance **3** a series of connected pipes in rows, layers, or windings **4** (a stamp from) a roll of postage stamps

[1]**coin** /koyn‖kɔɪn/ *n* **1** a usu thin round piece of metal issued as money **2** metal money [Middle French, wedge, corner, fr Latin *cuneus* wedge]

[2]**coin** *vt* **1a** to make (a coin), esp by stamping; mint **b** to convert (metal) into coins **2** to create, invent < ~ *a phrase*> **3** to make or earn (money) rapidly and in large quantity – often in *coin it*

coinage /ˈkoynij‖ˈkɔɪnɪdʒ/ *n* **1** coining or (a large number of) coins **2** sthg (e g a word) made up or invented

coincide /ˌkoh·inˈsied‖ˌkəʊɪnˈsaɪd/ *vi* **1** to occupy the same place in space or time **2** to correspond in nature, character, function, or position **3** to be in accord or agreement; concur

coincidence /kohˈinsid(ə)ns‖kəʊˈɪnsɪd(ə)ns; *sense 1 also* ˌkoh·inˈsied(ə)ns‖ˌkəʊɪnˈsaɪd(ə)ns/ *n* **1** the act or condition of coinciding; a correspondence **2** (an example of) the chance occurrence at the same time or place of 2 or more events that appear to be related or similar – **coincidental** *adj*, **coincidentally** *adv*

coincident /kohˈinsid(ə)nt‖kəʊˈɪnsɪd(ə)nt/ *adj* **1** occupying the same space or time < ~ *points*> **2** of similar nature; harmonious – **coincidently** *adv*

coir /ˈkoyə‖ˈkɔɪə/ *n* a stiff coarse fibre from the husk of a coconut

coition /kohˈish(ə)n‖kəʊˈɪʃ(ə)n/ *n* coitus – **coitional** *adj*

coitus /ˈkoytəs, ˈkoh·itəs‖ˈkɔɪtəs, ˈkəʊɪtəs/ *n* the natural conveying of semen to the female reproductive tract; *broadly* SEXUAL INTERCOURSE – **coital** *adj*, **coitally** *adv*

ˌcoitus interˈruptus /intəˈruptəs‖ɪntəˈrʌptəs/ *n* coitus which is purposely interrupted in order to prevent ejaculation of sperm into the vagina

[1]**coke** /kohk‖kəʊk/ *n* a solid porous fuel that remains after gases have been driven from coal by heating

[2]**coke** *vt* to convert (coal) into coke

[3]**coke** *n* cocaine – slang

col /kol‖kɒl/ *n* a depression or pass in a mountain ridge or range

col- – see COM-

[1]**cola** /ˈkohlə‖ˈkəʊlə/ *pl of* [1, 2]COLON

[2]**cola** *also* **kola** /ˈkohlə‖ˈkəʊlə/ *n* a carbonated soft drink flavoured with extract from coca leaves, kola nut, sugar, caramel, and acid and aromatic substances

colander /ˈkoləndə‖ˈkɒləndə; *also* ˈku-‖ˈkʌ-/, **cullender** /ˈkuləndə‖ˈkʌləndə/ *n* a perforated bowl-shaped utensil for washing or draining food

[1]**cold** /kohld‖kəʊld/ *adj* **1** having a low temperature, often below some normal temperature or below that compatible with human comfort **2a** marked by lack of warm feeling; unemotional; *also* unfriendly <*a* ~ *stare*> **b** marked by deliberation or calculation <*a* ~ *act of aggression*> **3a** previously cooked but served cold < ~ *meats*> **b** not (sufficiently) hot or heated **c** made cold < ~ *drinks*> **4a** depressing, cheerless **b** producing a sensation of cold; chilling < ~ *blank walls*> **c** COOL 5 **5a** dead **b** unconscious <*knocked out* ~ > **6a** retaining only faint scents, traces, or clues <*a* ~ *trail*> **b** far from a goal, object, or solution sought **c** stale, uninteresting < ~ *news*> **7** presented or regarded in a straightforward way; impersonal <*the* ~ *facts*> **8** unprepared **9** intense yet without the usual outward effects <*a* ~ *fury*> – **coldish** *adj*, **coldly** *adv*, **coldness** *n* – **in cold blood** with premeditation; deliberately

[2]**cold** *n* **1a** a condition of low temperature **b** cold weather **2** bodily sensation produced by relative lack of heat; chill **3** a bodily disorder popularly associated with chilling; *specif* COMMON COLD **4** a state of neglect or deprivation – esp in *come/bring in out of the cold*

[3]**cold** *adv* with utter finality; absolutely <*was turned down* ~ >

ˌcold-ˈblooded *adj* **1a** done or acting without consideration or compunction; ruthless < ~ *murder*> **b** concerned only with the facts; emotionless **2** having a body temperature not internally regulated but approximating to that of the environment – **cold-bloodedly** *adv*, **cold-bloodedness** *n*

cold call *n* an unsolicited visit or phone call made by a salesman to a prospective customer – **cold-call** *vt*

cold chisel *n* a chisel made of steel of a strength and temper suitable for chipping or cutting cold metal

ˌcold ˈcomfort *n* scant consolation

ˌcold ˈcream *n* a thick oily often perfumed cream for cleansing and soothing the skin of the neck, face, etc

ˌcold ˈfront *n* an advancing edge of a cold air mass

ˌcold ˈshoulder *n* intentionally cold or unsympathetic treatment – usu + *the* – **cold-shoulder** *vt*

ˈcold ˌsore *n* (herpes simplex when occurring as) 1 or more blisters appearing round or inside the mouth

ˌcold ˈstorage *n* a condition of being held or continued without being acted on; abeyance

ˈcold ˌwar *n* **1** a conflict carried on by methods short of military action **2** a hostile but nonviolent relationship – **cold warrior** *n*

coleslaw /ˈkohlˌslaw‖ˈkəʊlˌslɔː/ *n* a salad of raw sliced or chopped white cabbage [Dutch *koolsla*, fr *kool* cabbage + *sla* salad]

coley /ˈkohli‖ˈkəʊlɪ/ *n*, *Br* an important N Atlantic food fish closely related to the cod

colic /ˈkolik‖ˈkɒlɪk/ *n* a paroxysm of abdominal pain localized in the intestines or other hollow organ and caused by spasm, obstruction, or twisting – **colicky** *adj*

colitis /kəˈlietəs, koh-‖kəˈlaɪtəs, kəʊ-/ *n* inflammation of the colon

collaborate /kəˈlabərayt‖kəˈlæbəreɪt/ *vi* **1** to

work together or with another (e g in an intellectual endeavour) **2** to cooperate with an enemy of one's country – **collaborator** *n*, **collaborative** *adj*, **collaboration** *n*

collage /ˈkolahzh‖ˈkɒlɑːʒ/ *n* **1** an (abstract) composition made of pieces of paper, wood, cloth, etc fixed to a surface **2** an assembly of diverse fragments – **collagist** *n*

[1]**collapse** /kəˈlaps‖kəˈlæps/ *vi* **1** to break down completely; disintegrate **2** to fall in or give way abruptly and completely (e g through compression) **3** to lose force, value, or effect suddenly **4** to break down in energy, stamina, or self-control through exhaustion or disease; *esp* to fall helpless or unconscious **5** to fold down into a more compact shape ~*vt* to cause to collapse – **collapsible** *adj*, **collapsibility** *n*

[2]**collapse** *n* **1a** an (extreme) breakdown in energy, strength, or self-control **b** an airless state of (part of) a lung **2** the act or an instance of collapsing

[1]**collar** /ˈkolə‖ˈkɒlə/ *n* **1** a band, strip, or chain worn round the neck: e g **1a** a band that serves to finish or decorate the neckline of a garment; *esp* one that is turned over **b** a band fitted about the neck of an animal **c** a part of the harness of draught animals that fits over the shoulders and takes the strain when a load is drawn **d** a protective or supportive device worn round the neck **2** sthg resembling a collar (e g a ring or round flange to restrain motion or hold sthg in place) **3** any of various animal structures or markings similar to a collar in appearance or form **4** a cut of bacon from the neck of a pig – **collared** *adj*, **collarless** *adj*

[2]**collar** *vt* **1a** to seize by the collar or neck; *broadly* to apprehend **b** to get control of **2** to buttonhole *USE* infml

ˈ**collar**ˌ**bone** /-ˌbohn‖-ˌbəʊn/ *n* the clavicle

collate /kəˈlayt‖kəˈleɪt/ *vt* **1** to collect and compare carefully in order to verify and often to integrate or arrange in order **2** to appoint (a priest) to a Church of England benefice of which the bishop is the patron **3** to assemble in proper order < ~ *printed sheets*> – **collator** *n*

[1]**collateral** /kəˈlat(ə)rəl‖kəˈlæt(ə)rəl/ *adj* **1** accompanying as secondary or subordinate **2** belonging to the same ancestral stock but not in a direct line of descent – usu contrasted with *lineal* **3** parallel or corresponding in position, time, or significance **4** of or being collateral – **collaterally** *adv*, **collaterality** *n*

[2]**collateral** *n* **1** a collateral relative **2** property pledged by a borrower to protect the interests of the lender

collation /kəˈlaysh(ə)n‖kəˈleɪʃ(ə)n/ *n* **1** a light meal; *esp* one allowed on fast days in place of lunch or supper **2** the act, process, or result of collating

colleague /ˈkoleeg‖ˈkɒliːg/ *n* a fellow worker, esp in a profession

[1]**collect** /ˈkolikt‖ˈkɒlɪkt/ *n* a short prayer comprising an invocation, petition, and conclusion; *specif, often cap* one preceding the Epistle read at Communion

[2]**collect** /kəˈlekt‖kəˈlekt/ *vt* **1a** to bring together into 1 body or place; *specif* to assemble a collection of **b** to gather or exact from a number of sources < ~ *taxes*> **2** to accumulate, gather <*books* ~ *dust*> **3** to gain or regain control of < ~ *his thoughts*> **4** to claim as due and receive possession or payment of < ~ *social security*> **5** to provide transport or escort for < ~ *the children from school*> **6** *chiefly Br* to gain, obtain ~ *vi* **1** to come together in a band, group, or mass; gather <*the troops* ~ed> **2a** to assemble a collection **b** to receive payment < ~ing *on his insurance*> – **collectible, collectable** *adj*

[3]**collect** /kəˈlekt‖kəˈlekt/ *adv or adj, NAm* to be paid for by the receiver

collected /kəˈlektid‖kəˈlektɪd/ *adj* **1** exhibiting calmness and composure **2** *of a gait or horse* (performed) in a state of collection – **collectedly** *adv*, **collectedness** *n*

collection /kəˈleksh(ə)n‖kəˈlekʃ(ə)n/ *n* **1** sthg collected; *esp* an accumulation of objects gathered for study, comparison, or exhibition **2** the act of collecting

[1]**collective** /kəˈlektiv‖kəˈlektɪv/ *adj* **1** denoting a number of individuals considered as 1 group <flock *is a* ~ *word*> **2** *of a fruit* MULTIPLE 4 **3** of, made, or held in common by a group of individuals < ~ *responsibility*> **4** collectivized <*a* ~ *farm*> – **collectively** *adv*

[2]**collective** *n* **1** *sing or pl in constr* a collective body; a group **2** a cooperative organization; *specif* a collective farm

colˌ**lective** ˈ**bargaining** *n* negotiation between an employer and union representatives usu on wages, hours, and working conditions

collectivism /kəˈlektiˌviz(ə)m‖kəˈlektɪˌvɪz(ə)m/ *n* a political or economic theory advocating collective control, esp over production and distribution – **collectivist** *adj or n*, **collectivistic** *adj*, **collectivistically** *adv*

collectiv·ize, -ise /kəˈlektiviez‖kəˈlektɪvaɪz/ *vt* to organize under collective control – **collectivization** *n*

collector /kəˈlektə‖kəˈlektə/ *n* **1a** an official who collects funds, esp money **b** one who makes a collection <*a stamp* ~> **2** a conductor maintaining contact between moving and stationary parts of an electric circuit **3** a region in a transistor that collects charge carriers – **collectorship** *n*

colleen /koˈleen‖kɒˈliːn/ *n* **1** an Irish girl **2** *Irish* a girl

college /ˈkolij‖ˈkɒlɪdʒ/ *n* **1** a building used for an educational or religious purpose **2a** a self-governing endowed constituent body of a university offering instruction and often living quarters but not granting degrees **b** an institution offering vocational or technical instruction <*business* ~> **3** an organized body of people engaged in a common pursuit **4** *chiefly Br* a public school or private secondary school; *also* a state school for older pupils *USE* (except 1) sing. or pl in constr – **college** *adj*

collegiate /kəˈleeji·ət‖kəˈliːdʒɪət/ *adj* **1** of a collegiate church **2** of or comprising a college – **collegiately** *adv*

colˌ**legiate** ˈ**church** *n* a church other than a cathedral that has a chapter of canons

collide /kəˈlied‖kəˈlaɪd/ *vi* **1** to come together forcibly **2** to come into conflict

collie /ˈkoli‖ˈkɒlɪ/ *n* a large dog of any of several varieties of a breed developed in Scotland, esp for use in herding sheep and cattle

collier /ˈkolyə‖ˈkɒljə/ *n* **1** a coal miner **2** a ship for transporting coal

colliery /ˈkolyəri‖ˈkɒljərɪ/ *n* a coal mine and its associated buildings

collision /kəˈlizh(ə)n‖kəˈlɪʒ(ə)n/ *n* **1** an act or instance of colliding; a clash **2** an encounter between particles (e g atoms or molecules) resulting in exchange or transformation of energy – **collisional** *adj*

colˈlision ˌcourse *n* a course or approach that would result in collision or conflict if continued unaltered

collocate /ˈkoləkayt‖ˈkɒləkeɪt/ *vt* to set or arrange in a place or position; *esp* to set side by side – fml ~*vi, of a linguistic element* to form part of a collocation

collocation /ˌkoləˈkaysh(ə)n‖ˌkɒləˈkeɪʃ(ə)n/ *n* the act or result of placing or arranging together; *specif* a noticeable arrangement or joining together of linguistic elements (e g words) – **collocational** *adj*

colloid /ˈkoloyd‖ˈkɒlɔɪd/ *n* **1a** a substance composed of particles that are too small to be seen with a light microscope but too large to form a true solution and that will typically diffract a beam of light **b** a system consisting of a colloid together with the gaseous, liquid, or solid medium in which it is dispersed **2** a gelatinous substance found in tissues, esp in disease – **colloidal** *adj*, **colloidally** *adv*

colloquial /kəˈlohkwi·əl‖kəˈləʊkwɪəl/ *adj* used in, characteristic of, or using the style of familiar and informal conversation; conversational – **colloquial** *n*, **colloquially** *adv*, **colloquiality** *n*

colloquialism /kəˈlohkwi·əˌliz(ə)m‖kəˈləʊkwɪəˌlɪz(ə)m/ *n* **1** a colloquial expression **2** colloquial style

colloquy /ˈkoləkwi‖ˈkɒləkwɪ/ *n* a formal conversation or dialogue

collude /kəˈloohd‖kəˈluːd/ *vi* to conspire, plot

collusion /kəˈloohzh(ə)n‖kəˈluːʒ(ə)n/ *n* secret agreement or cooperation for an illegal or deceitful purpose – **collusive** *adj*, **collusively** *adv*

collywobbles /ˈkoliˌwoblz‖ˈkɒlɪˌwɒblz/ *n pl* **1** stomachache **2** qualms, butterflies *USE* + *the*; infml

cologne /kəˈlohn‖kəˈləʊn/ *n* TOILET WATER – **cologned** *adj*

[1]**colon** /ˈkohˌlon‖ˈkəʊˌlɒn/ *n, pl* **colons, cola** /-lə‖-lə/ the part of the large intestine that extends from the caecum to the rectum – **colonic** *adj*

[2]**colon** *n, pl* **colons, cola** /-lə‖-lə/ a punctuation mark : used chiefly a clause or phase that explains or illustrates what has gone before to introduce

colonel /ˈkuhnl‖ˈkɜːnl/ *n* an officer in the army or US airforce ranking below brigadier or brigadier general [alteration of earlier *coronel*, fr Middle French, fr Italian *colonnello* column of soldiers, colonel, fr *colonna* column, fr Latin *columna*] – **colonelcy** *n*

ˌColonel ˈBlimp /blimp‖blɪmp/ *n* a pompous person with out-of-date or ultraconservative views; *broadly* a reactionary – **Colonel Blimpism** *n*

[1]**colonial** /kəˈlohnyəl, -ni·əl‖kəˈləʊnjəl, -nɪəl/ *adj* **1** (characteristic) of a colony **2** *often cap* made or prevailing in America before 1776 **3** possessing or composed of colonies <*Britain's* ~ *empire*> – **colonialize** *vt*, **colonially** *adv*, **colonialness** *n*

[2]**colonial** *n* a member or inhabitant of a (British Crown) colony

colonialism /kəˈlohni·əˌliz(ə)m‖kəˈləʊnɪəˌlɪz(ə)m/ *n* (a policy based on) control by a state over a dependent area or people – **colonialist** *n or adj*, **colonialistic** *adj*

colonist /ˈkolənist‖ˈkɒlənɪst/ *n* **1** a member or inhabitant of a colony **2** one who colonizes or settles in a new country

colon·ize, -ise /ˈkoləniez‖ˈkɒlənaɪz/ *vt* to establish a colony in, on, or of to make or establish a colony; settle – **colonizer** *n*, **colonization** *n*

colonnade /ˌkoləˈnayd‖ˌkɒləˈneɪd/ *n* a row of columns, usu supporting an entablature – **colonnaded** *adj*

colonoscope /kohˈlonəˌskohp‖kəʊˈlɒnəˌskəʊp/ *n* a long medical instrument with which the colon can be examined and operated upon – **colonoscopy** *n*

colony /ˈkoləni‖ˈkɒlənɪ/ *n* **1** a body of settlers living in a new territory but subject to control by the parent state; *also* their territory **2** a distinguishable localized population within a species <*a* ~ *of termites*> **3a** a mass of microorganisms, usu growing in or on a solid medium **b** all the units of a compound animal (e g a coral) **4** (the area occupied by) a group of individuals with common interests living close together <*an artists'* ~> **5** a group of people segregated from the general public <*a leper* ~>

colophon /ˈkoləˌfon‖ˈkɒləˌfɒn/ *n* **1** a statement at the end of a book or manuscript that usu gives facts about its production **2** an identifying design used by a printer or publisher

color /ˈkulə‖ˈkʌlə/ *vb or n, chiefly NAm* (to) colour

ˌColoˌrado ˈbeetle /ˌkoləˈrahdoh‖ˌkɒləˈrɑːdəʊ/ *n* a black-and-yellow striped beetle that feeds on the leaves of the potato

coloration, *Br also* **colouration** /ˌkuləˈraysh(ə)n‖ˌkʌləˈreɪʃ(ə)n/ *n* **1** COLOURING 1c(1), COMPLEXION 1 **2** use or choice of colours (e g by an artist) **3** an arrangement or range of colours <*the brilliant* ~ *of a butterfly's wing*>

coloratura /ˌkolərəˈtyooərə‖ˌkɒlərəˈtjʊərə/ *n* (a singer who uses) elaborate embellishment in vocal music

colossal /kəˈlos(ə)l‖kəˈlɒs(ə)l/ *adj* of or like a colossus; *esp* of very great size or degree – **colossally** *adv*

colossus /kəˈlosəs‖kəˈlɒsəs/ *n, pl* **colossuses, colossi** /-sie‖-saɪ/ **1** a statue of gigantic size **2** sby or sthg remarkably preeminent

colostrum /kəˈlostrəm‖kəˈlɒstrəm/ *n* the milk that is secreted for a few days after giving birth and is characterized by high protein and antibody content – **colostral** *adj*

[1]**colour**, *NAm chiefly* **color** /ˈkulə‖ˈkʌlə/ *n* **1a**

the visual sensation (e g red or grey) caused by the wavelength of perceived light that enables one to differentiate otherwise identical objects **b** the aspect of objects and light sources that may be described in terms of hue, lightness, and saturation for objects and hue, brightness, and saturation for light sources **c** a hue, esp as opposed to black, white, or grey **2** an outward often deceptive show; an appearance (of authenticity) <*his wounds gave ~ to his story*> **3** the tint characteristic of good health **4a** an identifying badge, pennant, or flag (e g of a ship or regiment) **b** coloured clothing distinguishing one as a member of a usu specified group or as a representative of a usu specified person or thing **5** character, nature <*showed himself in his true ~s*> **6** the use or combination of colours (e g by painters) **7** vitality, interest <*the play had a good deal of ~ to it*> **8** a pigment **9** tonal quality in music **10** skin pigmentation other than white, characteristic of race **11** *Br* the award made to a regular member of a team <*got my cricket ~s*> *USE* (*4a, 4b, 5, & 11*) usu pl with sing. meaning

[2]**colour,** *NAm chiefly* **color** *vt* **1a** to give colour to **b** to change the colour of **2** to change as if by dyeing or painting: e g **2a** to misrepresent, distort **b** to influence, affect < *~ his judgment*> *~vi* to take on or impart colour; *specif* to blush – **colourant** *n*

'**colour ˌbar** *n* a social or legal barrier that prevents coloured people from participating with whites in various activities or restricts their opportunities

'**colour-ˌblind** *adj* (partially) unable to distinguish 1 or more colours – **colour blindness** *n*

[1]'**coloured** *adj* **1** having colour **2** marked by exaggeration or bias **3a** of a race other than the white; *esp* BLACK 2 **b** *often cap* of mixed race – esp of S Africans of mixed descent

[2]**coloured** *n, pl* **coloureds, coloured** *often cap* a coloured person

colourfast /'kuləˌfahst‖'kʌləˌfɑːst/ *adj* having colour that will not fade or run – **colourfastness** *n*

'**colourful** /-f(ə)l‖-f(ə)l/ *adj* **1** having striking colours **2** full of variety or interest – **colourfully** *adv*, **colourfulness** *n*

colouring /'kuləring‖'kʌlərɪŋ/ **1a** (the effect produced by combining or) applying colours **b** sthg that produces colour **c(1)** natural colour **c(2)** COMPLEXION 1 **2** an influence, bias **3** a timbre, quality

colourless /'kuləlis‖'kʌləlɪs/ *adj* lacking colour: e g **a** pallid **b** dull, uninteresting – **colourlessly** *adv*, **colourlessness** *n*

'**colour ˌscheme** *n* a systematic combination of colours

colt /kohlt, kolt‖kəʊlt, kɒlt/ *n* **1** a young male horse that is either sexually immature or has not attained an arbitrarily designated age **2** a novice; *esp* a cricketer or rugby player in a junior team

coltish /'kohltish, 'kol-‖'kəʊltɪʃ, 'kɒl-/ *adj* **1** frisky, playful **2** of or resembling a colt – **coltishly** *adv*, **coltishness** *n*

columbine /'koləmbien‖'kɒləmbaɪn/ *n* any of a genus of plants of the buttercup family with showy spurred flowers

column /'koləm‖'kɒləm/ *n* **1a** a vertical arrangement of items or a vertical section of printing on a page **b** a special and usu regular feature in a newspaper or periodical **2** a pillar that usu consists of a round shaft, a capital, and a base **3** sthg resembling a column in form, position, or function <*a ~ of water*> **4** a long narrow formation of soldiers, vehicles, etc in rows – **columned** *adj*

columnist /'koləmnist‖'kɒləmnɪst/ *n* one who writes a newspaper or magazine column

com-, col-, con- *prefix* with; together; jointly – usu *com-* before *b, p,* or *m* <*commingle*>, *col-* before *l* <*collinear*>, and *con-* before other sounds <*concentrate*>

[1]**coma** /'kohmə‖'kəʊmə/ *n* a state of deep unconsciousness caused by disease, injury, etc

[2]**coma** *n, pl* **comae** /'kohmi‖'kəʊmɪ/ **1** the head of a comet, usu containing a nucleus **2** an optical aberration in which the image of a point source becomes a comet-shaped blur – **comatic** *adj*

comatose /'kohməˌtohs, -ˌtohz‖'kəʊməˌtəʊs, -ˌtəʊz/ *adj* **1** of or suffering from coma **2** characterized by lethargy and sluggishness; torpid <*a ~ economy*>

[1]**comb** /kohm‖kəʊm/ *n* **1a** a toothed instrument used esp for adjusting, cleaning, or confining hair **b** a structure resembling such a comb; *esp* any of several toothed devices used in handling or ordering textile fibres **c** a currycomb **2** a fleshy crest on the head of a domestic fowl or a related bird **3** a honeycomb – **combed** *adj*, **comblike** *adj*

[2]**comb** *vt* **1** to draw a comb through for the purpose of arranging or cleaning **2** to pass across with a scraping or raking action **3a** to eliminate (e g with a comb) by a thorough going over – usu + *out* **b** to search or examine systematically **4** to use with a combing action *~vi, of a wave* to roll over or break into foam

[1]**combat** /'kombat, kəm'bat‖'kɒmbæt, kəm'bæt/ *vb* **-tt-** (*NAm* **-t-, -tt-**) *vi* to engage in combat; fight *~ vt* **1** to fight with; battle **2** to struggle against; *esp* to strive to reduce or eliminate < *~ inflation*>

[2]**combat** /'kombat‖'kɒmbæt/ *n* **1** a fight or contest between individuals or groups **2** a conflict, controversy **3** active fighting in a war – **combat** *adj*

combatant /'kombətənt, kəm'bat(ə)nt‖'kɒmbətənt, kəm'bæt(ə)nt/ *n* a person, nation, etc that is (ready to be) an active participant in combat – **combatant** *adj*

combative /'kombətiv‖'kɒmbətɪv/ *adj* marked by eagerness to fight or contend – **combatively** *adv*, **combativeness** *n*

comber /'kohmə‖'kəʊmə/ *n* ROLLER 2

combination /ˌkombi'naysh(ə)n‖ˌkɒmbɪ'neɪʃ(ə)n/ *n* **1a** a result or product of combining **b** a group of people working as a team **2** any of the different sets of a usu specified number of individuals that can be chosen from a group and are considered without regard to order within the set **3** *pl* any of various 1-piece undergarments for the upper and lower parts of the body and legs **4** a (process of) combining, esp to form a chemical compound – **combinational** *adj*

ˌcombiˈnation ˌlock *n* a lock with a mechanism operated by the selection of a specific combination of letters or numbers

[1]**combine** /kəmˈbien‖kəmˈbaɪn/ *vt* **1a** to bring into such close relationship as to obscure individual characters; merge **b** to cause to unite into a chemical compound **2** to cause to mix together **3** to possess in combination ~ *vi* **1a** to become one **b** to unite to form a chemical compound **2** to act together – **combiner** *n*, **combinable** *adj*, **combinability** *n*

[2]**combine** /ˈkombien‖ˈkɒmbaɪn/ *n* **1** a combination of people or organizations, esp in industry or commerce, to further their interests **2** **combine, combine harvester** a harvesting machine that cuts, threshes, and cleans grain while moving over a field

comˈbining ˌform /kəmˈbiening‖kəmˈbaɪnɪŋ/ *n* a linguistic form (e g *Franco-*) that cannot stand alone but forms compounds with other free or bound forms

combo /ˈkomboh‖ˈkɒmbəʊ/ *n, pl* **combos** a usu small jazz or dance band

combustible /kəmˈbustəbl‖kəmˈbʌstəbl/ *adj* **1** capable of (easily) being set on fire **2** easily excited – **combustible** *n*, **combustibly** *adv*, **combustibility** *n*

combustion /kəmˈbuschən‖kəmˈbʌstʃən/ *n* **1** a chemical reaction, esp an oxidation, in which light and heat are evolved **2** a slower chemical oxidation – **combustive** *adj*

[1]**come** /kum‖kʌm/ *vb* **came** /kaym‖keɪm/; **come** *vi* **1a** to move towards sthg nearer, esp towards the speaker; approach **b** to move or journey nearer, esp towards or with the speaker, with a specified purpose <he came *to see us*> **c(1)** to reach a specified position in a progression <*now we* ~ *to the section on health*> **c(2)** to arrive, appear,occur <*the time has* ~> <*they* came *by train*> **d(1)** to approach, reach, or fulfil a specified condition <*this* ~s *near perfection*> – often + *to* <came *to his senses*> **d(2)** – used with a following infinitive to express arrival at a condition <came *to regard him as a friend*> or chance occurrence <*how did you* ~ *to be invited?*> **2a** to happen, esp by chance <*no harm will* ~ *to you*> **b(1)** to extend, reach <*her dress* came *to her ankles*> **b(2)** to amount <*that* ~s *to 75p exactly*> **c** to originate, arise, or be the result *of* <*wine* ~s *from grapes*> **d** to fall within the specified limits, scope, or jurisdiction <*this* ~s *within the terms of the treaty*> **e** to issue *from* <*a sob* came *from her throat*> **f** to be available or turn out, usu as specified <*this model* ~s *in several sizes*> **g** to be or belong in a specified place or relation <*the address* ~s *above the date*>; *also* TAKE PLACE <*Monday* ~s *after Sunday*> **h** to take form <*the story won't* ~> **3** to become <*it* came *untied*> <*the handle* came *off*>; *esp* to reach a culminating state <*it all* came *right in the end*> **4** to experience orgasm – infml ~ *vt* **1a** to move nearer by traversing <*has* ~ *several miles*> **b** to reach some state after traversing <*has* ~ *a long way from humble beginnings*> **2** to take on the aspect of; play the role of – infml <*don't* ~ *the old soldier with me*> – infml – **as it comes** without stipulated additions; *specif* NEAT 1a – **come a cropper 1** *chiefly Br* to have a fall or an accident **2** to fail completely – slang – **come across** to meet with or find by chance – **come by** to get possession of; acquire – **come clean** to tell the whole story; confess – infml – **come home to roost** to rebound upon the perpetrator – **come into** to acquire as a possession or inheritance <came into *a fortune*> – **come off it** to cease foolish or pretentious talk or behaviour – usu used imperatively; infml – **come one's way** to fall to one's lot – **come over** to seize suddenly and strangely <*what's* come over *you?*> – **come through** to survive (e g an illness) – **come to** to be a question of <*hopeless when it* comes to *arithmetic*> – **come to a head** to arrive at a culminating point or crisis – **come to grief** to end badly; fail – **come to oneself 1** COME TO **2** to regain self-control – **come to pass** HAPPEN 2 – fml – **come unstuck** COME TO GRIEF – infml – **come upon** to meet with or find by chance – **to come** in the future; coming <*in years* to come>

[2]**come** *interj* – used to express encouragement or to urge reconsideration <~, ~, *it's not as bad as that*>

come about *vi* **1** to occur; TAKE PLACE **2** to change direction <*the wind has* come about *into the north*> **3** *of a ship* to turn onto a new tack

come across *vi* **1** to provide sthg demanded or expected, esp sex or money **2** to produce an impression <*he* comes across *as a persuasive speaker*>

ˌcome aˈgain *interj* – used as a request for a remark to be repeated; infml

come along *vi* **1** to appear <*wouldn't just marry the first man that* came along> **2** to hurry – usu imperative

ˈcomeˌback /-ˌbak‖-ˌbæk/ *n* **1a** a means of redress **b** a retrospective criticism of a decision **2** a return to a former state or condition **3** a sharp or witty reply; a retort – infml

come back *vi* **1** to return to memory <*it's all* coming back *to me now*> **2** to reply, retort **3** to regain a former condition or position

comedian /kəˈmeedi·ən‖kəˈmiːdɪən/, *fem* **comedienne** /kəˌmeediˈen‖kəˌmiːdɪˈen/ *n* **1** an actor who plays comic roles **2** one, esp a professional entertainer, who aims to be amusing

ˈcomeˌdown /-ˌdown‖-ˌdaʊn/ *n* a striking descent in rank or dignity – infml

come down *vi* **1** to formulate and express one's opinion or decision <came down *in favour of abortion on demand*> **2** *of an aircraft, missile, etc* to land; *esp* to crash **3** to become ill <*they* came down *with measles*> **4** *Br* to return from a university

comedy /ˈkomədi‖ˈkɒmədɪ/ *n* **1a** a drama of light and amusing character, typically with a happy ending **b** (a work in) the genre of (dramatic) literature dealing with comic or serious subjects in a light or satirical manner **2** a ludicrous or farcical event or series of events **3** the comic aspect of sthg [Middle French *comedie*, fr Latin *comoedia*, fr Greek *kōmōidia*, fr *kōmos* revel + *aeidein* to sing]

ˌcome-ˈhither *adj* sexually inviting <*that* ~ *look in his eyes*>

come in *vi* **1** to arrive <*I was there when the train* came in> **2** to finish as specified, esp in a competition <came in *third*> **3a** to function in a specified manner; be of use <*to* come in *handy*> **b** to make reply to a signal <came in *loud and clear*> **4** to assume a role or function <*that's where you* come in> – **come in for** to become subject to <coming in for *increasing criticism*>

comely /ˈkumli‖ˈkʌmlɪ/ *adj* of pleasing appearance; not plain – **comeliness** *n*

come off *vi* **1** to finish or emerge from sthg in a specified condition <came off *well in the contest*> **2** to succeed <*that didn't quite* come off> **3** to happen, occur **4** to become detached

ˈcome-ˌon *n* **1** *chiefly NAm* an attraction or enticement (e g in sales promotion) to induce an action **2** an instance of sexually provocative enticement – infml

come on *vi* **1** to advance or begin by degrees <*as darkness* came on, *it got harder to see*> **2** – used in cajoling, pleading, defiance, or encouraging <come on, *you can do it*> **3** COME ALONG 2 **4** to appear on the radio, television, or stage **5** *chiefly NAm* to project a specified appearance <comes on *as a Liberal in his speeches*>

come out *vi* **1a** to come to public notice; be published **b** to become evident <*this will* come out *in the full analysis*> **2a** to declare oneself, esp in public utterance <came out *in favour of the popular candidate*> **b** to present oneself openly as homosexual **3** to end up; TURN OUT <*everything will* come out *right*> **4** to make a debut; *specif* to make one's first appearance in society as a debutante – **come out in the wash 1** to become known in the course of time **2** to reach a satisfactory conclusion – **come out with** to utter or say, usu unexpectedly

come over *vi* **1a** to change from one side (e g of a controversy) to the other **b** to drop in casually <come over *any time; we're always in*> **2** COME ACROSS 2 <*she* comes over *as a very sincere person*> **3** *Br* to become <*she* came over *all queer*>

comer /ˈkumə‖ˈkʌmə/ *n* **1** sby who comes or arrives <*all* ~s> **2** *chiefly NAm* sby making rapid progress or showing promise

come round *vi* **1** COME TO **2** to accede to a particular opinion or course of action **3** COME ABOUT 2

comestible /kəˈmestəbl‖kəˈmestəbl/ *n* food – usu pl with sing. meaning; fml

comet /ˈkomit‖ˈkɒmɪt/ *n* a celestial body that follows a usu highly elliptical orbit round the sun and consists of an indistinct head usu surrounding a bright nucleus, often with a long tail which points away from the sun [Old English *cometa*, fr Latin, fr Greek *komētēs*, lit., long-haired, fr *komē* hair] – **cometary** *adj*

come through *vi* **1** to do what is needed or expected **2** to become communicated

ˌcome ˈto *vi* to recover consciousness

come up *vi* **1** to rise in rank or status **2** to arise inevitably or by chance <*any problems that* come up> **3** to appear before a magistrate <*he* came up *for speeding*> **4** to become, esp after cleaning <*the table* came up *like new*> – **come up with** to provide, esp in dealing with a problem or challenge <came up with *a better solution*>

ˌcome-ˈuppance /ˈup(ə)ns‖ˈʌp(ə)ns/ *n* a deserved rebuke or penalty

comfit /ˈkumfit‖ˈkʌmfɪt/ *n* a sweetmeat consisting of a nut, seed, piece of fruit, etc coated and preserved with sugar

[1]**comfort** /ˈkumfət‖ˈkʌmfət/ *n* **1** (sby or sthg that provides) consolation or encouragement in time of trouble or worry **2** contented well-being – **comfortless** *adj*

[2]**comfort** *vt* **1** to cheer up **2** to ease the grief or trouble of; console – **comfortingly** *adv*

comfortable /ˈkumftəbl‖ˈkʌmftəbl/ *adj* **1a** providing or enjoying contentment and security <*a* ~ *income*> **b** providing or enjoying physical comfort <*a* ~ *armchair*> **2a** causing no worry or doubt <~ *assumptions that require no thought*> **b** free from stress or tension <*a* ~ *routine*> – **comfortably** *adv*

comforter /ˈkumfətə‖ˈkʌmfətə/ *n* **1** *cap* HOLY SPIRIT **2a** a knitted scarf **b** *chiefly NAm* a quilt, eiderdown

ˈcomfort ˌstation *n, NAm* a public toilet (e g at a petrol station) – euph

comfrey /ˈkumfri‖ˈkʌmfrɪ/ *n* any of a genus of (tall) plants of the borage family whose coarse hairy leaves are much used in herbal medicine

comfy /ˈkumfi‖ˈkʌmfɪ/ *adj* comfortable – infml

[1]**comic** /ˈkomik‖ˈkɒmɪk/ *adj* **1** of or marked by comedy **2** causing laughter or amusement; funny

[2]**comic** *n* **1** a comedian **2** a magazine consisting mainly of strip-cartoon stories **3** *pl, NAm* the part of a newspaper devoted to strip cartoons

comical /ˈkomikl‖ˈkɒmɪkl/ *adj* being of a kind to excite laughter, esp because of a startlingly or unexpectedly humorous impact – **comically** *adv*

ˌcomic ˈopera *n* opera with humorous episodes and usu some spoken dialogue and a sentimental plot

ˈcomic ˌstrip *n* STRIP CARTOON

[1]**coming** /ˈkuming‖ˈkʌmɪŋ/ *n* an act or instance of arriving <~s *and goings*>

[2]**coming** *adj* **1** immediately due in sequence or development; next <*the* ~ *year*> **2** gaining in importance; up-and-coming

comity /ˈkomiti‖ˈkɒmɪtɪ/ *n* harmony, fellowship; *specif* the recognition by courts of one jurisdiction of the laws and decisions of another [Latin *comitas* courtesy, fr *comis* courteous]

ˌcomity of ˈnations *n* the courtesy and friendship of nations, marked esp by recognition of each other's laws

comma /ˈkomə‖ˈkɒmə/ *n* **1** a punctuation mark , used esp as a mark of separation within the sentence **2** a butterfly with a silvery comma-shaped mark on the underside of the hind wing

[1]**command** /kəˈmahnd‖kəˈmɑːnd/ *vt* **1** to direct authoritatively; order **2a** to have at one's immediate disposal **b** to be able to ask for and receive <~s *a high fee*> **c** to overlook or dominate (as if) from a strategic position **d** to have military command of as senior officer ~*vi* to be commander; be supreme – **commandable** *adj*

[2]**command** *n* **1** an order given **2** (the activation of a device by) an electrical signal **3a** the ability or power to control; the mastery **b** the

authority or right to command <*the officer in* ~> **c** facility in use <*a good* ~ *of French*> **4** *sing or pl in constr* the unit, personnel, etc under a commander

[3]**command** *adj* done on command or request <*a* ~ *performance*>

commandant /ˌkomən'dant, -'dahnt‖ˌkɒmən'dænt, -'dɑːnt/ *n* a commanding officer

commandeer /ˌkomən'diə‖ˌkɒmən'dɪə/ *vt* **1** to seize for military purposes **2** to take arbitrary or forcible possession of

commander /kə'mahndə‖kə'mɑːndə/ *n* an officer in the navy ranking below captain – **commandership** *n*

comˌmander-in-'chief *n* one who is in supreme command of an armed force

commanding /kə'mahnding‖kə'mɑːndɪŋ/ *adj* **1** having command; being in charge <*a* ~ *officer*> **2** dominating or having priority <*a* ~ *position of a castle*> **3** deserving or expecting respect and obedience <*a* ~ *voice*> – **commandingly** *adv*

com'mandment /-mənt‖-mənt/ *n* sthg commanded; *specif* any of the biblical Ten Commandments

commando /kə'mahndoh‖kə'mɑːndəʊ/ *n, pl* **commandos, commandoes** (a member of) a usu small military unit for surprise raids

com'mand ˌpaper *n* a government report laid before Parliament at the command of the crown

com'mand ˌpost *n* the headquarters of a military unit in the field

comme il faut /ˌkom eel 'foh‖ˌkɒm iːl 'fəʊ/ *adj* conforming to accepted standards; proper [French, lit., as it should be]

commemorate /kə'memərayt‖kə'meməreɪt/ *vt* **1** to call to formal remembrance **2** to mark by some ceremony or observation; observe **3** to serve as a memorial of – **commemorative** *adj*, **commemoration** *n*

commence /kə'mens‖kə'mens/ *vb* to start, begin – fml – **commencement** *n*

commend /kə'mend‖kə'mend/ *vt* **1** to entrust for care or preservation **2** to recommend as worthy of confidence or notice – **commendable** *adj*, **commendably** *adv*

commendation /ˌkomən'daysh(ə)n‖ˌkɒmən'deɪʃ(ə)n/ *n* sthg (e g a formal citation) that commends – **commendatory** *adj*

commensurable /kə'mensh(ə)rəbl‖kə'menʃ(ə)rəbl/ *adj* having a common measure; *esp* divisible by a common unit an integral number of times – **commensurably** *adv*, **commensurability** *n*

commensurate /kə'menshərət‖kə'menʃərət/ *adj* **1** (approximately) equal in measure or extent; coextensive **2** corresponding in size, extent, amount, or degree; proportionate <*was given a job* ~ *with his abilities*> – **commensurately** *adv*, **commensuration** *n*

[1]**comment** /'koment‖'kɒment/ *n* **1** a note explaining or criticizing the meaning of a piece of writing **2a** an observation or remark expressing an opinion or attitude **b** a judgment expressed indirectly <*this film is a* ~ *on current moral standards*>

[2]**comment** *vi* to explain or interpret sthg by comment; *broadly* to make a comment <~ed *on the match*>

commentary /'komənt(ə)ri‖'kɒmənt(ə)rɪ/ *n* **1** a systematic series of explanations or interpretations (e g of a piece of writing) **2** a series of spoken remarks and comments used as a broadcast description of some event

commentate /'koməntayt‖'kɒmənteɪt/ *vi* to act as a commentator; *esp* to give a broadcast commentary

commentator /'koménˌtaytə‖'kɒmənˌteɪtə/ *n* a person who provides a commentary; *specif* one who reports and discusses news or sports events on radio or television

commerce /'komuhs‖'kɒmɜːs/ *n* the exchange or buying and selling of commodities, esp on a large scale

[1]**commercial** /kə'muhsh(ə)l‖kə'mɜːʃ(ə)l/ *adj* **1a(1)** engaged in work designed for the market **a(2)** (characteristic) of commerce **a(3)** having or being a good financial prospect <*found oil in* ~ *quantities*> **b(1)** *esp of a chemical* average or inferior in quality **b(2)** producing work to a standard determined only by market criteria **2a** viewed with regard to profit <*a* ~ *success*> **b** designed for a large market **3** supported by advertisers <~ *TV*> – **commercially** *adv*

[2]**commercial** *n* an advertisement broadcast on radio or television

com'mercialˌism /-ˌiz(ə)m‖-ˌɪz(ə)m/ *n* **1** commercial spirit, institutions, or methods **2** excessive emphasis on profit – **commercialist** *n*, **commercialistic** *adj*

com'mercial·ˌize, -ise /-ˌiez‖-ˌaɪz/ *vt* **1a** to manage on a business basis for profit **b** to make commercial **2** to exploit for profit – **commercialization** *n*

comˌmercial 'traveller *n, Br* SALES REPRESENTATIVE

commie /'komi‖'kɒmɪ/ *n* a communist – chiefly derog

commiserate /kə'mizərayt‖kə'mɪzəreɪt/ *vi* to feel or express sympathy *with* sby; condole – **commiserative** *adj*, **commiseration** *n*

commissar /ˌkomi'sahr‖ˌkɒmɪ'sɑːr/ *n* **1** a Communist party official assigned to a military unit to teach party principles and ideals **2** the head of a government department in the USSR until 1946

commissariat /ˌkomi'seəri·ət‖ˌkɒmɪ'seərɪət/ *n* **1** the department of an army that organizes food supplies **2** a government department in the USSR until 1946

commissary /'komis(ə)ri‖'kɒmɪs(ə)rɪ/ *n* **1** an officer in charge of military supplies **2** *NAm* (a store for) equipment, food supplies, etc, esp of a military force

[1]**commission** /kə'mish(ə)n‖kə'mɪʃ(ə)n/ *n* **1a** a formal warrant granting various powers **b** (a certificate conferring) military rank above a certain level **2** an authorization or command to act in a prescribed manner or to perform prescribed acts; a charge **3** authority to act as agent for another; *also* sthg to be done by an agent **4a** *sing or pl in constr* a group of people directed to perform some duty **b** *often cap* a government agency **5** an act of committing sthg **6** a fee, esp a percentage, paid to an agent or employee for

transacting a piece of business or performing a service – **in/into commission 1** *of a ship* ready for active service **2** in use or in condition for use – **on commission** with commission serving as partial or full pay for work done – **out of commission 1** out of active service or use **2** out of working order

[2]**commission** *vt* **1a** to confer a formal commission on **b** to order, appoint, or assign to perform a task or function **2** to put (a ship) in commission

commissionaire /kə,mishə'neə||kə,mɪʃə'neə/ *n, chiefly Br* a uniformed attendant at a cinema, theatre, office, etc

commissioner /kə'mishənə||kə'mɪʃənə/ *n* **1** a member or the head of a commission **2** the government representative in a district, province, etc – **commissionership** *n*

commit /kə'mit||kə'mɪt/ *vt* **-tt- 1a** to entrust **b** to place in a prison or mental institution **c** to transfer, consign <~ *something to paper*> **2** to carry out (a crime, sin, etc) **3a** to obligate, bind **b** to assign to some particular course or use <*all available troops were* ~ted *to the attack*> – **committable** *adj*

com'mitment /-mənt||-mənt/ *n* **1** an act of committing to a charge or trust; *esp* a consignment to an institution **2a** an agreement or pledge to do sthg in the future **b** sthg pledged **c** loyalty to a system of thought or action

committal /kə'mitl||kə'mɪtl/ *n* commitment or consignment (e g to prison or the grave)

committee /kə'miti||kə'mɪtɪ/ *n sing or pl in constr* a body of people delegated **a** to report on, investigate, etc some matter **b** to organize or administrate a society, event, etc – **committeeman** *n*, **committeewoman** *n*

com'mittee ,stage *n* the stage in parliamentary procedure between the second reading and the third reading when a bill is discussed in detail in committee

commode /kə'mohd||kə'məʊd/ *n* **1** a low chest of drawers **2** a boxlike structure or chair with a removable seat covering a chamber pot

commodious /kə'mohdi·əs||kə'məʊdɪəs/ *adj* comfortably or conveniently spacious; roomy – fml – **commodiously** *adv*, **commodiousness** *n*

commodity /kə'modəti||kə'mɒdətɪ/ *n* **1** sthg useful or valuable **2a** a product possessing utility; sthg that can be bought and sold **b** an article of trade or commerce, esp when delivered for shipment

commodore /'komədaw||'kɒmədɔː/ *n* **1** an officer in the navy ranking below rear admiral **2** the senior captain of a merchant shipping line **3** the chief officer of a yacht club

[1]**common** /'komən||'kɒmən/ *adj* **1** of the community at large; public <*work for the* ~ *good*> **2a** belonging to or shared by 2 or more individuals or by all members of a group **b** belonging equally to 2 or more quantities <*a* ~ *denominator*> **3a** occurring or appearing frequently; familiar <*a* ~ *sight*> **b** of the familiar kind **4a** widespread, general <~ *knowledge*> **b** characterized by a lack of privilege or special status <*the* ~ *people*> **c** simply satisfying accustomed criteria (and no more); elementary <~ *decency*> **5a** falling below ordinary standards; second-rate **b** lacking refinement **6** either masculine or feminine in gender – **commonly** *adv*, **commonness** *n*

[2]**common** *n* **1** *pl* the common people – used chiefly in a historical context **2** *pl* food or provisions (shared jointly by all members of an institution) – esp in *short commons* **3** *pl but sing or pl in constr, often cap* **3a** the political group or estate made up of commoners **b** HOUSE OF COMMONS **4** a right which sby may have on another's land **5** a piece of land open to use by all: e g **5a** undivided land used esp for pasture **b** a more or less treeless expanse of undeveloped land available for recreation **6a** a religious service suitable for any of various festivals **b** the ordinary of the Mass **7** *Br* COMMON SENSE – slang – **in common** shared together – used esp of shared interests, attitudes, or experience

commonalty /'komənəlti||'kɒmənəltɪ/ *n* (the political estate formed by) the common people

,common 'cold *n* inflammation of the mucous membranes of the nose, throat, mouth, etc caused by a virus and lasting for a short time

commoner /'komənə||'kɒmənə/ *n* **1** a member of the common people; sby not of noble rank **2** a student (e g at Oxford) who is not supported by the college endowments

,common-'law *adj* **1** of the common law **2** recognized in law without solemnization of marriage <*his* ~ *wife*>

,common 'law *n* the body of uncodified English law that forms the basis of the English legal system

,common 'market *n* an economic unit formed to remove trade barriers among its members; *specif, often cap C&M the* European economic community

,common 'noun *n* a noun that may occur with limiting modifiers (e g *a* or *an, some, every,* and *my*) and that designates any one of a class of beings or things

,common or 'garden *adj* ordinary, everyday – infml

[1]**'common,place** /-,plays||-,pleɪs/ *n* **1** an obvious or trite observation **2** sthg taken for granted

[2]**commonplace** *adj* routinely found; ordinary, unremarkable – **commonplaceness** *n*

'common ,room *n* a room or set of rooms in a school, college, etc for the recreational use of the staff or students

,common 'sense *n* sound and prudent (but often unsophisticated) judgment – **commonsense** *adj*, **commonsensical** *adj*

'common,wealth /-,welth||-,welθ/ *n* **1** a political unit: e g **1a** one founded on law and united by agreement of the people for the common good **b** one in which supreme authority is vested in the people **2** *cap* the English state from 1649 to 1660 **3** a state of the USA **4** *cap* a federal union of states – used officially of Australia **5** *often cap* a loose association of autonomous states under a common allegiance; *specif* an association consisting of Britain and states that were formerly British colonies

commotion /kə'mohsh(ə)n||kə'məʊʃ(ə)n/ *n*

1 a state of civil unrest or insurrection **2** a disturbance, tumult **3** noisy confusion and bustle

communal /ˈkomyoonl‖ˈkɒmjʊnl/ *adj* **1** of a commune or communes **2** of a community **3** shared <~ *activity*> – **communalize** *vt*, **communally** *adv*, **communality** *n*

[1]**commune** /kəˈmyoohn‖kəˈmjuːn/ *vi* **1** to receive Communion **2** to communicate intimately

[2]**commune** /ˈkoˌmyoohn‖ˈkɒˌmjuːn/ *n* **1** the smallest administrative district of many (European) countries **2** *sing or pl in constr* an often rural community of unrelated individuals or families organized on a communal basis

communicable /kəˈmyoohnikəbl‖kəˈmjuːnɪkəbl/ *adj, esp of a disease* transmittable – **communicableness** *n*, **communicably** *adv*, **communicability** *n*

communicant /kəˈmyoohnikənt‖kəˈmjuːnɪkənt/ *n* **1** a church member who receives or is entitled to receive Communion **2** an informant – **communicant** *adj*

communicate /kəˈmyoohniˌkayt‖kəˈmjuːnɪˌkeɪt/ *vt* **1** to convey knowledge of or information about; make known **2** to cause to pass from one to another ~ *vi* **1** to receive Communion **2** to transmit information, thought, or feeling so that it is satisfactorily received or understood **3** to give access to each other; connect <*the rooms* ~> [Latin *communicare* to impart, participate, fr *communis* common] – **communicator** *n*, **communicatory** *adj*

communication /kəˌmyoohniˈkaysh(ə)n‖kəˌmjuːnɪˈkeɪʃ(ə)n/ *n* **1** a verbal or written message **2** (the use of a common system of symbols, signs, behaviour, etc for the) exchange of information **3** *pl* **3a** a system (e g of telephones) for communicating **b** a system of routes for moving troops, supplies, etc **4** *pl but sing or pl in constr* techniques for the effective transmission of information, ideas, etc – **communicational** *adj*

comˌmuniˈcation ˌcord *n, Br* a device (e g a chain or handle) in a railway carriage that may be pulled in an emergency to sound an alarm

communicative /kəˈmyoohnikətiv‖kəˈmjuːnɪkətɪv/ *adj* **1** tending to communicate; talkative **2** of communication – **communicatively** *adv*, **communicativeness** *n*

communion /kəˈmyoohnyən, -ni·ən‖kəˈmjuːnjən, -nɪən/ *n* **1a** *often cap* the religious service celebrating the Eucharist in Protestant churches **b** the act of receiving the Eucharist **2** intimate fellowship or rapport **3** a body of Christians having a common faith and discipline

communiqué /kəˈmyoohniˌkay‖kəˈmjuːnɪˌkeɪ/ *n* BULLETIN 1

communism /ˈkomyooniz(ə)m‖ˈkɒmjʊnɪz(ə)m/ *n* **1a** a theory advocating elimination of private property **b** a system in which goods are held in common and are available to all as needed **2** *cap* **2a** a doctrine based on revolutionary Marxian socialism and Marxism-Leninism that is the official ideology of the USSR **b** a system of government in which a single party controls state-owned means of production

communist /ˈkomyoonist‖ˈkɒmjʊnɪst/ *n*, *often cap* **1** an adherent or advocate of Communism **2** a left-wing revolutionary – **communist** *adj, often cap*, **communistic** *adj, often cap*

community /kəˈmyoohnəti‖kəˈmjuːnətɪ/ *n* **1** *sing or pl in constr* **1a** a group of people living in a particular area **b** all the interacting populations of various living organisms in a particular area **c** a group of individuals with some common characteristic (e g profession, religion, or status) **d** a body of people or nations having a common history or common interests <*the international* ~> **2** society in general **3a** joint ownership or participation **b** common character; likeness <*bound by* ~ *of interests*> **c** social ties; fellowship **d** the state or condition of living in a society

comˈmunity ˌcentre *n* a building or group of buildings for the educational and recreational activities of a community

commutation /ˌkomyooˈtaysh(ə)n‖ˌkɒmjʊˈteɪʃ(ə)n/ *n* **1** a replacement; *specif* a substitution of one form of payment or charge for another **2** an act or process of commuting **3** the process of converting an alternating current to a direct current

ˌcommuˈtation ˌticket *n, NAm* a ticket sold, usu at a reduced rate, for a fixed number of trips over the same route during a limited period

commutative /kəˈmyoohtətiv‖kəˈmjuːtətɪv/ *adj* **1** of or showing commutation **2** combining mathematical elements to produce a result that is independent of the order in which the elements are taken

commutator /ˈkomyooˌtaytə‖ˈkɒmjʊˌteɪtə/ *n* a device for reversing the direction of an electric current; *esp* a device on a motor or generator that converts alternating current to direct current

commute /kəˈmyooht‖kəˈmjuːt/ *vt* **1** to convert (e g a payment) into another form **2** to exchange (a penalty) for another less severe ~ *vi* **1** to travel back and forth regularly (e g between home and work) **2** *of 2 mathematical operators* to give a commutative result – **commutable** *adj*, **commuter** *n*

[1]**compact** /kəmˈpakt‖kəmˈpækt/ *adj* **1** having parts or units closely packed or joined **2** succinct, terse <*a* ~ *statement*> **3** occupying a small volume because of efficient use of space <*a* ~ *camera*> – **compactly** *adv*, **compactness** *n*

[2]**compact** *vt* **1a** to knit or draw together; combine, consolidate **b** to press together; compress **2** to make up by connecting or combining; compose – **compactible** *adj*, **compaction** *n*, **compactor** *n*

[3]**compact** /ˈkomˌpakt‖ˈkɒmˌpækt/ *n* sthg compact or compacted: e g **a** a small slim case for face powder **b** a medium-sized US motor car

[4]**compact** /ˈkomˌpakt‖ˈkɒmˌpækt/ *n* an agreement, contract

compact disc *n* a small plastic aluminium-coated disc on which sound is stored in digital form in microscopic pits and read by a laser beam mounted in a special record player

[1]**companion** /kəmˈpanyən‖kəmˈpænjən/ *n* one who accompanies another; a comrade [Old French *compagnon*, fr Late Latin *companion-, companio*, fr Latin *com-* with + *panis* bread,

food] – **companionate** *adj*, **companionship** *n*

[2]**companion** *n* (a covering at the top of) a companionway

companionable /kəmˈpanyənəbl‖kəmˈpænjənəbl/ *adj* marked by, conducive to, or suggestive of companionship; sociable – **companionableness** *n*, **companionably** *adv*

comˈpanionˌway /-ˌway‖-ˌweɪ/ *n* a ship's stairway from one deck to another

company /ˈkump(ə)ni‖ˈkʌmp(ə)nɪ/ *n* **1a** friendly association with another; fellowship <*I enjoy her* ~> **b** companions, associates <*know a person by the* ~ *he keeps*> **c** *sing or pl in constr* visitors, guests <*having* ~ *for dinner*> **2** *sing or pl in constr* **2a** a group of people or things <*a* ~ *of horsemen*> **b** a unit of soldiers composed usu of a headquarters and 2 or more platoons **c** an organization of musical or dramatic performers **d** the officers and men of a ship **3a** *sing or pl in constr* an association of people for carrying on a commercial or industrial enterprise **b** those members of a partnership firm whose names do not appear in the firm name <*John Smith and* Company>

ˌcompany ˈsecretary *n* a senior officer of a company who typically supervises its financial and legal aspects

comparable /ˈkomp(ə)rəbl‖ˈkɒmp(ə)rəbl/ *adj* **1** capable of or suitable for comparison **2** approximately equivalent; similar <*fabrics of* ~ *quality*> – **comparableness** *n*, **comparably** *adv*, **comparability** *n*

[1]**comparative** /kəmˈparətiv‖kəmˈpærətɪv/ *adj* **1** of or constituting the degree of grammatical comparison expressing increase in quality, quantity, or relation **2** considered as if in comparison to sthg else as a standard; relative <*a* ~ *stranger*> **3** characterized by the systematic comparison of phenomena <~ *anatomy*> – **comparatively** *adv*, **comparativeness** *n*

[2]**comparative** *n* the comparative degree or form in a language

[1]**compare** /kəmˈpeə‖kəmˈpeə/ *vt* **1** to represent as similar; liken **2** to examine the character or qualities of, esp in order to discover resemblances or differences **3** to inflect or modify (an adjective or adverb) according to the degrees of comparison ~ *vi* **1** to bear being compared <*it just doesn't* ~> **2** to be equal or alike – + *with*

[2]**compare** *n* COMPARISON 1b <*beauty beyond* ~>

comparison /kəmˈparis(ə)n‖kəmˈpærɪs(ə)n/ *n* **1a** the representing of one thing or person as similar to or like another **b** an examination of 2 or more items to establish similarities and dissimilarities **2** identity or similarity of features <*several points of* ~ *between the 2 authors*> **3** the modification of an adjective or adverb to denote different levels of quality, quantity, or relation

compartment /kəmˈpahtmənt‖kəmˈpɑːtmənt/ *n* **1** any of the parts into which an enclosed space is divided **2** a separate division or section – **compartment** *vt*, **compartmental** *adj*

compartmental·ize, -ise /ˌkompahtˈment(ə)lˌiez‖ˌkɒmpɑːtˈment(ə)lˌaɪz/ *vt* to separate into isolated compartments; *also* to keep in isolated categories <~d *knowledge*> – **compartmentalization** *n*

[1]**compass** /ˈkumpəs‖ˈkʌmpəs/ *vt* **1** to devise or contrive often with craft or skill; plot **2a** to encompass **b** to travel entirely round <~ *the earth*> **3** to achieve; BRING ABOUT **4** to comprehend *USE* fml – **compassable** *adj*

[2]**compass** *n* **1a** a boundary, circumference <*within the* ~ *of the city walls*> **b** range, scope <*the* ~ *of a voice*> **2a** an instrument that indicates directions, typically by means of a freely-turning needle pointing to magnetic north **b** an instrument for drawing circles or transferring measurements that consists of 2 legs joined at 1 end by a pivot – usu pl with sing. meaning

ˈcompass ˌcard *n* the circular card attached to the needles of a mariner's compass showing the 32 points of the compass

compassion /kəmˈpash(ə)n‖kəmˈpæʃ(ə)n/ *n* sympathetic consciousness of others' distress together with a desire to alleviate it – **compassionless** *adj*

compassionate /kəmˈpash(ə)nət‖kəmˈpæʃ(ə)nət/ *adj* **1** having or showing compassion; sympathetic **2** granted because of unusual, distressing circumstances affecting an individual – used of special privileges (e g extra leave of absence) – **compassionately** *adv*, **compassionateness** *n*

compatible /kəmˈpatəbl‖kəmˈpætəbl/ *adj* **1** capable of existing together in harmony **2** capable of being used together without modification; *esp* of or being equipment from one type of machine that can be used in a different machine – **compatibleness** *n*, **compatibly** *adv*, **compatibility** *n*

compatriot /kəmˈpatri·ət‖kəmˈpætrɪət/ *n* a fellow countryman – **compatriotic** *adj*

compeer /ˈkomˌpiə‖ˈkɒmˌpɪə/ *n* an equal, peer

compel /kəmˈpel‖kəmˈpel/ *vt* **-ll- 1** to drive or force irresistibly *to* do sthg **2** to cause to occur by overwhelming pressure – **compellable** *adj*

compendious /kəmˈpendi·əs‖kəmˈpendɪəs/ *adj* comprehensive but relatively brief – **compendiously** *adv*, **compendiousness** *n*

compendium /kəmˈpendi·əm‖kəmˈpendɪəm/ *n, pl* **compendiums, compendia** /-di·ə‖-dɪə/ **1** a brief summary of a larger work or of a field of knowledge; an abstract **2** a collection of indoor games and puzzles

compensate /ˈkompənsayt‖ˈkɒmpənseɪt/ *vt* **1** to have an equal and opposite effect to; counterbalance **2** to make amends to, esp by appropriate payment <~ *a neighbour for damage to his property*> ~ *vi* to supply an equivalent *for* – **compensative** *adj*, **compensator** *n*, **compensatory** *adj*

compensation /ˌkompenˈsaysh(ə)n, -pən-‖ˌkɒmpenˈseɪʃ(ə)n, -pən-/ *n* **1a** increased functioning or development of one organ to compensate for a defect in another **b** the alleviation of feelings of inferiority, frustration, failure, etc in one field by increased endeavour in another **2** a recompense; *specif* payment for damage or loss – **compensational** *adj*

[1]**compere** /ˈkompeə‖ˈkɒmpeə/ *n*, *Br* the presenter of a radio or television programme, esp a

light entertainment programme [French *compère*, lit., godfather, fr Medieval Latin *compater*, fr Latin *com-* with + *pater* father]

[2]**compere** *vb, Br* to act as compere (for)

compete /kəm'peet‖kəm'piːt/ *vi* to strive consciously or unconsciously for an objective; *also* to be in a state of rivalry

competence /'kompit(ə)ns‖'kɒmpɪt(ə)ns/ *also* **competency** /-si‖-sɪ/ *n* **1** the quality or state of being competent **2** a sufficiency of means for the necessities and conveniences of life – fml

competent /'kompit(ə)nt‖'kɒmpɪt(ə)nt/ *adj* **1a** having requisite or adequate ability <*a* ~ *workman*> **b** showing clear signs of production by a competent agent (e g a workman or writer) <*a* ~ *novel*> **2** legally qualified – **competently** *adv*

competition /ˌkompə'tish(ə)n‖ˌkɒmpə'tɪʃ(ə)n/ *n* **1** the act or process of competing; rivalry **2** a usu organized test of comparative skill, performance, etc; *also, sing or pl in constr* the others competing with one <*keep ahead of the* ~> **3** the competing of 2 or more parties to do business with a third party **4** competing demand by 2 or more (kinds of) organisms for some environmental resource in short supply

competitive /kəm'petətiv‖kəm'petətɪv/ *adj* **1** relating to, characterized by, or based on competition; *specif, of wages and prices* at least as good as those offered by competitors **2** inclined or desiring to compete – **competitively** *adv*, **competitiveness** *n*

competitor /kəm'petitə‖kəm'petɪtə/ *n* sby who or sthg that competes; a rival

compile /kəm'piel‖kəm'paɪl/ *vt* **1** to collect into 1 work **2** to compose out of materials from other documents – **compiler** *n*, **compilation** *n*

complacency /kəm'plays(ə)nsi‖kəm'pleɪs(ə)nsɪ/ *also* **complacence** *n* self-satisfaction accompanied by unawareness of actual dangers or deficiencies

complacent /kəm'plays(ə)nt‖kəm'pleɪs(ə)nt/ *adj* self-satisfied – **complacently** *adv*

complain /kəm'playn‖kəm'pleɪn/ *vi* **1** to express feelings of discontent **2** to make a formal accusation or charge – **complainer** *n*, **complainingly** *adv*

complainant /kəm'playnənt‖kəm'pleɪnənt/ *n* one who makes a complaint; *specif* the party in a legal action or proceeding who makes a complaint

complaint /kəm'playnt‖kəm'pleɪnt/ *n* **1** an expression of discontent **2a** sthg that is the cause or subject of protest or outcry **b** a bodily ailment or disease

complaisant /kəm'plays(ə)nt‖kəm'pleɪs(ə)nt/ *adj* **1** marked by an inclination to please or comply **2** tending to consent to others' wishes – **complaisance** *n*, **complaisantly** *adv*

[1]**complement** /'komplimənt‖'kɒmplɪmənt/ *n* **1a** sthg that fills up or completes **b** the quantity required to make sthg complete; *specif* COMPANY 2d **c** either of 2 mutually completing parts; a counterpart **2a** an angle or arc that when added to a given angle or arc equals 90° **b** a number that when added to another number of the same sign yields zero if the significant digit farthest to the left is discarded **3** an added word or expression by which a predication is made complete (e g *president* in 'they elected him president') **4** the protein in blood serum that in combination with antibodies causes the destruction of antigens (e g bacteria) – **complemental** *adj*

[2]**complement** *vt* to be complementary to

complementary /ˌkompli'ment(ə)ri‖ˌkɒmplɪ'ment(ə)rɪ/ *adj* **1** serving to fill out or complete **2** mutually supplying each other's lack **3** of or constituting either of a pair of contrasting colours that produce a neutral colour when combined **4** *of a pair of angles* having the sum of 90° – **complementary** *n*, **complementariness** *n*, **complementarily** *adv*, **complementarity** *n*

[1]**complete** /kəm'pleet‖kəm'pliːt/ *adj* **1** having all necessary parts, elements, or steps **2** whole or concluded <*after 2* ~ *revolutions about the sun*> **3** thoroughly competent; highly proficient **4a** fully carried out; thorough <*a* ~ *renovation*> **b** total, absolute <~ *silence*> – **completely** *adv*, **completeness** *n*, **completive** *adj*

[2]**complete** *vt* **1** to bring to an end; *esp* to bring to a perfected state <~ *a painting*> **2a** to make whole or perfect <*the church* ~s *the charm of this village*> **b** to mark the end of <*a rousing chorus* ~s *the show*> **c** to execute, fulfil <~ *a contract*> – **completion** *n*

[1]**complex** /'kompleks‖'kɒmpleks/ *adj* **1a** composed of 2 (or many) more parts **b** *of a sentence* consisting of a main clause and 1 or more subordinate clauses **2** hard to separate, analyse, or solve **3** of or being a complex number – **complexly** *adv*, **complexity** *n*

[2]**complex** *n* **1** a whole made up of complicated or interrelated parts **2a** a group of repressed related desires and memories that usu adversely affects personality and behaviour **b** an exaggerated reaction to sthg <*has a* ~ *about flying*>

complexion /kəm'pleksh(ə)n‖kəm'plekʃ(ə)n/ *n* **1** the appearance of the skin, esp of the face **2** overall aspect or character <*that puts a different* ~ *on things*> – **complexional** *adj*, **complexioned** *adj*

complex number *n* a number containing both real and imaginary parts

compliance /kəm'plie·əns‖kəm'plaɪəns/ *n* **1** the act or process of complying (readily) with the wishes of others **2** a disposition to yield to others **3** (a measure of) the ease of overcoming a restoring force (e g a spring) – **compliant** *adj*, **compliantly** *adv*

complicate /'komplikayt‖'kɒmplɪkeɪt/ *vt* **1** to combine, esp in an involved or inextricable manner **2** to make complex or difficult

complicated /'kompliˌkaytid‖'kɒmplɪˌkeɪtɪd/ *adj* **1** consisting of parts intricately combined **2** difficult to analyse, understand, or explain – **complicatedly** *adv*, **complicatedness** *n*

complication /ˌkompli'kaysh(ə)n‖ˌkɒmplɪ'keɪʃ(ə)n/ *n* **1a** intricacy, complexity **b** an instance of making difficult, involved, or intricate **c** a complex or intricate feature or element **d** a factor or issue that occurs unexpectedly and changes existing plans, methods, or attitudes – often pl **2** a secondary disease or condition developing in the course of a primary disease

complicity /kəm'plisəti‖kəm'plɪsətɪ/ *n* (an instance of) association or participation (as if) in a wrongful act

[1]**compliment** /'kompliment‖'kɒmplɪmənt/ *n* **1** an expression of esteem, affection, or admiration; *esp* a flattering remark **2** *pl* best wishes; regards [French, fr Italian *complimento*, fr Spanish *cumplimiento*, fr *cumplir* to be courteous]

[2]**compliment** /'kompli,ment‖'kɒmplɪ,ment/ *vt* **1** to pay a compliment to **2** to present with a token of esteem

complimentary /,kompli'ment(ə)ri‖,kɒmplɪ'ment(ə)rɪ/ *adj* **1** expressing or containing a compliment **2** given free as a courtesy or favour – **complimentarily** *adv*

compline /'komplin‖'kɒmplɪn/ *n, often cap* the last of the canonical hours, said before retiring at night

comply /kəm'plie‖kəm'plaɪ/ *vi* to conform or adapt one's actions to another's wishes or to a rule – **complier** *n*

[1]**component** /kəm'pohnənt‖kəm'pəʊnənt/ *n* a constituent part; an ingredient

[2]**component** *adj* serving or helping to constitute; constituent

comport /kəm'pawt‖kəm'pɔːt/ *vi* to be fitting; accord <*acts that ~ with ideals*> ~*vt* to behave (oneself) in a manner conformable to what is right, proper, or expected *USE* fml

compose /kəm'pohz‖kəm'pəʊz/ *vt* **1a** to form by putting together **b** to form the substance of; MAKE UP – chiefly passive <~d *of many ingredients*> **c** SET 11c **2a** to create by mental or artistic labour; produce <~ *a sonnet*> **b** to formulate and write (a piece of music) **3** to settle (a point of disagreement) **4** to free from agitation; calm, settle <~ *oneself*> ~*vi* to practise composition

composer /kəm'pohzə‖kəm'pəʊzə/ *n* a person who writes music

[1]**composite** /'kompəzit‖'kɒmpəzɪt/ *adj* made up of distinct parts: e g **a** *cap* of a Roman order of architecture that combines Ionic with Corinthian **b** of or belonging to a very large family of plants, including the dandelion, daisy, and sunflower, typically having florets arranged in dense heads that resemble single flowers – **compositely** *adv*

[2]**composite** *n* sthg composite; a compound

composition /,kompə'zish(ə)n‖,kɒmpə'zɪʃ(ə)n/ *n* **1a** the act or process of composing; *specif* arrangement into proper proportion or relation and esp into artistic form **b** (the production of) an arrangement of type for printing **2** the factors or parts which go to make sthg; *also* the way in which the factors or parts make up the whole **3** an agreement by which a creditor accepts partial payment **4** a product of mixing or combining various elements or ingredients **5** an intellectual creation: e g **5a** a piece of writing; *esp* a school essay **b** a written piece of music, esp of considerable size and complexity – **compositional** *adj*, **compositionally** *adv*

compositor /kəm'pozitə‖kəm'pɒzɪtə/ *n* sby who sets type

compos mentis /,kompəs 'mentis‖,kɒmpəs 'mentɪs/ *adj* of sound mind, memory, and understanding

[1]**compost** /'kompost‖'kɒmpɒst/ *n* a mixture of decayed organic matter used for fertilizing and conditioning land

[2]**compost** *vt* to convert (e g plant debris) to compost – **composter** *n*

composure /kəm'pohzhə‖kəm'pəʊʒə/ *n* calmness or repose, esp of mind, bearing, or appearance

compote /'kompot‖'kɒmpɒt/ *n* a dessert of fruit cooked in syrup and usu served cold

[1]**compound** /kəm'pownd‖kəm'paʊnd/ *vt* **1** to put together (parts) so as to form a whole; combine **2** to form by combining parts <~ *a medicine*> **3a** to pay (interest) on both the accumulated interest and the principal **b** to add to; augment <*to ~ an error*> **4** to agree for a consideration not to prosecute (an offence) <~ *a felony*> ~*vi* to become joined in a compound [Middle French *compondre*, fr Latin *componere*, fr *com-* with + *ponere* to put] – **compoundable** *adj*, **compounder** *n*

[2]**compound** /'kompownd‖'kɒmpaʊnd/ *adj* **1** composed of or resulting from union of (many similar) separate elements, ingredients, or parts **2** involving or used in a combination **3** *of a sentence* having 2 or more main clauses

[3]**compound** /'kompownd‖'kɒmpaʊnd/ *n* **1** a word consisting of components that are words, combining forms, or affixes (e g *houseboat, anthropology*) **2** sthg formed by a union of elements or parts; *specif* a distinct substance formed by combination of chemical elements in fixed proportion by weight

[4]**compound** /'kompownd‖'kɒmpaʊnd/ *n* a fenced or walled-in area containing a group of buildings, esp residences [Malay *kampong* group of buildings, village]

compound eye *n* an arthropod eye consisting of a number of separate visual units

,compound 'fracture *n* a bone fracture produced in such a way as to form an open wound

,compound 'interest *n* interest computed on the original principal plus accumulated interest

comprehend /,kompri'hend‖,kɒmprɪ'hend/ *vt* **1** to grasp the nature, significance, or meaning of; understand **2** to include <*the park* ~s *all of the land beyond the river*> – fml

comprehensible /,kompri'hensəbl‖,kɒmprɪ'hensəbl/ *adj* capable of being comprehended; intelligible – **comprehensibleness** *n*, **comprehensibly** *adv*, **comprehensibility** *n*

comprehension /,kompri'hensh(ə)n‖,kɒmprɪ'henʃ(ə)n/ *n* **1a** grasping with the intellect; understanding **b** knowledge gained by comprehending **c** the capacity for understanding fully **2** a school exercise testing understanding of a passage

[1]**comprehensive** /,kompri'hensiv‖,kɒmprɪ'hensɪv/ *adj* **1** covering completely or broadly; inclusive <~ *insurance*> **2** having or exhibiting wide mental grasp <~ *knowledge*> **3** *chiefly Br* of or being the principle of educating in 1 unified school nearly all children above the age of 11 from a given area regardless of ability – **comprehensively** *adv*, **comprehensiveness** *n*

[2]**comprehensive** *n, Br* a compre-

hensive school

[1]**compress** /kəm'pres||kəm'pres/ *vt* **1** to press or squeeze together **2** to reduce in size or volume as if by squeezing ~*vi* to be compressed – **compressible** *adj*, **compressibility** *n*

[2]**compress** /'kompres||'kɒmpres/ *n* a pad pressed on a body part (e g to ease the pain and swelling of a bruise)

compression /kəm'presh(ə)n||kəm'preʃ(ə)n/ *n* **1** a compressing or being compressed **2** (the quality of) the process of compressing the fuel mixture in a cylinder of an internal-combustion engine – **compressional** *adj*

compressor /kəm'presə||kəm'presə/ *n* sthg that compresses; *esp* a machine for compressing gases

comprise /kəm'priez||kəm'praɪz/ *vt* **1** to include, contain **2** to be made up of **3** to make up, constitute

[1]**compromise** /'komprəmiez||'kɒmprəmaɪz/ *n* **1a** the settling of differences through arbitration or through consent reached by mutual concessions **b** a settlement reached by compromise **c** sthg blending qualities of 2 different things <*a ~ solution*> **2** a concession to sthg disreputable or prejudicial <*a ~ of principles*>

[2]**compromise** *vt* **1** to adjust or settle by mutual concessions **2** to expose to discredit or scandal ~*vi* to come to agreement by mutual concession – **compromiser** *n*

Comptometer /komp'tomitə||kɒmp'tɒmɪtə/ *trademark* – used for a calculating machine

comptroller /kən'trohlə||kən'trəʊlə; *also* ˌkom(p)'trohlə||ˌkɒm(p)'trəʊlə/ *n* CONTROLLER 1 – **comptrollership** *n*

compulsion /kəm'pulsh(ə)n||kəm'pʌlʃ(ə)n/ *n* **1a** compelling or being compelled **b** a force or agency that compels **2** a strong impulse to perform an irrational act

compulsive /kəm'pulsiv||kəm'pʌlsɪv/ *adj* of, caused by, like, or suffering from a psychological compulsion or obsession – **compulsively** *adv*, **compulsiveness** *n*

compulsory /kəm'puls(ə)ri||kəm'pʌls(ə)rɪ/ *adj* **1** mandatory, enforced < ~ *arbitration*> **2** involving compulsion or obligation; coercive < ~ *legislation*> – **compulsorily** *adv*

compunction /kəm'pungksh(ə)n||kəm'pʌŋkʃ(ə)n/ *n* **1** anxiety arising from awareness of guilt; remorse **2** a twinge of misgiving; a scruple – **compunctious** *adj*

computation /ˌkompyoo'taysh(ə)n||ˌkɒmpjʊ'teɪʃ(ə)n/ *n* **1** the use or operation of a computer **2** (a system of) calculating; *also* the amount calculated – **computational** *adj*

compute /kəm'pyooht||kəm'pju:t/ *vt* to determine, esp by mathematical means; *also* to determine or calculate by means of a computer ~ *vi* **1** to make calculation; reckon **2** to use a computer – **computable** *adj*, **computability** *n*

computer /kəm'pyoohtə||kəm'pju:tə/ *n* a programmable electronic device that can store, retrieve, and process data

computerate /kəm'pyoohtərət/ *adj* able to use a computer competently – **computeracy** *n*

computer·ize, **-ise** /kəm'pyoohtəˌriez||kəm'pju:təˌraɪz/ *vt* **1** to carry out, control, or conduct by means of a computer **2** to equip with computers – **computerization** *n*

comrade /'komrid, -rayd||'kɒmrɪd, -reɪd/ *n* **1a** an intimate friend or associate; a companion **b** a fellow soldier **2** a communist [Middle French *camarade* group sleeping in one room, roommate, companion, fr Spanish *camarada*, fr *cámara* room, fr Late Latin *camera, camara* – see CHAMBER] – **comradely** *adj*, **comradeliness** *n*, **comradeship** *n*

[1]**con**, *NAm chiefly* **conn** /kon||kɒn/ *vt* **-nn-** to conduct or direct the steering of (e g a ship)

[2]**con**, *NAm chiefly* **conn** *n* the control exercised by one who cons a ship

[3]**con** *adv* on the negative side; in opposition <*so much has been written pro and ~*>

[4]**con** *n* (sby holding) the opposing or negative position

[5]**con** *vt* **-nn-** **1** to swindle, trick **2** to persuade, cajole *USE* slang – **con** *n*

[6]**con** *n* a convict – slang

con- – see COM-

concatenate /kon'katənayt||kɒn'kætəneɪt/ *vt* to link together in a series or chain – fml – **concatenation** *n*

concave /ˌkon'kayv, '--||ˌkɒn'keɪv, '--/ *adj* hollowed or rounded inwards like the inside of a bowl – **concavely** *adv*

concavity /kon'kavəti, kən-||kɒn'kævətɪ, kən-/ *n* **1** a concave line or surface or the space included in it **2** the quality or state of being concave

conceal /kən'seel||kən'si:l/ *vt* **1** to prevent disclosure or recognition of **2** to place out of sight – **concealable** *adj*, **concealer** *n*, **concealingly** *adv*, **concealment** *n*

concede /kən'seed||kən'si:d/ *vt* **1** to grant as a right or privilege **2a** to accept as true, valid, or accurate **b** to acknowledge grudgingly or hesitantly **3** to allow involuntarily < ~d *2 more goals*> ~ *vi* to yield – **conceder** *n*

conceit /kən'seet||kən'si:t/ *n* **1** excessively high opinion of oneself **2a** a fanciful idea **b** an elaborate figure of speech

con'ceited *adj* having an excessively high opinion of oneself – **conceitedly** *adv*, **conceitedness** *n*

conceivable /kən'seevəbl||kən'si:vəbl/ *adj* capable of being conceived; imaginable – **conceivableness** *n*, **conceivably** *adv*, **conceivability** *n*

conceive /kən'seev||kən'si:v/ *vt* **1** to become pregnant with (young) **2a** to cause to originate in one's mind < ~ *a prejudice against him*> **b** to form a conception of; evolve mentally; visualize **3** to be of the opinion – fml ~ *vi* to become pregnant

[1]**concentrate** /'kons(ə)ntrayt||'kɒns(ə)ntreɪt/ *vt* **1a** to bring or direct towards a common centre or objective; focus **b** to gather into 1 body, mass, or force <*power was* ~d *in a few able hands*> **2a** to make less dilute **b** to express or exhibit in condensed form ~ *vi* **1** to draw towards or meet in a common centre **2** to gather, collect **3** to concentrate one's powers, efforts, or attention – **concentrative** *adj*, **concentrator** *n*

[2]**concentrate** *n* sthg concentrated; *esp* a feed for animals rich in digestible nutrients

concentration /ˌkonsən'traysh(ə)n||ˌkɒnsən-

'treɪʃ(ə)n/ *n* **1** direction of attention to a single object **2** a concentrated mass or thing **3** the relative content of a (chemical) component; strength

concentration camp *n* a camp where political prisoners, refugees, etc are confined; *esp* any of the Nazi camps for the internment or mass execution of (Jewish) prisoners during WW II

concentric /kən'sentrik, kon-‖kən'sentrɪk, kɒn-/ *adj* having a common centre <~ *circles*> – **concentrically** *adv*, **concentricity** *n*

concept /'konsept‖'kɒnsept/ *n* **1** sthg conceived in the mind; a thought, notion **2** a generic idea abstracted from particular instances – **conceptual** *adj*, **conceptually** *adv*

conception /kən'sepsh(ə)n‖kən'sepʃ(ə)n/ *n* **1a** conceiving or being conceived **b** an embryo, foetus **2** a general idea; a concept **3** the originating of sthg in the mind – **conceptional** *adj*, **conceptive** *adj*

conceptual·ize, -ise /kən'septyooəliez, -choo-‖kən'septjʊəlaɪz, -tʃʊ-/ *vt* to form a concept of – **conceptualization** *n*

[1]**concern** /kən'suhn‖kən'sɜːn/ *vt* **1** to relate to; be about <*the novel* ~s *3 soldiers*> **2** to have an influence on; involve; *also* to be the business or affair of <*the problem* ~s *us all*> **3** to be a care, trouble, or distress to <*his ill health* ~s *me*> **4** to engage, occupy <~s *himself with trivia*>

[2]**concern** *n* **1** sthg that relates or belongs to one <*it's not my* ~> **2** matter for consideration **3** marked interest or regard, usu arising through a personal tie or relationship **4** a business or manufacturing organization or establishment

con'cerned *adj* **1** anxious **2a** interestedly engaged <~ *with books and music*> **b** (culpably) involved <*arrested all* ~>

concerning /kən'suhning‖kən'sɜːnɪŋ/ *prep* relating to; with reference to

concert /'konsuht, -sət‖'kɒnsɜːt, -sət; *sense 2 usu* 'konsət‖'kɒnsət/ *n* **1** an instance of working together; an agreement – esp in *in concert (with)* **2** a public performance of music or dancing; *esp* a performance, usu by a group of musicians, that is made up of several individual compositions

concerted /kən'suhtid‖kən'sɜːtɪd/ *adj* **1a** planned or done together; combined <*a* ~ *effort*> **b** performed in unison <~ *artillery fire*> **2** arranged in parts for several voices or instruments – **concertedly** *adv*, **concertedness** *n*

ˌconcert 'grand /'konsət‖'kɒnsət/ *n* a grand piano of the largest size for concerts

[1]**concertina** /ˌkonsə'teenə‖ˌkɒnsə'tiːnə/ *n* a small hexagonal musical instrument of the accordion family

[2]**concertina** *vi* **concertinaed** /-nəd‖-nəd/; **concertinaing** /-nə·ing‖-nəɪŋ/ *Br* to become compressed in the manner of a concertina being closed, esp as a result of a crash

concertmaster /'konsətˌmahstə‖'kɒnsətˌmɑːstə/ *n, chiefly NAm* LEADER 5a

concerto /kən'cheətoh, -'chuh-‖kən'tʃeətəʊ, -'tʃɜː-/ *n, pl* **concerti** /-ti‖-tɪ/, **concertos** a piece for 1 or more soloists and orchestra, usu with 3 contrasting movements

'concert ˌpitch /'konsət‖'kɒnsət/ *n* **1** a tuning standard of usu 440 Hz for A above middle C **2** a high state of fitness, tension, or readiness

concession /kən'sesh(ə)n‖kən'seʃ(ə)n/ *n* **1** the act or an instance of conceding **2** a grant of land, property, or a right made, esp by a government, in return for services or for a particular use **3** a reduction of demands or standards made esp to accommodate shortcomings – **concessional** *adj*, **concessionally** *adv*, **concessionary** *adj*

concessionaire /kənˌseshə'neə‖kənˌseʃə'neə/ *n* the owner or beneficiary of a concession

concessive /kən'sesiv‖kən'sesɪv/ *adj* denoting the yielding or admitting of a point <*a* ~ *clause beginning with 'although'*> – **concessively** *adv*

conch /konch, kongk‖kɒntʃ, kɒŋk/ *n, pl* **conches** /'konchiz‖'kɒntʃɪz/, **conchs** **1** (the spiral shell of) any of various large marine gastropod molluscs **2** (the plain semidome of) an apse

conchology /kong'koləji‖kɒŋ'kɒlədʒɪ/ *n* the branch of zoology that deals with shells – **conchologist** *n*

concierge /ˌkonsi'eəzh‖ˌkɒnsɪ'eəʒ/ *n* sby who is employed as doorkeeper, caretaker, etc, esp in France [French fr Latin *conservus* fellow slave, fr *com-* with + *servus* slave]

conciliate /kən'sili·ayt‖kən'sɪlɪeɪt/ *vt* **1** to reconcile **2** to appease – **conciliator** *n*, **conciliative** *adj*, **conciliatory** *adj*, **conciliation** *n*

concise /kən'sies‖kən'saɪs/ *adj* marked by brevity of expression or statement; free from all elaboration and superfluous detail – **concisely** *adv*, **conciseness, concision** *n*

conclave /'kongklayv, 'kon-‖'kɒŋkleɪv, 'kɒn-/ *n* a private meeting or secret assembly; *esp* the assembly of Roman Catholic cardinals secluded continuously while electing a pope

conclude /kən'kloohd‖kən'kluːd/ *vt* **1** to bring to an end, esp in a particular way or with a particular action <~ *a meeting with a prayer*> **2a** to arrive at as a logically necessary inference <~d *that her argument was sound*> **b** to decide <~d *he would wait a little longer*> **c** to come to an agreement on; effect <~ *a sale*> ~*vi* END 1

conclusion /kən'kloohzh(ə)n‖kən'kluːʒ(ə)n/ *n* **1** a reasoned judgment; an inference; *specif* the inferred proposition of a syllogism **2a** a result, outcome **b** a final summing up (e g of an essay) **3** an act or instance of concluding

conclusive /kən'kloohsiv, -ziv‖kən'kluːsɪv, -zɪv/ *adj* putting an end to debate or question, esp by reason of irrefutability – **conclusively** *adv*, **conclusiveness** *n*

concoct /kən'kokt‖kən'kɒkt/ *vt* to prepare (e g a meal, story, etc) by combining diverse ingredients – **concocter** *n*, **concoctive** *adj*, **concoction** *n*

[1]**concomitant** /kon'komit(ə)nt, kən-‖kɒn'kɒmɪt(ə)nt, kən-/ *adj* accompanying, esp in a subordinate or incidental way – **concomitance** *n*, **concomitantly** *adv*

[2]**concomitant** *n* sthg that accompanies or is collaterally connected with sthg else; an accompaniment

concord /'kongkawd, 'kon-‖'kɒŋkɔːd, 'kɒn-/

n **1a** a state of agreement; harmony **b** a harmonious combination of simultaneously heard notes **2** a treaty, covenant **3** grammatical agreement

concordance /kəng'kawd(ə)ns, kən-‖kəŋ-'kɔːd(ə)ns, kən-/ *n* **1** an alphabetical index of the principal words in a book or an author's works, with their immediate contexts **2** agreement

concordant /kəng'kawd(ə)nt, kən-‖kəŋ'kɔːd(ə)nt, kən-/ *adj* consonant, harmonious – **concordantly** *adv*

concordat /kon'kawdat, kən-‖kɒn'kɔːdæt, kən-/ *n* a compact, covenant; *specif* one between a pope and a sovereign or government

concourse /'kongkaws, 'kon-‖'kɒŋkɔːs, 'kɒn-/ *n* **1** a coming, gathering, or happening together <*a large ~ of people*> **2a** an open space where roads or paths meet **b** an open space or main hall (e g in a station)

1**concrete** /'kongkreet, 'kon-‖'kɒŋkriːt, 'kɒn-/ *adj* **1** *of a noun* naming a thing rather than a quality, state, or action **2a** characterized by or belonging to immediate experience of actual things or events **b** specific, particular <*~ proposals*> **c** real, tangible <*~ evidence*> **3** relating to or made of concrete – **concretely** *adv*, **concreteness** *n*

2**concrete** *n* a hard strong building material made by mixing a cementing material (e g portland cement) and a mineral aggregate (e g sand and gravel) with sufficient water to cause the cement to set and bind the entire mass

3**concrete** /kəng'kreet, kən-‖kəŋ'kriːt, kən-; *sense 2 usu* 'kongkreet, 'kon-‖'kɒŋkriːt, 'kɒn-/ *vt* **1** to form into a solid mass; solidify **2** to cover with, form of, or set in concrete *~vi* to become concreted

concretion /kəng'kreesh(ə)n, kən-‖kəŋ'kriːʃ(ə)n, kən-/ *n* **1** a hard usu inorganic mass formed (abnormally) in a living body **2** a mass of deposited mineral matter in a rock – **concretionary** *adj*

concubinage /'kongkyoobinij, kən'kyooh-‖'kɒŋkjʊbɪnɪdʒ, kən'kjuː-/ *n* being or having a concubine

concubine /'kongkyoobien, 'kon-‖'kɒŋkjʊbaɪn, 'kɒn-/ *n* a woman who lives with a man as his wife; MISTRESS 5; *esp* a woman who lives with a man in addition to his lawful wife or wives [Old French, fr Latin *concubina*, fr *com-* with + *cubare* to lie]

concupiscence /kəng'kyoohpis(ə)ns, kən-‖kəŋ'kjuːpɪs(ə)ns, kən-/ *n* strong desire; *esp* lust – **concupiscent** *adj*

concur /kən'kuh‖kən'kɜː/ *vi* **-rr-** **1** to happen together; coincide **2** to act together to a common end or single effect **3** to express agreement <*~ with an opinion*>

concurrence /kən'kurəns‖kən'kʌrəns/ *n* **1a** agreement or union in action **b(1)** agreement in opinion or design **b(2)** consent **2** a coming together; a conjunction

concurrent /kən'kurənt‖kən'kʌrənt/ *adj* **1a** meeting or intersecting in a point **b** running parallel **2** operating or occurring at the same time – **concurrent** *n*, **concurrently** *adv*

concuss /kən'kus‖kən'kʌs/ *vt* to affect with concussion

concussion /kən'kush(ə)n‖kən'kʌʃ(ə)n/ *n* **1** a hard blow or collision **2** (a jarring injury to the brain often resulting in unconsciousness caused by) a stunning or shattering effect from a hard blow – **concussive** *adj*, **concussively** *adv*

condemn /kən'dem‖kən'dem/ *vt* **1** to declare to be utterly reprehensible, wrong, or evil, usu after considering evidence **2a** to prescribe punishment for; *specif* to sentence to death **b** to sentence, doom **3** to declare unfit for use or consumption **4** to declare (e g contraband) convertible to public use – **condemnable** *adj*, **condemnatory** *adj*

condemnation /ˌkondəm'naysh(ə)n, -dem-‖ˌkɒndəm'neɪʃ(ə)n, -dem-/ *n* **1** censure, blame **2** the act of judicially convicting **3** the state of being condemned

con'demned ˌcell *n* a prison cell for people condemned to death

condensation /ˌkondən'saysh(ə)n, -den-‖ˌkɒndən'seɪʃ(ə)n, -den-/ *n* **1a** chemical combination between molecules with elimination of a simple molecule (e g water) to form a new, more complex compound **b** a change to a denser form (e g from vapour to liquid) **2** a product of condensing; *specif* an abridgment of a literary work – **condensational** *adj*

condense /kən'dens‖kən'dens/ *vt* to make denser or more compact; *esp* to subject to condensation *~vi* to undergo condensation – **condensable** *adj*

condenser /kən'densə‖kən'densə/ *n* **1a** a lens or mirror used to concentrate light on an object **b** an apparatus for condensing gas or vapour **2** a capacitor – now used chiefly in the motor trade

condescend /ˌkondi'send‖ˌkɒndɪ'send/ *vi* to waive the privileges of rank <*~ed to eat with subordinates*>; *broadly* to descend to less formal or dignified action or speech

condescension /ˌkondi'sensh(ə)n‖ˌkɒndɪ'senʃ(ə)n/ *n* **1** voluntary descent from one's rank or dignity in relations with an inferior **2** a patronizing attitude

condign /kən'dien‖kən'daɪn/ *adj* deserved, appropriate <*~ punishment*> – fml – **condignly** *adv*

condiment /'kondimənt‖'kɒndɪmənt/ *n* sthg used to enhance the flavour of food; *esp* seasoning

1**condition** /kən'dish(ə)n‖kən'dɪʃ(ə)n/ *n* **1** sthg essential to the appearance or occurrence of sthg else; a prerequisite **2** a favourable or unfavourable state of sthg <*delayed by the ~ of the road*> **3a** a state of being **b** social status; rank **c** a usu defective state of health or appearance <*a heart ~*> **d** a state of physical fitness or readiness for use <*the car was in good ~*> **e** *pl* attendant circumstances <*under present ~s*>

2**condition** *vt* **1** to put into a proper or desired state for work or use **2** to give a certain condition to **3a** to adapt to a surrounding culture **b** to modify so that an act or response previously associated with one stimulus becomes associated with another – **conditionable** *adj*, **conditioner** *n*

conditional /kən'dish(ə)nl‖kən'dɪʃ(ə)nl/ *adj* **1** subject to, implying, or dependent on a condition <*a ~ promise*> **2** expressing, containing, or implying a supposition <*the* ~ *clause* if he speaks> **3** CONDITIONED 3 – **conditional** *n*, **conditionally** *adv*, **conditionality** *n*

conditioned /kən'dish(ə)nd‖kən'dɪʃ(ə)nd/ *adj* **1** CONDITIONAL 1 **2** brought or put into a specified state **3** *esp of a reflex* determined or established by conditioning

condole /kən'dohl‖kən'dəʊl/ *vi* to express sympathetic sorrow – **condolatory** *adj*

condolence /kən'dohləns‖kən'dəʊləns/ *n* (an expression of) sympathy with another in sorrow

condom /'kondəm‖'kɒndəm/ *n* a sheath, usu of rubber, worn over the penis (e g to prevent conception or venereal infection during sexual intercourse)

condominium /ˌkondə'minyəm, -ni·əm‖ˌkɒndə'mɪnjəm, -nɪəm/ *n* **1** (a territory under) joint sovereignty by 2 or more nations **2** *NAm* (individual ownership of) a unit in a multi-unit structure (e g a block of flats)

condone /kən'dohn‖kən'dəʊn/ *vt* to pardon or overlook voluntarily; tacitly accept; *esp* to treat as if harmless or of no importance – **condoner** *n*, **condonable** *adj*, **condonation** *n*

condor /'kondaw‖'kɒndɔː/ *n* a very large vulture of the high Andes with bare head and neck

conduce /kən'dyoohs‖kən'djuːs/ *vi* to lead or tend *to* a particular and usu desirable result; contribute – **conducive** *adj*

[1]**conduct** /'kondukt‖'kɒndʌkt/ *n* **1** the act, manner, or process of carrying on; management **2** a mode or standard of personal behaviour, esp as based on moral principles

[2]**conduct** /kən'dukt‖kən'dʌkt/ *vt* **1** to bring (as if) by leading; guide **2** to carry on or out, usu from a position of command or control <~ *an experiment*> **3a** to convey in a channel, pipe, etc **b** to act as a medium for transmitting (e g heat or light) **4** to behave in a specified manner <~ed *himself appallingly*> **5** to direct the performance or execution of (e g a musical work or group of musicians) ~ *vi* **1** to act as leader or director, esp of an orchestra **2** to have the property of transmitting heat, sound, electricity, etc – **conductible** *adj*, **conductive** *adj*, **conductibility** *n*

conduction /kən'duksh(ə)n‖kən'dʌkʃ(ə)n/ *n* **1** the act of conducting or conveying **2** transmission through or by means of a conductor **3** the transmission of an electrical impulse through (nerve) tissue

conductivity /ˌkonduk'tivəti‖ˌkɒndʌk'tɪvətɪ/ *n* the quality or power of conducting or transmitting

conductor /kən'duktə‖kən'dʌktə/ *n* **1** a collector of fares on a public conveyance, esp a bus **2** one who directs the performance of musicians **3** a substance or body capable of transmitting electricity, heat, sound, etc **4** *chiefly NAm* GUARD 6 – **conductorial** *adj*

con'ductor ˌrail *n* a rail for conducting current to an electric locomotive or train

conduit /'kondit, 'kondwit, 'kondyoo·it‖'kɒndɪt, 'kɒndwɪt, 'kɒndjʊɪt/ *n* **1** a channel through which sthg (e g a fluid) is conveyed **2** a pipe, tube, or tile for protecting electric wires or cables

[1]**cone** /kohn‖kəʊn/ *n* **1** a mass of overlapping woody scales that, esp in trees of the pine family, are arranged on an axis and bear seeds between them; *broadly* any of several similar flower or fruit clusters **2a** a solid generated by rotating a right-angled triangle about a side other than its hypotenuse **b** a solid figure tapering evenly to a point from a circular base **3a** any of the relatively short light receptors in the retina of vertebrates that are sensitive to bright light and function in colour vision **b** any of many somewhat conical tropical gastropod molluscs **c** the apex of a volcano **d** a crisp cone-shaped wafer for holding a portion of ice cream

[2]**cone** *vt* **1** to bevel like the slanting surface of a cone **2** to mark off (e g a road) with cones

coney /'kohni‖'kəʊnɪ/ *n* **1** a cony **2** rabbit fur

confabulate /kən'fabyoolayt‖kən'fæbjʊleɪt/ *vi* **1** to chat **2** to hold a discussion *USE* humor – **confabulatory** *adj*, **confabulation** *n*

confection /kən'feksh(ə)n‖kən'fekʃ(ə)n/ *n* a fancy or rich dish (e g a cream cake or preserve) or sweetmeat – **confectionary** *adj*

confectioner /kən'fekshənə‖kən'fekʃənə/ *n* a manufacturer of or dealer in confectionery

confectionery /kən'fekshənri‖kən'fekʃənrɪ/ *n* **1** confections, sweets **2** the confectioner's art or business **3** a confectioner's shop

confederacy /kən'fed(ə)rəsi‖kən'fed(ə)rəsɪ/ *n* **1** a league or compact for mutual support or common action; an alliance **2** an unlawful association; a conspiracy **3** a league or alliance for common action; *esp, cap* the 11 states withdrawing from the USA in 1860 and 1861 – **confederal** *adj*, **confederalist** *n*

[1]**confederate** /kən'fed(ə)rət‖kən'fed(ə)rət/ *adj* **1** united in a league; allied **2** *cap* of or relating to the Confederacy

[2]**confederate** *n* **1** an ally, accomplice **2** *cap* an adherent of the Confederacy

[3]**confederate** /kən'fedəˌrayt‖kən'fedəˌreɪt/ *vt* to unite in a confederacy ~*vi* to band together – **confederative** *adj*

confederation /kənˌfedə'raysh(ə)n‖kənˌfedə'reɪʃ(ə)n/ *n* a league

confer /kən'fuh‖kən'fɜː/ *vb* **-rr-** *vt* to bestow (as if) from a position of superiority ~*vi* to come together to compare views or take counsel; consult – **conferrable** *adj*, **conferral** *n*, **conferrer** *n*, **conferee** *n*

conference /'konf(ə)rəns‖'kɒnf(ə)rəns/ *n* **1a** a usu formal interchange of views; a consultation **b** a meeting of 2 or more people for the discussion of matters of common concern **2** a representative assembly or administrative organization of a denomination, organization, association, etc – **conferential** *adj*

confess /kən'fes‖kən'fes/ *vt* **1** to make known (e g sthg wrong or damaging to oneself); admit **2a** to acknowledge (sin) to God or a priest **b** to receive the confession of (a penitent) **3** to declare faith in or adherence to ~ *vi* **1a** to acknowledge one's sins or the state of one's conscience to God or a priest **b** to hear a confession **2** to admit – **confessor** *n*

confession /kən'fesh(ə)n‖kən'feʃ(ə)n/ *n* **1** a disclosure of one's sins **2** a statement of what is confessed: e g **2a** a written acknowledgment of guilt by a party accused of an offence **b** a formal statement of religious beliefs **3** an organized religious body having a common creed – **confessional** *adj*, **confessionalism** *n*, **confessionalist** *n*, **confessionally** *adv*

confessional /kən'fesh(ə)nl‖kən'feʃ(ə)nl/ *n* **1** a place where a priest hears confessions **2** *the* practice of confessing to a priest

confetti /kən'feti‖kən'fetɪ/ *n* small bits of brightly coloured paper meant to be thrown (e g at weddings) [Italian, pl of *confetto* sweetmeat, deriv of Latin *confect-, conficere* to prepare]

confidant, *fem* **confidante** /'konfi,dant, ,- -'-‖'kɒnfɪ,dænt, ,- -'-/ *n* one to whom secrets are entrusted; *esp* an intimate

confide /kən'fied‖kən'faɪd/ *vi* to show confidence *in* by imparting secrets ~*vt* to tell confidentially

confidence /'konfid(ə)ns‖'kɒnfɪd(ə)ns/ *n* **1** faith, trust <*their ~ in God's mercy*> **2** a feeling or consciousness of one's powers being sufficient, or of reliance on one's circumstances **3** the quality or state of being certain <*they had every ~ of success*> **4a** a relationship of trust or intimacy <*took his friend into his ~*> **b** reliance on another's discretion <*their story was told in strictest ~*> **c** legislative support <*vote of ~*> **5** sthg said in confidence; a secret

'confidence ,trick *n* a swindle performed by a person who pretends to be sthg that he/she is not

confident /'konfid(ə)nt‖'kɒnfɪd(ə)nt/ *adj* **1** characterized by assurance; *esp* self-reliant **2** full of conviction; certain – **confidently** *adv*

confidential /,konfi'densh(ə)l‖,kɒnfɪ'denʃ(ə)l/ *adj* **1** private, secret **2** marked by intimacy or willingness to confide <*a ~ tone*> – **confidentially** *adv*, **confidentialness** *n*, **confidentiality** *n*

configuration /kən,figoo'raysh(ə)n, -,figyoo-‖kən,fɪgʊ'reɪʃ(ə)n, -,fɪgjʊ-/ *n* **1a** (relative) arrangement of parts **b** sthg (e g a figure, contour, pattern, or apparatus) produced by such arrangement **c** the relative positions in space of the atoms in a chemical compound **2** a gestalt <*personality ~*> – **configurational** *adj*, **configurationally** *adv*, **configurative** *adj*

[1]**confine** /kən'fien‖kən'faɪn/ *vt* **1** to keep within limits; restrict **2a** to shut up; imprison **b** to keep indoors or in bed, esp just before childbirth – usu passive – **confiner** *n*, **confinement** *n*

[2]**confine** /'konfien‖'kɒnfaɪn/ *n* **1** bounds, borders **2** outlying parts; limits ***USE*** usu pl with sing. meaning

confirm /kən'fuhm‖kən'fɜːm/ *vt* **1** to make firm or firmer; strengthen **2** to give approval to; ratify **3** to administer the rite of confirmation to **4** to make certain of; remove doubt about by authoritative act or indisputable fact – **confirmable** *adj*, **confirmability** *n*

confirmation /,konfə'maysh(ə)n‖,kɒnfə'meɪʃ(ə)n/ *n* **1** a rite admitting a person to full membership of a church **2** confirming proof; corroboration – **confirmational** *adj*, **confirmatory** *adj*

confirmed /kən'fuhmd‖kən'fɜːmd/ *adj* **1a** made firm; strengthened **b** being so fixed in habit as to be unlikely to change <*a ~ bachelor*> **2** having received the rite of confirmation – **confirmedly** *adv*, **confirmedness** *n*

confiscate /'konfiskayt‖'kɒnfɪskeɪt/ *vt* to seize (as if) by authority [Latin *confiscare*, fr *com-* with + *fiscus* treasury] – **confiscator** *n*, **confiscation** *n*, **confiscatory** *adj*

conflagration /,konflə'graysh(ə)n‖,kɒnflə'greɪʃ(ə)n/ *n* a (large disastrous) fire

conflate /kən'flayt‖kən'fleɪt/ *vt* to bring together; fuse <*~ 2 texts into 1*> – **conflation** *n*

[1]**conflict** /'konflikt‖'kɒnflɪkt/ *n* **1** a sharp disagreement or clash (e g between divergent ideas, interests, or people) **2** (distress caused by) mental struggle resulting from incompatible impulses **3** a hostile encounter (e g a fight, battle, or war)

[2]**conflict** /kən'flikt‖kən'flɪkt/ *vi* to be in opposition (to another or each other); disagree – **confliction** *n*

confluence /'konfloo·əns‖'kɒnflʊəns/, **confluency** /-si‖-sɪ/ *n* **1** a coming or flowing together; a meeting or gathering at 1 point **2** the (place of) union of 2 or more streams

conform /kən'fawm‖kən'fɔːm/ *vt* to give the same shape, outline, or contour to; bring into harmony or accord ~ *vi* **1** to be similar or identical **2** to be obedient or compliant; *esp* to adapt oneself to prevailing standards or customs – **conformer** *n*, **conformism** *n*, **conformist** *n*

conformable /kən'fawməbl‖kən'fɔːməbl/ *adj* **1** corresponding in form or character; similar – usu + *to* **2** *of geological strata* following in unbroken sequence – **conformably** *adv*

conformation /,konfə'maysh(ə)n‖,kɒnfə'meɪʃ(ə)n/ *n* **1** adaptation **2a** CONFORMITY 1 **b** the way in which sthg is formed; shape, structure – **conformational** *adj*

conformity /kən'fawməti‖kən'fɔːmətɪ/ *n* **1** correspondence in form, manner, or character; agreement <*behaved in ~ with his beliefs*> **2** an act or instance of conforming **3** action in accordance with a specified standard or authority; <*~ to social custom*>

confound /kən'fownd‖kən'faʊnd/ *vt* **1** to put to shame; discomfit **2** to refute **3** to damn – used as a mild interjection of annoyance <*~ him!*> **4** to throw into confusion or perplexity – **confounder** *n*

con'founded *adj* damned <*that ~ cat!*> – **confoundedly** *adv*

confraternity /,konfrə'tuhnəti‖,kɒnfrə'tɜːnətɪ/ *n* a society devoted to a religious or charitable cause

confront /kən'frunt‖kən'frʌnt/ *vt* **1** to face, esp in challenge; oppose **2a** to cause to meet; bring face to face *with* <*~ a reader with statistics*> **b** to be faced with <*the problems that one ~s are enormous*> – **confronter** *n*

confrontation /,konfrən'taysh(ə)n‖,kɒnfrən'teɪʃ(ə)n/ *n* **1** a face-to-face meeting **2** (an instance of) the clashing of forces or ideas; a conflict – **confrontational** *adj*, **confrontationism** *n*, **confrontationist** *n*

confuse /kən'fyoohz‖kən'fjuːz/ *vt* **1a** to make embarrassed; abash **b** to disturb or muddle in mind or purpose <*his question ~*d *me*> **2a** to make indistinct; blur <*stop* confusing *the issue*> **b** to mix indiscriminately; jumble **c** to fail to differentiate from another often similar or related thing <*~ Socialism with Communism*>

3 *archaic* to bring to ruin – **confused** *adj*, **confusedly** *adv*, **confusing** *adj*, **confusingly** *adv*

confusion /kən'fyoohzh(ə)n‖kən'fjuːʒ(ə)n/ *n* **1** an instance of confusing or being confused **2** (a) disorder, muddle

confute /kən'fyooht‖kən'fjuːt/ *vt* to overwhelm in argument; refute conclusively – **confutation** *n*

conga /'kong·gə‖'kɒŋgə/ *n* **1** a dance involving 3 steps followed by a kick and performed by a group, usu in single file **2** a tall narrow bass drum beaten with the hands

congeal /kən'jeel‖kən'dʒiːl/ *vb* to turn from a fluid to a solid state (as if) by cold; to coagulate – **congealable** *adj*, **congealment** *n*

congenial /kən'jeenyəl, -ni·əl‖kən'dʒiːnjəl, -nɪəl/ *adj* **1** existing or associated together harmoniously – often + *with* **2** pleasant; *esp* agreeably suited to one's nature, tastes, or outlook – **congenially** *adv*, **congeniality** *n*

congenital /kən'jenitl‖kən'dʒenɪtl/ *adj* **1a** existing at or dating from birth <~ *idiocy*> **b** constituting an essential characteristic; inherent <~ *fear of snakes*> **2** being such by nature <*a* ~ *liar*> – **congenitally** *adv*

conger /'kong·gə‖'kɒŋgə/, ˌ**conger** '**eel** *n* any of various related (large) edible sea eels

congest /kən'jest‖kən'dʒest/ *vt* **1** to cause an excessive fullness of the blood vessels of (e g an organ) **2** to clog <*traffic* ~ed *the highways*> – **congestion** *n*, **congestive** *adj*

[1]**conglomerate** /kən'glomərət‖kən'glɒmərət/ *adj* made up of parts from various sources or of various kinds

[2]**conglomerate** /kən'gloməraytǁkən - 'glɒməreɪt/ *vt* to accumulate ~*vi* to gather into a mass or coherent whole – **conglomerator** *n*, **conglomerative** *adj*

[3]**conglomerate** /kən'glomərət‖kən'glɒmərət/ *n* **1** a composite mixture; *specif* (a) rock composed of variously-sized rounded fragments in a cement **2** a widely diversified business company – **conglomeratic** *adj*

conglomeration /kənˌglomə'raysh(ə)n‖kənˌglɒmə'reɪʃ(ə)n/ *n* a mixed coherent mass

congrats /kən'grats‖kən'græts/ *n pl* congratulations – infml

congratulate /kən'gratyoolayt, -choo-‖kən'grætjʊleɪt, -tʃʊ-/ *vt* to express pleasure to (a person) on account of success or good fortune – **congratulator** *n*, **congratulatory** *adj*

congratulation /kənˌgratyoo'laysh(ə)n, -choo-‖kənˌgrætjʊ'leɪʃ(ə)n, -tʃʊ-/ *n* a congratulatory expression – usu pl with sing. meaning

congregate /'kong·griˌgayt‖'kɒŋgrɪˌgeɪt/ *vb* to (cause to) gather together

congregation /ˌkong·gri'gaysh(ə)n‖ˌkɒŋgrɪ'geɪʃ(ə)n/ *n* **1** an assembly of people; *esp* such an assembly for religious worship **2** a religious community; *esp* an organized body of believers in a particular locality

congregational /ˌkong·gri'gaysh(ə)nl‖ˌkɒŋgrɪ'geɪʃ(ə)nl/ *adj* **1** of a congregation **2** *often cap* of (a body of) Protestant churches governed by the assembly of the local congregation – **congregationalism** *n*, *often cap*, **congregationalist** *n or adj*, *often cap*

congress /'kong·gres, -gris‖'kɒŋgres, -grɪs/ *n* **1** a formal meeting of delegates for discussion and usu action on some question **2** the supreme legislative body of a nation; *esp*, *cap* that of the USA **3** an association, usu made up of delegates from constituent organizations **4** the act or action of coming together and meeting – fml – **congressional** *adj*, **congressionally** *adv*

congressman /'kong·gresmən, -gris-‖'kɒŋgresmən, -grɪs-/, *fem* '**congress**ˌ**woman** *n* a member of a congress

congruent /'kong·grooənt‖'kɒŋgrʊənt/ *adj* **1** congruous **2** being exactly the same in size and shape <~ *triangles*> – **congruently** *adv*

congruity /kən'grooh·əti‖kən'gruːətɪ/ *n* being congruent or congruous

congruous /'kong·grooəs‖'kɒŋgrʊəs/ *adj* **1** in agreement, harmony, or correspondence **2** conforming to the circumstances or requirements of a situation; appropriate – fml <*a* ~ *room to work in* – G B Shaw> – **congruously** *adv*, **congruousness** *n*

conic /'konik, 'kohnik‖'kɒnɪk, 'kəʊnɪk/, ˌ**conic** '**section** *n* **1** a plane curve, line, or point that is the intersection of a plane and a cone **2** a curve generated by a point which moves so that the ratio of its distance from a fixed point to its distance from a fixed line is constant

conical /'konikl‖'kɒnɪkl/, **conic** /'konik, 'kohnik‖'kɒnɪk, 'kəʊnɪk/ *adj* **1** resembling a cone in shape **2** of a cone – **conically** *adv*, **conicity** *n*

conifer /'konifə, 'koh-‖'kɒnɪfə, 'kəʊ-/ *n* any of an order of mostly evergreen trees and shrubs including pines, cypresses, and yews, that bear ovules naked on the surface of scales rather than enclosed in an ovary – **coniferous** *adj*

conjectural /kən'jekch(ə)rəl‖kən'dʒektʃ(ə)rəl/ *adj* of the nature of or involving or based on conjecture – **conjecturally** *adv*

[1]**conjecture** /kən'jekchə‖kən'dʒektʃə/ *n* **1** the drawing of conclusions from inadequate evidence **2** a conclusion reached by surmise or guesswork

[2]**conjecture** *vt* **1** to arrive at by conjecture **2** to make conjectures as to ~*vi* to form conjectures – **conjecturer** *n*

conjoin /kən'joyn‖kən'dʒɔɪn/ *vi* to join together, esp for a common purpose

conjoint /kən'joynt‖kən'dʒɔɪnt/ *adj* related to, made up of, or carried on by 2 or more in combination; joint, united – **conjointly** *adv*

conjugal /'konjoogl‖'kɒndʒʊgl/ *adj* of the married state or married people and their relationship [Latin *conjugalis*, fr *conjug-*, *conjux* husband, wife, fr *conjungere* to join, unite in marriage, fr *com-* with + *jungere* to join] – **conjugally** *adv*, **conjugality** *n*

[1]**conjugate** /'konjoogət, -gayt‖'kɒndʒʊgət, -geɪt/ *adj* **1** having features in common but opposite or inverse in some particular **2** derived from the same root <~ *words*> – **conjugately** *adv*, **conjugateness** *n*

[2]**conjugate** /'konjoogayt‖'kɒndʒʊgeɪt/ *vt* to give in prescribed order the various inflectional forms of (a verb) ~ *vi* **1** to become joined together **2** to pair and fuse in genetic conjugation

[3]**conjugate** /'konjoogət, -gayt‖'kɒndʒʊgət, -geɪt/ *n* sthg conjugate; a product of conjugating

conjugation /ˌkonjoo'gaysh(ə)n‖ˌkɒndʒʊ'geɪʃ(ə)n/ *n* **1a** (a diagrammatic arrangement of) the inflectional forms of a verb **b** a class of verbs having the same type of inflectional forms **2a** fusion of (similar) gametes with union of their nuclei that in algae, fungi, etc replaces the typical fertilization of higher forms **b** the one-way transfer of DNA between bacteria in cellular contact – **conjugational** *adj*, **conjugationally** *adv*, **conjugative** *adj*

conjunction /kən'jungksh(ə)n‖kən'dʒʌŋkʃ(ə)n/ *n* **1** joining together; being joined together **2** occurrence together in time or space; concurrence **3** the apparent meeting or passing of 2 or more celestial bodies **4** a word (e g *and* or *when*) that joins together sentences, clauses, phrases, or words – **conjunctional** *adj*, **conjunctionally** *adv*

conjunctiva /kən'jungktivə‖kən'dʒʌŋktɪvə/ *n, pl* **conjunctivas, conjunctivae** /-vi‖-vɪ/ the mucous membrane that lines the inner surface of the eyelids and is continued over part of the eyeball – **conjunctival** *adj*, **conjunctivitis** *n*

conjunctive /kən'jung(k)tiv‖kən'dʒʌŋ(k)tɪv/ *adj* **1** connective **2** being or functioning like a conjunction – **conjunctive** *n*, **conjunctively** *adv*

conjuncture /kən'jung(k)chə‖kən'dʒʌŋ(k)tʃə/ *n* a combination of circumstances or events usu producing a crisis; a juncture

conjure /'kunjə‖'kʌndʒə; *vt sense 2* kən'jooə‖kən'dʒʊə/ *vt* **1a** to summon by invocation or by uttering a spell, charm, etc **b(1)** to affect or effect (as if) by magical powers **b(2)** to imagine, contrive – often + *up* <*to* ~ *up imaginary dangers*> **2** *archaic* to charge or entreat earnestly or solemnly ~ *vi* **1** to make use of magical powers **2** to use a conjurer's tricks [Old French *conjurer*, fr Latin *conjurare* to swear together, fr *com-* with + *jurare* to swear]

conjurer, conjuror /'kunjərə‖'kʌndʒərə/ *n* one who performs tricks by sleight of hand or illusion

[1]**conk** /kongk‖kɒŋk/ *n* (a punch on) the nose – infml

[2]**conk** *vt* to hit (someone) on the head, esp the nose – infml

[3]**conk** *vi* **1** to break down; *esp* to stall <*the motor suddenly* ~ed *out*> **2** to faint *USE* usu + *out*; infml

conker /'kongkə‖'kɒŋkə/ *n* **1** *pl but sing in constr* a British game in which each player in turn swings a conker on a string to try to break one held on its string by his/her opponent **2** the large seed of the horse chestnut, esp as used in playing conkers

connect /kə'nekt‖kə'nekt/ *vt* **1** to join or fasten together, usu by some intervening thing **2** to place or establish in relationship ~ *vi* **1** to be or become joined – **connectable** *also* **connectible** *adj*, **connector** *also* **connecter** *n*

connected /kə'nektid‖kə'nektɪd/ *adj* **1** joined or linked together **2** having a social, professional, or commercial relationship – **connectedly** *adv*, **connectedness** *n*

con'necting rod /kə'nekting‖kə'nektɪŋ/ *n* a rod that transmits power from a part of a machine in reciprocating motion (e g a piston) to another that is rotating (e g a crankshaft)

connection, *chiefly Br* **connexion** /kə'neksh(ə)n‖kə'nekʃ(ə)n/ *n* **1a** causal or logical relationship <*the* ~ *between 2 ideas*> **b** contextual relations or associations <*in this* ~ *the word has a different meaning*> **2a** sthg that connects; a link **b** an arrangement that assists communication or transport; *specif* a train, aeroplane, etc that one should transfer to at a particular station, airport, etc **3** a person connected with others, esp by marriage, kinship, or common interest <*has powerful* ~s *in high places*> **4** a social, professional, or commercial relationship: e g **4a** an arrangement to execute orders or advance interests of another <*a firm's foreign* ~s> **b** a source of contraband (e g illegal drugs) **5** a religious denomination – **connectional** *adj* – **in connection with** with reference to; concerning

[1]**connective** /kə'nektiv‖kə'nektɪv/ *adj* tending to connect – **connectively** *adv*, **connectivity** *n*

[2]**connective** *n* sthg that connects; *esp* a conjunction

'conning ˌtower /'koning‖'kɒnɪŋ/ *n* a raised observation tower and usu entrance on the deck of a submarine

connivance /kə'niev(ə)ns‖kə'naɪv(ə)ns/ *n* knowledge of and active or passive consent to wrongdoing

connive /kə'niev‖kə'naɪv/ *vi* **1** to pretend ignorance of or fail to take action against sthg one ought to oppose **2a** to be indulgent or in secret sympathy **b** to cooperate secretly or have a secret understanding; conspire *USE* often + *at* – **conniver** *n*

connoisseur /ˌkonə'suh, -'sooə‖ˌkɒnə'sɜː, -'sʊə/ *n* **1** an expert judge in matters of taste or appreciation (e g of art) **2** one who enjoys with discrimination and appreciation of subtleties [obs French, fr Old French *connoisseor*, fr *connoistre* to know, fr Latin *cognoscere*] – **connoisseurship** *n*

connote /kə'noht‖kə'nəʊt/ *vt* **1** to convey in addition to exact explicit meaning <*all the misery that poverty* ~s> **2** to be associated with or inseparable from as a consequence or accompaniment <*the remorse so often* ~d *by guilt*> **3** to imply or indicate as a logically essential attribute of sthg denoted – **connotation** *n*, **connotational, connotative** *adj*

connubial /kə'nyoohbi·əl‖kə'njuːbɪ·əl/ *adj* conjugal – **connubially** *adv*, **connubiality** *n*

conquer /'kongkə‖'kɒŋkə/ *vt* **1** to gain or acquire by force of arms; subjugate **2** to overcome by force of arms; vanquish **3** to gain mastery over <~ed *the mountain*> <~ed *his fear*> ~*vi* to be victorious – **conqueror** *n*

conquest /'kon(g)kwest‖'kɒn(g)kwest/ *n* **1** conquering **2a** sthg conquered; *esp* territory taken in war – often pl **b** a person who has been won over, esp by love or sexual attraction

consanguineous /ˌkonsang'gwini·əs‖ˌkɒnsæŋ'gwɪnɪəs/ *adj* of the same blood or origin; *specif* descended from the same ancestor – **consanguineously** *adv*, **consanguinity** *n*

conscience /'konsh(ə)ns‖'kɒnʃ(ə)ns/ *n* **1** the consciousness of the moral quality of one's own conduct or intentions, together with a feeling of obligation to refrain from doing wrong **2** conformity to the dictates of conscience; conscientiousness – **conscienceless** *adj* – **in all conscience**

by any standard of fairness

conscience clause *n* a clause in a law exempting those who object on moral or religious grounds

ˈconscience ˌmoney *n* money paid usu anonymously to relieve the conscience

conscientious /ˌkonshiˈenshəs‖ˌkɒnʃɪˈenʃəs/ *adj* **1** governed by or conforming to the dictates of conscience; scrupulous **2** meticulous or careful, esp in one's work; *also* hard-working – **conscientiously** *adv*, **conscientiousness** *n*

consciˌentious obˈjector *n* one who refuses to serve in the armed forces or bear arms, esp on moral or religious grounds – **conscientious objection** *n*

[1]**conscious** /ˈkonshəs‖ˈkɒnʃəs/ *adj* **1** perceiving with a degree of controlled thought or observation **2** personally felt **3** capable of or marked by thought, will, intention, or perception **4** having mental faculties undulled by sleep, faintness, or stupor; awake **5** done or acting with critical awareness <*made a ~ effort to avoid the same mistakes*> **6** marked by awareness of or concern for sthg specified <*a fashion*-conscious *shopper*> – **consciously** *adv*

[2]**conscious** *n* CONSCIOUSNESS 3 – used in Freudian psychology

consciousness /ˈkonshəsnis‖ˈkɒnʃəsnɪs/ *n* **1** concern, awareness <*class ~*> **2** the totality of conscious states of an individual **3** the upper level of mental life of which sby is aware, as contrasted with unconscious processes

[1]**conscript** /ˈkonskript‖ˈkɒnskrɪpt/ *n or adj* (sby) conscripted

[2]**conscript** /kənˈskript‖kənˈskrɪpt/ *vt* to enlist compulsorily, esp for military service – **conscription** *n*

consecrate /ˈkonsikrayt‖ˈkɒnsɪkreɪt/ *vt* **1** to ordain to a religious office, esp that of bishop **2a** to make or declare sacred by a solemn ceremony **b** to prepare (bread and wine used at communion) to be received as Christ's body and blood **c** to devote to a purpose with deep solemnity or dedication **3** to make inviolable or venerable <*principles ~*d *by the weight of history*> – **consecrator** *n*, **consecration** *n*, **consecratory** *adj*

consecutive /kənˈsekyootiv‖kənˈsekjʊtɪv/ *adj* following one after the other in order without gaps – **consecutively** *adv*, **consecutiveness** *n*

consensus /kənˈsensəs‖kənˈsensəs/ *n* **1** general agreement; unanimity **2** the judgment arrived at by most of those concerned [Latin, fr *consensus*, past participle of *consentire* to agree in feeling, fr *com-* with + *sentire* to feel]

[1]**consent** /kənˈsent‖kənˈsent/ *vi* to give assent or approval; agree *to* – **consenter** *n*, **consentingly** *adv*

[2]**consent** *n* compliance in or approval of what is done or proposed by another; acquiescence

consequence /ˈkonsikwəns‖ˈkɒnsɪkwəns/ *n* **1** sthg produced by a cause or necessarily following from a set of conditions **2** a conclusion arrived at by reasoning **3a** importance in terms of power to produce an effect; moment **b** social importance – **in consequence** as a result; consequently

consequent /ˈkonsikwənt‖ˈkɒnsɪkwənt/ *adj* following as a result or effect

consequential /ˌkonsiˈkwensh(ə)l‖ˌkɒnsɪˈkwenʃ(ə)l/ *adj* **1** consequent **2** of the nature of a secondary result; indirect **3** having significant consequences; important – **consequentially** *adv*, **consequentialness, consequentiality** *n*

consequently /ˈkonsikwəntli‖ˈkɒnsɪkwəntlɪ/ *adv* as a result; in view of the foregoing

conservancy /kənˈsuhv(ə)nsi‖kənˈsɜːv(ə)nsɪ/ *n* **1a** conservation **b** (an area protected by) an organization designated to conserve and protect the environment **2** *Br* a board regulating a river or port

conservation /ˌkonsəˈvaysh(ə)n‖ˌkɒnsəˈveɪʃ(ə)n/ *n* careful preservation and protection, esp of a natural resource, the quality of the environment, or plant or animal species, to prevent exploitation, destruction, etc – **conservational** *adj*, **conservationist** *n*

conservatism /kənˈsuhvətiz(ə)m‖kənˈsɜːvətɪz(ə)m/ *n* **1** (a political philosophy based on) the disposition to preserve what is established **2** *cap* the principles and policies of a Conservative party **3** the tendency to prefer an existing situation to change

[1]**conservative** /kənˈsuhvətiv‖kənˈsɜːvətɪv/ *adj* **1a** of or being a philosophy of conservatism; traditional **b** *cap* advocating conservatism; *specif* of or constituting a British political party associated with support of established institutions and opposed to radical change **2a** moderate, cautious <*a ~ estimate*> **b** marked by or relating to traditional norms of taste, elegance, style, or manners <*a ~ suit*> – **conservatively** *adv*, **conservativeness** *n*

[2]**conservative** *n* **1** *cap* a supporter of a Conservative party **2** one who keeps to traditional methods or views

conservatoire /kənˈsuhvətwah‖kənˈsɜːvətwɑː/ *n* a school specializing in any one of the fine arts <*a ~ of music*>

conservatory /kənˈsuhvət(ə)ri‖kənˈsɜːvət(ə)rɪ/ *n* **1** a greenhouse, usu forming a room of a house, for growing or displaying ornamental plants **2** *chiefly NAm* a conservatoire

[1]**conserve** /kənˈsuhv‖kənˈsɜːv/ *vt* **1a** to keep in a state of safety or wholeness <*~ wild life*> **b** to avoid wasteful or destructive use of <*~ natural resources*> **2** to preserve, esp with sugar **3** to maintain (mass, energy, momentum, etc) constant during a process of chemical or physical change – **conserver** *n*

[2]**conserve** /kənˈsuhv, ˈkonsuhv‖kənˈsɜːv, ˈkɒnsɜːv/ *n* a preserve of fruit boiled with sugar that is used like jam

consider /kənˈsidə‖kənˈsɪdə/ *vt* **1** to think about with care or caution **2** to gaze on steadily or reflectively **3** to think of as specified; regard as being **4** to have as an opinion <*~*ed *that he was wrong*> *~vi* to reflect, deliberate <*paused a moment to ~*>

considerable /kənˈsid(ə)rəbl‖kənˈsɪd(ə)rəbl/ *adj* **1** worth consideration; significant **2** large in extent or degree <*a ~ number*> – **considerably** *adv*

considerate /kənˈsid(ə)rət‖kənˈsɪd(ə)rət/ *adj* marked by or given to consideration of the rights and feelings of others – **considerately** *adv*, **considerateness** *n*

consideration /kən,sidə'raysh(ə)n‖kən,sɪdə'reɪʃ(ə)n/ *n* **1** continuous and careful thought <*after long* ~> **2a** sthg considered as a basis for thought or action; a reason **b** a taking into account **3** thoughtful and sympathetic or solicitous regard **4a** a recompense, payment <*for a small* ~> **b** an element of inducement that distinguishes a legally binding contract from a mere promise – **in consideration of 1** in recompense or payment for **2** ON ACCOUNT OF, BECAUSE OF

con'sidered *adj* matured by extended thought <*his* ~ *opinion*>

[1]considering /kən'sid(ə)ring‖kən'sɪd(ə)rɪŋ/ *prep* taking into account <*he did well* ~ *his limitations*>

[2]considering *conj* in view of the fact that

consign /kən'sien‖kən'saɪn/ *vt* **1** to give over to another's care **2** to give, transfer, or deliver into the hands or control of another; *also* to assign *to* sthg as a destination or end – **consignable** *adj*, **consignor** *n*

consignee /,konsie'nee‖,kɒnsaɪ'niː/ *n* one to whom sthg is consigned

consignment /kən'sienmənt‖kən'saɪnmənt/ *n* sthg consigned, esp in a single shipment

consist /kən'sist‖kən'sɪst/ *vi* **1** to lie, reside *in* <*liberty* ~*s in the absence of obstructions* – A E Housman> **2** to be made up or composed *of* <*breakfast* ~ed *of cereal, milk, and fruit*>

consistency /kən'sist(ə)nsi‖kən'sɪst(ə)nsɪ/ *also* **consistence** *n* **1** internal constancy of constitution or character; persistency **2** degree of resistance of **2a** a liquid to movement <*the* ~ *of thick syrup*> **b** a soft solid to deformation <*the* ~ *of clay*> **3a** agreement or harmony of parts or features to one another or a whole; *specif* ability to be asserted together without contradiction **b** harmony of conduct or practice with past performance or stated intent

consistent /kən'sist(ə)nt‖kən'sɪst(ə)nt/ *adj* marked by harmonious regularity or steady continuity; free from irregularity, variation, or contradiction – **consistently** *adv*

consistory /kən'sist(ə)ri‖kən'sɪst(ə)rɪ/ *n* a church tribunal or governing body; *esp* one made up of the Pope and cardinals – **consistorial** *adj*

consol /kən'sol, 'kon,sol‖kən'sɒl, 'kɒn,sɒl/ *n* an interest-bearing government bond having no maturity date but redeemable on call – usu pl

,conso'lation ,prize /,konsə'laysh(ə)n‖,kɒnsə'leɪʃ(ə)n/ *n* a prize given to one who just fails to gain a major prize in a contest

[1]console /kən'sohl‖kən'səʊl/ *vt* to alleviate the grief or sense of loss of – **consolingly** *adv*, **consolable** *adj*, **consolation** *n*, **consolatory** *adj*

[2]console /'konsohl, 'konsl‖'kɒnsəʊl, 'kɒnsl/ *n* **1** a carved bracket projecting from a wall to support a shelf or cornice **2** the desk containing the keyboards, stops, etc of an organ **3a** a control panel; *also* a cabinet in which a control panel is mounted **b** the part of a computer used for communication between the operator and the computer **4** a cabinet (e g for a radio or television set) designed to rest directly on the floor

consolidate /kən'solidayt‖kən'sɒlɪdeɪt/ *vt* **1** to join together into 1 whole; unite **2** to make firm or secure; strengthen <~ *their hold on first place*> **3** to form into a compact mass ~ *vi* to become consolidated; *specif* to merge <*the 2 companies* ~d> – **consolidator** *n*

consommé /kən'somay, ,konsə'may‖kən'sɒmeɪ, ,kɒnsə'meɪ/ *n* a thin clear meat soup made from meat broth

consonance /'kons(ə)nəns‖'kɒns(ə)nəns/ *n* **1a** correspondence or recurrence of sounds, esp in words; assonance **b** an agreeable combination of musical notes in harmony **2** harmony or agreement among components – fml

[1]consonant /'kons(ə)nənt‖'kɒns(ə)nənt/ *n* (a letter or other symbol representing) any of a class of speech sounds (e g /p/, /g/, /n/, /l/, /s/, /r/) characterized by constriction or closure at 1 or more points in the breath channel – **consonantal** *adj*

[2]consonant *adj* **1** marked by musical consonances **2** having similar sounds <~ *words*> **3** in agreement or harmony; free from elements making for discord – fml – **consonantly** *adv*

[1]consort /'konsawt‖'kɒnsɔːt/ *n* **1** an associate **2** a spouse

[2]consort *n* **1** a conjunction, association <*he ruled in* ~ *with his father*> **2a** a group of musicians performing esp early music **b** a set of musical instruments (e g viols or recorders) of the same family played together

[3]consort /kən'sawt‖kən'sɔːt/ *vi* **1** to keep company *with* **2** to accord, harmonize *with USE* fml

consortium /kən'sawti·əm‖kən'sɔːtɪ·əm/ *n, pl* **consortia** /-ti·ə‖-tɪə/ *also* **consortiums** a business or banking agreement or combination

conspectus /kən'spektəs‖kən'spektəs/ *n, pl* **conspectuses** a survey, summary; *esp* a brief one providing an overall view

conspicuous /kən'spikyoo·əs‖kən'spɪkjʊəs/ *adj* **1** obvious to the eye or mind **2** attracting attention; striking – **conspicuously** *adv*, **conspicuousness** *n*

conspiracy /kən'spirəsi‖kən'spɪrəsɪ/ *n* **1** (the offence of) conspiring together **2a** an agreement among conspirators **b** *sing or pl in constr* a group of conspirators

con,spiracy of 'silence *n* an agreement to keep silent, esp in order to promote or protect selfish interests

conspirator /kən'spirətə‖kən'spɪrətə/ *n* one who conspires; a plotter

conspiratorial /kən,spirə'tawri·əl, ,kon-‖kən,spɪrə'tɔːrɪ·əl, ,kɒn-/ *adj* (suggestive) of a conspiracy or conspirator – **conspiratorially** *adv*

conspire /kən'spie·ə‖kən'spaɪ·ə/ *vi* **1a** to join in a plot **b** to scheme **2** to act together <*circumstances* ~d *to defeat his efforts*>

constable /'konstəbl, 'kun-‖'kɒnstəbl, 'kʌn-/ *n* **1** a high officer of a medieval royal or noble household **2** the warden or governor of a royal castle or a fortified town **3** *Br* a policeman; *specif* one ranking below sergeant [Old French *conestable*, fr Late Latin *comes stabuli*, lit., officer of the stable]

[1]constabulary /kən'stabyooləri‖kən'stæbjʊlərɪ/ *n sing or pl in constr* **1** the police force of a district or country **2** an armed police force organized on military lines

[2]**constabulary** *adj* of a constable or constabulary

constancy /'konstənsi‖'kɒnstənsɪ/ *n* **1** fidelity, loyalty **2** freedom from change

[1]**constant** /'konstənt‖'kɒnstənt/ *adj* **1** marked by steadfast resolution or faithfulness; exhibiting constancy of mind or attachment **2** invariable, uniform **3** continually occurring or recurring; regular – **constantly** *adv*

[2]**constant** *n* sthg invariable or unchanging: e g **a** a number that has a fixed value in a given situation or universally or that is characteristic of some substance or instrument **b** a number that is assumed not to change value in a given mathematical discussion

constellation /ˌkonstə'laysh(ə)n‖ˌkɒnstə'leɪʃ(ə)n/ *n* **1** any of many arbitrary configurations of stars supposed to fill the outlines of usu mythical figures **2** a cluster, group, or configuration; *esp* a large or impressive one – **constellatory** *adj*

consternation /ˌkonstə'naysh(ə)n‖ˌkɒnstə'neɪʃ(ə)n/ *n* amazed dismay that hinders or throws into confusion

constipate /'konstipayt‖'kɒnstɪpeɪt/ *vt* to cause constipation in

constipation /ˌkonsti'paysh(ə)n‖ˌkɒnstɪ'peɪʃ(ə)n/ *n* abnormally delayed or infrequent passage of faeces

constituency /kən'stityoo·ənsi, -'stichoo-‖kən'stɪtjʊənsɪ, -'stɪtʃʊ-/ *n* (the residents in) an electoral district

[1]**constituent** /kən'stityoo·ənt, -choo-‖kən'stɪtjʊənt, -tʃʊ-/ *n* **1** an essential part; a component **2** a resident in a constituency

[2]**constituent** *adj* **1** serving to form, compose, or make up a unit or whole; component **2** having the power to frame or amend a constitution <*a* ~ *assembly*> – **constituently** *adv*

constitute /'konstityooht, -chooht‖'kɒnstɪtju:t, -tʃu:t/ *vt* **1** to appoint to an often specified office, function, or dignity <~d *authorities*> **2** to establish; SET UP: e g **2a** to establish formally **b** to give legal form to **3** to form, make, be <*unemployment* ~s *a major problem*>

constitution /ˌkonsti'tyoohsh(ə)n‖ˌkɒnstɪ'tju:ʃ(ə)n/ *n* **1** the act of establishing, making, or setting up **2a** the physical and mental structure of an individual **b** the factors or parts which go to make sthg; composition; *also* the way in which these parts or factors make up the whole **3** the way in which a state or society is organized **4** (a document embodying) the fundamental principles and laws of a nation, state, or social group

[1]**constitutional** /ˌkonsti'tyoohsh(ə)nl‖ˌkɒnstɪ'tju:ʃ(ə)nl/ *adj* **1** relating to, inherent in, or affecting the constitution of body or mind **2** being in accordance with or authorized by the constitution of a state or society <*a* ~ *government*> **3** regulated according to a constitution <*a* ~ *monarchy*> **4** of a constitution – **constitutionalize** *vt*, **constitutionality** *n*

[2]**constitutional** *n* a walk taken for one's health

ˌconstiˈtutionalism /-iz(ə)m‖-ɪz(ə)m/ *n* adherence to constitutional principles; *also* a constitutional system of government – **constitutionalist** *n*

constitutionally /ˌkonsti'tyoohsh(ə)nl·i‖ˌkɒnstɪ'tju:ʃ(ə)nlɪ/ *adv* **1a** in accordance with one's mental or bodily constitution **b** in structure, composition, or physical constitution **2** in accordance with a constitution <*was not* ~ *eligible to fill the office*>

constitutive /kən'stityootiv‖kən'stɪtjʊtɪv/ *adj* having the power to enact or establish – **constitutively** *adv*

constrain /kən'strayn‖kən'streɪn/ *vt* **1** to force by imposed stricture or limitation <*the evidence* ~s *belief*> **2** to force or produce in an unnatural or strained manner <*a* ~ed *smile*> **3** to hold within narrow confines; *also* to clasp tightly – **constrainedly** *adv*

constraint /kən'straynt‖kən'streɪnt/ *n* **1a** constraining or being constrained **b** a constraining agency or force; a check **2a** repression of one's own feelings, behaviour, or actions **b** a sense of being constrained; embarrassment

constrict /kən'strikt‖kən'strɪkt/ *vt* **1a** to make narrow **b** to compress, squeeze <~ *a nerve*> **2** to set or keep within limits – **constrictive** *adj*, **constriction** *n*

constrictor /kən'striktə‖kən'strɪktə/ *n* **1** a muscle that contracts a cavity or orifice or compresses an organ **2** a snake (e g a boa constrictor) that kills prey by compressing it in its coils

[1]**construct** /kən'strukt‖kən'strʌkt/ *vt* **1** to make or form by combining parts; build **2** to set in logical order **3** to draw (a geometrical figure) with suitable instruments and under given conditions – **constructible** *adj*, **constructor** *n*

[2]**construct** /'konstrukt‖'kɒnstrʌkt/ *n* sthg constructed, esp mentally

construction /kən'struksh(ə)n‖kən'strʌkʃ(ə)n/ *n* **1** the arrangement and connection of words or groups of words into some higher unit (e g a phrase or clause) **2** the process, art, or manner of constructing; *also* sthg constructed **3** the act or result of construing, interpreting, or explaining – **constructional** *adj*, **constructionally** *adv*

constructive /kən'struktiv‖kən'strʌktɪv/ *adj* **1** (judicially) implied rather than explicit <~ *dismissal*> **2** of or involved in construction **3** suggesting improvement or development <~ *criticism*> – **constructively** *adv*, **constructiveness** *n*

construe /kən'strooh‖kən'stru:/ *vt* **1** to analyse the syntax of (e g a sentence or sentence part) **2** to understand or explain the sense or intention of <~d *my actions as hostile*> **3** to translate closely ~*vi* to construe a sentence or sentence part, esp in connection with translating – **construable** *adj*

consubstantiation /ˌkonsəbˌstanshi'aysh(ə)n, -si'aysh(ə)n‖ˌkɒnsəbˌstænʃɪ'eɪʃ(ə)n, -sɪ'eɪʃ(ə)n/ *n* (the Anglican doctrine of) the actual presence and combination of the body and blood of Christ with the bread and wine used at Communion

consul /'kons(ə)l‖'kɒns(ə)l/ *n* **1a** either of 2 elected chief magistrates of the Roman republic **b** any of 3 chief magistrates of France from 1799 to 1804 **2** an official appointed by a government to reside in a foreign country to look after the (commercial) interests of citizens of the appointing country – **consulship** *n*, **consular** *adj*

consulate /ˈkonsyooləṭ‖ˈkɒnsjʊlət/ *n* **1** a government by consuls **2** the residence, office, or jurisdiction of a consul

consult /kənˈsult‖kənˈsʌlt/ *vt* **1** to ask the advice or opinion of < ~ *a doctor*> **2** to refer to < ~ *a dictionary*> ~ *vi* **1** to deliberate together; confer **2** to serve as a consultant – **consulter** *n*

consultancy /kənˈsult(ə)nsi‖kənˈsʌlt(ə)nsɪ/ *n* **1** an agency that provides consulting services **2** consultation

consultant /kənˈsult(ə)nt‖kənˈsʌlt(ə)nt/ *n* **1** one who consults sby or sthg **2** an expert who gives professional advice or services **3** the most senior grade of British hospital doctor, usu having direct clinical responsibility for hospital patients – **consultantship** *n*

consultation /ˌkons(ə)lˈtaysh(ə)n‖ˌkɒns(ə)lˈteɪʃ(ə)n/ *n* **1** a council, conference **2** the act of consulting or conferring

consultative /kənˈsultətiv‖kənˈsʌltətɪv/ *adj* of or intended for consultation; advisory

consulting /kənˈsulting‖kənˈsʌltɪŋ/ *adj* **1** providing professional or expert advice <*a* ~ *architect*> **2** of a (medical) consultation or consultant

consume /kənˈsyoohm‖kənˈsjuːm/ *vt* **1** to do away with completely; destroy <*fire* ~d *several buildings*> **2a** to spend wastefully; squander **b** to use or use up <*furnaces* ~ *fuel*> **3** to eat or drink, esp in great quantity or eagerly **4** to engage fully; engross <*she was* ~d *with curiosity*> ~*vi* to waste or burn away; perish – **consumable** *adj*, **consumingly** *adv*

consumer /kənˈsyoohmə‖kənˈsjuːmə/ *n* a customer for goods or services – **consumership** *n*

[1]**consummate** /kənˈsumət, ˈkonsyoomət, -sə-, -su-‖kənˈsʌmət, ˈkɒnsjʊmət, -sə-, -sʌ-/ *adj* **1** extremely skilled and accomplished <*a* ~ *liar*> **2** of the highest degree < ~ *skill*> – **consummately** *adv*

[2]**consummate** /ˈkonsyoomayt, -sə-, -su-‖ˈkɒnsjʊmeɪt, -sə-, -sʌ-/ *vt* to make (a marriage) complete by sexual intercourse – **consummative** *adj*, **consummator** *n*

consummation /ˌkonsəˈmaysh(ə)n, -su-, -syoo-‖ˌkɒnsəˈmeɪʃ(ə)n, -sʌ-, -sjʊ-/ *n* **1** the consummating of a marriage **2** the ultimate end; a goal

consumption /kənˈsumsh(ə)n, -ˈsumpsh(ə)n‖kənˈsʌmʃ(ə)n, -ˈsʌmpʃ(ə)n/ *n* **1** the act or process of consuming **2** the utilization of economic goods in the satisfaction of wants or in the process of production, resulting chiefly in their destruction, deterioration, or transformation **3** (a progressive wasting of the body, esp from) lung tuberculosis

consumptive /kənˈsum(p)tiv‖kənˈsʌm(p)tɪv/ *adj* of or affected with consumption (of the lungs) – **consumptive** *n*, **consumptively** *adv*

[1]**contact** /ˈkontakt‖ˈkɒntækt/ *n* **1a** (an instance of) touching **b** (a part made to form) the junction of 2 electrical conductors through which a current passes **2a** association, relationship <*she needs human* ~> **b** connection, communication <*keep in* ~*!*> **c** the act of establishing communication with sby or observing or receiving a significant signal from a person or object **3** one serving as a carrier or source <*our* ~ *in Berlin*>

[2]**contact** /ˈkontakt, konˈtakt, kən-‖ˈkɒntækt, kɒnˈtækt, kən-/ *vt* **1** to bring into contact **2a** to enter or be in contact with; join **b** to get in communication with < ~ *your local agent*> ~*vi* to make contact

ˈ**contact** ˌ**lens** *n* a thin lens designed to fit over the cornea of the eye, esp for the correction of a visual defect

contagion /kənˈtayj(ə)n, -jyən‖kənˈteɪdʒ(ə)n, -dʒjən/ *n* **1a** the transmission of a disease by (indirect) contact **b** (a virus, bacterium, etc that causes) a contagious disease **2** corrupting influence or contact

contagious /kənˈtayjəs, -jyəs‖kənˈteɪdʒəs, -dʒjəs/ *adj* **1** communicable by contact; catching **2** bearing contagion **3** exciting similar emotions or conduct in others < ~ *enthusiasm*> – **contagiously** *adv*, **contagiousness** *n*

contain /kənˈtayn‖kənˈteɪn/ *vt* **1** to keep within limits; hold back or hold down: e g **1a** to restrain, control < ~ *yourself!*> **b** to check, halt < ~ *the enemy's attack*> **c** to follow successfully a policy of containment towards **d** to prevent (an enemy, opponent, etc) from advancing or attacking **2a** to have within; hold **b** to comprise, include <*the bill* ~s *several new clauses*> **3** to be divisible by, usu without a remainder – **containable** *adj*

container /kənˈtaynə‖kənˈteɪnə/ *n* a receptacle for the shipment of goods; *specif* a metal packing case, standardized for mechanical handling, usu forming a single lorry or rail-wagon load

container·ize, -ise /kənˈtaynəriez‖kənˈteɪnəraɪz/ *vt* **1** to ship by containerization **2** to convert to the use of containers <*plans to* ~ *the ports*>

conˈtainer ˌ**ship** *n* a ship for carrying cargo in containers

containment /kənˈtaynmənt‖kənˈteɪnmənt/ *n* preventing the expansion of a hostile power or ideology

contaminate /kənˈtaminayt‖kənˈtæmɪneɪt/ *vt* **1a** to soil, stain, or infect by contact or association **b** to make inferior or impure by adding sthg <*iron* ~d *with phosphorus*> **2** to make unfit for use by the introduction of unwholesome or undesirable elements – **contaminator** *n*, **contamination** *n*, **contaminative** *adj*

contemplate /ˈkontəmplayt‖ˈkɒntəmpleɪt/ *vt* **1** to view or consider with continued attention; meditate on **2** to have in view as contingent or probable or as an end or intention <*what do you* ~ *doing?*> ~*vi* to ponder, meditate – **contemplator** *n*

contemplation /ˌkontəmˈplaysh(ə)n, -tem-‖ˌkɒntəmˈpleɪʃ(ə)n, -tem-/ *n* **1** meditation on spiritual things as a private devotion **2** an act of considering with attention; a study **3** the act of regarding steadily

contemplative /ˈkontəmˌplaytiv, -tem-, kənˈtemplətiv‖ˈkɒntəmˌpleɪtɪv, -tem-, kənˈtemplətɪv/ *adj* **1** of or involving contemplation

2 of a religious order devoted to prayer and penance – **contemplative** *n*, **contemplatively** *adv*, **contemplativeness** *n*

contemporaneous /kən,tempə'raynyəs, kon-, -ni·əs‖kən,tempə'reɪnjəs, kɒn-, -nɪəs/ *adj* CONTEMPORARY 1 – **contemporaneously** *adv*, **contemporaneousness, contemporaneity** *n*

[1]**contemporary** /kən'temp(ə)rəri, -pri‖kən'temp(ə)rərɪ, -prɪ/ *adj* **1** happening, existing, living, or coming into being during the same period of time **2** marked by characteristics of the present period; modern [Latin *com-* with + *tempor-, tempus* time] – **contemporarily** *adv*

[2]**contemporary** *n* sby or sthg contemporary with another; *specif* one of about the same age as another

contempt /kən'tem(p)t‖kən'tem(p)t/ *n* **1a** the act of despising; the state of mind of one who despises **b** lack of respect or reverence for sthg **2** the state of being despised <*he is held in* ~> **3** obstruction of the administration of justice in court; *esp* wilful disobedience to or open disrespect of a court

contemptible /kən'tem(p)təbl‖kən'tem(p)təbl/ *adj* worthy of contempt – **contemptibleness** *n*, **contemptibly** *adv*

contemptuous /kən'tem(p)choo·əs, -tyoo·əs‖kən'tem(p)tʃʊəs, -tjʊəs/ *adj* showing, feeling, or expressing contempt – **contemptuously** *adv*, **contemptuousness** *n*

contend /kən'tend‖kən'tend/ *vi* **1** to strive or vie in contest or rivalry or against difficulties **2** to strive in debate; argue ~*vt* to maintain, assert – **contender** *n*

[1]**content** /kən'tent‖kən'tent/ *adj* happy, satisfied – **contentment** *n*

[2]**content** /kən'tent‖kən'tent/ *vt* **1** to appease the desires of; satisfy **2** to limit (oneself) in requirements, desires, or actions – usu + *with*

[3]**content** /kən'tent‖kən'tent/ *n* freedom from care or discomfort; satisfaction

[4]**content** /'kontent‖'kɒntent/ *n* **1a** that which is contained – usu pl with sing. meaning <*the jar's* ~s> **b** *pl* the topics or matter treated in a written work <*table of* ~s> **2a** the substance, gist <~ *as opposed to form*> **b** the events, physical detail, and information in a work of art **3** the matter dealt with in a field of study **4** the amount of specified material contained; proportion <*the lead* ~ *of paint*>

contented /kən'tentid‖kən'tentɪd/ *adj* happy, satisfied – **contentedly** *adv*, **contentedness** *n*

contention /kən'tensh(ə)n‖kən'tenʃ(ə)n/ *n* **1** (an act or instance of) contending **2** a point advanced or maintained in a debate or argument

contentious /kən'tenshəs‖kən'tenʃəs/ *adj* **1** exhibiting an often perverse and wearisome tendency to quarrels and disputes **2** likely to cause contention – **contentiously** *adv*, **contentiousness** *n*

[1]**contest** /kən'test‖kən'test/ *vt* to make the subject of dispute, contention, or litigation ~*vi* to strive, vie – **contestable** *adj*, **contester** *n*

[2]**contest** /'kontest‖'kɒntest/ *n* **1** a struggle for superiority or victory **2** a competitive event; COMPETITION 2; *esp* one adjudicated by a panel of specially chosen judges

contestant /kən'test(ə)nt‖kən'test(ə)nt/ *n* **1** one who participates in a contest **2** one who contests an award or decision

context /'kontekst‖'kɒntekst/ *n* **1** the parts surrounding a written or spoken word or passage that can throw light on its meaning **2** the interrelated conditions in which sthg exists or occurs – **contextual** *adj*, **contextually** *adv*

contiguous /kən'tigyoo·əs‖kən'tɪgjʊ·əs/ *adj* **1** in actual contact; touching along a boundary or at a point **2** next or near in time or sequence – **contiguously** *adv*, **contiguousness** *n*, **contiguity** *n*

continence /'kontinəns‖'kɒntɪnəns/ *n* **1** self-restraint from yielding to impulse or desire **2** ability to refrain from a bodily activity; the state of being continent

[1]**continent** /'kontinənt‖'kɒntɪnənt/ *adj* **1** exercising continence **2** not suffering from incontinence of the urine or faeces – **continently** *adv*

[2]**continent** *n* **1** any of the (7) great divisions of land on the globe **2** *cap the* continent of Europe as distinguished from the British Isles

[1]**continental** /,konti'nentl‖,kɒntɪ'nentl/ *adj* (characteristic) of a continent, esp Europe – **continentally** *adv*

[2]**continental** *n* an inhabitant of a continent, esp Europe

continental breakfast *n* a light breakfast, typically of bread rolls with preserves and coffee

,conti,nental 'drift *n* the (supposed) drifting apart of the continents from being a solid land mass

,conti,nental 'quilt *n* a duvet

,conti,nental 'shelf *n* the gently sloping part of the ocean floor that borders a continent and ends in a steeper slope to the ocean depths

contingency /kən'tinj(ə)nsi‖kən'tɪndʒ(ə)nsɪ/ *n* **1** an event that may occur; *esp* an undesirable one **2** an event that is liable to accompany another event

[1]**contingent** /kən'tinj(ə)nt‖kən'tɪndʒ(ə)nt/ *adj* **1** happening by chance or unforeseen causes **2** dependent *on* or conditioned by sthg else – **contingently** *adv*

[2]**contingent** *n* a quota or share, esp of people supplied from or representative of an area, group, or military force

continual /kən'tinyoo·əl, -yool‖kən'tɪnjʊəl, -jʊl/ *adj* **1** continuing indefinitely without interruption **2** recurring in steady rapid succession – **continually** *adv*

continuance /kən'tinyoo·əns‖kən'tɪnjʊəns/ *n* **1** the act or process of continuing in a state, condition, or course of action **2** *NAm* adjournment of court proceedings

continuation /kən,tinyoo'aysh(ə)n‖kən,tɪnjʊ'eɪʃ(ə)n/ *n* **1** the act or process of continuing in a state or activity **2** resumption after an interruption **3** sthg that continues, increases, or adds

continue /kən'tinyooh‖kən'tɪnju:/ *vi* **1** to maintain a condition, course, or action without interruption **2** to remain in existence; endure **3** to remain in a place or condition; stay **4** to resume an activity after interruption ~ *vt* **1a** to maintain (a condition, course, or action) without interruption; CARRY ON <~s *walking*> **b** to prolong; *specif* to resume after interruption **2** to cause to continue **3** to say further <*'We must* *fight for freedom'*, ~d *the speaker*> **4** *NAm* to postpone (a legal proceeding) – **continuer** *n*

continuity /ˌkonti'nyooh·əti‖ˌkɒntɪ'njuːətɪ/ *n* **1a** uninterrupted connection, succession, or union **b** persistence without essential change **c** uninterrupted duration in time **2** sthg that has, displays, or provides continuity: e g **2a** a script or scenario in the performing arts; *esp* one giving the details of the sequence of individual shots **b** speech or music used to link parts of an entertainment, esp a radio or television programme

continuo /kən'tinyooˌoh‖kən'tɪnjʊˌəʊ/ *n, pl* **continuos** a bass part for a keyboard or stringed instrument written as a succession of bass notes with figures that indicate the required chords

continuous /kən'tinyoo·əs‖kən'tɪnjʊəs/ *adj* marked by uninterrupted extension in space, time, or sequence – **continuously** *adv*, **continuousness** *n*

continuum /kən'tinyoo·əm‖kən'tɪnjʊəm/ *n, pl* **continua** /-nyoo·ə‖-njʊə/, **continuums** **1** sthg (e g duration or extension) absolutely continuous and homogeneous that can be described only by reference to sthg else (e g numbers) **2a** sthg in which a fundamental common character is discernible amid a series of imperceptible or indefinite variations <*the* ~ *of experience*> **b** an uninterrupted ordered sequence

contort /kən'tawt‖kən'tɔːt/ *vb* to twist in a violent manner; deform – **contortive** *adj*, **contortion** *n*

contortionist /kən'tawsh(ə)nist‖kən'tɔːʃ(ə)nɪst/ *n* **1** an acrobat who specializes in unnatural body postures **2** one who extricates him-/herself from a dilemma by complicated but doubtful arguments – **contortionistic** *adj*

[1]**contour** /'konˌtooə‖'kɒnˌtʊə/ *n* **1** (a line representing) an outline, esp of a curving or irregular figure **2 contour, contour line** a line (e g on a map) connecting points of equal elevation or height

[2]**contour** *vt* **1a** to shape the contour of **b** to shape so as to fit contours **2** to construct (e g a road) in conformity to a contour

contra- /kontrə-‖kɒntrə-/ *prefix* **1** against; contrary; contrasting <contra*distinction*> **2** pitched below normal <contra*bass*>

contraband /'kontrəˌband‖'kɒntrəˌbænd/ *n* goods or merchandise whose import, export, or possession is forbidden; *also* smuggled goods [Italian *contrabbando*, fr Medieval Latin *contrabannum*, fr *contra-* against + *bannum* decree] – **contraband** *adj*

contraception /ˌkontrə'sepsh(ə)n‖ˌkɒntrə'sepʃ(ə)n/ *n* prevention of conception or impregnation – **contraceptive** *adj*

contraceptive /ˌkontrə'septiv‖ˌkɒntrə'septɪv/ *n* a method or device used in preventing conception; *esp* a condom

[1]**contract** /'kontrakt‖'kɒntrækt/ *n* **1a** (a document containing) a legally binding agreement between 2 or more people or parties **b** a betrothal **2** an undertaking to win a specified number of tricks in bridge

[2]**contract** /kən'trakt‖kən'trækt; *vt sense 1 and vi sense 1 usu* 'kontrakt‖'kɒntrækt/ *vt* **1** to undertake by contract **2a** to catch (an illness) **b** to incur as an obligation <~ *a debt*> **3** to knit, wrinkle <*a frown* ~ed *his brow*> **4** to reduce to a smaller size (as if) by squeezing or forcing together **5** to shorten (e g a word) ~ *vi* **1** to make a contract **2** to draw together so as to become smaller or shorter <*metal* ~s *on cooling*> – **contractible** *adj*, **contractibility** *n*

ˌcontract 'bridge /'kontrakt‖'kɒntrækt/ *n* a form of bridge in which tricks made in excess of the contract do not count towards game bonuses

contractile /kən'traktiel‖kən'træktaɪl/ *adj* having the power or property of contracting – **contractility** *n*

contract in *vb* to agree to inclusion (of) in a particular scheme

contraction /kən'traksh(ə)n‖kən'trækʃ(ə)n/ *n* **1** the shortening and thickening of a muscle (fibre) **2** (a form produced by) a shortening of a word, syllable, or word group – **contractional** *adj*, **contractive** *adj*

contractor /kən'traktə, 'kontraktə‖kən'træktə, 'kɒntræktə/ *n* one who contracts to perform work or to provide supplies

contract out *vb* to agree to exclusion (of) from a particular scheme

contractual / kən'traktyoo·əl, -choo·əl‖kən'træktjʊəl, -tʃʊəl/ *adj* of or constituting a contract – **contractually** *adv*

contradict /ˌkontrə'dikt‖ˌkɒntrə'dɪkt/ *vt* **1** to state the contrary of (a statement or speaker) **2** to deny the truthfulness of (a statement or speaker) – **contradictable** *adj*, **contradictor** *n*

contradiction /ˌkontrə'diksh(ə)n‖ˌkɒntrə'dɪkʃ(ə)n/ *n* **1** a logical inconsistency **2** an opposition or conflict inherent in a system or situation

contradictory *adj* **1** given to or marked by contradiction **2** serving to contradict – **contradictorily** *adv*, **contradictoriness** *n*

ˌcontradi'stinction /-di'stingksh(ə)n‖-dɪ'stɪŋkʃ(ə)n/ *n* distinction by contrast – **contradistinctive** *adj*, **contradistinctively** *adv*

contraflow /ˌkontrə'floh/ *n* a diversion of traffic on a dual carriageway, so that all traffic uses one carriageway while the other is temporarily closed

contrail /'kontrayl‖'kɒntreɪl/ *n* a streak of condensed water vapour created in the air by the passage of an aircraft or rocket at high altitudes

ˌcontra'indicate /-'indikayt‖-'ɪndɪkeɪt/ *vt* to make (a treatment of procedure) inadvisable <*a drug that is* ~d *in pregnancy*> – **contraindication** *n* **contraindicative** *adj*

contralto /kən'traltoh, kən'trahltoh‖kən'træltəʊ, kən'trɑːltəʊ/ *n, pl* **contraltos** **1** (a person with) the lowest female singing voice **2** the part sung by a contralto

contraption /kən'trapsh(ə)n‖kən'træpʃ(ə)n/ *n* a newfangled or complicated device; a gadget

contrapuntal /ˌkontrə'puntl‖ˌkɒntrə'pʌntl/ *adj* of counterpoint – **contrapuntally** *adv*

contrariety /ˌkontrə'rie·əti‖ˌkɒntrə'raɪ·ətɪ/ *n* opposition, disagreement – fml

contrariwise /'kontrəriˌwiez, kən'treə-‖'kɒntrərɪˌwaɪz, kən'treə-/ *adv* conversely; VICE VERSA

[1]**contrary** /'kontrəri‖'kɒntrərɪ/ *n* **1** a fact or condition incompatible with another **2** either of

a pair of opposites **3** either of 2 terms (e g true and false) that cannot both simultaneously be said to be true of the same subject – **on the contrary** just the opposite; no – **to the contrary 1** to the opposite effect <*if I hear nothing* to the contrary *I'll accept that explanation*> **2** notwithstanding

[2]**contrary** /'kontrəri‖'kɒntrəri; *sense 4 often* kən'treəri‖kən'treərı/ *adj* **1** completely different or opposed **2** opposite in position, direction, or nature **3** *of wind or weather* unfavourable **4** obstinately self-willed; inclined to oppose the wishes of others – **contrarily** *adv*, **contrariness** *n*

'**contrary to** /'kontrəri‖'kɒntrərı/ *prep* in opposition to

[1]**contrast** /'kontrahst‖'kɒntrɑːst/ *n* **1a** juxtaposition of dissimilar elements (e g colour, tone, or emotion) in a work of art **b** degree of difference between the lightest and darkest parts of a painting, photograph, television picture, etc **2** comparison of similar objects to set off their dissimilar qualities **3** a person or thing against which another may be contrasted – **contrastive** *adj*, **contrastively** *adv*

[2]**contrast** /kən'trahst‖kən'trɑːst/ *vi* to exhibit contrast ~ *vt* **1** to put in contrast **2** to compare in respect to differences – **contrastable** *adj*

contravene /ˌkontrə'veen‖ˌkɒntrə'viːn/ *vt* to go or act contrary to <~ *a law*> – **contravener** *n*

contravention /ˌkontrə'vensh(ə)n‖ˌkɒntrə'venʃ(ə)n/ *n* a violation or infringement

contretemps /'kon(h)trəˌtonh, 'kawntrə-, -tong ‖'kɒntrəˌtɑ̃, 'kɔːntrə-, -tɒŋ (*Fr* kɔ̃trətɑ̃)/ *n, pl* **contretemps** /-(z) ‖-(z) (*Fr* ~)/ a minor setback, disagreement, or confrontation [French, fr *contre-* counter- + *temps* time, fr Latin *tempus*]

contribute /kən'tribyooht, 'kontri-‖kən'trɪbjuːt, 'kɒntrɪ-/ *vt* **1** to give in common with others **2** to supply (e g an article) for a publication ~ *vi* **1** to help bring about an end or result **2** to supply articles to a publication – **contributive** *adj*, **contributively** *adv*, **contributor** *n*

contribution /ˌkontri'byoohsh(ə)n‖ˌkɒntrɪ'bjuːʃ(ə)n/ *n* the act of contributing; *also* sthg contributed

contributory /kən'tribyoot(ə)ri‖kən'trɪbjʊt(ə)rɪ/ *adj* **1** contributing to a common fund or enterprise **2** of or forming a contribution **3** financed by contributions; *specif, of an insurance or pension plan* contributed to by both employers and employees

contrite /kən'triet‖kən'traɪt/ *adj* **1** grieving and penitent for sin or shortcoming **2** showing contrition – **contritely** *adv*, **contriteness** *n*

contrition /kən'trish(ə)n‖kən'trɪʃ(ə)n/ *n* sorrow for one's sins, arising esp from the love of God rather than fear of punishment

contrivance /kən'triev(ə)ns‖kən'traɪv(ə)ns/ *n* **1** contriving or being contrived **2** sthg contrived; *esp* a mechanical device

contrive /kən'triev‖kən'traɪv/ *vt* **1a** to devise, plan **b** to create in an inventive or resourceful manner **2** to bring about; manage – **contriver** *n*

con'trived *adj* unnatural and forced

[1]**control** /kən'trohl‖kən'trəʊl/ *vt* **-ll- 1** to check, test, or verify **2a** to exercise restraining or directing influence over **b** to have power over; rule – **controllable** *adj*, **controllability** *n*

[2]**control** *n* **1** power to control, direct, or command **2a** (an organism, culture, etc used in) an experiment in which the procedure or agent under test in a parallel experiment is omitted and which is used as a standard of comparison in judging experimental effects **b** a mechanism used to regulate or guide the operation of a machine, apparatus, or system – often pl **c** an organization that directs a space flight <*mission* ~> **d** a personality or spirit believed to be responsible for the actions of a spiritualistic medium at a séance

controller /kən'trohlə‖kən'trəʊlə/ *n* **1a** a public-finance official **b** a chief financial officer, esp of a business enterprise **2** one who controls or has power to control – **controllership** *n*

controversial /ˌkontrə'vuhsh(ə)l‖ˌkɒntrə'vɜːʃ(ə)l/ *adj* of, given to, or arousing controversy – **controversialism** *n*, **controversialist** *n*, **controversially** *adv*

controversy /'kontrəˌvuhsi‖'kɒntrəˌvɜːsɪ; *also* kən'trovəsi‖kən'trɒvəsɪ/ *n* (a) debate or dispute, esp in public or in the media [Latin *controversia*, fr *controversus* disputable, lit., turned opposite, fr *contra* against + *vers* , *vertere* to turn]

controvert /'kontrəˌvuht, ˌ--'-‖'kɒntrəˌvɜːt, ˌ--'-/ *vt* to deny or dispute – fml – **controverter** *n*, **controvertible** *adj*

contumacious /ˌkontyoo'mayshəs‖ˌkɒntjʊ'meɪʃəs/ *adj* stubbornly disobedient; rebellious – fml – **contumaciously** *adv*, **contumacy** *n*

contumely /kon'tyoohmili, 'kontyoomili‖kɒn'tjuːmɪlɪ, 'kɒntjʊmɪlɪ/ *n* abusive and contemptuous language or treatment – fml – **contumelious** *adj*, **contumeliously** *adv*

contuse /kən'tyoohz‖kən'tjuːz/ *vt* to bruise (tissue) – **contusion** *n*

conundrum /kə'nundrəm‖kə'nʌndrəm/ *n* **1** a riddle; *esp* one whose answer is or involves a pun **2** an intricate and difficult problem

conurbation /ˌkonuh'baysh(ə)n‖ˌkɒnɜː'beɪʃ(ə)n/ *n* a grouping of several previously separate towns to form 1 large community

convalesce /ˌkonvə'les‖ˌkɒnvə'les/ *vi* to recover gradually after sickness or weakness – **convalescence** *n*, **convalescent** *adj or n*

convection /kən'veksh(ə)n‖kən'vekʃ(ə)n/ *n* (the transfer of heat by) the circulatory motion that occurs in a gas or liquid at a nonuniform temperature owing to the variation of density with temperature – **convect** *vb*, **convectional** *adj*, **convective** *adj*

convector /kən'vektə‖kən'vektə/ *n* a heating unit from which heated air circulates by convection

convene /kən'veen‖kən'viːn/ *vi* to come together in a body ~ *vt* **1** to summon before a tribunal **2** to cause to assemble

convenience /kən'veenyəns, -ni·əns‖kən'viːnjəns, -nɪəns/ *n* **1** fitness or suitability **2** an appliance, device, or service conducive to comfort **3** a suitable time; an opportunity <*at your earliest* ~> **4** personal comfort or advantage **5** *Br* PUBLIC CONVENIENCE

convenient /kən'veenyənt, -ni·ənt‖kən'viːnjənt, -nɪənt/ *adj* **1** suited to personal comfort or to easy use **2** suited to a particular situation **3** near at hand; easily accessible – **conveniently** *adv*

convent /ˈkonv(ə)nt, -vent‖ˈkɒnv(ə)nt, -vent/ *n* a local community or house of a religious order or congregation; *esp* an establishment of nuns

conventicle /kənˈventikl‖kənˈventɪkl/ *n* **1** an (irregular or unlawful) assembly or meeting **2** a (clandestine) assembly for religious worship

convention /kənˈvensh(ə)n‖kənˈvenʃ(ə)n/ *n* **1a** an agreement or contract, esp between states or parties **b** an agreement between enemies (e g concerning the exchange of prisoners) **2** a generally agreed principle or practice **3** an assembly **4a** (an) accepted social custom or practice **b** an established artistic technique or practice **c** an agreed system of bidding or playing that conveys information between partners in bridge or another card game

conventional /kənˈvensh(ə)nl‖kənˈvenʃ(ə)nl/ *adj* **1a** conforming to or sanctioned by convention **b** lacking originality or individuality **2** *of warfare* not using atom or hydrogen bombs – **conventionalism** *n*, **conventionalist** *n*, **conventionalize** *vt*, **conventionally** *adv*, **conventionality** *n*

converge /kənˈvuhj‖kənˈvɜːdʒ/ *vi* **1** to move together towards a common point; meet **2** to come together in a common interest or focus ~*vt* to cause to converge – **convergent** *adj*, **convergence** *n*

conversant /kənˈvuhs(ə)nt‖kənˈvɜːs(ə)nt/ *adj* having knowledge or experience; familiar *with* – **conversantly** *adv*

conversation /ˌkonvəˈsaysh(ə)n‖ˌkɒnvəˈseɪʃ(ə)n/ *n* **1** (an instance of) informal verbal exchange of feelings, opinions, or ideas **2** an exchange similar to conversation; *esp* real-time interaction with a computer, esp through a keyboard – **conversational** *adj*, **conversationally** *adv*

conversationalist /ˌkonvəˈsaysh(ə)nl·ist‖ˌkɒnvəˈseɪʃ(ə)nlɪst/ *n* one who converses a great deal or who excels in conversation

conversazione /ˌkonvəsatsiˈohni‖ˌkɒnvəsætsɪˈəʊnɪ/ *n, pl* **conversaziones** /-neez‖-niːz/, **conversazioni** /-ni‖-nɪ/ a meeting for informal discussion of intellectual or cultural matters

[1]**converse** /kənˈvuhs‖kənˈvɜːs/ *vi* **1** to exchange thoughts and opinions in speech; talk **2** to carry on an exchange similar to a conversation; *esp* to interact with a computer

[2]**converse** /ˈkonˌvuhs‖ˈkɒnˌvɜːs/ *n* conversation – fml

[3]**converse** /ˈkonˌvuhs‖ˈkɒnˌvɜːs/ *adj* reversed in order, relation, or action; opposite – **conversely** *adv*

[4]**converse** /ˈkonˌvuhs‖ˈkɒnˌvɜːs/ *n* sthg opposite to another

conversion /kənˈvuhsh(ə)n‖kənˈvɜːʃ(ə)n/ *n* **1** converting or being converted **2** (an experience associated with) a definite and decisive adoption of a religious faith **3** sthg converted from one use to another **4** the alteration of a building to a different purpose; *also* a building so altered **5** (the score resulting from) an opportunity to kick a goal awarded to the scoring team after a try in rugby – **conversional** *adj*

[1]**convert** /kənˈvuht‖kənˈvɜːt/ *vt* **1a** to win over from one persuasion or party to another **b** to bring about a religious conversion in **2a** to alter the physical or chemical nature or properties of, esp in manufacturing **b** to change from one form or function to another; *esp* to make (structural) alterations to (a building or part of a building) **c** to exchange for an equivalent **3** to complete (a try) in rugby by successfully kicking a conversion ~*vi* to undergo conversion – **converter** *n*

[2]**convert** /ˈkonvuht‖ˈkɒnvɜːt/ *n* a person who has experienced an esp religious conversion

[1]**convertible** /kənˈvuhtəbl‖kənˈvɜːtəbl/ *adj* **1** capable of being converted **2** *of a motor vehicle* having a top that may be lowered or removed **3** capable of being exchanged for a specified equivalent (e g another currency) – **convertibleness** *n*, **convertibly** *adv*

[2]**convertible** *n* a convertible motor car

convex /ˌkonˈveks‖ˌkɒnˈveks; *not attrib* kənˈveks‖kənˈveks/ *adj* curved or rounded outwards like the outside of a bowl – **convexly** *adv*

convexity /kənˈveksəti‖kənˈveksətɪ/ *n* a convex line, surface, or part

convey /kənˈvay‖kənˈveɪ/ *vt* **1** to take or carry from one place to another **2** to impart or communicate (e g feelings or ideas) **3** to transmit, transfer; *specif* to transfer (property or the rights to property) to another

conveyance /kənˈvayəns‖kənˈveɪəns/ *n* **1** a document by which rights to property are transferred **2** a means of transport; a vehicle

conveyancing /kənˈvayənsing‖kənˈveɪənsɪŋ/ *n* the act or business of transferring rights to property – **conveyancer** *n*

conveyer, conveyor /kənˈvayə‖kənˈveɪə/ *n* a mechanical apparatus for carrying articles or bulk material (e g by an endless moving belt)

[1]**convict** /kənˈvikt‖kənˈvɪkt/ *vt* **1** to find or prove to be guilty **2** to convince of error or sinfulness

[2]**convict** /ˈkonvikt‖ˈkɒnvɪkt/ *n* a person serving a (long-term) prison sentence

conviction /kənˈviksh(ə)n‖kənˈvɪkʃ(ə)n/ *n* **1** convicting or being convicted, esp in judicial proceedings **2a** a strong persuasion or belief **b** the state of being convinced

convince /kənˈvins‖kənˈvɪns/ *vt* to cause to believe; persuade

convincing /kənˈvinsing‖kənˈvɪnsɪŋ/ *adj* having the power to overcome doubt or disbelief; plausible – **convincingly** *adv*, **convincingness** *n*

convivial /kənˈvivi·əl‖kənˈvɪvɪəl/ *adj* relating to or fond of eating, drinking, and good company – **convivially** *adv*, **conviviality** *n*

convocation /ˌkonvəˈkaysh(ə)n, -voh-‖ˌkɒnvəˈkeɪʃ(ə)n, -vəʊ-/ *n* **1** an assembly of people called together: e g **1a** either of the 2 provincial assemblies of bishops and representative clergy of the Church of England **b** a ceremonial assembly of graduates of a college or university **2** the act of calling together – **convocational** *adj*

convoke /kənˈvohk‖kənˈvəʊk/ *vt* to call together to a formal meeting

convoluted /ˌkonvəˈloohtid‖ˌkɒnvəˈluːtɪd/ *adj* **1** having convolutions **2** involved, intricate <*a ~ argument*>

convolution /ˌkonvəˈloohsh(ə)n‖ˌkɒnvəˈluːʃ-

(ə)n/ *n* **1** any of the irregular ridges on the surface of the brain, esp of the cerebrum of higher mammals **2** sthg intricate or complicated – **convolutional** *adj*

convolvulus /kən'volvyooləs‖kən'vɒlvjʊləs/ *n, pl* **convolvuluses, convolvuli** /-lie‖-laɪ/ any of a genus of usu twining plants (e g bindweed)

[1]**convoy** /'konvoy‖'kɒnvɔɪ/ *vt* to accompany or escort, esp for protection

[2]**convoy** *n* **1** convoying or being convoyed **2** *sing or pl in constr* a group of ships, military vehicles, etc moving together, esp with a protective escort; *also* such an escort

convulse /kən'vuls‖kən'vʌls/ *vt* **1** to shake or agitate violently, esp (as if) with irregular spasms **2** to cause to laugh helplessly

convulsion /kən'vulsh(ə)n‖kən'vʌlʃ(ə)n/ *n* **1** an abnormal violent and involuntary contraction or series of contractions of the muscles **2a** a violent disturbance **b** an uncontrolled fit; a paroxysm – **convulsive** *adj*, **convulsively** *adv*

cony, coney /'kohni‖'kəʊnɪ/ *n* **1** a rabbit **2** rabbit fur

[1]**coo** /kooh‖ku:/ *vi* **cooed, coo'd 1** to make (a sound similar to) the low soft cry characteristic of a dove or pigeon **2** to talk lovingly or appreciatively – **coo** *n*

[2]**coo** *interj, Br* – used to express surprise; infml

[1]**cook** /kook‖kʊk/ *n* sby who prepares food for eating

[2]**cook** *vi* **1** to prepare food for eating, esp by subjection to heat **2** to undergo the process of being cooked <*the rice is* ~ing *now*> **3** to occur, happen – infml <*what's* ~ing?> ~ *vt* **1** to prepare (e g food) for eating by a heating process **2** to subject to the action of heat or fire – **cook someone's goose** to ruin sby irretrievably – **cook the books** to falsify financial accounts in order to deceive

cooker /'kookə‖'kʊkə/ *n* **1** an apparatus, appliance, etc for cooking; *esp* one typically consisting of an oven, hot plates or rings, and a grill fixed in position **2** a variety, esp of fruit, not usu eaten raw

cookery /'kook(ə)ri‖'kʊk(ə)rɪ/ *n* the art or practice of cooking

'cookery ˌbook *n* a book of recipes and instructions for preparing and cooking food

'cookˌhouse /-ˌhows‖-ˌhaʊs/ *n* a kitchen set up outdoors, at a campsite, or on board ship

cookie, cooky /'kooki‖'kʊkɪ/ *n* **1a** *Scot* a plain bun **b** *NAm* a sweet flat or slightly leavened biscuit **2** *chiefly NAm* a person, esp of a specified type – infml <*a tough* ~> [Dutch *koekje* small cake, fr *koek* cake]

cooking /'kooking‖'kʊkɪŋ/ *adj* suitable for or used in cooking

'cook-ˌoff *n* accidental ignition of a cartridge in the chamber of a gun, caused by heat generated by frequent firing of the weapon

'cookˌout /-ˌowt‖-ˌaʊt/ *n, chiefly NAm* (the meal eaten at) an outing at which food is cooked and served in the open

cook up *vt* to concoct, improvise – infml

[1]**cool** /koohl‖ku:l/ *adj* **1** moderately cold; lacking in warmth **2a** dispassionately calm and self-controlled **b** lacking friendliness or enthusiasm **c** of or being an understated, restrained, and melodic style of jazz **3** disrespectful, impudent <*a* ~ *reply*> **4** bringing or suggesting relief from heat <*a* ~ *dress*> **5** *of a colour* producing an impression of being cool; *specif* in the range blue to green **6** showing sophistication by a restrained or detached manner **7** – used as an intensive; infml <*paid a* ~ *million for it*> **8** very good; excellent – slang – **coolish** *adj*, **coolly** *also* **cooly** *adv*, **coolness** *n*

[2]**cool** *vi* **1** to become cool; lose heat or warmth **2** to lose enthusiasm or passion ~ *vt* **1** to make cool; impart a feeling of coolness to – often + *off* or *down* **2** to moderate the excitement, force, or activity of – **cool it** to become calm or quiet; relax – infml – **cool one's heels** to wait or be kept waiting for a long time, esp (as if) from disdain or discourtesy

[3]**cool** *n* **1** a cool atmosphere or place **2** poise, composure – infml <*don't lose your* ~>

[4]**cool** *adv* in a casual and nonchalant manner – infml <*play it* ~>

coolant /'koohlənt‖'ku:lənt/ *n* a liquid or gas used in cooling, esp in an engine

cool down *vi* to allow a violent emotion (e g rage) to pass

cooler /'koohlə‖'ku:lə/ *n* **1a** a container for cooling liquids **b** *NAm* a refrigerator **2** a prison cell – slang

ˌcool'headed /-'hedid‖-'hedɪd/ *adj* not easily excited

coolie /'koohli‖'ku:lɪ/ *n* an unskilled labourer or porter, usu in or from the Far East, hired for low or subsistence wages

coon /koohn‖ku:n/ *n* **1** *chiefly NAm* a raccoon **2** a Negro – derog

[1]**coop** /koohp‖ku:p/ *n* **1** a cage or small enclosure or building, esp for housing poultry **2** a confined space

[2]**coop** *vt* **1** to confine in a restricted space – usu + *up* **2** to place or keep in a coop – often + *up*

co-op /'koh ˌop‖'kəʊ ˌɒp/ *n* a cooperative

cooper /'koohpə‖'ku:pə/ *n* a maker or repairer of barrels, casks, etc – **cooper** *vb*, **cooperage** *n*

cooperate /koh'opərayt‖kəʊ'ɒpəreɪt/ *vi* to act or work with another or others for a common purpose – **cooperator** *n*

cooperation /kohˌopə'raysh(ə)n‖kəʊˌɒpə'reɪʃ(ə)n/ *n* **1** a common effort **2** association for common benefit

[1]**cooperative** /koh'op(ə)rətiv‖kəʊ'ɒp(ə)rətɪv/ *adj* **1** showing cooperation or a willingness to work with others **2** of, or organized as, a cooperative – **cooperatively** *adv*, **cooperativeness** *n*

[2]**cooperative** *n* an enterprise (e g a shop) or organization (e g a society) owned by and operated for the benefit of those using its services

co-opt /ˌkoh 'opt‖ˌkəʊ 'ɒpt/ *vt* **1** to choose or elect as a member; *specif, of a committee* to draft onto itself as an additional member **2** to gain the participation or services of; assimilate – **co-optation** *n*, **co-optative** *adj*, **co-option** *n*, **co-optive** *adj*

[1]**coordinate** /koh'awd(ə)nət, -di-‖kəʊ'ɔ:d(ə)nət, -dɪ-/ *adj* **1** equal in rank, quality, or significance **2** relating to or marked by coordination – **coordinately** *adv*, **coordinateness** *n*

[2]**coordinate** *n* **1** any of a set of numbers used in specifying the location of a point on a line, on

a surface, or in space **2** *pl* outer garments, usu separates, in harmonizing colours, materials, and pattern

[3]**coordinate** /koh'awd(ə)nayt, -di-||kəʊ'ɔːd-(ə)neɪt, -dɪ-/ *vt* to combine in a common action; harmonize ~*vi* to be or become coordinate, esp so as to act together harmoniously – **coordination** *n*, **coordinative** *adj*, **coordinator** *n*

coot /kooht||kuːt/ *n* **1** any of various slaty-black water birds of the rail family that somewhat resemble ducks **2** a foolish person – infml

[1]**cop** /kop||kɒp/ *vt* **-pp-** to get hold of; catch; *specif*, *Br* to arrest – slang – **cop it** *Br* to be in serious trouble – slang

[2]**cop** *n*, *Br* a capture, arrest – esp in *a fair cop*; slang – **not much cop** *chiefly Br* fairly bad; worthless – slang

[3]**cop** *n* a policeman – infml

[1]**cope** /kohp||kəʊp/ *n* a long ecclesiastical vestment resembling a cape, worn on special occasions (e g processions)

[2]**cope** *vt* to supply or cover with a cope or coping

[3]**cope** *vi* to deal with a problem or task effectively – usu + *with*

copeck /'kohpek||'kəʊpek/ *n* a kopeck

Copernican /koh'puhnikən, kə'puh-||kəʊ-'pɜːnɪkən, kə'pɜː-/ *adj* of Copernicus or the belief that the earth rotates daily on its axis and the planets revolve in orbits round the sun

copier /'kopi·ə||'kɒpɪə/ *n* a machine for making copies, esp by photocopying or xeroxing

'**co-ˌpilot** /koh||kəʊ/ *n* a qualified aircraft pilot who assists or relieves the pilot but is not in command

coping /'kohping||'kəʊpɪŋ/ *n* the final, usu sloping, course of brick, stone, etc on the top of a wall

copious /'kohpi·əs, 'kohpyəs||'kəʊpɪ·əs, 'kəʊpjəs/ *adj* **1** plentiful, lavish <*a* ~ *harvest*> **2** profuse in words or expression – **copiously** *adv*, **copiousness** *n*

'**cop-ˌout** *n* an act of copping out – infml

cop out *vi* to avoid an unwanted responsibility or commitment – infml

[1]**copper** /'kopə||'kɒpə/ *n* **1** a common reddish metallic element that is ductile and malleable and one of the best conductors of heat and electricity **2** a coin or token made of copper or bronze and usu of low value **3** any of various small butterflies with usu copper-coloured wings **4** *chiefly Br* a large metal vessel used, esp formerly, for boiling clothes [Old English *coper*, fr a prehistoric Germanic word borrowed fr Late Latin *cuprum*, fr Latin (*aes*) *Cyprium*, lit., (metal) from Cyprus] – **coppery** *adj*

[2]**copper** *n* a policeman – infml

ˌ**copper 'beech** *n* a variety of beech with copper-coloured leaves

ˌ**copper-'bottomed** *adj*, *chiefly Br* completely safe; reliable – infml

'**copperˌplate** /-ˌplayt||-ˌpleɪt/ *n* handwriting modelled on engravings in copper and marked by lines of sharply contrasting thickness; *broadly* formal and ornate handwriting

'**copperˌsmith** /-ˌsmith||-ˌsmɪθ/ *n* sby who works in, or produces articles of, copper

coppice /'kopis||'kɒpɪs/ *n* a thicket, grove, etc of small trees (originating mainly from shoots or root suckers rather than seed)

copra /'koprə||'kɒprə/ *n* dried coconut meat yielding coconut oil

copse /kops||kɒps/ *n* a coppice

Copt /kopt||kɒpt/ *n* a member of a people descended from the ancient Egyptians

Coptic /'koptik||'kɒptɪk/ *adj* of the Copts, their Afro-Asiatic liturgical language, or their church – **Coptic** *n*

copula /'kopyoolə||'kɒpjʊlə/ *n* a verb (e g a form of *be* or *seem*) that links a subject and a complement

copulate /'kopyoolayt||'kɒpjʊleɪt/ *vi* to engage in sexual intercourse – **copulation** *n*, **copulatory** *adj*

[1]**copulative** /'kopyoolətiv||'kɒpjʊlətɪv/ *adj* **1a** joining together coordinate words or word groups and expressing addition of their meanings **b** functioning as a copula **2** of copulation – **copulatively** *adv*

[2]**copulative** *n* a copulative word

[1]**copy** /'kopi||'kɒpɪ/ *n* **1** an imitation, transcript, or reproduction of an original work **2** any of a series of esp mechanical reproductions of an original impression **3** (newsworthy) material ready to be printed or photoengraved

[2]**copy** *vt* **1** to make a copy of **2** to model oneself on ~ *vi* **1** to make a copy **2** to undergo copying <*the document did not* ~ *well*>

'**copyˌbook** /-ˌbook||-ˌbʊk/ *n* a book formerly used in teaching penmanship and containing models for imitation

'**copy-ˌbook** *adj*, *Br* completely correct; proper

'**copyˌcat** /-ˌkat||-ˌkæt/ *n* one who slavishly imitates the behaviour or practices of another – used chiefly by children

'**copy-ˌedit** *vb* to prepare (manuscript copy) for printing, esp by correcting errors and specifying style – **copy editor** *n*

'**copyˌhold** /-ˌhohld||-ˌhəʊld/ *n* (land held by) a former type of land tenure in England established by a transcript of the manorial records – **copyholder** *n*

copyist /'kopi·ist||'kɒpɪ·ɪst/ *n* one who makes copies

[1]'**copyˌright** /-ˌriet||-ˌraɪt/ *n* the exclusive legal right to reproduce, publish, and sell a literary, musical, or artistic work – **copyright** *adj*

[2]**copyright** *vt* to secure a copyright on

'**copyˌwriter** /-ˌrietə||-ˌraɪtə/ *n* a writer of advertising or publicity copy

coquetry /'kokətri, 'koh-||'kɒkətrɪ, 'kəʊ-/ *n* flirtatious behaviour or attitude

coquette /ko'ket, kə-, koh-||kɒ'ket, kə-, kəʊ-/ *n* a flirtatious woman – **coquettish** *adj*

cor /kaw||kɔː/ *interj*, *Br* – used to express surprise or incredulity; slang

coracle /'korəkl||'kɒrəkl/ *n* a small (nearly) circular boat of a traditional Welsh or Irish design made by covering a wicker frame with waterproof material [Welsh *corwgl*]

coral /'korəl||'kɒrəl/ *n* **1** (the hard esp red deposit produced as a skeleton chiefly by) a colony of polyps **2** a piece of (red) coral **3a** a bright reddish mass of ovaries (e g of a lobster or scallop) **b** deep orange-pink – **coral** *adj*, **coralloid, coralloidal** *adj*

cor anglais /ˌkawr 'ong·glay, ˌ- -'- ‖ˌkɔːr 'ɒŋgleɪ, ˌ- -'- (*Fr* kɔr ɑ̃glɛ)/ *n* a double-reed woodwind instrument similar to, and with a range a fifth lower than, the oboe [French, English horn]

[1]**corbel** /'kawbl‖'kɔːbl/ *n* a projection from a wall which supports a weight; *esp* one stepped upwards and outwards from a vertical surface

[2]**corbel** *vt* **-ll-** (*NAm* **-l-, -ll-**) to supply with or make into a corbel

[1]**cord** /kawd‖kɔːd/ *n* **1** (a length of) long thin flexible material consisting of several strands (e g of thread or yarn) woven or twisted together **2** a moral, spiritual, or emotional bond **3a** an anatomical structure (e g a nerve) resembling a cord **b** an electric flex **4** a unit of cut wood usu equal to 128ft^3 (about 3.63m^3) **5a** a rib like a cord on a textile **b(1)** a fabric made with such ribs **b(2)** *pl* trousers made of corduroy

[2]**cord** *vt* **1** to provide, bind, or connect with a cord **2** to pile up (wood) in cords – **corder** *n*

cordage /'kawdij‖'kɔːdɪdʒ/ *n* ropes, esp in a ship's rigging

[1]**cordial** /'kawdi·əl‖'kɔːdɪ·əl/ *adj* **1** warmly and genially affable **2** sincerely or deeply felt – **cordially** *adv*, **cordialness, cordiality** *n*

[2]**cordial** *n* **1** a stimulating medicine **2** a nonalcoholic sweetened fruit drink; a fruit syrup

cordite /'kawdiet‖'kɔːdaɪt/ *n* a smokeless explosive for propelling bullets, shells, etc made from nitroglycerine, guncotton, and petroleum jelly

[1]**cordon** /'kawd(ə)n‖'kɔːd(ə)n/ *n* **1a** *sing or pl in constr* a line of troops, police, etc enclosing an area **b** a line or ring of people or objects **2** a plant, esp a fruit-tree, trained to a single stem by pruning off all side shoots

[2]**cordon** *vt* to form a protective or restrictive cordon round – often + *off*

cordon bleu /ˌkawdonh 'bluh ‖ˌkɔːdɑ̃ 'blɜː (*Fr* kɔrdɔ̃ blø)/ *adj or n* (typical of or being) sby with great skill or distinction in (classical French) cookery [French, lit., blue cordon]

corduroy /'kawd(ə)roy‖'kɔːd(ə)rɔɪ/ *n* **1** a durable usu cotton pile fabric with lengthways ribs or wales **2** *chiefly NAm* a road built of logs laid side by side

[1]**core** /kaw‖kɔː/ *n* **1** a central or interior part, usu distinct from an enveloping part: e g **1a** the usu inedible central part of an apple, pineapple, etc **b** the portion of a foundry mould that shapes the interior of a hollow casting **c** a cylindrical portion removed from a mass for inspection; *specif* such a portion of rock got by boring **d(1)** a piece of ferromagnetic material (e g iron) serving to concentrate and intensify the magnetic field resulting from a current in a surrounding coil **d(2)** a tiny ring-shaped piece of magnetic material (e g ferrite) used in computer memories **d(3) core, core memory, core storage** a computer memory consisting of an array of cores strung on fine wires **e** the central part of a planet, esp the earth **f** a conducting wire with its insulation in an electric cable **g** a subject which is central in a course of studies **2** the essential, basic, or central part (e g of an individual, class, or entity)

[2]**core** *vt* to remove a core from – **corer** *n*

co-respondent /ˌkoh ri'spond(ə)nt‖ˌkəʊ rɪ'spɒnd(ə)nt/ *n* a person claimed to have committed adultery with the respondent in a divorce case

corgi /'kawgi‖'kɔːgɪ/ *n, pl* **corgis** (any of) either of 2 varieties of short-legged long-backed dogs with fox-like heads [Welsh, fr *cor* dwarf + *ci* dog]

coriander /ˌkori'andə‖ˌkɒrɪ'ændə/ *n* (the aromatic ripened dried fruits used for flavouring of) an Old World plant of the carrot family

Corinthian /kə'rinthi·ən‖kə'rɪnθɪən/ *adj* **1** (characteristic) of (inhabitants of) Corinth in ancient Greece **2** of the lightest and most ornate of the 3 Greek orders of architecture, characterized esp by a bell-shaped capital decorated with leaves – **Corinthian** *n*

[1]**cork** /kawk‖kɔːk/ *n* **1** the elastic tough outer tissue of a species of oak tree, used esp for stoppers and insulation **2** a usu cork stopper, esp for a bottle **3** an angling float – **corky** *adj*

[2]**cork** *vt* to fit or close with a cork

corkage /'kawkij‖'kɔːkɪdʒ/ *n* a charge made for serving alcoholic drink, esp wine, in a restaurant; *esp* one made for serving drink bought elsewhere

corked /'kawkt‖'kɔːkt/ *adj, of wine* having an unpleasant smell and taste as a result of being kept in a bottle sealed with a leaky cork

corker /'kawkə‖'kɔːkə/ *n* sthg or sby astonishing or superlative – infml; no longer in vogue – **corking** *adj or adv*

[1]**'cork,screw** /-ˌskrooh‖-ˌskruː/ *n* an implement for removing corks from bottles, typically consisting of a pointed spiral piece of metal attached to a handle

[2]**corkscrew** *vt* to twist into a spiral ~*vi* to move in a winding course

[3]**corkscrew** *adj* spiral <*a ~ staircase*>

corm /kawm‖kɔːm/ *n* a rounded thick underground plant stem base with buds and scaly leaves

cormorant /'kawmərənt‖'kɔːmərənt/ *n* a common dark-coloured web-footed European seabird with a long neck, hooked bill, and white throat and cheeks; *also* any of several related seabirds [Middle French, fr Old French *cormareng*, fr *corp* raven + *marenc* of the sea]

[1]**corn** /kawn‖kɔːn/ *n* **1** a small hard seed **2** (the seeds of) the important cereal crop of a particular region (e g wheat and barley in Britain) **3** SWEET CORN **4** sthg corny – infml

[2]**corn** *vt* to preserve or season with salt or brine <*~ed beef*>

[3]**corn** *n* a local hardening and thickening of skin (e g on the top of a toe)

'corn,cob /-ˌkob‖-ˌkɒb/ *n* **1** the axis on which the edible kernels of sweet corn are arranged **2** an ear of sweet corn

'corn ,cockle *n* a poisonous annual purple-flowered plant of the pink family that is a now rare weed of cornfields

'corn,crake /-ˌkrayk‖-ˌkreɪk/ *n* a common Eurasian short-billed rail

cornea /kaw'nee·ə, 'kawni·ə‖kɔː'niːə, 'kɔːnɪə/ *n* the hard transparent part of the coat of the eyeball that covers the iris and pupil – **corneal** *adj*

cornelian /kaw'neelyən‖kɔː'niːljən/ *n* a hard reddish chalcedony used in jewellery

[1]**corner** /'kawnə‖'kɔːnə/ *n* **1a** the point where converging lines, edges, or sides meet; an angle **b** the place of intersection of 2 streets or roads **c** a piece designed to form, mark, or protect a corner (e g of a book) **2** the angular space between meeting lines, edges, or borders: e g **2a** the area of a playing field or court near the intersection of the sideline and the goal line or baseline **b** any of the 4 angles of a boxing ring; *esp* that in which a boxer rests between rounds **3** *sing or pl in constr* a contestant's group of supporters, adherents, etc **4** CORNER KICK; *also* CORNER HIT **5a** a private, secret, or remote place **b** a difficult or embarrassing situation; a position from which escape or retreat is difficult <*talked himself into a tight* ~> **6** control or ownership of enough of the available supply of a commodity or security to permit manipulation of esp the price **7** a point at which significant change occurs – often in *turn a corner* – **cornered** *adj* – **round the corner** imminent; AT HAND

[2]**corner** *vt* **1a** to drive into a corner **b** to catch and hold the attention of, esp so as to force into conversation **2** to get a corner on < ~ *the wheat market*> ~*vi* to turn a corner <*this car* ~*s well*>

-cornered /-kawnəd‖-kɔːnəd/ *comb form* (→ *adj*) **1** having such or so many corners **2** having so many participants or contestants

'corner ˌhit *n* a free hit, esp in hockey, awarded to the attacking side when a member of the defending side has sent the ball over his/her own goal line

'corner ˌkick *n* a free kick in soccer that is taken from the corner of the field and is awarded to the attacking team when a member of the defending team has sent the ball behind his/her own goal line

'cornerˌstone /-ˌstohn‖-ˌstəʊn/ *n* **1** a block of stone forming a part of a corner or angle in a wall; *specif* FOUNDATION STONE **2** the most basic element; a foundation

[1]**cornet** /'kawnit‖'kɔːnɪt/ *n* **1** a valved brass instrument resembling a trumpet but with a shorter tube and less brilliant tone **2** sthg shaped like a cone: e g **2a** a piece of paper twisted for use as a container **b** an ice cream cone – **cornetist, cornettist** *n*

[2]**cornet** *n* the former fifth commissioned officer of a British cavalry troop who carried the standard

'cornˌflakes /-ˌflayks‖-ˌfleɪks/ *n pl* toasted flakes of maize eaten as a breakfast cereal

'cornˌflour /-ˌflowə‖-ˌflaʊə/ *n* a finely ground flour made from maize, rice, etc and used esp as a thickening agent in cooking

'cornˌflower /-ˌflowə‖-ˌflaʊə/ *n* **1** CORN COCKLE **2** a usu bright-blue-flowered European composite plant

cornice /'kawnis‖'kɔːnɪs/ *n* **1a** the ornamental projecting piece that forms the top edge of a building, pillar, etc; *esp* the top projecting part of an entablature **b** an ornamental plaster moulding between wall and ceiling **2** a decorative band of metal or wood used to conceal curtain fixtures **3** an overhanging mass of snow, ice, etc on a mountain – **corniced** *adj*

[1]**Cornish** /'kawnish‖'kɔːnɪʃ/ *adj* (characteristic) of Cornwall

[2]**Cornish** *n* the ancient Celtic language of Cornwall

Cornish pasty *n* a pasty consisting of a circular piece of pastry folded over a savoury filling of meat, potato, and other vegetables

cornucopia /ˌkawnyoo'kohpi·ə‖ˌkɔːnjʊ-'kəʊpɪə/ *n* **1** a goat's horn overflowing with fruit and corn used to symbolize abundance **2** an inexhaustible store; an abundance **3** a vessel shaped like a horn or cone [Late Latin, fr Latin *cornu copiae* horn of plenty] – **cornucopian** *adj*

corny /'kawni‖'kɔːnɪ/ *adj* **1** tiresomely simple and sentimental; trite **2** hackneyed – infml – **cornily** *adv*, **corniness** *n*

corolla /kə'rolə‖kə'rɒlə/ *n* the petals of a flower constituting the inner floral envelope – **corollate** *adj*

corollary /kə'roləri‖kə'rɒlərɪ/ *n* **1** a direct conclusion from a proved proposition **2** sthg that naturally follows or accompanies – **corollary** *adj*

corona /kə'rohnə‖kə'rəʊnə/ *n* **1** the concave moulding on the upper part of a classical cornice **2a** a usu coloured circle of usu diffracted light seen round and close to a luminous celestial body (e g the sun or moon) **b** the tenuous outermost part of the atmosphere of the sun and other stars appearing as a halo round the moon's black disc during a total eclipse of the sun **c** the upper portion of a bodily part (e g a tooth or the skull) **d** a circular appendage on the inner side of the corolla in the daffodil, jonquil, etc **3** a long straight-sided cigar with a roundly blunt sealed mouth end

[1]**coronary** /'korən(ə)ri‖'kɒrən(ə)rɪ/ *adj* (of or being the arteries or veins) of the heart

[2]**coronary** *n* CORONARY THROMBOSIS

ˌcoronary throm'bosis /throm'bohsis‖θrɒm'bəʊsɪs/ *n* the blocking of a coronary artery of the heart by a blood clot, usu causing death of heart muscle tissue

coronation /ˌkorə'naysh(ə)n‖ˌkɒrə'neɪʃ(ə)n/ *n* the act or ceremony of investing a sovereign or his/her consort with the royal crown

coroner /'korənə‖'kɒrənə/ *n* a public officer whose principal duty is to inquire into the cause of any death which there is reason to suppose might not be due to natural causes

coronet /'korənit‖'kɒrənɪt/ *n* **1** a small crown **2** an ornamental wreath or band for the head

corpora /'kawpərə‖'kɔːpərə/ *pl of* CORPUS

[1]**corporal** /'kawp(ə)rəl‖'kɔːp(ə)rəl/ *adj* of or affecting the body [Middle French, fr Latin *corporalis*, fr *corpor-, corpus* body] – **corporality** *n*, **corporally** *adv*

[2]**corporal** *n* a noncommissioned officer in the army, marines, or Royal Air Force, ranking below sergeant [Middle French, alteration of *caporal*, fr Italian *caporale*, fr *capo* head, fr Latin *caput*]

corporate /'kawp(ə)rət‖'kɔːp(ə)rət/ *adj* **1a** INCORPORATED 2 **b** of a company **2** of or formed into a unified body of individuals –

corporately *adv*

corporation /ˌkawpəˈraysh(ə)n‖ˌkɔːpəˈreɪʃ(ə)n/ *n* **1** *sing or pl in constr* the municipal authorities of a town or city **2** a body made up of more than 1 person which is formed and authorized by law to act as a single person with its own legal identity, rights, and duties **3** an association of employers and employees or of members of a profession in a corporate state **4** a potbelly – humor

ˌcorpoˈration ˌtax *n* tax levied on the profits of limited companies

corporeal /kawˈpawri·əl‖kɔːˈpɔːrɪəl/ *adj* having, consisting of, or relating to a physical material body: e g **a** not spiritual **b** not immaterial or intangible; substantial – **corporealness** *n*, **corporeally** *adv*, **corporeality** *n*

corps /kaw‖kɔː/ *n, pl* **corps** /kawz‖kɔːz/ **1** *sing or pl in constr* an army unit usu consisting of 2 or more divisions (organized for a particular purpose) **2** a group of people associated together, esp in a common activity or occupation

corps de ballet /ˌkaw də ˈbalay, ‖ˌkɔː də ˈbæleɪ, *NAm* baˈlay‖bæˈleɪ/ *n, pl* **corps de ballet** /~/ the ensemble of a ballet company

corpse /kawps‖kɔːps/ *n* a dead (human) body

corpulence /ˈkawpyooləns‖ˈkɔːpjʊləns/, **corpulency** /-si‖-sɪ/ *n* the state of being excessively fat; obesity – **corpulent** *adj*

corpus /ˈkawpəs‖ˈkɔːpəs/ *n, pl* **corpora** /ˈkawpərə‖ˈkɔːpərə/ **1** the body or corpse of a human or animal **2** the main body or corporeal substance of a thing; *esp* the main part of a bodily structure or organ <*the ~ of the uterus*> **3a** a collection or body of writings or works (e g of 1 author or artist), esp of a particular kind or on a particular subject **b** a body of spoken and/or written language for linguistic study

corpuscle /ˈkawpəsl, -pu-, kawˈpusl‖ˈkɔːpəsl, -pʌ-, kɔːˈpʌsl/ *n* **1** a minute particle **2a** a living (blood) cell **b** any of various very small multicellular parts of an organism – **corpuscular** *adj*

[1]**corral** /kəˈrahl, ko-, kaw-, -ral‖kəˈrɑːl, kɒ-, kɔː-, -ræl/ *n* **1** a pen or enclosure for confining livestock **2** an enclosure made with wagons for defence of an encampment

[2]**corral** *vt* **-ll-** **1** to enclose in a corral **2** to arrange (wagons) so as to form a corral

[1]**correct** /kəˈrekt‖kəˈrekt/ *vt* **1** to alter or adjust so as to counteract some imperfection or failing **2a** to punish (e g a child) with a view to reforming or improving **b** to point out the faults of <*~ing essays*> – **correctable** *adj*, **corrective** *adj or n*, **correctively** *adv*, **corrector** *n*

[2]**correct** *adj* **1** conforming to an approved or conventional standard **2** true, right – **correctly** *adv*, **correctness** *n*

correction /kəˈreksh(ə)n‖kəˈrekʃ(ə)n/ *n* **1a** an amendment **b** a rebuke, punishment **2a** sthg substituted, esp written, in place of what is wrong **b** a quantity applied by way of correcting (e g in adjusting an instrument) – **correctional** *adj*

[1]**correlate** /ˈkorilayt, -lət‖ˈkɒrɪleɪt, -lət/ *n* either of 2 things so related that one directly implies the other (e g husband and wife) – **correlate** *adj*

[2]**correlate** /ˈkorilayt‖ˈkɒrɪleɪt/ *vi* to have reciprocal or mutual relationship ~ *vt* **1** to establish a mutual or reciprocal relation of **2** to relate so that to each member of one set or series a corresponding member of another is assigned – **correlatable** *adj*

correlation /ˌkoriˈlaysh(ə)n‖ˌkɒrɪˈleɪʃ(ə)n/ *n* **1** a relation of phenomena as invariable accompaniments of each other **2** an interdependence between mathematical variables, esp in statistics – **correlational** *adj*

correlative /kəˈrelətiv, ko-‖kəˈrelətɪv, kɒ-/ *adj* naturally related; corresponding – **correlative** *n*, **correlatively** *adv*

correspond /ˌkoriˈspond‖ˌkɒrɪˈspɒnd/ *vi* **1a** to be in conformity or agreement; suit, match – usu + *to* or *with* **b** to be equivalent or parallel **2** to communicate *with* a person by exchange of letters

correspondence /ˌkoriˈspond(ə)ns‖ˌkɒrɪˈspɒnd(ə)ns/ *n* **1a** the agreement of things with one another **b** a particular similarity **c** an association of 1 or more members of one set with each member of another set **2a** (communication by) letters **b** the news, information, or opinion contributed by a correspondent to a newspaper or periodical

[1]**correspondent** /ˌkoriˈspond(ə)nt‖ˌkɒrɪˈspɒnd(ə)nt/ *adj* **1** corresponding **2** fitting, conforming *USE* + *with* or *to*

[2]**correspondent** *n* **1** one who communicates with another by letter **2** one who has regular commercial relations with another **3** one who contributes news or comment to a publication or radio or television network

corresponding /ˌkoriˈsponding‖ˌkɒrɪˈspɒndɪŋ/ *adj* **1** agreeing in some respect (e g kind, degree, position, or function) **2** related, accompanying – **correspondingly** *adv*

corridor /ˈkoridaw, -də‖ˈkɒrɪdɔː, -də/ *n*, **1** a passage (e g in a building or railway carriage) onto which compartments or rooms open **2** a usu narrow passageway or route: e g **2a** a narrow strip of land through foreign-held territory **b** a restricted path for air traffic **3** a strip of land that by geographical characteristics is distinct from its surroundings

corrie /kori‖kɒrɪ/ *n, chiefly Scot* a steep-sided bowl-like valley in the side of a mountain; a cwm, cirque

corrigendum /ˌkoriˈjendəm‖ˌkɒrɪˈdʒendəm/ *n, pl* **corrigenda** /-də‖-də/ an error in a printed work, shown with its correction on a separate sheet

corroborate /kəˈrobərayt‖kəˈrɒbəreɪt/ *vt* to support with evidence or authority; make more certain – **corroborative, corroboratory** *adj*, **corroborator** *n*, **corroboration** *n*

corroboree /kəˈrobəri‖kəˈrɒbərɪ/ *n* **1** a nocturnal Australian aboriginal festivity with songs and symbolic dances to celebrate important events **2** *Austr* **2a** a noisy festivity **b** a tumult

corrode /kəˈrohd‖kəˈrəʊd/ *vt* **1** to eat or wear (esp metal) away gradually, esp by chemical action **2** to weaken or destroy (as if) by corrosion ~*vi* to undergo corroding – **corrodible** *adj*

corrosion /kəˈrohzh(ə)n‖kəˈrəʊʒ(ə)n/ *n* the action or process of corroding; *also* the product of such a process

corrosive /kə'rohsiv, -ziv‖kə'rəʊsɪv, -zɪv/ *adj* **1** corroding **2** bitingly sarcastic – **corrosive** *n*, **corrosively** *adv*, **corrosiveness** *n*

corrugate /'korəgayt, -roo-‖'kɒrəgeɪt, -rʊ-/ *vb* to shape or become shaped into alternating ridges and grooves; furrow [Latin *corrugare*, fr *com-* with + *ruga* wrinkle] – **corrugation** *n*

[1]**corrupt** /kə'rupt‖kə'rʌpt/ *vt* **1a** to change from good to bad in morals, manners, or actions; *also* to influence by bribery **b** to degrade with unsound principles or moral values **2** to alter from the original or correct form or version ~ *vi* to become corrupt – **corrupter, corruptor** *n*, **corruptible** *adj*, **corruptibly** *adv*, **corruptibility** *n*, **corruptive** *adj*

[2]**corrupt** *adj* **1a** morally degenerate and perverted **b** characterized by bribery **2** having been vitiated by mistakes or changes <*a* ~ *text*> – **corruptly** *adv*, **corruptness** *n*

corruption /kə'rupsh(ə)n‖kə'rʌpʃ(ə)n/ *n* **1** impairment of integrity, virtue, or moral principle **2** decay, decomposition **3** inducement by bribery to do wrong **4** a departure from what is pure or correct

corsage /kaw'sahzh‖kɔː'sɑːʒ/ *n* an arrangement of flowers to be worn by a woman, esp on the bodice

corsair /'kawseə‖'kɔːseə/ *n* a pirate; *esp* a privateer of the Barbary coast

corselette /ˌkawsə'let‖ˌkɔːsə'let/, **corselet** /'kawslit‖'kɔːslɪt/ *n*, a one-piece undergarment combining girdle and bra

[1]**corset** /'kawsit‖'kɔːsɪt/ *n* a boned supporting undergarment for women, extending from beneath the bust to below the hips, and designed to give shape to the figure; *also* a similar garment worn by men and women, esp in cases of injury

[2]**corset** *vt* to restrict closely

cortege /kaw'tayzh‖kɔː'teɪʒ/ *also* **cortège** /kaw'tezh‖kɔː'teʒ/ *n* **1** a train of attendants; a retinue **2** a procession; *esp* a funeral procession [French *cortège*, fr Italian *corteggio*, fr *corte* court, fr Latin *cohort-, cohors* throng]

cortex /'kawteks‖'kɔːteks/ *n, pl* **cortices** /'kawtiseez‖'kɔːtɪsiːz/, **cortexes** **1** a plant bark (e g cinchona) used medicinally **2** the outer part of the kidney, adrenal gland, a hair, etc; *esp* the outer layer of grey matter of the brain **3** the layer of tissue between the inner vascular tissue and the outer epidermal tissue of a green plant

cortisone /'kawtisohn, -zohn‖'kɔːtɪsəʊn, -zəʊn/ *n* a steroid hormone that is produced by the cortex of the adrenal gland

corundum /kə'rundəm‖kə'rʌndəm/ *n* a very hard mineral that consists of aluminium oxide, exists in various colours, and is used as an abrasive and a gemstone

coruscate /'korəskayt‖'kɒrəskeɪt/ *vi* to sparkle, flash <*her* coruscating *wit*> – **coruscation** *n*

corvette /kaw'vet‖kɔː'vet/ *n* **1** a small sailing warship with a flush deck **2** a small highly manoeuvrable armed escort ship

[1]**cos** /kəz‖kəz; *strong* koz‖kɒz/ *conj* because – used in writing to represent a casual or childish pronunciation

[2]**cos** /koz‖kɒz/, **'cos ˌlettuce** *n* a long-leaved variety of lettuce [*Kos, Cos*, Greek island]

cosh /kosh‖kɒʃ/ *vt or n, chiefly Br* (to strike with) a short heavy rod often enclosed in a softer material and used as a hand weapon [perhaps fr Romany *kosh* stick]

cosine /'kohˌsien‖'kəʊˌsaɪn/ *n* the trigonometric function that for an acute angle in a right-angled triangle is the ratio between the side adjacent to the angle and the hypotenuse

[1]**cosmetic** /koz'metik‖kɒz'metɪk/ *n* a cosmetic preparation for external use

[2]**cosmetic** *adj* of or intended to improve beauty (e g of the hair or complexion); *broadly* intended to improve the outward appearance [Greek *kosmētikos*, fr *kosmein* to arrange, order, fr *kosmos* order] – **cosmetically** *adv*, **cosmetology** *n*, **cosmetologist** *n*

cosmetician /ˌkozmi'tish(ə)n‖ˌkɒzmɪ'tɪʃ(ə)n/ *n* sby who is professionally trained in the use of cosmetics

cosmic /'kozmik‖'kɒzmɪk/ *also* **cosmical** /-kl‖-kl/ *adj* **1** of the universe in contrast to the earth alone **2** great in extent, intensity, or comprehensiveness – **cosmically** *adv*

ˌcosmic 'ray *n* a stream of highly energetic radiation reaching the earth's atmosphere from space – usu pl with sing. meaning

cosmogony /koz'mogəni‖kɒz'mɒgənɪ/ *n* (a theory of) the creation or origin of the universe – **cosmogonist** *n*, **cosmogonic, cosmogonical** *adj*

cosmology /koz'moləji‖kɒz'mɒlədʒɪ/ *n* **1** a theoretical account of the nature of the universe **2** astronomy dealing with the origin, structure, and space-time relationships of the universe – **cosmologic, cosmological** *adj*, **cosmologically** *adv*, **cosmologist** *n*

cosmonaut /'kozməˌnawt‖'kɒzməˌnɔːt/ *n* a usu Soviet astronaut

[1]**cosmopolitan** /ˌkozmə'polit(ə)n‖ˌkɒzmə'pɒlɪt(ə)n/ *adj* **1** having worldwide rather than provincial scope or bearing **2** marked by a sophistication that comes from wide and often international experience **3** composed of people, constituents, or elements from many parts of the world **4** *of a plant, animal, etc* found in most parts of the world and under varied ecological conditions [French *cosmopolitain*, deriv of Greek *kosmos* world + *politēs* citizen] – **cosmopolitanism** *n*

[2]**cosmopolitan** *n* a cosmopolitan person or organism

cosmos /'kozmos‖'kɒzmɒs/ *n* **1** an orderly universe **2** a complex and orderly system that is complete in itself

cosset /'kosit‖'kɒsɪt/ *vt* to treat as a pet; pamper

[1]**cost** /kost‖kɒst/ *n* **1a** the price paid or charged for sthg **b** the expenditure (e g of effort or sacrifice) made to achieve an object **2** the loss or penalty incurred in gaining sthg **3** *pl* expenses incurred in litigation – **at all costs** regardless of the price or difficulties – **to one's cost** to one's disadvantage or loss

[2]**cost** *vb* **cost,** (*vt* 2) **costed** *vi* **1** to require a specified expenditure <*the best goods* ~ *more*> **2** to require the specified effort, suffering, or loss ~ *vt* **1** to cause to pay, suffer, or lose <*frequent*

absences ~ *him his job*> <*your suggestion would* ~ *us too much time*> **2** to estimate or set the cost of

'co-ˌstar /koh‖kəʊ/ *n* a star who has equal billing with another leading performer in a film or play – **co-star** *vb*

costermonger /'kostəˌmung·gə‖'kɒstə-ˌmʌŋgə/ *n, Br* a seller of articles, esp fruit or vegetables, from a street barrow or stall [alteration of obs *costardmonger*, fr *costard* large apple + *monger* trader]

costive /'kostiv‖'kɒstɪv/ *adj* affected with or causing constipation – **costively** *adv*, **costiveness** *n*

costly /'kostli‖'kɒstlɪ/ *adj* **1** valuable, expensive **2** made at great expense or with considerable sacrifice – **costliness** *n*

ˌcost of 'living *n* the cost of purchasing those goods and services which are included in an accepted standard level of consumption

[1]**costume** /'kostyoohm, 'kostyoom‖'kɒstju:m, 'kɒstjʊm/ *n* **1** a distinctive fashion in coiffure, jewellery, and apparel of a period, country, class, or group **2** a set of garments suitable for a specified occasion, activity, or season **3** a set of garments belonging to a specific time, place or, character, worn in order to assume a particular role (e g in a play or at a fancy-dress party) – **costumey** *adj*

[2]**costume** *vt* **1** to provide with a costume **2** to design costumes for <~ *a play*>

ˌcostume 'jewellery *n* inexpensive jewellery typically worn attached to clothing rather than on the body

costumier /ko'styoohmi·ə‖kɒ'stju:mɪə/, **costumer** /'kostyoohmə, -yoo-, ko'styoohmə‖'kɒstju:mə, -jʊ-, kɒ'stju:mə/ *n* sby who deals in or makes costumes (e g for theatrical productions)

[1]**cosy,** *NAm chiefly* **cozy** /'kohzi‖'kəʊzɪ/ *adj* **1** enjoying or affording warmth and ease; snug **2a** marked by the intimacy of the family or a close group **b** self-satisfied, complacent – **cosily** *adv*

[2]**cosy,** *NAm chiefly* **cozy** *n* a covering, esp for a teapot, designed to keep the contents hot

[1]**cot** /kot‖kɒt/ *n* a small house; a cottage – poetic

[2]**cot** *n* **1** a lightweight bedstead **2** a small bed with high enclosing sides, esp for a child **3** *chiefly NAm* CAMP BED [Hindi *khāṭ* bedstead, fr Sanskrit *khaṭvā*]

cotangent /koh'tanj(ə)nt, '-ˌ--‖kəʊ'tændʒ(ə)nt, '-ˌ--/ *n* the trigonometric function that is the reciprocal of the tangent

cot death *n* the sudden death of a baby, usu while sleeping, from no apparent disease

cote /koht‖kəʊt/ *n* a shed or coop for small domestic animals, esp pigeons

coterie /'kohtəri‖'kəʊtərɪ/ *n* a close group of people with a unifying common interest or purpose

coterminous /koh'tuhminəs‖kəʊ'tɜ:mɪnəs/ *adj* **1** having the same boundaries <~ *states*> **2** coextensive in scope or duration <~ *interests*> – **coterminously** *adv*

cottage /'kotij‖'kɒtɪdʒ/ *n* a small house, esp in the country – **cottager** *n*, **cottagey** *adj*

ˌcottage 'cheese *n* a soft white bland cheese made from the curds of skimmed milk

ˌcottage 'hospital *n, Br* a small hospital without resident doctors

cottage industry *n* an industry whose work force consists of family units working at home with their own equipment

ˌcottage 'pie *n* a shepherd's pie esp made with minced beef

[1]**cotton** /'kot(ə)n‖'kɒt(ə)n/ *n* **1** (a plant producing or grown for) a soft usu white fibrous substance composed of the hairs surrounding the seeds of various tropical plants of the mallow family **2a** fabric made of cotton **b** yarn spun from cotton [Middle French *coton*, fr Arabic *quṭn*]

[2]**cotton** *vi* to come to understand; CATCH ON 2 – usu + *on* or *onto*; infml

'cotton ˌgin *n* a machine for separating the seeds, seed cases, and foreign material from cotton

ˌcotton 'wool *n* **1** raw cotton; *esp* cotton pressed into sheets used esp for lining, cleaning, or as a surgical dressing **2** an overprotected comfortable environment

cotyledon /ˌkoti'leed(ə)n‖ˌkɒtɪ'li:d(ə)n/ *n* **1** a lobule of the placenta of a mammal **2** the first leaf or either of the first pair or whorl of leaves developed by the embryo of a seed plant – **cotyledonal** *adj*, **cotyledonary, cotyledonous** *adj*

[1]**couch** /kowch‖kaʊtʃ/ *vt* **1** to lower to and hold in an attacking position <~ed *his lance*> **2** to treat (a cataract) by displacing the lens of the eye **3** to phrase in a specified manner <~ed *in hostile terms*> – fml ~*vi, of an animal* to lie down to sleep; *also* to lie in ambush

[2]**couch** *n* **1** a piece of furniture for sitting or lying on **1a** with a back and usu armrests **b** with a low back and raised head-end **2** a long upholstered seat with a headrest for patients to lie on during medical examination or psychoanalysis **3** the den of an animal (e g an otter)

couchette /kooh'shet‖ku:'ʃet/ *n* a seat in a railway-carriage compartment that converts into a bunk

'couch ˌgrass /'kowch, 'koohch‖'kaʊtʃ, 'ku:tʃ/ *n* any of several grasses that spread rapidly by long creeping underground stems and are difficult to eradicate

cougar /'koohgə‖'ku:gə/ *n, chiefly NAm* a puma

[1]**cough** /kof‖kɒf/ *vi* **1** to expel air from the lungs suddenly with an explosive noise **2** to make a noise like that of coughing ~*vt* to expel by coughing <~ *up mucus*>

[2]**cough** *n* **1** a condition marked by repeated or frequent coughing **2** an act or sound of coughing

cough up *vb* to produce or hand over (esp money or information) unwillingly – infml

could /kəd‖kəd; *strong* kood‖kʊd/ *verbal auxiliary* **1** *past of* CAN – used in the past <*he found he* ~ *go*>, in the past conditional <*he said he would go if he* ~>, as an alternative to *can* suggesting less force or certainty <*you* ~ *be right*>, as a polite form in the present <~ *you do this for me*>, as an alternative to *might* expressing purpose in the past <*wrote it down so that I* ~ *remember it*>, and as an alternative to *ought* or *should <you ~ at least apologize>* **2** feel impelled to *<I ~ wring her neck>*

couldn't /'koodnt‖'kʊdnt/ could not

coulomb /'kooh,lom, -,lohm‖'ku:,lɒm, -,ləʊm/ *n* the SI unit of electric charge equal to the quantity of electricity transferred by a current of 1 amp in 1 second

coulter /'kohltə‖'kəʊltə/ *n* a blade or sharp disc attached to the beam of a plough that makes a vertical cut in the ground in front of the ploughshare

¹council /'kownsl, -sil‖'kaʊnsl, -sɪl/ *n* **1** an assembly, meeting **2a** *sing or pl in constr* an elected or appointed body with administrative, legislative, or advisory powers **b** a locally-elected body having power over a parish, district, county, etc

²council *adj* **1** used by a council *<a ~ chamber>* **2** *Br* provided, maintained, or operated by local government *<~ flats>*

councillor /'kowns(ə)lə, -silə‖'kaʊns(ə)lə, -sɪlə/, *NAm also* **councilor** *n* a member of a council

¹counsel /'kownsl‖'kaʊnsl/ *n, pl* **counsels**, *(4)* **counsel** **1** advice **2** deliberation, consultation **3** thoughts or intentions – chiefly in *keep one's own counsel* **4a** a barrister engaged in the trial of a case in court **b** a lawyer appointed to advise a client

²counsel *vt* **-ll-** (*NAm* **-l, -ll-**) to advise

counsellor, *NAm chiefly* **counselor** /'kownsl·ə‖'kaʊnslə/ *n* **1** an adviser **2** *NAm* a lawyer; *specif* a counsel

¹count /kownt‖kaʊnt/ *vt* **1a** to reckon or name by units or groups so as to find the total number of units involved – often + *up* **b** to name the numbers in order up to and including **c** to include in a tallying and reckoning *<about 100 copies if you ~ the damaged ones>* **2** to consider *<~ yourself lucky>* **3** to include or exclude (as if) by counting *<~ me in>* *~ vi* **1a** to name the numbers in order by units or groups *<~ in tens>* **b** to count the units in a group **2** to rely *on* or *upon* sby or sthg **3** to have value or significance *<these are the men who really ~>* – **countable** *adj*

²count *n* **1a** the action or process of counting **b** a total obtained by counting **2a** an allegation in an indictment *<guilty on all ~s>* **b** a specific point under consideration; an issue **3** the total number of individual things in a given unit or sample *<blood ~>* **4** the calling out of the seconds from 1 to 10 when a boxer has been knocked down during which he must rise or be defeated **5** any of various measures of the fineness of a textile yarn **6** *chiefly NAm the* score

³count *n* a European nobleman corresponding in rank to a British earl

'count,down /-,down‖-,daʊn/ *n* a continuous counting backwards to zero of the time remaining before an event, esp the launching of a space vehicle – **count down** *vi*

¹countenance /'kownt(ə)nəns‖'kaʊnt(ə)nəns/ *n* **1** composure *<keep one's ~>* **2** a face; *esp* the face as an indication of mood, emotion, or character **3** moral support; sanction *USE* fml

²countenance *vt* to extend approval or support to – fml

¹counter /'kowntə‖'kaʊntə/ *n* **1** a small disc of metal, plastic, etc used in counting or in games **2** sthg of value in bargaining; an asset **3** a level surface (e g a table) over which transactions are conducted or food is served or on which goods are displayed – **over the counter** without a prescription – **under the counter** by surreptitious means; in an illicit and private manner

²counter *n* a device for indicating a number or amount

³counter *vt* **1** to act in opposition to; oppose **2** to nullify the effects of; offset *~vi* to meet attacks or arguments with defensive or retaliatory steps

⁴counter *adv* in an opposite, contrary, or wrong direction

⁵counter *n* **1** the contrary, opposite **2** an overhanging stern of a vessel **3a** the (blow resulting from the) making of an attack while parrying (e g in boxing or fencing) **b** an agency or force that offsets; a check

⁶counter *adj* **1** marked by or tending towards an opposite direction or effect **2** showing opposition, hostility, or antipathy

counter- *prefix* **1a** contrary; in the opposite direction <counter*march*> **b** opposing; retaliatory <counter*offensive*> **2** complementary; corresponding <counter*part*> **3** duplicate; substitute <counter*foil*>

counteract /,kowntə'rakt‖,kaʊntə'rækt/ *vt* to lessen or neutralize the usu ill effects of by an opposing action – **counteraction** *n*, **counteractive** *adj*

,counterat'tack /-ə'tak‖-ə'tæk/ *vb* to make an attack (against) in reply to an enemy's attack – **counterattack** *n*

'counterat,traction /-ə,traksh(ə)n‖-ə,trækʃ(ə)n/ *n* an attraction that competes with another

¹'counter,balance /-,baləns‖-,bæləns/ *n* **1** a weight that balances another **2** a force or influence that offsets or checks an opposing force

²,counter'balance *vt* to oppose or balance with an equal weight or force

'counter,blast /-,blahst‖-,blɑ:st/ *n* an energetic and often vociferous reaction or response

'counter,claim /-,klaym‖-,kleɪm/ *n* an opposing claim, esp in law – **counterclaim** *vi*

,counter'clockwise /-'klokwiez‖-'klɒkwaɪz/ *adj or adv, chiefly NAm* anticlockwise

,counter'espionage /-'espi·ənahzh‖-'espɪənɑ:ʒ/ *n* espionage directed towards detecting and thwarting enemy espionage

¹counterfeit /'kowntəfit, -feet‖'kaʊntəfɪt, -fi:t/ *vb* to imitate or copy (sthg) closely, esp with intent to deceive or defraud – **counterfeiter** *n*

²counterfeit *adj* **1** made in imitation of sthg else with intent to deceive or defraud **2** insincere, feigned

³counterfeit *n* **1** a forgery **2** sthg likely to be mistaken for sthg of higher value

'counter,foil /-,foyl‖-,fɔɪl/ *n* a detachable part of a cheque, ticket, etc usu kept as a record or receipt

,counterin'telligence /-in'telij(ə)ns‖-ɪn-

'telɪdʒ(ə)ns/ *n* organized activity of an intelligence service designed to block an enemy's sources of information

[1]**countermand** /ˌkowntə'mahnd, '--ˌ-‖ ˌkaʊntə'mɑːnd, '--ˌ-/ *vt* **1** to revoke (a command) by a contrary order **2** to order back (e g troops) by a superseding contrary order

[2]**countermand** *n* (the giving of) a contrary order revoking an earlier one

'**counterˌmarch** /-ˌmahch‖-ˌmɑːtʃ/ *n* a movement in marching by which a unit of troops reverses direction while keeping the same order – **countermarch** *vi*

'**counterˌmeasure** /-ˌmezhə‖-ˌmeʒə/ *n* a measure designed to counter another action or state of affairs

ˌ**counterof'fensive** /-ə'fensiv‖-ə'fensɪv/ *n* a military offensive undertaken from a previously defensive position

'**counterˌpane** /-ˌpayn‖-ˌpeɪn/ *n* a bedspread [Middle English *countrepointe*, from Middle French *coute pointe*, lit., embroidered quilt]

'**counterˌpart** /-ˌpaht‖-ˌpɑːt/ *n* **1** a duplicate **2** sthg that completes; a complement **3** one having the same function or characteristics as another; an equivalent

[1]'**counterˌpoint** /-ˌpoynt‖-ˌpɔɪnt/ *n* **1a** one or more independent melodies added above or below a given melody **b** the combination of 2 or more independent melodies into a single harmonic texture **2a** a complementing or contrasting item **b** use of contrast or interplay of elements in a work of art

[2]**counterpoint** *vt* **1** to compose or arrange in counterpoint **2** to set off or emphasize by contrast or juxtaposition

'**counterˌpoise** /-ˌpoyz‖-ˌpɔɪz/ *n* **1** a counterbalance **2** a state of balance; equilibrium – **counterpoise** *vt*

ˌ**counterˌrevo'lution** /-ˌrevə'loohsh(ə)n‖-ˌrevə'luːʃ(ə)n/ *n* a revolution directed towards overthrowing the system established by a previous revolution – **counterrevolutionary** *adj or n*, **counterrevolutionist** *n*

[1]'**counterˌsign** /-ˌsien‖-ˌsaɪn/ *n* a password or secret signal given by one wishing to pass a guard

[2]**countersign** *vt* to add one's signature to (a document) as a witness of another signature – **countersignature** *n*

'**counterˌsink** /-ˌsingk‖-ˌsɪŋk/ *vt* **countersunk** /-ˌsungk‖-ˌsʌŋk/ **1** to enlarge (a hole), esp by bevelling, so that the head of a bolt, screw, etc will fit below or level with the surface **2** to set the head of (e g a screw) below or level with the surface

'**counterˌtenor** /-ˌtenə‖-ˌtenə/ *n* (a person with) an adult male singing voice higher than tenor

ˌ**counter'vail** /-'vayl‖-'veɪl/ *vt* to counterbalance, offset

countess /'kowntis, -tes‖'kaʊntɪs, -tes/ *n* **1** the wife or widow of an earl or count **2** a woman having in her own right the rank of an earl or count

countinghouse /'kowntingˌhows‖'kaʊntɪŋ ˌhaʊs/ *n* a building, room, or office used for keeping account books and transacting business

'**countless** /-lis‖-lɪs/ *adj* too numerous to be counted; innumerable

countrified *also* **countryfied** /'kuntrified‖'kʌntrɪfaɪd/ *adj* **1** rural, rustic **2** unsophisticated

country /'kuntri‖'kʌntrɪ/ *n* **1** an indefinite usu extended expanse of land; a region **2a** the land of a person's birth, residence, or citizenship **b** a political state or nation or its territory **3** *sing or pl in constr* **3a** *the* populace **b** *the* electorate <*the government was forced to go to the* ~> **4** rural as opposed to urban areas **5** COUNTRY MUSIC

ˌ**country and 'western** *n* COUNTRY MUSIC

'**country ˌclub** *n* a sporting or social club set in a rural area

ˌ**country 'cousin** *n* one who is unaccustomed to or confused by the bustle and sophistication of city life

ˌ**country 'dance** *n* any of various native or folk dances for several pairs of dancers typically arranged in square or circular figures or in 2 long rows facing a partner

'**countryman** /-mən‖-mən/, *fem* '**country ˌwoman** *n* **1** an inhabitant or native of a specified country **2** a compatriot **3** one living in the country or having country ways

'**country ˌmusic** *n* music derived from or imitating the folk style of the southern USA or the Western cowboy

ˌ**country 'seat** *n* a mansion or estate in the country that is the hereditary property of 1 family

'**countryˌside** /-ˌsied‖-ˌsaɪd/ *n* a rural area

[1]**county** /'kownti‖'kaʊntɪ/ *n* **1a** any of the territorial divisions of Britain and Ireland constituting the chief units for administrative, judicial, and political purposes **b** *sing or pl in constr* the people of a county **2** the largest local government unit in various countries (e g the USA)

[2]**county** *adj* **1** of a county **2** *Br* characteristic of or belonging to the English landed gentry <*a* ~ *accent*>

ˌ**county 'borough** *n* a borough which until 1974 had the local-government powers of a county

ˌ**county 'court** *n, often cap 1st C* a local civil court in England which is presided over by a judge and deals with relatively minor claims

ˌ**county 'town** *n, chiefly Br* a town that is the seat of the government of a county

coup /kooh‖kuː/ *n, pl* **coups** /koohz‖kuːz/ **1** a brilliant, sudden, and usu highly successful stroke or act **2** COUP D'ETAT

coup de grâce /ˌkooh də 'grahs, 'gras ‖ˌkuː də 'grɑːs, 'græs (*Fr* ku də gras)/ *n, pl* **coups de grâce** /~ ~ ~/ **1** a fatal blow or shot administered to end the suffering of a mortally wounded person or animal **2** a decisive finishing stroke [French, lit., stroke of mercy]

ˌ**coup d'é'tat** /day'tah ‖deɪ'tɑː (*Fr* deta)/ *n, pl* **coups d'état** /~ ~/ the violent overthrow of an existing government by a small group [French, lit., stroke of state]

coupé /'koohpay‖'kuːpeɪ; *sense 2 also* koohp‖kuːp/, **coupe** /koohp‖kuːp/ *n* **1** a 4-wheeled horse-drawn carriage for 2 passengers with an outside seat for the driver **2** a closed 2-door motor car with a sloping back

[1]**couple** /ˈkupl‖ˈkʌpl/ *vt* **1** to unite or link <~d *his praise with a request*> **2a** to fasten together; connect **b** to bring (2 electric circuits) into such close proximity as to permit mutual influence **3** to join in marriage ~ *vi* **1** to copulate **2** to join

[2]**couple** *n, pl* **couples, couple 1** *sing or pl in constr* 2 people paired together; *esp* a married or engaged couple **2a** 2 things considered together; a pair **b** an indefinite small number; a few <*a ~ of days ago*> – infml **3** 2 equal and opposite forces that act along parallel lines and cause rotation

[3]**couple** *adj* two – + *a* <*a ~ more drinks*>

couplet /ˈkuplit‖ˈkʌplɪt/ *n* a unit of 2 successive, usu rhyming, lines of verse

coupling /ˈkupling‖ˈkʌplɪŋ/ *n* a device that serves to connect the ends of adjacent parts or objects

coupon /ˈkoohpon‖ˈku:pɒn/ *n* a form handed over in order to obtain an article, service, or accommodation: e g **a** a detachable ticket or certificate that entitles the holder to sthg **b** a voucher given with a purchase that can be exchanged for goods **c** a part of a printed advertisement to be cut off for use as an order form or enquiry form **d** a printed entry form for a competition, esp the football pools

courage /ˈkurij‖ˈkʌrɪdʒ/ *n* mental or moral strength to confront and withstand danger, fear, or difficulty; bravery – **courageous** *adj*, **courageously** *adv*

courgette /kawˈzhet, kooə-‖kɔ:ˈʒet, kʊə-/ *n* (the plant that bears) a variety of small vegetable marrow

courier /ˈkoori·ə‖ˈkʊrɪə/ *n* **1a** a member of a diplomatic service who carries state or embassy papers **b** one who carries secret information, contraband, etc **2** a tourist guide employed by a travel agency

[1]**course** /kaws‖kɔ:s/ *n* **1** the act or action of moving in a path from point to point **2** the path over which sthg moves: e g **2a** a racecourse **b** the direction of travel, usu measured as a clockwise angle from north **c** WATERCOURSE **d** GOLF COURSE **3a** usual procedure or normal action <*the law must take its ~*> **b** a chosen manner of conducting oneself; a plan of action <*our wisest ~ is to retreat*> **c** progression through a series of acts or events or a development or period <*in the ~ of the year*> **4a** a series of educational activities relating to a subject, esp when constituting a curriculum <*a management ~*> **b** a particular medical treatment administered over a designated period **5a** a part of a meal served at one time **b** a row; *esp* a continuous horizontal layer of brick or masonry throughout a wall – **of course 1** as might be expected; naturally **2** admittedly; TO BE SURE

[2]**course** *vt* **1** to hunt or pursue (e g hares) with dogs that follow by sight **2** to follow close upon; pursue ~*vi of a liquid* to run or pass rapidly (as if) along an indicated path <*blood* coursing *through his veins*>

[3]**course** *adv* OF COURSE – infml

courser /ˈkawsə‖ˈkɔ:sə/ *n* **1** any of various African and Asian birds noted for their swift running **2** a swift powerful horse - poetic

[1]**court** /kawt‖kɔ:t/ *n* **1a** the residence or establishment of a dignitary, esp a sovereign **b** *sing or pl in constr* **b(1)** the sovereign and his officers and advisers who are the governing power **b(2)** the family and retinue of a sovereign **c** a reception held by a sovereign **2a** a manor house or large building (e g a block of flats) surrounded by usu enclosed grounds – archaic except in proper names <*Hampton* Court> **b** a space enclosed wholly or partly by a building **c** (a division of) a rectangular space walled or marked off for playing lawn tennis, squash, basketball, etc **d** a yard surrounded by houses, with only 1 opening onto a street **3a** (a session of) an official assembly for the transaction of judicial business **b** *sing or pl in constr* judicial officers in session **4** *sing or pl in constr* an assembly with legislative or administrative powers **5** conduct or attention intended to win favour <*pay ~ to the king*>

[2]**court** *vt* **1** to act so as to invite or provoke <~s *disaster*> **2a** to seek the affections of; woo **b** *of an animal* to perform actions to attract (a mate) **3** to seek to win the favour of ~*vi of a man and woman* to be involved in a relationship that may lead to marriage

ˈ**court** ˌ**card** *n* a king, queen, or jack in a pack of cards [alteration of *coat card*; fr the coats worn by the figures depicted]

courteous /ˈkuhtyəs, -ti·əs, ‖ˈkɜ:tjəs, -tɪəs,*also* ˈkaw-‖ˈkɔ:-/ *adj* showing respect and consideration for others – **courteously** *adv*, **courteousness** *n*

courtesan /ˌkawtiˈzan, ˈ--ˌ-‖ˌkɔ:tɪˈzæn, ˈ--ˌ-/ *n* a prostitute with a courtly, wealthy, or upper-class clientele

[1]**courtesy** /ˈkuhtəsi‖ˈkɜ:təsɪ/ *n* **1** courteous behaviour **2** a courteous act or expression – **by courtesy of** through the kindness, generosity, or permission granted by (a person or organization)

[2]**courtesy** *adj* granted, provided, or performed by way of courtesy <*made a ~ call on the ambassador*>

courthouse /ˈkawtˌhows‖ˈkɔ:tˌhaʊs/ *n, chiefly NAm* a building in which courts of law are regularly held

courtier /ˈkawtyə‖ˈkɔ:tjə/ *n* one in attendance at a royal court

courtly /ˈkawtli‖ˈkɔ:tlɪ/ *adj* of a quality befitting the court; elegant, refined – **courtliness** *n*

[1]ˌ**court-**ˈ**martial** *n, pl* **courts-martial** *also* **court-martials** (a trial by) a court of commissioned officers that tries members of the armed forces

[2]**court-martial** *vt* **-ll-** (*NAm* **-l-**, **-ll-**) to try by court-martial

ˌ**court of in**ˈ**quiry** *n* a board of people appointed to ascertain the causes of an accident, disaster, etc

ˌ**Court of** ˈ**Session** *n* the highest civil court in Scotland

ˈ**court**ˌ**ship** /-ˌship‖-ˌʃɪp/ *n* the act, process, or period of courting

ˈ**court**ˌ**yard** /-ˌyahd‖-ˌjɑ:d/ *n* an open court or enclosure adjacent to a building

couscous /ˈkoohsˌkoohs‖ˈku:sˌku:s/ *n* a N African dish of crushed or coarsely ground wheat steamed and served with meat, vegetables, and spices

cousin /ˈkuzn‖ˈkʌzn/ *n* **1a** a child of one's uncle or aunt **b** a relative descended from one's grandparent or more remote ancestor in a different line **2** – formerly used as a title by a sovereign in addressing a nobleman – **cousinhood** *n*, **cousinship** *n*

couture /ˌkoohˈtyooə‖ˌkuːˈtjʊə/ *n* **1** the business of designing and making fashionable custom-made women's clothing **2** HAUTE COUTURE

couturier /koohˈtyooəri·ə,-ri·ay‖kuː-ˈtjʊərɪə,-rɪeɪ/, *fem* **couturière** /koohˌtyooəriˈeə‖kuːˌtjʊərɪˈeə/ *n* (the proprietor of or designer for) an establishment engaged in couture

[1]**cove** /kohv‖kəʊv/ *n* **1** a small sheltered area; *esp* an inlet or bay **2** a (deep) recess in (the side of) a mountain **3** a concave moulding, esp at the point where a wall meets a ceiling or floor

[2]**cove** *vt* to make in a hollow concave form

[3]**cove** *n, Br* a man, fellow – slang; no longer in vogue

coven /ˈkuvn, ˈkovn‖ˈkʌvn, ˈkɒvn/ *n sing or pl in constr* an assembly or band of witches

[1]**covenant** /ˈkuv(ə)nənt, ˈkov-‖ˈkʌv(ə)nənt, ˈkɒv-/ *n* **1** a solemn agreement **2** a written promise

[2]**covenant** *vb* to promise by or enter into a covenant

Coventry /ˈkov(ə)ntri‖ˈkɒv(ə)ntrɪ; *also* ˈku-‖ˈkʌ-/ *n* a state of ostracism or exclusion – chiefly in *send to Coventry*

[1]**cover** /ˈkuvə‖ˈkʌvə/ *vt* **1a** to guard from attack **b(1)** to have within the range of one's guns **b(2)** to hold within range of an aimed firearm **c(1)** to insure **c(2)** to afford protection against or compensation for **d** to mark (an opponent) in order to obstruct play **e** to make sufficient provision for (a demand or charge) by means of a reserve or deposit <*his balance was insufficient to* ~ *his cheque*> **2a** to hide from sight or knowledge; conceal – usu + *up* **b** to lie or spread over; envelop <*snow* ~ed *the ground*> **3** to lay or spread sthg over **4** to extend thickly or conspicuously over the surface of <~ed *in spots*> **5** to place or set a cover or covering over **6a** *of a male animal* to copulate with (a female animal) **b** to sit on and incubate (eggs) **7** to invest with a large or excessive amount of sthg <~s *himself with glory*> **8** to play a higher-ranking card on (a previously played card) **9** to include, consider, or take in <*this book* ~s *modern physics*> **10a** to have as one's territory or field of activity <*one salesman* ~s *the whole county*> **b** to report news about **11** to pass over; traverse <~ed *5 miles at great speed*> ~ *vi* **1** to conceal sthg illicit, blameworthy, or embarrassing from notice – usu + *up* **2** to act as a substitute or replacement during an absence – chiefly in *cover for someone* – **cover one's tracks** to conceal evidence of one's past actions in order to elude pursuit or investigation – **cover the ground 1** to cover a distance with adequate speed **2** to deal with an assignment or examine a subject thoroughly

[2]**cover** *n* **1** sthg that protects, shelters, or guards: e g **1a** natural shelter for an animal **b(1)** a position affording shelter from attack **b(2)** (the protection offered by) a force supporting a military operation **b(3)** COVERAGE 3a **2** sthg that is placed over or about another thing: **2a** a lid, top **b** (the front or back part of) a binding or jacket of a book **c** an overlay or outer layer (e g for protection) <*a chair* ~> **d** a roof **e** a cloth (e g a blanket) used on a bed <*threw back the* ~s> **f** sthg (e g vegetation or snow) that covers the ground **g** the extent to which clouds obscure the sky **3a** sthg that conceals or obscures <*under* ~ *of darkness*> **b** a masking device; a pretext **4** an envelope or wrapper for postal use <*under separate* ~> **5a** cover-point, extra cover, or a cricket fielding position between them **b** *pl the* fielding positions in cricket that lie between point and mid-off

coverage /ˈkuv(ə)rij‖ˈkʌv(ə)rɪdʒ/ *n* **1** the act or fact of covering **2** inclusion within the scope of discussion or reporting <*news* ~> **3a** the total range of risks covered by the terms of an insurance contract **b** the number or percentage of people reached by a communications medium

ˈ**cover** ˌ**charge** *n* a charge (e g for service) made by a restaurant or nightclub in addition to the charge for food and drink

ˈ**cover** ˌ**girl** *n* an attractive girl whose picture appears on a magazine cover

[1]**covering** /ˈkuv(ə)ring‖ˈkʌv(ə)rɪŋ/ *n* sthg that covers or conceals

[2]**covering** *adj* containing an explanation of an accompanying item <*a* ~ *letter*>

ˈ**coverlet** /-lit‖-lɪt/ *n* a bedspread

ˈ**cover** ˌ**note** *n, Br* a provisional insurance document providing cover between acceptance of a risk and issue of a full policy

ˈ**cover-**ˌ**point** *n* a fielding position in cricket further from the batsman than point and situated between mid-off and point

[1]**covert** /ˈkuvət, -vuht, ˈko-‖ˈkʌvət, -vɜːt, ˈkɒ-/ *adj* not openly shown; secret – **covertly** *adv*, **covertness** *n*

[2]**covert** *n* **1a** a hiding place; a shelter **b** a thicket affording cover for game **2** a feather covering the bases of the wing or tail feathers of a bird

ˈ**cover-**ˌ**up** *n* a device or course of action that conceals sthg (e g sthg illegal)

covet /ˈkovit, ˈku-‖ˈkɒvɪt, ˈkʌ-/ *vt* to desire (what belongs to another) inordinately or culpably

covetous /ˈkovitəs, ˈku-‖ˈkɒvɪtəs, ˈkʌ-/ *adj* showing an inordinate desire for esp another's wealth or possessions – **covetously** *adv*, **covetousness** *n*

covey /ˈkuvi‖ˈkʌvɪ/ *n* **1** a mature bird or pair of birds with a brood of young; *also* a small flock **2** a company, group

[1]**cow** /kow‖kaʊ/ *n* **1** the mature female of cattle or of any animal the male of which is called *bull* **2** a domestic bovine animal regardless of sex or age **3** a woman; *esp* one who is unpleasant **4** *chiefly Austr* a cause of annoyance or difficulty *USE* (*3&4*) vulg – **till the cows come home** FOREVER 1

[2]**cow** *vt* to intimidate with threats or a show of strength

coward /ˈkowəd‖ˈkaʊəd/ *n* one who lacks

courage or resolve [Old French *coart*, fr *coe* tail, fr Latin *cauda*]

cowardice /'kowədis‖'kauədɪs/ *n* lack of courage or resolve

[1]'**cowardly** /-li‖-lɪ/ *adv* in a cowardly manner

[2]**cowardly** *adj* resembling or befitting a coward – **cowardliness** *n*

'**cow,bell** /-,bel‖-,bel/ *n* a bell hung round the neck of a cow to make a sound by which it can be located

'**cow,boy** /-,boy‖-,bɔɪ/, *fem* '**cow,girl** *n* **1** one who tends or drives cattle; *esp* a usu mounted cattle ranch hand in N America **2** one who employs irresponsible, irregular, or unscrupulous methods, esp in business

'**cow,catcher** /-,kachə‖-,kætʃə/ *n, chiefly NAm* an apparatus on the front of a locomotive or tram for removing obstacles from the track

cower /'kowə‖'kauə/ *vi* to crouch down or shrink away (e g in fear) from sthg menacing

'**cow,hand** /-,hand‖-,hænd/ *n* a cowherd or cowboy

'**cow,herd** /-,huhd‖-,hɜːd/ *n* one who tends cows

'**cow,hide** /-,hied‖-,haɪd/ *n* **1** leather made from the hide of a cow **2** *NAm* a coarse leather whip

cowl /kowl‖kaul/ *n* **1a** a hood or long hooded cloak, esp of a monk **b** a draped neckline on a garment resembling a folded-down hood **2a** a chimney covering designed to improve ventilation **b** a cowling – **cowled** *adj*

'**cow,lick** /-,lik‖-,lɪk/ *n* a tuft of hair that sticks up, esp over the forehead

cowling /'kowling‖'kaulɪŋ/ *n* a removable metal covering over an engine, esp in an aircraft

'**cowman** /-mən‖-mən/ *n* a cowherd or cowboy

,**co-'worker** /,koh‖,kəu/ *n* a fellow worker

'**cow,pat** /-,pat‖-,pæt/ *n* a small heap of cow dung

'**cow,pox** /-,poks‖-,pɒks/ *n* a mild disease of the cow that when communicated to humans gives protection against smallpox

cowrie, cowry /'kowri‖'kaurɪ/ *n* any of numerous marine gastropod molluscs with glossy and often brightly coloured shells, formerly used as money in parts of Africa and Asia

'**cow,slip** /-,slip‖-,slɪp/ *n* a common European plant of the primrose family with fragrant yellow or purplish flowers [Old English *cūslyppe*, lit., cow dung, fr *cū* cow + *slypa, slyppe* paste]

cox /koks‖kɒks/ *vb or n* (to) coxswain – **coxless** *adj*

coxcomb /'koks,kohm‖'kɒks,kəum/ *n* a conceited foolish person; a fop

coy /koy‖kɔɪ/ *adj* **1a** (affectedly) shy **b** provocatively playful or coquettish **2** showing reluctance to make a definite commitment or face unpalatable facts – **coyly** *adv*, **coyness** *n*

coyote /'koyoht, -'-, -'ohti, kie'ohti‖'kɔɪəut, -'-, -'əutɪ, kaɪ'əutɪ/ *n*, a small N American wolf

coypu /'koyp(y)ooh‖'kɔɪp(j)uː/ *n*, a S American aquatic rodent with webbed feet

[1]**cozy** /'kohzi‖'kəuzɪ/ *adj, NAm* cosy

[2]**cozy** *n, chiefly NAm* a cosy

[1]**crab** /krab‖kræb/ *n* **1** any of numerous chiefly marine crustaceans usu with the front pair of limbs modified as grasping pincers and a short broad flattened carapace; *also* the flesh of this cooked and eaten as food **2** *pl* infestation with crab lice

[2]**crab** *vb* **-bb-** *vt* **1** to cause to move sideways or in an indirect or diagonal manner **2** to head (an aircraft) by means of the rudder into a crosswind to counteract drift ~*vi* to move sideways indirectly or diagonally

[3]**crab** *n* CRAB APPLE

[4]**crab** *vb* **-bb-** *vt* to make sullen; sour <*old age has* ~bed *his nature*> ~*vi* to carp, grouse <*always* ~s *about the weather*> – infml

[5]**crab** *n* an ill-tempered person – infml

'**crab ,apple** *n* (a tree that bears) a small usu wild sour apple

crabbed /'krabid‖'kræbɪd/ *adj* **1** morose, peevish **2** difficult to read or understand <~ *handwriting*> – **crabbedly** *adv*, **crabbedness** *n*

crabby /'krabi‖'kræbɪ/ *adj* cross, ill-tempered – infml

'**crab ,louse** *n* a sucking louse that infests the pubic region of the human body

'**crab,wise** /-,wiez‖-,waɪz/ *adv* **1** sideways **2** in a sidling or cautiously indirect manner

[1]**crack** /krak‖kræk/ *vi* **1** to make a sudden sharp explosive noise **2a** to break or split apart **b** to develop fissures **3a** to lose control or effectiveness under pressure – often + *up* **b** to fail in tone, volume, etc <*his voice* ~ed> **4** *esp of hydrocarbons* to break up into simpler chemical compounds when heated, usu with a catalyst ~ *vt* **1a** to break so that fissures appear on the surface <~ *a mirror*> **b** to break with a crack <~ *nuts*> **2** to tell (a joke) **3a** to puzzle out and expose, solve, or reveal the mystery of <~ *a code*> **b** to break into <~ *a safe*> **c** to break through (e g a barrier) so as to gain acceptance or recognition **4** to cause to make a sudden sharp noise <~ *one's knuckles*> **5a** to subject (esp heavy hydrocarbons) to cracking, esp to produce petrol **b** to produce (e g petrol) by cracking **6** to open (e g a can or bottle) for drinking – infml

[2]**crack** *n* **1** a sudden sharp loud noise **2a** a line or narrow opening that marks a break; a fissure **b** a narrow opening; a chink **3** a broken tone of the voice **4** a sharp resounding blow **5** a witty remark; a quip – infml **6** an attempt, try *at* – infml

[3]**crack** *adj* of superior quality or ability <*a* ~ *shot*> – infml

'**crack,down** /-,down‖-,daun/ *n* an act or instance of cracking down

crack down *vi* to take regulatory or disciplinary action – usu + *on*

cracked *adj* **1** marked by harshness, dissonance, or failure to sustain a tone <*a* ~ *voice*> **2** mentally disordered; crazy – infml

cracker /'krakə‖'krækə/ *n* **1a** a (folded) usu paper cylinder containing an explosive that is discharged to make a noise **b** a brightly coloured paper and cardboard tube that makes a cracking noise when pulled sharply apart and usu contains a toy, paper hat, or other party item **2** *pl* a nutcracker **3** a thin often savoury biscuit **4** the equipment in which cracking, esp of petroleum, is carried out **5** *Br* sthg or sby exceptional; *esp* an outstandingly attractive girl or woman – infml

ˈcrackers *adj, chiefly Br* mad, crazy – infml

[1]**crackle** /ˈkrakl‖ˈkrækl/ *vi* **1** to make a crackle **2** CRAZE ~ *vt* **1** to crush or crack with a snapping sound **2** CRAZE 1

[2]**crackle** *n* **1** the noise of repeated small cracks or reports **2** a network of fine cracks on an otherwise smooth surface – **crackly** *adj*

crackling /ˈkrakling‖ˈkræklɪŋ/ *n* **1** the crisp skin of roast meat, esp pork **2** the crisp residue left after the rendering of animal fat, esp lard – usu pl with sing. meaning

ˈcrackˌpot /-ˌpot‖-ˌpɒt/ *n* sby with eccentric ideas; a crank – infml – **crackpot** *adj*

ˈcracksman /-mən‖-mən/ *n* a burglar – infml

ˈcrack-ˌup *n* **1** a mental collapse; NERVOUS BREAKDOWN **2** a collapse, breakdown

crack up *vt* to present in (excessively) favourable terms <*wasn't all that it was* cracked up *to be*> – infml ~*vi* to undergo a physical or mental collapse

-cracy /-krəsi‖-krəsɪ/ *comb form* (→ *n*) **1** rule; government <*demo*cracy> **2** powerful or dominant social or political class <*aristo*cracy> **3** state having a (specified) government or ruling class <*merito*cracy>

[1]**cradle** /ˈkraydl‖ˈkreɪdl/ *n* **1a** a baby's bed or cot, usu on rockers **b** a framework of wood or metal used as a support, scaffold, etc **2a** the earliest period of life; infancy **b** a place of origin <~ *of civilization*>

[2]**cradle** *vt* **1** to place or keep (as if) in a cradle **2** to shelter or hold protectively

[1]**craft** /krahft‖krɑːft/ *n, pl* **crafts**, (*5*) **craft** *also* **crafts 1** skill in planning, making, or executing; dexterity – often in combination <*stage*craft> **2** an activity or trade requiring manual dexterity or artistic skill; *broadly* a trade, profession **3** skill in deceiving to gain an end **4** *sing or pl in constr* the members of a trade or trade association **5a** a (small) boat **b** an aircraft **c** a spacecraft

[2]**craft** *vt* to make (as if) using skill and dexterity

ˈcraftsman /-mən‖-mən/, *fem* **ˈcraftsˌwoman** *n* **1** a workman who practises a skilled trade or handicraft **2** one who displays a high degree of manual dexterity or artistic skill – **craftsmanlike** *adj*, **craftsmanship** *n*

crafty /ˈkrahfti‖ˈkrɑːftɪ/ *adj* showing subtlety and guile – **craftily** *adv*, **craftiness** *n*

crag /krag‖kræg/ *n* a steep rugged rock or cliff

craggy /ˈkragi‖ˈkrægɪ/ *adj* rough, rugged <*a ~ face*> – **cragginess** *n*

crake /krayk‖kreɪk/ *n* a (short-billed) rail (e g the corncrake)

cram /kram‖kræm/ *vb* **-mm-** *vt* **1** to pack tight; jam <~ *a suitcase with clothes*> **2** to thrust forcefully **3** to prepare hastily for an examination **4** to eat voraciously; bolt – infml ~ *vi* **1** to study hastily and intensively for an examination **2** to eat greedily or until uncomfortably full – infml

ˌcram-ˈfull *adj* as full as can be

crammer /ˈkramə‖ˈkræmə/ *n, Br* a school or teacher that prepares students intensively for an examination – infml

[1]**cramp** /kramp‖kræmp/ *n* **1** a painful involuntary spasmodic contraction of a muscle **2** *pl* severe abdominal pain

[2]**cramp** *n* **1** a usu metal device bent at the ends and used to hold timbers or blocks of stone together **2** a clamp

[3]**cramp** *vt* **1** to affect with cramp **2a** to confine, restrain **b** to restrain from free expression – esp in *cramp someone's style* **3** to fasten or hold with a clamp

crampon /ˈkrampon‖ˈkræmpɒn/ *n* **1** a hooked mechanical device for lifting heavy objects – usu pl with sing. meaning **2** a metal frame with downward- and forward-pointing spikes that is fixed to the sole of a boot for climbing slopes of ice or hard snow

cranberry /ˈkranb(ə)ri‖ˈkrænb(ə)rɪ/ *n* any of various plants of the heath family; *also* the red acid berry of such plants used in making sauces and jellies

[1]**crane** /krayn‖kreɪn/ *n* **1** any of a family of tall wading birds **2** a machine for moving heavy weights by means of a projecting swinging arm or a hoisting apparatus supported on an overhead track

[2]**crane** *vt* **1** to raise or lift (as if) by a crane **2** to stretch (e g the neck), esp in order to see better ~*vi* to stretch one's neck, esp in order to see better

ˈcrane ˌfly *n* any of numerous long-legged slender two-winged flies that resemble large mosquitoes but do not bite

cranium /ˈkraynyəm, -ni·əm‖ˈkreɪnjəm, -nɪəm/ *n, pl* **craniums, crania** /-nyə, -ni·ə‖-njə, -nɪə/ the skull; *specif* the part that encloses the brain – **cranial** *adj*

[1]**crank** /krangk‖kræŋk/ *n* **1** a part of an axle or shaft bent at right angles by which reciprocating motion is changed into circular motion or vice versa **2** an eccentric person

[2]**crank** *vi* to turn a crank (e g in starting an engine) ~ *vt* **1** to bend into the shape of a crank **2** to provide or fasten with a crank **3a** to move or operate (as if) by a crank **b** to start by use of a crank – often + *up*

ˈcrankˌshaft /-ˌshahft‖-ˌʃɑːft/ *n* a shaft driven by or driving a crank

cranky /ˈkrangki‖ˈkræŋkɪ/ *adj* **1** *of machinery* working erratically; unpredictable **2** ECCENTRIC 2 **3** *NAm* bad-tempered – **crankily** *adv*, **crankiness** *n*

cranny /ˈkrani‖ˈkrænɪ/ *n* a small crack or slit; a chink – **crannied** *adj*

[1]**crap** /krap‖kræp/ *n* **1a** excrement **b** an act of defecation **2** nonsense, rubbish – slang; sometimes used as an interjection *USE* (*1*) vulg

[2]**crap** *vi* **-pp-** to defecate – vulg

crappy /ˈkrapi‖ˈkræpɪ/ *adj* of very poor quality – slang

craps /kraps‖kræps/ *n pl but sing or pl in constr* a gambling game played with 2 dice – **crap** *adj*

crapulous /ˈkrapyooləs‖ˈkræpjʊləs/ *adj* given to, or suffering the effects of, excessive drinking of alcohol [Late Latin *crapulosus*, fr Latin *crapula* drunkenness, fr Greek *kraipalē*]

[1]**crash** /krash‖kræʃ/ *vt* **1a** to break violently and noisily; smash **b** to damage (an aircraft) in landing **c** to damage (a vehicle) by collision **2a**

to cause to make a crashing sound **b** to force (e g one's way) with loud crashing noises **3** to enter without invitation or payment <~ *the party*> – infml **4** to cause (e g a computer system or program) to crash ~ *vi* **1a** to break or go to pieces (as if) with violence and noise **b** to crash an aircraft or vehicle **c** to be involved in a crash **2** to make a crashing noise **3** to move or go (as if) with a crash **4** to spend the night in a (makeshift) place; go to sleep <*can I* ~ *on your floor tonight?*> – sometimes + *out*; slang **5** *esp of a computer system or program* to become (suddenly) completely inoperative

[2]**crash** *n* **1** a loud noise (e g of things smashing) **2** a breaking to pieces (as if) by collision; *also* an instance of crashing <*a plane* ~> **3** a sudden decline or failure (e g of a business)

[3]**crash** *adj* designed to achieve an intended result in the shortest possible time <*a* ~ *diet*>

[4]**crash** *n* a coarse fabric made orig of linen, used for draperies, clothing, etc

'crash ˌbarrier *n* a barrier to prevent vehicles accidentally colliding or leaving the road

'crash-ˌdive *vb* (to cause) to descend or dive steeply and quickly – used esp with reference to an aircraft or submarine – **crashdive** *n*

'crash ˌhelmet *n* a helmet that is worn (e g by motorcyclists) to protect the head in the event of an accident

crashing /'krashing‖'kræʃɪŋ/ *adj* utter, absolute <*a* ~ *bore*>

ˌcrash-'land *vb* to land (an aircraft) under emergency conditions, usu with some damage to the craft – **crash landing** *n*

crass /kras‖kræs/ *adj* **1** insensitive, coarse <~ *behaviour*> **2** deplorably great; complete <~ *stupidity*> – **crassly** *adv*, **crassness** *n*

-crat /-krat‖-kræt/ *comb form* (→ *n*) **1** advocate or partisan of (a specified form of government) <*demo*crat> **2** member of (a specified ruling class) <*pluto*crat> – **-cratic** *comb form* (→ *adj*)

[1]**crate** /krayt‖kreɪt/ *n* **1** a usu wooden framework or box for holding goods (e g fruit, bottles, etc), esp during transit **2** the contents of a crate

[2]**crate** *vt* to pack in a crate

[1]**crater** /'kraytə‖'kreɪtə/ *n* **1** a (bowl-shaped) depression: e g **1a** round the mouth of a volcano **b** formed by the impact of a meteorite **2** a hole in the ground made by an explosion **3** a jar or vase with a wide mouth used in classical antiquity for mixing wine and water

[2]**crater** *vt* to form craters in

cravat /krə'vat‖krə'væt/ *n* a decorative band or scarf worn round the neck, esp by men [French *cravate*, fr *Cravate* Croatian; originally referring to the linen scarves worn by Croatian mercenaries]

crave /krayv‖kreɪv/ *vt* **1** to have a strong or urgent desire for **2** to ask for earnestly; beg – fml ~*vi* to have a strong desire; yearn <~s *after affection*>

craven /'krayv(ə)n‖'kreɪv(ə)n/ *adj* cowardly – **craven** *n*, **cravenly** *adv*, **cravenness** *n*

craving /'krayving‖'kreɪvɪŋ/ *n* a great desire or longing

[1]**crawl** /krawl‖krɔːl/ *vi* **1** to move slowly in a prone position (as if) without the use of limbs **2** to move or progress slowly or laboriously **3** CREEP 3b **4a** to be alive or swarming (as if) with creeping things **b** to have the sensation of insects creeping over one <*the story made her flesh* ~> **5** to behave in a servile manner – infml ~*vt* to move upon (as if) in a creeping manner <*the meanest man who ever* ~ed *the earth*>

[2]**crawl** *n* **1a** crawling **b** slow or laborious motion **2** the fastest swimming stroke, executed lying on the front and consisting of alternating overarm strokes combined with kicks with the legs

crawler /'krawlə‖'krɔːlə/ *n* **1** a vehicle (e g a crane) that travels on endless metal belts **2** a servile person – infml

crayfish /'krayˌfish‖'kreɪˌfɪʃ/ *n* **1** any of numerous freshwater crustaceans resembling the lobster but usu much smaller **2** SPINY LOBSTER [by folk etymology fr Middle French *crevice*, of Germanic origin]

crayon /'krayon, -ən‖'kreɪɒn, -ən/ *vt or n* (to draw or colour with) a stick of coloured chalk or wax used for writing or drawing

[1]**craze** /krayz‖kreɪz/ *vt* **1** to produce minute cracks on the surface or glaze of **2** to make (as if) insane ~*vi* to develop a mesh of fine cracks

[2]**craze** *n* **1** an exaggerated and often short-lived enthusiasm; a fad **2** fine cracks in a surface or coating of glaze, enamel, etc

crazy /'krayzi‖'kreɪzɪ/ *adj* **1** mad, insane **2a** impractical <*a* ~ *idea*> **b** unusual, eccentric **3** extremely enthusiastic *about*; very fond – **crazily** *adv*, **craziness** *n* – **like crazy** to an extreme degree <*everyone dancing* like crazy> – infml

ˌcrazy 'paving *n, Br* a paved surface made up of irregularly shaped paving stones

[1]**creak** /kreek‖kriːk/ *vi* to make a prolonged grating or squeaking noise

[2]**creak** *n* a prolonged rasping, grating, or squeaking noise (e g of an unoiled hinge) – **creaky** *adj*, **creakily** *adv*

[1]**cream** /kreem‖kriːm/ *n* **1** the yellowish part of milk containing butterfat, that forms a surface layer when milk is allowed to stand **2a** a food (e g a sauce or cake filling) prepared with or resembling cream in consistency, richness, etc **b** a biscuit, chocolate, etc filled with (a soft preparation resembling) whipped cream **c** sthg with the consistency of thick cream; *esp* a usu emulsified medicinal or cosmetic preparation **3** the choicest part **4** a pale yellowish white colour – **creamily** *adv*, **creaminess** *n*, **creamy** *adj*

[2]**cream** *vi* **1** to form cream or a surface layer like the cream on milk **2** to break into a creamy froth ~ *vt* **1a** SKIM 1c **b** to take away (the choicest part) – usu + *off* <~ *off the brightest students*> **2** to provide, prepare, or treat with cream or a cream sauce **3** to work or blend to the consistency of cream <~ *butter and sugar*> **4** to cause to form a surface layer of or like cream **5** *NAm* to defeat completely – infml

ˌcream 'cheese *n* a mild white soft unripened cheese made from whole milk enriched with cream

creamer /'kreemə‖'kriːmə/ *n* **1** a device for separating cream from milk **2** a small vessel (e g a jug) for serving cream

creamery /'kreemǝri‖'kri:mǝrɪ/ *n* an establishment where butter and cheese are made or where milk and milk products are prepared or sold

ˌcream of 'tartar /'tahtǝ‖'tɑ:tǝ/ *n* potassium hydrogen tartrate occurring as a white powder and used esp in baking powder

[1]**crease** /krees‖kri:s/ *n* **1** a line or mark made (as if) by folding a pliable substance **2a** an area surrounding the goal in lacrosse, hockey, etc into which an attacking player may not precede the ball or puck **b** the bowling crease, popping crease, or return crease of a cricket pitch – **creaseless** *adj*

[2]**crease** *vt* **1** to make a crease in or on; wrinkle **2** *chiefly Br* **2a** to cause much amusement to – often + *up* **b** to tire out ~*vi* to become creased *USE* (*2*) infml

create /kri'ayt‖krɪ'eɪt/ *vt* **1** to bring into existence **2a** to invest with a new form, office, or rank <*was* ~d *a peer of the realm*> **b** to produce, cause <~d *a disturbance*> **3** to design, invent ~*vi Br* to make a loud fuss about sthg – infml

creation /kri'aysh(ǝ)n‖krɪ'eɪʃ(ǝ)n/ *n* **1** *often cap* the act of bringing the world into ordered existence **2** sthg created: e g **2a** the world **b** creatures singly or collectively **c** an original work of art **d** a product of some minor art or craft (e g dressmaking or cookery) showing unusual flair or imagination – often derog

creative /kri'aytiv‖krɪ'eɪtɪv/ *adj* **1** marked by or requiring the ability or power to create; given to creating **2** having the quality of sthg imaginatively created <*the* ~ *arts*> – **creatively** *adv*, **creativeness** *n*

creator /kri'aytǝ‖krɪ'eɪtǝ/ *n* a person who creates, usu by bringing sthg new or original into being; *esp, cap* GOD 1

creature /'kreechǝ‖'kri:tʃǝ/ *n* **1a** sthg created <~s *of fantasy*> **b** a lower animal <*the* ~s *of the woods*> **2a** an animate being; *esp* a non-human one **b** a human being; a person **3** one who is the servile dependant or tool of another – **creatural** *adj*, **creatureliness** *n*, **creaturely** *adj*

creature comforts *n pl* material things that give bodily comfort

crèche /kresh‖kreʃ/ *n* **1** a representation of the Nativity scene **2** *chiefly Br* a centre where children under school age are looked after while their parents are at work

credence /'kreedǝns‖'kri:dǝns/ *n* acceptance of sthg as true or real

credential /kri'densh(ǝ)l‖krɪ'denʃ(ǝ)l/ *n* sthg, esp a letter, that gives proof of identity, status, or authority – usu pl with sing. meaning

ˌcredi'bility ˌgap /ˌkredǝ'bilǝti‖ˌkredǝ'bɪlǝtɪ/ *n* (a lack of credibility arising from) a discrepancy between what is claimed and what is perceived to be true

credible /'kredǝbl‖'kredǝbl/ *adj* offering reasonable grounds for belief – **credibly** *adv*, **credibility** *n*

[1]**credit** /'kredit‖'kredɪt/ *n* **1a** the balance in a person's favour in an account **b** an amount or sum placed at a person's disposal by a bank and usu to be repaid with interest **c** time given for payment for goods or services provided but not immediately paid for **d** an entry on the right-hand side of an account constituting an addition to a revenue, net worth, or liability account **2** credence **3** influence derived from enjoying the confidence of others; standing **4** a source of honour or repute <*a* ~ *to her parents*> **5** acknowledgment, approval <~ *where* ~ *is due*> **6a** a line, note, or name that acknowledges the source of an item **b** an acknowledgment of a contributor by name that appears at the beginning or end of a film or television programme **7a** recognition that a student has fulfilled a course requirement **b** the passing of an examination at a level well above the minimum though not with distinction – **on credit** with the cost charged to one's account and paid later

[2]**credit** *vt* **1** to believe **2a** to enter on the credit side of an account **b** to place to the credit of <~ *an account*> **3a** to ascribe some usu favourable characteristic to – + *with* <~ *me with some intelligence*> **b** to attribute *to* some person <*they* ~ *the invention to him*>

creditable /'kreditǝbl‖'kredɪtǝbl/ *adj* **1** worthy of esteem or praise **2** *NAm* capable of being attributed *to* – **creditably** *adv*

'credit ˌcard *n* a card provided by a bank, agency, or business allowing the holder to obtain goods and services on credit

creditor /'kreditǝ‖'kredɪtǝ/ *n* one to whom a debt is owed

credo /'kreedoh, 'kray-‖'kri:dǝʊ, 'kreɪ-/ *n, pl* **credos** **1** a creed **2** *cap* a musical setting of the creed in a sung mass

credulity /kri'dyoohlǝti‖krɪ'dju:lǝtɪ/ *n* undue willingness to believe; gullibility

credulous /'kredyoolǝs‖'kredjʊlǝs/ *adj* ready to believe, esp on slight evidence – **credulously** *adv*, **credulousness** *n*

creed /kreed‖kri:d/ *n* **1** a brief conventionalized statement of religious belief; *esp* such a statement said or sung as part of Christian worship **2** a set of fundamental beliefs [Old English *crēda*, fr Latin *credo* I believe (first word of the Apostles' and Nicene Creeds), fr *credere* to believe, trust, entrust] – **creedal** *adj*, **credal** *adj*

creek /kreek‖kri:k/ *n* **1** *chiefly Br* a small narrow inlet of a lake, sea, etc **2** *chiefly NAm & Austr* a brook – **up the creek 1** in trouble – infml **2** wrong, mistaken – infml

creel /kreel‖kri:l/ *n* a wickerwork container (e g for newly caught fish)

[1]**creep** /kreep‖kri:p/ *vi* **crept** /krept‖krept/ **1** to move along with the body prone and close to the ground **2a** to go very slowly **b** to go timidly or cautiously so as to escape notice **c** to enter, advance, or develop gradually or slowly <*a note of irritation* crept *into her voice*> **3a** CRAWL 4b **b** *of a plant* to spread or grow over a surface by clinging with tendrils, roots, etc or rooting at intervals **4** to change shape permanently due to prolonged stress or exposure to high temperatures

[2]**creep** *n* **1** a movement of or like creeping **2** the slow change of dimensions of an object due to prolonged exposure to high temperature or

stress **3** a distressing sensation, esp of apprehension or disgust, like that caused by insects creeping over one's flesh – usu pl with sing. meaning <*gives me the* ~s>; infml **4** *Br* an obnoxious or ingratiatingly servile person – infml

creeper /'kreepə‖'kriːpə/ *n* **1a** a creeping plant **b** a bird (e g a tree creeper) that creeps about on trees or bushes **c** a creeping insect or reptile **2** a grapnel

creepy /'kreepi‖'kriːpɪ/ *adj* producing a sensation of shivery apprehension

ˌcreepy-'crawly /'krawli‖'krɔːlɪ/ *n, Br* a small creeping or scuttling creature (e g a spider) – infml

cremate /kri'mayt‖krɪ'meɪt/ *vt* to reduce (a dead body) to ashes by burning – **cremation** *n*

crematorium /ˌkremə'tawri·əm‖ˌkremə'tɔːrɪəm/ *n, pl* **crematoriums, crematoria** /-ri·ə‖-rɪə/ a place where cremation is carried out

ˌcrème de 'menthe /ˌkrem də 'mont ‖ ˌkrem də 'mɒnt (*Fr* krɛm də mɑ̃ːt)/ *n* a sweet green or white mint-flavoured liqueur [French, lit., cream of mint]

crenellated /'krenəˌlaytid‖'krenəˌleɪtɪd/ *adj* having battlements

creole /'kreeˌohl‖'kriːˌəʊl/ *adj, often cap* of Creoles or their language

Creole *n* **1** a person of European descent in the W Indies or Spanish America **2** a white descendant of early French or Spanish settlers of the Gulf States of the USA **3** a person of mixed French or Spanish and Negro descent **4** *not cap* a language based on 2 or more languages that serves as the native language of its speakers

¹creosote /'kree·əˌsoht‖'kriːəˌsəʊt/ *n* **1** a clear or yellowish oily liquid obtained from wood tar and used as an antiseptic **2** a brownish oily liquid obtained from coal tar and used esp as a wood preservative [German *kreosot*, fr Greek *kreas* flesh + *sōtēr* preserver, fr *sōzein* to preserve, fr *sōs* safe]

²creosote *vt* to treat with creosote

crepe, crêpe /krayp‖kreɪp/ *n* **1** a light crinkled fabric woven from any of various fibres **2** a small very thin pancake – **crepey, crepy** *adj*

ˌcrepe 'paper *n* thin paper with a crinkled or puckered texture

crept /krept‖krept/ *past of* CREEP

crepuscular /kri'puskyoolə‖krɪ'pʌskjʊlə/ *adj* **1** active in the twilight <~ *insects*> **2** of or resembling twilight; dim – fml

¹crescendo /krə'shendoh‖krə'ʃendəʊ/ *n, pl* **crescendos, crescendoes 1** a gradual increase; *esp* a gradual increase in volume in a musical passage **2** a crescendo musical passage [Italian, lit., growing, fr *crescere* to increase, grow] – **crescendo** *vi*

²crescendo *adv or adj* with an increase in volume – used in music

crescent /'krezənt‖'krezənt/ *n* **1** the figure of the moon at any stage between new moon and first quarter or last quarter and the succeeding new moon **2** sthg shaped like a crescent and consisting of a concave and a convex curve

cress /kres‖kres/ *n* any of numerous plants of the mustard family that have mildly pungent leaves and are used in salads and as a garnish

¹crest /krest‖krest/ *n* **1a** a showy tuft or projection on the head of an animal, esp a bird **b** the plume, emblem, etc worn on a knight's helmet **c(1)** a symbol of a family, office, etc that appears as a figure on top of the helmet in a heraldic achievement **c(2)** COAT OF ARMS – not used technically in heraldry **d** the upper muscular ridge of a horse's neck from which the mane grows **2** the ridge or top, esp of a wave, roof, or mountain **3** *the* climax, culmination <*at the* ~ *of his fame*> – **crestless** *adj*

²crest *vt* **1** to provide with a crest; crown **2** to reach the crest of ~*vi of waves* to rise to a crest

crested /'krestid‖'krestɪd/ *adj* **1** having a crest **2** marked or decorated with a crest <~ *crockery*>

crestfallen /'krestˌfawlən‖'krestˌfɔːlən/ *adj* disheartened, dejected

cretaceous /kri'tayshəs‖krɪ'teɪʃəs/ *adj* **1** resembling or containing chalk **2** *cap* of or being the last period of the Mesozoic era – **cretaceous** *n*, **cretaceously** *adv*

cretin /'kretin‖'kretɪn/ *n* sby afflicted with cretinism; *broadly* an imbecile, idiot [French *crétin*, fr French dialect *cretin* Christian, human being, kind of idiot found in the Alps, fr Latin *christianus* Christian] – **cretinous** *adj*

cretinism /'kretiˌniz(ə)m‖'kretɪˌnɪz(ə)m/ *n* (congenital) physical stunting and mental retardation caused by severe deficiency of the thyroid gland in infancy

cretonne /'kreeˌton, kri'ton‖'kriːˌtɒn, krɪ'tɒn/ *n* a strong unglazed cotton or linen cloth used esp for curtains and upholstery [French, fr *Creton*, town in Normandy, France]

crevasse /krə'vas‖krə'væs/ *n* a deep fissure, esp in a glacier

crevice /'krevis‖'krevɪs/ *n* a narrow opening resulting from a split or crack

¹crew /krooh‖kruː/ *chiefly Br past of* CROW

²crew *n sing or pl in constr* **1** a company of men working on 1 job or under 1 foreman **2a** the personnel of a ship or boat (excluding the captain and officers) **b** members of a crew <*the captain and 50* ~> **c** the people who man an aircraft in flight **3** a number of people temporarily associated – infml

³crew *vb* to serve as a member of a crew (on)

'crew ˌcut *n* a very short bristly haircut, esp for a man

¹crib /krib‖krɪb/ *n* **1** a manger for feeding animals **2** an enclosure, esp with barred or slatted sides: e g **2a** a stall for a stabled animal **b** CRADLE 1a **c** a bin for storage **3a** a set of cards contributed to equally by each player in cribbage for the dealer to use in scoring **b** cribbage **4** a literal translation; *esp* one used surreptitiously by students **5** *Br* a building considered with a view to unlawful entry **6** *chiefly NAm* COT 2

²crib *vb* **-bb-** *vt* **1** to confine, cramp **2** to provide with or put into a crib **3** to pilfer, steal; *esp* to plagiarize ~ *vi* **1** to steal, plagiarize **2** to use a crib; cheat – **cribber** *n*

cribbage /'kribij‖'krɪbɪdʒ/ *n* a card game for 2 to 4 players each attempting to form various counting combinations of cards

¹crick /krik‖krɪk/ *n* a painful spasmodic condition of the muscles of the neck, back, etc

[2]**crick** *vt* to cause a crick in (the neck, back, etc)
[1]**cricket** /ˈkrikit‖ˈkrɪkɪt/ *n* a leaping insect noted for the chirping sounds produced by the male
[2]**cricket** *n* a game played with a bat and ball on a large field with 2 wickets near its centre by 2 sides of 11 players each – **cricketer** *n* – **not cricket** against the dictates of fair play; not honourable
crier /ˈkrie·ə‖ˈkraɪə/ *n* an officer who makes announcements in a court
crikey /ˈkrieki‖ˈkraɪkɪ/ *interj, chiefly Br* – used to express surprise; no longer in vogue
crime /kriem‖kraɪm/ *n* **1** (a) violation of law **2** a grave offence, esp against morality **3** criminal activity **4** sthg deplorable, foolish, or disgraceful <*it's a ~ to waste good food*> – infml
[1]**criminal** /ˈkriminl‖ˈkrɪmɪnl/ *adj* **1** involving or being a crime **2** relating to crime or its punishment **3** guilty of crime **4** disgraceful, deplorable – infml – **criminally** *adv*, **criminality** *n*
[2]**criminal** *n* one who has committed or been convicted of a crime
criminology /ˌkrimiˈnoləji‖ˌkrɪmɪˈnɒlədʒɪ/ *n* the study of crime, criminals, and penal treatment – **criminologist** *n*, **criminological** *adj*
crimp /krimp‖krɪmp/ *vt* **1** to make wavy or curly <*~ her hair*> **2** to roll or curl the edge of (e g a steel panel) **3** to pinch or press together in order to seal or join – **crimp** *n*, **crimper** *n*
Crimplene /ˈkrimpleen‖ˈkrɪmpliːn/ *trademark* – used for a textured continuous-filament polyester yarn
[1]**crimson** /ˈkrimz(ə)n‖ˈkrɪmz(ə)n/ *adj or n* (a) deep purplish red
[2]**crimson** *vb* to make or become crimson
cringe /krinj‖krɪndʒ/ *vi* **1** to shrink or wince, esp in fear or servility **2** to behave with fawning self-abasement
[1]**crinkle** /ˈkringkl‖ˈkrɪŋkl/ *vi* **1** to wrinkle **2** to rustle *~vt* to cause to crinkle
[2]**crinkle** *n* a wrinkle – **crinkly** *adj*
crinoline /ˈkrinəlin‖ˈkrɪnəlɪn/ *n* (a padded or hooped petticoat supporting) a full skirt as worn by women in the 19th c
cripes /krieps‖kraɪps/ *interj, Br* – used to express surprise; no longer in vogue
[1]**cripple** /ˈkripl‖ˈkrɪpl/ *n* a lame or partly disabled person or animal
[2]**cripple** *vt* **1** to make a cripple; lame **2** to deprive of strength, efficiency, wholeness, or capability for service
crisis /ˈkriesis‖ˈkraɪsɪs/ *n, pl* **crises** /-seez‖-siːz/ **1a** the turning point for better or worse in an acute disease (e g pneumonia) **b** a sudden attack of pain, distress, etc **2** an unstable or crucial time or situation; *esp* TURNING POINT
[1]**crisp** /krisp‖krɪsp/ *adj* **1a** easily crumbled; brittle **b** desirably firm and fresh <*a ~ apple*> **2** sharp, clean-cut, and clear <*a ~ illustration*> **3** decisive, sharp <*a ~ manner*> **4** *of weather* briskly cold; fresh; *esp* frosty – **crisply** *adv*, **crispness** *n*
[2]**crisp** *vt* **1** to curl, crimp **2** to make or keep crisp *~vi* to become crisp – **crisper** *n*
[3]**crisp** *n, chiefly Br* a thin slice of (flavoured or salted) fried potato, usu eaten cold
crispy /ˈkrispi‖ˈkrɪspɪ/ *adj* crisp – **crispiness** *n*
[1]**crisscross** /ˈkrisˌkros‖ˈkrɪsˌkrɒs/ *adj or n* (marked or characterized by) crisscrossing or a crisscrossed pattern
[2]**crisscross** *vt* **1** to mark with intersecting lines **2** to pass back and forth through or over *~vi* to go or pass back and forth
criterion /krieˈtiəri·ən‖kraɪˈtɪərɪən/ *n, pl* **criteria** /-ri·ə‖-rɪə/ *also* **criterions** a standard on which a judgment or decision may be based [Greek *kritērion*, fr *kritēs* judge, fr *krinein* to judge, decide] – **criterial** *adj*
criterium /krieˈtiəri·əm‖kraɪˈtɪərɪəm/ *n* a bicycle race consisting of several laps of a circuit on roads, esp in a town centre, closed for the occasion
critic /ˈkritik‖ˈkrɪtɪk/ *n* one who criticizes: e g **a** one who evaluates works of art, literature, or music, esp as a profession **b** one who tends to judge harshly or to be over-critical of minor faults
critical /ˈkritikl‖ˈkrɪtɪkl/ *adj* **1a** inclined to criticize severely and unfavourably **b** consisting of or involving criticism **c** exercising or involving careful judgment or judicious evaluation **2a** relating to or being a measurement, point, etc at which some quality, property, or phenomenon undergoes a marked change <*~ temperature*> **b** crucial, decisive <*~ test*> **c** being in or approaching a state of crisis **3** *of a nuclear reactor* sustaining an energy-producing chain reaction – **critically** *adv*, **criticality** *n*
criticism /ˈkritiˌsiz(ə)m‖ˈkrɪtɪˌsɪz(ə)m/ *n* **1a** the act of criticizing, usu unfavourably **b** a critical observation or remark **c** a critique **2** the art or act of analysing and evaluating esp the fine arts, literature, or literary documents
critic·ize, -ise /ˈkritiˌsiez‖ˈkrɪtɪˌsaɪz/ *vt* **1** to consider the merits and demerits of and judge accordingly; evaluate **2** to stress the faults of *~vi* to criticize sthg or sby
critique /kriˈteek‖krɪˈtiːk/ *n* an act of criticizing; *esp* a critical estimate or discussion (e g an article or essay)
critter /ˈkritə‖ˈkrɪtə/ *n, dial* a creature
[1]**croak** /krohk‖krəʊk/ *vi* **1a** to make a croak **b** to speak in a hoarse throaty voice **2** to die – slang *~ vt* **1** to utter (gloomily) in a hoarse raucous voice **2** to kill – slang
[2]**croak** *n* a deep hoarse cry characteristic of a frog or toad; *also* a similar sound – **croaky** *adj*
[1]**crochet** /ˈkrohshay‖ˈkrəʊʃeɪ/ *n* crocheted work
[2]**crochet** *vt* to form (e g a garment or design) by drawing a single continuous yarn or thread into a pattern of interlocked loops using a hooked needle *~vi* to do or make crochet work – **crocheter** *n*
[1]**crock** /krok‖krɒk/ *n* **1** a thick earthenware pot or jar **2** a piece of broken earthenware used esp to cover the bottom of a flowerpot
[2]**crock** *n* **1** an old (broken-down) vehicle **2** an (elderly) disabled person *USE* infml
[3]**crock** *vt* to cause to become disabled *~vi* BREAK DOWN 1a *USE* (*vt & vi*) sometimes + *up*; infml
crockery /ˈkrokəri‖ˈkrɒkərɪ/ *n* earthenware or china tableware, esp for everyday domestic use
crocodile /ˈkrokədiel‖ˈkrɒkədaɪl/ *n* **1** any of several tropical or subtropical large voracious

thick-skinned long-bodied aquatic reptiles; *broadly* a crocodilian **2** the skin of a crocodile; *also* leather prepared from this **3** *Br* a line of people (e g schoolchildren) walking in pairs [Latin *crocodilus*, fr Greek *krokodilos* lizard, crocodile, fr *krokē* pebble + *drilos* worm]

'crocodile ˌtears *n pl* false or affected tears; hypocritical sorrow

crocodilian /ˌkrokə'dili·ən‖ˌkrɒkə'dɪlɪən/ *n* a crocodile, alligator, or related (extinct) reptile – **crocodilian** *adj*

crocus /'krohkəs‖'krəʊkəs/ *n, pl* **crocuses** any of a large genus of usu early-flowering plants of the iris family bearing a single usu brightly-coloured long-tubed flower

croft /kroft‖krɒft/ *n, chiefly Br* **1** a small enclosed field usu adjoining a house **2** a small farm on often poor land, esp in Scotland, worked by a tenant – **crofter** *n*

croissant /'kwahsong ‖'kwɑːsɒŋ (*Fr* krwasɔ̃)/ *n* a usu flaky rich crescent-shaped roll of bread or yeast- leavened pastry

cromlech /'kromlək‖'krɒmlək/ *n* a dolmen

crone /'krohn‖'krəʊn/ *n* a withered old woman

crony /'krohni‖'krəʊnɪ/ *n* a close friend, esp of long standing; a chum – infml; often derog [alteration of obs *chrony*, prob fr Greek *chronios* long-lasting, fr *chronos* time]

[1]**crook** /krook‖krʊk/ *n* **1** an implement or part of sthg having a bent or hooked shape **2** a shepherd's staff **3** a bend, curve <*she carried the parcel in the ~ of her arm*> **4** a person given to criminal practices; a thief, swindler – infml

[2]**crook** *vt* BEND 1 <*I ~ed my neck so I could see*> *~vi* to curve, wind

[3]**crook** *adj, Austr & NZ* **1** ill, sick **2** not in correct working order **3** bad, unpleasant *USE* infml

crooked /'krookid‖'krʊkɪd/ *adj* **1** having a crook or curve; bent **2** not morally straightforward; dishonest **3** *Austr* bad-tempered; angry – **crookedly** *adv*, **crookedness** *n*

croon /kroohn‖kruːn/ *vi* to sing usu sentimental popular songs in a low or soft voice *~vt* to sing in a crooning manner – **croon** *n*, **crooner** *n*

[1]**crop** /krop‖krɒp/ *n* **1** (the stock or handle of) a riding whip, esp with a short stock and a loop on the end **2** a pouched enlargement of the gullet of many birds in which food is stored and prepared for digestion **3** a short haircut **4a** (the total production of) a plant or animal product that can be grown and harvested extensively **b** a group or quantity appearing at any one time <*a new ~ of students*>

[2]**crop** *vb* **-pp-** *vt* **1a** to remove the upper or outer parts of <*~ a hedge*> **b** to harvest <*~ trout*> **c** to cut short; trim **2** to grow as or to cause (land) to bear a crop <*~ more wheat next year*> *~ vi* **1** to feed by cropping sthg **2** to yield or bear a crop

[1]**cropper** /'kropə‖'krɒpə/ *n* a plant that yields a crop of a usu specified quality or amount

[2]**cropper** *n* **1** a severe fall **2** a sudden or complete disaster *USE* chiefly in *come a cropper*; infml

crop up *vi* to happen or appear unexpectedly or casually – infml

croquet /'krohkay‖'krəʊkeɪ/ *n* **1** a game in which wooden balls are driven by mallets through a series of hoops set out on a lawn **2** the driving away of an opponent's croquet ball by striking one's own ball placed against it – **croquet** *vt*

croquette /kroh'ket‖krəʊ'ket/ *n* a small (rounded) piece of minced meat, vegetable, etc coated with egg and breadcrumbs and fried in deep fat

crosier, crozier /'krohzhə‖'krəʊʒə/ *n* a staff resembling a shepherd's crook carried by bishops as a symbol of office

[1]**cross** /kros‖krɒs/ *n* **1a** an upright stake with a transverse beam used, esp by the ancient Romans, for execution **b** *often cap* the cross on which Jesus was crucified **2a** the Crucifixion **b** an affliction, trial **3** a figure or design consisting of an upright bar intersected by a horizontal one; *specif* one used as a Christian emblem **4** a monument shaped like or surmounted by a cross <*the market ~*> **5** a mark formed by 2 intersecting lines crossing at their midpoints that is used as a signature, to mark a position, to indicate that sthg is incorrect, or to indicate a kiss in a letter **6** a badge, emblem, or decoration shaped like a cross **7a** the crossing of dissimilar individuals; *also* the resulting hybrid **b** sby who or sthg that combines characteristics of 2 different types or individuals **8** a hook delivered over the opponent's lead in boxing **9** the act of crossing the ball in soccer – **on the cross** on the bias; diagonally

[2]**cross** *vt* **1a** to lie or be situated across **b** to intersect **2** to make the sign of the cross on or over **3** to cancel by marking a cross on or drawing a line through **4** to place or fold crosswise <*~ the arms*> **5** to run counter to; oppose **6** to go across **7a** to draw a line across <*~ one's* t's> **b** to draw 2 parallel lines across (a cheque) so that it can only be paid directly into a bank account **8** to cause (an animal or plant) to interbreed with one of a different kind; hybridize **9** to kick or pass (the ball) across the field in soccer, specif from the wing into the goal area *~ vi* **1** to move, pass, or extend across sthg – usu + *over* **2** *of letters, travellers, etc* to meet and pass **3** to interbreed, hybridize **4** to cross the ball in soccer – **cross the floor** *of a member of parliament* to transfer allegiance to the opposing party – **cross swords** to come into conflict – **cross one's mind** to occur to one

[3]**cross** *adj* **1** lying or moving across **2** mutually opposed <*~ purposes*> **3** involving mutual interchange; reciprocal **4a** irritable, grumpy **b** angry, annoyed **5** crossbred, hybrid – **crossly** *adv*, **crossness** *n*

[4]**cross** *adv* not parallel; crosswise

'crossˌbar /-ˌbah‖-ˌbɑː/ *n* a transverse bar (e g between goalposts)

'cross ˌbench *n* any of the benches in the House of Lords for members who belong to neither government nor opposition parties – usu pl – **crossbencher** *n*

crossbones /'krosˌbohnz‖'krɒsˌbəʊnz/ *n pl* 2 leg or arm bones placed or depicted crosswise

crossbow /'krosˌboh‖'krɒsˌbəʊ/ *n* a short

bow mounted crosswise near the end of a wooden stock and used to fire bolts and stones – **crossbowman** *n*

ˈcrossˌbred /-ˌbred‖-ˌbred/ *adj* hybrid; *specif* produced by interbreeding 2 pure but different breeds, strains, or varieties – **crossbred** *n*

[1]**ˈcrossˌbreed** *vb* **ˈcrossˌbred** *vt* to hybridize or cross (esp 2 varieties or breeds of the same species) ~*vi* to undergo crossbreeding

[2]**crossbreed** *n* a hybrid

ˌcross-ˈcheck *vb* to check (information) for validity or accuracy by reference to more than 1 source – **cross-check** *n*

[1]**ˌcross-ˈcountry** *adj* **1** proceeding over countryside and not by roads **2** racing or travelling over the countryside instead of over a track or run – **cross-country** *adv*

[2]**ˌcross-ˈcountry** *n* cross-country running, horse riding, etc

ˈcrossˌcurrent /-ˌkurənt‖-ˌkʌrənt/ *n* a conflicting tendency – usu pl

ˈcrossˌcut /-ˌkut‖-ˌkʌt/ *vt* to intersperse with contrasting images – **crosscut** *n*

ˈcrossˌcut ˌsaw *n* a saw designed to cut across the grain of wood

crosse /kros‖krɒs/ *n* the long-handled netted stick used in lacrosse

ˌcross-exˈamine *vt* to question closely (esp a witness in a law court) in order to check answers or elicit new information – **cross-examination** *n*, **cross-examiner** *n*

ˌcross-ˌfertil·iˈzation, -isation *n* **1a** fertilization by the joining of ova with pollen or sperm from a different individual **b** cross-pollination **2** interaction, esp of a broadening or productive nature – **cross-fertilize** *vb*

ˈcrossˌfire /-ˌfie·ə‖-ˌfaɪə/ *n* **1** firing from 2 or more points in crossing directions **2** rapid or heated interchange

ˌcross-ˈgrained *adj* **1** having the grain or fibres running diagonally, transversely, or irregularly **2** difficult to deal with; intractable

ˌcrossˈhatch /-ˈhach‖-ˈhætʃ/ *vt* to shade with a series of intersecting parallel lines – **cross-hatching** *n*

crossing /ˈkrosing‖ˈkrɒsɪŋ/ *n* **1** a traversing or travelling across **2a** a place or structure (e g on a street or over a river) where pedestrians or vehicles may cross **b** LEVEL CROSSING **c** a place where railway lines, roads, etc cross each other

ˌcross-ˈlegged /ˈlegid‖ˈlegɪd; *also* legd‖legd/ *adv or adj* **1** with legs crossed and knees spread wide apart <*sat ~ on the floor*> **2** with one leg placed over and across the other

crosspatch /ˈkrosˌpach‖ˈkrɒsˌpætʃ/ *n* a bad-tempered person – infml

ˈcrossˌpiece /-ˌpees‖-ˌpiːs/ *n* a horizontal member (e g of a structure)

crossply /ˈkrosˌplie‖ˈkrɒsˌplaɪ/ *n or adj* (a tyre) with the cords arranged crosswise to strengthen the tread

ˌcross-ˈpurposes *n pl* – **at cross purposes** having a mutual misunderstanding or deliberately conflicting approach

ˌcross-reˈfer *vb* **-rr-** *vt* **1** to direct (a reader) from one page or entry (e g in a book) to another **2** to refer from (a secondary entry) to a main entry ~*vi* to make a cross-reference

[1]**ˌcross-ˈreference** *n* an indication at one place (e g in a book or filing system) of the existence of relevant information at another place

[2]**ˌcross-ˈreference** *vb* to cross-refer

ˈcrossˌroad /-ˌrohd‖-ˌrəʊd/ *n* **1** the place where 2 or more roads intersect **2a** a central meeting place <*the ~s of the world*> **b** a crucial point, esp where a decision must be made <*at a ~s in her career*> *USE* usu pl with sing. meaning but sing. or pl in constr

ˈcross-ˌsection *n* **1** (a drawing of) a surface made by cutting across sthg, esp at right angles to its length **2** a representative sample – **cross-sectional** *adj*

ˈcross-ˌstitch *n* (needlework using) a stitch in the shape of an X formed by crossing one stitch over another – **cross-stitch** *vb*

ˈcross-ˌtalk *n* **1** unwanted signals in a communication channel that come from another channel **2** *Br* rapid exchange of repartee (e g between comedians)

ˈcrossˌtrees /-treez‖-triːz/ *n pl* a pair of horizontal crosspieces on a mast to which supporting ropes are attached

ˈcrossˌwind /-ˌwind‖-ˌwɪnd/ *n* a wind blowing in a direction not parallel to the course of a vehicle, aircraft, etc

ˈcrossˌwise /-ˌwiez‖-ˌwaɪz/ *adv* so as to cross sthg; across

ˈcrossˌword ˌpuzzle /ˈkrosˌwuhd‖ˈkrɒsˌwɜːd/ *n* a puzzle in which words are entered in a pattern of numbered squares in answer to correspondingly numbered clues in such a way that the words read across and down

crotch /kroch‖krɒtʃ/ *n* **1** an angle formed where 2 branches separate off from a tree trunk **2** the angle between the inner thighs where they meet the human body – **crotched** *adj*

crotchet /ˈkrochit‖ˈkrɒtʃɪt/ *n* a musical note with the time value of half a minim or 2 quavers

crotchety /ˈkrochiti‖ˈkrɒtʃɪtɪ/ *adj* bad-tempered – infml – **crotchetiness** *n*

crouch /krowch‖kraʊtʃ/ *vi* to lower the body by bending the legs – **crouch** *n*

[1]**croup** /kroohp‖kruːp/ *n* the rump of a quadruped

[2]**croup** *n* a spasmodic laryngitis, esp of infants, marked by periods of difficult breathing and a hoarse cough – **croupous** *adj*, **croupy** *adj*

croupier /ˈkroohpi·ə, -ay‖ˈkruːpɪə, -eɪ/ *n* an employee of a gambling casino who collects and pays out bets at the gaming tables

crouton /ˈkroohton‖ˈkruːtɒn/ *n* a small cube of crisp toasted or fried bread served with soup or used as a garnish

[1]**crow** /kroh‖krəʊ/ *n* **1** the carrion or hooded crow or a related large usu entirely glossy black bird **2** a crowbar – **as the crow flies** in a straight line

[2]**crow** *vi* **crowed**, (*1*) **crowed** *also* **crew** /krooh‖kruː/ **1** to make the loud shrill cry characteristic of a cock **2** *esp of an infant* to utter sounds of happiness or pleasure **3a** to exult gloatingly, esp over another's misfortune **b** to brag exultantly or blatantly

[3]**crow** *n* **1** the characteristic cry of the cock **2** a triumphant cry

crowbar /ˈkrohˌbah‖ˈkrəʊˌbɑː/ *n* an iron or

steel bar for use as a lever that is wedge-shaped at the working end

[1]**crowd** /krowd‖kraʊd/ *vi* **1** to press close <*people* ~ing *through the narrow gates*> **2** to collect in numbers; throng ~ *vt* **1a** to fill by pressing or thronging together <*people* ~ed *the hall*> **b** to force or thrust into a small space <~ed *books onto the shelves*> **2** to push, force <~ed *us off the pavement*> **3** to hoist more (sail) than usual for greater speed – usu + *on* **4** to press close to; jostle **5** to put pressure on – infml

[2]**crowd** *n sing or pl in constr* **1** a large number of people gathered together without order; a throng **2** people in general – + *the* **3** a large number of things close together and in disorder **4** a specified social group <*the in* ~>

crowded /'krowdid‖'kraʊdɪd/ **1** filled with numerous people, things, or events **2** pressed or forced into a small space <~ *spectators*>

crowd out *vt* **1** to exclude by depriving of space or time **2** to fill to capacity by coming or collecting together

crowfoot /'kroh,foot‖'krəʊ,fʊt/ *n, pl* **crowfoots** any of numerous plants, esp of the buttercup family, with lobed leaves shaped like a crow's foot

[1]**crown** /krown‖kraʊn/ *n* **1** a reward of victory or mark of honour; *esp* the title representing the championship in a sport **2** a (gold and jewel-encrusted) headdress worn as a symbol of sovereignty **3a** the topmost part of the skull or head **b** the summit of a slope, mountain, etc **c** the upper part of the foliage of a tree or shrub **d** the part of a hat or cap that covers the crown of the head **e** (an artificial substitute for) the part of a tooth visible outside the gum **4** a wreath, band, or circular ornament for the head, esp worn as a symbol of victory **5** *often cap* **5a** the sovereign as head of state; *also* sovereignty **b** the government under a constitutional monarchy **6** the high point or culmination **7a** a British coin worth 25 pence (formerly 5 shillings) **b** a size of paper usu 20 x 15in (508 × 381mm) **8** the part of a flowering plant at which stem and root merge – **crowned** *adj*

[2]**crown** *vt* **1a** to place a crown on the head of, esp as a symbol of investiture **b** to recognize, usu officially, as (the leader in a particular field) **2** to bestow sthg on as a mark of honour or reward **3** to surmount, top; *esp* to put a draughtsman on top of (another draughtsman) to make a king **4** to bring to a successful conclusion **5** to put an artificial crown on (a tooth) **6** to hit on the head – infml

,crown 'colony *n, often cap C&C* a colony of the Commonwealth over which the British government retains some control

,Crown 'Court *n* a local criminal court in England and Wales having jurisdiction over serious offences

,crown 'jewels *n pl* the jewels (e g crown and sceptre) belonging to a sovereign's regalia

,crown 'prince *n* an heir apparent to a crown or throne

,crown prin'cess *n* **1** the wife of a crown prince **2** a female heir apparent or heir presumptive to a crown or throne

'crow's-,foot *n, pl* **'crow's-,feet** **1** any of the wrinkles round the outer corners of the eyes – usu pl **2** crowfoot

'crow's ,nest *n* a partly enclosed high lookout platform (e g on a ship's mast)

crozier /'krohzhə‖'krəʊʒə/ *n* a crosier

crucial /'kroohshəl‖'kruːʃəl/ *adj* **1** important or essential to the resolving of a crisis; decisive **2** of the greatest importance or significance – **crucially** *adv*

crucible /'kroohsibl‖'kruːsɪbl/ *n* **1** a vessel for melting and calcining a substance at a very high temperature **2** a severe test

crucifix /'kroohsifiks‖'kruːsɪfɪks/ *n* a representation of Christ on the cross

crucifixion /,kroohsi'fiksh(ə)n‖,kruːsɪ'fɪkʃ(ə)n/ *n* **1** the act of crucifying **2** *cap* the crucifying of Christ

cruciform /'kroohsi,fawm‖'kruːsɪ,fɔːm/ *adj* forming or arranged in a cross – **cruciformly** *adv*

crucify /'kroohsi,fie‖'kruːsɪ,faɪ/ *vt* **1** to execute by nailing or binding the hands and feet to a cross and leaving to die **2** to treat cruelly; torture, persecute

[1]**crude** /kroohd‖kruːd/ *adj* **1** existing in a natural state and unaltered by processing **2** vulgar, gross **3** rough or inexpert in plan or execution – **crudely** *adv*, **crudeness** *n*

[2]**crude** *n* a substance, esp petroleum, in its natural unprocessed state

crudity /'kroohdəti‖'kruːdətɪ/ *n* **1** being crude **2** sthg crude

cruel /'krooh·əl‖'kruːəl/ *adj* **-ll-** (*NAm* **-l-**, **-ll-**) **1** liking to inflict pain or suffering; pitiless **2** causing suffering; painful – **cruelly** *adv*, **cruelness** *n*

'cruelty /-ti‖-tɪ/ *n* **1** being cruel **2** (an instance of) cruel behaviour

cruet /'krooh·it‖'kruːɪt/ *n* **1** a vessel to hold wine or water for the Eucharist **2** a small usu glass bottle or jug that holds oil or vinegar for use at table **3** a small container (e g a pot or shaker) for holding a condiment, esp salt, pepper, or mustard, at table **4** a set of cruets, usu on a stand

[1]**cruise** /kroohz‖kruːz/ *vi* **1** to travel by sea for pleasure **2** to go about or patrol the streets without any definite destination **3a** *of an aircraft* to fly at the most efficient operating speed **b** *of a vehicle* to travel at an economical speed that can be maintained for a long distance **4** to make progress easily **5** to search (e g in public places) for an esp homosexual partner – slang [Dutch *kruisen* to make a cross, sail to and fro, fr Middle Dutch *crucen*, fr *cruce* cross, fr Latin *cruc-*, *crux*]

[2]**cruise** *n* an act or instance of cruising; *esp* a sea voyage for pleasure

'cruise ,missile *n* a long-distance low-flying guided missile with small wings

cruiser /'kroohzə‖'kruːzə/ *n* **1** CABIN CRUISER **2** a large fast lightly armoured warship

[1]**crumb** /krum‖krʌm/ *n* **1** a small fragment, esp of bread **2** a small amount <*a* ~ *of comfort*> **3a** (loose crumbly soil or other material resembling) the soft part of bread inside the crust **b** a small lump consisting of soil particles **4** a worthless person – slang

[2]**crumb** *vt* **1** to break up into crumbs **2** to cover or thicken with crumbs

[1]**crumble** /ˈkrumbl‖ˈkrʌmbl/ *vb* to break or fall into small pieces; disintegrate – often + *away* – **crumbly** *adj*

[2]**crumble** *n* a dessert of stewed fruit topped with a crumbly mixture of fat, flour, and sugar

crummy, crumby /ˈkrumi‖ˈkrʌmɪ/ *adj* **1** miserable, filthy **2** of poor quality; worthless ***USE*** slang

crumpet /ˈkrumpit‖ˈkrʌmpɪt/ *n* **1** a small round cake made from an unsweetened leavened batter that is cooked on a griddle and usu toasted before serving **2** *Br* women collectively as sexual objects – slang <*a piece of* ~>

[1]**crumple** /ˈkrumpl‖ˈkrʌmpl/ *vt* to press, bend, or crush out of shape; rumple ~ *vi* **1** to become crumpled **2** to collapse <*her face* ~d *at the news*> – often + *up*

[2]**crumple** *n* a wrinkle or crease made by crumpling

[1]**crunch** /krunch‖krʌntʃ/ *vb* **1** to chew or bite (sthg) with a noisy crushing sound **2** to (cause to) make a crushing sound **3** to make (one's way) with a crushing sound

[2]**crunch** *n* **1** an act or sound of crunching **2** *the* critical or decisive situation or moment – infml

crupper /ˈkrupə‖ˈkrʌpə/ *n* a leather loop passing under a horse's tail and buckled to the saddle to prevent the saddle from slipping forwards

crusade /kroohˈsayd‖kruːˈseɪd/ *n* **1** *cap* any of the medieval Christian military expeditions to win the Holy Land from the Muslims **2** a reforming enterprise undertaken with zeal and enthusiasm [Middle French *croisade* and Spanish *cruzada*, fr Latin *cruc-*, *crux* cross] – **crusade** *vi*

cruse /kroohz, kroohs‖kruːz, kruːs/ *n* a small earthenware jar or pot for holding oil, water, etc

[1]**crush** /krush‖krʌʃ/ *vt* **1** to alter or destroy the structure of by pressure or compression **2** to reduce to particles by pounding or grinding **3** to subdue, overwhelm <*a* ~*ing remark*> **4** to crowd, push ~*vi* to become crushed – **crushable** *adj*, **crusher** *n*

[2]**crush** *n* **1** a crowding together, esp of many people **2** (the object of) an intense usu brief infatuation – infml

ˈ**crush ˌbarrier** *n* a barrier erected to control crowds

crust /krust‖krʌst/ *n* **1a** the hardened exterior of bread **b** a piece of this or of bread grown dry or hard **2** the pastry cover of a pie **3a** a hard or brittle surface layer (e g of soil or snow) **b** the outer rocky layer of the earth **c** a deposit built up on the inside of a wine bottle during long aging **d** a hard deposit (on the skin); *esp* a scab **4** a superficial hardness of behaviour <*break through her* ~ *of reserve*> – **crust** *vb*, **crustal** *adj*

crustacean /kruˈstaysh(ə)n‖krʌˈsteɪʃ(ə)n/ *n*, *pl* **crustaceans, crustacea** /-shə‖-ʃə/ any of a large class of mostly aquatic arthropods with a carapace, a pair of appendages on each segment, and 2 pairs of antennae, including the lobsters, crabs, woodlice, etc – **crustacean** *adj*

crusty /ˈkrusti‖ˈkrʌstɪ/ *adj* **1** having a hard well-baked crust **2** surly, uncivil – **crustily** *adv*, **crustiness** *n*

crutch /kruch‖krʌtʃ/ *n* **1a** a staff of wood or metal typically fitting under the armpit to support a disabled person in walking **b** a prop, stay **2** the crotch of an animal or human **3** the part of a garment that covers the human crotch

crux /kruks, krooks‖krʌks, krʊks/ *n, pl* **cruxes** *also* **cruces** /ˈkroohˌseez‖ˈkruːˌsiːz/ **1** a puzzling or difficult problem **2** an essential or decisive point <*the* ~ *of the matter*>

[1]**cry** /krie‖kraɪ/ *vi* **1** to call loudly; shout (e g in fear or pain) **2** to weep, sob **3** *of a bird or animal* to utter a characteristic sound or call **4** to require or suggest strongly a remedy – usu + *out for*; infml ~ *vt* **1** to utter loudly; shout **2** to proclaim publicly; advertise <~ *their wares*> [Old French *crier*, fr Latin *quiritare* to make a public outcry, fr *Quirit-*, *Quiris* Roman citizen] – **cry over spilt milk** to express vain regrets for what cannot be recovered or undone – **cry wolf** to raise a false alarm and risk the possibility that a future real need will not be taken seriously – **for crying out loud** used to express exasperation and annoyance; infml

[2]**cry** *n* **1** an inarticulate utterance of distress, rage, pain, etc **2** a loud shout **3** a watchword, slogan <*'death to the invader' was the* ~> **4** a general public demand or complaint **5** a spell of weeping <*have a good* ~> **6** the characteristic sound or call of an animal or bird **7** pursuit – in *in full cry*

ˈ**cryˌbaby** /-ˌbaybi‖-ˌbeɪbɪ/ *n* one who cries or complains too easily or frequently – infml

cry down *vt* to disparage, depreciate

cry off *vt* to call off (e g an agreement) ~*vi*, *chiefly Br* to withdraw; BACK OUT

cryogen /ˈkrie·əjən‖ˈkraɪədʒən/ *n* a substance used in producing low temperatures – **cryogenic** *adj*

crypt /kript‖krɪpt/ *n* a chamber (e g a vault) wholly or partly underground; *esp* a vault under the main floor of a church [Latin *crypta*, fr Greek *kryptē*, fr *kryptos* hidden, fr *kryptein* to hide] – **cryptal** *adj*

crypt- /kript-‖krɪpt-/, **crypto-** *comb form* **1** hidden; obscure <crypto*genic*> **2** secret; unavowed <crypto*fascist*>

cryptic /ˈkriptik‖ˈkrɪptɪk/ *adj* **1** secret, occult **2** intended to be obscure or mysterious **3** serving to conceal **4** making use of cipher or code – **cryptically** *adv*

cryptogram /ˈkriptəˌgram‖ˈkrɪptəˌgræm/ *n* a communication in cipher or code – **cryptogrammic** *adj*

cryptography /kripˈtogrəfi‖krɪpˈtɒgrəfɪ/ *n* **1** secret writing **2** the preparation of cryptograms, ciphers, or codes – **cryptographer** *n*, **cryptographic** *adj*

[1]**crystal** /ˈkristl‖ˈkrɪstl/ *n* **1** (almost) transparent and colourless quartz **2** sthg resembling crystal in transparency and colourlessness **3** a chemical substance in a form that has a regularly repeating internal arrangement of atoms and often regularly arranged external plane faces **4** (an object made of) a clear colourless glass of superior quality **5** the transparent cover over a watch or clock dial **6** an electronic component containing crystalline material used as a frequency-determining element

[2]**crystal** *adj* **1** consisting of or resembling crystal; clear, lucid **2** relating to or using a crystal
ˈ**crystal** ˌ**gazing** *n* **1** the art or practice of concentrating on a crystal ball to aid divination **2** the attempt to predict future events or make difficult judgments, esp without adequate data – **crystal gazer** *n*
crystalline /ˈkristlˌien‖ˈkrɪstlˌaɪn/ *adj* composed of crystal or crystals – **crystallinity** *n*
crystall·ize, -ise *also* **crystal·ize, -ise** /ˈkristlˌiez‖ˈkrɪstḷˌaɪz/ *vt* **1** to cause to form crystals or assume crystalline form **2** to cause to take a definite form **3** to coat (e g fruit) with (sugar) crystals ~*vi* to become crystallized – **crystallizer** *n*, **crystallization** *n*
cry up *vt* to praise highly; extol
cub /kub‖kʌb/ *n* **1** the young of a flesh-eating mammal (e g a bear or lion) **2** an inexperienced newspaper reporter **3** CUB SCOUT
cubby /ˈkubi‖ˈkʌbɪ/, ˈ**cubby**ˌ**hole** /-ˌhohl‖-ˌhəʊl/ *n* a snug or cramped space
[1]**cube** /kyoohb‖kjuːb/ *n* **1a** the regular solid of 6 equal square sides **b** a block of anything so shaped **2** the product got by multiplying together 3 equal numbers
[2]**cube** *vt* **1** to raise to the third power **2** to cut into cubes
ˌ**cube** ˈ**root** *n* a number whose cube is a given number
cubic /ˈkyoohbik‖ˈkjuːbɪk *also* **cubical**/-kl/ *adj* **1** cube-shaped **2** of or being a crystal system characterized by 3 equal axes at right angles **3a** three-dimensional **b** being the volume of a cube whose edge is a specified unit < ~ *metre*> **4** of or involving (terms of) the third power or order – **cubicly** *adv*, **cubic** *n*, **cubically** *adv*
cubicle /ˈkyoohbikl‖ˈkjuːbɪkl/ *n* **1** a sleeping compartment partitioned off from a large room **2** a small partitioned space or compartment
cubism /ˈkyoohˌbiz(ə)m‖ˈkjuːˌbɪz(ə)m/ *n* a 20th-c art movement that stresses abstract form, esp by displaying several aspects of the same object simultaneously – **cubist** *n*, **cubist, cubistic** *adj*
cubit /ˈkyoohbit‖ˈkjuːbɪt/ *n* any of various ancient units of length based on the length of the forearm from the elbow to the tip of the middle finger
ˈ**cub** ˌ**scout** *n* a member of the most junior section of the (British) Scout movement
[1]**cuckold** /ˈkukohld, ˈkookohld‖ˈkʌkəʊld, ˈkʊkəʊld/ *n* a man whose wife is adulterous
[2]**cuckold** *vt* to make a cuckold of (a husband) – **cuckolder** *n*, **cuckoldry** *n*
[1]**cuckoo** /ˈkookooh‖ˈkʊkuː/ *n, pl* **cuckoos** **1** (any of a large family of birds including) a greyish brown European bird that lays its eggs in the nests of other birds which hatch them and rear the offspring **2** the characteristic call of the cuckoo
[2]**cuckoo** *adj* deficient in sense or intelligence; silly – infml
ˈ**cuckoo** ˌ**clock** *n* a clock that announces the hours by sounds resembling a cuckoo's call
ˈ**cuckoo** ˌ**spit** *n* (a frothy secretion exuded on plants by the larva of) a froghopper
cucumber /ˈkyoohkumbə‖ˈkjuːkʌmbə/ *n* (a climbing plant with) a long green edible fruit cultivated as a garden vegetable and eaten esp in salads
cud /kud‖kʌd/ *n* food brought up into the mouth by a ruminating animal from its first stomach to be chewed again
[1]**cuddle** /ˈkudl‖ˈkʌdl/ *vt* to hold close for warmth or comfort or in affection ~*vi* to lie close; nestle, snuggle
[2]**cuddle** *n* an act of cuddling
ˈ**cuddlesome** /-s(ə)m‖-s(ə)m/ *adj* cuddly
cuddly /ˈkudli, ˈkudl·i‖ˈkʌdlɪ, ˈkʌdlɪ/ *adj* suitable for cuddling; lovable
[1]**cudgel** /ˈkuj(ə)l‖ˈkʌdʒ(ə)l/ *n* a short heavy club
[2]**cudgel** *vt* **-ll-** (*NAm* **-l-, -ll-**) to beat (as if) with a cudgel
[1]**cue** /kyooh‖kjuː/ *n* **1a** a signal to a performer to begin a specific speech or action **b** sthg serving a comparable purpose; a hint **2** a feature of sthg that determines the way in which it is perceived [prob fr *qu*, abbreviation (used as a direction in actors' copies of plays) of Latin *quando* when]
[2]**cue** *vt* **cuing, cueing** to give a cue to; prompt
[3]**cue** *n* a leather-tipped tapering rod for striking the ball in billiards, snooker, etc [French *queue*, lit., tail, fr Latin *cauda*]
[4]**cue** *vb* **cuing, cueing** *vt* to strike with a cue ~*vi* to use a cue
[1]**cuff** /kuf‖kʌf/ *n* **1** a fold or band at the end of a sleeve which encircles the wrist **2** a turned-up hem of a trouser leg **3** a handcuff – usu pl; infml – **cuffless** *adj* – **off the cuff** without preparation
[2]**cuff** *vt* to strike, esp (as if) with the palm of the hand
[3]**cuff** *n* a blow with the hand, esp when open; a slap
ˈ**cuff** ˌ**link** *n* a usu ornamental device consisting of 2 linked parts used to fasten a shirt cuff
cuirass /kwiˈras‖kwɪˈræs/ *n* a piece of armour consisting of a (joined backplate and) breastplate
cuisine /kwiˈzeen‖kwɪˈziːn/ *n* a manner of preparing or cooking food; *also* the food prepared
cul-de-sac /ˈkul di ˌsak‖ˈkʌl dɪ ˌsæk/ *n, pl* **culs-de-sac** /~/ *also* **cul-de-sacs** /saks‖sæks/ **1** an (anatomical) pouch or tube with only 1 opening **2** a street, usu residential, closed at 1 end [French, lit., bottom of the bag]
culinary /ˈkulin(ə)ri‖ˈkʌlɪn(ə)rɪ/ *adj* of the kitchen or cookery
[1]**cull** /kul‖kʌl/ *vt* **1** to select from a group; choose **2** to identify and remove the rejects from (a flock, herd, etc) **3** to control the size of a population of (animals) by killing a limited number – **culler** *n*
[2]**cull** *n* **1** culling **2** a culled animal
cullender /ˈkuləndə‖ˈkʌləndə/ *n* a colander
culminate /ˈkulminayt‖ˈkʌlmɪneɪt/ *vi* **1** *of a celestial body* to be at the meridian; be directly overhead **2** to reach the highest or a climactic or decisive point – often + *in* – **culmination** *n*
culottes /kooˈlots‖kʊˈlɒts/ *n pl* women's short trousers having the appearance of a skirt
culpable /ˈkulpəbl‖ˈkʌlpəbl/ *adj* deserving condemnation or blame – **culpableness** *n*, **culpably** *adv*, **culpability** *n*
culprit /ˈkulprit‖ˈkʌlprɪt/ *n* one guilty of a

crime or a fault [Anglo French *cul* (abbr of *culpable* guilty) + *prest, prit* ready (i e to prove it)]

cult /kult‖kʌlt/ *n* **1** (the body of adherents of) **1a** a system of religious beliefs and ritual <*the ~ of the Virgin Mary*> **b** a religion regarded as unorthodox or spurious **2** (a group marked by) great devotion, often regarded as a fad, to a person, idea, or thing – **cultic** *adj*, **cultism** *n*, **cultist** *n*

cultivar /'kulti,vah‖'kʌltɪ,vɑː/ *n* a variety of a plant or other organism produced and kept under cultivation

cultivate /'kultivayt‖'kʌltɪveɪt/ *vt* **1** to prepare or use (land, soil, etc) for the growing of crops; *also* to break up the soil about (growing plants) **2a** to foster the growth of (a plant or crop) **b** CULTURE 2a **c** to improve by labour, care, or study; refine <~ *the mind*> **3** to further, encourage <~ *a friendship*> – **cultivatable** *adj*, **cultivation** *n*

'cultivated *adj* refined, educated

cultivator /'kultivaytə‖'kʌltɪveɪtə/ *n* an implement to break up the soil (while crops are growing)

¹culture /'kulchə‖'kʌltʃə/ *n* **1** cultivation, tillage **2** the development of the mind, esp by education **3a** enlightenment and excellence of taste acquired by intellectual and aesthetic training **b** intellectual and artistic enlightenment as distinguished from vocational and technical skills **4a** the socially transmitted pattern of human behaviour that includes thought, speech, action, institutions, and artefacts **b** the customary beliefs, social forms, etc of a racial, religious, or social group **5** (a product of) the cultivation of living cells, tissue, viruses, etc in prepared nutrient media – **cultural** *adj*, **culturally** *adv*

²culture *vt* **1** to cultivate **2a** to grow (bacteria, viruses, etc) in a culture **b** to start a culture from <~ *a specimen of urine*>

cultured /'kulchəd‖'kʌltʃəd/ *adj* cultivated

culvert /'kulvət‖'kʌlvət/ *n* a construction that allows water to pass over or under an obstacle (e g a road or canal)

cum /kum‖kʌm/ *prep* with; combined with; along with <*lounge ~ dining room*>

cumber /'kumbə‖'kʌmbə/ *vt* **1** to clutter up; hamper **2** to burden *USE* fml

'cumbersome /-s(ə)m‖-s(ə)m/ *adj* unwieldy because of heaviness and bulk – **cumbersomely** *adv*, **cumbersomeness** *n*

cumin /'kumin, 'kyoohmin‖'kʌmɪn, 'kjuːmɪn/ *n* a plant cultivated for its aromatic seeds used as a flavouring

cummerbund /'kumə,bund‖'kʌmə,bʌnd/ *n* a broad waistsash worn esp with men's formal evening wear [Hindi *kamarband*, fr Persian, fr *kamar* waist + *band* band]

cumulative /'kyoohmyooləttiv‖'kjuːmjʊlətɪv/ *adj* **1a** made up of accumulated parts **b** increasing by successive additions **2** formed by adding new material of the same kind <*a ~ book index*> – **cumulatively** *adv*, **cumulativeness** *n*

cumulonimbus /,kyoohmyooloh'nimbəs‖,kjuːmjʊləʊ'nɪmbəs/ *n* a cumulus cloud formation often in the shape of an anvil, extending to great heights and characteristic of thunderstorm conditions

cumulus /'kyoohmyooləs‖'kjuːmjʊləs/ *n, pl* **cumuli** /-lie, -li‖-laɪ, -lɪ/ a massive cloud formation with a flat base and rounded outlines often piled up like a mountain

¹cuneiform /'kyoohni,fawm‖'kjuːnɪ,fɔːm/ *adj* **1** wedge-shaped **2** composed of or written in the wedge-shaped characters used in ancient Assyrian, Babylonian, and Persian inscriptions

²cuneiform *n* **1** cuneiform writing **2** a cuneiform part

,cunni'lingus /-'ling·gəs‖-'lɪŋgəs/ *n* oral stimulation of the vulva or clitoris

¹cunning /'kuning‖'kʌnɪŋ/ *adj* **1** dexterous, ingenious **2** devious, crafty **3** *NAm* prettily appealing; cute – **cunningly** *adv*, **cunningness** *n*

²cunning *n* craft, slyness

cunt /kunt‖kʌnt/ *n* **1** the female genitals **2** sexual intercourse – used by men **3** *Br* an unpleasant person *USE* vulg

¹cup /kup‖kʌp/ *n* **1** a small open drinking vessel that is usu bowl-shaped and has a handle on 1 side **2** the consecrated wine of the Communion **3** that which comes to one in life (as if) by fate <~ *of happiness*> **4** (a competition or championship with) an ornamental usu metal cup offered as a prize **5a** sthg resembling a cup **b** either of 2 parts of a garment, esp a bra, that are shaped to fit over the breasts **6** any of various usu alcoholic and cold drinks made from mixed ingredients **7** the capacity of a cup; *specif, chiefly NAm* CUPFUL 2 – **cuplike** *adj* – **in one's cups** ²DRUNK 1

²cup *vt* **-pp- 1** to treat or draw blood from by cupping **2** to form into the shape of a cup <~*ped his hands*>

cupboard /'kubəd‖'kʌbəd/ *n* a shelved recess or freestanding piece of furniture with doors, for storage of utensils, food, clothes, etc

'cupboard ,love *n* insincere love professed for the sake of gain

cupful /'kupf(ə)l‖'kʌpf(ə)l/ *n, pl* **cupfuls** *also* **cupsful 1** as much as a cup will hold **2** *chiefly NAm* a unit of measure equal to 8 fl oz (about 0.23l)

cupidity /kyooh'pidəti‖kjuː'pɪdətɪ/ *n* inordinate desire for wealth; avarice, greed

cupola /'kyoohpələ‖'kjuːpələ/ *n* **1** a small domed structure built on top of a roof **2** a vertical cylindrical furnace for melting pig iron

cuppa /'kupə‖'kʌpə/ *n, chiefly Br* a cup of tea – infml

cupping /'kuping‖'kʌpɪŋ/ *n* the application to the skin of a previously heated glass vessel, in which a partial vacuum develops, in order to draw blood to the surface (e g for bleeding)

cupric /'kyoohprik‖'kjuːprɪk/ *adj* of or containing (bivalent) copper

'cup-,tie *n* a match in a knockout competition for a cup

cur /kuh‖kɜː/ *n* **1** a mongrel or inferior dog **2** a surly or cowardly fellow

curaçao *also* **curaçoa** /kyooərə'sow, -'soh, '---‖kjʊərə'saʊ, -'səʊ, '---/ *n* a liqueur flavoured with the peel of bitter oranges

curacy /'kyooərəsi‖'kjʊərəsɪ/ *n* the (term of) office of a curate

curate /'kyooərət‖'kjʊərət/ *n* a clergyman serving as assistant (e g to a rector) in a parish

curative /'kyooərətiv‖'kjʊərətɪv/ *adj* relating

to or used in the cure of diseases – **curative** *n*, **curatively** *adv*

curator /kyoo'raytə‖kjʊ'reɪtə/ *n* sby in charge of a place of exhibition (e g a museum or zoo) – **curatorship** *n*, **curatorial** *adj*

[1]**curb** /kuhb‖kɜːb/ *n* **1a** a chain or strap that is used to restrain a horse and is attached to the sides of the bit and passes below the lower jaw **b** a bit used esp with a curb chain or strap, usu in a double bridle **2** a sprain in a ligament just below a horse's hock **3** a check, restraint **4** an edge or margin that strengthens or confines **5** *chiefly NAm* a kerb

[2]**curb** *vt* **1** to put a curb on **2** to check, control

curd /kuhd‖kɜːd/ *n* **1** the thick casein-rich part of coagulated milk used as a food or made into cheese **2** a rich thick fruit preserve made with eggs, sugar, and butter **3** the edible head of a cauliflower or a similar related plant – **curdy** *adj*

curdle /'kuhdl‖'kɜːdl/ *vb* **1** to form curds (in); *specif* to separate into solid curds and liquid **2** to spoil, sour

[1]**cure** /kyooə‖kjʊə/ *n* **1** spiritual or pastoral charge **2** (a drug, treatment, etc that gives) relief or esp recovery from a disease **3** sthg that corrects a harmful or troublesome situation; a remedy **4** a process or method of curing – **cureless** *adj*

[2]**cure** *vt* **1a** to restore to health, soundness, or normality **b** to bring about recovery from **2a** to rectify **b** to free (sby) from sthg objectionable or harmful **3** to prepare by chemical or physical processing; *esp* to preserve (meat, fish, etc) by salting, drying, smoking, etc ~ *vi* **1** to undergo a curing process **2** to effect a cure – **curable** *adj*, **curableness** *n*, **curably** *adv*, **curer** *n*, **curability** *n*

curé /'kyooəray‖'kjʊəreɪ/ *n* a French parish priest

'cure-ˌall *n* a remedy for all ills; a panacea

curettage /kyoo'retij‖kjʊ'retɪdʒ/ *n* a surgical scraping or cleaning (e g of the womb) by means of a curette

curette, **curet** /kyoo'ret‖kjʊ'ret/ *n* a scoop, loop, or ring used in curettage – **curette** *vt*

curfew /'kuhfyooh‖'kɜːfjuː/ *n* **1** a regulation imposed on all or particular people, esp during times of civil disturbance, requiring their withdrawal from the streets by a stated time **2** a signal (e g the sounding of a bell) announcing the beginning of a time of curfew **3a** the hour at which a curfew becomes effective **b** the period during which a curfew is in effect [Middle French *covrefeu* signal given to bank the hearth fire, curfew, fr *covrir* to cover + *feu* fire]

Curia /'kyooəri·ə‖'kjʊərɪə/ *n*, the administration and governmental apparatus of the Roman Catholic church

curio /'kyooərioh‖'kjʊərɪəʊ/ *n*, *pl* **curios** sthg considered novel, rare, or bizarre

curiosity /ˌkyooəri'osəti‖ˌkjʊərɪ'ɒsətɪ/ *n* **1** desire to know **2** inquisitiveness, nosiness **3** a strange, interesting, or rare object, custom, etc

curious /'kyooəri·əs‖'kjʊərɪəs/ *adj* **1** eager to investigate and learn **2** inquisitive, nosy **3** strange, novel, or odd – **curiously** *adv*, **curiousness** *n*

curium /'kyooəri·əm‖'kjʊərɪəm/ *n* an artificially produced radioactive metallic element [Marie *Curie* (1867-1934) & Pierre *Curie* (1859-1906), French chemists]

[1]**curl** /kuhl‖kɜːl/ *vt* **1** to form into waves or coils **2** to form into a curved shape; twist **3** to provide with curls ~ *vi* **1a** to grow in coils or spirals **b** to form curls or twists **2** to move or progress in curves or spirals **3** to play the game of curling

[2]**curl** *n* **1** a curled lock of hair **2** sthg with a spiral or winding form; a coil **3** curling or being curled <*a ~ of the lip*> **4** a (plant disease marked by the) rolling or curling of leaves

curler /'kuhlə‖'kɜːlə/ *n* a small cylinder on which hair is wound for curling

curlew /'kuhlyooh‖'kɜːljuː/ *n*, any of various largely brownish (migratory) wading birds with long legs and a long slender down-curved bill

curlicue *also* **curlycue** /'kuhliˌkyooh‖'kɜːlɪˌkjuː/ *n* a decorative curve or flourish (e g in handwriting)

curling /'kuhling‖'kɜːlɪŋ/ *n* a game in which 2 teams, of 4 players each, slide heavy round flat-bottomed stones over ice towards a target circle marked on the ice – **curler** *n*

curly /'kuhli‖'kɜːlɪ/ *adj* tending to curl; having curls – **curliness** *n*

curmudgeon /kə'mujən‖kə'mʌdʒən/ *n* a crusty ill-tempered (old) man – **curmudgeonly** *adj*

currant /'kurənt‖'kʌrənt/ *n* **1** a small seedless type of dried grape used in cookery **2** (a shrub of the gooseberry family bearing) a redcurrant, blackcurrant, or similar acid edible fruit [Middle English *raison of Coraunte*, lit., raisin of Corinth, fr *Corinth*, region & city of Greece]

currency /'kurənsi‖'kʌrənsɪ/ *n* **1a** circulation as a medium of exchange <*sixpences are no longer in ~*> **b** (the state of being in) general use, acceptance, or prevalence **2** sthg (e g coins and bank notes) that is in circulation as a medium of exchange

[1]**current** /'kurənt‖'kʌrənt/ *adj* **1a** in progress now <*during the ~ week*> **b** occurring in or belonging to the present time **2** used as a medium of exchange **3** generally accepted, used, or practised at the moment [Old French *curant*, present participle of *courre* to run, fr Latin *currere*] – **currently** *adv*, **currentness** *n*

[2]**current** *n* **1a** the part of a body of gas or liquid that moves continuously in a certain direction **b** the swiftest part of a stream **c** a (tidal) movement of lake, sea, or ocean water **2** a tendency to follow a certain or specified course **3** a flow of electric charge; *also* the rate of such flow

current account *n*, *chiefly Br* a bank account against which cheques may be drawn and on which interest is usu not payable

curriculum /kə'rikyooləm‖kə'rɪkjʊləm/ *n*, *pl* **curricula** /-lə‖-lə/ *also* **curriculums** the courses offered by an educational institution or followed by an individual or group – **curricular** *adj*

curˌriculum 'vitae /'veetie‖'viːtaɪ/ *n*, *pl* **curricula vitae** /-lə‖-lə/ a summary of sby's career and qualifications, esp as relevant to a job application [Latin, course of (one's) life]

currish /'kuhrish‖'kɜːrɪʃ/ *adj* ignoble – **currishly** *adv*

[1]**curry** /'kuri‖'kʌrɪ/ *vt* **1** to dress the coat of (e g a horse) with a currycomb **2** to dress (tanned leather) – **currier** *n* – **curry favour** to seek to gain

favour by flattery or attention

[2]**curry** *also* **currie** /'kuri||'kʌrɪ/ *n* a food or dish seasoned with a mixture of spices or curry powder

[3]**curry** *vt* to flavour or cook with curry powder or sauce

currycomb /'kuri,kohm||'kʌrɪ,kəʊm/ *n* a metal comb with rows of teeth or serrated ridges, used esp to clean grooming brushes or to curry horses – **currycomb** *vt*

'**curry ,powder** *n* a condiment consisting of several pungent ground spices (e g cayenne pepper, fenugreek, and turmeric)

[1]**curse** /kuhs||kɜːs/ *n* **1** an utterance (of a deity) or a request (to a deity) that invokes harm or injury; an imprecation **2** an evil or misfortune that comes (as if) in response to imprecation or as retribution **3** a cause of misfortune **4** menstruation – + *the*; infml

[2]**curse** *vt* **1** to call upon divine or supernatural power to cause harm or injury to; *also* to doom, damn **2** to use profanely insolent language against **3** to bring great evil upon; afflict ~*vi* to utter curses; swear

cursed /kuhsid, kuhst||kɜːsɪd, kɜːst/ *also* **curst** /kuhst||kɜːst/ *adj* under or deserving a curse – **cursedly** *adv*, **cursedness** *n*

[1]**cursive** /'kuhsiv||'kɜːsɪv/ *adj* running, coursing; *esp* written in flowing, usu slanted, strokes with the characters joined in each word – **cursively** *adv*, **cursiveness** *n*

[2]**cursive** *n* cursive writing

cursor /'kuhsə||'kɜːsə/ *n* **1** a sliding part of an instrument **2** a movable pointer (e g a flashing square of light) on a VDU, radar screen, etc for indicating a specific position

cursory /'kuhsəri||'kɜːsərɪ/ *adj* rapid and often superficial; hasty – **cursorily** *adv*, **cursoriness** *n*

curt /kuht||kɜːt/ *adj* marked by rude or peremptory shortness; brusque – **curtly** *adv*, **curtness** *n*

curtail /kuh'tayl||kɜː'teɪl/ *vt* to cut short, limit – **curtailer** *n*, **curtailment** *n*

[1]**curtain** /'kuht(ə)n||'kɜːt(ə)n/ *n* **1** a hanging fabric screen that can usu be drawn back or up; *esp* one used at a window **2** a device or agency that conceals or acts as a barrier **3a** a castle wall between 2 neighbouring bastions **b** an exterior wall that carries no load **4a** the movable screen separating the stage from the auditorium of a theatre **b** the ascent or opening (e g at the beginning of a play) of a stage curtain; *also* its descent or closing **c** CURTAIN CALL **d** *pl* the end; *esp* death – infml

[2]**curtain** *vt* **1** to furnish (as if) with curtains **2** to veil or shut off (as if) with a curtain

'**curtain ,call** *n* an appearance by a performer after the final curtain of a play in response to the applause of the audience

'**curtain ,raiser** *n* **1** a short play presented before the main full-length drama **2** a usu short preliminary to a main event

[1]**curtsy, curtsey** /'kuhtsi||'kɜːtsɪ/ *n* an act of respect on the part of a woman, made by bending the knees and lowering the head and shoulders

[2]**curtsy, curtsey** *vi* to make a curtsy

curvaceous *also* **curvacious** /kuh'vayshəs||kɜː'veɪʃəs/ *adj, of a woman* having a pleasingly well-developed figure with attractive curves – infml

curvature /'kuhvəchə||'kɜːvətʃə/ *n* **1** (a measure or amount of) curving or being curved **2a** an abnormal curving (e g of the spine) **b** a curved surface of an organ (e g the stomach)

[1]**curve** /kuhv||kɜːv/ *vi* to have or make a turn, change, or deviation from a straight line without sharp breaks or angularity ~*vt* to cause to curve

[2]**curve** *n* **1** a curving line or surface **2** sthg curved (e g a curving line of the human body) **3** a representation on a graph of a varying quantity (e g speed, force, or weight) **4** a distribution indicating the relative performance of individuals measured against one another – **curvy** *adj*

[1]**cushion** /'kooshən||'kʊʃən/ *n* **1** a soft pillow or padded bag; *esp* one used for sitting, reclining, or kneeling on **2** a bodily part resembling a pad **3** a pad of springy rubber along the inside of the rim of a billiard table off which balls bounce **4** sthg serving to mitigate the effects of disturbances or disorders

[2]**cushion** *vt* **1** to furnish with a cushion **2a** to mitigate the effects of **b** to protect against force or shock **3** to slow gradually so as to minimize the shock or damage to moving parts

cushy /'kooshi||'kʊʃɪ/ *adj* entailing little hardship or effort; easy <*a ~ job*> – infml [Hindi *khush* pleasant, fr Persian *khūsh*] – **cushily** *adv*, **cushiness** *n*

cusp /kusp||kʌsp/ *n* a point, apex: e g **a** either horn of a crescent moon **b** a pointed projection formed by or arising from the intersection of 2 arcs or foils **c(1)** a point on the grinding surface of a tooth **c(2)** a fold or flap of a heart valve – **cuspate** *adj*

cuspidor /'kuspidaw||'kʌspɪdɔː/ *n* a spittoon

[1]**cuss** /kus||kʌs/ *n* **1** a curse **2** a fellow <*a harmless old ~*> *USE* infml

[2]**cuss** *vb* to curse – infml – **cusser** *n*

cussed /'kusid||'kʌsɪd/ *adj* **1** cursed **2** obstinate, cantankerous *USE* infml – **cussedly** *adv*, **cussedness** *n*

custard /'kustəd||'kʌstəd/ *n* **1** a semisolid usu sweetened and often baked mixture made with milk and eggs **2** a sweet sauce made with milk and eggs or a commercial preparation of coloured cornflour

custodial /ku'stohdi·əl||kʌ'stəʊdɪəl/ *adj* **1** of guardianship or custody **2** of or involving legal detention <*a ~ sentence*>

custodian /ku'stohdi·ən||kʌ'stəʊdɪən/ *n* one who guards and protects or maintains; *esp* the curator of a public building – **custodianship** *n*

custody /'kustədi||'kʌstədɪ/ *n* **1a** the state of being cared for or guarded **b** imprisonment, detention **2** the act or right of caring for a minor, esp when granted by a court of law; guardianship

[1]**custom** /'kustəm||'kʌstəm/ *n* **1a** an established socially accepted practice **b** long-established practice having the force of law **c** the usual practice of an individual **d** the usages that regulate social life **2a** *pl* duties or tolls imposed on imports or exports **b** *pl but sing or pl in constr* the agency, establishment, or procedure for collecting such customs **3** *chiefly Br* business patronage

[2]**custom** *adj, chiefly NAm* made or performed according to personal order <~ *clothes*>

customary /'kustəm(ə)ri‖'kʌstəm(ə)rɪ/ *adj* established by or according to custom; usual – **customarily** *adv*, **customariness** *n*

customer /'kustəmə‖'kʌstəmə/ *n* **1** one who purchases a commodity or service **2** an individual, usu having some specified distinctive trait <*a tough* ~>

'**customs,house** /-,hows‖-,haʊs/ *n* a building where customs are collected and where vessels are entered and cleared

[1]**cut** /kut‖kʌt/ *vb* **-tt-; cut** *vt* **1a(1)** to penetrate (as if) with an edged instrument **a(2)** to castrate (a usu male animal) **b** to hurt the feelings of <*his cruel remark* ~ *me deeply*> **c** [1]CHOP 2 **d** to experience the emergence of (a tooth) through the gum **2a** to trim, pare **b** to shorten by omissions **c** to dilute, adulterate **d** to reduce in amount <~ *costs*> **e** EDIT 1b **3a** to mow or reap <~ *hay*> **b(1)** to divide into parts with an edged instrument <~ *bread*> **b(2)** to fell, hew <~ *timber*> **c** to play a cut in cricket at (a ball) or at the bowling of (a bowler) **4a** to divide into segments **b** to intersect, cross **c** to break, interrupt <~ *our supply lines*> **d(1)** to divide (a pack of cards) into 2 portions **d(2)** to draw (a card) from the pack **5a** to refuse to recognize (an acquaintance) **b** to stop (a motor) by opening a switch **c** to terminate the filming of (a scene in a film) **6a** to make or give shape to (as if) with an edged tool <~ *a diamond*> **b** to record sounds on (a gramophone record) **7a** to perform, make <~ *a caper*> **b** to give the appearance or impression of <~ *a fine figure*> **8a** to stop, cease <~ *the nonsense*> – infml **b** to absent oneself from (e g a class) – infml ~ *vi* **1a** to function (as if) as an edged tool **b** to be able to be separated, divided, or marked with a sharp instrument <*cheese* ~s *easily*> **c** to perform the operation of dividing, severing, incising, or intersecting **d(1)** to make a stroke with a whip, sword, etc **d(2)** to play a cut in cricket **e** to wound feelings or sensibilities **f** to cause constriction or chafing **g** to be of effect, influence, or significance <*an analysis that* ~s *deep*> **2a** to cut a pack of cards, esp in order to decide who deals **b** to draw a card from the pack **3a** to move swiftly <*a yacht* ~ting *through the water*> **b** to describe an oblique or diagonal line **c** to change sharply in direction; swerve **d** to make an abrupt transition from one sound or image to another in film, radio, or television **4** to stop filming or recording – **cut corners** to perform some action in the quickest, easiest, or cheapest way – **cut no ice** to fail to impress; have no importance or influence – infml – **cut short 1** to abbreviate **2** INTERRUPT 1

[2]**cut** *n* **1** sthg cut (off): e g **1a** a length of cloth varying from 40 to 100yd (44 to 109m) in length **b** the yield of products cut, esp during 1 harvest **c** a (slice cut from a) piece from a meat carcass or a fish **d** a share <*took his* ~ *of the profits*> **2a** a canal, channel, or inlet made by excavation or worn by natural action **b(1)** an opening made with an edged instrument **b(2)** a gash, wound **c** a surface or outline left by cutting **d** a passage cut as a roadway **3a** a gesture or expression that hurts the feelings **b** a stroke or blow with the edge of sthg sharp **c** a lash (as if) with a whip **d** the act of reducing or removing a part <*a* ~ *in pay*> **e** (the result of) a cutting of playing cards **4a** a sharp downward blow or stroke; *also* backspin **b** an attacking stroke in cricket played with the bat held horizontally and sending the ball on the off side **5** an abrupt transition from one sound or image to another in film, radio, or television **6a** the shape and style in which a thing is cut, formed, or made <*clothes of a good* ~> **b** a pattern, type **c** a haircut – **a cut above** superior (to); of higher quality or rank (than)

,**cut-and-'dried** *adj* completely decided; not open to further discussion

cutaway /'kutəway‖'kʌtəweɪ/ *adj* having or showing parts cut away or absent

'**cut,back** /-,bak‖-,bæk/ *n* **1** sthg cut back **2** a reduction

cut back *vt* **1** to shorten by cutting; prune <cut back *a rose tree*> **2** to reduce, decrease <cut back *expenditure*> ~ *vi* **1** to interrupt the sequence of a plot (e g of a film) by returning to events occurring previously **2** CUT DOWN; *esp* to economize

cut down *vt* **1** to strike down and kill or incapacitate **2** to reduce, curtail <cut down *expenses*> ~*vi* to reduce or curtail volume or activity <cut down *on his smoking*> – **cut down to size** to reduce from an exaggerated importance to true or suitable stature

cute /kyooht‖kju:t/ *adj* attractive or pretty, esp in a dainty or delicate way – infml – **cutely** *adv*, **cuteness** *n*

,**cut 'glass** *n* glass ornamented with patterns cut into its surface by an abrasive wheel and then polished

cuticle /'kyoohtikl‖'kju:tɪkl/ *n* a skin or outer covering: e g **a** the (dead or horny) epidermis of an animal **b** a thin fatty film on the external surface of many higher plants – **cuticular** *adj*

cut in *vi* **1** to thrust oneself into a position between others or belonging to another **2** to join in sthg suddenly <cut in *on the conversation*> **3** to take 1 of a dancing couple as one's partner **4** to become automatically connected or started in operation ~ *vt* **1** to introduce into a number, group, or sequence **2** to include, esp among those benefiting or favoured <cut *them* in *on the profits*>

cutlass *also* **cutlas** /'kutləs‖'kʌtləs/ *n* a short curved sword, esp as used formerly by sailors

cutler /'kutlə‖'kʌtlə/ *n* one who deals in, makes, or repairs cutlery

cutlery /'kutləri‖'kʌtlərɪ/ *n* **1** edged or cutting tools; *esp* implements (e g knives, forks, and spoons) for cutting and eating food **2** the business of a cutler

cutlet /'kutlit‖'kʌtlɪt/ *n* **1** (a flat mass of minced food in the shape of) a small slice of meat from the neck of lamb, mutton, or veal **2** a cross-sectional slice from between the head and centre of a large fish

'**cut,off** /-,of‖-,ɒf/ *n* **1** (a device for) cutting off **2** the point, date, or period for a cutoff – **cutoff** *adj*

cut off *vt* **1** to strike off; sever **2** to bring to an untimely end **3** to stop the passage of <cut off *supplies*> **4** to shut off, bar <*the fence* cut off *his view*> **5** to separate, isolate <cut *himself* off *from his family*> **6** to disinherit **7a** to stop the operation of; turn off **b** to stop or interrupt while in communication <*the operator* cut *me* off>

ˈcutˌout /-ˌowt‖-ˌaʊt/ *n* **1** sthg cut out or off from sthg else **2** a device that cuts out; *esp* one that is operated automatically by an excessive electric current – **cutout** *adj*

[1]**cut out** *vt* **1** to form or shape by cutting, erosion, etc **2** to take the place of; supplant **3** to put an end to; desist from <cut out *smoking*> **4a** to remove or exclude (as if) by cutting **b** to make inoperative ~*vi* to cease operating

[2]**ˌcut ˈout** *adj* naturally fitted or suited <*not* ~ *to be an actor*>

ˌcut-ˈprice *adj* selling or sold at a discount

cutter /ˈkutə‖ˈkʌtə/ *n* **1a** one whose work is cutting or involves cutting (e g of cloth or film) **b** an instrument, machine, machine part, or tool that cuts **2a** a ship's boat for carrying stores or passengers **b** a fore-and-aft rigged sailing boat with a single mast and 2 foresails **c** a small armed boat in the US coastguard

[1]**ˈcutˌthroat** /-ˌthroht‖-ˌθrəʊt/ *n* a murderous thug

[2]**cutthroat** *adj* **1** murderous, cruel **2** ruthless, unprincipled <~ *competition*>

[1]**cutting** /ˈkuting‖ˈkʌtɪŋ/ *n* **1** sthg cut (off or out): e g **1a** a part of a plant stem, leaf, root, etc capable of developing into a new plant **b** a harvest **c** *chiefly Br* an excavation or cut, esp through high ground, for a canal, road, etc **d** *chiefly Br* an item cut out of a publication **2** sthg made by cutting

[2]**cutting** *adj* **1** designed for cutting; sharp, edged **2** *of wind* marked by sharp piercing cold **3** likely to wound the feelings of another; *esp* sarcastic – **cuttingly** *adv*

cuttlefish /ˈkutlˌfish‖ˈkʌtlˌfɪʃ/ *n* a 10-armed marine cephalopod mollusc differing from the related squids in having a hard internal shell

[1]**cut up** *vt* **1** to cut into parts or pieces **2** to subject to hostile criticism; censure ~*vi NAm* to behave in a comic, boisterous, or unruly manner – **cut up rough** to express often obstreperous resentment

[2]**ˌcut ˈup** *adj* deeply distressed; grieved – infml

ˈcutˌworm /-ˌwuhm‖-ˌwɜːm/ *n* any of various chiefly nocturnal caterpillars (that feed on plant stems near ground level)

cwm /koohm‖kuːm/ *n* CIRQUE 1

-cy /-si‖-sɪ/ *suffix* (*n, adj* → *n*) **1** action or practice of <*piracy*> **2** rank or office of <*baronetcy*> **3** body or class of <*magistracy*> **4** quality or state of <*bankruptcy*> *USE* often replacing a final *-t* or *-te* of the base word

cyanide /ˈsie·ənied‖ˈsaɪənaɪd/ *n* (a usu extremely poisonous salt of hydrocyanic acid or a nitrile, containing) the chemical radical -CN

cybernetics /ˌsiebəˈnetiks‖ˌsaɪbəˈnetɪks/ *n pl but sing or pl in constr* the comparative study of the automatic control systems formed by the nervous system and brain and by mechanical-electrical communication systems [Greek *kybernētēs* pilot, governor fr *kybernan* to steer, govern] – **cybernetic** *adj*

cyclamate /ˈsiekləmayt, -mət, ˈsiklə-‖ˈsaɪkləmeɪt, -mət, ˈsɪklə-/ *n* a synthetic compound used, esp formerly, as an artificial sweetener

cyclamen /ˈsikləmən‖ˈsɪkləmən/ *n* any of a genus of plants of the primrose family with showy drooping flowers

[1]**cycle** /ˈsiekl‖ˈsaɪkl/ *n* **1a** (the time needed to complete) a series of related events happening in a regularly repeated order **b** one complete performance of a periodic process (e g a vibration or electrical oscillation) **2** a group of poems, plays, novels, or songs on a central theme **3** a bicycle, motorcycle, tricycle, etc

[2]**cycle** *vi* **1a** to pass through a cycle **b** to recur in cycles **2** to ride a cycle – **cycler** *n*

cyclic /ˈsiklik, ˈsieklik‖ˈsɪklɪk, ˈsaɪklɪk/, **cyclical** /-kl‖-kl/ *adj* **1** of or belonging to a cycle **2** of or containing a ring of atoms <*benzene is a* ~ *compound*> – **cyclically, cyclicly** *adv*

cyclist /ˈsieklist‖ˈsaɪklɪst/ *n* one who rides a cycle

cyclo-cross /ˈsiekloh ˌkros‖ˈsaɪkləʊ ˌkrɒs/ *n* the sport of racing bicycles on cross-country courses that usu require the contestants to carry the bicycle over obstacles, up steep banks, etc

cyclone /ˈsieklohn‖ˈsaɪkləʊn/ *n* **1a** a storm or system of winds that rotates about a centre of low atmospheric pressure, advances at high speeds, and often brings abundant rain **b** a tornado **c** [3]LOW 1b **2** any of various centrifugal devices for separating materials (e g solid particles from gases or liquids) – **cyclonic** *adj*, **cyclonically** *adv*

cyclopedia, cyclopaedia /ˌsiekləˈpeedi·ə‖ˌsaɪkləˈpiːdɪə/ *n* an encyclopedia – **cyclopedic** *adj*

[1]**cyclostyle** /ˈsiekləˌstiel‖ˈsaɪkləˌstaɪl/ *n* a duplicating machine that uses a stencil cut by a pen whose tip is a small rowel

[2]**cyclostyle** *vt* to duplicate by using a cyclostyle

cyclotron /ˈsiekləˌtron‖ˈsaɪkləˌtrɒn/ *n* a particle accelerator in which protons, ions, etc are propelled by an alternating electric field in a constant magnetic field

cyder /ˈsiedə‖ˈsaɪdə/ *n, Br* cider

cygnet /ˈsignit‖ˈsɪgnɪt/ *n* a young swan

cylinder /ˈsilində‖ˈsɪlɪndə/ *n* **1a** a surface traced by a straight line moving in a circle or other closed curve round and parallel to a fixed straight line **b** the space bounded by a cylinder and 2 parallel planes that cross it **c** a hollow or solid object with the shape of a cylinder and a circular cross-section **2a** the piston chamber in an engine **b** any of various rotating parts (e g in printing presses) – **cylindered** *adj*

cylindrical /siˈlindrikl‖sɪˈlɪndrɪkl/, **cylindric** /-drik‖-drɪk/ *adj* (having the form) of a cylinder – **cylindrically** *adv*

cymbal /ˈsimbl‖ˈsɪmbl/ *n* a concave brass plate that produces a clashing tone when struck with a drumstick or against another cymbal – **cymbalist** *n*

cynic /ˈsinik‖ˈsɪnɪk/ *n* **1** *cap* an adherent of an ancient Greek school of philosophers who held that virtue is the highest good and that its essence lies in mastery over one's desires and wants

2a one who is habitually pessimistic or sardonic **b** one who sarcastically doubts the existence of human sincerity or of any motive other than self-interest [Latin *cynicus*, fr Greek *kynikos*, lit., like a dog, fr *kyn-*, *kyōn* dog] – **cynic, cynical** *adj*, **cynically** *adv*, **cynicism** *n*

cynosure /ˈsinə,zyooə, ˈsie-, -,shooə‖ˈsɪnə-,zjʊə, ˈsaɪ-, -,ʃʊə/ *n* a centre of attraction or attention

cypher /ˈsiefə‖ˈsaɪfə/ *vb or n, chiefly Br* (to) cipher

cypress /ˈsieprəs‖ˈsaɪprəs/ *n* (the wood of) any of a genus of evergreen gymnospermous trees with aromatic overlapping leaves resembling scales

Cyrillic /siˈrilik‖sɪˈrɪlɪk/ *adj* of or constituting an alphabet used for writing various Slavic languages (e g Old Church Slavonic and Russian)

cyst /sist‖sɪst/ *n* **1** a closed sac (e g of watery liquid or gas) with a distinct membrane, developing (abnormally) in a plant or animal **2** a body resembling a cyst: e g **2a** (a capsule formed about) a microorganism in a resting or spore stage **b** a resistant cover about a parasite when inside the host – **cystoid** *adj or n*

cystitis /siˈstietəs‖sɪˈstaɪtəs/ *n* inflammation of the urinary bladder

cytology /sieˈtoləji‖saɪˈtɒlədʒɪ/ *n* the biology of (the structure, function, multiplication, pathology, etc of) cells – **cytologist** *n*, **cytological, cytologic** *adj*, **cytologically** *adv*

cytoplasm /ˈsietə,plaz(ə)m‖ˈsaɪtə,plæz(ə)m/ *n* the substance of a plant or animal cell outside the organelles (e g the nucleus and mitochondria) – **cytoplasmic** *adj*, **cytoplasmically** *adv*

czar /zah‖zɑː/ *n* a tsar

Czech /chek‖tʃek/ *n* **1** a native or inhabitant of Czechoslovakia; *specif* a Slav of W Czechoslovakia **2** the Slavonic language of the Czechs – **Czech** *adj*

d /dee‖diː/ *n, pl* **d's, ds** *often cap* **1** (a graphic representation of or device for reproducing) the 4th letter of the English alphabet **2** five hundred **3** the 2nd note of a C-major scale **4** one designated *d*, esp as the 4th in order or class **5** sthg shaped like the letter D: e g **5a** a semicircle on a billiard table used chiefly when returning a potted cue ball to the table **b** the metal loop on the cheek piece of the bit of a bridle

[1]**-d** *suffix* **1** – used to form the past participle of regular weak verbs that end in *e* <*loved*>; compare [1]-ED 1 **2** – used to form adjectives of identical meaning from Latin-derived adjectives ending in *-ate* <*crenulated*> **3** [1]-ED 2 – used to form adjectives from nouns ending in *e* <*bow-tied*>

[2]**-d** *suffix* (→ *vb*) – used to form the past tense of regular weak verbs that end in *e*; compare [2]-ED

[3]**-d** *suffix* (→ *adj*), *NAm* – used after the figure 2 or 3 to indicate the ordinal number second or third <*2d*>

d' *vb* do <*d'you know*>

'd *vb* **1** had **2** would **3** did – used in questions; infml

[1]**dab** /dab‖dæb/ *n* **1** a sudden feeble blow or thrust; a poke **2** a gentle touch or stroke (e g with a sponge); a pat

[2]**dab** *vb* **-bb-** *vt* **1** to touch lightly, and usu repeatedly; pat **2** to apply lightly or irregularly; daub ~ *vi* to make a dab

[3]**dab** *n* **1** a daub, patch **2** *pl, Br* fingerprints – infml

[4]**dab** *n* a flatfish; *esp* any of several flounders

[5]**dab** *n* DAB HAND – infml

dabble /ˈdabl‖ˈdæbl/ *vt* to wet slightly or intermittently by dipping in a liquid ~ *vi* **1** to paddle, splash, or play (as if) in water **2** to work or concern oneself superficially <~*s in art*>

dabchick /ˈdab,chik‖ˈdæb,tʃɪk/ *n* any of several small grebes

,dab ˈhand /dab‖dæb/ *n, chiefly Br* sby skilful *at*; an expert – infml

dace /days‖deɪs/ *n, pl* **dace** a small freshwater European fish

dachshund /ˈdaksənd‖ˈdæksənd/ *n* (any of) a breed of dogs of German origin with a long body, short legs, and long drooping ears [German, fr *dachs* badger + *hund* dog]

dactyl /ˈdaktil‖ˈdæktɪl/ *n* a metrical foot consisting of 1 long and 2 short, or 1 stressed and 2 unstressed, syllables (e g in *tenderly*) – **dactylic** *adj or n*

dad /dad‖dæd/ *n* a father – infml

daddy /ˈdadi‖ˈdædɪ/ *n* a father – infml

,daddy ˈlonglegs /ˈlong,legz‖ˈlɒŋ,legz/ *n, pl* **daddy longlegs** CRANE FLY

dado /ˈdaydoh‖ˈdeɪdəʊ/ *n, pl* **dadoes 1** the part of a pedestal or plinth between the base and the cornice **2** the lower part of an interior wall when specially decorated or faced

daemon /ˈdeemən‖ˈdiːmən/ *n* **1** an attendant power or spirit; a genius **2** a supernatural being of Greek mythology **3** DEMON 1

daffodil /ˈdafədil‖ˈdæfədɪl/ *n* any of various plants with flowers that have a large typically yellow corona elongated into a trumpet shape; *also* a related bulb-forming plant

daft /dahft‖dɑːft/ *adj* **1** silly, foolish **2** *chiefly Br* fanatically enthusiastic *USE* infml – **daft** *adv*, **daftly** *adv*, **daftness** *n*

dagger /ˈdagə‖ˈdægə/ *n* **1** a short sharp pointed weapon for stabbing **2** a sign † used as a reference mark or to indicate a death date – **at daggers drawn** in bitter conflict

dago /ˈdaygoh‖ˈdeɪgəʊ/ *n, pl* **dagos, dagoes** sby of Italian, Spanish, or Portuguese birth or descent – derog

daguerreotype /dəˈger(i)ə,tiep‖dəˈger(ɪ)ə-,taɪp/ *n* an early photograph produced on a silver or a silver-covered copper plate

dahlia /ˈdayli·ə, ˈdah-‖ˈdeɪlɪə, ˈdɑː-/ *n* any of an American genus of plants with showy flower heads and roots that form tubers [Anders *Dahl* (died 1789), Swedish botanist]

Dáil /doyl, diel‖dɔɪl, daɪl/, **Dáil Eireann** /~ ˈeərən‖~ ˈeərən/ *n* the lower house of parliament in the Irish Republic

[1]**daily** /ˈdayli‖ˈdeɪlɪ/ *adj* **1a** occurring, made, or

acted on every day **b** *of a newspaper* issued every weekday **c** of or providing for every day **2** covering the period of or based on a day

[2]**daily** *adv* every day; every weekday

[3]**daily** *n* **1** a newspaper published daily from Monday to Saturday **2** *Br* a charwoman who works on a daily basis

[1]**dainty** /'daynti||'deɪntɪ/ *n* sthg particularly nice to eat; a delicacy

[2]**dainty** *adj* **1** attractively prepared and served **2** delicately beautiful **3a** fastidious **b** showing avoidance of anything rough – **daintily** *adv*, **daintiness** *n*

daiquiri /die'kiəri, də-, 'dakiri||daɪ'kɪərɪ, də-, 'dækɪrɪ/ *n* a cocktail made of rum, lime juice, and sugar [*Daiquiri*, town in Cuba]

[1]**dairy** /'deəri||'deərɪ/ *n* **1** a room, building, etc where milk is processed and butter or cheese is made **2** farming concerned with the production of milk, butter, and cheese **3** an establishment for the sale or distribution of milk and milk products

[2]**dairy** *adj* of or concerned with (the production of) milk (products)

'**dairying** /-ing||-ɪŋ/ *n* the business of operating a dairy or producing milk products

dairyman /-mən||-mən/, *fem* '**dairy,maid** / -,mayd||-,meɪd/ *n* one who operates or works for a dairy (farm)

dais /'day·is||'deɪɪs/ *n* a raised platform; *esp* one at the end of a hall

daisy /'dayzi||'deɪzɪ/ *n* a composite plant with well-developed ray flowers in its flower head: e g **a** a common short European plant with a yellow disc and white or pink ray flowers **b** OX-EYE DAISY [Old English *dægesēage*, fr *dæg* day + *ēage* eye]

daisy wheel *n* a disc that carries the letter type in some kinds of typewriter or printer

Dalai Lama /,dalie'lahmə||,dælaɪ'lɑːmə/ *n* the spiritual head of Tibetan Buddhism

dale /dayl||deɪl/ *n* a vale, valley

dalliance /'dali·əns||'dælɪəns/ *n* a dallying: e g **a** amorous or erotically stimulating activity **b** a frivolous action

dally /'dali||'dælɪ/ *vi* **1a** to act playfully; *esp* to flirt **b** to deal lightly; toy **2** to waste time; dawdle – **dallier** *n*

dalmatian /dal'maysh(ə)n||dæl'meɪʃ(ə)n/ *n, often cap* (any of) a breed of medium-sized dogs with a white short-haired coat with black or brown spots [*Dalmatia*, region of Yugoslavia where the breed supposedly originated]

[1]**dam** /dam||dæm/ *n* a female parent – used esp with reference to domestic animals

[2]**dam** *n* **1** a barrier preventing the flow of a fluid; *esp* a barrier across a watercourse **2** a body of water confined by a dam

[3]**dam** *vt* **-mm- 1** to provide or restrain with a dam **2** to stop up; block

[1]**damage** /'damij||'dæmɪdʒ/ *n* **1** loss or harm resulting from injury to person, property, or reputation **2** *pl* compensation in money imposed by law for loss or injury **3** expense, cost – infml <*what's the* ~?>

[2]**damage** *vt* to cause damage to ~*vi* to become damaged – **damager** *n*

damascene *vt* to ornament (e g iron or steel) with wavy patterns like those of watered silk or with inlaid work of precious metals

[1]**damask** /'daməsk||'dæməsk/ *n* **1** a reversible lustrous fabric (e g of linen, cotton, or silk) having a plain background woven with patterns **2** greyish red

[2]**damask** *adj* **1** made of or resembling damask **2** of the colour damask

,**damask 'rose** *n* a large fragrant pink rose cultivated esp as a source of attar of roses

dame /daym||deɪm/ *n* **1** a woman of rank, station, or authority: e g **1a** the wife or daughter of a lord **b** a female member of an order of knighthood – used as a title preceding the Christian name **2a** an elderly woman; *specif* a comic one in pantomime played usu by a male actor **b** *chiefly NAm* a woman – infml

[1]**damn** /dam||dæm/ *vt* **1** to condemn to a punishment or fate; *esp* to condemn to hell **2** to condemn as a failure by public criticism **3** to bring ruin on **4** to curse – often used as an interjection to express annoyance ~*vi* to curse, swear – **I'll be damned** – used to express astonishment – **I'll be damned if** I emphatically do not or will not <I'll be damned if *I'll go*>

[2]**damn** *n* **1** the utterance of the word *damn* as a curse **2** the slightest bit <*I couldn't care a* ~> – chiefly in negative phrases

[3]**damn** *adj or adv* – used as an intensive – **damn well** beyond doubt or question; certainly

damnable /'damnəbl||'dæmnəbl/ *adj* **1** liable to or deserving condemnation **2** very bad; detestable – **damnableness** *n*, **damnably** *adv*

damnation /dam'naysh(ə)n||dæm'neɪʃ(ə)n/ *n* damning or being damned

damnedest, damndest /'damdist||'dæmdɪst/ *n* utmost, best – chiefly in *do one's damnedest*; infml

damning /'daming||'dæmɪŋ/ *adj* causing or leading to condemnation or ruin <*presented some* ~ *testimony*> – **damningly** *adv*

[1]**damp** /damp||dæmp/ *n* **1** a noxious gas, esp in a coal mine **2** moisture, humidity **3** DAMPER 2 **4** *archaic* fog, mist – **damp-proof** *adj*

[2]**damp** *vt* **1a** to diminish the activity or intensity of <~ *the fire in the furnace*> – often + *down* **b** to reduce progressively the vibration or oscillation of (e g sound waves) **2** to dampen ~*vi* to diminish progressively in vibration or oscillation

[3]**damp** *adj* slightly or moderately wet – **damply** *adv*, **dampness** *n*, **dampish** *adj*

'**damp ,course** *n* a horizontal damp-resistant layer near the ground in a masonry wall

dampen /'dampən||'dæmpən/ *vt* **1** to check or diminish the activity or vigour of (esp feelings) <*nothing could* ~ *his spirits*> **2** to make damp **3** DAMP 1b – **dampener** *n*

damper /'dampə||'dæmpə/ *n* **1** a device that damps: e g **1a** a valve or plate (e g in the flue of a furnace) for regulating the draught **b** a small felted block which prevents or stops the vibration of a piano string **c** a device (e g a shock absorber) designed to bring a mechanism to rest with minimum oscillation **2** a dulling or deadening influence <*put a* ~ *on the celebration*>

damsel /ˈdamzəl‖ˈdæmzəl/ *n, archaic* a young woman; a girl

damson /ˈdamzən‖ˈdæmzən/ *n* (the small acid purple fruit of) an Asiatic plum [Latin (*prunum*) *damascenum*, lit., (plum) from Damascus]

[1]**dance** /dahns‖dɑːns/ *vi* **1** to engage in or perform a dance **2** to move quickly up and down or about ~ *vt* to perform or take part in as a dancer – **danceable** *adj*, **dancer** *n*

[2]**dance** *n* **1** (an act or instance or the art of) a series of rhythmic and patterned bodily movements usu performed to music **2** a social gathering for dancing **3** a piece of music for dancing to

dandelion /ˈdandi,lie·ən‖ˈdændɪ,laɪən/ *n* any of a genus of yellow-flowered composite plants including one that occurs virtually worldwide as a weed [Middle French *dent de lion*, lit., lion's tooth]

dander /ˈdandə‖ˈdændə/ *n* anger, temper – chiefly in *have/get one's dander up*; infml

dandify /ˈdandifie‖ˈdændɪfaɪ/ *vt* to cause to resemble a dandy – **dandification** *n*

dandle /ˈdandl‖ˈdændl/ *vt* to move (e g a baby) up and down in one's arms or on one's knee in affectionate play

dandruff /ˈdandruf, -drəf‖ˈdændrʌf, -drəf/ *n* a scurf that comes off the scalp in small white or greyish scales – **dandruffy** *adj*

[1]**dandy** /ˈdandi‖ˈdændɪ/ *n* a man who gives exaggerated attention to dress and demeanour – **dandyish** *adj*, **dandyishly** *adv*, **dandyism** *n*

[2]**dandy** *adj, NAm* very good; first-rate – infml; not now in vogue

Dane /dayn‖deɪn/ *n* a native or inhabitant of Denmark

danger /ˈdaynjə‖ˈdeɪndʒə/ *n* **1** exposure to the possibility of injury, pain, or loss **2** a case or cause of danger <*the* ~s *of mining*>

ˈ**danger ,money** *n* extra pay for dangerous work

dangerous /ˈdaynj(ə)rəs‖ˈdeɪndʒ(ə)rəs/ *adj* **1** exposing to or involving danger **2** able or likely to inflict injury – **dangerously** *adv*, **dangerousness** *n*

dangle /ˈdang·gl‖ˈdæŋgl/ *vi* to hang or swing loosely ~ *vt* **1** to cause to dangle; swing **2** to display enticingly <~d *the possibility before them*> – **dangler** *n*, **danglingly** *adv*

[1]**Danish** /ˈdaynish‖ˈdeɪnɪʃ/ *adj* (characteristic) of Denmark

[2]**Danish** *n* the Germanic language of the Danes

,**Danish** ˈ**pastry** *n* (a piece of) confectionery made from a rich yeast dough with a sweet filling

dank /dangk‖dæŋk/ *adj* unpleasantly moist or wet – **dankly** *adv*, **dankness** *n*

dapper /ˈdapə‖ˈdæpə/ *adj, esp of a small man* neat and spruce as regards clothing and demeanour – **dapperly** *adv*, **dapperness** *n*

dapple /ˈdapl‖ˈdæpl/ *vb* to mark or become marked with rounded patches of varying shade – **dapple** *n*

Darby and Joan /,dahbi ənd ˈjohn‖,dɑːbɪ ənd ˈdʒəʊn/ *n* a happily married elderly couple

[1]**dare** /deə‖deə/ *vb* **dared,** *archaic* **durst** /duhst‖dɜːst/ *vi* to have sufficient courage or impudence (to) <*no one* ~d *say a word*> ~ *vt* **1a** to challenge to perform an action, esp as a proof of courage <~d *him to jump*> **b** to confront boldly; defy <~d *the anger of her family*> **2** to have the courage to contend against, venture, or try – **darer** *n*

[2]**dare** *n* a challenge to a bold act <*foolishly took a* ~>

daredevil /ˈdeə,devl‖ˈdeə,devl/ *n or adj* (sby) recklessly bold – **daredevilry** *n*

daren't /deənt‖deənt/ dare not

daresay /,deəˈsay‖,deəˈseɪ/ *vb pres 1 sing* venture to say (so); think (it) probable; suppose (so)

[1]**daring** /ˈdeəring‖ˈdeərɪŋ/ *adj* adventurously bold in action or thought – **daringly** *adv*, **daringness** *n*

[2]**daring** *n* venturesome boldness

[1]**dark** /dahk‖dɑːk/ *adj* **1** (partially) devoid of light **2a** (partially) black **b** *of a colour* of (very) low lightness **3a** arising from or showing evil traits or desires; evil **b** dismal, sad <*took a* ~ *view of the future*> **c** lacking knowledge or culture **4** not fair; swarthy <*her* ~ *good looks*> **5** secret <*kept his plans* ~> – **darkish** *adj*, **darkly** *adv*, **darkness** *n*

[2]**dark** *n* **1a** the absence of light; darkness **b** a place or time of little or no light; night, nightfall <*after* ~> **2** a dark or deep colour – **in the dark** in ignorance <*kept the public* in the dark *about the agreement*>

ˈ**Dark ,Ages** *n pl* the period from about AD 476 to about 1000

darken /ˈdahkən‖ˈdɑːkən/ *vb* to make or become dark or darker – **darkener** *n*

,**dark** ˈ**horse** *n* sby or sthg (e g a contestant) little known, but with a potential much greater than the evidence would suggest

ˈ**darkroom** /-,roohm, -room‖-,ruːm, -rʊm/ *n* a room with no light or with a safelight for handling and processing light-sensitive photographic materials

darky, darkey /ˈdahki‖ˈdɑːkɪ/ *n* a Negro – derog

[1]**darling** /ˈdahling‖ˈdɑːlɪŋ/ *n* **1a** a dearly loved person **b** DEAR 1b **2** a favourite <*the critics'* ~>

[2]**darling** *adj* **1** dearly loved; favourite **2** charming <*a* ~ *little house*> – used esp by women

[1]**darn** /dahn‖dɑːn/ *vt* to mend (sthg) with interlacing stitches woven across a hole or worn part <~ *a sock*> – **darner** *n*

[2]**darn** *n* a place that has been darned <*a sweater full of* ~s>

[3]**darn** *vb* to damn – **darned** *adj or adv*

[4]**darn** *adj or adv* damned

[1]**dart** /daht‖dɑːt/ *n* **1a** a small projectile with a pointed shaft at one end and flights of feather, plastic, etc at the other **b** *pl but sing in constr* a game in which darts are thrown at a dartboard **2** sthg with a slender pointed shaft or outline; *specif* a stitched tapering fold put in a garment to shape it to the figure **3** a quick movement; a dash

[2]**dart** *vt* **1** to throw with a sudden movement **2** to thrust or move with sudden speed **3** to put a dart or darts in (a garment or part of a garment) ~*vi* to move suddenly or rapidly <~

ed *across the road*>

ˈdartˌboard /-ˌbawd‖-ˌbɔːd/ *n* a circular target used in darts that is divided, usu by wire, into different scoring areas

[1]**dash** /dash‖dæʃ/ *vt* **1** to strike or knock violently **2** to break by striking or knocking **3** to destroy, ruin <*the news* ~ed *her hopes*> **4** *Br* DAMN 4 – euph <~ *it all*> ~ *vi* **1** to move with sudden speed <~ed *through the rain*> **2** to smash

[2]**dash** *n* **1** (the sound produced by) a sudden burst or splash **2a** a stroke of a pen **b** a punctuation mark – used esp to indicate a break in the thought or structure of a sentence **3** a small but significant addition <*a* ~ *of salt*> **4** liveliness of style and action; panache **5** a sudden onset, rush, or attempt **6** a signal (e g a flash or audible tone) of relatively long duration that is one of the 2 fundamental units of Morse code

dashboard /ˈdashˌbawd‖ˈdæʃˌbɔːd/ *n* a panel extending across a motor car, aeroplane, or motorboat below the windscreen and usu containing dials and controls

dashing /ˈdashing‖ˈdæʃɪŋ/ *adj* **1** marked by vigorous action; spirited **2** marked by smartness, esp in dress and manners – **dashingly** *adv*

dash off *vt* to complete or execute (e g writing or drawing) hastily

data /ˈdahtə, ˈdaytə‖ˈdɑːtə, ˈdeɪtə/ *n pl but sing or pl in constr* factual information (e g measurements or statistics) used as a basis for reasoning, discussion, or calculation

ˈdataˌbank *n* a collection of data organized esp for rapid search and retrieval (e g by computer)

ˈdataˌbase *n* the data that is accessible to a data-processing system (e g a computer)

ˌdata ˈprocessing *n* the conversion (e g by computer) of crude information into usable or storable form – **data processor** *n*

[1]**date** /dayt‖deɪt/ *n* (the oblong edible fruit of) a tall palm [Old French, deriv of Latin *dactylus*, fr Greek *daktylos*, lit., finger]

[2]**date** *n* **1a** the time reckoned in days or larger units at which an event occurs <*the* ~ *of her birth*> **b** a statement of such a time <*the* ~ *on the letter*> **2** the period of time to which sthg belongs **3a** an appointment for a specified time; *esp* a social engagement between 2 people of opposite sex – infml **b** *NAm* a person of the opposite sex with whom one has a date – infml [Middle French, fr Late Latin *data*, fr *data* given (used in showing when and where a document was written, e g in *data Romae* given at Rome), fr Latin *dare* to give] – **to date** up to the present moment

[3]**date** *vt* **1** to determine the date of <~ *an antique*> **2** to record the date of **3a** to mark with characteristics typical of a particular period **b** to show up plainly the age of <*his knickerbockers* ~ *him*> **4** *chiefly NAm* to make or have a date with (a person of the opposite sex) – infml ~ *vi* **1** to have been in existence – usu + *from* **2** to become old-fashioned <*clothes that never* ~> – **datable, dateable** *adj*, **dater** *n*

ˈdated *adj* **1** provided with a date <*a* ~ *document*> **2** out-of-date, old-fashioned – **datedly** *adv*, **datedness** *n*

dateless /ˈdaytlis‖ˈdeɪtlɪs/ *adj* **1** having no date **2** timeless

ˈdateˌline /-ˌlien‖-ˌlaɪn/ *n* **1** a line in a written document or publication giving the date and place of composition or issue **2** INTERNATIONAL DATE LINE – **dateline** *vt*

dative /ˈdaytiv‖ˈdeɪtɪv/ *n* (a form in) a grammatical case expressing typically the indirect object of a verb, the object of some prepositions, or a possessor – **dative** *adj*

[1]**daub** /dawb‖dɔːb/ *vt* **1** to cover or coat with soft adhesive matter; plaster **2** to coat with a dirty substance **3** to apply (e g colouring material) crudely (to) ~*vi* to paint without much skill – **dauber** *n*

[2]**daub** *n* **1** material used to daub walls **2** a daubing **3** sthg daubed on; a smear **4** a crude picture

[1]**daughter** /ˈdawtə‖ˈdɔːtə/ *n* **1a** a human female having the relation of child to parent **b** a female descendant – often pl **2a** a human female having a specified origin or affiliation <*a* ~ *of the Church*> **b** sthg considered as a daughter <*French is a* ~ *(language) of Latin*> – **daughterly** *adj*

[2]**daughter** *adj* **1** having the characteristics or relationship of a daughter **2** of the first generation of offspring, molecules, etc produced by reproduction, division, or replication <*the* ~ *cells*>

ˈdaughter-in-ˌlaw *n, pl* **daughters-in-law** the wife of one's son

daunt /dawnt‖dɔːnt/ *vt* to lessen the courage of; inspire awe in

ˈdauntless /-lis‖-lɪs/ *adj* fearless – **dauntlessly** *adv*, **dauntlessness** *n*

dauphin /ˈdawfin‖dɔːfɪn (*Fr* dofɛ̃)/ *n, often cap* the eldest son of a king of France

davit /ˈdavit‖ˈdævɪt/ *n* any of 2 or more projecting arms on a vessel which are used as cranes, esp for lowering boats

Davy Jones's locker /ˌdayvi ˈjohnziz‖ˌdeɪvɪ ˈdʒəʊnzɪz/ *n* the bottom of the sea

ˈDavy ˌlamp /ˈdayvi‖ˈdeɪvɪ/ *n* an early safety lamp used in mines [Sir Humphry *Davy* (1778-1829), English chemist & inventor]

dawdle /ˈdawdl‖ˈdɔːdl/ **1** to spend time idly **2** to move lackadaisically – **dawdle** *n*, **dawdler** *n*

[1]**dawn** /dawn‖dɔːn/ *vi* **1** to begin to grow light as the sun rises **2** to begin to appear or develop **3** to begin to be perceived or understood <*the truth finally* ~ed *on him*>

[2]**dawn** *n* **1** the first appearance of light in the morning **2** a first appearance; a beginning <*the* ~ *of the space age*>

day /day‖deɪ/ *n* **1** the time of light when the sun is above the horizon between one night and the next **2** the time required by a celestial body, specif the earth, to turn once on its axis **3** the solar day of 24 hours beginning at midnight **4** a specified day or date <*wash* ~> **5** a specified time or period <*in grandfather's* ~> **6** the conflict or contention of the day <*played hard and won the* ~> **7** the time established by usage or law for work, school, or business <*an 8-hour* ~> **8** an era – **day in, day out** DAY AFTER DAY – **from day to day** [2]DAILY

ˌday after ˈday *adv* for an indefinite or

seemingly endless number of successive days

ˈdayˌbreak /-ˌbrayk‖-ˌbreɪk/ *n* DAWN 1

ˈdayˌdream /-ˌdreem‖-ˌdriːm/ *n* a visionary, usu wish-fulfilling, creation of the waking imagination – **daydream** *vi*

ˈdayˌlight /-ˌliet‖-ˌlaɪt/ *n* **1** DAWN 1 **2** knowledge or understanding of sthg that has been obscure <*began to see* ~ *on the problem*> **3** *pl* mental soundness or stability; wits <*scared the* ~*s out of her*> – infml

daylight saving time *n, chiefly NAm* time usu 1 hour ahead of standard time and used esp during the summer

day nursery *n* a public centre for the care of young children

ˌday of ˈreckoning *n* a time when the results of mistakes or misdeeds are felt, or when offences are punished

ˌday-reˈturn *n, Br* a ticket sold for a return journey on the same day and usu at a reduced rate if used outside rush hours

days /dayz‖deɪz/ *adv, chiefly NAm* by day repeatedly; on any day

ˌday-to-ˈday *adj* **1** taking place, made, or done in the course of successive days <~ *problems*> **2** providing for a day at a time with little thought for the future <*lived an aimless* ~ *existence*>

daze /dayz‖deɪz/ *vt* to stupefy, esp by a blow; stun – **daze** *n*, **dazedly** *adv*, **dazedness** *n*

dazzle /ˈdazl‖ˈdæzl/ *vi* **1** to lose clear vision, esp from looking at bright light **2a** to shine brilliantly **b** to arouse admiration by an impressive display ~ *vt* **1** to overpower or temporarily blind (the sight) with light **2** to impress deeply, overpower, or confound with brilliance – **dazzle** *n*, **dazzler** *n*, **dazzlingly** *adv*

ˈD ˌday /dee‖diː/ *n* a day set for launching an operation; *specif* June 6, 1944, on which the Allies began the invasion of France in WW II

DDT *n* a synthetic chlorinated water-insoluble insecticide that tends to accumulate in food chains and is poisonous to many vertebrates [*d*ichloro-*d*iphenyl-*t*richloro-ethane]

de- /dee-‖diː-/ *prefix* **1a** do the opposite of (a specified action) <de*compose*> **b** reverse of <de-*emphasis*> **2a** remove (sthg specified) from <de*louse*> **b** remove from (sthg specified) <de*throne*> **3** reduce <de*value*> **4** alight from (a specified thing) <de*train*>

deacon /ˈdeekən‖ˈdiːkən/ *n* a subordinate officer in a Christian church: e g **a** a clergyman ranking below a priest and, in the Anglican and Roman Catholic churches, usu a candidate for ordination as priest **b** an assistant minister in a Lutheran parish **c** any of a group of laymen with administrative and sometimes spiritual duties in various Protestant churches

[1]**dead** /ded‖ded/ *adj* **1** deprived of life; having died **2a(1)** having the appearance of death; deathly <*in a* ~ *faint*> **a(2)** lacking power to move, feel, or respond; numb **b** very tired **c** grown cold; extinguished <~ *coals*> **3a** inanimate, inert <~ *matter*> **b** barren, infertile <~ *soil*> **4a(1)** no longer having power or effect <*a* ~ *law*> **a(2)** no longer having interest, relevance, or significance <*a* ~ *issue*> **b** no longer used; obsolete <*a* ~ *language*> **c** no longer existing <*charity is* ~> **d** lacking in activity **e** lacking elasticity or springiness **f** out of action or use; *specif* free from any connection to a source of voltage and free from electric charges **g** temporarily out of play <*a* ~ *ball*> **5** not imparting motion or power although otherwise functioning <*a* ~ *rear axle*> **6** lacking warmth, odour, vigour, or taste **7a** absolutely uniform <~ *level*> **b** exact <~ *centre of the target*> **c** abrupt <*brought to a* ~ *stop*> **d** complete, absolute <*a* ~ *silence*> <*a* ~ *loss*> <*a* ~ *giveaway*> **8** lacking in gaiety or animation – chiefly infml – **deadness** *n*

[2]**dead** *n* **1** *pl in constr* dead people or animals **2** the state of being dead <*raised him from the* ~> **3** the time of greatest quiet or inactivity <*the* ~ *of night*>

[3]**dead** *adv* **1** absolutely, utterly <~ *certain* > **2** suddenly and completely <*stopped* ~> **3** directly, exactly <~ *ahead*> **4** *Br* very, extremely <~ *lucky*> – infml

deadbeat /ˈdedˌbeet‖ˈdedˌbiːt/ *n, chiefly NAm* a loafer

deaden /ˈdedən‖ˈdedən/ *vt* **1** to deprive of liveliness, brilliance, sensation, or force **2** to make (e g a wall) impervious to sound – **deadener** *n*, **deadeningly** *adv*

ˌdead-ˈend *adj* **1a** lacking opportunities for advancement <*a* ~ *job*> **b** lacking an exit <*a* ~ *street*> **2** made aggressively antisocial by a dead-end existence <~ *kids*>

ˌdead ˈend *n* **1** an end (e g of a street) without an exit **2** a position, situation, or course of action that leads no further

ˌdead ˈheat *n* an inconclusive finish to a race or other contest, in which the fastest time, highest total, etc is achieved by more than one competitor – **dead-heat** *vi*

ˌdead ˈletter *n* **1** a law that has lost its force without being formally abolished **2** an undeliverable and unreturnable letter

deadline /ˈdedlien‖ˈdedlaɪn/ *n* **1** a boundary beyond which it is not possible or permitted to pass **2** a date or time before which sthg (e g the presentation of copy for publication) must be done

deadlock /ˈdedlok‖ˈdedlɒk/ *n* **1** a lock that can be opened and shut only by a key **2** inaction or neutralization resulting from the opposition of equally powerful and uncompromising people or factions; a standstill **3** a tied score – **deadlock** *vt*

[1]**deadly** /ˈdedli‖ˈdedlɪ/ *adj* **1** likely to cause or capable of producing death **2a** aiming to kill or destroy; implacable <*a* ~ *enemy*> **b** unerring <~ *accuracy*> **c** marked by determination or extreme seriousness <*she was in* ~ *earnest*> **3** lacking animation; dull **4** intense, extreme <~ *fear*> – **deadliness** *n*

[2]**deadly** *adv* **1** suggesting death <~ *pale*> **2** extremely <~ *serious*>

ˌdeadly ˈnightˌshade /ˈnietˌshayd‖ˈnaɪtˌʃeɪd/ *n* a European poisonous nightshade that has dull purple flowers and black berries

ˌdead ˌman's ˈhandle *n, Br* a handle that requires constant pressure to allow operation (e g of a train or tram)

[1]**deadpan** /dedˈpan‖ dedˈpæn/ *adj*

impassive, expressionless

[2]**deadpan** *adv* in a deadpan manner

ˌ**dead ˈreckoning** *n* the calculation without celestial observations of the position of a ship or aircraft, from the record of the courses followed, the distance travelled, etc – **dead reckon** *vb*, **dead reckoner** *n*

ˈ**deadˌweight** /-ˌwayt‖-ˌweɪt/ *n* **1** the unrelieved weight of an inert mass **2** a ship's total weight including cargo, fuel, stores, crew, and passengers

ˈ**deadˌwood** /-ˌwood‖-ˌwʊd/ *n* useless personnel or material

deaf /def‖def/ *adj* **1** (partially) lacking the sense of hearing **2** unwilling to hear or listen *to*; not to be persuaded <~ *to reason*> – **deafish** *adj*, **deafly** *adv*, **deafness** *n*

ˈ**deaf-ˌaid** *n, Br* HEARING AID

deafen /ˈdefən‖ˈdefən/ *vt* to make deaf ~*vi* to cause deafness or stun sby with noise – **deafeningly** *adv*

ˌ**deaf-ˈmute** *n or adj* (one who is) deaf and dumb

[1]**deal** /deel‖diːl/ *n* **1** a usu large or indefinite quantity or degree; a lot **2a** the act or right of distributing cards to players in a card game **b** HAND 9b

[2]**deal** *vb* **dealt** /delt‖delt/ *vt* **1a** to give as sby's portion; apportion **b** to distribute (playing cards) to players in a game **2** to administer, bestow <~t *him a blow*> ~ *vi* **1** to distribute the cards in a card game **2** to concern oneself or itself <*the book* ~s *with education*> **3a** to trade **b** to sell or distribute sthg as a business <~ *in insurance*> **4** to take action with regard to sby or sthg <~ *with an offender*>

[3]**deal** *n* **1** a transaction **2** treatment received <*a raw* ~> **3** an arrangement for mutual advantage

[4]**deal** *n* (a sawn piece of) fir or pine timber – **deal** *adj*

dealer /ˈdeelə‖ˈdiːlə/ *n* **1** sby who deals in goods or services **2** sby or sthg that deals playing cards

dealing /ˈdeeling‖ˈdiːlɪŋ/ *n* **1** *pl* friendly or business interactions **2** a method of business; a manner of conduct

[1]**dean**, **dene** /deen‖diːn/ *n, Br* a narrow wooded valley containing a stream

[2]**dean** *n* **1a** the head of the chapter of a collegiate or cathedral church – often used as a title **b** RURAL DEAN **2** the head of a university division, faculty, or school **3** a doyen [Middle French *deien*, fr Late Latin *decanus*, lit., chief of ten, fr Latin *decem* ten] – **deanship** *n*

deanery /ˈdeenəri‖ˈdiːnərɪ/ *n* the office, jurisdiction, or official residence of a clerical dean

[1]**dear** /diə‖dɪə/ *adj* **1** highly valued; much loved – often used in address <~ *Sir*> **2** expensive **3** heartfelt <*her* ~est *wish*> – **dear** *adv*, **dearly** *adv*, **dearness** *n*

[2]**dear** *n* **1a** a loved one; a sweetheart **b** – used as a familiar or affectionate form of address **2** a lovable person

[3]**dear** *interj* – used typically to express annoyance or dismay <*oh* ~>

dearth /duhth‖dɜːθ/ *n* an inadequate supply; a scarcity

deary /ˈdiəri‖ˈdɪərɪ/ *n* a dear person – used chiefly in address

death /deth‖deθ/ *n* **1** a permanent cessation of all vital functions; the end of life **2** the cause or occasion of loss of life <*drinking was the* ~ *of him*> **3** *cap* death personified, usu represented as a skeleton with a scythe **4** the state of being dead **5** extinction, disappearance – **at death's door** seriously ill – **to death** beyond all acceptable limits; excessively <*bored* to death>

ˈ**deathˌblow** /-ˌbloh‖-ˌbləʊ/ *n* a destructive or killing stroke or event

ˈ**death ˌduty** *n, chiefly Br* tax levied on the estate of a dead person – often pl with sing. meaning

ˈ**deathless** /-lis‖-lɪs/ *adj* immortal, imperishable – **deathlessly** *adv*, **deathlessness** *n*

ˈ**deathly** /-li‖-lɪ/ *adj* (suggestive) of death – **deathly** *adv*

ˈ**death ˌmask** *n* a cast taken from the face of a dead person

ˈ**death ˌrate** *n* the number of deaths per 1000 people in a population over a given period

ˈ**death ˌrattle** *n* a gurgling sound produced by air passing through mucus in the lungs and throat of a dying person

ˈ**death's-ˌhead** *n* a human skull symbolic of death

ˈ**death ˌtrap** *n* a potentially lethal structure or place

ˈ**deathˌwatch** /-ˌwoch‖-ˌwɒtʃ/ *n* a vigil kept with the dead or dying

ˈ**death-ˌwish** *n* a usu unconscious desire for the death of another or oneself

deb /deb‖deb/ *n* a debutante – infml – **debby** *adj*

debacle /diˈbahkəl‖dɪˈbɑːkəl/ *n* **1** a tumultuous breakup of ice in a river **2** a violent disruption (e g of an army); a rout **3** a complete failure; a fiasco

debar /ˌdeeˈbah‖ˌdiːˈbɑː/ *vt* **-rr-** to bar *from* having, doing, or undergoing sthg; preclude – **debarment** *n*

debark /ˌdeeˈbahk‖ˌdiːˈbɑːk/ *vt* to remove the bark from (a tree)

debase /diˈbays‖dɪˈbeɪs/ *vt* **1** to lower in status, esteem, quality, or character **2a** to reduce the intrinsic value of (a coin) by increasing the content of low-value metal **b** to reduce the exchange value of (a monetary unit) – **debasement** *n*, **debaser** *n*

debatable /diˈbaytəbl‖dɪˈbeɪtəbl/ *adj* **1** claimed by more than 1 country <~ *territory*> **2** open to debate; questionable

[1]**debate** /diˈbayt‖dɪˈbeɪt/ *n* a contention by words or arguments; *esp* the formal discussion of a motion **a** in parliament **b** between 2 opposing sides

[2]**debate** *vi* **1a** to contend in words **b** to discuss a question by considering opposed arguments **2** to participate in a debate ~ *vt* **1** to argue about **2** to consider – **debater** *n*

[1]**debauch** /diˈbawch‖dɪˈbɔːtʃ/ *vt* **1** to lead away from virtue or excellence **2** to make excessively intemperate or sensual – **debaucher** *n*

[2]**debauch** *n* **1** an act or occasion of debauchery **2** an orgy

debauchee /diˌbawˈchee‖dɪˌbɔːˈtʃiː/ *n* one given to debauchery

debauchery /di'bawchəri||dɪ'bɔːtʃərɪ/ *n* excessive indulgence in the pleasures of the flesh

debenture /di'benchə||dɪ'bentʃə/ *n, Br* a loan secured on the assets of a company in respect of which the company must pay a fixed interest before any dividends are paid to its own shareholders

debilitate /di'bilitayt||dɪ'bɪlɪteɪt/ *vt* to impair the strength of; enfeeble – **debilitation** *n*

debility /di'biləti||dɪ'bɪlətɪ/ *n* a weakness or infirmity

[1]**debit** /'debit||'debɪt/ *n* **1a** (an entry in an account that is) a record of money owed **b** the sum of the items so entered **2** a charge against a bank account

[2]**debit** *vt* **1** to enter as a debit **2** to charge to the debit of <~ *an account*>

debit card *n* a card issued by a bank authorizing the purchase of goods or services which are charged directly to the holder's account

debonair /,debə'neə||,debə'neə/ *adj* **1** suave, urbane **2** lighthearted, nonchalant – **debonairly** *adv*, **debonairness** *n*

debouch /di'bowch||dɪ'baʊtʃ/ *vi* to emerge or issue, esp from a narrow place into a wider place

debrief /,dee'breef||,diː'briːf/ *vt* to interrogate (a person) on return from a mission in order to obtain useful information

debris /'debri||'debrɪ/ *n* **1** the remains of sthg broken down or destroyed **2a** an accumulation of fragments of rock **b** accumulated rubbish or waste [French *débris*, fr Middle French, fr *debriser* to break to pieces]

debt /det||det/ *n* **1** a state of owing <*heavily in* ~> **2** sthg owed; an obligation <*couldn't pay her* ~s> – **in someone's debt** owing sby gratitude; indebted to sby

debtor /'detə||'detə/ *n* one who owes a debt

debug /,dee'bug||,diː'bʌg/ *vt* **-gg- 1** to eliminate errors in or malfunctions of <~ *a computer program*> **2** to remove a concealed microphone or wiretapping device from

debunk /,dee'bungk||,diː'bʌŋk/ *vt* to expose the falseness of – **debunker** *n*

debut /'dayb(y)ooh||'deɪb(j)uː/ *n* **1** a first public appearance **2** a formal entrance into society – **debut** *vi*

debutante /'debyoo,tont||'debjʊ,tɒnt/ *n* a woman making a debut; *esp* a young woman making her formal entrance into society

deca- /dekə-||dekə-/, **dec-, deka-, dek-** *comb form* ten (10^1) <deca*hedron*>

decade /'dekayd||'dekeɪd; *also* di'kayd||dɪ'keɪd/ *n* **1** a group, set, or sequence of 10 **2** a period of 10 years **3** a division of the rosary containing 10 Hail Marys [Middle French *décade*, deriv of Greek *deka* ten]

decadence /'dekədəns||'dekədəns/ *n* **1** being decadent **2** a period of decline

decadent /'dekədənt||'dekədənt/ *adj* **1** marked by decay or decline, esp in moral or cultural standards **2** tending to gratify one's desires, appetites, or whims in an excessive or unrestrained manner – **decadently** *adv*

Decalogue /'dekəlog||'dekəlɒg/ *n* TEN COMMANDMENTS

decamp /,dee'kamp||,diː'kæmp/ *vi* **1** to break up a camp **2** to depart suddenly; abscond – **decampment** *n*

decant /di'kant||dɪ'kænt/ *vt* **1** to pour from one vessel into another, esp a decanter **2** to draw off without disturbing the sediment – **decantation** *n*

decanter /di'kantə||dɪ'kæntə/ *n* an ornamental glass bottle used for serving an alcoholic drink, esp wine

decapitate /di'kapitayt||dɪ'kæpɪteɪt/ *vt* to cut off the head of – **decapitator** *n*, **decapitation** *n*

decathlon /di'kathlon||dɪ'kæθlɒn/ *n* a men's athletic contest in which each competitor competes in 10 running, jumping, and throwing events – **decathlete** *n*

[1]**decay** /di'kay||dɪ'keɪ/ *vi* **1** to decline from a sound or prosperous condition **2** to decrease gradually in quantity, activity, or force; *specif* to undergo radioactive decay **3** to fall into ruin **4** to decline in health, strength, or vigour **5** to undergo decomposition ~*vt* to destroy by decomposition – **decayer** *n*

[2]**decay** *n* **1** a gradual decline in strength, soundness, prosperity, or quality **2** a wasting or wearing away; ruin **3** (a product of) rot; *specif* decomposition of organic matter (e g proteins), chiefly by bacteria in the presence of oxygen **4** a decline in health or vigour **5** decrease in quantity, activity, or force; *esp* spontaneous disintegration of an atom or particle (e g a meson) usu with the emission of radiation

decease /di'sees||dɪ'siːs/ *n* death – fml – **decease** *vi*

de'ceased *n or adj, pl* **deceased** (sby) no longer living; *esp* (sby) recently dead

deceit /di'seet||dɪ'siːt/ *n* **1** the act or practice of deceiving; deception **2** the quality of being deceitful

de'ceitful /-f(ə)l||-f(ə)l/ *adj* having a tendency or disposition to deceive: **a** not honest **b** deceptive, misleading – **deceitfully** *adv*, **deceitfulness** *n*

deceive /di'seev||dɪ'siːv/ *vt* to cause to accept as true or valid what is false or invalid; delude ~*vi* to practise deceit – **deceivable** *adj*, **deceiver** *n*, **deceivingly** *adv*

decelerate /,dee'selərayt||,diː'seləreɪt/ *vb* to (cause to) move at decreasing speed – **decelerator** *n*, **deceleration** *n*

December /di'sembə||dɪ'sembə/ *n* the 12th month of the Gregorian calendar [Latin *December* (tenth month of the early Roman calendar), fr *decem* ten]

decency /'deesənsi||'diːsənsɪ/ *n* **1** propriety, decorum **2** a standard of propriety – usu pl

decent /'dees(ə)nt||'diːs(ə)nt/ *adj* **1** conforming to standards of propriety, good taste, or morality; *specif* clothed according to standards of propriety **2** free from obscenity **3** adequate, tolerable <~ *wages*> **4** *chiefly Br* obliging, considerate <*jolly* ~ *of you*> – infml – **decently** *adv*

decentral·ization, -isation /dee,sentrəlie'zaysh(ə)n||diː,sentrəlaɪ'zeɪʃ(ə)n/ *n* **1** the distribution of functions and powers from a central authority to regional authorities, departments, etc **2** the redistribution of population and industry from urban centres to outlying areas – **decentralizationist** *n*

decentral·ize, -ise /ˌdee'sentrəliez‖ˌdiː'sentrəlaɪz/ *vt* to bring about the decentralization of ~*vi* to undergo decentralization

deception /di'sepsh(ə)n‖dɪ'sepʃ(ə)n/ *n* **1a** the act of deceiving **b** the fact or condition of being deceived **2** sthg that deceives; a trick – **deceptional** *adj*

deceptive /di'septiv‖dɪ'septɪv/ *adj* tending or having power to deceive; misleading – **deceptively** *adv*, **deceptiveness** *n*

deci- /desi-, desə‖desɪ-, desə/ *comb form* one tenth part of (a specified unit) <deci*litre*>

decibel /'desibel‖'desɪbel/ *n* **1** a unit for expressing the ratio of 2 amounts of electric or acoustic signal power equal to 10 times the common logarithm of this ratio **2** a unit for expressing the intensity of sounds on a scale from zero for the average least perceptible sound to about 130 for the average pain level

decide /di'sied‖dɪ'saɪd/ *vt* **1** to arrive at a solution that ends uncertainty or dispute about **2** to bring to a definitive end **3** to induce to come to a choice ~*vi* to make a choice or judgment – **decider** *n*, **decidable** *adj*, **decidability** *n*

de'cided *adj* **1** unquestionable <*a* ~ *advantage*> **2** free from doubt or hesitation <*a woman of* ~ *opinions*> – **decidedly** *adv*, **decidedness** *n*

deciduous /di'sidyoo·əs‖dɪ'sɪdjʊəs/ *adj* (having parts) that fall off or are shed seasonally or at a particular stage in development <*a* ~ *tree*> – **deciduously** *adv*, **deciduousness** *n*

[1]**decimal** /'desiməl‖'desɪməl/ *adj* **1** numbered or proceeding by tens: **1a** based on the number 10 **b** subdivided into units which are tenths, hundredths, etc of another unit **c** expressed in a decimal fraction **2** using a decimal system (e g of coinage) <*when Britain went* ~> [Latin *decima* tenth part, fr *decimus* tenth, fr *decem* ten] – **decimally** *adv*

[2]**decimal, ˌdecimal 'fraction** *n* a fraction that is expressed as a sum of integral multiples of powers of $^1/_{10}$ by writing a dot followed by 1 digit for the number of tenths, 1 digit for the number of hundredths, and so on (e g $0.25 = {}^{25}/_{100}$)

decimal·ize, -ise /'desiməˌliez‖'desɪməˌlaɪz/ *vt* to convert to a decimal system <~ *currency*> – **decimalization** *n*

ˌdecimal 'point *n* the dot at the left of a decimal fraction

decimate /'desimayt‖'desɪmeɪt/ *vt* **1** to kill every tenth man of (e g mutinous soldiers) **2** to destroy a large part of – disapproved of by some speakers [Latin *decimare*, fr *decimus* tenth, fr *decem* ten] – **decimation** *n*

decipher /di'siefə‖dɪ'saɪfə/ *vt* **1a** to convert into intelligible form **b** to decode **2** to make out the meaning of despite obscurity – **decipherable** *adj*, **decipherer** *n*, **decipherment** *n*

decision /di'sizh(ə)n‖dɪ'sɪʒ(ə)n/ *n* **1a** deciding **b** a conclusion arrived at after consideration **2** a report of a conclusion **3** promptness and firmness in deciding – **decisional** *adj*

decisive /di'siesiv‖dɪ'saɪsɪv/ *adj* **1** having the power or quality of deciding; conclusive **2** marked by or indicative of determination or firmness; resolute **3** unmistakable, unquestionable <*a* ~ *victory*> – **decisively** *adv*, **decisiveness** *n*

[1]**deck** /dek‖dek/ *n* **1** a platform in a ship serving usu as a structural element and forming the floor for its compartments **2** sthg resembling the deck of a ship: e g **2a** a level or floor of a bus with more than 1 floor **b** the roadway of a bridge **c** TAPE DECK **d** RECORD DECK **3** *NAm* a pack of playing cards **4** *the* ground – infml; chiefly in *hit the deck* – **decked** *adj*

[2]**deck** *vt* to array, decorate – often + *out*

'deck ˌchair *n* an adjustable folding chair made of canvas stretched over a wooden frame

decker /'dekə‖'dekə/ *n* sthg with a deck or a specified number of levels, floors, or layers – often in combination <*double*-decker *bus*>

'deckˌhand /-ˌhand‖-ˌhænd/ *n* a seaman who performs manual duties

deckle /'dekl‖'dekl/ *n* a part of a paper-making machine that determines the width of the web

deckle edge *n* a rough untrimmed edge of paper – **deckle-edged** *adj*

declaim /di'klaym‖dɪ'kleɪm/ *vi* **1** to speak rhetorically **2** to speak pompously or bombastically ~*vt* to deliver rhetorically; *specif* to recite in elocution – **declaimer** *n*, **declamation** *n*

declaration /ˌdeklə'raysh(ə)n‖ˌdeklə'reɪʃ(ə)n/ *n* **1** sthg declared **2** a document containing such a declaration

declare /di'kleə‖dɪ'kleə/ *vt* **1** to make known formally or explicitly **2** to make evident; show **3** to state emphatically; affirm <~s *his innocence*> **4** to make a full statement of (one's taxable or dutiable income or property) **5a** to announce (e g a trump suit) in a card game **b** to meld (a combination of playing cards) in canasta, rummy, etc ~ *vi* **1** to make a declaration **2** to avow one's support **3** *of a captain or team* to announce one's decision to end one's side's innings in cricket before all the batsmen are out – **declarable** *adj* – **declare war** to commence hostilities; *specif* to make a formal declaration of intention to go to war

declassify /ˌdee'klasifie‖ˌdiː'klæsɪfaɪ/ *vt* to declare (e g information) no longer secret

declension /di'klensh(ə)n‖dɪ'klenʃ(ə)n/ *n* **1** a schematic arrangement of noun, adjective, or pronoun inflections **2** a class of nouns or adjectives having the same type of inflectional forms – **declensional** *adj*

declination /ˌdekli'naysh(ə)n‖ˌdeklɪ'neɪʃ(ə)n/ *n* **1** angular distance (e g of a star) N or S from the celestial equator **2** a formal refusal **3** the angle between a compass needle and the geographical meridian, equal to the difference between magnetic and true north – **declinational** *adj*

[1]**decline** /di'klien‖dɪ'klaɪn/ *vi* **1a** to slope downwards; descend **b** to bend down; droop **2a** *of a celestial body* to sink towards setting **b** to draw towards a close; wane **3** to refuse ~ *vt* **1** to give in prescribed order the grammatical forms of (a noun, pronoun, or adjective) **2a** to refuse to undertake, engage in, or comply with <~ *battle*> **b** to refuse courteously <~ *an invitation*> – **declinable** *adj*

[2]**decline** *n* **1** the process of declining: **1a** a gradual physical or mental decay **b** a change to a lower state or level **2** the period during which

sthg is approaching its end **3** a downward slope

declivity /di'klivəti‖dɪ'klɪvətɪ/ *n* **1** downward inclination **2** a descending slope *USE* fml – **declivitous** *adj*

decoct /di'kokt‖dɪ'kɒkt/ *vt* **1** to extract the essence of by boiling **2** to boil down; concentrate – **decoction** *n*

decode /ˌdee'kohd‖ˌdiː'kəʊd/ *vt* to convert (a coded message) into intelligible language – **decoder** *n*

décolletage /ˌdaykol'tahzh ‖ˌdeɪkɒl'tɑːʒ (*Fr* dekɔltaːʒ)/ *n* the low-cut neckline of a dress

décolleté /ˌdaykol'tay, -'-- ‖ˌdeɪkɒl'teɪ, -'-- (*Fr* dekɔlte)/ *adj* **1** wearing a strapless or low-necked dress **2** low-necked

decolon·ize, -ise /ˌdee'koləniez‖ˌdiː'kɒlənaɪz/ *vt* to free from colonial status – **decolonization** *n*

decompose /ˌdeekəm'pohz‖ˌdiːkəm'pəʊz/ *vt* **1** to separate into constituent parts, elements, atoms, etc **2** to rot ~*vi* to undergo chemical breakdown; decay, rot – **decomposer** *n*, **decomposable** *adj*, **decomposability** *n*, **decomposition** *n*, **decompositional** *adj*

decompress /ˌdeekəm'pres‖ˌdiːkəm'pres/ *vt* to release from pressure or compression – **decompression** *n*

decongestant /ˌdeekən'jest(ə)nt‖ˌdiːkən'dʒest(ə)nt/ *n* sthg (e g a drug) that relieves congestion

decontaminate /ˌdeekən'taminayt‖ˌdiːkən'tæmɪneɪt/ *vt* to rid of contamination (e g radioactivity) – **decontamination** *n*

decor, décor /'dekaw, 'daykaw‖'dekɔː, 'deɪkɔː/ *n* **1** the style and layout of interior decoration and furnishings **2** a stage setting

decorate /'dekərayt‖'dekəreɪt/ *vt* **1a** to add sthg ornamental to **b** to apply new coverings of paint, wallpaper, etc to the interior or exterior surfaces of **2** to award a mark of honour to – **decorator** *n*

decoration /ˌdekə'raysh(ə)n‖ˌdekə'reɪʃ(ə)n/ *n* **1** an ornament **2** a badge of honour (e g a medal)

decorative /'dek(ə)rətiv‖'dek(ə)rətɪv/ *adj* serving to decorate; *esp* purely ornamental rather than functional – **decoratively** *adv*, **decorativeness** *n*

decorous /'dekərəs‖'dekərəs/ *adj* marked by propriety and good taste; correct – **decorously** *adv*, **decorousness** *n*

decorum /di'kawrəm‖dɪ'kɔːrəm/ *n* propriety and good taste in conduct or appearance

[1]**decoy** /'deekoy, di'koy‖'diːkɔɪ, dɪ'kɔɪ/ *n* **1** a pond into which wild fowl are lured for capture **2** sthg used to lure or lead another into a trap **3** sby or sthg used to distract or divert the attention (e g of an enemy)

[2]**decoy** *vt* to lure or entice (as if) by a decoy

[1]**decrease** /di'krees‖dɪ'kriːs/ *vb* to (cause to) grow progressively less (e g in size, amount, number, or intensity) – **decreasingly** *adv*

[2]**decrease** /'deeˌkrees, di'krees‖'diːˌkriːs, dɪ'kriːs/ *n* **1** the process of decreasing **2** the amount by which sthg decreases

[1]**decree** /di'kree‖dɪ'kriː/ *n* **1** an order usu having legal force **2a** a religious rule made by a council or titular head **b** a foreordaining will **3** a judicial decision, esp in an equity, probate, or divorce court

[2]**decree** *vt* to command or impose by decree – **decreer** *n*

decree nisi /diˌkree 'neezi, -zie, 'niesie‖dɪˌkriː 'niːzɪ, -zaɪ, 'naɪsaɪ/ *n* a provisional decree of divorce that is made absolute after a fixed period unless cause to the contrary is shown [Latin *nisi* unless, fr *ne-* not + *si* if]

decrepit /di'krepit‖dɪ'krepɪt/ *adj* **1** wasted and weakened (as if) by the infirmities of old age **2a** worn-out **b** fallen into ruin or disrepair – **decrepitly** *adv*, **decrepitude** *n*

decry /di'krie‖dɪ'kraɪ/ *vt* **1** to depreciate (e g a coin) officially or publicly **2** to express strong disapproval of – **decrier** *n*

dedicate /'dedikayt‖'dedɪkeɪt/ *vt* **1** CONSECRATE 2A **2a** to set apart to a definite use **b** to assign permanently to a goal or way of life **3** to inscribe or address (a book, song, etc) to somebody or something as a mark of esteem or affection – **dedicator** *n*, **dedicatee** *n*

'**dedicated** *adj* **1** devoted to a cause, ideal, or purpose; zealous <*a ~ scholar*> **2** given over to a particular purpose <*a ~ process control computer*> – **dedicatedly** *adv*

dedication /ˌdedi'kaysh(ə)n‖ˌdedɪ'keɪʃ(ə)n/ *n* **1** a devoting or setting aside for a particular, specif religious, purpose **2** a phrase or sentence that dedicates **3** self-sacrificing devotion – **dedicative** *adj*, **dedicatory** *adj*

deduce /di'dyoohs‖dɪ'djuːs/ *vt* to establish by deduction; *specif* to infer from a general principle – **deducible** *adj*

deduct /di'dukt‖dɪ'dʌkt/ *vt* to subtract (an amount) from a total – **deductible** *adj*, **deductibility** *n*

deduction /di'duksh(ə)n‖dɪ'dʌkʃ(ə)n/ *n* **1a** an act of taking away **b** sthg that is or may be subtracted **2** (the deriving of) a necessary conclusion reached by reasoning; *specif* an inference in which a particular conclusion is drawn from general premises

deductive /di'duktiv‖dɪ'dʌktɪv/ *adj* **1** of or employing mathematical or logical deduction **2** capable of being deduced from premises; inferential – **deductively** *adv*

[1]**deed** /deed‖diːd/ *n* **1** sthg that is done <*evil ~s*> **2** an illustrious act or action; a feat, exploit **3** the act of performing <*never mistake the word for the ~*> **4** a signed (and sealed) written document containing some legal transfer, bargain, or contract – **deedless** *adj*

[2]**deed** *vt, NAm* to convey or transfer by deed

'**deed ˌpoll** *n, pl* **deeds poll** a deed made and executed by 1 party only

deem /deem‖diːm/ *vt* to judge, consider – fml <*would ~ it an honour*>

[1]**deep** /deep‖diːp/ *adj* **1** extending far from some surface or area: e g **1a** extending far downwards <*a ~ well*> **b** (extending) far from the surface of the body **c** extending well back from a front surface <*a ~ cupboard*> **d(1)** near the outer limits of the playing area or far from an attacking movement **d(2)** of or occupying a fielding position in cricket far from the batsman

2 having a specified extension in an implied direction <*shelf 20 inches* ~> **3a** difficult to understand **b** capable of profound thought <*a* ~ *thinker*> **c** engrossed, involved <*a man* ~ *in debt*> **d** intense, extreme <~ *sleep*> **4a** *of a colour* high in saturation and low in lightness **b** having a low musical pitch or pitch range **5** remote in time or space – **deeply** *adv*, **deepness** *n* – **in deep water** in difficulty or distress; unable to manage

[2]**deep** *adv* **1a(1)** to a great depth **a(2)** deep to a specified degree – usu in combination <*ankle*-deep *in mud*> **b** well within the boundaries <*a house* ~ *in the woods*> **2** far on; late <*danced* ~ *into the night*> **3** in a deep position <*the wingers were playing* ~> **4** far back in space or time <*had its roots* ~ *in the Dark Ages*>

[3]**deep** *n* **1** a vast or immeasurable extent; an abyss **2a** *the* sea **b** any of the very deep portions of a body of water, esp the sea

deepen /ˈdeep(ə)n‖ˈdiːp(ə)n/ *vb* to make or become deeper or more profound

ˌdeep-ˈfreeze *vt* **-froze** /frohz‖frəʊz/; **-frozen** /ˈfrohz(ə)n‖ˈfrəʊz(ə)n/ to freeze or store (e g food) in a freezer

deep freeze *n* a freezer

ˌdeep-ˈfry *vt* to fry (food) by complete immersion in hot fat or oil – **deep-fryer** *n*

ˌdeep-ˈrooted *adj* firmly established <*a* ~ *loyalty*>

ˌdeep-ˈseated *adj* **1** situated far below the surface <*a* ~ *inflammation*> **2** firmly established <*a* ~ *tradition*>

deer /diə‖dɪə/ *n, pl* **deer** *also* **deers** any of several ruminant mammals of which most of the males and some of the females bear antlers

ˈdeerˌstalker /-ˌstawkə‖-ˌstɔːkə/ *n* a close-fitting hat with peaks at the front and the back and flaps that may be folded down as coverings for ears

deface /diˈfays‖dɪˈfeɪs/ *vt* to mar the external appearance of – **defacement** *n*, **defacer** *n*

[1]**de facto** /di ˈfaktoh, day‖dɪ ˈfæktəʊ, deɪ/ *adv* in reality; actually

[2]**de facto** *adj* existing in fact; effective <*a* ~ *state of war*>

defame /diˈfaym‖dɪˈfeɪm/ *vt* to injure the reputation of by libel or slander – **defamation** *n*, **defamatory** *adj*, **defamer** *n*

[1]**default** /diˈfawlt‖dɪˈfɔːlt/ *n* failure to act, pay, appear, or compete – **in default of** in the absence of

[2]**default** *vi* to fail to meet an esp financial obligation ~ *vt* **1** to fail to perform, pay, or make good **2** to declare to be in default – **defaulter** *n*

[1]**defeat** /diˈfeet‖dɪˈfiːt/ *vt* **1a** to nullify <~ *an estate*> **b** to frustrate <~ *a hope*> **2** to win victory over <~ *the opposing team*>

[2]**defeat** *n* **1** an overthrow, esp of an army in battle **2** the loss of a contest

defeatism /diˈfeetiz(ə)m‖dɪˈfiːtɪz(ə)m/ *n* acceptance of or resignation to defeat – **defeatist** *n or adj*

defecate, *Br also* **defaecate** /ˈdefəkayt‖ˈdefəkeɪt/ *vb* to discharge (esp faeces) from the bowels – **defecation** *n*

[1]**defect** /ˈdeefekt‖ˈdiːfekt/ *n* an imperfection that impairs worth or usefulness

[2]**defect** /diˈfekt‖dɪˈfekt/ *vi* to desert a cause or party, often in order to espouse another – **defector** *n*, **defection** *n*

[1]**defective** /diˈfektiv‖dɪˈfektɪv/ *adj* **1** lacking sthg essential; faulty **2** lacking 1 or more of the usual grammatical inflections – **defectively** *adv*, **defectiveness** *n*

[2]**defective** *n* one who is subnormal physically or mentally

defence, *NAm chiefly* **defense** /diˈfens‖dɪˈfens/ *n* **1** the act or action of defending **2a** a means or method of defending; *also, pl* a defensive structure **b** an argument in support or justification **c** a defendant's denial, answer, or strategy **3** *sing or pl in constr* **3a** a defending party or group (e g in a court of law) **b** defensive players, acts, or moves in a game or sport **4** the military resources of a country <~ *budget*> – **defenceless** *adj*, **defencelessly** *adv*, **defencelessness** *n*

defend /diˈfend‖dɪˈfend/ *vt* **1a** to protect from attack **b** to maintain by argument in the face of opposition or criticism **c** to attempt to prevent an opponent from scoring in (e g a goal) **2** to act as legal representative in court for ~ *vi* **1** to take action against attack or challenge **2** to play or be in defence – **defendable** *adj*

defendant /diˈfend(ə)nt‖dɪˈfend(ə)nt/ *n* a person, company, etc against whom a criminal charge or civil claim is made

defensible /diˈfensəbl‖dɪˈfensəbl/ *adj* capable of being defended – **defensibly** *adv*, **defensibility** *n*

[1]**defensive** /diˈfensiv‖dɪˈfensɪv/ *adj* **1** serving to defend **2a** devoted to resisting or preventing aggression or attack; *also* disposed (as if) to ward off expected criticism or critical inquiry **b** of or relating to the attempt to keep an opponent from scoring – **defensively** *adv*, **defensiveness** *n*

[2]**defensive** *n* – **on the defensive** being prepared for expected aggression, attack, or criticism

[1]**defer** /diˈfuh‖dɪˈfɜː/ *vt* **-rr-** to delay; PUT OFF 2a – **deferment** *n*, **deferrable** *adj*, **deferral** *n*, **deferrer** *n*

[2]**defer** *vi* **-rr-** to submit *to* another's opinion, usu through deference or respect

deference /ˈdef(ə)rəns‖ˈdef(ə)rəns/ *n* respect and esteem due a superior or an elder – **in deference to** because of respect for

defiance /diˈfie·əns‖dɪˈfaɪəns/ *n* a disposition to resist; contempt of opposition – **defiant** *adj*, **defiantly** *adv* – **in defiance of** despite; CONTRARY TO

deficiency /diˈfish(ə)nsi‖dɪˈfɪʃ(ə)nsɪ/ *n* **1** being deficient **2** a shortage of substances necessary to health

deficiency disease *n* a disease (e g scurvy) caused by a lack of essential vitamins, minerals, etc in the diet

deficient /diˈfish(ə)nt‖dɪˈfɪʃ(ə)nt/ *adj* **1** lacking in some necessary quality or element **2** not up to a normal standard or complement – **deficiently** *adv*

deficit /ˈdefəsit‖ˈdefəsɪt/ *n* **1** a deficiency in amount or quality **2** an excess of expenditure over revenue [French *déficit*, fr Latin *deficit* it is wanting, fr *deficere* to be wanting]

[1]**defile** /diˈfiel‖dɪˈfaɪl/ *vt* **1** to make unclean or impure **2** to deprive of virginity –

defilement *n*, **defiler** *n*

[2]**defile** *vi* to march off in a file

[3]**defile** *n* a narrow passage or gorge

define /di'fien‖dɪ'faɪn/ *vt* **1a** to fix or mark the limits of; demarcate **b** to make clear or precise in outline <*the issues aren't too well* ~d> **2a** to be the essential quality or qualities of; identify <*whatever* ~s *us as human*> **b** to set forth the meaning of <~ *a word*> ~*vi* to make a definition – **definable** *adj*, **definer** *n*

definite /'definət‖'defɪnət/ *adj* **1** having distinct or certain limits **2a** free of all ambiguity, uncertainty, or obscurity **b** unquestionable, decided <*a* ~ *advantage*> **3** designating an identified or immediately identifiable person or thing <*the* ~ *article* the> – **definitely** *adv*, **definiteness** *n*

definition /,defi'nish(ə)n‖,defɪ'nɪʃ(ə)n/ *n* **1a** a word or phrase expressing the essential nature of a person, word, or thing; a meaning **b** the action or process of stating such a meaning **2a** the action or power of making definite and clear **b(1)** distinctness of outline or detail (e g in a photograph) **b(2)** clarity, esp of musical sound in reproduction – **definitional** *adj*

definitive /di'finətiv‖dɪ'fɪnətɪv/ *adj* **1** serving to provide a final solution <*a* ~ *victory*> **2** authoritative and apparently exhaustive <*a* ~ *biography*> – **definitively** *adv*, **definitiveness** *n*

deflate /di'flayt, ,dee-‖dɪ'fleɪt, ,diː-/ *vt* **1** to release air or gas from **2a** to reduce in size or importance **b** to reduce in self-confidence or self-importance, esp suddenly **3** to reduce (a price level) or cause (the availability of credit or the economy) to contract ~*vi* to lose firmness (as if) through the escape of contained gas – **deflator** *n*

deflation /di'flaysh(ə)n, ,dee-‖dɪ'fleɪʃ(ə)n, ,diː-/ *n* **1a** a contraction in the volume of available money and credit, and thus in the economy, esp as a result of government policy **b** a decline in the general level of prices **2** the erosion of soil by the wind – **deflationary** *adj*

deflect /di'flekt‖dɪ'flekt/ *vb* to turn from a straight course or fixed direction – **deflective** *adj*, **deflector** *n*

deflection, *Br also* **deflexion** /di'fleksh(ə)n‖dɪ'flekʃ(ə)n/ *n* (the amount or degree of) deflecting

deflower /,dee'flowə‖,diː'flaʊə/ *vt* to deprive of virginity; ravish – **deflowerer** *n*

defoliant /,dee'fohli·ənt‖,diː'fəʊlɪənt/ *n* a chemical applied to plants to cause the leaves to drop off prematurely – **defoliate** *vt or adj*, **defoliation** *n*, **defoliator** *n*

deforest /di'forist‖dɪ'fɒrɪst/ *vt* to clear of forests – **deforestation** *n*

deform /di'fawm‖dɪ'fɔːm/ *vt* **1** to spoil the form or appearance of **2** to make hideous or monstrous **3** to alter the shape of by stress ~*vi* to become misshapen or changed in shape – **deformation** *n*, **deformational** *adj*

deformity /di'fawməti‖dɪ'fɔːmətɪ/ *n* **1** the state of being deformed **2** a physical blemish or distortion; a disfigurement

defraud /di'frawd‖dɪ'frɔːd/ *vt* to cheat of sthg – **defrauder** *n*, **defraudation** *n*

defray /di'fray‖dɪ'freɪ/ *vt* to provide for the payment of – **defrayable** *adj*, **defrayal** *n*

defrock /,dee'frok‖,diː'frɒk/ *vt* to unfrock

defrost /,dee'frost‖,diː'frɒst/ *vt* **1** to thaw out from a frozen state <~ *meat*> **2** to free from ice <~ *the refrigerator*> **3** *NAm* to demist ~*vi* to thaw out, esp from a deep-frozen state – **defroster** *n*

deft /deft‖deft/ *adj* marked by facility and skill – **deftly** *n*, **deftness** *n*

defunct /di'fungkt‖dɪ'fʌŋkt/ *adj* no longer existing or in use; *esp* dead

defuse /,dee'fyoohz‖,diː'fjuːz/ *vt* **1** to remove the fuse from (a mine, bomb, etc) **2** to make less harmful, potent, or tense <~ *the crisis*>

defy /di'fie‖dɪ'faɪ/ *vt* **1** to challenge to do sthg considered impossible; dare **2** to face with assured power of resistance; show no fear of nor respect for <~ *public opinion*> **3** to resist attempts at <*the paintings* ~ *classification*> – **defier** *n*

[1]**degenerate** /di'jen(ə)rət‖dɪ'dʒen(ə)rət/ *adj* **1** having declined in nature, character, structure, function, etc from an ancestral or former state **2** having sunk to a condition below that which is normal to a type; *esp* having sunk to a lower and usu peculiarly corrupt state – **degenerately** *adv*, **degenerateness** *n*, **degeneracy** *n*

[2]**degenerate** *n* sthg or esp sby degenerate; *esp* one showing signs of reversion to an earlier cultural or evolutionary stage

[3]**degenerate** /di'jenərayt‖dɪ'dʒenəreɪt/ *vi* **1** to pass from a higher to a lower type or condition; deteriorate **2** to sink into a low intellectual or moral state **3** to decline from a former thriving or healthy condition – **degenerative** *adj*, **degeneration** *n*

degrade /di'grayd‖dɪ'greɪd/ *vt* **1a** to lower in grade, rank, or status; demote **b** to reduce the quality of; *specif* to impair with respect to some physical property **2** to bring to low esteem or into disrepute <degrading *vices*> **3** ERODE 1c **4** to decompose (a chemical compound) ~ *vi* **1** to degenerate **2** *of a chemical compound* to decompose – **degradable** *adj*, **degrader** *n*, **degradingly** *adv*, **degradation** *n*

degree /di'gree‖dɪ'griː/ *n* **1** a step or stage in a process, course, or order of classification <*advanced by* ~s> **2a** the extent or measure of an action, condition, or relation **b** any of the (sets of) forms used in the comparison of an adjective or adverb **c** a legal measure of guilt or negligence <*guilty of murder in the first* ~> **d** a positive and esp considerable amount <*eccentric to a* ~> **3** the civil condition or status of a person <*people of high* ~> **4** an academic title conferred **4a** on students in recognition of proficiency **b** honorarily **5** a division or interval of a scale of measurement; *specif* any of various units for measuring temperature **6** a 360th part of the circumference of a circle – **to a degree 1** to a remarkable extent **2** in a small way

dehuman·ize, **-ise** /,dee'hyoohməniez‖,diː'hjuːmənaɪz/ *vt* to divest of human qualities or personality – **dehumanization** *n*

dehydrate /,deehie'drayt‖,diːhaɪ'dreɪt/ *vt* **1** to remove (bound) water from (a chemical compound, foods, etc) **2** to make dry and uninteresting in style or character ~*vi* to lose water or body fluids (abnormally) – **dehydrator** *n*, **dehydration** *n*

deify /ˈdee·ifie, ˈday-‖ˈdiːɪfaɪ, ˈdeɪ-/ *vt* **1a** to make a god of **b** to take as an object of worship **2** to glorify as of supreme worth <~ *money*> – **deification** *n*

deign /dayn‖deɪn/ *vi* to condescend ~*vt* to condescend to give or offer

deism /ˈdee·iz(ə)m, ˈday-‖ˈdiːɪz(ə)m, ˈdeɪ-/ *n, often cap* a movement or system of thought advocating natural religion based on human reason rather than revelation; *specif* a chiefly 18th-c doctrine asserting that although God created the universe he does not intervene in its functioning – **deist** *n, often cap*, **deistic** *adj*, **deistically** *adv*

deity /ˈdee·əti, ˈday-‖ˈdiːətɪ, ˈdeɪ-/ *n* **1a** the rank or essential nature of a god **b** *cap the* Supreme Being; GOD 1 **2** a god or goddess **3** one exalted or revered as supremely good or powerful

déjà vu /ˌdayzhah ˈvooh ‖ˌdeɪʒɑː ˈvuː (*Fr* deʒa vy)/ *n* **1** the illusion of remembering scenes and events when they are experienced for the first time **2** sthg excessively or unpleasantly familiar [French, already seen]

dejected /diˈjektid‖dɪˈdʒektɪd/ *adj* cast down in spirits; depressed – **dejectedly** *adv*, **dejectedness** *n*

dejection /diˈjeksh(ə)n‖dɪˈdʒekʃ(ə)n/ *n* lowness of spirits

de jure /ˌdi ˈjooəri‖ˌdɪ ˈdʒʊərɪ/ *adv or adj* by (full legal) right <*recognition extended* ~ *to the new government*>

dekko /ˈdekoh‖ˈdekəʊ/ *n, Br* a look, glance – slang [Hindi *dekho* look!, imperative pl of *dekhnā* to see, fr Sanskrit *dṛś* to see]

[1]**delay** /diˈlay‖dɪˈleɪ/ *n* **1** delaying or (an instance of) being delayed **2** the time during which sthg is delayed

[2]**delay** *vt* **1** to postpone **2** to stop, detain, or hinder for a time ~ *vi* **1** to move or act slowly **2** to pause momentarily – **delayer** *n*, **delaying** *adj*

delectable /diˈlektəbl‖dɪˈlektəbl/ *adj* **1** highly pleasing; delightful **2** delicious – **delectableness** *n*, **delectably** *adv*, **delectability** *n*

delectation /ˌdelekˈtaysh(ə)n, ˌdee-‖ˌdelekˈteɪʃ(ə)n, ˌdiː-/ *n* **1** DELIGHT 1 **2** enjoyment

delegacy /ˈdeligəsi‖ˈdelɪgəsɪ/ *n* **1a** the act of delegating **b** an appointment as delegate **2** *sing or pl in constr* a body of delegates; a board

[1]**delegate** /ˈdeligət‖ˈdelɪgət/ *n* a person delegated to act for another; *esp* a representative to a conference

[2]**delegate** /ˈdeligayt‖ˈdelɪgeɪt/ *vt* **1** to entrust (e g a duty or responsibility) to another **2** to appoint as one's representative ~*vi* to assign responsibility or authority

delegation /ˌdeliˈgaysh(ə)n‖ˌdelɪˈgeɪʃ(ə)n/ *n* **1** the act of empowering to act for another **2** *sing or pl in constr* a group of people chosen to represent others

delete /diˈleet‖dɪˈliːt/ *vt* to eliminate, esp by blotting out, cutting out, or erasing

deleterious /ˌdeliˈtiəri·əs‖ˌdelɪˈtɪərɪəs/ *adj* harmful, detrimental – fml – **deleteriously** *adv*, **deleteriousness** *n*

deletion /diˈleesh(ə)n‖dɪˈliːʃ(ə)n/ *n* sthg deleted

delft /delft‖delft/ *n* tin-glazed Dutch earthenware with blue and white or polychrome decoration [*Delft*, town in the Netherlands]

[1]**deliberate** /diˈlib(ə)rət‖dɪˈlɪb(ə)rət/ *adj* **1** characterized by or resulting from careful and thorough consideration **2** characterized by awareness of the consequences; wilful **3** slow, unhurried <*walked with a* ~ *step*> – **deliberately** *adv*, **deliberateness** *n*

[2]**deliberate** /diˈlibərayt‖dɪˈlɪbəreɪt/ *vt* to think about deliberately and often with formal discussion before reaching a decision ~*vi* to ponder issues and decisions carefully

deliberation /diˌlibəˈraysh(ə)n‖dɪˌlɪbəˈreɪʃ(ə)n/ *n* **1** deliberating or being deliberate **2** a discussion and consideration of pros and cons – **deliberative** *adj*, **deliberatively** *adv*, **deliberativeness** *n*

delicacy /ˈdelikəsi‖ˈdelɪkəsɪ/ *n* **1** sthg pleasing to eat that is considered rare or luxurious **2** the quality or state of being dainty <*lace of great* ~> **3** frailty, fragility **4** precise and refined perception or discrimination **5a** refined sensibility in feeling or conduct **b** avoidance of anything offensive or disturbing

delicate /ˈdelikət‖ˈdelɪkət/ *adj* **1a** pleasing to the senses in a mild or subtle way **b** marked by daintiness or charm of colour, line, or proportion **2a** marked by keen sensitivity or subtle discrimination <~ *perception*> **b** fastidious, squeamish **3a** marked by extreme precision **b** having or showing extreme sensitivity <*a* ~ *instrument*> **4** calling for or involving meticulously careful treatment <*the* ~ *balance of power*> **5a** very finely made **b(1)** fragile **b(2)** weak, sickly **c** marked by or requiring tact <*touches on a* ~ *subject*> – **delicately** *adv*, **delicateness** *n*

delicatessen /ˌdelikəˈtes(ə)n‖ˌdelɪkəˈtes(ə)n/ *n* **1** *pl in constr* (delicacies and foreign) foods ready for eating (e g cooked meats) **2** a shop where delicatessen are sold

delicious /diˈlishəs‖dɪˈlɪʃəs/ *adj* **1** affording great pleasure; delightful **2** highly pleasing to one of the bodily senses, esp of taste or smell – **deliciously** *adv*, **deliciousness** *n*

[1]**delight** /diˈliet‖dɪˈlaɪt/ *n* **1** great pleasure or satisfaction; joy **2** sthg that gives great pleasure

[2]**delight** *vi* to take great pleasure *in* doing sthg ~*vt* to give enjoyment or satisfaction to – **delighter** *n*

deˈlightful /-f(ə)l‖-f(ə)l/ *adj* highly pleasing – **delightfully** *adv*, **delightfulness** *n*

delimit /diˈlimit‖dɪˈlɪmɪt/ *vt* to fix the limits of

delineate /diˈliniayt‖dɪˈlɪnɪeɪt/ *vt* **1** to show by drawing lines in the shape of **2** to describe in usu sharp or vivid detail – **delineator** *n*, **delineative** *adj*, **delineation** *n*

delinquency /diˈlingkwənsi‖dɪˈlɪŋkwənsɪ/ *n* (the practice of engaging in) antisocial or illegal conduct – used esp when emphasis is placed on maladjustment rather than criminal intent

[1]**delinquent** /diˈlingkwənt‖dɪˈlɪŋkwənt/ *n* a delinquent person

[2]**delinquent** *adj* **1** guilty of wrongdoing or of neglect of duty **2** marked by delinquency [Latin *delinquere* to fail, offend, fr *de* from, away + *linquere* to leave] – **delinquently** *adv*

deliquesce /ˌdeliˈkwes‖ˌdelɪˈkwes/ *vi* to melt

away; *specif, of a compound* to dissolve gradually in water attracted and absorbed from the air – **deliquescence** *n*, **deliquescent** *adj*

delirious /di'liəri·əs‖dɪ'lɪərɪəs/ *adj* (characteristic) of or affected by delirium – **deliriously** *adv*, **deliriousness** *n*

delirium /di'liəri·əm‖dɪ'lɪərɪəm/ *n* **1** confusion, frenzy, disordered speech, hallucinations, etc occurring as a (temporary) mental disturbance **2** frenzied excitement

de,lirium 'tremens /'tremenz‖'tremenz/ *n* a violent delirium with tremors induced by chronic alcoholism

deliver /di'livə‖dɪ'lɪvə/ *vt* **1** to set free **2** to hand over; convey <~ *the milk*> **3a** to assist in giving birth <*she was* ~ed *of a fine boy*> **b** to aid in the birth of **c** to give birth to **4** to utter <~ed *her speech effectively*> **5** to aim or guide (e g a blow) to an intended target or destination ~*vi* to produce the promised, desired, or expected results – infml – **deliverable** *adj*, **deliverer** *n*

deliverance /di'liv(ə)rəns‖dɪ'lɪv(ə)rəns/ *n* **1** liberation, rescue **2** an opinion or verdict expressed publicly

delivery /di'liv(ə)ri‖dɪ'lɪv(ə)rɪ/ *n* **1** DELIVERANCE 1 **2a** the act of handing over **b** a physical or legal transfer **c** sthg delivered at 1 time or in 1 unit <*milk* deliveries> **3** the act of giving birth **4** the uttering of a speech; *also* the manner or style of uttering in speech or song **5** the act or manner or an instance of sending forth, throwing, or bowling

de'liveryman /-mən, -,man‖-mən, -,mæn/ *n*, *pl* **deliverymen** /-mən, -,men‖-mən, -,men/ a van driver who delivers wholesale or retail goods to customers, usu over a regular local route

dell /del‖del/ *n* a small secluded hollow or valley, esp in a forest

delouse /,dee'lows‖,di:'laʊs/ *vt* to remove lice from

Delphic /'delfik‖'delfɪk/, **Delphian** /'delfi·ən‖'delfɪən/ *adj* **1** of ancient Delphi in Greece or its oracle **2a** ambiguous **b** obscure, enigmatic – **delphically** *adv*

delphinium /del'fini·əm‖del'fɪnɪəm/ *n* any of a genus of plants of the buttercup family with deeply cut leaves and flowers in showy spikes

delta /'deltə‖'deltə/ *n* **1** the 4th letter of the Greek alphabet **2** a triangular alluvial deposit at the mouth of a river – **deltaic** *adj*

'delta ,wing *n* an approximately triangular aircraft wing with a (nearly) straight rearmost edge – **delta-winged** *adj*

delude /di'loohd‖dɪ'lu:d/ *vt* to mislead the mind or judgment of; deceive, trick – **deluder** *n*, **deludingly** *adv*

[1]**deluge** /'delyoohj, -yoohzh‖'delju:dʒ, -ju:ʒ/ *n* **1a** a great flood; *specif, cap the* Flood recorded in the Old Testament (Gen 6:8) **b** a drenching fall of rain **2** an overwhelming amount or number <*a* ~ *of criticism*>

[2]**deluge** *vt* **1** to overflow with water; inundate **2** to overwhelm, swamp

delusion /di'loohzh(ə)n‖dɪ'lu:ʒ(ə)n/ *n* **1** deluding or being deluded **2a** sthg delusively believed **b** (a mental state characterized by) a false belief (about the self or others) that persists despite the facts and occurs esp in psychotic states – **delusional** *adj*, **delusionary** *adj*

delusive /di'loohsiv, -ziv‖dɪ'lu:sɪv, -zɪv/ *adj* **1** likely to delude **2** constituting a delusion – **delusively** *adv*, **delusiveness** *n*

de luxe /di 'luks‖dɪ 'lʌks/ *adj* notably luxurious or elegant [French, lit., of luxury]

delve /delv‖delv/ *vi* **1** to dig or work (as if) with a spade **2** to make a careful or detailed search for information <~d *into the past*> – **delver** *n*

demagnet·ize, -ise /,dee'magnitiez‖,di:'mægnɪtaɪz/ *vt* to cause not to have magnetic properties or a magnetic field – **demagnetizer** *n*, **demagnetization** *n*

demagogue, *NAm also* **demagog** /'deməgog‖'deməgɒg/ *n* **1** a leader of the common people in ancient times **2** an agitator who makes use of popular prejudices in order to gain power [Greek *dēmagōgos*, fr *dēmos* people + *agōgos* leading, fr *agein* to lead] – **demagoguery** *n*, **demagogy** *n*, **demagogic**, **demagogical** *adj*, **demagogically** *adv*

[1]**demand** /di'mahnd‖dɪ'mɑ:nd/ *n* **1** an act of demanding or asking, esp with authority; a claim **2a** an expressed desire for ownership or use **b** willingness and ability to purchase a commodity or service **c** the quantity of a commodity or service wanted at a specified price and time **3** a desire or need *for*; the state of being sought after <*gold is in great* ~> – **on demand** whenever the demand is made

[2]**demand** *vi* to make a demand; ask ~ *vt* **1** to ask or call for with authority; claim as due or just **2** to call for urgently, peremptorily, or insistently **3** to ask authoritatively or earnestly to be informed of **4** to require – **demandable** *adj*, **demander** *n*

demanding /di'mahnding‖dɪ'mɑ:ndɪŋ/ *adj* exacting – **demandingly** *adv*

demarcate /'deemah,kayt‖'di:mɑ:,keɪt/ *vt* **1** to mark the limits of **2** to set apart; separate

demarcation *also* **demarkation** /,deemah'kaysh(ə)n‖,di:mɑ:'keɪʃ(ə)n/ *n* the marking of limits or boundaries, esp between areas of work to be carried out by members of particular trade unions <*a* ~ *dispute*>

demean /di'meen‖dɪ'mi:n/ *vt* to degrade, debase

demeanour, *NAm chiefly* **demeanor** /di'meenə‖dɪ'mi:nə/ *n* behaviour towards others; outward manner

demented /di'mented‖dɪ'mented/ *adj* insane; *also* crazy – **dementedly** *adv*, **dementedness** *n*

dementia /di'mensh(y)ə‖dɪ'menʃ(j)ə/ *n* **1** deteriorated mentality due to damage to or (natural) deterioration of the brain **2** madness, insanity – **demential** *adj*

demerara sugar /,demə'reərə‖,demə'reərə/ *n* brown crystallized unrefined cane sugar from the W Indies [*Demerara*, region of Guyana]

demerit /,dee'merit, '-,--‖,di:'merɪt, '-,--/ *n* **1** a quality that deserves blame or lacks merit; a fault, defect **2** *NAm* a bad mark given to an offender

demesne /di'mayn, -'meen‖dɪ'meɪn, -'mi:n/ *n* **1** legal possession of land as one's own **2** land actually occupied by the owner and not held by tenants **3a** the land attached to a mansion **b** landed property; an estate **c** a region, realm

demi- /demi-‖demɪ-/ *prefix* **1** half <demi*semiquaver*> **2** partly belonging to (a specified type or class) <demi*god*>

demigod /ˈdemi͵god‖ˈdemɪ͵gɒd/, *fem* **ˈdemi͵goddess** *n* **1a** a mythological superhuman being with less power than a god **b** an offspring of a union between a mortal and a god **2** a person so outstanding that he/she seems to approach the divine

demijohn /ˈdemi͵jon‖ˈdemɪ͵dʒɒn/ *n* a narrow-necked large bottle of glass or stoneware

demilitar·ize, -ise /͵deeˈmilitəriez‖͵diːˈmɪlɪtəraɪz/ *vt* to strip of military forces, weapons, etc – **demilitarization**

1**demise** /diˈmiez‖dɪˈmaɪz/ *vt* **1** to convey (e g an estate) by will or lease **2** to transmit by succession or inheritance ~*vi* to pass by descent or bequest <*the property* ~d *to the king*>

2**demise** *n* **1** the conveyance of an estate or transfer of sovereignty by demising **2a** death – technical, euph, or humor **b** a cessation of existence or activity – fml or humor

demist /͵deeˈmist‖͵diːˈmɪst/ *vt, Br* to remove mist from (e g a car windscreen) – **demister** *n*

demo /ˈdemoh‖ˈdeməʊ/ *n, pl* **demos 1** DEMONSTRATION 4 **2** *cap NAm* DEMOCRAT 2

1**demob** /͵deeˈmob‖͵diːˈmɒb/ *vt, chiefly Br* to demobilize

2**demob** *n, chiefly Br* a demobilization

demobil·ize, -ise /͵deeˈmohbiliez‖͵diːˈməʊbɪlaɪz/ *vt* **1** to disband **2** to discharge from military service – **demobilization** *n*

democracy /diˈmokrəsi‖dɪˈmɒkrəsɪ/ *n* **1a** government by the people **b** (a political unit with) a government in which the supreme power is exercised by the people directly or indirectly through a system of representation usu involving free elections **2** the absence of class distinctions or privileges [Middle French *democratie*, deriv of Greek *dēmokratia*, fr *dēmos* people + *-kratia* government, fr *kratos* strength, power]

democrat /ˈdeməkrat‖ˈdeməkræt/ *n* **1a** an adherent of democracy **b** one who practises social equality **2** *cap* a member of the Democratic party of the USA

democratic /͵deməˈkratik‖͵deməˈkrætɪk/ *adj* **1** of or favouring democracy or social equality **2** *often cap* of or constituting a political party of the USA associated with policies of social reform and internationalism – **democratically** *adv*, **democratize** *vt*, **democratization** *n*, **democratizer** *n*

démodé /͵daymohˈday‖͵deɪməʊˈdeɪ/ *adj* no longer fashionable; out-of-date

demography /diˈmogrəfi‖dɪˈmɒgrəfɪ/ *n* the statistical study of human populations, esp with reference to size and density, distribution, and vital statistics – **demographer** *n*, **demographic** *adj*, **demographically** *adv*

demolish /diˈmolish‖dɪˈmɒlɪʃ/ *vt* **1** to destroy, smash, or tear down **2** to eat up – infml – **demolisher** *n*

demolition /͵deməˈlish(ə)n‖͵deməˈlɪʃ(ə)n/ *n* the act or an instance of demolishing – **demolitionist** *n*

demon /ˈdeemən‖ˈdiːmən/ *n* **1a** an evil spirit **b** an evil or undesirable emotion, trait, or state **2** DAEMON 1, 2 **3** one who has unusual drive or effectiveness <*a* ~ *for work*> – **demonism** *n*, **demonize** *vt*, **demonization** *n*, **demonology** *n*

demonet·ize, -ise /͵deeˈmunitiez‖͵diːˈmʌnɪtaɪz/ *vt* to stop using (a metal) as a money standard – **demonetization**

1**demoniac** /diˈmohniak‖dɪˈməʊnɪæk/ *also* **demoniacal** /͵deemohˈnie·əkl‖͵diːməʊˈnaɪəkl/ *adj* **1** possessed or influenced by a demon **2** demonic – **demoniacally** *adv*

2**demoniac** *n* one regarded as possessed by a demon

demonic /diˈmonik‖dɪˈmɒnɪk/ *also* **demonical** /-kl‖-kl/ *adj* (suggestive) of a demon; fiendish – **demonically** *adv*

demonstrable /diˈmonstrəbl‖dɪˈmɒnstrəbl/ *adj* **1** capable of being demonstrated **2** apparent, evident – **demonstrableness** *n*, **demonstrably** *adv*, **demonstrability** *n*

demonstrate /ˈdemənstrayt‖ˈdemənstreɪt/ *vt* **1** to show clearly **2a** to prove or make clear by reasoning or evidence **b** to illustrate and explain, esp with many examples **3** to show or prove the application, value, or efficiency of to a prospective buyer ~ *vi* **1** to make or give a demonstration **2** to take part in a demonstration

demonstration /͵demənˈstraysh(ə)n‖͵demənˈstreɪʃ(ə)n/ *n* **1** an outward expression or display **2a(1)** conclusive evidence; proof **a(2)** a proof in which the conclusion is the immediate sequence of reasoning from premises **b** a showing and explanation of the merits of a product to a prospective buyer **c** a display of an action or process <*cooking* ~> **3** a show of armed force **4** a mass meeting, procession, etc to display group feelings (e g about grievances or political issues) – **demonstrational** *adj*

demonstrative /diˈmonstrətiv‖dɪˈmɒnstrətɪv/ *adj* **1** demonstrating sthg to be real or true **2** pointing out the one referred to and distinguishing it from others of the same class <~ *pronouns*> **3** given to or marked by display of feeling – **demonstratively** *adv*, **demonstrativeness** *n*

demonstrator /ˈdemən͵straytə‖ˈdemən͵streɪtə/ *n* one who demonstrates: e g **a** a junior staff member who demonstrates experiments in a university science department **b** sby who participates in a demonstration

demoral·ize, -ise /diˈmorə͵liez‖dɪˈmɒrə͵laɪz/ *vt* to weaken the morale or self-respect of; discourage, dispirit – **demoralizingly** *adv*, **demoralization** *n*

demote /diˈmoht‖dɪˈməʊt/ *vt* to reduce to a lower grade or rank – **demotion** *n*

demotic /diˈmotik‖dɪˈmɒtɪk/ *adj* **1** of the people **2** of or written in a simplified form of the ancient Egyptian hieratic writing **3** of the Modern Greek vernacular – **demotic** *n*

1**demur** /diˈmuh‖dɪˈmɜː/ *vi* **-rr-** to take exception; (mildly) object – **demurral** *n*, **demurrable** *adj*

2**demur** *n* **1** a hesitation <*men who follow fashion without* ~> **2** objection, protest

demure /diˈmyooə‖dɪˈmjʊə/ *adj* **1** reserved, modest **2** affectedly modest, reserved, or serious; coy – **demurely** *adv*, **demureness** *n*

demystify /deeˈmistifie‖diːˈmɪstɪfaɪ/ *vt* to

eliminate the mystery from; clarify <~ *the law*> – **demystification** *n*

den /den‖den/ *n* **1** the lair of a wild, usu predatory, animal **2** a centre of secret, esp unlawful, activity <*an opium* ~> **3** a comfortable usu secluded room

denational·ize, -ise /dee'nashən(ə)l,iez‖diː'næʃən(ə)l,aɪz/ *vt* **1** to divest of national status, character, or rights **2** to remove from ownership or control by the state – **denationalization** *n*

denial /di'nie·əl‖dɪ'naɪəl/ *n* **1** a refusal to satisfy a request or desire **2a** a refusal to admit the truth or reality (e g of a statement or charge) **b** an assertion that an allegation is false **3** a refusal to acknowledge sby or sthg; a disavowal

denier /'deni·ə, 'denyə‖'denɪə, 'denjə/ *n* a unit of fineness for silk, rayon, or nylon yarn equal to the fineness of a yarn weighing 1g for each 9000m

denigrate /'denigrayt‖'denɪgreɪt/ *vt* **1** to cast aspersions on; defame **2** to belittle – **denigrator** *n*, **denigratory** *adj*, **denigration** *n*

denim /'denəm‖'denəm/ *n* **1** a firm durable twilled usu blue cotton fabric used esp for jeans **2** *pl* denim trousers; *esp* blue jeans [French (*serge*) *de Nîmes* (serge) of Nîmes, town in France]

denizen /'deniz(ə)n‖'denɪz(ə)n/ *n* **1** an inhabitant **2** a naturalized plant or animal

denominate /di'nominayt‖dɪ'nɒmɪneɪt/ *vt* to give a name to – fml

denomination /di,nomi'naysh(ə)n‖dɪ,nɒmɪ'neɪʃ(ə)n/ *n* **1** a name, designation; *esp* a general name for a category **2** a religious organization or sect **3** a grade or degree in a series of values or sizes (e g of money)

denominational /di,nomi'naysh(ə)nl‖dɪ,nɒmɪ'neɪʃ(ə)nl/ *adj* of a particular religious denomination

denominator /di'nomi,naytə‖dɪ'nɒmɪ,neɪtə/ *n* the part of a vulgar fraction that is below the line and that in fractions with 1 as the numerator indicates into how many parts the unit is divided; a divisor

denotation /,deenoh'taysh(ə)n‖,diːnəʊ'teɪʃ(ə)n/ *n* **1** a direct specific meaning as distinct from a connotation **2** a denoting term; a name

denote /di'noht‖dɪ'nəʊt/ *vt* **1** to indicate; be a sign or mark for **2** to have the meaning of; mean – **denotative** *adj*

denouement /day'noohmonh‖deɪ'nuːmɑ̃/ *n* **1** the resolution of the main complication in a literary work **2** the outcome of a complex sequence of events [French *dénouement*, lit., untying, fr *dénouer* to untie, deriv of Latin *de* from, away + *nodus* knot]

denounce /di'nowns‖dɪ'naʊns/ *vt* **1** to condemn, esp publicly, as deserving censure or punishment **2** to inform against; accuse **3** to announce formally the termination of (e g a treaty) – **denouncement** *n*, **denouncer** *n*

dense /dens‖dens/ *adj* **1** marked by high density, compactness, or crowding together of parts <~ *undergrowth*> **2** sluggish of mind; stupid **3** demanding concentration to follow or comprehend <~ *prose*> – **densely** *adv*, **denseness** *n*

density /'densəti‖'densətɪ/ *n* **1** the quantity per unit volume, unit area, or unit length: e g **1a** the mass of a substance or distribution of a quantity per unit of volume or space **b** the average number of individuals or units per unit of space <*a population* ~> **2** the degree of opaqueness of sthg translucent

[1]dent /dent‖dent/ *n* **1** a depression or hollow made by a blow or by pressure **2** an adverse effect <*made a* ~ *in the weekly budget*>

[2]dent *vt* to make a dent in or on

dental /'dentl‖'dentl/ *adj* **1** of the teeth or dentistry **2** articulated with the tip or blade of the tongue against or near the upper front teeth [Latin *dentalis*, fr *dent-*, *dens* tooth] – **dentalize** *vt*, **dentally** *adv*

dentifrice /'denti,fris‖'dentɪ,frɪs/ *n* a powder, paste, or liquid for cleaning the teeth

dentist /'dentist‖'dentɪst/ *n* one who treats diseases, malformations, and injuries to the teeth, mouth, etc and who makes and inserts false teeth – **dentistry** *n*

denture /'denchə, -chooə‖'dentʃə, -tʃʊə/ *n* an artificial replacement for 1 or more teeth; *esp, pl* a set of false teeth

denude /di'nyoohd‖dɪ'njuːd/ *vt* to strip of all covering; to lay bare by erosion – **denudation** *n*

denunciation /di,nunsi'aysh(ə)n‖dɪ,nʌnsɪ'eɪʃ(ə)n/ *n* a (public) condemnation

deny /di'nie‖dɪ'naɪ/ *vt* **1** to declare to be untrue or invalid; refuse to accept **2** to disown, repudiate **3a** to give a negative answer to **b** to refuse to grant <~ *a request*> **c** to restrain (oneself) from self-indulgence

deodorant /dee'ohdərənt‖diː'əʊdərənt/ *n* a preparation that destroys or masks unpleasant smells – **deodorant** *adj*

deodor·ize, -ise /dee'ohdəriez‖diː'əʊdəraɪz/ *vt* to destroy or prevent the unpleasant smell of – **deodorizer** *n*, **deodorization**

depart /di'paht‖dɪ'pɑːt/ *vi* **1** to go away; leave **2** to turn aside; deviate *from* ~*vt* to go away from; leave

de'parted *adj* **1** bygone **2** having died, esp recently – euph

department /di'pahtmənt‖dɪ'pɑːtmənt/ *n* **1a** a major division of a government **b** a division of an institution or business that provides a specified service or deals with a specified subject **c** a major administrative subdivision (e g in France) **d** a section of a department store **2** a distinct sphere (e g of activity or thought) – infml <*that's not my* ~> – **departmental** *adj*, **departmentally** *adv*, **departmentalize** *vt*, **departmentalization** *n*

de'partment ,store *n* a large shop, selling a wide variety of goods, arranged in several departments

departure /di'pahchə‖dɪ'pɑːtʃə/ *n* **1a** the act of going away **b** a setting out (e g on a new course of action) **2** the distance due east or west travelled by a ship in its course **3** deviation, divergence

depend /di'pend‖dɪ'pend/ *vi* **1** to be determined by or based on some condition or action **2a** to place reliance or trust **b** to be dependent, esp for financial support **3** to hang down *USE* (*1&2*) + *on* or *upon*

dependable /di'pendəbl‖dɪ'pendəbl/ *adj* reliable – **dependableness** *n*, **dependably** *adv*, **dependability** *n*

dependant, *NAm chiefly* **dependent** /di'pendənt‖dɪ'pendənt/ *n* a person who relies on another for esp financial support

dependence *also* **dependance** /di'pendəns‖dɪ'pendəns/ *n* **1** being influenced by or subject to another **2** reliance, trust **3** a need for or reliance on a drug: **3a** compulsive physiological need for a habit-forming drug (e g heroin); addiction **b** psychological need for a drug after a period of use; habituation

dependency /di'pend(ə)nsi‖dɪ'pend(ə)nsɪ/ *n* sthg that is dependent on sthg else; *specif* a territorial unit under the jurisdiction of a nation but not formally annexed to it

dependent /di'pend(ə)nt‖dɪ'pend(ə)nt/ *adj* **1** determined or conditioned by another; contingent **2** relying on another for support **3** subject to another's jurisdiction **4** SUBORDINATE 3 *USE* (*1&2*) + *on* or *upon* – **dependently** *adv*

depict /di'pikt‖dɪ'pɪkt/ *vt* **1** to represent by a picture **2** to describe – **depicter** *n*, **depiction** *n*

depilate /'depilayt‖'depɪleɪt/ *vt* to remove hair from – **depilation** *n*, **depilatory** *adj or n*

deplete /di'pleet‖dɪ'pliːt/ *vt* to reduce in amount by using up; exhaust, esp of strength or resources – **depletion** *n*

deplorable /di'plawrəbl‖dɪ'plɔːrəbl/ *adj* **1** lamentable **2** extremely bad – **deplorableness** *n*, **deplorably** *adv*

deplore /di'plaw‖dɪ'plɔː/ *vt* **1** to feel or express grief for **2** to regret or disapprove of strongly – **deploringly** *adv*

deploy /di'ploy‖dɪ'plɔɪ/ *vt* **1** to spread out (e g troops or ships), esp in battle formation **2** to utilize or arrange as if deploying troops ~*vi* to move in being deployed – **deployable** *adj*, **deployment** *n*

depopulate /ˌdee'popyoolayt‖ˌdiː'pɒpjʊleɪt/ *vt* to reduce greatly the population of ~*vi* to decrease in population – **depopulator** *n*, **depopulation** *n*

deport /di'pawt‖dɪ'pɔːt/ *vt* **1a** to expel (e g an alien) legally from a country **b** to transport (e g a convicted criminal) to a penal colony or place of exile **2** to behave or conduct (oneself) in a specified manner – fml – **deportation** *n*, **deportee** *n*

de'portment /-mənt‖-mənt/ *n* **1** *Br* the manner in which one stands, sits, or walks; posture **2** *NAm* behaviour, conduct

depose /di'pohz‖dɪ'pəʊz/ *vt* **1** to remove from a position of authority (e g a throne) **2** to testify under oath or by affidavit ~*vi* to bear witness

¹deposit /di'pozit‖dɪ'pɒzɪt/ *vt* **1** to place, esp for safekeeping or as a pledge; *esp* to put in a bank **2a** to lay down; place **b** to let fall (e g sediment) – **depositor** *n*

²deposit *n* **1** depositing or being deposited **2a** money deposited in a bank **b** money given as a pledge or down payment **3** a depository **4** sthg laid down; *esp* (an accumulation of) matter deposited by a natural process

de'posit acˌcount *n*, *chiefly Br* an account (e g in a bank) on which interest is usu payable and from which withdrawals can be made usu only by prior arrangement

depositary /di'pozit(ə)ri‖dɪ'pɒzɪt(ə)rɪ/ *n* a person to whom sthg is entrusted

deposition /ˌdepə'zish(ə)n, ˌdee-‖ˌdepə'zɪʃ(ə)n, ˌdiː-/ *n* **1** removal from a position of authority **2** a (written and sworn) statement presented as evidence **3** an act or process of depositing – **depositional** *adj*

depository /di'pozit(ə)ri‖dɪ'pɒzɪt(ə)rɪ/ *n* **1** a depositary **2** a place where sthg is deposited, esp for safekeeping

depot /'depoh‖'depəʊ/ *n* **1a** a place for the storage of military supplies **b** a place for the reception and training of military recruits; a regimental headquarters **2a** a place for storing goods **b** a store, depository **3a** *Br* an area (e g a garage) in which buses or trains are stored, esp for maintenance **b** *NAm* a railway station

deprave /di'prayv‖dɪ'preɪv/ *vt* to corrupt morally; pervert [Middle French *depraver*, fr Latin *depravare* to pervert, fr *de* from, away + *pravus* crooked, bad] – **depravedly** *adv*, **depraver** *n*, **depravation** *n*

depravity /di'pravəti‖dɪ'prævətɪ/ *n* (an instance of) moral corruption

deprecate /'deprikayt‖'deprɪkeɪt/ *vt* to express disapproval of, esp mildly or regretfully [Latin *deprecari* to avert by prayer, fr *de* from, away + *precari* to pray, fr *prec-, prex* request, prayer] – **deprecatingly** *adv*, **deprecation** *n*

deprecatory /'deprikayt(ə)ri‖'deprɪkeɪt(ə)rɪ/ *adj* **1** apologetic **2** disapproving – **deprecatorily** *adv*

depreciate /di'prees(h)iayt‖dɪ'priːsɪeɪt,-ʃɪeɪt/ *vt* **1** to lower the price or estimated value of **2** to belittle, disparage ~*vi* to lessen in value; fall [Late Latin *depretiare*, fr Latin *de* from, away + *pretium* price] – **depreciable** *adj*, **depreciator** *n*, **depreciative**, **depreciatory** *adj*, **depreciation**

depredate /'depridayt‖'deprɪdeɪt/ *vb* to plunder, ravage – **depredator** *n*, **depredatory** *adj*, **depredation** *n*

depress /di'pres‖dɪ'pres/ *vt* **1** to push or press down **2** to lessen the activity or strength of **3** to sadden, dispirit **4** to decrease the market value or marketability of – **depressingly** *adv*

de'pressed *adj* **1** low in spirits; sad **2** lowered or sunken, esp in the centre **3** suffering from economic depression

depression /di'presh(ə)n‖dɪ'preʃ(ə)n/ *n* **1** the angular distance of a celestial body below the horizon **2a** a pressing down; a lowering **b** (a mental disorder marked by inactivity, difficulty in thinking and concentration, and esp by) sadness or dejection **c** a lowering of activity, vitality, amount, force, etc **3** a depressed place or part; a hollow **4** ³LOW 1b **5** a period of low general economic activity marked esp by rising levels of unemployment

deprivation /ˌdepri'vaysh(ə)n‖ˌdeprɪ'veɪʃ(ə)n/ *n* **1** an act of depriving; a loss **2** being deprived; privation

deprive /di'priev‖dɪ'praɪv/ *vt* **1** to take sthg away from **2** to remove (e g a clergyman) from office **3** to withhold sthg from <*he threatened to ~ them of their rights*> *USE* (*1&3*) + *of*

de'prived *adj* lacking the necessities of life or a good environment

depth /depth‖depθ/ *n* **1a(1)** a deep place in a

body of water **a(2)** a part that is far from the outside or surface <*the* ~s *of the woods*> **b(1)** a profound or intense state (e g of thought or feeling) **b(2)** the worst, most intensive, or severest part <*the* ~s *of winter*> **2a** the perpendicular measurement downwards from a surface **b** the distance from front to back **3** the quality of being deep **4** the degree of intensity <~ *of a colour*> – **in depth** with great thoroughness <*haven't studied it* in depth> – **out of one's depth 1** in water that is deeper than one's height **2** beyond one's ability to understand

'depth ˌcharge *n* an explosive projectile for use underwater, esp against submarines

deputation /ˌdepyooˈtaysh(ə)n‖ˌdepjʊˈteɪʃ(ə)n/ *n sing or pl in constr* a group of people appointed to represent others

1depute /diˈpyooht‖dɪˈpjuːt/ *vt* to delegate

2depute *n, Scot* a deputy

deput·ize, -ise /ˈdepyooˌtiez‖ˈdepjʊˌtaɪz/ *vi* to act as a deputy *for*

deputy /ˈdepyooti‖ˈdepjʊtɪ/ *n* **1** a person (e g a second-in-command) appointed as a substitute with power to act for another **2** a member of the lower house of some legislative assemblies

derail /ˌdeeˈrayl‖ˌdiːˈreɪl/ *vt* to cause (e g a train) to leave the rails ~*vi* to be derailed – **derailment** *n*

derange /diˈraynj‖dɪˈreɪndʒ/ *vt* to disturb the operation or functions of – **derangement** *n*

derby /ˈdahbi‖ˈdɑːbɪ/ *n* **1** *cap* a flat race for 3-year-old horses over $1^1/_2$mi (about 2.9km) held annually at Epsom in England **2** a usu informal race or contest for a specified category of contestant <*a donkey* ~> **3** a sporting match against a major local rival **4** *chiefly NAm* ²BOWLER

1derelict /ˈderəlikt‖ˈderəlɪkt/ *adj* **1** left to decay **2** *chiefly NAm* lacking a sense of duty; negligent

2derelict *n* **1** sthg voluntarily abandoned; *specif* a ship abandoned on the high seas **2** a down-and-out

dereliction /ˌderəˈliksh(ə)n‖ˌderəˈlɪkʃ(ə)n/ *n* **1** (intentional) abandonment or being abandoned **2** a recession of water leaving permanently dry land **3a** conscious neglect <~ *of duty*> **b** a fault, shortcoming

deride /diˈried‖dɪˈraɪd/ *vt* to mock, scorn

de rigueur /də riˈguh ‖də rɪˈgɜː (*Fr* də rigœːr)/ *adj* required by fashion, etiquette, or custom [French, compulsory, lit., of strictness]

derision /diˈrizh(ə)n‖dɪˈrɪʒ(ə)n/ *n* deriding or being derided

derisive /diˈriesiv, -ziv‖dɪˈraɪsɪv, -zɪv/ *adj* showing derision; mocking, scornful – **derisively** *adv*

derisory /diˈriez(ə)ri‖dɪˈraɪz(ə)rɪ/ *adj* **1** derisive **2** worthy of derision; ridiculous; *specif* contemptibly small <*a* ~ *pay offer*>

derivation /ˌderiˈvaysh(ə)n‖ˌderɪˈveɪʃ(ə)n/ *n* **1a** the formation of a word from another word or root, esp with an affix **b** an act of tracing or stating the derivation of a word **c** ETYMOLOGY 1 **2a** the source, origin **b** descent <*a family of Scottish* ~> **3** DERIVATIVE 2 **4** an act of deriving – **derivational** *adj*

1derivative /diˈrivətiv‖dɪˈrɪvətɪv/ *adj* **1** formed by derivation **2** made up of derived elements; not original – **derivatively** *adv*

2derivative *n* **1** a word formed by derivation **2** sthg derived **3** the limit of the ratio of the change in a function to the corresponding change in its independent variable as the latter change approaches zero **4** a chemical related structurally to and (theoretically) derivable from another

derive /diˈriev‖dɪˈraɪv/ *vt* **1a** to obtain or receive, esp from a specified source **b** to obtain (a chemical) from a parent substance **2** to infer, deduce **3a** to trace the derivation of **b** to form by derivation ~*vi* to come as a derivative *from* – **derivable** *adj*

derm /duhm‖dɜːm/ *n* **1** the dermis **2** SKIN 2a

dermatitis /ˌduhməˈtietəs‖ˌdɜːməˈtaɪtəs/ *n* a disease or inflammation of the skin

dermatology /ˌduhməˈtoləji‖ˌdɜːməˈtɒlədʒɪ/ *n* a branch of medicine dealing with (diseases of) the skin – **dermatologist** *n*, **dermatologic, dermatological** *adj*

dermis /ˈduhmis‖ˈdɜːmɪs/ *n* (the sensitive vascular inner layer of) the skin – **dermal** *adj*

derogate /ˈderəgayt‖ˈderəgeɪt/ *vb* – **derogation** *n*, **derogative** *adj* – **derogate from** to impair by taking away a part; detract from – fml

derogatory /diˈrogət(ə)ri‖dɪˈrɒgət(ə)rɪ/ *adj* expressing a low opinion; disparaging – **derogatorily** *adv*

derrick /ˈderik‖ˈderɪk/ *n* **1** a hoisting apparatus employing a tackle rigged at the end of a beam **2** a framework over an oil well or similar hole, for supporting drilling tackle [obs *derrick* hangman, gallows, fr *Derick*, surname of a 17th-c English hangman]

derring-do /ˌdering ˈdooh‖ˌderɪŋ ˈduː/ *n* daring action <*deeds of* ~>

derv /duhv‖dɜːv/ *n* fuel oil for diesel engines [*d*iesel-*e*ngined *r*oad *v*ehicle]

dervish /ˈduhvish‖ˈdɜːvɪʃ/ *n* a member of a Muslim religious order noted for devotional exercises (e g bodily movements leading to a trance) [Turkish *derviş*, lit., beggar, fr Persian *darvēsh*]

desalinate /ˌdeeˈsalinayt‖ˌdiːˈsælɪneɪt/ *vt* to remove salt from (esp sea water) – **desalinator** *n*, **desalination** *n*

1descant /ˈdesˌkant‖ˈdesˌkænt/ *n* a counterpoint superimposed on a simple melody and usu sung by some or all of the sopranos

2descant /desˈkant, dis-‖desˈkænt, dɪs-/ *vi* **1** to sing or play a descant **2** to talk or write at considerable length *on* or *upon*

descend /diˈsend‖dɪˈsend/ *vi* **1** to pass from a higher to a lower level **2** to pass from the general to the particular **3** to pass by inheritance **4** to incline, lead, or extend downwards <*the road* ~s *to the river*> **5a** to come down or make a sudden attack – usu + *on* or *upon* **b** to make a sudden disconcerting visit or appearance – usu + *on* or *upon*; chiefly humor **6** to proceed from higher to lower in a sequence or gradation **7** to sink in status or dignity; stoop ~*vt* to pass, move, or extend down or down along <*he* ~ed *the steps*>

descendant, *NAm also* **descendent** /diˈsend(ə)nt‖dɪˈsend(ə)nt/ *n* sby or sthg descended or deriving from another

de'scended *adj* having as an ancestor; sprung *from*
descent /di'sent||dɪ'sent/ *n* **1** the act or process of descending **2** a downward step (e g in status or value) **3a** derivation from an ancestor; birth, lineage **b** transmission of an estate by inheritance **c** a transmission from a usu earlier source; a derivation **4a** a downward inclination; a slope **b** a descending way (e g a staircase) **5** a sudden hostile raid or attack
describe /di'skrieb||dɪ'skraɪb/ *vt* **1** to give an account of in words **2** to trace the outline of – **describable** *adj*
description /di'skripsh(ə)n||dɪ'skrɪpʃ(ə)n/ *n* **1** an account intended to convey a mental image of sthg experienced **2** kind, sort <*people of every* ~>
descriptive /di'skriptiv||dɪ'skrɪptɪv/ *adj* serving to describe, esp vividly – **descriptively** *adv*
descry /di'skrie||dɪ'skraɪ/ *vt* to notice or see, esp at a distance – fml
desecrate /'desikrayt||'desɪkreɪt/ *vt* to violate the sanctity of; profane – **desecrator** *n*, **descration** *n*
desegregate /ˌdee'segrigayt||ˌdiː'segrɪgeɪt/ *vt* to eliminate (racial) segregation in – **desegregation** *n*
desensit·ize, -ise /ˌdee'sensətiez||ˌdiː'sensətaɪz/ *vt* **1** to make (sby previously sensitive) insensitive or nonreactive to a sensitizing agent **2** to make (a photographic material) less sensitive or completely insensitive to radiation – **desensitizer** *n*, **desensitization** *n*
[1]**desert** /'dezət||'dezət/ *n* **1** (a desolate region like) a dry barren region incapable of supporting much life **2** an area or place that is deprived of or devoid of sthg important <*a cultural* ~>
[2]**desert** /di'zuht||dɪ'zɜːt/ *n* deserved reward or punishment – usu pl with sing. meaning <*got her just* ~s>
[3]**desert** /di'zuht||dɪ'zɜːt/ *vt* **1** to leave, usu without intending to return **2a** to abandon or forsake, esp in time of need **b** to abandon (military service) without leave ~*vi* to quit one's post, (military) service, etc without leave or justification – **deserter** *n*
Desert /'dezət||'dezət/ *trademark* – used for an ankle-high laced suede boot with a rubber sole
desertion /di'zuhsh(ə)n||dɪ'zɜːʃ(ə)n/ *n* the abandonment of a post or relationship and the moral and legal obligations attached to it
deserve /di'zuhv||dɪ'zɜːv/ *vb* to be worthy of or suitable for (some recompense or treatment) – **deservedly** *adv*
deserving /di'zuhving||dɪ'zɜːvɪŋ/ *adj* meriting (financial) aid
deshabille /ˌdayza'beel, dis-||ˌdeɪzæ'biːl, dɪs-/, **déshabillé** /ˌdayza'beeˌay||ˌdeɪzæ'biːˌeɪ/ *n* the state of being only partially or carelessly dressed
desiccate /'desikayt||'desɪkeɪt/ *vt* **1** to dry up **2** to preserve (a food) by drying to dehydrate – **desiccant** *n*, **desiccator** *n*, **desiccative** *adj*, **desiccation** *n*
desideratum /diˌzidə'raytəm, -'rah-||dɪˌzɪdə'reɪtəm, -'rɑː-/ *n, pl* **desiderata** /-tə||-tə/ sthg desired as necessary – fml
[1]**design** /di'zien||dɪ'zaɪn/ *vt* **1a** to conceive and plan out in the mind **b** to devise for a specific function or end **2a** to draw the plans for **b** to create or execute according to a plan; devise ~ *vi* **1** to conceive or execute a plan **2** to draw, lay out, or prepare a design – **designer** *n*, **designedly** *adv*
[2]**design** *n* **1** a mental plan or scheme **2a** a particular purpose held in view **b** deliberate purposeful planning <*more by accident than by* ~> **3** *pl* dishonest, hostile, or acquisitive intent – + *on* **4** (the act of producing) a drawing, plan, or pattern showing the details of how sthg is to be constructed **5** the arrangement of the elements of a work of art or artefact **6** a decorative pattern
[1]**designate** /'dezignət, -nayt||'dezɪgnət, -neɪt/ *adj* chosen for an office but not yet installed <*ambassador* ~>
[2]**designate** /'dezignayt||'dezɪgneɪt/ *vt* **1** to indicate; POINT OUT **2** to call by a distinctive name or title **3** to nominate for a specified purpose, office, or duty – **designator** *n*, **designatory** *adj*, **designation** *n*
designing /di'ziening||dɪ'zaɪnɪŋ/ *adj* crafty, scheming
desirable /di'zie·ərəbl||dɪ'zaɪərəbl/ *adj* **1** causing (sexual) desire; attractive **2** worth seeking or doing as advantageous, beneficial, or wise – **desirableness** , **desirably** *adv*, **desirability** *n*
[1]**desire** /di'zie·ə||dɪ'zaɪə/ *vt* **1** to long or hope for **2** to express a wish for; request **3** to wish to have sexual relations with
[2]**desire** *n* **1** a conscious impulse towards an object or experience promising enjoyment or satisfaction **2** a (sexual) longing or craving
desirous /di'zie·ərəs||dɪ'zaɪərəs/ *adj* eagerly wanting; desiring – fml
desist /di'zist||dɪ'zɪst/ *vi* to cease to proceed or act – fml – **desistance** *n*
desk /desk||desk/ *n* **1a** a table with a sloping or horizontal surface and often drawers and compartments, that is designed esp for writing and reading **b** a church lectern **c** a table, counter, or booth at which cashiers, clerks, etc work **d** a music stand **2** a division of an organization specializing in a usu specified phase of activity
desktop /'deskˌtop/ *adj* being or using a small computer unit for office or home use
[1]**desolate** /'dezələt||'dezələt/ *adj* **1** deserted, uninhabited **2** forsaken, forlorn **3** barren, lifeless <*a* ~ *landscape*> – **desolately** *adv*, **desolateness** *n*
[2]**desolate** /'dezəlayt||'dezəleɪt/ *vt* **1** to deprive of inhabitants **2** to lay waste – **desolator** *n*
[1]**despair** /di'speə||dɪ'speə/ *vi* to lose all hope or confidence <~ *of winning*> [Middle French *desperer*, fr Latin *desperare*, fr *de* from, away + *sperare* to hope] – **despairingly** *adv*
[2]**despair** *n* **1** utter loss of hope **2** a cause of hopelessness <*that child is the* ~ *of his parents*>
despatch /di'spach||dɪ'spætʃ/ *vb or n* (to) dispatch
desperado /ˌdespə'rahdoh||ˌdespə'rɑːdəʊ/ *n, pl* **desperadoes, desperados** a bold, reckless, or violent person, esp a criminal

desperate /ˈdesp(ə)rət‖ˈdesp(ə)rət/ *adj* **1** being (almost) beyond hope **2a** reckless because of despair **b** undertaken as a last resort <*a* ~ *remedy*> **3** suffering extreme need or anxiety <~ *for money*> **4** fraught with extreme danger or impending disaster – **desperately** *adv*, **desperateness** *n*

desperation /ˌdespəˈraysh(ə)n‖ˌdespəˈreɪʃ-(ə)n/ *n* **1** loss of hope and surrender to despair **2** extreme recklessness caused by hopelessness

despicable /diˈspikəbl‖dɪˈspɪkəbl/ *adj* morally contemptible – **despicableness** *n*, **despicably** *adv*

despise /diˈspiez‖dɪˈspaɪz/ *vt* **1** to regard with contempt or distaste **2** to regard as negligible or worthless – **despiser** *n*

despite /diˈspiet‖dɪˈspaɪt/ *prep* notwithstanding; IN SPITE OF

despoil /diˈspoyl‖dɪˈspɔɪl/ *vt* to plunder, pillage – **despoiler** *n*, **despoilment** *n*

despondent /diˈspond(ə)nt‖dɪˈspɒnd(ə)nt/ *adj* feeling extreme discouragement or dejection – **despondently** *adv*, **despondency** *n*

despot /ˈdespot‖ˈdespɒt/ *n* **1** a ruler with absolute power **2** a person exercising power abusively or tyrannically – **despotic** *adj*, **despotically** *adv*

despotism /ˈdespəˌtiz(ə)m‖ˈdespəˌtɪz(ə)m/ *n* **1** rule by a despot; absolutism **2** despotic exercise of power

dessert /diˈzuht‖dɪˈzɜːt/ *n* a usu sweet course or dish served at the end of a meal

desˈsertˌspoon /-ˌspoohn‖-ˌspuːn/ *n* **1** a spoon intermediate in size between a teaspoon and a tablespoon and used for eating dessert **2** a dessertspoonful

desˈsertˌspoonful /-f(ə)l‖-f(ə)l/ *n* **1** as much as a dessertspoon can hold **2** a unit of measure equal to about $8.9cm^3$ (about $2^1/_2$ fluid drachms)

dessert wine *n* a usu sweet wine often served with dessert

destination /ˌdestiˈnaysh(ə)n‖ˌdestɪˈneɪʃ(ə)n/ *n* a place which is set for the end of a journey or to which sthg is sent

destine /ˈdestin‖ˈdestɪn/ *vt* **1** to designate or dedicate in advance **2** to direct or set apart for a specified purpose or goal <*freight* ~d *for English ports*> *USE* usu pass

destiny /ˈdestini‖ˈdestɪnɪ/ *n* **1** the power or agency held to determine the course of events **2** sthg to which a person or thing is destined; fortune **3** a predetermined course of events

destitute /ˈdestityooht‖ˈdestɪtjuːt/ *adj* **1** lacking sthg necessary or desirable – + *of* <*a heart* ~ *of feeling*> **2** lacking the basic necessities of life; extremely poor – **destitution** *n*

destroy /diˈstroy‖dɪˈstrɔɪ/ *vt* **1** to demolish, ruin **2a** to put an end to; kill **b** to make ineffective; neutralize

destroyer /diˈstroyə‖dɪˈstrɔɪə/ *n* a fast multi-purpose warship smaller than a cruiser

destruction /diˈstruksh(ə)n‖dɪˈstrʌkʃ(ə)n/ *n* **1** destroying or being destroyed **2** a cause of ruin or downfall

destructive /diˈstruktiv‖dɪˈstrʌktɪv/ *adj* **1** causing destruction **2** designed or tending to destroy; negative <~ *criticism*> – **destructively** *adv*, **destructiveness** *n*, **destructivity** *n*

desuetude /ˈdeswityoohd, diˈsyooh·iˌtyoohd‖ˈdeswɪtjuːd, dɪˈsjuːɪˌtjuːd/ *n* discontinuance from use; disuse – fml

desultory /ˈdesəlt(ə)ri, ˈdez-‖ˈdesəlt(ə)rɪ, ˈdez-/ *adj* passing aimlessly from one subject or activity to another – **desultorily** *adv*, **desultoriness** *n*

detach /diˈtach‖dɪˈtætʃ/ *vt* **1** to separate, esp from a larger mass and usu without causing damage **2** to separate from a parent organization for a special purpose <~ *a ship from the fleet*> – **detachable** *adj*, **detachably** *adv*, **detachability** *n*

deˈtached *adj* **1** standing by itself; *specif* not sharing any wall with another building **2** free from prejudice or emotional involvement; aloof – **detachedly** *adv*

deˈtachment /-mənt‖-mənt/ *n* **1** a detaching, separation **2** *sing or pl in constr* a body of troops, ships, etc separated from the main body for a special mission **3** freedom from bias

[1]detail /ˈdeeˌtayl‖ˈdiːˌteɪl/ *n* **1** extended treatment of or attention to particular items **2a** a small and subordinate part; *specif* part of a work of art considered or reproduced in isolation **b** a part considered separately from the whole **c** an individual relevant part or fact – usu pl <*can you let me have the* ~s *by tonight*> **3a** *sing or pl in constr* a small military detachment selected for a particular task **b** the task to be performed by a military detail – **in detail** item by item; thoroughly

[2]detail *vt* **1** to report in detail **2** to assign to a particular task or place

ˈdeˌtailed *adj* marked by abundant detail or thorough treatment

detain /diˈtayn‖dɪˈteɪn/ *vt* **1** to hold or retain (as if) in custody **2** to delay; HOLD BACK 1

detainee /ˌdeetayˈnee‖ˌdiːteɪˈniː/ *n* a person held in custody, esp for political reasons

detect /diˈtekt‖dɪˈtekt/ *vt* to discover the existence or presence of – **detectable** *adj*, **detection** *n*, **detectability** *n*

[1]detective /diˈtektiv‖dɪˈtektɪv/ *adj* **1** used in detecting sthg **2** of detectives or their work <*a* ~ *novel*>

[2]detective *n* a policeman or other person engaged in investigating crimes, detecting lawbreakers, or getting information that is not readily accessible

detector /diˈtektə‖dɪˈtektə/ *n* an electrical circuit for separating an (audio) signal from a (radio) carrier

détente, **detente** /dayˈtonht‖deɪˈtɑ̃t/ *n* a relaxation of strained relations (e g between ideologically opposed nations) [French, lit., slackening, fr *déstendre* to slacken, release, deriv of Latin *de* from, away + *tendere* to stretch]

detention /diˈtensh(ə)n‖dɪˈtenʃ(ə)n/ *n* **1** detaining or being detained, esp in custody **2** *chiefly Br* the keeping in of a pupil after school hours as a punishment

deter /diˈtuh‖dɪˈtɜː/ *vt* **-rr-** to discourage or prevent from acting – **determent** *n*, **deterable** *adj*

detergent /diˈtuhj(ə)nt‖dɪˈtɜːdʒ(ə)nt/ *n* a cleansing agent; *specif* any of various synthetic (water-soluble) compounds that are chemically different from soaps and are able to keep oils, dirt, etc in suspension and act as wetting agents [French *détergent*, fr Latin *detergēre* to wipe off, cleanse, fr *de* from, away + *tergēre* to wipe off]

deteriorate /di'tiəri·ə,rayt‖dɪ'tɪərɪə,reɪt/ *vb* to grow or make or worse – **deteriorative** *adj*, **deterioration** *n*

determinant /di'tuhminənt‖dɪ'tɜːmɪnənt/ *n* sthg that determines, fixes, or conditions

determination /di,tuhmi'naysh(ə)n‖dɪ-,tɜːmɪ'neɪʃ(ə)n/ *n* **1** a judicial decision settling a controversy **2a** firm intention **b** the ability to make and act on firm decisions; resoluteness

determine /di'tuhmin‖dɪ'tɜːmɪn/ *vt* **1a** to fix conclusively or authoritatively **b** to settle, decide <~ *the rights and wrongs of a case*> **2a** to fix beforehand **b** to regulate <*demand* ~s *the price*> **3a** to ascertain the intent, nature, or scope of **b** to set an end to <~ *an estate*> ~ *vi* **1** to come to a decision **2** to come to an end or become void

de'termined *adj* **1** decided, resolved <*was* ~ *to learn to drive*> **2** firm, resolute <*a very* ~ *woman*> – **determinedly** *adv*, **determinedness** *n*

determinism /di'tuhmi,niz(ə)m‖dɪ'tɜːmɪ,nɪz(ə)m/ *n* **1** a doctrine that all phenomena are determined by preceding occurrences; *esp* the doctrine that all human acts, choices, etc are causally determined and that free will is illusory **2** a belief in predestination – **determinist** *n or adj*, **deterministic** *adj*, **deterministically** *adv*

[1]**deterrent** /di'terənt‖dɪ'terənt/ *adj* serving to deter – **deterrence** *n*, **deterrently** *adv*

[2]**deterrent** *n* sthg that deters; *esp* a (nuclear) weapon that is held in readiness by one nation or alliance in order to deter another from attacking

detest /di'test‖dɪ'test/ *vt* to feel intense dislike for; loathe – **detestable** *adj*, **detestably** *adv*

detestation /,deete'staysh(ə)n‖,diːte'steɪʃ(ə)n/ *n* extreme dislike; abhorrence

dethrone /,dee'throhn‖,diː'θrəʊn/ *vt* DEPOSE 1 – **dethronement** *n*

detonate /'detənayt‖'detəneɪt/ *vb* to (cause to) explode with sudden violence <~ *an atom bomb*> – **detonatable** *adj*, **detonative** *adj*

detonation /,detə'naysh(ə)n‖,detə'neɪʃ(ə)n/ *n* **1** the action or process of detonating **2** premature combustion in an internal-combustion engine that results in knocking

detonator /'detənaytə‖'detəneɪtə/ *n* **1** a device used for detonating a high explosive **2** a device, clipped on to a railway line, that detonates as a train passes to warn of esp fog or emergency

[1]**detour** /'dee,tooə‖'diː,tʊə/ *n* a deviation from a course or procedure; *specif* a way that is an alternative to a shorter or planned route

[2]**detour** *vi* to make a detour ~*vt* to send by a roundabout route

detract /di'trakt‖dɪ'trækt/ *vi* to take away sthg desirable – usu + *from*

detractor /di'traktə‖dɪ'træktə/ *n* one who denigrates sby or his/her ideas or beliefs

detrain /,dee'trayn‖,diː'treɪn/ *vb* to alight or remove from a railway train – **detrainment** *n*

detriment /'detrimənt‖'detrɪmənt/ *n* (a cause of) injury or damage

detrimental /,detri'mentl‖,detrɪ'mentl/ *adj* harmful, damaging – **detrimentally** *adv*

detritus /di'trietəs‖dɪ'traɪtəs/ *n, pl* **detritus** /~/ **1** loose material (e g rock fragments or organic particles) produced by disintegration **2** debris caused by disintegration – **detrital** *adj*

de trop /də'troh ‖də'trəʊ (*Fr* də tro)/ *adj* not wanted or needed; superfluous

deuce /dyoohs‖djuːs/ *n* **1** a playing card or the face of a dice representing the number 2 **2** a tie in a game (e g tennis) after which a side must score 2 consecutive clear points to win **3a** the devil, the dickens – formerly used as an interjection or intensive **b** sthg very bad or remarkable of its kind <*a* ~ *of a mess*>

deuced /dyoohst, 'dyoohsid‖djuːst, 'djuːsɪd/ *adj* damned, confounded – **deuced, deucedly** *adv*

devaluation /,dee,valyoo'aysh(ə)n‖,diː-,væljʊ'eɪʃ(ə)n/ *n* **1** a reduction in the exchange value of a currency **2** a lessening, esp of status or stature

devalue /,dee'valyooh‖,diː'væljuː/, **devaluate** /dee'valyoo,ayt‖diː'væljʊ,eɪt/ *vt* **1** to reduce the exchange value of (money) **2** to lessen the value or reputation of ~*vi* to institute devaluation

devastate /'devəstayt‖'devəsteɪt/ *vt* **1** to reduce to ruin; lay waste **2** to have a shattering effect on; overwhelm <*a* devastating *attack on his work*> – **devastatingly** *adv*, **devastator** *n*, **devastation** *n*

develop /di'veləp‖dɪ'veləp/ *vt* **1a** to unfold gradually or in detail; expound **b** to show signs of <~ *an illness*> **c** to subject (exposed photograph material) esp to chemicals, in order to produce a visible image; *also* to make visible by such a method **d** to elaborate by the unfolding of a musical idea and by the working out of rhythmic and harmonic changes in the theme **2** to bring out the possibilities of **3a** to promote the growth of <~ed *her muscles*> **b** to make more available or usable <~ *its resources*> **c** to build on or change the use of (a tract of land) **d** to move (a chess piece) to a position providing more opportunity for effective use **4** to cause to grow, mature, or increase **5** to acquire gradually <~ *a taste for good wine*> ~ *vi* **1a** to go through a process of natural growth, differentiation, or evolution by successive changes **b** to evolve; *broadly* to grow **2** to become gradually visible or apparent **3** to develop one's pieces in chess – **developable** *adj*

developer /di'veləpə‖dɪ'veləpə/ *n* **1** a chemical used to develop exposed photographic materials **2** a person who develops real estate; *esp* sby who improves and subdivides land and builds and sells houses on it

de'velopment /-mənt‖-mənt/ *n* **1** the act, process, or result of developing **2** being developed – **developmental** *adj*, **developmentally** *adv*

[1]**deviant** /'deevi·ənt‖'diːvɪənt/ *adj* **1** deviating, esp from a norm **2** characterized by deviation – **deviance, deviancy** *n*

[2]**deviant** *n* a person whose behaviour differs markedly from the norm

[1]**deviate** /'deevi,ayt‖'diːvɪ,eɪt/ *vi* to stray, esp from a topic, principle, or accepted norm or from a straight course – **deviator** *n*, **deviatory** *adj*

[2]**deviate** /'deevi·ət, -ayt‖'diːvɪət, -eɪt/ *n, chiefly NAm* a deviant

deviation /ˌdeeviˈaysh(ə)n‖ˌdiːvɪˈeɪʃ(ə)n/ *n* **1** deflection of a compass needle caused by local magnetic influences **2** the difference between a value in a frequency distribution and a fixed number **3** departure from an established party line **4** departure from accepted norms of behaviour <*sexual* ~> – **deviationism** *n*, **deviationist** *n*

device /diˈvies‖dɪˈvaɪs/ *n* **1a** a scheme to trick or deceive **b** sthg elaborate or intricate in design **c** sthg (e g a figure of speech or a dramatic convention) designed to achieve a particular artistic effect **d** a piece of equipment or a mechanism designed for a special purpose or function **2** *pl* desire, will <*left to her own* ~s> **3a** an emblematic design used in a heraldic achievement **b** a motto

[1]**devil** /ˈdevl‖ˈdevl/ *n* **1** *often cap* the supreme spirit of evil in Jewish and Christian belief, the tempter of mankind, the leader of all apostate angels, and the ruler of hell **2** a malignant spirit; a demon **3** an extremely cruel or wicked person; a fiend **4** a high-spirited, reckless, or energetic person **5** a junior legal counsel working without payment to gain experience **6a** a person of the specified type <*lucky* ~> **b** sthg provoking, difficult, or trying <*this type of bottle is the very* ~ *to open*> **c** – used as an interjection or intensive <*what the* ~ *is that?*> ***USE*** (6) infml [Old English *dēofol*, fr Late Latin *diabolus*, fr Greek *diabolos*, lit., slanderer, fr *diaballein* to throw across, slander, fr *dia* through + *ballein* to throw]

[2]**devil** *vb* **-ll-** (*NAm* **-l-**, **-ll-**) *vt* to season (food) highly, esp with peppery condiments ~*vi* to serve or function as a legal devil

devilish /ˈdevl·ish‖ˈdevlɪʃ/ *adj* (characteristic) of a devil – **devilishly** *adv*

ˌdevil-may-ˈcare *adj* heedless of authority or convention

devilment /ˈdevlmənt‖ˈdevlmənt/ *n* wild mischief

ˌdevil's ˈadvocate *n* **1** the Roman Catholic official who presents the possible objections to claims to canonization or to the title 'Blessed' **2** a person who champions the less accepted or approved cause, esp for the sake of argument

devious /ˈdeevi·əs, -vyəs‖ˈdiːvɪəs, -vjəs/ *adj* **1** deviating from a fixed or straight course **2** deviating from a right, accepted, or common course **3** not straightforward or wholly sincere – **deviously** *adv*, **deviousness** *n*

[1]**devise** /diˈviez‖dɪˈvaɪz/ *vt* **1a** to formulate in the mind; invent **b** to plan, plot **2** to give or leave (real property) by will – **devisable** *adj*, **devisal** *n*, **diviser** *n*

[2]**devise** *n* **1** a devising act or clause **2** property devised by will

devital·ize, -ise /ˌdeeˈvietlˌiez‖ˌdiːˈvaɪtlˌaɪz/ *vt* to deprive of life, vigour, or effectiveness

devoid /diˈvoyd‖dɪˈvɔɪd/ *adj* not having or using; lacking – + *of*

devolution /ˌdeevəˈloohsh(ə)n‖ˌdiːvəˈluːʃ(ə)n/ *n* **1** the passage of rights, property, etc to a successor **2** delegation or conferral to a subordinate **3** the surrender of functions and powers to regional or local authorities by a central government; *specif* such a surrender of powers to Scottish and Welsh authorities by the UK government – **devolutionary** *adj*, **devolutionist** *n*

devolve /diˈvolv‖dɪˈvɒlv/ *vt* **1** to transfer from one person to another; HAND DOWN 1, 2 **2** to surrender by devolution ~ *vi* **1** to pass by transmission or succession **2** to fall or be passed, usu as an obligation or responsibility ***USE*** (*vi*) usu + *on* or *upon*

devote /diˈvoht‖dɪˈvəʊt/ *vt* **1** to set apart for a special purpose; dedicate *to* **2** to give (oneself) over wholly *to*

deˈvoted *adj* loyally attached <*a* ~ *friend*> – **devotedly** *adv*

devotee /ˌdevəˈtee‖ˌdevəˈtiː/ *n* **1** a deeply religious person **2** a keen follower or supporter; an enthusiast

devotion /diˈvohsh(ə)n‖dɪˈvəʊʃ(ə)n/ *n* **1a** piety **b** a special act of prayer or supplication – usu pl **2a** devoting or being devoted **b** ardent love, affection, or dedication – **devotional** *adj*, **devotionally** *adv*

devour /diˈvowə‖dɪˈvaʊə/ *vt* **1** to eat up greedily or ravenously **2** to swallow up; consume <~ed *by fire*> **3** to preoccupy, absorb <~ed *by guilt*> **4** to take in eagerly through the mind or senses <~s *books*> – **devourer** *n*

devout /diˈvowt‖dɪˈvaʊt/ *adj* **1** devoted to religion; pious **2** sincere, genuine <*a* ~ *hope*> – **devoutly** *adv*, **devoutness** *n*

dew /dyooh‖djuː/ *n* moisture that condenses on the surfaces of cool bodies, esp at night

dewlap /ˈdyoohlap‖ˈdjuːlæp/ *n* a hanging fold of skin under the neck of an animal (e g a cow) – **dewlapped** *adj*

ˈdew ˌpond *n* a shallow usu artificial pond thought to be filled by the condensation of dew

dewy /ˈdyooh·i‖ˈdjuːɪ/ *adj* moist (as if) with dew – **dewily** *adv*, **dewiness** *n*

dexterity /dekˈsterəti‖dekˈsterətɪ/ *n* **1** skill and ease in using the hands **2** mental quickness

dexterous, dextrous /ˈdekstrəs‖ˈdekstrəs/ *adj* **1** skilful with the hands **2** mentally adroit [Latin *dextr-, dexter* on the right-hand, skilful] – **dexterously** *adv*

dextrorotatory /ˌdekstrohˈrohtətri, -rohˈtaytəri‖ˌdekstrəʊˈrəʊtətrɪ, -rəʊˈteɪtərɪ/ *adj* turning clockwise or towards the right; *esp* rotating the plane of polarization of light towards the right <~ *crystals*> – **dextrorotation** *n*

dextrose /ˈdekstrohz, ˈdekstrohs‖ˈdekstrəʊz, ˈdekstrəʊs/ *n* dextrorotatory glucose

dhoti /ˈdohti‖ˈdəʊtɪ/ *n, pl* **dhotis** a loincloth worn by Hindu men

dhow /dow‖daʊ/ *n* an Arab lateen-rigged boat, usu having a long overhanging bow and a high poop

di- /die-‖daɪ-/ *comb form* **1** twice; twofold; double <di*chromatic*> **2** containing 2 atoms, groups, or chemical equivalents in the molecular structure <di*chloride*>

dia- /die·ə-‖daɪə-/ *also* **di-** *prefix* through <dia*positive*>; across <dia*meter*>

diabetes /ˌdie·əˈbeetis, -teez‖ˌdaɪəˈbiːtɪs, -tiːz/ *n* any of various abnormal conditions characterized by the secretion and excretion of excessive amounts of urine; *specif* DIABETES MELLITUS [Latin, fr Greek *diabētēs*, fr *diabainein* to cross over, fr *dia* through + *bainein* to go]

ˌdiaˌbetes ˈmellitus /ˈmelitəs‖ˈmelɪtəs/ *n* a disorder of the process by which the body uses sugars and other carbohydrates in which not enough insulin is produced or the cells become resistant to its action and which is characterized typically by abnormally great amounts of sugar in the blood and urine

¹diabetic /ˌdie·əˈbetik‖ˌdaɪəˈbetɪk/ *adj* **1** of diabetes or diabetics **2** affected with diabetes

²diabetic *n* a person affected with diabetes

diabolic /ˌdie·əˈbolik‖ˌdaɪəˈbɒlɪk/ *adj* **1** (characteristic) of the devil; fiendish **2** DIABOLICAL 2 – **diabolically** *adv*, **diabolicalness** *n*

diabolical /ˌdie·əˈbolikl‖ˌdaɪəˈbɒlɪkl/ *adj* **1** DIABOLIC 1 **2** *chiefly Br* dreadful, appalling – infml

diacritic /ˌdie·əˈkritik‖ˌdaɪəˈkrɪtɪk/ *n* a mark near or through an orthographic or phonetic character or combination of characters indicating a changed phonetic value

diacritical /ˌdie·əˈkritikl‖ˌdaɪəˈkrɪtɪkl/ *also* **diacritic** *adj* **1** serving as a diacritic **2** serving to distinguish; distinctive

diadem /ˈdie·əˌdem‖ˈdaɪəˌdem/ *n* **1** a crown; *specif* a headband worn as a badge of royalty **2** regal power or dignity

diaeresis, *chiefly NAm* **dieresis** /dieˈerisis, -ˈiərisis‖daɪˈerɪsɪs, -ˈɪərɪsɪs/ *n, pl* **diaereses** /-ˌseez‖-ˌsiːz/ a mark¨ placed over a vowel to indicate pronunciation as a separate syllable (e g in *naïve*) – **diaeretic** *adj*

diagnose /ˈdie·əgnohz‖ˈdaɪəgnəʊz/ *vt* to recognize (e g a disease) by signs and symptoms – **diagnosable, diagnoseable** *adj*

diagnosis /ˌdie·əgˈnohsis‖ˌdaɪəgˈnəʊsɪs/ *n, pl* **diagnoses** /-seez‖-siːz/ **1** the art or act of identifying a disease from its signs and symptoms **2** (a statement resulting from) the investigation of the cause or nature of a problem or phenomenon

¹diagnostic /ˌdie·əgˈnostik‖ˌdaɪəgˈnɒstɪk/ *also* **diagnostical** /-kl‖-kl/ *adj* of or involving diagnosis – **diagnostically** *adv*

²diagnostic *n* the art or practice of diagnosis – often pl with sing. meaning – **diagnostician** *n*

¹diagonal /dieˈag(ə)nl‖daɪˈæg(ə)nl/ *adj* **1** joining 2 nonadjacent angles of a polygon or polyhedron **2** running in an oblique direction from a reference line (e g the vertical) – **diagonalize** *vt*, **diagonally** *adv*

²diagonal *n* **1** a diagonal straight line or plane **2** a diagonal direction **3** SOLIDUS 2

¹diagram /ˈdie·əˌgram‖ˈdaɪəˌgræm/ *n* **1** a line drawing made for mathematical or scientific purposes **2** a drawing or design that shows the arrangement and relations (e g of parts) – **diagrammatic** *also* **diagrammatical** *adj*, **diagrammatically** *adv*

²diagram *vt* **-mm-** (*NAm* **-m-**, **-mm-**) to represent in the form of a diagram

¹dial /die·əl‖daɪəl/ *n* **1** a sundial **2** the graduated face of a timepiece **3a** a face on which some measurement is registered, usu by means of numbers and a pointer **b** a disc-shaped control on an electrical or mechanical device <*a telephone* ~> **4** *Br* a person's face – slang

²dial *vb* **-ll-** (*NAm* **-l-**, **-ll-**) *vt* to operate a dial so as to select <~led *the number*> ~ *vi* **1** to manipulate a dial **2** to make a call on a dial telephone

dialect /ˈdie·əlekt‖ˈdaɪəlekt/ *n* a regional, social, or subordinate variety of a language, usu differing distinctively from the standard or original language – **dialectal** *adj*, **dialectally** *adv*

dialectic /ˌdie·əˈlektik‖ˌdaɪəˈlektɪk/ *n* a systematic reasoning, exposition, or argument that juxtaposes opposed or contradictory ideas and usu seeks to resolve their conflict – usu pl with sing. meaning but sing. or pl in constr

dialectical /ˌdie·əˈlektikl‖ˌdaɪəˈlektɪkl/ *also* **dialectic** *adj* **1** of or in accordance with dialectic **2** (characteristic) of a dialect – **dialectically** *adv*

dialectician /ˌdie·əlekˈtish(ə)n‖ˌdaɪəlekˈtɪʃ(ə)n/ *n* **1** one who is skilled in or practises dialectic **2** a student of dialects

dialogue, *NAm also* **dialog** /ˈdie·əlog‖ˈdaɪəlɒg/ *n* **1** a literary work in conversational form **2a** a conversation between 2 or more people or between a person and sthg else (e g a computer) **b** an exchange of ideas and opinions **3** the conversational element of literary or dramatic composition **4** discussion or negotiation between 2 nations, factions, groups, etc with conflicting interests [deriv of Greek *dialogos*, fr *dialegesthai* to converse, fr *dia* through + *legein* to speak]

diameter /dieˈamitə‖daɪˈæmɪtə/ *n* **1** a line passing through the centre of a geometrical figure or body **2** the length of a straight line through the centre of an object (e g a circle) – **diametral** *adj*

diametric /ˌdie·əˈmetrik‖ˌdaɪəˈmetrɪk/, **diametrical** /-kl‖-kl/ *adj* **1** of or constituting a diameter **2** completely opposed or opposite – **diametrically** *adv*

¹diamond /ˈdie·əmənd‖ˈdaɪəmənd/ *n* **1** a (piece of) very hard crystalline carbon that is highly valued as a precious stone, esp when flawless and transparent, and is used industrially as an abrasive and in rock drills **2** a square or rhombus orientated so that the diagonals are horizontal and vertical **3a** a playing card marked with 1 or more red diamond-shaped figures **b** *pl but sing or pl in constr* the suit comprising cards identified by this figure **4** the entire playing field or the area enclosed by the bases in baseball

²diamond *adj* of, marking, or being a 60th or 75th anniversary <~ *wedding*>

¹diaper /ˈdiepə, ˈdie·əpə‖ˈdaɪpə, ˈdaɪəpə/ *n* **1** a soft usu white linen or cotton fabric used for tablecloths or towels **2** an ornamental pattern consisting of one or more small repeated units of design (e g geometric figures) **3** *chiefly NAm* a nappy

²diaper *vt* to ornament with diaper designs

diaphanous /dieˈafənəs‖daɪˈæfənəs/ *adj* so fine as to be almost transparent – **diaphanously** *adv*, **diaphanousness** *n*

diaphragm /ˈdie·əˌfram‖ˈdaɪəˌfræm/ *n* **1** the partition separating the chest and abdominal cavities in mammals **2** a dividing membrane or thin partition, esp in a tube **3** a partition in a plant or the body or shell of an invertebrate animal **4** a device that limits the aperture of a lens or optical system **5** a thin flexible disc that is free to vibrate (e g in an earphone) **6** DUTCH CAP – **diaphragmatic** *adj*, **diaphragmatically** *adv*

diarist /ˈdie·ərist‖ˈdaɪərɪst/ *n* one who keeps a diary

diarrhoea, *NAm chiefly* **diarrhea** /ˌdie·əˈriə‖ˌdaɪəˈrɪə/ *n* abnormally frequent intestinal evacuations with more or less fluid faeces – **diarrhoeal, diarrhoeic** *also* **diarrhoetic** *adj*

diary /ˈdie·əri‖ˈdaɪərɪ/ *n* **1** (a book containing) a daily record of personal experiences or observations **2** *chiefly Br* a book with dates marked in which memoranda can be noted [Latin *diarium*, fr *dies* day]

Diaspora /dieˈaspərə‖daɪˈæspərə/ *n* **1** the settling, or area of settlement, of Jews outside Palestine after the Babylonian exile **2** *sing or pl in constr* the Jews living outside Palestine or modern Israel

diatom /ˈdie·ətəm, -ˌtom‖ˈdaɪətəm, -ˌtɒm/ *n* any of a class of minute single-celled algae with hard shell-like skeletons that are composed of silica

diatonic /ˌdie·əˈtonik‖ˌdaɪəˈtɒnɪk/ *adj* relating to a major or minor musical scale of 8 notes to the octave without chromatic deviation – **diatonically** *adv*

diatribe /ˈdie·əˌtrieb‖ˈdaɪəˌtraɪb/ *n* a (lengthy) piece of bitter and abusive criticism

[1]**dibble** /ˈdibl‖ˈdɪbl/ *n* a small pointed hand implement used to make holes in the ground for plants, seeds, or bulbs

[2]**dibble** *vt* **1** to plant with a dibble **2** to make holes in (soil) (as if) with a dibble

[1]**dice** /dies‖daɪs/ *n, pl* **dice** /~/ **1a** a small cube that is marked on each face with from 1 to 6 spots and that is used to determine arbitrary values in various games **b** a gambling game played with dice **2** a small cubical piece (e g of food) – **no dice** of no avail; no use – infml

[2]**dice** *vt* **1** to cut (e g food) into small cubes **2** to gamble using dice < ~ *his money away*> ~ *vi* **1** to play games with dice **2** to take a chance < ~ *with death*> – **dicer** *n*

dicey /ˈdiesi‖ˈdaɪsɪ/ *adj* risky, unpredictable – infml

dichotomy /dieˈkotəmi‖daɪˈkɒtəmɪ/ *n* **1** a division into 2 esp mutually exclusive or contradictory groups **2** a (repeated) branching (into 2 branches)

dick /dik‖dɪk/ *n* **1** *chiefly Br* a person <*clever* ~> **2** a detective **3** the penis – vulg *USE* (*1&2*) infml

dickens /ˈdikinz‖ˈdɪkɪnz/ *n* devil, deuce – used as an interjection or intensive

dicker /ˈdikə‖ˈdɪkə/ *vi* **1** to bargain, haggle **2** to hesitate, dither /ˈdikiˌbuhd‖ˈdɪkɪˌbɜːd/

dickeybird /ˈdikiˌbuhd‖ˈdɪkɪˌbɜːd/ *n* **1** a small bird – used by or to children **2** so much as a single word <*never said a* ~> – infml

dicky /ˈdiki‖ˈdɪkɪ/ *adj, Br* in a weak or unsound condition – infml <*a* ~ *heart*>

Dictaphone /ˈdiktəˌfohn‖ˈdɪktəˌfəʊn/ *trademark* – used for a dictating machine

[1]**dictate** /dikˈtayt‖dɪkˈteɪt/ *vi* **1** to give dictation **2** to speak or act with authority; prescribe ~ *vt* **1** to speak or read for a person to transcribe or for a machine to record **2** to impose, pronounce, or specify with authority

[2]**dictate** /ˈdiktayt‖ˈdɪkteɪt/ *n* **1** an authoritative rule, prescription, or command **2** a ruling principle – usu pl <*according to the* ~s *of his conscience*>

dictation /dikˈtaysh(ə)n‖dɪkˈteɪʃ(ə)n/ *n* **1** PRESCRIPTION 2 **2a** the act or manner of uttering words to be transcribed **b** material that is dictated or transcribed

dictator /dikˈtaytə‖dɪkˈteɪtə/ *n* **1** a person granted absolute emergency power, esp in ancient Rome **2** an absolute ruler; *esp* one who has seized power unconstitutionally and uses it oppressively

dictatorial /ˌdiktəˈtawri·əl‖ˌdɪktəˈtɔːrɪəl/ *adj* **1** of a dictator **2** arrogantly domineering – **dictatorially** *adv*, **dictatorialness** *n*

dicˈtatorˌship /-ˌship‖-ˌʃɪp/ *n* **1** the office of dictator **2** total or absolute control; leadership, rule **3** a state or form of government where absolute power is concentrated in one person or a small clique

diction /ˈdiksh(ə)n‖ˈdɪkʃ(ə)n/ *n* **1** choice of words, esp with regard to correctness or clearness **2** pronunciation and enunciation of words in speaking or singing

dictionary /ˈdikshən(ə)ri‖ˈdɪkʃən(ə)rɪ/ *n* **1** a reference book containing words, terms, or names, usu alphabetically arranged, together with information about them **2** a reference book giving for words of one language equivalents in another **3** a list (e g of synonyms or hyphenation instructions) stored in machine-readable form (e g on a computer disk) for reference by an automatic system (e g for computerized typesetting)

dictum /ˈdiktəm‖ˈdɪktəm/ *n, pl* **dicta** /-tə‖-tə/ *also* **dictums** **1** an authoritative statement on some topic; a pronouncement **2** OBITER DICTUM 1

did /did‖dɪd/ *past of* DO

didactic /dieˈdaktik‖daɪˈdæktɪk/ *adj* **1** intended to teach sthg, esp a moral lesson **2** having a tendency to teach in an authoritarian manner – **didactically** *adv*, **didacticism** *n*

diddle /ˈdidl‖ˈdɪdl/ *vt* to cheat, swindle – infml – **diddler** *n*

didn't /ˈdidnt‖ˈdɪdnt/ did not

didst /didst‖dɪdst/ *archaic past 2 sing of* DO

[1]**die** /die‖daɪ/ *vi* **dying** **1** to stop living; suffer the end of physical life **2** to pass out of existence, cease <*his anger* ~d> **3** to long keenly or desperately <dying *to go*> **4** to stop <*the motor* ~d>

[2]**die** *n, pl* (*1*) **dice** /dies‖daɪs/, (*2&3*) **dies** /diez‖daɪz/ **1** a dice **2** DADO 1 **3** any of various tools or devices for giving a desired shape, form, or finish to a material or for impressing an object or material – **the dice are loaded** all the elements of a situation are combined to work – usu + *against* or *in favour of* – **the die is cast** the irrevocable decision or step has been taken

die down *vi* **1** *of a plant* to undergo death of the parts lying above ground **2** to diminish, subside

ˈ**die-ˌhard** *n or adj* (one) strongly resisting change

die out *vi* to become extinct

dieresis /ˌdie'erisis, -ərisis‖ˌdaɪ'erɪsɪs, -'ɪərɪsɪs/ *n, chiefly NAm* a diaeresis

diesel /'deezl‖'di:zl/ *n* **1** (a vehicle driven by) a diesel engine **2** a heavy mineral oil used as fuel in diesel engines [Rudolph *Diesel* (1858-1913), German mechanical engineer]

'**diesel** ˌ**engine** *n* an internal-combustion engine in which fuel is ignited by air compressed to a sufficiently high temperature

¹**diet** /'die·ət‖'daɪət/ *n* **1** the food and drink habitually taken by a group, animal, or individual **2** the kind and amount of food prescribed for a person or animal for a special purpose (e g losing weight)

²**diet** *vb* to (cause to) eat and drink sparingly or according to prescribed rules – **dieter** *n*

³**diet** *n* any of various national or provincial legislatures

¹**dietary** /'die·ət(ə)ri‖'daɪət(ə)rɪ/ *n* the kinds and amounts of food available to or eaten by an individual, group, or population

²**dietary** *adj* of (the rules of) a diet – **dietarily** *adv*

dietetic /ˌdie·ə'tetik‖ˌdaɪə'tetɪk/ *adj* **1** of diet **2** adapted for use in special diets – **dietetically** *adv*

ˌ**die'tetics** *n pl but sing or pl in constr* the application of the principles of nutrition to feeding

dietitian, **dietician** /ˌdie·ə'tish(ə)n‖ˌdaɪə'tɪʃ(ə)n/ *n* a specialist in dietetics

differ /'difə‖'dɪfə/ *vi* **1a** to be unlike; be distinct *from* **b** to change from time to time; vary **2** to disagree <*people who ~ on religious matters*>

difference /'difrəns‖'dɪfrəns/ *n* **1a** unlikeness between 2 or more people or things **b** the degree or amount by which things differ **2** a disagreement, dispute; dissension **3** the degree or amount by which things differ in quantity or measure; *specif* REMAINDER 2b(1) **4** a significant change in or effect on a situation

different /'difrənt‖'dɪfrənt/ *adj* **1** partly or totally unlike; dissimilar – + *from*, chiefly Br *to*, or chiefly NAm *than* **2a** distinct **b** various **c** another **3** unusual, special – **differently** *adv*, **differentness** *n*

¹**differential** /ˌdifə'renshəl‖ˌdɪfə'renʃəl/ *adj* **1a** of or constituting a difference **b** based on or resulting from a differential <*~ freight charges*> **c** functioning or proceeding differently or at a different rate **2** of or involving a differential or differentiation **3** of quantitative differences – **differentially** *adv*

²**differential** *n* **1** the product of the derivative of a function of one variable with the increment of the independent variable **2** the amount of a difference between comparable individuals or classes; *specif* the amount by which the remuneration of distinct types of worker differs **3** (a case covering) a differential gear

diffeˌrential '**calculus** *n* a branch of mathematics dealing chiefly with the rate of change of functions with respect to their variables

differential gear *n* an arrangement of gears in a vehicle that allows one of the wheels imparting motion to turn (e g in going round a corner) faster than the other

differentiate /ˌdifə'renshiayt‖ˌdɪfə'renʃɪeɪt/ *vt* **1** to obtain the mathematical derivative of **2** to mark or show a difference in **3** to cause differentiation of in the course of development **4** to express the specific difference of ~ *vi* **1** to recognize a difference *between* **2** to become distinct or different in character **3** to undergo differentiation – **differentiability** *n*, **differentiable** *adj*

differentiation /ˌdifəˌrenshi'aysh(ə)n‖ˌdɪfəˌrenʃɪ'eɪʃ(ə)n/ *n* **1** development into more complex, numerous, or varied forms **2a** modification of body parts for performance of particular functions **b** all the processes whereby apparently similar cells, tissues, and structures attain their adult forms and functions

difficult /'difik(ə)lt‖'dɪfɪk(ə)lt/ *adj* **1** hard to do, make, carry out, or understand **2a** hard to deal with, manage, or please <*a ~ child*> **b** puzzling – **difficultly** *adv*

difficulty /'difik(ə)lti‖'dɪfɪk(ə)ltɪ/ *n* **1** being difficult **2** an obstacle or impediment **3** a cause of (financial) trouble or embarrassment – usu pl with sing. meaning

diffident /'difid(ə)nt‖'dɪfɪd(ə)nt/ *adj* **1** lacking in self-confidence **2** reserved, unassertive – **diffidently** *adv*, **diffidence** *n*

diffract /di'frakt‖dɪ'frækt/ *vt* to cause (a beam of light) to become a set of light and dark or coloured bands in passing by the edge of an opaque body, through narrow slits, etc – **diffraction** *n*

¹**diffuse** /di'fyoohs‖dɪ'fju:s/ *adj* **1** not concentrated or localized; scattered **2** lacking conciseness; verbose – **diffusely** *adv*, **diffuseness** *n*

²**diffuse** /di'fyoohz‖dɪ'fju:z/ *vt* **1** to spread out freely in all directions **2** to break up and distribute (incident light) by reflection ~ *vi* **1** to spread out or become transmitted **2** to undergo diffusion – **diffuser** *n*, **diffusible** *adj*, **diffusive** *adj*

diffusion /di'fyoohzh(ə)n‖dɪ'fju:ʒ(ə)n/ *n* **1** diffusing or being diffused **2** being long-winded **3a** the process whereby particles of liquids, gases, or solids intermingle as the result of their spontaneous movement **b** reflection of light by a rough reflecting surface – **diffusional** *adj*

¹**dig** /dig‖dɪg/ *vb* **-gg-; dug** /dug‖dʌg/ *vi* **1** to turn up, loosen, or remove earth **2** to understand ~ *vt* **1** to break up, turn, or loosen (earth) with an implement **2** to bring to the surface (as if) by digging; unearth **3** to hollow out by removing earth; excavate <*~ a hole*> **4** to drive down into; thrust **5** to poke, prod <*~ him in the ribs*> **6a** to pay attention to; notice **b** to understand, appreciate *USE* (*vi 2; vt 6*) slang

²**dig** *n* **1a** a thrust, poke **b** a cutting or snide remark **2** an archaeological excavation (site) **3** *pl, chiefly Br* LODGING 2b

¹**digest** /'diejest‖'daɪdʒest/ *n* **1** a systematic compilation of laws **2** a literary abridgment

²**digest** /di'jest, die-‖dɪ'dʒest, daɪ-/ *vt* **1** to distribute or arrange systematically **2** to convert (food) into a form the body can use **3** to assimilate mentally **4** to soften or decompose or extract soluble ingredients from by heat and moisture or chemicals **5** to compress into a short summary ~*vi* to become digested – **digester** *n*, **digestible** *adj*, **digestibility** *n*

digestion /di'jeschən||dɪ'dʒestʃən/ *n* the process or power of digesting sthg, esp food

[1]**digestive** /di'jestiv||dɪ'dʒestɪv/ *n* sthg that aids digestion

[2]**digestive** *adj* of, causing, or promoting digestion – **digestively** *adv*, **digestiveness** *n*

digger /'digə||'dɪgə/ *n* **1** a tool or machine for digging **2** a private soldier from Australia or New Zealand, esp in WW I – infml

diggings /'digingz||'dɪgɪŋz/ *n pl* **1** material dug out **2** a place of excavating, esp for ore, metals, or precious stones

dig in *vt* to incorporate by burying in the soil ~ *vi* **1** to dig defensive positions **2** to hold stubbornly to a position; defend doggedly (e g when batting in cricket) **3** to begin eating – infml – **dig one's heels in** to refuse to move or change one's mind; be stubborn

digit /'dijit||'dɪdʒɪt/ *n* **1a** any of the Arabic numerals from 1 to 9, usu also including 0 **b** any of the elements that combine to form numbers in a system other than the decimal system **2** a finger or toe **3** a unit of measurement equal to $^3/_4$in (about 1.9cm)

digital /'dijitl||'dɪdʒɪtl/ *adj* **1** of or with the fingers or toes **2** of calculation by numerical methods which use discrete units **3** of data in the form of numerical digits **4** *of an automatic device* presenting information in the form of numerical digits – **digitally** *adv*

ˌdigital comˈputer *n* a computer that operates with numbers expressed as discrete pulses representing digits

dignified /'dignified||'dɪgnɪfaɪd/ *adj* showing or having dignity

dignify /'dignifie||'dɪgnɪfaɪ/ *vt* to confer dignity or distinction on

dignitary /'dignit(ə)ri||'dɪgnɪt(ə)rɪ/ *n* a person of high rank or holding a position of dignity or honour – **dignitary** *adj*

dignity /'dignəti||'dɪgnətɪ/ *n* **1** being worthy, honoured, or esteemed **2** high rank, office, or position **3** stillness of manner; gravity

dig out *vt* to find, unearth

digraph /'dieˌgrahf, -ˌgraf||'daɪˌgrɑːf, -ˌgræf/ *n* a group of 2 successive letters, esp whose phonetic value is a single sound

digress /di'gres, die-||dɪ'gres, daɪ-/ *vi* to turn aside, esp from the main subject in writing or speaking – **digressive** *adj*, **digressively** *adv*, **digressiveness** *n*

digression /di'gresh(ə)n, die-||dɪ'greʃ(ə)n, daɪ-/ *n* (an instance of) digressing – **digressional** *adj*, **digressionary** *adj*

[1]**dike** /diek||daɪk/ *vb or n* (to) dyke

[2]**dike** *n* a lesbian – derog

dilapidated /di'lapidaytid||dɪ'læpɪdeɪtɪd/ *adj* decayed or fallen into partial ruin, esp through neglect or misuse [Latin *dilapidare* to pelt with stones, destroy, fr *dis-* apart + *lapidare* to throw stones, fr *lapid-, lapis* stone] – **dilapidation** *n*

dilate /di'layt, die-||dɪ'leɪt, daɪ-/ *vt* to distend ~ *vi* **1** to comment at length *on* or *upon* **2** to become wide – **dilatable** *adj*, **dilator** *n*, **dilative** *adj*, **dilatability** *n*

dilatory /'dilət(ə)ri||'dɪlət(ə)rɪ/ *adj* **1** tending or intended to cause delay **2** slow, tardy – **dilatorily** *adv*, **dilatoriness** *n*

dildo /'dildoh||'dɪldəʊ/ *n, pl* **dildos** an object serving as an artificial penis for inserting into the vagina

dilemma /di'lemə, die-||dɪ'lemə, daɪ-/ *n* **1** an argument in which an opponent's position is refuted by being shown to lead to 2 or more unacceptable alternatives **2** a situation involving choice between 2 equally unsatisfactory alternatives [Late Latin, *d*eriv of Greek *di-* double + *lēmma* assumption, fr *lambanein* to take] – **dilemmatic** *adj*

dilettante /ˌdili'tanti||ˌdɪlɪ'tæntɪ/ *n, pl* **dilettanti** /ˌdili'tanti||ˌdɪlɪ'tæntɪ/ **dilettantes** /-tiz||-tɪz/ a person with a superficial interest in an art or a branch of knowledge [Italian, fr *dilettare* to delight, fr L *delectare*] – **dilettante** *adj*, **dilettantish** *adj*, **dilettantism** *n*

diligence /'dilij(ə)ns||'dɪlɪdʒ(ə)ns/ *n* steady application and effort

diligent /'dilij(ə)nt||'dɪlɪdʒ(ə)nt/ *adj* showing steady application and effort – **diligently** *adv*

dill /dil||dɪl/ *n* a European plant with aromatic foliage and seeds, both of which are used in flavouring foods (e g pickles)

dillydally /'diliˌdali||'dɪlɪˌdælɪ/ *vi* to waste time by loitering; dawdle – infml

[1]**dilute** /die'looht, -'lyooht||daɪ'luːt, -'ljuːt/ *vt* **1** to make thinner or more liquid by adding another liquid **2** to diminish the strength or brilliance of by adding more liquid, light, etc **3** to attenuate – **diluter, dilutor** *n*, **dilutive** *adj*, **dilution** *n*

[2]**dilute** *adj* weak, diluted – **diluteness** *n*

[1]**dim** /dim||dɪm/ *adj* **-mm- 1** giving out a weak or insufficient light **2a** seen indistinctly <*a ~ shape loomed out of the fog*> **b** characterized by an unfavourable or pessimistic attitude – esp in *take a dim view of* **3** not seeing clearly <*the old man's eyes were ~*> **4** lacking intelligence; stupid – infml – **dimly** *adv*, **dimness** *n*

[2]**dim** *vb* **-mm-** *vt* **1** to make dim **2** *NAm* DIP 4 ~*vi* to become dim

dime /diem||daɪm/ *n* a coin worth $^1/_{10}$ of a US dollar

[1]**dimension** /di'mensh(ə)n, die-||dɪ'menʃ(ə)n, daɪ-/ *n* **1a(1)** extension in 1 direction **a(2)** any of a group of parameters necessary and sufficient to determine uniquely each element of a system of usu mathematical entities <*the surface of a sphere has 2 ~s*> **b** the size of extension in 1 or all directions **c** the range over which sthg extends; the scope – usu pl with sing. meaning **d** an aspect <*gave a whole new ~ to the problem*> **2** any of the fundamental quantities, specif mass, length, and time, which combine to make a derived unit – usu pl – **dimensional** *adj*, **dimensionally** *adv*, **dimensionless** *adj*, **dimensionality** *n*

[2]**dimension** *vt* to indicate the dimensions on (a drawing)

diminish /di'minish||dɪ'mɪnɪʃ/ *vt* **1** to make or cause to appear less **2** to lessen the reputation of; belittle ~*vi* to become gradually less; dwindle – **diminishable** *adj*, **diminishment** *n*

diminuendo /diˌminyoo'endoh||dɪˌmɪnjʊ'endəʊ/ *n, adv, or adj, pl* **diminuendos** (a musical passage played) with a decrease in volume

diminution /ˌdimi'nyoohsh(ə)n||ˌdɪmɪ'njuːʃ(ə)n/ *n* a diminishing or decrease –

diminutional *adj*

[1]**diminutive** /di'minyootiv‖dɪ'mɪnjʊtɪv/ *n* a diminutive word, affix, or name

[2]**diminutive** *adj* **1** indicating small size and sometimes lovableness or triviality – used in connection with affixes and words formed with them (e g *duckling*), with clipped forms (e g *Jim*), and with altered forms (e g *Peggy*) **2** exceptionally small; tiny – **diminutively** *adv*, **diminutiveness** *n*

dimity /'dimiti‖'dɪmɪtɪ/ *n* a corded cotton fabric woven with checks or stripes

[1]**dimple** /'dimpl‖'dɪmpl/ *n* **1** a slight natural indentation in the cheek or another part of the human body **2** a depression or indentation on a surface – **dimply** *adj*

[2]**dimple** *vb* to mark with or form dimples

dimwit /'dim,wit‖'dɪm,wɪt/ *n* a stupid or mentally slow person – infml – **dim-witted** *adj*, **dim-wittedly** *adv*, **dim-wittedness** *n*

[1]**din** /din‖dɪn/ *n* a loud continued discordant noise

[2]**din** *vi* **-nn-** to make a din – **din into** to instil into by perpetual repetition

dinar /'dee,nah‖'diː,nɑː/ *n* (a coin or note representing) a money unit of certain Arab countries and Yugoslavia

dine /dien‖daɪn/ *vi* to eat dinner ~*vt* to entertain to dinner <*wined and* ~d *us splendidly*> – **dine off/on/upon** to eat (sthg) as one's meal, esp one's dinner

diner /'dienə‖'daɪnə/ *n* **1** sby who is dining **2a** *NAm* a small restaurant, often beside the road **b** *chiefly NAm* DINING CAR

[1]**dingdong** /'ding,dong‖'dɪŋ,dɒŋ/ *n* **1** the ringing sound produced by repeated strokes, esp on a bell **2** a rapid heated exchange of words or blows – infml

[2]**dingdong** *adj* **1** of or resembling the sound of a bell **2** with the advantage (e g in an argument or race) passing continually back and forth from one participant, side, etc to the other – infml

dinghy /'ding·gi‖'dɪŋgɪ/ *n* **1** a small boat often carried on a ship and used esp as a lifeboat or to transport passengers to and from shore **2** a small open sailing boat **3** a rubber life raft [Bengali *diṅgi* & Hindi *ḍiṅgī*]

dingo /'ding·goh‖'dɪŋgəʊ/ *n, pl* **dingoes** a wild dog of Australia

dingy /'dinji‖'dɪndʒɪ/ *adj* **1** dirty, discoloured **2** shabby, squalid – **dingily** *adv*, **dinginess** *n*

'**dining ,car** /'diening‖'daɪnɪŋ/ *n* a railway carriage where meals are served

dining room *n* a room set aside for eating meals in

dinkum /'dingkəm‖'dɪŋkəm/ *adj*, *Austr* real, genuine – infml

dinky /'dingki‖'dɪŋkɪ/ *adj* **1** *chiefly Br* neat and dainty **2** *chiefly NAm* small, insignificant *USE* infml

dinner /'dinə‖'dɪnə/ *n* **1** (the food eaten for) the principal meal of the day taken either in the evening or at midday **2** a formal evening meal or banquet

'**dinner ,jacket** *n* a usu black jacket for men's semiformal evening wear

dinosaur /'dienə,saw‖'daɪnə,sɔː/ *n* any of a group of extinct, typically very large flesh- or plant-eating reptiles, most of which lived on the land; *broadly* any large extinct reptile [deriv of Greek *deinos* terrible + *sauros* lizard] – **dinosaurian** *adj or n*, **dinosauric** *adj*

dint /dint‖dɪnt/ *n* – **by dint of** by means or application of

diocese /'die·əsis‖'daɪəsɪs/ *n* the area under the jurisdiction of a bishop – **diocesan** *adj*

diode /'die,ohd‖'daɪ,əʊd/ *n* **1** a thermionic valve having only an anode and a cathode **2** a semiconductor device having only 2 terminals

dioxide /,die'oksied‖,daɪ'ɒksaɪd/ *n* an oxide containing 2 atoms of oxygen

dioxin /die'oksin‖daɪ'ɒksɪn/ *n* a poisonous chemical compound contained as an impurity in various weedkillers

[1]**dip** /dip‖dɪp/ *vb* **-pp-** *vt* **1** to plunge or immerse in a liquid (e g in order to moisten or dye) **2** to lift up (water, grain etc) by scooping or ladling **3** to lower and then raise again < ~ *a flag in salute*> **4** to lower (the beam of a vehicle's headlights) so as to reduce glare ~ *vi* **1a** to plunge into a liquid and quickly emerge **b** to immerse sthg in a processing liquid or finishing material **2** to drop down or decrease suddenly **3** to reach inside or below sthg, esp so as to take out part of the contents – usu + *in* or *into* **4** to incline downwards from the plane of the horizon – **dip into 1** to make inroads into for funds <dipped into *the family's savings*> **2** to read superficially or in a random manner <dipped into *a book while he was waiting*>

[2]**dip** *n* **1** a brief bathe for sport or exercise **2a** a sharp downward course; a drop **b** the angle that a stratum or similar geological feature makes with a horizontal plane **3** the angle formed with the horizon by a magnetic needle rotating in the vertical plane **4** a hollow, depression **5a** a sauce or soft mixture into which food is dipped before being eaten **b** a liquid preparation into which an object or animal may be dipped (e g for cleaning or disinfecting) **6** a pickpocket – slang

diphtheria /dif'thiəri·ə, dip-‖dɪf'θɪərɪə, dɪp-/ *n* an acute infectious disease caused by a bacterium and marked by fever and the formation of a false membrane, esp in the throat, causing difficulty in breathing – **diphtherial, diphtherian** *adj*, **diphtheritic** *adj*

diphthong /'difthong, 'dip-‖'dɪfθɒŋ, 'dɪp-/ *n* **1** a gliding monosyllabic vowel sound (e g /oy/ in *toy*) that starts at or near the articulatory position for one vowel and moves to or towards the position of another **2** a digraph **3** either of the ligatures æ or œ – **diphthongal** *adj*

diploma /di'plohmə‖dɪ'pləʊmə/ *n* **1** an official or state document **2** a document conferring some honour or privilege **3** (a certificate of) a qualification, usu in a more specialized subject or at a lower level than a degree [Latin, passport, diploma, fr Greek *diplōma* folded paper, passport, fr *diploun* to double, fr *diploos* double]

diplomacy /di'plohməsi‖dɪ'pləʊməsɪ/ *n* **1** the art and practice of conducting international relations **2** skill and tact in handling affairs

diplomat /'dipləmat‖'dɪpləmæt/ *n* **1** one (e g an ambassador) employed in diplomacy **2** one skilled in dealing with people tactfully and adroitly

diplomatic /ˌdiplə'matik‖ˌdɪplə'mætɪk/ *adj* **1** exactly reproducing the original <*a* ~ *edition*> **2** of diplomats or international relations **3** employing tact and conciliation – **diplomatically** *adv*

diplomatist /di'plohmətist‖dɪ'pləʊmətɪst/ *n* a person skilled or employed in diplomacy

dipper /'dipə‖'dɪpə/ *n* **1** sthg (e g a long-handled cup) used for dipping **2** any of several diving birds **3** *cap, chiefly NAm* **3a Dipper, Big Dipper** URSA MAJOR **b** URSA MINOR

dipsomania /ˌdipsoh'maynyə, -ni·ə, ˌdipsə-‖ˌdɪpsəʊ'meɪnjə, -nɪə, ˌdɪpsə-/ *n* an uncontrollable craving for alcoholic drinks – **dipsomaniac** *n*, **dipsomaniacal** *adj*

dipstick /'dipˌstik‖'dɪpˌstɪk/ *n* a graduated rod for measuring the depth of a liquid (e g the oil in a car's engine)

diptych /'diptik‖'dɪptɪk/ *n* **1** a 2-leaved hinged writing tablet **2** a painting or carving done on 2 hinged panels and used esp as an altarpiece

dire /die·ə‖daɪə/ *adj* **1** dreadful, awful **2** warning of disaster; ominous <*a* ~ *forecast*> **3** desperately urgent <~ *need*> – **direly** *adv*, **direness** *n*

[1]**direct** /di'rekt, die-‖dɪ'rekt, daɪ-/ *vt* **1a** to mark (e g a letter or parcel) with a name and address **b** to address or aim (e g a remark) **2** to cause to turn, move, point, or follow a straight course <~ed *her eyes heavenward*> **3** to show or point out the way for **4a** to control and regulate the activities or course of **b** to control the organization and performance of; supervise <~ed *the latest science fiction film*> **c** to order or instruct with authority <*police* ~ed *the crowd to move back*> **d** to train and usu lead performances of; *specif, chiefly NAm* to conduct ~*vi* to act as director

[2]**direct** *adj* **1a** going from one point to another in time or space without deviation or interruption; straight **b** going by the shortest way <*the* ~ *route*> **2a** stemming immediately from a source, cause, or reason <~ *result*> **b** passing in a straight line of descent from parent to offspring <~ *ancestor*> **3** frank, straightforward **4a** operating without an intervening agency **b** effected by the action of the people or the electorate and not by representatives **5** consisting of or reproducing the exact words of a speaker or writer <~ *speech*> **6** diametric, exact <*was a* ~ *contradiction of all he'd said before*> – **directness** *n*

[3]**direct** *adv* **1** from point to point without deviation; by the shortest way **2** without an intervening agency or stage

direct action *n* action that seeks to achieve an end by the most immediately effective means (e g boycott or strike)

direct current *n* an electric current flowing in 1 direction only; *esp* such a current that is substantially constant in value

direct 'debit *n* an instruction to a bank to accept debits to an account from another named account at regular times

direction /di'reksh(ə)n, die-‖dɪ'rekʃ(ə)n, daɪ-/ *n* **1** guidance or supervision of action **2a** the act, art, or technique of directing an orchestra, film, or theatrical production **b** a word, phrase, or sign indicating the appropriate tempo, mood, or intensity of a passage or movement in music **3** *pl* explicit instructions on how to do sthg or get to a place <*read the* ~s *on the packet*> <*asked for* ~s *to King's Cross*> **4a** the line or course along which sby or sthg moves or is aimed <*drove off in the* ~ *of London*> **b** the point towards which sby or sthg faces

directional /di'reksh(ə)nl, die-‖dɪ'rekʃ(ə)nl, daɪ-/ *adj* **1** of or indicating direction in space: e g **1a** suitable for detecting the direction from which radio signals come, or for sending out signals in 1 direction only <*a* ~ *aerial*> **b** of or being a device that operates more efficiently in one direction than in others **2** relating to direction or guidance, esp of thought or effort – **directionality** *n*

di'rection ˌfinder *n* an aerial used to determine the direction of incoming radio waves

[1]**directive** /di'rektiv, die-‖dɪ'rektɪv, daɪ-/ *adj* **1** serving to direct, guide, or influence **2** serving to provide a direction

[2]**directive** *n* an authoritative instruction issued by a high-level body or official

[1]**di'rectly** /-li‖-lɪ/ *adv* **1** in a direct manner **2a** without delay; immediately **b** soon, shortly

[2]**directly** *conj, chiefly Br* immediately after; as soon as – infml

direct object *n* a grammatical object representing the primary goal or the result of the action of its verb (e g *me* in 'he hit me' and *house* in 'we built a house')

director /di'rektə, die-‖dɪ'rektə, daɪ-/ *n* **1** the head of an organized group or administrative unit **2** a member of a governing board entrusted with the overall direction of a company **3** sby who has responsibility for supervising the artistic and technical aspects of a film or play – **directorship** *n*, **directorial** *adj*

directorate /di'rektərət, die-‖dɪ'rektərət, daɪ-/ *n* **1** the office of director **2** a board of directors (e g of a company)

directory /di'rekt(ə)ri, die-‖dɪ'rekt(ə)rɪ, daɪ-/ *n* **1** a book or collection of directions or rules, esp concerning forms of worship **2** an alphabetical or classified list (e g of names, addresses, telephone numbers, etc)

direct tax *n* a tax (e g income tax) exacted directly from the person, organization, etc on whom it is levied

dirge /duhj‖dɜːdʒ/ *n* **1** a song or hymn of grief or lamentation **2** a slow mournful piece of music

[1]**dirigible** /'dirijəbl, -'---‖'dɪrɪdʒəbl, -'---/ *adj* capable of being steered

[2]**dirigible** *n* an airship

dirk /duhk‖dɜːk/ *n* a long straight-bladed dagger, used esp by Scottish Highlanders

dirndl /'duhndl‖'dɜːndl/ *n* a full skirt with a tight waistband

dirt /duht‖dɜːt/ *n* **1a** excrement **b** a filthy or soiling substance (e g mud or grime) **c** sby or sthg worthless or contemptible **2** [3]SOIL 2a **3a** obscene or pornographic speech or writing **b**

scandalous or malicious gossip

[1]**dirty** /ˈduhti‖ˈdɜːtɪ/ *adj* **1a** not clean or pure; marked or contaminated with dirt **b** causing sby or sthg to become soiled or covered with dirt <~ *jobs*> **2a** base, sordid <*war is a ~ business*> **b** unsportsmanlike, unfair <~ *players*> **c** low, despicable <~ *tricks*> **3a** indecent, obscene <~ *language*> **b** sexually illicit <*a ~ weekend*> **4** *of weather* rough, stormy **5** *of colour* not clear and bright; dull <*drab* dirty-*pink walls*> **6** conveying resentment or disgust <*gave him a ~ look*> **7** producing considerable fallout <~ *bombs*> – **dirtily** *adv*, **dirtiness** *n*

[2]**dirty** *vb* to make or become dirty

dis- /dis-‖dɪs-/ *prefix* **1a** do the opposite of (a specified action) <dis*establish*> **b** deprive of, remove (sthg specified) from <dis*arm*> **c** exclude or expel from <dis*bar*> **2** opposite or absence of <dis*belief*> **3** not <dis*agreeable*> **4** completely <dis*annul*> **5** dys- <dis*function*>

disability /ˌdisəˈbiləti‖ˌdɪsəˈbɪlətɪ/ *n* **1a** the condition of being disabled; *specif* inability to do sthg (e g pursue an occupation) because of physical or mental impairment **b** sthg that disables; a handicap **2** a legal disqualification

disable /disˈaybl‖dɪsˈeɪbl/ *vt* **1** to deprive of legal right, qualification, or capacity **2** to make incapable or ineffective; *esp* to deprive of physical soundness; cripple – **disablement** *n*

disabuse /ˌdisəˈbyoohz‖ˌdɪsəˈbjuːz/ *vt* to free from a mistaken impression or judgment

disaccharide /ˌdieˈsakəried‖ˌdaɪˈsækəraɪd/ *n* any of a class of sugars (e g sucrose) that, on hydrolysis, yield 2 monosaccharide molecules

[1]**disadvantage** /ˌdisədˈvahntij‖ˌdɪsədˈvɑːntɪdʒ/ *n* **1** loss or damage, esp to reputation or finances **2a** an unfavourable, inferior, or prejudicial situation **b** sby or sthg which causes one to be in an unfavourable condition or position; a handicap

[2]**disadvantage** *vt* to place at a disadvantage

disadvantageous /ˌdisadvənˈtayjəs‖ˌdɪsædvənˈteɪdʒəs/ *adj* **1** prejudicial, unfavourable **2** derogatory, disparaging – **disadvantageously** *adv*, **disadvantageousness** *n*

disaffect /ˌdisəˈfekt‖ˌdɪsəˈfekt/ *vt* to alienate the affection or loyalty of – **disaffection** *n*

ˌdisafˈfected *adj* discontented and resentful, esp towards authority

disaffiliate /ˌdisəˈfiliayt‖ˌdɪsəˈfɪlieɪt/ *vb* to end, or separate from, an affiliation or connection – **disaffiliation** *n*

disagree /ˌdisəˈgree‖ˌdɪsəˈgriː/ *vi* **1** to be unlike or at variance **2** to differ in opinion – usu + *with* **3** to have a bad effect – usu + *with* <*fried foods ~ with me*>

disagreeable /disəˈgree·əbl‖dɪsəˈgriːəbl/ *adj* **1** unpleasant, objectionable **2** peevish, ill-tempered – **disagreeableness** *n*, **disagreeably** *adv*, **disagreeability** *n*

ˌdisaˈgreement /-mənt‖-mənt/ *n* **1** a lack of correspondence; a disparity **2** a difference of opinion; an argument

disallow /ˌdisəˈlow‖ˌdɪsəˈlaʊ/ *vt* to refuse to admit or recognize – **disallowance** *n*

disappear /ˌdisəˈpiə‖ˌdɪsəˈpɪə/ *vi* **1** to pass from view suddenly or gradually **2** to cease to be or to be known **3** to leave or depart, esp secretly – infml – **disappearance** *n*

disappoint /ˌdisəˈpoynt‖ˌdɪsəˈpɔɪnt/ *vt* to fail to meet the expectation or hope of; *also* to sadden by so doing – **disappointing** *adj*, **disappointingly** *adv*

ˌdisapˈpointed *adj* defeated in expectation or hope; thwarted – **disappointedly** *adv*

ˌdisapˈpointment /-mənt‖-mənt/ *n* **1** disappointing or being disappointed **2** sby or sthg that disappoints

disapprobation /ˌdisˌaprəˈbaysh(ə)n‖ˌdɪsˌæprəˈbeɪʃ(ə)n/ *n* disapproval – fml

disapproval /ˌdisəˈproohv(ə)l‖ˌdɪsəˈpruːv(ə)l/ *n* unfavourable opinion; censure

disapprove /ˌdisəˈproohv‖ˌdɪsəˈpruːv/ *vt* to refuse approval to; reject ~*vi* to have or express an unfavourable opinion *of* – **disapprover** *n*, **disapprovingly** *adv*

disarm /disˈahm‖dɪsˈɑːm/ *vt* **1a** to deprive of a weapon or weapons **b** to deprive of a means of attack or defence **c** to make (e g a bomb) harmless, esp by removing a fuse or warhead **2** to dispel the hostility or suspicion of ~ *vi* **1** to lay aside arms **2** to reduce or abolish weapons and armed forces – **disarmament** *n*

disarrange /ˌdisəˈraynj‖ˌdɪsəˈreɪndʒ/ *vt* to disturb the arrangement or order of – **disarrangement** *n*

[1]**disarray** /ˌdisəˈray‖ˌdɪsəˈreɪ/ *n* a lack of order or sequence; disorder

[2]**disarray** *vt* to throw or place into disorder

disassociate /ˌdisəˈsohs(h)iayt‖ˌdɪsəˈsəʊsɪeɪt,-ʃɪeɪt/ *vt* to dissociate – **disassociation** *n*

disaster /diˈzahstə‖dɪˈzɑːstə/ *n* **1** a sudden event bringing great damage, loss, or destruction; *broadly* an unfortunate occurrence **2** a failure <*was a complete ~ as a teacher*> – infml [Middle French *desastre*, fr Italian *disastro*, lit., unfavourable aspect of a star, fr Latin *dis-* apart + *astrum* star] – **disastrous** *adj*, **disastrously** *adv*

disavow /ˌdisəˈvow‖ˌdɪsəˈvaʊ/ *vt* to deny knowledge of or responsibility for; repudiate – fml – **disavowal** *n*

disband /disˈband‖dɪsˈbænd/ *vb* to (cause to) break up and separate; disperse – **disbandment** *n*

disbar /disˈbah‖dɪsˈbɑː/ *vt* to deprive (a barrister) of the right to practise; expel from the bar – **disbarment** *n*

disbelief /ˌdisbiˈleef‖ˌdɪsbɪˈliːf/ *n* mental rejection of sthg as untrue

disbelieve /ˌdisbiˈleev‖ˌdɪsbɪˈliːv/ *vb* to reject or withhold belief (in) – **disbeliever** *n*

disburden /disˈbuhd(ə)n‖dɪsˈbɜːd(ə)n/ *vt* to unburden – **disburdenment** *n*

disburse /disˈbuhs‖dɪsˈbɜːs/ *vt* **1** to pay out, esp from a fund **2** to make a payment in settlement of; defray – fml – **disbursement** *n*, **disburser** *n*

disc, *NAm chiefly* **disk** /disk‖dɪsk/ *n* **1a** a thin flat circular object **b** an apparently flat figure or surface (e g of a planet) <*the solar ~*> **2** any of various round flat anatomical structures; *esp* any of the cartilaginous discs between the spinal vertebrae **3** a gramophone record **4** DISK 1a **5** any of the sharp-edged concave circular cutting blades of a harrow

[1]**discard** /disˈkahd‖dɪsˈkɑːd/ *vt* **1a** to throw out (a playing card) from one's hand **b** to play (any

card from a suit different from the one led except a trump) when unable to follow suit **2** to get rid of as useless or superfluous ~*vi* to discard a playing card

[2]**discard** *n* **1** the act of discarding in a card game **2** sby or sthg discarded; *esp* a discarded card

ˈdisc ˌbrake *n* a brake that operates by the friction of a calliper pressing against the sides of a rotating disc

discern /diˈsuhn‖dɪˈsɜːn/ *vt* **1** to detect with one of the senses, esp vision **2** to perceive or recognize mentally – **discerner** *n*, **discernible** *also* **discernable** *adj*, **discernibly** *adv*

discerning /diˈsuhning‖dɪˈsɜːnɪŋ/ *adj* showing insight and understanding; discriminating – **discerningly** *adv*

diˈscernment /-mənt‖-mənt/ *n* skill in discerning; keen insight

[1]**discharge** /disˈchahj‖dɪsˈtʃɑːdʒ/ *vt* **1a** to unload **b** to release from an obligation **2a** to shoot < ~ *a gun*> **b** to release from custody or care **c** to send or pour out; emit **3a** to dismiss from employment or service **b** to fulfil (e g a debt or obligation) by performing an appropriate action **c** to annul legally **4** to remove an electric charge from or reduce the electric charge of ~ *vi* **1** to throw off or deliver a load, charge, or burden **2a** *of a gun* to be fired **b** to pour out (fluid) contents **3** to lose or reduce an electric charge

[2]**discharge** /ˈdischahj, -ˈ-‖ˈdɪstʃɑːdʒ, -ˈ-/ *n* **1a** the relieving of an obligation, accusation, or penalty **b** a certificate of release or payment **2** the act of discharging or unloading **3a** legal release from confinement **b** an acquittal **4** the act or an instance of firing a missile or missiles **5a** a flowing or pouring out **b** sthg that is discharged or emitted <*a purulent* ~> **6** release or dismissal, esp from an office or employment **7a** a usu brief flow of an electric charge through a gas, usu with associated light emission **b** the conversion of the chemical energy of a battery into electrical energy

disciple /diˈsiepl‖dɪˈsaɪpl/ *n* **1** one who accepts and assists in spreading another's doctrines; a follower **2** any of the followers of Christ during his life on earth; *esp* any of Christ's 12 appointed followers – **discipleship** *n*, **discipular** *adj*

disciplinarian /ˌdisipliˈneəri·ən‖ˌdɪsɪplɪˈneərɪən/ *n* one who enforces or advocates (strict) discipline or order – **disciplinarian** *adj*

disciplinary /ˌdisiˈplinəri‖ˌdɪsɪˈplɪnərɪ/ *adj* **1** of or involving discipline; corrective < ~ *action*> **2** of a particular field of study

[1]**discipline** /ˈdisiplin‖ˈdɪsɪplɪn/ *n* **1** a field of study **2** training of the mind and character designed to produce obedience and self-control **3** punishment, chastisement **4a** order obtained by enforcing obedience (e g in a school or army) **b** self-control **5** a system of rules governing conduct [Latin *disciplina* teaching, learning, fr *discipulus* pupil] – **disciplinal** *adj*

[2]**discipline** *vt* **1** to punish or penalize for the sake of discipline **2** to train by instruction and exercise, esp in obedience and self-control **3** to bring (a group) under control – **disciplinable** *adj*, **discipliner** *n*

ˈdisc ˌjockey *n* one who introduces records of popular usu contemporary music (e g on a radio programme or at a discotheque)

disclaim /disˈklaym‖dɪsˈkleɪm/ *vi* to make a disclaimer ~ *vt* **1** to renounce a legal claim to **2** to deny, disavow

disclaimer /disˈklaymə‖dɪsˈkleɪmə/ *n* **1** a denial of legal responsibility **2** a denial, repudiation

disclose /disˈklohz‖dɪsˈkləʊz/ *vt* **1** to expose to view **2** to make known; reveal to public knowledge – **discloser** *n*

disclosure /disˈklohzhə‖dɪsˈkləʊʒə/ *n* **1** (an instance of) disclosing; an exposure **2** sthg disclosed; a revelation

disco /ˈdiskoh‖ˈdɪskəʊ/ *n, pl* **discos** **1** a collection of popular records together with the equipment for playing them **2** a discotheque – infml

discolour /disˈkulə‖dɪsˈkʌlə/ *vb* to (cause to) change colour for the worse; stain – **discoloration** *n*

discomfit /disˈkumfit‖dɪsˈkʌmfɪt/ *vt* **1** to frustrate the plans of; thwart **2** to cause perplexity and embarrassment to; disconcert – **discomfiture** *n*

[1]**discomfort** /disˈkumfət‖dɪsˈkʌmfət/ *vt* to make uncomfortable or uneasy

[2]**discomfort** *n* (sthg causing) mental or physical unease

discompose /ˌdiskəmˈpohz‖ˌdɪskəmˈpəʊz/ *vt* to destroy the composure of – fml – **discomposure** *n*

disconcert /ˌdiskənˈsuht‖ˌdɪskənˈsɜːt/ *vt* to disturb the composure of; fluster – **disconcerting** *adj*, **disconcertingly** *adv*

disconnect /ˌdiskəˈnekt‖ˌdɪskəˈnekt/ *vt* to sever the connection of or between; *specif* CUT OFF 7b – **disconnection** *n*

ˌdisconˈnected *adj* disjointed, incoherent – **disconnectedly** *adv*, **disconnectedness** *n*

disconsolate /disˈkonsələt‖dɪsˈkɒnsələt/ *adj* dejected, downcast – **disconsolately** *adv*, **disconsolateness** *n*, **disconsolation** *n*

[1]**discontent** /ˌdiskənˈtent‖ˌdɪskənˈtent/ *n* **1** lack of contentment; dissatisfaction **2** one who is discontented; a malcontent

[2]**discontent** *vt* to make discontented

ˌdisconˈtented *also* **discontent** *adj* restlessly unhappy; dissatisfied

discontinue /ˌdiskənˈtinyooh‖ˌdɪskənˈtɪnjuː/ *vt* to cease, stop; *specif* to cease production of <*this line has been* ~d> ~*vi* to come to an end – **discontinuance** *n*

discontinuous /ˌdiskənˈtinyoo·əs‖ˌdɪskənˈtɪnjʊəs/ *adj* lacking sequence, coherence, or continuity – **discontinuously** *adv*, **discontinuity** *n*

discord /ˈdiskawd‖ˈdɪskɔːd/ *n* **1** lack of agreement or harmony; conflict **2a** dissonance **b** a harsh unpleasant combination of sounds

discordant /disˈkawd(ə)nt‖dɪsˈkɔːd(ə)nt/ *adj* **1** disagreeing; AT VARIANCE **2** relating to a discord; dissonant < ~ *tones*> – **discordance, discordancy** *n*, **discordantly** *adv*

discotheque /ˈdiskəˌtek‖ˈdɪskəˌtek/ *n* a nightclub for dancing to usu recorded music

[1]**discount** /ˈdiskownt‖ˈdɪskaʊnt/ *n* a reduction made from the gross amount or value of sthg:

e g **a** a reduction in the price of goods, accorded esp to special or trade customers **b** a reduction in the amount due on a bill of exchange, debt, etc when paid promptly or before the specified date

[2]**discount** /'diskownt‖'dıskaʊnt; *sense 2* dis'kownt‖dıs'kaʊnt/ *vt* **1a** to make a deduction from, usu for cash or prompt payment **b** to sell or offer for sale at a discount **c** to buy or sell (a bill of exchange) before maturity at below the stated price **2a** to leave out of account as unimportant, unreliable, or irrelevant; disregard **b** to underestimate the importance of; minimize **3** to take (e g a future event) into account in present arrangements or calculations – **discountable** *adj*

discountenance /dis'kownt(ə)nəns‖dıs'kaʊnt(ə)nəns/ *vt* **1** to abash, disconcert **2** to discourage by showing disapproval – fml

discourage /dis'kurij‖dıs'kʌrıdʒ/ *vt* **1** to deprive of confidence; dishearten **2a** to hinder, deter *from* **b** to attempt to prevent, esp by showing disapproval – **discouragement** *n*

[1]**discourse** /'diskaws‖'dıskɔːs/ *n* **1** a talk, conversation **2** (orderly expression of ideas in) a formal speech or piece of writing

[2]**discourse** /'--, -'-/ *vi* **1** to express one's ideas in speech or writing **2** to talk, converse *USE* usu + *on* or *upon* – **discourser** *n*

discourteous /dis'kuhtyəs, -'kaw-, -ti·əs‖dıs'kɜːtjəs, -'kɔː-, -tıəs/ *adj* rude, impolite – **discourteously** *adv*, **discourteousness** *n*

discourtesy /dis'kuhtəsi, -'kaw-‖dıs'kɜːtəsı, -'kɔː-/ *n* (an instance of) rudeness; (an) incivility

discover /di'skuvə‖dı'skʌvə/ *vt* **1** to obtain sight or knowledge of for the first time **2** to make known or visible – fml – **discoverable** *adj*, **discoverer** *n*

discovery /di'skuv(ə)ri‖dı'skʌv(ə)rı/ *n* **1a** the act or an instance of discovering or revealing **b** an obligatory disclosure of documents or facts by a party to a legal action **2** sby or sthg discovered

[1]**discredit** /dis'kredit‖dıs'kredıt/ *vt* **1** to refuse to accept as true or accurate **2** to cast doubt on the accuracy, authority, or reputation of

[2]**discredit** *n* **1** (sby or sthg causing) loss of credit or reputation **2** loss of belief or confidence; doubt

discreditable /dis'kreditəbl‖dıs'kredıtəbl/ *adj* bringing discredit or disgrace – **discreditably** *adv*

discreet /di'skreet‖dı'skriːt/ *adj* **1** judicious in speech or conduct; *esp* capable of maintaining a prudent silence **2** unpretentious, modest <*the house was furnished with ~ elegance*> – **discreetly** *adv*, **discreetness** *n*

discrepant /di'skrep(ə)nt‖dı'skrep(ə)nt/ *adj* disagreeing; AT VARIANCE [Latin *discrepare* to sound discordantly, fr *dis-* apart + *crepare* to rattle, creak] – **discrepancy** *n*, **discrepantly** *adv*

discrete /di'skreet‖dı'skriːt/ *adj* **1** individually distinct **2** consisting of distinct or unconnected elements – **discretely** *adv*, **discreteness** *n*

discretion /di'skresh(ə)n‖dı'skreʃ(ə)n/ *n* **1** the quality of being discreet **2** the ability to make responsible decisions **3a** individual choice or judgment <*left the decision to his ~*> **b** power of free decision within legal bounds <*reached the age of ~*>

discretionary /di'skresh(ə)nri‖dı'skreʃ(ə)nrı/ *adj* **1** left to or exercised at one's own discretion <*~ powers*> **2** subject to the discretion of another

discriminate /di'skrimi,nayt‖dı'skrımı,neıt/ *vt* to distinguish (e g objects or ideas) by noting differences ~ *vi* **1a** to make a distinction <*~ between fact and fancy*> **b** to show good judgment or discernment **2** to treat sby differently and esp unfavourably on the grounds of race, sex, religion, etc – **discriminator** *n*

discriminating /di'skrimi,nayting‖dı'skrımı,neıtıŋ/ *adj* **1** discerning, judicious **2** discriminatory – **discriminatingly** *adv*

discrimination /di,skrimi'naysh(ə)n‖dı,skrımı'neıʃ(ə)n/ *n* **1** the act or process of responding to different sensory stimuli in different ways **2** discernment and good judgment, esp in matters of taste **3** prejudicial treatment (e g on the grounds of race or sex) – **discriminational** *adj*

discriminatory /di'skriminət(ə)ri‖dı'skrımınət(ə)rı/ *adj* showing esp unfavourable discrimination – **discriminatorily** *adv*

discursive /di'skuhsiv, -ziv‖dı'skɜːsıv, -zıv/ *adj* **1** passing usu unmethodically from one topic to another; digressive **2** proceeding by logical argument or reason – **discursively** *adv*, **discursiveness** *n*

discus /'diskəs‖'dıskəs/ *n, pl* **discuses** (the athletic field event involving the throwing of) a solid disc, between 180mm and 219mm (about 7 to 9in) in diameter, that is thicker in the centre than at the edge

discuss /di'skus‖dı'skʌs/ *vt* to consider or examine (a topic) in speech or writing – **discussable, discussible** *adj*

discussion /di'skush(ə)n‖dı'skʌʃ(ə)n/ *n* (an instance of) consideration of a question in open debate or conversation

[1]**disdain** /dis'dayn‖dıs'deın/ *n* contempt for sthg regarded as worthless or insignificant; scorn

[2]**disdain** *vt* **1** to regard with disdain **2** to refuse or abstain from because of disdain <*she ~ed to answer him*>

dis'dainful /-f(ə)l‖-f(ə)l/ *adj* feeling or showing disdain – **disdainfully** *adv*, **disdainfulness** *n*

disease /di'zeez‖dı'ziːz/ *n* **1** a condition of (a part of) a living animal or plant body that impairs the performance of a vital function; (a) sickness, malady **2** a harmful or corrupt development, situation, condition, etc <*the ~ of prejudice*> [Middle French *desaise* uneasiness, sickness, fr *des-* not- + *aise* ease] – **diseased** *adj*

disembark /,disim'bahk‖,dısım'bɑːk/ *vb* to (cause to) alight from a ship, plane, etc – **disembarkation** *n*

disembody /,disim'bodi‖,dısım'bɒdı/ *vt* to divest of a body or material existence

disembowel /,disim'bowəl‖,dısım'baʊəl/ *vt* to remove the bowels or entrails of; eviscerate – **disembowelment** *n*

disembroil /,disim'broyl‖,dısım'brɔıl/ *vt* to free from a confused or entangled state or situation

disenchant /,disin'chahnt‖,dısın'tʃɑːnt/ *vt* to rid of an illusion – **disenchanter** *n*, **disenchanting** *adj*, **disenchantingly** *adv*, **disenchantment** *n*

disencumber /,disin'kumbə‖,dısın'kʌmbə/

vt to free from an encumbrance

disendow /ˌdisin'dow‖ˌdɪsɪn'daʊ/ *vt* to strip of an endowment – **disendowment** *n*

disengage /ˌdising'gayj‖ˌdɪsɪŋ'geɪdʒ/ *vt* **1** to release or detach from sthg that engages or entangles **2** to remove (e g troops) from combat areas ~ *vi* **1** to detach or release oneself; *specif, esp of troops* to withdraw **2** to move one's fencing sword to the other side of an opponent's sword in order to attack – **disengagement** *n*

disentangle /ˌdisin'tang·gl‖ˌdɪsɪn'tæŋgl/ *vb* to (cause to) become free from entanglements: unravel – **disentanglement** *n*

disequilibrium /ˌdiseekwi'libri·əm, -ekwi-‖ˌdɪsiːkwɪ'lɪbrɪəm, -ekwɪ-/ *n* loss or lack of equilibrium

disestablish /ˌdisi'stablish‖ˌdɪsɪ'stæblɪʃ/ *vt* to deprive (esp a national church) of established status – **disestablishment** *n*

[1]**disfavour** /dis'fayvə‖dɪs'feɪvə/ *n* **1** disapproval, dislike **2** the state of being disapproved of <*fell into* ~>

[2]**disfavour** *vt* to regard or treat with disfavour

disfigure /dis'figə‖dɪs'fɪgə/ *vt* to spoil the appearance or quality of; mar – **disfigurement** *n*

disfranchise /dis'frahnchiez, -'fran-‖dɪs'frɑːntʃaɪz, -'fræn-/ *vt* to disenfranchise – **disfranchisement**

disfrock /dis'frok‖dɪs'frɒk/ *vt* to unfrock

disgorge /dis'gawj‖dɪs'gɔːdʒ/ *vt* **1a** to discharge with force; *specif* to vomit **b** to give up on request or under pressure **2** to discharge the contents of (e g one's stomach) ~*vi* to discharge contents <*where the river* ~s *into the sea*>

[1]**disgrace** /dis'grays‖dɪs'greɪs/ *vt* **1** to bring reproach or shame to **2** to cause to lose favour or standing

[2]**disgrace** *n* **1a** loss of favour, honour, or respect; shame **b** the state of being out of favour <*she's in* ~> **2** sby or sthg shameful <*his manners are a* ~>

dis'graceful /-f(ə)l‖-f(ə)l/ *adj* shameful, shocking – **disgracefully** *adv*, **disgracefulness** *n*

disgruntled /dis'gruntld‖dɪs'grʌntld/ *adj* aggrieved and dissatisfied

[1]**disguise** /dis'giez‖dɪs'gaɪz/ *vt* **1** to change the appearance or nature of in order to conceal identity <~d *himself as a tramp*> **2** to hide the true state or character of – **disguisedly** *adv*, **disguisement** *n*

[2]**disguise** *n* **1** (the use of) sthg (e g clothing) to conceal one's identity **2** an outward appearance that misrepresents the true nature of sthg <*a blessing in* ~>

[1]**disgust** /dis'gust‖dɪs'gʌst/ *n* strong aversion aroused by sby or sthg physically or morally distasteful

[2]**disgust** *vt* to arouse repugnance or aversion in – **disgusted** *adj*, **disgustedly** *adv*

[1]**dish** /dish‖dɪʃ/ *n* **1a** a shallow open often circular or oval vessel used esp for holding or serving food; *broadly* any vessel from which food is eaten or served **b** a dishful **c** *pl the* utensils and tableware used in preparing, serving, and eating a meal <*wash the* ~es> **2** a type of food prepared in a particular way <*a delicious meat* ~> **3** sthg resembling a dish in shape: e g **3a** a directional aerial, esp for receiving radio or television transmissions or microwaves, having a concave usu parabolic reflector **b** a hollow or depression **4** an attractive person – infml

[2]**dish** *vt* **1** to make concave like a dish **2** *chiefly Br* to ruin or spoil (e g a person or his/her hopes) – infml

dishabille /ˌdisə'beel‖ˌdɪsə'biːl/ *n* deshabille

disharmony /dis'hahməni‖dɪs'hɑːmənɪ/ *n* lack of harmony; discord – **disharmonious** *adj*

dishcloth /-ˌkloth‖-ˌklɒθ/ *n* a cloth for washing or drying dishes

dishearten /dis'haht(ə)n‖dɪs'hɑːt(ə)n/ *vt* to cause to lose enthusiasm or morale; discourage – **disheartening** *adj*, **dishearteningly** *adv*, **disheartenment** *n*

dishevel /di'shevl‖dɪ'ʃevl/ *vt* **-ll-** (*NAm* **-l-**, **-ll-**) to make untidy or disordered

di'shevelled, *NAm chiefly* **disheveled** *adj, esp of a person's hair or appearance* unkempt, untidy

'**dishful** /-f(ə)l‖-f(ə)l/ *n* the amount a dish contains or will hold

dishonest /dis'onist‖dɪs'ɒnɪst/ *adj* not honest, truthful, or sincere – **dishonestly** *adv*

dishonesty /dis'onisti‖dɪs'ɒnɪstɪ/ *n* (an instance of) lack of honesty or integrity

[1]**dishonour** /dis'onə‖dɪs'ɒnə/ *n* **1** (sby or sthg causing) loss of honour or reputation **2** a state of shame or disgrace

[2]**dishonour** *vt* **1** to treat in a degrading or disrespectful manner **2** to bring shame on **3** to refuse to accept or pay (e g a cheque)

dishonourable /dis'on(ə)rəbl‖dɪs'ɒn(ə)rəbl/ *adj* base, shameful – **dishonourably** *adv*

dish out *vt* to give or distribute freely – infml

dish up *vt* **1** to put (a meal, food, etc) onto dishes; serve **2** to produce or present (e g facts) <*has been* dishing up *the same lessons for years*> – infml ~*vi* to put food onto dishes ready to be eaten <*I'm* dishing up *now*>

'**dish,washer** /-ˌwoshə‖-ˌwɒʃə/ *n* a person or electrical machine that washes dishes

'**dish,water** /-ˌwawtə‖-ˌwɔːtə/ *n* water in which dishes have been washed

dishy /'dishi‖'dɪʃɪ/ *adj, chiefly Br, of a person* attractive – infml

[1]**disillusion** /ˌdisi'loohzh(ə)n, -'lyooh-‖ˌdɪsɪ'luːʒ(ə)n, -'ljuː-/ *n* the state of being disillusioned

[2]**disillusion** *vt* to reveal the usu unpleasant truth (e g about sby or sthg admired) to; disenchant – **disillusionment** *n*

ˌ**disil'lusioned** *adj* bitter or depressed as a result of having been disillusioned

disincentive /ˌdisin'sentiv‖ˌdɪsɪn'sentɪv/ *n* sthg that discourages action or effort; a deterrent

disinclination /ˌdisingkli'naysh(ə)n‖ˌdɪsɪŋklɪ'neɪʃ(ə)n/ *n* (an) unwillingness to do sthg; mild dislike

disinclined /ˌdisin'kliend‖ˌdɪsɪn'klaɪnd/ *adj* unwilling

disinfect /ˌdisin'fekt‖ˌdɪsɪn'fekt/ *vt* to cleanse of infection, esp by destroying harmful microorganisms – **disinfection** *n*

disinfectant /ˌdisin'fekt(ə)nt‖ˌdɪsɪn'fekt(ə)nt/ *n* a chemical that destroys harmful microorganisms

disinfest /ˌdisin'fest‖ˌdɪsɪn'fest/ *vt* to rid of

insects, rodents, or other pests – **disinfestation** *n*

disingenuous /ˌdisinˈjenyoo·əs‖ˌdɪsɪnˈdʒenjʊəs/ *adj* insincere; *also* falsely frank or naive in manner – **disingenuously** *adv*, **disingenuousness** *n*

disinherit /ˌdisinˈherit‖ˌdɪsɪnˈherɪt/ *vt* to deprive (an heir) of the right to inherit; *broadly* to deprive of a special right or privilege – **disinheritance** *n*

disintegrate /disˈintigrayt‖dɪsˈɪntɪgreɪt/ *vt* **1** to break up into fragments or constituent elements **2** to destroy the unity or cohesion of ~ *vi* **1** to break into fragments or constituent elements **2** to lose unity or cohesion **3** *esp of a nucleus* to undergo a change in composition (e g by emitting radioactive particles or dividing into smaller units) – **disintegrator** *n*, **disintegrative** *adj*, **disintegration** *n*

disinter /ˌdisinˈtuh‖ˌdɪsɪnˈtɜː/ *vt* **1** to remove from a grave or tomb **2** to bring to light; unearth – **disinterment** *n*

disˈinterested *adj* **1** uninterested – disapproved of by some speakers **2** free from selfish motive or interest; impartial – **disinterestedly** *adv*, **disinterestedness** *n*

disjoint /disˈjoynt‖dɪsˈdʒɔɪnt/ *vt* **1** to disturb the orderly arrangement of **2** to take apart at the joints

disˈjointed *adj* lacking orderly sequence; incoherent – **disjointedly** *adv*, **disjointedness** *n*

disk /disk‖dɪsk/ *n* **1a** *Br also* **disc** a round flat plate coated with a magnetic substance on which data for a computer is stored **b disk, disk pack** a computer storage device consisting of a stack of disks rotating at high speed, each disk having its own head to read and write data **2** *chiefly NAm* a disc

disk drive *n* a device for a computer which transfers data to and from magnetic disks

[1]**dislike** /disˈliek‖dɪsˈlaɪk/ *vt* to regard with dislike

[2]**dislike** *n* (an object of) a feeling of aversion or disapproval

dislocate /ˈdisləˌkayt‖ˈdɪsləˌkeɪt/ *vt* **1** to put out of place; *esp* to displace (e g a bone or joint) from normal connection **2** to put (plans, machinery, etc) out of order; disrupt

dislocation /ˌdisləˈkaysh(ə)n‖ˌdɪsləˈkeɪʃ(ə)n/ *n* **1** displacement of 1 or more bones at a joint **2** disruption of an established order or course

dislodge /disˈloj‖dɪsˈlɒdʒ/ *vt* to force out of or remove from a fixed or entrenched position

disloyal /disˈloyəl‖dɪsˈlɔɪəl/ *adj* untrue to obligations or ties; unfaithful – **disloyally** *adv*, **disloyalty** *n*

dismal /ˈdizm(ə)l‖ˈdɪzm(ə)l/ *adj* causing or expressing gloom or sadness [Middle English *dismal* days marked as unlucky in medieval calendars, fr Medieval Latin *dies mali*, lit., evil days] – **dismally** *adv*, **dismalness** *n*

dismantle /disˈmantl‖dɪsˈmæntl/ *vt* **1** to strip of furniture, equipment, etc **2** to take to pieces – **dismantlement** *n*

dismast /disˈmahst‖dɪsˈmɑːst/ *vt* to remove or break off the mast of (a ship)

[1]**dismay** /diˈsmay, diz-‖dɪˈsmeɪ, dɪz-/ *vt* to fill with dismay – **dismayingly** *adv*

[2]**dismay** *n* sudden consternation or apprehension

dismember /disˈmembə‖dɪsˈmembə/ *vt* **1** to cut or tear off the limbs or members of **2** to divide up (e g a territory) into parts – **dismemberment** *n*

dismiss /disˈmis‖dɪsˈmɪs/ *vt* **1** to allow to leave; send away **2** to remove or send away from employment or service **3a** to put out of one's mind; reject as unworthy of serious consideration **b** to put out of judicial consideration; refuse a further hearing to (e g a court case) **4** to bowl out (a batsman or side) in cricket – **dismissal** *n*, **dismissible** *adj*

dismount /disˈmownt‖dɪsˈmaʊnt/ *vi* to alight from a horse, bicycle, etc ~ *vt* **1** to throw down or remove from horseback **2** to remove from a mounting

disobedient /ˌdisəˈbeedi·ənt‖ˌdɪsəˈbiːdɪənt/ *adj* refusing or failing to obey – **disobedience** *n*, **disobediently** *adv*

disobey /ˌdisəˈbay‖ˌdɪsəˈbeɪ/ *vb* to fail to obey

disoblige /ˌdisəˈbliej‖ˌdɪsəˈblaɪdʒ/ *vt* **1** to go counter to the wishes of **2** to inconvenience

[1]**disorder** /disˈawdə‖dɪsˈɔːdə/ *vt* **1** to throw into confusion or disorder **2** to disturb the good health of; upset

[2]**disorder** *n* **1** lack of order; confusion **2** breach of the peace or public order **3** an abnormal physical or mental condition; an ailment

disˈorderly /-li‖-lɪ/ *adj* **1a** untidy, disarranged **b** unruly, violent **2** offensive to public order <*charged with being drunk and ~*> – **disorderliness** *n*

disorderly house *n* a brothel

disorgan·ize, -ise /disˈawgəniez‖dɪsˈɔːgənaɪz/ *vt* to throw into disorder or confusion – **disorganization** *n*

disorientate /disˈawri·ənˌtayt‖dɪsˈɔːrɪənˌteɪt/ *vt* **1** to deprive of the normal sense of position, relationship, or identity **2** to confuse – **disorientation** *n*

disown /disˈohn‖dɪsˈəʊn/ *vt* **1** to refuse to acknowledge as one's own **2** to repudiate any connection with

disparage /diˈsparij‖dɪˈspærɪdʒ/ *vt* to speak slightingly of; belittle – **disparagement** *n*, **disparaging** *adj*, **disparagingly** *adv*

disparate /ˈdispərət‖ˈdɪspərət/ *adj* markedly distinct in quality or character – **disparately** *adv*, **disparateness** *n*

disparity /diˈsparəti‖dɪˈspærətɪ/ *n* (a) difference or inequality

dispassionate /disˈpash(ə)nət‖dɪsˈpæʃ(ə)nət/ *adj* not influenced by strong feeling; *esp* calm, impartial – **dispassionately** *adv*, **dispassionateness** *n*

[1]**dispatch** /diˈspach‖dɪˈspætʃ/ *vt* **1** to send off or away promptly, esp to a particular place or to carry out a particular, usu official, task **2a** to carry out or complete (e g a task) rapidly or efficiently **b** to get through; consume quickly – infml <*soon* ~ed *that chocolate cake*> **3** to kill, esp with quick efficiency – euph – **dispatcher** *n*

[2]**dispatch** *n* **1** a sending off (e g of a communication or messenger) **2a** a message; *esp* an important official diplomatic or military message **b** a news item sent in by a correspondent to a newspaper **3** promptness and efficiency **4** an act

of killing; *specif* a murder – euph

dispel /di'spel‖dɪ'spel/ *vt* **-ll-** to drive away; disperse

dispensable /di'spensəbl‖dɪ'spensəbl/ *adj* that can be dispensed with; inessential – **dispensability** *n*

dispensary /di'spens(ə)ri‖dɪ'spens(ə)rɪ/ *n* a part of a hospital or chemist's shop where drugs, medical supplies, etc are dispensed

dispensation /ˌdispen'saysh(ə)n‖ˌdɪspen'seɪʃ(ə)n/ *n* **1a** an esp divine ordering of human affairs **b** a particular arrangement or provision made by God, providence, or nature **c** a usu specified religious system, esp considered as controlling human affairs during a particular period **2a** an exemption from a law, vow, etc; *specif* permission to disregard or break a rule of Roman Catholic church law **b** a formal authorization – **dispensational** *adj*

dispense /di'spens‖dɪ'spens/ *vt* **1a** to deal out, distribute **b** to administer (e g law or justice) **2** to give a dispensation to; exempt *from* **3** to prepare and give out (drugs, medicine, etc on prescription) – **dispense with 1** DISCARD 2 **2** to do without

dispenser /di'spensə‖dɪ'spensə/ *n* **1** a container or machine that dispenses items (e g of food) or usu fixed quantities (e g of drink) **2** a person who dispenses medicines

disperse /di'spuhs‖dɪ'spɜːs/ *vt* **1a** to cause to break up or scatter <*they* ~d *the meeting*> **b** to spread over a wide area **c** to cause to evaporate or vanish **2a** to subject (e g light) to dispersion **b** to distribute (e g fine particles) more or less evenly throughout a liquid ~ *vi* **1** to break up in random fashion; scatter **2** to become dispersed; dissipate – **dispersal** *n*, **dispersedly** *adv*, **disperser** *n*, **dispersible** *adj*, **dispersive** *adj*, **dispersively** *adv*, **dispersiveness** *n*

dispersion /di'spuhsh(ə)n‖dɪ'spɜːʃ(ə)n/ *n* **1** *cap the* Diaspora **2** the extent to which the values of a frequency distribution are scattered around an average **3** the separation of light into colours by refraction or diffraction with formation of a spectrum; *also* the separation of nonhomogeneous radiation into components in accordance with some characteristic (e g energy, wavelength, or mass) **4a** a dispersed substance **b** a system consisting of a dispersed substance and the medium in which it is dispersed; COLLOID 1b

dispirit /di'spirit‖dɪ'spɪrɪt/ *vt* to dishearten, discourage – **dispirited** *adj*, **dispiritedly** *adv*, **dispiritedness** *n*

displace /dis'plays‖dɪs'pleɪs/ *vt* **1a** to remove from or force out of the usual or proper place **b** to remove from office **2** to take the place of; replace; *specif* to take the place of (e g an atom) in a chemical reaction – **displaceable** *adj*

disˌplaced 'person *n* sby who has been forced to leave his/her country because of war, revolution, etc; a refugee

dis'placement /-mənt‖-mənt/ *n* **1a** the volume or weight of a fluid (e g water) displaced by a body of equal weight floating in it **b** the difference between the initial position of a body and any later position **2** the transfer of emotions from the object that orig evoked them to a substitute (e g in dreams)

[1]**display** /di'splay‖dɪ'spleɪ/ *vt* **1** to expose to view; show **2** to exhibit, esp ostentatiously ~*vi* to make a breeding display

[2]**display** *n* **1a(1)** a presentation or exhibition of sthg in open view <*a fireworks* ~> **a(2)** an esp ostentatious show or demonstration **b** an arrangement of type or printing designed to catch the eye (e g in headlines and title pages) **c** an eye-catching arrangement exhibiting sthg (e g goods for sale) **d** a device (e g a cathode-ray tube screen) that presents information in visual form <*a visual* ~ *unit*> **2** a pattern of behaviour exhibited esp by male birds in the breeding season

displease /dis'pleez‖dɪs'pliːz/ *vb* to cause annoyance or displeasure (to)

displeasure /dis'plezhə‖dɪs'pleʒə/ *n* disapproval, annoyance

disport /di'spawt‖dɪ'spɔːt/ *vt* to divert or amuse (oneself) actively ~*vi* to frolic, gambol

[1]**disposable** /di'spohzəbl‖dɪ'spəʊzəbl/ *adj* **1** available for use; *specif* remaining after deduction of taxes <~ *income*> **2** designed to be used once and then thrown away – **disposability** *n*

[2]**disposable** *n* a disposable article

disposal /di'spohzl‖dɪ'spəʊzl/ *n* **1a** orderly arrangement or distribution **b** management, administration **c** bestowal **d** the act or action of getting rid of sthg; *specif* the destruction or conversion of waste matter **2** the power or right to use freely <*the car was at my* ~>

dispose /di'spohz‖dɪ'spəʊz/ *vt* **1** to incline *to* – <~d *to ill-health*> **2** to put in place; arrange **3** to cause to have a specified attitude *towards* <*unfavourably* ~d *towards her in-laws*> ~*vi* to settle a matter finally – **dispose of 1** to get rid of (e g by finishing, selling, eating, or killing) **2** to deal with conclusively <disposed of *the matter efficiently*>

disposition /ˌdispə'zish(ə)n‖ˌdɪspə'zɪʃ(ə)n/ *n* **1a** final arrangement; settlement **b** transfer of property, esp by will or deed **c** orderly arrangement **2a** natural temperament **b** a tendency, inclination

dispossess /ˌdispə'zes‖ˌdɪspə'zes/ *vt* to deprive of possession or occupancy – **dispossessor** *n*, **dispossession** *n*

disproof /dis'proohf‖dɪs'pruːf/ *n* **1** the act or action of disproving **2** evidence that disproves

disproportion /ˌdisprə'pawsh(ə)n‖ˌdɪsprə'pɔːʃ(ə)n/ *n* (a) lack of proportion, symmetry, or proper relation – **disproportional** *adj*

disproportionate /ˌdisprə'pawsh(ə)nət‖ˌdɪsprə'pɔːʃ(ə)nət/ *adj* out of proportion – **disproportionately** *adv*

disprove /dis'proohv‖dɪs'pruːv/ *vt* to prove to be false; refute – **disprovable** *adj*

disputant /di'spyooht(ə)nt, 'dispyoot(ə)nt‖dɪ'spjuːt(ə)nt, 'dɪspjʊt(ə)nt/ *n* one engaged in a dispute

disputation /ˌdispyooh'taysh(ə)n‖ˌdɪspjuː'teɪʃ(ə)n/ *n* **1** a debate, argument **2** the oral defence of a thesis by formal logic

disputatious /ˌdispyoo'tayshəs‖ˌdɪspjʊ'teɪʃəs/ *adj* inclined to dispute; argumentative – **disputatiously** *adv*, **disputatiousness** *n*

[1]**dispute** /di'spyooht‖dɪ'spjuːt/ *vi* to argue, esp angrily and persistently – often + *about* ~ *vt* **1a** to make the subject of disputation; discuss angrily **b** to call into question **2a** to struggle against; resist **b** to struggle over; contest – **disputable** *adj*, **disputably** *adv*, **disputer** *n*

[2]**dispute** *n* **1** controversy, debate <*his honesty is beyond* ~> **2** a quarrel, disagreement

disqualification /dis,kwolifi'kaysh(ə)n, ,---'--‖dɪs,kwɒlɪfɪ'keɪʃ(ə)n, ,---'--/ *n* **1** disqualifying or being disqualified **2** sthg that disqualifies

disqualify /dis'kwolifie‖dɪs'kwɒlɪfaɪ/ *vt* **1** to make or declare unfit or unsuitable to do sthg **2** to declare ineligible (e g for a prize) because of violation of the rules

disquiet /dis'kwie·ət‖dɪs'kwaɪət/ *vt or n* (to cause) anxiety or worry – **disquieting** *adj*, **disquietingly** *adv*

disquietude /dis'kwie·ətyoohd, -choohd‖dɪs'kwaɪətjuːd, -tʃuːd/ *n* disquiet – fml

disquisition /,diskwi'zish(ə)n‖,dɪskwɪ'zɪʃ(ə)n/ *n* a long or elaborate discussion or essay on a subject

[1]**disregard** /,disri'gahd‖,dɪsrɪ'gɑːd/ *vt* **1** to pay no attention to **2** to treat as not worthy of regard or notice

[2]**disregard** *n* lack of attention or regard; neglect – **disregardful** *adj*

disrepair /,disri'peə‖,dɪsrɪ'peə/ *n* the state of being in need of repair

disreputable /dis'repyootəbl‖dɪs'repjʊtəbl/ *adj* **1** having a bad reputation; not respectable **2** dirty or untidy in appearance – **disreputableness** *n*, **disreputably** *adv*, **disreputability** *n*

disrepute /,disri'pyooht‖,dɪsrɪ'pjuːt/ *n* lack of good reputation or respectability

disrespect /,disri'spekt‖,dɪsrɪ'spekt/ *n* lack of respect or politeness – **disrespectful** *adj*, **disrespectfully** *adv*, **disrespectfulness** *n*

disrobe /dis'rohb‖dɪs'rəʊb/ *vi* to take off (esp ceremonial outer) clothing – fml or humor

disrupt /dis'rupt‖dɪs'rʌpt/ *vt* **1** to break apart forcibly; rupture **2a** to throw into disorder **b** to interrupt the continuity of – **disruption** *n*, **disruptive** *adj*, **disruptively** *adv*, **disruptiveness** *n*

dissatisfaction /di,satis'faksh(ə)n, ,---'--‖dɪ,sætɪs'fækʃ(ə)n, ,---'--/ *n* lack of satisfaction; discontent – **dissatisfactory** *adj*

dissatisfy /di'satisfie, dis'sa-‖dɪ'sætɪsfaɪ, dɪs'sæ-/ *vt* to make displeased, discontented, or disappointed

dissect /di'sekt, die-‖dɪ'sekt, daɪ-/ *vt* **1** to cut (e g an animal or plant) into pieces, esp for scientific examination **2** to analyse and interpret in detail – **dissection** *n*, **dissector** *n*

dissemble /di'sembl‖dɪ'sembl/ *vt* to disguise, conceal ~ *vi* to conceal facts, intentions, or feelings under some pretence – **dissembler** *n*

disseminate /di'seminayt‖dɪ'semɪneɪt/ *vt* to spread about freely or widely <~ *ideas*> – **disseminator**, **dissemination n**

dissension /di'sensh(ə)n‖dɪ'senʃ(ə)n/ *n* disagreement in opinion; discord

[1]**dissent** /di'sent‖dɪ'sent/ *vi* **1** to withhold assent **2** to differ in opinion; *specif* to reject the doctrines of an established church – **dissenter** *n*

[2]**dissent** *n* difference of opinion; *esp* religious or political nonconformity

Dissenter /di'sentə‖dɪ'sentə/ *n* an English Nonconformist

dissenting /di'senting‖dɪ'sentɪŋ/ *adj, often cap* Nonconformist

dissertation /,disə'taysh(ə)n‖,dɪsə'teɪʃ(ə)n/ *n* a long, detailed, usu written treatment of a subject; *specif* one submitted for a (higher) degree

disservice /di'suhvis, dis'suh-‖dɪ'sɜːvɪs, dɪs'sɜː-/ *n* an action or deed which works to sby's disadvantage

dissever /di'sevə, dis'sevə‖dɪ'sevə, dɪs'sevə/ *vb* to (cause to) separate or come apart – fml – **disseverance** *n*, **disseverment** *n*

dissident /'disid(ə)nt‖'dɪsɪd(ə)nt/ *n or adj* (sby) disagreeing strongly or rebelliously with an established opinion, group, government, etc [Latin *dissidēre* to sit apart, disagree, fr *dis-* apart + *sedēre* to sit] – **dissidence** *n*

dissimilar /di'similə, dis'si-‖dɪ'sɪmɪlə, dɪs'sɪ-/ *adj* not similar; unlike – **dissimilarly** *adv*, **dissimilarity** *n*

dissimulate /di'simyoolayt, dis'si-‖dɪ'sɪmjʊleɪt, dɪs'sɪ-/ *vb* to dissemble – **dissimulator** *n*, **dissimulation** *n*

dissipate /'disipayt‖'dɪsɪpeɪt/ *vt* **1a** to cause to disappear or scatter; dispel **b** to lose (e g heat or electricity) irrecoverably **2** to spend or use up (money, energy, etc) aimlessly or foolishly ~*vi* to separate and scatter or vanish – **dissipater** *n*, **dissipative** *adj*

dissipated *adj* given to dissipation; dissolute – **dissipatedly** *adv*, **dissipatedness** *n*

dissipation /,disi'paysh(ə)n‖,dɪsɪ'peɪʃ(ə)n/ *n* **1** dispersion, diffusion **2** wasteful expenditure **3** dissolute living; debauchery; *specif* excessive indulgence in alcohol

dissociate /di'sohs(h)i,ayt‖dɪ'səʊsɪ,eɪt, -ʃɪeɪt/ *vt* to separate from association or union with sby or sthg else; disconnect – **dissociation** *n*, **dissociative** *adj*

dissoluble /di'solyoobl‖dɪ'sɒljʊbl/ *adj* capable of being dissolved or disintegrated – **dissolubility** *n*

dissolute /'disəlooht, -lyooht‖'dɪsəluːt, -ljuːt/ *adj* loose in morals; debauched – **dissolutely** *adv*, **dissoluteness** *n*

dissolution /,disə'loohsh(ə)n, -'lyooh‖,dɪsə'luːʃ(ə)n, -'ljuː/ *n* **1** separation into component parts **2** disintegration, decay **3** the termination of an association, union, etc **4** the breaking up or dispersal of a group, assembly, etc

[1]**dissolve** /di'zolv‖dɪ'zɒlv/ *vt* **1a** to terminate officially <*the marriage was* ~d> **b** to cause to break up; dismiss <*Parliament was* ~d *before the election*> **2a** to cause to pass into solution <~ *sugar in water*> **b** to melt, liquefy **3** to fade out (one film or television scene) whilst fading in another ~ *vi* **1a** to pass into solution **b** to become fluid; melt **2** to fade away; disperse <*the vision* ~d *before his eyes*> **3** to be emotionally overcome – **dissolvable** *adj*, **dissolver** *n*

[2]**dissolve** *n* an effect used in films and television in which one scene is dissolved into the next

dissonance /'disənəns‖'dɪsənəns/ *n* **1** a combination of discordant sounds **2** lack of agreement **3** (the sound produced by playing) an unresolved musical note or chord; *specif* an interval not included in a major or minor triad or its inversions

dissonant /ˈdisənənt‖ˈdɪsənənt/ *adj* **1** marked by dissonance **2** incongruous – **dissonantly** *adv*

dissuade /diˈswayd‖dɪˈsweɪd/ *vt* to deter or discourage *from* a course of action by persuasion

distaff /ˈdistahf‖ˈdɪstɑːf/ *n* **1** a staff for holding the flax, tow, wool, etc in spinning **2** woman's work or domain

[1]**distance** /ˈdist(ə)ns‖ˈdɪst(ə)ns/ *n* **1a** (the amount of) separation in space or time between 2 points or things **b** an extent of space or an advance along a route measured linearly; *specif* a usu particular length covered in a race <*a world class runner over all* ~s> **c** a distant point or place **2a** remoteness in space **b** reserve, coldness **c** difference, disparity

[2]**distance** *vt* **1** to place or keep physically or mentally at a distance **2** to outstrip

distant /ˈdist(ə)nt‖ˈdɪst(ə)nt/ *adj* **1a** separated in space or time by a specified distance <*a few miles* ~> **b** far-off or remote in space or time <*the* ~ *hills*> **2** not closely related <*a* ~ *cousin*> **3** different in kind **4** reserved, aloof **5** coming from or going to a remote place <~ *voyages*> – **distantly** *adv*, **distantness** *n*

distaste /disˈtayst‖dɪsˈteɪst/ *n* (a) dislike, aversion

disˈtasteful /-f(ə)l‖-f(ə)l/ *adj* showing or causing distaste; offensive – **distastefully** *adv*, **distastefulness** *n*

[1]**distemper** /diˈstempə‖dɪˈstempə/ *n* any of various animal diseases; *esp* a highly infectious virus disease occurring esp in dogs

[2]**distemper** *vt* to paint in or with distemper

[3]**distemper** *n* **1** a method of painting in which pigments are mixed with white or yolk of egg or size, esp for mural decoration **2** the paint used in the distemper process; *broadly* any of numerous water-based paints for general, esp household, use

distend /diˈstend‖dɪˈstend/ *vb* to (cause to) swell from internal pressure – **distensible** *adj*, **distensibility** *n*, **distension** *n*

distil, *NAm chiefly* **distill** /diˈstil‖dɪˈstɪl/ *vb* **-ll-** *vt* **1** to cause to fall or exude in drops or a fine mist **2a** to subject to or transform by distillation **b** to obtain or separate *out* or *off* (as if) by distillation **c** to extract the essence of (e g an idea or subject) ~ *vi* **1** to undergo distillation **2** to condense or drop from a still after distillation **3** to appear slowly or in small quantities at a time

distillate /ˈdistilət, -ˌlayt‖ˈdɪstɪlət, -ˌleɪt/ *n* **1** a product of distillation **2** a concentrated form

distillation /ˌdistiˈlaysh(ə)n‖ˌdɪstɪˈleɪʃ(ə)n/ *n* a process that consists of condensing the gas or vapour obtained from heated liquids or solids and that is used esp for purification, fractionation, or the formation of new substances

distiller /diˈstilə‖dɪˈstɪlə/ *n* a person or company that makes alcohol, esp spirits, by distilling – **distillery** *n*

distinct /diˈstingkt‖dɪˈstɪŋkt/ *adj* **1** different, separate *from* **2** readily perceptible to the senses or mind; clear **3** definite, decided <*a* ~ *possibility of rain*> – **distinctly** *adv*, **distinctness** *n*

distinction /diˈstingksh(ə)n‖dɪˈstɪŋkʃ(ə)n/ *n* **1a** discrimination, differentiation **b** a difference made or marked; a contrast **2** a distinguishing quality or mark **3a** outstanding merit, quality, or worth <*a writer of some* ~> **b** special honour or recognition <*passed her exam with* ~>

distinctive /diˈstingktiv‖dɪˈstɪŋktɪv/ *adj* clearly marking sby or sthg as different from others; characteristic – **distinctively** *adv*, **distinctiveness** *n*

distinguish /diˈsting·gwish‖dɪˈstɪŋgwɪʃ/ *vt* **1a** to mark or recognize as separate or different – often + *from* **b** to separate into kinds, classes, or categories **c** to make (oneself) outstanding or noteworthy **d** to mark as different; characterize **2** to discern; MAKE OUT 3, 5 ~*vi* to recognize the difference *between* – **distinguishable** *adj*, **distinguishably** *adv*, **distinguishability** *n*

diˈstinguished *adj* **1** marked by eminence, distinction, or excellence **2** dignified in manner, bearing, or appearance

distort /diˈstawt‖dɪˈstɔːt/ *vt* **1** to alter the true meaning of; misrepresent **2** to cause to take on an unnatural or abnormal shape **3** to reproduce or broadcast (radio sound, a television picture, etc) poorly or inaccurately owing to a change in the wave form of the original signal – **distortion** *n*, **distortional** *adj*

distract /diˈstrakt‖dɪˈstrækt/ *vt* **1** to turn aside; divert **2** to draw (e g one's attention) to a different object – **distractingly** *adv*, **distractible** *adj*, **distractibility** *n*

diˈstracted *adj* **1** confused, perplexed **2** agitated – **distractedly** *adv*

distraction /diˈstraksh(ə)n‖dɪˈstrækʃ(ə)n/ *n* **1** extreme agitation or mental confusion **2** sthg that distracts; *esp* an amusement – **distractive** *adj*

distrain /diˈstrayn‖dɪˈstreɪn/ *vb* to impose a distress (upon); *also* to seize (goods, property, etc) by way of distress – **distrainable** *adj*, **distrainer** *n*, **distrainment** *n*, **distrainee** *n*

distraint /diˈstraynt‖dɪˈstreɪnt/ *n* distraining; DISTRESS 1a

distrait /diˈstray ‖dɪˈstreɪ (*Fr* distrɛ)/ *adj* absentminded

distraught /diˈstrawt‖dɪˈstrɔːt/ *adj* mentally agitated; frantic – **distraughtly** *adv*

[1]**distress** /diˈstres‖dɪˈstres/ *n* **1a** (a) seizure of goods, property, etc as a pledge or to obtain satisfaction of a claim **b** sthg distrained **2a** mental or physical anguish **b** hardship or suffering caused esp by lack of money or the necessities of life **3** a state of danger or desperate need <*a ship in* ~> – **distressful** *adj*

[2]**distress** *vt* to cause distress to – **distressingly** *adv*

distribute /diˈstribyooht‖dɪˈstrɪbjuːt/ *vt* **1** to divide among several or many **2a** to disperse or scatter over an area **b** to give out, deliver **3** to return (e g used type) to the proper storage places

distribution /ˌdistriˈbyoohsh(ə)n‖ˌdɪstrɪˈbjuːʃ(ə)n/ *n* **1a** distributing, apportioning **b** sthg distributed **2a** the position, arrangement, or frequency of occurrence (e g of the members of a group) over a usu specified area or length of time **b** the natural geographical range of an organism **3** an arrangement of statistical data that shows the frequency of occurrence of the values of a variable **4** the transport and marketing of goods between manufacturer or wholesaler and retailer – **distributional** *adj*

[1]**distributive** /di'stribyootiv‖dɪ'strɪbjʊtɪv/ *adj* **1** of distribution **2** denoting a word (e g *each, either,* or *none*) referring singly to all the members of a group – **distributively** *adv*, **distributiveness** *n*

[2]**distributive** *n* a distributive word

distributor /di'stribyootə‖dɪ'strɪbjʊtə/ *n* **1** sby employed to manage the distribution of goods **2** an apparatus for directing current to the various sparking plugs of an internal-combustion engine

district /'distrikt‖'dɪstrɪkt/ *n* **1** a territorial division made esp for administrative purposes **2** an area or region with a specified character or feature <*a residential* ~>

distrust /dis'trust‖dɪs'trʌst/ *vt or n* (to view with) suspicion or lack of trust – **distrustful** *adj*, **distrustfully** *adv*, **distrustfulness** *n*

disturb /di'stuhb‖dɪ'stɜːb/ *vt* **1a** to break in upon; interrupt **b** to alter the position or arrangement of **2a** to destroy the peace of mind or composure of **b** to throw into disorder **c** to put to inconvenience – **disturbingly** *adv*

disturbance /di'stuhb(ə)ns‖dɪ'stɜːb(ə)ns/ *n* **1** disturbing or being disturbed **2** sthg that disturbs

di'sturbed *adj* having or showing symptoms of emotional or mental instability

disunion /dis'yoohnyən, -ni·ən‖dɪs'juːnjən, -nɪən/ *n* **1** the termination of union; separation **2** disunity

disunite /ˌdisyoo'niet‖ˌdɪsjʊ'naɪt/ *vt* to divide, separate

disunity /dis'yoohnəti‖dɪs'juːnətɪ/ *n* lack of unity; *esp* dissension

disuse /dis'yoohs‖dɪs'juːs/ *n* the state of no longer being used <*that word has fallen into* ~>

disused /dis'yoohzd‖dɪs'juːzd/ *adj* no longer used; abandoned

[1]**ditch** /dich‖dɪtʃ/ *n* a long narrow excavation dug in the earth for defence, drainage, irrigation, etc

[2]**ditch** *vt* **1a** to enclose with a ditch **b** to dig a ditch in **2** to make a forced landing of (an aircraft) on water **3** to get rid of; abandon *USE* (2&3) infml – **ditch** *n*

[1]**dither** /'didhə‖'dɪðə/ *vi* to act nervously or indecisively; vacillate – **ditherer** *n*

[2]**dither** *n* a state of indecision or nervous excitement – **dithery** *adj*

[1]**ditto** /'ditoh‖'dɪtəʊ/ *n* **1** a thing mentioned previously or above; the same – used to avoid repeating a word **2** *also* **ditto mark** a mark ,, or ' used as a sign indicating repetition usu of a word directly above in a previous line

[2]**ditto** *vt* to repeat the action or statement of

ditty /'diti‖'dɪtɪ/ *n* a short simple song

diuretic /ˌdieyoo'retik‖ˌdaɪjʊ'retɪk/ *n or adj* (a drug) acting to increase the flow of urine – **diuretically** *adv*

diurnal /die'uhnl‖daɪ'ɜːnl/ *adj* **1** having a daily cycle **2a** occurring during the day or daily **b** opening during the day and closing at night <~ *flowers*> **c** active during the day – **diurnally** *adv*

divagate /'dievəˌgayt‖'daɪvəˌgeɪt/ *vi* to wander from one place or subject to another; stray – fml – **divagation** *n*

divan /di'van, 'dievan‖dɪ'væn, 'daɪvæn; *sense 3* di'van‖dɪ'væn/ *n* **1** the privy council of the Ottoman Empire **2** a council chamber in some Muslim countries, esp Turkey **3a** a long low couch, usu without arms or back, placed against a wall **b** a bed of a similar style without a head or foot board [Turkish, fr Persian *dīwān* account book]

[1]**dive** /diev‖daɪv/ *vb* **dived,** *NAm also* **dove** /dohv‖dəʊv/ *vi* **1a** to plunge into water headfirst **b** to engage in the sport of prescribed dives into water **c** to submerge <*the submarine* ~d> **2a** to descend or fall steeply **b** to plunge one's hand quickly *into* **c** *of an aircraft* to descend in a dive **3** to lunge or dash headlong <~d *for cover*> ~ *vt* **1** to cause to descend <~d *his plane through the sound barrier*> **2** to dip or plunge (one's hand) *into*

[2]**dive** *n* **1a(1)** a headlong plunge into water; *esp* one executed in a prescribed manner **a(2)** an act or instance of submerging (e g by a submarine) **a(3)** a steep descent of an aeroplane at greater than the maximum horizontal speed **b** a sharp decline **2** a disreputable bar, club, etc **3** a faked knockout – chiefly in *take a dive* **4** a ploy in soccer in which a player makes it appear that he has been fouled by falling over deliberately after a tackle *USE* (*except 1a*) infml

'dive-ˌbomb *vt* to bomb from an aeroplane while making a steep dive towards the target – **dive-bomber** *n*

diver /'dievə‖'daɪvə/ *n* **1** sby who dives; *esp* a person who works or explores underwater for long periods, either carrying a supply of air or having it sent from the surface **2** any of various diving birds; *specif* a loon

diverge /die'vuhj‖daɪ'vɜːdʒ/ *vi* **1a** to move in different directions from a common point **b** to differ in character, form, or opinion – often + *from* **2** to turn aside from a path or course – often + *from* **3** to be mathematically divergent

divergence /die'vuhj(ə)ns, di-‖daɪ'vɜːdʒ(ə)ns, dɪ-/ *also* **divergency** /-si‖-sɪ/ *n* **1a** (an instance of) diverging or being divergent **b** the amount by which sthg diverges; DIFFERENCE 3 **2** the acquisition of dissimilar characteristics by related organisms living in different environments

divergent /die'vuhj(ə)nt, di-‖daɪ'vɜːdʒ(ə)nt, dɪ-/ *adj* **1** diverging or differing from each other **2** *of a mathematical series* having a sum that continues to increase or decrease as the number of terms increases without limit **3** causing divergence of rays <*a* ~ *lens*> – **divergently** *adv*

divers /'dievəz‖'daɪvəz/ *adj, archaic* various

diverse /'dieˌvuhs, -'-‖'daɪˌvɜːs, -'-/ *adj* **1** different, unlike **2** varied, assorted – **diversely** *adv*, **diverseness** *n*

diversify /ˌdie'vuhsiˌfie‖ˌdaɪ'vɜːsɪˌfaɪ/ *vt* **1** to make diverse; vary **2** to divide (e g investment of funds) among different securities to reduce risk ~*vi* to engage in varied business operations in order to reduce risk – **diversifier** *n*, **diversification** *n*

diversion /di'vuhsh(ə)n, die-‖dɪ'vɜːʃ(ə)n, daɪ-/ *n* **1** a turning aside from a course, activity, or use; *specif* a detour used by traffic when the usual route is closed **2** an amusement, pastime **3**

sthg that draws the attention away from the main scene of activity or operations – **diversionary** *adj*

diversity /di'vuhsəti, die-‖dɪ'vɜːsətɪ, daɪ-/ *n* **1** the condition of being different or having differences **2** a variety, assortment

divert /die'vuht‖daɪ'vɜːt/ *vt* **1a** to turn aside from one course or use to another **b** to distract **2** to entertain, amuse

divertimento /diˌvuhti'mentoh‖dɪˌvɜːtɪ'mentəʊ/ *n, pl* **divertimenti** /-ti‖-tɪ/, **divertimentos** an instrumental chamber work in several movements and usu light in character

divertissement /di'vuhtismənt ‖dɪ'vɜːtɪsmənt (*Fr* divɛrtismɑ̃)/ *n, pl* **divertissements** /-mənt(s)‖-mənt(s) (*Fr* ~)/ **1** a ballet suite serving as an interlude **2** a divertimento **3** a diversion, entertainment

divest /die'vest‖daɪ'vest/ *vt* **1a** to deprive or dispossess *of* property, authority, title, etc **b** to rid or free (oneself) *of* **c** to strip *of* clothing, equipment, etc **2** to take away (e g property or vested rights) *USE* (1c&2) fml – **divestiture** *n*, **divestment** *n*

[1]**divide** /di'vied‖dɪ'vaɪd/ *vt* **1** to separate into 2 or more parts, categories, divisions, etc **2a** to give out in shares; distribute **b** to set aside for different purposes < ~d *his time between work and play*> **3a** to cause to be separate; serve as a boundary between **b** to separate into opposing sides or parties **c** to cause (a parliamentary body) to vote by division **4a** to mark divisions on < ~ *a sextant*> **b** to determine how many times (a number or quantity) contains another number or quantity by means of a mathematical operation < ~ *42 by 14*> ~ *vi* **1** to perform mathematical division **2a(1)** to become separated into parts **a(2)** to diverge **b** to vote by division – **dividable** *adj* – **divide into** to use as a divisor of <divide *14* into *42*>

[2]**divide** *n* **1** WATERSHED 1 **2** a point or line of division

dividend /'dividend, -dənd‖'dɪvɪdend, -dənd/ *n* **1** (a pro rata share in) the part of a company's profits payable to shareholders **2** a reward, benefit <*her action will pay great* ~s> **3a** a number to be divided by another **b** a sum or fund to be divided and distributed

divider /di'viedə‖dɪ'vaɪdə/ *n* **1** *pl* a compasslike instrument with 2 pointed ends used for measuring or marking off lines, angles, etc **2** a partition or screen used to separate parts of a room, hall, etc

divination /ˌdivi'naysh(ə)n‖ˌdɪvɪ'neɪʃ(ə)n/ *n* **1** the art or practice that seeks to foresee the future or discover hidden knowledge (e g by using supernatural powers) **2** (an instance of) unusual insight or perception – **divinatory** *adj*

[1]**divine** /di'vien‖dɪ'vaɪn/ *adj* **1a** of, being, or proceeding directly from God or a god **b** devoted to the worship of God or a god; sacred **2** delightful, superb – infml – **divinely** *adv*, **divineness** *n*

[2]**divine** *n* a clergyman; *esp* one skilled in theology

[3]**divine** *vt* **1** to discover, perceive, or foresee intuitively or by supernatural means **2** to discover or locate (e g water or minerals) by means of a divining rod ~ *vi* to practise divination – **divinable** *adj*, **diviner** *n*

Diˌvine 'Office *n* the prescribed forms of prayer and ritual for daily worship used by Roman Catholic priests

diˌvine 'right *n* the right of a sovereign to rule, held to derive directly from God; *broadly* a right which cannot be transferred

diˌvine 'service *n* an esp nonsacramental service of Christian worship

'diving ˌbell /'dieving‖'daɪvɪŋ/ *n* a bell-shaped metal container open only at the bottom and supplied with compressed air through a tube, in which a person can be let down under water

'diving ˌsuit *n* a waterproof diver's suit with a helmet that is supplied with air pumped through a tube

di'vining ˌrod /di'viening‖dɪ'vaɪnɪŋ/ *n* a forked rod (e g a twig) believed to dip downwards when held over ground concealing water or minerals

divinity /di'vinəti‖dɪ'vɪnətɪ/ *n* **1** the quality or state of being divine **2a** *often cap* GOD 1 **b** a male or female deity **3** theology

divisible /di'vizəbl‖dɪ'vɪzəbl/ *adj* capable of being divided, esp without a remainder – **divisibility** *n*

division /di'vizh(ə)n‖dɪ'vɪʒ(ə)n/ *n* **1a** dividing or being divided **b** (a) distribution **2** any of the parts or sections into which a whole is divided **3** *sing or pl in constr* **3a** a major army formation having the necessary tactical and administrative services to act independently **b** a naval unit of men under a single command **4a** an administrative territorial unit **b** an administrative or operating unit of an organization **5** a group of organisms forming part of a larger group; *specif* a primary category of the plant kingdom equivalent to a phylum of the animal kingdom **6** a competitive class or category (e g of a soccer league) **7** sthg that divides, separates, or marks off **8** disagreement, disunity **9** the physical separation into different lobbies of the members of a parliamentary body voting for and against a question **10** the mathematical operation of dividing one number by another – **divisional** *adj*

diˌvision of 'labour *n* the distribution of various parts of the process of production among different people, groups, or machines, each specializing in a particular job, to increase efficiency

divisive /di'viesiv, -ziv‖dɪ'vaɪsɪv, -zɪv/ *adj* tending to cause disunity or dissension – **divisively** *adv*, **divisiveness** *n*

divisor /di'viezə‖dɪ'vaɪzə/ *n* the number by which another number or quantity is divided

[1]**divorce** /di'vaws‖dɪ'vɔːs/ *n* **1** (a decree declaring) a legal dissolution of a marriage **2** a separation, severance

[2]**divorce** *vt* **1a** to end marriage with (one's spouse) by divorce **b** to dissolve the marriage between **2** to end the relationship or union of; separate – usu + *from* ~ *vi* to obtain a divorce

divorcé /divaw'say, -'see‖dɪvɔː'seɪ, -'siː/, *fem* **divorcée** /-'see‖-'siː/ *n* a divorced person

divot /'divət‖'dɪvət/ *n* **1** a piece of turf dug out in making a golf shot **2** *Scot* a piece of turf

divulge /die'vulj, di-‖daɪ'vʌldʒ, dɪ-/ *vt* to make

known (e g a confidence or secret); reveal – **divulgence** *n*

divvy /ˈdivi‖ˈdɪvɪ/ *n, Br* DIVIDEND 1; *esp* one paid by a Cooperative Wholesale Society – infml

dixie /ˈdiksi‖ˈdɪksɪ/ *n, Br* a large metal pot in which food and drink is made or carried, esp by soldiers

Dixie *n* the Southern states of the USA

ˈ**dixie,land** /-ˌland‖-ˌlænd/ *n* jazz music in duple time characterized by collective improvisation

[1]**dizzy** /ˈdizi‖ˈdɪzɪ/ *adj* **1a** experiencing a whirling sensation in the head with a tendency to lose balance **b** mentally confused **2** causing or feeling giddiness or mental confusion <*a* ~ *height*> **3** foolish, silly – infml – **dizzily** *adv*, **dizziness** *n*

[2]**dizzy** *vt* to make dizzy; bewilder – **dizzyingly** *adv*

DJ /ˈdee,jay‖ˈdiːˌdʒeɪ/ *n* **1** DISC JOCKEY **2** DINNER JACKET

djin, djinn /jin‖dʒɪn/ *n, pl* **djin, djinn** a jinn

DNA *n* any of various nucleic acids that are found esp in cell nuclei and are responsible for transmitting genetic information [*d*eoxyribo*n*ucleic *a*cid]

[1]**do** /dooh‖duː/ *vb* **does** /dəz‖dəz; *strong* duz‖dʌz/; **did** /did‖dɪd/; **done** /dun‖dʌn/ *vt* **1** to carry out the task of; effect, perform <~ *some washing*> **2** to put into a specified condition <~ *him to death*> **3** to have as a function <*what's that book* ~ing *on the floor?*> **4** to cause, impart <*sleep will* ~ *you good*> **5** to bring to an esp unwanted conclusion; finish – used esp in the past participle <*that's* done *it*> **6** to expend, exert <did *their damnedest to hog the game*> **7a** to provide <*they* ~ *a mail-order service*> **b** to have available for purchase; sell <*they* ~ *teas here*> **8** to bring into existence; produce <~ *a biography of the general*> **9a** to put on; perform <*are* ~ing *'The Merchant of Venice' tomorrow night*> **b** to play the part of; act <*can* ~ *Harold Wilson very well*> **c** to behave like <did *a Houdini and escaped from his chains*> **10a** to put in order; arrange <*had his hair* done> **b** to clean, wash <~ *the dishes*> **c** to cook <*likes her steak well* done> **d** to decorate, furnish <did *the living room in blue*> **11a** to execute an artistic representation of <did *her in oils*> **b** to perform the appropriate professional service or services for <*the barber will* ~ *you now*> **12a** to work at, esp as a course of study or occupation <~ *classics*> <*what are you* ~ing *nowadays?*> **b** to solve; WORK OUT <~ *a sum*> **13a** to pass over; cover <~ *30 miles to the gallon*> **b** to travel at a (maximum) speed of <~ *70 on the motorway*> **14** to see the sights of; tour <~ *12 countries in 12 days*> **15** to serve out, esp as a prison sentence <did *3 years*> **16** to suffice, suit <*worms will* ~ *us for bait*> **17** – used as a substitute verb to avoid repetition <*if you must make such a racket,* ~ *it somewhere else*> **18a** *chiefly Br* to arrest, convict – slang <*get* done *for theft*> **b** *chiefly Br* to attack, hurt – slang **c** to treat unfairly; *esp* to cheat, deprive <did *him out of his inheritance*> – infml **d** to rob – slang <~ *a shop*> **19** to have sexual intercourse with (a woman or passive partner) – slang ~ *vi* **1** to act, behave <~ *as I say*> **2a** to fare; GET ALONG <*how do you* ~*?*> **b** to carry on business or affairs; manage <*we can* ~ *without your help*> **3** to be in progress; happen <*there's nothing* ~ing> **4** to come to or make an end; finish – used in the past participle <*have you* done *with the newspaper?*> **5** to be active or busy **6** to suffice, serve <*half of that will* ~> **7** to be fitting; conform to custom or propriety <*won't* ~ *to be late*> **8a** – used as a substitute verb to avoid repetition <*you sing,* ~ *you?*> and, esp in British English, after a modal auxiliary <*haven't heard of her yet but you will* ~> **b** – used as a substitute for verb and object <*he likes it and so* ~ *I*> **9** – used in the imperative after another imperative to add emphasis <*be quiet,* ~> – used with the infinitive without *to* **9a** to form present and past tenses in legal and parliamentary language <~ *hereby bequeath*> and in poetry <*give what she* did *crave* – Shak> **b** to form present and past tenses in declarative sentences with inverted word order <*fervently* ~ *we pray* – Abraham Lincoln> or in questions or negative sentences <did *you hear that?*> <*we* don't *know*> <don't *go*> **c** to form present and past tenses expressing emphasis <~ *be careful*> – **doable** *adj* – **do away with 1** to put an end to; abolish **2** to put to death; kill – **do duty for** to act as a substitute for; serve as – **do for 1** *chiefly Br* to keep house for **2a** to wear out, exhaust **b** to bring about the death or ruin of – **do justice (to) 1a** to treat fairly or adequately **b** to show due appreciation for **2** to show in the best light <*I hope he* did *himself* justice *in the examinations*> – **do one's bit** *Br* to make one's personal contribution, esp to a cause – **do one's nut** to become frantic or angry – infml – **do proud** to treat or entertain splendidly – **do the dirty on** to play a sly trick on – **do the trick** to achieve the desired result – infml – **to do with** concerned with; of concern to <*nothing* to do with *you*>

[2]**do** *n, pl* **dos, do's** /doohz‖duːz/ **1** sthg one ought to do – usu pl <*gave her a list of* ~s *and don'ts*> **2** *chiefly Br* a festive party or occasion – infml

[3]**do, doh** /doh‖dəʊ/ *n* the 1st note of the diatonic scale in solmization

doc /dok‖dɒk/ *n* a doctor – often used as an informal term of address

docile /ˈdoh,siel‖ˈdəʊˌsaɪl/ *adj* easily led or managed; tractable – **docilely** *adv*, **docility** *n*

[1]**dock** /dok‖dɒk/ *n* any of a genus of coarse weeds whose leaves are used to alleviate nettle stings

[2]**dock** *n* the solid bony part of an animal's tail as distinguished from the hair

[3]**dock** *vt* **1a** to remove part of the tail of **b** to cut (e g a tail) short **2** to make a deduction from (e g wages) **3** to take away (a specified amount) *from*

[4]**dock** *n* **1a** a usu artificially enclosed body of water in a port or harbour, where a ship can moor (e g for repair work to be carried out) **b** *pl the* total number of such enclosures in a harbour, together with wharves, sheds, etc **2** *chiefly NAm* a wharf – **in dock** in a garage or repair shop

[5]**dock** *vt* **1** to haul or guide into a dock **2** to join

(e g 2 spacecraft) together while in space ~ *vi* **1** to come or go into dock **2** *of spacecraft* to join together while in space

[6]**dock** *n* the prisoner's enclosure in a criminal court – **in the dock** on trial

docker /ˈdokə‖ˈdɒkə/ *n* sby employed in loading and unloading ships, barges, etc

[1]**docket** /ˈdokit‖ˈdɒkɪt/ *n* **1** a brief written summary of a document **2a** a document recording the contents of a shipment or the payment of customs duties **b** a label attached to goods bearing identification or instructions **c** (a copy of) a receipt **3a** *NAm* **3a(1)** a formal record of legal proceedings **a(2)** a list of legal causes to be tried **b** *chiefly NAm* a list of business matters to be acted on

[2]**docket** *vt* **1** to put an identifying statement or label on **2** to make an abstract of (e g legal proceedings) **3** *NAm* to place on the docket for legal action

ˈ**dock,yard** /-ˌyahd‖-ˌjaːd/ *n* a place or enclosure in which ships are built or repaired

[1]**doctor** /ˈdoktə‖ˈdɒktə/ *n* **1a** *also* **Doctor of the Church**, *often cap* a theologian whose doctrines the Roman Catholic church holds to be authoritative **b** a holder of the highest level of academic degree conferred by a university **2a** one qualified to practise medicine; a physician or surgeon **b** *NAm* a licensed dentist or veterinary surgeon **3** sby skilled in repairing or treating a usu specified type of machine, vehicle, etc **4** *archaic* a learned or authoritative teacher – **doctoral** *adj*, **doctorate** *n*, **doctorship** *n*

[2]**doctor** *vt* **1a** to give medical treatment to **b** to repair, mend **2a** to adapt or modify for a desired end <~ed *the play to suit the audience*> **b** to alter in a dishonest way **3** to castrate or spay – euph ~*vi* to practise medicine – infml

doctrinaire /ˌdoktriˈneə‖ˌdɒktrɪˈneə/ *n or adj* (one) concerned with abstract theory to the exclusion of practical considerations – chiefly derog

doctrinal /dokˈtrienl‖dɒkˈtraɪnl/ *adj* of or concerned with doctrine – **doctrinally** *adv*

doctrine /ˈdoktrin‖ˈdɒktrɪn/ *n* **1** sthg that is taught **2** a principle or the body of principles in a branch of knowledge or system of belief

[1]**document** /ˈdokyoomənt‖ˈdɒkjʊmənt/ *n* an original or official paper that gives information about or proof of sthg

[2]**document** /ˈdokyooˌment‖ˈdɒkjʊˌment/ *vt* **1** to provide documentary evidence of **2a** to support with factual evidence, references, etc **b** to be or provide a documentary account of **3** to provide (a ship) with papers required by law recording ownership, cargo, etc

[1]**documentary** /ˌdokyooˈment(ə)ri‖ˌdɒkjʊˈment(ə)rɪ/ *adj* **1** being or consisting of documents; contained or certified in writing <~ *evidence*> **2** presenting or based on factual material

[2]**documentary** *n* a broadcast or film that presents a factual account of a person or topic using a variety of techniques (e g narrative and interview)

documentation /ˌdokyoomenˈtaysh(ə)n‖ˌdɒkjʊmenˈteɪʃ(ə)n/ *n* (the provision or use of) documents or documentary evidence – **documentational** *adj*

[1]**dodder** /ˈdodə‖ˈdɒdə/ *n* any of a genus of leafless plants of the bindweed family that are wholly parasitic on other plants

[2]**dodder** *vi* **1** to tremble or shake from weakness or age **2** to walk feebly and unsteadily – **dodderer** *n*

doddering /ˈdodəring‖ˈdɒdərɪŋ/, **doddery** /ˈdod(ə)ri‖ˈdɒd(ə)rɪ/ *adj* weak, shaky, and slow, esp because of old age

doddle /ˈdodl‖ˈdɒdl/ *n, chiefly Br* a very easy task – infml

[1]**dodge** /doj‖dɒdʒ/ *vi* to shift position suddenly and usu repeatedly (e g to avoid a blow or a pursuer) ~ *vt* **1** to evade (e g a duty) usu by trickery **2a** to avoid by a sudden or repeated shift of position **b** to avoid an encounter with

[2]**dodge** *n* **1** a sudden movement to avoid sthg **2** a clever device to evade or trick <*a tax* ~>

dodgem /ˈdojəm‖ˈdɒdʒəm/, ˈ**dodgem ˌcar** *n, Br* any of a number of small electric cars designed to be steered about and bumped into one another as a fun-fair amusement

dodger /ˈdojə‖ˈdɒdʒə/ *n* one who uses clever and often dishonest methods, esp to avoid payment (e g of taxes) or responsibility

dodgy /ˈdoji‖ˈdɒdʒɪ/ *adj, chiefly Br* **1** shady, dishonest <*a* ~ *person*> **2** risky, dangerous <*a* ~ *plan*> **3** liable to collapse, fail, or break down <*that chair's a bit* ~> *USE* infml

dodo /ˈdohˌdoh‖ˈdəʊˌdəʊ/ *n, pl* **dodoes, dodos** an extinct heavy flightless bird that formerly lived on the island of Mauritius [Portuguese *doudo*, fr *doudo* silly, stupid]

do down *vt, chiefly Br* **1** to cheat **2** to speak badly of; belittle

doe /doh‖dəʊ/ *n*, the adult female fallow deer; *broadly* the adult female of any of various mammals (e g the rabbit) or birds (e g the guinea fowl) of which the male is called a buck

doer /ˈdooh·ə‖ˈduːə/ *n* one who takes action or participates actively in sthg, rather than theorizing

does /dəz‖dəz; *strong* duz‖dʌz/ *pres 3rd sing of* DO

doeskin /ˈdohˌskin‖ˈdəʊˌskɪn/ *n* **1** (leather made from) the skin of a doe **2** a smooth closely woven woollen fabric

doff /dof‖dɒf/ *vt* to take off (one's hat) in greeting or as a sign of respect

[1]**dog** /dog‖dɒg/ *n* **1a** a 4-legged flesh-eating domesticated mammal occurring in a great variety of breeds and prob descended from the common wolf **b** any of a family of carnivores to which the dog belongs **c** a male dog **2a** any of various usu simple mechanical devices for holding, fastening, etc that consist of a spike, rod, or bar **b** an andiron **3** *chiefly NAm* sthg inferior of its kind **4** an esp worthless man or fellow <*a lazy* ~> **5** *pl* ruin <*go to the* ~s> *USE* (4,5) infml

[2]**dog** *vt* -gg- to pursue closely like a dog; hound

[3]**dog** *adj* male <*a* ~ *fox*>

ˈ**dog ˌbiscuit** *n* a hard dry biscuit for dogs

ˈ**dog ˌcollar** *n* CLERICAL COLLAR – infml

ˈ**dog ˌdays** *n pl* the hottest days in the year

doge /dohj‖dəʊdʒ/ *n* the chief magistrate of the former republics of Venice and Genoa

ˈ**dog-ˌeared** *adj* having dog-ears; *broadly* worn, shabby

ˌdog-eat-ˈdog *adj* marked by ruthless self-interest; cutthroat

ˈdogˌfight /-ˌfiet‖-ˌfaɪt/ *n* **1** a viciously fought contest **2** a fight between aircraft, usu at close quarters – **dogfight** *vi*

ˈdogˌfish /-ˌfish‖-ˌfɪʃ/ *n* any of various small sharks

dogged /ˈdogid‖ˈdɒgɪd/ *adj* stubbornly determined – **doggedly** *adv*, **doggedness** *n*

doggerel /ˈdog(ə)rəl‖ˈdɒg(ə)rəl/ *n* (an example of) verse that is loosely styled and irregular in measure, esp for comic effect

doggo /ˈdogoh‖ˈdɒgəʊ/ *adv, Br* in hiding and without moving – infml; chiefly in *lie doggo*

doggoned /ˈdogond‖ˈdɒgɒnd/, **doggone** /ˈdoˌgon‖ˈdɒˌgɒn/ *adj or adv, chiefly NAm* damned – euph

[1]**doggy** /ˈdogi‖ˈdɒgɪ/ *adj* **1** resembling or suggestive of a dog <*a ~ odour*> **2** concerned with or fond of dogs <*a ~ person*> *USE* infml

[2]**doggy, doggie** /ˈdogi‖ˈdɒgɪ/ *n* a dog – used esp by or to children

ˈdogˌhouse /-ˌhows‖-ˌhaʊs/ *n, chiefly NAm* a dog kennel – **in the doghouse** in a state of disfavour – infml

[1]**ˈdogˌleg** /-ˌleg‖-ˌleg/ *n* **1** a sharp bend (e g in a road) **2** an angled fairway on a golf course

[2]**dogleg** *adj* bent like a dog's hind leg

dogma /ˈdogmə‖ˈdɒgmə/ *n* **1** an authoritative tenet or principle **2** a doctrine or body of doctrines formally and authoritatively stated by a church **3** a point of view or tenet put forth as authoritative without adequate grounds – chiefly derog

dogmatic /dogˈmatik‖dɒgˈmætɪk/ *also* **dogmatical** /-kl‖-kl/ *adj* **1** of dogma or dogmatics **2** characterized by or given to the use of dogmatism – chiefly derog – **dogmatically** *adv*, **dogmaticalness** *n*

dogˈmatics *n pl but sing or pl in constr* a branch of theology that seeks to interpret the dogmas of a religious faith

dogmatism /ˈdogməˌtiz(ə)m‖ˈdɒgməˌtɪz(ə)m/ *n* (unwarranted or arrogant) assertion of opinion – **dogmatist** *n*

do-gooder /ˌdooh ˈgoodə‖ˌduː ˈgʊdə/ *n* an earnest often naive and ineffectual humanitarian or reformer

ˈdog ˌpaddle *n* an elementary form of swimming in which the arms paddle and the legs kick – **dog-paddle** *vi*

ˈdogsˌbody /-ˌbodi‖-ˌbɒdɪ/ *n, chiefly Br* a person who carries out routine or menial work – infml

ˌdog-ˈtired *n* extremely tired – infml

ˈdogˌwood /-ˌwood‖-ˌwʊd/ *n* any of several trees and shrubs with heads of small flowers

doh /doh‖dəʊ/ *n* [3]DO

doily, doyley, doyly /ˈdoyli‖ˈdɔɪlɪ/ *n* a small decorative mat, esp of paper, cloth, or plastic openwork, often placed under food, esp cakes, on a plate or stand

do in *vt* **1** to kill <*tried to* do *him* in *with a club*> **2** to wear out, exhaust <*walking all day nearly* did *us* in> *USE* infml

doings /ˈdooh·ings‖ˈduːɪŋs/ *n, pl* **doings** *also* **doingses** /-ziz‖-zɪz/, *chiefly Br* a small object, esp one whose name is forgotten or not known – infml

Dolby /ˈdolbi‖ˈdɒlbɪ/ *trademark* – used for a sound recording system that reduces unwanted noise by electronic processing

doldrums /ˈdoldrəmz‖ˈdɒldrəmz/ *n pl* **1** a depressed state of mind; *the* blues **2** an equatorial ocean region where calms, squalls, and light shifting winds prevail **3** a state of stagnation or slump

dole /dohl‖dəʊl/ *n* **1** a distribution of food, money, or clothing to the needy **2** *the* government unemployment benefit

doleful /ˈdohlf(ə)l‖ˈdəʊlf(ə)l/ *adj* sad, mournful – **dolefully** *adv*, **dolefulness** *n*

dole out *vt* to give, distribute, or deliver, esp in small portions

doll /dol‖dɒl/ *n* **1** a small-scale figure of a human being used esp as a child's toy **2a** a (pretty but often silly) young woman – infml **b** an attractive person – slang – **dollish** *adj*, **dollishly** *adv*

dollar /ˈdolə‖ˈdɒlə/ *n* (a coin or note representing) the basic money unit of the USA, Canada, Australia, etc [Dutch or Low German *daler*, a silver coin, fr German *taler*, short for *joachimstaler*, fr Sankt *Joachimsthal*, town in Bohemia where the coins were first minted]

[1]**dollop** /ˈdoləp‖ˈdɒləp/ *n* a soft shapeless blob; *esp* a serving of mushy or semiliquid food

[2]**dollop** *vt* to serve *out* carelessly or clumsily

ˈdoll's ˌhouse *n* a child's small-scale toy house

doll up *vt* to dress prettily or showily – infml

[1]**dolly** /ˈdoli‖ˈdɒlɪ/ *n* **1** DOLL 1 – used chiefly by or to children **2** a wooden-pronged instrument for beating and stirring clothes while washing them in a tub **3a** a platform on a roller or on wheels or castors for moving heavy objects **b** a wheeled platform for a film or television camera

[2]**dolly** *vi* to move a film or television camera on a dolly towards or away from a subject – usu + *in* or *out*

ˈdolly ˌbird *n, chiefly Br* a pretty young woman, esp one who is a slavish follower of fashion and not regarded as intelligent

dolmen /ˈdolmən‖ˈdɒlmən/ *n* a prehistoric monument consisting of 2 or more upright stones supporting a horizontal slab [French, fr Breton *tolmen*, fr *tol* table + *men* stone]

dolorous /ˈdolərəs‖ˈdɒlərəs/ *adj* causing or expressing misery or grief – **dolorously** *adv*, **dolorousness** *n*

dolour, *NAm chiefly* **dolor** /ˈdohlə, ˈdolə‖ˈdəʊlə, ˈdɒlə/ *n* mental suffering or anguish

dolphin /ˈdolfin‖ˈdɒlfɪn/ *n* any of various small toothed whales with the snout elongated into a beak to varying extents

dolt /dohlt‖dəʊlt/ *n* an extremely dull or stupid person – **doltish** *adj*, **doltishly** *adv*, **doltishness** *n*

Dom /dom‖dɒm/ *n* **1** – used as a title for Benedictine, Carthusian, and Cistercian monks and some canons regular **2** – used formerly as a title preceding the Christian name of a Portuguese or Brazilian man of rank

-dom /-d(ə)m‖-d(ə)m/ *suffix* (→ *n*) **1a** rank or office of <*duke*dom> **b** realm or jurisdiction of <*king*dom> **2** state or fact of being <*free*dom> **3** group or class of people having (a specified office, occupation, interest, or character) <*official*dom>

domain /də'mayn‖də'meɪn/ *n* **1** a territory over which control is exercised **2** a sphere of influence or activity

[1]**dome** /dohm‖dəʊm/ *n* **1** a (nearly) hemispherical roof or vault **2** a dome-shaped (geological) structure **3** *archaic* a stately building; a mansion – **domal** *adj*

[2]**dome** *vt* to cover with or form into a dome

'**Domesday** ˌ**Book** /'doohmzˌday, -di‖'du:mzˌdeɪ, -dɪ/ *n* a record of a survey of English lands made by order of William I about 1086

[1]**domestic** /də'mestik‖də'mestɪk/ *adj* **1** of or devoted to the home or the family **2** of one's own or some particular country; not foreign <~ *politics*> **3a** living near or about the habitations of human beings **b** tame; *also* bred by human beings for some specific purpose (e g food, hunting, etc) [Middle French *domestique*, fr Latin *domesticus*, fr *domus* house, home] – **domestically** *adv*

[2]**domestic** *n* a household servant

domesticate /də'mestikayt‖də'mestɪkeɪt/ *vt* **1** to bring (an animal or species) under human control for some specific purpose (e g for carrying loads, hunting, food, etc) **2** to cause to be fond of or adapted to household duties or pleasures – **domestication**

domestic fowl *n* a chicken, turkey, or other bird developed from the jungle fowl, esp for meat or egg production

domesticity /ˌdome'stisəti‖ˌdɒme'stɪsətɪ/ *n* (devotion to) home or family life

doˌmestic '**science** *n* instruction in the household arts

[1]**domicile** /'domisiel‖'dɒmɪsaɪl/ *also* **domicil** /-s(i)l‖-s(ɪ)l/ *n* a home; *esp* a person's permanent and principal home for legal purposes

[2]**domicile** *vt* to establish in or provide with a domicile

domiciliary /ˌdomi'silyəri‖ˌdɒmɪ'sɪljərɪ/ *adj* **1** of or being a domicile **2** taking place or attending in the home <~ *visit*>

[1]**dominant** /'dominənt‖'dɒmɪnənt/ *adj* **1** commanding, controlling, or prevailing over all others **2** overlooking and commanding from a superior height **3** being the one of a pair of bodily structures that is the more effective or predominant in action <*the* ~ *eye*> **4** being the one of a pair of (genes determining) contrasting inherited characteristics that predominates – **dominance** *n*, **dominantly** *adv*

[2]**dominant** *n* **1** a socially dominant individual **2** the fifth note of a diatonic scale

dominate /'dominayt‖'dɒmɪneɪt/ *vt* **1** to exert controlling influence or power over **2** to overlook from a superior height **3** to occupy a commanding or preeminent position in ~ *vi* **1** to have or exert mastery or control **2** to occupy a higher or superior position **dominator** *n*, **dominative** *adj*, **domination** *n*

domineer /ˌdomi'niə‖ˌdɒmɪ'nɪə/ *vi* to exercise arbitrary or overbearing control <*a* ~*ing husband*> – **domineeringly** *adv*

Dominican /də'minikən‖də'mɪnɪkən/ *n or adj* (a member) of a preaching order of mendicant friars founded by St Dominic in 1215

dominion /də'minyən, -ni·ən‖də'mɪnjən, -nɪən/ *n* **1** the power or right to rule; sovereignty **2** absolute ownership **3** *often cap* a self-governing nation of the Commonwealth other than the United Kingdom

domino /'dominoh‖'dɒmɪnəʊ/ *n, pl* **dominoes, dominos** **1a(1)** a long loose hooded cloak worn with a mask as a masquerade costume **a(2)** a half mask worn with a masquerade costume **b** sby wearing a domino **2a** a flat rectangular block whose face is divided into 2 equal parts that are blank or bear from 1 to usu 6 dots arranged as on dice faces **b** *pl but usu sing in constr* any of several games played with a set of usu 28 dominoes

[1]**don** /don‖dɒn/ *n* **1** a Spanish nobleman or gentleman – used as a title preceding the Christian name **2** a head, tutor, or fellow in a college of Oxford or Cambridge university; *broadly* a university teacher

[2]**don** *vt* **-nn-** PUT ON 1a, b

donate /doh'nayt‖dəʊ'neɪt/ *vb* **1** to make a gift or donation (of), esp to a public or charitable cause **2** to give off or transfer (e g electrons) – **donator** *n*

donation /doh'naysh(ə)n‖dəʊ'neɪʃ(ə)n/ *n* **1** the act of donating **2** sthg donated

[1]**done** /dun‖dʌn/ **1** *past part of* DO **2** *chiefly dial & NAm past of* DO

[2]**done** *adj* **1** conformable to social convention <*it's not* ~ *to eat peas off your knife*> **2** arrived at or brought to an end; completed **3** physically exhausted; spent **4** no longer involved; through <*I'm* ~ *with the Army*> **5** doomed to failure, defeat, or death **6** cooked sufficiently **7** arrested, imprisoned – slang <*robbed a bank and got* ~ *for 10 years*>

[3]**done** *interj* – used in acceptance of a bet or transaction

ˌ**done** '**in** *adj* physically exhausted – infml

donga /'dong·gə‖'dɒŋgə/ *n, SAfr* a narrow steep-sided ravine

donjon /'dunj(ə)n, 'don-‖'dʌndʒ(ə)n, 'dɒn-/ *n* a massive inner tower in a medieval castle

Don Juan /don 'jooh·ən ‖dɒn 'dʒu:ən (*Sp* don Xwan)/ *n* a promiscuous man; *broadly* a lady-killer

donkey /'dongki‖'dɒŋkɪ/ *n* **1** the domestic ass **2** a stupid or obstinate person

'**donkey** ˌ**engine** *n* a small, usu portable, auxiliary engine

'**donkey** ˌ**jacket** *n* a thick hip-length hard-wearing jacket, usu blue and with a strip of (imitation) leather across the shoulders

'**donkey's** ˌ**years** *n pl, chiefly Br* a very long time – infml

'**donkeyˌwork** /-ˌwuhk‖-ˌwɜ:k/ *n* hard, monotonous, and routine work – infml

donnish /'donish‖'dɒnɪʃ/ *adj* pedantic – **donnishly** *adv*, **donnishness** *n*

donor /'dohnə‖'dəʊnə/ *n* **1** a person who gives, donates, or presents **2** sby used as a source of biological material <*a blood* ~> **3a** a compound capable of giving up a part (e g an atom, radical, or elementary particle) for combination with an acceptor **b** an impurity that is added to a semiconductor to increase the number of mobile electrons

[1]**don't** /dohnt‖dəʊnt/ **1** do not **2** does not – nonstandard, though sometimes used by educated speakers

[2]**don't** *n* a prohibition – usu pl <*a list of dos and* ~s>

doodle /ˈdoohdl‖ˈduːdl/ *vi or n* (to make) an aimless scribble or sketch – **doodler** *n*

ˈ**doodle,bug** /-ˌbug‖-ˌbʌg/ *n* FLYING BOMB – infml

[1]**doom** /doohm‖duːm/ *n* **1** a law in Anglo-Saxon England **2a** JUDGMENT 2a; *also, archaic* a judicial condemnation **b** JUDGMENT DAY **3a** an (unhappy) destiny **b** unavoidable death or destruction

[2]**doom** *vt* **1** to destine, esp to failure or destruction **2** *archaic* to give judgment against; condemn

doomsday /ˈdoohmz,day, -di‖ˈduːmz,deɪ, -dɪ/ *n, often cap* JUDGMENT DAY; *broadly* some remote point in the future <*if you expect people to work harder for less money, you'll have to wait* from now till ~>

door /daw‖dɔː/ *n* **1** a usu swinging or sliding barrier by which an entry is closed and opened; *also* a similar part of a piece of furniture **2** a doorway **3** a means of access – **at someone's door** as a charge against sby as being responsible <*laid the blame* at our door>

ˈ**door,frame** /-ˌfraym‖-ˌfreɪm/ *n* **1** a frame round the opening in which a door is fitted **2** the framework in which the panels of a door are fitted

ˈ**door,keeper** /-ˌkeepə‖-ˌkiːpə/ *n* a person who guards the main door to a building and lets people in and out

ˈ**door,knob** /-ˌnob‖-ˌnɒb/ *n* a knob that when turned releases a door latch

ˈ**doorman** /-mən‖-mən/ *n* a (uniformed) person who tends the entrance to a hotel, theatre, etc and assists people (e g in calling taxis)

ˈ**door,mat** /-ˌmat‖-ˌmæt/ *n* **1** a mat (e g of bristles) placed before or inside a door for wiping dirt from the shoes **2** a person who submits to bullying and indignities – infml

ˈ**door,nail** /-ˌnayl‖-ˌneɪl/ *n* a large-headed nail formerly used for the strengthening or decoration of doors – chiefly in *dead as a doornail*

ˈ**door,step** /-ˌstep‖-ˌstep/ *n* **1** a step in front of an outer door **2** *Br* a very thick slice of bread – infml

[1]ˌ**door-to-ˈdoor** *adj* **1** making a usu unsolicited call (e g for selling or canvassing) at every home in an area **2** providing delivery to a specified address

[2]**door-to-door** *adv* from the precise point of departure to the final point of arrival <*a journey of 2 hours* ~>

ˈ**door,way** /-ˌway‖-ˌweɪ/ *n* an entrance into a building or room that is closed by means of a door

do over *vt, Br* to attack and injure – slang

[1]**dope** /dohp‖dəʊp/ *n* **1a** a thick liquid or pasty preparation **b** a preparation for giving a desired quality to a substance or surface **c** a coating (e g a cellulose varnish) applied to a surface or fabric (e g of an aeroplane or balloon) to improve strength, impermeability, or tautness **2** absorbent or adsorbent material used in various manufacturing processes (e g the making of dynamite) **3a** marijuana, opium, or another drug **b** a preparation given illegally to a racing horse, greyhound, etc to make it run faster or slower **4** a stupid person – infml **5** information, esp from a reliable source – infml [Dutch *doop* sauce, fr *dopen* to dip]

[2]**dope** *vt* **1** to treat or affect with dope; *esp* to give a narcotic to **2** to add an impurity to (a semiconductor) so as to give the required electrical properties ~*vi* to take dope – **doper** *n*

dopey, dopy /ˈdohpi‖ˈdəʊpɪ/ *adj* **1a** dulled by alcohol or a narcotic **b** stupefied (e g by a drug or sleep) **2** dull, stupid – infml – **dopiness** *n*

doppelgänger /ˈdopl,gengə‖ˈdɒpl,geŋə/, **doppleganger** /-ˌgangə‖-ˌgæŋə/ *n* a ghostly counterpart of a living person [German *doppelgänger*, lit., double goer]

[1]**Doric** /ˈdorik‖ˈdɒrɪk/ *adj* **1** (characteristic) of the ancient Dorians or their language **2** of the oldest and simplest of the 3 Greek orders of architecture

[2]**Doric** *n* **1** a dialect of ancient Greek **2** a broad rustic dialect of English, esp a Scots one

dormant /ˈdawmənt‖ˈdɔːmənt/ *adj* **1** marked by a suspension of activity: e g **1a** temporarily devoid of external activity <*a* ~ *volcano*> **b** temporarily in abeyance <*the law lay* ~ *for several years*> **2** (appearing to be) asleep or inactive, esp throughout winter – **dormancy** *n*

dormer /ˈdawmə‖ˈdɔːmə/ *n* a window set vertically in a structure projecting through a sloping roof

dormitory /ˈdawmət(ə)ri‖ˈdɔːmət(ə)rɪ/ *n* **1** a large room containing a number of beds **2** a residential community from which the inhabitants commute to their places of employment [Latin *dormitorium*, fr *dormire* to sleep]

dormouse /ˈdaw,mows‖ˈdɔː,maʊs/ *n* any of numerous small Old World rodents having a long bushy tail

dorp /dawp‖dɔːp/ *n, SAfr* a village

dorsal /ˈdawsl‖ˈdɔːsl/ *adj* relating to or situated near or on the back or top surface esp of an animal or aircraft or of any of its parts – **dorsally** *adv*

dosage /ˈdohsij‖ˈdəʊsɪdʒ/ *n* **1a** the amount of a dose of medicine **b** the giving of such a dose **2** the presence and relative representation or strength of a factor or agent

dose /dohs‖dəʊs/ *n* **1a** the measured quantity of medicine to be taken at one time **b** the quantity of radiation administered or absorbed **2** a part of an experience to which one is exposed <*a* ~ *of hard work*> **3** an infection with a venereal disease – slang – **dose** *vt*

[2]**dose** *vt* to give a dose, esp of medicine, to

doss /dos‖dɒs/ *n, chiefly Br* **1** a crude or makeshift bed, esp one in a dosshouse **2** a short sleep *USE* slang

doss down *vi, chiefly Br* to sleep or bed down in a makeshift bed – infml

dosser /ˈdosə‖ˈdɒsə/ *n, chiefly Br* a down-and-out, esp one who is forced to sleep in dosshouses

ˈ**doss,house** /-ˌhows‖-ˌhaʊs/ *n, chiefly Br* a

hostel for derelicts

dossier /'dosi·ə, 'dosiay||'dɒsɪə, 'dɒsɪeɪ/ *n* a file of papers containing a detailed report or information [French, bundle of documents labelled on the back, dossier, fr *dos* back, fr Latin *dorsum*]

dost /dust||dʌst/ *archaic pres 2 sing of* DO

[1]**dot** /dot||dɒt/ *n* **1** a small spot; a speck **2a(1)** a small point made with a pointed instrument **a(2)** a small round mark used in spelling or punctuation **b(1)** a point after a note or rest in music indicating augmentation of the time value by one half **b(2)** a point over or under a note indicating that it is to be played staccato **3** a precise point, esp in time <*arrived at 6 on the* ~> **4** a signal (e g a flash or audible tone) of relatively short duration that is one of the 2 fundamental units of Morse code

[2]**dot** *vb* **-tt-** *vt* **1** to mark with a dot **2** to intersperse with dots or objects scattered at random <*boats* ~ting *the lake*> ~*vi* to make a dot

dotage /'dohtij||'dəʊtɪdʒ/ *n* a state or period of senile mental decay resulting in feeblemindedness

dote /doht||dəʊt/ *vi* **1** to exhibit mental decline of or like that of old age **2** to show excessive or foolish fondness – usu + *on* – **doter** *n*, **dotingly** *adv*

doth /duth||dʌθ/ *archaic pres 3 sing of* DO

dottle /'dotl||'dɒtl/ *n* (partially) unburnt tobacco left in the bowl of a pipe

dotty /'doti||'dɒtɪ/ *adj* **1** crazy, mad **2** amiably eccentric or absurd ***USE*** infml – **dottily** *adv*, **dottiness** *n*

[1]**double** /'dubl||'dʌbl/ *adj* **1** twofold, dual **2** consisting of 2, usu combined, similar members or parts <*an egg with a* ~ *yolk*> **3** being twice as great or as many <~ *the number of expected applicants*> **4** marked by duplicity; deceitful **5** folded in 2 **6** of twofold or extra size, strength, or value <*a* ~ *Scotch*> **7** *of a plant or flower* having more than the normal number of petals or ray flowers – **doubleness** *n*

[2]**double** *n* **1** a double amount; *esp* a double measure of spirits **2a** a living person who closely resembles another living person **b** a wraith; a doppelgänger **c(1)** an understudy **c(2)** one who resembles an actor and takes his/her place in scenes calling for special skills **3** a sharp turn or twist **4a** a bet in which the winnings and stake from a first race are bet on a second race **b** two wins in or on horse races, esp in a single day's racing **5** an act of doubling in a card game **6** the outermost narrow ring on a dartboard counting double the stated score; *also* a throw in darts that lands there – **at the double** at a fast rate between running and walking; *specif, of a military order to move* in double time

[3]**double** *adv* **1** to twice the extent or amount **2** two together

[4]**double** *vt* **1a** to increase by adding an equal amount **b** to amount to twice the number of **c** to make a call in bridge that increases the value of tricks won or lost on (an opponent's bid) **2a** to make into 2 thicknesses; fold **b** to clench <~d *his fist*> **c** to cause to stoop or bend over – usu + *up* or *over* **3** to cause (troops) to move in double time **4** to cause (a billiard ball) to rebound ~ *vi* **1a** to become twice as much or as many **b** to double a bid (e g in bridge) **2** to turn back on one's course – usu + *back* **3** to become bent or folded, usu in the middle – usu + *up* or *over* **4** to serve an additional purpose – usu + *as* **5** to hurry along; *esp, of troops* to move in double time **6** *of a billiard ball* to rebound

,double-'barrelled *adj* **1** *of a firearm* having 2 barrels **2** having a double purpose <*asked a* ~ *question*> **3** *of a surname* having 2 parts

,double 'bass *n* the largest instrument in the violin family tuned a fifth below the cello – **double bassist** *n*

,double 'bed *n* a bed for 2 people

,double-'breasted *adj* having a front fastening with one half of the front overlapping the other and usu a double row of buttons and a single row of buttonholes <*a* ~ *coat*>

double check *vb or n* (to make or subject to) a careful check, esp for a second time

,double 'chin *n* a chin with a fleshy fold under it

,double 'cream *n* thick heavy cream that contains 48 per cent butterfat and is suitable for whipping

,double-'cross *vt or n* (to deceive by) an act of betraying or cheating – **double-crosser** *n*

,double-'dealing *adj or n* underhand or deceitful (action) – **double-dealer** *n*

,double-'decker /'dekə||'dekə/ *n* sthg that has 2 decks, levels, or layers; *esp* a bus with seats on 2 floors

,double de'clutch /dee'kluch||diː'klʌtʃ/ *vi, Br* to change gear in a motor vehicle by disengaging the gear twice, first to pass to neutral, then to pass to the desired gear

,double 'dutch *n, often cap 2nd D* unintelligible or nonsensical speech or writing; gibberish – infml

,double-'edged *adj* having 2 purposes or possible interpretations; *specif, of a remark* seeming innocent, but capable of a malicious interpretation

double entendre /,doohbl on'ton(h)dr||,duːbl ɒn'tɒndr, ɒn'tɑ̃dr (*Fr* dubl ɑ̃tɑ̃ːdr)/ *n, pl* **double entendres** /~/ an ambiguous word or expression one of whose meanings is usu risqué [obs French, lit., double meaning]

,double 'first *n, Br* first-class honours gained in 2 university examinations or subjects

,double 'glazing *n* a system of glazing in which 2 panes of glass are separated by an air space providing heat and sound insulation; *also* the 2 panes of glass so used – **double-glaze** *vt*

,double-'jointed *adj* having or being a joint that permits an exceptional degree of flexibility of the parts joined

,double-'park *vi* to park beside a row of vehicles already parked parallel to the kerb

,double-'quick *adj* very quick – **double-quick** *adv*

doubles /'dublz||'dʌblz/ *n, pl* **doubles** a game between 2 pairs of players

double stopping *n* the simultaneous playing of 2 strings of a bowed instrument (e g a violin)

doublet /'dublit||'dʌblɪt/ *n* **1** a man's

close-fitting jacket, with or without sleeves, worn in Europe, esp in the 15th to 17th c **2** either of a pair; *specif* either of 2 words (e g *guard* and *ward*) in a language having the same derivation but a different meaning

ˈdouble ˌtake *n* a delayed reaction to a surprising or significant situation – esp in *do a double take*

ˈdouble-ˌtalk *n* involved and often deliberately ambiguous language – **double-talk** *vi*, **double-talker** *n*

ˈdoubleˌthink /-ˌthingk‖-ˌθɪŋk/ *n* a simultaneous belief in 2 contradictory ideas

ˌdouble ˈtime *n* **1** a rate of marching of twice the number of steps per minute as the normal slow rate **2** payment of a worker at twice his/her regular wage rate

double up *vi* to share accommodation designed for one

doubloon /dubˈloohn‖dʌbˈluːn/ *n* a former gold coin of Spain and Spanish America

doubly /ˈdubli‖ˈdʌblɪ/ *adv* **1** to twice the degree < ~ *pleased*> **2** in 2 ways

[1]**doubt** /dowt‖daʊt/ *vt* **1** to be in doubt about <*he* ~s *everyone's word*> **2a** to lack confidence in; distrust **b** to consider unlikely ~*vi* to be uncertain – **doubtable** *adj*, **doubter** *n*, **doubtingly** *adv*

[2]**doubt** *n* **1** (a state of) uncertainty of belief or opinion **2** a lack of confidence; distrust **3** an inclination not to believe or accept; a reservation – **in doubt** uncertain – **no doubt** doubtless

ˈdoubtful /-f(ə)l‖-f(ə)l/ *adj* **1** causing doubt; open to question **2a** lacking a definite opinion; hesitant **b** uncertain in outcome; not settled **3** of questionable worth, honesty, or validity – **doubtfully** *adv*, **doubtfulness** *n*

ˌdoubting ˈThomas /ˈtoməs‖ˈtɒməs/ *n* a habitually doubtful person [*Thomas*, apostle of Jesus who doubted Jesus' resurrection until he had proof of it (John 20:24-29)]

ˈdoubtless /-lis‖-lɪs/ *adv* **1** without doubt **2** probably

douche /doohsh‖duːʃ/ *n* (a device for giving) a jet or current of fluid, directed against a part or into a cavity of the body, esp the vagina – **douche** *vb*

dough /doh‖dəʊ/ *n* **1** a mixture that consists essentially of flour or meal and milk, water, or another liquid and is stiff enough to knead or roll **2** money – slang – **doughlike** *adj*

doughnut /ˈdohˌnut‖ˈdəʊˌnʌt/ *n* a small round or ring-shaped cake that is often made with a yeast dough, filled with jam, and deep-fried

doughty /ˈdowti‖ˈdaʊtɪ/ *adj* valiant, bold – poetic – **doughtily** *adv*, **doughtiness** *n*

doughy /ˈdoh·i‖ˈdəʊɪ/ *adj* unhealthily pale; pasty

do up *vt* **1** to repair, restore <do up *old furniture*> **2** to wrap up <do up *a parcel*> **3** to fasten (clothing or its fastenings) together <*she* did *her blouse* up> **4** to make more beautiful or attractive <*she's* done *herself* up *for the party*> – infml

dour /dooə, dowə‖dʊə, daʊə/ *adj* **1** stern, harsh **2** gloomy, sullen – **dourly** *adv*, **dourness** *n*

[1]**douse, dowse** /dows‖daʊs/ *vt* to take (a sail) in or down

[2]**douse, dowse** *vt* **1** to plunge into or drench with water **2** to extinguish < ~ *the lights*> – **douser** *n*

[1]**dove** /duv‖dʌv/ *n* **1** any of various (smaller and slenderer) types of pigeon **2** an advocate of negotiation and compromise; *esp* an opponent of war – usu contrasted with *hawk* – **dovish** *adj*, **dovishness** *n*

[2]**dove** /dohv‖dəʊv/ *NAm past of* DIVE

dovecot, dovecote /ˈduvˌkot‖ˈdʌvˌkɒt/ *n* a small compartmented raised house or box for domestic pigeons

[1]**dovetail** /ˈduvˌtayl‖ˈdʌvˌteɪl/ *n* a tenon like a dove's tail and the mortise into which it fits to form a joint

[2]**dovetail** *vb* **1** to join (as if) by means of dovetails **2** to fit skilfully together to form a whole

dowager /ˈdowəjə‖ˈdaʊədʒə/ *n* **1** a widow holding property or a title received from her deceased husband **2** a dignified elderly woman

dowdy /ˈdowdi‖ˈdaʊdɪ/ *adj* **1** not neat or smart in appearance **2** old-fashioned, frumpy – **dowdily** *adv*, **dowdiness** *n*, **dowdyish** *adj*

[1]**dowel** /ˈdowəl‖ˈdaʊəl/ *n* a usu metal or wooden pin fitting into holes in adjacent pieces to preserve their relative positions; *also* rods of wood or metal for sawing into such pins

[2]**dowel** *vt* **-ll-** (*NAm* **-l-**, **-ll-**) to fasten by dowels

dower /ˈdowə‖ˈdaʊə/ *n* a widow's legal share during her life of her deceased husband's property – no longer used technically

[1]**down** /down‖daʊn/ *n* (a region of) undulating treeless usu chalk uplands, esp in S England – usu pl with sing. meaning

[2]**down** *adv* **1a** at or towards a relatively low level < ~ *into the cellar*> **b** downwards from the surface of the earth or water **c** below the horizon **d** downstream **e** in or into a lying or sitting position <*lie* ~ > **f** to or on the ground, surface, or bottom <*house burnt* ~ > **g** so as to conceal a particular surface <*turned it face* ~ > **h** downstairs **2** ON THE SPOT 2; *esp* as an initial payment <*paid £10* ~ > **3a(1)** in or into a relatively low condition or status <*family has come* ~ *in the world*> – sometimes used interjectionally to express opposition < ~ *with the oppressors!*> **a(2)** to prison – often + *go* or *send* **b(1)** in or into a state of relatively low intensity or activity <*turn the radio* ~ > **b(2)** into silence <*shouted him* ~ > **b(3)** into a slower pace or lower gear <*changed* ~ *into second*> **c** lower in amount, price, figure, or rank <*prices are coming* ~ > **d** behind an opponent <*we're 3 points* ~ > **4a** so as to be known, recognized, or recorded, esp on paper <*scribbled it* ~ > **b** so as to be firmly held in position <*stick* ~ *the flap of the envelope*> **c** to the moment of catching or discovering <*track the criminal* ~ > **5** in a direction conventionally the opposite of up: e g **5a** to leeward **b** in or towards the south **c** *chiefly Br* away from the capital of a country or from a university city **d** to or at the front of a theatrical stage **6** DOWNWARDS 3, 4 <*jewels handed* ~ *in the family*> **7a** to a concentrated state <*got his report* ~ *to 3 pages*> **b** so as to be flattened, reduced, eroded, or diluted <*water* ~ *the gin*> **c** completely from top to bottom

[3]**down** *adj* **1** directed or going downwards <*the ~ escalator*> **2a** depressed, dejected **b** ill <*~ with flu*> **3** having been finished or dealt with <*eight ~ and two to go*> **4** with the rudder to windward – used with reference to a ship's helm **5** *chiefly Br* bound in a direction regarded as down; *esp* travelling away from a large town, esp London

[4]**down** *prep* **1a** down along, round, through, towards, in, into, or on **b** at the bottom of <*the bathroom is ~ those stairs*> **2** *Br* down to; to <*going ~ the shops*> – nonstandard

[5]**down** *n* a grudge, prejudice – often in *have a down on*

[6]**down** *vt* **1** to cause to go or come down **2** to drink down; swallow quickly – infml **3** to defeat

[7]**down** *n* a covering of soft fluffy feathers

ˌdown-and-ˈout *n or adj* (sby) destitute or impoverished

[1]**ˈdownˌbeat** /-ˌbeet‖-ˌbiːt/ *n* the principally accented (e g the first) note of a bar of music

[2]**downbeat** *adj* **1** pessimistic, gloomy **2** relaxed, informal

ˈdownˌcast /-ˌkahst‖-ˌkɑːst/ *adj* **1** dejected, depressed **2** directed downwards <*with ~ eyes*>

ˈdownˌdraught /-ˌdrahft‖-ˌdrɑːft/ *n* a downward movement of gas, esp air (e g in a chimney)

downer /ˈdownə‖ˈdaʊnə/ *n* a depressing experience or situation – infml

ˈdownˌfall /-ˌfawl‖-ˌfɔːl/ *n* **1** (a cause of) a sudden fall (e g from high rank or power) **2** an often heavy fall of rain or esp snow – **downfallen** *adj*

ˌdownˈgrade /-ˈgrayd‖-ˈgreɪd/ *vt* **1** to lower in rank, value, or importance **2** to alter the status of (a job) so as to lower the rate of pay

ˌdownˈhearted /-ˈhahtid‖-ˈhɑːtɪd/ *adj* downcast, dejected – **downheartedly** *adv*, **downheartedness** *n*

[1]**ˈdownˌhill** /-ˌhil‖-ˌhɪl/ *n* a skiing race downhill against time

[2]**ˌdownˈhill** *adv* **1** towards the bottom of a hill **2** towards a lower or inferior state or level

[3]**ˌdownˈhill** *adj* sloping downhill

download *vb* to transfer (programs or data) from one computer to another

ˌdown-ˈmarket *adj* being or using goods designed to appeal to the lower social end of a market – **down-market** *adv*

ˈdown ˌpayment *n* a deposit paid at the time of purchase or delivery

ˈdownˌpour /-ˌpaw‖-ˌpɔː/ *n* a heavy fall of rain

[1]**ˈdownˌright** /-ˌriet‖-ˌraɪt/ *adv* thoroughly, outright <*~ mean*>

[2]**downright** *adj* **1** absolute, thorough <*a ~ lie*> **2** plain, blunt <*a ~ man*> – **downrightly** *adv*, **downrightness** *n*

ˈDown's ˌsyndrome /downz‖daʊnz/ *n* a form of congenital mental deficiency in which a child is born with slanting eyes, a broad short skull, and broad hands with short fingers; mongolism [J L H *Down* (1828-96), English physician]

ˌdownˈstage /-ˈstayj‖-ˈsteɪdʒ/ *adv or adj* at the front of a theatrical stage; *also* towards the audience or camera

[1]**ˌdownˈstairs** /-ˈsteəz‖-ˈsteəz/ *adv* down the stairs; on or to a lower floor

[2]**downstairs** *adj* situated on the main, lower, or ground floor of a building

[3]**downstairs** *n, pl* **downstairs** the lower floor of a building

ˌdownˈstream /-ˈstreem‖-ˈstriːm/ *adv or adj* in the direction of the flow of a stream

ˌdown-to-ˈearth *adj* practical, realistic

ˈdownˌtown /-ˌtown‖-ˌtaʊn/ *adv, adj, or n, chiefly NAm* (to, towards, or in) the lower part or main business district of a town or city

ˈdownˌtrodden /-ˌtrod(ə)n‖-ˌtrɒd(ə)n/ *adj* oppressed by those in power

downward /ˈdownwood‖ˈdaʊnwʊd/ *adj* **1** moving or extending downwards <*the ~ path*> **2** descending to a lower pitch **3** descending from a head, origin, or source – **downwardly** *adv*, **downwardness** *n*

ˈdownwards /-woodz‖-wʊdz/ *adv* **1a** from a higher to a lower place or level; in the opposite direction from up <*sun sank ~*> **b** downstream **c** so as to conceal a particular surface <*turned it face ~*> **2a** from a higher to a lower condition **b** going down in amount, price, figure, or rank <*from the fourth form ~*> **3** from an earlier time **4** from an ancestor or predecessor

ˌdownˈwind /-ˈwind‖-ˈwɪnd/ *adv or adj* in the direction that the wind is blowing

downy /ˈdowni‖ˈdaʊnɪ/ *adj* **1** resembling or covered in down **2** made of down

dowry /ˈdowri‖ˈdaʊrɪ/ *n* the money, goods, or estate that a woman brings to her husband in marriage

[1]**dowse** /dows‖daʊs/ *vt* to douse

[2]**dowse** /dowz‖daʊz/ *vi* to search for hidden water or minerals with a divining rod

ˈdowsing ˌrod /ˈdowzing‖ˈdaʊzɪŋ/ *n* a divining rod

doxology /dokˈsoləji‖dɒkˈsɒlədʒɪ/ *n* a liturgical expression of praise to God

doyen /ˈdoyən ‖ˈdɔɪən (*Fr* dwajɛ̃)/, *fem* **doyenne** /doyˈen ‖dɔɪˈen (*Fr* dwajɛn)/ *n* the senior or most experienced member of a body or group [French, fr Late Latin *decanus* dean – see [2]DEAN]

doyley, doyly /ˈdoyli‖ˈdɔɪlɪ/ *n* a doily

doze /dohz‖dəʊz/ *vi* **1** to sleep lightly **2** to fall into a light sleep – usu + *off* – **doze** *n*, **dozer** *n*

doze away *vt* to pass (time) drowsily

dozen /ˈduzən‖ˈdʌzən/ *n, pl* **dozens, dozen** **1** a group of 12 **2** an indefinitely large number – usu pl with sing. meaning [Old French *dozaine*, fr *doze* twelve, fr Latin *duodecim*, fr *duo* two + *decem* ten] – **dozen** *adj*, **dozenth** *adj*

dozy /ˈdohzi‖ˈdəʊzɪ/ *adj* **1** drowsy, sleepy **2** *chiefly Br* stupid and slow-witted – infml – **doziness** *n*

[1]**drab** /drab‖dræb/ *adj* **-bb-** **1** of a dull brown colour **2** dull, cheerless – **drably** *adv*, **drabness** *n*

[2]**drab** *n* – see DRIBS AND DRABS

drachm /dram‖dræm/ *n* **1** a drachma **2** a unit of weight equal to $^1/_8$oz apothecary (about 3.89g)

drachma /ˈdrakmə‖ˈdrækmə/ *n, pl* **drachmas, drachmae** /-mi‖-mɪ/, **drachmai** /-mie‖-maɪ/ **1**

any of various ancient Greek units of weight **2a** an ancient Greek silver coin **b** the basic money unit of modern Greece

draconian /dray'kohnyən, -ni·ən, drə-‖dreɪ-'kəʊnjən, -nɪən, drə-/, **draconic** /dray'konik, drə-‖dreɪ'kɒnɪk, drə-/ *adj, often cap, esp of a law* extremely severe; drastic [*Draco* (fl 621BC), Athenian lawgiver]

[1]**draft** /drahft‖drɑːft/ *n* **1** the act, result, or plan of drawing out or sketching: e g **1a** a construction plan **b** a preliminary sketch, outline, or version <*a rough ~ of a book*> **2a** a group of individuals selected for a particular job **b** (the group of individuals resulting from) the selecting of certain animals from a herd or flock **3a** an order for the payment of money drawn by one person or bank on another **b** (an instance of) drawing from or making demands on sthg **4** *chiefly NAm* conscription – usu + *the* **5** *NAm* a draught

[2]**draft** *adj* **1** *esp of livestock* chosen from a group **2** *NAm* draught

[3]**draft** *vt* **1** to draw the preliminary sketch, version, or plan of **2** *NAm* to conscript for military service – **draftable** *adj*, **draftee** *n*, **drafter** *n*

draftsman /'drahftsmən‖'drɑːftsmən/ *n* sby who draws up legal documents or other writings

[1]**drag** /drag‖dræg/ *n* **1** a device for dragging under water to search for objects **2a** sthg that retards motion, action, or progress **b** the retarding force acting on a body (e g an aircraft) moving through a fluid (e g air), parallel and opposite to the direction of motion **c** a burden, encumbrance **3** an object drawn over the ground to leave a scented trail (e g for dogs to follow) **4a** a drawing along or over a surface with effort or pressure **b** motion effected with slowness or difficulty **c** a drawing into the mouth of pipe, cigarette, or cigar smoke – infml **5a** woman's clothing worn by a man – slang; often in *in drag* **b** clothing – slang **6** a dull or boring person or experience – slang

[2]**drag** *vb* **-gg-** *vt* **1a** to draw slowly or heavily; haul **b** to cause to move with painful or undue slowness or difficulty **2a** to search (a body of water) with a drag **b** to catch with a dragnet or trawl **3** to bring by force or compulsion – infml <*had to ~ her husband to the opera*> ~ *vi* **1** to hang or lag behind **2** to trail along on the ground **3** to move or proceed laboriously or tediously – infml **4** to draw tobacco smoke into the mouth – usu + *on* <*~ on a cigarette*>; infml – **draggingly** *adv* – **drag one's feet/heels** to act in a deliberately slow, dilatory, or ineffective manner

draggle /'dragl‖'drægl/ *vt* to make wet and dirty ~ *vi* **1** to trail on the ground **2** to straggle

'drag,net /-,net‖-,net/ *n* **1** a net drawn along the bottom of a body of water or the ground to catch fish or small game **2** a network of measures for apprehension (e g of criminals)

dragon /'dragən‖'drægən/ *n* **1** a mythical winged and clawed monster, often breathing fire **2** a fierce, combative, or very strict person – **dragonish** *adj*

'dragon,fly /-,flie‖-,flaɪ/ *n* any of a suborder of long slender-bodied often brightly coloured insects that have a fine network of veins in their wings and often live near water

[1]**dragoon** /drə'goohn‖drə'guːn/ *n* a member of a European military unit formerly composed of mounted infantrymen armed with carbines

[2]**dragoon** *vt* **1** to reduce to subjection by harsh use of troops **2** to (attempt to) force into submission by persecution

[1]**drain** /drayn‖dreɪn/ *vt* **1a** to draw off (liquid) gradually or completely **b** to exhaust physically or emotionally **2a** to make gradually dry <*~ a swamp*> **b** to carry away the surface water of **c** to deplete or empty (as if) by drawing off gradually <*war that ~s a nation of youth and wealth*> **d** to empty by drinking the contents of <*~ed his glass*> ~ *vi* **1** to flow off gradually **2** to become gradually dry – **drainer** *n*

[2]**drain** *n* **1** a means (e g a pipe) by which usu liquid matter is drained away **2** a gradual outflow or withdrawal **3** sthg that causes depletion; a burden – **down the drain** being used wastefully or brought to nothing

drainage /'draynij‖'dreɪnɪdʒ/ *n* **1a** draining **b** sthg drained off **2** a system of drains

'draining ,board /'drayning‖'dreɪnɪŋ/ *n, Br* a usu grooved and often slightly sloping surface at the side of a sink unit on which washed dishes are placed to drain

'drain,pipe /-,piep‖-,paɪp/ *n* a pipe that carries waste, liquid sewage, excess water, etc away from a building

,drainpipe 'trousers, **'drain,pipes** *n pl* tight trousers with narrow legs

[1]**drake** /drayk‖dreɪk/ *n* a mayfly; *esp* an artificial one used as bait in angling

[2]**drake** *n* a male duck

dram /dram‖dræm/ *n* **1** a unit of mass equal to 1/16oz avoirdupois (about 1.77g) **2** *chiefly Scot* a tot of spirits, usu whisky

drama /'drahmə‖'drɑːmə/ *n* **1** a composition in verse or prose intended to portray life or character or to tell a story through action and dialogue; *specif* a play **2** dramatic art, literature, or affairs **3** a situation or set of events having the qualities of a drama

dramatic /drə'matik‖drə'mætɪk/ *adj* **1** of drama **2a** suitable to or characteristic of drama; vivid **b** striking in appearance or effect – **dramatically** *adv*

dra,matic 'irony *n* incongruity between a situation developed in a play and the accompanying words or actions that is understood by the audience but not by the characters

dra'matics *n pl* **1** *sing or pl in constr* the study or practice of theatrical arts (e g acting and stagecraft) **2** dramatic behaviour; *esp* an exaggerated display of emotion

dramatis personae /,drahmətis puh'sohnie‖,drɑːmətɪs pɜː'səʊnaɪ/ *n pl* (a list of) the characters or actors in a play

dramatist /'drahmətist, 'dra-‖'drɑːmətɪst, 'dræ-/ *n* a playwright

dramat·ize, -ise /'drahmətiez, dra-‖'drɑːmətaɪz, dræ-/ *vt* **1** to adapt (e g a novel) for theatrical presentation **2** to present in a dramatic manner ~ *vi* **1** to be suitable for dramatization **2** to behave dramatically – **dramatizable** *adj*, **dramatization** *n*

drank /drangk‖dræŋk/ *past of* DRINK

[1]**drape** /drayp‖dreɪp/ *vt* **1** to cover or decorate (as if) with folds of cloth **2** to hang or stretch loosely or carelessly <~d *his legs over the chair*> **3** to arrange in flowing lines or folds – **drapable** *also* **drapeable** *adj*, **drapability** *also* **drapeability** *n*

[2]**drape** *n* a piece of drapery; *esp, chiefly NAm* a curtain

draper /ˈdraypə‖ˈdreɪpə/ *n, chiefly Br* a dealer in cloth and sometimes also in clothing, haberdashery, and soft furnishings

drapery /ˈdrayp(ə)ri‖ˈdreɪp(ə)rɪ/ *n* **1a** (a piece of) cloth or clothing arranged or hung gracefully, esp in loose folds **b** cloth or textile fabrics used esp for clothing or soft furnishings; *also, NAm* hangings of heavy fabric used as a curtain **2** the draping or arranging of materials **3a** *Br* the trade of a draper **b** the goods sold by a draper

drastic /ˈdrastik‖ˈdræstɪk/ *adj* **1** acting rapidly or violently <*a* ~ *purgative*> **2** radical in effect or action; severe – **drastically** *adv*

drat /drat‖dræt/ *vt* **-tt-** to damn – euph; used as a mild oath

[1]**draught**, *NAm chiefly* **draft** /drahft‖drɑːft/ *n* **1** (the quantity of fish taken by) the act of drawing a net **2** a team of animals together with what they draw **3** the act or an instance of drinking; *also* the portion drunk in such an act **4** the act of drawing (e g from a cask); *also* a quantity of liquid so drawn **5** the depth of water a ship requires to float in, esp when loaded **6** a current of air in a closed-in space – **on draught** *of beer or cider* ready to be served from the cask or barrel with or without the use of added gas in serving

[2]**draught**, *NAm chiefly* **draft** *adj* **1** used for drawing loads <~ *oxen*> **2** served from the barrel or cask <~ *beer*>

ˈ**draught,board** /-ˌbawd‖-ˌbɔːd/ *n* a chessboard

draughts /drahfts‖drɑːfts/ *n pl but sing or pl in constr, Br* a game for 2 players each of whom moves his/her usu 12 draughtsmen according to fixed rules across a chessboard usu using only the black squares

draughtsman /ˈdrahftsmən‖ˈdrɑːftsmən/ *n* **1a** an artist skilled in drawing **b** *fem* **draughtswoman** sby who draws plans and sketches (e g of machinery or structures) **2** *Br* a disc-shaped piece used in draughts

draughty /ˈdrahfti‖ˈdrɑːftɪ/ *adj* having a cold draught blowing through

[1]**draw** /draw‖drɔː/ *vb* **drew** /drooh‖druː/; **drawn** /drawn‖drɔːn/ *vt* **1** to pull, haul **2** to cause to go in a certain direction <drew *him aside*> **3a** to attract <*honey* ~s *flies*> **b** to bring in, gather, or derive from a specified source <drew *inspiration from his teacher*> **c** to bring on oneself; provoke <drew *enemy fire*> **d** to bring out by way of response; elicit <drew *cheers from the audience*> **4** to inhale <drew *a deep breath*> **5a** to bring or pull out, esp with effort <~ *a tooth*> **b** to extract the essence from <~ *tea*> **c** to disembowel <*pluck and* ~ *a goose*> **d** to cause (blood) to flow **6** to require (a specified depth) to float in **7a** to accumulate, gain <~ing *interest*> **b** to take (money) from a place of deposit – often + *out* **c** to use in making a cash demand <~ing *a cheque on his account*> **d** to receive regularly, esp from a particular source <~ *a salary*> **8a** to take (cards) from a dealer or pack **b** to receive or take at random <drew *a winning number*> **9** to bend (a bow) by pulling back the string **10** to strike (a ball) so as to impart a curved motion or backspin **11** to leave undecided or have equal scores in (a contest) **12** to produce a likeness of (e g by making lines on a surface); portray, delineate **13** to formulate or arrive at by reasoning <~ *a conclusion*> **14** to pull together and close (e g curtains) **15** to stretch or shape (esp metal) by pulling through dies; *also* to produce (e g a wire) thus **16** to drive game out of ~ *vi* **1** to come or go steadily or gradually <*night* ~s *near*> **2** to advance as far as a specified position <drew *level*> **3a** to pull back a bowstring **b** to bring out a weapon **4a** to produce or allow a draught <*the chimney* ~s *well*> **b** *of a sail* to swell out in a wind **5** to steep, infuse <*give the tea time to* ~> **6** to sketch **7** to finish a competition or contest without either side winning **8a** to make a written demand for payment of money on deposit **b** to obtain resources (e g of information) <~ing *from a common fund of knowledge*> **9** *chiefly NAm* to suck in sthg, esp tobacco smoke – usu + *on* – **draw a blank** to fail to gain the desired object (e g information sought) – **draw lots** to decide an issue by lottery in which objects of unequal length or with different markings are used – **draw on/upon** to use as source of supply – **draw rein** to bring a horse to a stop while riding – **draw the/a line 1** to fix an arbitrary boundary between things that tend to merge **2** to fix a boundary excluding what one will not tolerate or engage in – usu + *at*

[2]**draw** *n* **1a** a sucking pull on sthg held between the lips <*took a* ~ *on his pipe*> **b** *the* removing of a handgun from its holster in order to shoot **2** a drawing of lots; a raffle **3** a contest left undecided; a tie **4** sthg that draws public attention or patronage **5** the usu random assignment of starting positions in a competition, esp a competitive sport **6** *NAm* the movable part of a drawbridge

draw away *vi* to move ahead (e g of an opponent in a race) gradually

ˈ**draw,back** /-ˌbak‖-ˌbæk/ *n* an objectionable feature; a disadvantage

draw back *vi* to avoid an issue or commitment; retreat

ˈ**draw,bridge** /-ˌbrij‖-ˌbrɪdʒ/ *n* a bridge made to be raised up, let down, or drawn aside so as to permit or hinder passage

drawer /*sense 1* ˈdraw·ə‖ˈdrɔːə; *senses 2, 3* draw‖drɔː/ *n* **1** one who draws a bill of exchange or order for payment or makes a promissory note **2** an open-topped box in a piece of furniture which to open and close slides back and forth in its frame **3** *pl* an undergarment for the lower body – now usu humor

draw in *vt* **1** to cause or entice to enter or participate **2** to sketch roughly <drawing in *the first outlines*> ~ *vi* **1** *of a train* to come into a station **2** *of successive days* to grow shorter (e g in winter)

drawing /ˈdraw·ing‖ˈdrɔːɪŋ/ *n* **1** the art or technique of representing an object, figure, or plan by means of lines **2** sthg drawn or subject to drawing: e g **2a** an amount drawn from a fund **b** a representation formed by drawing

ˈ**drawing ˌboard** *n* **1** a board to which paper is attached for drawing on **2** a planning stage

ˈ**drawing ˌpin** *n, Br* a pin with a broad flat head for fastening esp sheets of paper to boards

ˈ**drawing ˌroom** *n* **1** a formal reception room **2** LIVING ROOM – fml

[1]**drawl** /drawl‖drɔːl/ *vb* to speak or utter slowly and often affectedly, with vowels greatly prolonged – **drawler** *n*, **drawlingly** *adv*

[2]**drawl** *n* a drawling manner of speaking – **drawly** *adj*

draw off *vt* to remove (liquid) ~*vi of troops* to move apart (and form new groups)

draw on *vi* to approach <*night* draws on> ~ *vt* **1** to cause; BRING ON 1 **2** to put on <*she* drew on *her gloves*>

draw out *vt* **1** to remove, extract **2** to extend beyond a minimum in time; prolong **3** to cause to speak freely

ˈ**drawˌstring** /-ˌstring‖-ˌstrɪŋ/ *n* a string or tape threaded through fabric, which when pulled closes an opening (e g of a bag) or gathers material (e g of curtains or clothes)

draw up *vt* **1** to bring (e g troops) into array **2** DRAFT 1 **3** to straighten (oneself) to an erect posture, esp as an assertion of dignity or resentment **4** to bring to a halt ~*vi* to come to a halt

[1]**dray** /dray‖dreɪ/ *n* a strong low cart or wagon without sides, used esp by brewers

[2]**dray** a drey

[1]**dread** /dred‖dred/ *vt* **1** to fear greatly **2** to be extremely apprehensive about

[2]**dread** *n* (the object of) great fear, uneasiness, or apprehension

[3]**dread** *adj* causing or inspiring dread

ˈ**dreadful** /-f(ə)l‖-f(ə)l/ *adj* **1** inspiring dread; causing great and oppressive fear **2a** extremely unpleasant or shocking **b** very disagreeable (e g through dullness or poor quality) – **dreadfully** *adv*, **dreadfulness** *n*

dreadlocks /ˈdredˌloks‖ˈdredˌlɒks/ *n pl* long matted locks of hair, often dyed with henna, that are worn by male Rastafarians

dreadnought /ˈdredˌnawt‖ˈdredˌnɔːt/ *n* a battleship whose main armament consists of big guns of the same calibre

[1]**dream** /dreem‖driːm/ *n* **1** a series of thoughts, images, or emotions occurring during sleep **2** a daydream, reverie <*walked round in a* ~ *all day*> **3** sthg notable for its beauty, excellence, or enjoyable quality <*the new car goes like a* ~> **4** a strongly desired goal; an ambition <*his* ~ *of becoming president*>; *also* a realization of an ambition – often used attributively <*a* ~ *house*> – **dreamless** *adj*, **dreamlessly** *adv*, **dreamlessness** *n*, **dreamlike** *adj*

[2]**dream** *vb* **dreamed** /dreemd, dremt‖driːmd, dremt/, **dreamt** /dremt‖dremt/ *vi* **1** to have a dream **2** to indulge in daydreams or fantasies ~ *vt* **1** to have a dream of **2** to consider as a possibility; imagine **3** to pass (time) in reverie or inaction – usu + *away* – **dreamer** *n* – **dream of** to consider even the possibility of – in neg constructions <*wouldn't* dream *of disturbing you*>

ˈ**dreamˌland** /-ˌland‖-ˌlænd/ *n* an unreal delightful region existing only in imagination or in fantasy; NEVER-NEVER LAND

dream up *vt* to devise, invent – infml

dreamy /ˈdreemi‖ˈdriːmɪ/ *adj* **1** pleasantly abstracted from immediate reality **2** given to dreaming or fantasy <*a* ~ *child*> **3a** suggestive of a dream in vague or visionary quality **b** delightful, pleasing; *esp, of a man* sexually attractive – infml – **dreamily** *adv*, **dreaminess** *n*

drear /driə‖drɪə/ *adj* dreary – poetic

dreary /ˈdriəri‖ˈdrɪərɪ/ *adj* causing feelings of cheerlessness or gloom; dull [Old English *drēorig* sad, bloody, fr *drēor* gore] – **drearily** *adv*, **dreariness** *n*

[1]**dredge** /drej‖dredʒ/ *n* **1** an oblong frame with an attached net for gathering fish, shellfish, etc from the bottom of the sea, a river, etc **2** a machine for removing earth, mud, etc usu by buckets on an endless chain or a suction tube

[2]**dredge** *vt* **1a** to dig, gather, or pull out with a dredge – often + *up* or *out* **b** to deepen (e g a waterway) with a dredging machine **2** to bring to light by thorough searching – usu + *up* <dredging *up memories*>; infml ~*vi* to use a dredge

[3]**dredge** *vt* to coat (e g food) by sprinkling (e g with flour) – **dredger** *n*

dredger /ˈdrejə‖ˈdredʒə/ *n* a barge with an apparatus for dredging harbours, waterways, etc

dreg /dreg‖dreg/ *n* **1** sediment; lees **2** the most undesirable part <*the* ~s *of society*> *USE* usu pl with sing. meaning

[1]**drench** /drench‖drentʃ/ *n* a poisonous or medicinal drink, esp put down the throat of an animal

[2]**drench** *vt* **1** to administer a drench to (an animal) **2** to make thoroughly wet (e g with falling water or by immersion); saturate

[1]**dress** /dres‖dres/ *vt* **1** to arrange (e g troops) in the proper alignment **2a** to put clothes on **b** to provide with clothing **3** to add decorative details or accessories to; embellish <~ *a Christmas tree*> **4** to prepare for use or service; *esp* to prepare (e g a chicken) for cooking or eating **5a** to apply dressings or medicaments to (e g a wound) **b(1)** to arrange (the hair) **b(2)** to groom and curry (an animal) **c** to kill and prepare for market **d** to cultivate, esp by applying manure or fertilizer **e** to finish the surface of (e g timber, stone, or textiles) **f** to arrange goods on a display in (e g a shop window) ~ *vi* **1a** to put on clothing **b** to put on or wear formal, elaborate, or fancy clothes **2** to align oneself properly in a line

[2]**dress** *n* **1** utilitarian or ornamental covering for the human body; *esp* clothing suitable for a particular purpose or occasion **2** a 1-piece outer garment including both top and skirt usu for a woman or girl **3** covering, adornment, or appearance appropriate or peculiar to a specified time <*18th-century* ~>

[3]**dress** *adj* of, being, or suitable for an occasion requiring or permitting formal dress <*a* ~ *affair*>

dressage /ˈdresahzh, -ˈ-‖ˈdresɑːʒ, -ˈ-/ *n* the

execution by a trained horse of precise movements in response to its rider

ˈdress ˌcircle *n* the first or lowest curved tier of seats in a theatre

dress down *vt* to reprove severely – **dressing down** *n*

[1]**dresser** /ˈdresə‖ˈdresə/ *n* **1** a piece of kitchen furniture resembling a sideboard with a high back and having compartments and shelves for holding dishes and cooking utensils **2** *chiefly NAm* a chest of drawers or bureau with a mirror

[2]**dresser** *n* a person who looks after stage costumes and helps actors to dress

dressing /ˈdresing‖ˈdresɪŋ/ *n* **1** a seasoning, sauce, or stuffing **2** material applied to cover a wound, sore, etc **3** manure or compost to improve the growth of plants

ˈdressing ˌgown *n* a loose robe worn esp over nightclothes or when not fully dressed

ˈdressing ˌtable *n* a table usu fitted with drawers and a mirror for use while dressing and grooming oneself

ˈdressˌmaker /-ˌmaykə‖-ˌmeɪkə/ *n* sby who makes dresses – **dressmaking** *n*

ˈdress reˌhearsal *n* **1** a full rehearsal of a play in costume and with stage props shortly before the first performance **2** a full-scale practice; DRY RUN 2

dress up *vt* **1a(1)** to clothe in best or formal clothes **a(2)** to make suitable for a formal occasion (e g by adding accessories) <dressing up *a smock with a gilt belt and scarves*> **b** to dress in clothes suited to a particular assumed role **2** to present or cause to appear in a certain light (e g by distortion or exaggeration) ~*vi* to get dressed up

dressy /ˈdresi‖ˈdresɪ/ *adj* **1** *of a person* showy in dress **2** *of clothes* stylish, smart **3** overly elaborate in appearance – **dressiness** *n*

drew /drooh‖druː/ *past of* DRAW

drey, dray /dray‖dreɪ/ *n* a squirrel's nest

[1]**dribble** /ˈdribl‖ˈdrɪbl/ *vi* **1** to fall or flow in drops or in a thin intermittent stream; trickle **2** to let saliva trickle from the mouth; drool **3** to come or issue in piecemeal or disconnected fashion **4a** to dribble a ball or puck **b** to proceed by dribbling **c** *of a ball* to move with short bounces ~*vt* to propel (a ball or puck) by successive slight taps or bounces with hand, foot, or stick – **dribbler** *n*

[2]**dribble** *n* **1** a small trickling stream or flow **2** a tiny or insignificant bit or quantity **3** an act or instance of dribbling

dribs and drabs /ˌdribz ən ˈdrabz‖ˌdrɪbz ən ˈdræbz/ *n pl* small usu scattered amounts – infml

ˌdried-ˈup *adj* wizened, shrivelled

drier *also* **dryer** /ˈdrie·ə‖ˈdraɪə/ *n* **1** a substance that accelerates drying (e g of oils and printing inks) **2** any of various machines for drying sthg (e g the hair or clothes)

[1]**drift** /drift‖drɪft/ *n* sthg driven, propelled, or urged along or drawn (as if) by a natural agency: e g **1a** a mass of sand, snow, etc deposited (as if) by wind or water **b** rock debris deposited by natural wind, water, etc; *specif* a deposit of clay, sand, gravel, and boulders transported by (running water from) a glacier **2** a general underlying tendency or meaning, esp of what is spoken or written **3** a tool for ramming down or driving sthg, usu into or out of a hole **4** the motion or action of drifting: e g **4a** a ship's deviation from its course caused by currents **b** a slow-moving ocean current **c** the lateral motion of an aircraft due to air currents **d** an easy, moderate, more or less steady flow along a spatial course **e** a gradual shift in attitude, opinion, or emotion **f** an aimless course, with no attempt at direction or control **g** a deviation from a true reproduction, representation, or reading

[2]**drift** *vi* **1a** to become driven or carried along by a current of water or air **b** to move or float smoothly and effortlessly **2a** to move in a random or casual way **b** to become carried along aimlessly <*the conversation* ~ed *from one topic to another*> **3** to pile up under the force of wind or water **4** to deviate from a set adjustment ~*vt* to pile up in a drift

drifter /ˈdriftə‖ˈdrɪftə/ *n* **1** sby or sthg that travels or moves about aimlessly **2** a coastal fishing boat equipped with drift nets

ˈdrift ˌnet *n* a large fishing net that hangs vertically and is arranged to drift with the tide, currents, etc

ˈdriftˌwood /-ˌwood‖-ˌwʊd/ *n* wood cast up on a shore or beach

[1]**drill** /dril‖drɪl/ *vb* **1a** to bore or drive a hole in (as if) by the piercing action of a drill **b** to make (e g a hole) by piercing action **2a** to instruct and exercise by repeating **b** to train or exercise in military drill ~ *vi* **1** to make a hole with a drill **2** to engage in esp military drill – **drillable** *adj*

[2]**drill** *n* **1** (a device or machine for rotating) a tool with an edged or pointed end for making a hole in a solid substance by revolving or by a succession of blows **2** training in marching and the manual of arms **3** a physical or mental exercise aimed at improving facility and skill by regular practice **4** *chiefly Br* the approved or correct procedure for accomplishing sthg efficiently – infml

[3]**drill** *n* **1a** a shallow furrow into which seed is sown **b** a row of seed sown in such a furrow **2** a planting implement that makes holes or furrows, drops in the seed and sometimes fertilizer, and covers them with earth

[4]**drill** *vt* **1** to sow (seeds) by dropping along a shallow furrow **2** to sow with seed or set with seedlings inserted in drills

[5]**drill** *n* a durable cotton fabric in twill weave

drily /ˈdrieli‖ˈdraɪlɪ/ *adv* dryly

[1]**drink** /dringk‖drɪŋk/ *vb* **drank** /drangk‖dræŋk/; **drunk** /drungk‖drʌŋk/, **drank** *vt* **1a** to swallow (a liquid); *also* to swallow the liquid contents of (e g a cup) **b** to take in or suck up; absorb <~ing *air into his lungs*> **c** to take in or receive avidly – usu + *in* <drank *in every word of the lecture*> **2** to join in (a toast) **3** to bring to a specified state by taking drink <drank *himself into oblivion*> ~ *vi* **1** to take liquid into the mouth for swallowing **2** to drink alcoholic beverages, esp habitually or to excess – **drink like a fish** to habitually drink alcohol to excess – **drink to** to drink a toast to

[2]**drink** *n* **1a** liquid suitable for swallowing **b** alcoholic drink **2** a draught or portion of liquid

for drinking **3** excessive consumption of alcoholic beverages <*drove him to* ~> **4** OCEAN 1; *broadly* any sizable body of water – + *the*; infml

drinkable /ˈdringkəbl‖ˈdrɪŋkəbl/ *adj* suitable or safe for drinking

drinker /ˈdringkə‖ˈdrɪŋkə/ *n* one who drinks alcoholic beverages to excess

[1]**drip** /drip‖drɪp/ *vb* **-pp-** *vt* to let fall in drops ~ *vi* **1a** to let fall drops of moisture or liquid **b** to overflow (as if) with moisture <*a novel that* ~s *with sentimentality*> **2** to fall (as if) in drops – **dripper** *n*

[2]**drip** *n* **1a** the action or sound of falling in drops **b** liquid that falls, overflows, or is forced out in drops **2** a projection for throwing off rainwater **3a** a device for the administration of a liquid at a slow rate, esp into a vein **b** a substance administered by means of a drip <*a saline* ~> **4** a dull or inconsequential person – infml – **dripless** *adj*, **drippy** *adj*

[1]ˌ**drip-ˈdry** *vb* to dry with few or no wrinkles when hung dripping wet

[2]ˌ**drip-ˈdry** *adj* made of a washable fabric that drip-dries

dripping /ˈdriping‖ˈdrɪpɪŋ/ *n* the fat that runs out from meat during roasting

[1]**drive** /driev‖draɪv/ *vb* **drove** /drohv‖drəʊv/; **driven** /ˈdriv(ə)n‖ˈdrɪv(ə)n/ *vt* **1a** to set in motion by physical force **b** to force into position by blows <~ *a nail into the wall*> **c** to repulse or cause to go by force, authority, or influence <~ *the enemy back*> **d** to set or keep in motion or operation <~ *machinery by electricity*> **2a** to control and direct the course of (a vehicle or draught animal) **b** to convey or transport in a vehicle **3** to carry on or through energetically <driving *a hard bargain*> **4a** to exert inescapable or persuasive pressure on; force **b** to compel to undergo or suffer a change (e g in situation, awareness, or emotional state) <drove *him crazy*> **c** to urge relentlessly to continuous exertion **5** to cause (e g game or cattle) to move in a desired direction **6** to bore (e g a tunnel or passage) **7a** to propel (an object of play) swiftly **b** to play a drive in cricket at (a ball) or at the bowling of (a bowler) ~ *vi* **1** to rush or dash rapidly or with force against an obstruction <*rain* driving *against the windscreen*> **2** to operate a vehicle **3** to drive an object of play (e g a golf ball) – **drive at** to imply as an ultimate meaning or conclusion <*couldn't work out what she was* driving at> – **drive up the wall** to infuriate or madden (sby)

[2]**drive** *n* **1** an act of driving: e g **1a** a trip in a carriage or motor vehicle **b** a shoot in which the game is driven within the range of the guns **2** a private road giving access from a public way to a building on private land **3** a (military) offensive, aggressive, or expansionist move **4** a strong systematic group effort; a campaign **5a** a motivating instinctual need or acquired desire <*a sexual* ~> <*a* ~ *for perfection*> **b** great zeal in pursuing one's ends **6a** the means for giving motion to a machine (part) <*a chain* ~> **b** the means by or position from which the movement of a motor vehicle is controlled or directed **7** a device including a transport and heads for reading information from or writing information onto a tape, esp magnetic tape, or disc **8** the act or an instance of driving an object of play; *esp* an attacking cricket stroke played conventionally with a straight bat and designed to send the ball in front of the batsman's wicket

ˈ**drive-ˌin** *adj or n* (being) a place (e g a bank, cinema, or restaurant) that people can use while remaining in their cars

[1]**drivel** /ˈdrivl‖ˈdrɪvl/ *vi* **-ll-** (*NAm* **-l-**, **-ll-**) **1** to let saliva dribble from the mouth or mucus run from the nose **2** to talk stupidly and childishly or carelessly – **driveller** *n*

[2]**drivel** *n* foolish or childish nonsense

driver /ˈdrievə‖ˈdraɪvə/ *n* **1** a coachman **2** the operator of a motor vehicle **3** an implement (e g a hammer) for driving **4** a mechanical piece for imparting motion to another piece **5** a golf club with a wooden head used in hitting the ball long distances, esp off the tee – **driverless** *adj*

ˈ**driveˌway** /-ˌway‖-ˌweɪ/ *n* DRIVE 2

driving /ˈdrieving‖ˈdraɪvɪŋ/ *adj* **1** that communicates force <*a* ~ *wheel*> **2a** having great force <~ *rain*> **b** acting with vigour; energetic

[1]**drizzle** /ˈdriz(ə)l‖ˈdrɪz(ə)l/ *vi* to rain in very small drops or very lightly ~*vt* to shed or let fall in minute drops

[2]**drizzle** *n* a fine misty rain – **drizzly** *adj*

drogue /drohg‖drəʊg/ *n* **1** SEA ANCHOR **2** a small parachute for stabilizing or decelerating sthg or for pulling a larger parachute out of stowage

droll /drohl‖drəʊl/ *adj* humorous, whimsical, or odd – **drollness** *n*, **drolly** *adv*

drollery /ˈdrohləri‖ˈdrəʊlərɪ/ *n* **1** the act or an instance of jesting or droll behaviour **2** droll humour

dromedary /ˈdroməd(ə)ri, ˈdrum-‖ˈdrɒməd(ə)rɪ, ˈdrʌm-/ *n* a (1-humped) camel bred esp for riding

[1]**drone** /ˈdrohn‖ˈdrəʊn/ *n* **1** the male of a bee (e g the honeybee) that has no sting and gathers no honey **2** sby who lives off others **3** a remotely-controlled pilotless aircraft, missile, or ship

[2]**drone** *vi* **1** to make a sustained deep murmuring or buzzing sound **2** to talk in a persistently monotonous tone – **droner** *n*, **droningly** *adv*

[3]**drone** *n* **1** any of the usu 3 pipes on a bagpipe that sound fixed continuous notes **2** a droning sound **3** an unvarying sustained bass note

drool /droohl‖druːl/ *vi* **1a** to secrete saliva in anticipation of food **b** DRIVEL 1 **2** to make a foolishly effusive show of pleasure ~*vt* to express sentimentally or effusively

[1]**droop** /droohp‖druːp/ *vi* **1** to hang or incline downwards **2** to become depressed or weakened; languish ~*vt* to let droop – **droopingly** *adv*

[2]**droop** *n* the condition or appearance of drooping – **droopy** *adj*

[1]**drop** /drop‖drɒp/ *n* **1a(1)** the quantity of fluid that falls in 1 spherical mass **a(2)** *pl* a dose of medicine measured by drops **b** a minute quantity <*not a* ~ *of pity in him*> **2** sthg that resembles a liquid drop: e g **2a** an ornament that hangs from a piece of jewellery (e g an earring) **b** a small globular often medicated sweet or lozenge **3a** the act or an instance of dropping; a fall

b a decline in quantity or quality **c** (the men or equipment dropped by) a parachute descent **4a** the distance from a higher to a lower level or through which sthg drops **b** a decrease of electric potential **5** sthg that drops, hangs, or falls: e g **5a** an unframed piece of cloth stage scenery **b** a hinged platform on a gallows **6** *NAm* a central point or depository to which sthg (e g mail) is brought for distribution **7** a small quantity of drink, esp alcohol; *broadly* an alcoholic drink – infml **8** (a secret place used for the deposit and collection of) letters or stolen or illegal goods – slang – **droplet** *n* – **at the drop of a hat** without hesitation; promptly – **have/get the drop on** *NAm* to have or get at a disadvantage – slang

²**drop** *vb* **-pp-** *vi* **1** to fall in drops **2a(1)** to fall, esp unexpectedly or suddenly **a(2)** to descend from one level to another <*his voice* ~ped> **b** to fall in a state of collapse or death <*he'll work until he* ~s> **c** *of a card* to become played by reason of the obligation to follow suit **3a** to cease to be of concern; lapse <*let the matter* ~> **b** to become less <*production* ~ped> ~ *vt* **1a** to let fall; cause to fall **b** to drop a catch offered by (a batsman) **2a** to lower from one level or position to another **b** to cause to lessen or decrease; reduce <~ped *his speed*> **3** to set down from a ship or vehicle; unload; *also* to airdrop **4a** to bring down with a shot or blow **b** to cause (a high card) to drop **c** to score (a goal) with a dropkick **5a** to give up (e g an idea) **b** to leave incomplete; cease <~ped *what he was doing*> **c** to break off an association or connection with <~ped *his old friends*>; *also* to leave out of a team or group **6** to leave (a letter representing a speech sound) unsounded <~ *the* h *in* have> **7a** to utter or mention in a casual way <~ *a hint*> **b** to send through the post <~ *us a line soon*> **8** to lose <~ped *£500 on the stock market*> – infml – **drop a brick/clanger** to make an embarrassing error or mistaken remark – infml

drop behind *vb* to fail to keep up (with)

drop in *vi* to pay a usu brief, casual, or unexpected visit

ˈ**dropˌkick** /-ˌkik‖-ˌkɪk/ *n* a kick made (e g in rugby) by dropping a football to the ground and kicking it at the moment it starts to rebound – **drop-kick** *vb*, **drop kicker** *n*

ˈ**drop-ˌoff** *n* a marked dwindling or decline <*a* ~ *in attendance*>

drop off *vi* **1** to fall asleep **2** to decline, slump

ˈ**dropˌout** /-ˌowt‖-ˌaʊt/ *n* **1** one who rejects or withdraws from participation in conventional society **2** a student who fails to complete or withdraws from a course, usu of higher education **3** a dropkick awarded to the defending team in rugby (e g after an unconverted try)

drop out *vi* **1** to withdraw from participation **2** to make a dropout in rugby

dropper /ˈdropə‖ˈdrɒpə/ *n* a short usu glass tube fitted with a rubber bulb and used to measure or administer liquids by drops – **dropperful** *n*

droppings /ˈdropingz‖ˈdrɒpɪŋz/ *n pl* animal dung

dropsy /ˈdropsi‖ˈdrɒpsɪ/ *n* oedema – **dropsical** *adj*

dross /dros‖drɒs/ *n* **1** the scum on the surface of molten metal **2** waste, rubbish, or foreign matter; impurities – **drossy** *adj*

drought /drowt‖draʊt/ *n* **1** a prolonged period of dryness **2** a prolonged shortage of sthg – **droughty** *adj*

¹**drove** /drohv‖drəʊv/ *n* **1** a group of animals driven or moving in a body **2** a crowd of people moving or acting together

²**drove** *past of* DRIVE

drover /ˈdrohvə‖ˈdrəʊvə/ *n* one who drives cattle or sheep

drown /drown‖draʊn/ *vi* to become drowned ~ *vt* **1a** to suffocate by submergence, esp in water **b** to submerge, esp by a rise in the water level **c** to wet thoroughly; drench <~ed *the chips with ketchup*> **2** to engage (oneself) deeply and strenuously <~ed *himself in work*> **3** to blot out (a sound) by making a loud noise **4** to destroy (e g a sensation or an idea) as if by drowning <~ed *his sorrows in drink*>

¹**drowse** /drowz‖draʊz/ *vi* to doze ~*vt* to pass (time) drowsily or in dozing – usu + *away*

²**drowse** *n* the act or an instance of dozing

drowsy /ˈdrowzi‖ˈdraʊzɪ/ *adj* **1a** sleepy **b** tending to induce sleepiness <*a* ~ *summer afternoon*> **c** indolent, lethargic **2** giving the appearance of peaceful inactivity – **drowsily** *adv*, **drowsiness** *n*

drub /drub‖drʌb/ *vt* **-bb-** **1** to beat severely **2** to defeat decisively

¹**drudge** /druj‖drʌdʒ/ *vi* to do hard, menial, routine, or monotonous work – **drudger** *n*, **drudgery** *n*

²**drudge** *n* one who drudges

¹**drug** /drug‖drʌg/ *n* **1** a substance used as (or in the preparation of) a medication **2** a substance that causes addiction or habituation

²**drug** *vt* **-gg-** **1** to affect or adulterate with a drug **2** to administer a drug to **3** to lull or stupefy (as if) with a drug

drugget /ˈdrugit‖ˈdrʌgɪt/ *n* a coarse durable cloth used chiefly as a floor covering

druggist /ˈdrugist‖ˈdrʌgɪst/ *n* **1** one who deals in or dispenses drugs and medicines; a pharmacist **2** *NAm* the owner or manager of a drugstore

ˈ**drugˌstore** /-ˌstaw‖-ˌstɔː/ *n, chiefly NAm* a chemist's shop; *esp* one that also sells sweets, magazines, and refreshments

druid /ˈdrooh·id‖ˈdruːɪd/, *fem* **druidess** /-dis‖-dɪs/ *n, often cap* **1** a member of a pre-Christian Celtic order of priests associated with a mistletoe cult **2** an officer of the Welsh Gorsedd, the institution that governs an eisteddfod – **druidic, druidical** *adj, often cap*

¹**drum** /drum‖drʌm/ *n* **1** a percussion instrument usu consisting of a hollow cylinder with a drumhead stretched over each end, that is beaten with a stick or a pair of sticks in playing **2** the tympanic membrane of the ear **3** the sound made by striking a drum; *also* any similar sound **4** sthg resembling a drum in shape: e g **4a** a cylindrical machine or mechanical device or part; *esp* a metal cylinder coated with magnetic material on which data (e g for a computer) may be recorded **b** a cylindrical container; *specif* a large

usu metal container for liquids **5** a dwelling; PAD 6 – slang

[2]**drum** *vb* **-mm-** *vi* **1** to beat a drum **2** to make a succession of strokes, taps, or vibrations that produce drumlike sounds **3** to throb or sound rhythmically <*blood* ~med *in his ears*> ~ *vt* **1** to summon or enlist (as if) by beating a drum <~med *them into service*> **2** to instil (an idea or lesson) by constant repetition – usu + *into* or *out of* <~med *the idea into them*> **3a** to strike or tap repeatedly **b** to produce (rhythmic sounds) by such action

'drum,beat /-ˌbeet‖-ˌbiːt/ *n* a stroke on a drum or its sound

'drum,fire /-ˌfie·ə‖-ˌfaɪə/ *n* artillery fire so continuous as to sound like a roll on a drum

'drum,head /-ˌhed‖-ˌhed/ *n* the material stretched over the end of a drum

drumhead court-martial *n* a summary court-martial

,drum 'major *n* the marching leader of a band

drummer /'drumə‖'drʌmə/ *n* **1** one who plays a drum **2** *chiefly NAm* SALES REPRESENTATIVE

drum out *vt* to dismiss ignominiously; expel <drummed *him* out *of the army*>

'drum,stick /-ˌstik‖-ˌstɪk/ *n* **1** a stick for beating a drum **2** the part of a fowl's leg between the thigh and tarsus when cooked as food

drum up *vt* **1** to bring about by persistent effort <drum up *some business*> **2** to invent, originate <drum up *a new time-saving method*>

[1]**drunk** /drungk‖drʌŋk/ *past part of* DRINK

[2]**drunk** *adj* **1** under the influence of alcohol **2** dominated by an intense feeling <~ *with power*> **3** DRUNKEN 2b

[3]**drunk** *n* a person who is (habitually) drunk

drunkard /'drungkəd‖'drʌŋkəd/ *n* a person who is habitually drunk

drunken /'drungkən‖'drʌŋkən/ *adj* **1** DRUNK 1 **2a** given to habitual excessive use of alcohol **b** of, characterized by, or resulting from alcoholic intoxication <*a* ~ *brawl*> **3** unsteady or lurching as if from alcoholic intoxication – **drunkenly** *adv*, **drunkenness** *n* – **drunk in charge** driving while intoxicated

drupe /droohp‖druːp/ *n* a fruit (e g a cherry or almond) that has a stone enclosed by a fleshy layer and is covered by a flexible or stiff outermost layer – **drupaceous** *adj*

[1]**dry** /drie‖draɪ/ *adj* **1a** (relatively) free from a liquid, esp water **b** not in or under water <~ *land*> **c** lacking precipitation or humidity <*a* ~ *climate*> **2a** characterized by exhaustion of a supply of water or liquid <*the barrel ran* ~> **b** devoid of natural moisture <~ *mouth*>; *also* thirsty **c** no longer sticky or damp <*the paint is* ~> **d** *of a mammal* not giving milk <*a* ~ *cow*> **e** lacking freshness; stale **3a** marked by the absence or scantiness of secretions <*a* ~ *cough*> **b** not shedding or accompanied by tears <*no* ~ *eyes*> **4** prohibiting the manufacture or distribution of alcoholic beverages <*a* ~ *county*> **5** lacking sweetness; sec **6** solid as opposed to liquid <~ *groceries*> **7** functioning without lubrication <*a* ~ *clutch*> **8** built or constructed without a process which requires water **9a** not showing or communicating warmth, enthusiasm, or feeling; impassive **b** uninteresting <~ *passages of description*> **c** lacking embellishment, bias, or emotional concern; plain <*the* ~ *facts*> **10** not yielding what is expected or desired; unproductive <*a* ~ *oil field*> **11** marked by a matter-of-fact, ironic, or terse manner of expression <~ *wit*> – **dryish** *adj*, **dryishly** *adv*, **dryly** *adv*, **dryness** *n*

[2]**dry** *vb* to make or become dry – often + *out* – **dryable** *adj*

dryad /'drie·ad, -əd‖'draɪæd, -əd/ *n* a nymph of the woods in Greek mythology [Latin *dryad-*, *dryas*, fr Greek, fr *drys* tree]

dry cell *n* a primary cell whose electrolyte is not a liquid

,dry-'clean *vb* to subject to or undergo dry cleaning – **dry-cleanable** *adj*, **dry cleaner** *n*

,dry 'cleaning *n* **1** the cleaning of fabrics or garments with organic solvents and without water **2** that which is dry-cleaned

dry dock *n* a dock from which the water can be pumped to allow ships to be repaired

dryer /'drie·ə‖'draɪə/ *n* a drier

dry goods *n pl*, *NAm* drapery as distinguished esp from hardware and groceries

,dry 'ice *n* solidified carbon dioxide

dry out *vi* to undergo treatment for alcoholism or drug addiction

,dry 'rot *n* **1** (a fungus causing) a decay of seasoned timber **2** decay from within, caused esp by resistance to new forces

dry run *n* **1** a firing practice without ammunition **2** a practice exercise; a rehearsal, trial

,dry-'shod *adj* having or keeping dry shoes or feet

dry up *vi* **1** to disappear or cease to yield (as if) by evaporation, draining, or the cutting off of a source of supply **2** to wither or die through gradual loss of vitality **3** to wipe dry dishes, cutlery, etc by hand after they have been washed **4** to stop talking; SHUT UP – infml ~*vt* to cause to dry up

dt's /ˌdee 'teez‖ˌdiː 'tiːz/ *n pl, often cap D&T* DELIRIUM TREMENS

dual /'dyooh·əl‖'djuːəl/ *adj* **1** consisting of 2 (like) parts or elements **2** having a double character or nature – **dual** *n*, **duality** *n*, **dualize** *vt*, **dually** *adv*

,dual 'carriage,way *n, chiefly Br* a road that has traffic travelling in opposite directions separated by a central reservation

[1]**dub** /dub‖dʌb/ *vt* **-bb-** **1a** to confer knighthood on **b** to call by a descriptive name or epithet; nickname **2** *Br* to dress (a fishing fly) – **dubber** *n*

[2]**dub** *vt* **-bb-** **1** to make alterations to the original sound track of (a film): e g **1a** to provide with a sound track in which the voices are not those of the actors on the screen **b** to provide with a sound track in a new language **2** to transpose (a previous recording) to a new record **3** *chiefly Br* MIX 1b(2) – **dubber** *n*

dubbin /'dubin‖'dʌbɪn/ *also* **dubbing** /'dubing‖'dʌbɪŋ/ *n* a dressing of oil and tallow for leather – **dubbin** *vt*

dubiety /dyooh'bie·əti‖djuː'baɪətɪ/ *n* **1** the state of being doubtful **2** a doubtful matter *USE* fml

dubious /ˈdyoohbi·əs‖ˈdju:bɪəs/ *adj* **1** giving rise to doubt; uncertain **2** unsettled in opinion; undecided **3** of questionable value, quality, or origin – **dubiously** *adv*, **dubiousness** *n*

ducal /ˈdyoohkl‖ˈdju:kl/ *adj* of or relating to a duke or duchy – **ducally** *adv*

ducat /ˈdukət‖ˈdʌkət/ *n* a usu gold coin formerly used in many European countries

duchess /ˈduchis‖ˈdʌtʃɪs/ *n* **1** the wife or widow of a duke **2** a woman having in her own right the rank of a duke

duchy /ˈduchi‖ˈdʌtʃɪ/ *n* a dukedom

[1]**duck** /duk‖dʌk/ *n*, **1a** any of various swimming birds in which the neck and legs are short, the bill is often broad and flat, and the sexes are almost always different from each other in plumage **b** the flesh of any of these birds used as food **2** a female duck **3** *chiefly Br* DEAR 1b – often pl with sing. meaning but sing. in constr; infml

[2]**duck** *vt* **1** to thrust momentarily under water **2** to lower (e g the head), esp quickly as a bow or to avoid being hit **3** to avoid, evade < ~ *the issue*> ~ *vi* **1** to plunge at least one's head under the surface of water **2a** to move the head or body suddenly; dodge **b** to bow, bob **3** to evade a duty, question, or responsibility – **duck** *n*

[3]**duck** *n* a durable closely woven usu cotton fabric

[4]**duck** *n* a score of nought, esp in cricket

ˌ**duckˌbilled ˈplatypus** *n* the platypus

ˈ**duckˌboard** /-ˌbawd‖-ˌbɔ:d/ *n* a usu wooden board or slat used to make a path over wet or muddy ground – usu pl

ˈ**ducking ˌstool** /ˈduking‖ˈdʌkɪŋ/ *n* a seat attached to a plank and formerly used to plunge culprits into water

duckling /ˈdukling‖ˈdʌklɪŋ/ *n* a young duck

ˌ**ducks and ˈdrakes** *n pl but sing in constr* the pastime of skimming flat stones or shells along the surface of calm water

ˈ**duckˌweed** /-ˌweed‖-ˌwi:d/ *n* any of several small free-floating stemless plants that often cover large areas of the surface of still water

[1]**ducky** /ˈduki‖ˈdʌkɪ/ *adj* darling, sweet – infml

[2]**ducky**, **duckie** *n* DEAR 1b – infml

[1]**duct** /dukt‖dʌkt/ *n* **1** a bodily tube or vessel, esp when carrying the secretion of a gland **2a** a pipe, tube, or channel that conveys a substance **b** a pipe or tubular runway for carrying an electric power line, telephone cables, or other conductors **3** a continuous tube in plant tissue – **ducting** *n*

[2]**duct** *vt* to convey (e g a gas) through a duct

ductile /ˈduktiel‖ˈdʌktaɪl/ *adj* **1** capable of being easily fashioned into a new form **2** *of metals* capable of being drawn out or hammered thin **3** easily led or influenced; tractable <*the ~ masses*> – infml – **ductility** *n*

ˌ**ductless ˈgland** /-lis‖-lɪs/ *n* ENDOCRINE 2

[1]**dud** /dud‖dʌd/ *n* **1** a bomb, missile, etc that fails to explode **2** *pl* personal belongings; *esp* clothes **3** a failure **4** a counterfeit, fake *USE* (*2, 3, & 4*) infml

[2]**dud** *adj* valueless < ~ *cheques*> – infml

dude /d(y)oohd‖d(j)u:d/ *n*, *chiefly NAm* **1** a dandy **2** a city-dweller; *esp* a man from the eastern USA holidaying (on a ranch) in the western USA *USE* infml – **dudish** *adj*, **dudishly** *adv*

dudgeon /ˈdujən‖ˈdʌdʒən/ *n* indignation, resentment – esp in *in high dudgeon*

[1]**due** /dyooh‖dju:/ *adj* **1** owed or owing as a debt **2a** owed or owing as a natural or moral right <*got his ~ reward*> **b** appropriate <*after ~ consideration*> **3a** (capable of) satisfying a need, obligation, or duty **b** regular, lawful < ~ *proof of loss*> **4** ascribable – + *to* <*this bad weather is ~ to an anticyclone*> **5** payable **6** required or expected in the prearranged or normal course of events < ~ *to arrive at any time*> – **in due course** after a normal passage of time; in the expected or allocated time

[2]**due** *n* sthg due or owed: e g **a** sthg esp nonmaterial that rightfully belongs to one <*I don't like him, but to give him his ~ he's a good singer*> **b** *pl* fees, charges

[3]**due** *adv* directly, exactly – used before points of the compass < ~ *north*>

[1]**duel** /ˈdyooh·əl‖ˈdju:əl/ *n* **1** a formal combat with weapons fought between 2 people in the presence of witnesses in order to settle a quarrel **2** a conflict between usu evenly matched antagonistic people, ideas, or forces

[2]**duel** *vi* **-ll-** (*NAm* **-l-**, **-ll-**) to fight a duel – **dueller** *n*, **duellist** *n*

duenna /dyoohˈenə‖dju:ˈenə/ *n* **1** an older woman serving as governess and companion to the younger ladies in a Spanish or Portuguese family **2** a chaperon – **duennaship** *n*

duet /dyoohˈet‖dju:ˈet/ *n* a (musical) composition for 2 performers

ˈ**due to** *prep* BECAUSE OF 1 – though disapproved by many, now used by numerous educated speakers and writers; compare [1]DUE 4

[1]**duff** /duf‖dʌf/ *n* a boiled or steamed pudding, often containing dried fruit

[2]**duff** *adj*, *Br* not working; worthless, useless – slang

duffel, **duffle** /ˈduf(ə)l‖ˈdʌf(ə)l/ *n* a coarse heavy woollen material with a thick nap [*Duffel*, town in Belgium]

ˈ**duffel ˌbag** *n* a cylindrical fabric bag, closed by a drawstring, used for carrying personal belongings

ˈ**duffel ˌcoat** *n* a coat made of duffel that is usu thigh- or knee-length, hooded, and fastened with toggles

duffer /ˈdufə‖ˈdʌfə/ *n* an incompetent, ineffectual, or clumsy person

[1]**dug** /dug‖dʌg/ *past of* DIG

[2]**dug** /dug‖dʌg/ *n* an udder; *also* a teat – usu used with reference to animals but derog when used of a woman

dugout /ˈdugˌowt‖ˈdʌgˌaʊt/ *n* **1** a boat made by hollowing out a large log **2** a shelter dug in the ground or in a hillside, esp for troops

duke /dyoohk‖dju:k/ *n* **1** a sovereign ruler of a European duchy **2** a nobleman of the highest hereditary rank; *esp* a member of the highest rank of the British peerage **3** a fist – usu pl; slang – **dukedom** *n*

dulcet /ˈdulsit‖ˈdʌlsɪt/ *adj*, *esp of sounds* sweetly pleasant or soothing – **dulcetly** *adv*

dulcimer /ˈdulsimə‖ˈdʌlsɪmə/ *n* a stringed instrument having strings of graduated length stretched over a sounding board and played with light hammers

[1]**dull** /dul‖dʌl/ *adj* **1** mentally slow; stupid **2a** slow in perception or sensibility; insensible **b** lacking zest or vivacity; listless **3** lacking sharpness of cutting edge or point; blunt **4** not resonant or ringing <*a ~ booming sound*> **5** *of a colour* low in saturation and lightness **6** cloudy, overcast **7** boring, uninteresting – **dullness, dulness** *n*, **dully** *adv*

[2]**dull** *vb* to make or become dull

dullard /'duləd‖'dʌləd/ *n* a stupid or insensitive person

duly /'dyoohli‖'dju:lɪ/ *adv* in a due manner, time, or degree; properly <*your suggestion has been ~ noted*>

dumb /dum‖dʌm/ *adj* **1** devoid of the power of speech **2** naturally incapable of speech <~ *animals*> **3** not expressed in uttered words <~ *insolence*> **4a** not willing to speak **b** temporarily unable to speak (e g from astonishment) <*struck* ~> **5** lacking some usual attribute or accompaniment **6** stupid – **dumbly** *adv*, **dumbness** *n*

dumbbell /'dum,bel‖'dʌm,bel/ *n* **1** a short bar with adjustable weights at each end used usu in pairs for weight training **2** *NAm* DUMMY 6

dumbfound, dumfound /dum'fownd‖dʌm'faʊnd/ *vt* to strike dumb with astonishment; amaze

'dumb ,show *n* (a play or part of a play presented by) movement, signs, and gestures without words

,dumb 'waiter *n* **1** a movable table or stand often with revolving shelves for holding food or dishes **2** a small lift for conveying food and dishes (e g from the kitchen to the dining area of a restaurant)

dumdum /'dum,dum‖'dʌm,dʌm/ *n* a bullet that expands on impact and inflicts a severe wound [*Dum-Dum*, arsenal near Calcutta, India]

[1]**dummy** /'dumi‖'dʌmɪ/ *n* **1** the exposed hand in bridge played by the declarer in addition to his/her own hand; *also* the player whose hand is a dummy **2** an imitation or copy of sthg used to reproduce some of the attributes of the original; e g **2a** *chiefly Br* a rubber teat given to babies to suck in order to soothe them **b** a large puppet in usu human form, used by a ventriloquist **c** a model of the human body, esp the torso, used for fitting or displaying clothes **3** a person or corporation that seems to act independently but is in reality acting for or at the direction of another **4** a pattern for a printing job showing the position of typographic elements (e g text and illustrations) **5** an instance of dummying an opponent in sports **6** a dull or stupid person – infml

[2]**dummy** *adj* resembling or being a dummy: e g **a** sham, artificial **b** existing in name only; fictitious

[3]**dummy** *vi* **1** to deceive an opponent (e g in rugby or soccer) by pretending to pass or release the ball while still retaining possession of it **2** *NAm* to refuse to talk – usu + *up*; slang ~*vt* to deceive (an opponent) by dummying

'dummy ,run *n* a rehearsal; TRIAL RUN

[1]**dump** /dump‖dʌmp/ *vt* **1a** to unload or let fall in a heap or mass **b** to get rid of unceremoniously or irresponsibly; abandon **2** to sell in quantity at a very low price; *specif* to sell abroad at less than the market price at home **3** to copy (data in a computer's internal storage) onto an external storage medium – **dumper** *n*

[2]**dump** *n* **1a** an accumulation of discarded materials (e g refuse) **b** a place where such materials are dumped **2** a quantity of esp military reserve materials accumulated in 1 place **3** an instance of dumping data stored in a computer **4** a disorderly, slovenly, or dilapidated place – infml

'dumper ,truck /'dumpə‖'dʌmpə/, **'dump ,truck** *n* a lorry whose body may be tilted to empty the contents

dumpling /'dumpling‖'dʌmplɪŋ/ *n* **1** a small usu rounded mass of leavened dough cooked by boiling or steaming often in stew **2** a short round person – humor

dumps /dumps‖dʌmps/ *n pl* a gloomy state of mind; despondency – esp in *in the dumps*; infml

dumpy /'dumpi‖'dʌmpɪ/ *adj* short and thick in build; squat – **dumpily** *adv*, **dumpiness** *n*

[1]**dun** /dun‖dʌn/ *adj* **1** of the colour dun **2** *of a horse* having a greyish or light brownish colour

[2]**dun** *n* **1** a dun horse **2** a slightly brownish dark grey

[3]**dun** *vt* **-nn-** to make persistent demands upon for payment

[4]**dun** *n* **1** one who duns **2** an urgent request; *esp* a demand for payment

dunce /duns‖dʌns/ *n* a dull or stupid person [John *Duns* Scotus (1265?-1308), Scottish theologian whose once accepted writings were ridiculed in the 16th c]

dunce's cap *n* a conical cap formerly used to humiliate slow learners at school

dunderhead /'dundə,hed‖'dʌndə,hed/ *n* a dunce, blockhead – **dunderheaded** *adj*

dune /dyoohn‖dju:n/ *n* a hill or ridge of sand piled up by the wind

[1]**dung** /dung‖dʌŋ/ *n* the excrement of an animal – **dungy** *adj*

[2]**dung** *vt* to fertilize or dress with manure ~*vi*, *of an animal* to defecate

dungaree /,dung·gə'ree‖,dʌŋgə'ri:/ *n* a heavy coarse durable cotton twill woven from coloured yarns; *specif* blue denim [Hindi *dūgrī*]

,dunga'rees /-reez‖-ri:z/ *n pl* a 1-piece outer garment consisting of trousers and a bib with shoulder straps fastened at the back – **dungaree** *adj*

dungeon /'dunjən‖'dʌndʒən/ *n* a dark usu underground prison or vault, esp in a castle

'dung,hill /-,hil‖-,hɪl/ *n* a heap of dung (e g in a farmyard)

dunk /dungk‖dʌŋk/ *vt* to dip (e g a piece of bread) into liquid (e g soup) before eating

dunny /'duni‖'dʌnɪ/ *n*, *chiefly Austr & NZ* a toilet – infml

duo /'dyooh,oh‖'dju:,əʊ/ *n*, *pl* **duos** a pair (of performers); *also* a piece (e g of music) written for 2 players

duo- *comb form* two

duodecimal /,dyooh·oh'desim(ə)l‖,dju:əʊ'desɪm(ə)l/ *adj* proceeding by or based on the number of 12 [Latin *duodecim* twelve – see DOZEN] – **duodecimal** *n*

duodenum /,dyooh·ə'deenəm‖,dju:ə'di:nəm/

n, pl **duodena** /-nə||-nə/, **duodenums** the first part of the small intestine extending from the stomach to the jejunum – **duodenal** *adj*

duologue /'dyooh·ə,log||'dju:ə,lɒg/ *n* a (theatrical) dialogue between 2 people

[1]**dupe** /dyoohp||dju:p/ *n* one who is easily deceived or cheated

[2]**dupe** *vt* to make a dupe of; deceive – **duper** *n*, **dupery** *n*

duple /'dyoohpl||'dju:pl/ *adj* **1** having 2 elements; twofold **2** marked by 2 or a multiple of 2 beats per bar of music

[1]**duplex** /'dyooh,pleks||'dju:,pleks/ *adj* **1** double, twofold **2** allowing telecommunication in opposite directions simultaneously

[2]**duplex** *n* sthg duplex: e g **a** *NAm* a 2-family house **b** *NAm* a flat on 2 floors

[1]**duplicate** /'d(y)oohplikət||'d(j)u:plɪkət/ *adj* **1a** consisting of or existing in 2 corresponding or identical parts or examples < ~ *invoices*> **b** being the same as another <*a ~ key*> **2** being a card game, specif bridge, in which different players play identical hands in order to compare scores

[2]**duplicate** *n* **1** either of 2 things that exactly resemble each other; *specif* an equally valid copy of a legal document **2** a copy – **in duplicate** with an original and 1 copy <*typed ~*>; *also* with 2 identical copies

[3]**duplicate** /'d(y)oohpli,kayt||'d(j)u:plɪ,keɪt/ *vt* **1** to make double or twofold **2** to make an exact copy of < ~ *the document*> ~*vi* to replicate <*DNA in chromosomes* ~s> – **duplication** *n*, **duplicative** *adj*

duplicator /'d(y)oohpli,kaytə||'d(j)u:plɪ,keɪtə/ *n* a machine for making copies, esp by means other than photocopying or xeroxing

duplicity /dyooh'plisəti||dju:'plɪsətɪ/ *n* malicious deception in thought, speech, or action – **duplicitous** *adj*, **duplicitously** *adv*

durable /'dyooərəbl||'djʊərəbl; *also* j-||dʒ-/ *adj* able to exist or be used for a long time without significant deterioration – **durableness** *n*, **durably** *adv*, **durability** *n*

duration /dyoo(ə)'raysh(ə)n||djʊ(ə)'reɪʃ(ə)n/ *n* **1** continuance in time **2** the time during which sthg exists or lasts

duress /dyoo(ə)'res||djʊ(ə)'res; *also* j-||dʒ-/ *n* **1** forcible restraint or restriction **2** compulsion by threat, violence, or imprisonment

Durex /'dyooəreks||'djʊəreks/ *trademark* – used for a condom

during /'dyooəring||'djʊərɪŋ; *also* j-||dʒ-/ *prep* **1** throughout the whole duration of <*swims every day ~ the summer*> **2** at some point in the course of <*takes his holiday ~ July*>

dusk /dusk||dʌsk/ *n* (the darker part of) twilight

dusky /'duski||'dʌskɪ/ *adj* **1** somewhat dark in colour; *esp* dark-skinned **2** shadowy, gloomy – **duskily** *adv*, **duskiness** *n*

[1]**dust** /dust||dʌst/ *n* **1** fine dry particles of any solid matter, esp earth; *specif* the fine particles of waste that settle esp on household surfaces **2** the particles into which sthg, esp the human body, disintegrates or decays **3** sthg worthless <*worldly success was ~ to him*> **4** the surface of the ground **5a** a cloud of dust <*the cars raised quite a ~*> **b** confusion, disturbance – esp in *kick up/raise a dust*

[2]**dust** *vt* **1** to make free of dust (e g by wiping or beating) **2** to prepare to use again – usu + *down* or *off* **3a** to sprinkle with fine particles <~ *a cake with icing sugar*> **b** to sprinkle in the form of dust <~ *sugar over a cake*> ~ *vi* **1** *of a bird* to work dust into the feathers **2** to remove dust (e g from household articles), esp by wiping or brushing

'**dust,bin** /-,bin||-,bɪn/ *n*, *Br* a container for holding household refuse until collection

'**dust ,bowl** *n* a region that suffers from prolonged droughts and dust storms

'**dust,cart** /-,kaht||-,kɑ:t/ *n*, *Br* a vehicle for collecting household waste

'**dust,coat** /-,koht||-,kəʊt/ *n*, *chiefly Br* a loose lightweight coat worn to protect clothing

duster /'dustə||'dʌstə/ *n* sthg that removes dust; *specif* a cloth for removing dust from household articles

'**dust ,jacket** *n* a removable outer paper cover for a book

'**dustman** /-mən||-mən/ *n*, *Br* one employed to remove household refuse

'**dust,pan** /-,pan||-,pæn/ *n* a shovel-like utensil with a handle into which household dust and litter is swept

'**dust,sheet** /-,sheet||-,ʃi:t/ *n* a large sheet (e g of cloth) used as a cover to protect sthg, esp furniture, from dust

'**dust-,up** *n* a quarrel, row – infml

dusty /'dusti||'dʌstɪ/ *adj* **1** covered with or full of dust **2** consisting of dust; powdery **3** resembling dust, esp in consistency or colour **4** lacking vitality; dry <~ *scholarship*> – **dustily** *adv*, **dustiness** *n* – **not so dusty** fairly good

[1]**dutch** /duch||dʌtʃ/ *adv*, *often cap* with each person paying for him-/herself <*we always go ~*>

[2]**dutch** *n*, *Br* one's wife – slang

Dutch *n* **1** the Germanic language of the Netherlands **2** *pl in constr* the people of the Netherlands – **Dutch** *adj*, **Dutchman** *n*

,**Dutch 'auction** *n* an auction in which the auctioneer gradually reduces the bidding price until a bid is received

,**Dutch 'barn** *n* a large barn with open sides used esp for storage of hay

,**Dutch 'cap** *n* a moulded cap, usu of thin rubber, that fits over the uterine cervix to act as a mechanical contraceptive barrier

,**Dutch 'courage** *n* courage produced by intoxication rather than inherent resolution

,**Dutch 'elm di,sease** *n* a fatal disease of elms caused by a fungus, spread from tree to tree by a beetle, and characterized by yellowing of the foliage and defoliation

,**Dutch 'oven** *n* **1** a 3-walled metal shield used for roasting before an open fire **2** a brick oven in which food is cooked by heat radiating from the prewarmed walls

,**Dutch 'treat** *n* a meal or entertainment for which each person pays for him-/herself

,**Dutch 'uncle** *n* one who admonishes sternly and bluntly

dutiable /'dyoohti·əbl, -tyəbl||'dju:tɪəbl, -tjəbl/ *adj* subject to a duty <~ *imports*>

dutiful /ˈdyoohtif(ə)l‖ˈdjuːtɪf(ə)l/ *adj* **1** filled with or motivated by a sense of duty **2** proceeding from or expressive of a sense of duty <~ *affection*> – **dutifully** *adv*, **dutifulness** *n*

duty /ˈdyoohti‖ˈdjuːtɪ/ *n* **1** conduct due to parents and superiors; respect **2a** tasks, conduct, service, or functions that arise from one's position, job, or moral obligations **b** assigned (military) service or business **3a** a moral or legal obligation **b** the force of moral obligation **4** a tax, esp on imports

ˌduty-ˈfree *adj* exempted from duty

duvet /ˈdoohvay‖ˈduːveɪ/ *n* a large quilt filled with insulating material (e g down, feathers, or acrylic fibre), usu placed inside a removable fabric cover and used in place of bedclothes

[1]**dwarf** /dwawf‖dwɔːf/ *n, pl* **dwarfs, dwarves** /dwawvz‖dwɔːvz/ **1** a person of unusually small stature; *esp* one whose bodily proportions are abnormal **2** an animal or plant much below normal size **3** a small manlike creature in esp Norse and Germanic mythology who was skilled as a craftsman – **dwarfish** *adj*, **dwarfishness** *n*, **dwarflike** *adj*, **dwarfness** *n*

[2]**dwarf** *vt* **1** to stunt the growth of **2** to cause to appear smaller <*the other buildings are* ~ed *by the skyscraper*>

dwell /dwel‖dwel/ *vi* **dwelt** /dwelt‖dwelt/, **dwelled** /dweld, dwelt‖dweld, dwelt/ **1** to remain for a time **2** to keep the attention directed, esp in speech or writing; linger – + *on* or *upon* <dwelt *on the weaknesses in his opponent's arguments*> **3** to live as a resident; reside – fml – **dweller** *n*

dwelling /ˈdweling‖ˈdwelɪŋ/ *n* a place (e g a house or flat) in which people live – fml or humor

dwindle /ˈdwindl‖ˈdwɪndl/ *vi* to become steadily less in quantity; shrink, diminish

[1]**dye** /die‖daɪ/ *n* **1** a colour or tint produced by dyeing **2** a soluble or insoluble colouring matter

[2]**dye** *vt* **dyeing** to impart a new and often permanent colour to, esp by impregnation with a dye – **dyer** *n*, **dyeable** *adj*, **dyeability** *n*

ˌdyed-in-the-ˈwool *adj* thoroughgoing, uncompromising <*a* ~ *conservative*>

ˈdyeˌstuff /-ˌstuf‖-ˌstʌf/ *n* DYE 2

[1]**dyke, dike** /diek‖daɪk/ *n* **1** an artificial watercourse; a ditch **2** a bank, usu of earth, constructed to control or confine water **3** a barrier preventing passage, esp of sthg undesirable **4** a raised causeway **5** a body of intrusive igneous rock running across the strata **6** *chiefly Br* a natural watercourse **7** *dial Br* a wall or fence of turf or stone

[2]**dyke, dike** *vt* to surround or protect with a dyke

dynamic /dieˈnamik, di-‖daɪˈnæmɪk, dɪ-/ *adj* **1a** of physical force or energy in motion **b** of dynamics **2a** marked by continuous activity or change <*a* ~ *population*> **b** energetic, forceful <*a* ~ *personality*> [French *dynamique*, fr Greek *dynamikos* powerful, fr *dynamis* power, fr *dynasthai* to be able] – **dynamical** *adj*, **dynamically** *adv*

dyˈnamics *n pl but sing or pl in constr* **1** a branch of mechanics that deals with forces and their relation to the motion of bodies **2** a pattern of change or growth <*population* ~> **3** variation and contrast in force or intensity (e g in music)

dynamism /ˈdienəˌmiz(ə)m‖ˈdaɪnəˌmɪz(ə)m/ *n* **1a** a philosophical system that describes the universe in terms of the interplay of forces **b** DYNAMICS 2 **2** dynamic quality – **dynamist** *n*, **dynamistic** *adj*

[1]**dynamite** /ˈdienəˌmiet‖ˈdaɪnəˌmaɪt/ *n* **1** a blasting explosive that is made of nitroglycerine absorbed in a porous material **2** sby or sthg that has explosive force or effect – infml

[2]**dynamite** *vt* to destroy with dynamite – **dynamiter** *n*

dynamo /ˈdienəmoh‖ˈdaɪnəməʊ/ *n, pl* **dynamos** **1** a machine by which mechanical energy is converted into electrical energy; *specif* such a device that produces direct current (e g in a motor car) **2** a forceful energetic person

dynasty /ˈdinəsti‖ˈdɪnəstɪ/ *n* a succession of hereditary rulers; *also* the time during which such a dynasty rules – **dynastic** *adj*, **dynastically** *adv*

dys- /dis-‖dɪs-/ *prefix* **1** abnormal; impaired <dys*function*> **2** difficult; painful <dys*uria*>

dysentery /ˈdis(ə)ntri‖ˈdɪs(ə)ntrɪ/ *n* any of several infectious diseases characterized by severe diarrhoea, usu with passing of mucus and blood – **dysenteric** *adj*

dysˈlexia /-ˈleksi·ə‖-ˈleksɪə/ *n* a maldevelopment of reading ability in otherwise normal children due to a neurological disorder [deriv of Greek *dys* difficult, bad + *lexis* word, speech] – **dyslexic** *adj*

dysˈpepsia /-ˈpepsi·ə‖-ˈpepsɪə/ *n* indigestion

dysˈpeptic /-ˈpeptik‖-ˈpeptɪk/ *adj* **1** relating to or having dyspepsia **2** showing a sour disposition; ill-tempered – **dyspeptic** *n*, **dyspeptically** *adv*

E

e /ee‖iː/ *n, pl* **e's, es** *often cap* **1** (a graphic representation of or device for reproducing) the 5th letter of the English alphabet **2** the 3rd note of a C-major scale **3** one designated *e*: e g **3a** the 5th in order or class **b** the base of the system of natural logarithms having the approximate numerical value 2.71828

e- *prefix* **1a** deprive of; remove (a specified quality or thing) <*emasculate*> **b** lacking; without <*edentate*> **2** out; on the outside <*evert*> **3** forth <*emanate*>

[1]**each** /eech‖iːtʃ/ *adj* being one of 2 or more distinct individuals considered separately and often forming a group

[2]**each** *pron* each one

[3]**each** *adv* to or for each; apiece

ˌeach ˈother *pron* each of 2 or more in reciprocal action or relation – not used as subject of a clause <*wore* each other's *shirts*> <*looked at* ~ *in surprise*>

ˌeach ˈway *adj or adv, Br, of a bet* backing a horse, dog, etc to finish in the first two, three, or four in a race as well as to win

eager /ˈeegə‖ˈiːgə/ *adj* marked by keen, enthusiastic, or impatient desire or interest – **eagerly** *adv*, **eagerness** *n*

eagle /ˈeegl‖ˈiːgl/ *n* **1** any of various large birds of prey noted for their strength, size, gracefulness, keenness of vision, and powers of flight **2** a 10-dollar gold coin of the USA **3** a golf score for 1 hole of 2 strokes less than par

ˌeagle-ˈeyed *adj* **1** having very good eyesight **2** looking very keenly at sthg **3** good at noticing details; observant

eaglet /ˈeeglit‖ˈiːglɪt/ *n* a young eagle

[1]**ear** /iə‖ɪə/ *n* **1a** (the external part of) the characteristic vertebrate organ of hearing and equilibrium **b** any of various organs capable of detecting vibratory motion **2** the sense or act of hearing **3** sensitivity to musical tone and pitch **4** sthg resembling an ear in shape or position; *esp* a projecting part (e g a lug or handle) **5a** sympathetic attention <*gained the* ~ *of the managing director*> **b** *pl* notice, awareness <*it has come to my* ~s *that you are discontented*> – **by ear** from memory of the sound without having seen the written music – **in one ear and out the other** through one's mind without making an impression – **up to one's ears** deeply involved; heavily implicated

[2]**ear** *n* the fruiting spike of a cereal, including both the seeds and protective structures

earache /ˈiəˌrayk‖ˈɪəˌreɪk/ *n* an ache or pain in the ear

ˈearˌdrum /-ˌdrum‖-ˌdrʌm/ *n* TYMPANIC MEMBRANE

eared /iəd‖ɪəd/ *adj* having ears, esp of a specified kind or number <*long*-eared *owl*>

ˈearful /-f(ə)l‖-f(ə)l/ *n* **1** an outpouring of news or gossip **2** a sharp verbal reprimand *USE* infml

earl /uhl‖ɜːl/ *n* a member of the British peerage ranking below a marquess and above a viscount – **earldom** *n*

ˈearˌlobe /-ˌlohb‖-ˌləʊb/ *n* the pendent part of the ear of humans or of some fowls

[1]**early** /ˈuhli‖ˈɜːlɪ/ *adv* **1** at or near the beginning of a period of time, a development, or a series **2** before the usual or proper time

[2]**early** *adj* **1a** of or occurring near the beginning of a period of time, a development, or a series **b(1)** distant in past time **b(2)** primitive **2a** occurring before the usual time **b** occurring in the near future – **earliness** *n*

ˌearly ˈclosing *n* **1** the closing of shops in a British town or district on 1 afternoon a week **2** the day on which shops close early

[1]**earmark** /ˈiəˌmahk‖ˈɪəˌmɑːk/ *n* **1** a mark of identification on the ear of an animal **2** a distinguishing or identifying characteristic

[2]**ˈearˌmark** *vt* **1** to mark (livestock) with an earmark **2** to designate (e g funds) for a specific use or owner

ˈearˌmuffs /-ˌmufs‖-ˌmʌfs/ *n pl* a pair of ear coverings connected by a flexible band and worn as protection against cold or noise

earn /uhn‖ɜːn/ *vt* **1** to receive (e g money) as return for effort, esp for work done or services rendered **2** to bring in as income **3** to gain or deserve because of one's behaviour or qualities

[1]**earnest** /ˈuhnist‖ˈɜːnɪst/ *n* a serious and intent mental state – esp in *in earnest*

[2]**earnest** *adj* determined and serious – **earnestly** *adv*, **earnestness** *n*

[3]**earnest** *n* **1** sthg of value, esp money, given by a buyer to a seller to seal a bargain **2** a token of what is to come; a pledge

earnings /ˈuhningz‖ˈɜːnɪŋz/ *n pl* money earned; *esp* gross revenue

earphone /ˈiəˌfohn‖ˈɪəˌfəʊn/ *n* a device that converts electrical energy into sound waves and is worn over or inserted into the ear

ˈearˌpiece /-ˌpees‖-ˌpiːs/ *n* a part of an instrument (e g a telephone) to which the ear is applied for listening; *esp* an earphone

ˈearˌplug /-ˌplug‖-ˌplʌg/ *n* a device inserted into the outer opening of the ear for protection against water, loud noise, etc

ˈearˌring /-ˌring‖-ˌrɪŋ/ *n* an ornament for the ear that is attached to the earlobe

ˈearˌshot /-ˌshot‖-ˌʃɒt/ *n* the range within which sthg, esp the unaided voice, may be heard

[1]**earth** /uhth‖ɜːθ/ *n* **1** [3]SOIL 2a **2** the sphere of mortal or worldly existence as distinguished from spheres of spiritual life **3a** areas of land as distinguished from sea and air **b** the solid ground **4** *often cap* the planet on which we live that is third in order from the sun **5** the people of the planet earth **6** the lair of a fox, badger, etc **7** a metallic oxide formerly classed as an element **8** *chiefly Br* **8a** an electrical connection to earth **b** a large conducting body (e g the earth) used as the arbitrary zero of potential **9** a huge amount of money <*his suit must have cost the* ~*!*> – infml – **earthward** *adj or adv*, **earthwards** *adv* – **on earth** – used to intensify an interrogative pronoun <*where* on earth *is it?*>

[2]**earth** *vt* **1** to drive (e g a fox) to hiding in its earth **2** to draw soil about (plants) – usu + *up* **3** *chiefly Br* to connect electrically with earth ~ *vi, of a hunted animal* to hide in its lair

ˈearthˌbound /-ˌbownd‖-ˌbaʊnd/ *adj* **1a** restricted to the earth **b** heading or directed towards the planet earth <*an* ~ *spaceship*> **2a** bound by worldly interests; lacking spiritual quality **b** pedestrian, unimaginative

earthen /ˈuhdh(ə)n, -th(ə)n‖ˈɜːð(ə)n, -θ(ə)n/ *adj* made of earth or baked clay

ˈearthenˌware /-ˌweə‖-ˌweə/ *n* ceramic ware made of slightly porous opaque clay fired at a low temperature

ˈearthˌling /-ˌling‖-ˌlɪŋ/ *n* an inhabitant of the earth, esp as contrasted with inhabitants of other planets

[1]**ˈearthly** /-li‖-lɪ/ *adj* **1a** characteristic of or belonging to this earth **b** relating to human beings' actual life on this earth; worldly **2** possible – usu + neg or interrog <*there is no* ~ *reason for such behaviour*> – **earthliness** *n*

[2]**earthly** *n* a chance of success – usu + neg; infml

ˈearthˌnut /-ˌnut‖-ˌnʌt/ *n* the pignut

ˈearthˌquake /-ˌkwayk‖-ˌkweɪk/ *n* a (repeated) usu violent earth tremor caused by volcanic action or processes within the earth's crust

ˈearthˌshaking /-ˌshayking‖-ˌʃeɪkɪŋ/ *adj* having tremendous importance or a widespread often violent effect – chiefly infml

ˈ**earthˌwork** /-ˌwuhk‖-ˌwɜːk/ *n* (the construction of) an embankment, field fortification, etc made of earth

ˈ**earthˌworm** /-ˌwuhm‖-ˌwɜːm/ *n* any of numerous widely distributed hermaphroditic worms that live in the soil

earthy /ˈuhthi‖ˈɜːθɪ/ *adj* **1** consisting of, resembling, or suggesting earth <*an* ~ *flavour*> **2** crude, coarse <~ *humour*> – **earthily** *adv*, **earthiness** *n*

earwig /ˈiəˌwig‖ˈɪəˌwɪg/ *n* any of numerous insects that have slender many-jointed antennae and a pair of appendages resembling forceps [Old English *ēarwicga*, fr *ēare* ear + *wicga* insect; so called fr the insect's reputed habit of creeping into people's ears]

[1]**ease** /eez‖iːz/ *n* **1** being comfortable: e g **1a** freedom from pain, discomfort, or anxiety **b** freedom from labour or difficulty **c** freedom from embarrassment or constraint; naturalness **2** facility, effortlessness **3** easing or being eased – **easeful** *adj*, **easefully** *adv* – **at ease 1** free from pain or discomfort **2** free from restraint or formality <*he's quite* at *his* ease *in any kind of company*> **3** standing with the feet apart and usu 1 or both hands behind the body – used esp as a military command

[2]**ease** *vt* **1** to free from sthg that pains, disquiets, or burdens – + *of* **2** to alleviate **3** to lessen the pressure or tension of, esp by slackening, lifting, or shifting **4** to make less difficult **5** to manoeuvre gently or carefully in a specified way <~d *the heavy block into position*> **6** to put the helm of (a ship) towards the lee ~ *vi* **1** to decrease in activity, intensity, or severity – often + *off* or *up* <*the rain is* easing *off*> **2** to manoeuvre oneself gently or carefully <~d *through a hole in the fence*>

easel /ˈeezl‖ˈiːzl/ *n* a frame for supporting sthg (e g an artist's canvas) [Dutch *ezel*, lit., ass]

easily /ˈeezəli‖ˈiːzəlɪ/ *adv* **1** without difficulty <*my car will do a hundred* ~> **2** without doubt; by far <~ *the best*>

[1]**east** /eest‖iːst/ *adj or adv* towards, at, belonging to, or coming from the east

[2]**east** *n* **1** (the compass point corresponding to) the direction 90° to the right of north that is the general direction of sunrise **2a** *often cap* regions or countries lying to the east of a specified or implied point of orientation **b** *cap* regions lying to the east of Europe **3** the altar end of a church **4** sby (e g a bridge player) occupying a position designated east – **eastward** *adj or n*, **eastwards** *adv*

Easter /ˈeestə‖ˈiːstə/ *n* a feast that commemorates Christ's resurrection and is observed on the first Sunday after the first full moon following March 21

ˈ**Easter ˌegg** *n* a (chocolate or painted and hard-boiled) egg given as a present and eaten at Easter

[1]ˈ**easterly** /-li‖-lɪ/ *adj or adv* east

[2]**easterly** *n* a wind from the east

eastern /ˈeest(ə)n‖ˈiːst(ə)n/ *adj* **1** *often cap* (characteristic) of a region conventionally designated east **2** east **3 Eastern, Eastern Orthodox** ORTHODOX 2a – **easternmost** *adj*

Easterner /ˈeest(ə)nə‖ˈiːst(ə)nə/ *n*, *chiefly NAm* a native or inhabitant of the East, esp the E USA

[1]**easy** /ˈeezi‖ˈiːzɪ/ *adj* **1** causing or involving little difficulty or discomfort **2a** not severe; lenient **b** readily prevailed on; compliant **3a** plentiful in supply at low or declining interest rates <~ *money*> **b** less in demand and usu lower in price <*gilts were* easier> **4a** marked by peace and comfort <*the* ~ *course of his life*> **b** not hurried or strenuous <*an* ~ *pace*> **c** free from pain, annoyance, or anxiety **5** marked by social ease <~ *manners*> **6** not burdensome or straitened <*bought on* ~ *terms*> **7** marked by ready facility and freedom from constraint <*an* ~ *flowing style*> **8** *chiefly Br* not having marked preferences on a particular issue – infml – **easiness** *n*

[2]**easy** *adv* **1** easily <*promises come* ~> **2** without undue speed or excitement; slowly, cautiously <*take it* ~> – **easy on 1** leniently with <*go* easy on *the boy*> **2** not too lavishly with <*go* easy on *the ice, bartender*>

ˈ**easy ˌchair** *n* a large usu upholstered armchair designed for comfort and relaxation

ˌ**easyˈgoing** /-ˈgoh·ing‖-ˈgəʊɪŋ/ *adj* taking life easily: e g **a** placid and tolerant **b** indolent and careless – **easygoingness** *n*

eat /eet‖iːt/ *vb* **ate** /et, ayt‖et, eɪt/; **eaten** /ˈeet(ə)n‖ˈiːt(ə)n/ *vt* **1** to take in through the mouth and swallow as food **2** to consume gradually; corrode <*the acid has* ~en *away the battery terminals*> **3** to vex, bother – infml <*what's* ~ing *you?*> ~ *vi* to take food or a meal – **eatable** *adj*, **eater** *n* – **eat humble pie** to apologize or retract under pressure – **eat one's heart out** to grieve bitterly, esp for sthg desired but unobtainable – **eat one's words** to retract what one has said – **eat out of someone's hand** to accept sby's domination

eatables /ˈeetəblz‖ˈiːtəblz/ *n pl* food

eats /eets‖iːts/ *n pl* food – infml

eau de cologne /ˌoh də kəˈlohn‖ˌəʊ də kəˈləʊn/ *n, pl* **eaux de cologne** /~/ TOILET WATER [French, lit., Cologne water, fr *Cologne*, city in Germany]

eaves /eevz‖iːvz/ *n pl* the lower border of a roof that overhangs the wall

eavesdrop /ˈeevzˌdrop‖ˈiːvzˌdrɒp/ *vi* to listen secretly to what is said in private – **eavesdropper** *n*

[1]**ebb** /eb‖eb/, ˈ**ebb ˌtide** *n* **1** the flowing out of the tide towards the sea **2** a point or condition of decline <*relations were at a low* ~>

[2]**ebb** *vi* **1** *of tidal water* to recede from the flood state **2** to decline from a higher to a lower level or from a better to a worse state

[1]**ebony** /ˈebəni‖ˈebənɪ/ *n* (any of various tropical trees that yield) a hard heavy black wood

[2]**ebony** *adj* **1** made of or resembling ebony **2** black, dark – usu apprec

ebullience /iˈbuli·əns, -yəns‖ɪˈbʌlɪəns, -jəns/, **ebulliency** /-si‖-sɪ/ *n* the quality of being full of liveliness and enthusiasm; exuberance

ebullient /iˈbuli·ənt, -yənt‖ɪˈbʌlɪənt, -jənt/ *adj* **1** boiling, agitated **2** characterized by ebullience – **ebulliently** *adv*

[1]**eccentric** /ikˈsentrik‖ɪkˈsentrɪk/ *adj* **1** not

having the same centre <~ *spheres*> **2** deviating from established convention; odd <~ *behaviour*> **3a** deviating from a circular path <*an* ~ *orbit*> **b** located elsewhere than at the geometrical centre; *also* having the axis or support so located <*an* ~ *wheel*> – **eccentrically** *adv*, **eccentricity** *n*

[2]**eccentric** *n* **1** a mechanical device using eccentrically mounted parts to transform circular into reciprocating motion **2** an eccentric person

ecclesiastic /iˌkleeziˈastik‖ɪˌkliːzɪˈæstɪk/ *n* a clergyman

ecclesiastical /iˌkleeziəˈastikl‖ɪˌkliːzɪəˈæstɪkl/ *adj* **1** of a church, esp as a formal and established institution **2** suitable for use in a church <~ *vestments*> – **ecclesiastically** *adv*

echelon /ˈeshəlon, ˈay-‖ˈeʃəlɒn, ˈeɪ-/ *n* **1** an arrangement of units (e g of troops or ships) resembling a series of steps **2** a particular division of a headquarters or supply organization in warfare **3** any of a series of levels or grades (e g of authority or responsibility) in some organized field of activity [French *échelon*, lit., rung of a ladder, fr *échelle* ladder]

echinoderm /iˈkienohˌduhm‖ɪˈkaɪnəʊˌdɜːm/ *n* any of a phylum of radially symmetrical marine animals consisting of the starfishes, sea urchins, and related forms – **echinodermatous** *adj*

[1]**echo** /ˈekoh‖ˈekəʊ/ *n, pl* **echoes** **1a** the repetition of a sound caused by the reflection of sound waves **b** the repeated sound due to such reflection **2** sby or sthg that repeats or imitates another **3** a repercussion, result **4** a soft repetition of a musical phrase **5a** the reflection by an object of transmitted radar signals **b** a blip – **echoey** *adj*

[2]**echo** *vi* **1** to resound with echoes **2** to produce an echo ~ *vt* **1** to repeat, imitate **2** to send back or repeat (a sound) as an echo

éclair /iˈkleə, ay-‖ɪˈkleə, eɪ-/ *n* a small light oblong cake of choux pastry that is split and filled with cream and usu topped with (chocolate) icing [French, lit., lightning]

éclat /ayˈklah ‖eɪˈklɑː (*Fr* ekla)/ *n* **1** ostentatious display **2** brilliant or conspicuous success **3** acclaim, applause [French, splinter, burst, ostentation]

[1]**eclectic** /eˈklektik, i-‖eˈklektɪk, ɪ-/ *adj* **1** selecting or using elements from various doctrines, methods, or styles **2** composed of elements drawn from various sources – **eclectically** *adv*, **eclecticism** *n*

[2]**eclectic** *n* one who uses an eclectic method or approach

[1]**eclipse** /iˈklips‖ɪˈklɪps/ *n* **1a** the total or partial obscuring of one celestial body by another **b** passage into the shadow of a celestial body **2** a falling into obscurity or decay; a decline

[2]**eclipse** *vt* to cause an eclipse of: e g **a** to obscure, darken **b** to surpass

[1]**ecliptic** /iˈkliptik‖ɪˈklɪptɪk/ *n* **1** the plane of the earth's orbit extended to meet the celestial sphere **2** a great circle drawn on a terrestrial globe making an angle of about 23° 27′ with the equator and used for illustrating and solving astronomical problems

[2]**ecliptic** *adj* of the ecliptic or an eclipse

eclogue /ˈekˌlog‖ˈekˌlɒg/ *n* a short poem; *esp* a pastoral dialogue

ecology /iˈkoləji, ee-‖ɪˈkɒlədʒɪ, iː-/ *n* (a science concerned with) the interrelationship of living organisms and their environments [deriv of Greek *oikos* house + *logos* speech, reason] – **ecological** *adj*, **ecologically** *adv*, **ecologist** *n*

economic /ˌekəˈnomik, ˌee-‖ˌekəˈnɒmɪk, ˌiː-/ *adj* **1** of economics **2** of or based on the production, distribution, and consumption of goods and services **3** of an economy **4** having practical or industrial significance or uses; affecting material resources <~ *pests*> **5** profitable – **economically** *adv*

economical /ˌekəˈnomikl, ˌee-‖ˌekəˈnɒmɪkl, ˌiː-/ *adj* thrifty – **economically** *adv*

ˌecoˈnomics *n pl but sing or pl in constr* **1** a social science concerned chiefly with the production, distribution, and consumption of goods and services **2** economic aspect or significance – **economist** *n*

econom·ize, -ise /iˈkonəˌmiez‖ɪˈkɒnəˌmaɪz/ *vi* to practise economy; be frugal – often + *on* <~ *on oil*> ~*vt* to use more economically; save <~ *oil*> – **economizer** *n*

economy /iˈkonəmi‖ɪˈkɒnəmɪ/ *n* **1** thrifty and efficient use of material resources; frugality in expenditure; *also* an instance or means of economizing **2** efficient and sparing use of nonmaterial resources (e g effort, language, or motion) **3** the structure of economic life in a country, area, or period; *specif* an economic system [deriv of Greek *oikonomia*, fr *oikos* house + *nemein* to manage]

ˈecoˌsystem /-ˌsistəm‖-ˌsɪstəm/ *n* a complex consisting of a community and its environment functioning as a reasonably self-sustaining ecological unit in nature

ecstasy /ˈekstəsi‖ˈekstəsɪ/ *n* **1** a state of very strong feeling, esp of joy or happiness **2** a (mystic or prophetic) trance

ecstatic /ikˈstatik, ek-‖ɪkˈstætɪk, ek-/ *adj* subject to, causing, or in a state of ecstasy – **ecstatic** *n*, **ecstatically** *adv*

ˈectoˌderm /-ˌduhm‖-ˌdɜːm/ *n* **1** the outer cellular membrane of an animal having only 2 germ layers in the embryo (e g a jellyfish) **2** (a tissue derived from) the outermost of the 3 primary germ layers of an embryo – **ectodermal, ectodermic** *adj*

ectoplasm /ˈektəˌplaz(ə)m, ˈektoh-‖ˈektə-ˌplæz(ə)m, ˈektəʊ-/ *n* **1** the outer relatively rigid granule-free layer of the cytoplasm of a cell **2** a substance supposed to emanate from a spiritualist medium in a state of trance – **ectoplasmic** *adj*

ecumenical *also* **oecumenical** /ˌekyooˈmenikl, ˌeek-‖ˌekjʊˈmenɪkl, ˌiːk-/ *adj* **1** of or representing the whole of a body of churches <*an* ~ *council*> **2** promoting or tending towards worldwide Christian unity or cooperation <~ *discussions*> – **ecumenicalism** *n*, **ecumenically** *adv*, **ecumenism** *n*, **ecumenist** *n*

eczema /ˈeks(i)mə‖ˈeks(ɪ)mə/ *n* an inflammatory condition of the skin characterized by itching and oozing blisters [Greek *ekzema*, fr *ekzein* to erupt, fr *ex* out + *zein* to boil] – **eczematous** *adj*

[1]**-ed** /-d‖-d *after vowels and m,n,ng,v,z,zh,j,dh,r,l,b,g;* -id‖-ɪd *after d,t;* -t *after all others. Exceptions are given at their own entry*

suffix **1** – used to form the past participle of regular weak verbs that end in a consonant <*end*ed>, a vowel other than *e* <*halo*ed>, or a final *y* that changes to *i* <*cri*ed>; compare ¹-D 1 **2a** having; characterized by; provided with <*polo-neck*ed> <*2-legg*ed> **b** wearing; dressed in <*bowler-hatt*ed> **c** having the characteristics of <*bigot*ed> ***USE*** (*2*) used to form adjectives from nouns that end in a consonant, a vowel other than *e*, or a final *y* that changes to *i*; compare ¹-D 2

2**-ed** *suffix* – used to form the past tense of regular weak verbs that end in a consonant, a vowel other than *e*, or a final *y* that changes to *i*; compare ²-D

Edam /ˈeedam‖ˈiːdæm/ *n* a yellow mild cheese of Dutch origin usu made in flattened balls coated with red wax [*Edam*, town in the Netherlands]

1**eddy** /ˈedi‖ˈedɪ/ *n* **1** a current of water or air running contrary to the main current; *esp* a small whirlpool **2** sthg (e g smoke or fog) moving in the manner of an eddy or whirlpool

2**eddy** *vb* to (cause to) move in or like an eddy <*the crowd* eddied *about in the marketplace*>

edelweiss /ˈaydlˌvies‖ˈeɪdlˌvaɪs/ *n* a small perennial plant that is covered in dense fine white hairs and grows high in the Alps [German, fr *edel* noble + *weiss* white]

Eden /ˈeedn‖ˈiːdn/ *n* **1** the garden where, according to the account in Genesis, Adam and Eve lived before the Fall **2** PARADISE 2 – **Edenic** *adj*

1**edge** /ej‖edʒ/ *n* **1a** the cutting side of a blade **b** the (degree of) sharpness of a blade **c** penetrating power; keenness <*took the* ~ *off the criticism*> **2a** the line where an object or area begins or ends; a border <*the town stands on the* ~ *of a plain*> **b** the narrow part adjacent to a border; the brink, verge **c** a point that marks a beginning or transition; a threshold – esp in *on the edge of* <*felt herself to be on the* ~ *of insanity*> **d** a favourable margin; an advantage <*had the* ~ *on the competition*> **3** a line where 2 planes or 2 plane faces of a solid body meet or cross **4** the edging of a cricket ball – **on edge** anxious, nervous

2**edge** *vt* **1** to give or supply an edge to **2** to move or force gradually in a specified way <~d *him off the road*> **3** to incline (a ski) sideways so that 1 edge cuts into the snow **4** to hit (a ball) or the bowling of (a bowler) in cricket with the edge of the bat ~*vi* to advance cautiously (e g by short sideways steps) – **edger** *n*

edged /ejd‖edʒd/ *adj* having a specified kind of edge, boundary, or border or a specified number of edges – usu in combination <*rough*-edged>

ˈ**edgeways** /-ˌwayz, -wiz‖-ˌweɪz, -wɪz/, **edgewise** /-ˌwiez‖-ˌwaɪz/ *adv* with the edge foremost; sideways

edging /ˈejing‖ˈedʒɪŋ/ *n* sthg that forms an edge or border

edgy /ˈeji‖ˈedʒɪ/ *adj* tense, irritable; ON EDGE – **edgily** *adv*, **edginess** *n*

edible /ˈedəbl‖ˈedəbl/ *adj* fit to be eaten as food – **edible** *n*, **edibleness** *n*, **edibility** *n*

edict /ˈeedikt‖ˈiːdɪkt/ *n* **1** an official public decree **2** the order or command of an authority – **edictal** *adj*

edification /ˌedifiˈkaysh(ə)n‖ˌedɪfɪˈkeɪʃ(ə)n/ *n* the improvement of character or the mind – fml – **edificatory** *adj*

edifice /ˈedifis‖ˈedɪfɪs/ *n* **1** a building; *esp* a large or massive structure **2** a large abstract structure or organization

edify /ˈediˌfie‖ˈedɪˌfaɪ/ *vt* to instruct and improve, esp in moral and spiritual knowledge

edit /ˈedit‖ˈedɪt/ *vt* **1a** to prepare an edition of **b** to assemble (e g a film or tape recording) by deleting, inserting, and rearranging material **c** to alter or adapt (e g written or spoken words), esp to make consistent with a particular standard or purpose **2** to direct the publication of <~s *the local newspaper*> **3** to delete – usu + *out* – **editable** *adj*

edition /iˈdish(ə)n‖ɪˈdɪʃ(ə)n/ *n* **1a** the form in which a text is published <*paperback* ~> **b** the whole number of copies published at one time **c** the issue of a newspaper or periodical for a specified time or place **2** the whole number of articles of one style put out at one time <*a limited* ~ *of collectors' pieces*> **3** a copy, version <*she's a friendlier* ~ *of her mother*>

editor /ˈeditə‖ˈedɪtə/ *n* **1** one who edits written material, films, etc, esp as an occupation **2** a person responsible for the editorial policy and content of a (section of a) newspaper or periodical – **editorship** *n*

1**editorial** /ˌediˈtawri·əl‖ˌedɪˈtɔːrɪəl/ *adj* of or written by an editor – **editorially** *adv*

2**editorial** *n* a newspaper or magazine article that gives the opinions of the editors or publishers

ˌ**ediˈtorial·ˌize, -ise** /-ˌiez‖-ˌaɪz/ *vi* **1** to express an opinion in the form of an editorial **2** to introduce personal opinion into an apparently objective report (e g by direct comment or hidden bias) – **editorializer** *n*, **editorialization** *n*

educate /ˈedyooˌkayt, ˈejoo-‖ˈedjʊˌkeɪt, ˈedʒʊ-/ *vt* **1** to provide schooling for **2** to develop mentally or morally, esp by instruction **3** to train or improve (faculties, judgment, skills, etc) – **educable** *adj*, **educative** *adj*, **educator** *n*

ˈ**eduˌcated** *adj* **1** having an education, esp one beyond the average **2a** trained, skilled <*an* ~ *palate*> **b** befitting sby educated <~ *conversation*> **c** based on some knowledge of fact <*an* ~ *guess*> – **educatedly** *adv*, **educatedness** *n*

education /ˌedyooˈkaysh(ə)n, -joo-‖ˌedjʊˈkeɪʃ(ə)n, -dʒʊ-/ *n* **1** educating or being educated **2** the field of study that deals with methods of teaching and learning – **educational** *adj*, **educationally** *adv*

educationalist /ˌedyooˈkaysh(ə)nl·ist, -joo-‖ˌedjʊˈkeɪʃ(ə)nlɪst, -dʒʊ-/, **educationist** /-ist‖-ɪst/ *n* an educational theorist or administrator

educe /iˈdyoohs‖ɪˈdjuːs; *also* ij-‖ɪdʒ-/ *vt* **1** to elicit, develop **2** to arrive at through a consideration of the facts or evidence; infer ***USE*** fml – **educible** *adj*, **eduction** *n*

1**-ee** /-ee‖-iː/ *suffix* **1** (*vt* → *n*) one to whom (a specified action) is done <*train*ee> **2** (*n, adj, vb* → *n*) one who acts (in a specified way) <*escap*ee>

2**-ee** *suffix* (*n* → *n*) a particular, esp small, kind of <*boot*ee>

eel /eel‖iːl/ *n* any of numerous long snakelike

fishes with a smooth slimy skin and no pelvic fins – **eellike** *adj*, **eely** *adj*

e'en /een‖iːn/ *adv* even – chiefly poetic

-eer /-iə‖-ɪə/ *suffix* (*n* → *n*) person engaged in (a specified occupation or activity) <*auctioneer*> – often derog <*profiteer*>

e'er /eə‖eə/ *adv* ever – chiefly poetic

eerie *also* **eery** /ˈiəri‖ˈɪərɪ/ *adj* frighteningly strange or gloomy; weird – **eerily** *adv*, **eeriness** *n*

efface /iˈfays‖ɪˈfeɪs/ *vt* **1** to eliminate or make indistinct (as if) by wearing away a surface; obliterate **2** to make (oneself) modestly or shyly inconspicuous – **effaceable** *adj*, **effacement** *n*, **effacer** *n*

[1]**effect** /iˈfekt‖ɪˈfekt/ *n* **1a** the result of a cause or agent **b** the result of purpose or intention <*employed her knowledge to good* ~> **2** the basic meaning; intent – esp in *to that effect* and *to the effect* **3** power to bring about a result; efficacy **4** *pl* personal movable property; goods **5a** a distinctive impression on the human senses <*the use of colour produces a very striking* ~> **b** the creation of an often false desired impression <*her tears were purely for* ~> **c** sthg designed to produce a distinctive or desired impression – often pl <*special lighting* ~s> **6** the quality or state of being operative; operation <*the law comes into* ~ *next week*> **7** an experimental scientific phenomenon named usu after its discoverer – **in effect** for all practical purposes; actually although not appearing so

[2]**effect** *vt* **1** to bring about, often by surmounting obstacles; accomplish **2** to put into effect; CARRY OUT

effective /iˈfektiv‖ɪˈfektɪv/ *adj* **1a** producing a decided, decisive, or desired effect **b** impressive, striking **2** ready for service or action <~ *manpower*> **3** actual, real **4** being in effect; operative – **effectiveness** *n*

efˈfectively /-li‖-lɪ/ *adv* IN EFFECT

effectual /iˈfektyooəl, -chooəl‖ɪˈfektjʊəl, -tʃʊəl/ *adj* producing or able to produce a desired effect; adequate, effective – **effectualness** *n*, **effectuality** *n*

efˈfectually /-li‖-lɪ/ *adv* IN EFFECT

effectuate /iˈfektyoo,ayt, -choo-‖ɪˈfektjʊ,eɪt, -tʃʊ-/ *vt* EFFECT 2 – **effectuation** *n*

effeminate /iˈfeminət‖ɪˈfemɪnət/ *adj* **1** *of a man* having qualities usu thought of as feminine; not manly in appearance or manner **2** marked by an unbecoming delicacy or lack of vigour <~ *art*> – **effeminate** *n*, **effeminacy** *n*

effervesce /,efəˈves‖,efəˈves/ *vi* **1** *of a liquid* to bubble, hiss, and foam as gas escapes **2** to show liveliness or exhilaration – **effervescence** *n*, **effervescent** *adj*, **effervescently** *adv*

effete /iˈfeet‖ɪˈfiːt/ *adj* **1** worn out; exhausted **2** marked by weakness or decadent overrefinement – **effetely** *adv*, **effeteness** *n*

efficacious /,efiˈkayshəs‖,efɪˈkeɪʃəs/ *adj* having the power to produce a desired effect – **efficacity** *n*, **efficacy** *n*, **efficaciously** *adv*, **efficaciousness** *n*

efficiency /iˈfish(ə)nsi‖ɪˈfɪʃ(ə)nsɪ/ *n* **1** the quality or degree of being efficient **2a** efficient operation **b** the ratio of the useful energy delivered by a dynamic system to the energy supplied to it

efficient /iˈfish(ə)nt‖ɪˈfɪʃ(ə)nt/ *adj* **1** *of a person* able and practical; briskly competent **2** productive of desired effects, esp with minimum waste – **efficiently** *adv*

effigy /ˈefəji‖ˈefədʒɪ/ *n* an image or representation, esp of a person; *specif* a crude figure representing a hated person

efflorescence /,eflawˈres(ə)ns‖,eflɔːˈres(ə)ns/ *n* **1** the period or state of flowering **2** the action, process, period, or result of developing and unfolding as if coming into flower; blossoming – **efflorescent** *adj*

[1]**effluent** /ˈefloo·ənt‖ˈeflʊənt/ *adj* flowing out; emanating <*an* ~ *river*>

[2]**effluent** *n* sthg that flows out: e g **a** an outflowing branch of a main stream or lake **b** smoke, liquid industrial refuse, sewage, etc discharged into the environment, esp when causing pollution

effluvium /eˈfloohvi·əm, -vyəm‖eˈfluːvɪəm, -vjəm/ *n, pl* **effluvia** /-vi·ə‖-vɪə/, **effluviums** **1** an offensive exhalation or smell (e g from rotting vegetation) **2** a by-product, esp in the form of waste

efflux /ˈefluks‖ˈeflʌks/ *n* an outflow, esp of liquid or gas – **effluxion** *n*

effort /ˈefət‖ˈefət/ *n* **1** conscious exertion of physical or mental power **2** a serious attempt; a try **3** sthg produced by exertion or trying – **effortful** *adj*, **effortless** *adj*, **effortlessly** *adv*, **effortlessness** *n*

effrontery /iˈfrunt(ə)ri‖ɪˈfrʌnt(ə)rɪ/ *n* the quality of being shamelessly bold; insolence

effulgence /iˈfulj(ə)ns‖ɪˈfʌldʒ(ə)ns/ *n* radiant splendour; brilliance – fml – **effulgent** *adj*

effuse /iˈfyoohz‖ɪˈfjuːz/ *vt* **1** to pour out (e g a liquid) **2** to radiate, emit ~ *vi* to flow out, emanate *USE* fml

effusion /iˈfyoohzh(ə)n‖ɪˈfjuːʒ(ə)n/ *n* **1** an act of effusing **2** unrestrained expression of words or feelings **3** the escape of a fluid from a containing vessel; *also* the fluid that escapes

effusive /iˈfyoohsiv‖ɪˈfjuːsɪv/ *adj* **1** unduly emotionally demonstrative; gushing **2** *of rock* characterized or formed by a nonexplosive outpouring of lava – **effusively** *adv*, **effusiveness** *n*

eft /eft‖eft/ *n* a newt

egalitarian /i,galiˈteəri·ən‖ɪ,gælɪˈteərɪən/ *adj* marked by or advocating social, political, and economic equality between human beings – **egalitarian** *n*, **egalitarianism** *n*

[1]**egg** /eg‖eg/ *vt* to incite to action – usu + *on* <~ed *the mob on to riot*>

[2]**egg** *n* **1a** the hard-shelled reproductive body produced by a bird; *esp* that produced by domestic poultry and used as a food **b** an animal reproductive body consisting of an ovum together with its nutritive and protective envelopes that is capable of developing into a new individual **c** an ovum **2** sthg resembling an egg in shape **3** a person – infml; not now in vogue <*he's a good* ~*!*>

ˈegg,cup /-,kup‖-,kʌp/ *n* a small cup without a handle used for holding a boiled egg

ˈegg,head /-,hed‖-,hed/ *n* an intellectual, highbrow – derog or humor – **eggheaded** *adj*

ˈegg,nog /-,nog‖-,nɒg/ *n* a drink consisting of eggs beaten up with sugar, milk or cream, and

often spirits
'egg,plant /-ˌplahnt‖-ˌplɑːnt/ *n* a widely cultivated plant of the nightshade family; *also, chiefly NAm* its fruit, the aubergine
[1]'egg,shell /-ˌshel‖-ˌʃel/ *n* the hard exterior covering of an egg
[2]'egg,shell *adj* **1** *esp of china* thin and fragile **2** *esp of paint* having a slight sheen
'egg ,timer *n* an instrument like a small hourglass that runs for about 3 minutes and is used for timing the boiling of eggs
egis /'eejis‖'iːdʒɪs/ *n* an aegis
eglantine /'eglәntien, -teen‖'eglәntaɪn, -tiːn/ *n* sweetbrier
ego /'eegoh, 'egoh‖'iːgәʊ, 'egәʊ/ *n, pl* **egos 1** the self, esp as contrasted with another self or the world **2** SELF-ESTEEM 1 **3** the one of the 3 divisions of the mind in psychoanalytic theory that serves as the organized conscious mediator between the person and reality, esp in the perception of and adaptation to reality
,ego'centric /-'sentrik‖-'sentrɪk/ *adj* limited in outlook or concern to one's own activities or needs; self-centred, selfish – **egocentric** *n*, **egocentrically** *adv*, **egocentricity** *n*, **egocentrism** *n*
'ego,ism /-ˌiz(ә)m‖-ˌɪz(ә)m/ *n* **1** (conduct based on) a doctrine that individual self-interest is or should be the foundation of morality **2** egotism
'egoist /-ist‖-ɪst/ *n* **1** a believer in egoism **2** an egocentric or egotistic person – **egoistic** *also* **egoistical** *adj*, **egoistically** *adv*
egotism /'eegәˌtiz(ә)m, 'egә-‖'iːgәˌtɪz(ә)m, 'egә-/ *n* **1** the practice of talking about oneself too much **2** an extreme sense of self-importance – **egotist** *n*, **egotistic, egotistical** *adj*, **egotistically** *adv*
'ego ,trip *n* an act or series of acts that selfishly enhances and satisfies one's ego – infml – **ego-trip** *vi*, **ego-tripper** *n*
egregious /i'greej(y)әs‖ɪ'griːdʒ(j)әs/ *adj* conspicuously or shockingly bad; flagrant – fml [Latin *egregius* outstanding, distinguished, fr *e-* out, away + *greg-, grex* herd] – **egregiously** *adv*, **egregiousness** *n*
egress /'eegres‖'iːgres/ *n* **1** going or coming out; *specif* the emergence of a celestial object from eclipse, transit, or occultation **2** a place or means of going out; an exit – fml – **egress** *vi*, **egression** *n*
egret /'eegrit, -gret‖'iːgrɪt, -gret/ *n* any of various herons that bear long plumes during the breeding season
[1]Egyptian /ee'jipsh(ә)n‖iː'dʒɪpʃ(ә)n/ *adj* (characteristic) of Egypt
[2]Egyptian *n* **1** a native or inhabitant of Egypt **2** the language of the ancient Egyptians to about the 3rd c AD
eh /ay‖eɪ/ *interj* – used to ask for confirmation or to express inquiry
eiderdown /'iedәˌdown‖'aɪdәˌdaʊn/ *n* **1** the down of the eider duck **2** a thick warm quilt filled with eiderdown or other insulating material
'eider ,duck *n* any of several large northern sea ducks having fine soft down
eight /ayt‖eɪt/ *n* **1** (the number) 8 **2** the eighth in a set or series **3** sthg having 8 parts or members or a denomination of 8; *esp* (the crew of) an 8-person racing boat – **eight** *adj or pron*, **eightfold** *adj or adv*
eighteen /ˌay'teen‖ˌeɪ'tiːn/ *n* (the number) 18 – **eighteen** *adj or pron*, **eighteenth** *adj or n*
eighth /ayt·th‖eɪtθ/ *adj or n* (of or being) number eight in a countable series
eighth note *n, NAm* a quaver
'eightsome reel /-s(ә)m‖-s(ә)m/ *n* a Scottish reel for eight dancers
eighty /'ayti‖'eɪtɪ/ *n* **1** (the number) 80 **2** *pl* the numbers 80 to 89; *specif* a range of temperatures, ages, or dates within a century characterized by those numbers – **eightieth** *adj or n*, **eighty** *adj or pron*, **eightyfold** *adj or adv*
eisteddfod /ie'stedhvod,ie'stedfәd‖aɪ'steðvɒd, aɪ'stedfәd/ *n, pl* **eisteddfods, eisteddfodau** /-ˌdie‖-ˌdaɪ/ a Welsh-language competitive festival of the arts, esp music and poetry [Welsh, lit., session, fr *eistedd* to sit + *bod* being] – **eisteddfodic** *adj*
[1]either /'iedhә, 'ee-‖'aɪðә, 'iː-/ *adj* **1** being the one and the other of 2 <*flowers blooming on ~ side of the path*> **2** being the one or the other of 2 <*take ~ road*>
[2]either *pron* the one or the other <*could be happy with ~ of them*>
[3]either *conj* – used before 2 or more sentence elements of the same class or function joined usu by *or* to indicate that what immediately follows is the first of 2 or more alternatives <*~ sink or swim*>
[4]either *adv* for that matter, likewise – used for emphasis after a negative or implied negation <*not wise or handsome ~*>
,either-'or *adj or n* (involving) an unavoidable choice between only 2 possibilities
[1]ejaculate /i'jakyooˌlayt‖ɪ'dʒækjʊˌleɪt/ *vt* **1** to eject from a living body; *specif* to eject (semen) in orgasm **2** to utter suddenly and vehemently – fml – **ejaculation** *n*, **ejaculatory** *adj*
[2]ejaculate /i'jakyoolәt‖ɪ'dʒækjʊlәt/ *n* the semen released by a single ejaculation
eject /i'jekt‖ɪ'dʒekt/ *vt* **1** to drive out, esp by physical force <*the hecklers were ~ed*> **2** to evict from property ~*vi* to escape from an aircraft by using the ejector seat – **ejectable** *adj*, **ejection** *n*, **ejective** *adj*, **ejector** *n*
e'jector ,seat *n* an emergency escape seat that propels an occupant out and away from an aircraft by means of an explosive charge
,eke 'out /eek‖iːk/ *vt* **1a** to make up for the deficiencies of; supplement <eked out *his income by getting a second job*> **b** to make (a supply) last by economy **2** to make (e g a living) by laborious or precarious means
el /el‖el/ *n, NAm* an elevated railway
[1]elaborate /i'lab(ә)rәt‖ɪ'læb(ә)rәt/ *adj* **1** planned or carried out with great care and attention to detail <*~ preparations*> **2** marked by complexity, wealth of detail, or ornateness; intricate <*a highly ~ coiffure*> – **elaborately** *adv*, **elaborateness** *n*
[2]elaborate /i'labәˌrayt‖ɪ'læbәˌreɪt/ *vt* **1** to build up (complex organic compounds) from simple ingredients **2** to work out in detail; develop ~*vi* to go into detail; add further information – often + *on* <*urged him to ~ on his scheme*> – **elaboration** *n*, **elaborative** *adj*

élan /ay'lonh, -'lan ‖eɪ'lɑ̃, -'læn (*Fr* elɑ̃)/ *n* vigorous spirit or enthusiasm; verve [French, fr Middle French *eslan* rush, fr *(s')eslancer* to rush]

eland /'eelənd‖'iːlənd/ *n* either of 2 large African antelopes

elapse /i'laps‖ɪ'læps/ *vi, of a period of time* to pass by

[1]**elastic** /i'lastik, i'lah-‖ɪ'læstɪk, ɪ'lɑː-/ *adj* **1a** *of a solid* capable of recovering size and shape after deformation **b** *of a gas* capable of indefinite expansion **2** buoyant, resilient **3** capable of being easily stretched or expanded and resuming its former shape **4** capable of ready change; flexible, adaptable <*an* ~ *conscience*> – **elastically** *adv*, **elasticity** *n*, **elasticize** *vt*

[2]**elastic** *n* **1** an elastic fabric usu made of yarns containing rubber **2** easily stretched rubber, usu prepared in cords, strings, or bands

elasticated /i'lasti,kaytid‖ɪ'læstɪ,keɪtɪd/ *adj* **1** *of fabric* made stretchy by the insertion or interweaving of elastic **2** elasticized

e,lastic 'band *n, Br* RUBBER BAND

Elastoplast /i'lastə,plahst‖ɪ'læstə,plɑːst/ *trademark* – used for an elastic adhesive plaster

elate /i'layt‖ɪ'leɪt/ *vt* to fill with joy or pride; put in high spirits – **elated** *adj*, **elatedly** *adv*, **elation** *n*

[1]**elbow** /'elboh‖'elbəʊ/ *n* **1a** the joint between the human forearm and upper arm **b** a corresponding joint in the forelimb of a vertebrate animal **2** an elbow-like pipe fitting **3** the part of a garment that covers the elbow – **out at elbows 1** shabbily dressed **2** POOR 1 – **up to the elbows in/with** busily engaged in

[2]**elbow** *vt* **1** to push or shove aside (as if) with the elbow; jostle **2** to force (e g one's way) rudely or roughly (as if) by pushing with the elbow <~ed *his way into the best circles*> ~*vi* to advance by elbowing one's way

'elbow ,grease *n* hard physical effort – infml

'elbowroom /-,roohm, -room‖-,ruːm, -rʊm/ *n* adequate space or scope for movement, work, or operation

[1]**elder** /'eldə‖'eldə/ *n* any of several shrubs or small trees of the honeysuckle family

[2]**elder** *adj* of earlier birth or greater age, esp than another related person or thing

[3]**elder** *n* **1** one who is older; a senior **2** one having authority by virtue of age and experience <*the village* ~s> **3** an official of the early church or of a Presbyterian congregation – **eldership** *n*

'elderberry /-b(ə)ri, -,beri‖-b(ə)rɪ, -,berɪ/ *n* (the black or red berry of) an elder

'elderly /-li‖-lɪ/ *adj* rather old – **elderliness** *n*

,elder 'statesman *n* an eminent senior or retired member of a group whose advice is often sought unofficially

eldest /'eldist‖'eldɪst/ *adj* of the greatest age or seniority; oldest

El Dorado /,el də'rahdoh, do'rah-‖,el də-'rɑːdəʊ, dɒ'rɑː-/ *n* a place of fabulous wealth, abundance, or opportunity

[1]**elect** /i'lekt‖ɪ'lekt/ *adj* **1** SELECT 1, 2 **2** chosen for salvation through divine mercy **3** chosen for office or position but not yet installed <*the president*-elect>

[2]**elect** *vt* **1** to select by vote for an office, position, or membership <~ed *him president*> **2** *of God* to choose or predestine (sby) to receive salvation **3** *chiefly NAm* to make a selection of ~*vi* to choose, decide – fml – **election** *n*

electioneer /i,leksh(ə)n'iə‖ɪ,lekʃ(ə)n'ɪə/ *vi* to work for a candidate or party in an election – **electioneer** *n*

elective /ilektiv‖ɪlektɪv/ *adj* **1a** chosen or filled by popular election <*an* ~ *office*> **b** of election **2** permitting a choice; optional – **electively** *adv*, **electiveness** *n*

elector /i'lektə‖ɪ'lektə/ *n* **1** sby qualified to vote in an election **2** sby entitled to participate in an election: e g **2a** *often cap* any of the German princes entitled to elect the Holy Roman Emperor **b** a member of the electoral college in the USA

electoral /i'lekt(ə)rəl‖ɪ'lekt(ə)rəl/ *adj* of (an) election or electors

e,lectoral 'college *n sing or pl in constr* a body of electors chosen in each state to elect the president and vice-president of the USA

electorate /i'lekt(ə)rət‖ɪ'lekt(ə)rət/ *n* **1** *often cap* the territory, jurisdiction, etc of a German elector **2** *sing or pl in constr* a body of electors

electr- /ilektr-‖ɪlektr-/, **electro-** *comb form* **1a** (caused by) electricity <electro*magnetism*> **b** electric <electr*ode*>; electric and <electro*mechanical*>; electrically <electro*positive*> **2** electrolytic <electro*analysis*> **3** electron <electro*phile*>

[1]**electric** /i'lektrik‖ɪ'lektrɪk/ *adj* **1a** of, being, supplying, producing, or produced by electricity <~ *current*> **b** operated by or using electricity <*an* ~ *motor*> **2** producing an intensely stimulating effect; thrilling <*an* ~ *performance*> **3** *of a musical instrument* electronically producing or amplifying sound [deriv of Latin *electrum* amber, alloy of gold and silver, fr Gk *ēlektron*]

[2]**electric** *n* **1** *pl* electrical parts; electric circuitry **2** electricity – sometimes pl with sing. meaning; infml

electrical /i'lektrikl‖ɪ'lektrɪkl/ *adj* **1** of or connected with electricity **2** ELECTRIC 1 <~ *appliances*> – **electrically** *adv*

e,lectric 'blanket *n* a blanket containing an electric heating element that is used to warm a bed

e,lectric 'chair *n* **1** a chair used in legal electrocution **2** *the* penalty of death by electrocution

e,lectric 'eye *n* PHOTOELECTRIC CELL

electrician /,elək'trish(ə)n, i,lek-‖,elək'trɪʃ-(ə)n, ɪ,lek-/ *n* one who installs, maintains, operates, or repairs electrical equipment

electricity /i,lek'trisəti, ,ee-‖ɪ,lek'trɪsətɪ, ,iː-/ *n* **1** (the study of) the phenomena due to (the flow or accumulation of) positively and negatively charged particles (e g protons and electrons) **2** electric current; *also* electric charge

e,lectric 'ray *n* any of various rays found in warm seas that can give elctric shocks

e,lectric 'shock *n* [2]SHOCK 4

electrify /i'lekrifie‖ɪ'lekrɪfaɪ/ *vt* **1a** to charge (a body) with electricity **b** to equip for use of or supply with electric power **2** to excite, thrill – **electrification** *n*

electro- /ilektroh-‖ɪlektrəʊ-/ – see ELECTR-

electrocardiogram /i,lektroh'kahdi·ə-,gram‖ɪ,lektrəʊ'kɑːdɪə,græm/ *n* the tracing made by an electrocardiograph

,electro'cardio,graph /-,grahf, -,graf‖-,grɑːf, -,græf/ *n* an instrument for recording the changes of electrical potential difference occurring during the heartbeat – **electrocardiographic** *adj*, **electrocardiographically** *adv*, **electrocardiography** *n*

electroconvulsive therapy /i,lektrohkən'vulsiv‖ɪ,lektrəʊkən'vʌlsɪv/ *n* a treatment for serious mental disorder, esp severe depression, in which a fit is induced by passing an electric current through the brain

electrocute /i'lektrə,kyooht‖ɪ'lektrə,kjuːt/ *vt* to execute or kill by electricity – **electrocution** *n*

electrode /i'lektrohd‖ɪ'lektrəʊd/ *n* a conductor used to establish electrical contact with a nonmetallic part of a circuit (e g the acid in a car battery)

e,lectroen'cephalo,gram /-in'sef(ə)lə-,gram‖-ɪn'sef(ə)lə,græm/ *n* the tracing made by an electroencephalograph

e,lectroen'cephalo,graph /-in'sef(ə)lə-,grahf, -,graf‖-ɪn'sef(ə)lə,grɑːf, -,græf/ *n* an instrument for detecting and recording brain waves – **electroencephalographic** *adj*, **electroencephalography** *n*

electrolysis /,elek'troləsis, i,lek-‖,elek'trɒləsɪs, ɪ,lek-/ *n* **1** the passage of an electric current through an electrolyte to generate a gas, deposit a metal on (an object serving as) an electrode, etc **2** the destruction of hair roots, warts, moles, etc by means of an electric current – **electrolyse** *vt*

electrolyte /i'lektrə,liet‖ɪ'lektrə,laɪt/ *n* **1** a nonmetallic electric conductor (e g a salt solution) in which current is carried by the movement of ions **2** a substance that becomes an ionic conductor when dissolved in a suitable solvent or melted

electromagnetic spectrum *n* the entire range of wavelengths or frequencies of electromagnetic radiation extending from gamma rays to the longest radio waves and including visible light

electromagnetism /i,lektroh'magnətiz(ə)m‖ɪ,lektrəʊ'mægnətɪz(ə)m/ *n* **1** magnetism developed by a current of electricity **2** physics dealing with the physical relations between electricity and magnetism – **electromagnetic** *adj*, **electromagnetically** *adv*

electromotive force /i,lektrə'mohtiv‖ɪ,lektrə'məʊtɪv/ *n* the amount of energy derived from an electrical source per unit current of electricity passing through the source (e g a cell or generator)

electron /i'lektron‖ɪ'lektrɒn/ *n* a negatively charged elementary particle that occurs in atoms outside the nucleus and the mass movement of which constitutes an electric current in a metal

electronic /i,lek'tronik, ,eelek-‖ɪ,lek'trɒnɪk, ,iːlek-/ *adj* **1** of electrons **2** of, being, or using devices constructed or working by the methods or principles of electronics – **electronically** *adv*

electronic mail *n* messages transmitted and received by electronic means (e g by computer or telex)

,elec'tronics *n pl but sing in constr* physics or technology dealing with the emission, behaviour, and effects of electrons in thermionic valves, transistors, or other electronic devices

e,lectron 'micro,scope *n* an instrument in which a beam of electrons is used to produce an enormously enlarged image of a minute object – **electron microscopist** *n*, **electron microscopy** *n*

e'lectron ,tube *n* an electronic device (e g a thermionic valve) consisting of a sealed container containing a vacuum or gas through which the flow of electrons is controlled

electroplate /i'lektroh,playt‖ɪ'lektrəʊ,pleɪt/ *vt* to plate with a continuous metallic coating by electrolysis

e,lectro'positive /-'pozətiv‖-'pɒzətɪv/ *adj* **1** charged with positive electric particles **2** having a tendency to release electrons

electroshock therapy /i,lektrə'shok‖ɪ-,lektrə'ʃɒk/ *n* ELECTROCONVULSIVE THERAPY

eleemosynary /,eli·i'mosin(ə)ri‖,elɪɪ'mɒsɪn-(ə)rɪ/ *adj* of, supported by, or giving charity

elegant /'elig(ə)nt‖'elɪg(ə)nt/ *adj* **1** gracefully refined or dignified (e g in manners, taste, or style) **2** tastefully rich or luxurious, esp in design or ornamentation <~ *furnishings*> **3** *of ideas* neat and simple <*an* ~ *piece of reasoning*> – **elegance** *n*, **elegantly** *adv*

,ele,giac 'couplet /,eli'jie·ək‖,elɪ'dʒaɪək/ *n* a classical verse form in which dactylic hexameters alternate with pentameters

elegy /'eləji‖'elədʒɪ/ *n* **1a** a song, poem, or other work expressing sorrow or lamentation, esp for one who is dead **b** a pensive or reflective poem that is usu nostalgic or melancholy **2** a poem in elegiac couplets – **elegize** *vb*, **elegiac** *adj*, **elegiacal** *adj*, **elegiacally** *adv*

element /'eləmənt‖'eləmənt/ *n* **1a** any of the 4 substances air, water, fire, and earth formerly believed to constitute the physical universe **b** *pl* forces of nature; *esp* violent or severe weather **c** the state or sphere natural or suited to sby or sthg <*at school she was in her* ~> **2** a constituent part: e g **2a** *pl* the simplest principles of a subject of study; the rudiments **b** any of the numbers or symbols in an array (e g a matrix) **c** a constituent of a mathematical set **d** a specified group within a human community <*the rowdy* ~ *in the classroom*> – often pl with sing. meaning **e** any of the factors determining an outcome **f** a distinct part of a composite device; *esp* a resistor in an electric heater, kettle, etc **3** any of more than 100 fundamental substances that consist of atoms of only one kind **4** *pl* the bread and wine used at Communion

elemental /,eli'mentl‖,elɪ'mentl/ *adj* **1** existing as an uncombined chemical element **2** of or resembling a great force of nature <~ *passions*> – **elemental** *n*, **elementally** *adv*

elementary /,eli'ment(ə)ri‖,elɪ'ment(ə)rɪ/ *adj* **1** of or dealing with the basic elements or principles of sthg; simple **2** ELEMENTAL 1 – **elementarily** *adv*, **elementariness** *n*

,ele,mentary 'particle *n* any of the constituents of matter and energy (e g the electron, proton, or photon) whose nature has not yet been proved to be due to the combination of other more fundamental entities

elephant /ˈelifənt‖ˈelɪfənt/ *n* a very large nearly hairless mammal having the snout prolonged into a muscular trunk and 2 upper incisors developed into long tusks which provide ivory

elephantiasis /ˌelifənˈtie·əsis‖ˌelɪfənˈtaɪəsɪs/ *n, pl* **elephantiases** /-ˌseez‖-ˌsiːz/ enormous enlargement of a limb or the scrotum caused by lymphatic obstruction

elephantine /ˌeliˈfantien‖ˌelɪˈfæntaɪn/ *adj* **1a** huge, massive **b** clumsy, ponderous **2** of an elephant

elevate /ˈeliˌvayt‖ˈelɪˌveɪt/ *vt* **1** to lift up; raise **2** to raise in rank or status; exalt **3** to improve morally, intellectually, or culturally. **4** to raise the spirits of; elate

ˈ**elevated** *adj* **1** raised, esp above a surface (e g the ground) <*an ~ road*> **2** morally or intellectually on a high plane; lofty <*~ thoughts*> **3** exhilarated in mood or feeling **4** slightly tipsy – not now in vogue

elevation /ˌeliˈvaysh(ə)n‖ˌelɪˈveɪʃ(ə)n/ *n* **1** the height to which sthg is elevated: e g **1a** the angle to which a gun is aimed above the horizon **b** the height above sea level **2** (the ability to achieve) a ballet dancer's or a skater's leap and seeming suspension in the air **3** an elevated place **4** being elevated **5** a geometrical projection (e g of a building) on a vertical plane – **elevational** *adj*

elevator /ˈeliˌvaytə‖ˈelɪˌveɪtə/ *n* **1** sby or sthg that raises or lifts sthg up: e g **1a** an endless belt or chain conveyer for raising grain, liquids, etc **b** *chiefly NAm* LIFT 9 **c** *NAm* a building for elevating, storing, discharging, and sometimes processing grain **2** a movable horizontal control surface, usu attached to the tailplane of an aircraft for controlling climb and descent

eleven /iˈlev(ə)n‖ɪˈlev(ə)n/ *n* **1** (the number) 11 **2** the eleventh in a set or series **3** *sing or pl in constr* sthg having 11 parts or members or a denomination of 11; *esp* a cricket, soccer, or hockey team – **eleven** *adj or pron*, **elevenfold** *adj or adv*, **eleventh** *adj or n*

eˌleven-ˈplus, 11-plus *n* an examination taken, esp formerly, at the age of 10-11 to determine which type of British state secondary education a child should receive

eˈlevenses *n pl but sometimes sing in constr, Br* light refreshment taken in the middle of the morning

eˌleventh ˈhour *n the* latest possible time <*won his reprieve at the ~*> – **eleventh-hour** *adj*

elf /elf‖elf/ *n, pl* **elves** /elvz‖elvz/ a (mischievous) fairy – **elfish** *adj*, **elfishly** *adv*

elfin /ˈelfin‖ˈelfɪn/ *adj* of or resembling an elf, esp in being small, sprightly, or impish

elicit /iˈlisit‖ɪˈlɪsɪt/ *vt* **1** to draw forth or bring out (sthg latent or potential) **2** to call forth or draw out (a response or reaction); evoke – **elicitor** *n*, **elicitation** *n*

elide /iˈlied‖ɪˈlaɪd/ *vt* to suppress or alter (e g a vowel or syllable) by elision

eligible /ˈelijəbl‖ˈelɪdʒəbl/ *adj* **1** qualified to be chosen; *also* entitled <*~ for promotion*> <*~ to retire*> **2** worthy or desirable, esp as a marriage partner <*an ~ young bachelor*> – **eligible** *n*, **eligibly** *adv*, **eligibility** *n*

eliminate /iˈlimiˌnayt‖ɪˈlɪmɪˌneɪt/ *vt* **1a** to cast out or get rid of completely; eradicate <*the need to ~ poverty*> **b** to set aside as unimportant; ignore **2** to expel (e g waste) from the living body **3a** to kill (a person), esp so as to remove as an obstacle **b** to remove (a competitor, team, etc) from a competition, usu by defeat – **elimination** *n*, **eliminative** *adj*, **eliminator** *n*

elision /iˈlizh(ə)n‖ɪˈlɪʒ(ə)n/ *n* an omission; *specif* omission of a vowel or syllable in pronunciation

élite, elite /iˈleet, ay-‖ɪˈliːt, eɪ-/ *n* **1** *sing or pl in constr* a small superior group; *esp* one that has a power out of proportion to its size **2** a typewriter type producing 12 characters to the inch [French *élite*, fr Old French *eslite*, lit., chosen, fr *eslire* to choose, fr Latin *eligere*] – **élite** *adj*

éˈliˌtism, elitism /-ˌtiz(ə)m‖-ˌtɪz(ə)m/ *n* (advocacy of) leadership by an élite – **élitist** *n or adj*

elixir /iˈliksə, -siə‖ɪˈlɪksə, -sɪə/ *n* **1** an alchemist's substance supposedly capable of changing base metals into gold **2a elixir, elixir of life** a substance held to be capable of prolonging life indefinitely **b** a cure-all **3** a sweetened liquid (e g a syrup) containing a drug or medicine

Elizabethan /iˌlizəˈbeeth(ə)n‖ɪˌlɪzəˈbiːθ(ə)n/ *adj* (characteristic) of (the age of) Elizabeth I – **Elizabethan** *n*

elk /elk‖elk/ *n*, **1** the largest existing deer of Europe and Asia **2** *NAm* the wapiti

ˈ**elkˌhound** /-ˌhownd‖-ˌhaʊnd/ *n* any of a large Norwegian breed of hunting dogs with a very heavy coat

ell /el‖el/ *n* a former English unit of length equal to 45in (about 1.14m)

ellipse /iˈlips‖ɪˈlɪps/ *n* a closed plane curve generated by a point moving in such a way that the sums of its distances from 2 fixed points is a constant; a closed plane curve obtained by plane section of a right circular cone

ellipsis /iˈlipsis‖ɪˈlɪpsɪs/ *n, pl* **ellipses** /-ˌseez‖-ˌsiːz/ **1** the omission of 1 or more words needed to make a construction grammatically complete **2** marks or a mark (e g ... or *** or –) indicating the omission of letters or words

elliptical /iˈliptikl‖ɪˈlɪptɪkl/, **elliptic** /-tik‖-tɪk/ *adj* **1a** of or shaped like an ellipse **b** of or marked by ellipsis or an ellipsis **2** *of speech or writing* extremely or excessively concise – **elliptically** *adv*, **ellipticity** *n*

elm /elm‖elm/ *n* (the wood of) any of a genus of large graceful trees

elocution /ˌeləˈkyoohsh(ə)n‖ˌeləˈkjuːʃ(ə)n/ *n* the art of effective public speaking, esp of good diction – **elocutionary** *adj*, **elocutionist** *n*

[1]**elongate** /ˈelongˌgayt, ˈee-‖ˈelɒŋˌgeɪt, ˈiː-/ *vt* to extend the length of ~ *vi* to grow in length

[2]**elongate, elongated** *adj* long in proportion to width – used esp in botany and zoology

elongation /ˌelongˈgaysh(ə)n, ˌee-‖ˌelɒŋˈgeɪʃ(ə)n, ˌiː-/ *n* the angular distance of one celestial body from another round which it revolves or from a particular point in the sky as viewed from earth

elope /iˈlohp‖ɪˈləʊp/ *vi* to run away secretly with the intention of getting married or cohabiting, usu without parental consent –

elopement *n*, **eloper** *n*

eloquent /'eləkwənt‖'eləkwənt/ *adj* **1** characterized by fluent, forceful, and persuasive use of language **2** vividly or movingly expressive or revealing <*an ~ gesture of reassurance*> – **eloquence** *n*, **eloquently** *adv*

else /els‖els/ *adv* **1** apart from the person, place, manner, or time mentioned or understood <*how ~ could he have acted*> <*everybody ~ but me*> **2** also, besides <*there's nothing ~ to eat*> **3** if not, otherwise <*do what you are told or ~ you'll be sorry*> – used absolutely to express a threat <*do what I tell you or ~*>

,else'where /-'weə‖-'weə/ *adv* in or to another place <*took his business ~*>

elucidate /i'loohsi,dayt‖ɪ'luːsɪ,deɪt/ *vb* to make (sthg) lucid, esp by explanation – **elucidative** *adj*, **elucidator** *n*, **elucidation** *n*

elude /i'loohd‖ɪ'luːd/ *vt* **1** to avoid cunningly or adroitly **2** to escape the memory, understanding, or notice of

elusive /i'loohsiv‖ɪ'luːsɪv/ *adj* tending to elude – **elusively** *adv*, **elusiveness** *n*, **elusion** *n*

elver /'elvə‖'elvə/ *n* a young eel

elves /elvz‖elvz/ *pl of* ELF

elvish /'elvish‖'elvɪʃ/ *adj* elfish

Elysium /i'lizi·əm‖ɪ'lɪzɪəm/ *n, pl* **Elysiums, Elysia** /-zi·ə‖-zɪə/ **1** the home of the blessed after death in Greek mythology **2** PARADISE 2 – **Elysian** *adj*

em, m /em‖em/ *n* **1** the width of the body of a piece of type bearing the letter M used as a unit of measure of printed matter **2** 'PICA 2

em- /im-, em-‖ɪm-, em-/ – see EN-

'em /(ə)m‖(ə)m/ *pron* them – used in writing to suggest casual speech

emaciate /i'maysi,ayt‖ɪ'meɪsɪ,eɪt/ *vb* to make or become excessively thin or feeble – **emaciation** *n*

emanate /'emə,nayt‖'emə,neɪt/ *vi* to come out from a source <*a foul smell* ~d *from the sewer*> ~*vt* EMIT 1

emancipate /i'mansi,payt‖ɪ'mænsɪ,peɪt/ *vt* to free from restraint, control, or esp slavery – **emancipator** *n*, **emancipation** *n*, **emancipationist** *n*

emasculate /i'maskyoo,layt‖ɪ'mæskjʊ,leɪt/ *vt* **1** to castrate **2** to deprive of strength, vigour, or spirit; weaken – **emasculate** *adj*, **emasculation** *n*, **emasculator** *n*

embalm /im'bahm‖ɪm'bɑːm/ *vt* **1** to treat (a dead body) so as to give protection against decay **2** to preserve from oblivion – **embalmer** *n*, **embalmment** *n*

embankment /im'bangkmənt‖ɪm'bæŋkmənt/ *n* a raised structure to hold back water or to carry a roadway or railway – **embank** *vt*

embargo /im'bahgoh‖ɪm'bɑːgəʊ/ *n, pl* **embargoes** **1** an order of a government prohibiting the departure or entry of commercial ships **2** a legal prohibition on commerce **3** a stoppage, impediment; *esp* a prohibition – **embargo** *vt*

embark /im'bahk‖ɪm'bɑːk/ *vi* **1** to go on board a boat or aircraft **2** to make a start; commence – usu + *on* or *upon* <~ed *on a new career*> ~*vt* to cause to go on board a boat or aircraft – **embarkment** *n*, **embarkation** *n*

embarrass /im'barəs‖ɪm'bærəs/ *vt* **1** to involve in financial difficulties, esp debt **2** to cause to experience a state of self-conscious distress; disconcert – **embarrassedly** *adv*, **embarrassingly** *adv*, **embarrassment** *n*

embassy /'embəsi‖'embəsɪ/ *n* **1a** the position of an ambassador **b** an ambassador's official mission abroad **2** (the residence of) a diplomatic body headed by an ambassador

em'battled *adj* involved in battle or conflict

embed /im'bed‖ɪm'bed/ *vt* **-dd-** to place or fix firmly (as if) in surrounding matter <*a splinter was* ~ded *in his finger*>

embellish /im'belish‖ɪm'belɪʃ/ *vt* **1** to make beautiful by adding ornaments; decorate **2** to make (speech or writing) more interesting by adding fictitious or exaggerated detail – **embellisher** *n*, **embellishment** *n*

ember /'embə‖'embə/ *n* **1** a glowing fragment (e g of coal or wood) in a (dying) fire **2** *pl* the smouldering remains of a fire **3** *pl* slowly fading emotions, memories, ideas, or responses

'ember ,day *n* a day set aside for fasting and prayer in Anglican and Roman Catholic churches that falls on the Wednesday, Friday, or Saturday following the first Sunday in Lent, Whitsunday, September 14, or December 13

embezzle /im'bezl‖ɪm'bezl/ *vt* to appropriate (e g property entrusted to one's care) fraudulently to one's own use – **embezzlement** *n*, **embezzler** *n*

embitter /im'bitə‖ɪm'bɪtə/ *vt* **1** to make bitter **2** to excite bitter feelings in – **embitterment** *n*

emblazon /im'blayz(ə)n‖ɪm'bleɪz(ə)n/ *vt* **1** to display conspicuously **2a(1)** to deck in bright colours **a(2)** to inscribe, adorn, or embellish (as if) with heraldic bearings or devices **b** to celebrate, extol – **emblazonment** *n*, **emblazonry** *n*

emblem /'embləm‖'embləm/ *n* **1** an object or a typical representation of an object symbolizing another object or idea **2** a device, symbol, or figure adopted and used as an identifying mark

emblematic /,emblə'matik‖,emblə'mætɪk/ *also* **emblematical** /-tikl‖-tɪkl/ *adj* of or constituting an emblem; symbolic – **emblematically** *adv*

embody /im'bodi‖ɪm'bɒdɪ/ *vt* **1** to give a body to (a spirit); incarnate **2** to make (e g ideas or concepts) concrete and perceptible <*a chapter which* embodies *his new theory*> **3** to make (e g connected ideas or principles) a part of a body or system; incorporate, include – usu + *in* <*their way of life is* embodied *in their laws*> **4** to represent in human or animal form; personify <*men who* embodied *the idealism of the revolution*> – **embodier** *n*, **embodiment** *n*

embolden /im'bohld(ə)n‖ɪm'bəʊld(ə)n/ *vt* to make bold or courageous

embolism /'embəliz(ə)m‖'embəlɪz(ə)m/ *n* (the sudden obstruction of a blood vessel by) an embolus – **embolismic** *adj*

embolus /'embələs‖'embələs/ *n, pl* **emboli** /-lie‖-laɪ/ a blood clot, air bubble, or other particle circulating abnormally in the blood

emboss /im'bos‖ɪm'bɒs/ *vt* **1** to ornament with raised work **2** to raise in relief from a surface – **embosser** *n*, **embossment** *n*

embouchure /,ombooh'shooə‖,ɒmbuː'ʃʊə/ *n* the position and use of the lips in playing a musical wind instrument

[1]**embrace** /im'brays‖ɪm'breɪs/ *vt* **1** to take and hold closely in the arms as a sign of affection; hug **2** to encircle, enclose **3a** to take up, esp readily or eagerly; adopt <~ *a cause*> **b** to avail oneself of; welcome <~d *the opportunity to study further*> **4** to include as a part or element of a more inclusive whole ~*vi* to join in an embrace; hug one another – **embracer** *n*, **embracingly** *adv*, **embracive** *adj*

[2]**embrace** *n* an act of embracing or gripping

embrasure /im'brayzhə‖ɪm'breɪʒə/ *n* **1** a door or window aperture, esp with splayed sides that increase the width of the opening on the inside **2** an opening with sides flaring outwards in a wall or parapet, usu for a gun

embrocation /ˌembrə'kaysh(ə)n‖ˌembrə'keɪʃ(ə)n/ *n* a liniment

embroider /im'broydə‖ɪm'brɔɪdə/ *vt* **1a** to ornament (e g cloth or a garment) with decorative stitches made by hand or machine **b** to form (e g a design or pattern) in ornamental needlework **2** to elaborate on (a narrative); embellish with exaggerated or fictitious details ~ *vi* **1** to do or make embroidery **2** to provide embellishments; elaborate – + *on* or *upon* – **embroiderer** *n*, **embroidery** *n*

embroil /im'broyl‖ɪm'brɔɪl/ *vt* **1** to throw (e g a person or affairs) into disorder or confusion **2** to involve in conflict or difficulties – **embroilment** *n*

embryo /'embrioh‖'embrɪəʊ/ *n, pl* **embryos** **1a** an animal in the early stages of growth before birth or hatching **b** the developing human individual during the first 8 weeks after conception **2** a rudimentary plant within a seed **3a** sthg as yet undeveloped **b** a beginning or undeveloped state of sthg – esp in *in embryo* <*plans still in* ~> [Medieval Latin, fr Greek *embryon*, fr *en* in + *bryein* to swell]

embryonic /ˌembri'onik‖ˌembrɪ'ɒnɪk/ *also* **embryonal** /em'brie·ənl‖em'braɪənl/ *adj* **1** of an embryo **2** in an early stage of development – **embryonically** *adv*

emend /i'mend‖ɪ'mend/ *vt* to correct, usu by textual alterations – **emendable** *adj*, **emender** *n*

emendation /ˌeemen'daysh(ə)n‖ˌiːmen'deɪʃ(ə)n/ *n* (an alteration made by) the act of emending

emerald /'em(ə)rəld‖'em(ə)rəld/ *adj or n* (of the bright green colour of) a beryl used as a gemstone

emerge /i'muhj‖ɪ'mɜːdʒ/ *vi* **1** to rise (as if) from an enveloping fluid; come out into view **2** to become manifest or known **3** to rise from an obscure or inferior condition – **emergence** *n*

emergency /i'muhj(ə)nsi‖ɪ'mɜːdʒ(ə)nsɪ/ *n* an unforeseen occurrence or combination of circumstances that calls for immediate action

emergent /i'muhj(ə)nt‖ɪ'mɜːdʒ(ə)nt/ *adj* emerging; *esp* in the early stages of formation or development

emeritus /i'meritəs‖ɪ'merɪtəs/, *fem* **emerita** /-tə‖-tə/ *adj* holding an honorary title after retirement

emery /'em(ə)ri‖'em(ə)rɪ/ *n* a dark granular mineral consisting mainly of corundum which is used for grinding and polishing

emetic /i'metik‖ɪ'metɪk/ *n or adj* (sthg) that induces vomiting – **emetically** *adv*

emigrant /'emigrənt‖'emɪgrənt/ *n* one who emigrates – **emigrant** *adj*

emigrate /'emiˌgrayt‖'emɪˌgreɪt/ *vi* to leave one's home or country for life or residence elsewhere – **emigration** *n*

émigré, **emigré** /'emigray ‖'emɪgreɪ (*Fr* emigre)/ *n* a (political) emigrant

eminence /'eminəns‖'emɪnəns/ *n* **1** a position of prominence or superiority – used as a title for a cardinal **2** sby or sthg high, prominent, or lofty: e g **2a** a person of high rank or attainments **b** a natural geographical elevation; a height

eminent /'eminənt‖'emɪnənt/ *adj* **1** standing out so as to be readily seen or noted; conspicuous, notable **2** exhibiting eminence, esp in position, fame, or achievement – **eminently** *adv*

emir /'emiə, -'-‖'emɪə, -'-/ *n* **1** a ruler of any of various Muslim states **2** a high-ranking Turkish official of former times **3** a male descendant of Muhammad [Arabic *amīr* commander]

emirate /'emirət‖'emɪrət/ *n* the position, state, power, etc of an emir

emissary /'emis(ə)ri‖'emɪs(ə)rɪ/ *n* one sent on an often secret mission as the agent of another

emission /i'mish(ə)n‖ɪ'mɪʃ(ə)n/ *n* **1** an act or instance of emitting **2a** sthg (e g electromagnetic waves, smoke, electrons, noise, etc) sent forth by emitting **b** an effluvium – **emissive** *adj*

emit /i'mit‖ɪ'mɪt/ *vt* **-tt-** **1a** to throw or give off or out (e g light) **b** to send out; eject **2** to give utterance or voice to <~ted *a groan*>

Emmenthal, **Emmental** /'emənˌtahl‖'emənˌtɑːl/ *n* a pale yellow Swiss cheese with many holes that form during ripening

emollient /i'mohli·ənt, i'mo-, -yənt‖ɪ'məʊlɪənt, ɪ'mɒ-, -jənt/ *n or adj* (a substance) that makes soft or gives relief

emolument /i'molyoomənt‖ɪ'mɒljʊmənt/ *n* the returns arising from office or employment; a salary [Latin *emolumentum*, lit., miller's fee, fr *emolere* to grind up, fr *e-* out + *molere* to grind]

emote /i'moht‖ɪ'məʊt/ *vi* to give expression to emotion, esp theatrically

emotion /i'mohsh(ə)n‖ɪ'məʊʃ(ə)n/ *n* **1** excitement **2** a mental and physical reaction (e g anger, fear, or joy) marked by strong feeling and often physiological changes that prepare the body for immediate vigorous action [Middle French, fr *emouvoir* to stir up, fr Latin *emovēre* to remove, disturb, fr *e-* out + *movēre* to move] – **emotionless** *adj*

emotional /i'mohsh(ə)nl‖ɪ'məʊʃ(ə)nl/ *adj* **1** of the emotions <*an* ~ *disorder*> **2** inclined to show (excessive) emotion **3** EMOTIVE 2 – **emotionalism** *n*, **emotionalist** *n*, **emotionalize** *vt*, **emotionally** *adv*, **emotionality** *n*

emotive /i'mohtiv‖ɪ'məʊtɪv/ *adj* **1** EMOTIONAL 1 **2** appealing to, expressing, or arousing emotion rather than reason – **emotively** *adv*, **emotivity** *n*

empanel /im'panl‖ɪm'pænl/ *vt* **-ll-** (*NAm* **-l-**, **-ll-**) to enrol in or on a panel <~ *a jury*>

empathy /'empəthi‖'empəθɪ/ *n* **1** the imaginative projection of a subjective state into an object, esp a work of art, so allowing it to be better understood and appreciated **2** the capacity for participation in another's feelings or ideas – **empathize** *vi*, **empathic** *adj*

emperor /'emp(ə)rə||'emp(ə)rə/ *n* the supreme ruler of an empire – **emperorship** *n*

emphasis /'emfəsis||'emfəsɪs/ *n, pl* **emphases** /-,seez||-,si:z/ **1a** force or intensity of expression that gives special impressiveness or importance to sthg **b** a particular prominence given in speaking or writing to 1 or more words or syllables **2** special consideration of or stress on sthg <*the school's ~ on examinations*>

emphas·ize, -ise /'emfə,siez||'emfə,saɪz/ *vt* to give emphasis to; place emphasis or stress on

emphatic /im'fatik||ɪm'fætɪk/ *adj* **1** spoken with or marked by emphasis **2** tending to express oneself in forceful speech or to take decisive action – **emphatically** *adv*

emphysema /,emfi'seemə||,emfɪ'si:mə/ *n* a disorder characterized by air-filled expansions of body tissues, esp in the lungs

empire /'empie·ə||'empaɪə/ *n* **1a** (the territory of) a large group of countries or peoples under 1 authority **b** sthg resembling a political empire; *esp* an extensive territory or enterprise under single domination or control **2** imperial sovereignty

empirical /em'pirikl||em'pɪrɪkl/ *also* **empiric** *adj* originating in, based, or relying on observation or experiment rather than theory – **empirically** *adv*

empiricism /em'pirisiz(ə)m||em'pɪrɪsɪz(ə)m/ *n* **1** quackery **2** the practice of discovery by observation and experiment **3** a theory that all knowledge is dependent on experience of the external world – **empiricist** *n*

emplacement /im'playsmənt||ɪm'pleɪsmənt/ *n* **1** the situation or location of sthg **2** a prepared position for weapons or military equipment – **emplace** *vt*

emplane /im'playn||ɪm'pleɪn/ *vb* to (cause to) board an aircraft

[1]**employ** /im'ploy||ɪm'plɔɪ/ *vt* **1a** to use in a specified way or for a specific purpose **b** to spend (time) **c** to use **2a** to engage the services of **b** to provide with a job that pays wages or a salary ***USE*** (1b,c) fml – **employable** *adj*, **employer** *n*, **employability** *n*

[2]**employ** *n* the state of being employed, esp for wages or a salary <*in the government's ~*> – fml

employee, *NAm also* **employe** /,employ'ee, im,ploy'ee||,emplɔɪ'i:, ɪm,plɔɪ'i:/ *n* one employed by another, esp for wages or a salary and in a position below executive level

employment /im'ploymənt||ɪm'plɔɪmənt/ *n* (an) activity in which one engages or is employed

em'ployment ,agency *n* an agency whose business is to find jobs for people seeking them or to find people to fill vacant jobs

em'ployment ex,change *n* LABOUR EXCHANGE

emporium /im'pawri·əm||ɪm'pɔ:rɪəm/ *n, pl* **emporiums, emporia** /-ri·ə||-rɪə/ a place of trade; *esp* a commercial centre or large shop

empower /im'powə||ɪm'paʊə/ *vt* to give official authority or legal power to – **empowerment** *n*

empress /'empris||'emprɪs/ *n* **1** the wife or widow of an emperor **2** a woman having in her own right the rank of emperor

[1]**empty** /'empti||'emptɪ/ *adj* **1a** containing nothing; *esp* lacking typical or expected contents **b** not occupied, inhabited, or frequented **2a** lacking reality or substance; hollow <*an ~ pleasure*> **b** lacking effect, value, or sincerity <*~ threats*> **c** lacking sense; foolish <*his ~ ideas*> **3** hungry – infml – **emptily** *adv*, **emptiness** *n* – **on an empty stomach** not having eaten anything

[2]**empty** *vt* **1a** to make empty; remove the contents of **b** to deprive, divest <*acting* emptied *of all emotion*> **c** to discharge (itself) of contents **2** to remove from what holds, encloses, or contains **3** to transfer by emptying <emptied *the biscuits onto the plate*> ~ *vi* **1** to become empty **2** to discharge contents <*the river* empties *into the ocean*> – **emptier** *n*

[3]**empty** *n* a bottle, container, vehicle, etc that has been emptied

,empty-'handed *adj* having or bringing nothing, esp because nothing has been gained or obtained

,empty-'headed *adj* foolish, silly

empyreal /,empie'ree·əl||,empaɪ'ri:əl/ *adj* celestial

empyrean /,empie'ree·ən||,empaɪ'ri:ən/ *adj or n* (of) the highest heavenly sphere in ancient and medieval cosmology

emu /'eemyooh||'i:mju:/ *n* a swift-running Australian flightless bird

emulate /'emyoo,layt||'emjʊ,leɪt/ *vt* **1** RIVAL 2 **2** to imitate closely; approach equality with; *specif* to imitate by means of an emulator – **emulation** *n*, **emulative** *adj*

emulsify /i'mulsifie||ɪ'mʌlsɪfaɪ/ *vt* to convert (e g an oil) into an emulsion – **emulsifiable** *adj*, **emulsifier** *n*, **emulsification** *n*

[1]**emulsion** /i'mulsh(ə)n||ɪ'mʌlʃ(ə)n/ *n* **1** (the state of) a substance (e g fat in milk) consisting of one liquid dispersed in droplets throughout another liquid **2** SUSPENSION 2b; *esp* a suspension of a silver compound in a gelatin solution or other solid medium for coating photographic plates, film, etc – **emulsive** *adj*

[2]**emulsion** *vt* to paint (e g a wall) with emulsion paint

en, n /en||en/ *n* the width of the body of a piece of type bearing the letter *n* used as a unit of measure of printed matter; one half of an em

[1]**en-** *also* **em-** *prefix* (→ *vb*) **1** put into or onto <en*throne*>; go into or onto <em*bus*> **2** cause to be <en*slave*> **3** provide with <em*power*> **4** so as to cover <en*gulf*>; thoroughly <en*tangle*> ***USE*** usu *em* before *b, m,* or *p*

[2]**en-** *also* **em-** *prefix* in; within <en*ergy*> – usu *em-* before *b, m,* or *p* <em*pathy*>

[1]**-en** *also* **-n** /-(ə)n||-(ə)n/ *suffix* (*n* → *adj*) made of; consisting of <*wood*en>

[2]**-en** *suffix* (*n, adj* → *vb*) **1a** cause to be <*sharp*en> **b** cause to have <*height*en> **2a** become <*steep*en> **b** come to have <*length*en>

enable /in'aybl||ɪn'eɪbl/ *vt* **1** to provide with the means or opportunity **2** to make possible, practical, or easy

enact /in'akt‖ɪn'ækt/ *vt* **1** to make into law **2** to act out, play – **enaction** *n*, **enactment** *n*

[1]**enamel** /i'naml‖ɪ'næml/ *vt* **-ll-** (*NAm* **-l-**, **-ll-**) to cover, inlay, or decorate with enamel – **enameler** *n*, **enamelist** *n*

[2]**enamel** *n* **1** a usu opaque glassy coating applied to the surface of metal, glass, or pottery **2** sthg enamelled; *esp* enamelware **3** a substance composed of calcium phosphate that forms a thin hard layer capping the teeth **4** a paint that dries with a glossy appearance **5** *chiefly NAm* an often coloured coating applied to the nails to give them a smooth or glossy appearance; nail varnish

e'namel,ware /-,weə‖-,weə/ *n* metal household or kitchen utensils coated with enamel

enamour, *NAm chiefly* **enamor** /i'namə‖ɪ'næmə/ *vt* to inspire with love or liking – usu pass + *of*

encamp /in'kamp‖ɪn'kæmp/ *vt* to place or establish in a camp ~*vi* to set up or occupy a camp

en'campment /-mənt‖-mənt/ *n* the place where a group (e g a body of troops) is encamped; a camp

encapsulate /in'kapsyoo,layt‖ɪn'kæpsjʊ,leɪt/ *vt* **1** to enclose (as if) in a capsule **2** to epitomize, condense ~*vi* to become encapsulated – **encapsulation** *n*

encase /in'kays‖ɪn'keɪs/ *vt* to enclose (as if) in a case – **encasement** *n*

encaustic /en'kawstik, -'kos-‖en'kɔːstɪk, -'kɒs-/ *n* (a decorative technique using) a paint made from pigment mixed with melted beeswax and resin and fixed by heat after application – **encaustic** *adj*

-ence /-(ə)ns‖-(ə)ns/ *suffix* (*vb* → *n*) **1** action or process of <*emerg*ence>; *also* instance of (a specified action or process) <*refer*ence> **2** quality or state of <*depend*ence> – **-ent** *suffix* (*vb* → *adj* or *n*)

encephalitis /,in,sefə'lietəs‖,ɪn,sefə'laɪtəs/ *n*, *pl* **encephalitides** /-'litə,deez‖-'lɪtə,diːz/ inflammation of the brain, usu caused by infection – **encephalitic** *adj*

enchant /in'chahnt‖ɪn'tʃɑːnt/ *vt* **1** to bewitch **2** to attract and move deeply; delight – **enchantment** *n*

enchanter /in'chahntə‖ɪn'tʃɑːntə/ *n* a sorcerer

enchanting /in'chahnting‖ɪn'tʃɑːntɪŋ/ *adj* charming – **enchantingly** *adv*

encipher /in'siefə‖ɪn'saɪfə/ *vt* to convert (a message) into a cipher

encircle /in'suhkl‖ɪn'sɜːkl/ *vt* **1** to form a circle round; surround **2** to move or pass completely round – **encirclement** *n*

enclave /'enklayv‖'enkleɪv/ *n* a territorial or culturally distinct unit enclosed within foreign territory

enclose *also* **inclose** /in'klohz‖ɪn'kləʊz/ *vt* **1a(1)** to close in completely; surround <~d *the field with a high fence*> **a(2)** to fence off (common land) for individual use **b** to hold in; confine **2** to include in a package or envelope, esp along with sthg else <*a cheque is* ~d *herewith*>

enclosure /in'klohzhə‖ɪn'kləʊʒə/ *n* **1** enclosing or being enclosed **2** sthg that encloses **3** sthg enclosed: e g **3a** sthg included in the same envelope or package as a letter **b** an area of enclosed ground; *esp* one reserved for a certain class of spectator in a sports ground

encode /in'kohd‖ɪn'kəʊd/ *vt* to convert (e g a body of information) from one system of communication into another; *esp* to convert (a message) into code – **encoder** *n*

encomium /en'kohmi·əm, -myəm‖en'kəʊmɪəm, -mjəm/ *n*, *pl* **encomiums, encomia** /-mi·ə, -myə‖-mɪə, -mjə/ a usu formal expression of warm or high praise; a eulogy

encompass /in'kumpəs‖ɪn'kʌmpəs/ *vt* **1** to form a circle about; enclose **2** to include <*a plan that* ~es *a number of aims*> – **encompassment** *n*

[1]**encore** /'ong,kaw‖'ɒŋ,kɔː/ *n* (an audience's appreciative demand for) a performer's reappearance to give an additional or repeated performance

[2]**encore** *vt* to call for an encore of or by

[1]**encounter** /in'kowntə‖ɪn'kaʊntə/ *vt* **1a** to meet as an adversary or enemy **b** to engage in conflict with **2** to meet or come across, esp unexpectedly

[2]**encounter** *n* **1** a meeting or clash between hostile factions or people **2** a chance meeting

encourage /in'kurij‖ɪn'kʌrɪdʒ/ *vt* **1** to inspire with courage, spirit, or hope **2** to spur on <*they were* ~d *to paint by their parents*> **3** to give help or patronage to (e g a process or action); promote <*many companies* ~ *union membership*> – **encouragement** *n*, **encouragingly** *adv*

encroach /in'krohch‖ɪn'krəʊtʃ/ *vi* **1** to enter gradually or by stealth into the possessions or rights of another; intrude, trespass **2** to advance beyond the usual or proper limits *USE* usu + *on* or *upon* – **encroachment** *n*

encrust *also* **incrust** /in'krust‖ɪn'krʌst/ *vt* to cover, line, or overlay with a crust, esp of jewels or precious metal ~*vi* to form a crust

encumber /in'kumbə‖ɪn'kʌmbə/ *vt* **1** to weigh down, burden **2** to impede or hamper the function or activity of **3** to burden with a legal claim <~ *an estate*>

encumbrance /in'kumbrəns‖ɪn'kʌmbrəns/ *n* **1** sthg that encumbers; an impediment **2** a claim (e g a mortgage) against property

-ency /-(ə)nsi‖-(ə)nsɪ/ *suffix* (→ *n*) quality or state of <*despond*ency>

encyclical /en'siklikl‖en'sɪklɪkl/ *n* a papal letter to the bishops of the church as a whole or to those in 1 country

encyclopedia, **encyclopaedia** /in,sieklə'peedi·ə, -dyə‖ɪn,saɪklə'piːdɪə, -djə/ *n* a work containing general information on all branches of knowledge or comprehensive information on 1 branch, usu in articles arranged alphabetically by subject [Medieval Latin *encyclopaedia* course of general education, fr Greek *enkyklios paideia* general education] – **encyclopedist** *n*

encyclopedic, **encyclopaedic** /in,sieklə'peedik‖ɪn,saɪklə'piːdɪk/ *adj* (suggestive) of an encyclopedia or its methods of treating a subject; comprehensive – **encyclopedically** *adv*

[1]**end** /end‖end/ *n* **1a** the part of an area that lies at the boundary <*the north* ~ *of the village*>; *also* the farthest point from where one is <*it's at the other* ~ *of the garden*> **b(1)** the point that marks the extent of sthg in space or time; the limit <*at the* ~ *of the day*> **b(2)** the point where sthg ceases to exist <*world without* ~> **c** either of the extreme or last parts lengthways of an object that is appreciably longer than it is broad <*a pencil with a point at either* ~> **2a** (the events, sections, etc immediately preceding) the cessation of action, activity, or existence <*at the* ~ *of the war*> **b** the final condition; *esp* death **3** sthg left over; remnant **4** an aim or purpose **5** sthg or sby extreme of a kind; *the* ultimate **6a** either half of a games pitch, court, etc <*change* ~s *at halftime*> **b** a period of action or turn to play in bowls, curling, etc **7** a particular part of an undertaking or organization <*the advertising* ~ *of a business*> *USE* (*5 & 7*) infml – **ended** *adj* – **in the end** ultimately – **no end 1** exceedingly **2** an endless amount; a huge quantity – **on end 1** [2]UPRIGHT **2** without a stop

[2]**end** *vt* **1** to bring to an end **2** to destroy ~ *vi* **1** to come to an end **2** to reach a specified ultimate situation, condition, or rank – often + *up*

[3]**end** *adj* final, ultimate <~ *results*> <~ *markets*>

endanger /in'daynjə‖ɪn'deɪndʒə/ *vt* to bring into danger or peril – **endangerment** *n*

endear /in'diə‖ɪn'dɪə/ *vt* to cause to become beloved or admired – often + *to* – **endearingly** *adv*

en'dearment /-mənt‖-mənt/ *n* a word or act (e g a caress) expressing affection

[1]**endeavour,** *NAm chiefly* **endeavor** /in'devə‖ɪn'devə/ *vt* to attempt by exertion or effort; TRY 4 – usu + infin; fml

[2]**endeavour,** *NAm chiefly* **endeavor** *n* serious determined effort; *also* an instance of this – fml

[1]**endemic** /en'demik‖en'demɪk/ *adj* **1** belonging or native to a particular people or region; not introduced or naturalized <~ *diseases*> **2** regularly occurring in or associated with a particular topic or sphere of activity – **endemically** *adv*, **endemicity** *n*, **endemism** *n*

[2]**endemic** *n* an endemic disease or species

'end ˌgame *n* the final stage of a (specif chess) game, esp when forces have been greatly reduced

ending /'ending‖'endɪŋ/ *n* **1** the last part of a book, film, etc **2** one or more letters or syllables added to a word base, esp as an inflection

endive /'enˌdiev‖'enˌdaɪv/ *n* **1** an annual or biennial composite plant that resembles a lettuce and has bitter leaves used in salads **2** *NAm* the developing crown of chicory when blanched for use as a salad plant

endless /'endlis‖'endlɪs/ *adj* **1** (seeming) without end **2** extremely numerous **3** *of a belt, chain, etc* that is joined to itself at its ends – **endlessly** *adv*, **endlessness** *n*

[1]**endocrine** /'endohkrin, -krien, -də-‖'endəʊkrɪn, -kraɪn, -də-/ *adj* **1** producing secretions that are discharged directly into the bloodstream <~ *system*> **2** of or being an endocrine gland or its secretions <~ *hormone*>

[2]**endocrine** *n* **1** a hormone – no longer in technical use **2 endocrine, endocrine gland** the thyroid, pituitary, or other gland that produces an endocrine secretion

endoderm /'endohˌduhm‖'endəʊˌdɜːm/ *n* the innermost of the germ layers of an embryo that is the source of the epithelium of the digestive tract and its derivatives – **endodermal** *adj*, **endodermally** *adv*

endogenous /en'dojinəs‖en'dɒdʒɪnəs/ *also* **endogenic** /ˌendoh'jenik‖ˌendəʊ'dʒenɪk/ *adj* **1** growing from or on the inside **2** originating within the body – **endogenously** *adv*

endorse /in'daws‖ɪn'dɔːs/ *vt* **1a** to write on the back of **b** to write (one's signature) on a cheque, bill, or note **2** to express approval of; support; *specif, chiefly NAm* to express support for (e g a political candidate) publicly **3** *Br* to record on (e g a driving licence) particulars of an offence committed by the holder – **endorsable** *adj*, **endorsement** *n*, **endorser** *n*, **endorsee** *n*

endosperm /'endohˌspuhm‖'endəʊˌspɜːm/ *n* a nourishing tissue in seed plants that is formed within the embryo sac – **endospermic** *adj*, **endospermous** *adj*

endow /in'dow‖ɪn'daʊ/ *vt* **1** to provide with a continuing source of income <~ *a hospital*> **2a** to provide *with* an ability or attribute <~ed *with a natural grace*> **b** CREDIT 3a – usu + *with*

[1]**en'dowment** /-mənt‖-mənt/ *n* **1** sthg endowed; *specif* the part of an institution's income derived from donations **2** a natural quality with which a person is endowed

[2]**endowment** *adj* of, being, or involving life insurance under which a certain sum is paid to the insured at the end of an agreed period or to a specified beneficiary if the insured dies within that period

'endˌpaper /-ˌpaypə‖-ˌpeɪpə/ *n* a folded sheet of paper forming the front or back inside cover and flyleaf of a book

endue /in'dyooh‖ɪn'djuː/ *vt* to provide, endow; *also* to imbue – usu pass + *with*; fml

endurance /in'dyooərəns‖ɪn'djʊərəns/ *n* the ability to withstand hardship, adversity, or stress

endure /in'dyooə‖ɪn'djʊə/ *vi* to continue in the same state; last ~ *vt* **1** to undergo (e g a hardship), esp without giving in **2** to tolerate, permit – **endurable** *adj*, **endurably** *adv*

'end ˌuser *n* the final recipient of goods or services produced by a complex process; *esp* sby who uses a computer program in its completed form

'endˌways /-ˌways‖-ˌweɪs/, **'endˌwise** /-ˌwiez‖-ˌwaɪz/ *adv or adj* **1** with the end forwards (e g towards the observer) **2** in or towards the direction of the ends; lengthways **3** upright; ON END <*boxes set* ~> **4** end to end <*put the tables together* ~>

enema /'enimə‖'enɪmə/ *n, pl* **enemas** *also* **enemata** /ˌeni'mahtə‖ˌenɪ'mɑːtə/ **1** injection of liquid into the intestine by way of the anus (e g to ease constipation) **2** material for injection as an enema

enemy /'enəmi‖'enəmɪ/ *n* **1** one who is antagonistic to another; *esp* one seeking to injure, overthrow, or confound an opponent **2** sthg harmful or deadly **3a** *sing or pl in constr* a military adversary **b** a hostile military unit or force [Old French *enemi*, fr Latin *inimicus*, fr *in-* not- + *amicus* friend]

energetic /ˌenəˈjetik‖ˌenəˈdʒetɪk/ *adj* **1** marked by energy, activity, or vigour **2** operating with power or effect; forceful **3** of energy <~ *equation*> – **energetically** *adv*

energ·ize, -ise /ˈenəˌjiez‖ˈenəˌdʒaɪz/ *vt* **1** to give energy to; make energetic or vigorous **2** to apply energy to so as to facilitate normal operation – **energizer** *n*

energy /ˈenəji‖ˈenədʒɪ/ *n* **1** the capacity of acting or being active <*great intellectual* ~> **2** natural power vigorously exerted <*devoted all his* energies *to it*> **3** the capacity for doing work <*solar* ~> [Late Latin *energia*, fr Greek *energeia* activity, fr *en* in + *ergon* work]

enervate /ˈenəˌvayt‖ˈenəˌveɪt/ *vt* to lessen the mental or physical strength or vitality of; weaken – **enervate, enervated** *adj*, **enervation** *n*

en famille /on faˈmee ‖ɒn fæˈmiː (*Fr* ɑ̃ famiːj)/ *adv* all together as a family

enfant terrible /ˌonfonh teˈreeblə ‖ˌɒnfɑ̃ teˈriːblə (*Fr* ɑ̃fɑ̃ tɛribl)/ *n, pl* **enfants terribles** /~/ a person whose remarks or unconventional actions cause embarrassment [French, lit., terrifying child]

enfeeble /inˈfeebl‖ɪnˈfiːbl/ *vt* to make feeble – **enfeeblement** *n*

enfilade /ˌenfiˈlayd‖ˌenfɪˈleɪd/ *vt or n* (to subject to) gunfire directed along the length of an enemy battle line

enfold /inˈfohld‖ɪnˈfəʊld/ *vt* **1** to wrap up; envelop **2** to clasp in the arms; embrace

enforce /inˈfaws‖ɪnˈfɔːs/ *vt* **1** to give greater force to (e g an argument); reinforce **2** to impose, compel <~ *obedience from them*> **3** to cause (a rule or law) to be carried out effectively – **enforceable** *adj*, **enforcement** *n*, **enforcer** *n*, **enforceability** *n*

enfranchise /inˈfranchiez‖ɪnˈfræntʃaɪz/ *vt* **1** to set free (e g from slavery) **2a** to admit to the right of voting **b** to admit (a municipality) to political privileges, esp the right of Parliamentary representation – **enfranchisement** *n*

engage /inˈgayj‖ɪnˈgeɪdʒ/ *vt* **1a** to attract and hold (sby's thoughts, attention, etc) **b** to interlock with; cause to mesh **2a** to arrange to employ (sby) **b** to arrange to obtain the services of **c** to order (a room, seat, etc) to be kept for one; reserve **3a** to hold the attention of; engross **b** to induce to participate, esp in conversation **4a** to enter into contest with <~ *the enemy fleet*> **b** to bring together or interlock (e g weapons) ~ *vi* **1** to pledge oneself; promise **2** to occupy one's time; participate <*at university he* ~d *in gymnastics*> **3** to enter into conflict <*the fleets* ~d *in the Atlantic*> **4** to be or become interlocked or meshed

engagé /ˌong·gaˈzhay ‖ˌɒŋgæˈʒeɪ (*Fr* ɑ̃gaʒe)/ *adj* actively involved or committed (politically)

engaged /inˈgayjd‖ɪnˈgeɪdʒd/ *adj* **1** involved in activity; occupied **2** pledged to be married **3** *chiefly Br* **3a** in use <*the telephone is* ~> **b** reserved, booked <*this table is* ~>

enˈgagement /-mənt‖-mənt/ *n* **1** an agreement to marry; a betrothal **2** a pledge **3a** a promise to be present at a certain time and place **b** employment, esp for a stated time **4** a hostile encounter between military forces

engaging /inˈgayjing‖ɪnˈgeɪdʒɪŋ/ *adj* attractive, pleasing – **engagingly** *adv*

engender /inˈjendə‖ɪnˈdʒendə/ *vt* to cause to exist or develop; produce

engine /ˈenjin‖ˈendʒɪn/ *n* **1** a mechanical tool <*a terrible* ~ *of war*> **2** a machine for converting any of various forms of energy into mechanical force and motion **3** a railway locomotive [Old French *engin*, fr Latin *ingenium* natural disposition, talent, ingenuity, fr *in* in + *gignere* to beget] – **engineless** *adj*

-engined /-enjind‖-endʒɪnd/ *comb form* (→ *adj*) having (such or so many) engines <*front*-engined *cars*>

[1]engineer /ˌenjiˈniə‖ˌendʒɪˈnɪə/ *n* **1** a soldier who carries out engineering work **2a** a designer or builder of engines **b** a person who is trained in or follows as a profession a branch of engineering **c** a person who starts or carries through an enterprise, esp by skilful or artful contrivance <*the* ~ *of the agreement*> **3** a person who runs or supervises an engine or apparatus

[2]engineer *vt* **1** to lay out, construct, or manage as an engineer **2** to contrive, plan, or guide, usu with subtle skill and craft

engineering /ˌenjiˈniəring‖ˌendʒɪˈnɪərɪŋ/ *n* **1** the art of managing engines **2** the application of science and mathematics by which the properties of matter and the sources of energy in nature are made useful to human beings

[1]English /ˈing·glish‖ˈɪŋglɪʃ/ *adj* (characteristic) of England – **Englishman** *n*, **Englishness** *n*

[2]English *n* **1a** the Germanic language of the people of Britain, the USA, and most Commonwealth countries **b** English language, literature, or composition as an academic subject **2** *pl in constr* the people of England

ˌEnglish ˈhorn *n, chiefly NAm* COR ANGLAIS

ˌEnglish ˈsetter *n* any of a breed of gundogs characterized by a moderately long silky coat

engrave /inˈgrayv‖ɪnˈgreɪv/ *vt* **1a** to cut (a design or lettering) on a hard surface (e g metal or stone) with a sharp tool **b** to impress deeply, as if by engraving <*the incident was* ~d *in his memory*> **2a** to cut a design or lettering on (a hard surface) for printing; *also* to print from an engraved plate **b** to photoengrave – **engraver** *n*

engraving /inˈgrayving‖ɪnˈgreɪvɪŋ/ *n* (a print made from) an engraved printing surface

engross /inˈgrohs‖ɪnˈgrəʊs/ *vt* **1a** to copy or write in a large hand **b** to prepare the final text of (an official document) **2** to occupy fully the time and attention of; absorb <*an* ~ing *problem*> – **engrosser** *n*, **engrossment** *n*

engulf /inˈgulf‖ɪnˈgʌlf/ *vt* **1** to flow over and enclose; overwhelm <*the mounting seas threatened to* ~ *the island*> **2** *of an amoeba, phagocytic cell, etc* to take in (food) by flowing over and enclosing – **engulfment** *n*

enhance /inˈhahns‖ɪnˈhɑːns/ *vt* to improve (e g in value, desirability, or attractiveness); heighten – **enhancement** *n*

enigma /iˈnigmə‖ɪˈnɪgmə/ *n* **1** intentionally obscure speech or writing; a riddle **2** sby or sthg hard to understand or explain; a puzzle [Latin *aenigma*, fr Greek *ainigma*, fr *ainissesthai* to speak in riddles, fr *ainos* fable] – **enigmatic** *adj*, **enigmatically** *adv*

enjoin /in'joyn‖ɪn'dʒɔɪn/ *vt* **1** to order (sby) to do sthg; command **2** to impose (a condition or course of action) on sby **3** to forbid by law; prohibit ***USE*** fml

enjoy /in'joy‖ɪn'dʒɔɪ/ *vt* **1** to take pleasure or satisfaction in **2a** to have the use or benefit of **b** to experience <*he* ~ed *good health*> – **enjoyable** *adj*, **enjoyableness** *n*, **enjoyably** *adv*, **enjoyment** *n*

enlarge /in'lahj‖ɪn'lɑːdʒ/ *vt* **1** to make larger **2** to reproduce in a larger form; *specif* to make a photographic enlargement of ~ *vi* **1** to grow larger **2** to speak or write at length; elaborate – often + *on* or *upon* – **enlarger** *n*

en'largement /-mənt‖-mənt/ *n* a photographic print that is larger than the negative

enlighten /in'liet(ə)n‖ɪn'laɪt(ə)n/ *vt* to cause to understand; free from false beliefs

en'lightenment /-mənt‖-mənt/ *n* **1** *cap* an 18th-c movement marked by a belief in universal human progress and the importance of reason and the sciences – + *the* **2** NIRVANA 1

enlist /in'list‖ɪn'lɪst/ *vt* **1** to engage (a person) for duty in the armed forces **2a** to secure the support and aid of <~ *you in a good cause*> ~*vi* to enrol oneself in the armed forces – **enlistment** *n*

enlisted man *n* a person in the US armed forces ranking below a commissioned or warrant officer

enliven /in'liev(ə)n‖ɪn'laɪv(ə)n/ *vt* to give life, action, spirit, or interest to; animate – **enlivenment** *n*

en masse /ˌom 'mas ‖ˌɒm 'mæs (*Fr* ɑ̃ mas)/ *adv* in a body; as a whole

enmesh /in'mesh‖ɪn'meʃ/ *vt* to catch or entangle (as if) in a net or mesh – **enmeshment** *n*

enmity /'enmiti‖'enmɪtɪ/ *n* (a state of) hatred or ill will

ennoble /in'nohbl‖ɪn'nəʊbl/ *vt* **1** to make noble; elevate <*believes that hard work* ~s *the human spirit*> **2** to raise to the rank of the nobility – **ennoblement** *n*

ennui /on'wi ‖ɒn'wɪ (*Fr* ɑ̃nɥi)/ *n* weariness and dissatisfaction resulting from lack of interest or boredom

enormity /i'nawməti‖ɪ'nɔːmətɪ/ *n* **1** great wickedness <*the sheer* ~ *of the crime*> **2** a terribly wicked or evil act **3** the quality or state of being enormous

enormous /i'nawməs‖ɪ'nɔːməs/ *adj* marked by extraordinarily great size, number, or degree – **enormously** *adv*, **enormousness** *n*

[1]**enough** /i'nuf‖ɪ'nʌf/ *adj* fully adequate in quantity, number, or degree

[2]**enough** *adv* to a fully adequate degree; sufficiently

[3]**enough** *pron, pl* **enough** a sufficient quantity or number <*had* ~ *of their foolishness*>

en passant /ˌon pa'sonh ‖ˌɒn pæ'sɑ̃ (*Fr* ɑ̃ pasɑ̃)/ *adv* in passing – used in chess of the capture of a pawn as it makes a first move of 2 squares by an enemy pawn in a position to threaten the first of these squares

enplane /en'playn‖en'pleɪn/ *vi, chiefly NAm* to emplane

enquire /in'kwie·ə‖ɪn'kwaɪə/ *vb* to inquire

enquiry /in'kwie·əri‖ɪn'kwaɪərɪ/ *n* an inquiry

enrage /in'rayj‖ɪn'reɪdʒ/ *vt* to fill with rage; anger

enrapture /in'rapchə‖ɪn'ræptʃə/ *vt* to fill with delight

enrich /in'rich‖ɪn'rɪtʃ/ *vt* **1** to make rich or richer, esp in some desirable quality <*the experience greatly* ~ed *his life*> **2** to adorn, ornament <~ing *the ceiling with frescoes*> **3a** to make (soil) more fertile **b** to improve (a food) in nutritive value by adding nutrients (lost in processing) **c** to increase the proportion of a valuable or desirable ingredient in <~ *uranium with uranium 235*>; *also* to add a desirable substance to <~ *natural gas*> – **enricher** *n*, **enrichment** *n*

enrol, *NAm also* **enroll** /in'rohl‖ɪn'rəʊl/ *vb* **-ll-** *vt* **1** to enter on a list, roll, etc **2** to prepaıe a final perfect copy of (a bill passed by a legislature) in written or printed form ~*vi* to enrol oneself <~ *in the history course*> – **enrolment** *n*

en route /ˌon 'rooht ‖ˌɒn 'ruːt (*Fr* ɑ̃ rut)/ *adv or adj* on or along the way <*soon they were* ~ *to the border*>

ensconce /in'skons‖ɪn'skɒns/ *vt* to settle (e g oneself) comfortably or snugly

ensemble /on'sombl ‖ɒn'sɒmbl (*Fr* ɑ̃sɑ̃ːbl)/ *n* **1** a group constituting an organic whole or together producing a single effect: e g **1a** concerted music of 2 or more parts **b** a complete outfit of matching garments **c** *sing or pl in constr* **c(1)** the musicians engaged in the performance of a musical ensemble **c(2)** a group of supporting players, singers, or dancers **2** the quality of togetherness in performance <*the quartet's* ~ *was poor*>

enshrine /in'shrien‖ɪn'ʃraɪn/ *vt* **1** to enclose (as if) in a shrine **2** to preserve or cherish, esp as sacred <*they* ~d *their leader's memory in their hearts*> – **enshrinement** *n*

enshroud /in'shrowd‖ɪn'ʃraʊd/ *vt* to shroud

ensign /'ensien‖'ensaɪn; *sense 1 naval* 'ensən‖'ensən/ *n* **1** a flag that is flown (e g by a ship) as the symbol of nationality **2a** a standard-bearer **b** an officer of the lowest rank in the US navy

enslave /in'slayv‖ɪn'sleɪv/ *vt* to reduce (as if) to slavery; subjugate – **enslavement** *n*, **enslaver** *n*

ensnare /in'sneə‖ɪn'sneə/ *vt* to take (as if) in a snare

ensue /in'syooh‖ɪn'sjuː/ *vi* to take place afterwards or as a result

ensure /in'shooə, -'shaw‖ɪn'ʃʊə, -'ʃɔː/ *vt* to make sure, certain, or safe; guarantee

entablature /en'tabləchə‖en'tæblətʃə/ *n* the upper section of a wall or storey, usu supported on columns or pilasters, and in classical orders consisting of architrave, frieze, and cornice

[1]**entail** /in'tayl‖ɪn'teɪl/ *vt* **1** to settle (property) so that sale or bequeathal is not permitted and inheritance is limited to (a specified class of) the owner's lineal descendants **2** to involve or imply as a necessary accompaniment or result <*the project will* ~ *considerable expense*> – **entailer** *n*, **entailment** *n*

[2]**entail** *n* **1** (the rule fixing) an entailing

2 sthg entailed

entangle /in'tang·gl‖ɪn'tæŋgl/ *vt* **1** to make tangled, complicated, or confused **2** to involve in a tangle – **entangler** *n*

en'tanglement /-mənt‖-mənt/ *n* **1** sthg that entangles, confuses, or ensnares **2** the condition of being deeply involved

entente /on'tont ‖ɒn'tɒnt (*Fr* ɑ̃tɑ̃:t)/ *n* **1** a friendly relationship between 2 or more countries **2** *sing or pl in constr* the countries having an entente [French, understanding, agreement, fr *entendre* to intend, hear, understand]

enter /'entə‖'entə/ *vi* **1** to go or come in **2** to register as candidate in a competition <*decided to* ~ *for the race*> **3** to make a beginning <~d ing *upon a career*> ~ *vt* **1** to go or come into <~ *a room*> <~ing *her early thirties*> **2** to inscribe, register <~ *the names of qualified voters in the rolls*> **3** to cause to be received, admitted, or considered – often + *for* <~ *a child for a public school*> **4** to put in; insert **5** to become a member of or an active participant in <~ *university*> <~ *a race*> **6** to put on record <~ *a complaint against his partner*> – **enterable** *adj* – **enter into 1** to make oneself a party to or in <enter into *an important agreement*> **2** to participate or share in <*cheerfully* entering into *the household tasks*>

enteritis /,entə'rietəs‖,entə'raɪtəs/ *n* inflammation of the intestines, esp the human ileum, usu marked by diarrhoea

enteron /'entəron‖'entərɒn/ *n* the alimentary canal or system, esp of the embryo

enterprise /'entə,priez‖'entə,praɪz/ *n* **1** a (difficult or complicated) project or undertaking **2** a unit of economic organization or activity; *esp* a business organization **3** readiness to engage in enterprises – **enterpriser** *n*

enterprising /'entə,priezing‖'entə,praɪzɪŋ/ *adj* marked by initiative and readiness to engage in enterprises

entertain /,entə'tayn‖,entə'teɪn/ *vt* **1** to show hospitality to **2** to be ready and willing to think about (an idea, doubt, suggestion, etc) **3** to hold the attention of, usu pleasantly or enjoyably; divert **4** to play against (an opposing team) on one's home ground ~*vi* to invite guests to esp one's home – **entertainer** *n*

,enter'tainment /-mənt‖-mənt/ *n* **1** sthg entertaining, diverting, or engaging **2** a public performance

enthral, *NAm also* **enthrall** /in'thrawl‖ɪn'θrɔ:l/ *vt* **-ll-** to hold the complete interest and attention of; captivate – **enthralment** *n*

enthrone /in'throhn‖ɪn'θrəʊn/ *vt* to seat, esp ceremonially, (as if) on a throne – **enthronement** *n*

enthuse /in'thyoohz‖ɪn'θju:z/ *vt* to make enthusiastic ~*vi* to show enthusiasm

enthusiasm /in'thyoohzi,az(ə)m‖ɪn'θju:zɪ-,æz(ə)m/ *n* **1** keen and eager interest and admiration – usu + *for* or *about* **2** an object of enthusiasm

enthusiast /in'thyoohzi,ast‖ɪn'θju:zɪ,æst/ *n* sby filled with enthusiasm; *esp* sby ardently attached to a usu specified cause, object, or pursuit <*a cycling* ~> – **enthusiastic** *adj*, **enthusiastically** *adv*

entice /in'ties‖ɪn'taɪs/ *vt* to tempt or persuade by arousing hope or desire – **enticement** *n*

entire /in'tie·ə‖ɪn'taɪə/ *adj* **1** having no element or part left out <*was alone the* ~ *day*> **2** complete in degree; total <*his* ~ *devotion to his family*> **3a** consisting of 1 piece; homogeneous <*the book is* ~ *in style*> **b** intact <*strove to keep the collection* ~> **4** not castrated – **entire** *adv*, **entireness** *n*

en'tirely /-li‖-lɪ/ *adv* **1** wholly, completely <*agreed with me* ~> **2** in an exclusive manner; solely <*it is his fault* ~>

entirety /in'tie·ərəti‖ɪn'taɪərətɪ/ *n* **1** the state of being entire or complete **2** the whole or total

entitle /in'tietl‖ɪn'taɪtl/ *vt* **1** to title **2** to give (sby) the right *to* (do or have) sthg <*this ticket* ~s *the bearer to free admission*> – **entitlement** *n*

entity /'entəti‖'entətɪ/ *n* **1a** being, existence; *esp* independent, separate, or self-contained existence **b** the existence of a thing as contrasted with its attributes **2** sthg that has separate and distinct existence

entomb /in'toohm‖ɪn'tu:m/ *vt* **1** to deposit (as if) in a tomb; bury **2** to serve as a tomb for – **entombment** *n*

entomology /,entə'moləji‖,entə'mɒlədʒɪ/ *n* zoology that deals with insects – **entomologist** *n*, **entomological** *adj*, **entomologically** *adv*

entourage /'ontoo,rahzh ‖'ɒntʊ,rɑ:ʒ (*Fr* ɑ̃tura:ʒ)/ *n sing or pl in constr* a group of attendants or associates, esp of sby of high rank

entr'acte /'ontrakt, -'- ‖'ɒntrækt, -'- (*Fr* ɑ̃trakt)/ *n* (a performance or interlude in) the interval between 2 acts of a play

entrails /'entraylz‖'entreɪlz/ *n pl* internal parts; *esp* the intestines

[1]**entrain** /in'trayn‖ɪn'treɪn/ *vt, of a fluid* to draw in and transport (e g solid particles or gas) – **entrainment** *n*

[2]**entrain** *vb* to put or go aboard a train

[1]**entrance** /'entrəns‖'entrəns/ *n* **1** the act of entering **2** the means or place of entry **3** power or permission to enter; admission **4** an arrival of a performer onto the stage or before the cameras

[2]**entrance** /in'trahns‖ɪn'trɑ:ns/ *vt* **1** to put into a trance **2** to fill with delight, wonder, or rapture – **entrancement** *n*

entrant /'entrənt‖'entrənt/ *n* sby or sthg that enters or is entered; *esp* one who enters a contest

entrap /in'trap‖ɪn'træp/ *vt* **-pp- 1** to catch (as if) in a trap **2** to lure into a compromising statement or act – **entrapment** *n*

entreat /in'treet‖ɪn'tri:t/ *vt* to ask urgently or plead with (sby) *for* (sthg); beg ~*vi* to make an earnest request; plead – **entreatingly** *adv*, **entreatment** *n*

entreaty /in'treeti‖ɪn'tri:tɪ/ *n* an act of entreating; a plea

entrée, entree /'ontray ‖'ɒntreɪ (*Fr* ɑ̃tre)/ *n* **1** freedom of entry or access <*had an* ~ *into the highest circles*> **2a** *chiefly Br* a dish served between the usual (fish and meat) courses of a dinner **b** *chiefly NAm* the principal dish of a meal

entrench /in'trench‖ɪn'trentʃ/ *vt* **1a** to surround with a (defensive) trench **b** to place (oneself) in a strong defensive position **2** to establish solidly, esp so as to make change difficult ~*vi* to dig or occupy a (defensive) trench – **entrenchment** *n*

entrepreneur /ˌontrəprəˈnuh ‖ˌɒntrəprəˈnɜː (*Fr* ɑ̃trəprənœːr)/ *n* one who organizes, manages, and assumes the risks of a business or enterprise [French, fr *entreprendre* to undertake] – **entrepreneurial** *adj*, **entrepreneurship** *n*

entresol /ˈontrəˌsol‖ˈɒntrəˌsɒl (*Fr* ɑ̃trəsɔl)/ *n* a mezzanine

entropy /ˈentrəpi‖ˈentrəpɪ/ *n* **1** a measure of the unavailable energy in a closed thermodynamic system **2** the degradation of the matter and energy in the universe to an ultimate state of inert uniformity – **entropic** *adj*

entrust /inˈtrust‖ɪnˈtrʌst/ *vt* **1** to confer a trust on; *esp* to deliver sthg in trust to – + *with* <~ed *the bank with his savings*> **2** to commit to another with confidence – + *to* <~ed *his savings to the bank*> – **entrustment** *n*

entry /ˈentri‖ˈentrɪ/ *n* **1** the act of entering; entrance **2** the right or privilege of entering **3** a door, gate, hall, vestibule, or other place of entrance **4a** the act of registering a record **b** a record made in a diary, account book, index, etc **c** a dictionary headword, often with its definition **5** a person, thing, or group entered in a contest; an entrant **6** the total of those entered or admitted

entwine /inˈtwien‖ɪnˈtwaɪn/ *vb* to twine together or round

E number *n* a number, preceded by the letter E, which is found in lists of food ingredients and denotes a certain food additive

enumerate /iˈnyoohmərayt‖ɪˈnjuːməreɪt/ *vt* **1** to count **2** to specify one after another; list – **enumerator** *n*, **enumerative** *adj*, **enumeration** *n*

enunciate /iˈnunsiˌayt‖ɪˈnʌnsɪˌeɪt/ *vt* **1a** to make a definite or systematic statement of; formulate **b** to announce, proclaim **2** to articulate, pronounce ~ *vi* to utter articulate sounds – **enunciator** *n*, **enunciable** *adj*. **enunciation** *n*

envelop /inˈveləp‖ɪnˈveləp/ *vt* **1** to enclose or enfold completely (as if) with a covering **2** to surround so as to cut off – **envelopment** *n*

envelope /ˈenvəlohp, ˈon-‖ˈenvələʊp, ˈɒn-/ *n* **1** sthg that envelops; a wrapper, covering **2** a flat container, usu of folded and gummed paper (e g for a letter) **3** a membrane or other natural covering that encloses

envenom /inˈvenəm‖ɪnˈvenəm/ *vt* **1** to put poison into or onto <~ *a weapon*> **2** to embitter <*jealousy* ~ing *his mind*>

enviable /ˈenvi·əbl‖ˈenvɪəbl/ *adj* highly desirable – **enviableness** *n*, **enviably** *adv*

envious /ˈenvi·əs‖ˈenvɪəs/ *adj* feeling or showing envy – **enviously** *adv*, **enviousness** *n*

environ /inˈvie(ə)rən‖ɪnˈvaɪ(ə)rən/ *vt* to encircle, surround – fml

enˈvironment /-mənt‖-mənt/ *n* **1** the circumstances, objects, or conditions by which one is surrounded **2** the complex of climatic, soil, and biological factors that acts upon an organism or an ecological community – **environmental** *adj*, **environmentally** *adv*

enˌvironˈmentalist /-ist‖-ɪst/ *n* sby concerned about the quality of the human environment – **environmentalism** *n*, **environmentalist, environmentalistic** *adj*

environs /inˈvie(ə)rənz‖ɪnˈvaɪ(ə)rənz/ *n pl* the neighbourhood surrounding sthg, esp a town

envisage /inˈvizij‖ɪnˈvɪzɪdʒ/ *vt* to have a mental picture of; visualize, esp in advance of an expected or hoped-for realization

[1]**envoy, envoi** /ˈenvoy‖ˈenvɔɪ/ *n* the concluding remarks to a poem, essay, or book; *specif* a short fixed final stanza of a ballade

[2]**envoy** *n* **1** a diplomatic agent, esp one who ranks immediately below an ambassador **2** a messenger, representative

[1]**envy** /ˈenvi‖ˈenvɪ/ *n* painful, resentful, or admiring awareness of an advantage enjoyed by another, accompanied by a desire to possess the same advantage; *also* an object of such a feeling

[2]**envy** *vt* to feel envy towards or on account of – **envier** *n*, **envyingly** *adv*

enzyme /ˈenziem‖ˈenzaɪm/ *n* any of numerous complex proteins that are produced by living cells and catalyse specific biochemical reactions at body temperatures [German *enzym*, deriv of Greek *en* in + *zymē* leaven] – **enzymatic** *adj*, **enzymatically** *adv*, **enzymic** *adj*

eon /ˈeeon, ˈee·ən‖ˈiːɒn, ˈiːən/ *n* an aeon

epaulette, *NAm chiefly* **epaulet** /ˌepəˈlet‖ˌepəˈlet/ *n* an ornamental (fringed) strip or pad attached to the shoulder of a garment, esp a military uniform

épée /ˈepay ‖ˈepeɪ (*Fr* epe)/ *n* (the sport of fencing with) a sword having a bowl-shaped guard and a rigid tapering blade of triangular cross-section with no cutting edge – **épéeist** *n*

ephemeral /iˈfemərəl‖ɪˈfemərəl/ *adj* **1** lasting 1 day only <*an* ~ *fever*> **2** lasting a very short time <~ *pleasures*> [Greek *ephēmeros* lasting a day, daily, fr *epi* on, at + *hēmera* day] – **ephemerally** *adv*, **ephemerality** *n*

epi- /epi-‖epɪ-/, **ep-** /ep-‖ep-/ *prefix* **1** outer; external <epi*dermis*> **2** besides; IN ADDITION <epi*logue*> **3** over; above <epi*graph*>

[1]**epic** /ˈepik‖ˈepɪk/ *adj* **1** (having the characteristics) of an epic **2a** extending beyond the usual or ordinary, esp in size or scope **b** heroic – **epical** *adj*, **epically** *adv*

[2]**epic** *n* **1** a long narrative poem recounting the deeds of a legendary or historical hero **2** a series of events or body of legend or tradition fit to form the subject of an epic

epicentre /ˈepiˌsentə‖ˈepɪˌsentə/ *n* **1** the part of the earth's surface directly above the place of origin of an earthquake **2** CENTRE 2 – **epicentral** *adj*

epicure /ˈepikyooə‖ˈepɪkjʊə/ *n* sby with sensitive and discriminating tastes, esp in food or wine [*Epicurus* (342–270 BC), Greek philosopher] – **epicurism** *n*

Epicurean /ˌepikyooˈree·ən, -ˈkyooəri·ən‖ˌepɪkjʊˈriːən, -ˈkjʊərɪən/ *n or adj* **1** (a follower) of the doctrine of the Greek philosopher Epicurus who advocated the superiority of emotional calm and intellectual pleasures **2** *often not cap* (of or suited to) an epicure – **Epicureanism** *n*

epidemic /ˌepiˈdemik‖ˌepɪˈdemɪk/ *n or adj* (an

outbreak of a disease) affecting many individuals within a population, community, or region at the same time – **epidemical** *adj*, **epidemically** *adv*, **epidemicity** *n*

epidermis /ˌepiˈduhmis‖ˌepɪˈdɜːmɪs/ *n* **1a** the thin outer epithelial layer of the animal body that is derived from ectoderm and forms in vertebrates an insensitive layer over the dermis **b** any of various covering layers resembling the epidermis **2** a thin surface layer of tissue in higher plants – **epidermal** *adj*, **epidermic** *adj*, **epidermoid** *adj*

epidiascope /ˌepiˈdie·əˌskohp‖ˌepɪˈdaɪəˌskəʊp/ *n* a projector for images of opaque objects or for transparencies

epiglottis /ˌepiˈglotis‖ˌepɪˈglɒtɪs/ *n* a thin plate of flexible cartilage in front of the glottis that folds back over and protects the glottis during swallowing – **epiglottal** *also* **epiglottic** *adj*

epigram /ˈepiˌgram‖ˈepɪˌgræm/ *n* **1** a short often satirical poem **2** a neat, witty, and often paradoxical remark or saying – **epigrammatic, epigrammatical** *adj*, **epigrammatically** *adv*, **epigrammatism** *n*, **epigrammatist** *n*, **epigrammatize** *vb*

epigraph /ˈepiˌgrahf, -ˌgraf‖ˈepɪˌgrɑːf, -ˌgræf/ *n* **1** an engraved inscription **2** a quotation at the beginning of a book, chapter, etc suggesting its theme

epilepsy /ˈepiˌlepsi‖ˈepɪˌlepsɪ/ *n* any of various disorders marked by disturbed electrical rhythms of the brain and spinal chord and typically manifested by convulsive attacks often with clouding of consciousness

epileptic /ˌepiˈleptik‖ˌepɪˈleptɪk/ *adj* of, affected with, or having the characteristics of epilepsy – **epileptic** *n*, **epileptically** *adv*

epilogue /ˈepiˌlog‖ˈepɪˌlɒg/ *n* **1** a concluding section of a literary or dramatic work that comments on or summarizes the main action or plot **2** a speech or poem addressed to the audience by an actor at the end of a play

epiphany /iˈpifəni‖ɪˈpɪfənɪ/ *n* **1** *cap* (January 6 observed as a church festival in commemoration of) the coming of the Magi **2** a usu sudden manifestation or perception of the essential nature or meaning of sthg – **epiphanic** *adj*

episcopacy /iˈpiskəpəsi‖ɪˈpɪskəpəsɪ/ *n* **1** government of the church by bishops or by a hierarchy **2** an episcopate

episcopal /iˈpiskəpl‖ɪˈpɪskəpl/ *adj* **1** of a bishop **2** of, having, or constituting government by bishops **3** *cap* Anglican; *esp* of an Anglican church that is not established (e g in the USA or Scotland) – **episcopally** *adv*, **Episcopalian** *n or adj*, **Episcopalianism** *n*

episode /ˈepisohd‖ˈepɪsəʊd/ *n* **1a** the part of an ancient Greek tragedy between 2 choric songs **b** a developed situation or incident that is integral to but separable from a continuous narrative (e g a play or novel) **c** the part of a serial presented at 1 performance **2** an event that is distinctive and separate although part of a larger series (e g in history or in sby's life)

episodic /ˌepiˈsodik‖ˌepɪˈsɒdɪk/ *also* **episodical** /-kl‖-kl/ *adj* **1** made up of separate, esp loosely connected, episodes <*an ~ narrative*> **2** of or limited in duration or significance to a particular episode **3** occasional, sporadic – **episodically** *adv*

epistle /iˈpisl‖ɪˈpɪsl/ *n* **1** *cap* (a liturgical reading from) any of the letters (e g of St Paul) adopted as books of the New Testament **2** an esp formal letter

epistolary /iˈpistəl(ə)ri‖ɪˈpɪstəl(ə)rɪ/ *adj* **1** of or suitable to a letter **2** carried on by or in the form of letters <*~ love affairs – TLS*> **3** written in the form of a series of letters <*~ novel*>

epitaph /ˈepiˌtahf, -taf‖ˈepɪˌtɑːf, -tæf/ *n* **1** a commemorative inscription on a tombstone or monument **2** a brief statement commemorating a deceased person or past event

epithelium /ˌepiˈtheeli·əm, -lyəm‖ˌepɪˈθiːlɪəm, -ljəm/ *n, pl* **epithelia** /-li·ə, -lyə‖-lɪə, -ljə/ **1** a membranous cellular tissue that covers a free surface or lines a tube or cavity of an animal body and serves esp to enclose and protect other parts of the body, to produce secretions and excretions, and to function in assimilation **2** a usu thin layer of cells that lines a cavity or tube of a plant – **epithelial** *adj*, **epithelioid** *adj*

epithet /ˈepithet‖ˈepɪθet/ *n* **1** a descriptive word or phrase accompanying or occurring in place of the name of a person or thing **2** a disparaging or abusive word or phrase – **epithetic, epithetical** *adj*

epitome /iˈpitəmi‖ɪˈpɪtəmɪ/ *n* **1** a condensed account or summary, esp of a literary work **2** a typical or ideal example; an embodiment

epitom·ize, -ise /iˈpitəmiez‖ɪˈpɪtəmaɪz/ *vt* to make or serve as an epitome of

epoch /ˈeepok‖ˈiːpɒk/ *n* **1** a date or time selected as a point of reference (e g in astronomy) **2** a memorable event or date; *esp* TURNING POINT **3a** an extended period of time, usu characterized by a distinctive development or by a memorable series of events **b** a division of geological time less than a period and greater than an age – **epochal** *adj*, **epochally** *adv*

ˈ**epoch-ˌmaking** *adj* uniquely or highly significant <*the steam engine was an ~ invention*>

eponym /ˈepohˌnim, ˈepə-‖ˈepəʊˌnɪm, ˈepə-/ *n* the person after whom sthg is (believed to be) named – **eponymic** *adj*, **eponymous** *adj*

Epsom salts /ˈeps(ə)m‖ˈeps(ə)m/ *n pl but sing or pl in constr* hydrated magnesium sulphate used as a purgative

equable /ˈekwəbl‖ˈekwəbl/ *adj* uniform, even; *esp* free from extremes or sudden changes <*an ~ climate*> – **equably** *adv*, **equability** *n*

[1]**equal** /ˈeekwəl‖ˈiːkwəl/ *adj* **1a** of the same quantity, amount, or number as another **b** identical in value; equivalent **2a** like in quality, nature, or status **b** like for each member of a group, class, or society <*~ rights*> **3** evenly balanced or matched <*the 2 opponents were ~*> **4** capable of meeting the requirements of sthg (e g a situation or task) – + *to* <*he is quite ~ to the job*>

[2]**equal** *n* sby or sthg equal <*she is anyone's ~*>

[3]**equal** *vt* **-ll-** (*NAm* **-l-, -ll-**) **1** to be equal to; *esp* to be identical in value to **2** to make or produce sthg equal to

equalitarian /iˌkwoliˈteəri·ən‖ɪˌkwɒlɪ-

ˈteərɪən/ *n or adj* (an) egalitarian – **equalitarianism** *n*

equality /iˈkwoləti‖ɪˈkwɒlətɪ/ *n* the quality or state of being equal

equal·ize, -ise /ˈeekwəˌliez‖ˈiːkwəˌlaɪz/ *vt* **1** to make equal **2** to make uniform; *esp* to distribute evenly or uniformly ~*vi chiefly Br* to make sthg equal; *esp* to bring the scores level (e g in a football match) – **equalizer** *n*, **equalization** *n*

equally /ˈeekwəli‖ˈiːkwəlɪ/ *adv* **1** in an equal or uniform manner; evenly **2** to an equal degree; alike <*respected ~ by young and old*>

equanimity /ˌeekwəˈniməti, ˌekwə-‖ˌiːkwəˈnɪmətɪ, ˌekwə-/ *n* evenness of mind or temper, esp under stress

equate /iˈkwayt‖ɪˈkweɪt/ *vt* **1** to make or set equal **2** to treat, represent, or regard as equal, equivalent, or comparable <~s *dissension with disloyalty*>

equation /iˈkwayzh(ə)n‖ɪˈkweɪʒ(ə)n; *sense 1* iˈkwaysh(ə)n‖ɪˈkweɪʃ(ə)n/ *n* **1** equating or being equated **2** a statement of the equality of 2 mathematical expressions – **equational** *adj*, **equationally** *adv*

equator /iˈkwaytə‖ɪˈkweɪtə/ *n* **1** the great circle of the celestial sphere whose plane is perpendicular to the rotational axis of the earth **2** GREAT CIRCLE; *specif* the one that is equidistant from the 2 poles of the earth and divides the earth's surface into the northern and southern hemispheres **3** a circle or circular band dividing the surface of a body into 2 usu equal and symmetrical parts

equatorial /ˌekwəˈtawri·əl‖ˌekwəˈtɔːrɪəl/ *adj* **1a** of, at, or in the plane of the (earth's) equator **b** *of the climate* characterized by consistently high temperatures and rainfall throughout the year **2** being or having a support (e g for a telescope) that includes 2 axles at right angles to each other and allows a celestial body to be kept in view as the earth rotates

equerry /iˈkweri, ˈekwəri‖ɪˈkwerɪ, ˈekwərɪ/ *n* **1** an officer of a prince or noble charged with the care of horses **2** an officer of the British royal household in personal attendance on a member of the royal family

[1]**equestrian** /iˈkwestri·ən‖ɪˈkwestrɪən/ *adj* **1a** of or featuring horses, horsemen, or horsemanship **b** representing a person on horseback **2** (composed) of knights – **equestrianism** *n*

[2]**equestrian** *n* sby who rides or performs on horseback

equi- *comb form* equal <equi*poise*>; equally <equi*probable*>

equidistant /ˌeekwiˈdist(ə)nt, ˌekwi-‖ˌiːkwɪˈdɪst(ə)nt, ˌekwɪ-/ *adj* equally distant – **equidistantly** *adv*, **equidistance** *n*

equilateral /ˌeekwiˈlat(ə)rəl, ˌekwi-‖ˌiːkwɪˈlæt(ə)rəl, ˌekwɪ-/ *adj* having all sides equal <~ *triangle*>

equilibrium /ˌeekwiˈlibri·əm, ˌekwi-‖ˌiːkwɪˈlɪbrɪəm, ˌekwɪ-/ *n, pl* **equilibriums, equilibria** /-bri·ə‖-brɪə/ **1** a state of balance between opposing forces, actions, or processes (e g in a reversible chemical reaction) **2a** a state of adjustment between opposing or divergent influences or elements **b** a state of intellectual or emotional balance **3** the normal state of the animal body in respect to its environment that involves adjustment to changing conditions

equine /ˈekwien‖ˈekwaɪn/ *adj* of or resembling the horse (family) – **equine** *n*, **equinely** *adv*

[1]**equinoctial** /ˌeekwiˈnoksh(ə)l, ˌekwi-‖ˌiːkwɪˈnɒkʃ(ə)l, ˌekwɪ-/ *adj* **1** relating to (the time when the sun passes) an equinox **2** relating to the regions or climate of the equinoctial circle or equator

[2]**equinoctial, equinoctial circle** *n* EQUATOR 1

equinox /ˈekwiˌnoks‖ˈekwɪˌnɒks/ *n* **1** either of the 2 times each year that occur about March 21st and September 23rd when the sun crosses the equator and day and night are of equal length everywhere on earth **2** either of the 2 points on the celestial sphere where the celestial equator intersects the ecliptic [Middle French *equinoxe*, fr Latin *aequinoctium*, fr *aequus* equal + *noct-, nox* night]

equip /iˈkwip‖ɪˈkwɪp/ *vt* **-pp- 1** to make ready for service, action, or use; provide with appropriate supplies **2** to dress, array

equipage /ˈekwipij‖ˈekwɪpɪdʒ/ *n* **1** material or articles used in equipment **2a** an etui **b** trappings **3** a horse-drawn carriage (with its servants)

equipment /iˈkwipmənt‖ɪˈkwɪpmənt/ *n* **1** the set of articles, apparatus, or physical resources serving to equip a person, thing, enterprise, expedition, etc **2** mental or emotional resources

equipoise /ˈekwiˌpoyz, ˈeekwi-‖ˈekwɪˌpɔɪz, ˈiːkwɪ-/ *n* **1** a state of equilibrium **2** a counterbalance

equitable /ˈekwitəbl‖ˈekwɪtəbl/ *adj* **1** fair and just **2** valid in equity as distinguished from law – **equitableness** *n*, **equitably** *adv*, **equitability** *n*

equitation /ˌekwiˈtaysh(ə)n‖ˌekwɪˈteɪʃ(ə)n/ *n* the act or art of riding on horseback

equity /ˈekwiti‖ˈekwɪtɪ/ *n* **1** justice according to natural law or right; fairness **2** a system of justice originally developed in the Chancery courts on the basis of conscience and fairness to supplement or override the more rigid common law **3a** a right, claim, or interest existing or valid in equity **b** the money value of a property or of an interest in a property in excess of claims against it **4** a share that does not bear fixed interest – usu pl

equivalent /iˈkwivəl(ə)nt‖ɪˈkwɪvəl(ə)nt/ *adj* **1** equal in force, amount, or value **2** corresponding or virtually identical, esp in effect, function, or meaning – **equivalence** *also* **equivalency** *n*, **equivalent** *n*, **equivalently** *adv*

equivocal /iˈkwivəkl‖ɪˈkwɪvəkl/ *adj* **1** subject to 2 or more interpretations; ambiguous <~ *evidence*> **2** questionable, suspicious – **equivocally** *adv*, **equivocalness** *n*, **equivocality** *n*

equivocate /iˈkwivəˌkayt‖ɪˈkwɪvəˌkeɪt/ *vi* to use equivocal language, esp with intent to deceive or avoid committing oneself – **equivocation** *n*, **equivocator** *n*

er, ur /uh‖ɜː/ *interj* – used to express hesitation or doubt

[1]**-er** /-ə‖-ə/ *suffix* (→ *adj or adv*) – used to form the comparative degree of adjectives and adverbs of 1 syllable, and of some adjectives and

adverbs of 2 or more syllables, that end in a consonant <*hott*er>, a vowel other than *e*, or a final *y* that changes to *i* <*dri*er>; compare [1]-R

[2]**-er, -ar, -ier, -r, -yer** *suffix* **1** (*n* → *n*) **1a** one engaged in the occupation of <*geographer*> **b** one belonging to or associated with <*sixth-former*> **c** native of; resident of <*cottager*> <*Londoner*> **d** sthg that has <*three-wheeler*> <*four-poster*> **2** (*vb* → *n*) **2a** one who or that which does or performs (a specified action) <*reporter*> <*eye-opener*> **b** sthg that is a suitable object of (a specified action) <*broiler*> <*cooker*> **3** (*adj* → *n*) sby or sthg that is <*foreigner*> *USE -yer* in a few words after *w*, *-ier* in a few words after other letters, *-r* in words after *e*, otherwise *-er*

era /ˈiərə‖ˈɪərə/ *n* **1** a system of chronological notation computed from a given date as a basis <*Christian* ~> **2** EPOCH 2 **3a** a usu historical period set off or typified by some distinctive figure or characteristic feature <*the* ~ *of space flight*> **b** any of the 5 major divisions of geological time

eradicate /iˈradi,kayt‖ɪˈrædɪ,keɪt/ *vt* **1** to pull up by the roots **2** to eliminate; DO AWAY WITH – **eradicator** *n*, **eradicable** *adj*, **eradication** *n*, **eradicative** *adj*,

erase /iˈrayz‖ɪˈreɪz/ *vt* **1a** to obliterate or rub out (e g written, painted, or engraved letters) **b** to remove (recorded matter) from a magnetic tape or wire **c** to delete from a computer storage device **2** to remove from existence or memory as if by erasing ~*vi* to yield to being erased <*pencil* ~s *easily*> – **erasability** *n*, **erasable** *adj*, **erasure** *n*

eraser /iˈrayzə‖ɪˈreɪzə/ *n* [1]RUBBER 1b

[1]**ere** /eə‖eə/ *prep* [2]BEFORE 2 – poetic

[2]**ere** *conj* before – poetic

[1]**erect** /iˈrekt‖ɪˈrekt/ *adj* **1a** vertical in position; upright **b** standing up or out from the body <~ *hairs*> **c** characterized by firm or rigid straightness (e g in bodily posture) <*an* ~ *bearing*> **2** in a state of physiological erection – **erectly** *adv*, **erectness** *n*

[2]**erect** *vt* **1a** to put up by the fitting together of materials or parts; build **b** to fix in an upright position **2** to elevate in status <~s *a few odd notions into a philosophy*> **3** to establish; SET UP 6a **4** to construct (e g a perpendicular) on a given base – **erectable** *adj*, **erector** *n*

erectile /iˈrektiel‖ɪˈrektaɪl/ *adj* **1** capable of being raised to an erect position; *esp, of animal tissue* capable of becoming swollen with blood to bring about the erection of a body part **2** of or involving the erection of the penis – **erectility** *n*

erection /iˈreksh(ə)n‖ɪˈrekʃ(ə)n/ *n* **1** (an occurrence in the penis or clitoris of) the dilation with blood and resulting firmness of a previously flaccid body part **2** sthg erected

eremite /ˈerəmiet‖ˈerəmaɪt/ *n* a usu Christian hermit or recluse – **eremitic, eremitical** *adj*

erg /uhg‖ɜːg/ *n* the cgs unit of work or energy; 10^{-7} joules [Greek *ergon* work]

ergo /ˈuhgoh‖ˈɜːgəʊ/ *adv* therefore, hence

ergonomics /,uhgəˈnomiks‖,ɜːgəˈnɒmɪks/ *n pl but sing or pl in constr* a science concerned with the relationship between human beings, the machines they use, and the working environment – **ergonomic** *adj*, **ergonomist** *n*

ergot /ˈuhgət, -got‖ˈɜːgət, -gɒt/ *n* **1** (a fungus bearing) a black or dark purple club-shaped sclerotium that develops in place of the seed of a grass (e g rye) **2** a disease of rye and other cereals caused by an ergot fungus **3** the dried sclerotia of an ergot fungus containing alkaloids used medicinally (e g to treat migraine) – **ergotic** *adj*

ermine /ˈuhmin‖ˈɜːmɪn/ *n*, (the winter fur of) a stoat or related weasel that has a white winter coat usu with black on the tail

erode /iˈrohd‖ɪˈrəʊd/ *vt* **1a** to diminish or destroy by degrees **b** to eat into or away by slow destruction of substance; corrode **c** to wear away by the action of water, wind, glacial ice, etc **2** to produce or form by eroding ~*vi* to undergo erosion – **erodible** *adj*

erogenous /iˈrojənəs‖ɪˈrɒdʒənəs/ *also* **erogenic** /,erəˈjenik‖,erəˈdʒenɪk/ *adj* of or producing sexual excitement (when stimulated)

erosion /iˈrohzh(ə)n‖ɪˈrəʊʒ(ə)n/ *n* (an instance or product of) eroding or being eroded – **erosional** *adj*, **erosionally** *adv*, **erosive** *adj*

erotic /iˈrotik‖ɪˈrɒtɪk/ *adj* **1** of, concerned with, or tending to arouse sexual desire **2** strongly affected by sexual desire [Greek *erōtikos*, fr *erōt-, erōs* love] – **erotic** *n*, **erotical** *adj*, **erotically** *adv*, **eroticize** *vt*

erotica /iˈrotikə‖ɪˈrɒtɪkə/ *n pl but sing or pl in constr* literature or art with an erotic theme or quality

eroticism /iˈrotə,siz(ə)m‖ɪˈrɒtə,sɪz(ə)m/ *n* **1** an erotic theme, quality, or character **2** EROTISM 1 **3** (insistent) sexual impulse or desire – **eroticist** *n*

erotism /ˈerə,tiz(ə)m‖ˈerə,tɪz(ə)m/ *n* **1** sexual exitement or arousal **2** EROTICISM 1, 3

err /uh‖ɜː/ *vi* **1a** to make a mistake **b** to do wrong; sin **2** to be inaccurate or incorrect

errand /ˈerənd‖ˈerənd/ *n* (the object or purpose of) a short trip taken to attend to some business, often for another

errant /ˈerənt‖ˈerənt/ *adj* **1** (given to) travelling, esp in search of adventure **2** going astray <*an* ~ *calf*>; *esp* doing wrong; erring <*an* ~ *child*> – **errant** *n*, **errantly** *adv*

erratic /iˈratik‖ɪˈrætɪk/ *adj* **1** having no fixed course <*an* ~ *comet*> **2** *esp of a boulder* transported from an original resting place, esp by a glacier **3** characterized by lack of consistency, regularity, or uniformity, esp in behaviour – **erratic** *n*, **erratically** *adv*, **erraticism** *n*

erratum /iˈrahtəm‖ɪˈrɑːtəm/ *n, pl* **errata** /-tə‖-tə/ a corrigendum

erroneous /iˈrohnyəs, -ni·əs‖ɪˈrəʊnjəs, -nɪəs/ *adj* containing or characterized by error; incorrect – **erroneously** *adv*, **erroneousness** *n*

error /ˈerə‖ˈerə/ *n* **1a** a mistake or inaccuracy in speech, opinion, or action **b** the state of being wrong in behaviour or beliefs <*he realized the* ~ *of his ways*> **c** an act that fails to achieve what was intended **2** the difference between an observed or calculated value and a true value – **errorless** *adj* – **in error** by mistake

ersatz /ˈeəzatz, ˈuh-‖ˈeəzætz, ˈɜː-/ *adj* being a usu artificial and inferior substitute; an imitation – **ersatz** *n*

Erse /uhs‖ɜːs/ *n* Scottish Gaelic – no longer used technically – **Erse** *adj*

eructation /iˌruk'taysh(ə)n, ˌeeruk-‖ɪˌrʌk'teɪʃ-(ə)n, ˌiːrʌk-/ *n* belching

erudite /'eroodiet‖'erudaɪt/ *adj* possessing or displaying extensive or profound knowledge; learned – **eruditely** *adv*, **erudition** *n*

erupt /i'rupt‖ɪ'rʌpt/ *vi* **1a** *esp of a volcano* to release lava, steam, etc suddenly and usu violently **b(1)** to burst violently from limits or restraint **b(2)** *of a tooth* to emerge through the gum **c** to become suddenly active or violent; explode **2** to break out (e g in a rash) ~*vt* to force out or release suddenly or violently [Latin *eruptus*, past participle of *erumpere* to burst forth, fr *e-* out + *rumpere* to break] – **eruptible** *adj*, **eruptive** *adj*, **eruptively** *adv*

eruption /i'rupsh(ə)n‖ɪ'rʌpʃ(ə)n/ *n* (a product of) erupting

-ery /-(ə)ri‖-(ə)rɪ/, **-ry** *suffix* (→ *n*) **1** quality or state of having (a specified trait or mode of behaviour) <*snobb*ery> **2** art or practice of <*cook*ery> **3** place of doing, keeping, producing, or selling (a specified thing) <*fish*ery> <*bak*ery> **4a** collection or body of <*fin*ery> **b** class of (specified) goods <*confectio*nery> **5** state or condition of <*slav*ery> **6** all that is concerned with or characteristic of – chiefly derog <*tomfool*ery> *USE -ry* often after *d, t, l,* or *n*, otherwise *-ery*

erysipelas /ˌeri'sipələs‖ˌerɪ'sɪpələs/ *n* a feverish disease with intense deep red local inflammation of the skin, caused by infection by a streptococcal bacterium

[1]**-es** /-əz, -iz‖-əz, -ɪz *after* s,z,sh,ch; -z *after* v *or a vowel*/ *suffix* (→ *n pl*) **1** – used to form the plural of most nouns that end in *s* <*glass*es>, *z* <*fuzz*es>, *sh* <*bush*es>, *ch* <*peach*es>, or a final *y* that changes to *i* <*ladi*es> and some nouns ending in *f* that changes to *v* <*loav*es>; compare [1]-s 1 **2** [1]-s 2

[2]**-es** *suffix* (→ *vb*) – used to form the third person singular present of most verbs that end in *s* <*bless*es>, *z* <*fizz*es>, *sh* <*hush*es>, *ch* <*catch*es>, or a final *y* that changes to *i* <*defi*es>; compare [2]-s

escalate /'eskəlayt‖'eskəleɪt/ *vi* **1** EXPAND 1a **2** RISE 10b <escalating *prices*> ~*vt* EXPAND 1 – **escalation** *n*, **escalatory** *adj*

escalator /'eskəlaytə‖'eskəleɪtə/ *n* a power-driven set of stairs arranged like an endless belt that ascend or descend continuously

escalope /'eskəˌlop‖'eskəˌlɒp/ *n* a thin boneless slice of meat; *esp* a slice of veal from the leg

escapade /'eskəpayd‖'eskəpeɪd/ *n* a wild, reckless, and often mischievous adventure, esp one that flouts rules or convention

[1]**escape** /i'skayp‖ɪ'skeɪp/ *vi* **1a** to get away, esp from confinement or restraint **b** *of gases, liquids, etc* to leak out gradually; seep **c** *of a plant* to run wild from cultivation **2** to avoid a threatening evil ~ *vt* **1** to get or stay out of the way of; avoid **2** to fail to be noticed or recallable by <*his name* ~s *me*> **3** to be produced or made by (esp a person), usu involuntarily <*a yawn* ~d *him*> – **escapable** *adj*, **escaper** *n*, **escapee** *n*

[2]**escape** *n* **1** an act or instance of escaping **2** a means of escape **3** a cultivated plant run wild

[3]**escape** *adj* **1** providing a means of escape **2** providing a means of evading a regulation, claim, or commitment <*an* ~ *clause in a contract*>

escapement /i'skaypmənt‖ɪ'skeɪpmənt/ *n* a device in a timepiece through which the energy of the power source is delivered to the regulatory mechanism that controls the motion of the cogwheels

escapism /i'skayˌpiz(ə)m‖ɪ'skeɪˌpɪz(ə)m/ *n* habitual diversion of the mind to purely imaginative activity or entertainment as an escape from reality or routine – **escapist** *adj or n*

escapology /ˌeskə'poləji‖ˌeskə'pɒlədʒɪ/ *n* the art or practice of escaping, esp as a theatrical performance – **escapologist** *n*

escarpment /i'skahpmənt‖ɪ'skɑːpmənt/ *n* a long cliff or steep slope separating 2 more gently sloping surfaces

eschatology /ˌeskə'toləji‖ˌeskə'tɒlədʒɪ/ *n* **1** a branch of theology or religious belief concerned with the ultimate destiny of the universe or of mankind **2** the Christian doctrine concerning death, judgment, heaven, and hell – **eschatological** *adj*, **eschatologically** *adv*

[1]**escheat** /is'cheet‖ɪs'tʃiːt/ *n* the reversion of property to a government or feudal lord on the owner's dying without having made a will and without heirs; *also* property that has so reverted

[2]**escheat** *vb* to (cause to) revert by escheat – **escheatable** *adj*

eschew /is'chooh‖ɪs'tʃuː/ *vt* to avoid habitually, esp on moral or practical grounds; shun – fml

[1]**escort** /'eskawt‖'eskɔːt/ *n* **1** a person, group of people, ship, aircraft, etc accompanying sby or sthg to give protection or show courtesy **2** one who accompanies another socially

[2]**escort** /i'skawt‖ɪ'skɔːt/ *vt* to accompany as an escort

escritoire /ˌeskri'twah‖ˌeskrɪ'twɑː/ *n* a writing table or desk

escutcheon /i'skuchən‖ɪ'skʌtʃən/ *n* **1** a shield on which a coat of arms is displayed **2** a protective or ornamental shield or plate (e g round a keyhole)

[1]**-ese** /-eez‖-iːz/ *suffix* (*n* → *adj*) of or originating in (a specified place or country) <*Japan*ese> <*Vienn*ese>

[2]**-ese** *suffix pl* **-ese** (*n* → *n*), **1** inhabitant of <*Chin*ese> **2a** language of <*Portugu*ese> <*Canton*ese> **b** speech, literary style, or diction peculiar to (a specified place, person, or group) – chiefly derog <*journal*ese> <*official*ese>

Eskimo *also* **Esquimau** /'eskimoh‖'eskɪməʊ/ *n* (a member or the language of) any of a group of peoples of N Canada, Greenland, Alaska, and E Siberia – **Eskimoan** *adj*

Eskimo dog *n* (any of) a breed of broad-chested powerful sledge dogs native to Greenland and Labrador

esoteric /ˌeesə'terik, ˌesoh-‖ˌiːsə'terɪk, ˌesəʊ-/ *adj* **1** designed for, understood by, or restricted to a small group, esp of the specially initiated <~ *knowledge*> **2** private, confidential <*an* ~ *purpose*> – **esoterically** *adv*, **esotericism** *n*

ESP *n* extrasensory perception

espalier /iˈspalyə‖ɪˈspæljə/ *n* (a fruit tree or shrub trained to grow flat against) a railing, trellis, etc

especial /iˈspesh(ə)l‖ɪˈspeʃ(ə)l/ *adj* (distinctively or particularly) special – **especially** *adv*

Esperanto /ˌespəˈrantoh‖ˌespəˈræntəʊ/ *n* an artificial international language – **Esperantist** *n or adj*

espionage /ˈespi·ənahzh, ˌ---ˈ-, -nij, iˈspie-‖ˈespɪənɑːʒ, ˌ---ˈ-, -nɪdʒ, ɪˈspaɪ-/ *n* spying or the use of spies to obtain information

esplanade /ˌespləˈnahd, -nayd‖ˌespləˈnɑːd, -neɪd/ *n* a level open stretch of paved or grassy ground, esp along a shore

espousal /iˈspowzl‖ɪˈspaʊzl/ *n* **1** a betrothal; *also* a marriage – often pl with sing. meaning; fml **2** the adoption or support of a cause or belief

espouse /iˈspowz‖ɪˈspaʊz/ *vt* **1** to marry – fml **2** to take up and support as a cause; become attached to – **espouser** *n*

espresso /iˈspresoh‖ɪˈspresəʊ/ *n, pl* **espressos** (an apparatus for making) coffee brewed by forcing steam through finely ground coffee beans

eˌsprit de ˈcorps /də ˈkaw‖də ˈkɔː/ *n* the common spirit and loyalty existing among the members of a group

espy /iˈspie‖ɪˈspaɪ/ *vt* to catch sight of

-esque /-ˈesk‖-ˈesk/ *suffix* (*n* → *adj*) in the manner or style of; like <*statu*esque> <*Kafka*esque>

esquire /iˈskwie·ə‖ɪˈskwaɪə/ *n* **1** a member of the English gentry ranking below a knight **2** – used instead of Mr as a man's courtesy title and usu placed in its abbreviated form *Esq* after the surname

-ess /-is, -əs, -es‖-ɪs, -əs, -es/ *suffix* (*n* → *n*) female <*actr*ess> <*lion*ess> – often derog <*Negr*ess> <*poet*ess>

[1]**essay** /eˈsay‖eˈseɪ/ *vt* to attempt – fml – **essayer** *n*

[2]**essay** /ˈesay‖ˈeseɪ/ *n* **1** a usu short piece of prose writing on a specific topic **2** an (initial tentative) effort or attempt – fml – **essayist** *n*, **essayistic** *adj*

essence /ˈes(ə)ns‖ˈes(ə)ns/ *n* **1a** the real or ultimate nature of an individual being or thing, esp as opposed to its existence or its accidental qualities **b** the properties or attributes by means of which sthg can be categorized or identified **2** sthg that exists, esp in an abstract form; an entity **3a** (an alcoholic solution or other preparation of) an extract, essential oil, etc possessing the special qualities of a plant, drug, etc in concentrated form **b** an odour, perfume **c** one who or that which resembles an extract in possessing a quality in concentrated form – **in essence** in or by its very nature; essentially – **of the essence** of the utmost importance; essential

[1]**essential** /iˈsensh(ə)l‖ɪˈsenʃ(ə)l/ *adj* **1** of or being (an) essence; inherent **2** of the utmost importance; basic, necessary – **essentially** *adv*, **essentialness, essentiality** *n*

[2]**essential** *n* sthg basic, indispensable, or fundamental

[1]**-est** /-ist‖-ɪst/ *suffix* (*adj or adv* → *adj or adv*) – used to form the superlative degree of adjectives and adverbs of 1 and sometimes 2 or more syllables that end in a consonant <*fat*test> <*dear*est>, a vowel other than *e*, or a final *y* that changes to *i* <*drear*iest>; compare [1]-ST

[2]**-est, -st** /-ist‖-ɪst/ *suffix* (→ *vb*) – used to form the archaic second person singular of verbs (with *thou*)

establish /iˈstablish‖ɪˈstæblɪʃ/ *vt* **1** to make firm or stable **2** to enact permanently <~ *a law*> **3** to bring into existence; found <~ed *a republic*> **4a** to set on a firm basis; place (e g oneself) in a permanent or firm usu favourable position <~ed *himself as the leader*> **b** to gain full recognition or acceptance of <*she* ~ed *her fame as an actress*> **5** to make (a church or religion) a national institution supported by civil authority **6** to put beyond doubt; prove <~ed *his innocence*> **7** to cause (a plant) to grow and multiply in a place where previously absent – **establishable** *adj*, **establisher** *n*

eˈstablishment /-mənt‖-mənt/ *n* **1** sthg established: e g **1a** a usu large organization or institution **b** a place of business or residence with its furnishings and staff **2** an established order of society: e g **2a** *sing or pl in constr, often cap the* entrenched social, economic, and political leaders of a nation **b** *often cap* a controlling group <*the literary* ~>

estate /iˈstayt‖ɪˈsteɪt/ *n* **1** a social or political class (e g the nobility, clergy, or commons) **2a(1)** the whole of sby's real or personal property **a(2)** the assets and liabilities left by sby at death **b** a large landed property, esp in the country, usu with a large house on it **3** *Br* a part of an urban area devoted to a particular type of development <*a housing* ~ *next to an industrial* ~>; *specif* one devoted to housing **4** a state, condition – fml <*men of low* ~>

eˈstate ˌagent *n, Br* **1** an agent who is involved in the buying and selling of land and property (e g houses) **2** one who manages an estate; a steward

eˈstate ˌcar *n, Br* a relatively large motor car with a nearly vertical rear door and 1 compartment in which both passengers and bulky luggage can be carried

[1]**esteem** /iˈsteem‖ɪˈstiːm/ *n* favourable regard <*held in high* ~ *by his colleagues*>

[2]**esteem** *vt* **1** to consider, deem <*would* ~ *it a privilege*> **2** to set a high value on; regard highly and prize accordingly

ester /ˈestə‖ˈestə/ *n* a (fragrant) compound formed by the reaction between an acid and an alcohol usu with elimination of water

esthete /ˈeestheet‖ˈiːsθiːt/ *n, NAm* an aesthete – **esthetic** *adj*, **esthetics** *n*

estimable /ˈestiməbl‖ˈestɪməbl/ *adj* worthy of esteem – **estimableness** *n*

[1]**estimate** /ˈestimayt‖ˈestɪmeɪt/ *vt* **1a** to judge approximately the value, worth, or significance of **b** to determine roughly the size, extent, or nature of **c** to produce a statement of the approximate cost of **2** to judge, conclude – **estimative** *adj*, **estimator** *n*

[2]**estimate** /ˈestimət‖ˈestɪmət/ *n* **1** the act of appraising or valuing; a calculation **2** an opinion or judgment of the nature, character, or quality

of sby or sthg **3** (the numerical value of) a rough or approximate calculation **4** a statement of the expected cost of a job

estimation /ˌestiˈmaysh(ə)n‖ˌestɪˈmeɪʃ(ə)n/ *n* **1** ESTIMATE 2 **2a** estimating **b** the value, amount, or size arrived at in an estimate **3** esteem

estrange /iˈstraynj‖ɪˈstreɪndʒ/ *vt* to arouse enmity or indifference in (sby) in place of affection; alienate – usu + *from* <~d *from her husband*> – **estrangement** *n*, **estranger** *n*

estuary /ˈestyooəri‖ˈestjʊərɪ/ *n* a water passage where the tide meets a river; *esp* a sea inlet at the mouth of a river

et al /ˌet ˈal‖ˌet ˈæl/ *adv* and others

etc /it ˈsetrə‖ɪt ˈsetrə/ *adv* ET CETERA

et cetera /it ˈsetrə‖ɪt ˈsetrə/ *adv* and other things, esp of the same kind; *broadly* and so forth

[1]**etch** /ech‖etʃ/ *vt* **1a** to produce (e g a picture or letters), esp on a plate of metal or glass, by the corrosive action of an acid **b** to subject (metal, glass, etc) to such etching **2** to delineate or impress clearly <*scenes that are indelibly* ~ed *in our minds*> ~*vi* to practise etching – **etcher** *n*

[2]**etch** *n* (the action or effect of) an etching acid (on a surface)

etching /ˈeching‖ˈetʃɪŋ/ *n* **1** the art of producing pictures or designs by printing from an etched metal plate **2** an impression from an etched plate

[1]**eternal** /iˈtuhnl‖ɪˈtɜːnl/ *adj* **1** having infinite duration; everlasting <~ *life*> **2** incessant, interminable **3** timeless <*the* ~ *truths*> – **eternalize** *vt*, **eternally** *adv*, **eternalness** *n*, **eternize** *vt*

[2]**eternal** *n* **1** *cap* GOD 1 – + *the* **2** sthg eternal

eternal triangle *n* a conflict that results from the sexual attraction between 2 people of one sex and 1 person of the other

eternity /iˈtuhnəti‖ɪˈtɜːnətɪ/ *n* **1** the quality or state of being eternal **2** infinite time **3** the eternal life after death **4** a (seemingly) endless or immeasurable time <*we waited an* ~ *for the train*>

ethane /ˈeethayn‖ˈiːθeɪn/ *n* an odourless gaseous hydrocarbon of the alkane group found in natural gas and used esp as a fuel

ether /ˈeethə‖ˈiːθə/ *n* **1 ether, aether** (the rarefied element formerly believed to fill) the upper regions of space; the heavens **2 ether, aether** a medium formerly held to permeate all space and transmit electromagnetic waves (e g light and radio waves) **3a** a volatile inflammable liquid used esp as a solvent and formerly as a general anaesthetic **b** any of various organic compounds characterized by an oxygen atom attached to 2 carbon atoms – **etherish** *adj*, **etheric** *adj*

ethereal /iˈthiəri·əl‖ɪˈθɪərɪəl; *sense 3* ˌethəˈree·əl‖ˌeθəˈriːəl/ *adj* **1** of the regions beyond the earth **2a** lacking material substance; intangible **b** marked by unusual delicacy, lightness, and refinement **3** of, containing, or resembling a chemical ether **4** celestial, heavenly – poetic – **ethereally** *adv*, **ethereality, etherealness** *n*, **etherealize** *vt*, **etherealization** *n*

ethic /ˈethik‖ˈeθɪk/ *n* **1** *pl but sing or pl in constr* inquiry into the nature and basis of moral principles and judgments **2** a set of moral principles or values **3** *pl but sing or pl in constr* the principles of conduct governing an individual or a group

ethical /ˈethikl‖ˈeθɪkl/ *also* **ethic** *adj* **1** conforming to accepted, esp professional, standards of conduct or morality **2** *of a drug* available to the general public only on a doctor's or dentist's prescription – **ethically** *adv*, **ethicality, ethicalness** *n*

[1]**ethnic** /ˈethnik‖ˈeθnɪk/ *adj* **1** of or being human races or large groups classed according to common traits **2** of an exotic, esp peasant, culture – **ethnicity** *n*

[2]**ethnic** *n, chiefly NAm* a member of an ethnic (minority) group

ethnical /ˈethnikl‖ˈeθnɪkl/ *adj* **1** ethnic **2** ethnological – **ethnically** *adv*

ethnography /ethˈnogrəfi‖eθˈnɒgrəfɪ/ *n* ethnology; *specif* descriptive anthropology – **ethnographer** *n*, **ethnographic, ethnographical** *adj*, **ethnographically** *adv*

ethnology /ethˈnoləji‖eθˈnɒlədʒɪ/ *n* a science that deals with the various forms of social relationships (e g kinship, law, religion, etc) found in esp preliterate human societies – **ethnologist** *n*, **ethnologic, ethnological** *adj*, **ethnologically** *adv*

ethos /ˈeethos‖ˈiːθɒs/ *n* the distinguishing character or guiding beliefs of a person, institution, etc

ethyl /ˈethil, ˈeethil, -thiel‖ˈeθɪl, ˈiːθɪl, -θaɪl/ *n* a hydrocarbon radical C_2H_5 derived from ethane

ethyl alcohol *n* ALCOHOL 1

ethylene /ˈethiˌleen‖ˈeθɪˌliːn/ *n* **1** an inflammable gaseous unsaturated hydrocarbon of the alkene group, found in coal gas and used esp in organic chemical synthesis **2** a hydrocarbon radical C_2H_4 derived from ethane

etiolate /ˈeeti·əˌlayt, -tioh-‖ˈiːtɪəˌleɪt, -tɪəʊ-/ *vt* **1** to bleach and alter the natural development of (a green plant) by excluding sunlight **2** to make weak, pale, or sickly – **etiolation** *n*

etiology /ˌeetiˈoləji‖ˌiːtɪˈɒlədʒɪ/ *n, NAm* aetiology – **etiologic, etiological** *adj*, **etiologically** *adv*

etiquette /ˈetiˌket‖ˈetɪˌket/ *n* the conventionally accepted standards of proper social or professional behaviour [French *étiquette*, lit., ticket – see TICKET]

Etruscan /iˈtruskən‖ɪˈtrʌskən/ *n or adj* (a native or inhabitant or the language) of the ancient country of Etruria in Italy

-ette /-ˈet‖-ˈet/ *suffix* (*n* → *n*) **1** small or lesser kind of <*kitchen*ette> **2** female <*usher*ette> **3** imitation; substitute <*leather*ette>

etui /eˈtwee‖eˈtwiː/ *n, pl* **etuis** /eˈtwee(z)‖eˈtwiː(z)/ a small ornamental case, esp for needles

etymology /ˌetiˈmoləji‖ˌetɪˈmɒlədʒɪ/ *n* **1** the history of the origin and development of a word or other linguistic form **2** a branch of linguistics dealing with etymologies – **etymologist** *n*, **etymological** *adj*, **etymologically** *adv*

eucalyptus /ˌyoohkəˈliptəs‖ˌjuːkəˈlɪptəs/ *n, pl* **eucalyptuses, eucalypti** /-ˈliptie‖-ˈlɪptaɪ/ any of a genus of mostly Australian evergreen trees that are widely cultivated for their gums, resins, oils, and wood

Eucharist /ˈyoohkərist‖ˈjuːkərɪst/ *n* (the

bread and wine consecrated in) the Christian sacrament in which bread and wine, being or representing the body and blood of Christ, are ritually consumed in accordance with Christ's injunctions at the Last Supper – **eucharistic** *adj, often cap*

eugenic /yooh'jenik||ju:'dʒenɪk/ *adj* **1** relating to or fit for the production of good offspring **2** of eugenics – **eugenically** *adv*

eu'genics *n pl but sing in constr* a science dealing with the improvement (e g by control of human mating) of the hereditary qualities of a race or breed – **eugenicist** *n*

eulog·ize, -ise /'yoohlə,jiez||'ju:lə,dʒaɪz/ *vt* to praise highly – **eulogizer** *n*

eulogy /'yoohləji||'ju:lədʒɪ/ *n* **1** a (formal) speech or piece of writing in praise of a person or thing **2** high praise – **eulogist** *n*, **eulogistic** *adj*, **eulogistically** *adv*

eunuch /'yoohnək||'ju:nək/ *n* **1** a castrated man employed, esp formerly, in a harem or as a chamberlain in a palace **2** a man or boy deprived of the testes or external genitals [Latin *eunuchus*, fr Greek *eunouchos*, fr *eunē* bed + *echein* to have, have charge of] – **eunuchism** *n*, **eunuchoid** *adj or n*

euphemism /'yoohfə,miz(ə)m||'ju:fə,mɪz(ə)m/ *n* the substitution of a mild, indirect, or vague expression for an offensive or unpleasant one; *also* the expression so substituted <fall asleep *is a* ~ *for* die> – **euphemistic** *adj*, **euphemistically** *adv*

euphonious /yooh'fohnyəs, -ni·əs||ju:'fəʊnjəs, -nɪəs/ *adj* pleasing to the ear – **euphoniously** *adv*

euphonium /yooh'fohnyəm, -ni·əm||ju:'fəʊnjəm, -nɪəm/ *n* a brass instrument smaller than but resembling a tuba

euphony /'yoohfəni||'ju:fənɪ/ *n* a pleasing or sweet sound, esp in speech – **euphonic** *adj*, **euphonically** *adv*

euphoria /yooh'fawri·ə||ju:'fɔ:rɪə/ *n* an (inappropriate) feeling of well-being or elation – **euphoric** *adj*, **euphorically** *adv*

euphuism /'yoohfyooh,iz(ə)m||'ju:fju:,ɪz(ə)m/ *n* an artificial and ornate style of writing or speaking – **euphuist** *n*, **euphuistic** *adj*, **euphuistically** *adv*

Eurasian /yooə'rayzh(ə)n, yoo'ray-||jʊə'reɪʒ(ə)n, jʊ'reɪ-/ *adj* **1** of, growing in, or living in Europe and Asia **2** of mixed European and Asian origin – **Eurasian** *n*

eureka /yoo(ə)'reekə||jʊ(ə)'ri:kə/ *interj* – used to express triumph at a discovery [Greek *heurēka* I have found, fr *heuriskein* to find; fr the exclamation attributed to Archimedes (287–212 BC), Greek mathematician & inventor, on finding a method for determining the purity of gold]

eurhythmic, eurythmic /yoo(ə)'ridhmik||jʊ(ə)'rɪðmɪk/ *adj* **1** harmonious **2** of eurhythmics

eu'rhythmics, eurythmics *n pl but sing or pl in constr* the art of harmonious bodily movement, esp through expressive timed movements in response to music

'Euro,crat /-,krat||-,kræt/ *n* a staff member of the administrative commission of the European Economic Community – infml

'Euro,dollar /-,dolə||-,dɒlə/ *n* a US dollar held (e g by a bank) outside the USA, esp in Europe

¹European /,yooərə'pee·ən||,jʊərə'pi:ən/ *adj* **1** native to Europe **2** of European descent or origin **3** concerned with or affecting the whole of Europe **4** advocating European unity or alliance – **Europeanism** *n*, **Europeanize** *vt*, **Europeanization** *n*

²European *n* a native or inhabitant of (the mainland of) Europe

eu,stachian 'tube /yooh'stayshyən, -shən||ju:'steɪʃjən, -ʃən/ *n, often cap E* a tube connecting the middle ear with the pharynx that equalizes air pressure on both sides of the eardrum [Bartolommeo *Eustachio* (1520-74), Italian anatomist]

euthanasia /,yoohthə'nayzyə, -zhə, -zi·ə||,ju:θə'neɪzjə, -ʒə, -zɪə/ *n* the act or practice of killing (hopelessly sick or injured) individuals for reasons of mercy [Greek, easy death, fr *eu-* easy, good, + *thanatos* death] – **euthanasic** *adj*

evacuate /i'vakyoo,ayt||ɪ'vækjʊ,eɪt/ *vt* **1** EMPTY 1a **2** to discharge from the body as waste **3** to remove gas, water, etc from, esp by pumping; *esp* to produce a vacuum in **4a** to remove, esp from a dangerous area **b** to withdraw from military occupation of **c** to vacate <*rapidly* ~d *the burning building*> ~ *vi* **1** to withdraw from a place in an organized way, esp for protection **2** to pass urine or faeces from the body – **evacuation** *n*, **evacuative** *adj*

evacuee /i,vakyoo'ee||ɪ,vækjʊ'i:/ *n* a person evacuated from a dangerous place

evade /i'vayd||ɪ'veɪd/ *vi* to take refuge by evading sthg ~ *vt* **1** to get away from or avoid, esp by deception **2a** to avoid facing up to <~d *the issue*> **b** to fail to pay <~ *taxes*> **3** to baffle, foil <*the problem* ~s *all efforts at solution*> – **evadable** *adj*, **evader** *n*

evaluate /i'valyoo,ayt||ɪ'væljʊ,eɪt/ *vt* to determine the amount, value, or significance of, esp by careful appraisal and study – **evaluation** *n*, **evaluative** *adj*, **evaluator** *n*

evanescent /,evə'nes(ə)nt||,evə'nes(ə)nt/ *adj* tending to dissipate or vanish like vapour – **evanescence** *n*, **evanesce** *vi*

evangelical /,eevan'jelikl||,i:væn'dʒelɪkl/ *also* **evangelic** /-'jelik||-'dʒelɪk/ *adj* **1** of or in agreement with the Christian message as presented in the 4 Gospels **2** *often cap* Protestant; *specif* of the German Protestant church **3** *often cap* (of or being a usu Protestant denomination) emphasizing salvation by faith in the atoning death of Jesus Christ, personal conversion, and the authority of Scripture **4a** of, adhering to, or marked by fundamentalism **b** LOW CHURCH **5** evangelistic, zealous <~ *ardour*> – **Evangelical** *n*, **Evangelicalism** *n*, **evangelically** *adv*

evangelist /i'vanjəlist||ɪ'vændʒəlɪst/ *n* **1** *often cap* a writer of any of the 4 Gospels **2** one who evangelizes; *specif* a Protestant minister or layman who preaches at special services

evangel·ize, -ise /i'vanjə,liez||ɪ'vændʒə,laɪz/ *vb* to preach the Christian gospel (to), esp with the intention of converting to Christianity – **evangelization** *n*

evaporate /i'vapərayt||ɪ'væpəreɪt/ *vi* **1a** to

pass off in vapour **b** to pass off or away; disappear, fade <*his fears* ~d> **2** to give out vapour ~ *vt* **1** to convert into vapour **2a** to expel moisture, esp water, from <~d *milk*> **b** to cause to disappear or fade – **evaporatable** *adj*, **evaporation** *n*, **evaporative** *adj*, **evaporator** *n*

evasion /i'vayzh(ə)n‖ɪ'veɪʒ(ə)n/ *n* an act, instance, or means of evading <*suspected of tax* ~>

evasive /i'vaysiv, -ziv‖ɪ'veɪsɪv, -zɪv/ *adj* tending or intended to evade – **evasively** *adv*, **evasiveness** *n*

eve /eev‖iːv/ *n* **1** the evening or the day before a special day, esp a religious holiday **2** the period immediately preceding an event <*the* ~ *of the election*> **3** the evening – chiefly poetic

[1]**even** /'eev(ə)n‖'iːv(ə)n/ *n, archaic* the evening – poetic

[2]**even** *adj* **1a** having a horizontal surface; flat, level <~ *ground*> **b** without break or irregularity; smooth **c** in the same plane or line – + *with* <~ *with the ground*> **2a** without variation; uniform <*an* ~ *disposition*> **b** LEVEL 3 **3a** equal <*we were* ~ *after the 4th game, having won 2 each*>; *also* fair <*an* ~ *exchange*> **b** being in equilibrium **4** exactly divisible by 2 <*an* ~ *number*> **5** exact, precise <*an* ~ *pound*> **6** fifty-fifty <*she stands an* ~ *chance of winning*> – **evenly** *adv*, **evenness** *n*

[3]**even** *adv* **1** at the very time – + *as* **2a** – used as an intensive to emphasize the contrast with a less strong possibility <*he looks content,* ~ *happy*> **b** – used as an intensive to emphasize the comparative degree <~ *better than last time*> – **even if** in spite of the possibility or fact that – **even now 1** at this very moment **2** in spite of what has happened – **even so** in spite of that

[4]**even** *vb* to make or become even – often + *up* or *out* – **evener** *n*

ˌ**even'handed** /-'handid‖-'hændɪd/ *adj* fair, impartial – **evenhandedly** *adv*, **evenhandedness** *n*

evening /'eevning‖'iːvnɪŋ/ *n* **1** the latter part of the day and the early part of the night; the time between sunset and bedtime **2** a late period (e g of time or life); the end **3** (the period of) an evening's entertainment

'**evening** ˌ**dress** *n* **1** clothes for formal or semiformal evening occasions **2** a dress, esp with a floor-length skirt, for wear on formal or semiformal occasions

ˌ**evening** '**prayer** *n, often cap E&P* the daily evening office of the Anglican church

'**evenings** *adv, chiefly NAm* in the evening repeatedly; on any evening

ˌ**evening** '**star** *n* a bright planet, specif Venus, seen in the western sky at sunset

'**even**ˌ**song** /-ˌsong‖-ˌsɒŋ/ *n, often cap* **1** VESPERS 1 **2** EVENING PRAYER

event /i'vent‖ɪ'vent/ *n* **1a** a qualitative or quantitative change or complex of changes located in a restricted portion of time and space **b** a (noteworthy or important) happening or occurrence **c** a social occasion or activity **2** a contingency, case – esp in *in the event of* <*in the* ~ *of my death*> and (*chiefly NAm*) *in the event that* <*in the* ~ *that I die*> **3** any of the contests in a sporting programme or tournament – **eventful** *adj*, **eventfully** *adv*, **eventfulness** *n*, **eventless** *adj* – **in any event, at all events** ANYWAY 1 – **in the event** *Br* when it actually happens or happened

eventide /'eev(ə)nˌtied‖'iːv(ə)nˌtaɪd/ *n* the evening – chiefly poetic

eventual /i'ventyooəl, -chəl, -chooəl‖ɪ'ventjʊəl, -tʃəl, -tʃʊəl/ *adj* taking place at an unspecified later time; ultimately resulting <*they counted on his* ~ *success*> – **eventually** *adv*

eventuality /iˌventyoo'aləti, -choo-‖ɪˌventjʊ'ælətɪ, -tʃʊ-/ *n* a possible, esp unwelcome, event or outcome

eventuate /i'ventyooayt, -choo-‖ɪ'ventjʊeɪt, -tʃʊ-/ *vi* to result – fml

ever /'evə‖'evə/ *adv* **1** always – now chiefly in certain phrases and in combination <~ *yours, John*> <*an* ever-*growing need*> **2** at any time <*faster than* ~> – chiefly in negatives and questions <*have you* ~ *met?*> <*he won't* ~ *do it*> **3** – used as an intensive <*looks* ~ *so angry*> <~ *since Monday*> <*why* ~ *not?*> – **ever so/such** *chiefly Br* very much – infml <ever such *a nice girl*> <*thanks* ever so>

[1]'**ever**ˌ**green** /-ˌgreen‖-ˌgriːn/ *adj* **1** having leaves that remain green and functional through more than 1 growing season **2** always retaining freshness, interest, or popularity

[2]**evergreen** *n* an evergreen plant; *also* a conifer

[1]**everlasting** /-'lahsting‖-'lɑːstɪŋ/ *adj* **1** lasting or enduring through all time **2a(1)** continuing long or indefinitely; perpetual **a(2)** *of a plant* retaining its form or colour for a long time when dried **b** tediously persistent; ETERNAL 2 **3** lasting or wearing for a long time; durable – **everlastingly** *adv*, **everlastingness** *n*

[2]**everlasting** *n* **1** *cap* GOD 1 – + *the* **2** eternity

ˌ**ever'more** /-'maw‖-'mɔː/ *adv* **1** always, forever **2** in the future

every /'evri‖'evrɪ/ *adj* **1** being each member without exception, of a group larger than 2 <*enjoyed* ~ *minute*> <*his* ~ *word*> **2** being each or all possible <*was given* ~ *chance*> <*have* ~ *confidence in him*> **3** being once in each <*go* ~ *third day*> – **every now and then/again, every so often** at intervals; occasionally

'**every**ˌ**body** /-ˌbodi‖-ˌbɒdɪ/ *pron* every person

'**every**ˌ**day** /-ˌday‖-ˌdeɪ/ *adj* encountered or used routinely or typically; ordinary <*clothes for* ~ *wear*> – **everydayness** *n*

'**every**ˌ**one** /-ˌwun‖-ˌwʌn/ *pron* everybody

'**every**ˌ**thing** /-ˌthing‖-ˌθɪŋ/ *pron* **1a** all that exists **b** all that is necessary or that relates to the subject <*my new car has* ~> **2** sthg of the greatest importance; all that counts <*he meant* ~ *to her*>

'**every**ˌ**where** /-ˌweə‖-ˌweə/ *adv or n* (in, at, or to) every place or the whole place

ˌ**every** '**which** ˌ**way** *adv, NAm* in every direction; all over the place

evict /i'vikt‖ɪ'vɪkt/ *vt* **1a** to recover (property) from a person by a legal process **b** to remove (a tenant) from rented accommodation or land by a legal process **2** to force out – **evictor** *n*, **eviction** *n*

[1]**evidence** /'evid(ə)ns‖'evɪd(ə)ns/ *n* **1** an outward sign; an indication **2** sthg, esp a fact, that

gives proof or reasons for believing or agreeing with sthg; *specif* information used (by a tribunal) to arrive at the truth – **evidential** *adj*, **evidentially** *adv*, **evidentiary** *adj* – **in evidence** to be seen; conspicuous

[2]**evidence** *vt* to offer evidence of; show

evident /'evid(ə)nt‖'evɪd(ə)nt/ *adj* clear to the vision or understanding

'**evidently** /-li‖-lɪ/ *adv* **1** clearly, obviously **2** on the basis of available evidence; as seems evident

[1]**evil** /'eevl‖'i:vl/ *adj* **-ll-** (*NAm* **-l-**, **-ll-**) **1** not good morally; sinful, wicked **2a** causing discomfort or repulsion; offensive <*an* ~ *smell*> **b** disagreeable <*an* ~ *temper*> **3a** pernicious, harmful **b** marked by misfortune <*an* ~ *day*> – **evil** *adv, archaic*, **evilly** *adv*, **evilness** *n*

[2]**evil** *n* **1** sthg evil; sthg that brings sorrow, distress, or calamity **2a** the fact of suffering, misfortune, or wrongdoing **b** wickedness, sin

ˌ**evil** '**eye** *n* (a spell put on sby with) a look believed to be capable of inflicting harm

evince /i'vins‖ɪ'vɪns/ *vt* to show clearly; reveal – fml – **evincible** *adj*

eviscerate /i'visərayt‖ɪ'vɪsəreɪt/ *vt* **1** to disembowel **2** to remove an organ from (a patient); *also* to remove the contents of (an organ) **3** to deprive of vital content or force – fml – **evisceration** *n*

evoke /i'vohk‖ɪ'vəʊk/ *vt* to call forth or up: e g **a** CONJURE 1a **b** to cite, esp with approval or for support; invoke **c** to bring to mind or recollection, esp imaginatively or poignantly <*this place* ~s *memories of happier years*> – **evocation** *n*, **evocative** *adj*, **evocatively** *adv*, **evocator** *n*

evolution /ˌeevə'loohsh(ə)n‖ˌi:və'lu:ʃ(ə)n/ *n* **1a** a process of change and development, esp from a lower or simpler state to a higher or more complex state **b** the action or an instance of forming and giving sthg off; emission **c** a process of gradual and relatively peaceful social, political, economic, etc advance **d** sthg evolved **2** the process of working out or developing **3a** the historical development of a biological group (e g a race or species) **b** a theory that the various types of animals and plants derived from preexisting types and that the distinguishable differences are due to natural selection – **evolutionism** *n*, **evolutionist** *n or adj*, **evolutionary** *adj*, **evolutionarily** *adv*

evolve /i'volv‖ɪ'vɒlv/ *vt* **1** EMIT 1a **2a** to work out, develop **b** to produce by natural evolutionary processes ~*vi* to undergo evolutionary change – **evolvable** *adj*, **evolvement** *n*

ewe /yooh‖ju:/ *n* the female of the (mature) sheep or a related animal

ewer /'yooh·ə‖'ju:ə/ *n* a wide-mouthed pitcher or jug; *esp* one used to hold water for washing or shaving

[1]**ex** /eks, egz‖eks, egz/ *adj* former – often in combination <*the* ex-*president*>

[2]**ex** *prep* **1** from a specified place or source **2a** *esp of securities* without an indicated value or right **b** free of charges until the time of removal from (a place) <~ *dock*>

[3]**ex** *n* a former spouse, boyfriend, or girl friend – infml

ex- /eks-, egz-‖eks-, egz-/ *prefix* **1** out of; outside <ex*clude*> **2** cause to be <ex*acerbate*> **3** not <ex*animate*> **4** deprive of <ex*communicate*>

exacerbate /ek'sasəbayt, ig'za-‖ek'sæsəbeɪt, ɪg'zæ-/ *vt* to make (sthg bad) worse; aggravate – **exacerbation** *n*

[1]**exact** /ig'zakt‖ɪg'zækt/ *vt* to demand and obtain by force, threats, etc; require – **exactable** *adj*, **exactor** *also* **exacter** *n*

[2]**exact** *adj* **1** exhibiting or marked by complete accordance with fact **2** marked by thorough consideration or minute measurement of small factual details – **exactness** *n*

exacting /ig'zakting‖ɪg'zæktɪŋ/ *adj* making rigorous demands; *esp* requiring careful attention and precise accuracy – **exactingly** *adv*, **exactingness** *n*

exaction /ig'zaksh(ə)n‖ɪg'zækʃ(ə)n/ *n* **1a** exacting **b** extortion **2** sthg exacted; *esp* a fee, reward, or contribution demanded or levied with severity or injustice

exactly /ig'zaktli‖ɪg'zæktlɪ/ *adv* **1** altogether, entirely <*not* ~ *what I had in mind*> **2** quite so – used to express agreement

exaggerate /ig'zajərayt‖ɪg'zædʒəreɪt/ *vt* **1** to say or believe more than the truth about **2** to make greater or more pronounced than normal; overemphasize ~*vi* to make an exaggeration – **exaggeratedly** *adv*, **exaggeratedness** *n*, **exaggerative, exaggeratory** *adj*, **exaggerator** *n*, **exaggeration** *n*

exalt /ig'zawlt‖ɪg'zɔ:lt/ *vt* **1** to raise high, esp in rank, power, or character **2** to praise highly; glorify – **exaltedly** *adv*, **exalter** *n*

exaltation /ˌegzawl'taysh(ə)n‖ˌegzɔ:l'teɪʃ(ə)n/ *n* an excessively intensified sense of well-being, power, or importance

exam /ig'zam, ik'sam‖ɪg'zæm, ɪk'sæm/ *n* an examination

examination /igˌzami'naysh(ə)n‖ɪgˌzæmɪ'neɪʃ(ə)n/ *n* **1** (an) examining <*a medical* ~> **2** (the taking by a candidate for a university degree, Advanced level, Ordinary level, etc of) a set of questions designed to test knowledge **3** a formal interrogation (in a law court) – **examinational** *adj*, **examinatorial** *adj*

examine /ig'zamin‖ɪg'zæmɪn/ *vt* **1** to inspect closely; investigate **2a** to interrogate closely <~ *a prisoner*> **b** to test (e g a candidate for a university degree) by an examination in order to determine knowledge – **examinable** *adj*, **examinee** *n*, **examiner** *n*

example /ig'zahmpl‖ɪg'zɑ:mpl/ *n* **1** sthg representative of all of the group or type to which it belongs **2** sby or sthg that may be copied by other people <*a good or bad* ~> <*set an* ~> **3** (the recipient of) a punishment inflicted as a warning to others <*make an* ~ *of them*> **4** a problem to be solved to illustrate a rule (e g in arithmetic) – **for example** as an example

exasperate /ig'zahspəˌrayt, -zas-‖ɪg'zɑ:spəˌreɪt, -zæs-/ *vt* to anger or irritate (sby) – **exasperatedly** *adv*, **exasperatingly** *adv*, **exasperation** *n*

ex cathedra /ˌeks kə'theedrə‖ˌeks kə'θi:drə/ *adv or adj* with authority <~ *pronouncements*>

excavate /'ekskəvayt‖'ekskəveɪt/ *vt* **1** to form a cavity or hole in **2** to form by hollowing **3** to dig out and remove **4** to expose to view by digging away a covering ~*vi* to make excavations – **excavator** *n*, **excavation** *n*

exceed /ik'seed‖ɪk'si:d/ *vt* **1** to extend beyond **2** to be greater than or superior to **3** to act or go beyond the limits of <~ *the speed limit*>

exceedingly /ik'seedingli‖ɪk'si:dɪŋlɪ/, **exceeding** *adv* very, extremely

excel /ik'sel‖ɪk'sel/ *vb* **-ll-** to be superior (to); surpass (others) in accomplishment or achievement – often + *at* or *in*

excellence /'eks(ə)ləns‖'eks(ə)ləns/ *n* **1** *also* **excellency** being excellent **2** *also* **excellency** an excellent or valuable quality; a virtue **3 Excellency, Excellence** – used as a title for certain high dignitaries (e g ambassadors) of state and church

excellent /'eksəl(ə)nt‖'eksəl(ə)nt/ *adj* outstandingly good – **excellently** *adv*

[1]**except** /ik'sept‖ɪk'sept/ *vt* to take or leave out from a number or a whole; exclude

[2]**except** *also* **excepting** *prep* with the exclusion or exception of

[3]**except** *also* **excepting** *conj* **1** only, but <*would go* ~ *it's too far*> <*would have protested* ~ *that he was afraid*> **2** unless <~ *you repent*> – fml

ex'cept for *prep* **1** but for; were it not for <*couldn't have done it* ~ *your help*> **2** with the exception of <*all here* ~ *Mary*>

exception /ik'sepsh(ə)n‖ɪk'sepʃ(ə)n/ *n* **1** excepting or excluding **2** sby or sthg excepted; *esp* a case to which a rule does not apply **3** question, objection <*witnesses whose authority is beyond* ~ – T B Macaulay>

ex'ceptionable /-əbl‖-əbl/ *adj* likely to cause objection; objectionable – **exceptionably** *adv*, **exceptionability** *n*

exceptional /ik'sepsh(ə)nl‖ɪk'sepʃ(ə)nl/ *adj* **1** forming an exception; unusual **2** not average; *esp* superior – **exceptionally** *adv*, **exceptionality** *n*

[1]**excerpt** /ek'suhpt‖ek'sɜ:pt/ *vt* **1** to select (a passage) for quoting, copying, or performing **2** to take excerpts from (e g a book) – **excerpter** *also* **excerptor** *n*, **excerption** *n*

[2]**excerpt** /'ek,suhpt‖'ek,sɜ:pt/ *n* a passage taken from a book, musical composition, etc

[1]**excess** /ik'ses‖ɪk'ses/ *n* **1a** the exceeding of usual, proper, or specified limits **b** the amount or degree by which one thing or quantity exceeds another **2** (an instance of) undue or immoderate indulgence; intemperance **3** an amount an insured person agrees to pay him-/herself out of each claim made on an insurance policy in return for a lower premium – **excessive** *adj*, **excessively** *adv*, **excessiveness** *n* – **in excess of** more than

[2]**excess** /'ekses, ik'ses‖'ekses, ɪk'ses/ *adj* more than the usual, proper, or specified amount; extra <*charges for* ~ *baggage*>

[1]**exchange** /iks'chaynj‖ɪks'tʃeɪndʒ/ *n* **1a** the act of exchanging one thing for another; a trade <*an* ~ *of prisoners*> **b** a usu brief interchange of words or blows **2** sthg offered, given, or received in an exchange **3a** (the system of settling, usu by bills of exchange rather than money) debts payable currently, esp in a foreign country **b(1)** change or conversion of one currency into another **b(2) exchange, exchange rate** the value of one currency in terms of another **4** a place where things or services are exchanged: e g **4a** an organized market for trading in securities or commodities **b** a centre or device controlling the connection of telephone calls between many different lines

[2]**exchange** *vt* **1a** to part with, give, or transfer in return for sthg received as an equivalent <*where can I* ~ *my dollars for pounds?*> <*John* ~d *books with Peter*> **b** *of 2 parties* to give and receive (things of the same type) <*the 2 armies* ~d *prisoners*> <*they* ~d *blows*> **2** to replace by other goods <*will they* ~ *clothes that don't fit?*> ~ *vi* **1** to pass or become received in exchange **2** to engage in an exchange – **exchangeable** *adj*, **exchanger** *n*, **exchangeability** *n*

exchequer /iks'chekə‖ɪks'tʃekə/ *n* **1** *cap* a former civil court having jurisdiction primarily over revenue and now merged with the Queen's Bench Division **2** *often cap* the department of state in charge of the national revenue **3** the (national or royal) treasury

[1]**excise** /'ek,siez, ,-'-‖'ek,saɪz, ,-'-/ *n* **1** an internal tax levied on the manufacture, sale, or consumption of a commodity within a country **2** any of various taxes on privileges, often levied in the form of a licence that must be bought

[2]**excise** /ek'siez‖ek'saɪz/ *vt* to impose an excise on – **excisable** *adj*

[3]**excise** *vt* to remove (as if) by cutting out – **excision** *n*

excitable /ik'sietəbl‖ɪk'saɪtəbl/ *adj* capable of being readily activated or roused into a state of excitement or irritability; *specif* capable of being activated by and reacting to stimuli – **excitableness, excitability** *n*

excite /ik'siet‖ɪk'saɪt/ *vt* **1a** to provoke or stir up (action) <~ *a rebellion*> **b** to rouse to strong, esp pleasurable, feeling **c** to arouse (e g an emotional response) <*her late arrival* ~d *much curiosity*> **2** to induce a magnetic field or electric current in; *also* to induce (e g a magnetic field or an electric current) **3** to raise (e g an atom or a molecule) to a higher energy level – **excitant** *n or adj*, **excitative, excitatory** *adj*, **excitedly** *adv*, **excitement** *n*, **exciter** *n*, **exciting** *adj*, **excitingly** *adv*, **excitation** *n*

exclaim /ik'sklaym‖ɪk'skleɪm/ *vi* to cry out or speak in strong or sudden emotion ~*vt* to utter sharply, passionately, or vehemently – **exclaimer** *n*

exclamation /,ekskla'maysh(ə)n‖,ekskla'meɪʃ(ə)n/ *n* exclaiming or the words exclaimed – **exclamatory** *adj*

,excla'mation ,mark *n* a punctuation mark ! used esp after an interjection or exclamation

exclude /ik'skloohd‖ɪk'sklu:d/ *vt* **1a** to shut out **b** to bar from participation, consideration, or inclusion **2** to expel, esp from a place or position previously occupied – **excludable** *adj*, **excluder** *n*, **exclusion** *n*, **exclusionary** *adj*

[1]**exclusive** /ik'skloohsiv, -ziv‖ɪk'sklu:sɪv, -zɪv/ *adj* **1a** excluding or having power to exclude **b** limiting or limited to possession, control, use, etc by a single individual, group, etc <*an* ~ *interview*> **2a** excluding others (considered to be

inferior) from participation, membership, or entry *<an ~ club>* **b** snobbishly aloof **3** stylish and expensive **4a** SOLE 1, 2 *<~ jurisdiction>* **b** whole, undivided *<his ~ attention>* **5** not inclusive *<Monday to Friday ~>* – **exclusively** *adv*, **exclusiveness, exclusivity** *n*

[2]**exclusive** *n* **1** a newspaper story printed by only 1 newspaper **2** an exclusive right (e g to sell a particular product in a certain area)

excogitate /eks'kojitayt‖eks'kɒdʒɪteɪt/ *vt* to think out; devise – fml – **excogitative** *adj*, **excogitation** *n*

[1]**excommunicate** /ˌekskə'myoohniˌkayt‖ˌekskə'mju:nɪˌkeɪt/ *vt* **1** to deprive officially of the rights of church membership **2** to exclude from fellowship of a group or community – **excommunicative, excommunicatory** *adj*, **excommunication** *n*

[2]**excommunicate** /ˌekskə'myoohnikət, -ˌkayt‖ˌekskə'mju:nɪkət, -ˌkeɪt/ *n or adj* (one who is) excommunicated

excoriate /ik'skawriayt‖ɪk'skɔ:rɪeɪt/ *vt* **1** to wear away the skin of; abrade **2** to censure scathingly – fml – **excoriation** *n*

excrement /'ekskrəmənt‖'ekskrəmənt/ *n* faeces or other waste matter discharged from the body – **excremental** *adj*, **excrementitious** *adj*

excrescence /ik'skres(ə)ns‖ɪk'skres(ə)ns/, **excrescency** /-si‖-sɪ/ *n* an excessive or abnormal outgrowth or enlargement – **excrescent** *adj*

excreta /ik'skreetə‖ɪk'skri:tə/ *n pl* excrement – **excretal** *adj*

excrete /ik'skreet‖ɪk'skri:t/ *vt* to separate and eliminate or discharge (waste) from blood or living tissue – **excreter** *n*, **excretory** *adj*, **excretion** *n*

excruciating /ik'skroohshiˌayting‖ɪk'skru:ʃɪˌeɪtɪŋ/ *adj* causing great pain or anguish; agonizing, tormenting – **excruciate** *vt*, **excruciatingly** *adv*, **excrutiation** *n*

exculpate /'ekskulˌpayt, ik'skulˌpayt‖'ekskʌlˌpeɪt, ɪk'skʌlˌpeɪt/ *vt* to clear from alleged fault, blame, or guilt – **exculpation** *n*, **exculpatory** *adj*

excursion /ik'skuhsh(ə)n‖ɪk'skɜ:ʃ(ə)n/ *n* **1** a (brief) pleasure trip, usu at reduced rates **2** a deviation from a direct, definite, or proper course; *esp* a digression – **excursionist** *n*

[1]**excuse** /ik'skyoohz‖ɪk'skju:z/ *vt* **1a** to make apology for *<quietly ~d his clumsiness>* **b** to try to remove blame from *<~d himself for being so careless>* **2** to forgive entirely or overlook as unimportant *<she graciously ~d his thoughtlessness>* **3** to allow to leave; dismiss *<the class was ~d>* **4** to be an acceptable reason for; justify – usu neg *<nothing can ~ his cruelty>* **5** *Br* to free from (a duty) – usu pass *<the class was ~d homework>* – **excusal** *n*, **excusable** *adj*, **excusably** *adv*, **excusatory** *adj*, **excuser** *n*

[2]**excuse** /ik'skyoohs‖ɪk'skju:s/ *n* **1** sthg offered as grounds for being excused *<he had a good ~ for being late>* **2** *pl* an expression of regret for failure to do sthg or esp for one's absence *<make my ~s at the party tomorrow>*

ˌex-diˈrectory *adj, Br* intentionally not listed in a telephone directory

execrable /'eksikrəbl‖'eksɪkrəbl/ *adj* detestable, appalling – chiefly fml – **execrably** *adv*

execrate /'eksiˌkrayt‖'eksɪˌkreɪt/ *vt* **1** to declare to be evil or detestable; denounce **2** to detest utterly; abhor *USE* chiefly fml – **execrator** *n*, **execration** *n*, **execrative** *adj*

executant /ig'zekyoot(ə)nt‖ɪg'zekjʊt(ə)nt/ *n* one who executes or performs; *esp* one skilled in the technique of an art

execute /'eksiˌkyooht‖'eksɪˌkju:t/ *vt* **1** to carry out fully; put completely into effect **2** to put to death (legally) as a punishment **3** to make or produce (e g a work of art), esp by carrying out a design **4** to (do what is required to) make valid *<~ a deed>* **5** to play, perform *<~ a piece of music>* – **executable** *adj*

execution /ˌeksi'kyoohsh(ə)n‖ˌeksɪ'kju:ʃ(ə)n/ *n* **1** a putting to death as a punishment **2** a judicial writ directing the enforcement of a judgment **3** the act, mode, or result of performance *<the ~ was perfect but the piece lacked expression>*

executioner /ˌeksi'kyoohsh(ə)nə‖ˌeksɪ'kju:ʃ(ə)nə/ *n* one who puts to death; *specif* one legally appointed to perform capital punishment

[1]**executive** /ig'zekyootiv‖ɪg'zekjʊtɪv/ *adj* **1** concerned with making and carrying out laws, decisions, etc; *specif, Br* of or concerned with the detailed application of policy or law rather than its formulation **2** of, for, or being an executive *<the ~ offices are on the top floor>*

[2]**executive** *n* **1** the executive branch of a government **2** an individual or group that controls or directs an organization **3** one who holds a position of administrative or managerial responsibility

executor /'eksiˌkyoohtə, ig'zekyootə‖'eksɪˌkju:tə, ɪg'zekjʊtə/, *fem* **executrix** /ig'zekyooˌtriks‖ɪg'zekjʊˌtrɪks/ *n, pl* **executors,** *fem* **executrices** /-ˌtrieseez‖-ˌtraɪsi:z/ one appointed to carry out the provisions of a will – **executory, executorial** *adj*

exegesis /ˌeksi'jeesis‖ˌeksɪ'dʒi:sɪs/ *n, pl* **exegeses** /-seez‖-si:z/ an explanation or critical interpretation of an esp biblical text; *broadly* an exposition – **exegetic, exegetical** *adj*

exemplar /ig'zemplə, -ˌplah‖ɪg'zemplə, -ˌplɑ:/ *n* sthg that serves as a model or example; *also* a copy of a book or text

exemplary /ig'zempləri‖ɪg'zemplərɪ/ *adj* **1** deserving imitation; commendable *<his conduct was ~>* **2** serving as a warning *<~ punishments>* **3** serving as an example, instance, or illustration – **exemplarily** *adv*, **exemplariness, exemplarity** *n*

exemplify /ig'zemplifie‖ɪg'zemplɪfaɪ/ *vt* **1** to show or illustrate by example **2** to be an instance of or serve as an example of; typify, embody – **exemplification** *n*

[1]**exempt** /ig'zempt‖ɪg'zempt/ *adj* freed from some liability or requirement to which others are subject *<~ from jury service>*

[2]**exempt** *vt* to make exempt; excuse *<~ed from jury service>* – **exemption** *n*

[1]**exercise** /'eksəˌsiez‖'eksəˌsaɪz/ *n* **1** the use of a specified power or right *<the ~ of his authority>* **2a** regular or repeated use of a faculty or body part **b** bodily exertion for the sake of developing and maintaining physical fitness **3** sthg performed or practised in order to develop, improve, or display a specific power or skill **4** a manoeuvre or drill carried out for

training and discipline

[2]**exercise** *vt* 1 to make effective in action; use, exert <*didn't* ~ *good judgment*> **2a** to use repeatedly in order to strengthen or develop **b** to train (e g troops) by drills and manoeuvres **c** to give exercise to <~ *the horses*> **3a** to engage the attention and effort of <*the problem greatly* ~d *his mind*> **b** to cause anxiety, alarm, or indignation in <*citizens* ~d *about pollution*> ~*vi* to take exercise; *esp* to train – **exercisable** *adj*, **exerciser** *n*

exert /ig'zuht‖ɪg'zɜːt/ *vt* **1** to bring (e g strength or authority) to bear, esp with sustained effort; employ, wield **2** to take upon (oneself) the effort of doing sthg <*he never* ~s *himself to help anyone*> – **exertion** *n*

exeunt /'eksi,oont‖'eksɪ,ʊnt/ – used as a stage direction to specify that all or certain named characters leave the stage

ex gratia /,eks 'graysh(i)ə‖,eks 'greɪʃ(ɪ)ə/ *adj or adv* as a favour; not compelled by legal right <~ *payments*>

exhalation /,eksə'laysh(ə)n, ,eks·hə-‖,eksə-'leɪʃ(ə)n, ,ekshə-/ *n* **1** exhaling **2** sthg exhaled or given off; an emanation

exhale /eks'hayl, ig'zayl‖eks'heɪl, ɪg'zeɪl/ *vt* **1** to breathe out **2** to give forth (gas or vapour); emit ~ *vi* **1** to rise or be given off as vapour **2** to emit breath or vapour

[1]**exhaust** /ig'zawst‖ɪg'zɔːst/ *vt* **1a** to draw off or let out completely **b** to empty by drawing off the contents; *specif* to create a vacuum in **2a** to consume entirely; USE UP <~ed *our funds in a week*> **b** to tire out <~ed *by their efforts*> **3a** to develop or deal with (a subject) to the fullest possible extent **b** to try out the whole number of <~ed *all the possibilities*> – **exhauster** *n*, **exhaustible** *adj*, **exhaustibility** *n*

[2]**exhaust** *n* **1** (the escape of) used gas or vapour from an engine **2** the conduit or pipe through which used gases escape

exhaustion /ig'zawschən‖ɪg'zɔːstʃən/ *n* extreme tiredness

exhaustive /ig'zawstiv‖ɪg'zɔːstɪv/ *adj* comprehensive, thorough <*conducted an* ~ *investigation*> – **exhaustively** *adv*, **exhaustiveness** *n*, **exhaustivity** *n*

[1]**exhibit** /ig'zibit‖ɪg'zɪbɪt/ *vt* to present to view: e g **a** to show or display outwardly, esp by visible signs or actions; reveal, manifest <~ed *no fear*> **b** to show publicly, esp for purposes of competition or demonstration ~*vi* to display sthg for public inspection – **exhibitive** *adj*, **exhibitor** *n*, **exhibitory** *adj*

[2]**exhibit** *n* **1** sthg exhibited **2** sthg produced as evidence in a lawcourt **3** *chiefly NAm* EXHIBITION 1

exhibition /,eksi'bish(ə)n‖,eksɪ'bɪʃ(ə)n/ *n* **1** an act or instance of exhibiting <*an* ~ *of ill-temper*> **2** a public showing (e g of works of art or objects of manufacture) **3** *Br* a grant drawn from the funds of a school or university to help to maintain a student

,exhi'bitionism /-iz(ə)m‖-ɪz(ə)m/ *n* **1** a perversion marked by a tendency to indecent exposure **2** the act or practice of behaving so as to attract attention to oneself – **exhibitionist** *n or adj*, **exhibitionistic** *adj*

exhilarate /ig'zilərayt‖ɪg'zɪləreɪt/ *vt* **1** to make cheerful **2** to enliven, invigorate – **exhilarative** *adj*, **exhilaration** *n*

exhort /ig'zawt‖ɪg'zɔːt/ *vt* to urge or advise strongly ~*vi* to give warnings or advice; make urgent appeals – **exhortative** *adj*, **exhorter** *n*

exhortation /,egzaw'taysh(ə)n‖,egzɔː'teɪʃ-(ə)n/ *n* language intended to incite and encourage; *esp* an inspiring or encouraging speech or passage of writing

exhume /eks'hyoohm, ek'syoohm, ik-‖eks-'hjuːm, ek'sjuːm, ɪk-/ *vt* **1** to disinter **2** to bring back from neglect or obscurity – **exhumer** *n*, **exhumation** *n*

exigency /'eksij(ə)nsi, ig'zij(ə)nsi‖'eksɪdʒ-(ə)nsɪ, ɪg'zɪdʒ(ə)nsɪ/, **exigence** /'eksij(ə)ns, 'egz-‖'eksɪdʒ(ə)ns, 'egz-/ *n* **1** an emergency **2** such need or necessity as belongs to the occasion; a requirement – usu pl with sing. meaning ***USE*** fml

exigent /'eksij(ə)nt, 'egz-‖'eksɪdʒ(ə)nt, 'egz-/ *adj* **1** requiring immediate aid or action **2** exacting, demanding ***USE*** fml – **exigently** *adv*

exiguous /ig'zigyoo·əs‖ɪg'zɪgjʊəs/ *adj* excessively scanty; inadequate, meagre – fml – **exiguously** *adv*, **exiguousness** *n*, **exiguity** *n*

[1]**exile** /'eksiel, 'egziel‖'eksaɪl, 'egzaɪl/ *n* **1** enforced or voluntary absence from one's country or home **2** one who is exiled voluntarily or by authority

[2]**exile** *vt* to send into exile

exist /ig'zist‖ɪg'zɪst/ *vi* **1a** to have being in the real world; be **b** to have being in specified conditions <*some chemical compounds* ~ *only in solution*> **2** to continue to be <*Nazism still* ~s> **3a** to have life or the functions of vitality <*man cannot* ~ *without water*> **b** to live at an inferior level or under adverse circumstances <*starving people* ~ing *from one day to the next*>

existence /ig'zist(ə)ns‖ɪg'zɪst(ə)ns/ *n* **1a** the totality of existent things **b** the state or fact of existing; life **2** manner of living or being <*pursued a solitary* ~>

existent /ig'zist(ə)nt‖ɪg'zɪst(ə)nt/ *adj* **1** having being; existing **2** extant – **existent** *n*

existential /,egzi'stensh(ə)l‖,egzɪ'stenʃ(ə)l/ *adj* **1** of or grounded in existence <~ *propositions*> **2** existentialist – **existentially** *adv*

,exi'stential,ism /-,iz(ə)m‖-,ɪz(ə)m/ *n* a philosophical movement characterized by inquiry into human beings' experience of themselves in relation to the world, esp with reference to their freedom, responsibility, and isolation and the experiences (e g of anxiety and despair) in which these are revealed – **existentialist** *n or adj*

[1]**exit** /'eksit, 'egzit‖'eksɪt, 'egzɪt/ – used as a stage direction to specify who goes off stage

[2]**exit** *n* **1** a departure of a performer from a scene **2** the act of going out or away **3** a way out of an enclosed place or space **4** death – euph – **exit** *vi*

ex libris /,eks 'leebris‖,eks 'liːbrɪs/ *n*, *pl* **ex libris** a bookplate

Exocet /'eksoh,set‖'eksəʊ,set/ *trademark* – used for an air- or ground-launched radar-guided missile, deployed esp in attacks on ships

exodus /'eksədəs‖'eksədəs/ *n* a mass departure; an emigration

ex officio /ˌeks əˈfis(h)ioh‖ˌeks əˈfɪsɪəʊ,-ʃɪəʊ/ *adv or adj* by virtue or because of an office <*the president is an* ~ *member of the committee*>
exogamy /ekˈsogəmi‖ekˈsɒgəmɪ/ *n* marriage outside one's tribe – **exogamous, exogamic** *adj*
exonerate /igˈzonərayt‖ɪgˈzɒnəreɪt/ *vt* **1** to relieve of a responsibility, obligation, or hardship **2** to free from blame; exculpate – **exonerative** *adj*, **exoneration** *n*
exorbitant /igˈzawbit(ə)nt‖ɪgˈzɔːbɪt(ə)nt/ *adj, of prices, demands, etc* much greater than is reasonable; excessive – **exorbitance** *n*, **exorbitantly** *adv*
exorc·ise, -ize /ˈeksawˌsiez‖ˈeksɔːˌsaɪz/ *vt* **1a** to expel (an evil spirit) by solemn command (e g in a religious ceremony) **b** to get rid of (e g an unpleasant thought or emotion) as if by exorcism **2** to free (e g a person or place) of an evil spirit – **exorciser** *n*
exorcism /ˈeksawˌsiz(ə)m‖ˈeksɔːˌsɪz(ə)m/ *n* (a spell used in) the act of exorcising – **exorcist** *n*
exotic /igˈzotik‖ɪgˈzɒtɪk/ *adj* **1** introduced from another country; not native to the place where found <*an* ~ *plant*> **2** strikingly or excitingly different or unusual <*an* ~ *dish*> [Latin *exoticus*, fr Greek *exōtikos*, fr *exō* outside] – **exotic** *n*, **exotically** *adv*, **exoticness** *n*, **exoticism** *n*
expand /ikˈspand‖ɪkˈspænd/ *vt* **1a** to increase the size, extent, number, volume, or scope of <*the company has* ~ed *its interests overseas*> **b** to introduce gas into (a plastic or resin) <~ed *vinyl*> **2** to express in detail or in full <~ *an argument*> ~ *vi* **1** to become expanded <*iron* ~s *when heated*> **2** ENLARGE 2 **3** to grow genial; become more sociable <*only* ~s *among friends*> – **expandable** *adj*
expanse /ikˈspans‖ɪkˈspæns/ *n* **1** sthg spread out, esp over a wide area **2** the extent to which sthg is spread out
expansion /ikˈspansh(ə)n‖ɪkˈspænʃ(ə)n/ *n* **1** expanding or being expanded <*territorial* ~> **2** the increase in volume of working fluid (e g steam) in an engine cylinder **3** sthg expanded: e g **3a** an expanded part **b** a fuller treatment of an earlier theme or work – **expansional** *adj*, **expansionary** *adj*
expansive /ikˈspansiv‖ɪkˈspænsɪv/ *adj* **1** having a capacity or tendency to expand or cause expansion **2** freely communicative; genial, effusive **3** having wide expanse or extent **4** characterized by largeness or magnificence of scale <~ *living*> – **expansively** *adv*, **expansiveness** *n*
expatiate /ikˈspayshiˌayt, ek-‖ɪkˈspeɪʃɪˌeɪt, ek-/ *vi* to speak or write at length or in detail, usu on a single subject – usu + on or upon – **expatiation** *n*
[1]**expatriate** /eksˈpatriayt‖eksˈpætrɪeɪt/ *vt* **1** to exile, banish **2** to withdraw (oneself) from residence in or allegiance to one's native country – **expatriation** *n*
[2]**expatriate** /ˌeksˈpatri·ət‖ˌeksˈpætrɪət/ *n* one who lives in a foreign country – **expatriate** *adj*
expect /ikˈspekt‖ɪkˈspekt/ *vi* **1** to look forward with anticipation **2** to be pregnant ~ *vt* **1** to anticipate or look forward to <~ed *a telephone call*> **2a** to consider (an event) probable or certain <~ *to be forgiven*> **b** to consider reasonable, due, or necessary <*he* ~ed *respect from his children*> **c** to consider bound in duty or obligated <*they* ~ed *him to pay his dues*> **3** to suppose, think <*I* ~ *that's true*> – infml – **expectable** *adj*, **expectably** *adv*, **expectance, expectancy** *n*, **expectedly** *adv*, **expectedness** *n*
expectant /ikˈspekt(ə)nt‖ɪkˈspekt(ə)nt/ *adj* **1** characterized by expectation **2** *of a pregnant woman* expecting the birth of a child – **expectantly** *adv*
expectation /ˌekspekˈtaysh(ə)n‖ˌekspekˈteɪʃ(ə)n/ *n* **1** expecting or sthg expected **2** prospects of inheritance – usu pl with sing. meaning **3** an expected amount or number (e g of years of life) based on statistical probability
expectorate /ikˈspektərayt‖ɪkˈspektəreɪt/ *vb* **1** to eject (matter) from the throat or lungs by coughing or spitting **2** to spit (e g saliva) – **expectoration** *n*
expediency /ikˈspeedi·ənsi, -dyənsi‖ɪkˈspiːdɪənsɪ, -djənsɪ/ *n* **1 expediency, expedience** suitability, fitness **2** cultivation of or adherence to expedient means and methods **3** an expedient
[1]**exˈpedient** /-ənt‖-ənt/ *adj* **1** suitable for achieving a particular end **2** characterized by concern with what is opportune and esp by self-interest, rather than by concern with what is moral – **expediently** *adv*
[2]**expedient** *n* a means to an end; *esp* one devised or used in case of urgent need
expedite /ˈekspiˌdiet‖ˈekspɪˌdaɪt/ *vt* **1** to execute promptly **2** to hasten the process or progress of; facilitate *USE* fml – **expediter** *n*
expedition /ˌekspiˈdish(ə)n‖ˌekspɪˈdɪʃ(ə)n/ *n* **1** a journey or excursion undertaken for a specific purpose (e g for war or exploration) **2** efficient promptness; speed – fml
ˌexpeˈditionary /-ri‖-rɪ/ *adj* of or constituting an expedition; *also* sent on military service abroad
ˌexpeˈditious /-shəs‖-ʃəs/ *adj* speedy – fml – **expeditiously** *adv*, **expeditiousness** *n*
expel /ikˈspel‖ɪkˈspel/ *vt* **-ll-** **1** to drive or force out <~led *air from the lungs*> **2** to drive away; *esp* to deport **3** to cut off from membership <~led *from school*> – **expellable** *adj*, **expeller** *n*, **expellee** *n*
expend /ikˈspend‖ɪkˈspend/ *vt* **1** to pay out <*the new roads on which so much public money is* ~ed> **2** to consume (e g time, care, or attention) by use; USE UP <*projects on which he* ~ed *great energy*> – **expender** *n*
exˈpendable /-dəbl‖-dəbl/ *adj* **1** normally used up in service; not intended to be kept or reused <~ *supplies like pencils and paper*> **2** regarded as available for sacrifice or destruction in order to accomplish an objective <~ *troops*> – **expendability** *n*
expenditure /ikˈspendichə‖ɪkˈspendɪtʃə/ *n* **1** the act or process of expending **2** the amount expended
expense /ikˈspens‖ɪkˈspens/ *n* **1a** sthg expended to secure a benefit or bring about a result **b** financial burden or outlay **c** *pl* the charges incurred by an employee in performing his/her duties **d** an item of business outlay chargeable against revenue in a specific period **2** a cause or occasion of usu high expenditure <*a car is a*

great ~> – **at somebody's expense** in a manner that causes sby to be ridiculed <*made a joke* at my expense> – **at the expense of** to the detriment of <*develop a boy's physique* at the expense of *his intelligence* – Bertrand Russell>

ex'pense ac,count *n* an account of expenses reimbursable to an employee – **expense-account** *adj*

expensive /ik'spensiv‖ɪk'spensɪv/ *adj* **1** involving great expense **2** commanding a high price; dear – **expensively** *adv*, **expensiveness** *n*

[1]**experience** /ik'spiəri·əns‖ɪk'spɪərɪəns/ *n* **1** (the facts or events perceived by) the usu conscious perception or apprehension of reality or of an external, bodily, or mental event **2** (the knowledge, skill, or practice derived from) direct participation or observation **3** the sum total of conscious events that make up an individual life or the collective past of a community, nation, or humankind generally **4** sthg personally encountered or undergone <*a terrifying* ~>

[2]**experience** *vt* to have experience of <~d *severe hardships as a child*>

ex'perienced *adj* skilful or wise as a result of experience of a particular activity or of life as a whole

experiment /ik'sperimənt‖ɪk'sperɪmənt/ *n* **1** a tentative procedure or policy that is on trial **2** an operation carried out under controlled conditions in order to test or establish a hypothesis or to illustrate a known law <*a scientific* ~> **3** the process of making experiments – **experiment** *vi*, **experimentation** *n*, **experimenter** *n*

experimental /ik,speri'mentl‖ɪk,sperɪ'mentl/ *adj* **1** experiential **2** based on or derived from experiment – **experimentalism** *adj*, **experimentally** *adv*

expert /'ekspuht‖'ekspɜːt/ *n or adj* (sby or sthg) having or showing special skill or knowledge derived from training or experience – **expertly** *adv*, **expertness** *n*

expertise /,ekspuh'teez‖,ekspɜː'tiːz/ *n* skill in or knowledge of a particular field; know-how

expiate /'ekspi,ayt‖'ekspɪ,eɪt/ *vt* **1a** to eradicate the guilt incurred by (e g a sin) **b** to pay the penalty for (e g a crime) **2** to make amends for – **expiation** *n*, **expiator** *n*, **expiatory** *adj*

expiration /,ekspie·ə'raysh(ə)n, -spi-‖,ekspaɪə'reɪʃ(ə)n, -spɪ-/ *n* **1** the release of air from the lungs through the nose or mouth **2** expiry, termination

expire /ik'spie·ə‖ɪk'spaɪə/ *vi* **1** to come to an end <*his term of office* ~s *this year*> **2** to emit the breath **3** to die – fml ~*vt* to breathe out (as if) from the lungs

explain /ik'splayn‖ɪk'spleɪn/ *vt* **1** to make plain or understandable **2** to give the reason for or cause of <*unwilling to* ~ *his conduct*> ~*vt* to make sthg plain or understandable [Latin *explanare*, lit., to make level, fr *ex-* out, throughly + *planus* level, flat] – **explainable** *adj*, **explainer** *n* – **explain oneself** to clarify one's statements or the reasons for one's conduct

explain away *vt* to avoid blame for or cause to appear insignificant by making excuses <*tried to* explain away *the corruption in his department*>

explanation /,eksplə'naysh(ə)n‖,eksplə'neɪʃ(ə)n/ *n* the act or process of explaining; sthg, esp a statement, that explains

explanatory /ik'splanət(ə)ri‖ɪk'splænət(ə)rɪ/ *adj* serving to explain – **explanatorily** *adv*

[1]**expletive** /ek'spleetiv‖ek'spliːtɪv/ *adj* serving to fill up <~ *phrases*>

[2]**expletive** *n* **1** a word, phrase, etc inserted to fill a space without adding to the sense **2** a usu meaningless exclamatory word or phrase; *specif* one that is obscene or profane

explicable /'eksplikəbl, ek'splikəbl‖'eksplɪkəbl, ek'splɪkəbl/ *adj* capable of being explained – **explicably** *adv*

explicate /'eksplikayt‖'eksplɪkeɪt/ *vt* **1** to give a detailed explanation of **2** to develop the implications of; analyse logically – **explicator** *n*, **explicative** *adj*, **explicatory** *adj*, **explication** *n*

explicit /ik'splisit‖ɪk'splɪsɪt/ *adj* **1** clear, unambiguous <~ *instructions*>; *also* graphically frank <~ *sex scenes*> **2** fully developed or formulated – **explicitly** *adv*, **explicitness** *n*

explode /ik'splohd‖ɪk'spləʊd/ *vt* **1** to bring (e g a belief or theory) into discredit by demonstrating falsity <~ *a rumour*> **2** to cause to explode or burst noisily ~ *vi* **1** to give expression to sudden, violent, and usu noisy emotion <~ *with anger*> **2a** to undergo a rapid chemical or nuclear reaction with the production of noise, heat, and violent expansion of gases **b** to burst or expand violently as a result of pressure <*the boiler* ~d> <*the* exploding *population*> – **exploder** *n*

[1]**exploit** /'eksployt‖'eksplɔɪt/ *n* a deed, act; *esp* a notable or heroic one

[2]**exploit** /ik'sployt‖ɪk'splɔɪt/ *vt* **1** to turn to economic account <~ *a mine*>; *also* to utilize **2** to take unfair advantage of for financial or other gain <~s *the workers by paying low wages*> – **exploitation** *n* **exploitable** *adj*, **exploiter** *n*, **exploitability** *n*

explore /ik'splaw‖ɪk'splɔː/ *vt* **1** to examine or inquire into thoroughly **2** to examine minutely, esp for diagnostic purposes **3** to travel into or through for purposes of geographical discovery ~*vi* to make or conduct a search – **explorer** *n*, **exploration** *n*, **explorative** *adj*, **exploratively** *adv*, **exploratory** *adj*

explosion /ik'splohzh(ə)n‖ɪk'spləʊʒ(ə)n/ *n* exploding: e g **a** a rapid large-scale expansion, increase, or upheaval <*the population* ~> **b** a sudden violent outburst of emotion

[1]**explosive** /ik'splohsiv, -ziv‖ɪk'spləʊsɪv, -zɪv/ *adj* **1** tending or threatening to burst forth with sudden violence or noise **2** tending to arouse strong reactions; controversial – **explosively** *adv*, **explosiveness** *n*

[2]**explosive** *n* an explosive substance

exponent /ik'spohnənt‖ɪk'spəʊnənt/ *n* **1** a symbol written above and to the right of a mathematical expression to indicate the operation of raising to a power <*in the expression* a^3, *the* ~ 3 *indicates that* a *is cubed*> **2a** sby or sthg that expounds or interprets **b** sby who advocates or exemplifies *USE* (2) usu + *of* – **exponential** *adj*

[1]**export** /ik'spawt‖ɪk'spɔːt/ *vt* to carry or send (e g a commodity) to some other place (e g another country) for purposes of trade ~*vi* to export sthg abroad – **exportable** *adj*, **exportability**

n, **exporter** *n*

2**export** /'ekspawt‖'ekspɔːt/ *n* **1** sthg exported **2** an act of exporting

ˌ**expor'tation** /-'taysh(ə)n‖-'teɪʃ(ə)n/ *n* an act of exporting; *also, chiefly NAm* a commodity exported

expose /ik'spohz‖ɪk'spəʊz/ *vt* **1a** to deprive of shelter or protection; lay open to attack or distressing influence <~s *himself to ridicule*> **b** to submit or subject to an action or influence; *specif* to subject (a photographic film, plate, or paper) to the action of radiant energy **c** to abandon (an infant) in an unsheltered place **2** to lay open to view; display: e g **2a** to exhibit for public veneration **b** to reveal the face of (a playing card) **c** to engage in indecent exposure of (oneself) **3** to bring (sthg shameful) to light – **exposer** *n*

exposé, expose /ek'spohzay ‖ek'spəʊzeɪ (*Fr* ɛkspoze)/ *n* **1** a formal recital or exposition of facts; a statement **2** an exposure of sthg discreditable

exposition /ˌekspə'zish(ə)n‖ˌekspə'zɪʃ(ə)n/ *n* **1** the art or practice of expounding or explaining the meaning or purpose of sthg (e g a text) **2a** a detailed explanation or elucidation, esp of sthg difficult to understand **b** the first part of a musical composition in which the theme is presented **3** a usu international public exhibition or show (e g of industrial products) – **expositional** *adj*, **expositor** *n*, **expository** *adj*

ex post facto /ˌeks ˌpohst 'faktoh‖ˌeks ˌpəʊst 'fæktəʊ/ *adj or adv* **1** after the fact <~ *approval*> **2** applied retrospectively <~ *laws*>

expostulate /ik'spostyoolayt, -chəlayt‖ɪk'spɒstjʊleɪt, -tʃəleɪt/ *vi* to reason earnestly *with* sby in order to dissuade or remonstrate – fml – **expostulation** *n*

exposure /ik'spohzh(ə)‖ɪk'spəʊʒ(ə)/ *n* **1a** a disclosure, esp of a weakness or sthg shameful or criminal; an exposé, unmasking **b** presentation or exposition, esp to the public by means of the mass media **c(1)** the act of exposing a sensitized photographic film, plate, or paper; *also* the duration of such an exposure **c(2)** a section of a film with 1 picture on it **2a** being exposed, specif to the elements **b** the specified direction in which a building, room, etc faces

expound /ik'spownd‖ɪk'spaʊnd/ *vt* to set forth, esp in careful or elaborate detail; state, explain – **expounder** *n*

1**express** /ik'spres‖ɪk'spres/ *adj* **1** firmly and explicitly stated <*he disobeyed my* ~ *orders*> **2** of a particular sort; specific <*he came for that* ~ *purpose*> **3a** (adapted or suitable for) travelling at high speed <*an* ~ *highway*> **b** *Br* designated to be delivered without delay by special messenger <~ *mail*>

2**express** *adv* by express

3**express** *n* **1** an express vehicle **2** *Br* express mail

4**express** *vt* **1a** to show or represent, esp in words; state **b** to make known the opinions, feelings, etc of (oneself) <~es *himself through his work*> **c** to represent by a sign or symbol **2** to force out (e g the juice of a fruit) by pressure – **expresser** *n*, **expressible** *adj*

expression /ik'spresh(ə)n‖ɪk'spreʃ(ə)n/ *n* **1a** expressing, esp in words <*freedom of* ~> **b(1)** an outward manifestation or symbol <*this gift is an* ~ *of my admiration for you*> **b(2)** a significant word or phrase **b(3)** a mathematical or logical symbol or combination of symbols serving to express sthg **2a** a means or manner of expressing sthg; *esp* sensitivity and feeling in communicating or performing <*read the poem with* ~> **b(1)** the quality or fact of being expressive **b(2)** facial aspect or vocal intonation indicative of feeling **3** (a product of) pressing out – **expressional** *adj*, **expressionless** *adj*, **expressionlessly** *adv*, **expressionlessness** *n*

ex'pressionˌism /-ˌiz(ə)m‖-ˌɪz(ə)m/ *n* a mode of artistic expression that attempts to depict the artist's subjective emotions and responses to objects and events – **expressionist** *n or adj*, **expressionistic** *adj*, **expressionistically** *adv*

expressive /ik'spresiv‖ɪk'spresɪv/ *adj* **1** of expression <*the* ~ *function of language*> **2** serving to express or represent **3** full of expression; significant <*an* ~ *silence*> – **expressively** *adv*, **expressiveness** *n*, **expressivity** *n*

expressly /ik'spresli‖ɪk'spreslɪ/ *adv* **1** explicitly **2** for the express purpose; specially <*needed a clinic* ~ *for the treatment of addicts*>

ex'pressˌway *n, chiefly NAm* a motorway

expropriate /ek'sprohpriˌayt‖ek'sprəʊprɪˌeɪt/ *vt* **1** to dispossess **2** to transfer to one's own possession <~d *all the land within a 10-mile radius*> – **expropriator** *n*, **expropriation** *n*

expulsion /ik'spulsh(ə)n‖ɪk'spʌlʃ(ə)n/ *n* expelling or being expelled – **expulsive** *adj*

expunge /ik'spunj‖ɪk'spʌndʒ/ *vt* **1** to strike out; obliterate, erase **2** to efface completely; destroy <*nothing can* ~ *his shame*> *USE* fml – **expunction** *n*, **expunger** *n*

expurgate /'ekspuhˌgayt‖'ekspɜːˌgeɪt/ *vt* to rid of sthg morally offensive; *esp* to remove objectionable parts from, before publication or presentation – **expurgator** *n*, **expurgation** *n*, **expurgatorial** *adj*, **expurgatory** *adj*

exquisite /ik'skwizit, 'ekskwizit‖ɪk'skwɪzɪt, 'ekskwɪzɪt/ *adj* **1a** marked by flawless, beautiful, and usu delicate craftsmanship **b** keenly sensitive, esp in feeling; discriminating <~ *taste*> **2a** extremely beautiful; delightful <*an* ~ *white blossom*> **b** acute, intense <~ *pain*> – **exquisitely** *adv*, **exquisiteness** *n*

extant /ek'stant‖ek'stænt/ *adj* still or currently existing <~ *manuscripts*>

extemporaneous /ikˌstempə'raynyəs, -ni·əs‖ɪkˌstempə'reɪnjəs, -nɪəs/ *adj* **1** done, spoken, performed, etc on the spur of the moment; impromptu **2** provided, made, or put to use as an expedient; makeshift – **extemporaneously** *adv*, **extemporaneousness** *n*, **extemporaneity** *n*

extempore /ik'stempəri‖ɪk'stempərɪ/ *adj or adv* (spoken or done) in an extemporaneous manner <*speaking* ~> [Latin *ex tempore*, fr *ex* out of, from + *tempor-*, *tempus* time]

ex'tempor·ize, -ise /ik'stempəˌriez‖ɪk'stempəˌraɪz/ *vi* to speak, or perform sthg, extemporaneously; improvise ~ *vt* to compose, perform, or utter extemporaneously – **extemporizer** *n*, **extemporization** *n*

extend /ik'stend‖ɪk'stend/ *vt* **1** to spread or

stretch forth; unfold < ~ed *both her arms* > **2a** to stretch out to fullest length < ~ed *the sail* > **b** to exert (e g a horse or oneself) to full capacity < *won the race without* ~ing *himself* > **3** to give or offer, usu in response to need; proffer < ~ing *aid to the needy* > **4a** to cause to reach (e g in distance or scope) < *national authority was* ~ed *over new territories* > < ~ed *the road to the coast* > **b** to prolong in time **c** to advance, further < ~ing *human knowledge* > **5a** to enlarge **b** to increase the scope, meaning, or application of; broaden ~ *vi* **1** to stretch out in distance, space, or time < *his jurisdiction* ~ed *over the whole area* > **2** to reach in scope or application – **extendable, extendible** *adj*

extension /ik'stensh(ə)n‖ɪk'stenʃ(ə)n/ *n* **1a** extending or being extended **b** sthg extended **2** extent, scope **3** a straightening of (a joint between the bones of) a limb **4** an increase in length of time **5** a programme of instruction for nonresident students of a university **6a** a part added (e g to a building) **b** an extra telephone connected to the principal line

extensive /ik'stensiv, -ziv‖ɪk'stensɪv, -zɪv/ *adj* **1** having wide or considerable extent < ~ *reading* > **2** of or being farming in which large areas of land are used with minimum outlay and labour – **extensively** *adv*, **extensiveness** *n*

extent /ik'stent‖ɪk'stent/ *n* **1** the range or distance over which sthg extends **2** the point or limit to which sthg extends < *the* ~ *of our patience* >

extenuate /ik'stenyoo,ayt‖ɪk'stenjʊ,eɪt/ *vt* to (try to) lessen the seriousness or extent of (e g a crime) by giving excuses – **extenuator** *n*, **extenuatory** *adj*, **extenuation** *n*

[1]**exterior** /ik'stiəri·ə‖ɪk'stɪərɪə/ *adj* **1** on the outside or an outside surface; external **2** suitable for use on outside surfaces – **exteriorize** *vt*, **exteriorly** *adv*, **exteriorization** *n*, **exteriority** *n*

[2]**exterior** *n* **1a** an exterior part or surface; outside **b** an outward manner or appearance < *a deceptively friendly* ~ > **2** a representation of an outdoor scene

exterminate /ik'stuhmi,nayt‖ɪk'stɜːmɪ,neɪt/ *vt* to destroy completely; *esp* to kill all of < ~d *the mice* > – **exterminator** *n*, **extermination** *n*, **exterminatory** *adj*

[1]**external** /ik'stuhnl‖ɪk'stɜːnl/ *adj* **1a** capable of being perceived outwardly < ~ *signs of a disease* > **b(1)** superficial **b(2)** not intrinsic or essential < ~ *circumstances* > **2** of, connected with, or intended for the outside or an outer part **3a(1)** situated outside, apart, or beyond **a(2)** arising or acting from outside < *an* ~ *force* > **b** of dealings with foreign countries **c** having existence independent of the mind < ~ *reality* > – **externally** *adv*, **externality** *n*

[2]**external** *n* an external feature or aspect – usu pl

external·ize, -ise /ik'stuhnl,iez‖ɪk'stɜːnl,aɪz/ *vt* **1** to make external or externally visible **2** to attribute to causes outside the self; rationalize < ~s *his failure* > – **externalization** *n*

extinct /ik'stingkt‖ɪk'stɪŋkt/ *adj* **1a** no longer burning **b** no longer active < *an* ~ *volcano* > **2** no longer existing < *an* ~ *animal* > **3** having no qualified claimant < *an* ~ *title* >

extinction /ik'stingksh(ə)n‖ɪk'stɪŋkʃ(ə)n/ *n* **1** making or being extinct or (causing to be) extinguished **2** elimination or reduction of a conditioned response by not reinforcing it – **extinctive** *adj*

extinguish /ik'sting·gwish‖ɪk'stɪŋgwɪʃ/ *vt* **1a** to cause to cease burning; quench **b** to bring to an end < *hope for their safety was slowly* ~ed > **c** to cause extinction of (a conditioned response) **2a** to make void < ~ *a claim* > **b** to abolish (a debt) by payment – **extinguishable** *adj*, **extinguisher** *n*, **extinguishment** *n*

extirpate /'ekstuh,payt‖'ekstɜː,peɪt/ *vt* **1** to destroy completely (as if) by uprooting; annihilate **2** to cut out by surgery – **extirpator** *n*, **extirpation** *n*, **extirpative** *adj*

extol, *NAm also* **extoll** /ik'stohl, -'stol‖ɪk'stəʊl, -'stɒl/ *vt* **-ll-** to praise highly; glorify

extort /ik'stawt‖ɪk'stɔːt/ *vt* to obtain from sby by force or threats < ~ *money* > < ~ *a confession* > – **extorter** *n*, **extortive** *adj*

extortion /ik'stawsh(ə)n‖ɪk'stɔːʃ(ə)n/ *n* extorting; *specif* the unlawful extorting of money – **extortioner** *n*, **extortionist** *n*

extortionate /ik'stawsh(ə)nət‖ɪk'stɔːʃ(ə)nət/ *adj* excessive, exorbitant – **extortionately** *adv*

[1]**extra** /'ekstrə‖'ekstrə/ *adj* **1** more than is due, usual, or necessary; additional < ~ *work* > **2** subject to an additional charge < *room service is* ~ >

[2]**extra** *n* sthg or sby extra or additional: e g **a** an added charge **b** a specified edition of a newspaper **c** a run in cricket (e g a bye, leg bye, no-ball, or wide) that is not scored by a stroke of the bat and is not credited to a batsman's individual score **d** an additional worker; *specif* one hired to act in a group scene in a film or stage production

[3]**extra** *adv* beyond or above the usual size, extent, or amount

extra- /ekstrə-‖ekstrə-/ *prefix* outside; beyond < extra*mural* >

[1]**extract** /ik'strakt‖ɪk'strækt/ *vt* **1** to draw forth or pull out, esp against resistance or with effort **2** to withdraw (e g a juice) by physical or chemical process **3** to separate (a metal) from an ore **4** to find (a mathematical root) by calculation **5** to excerpt – **extractable, extractible** *adj*, **extractor** *n*, **extractability** *n*

[2]**extract** /'ekstrakt‖'ekstrækt/ *n* **1** an excerpt **2 extract, extractive** (a solution of) the essential constituents of a complex material (e g an aromatic plant) prepared by extraction

extraction /ik'straksh(ə)n‖ɪk'strækʃ(ə)n/ *n* **1** extracting **2** ancestry, origin **3** sthg extracted

extracurricular /,ekstrəkə'rikyoolə‖,ekstrəkə'rɪkjʊlə/ *adj* **1** not falling within the scope of a regular curriculum **2** lying outside one's normal activities

extraditable /'ekstrə,dietəbl‖'ekstrə,daɪtəbl/ *adj* liable to or warranting extradition

extradite /'ekstrə,diet‖'ekstrə,daɪt/ *vt* **1** to hand over for extradition **2** to obtain by extradition

extradition /,ekstrə'dish(ə)n‖,ekstrə'dɪʃ(ə)n/ *n* the surrender of an alleged criminal by one state to another having jurisdiction to try the charge

extrajudicial /ˌekstrəjoohˈdish(ə)l‖ˌekstrədʒuːˈdɪʃ(ə)l/ *adj* **1** not forming part of regular legal proceedings **2** in contravention of law – **extrajudicially** *adv*

extramarital /ˌekstrəˈmaritl‖ˌekstrəˈmærɪtl/ *adj, esp of sexual relations* involving sby other than one's spouse

extramural /ˌekstrəˈmyooərəl‖ˌekstrə-ˈmjʊərəl/ *adj* **1** outside (the walls or boundaries of) a place or organization **2** *chiefly Br* of extension courses or facilities <*university* ~ *department*> – **extramurally** *adv*

extraneous /ikˈstraynyəs, -ni·əs‖ɪkˈstreɪnjəs, -nɪəs/ *adj* **1** on or coming from the outside **2** not forming an essential or vital part; irrelevant – **extraneously** *adv*, **extraneousness** *n*

extraordinary /ikˈstrawdin(ə)ri‖ɪkˈstrɔːdɪn-(ə)rɪ/ *adj* **1a** going beyond what is usual, regular, or customary **b** highly exceptional; remarkable **2** on or for a special function or service <*an* ~ *general meeting*> – **extraordinarily** *adv*, **extraordinariness** *n*

extrapolate /ekˈstrapəˌlayt‖ekˈstræpəˌleɪt/ *vt* **1** to use or extend (known data or experience) in order to surmise or work out sthg unknown **2** to predict by extrapolating known data or experience – **extrapolator** *n*, **extrapolative** *adj*, **extrapolation** *n*

extrasensory /ˌekstrəˈsens(ə)ri‖ˌekstrəˈsens-(ə)rɪ/ *adj* residing beyond or outside the ordinary physical senses <*instances of* ~ *perception*>

extraterrestrial /ˌekstrətəˈrestri·əl‖ˌekstrətəˈrestrɪəl/ *adj* originating, existing, or occurring outside the earth or its atmosphere

extraterritorial /ˌekstrəˌteriˈtawri·əl‖ˌekstrəˌterɪˈtɔːrɪəl/ *adj* outside the territorial limits of a jurisdiction

extravagance /ikˈstravəgəns‖ɪk-ˈstrævəgəns/, **extravagancy** /-si‖-sɪ/ *n* **1** an extravagant act; *specif* an excessive outlay of money **2** sthg extravagant

exˈtravagant /-gənt‖-gənt/ *adj* **1a** lacking in moderation, balance, and restraint; excessive **b** excessively elaborate or showy **2a** wasteful, esp of money **b** profuse **3** exorbitant [Middle French, wandering, irregular, fr Latin *extra* outside, beyond + *vagari* to wander about] – **extravagantly** *adv*

extravaganza /ikˌstravəˈganzə‖ɪkˌstrævə-ˈgænzə/ *n* **1** a literary or musical work marked by extreme freedom of style and structure **2** a lavish or spectacular show or event

extravert /ˈekstrəˌvuht‖ˈekstrəˌvɜːt/ *n or adj* (an) extrovert

1**extreme** /ikˈstreem‖ɪkˈstriːm/ *adj* **1a** existing in a very high degree <~ *poverty*> **b** going to great or exaggerated lengths; not moderate <*an* ~ *right-winger*> **c** exceeding the usual or expected; severe <*took* ~ *measures*> **2** situated at the farthest possible point from a centre or the nearest to an end <*the country's* ~ *north*> **3a** most advanced or thoroughgoing <*the* ~ *avant-garde*> **b** maximum <*the* ~ *penalty*> – **extremely** *adv*, **extremeness** *n*

2**extreme** *n* **1a** sthg situated at or marking one or other extreme point of a range <~*s of heat and cold*> **b** the first term or the last term of a mathematical proportion **2** a very pronounced or extreme degree <*his enthusiasm was carried to an* ~> **3** an extreme measure or expedient <*going to* ~*s*> – **in the extreme** to the greatest possible extent <*boring* in the extreme>

exˌtreme ˈunction *n* the (Roman Catholic) sacrament of anointing and praying over sby who is dying

extremism /ikˈstreeˌmiz(ə)m‖ɪkˈstriːˌmɪz-(ə)m/ *n* advocacy of extreme political measures; radicalism – **extremist** *n or adj*

extremity /ikˈstreməti‖ɪkˈstremətɪ/ *n* **1a** the most extreme part, point, or degree **b** a (human) hand, foot, or other limb **2** (a moment marked by) extreme misfortune and esp danger of destruction or death **3** a drastic or desperate act or measure

extricate /ˈekstriˌkayt‖ˈekstrɪˌkeɪt/ *vt* to disentangle, esp with considerable effort – **extricable** *adj*, **extrication** *n*

extrinsic /ekˈstrinsik, -zik‖ekˈstrɪnsɪk, -zɪk/ *adj* **1** not forming part of or belonging to a thing; extraneous **2** originating from or on the outside – **extrinsically** *adv*

extrovert *also* **extravert** /ˈekstrəˌvuht‖ˈekstrə-ˌvɜːt/ *n* one whose attention and interests are directed wholly or predominantly towards what is outside the self [deriv of Latin *extra* outside + *vertere* to turn] – **extrovert** *adj*, **extroverted** *adj*, **extroversion** *n*

extrude /ikˈstroohd‖ɪkˈstruːd/ *vt* **1** to force or push out **2** to shape (e g metal or plastic) by forcing through a die ~ *vi* to become extruded – **extruder** *n*, **extrudable** *adj*, **extrudability** *n*, **extrusion** *n*

exuberant /igˈzyoohb(ə)rənt‖ɪgˈzjuːb(ə)rənt/ *adj* **1a** joyously unrestrained and enthusiastic <~ *high spirits*> **b** lavish and flamboyant <~ *metaphors*> **2** great or extreme in degree, size, or extent **3** abundant, luxuriant <~ *vegetation*> – **exuberance** *n*, **exuberantly** *adv*

exude /igˈzyoohd‖ɪgˈzjuːd/ *vi* to ooze out ~ *vt* **1** to allow or cause to ooze or spread out in all directions **2** to radiate an air of <~*s charm*> – **exudation** *n*

exult /igˈzult‖ɪgˈzʌlt/ *vi* to be extremely joyful; rejoice openly – usu + *at*, *in*, or *over* – **exultance** *n*, **exultancy** *n*, **exultant** *adj*, **exultingly** *adv*, **exultation** *n*, **exultantly** *adv*

-ey /-i‖-ɪ/ – see 1Y-

1**eye** /ie‖aɪ/ *n* **1a** any of various usu paired organs of sight; *esp* a nearly spherical liquid-filled organ that is lined with a light-sensitive retina and housed in a bony socket in the skull **b** the visible parts of the eye with its surrounding structures (e g eyelashes and eyebrows) **c(1)** the faculty of seeing with eyes <*a keen* ~ *for detail*> **c(2)** the faculty of intellectual or aesthetic perception or appreciation <*an* ~ *for beauty*> **d** a gaze, glance <*caught his* ~> **e** view, attention <*in the public* ~> **2a** the hole through the head of a needle **b** a (nearly) circular mark (e g on a peacock's tail) **c** a loop; *esp* one of metal or thread into which a hook is inserted **d** an undeveloped bud (e g on a potato) **e** a calm area in the centre of a tropical cyclone **f** the (differently coloured or marked) centre of a flower – **in the eye/eyes of** in the judgment or opinion of – **my eye** – used to express mild disagreement or sometimes surprise; infml – **set/clap eyes on** to catch sight of – **with an eye to** having as an aim or purpose

[2]**eye** *vt* **eyeing, eying** to watch closely – **eyer** *n*

'eyeˌball *n* the capsule of the eye of a vertebrate formed by the sclera and cornea that cover it, together with the structures they contain

'eyeˌbrow *n* (hair growing on) the ridge over the eye

'eye-ˌcatching *adj* strikingly visually attractive – **eye-catcher** *n*

eyed /ied‖aɪd/ *adj* having an eye or eyes, esp of a specified kind or number – often in combination <*an almond-*eyed *girl*>

'eyeful /-f(ə)l‖-f(ə)l/ *n* a pleasing sight; *specif* an attractive woman – infml

'eyeˌglass *n* **1** an eyepiece **2** a lens worn to aid vision; *specif* a monocle **3** *pl* glasses, spectacles

'eyeˌlash *n* (a single hair of) the fringe of hair edging the eyelid

'eyelet /-lit‖-lɪt/ *n* **1** a small usu reinforced hole designed so that a cord, lace, etc may be passed through it, or used in embroidery **2** a small typically metal ring to reinforce an eyelet

'eyeˌlid *n* a movable lid of skin and muscle that can be closed over the eyeball

'eyeˌliner *n* a cosmetic for emphasizing the contours of the eyes

'eye-ˌopener *n* **1** *chiefly NAm* a drink intended to stop one feeling sleepy on waking up **2** sthg surprising and esp revelatory – infml <*his behaviour was a real* ~ *to me*> – **eye-opening** *adj*

'eyeˌpiece *n* the lens or combination of lenses at the eye end of an optical instrument

'eye ˌshadow *n* a coloured cream or powder applied to the eyelids to accentuate the eyes

'eyeˌsight *n* SIGHT 5

'eyeˌsore *n* sthg offensive to the sight

ˌeye'tooth *n* a canine tooth of the upper jaw

'eyeˌwash *n* deceptive statements or actions; rubbish, claptrap – infml

'eyeˌwitness *n* one who sees an occurrence and can bear witness to it (e g in court)

eyrie /'iəri, 'eəri, 'ie·əri‖'ɪərɪ, 'eərɪ, 'aɪərɪ/ *n* **1** the nest of a bird (of prey) on a cliff or a mountain top **2** a room or dwelling situated high up

F

f /ef‖ef/ *n, pl* **f's, fs** *often cap* **1** (a graphic representation of or device for reproducing) the 6th letter of the English alphabet **2** the 4th note of a C-major scale

fa, fah /fah‖fɑː/ *n* the 4th note of the diatonic scale in solmization

FA /ˌe'fay‖ˌe'feɪ/ *n, Br* fuck-all – euph; often in *sweet FA*

Fabian /'faybi·ən, -byən‖'feɪbɪən, -bjən/ *adj* of or being a society founded in England in 1884 to work for the gradual establishment of socialism [Quintus *Fabius* Maximus (died 203 BC), Roman general who wore down his enemies while avoiding open battles] – **Fabian** *n*, **Fabianism** *n*

fable /'faybl‖'feɪbl/ *n* **1a** a legendary story of supernatural happenings **b** myths or legendary tales collectively **2** a fictitious account; a lie **3** a story intended to convey a moral; *esp* one in which animals speak and act like human beings [Middle French, fr Latin *fabula* conversation, story, play, fr *fari* to speak]

'fabled *adj* **1** fictitious **2** told or celebrated in fables; legendary

fabric /'fabrik‖'fæbrɪk/ *n* **1a** the basic structure of a building <*the* ~ *of the theatre*> **b** an underlying structure; a framework <*the* ~ *of society*> **2** an act of constructing; an erection **3** texture, quality – used chiefly with reference to textiles **4a** CLOTH 1 **b** a material that resembles cloth [Middle French *fabrique*, fr Latin *fabrica* workshop, structure, fr *fabr-, faber* smith]

'fabricate /-kayt‖-keɪt/ *vt* **1** to construct or manufacture from many parts **2** to invent or create, esp in order to deceive – **fabricator** *n*, **fabrication** *n*

fabulous /'fabyooləs‖'fæbjʊləs/ *adj* **1** resembling things told of in fables, esp in incredible or exaggerated quality; extraordinary <~ *wealth*> **2** told in or based on fable **3** marvellous, great – infml <*a* ~ *party*> – **fabulously** *adv*, **fabulousness** *n*

facade *also* **façade** /fə'sahd‖fə'sɑːd/ *n* **1** a face, esp the front or principal face, of a building given special architectural treatment **2** a false or superficial appearance

[1]**face** /fays‖feɪs/ *n* **1** the front part of the (human) head including the chin, mouth, nose, eyes, etc and usu the forehead **2a** a facial expression; *specif* a grimace <*he pulled a* ~> **b** MAKE-UP 2a, b <*she put her* ~ *on*> **3a** an outward appearance <*put a good* ~ *on it*> **b** effrontery, impudence <*had the* ~ *to ask for his money back*> **c** dignity, reputation <*afraid to lose* ~> **4a(1)** a front, upper, or outer surface **a(2)** the front of sthg with 2 or 4 sides **a(3)** an exposed surface of rock **a(4)** any of the plane surfaces of a geometric solid **b** a surface specially prepared: e g **b(1)** the right side (e g of cloth or leather) **b(2)** an inscribed, printed, or marked surface **c** the surface (e g of type) that receives the ink and transfers it to the paper **5** the exposed working surface of a mine, drift, or excavation [Old French, deriv of Latin *facies* make, form, face, fr *facere* to make, do] – **in the face of/in face of** in opposition to; despite – **to someone's face** candidly in sby's presence and to his/her knowledge

[2]**face** *vt* **1** to meet or deal with firmly and without evasion <~ *the situation calmly*> **2a** to apply a facing to **b** to cover the front or surface of <~d *the building with marble*> **3** to have the face towards <~ *the wall*>; *also* to front on <*a house* facing *the park*> **4** to turn (e g a playing card) face-up **5** to make the surface of (e g a stone) flat or smooth **6** to cause (troops) to face in a particular direction on command ~ *vi* **1** to have the face or front turned in a specified direction <*the house* ~s *towards the east*> **2** to turn the face in a specified direction – **face the music** to confront and endure the unpleasant

consequences of one's actions – **face up to** to confront without shrinking – **face with** to confront with <faced *him* with *the evidence*>

'face,cloth *n* FLANNEL 3

-faced /-fayst‖-feɪst/ *comb form* (*adj, n → adj*) having (such) a face or (so many) faces <*two*-faced>

'faceless /-lis‖-lɪs/ *adj* lacking identity; anonymous – **facelessness** *n*

'face-,lift *n* **1** plastic surgery to remove facial defects (e g wrinkles) typical of aging **2** an alteration intended to improve appearance or utility – **face-lift** *vt*

face out *vt* to confront defiantly or impudently <faced out *the opposition*>

'face-,pack *n* a cream, paste, etc applied to the face to improve the complexion and remove impurities

'face-,saving *adj* serving to preserve one's dignity or reputation – **face-saver** *n*

facet /'fasit‖'fæsɪt/ *n* **1** a small plane surface (e g of a cut gem) **2** any of the aspects from which sthg specified may be considered <*another ~ of his genius*> **3** the external surface of any of the usu many optical elements of the compound eye of an insect or other arthropod – **faceted, facetted** *adj*

facetious /fə'seeshəs‖fə'siːʃəs/ *adj* **1** inappropriately lacking seriousness in manner; flippant **2** intended to be amusing – **facetiously** *adv*, **facetiousness** *n*

,face-to-'face *adj* in each other's usu hostile presence <*a ~ encounter*>

,face to 'face *adv* **1** in or into the usu hostile presence of (one) another **2** in or into confrontation with sthg which calls for immediate action

'face ,value *n* **1** the value indicated on the face (e g of a postage stamp or a share certificate) **2** the apparent value or significance <*if their results may be taken at ~*>

¹facial /'faysh(ə)l‖'feɪʃ(ə)l/ *adj* of the face – **facially** *adv*

²facial *n* a facial beauty treatment

facile /'fasiel‖'fæsaɪl/ *adj* **1a** easily or readily accomplished or performed **b** specious, superficial **2** used, done, or understood with ease – **facilely** *adv*, **facileness** *n*

facilitate /fə'silitayt‖fə'sɪlɪteɪt/ *vt* to make easier – fml – **facilitative** *adj*, **facilitator** *n*

facility /fə'siləti‖fə'sɪlətɪ/ *n* **1** the quality of being easily performed **2** the ability to perform sthg easily; aptitude **3** sthg (e g equipment) that promotes the ease of an action or operation – usu pl <*provide books and other* facilities *for independent study*>

facing /'faysing‖'feɪsɪŋ/ *n* **1a** a lining at the edge of sthg, esp a garment, for stiffening or ornament **b** *pl* the collar, cuffs, and trimmings of a uniform coat **2** an ornamental or protective layer **3** material used for facing

facsimile /fak'siməli‖fæk'sɪməlɪ/ *n* **1** an exact copy, esp of printed material **2** the transmission and reproduction of graphic material (e g typescript or pictures) by wire or radio [Latin *fac* make + *simile* similar] – **facsimile** *vt*

fact /fakt‖fækt/ *n* **1** a thing done; *esp* a criminal act **2** the quality of having actual existence in the real world; *also* sthg having such existence **3** an event, esp as distinguished from its legal effect **4** a piece of information presented as having objective reality <*that's a ~*> – **factless** *adj*, **facticity** *n* – **in fact 1** really; AS A MATTER OF FACT **2** briefly; IN SHORT

¹faction /'faksh(ə)n‖'fækʃ(ə)n/ *n* **1** a party or minority group within a party **2** dissension with a party or group – **factional** *adj*, **factionalism** *n*, **factionally** *adv*

²faction *n* the dramatized reconstruction of some real historical situation or event

-faction /-'faksh(ə)n‖-'fækʃ(ə)n/ *comb form* (→ *n*) **1** making; -fication <*lique*faction> **2** state <*satis*faction> – **-factive** *comb form* (→ *adj*)

factious /'fakshəs‖'fækʃəs/ *adj* **1** caused by or inclined to faction **2** seditious – **factiously** *adv*, **factiousness** *n*

factitious /fak'tishəs‖fæk'tɪʃəs/ *adj* **1** produced by human beings rather than by natural forces **2** produced artificially; sham, unreal – **factitiously** *adv*, **factitiousness** *n*

,fact of 'life *n, pl* **facts of life 1** *pl* the processes and behaviour involved in (human) sex and reproduction **2** sthg that exists and must be taken into consideration

¹factor /'faktə‖'fæktə/ *n* **1** one who acts for another; an agent **2** a condition, force, or fact that actively contributes to a result **3** a gene **4** any of the numbers or symbols that when multiplied together form a product – **factorship** *n*

²factor *vt* to express as the product of factors – **factorable** *adj*

factor·ize, -ise /'faktəriez‖'fæktəraɪz/ *vt* to factor – **factorization** *n*

factory /'fakt(ə)ri‖'fækt(ə)rɪ/ *n* a building or set of buildings with facilities for manufacturing

factotum /fak'tohtəm‖fæk'təʊtəm/ *n* a servant employed to carry out many types of work [Latin *fac* do + *totum* everything]

factual /'faktyooəl, -chooəl‖'fæktjʊəl, -tʃʊəl/ *adj* **1** of facts **2** restricted to or based on fact – **factually** *adv*, **factualness** *n*, **factuality** *n*

faculty /'fakəlti‖'fækəltɪ/ *n* **1a** an inherent capability, power, or function of the body <*the ~ of hearing*> **b** a natural aptitude; a talent <*has a ~ for saying the right things*> **2** a group of related subject departments in a university **3** *sing or pl in constr* the members of a profession **4** (conferred) power or prerogative

fad /fad‖fæd/ *n* **1** a usu short-lived but enthusiastically pursued practice or interest; a craze **2** an idiosyncratic taste or habit – **faddish** *adj*, **faddishness** *n*, **faddism** *n*, **faddist** *n*, **faddy** *adj*

¹fade /fayd‖feɪd/ *vi* **1** to lose freshness or vigour; wither **2** *of a brake* to lose braking power gradually, esp owing to prolonged use **3** to lose freshness or brilliance of colour **4** to disappear gradually; vanish – often + *away* <*the smile ~d from his face*> **5** to change gradually in loudness, strength, or visibility – often used of electronic signals or sounds; usu + *in* or *out* ~ *vt* to cause to fade

²fade *n* an effect consisting of a fade-out or a fade-in or a combination of both

'fade-,in *n* the gradual appearance of a sound or picture, usu in broadcasting or on film

ˈ**fade-ˌout** *n* the gradual disappearance of esp a sound or picture, usu in broadcasting or on film

faeces, *NAm chiefly* **feces** /ˈfeeseez‖ˈfiːsiːz/ *n pl* bodily waste discharged through the anus – **faecal** *adj*

faerie *also* **faery** /ˈfayəri, ˈfeəri‖ˈfeɪərɪ, ˈfeərɪ/ *n* **1** fairyland **2** a fairy *USE* poetic – **faery** *adj*

[1]**fag** /fag‖fæg/ *vi* **-gg-** **1** to act as a fag, esp in a British public school **2** to work hard; toil – infml

[2]**fag** *n* **1** a British public-school pupil who acts as servant to an older schoolmate **2** *chiefly Br* a tiring or boring task – infml

[3]**fag** *n* a cigarette – infml

[4]**fag** *n, chiefly NAm* FAGGOT 2

ˈ**fag ˌend** *n* **1** a poor or worn-out end; a remnant **2** the extreme end <*the* ~ *of one quarrel* – William Golding> USE infml

ˌ**fagged** ˈ**out** *adj* tired, exhausted – infml

faggot /ˈfagət‖ˈfægət/ *n* **1** *NAm chiefly* **fagot** **1a** a bundle: e g **1a(1)** a bundle of sticks **a(2)** a bundle of pieces of wrought iron to be shaped by hammering or rolling at high temperature **a(3)** a bunch of herbs tied together; BOUQUET GARNI **b** a round mass of minced meat (e g pig's liver) mixed with herbs and usu breadcrumbs **2** *chiefly NAm* a usu male homosexual – derog

Fahrenheit /ˈfarənˌhiet‖ˈfærənˌhaɪt/ *adj* relating to, conforming to, or being a scale of temperature on which water freezes at 32° and boils at 212° under standard conditions [Gabriel *Fahrenheit* (1686-1736), German physicist]

faience, faïence /fieˈahns, -ˈonhs ‖faɪˈɑːns, -ˈɑ̃s (*Fr* fajɑ̃ːs)/ *n* tin-glazed decorated earthenware

[1]**fail** /fayl‖feɪl/ *vi* **1a** to lose strength; weaken <*her health was* ~ing> **b** to fade or die away <*until the light* ~s> **c** to stop functioning **2a** to fall short <~ed *in his duty*> **b** to be or become absent or inadequate <*the water supply* ~ed> **c** to be unsuccessful (e g in passing a test) **d** to become bankrupt or insolvent ~ *vt* **1a** to disappoint the expectations or trust of <*his friends* ~ed *him*> **b** to prove inadequate for or incapable of carrying out an expected service or function for <*for once his wit* ~ed *him*> **2** to be deficient in; lack **3** to leave undone; neglect **4a** to be unsuccessful in passing (e g a test) **b** to grade (e g a student) as not passing – **failingly** *adv*

[2]**fail** *n* **1** failure – chiefly in *without fail* **2** an examination failure

[1]**failing** /ˈfayling‖ˈfeɪlɪŋ/ *n* a usu slight or insignificant defect in character; *broadly* a fault, imperfection

[2]**failing** *prep* in absence or default of <~ *specific instructions, use your own judgment*>

ˈ**failˌsafe** /-ˌsayf‖-ˌseɪf/ *adj* designed so as to counteract automatically the effect of an anticipated possible source of failure

failure /ˈfaylyə‖ˈfeɪljə/ *n* **1a** nonoccurrence or nonperformance; *specif* a failing to perform a duty or expected action **b** inability to perform a normal function <*heart* ~> **2** lack of success **3a** a falling short; a deficiency <*a* ~ *in the supply of raw materials*> **b** deterioration, decay **4** sby or sthg unsuccessful

fain /fayn‖feɪn/ *adv, archaic* **1** with pleasure **2** rather

[1]**faint** /faynt‖feɪnt/ *adj* **1** cowardly, timid – chiefly in *faint heart* **2** weak, dizzy, and likely to faint <*felt* ~> **3** performed, offered, or accomplished weakly or languidly; feeble <*made a* ~ *attempt at a smile*> **4** lacking distinctness; *esp* dim <*a* ~ *light*> – **faintly** *adv*, **faintness** *n*

[2]**faint** *vi* to lose consciousness because of a temporary decrease in the blood supply to the brain (e g through exhaustion or shock)

[3]**faint** *n* (a condition of) fainting

ˌ**faintˈhearted** *adj* lacking courage or resolution; timid – **faintheartedly** *adv*, **faintheartedness** *n*

[1]**fair** /feə‖feə/ *adj* **1** attractive, beautiful **2** superficially pleasing; specious <*she trusted his* ~ *promises*> **3** clean, clear <*a* ~ *copy*> **4** not stormy or foul; fine <~ *weather*> **5a** free from self-interest or prejudice; honest **b** conforming with the established rules; allowed <*a* ~ *tackle*> **6** favourable to a ship's course <*a* ~ *wind*> **7** light in colour; blond **8** moderately good or large; adequate <*a* ~ *understanding of the work*> – **fairness** *n* – **in a fair way to** likely to

[2]**fair** *adv* fairly

[3]**fair** *vi, of the weather* to clear ~*vt* to join so that the external surfaces blend smoothly

[4]**fair** *n* **1** a periodic gathering of buyers and sellers at a particular place and time for trade or a competitive exhibition, usu accompanied by entertainment and amusements **2a** *Br* FUN FAIR **b** an exhibition usu designed to acquaint prospective buyers or the general public with a product **3** a sale of a collection of articles usu for a charitable purpose

ˌ**fair and** ˈ**square** *adv* **1** in an honest manner <*won the match* ~> **2** exactly, directly <*hit him* ~ *on the nose*> – **fair and square** *adj*

ˌ**fair** ˈ**game** *n* sby or sthg open to legitimate pursuit, attack, or ridicule

ˈ**fairˌground** *n* an area where outdoor fairs, circuses, or exhibitions are held

ˈ**fairly** /-li‖-lɪ/ *adv* **1** completely, quite <~ *bursting with pride*> **2a** in a proper or legal manner <~ *priced stocks*> **b** impartially, honestly <*a story told* ~ *and objectively*> **3** to a full degree or extent; plainly, distinctly <*had* ~ *caught sight of him*> **4** for the most part; quite <*a* ~ *easy job*>

ˌ**fair** ˈ**play** *n* equitable or impartial treatment; justice

ˈ**fairˌway** *n* **1** a navigable channel in a river, bay, or harbour **2** the mowed part of a golf course between a tee and a green

ˈ**fair-ˌweather** *adj* present or loyal only in untroubled times – chiefly in *fair-weather friend*

fairy /ˈfeəri‖ˈfeərɪ/ *n* **1** a small mythical being having magic powers and usu human form **2** an effeminate male (homosexual) – derog – **fairy** *adj*, **fairylike** *adj*

ˈ**fairyˌland** *n* **1** the land of fairies **2** a place of magical charm

ˈ**fairy ˌlights** *n pl, chiefly Br* small coloured electric lights for decoration, esp outdoors or on a Christmas tree

ˈ**fairy-ˌtale** *adj* marked by **a** unusual grace or beauty **b** apparently magical success or good fortune <*a* ~ *start to his career*>

'fairy ˌtale *n* **1** a story which features supernatural or imaginary forces and beings **2** a made-up story, usu designed to mislead; a fabrication

fait accompli /ˌfayt əˈkompli, ˌfet əkomˈpli ‖ ˌfeɪt əˈkɒmplɪ, ˌfet əkɒmˈplɪ (*Fr* fɛt akɔ̃pli)/ *n, pl* **faits accomplis** /~/ sthg already accomplished and considered irreversible [French, accomplished fact]

faith /fayth‖feɪθ/ *n* **1a** allegiance to duty or a person; loyalty – chiefly in *good/ bad faith* **b** fidelity to one's promises – chiefly in *keep/ break faith* **2a** belief and trust in and loyalty to God or the doctrines of a religion **b(1)** firm belief in sthg for which there is no objective proof **b(2)** complete confidence **3** sthg believed with strong conviction; *esp* a system of religious beliefs

1'faithful /-f(ə)l‖-f(ə)l/ *adj* **1** showing faith; loyal, steadfast; *specif* loyal to one's spouse in having no sexual relations outside marriage **2** firm in adherence to promises or in observance of duty; conscientious **3** true to the facts or to an original; accurate <*the portrait is a* ~ *likeness*> – **faithfully** *adv*, **faithfulness** *n*

2faithful *n pl* **1** *the* full church members **2** *the* body of adherents of a religion (e g Islam) **3 faithful, faithfuls** loyal followers or members <*party* ~s>

'faith ˌhealing *n* a practice of attempting the cure of illnesses by prayer rather than medical techniques – **faith healer** *n*

'faithless /-lis‖-lɪs/ *adj* **1a** lacking faith, esp religious faith **b** heedless of duty or allegiance; disloyal **2** that may not be relied on; untrustworthy <*a* ~ *friend*> – **faithlessly** *adv*, **faithlessness** *n* to feign <~d *an illness*>

1fake *vt* **1** to alter or treat so as to impart a false character or appearance; falsify <~d *all the results to suit his theories*> **2a** to counterfeit, simulate **b** to feign <~d *an illness*> ~ *vi* **1** to engage in faking sthg; pretend **2** *NAm* to dummy – **faker** *n*, **fakery** *n*

2fake *n* **1** a worthless imitation passed off as genuine **2** an impostor, charlatan

3fake *adj* counterfeit, phoney

fakir /ˈfaykiə, fəˈkiə, ˈfahkiə, -kə‖ˈfeɪkɪə, fəˈkɪə, ˈfɑːkɪə, -kə/ *n* **1** a Muslim mendicant **2** an itinerant Hindu ascetic holy man [Arabic *faqīr*, lit., poor man]

falcon /faw(l)kən‖fɔː(l)kən/ *n* **1** any of various hawks distinguished by long wings **2** 1HAWK 1

'falconer /-nə‖-nə/ *n* one who hunts with hawks or who breeds or trains hawks for hunting

'falconry /-ri‖-rɪ/ *n* the art of training or the sport of using falcons to pursue game

1fall /fawl‖fɔːl/ *vi* **fell** /fel‖fel/; **fallen** /ˈfawlən‖ˈfɔːlən/ **1a** to descend freely by the force of gravity **b** to hang freely <*her hair* ~s *over her shoulders*> **c** to come as if by descending <*a hush* fell *on the audience*> **2a** to become less or lower in degree, level, pitch, or volume <*their voices* fell *to a whisper*> **b** to be uttered; issue <*let* ~ *a remark*> **c** to look down <*her glance* fell *on me*> **3a** to come down from an erect to a usu prostrate position suddenly and esp involuntarily <*slipped and* fell *on the ice*> **b** to enter an undesirable state, esp unavoidably or unwittingly; stumble, stray <fell *into error*> <fell *ill*> **c** to drop because wounded or dead; *esp* to die in battle – euph **d** to suffer military capture <*after a long siege the city* fell> **e** to lose office <*the government* fell> **f** to suffer ruin or defeat <*we must stand or* ~ *together*> **4a** to yield to temptation; sin **b** *of a woman* to lose one's virginity, esp outside marriage **5a** to move or extend in a downward direction – often + *off* or *away* <*the land* ~s *away to the east*> **b** to decline in quality or quantity; abate, subside – often + *off* or *away* <*production* fell *off because of the strike*> **c** to assume a look of disappointment or dismay <*his face* fell> **d** to decline in financial value <*shares* fell *sharply today*> **6a** to occur at a specified time or place <*Christmas* ~s *on a Thursday this year*> **b** to come (as if) by chance – + *in* or *into* **c** to come or pass by lot, assignment, or inheritance; devolve – usu + *on, to*, or *upon* <*it* fell *to me to break the news*> **7** to come within the limits, scope, or jurisdiction of sthg <~s *within our borders*> **8** to pass, esp involuntarily and suddenly, into a new state or condition <~ *in love*> <*the book* fell *apart*> **9** to begin heartily or actively – usu + *to* <fell *to work*> – **fall behind** DROP BEHIND – **fall between two stools** to fail because of inability to choose between or reconcile 2 alternative or conflicting courses of action – **fall flat** to produce no response or result <*the joke* fell flat> – **fall for 1** to fall in love with **2** to be deceived by <*he* fell for *the trick*> – **fall foul of** to arouse aversion in; clash with – **fall on/upon 1** to descend upon; attack <fell *hungrily* on *the pie*> **2** to meet with <*he* fell on *hard times*> **3** to hit on – **fall over oneself** to display almost excessive eagerness – **fall short** to fail to attain a goal or target

2fall *n* **1** the act of falling by the force of gravity **2a** a falling out, off, or away; a dropping <*a* ~ *of snow*> **b** sthg or a quantity that falls or has fallen <*a* ~ *of rock*> **3** a rope or chain for a hoisting tackle **4a** a loss of greatness or power; a collapse <*the* ~ *of the Roman Empire*> **b** the surrender or capture of a besieged place <*the* ~ *of Troy*> **c** *often cap* mankind's loss of innocence through the disobedience of Adam and Eve **5a** a downward slope **b** CATARACT 2a – usu pl with sing. meaning but sing. or pl in constr **6** a decrease in size, quantity, degree, or value **7** the distance which sthg falls **8a** an act of forcing a wrestler's shoulders to the mat for a prescribed time **b** a bout of wrestling **9** *chiefly NAm* autumn

fall about *vi* to be convulsed (with laughter) – infml

fallacy /ˈfaləsi‖ˈfæləsɪ/ *n* **1** deceptive appearance or nature; deception, delusiveness **2** a false idea <*the popular* ~ *that scientists are illiterate*> **3** an argument failing to satisfy the conditions of valid inference – **fallacious** *adj*, **fallaciously** *adv*, **fallaciousness** *n*

fall back *vi* to retreat, recede – **fallback** *n* – **fall back on/upon** to have recourse to <*when facts were scarce he* fell back on *his imagination*>

fall down *vi* to fail to meet expectations or requirements; be inadequate <*she* fell down *on the job*> – infml

'fall ˌguy *n* **1** one who is easily cheated or

tricked **2** a scapegoat *USE* infml

fallible /'faləbl‖'fæləbl/ *adj* capable of being or likely to be wrong – **fallibly** *adv*, **fallibility** *n*

fall in *vi* **1** to sink or collapse inwards **2** to take one's proper place in a military formation – **fall in with** to concur with <*had to* fall in with *her wishes*>

ˌfalling ˈstar *n* a meteor when falling into the earth's atmosphere and producing a bright streak of light

ˈfallˌoff *n* a decline, esp in quantity or quality

falˌlopian ˈtube /fə'lohpi·ən, -pyən‖fə-'ləʊpɪən, -pjən/ *n, often cap F* either of the pair of tubes conducting the egg from the ovary to the uterus in mammals [Gabriel *Fallopius* (1523-62), Italian anatomist]

ˈfallˌout *n* **1a** polluting particles, esp radioactive particles resulting from a nuclear explosion, descending through the atmosphere **b** descent of fallout through the atmosphere **2** secondary results or products

fall out *vi* **1** to have a disagreement; quarrel **2** to leave one's place in the ranks of a military formation **3** to happen; COME ABOUT – fml or poetic <*as it* fell out *upon a day*>

[1]**fallow** /'faloh‖'fæləʊ/ *adj* light yellowish brown

[2]**fallow** *n* **1** (ploughed and harrowed) land that is allowed to lie idle during the growing season **2** (the period of) being fallow

[3]**fallow** *vt* to plough, harrow, etc (land) without seeding, esp so as to destroy weeds

[4]**fallow** *adj* **1** *of land* left unsown after ploughing **2** dormant, inactive – chiefly in *to lie fallow* – **fallowness** *n*

fallow deer *n* a small European deer with broad antlers and a pale yellow coat spotted with white in the summer

fall through *vi* to fail to be carried out

fall to *vi* to begin doing sthg (e g working or eating), esp vigorously – often imper

false /fawls‖fɔːls/ *adj* **1** not genuine <~ *documents*> **2a** intentionally untrue; lying <~ *testimony*> **b** adjusted or made so as to deceive <*a suitcase with a* ~ *bottom*> **3** not based on reality; untrue <~ *premises*> <*a* ~ *sense of security*> **4** disloyal, treacherous <*a* ~ *friend*> **5a** fitting over a main part as strengthening, protection, or disguise **b** appearing forced or artificial; unconvincing **6** resembling or related to a more widely known kind <~ *oats*> **7** inaccurate in pitch or vowel length **8** imprudent, unwise <*a* ~ *move*> – **falsely** *adv*, **falseness** *n*, **falsity** *n*

ˌfalse aˈlarm *n* an occurrence that raises but fails to meet expectations

ˈfalsehood /-hood‖-hʊd/ *n* **1** an untrue statement; a lie **2** absence of truth or accuracy; falsity **3** the practice of telling lies

ˌfalse ˈstart *n* **1** an incorrect and esp illegally early start by a competitor in a race **2** an abortive beginning to an activity or course of action

falsetto /fawl'setoh‖fɔːl'setəʊ/ *n, pl* **falsettos** (a singer who uses) an artificially high voice, specif an artificially produced male singing voice that extends above the range of the singer's full voice [Italian, fr *falso* false, fr Latin *falsus*] – **falsetto** *adv*

falsies /'fawlsiz‖'fɔːlsɪz/ *n pl* pads of foam rubber or other material worn to enlarge the apparent size of the breasts

falsify /'fawlsiˌfie‖'fɔːlsɪˌfaɪ/ *vt* **1** to prove or declare false **2a** to make false by fraudulent alteration <*his accounts were* falsified *to conceal a theft*> **b** to represent falsely; misrepresent – **falsifier** *n*, **falsification** *n*

falter /'fawltə‖'fɔːltə/ *vi* **1** to walk or move unsteadily or hesitatingly; stumble **2** to speak brokenly or weakly; stammer **3a** to hesitate in purpose or action; waver **b** to lose strength, purpose, or effectiveness; weaken <*the business was* ~ing> ~*vt* to utter in a hesitant or broken manner – **falterer** *n*, **falteringly** *adv*

fame /faym‖feɪm/ *n* **1** public estimation; reputation **2** popular acclaim; renown

famed *adj* well-known, famous

familial /fə'mili·əl, -yəl‖fə'mɪlɪəl, -jəl/ *adj* (characteristic) of a family or its members

[1]**familiar** /fə'mili·ə, -yə‖fə'mɪlɪə, -jə/ *n* **1** an intimate associate; a companion **2** FAMILIAR SPIRIT

[2]**familiar** *adj* **1** closely acquainted; intimate <*a subject I am* ~ *with*> **2a** casual, informal **b** too intimate and unrestrained; presumptuous **3** frequently seen or experienced; common – **familiarly** *adv*, **familiarness** *n*

familiarity /fəˌmili'arəti‖fəˌmɪlɪ'ærətɪ/ *n* **1a** absence of ceremony; informality **b** an unduly informal act or expression; an impropriety **2** close acquaintance *with* or knowledge of sthg

familiar·ize, -ise /fə'mili·əˌriez, -yəˌriez‖fə-'mɪlɪəˌraɪz, -jəˌraɪz/ *vt* **1** to make known or familiar **2** to make well acquainted <~ *yourselves with the rules*> – **familiarization** *n*

familiar spirit *n* a spirit or demon that waits on an individual (e g a witch)

[1]**family** /'faməli‖'fæməlɪ/ *n sing or pl in constr* **1** a group of people united by their common convictions (e g of religion or philosophy); a fellowship, brotherhood **2** a group of people of common ancestry or deriving from a common stock **3** a group of people living under 1 roof; *esp* a set of 2 or more adults living together and rearing their children **4a** a closely related series of elements or chemical compounds **b** a group of related languages descended from a single ancestral language **5** a category in the biological classification of living things ranking above a genus and below an order [Latin *familia* household (including servants as well as kin of the householder), fr *famulus* servant]

[2]**family** *adj* of or suitable for a family or all of its members <~ *entertainment*>

ˌfamily alˈlowance *n* CHILD BENEFIT

ˈfamily ˌman *n* **1** a man with a wife and children dependent on him **2** a man of domestic habits

ˌfamily ˈplanning *n* a system of achieving planned parenthood by contraception; BIRTH CONTROL

ˌfamily ˈtree *n* (a diagram of) a genealogy

famine /'famin‖'fæmɪn/ *n* an extreme scarcity of food; *broadly* any great shortage

famish /'famish‖'fæmɪʃ/ *vt* to cause to suffer

severely from hunger – usu pass <*I'm* ~ed>

famous /ˈfayməs‖ˈfeɪməs/ *adj* well-known – **famously** *adv*, **famousness** *n*

[1]**fan** /fan‖fæn/ *n* **1** a device for winnowing grain **2** an instrument for producing a current of air: e g **2a** a folding circular or semicircular device that consists of material (e g paper or silk) mounted on thin slats that is waved to and fro by hand to produce a cooling current of air **b** a device, usu a series of vanes radiating from a hub rotated by a motor, for producing a current of air – **fanlike** *adj*

[2]**fan** *vb* **-nn-** *vt* **1a** to winnow (grain) **b** to eliminate (e g chaff) by winnowing **2** to move or impel (air) with a fan **3a** to direct or blow a current of air on (as if) with a fan **b** to stir up to activity as if by fanning a fire; stimulate <*he was* ~ning *the mob's fury with an emotive speech*> **4** to spread like a fan <~ned *the pack of cards*> **5** to fire (a revolver) by squeezing the trigger and striking the hammer to the rear with the free hand ~ *vi* **1** to move like a fan; flutter **2** to spread like a fan – often + *out* <*tanks* ~ning *out across the plain*>

[3]**fan** *n* an enthusiastic supporter or admirer (e g of a sport, pursuit, or celebrity)

fanatic /fəˈnatik‖fəˈnætɪk/ *n or adj* (one who is) excessively and often uncritically enthusiastic, esp in religion or politics [Latin *fanaticus* inspired by a deity, frenzied, fr *fanum* temple] – **fanatical** *adj*, **fanatically** *adv*, **fanaticism** *n*, **fanaticize** *vt*

ˈ**fan ˌbelt** *n* an endless belt driving a cooling fan for a radiator

fancier /ˈfansi·ə‖ˈfænsɪə/ *n* one who breeds or grows a usu specified animal or plant for points of excellence <*a pigeon* ~>

fanciful /ˈfansif(ə)l‖ˈfænsɪf(ə)l/ *adj* **1** given to or guided by fancy or imagination rather than by reason and experience **2** existing in fancy only; imaginary **3** marked by fancy or whim; *specif* elaborate, contrived – **fancifully** *adv*, **fancifulness** *n*

[1]**fancy** /ˈfansi‖ˈfænsɪ/ *n* **1** a liking based on whim rather than reason; an inclination <*took a* ~ *to her*> **2a** a notion, whim **b** a mental image or representation of sthg **3a** imagination, esp of a capricious or delusive sort **b** the power of mental conception and representation, used in artistic expression (e g by a poet) **4a** *sing or pl in constr* *the* group of fanciers or of devotees of a particular sport, esp boxing **b** sby or sthg considered likely to do well (e g in a race) – infml

[2]**fancy** *vt* **1** to believe without knowledge or evidence <*I* ~ *I've seen you somewhere before*> **2a** to have a fancy for; like, desire <*I really* ~ *blond men*> **b** to consider likely to do well <*which horse do you* ~*?*> **3** to form a conception of; imagine – often imper <*just* ~ *that!*> *USE* (*2&3*) infml – **fanciable** *adj*

[3]**fancy** *adj* **1** based on fancy or the imagination; whimsical **2a** not plain or ordinary <~ *cakes*>; *esp* fine, quality **b** ornamental <~ *goods*> **c** *of an animal or plant* bred esp for bizarre or ornamental qualities **d** parti-coloured <~ *carnations*> **3** extravagant, exorbitant <~ *prices*> – infml

ˌ**fancy ˈdress** *n* unusual or amusing dress (e g representing a historical or fictional character) worn for a party or other special occasion

ˌ**fancy-ˈfree** *adj* free to do what one wants, esp because not involved in a relationship – chiefly in *footloose and fancy-free*

ˈ**fancy ˌman** *n* a woman's lover – derog; infml

ˈ**fancy ˌwoman** *n* **1** MISTRESS 4 – derog **2** a prostitute *USE* infml

ˈ**fancyˌwork** *n* decorative needlework

fandango /fanˈdang·goh‖fænˈdæŋgəʊ/ *n, pl* **fandangos** (music for) a lively Spanish dance, usu performed by a couple to the accompaniment of guitar and castanets

fanfare /ˈfanˌfeə‖ˈfænˌfeə/ *n* **1** a flourish of trumpets **2** a showy outward display

fang /fang‖fæŋ/ *n* **1a** a tooth by which an animal's prey is seized and held or torn **b** any of the long hollow or grooved teeth of a venomous snake **2** the root of a tooth or any of the prongs into which a root divides **3** a projecting tooth or prong – **fanged** *adj*

ˈ**fanˌlight** *n* an esp semicircular window with radiating divisions over a door or window

fanny /ˈfani‖ˈfænɪ/ *n* **1** *Br* the female genitals – vulg **2** *NAm* the buttocks – infml

fantasia /fanˈtayzyə, -zh(y)ə‖fænˈteɪzjə, -ʒ(j)ə/ *n* a free instrumental or literary composition not in strict form (comprising familiar tunes)

fantastic /fanˈtastik‖fænˈtæstɪk/ *adj* **1a** unreal, imaginary **b** so extreme as to challenge belief; incredible; *specif* exceedingly large or great **2** marked by extravagant fantasy or eccentricity **3** – used as a generalized term of approval – **fantastical** *adj*, **fantastically** *adv*, **fantasticalness** *n*, **fantasticality** *n*

[1]**fantasy** /ˈfantəsi‖ˈfæntəsɪ/ *n* **1** unrestricted creative imagination; fancy **2a** a creation of the unrestricted imagination whether expressed or merely conceived (e g a fantastic design or idea) **b** a fantasia **c** imaginative fiction or drama characterized esp by strange, unrealistic, or grotesque elements **3** (the power or process of creating) a usu extravagant mental image or daydream

[2]**fantasy** *vb* to fantasize

[1]**far** /fah‖fɑː/ *adv* **farther** /ˈfahdhə‖ˈfɑːðə/, **further** /ˈfuhdhə‖ˈfɜːðə/; **farthest** /ˈfahdhist‖ˈfɑːðɪst/, **furthest** /ˈfuhdhist‖ˈfɜːðɪst/ **1** to or at a considerable distance in space <*wandered* ~ *into the woods*> **2a** by a broad interval <*the* ~ *distant future*> **b** in total contrast – + *from* <~ *from criticizing you, I'm delighted*> **3** to or at an extent or degree <*as* ~ *as I know*> **4a** to or at a considerable distance or degree <*a bright student will go* ~> **b** MUCH 1c <~ *too hot*> **5** to or at a considerable distance in time <*worked* ~ *into the night*> – **by far** FAR AND AWAY – **far and away** by a considerable margin <*was* far and away *the best team*> – **how far** to what extent, degree, or distance <*didn't know* how far *to trust him*> – **so far 1** to a certain extent, degree, or distance <*when the water rose* so far, *the villagers sought higher ground*> **2** up to the present <*has written only one novel* so far>

[2]**far** *adj* **farther** /ˈfahdhə‖ˈfɑːðə/, **further** /ˈfuhdhə‖ˈfɜːðə/; **farthest** /ˈfahdhist‖ˈfɑːðɪst/, **furthest** /ˈfuhdhist‖ˈfɜːðɪst/ **1** remote in space,

time, or degree <*in the ~ distance*> **2** long <*a ~ journey*> **3** being the more distant of 2 <*the ~ side of the lake*> **4** *of a political position* extreme <*the ~ left*>

faraway /ˌfahrə'way‖ˌfɑːrə'weɪ/ *adj* **1** lying at a great distance; remote **2** dreamy, abstracted <*a ~ look in her eyes*>

farce /fahs‖fɑːs/ *n* **1** forcemeat **2** a comedy with an improbable plot that is concerned more with situation than characterization **3** the broad humour characteristic of farce **4** a ridiculous or meaningless situation or event [Middle French, deriv of Latin *farcire* to stuff] – **farcical** *adj*, **farcically** *adv*, **farcicality** *n*

[1]**fare** /feə‖feə/ *vi* to get along; succeed, do <*how did you ~ in your exam?*>

[2]**fare** *n* **1a** the price charged to transport sby **b** a paying passenger **2** food provided for a meal <*good simple ~*>

[1]**farewell** /feə'wel‖feə'wel/ *interj* goodbye

[2]**farewell** *n* **1** a parting wish for good luck; a goodbye **2** an act of departure or leave-taking – **farewell** *adj*

[3]**farewell** *vt, NAm, Austr, & NZ* to bid farewell

ˌfar'fetched *adj* not easily or naturally deduced; improbable – **farfetchedness** *n*

ˌfar-'flung *adj* **1** widely spread or distributed **2** remote <*a ~ outpost of the Empire*>

ˌfar-'gone *adj* in an advanced state, esp of sthg unpleasant (e g drunkenness or madness)

farina /fə'reenə‖fə'riːnə/ *n* **1** a starchy flour or fine meal of vegetable matter (e g cereal grains) used chiefly as a cereal or for making puddings **2** any of various powdery or mealy substances – **farinaceous** *adj*

[1]**farm** /fahm‖fɑːm/ *n* **1** an area of land devoted to growing crops or raising (domestic) animals **2** FISH FARM [Middle English *ferme* rent, lease, fr Old French, lease, fr *fermer* to fix, make a contract, fr Latin *firmare* to make firm, fr *firmus* firm]

[2]**farm** *vt* **1a** to collect and take the proceeds of (e g taxation or a business) on payment of a fixed sum **b** to give up the proceeds of (e g an estate or a business) to another on condition of receiving in return a fixed sum **2a** to cultivate or rear (crops or livestock) on a farm **b** to manage and cultivate (land) as farmland or as a farm **3** to attempt to receive (all the balls bowled) (e g so as to protect the other batsman from dismissal) *~vi* to engage in the production of crops or livestock

farmer /'fahmə‖'fɑːmə/ *n* **1** sby who pays a fixed sum for some privilege or source of income **2** sby who cultivates land or crops or raises livestock

'farmˌhand *n* a farm worker

'farmˌhouse *n* a dwelling house on a farm

farm out /-ˌsted, -stid‖-ˌsted, -stɪd/ *vt* **1** to turn over for performance or use, usu on contract **2** to put (e g children) into sby's care in return for a fee

'farmˌyard *n* the area round or enclosed by farm buildings

ˌfar-'off *adj* remote in time or space

ˌfar-'out *adj* **1** extremely unconventional; weird <*~ clothes*> **2** – used as a generalized term of approval <*~, man!*> *USE* infml; no longer in vogue – **far-outness** *n*

farrago /fə'rahgoh‖fə'rɑːgəʊ/ *n, pl* **farragoes** a confused collection; a hotchpotch

ˌfar-'reaching *adj* having a wide range, influence, or effect

farrier /'fari·ə‖'færɪə/ *n* **1** a horse doctor **2** a blacksmith who shoes horses – **farriery** *n*

[1]**farrow** /'faroh‖'færəʊ/ *vb* to give birth to (pigs) – often + *down*

[2]**farrow** *n* (farrowing) a litter of pigs

ˌfar'sighted *adj* **1a** seeing or able to see to a great distance **b** having foresight or good judgment; sagacious **2** hypermetropic – **farsightedly** *adv*, **farsightedness** *n*

[1]**fart** /faht‖fɑːt/ *vi* to expel wind from the anus – vulg

[2]**fart** *n* **1** an expulsion of intestinal wind **2** an unpleasant person *USE* vulg

[1]**farther** /'fahdhə‖'fɑːðə/ *adv* **1** at or to a greater distance or more advanced point <*~ down the corridor*> **2** [1]FURTHER 3

[2]**farther** *adj* **1a** more distant; remoter **b** FAR 3 <*the ~ side*> **2** [2]FURTHER 2

[1]**farthest** /'fahdhist‖'fɑːðɪst/ *adj* most distant in space or time

[2]**farthest** *adv* **1** to or at the greatest distance in space, time, or degree **2** by the greatest degree or extent; most

farthing /'fahdhing‖'fɑːðɪŋ/ *n* **1** (a coin representing) a former British money unit worth $^1/_4$ of an old penny **2** sthg of small value; a mite

fascia /'fayshə‖'feɪʃə; *med* 'fashi·ə‖'fæʃɪə/ *n, pl* **fasciae** /-iˌee, -iˌie‖-ɪˌiː, -ɪˌaɪ/, **fascias** **1a** a flat horizontal piece (e g of stone or board) under projecting eaves **b** a nameplate over the front of a shop **2** a broad well-defined band of colour **3** (a sheet of) connective tissue covering or binding together body structures **4** *Br* the dashboard of a motor car – **fascial** *adj*

fascinate /'fasinayt‖'fæsɪneɪt/ *vt* **1** to transfix by an irresistible mental power <*believed that the serpent could ~ its prey*> **2** to attract strongly, esp by arousing interest; captivate *~vi* to be irresistibly attractive – **fascinator** *n*, **fascinatingly** *adv*, **fascination** *n*

fascism /'fashiz(ə)m‖'fæʃɪz(ə)m/ *n* **1** a political philosophy, movement, or regime that is usu hostile to socialism, exalts nation and race, and stands for a centralized government headed by a dictatorial leader, severe regimentation, and forcible suppression of opposition **2** brutal dictatorial control [Italian *fascismo*, fr *fascio* bundle, fasces, group, fr Latin *fascis* bundle & *fasces* bundle of rods used as a symbol of power] – **fascist** *n or adj, often cap*, **fascistic** *adj, often cap*

[1]**fashion** /'fash(ə)n‖'fæʃ(ə)n/ *n* **1** the make or form of sthg **2** a manner, way <*the people assembled in an orderly ~*> **3a** a prevailing and often short-lived custom or style **b** the prevailing style or custom, esp in dress **c** an affluent and fashionable life style <*women of ~*> – **after a fashion** in an approximate or rough way <*became an artist* after a fashion>

[2]**fashion** *vt* **1** to give shape or form to, esp by using ingenuity; mould, construct **2** to mould into a particular character by influence or training; transform, adapt – **fashioner** *n*

fashionable /ˈfash(ə)nəbl‖ˈfæʃ(ə)nəbl/ *adj* **1** conforming to the latest custom or fashion **2** of the world of fashion; used or patronized by people of fashion – **fashionableness** *n*, **fashionably** *adv*

[1]**fast** /fahst‖fɑːst/ *adj* **1a** firmly fixed or attached **b** tightly closed or shut **2** firm, steadfast – chiefly in *fast friends* **3a(1)** moving or able to move rapidly; swift **a(2)** taking a comparatively short time **a(3)** *of a suburban train* EXPRESS 3a **a(4)** accomplished quickly **a(5)** quick to learn **b** conducive to rapidity of play or action or quickness of motion <*a ~ pitch*> **c** indicating in advance of what is correct <*the clock was ~*> **d** having or being a high photographic speed <*~ film*> <*~ lens*> **4** *of a colour* permanently dyed; not liable to fade **5a** dissipated, wild <*a very ~ set*> **b** *esp of a woman* FORWARD 3b; *also* promiscuous **6** resistant to change from destructive action, fading, etc – often in combination <*colour*fast> <*acid*-fast *bacteria*> **7** dishonest, shady; *also* acquired by dishonest means or with little effort – infml <*made a ~ buck*>

[2]**fast** *adv* **1** in a firm or fixed manner **2** sound, deeply <*fell ~ asleep*> **3a** in a rapid manner; quickly **b** in quick succession <*orders came in thick and ~*> **4** in a reckless or dissipated manner **5** ahead of a correct time or posted schedule

[3]**fast** *vi* to abstain from some or all foods or meals

[4]**fast** *n* an act or time of fasting

fasten /ˈfahs(ə)n‖ˈfɑːs(ə)n/ *vt* **1** to attach or secure, esp by pinning, tying, or nailing **2** to fix or direct steadily <*~ed his eyes on the awful sight*> **3** to attach, impose *on* <*~ed the blame on me*> *~vi* to become fast or fixed – **fastener** *n* – **fasten on/upon/onto 1** to take a firm grip or hold on **2** to focus attention on

fastening /ˈfahs(ə)ning‖ˈfɑːs(ə)nɪŋ/ *n* a fastener

fastidious /faˈstidi·əs, -dyəs‖fæˈstɪdɪəs, -djəs/ *adj* **1** excessively difficult to satisfy or please **2** showing or demanding great delicacy or care – **fastidiously** *adv*, **fastidiousness** *n*

fastness /ˈfahstnis‖ˈfɑːstnɪs/ *n* **1a** the quality of being fixed **b** colourfast quality **2** a fortified, secure, or remote place

[1]**fat** /fat‖fæt/ *adj* **-tt- 1** having an unusually large amount of fat: **1a** plump **b** obese **c** *of a meat animal* fattened for market **2a** well filled out; thick, big <*a ~ volume of verse*> **b** prosperous, wealthy <*grew ~ on the war – Time*> **3** richly rewarding or profitable; substantial <*a ~ part in a new play*> **4** productive, fertile <*a ~ year for crops*> **5** practically nonexistent <*a ~ chance*> <*a ~ lot of good it did him*> – infml **6** foolish, thick <*get that idea out of your ~ head*> – infml – **fatly** *adv*, **fatness** *n*, **fattish** *adj*

[2]**fat** *n* **1** (animal tissue consisting chiefly of cells distended with) greasy or oily matter **2a** any of numerous compounds of carbon, hydrogen, and oxygen that are a major class of energy-rich food and are soluble in organic solvents (e g ether) but not in water **b** a solid or semisolid fat as distinguished from an oil **3** the best or richest part <*the ~ of the land*> **4** excess <*we must trim the ~ off this budget*>

[3]**fat** *vt* **-tt-** to fatten

fatal /ˈfaytl‖ˈfeɪtl/ *adj* **1** fateful, decisive **2a** of fate **b** like fate in proceeding according to a fixed sequence; inevitable **3a** causing death **b** bringing ruin **c** productive of disagreeable or contrary results – infml <*it's ~ to offer him a drink*>

ˈ**fatalˌism** /-ˌiz(ə)m‖-ˌɪz(ə)m/ *n* the belief that all events are predetermined and outside the control of human beings – **fatalist** *n*, **fatalistic** *adj*, **fatalistically** *adv*

fatality /fəˈtaləti‖fəˈtæləti/ *n* **1** sthg established by fate **2a** the quality or state of causing death or destruction **b** the quality or condition of being destined for disaster **3** FATE 1 **4a** death resulting from a disaster **b** one who experiences or is subject to a fatal outcome

fatally /ˈfaytl·i‖ˈfeɪtlɪ/ *adv* **1** in a fatal manner; *esp* mortally **2** as is or was fatal

ˌ**fat** ˈ**cat** *n, chiefly NAm* a wealthy, privileged, and usu influential person; *esp* one who contributes to a political campaign fund

[1]**fate** /fayt‖feɪt/ *n* **1** the power beyond human control that determines events; destiny **2a** a destiny apparently determined by fate **b** a disaster; *esp* death **3a** an outcome, end; *esp* one that is adverse and inevitable **b** the expected result of normal development <*prospective ~ of embryonic cells*> [Middle French fr Latin *fatum*, lit., what has been spoken, fr *fari* to speak]

[2]**fate** *vt* to destine; *also* to doom – usu pass <*the plan was ~*d *to fail*>

ˈ**fateful** /-f(ə)l‖-f(ə)l/ *adj* **1** having a quality of ominous prophecy <*a ~ remark*> **2a** having momentous and often unpleasant consequences; decisive <*the ~ decision to declare war*> **b** deadly, catastrophic **3** controlled by fate; foreordained – **fatefully** *adv*, **fatefulness** *n*

Fates /fayts‖feɪts/ *n pl* the 3 goddesses of classical mythology who determine the course of human life

ˈ**fatˌhead** *n* a slow-witted or stupid person; a fool – infml – **fatheaded** *adj*, **fatheadedly** *adv*, **fatheadedness** *n*

[1]**father** /ˈfahdhə‖ˈfɑːðə/ *n* **1a** a male parent of a child; *also* SIRE 3 **b** *cap* **b(1)** GOD 1 **b(2)** the first person of the Trinity **2** a forefather **3a** a man who relates to another in a way suggesting the relationship of father and child, esp in receiving filial respect **b** *often cap* **b(1)** an old man – used as a respectful form of address **b(2)** sthg personified as an old man <Father *Time*> **4** *often cap* an early Christian writer accepted by the church as authoritative **5a** sby who originates or institutes <*the ~ of radio*> **b** a source, origin **6** a priest of the regular clergy – used esp as a title in the Roman Catholic church **7** any of the leading men (e g of a city) – usu pl – **fatherhood** *n*, **fatherless** *adj*, **fatherly** *adj*

[2]**father** *vt* **1a** to beget **b** to give rise to; initiate **c** to accept responsibility for **2** to fix the paternity of *on*

ˌ**Father** ˈ**Christmas** *n, Br* an old man with a white beard and red suit believed by children to deliver their presents at Christmas time

ˈ**father-in-ˌlaw** *n, pl* **fathers-in-law** the father of one's spouse

[1]**fathom** /ˈfadh(ə)m‖ˈfæð(ə)m/ *n* a unit of length equal to 6ft (about 1.83m) used esp for measuring the depth of water

[2]**fathom** *vt* **1** to measure by a sounding line **2** to penetrate and come to understand – often + *out* – **fathomable** *adj*

ˈ**fathomless** /-lis‖-lɪs/ *adj* incapable of being fathomed – **fathomlessly** *adv*, **fathomlessness** *n*

[1]**fatigue** /fəˈteeg‖fəˈtiːg/ *n* **1a** physical or nervous exhaustion **b** the temporary loss of power to respond induced in a sensory receptor or motor end organ by continued stimulation **2a** manual or menial military work **b** *pl* the uniform or work clothing worn on fatigue **3** the tendency of a material to break under repeated stress

[2]**fatigue** *vt* **1** to weary, exhaust **2** to induce a condition of fatigue in ~*vi, esp of a metal* to suffer fatigue – **fatigable** *adj*, **fatigability** *n*, **fatiguingly** *adv*

[3]**fatigue** *adj* being part of fatigues <*a ~ cap*>

fatten /ˈfat(ə)n‖ˈfæt(ə)n/ *vt* **1** to make fat, fleshy, or plump; *esp* to feed (e g a stock animal) for slaughter – often + *up* **2** to make fertile ~*vi* to become fat – **fattener** *n*

[1]**fatty** /ˈfati‖ˈfætɪ/ *adj* **1** containing (large amounts of) fat; *also* corpulent **2** GREASY 2 <~ *food*> **3** derived from or chemically related to fat – **fattiness** *n*

[2]**fatty** *n* a fat person or animal – infml

fatuous /ˈfatyoo·əs‖ˈfætjʊəs/ *adj* complacently or inanely foolish; idiotic – **fatuously** *adv*, **fatuousness** *n*, **fatuity** *n*

faucet /ˈfawsit‖ˈfɔːsɪt/ *n, NAm* a tap

[1]**fault** /fawlt‖fɔːlt/ *n* **1a** a failing **b** an imperfection, defect <*a ~ in the computer*> **c** an action, esp a service that does not land in the prescribed area, which loses a rally in tennis, squash, etc **2a** a misdemeanour **b** a mistake **3** responsibility for wrongdoing or failure <*the accident was the driver's ~*> **4** a fracture in the earth's crust accompanied by displacement (e g of the strata) along the fracture line – **faultless** *adj*, **faultlessly** *adv*, **faultlessness** *n*, **faulty** *adj*, **faultily** *adv*, **faultiness** *n* – **at fault** in the wrong; liable for blame

[2]**fault** *vi* **1** to commit a fault; err **2** to produce a geological fault ~ *vt* **1** to find a fault in <*can't ~ his logic*> **2** to produce a geological fault in

ˈ**faultˌfinding** *adj* overinclined to criticize – **faultfinder** *n*, **faultfinding** *n*

fauna /ˈfawnə‖ˈfɔːnə/ *n, pl* **faunas** *also* **faunae** /-ni, -nie‖-nɪ, -naɪ/ the animals or animal life of a region, period, or special environment – **faunal** *adj*, **faunally** *adv*, **faunistic** *adj*

faux pas /ˌfoh ˈpah‖ˌfəʊ ˈpɑː/ *n, pl* **faux pas** /ˌfoh ˈpah(z)‖ˌfəʊ ˈpɑː(z)/ an esp social blunder [French, lit., false step]

[1]**favour**, *NAm chiefly* **favor** /ˈfayvə‖ˈfeɪvə/ *n* **1a(1)** friendly regard shown towards another, esp by a superior **a(2)** approving consideration or attention; approbation <*looked with ~ on our project*> **b** partiality, favouritism **c** popularity **2** (an act of) kindness beyond what is expected or due **3** a token of allegiance or love (e g a ribbon or badge), usu worn conspicuously **4** consent to sexual activities, esp given by a woman – usu pl with sing. meaning; euph <*granted her ~s*> – **in favour of 1** in agreement or sympathy with; on the side of **2** to the advantage of <*John gave up his rights in the house* in favour of *his wife*> **3** in order to choose; out of preference for <*gave up his job* in favour of *travelling*> – **in someone's favour 1** liked or esteemed by sby <*doing extra work to get back* in his boss's favour> **2** to sby's advantage <*the odds were* in his favour> – **out of favour** unpopular, disliked

[2]**favour**, *NAm chiefly* **favor** *vt* **1a** to regard or treat with favour **b** to do a favour or kindness for; oblige – usu + *by* or *with* <~ed *them with a smile*> **2** to show partiality towards; prefer **3a** to give support or confirmation to; sustain <*this evidence* ~s *my theory*> **b** to afford advantages for success to; facilitate <*good weather* ~ed *the outing*> **4** to look like (e g a relation) <*he* ~s *his father*>

favourable /ˈfayv(ə)rəbl‖ˈfeɪv(ə)rəbl/ *adj* **1a** disposed to favour; partial **b** expressing or winning approval; *also* giving a result in one's favour <*a ~ comparison*> **2a** tending to promote; helpful, advantageous <~ *wind*> **b** successful – **favourably** *adv*

ˈ**favoured** *adj* **1** endowed with special advantages or gifts **2** having an appearance or features of a specified kind – usu in combination <*an ill-*favoured *child*> **3** receiving preferential treatment

[1]**favourite** /ˈfayv(ə)rit‖ˈfeɪv(ə)rɪt/ *n* **1** sby or sthg favoured or preferred above others **2** the competitor judged most likely to win

[2]**favourite** *adj* constituting a favourite

favouritism /ˈfayv(ə)riˌtiz(ə)m‖ˈfeɪv(ə)rɪˌtɪz(ə)m/ *n* the showing of unfair favour; partiality

[1]**fawn** /fawn‖fɔːn/ *vi* **1** *esp of a dog* to show affection **2** to court favour by acting in a servilely flattering manner *USE* usu + *on* or *upon* – **fawner** *n*, **fawningly** *adv*

[2]**fawn** *n* **1** a young (unweaned) deer **2** light greyish brown

[1]**fax** /faks/ FACSIMILE (2)

[2]**fax** *vt* to send by facsimile transmission

fay /fay‖feɪ/ *n* a fairy – poetic

faze /fayz‖feɪz/ *vt, chiefly NAm* to disturb the composure of; disconcert, daunt – infml

fealty /ˈfee·əlti‖ˈfiːəltɪ/ *n* **1** fidelity to one's feudal lord **2** allegiance, faithfulness

[1]**fear** /fiə‖fɪə/ *n* **1** (an instance of) an unpleasant often strong emotion caused by anticipation or awareness of (a specified) danger; *also* a state marked by this emotion <*in ~ of their lives*> **2** anxiety, solicitude **3** profound reverence and awe, esp towards God **4** reason for alarm; danger – **fearless** *adj*, **fearlessly** *adv*, **fearlessness** *n* – **for fear of** because of anxiety about; IN CASE OF

[2]**fear** *vt* **1** to have a reverential awe of <~ *God*> **2** to be afraid of; consider or expect with alarm ~*vi* to be afraid or apprehensive – **fearer** *n*

ˈ**fearful** /-f(ə)l‖-f(ə)l/ *adj* **1** causing or likely to cause fear **2a** full of fear <~ *of reprisals*> **b** showing or arising from fear <*a ~ glance*> **c** timid, timorous <*a ~ child*> **3** extremely bad, large, or intense <*a ~ waste*> – infml – **fearfully** *adv*, **fearfulness** *n*

ˈfearsome /-s(ə)m‖-s(ə)m/ *adj* FEARFUL 1, 2c – **fearsomely** *adv*, **fearsomeness** *n*

feasible /ˈfeezəbl‖ˈfiːzəbl/ *adj* **1** capable of being done or carried out <*a ~ plan*> **2** capable of being used or dealt with successfully; suitable <*our ~ sources of energy are limited*> **3** reasonable, likely – **feasibleness** *n*, **feasibly** *adv*, **feasibility** *n*

[1]feast /feest‖fiːst/ *n* **1a** an elaborate often public meal, sometimes accompanied by a ceremony or entertainment; a banquet **b** sthg that gives abundant pleasure <*a ~ for the eyes*> **2** a periodic religious observance commemorating an event or honouring a deity, person, or thing

[2]feast *vi* to have or take part in a feast ~ *vt* **1** to give a feast for **2** to delight, gratify <~ *your eyes on her beauty*> – **feaster** *n*

feat /feet‖fiːt/ *n* **1** a notable and esp courageous act **2** an act or product of skill, endurance, or ingenuity

[1]feather /ˈfedhə‖ˈfeðə/ *n* **1** any of the light horny outgrowths that form the external covering of a bird's body and consist of a shaft that bears 2 sets of barbs that interlock to form a continuous vane **2** plumage **3** the act of feathering an oar – **feathered** *adj*, **feathery** *adj* – **a feather in one's cap** a deserved honour or mark of distinction in which one can take pride

[2]feather *vt* **1a** to fit (e g an arrow) with feathers **b** to cover, clothe, or adorn with feathers **2a** to turn (an oar blade) almost horizontal when lifting from the water **b** to change the angle at which (a propeller blade) meets the air so as to have the minimum wind resistance; *also* to feather the propeller blades attached to (a propeller or engine) – **feather one's nest** to provide for oneself, esp dishonestly, through a job in which one is trusted

featherbed /ˌ--ˈ-, ˈ--ˌ-/ *vt* **-dd- 1** to cushion or protect from hardship, worry, etc; to pamper **2** to assist (e g an industry) with government subsidies

ˌfeather ˈbed *n* (a bed with) a feather mattress

ˈfeatherˌbrain /-ˌbrayn‖-ˌbreɪn/ *n* a foolish scatterbrained person – **featherbrained** *adj*

ˈfeatherˌweight /-ˌwayt‖-ˌweɪt/ *n* **1** a boxer who weighs not more than 9st (57.2kg) if professional or more than 54kg (about 8st 7lb) but not more than 57kg (about 8st 13lb) if amateur **2** sby or sthg of limited importance or effectiveness

[1]feature /ˈfeechə‖ˈfiːtʃə/ *n* **1a** the make-up or appearance of the face or its parts <*gentle of ~*> **b** a part of the face <*her nose was not her best ~*>; *also, pl* the face <*an embarrassed look on his ~s*> **2** a prominent or distinctive part or characteristic **3a** a full-length film; *esp* the main film on a cinema programme **b** a distinctive article, story, or special section in a newspaper or magazine **c** *Br* a radio documentary – **featureless** *adj*

[2]feature *vt* **1** to give special prominence to (e g in a performance or newspaper) **2** to have as a characteristic or feature ~ *vi* to play an important part; be a feature – usu + *in*

febrile /ˈfeebriel‖ˈfiːbraɪl/ *adj* of fever; feverish

February /ˈfebrooəri, -ˌeri‖ˈfebrʊərɪ, -ˌerɪ/ *n* the 2nd month of the Gregorian calendar [Latin *Februarius*, fr *Februa*, pl, an annual feast of purification held on 15 February]

feces /ˈfeeseez‖ˈfiːsiːz/ *n pl, NAm* faeces – **fecal** *adj*

feckless /ˈfeklis‖ˈfeklɪs/ *adj* **1** ineffectual, weak **2** worthless, irresponsible – **fecklessly** *adv*, **fecklessness** *n*

fecund /ˈfeekənd, ˈfekənd‖ˈfiːkənd, ˈfekənd/ *adj* **1** fruitful in offspring or vegetation; prolific **2** very intellectually productive or inventive to a marked degree ***USE*** fml – **fecundity** *n*

[1]fed *past of* FEED

[2]fed /fed‖fed/ *n, often cap, NAm* a federal agent or officer – infml

federal /ˈfed(ə)rəl‖ˈfed(ə)rəl/ *adj* **1a** formed by agreement between political units that surrender their individual sovereignty to a central authority but retain limited powers of government; *also* of or constituting a government so formed **b** of the central government of a federation as distinguished from those of the constituent units **2** of or loyal to the federal government of the USA in the American Civil War – **federally** *adv*

Federal *n* a supporter or soldier of the North in the American Civil War

federalism /ˈfedrəliz(ə)m‖ˈfedrəlɪz(ə)m/ *n, often cap* (advocacy of) the federal principle – **federalist** *n*

federate /ˈfedərayt‖ˈfedəreɪt/ *vt* to join in a federation – **federative** *adj*

federation /ˌfedəˈraysh(ə)n‖ˌfedəˈreɪʃ(ə)n/ *n* **1** federating; *esp* the formation of a federal union **2** sthg formed by federating: e g **2a** a country formed by the federation of separate states **b** a union of organizations

ˌfed ˈup *adj* discontented, bored – infml

fee /fee‖fiː/ *n* **1a** an estate in land held in feudal law from a lord **b** an inherited or heritable estate in land **2a(1)** a sum of money paid esp for entrance or for a professional service – often pl with sing. meaning **a(2)** money paid for education – usu pl with sing. meaning **b** a gratuity – **in fee** in absolute and legal possession

feeble /ˈfeebl‖ˈfiːbl/ *adj* **1** lacking in strength or endurance; weak **2** deficient in authority, force, or effect [Old French *feble*, fr Latin *flebilis* lamentable, wretched, fr *flēre* to weep] – **feebleness** *n*, **feeblish** *adj*, **feebly** *adv*

ˌfeebleˈminded /-ˈmiendid‖-ˈmaɪndɪd/ *adj* **1** mentally deficient **2** foolish, stupid – **feeblemindedly** *adv*, **feeblemindedness** *n*

[1]feed /feed‖fiːd/ *vb* **fed** /fed‖fed/ *vt* **1a** to give food to **b** to give as food **2** to provide sthg essential to the growth, sustenance, maintenance, or operation of **3** to produce or provide food for **4a** to satisfy, gratify **b** to support, encourage **5a(1)** to supply for use, consumption, or processing, esp in a continuous manner <fed *the tape into the machine*> **a(2)** to supply material to (e g a machine), esp in a continuous manner **b** to supply (a signal or power) to an electronic circuit ~ *vi* **1a** to consume food; eat **b** to prey **2** to become nourished or satisfied as if by food **3**

to be moved into a machine or opening for use, processing, or storage <*the grain* fed *into the silo*> *USE* (*vi 1*) usu + *off, on,* or *upon*

[2]**feed** *n* **1** an act of eating **2a** (a mixture or preparation of) food for livestock **b** the amount given at each feeding **3a** material supplied (e g to a furnace) **b** a mechanism by which the action of feeding is effected **4** one who supplies cues for another esp comic performer's lines or actions **5** an esp large meal – infml

ˈfeedˌback /-ˌbak‖-ˌbæk/ *n* **1** the return to the input of a part of the output of a machine, system, or process **2** (the return to a source of) information about the results of an action or process, usu in response to a request

feeder /ˈfeedə‖ˈfiːdə/ *n* **1** a device or apparatus for supplying food (e g to a caged animal) **2a** a device feeding material into or through a machine **b** a heavy wire conductor supplying electricity to a point of an electric distribution system **c** a transmission line running from a radio transmitter to an antenna **d** a road, railway, airline, or aircraft that links remote areas with the main transport system **3** an animal being fattened or suitable for fattening

ˈfeeding ˌbottle *n* a bottle with a teat, designed to hold milk and used for feeding babies

feed up *vt* to fatten by plentiful feeding

[1]**feel** /feel‖fiːl/ *vb* **felt** /felt‖felt/ *vt* **1a** to handle or touch in order to examine or explore **b** to perceive by a physical sensation coming from discrete end organs (e g of the skin or muscles) <~ *a draught*> **2** to experience actively or passively; be affected by <*he shall* ~ *my wrath*> **3** to ascertain or explore by cautious trial <~ing *their way*> – often + *out* <felt *out the opposition*> **4a** to be aware of by instinct or by drawing conclusions from the evidence available <felt *the presence of a stranger in the room*> **b** to believe, think <*is generally* felt *that such action is inadvisable*> ~ *vi* **1a** to (be able) to receive the sensation of touch **b** to search for sthg by using the sense of touch **2a** to be conscious of an inward impression, state of mind, or physical condition <~s *much better now*> **b** to believe oneself to be <*I did* ~ *a fool*> **3** to have sympathy or pity <*really* ~s *for the underprivileged*> – **feel like 1** to resemble or seem to be on the evidence of touch <*it* feels like *velvet*> **2** to wish for; be in the mood for <*do you* feel like *a drink?*>

[2]**feel** *n* **1** the sense of feeling; touch **2** sensation, feeling **3a** the quality of a thing as imparted through touch <*the material had a velvety* ~> **b** typical or peculiar quality or atmosphere <*the* ~ *of an old country pub*> **4** intuitive skill, knowledge, or ability – usu + *for* <*a* ~ *for words*>

feeler /ˈfeelə‖ˈfiːlə/ *n* **1** a tactile appendage (e g a tentacle) of an animal **2** sthg (e g a proposal) ventured to ascertain the views of others

[1]**feeling** /ˈfeeling‖ˈfiːlɪŋ/ *n* **1** (a sensation experienced through) the one of the 5 basic physical senses by which stimuli, esp to the skin and mucous membranes, are interpreted by the brain as touch, pressure, and temperature **2a** an emotional state or reaction <*a* ~ *of loneliness*> **b** *pl* susceptibility to impression; sensibility <*the remark hurt her* ~s> **3** a conscious recognition; a sense <*the harsh sentence left him with a* ~ *of injustice*> **4a** an opinion or belief, esp when unreasoned; a sentiment <*what are your* ~s *on the matter?*> **b** a presentiment <*I've a* ~ *he won't come*> **5** capacity to respond emotionally, esp with the higher emotions <*a man of noble* ~> **6** FEEL 3, 4 **7** the quality of a work of art that embodies and conveys the emotion of the artist

[2]**feeling** *adj* **1a** having the capacity to feel or respond emotionally; sensitive **b** easily moved emotionally; sympathetic **2** expressing emotion or sensitivity – **feelingly** *adv*

feet /feet‖fiːt/ *pl of* [1]FOOT

feign /fayn‖feɪn/ *vt* to give a false appearance or impression of deliberately; *also* to pretend ~*vi* to pretend, dissemble – **feigner** *n*

[1]**feint** /faynt‖feɪnt/ *n* sthg feigned; *specif* a mock blow or attack directed away from the point one really intends to attack

[2]**feint** *vi* to make a feint ~*vt* to make a pretence of

[3]**feint** *adj, of rulings on paper* faint, pale

feldspar /ˈfel(d)spah‖ˈfel(d)spɑː/, **felspar** /ˈfelspah‖ˈfelspɑː/ *n* any of a group of minerals that consist of aluminium silicates with either potassium, sodium, calcium, or barium, and are an essential constituent of nearly all crystalline rocks

felicitate /fəˈlisitayt‖fəˈlɪsɪteɪt/ *vt* to offer congratulations or compliments to – usu + *on* or *upon*; fml – **felicitator** *n*, **felicitation** *n*

felicitous /fəˈlisitəs‖fəˈlɪsɪtəs/ *adj* **1** very well suited or expressed; apt <*a* ~ *remark*>; *also* marked by or given to such expression <*a* ~ *speaker*> **2** pleasant, delightful *USE* fml – **felicitously** *adv*, **felicitousness** *n*

felicity /fəˈlisiti‖fəˈlɪsɪtɪ/ *n* **1** (sthg causing) great happiness **2** a felicitous faculty or quality, esp in art or language; aptness **3** a felicitous expression *USE* fml

feline /ˈfeelien‖ˈfiːlaɪn/ *adj* **1** of cats or the cat family **2** resembling a cat; having the characteristics generally attributed to cats, esp grace, stealth, or slyness – **feline** *n*, **felinely** *adv*, **felinity** *n*

[1]**fell** /fel‖fel/ *vt* **1** to cut, beat, or knock down <~ing *trees*> **2** to kill – **fellable** *adj*, **feller** *n*

[2]**fell** *past of* FALL

[3]**fell** *n* a steep rugged stretch of high moorland, esp in northern England and Scotland – often pl with sing. meaning

[4]**fell** *adj* **1** fierce, cruel **2** very destructive; deadly *USE* poetic – **fellness** *n*, **felly** *adv* – **at one fell swoop** all at once; *also* with a single concentrated effort

fellah /ˈfelə‖ˈfelə/ *n, pl* **fellahin, fellaheen** /-ˈheen‖-ˈhiːn/ a peasant or agricultural labourer in an Arab country

fellatio /fəˈlayshioh‖fəˈleɪʃɪəʊ/ *n* oral stimulation of the penis – **fellate** *vt*, **fellation** *n*, **fellator** *n*

[1]**fellow** /ˈfeloh‖ˈfeləʊ/ *n* **1** a comrade, associate – usu pl **2a** an equal in rank, power, or character; a peer **b** either of a pair; a mate **3** a member of an incorporated literary or scientific society **4** a man; *also* a boy **5** an incorporated member of a collegiate foundation **6** a person appointed to a salaried position allowing for advanced research **7** a boyfriend – infml

[2]fellow *adj* being a companion or associate; belonging to the same group – used before a noun <~ *traveller*>

fellow feeling *n* a feeling of community of interest or of mutual understanding; *specif* sympathy

fellowship /-ship‖-ʃɪp/ *n* **1** the condition of friendly relations between people; companionship **2a** community of interest, activity, feeling, or experience **b** the state of being a fellow or associate **3** *sing or pl in constr* a group of people with similar interests; an association **4a** the position of a fellow (e g of a university) **b** (a foundation for the provision of) the salary of a fellow

fellow traveller *n* a nonmember who sympathizes with and often furthers the ideals and programme of an organized group, esp the Communist party – chiefly derog

felon /ˈfelən‖ˈfelən/ *n* **1** sby who has committed a felony **2** a whitlow

felony /ˈfeləni‖ˈfelənɪ/ *n* a grave crime (e g murder or arson) that was formerly regarded in law as more serious than a misdemeanour and involved forfeiture of property in addition to any other punishment – **felonious** *adj*, **feloniously** *adv*

felspar /ˈfel,spah‖ˈfel,spɑː/ *n* feldspar

[1]felt /felt‖felt/ *n* **1** a nonwoven cloth made by compressing wool or fur often mixed with natural or synthetic fibres **2** an article made of felt **3** a material resembling felt

[2]felt *vt* **1** to make into or cover with felt **2** to cause to stick and mat together

[3]felt *past of* FEEL

[1]female /ˈfeemayl‖ˈfiːmeɪl/ *n* **1** an individual that bears young or produces eggs; *esp* a woman or girl as distinguished from a man or boy **2** a plant or flower with an ovary but no stamens

[2]female *adj* **1** of or being a female **2** designed with a hole or hollow into which a corresponding male part fits <*a* ~ *plug*> – **femaleness** *n*

[1]feminine /ˈfemənin‖ˈfemənɪn/ *adj* **1** of or being a female person **2** characteristic of, appropriate to, or peculiar to women; womanly **3** of or belonging to the gender that normally includes most words or grammatical forms referring to females **4a** having or occurring in an extra unstressed final syllable <~ *rhyme*> **b** having the final chord occurring on a weak beat – **femininely** *adv*, **feminineness** *n*, **femininity** *n*

[2]feminine *n* **1** the feminine principle in human nature – esp in *eternal feminine* **2** (a word or morpheme of) the feminine gender

feminism /ˈfeminiz(ə)m‖ˈfemɪnɪz(ə)m/ *n* the advocacy or furtherance of women's rights, interests, and equality with men in political, economic, and social spheres – **feminist** *n or adj*, **feministic** *adj*

femme fatale /,fam faˈtahl ‖,fæm fæˈtɑːl (*Fr* fam fatal)/ *n, pl* **femmes fatales** /fatahl(z) ‖ fætɑːl(z) (*Fr* ~)/ a seductive and usu mysterious woman; *esp* one who lures men into dangerous or compromising situations [French, lit., fatal woman]

femur /ˈfeemə‖ˈfiːmə/ *n, pl* **femurs, femora** /ˈfemərə‖ˈfemərə/ **1** the bone of the hind or lower limb nearest the body; the thighbone **2** the third segment of an insect's leg counting from the base – **femoral** *adj*

fen /fen‖fen/ *n* an area of low wet or flooded land

[1]fence /fens‖fens/ *n* **1** a barrier (e g of wire or boards) intended to prevent escape or intrusion or to mark a boundary <*a garden* ~> **2a** a receiver of stolen goods **b** a place where stolen goods are bought – **fenceless** *adj* – **on the fence** in a position of neutrality or indecision

[2]fence *vt* **1a** to enclose with a fence – usu + *in* **b** to separate *off* or keep *out* (as if) with a fence **2** to provide a defence for; shield, protect **3** to receive or sell (stolen goods) ~ *vi* **1a** to practise fencing **b(1)** to use tactics of attack and defence (e g thrusting and parrying) resembling those of fencing **b(2)** *of a batsman* to play at and miss the ball in cricket, esp outside the off stump – usu + *at* **2** to deal in stolen goods – **fencer** *n*

fencing /ˈfensing‖ˈfensɪŋ/ *n* **1** the art of attack and defence with a sword (e g the foil, épée, or sabre) **2** (material used for building) fences

fend /fend‖fend/ *vi* – **fend for** to provide a livelihood for; support

fender /ˈfendə‖ˈfendə/ *n* a device that protects: e g **a** a cushion (e g of rope or wood) hung over the side of a ship to absorb impact **b** a low metal guard for a fire used to confine the coals **c** *NAm* a wing or mudguard

fend off *vt* to keep or ward off; repel

fennel /ˈfenl‖ˈfenl/ *n* a European plant of the carrot family cultivated for its aromatic seeds and foliage

feral /ˈfiərəl‖ˈfɪərəl/ *adj* **1** (suggestive) of a wild beast; savage **2a** not domesticated or cultivated; WILD 1a **b** having escaped from domestication and become wild <~ *pigeons*>

[1]ferment /fəˈment‖fəˈment/ *vb* **1** to (cause to) undergo fermentation **2** to (cause to) be in a state of agitation or intense activity – **fermentable** *adj*, **fermenter** *n*

[2]ferment /ˈfuhment‖ˈfɜːment/ *n* **1** an agent (e g an enzyme or organism) capable of bringing about fermentation **2a** FERMENTATION 1 **b** a state of unrest or upheaval; agitation, tumult

fermentation /,fuhmenˈtaysh(ə)n‖,fɜːmen-ˈteɪʃ(ə)n/ *n* **1a** a chemical change with effervescence **b** an enzymatically controlled anaerobic breakdown of an energy-rich compound (e g a carbohydrate to carbon dioxide and alcohol); *broadly* an enzymatically controlled transformation of an organic compound **2** FERMENT 2b – **fermentative** *adj*

fermion /ˈfuhmyən, ˈfeə-, -mi·ən‖ˈfɜːmjən, ˈfeə-, -mɪən/ *n* a particle (e g an electron) that interacts with other particles in a way described by Fermi and Dirac – **fermionic** *adj*

fern /fuhn‖fɜːn/ *n* any of a class of flowerless seedless lower plants; *esp* any of an order resembling flowering plants in having a root, stem, and leaflike fronds but differing in reproducing by spores – **fernlike** *adj*, **ferny** *adj*

ferocious /fəˈrohshəs‖fəˈrəʊʃəs/ *adj* extremely fierce or violent – **ferociously** *adv*, **ferociousness** *n*

ferocity /fəˈrosəti‖fəˈrɒsətɪ/ *n* the quality or state of being ferocious

¹ferret /ˈferit‖ˈferɪt/ *n* **1** a partially domesticated usu albino European polecat used esp for hunting small rodents (e g rats) **2** an active and persistent searcher [Middle French *furet*, deriv of Latin *fur* thief] – **ferrety** *adj*

²ferret *vi* **1** to hunt with ferrets **2** to search *about* or *around* – infml ~ *vt* **1** to hunt (e g rats) with ferrets **2** to drive (game), esp from covert or burrows – **ferreter** *n*

ferret out *vt* to find and bring to light by searching <ferret out *the answers*> – infml

ferric /ˈferik‖ˈferɪk/ *adj* of, containing, or being (trivalent) iron

ferro- /feroh-‖ferəʊ-/ *comb form* **1** (containing) iron <ferro*concrete*>; iron and <fero*nickel*> – chiefly in names of alloys **2** ferrous iron <ferro*cyanide*>

ˌferromagˈnetic /-magˈnetik‖-mægˈnetɪk/ *adj* of or being a substance, esp iron, characterized by strong magnetization in which all the magnetic ions are polarized in the same direction – **ferromagnetic** *n*, **ferromagnetism** *n*

ferrous /ˈferəs‖ˈferəs/ *adj* of, containing, or being (bivalent) iron

ferrule /ˈferoohl, -rəl‖ˈferuːl, -rəl/ *n* **1** a ring or cap, usu of metal, strengthening a cane, tool handle, etc **2** a short tube or bush for making a tight joint (e g between pipes)

¹ferry /ˈferi‖ˈferɪ/ *vt* **1** to carry by boat over a body of water **2** to convey (e g by car) from one place to another ~*vi* to cross water in a boat

²ferry *n* (a boat used at) a place where people or things are carried across a body of water (e g a river)

fertile /ˈfuhtiel‖ˈfɜːtaɪl/ *adj* **1a** (capable of) producing or bearing fruit (in great quantities); productive **b** characterized by great resourcefulness and activity; inventive <*a* ~ *imagination*> **2a(1)** capable of sustaining abundant plant growth <~ *soil*> **a(2)** affording abundant possibilities for development <*a* ~ *area for research*> **b** capable of growing or developing <~ *egg*> **c** capable of breeding or reproducing **3** capable of being converted into fissile material – **fertilely** *adv*, **fertileness** *n*, **fertility** *n*

fertil·ize, -ise /ˈfuhtiliez‖ˈfɜːtɪlaɪz/ *vt* to make fertile: e g **a(1)** to inseminate, impregnate, or pollinate **a(2)** to make (an ovule, egg, etc) capable of developing into a new individual by uniting with a male germ cell **b** to apply a fertilizer to <~ *land*> – **fertilizable** *adj*, **fertilization** *n*, **fertilizational** *adj*,

ˈfertil·izer, -iser /-zə‖-zə/ *n* a substance (e g manure) used to make soil more fertile

ferule /ˈferoohl‖ˈferuːl/ *n* a flat ruler used to punish children

fervent /ˈfuhv(ə)nt‖ˈfɜːv(ə)nt/ *adj* exhibiting deep sincere emotion; ardent – **fervently** *adv*

fervid /ˈfuhvid‖ˈfɜːvɪd/ *adj* passionately intense; ardent – **fervidly** *adv*, **fervidness** *n*

fervour, *NAm chiefly* **fervor** /ˈfuhvə‖ˈfɜːvə/ *n* the quality or state of being fervent or fervid

festal /ˈfestl‖ˈfestl/ *adj* festive – **festally** *adv*

fester /ˈfestə‖ˈfestə/ *vi* **1** to generate pus **2** to putrefy, rot **3** to rankle ~*vt* to make inflamed or corrupt

¹festival /ˈfestivl‖ˈfestɪvl/ *adj* of, appropriate to, or set apart as a festival

²festival *n* **1a** a time marked by special (e g customary) celebration **b** FEAST 2 **2** a usu periodic programme or season of cultural events or entertainment <*the Edinburgh* ~> **3** gaiety, conviviality

festive /ˈfestiv‖ˈfestɪv/ *adj* **1** of or suitable for a feast or festival **2** joyous, gay – **festively** *adv*, **festiveness** *n*

festivity /feˈstivəti‖feˈstɪvətɪ/ *n* **1** FESTIVAL 1 **2** festive activity – often pl with sing. meaning

¹festoon /feˈstoohn‖feˈstuːn/ *n* a decorative chain or strip hanging between 2 points; *also* a carved, moulded, or painted ornament representing this

²festoon *vt* **1** to hang or form festoons on **2** to cover profusely and usu gaily

fetal /ˈfeetl‖ˈfiːtl/ *adj* foetal

fetch /fech‖fetʃ/ *vt* **1** to go or come after and bring or take back **2a** to cause to come; bring **b** to produce as profit or return; realize **3** to reach by sailing, esp against the wind or tide and without having to tack **4** to strike or deal (a blow, slap, etc) <~ed *him one in the face*> – infml ~ *vi* **1** to go after sthg and bring it back **2** to take a roundabout way **3** to hold course on a body of water – **fetcher** *n*

fetching /ˈfeching‖ˈfetʃɪŋ/ *adj* attractive, becoming – **fetchingly** *adv*

fetch up *vt* **1** to bring up or out; produce **2** to bring to a stop **3** to vomit ~*vi* to come to a specified standstill, stopping place, or result; arrive *USE* infml

¹fete, fête /fayt, fet‖feɪt, fet/ *n* **1** a festival **2** *Br* a usu outdoor bazaar or other entertainment held esp to raise money for a particular purpose

²fete, fête *vt* to honour or commemorate (sby or sthg) with a fete or other ceremony

fetid, foetid /ˈfeetid‖ˈfiːtɪd/ *adj* having a heavy offensive smell; stinking – **fetidly** *adv*, **fetidness** *n*

fetish *also* **fetich** /ˈfetish‖ˈfetɪʃ/ *n* **1** an object believed among a primitive people to have magical power; *broadly* a material object regarded with superstitious trust or reverence **2** an object of irrational reverence or obsessive devotion **3** an object or bodily part whose presence in reality or fantasy is psychologically necessary for sexual gratification

fetishism *also* **fetichism** /ˈfetishiz(ə)m‖ˈfetɪʃɪz(ə)m/ *n* **1** belief in magical fetishes **2** the displacement of erotic interest and satisfaction to a fetish – **fetishist** *n*, **fetishistic** *adj*

fetlock /ˈfetˌlok‖ˈfetˌlɒk/ *n* **1** a projection bearing a tuft of hair on the back of the leg above the hoof of an animal of the horse family **2** the joint of the limb or tuft of hair at the fetlock

¹fetter /ˈfetə‖ˈfetə/ *n* **1** a shackle for the feet **2** sthg that confines; a restraint – usu pl with sing. meaning

²fetter *vt* **1** to put fetters on **2** to bind (as if) with fetters; shackle, restrain

fettle /ˈfetl‖ˈfetl/ *n* a state of physical or mental fitness or order; condition <*in fine* ~>

fetus /ˈfeetəs‖ˈfiːtəs/ *n* a foetus

feud /fyoohd‖fjuːd/ *n* a lasting state of hostilities, esp between families or clans – **feud** *vi*

feudal /ˈfyoohdl‖ˈfjuːdl/ *adj* of feudalism or a medieval fee; *also* suggestive of feudalism (e g in servility) – **feudally** *adv*, **feudalize** *vt*, **feudalization** *n*

ˈfeudalˌism /-ˌiz(ə)m‖-ˌɪz(ə)m/ *n* a medieval system of political organization involving the relationship of lord to vassal with all land held in fee, homage, the service of tenants under arms and in court, wardship, and forfeiture – **feudalist** *n*, **feudalistic** *adj*

feudatory /ˈfyoohdət(ə)ri‖ˈfju:dət(ə)rɪ/ *adj* **1** owing feudal allegiance **2** under a foreign overlord

fever /ˈfeevə‖ˈfi:və/ *n* **1** (any of various diseases characterized by) a rise of body temperature above the normal **2a** a state of intense emotion or activity **b** a contagious usu transient enthusiasm; a craze

feverish /ˈfeevərish‖ˈfi:vərɪʃ/ *also* **feverous** /-rəs‖-rəs/ *adj* **1a** having the symptoms of a fever **b** indicating, relating to, or caused by (a) fever **c** tending to cause or infect with fever **2** marked by intense emotion, activity, or instability – **feverishly** *adv*, **feverishness** *n*, **feverously** *adv*

ˈfever ˌpitch *n* a state of intense excitement and agitation

[1]few /fyooh‖fju:/ *adj* **1** amounting to only a small number <*one of his* ~ *pleasures*> **2** at least some though not many – + *a* <*a good* ~ *drinks*> – **fewness** *n*

[2]few *n pl in constr* **1** not many <~ *were present*> **2** at least some though not many – + *a* <*a* ~ *of them*> **3** a select or exclusive group of people; an elite <*the* ~>

fey /fay‖feɪ/ *adj* **1a** able to see into the future **b** marked by an otherworldly and irresponsible air **2** *chiefly Scot* **2a** fated to die; doomed **b** marked by an excited or elated state – **feyness** *n*

fez /fez‖fez/ *n, pl* **-zz-** *also* **-z-** a brimless hat shaped like a truncated cone, usu red and with a tassel, which is worn by men in southern and eastern Mediterranean countries [*Fez*, city in Morocco]

fiancé, *fem* **fiancée** /fiˈonsay‖fɪˈɒnseɪ/ *n* sby engaged to be married [French, fr Middle French, fr *fiancer* to promise, betroth, deriv of Latin *fidere* to trust]

fiasco /fiˈaskoh‖fɪˈæskəʊ/ *n, pl* **fiascoes** a complete and ignominious failure

fiat /ˈfie·ət, -at‖ˈfaɪət, -æt/ *n* an authoritative and often arbitrary order; a decree <*government by* ~>

fib /fib‖fɪb/ *vi or n* **-bb-** (to tell) a trivial or childish lie – infml – **fibber** *n*

fibre, *NAm chiefly* **fiber** /ˈfiebə‖ˈfaɪbə/ *n* **1a** an elongated tapering supportive thick-walled plant cell **b(1)** NERVE 2 **b(2)** any of the filaments composing most of the intercellular matrix of connective tissue **b(3)** any of the elongated contractile cells of muscle tissue **c** a slender natural or man-made thread or filament (e g of wool, cotton, or asbestos) **2** material made of fibres **3** essential structure or character <*the very* ~ *of his being*>; *also* strength, fortitude <*a man of great moral* ~>

ˈfibreˌboard /-ˌbawd‖-ˌbɔ:d/ *n* a material made by compressing fibres (e g of wood) into stiff boards

ˈfibreˌglass /-ˌglahs‖-ˌglɑ:s/ *n* **1** glass in fibrous form used in making various products (e g textiles and insulation materials) **2** a combination of synthetic resins and fibreglass

ˌfibre ˈoptics *n pl* the use of very thin glass or plastic fibres that transmit light throughout their length by internal reflection, as a means of seeing what is hidden (e g in surgery) or conveying signals (e g telephone messages)

fibrositis /ˌfiebrəˈsietəs‖ˌfaɪbrəˈsaɪtəs/ *n* a painful muscular condition prob resulting from inflammation of fibrous tissue (e g muscle sheaths)

fibrous /ˈfiebrəs‖ˈfaɪbrəs/ *adj* **1** containing, consisting of, or resembling fibres **2** tough, stringy – **fibrously** *adv*, **fibrousness** *n*

fibula /ˈfibyoolə‖ˈfɪbjʊlə/ *n, pl* **fibulae** /-li‖-lɪ/, **fibulas** **1** an ornamented clasp used esp by the ancient Greeks and Romans **2** the (smaller) outer of the 2 bones between the knee and ankle – **fibular** *adj*

fickle /ˈfikl‖ˈfɪkl/ *adj* inconstant, capricious – **fickleness** *n*

fiction /ˈfiksh(ə)n‖ˈfɪkʃ(ə)n/ *n* **1a** sthg invented by the imagination; *specif* an invented story **b** literature (e g novels or short stories) describing imaginary people and events **2** an assumption of a possibility as a fact, irrespective of the question of its truth <*a legal* ~> – **fictional** *adj*, **fictionally** *adv*, **fictionality** *n*, **fictionalize** *vt*, **fictionalization** *n*

fictitious /fikˈtishəs‖fɪkˈtɪʃəs/ *adj* **1** (characteristic) of fiction **2** *of a name* false, assumed **3** not genuinely felt; feigned – **fictitiously** *adv*, **fictitiousness** *n*

[1]fiddle /ˈfidl‖ˈfɪdl/ *n* **1** a violin **2** a device to keep objects from sliding off a table on board ship **3** *Br* a dishonest practice; a swindle – infml **4** *Br* an activity involving intricate manipulation – infml

[2]fiddle *vi* **1** to play on a fiddle **2a** to move the hands or fingers restlessly **b** to spend time in aimless or fruitless activity – often + *about* or *around* ~ *vt* **1** *Br* to falsify (e g accounts), esp so as to gain financial advantage **2** *Br* to get or contrive by cheating or deception *USE* (*vi 2 &vt*) infml – **fiddler** *n*

ˈfiddle-ˌfaddle /ˌfadl‖ˌfædl/ *n* nonsense – often used as an interjection; infml

fiddlesticks /ˈfidlˌstiks‖ˈfɪdlˌstɪks/ *n pl* nonsense – used as an interjection; infml

fiddling /ˈfidling‖ˈfɪdlɪŋ/ *adj* trifling, petty <*made some* ~ *excuse*>

fidelity /fiˈdeləti‖fɪˈdelətɪ/ *n* **1a** the quality or state of being faithful; loyalty **b** accuracy in details; exactness **2** the degree of similarity between some reproduced (e g recorded) material and its original source

[1]fidget /ˈfijit‖ˈfɪdʒɪt/ *n* **1** uneasiness or restlessness shown by nervous movements – usu pl with sing. meaning **2** sby who fidgets *USE* infml

[2]fidget *vb* to (cause to) move or act restlessly or nervously – **fidgety** *adj*

fief /feef‖fi:f/ *n* **1** a feudal estate **2** sthg over which one has rights or exercises control <*a politician's* ~> – **fiefdom** *n*

[1]field /feeld‖fi:ld/ *n* **1a** an (enclosed) area of

land free of woods and buildings (used for cultivation or pasture) **b** an area of land containing a natural resource <*coal* ~> **c** (the place where) a battle is fought; *also* a battle **d** a large unbroken expanse (e g of ice) **2a** an area or division of an activity <*a lawyer eminent in his* ~> **b** the sphere of practical operation outside a place of work (e g a laboratory) <*geologists working in the* ~> **c** an area in which troops are operating (e g in an exercise or theatre of war) **d(1)** an area constructed, equipped, or marked for sports **d(2)** the part of a sports area enclosed by the running track and used for athletic field events **3** a space on which sthg is drawn or projected; *esp* the surface, esp a shield, on which a coat of arms is displayed **4** the participants in a sports activity, esp with the exception of the favourite or winner **5** a region or space in which a given effect (e g magnetism) exists **6** *also* **field of view** the area visible through the lens of an optical instrument

[2]**field** *vt* **1a** to stop and pick up (a batted ball) **b** to deal with by giving an impromptu answer <*the Minister* ~ed *the reporters' questions*> **2** to put into the field of play or battle <~ *a team*> ~*vi* to play as a fielder in cricket, baseball, etc

ˈfield ˌday *n* **1a** a day for military exercises or manoeuvres **b** an outdoor meeting or social gathering **2** a time of unusual pleasure and unrestrained action <*the newspaper had a* ~ *with the scandal*>

fielder /ˈfeeldə||ˈfiːldə/ *n* any of the players whose job is to field the ball (e g in cricket)

ˈfield ˌevent *n* an athletic event (e g discus, javelin, or jumping) other than a race

ˈfield ˌglasses *n pl* an optical instrument usu consisting of 2 telescopes on a single frame with a focussing device

ˈfield ˌhockey *n, chiefly NAm* HOCKEY 1

field marshal *n* an officer holding the highest rank in the British army

ˈfield ˌmouse *n* any of various mice or voles that inhabit fields

ˈfield ˌofficer *n* a commissioned army officer of the rank of colonel, lieutenant colonel, or major

ˈfieldˌwork /-ˌwuhk||-ˌwɜːk/ *n* **1** a temporary fortification in the field **2** work done in the field (e g by students) to gain practical experience through firsthand observation **3** the gathering of data in anthropology, sociology, etc through the observation or interviewing of subjects in the field – **field-worker** *n*

fiend /feend||fiːnd/ *n* **1a** DEVIL 1 **b** a demon **c** a person of great wickedness or cruelty **2** sby excessively devoted to a specified activity or thing; a fanatic, devotee <*a golf* ~> **3** one who uses immoderate quantities of sthg (specified); an addict <*a dope* ~> **4** sby remarkably clever at a specified activity; WIZARD 2 <*a* ~ *at arithmetic*> *USE* (*2 & 4*) infml

fiendish /ˈfeendish||ˈfiːndɪʃ/ *adj* **1** perversely diabolical **2** extremely cruel or wicked **3** excessively bad, unpleasant, or difficult – **fiendishly** *adv*, **fiendishness** *n*

fierce /fiəs||fɪəs/ *adj* **1** violently hostile or aggressive; combative, pugnacious **2a** lacking restraint or control; violent, heated <*a* ~ *argument*> **b** extremely intense or severe <~ *pain*> **3** furiously active or determined <*make a* ~ *effort*> **4** wild or menacing in appearance – **fiercely** *adv*, **fierceness** *n*

fiery /ˈfie·əri||ˈfaɪərɪ/ *adj* **1a** consisting of fire **b** burning, blazing <~ *cross*> **c** liable to catch fire or explode **2** very hot <*a* ~ *chilli sauce*> **3** of the colour of fire; *esp* red **4a** full of or exuding strong emotion or spirit; passionate <*a* ~ *speech*> **b** easily provoked; irascible <*a* ~ *temper*> – **fierily** *adv*, **fieriness** *n*

fiesta /fiˈestə||fɪˈestə/ *n* a saint's day in Spain and Latin America, often celebrated with processions and dances

fife /fief||faɪf/ *n* a small flute used chiefly to accompany the drum

fifteen /fifˈteen||fɪfˈtiːn/ *n* **1** (the number) 15 **2** the fifteenth in a set or series **3** *sing or pl in constr* sthg having 15 parts or members or a denomination of 15; *esp* a Rugby Union football team – **fifteen** *adj or pron*, **fifteenth** *adj or n*

fifth /fifth||fɪfθ; *also* fith||fɪθ/ *n* **1** number five in a countable series **2a** (the combination of 2 notes at) a musical interval of 5 diatonic degrees **b** DOMINANT 2 – **fifth** *adj or adv*, **fifthly** *adv*

ˌfifth ˈcolumn *n* a group within a nation or faction that sympathizes with and works secretly for an enemy or rival [name applied to rebel sympathizers in Madrid in 1936 when four rebel columns were advancing on the city] – **fifth columnist** *n*

fifty /ˈfifti||ˈfɪftɪ/ *n* **1** (the number) 50 **2** *pl* the numbers 50 to 59; *specif* a range of temperatures, ages, or dates within a century characterized by those numbers – **fiftieth** *adj or n*, **fifty** *adj or pron*, **fiftyfold** *adj or adv*

[1]**ˌfifty-ˈfifty** *adv* evenly, equally <*they shared the money* ~>

[2]**fifty-fifty** *adj* half favourable and half unfavourable; even <*a* ~ *chance*>

[1]**fig** /fig||fɪg/ *n* **1** (any of a genus of trees that bear) a many-seeded fleshy usu pear-shaped or oblong edible fruit **2** a contemptibly worthless trifle <*not worth a* ~>

[2]**fig** *n* dress, array <*in full* ~>

[1]**fight** /fiet||faɪt/ *vb* **fought** /fawt||fɔːt/ *vi* **1a** to contend in battle or physical combat; *esp* to strive to overcome a person by blows or weapons **b** [5]BOX **2** to strive, struggle <~ing *for his life*> ~ *vt* **1a(1)** to contend against (as if) in battle or physical combat **a(2)** to engage in a boxing match with **b** to attempt to prevent the success, effectiveness, or development of <*the company* fought *the strike for months*> **2a** to wage <~ *a war*> **b** to take part in (a boxing match) **c** to stand as a candidate for (e g a constituency) in an election **3** to struggle to endure or surmount <*he* fought *his illness for a year before he died*> **4a** to make (one's way) by fighting **b** to resolve or control by fighting – + *out* or *down* <fought *down her fear*> – **fight shy of** to avoid facing or meeting

[2]**fight** *n* **1a** an act of fighting; a battle, combat **b** a boxing match **c** a verbal disagreement; an

argument **2** a usu protracted struggle for an objective **3** strength or disposition for fighting; pugnacity

fight back *vi* to struggle to recover from a losing or disadvantageous position; resist – **fightback** *n*

fighter /'fietə‖'faɪtə/ *n* **1a** a pugnacious or boldly determined individual **b** ¹BOXER **2** a fast manoeuvrable aeroplane designed to destroy enemy aircraft

fighting chance *n* a small chance that may be realized through struggle

fight off *vt* to ward off (as if) by fighting; repel

fight out *vt* to settle (e g an argument) by fighting – esp in *fight it out*

figment /'figmənt‖'fɪgmənt/ *n* sthg fabricated or imagined <*a* ~ *of the author's imagination*>

figurative /'figyoorətiv‖'fɪgjʊrətɪv/ *adj* **1a** representing by a figure or likeness; emblematic **b** representational <~ *sculpture*> **2** characterized by or using figures of speech, esp metaphor – **figuratively** *adv*, **figurativeness** *n*

¹figure /'figə‖'fɪgə/ *n* **1a** an (Arabic) number symbol <*a salary running into 6* ~s> **b** *pl* arithmetical calculations <*good at* ~s> **c** a written or printed character **d** value, esp as expressed in numbers <*the house sold at a low* ~> **2** bodily shape or form, esp of a person <*a slender* ~> **3a** the graphic representation of an esp human form **b** a diagram or pictorial illustration in a text **c** a geometrical diagram or shape **4** an intentional deviation from the usual form or syntactic relation of words **5** the form of a syllogism with respect to the position of the middle term **6** an often repetitive pattern in a manufactured article (e g cloth) or natural substance (e g wood) **7** an appearance made; a usu favourable impression produced <*the couple cut quite a* ~> **8a** a series of movements in a dance **b** an outline representation of a form traced by a series of evolutions (e g by a skater on an ice surface) **9** a personage, personality <*great political* ~s> **10** a short musical phrase

²figure *vt* **1** to represent (as if) by a figure or outline; portray **2a** to decorate with a pattern **b** to write figures over or under (the bass) in order to indicate the accompanying chords **3** to indicate or represent by numerals **4a** to calculate **b** *chiefly NAm* to conclude, decide <*he* ~d *there was no use in further effort*> **c** *chiefly NAm* to regard, consider ~ *vi* **1** to take an esp important or conspicuous part – often + *in* **2** to calculate **3** to seem reasonable or expected – infml; esp in *that figures* – **figurer** *n* – **figure on** *NAm* to take into consideration (e g in planning) <figure on *$50 a month extra income*>

figured /'figəd‖'fɪgəd/ *adj* **1** represented, portrayed **2** adorned with or formed into a figure <~ *muslin*> <~ *wood*> **3** indicated by figures

figured bass *n* a continuo

'figure,head /-,hed‖-,hed/ *n* **1** an ornamental carved figure on a ship's bow **2** a head or chief in name only

,figure of 'eight *n* sthg (e g a skater's figure) resembling the Arabic numeral 8 in form or shape

,figure of 'speech *n* a form of expression (e g a hyperbole or metaphor) used to convey meaning or heighten effect

figure out *vt* **1** to discover, determine <*try to* figure out *a solution*> **2** to solve, fathom <*I just can't* figure *him* out>

figurine /figyoo'reen, '---‖fɪgjʊ'ri:n, '---/ *n* a statuette

figwort /'fig,wuht‖'fɪg,wɜ:t/ *n* any of a genus of chiefly herbaceous plants with an irregular 2-lipped corolla

filament /'filəmənt‖'fɪləmənt/ *n* a single thread or a thin flexible threadlike object or part: e g **a** a slender conductor (e g in an electric light bulb) made incandescent by the passage of an electric current; *specif* such a conductor that heats the cathode of a thermionic device **b** an elongated thin series of attached cells or a very long thin cylindrical single cell (e g of some algae, fungi, or bacteria) **c** the anther-bearing stalk of a stamen – **filamentary** *adj*, **filamentous** *adj*

filbert /'filbət‖'fɪlbət/ *n* (the sweet thick-shelled nut of) either of 2 European hazels

filch /filch‖fɪltʃ/ *vt* to steal (sthg of small value); pilfer

¹file /fiel‖faɪl/ *n* a tool, usu of hardened steel, with many cutting ridges for shaping or smoothing objects or surfaces

²file *vt* to rub, smooth, or cut away (as if) with a file

³file *vt* **1** to arrange in order (e g alphabetically) for preservation and reference **2** to submit or record officially <~ *a lawsuit*> ~ *vi* to place items, esp papers, in a file

⁴file *n* **1** a folder, cabinet, etc in which papers are kept in order **2** a collection of papers or publications on a subject, usu arranged or classified

⁵file *n* **1** a row of people, animals, or things arranged one behind the other **2** any of the rows of squares that extend across a chessboard from white's side to black's side

⁶file *vi* to march or proceed in file

filet *n, chiefly NAm* a fillet

filial /'fili·əl, -yəl‖'fɪlɪəl, -jəl/ *adj* **1** of or befitting a son or daughter, esp in his/her relationship to a parent <~ *obedience*> **2** having or assuming the relation of a child or offspring – **filially** *adv*

filibuster /'fili,bustə‖'fɪlɪ,bʌstə/ *vi or n, chiefly NAm* (to engage in) the use of extreme delaying tactics in a legislative assembly [Spanish *filibustero*, lit., freebooter]

filigree /'filigree‖'fɪlɪgri:/ *vt or n* (to decorate with) **a** ornamental openwork of delicate or intricate design **b** a pattern or design resembling such openwork <*a* ~ *of frost on a window*>

filing /'fieling‖'faɪlɪŋ/ *n* a usu metal fragment rubbed off in filing – usu pl

¹fill /fil‖fɪl/ *vt* **1a** to put into as much as can be held or conveniently contained <~ *a cup with water*> **b** to supply with a full complement <*the class is already* ~ed> **c(1)** to cause to swell or billow <*wind* ~ed *the sails*> **c(2)** to trim (a sail) to catch the wind **d** to repair the cavities of (a tooth) **e** to stop up; obstruct, plug **2a** to feed, satiate **b** to satisfy, fulfil <~s *all requirements*> **3a** to occupy the whole of <*smoke* ~ed *the room*> **b** to spread through

4a to possess and perform the duties of; hold < ~ *an office*> **b** to place a person in < ~ *a vacancy*> ~*vi* to become full – **fill somebody's shoes** to take over sby's job, position, or responsibilities – **fill the bill** to suffice

[2]**fill** *n* **1a** the quantity needed to fill sthg <*a ~ of pipe tobacco*>; *esp* as much as one can eat or drink <*eat your ~* > **b** as much as one can bear <*I've had my ~ of them for today*> **2** material used to fill a receptacle, cavity, passage, or low place

filler /ˈfilə‖ˈfɪlə/ *n* **1** a substance added to a product (e g to increase bulk or strength) **2** a composition or material used to fill holes before painting or varnishing **3** a piece (e g a plate) used to cover or fill a space between 2 parts of a structure

[1]**fillet,** *chiefly NAm* **filet** /ˈfilit‖ˈfɪlɪt/ *n* **1** a ribbon or narrow strip of material used esp as a headband **2a** a thin narrow strip of material **b(1)** a fleshy boneless piece of meat cut from the hind loin or upper hind leg **b(2)** a long slice of boneless fish **3** a narrow flat architectural moulding

[2]**fillet** *vt* **1** to bind, provide, or adorn (as if) with a fillet **2a** to cut (meat or fish) into fillets **b** to remove the bones from (esp fish) **3** to remove inessential parts from

fill in *vt* **1** to give necessary or recently acquired information to <*friends* filled *him* in *on the latest gossip*> **2** to add what is necessary to complete; MAKE OUT 2 <fill in *this form, please*> **3** to enrich (e g a design) with detail ~*vi* to take sby's place, usu temporarily; substitute <*he often* filled in *in emergencies*>

filling /ˈfiling‖ˈfɪlɪŋ/ *n* **1** sthg used to fill a cavity, container, or depression **2** a food mixture used to fill cakes, sandwiches, etc

ˈ**filling ˌstation** *n* a retail establishment for selling fuel, oil, etc to motorists

[1]**fillip** /ˈfilip‖ˈfɪlɪp/ *n* sthg that arouses or boosts; a stimulus

[2]**fillip** *vt* to stimulate

fill out *vi* to put on flesh ~*vt, chiefly NAm* FILL IN 2

filly /ˈfili‖ˈfɪlɪ/ *n* a young female horse, usu of less than 4 years

[1]**film** /film‖fɪlm/ *n* **1a** a thin skin or membranous covering **b** (dimness of sight resulting from) an abnormal growth on or in the eye **2a** a thin layer or covering <*a ~ of ice on the pond*> **b(1)** a thin flexible transparent sheet (e g of plastic) used as a wrapping **b(2)** a roll or strip of cellulose acetate or cellulose nitrate coated with a light-sensitive emulsion for taking photographs **3a** a series of pictures recorded on film for the cinema and projected rapidly onto a screen so as to create the illusion of movement **b** a representation (e g of an incident or story) on film **c** CINEMA 2 – often pl with sing. meaning – **filmic** *adj*, **filmically** *adv*, **filmy** *adj*, **filminess** *n*

[2]**film** *vt* to make a film of or from ~ *vi* **1** to be suitable for photographing **2** to make a film

ˈ**filmˌstrip** /-ˌstrip‖-ˌstrɪp/ *n* a strip of film containing photographs, diagrams, or graphic matter for still projection

Filofax /ˈfieloh,faks/ *trademark* – used for a loose-leaf file holding a diary, address book, and other aids to personal organization

[1]**filter** /ˈfiltə‖ˈfɪltə/ *n* **1** a porous article or mass (e g of paper, sand, etc) through which a gas or liquid is passed to separate out matter in suspension **2** an apparatus containing a filter medium <*a car's oil* ~ > **3a** a device or material for suppressing or minimizing waves or oscillations of certain frequencies (e g of electricity, light, or sound) **b** a transparent material (e g coloured glass) that absorbs light of certain colours selectively

[2]**filter** *vt* **1** to subject to the action of a filter **2** to remove by means of a filter ~ *vi* **1** to pass or move (as if) through a filter **2** to move gradually <*the children* ~ed *out of assembly*> **3** to become known over a period of time <*the news soon* ~ed *through to the public*> **4** *Br, of traffic* to turn left or right in the direction of the green arrow while the main lights are still red – **filterable** *also* **filtrable** *adj*, **filterability** *n*

ˌ**filter ˈtip** *n* (a cigar or cigarette with) a tip of porous material that filters the smoke before it enters the smoker's mouth – **filter-tipped** *adj*

filth /filth‖fɪlθ/ *n* **1** foul or putrid matter, esp dirt or refuse **2** sthg loathsome or vile; *esp* obscene or pornographic material

filthy /ˈfilthi‖ˈfɪlθɪ/ *adj* **1** covered with or containing filth; offensively dirty **2** vile, obscene – **filthily** *adv*, **filthiness** *n*

[1]**fin** /fin‖fɪn/ *n* **1** an external membranous part of an aquatic animal (e g a fish or whale) used in propelling or guiding the body **2a(1)** an appendage of a boat (e g a submarine) **a(2)** a vertical aerofoil attached to an aircraft for directional stability **b** FLIPPER 1 **c** any of the projecting ribs on a radiator or an engine cylinder – **finlike** *adj*, **finned** *adj*

[2]**fin** *vb* **-nn-** *vi* to lash or move through the water (as if) using fins ~*vt* to equip with fins

[1]**final** /ˈfienl‖ˈfaɪnl/ *adj* **1** not to be altered or undone; conclusive **2** being the last; occurring at the end <*the ~ chapter of a book*> **3** of or relating to the ultimate purpose or result of a process <*the ~ goal of life*> [Middle French, fr Latin *finalis*, fr *finis* boundary, end] – **finally** *adv*

[2]**final** *n* **1** a deciding match, game, trial, etc in a sport or competition; *also, pl* a round made up of these **2** the last examination in a course – usu pl

finale /fiˈnahli‖fɪˈnɑːlɪ/ *n* **1** the last section of an instrumental musical composition **2** a final scene or number in (an act of) a public performance **3** the last and often climactic event or item in a sequence

finalist /ˈfienl·ist‖ˈfaɪnlɪst/ *n* a contestant in the finals of a competition

finality /fiˈnaləti, fie-‖fɪˈnælətɪ, faɪ-/ *n* **1** the condition of being at an ultimate point, esp of development or authority **2** a fundamental fact, action, or belief

final·ize, -ise /ˈfienl·iez‖ˈfaɪnlaɪz/ *vt* **1** to put in final or finished form **2** to give final approval to – **finalization** *n*

[1]**finance** /ˈfienans‖ˈfaɪnæns/ *n* **1** *pl* resources of money **2** the system that includes the circulation of money and involves banking, credit, and investment **3** the science of the management of

funds **4** the obtaining of funds [Middle French payment, ransom, fr *finer* to end, pay, fr *fin* end fr Latin *finis*] – **financial** *adj*, **financially** *adv*

[2]**finance** *vt* to raise or provide money for

financier /fi'nansi·ə, fie-‖fi'nænsɪə, faɪ-/ *n* one skilled in dealing with finance or investment

finch /finch‖fɪntʃ/ *n* any of numerous songbirds with a short stout conical beak adapted for crushing seeds

[1]**find** /fiend‖faɪnd/ *vb* **found** /fownd‖faʊnd/ *vt* **1a** to come upon, esp accidentally; encounter **b** to meet with (a specified reception) <*hoped to ~ favour*> **2a** to come upon or discover by searching, effort, or experiment; obtain **b** to obtain by effort or management <*~ the time to study*> **c** to attain, reach <*water ~s its own level*> **3a** to experience, feel <found *much pleasure in their company*> **b** to perceive (oneself) to be in a specified place or condition <found *himself in a dilemma*> **c** to gain or regain the use or power of <*trying to ~ his tongue*> **d** to bring (oneself) to a realization of one's powers or of one's true vocation <*he must be helped to ~ himself as an individual*> **4** to provide, supply <*the parents must ~ all the school fees themselves*> **5** to determine and announce <*~ a verdict*> *~vi* to determine a case judicially by a verdict <*~ for the defendant*> – **find fault** to criticize unfavourably

[2]**find** *n* **1** an act or instance of finding sthg, esp sthg valuable **2** sby or sthg found; *esp* a valuable object or talented person discovered

finder /'fiendə‖'faɪndə/ *n* **1** one who finds **2** a small astronomical telescope attached to a larger telescope for finding an object

fin de siècle /'fan də see'eklə ‖'fæn də si:'eklə (*Fr* fɛ̃ də sjɛkl)/ *adj* (characteristic) of the close of the 19th c and esp its literary and artistic climate of sophisticated decadence and world-weariness [French, end of the century]

finding /'fiending‖'faɪndɪŋ/ *n* **1** FIND 2 **2a** the result of a judicial inquiry **b** the result of an investigation – usu pl with sing. meaning <*the ~s of the welfare committee*>

find out *vt* **1** to learn by study, observation, or search; discover **2a** to detect in an offence <*the culprits were soon* found out> **b** to ascertain the true character or identity of; unmask *~vi* to discover, learn, or verify sthg

[1]**fine** /fien‖faɪn/ *n* **1** a sum payable as punishment for an offence **2** a forfeiture or penalty paid to an injured party in a civil action – **in fine** IN SHORT

[2]**fine** *vt* to punish by a fine

[3]**fine** *adj* **1** free from impurity **2a** very thin in gauge or texture <*~ thread*> **b** consisting of relatively small particles **c** very small <*~ print*> **d** keen, sharp <*a knife with a ~ edge*> **3a(1)** having a delicate or subtle quality <*a wine of ~ bouquet*> **a(2)** subtle or sensitive in perception or discrimination <*a ~ distinction*> **b** performed with extreme care and accuracy <*~ workmanship*> **4** in, at, or through a fielding position in cricket behind the batsman and near an extension of the line between the wickets **5a** superior in quality, conception, or appearance; excellent <*a ~ musician*> **b** bright and sunny **6** marked by or affecting often excessive elegance or refinement <*~ manners*> **7** very well <*feel ~*> **8** awful – used as an intensive <*a ~ mess we're in!*> – **fine** *adv*, **finely** *adv*, **fineness** *n*

[4]**fine** *vt* **1** to purify, clarify – often + *down* **2** to make finer in quality or size – often + *down* ~ *vi* **1** to become pure or clear <*the ale will ~*> **2** to become finer or smaller in lines or proportions; diminish – often + *away* or *down*

,fine 'art *n* (an) art (e g painting, sculpture, or music) concerned primarily with beauty rather than utility – usu pl

finery /'fienəri‖'faɪnərɪ/ *n* dressy or showy clothing and jewels

fines herbes /,feenz 'eəb ‖,fi:nz 'eəb (*Fr* fin zɛrb)/ *n pl* a mixture of finely chopped herbs used esp as a seasoning

[1]**finesse** /fi'nes‖fɪ'nes/ *n* **1** refinement or delicacy of workmanship **2** skilful handling of a situation; adroitness **3** the withholding of one's highest card in the hope that a lower card will take the trick because the only opposing higher card is in the hand of an opponent who has already played

[2]**finesse** *vi* to make a finesse in playing cards ~ *vt* **1** to play (a card) in a finesse **2a** to bring about by finesse **b** to evade or trick by finesse

[1]**finger** /'fing·gə‖'fɪŋgə/ *n* **1** any of the 5 parts at the end of the hand or forelimb; *esp* one other than the thumb **2a** sthg that resembles a finger, esp in being long, narrow, and often tapering in shape <*a ~ of toast*> **b** a part of a glove into which a finger is inserted **3** the breadth of a finger – **have a finger in the/every pie** to be involved or have an interest in sthg/everything – infml – **pull/take one's finger out** *Br* to start working hard; get cracking – slang

[2]**finger** *vt* **1a** to play (a musical instrument) with the fingers **b** to play (e g notes or chords) with a specific fingering **c** to mark fingerings on (a music score) as a guide in playing **2** to touch or feel with the fingers; handle *~vi* to touch or handle sthg <*~s through the cards*>

'finger,board /-,bawd‖-,bɔ:d/ *n* the part of a stringed instrument against which the fingers press the strings to vary the pitch

'finger ,bowl *n* a small water bowl for rinsing the fingers at table

[1]**fingering** /'fing·gəring‖'fɪŋgərɪŋ/ *n* (the marking indicating) the use or position of the fingers in sounding notes on an instrument

[2]**fingering** *n* a fine wool yarn for knitting

'finger,plate /-,playt‖-,pleɪt/ *n* a protective plate fastened to a door usu near the handle to protect the door surface from finger marks

'finger,post /-,pohst‖-,pəʊst/ *n* a signpost whose signs are or terminate in the shape of a pointing finger

'finger,print /-,print‖-,prɪnt/ *n* **1** the impression of a fingertip on any surface; *esp* an ink impression of the lines upon the fingertip taken for purposes of identification **2** unique distinguishing characteristics (e g of a recording machine or infrared spectrum) – **fingerprint** *vt*, **fingerprinting** *n*

'finger,stall /-,stawl‖-,stɔ:l/ *n* a protective cover for an injured finger

'finger,tip /-,tip‖-,tɪp/ *adj* readily accessible;

being in close proximity

finicky /ˈfiniki‖ˈfɪnɪkɪ/ *adj* **1** excessively exacting or meticulous in taste or standards; fussy **2** requiring delicate attention to detail <*a ~ job*> – **finickiness** *n*

finis /ˈfinis‖ˈfɪnɪs/ *n* the end, conclusion – used esp to mark the end of a book or film

[1]**finish** /ˈfinish‖ˈfɪnɪʃ/ *vt* **1a** to end, terminate **b** to eat, drink, or use entirely – often + *off* or *up* **2a** to bring to completion or issue; complete, perfect <~ed *her new novel*> – often + *off* **b** to put a final coat or surface on **c** to neaten (the raw edge of a piece of sewing) to prevent fraying **d** to complete the schooling of (a girl), esp in the social graces **3a** to bring to an end the significance or effectiveness of <*the scandal* ~ed *his career*> **b** to bring about the death of ~ *vi* **1** to end, terminate **2a** to come to the end of a course, task, or undertaking in a specified manner <~ed *with a song*> **b** to come to the end of a relationship <*David and I have* ~ed> **3** to arrive, end, or come to rest in a specified position or manner – often + *up* <*we* ~ed *up in Paris*>; *specif* to end a competition in a specified manner or position <~ed *third in the race*> – **finisher** *n* – **finish with** to end a relationship or affair with

[2]**finish** *n* **1a** the final stage; the end **b** the cause of one's ruin; downfall **2** the texture or appearance of a surface, esp after a coating has been applied **3** the result or product of a finishing process **4** the quality or state of being perfected, esp in the social graces

ˈ**finishing ˌschool** /ˈfinishing‖ˈfɪnɪʃɪŋ/ *n* a private school for girls that prepares its students esp for social activities

finite /ˈfieniet‖ˈfaɪnaɪt/ *adj* **1a** having definite or definable limits <*a ~ number of possibilities*> **b** subject to limitations, esp those imposed by the laws of nature <~ *beings*> **2** completely determinable in theory or in fact by counting, measurement, or thought <*a ~ distance*> **3** neither infinite nor infinitesimal **4** *of a verb form* showing distinction of grammatical person and number – **finite** *n*, **finitely** *adv*, **finiteness** *n*, **finitude** *n*

fink /fingk‖fɪŋk/ *n*, *NAm* **1** an informer **2** a contemptible person *USE* infml

finnan haddie /ˌfinən ˈhadi‖ˌfɪnən ˈhædɪ/ *n*, *chiefly Scot* FINNAN HADDOCK

finnan haddock *n* a haddock that is split and smoked until pale yellow

[1]**Finnish** /ˈfinish‖ˈfɪnɪʃ/ *adj* (characteristic) of Finland

[2]**Finnish** *n* a language of Finland, Karelia, and parts of Sweden and Norway

fiord, fjord /fyawd, ˈfeeˌawd‖fjɔːd, ˈfiːˌɔːd/ *n* a narrow inlet of the sea between cliffs (e g in Norway) [Norwegian *fjord*, fr Old Norse *fjörthr*]

ˈ**fipple ˌflute** /ˈfipl‖ˈfɪpl/ *n* a tubular wind instrument characterized mainly by a whistle mouthpiece and finger holes

fir /fuh‖fɜː/ *n* (the wood of) any of various related evergreen trees of the pine family that have flattish leaves and erect cones

[1]**fire** /fie·ə‖faɪə/ *n* **1a** the phenomenon of combustion manifested in light, flame, and heat **b(1)** burning passion or emotion; ardour **b(2)** liveliness of imagination; inspiration **2** fuel in a state of combustion (e g in a fireplace or furnace) **3a** a destructive burning (e g of a building or forest) **b** a severe trial or ordeal **4** brilliance, luminosity <*the ~ of a diamond*> **5** the discharge of firearms **6** *Br* a small usu gas or electric domestic heater – **fireless** *adj* – **on fire** eager, burning – **under fire** under attack

[2]**fire** *vt* **1a** to set on fire; kindle; *also* to ignite <~ *a rocket engine*> **b(1)** to give life or spirit to; inspire <~d *the poet's imagination*> **b(2)** to fill with passion; inflame **c** to light up as if by fire **2a** to drive out or away (as if) by fire – usu + *out* **b** to dismiss from a position **3a(1)** to cause to explode **a(2)** to propel (as if) from a gun <~ *a rocket*> **b** to throw with speed; hurl **4** to apply fire or fuel to: e g **4a** to process by applying heat **b** to feed or serve the fire of ~ *vi* **1a** to catch fire; ignite **b** *of an internal-combustion engine* to undergo ignition of the explosive charge **2** to become filled with excitement or anger – often + *up* **3a** to discharge a firearm **b** to emit or let fly an object – **firer** *n*

ˈ**fireˌarm** /-ˌahm‖-ˌɑːm/ *n* a weapon from which a shot is discharged by gunpowder – usu used only with reference to small arms

fire away *vi* to go ahead; begin – usu imper; infml

ˈ**fireˌball** /-ˌbawl‖-ˌbɔːl/ *n* **1** a large brilliant meteor **2** BALL LIGHTNING **3** the bright cloud of vapour and dust created by a nuclear explosion **4** a highly energetic person – infml

ˈ**fireˌbomb** /-ˌbom‖-ˌbɒm/ *n* an incendiary bomb – **firebomb** *vt*

ˈ**fireˌbox** /-ˌboks‖-ˌbɒks/ *n* a chamber (e g of a furnace or steam boiler) that contains a fire

ˈ**fireˌbrand** /-ˌbrand‖-ˌbrænd/ *n* **1** a piece of burning material, esp wood **2** one who creates unrest or strife; an agitator, troublemaker

ˈ**fireˌbreak** /-ˌbrayk‖-ˌbreɪk/ *n* a strip of cleared or unplanted land intended to check a forest or grass fire

ˈ**fireˌbrick** /-ˌbrik‖-ˌbrɪk/ *n* a brick that is resistant to high temperatures and is used in furnaces, fireplaces, etc

ˈ**fire briˌgade** *n* an organization for preventing or extinguishing fires; *esp* one maintained in Britain by local government

ˈ**fireˌbug** /-ˌbug‖-ˌbʌg/ *n* a pyromaniac, fire-raiser – infml

ˈ**fireˌclay** /-ˌklay‖-ˌkleɪ/ *n* clay that is resistant to high temperatures and is used esp for firebricks and crucibles

ˈ**fireˌdamp** /-ˌdamp‖-ˌdæmp/ *n* (the explosive mixture of air with) a combustible mine gas that consists chiefly of methane

ˈ**fireˌdog** /-ˌdog‖-ˌdɒg/ *n* an andiron

ˈ**fire ˌdrill** *n* a practice drill in extinguishing or escaping from fires

ˈ**fire-ˌeater** *n* **1** a performer who pretends to eat fire **2** one who is quarrelsome or violent – **fire-eating** *adj*

ˈ**fire ˌengine** *n* a vehicle equipped with fire-fighting equipment

ˈ**fire eˌscape** *n* a device, esp an external staircase, for escape from a burning building

ˈ**fire exˌtinguisher** *n* an apparatus for putting out fires with chemicals

ˈ**fire ˌfighter** *n* sby who fights fires – **fire fighting** *n*

ˈ**fireˌfly** /-ˌflie‖-ˌflaɪ/ *n* any of various night-flying beetles that produce a bright intermittent light

ˈ**fireˌguard** /-ˌgahd‖-ˌgɑːd/ *n* a protective metal framework placed in front of an open fire

ˈ**fire ˌirons** *n pl* utensils (e g tongs, poker, and shovel) for tending a household fire

ˈ**fireˌlight** /-ˌliet‖-ˌlaɪt/ *n* the light of a fire, esp of one in a fireplace

ˈ**fire ˌlighter** *n* a piece of inflammable material used to help light a fire (e g in a grate)

ˈ**fireman** /-mən‖-mən/ *n, pl* **firemen 1** sby employed to extinguish fires **2** sby who tends or feeds fires or furnaces

ˈ**fireˌplace** /-ˌplays‖-ˌpleɪs/ *n* a usu framed opening made in a chimney to hold a fire; a hearth

ˈ**fireˌpower** /-ˌpowə‖-ˌpaʊə/ *n* the capacity (e g of a military unit) to deliver effective fire on a target

ˈ**fireˌproof** /-ˌproohf‖-ˌpruːf/ *adj* proof against or resistant to fire; *also* heatproof – **fireproof** *vt*, **fireproofing** *n*

ˈ**fire-ˌraising** *n, Br* arson – **fire-raiser** *n*

ˈ**fireˌside** /-ˌsied‖-ˌsaɪd/ *n* **1** a place near the fire or hearth **2** home – **fireside** *adj*

ˈ**fire ˌstation** *n* a building housing fire apparatus and usu firemen

ˈ**fire ˌstorm** *n* a huge uncontrollable fire that is started typically by bombs and that causes and is kept in being by an inrush of high winds

ˈ**fireˌtrap** /-ˌtrap‖-ˌtræp/ *n* a building difficult to escape from in case of fire

ˈ**fire-ˌwatcher** *n* sby who watches for the outbreak of fire (e g during an air raid) – **fire-watching** *n*

ˈ**fireˌwater** /-ˌwawtə‖-ˌwɔːtə/ *n* strong alcoholic drink – infml

ˈ**fireˌwood** /-ˌwood‖-ˌwʊd/ *n* wood cut for fuel

ˈ**fireˌwork** /-ˌwuhk‖-ˌwɜːk/ *n* **1** a device for producing a striking display (e g of light or noise) by the combustion of explosive or inflammable mixtures **2** *pl* a display of fireworks **3** *pl* **3a** a display of temper or intense conflict **b** PYROTECHNICS 2

ˈ**firing ˌline** *n* **1** a line from which fire is delivered against a target; *also* the troops stationed in a firing line **2** the forefront of an activity, esp one involving risk or difficulty – esp in *in the firing line*

ˈ**firing ˌsquad** *n* a detachment detailed to fire a salute at a military burial or carry out an execution

firkin /ˈfuhkin‖ˈfɜːkɪn/ *n* **1** a small wooden vessel or cask of usu 9 gall capacity **2** any of various British units of capacity usu equal to a quarter of a barrel (about 41l)

[1]**firm** /fuhm‖fɜːm/ *adj* **1a** securely or solidly fixed in place **b** not weak or uncertain; vigorous <*a* ~ *handshake*> **c** having a solid or compact structure that resists stress or pressure **2** not subject to change, unsteadiness, or disturbance; steadfast <*a* ~ *price*> **3** indicating firmness or resolution <*a* ~ *mouth*> – **firm** *adv*, **firmish** *adj*, **firmly** *adv*, **firmness** *n*

[2]**firm** *vt* **1** to make solid, compact, or firm <~ing *his grip on the racket*> **2** to put into final form; settle <~ *a contract*> **3** to support, strengthen <*help* ~ *up the franc*> ~ *vi* **1** to become firm; harden **2** to recover from a decline; improve <*the market* ~ed *slightly*> ***USE*** (*vt 2 & 3, vi*) often + *up*

[3]**firm** *n* a business partnership not usu recognized as a legal person distinct from the members composing it; *broadly* any business unit or enterprise

firmament /ˈfuhməmənt‖ˈfɜːməmənt/ *n* the vault or arch of the sky; the heavens – **firmamental** *adj*

[1]**first** /fuhst‖fɜːst/ *adj* **1** preceding all others in time, order, or importance: e g **1a** earliest **b** being the lowest forward gear or speed of a motor vehicle **c** relating to or having the (most prominent and) usu highest part among a group of instruments or voices **2** least, slightest <*hasn't the* ~ *idea what to do*> – **at first hand** directly from the original source

[2]**first** *adv* **1** before anything else; at the beginning **2** for the first time **3** in preference to sthg else <*I'll see him dead* ~>

[3]**first** *n, pl* (*2a*) **first,** (*2b, c, & d*) **firsts 1** number one in a countable series **2** sthg or sby that is first: e g **2a** the first occurrence or item of a kind <*was one of the* ~ *to know*> **b** the first and lowest forward gear or speed of a motor vehicle **c** the winning place in a contest **d first, first class** *often cap* the highest level of British honours degree <*got a* ~ *in history*> – **at first** at the beginning; initially – **from the first** from the beginning

ˌ**first ˈaid** *n* **1** emergency care or treatment given to an ill or injured person before proper medical aid can be obtained **2** temporary emergency measures taken to alleviate a problem before a permanent solution can be found – **first-aider** *n*

ˌ**firstˈborn** *adj* born before all others; eldest – **firstborn** *n*

[1]ˌ**first ˈclass** *n* the first or highest group in a classification: e g **a** the highest of usu 3 classes of travel accommodation **b** FIRST 2d – **first-class** *adj*

[2]**first class** *adv* **1** in the highest quality of accommodation <*travel* ~> **2** as mail that is delivered as fast as possible <*send a letter* ~>

ˌ**first ˈfloor** *n* **1** *Br* the floor immediately above the ground floor **2** *NAm* GROUND FLOOR

ˌ**firstˈfruits** *n pl* **1** agricultural produce offered to God in thanksgiving **2** the earliest products or results of an enterprise

ˌ**firstˈhand** *adj* of or coming directly from the original source – **firsthand** *adv*

ˌ**first ˈlady** *n, often cap F&L* the wife or hostess of a US president or state governor

ˌ**first lieuˈtenant** *n* an officer holding the second lowest rank in the US army, airforce, or marines

ˈ**firstly** /-li‖-lɪ/ *adv* in the first place; first

first name *n* the name that stands first in a person's full name

ˌ**first ˈnight** *n* the night on which a theatrical production is first performed at a given place

ˌ**first ofˈfender** *n* sby convicted of an offence for the first time

ˌ**first ˈperson** *n* (a member of) a set of linguistic forms (e g verb forms and pronouns) referring to the speaker or writer of the utterance in which they occur

ˌ**first-ˈrate** *adj* of the first or greatest order of size, importance, or quality – **first-rater** *n*

firth /fuhth‖fɜːθ/ *n* a sea inlet or estuary (e g in Scotland)

[1]**fiscal** /ˈfiskl‖ˈfɪskl/ *adj* of taxation, public revenues, or public debt < ~ *policy*> [Latin *fiscalis*, fr *fiscus* basket, treasury] – **fiscally** *adv*

[2]**fiscal** *n* a procurator-fiscal

[1]**fish** /fish‖fɪʃ/ *n, pl* **fish, fishes 1a** an aquatic animal – usu in combination <*star*fish> **b** (the edible flesh of) any of numerous cold-blooded aquatic vertebrates that typically have an elongated scaly body, limbs, when present, in the form of fins, and gills **2** a person; *esp* a fellow – usu derog <*a queer* ~> – **fish out of water** a person who is out of his/her proper sphere or element

[2]**fish** *vi* **1** to try to catch fish **2** to seek sthg by roundabout means <~ing *for compliments*> **3a** to search for sthg underwater <~ *for pearls*> **b** to search (as if) by groping or feeling <~ing *around under the bed for his shoes*> ~ *vt* **1a** to (try to) catch (fish in) <~ *the stream*> <~ *salmon*> **b** to use (e g a net, type of rod, or bait) in fishing **2** to draw *out* as if fishing *USE* (*vi 2 & 3*) usu + *for*; (*vi 2 & 3b, vt 2*) infml – **fisher** *n*

[3]**fish** *n* a piece of wood or iron fastened alongside another member to strengthen it

ˈ**fisherman** /ˈfishəmən‖ˈfɪʃəmən/ *n* **1** *fem* **fisherwoman** one who engages in fishing as an occupation or for pleasure **2** a ship used in commercial fishing

fishery /ˈfishəri‖ˈfɪʃərɪ/ *n* **1** the activity or business of catching fish and other sea animals **2** a place or establishment for catching fish and other sea animals

ˈ**fish ˌfarm** *n* a tract of water used for the artificial cultivation of an aquatic life form (e g fishes)

ˌ**fish ˈfinger** *n* a small oblong of fish coated with breadcrumbs

fishing /ˈfishing‖ˈfɪʃɪŋ/ *n* the sport or business of or a place for catching fish

ˈ**fishˌmonger** /-ˌmung·gə‖-ˌmʌŋgə/ *n, chiefly Br* a retail fish dealer

fish out *vt* to exhaust the supply of fish in by overfishing

ˈ**fishˌplate** /-ˌplayt‖-ˌpleɪt/ *n* a usu metal plate used to lap a butt joint

ˈ**fish ˌslice** *n* **1** a broad-bladed knife for cutting and serving fish at table **2** a kitchen implement with a broad blade and long handle used esp for turning or lifting food in frying

ˈ**fishˌwife** /-ˌwief‖-ˌwaɪf/ *n* **1** a woman who sells or guts fish **2** a vulgar abusive woman

fishy /ˈfishi‖ˈfɪʃɪ/ *adj* **1** of or like fish, esp in taste or smell **2** creating doubt or suspicion; questionable – infml

fissile /ˈfisiel‖ˈfɪsaɪl/ *adj* **1** capable of being split or cleft; having the property of cleavage **2** capable of undergoing (nuclear) fission – **fissility** *n*

fission /ˈfish(ə)n‖ˈfɪʃ(ə)n/ *n* **1** a splitting or breaking up into parts **2** reproduction by spontaneous division into 2 or more parts each of which grows into a complete organism **3** the splitting of an atomic nucleus with the release of large amounts of energy [Latin *fission-, fissio*, fr *fiss-, findere* to split] – **fission** *vb*, **fissionable** *adj*, **fissional** *adj*, **fissionability** *n*

[1]**fissure** /ˈfishə‖ˈfɪʃə/ *n* **1** a narrow, long, and deep opening, usu caused by breaking or parting **2** a natural cleft between body parts or in the substance of an organ (e g the brain)

[2]**fissure** *vb* to break into fissures

[1]**fist** /fist‖fɪst/ *n* **1** the hand clenched with the fingers doubled into the palm and the thumb across the fingers **2** HAND 1a <*get your* ~s *off my book*> **3** an attempt that meets with the specified degree of success *USE* (*2 & 3*) infml

[2]**fist** *vt* to hit with the fist

-fisted /-fistid‖-fɪstɪd/ *comb form* (*adj, n* → *adj*) having (such or so many) fists <*two*-fisted> <*tight*fisted>

fisticuffs /ˈfistiˌkufs‖ˈfɪstɪˌkʌfs/ *n pl* the act or practice of fighting with the fists – no longer in vogue; humor

fistula /ˈfistyoolə‖ˈfɪstjʊlə/ *n, pl* **fistulas, fistulae** /-lii‖-lɪ/ an abnormal or surgically made passage leading from an abscess or hollow organ to the body surface or between hollow organs

[1]**fit** /fit‖fɪt/ *n, archaic* a division of a poem or song

[2]**fit** *n* **1a** a sudden violent attack of a disease (e g epilepsy), esp when marked by convulsions or unconsciousness **b** a sudden but transient attack of a specified physical disturbance <*a* ~ *of shivering*> **2** a sudden outburst or flurry, esp of a specified activity or emotion <*a* ~ *of letter-writing*> – **by/in fits and starts** in a jerky, impulsive, or irregular manner

[3]**fit** *adj* **-tt- 1a(1)** adapted or suited to an end or purpose **a(2)** adapted to the environment so as to be capable of surviving **b** acceptable from a particular viewpoint (e g of competence, morality, or qualifications) **2a** in a suitable state; ready **b** in such a distressing state as to be ready to do or suffer sthg specified <*so tired I was* ~ *to drop*> **3** HEALTHY 1 – **fitly** *adv*, **fitness** *n*

[4]**fit** *vb* **fitted** *also* **fit**; **-tt-** *vt* **1** to be suitable for or to; harmonize with **2a** to be of the correct size or shape for **b** to insert or adjust until correctly in place **c(1)** to cause to try on (clothes) in order to make adjustments in size **c(2)** to make or find clothes of the right size for <*it's difficult to* ~ *him because he's so short*> **d** to make a place or room for; accommodate **3** to be in agreement or accord with <*the theory* ~s *all the facts*> **4a** to put into a condition of readiness **b** to bring to a required form and size; adjust **c** to cause to conform to or suit sthg **5** to supply, equip –often + *out* ~ *vi* **1** to conform to a particular shape or size **2** to be in harmony or accord; belong

[5]**fit** *n* **1** the manner in which clothing fits the wearer **2** the degree of closeness with which surfaces are brought together in an assembly of parts

fitful /ˈfitf(ə)l‖ˈfɪtf(ə)l/ *adj* having a spasmodic

or intermittent character; irregular <~ *sleep*> – **fitfully** *adv*, **fitfulness** *n*

fitment /ˈfitmənt‖ˈfɪtmənt/ *n* **1** a piece of equipment; *esp* an item of built-in furniture **2** *pl* FITTINGS 2

fitter /ˈfitə‖ˈfɪtə/ *n* sby who assembles or repairs machinery or appliances

[1]**fitting** /ˈfiting‖ˈfɪtɪŋ/ *adj* appropriate to the situation <*made a* ~ *answer*> – **fittingly** *adv*, **fittingness** *n*

[2]**fitting** *n* **1** a trying on of clothes which are in the process of being made or altered **2** a small often standardized part <*an electrical* ~>

fit up *vt* **1** FIX UP **2** *Br* FRAME 4a <*was* fitted up *for the murder of the policeman*> – slang – **fit-up** *n*

five /fiev‖faɪv/ *n* **1** (the number) 5 **2** the fifth in a set or series <*the* ~ *of clubs*> **3** sthg having 5 parts or members or a denomination of 5 **4** *pl but sing in constr* any of several games in which players hit a ball with their hands against the front wall of a 3- or 4-walled court – **five** *adj or pron*, **fivefold** *adj or adv*

ˌ**five oʼclock ˈshadow** *n* a just visible beard-growth

fiver /ˈfievə‖ˈfaɪvə/ *n* a £5 or $5 note; *also* the sum of £5 – infml

[1]**fix** /fiks‖fɪks/ *vt* **1a** to make firm, stable, or stationary **b(1)** to change into a stable compound or available form <*bacteria that* ~ *nitrogen*> **b(2)** to kill, harden, and preserve for microscopic study **b(3)** to make the image of (a photographic film) permanent by removing unused sensitive chemicals **c** to fasten, attach **2** to hold or direct steadily <~es *his eyes on the horizon*> **3a** to set or place definitely; establish **b** to assign <~ *the blame*> **4** to set in order; adjust **5a** to repair, mend <~ *the clock*> **b** to restore, cure **c** to spay, castrate **6** *chiefly NAm* to get ready or prepare (esp food or drink) <*can I* ~ *you a drink?*> **7a** to get even with – infml **b** to influence by illicit means <*the jury had been* ~ed> – infml ~ *vi* **1** to become firm, stable, or fixed **2** *chiefly NAm* to get ready; be about *to* <*weʼre* ~ing *to leave soon*> – **fixable** *adj*

[2]**fix** *n* **1** a position of difficulty or embarrassment; a trying predicament **2** (a determination of) the position (e g of a ship) found by bearings, radio, etc **3** sthg influenced by illicit means <*the election was a* ~> – infml **4** a shot of a narcotic – slang

fixation /fikˈsaysh(ə)n‖fɪkˈseɪʃ(ə)n/ *n* **1** an (obsessive or unhealthy) attachment or preoccupation **2** a concentration of the libido on infantile forms of gratification <~ *at the oral stage*>

fixative /ˈfiksətiv‖ˈfɪksətɪv/ *n* sthg that fixes or sets: e g **a** a substance added to a perfume, esp to prevent too rapid evaporation **b** a varnish used esp to protect crayon drawings **c** a substance used to fix living tissue – **fixative** *adj*

fixed /fikst‖fɪkst/ *adj* **1a** securely placed or fastened; stationary **b** formed into a chemical compound <~ *nitrogen*> **c** not subject to or capable of change or fluctuation; settled <*a* ~ *income*> **d** intent; IMMOBILE 2 <*a* ~ *stare*> **2** supplied with sthg needed or desirable (e g money) <*how are you* ~?> – infml – **fixedly** *adv*, **fixedness** *n* –**no fixed abode** no regular home

fixed star *n* any of the stars so distant that they appear to remain fixed relative to one another

fixity /ˈfiksəti‖ˈfɪksətɪ/ *n* the quality or state of being fixed or stable

fixture /ˈfikschə‖ˈfɪkstʃə/ *n* **1** fixing or being fixed **2a** sthg fixed (e g to a building) as a permanent appendage or as a structural part **b** sthg so annexed to land or a building that it is regarded as legally a part of it **3** sby or sthg invariably present in a specified setting or long associated with a specified place or activity **4** (an esp sporting event held on) a settled date or time

fix up *vt* to provide *with*; make the arrangements for – infml <*she* fixed *him* up *with a good job*>

[1]**fizz** /fiz‖fɪz/ *vi* to make a hissing or sputtering sound

[2]**fizz** *n* **1a** a fizzing sound **b** spirit, liveliness **2** an effervescent beverage (e g champagne) – infml – **fizzy** *adj*

fizzle /ˈfizl‖ˈfɪzl/ *vi or n* (to make) a weak fizzing sound

fizzle out *vi* to fail or end feebly, esp after a promising start – infml

fjord /fyawd, ˈfeeˌawd‖fjɔːd, ˈfiːˌɔːd/ *n* a fiord

flabbergast /ˈflabəˌgahst‖ˈflæbəˌgɑːst/ *vt* to overwhelm with shock or astonishment – infml

flabby /ˈflabi‖ˈflæbɪ/ *adj* **1** (having flesh) lacking resilience or firmness **2** ineffective, feeble – **flabbily** *adv*, **flabbiness** *n*

flaccid /ˈflaksid‖ˈflæksɪd/ *adj* **1a** lacking normal or youthful firmness; flabby <~ *muscles*> **b** LIMP 1 **2** lacking vigour or force – **flaccidly** *adv*, **flaccidity** *n*

[1]**flag** /flag‖flæg/ *n* a (wild) iris or similar plant of damp ground with long leaves

[2]**flag** *n* a (slab of) hard evenly stratified stone that splits into flat pieces suitable for paving

[3]**flag** *vt* **-gg-** to lay (e g a pavement) with flags

[4]**flag** *n* **1** a usu rectangular piece of fabric of distinctive design that is used as a symbol (e g of a nation) or as a signalling device; *esp* one flown from a single vertical staff **2** NATIONALITY 3; *esp* the nationality of registration of a ship, aircraft, etc

[5]**flag** *vt* **-gg-** **1** to put a flag on (e g for identification) **2a** to signal to (as if) with a flag **b** to signal to stop – usu + *down*

[6]**flag** *vi* **-gg-** **1** to hang loose without stiffness **2** to become feeble, less interesting, or less active; decline

ˈ**flag ˌday** *n*, *Br* a day on which charitable contributions are solicited in exchange for small paper flags on pins or, more recently, stickers

flagellant /ˈflajilənt‖ˈflædʒɪlənt/ *n* **1** a person who scourges him-/herself as a public penance **2** a person who responds sexually to being beaten by or to beating another person – **flagellant** *adj*, **flagellantism** *n*

[1]**flagellate** /ˈflajilayt‖ˈflædʒɪleɪt/ *vt* to whip or flog, esp as a religious punishment or for sexual gratification [Latin *flagellare*, fr *flagellum*, diminutive of *flagrum* whip] – **flagellation** *n*

[2]**flagellate** /ˈflajilət‖ˈflædʒɪlət/, **flagellated** /-laytid‖-leɪtɪd/ *adj* **1** having flagella **2** shaped like a flagellum

[3]**flagellate** /ˈflajilət‖ˈflædʒɪlət/ *n* a protozoan or algal cell that has a flagellum

flagellum /fləˈjeləm‖fləˈdʒeləm/ *n, pl* **flagella** /-lə‖-lə/ *also* **flagellums** any of various elongated filament-shaped appendages of plants or animals; *esp* one that projects singly or in groups and powers the motion of a microorganism – **flagellar** *adj*

flageolet /ˌflajəˈlet‖ˌflædʒəˈlet/ *n* a small fipple flute

ˌflag of conˈvenience *n* the flag of a country in which a ship is registered in order to avoid the taxes and regulations of the ship-owner's home country

flagon /ˈflagən‖ˈflægən/ *n* **1a** a large usu metal or pottery vessel with handle and spout and often a lid, used esp for holding liquids at table **b** a large squat short-necked bottle, often with 1 or 2 ear-shaped handles, in which cider, wine, etc are sold **2** the contents of or quantity contained in a flagon

flagrant /ˈflaygrənt‖ˈfleɪgrənt/ *adj* conspicuously scandalous; outrageous – **flagrance, flagrancy** *n*, **flagrantly** *adv*

ˈflagˌship /-ˌship‖-ʃɪp/ *n* **1** the ship that carries the commander of a fleet or subdivision of a fleet and flies his flag **2** the finest, largest, or most important one of a set

ˈflag-ˌwaving *n* passionate appeal to patriotic or partisan sentiment; jingoism – **flag-waver** *n*

[1]**flail** /flayl‖fleɪl/ *n* a threshing implement consisting of a stout short free-swinging stick attached to a wooden handle

[2]**flail** *vt* **1a** to strike (as if) with a flail **b** to swing or beat as though wielding a flail <~ing *his arms to ward off the insects*> **2** to thresh (grain) with a flail ~*vi* to wave, thrash – often + *about*

flair /fleə‖fleə/ *n* **1** discriminating sense; intuitive discernment, esp in a specified field <*a* ~ *for style*> **2** natural aptitude; talent <*shows little* ~ *for the subject*> **3** a uniquely attractive quality; *esp* sophistication or smartness <*she has a certain* ~ *about her*> ***USE*** (*1 & 2*) usu + *for*

flak /flak‖flæk/ *n* **1** the fire from antiaircraft guns **2** heavy criticism or opposition – infml [German, fr *flieger*a*bwehrk*anonen, fr *flieger* flyer + *abwehr* defence + *kanonen* cannons]

[1]**flake** *n* **1** a small loose mass or particle **2** a thin flattened piece or layer; a chip **3** a pipe tobacco of small irregularly cut pieces

[2]**flake** *vi* to come away in flakes – usu + *off* ~*vt* **1** to form or separate into flakes; chip **2** to cover (as if) with flakes – **flaker** *n*

flake out *vi* to collapse or fall asleep from exhaustion – infml

flaky /ˈflayki‖ˈfleɪkɪ/ *adj* **1** consisting of flakes **2** tending to flake – **flakiness** *n*

flambeau /ˈflamboh‖ˈflæmbəʊ/ *n, pl* **flambeaux, flambeaus** /-boh(z)‖-bəʊ(z)/ a flaming torch; *broadly* TORCH 1

flamboyant /flamˈboyənt‖flæmˈbɔɪənt/ *adj* **1** *often cap, of architecture* characterized by waving curves suggesting flames **2** ornate, florid; *also* resplendent **3** given to dashing display; ostentatious [French, fr *flamboyer* to flame, fr Old French, fr *flambe* flame] – **flamboyance, flamboyancy** *n*, **flamboyantly** *adv*

[1]**flame** /flaym‖fleɪm/ *n* **1** (a tongue of) the glowing gaseous part of a fire **2a** a state of blazing usu destructive combustion – often pl with sing. meaning <*the whole city was in* ~s> **b** a condition or appearance suggesting a flame, esp in having red, orange, or yellow colour **c** bright reddish orange **d** brilliance, brightness **3** burning passion or love **4** a sweetheart – usu in *old flame* – **flameless** *adj*, **flameproof** *adj or vt*, **flamy** *adj*

[2]**flame** *vi* **1** to burn with a flame; blaze **2** to break out violently or passionately <flaming *with indignation*> **3** to shine brightly like flame; glow ~ *vt* **1** to treat or affect with flame: e g **1a** to cleanse, sterilize, or destroy by fire **b** to flambé – **flamer** *n*

flamenco /fləˈmengkoh‖fləˈmeŋkəʊ/ *n, pl* **flamencos** (music suitable for) a vigorous rhythmic dance (style) of the Andalusian gypsies

ˈflameˌthrower /-ˌthroh·ə‖-ˌθrəʊə/ *n* a weapon that expels a burning stream of liquid

flaming /ˈflayming‖ˈfleɪmɪŋ/ *adj* **1** being in flames or on fire; blazing **2** resembling or suggesting a flame in colour, brilliance, or shape <~ *red hair*> **3** ardent, passionate <*had a* ~ *row with the boss*> **4** BLOODY 4 – slang – **flamingly** *adv*

flamingo /fləˈming·goh‖fləˈmɪŋgəʊ/ *n, pl* **flamingos** *also* **flamingoes** any of several web-footed broad-billed aquatic birds with long legs and neck and rosy-white plumage with scarlet and black markings

flammable /ˈflaməbl‖ˈflæməbl/ *adj* INFLAMMABLE 1 – **flammable** *n*, **flammability** *n*

flan /flan‖flæn/ *n* **1** a pastry or cake case containing a sweet or savoury filling **2** the metal disc from which a coin, medal, etc is made

[1]**flange** /flanj‖flændʒ/ *n* a rib or rim for strength, for guiding, or for attachment to another object <*a* ~ *on a pipe*>

[2]**flange** *vt* to provide with a flange – **flanger** *n*

[1]**flank** /flangk‖flæŋk/ *n* **1** the (fleshy part of the) side, esp of a quadruped, between the ribs and the hip **2a** a side **b** the right or left of a formation

[2]**flank** *vt* **1** to protect a flank of **2** to attack or threaten the flank of **3** to be situated at the side of; border

[1]**flannel** /ˈflanl‖ˈflænl/ *n* **1a** a twilled loosely woven wool or worsted fabric with a slightly napped surface **b** a stout cotton fabric usu napped on 1 side **2** *pl* garments of flannel; *esp* men's trousers **3** *Br* a cloth used for washing the skin, esp of the face **4** *chiefly Br* flattering talk; *also* nonsense – infml – **flannel** *adj*, **flannelly** *adj*

[2]**flannel** *vb* **-ll-** (*NAm* **-l-**, **-ll-**) *chiefly Br vi* to speak or write flannel, esp with intent to deceive ~*vt* to make (one's way) or persuade (sby) to one's advantage by flannelling ***USE*** infml

flannelette /ˌflanlˈet‖ˌflænlˈet/ *n* a napped cotton flannel

[1]**flap** /flap‖flæp/ *n* **1** a stroke with sthg broad; a slap **2** sthg broad or flat, flexible or hinged, and usu thin, that hangs loose or projects freely: e g **2a** an extended part forming a closure (e g of an envelope or carton) **b** a movable control surface on an aircraft wing for increasing lift or lift

and drag **3** the motion of sthg broad and flexible (e g a sail); *also* an instance of the up-and-down motion of a wing (e g of a bird) **4** a state of excitement or panicky confusion; an uproar – infml

[2]flap *vb* **-pp-** *vt* **1** to beat (as if) with a flap **2** to (cause to) move in flaps ~ *vi* **1** to sway loosely, usu with a noise of striking and esp when moved by the wind **2a** to beat (sthg suggesting) wings **b** *esp of wings* to beat **c** to progress by flapping **d** to flutter ineffectively **3** to be in a flap or panic – infml

ˈflapˌjack /-ˌjak‖-ˌdʒæk/ *n* **1** a thick pancake **2** a biscuit made with oats and syrup

flapper /ˈflapə‖ˈflæpə/ *n* **1a** an implement that can be flapped (e g to scare birds or swat flies) **b** FLIPPER 1 **2** a young woman; *specif* an emancipated girl of the period of WW I and the twenties – infml

[1]flare /fleə‖fleə/ *vi* **1** to burn with an unsteady flame **2a** to shine or blaze with a sudden flame **b** to become suddenly and often violently excited, angry, or active **3** to open or spread outwards; *esp* to widen gradually towards the lower edge ~ *vt* **1** to cause to flare **2** to provide with a flare <*a* ~d *skirt*> USE (*vi 2*) usu + up

[2]flare *n* **1** a (sudden) unsteady glaring light or flame **2a** (a device or substance used to produce) a fire or blaze of light used to signal, illuminate, or attract attention **b** a temporary outburst of energy **b(1)** from a small area of the sun's surface **b(2)** from a star **3** a sudden outburst (e g of sound, excitement, or anger) **4** a spreading outwards; *also* a place or part that spreads <*jeans with wide* ~s> **5** light resulting from reflection (e g between lens surfaces)

ˈflare-ˌup *n* an instance of sudden activity, emotion, etc

[1]flash /flash‖flæʃ/ *vi* **1** *of flowing water* to rush, dash **2a** to burst violently into flames **b** to break forth in or like a sudden flame or flare <*lightning* ~ing *in the sky*> **3a** to appear suddenly <*an idea* ~es *into her mind*> **b** to move (as if) with great speed **4a** to break forth or out so as to make a sudden display <*the sun* ~ed *from behind a cloud*> **b** to act or speak vehemently and suddenly, esp in anger – often + *out* **5a** to give off light suddenly or in transient bursts **b** to glow or gleam, esp with animation or passion <*his eyes* ~ed *in a sinister fashion*> **6** to commit the offence of indecent exposure – slang ~ *vt* **1a** to cause the sudden appearance or reflection of (esp light) **b(1)** to cause (e g a mirror) to reflect light **b(2)** to cause (a light) to flash **c** to convey by means of flashes of light **2a** to make known or cause to appear with great speed <~ *a message on the screen*> **b** to display ostentatiously <*always* ~ing *his money around*> **c** to expose to view suddenly and briefly <~ing *a shy smile*>

[2]flash *n* **1** a sudden burst of light <*a* ~ *of lightning*> **2** a sudden burst of perception, emotion, etc <*had a* ~ *of intuition*> **3** a short time <*I'll be back in a* ~> **4** an esp vulgar or ostentatious display **5** a rush of water released to permit passage of a boat **6a** a brief look; a glimpse **b** a brief news report, esp on radio or television **c** FLASHLIGHT 2; *also* flashlight photography **d** a quick-spreading flame or momentary intense outburst of radiant heat **7** a thin ridge on a cast or forged article, resulting from the hot metal, plastic, etc penetrating between the 2 parts of the mould **8** an immediate brief pleasurable feeling resulting from an intravenous injection (e g of heroin) **9** an indecent exposure of the genitals USE (*8 & 9*) slang

[3]flash *adj* **1** of sudden origin or onset and usu short duration <*a* ~ *fire*>; *also* carried out very quickly <~ *freezing*> **2** flashy, showy – infml

ˈflashˌback /-ˌbak‖-ˌbæk/ *n* **1** (an) interruption of chronological sequence in a literary, theatrical, or cinematic work by the evocation of earlier events **2** a burst of flame back or out to an unwanted position (e g in a furnace)

ˈflashˌbulb /-ˌbulb‖-ˌbʌlb/ *n* an electric flash lamp in which metal foil or wire is burned

ˈflashˌcube /-ˌkyoohb‖-ˌkju:b/ *n* a small cube incorporating 4 flashbulbs for taking 4 photographs in succession

flasher /ˈflashə‖ˈflæʃə/ *n* **1a** a light (e g a traffic signal or car light) that catches the attention by flashing **b** a device for automatically flashing a light **2** one who commits the offence of indecent exposure – slang

ˈflashˌgun /-ˌgun‖-ˌgʌn/ *n* a device for holding and operating a photographic flashlight

ˈflashˌlight /-ˌliet‖-ˌlaɪt/ *n* **1** a usu regularly flashing light used for signalling (e g in a lighthouse) **2** (a photograph taken with) a sudden bright artificial light used in taking photographic pictures **3** *chiefly NAm* an electric torch

ˈflash ˌpoint *n* **1** the temperature at which vapour from a volatile substance ignites **2** a point at which sby or sthg bursts suddenly into (violent) action

flashy /ˈflashi‖ˈflæʃɪ/ *adj* **1** superficially attractive; temporarily brilliant or bright **2** ostentatious or showy, esp beyond the bounds of good taste – **flashily** *adv*, **flashiness** *n*

flask /flahsk‖flɑ:sk/ *n* **1** a broad flat bottle, usu of metal or leather-covered glass, used to carry alcohol or other drinks on the person **2** any of several conical, spherical, etc narrow-necked usu glass containers used in a laboratory **3** VACUUM FLASK

[1]flat /flat‖flæt/ *adj* **-tt-** **1** having a continuous horizontal surface **2a** lying at full length or spread out on a surface; prostrate **b** resting with a surface against sthg **3** having a broad smooth surface and little thickness; *also* shallow <*a* ~ *dish*> **4a** clearly unmistakable; downright <*gave a* ~ *denial*> **b(1)** fixed, absolute <*charged a* ~ *rate*> **b(2)** exact <*got to work in 10 minutes* ~> **5a** lacking animation; dull, monotonous; *also* inactive <*trade is a bit* ~ *just now*> **b** having lost effervescence or sparkle <~ *beer*> **6a** *of a tyre* lacking air; deflated **b** *of a battery* completely or partially discharged **7a** *of a musical note* lowered a semitone in pitch **b** lower than the proper musical pitch **8a** having a low trajectory <*threw a fast* ~ *ball*> **b** *of a tennis ball or shot* hit squarely without spin **9a** uniform in colour **b** *of a painting* lacking illusion of depth **c(1)** *of a photograph* lacking contrast

c(2) *of lighting for photography* not emphasizing shadows or contours **d** *esp of paint* having a matt finish – **flatly** *adv*, **flatness** *n*, **flattish** *adj*

[2]**flat** *n* **1** an area of level ground; a plain – often pl with sing. meaning **2** a flat part or surface <*the ~ of one's hand*> **3** (a character indicating) a musical note 1 semitone lower than a specified or particular note **4a** a flat piece of theatrical scenery **b** any of the sides of a nut or bolt head **5** a flat tyre **6** *often cap* the flat-racing season <*the end of the ~*>

[3]**flat** *adv* **1** positively, uncompromisingly <*turned the offer down ~*> **2a** on or against a flat surface **b** so as to be spread out; at full length <*fell ~ on the ground*> **3** below the proper musical pitch **4** wholly, completely <*~ broke*> – infml

[4]**flat** *n* a self-contained set of rooms used as a dwelling – **flatlet** *n*

ˌflatˈfeet *n pl but sing or pl in constr* a condition in which the arches of the insteps of the feet are flattened so that the entire sole rests on the ground

ˈflatˌfish /-ˌfish‖-ˌfɪʃ/ *n* any of an order of marine fishes (e g the flounders and soles) that swim on one side of the flattened body and have both eyes on the upper side

ˈflatˌfoot /-ˌfoot‖-ˌfʊt/ *n, pl* **flatfeet** /-ˌfeet‖-ˌfiːt/ a policeman – slang

ˌflat-ˈfooted /-ˈfootid‖-ˈfʊtɪd/ *adj* affected with flat feet – **flat-footedly** *adv*

ˈflatˌiron /-ˌie·ən‖-ˌaɪən/ *n* IRON 2c; *esp* one heated on a fire, stove, etc

ˌflat ˈout *adv* at maximum speed, capacity, or performance – **flat-out** *adj, chiefly Br*

ˈflat ˌrace *n* a race, usu for horses, on a level course without obstacles – **flat-racing** *n*

flat spin *n* **1** an aerial manoeuvre or flight condition consisting of a spin in which the aircraft is roughly horizontal **2** a state of extreme agitation – infml

flatten /ˈflat(ə)n‖ˈflæt(ə)n/ *vt* **1** to make flat **2** to lower in pitch, esp by a semitone **3** to beat or overcome utterly – infml *~vi* to become flat or flatter: e g **3a** to extend in or into a flat position or form <*hills ~ing into coastal plains*> – often + *out* **b** to become uniform or stabilized, often at a new lower level – usu + *out* – **flattener** *n*

flatter /ˈflatə‖ˈflætə/ *vt* **1** to praise excessively, esp from motives of self-interest or in order to gratify another's vanity **2** to raise the hope of or gratify, often groundlessly or with intent to deceive <*I was ~ed by the invitation*> **3a(1)** to portray or represent (too) favourably <*always paints pictures that ~ his subjects*> **a(2)** to display to advantage <*candlelight often ~s the face*> **b** to judge (oneself) (too) favourably <*I ~ myself I am not a fool*> *~vi* to flatter sby or sthg – **flatterer** *n*, **flatteringly** *adv*, **flattery** *n*

ˈflatˌtop /-ˌtop‖-ˌtɒp/ *n, chiefly NAm* AIRCRAFT CARRIER

flatulent /ˈflatyoolənt‖ˈflætjʊlənt/ *adj* **1** causing, marked by, or affected with accumulation of gas in the stomach or intestines **2** pretentious without real worth or substance; turgid – **flatulence, flatulency** *n*, **flatulently** *adv*

flaunt /flawnt‖flɔːnt/ *vi* **1** to wave or flutter proudly <*the flag ~s in the breeze*> **2** to parade or display oneself to public notice *~ vt* **1** to display ostentatiously or impudently; parade <*~ing his superiority*> **2** to flout – nonstandard – **flauntingly** *adv*, **flaunty** *adj*

flautist /ˈflawtist‖ˈflɔːtɪst/ *n* one who plays a flute

[1]**flavour**, *NAm chiefly* **flavor** /ˈflayvə‖ˈfleɪvə/ *n* **1** the blend of taste and smell sensations evoked by a substance in the mouth; *also* a distinctive flavour **2** characteristic or predominant quality <*the newspaper retains a sporting ~*> – **flavourful** *adj*, **flavourless** *adj*, **flavoursome** *adj*

[2]**flavour**, *NAm chiefly* **flavor** *vt* to give or add flavour to – **flavouring** *n*

flaw /flaw‖flɔː/ *n* **1** a blemish, imperfection **2** a usu hidden defect (e g a crack) that may cause failure under stress <*a ~ in a bar of steel*> **3** a weakness in sthg immaterial <*a ~ in his argument*> – **flaw** *vb*, **flawless** *adj*, **flawlessly** *adv*, **flawlessness** *n*

flax /flaks‖flæks/ *n* **1** (a plant related to or resembling) a slender erect blue-flowered plant cultivated for its strong woody fibre and seed **2** the fibre of the flax plant, esp when prepared for spinning

flaxen /ˈflaks(ə)n‖ˈflæks(ə)n/ *adj* **1** made of flax **2** resembling flax, esp in being a pale soft straw colour <*~ hair*>

flay /flay‖fleɪ/ *vt* **1** to strip off the skin or surface of; *also* to whip savagely **2a** to strip of possessions; SKIN 3 **b** to criticize or censure harshly

flea /flee‖fliː/ *n* **1** any of an order of wingless bloodsucking jumping insects that feed on warm-blooded animals **2** FLEA BEETLE – **with a flea in one's ear** with a usu embarrassing reprimand <*sent off* with a flea in his ear>

ˈfleaˌbag /-ˌbag‖-ˌbæg/ *n* **1** a dirty or neglected person or animal **2** *chiefly NAm* an inferior hotel or lodging *USE* infml

flea beetle *n* a small jumping beetle that feeds on foliage

ˈfleaˌbite /-ˌbiet‖-ˌbaɪt/ *n* a trifling problem or expense – infml

ˈflea ˌmarket *n* a usu open-air market selling secondhand articles and antiques

ˈfleaˌpit /-ˌpit‖-ˌpɪt/ *n, chiefly Br* a shabby cinema or theatre – infml or humor

[1]**fleck** /flek‖flek/ *vt* to mark or cover with flecks; streak

[2]**fleck** *n* **1** a small spot or mark, esp of colour **2** a grain, particle

fledge /flej‖fledʒ/ *vt* **1** to rear until ready for flight or independent activity **2** to cover (as if) with feathers or down **3** to feather (esp an arrow)

fledgling, fledgeling /ˈflejling‖ˈfledʒlɪŋ/ *n* **1** a young bird just fledged **2** an inexperienced person

flee /flee‖fliː/ *vb* **fled** /fled‖fled/ *vi* **1** to run away from danger, evil, etc **2** to pass away swiftly; vanish <*mists ~ing before the rising sun*> *~vt* to run away from; shun

[1]**fleece** /flees‖fliːs/ *n* **1a** the coat of wool covering a sheep or similar animal **b** the wool obtained from a sheep at 1 shearing **2a** a soft or woolly covering like a sheep's fleece <*a ~ of*

snow lay on the ground> **b** a soft bulky deep-piled fabric used chiefly for lining coats – **fleeced** *adj*, **fleecy** *adj*

[2]**fleece** *vt* to strip of money or property, usu by fraud or extortion; *esp* to overcharge – infml

[1]**fleet** /fleet‖fli:t/ *vi* to fly swiftly; pass rapidly *<clouds* ~ing *across the sky>*

[2]**fleet** *n* **1** a number of warships under a single command **2** *often cap* a country's navy – usu + *the* **3** a group of ships, aircraft, lorries, etc owned or operated under one management

[3]**fleet** *adj* swift in motion; nimble – **fleetly** *adv*, **fleetness** *n*

fleet admiral *n* an officer holding the highest rank in the US navy

fleeting /'fleeting‖'fli:tɪŋ/ *adj* passing swiftly; transitory – **fleetingly** *adv*, **fleetingness** *n*

'Fleet ˌStreet *n* the national London-based press

[1]**flesh** /flesh‖fleʃ/ *n* **1a** the soft, esp muscular, parts of the body of a (vertebrate) animal as distinguished from visceral structures, bone, hide, etc **b** excess weight; fat **2** the edible parts of an animal; *esp* the muscular tissue of any animal usu excluding fish and sometimes fowl **3a** the physical being of humans *<the spirit indeed is willing, but the ~ is weak>* **b** the physical or sensual aspect of human nature *<pleasures of the ~>* **4a** human beings; humankind – esp in *all flesh* **b** living beings generally **c** kindred, stock *<one's own ~>* **5** a fleshy (edible) part of a plant or fruit – **in the flesh** in bodily form; IN PERSON

[2]**flesh** *vt* **1** to feed (e g a hawk or hound) with flesh from the kill to encourage interest in the chase; *broadly* to initiate or habituate, esp by giving a foretaste **2** to clothe or cover (as if) with flesh; *broadly* to give substance to *<~ed his argument out with solid fact>* – usu + *out* ~ *vi* to become (more) fleshy or substantial – usu + *out*

fleshings /'fleshingz‖'fleʃɪŋz/ *n pl* flesh-coloured tights worn by dancers and actors

fleshly /'fleshli‖'fleʃlɪ/ *adj* carnal

'fleshˌpot /-ˌpot‖-ˌpɒt/ *n* **1** *pl* bodily comfort or good living; luxury – usu + *the* **2** a nightclub or similar place of entertainment *<a tour of the city's ~s>* – usu pl

'flesh ˌwound *n* an injury involving penetration of body muscle without damage to bones or internal organs

fleshy /'fleshi‖'fleʃɪ/ *adj* **1a** consisting of or resembling flesh **b** marked by (abundant) flesh; *esp* corpulent **2** succulent, pulpy – **fleshiness** *n*

fleur-de-lis, fleur-de-lys /ˌfluh də 'lee‖ˌflɜ: də 'li:/ *n, pl* **fleurs-de-lis, fleur-de-lis, fleurs-de-lys, fleur-de-lys** /lee(z)‖li:(z)/ **1** IRIS 2 **2** a conventionalized iris in art and heraldry

flew /flooh‖flu:/ *past of* FLY

[1]**flex** /fleks‖fleks/ *vt* **1** BEND 1 **2a** to bend (a limb or joint) **b** to move (a muscle or muscles) so as to flex a limb or joint

[2]**flex** *n, chiefly Br* a length of flexible insulated electrical cable used in connecting a portable electrical appliance to a socket

flexible /'fleksəbl‖'fleksəbl/ *adj* **1** capable of being bent; pliant **2** yielding to influence; tractable **3** capable of changing in response to new conditions; versatile *<a highly ~ curriculum>* – **flexibility** *n*, **flexibly** *adv*

flexitime /'fleksitiem/ *n* a system by which employees work a set number of hours but can choose from a usu limited range of daily starting and finishing times

flibbertigibbet /ˌflibəti'jibit‖ˌflɪbətɪ'dʒɪbɪt/ *n* a flighty or garrulous woman – infml

[1]**flick** /flik‖flɪk/ *n* a light jerky movement or blow

[2]**flick** *vt* **1a** to strike lightly with a quick sharp motion **b** to remove with flicks – usu + *away* or *off* **2** to cause to move with a flick ~ *vi* **1** to move lightly or jerkily; dart **2** to direct a flick at sthg

[3]**flick** *n* **1** FILM 4b **2** (a showing of a film at) a cinema – + *the*; usu pl *USE* infml

[1]**flicker** /'flikə‖'flɪkə/ *vi* **1** to move irregularly or unsteadily; quiver **2** to burn fitfully or with a fluctuating light **3** to appear or be present irregularly or indistinctly **4** *of a light* to fluctuate in intensity ~ *vt* to cause to flicker – **flickeringly** *adv*

[2]**flicker** *n* **1** a flickering (movement or light) **2** a momentary quickening or stirring *<a ~ of interest>* – **flickery** *adj*

'flick-ˌknife *n* a pocket knife with a blade that flicks open when required

flier, flyer /'flie·ə‖'flaɪə/ *n* **1** sby or sthg that moves very fast **2** an airman

[1]**flight** /fliet‖flaɪt/ *n* **1a** a passage through the air using wings **b** the ability to fly **2a(1)** a passage or journey through air or space; *specif* any such flight scheduled by an airline **a(2)** the distance covered in such a flight **b** the trajectory of a struck or bowled ball **c** swift movement **3** a group of similar creatures or objects flying through the air **4** a brilliant exercise or display *<a ~ of fancy>* **5** a continuous series of stairs from one landing or floor to another **6** any of the vanes or feathers at the tail of a dart, arrow, etc that provide stability **7** a small unit of (military) aircraft or personnel in the Royal Air Force – **flightless** *adj*

[2]**flight** *vt* **1** [1]FLUSH 2 **2** to impart flight to (a bowled ball)

[3]**flight** *n* an act or instance of fleeing

'flight ˌdeck *n* **1** the deck of a ship used for the takeoff and landing of aircraft **2** the compartment housing the controls and those crew who operate them in an aircraft

flight lieutenant *n* an officer in the Royal Air Force ranking below squadron leader

'flight reˌcorder *n* a robust device fitted to an aircraft that records details of its flight, esp for use in investigating accidents

flight sergeant *n* a high-ranking noncommissioned officer in the Royal Air Force

flighty /'flieti‖'flaɪtɪ/ *adj* **1** easily excited or upset; skittish **2** irresponsible, silly; *also* flirtatious – **flightily** *adv*, **flightiness** *n*

[1]**flimsy** /'flimzi‖'flɪmzɪ/ *adj* **1a** lacking in strength or substance **b** of inferior materials or workmanship; easily destroyed or broken **2** having little worth or plausibility *<a ~ excuse>* – **flimsily** *adj*, **flimsiness** *n*

[2]**flimsy** *n* (a document printed on) a lightweight paper used esp for multiple copies

flinch /flinch‖flɪntʃ/ *vi* to shrink (as if) from

physical pain; *esp* to tense the muscles involuntarily in fear – **flinch** *n*, **flinchingly** *adv*

[1]**fling** /fling‖flɪŋ/ *vb* **flung** /flung‖flʌŋ/ *vi* **1** to move in a hasty or violent manner <~ing *out of the room in a rage*> **2** *of an animal* to kick or plunge vigorously – usu + *out* ~ *vt* **1** to throw or cast (aside), esp with force or recklessness <flung *the books on the table*> <~ing *his arms out*> <flung *off all restraint*> **2** to place or send suddenly and unceremoniously <*the attack* flung *the enemy force into confusion*> **3** to ejaculate or utter vigorously **4** to cast or direct (oneself or one's efforts) vigorously or unrestrainedly <flung *herself into her work*>

[2]**fling** *n* **1** a period devoted to self-indulgence **2** a casual attempt – chiefly infml

flint /flint‖flɪnt/ *n* **1** a hard quartz found esp in chalk or limestone **2** a flint implement used by primitive human beings **3** a material (e g an alloy of iron and cerium) used for producing a spark (e g in a cigarette lighter) – **flintlike** *adj*, **flinty** *adj*

ˈ**flintˌlock** /-ˌlok‖-ˌlɒk/ *n* (a gun having) a gunlock used in the 17th and 18th c, in which the charge is ignited by sparks struck from flint

[1]**flip** /flip‖flɪp/ *vb* **-pp-** *vt* **1** to toss or cause to move with a sharp movement, esp so as to be turned over in the air <~ *a coin*> **2** FLICK 1a **3** to turn *over* ~ *vi* **1** to lose one's sanity or self-control **2** to become extremely enthusiastic; go wild <*I just* ~ped *over that new record*> *USE* (*vi*) slang – **flip through** LEAF THROUGH

[2]**flip** *n* **1** a (motion used in) flipping or a flick **2** a somersault, esp when performed in the air **3** a mixed drink usu consisting of a sweetened spiced alcoholic drink to which beaten eggs have been added

[3]**flip** *adj* **-pp-** flippant, impertinent – infml

flip-flop /ˈflip ˌflop‖ˈflɪp ˌflɒp/ *n* **1** a backward handspring **2** a usu electronic device or circuit (e g in a computer) capable of assuming either of 2 stable states **3** a rubber sandal consisting of a sole and a strap fixed between the toes – **flip-flop** *vi*

flippant /ˈflip(ə)nt‖ˈflɪp(ə)nt/ *adj* lacking proper respect or seriousness, esp in the consideration of grave matters – **flippancy** *n*, **flippantly** *adv*

flipper /ˈflipə‖ˈflɪpə/ *n* **1** a broad flat limb (e g of a seal) adapted for swimming **2** a flat rubber shoe with the front expanded into a paddle used for underwater swimming

flipping /ˈfliping‖ˈflɪpɪŋ/ *adj or adv, Br* [1]BLOODY 4, [3]BLOODY – euph

ˈ**flip ˌside** *n* the side of a gramophone record which is not the principal marketing attraction

[1]**flirt** /fluht‖flɜːt/ *vi* to behave amorously without serious intent – **flirty** *adj*, **flirtation** *n*, **flirtatious** *adj*, **flirtatiously** *adv*, **flirtatiousness** *n* – **flirt with** to show superficial or casual interest in or liking for

[2]**flirt** *n* **1** an act or instance of flirting **2** one, esp a woman, who flirts

flit /flit‖flɪt/ *vi* **-tt-** **1** to pass lightly and quickly or irregularly from one place or condition to another; *esp* to fly in this manner **2** *chiefly Scot & NEng* to move house, esp rapidly and secretly – **flit** *n*

flitch /flich‖flɪtʃ/ *n* a salted and often smoked side of pork

[1]**float** /floht‖fləʊt/ *n* **1a** a cork or other device used to keep the baited end of a fishing line afloat **b** a floating platform for swimmers or boats **c** sthg (e g a hollow ball) that floats at the end of a lever in a cistern, tank, or boiler and regulates the liquid level **d** a sac containing air or gas and buoying up the body of a plant or animal **e** a watertight structure enabling an aircraft to float on water **2** a tool for smoothing a surface of plaster, concrete, etc **3** (a vehicle with) a platform supporting an exhibit in a parade **4** a sum of money available for day-to-day use (e g for expenses or for giving change)

[2]**float** *vi* **1** to rest on the surface of or be suspended in a fluid **2a** to drift (as if) on or through a liquid <*yellow leaves* ~ed *down*> **b** to wander aimlessly **3** to lack firmness of purpose; vacillate **4** *of a currency* to find a level in the international exchange market in response to the law of supply and demand and without artificial support or control ~ *vt* **1** to cause to float in or on the surface of a liquid; *also* to carry along in this manner **2** to smooth (e g plaster) with a float **3** to present (e g an idea) for acceptance or rejection **4** to cause (currency) to float

floatation /flohˈtaysh(ə)n‖fləʊˈteɪʃ(ə)n/ *n* flotation

floating /ˈflohting‖ˈfləʊtɪŋ/ *adj* **1** located out of the normal position <*a* ~ *kidney*> **2a** continually changing position or abode <*a large* ~ *population*> **b** not presently committed or invested <~ *capital*> **c** short-term and usu not funded <~ *debt*> **3** connected or constructed so as to operate and adjust smoothly

floating rib *n* a rib (e g any of the last 2 pairs in human beings) that has no attachment to the sternum

[1]**flock** /flok‖flɒk/ *n sing or pl in constr* **1** a group of birds or mammals assembled or herded together **2** a church congregation, considered in relation to its pastor **3** a large group

[2]**flock** *vi* to gather or move in a crowd

[3]**flock** *n* **1** a tuft of wool or cotton fibre **2** woollen or cotton refuse used for stuffing furniture, mattresses, etc **3** very short or pulverized fibre used esp to form a velvety pattern on cloth or paper or a protective covering on metal

floe /floh‖fləʊ/ *n* (a sheet of) floating ice, esp on the sea

flog /flog‖flɒg/ *vt* **-gg-** **1** to beat severely with a rod, whip, etc **2** to force into action; drive **3** to repeat (sthg) so frequently as to make uninteresting – esp in *flog something to death*; infml **4** *Br* SELL 2a – slang [perhaps deriv of Latin *flagellare* to whip – see [1]FLAGELLATE] – **flog a dead horse** to waste time or energy on worn-out or previously settled subjects

[1]**flood** /flud‖flʌd/ *n* **1** an overflowing of a body of water, esp onto normally dry land **2** FLOW 2 **3** an overwhelming quantity or volume **4** a floodlight

[2]**flood** *vt* **1** to cover with a flood; inundate **2a** to fill abundantly or excessively **b** to supply (a carburettor) with an excess of fuel **3** to drive *out* of a house, village, etc by flooding ~ *vi* **1** to pour forth in a flood **2** to become

filled with a flood

ˈflood,gate /-,gayt‖-,geɪt/ *n* **1** a gate for shutting out or admitting water **2** sthg serving to restrain an outburst

ˈflood,light /-,liet‖-,laɪt/ *n* (a source of) a broad beam of light for artificial illumination – **floodlight** *vt*

ˈflood ,tide *n* the tide while flowing in or at its highest point

¹floor /flaw‖flɔː/ *n* **1** the level base of a room **2a** the lower inside surface of a hollow structure (e g a cave or bodily part) **b** a ground surface <*the ocean* ~> **3** a structure between 2 storeys of a building; *also* a storey **4a** the part of an assembly in which members sit and speak **b** the right to address an assembly **5** a lower limit – **flooring** *n*

²floor *vt* **1** to cover with a floor **2a** to knock to the floor or ground **b** to reduce to silence or defeat; nonplus *USE* (*2*) infml

ˈfloor ,show *n* a series of acts presented in a nightclub

floozy, floozie, floosie /ˈfloohzi‖ˈfluːzɪ/ *n* **1** a (disreputable) woman or girl **2** a female companion – derog

¹flop /flop‖flɒp/ *vi* **-pp- 1** to swing or hang loosely but heavily **2** to fall, move, or drop in a heavy, clumsy, or relaxed manner **3** to relax completely; slump **4** to fail completely *USE* (*3&4*) infml

²flop *n* **1** (the dull sound of) a flopping motion **2** a complete failure – infml

³flop *adv* with a flop

floppy /ˈflopi‖ˈflɒpɪ/ *adj* tending to hang loosely; *esp* being both soft and flexible – **floppily** *adv*, **floppiness** *n*

floppy disk, floppy *n* a flexible disk, coated with a magnetic substance, that is used to store data for a computer

flora /ˈflawrə‖ˈflɔːrə/ *n, pl* **floras** *also* **florae** /ˈflawri‖ˈflɔːrɪ/ **1** a treatise on, or a work used to identify, the plants of a region **2** plant life (of a region, period, or special environment)

floral /ˈflawrəl, ˈflorəl‖ˈflɔːrəl, ˈflɒrəl/ *adj* of flowers or a flora [Latin *flor-, flos* flower] – **florally** *adv*

floret /ˈflawrit, ˈflo-‖ˈflɔːrɪt, ˈflɒ-/ *n* any of the small flowers forming the head of a (composite) plant

florid /ˈflorid‖ˈflɒrɪd/ *adj* **1** excessively flowery or ornate in style **2** tinged with red; ruddy <*a* ~ *complexion*> – **floridly** *adv*, **floridness** *n*, **floridity** *n*

florin /ˈflorin‖ˈflɒrɪn/ *n* **1** any of various former gold coins of European countries **2** a former British or Commonwealth silver coin worth 2 shillings **3** a gulden

florist /ˈflorist‖ˈflɒrɪst/ *n* one who deals in or grows flowers and ornamental plants for sale – **floristry** *n*

floss /flos‖flɒs/ *n* **1** waste or short silk or silky fibres, esp from the outer part of a silkworm's cocoon **2** soft thread of silk or cotton for embroidery – **flossy** *adj*

flotation, floatation /flohˈtaysh(ə)n‖fləʊˈteɪʃ(ə)n/ *n* **1** the act, process, or state of floating **2** the launching, esp by financing, of a company, enterprise, etc

flotilla /fləˈtilə‖fləˈtɪlə/ *n* a small fleet of ships, esp warships [Spanish, diminutive of *flota* fleet, fr Old French *flote*, fr Old Norse *floti*]

flotsam /ˈflots(ə)m‖ˈflɒts(ə)m/ *n* **1** floating wreckage, esp of a ship or its cargo **2** FLOTSAM AND JETSAM [Anglo-French *floteson*, fr Old French *floter* to float]

,flotsam and ˈjetsam /ˈjets(ə)m‖ˈdʒets(ə)m/ *n* **1** vagrants **2** unimportant miscellaneous material; ODDS AND ENDS

¹flounce /flowns‖flaʊns/ *vi* to move in a violent or exaggerated fashion – **flounce** *n*, **flouncy** *adj*

²flounce *n* a wide gathered strip of fabric attached by the gathered edge (e g to the hem of a skirt or dress) – **flouncy** *adj*

³flounce *vt* to trim with a flounce or flounces

¹flounder /ˈflowndə‖ˈflaʊndə/ *n* any of various flatfishes including some marine food fishes

²flounder *vi* **1** to struggle to move or obtain footing **2** to proceed or act clumsily or ineffectually – **flounder** *n*

¹flour /flowə‖flaʊə/ *n* **1** finely ground meal, esp of wheat **2** a fine soft powder – **floury** *adj*

²flour *vt* **1** to coat (as if) with flour **2** to make (e g grain) into flour

¹flourish /ˈflurish‖ˈflʌrɪʃ/ *vi* **1** to grow luxuriantly; thrive **2a** to achieve success; prosper **b** to be in good health **c** to reach a height of activity, development, or influence ~*vt* to wave or wield with dramatic gestures; brandish

²flourish *n* **1** a showy or flowery embellishment (e g in literature or handwriting) or passage (e g in music) **2a** an act of brandishing **b** an ostentatious or dramatic action

flout /flowt‖flaʊt/ *vt* to treat with contemptuous disregard; scorn <*openly* ~ing *the rules*> – **flouter** *n*

¹flow /floh‖fləʊ/ *vi* **1a** to issue or move (as if) in a stream <*rivers* ~ing *to the sea*> **b** to circulate <*blood* ~ing *round the body*> **2** *of the tide* to rise **3** to abound <~ing *with milk and honey*> **4a** to proceed smoothly and readily <*conversation began to* ~> **b** to have a smooth graceful continuity <*the* ~ing *lines of the car*> **5** to hang loose or freely

²flow *n* **1** a flowing **2** the flowing in of the tide towards the land **3a** a smooth uninterrupted movement or supply <*a steady* ~ *of ideas*> **b** a stream or gush of fluid **c** the direction of (apparent) movement **4** the quantity that flows in a certain time **5** menstruation **6a** the motion characteristic of fluids **b** a continuous transfer of energy

flowchart /-,chaht‖-,tʃɑːt/ *n* a diagram consisting of a set of symbols and connecting lines that shows step-by-step progression through a procedure or system

¹flower /ˈflowə‖ˈflaʊə/ *n* **1a** a blossom, inflorescence **b** a shoot of a higher plant bearing leaves modified for reproduction to form petals, sepals, ovaries, and anthers **c** a plant cultivated for its blossoms **2a** the finest or most perfect part or example <*the* ~ *of a nation's youth destroyed in war*> **b** the finest most vigorous period; prime **c** a state of blooming or flourishing – esp in *in flower* **3** *pl* a finely divided powder produced esp by condensation or sublimation

< ~s *of sulphur*>

^{2}**flower** *vi* **1** to produce flowers; blossom **2** to reach a peak condition; flourish ~ *vt* **1** to cause to bear flowers **2** to decorate with a floral design – **flowerer** *n*, **flowering** *adj*

ˈ**flower** ˌ**girl** *n* a girl or woman who sells flowers, esp in a market or the street

ˈ**flower**ˌ**pot** /-ˌpot‖-ˌpɒt/ *n* a pot, typically the shape of a small bucket, in which to grow plants

flowery /ˈflowəri‖ˈflaʊərɪ/ *adj* **1** of or resembling flowers **2** containing or using highly ornate language – **floweriness** *n*

flown /flohn‖fləʊn/ *past part of* FLY

flu /flooh‖fluː/ *n* influenza

fluctuate /ˈfluktyooˌayt, -chooˌayt‖ˈflʌktjʊˌeɪt, -tʃʊˌeɪt/ *vi* **1** to rise and fall; swing back and forth **2** to change continually and irregularly; waver – **fluctuant** *adj*, **fluctuation** *n*

flue /flooh‖fluː/ *n* **1** a channel in a chimney for flame and smoke **2** a pipe for conveying heat (e g to water in a steam boiler)

fluent /ˈflooh·ənt‖ˈfluːənt/ *adj* **1** capable of flowing; fluid **2a** able to speak or write with facility; *also* spoken or written in this way **b** effortlessly smooth and rapid; polished <*a ~ performance*> – **fluency** *n*, **fluently** *adv*

^{1}**fluff** /fluf‖flʌf/ *n* **1a** small loose bits of waste material (e g hairs and threads) that stick to clothes, carpets, etc **b** soft light fur, down, etc **2** a blunder; *esp* an actor's lapse of memory – chiefly infml

^{2}**fluff** *vi* **1** to become fluffy – often + *out* or *up* **2** to make a mistake, esp in a performance ~ *vt* **1** to make fluffy – often + *out* or *up* <*the bird ~ed out its feathers*> **2a** to fail to perform or achieve successfully; bungle <*he ~ed his exam*> **b** to deliver badly or forget (one's lines) in a play *USE* (*vi 2; vt 2*) chiefly infml

fluffy /ˈflufi‖ˈflʌfɪ/ *adj* **1** like or covered with fluff **2** light and soft or airy <*a ~ sponge cake*> – **fluffiness** *n*

^{1}**fluid** /ˈflooh·id‖ˈfluːɪd/ *adj* **1a** having particles that easily change their relative position without separation of the mass; able to flow **b** likely or tending to change or move; not fixed **2** characterized by or employing a smooth easy style <*the ballerina's ~ movements*> **3a** available for a different use **b** easily converted into cash <*~ assets*> – **fluidly** *adv*, **fluidity** *also* **fluidness** *n*

^{2}**fluid** *n* **1** sthg capable of flowing to conform to the outline of its container; *specif* a liquid or gas **2** a liquid in the body of an animal or plant – **fluidal** *adj*

ˌ**fluid** ˈ**ounce**, *NAm* **fluidounce** /ˌflooh·iˈdowns‖ˌfluːɪˈdaʊns/ *n* **1** a British unit of liquid capacity equal to $^{1}/_{20}$ imperial pt (about $28.41cm^3$) **2** a US unit of liquid capacity equal to $^{1}/_{16}$ US pt (about $29.54cm^3$)

^{1}**fluke** /floohk‖fluːk/ *n* **1** a flatfish **2** a liver fluke or related trematode worm

^{2}**fluke** *n* **1** the part of an anchor that digs into the sea, river, etc bottom **2** a barbed end (e g of a harpoon) **3** either of the lobes of a whale's tail

^{3}**fluke** *n* an accidentally successful stroke or action

fluky *also* **flukey** /ˈfloohki‖ˈfluːkɪ/ *adj* **1** happening by or depending on chance rather than skill **2** *esp of wind* unsteady, changeable

flume /floohm‖fluːm/ *n* an inclined channel for conveying water (e g for power generation)

flummery /ˈfluməri‖ˈflʌmərɪ/ *n* **1** a sweet dish typically made with flour or oatmeal, eggs, honey, and cream **2** pretentious humbug [Welsh *llymru*]

flummox /ˈfluməks‖ˈflʌməks/ *vt* to bewilder or confuse completely

flung /flung‖flʌŋ/ *past of* FLING

flunk /flungk‖flʌŋk/ *vb, chiefly NAm vi* **1** to fail, esp in an examination or course **2** to be turned *out* of a school or college for failure ~ *vt* **1** to give a failing mark to **2** to get a failing mark in *USE* infml

flunky, flunkey /ˈflungki‖ˈflʌŋkɪ/ *n* **1** a liveried servant **2** a yes-man **3** *chiefly NAm* a person performing menial duties

fluorescence /flooəˈres(ə)ns‖flʊəˈres(ə)ns/ *n* the emitting of electromagnetic radiation, usu as visible light, as a result of the simultaneous absorption of radiation of shorter wavelength; *also* the radiation emitted – **fluoresce** *vi*, **fluorescer** *n*

fluorescent /flooəˈres(ə)nt‖flʊəˈres(ə)nt/ *adj* **1** of or having fluorescence **2** bright and glowing as a result of fluorescence

fluoridate /ˈflooəriˌdayt‖ˈflʊərɪˌdeɪt/ *vt* to add a fluoride to (e g drinking water) – **fluoridation** *n*

fluoride /ˈflooəried‖ˈflʊəraɪd/ *n* a compound of fluorine

fluorine /ˈflooəreen‖ˈflʊəriːn/ *n* a nonmetallic halogen element that is normally a pale yellowish toxic gas

^{1}**flurry** /ˈfluri‖ˈflʌrɪ/ *n* **1a** a gust of wind **b** a brief light fall of snow **2** a state of nervous excitement or bustle **3** a short-lived outburst of trading activity

^{2}**flurry** *vb* to (cause to) become agitated and confused

^{1}**flush** /flush‖flʌʃ/ *vi* to take wing suddenly ~ *vt* **1** to cause (a bird) to flush **2** to expose or chase from a place of concealment – often + *out* <*~ out the criminals*>

^{2}**flush** *n* **1** (a cleansing with) a sudden flow, esp of water **2a** a sudden increase, esp of new plant growth **b** a surge of emotion <*felt a ~ of anger at the insult*> **3a** a tinge of red, esp in the cheeks; a blush **b** a fresh and vigorous state <*in the first ~ of womanhood*> **4** a transitory sensation of extreme heat; *specif* HOT FLUSH **5** *Br* a device for flushing toilets or drains

^{3}**flush** *vi* **1** to flow and spread suddenly and freely **2a** to glow brightly with a ruddy colour **b** to blush **3** to produce new growth <*the plants ~ed twice during the year*> ~ *vt* **1a** to cause to flow or be carried along on a stream of liquid; *specif* to dispose of thus **b** to pour liquid over or through; *esp* to cleanse (as if) with a rush of liquid <*~ the toilet*> **2** to inflame, excite – usu pass <*was ~ed with victory*> **3** to cause to blush

^{4}**flush** *adj* **1** filled to overflowing **2a** having or forming a continuous edge or plane surface; not indented, recessed, or projecting <*panelling ~ with the wall*> **b** arranged edge to edge so as to fit snugly **3** readily available; abundant – chiefly infml **4** having a plentiful supply of money – infml – **flushness** *n*

[5]**flush** *adv* **1** so as to form a level or even surface or edge **2** squarely <*hit him* ~ *on the chin*>

[6]**flush** *vt* to make flush <~ *the headings on a page*>

[7]**flush** *n* a hand of playing cards, esp in a gambling game, all of the same suit

[1]**fluster** /ˈflustə‖ˈflʌstə/ *vb* to make or become agitated, nervous, or confused

[2]**fluster** *n* a state of agitated confusion

[1]**flute** /flooht‖fluːt/ *n* **1** a keyed woodwind instrument that consists of a cylindrical tube stopped at one end, and is played by blowing air across a side hole **2a** a grooved pleat **b** any of the vertical parallel grooves on the shaft of a classical column – **fluting** *n*

[2]**flute** *vi* to produce a flutelike sound ~ *vt* **1** to utter with a flutelike sound **2** to form flutes in – **fluter** *n*

flutist /ˈfloohtist‖ˈfluːtɪst/ *n, chiefly NAm* a flautist

[1]**flutter** /ˈflutə‖ˈflʌtə/ *vi* **1** to flap the wings rapidly **2a** to move with quick wavering or flapping motions <*flags* ~ing *in the wind*> **b** to beat or vibrate in irregular spasms <*his pulse* ~ed> **3** to move about or behave in an agitated aimless manner ~*vt* to cause to flutter – **flutterer** *n*, **fluttery** *adj*

[2]**flutter** *n* **1** a fluttering **2a** a state of (nervous) confusion, excitement, or commotion **b** abnormal spasmodic fluttering of a body part **3** a distortion in reproduced sound similar to but at a faster rate than wow **4** an unwanted oscillation (e g of an aircraft part or bridge) set up by natural forces **5** *chiefly Br* a small gamble or bet

fluvial /ˈfloohvi·əl, -vyəl‖ˈfluːvɪəl, -vjəl/ *adj* of, produced by, or living in a stream or river

[1]**flux** /fluks‖flʌks/ *n* **1** a continuous flow or flowing **2a** an influx **b** continual change; fluctuation <*the programme was in a state of* ~> **3** a substance used to promote fusion of metals (e g in soldering or brazing) **4** the rate of transfer of a fluid, particles, or energy across a given surface **5** *archaic* an (abnormal) flowing of fluid, esp excrement, from the body

[2]**flux** *vt* **1** to cause to become fluid **2** to treat with a flux ~*vi* to become fluid

[1]**fly** /flie‖flaɪ/ *vb* **flew** /flooh‖fluː/; **flown** /flohn‖fləʊn/ *vi* **1a** to move in or through the air by means of wings **b** to move through the air or space **c** to float, wave, or soar in the air <*flags* ~ing *at half-mast*> **2a** to take flight; flee **b** to fade and disappear; vanish <*the shadows have* flown> **3a** to move, act, or pass swiftly <*he* flew *past me*> **b** to move or pass suddenly and violently into a specified state <flew *into a rage*> **c** to seem to pass quickly <*our holiday simply* flew> **4** to operate or travel in an aircraft or spacecraft **5** to depart in haste; dash – chiefly infml ~ *vt* **1a** to cause to fly <~ *a kite*> **b** to operate (a flying machine or spacecraft) in flight **c** to journey over by flying <~ *the Atlantic*> **2** to flee or escape from **3** to transport by aircraft – **flyable** *adj*, **flying** *n* – **fly at/on, fly out at** to assail suddenly and violently – **fly in the face/teeth of** to act in open defiance or disobedience of – **fly off the handle** to lose one's temper, esp suddenly

[2]**fly** *n* **1** an act or process of flying **2** *pl* the space over a stage where scenery and equipment can be hung **3a** a (garment) opening concealed by a fold of cloth extending over the fastener; *esp, pl* such an opening in the front of a pair of trousers **b** FLY SHEET 2 **c(1)** the length of an extended flag from its staff or support **c(2)** the outer or loose end of a flag **4** *chiefly Br* a light covered horse-drawn carriage

[3]**fly** *adj, chiefly Br* keen, artful – infml

[4]**fly** *n* **1** a winged insect – often in combination <*may*fly> **2** TWO-WINGED FLY **3** a natural or artificial fly attached to a fishhook for use as bait – **fly in the ointment** a detracting factor or element

flyaway /ˈflie·əˌway‖ˈflaɪəˌweɪ/ *adj* **1** lacking practical sense; flighty **2** *esp of the hair* tending not to stay in place

flyblow /ˈflieˌbloh‖ˈflaɪˌbləʊ/ *n* (infestation, esp of meat, with) an egg or young larva deposited by various flies

ˈflyˌblown /-ˌblohn‖-ˌbləʊn/ *adj* **1** infested with flyblows **2** impure, tainted; *also* not new; used

flyby /ˈflieˌbie‖ˈflaɪˌbaɪ/ *n, pl* **flybys** /-ˌbiez‖-ˌbaɪz/ **1** a flypast **2** a flight of a spacecraft close to a celestial body (e g Mars), esp to obtain scientific data

[1]**ˈfly-by-ˌnight** *n* **1** one who seeks to evade responsibilities or debts by flight **2** a shaky business enterprise *USE* chiefly infml

[2]**ˈfly-by-ˌnight** *adj* **1** given to making a quick profit, usu by disreputable or irresponsible acts; *broadly* untrustworthy **2** transitory, passing *USE* chiefly infml

ˈflyˌcatcher /-ˌkachə‖-ˌkætʃə/ *n* any of several small birds that feed on insects caught while flying

flyer /ˈflie·ə‖ˈflaɪə/ *n* a flier

ˈfly-ˌfishing *n* fishing (e g for salmon or trout) using artificial flies as bait

ˈfly-ˌhalf *n* STAND-OFF HALF

flying /ˈflie·ing‖ˈflaɪɪŋ/ *adj* **1a** (capable of) moving in the air **b** rapidly moving <~ *feet*> **c** very brief; hasty <*a* ~ *visit*> **2** intended for ready movement or action <~ *pickets*> **3** of (the operation of) or using an aircraft **4** (to be) traversed after a flying start – **with flying colours** with complete or eminent success

ˈflying ˌboat *n* a seaplane with a hull adapted for floating

ˌflying ˈbomb *n* a pilotless aircraft carrying explosives

ˌflying ˈbuttress *n* a projecting arched structure that supports a wall or building

ˈflying ˌfish *n* any of numerous (tropical) fishes that have long pectoral fins and are able to glide some distance through the air

ˌflying ˈfox *n* FRUIT BAT

ˈflying ˌofficer *n* an officer in the Royal Air Force ranking below flight lieutenant

ˌflying ˈsaucer *n* any of various unidentified flying objects reported as being saucer- or disc-shaped

ˈflying ˌsquad *n, often cap F&S* a standby

group of people, esp police, ready to move or act swiftly in an emergency

ˌflying ˈstart *n* **1** a start to a race in which the participants are already moving when they cross the starting line or receive the starting signal **2** a privileged or successful beginning <*she got off to a ~ at school*>

ˈflyˌleaf /-ˌleef‖-ˌliːf/ *n* a blank leaf at the beginning or end of a book that is fastened to the cover

ˈflyˌover /-ˌohvə‖-ˌəʊvə/ *n, Br* (the upper level of) a crossing of 2 roads, railways, etc at different levels

ˈflyˌpaper /-ˌpaypə‖-ˌpeɪpə/ *n* paper coated with a sticky, often poisonous, substance for killing flies

ˈflyˌpast /-ˌpahst‖-ˌpɑːst/ *n, Br* a ceremonial usu low-altitude flight by (an) aircraft over a person or public gathering

ˈfly ˌsheet *n* **1** a small pamphlet or circular **2** an outer protective sheet covering a tent

ˈflyˌswatter /-ˌswotə‖-ˌswɒtə/ *n* a implement for killing insects that consists of a flat piece of usu rubber or plastic attached to a handle

ˈflyˌweight /-ˌwayt‖-ˌweɪt/ *n* a boxer who weighs not more than 8st (50.8kg) if professional or more than 48kg (about 7st 7lb) but not more than 51kg (about 8st) if amateur

ˈflyˌwheel /-ˌweel‖-ˌwiːl/ *n* a wheel with a heavy rim that when revolving can either reduce speed fluctuations in the rotation of an engine or store energy

FM /ˌef ˈem‖ˌef ˈem/ *adj* of or being a broadcasting or receiving system using frequency modulation and usu noted for lack of interference

[1]foal /fohl‖fəʊl/ *n* a young animal of the horse family

[2]foal *vb* to give birth to (a foal)

[1]foam /fohm‖fəʊm/ *n* **1a** (a substance in the form of) a light frothy mass of fine bubbles formed in or on the surface of a liquid (e g by agitation or fermentation) **b** a frothy mass formed in salivating or sweating **c** a chemical froth discharged from fire extinguishers **2** a material in a lightweight cellular form resulting from introduction of gas bubbles during manufacture – **foamless** *adj*, **foamy** *adj*, **foamily** *adv*, **foaminess** *n*

[2]foam *vi* **1a** to produce or form foam **b** to froth at the mouth, esp in anger; *broadly* to be angry **2** to gush out in foam **3** to become covered (as if) with foam ~ *vt* **1** to cause air bubbles to form in **2** to convert (e g a plastic) into a foam

ˌfoam ˈrubber *n* fine-textured spongy rubber made by introducing air bubbles before solidification

fob /fob‖fɒb/ *n* **1** a small pocket on or near the waistband of a man's trousers, orig for holding a watch **2** a short strap or chain attached to a watch carried in a fob or a waistcoat pocket

fob off *vt* **-bb- 1** to put off with a trick or excuse – usu + *with* **2** to pass or offer (sthg spurious or inferior) as genuine or perfect – usu + *on*

fob watch *n* a large circular watch often with a cover for the face that is usu carried in a (fob) pocket

focal length /ˈfohk(ə)l‖ˈfəʊk(ə)l/ *n* the distance between the optical centre of a lens or mirror and the focal point

focal point *n* **1** the focus for a beam of incident rays parallel to the axis of a lens or mirror **2** FOCUS 5

fo'c'sle /ˈfohks(ə)l‖ˈfəʊks(ə)l/ *n* a forecastle

[1]focus /ˈfohkəs‖ˈfəʊkəs/ *n, pl* **focuses, foci** /ˈfohkie, -sie‖ˈfəʊkaɪ, -saɪ/ **1a** a point at which rays (e g of light, heat, or sound) converge or from which they (appear to) diverge after reflection or refraction **b** the point at which an object must be placed for an image formed by a lens or mirror to be sharp **2a** FOCAL LENGTH **b** adjustment (e g of the eye) necessary for distinct vision **c** a state in which sthg must be placed in order to be clearly perceived <*tried to bring the issues into* ~> **3** a fixed point that together with a straight line forms a reference system for generating a conic section in plane geometry; *also* either of 2 fixed points used in generating an ellipse or hyperbola **4** a localized area of disease or the chief site of a generalized disease **5** a centre of activity or attention **6** the place of origin of an earthquake – **focal** *adj*, **focally** *adv* – **out of/in focus** not/having or giving the proper sharpness of outline due to good focussing

[2]focus *vb* **-ss-, -s-** *vt* **1** to bring to a focus **2** to cause to be concentrated <~sed *their attention on the most urgent problems*> **3a** to adjust the focus of **b** to bring into focus ~ *vi* **1** to come to a focus; converge **2** to bring one's eyes or a camera to a focus

fodder /ˈfodə‖ˈfɒdə/ *n* **1** (coarse) food for cattle, horses, sheep, or other domestic animals **2** sthg used to supply a constant demand <*collected data which became computer* ~> – **fodder** *vt*

foe /foh‖fəʊ/ *n* an enemy, adversary

foetus, fetus /ˈfeetəs‖ˈfiːtəs/ *n* an unborn or unhatched vertebrate; *specif* a developing human from usu 3 months after conception to birth – **foetal** *adj*

[1]fog /fog‖fɒg/ *n* **1** dead or decaying grass on land in the winter **2** a second growth of grass; an aftermath

[2]fog *n* **1** (a murky condition of the atmosphere caused esp by) fine particles, specif of water, suspended in the lower atmosphere **2a** a state of confusion or bewilderment **b** sthg that confuses or obscures <*hid behind a* ~ *of rhetoric*> **3** cloudiness on a developed photograph caused by chemical action or radiation (e g from X rays)

[3]fog *vb* **-gg-** *vt* **1** to envelop or suffuse (as if) with fog **2** to make confused or confusing **3** to produce fog on (e g a photographic film) during development ~ *vi* **1** to become covered or thick with fog **2** to become blurred (as if) by a covering of fog or mist

ˈfogˌbound /-ˌbownd‖-ˌbaʊnd/ *adj* **1** covered with or surrounded by fog <*a* ~ *coast*> **2** unable to move because of fog

fogey, fogy /ˈfohgi‖ˈfəʊgɪ/ *n* a person with old-fashioned ideas – chiefly in *old fogey*; chiefly infml – **fogeyish** *adj*, **fogeyism** *n*

foggy /ˈfogi‖ˈfɒgɪ/ *adj* **1a** thick with fog **b** covered or made opaque by moisture or grime **2** blurred, obscured <*hadn't the* foggiest *notion* *what they were voting for*> – **foggily** *adv*, **fogginess** *n*

ˈ**fogˌhorn** /-ˌhawn‖-ˌhɔːn/ *n* a horn (e g on a ship) sounded in a fog to give warning

foible /ˈfoybl‖ˈfɔɪbl/ *n* **1** the part of a sword blade between the middle and point **2** a minor weakness or shortcoming in personal character or behaviour; *also* a quirk

[1]**foil** /foyl‖fɔɪl/ *vt* **1** *esp of a hunted animal* to spoil (a trail or scent) by crossing or retracing **2** to prevent from attaining an end; frustrate, defeat

[2]**foil** *n* **1** (fencing with) a light fencing sword with a circular guard and a flexible blade tapering to a blunted point **2** *archaic* the track or trail of an animal

[3]**foil** *n* **1a** a curved recess between cusps (e g in Gothic tracery) **b** any of several arcs that enclose a complex design **2a** very thin sheet metal <*silver* ~> **b** a thin coat of tin or silver laid on the back of a mirror **3** a thin piece of metal put under a gem or inferior stone to add colour or brilliance **4** sby or sthg that serves as a contrast to another <*acted as a* ~ *for a comedian*> **5** a hydrofoil

[4]**foil** *vt* to back or cover with foil

foist /foyst‖fɔɪst/ *vt* **1a** to introduce or insert surreptitiously or without warrant – + *in* or *into* **b** to force another to accept or tolerate, esp by stealth or deceit **2** to pass off as genuine or worthy *USE* (*1b&2*) usu + *off on, on,* or *upon*

[1]**fold** /fohld‖fəʊld/ *n* **1** an enclosure for sheep; *also* a flock of sheep **2** *sing or pl in constr* a group of people adhering to a common faith, belief, or enthusiasm

[2]**fold** *vt* **1** to pen (e g sheep) in a fold **2** to pen sheep for the fertilization of (land)

[3]**fold** *vt* **1** to lay one part of over another part **2** to reduce the length or bulk of by doubling over – often + *up* **3a** to clasp together; entwine <~ed *his arms*> **b** to bring (limbs) to rest close to the body <*the bird* ~ed *its wings*> **4a** to clasp closely; embrace **b** to wrap, envelop **5** to bend (e g a layer of rock) into folds **6** to gently incorporate (a food ingredient) into a mixture without thorough stirring or beating – usu + *in* ~ *vi* **1** to become or be capable of being folded <*a* ~ing *chair*> **2** to fail completely; *esp* to stop production or operation because of lack of business or capital – often + *up*; chiefly infml **3** to succumb to fatigue – infml – **foldable** *adj*

[4]**fold** *n* **1** (a crease made by) a doubling or folding over **2** a part doubled or laid over another part; a pleat **3** (a hollow inside) sthg that is folded or that enfolds **4a** a bend in rock strata produced usu by compression **b** *chiefly Br* an undulation in the landscape

-fold /-fohld‖-fəʊld/ *suffix* (→ *adj or adv*) **1** multiplied by (a specified number); times <*a twelve*fold *increase*> **2** having (so many) parts <*three*fold *aspect of the problem*>

ˈ**foldˌaway** /-əˌway‖-əˌweɪ/ *adj* designed to fold out of the way or out of sight <*a* ~ *bed*>

folder /ˈfohldə‖ˈfəʊldə/ *n* a folded cover or large envelope for holding or filing loose papers

foliage /ˈfohli·ij‖ˈfəʊlɪɪdʒ/ *n* **1** the leaves of a plant or clump of plants **2** (an ornamental representation of) a cluster of leaves, branches, etc – **foliaged** *adj*, **foliar** *adj*

[1]**foliate** /ˈfohli·ət‖ˈfəʊlɪət/ *adj* **1** having leaves or leaflets; *also* leaf-shaped – often in combination <*tri*foliate> **2** foliated

[2]**foliate** /ˈfohliˌayt‖ˈfəʊlɪˌeɪt/ *vt* **1** to beat (metal) into a leaf or thin foil **2** to number the leaves of (e g a manuscript) **3** to decorate (e g an arch or pedestal) with foils ~*vi* to divide into thin layers or leaves – **foliation** *n*

foliated *adj* composed of (easily separable) thin layers

[1]**folio** /ˈfohlioh‖ˈfəʊlɪəʊ/ *n, pl* **folios 1a** a leaf of a manuscript or book **b** a page or leaf number **2a(1)** (the size of each of the 2 leaves formed from) a sheet of paper folded once **a(2)** a book printed on pages of this size **b** a book of the largest size **3** a case or folder for loose papers **4** a certain number of words taken as a unit in measuring the length of a document

[2]**folio** *vt* **folios; folioing; folioed** FOLIATE 2

[1]**folk** /fohk‖fəʊk/ *n* **1** *pl in constr* the great proportion of a people that tends to preserve its customs, superstitions, etc **2** *pl in constr* a specified kind or class of people <*old* ~> – often pl with sing. meaning <*just plain* ~s> **3** simple music, usu song, of traditional origin or style **4** *pl in constr* people generally – infml; often pl with sing. meaning **5** *pl* the members of one's own family; relatives – infml

[2]**folk** *adj* **1** originating or traditional with the common people **2** of (the study of) the common people

ˈ**folk etyˌmology** *n* the transformation of words so as to bring them into an apparent relationship with other more familiar words (e g in the change of Spanish *cucaracha* to *cockroach*)

ˈ**folkˌlore** /-law‖-lɔː/ *n* **1** traditional customs and beliefs of a people preserved by oral tradition **2** the study of the life and spirit of a people through their folklore – **folklorist** *n*, **folkloric** *adj*

folksy /ˈfohksi‖ˈfəʊksɪ/ *adj* **1** informal or familiar in manner or style **2** having or affecting a lack of sophistication – chiefly derog *USE* infml – **folksily** *adv*, **folksiness** *n*

ˈ**folkˌway** /-ˌway‖-ˌweɪ/ *n* a traditional social custom

follicle /ˈfolikl‖ˈfɒlɪkl/ *n* **1a** a small anatomical cavity or deep narrow depression **b** GRAAFIAN FOLLICLE **2** a dry 1-celled many-seeded fruit that has a single carpel and opens along 1 line only – **follicular, folliculate** *also* **folliculated** *adj*

follow /ˈfoloh‖ˈfɒləʊ/ *vt* **1** to go, proceed, or come after <~ed *the guide*> **2a** to pursue, esp in an effort to overtake **b** to seek to attain; strive after <~ *knowledge*> **3a** to accept as a guide or leader **b** to obey or act in accordance with <*he* ~ed *the advice*> **4** to copy, imitate **5a** to walk or proceed along <~ *a path*> **b** to engage in as a calling or way of life; pursue (e g a course of action) **6a** to come or take place after in time or order **b** to cause to be followed – usu + *with* <~ed *dinner with a liqueur*> **7** to come into existence or take place as a result or consequence of **8a** to watch steadily <~ed *the ball over the fence*> **b** to keep the mind on <~ *a speech*> **c** to attend closely to; keep abreast of <*she* ~ed *his career with interest*> **d** to understand the logic of (e g an argument) <*I don't* *quite* ~ *you*> ~ *vi* 1 to go or come after sby or sthg in place, time, or sequence **2** to result or occur as a consequence or inference **3** *chiefly Br* to understand the logic of a line of thought – **follow one's nose** to go in a straight or obvious course – **follow suit 1** to play a card of the same suit as the card led **2** to follow an example set

follower /'foloh·ə‖'fɒləʊə/ *n* **1a** one who follows the opinions or teachings of another **b** one who imitates another **2** [3]FAN

[1]'**following** /-ing‖-ɪŋ/ *adj* **1** next after; succeeding <*the* ~ *day*> **2** now to be stated <*trains will leave at the* ~ *times*> **3** *of a wind* blowing in the direction in which sthg is travelling

[2]**following** *n, pl (1)* **following,** *(2)* **followings 1** sthg that comes immediately after or below in writing or speech **2** *sing or pl in constr* a group of followers, adherents, or partisans

[3]**following** *prep* subsequent to < ~ *the lecture tea was served*>

,**follow-my-'leader** *n, Br* **1** a game in which the actions of a designated leader must be copied by the other players **2** the slavish following by the majority of people of an example set by an individual

follow on *vi, of a side in cricket* to bat a second time immediately after making a score that is less, by more than a predetermined limit, than that of the opposing team in its first innings – **follow-on** *n*

follow through *vi* to continue the movement of a stroke after a cricket, golf, etc ball has been struck ~*vt* to pursue (an activity or process), esp to a conclusion – **follow-through** *n*

follow up *vt* **1a** to follow with sthg similar, related, or supplementary <following up *his promises with action*> **b** to take appropriate action about <follow up *complaints*> **2** to maintain contact with or reexamine (a person) at usu prescribed intervals in order to evaluate a diagnosis or treatment – **follow-up** *n*

folly /'foli‖'fɒlɪ/ *n* **1** lack of good sense or prudence **2** a foolish act or idea **3** (criminally or tragically) foolish actions or conduct **4** a usu fanciful structure (e g a summerhouse) built esp for scenic effect or to satisfy a whim

foment /foh'ment‖fəʊ'ment/ *vt* **1** to treat with moist heat (e g for easing pain) **2** to promote the growth or development of; incite < ~ *a rebellion*> – **fomenter** *n*

fomentation /,fohmen'taysh(ə)n‖,fəʊmen'teɪʃ(ə)n/ *n* **1** (the application to the body of) hot moist substances **2** fomenting, instigation

fond /fond‖fɒnd/ *adj* **1** foolish, silly < ~ *pride*> **2** having an affection or liking for sthg specified – + *of* < ~ *of music*> **3a** foolishly tender; indulgent **b** affectionate, loving **4** doted on; cherished <*his* ~est *hopes*>. – **fondness** *n*

fondant /'fondənt ‖'fɒndənt (*Fr* fɔ̃dɑ̃)/ *n* (a sweet made from) a soft creamy preparation of flavoured sugar and water

fondle /'fondl‖'fɒndl/ *vt* to handle tenderly or lingeringly ~*vi* to show affection or desire by caressing

fondly /'fondli‖'fɒndlɪ/ *adv* **1** affectionately **2** in a willingly credulous manner <*government* ~ *imagine that cutting taxes will reduce wage demands*>

fondue /'fond(y)ooh ‖'fɒnd(j)uː (*Fr* fɔ̃dy)/ *n* a dish consisting of a hot liquid (e g oil or a thick sweet or savoury sauce) into which small pieces of food are dipped for cooking or coating; *esp* one made with melted cheese and usu white wine

[1]**font** /font‖fɒnt/ *n* **1a** a receptacle for holy water; *esp* one used in baptism **b** a receptacle for oil in a lamp **2** *chiefly NAm* [1]FOUNT – **fontal** *adj*

[2]**font** *n, chiefly NAm* [2]FOUNT

food /foohd‖fuːd/ *n* **1a** (minerals, vitamins, etc together with) material consisting essentially of protein, carbohydrate, and fat taken into the body of a living organism and used to provide energy and sustain processes (e g growth and repair) essential for life **b** inorganic substances absorbed (e g in gaseous form or in solution) by plants **2** nutriment in solid form **3** sthg that sustains or supplies < ~ *for thought*>

'**food** ,**poisoning** *n* an acute gastrointestinal disorder caused by (the toxic products of) bacteria or by chemical residues in food

'**food,stuff** /-,stuf‖-,stʌf/ *n* a substance with food value; *esp* the raw material of food before or after processing

[1]**fool** /foohl‖fuːl/ *n* **1** a person lacking in prudence, common sense, or understanding **2a** a jester **b** a person who is victimized or made to appear foolish; a dupe **3** a cold dessert of fruit puree mixed with whipped cream or custard [Old French *fol*, fr Late Latin *follis*, fr Latin, bellows, bag] – **foolery** *n*

[2]**fool** *vi* **1a** to act or spend time idly or aimlessly **b(1)** to meddle, play, or trifle *with* <*a dangerous man to* ~ *with*> **b(2)** to philander *with* <*stop* ~ing *about with my wife*> **2** to play or improvise a comic role; *specif* to joke ~*vt* to make a fool of; deceive *USE* (*vi 1*) often + *around* or *about*

'**fool,hardy** /-,hahdi‖-,hɑːdɪ/ *adj* foolishly adventurous and bold; rash – **foolhardily** *adv*, **foolhardiness** *n*

foolish /'foohlish‖'fuːlɪʃ/ *adj* **1** marked by or proceeding from folly **2** absurd, ridiculous – **foolishly** *adv*, **foolishness** *n*

'**fool,proof** /-,proohf‖-,pruːf/ *adj* so simple or reliable as to leave no opportunity for error, misuse, or failure

foolscap /'foohlskap, 'fool-‖'fuːlskæp, 'fʊl-/ *n* a size of paper usu 17 × 13 1/2in (432 × 343mm) [fr the watermark of a fool's cap formerly applied to such paper]

'**fool's** ,**errand** *n* a needless or fruitless errand

'**fool's** ,**gold** *n* IRON PYRITES

,**fool's** '**paradise** *n* a state of illusory happiness

[1]**foot** /foot‖fʊt/ *n, pl* **feet** /feet‖fiːt/, *(3)* **feet** *also* **foot,** *(9)* **foot 1** the end part of the vertebrate leg on which an animal stands **2** an organ of locomotion or attachment of an invertebrate animal, esp a mollusc **3** a unit of length equal to 1/3yd (0.305m) **4** the basic unit of verse metre consisting of any of various fixed combinations of stressed and unstressed or long and short syllables **5** manner or motion of walking or running; step <*fleet of* ~ > **6a** the lower end of the leg of a chair, table, etc **b** the piece on a sewing

machine that presses the cloth against the feed **7** the lower edge or lowest part; the bottom *<the ~ of a page>* *<the ~ of the stairs>* **8a** the end that is opposite the head or top or nearest to the human feet *<the ~ of the bed>* **b** the part (e g of a stocking) that covers the human foot **9** *chiefly Br, sing or pl in constr* the infantry – **my foot** MY EYE – infml – **on foot** by walking or running *<tour the city* on foot> – **on one's feet 1** standing **2** in a recovered condition (e g from illness) **3** in an impromptu manner *<good debaters can think* on their feet>

[2]**foot** *vi* to dance ~ *vt* **1a** to perform the movements of (a dance) **b** to walk, run, or dance on, over, or through **2** to pay or stand credit for *<agreed to ~ the bill>* **3** to make or renew the foot of (e g a stocking) – **foot it 1** to dance **2** to travel on foot

footage /ˈfootij‖ˈfʊtɪdʒ/ *n* **1** length or quantity expressed in feet **2** (the length in feet of) exposed film

ˌfoot-and-ˈmouth, foot-and-mouth disease *n* a contagious virus disease, esp of cloven-footed animals, marked by small ulcers in the mouth, about the hoofs, and on the udder and teats

ˈfootˌball /-ˌbawl‖-ˌbɔːl/ *n* **1** (the inflated round or oval ball used in) any of several games, esp soccer, that are played between 2 teams on a usu rectangular field having goalposts at each end and whose object is to get the ball over a goal line or between goalposts by running, passing, or kicking **2** sthg treated as a basis for contention *<the bill became a political ~ in Parliament>* – **footballer** *n*

ˈfootball ˌpools *n* a form of organized gambling based on forecasting the results of football matches

ˈfootˌbath /-ˌbahth‖-ˌbɑːθ/ *n* a bath for cleansing, warming, or disinfecting the feet

ˈfootˌboard /-ˌbawd‖-ˌbɔːd/ *n* **1** a narrow platform on which to stand or brace the feet **2** a board forming the foot of a bed

ˈfootˌbridge /-ˌbrij‖-ˌbrɪdʒ/ *n* a bridge for pedestrians

ˈfooted *adj* having a foot or feet, esp of a specified kind or number – usu in combination *<a 4-*footed *animal>*

footer /ˈfootə‖ˈfʊtə/ *n, chiefly Br* soccer – infml; no longer in vogue

-footer /-footə‖-fʊtə/ *comb form* (→ *n*) sby or sthg that is a (specified) number of feet in height, length, or breadth

ˈfootˌfall /-ˌfawl‖-ˌfɔːl/ *n* the sound of a footstep

ˈfoot ˌfault *vi or n* (to make) a fault in tennis made when a server's feet are not behind the baseline

ˈfootˌhill /-ˌhil‖-ˌhɪl/ *n* a hill at the foot of mountains

ˈfootˌhold /-ˌhohld‖-ˌhəʊld/ *n* **1** FOOTING 1 **2** an (established) position or basis from which to progress

footing /ˈfooting‖ˈfʊtɪŋ/ *n* **1** a stable position or placing of or for the feet **2** a (condition of a) surface with respect to its suitability for walking or running on **3a** an established position; FOOTHOLD 2 **b** a position or rank in relation to others *<they all started off on an equal ~>* **4** an enlargement at the lower end of a foundation, wall, pier, or column to distribute the load; *also* a trench dug to accommodate this – often pl

footle /ˈfoohtl‖ˈfuːtl/ *vi* to mess or potter *around* or *about*; *also* to waste time – infml

ˈfootˌlights /-ˌliets‖-ˌlaɪts/ *n pl* a row of lights set across the front of a stage floor

footling /ˈfoohtling‖ˈfuːtlɪŋ/ *adj* **1** bungling, inept **2** unimportant, trivial; *also* pettily fussy *USE* infml

ˈfootˌloose /-ˌloohs‖-ˌluːs/ *adj* having no ties; free to go or do as one pleases

ˈfootman /-mən‖-mən/ *n* a servant in livery hired chiefly to wait, receive visitors, etc

footnote /-ˌnoht‖-ˌnəʊt/ *n* **1** a note of reference, explanation, or comment typically placed at the bottom of a printed page **2** sthg subordinately related to a larger event or work *<that biography is an illuminating ~ to the history of our times>* – **footnote** *vt*

[1]**ˈfootˌpad** /-ˌpad‖-ˌpæd/ *n, archaic* one who robs a pedestrian

[2]**footpad** *n* a broad foot on the leg of a spacecraft

ˈfootˌpath /-ˌpahth‖-ˌpɑːθ/ *n* a narrow path for pedestrians; *also* PAVEMENT a

ˈfootˌplate /-ˌplayt‖-ˌpleɪt/ *n, Br* the platform on which the crew stand in a locomotive

ˈfootˌprint /-ˌprint‖-ˌprɪnt/ *n* **1** an impression left by the foot **2** an area within which a spacecraft is intended to land

ˈfoot ˌrot *n* a progressive inflammation of the feet of sheep or cattle

ˌfootˈrule /-ˈroohl‖-ˈruːl/ *n* a ruler 1ft long; *also* a ruler graduated in feet and inches

footsie /ˈfootsi‖ˈfʊtsɪ/ *n* **1** surreptitious amorous caresses with the feet **2** clandestine dealings *USE* chiefly in *play footsie with*; infml

ˈfootˌslog /-ˌslog‖-ˌslɒg/ *vi* **-gg-** to march or tramp laboriously – infml – **footslog** *n*, **footslogger** *n*

ˈfootˌsore /-ˌsaw‖-ˌsɔː/ *adj* having sore or tender feet (e g from much walking) – **footsoreness** *n*

ˈfootˌstep /-ˌstep‖-ˌstep/ *n* **1a** the sound of a step or tread **b** distance covered by a step **2** FOOTPRINT 1 **3** a way of life, conduct, or action – usu pl with sing. meaning *<followed in his father's ~s>*

ˈfootˌwear /-ˌweə‖-ˌweə/ *n* articles (e g shoes or boots) worn on the feet

ˈfootˌwork /-ˌwuhk‖-ˌwɜːk/ *n* **1** the control and placing of the feet, esp in sport (e g in boxing or batting) **2** the activity of moving from place to place on foot *<the investigation entailed a lot of ~>*

fop /fop‖fɒp/ *n* a dandy – **foppish** *adj*, **foppishly** *adv*, **foppishness** *n*

[1]**for** /fə‖fə; *strong* faw‖fɔː/ *prep* **1a** – used to indicate purpose *<a grant ~ studying medicine>* *<what's this knob ~?>*, goal or direction *<left ~ home>* *<getting on ~ 5>*, or that which is to be had or gained *<now ~ a good rest>* *<run ~ your life>* **b** to belong to *<the flowers are ~ you>* **2** as being or constituting *<take him ~ a fool>* *<ate it ~ breakfast>* **3a** BECAUSE OF 1 *<cried ~ joy>* **b**

because of the hindrance of <*couldn't speak* ~ *laughing*> **4a** in place of <*change* ~ *a pound*> **b** on behalf of; representing <*acting* ~ *my client*> **c** in support of; IN FAVOUR OF 1 <*he played* ~ *England*> **5** considered as; considering <*tall* ~ *her age*> **6** with respect to; concerning <*famous* ~ *its scenery*> <*eggs are good* ~ *you*> **7** – used to indicate cost, payment, equivalence, or correlation <*£7* ~ *a hat*> <*punished* ~ *talking*> <*wouldn't hurt her* ~ *the world*> **8** – used to indicate duration of time or extent of space <~ *10 miles*> <*the worst accident* ~ *months*> **9** on the occasion or at the time of <*came home* ~ *Christmas*> <*invited them* ~ *9 o'clock*> **10** – used to introduce a clause with a nonfinite verb <*no need* ~ *you to worry*> <*it's dangerous* ~ *George to hurry*> **11** *chiefly NAm* AFTER 5 – **for all 1** IN SPITE OF <*couldn't open it* for all *their efforts*> **2** to the extent that <*dead* for all *I know*> **3** considering how little <*might as well stop talking* for all *the good it does*> – **for all one is worth** with all one's might – **for it** *chiefly Br* likely to get into trouble – infml – **for what it is worth** without guarantee of wisdom or accuracy – **for you** – used after *there* or *that* in exclamations of enthusiasm or exasperation <*that's country hotels* for you!>

[2]**for** *conj* **1** and the reason is that **2** BECAUSE 2

[3]**for** *adj* being in favour of a motion or measure

for- *prefix* **1a** so as to involve prohibition or exclusion <for*bid*> **b** so as to involve omission, refraining, or neglect <for*go*> <for*get*> **2** destructively; detrimentally <for*do*> **3** completely; excessively <for*spent*>

[1]**forage** /ˈforij‖ˈfɒrɪdʒ/ *n* **1** food for animals, esp when taken by browsing or grazing **2** a foraging for provisions; *broadly* a search

[2]**forage** *vt* **1** to collect or take provisions or forage from **2** to secure by foraging <~d *a chicken for the feast*> ~ *vi* **1** to wander in search of forage or food **2** to make a search *for*; rummage – **forager** *n*

forasˈmuch as /fərəzˈmuch‖fərəzˈmʌtʃ/ *conj, archaic* in view of the fact that; since

[1]**foray** /ˈforay‖ˈfɒreɪ/ *vi* to make a raid or incursion – **forayer** *n*

[2]**foray** *n* **1** a sudden invasion, attack, or raid **2** a brief excursion or attempt, esp outside one's accustomed sphere

[1]**forbear** /fawˈbeə‖fɔːˈbeə/ *vb* **forbore** /fawˈbaw‖fɔːˈbɔː/; **forborne** /fawˈbawn‖fɔːˈbɔːn/ *vt* to hold oneself back from, esp with an effort of self-restraint <*he* forbore *to answer the slander*> ~ *vi* **1** to hold back, abstain – usu + *from* <*he* forbore *from expressing his disagreement*> **2** to control oneself when provoked; be patient – chiefly fml

[2]**forbear** /ˈfawˌbeə‖ˈfɔːˌbeə/ *n* a forebear

forbearance /fawˈbeərəns‖fɔːˈbeərəns/ *n* **1** a refraining from the enforcement of sthg (e g a debt, right, or obligation) that is due **2** patience **3** leniency

forbid /fəˈbid‖fəˈbɪd/ *vt* **forbidding; forbade** /fəˈbad, -ˈbayd‖fəˈbæd, -ˈbeɪd/, **forbad; forbidden /fəˈbid(ə)n‖feˈbɪd(ə)n/** **1a** to refuse (e g by authority) to allow; command against <*the law* ~s *shops to sell alcohol to minors*> **b** to refuse access to or use of <*her father* forbade *him the house*> **2** to make impracticable; hinder, prevent <*space* ~s *further treatment of the subject here*> – **forbidder** *n*

forbidding /fəˈbiding‖fəˈbɪdɪŋ/ *adj* having a menacing, dangerous, or stern appearance – **forbiddingly** *adv*, **forbiddingness** *n*

[1]**force** /faws‖fɔːs/ *n* **1a** strength or energy exerted or brought to bear; active power <*the* ~s *of nature*> **b** moral or mental strength **c** capacity to persuade or convince <*couldn't resist the* ~ *of his argument*> **d** (legal) validity; operative effect <*an agreement having the* ~ *of law*> **2a(1)** a body (e g of troops or ships) assigned to a military purpose **a(2)** *pl* the armed services of a nation or commander **b(1)** a body of people or things fulfilling an often specified function <*a labour* ~> **b(2)** POLICE FORCE – often + *the* **c** an individual or group having the power of effective action <*he was the driving* ~ *behind the passing of that bill*> **3** violence, compulsion, or constraint exerted on or against a person or thing **4a** (the intensity of) an agency that if applied to a free body results chiefly in an acceleration of the body and sometimes in elastic deformation and other effects **b** an agency or influence analogous to a physical force <*economic* ~s> **5** the quality of conveying impressions intensely in writing or speech **6** *cap* a measure of wind strength as expressed by a number on the Beaufort scale <*a* Force *9 gale*> – **in force 1** in great numbers <*police were summoned* in force> **2** valid, operative <*the new law is now* in force>

[2]**force** *vt* **1** to compel by physical, moral, or intellectual means <~d *labour*> **2** to make or cause through natural or logical necessity <*his arguments* ~d *them to admit he was right*> **3a** to press, drive, or effect against resistance or inertia <~d *his way through the crowd*> **b** to impose or thrust urgently, importunately, or inexorably <~ *unwanted attentions on a woman*> **4a** to capture or penetrate by force <~ *a castle*> **b** to break open or through <~ *a lock*> **5a** to raise or accelerate to the utmost <forcing *the pace*> **b** to produce only with unnatural or unwilling effort <*a* ~d *laugh*> **6** to hasten the growth, onset of maturity, or rate of progress of <forcing *rhubarb*> **7** to induce (e g a particular bid from one's partner) in a card game by some conventional act, bid, etc **8** *of a batsman in cricket* to play an aggressive shot at (a delivery), esp off the back foot – **forcedly** *adv*, **forcer** *n* – **force someone's hand** to cause sby to act precipitously or reveal his/her purpose or intention

ˈforce-ˌfeed *vt* to feed forcibly

ˈforceful /-f(ə)l‖-f(ə)l/ *adj* possessing or filled with force; effective – **forcefully** *adv*, **forcefulness** *n*

ˌforce maˈjeure /maˈzhuh ‖mæˈʒɜː (*Fr* fɔrs maʒœːr)/ *n* a disruptive event (e g war) that cannot be reasonably anticipated

ˈforceˌmeat /-ˌmeet‖-ˌmiːt/ *n* a savoury highly seasoned stuffing, esp of breadcrumbs and meat

forceps /ˈfawsips, -seps‖ˈfɔːsɪps, -seps/ *n, pl*

forceps an instrument used (e g in surgery and watchmaking) for grasping, holding firmly, or pulling – usu pl with sing. meaning [Latin, fr *formus* warm + *capere* to take]

forcible /ˈfawsəbl‖ˈfɔːsəbl/ *adj* **1** effected by force used against opposition or resistance **2** powerful, forceful <*a* ~ *argument*> – **forcibleness** *n*, **forcibly** *adv*

[1]**ford** /fawd‖fɔːd/ *n* a shallow part of a river or other body of water that can be crossed by wading, in a vehicle, etc

[2]**ford** *vt* to cross (a river, stream, etc) at a ford – **fordable** *adj*

[1]**fore** /faw‖fɔː/ *adj or adv* (situated) in, towards, or adjacent to the front

[2]**fore** *n* sthg that occupies a forward position – **to the fore** in or into a position of prominence

[3]**fore** *interj* – used by a golfer to warn anyone in the probable line of flight of his/her ball

fore- /faw-‖fɔː-/ *comb form* **1** (occurring) earlier or beforehand <fore*payment*> **2a** situated at the front; in front <fore*leg*> **b** front part of <fore*arm*>

ˌ**fore-and-ˈaft** /ahft‖ɑːft/ *adj* **1** lying, running, or acting in the general line of the length of a ship or other construction **2** having no square sails

ˌ**fore and ˈaft** *adv* from stem to stern

[1]**forearm** /fawˈrahm, fawˈahm‖fɔːˈrɑːm, fɔː-ˈɑːm/ *vt* to arm in advance; prepare

[2]**forearm** /ˈfawˌrahm‖ˈfɔːˌrɑːm/ *n* (the part in other vertebrates corresponding to) the human arm between the elbow and the wrist

forebear, forbear /ˈfawˌbeə‖ˈfɔːˌbeə/ *n* an ancestor, forefather

forebode /fawˈbohd, fə-‖fɔːˈbəʊd, fə-/ *vt* **1** to foretell, portend **2** to have a premonition of (evil, misfortune, etc) – **foreboder** *n*

foreˈboding /-ˈbohding‖-ˈbəʊdɪŋ/ *n* an omen, prediction, or presentiment, esp of coming evil

[1]**forecast** /ˈfawˌkahst‖ˈfɔːˌkɑːst/ *vb* **forecast, forecasted** *vt* **1** to estimate or predict (some future event or condition), esp as a result of rational study and analysis of available pertinent data **2** to serve as a forecast of; presage ~*vi* to calculate or predict the future – **forecaster** *n*

[2]**forecast** *n* a prophecy, estimate, or prediction of a future happening or condition; *esp* a weather forecast

forecastle, fo'c'sle /ˈfohks(ə)l‖ˈfəʊks(ə)l/ *n* **1** a short raised deck at the bow of a ship **2** a forward part of a merchant ship having the living quarters

foreclose /fawˈklohz‖fɔːˈkləʊz/ *vt* **1** to take away the right to redeem (e g a mortgage), usu because of nonpayment **2** to take away the right to redeem a mortgage or other debt from ~*vi* to foreclose a mortgage or other debt – **foreclosure** *n*

ˈ**foreˌcourt** /-ˌkawt‖-ˌkɔːt/ *n* an open or paved area in front of a building; *esp* that part of a petrol station where the petrol pumps are situated

ˈ**foreˌfather** /-ˌfahdhə‖-ˌfɑːðə/ *n* **1** ANCESTOR 1a **2** a person of an earlier period and common heritage

ˈ**foreˌfinger** /-ˌfing·gə‖-ˌfɪŋgə/ *n* the finger next to the thumb

ˈ**foreˌfoot** /-ˌfoot‖-ˌfʊt/ *n* the forward part of a ship where the stem and keel meet

ˈ**foreˌfront** /-ˌfrunt‖-ˌfrʌnt/ *n* the foremost part or place; the vanguard

forego /fəˈgoh, faw-‖fəˈgəʊ, fɔː-/ *vt* **foregoes; foregoing; forewent** /fawˈwent‖fɔːˈwent/; **foregone** /fawˈgon‖fɔːˈgɒn/ to forgo

foregoing /ˈfawˌgoh·ing‖ˈfɔːˌgəʊɪŋ/ *adj* going before; that immediately precedes <*the* ~ *statement is open to challenge*>

ˌ**foregone conˈclusion** *n* an inevitable result; a certainty

ˈ**foreˌground** /-ˌgrownd‖-ˌgraʊnd/ *n* **1** the part of a picture or view nearest to and in front of the spectator **2** a position of prominence; the forefront

[1]ˈ**foreˌhand** /-ˌhand‖-ˌhænd/ *n* **1** the part of a horse in front of the rider **2** a forehand stroke in tennis, squash, etc; *also* the side or part of the court on which such strokes are made

[2]**forehand** *adj or adv* (made) with the palm of the hand turned in the direction of movement

forehead /ˈfawˌhed, ˈforid‖ˈfɔːˌhed, ˈfɒrɪd/ *n* the part of the face above the eyes

foreign /ˈforən‖ˈfɒrən; *also* ˈforin‖ˈfɒrɪn/ *adj* **1** (situated) outside a place or country; *esp* (situated) outside one's own country **2** born in, belonging to, or characteristic of some place or country other than the one under consideration **3** of or proceeding from some other person or material thing than the one under consideration **4** alien in character; not connected or pertinent *to* **5** of, concerned with, or dealing with other nations <~ *trade*> **6** occurring in an abnormal situation in the living body and commonly introduced from outside [Old French *forein*, fr Late Latin *foranus* on the outside, fr Latin *foris* outside] – **foreignism** *n*, **foreignness** *n*

ˌ**foreign ˈaid** *n* (economic) assistance provided by one nation to another

ˈ**foreigner** /-nə‖-nə/ *n* **1** a person belonging to or owing allegiance to a foreign country; an alien **2** *chiefly dial* STRANGER 1b; *esp* a person not native to a community

ˈ**foreign ˌoffice** *n* the government department for foreign affairs

foreˈknow *vt* **foreknew** /-ˈnyooh‖-ˈnjuː/; **foreknown** /-ˈnohn‖-ˈnəʊn/ to have previous knowledge of; know beforehand, esp by paranormal means or by revelation – **foreknowledge** *n*

ˈ**foreland** /-lənd‖-lənd/ *n* a promontory, headland

ˈ**foreˌleg** /-ˌleg‖-ˌleg/ *n* a front leg, esp of a quadruped

ˈ**foreˌlock** /-ˌlok‖-ˌlɒk/ *n* a lock of hair growing just above the forehead

ˈ**foreman** /-mən‖-mən/, *fem* ˈ**foreˌwoman** *n, pl* **foremen** /-mən‖-mən/ **1** the chairman and spokesman of a jury **2** a person, often a chief worker, who supervises a group of workers, a particular operation, or a section of a plant

ˈ**foreˌmast** /-ˌmahst‖-ˌmɑːst/ *n* the (lower part of the) mast nearest the bow of a ship

[1]ˈ**foreˌmost** /-ˌmohst, -məst‖-ˌməʊst, -məst/ *adj* **1** first in a series or progression **2** of first rank or position; preeminent

[2]**foremost** *adv* most importantly

<*first and* ~>

'foreˌname /-ˌnaym‖-ˌneɪm/ *n* a name that precedes a person's surname

'foreˌnoon /-ˌnoohn‖-ˌnuːn/ *n the* morning – fml

forensic /fə'renzik‖fə'renzɪk/ *adj* **1** belonging to or used in courts of law **2** of or being the scientific investigation of crime – **forensically** *adv*

ˌforeor'dain /-aw'dayn‖-ɔː'deɪn/ *vt* to settle, arrange, or appoint in advance; predestine – **foreordination** *n*

'foreˌpart /-ˌpaht‖-ˌpɑːt/ *n* the front part of sthg

'foreˌplay /-ˌplay‖-ˌpleɪ/ *n* erotic stimulation preceding sexual intercourse

'foreˌrunner /-ˌrunə‖-ˌrʌnə/ *n* **1** a premonitory sign or symptom **2a** a predecessor, forefather **b** PROTOTYPE 1

'foreˌsail /-ˌsayl‖-ˌseɪl/ *n* **1** the lowest square sail on the foremast of a square-rigged ship **2** the principal fore-and-aft sail set on a schooner's foremast

foresee /faw'see‖fɔː'siː/ *vt* **foreseeing; foresaw** /-'saw‖-'sɔː/; **foreseen** /-'seen‖-'siːn/ to be aware of (e g a development) beforehand – **foreseeable** *adj*, **foreseer** *n*

fore'shadow /-'shadoh‖-'ʃædəʊ/ *vt* to represent or typify beforehand; prefigure, suggest <*present trends* ~ *future events*> – **foreshadower** *n*

'foreˌshore /-ˌshaw‖-ˌʃɔː/ *n* **1** a strip of land bordering a body of water **2** the part of a seashore between high-tide and low-tide marks

fore'shorten /-'shawt(ə)n‖-'ʃɔːt(ə)n/ *vt* **1** to shorten (a detail in a drawing or painting) so as to create an illusion of depth **2** to make more compact

'foreˌsight /-ˌsiet‖-ˌsaɪt/ *n* **1** foreseeing, prescience **2** provident care; prudence **3** the sight nearest the muzzle on a firearm – **foresighted** *adj*, **foresightedly** *adv*, **foresightedness** *n*

'foreˌskin /-ˌskin‖-ˌskɪn/ *n* a fold of skin that covers the glans of the penis

[1]**forest** /'forist‖'fɒrɪst/ *n* **1** a tract of wooded land in Britain formerly owned by the sovereign and used for hunting game **2** a dense growth of trees and underbrush covering a large tract of land **3** sthg resembling a profusion of trees <*a* ~ *of TV aerials*>

[2]**forest** *vt* to cover with trees or forest – **forestation** *n*

fore'stall /-'stawl‖-'stɔːl/ *vt* **1** to exclude, hinder, or prevent by prior measures **2** to get ahead of; anticipate – **forestaller** *n*, **forestallment** *n*

forester /'foristə‖'fɒrɪstə/ *n* **1** a person trained in forestry **2** a person, animal, moth, etc that inhabits forest land

forestry /'foristri‖'fɒrɪstrɪ/ *n* **1** forest land **2** the scientific cultivation or management of forests

foretaste /'fawˌtayst‖'fɔːˌteɪst/ *n* **1** an advance indication or warning **2** a small anticipatory sample

fore'tell /-'tel‖-'tel/ *vt* **foretold** /-'tohld‖-'təʊld/ to tell beforehand; predict – **foreteller** *n*

'foreˌthought /-ˌthawt‖-ˌθɔːt/ *n* **1** a thinking or planning out in advance; premeditation **2** consideration for the future

[1]**forever** /fə'revə‖fə'revə/ *adv* **1 forever, forevermore** for all future time; indefinitely <*wants to live* ~> **2** persistently, incessantly <*is* ~ *whistling out of tune*>

[2]**forever** *n* a seemingly endless length of time

fore'warn /-'wawn‖-'wɔːn/ *vt* to warn in advance

'foreˌwoman /-ˌwoomən‖-ˌwʊmən/ *n, pl* **forewomen** /-wimin‖-wɪmɪn/ a woman who acts as a foreman

'foreˌword /-ˌwuhd‖-ˌwɜːd/ *n* a preface; *esp* one written by sby other than the author of the text

[1]**forfeit** /'fawfit‖'fɔːfɪt/ *n* **1** sthg lost, taken away, or imposed as a penalty **2** the loss or forfeiting of sthg, esp of civil rights [Middle French *forfait*, fr *forfaire* to commit a crime, forfeit, prob fr *fors* outside + *faire* to do] – **forfeit** *adj*

[2]**forfeit** *vt* **1** to lose the right to by some error, offence, or crime **2** to subject to confiscation as a forfeit – **forfeitable** *adj*, **forfeiture** *n*

forgather, foregather /faw'gadhə‖fɔː'gæðə/ *vi* to come together; assemble

[1]**forge** /fawj‖fɔːdʒ/ *n* (a workshop with) an open furnace where metal, esp iron, is heated and wrought

[2]**forge** *vt* **1** to shape (metal or a metal object) by heating and hammering or with a press **2** to form or bring into being, esp by an expenditure of effort <*made every effort to* ~ *party unity*> **3** to counterfeit (esp a signature, document, or bank note) ~*vi* to commit forgery – **forgeable** *adj*, **forger** *n*

[3]**forge** *vi* **1** to move forwards slowly and steadily but with effort <*the great ship* ~d *through the waves*> **2** to move with a sudden increase of speed and power <*the horse* ~d *ahead to win the race*>

forgery /'fawjəri‖'fɔːdʒərɪ/ *n* **1** (the crime of) forging **2** a forged document, bank note, etc

forget /fə'get‖fə'get/ *vb* **forgetting; forgot** /-'got‖-'gɒt/; **forgotten** /-'got(ə)n‖-'gɒt(ə)n/, *archaic or NAm* **forgot** *vt* **1** to fail to remember; lose the remembrance of **2** to fail to give attention to; disregard <forgot *his old friends*> ~ *vi* **1** to cease remembering or noticing <*forgive and* ~> **2** to fail to remember at the proper time – usu + *about* <~ *about paying the bill*> – **forgetter** *n* – **forget oneself** to lose one's dignity, temper, or self-control; act unsuitably or unworthily

for'getful /-f(ə)l‖-f(ə)l/ *adj* **1** likely or apt to forget **2** characterized by negligent failure to remember; neglectful – usu + *of* <~ *of his manners*> – **forgetfully** *adv*, **forgetfulness** *n*

for'get-me-ˌnot *n* any of a genus of small plants with white or bright blue flowers usu arranged in a spike

forgive /fə'giv‖fə'gɪv/ *vb* **forgave** /-'gayv‖-'geɪv/; **forgiven** /-'giv(ə)n‖-'gɪv(ə)n/ *vt* **1** to cease to resent <~ *an insult*> **2** to pardon <~ *us our trespasses*> ~*vi* to grant forgiveness – **forgivable** *adj*, **forgivably** *adv*, **forgiver** *n*, **forgiving** *adj*, **forgivingly** *adv*

for'giveness /-nis‖-nɪs/ *n* forgiving or being forgiven; pardon

forgo, **forego** /fə'goh, faw-‖fə'gəʊ, fɔː-/ *vt* **forgoes; forgoing; forwent** /faw'went‖fɔː'went/; **forgone** /faw'gon‖fɔː'gɒn/ to abstain or refrain from

1fork /fawk‖fɔːk/ *n* **1** a tool or implement with 2 or more prongs set on the end of a handle: e g **1a** an agricultural or gardening tool for digging, carrying, etc **b** a small implement for eating or serving food **2a** a forked part, or piece of equipment **b** a forked support for a cycle wheel – often pl with sing. meaning **3** (a part containing) a division into branches **4** any of the branches into which sthg forks **5** an attack by a chess piece (e g a knight) on 2 pieces simultaneously – **forkful** *n*

2fork *vi* **1** to divide into 2 or more branches **2** to make a turn into one of the branches of a fork <*we* ~ed *left at the inn*> **3** to make a payment or contribution – + *out* or *up* ~ *vt* **1** to raise, pitch, dig, or work with a fork <~ *hay*> **2** to attack (2 chessmen) simultaneously **3** to pay, contribute – + *out, over,* or *up* <~ed *out half of his salary for a new car*> *USE* (*vi 3; vt 3*) infml

forked *adj* having one end divided into 2 or more branches or points <~ *lightning*>

'fork,lift, **,forklift 'truck** *n* a vehicle for hoisting and transporting heavy objects by means of steel prongs inserted under the load

forlorn /fə'lawn‖fə'lɔːn/ *adj* **1a** bereft or forsaken *of* **b** sad and lonely because of isolation or desertion; desolate **2** in poor condition; miserable, wretched <~ *tumbledown buildings*> **3** nearly hopeless <*a* ~ *attempt*> – **forlornly** *adv*

for,lorn 'hope *n* a desperate or extremely difficult enterprise [by folk etymology fr Dutch *verloren hoop*, lit., lost troop]

1form /fawm‖fɔːm/ *n* **1a** the shape and structure of sthg as distinguished from its material **b** a body (e g of a person), esp in its external appearance or as distinguished from the face **2** the essential nature of a thing as distinguished from the matter in which it is embodied **3a** established or correct method of proceeding or behaving <*I must ask for your name as a matter of* ~> **b** a prescribed and set order of words <*the* ~ *of the marriage service*> **4** a printed or typed document; *esp* one with blank spaces for insertion of required or requested information **5a** conduct regulated by external controls (e g custom or etiquette); ceremony **b** manner or conduct of a specified sort, as tested by a prescribed or accepted standard <*rudeness is simply bad* ~> **6a** the bed or nest of a hare **b** a long seat; a bench **7** sthg (e g a frame) that holds, supports, and determines shape **8a** the way in which sthg is arranged, exists, or shows itself <*written in the* ~ *of a letter*> **b** a kind, variety <*one* ~ *of respiratory disorder*> **9a** orderly method of arrangement (e g in the presentation of ideas); manner of coordinating elements (e g of an artistic production or line of reasoning) <*his work lacks* ~> **b** the structural element, plan, or design of a work of art **10** *sing or pl in constr* a class organized for the work of a particular year, esp in a British school **11a** the past performances of a competitor considered as a guide to its future performance **b** known ability to perform <*a singer at the top of his* ~> **c** condition suitable for performing, esp in sports – often + *in, out of,* or *off* <*was out of* ~ *all season*> **12** *Br* a criminal record – slang – **formless** *adj*, **formlessly** *adv*, **formlessness** *n*

2form *vt* **1** to give form, shape, or existence to; fashion <~ed *from clay*> <~ *a judgment*> **2a** to give a particular shape to; shape or mould into a certain state or after a particular model <*a state* ~ed *along the lines of the Roman Republic*> **b** to arrange themselves in <*the women* ~ed *a line*> **c** to model or train by instruction and discipline <*a mind* ~ed *by classical education*> **3** to develop, acquire <~ *a habit*> **4** to serve to make up or constitute; be a usu essential or basic element of **5a** to produce (e g a tense) by inflection <~s *the past in* -ed> **b** to combine to make (a compound word) **6** to arrange in order; DRAW UP 1 ~ *vi* **1** to become formed or shaped <*a scab* ~ed *over the wound*> **2** to take (a definite) form; come into existence <*thunderclouds were* ~ing *over the hills*> – **formable** *adj*

formal /'fawml‖'fɔːml/ *adj* **1a** determining or being the essential constitution or structure <~ *cause*> **b** of, concerned with, or being the (outward) form of sthg as distinguished from its content **2** following or according with established form, custom, or rule; conventional <*lacked* ~ *qualifications for the job*> **3a** based on conventional forms and rules <~ *landscaping*> **b** characterized by punctilious respect for correct procedure <*very* ~ *in all his dealings*> **c** rigidly ceremonious; prim **4** having the appearance without the substance; ostensible <~ *Christians who go to church only at Easter*> – **formally** *adv*

formaldehyde /faw'maldi,hied‖fɔː'mældɪ,haɪd/ *n* a pungent irritating gas used chiefly as a disinfectant and preservative and in chemical synthesis

formalin /'fawməlin‖'fɔːməlɪn/ *n* a clear aqueous solution of formaldehyde

formalism /'fawml,iz(ə)m‖'fɔːml,ɪz(ə)m/ *n* the practice or doctrine of strict adherence to or sole consideration of prescribed or external forms (e g in mathematics, religion, or art) – **formalist** *n or adj*, **formalistic** *adj*

formality /faw'maləti‖fɔː'mælətɪ/ *n* **1** compliance with or observance of formal or conventional rules **2** an established form that is required or conventional

formal·ize, -ise /'fawml,iez‖'fɔːml,aɪz/ *vt* **1** to make formal **2** to give formal status or approval to – **formalization** *n*

1format /'fawmat‖'fɔːmæt/ *n* **1** the shape, size, and general make-up (e g of a book) **2** the general plan of organization or arrangement

2format *vt* **-tt-** to arrange (e g a book or data) in a particular format or style

formation /faw'maysh(ə)n‖fɔː'meɪʃ(ə)n/ *n* **1** giving form or shape to sthg or taking form; development **2** sthg formed <*new word* ~s> **3** the manner in which a thing is formed; structure **4** a body or series of rocks represented as a unit in geological mapping **5** an arrangement of a group of people or things in some prescribed manner or for a particular purpose; *also, sing or* *pl in constr* such a group – **formational** *adj*

formative /ˈfawmətiv‖ˈfɔːmətɪv/ *adj* **1** (capable of) giving form; constructive <*a ~ influence*> **2** capable of alteration by growth and development <*~ tissues*> **3** of or characterized by formative effects or formation <*~ years*> – **formatively** *adv*

forme, *NAm* **form** /fawm‖fɔːm/ *n* a frame enclosing metal type or blocks ready for printing

[1]**former** /ˈfawmə‖ˈfɔːmə/ *adj* **1** of or occurring in the past <*in ~ times*> **2** preceding in time or order <*the ~ Prime Minister*> **3** first of 2 things (understood to have been) mentioned

[2]**former** *n, pl* **former** the first mentioned; first <*of puppies and kittens the ~ are harder to train*>

[3]**former** *n, chiefly Br* a member of a specified school form or year <*a sixth ~*> – often in combination

formerly /ˈfawməli‖ˈfɔːməlɪ/ *adv* at an earlier time; previously

Formica /fawˈmiekə‖fɔːˈmaɪkə/ *trademark* – used for any of various laminated plastics used for surfaces, esp on wood

ˌformic ˈacid /ˈfawmik‖ˈfɔːmɪk/ *n* a pungent corrosive liquid acid naturally produced by ants

formidable /ˈfawmidəbl‖ˈfɔːmɪdəbl; *also* fəˈmidəbl‖fəˈmɪdəbl/ *adj* **1** causing fear, dread, or apprehension <*a ~ prospect*> **2** difficult to overcome; discouraging approach **3** tending to inspire respect or awe [Latin *formidabilis*, fr *formidare* to fear, fr *formido* fear] – **formidableness** *n*, **formidably** *adv*

formula /ˈfawmyoolə‖ˈfɔːmjʊlə/ *n, pl* **formulas, formulae** /-lee, -lie‖-liː, -laɪ/ **1a** a set form of words for use in a ceremony or ritual **b** (a conventionalized statement intended to express) a truth, principle, or procedure, esp as a basis for negotiation or action <*a peace ~*> <*the ~ for a good marriage*> **2** (a list of ingredients used in) a recipe **3a** a fact, rule, or principle expressed in symbols **b** a symbolic expression of the chemical composition of a substance **c** a group of numerical symbols associated to express a single concept **4** a prescribed or set form or method (e g of writing); an established rule or custom <*unimaginative television programmes written to a ~*> **5** a classification of racing cars specifying esp size, weight, and engine capacity – **formulaic** *adj*, **formulaically** *adv*

formulate /ˈfawmyoolayt‖ˈfɔːmjʊleɪt/ *vt* **1** to state in or reduce to a formula **2** to devise or develop <*~ policy*> <*~*d *a new soap*> – **formulation** *n*, **formulator** *n*

fornicate /ˈfawnikayt‖ˈfɔːnɪkeɪt/ *vi* to commit fornication [Late Latin *fornicare*, fr Latin *fornic-, fornix* arch, vault, brothel] – **fornicator** *n*

fornication /ˌfawniˈkaysh(ə)n‖ˌfɔːnɪˈkeɪʃ(ə)n/ *n* voluntary sexual intercourse outside marriage

forsake /fəˈsayk‖fəˈseɪk/ *vt* **forsook** /fəˈsook‖fəˈsʊk/ ; **forsaken** /fəˈsaykən‖fəˈseɪkən/ **1** to renounce (e g sthg once cherished) without intent to recover or resume <forsook *her family ties*> **2** to desert, abandon <*false friends ~ us in adversity*>

forsooth /fəˈsoohth‖fəˈsuːθ/ *adv* indeed, actually – now often used to imply contempt or doubt

forswear /fawˈsweə‖fɔːˈsweə/ *vb* **forswear; forsworn** /-ˈswawn‖-ˈswɔːn/ *vt* **1a** to reject or deny under oath **b** to (solemnly) renounce **2** to make a liar of (oneself) (as if) under oath *~vi* to swear falsely

forsythia /fawˈsiethi·ə, -thyə‖fɔːˈsaɪθɪə, -θjə/ *n* any of a genus of ornamental shrubs with bright yellow bell-shaped flowers appearing in early spring before the leaves [William *Forsyth* (1737-1804), British gardener]

fort /fawt‖fɔːt/ *n* a strong or fortified place

[1]**forte** /ˈfawtay, fawt‖ˈfɔːteɪ, fɔːt/ *n* the area or skill in which a person excels

[2]**forte** /ˈfawti, -tay‖ˈfɔːtɪ, -teɪ/ *n, adv, or adj* (a note or passage played) in a loud and often forceful manner – used in music

forth /fawth‖fɔːθ/ *adv* **1** onwards in time, place, or order; forwards <*from that day ~*> **2** out into notice or view <*put ~ leaves*> **3** away from a centre; abroad <*went ~ to preach*>

forthˈcoming /-ˈkuming‖-ˈkʌmɪŋ/ *adj* **1** approaching **2a** made available <*new funds will be ~ next year*> **b** willing to give information; responsive

ˈforthˌright /-ˌriet‖-ˌraɪt/ *adj* going straight to the point without ambiguity or hesitation – **forthrightly** *adv*, **forthrightness** *n*

forthˈwith /-ˈwidh‖-ˈwɪð/ *adv* immediately

fortification /ˌfawtifiˈkaysh(ə)n‖ˌfɔːtɪfɪˈkeɪʃ(ə)n/ *n* **1a** fortifying **b** the science or art of providing defensive works **2** sthg that fortifies, defends, or strengthens; *esp* works erected to defend a place or position

ˌfortified ˈwine /ˈfawtiˌfied‖ˈfɔːtɪˌfaɪd/ *n* a wine to which alcohol has been added during or after fermentation

fortify /ˈfawtifie‖ˈfɔːtɪfaɪ/ *vt* to make strong: e g **a** to strengthen and secure by military defences **b** to give strength, courage, or endurance to; strengthen **c** to add material to for strengthening or enriching *~vi* to erect fortifications – **fortifier** *n*

fortissimo /fawˈtisimoh‖fɔːˈtɪsɪməʊ/ *adv or adj* very loud – used in music

fortitude /ˈfawtityoohd, -choohd‖ˈfɔːtɪtjuːd, -tʃuːd/ *n* patient courage in pain or adversity

fortnight /ˈfawtˌniet‖ˈfɔːtˌnaɪt/ *n, chiefly Br* two weeks [Middle English *fourtenight*, alteration of *fourtene night*, fr Old English *fēowertȳne niht* fourteen nights]

[1]**ˈfortˌnightly** /-li‖-lɪ/ *adj* occurring or appearing once a fortnight

[2]**fortnightly** *adv, chiefly Br* once in a fortnight; every fortnight

[3]**fortnightly** *n* a publication issued fortnightly

fortress /ˈfawtris‖ˈfɔːtrɪs/ *n* a fortified place; *esp* a large and permanent fortification, sometimes including a town

fortuitous /fawˈtyooh·itəs, -ˈchooh-‖fɔːˈtjuːɪtəs, -ˈtʃuː-/ *adj* **1** occurring by chance **2** fortunate, lucky – **fortuitously** *adv*, **fortuitousness** *n*

fortunate /ˈfawch(ə)nət‖ˈfɔːtʃ(ə)nət/ *adj* **1** unexpectedly bringing some good; auspicious **2** lucky – **fortunately** *adv*, **fortunateness** *n*

fortune /ˈfawchoohn, -chən‖ˈfɔːtʃuːn, -tʃən/ *n* **1** *often cap* a supposed (personified) power that unpredictably determines events and issues **2a** prosperity attained partly through luck **b** LUCK 1 **c** *pl* the favourable or unfavourable events that accompany the progress of an individual or thing **3** destiny, fate <*tell his ~ with cards*> **4a** material possessions or wealth **b** a very large sum of money <*won a ~ on the pools*> – infml

ˈfortune ˌhunter *n* a person who seeks wealth, esp by marriage

ˈfortune-ˌteller *n* a person who claims to foretell future events – **fortune-telling** *n or adj*

forty /ˈfawti‖ˈfɔːtɪ/ *n* **1** (the number) 40 **2** *pl* the numbers 40 to 49; *specif* a range of temperatures, ages, or dates in a century characterized by those numbers – **fortieth** *adj or n*, **forty** *adj or pron*, **fortyfold** *adj or adv*

ˌforty-ˈfive *n* **1** (the number) 45 **2** a gramophone record that plays at 45 revolutions per minute – usu written 45 – **forty-five** *adj or pron*

ˌforty ˈwinks *n pl but sing or pl in constr* [2]NAP – infml

forum /ˈfawrəm‖ˈfɔːrəm/ *n, pl* **forums** *also* **fora** /-rə‖-rə/ **1a** the marketplace or public place of an ancient Roman city forming the public centre **b** a public meeting place or medium for open discussion **2a** a public meeting or lecture involving audience discussion **b** a programme (e g on radio or television) based around the discussion of problems

[1]**forward** /ˈfaw·wood‖ˈfɔːwʊd; *sense 1 also* ˈforəd ‖ˈfɒrəd *when referring to ships and aeroplanes*/ *adj* **1a** located at or directed towards the front **b** situated in advance **2** of or occupying a fielding position in cricket in front of the batsman's wicket **3a** eager, ready **b** lacking modesty or reserve; pert **4** advanced in development; precocious **5** moving, tending, or leading towards a position in (or at the) front **6** advocating an advanced policy in the direction of what is considered progress **7** of or getting ready for the future <*~ planning*> – **forwardly** *adv*, **forwardness** *n*

[2]**forward** *adv* **1** to or towards what is ahead or in front **2** to or towards an earlier time <*bring the date of the meeting ~*> **3** into prominence

[3]**forward** /ˈfaw·wood‖ˈfɔːwʊd/ *n* a mainly attacking player in hockey, soccer, etc stationed at or near the front of his/her side or team

[4]**forward** *vt* **1** to help onwards; promote **2a** to send (forwards) <*will ~ the goods on payment*> **b** to send onwards from an intermediate point in transit – **forwarder** *n*

forwards *adv* forward; *esp* forward in space

fosse, foss /fos‖fɒs/ *n* a ditch, moat

[1]**fossil** /ˈfosl‖ˈfɒsl/ *n* **1** a relic of an animal or plant of a past geological age, preserved in the earth's crust **2a** a person with outmoded views **b** sthg that has become rigidly fixed [Latin *fossilis* dug up, fr *foss-*, *fodere* to dig] – **fossiliferous** *adj*

[2]**fossil** *adj* **1a** extracted from the earth and derived from the remains of living things <*coal is a ~ fuel*> **b** preserved in a mineralized or petrified form from a past geological age **2** outmoded

fossil·ize, -ise /ˈfoslˌiez‖ˈfɒslˌaɪz/ *vt* **1** to convert into a fossil **2** to make outmoded, rigid, or fixed ~*vi* to become fossilized – **fossilization** *n*

[1]**foster** /ˈfostə‖ˈfɒstə/ *adj* giving, receiving, or sharing parental care though not related by blood <*a ~ child*>

[2]**foster** *vt* **1** to give parental care to; nurture **2** to promote the growth or development of – **fosterer** *n*

fought /fawt‖fɔːt/ *past of* FIGHT

[1]**foul** /fowl‖faʊl/ *adj* **1a** offensive to the senses **b** dirty, stained <*~ linen*> **2** notably unpleasant or distressing; detestable **3** obscene, abusive <*~ language*> **4a** treacherous, dishonourable <*fair means or ~*> **b** constituting a foul in a game or sport **5** defaced by changes <*~ manuscript*> **6** encrusted, clogged, or choked with a foreign substance <*a ~ ship's bottom*> **7** polluted <*~ air*> **8** entangled <*a ~ anchor*> – **foulness** *n*

[2]**foul** *n* **1** an entanglement or collision in angling, sailing, etc **2** an infringement of the rules in a game or sport

[3]**foul** *vi* **1** to become or be foul; *esp* to become clogged, choked up, or entangled **2** to commit a foul in a sport or game ~ *vt* **1a** to pollute **b** to become entangled with **c** to encrust with a foreign substance **d** to obstruct, block **2** to dishonour, discredit **3** to commit a foul against

ˌfoulˈmouthed /-ˈmowdhd‖-ˈmaʊðd/ *adj* given to the use of obscene, profane, or abusive language

ˌfoul ˈplay *n* violence; *esp* murder

ˈfoul-ˌup *n* **1** a state of confusion caused by ineptitude, carelessness, or mismanagement **2** a mechanical difficulty *USE* infml

foul up *vt* **1** *chiefly NAm* to contaminate **2** *chiefly NAm* to spoil or confuse by making mistakes or using poor judgment **3** to entangle, block <fouled up *the communications*> *USE* (*2 & 3*) infml

[1]**found** /fownd‖faʊnd/ *past of* FIND

[2]**found** *adj* having all usual, standard, or reasonably expected equipment <*the boat comes fully ~, ready to go*>

[3]**found** *vt* **1** to take the first steps in building **2** to set or ground on sthg solid – often + *on* or *upon* **3** to establish (e g an institution), often with provision for continued financial support – **founder** *n*

[4]**found** *vt* to melt (metal) and pour into a mould – **founder** *n*

foundation /fownˈdaysh(ə)n‖faʊnˈdeɪʃ(ə)n/ *n* **1** the act of founding **2** the basis on which sthg stands or is supported **3** an organization or institution established by endowment with provision for future maintenance **4** an underlying natural or prepared base or support; *esp* the whole masonry substructure on which a building rests **5** a body or ground on which sthg is built up or overlaid **6** a cream, lotion, etc applied as a base for other facial make-up – **foundational** *adj*, **foundationally** *adv*, **foundationless** *adj*

founˈdation ˌgarment *n* a girdle, corset, or other supporting undergarment

founˈdation ˌstone *n* a stone in the foundation of a building, esp when laid with public ceremony

founder /ˈfowndə‖ˈfaʊndə/ *vi* **1** to become disabled; *esp* to go lame **2** to collapse; GIVE WAY 3a **3** to sink **4** to come to grief; fail ~*vt* to disable (e g a horse), esp by overwork

ˌfounding ˈfather *n* **1** a founder **2** *cap both Fs* a member of the American Constitutional Convention of 1787

ˈfoundling /-ling‖-lɪŋ/ *n* an infant found abandoned by unknown parents

foundry /ˈfowndri‖ˈfaʊndrɪ/ *n* (a place for) casting metals

¹fount /fownt‖faʊnt/ *n* a fountain, source

²fount, *chiefly NAm* **font** /font‖fɒnt/ *n, Br* a complete set of matrices of characters (e g for photocomposition) in 1 style

fountain /ˈfowntən‖ˈfaʊntən/ *n* **1** a spring of water issuing from the earth **2** a source **3** (the structure providing) an artificially produced jet of water

ˈfountainˌhead /-ˌhed‖-ˌhed/ *n* **1** a spring that is the source of a stream **2** a principal source

ˈfountain ˌpen *n* a pen containing a reservoir that automatically feeds the nib with ink

four /faw‖fɔː/ *n* **1** (the number) 4 **2** the fourth in a set or series <*the ~ of hearts*> **3** sthg having 4 parts or members or a denomination of 4; *esp* (the crew of) a 4-person racing rowing boat **4** a shot in cricket that crosses the boundary after having hit the ground and scores 4 runs – **four** *adj or pron*, **fourfold** *adj or adv*

ˌfour-in-ˈhand *n* (a vehicle drawn by) a team of 4 horses driven by 1 person

ˌfour-leaf ˈclover, **ˌfour-leaved ˈclover** *n* a clover leaf that has 4 leaflets instead of 3 and is held to bring good luck

ˌfour-letter ˈword *n* any of a group of vulgar or obscene words typically made up of 4 letters

ˈfourpenny /-p(ə)ni‖-p(ə)nɪ/ *adj* costing or worth fourpence

ˌfour-ˈposter /ˈpohstə‖ˈpəʊstə/ *n* a bed with 4 tall often carved corner posts designed to support curtains or a canopy

¹ˌfourˈsquare /-ˈskweə‖-ˈskweə/ *adj* forthright

²foursquare *adv* **1** in a solidly based and steady way **2** resolutely

fourteen /fawˈteen‖fɔːˈtiːn/ *n* (the number) 14 – **fourteen** *adj or pron*, **fourteenth** *adj or n*

fourth /fawth‖fɔːθ/ *n* **1** number four in a countable series **2a** (the combination of 2 notes at) a musical interval of 4 diatonic degrees **b** a subdominant **3** the 4th and usu highest forward gear or speed of a motor vehicle – **fourth** *adj or adv*, **fourthly** *adv*

fourth dimension *n* **1** a dimension in addition to length, breadth, and depth; *specif* a coordinate in addition to 3 rectangular coordinates, esp when interpreted as the time coordinate in a space-time continuum **2** sthg outside the range of ordinary experience – **fourth-dimensional** *adj*

fourth estate *n, often cap F&E* PRESS 6a

¹fowl /fowl‖faʊl/ *n* **1** BIRD 1 **2** DOMESTIC FOWL; *esp* an adult hen **3** the flesh of birds used as food

²fowl *vi* to hunt, catch, or kill wildfowl – **fowler** *n*

ˈfowling ˌpiece *n* a light gun for shooting birds or small animals

ˈfowl ˌpest *n* a fatal infectious virus disease of domestic poultry

¹fox /foks‖fɒks/ *n* **1** (the fur of) a red fox or related flesh-eating mammal of the dog family with a pointed muzzle, large erect ears, and a long bushy tail **2** a clever crafty person

²fox *vt* **1** to outwit **2** to baffle

ˈfoxˌglove /-ˌgluv‖-ˌglʌv/ *n* a common tall European plant that has showy white or purple tubular flowers and is a source of digitalis

ˈfoxˌhole /-ˌhohl‖-ˌhəʊl/ *n* a pit dug, usu hastily, for individual cover against enemy fire

ˈfoxˌhound /-ˌhownd‖-ˌhaʊnd/ *n* any of various large swift powerful hounds of great endurance used in hunting foxes

ˈfoxˌhunting /-ˌhunting‖-ˌhʌntɪŋ/ *n* the practice of hunting foxes on horseback with a pack of hounds – **foxhunter** *n*

ˌfox ˈterrier *n* a small lively smooth-haired or wirehaired terrier formerly used to dig out foxes

fox-trot *vi or n* (to dance) a ballroom dance that includes slow walking and quick running steps

foxy /ˈfoksi‖ˈfɒksɪ/ *adj* **1** cunningly shrewd in conniving and contriving **2** warmly reddish brown **3** *NAm* physically attractive – **foxily** *adv*, **foxiness** *n*

foyer /ˈfoyˌay, -ə ‖ˈfɔɪˌeɪ, -ə (*Fr* fwaje)/ *n* an anteroom or lobby (e g of a theatre); *also* an entrance hallway [French, lit., fireplace, fr Medieval Latin *focarius*, fr Latin *focus* hearth]

fracas /ˈfrakah‖ˈfrækɑː/ *n, pl* **fracas**/-ah(z)‖-ɑː(z)/, *NAm* **fracases** /-siz‖-sɪz/ a noisy quarrel; a brawl

fraction /ˈfraksh(ə)n‖ˈfrækʃ(ə)n/ *n* **1a** a number (e g $^3/_4$, $^5/_8$, 0.234) that is expressed as the quotient of 2 numbers **b** a (small) portion or section **2** an act of breaking up; *specif* the breaking of the bread by a priest in the Eucharist **3** a tiny bit; a little <*a ~ closer*> [Late Latin *fraction-, fractio* act of breaking, fr Latin *fract-, frangere* to break]

fractional /ˈfraksh(ə)nl‖ˈfrækʃ(ə)nl/ *adj* **1** of or being a fraction **2** relatively tiny or brief **3** of or being a process for separating components of a mixture through differences in physical or chemical properties <*~ distillation*>

ˈfractionally /-li‖-lɪ/ *adv* to a very small extent

ˈfractionate /-ayt‖-eɪt/ *vt* to separate (e g a mixture) into different portions – **fractionation** *n*, **fractionator** *n*

fractious /ˈfrakshəs‖ˈfrækʃəs/ *adj* irritable and restless; hard to control – **fractiously** *adv*, **fractiousness** *n*

¹fracture /ˈfrakchə‖ˈfræktʃə/ *n* **1** a break or breaking, esp of hard tissue (e g bone) **2** the appearance of a broken surface of a mineral

²fracture *vt* **1** to cause a fracture in **2** to damage or destroy as if by breaking apart; break up *~ vi* to undergo fracture

fragile /ˈfrajiel‖ˈfrædʒaɪl/ *adj* **1** easily shattered **2** lacking in strength; delicate – **fragility** *n*

¹fragment /ˈfragmənt‖ˈfrægmənt/ *n* an incomplete, broken off, or detached part

²fragment /fragˈment‖frægˈment/ *vt* to break up or apart into fragments *~ vi* to fall to pieces – **fragmentation** *n*

fragmentary /ˈfragmənt(ə)ri‖ˈfrægmənt(ə)rɪ/ *adj* consisting of fragments; incomplete – **fragmentarily** *adv*, **fragmentariness** *n*

fragrance /ˈfraygrəns‖ˈfreɪgrəns/ *n* **1** (the quality or state of having) a sweet or pleasant smell **2** the smell of perfume, cologne, or toilet water – **fragrant** *adj*, **fragrantly** *adv*

frail /frayl‖freɪl/ *adj* **1** morally or physically weak **2** easily broken or destroyed **3** slight, insubstantial – **frailly** *adv*, **frailness** *n*

frailty /ˈfraylti‖ˈfreɪltɪ/ *n* a (moral) fault due to weakness

[1]frame /fraym‖freɪm/ *vt* **1a** to plan; WORK OUT 1b, c **b** to shape, construct **2** to fit or adjust for a purpose **3** to construct by fitting and uniting the parts of **4a** to contrive evidence against (an innocent person) **b** to prearrange the outcome of (e g a contest) – **framer** *n*

[2]frame *n* **1** sthg composed of parts fitted together and joined; *esp* the physical structure of a human body **2** a structure that gives shape or strength (e g to a building) **3a** an open case or structure made for admitting, enclosing, or supporting sthg <*a window* ~> **b** a machine built on or within a framework <*a spinning* ~> **c** the rigid part of a bicycle **d** the outer structure of a pair of glasses that holds the lenses **e** a framework covered with transparent material, used for protecting plants growing outdoors **4a** an enclosing border **b** the matter or area enclosed in such a border: e g **b(1)** any of the squares in which scores for each round are recorded (e g in bowling) **b(2)** a box of a strip cartoon **b(3)** a single picture of the series on a length of film **b(4)** a single complete television picture made up of lines **c** a limiting, typical, or esp appropriate set of circumstances; a framework **5** one round of play in snooker, bowling, etc **6** a frame-up – infml

ˌframe of ˈmind *n* a particular mental or emotional state

ˌframe of ˈreference *n* **1** an arbitrary set of axes used as a reference to describe the position or motion of sthg or to formulate physical laws **2** a set or system of facts, ideas, etc serving to orient or give particular meaning to a statement, a point of view, etc

ˈframe-ˌup *n* a conspiracy to frame sby or sthg – infml

ˈframeˌwork /-ˌwuhk‖-ˌwɜːk/ *n* **1** a skeletal, openwork, or structural frame **2** a basic structure (e g of ideas)

franc /frangk‖fræŋk/ *n* (a note or coin representing) the basic money unit of France, Belgium, Switzerland, and certain other French-speaking countries

[1]franchise /ˈfrahnchiez, ˈfran-‖ˈfrɑːntʃaɪz, ˈfræn-/ *n* **1** freedom from some burden or restriction **2a** a special privilege granted to an individual or group **b** a right or privilege; *specif* the right to vote **c** the right granted to an individual or group to market a company's goods or services in a particular territory; *also* the territory involved in such a right

[2]franchise *vt* to grant a franchise to

Franciscan /franˈsiskən‖frænˈsɪskən/ *n* a member of the Order of missionary friars founded by St Francis of Assisi in 1209 – **Franciscan** *adj*

Franco- /frangkoh-‖fræŋkəʊ-/ *comb form* **1** French nation, people, or culture <Franco*phile*> **2** French and <Franco-*German*>

[1]frank /frangk‖fræŋk/ *adj* marked by free, forthright, and sincere expression <*a* ~ *reply*>; *also* undisguised <~ *admiration*> – **frankness** *n*

[2]frank *vt* **1a** to send (a piece of mail) without charge **b** to put a frank on (a piece of mail) **2** to enable to pass or go freely or easily <*the delegates will* ~ *the policy*>

[3]frank *n* **1** an official signature or sign on a piece of mail indicating exemption from postal charges **2** a mark or stamp on a piece of mail indicating postage paid **3** a franked envelope

Frank *n* a member of a W Germanic people that established themselves in the Netherlands and Gaul and on the Rhine in the 3rd and 4th c – **Frankish** *adj*

frankfurter /ˈfrangkˌfuhtə‖ˈfræŋkˌfɜːtə/ *n* a cured cooked, usu beef and pork, sausage [German *frankfurter* of Frankfurt, fr *Frankfurt* (*am Main*), city in Germany]

frankincense /ˈfrangkinˌsens‖ˈfræŋkɪnˌsens/ *n* a fragrant gum resin chiefly from E African or Arabian trees that is burnt as incense

franklin /ˈfrangklin‖ˈfræŋklɪn/ *n* a medieval English landowner of free but not noble birth

frankly /ˈfrangkli‖ˈfræŋklɪ/ *adv* to tell the truth; actually <~, *I couldn't care less*>

frantic /ˈfrantik‖ˈfræntɪk/ *adj* **1** emotionally out of control <~ *with anger and frustration*> **2** marked by fast and nervous, disordered, or anxiety-driven activity – **frantically** *adv*, **franticly** *adv*, **franticness** *n*

frappé /ˈfrapay ‖ˈfræpeɪ (*Fr* frape)/ *n or adj* (a drink that is) chilled or partly frozen

fraternal /frəˈtuhnl‖frəˈtɜːnl/ *adj* **1a** of or involving brothers **b** of or being a fraternity or society **2** *of twins* derived from 2 ova **3** friendly, brotherly [Latin *fraternus*, fr *frater* brother] – **fraternalism** *n*, **fraternally** *adv*

fraternity /frəˈtuhnəti‖frəˈtɜːnətɪ/ *n* **1** *sing or pl in constr* a group of people associated or formally organized for a common purpose, interest, or pleasure: e g **1a** a fraternal order **b** a club for male students in some American universities **2** brotherliness **3** *sing or pl in constr* men of the same usu specified class, profession, character, or tastes

fratern·ize, -ise /ˈfratəˌniez‖ˈfrætəˌnaɪz/ *vi* **1** to associate or mingle on friendly terms **2** to associate on close terms with citizens or troops of a hostile country – **fraternization** *n*

fratricide /ˈfratriˌsied, ˈfray-‖ˈfrætrɪˌsaɪd, ˈfreɪ-/ *n* (the act of) sby who kills his/her brother or sister – **fratricidal** *adj*

Frau /frow ‖fraʊ / *n, pl* **Frauen** /-ən‖-ən/ a German-speaking married woman – used as a title equivalent to *Mrs*

fraud /frawd‖frɔːd/ *n* **1a** deception, esp for unlawful gain **b** a trick **2a** a person who is not what he/she pretends to be **b** sthg that is not what it seems or is represented to be

fraudulent /ˈfrawdyoolənt‖ˈfrɔːdjʊlənt/ *adj* characterized by, involving, or done by fraud –

fraudulence *n*, **fraudulently** *adv*

fraught /frawt||frɔːt/ *adj* **1** filled or charged *with* sthg specified <*the situation is* ~ *with danger*> **2** *Br* characterized by anxieties and tensions <~ *and complex relationships*>

fräulein /ˈfrawlien ||ˈfrɔːlaɪn (Ger frɔɪlaɪn)/ *n* an unmarried German-speaking woman – used as a title equivalent to *Miss*

[1]**fray** /fray||freɪ/ *n* a brawl, fight

[2]**fray** *vt* **1** to separate the threads at the edge of (e g fabric) **2** to strain, irritate <*his temper became a bit* ~ed> ~*vi* to wear out or into shreds

[1]**frazzle** /ˈfrazl||ˈfræzl/ *vt* to put in a state of extreme physical or nervous fatigue; upset – infml

[2]**frazzle** *n* a frazzled condition <*worn to a* ~> – infml

[1]**freak** /freek||friːk/ *n* **1a** a sudden and odd or seemingly pointless idea or whim **b** a seemingly capricious action or event **2** a person or animal with a physical oddity who appears in a circus, funfair, etc **3** a person seen as being highly unconventional, esp in dress or ideas **4** an ardent enthusiast <*a jazz* ~> **5a** a sexual pervert **b** HEAD 19 – often in combination <*speed*freak>; slang *USE* (*3 & 4*) infml

[2]**freak** *vb* FREAK OUT – slang

freakish /ˈfreekish||ˈfriːkɪʃ/ *adj* whimsical, capricious – **freakishly** *adv*, **freakishness** *n*

freak of ˈnature *n* FREAK 2

ˈ**freakˌout** *n* a drug-induced state of mind – slang

freak out *vt* **1** to put under the influence of a (hallucinogenic) drug **2** to put into a state of great excitement ~ *vi* **1** to experience hallucinations or withdraw from reality, esp by taking drugs **2** to behave in an irrational or uncontrolled manner (as if) under the influence of drugs **USE** slang

[1]**freckle** /ˈfrekl||ˈfrekl/ *n* any of the small brownish spots on the skin, esp of white people, that increase in number and intensity on exposure to sunlight – **freckly** *adj*

[2]**freckle** *vb* to mark or become marked with freckles or small spots

[1]**free** /free||friː/ *adj* **1a** enjoying civil and political liberty **b** politically independent **c** not subject to the control or domination of another **2a** not determined by external influences <*a* ~ *agent*> **b** voluntary, spontaneous **3a** exempt, relieved, or released, esp from an unpleasant or unwanted condition or obligation <~ *from pain*> – often in combination <*trouble*-free> <*duty*-free> **b** not bound, confined, or detained by force <*prisoner was now* ~> **4a** having no trade restrictions **b** not subject to government regulation **5** having or taken up with no obligations or commitments <*I'll be* ~ *this evening*> **6** having an unrestricted scope <*a* ~ *variable*> **7a** not obstructed or impeded **b** not being used or occupied <*used a* ~ *hand*> **c** not hampered or restricted; unfettered <~ *speech*> **8** not fastened <*the* ~ *end of the rope*> **9a** lavish, unrestrained <*very* ~ *with her praises*> **b** outspoken **c** too familiar or forward **10** not costing or charging anything **11a** not (permanently) united with, attached to, or combined with sthg else; separate <~ *oxygen*> **b** capable of being used alone as a meaningful linguistic form <hats *is a* ~ *form*> **12a** not literal or exact <~ *translation*> **b** not restricted by or conforming to conventional forms <~ *jazz*> **13** open to all comers – **freely** *adv*

[2]**free** *adv* **1** in a free manner **2** without charge <*admitted* ~> **3** not close-hauled <*sailing* ~>

[3]**free** *vt* **1** to cause to be free **2** to relieve or rid of sthg that restrains, confines, restricts, or embarrasses <~ *her husband from debt*> **3** to disentangle, clear – **freer** *n*

ˌ**free asˌsociˈation** *n* the expression of conscious thoughts, ideas, etc used esp in psychoanalysis to reveal unconscious processes; *esp* (the reporting of) the first thought, image, etc that comes to mind in response to a given stimulus (e g a word)

freebie, freebee /ˈfreebi||ˈfriːbɪ/ *n, chiefly NAm* sthg (e g a theatre ticket) given or received without charge – infml

ˈ**freeˌboard** /-ˌbawd||-ˌbɔːd/ *n* the vertical distance between the waterline and the deck of a ship

ˈ**freeˌbooter** /-ˌboohtə||-ˌbuːtə/ *n* a pirate, plunderer

ˈ**freeˌborn** /-ˌbawn||-ˌbɔːn/ *adj* not born in slavery

Free Church *n, chiefly Br* a British Nonconformist church

ˈ**freedˌman** /-man||-mæn/, *fem* ˈ**freedˌwoman** *n* sby freed from slavery

freedom /ˈfreedəm||ˈfriːdəm/ *n* **1a** the absence of necessity or constraint in choice or action **b** liberation from slavery or restraint **c** being exempt or released *from* sthg (onerous) <~ *from care*> **2a** ease, facility **b** being frank, open, or outspoken **c** improper familiarity **3** boldness of conception or execution **4** unrestricted use *of* <*gave him the* ~ *of their home*> **5** a right or privilege, esp political

free enterprise *n* an economic system that relies on private business operating competitively for profit to satisfy consumer demands and in which government action is restricted to protecting public interest and to keeping the national economy in balance

ˈ**free-ˌfall** *n* **1** (the condition of) unrestrained motion in a gravitational field **2** the part of a parachute jump before the parachute opens

ˌ**free-ˈfloating** *adj* relatively uncommitted to a particular course of action, party, etc

ˈ**free-for-ˌall** *n* **1** a fight or competition open to all comers and usu with no rules **2** an often vociferous quarrel or argument involving several participants

ˈ**freeˌhand** /-ˌhand||-ˌhænd/ *adj* done without the aid of drawing or measuring instruments – **freehand** *adv*

ˌ**free ˈhand** *n* freedom of action or decision <*gave her a* ~>

ˌ**freeˈhanded** /-ˈhandid||-ˈhændɪd/ *adj* openhanded, generous – **freehandedly** *adv*

ˈ**freeˌhold** /-ˌhohld||-ˌhəʊld/ *n* a tenure in absolute possession; *also* a property held by such tenure – **freeholder** *n*

ˈ**free ˌhouse** *n* a public house in Britain that

is entitled to sell drinks supplied by more than 1 brewery

,free 'kick *n* an unhindered kick in soccer, rugby, etc awarded because of a breach of the rules by an opponent

[1]**'free,lance** /-,lahns‖-,lɑːns/ *n* a person who pursues a profession without long-term contractual commitments to any one employer – **free-lance** *adj*

[2]**freelance** *vi* to act as a freelance

,free-'living *adj, of a living organism* neither parasitic nor symbiotic – **free-liver** *n*

'free,load /-,lohd‖-,ləʊd/ *vi* to take advantage of another's generosity or hospitality without sharing in the cost or responsibility involved – infml – **freeloader** *n*

,free 'love *n* the concept or practice of sexual relations without legal commitment

'free,man /-man‖-mæn/ *n* **1** sby enjoying civil or political liberty **2** sby who has the full rights of a citizen

'Free,mason /-,mays(ə)n‖-,meɪs(ə)n/ *n* a member of an ancient and widespread secret fraternity called Free and Accepted Masons

'free,masonry /-,mays(ə)nri‖-,meɪs(ə)nrɪ/ *n* **1** *cap* the principles, institutions, or practices of Freemasons **2** natural or instinctive fellowship

'free ,port *n* an enclosed (section of a) port where goods are received and shipped free of customs duty

,free-'range *adj* of, being, or produced by poultry reared in the open air rather than in a battery

,free 'rein *n* unrestricted liberty or scope

freesheet /'freesheet/ *n* a newspaper that is financed by advertising and distributed free of charge

freesia /'freezh(y)ə, -zyə‖'friːʒ(j)ə, -zjə/ *n* any of a genus of sweet-scented African plants of the iris family with red, white, yellow, or purple flowers [F H T *Freese* (died 1876) German physician]

,free'standing /-'standing‖-'stændɪŋ/ *adj* standing without lateral support or attachment <*a ~ column*>

'free,stone /-,stohn‖-,stəʊn/ *n* **1** a stone that can be cut without splitting **2** (a fruit with) a stone to which the flesh does not cling

'free,style /-,stiel‖-,staɪl/ *n* **1** (a style used in) a competition in which a contestant uses a style (e g of swimming) of his/her choice **2** catch-as-catch-can **3** CRAWL 2

,free'thinker /-'thingkə‖-'θɪŋkə/ *n* a person who forms opinions on the basis of reason; *esp* one who rejects religious dogma – **freethinking** *n or adj*

,free 'thought *n* freethinking; *specif* 18th-c deism

,free 'trade *n* trade based on the unrestricted international exchange of goods

free verse *n* verse without fixed metrical form

'free,way /-,way‖-,weɪ/ *n, NAm* a motorway

[1]**,free'wheel** /-'weel‖-'wiːl/ *n* a device fitted to a vehicle wheel allowing forward motion when the motive power is removed

[2]**freewheel** *vi* **1** *of a bicycle, cyclist, or motor car* to coast freely without power from the pedals or engine **2** to move, live, or drift along freely or irresponsibly – **freewheeler** *n*

,free 'will *n* the power of choosing without the constraint of divine necessity or causal law

[1]**freeze** /freez‖friːz/ *vb* **froze** /frohz‖frəʊz/; **frozen** /'frohz(ə)n‖'frəʊz(ə)n/ *vi* **1** to become congealed into a solid (e g ice) by cold **2** to become chilled with cold <*almost* froze *to death*> **3** to stick solidly (as if) by freezing **4** to become clogged with ice <*the water pipes* froze> **5** to become fixed or motionless; *esp* to abruptly cease acting or speaking **6** to be capable of undergoing freezing for preservation <*do strawberries ~ well?*> ~ *vt* **1** to convert from a liquid to a solid by cold **2** to make extremely cold **3a** to act on, usu destructively, by frost **b** to anaesthetize (as if) by cold <*the injection* froze *her gum*> **4** to cause to become fixed, immovable, or unalterable, as if paralysed **5** to immobilize the expenditure, withdrawal, or exchange of (foreign-owned bank balances) by government regulation **6** to preserve (e g food) by freezing the water content and maintaining at a temperature below 0°C – **freezingly** *adv*

[2]**freeze** *n* **1** freezing cold weather **2a** an act or period of freezing sthg, esp wages or prices at a certain level **b** being frozen

freeze-dry *vb* to dehydrate (sthg) while in a frozen state in a vacuum, esp for preservation – **freeze-dried** *adj*

freeze out *vt* to deliberately ignore or fail to respond to (sby) – infml

freezer /'freezə‖'friːzə/ *n* an apparatus that freezes or keeps cool; *esp* an insulated cabinet or room for storing frozen food or for freezing food rapidly

'freeze-,up *n* a spell of very cold weather – infml

[1]**freight** /frayt‖freɪt/ *n* **1** the charge made for transporting goods **2** a cargo **3** a goods train

[2]**freight** *vt* to load (esp a ship) with goods for transport

freighter /'fraytə‖'freɪtə/ *n* **1** a person or company that (charters and) loads a ship **2** a ship or aircraft used chiefly to carry freight

'freight,liner /-,lienə‖-,laɪnə/ *n, Br* a train designed for carrying containerized cargo

[1]**French** /french‖frentʃ/ *adj* of France, its people, or their language – **Frenchman** *n*, **Frenchness** *n*

[2]**French** *n* **1** the Romance language of the people of France and of parts of Belgium, Switzerland, and Canada **2** *pl in constr* the people of France

,French 'bean *n, chiefly Br* (the seed or pod of) a common bean often cultivated for its slender edible green pods

,French 'bread *n* crusty white bread made in long thin loaves

,French 'chalk *n* a soft white granular variety of soapstone used esp for drawing lines on cloth and as a dry lubricant

,French 'dressing *n* a salad dressing of oil, vinegar, and seasonings

,french 'fry *n, chiefly NAm* [1]CHIP 6a – usu pl

,French 'horn *n* a circular valved brass instrument

ˌ**French ˈkiss** *n* a kiss made with open mouths and usu with tongue-to-tongue contact – **French-kiss** *vb*

ˌ**French ˈleave** *n* leave taken without permission

ˌ**French ˈletter** *n, Br* a condom – infml

French-polish *vt* to apply French polish to (wood or furniture) in order to obtain a high gloss finish

ˌ**French ˈpolish** *n* a solution of shellac used as a wood polish

ˌ**French ˈwindows** *n pl* a pair of doors with full length glazing

frenetic /frəˈnetik‖frəˈnetɪk/ *adj* frenzied, frantic – **frenetically** *adv*

frenzied /ˈfrenzid‖ˈfrenzɪd/ *adj* marked by frenzy <*the dog's ~ barking*> – **frenziedly** *adv*

frenzy /ˈfrenzi‖ˈfrenzɪ/ *n* **1** a temporary madness **2** (a spell of) wild, compulsive, or agitated behaviour

frequency /ˈfreekwənsi‖ˈfriːkwənsɪ/ *n* **1 frequency, frequence** the fact or condition of occurring frequently **2a** the number of times that a periodic function repeats the same sequence of values during a unit variation of the independent variable **b** the number or proportion of individuals in a single class when objects are classified according to variations in a set of attributes **3a** the number of complete alternations per second of an alternating current **b** the number of sound waves per second produced by a sounding body **c** the number of complete oscillations per second of an electromagnetic wave

frequency modulation *n* a modulation of the frequency of a wave, esp a radio carrier wave, by the characteristics of the signal carried

[1]**frequent** /ˈfreekwənt‖ˈfriːkwənt/ *adj* **1** often repeated or occurring **2** habitual, persistent – **frequently** *adv*

[2]**frequent** /friˈkwent‖frɪˈkwent/ *vt* to be in or visit often or habitually – **frequenter** *n*, **frequentation** *n*

fresco /ˈfreskoh‖ˈfreskəʊ/ *n, pl* **frescoes, frescos** (a painting made by) the application of water colours to moist plaster [Italian, fr *fresco* fresh, of Germanic origin]

[1]**fresh** /fresh‖freʃ/ *adj* **1a** not salt <*~ water*> **b** free from taint; clean **c** *of wind* rather strong **d** *of weather* cool and windy **2a** *of food* not preserved **b** refreshed <*rose ~ from a good night's sleep*> **c** not stale, sour, or decayed **3a** (different or alternative and) new <*make a ~ start*> **b** newly or just come or arrived <*~ from school*> **4** too forward with a person of the opposite sex <*slapped his face when he got ~ with me*> – infml – **freshly** *adv*, **freshness** *n*

[2]**fresh** *adv* **1** just recently; newly <*a ~ laid egg*> **2** *chiefly NAm* as of a very short time ago <*we're ~ out of tomatoes*>

freshen /ˈfresh(ə)n‖ˈfreʃ(ə)n/ *vi* **1** *of wind* to increase in strength **2** *of water* to lose saltiness ~ *vt* to make fresh; *also* to refresh, revive – often + *up*

freshen up *vb* to make (oneself) fresher or more comfortable, esp by washing, changing one's clothes, etc

fresher /ˈfreshə‖ˈfreʃə/ *n, chiefly Br* a student in the first term at college or university – infml

freshet /ˈfreshit‖ˈfreʃɪt/ *n* STREAM 1

freshman /ˈfreshmən‖ˈfreʃmən/ *n* a fresher

ˌ**freshˈwater** /-ˈwawtə‖-ˈwɔːtə/ *adj* of or living in fresh water

[1]**fret** /fret‖fret/ *vb* **-tt-** *vt* **1** to torment with anxiety or worry; vex **2a** to eat or gnaw into; corrode **b** to rub, chafe **c** to make (e g a channel) by wearing away **3** to agitate, ripple ~ *vi* **1** to eat into sthg; corrode **2** to chafe **3a** to become vexed or worried **b** *of running water* to become agitated

[2]**fret** *n* **1** (a spot that has been subject to) wearing away **2** a state of (querulous) mental agitation or irritation

[3]**fret** *vt* **-tt- 1** to decorate with interlaced designs **2** to decorate (e g a ceiling) with embossed or carved patterns

[4]**fret** *n* an ornamental pattern or decoration consisting of small straight bars intersecting usu at right angles

[5]**fret** *n* any of a series of ridges fixed across the fingerboard of a stringed musical instrument (e g a guitar)

ˈ**fretful** /-f(ə)l‖-f(ə)l/ *adj* **1** tending to fret; in a fret **2** *of water* having the surface agitated – **fretfully** *adv*, **fretfulness** *n*

fretsaw /ˈfretˌsaw‖ˈfretˌsɔː/ *n* a narrow-bladed fine-toothed saw held under tension in a frame and used for cutting intricate patterns in thin wood

ˈ**fretˌwork** /-ˌwuhk‖-ˌwɜːk/ *n* **1** decoration consisting of frets **2** ornamental openwork, esp in thin wood; *also* ornamental work in relief

Freudian /ˈfroydi·ən, -dyən‖ˈfrɔɪdɪən, -djən/ *adj* of or conforming to the psychoanalytic theories or practices of Sigmund Freud [Sigmund *Freud* (1856-1939), Austrian psychologist] – **Freudian** *n*

Freudian slip *n* a slip of the tongue that is held to reveal some unconscious aspect of the speaker's mind

friable /ˈfrie·əbl‖ˈfraɪəbl/ *adj* easily crumbled – **friableness** *n*, **friability** *n*

friar /ˈfrie·ə‖ˈfraɪə/ *n* a member of a religious order combining monastic life with outside religious activity and orig owning neither personal nor community property

friary /ˈfrie·əri‖ˈfraɪərɪ/ *n* (a building housing) a community of friars

fricassee /ˈfrikəˌsee, ˌ--ˈ-‖ˈfrɪkəˌsiː, ˌ--ˈ-/ *n* a dish of small pieces of stewed chicken, rabbit, etc served in a white sauce – **fricassee** *vt*

friction /ˈfriksh(ə)n‖ˈfrɪkʃ(ə)n/ *n* **1a** the rubbing of one body against another **b** resistance to relative motion between 2 bodies in contact **2** disagreement between 2 people or parties of opposing views – **frictional** *adj*

Friday /ˈfrieday, -di‖ˈfraɪdeɪ, -dɪ/ *n* the day of the week following Thursday [Old English *frīgedæg*, fr *Frīa*, Germanic goddess of love + *dæg* day]

fridge /frij‖frɪdʒ/ *n, chiefly Br* a refrigerator

friend /frend‖frend/ *n* **1a** a person whose company, interests, and attitudes one finds sympathetic and to whom one is not closely related **b** an acquaintance **2a** sby or sthg not hostile **b** sby or sthg of the same nation, party, or group **c** sby or sthg that favours or encourages sthg (e g a charity) <*a ~ of the poor*> **3** *cap* a Quaker – **friendless** *adj*

1'**friendly** /-li‖-lɪ/ *adj* **1a** having the relationship of friends **b** showing interest and goodwill **c** not hostile **d** inclined to be favourable – usu + *to* **2** cheerful, comforting **3** engaged in only for pleasure or entertainment and not hotly contested <*a ~ game of poker*> – **friendliness** *n*

2**friendly** *n, chiefly Br* a match played for practice or pleasure and not as part of a competition

'**friendly soˌciety** *n, often cap F&S, Br* a mutual insurance association providing its subscribers with benefits during sickness, unemployment, and old age

ˌ**friendship** /-ship‖-ʃɪp/ *n* being friends or being friendly

frier /'frie·ə‖'fraɪə/ *n* a fryer

Friesian /'freezh(ə)n, -zyən‖'fri:ʒ(ə)n, -zjən/ *n, chiefly Br* any of a breed of large black-and-white dairy cattle from N Holland and Friesland

1**frieze** /freez‖fri:z/ *n* a heavy coarse fabric made of wool and shoddy

2**frieze** *n* **1** the part of an entablature between the architrave and the cornice **2** a sculptured or ornamented band (e g on a building)

frig /frig‖frɪg/ *vi* **-gg- 1** to masturbate **2** to have sexual intercourse *USE* vulg

frigate /'frigət‖'frɪgət/ *n* **1** a square-rigged 3-masted warship next in size below a ship of the line **2** a general-purpose naval escort vessel between a corvette and a cruiser in size

1**fright** /friet‖fraɪt/ *n* **1** fear excited by sudden danger or shock **2** sthg unsightly, strange, ugly, or shocking – infml

2**fright** *vt* to frighten – chiefly poetic

frighten /'friet(ə)n‖'fraɪt(ə)n/ *vb* to make or become afraid; scare – **frighteningly** *adv*

'**frightful** /-f(ə)l‖-f(ə)l/ *adj* **1** causing intense fear, shock, or horror **2** unpleasant, difficult <*had a ~ morning*> – infml – **frightfully** *adv*

frigid /'frijid‖'frɪdʒɪd/ *adj* **1a** intensely cold **b** lacking warmth or intensity of feeling **2** *esp of a woman* abnormally averse to sexual contact, esp intercourse – **frigidly** *adv*, **frigidness** *n*, **frigidity** *n*

frill /fril‖frɪl/ *n* **1a** a gathered or pleated fabric edging used on clothing **b** a small fringed or fluted roll of paper for decorating the bone end of a chop, chicken leg, etc **2** a ruff of hair or feathers round the neck of an animal **3a** an affectation, air **b** sthg decorative but not essential *USE* (*3*) usu pl – **frilly** *adj*

1**fringe** /frinj‖frɪndʒ/ *n* **1** an ornamental border (e g on a curtain or garment) consisting of straight or twisted threads or tassels **2a** sthg resembling a fringe; a border **b** the hair that falls over the forehead **c** any of the alternating light or dark bands produced by interference or diffraction of light **3a** sthg marginal, additional, or secondary **b** *sing or pl in constr* a group with marginal or extremist views **c** *often cap* a part of the British professional theatre featuring small-scale avant-garde productions

2**fringe** *vt* **1** to provide or decorate with a fringe **2** to serve as a fringe for <*a clearing* ~d *with trees*>

fringe benefit *n* a benefit (e g a pension) granted by an employer to an employee that involves a money cost without affecting basic wage rates

1**frippery** /'fripəri‖'frɪpərɪ/ *n* **1** nonessential ornamentation, esp of a showy or tawdry kind **2** affected elegance

2**frippery** *adj* trifling, tawdry

Frisbee /'frizbi‖'frɪzbɪ/ *trademark* – used for a plastic disc thrown between players by a flip of the wrist

Frisian /'freezh(ə)n, -zyən‖'fri:ʒ(ə)n, -zjən/ *n* **1** a member of a Germanic people inhabiting Friesland and the Frisian islands **2** the language of the Frisian people – **Frisian** *adj*

1**frisk** /frisk‖frɪsk/ *vi* to leap, skip, or dance in a lively or playful way ~*vt* to search (a person) for sthg, esp a hidden weapon, by passing the hands over his/her body – infml

2**frisk** *n* **1** a gambol, romp **2** an act of frisking

frisky /'friski‖'frɪskɪ/ *adj* lively, playful – **friskiness** *n*

fritter /'fritə‖'frɪtə/ *n* a piece of fried batter often containing fruit, meat, etc

fritter away *vt* to waste bit by bit

frivolous /'frivələs‖'frɪvələs/ *adj* **1** lacking in seriousness; irresponsibly self-indulgent **2** lacking practicality or serious purpose; unimportant – **frivolity** *n*, **frivolously** *adv*, **frivolousness** *n*

frizz /friz‖frɪz/ *n* (hair in) a mass of small tight curls – **frizz** *vb*, **frizzy** *adj*, **frizziness** *n*

1**frizzle** /'friz!‖'frɪzl/ *vb* to frizz or curl (the hair) – **frizzle** *n*, **frizzly** *adj*

2**frizzle** *vt* **1** to fry (e g bacon) until crisp and curled **2** to burn, scorch ~*vi* to cook with a sizzling noise

fro /froh‖frəʊ/ *prep, dial* from

frock /frok‖frɒk/ *n* **1** a monk's or friar's habit **2** a workman's outer shirt; *esp* SMOCK FROCK **3** a woman's dress

'**frock ˌcoat** *n* a usu double-breasted coat with knee-length skirts worn by men, esp in the 19th c

frog /frog‖frɒg/ *n* **1** any of various tailless smooth-skinned web-footed largely aquatic leaping amphibians **2** the triangular horny pad in the middle of the sole of a horse's foot **3a** a loop attached to a belt to hold a weapon or tool **b** a usu ornamental fastening for the front of a garment consisting of a button and a loop **4** a condition in the throat that produces hoarseness <*had a ~ in her throat*> – infml **5** often *cap* a French person - chiefly derog; infml

'**frogˌhopper** /-ˌhopə‖-ˌhɒpə/ *n* any of numerous leaping insects whose larvae secrete froth

'**frogman** /-mən‖-mən/ *n* a person equipped with face mask, flippers, rubber suit, etc and an air supply for swimming underwater for extended periods

'**frogˌmarch** /-ˌmahch‖-ˌmɑ:tʃ/ *vt* **1** to carry (a person) face downwards by the arms and legs **2** to force (a person) to move forwards with the arms held firmly behind

'**frogˌspawn** /-ˌspawn‖-ˌspɔ:n/ *n* (a gelatinous mass of) frog's eggs

1**frolic** /'frolik‖'frɒlɪk/ *vi* **-ck- 1** to play and run about happily **2** to make merry [Dutch *vroolijk* merry]

2**frolic** *n* **1** (a) playful expression of high spirits;

gaiety **2** a lighthearted entertainment or game – **frolicsome** *adj*

from /frəm||frəm; *strong* from||frɒm/ *prep* **1** – used to indicate a starting point: e g **1a** a place where a physical movement, or an action or condition suggestive of movement, begins <*came here ~ the city*> <*shot ~ above*> **b** a starting point in measuring or reckoning or in a statement of extent or limits <*cost ~ £5 to £10*> <*lives 5 miles ~ the coast*> **c** a point in time after which a period is reckoned <*a week ~ today*> **d** a viewpoint <*~ a practical standpoint*> **2** – used to indicate separation: e g **2a** physical separation <*absent ~ school*> **b** removal, refraining, exclusion, release, or differentiation <*protection ~ the sun*> <*saved ~ drowning*> **3** – used to indicate the source, cause, agent, or basis <*a call ~ my lawyer*> <*made ~ flour*>

frond /frond||frɒnd/ *n* a leaf, esp of a palm or fern – **fronded** *adj*

[1]**front** /frunt||frʌnt/ *n* **1** (feigned) demeanour or bearing, esp in the face of a challenge, danger, etc <*put up a brave ~*> **2a** the vanguard **b** *often cap* a zone of conflict between armies **c** the lateral space occupied by a military unit **3a** a sphere of activity <*progress on the educational ~*> **b** a movement linking divergent elements to achieve certain common objectives; *esp* a political coalition **4a** the (main) face of a building **b** the forward part or surface: e g **b(1)** the part of the human body opposite to the back **b(2)** the part of a garment covering the chest **c** a frontage **d** *the* beach promenade at a seaside resort **5** the boundary between 2 dissimilar air masses **6a** a position ahead of a person or of the foremost part of a thing **b** a position of importance, leadership, or advantage **7a** a person, group, or thing used to mask the identity or true character of the actual controlling agent **b** a person who serves as the nominal head or spokesman of an enterprise or group to lend it prestige – **in front of 1** directly ahead of <*watching the road* in front of *him*> **2** in the presence of <*don't swear* in front of *the children*>

[2]**front** *vi* **1** to face – often + *on* or *onto* <*garden ~ing on a lake*> **2** to serve as a front – often + *for* **3** *Austr & NZ* to appear; TURN UP 2 – often + *up* ~ *vt* **1** to be in front of **2** to supply a front to **3** to face towards

[3]**front** *adj* of or situated at the front – **front** *adv*

frontage /'fruntij||'frʌntɪdʒ/ *n* **1a** a piece of land that fronts **b** the land between the front of a building and the street **2** (the width of) the front face of a building

[1]**frontal** /'fruntl||'frʌntl/ *n* a facade

[2]**frontal** *adj* **1** of or adjacent to the forehead <*~ bone*> **2a** of, situated at, or showing the front <*full ~ nudity*> **b** direct <*~ assault*> **3** of a meteorological front – **frontally** *adv*

front bench *n* either of 2 rows of benches in Parliament on which party leaders sit

ˌfront-'end *adj* required or provided at the outset of a project or enterprise

frontier /frun'tiə||frʌn'tɪə/ *n* **1** a border between 2 countries **2** the boundary between the known and the unknown – often pl with sing. meaning <*the ~s of medicine*> **3** *NAm* a region that forms the margin of settled or developed territory – **frontier** *adj*

fron'tiersman /-mən||-mən/ *n* a man living on the frontier

frontispiece /'fruntis,pees||'frʌntɪsˌpiːs/ *n* an illustration preceding and usu facing the title page of a book or magazine [Middle French *frontispice*, fr Late Latin *frontispicium*, lit., view of the front, fr Latin *front-, frons* front + *specere* to look at]

front line *n* **1** a military front **2** the most advanced, responsible, or significant position in a field of activity – **front-line** *adj*

ˌfront-'page *adj* very newsworthy

'front-ˌrunner *n* **1** a contestant who runs best when in the lead **2** a leading contestant in a competition

[1]**frost** /frost||frɒst/ *n* **1a** (the temperature that causes) freezing **b** a covering of minute ice crystals on a cold surface **2a** coldness of attitude or manner **b** a failure – *chiefly infml*

[2]**frost** *vt* **1a** to cover (as if) with frost **b** to produce a fine-grained slightly roughened surface on (metal, glass, etc) **c** to cover (e g a cake or grapes) with sugar; *also, chiefly NAm* to ice (a cake) **2** to injure or kill (e g plants) by frost ~ *vi* to freeze – often + *over*

'frostˌbite /-ˌbiet||-ˌbaɪt/ *n* (gangrene or other local effect of a partial) freezing of some part of the body

'frostˌbitten /-ˌbit(ə)n||-ˌbɪt(ə)n/ *adj* afflicted with frostbite

frosting /'frosting||'frɒstɪŋ/ *n* **1** a dull or roughened finish on metal or glass **2a** *Br* thick fluffy cooked icing **b** *chiefly NAm* icing

frosty /'frosti||'frɒstɪ/ *adj* **1** marked by or producing frost **2** (appearing as if) covered with frost **3** marked by coolness or extreme reserve in manner – **frostily** *adv*, **frostiness** *n*

[1]**froth** /froth||frɒθ/ *n* **1a** a mass of bubbles formed on or in a liquid **b** a foamy saliva sometimes accompanying disease or exhaustion **2** sthg insubstantial or of little value

[2]**froth** *vt* to cause to foam – often + *up* ~ *vi* to produce or emit froth – often + *up*

frothy /'frothi||'frɒθɪ/ *adj* gaily frivolous or light – **frothily** *adv*, **frothiness** *n*

[1]**frown** /frown||fraʊn/ *vi* **1** to contract the brow in a frown **2** to give evidence of displeasure or disapproval – often + *on* or *upon* ~ *vt* to express by frowning – **frowner** *n*, **frowningly** *adv*

[2]**frown** *n* **1** a wrinkling of the brow in displeasure, concentration, or puzzlement **2** an expression of displeasure

frowst /frowst||fraʊst/ *vi, chiefly Br* to remain indoors in a hot airless room

frowsty /'frowsti||'fraʊstɪ/ *adj, chiefly Br* STUFFY 1a

frowsy, frowzy /'frowzi||'fraʊzɪ/ *adj* **1** having a slovenly or uncared-for appearance **2** musty, stale

froze /frohz||frəʊz/ *past of* FREEZE

frozen /'frohz(ə)n||'frəʊz(ə)n/ *adj* **1a** treated, affected, solidified, or crusted over by freezing **b** subject to long and severe cold <*the ~ north*> **2a** drained or incapable of emotion **b** incapable of being changed, moved, or undone

c not available for present use *<~ capital>* – **frozenly** *adv*, **frozenness** *n*

fructification /ˌfruktifiˈkaysh(ə)n‖ˌfrʌktɪfɪ-ˈkeɪʃ(ə)n/ *n* **1** forming or producing fruit **2** FRUIT 1d

fructify /ˈfruktifie‖ˈfrʌktɪfaɪ/ *vi* to bear fruit – fml ~*vt* to make fruitful or productive – fml

frugal /ˈfroohg(ə)l‖ˈfruːg(ə)l/ *adj* economical in the expenditure of resources; sparing – **frugally** *adv*, **frugality** *n*

[1]**fruit** /frooht‖fruːt/ *n* **1a** a product of plant growth (e g grain or vegetables) *<the ~s of the field>* **b(1)** the (edible) reproductive body of a flowering plant; *esp* one having a sweet pulp associated with the seed **b(2)** a succulent edible plant part used chiefly in a dessert or sweet dish **c** a dish, quantity, or diet of fruits *<please pass the ~>* **d** the ripened fertilized ovary of a flowering plant together with its contents **2** offspring, progeny **3a** the state of bearing fruit *<a tree in ~>* **b** a (favourable) product or result – often pl with sing. meaning **4** *Br* a fellow – in *old fruit*; infml [Old French, fr Latin *fructus* fruit, use, fr *fruct-*, *frui* to enjoy, have the use of] – **fruited** *adj*

[2]**fruit** *vb* to (cause to) bear fruit

ˈ**fruit** ˌ**bat** *n* any of various large Old World fruit-eating bats of warm regions

fruiterer /ˈfroohtərə‖ˈfruːtərə/ *n* one who deals in fruit

ˈ**fruit** ˌ**fly** *n* any of various small flies whose larvae feed on fruit or decaying vegetable matter

fruitful /ˈfroohtf(ə)l‖ˈfruːtf(ə)l/ *adj* **1** (conducive to) yielding or producing (abundant) fruit **2** abundantly productive – **fruitfully** *adv*, **fruitfulness** *n*

fruition /froohˈish(ə)n‖fruːˈɪʃ(ə)n/ *n* **1** bearing fruit **2** realization, fulfilment

fruitless /ˈfroohtlis‖ˈfruːtlɪs/ *adj* **1** lacking or not bearing fruit **2** useless, unsuccessful – **fruitlessly** *adv*, **fruitlessness** *n*

ˈ**fruit maˌchine** *n, Br* a coin-operated gambling machine that pays out according to different combinations of symbols (e g different types of fruit) visible on wheels

fruity /ˈfroohti‖ˈfruːtɪ/ *adj* **1** having the flavour of the unfermented fruit *<~ wine>* **2** *of a voice* marked by richness and depth **3** amusing in a sexually suggestive way *<a ~ story>* – infml – **fruitily** *adv*, **fruitiness** *n*

frump /frump‖frʌmp/ *n* **1** a dowdy unattractive girl or woman **2** a staid drab old-fashioned person *USE* chiefly infml – **frumpish** *adj*, **frumpy** *adj*

frustrate /fruˈstrayt‖frʌˈstreɪt/ *vt* **1a** to balk or defeat in an endeavour; foil **b** to induce feelings of discouragement and vexation in **2** to make ineffectual; nullify [Latin *frustrare* to deceive, frustrate, fr *frustra* in error, in vain] – **frustrating** *adj*, **frustratingly** *adv*

frustration /fruˈstraysh(ə)n‖frʌˈstreɪʃ(ə)n/ *n* **1a** frustrating or being frustrated **b** a deep sense of insecurity, tension, and dissatisfaction arising from unresolved problems or unfulfilled needs **2** sthg that frustrates

[1]**fry** /frie‖fraɪ/ *vb* to cook in hot fat

[2]**fry** *n* **1** a dish of fried food **2** *NAm* a social gathering (e g a picnic) at which food is fried and eaten

[3]**fry** *n, pl* **fry** **1a** recently hatched or very small (adult) fishes **b** the young of other animals, esp when occurring in large numbers **2** a member of a group or class; *esp* a person *<books for small ~>*

fryer /ˈfrie·ə‖ˈfraɪə/ *n* sthg intended for or used in frying; *esp* a deep vessel for frying foods

ˈ**frying** ˌ**pan** *n* a shallow metal pan with a handle that is used for frying foods – **out of the frying pan into the fire** clear of one difficulty only to fall into a greater one

ˈ**fry-**ˌ**up** *n, Br* (a dish prepared by) the frying of food for a simple impromptu meal – chiefly infml

fuchsia /ˈfyoohshə‖ˈfjuːʃə/ *n* any of a genus of decorative shrubs with showy nodding flowers usu in deep pinks, reds, and purples [Leonhard *Fuchs* (1501-66), German botanist]

fuchsine /ˌfoohkˌseen‖ˈfuːkˌsiːn/ *n* a brilliant bluish-red dye

[1]**fuck** /fuk‖fʌk/ *vi* **1** to have sexual intercourse **2** to mess *about* or *around* ~*vt* to have sexual intercourse with *USE* (*vi, vt*) vulg

[2]**fuck** *n* **1** an act of sexual intercourse **2** the slightest amount *<didn't care a ~>* *USE* vulg

[3]**fuck** *interj* – used to express annoyance; vulg

fucker /ˈfukə‖ˈfʌkə/ *n* a fool – vulg

fuck off *vi* **1** to go away **2** *NAm* to fuck about *USE* vulg

fuddle /ˈfudl‖ˈfʌdl/ *vt* **1** to make drunk **2** to make confused

fuddy-duddy /ˈfudi ˌdudi‖ˈfʌdɪ ˌdʌdɪ/ *n* a person who is old-fashioned, pompous, unimaginative, or concerned about trifles – infml – **fuddy-duddy** *adj*

[1]**fudge** /fuj‖fʌdʒ/ *vi* to avoid commitment; hedge – usu + *on* ~ *vt* **1a** to devise or put together roughly or without adequate basis *<she could always ~ up an excuse>* **b** to falsify *<~d the figures>* **2** to fail to come to grips with; dodge

[2]**fudge** *n* **1** a soft (creamy) sweet made typically of sugar, milk, butter, and flavouring **2** foolish nonsense – infml; sometimes used interjectionally

[1]**fuel** /ˈfyooh·əl‖ˈfjuːəl/ *n* **1a** a material used to produce heat or power by combustion **b** nutritive material **c** a material from which atomic energy can be liberated, esp in a reactor **2** a source of sustenance, strength, or encouragement

[2]**fuel** *vb* **-ll-** (*NAm* **-l-**, **-ll-**) *vt* **1** to provide with fuel **2** to support, stimulate *<inflation ~led by massive wage awards>* ~*vi* to take in fuel – often + *up*

fug /fug‖fʌg/ *n* the stuffy atmosphere of a poorly ventilated space – chiefly infml – **fuggy** *adj*

[1]**fugitive** /ˈfyoohjətiv‖ˈfjuːdʒətɪv/ *adj* **1** running away or trying to escape **2a** elusive **b** likely to change, fade, or disappear **3** fleeting, ephemeral – **fugitively** *adv*, **fugitiveness** *n*

[2]**fugitive** *n* a person who flees or tries to escape, esp from danger, justice, or oppression

fugue /fyoohg‖fjuːg/ *n* **1** a musical composition in which 1 or 2 themes are repeated or imitated by successively entering voices and are developed in a continuous interweaving of the voice parts **2** a disturbed state in which a person performs acts of which on recovery he/she has no recollection and which usu involves disappearance from his/her usual environment – **fuguist** *n*

führer, fuehrer /ˈfyooərə ‖ ˈfjʊərə (*Ger* fyrə)/ *n* **1** LEADER 2c(3) **2** a leader exercising tyrannical authority [German leader, guide, fr *führen* to lead]

[1]**-ful** /-f(ə)l ‖ -f(ə)l/ *suffix* **1** (*n* → *adj*) full of <*event*ful> **2** (*n* → *adj*) characterized by <*peace*ful> **3** (*n* → *adj*) having the qualities of <*master*ful> **4** (*vb* → *adj*) tending to or able to <*mourn*ful>

[2]**-ful** *suffix* (*n* → *n*) number or amount that (a specified thing) holds or can hold <*hand*ful>

fulcrum /ˈfulkrəm, ˈfool- ‖ ˈfʌlkrəm, ˈfʊl-/ *n, pl* **fulcrums, fulcra** /-krə ‖ -krə/ the support about which a lever turns [Late Latin, fr Latin, bedpost, fr *fulcire* to prop]

fulfil, *NAm chiefly* **fulfill** /foolˈfil ‖ fʊlˈfɪl/ *vt* **-ll-** **1a** to cause to happen as appointed or predicted – usu pass **b** to put into effect; CARRY OUT 1 **c** to measure up to; satisfy **2** to develop the full potential of – **fulfiller** *n*, **fulfilment** *n*

fulgent /ˈfulj(ə)nt ‖ ˈfʌldʒ(ə)nt/ *adj* dazzlingly bright – fml – **fulgently** *adv*

[1]**full** /fool ‖ fʊl/ *adj* **1** possessing or containing a great amount or as much or as many as is possible or normal **2a** complete, esp in detail, number, or duration **b** lacking restraint, check, or qualification <~ *support*> **c** having all distinguishing characteristics; enjoying all authorized rights and privileges **3a** at the highest or greatest degree; maximum **b** at the height of development <~ *bloom*> **4** rounded in outline; *also* well filled out or plump **5a** having an abundance of material (e g in the form of gathers or folds) <*a* ~ *skirt*> **b** rich in experience <*a* ~ *life*> **6** satisfied, esp with food or drink, often to the point of discomfort – usu + *up* **7** having both parents in common <~ *sisters*> **8a** with the attention completely occupied by or centred on sthg <*always* ~ *of his own importance*> **b** filled with excited anticipation or pleasure <~ *of her plans for a holiday in Fiji*> **9** possessing a rich or pronounced quality **10** – used as an intensive <*won by a* ~ *4 shots*> – **fullness** *also* **fulness** *n* – **full of oneself** bumptiously self-centred or conceited

[2]**full** *adv* exactly, squarely

[3]**full** *n* **1** the highest or fullest state, extent, or degree **2** the requisite or complete amount – chiefly in *in full*

[4]**full** *vi, of the moon* to become full ~*vt* to make full in sewing

[5]**full** *vt* to cleanse and finish (woollen cloth) by moistening, heating, and pressing – **fuller** *n*

ˈ**fullˌback** /-ˌbak ‖ -ˌbæk/ *n* a primarily defensive player in soccer, rugby, etc, usu stationed nearest the defended goal

ˌ**full-ˈblooded** *adj* **1** of unmixed ancestry; purebred **2a** forceful, vigorous **b** virile **3** being the specified thing to a great extent <*a* ~ *socialist*> – **full-bloodedness** *n*

ˌ**full-ˈblown** *adj* **1** at the height of bloom **2** fully developed or mature

ˌ**full-ˈbodied** *adj* marked by richness and fullness, esp of flavour <*a* ~ *wine*>

ˌ**full ˈcircle** *adv* through a series of developments that lead back to the original source, position, or situation

ˌ**full-ˈdress** *adj* **1** complete, full-scale **2** of or being full dress <~ *uniform*>

full dress *n* the style of dress prescribed for ceremonial or formal social occasions

fuller /ˈfoolə ‖ ˈfʊlə/ *n* a blacksmith's hammer for grooving and spreading iron

ˌ**fuller's ˈearth** /ˈfooləz ‖ ˈfʊləz/ *n* a clayey substance used in fulling cloth and as a catalyst

ˌ**full-ˈfledged** *adj, chiefly NAm* fully-fledged

ˌ**full ˈhouse** *n* a poker hand containing 3 of a kind and a pair

ˌ**full-ˈlength** *adj* **1** showing or adapted to the entire length, esp of the human figure **2** having a normal or standard length; unabridged

ˌ**full ˈmoon** *n* the moon when its whole apparent disc is illuminated

ˌ**full ˈnelson** /ˈnels(ə)n ‖ ˈnels(ə)n/ *n* a wrestling hold in which both arms are thrust under the corresponding arms of an opponent and the hands clasped behind the opponent's head

ˌ**full-ˈscale** *adj* **1** identical to an original in proportion and size **2** involving full use of available resources <*a* ~ *biography*>

ˌ**full ˈstop** *n* a punctuation mark . used to mark the end (e g of a sentence or abbreviation)

ˌ**full-ˈtime** *adj* employed for or involving full time – **full time** *adv*

ˌ**full ˈtime** *n* **1** the amount of time considered the normal or standard amount for working during a given period, esp a week **2** the end of a sports, esp soccer, match

ˌ**full ˈtoss** *n* a throw, esp a bowled ball in cricket, that has not hit the ground by the time it arrives at the point at which it was aimed

fully /ˈfooli ‖ ˈfʊlɪ/ *adv* **1** completely **2** AT LEAST 1 <~ *nine tenths of us*>

ˌ**fully-ˈfashioned** *adj* employing or produced by a knitting process for shaping to body lines <~ *tights*>

ˌ**fully-ˈfledged,** *NAm* ˌ**full-ˈfledged** *adj* having attained complete status

fulmar /ˈfoolmə ‖ ˈfʊlmə/ *n* a seabird of colder regions closely related to the petrels

ˈ**fulminate** /-nayt ‖ -neɪt/ *vt* to utter or thunder out with denunciation ~ *vi* to thunder forth censure or invective – usu + *against* or *at* – **fulminator** *n*, **fulmination** *n*

fulsome /ˈfools(ə)m ‖ ˈfʊls(ə)m/ *adj* **1** overabundant, copious <*described in* ~ *detail*> **2a** unnecessarily effusive **b** obsequious – **fulsomely** *adv*, **fulsomeness** *n*

fumble /ˈfumbl ‖ ˈfʌmbl/ *vi* **1a** to grope for or handle sthg clumsily or awkwardly **b** to make awkward attempts to do or find sthg **2** to feel one's way or move awkwardly ~ *vt* **1** to feel or handle clumsily **2** to deal with awkwardly or clumsily – **fumble** *n*, **fumbler** *n*, **fumblingly** *adv*

[1]**fume** /fyoohm ‖ fjuːm/ *n* **1** an (irritating or offensive) smoke, vapour, or gas – often pl with sing. meaning **2** a state of unreasonable excited irritation or anger – **fumy** *adj*

[2]**fume** *vt* to expose to or treat with fumes ~ *vi* **1a** to emit fumes **b** to be in a state of excited irritation or anger <*she fretted and* ~d *over the delay*> **2** to rise (as if) in fumes

fumigate /'fyoohmigayt‖'fjuːmɪgeɪt/ *vt* to apply smoke, vapour, or gas to, esp in order to disinfect or destroy pests – **fumigator** *n*, **fumigant** *n*, **fumigation** *n*

[1]**fun** /fun‖fʌn/ *n* **1** (a cause of) amusement or enjoyment **2** derisive jest; ridicule <*made him a figure of* ~>

[2]**fun** *adj, chiefly NAm* providing entertainment, amusement, or enjoyment <*a* ~ *person to be with*> – infml

[1]**function** /'fungksh(ə)n‖'fʌŋkʃ(ə)n/ *n* **1** an occupational duty **2** the action characteristic of a person or thing or for which a thing exists <*examining the* ~ *of poetry in modern society*> **3** any of a group of related actions contributing to a larger action **4** an impressive, elaborate, or formal ceremony or social gathering **5a** a mathematical relationship between each element of one set and at least one element of the same or another set **b** a quality, trait, or fact dependent on and varying with another **c** a facility on a computer or similar device corresponding to a mathematical function or operation – **functionless** *adj*

[2]**function** *vi* **1** to have a function; serve **2** to operate <*a government* ~s *through numerous divisions*>

functional /'fungksh(ə)nl‖'fʌŋkʃ(ə)nl/ *adj* **1a** of, connected with, or being a function **b** affecting physiological or psychological functions but not organic structure <~ *heart disease*> **2** designed or developed for practical use without ornamentation **3** (capable of) performing a function – **functionally** *adv*

'**functional,ism** /-,iz(ə)m‖-,ɪz(ə)m/ *n* **1** a theory that stresses the interdependence of the institutions of a society **2** a theory or practice that emphasizes practical utility or functional relations to the exclusion of ornamentation – **functionalist** *n*, **functionalist, functionalistic** *adj*

functionary /'fungksh(ə)nəri‖'fʌŋkʃ(ə)nərɪ/ *n* **1** sby who serves in a certain function **2** sby holding office

'**function ,word** *n* a word (e g a preposition or conjunction) chiefly expressing grammatical relationship

[1]**fund** /fund‖fʌnd/ *n* **1** an available quantity of material or intangible resources <~ *of knowledge*> **2** (an organization administering) a resource, esp a sum of money, whose principal or interest is set apart for a specific objective **3** *pl* an available supply of money

[2]**fund** *vt* **1** to make provision of resources for discharging the interest or principal of **2** to provide funds for <*research* ~ed *by the government*>

[1]**fundamental** /,fundə'mentl‖,fʌndə'mentl/ *adj* **1** serving as a basis to support existence or to determine essential structure or function – often + *to* **2** of essential structure, function, or facts <~ *change*> **3** of, being, or produced by the lowest component of a complex vibration **4** of central importance; principal <~ *purpose*> **5** belonging to one's innate or ingrained characteristics – **fundamentally** *adv*

[2]**fundamental** *n* **1** a minimum constituent without which a thing or system would not be what it is **2** the prime tone of a harmonic series **3** the harmonic component of a complex wave that has the lowest frequency

,**funda'mentalism** /-iz(ə)m‖-ɪz(ə)m/ *n* (adherence to) a belief in the literal truth of the Bible – **fundamentalist** *n or adj*

funeral /'fyoohn(ə)rəl‖'fjuːn(ə)rəl/ *n* **1** (a procession connected with) a formal and ceremonial disposing of dead body, esp by burial or cremation; *also, NAm* a funeral service **2** a matter, esp a difficulty, that is of concern only to the specified person <*if you get lost, that's your* ~> – infml

'**funeral di,rector** *n* an undertaker

'**funeral ,parlour** *n* an undertaker's establishment

funerary /'fyoohnərəri‖'fjuːnərərɪ/ *adj* of, used for, or associated with burial

funereal /fyooh'niəri·əl‖fjuː'nɪərɪəl/ *adj* **1** of a funeral **2** gloomy, solemn – **funereally** *adv*

'**fun ,fair** *n, chiefly Br* a usu outdoor show offering amusements (e g sideshows, rides, or games of skill)

fungicide /'funjisied‖'fʌndʒɪsaɪd/ *n* a substance used for destroying or preventing fungus – **fungicidal** *adj*, **fungicidally** *adv*

fungoid /'fung·goyd‖'fʌŋgɔɪd/ *adj* resembling, characteristic of, or being a fungus – **fungoid** *n*

fungous /'fung·gəs‖'fʌŋgəs/ *adj* of, like, or caused by a fungus or fungi

fungus /'fung·gəs‖'fʌŋgəs/ *n, pl* **fungi** /-gie, -gi‖-gaɪ, -gɪ/ *also* **funguses** any of a major group of often parasitic organisms lacking chlorophyll and including moulds, rusts, mildews, smuts, mushrooms, and toadstools – **fungal** *adj*

[1]**funicular** /fyooh'nikyoolə‖fjuː'nɪkjʊlə/ *adj* **1** dependent on the tension of a cord or cable **2** (of the form) of or associated with a cord

[2]**funicular** *n* a cable railway in which an ascending carriage counterbalances a descending carriage

[1]**funk** /fungk‖fʌŋk/ *n* **1a** a state of paralysing fear **b** a fit of inability to face difficulty **2** a coward *USE* infml

[2]**funk** *vt* **1** to be afraid of **2** to avoid doing or facing (sthg) because of lack of determination *USE* infml

[3]**funk** *n* funky music – slang

funky /'fungki‖'fʌŋkɪ/ *adj* **1** having an offensive smell – chiefly infml **2** having an earthy unsophisticated style and feeling (as in the blues) **3** having an earthily sexual quality **4** – used to approve sthg or sby, esp in pop culture *USE* (*2, 3, & 4*) slang – **funkiness** *n*

[1]**funnel** /'funl‖'fʌnl/ *n* **1** a utensil usu having the shape of a hollow cone with a tube extending from the smaller end, designed to direct liquids or powders into a small opening **2** a shaft, stack, or flue for ventilation or the escape of smoke or steam

[2]**funnel** *vb* **-ll-** (*NAm* **-l-**, **-ll-**) *vi* **1** to have or take the shape of a funnel **2** to pass (as if) through a funnel <*the crowd* ~led *out of the football ground*> ~ *vt* **1** to form in the shape of a funnel <~led *his hands and shouted through them*> **2** to move to a focal point or into a central channel <*contributions were* ~led *into 1 account*>

[1]**funny** /'funi‖'fʌnɪ/ *adj* **1** causing mirth and

laughter; seeking or intended to amuse **2** peculiar, strange, or odd **3** involving trickery, deception, or dishonesty <*told the prisoner not to try anything* ~> **4** unwilling to be helpful; difficult **5a** slightly unwell **b** slightly mad <~ *in the head*> *USE* (*3, 4, 5*) infml – **funnily** *adv*, **funniness** *n*, **funny** *adv*

[2]**funny** *n* a comic strip or comic section in a periodical – usu pl

ˈ**funny ˌbone** *n* the place at the back of the elbow where the nerve supplying the hand and forearm rests against the bone [fr the tingling felt when it is struck]

ˈ**funny ˌfarm** *n, chiefly NAm* a mental hospital – chiefly humor

[1]**fur** /fuh‖fɜː/ *vb* **-rr-** to (cause to) become coated or clogged (as if) with fur – often + *up*

[2]**fur** *n* **1** a piece of the dressed pelt of an animal used to make, trim, or line garments **2** an article of clothing made of or with fur **3** the hairy coat of a mammal, esp when fine, soft, and thick; *also* such a coat with the skin **4** a coating resembling fur: e g **4a** a coating of dead cells on the tongue of sby who is unwell **b** the thick pile of a fabric (e g chenille) **c** a coating formed in vessels (e g kettles or pipes) by deposition of scale from hard water **5** any of the heraldic representations of animal pelts or their colours that have a stylized pattern of tufts or patches – **furless** *adj*, **furred** *adj*

furbelow /ˈfuhbiˌloh‖ˈfɜːbɪˌləʊ/ *n* **1** a pleated or gathered piece of material; *specif* a flounce on women's clothing **2** sthg that suggests a furbelow, esp in being showy or superfluous – often in *frills and furbelows* – **furbelow** *vt*

furbish /ˈfuhbish‖ˈfɜːbɪʃ/ *vt* **1** to polish **2** to renovate – often + *up* – **furbisher** *n*

furious /ˈfyooəri·əs‖ˈfjʊərɪəs/ *adj* **1a** exhibiting or goaded by uncontrollable anger **b** giving a stormy or turbulent appearance <~ *bursts of flame from the fire*> **c** marked by (violent) noise, excitement, or activity **2** INTENSE 1a – **furiously** *adv*

furl /fuhl‖fɜːl/ *vt* to fold or roll (e g a sail or umbrella) close to or round sthg ~ *vi* to curl or fold as in being furled – **furl** *n*

furlong /ˈfuhlong‖ˈfɜːlɒŋ/ *n* a unit of length equal to 220yd (about 0.201km)

[1]**furlough** /ˈfuhloh‖ˈfɜːləʊ/ *n* a leave of absence from duty granted esp to a soldier

[2]**furlough** *vt, chiefly NAm* to grant a furlough to

furnace /ˈfuhnis‖ˈfɜːnɪs/ *n* an enclosed apparatus in which heat is produced (e g for heating a building or reducing ore)

furnish /ˈfuhnish‖ˈfɜːnɪʃ/ *vt* to provide or supply (with what is needed); *esp* to equip with furniture – **furnisher** *n*

furnishing /ˈfuhnishing‖ˈfɜːnɪʃɪŋ/ *n* an object that tends to increase comfort or utility; *specif* an article of furniture for the interior of a building – usu pl

furniture /ˈfuhnichə‖ˈfɜːnɪtʃə/ *n* necessary, useful, or desirable equipment: e g **a** the movable articles (e g tables, chairs, and beds) that make an area suitable for living in or use **b** accessories <*door* ~> **c** the whole movable equipment of a ship

furore /fyooˈrawri‖fjʊˈrɔːrɪ/ *n* an outburst of general excitement or indignation

furphy /ˈfuhfi‖ˈfɜːfɪ/ *n, Austr* an unlikely or absurd rumour – infml

furrier /ˈfuri·ə‖ˈfʌrɪə/ *n* a fur dealer

[1]**furrow** /ˈfuroh‖ˈfʌrəʊ/ *n* **1** a trench in the earth made by a plough **2** sthg like the track of a plough: e g **2a** a groove **b** a deep wrinkle

[2]**furrow** *vb* to make or form furrows, grooves, lines, etc (in)

furry /ˈfuhri‖ˈfɜːrɪ/ *adj* like, made of, or covered with fur

[1]**further** /ˈfuhdhə‖ˈfɜːðə/ *adv* **1** FARTHER 1 **2** moreover **3** to a greater degree or extent

[2]**further** *adj* **1** FARTHER 1 **2** additional

[3]**further** *vt* to help forward <*this will* ~ *your chances of success*> – **furtherance** *n*, **furtherer** *n*

further education *n, Br* vocational, cultural, or recreational education for people who have left school

ˌ**furtherˈmore** /-ˈmaw‖-ˈmɔː/ *adv* moreover

ˈ**furtherˌmost** /-ˌmohst‖-ˌməʊst/ *adj* most distant

ˈ**further to** *prep* following up <~ *your letter of the 4th July*>

furthest /ˈfuhdhist‖ˈfɜːðɪst/ *adv or adj* farthest

furtive /ˈfuhtiv‖ˈfɜːtɪv/ *adj* expressing or done by stealth [Latin *furtivus*, fr *furtum* theft, fr *fur* thief]

fury /ˈfyooəri‖ˈfjʊərɪ/ *n* **1** intense, disordered, and often destructive rage **2a** *cap* any of the 3 avenging deities who in Greek mythology punished crimes **b** (one who resembles) an avenging spirit **3** wild disordered force or activity **4** a frenzy

furze /fuhz‖fɜːz/ *n* gorse – **furzy** *adj*

[1]**fuse** /fyoohz‖fjuːz/ *n* **1** a combustible substance enclosed in a cord or cable for setting off an explosive charge by transmitting fire to it **2** *NAm chiefly* **fuze** the detonating device for setting off the charge in a projectile, bomb, etc

[2]**fuse**, *NAm also* **fuze** *vt* to equip with a fuse

[3]**fuse** *vt* **1** to reduce to a liquid or plastic state by heat **2** to blend thoroughly (as if) by melting together **3** to cause (e g a light bulb) to fail by fusing ~ *vi* **1** to become fluid with heat **2** to become blended (as if) by melting together **3** to fail because of the melting of a fuse – **fusible** *adj*, **fusibility** *n*

[4]**fuse** *n* (a device that includes) a wire or strip of fusible metal that melts and interrupts the circuit when the current exceeds a particular value

fuselage /ˈfyoohziˌlahzh‖ˈfjuːzɪˌlɑːʒ/ *n* the central body portion of an aeroplane designed to accommodate the crew and the passengers or cargo [French, fr *fuselé* spindle-shaped, deriv of Latin *fusus* spindle]

fusil /ˈfyoohzil‖ˈfjuːzɪl/ *n* a light flintlock musket

fusilier /ˌfyoohzəˈliə‖ˌfjuːzəˈlɪə/ *n* a member of a British regiment formerly armed with fusils

[1]**fusillade** /ˌfyoohzəˈlayd‖ˌfjuːzəˈleɪd/ *n* **1** a number of shots fired simultaneously or in rapid succession **2** a spirited outburst, esp of criticism

[2]**fusillade** *vt* to attack or shoot down by a fusillade

fusion /ˈfyoohzh(ə)n‖ˈfjuːʒ(ə)n/ *n* **1** fusing or

rendering plastic by heat **2** a union (as if) by melting: e g **2a** a merging of diverse elements into a unified whole **b** the union of light atomic nuclei to form heavier nuclei resulting in the release of enormous quantities of energy

[1]**fuss** /fus‖fʌs/ *n* **1a** needless or useless bustle or excitement **b** a show of (affectionate) attention – often in *make a fuss of* **2a** a state of agitation, esp over a trivial matter **b** an objection, protest

[2]**fuss** *vi* **1a** to create or be in a state of restless activity; *specif* to shower affectionate attentions **b** to pay close or undue attention to small details **2** to become upset; worry ~*vt* to agitate, upset – **fusser** *n*

ˈ**fuss,pot** /-ˌpot‖-ˌpɒt/ *n* a person who fusses about trifles – infml

fussy /ˈfusi‖ˈfʌsɪ/ *adj* **1** nervous and excitable (about small matters) **2a** showing too much concern over details **b** fastidious **3** having too much or too detailed ornamentation – **fussily** *adv*, **fussiness** *n*

fustian /ˈfusti·ən, ˈfuschən‖ˈfʌstɪən, ˈfʌstʃən/ *n* **1** a strong cotton or linen fabric (e g corduroy or velveteen) **2** pretentious and banal writing or speech – **fustian** *adj*

fusty /ˈfusti‖ˈfʌstɪ/ *adj* **1** stale or musty from being left undisturbed for a long time **2** out-of-date **3** rigidly old-fashioned or reactionary – **fustily** *adv*, **fustiness** *n*

futile /ˈfyoohtiel‖ˈfjuːtaɪl/ *adj* **1** completely ineffective **2** *of a person* ineffectual – **futilely** *adv*, **futileness** *n*, **futility** *n*

[1]**future** /ˈfyoohchə‖ˈfjuːtʃə/ *adj* **1** that is to be; *specif* existing after death **2** of or constituting the verb tense that expresses action or state in the future

[2]**future** *n* **1a** time that is to come **b** that which is going to occur **2** likelihood of success <*not much* ~ *in trying to sell furs in a hot country*> **3** sthg (e g a bulk commodity) bought for future acceptance or sold for future delivery – usu pl **4** (a verb form in) the future tense of a language – **futureless** *adj*

futurism /ˈfyoohchəˌriz(ə)m‖ˈfjuːtʃəˌrɪz(ə)m/ *n often cap* a movement in art, music, and literature begun in Italy about 1910 and seeking to express the dynamic energy and movement of mechanical processes – **futurist** *n or adj*

futuristic /ˌfyoohchəˈristik‖ˌfjuːtʃəˈrɪstɪk/ *adj* of the future or futurism; *esp* bearing no relation to known or traditional forms – **futuristically** *adv*

futurity /fyoohˈtyooərəti, -ˈchooə-‖fjuːˈtjʊərətɪ, -ˈtʃʊə-/ *n* **1** FUTURE 1a **2** *pl* future events or prospects **3** *chiefly NAm* a competition, esp a horse race, for which entries are made well in advance of the event

[1]**fuzz** /fuz‖fʌz/ *n* fine light particles or fibres (e g of down or fluff)

[2]**fuzz** *n sing or pl in constr* the police – slang

fuzzy /ˈfuzi‖ˈfʌzɪ/ *adj* **1** marked by or giving a suggestion of fuzz <*a* ~ *covering of felt*> **2** not clear; indistinct – **fuzzily** *adv*, **fuzziness** *n*

-fy /-fie‖-faɪ/, **-ify** *suffix* (→ *vb*) **1** become or cause to be <*puri*fy> **2** fill with <*horri*fy> **3** give the characteristics of; make similar to <*dandi*fy> **4** engage in (a specified activity) <*speechi*fy> – often humor or derog

g /jee‖dʒiː/ *n, pl* **g's, gs** *often cap* **1** (a graphic representation of or device for reproducing) the 7th letter of the English alphabet **2** the 5th note of a C-major scale **3** a unit of force equal to the force exerted by gravity on a body at rest and used to indicate the force to which a body is subjected when accelerated **4** *chiefly NAm* a sum of $1000 – slang

[1]**gab** /gab‖gæb/ *vi* **-bb-** to chatter, blab – infml – **gabber** *n*

[2]**gab** *n* (idle) talk – infml

gabardine /ˌgabəˈdeen, ˈ--ˌ-‖ˌgæbəˈdiːn, ˈ--ˌ-/ *n* **1** GABERDINE 1 **2a** a firm durable fabric (e g of wool or rayon) twilled with diagonal ribs on the right side **b** *chiefly Br* a waterproof coat made of gabardine

gabble /ˈgabl‖ˈgæbl/ *vb* to talk or utter rapidly or unintelligibly – **gabble** *n*, **gabbler** *n*

gaberdine /ˈgabəˌdeen, ˌ--ˈ-‖ˈgæbəˌdiːn, ˌ--ˈ-/ *n* **1** a coarse long coat or smock worn chiefly by Jews in medieval times **2** GABARDINE 2

gable /ˈgaybl‖ˈgeɪbl/ *n* the vertical triangular section of wall between 2 slopes of a pitched roof – **gabled** *adj*

[1]**gad** /gad‖gæd/ *vi* **-dd-** to go or travel in an aimless or restless manner or in search of pleasure – usu + *about* – **gadder** *n*

[2]**gad** *interj, archaic* – used as a mild oath

ˈ**gad,fly** /-ˌflie‖-ˌflaɪ/ *n* **1** any of various flies (e g a horsefly or botfly) that bite or annoy livestock **2** a person who stimulates or provokes others, esp by persistent irritating criticism

gadget /ˈgajit‖ˈgædʒɪt/ *n* a usu small and often novel mechanical or electronic device – **gadgetry** *n*

Gaelic /ˈgaylik‖ˈgeɪlɪk; *Scots* ˈgahlik‖ˈgɑːlɪk; *Irish* ˈgalik‖ˈgælɪk/ *adj* of or being (the language of) the Celts in Ireland, the Isle of Man, and the Scottish Highlands – **Gaelic** *n*

[1]**gaff** /gaf‖gæf/ *n* **1a** a spear or spearhead for killing fish or turtles **b** a pole with a hook for holding or landing heavy fish **2** a spar on which the head of a fore-and-aft sail is extended

[2]**gaff** *vt* to strike or secure (e g a fish) with a gaff

gaffe /gaf‖gæf/ *n* a social blunder; FAUX PAS

gaffer /ˈgafə‖ˈgæfə/ *n* **1** the chief lighting electrician in a film or television studio **2** *Br* a foreman or overseer **3** *dial* an old man [prob alteration of *godfather*]

[1]**gag** /gag‖gæg/ *vb* **-gg-** *vt* **1** to apply a gag to or put a gag in the mouth of (to prevent speech) **2** to cause to retch **3** to obstruct, choke <~ *a valve*> **4** to prevent from having free speech or expression – chiefly journ ~ *vi* **1** to heave, retch **2** to tell jokes

[2]**gag** *n* **1** sthg thrust into the mouth to keep it open or prevent speech or outcry **2** JOKE 1a **3** a hoax, trick **4** a check to free speech – chiefly journ

gaga /ˈgahˌgah‖ˈgɑːˌgɑː/ *adj* **1a** senile **b** slightly mad **2** infatuated – often + *about USE* infml

[1]**gage** /gayj‖geɪdʒ/ *n* **1** a token of defiance; *specif* a glove, cap, etc thrown on the ground in

former times as a challenge to a fight **2** sthg deposited as a pledge of performance

[2]**gage** *n* **1** GAUGE 3 **2** *NAm* GAUGE 1, 2, 4, 5, 6

[3]**gage** *vt, NAm* to gauge

[4]**gage** *n* a greengage

gaggle /'gagl‖'gægl/ *n* **1** a flock (of geese) **2** *sing or pl in constr* a typically noisy or talkative group or cluster – chiefly infml

gaiety /'gayəti‖'geɪətɪ/ *n* **1** merrymaking; *also* festive activity **2** gay quality, spirits, manner, or appearance

gaily /'gayli‖'geɪlɪ/ *adv* in a gay manner

[1]**gain** /gayn‖geɪn/ *n* **1** resources or advantage acquired or increased; a profit **2** the obtaining of profit or possessions **3** an increase in amount, magnitude, or degree

[2]**gain** *vt* **1a(1)** to get possession of or win, usu by industry, merit, or craft **a(2)** to increase a lead over or catch up a rival by (esp time or distance) **b** to get by a natural development or process <~ *strength*> **c** to acquire <~ *a friend*> **d** to arrive at <~ed *the river that night*> **2** to increase in <~ *momentum*> **3** *of a timepiece* to run fast by the amount of <*the clock* ~s *a minute a day*> ~ *vi* **1** to get advantage; profit **2** to increase, specif in weight **3** *of a timepiece* to run fast – **gainer** *n* – **gain ground** to make progress

'**gainful** /-f(ə)l‖-f(ə)l/ *adj* profitable – **gainfully** *adv*

gainsay /gayn'say‖geɪn'seɪ/ *vt* **gainsays** /-'sez‖-'sez/; **gainsaid** /-'sed‖-'sed/ **1** to deny, dispute **2** to oppose, resist – **gainsayer** *n*

gait /gayt‖geɪt/ *n* **1** a manner of walking or moving on foot **2** a sequence of foot movements (e g a walk, trot, or canter) by which a horse moves forwards

gaiter /'gaytə‖'geɪtə/ *n* a cloth or leather covering reaching from the instep to ankle, mid-calf, or knee

gal /gal‖gæl/ *n* a girl – used in writing to represent esp a US or upper-class pronunciation

gala /'gahlə‖'gɑːlə/ *n* **1** a festive gathering (that constitutes or marks a special occasion) **2** *Br* a special sports meeting [Italian, fr Middle French *gale* merrymaking, festivity, pleasure]

galactic /gə'laktik‖gə'læktɪk/ *adj* of a galaxy, esp the Milky Way galaxy

galantine /'galənteen‖'gælənti:n/ *n* a cold dish of boned and usu stuffed cooked meat glazed with aspic

galaxy /'galəksi‖'gæləksɪ/ *n* **1a** *often cap* MILKY WAY **b** any of many independent systems composed chiefly of stars, dust, and gases and separated from each other in the universe by vast distances **2** an assemblage of brilliant or notable people or things [Late Latin *galaxias*, fr Greek, fr *galakt-*, *gala* milk]

gale /gayl‖geɪl/ *n* **1** a strong wind **2** a noisy outburst <~s *of laughter*>

[1]**gall** /gawl‖gɔːl/ *n* **1a** BILE 1 **b** sthg bitter to endure **c** rancour **2** brazen and insolent audacity

[2]**gall** *n* a skin sore caused by rubbing

[3]**gall** *vt* **1a** to wear (away) by rubbing; chafe **b** to cause feelings of mortification and irritation in; vex acutely **2** to harass ~*vi* to become sore or worn by rubbing – **gallingly** *adv*

[4]**gall** *n* a diseased swelling of plant tissue produced by infection with fungi, insect parasites, etc

[1]**gallant** /'galənt, gə'lahnt, gə'lant‖'gælənt, gə'lɑːnt, gə'lænt/ *n* a (young) man of fashion (who is particularly attentive to women)

[2]**gallant** /*sense 1* 'galənt‖'gælənt; *sense 2* 'galənt, gə'lahnt, gə'lant‖'gælənt, gə'lɑːnt, gə'lænt/ *adj* **1a** splendid, stately <*a* ~ *ship*> **b** nobly chivalrous and brave **2** courteously and elaborately attentive, esp to ladies [Middle French *galant*, fr *galer* to have a good time, fr *gale* pleasure] – **gallantly** *adv*

gallantry /'galəntri‖'gæləntrɪ/ *n* **1a** an act of marked courtesy **b** courteous attention to a lady **2** spirited and conspicuous bravery

'**gall ˌbladder** *n* a membranous muscular sac in which bile from the liver is stored

galleon /'gali·ən‖'gælɪən/ *n* a heavy square-rigged sailing ship of the 15th to early 18th c used (by the Spanish) for war or commerce

gallery /'galəri‖'gælərɪ/ *n* **1** a covered passage for walking; a colonnade **2** an outdoor balcony **3a** a long and narrow passage, room, or corridor <*a shooting* ~> **b** a horizontal subterranean passage in a cave or (military) mining system **c** a passage, esp in the ground or wood, made by a mole or insect **4a** (a collection worthy of being displayed as if in) a room or building devoted to the exhibition of works of art **b** an institution or business exhibiting or dealing in works of art **5** *sing or pl in constr* **5a** (the occupants of) a balcony projecting from 1 or more interior walls of a hall, auditorium, or church, to accommodate additional people, or reserved for musicians, singers, etc **b** the undiscriminating general public **c** the spectators at a tennis, golf, etc match – **galleried** *adj*

galley /'gali‖'gælɪ/ *n* **1** a large low usu single-decked ship propelled by oars and sails and used esp in the Mediterranean in the Middle Ages and in classical antiquity **2** a kitchen on a ship or aircraft **3a** a long oblong tray with upright sides for holding set type **b galley, galley proof** a proof in the form of a long sheet (taken from type on a galley)

'**galley ˌslave** *n* a drudge

Gallic /'galik‖'gælɪk/ *adj* (characteristic) of Gaul or France

gallicism /'galisiz(ə)m‖'gælɪsɪz(ə)m/ *n, often cap* a characteristic French word or expression (occurring in another language)

gallivant /'galivant‖'gælɪvænt/ *vi* to travel energetically or roam about for pleasure

gallon /'galən‖'gælən/ *n* either of 2 units of liquid capacity equal to 8pt: **a** a British unit equal to about 4.546l **b** a US unit equal to about 3.785l – **gallonage** *n*

[1]**gallop** /'galəp‖'gæləp/ *n* **1** a fast bounding gait of a quadruped; *specif* the fastest natural 3-beat gait of the horse **2** a ride or run at a gallop **3** a rapid or hasty progression

[2]**gallop** *vb* to (cause to) progress or ride at a gallop – **galloper** *n*

gallows /'galohz‖'gæləʊz/ *n, pl* **gallows** *also* **gallowses** **1 gallows, gallows tree** a frame, usu of 2 upright posts and a crosspiece, for hanging criminals **2** *the* punishment of hanging

gallows humour *n* grim humour that makes fun of a very serious or terrifying situation

gallstone /ˈgawlˌstohn‖ˈgɔːlˌstəʊn/ *n* a calculus formed in the gall bladder or bile ducts

ˈGallup ˌpoll /ˈgaləp‖ˈgæləp/ *n* a survey of public opinion frequently used as a means of forecasting sthg (e g an election result) [George *Gallup* (born 1901), US public opinion statistician]

galore /gəˈlaw‖gəˈlɔː/ *adj* abundant, plentiful – used after a noun *<bargains ~>* [Irish Gaelic *go leor* enough]

galosh /gəˈlosh‖gəˈlɒʃ/ *n* a rubber overshoe – **galoshed** *adj*

galumph /gəˈlum(p)f‖gəˈlʌm(p)f/ *vi* to move with a clumsy heavy tread – infml

galvanic /galˈvanik‖gælˈvænɪk/ *adj* **1** of, being, or producing a direct current of electricity resulting from chemical action **2** having an electric effect; stimulating vigorous activity or vitality – **galvanically** *adv*

galvanism /ˈgalvənˌiz(ə)m‖ˈgælvənˌɪz(ə)m/ *n* **1** (the therapeutic use of) direct electric current produced by chemical action **2** vital or forceful activity [Luigi *Galvani* (1737-98), Italian physician & physicist who first described it]

ˈgalvan·ize, -ise /-iez‖-aɪz/ *vt* **1** to subject to or stimulate, rouse, or excite (as if) by the action of an electric current **2** to coat (iron or steel) with zinc as a protection from rust – **galvanizer** *n*, **galvanization** *n*

gambit /ˈgambit‖ˈgæmbɪt/ *n* **1** a chess opening, esp in which a player risks (several) minor pieces to gain an advantage **2a** a remark intended to start a conversation or make a telling point **b** a calculated move; a stratagem [Italian *gambetto*, lit., act of tripping someone, fr *gamba* leg]

[1]gamble /ˈgambl‖ˈgæmbl/ *vi* **1a** to play a game (of chance) for money or property **b** to bet or risk sthg on an uncertain outcome **2** SPECULATE 2 ~ *vt* **1** to risk by gambling; wager **2** to venture, hazard – **gambler** *n*

[2]gamble *n* **1** the playing of a game (of chance) for stakes **2** (sthg involving) an element of risk

gamboge /gamˈbohj, -ˈboozh‖gæmˈbəʊdʒ, -ˈbuʒ/ *n* **1** a gum resin from some SE Asian trees that is used as a yellow pigment **2** a strong yellow

gambol /ˈgambl‖ˈgæmbl/ *vb or n* **-ll-** (*NAm* **-l-**, **-ll-**) (to engage in) skipping or leaping about in play

[1]game /gaym‖geɪm/ *n* **1a(1)** activity engaged in for diversion or amusement; play **a(2)** the equipment for a particular esp indoor game **b** often derisive or mocking jesting *<make ~ of a nervous player>* **2a** a course or plan consisting of (secret) manoeuvres directed towards some end *<playing a waiting ~>* **b** a specified type of activity seen as competitive or governed by rules (and pursued for financial gain) *<the newspaper ~>* **3a(1)** (the quality of play in) a physical or mental competition conducted according to rules with the participants in direct opposition to each other; a match **a(2)** a division of a larger contest **a(3)** the number of points necessary to win a game **b** *pl* organized sports, esp athletics **c** a situation that involves contest, rivalry, or struggle *<got into microelectronics early in the ~>* **4a** animals under pursuit or taken in hunting; *specif* (the edible flesh of) certain wild mammals, birds, and fish (e g deer and pheasant), hunted for sport or food **b** an object of ridicule or attack – often in *fair game* **5** prostitution – slang; often in *on the game*

[2]game *vi* GAMBLE 1 ~*vt archaic* to lose or squander by gambling

[3]game *adj* **1** having a resolute unyielding spirit *<~ to the end>* **2** ready to take risks or try sthg new – **gamely** *adv*, **gameness** *n*

[4]game *adj* injured, crippled, or lame *<a ~ leg>*

ˈgameˌkeeper /-ˌkeepə‖-ˌkiːpə/ *n* one who has charge of the breeding and protection of game animals or birds on a private preserve

gamesmanship /ˈgaymzmənˌship‖ˈgeɪmzmənˌʃɪp/ *n* the art or practice of winning games by means other than superior skill without actually violating the rules

gamete /ˈgameet, gəˈmeet‖ˈgæmiːt, gəˈmiːt/ *n* a mature germ cell with a single set of chromosomes capable of fusing with another gamete of the other sex to form a zygote from which a new organism develops – **gametic** *adj*, **gametically** *adv*

gamin /ˈgamin‖ˈgæmɪn/, *fem* **gamine** /ˈgameen‖ˈgæmiːn/ *n* URCHIN 2

gamma /ˈgamə‖ˈgæmə/ *n* the 3rd letter of the Greek alphabet

gamma globulin *n* any of several immunoglobulins in blood or serum including most antibodies

ˈgamma ˌray *n* (a quantum of) electromagnetic radiation of shorter wavelength than X rays emitted in some radioactive decay processes – usu pl

[1]gammon /ˈgamən‖ˈgæmən/ *n* (the meat of) the lower end including the hind leg of a side of bacon removed from the carcass after curing with salt

[2]gammon *n* nonsense, humbug – not now in vogue

gammy /ˈgami‖ˈgæmɪ/ *adj, Br* [4]GAME – infml

gamp /gamp‖gæmp/ *n, Br* a large, esp loosely tied, umbrella – infml [Sarah *Gamp*, nurse with a large umbrella in the novel *Martin Chuzzlewit* by Charles Dickens (1812-70), English writer]

gamut /ˈgamət‖ˈgæmət/ *n* **1** the whole series of recognized musical notes **2** an entire range or series

gamy, gamey /ˈgaymi‖ˈgeɪmɪ/ *adj* having the strong flavour or smell of game (that has been hung until high) – **gamily** *adv*, **gaminess** *n*

[1]gander /ˈgandə‖ˈgændə/ *n* **1** an adult male goose **2** a simpleton

[2]gander *n* a look, glance – infml

[1]gang /gang‖gæŋ/ *n* **1** a combination of similar implements or devices arranged to act together **2** *sing or pl in constr* a group of people **2a** working together **b** associating for criminal, disreputable, etc ends; *esp* a group of adolescents who (disreputably) spend leisure time together **c** that have informal and usu close social relations *<have the ~ over for a party>*

[2]gang *vt* to assemble or operate (e g mechanical

parts) simultaneously as a group ~*vi* to move or act as a gang <*the children* ~ed *together*>

[3]**gang** *vi, Scot* to go

ganger /ˈgang·ə‖ˈgæŋə/ *n, Br* the foreman of a gang of workmen

gangling /ˈgang·gling‖ˈgæŋglɪŋ/, **gangly** /-gli‖-glɪ/ *adj* tall, thin, and awkward in movement

ganglion /ˈgang·glion, -ən‖ˈgæŋglɪɒn, -ən/ *n, pl* **ganglia** /-gli·ə‖-glɪə/ *also* **ganglions** **1a** a small cyst on a joint membrane or tendon sheath **b** a mass of nerve cells outside the brain or spinal cord; *also* NUCLEUS 2b **2** a focus of strength, energy, or activity – **ganglionated** *adj*, **ganglionic** *adj*

gangplank /ˈgang,plangk‖ˈgæŋ,plæŋk/ *n* a movable board, plank, etc used to board a ship from a quay or another ship

[1]**gangrene** /ˈgang,green‖ˈgæŋ,griːn/ *n* **1** local death of the body's soft tissues due to loss of blood supply **2** a pervasive moral evil – **gangrenous** *adj*

[2]**gangrene** *vb* to make or become gangrenous

gangster /ˈgangstə‖ˈgæŋstə/ *n* a member of a criminal gang – **gangsterism** *n*

gang up *vi* **1** to combine as a group for a specific (disreputable) purpose **2** to make a joint assault *on*

ˈ**gang,way** /-,way‖-,weɪ/ *n* **1** a (temporary) passageway (constructed of planks) **2a** the opening in a ship's side or rail through which it is boarded **b** a gangplank **3** a clear passage through a crowd – often used interjectionally **4** *Br* a narrow passage between sections of seats in a theatre, storage bays in a warehouse, etc

gannet /ˈganit‖ˈgænɪt/ *n* any of several related large fish-eating seabirds that breed in large colonies chiefly on offshore islands

gantry /ˈgantri‖ˈgæntrɪ/ *n* **1** a frame for supporting barrels **2** a frame structure raised on side supports that spans over or round sthg and is used for railway signals, as a travelling crane, for servicing a rocket before launching, etc

gaol /jay(ə)l‖dʒeɪ(ə)l/ *vb or n, chiefly Br* (to) jail

gap /gap‖gæp/ *n* **1** a break in a barrier (e g a wall or hedge) **2a** a mountain pass **b** a ravine **3** an empty space between 2 objects or 2 parts of an object **4** a break in continuity <*unexplained* ~s *in his story*> **5** a disparity or difference <*the* ~ *between imports and exports*> **6** a wide difference in character or attitude <*the generation* ~> – **gappy, gapped** *adj*

[1]**gape** /gayp‖geɪp/ *vi* **1a** to open the mouth wide **b** to open or part widely <*holes* ~d *in the pavement*> **2** to gaze stupidly or in open-mouthed surprise or wonder **3** to yawn – **gapingly** *adv*

[2]**gape** *n* **1** an act of gaping; *esp* an open-mouthed stare **2** the average width of the open mouth or beak **3** a fit of yawning

[1]**garage** /ˈgarahzh, ˈgarij‖ˈgærɑːʒ, ˈgærɪdʒ/ *n* **1** a building for the shelter of motor vehicles **2** an establishment for providing essential services (e g the supply of petrol or repair work) to motor vehicles

[2]**garage** *vt* to keep or put in a garage

garb /gahb‖gɑːb/ *n* **1** a style of clothing; dress **2** an outward form; appearance – **garb** *vt*

garbage /ˈgahbij‖ˈgɑːbɪdʒ/ *n* **1** worthless writing or speech **2** *chiefly NAm* RUBBISH 1

garble /ˈgahbl‖ˈgɑːbl/ *vt* to distort or confuse, giving a false impression of the facts <*a* ~d *message*> – **garbler** *n*

[1]**garden** /ˈgahd(ə)n‖ˈgɑːd(ə)n/ *n* **1a** a plot of ground where herbs, fruits, vegetables, or typically flowers are cultivated **b** a rich well-cultivated region <*the* ~ *of England*> **2a** a public recreation area or park <*a botanical* ~> **b** an open-air eating or drinking place <*beer* ~> – **gardenful** *n*

[2]**garden** *vi* to work in, cultivate, or lay out a garden – **gardener** *n*

[3]**garden** *adj* of a cultivated as distinguished from a wild kind grown in the open <*a* ~ *plant*>

garden city *n* a planned town with spacious residential areas including public parks and considerable garden space

ˈ**garden ,party** *n* a usu formal party held on the lawns of a garden

gargantuan /gahˈgantyoo·ən‖gɑːˈgæntjʊən/ *adj, often cap* gigantic, colossal <*a* ~ *meal*> [*Gargantua*, gigantic king in the novel *Gargantua* by François Rabelais (1494?-1553), French humorist]

[1]**gargle** /ˈgahgl‖ˈgɑːgl/ *vt* **1** to blow air from the lungs through (a liquid) held in the mouth or throat **2** to cleanse (the mouth or throat) in this manner ~ *vi* **1** to use a gargle **2** to speak or sing as if gargling

[2]**gargle** *n* **1** a liquid used in gargling **2** a bubbling liquid sound produced by gargling

gargoyle /ˈgah,goyl‖ˈgɑː,gɔɪl/ *n* a spout in the form of a grotesque human or animal figure projecting from a roof gutter to throw rainwater clear of a building – **gargoyled** *adj*

garish /ˈgeərish‖ˈgeərɪʃ/ *adj* **1** excessively and gaudily bright or vivid **2** tastelessly showy – **garishly** *adv*, **garishness** *n*

[1]**garland** /ˈgahlənd‖ˈgɑːlənd/ *n* **1** a wreath of flowers or leaves worn as an ornament or sign of distinction **2** an anthology or collection

[2]**garland** *vt* to form into or deck with a garland

garlic /ˈgahlik‖ˈgɑːlɪk/ *n* (the pungent compound bulb, much used as a flavouring in cookery, of) a European plant of the lily family – **garlicky** *adj*

garment /ˈgahmənt‖ˈgɑːmənt/ *n* an article of clothing

[1]**garner** /ˈgahnə‖ˈgɑːnə/ *n* **1** a granary **2** a grain bin *USE* fml or poetic

[2]**garner** *vt* to gather, store – fml or poetic

garnet /ˈgahnit‖ˈgɑːnɪt/ *n* **1** a hard brittle silicate mineral used as an abrasive and in its transparent deep red form as a gem **2** a dark red

[1]**garnish** /ˈgahnish‖ˈgɑːnɪʃ/ *vt* **1** to decorate, embellish **2** to add decorative or savoury touches to (food)

[2]**garnish** *n* **1** an embellishment, ornament **2** an edible savoury or decorative addition (e g watercress) to a dish

garret /ˈgarit‖ˈgærɪt/ *n* a small room just under the roof of a house

[1]**garrison** /ˈgaris(ə)n‖ˈgærɪs(ə)n/ *n* **1** a (fortified) town or place in which troops are stationed **2** *sing or pl in constr* the troops stationed at a garrison

[2]**garrison** *vt* **1** to station troops in **2a** to assign (troops) as a garrison **b** to occupy with troops

[1]**garrotte, garotte,** *chiefly NAm* **garrote** /gəˈrot‖gəˈrɒt/ *n* **1** (a Spanish method of execution using) an iron collar for strangling sby **2** strangling, esp with robbery as the motive

[2]**garrotte , garotte,** *chiefly NAm* **garrote** *vt* **1** to execute with a garrotte **2** to strangle and rob – **garrotter** *n*

garrulous /ˈgar(y)ooləs‖ˈgær(j)ʊləs/ *adj* excessively talkative, esp about trivial things – **garrulously** *adv*, **garrulousness** *n*, **garrulity** *n*

garter /ˈgahtə‖ˈgɑːtə/ *n* **1** a band, usu of elastic, worn to hold up a stocking or sock **2** *cap* (the blue velvet garter that is the badge of) the Order of the Garter; *also* membership of the Order

[1]**gas** /gas‖gæs/ *n, pl* **-s-** *also* **-ss-** **1** a fluid (e g air) that has neither independent shape nor volume and tends to expand indefinitely **2a** a gas or gaseous mixture used to produce general anaesthesia, as a fuel, etc **b** a substance (e g tear gas or mustard gas) that can be used to produce a poisonous, asphyxiating, or irritant atmosphere **3** *NAm* petrol **4** empty talk – chiefly infml [alteration of Latin *chaos* space, chaos; coined by J. B. van Helmont (1577-1644), Dutch chemist] – **gaseous** *adj*, **gaseousness** *n*

[2]**gas** *vb* **-ss-** *vt* **1** to treat chemically with a gas **2** to poison or otherwise affect adversely with gas ~ *vi* **1** to give off gas **2** to talk idly – chiefly infml

ˈgasˌbag /-ˌbag‖-ˌbæg/ *n* an idle talker – infml

ˈgas ˌchamber *n* a chamber in which prisoners are executed or animals killed by poison gas

gas-guzzler *n, chiefly NAm* a usu large motor car having a high consumption of petrol

[1]**gash** /gash‖gæʃ/ *vt or n* (to injure with) a deep long cut or cleft, esp in flesh

[2]**gash** *n* sthg, specif rubbish on board ship, superfluous or extra – infml

gasholder /ˈgasˌhohldə‖ˈgæsˌhəʊldə/ *n* a gasometer

gasify /ˈgasifie, ˈgay-‖ˈgæsɪfaɪ, ˈgeɪ-/ *vb* to change into gas – **gasifier** *n*, **gasification** *n*

gasket /ˈgaskit‖ˈgæskɪt/ *n* (a specially shaped piece of) sealing material for ensuring that a joint, esp between metal surfaces, does not leak liquid or gas

gaslight /ˈgasˌliet‖ˈgæsˌlaɪt/ *n* (light from) a gas flame or gas lighting fixture

ˈgas ˌmask *n* a mask connected to a chemical air filter and used as a protection against noxious fumes or gases

gasoline, gasolene /ˌgasəˈleen, ˈ--ˌ-‖ˌgæsəˈliːn, ˈ--ˌ-/ *n, NAm* petrol – **gasolinic** *adj*

gasometer /gaˈsomitə‖gæˈsɒmɪtə/ *n* a (large cylindrical storage) container for gas

gasp /gahsp‖gɑːsp/ *vi* **1** to catch the breath suddenly and audibly (e g with shock) **2** to breathe laboriously ~*vt* to utter with gasps – usu + *out* <*he* ~ed *out his message*> – **gasp** *n*

ˈgas ˌring *n* a hollow metal perforated ring through which jets of gas issue and over which food is cooked

gassy /ˈgasi‖ˈgæsɪ/ *adj* full of, containing, or like gas – **gassiness** *n*

gastric /ˈgastrik‖ˈgæstrɪk/ *adj* of the stomach [Greek *gastr-, gastēr* stomach, fr *gran* to gnaw, eat]

gastroenteritis /ˌgastrohˌentəˈrietəs‖ˌgæstrəʊˌentəˈraɪtəs/ *n* inflammation of the lining of the stomach and the intestines, usu causing painful diarrhoea

gastronomy /gaˈstronəmi‖gæˈstrɒnəmɪ/ *n* the art or science of good eating – **gastronomic** *also* **gastronomical** *adj*, **gastronomically** *adv*

gastropod /ˈgastrəˌpod‖ˈgæstrəˌpɒd/ *n* any of a large class of molluscs (e g snails) usu with a distinct head bearing sensory organs – **gastropod** *adj*, **gastropodan** *adj or n*

ˈgasˌworks /-ˌwuhks‖-ˌwɜːks/ *n, pl* **gasworks** a plant for manufacturing gas – often pl with sing. meaning

[1]**gate** /gayt‖geɪt/ *n* **1** (the usu hinged frame or door that closes) an opening in a wall or fence **2** a city or castle entrance, often with defensive structures **3a** a means of entrance or exit **b** a mountain pass **c** a space between 2 markers through which a skier, canoeist, etc must pass in a slalom race **d** a mechanically operated barrier used as a starting device for a race **e** either of a pair of barriers that **e(1)** let water in and out of a lock **e(2)** close a road at a level crossing **4** an (electronic) device (e g in a computer) that produces a signal when specified input conditions are met <*a logic* ~> **5** the set of notches in a manually worked gearbox into which the gear lever is pushed to select the gears **6** the total admission receipts or the number of spectators at a sporting event

[2]**gate** *vt, Br* to punish by confinement to the premises of a school or college

gateau /ˈgatoh‖ˈgætəʊ/ *n, pl* **gateaux, gateaus** /-tohz‖-təʊz/ any of various rich often filled elaborate (cream) cakes

ˈgate-ˌcrasher *n* one who enters, attends, or participates without a ticket or invitation – **gate-crash** *vb*

ˈgateˌhouse /-ˌhows‖-ˌhaʊs/ *n* **1** a structure above or beside a gate (e g of a city wall or castle) often used in former times as a guardroom or prison **2** a lodge at the entrance to the grounds of a large house **3** a building at a dam or lock from which the sluices or gates are controlled

ˈgateˌkeeper /-ˌkeepə‖-ˌkiːpə/ *n* sby who or sthg that tends or guards a gate

ˌgateleg ˈtable /ˈgaytleg‖ˈgeɪtleg/ *n* a table with drop leaves supported by 2 movable legs

ˈgateˌpost /-ˌpohst‖-ˌpəʊst/ *n* the post on which a gate is hung or against which it closes

ˈgateˌway /-ˌway‖-ˌweɪ/ *n* **1** an opening for a gate **2** GATE 3a

[1]**gather** /ˈgadhə‖ˈgæðə/ *vt* **1** to bring together; collect (*up*) **2** to pick, harvest **3a** to summon up <~ed *his courage*> **b** to accumulate <~ *speed*> **c** to prepare (e g oneself) for an effort **4a** to bring together the parts of **b** to draw about or close to sthg <~ing *her cloak about her*> **c** to pull (fabric) together, esp along a line of stitching, to create small tucks **5** to infer <*I* ~ *you're ready to leave*> ~*vi* to come together in a body – **gatherer** *n*

[2]**gather** *n* sthg gathered; *esp* a tuck in cloth made by gathering

ˈ**gathering** /-ring‖-rɪŋ/ *n* **1** an assembly, meeting; *also* a compilation **2** an abscess **3** a gather or series of gathers in cloth **4** SECTION 11

gauche /gohsh‖gəʊʃ/ *adj* lacking social experience or grace [French, lit., left, fr *gauchir* to turn aside] – **gauchely** *adv*, **gaucheness** *n*

gaucherie /ˈgohsh(ə)ri‖ˈgəʊʃ(ə)rɪ/ *n* (an instance of) tactless or awkward manner or behaviour

gaucho /ˈgowchoh‖ˈgaʊtʃəʊ/ *n, pl* **gauchos** a cowboy of the pampas

[1]**gaudy** /ˈgawdi‖ˈgɔːdɪ/ *adj* ostentatiously or tastelessly (and brightly) ornamented – **gaudily** *adv*, **gaudiness** *n*

[2]**gaudy** *n* a feast, esp a dinner for ex-students, in some British universities

[1]**gauge**, *NAm also* **gage** /gayj‖geɪdʒ/ *n* **1a** measurement according to some standard or system **b** dimensions, size **2** an instrument for or a means of measuring or testing sthg (e g a dimension or quantity) **3 gauge, gage** relative position of a ship with reference to another ship and the wind **4** the distance between the rails of a railway, wheels on an axle, etc **5** a measure of the size of the bore of a shotgun **6a** the thickness of a thin sheet of metal, plastic, film, etc **b** the diameter of wire, a hypodermic needle, a screw, etc **c** (a measure of) the fineness of a knitted fabric

[2]**gauge**, *NAm also* **gage** *vt* **1a** to measure (exactly) the size, dimensions, capacity, or contents of **b** to estimate, judge **2** to check for conformity to specifications or limits – **gaugeable** *adj*, **gaugeably** *adv*

gaunt /gawnt‖gɔːnt/ *adj* **1** excessively thin and angular as if from suffering **2** barren, desolate – **gauntly** *adv*, **gauntness** *n*

[1]**gauntlet** /ˈgawntlit‖ˈgɔːntlɪt/ *n* **1** a glove to protect the hand, worn with medieval armour **2** a strong protective glove with a wide extension above the wrist, used esp for sports and in industry **3** a challenge to combat – esp in *take up/throw down the gauntlet* [Middle French *gantelet*, diminutive of *gant* glove, of Germanic origin] – **gauntleted** *adj*

[2]**gauntlet** *n* a double file of men armed with weapons with which to strike at sby made to run between them; *broadly* criticism or an ordeal or test – usu in *run the gauntlet* [by folk etymology fr *gantelope*, modif of Swedish *gatlopp*, fr Old Swedish *gatulop*, fr *gata* road, lane + *lop* course, run]

gauze /gawz‖gɔːz/ *n* **1a** a thin often transparent fabric used chiefly for clothing or draperies **b** a loosely woven cotton surgical dressing **c** a fine mesh of metal or plastic filaments **2** a thin haze or mist [Middle French *gaze*, prob fr *Gaza*, town in Palestine] – **gauzily** *adv*, **gauziness** *n*, **gauzy** *adj*

gave /gayv‖geɪv/ *past of* GIVE

gavel /ˈgavl‖ˈgævl/ *n* a small mallet with which a chairman, judge, or auctioneer commands attention or confirms a vote, sale, etc

gavotte /gəˈvot‖gəˈvɒt/ *n* **1** an 18th-c dance in which the feet are raised rather than slid **2** a composition or movement of music in moderately quick $\frac{4}{4}$ time – **gavotte** *vi*

[1]**gawk** /gawk‖gɔːk/ *vi* to gawp – infml – **gawker** *n*

[2]**gawk** *n* a clumsy awkward person – **gawkish** *adj*, **gawkishly** *adv*, **gawkishness** *n*

gawky /ˈgawki‖ˈgɔːkɪ/ *adj* awkward and usu lanky <*a ~ child*> – **gawkily** *adv*, **gawky** *n*

gawp /gawp‖gɔːp/ *vi* to gape or stare stupidly – infml

[1]**gay** /gay‖geɪ/ *adj* **1** happily excited **2** bright, attractive <*~ sunny meadows*> **3** given to social pleasures <*the ~ life*> **4** homosexual – **gayness** *n*

[2]**gay** *n* a homosexual

gaze /gayz‖geɪz/ *vi or n* (to fix the eyes in) a steady and intent look – **gazer** *n*

gazebo /gəˈzeeboh‖gəˈziːbəʊ/ *n, pl* **gazebos** a structure placed to command a view

gazelle /gəˈzel‖gəˈzel/ *n* any of numerous small, graceful, and swift African and Asian antelopes noted for their soft lustrous eyes

[1]**gazette** /gəˈzet‖gəˈzet/ *n* **1** a newspaper – usu in newspaper titles **2** an official journal containing announcements of honours and government appointments

[2]**gazette** *vt, Br* to announce (the appointment or status of) in an official gazette <*he was* ~d *major*>

gazetteer /ˌgazəˈtiə‖ˌgæzəˈtɪə/ *n* a dictionary of place names

gazump /gəˈzump‖gəˈzʌmp/ *vb, Br* to thwart (a would-be house purchaser) by raising the price after agreeing to sell at a certain price – **gazumper** *n*

ge-, **geo-** *comb form* **1a** ground; soil <ge*ophyte*> **b** earth; earth's surface <geo*physics*> **2** geographical; geography and <geo*politics*>

[1]**gear** /giə‖gɪə/ *n* **1a** clothing, garments **b** movable property; goods **2** a set of equipment usu for a particular purpose <*fishing ~*> **3a(1)** a mechanism that performs a specific function <*the steering ~*> **a(2)** a toothed wheel (that is one of a set of interlocking wheels) **a(3)** working relation, position, or adjustment <*out of ~*> **b** any of 2 or more adjustments of a transmission (e g of a bicycle or motor vehicle) that determine direction of travel or ratio of engine speed to vehicle speed

[2]**gear** *vt* **1a** to provide with or connect by gearing **b** to put into gear **2** to adjust *to* so as to match, blend with, or satisfy sthg

ˈ**gearˌbox** /-ˌboks‖-ˌbɒks/ *n* (a protective casing enclosing) a set of (car) gears

ˈ**gear ˌlever** *n* a control, esp a rod, on a gear-changing mechanism (e g a gearbox) used to engage the different gears

gear up *vt* to make ready for effective operation; *also* to put (e g oneself) into a state of anxious excitement or nervous anticipation

gecko /ˈgekoh‖ˈgekəʊ/ *n, pl* **geckos, geckoes** any of numerous small chiefly tropical lizards

gee /jee‖dʒiː/ *interj, chiefly NAm* – used as an introductory expletive or to express surprise or enthusiasm

gee-gee /ˈjee-ˌjee‖ˈdʒiː-ˌdʒiː/ *n* a horse – used esp by or to children or in racing slang

geese /gees‖giːs/ *pl of* GOOSE

ˌ**gee-ˈup** *interj* – used as a direction, esp to a horse, to move ahead

geezer /ˈgeezə‖ˈgiːzə/ *n* a man (who is thought

a little odd or peculiar) – chiefly infml; esp in *old geezer*

ˈGeiger ˌcounter /ˈgiegə‖ˈgaɪgə/ *n* an electronic instrument for detecting the presence and intensity of ionizing radiations (e g cosmic rays or particles from a radioactive substance) [H W *Geiger* (1881-1945), German physicist]

geisha /ˈgayshə‖ˈgeɪʃə/, **ˈgeisha ˌgirl** *n, pl* **geisha, geishas** a Japanese girl who is trained to provide entertaining and lighthearted company, esp for men [Japanese, fr *gei* art + *-sha* person]

¹gel /jel‖dʒel/ *n* **1** a colloid in a more solid form than a sol **2** JELLY 3

²gel, *chiefly NAm* **jell** *vb* **-ll- 1** to change (from a sol) into a gel **2** to (cause to) take shape or become definite – **gelable** *adj*, **gelation** *n*

³gel /gel‖gel/ *n* a girl – used in writing to represent an upper-class pronunciation

gelatin, gelatine /ˈjelətin, -teen‖ˈdʒelətɪn, -tiːn/ *n* **1** a glutinous material obtained from animal tissues by boiling; *esp* a protein used esp in food (e g to set jellies) and photography **2** a thin coloured transparent sheet used to colour a stage light – **gelatinize** *vb*, **gelatinization** *n*

gelatinous /jiˈlatinəs‖dʒɪˈlætɪnəs/ *adj* resembling gelatin or jelly, esp in consistency; viscous – **gelatinously** *adv*, **gelatinousness** *n*

geld /geld‖geld/ *vt* to castrate – used esp with reference to male animals

gelding /ˈgelding‖ˈgeldɪŋ/ *n* a castrated male horse

gelignite /ˈjeligniet‖ˈdʒelɪgnaɪt/ *n* a dynamite in which the adsorbent base is a mixture of potassium or sodium nitrate usu with wood pulp

gem /jem‖dʒem/ *n* **1** a precious or sometimes semiprecious stone, esp when cut and polished for use in jewellery **2** sby or sthg highly prized or much beloved

Gemini /ˈjemini, -nie‖ˈdʒemɪnɪ, -naɪ/ *n* (sby born under) the 3rd sign of the zodiac in astrology, which is pictured as twins – **Geminian** *adj or n*

gen /jen‖dʒen/ *n, Br* the correct or complete information – infml [short for *general (information)*]

gen-, geno- *comb form* **1** race <geno*cide*> **2** genus; kind <geno*type*>

-gen /-jən‖-dʒən/ *also* **-gene** /-jeen‖-dʒiːn/ *comb form* (*n* → *n*) **1** sthg that produces <*carcino*gen> **2** sthg that is (so) produced <*phos*gene>

gendarme /ˈzhonˌdahm ‖ˈʒɒnˌdɑːm (*Fr* ʒɑ̃darm)/ *n* a member of a corps of armed police, esp in France

gender /ˈjendə‖ˈdʒendə/ *n* **1** sex **2a** a system of subdivision within a grammatical class of a language (e g noun or verb) that determines agreement with and selection of other words or grammatical forms **b** (membership of) a subclass within such a system

gene /jeen‖dʒiːn/ *n* a unit of inheritance that is carried on a chromosome, controls transmission of hereditary characters, and consists of DNA or, in some viruses, RNA [German *gen*, short for *pangen*, fr Greek *pan-* all + *-genēs* born] – **genic** *adj*, **genically** *adv*

genealogy /ˌjeeniˈaləji‖ˌdʒiːnɪˈælədʒɪ/ *n* **1** (an account of) the descent of a person, family, or group from an ancestor or from older forms **2** the study of family pedigrees – **genealogist** *n*, **genealogical** *adj*, **genealogically** *adv*

genera /ˈjenərə‖ˈdʒenərə/ *pl of* GENUS

¹general /ˈjen(ə)rəl‖ˈdʒen(ə)rəl/ *adj* **1** involving or applicable to the whole **2** of, involving, or applicable to (what is common to) every member of a class, kind, or group **3a** applicable to or characteristic of the majority of individuals involved; prevalent **b** concerned or dealing with universal rather than particular aspects **4** approximate rather than strictly accurate **5** not confined by specialization or careful limitation **6** holding superior rank <*the ~ manager*> – **in general** usually; FOR THE MOST PART

²general *n* **1** the chief of a religious order or congregation **2** a high-ranking officer in the army or US airforce

ˌgeneral eˈlection *n* an election in which candidates are elected in all constituencies of a nation or state

generalissimo /ˌjen(ə)rəˈlisimoh‖ˌdʒen(ə)rəˈlɪsɪməʊ/ *n, pl* **generalissimos** the supreme commander of several armies acting together or of a nation's armed forces

generality /ˌjenəˈraləti‖ˌdʒenəˈrælətɪ/ *n* **1** total applicability **2** generalization **3** *the* greatest part; *the* bulk

general·ization, -isation /ˌjen(ə)rəlieˈzaysh(ə)n‖ˌdʒen(ə)rəlaɪˈzeɪʃ(ə)n/ *n* **1** generalizing **2** a general statement, law, principle, or proposition (that does not take adequate account of the facts)

general·ize, -ise /ˈjen(ə)rəˌliez‖ˈdʒen(ə)rəˌlaɪz/ *vt* **1** to give a general form to **2** to derive or induce (a general conception or principle) from particulars **3** to give general applicability to <*~ a law*> *~vi* to make generalizations or vague or indefinite statements – **generalizable** *adj*, **generalizer** *n*

generally /ˈjen(ə)rəli‖ˈdʒen(ə)rəlɪ/ *adv* **1** without regard to specific instances <*~ speaking*> **2** usually; AS A RULE <*he ~ drinks tea*> **3** collectively; AS A WHOLE <*of interest to children ~*>

general practitioner *n* a medical doctor who treats all types of disease and is usu the first doctor consulted by a patient

general staff *n* a group of officers who aid a commander in administration, training, supply, etc

ˌgeneral ˈstrike *n* a strike in all or many of the industries of a region or country

generate /ˈjenəˌrayt‖ˈdʒenəˌreɪt/ *vt* **1** to bring into existence or originate (e g by a life-giving, physical, or chemical process); produce <*~ electricity*> **2** to be the cause of (a situation, action, or state of mind)

generation /ˌjenəˈraysh(ə)n‖ˌdʒenəˈreɪʃ(ə)n/ *n* **1** *sing or pl in constr* **1a** a group of living organisms constituting a single step in the line of descent from an ancestor **b** a group of individuals born and living at the same time **c** a group of individuals sharing a usu specified status for a limited period <*the next ~ of students*> **d** a type or class of objects usu developed from an earlier type <*a new ~ of computers*> **2** the average time between the birth of parents and that of their offspring **3a** the producing of offspring; procreation **b** the process of coming or bringing into being < ~ *of electricity*> – **generational** *adj*

generative /'jen(ə)rətiv‖'dʒen(ə)rətɪv/ *adj* having the power or function of generating, originating, producing, reproducing, etc

generator /'jenə,raytə‖'dʒenə,reɪtə/ *n* **1** an apparatus for producing a vapour or gas **2** DYNAMO 1; *also* an alternator

generic /ji'nerik‖dʒɪ'nerɪk/ *adj* **1** (characteristic) of or applied to (members of) a whole group or class **2** (having the rank) of a biological genus – **generically** *adv*

generous /'jen(ə)rəs‖'dʒen(ə)rəs/ *adj* **1** magnanimous, kindly **2** liberal in giving (e g of money or help) **3** marked by abundance, ample proportions, or richness – **generously** *adv*, **generousness** *n*, **generosity** *n*

genesis /'jenəsis‖'dʒenəsɪs/ *n, pl* **geneses** /-,seez‖-,siːz/ the origin or coming into being of sthg

genetic /jə'netik‖dʒə'netɪk/ *adj* **1** of or determined by the origin or development of sthg **2** of or involving genetics – **genetically** *adv*

ge'netics *n pl but sing in constr* **1** the biology of (the mechanisms and structures involved in) the heredity and variation of organisms **2** the genetic make-up of an organism, type, group, or condition – **geneticist** *n*

[1]**genial** /'jeenyəl, ni·əl‖'dʒiːnjəl, nɪəl/ *adj* **1** favourable to growth or comfort; mild < ~ *sunshine*> **2** cheerfully good-tempered; kindly – **genially** *adv*, **genialness** *n*, **geniality** *n*

[2]**genial** /jə'nee·əl‖dʒə'niːəl/ *adj* of the chin

genie /'jeeni‖'dʒiːnɪ/ *n, pl* **genies** *also* **genii** /-ni,ie‖-nɪ,aɪ/ a jinn

genital /'jenitl‖'dʒenɪtl/ *adj* **1** of or being the genitalia or another sexual organ **2** of or characterized by the final stage of sexual development in which oral and anal impulses are replaced by gratification obtained from (sexual) relationships – **genitally** *adv*

genitalia /,jeni'tayli·ə, -lyə‖,dʒenɪ'teɪlɪə, -ljə/ *n pl* the (external) reproductive and sexual organs

genitals /'jenitlz‖'dʒenɪtlz/ *n pl* the genitalia

genitive /'jenitiv‖'dʒenɪtɪv/ *adj or n* (of or in) a grammatical case expressing typically a relationship of possessor or source; *also* sthg in this case – **genitival** *adj*, **genitivally** *adv*

genius /'jeenyəs, -ni·əs‖'dʒiːnjəs, -nɪəs/ *n, pl* (*1a*) **genii** /-ni,ie‖-nɪ,aɪ/, (*1b & 3*) **genii** *also* **geniuses**, (*4*) **geniuses** *also* **genii** **1a** an attendant spirit of a person or place **b** one who influences another for good or bad **2a** a peculiar, distinctive, or identifying character or spirit <*optimism was the* ~ *of the Victorian era*> **b** the associations and traditions of a place **3** a spirit or jinn **4a** a single strongly marked capacity or aptitude <*had a* ~ *for teaching maths*> **b** (a person endowed with) extraordinary intellectual power (as manifested in creative activity)

,genius 'loci /'lohsie‖'ləʊsaɪ/ *n, pl* **genii loci** /'jeeni,ee‖'dʒiːnɪ,iː/ the pervading spirit of a place

genocide /'jenə,sied‖'dʒenə,saɪd/ *n* the deliberate murder of a racial or cultural group – **genocidal** *adj*

genotype /'jenoh,tiep‖'dʒenəʊ,taɪp/ *n* the genetic constitution of an individual or group – **genotypic** *also* **genotypical** *adj*, **genotypically** *adv*

genre /'zhonh·rə‖'ʒɑ̃rə (*Fr* ʒɑ̃ːr)/ *n* **1** a sort, type **2** a category of artistic, musical, or literary composition characterized by a particular style, form, or content

gent /jent‖dʒent/ *n* a gentleman – nonstandard or humor

genteel /jen'teel‖dʒen'tiːl/ *adj* **1a** of or appropriate to (the status or manners of) the gentry or upper class **b** free from vulgarity or rudeness; polite **2a** maintaining or striving to maintain the appearance of superior social status or respectability **b** marked by false delicacy, prudery, or affectation – **genteelly** *adv*, **genteelness** *n*

gentian /'jensh(ə)n‖'dʒenʃ(ə)n/ *n* any of several related esp mountain plants with showy usu blue flowers

gentile /'jentiel‖'dʒentaɪl/ *adj or n, often cap* (of) a non-Jewish person

gentility /jen'tiləti‖dʒen'tɪlətɪ/ *n* **1** *sing or pl in constr* the members of the upper class **2a** genteel attitudes, behaviour, or activity **b** superior social status or prestige indicated by manners, possessions, etc

[1]**gentle** /'jentl‖'dʒentl/ *adj* **1a** honourable, distinguished; *specif* of or belonging to a gentleman <*of* ~ *birth*> **b** kind, amiable <*bear with me,* ~ *reader*> **2** free from harshness, sternness, or violence; mild, soft; *also* tractable **3** MODERATE 1, 2a – **gentleness** *n*, **gently** *adv*

[2]**gentle** *n* a maggot, esp when used as bait for fish

[3]**gentle** *vt* to make mild, docile, soft, or moderate

'gentle,folk /-,fohk‖-,fəʊk/ *also* **gentlefolks** *n pl* people of good family and breeding

gentleman /'jentlmən‖'dʒentlmən/ *n, pl* **gentlemen** /~/ **1a** a man belonging to the landed gentry or nobility **b** a man who is chivalrous, well-mannered, and honourable (and of good birth or rank) **c** a man of independent wealth who does not work for gain **2** a valet – usu in *gentleman's gentleman* **3** a man of any social class or condition <*ladies and* gentlemen> – often as a courteous reference <*show this* ~ *to a seat*> – **gentlemanlike** *adj*

,gentleman-at-'arms *n, pl* **gentlemen-at-arms** any of a bodyguard of 40 gentlemen who attend the British sovereign on state occasions

'gentlemanly /-li‖-lɪ/ *adj* characteristic of or having the character of a gentleman – **gentlemanliness** *n*

gentleman's agreement **gentlemen's agreement**, *n* an unwritten agreement secured only by the honour of the participants

'gentle ,sex *n* the female sex

'gentle,woman *n, pl* **gentlewomen** /-,wimin‖-,wɪmɪn/ **1a** a woman of noble or gentle birth **b** a woman attendant on a lady of rank **2** a lady

gentry /'jentri‖'dʒentrɪ/ *n, sing or pl in constr* **1** the upper class **2** a class whose members are (landed proprietors) entitled to bear a coat of arms though not of noble rank

gents /jents‖dʒents/ *n, pl* **gents** *often cap, Br* a public lavatory for men – chiefly infml

genuflect /ˈjenyoo͵flekt‖ˈdʒenjʊ͵flekt/ *vi* to bend the knee, esp in worship or as a gesture of respect (to sacred objects) [Late Latin *genuflectere*, fr Latin *genu* knee + *flectere* to bend] – **genuflector** *n*, **genuflection, genuflexion** *n*

genuine /ˈjenyooin‖ˈdʒenjʊɪn/ *adj* **1** actually produced by or proceeding from the alleged source or author or having the reputed qualities or character <*this is a ~ antique*> **2** free from pretence; sincere – **genuinely** *adv*, **genuineness** *n*

genus /ˈjeenəs‖ˈdʒiːnəs/ *n, pl* **genera** /ˈjenərə‖ˈdʒenərə/ **1** a category in the classification of living things ranking between the family and the species **2** a class divided into several subordinate classes

geo- – see GE-

geocentric /͵jeeohˈsentrik‖͵dʒiːəʊˈsentrɪk/ *adj* **1** measured from or observed as if from the earth's centre **2** having or relating to the earth as centre – **geocentrically** *adv*

geography /jiˈogrəfi‖dʒɪˈɒgrəfɪ/ *n* **1** a science that deals with the earth and its life; *esp* the description of land, sea, air, and the distribution of plant and animal life including human beings and their industries **2** the geographical features of an area [Latin *geographia*, fr Greek *geōgraphia*, fr *geōgraphein* to describe the earth's surface, fr *gē* earth + *graphein* to write] – **geographer** *n*, **geographic, geographical** *adj*, **geographically** *adv*

geology /jiˈoləji‖dʒɪˈɒlədʒɪ/ *n* **1a** a science that deals with the history of the earth's crust, esp as recorded in rocks **b** a study of the solid matter of a celestial body (e g the moon) **2** the geological features of an area – **geologist** *n*, **geologize** *vi*, **geological, geologic** *adj*, **geologically** *adv*

geometric /͵ji·əˈmetrik‖͵dʒɪəˈmetrɪk/, **geometrical** /-kl‖-kl/ *adj* **1a** of or according to (the laws of) geometry **b** increasing in a geometric progression <*~ population growth*> **2a** *cap* of or being (a style of) ancient Greek pottery decorated with geometric patterns **b** using, being, or decorated with patterns formed from straight and curved lines – **geometrically** *adv*

geometric progression *n* a sequence (e g 1, $^1/_2$, $^1/_4$) in which the ratio of any term to its predecessor is constant

geometry /jiˈomətri‖dʒɪˈɒmətrɪ/ *n* **1a** a branch of mathematics that deals with the measurement, properties, and relationships of points, lines, angles, surfaces, and solids **b** a particular type or system of geometry **2** (surface) shape **3** an arrangement of objects or parts that suggests geometrical figures [deriv of Greek *geōmetria*, fr *geōmetrein* to measure the earth, fr *gē* earth + *metron* measure]

geophysics /͵jeeohˈfiziks‖͵dʒiːəʊˈfɪzɪks/ *n pl but sing or pl in constr* the physics of the earth including meteorology, oceanography, seismology, etc – **geophysical** *adj*, **geophysically** *adv*, **geophysicist** *n*

͵geoˈpolitics /-ˈpolitiks‖-ˈpɒlɪtɪks/ *n pl but sing in constr* the study of the influence of geography, economics, and demography on politics – **geopolitical** *adj*, **geopolitically** *adv*

georgette /jawˈjet‖dʒɔːˈdʒet/ *n* a thin strong clothing crepe of silk or of other material with a dull pebbly surface

1**Georgian** /ˈjawj(ə)n‖ˈdʒɔːdʒ(ə)n/ *n or adj* (a native or inhabitant or the language) of Georgia in the Caucasus

2**Georgian** *n or adj* (a native or inhabitant) of Georgia in the USA

3**Georgian** *adj* **1** (characteristic) of (the time of) the reigns of the first 4 Georges (1714 to 1830) **2** (characteristic) of the reign of George V (1910 to 1936) – **Georgian** *n*

geranium /jəˈraynyəm, -nyi·əm‖dʒəˈreɪnjəm, -njɪəm/ *n* **1** any of a widely distributed genus of plants having radially symmetrical flowers with glands that alternate with the petals **2** a pelargonium

geriatric /͵jeriˈatrik‖͵dʒerɪˈætrɪk/ *adj* **1** of geriatrics, the aged, or the process of aging **2** aged, decrepit – derog [Greek *gēras* old age + *iatreia* art of healing] – **geriatric** *n*

͵geriˈatrics *n pl but sing in constr* a branch of medicine that deals with (the diseases of) old age – **geriatrician** *n*

germ /juhm‖dʒɜːm/ *n* **1a** a small mass of cells capable of developing into (a part of) an organism **b** the embryo of a cereal grain that is usu separated from the starchy endosperm during milling **2** sthg that serves as an origin **3** a (disease-causing) microorganism – **germproof** *adj*, **germy** *adj*

german /ˈjuhmən‖ˈdʒɜːmən/ *adj* having the same parents, or the same grandparents, on either the maternal or paternal side – usu in comb <*cousin*-german>

1**German** *n* **1a** a native or inhabitant of Germany **b** one (e g a Swiss German) who speaks German as his/her native language outside Germany **2** the Germanic language of the people of Germany, Austria, and parts of Switzerland

2**German** *adj* (characteristic) of Germany, the Germans, or German

germane /juhˈmayn‖dʒɜːˈmeɪn/ *adj* both relevant and appropriate – **germanely** *adv*

1**Germanic** /juhˈmanik‖dʒɜːˈmænɪk/ *adj* **1** German **2** (characteristic) of the Germanic-speaking peoples **3** of Germanic

2**Germanic** *n* a branch of the Indo-European language family containing English, German, Dutch, Afrikaans, Flemish, Frisian, the Scandinavian languages, and Gothic

͵German ˈmeasles *n pl but sing or pl in constr* a virus disease that is milder than typical measles but is damaging to the foetus when occurring early in pregnancy

germicide /ˈjuhmi͵sied‖ˈdʒɜːmɪ͵saɪd/ *n* sthg that kills germs – **germicidal** *adj*, **germicidally** *adv*

germinal /ˈjuhminl‖ˈdʒɜːmɪnl/ *adj* **1a** in the earliest stage of development **b** creative, seminal **2** (having the characteristics) of a germ cell or early embryo – **germinally** *adv*

germinate /ˈjuhminayt‖ˈdʒɜːmɪneɪt/ *vt* to cause to sprout or develop ~ *vi* **1** to begin to grow; sprout **2** to come into being – **germinative** *adj*, **germination** *n*

gerontology /jeronˈtoləji‖dʒerɒnˈtɒlədʒɪ/ *n* the biology and medicine of aging and the problems of the aged – **gerontologist** *n*, **gerontological, gerontologic** *adj*

1**gerrymander** /ˈjeri͵mandə‖ˈdʒerɪ͵mændə/ *n*

(a pattern of districts resulting from) gerrymandering [Elbridge *Gerry* (1744-1814), US statesman + sala*mander*; fr the shape of an election district formed during Gerry's governorship of Massachusetts]

[2]**gerrymander** *vt* to divide (an area) into election districts to give one political party an electoral advantage – **gerrymandering** *n*

gerund /ˈjerənd‖ˈdʒerənd/ *n* a verbal noun in Latin that expresses generalized or uncompleted action, *also* the English verbal noun ending in *-ing*

gestalt /gəˈshtalt‖gəˈʃtælt/ *n, pl* **gestalten** /-tn‖-tn/, **gestalts** a structure, pattern, etc (e g a melody) that as an object of perception constitutes a functional unit with properties not derivable from the sum of its parts

gestapo /gəˈs(h)tahpoh‖gəˈstɑːpəʊ, -ʃtɑːpəʊ/ *n, pl* **gestapos** a secret-police organization operating esp against suspected traitors; *specif, cap* that of Nazi Germany [German, fr *Ge*heime *Sta*ats*po*lizei secret state police]

gestation /jeˈstaysh(ə)n‖dʒeˈsteɪʃ(ə)n/ *n* **1** the carrying of young in the uterus; pregnancy **2** conception and development, esp in the mind – **gestational** *adj*

gesticulate /jeˈstikyoo͵layt‖dʒeˈstɪkjʊ͵leɪt/ *vi* to make expressive gestures, esp when speaking – **gesticulator** *n*, **gesticulative** *adj*, **gesticulatory** *adj*, **gesticulation***n*

[1]**gesture** /ˈjeschə‖ˈdʒestʃə/ *n* **1a** a movement, usu of the body or limbs, that expresses or emphasizes an idea, sentiment, or attitude **b** the use of gestures **2** sthg said or done for its effect on the attitudes of others or to convey a feeling (e g friendliness) – **gestural** *adj*

[2]**gesture** *vb* to make or express (by) a gesture

[1]**get** /get‖get/ *vb* **-tt-; got; got** /got‖gɒt/, *NAm also* **gotten** /ˈgotn‖ˈgɒtn/; *nonstandard pres pl & 1 & 2 sing* **got** *vt* **1** to gain possession of: e g **1a** to obtain by way of benefit or advantage <got *little for his trouble*> **b** to obtain by concession or entreaty <~ *your mother's permission to go*> **c** to seek out and fetch or provide <~ *blackberries in the wood*> **d** to acquire by memorizing or calculation <~ *the answer to a problem*> **e** to seize **2a** to receive as a return; earn <*he* got *a bad reputation for carelessness*> **b** to become affected by; catch <got *measles from his sister*> **c** to be subjected to <~ *the sack*> **3** to beget **4a** to cause to come, go, or move <*grumbling won't* ~ *you anywhere*> **b** to bring into a specified condition by direct action <~ *my shoes mended*> **c** to prevail on; induce <~ *the Russians to give an English broadcast*> **5** to make ready; prepare <~ *dinner*> **6a** to overcome <*I'll* ~ *him on that point*> **b** to take vengeance on; *specif* to kill <*out to* ~ *his man*> **7a** to have – used in the present perfect tense form with present meaning <*I've* got *no money*> **b** to have as an obligation or necessity – used in the present perfect tense form with present meaning; + *to* and an understood or expressed infinitive <*he has* got *to come*> <*I won't if I haven't* got *to*> **8a** to hear <*I didn't quite* ~ *that for the noise*> **b** to establish communication with <~ *her on the telephone*> **9a** to puzzle <*you've really* got *me there*> **b** to irritate <*his superior attitude really* ~s *me*> **10** to hit <~ *him on the ear with a potato*> **11** to understand <*don't* ~ *me wrong*> **12** to affect emotionally <*the sight of her tears* got *him*> ~ *vi* **1** to reach or enter into the specified condition or activity <~ *drunk*> <*they* got *married last week*> – used as a verbal auxiliary instead of *be* to form the passive <*the risk of* ~ting *trapped*> **2a** to reach, arrive <*where's my pen* got *to?*> **b** to succeed in coming or going <*at last we're* ~ting *somewhere*> <~ *to sleep after midnight*> **c** to contrive by effort, luck, or permission – + *to* and an infinitive <*when you* ~ *to know him*> <*she never* ~s *to drive the car*> *USE* (*vt* 9a, 9b, 10, 11, & 12) infml – **get ahead** to achieve success – **get a move on** to hurry up – **get at 1** to reach effectively <get at *the truth*> **2** to influence corruptly; bribe **3** to nag, tease **4** to mean, imply <*what's he* getting at?> – **get away with** to do (a reprehensible act) without criticism or penalty – **get cracking/weaving** to make a start; get going – infml – **get even with** to repay in kind; revenge oneself on – **get into** to possess, dominate <*what's* got into *you?*> – **get it** CATCH IT – **get one's eye in** *chiefly Br* to get into practice; *specif* to gain ability to judge the speed and direction of a moving ball – **get one's goat** to make one angry or annoyed – infml – **get one's own back** to revenge oneself – **get on one's high horse** to adopt an unyielding and usu arrogant attitude – **get over 1** to overcome, surmount **2** to recover from **3** to accept calmly <*can't* get over *your beard*> – **get rid of** to rid oneself of; disencumber oneself of by eliminating, dismissing, or clearing away – **get round 1** to circumvent, evade **2** to cajole, persuade – **get the better of** to overcome – **get there 1** to be successful **2** to understand what is meant – **get the wind up** to become frightened – infml – **get the wrong end of the stick** to misunderstand sthg – **get through 1** to reach the end of; complete **2a** USE UP 1 <got through *a lot of money*> **b** WHILE AWAY <*hardly knew how to* get through *his days*> – **get under one's skin** to cause one persistent and often troublesome irritation, stimulation, or excitement – **get up someone's nose** to irritate sby intensely – infml – **get wind of** to become aware of

[2]**get** *n* **1** sthg begotten **2** a successful return of a difficult shot in tennis, squash, etc **3** *Br* a git – slang

get about *vi* **1** to be up and about; be well enough to walk **2** to become circulated, esp orally <*the news soon* got about>

get across *vb* to make or become clear or convincing

get along *vi* **1** to move away; leave for another destination **2** to manage **3** to be or remain on congenial terms

getaway /ˈgetə͵way‖ˈgetə͵weɪ/ *n* a departure, escape

get back *vi* to return, revert – **get back at** to gain revenge on; retaliate against

get by *vi* **1** to manage, survive <*we'll* get by *without your help*> **2** to succeed by a narrow margin; be just about acceptable

get down *vi* to leave or descend (e g from a vehicle) ~ *vt* **1** to depress <*the weather was* getting *her* down> **2** to swallow <get *this*

medicine down> **3** to record in writing <get down *the details*> – **get down to** to apply serious attention or consideration to; concentrate one's efforts on

get off *vi* **1** to start, leave **2** to escape from a dangerous situation or from punishment <*won't* get off *lightly*> **3** to leave work with permission **4** *Br* to start an amorous or sexual relationship – often + *with*; slang ~ *vt* **1** to secure the release of or procure a modified penalty for <*his lawyers* got *him* off *with little difficulty*> **2** to send, post

get on *vi* **1** GET ALONG **2** to become late or old – **get on for** to come near; approach <*he's* getting on for *90*>

get out *vi* **1** to emerge, escape <*doubted that he would* get out *alive*> **2** to become known; LEAK 2 <*their secret* got out> ~ *vt* **1** to cause to emerge or escape **2** to bring before the public; *esp* to publish <get *a new book* out>

get round *vi* GET ABOUT 2 – **get round to** to give esp overdue attention or consideration

ˈget-toˌgether *n* an (informal social) gathering or meeting

get together *vt* to bring together; accumulate ~ *vi* **1** to come together; assemble **2** to unite in discussion or promotion of a project

getup /ˈgetˌup‖ˈgetˌʌp/ *n* the outer appearance; *specif* an outfit, clothing – infml

get up *vi* **1a** to arise from bed **b** to rise to one's feet **2** to go ahead or faster – used in the imperative as a command, esp to driven animals ~ *vt* **1** to organize <got up *a party for the newcomers*> **2** to arrange the external appearance of; dress **3** to acquire a knowledge of **4** to create in oneself <*can't* get up *an atom of sympathy for them*>

gewgaw /ˈgyoohˌgaw‖ˈgjuːˌgɔː/ *n* a bauble, trinket

geyser /ˈgeezə‖ˈgiːzə; *sense 1 also* ˈgiezə‖ˈgaɪzə/ *n* **1** a spring that intermittently throws out jets of heated water and steam **2** *Br* an apparatus with a boiler in which water (e g for a bath) is rapidly heated by a gas flame and may be stored [Icelandic *Geysir*, name of a hot spring in Iceland, fr *geysir* gusher, fr *geysa* to rush forth, fr Old Norse]

ghastly /ˈgahstli‖ˈgɑːstlɪ/ *adj* **1a** (terrifyingly) horrible <*a ~ crime*> **b** intensely unpleasant, disagreeable, or objectionable **2** pale, wan – **ghastliness** *n*

ghee, ghi /gee‖giː/ *n* a semifluid clarified butter made, esp in India, from cow's or buffalo's milk

gherkin /ˈguhkin‖ˈgɜːkɪn/ *n* **1** (a slender annual climbing plant of the cucumber family that bears) a small prickly fruit used for pickling **2** the small immature fruit of the cucumber used for pickling

ghetto /ˈgetoh‖ˈgetəʊ/ *n, pl* **ghettos, ghettoes** **1** part of a city in which Jews formerly lived **2** an often slum area of a city in which a minority group live, esp because of social, legal, or economic pressures; *broadly* an area with 1 predominant type of resident [Italian, perhaps fr *getto* foundry, referring to a ghetto established on the site of a foundry in Venice in 1516]

ghetto blaster *n* a large portable radio, usu incorporating a cassette tape recorder

[1]**ghost** /gohst‖gəʊst/ *n* **1** the seat of life or intelligence <*give up the ~*> **2** a disembodied soul; *esp* the soul of a dead person haunting the living **3a** a faint shadowy trace <*a ~ of a smile*> **b** the least bit <*didn't have a ~ of a chance*> **4** a false image in a photographic negative or on a television screen **5** a ghost-writer **6** a red blood cell that has lost its haemoglobin – **ghostlike** *adj*

[2]**ghost** *vb* to ghostwrite

ˈghostly /-li‖-lɪ/ *adj* of, like, or being a ghost; spectral – **ghostliness** *n*

ˈghost ˌtown *n* a once-flourishing but now deserted town

ˈghostˌwrite /-ˌriet‖-ˌraɪt/ *vb* **ghostwrote** /-ˌroht‖-ˌrəʊt/, **ghostwritten** /-ˌrit(ə)n‖-ˌrɪt(ə)n/ to write (e g a speech) for another who is the presumed author – **ghost-writer** *n*

ghoul /goohl‖guːl/ *n* **1** a evil being of Arabic legend that robs graves and feeds on corpses **2** one who enjoys the macabre [Arabic *ghūl*, fr *ghāla* to seize] – **ghoulish** *adj*, **ghoulishly** *adv*, **ghoulishness** *n*

ghyll /gil‖gɪl/ *n* [3]GILL

[1]**GI** /ˌjee ˈie‖ˌdʒiː ˈaɪ/ *adj* (characteristic) of US military personnel or equipment [galvanized *i*ron; fr the abbreviation used in listing articles such as rubbish bins, but taken to stand for *government issue* or *general issue*]

[2]**GI** *n, pl* **GI's, GIs** a member of the US army, esp a private

[1]**giant** /ˈjie·ənt‖ˈdʒaɪənt/ *n* **1** *fem* **giantess** /-tis/ a legendary humanoid being of great stature and strength **2** sby or sthg extraordinarily large **3** a person of extraordinary powers <*a literary ~*> – **giantlike** *adj*

[2]**giant** *adj* extremely large

ˌgiant ˈpanda *n* PANDA 2

gibber /ˈjibə‖ˈdʒɪbə/ *vi* to make rapid, inarticulate, and usu incomprehensible utterances <*a* ~ing *idiot*>

gibberish /ˈjibərish‖ˈdʒɪbərɪʃ/ *n* unintelligible or meaningless language

gibbet /ˈjibit‖ˈdʒɪbɪt/ *n* an upright post with an arm for hanging the bodies of executed criminals

gibbon /ˈgib(ə)n‖ˈgɪb(ə)n/ *n* any of several tailless Asian anthropoid tree-dwelling apes

gibbous /ˈgibəs‖ˈgɪbəs/ *adj* **1a** *of the moon or a planet* seen with more than half but not all of the apparent disc illuminated **b** swollen on 1 side; convex, protuberant **2** having a hump; humpbacked – **gibbously** *adv*, **gibbousness** *n*, **gibbosity** *n*

gibe, jibe /jieb‖dʒaɪb/ *vb* to jeer (at) – **gibe** *n*, **giber** *n*

giblets /ˈjiblits‖ˈdʒɪblɪts/ *n pl* a fowl's heart, liver, or other edible internal organs

giddy /ˈgidi‖ˈgɪdɪ/ *adj* **1** lightheartedly frivolous **2a** feeling, or causing to feel, a sensation of unsteadiness and lack of balance as if everything is whirling round **b** whirling rapidly – **giddily** *adv*, **giddiness** *n*

[1]**gift** /gift‖gɪft/ *n* **1** a natural capacity or talent **2** sthg freely given by one person to another **3** the act, right, or power of giving – **gift of the gab** the ability to talk glibly and persuasively – infml

[2]**gift** *vt* to present

¹gifted *adj* having or revealing great natural ability – **giftedly** *adv*, **giftedness** *n*

¹gig /gig‖gɪg/ *n* **1** a long light ship's boat propelled by oars, sails, etc **2** a light 2-wheeled one-horse carriage

²gig *n* a pronged spear for catching fish

³gig *n* a musician's engagement for a specified time; *esp* such an engagement for 1 performance

gigantic /jie'gantik‖dʒaɪ'gæntɪk/ *adj* unusually great or enormous – **gigantically** *adv*

¹giggle /'gigl‖'gɪgl/ *vi* to laugh with repeated short catches of the breath (and in a silly manner) – **giggler** *n*, **gigglingly** *adv*

²giggle *n* **1** an act or instance of giggling **2** *chiefly Br* sthg that amuses or diverts – chiefly infml <*did it for a* ~> – **giggly** *adj*

gigolo /'zhigəloh‖'ʒɪgələʊ/ *n, pl* **gigolos 1** a man paid by a usu older woman for companionship or sex **2** a professional dancing partner or male escort [French, fr *gigolette* girl who frequents public dances, prostitute, fr *giguer* to dance]

¹gild /gild‖gɪld/ *vt* **gilded, gilt** /gilt‖gɪlt/ **1** to overlay (as if) with a thin covering of gold **2** to give an attractive but often deceptive appearance to – **gilder** *n*, **gilding** *n* – **gild the lily** to add unnecessary ornamentation to sthg beautiful in its own right

²gild *n* a guild

¹gill /jil‖dʒɪl/ *n* a unit of liquid capacity equal to ¼ pint

²gill /gil‖gɪl/ *n* **1** an organ, esp of a fish, for oxygenating blood using the oxygen dissolved in water **2** the flesh under or about the chin or jaws – usu pl with sing. meaning **3** any of the radiating plates forming the undersurface of the cap of some fungi (e g mushrooms) – **gilled** *adj*

³gill, ghyll /gil‖gɪl/ *n, Br* **1** a ravine **2** a narrow mountain stream or rivulet

gillie, gilly, ghillie /'gili‖'gɪlɪ/ *n* an attendant to sby who is hunting or fishing in Scotland [Scottish Gaelic *gille* & Irish Gaelic *giolla* boy, servant]

¹gilt /gilt‖gɪlt/ *adj* covered with gold or gilt; of the colour of gold

²gilt *n* **1** (sthg that resembles) gold laid on a surface **2** superficial brilliance; surface attraction **3** a gilt-edged security – usu pl

³gilt *n* a young female pig

ˌgilt-'edged, gilt-edge *adj* **1** of the highest quality or reliability **2** *of government securities* having a guaranteed fixed interest rate and redeemable at face value

gimcrack /'jimˌkrak‖'dʒɪmˌkræk/ *n* a showy unsubstantial object of little use or value – **gimcrack** *adj*, **gimcrackery** *n*

¹gimlet /'gimlit‖'gɪmlɪt/ *n* **1** a tool for boring small holes in wood, usu consisting of a crosswise handle fitted to a tapered screw **2** a cocktail consisting of lime juice, gin or vodka, and soda water

²gimlet *adj, of eyes* piercing, penetrating <*give him a* gimlet-*eyed stare*>

gimmick /'gimik‖'gɪmɪk/ *n* a scheme, device, or object devised to gain attention or publicity – **gimmickry** *n*, **gimmicky** *adj*

¹gin /jin‖dʒɪn/ *n* any of various tools or mechanical devices: e g **a** a snare or trap for game **b** a machine for raising or moving heavy weights **c** COTTON GIN [Old French *engin* – see ENGINE]

²gin *vt* **-nn- 1** to snare **2** to separate (cotton fibre) from seeds and waste material – **ginner** *n*, **ginning** *n*

³gin *n* a spirit made by distilling a mash of grain with juniper berries [alteration of *geneva*, fr obs Dutch *genever*, lit., juniper, fr Latin *juniperus*]

ginger /'jinjə‖'dʒɪndʒə/ *n* **1a** (any of several cultivated tropical plants with) a thickened pungent aromatic underground stem used (dried and ground) as a spice, or candied as a sweet **b** the spice usu prepared by drying and grinding ginger **2** a strong brown colour – **gingery** *adj*

ˌginger 'ale *n* a sweet yellowish carbonated nonalcoholic drink flavoured with ginger

'gingerˌbread /-ˌbred‖-ˌbred/ *n* a thick biscuit or cake made with treacle or syrup and flavoured with ginger

'ginger ˌgroup *n, Br* a pressure group (e g within a political party) urging stronger action

gingerly /'jinjəli‖'dʒɪndʒəlɪ/ *adj* very cautious or careful – **gingerliness** *n*, **gingerly** *adv*

'ginger ˌnut *n* a hard brittle biscuit flavoured with ginger

ginger up *vt* to stir to activity; vitalize

gingham /'ging·əm‖'gɪŋəm/ *n* a plain-weave often checked clothing fabric usu of yarn-dyed cotton [Malay *genggang* checkered cloth]

ginkgo /'gingkˌgoh, 'gingˌkoh‖'gɪŋkˌgəʊ, 'gɪŋˌkəʊ/, **gingko** /'gingˌkoh‖'gɪŋˌkəʊ/ *n, pl* **ginkgoes, gingkoes** a showy Chinese gymnospermous tree with fan-shaped leaves and yellow fruit

'gin ˌpalace *n, Br* a gaudy public house – derog

ginseng /'jinˌseng‖'dʒɪnˌseŋ/ *n* (the aromatic root, widely valued as a tonic, of) a Chinese or American plant of the ivy family

gipsy, *chiefly NAm* **gypsy** /'jipsi‖'dʒɪpsɪ/ *n* **1** *often cap* a member of a dark Caucasian people coming orig from India to Europe in the 14th or 15th c and leading a migratory way of life **2** a person who moves from place to place; a wanderer [alteration of *Egyptian*; fr the former belief that gipsies came from Egypt]

giraffe /ji'raf, ji'rahf‖dʒɪ'ræf, dʒɪ'rɑːf/ *n* a large African ruminant mammal with a very long neck and a beige coat marked with brown or black patches

gird /guhd‖gɜːd/ *vb* **girded, girt** /guht‖gɜːt/ *vt* **1a** to encircle or bind with a flexible band (e g a belt) **b** to surround **2** to provide or equip with a sword **3** to prepare (oneself) for action ~ *vi* to prepare for action – **gird one's loins, gird up one's loins** to prepare for action; muster one's resources

girder /'guhdə‖'gɜːdə/ *n* a horizontal main supporting beam

¹girdle /'guhdl‖'gɜːdl/ *n* **1** sthg that encircles or confines: e g **1a** a belt or cord encircling the body, usu at the waist **b** a woman's tightly fitting undergarment that extends from the waist to below the hips **c** a bony ring at the front and rear end of the trunk of vertebrates supporting the arms or legs **2** the edge of a cut gem that is grasped by the setting

²girdle *vt* to encircle (as if) with a girdle

³girdle *n, Scot & dial Eng* a griddle

girl /guhl‖gɜːl/ *n* **1a** a female child **b** a young unmarried woman **2a** a sweetheart, girlfriend **b** a daughter **3** a woman – chiefly infml – **girlhood** *n*, **girlish** *adj*, **girlishness** *n*

ˈgirlˌfriend /-ˌfrend‖-ˌfrend/ *n* **1** a frequent or regular female companion of a boy or man; *esp* one with whom he is romantically involved **2** a female friend

ˌgirl ˈguide *n, chiefly Br* GUIDE 3 – not now used technically

girlie, girly /ˈguhli‖ˈgɜːlɪ/ *adj* featuring nude or scantily clothed young women < ~ *magazines*>

giro /ˈjie(ə)roh‖ˈdʒaɪ(ə)rəʊ/ *n* a computerized low-cost system of money transfer comparable to a current account that is one of the national post office services in many European countries

girt /guht‖gɜːt/ *vb* to gird

[1]**girth** /guhth‖gɜːθ/ *n* **1** a strap that passes under the body of a horse or other animal to fasten esp a saddle on its back **2** a measurement of thickness round a body

[2]**girth** *vt* **1** to encircle **2** to bind or fasten with a girth

gist /jist‖dʒɪst/ *n the* main point of a matter; *the* essence

git /git‖gɪt/ *n, chiefly Br* a worthless, contemptible, or foolish person – slang

[1]**give** /giv‖gɪv/ *vb* **gave** /gayv‖geɪv/; **given** /ˈgiv(ə)n‖ˈgɪv(ə)n/ *vt* **1** to make a present of < ~ *a doll to a child*> **2a** to grant, bestow, or allot (by formal action) **b** to accord or yield to another < ~ *him her confidence*> **3a** to administer as a sacrament or medicine **b** to commit to another as a trust or responsibility <gave *her his coat to hold*> **c** to convey or express to another < ~ *an order*> **4a** to proffer, present (for another to use or act on) <gave *his hand to the visitor*> **b** to surrender (oneself) to a partner in sexual intercourse **5** to present to view or observation <gave *a signal*> **6a** to present for, or provide by way of, entertainment < ~ *a party*> **b** to present, perform, or deliver in public < ~ *a lecture*> **7** to propose as a toast <*I* ~ *you the Queen*> **8** to attribute, ascribe <gave *all the glory to God*> **9** to yield as a product or effect <*cows* ~ *milk*> <*84 divided by 12* ~s *7*> **10** to make known; show <*the thermometer* ~s *the temperature*> **11** to yield possession of by way of exchange; pay **12** to make, execute, or deliver (e g by some bodily action) <gave *him a push*> **13a** to inflict as punishment <gave *the boy a whipping*> **b** to cause to undergo; impose < ~ *them a spelling test*> **14a** to award by formal verdict < ~ *judgment against the plaintiff*> **b** to make a specified ruling on the status of (a player) <*Bowles was* ~n *offside*> **15a** to offer for consideration, acceptance, or use <*don't* ~ *me that old line*> **b** to agree to act in accordance with <*I* ~ *you my word*> **16a** to cause to have or receive <*mountains always* gave *him pleasure*> **b** to cause to catch or contract <*digging* ~s *me backache*> **c** to cause (sby) (to think or wonder) <*I was* given *to understand that he was ill*> **17** to apply freely or fully; devote < ~ *one's time to the service of others*> **18** to allow, concede <*it's late, I* ~ *you that*> **19** to care to the extent of <*didn't* ~ *a hang*> ~ *vi* **1** to make gifts **2** to yield or collapse in response to pressure <*the fence* gave *under his weight*> **3** to afford a view or passage; open <*the door* ~s *directly upon the garden*> – **giver** *n* – **give a dog a bad name** to implant prejudice by slander – **give a good account of** to acquit (oneself) well – **give a miss** *chiefly Br* to avoid, bypass – **give as good as one gets** to counterattack with equal vigour – **give birth to 1** to bring forth as a mother **2** to be the cause or origin of – **give chase** to go in pursuit – **give ground** to withdraw before superior force; retreat – **give me** I prefer <give me *London any day!*> – **give or take** allowing for a specified imprecision <*three hours,* give or take *a few minutes either way*> – **give place** to yield by way of being superseded – **give someone a wide berth** to stay at a safe distance from sby – **give someone/something his/her/its head 1** to give sby or sthg greater freedom and responsibility **2** to allow (a horse) to gallop – **give the lie to** to belie – **give way 1a** to retreat; GIVE GROUND **b** to yield the right of way <gave way *to oncoming traffic*> **2** to yield oneself without restraint or control <give way *to tears*> **3a** to yield (as if) to physical stress <*the wind caused the roof to* give way> **b** to yield to entreaty or insistence **4** GIVE PLACE

[2]**give** *n* the capacity or tendency to yield to pressure; resilience, elasticity

ˌgive-and-ˈtake *n* **1** the practice of making mutual concessions **2** the good-natured exchange of ideas or words

ˈgiveˌaway /-əˌway‖-əˌweɪ/ *n* **1** an unintentional revelation or betrayal **2** sthg given free or at a reduced price

give away *vt* **1** to make a present of **2** to hand over (a bride) to the bridegroom at a wedding **3a** to betray **b** to disclose, reveal – esp in **give the game/show away 4** to be at a disadvantage in a sporting contest by (e g a weight or age) compared with an opponent <giving away *4 years to the junior champion*>

give in *vt* to hand in; deliver <gave in *the money he'd found*> ~ *vi* to yield under insistence or entreaty

given /ˈgiv(ə)n‖ˈgɪv(ə)n/ *adj* **1** prone, disposed < ~ *to swearing*> **2** *of an official document* executed on the date specified **3a** fixed, specified <*at a* ~ *time*> **b** assumed as actual or hypothetical < ~ *that all men are equal before the law*> – **given** *n*

ˈgiven ˌname *n, chiefly NAm* CHRISTIAN NAME

give off *vt* to emit <gave off *an unpleasant smell*>

give out *vt* **1** to declare, publish <giving out *that he required complete rest*> **2** to emit <gave out *a constant hum*> **3** to issue, distribute <gave out *new uniforms*> ~ *vi* to come to an end; fail <*finally their patience* gave out *and they came to blows*>

give over *vt* **1** to set apart for a particular purpose or use **2** to deliver to sby's care ~ *vi* to bring an activity to an end <give over *and let me alone*> – infml

give up *vt* **1** to surrender, esp as a prisoner <*he* gave *himself* up> **2** to desist from <*refused to* give up *trying*> **3a** to abandon (oneself) to a particular feeling, influence, or activity <gave *himself* up *to despair*> **b** to renounce <*I must* give up *sugar*> **4** to declare incurable or insoluble <*the doctors* gave *her* up *for dead*> **5** to stop having a relationship with <*she's* given *me* up> ~*vi* to abandon an activity or course of action; *esp* to stop trying – **give up the ghost** to die

gizzard /'gizəd||'gɪzəd/ *n* **1** a muscular enlargement of the alimentary canal of birds that immediately follows the crop and has a tough horny lining for grinding food **2** a thickened part of the alimentary canal of some animals (e g an earthworm) similar in function to the crop of a bird

glacé /'glasay||'glæseɪ/ *adj* **1** made or finished so as to have a smooth glossy surface <~ *silk*> **2** coated with a glaze; candied <~ *cherries*>

glacial /'glays(h)yəl||'gleɪsjəl,-ʃjəl/ *adj* **1a** extremely cold <*a* ~ *wind*> **b** devoid of warmth and cordiality <*a* ~ *smile*> **2a** of or produced by glaciers **b** of or being any of those parts of geological time when much of the earth was covered by glaciers – **glacially** *adv*

glacier /'glasi·ə, 'glay-||'glæsɪə, 'gleɪ-/ *n* a large body of ice moving slowly down a slope or spreading outwards on a land surface

[1]**glad** /glad||glæd/ *adj* **-dd-** **1** expressing or experiencing pleasure, joy, or delight **2** very willing <~ *to do it*> **3** causing happiness and joy <~ *tidings*> – **gladden** *vt*, **gladly** *adv*, **gladness** *n*

[2]**glad** *n* a gladiolus – infml

glade /glayd||gleɪd/ *n* an open space within a wood or forest

glad eye *n* an amorous or sexually inviting look – infml

glad hand *n* a warm welcome or greeting often prompted by ulterior motives – infml – **glad hand** *vt*

gladiator /'gladi,aytə||'glædɪ,eɪtə/ *n* sby trained to fight in the arena for the entertainment of ancient Romans [Latin, fr *gladius* sword, of Celtic origin] – **gladiatorial** *adj*

gladiolus /gladi'ohləs||glædɪ'əʊləs/ *n, pl* **gladioli** /-lie||-laɪ/ any of a genus of (African) plants of the iris family with spikes of brilliantly coloured irregular flowers

'glad ,rags *n pl* smart clothes – infml

glamor·ize, -ise *also* **glamour·ize, -ise** /'glamə,riez||'glæmə,raɪz/ *vt* **1** to make glamorous <~ *the living room*> **2** to romanticize <*the novel* ~s *war*>

glamour, *NAm also* **glamor** /'glamə||'glæmə/ *n* a romantic, exciting, and often illusory attractiveness; *esp* alluring or fascinating personal attraction [Scots *glamour* magic spell, alteration of English *grammar*; fr the popular association of learning with occult practices] – **glamorous** *also* **glamourous** *adj*, **glamorously** *also* **glamourously** *adv*

[1]**glance** /glahns||glɑːns/ *vi* **1** to strike a surface obliquely so as to go off at an angle <*the bullet* ~d *off the wall*> – often + *off* **2a** to flash or gleam with intermittent rays of reflected light <*brooks* glancing *in the sun*> **b** to make sudden quick movements <*dragonflies* glancing *over the pond*> **3** to touch on a subject or refer to it briefly or indirectly <*the work* ~s *at the customs of ancient cultures*> **4a** *of the eyes* to move swiftly from one thing to another **b** to take a quick look at sthg < ~ d *at his watch*> ~ *vt* to cause to glance off a surface by throwing or shooting

[2]**glance** *n* **1** a quick intermittent flash or gleam **2** a deflected impact or blow **3a** a swift movement of the eyes **b** a quick or cursory look **4** an allusion – **at first glance** on first consideration

glancing /'glahnsing||'glɑːnsɪŋ/ *adj* having a slanting direction <*a* ~ *blow*> – **glancingly** *adv*

[1]**gland** /gland||glænd/ *n* **1** (an animal structure that does not secrete but resembles) an organ that selectively removes materials from the blood, alters them, and secretes them esp for further use in the body or for elimination **2** any of various secreting organs (e g a nectary) of plants – **glandless** *adj*

[2]**gland** *n* **1** a device for preventing leakage of fluid past a joint in machinery **2** the movable part of a stuffing box by which the packing is compressed

glandular /'glandyoolə||'glændjʊlə/ *adj* of, involving, or being (the cells or products of) glands – **glandularly** *adv*

[1]**glare** /gleə||gleə/ *vi* **1** to shine with a harsh uncomfortably brilliant light **2** to stare angrily or fiercely ~*vt* to express (e g hostility) by staring fiercely

[2]**glare** *n* **1a** a harsh uncomfortably bright light; *specif* painfully bright sunlight **b** garishness **2** an angry or fierce stare

glaring /'gleəring||'gleərɪŋ/ *adj* painfully and obtrusively evident – **glaringly** *adv*, **glaringness** *n*

glasnost /'glas, nost/ *n* exposure to public knowledge and discussion; openness – used esp of USSR policy

glass /glahs||glɑːs/ *n* **1a** a hard brittle usu transparent or translucent inorganic substance formed by fusing a mixture of silica sand, metallic oxides, and other ingredients **b** a substance resembling glass, esp in hardness and transparency **c** a substance (e g pumice) produced by the quick cooling of molten rock from the earth's core **2a** sthg made of glass: e g **2a(1)** a glass drinking vessel (e g a tumbler or wineglass) **a(2)** a mirror; LOOKING GLASS **a(3)** a barometer **b(1)** an optical instrument (e g a magnifying glass) for viewing objects not readily seen **b(2)** *pl* a pair of lenses together with a frame to hold them in place for correcting defects of vision or protecting the eyes **3** the quantity held by a glass container or drinking vessel **4** glassware – **glassful** *n*, **glassless** *adj*

'glass,blowing /-,bloh·ing||-,bləʊɪŋ/ *n* the art of shaping a mass of semimolten glass by blowing air into it through a tube – **glassblower** *n*

'glass,house /-,hows||-,haʊs/ *n, chiefly Br* **1** a greenhouse **2** a military prison – slang

'glass,ware /-,weə||-,weə/ *n* articles made of glass

,glass 'wool *n* glass fibres in a mass resembling wool used esp for thermal insulation

'glass,works /-,wuhks||-,wɜːks/ *n, pl* **glassworks** a place where glass is made – often pl with sing. meaning

glassy /ˈglahsi‖ˈglɑːsɪ/ *adj* dull, lifeless <~ *eyes*> – **glassily** *adv*, **glassiness** *n*

glaucoma /glawˈkohmə‖glɔːˈkəʊmə/ *n* increased pressure within the eyeball (leading to damage to the retina and gradual loss of vision)

glaucous /ˈglawkəs‖ˈglɔːkəs/ *adj* **1a** pale yellowy green **b** *esp of plants or plant parts* of a dull blue or bluish-green colour **2** *of a plant or fruit* having a powdery or waxy coating giving a frosted appearance – **glaucousness** *n*

[1]**glaze** /glayz‖gleɪz/ *vt* **1** to provide or fit with glass **2** to coat (as if) with a glaze <~ *apple tarts*> **3** to give a smooth glossy surface to ~ *vi* **1** to become glazed or glassy <*his eyes* ~d *over*> **2** to form a glaze – **glazer** *n*

[2]**glaze** *n* **1a** a liquid preparation that gives a glossy coating to food **b** a mixture predominantly of oxides (e g silica and alumina) applied to the surface of ceramic wares as decoration and to make them nonporous **c** a transparent or translucent colour applied to a printed surface to modify its tone **d** a smooth glossy or lustrous surface or finish **2** a glassy film (e g of ice)

glazier /ˈglayzi·ə, -zyə‖ˈgleɪzɪə, -zjə/ *n* one who fits glass, esp into windows, as an occupation – **glaziery** *n*

[1]**gleam** /gleem‖gliːm/ *n* **1a** a transient appearance of subdued or partly obscured light **b** a glint <*a* ~ *of anticipation in his eyes*> **2** a brief or faint appearance or occurrence <*a* ~ *of hope*> – **gleamy** *adj*

[2]**gleam** *vi* **1** to shine with subdued steady light or moderate brightness **2** to appear briefly or faintly

glean /gleen‖gliːn/ *vi* **1** to gather produce, esp grain, left by reapers **2** to gather material (e g information) bit by bit ~ *vt* **1a** to pick up (e g grain) after a reaper **b** to strip (e g a field) by gleaning **2a** to gather (e g information) bit by bit **b** to pick over in search of relevant material – **gleanable** *adj*, **gleaner** *n*

gleanings /ˈgleeningz‖ˈgliːnɪŋz/ *n pl* things acquired by gleaning

glebe /gleeb‖gliːb/ *n* **1** land belonging to an ecclesiastical benefice **2** *archaic* (a plot of cultivated) land

glee /glee‖gliː/ *n* **1** a feeling of merry high-spirited joy or delight **2** an unaccompanied song for 3 or more usu male solo voices – **gleeful** *adj*, **gleefully** *adv*, **gleefulness** *n*

glen /glen‖glen/ *n* a secluded narrow valley

glengarry /glenˈgari‖glenˈgærɪ/ *n, often cap* a straight-sided woollen cap coming to a rounded point over the brow and having 2 short ribbons hanging down behind, worn esp as part of Highland military uniform

glib /glib‖glɪb/ *adj* **-bb- 1** showing little forethought or preparation; lacking depth and substance <~ *solutions to problems*> **2** marked by (superficial or dishonest) ease and fluency in speaking or writing – **glibly** *adv*, **glibness** *n*

[1]**glide** /glied‖glaɪd/ *vi* **1** to move noiselessly in a smooth, continuous, and effortless manner **2** to pass gradually and imperceptibly **3a** *of an aircraft* to fly without the use of engines **b** to fly in a glider ~*vt* to cause to glide

[2]**glide** *n* **1** the act or action of gliding **2** GLANCE 5

glider /ˈgliedə‖ˈglaɪdə/ *n* an aircraft similar to an aeroplane but without an engine

[1]**glimmer** /ˈglimə‖ˈglɪmə/ *vi* **1** to shine faintly or unsteadily **2** to appear indistinctly with a faintly luminous quality

[2]**glimmer** *n* **1** a feeble or unsteady light **2a** a dim perception or faint idea **b** a small sign or amount <*a* ~ *of intelligence*>

glimmering /ˈglimərings‖ˈglɪmərɪŋ/ *n* a glimmer

[1]**glimpse** /glimps‖glɪmps/ *vt* to get a brief look at

[2]**glimpse** *n* a brief fleeting view or look

[1]**glint** /glint‖glɪnt/ *vi* **1** *of rays of light* to strike a reflecting surface obliquely and dart out at an angle **2** to shine with tiny bright flashes; sparkle or glitter, esp by reflection ~*vt* to cause to glint

[2]**glint** *n* **1** a tiny bright flash of light; a sparkle **2** a brief or faint manifestation <*detected a* ~ *of recognition in her expression*>

[1]**glissade** /gliˈsahd, -ˈsayd‖glɪˈsɑːd, -ˈseɪd/ *vi* to slide usu in a standing or squatting position down a slope, esp one that is snow-covered

[2]**glissade** *n* **1** the action of glissading **2** a gliding step in ballet

glissando /gliˈsandoh‖glɪˈsændəʊ/ *n, pl* **glissandi** /-di‖-dɪ/, **glissandos** a rapid sliding up or down the musical scale

glisten /ˈglis(ə)n‖ˈglɪs(ə)n/ *vi* to shine, usu by reflection, with a sparkling radiance or with the lustre of a wet or oiled surface

glister /ˈglistə‖ˈglɪstə/ *vi* to glitter – chiefly poetic – **glister** *n*

glitch /glich‖glɪtʃ/ *n* **1a** an unwanted brief surge of electrical power **b** a false or spurious electronic signal **2** a technical hitch or malfunction – infml

[1]**glitter** /ˈglitə‖ˈglɪtə/ *vi* **1a** to shine by reflection with a brilliant or metallic lustre <~ing *sequins*> **b** to shine with a hard cold glassy brilliance <~ing *eyes*> **2** to be brilliantly attractive in a superficial or deceptive way <*the chance of success* ~ed *before them*> – **glitteringly** *adv*

[2]**glitter** *n* **1** sparkling brilliance, showiness, or attractiveness **2** small glittering particles used for ornamentation – **glittery** *adj*

glitz /glits‖glɪts/ *n* conspicuous showiness; glitter – **glitzy** *adj*

gloaming /ˈglohming‖ˈgləʊmɪŋ/ *n* *the* twilight, dusk

[1]**gloat** /gloht‖gləʊt/ *vi* to observe or think about sthg with great and often malicious satisfaction, gratification, or relish – **gloater** *n*, **gloatingly** *adv*

[2]**gloat** *n* a gloating feeling

global /ˈglohbl‖ˈgləʊbl/ *adj* **1** spherical **2** of or involving the entire world **3** general, comprehensive – **globally** *adv*

globe /glohb‖gləʊb/ *n* sthg spherical or rounded: e g **a** a spherical representation of the earth, a heavenly body, or the heavens **b** EARTH 4

globe artichoke *n* ARTICHOKE 1b

ˈ**globe,fish** /-ˌfish‖-ˌfɪʃ/ *n* any of a family of (tropical) poisonous marine fishes which can distend themselves to a globular form

ˈ**globe-,trotter** *n* one who travels widely – **globe-trotting** *n or adj*

globular /ˈglobyoolə‖ˈglɒbjʊlə/ *adj* **1** globe-

or globule-shaped **2** having or consisting of globules – **globularly** *adv*, **globularness** *n*

globule /ˈglobyoohl‖ˈglɒbjuːl/ *n* a tiny globe or ball (e g of liquid or melted solid)

glockenspiel /ˈglokənˌspeel, -ˌshpeel‖ˈglɒkənˌspiːl, -ˌʃpiːl/ *n* a percussion instrument consisting of a series of graduated metal bars played with 2 hammers [German, fr *glocke* bell + *spiel* play]

[1]**gloom** /gloohm‖gluːm/ *vi* **1** to mope **2** to loom up dimly or sombrely <*the castle* ~ed *before them*> ~*vt* to make dark, murky, or sombre

[2]**gloom** *n* **1** partial or total darkness **2a** lowness of spirits **b** an atmosphere of despondency

gloomy /ˈgloohmi‖ˈgluːmɪ/ *adj* **1a** partially or totally dark; *esp* dismally and depressingly dark **b** low in spirits **2** causing gloom – **gloomily** *adv*, **gloominess** *n*

glorify /ˈglawriˌfie‖ˈglɔːrɪˌfaɪ/ *vt* **1a** to make glorious by bestowing honour, praise, or admiration **b** to elevate to celestial glory **2** to shed radiance or splendour on **3** to cause to appear better, more appealing, or more important than in reality **4** to give glory to (e g in worship) – **glorifier** *n*, **glorification** *n*

glorious /ˈglawri·əs‖ˈglɔːrɪəs/ *adj* **1a** possessing or deserving glory **b** conferring glory **2** marked by great beauty or splendour **3** delightful, wonderful <*had a* ~ *weekend*> – **gloriously** *adv*, **gloriousness** *n*

[1]**glory** /ˈglawri‖ˈglɔːrɪ/ *n* **1a** (sthg that secures) praise or renown **b** worshipful praise, honour, and thanksgiving <*giving* ~ *to God*> **2** a (most) commendable asset <*her hair was her crowning* ~> **3a** (sthg marked by) resplendence or magnificence **b** the splendour, blessedness, and happiness of heaven; *broadly* eternity **4** a state of great gratification or exaltation **5** a ring or spot of light: e g **5a** an aureole **b** CORONA 2a, b

[2]**glory** *vi* to rejoice proudly <~ing *in their youth and vigour*>

[1]**gloss** /glos‖glɒs/ *n* **1** (sthg that gives) surface lustre or brightness **2** a deceptively attractive outer appearance **3** paint to which varnish has been added to give a gloss finish

[2]**gloss** *n* **1a** a brief explanation (e g in the margin of a text) of a difficult word or expression **b** a false interpretation (e g of a text) **2a** a glossary **b** an interlinear translation **c** a continuous commentary accompanying a text

[3]**gloss** *vt* to supply glosses for

glossary /ˈglosəri‖ˈglɒsərɪ/ *n* a list of terms (e g those used in a particular text or in a specialized field), usu with their meanings

gloss over *vt* **1** to make appear right and acceptable **2** to veil or hide by treating rapidly or superficially

[1]**glossy** /ˈglosi‖ˈglɒsɪ/ *adj* **1** having a surface lustre or brightness **2** attractive in an artificially opulent, sophisticated, or smoothly captivating manner – **glossily** *adv*, **glossiness** *n*

[2]**glossy** *n*, *chiefly Br* a magazine expensively produced on glossy paper and often having a fashionable or sophisticated content

ˌglottal ˈstop /ˈglotl‖ˈglɒtl/ *n* a speech sound produced by sudden closure of the glottis

glottis /ˈglotis‖ˈglɒtɪs/ *n*, *pl* **glottises, glottides** /-tiˌdeez‖-tɪˌdiːz/ (the structures surrounding) the elongated space between the vocal cords – **glottal** *adj*

[1]**glove** /gluv‖glʌv/ *n* **1** a covering for the hand having separate sections for each of the fingers and the thumb and often extending part way up the arm **2** BOXING GLOVE

[2]**glove** *vt* to cover (as if) with a glove

ˈglove comˌpartment *n* a small storage compartment in the dashboard of a motor vehicle

[1]**glow** /gloh‖gləʊ/ *vi* **1** to shine (as if) with an intense heat **2a** to experience a sensation (as if) of heat; show a ruddy colour (as if) from being too warm <~ing *with rage*> **b** to show satisfaction or elation <~ *with pride*> – **glowingly** *adv*

[2]**glow** *n* **1** brightness or warmth of colour <*the* ~ *of his cheeks*> **2a** warmth of feeling or emotion **b** a sensation of warmth **3a** the state of glowing with heat and light **b** light (as if) from sthg burning without flames or smoke

glower /ˈglowə‖ˈglaʊə/ *vi* to look or stare with sullen annoyance or anger – **glower** *n*

ˈglowˌworm /-ˌwuhm‖-ˌwɜːm/ *n* a luminescent wingless insect; *esp* a larva or wingless female of a firefly that emits light from the abdomen

glucose /ˈgloohkohz, -kohs‖ˈgluːkəʊz, -kəʊs/ *n* a sweet (dextrorotatory form of a) sugar that occurs widely in nature and is the usual form in which carbohydrate is assimilated by animals [French, fr Greek *gleukos* must, sweet wine]

[1]**glue** /glooh‖gluː/ *n* **1** any of various strong adhesives; *esp* a gelatinous protein substance that forms a strongly adhesive solution and is obtained by boiling hides, bones, etc **2** a solution of glue used for sticking things together – **gluey** *adj*, **gluily** *adv*

[2]**glue** *vt* **gluing** *also* **glueing** **1** to cause to stick tightly with glue <~ *the wings onto the model aeroplane*> **2** to fix (e g the eyes) on an object steadily or with deep concentration <*kept her eyes* ~d *to the TV*>

glum /glum‖glʌm/ *adj* **-mm-** **1** broodingly morose **2** dreary, gloomy – **glumly** *adv*, **glumness** *n*

[1]**glut** /glut‖glʌt/ *vt* **-tt-** **1** to fill, esp with food, to beyond capacity **2** to flood (the market) with goods so that supply exceeds demand

[2]**glut** *n* an excessive supply (e g of a harvested crop) which exceeds market demand

gluten /ˈgloohtin‖ˈgluːtɪn/ *n* an elastic protein substance, esp of wheat flour, that gives cohesiveness to dough – **glutenous** *adj*

glutinous /ˈgloohtinəs‖ˈgluːtɪnəs/ *adj* (thick and) sticky; gummy – **glutinously** *adv*, **glutinousness** *n*

glutton /ˈglut(ə)n‖ˈglʌt(ə)n/ *n* **1** one given habitually to greedy and voracious eating and drinking **2** one who has a great capacity for accepting or enduring sthg <*he's a* ~ *for punishment*> – **gluttonous** *adj*, **gluttonousness** *n*

gluttony /ˈglut(ə)n·i‖ˈglʌt(ə)nɪ/ *n* excess in eating or drinking

glycerin /ˈglisərin‖ˈglɪsərɪn/, **glycerine** /ˈglisəreen, --ˈ-‖ˈglɪsəriːn, --ˈ-/ *n* glycerol [French *glycérine*, fr Greek *glykeros* sweet]

glycerol /'glisərol‖'glɪsərɒl/ *n* a sweet syrupy alcohol usu obtained from fats and used esp as a solvent and plasticizer

glycoside /'gliekə͵sied, -koh-‖'glaɪkə͵saɪd, -kəʊ-/ *n* any of numerous sugar derivatives in which a nonsugar group is attached by an oxygen or nitrogen atom and that on hydrolysis yield a sugar – **glycosidic** *adj*, **glycosidically** *adv*

gnarled /nahld‖nɑːld/ *adj* **1** full of or covered with knots or protuberances **2** crabbed in disposition, aspect, or character

gnash /nash‖næʃ/ *vt* to strike or grind (esp the teeth) together – **gnash** *n*

gnat /nat‖næt/ *n* any of various small usu biting 2-winged flies – **gnatty** *adj*

gnaw /naw‖nɔː/ *vt* **1a** to bite or chew on with the teeth; *esp* to wear away by persistent biting or nibbling <*a dog* ~ing *a bone*> **b** to make by gnawing <*rats* ~ed *a hole*> **2** to affect as if by continuous eating away; plague **3** to erode, corrode ~ *vi* **1** to bite or nibble persistently **2** to destroy or reduce sthg (as if) by gnawing <*waves* ~ing *away at the cliffs*> – **gnawer** *n*

gneiss /nies‖naɪs/ *n* a metamorphic rock usu composed of light bands of feldspar and quartz and dark bands of mica or hornblende – **gneissic** *adj*, **gneissoid** *adj*, **gneissose** *adj*

gnome /nohm‖nəʊm/ *n* a dwarf of folklore who lives under the earth and guards treasure [French, fr Modern Latin *gnomus*, coined by Paracelsus (1493-1541), Swiss alchemist] – **gnomish** *adj*

gnomic /'nohmik‖'nəʊmɪk/ *adj* resembling a pithy saying; aphoristic

gnu /nooh‖nuː/ *n*, any of several large horned African antelopes with an oxlike head, a short mane, and a long tail

[1]**go** /goh‖gəʊ/ *vb* **went** /went‖went/; **gone** /gon‖gɒn/ *vi* **1** to proceed on a course <~ *slow*> <went *by train*> <went *to France*> **2a** to move out of or away from a place; leave <*I must* ~> <*the ferry* ~es *every hour*> – sometimes used with a further verb to express purpose <*I* went *to see them*> <*I'll* ~ *and look*> **b** to make an expedition for a specified activity <~ *shopping*> **3a** to pass by means of a specified process or according to a specified procedure <*your suggestion will* ~ *before the committee*> **b(1)** to proceed in a thoughtless or reckless manner – used to intensify a complementary verb <*don't* ~ *saying that*> **b(2)** to proceed to do sthg surprising – used with *and* to intensify a complementary verb <*she* went *and won first prize*> **c(1)** to extend <*it's true as far as it* ~es> **c(2)** to speak, proceed, or develop in a specified direction or up to a specified limit <*you've* gone *too far*> **4** to travel on foot or by moving the feet **5** to be, esp habitually <~ *bareheaded*> **6a** to become lost, consumed, or spent <*half their income* ~es *in rent*> **b** to die **c** to elapse <*only three weeks to* ~> **d** to be got rid of (e g by sale or removal) <*these slums must* ~> **e** to fail <*his hearing started to* ~> **f** to succumb; GIVE WAY <*at last the dam* went> **7a** to happen, progress – often + *on* <*what's* ~ing *on*> **b** to be in general or on an average <*cheap, as yachts* ~> **c** to pass or be granted by award, assignment, or lot <*the prize* went *to a French girl*> **d** to turn out (well) <*worked hard to make the party* ~> **8** to put or subject oneself <went *to unnecessary expense*> **9a** to begin an action, motion, or process <*here* ~es> **b** to maintain or perform an action or motion <*his tongue* went *nineteen to the dozen*> **c** to function in a proper or specified way <*trying to get the motor to* ~> **d** to make a characteristic noise <*the telephone* went> **e** to perform a demonstrated action <~ *like this with your left foot*> **10a** to be known or identified as specified <*now* ~es *by another name*> **b(1)** to be in phrasing or content <*as the saying* ~es> **b(2)** to be sung or played in a specified manner <*the song* ~es *to the tune of 'Greensleeves'*> **11a** to act or occur in accordance or harmony <*a good rule to* ~ *by*> **b** to contribute to a total or result <*taxes that* ~ *for education*> **12** to be about, intending, or destined – + *to* and an infinitive <*is* ~ing *to leave town*> **13a** to come or arrive at a specified state or condition <~ *to sleep*> **b** to join a specified institution professionally or attend it habitually <*does she* ~ *to school?*> **c** to come to be; turn <*he* went *broke*> **d(1)** to become voluntarily <~ *bail for his friend*> **d(2)** to change to a specified system or tendency <*the company* went *public*> **e** to continue to be; remain <~ *hungry*> **14** to be compatible *with*, harmonize <*claret* ~es *with beef*> **15a** to be capable of passing, extending, or being contained or inserted <*it won't* ~ *round my waist*> **b** to belong <*these books* ~ *on the top shelf*> **16a** to carry authority <*what she said* went> **b** to be acceptable, satisfactory, or adequate <*anything* ~es *here*> **c** to be the case; be valid <*and that* ~es *for you too*> ~ *vt* **1** to proceed along or according to <~ *one's own way*> **2** to traverse <~ *ten miles*> **3** to undertake by travelling <~ *errands*> **4** to emit (a sound) <*the bell* ~es *ding dong*> **5** to participate to the extent of <~ *shares*> **6** to perform, effect <~ *the limit*> – **go about** to undertake; SET ABOUT – **go after** to seek, pursue – **go against 1** to act in opposition to; offend **2** to turn out unfavourably to – **go ahead 1** to begin **2** to continue, advance – **go all the way 1** to enter into complete agreement **2** to engage in actual sexual intercourse – **go along with 1** to occur as a natural accompaniment of **2** to agree with; support – **go ape** to run amok; lose control – **go at 1** to attack, assail **2** to undertake energetically – **go back on 1** to fail to keep (e g a promise) **2** to be disloyal to; betray – **go begging** to be available but in little demand – **go by the board** to be discarded – **go for 1** to serve or be accounted as <*it all* went for *nothing*> **2** to try to secure <*he* went for *the biggest mango*> **3a** to favour, accept <*cannot* go for *your idea*> **b** to have an interest in or liking for <*she* went for *him in a big way*> **4** to attack, assail <went for *him when his back was turned*> – **go for a burton** *Br* to get lost, broken, or killed – slang – **go great guns** to achieve great success – **go hang** to cease to be of interest or concern – **go into 1** to be contained in <*5* goes into *60 12 times*> **2** to investigate **3** to explain in depth <*the book doesn't* go into *the moral aspects*> –

go it 1 to behave in a reckless, excited, or impromptu manner **2** to proceed rapidly or furiously **3** to conduct one's affairs; act <*insists on* going it *alone*> – **go missing** *chiefly Br* to disappear – **go off the deep end 1** to enter recklessly on a course of action **2** to become very excited or perturbed – **go one better** to outdo or surpass another – **go out of one's way** to take extra trouble – **go over 1** EXAMINE 1 **2a** REPEAT 1 **b** to study, revise – **go places** to be on the way to success – **go slow** to hold a go-slow – **go steady** to be the constant and exclusive boyfriend or girl friend of another or each other – **go straight** to abandon a life of crime – **go through 1** to subject to thorough examination, study, or discussion; GO OVER **2** to experience, undergo **3** to perform <went through *his work in a daze*> – compare GO THROUGH *vi* – **go to bed with** to have sexual intercourse with – **go to one's head 1** to make one confused, excited, or dizzy **2** to make one conceited or overconfident – **go to pieces** to become shattered (e g in nerves or health) – **go to pot** to deteriorate, collapse – infml – **go to sleep** to lose sensation; become numb <*my foot has* gone to sleep> – **go to town 1** to work or act rapidly or efficiently **2** to indulge oneself ostentatiously – **go west** to die or become destroyed or expended – humor – **go with 1** GO ALONG WITH 1 <*the responsibility that* goes with *parenthood*> **2** to be the social or esp sexual companion of

[2]**go** *n, pl* **goes 1** the act or manner of going **2** energy, vigour <*full of get up and* ~> **3a** a turn in an activity (e g a game) **b** an attempt, try <*have a* ~ *at painting*> **c** chance, opportunity <*a fair* ~ *at work for everyone – The Listener*> **4** a spell of activity <*finished the job at one* ~> **5** a success <*made a* ~ *of the business*> **6** *the* height of fashion; *the* rage <*shawls are all the* ~ *at the moment*> – chiefly infml **7** an often unexpected or awkward turn of affairs – chiefly infml <*it's a rum* ~> – **on the go** constantly or restlessly active – infml

[3]**go** *adj* functioning properly <*declared all systems* ~ *for the rocket launch*>

[4]**go** *n* an Oriental board game of capture and territorial domination played by 2 players

go about *vi* to change tack when sailing

[1]**goad** /gohd‖gəʊd/ *n* **1** a pointed rod used to urge on an animal **2** sthg that pricks, urges, or stimulates (into action)

[2]**goad** *vt* **1** to drive (e g cattle) with a goad **2** to incite or rouse by nagging or persistent annoyance

[1]**go-aˈhead** *adj* energetic and progressive

[2]**ˈgo-aˌhead** *n* a sign, signal, or authority to proceed

goal /gohl‖gəʊl/ *n* **1** an end towards which effort is directed **2a** an area or object through or into which players in various games attempt to put a ball or puck against the defence of the opposing side **b** (the points gained by) the act of putting a ball or puck through or into a goal

ˈgoalˌkeeper /-ˌkeepə‖-ˌkiːpə/ *n* a player who defends the goal in soccer, hockey, lacrosse, etc – **goalkeeping** *n*

ˈgoal ˌline *n* a line at either end and usu running the width of a playing area on which a goal or goal post is situated

ˈgoalˌmouth /-ˌmowth‖-ˌmaʊθ/ *n* the area of a playing field directly in front of the goal

go along *vi* **1** to move along; proceed **2** to go or travel as a companion **3** to agree, cooperate <*I'd* go along *with your suggestion*>

ˈgoalˌpost /-ˌpohst‖-ˌpəʊst/ *n* either of usu 2 vertical posts that with or without a crossbar constitute the goal in soccer, rugby, etc

go around *vi* **1** to go here and there, esp in company <*the friends she* goes around *with*> **2** GO ROUND 1, 2

goat /goht‖gəʊt/ *n* **1** any of various long-legged (horned) ruminant mammals smaller than cattle and related to the sheep **2** a lecherous man **3** a foolish person – infml – **goatish** *adj*, **goatlike** *adj*

goatee /ˈgohˌtee‖ˈgəʊˌtiː/ *n* a small pointed beard

ˈgoatˌskin /-ˌskin‖-ˌskɪn/ *n* (leather made from) the skin of a goat

[1]**gob** /gob‖gɒb/ *n* a shapeless or sticky lump

[2]**gob** *n, Br* MOUTH 1a – slang

gobbet /ˈgobit‖ˈgɒbɪt/ *n* a piece, portion

[1]**gobble** /ˈgobl‖ˈgɒbl/ *vt* **1** to swallow or eat greedily or noisily **2** to take, accept, or read eagerly – often + *up*

[2]**gobble** *vi* to make the guttural sound of a male turkey or a similar sound – **gobble** *n*

gobbledygook, gobbledegook /ˈgobldiˌgoohk‖ˈgɒbldɪˌguːk/ *n* wordy and generally unintelligible jargon

gobbler /ˈgoblə‖ˈgɒblə/ *n* a male turkey – infml

ˈgo-beˌtween *n* an intermediate agent

goblet /ˈgoblit‖ˈgɒblɪt/ *n* a drinking vessel that has a usu rounded bowl, a foot, and a stem and is used esp for wine

goblin /ˈgoblin‖ˈgɒblɪn/ *n* a grotesque mischievous elf

goby /ˈgohbi‖ˈgəʊbɪ/ *n* any of numerous spiny-finned fishes with the pelvic fins often united to form a sucking disc

go-by /ˈgoh ˌbie‖ˈgəʊ ˌbaɪ/ *n* an act of avoidance; a miss <*give them the* ~>

go by *vi* to pass <*as time* goes by>

god /god‖gɒd/ *n* **1** *cap* the supreme or ultimate reality; the being perfect in power, wisdom, and goodness whom human beings worship as creator and ruler of the universe **2** a being or object believed to have more than natural attributes and powers (e g the control of a particular aspect of reality) and to require human beings' worship **3** sby or sthg of supreme value **4** a very influential person **5** *pl* the highest gallery in a theatre, usu with the cheapest seats – **godlike** *adj*

ˈgodˌchild /-ˌchield‖-ˌtʃaɪld/ *n* sby for whom sby else becomes sponsor at baptism

[1]**goddamn, goddam** /go(d)ˈdam‖gɒ(d)ˈdæm/ *n, often cap* a damn <*he doesn't give a* ~ *about anything*>

[2]**goddamn, goddam** /go(d)ˈdam‖gɒ(d)ˈdæm/ *vb, often cap* to damn

goddess /ˈgodes, -dis‖ˈgɒdes, -dɪs/ *n* **1** a female deity **2** a woman whose great charm or beauty arouses adoration

ˈGod-ˌfearing *adj* devout

ˈgodforˌsaken /-fəˌsaykən‖-fəˌseɪkən/ *adj* **1** remote, desolate **2** neglected, dismal

'god,head /-,hed||-,hed/ *n* **1** divine nature or essence **2** *cap* **2a** GOD 1 – usu + *the* **b** *the* nature of God, esp as existing in 3 persons

'godless /-lis||-lɪs/ *adj* not acknowledging a deity; impious – **godlessness** *n*

'godly /-li||-lɪ/ *adj* **1** divine **2** pious, devout – **godliness** *n*

godown /'goh,down||'gəʊ,daʊn/ *n* a warehouse in an Asian country, esp India

go down *vi* **1a** to fall (as if) to the ground <*the plane* went down *in flames*> **b** to go below the horizon <*the sun* went down> **c** to sink <*the ship* went down *with all hands*> **2** to be capable of being swallowed <*the medicine* went down *easily*> **3** to undergo defeat **4a** to find acceptance <*will the plan* go down *well with the farmers?*> **b** to come to be remembered, esp by posterity <*he will* go down *in history as a great general*> **5a** to undergo a decline or decrease <*the market is* going down> **b** *esp of a computer system or program* to crash **6** to become ill – usu + *with* <*he* went down *with flu*> **7** *Br* to leave a university **8** to be sent to prison – slang

'god,parent /-,peərənt||-,peərənt/ *n* a sponsor at baptism

godsend /'god,send||'gɒd,send/ *n* a desirable or needed thing or event that comes unexpectedly

,God'speed /-'speed||-'spi:d/ *n* a prosperous journey; success <*bade him* ~>

goer /'goh·ə||'gəʊə/ *n* **1** a regular attender – usu in combination <*a theatre*goer> **2** sby or sthg that moves or does things fast or actively; *esp* a swinger – infml

,go-'getter *n* an aggressively enterprising person – **go-getting** *adj or n*

goggle /'gogl||'gɒgl/ *vi* to stare with wide or protuberant eyes – **goggler** *n*

'goggle-,box *n, Br* a television set – infml

,goggle-'eyed *adj or adv* with the eyes wide or bulging (in amazement or fascination)

goggles /'goglz||'gɒglz/ *n pl* protective glasses set in a flexible frame that fits snugly against the face

go-go /'goh ,goh||'gəʊ ,gəʊ/ *adj* of or being the music or a style of dance performed or a dancer performing at a disco

go in *vi* **1** to enter **2** *of a celestial body* to become obscured by a cloud **3** to form a union or alliance – often + *with* <*asked the rest of us to* go in *with them on the project*> – **go in for 1** to engage in, esp as a hobby or for enjoyment **2** to enter and compete in (e g a test or race)

[1]**going** /'goh·ing||'gəʊɪŋ/ *n* **1** an act or instance of going – often in combination <*theatre*going> **2** the condition of the ground (e g for horse racing) **3** advance, progress <*found the* ~ *too slow and gave up the job*> **4** the depth of the tread of a stair

[2]**going** *adj* **1a** living, existing <*the best novelist* ~> **b** available for use or enjoyment <*asked if there were any jobs* ~> **2a** current, prevailing <~ *price*> **b** profitable, thriving <~ *concern*> – **going for** favourable to <*had everything* going for *me*>

,going-'over *n, pl* **goings-over 1** a thorough examination or investigation **2** a severe scolding

,goings-'on *n pl* **1** actions, events <*coming-out parties and sundry* ~> **2** reprehensible happenings or conduct <*tales of scandalous* ~ *in high circles*>

goitre, *NAm chiefly* **goiter** /'goytə||'gɔɪtə/ *n* an abnormal enlargement of the thyroid gland visible as a swelling of the front of the neck

go-kart /'goh ,kaht||'gəʊ ,kɑ:t/ *n* a tiny racing car with small wheels

gold /gohld||gəʊld/ *n* **1** a malleable ductile yellow metallic element that occurs chiefly free or in a few minerals and is used esp in coins and jewellery and as a currency reserve **2a(1)** gold coins **a(2)** GOLD MEDAL <*won a* ~ *in the 100m*> **b** money **c** GOLD STANDARD **d** gold as a commodity **3** a deep metallic yellow **4** sthg valued as excellent or the finest of its kind <*a heart of* ~>

'gold,beater /-,beetə||-,bi:tə/ *n* sby who beats gold into gold leaf – **goldbeating** *n*

'gold ,digger *n* a woman who uses charm to extract money or gifts from men – infml

golden /'gohld(ə)n||'gəʊld(ə)n/ *adj* **1** consisting of, relating to, or containing gold **2a** of the colour of gold **b** BLOND 1a **3** prosperous, flourishing <~ *days*> **4** highly favoured and promising (worldly) success – often in *golden boy/girl* **5** favourable, advantageous <*a* ~ *opportunity*> **6** of or marking a 50th anniversary <~ *wedding*> – **goldenly** *adv*, **goldenness** *n*

'golden ,age *n* a period of great happiness, prosperity, and achievement

,golden 'hand,shake *n* a large ex gratia money payment given by a company to an employee, esp on retirement

,golden 'mean *n* the medium between extremes; moderation

,golden 'oriole *n* an Old World oriole of which the male is brilliant yellow

,golden 'rule *n* **1** the precept that one should treat others as one would wish to be treated by them **2** a guiding principle

,golden 'syrup *n* the pale yellow syrup derived from cane sugar refining and used in cooking

'gold,finch /-,finch||-,fɪntʃ/ *n* a small red, black, yellow, and white European finch

'gold,fish /-,fish||-,fɪʃ/ *n* a small (golden yellow) fish related to the carps and widely kept in aquariums and ponds

,gold 'leaf *n* gold beaten into very thin sheets and used esp for gilding

,gold 'medal *n* a medal of gold awarded to sby who comes first in a competition

'gold ,mine *n* a rich source of sthg desired (e g information)

'gold ,rush *n* a rush to newly discovered goldfields in pursuit of riches

'gold,smith /-,smith||-,smɪθ/ *n* one who works in gold or deals in articles of gold

'gold ,standard *n* a standard of money under which the basic unit of currency is defined by a stated quantity of gold of a fixed fineness

golf /golf||gɒlf/ *n* a game in which a player using special clubs attempts to hit a ball into each of the 9 or 18 successive holes on a course with as few strokes as possible [perhaps fr Middle Dutch *colf, colve* club, bat] – **golf** *vi*

ˈ**golf ˌcourse** *n* an area of land laid out for playing golf consisting of a series of 9 or 18 holes each with a tee, fairway, and putting green

golfer /ˈgolfə‖ˈgɒlfə/ *n* sby who plays golf

ˈ**golf ˌlinks** *n* a golf course, esp near the sea – often pl with sing. meaning

golliwog, gollywog /ˈgoliˌwog‖ˈgɒlɪˌwɒg/ *n* a child's soft doll with a black face and black hair standing out round its head [*Golliwogg*, an animated doll in children's fiction by Bertha Upton (died 1912), US writer]

[1]**golly** /ˈgoli‖ˈgɒlɪ/ *interj* – used to express surprise

[2]**golly** *n* a golliwog

-gon /-gon, -gən‖-gɒn, -gən/ *comb form* (→ *n*) geometrical figure having (so many) angles <*deca*gon>

gonad /ˈgohnad‖ˈgəʊnæd; *also* ˈgo-‖ˈgɒ-/ *n* any of the primary sex glands (e g the ovaries or testes) – **gonadal** *adj*

gondola /ˈgondələ‖ˈgɒndələ/ *n* **1** a long narrow flat-bottomed boat used on the canals of Venice **2a** an enclosure suspended from a balloon for carrying passengers or instruments **b** a cabin suspended from a cable and used for transporting passengers (e g up a ski slope)

gondolier /ˌgondəˈliə‖ˌgɒndəˈlɪə/ *n* a boatman who propels a gondola

[1]**gone** /gon‖gɒn/ *adj* **1a** involved, absorbed <*far ~ in hysteria*> **b** pregnant by a specified length of time <*she's 6 months ~*> **c** infatuated – often + *on*; infml <*was real ~ on that man*> **2** dead – euph

[2]**gone** *adv, Br* past, turned <*it's ~ 3 o'clock*>

goner /ˈgonə‖ˈgɒnə/ *n* one whose case or state is hopeless or lost – infml

gong /gong‖gɒŋ/ *n* **1** a disc-shaped percussion instrument that produces a resounding tone when struck with a usu padded hammer **2** a flat saucer-shaped bell **3** a medal or decoration – slang [Malay & Javanese, of imitative origin] – **gong** *vi*

gonna /ˈgonə, gənə‖ˈgɒnə, gənə/ *verbal auxiliary pres* to be going to <*I'm ~ wash that man right out of my hair* – Oscar Hammerstein> – nonstandard

gonorrhoea, *chiefly NAm* **gonorrhea** /ˌgonəˈriə‖ˌgɒnəˈrɪə/ *n* a venereal disease in which there is inflammation of the mucous membranes of the genital tracts – **gonorrhoeal** *adj*

goo /gooh‖guː/ *n* **1** sticky matter **2** cloying sentimentality *USE* infml – **gooey** *adj*

[1]**good** /good‖gʊd/ *adj* **better** /ˈbetə‖ˈbetə/; **best** /best‖best/ **1a(1)** of a favourable character or tendency <*~ news*> **a(2)** bountiful, fertile <*~ land*> **a(3)** handsome, attractive <*~ looks*> **b(1)** suitable, fit <*it's a ~ day for planting roses*> **b(2)** free from injury or disease; whole <*1 ~ arm*> **b(3)** not depreciated <*bad money drives out ~*> **b(4)** commercially sound <*a ~ risk*> **b(5)** certain to last or live <*~ for another year*> **b(6)** certain to pay or contribute <*~ for a few quid*> **b(7)** certain to elicit a specified result <*always ~ for a laugh*> **c(1)** agreeable, pleasant; *specif* amusing **c(2)** beneficial to the health or character <*spinach is ~ for you*> **c(3)** not rotten; fresh <*the beef is still ~*> **d** ample, full **e(1)** well-founded, true <*~ reasons*> **e(2)** deserving of respect; honourable <*in ~ standing*> **e(3)** legally valid <*~ title*> **f(1)** adequate, satisfactory; *also* strong, robust **f(2)** conforming to a standard <*~ English*> **f(3)** choice, discriminating <*~ taste*> **2a(1)** morally commendable; virtuous <*a ~ man*> **a(2)** correct; *specif* well-behaved **a(3)** kind, benevolent <*~ intentions*> **b** reputable; *specif* wellborn <*a ~ family*> **c** competent, skilful <*a ~ doctor*> **d** loyal <*a ~ Catholic*> – **goodish** *adj* – **as good as** virtually; IN EFFECT – **as good as gold** extremely well-behaved – **good and** very, entirely – infml <*should be* good and *ready by Tuesday*> – **in someone's good books** in sby's favour

[2]**good** *n* **1a** sthg good <*it's no ~ complaining*> **b** the quality of being good <*to know ~ from evil*> **c** a good element or portion <*recognized the ~ in him*> **2** prosperity, benefit <*for the ~ of the community*> **3a** sthg that has economic utility or satisfies an economic want – usu pl **b** *pl* personal property having intrinsic value but usu excluding money, securities, and negotiable instruments **c** *pl* wares, merchandise <*tinned ~*s> **4** *pl but sing or pl in constr* the desired or necessary article <*came up with the ~*s> – infml **5** *pl* proof of wrongdoing – slang <*the police have got the ~*s *on him*> – **for good** forever, permanently – **to the good 1** for the best; beneficial <*this rain is all* to the good> **2** in a position of net gain or profit <*he ended the game £10* to the good>

[3]**good** *adv* well – infml

ˌ**good ˈbook** *n, often cap G&B the* Bible

[1]**goodbye,** *NAm also* **goodby** /goodˈbie‖gʊdˈbaɪ/ *interj* – used to express farewell [alteration of *God be with you*]

[2]**goodbye,** *NAm also* **goodby** *n* a concluding remark or gesture at parting

[1]ˈ**good-for-ˌnothing** *adj* of no value; worthless

[2]**good-for-nothing** *n* an idle worthless person

ˌ**Good ˈFriday** *n* the Friday before Easter, observed in churches as the anniversary of the crucifixion of Christ

ˌ**good-ˈhumoured** *adj* good-natured, cheerful – **good-humouredly** *adv*

ˌ**good-ˈlooking** *adj* having a pleasing or attractive appearance – **good-looker** *n*

goodly /ˈgoodli‖ˈgʊdlɪ/ *adj* **1** significantly large in amount; considerable <*a ~ number*> **2** *archaic* pleasantly attractive; handsome

ˌ**good-ˈnatured** *adj* of a cheerful and cooperative disposition – **goodnaturedly** *adv*, **good-naturedness** *n*

goodness /ˈgoodnis‖ˈgʊdnɪs/ *n* **1** the quality or state of being good **2** the nutritious or beneficial part of sthg

ˌ**good ˈoffices** *n pl* power or action that helps sby out of a difficulty – often in *through the good offices of*

ˌ**goodˈwill** /-ˈwil‖-ˈwɪl/ *n* **1a** a kindly feeling of approval and support; benevolent interest or concern **b** the favour or prestige that a business has acquired beyond the mere value of what it sells **2a** cheerful consent **b** willing effort – **good-willed** *adj*

goody, goodie /ˈgoodi‖ˈgʊdɪ/ *n* **1** sthg particularly attractive, pleasurable, or desirable **2** a good person or hero *USE* infml

ˈ**goody-ˌgoody** *n or adj* (sby) affectedly or ingratiatingly prim or virtuous – infml

[1]**goof** /goohf‖gu:f/ *n* **1** a ridiculous stupid person **2** *chiefly NAm* a blunder *USE* infml

[2]**goof** *vb, chiefly NAm vi* to make a goof; blunder ~*vt* to make a mess of; bungle – often + *up USE* infml

go off *vi* **1** to explode **2** to go forth or away; depart **3** to undergo decline or deterioration; *specif, of food or drink* to become rotten or sour **4** to follow a specified course; proceed <*the party* went off *well*> **5** to make a characteristic noise; sound <*the alarm* went off>

goofy /ˈgoohfi‖ˈgu:fɪ/ *adj* silly, daft – infml – **goofily** *adv*, **goofiness** *n*

googly /ˈgoohgli‖ˈgu:glɪ/ *n* a usu slow delivery by a right-handed bowler in cricket that is an off break as viewed by a right-handed batsman although apparently delivered with a leg-break action

gooly, goolie /ˈgoohli‖ˈgu:lɪ/ *n, Br* a testicle – slang

goon /goohn‖gu:n/ *n* **1** *NAm* a man hired to terrorize or eliminate opponents **2** an idiot, dope – slang – **goony** *adj*

go on *vi* **1** to continue; CARRY ON 2 **2a** to proceed (as if) by a logical step <*he* went on *to explain why*> **b** *of time* to pass **3** to take place; happen <*what's* going on?> **4** to be capable of being put on <*her gloves wouldn't* go on> **5a** to talk, esp in an effusive manner <*the way people* go on *about pollution*> **b** to criticize constantly; nag <*you're always* going on *at me*> **6a** to come into operation, action, or production <*the lights* went on *at sunset*> **b** to appear on the stage **7** *Br* to manage; GET ALONG <*how did you* go on *for money?*>

[1]**goose** /goohs‖gu:s/ *n, pl* (*1 & 2*) **geese** /gees‖gi:s/, (*3*) **gooses** **1** (the female of) any of numerous large long-necked web-footed waterfowl **2** a simpleton, dolt **3** a tailor's smoothing iron with a handle like a goose's neck – **goosey** *adj*

[2]**goose** *vt, chiefly NAm* to poke between the buttocks – vulg

gooseberry /ˈgoozb(ə)ri‖ˈgʊzb(ə)rɪ/ *n* **1** (the shrub that bears) an edible acid usu prickly green or yellow fruit **2** an unwanted companion to 2 lovers – chiefly in *to play gooseberry*

ˈ**gooseˌflesh** /-ˌflesh‖-ˌfleʃ/ *n* a bristling roughness of the skin, produced usu by cold or fear

ˈ**gooseˌfoot** /-ˌfoot‖-ˌfʊt/ *n, pl* **goosefoots** any of several plants with small green flowers that grow esp on disturbed or cultivated land

ˈ**goose ˌpimples** *n pl* gooseflesh

ˈ**goose ˌstep** *n* a straight-legged marching step – **goose-stepper** *n*

go out *vi* **1a** to leave a room, house, country, etc **b** to fight in a duel **c** to travel to a distant place <*they* went out *to Africa*> **d** to work away from home <*she* went out *charring*> **2a** to become extinguished <*the hall light* went out> **b** to become obsolete or unfashionable **3** to spend time regularly *with* sby of esp the opposite sex **4** to be broadcast <*the programme* went out *at 9 o'clock*>

go over *vi* **1** to become converted (e g to a religion or political party) **2** to receive approval; succeed <*my play should* go over *well in Scotland*>

gopher /ˈgohfə‖ˈgəʊfə/ *n* **1** any of several American burrowing rodents that are the size of a large rat and have large cheek pouches **2** any of numerous small N American ground squirrels closely related to the chipmunks

ˈ**Gordian ˌknot** /ˈgawdi·ən, -dyən‖ˈgɔ:dɪən, -djən/ *n* an intricate problem; *esp* one insoluble in its own terms [*Gordius*, King of Phrygia, who tied an intricate knot which supposedly could be undone only by the future ruler of Asia, and which Alexander the Great cut with his sword]

[1]**gore** /gaw‖gɔ:/ *n* (clotted) blood

[2]**gore** *n* a tapering or triangular piece of material (e g cloth) used to give shape to sthg (e g a garment or sail) – **gored** *adj*

[3]**gore** *vt* to pierce or wound with a horn or tusk

[1]**gorge** /gawj‖gɔ:dʒ/ *n* **1** the throat **2** the (contents of the) stomach or belly **3** the entrance into an outwork of a fort **4** a narrow steep-walled valley, often with a stream flowing through it

[2]**gorge** *vi* to eat greedily or until full ~ *vt* **1** to fill completely or to the point of making distended <*veins* ~d *with blood*> **2** to swallow greedily – **gorger** *n*

gorgeous /ˈgawjəs‖ˈgɔ:dʒəs/ *adj* **1** splendidly beautiful or magnificent **2** very fine; pleasant <*it was a* ~ *day for a picnic*> – **gorgeously** *adv*, **gorgeousness** *n*

gorgon /ˈgawgən‖ˈgɔ:gən/ *n* **1** *cap* any of 3 sisters in Greek mythology who had live snakes in place of hair and whose glance turned the beholder to stone **2** an ugly or repulsive woman – **Gorgonian** *adj*

Gorgonzola /ˌgawgənˈzohlə‖ˌgɔ:gənˈzəʊlə/ *n* a blue-veined strongly flavoured cheese of Italian origin [*Gorgonzola*, town in Italy]

gorilla /gəˈrilə‖gəˈrɪlə/ *n* **1** an anthropoid ape of western equatorial Africa related to the chimpanzee but less erect and much larger **2** an ugly or brutal man [deriv of Greek *Gorillai*, a mythical African tribe of hairy women]

gormand·ize, -ise /ˈgawmənˌdiez‖ˈgɔ:mənˌdaɪz/ *vb* to eat voraciously; gorge – **gormandizer** *n*

gormless /ˈgawmlis‖ˈgɔ:mlɪs/ *adj, Br* lacking understanding and intelligence; stupid – infml

go round *vi* **1** to spread, circulate <*there's a rumour* going round> **2** to satisfy demand; meet the need <*not enough jobs to* go round> **3** GO AROUND 1

gorse /gaws‖gɔ:s/ *n* a spiny yellow-flowered evergreen leguminous European shrub – **gorsy** *adj*

gory /ˈgawri‖ˈgɔ:rɪ/ *adj* **1** covered with gore; bloodstained **2** full of violence; bloodcurdling <*a* ~ *film*>

gosh /gosh‖gɒʃ/ *interj* – used to express surprise

gosling /ˈgozling‖ˈgɒzlɪŋ/ *n* a young goose

ˌ**go-ˈslow** *n, Br* a deliberate slowing down of production by workers as a means of forcing management's compliance with their demands

[1]**gospel** /'gospl‖'gɒspl/ *n* **1** *often cap* the message of the life, death, and resurrection of Jesus Christ; *esp* any of the first 4 books of the New Testament, or any similar apocryphal book, relating this **2** *cap* a liturgical reading from any of the New Testament Gospels **3** the message or teachings of a religious teacher or movement **4a** sthg accepted as a guiding principle <*the ~ of hard work*> **b** sthg so authoritative as not to be questioned <*they took his word as ~*> [Old English *gōdspel*, fr *gōd* good + *spell* tale, news]

[2]**gospel** *adj* **1** of the Christian gospel; evangelical **2** of or being usu evangelistic religious songs of American origin

gossamer /'gosəmə‖'gɒsəmə/ *n* **1** a film of cobwebs floating in air in calm clear weather **2** sthg light, insubstantial, or tenuous – **gossamer** *adj*, **gossamery** *adj*

[1]**gossip** /'gosip‖'gɒsɪp/ *n* **1** sby who habitually reveals usu sensational facts concerning other people's actions or lives **2a** (rumour or report of) the facts related by a gossip **b** a chatty talk – **gossipry** *n*, **gossipy** *adj*

[2]**gossip** *vi* to relate gossip – **gossiper** *n*

got /got‖gɒt/ **1** *past of* GET **2** *pres pl & 1&2 sing of* GET <*I ~ news for you*> – nonstandard

Goth /goth‖gɒθ/ *n* a member of a Germanic people that invaded parts of the Roman Empire between the 3rd and 5th centuries AD

[1]**Gothic** /'gothik‖'gɒθɪk/ *adj* **1** of the Goths, their culture, or Gothic **2** of a style of architecture prevalent from the middle of the 12th c to the early 16th c characterized by vaulting and pointed arches **3** *often not cap* of or like a class of novels of the late 18th and early 19th c dealing with macabre or mysterious events – **gothically** *adv*, **Gothicism** *n*, **gothicize** *vt*

[2]**Gothic** *n* **1** the E Germanic language of the Goths **2** Gothic architectural style **3a** BLACK LETTER **b** SANS SERIF

go through *vi* **1** to continue firmly or obstinately to the end – often + *with* <*can't* go through *with the wedding*> **2a** to receive approval or sanction **b** to come to a desired or satisfactory conclusion

[1]**gotta** /'gotə‖'gɒtə/ *vt pres* to have a <*I ~ horse*> – nonstandard

[2]**gotta** *verbal auxiliary pres* to have to; must <*we ~ go*> – nonstandard

gotten /'gotn‖'gɒtn/ *NAm past part of* GET

gouache /goo'ahsh ‖gʊ'ɑːʃ (*Fr* gwaʃ)/ *n* a method of painting with opaque watercolours that have been ground in water and mixed with a gum preparation

Gouda /'gowdə‖'gaʊdə/ *n* a mild cheese of Dutch origin that is similar to Edam but contains more fat [*Gouda*, town in the Netherlands]

[1]**gouge** /gowj‖gaʊdʒ/ *n* **1** a chisel with a curved cross section and bevel on the concave side of the blade **2** *chiefly NAm* overcharging, extortion – infml

[2]**gouge** *vt* **1** to scoop out (as if) with a gouge **2** to force *out* (an eye), esp with the thumb **3** *chiefly NAm* to subject to extortion; overcharge – infml – **gouger** *n*

goulash /'goohlash‖'guːlæʃ/ *n* a meat stew made usu with veal or beef and highly seasoned with paprika [Hungarian *gulyás* herdsman's stew]

go under *vi* to be destroyed or defeated; fail

go up *vi, Br* to enter or return to a university

gourd /gooəd‖gʊəd/ *n* (the fruit of) any of the cucumber family of typically tendril-bearing climbing plants (e g the melon, squash, and pumpkin); *esp* any of various hard-rinded inedible fruits used for ornament or for vessels and utensils

gourmand /'gawmənd, 'gooə- ‖'gɔːmənd, 'gʊə- (*Fr* gurmɑ̃)/ *n* one who is excessively fond of or heartily interested in food and drink – **gourmandism** *n*

gourmet /'gawmay, 'gooə- ‖'gɔːmeɪ, 'gʊə- (*Fr* gurmɛ)/ *n* a connoisseur of food and drink – **gourmet** *adj*

gout /gowt‖gaʊt/ *n* **1** painful inflammation of the joints, esp that of the big toe, resulting from a metabolic disorder in which there is an excessive amount of uric acid in the blood **2** a sticky blob – **gouty** *adj*

govern /'guv(ə)n‖'gʌv(ə)n/ *vt* **1** to exercise continuous sovereign authority over **2a** to control, determine, or strongly influence <*availability often ~s choice*> **b** to hold in check; restrain **3** to require (a word) to be in a usu specified case <*in English a transitive verb ~s a pronoun in the accusative*> **4** to serve as a precedent or deciding principle for <*habits and customs that ~ human decisions*> ~ *vi* **1** to prevail **2** to exercise authority [Old French *governer*, fr Latin *gubernare* to steer, govern, fr Greek *kybernan*] – **governable** *adj*

governance /'guv(ə)nəns‖'gʌv(ə)nəns/ *n* governing or being governed – fml

governess /'guv(ə)nis‖'gʌv(ə)nɪs/ *n* a woman entrusted with the private teaching and often supervision of a child

government /'guv(ə)nmənt, 'guvəmənt‖'gʌv(ə)nmənt, 'gʌvəmənt/ *n* **1** governing; *specif* authoritative direction or control **2** the office, authority, or function of governing **3** policy making as distinguished from administration **4** the machinery through which political authority is exercised **5** *sing or pl in constr* the body of people that constitutes a governing authority – **governmental** *adj*, **governmentally** *adv*

governor /'guv(ə)nə‖'gʌv(ə)nə/ *n* **1a** a ruler, chief executive, or nominal head of a political unit **b** a commanding officer **c** the managing director and usu the principal officer of an institution or organization **d** a member of a group (e g the governing body of a school) that controls an institution **2** a device giving automatic control of pressure, fuel, steam, etc, esp to regulate speed **3a** sby (e g a father, guardian, or employer) looked on as governing – slang **b** Mister, Sir – slang; used as a familiar form of address – **governorate** *n*, **governorship** *n*

ˌgovernor-'general *n, pl* **governors-general, governor-generals** a governor of high rank; *esp* one representing the Crown in a Commonwealth country – **governor-generalship** *n*

gown /gown‖gaʊn/ *n* **1a** a loose flowing robe worn esp by a professional or academic person when acting in an official capacity **b** a woman's dress, esp one that is elegant or for formal wear

c an outer garment worn in an operating theatre **2** the body of students and staff of a college or university <*riots between town and* ~ >

goy /goy‖gɔɪ/ *n, pl* **goyim** /-əm, -eem‖-əm, -iːm/, **goys** a gentile – chiefly derog – **goyish** *adj*

ˌ**Graafian** ˈ**follicle** /ˈgrahfi·ən‖ˈgrɑːfɪən/ *n* a vesicle in the ovary of a mammal enclosing a developing egg [Regnier de *Graaf* (1641-73), Dutch anatomist]

[1]**grab** /grab‖græb/ *vb* **-bb-** *vt* **1** to take or seize hastily or by a sudden motion or grasp **2** to obtain unscrupulously **3** to forcefully engage the attention of – infml <*he* ~s *an audience*> ~ *vi* to make a grab; snatch – **grabber** *n*

[2]**grab** *n* **1a** a sudden snatch **b** an unlawful or unscrupulous seizure **c** sthg intended to be grabbed – often in combination <*a* grab-*rail*> **2a** a mechanical device for clutching an object – **up for grabs** available for anyone to take or win – infml

[1]**grace** /grays‖greɪs/ *n* **1a** unmerited divine assistance given to human beings for their regeneration or sanctification **b** a state of being pleasing to God **2** a short prayer at a meal asking a blessing or giving thanks **3a** disposition to or an act or instance of kindness or clemency **b** a special favour **c** a temporary exemption; a reprieve **d** approval, favour **4a** a charming trait or accomplishment **b** an elegant appearance or effect; charm **c** ease and suppleness of movement or bearing **5** – used as a title for a duke, duchess, or archbishop **6** consideration, decency <*had the* ~ *to blush*> – **with bad/good grace** (un)willingly or (un)happily

[2]**grace** *vt* **1** to confer dignity or honour on **2** to adorn, embellish

graceful /ˈgraysf(ə)l‖ˈgreɪsf(ə)l/ *adj* displaying grace in form, action, or movement – **gracefully** *adv*, **gracefulness** *n*

graceless /ˈgrayslis‖ˈgreɪslɪs/ *adj* **1** lacking a sense of propriety **2** devoid of elegance; awkward – **gracelessly** *adv*, **gracelessness** *n*

Graces /ˈgraysiz‖ˈgreɪsɪz/ *n pl* the 3 beautiful sister goddesses in Greek mythology who are the givers of charm and beauty

gracious /ˈgrayshəs‖ˈgreɪʃəs/ *adj* **1a** marked by kindness and courtesy **b** marked by tact and delicacy **c** having those qualities (e g comfort, elegance, and freedom from hard work) made possible by wealth < ~ *living*> **2** merciful, compassionate – used conventionally of royalty and high nobility – **graciously** *adv*, **graciousness** *n*

gradation /grəˈdaysh(ə)n‖grəˈdeɪʃ(ə)n/ *n* **1** (a step or place in) a series forming successive stages **2** a gradual passing from one tint or shade to another (e g in a painting) **3** ablaut – **gradational** *adj*, **gradationally** *adv*

[1]**grade** /grayd‖greɪd/ *n* **1a(1)** a stage in a process **a(2)** a position in a scale of ranks or qualities **b** a degree of severity of illness **2** a class of things of the same stage or degree **3** a gradient **4** a domestic animal with one parent purebred and the other of inferior breeding **5** *NAm* a school form; a class **6** *NAm* a mark indicating a degree of accomplishment at school – **gradeless** *adj*

[2]**grade** *vt* **1a** to arrange in grades; sort **b** to arrange in a scale or series **2** to improve (e g cattle) by breeding with purebred animals – often + *up* **3** *NAm* to assign a mark to – **grader** *n*

ˈ**grade** ˌ**crossing** *n, chiefly NAm* LEVEL CROSSING

gradient /ˈgraydi·ənt, -dyənt‖ˈgreɪdɪənt, -djənt/ *n* **1** the degree of inclination of a road or slope; *also* a sloping road or railway **2** change in the value of a (specified) quantity with change in a given variable, esp distance <*a vertical temperature* ~ >

gradual /ˈgradyooəl, -jooəl, -jəl‖ˈgrædjʊəl, -dʒʊəl, -dʒəl/ *adj* proceeding or happening by steps or degrees – **gradually** *adv*, **gradualness** *n*

[1]**graduate** /ˈgradyoo·ət, -joo-‖ˈgrædjʊət, -dʒʊ-/ *n* **1** the holder of an academic degree **2** *chiefly NAm* one who has completed a course of study

[2]**graduate** *adj* **1** holding an academic degree or diploma **2** postgraduate

[3]**graduate** /ˈgradyooˌayt, -joo-‖ˈgrædjʊˌeɪt, -dʒʊ-/ *vt* **1** to mark with degrees of measurement **2** to divide into grades or intervals ~ *vi* **1** to receive an academic degree **2** to move up to a usu higher stage of experience, proficiency, or prestige **3** to change gradually **4** *NAm* to complete a course of study – **graduator** *n*

graduation /ˌgradyooˈaysh(ə)n, -joo-‖ˌgrædjʊˈeɪʃ(ə)n, -dʒʊ-/ *n* **1** a mark (e g on an instrument or vessel) indicating degrees or quantity **2** the award of an academic degree

Graeco-, *chiefly NAm* **Greco-** /greekoh-‖griːkəʊ-/ *comb form* **1** Greek nation, people, or culture <Graeco*mania*> **2** Greek and <Graeco-*Roman*>

graffito /grəˈfeetoh, gra-‖grəˈfiːtəʊ, græ-/ *n, pl* **graffiti** /-ti‖-tɪ/ an inscription or drawing, usu of a crude or political nature, made on a wall, rock, etc – usu pl [Italian, diminutive of *graffio* scratch, fr *graffiare* to scratch]

[1]**graft** /grahft‖grɑːft/ *vt* **1a** to cause (a plant scion) to unite with a stock; *also* to unite (plants or scion and stock) to form a graft **b** to propagate (a plant) by grafting **2** to attach, add **3** to implant (living tissue) surgically ~ *vi* **1** to become grafted **2** to perform grafting **3** *NAm* to practise graft – **grafter** *n*

[2]**graft** *n* **1a** a grafted plant **b** (the point of insertion upon a stock of) a scion **2** (living tissue used in) grafting **3a** the improper use of one's position (e g public office) to one's private, esp financial, advantage **b** sthg acquired by graft

[3]**graft** *vi, Br* to work hard – slang – **graft** *n*

Grail /grayl‖greɪl/ *n* HOLY GRAIL

[1]**grain** /grayn‖greɪn/ *n* **1** a seed or fruit of a cereal grass; *also* (the seeds or fruits collectively of) the cereal grasses or similar food plants **2a** a discrete (small hard) particle or crystal (e g of sand, salt, or a metal) **b** the least amount possible <*not a* ~ *of truth in what he said*> **c** fine crystallization (e g of sugar) **3** a unit of weight equal to 0.0648 gram **4a** the arrangement of the fibres in wood **b** the direction, alignment, or texture of the constituent particles, fibres, or threads <*the* ~ *of a rock*> **5** natural disposition or character; temper **6** (a brilliant scarlet dye made from) either kermes or cochineal – not now used technically – **grained** *adj*, **grainy** *adj*,

graininess *n* – **against the grain** counter to one's inclination, disposition, or feeling

[2]**grain** *vt* **1** to form into grains; granulate **2** to paint in imitation of the grain of wood or stone ~*vi* to become granular; granulate – **grainer** *n*

[1]**gram** /gram‖græm/ *n* a leguminous plant (e g the chick-pea) grown esp for its seed

[2]**gram, gramme** *n* one thousandth of a kilogram (about 0.04oz)

-gram /-gram‖-græm/ *comb form* (→ *n*) drawing; writing; record <*tele*gram>

grammar /ˈgramə‖ˈgræmə/ *n* **1** the study of the classes of words, their inflections, and their functions and relations in the sentence; *broadly* this study when taken to include that of phonology and sometimes of usage **2** the characteristic system of inflections and syntax of a language **3a** a grammar textbook **b** speech or writing evaluated according to its conformity to grammatical rules **4** the principles or rules of an art, science, or technique – **grammarian** *n*

ˈ**grammar** ˌ**school** *n* **1** a secondary school that emphasized the study of the classics **2** *Br* a secondary school providing an academic type of education from the age of 11 to 18

grammatical /grəˈmatikl‖grəˈmætɪkl/ *adj* **1** of grammar **2** conforming to the rules of grammar – **grammatically** *adv*, **grammaticalness** *n*, **grammaticality** *n*

gramophone /ˈgraməfohn‖ˈgræməfəʊn/ *n* a device for reproducing sounds from the vibrations of a stylus resting in a spiral groove on a rotating disc; *specif, chiefly Br* RECORD PLAYER

grampus /ˈgrampəs‖ˈgræmpəs/ *n* any of various (dolphinlike) small whales (e g the killer whale) [Middle French *graspeis*, fr *gras* fat (fr Latin *crassus*) + *peis* fish (fr Latin *piscis*)]

gran /gran‖græn/ *n, chiefly Br* a grandmother – infml

granary /ˈgranəri‖ˈgrænərɪ/ *n* **1** a storehouse for threshed grain **2** a region producing grain in abundance

[1]**grand** /grand‖grænd/ *adj* **1** having more importance than others; foremost **2** complete, comprehensive <*the ~ total of all money paid out*> **3** main, principal **4** large and striking in size, extent, or conception <*a ~ design*> **5a** lavish, sumptuous <*a ~ celebration*> **b** marked by regal form and dignity; imposing **c** lofty, sublime <*writing in the ~ style*> **6** intended to impress <*a man of ~ gestures and pretentious statements*> **7** very good; wonderful – infml <*a ~ time*> – **grandly** *adv*, **grandness** *n*

[2]**grand** *n* **1** GRAND PIANO **2a** *Br* a thousand pounds **b** *NAm* a thousand dollars *USE* (*2*) slang

grandchild /ˈgranˌchield‖ˈgrænˌtʃaɪld/ *n* a child of one's son or daughter

granddad, grandad /ˈgranˌdad‖ˈgrænˌdæd/ *n* a grandfather – infml

granddaughter /ˈgranˌdawtə‖ˈgrænˌdɔːtə/ *n* a daughter of one's son or daughter

grandee /granˈdee‖grænˈdiː/ *n* a Spanish or Portuguese nobleman of the highest rank

grandeur /ˈgranjə, -dyə‖ˈgrændʒə, -djə/ *n* **1** the quality of being large or impressive; magnificence **2** personal greatness marked by nobility, dignity, or power

grandfather /ˈgran(d)ˌfahdhə‖ˈgræn(d)ˌfɑːðə/ *n* the father of one's father or mother; *broadly* a male ancestor – **grandfatherly** *adj*

ˌ**grand**ˌ**father** ˈ**clock** *n* a tall pendulum clock standing directly on the floor

grandiloquence /granˈdiləkwəns‖grænˈdɪləkwəns/ *n* lofty or pompous eloquence; bombast [Latin *grandiloquus* using lofty language, fr *grandis* grand + *loqui* to speak] – **grandiloquent** *adj*, **grandiloquently** *adv*

grandiose /ˈgrandiohs, -ohz‖ˈgrændɪəʊs, -əʊz/ *adj* **1** impressive because of uncommon largeness, scope, or grandeur **2** characterized by affectation of grandeur or by absurd exaggeration – **grandiosely** *adv*, **grandioseness, grandiosity** *n*

grandma /ˈgranˌmah, ˈgramˌmah‖ˈgrænˌmɑː, ˈgræmˌmɑː/ *n* a grandmother – infml

grand mal /ˌgronhˈmal ‖ˌgrɑ̃ˈmæl (*Fr* grɑ̃ mal)/ *n* (an attack of) the severe form of epilepsy [French, lit., great illness]

ˌ**grand** ˈ**master** *n* a chess player who has consistently scored higher than a standardized score in international competition

grandmother /ˈgranˌmudhə, ˈgrand-, ˈgram-‖ˈgrænˌmʌðə, ˈgrænd-, ˈgræm-/ *n* the mother of one's father or mother; *broadly* a female ancestor – **grandmotherly** *adj*

ˌ**Grand** ˈ**National** *n* the major British steeplechase for horses that is run annually at Aintree near Liverpool

ˌ**grand** ˈ**opera** *n* opera with a serious dramatic plot and no spoken dialogue

grandpa /ˈgranˌpah, ˈgram-‖ˈgrænˌpɑː, ˈgræm-/ *n* a grandfather – infml

grandparent /ˈgran(d)ˌpeərənt‖ˈgræn(d)ˌpeərənt/ *n* the parent of one's father or mother – **grandparenthood** *n*, **grandparental** *adj*

ˌ**grand pi**ˈ**ano** *n* a piano with horizontal frame and strings

grand prix /ˌgronh ˈpree ‖ˌgrɑ̃ ˈpriː (*Fr* grɑ̃ pri)/ *n, pl* **grand prix** *often cap G&P* **1** any of a series of long-distance races for formula cars, held consecutively in different countries **2** a series of sporting tournaments producing an overall winner

ˌ**grand** ˈ**slam** *n* **1** the winning of all the tricks in 1 hand of a card game, specif bridge **2** a clean sweep or total success, esp in a sport

grandson /ˈgran(d)ˌsun‖ˈgræn(d)ˌsʌn/ *n* a son of one's son or daughter

[1]ˈ**grand**ˌ**stand** /-ˌstand‖-ˌstænd/ *n* a usu roofed stand for spectators at a racecourse, stadium, etc in an advantageous position for viewing the contest

[2]**grandstand** *vi, NAm* to play or act so as to impress onlookers – infml – **grandstander** *n*

ˌ**grand** ˈ**tour** *n* **1** an extended tour of the Continent, formerly a usual part of the education of young British gentlemen – usu + *the* **2** an extensive and usu educational tour

grange /graynj‖greɪndʒ/ *n* a farm; *esp* a farmhouse with outbuildings

granite /ˈgranit‖ˈgrænɪt/ *n* **1** a very hard granular igneous rock formed of quartz, feldspar, and mica and used esp for building **2** unyielding firmness or endurance – **granitelike** *adj*, **granitoid** *adj*, **granitic** *adj*

[1]**granny**, **grannie** /ˈgrani‖ˈgrænɪ/ *n* a grandmother – infml

[2]**granny**, **grannie** *adj* designed for use by an older relative – infml < ~ *flat*>

[1]**grant** /grahnt‖grɑːnt/ *vt* **1a** to consent to carry out or fulfil (e g a wish or request) < ~ *a child his wish*> **b** to permit as a right, privilege, or favour <*luggage allowances* ~ed *to passengers*> **2** to bestow or transfer formally **3a** to be willing to concede **b** to assume to be true – **grantable** *adj*, **granter** *n*, **grantor** *n*

[2]**grant** *n* **1** sthg granted; *esp* a gift for a particular purpose **2** a transfer of property; *also* the property so transferred

granular /ˈgranyoolə‖ˈgrænjʊlə/ *adj* (apparently) consisting of granules; having a grainy texture – **granularly** *adv*, **granularity** *n*

granulate /ˈgranyooˌlayt‖ˈgrænjʊˌleɪt/ *vt* to form or crystallize into grains or granules < ~d *sugar*> ~*vi, esp of a wound* (to form minute granules of new capillaries while beginning) to heal – **granulator** *n*, **granulation** *n*, **granulative** *adj*

granule /ˈgranyoohl‖ˈgrænjuːl/ *n* a small grain

grape /grayp‖greɪp/ *n* **1** (any of a genus of widely cultivated woody vines that bear, in clusters,) a smooth-skinned juicy greenish white to deep red or purple berry eaten as a fruit or fermented to produce wine **2** grapeshot – **grapy** *adj*

ˈ**grapeˌfruit** /-ˌfrooht‖-ˌfruːt/ *n* (a small tree that bears) a large round citrus fruit with a bitter yellow rind and a somewhat acid juicy pulp

ˈ**grapeˌshot** /-ˌshot‖-ˌʃɒt/ *n* a cluster of small iron balls used as a charge for a cannon

ˈ**grapeˌvine** /-ˌvien‖-ˌvaɪn/ *n* a secret or unofficial means of circulating information or gossip

[1]**graph** /grahf, graf‖grɑːf, græf/ *n* **1** a diagram (e g a series of points, a line, a curve, or an area) expressing a relation between quantities or variables **2** the collection of all points whose coordinates satisfy a given relation (e g the equation of a function)

[2]**graph** *vt* to plot on or represent by a graph

-graph /-ˌgrahf, -ˌgraf‖-ˌgrɑːf, -ˌgræf/ *comb form* (→ *n*) **1** sthg written or represented <*mono*graph> **2** instrument for recording or transmitting (sthg specified or by a specified means) <*seismo*graph>

[1]**graphic** /ˈgrafik‖ˈgræfɪk/ *also* **graphical** /-kl‖-kl/ *adj* **1** formed by writing, drawing, or engraving **2** marked by clear and vivid description; sharply outlined **3a** of the pictorial arts **b** of or employing engraving, etching, lithography, photography, or other methods of reproducing material in the graphic arts **c** of or according to graphics **4** of or represented by a graph **5** of writing [Latin *graphicus*, fr Greek *graphikos*, fr *graphein* to write] – **graphically** *adv*, **graphicness** *n*

[2]**graphic** *n* **1** a product of graphic art **2** a picture, map, or graph used for illustration or demonstration **3** a graphic representation displayed by a computer (e g on a VDU)

-graphic /-ˈgrafik‖-ˈgræfɪk/, **-graphical** /-kl‖-kl/ *comb form* (→ *adj*) **1** written, represented, or transmitted in (such) a way <*ideo*graphic> **2** of writing on a (specified) subject <*autobio*graphic>

graphite /ˈgrafiet‖ˈgræfaɪt/ *n* a soft black lustrous form of carbon that conducts electricity and is used esp in lead pencils and as a lubricant – **graphitize** *vt*, **graphitic** *adj*

graphology /graˈfoləji‖græˈfɒlədʒɪ/ *n* the study of handwriting, esp for the purpose of character analysis – **graphologist** *n*, **graphological** *adj*

ˈ**graph ˌpaper** *n* paper ruled for drawing graphs

-graphy /-grəfi‖-grəfɪ/ *comb form* (→ *n*) **1** writing or representation in (such) a manner or on (a specified subject) or by (a specified means) <*bio*graphy> **2** art or science of <*choreo*graphy> – **-grapher** *comb form* (→ *n*)

grapnel /ˈgrapnəl‖ˈgræpnəl/ *n* an instrument with several claws that is hurled with a line attached in order to hook onto a ship, the top of a wall, etc

[1]**grapple** /ˈgrapl‖ˈgræpl/ *n* **1** a grapnel **2** a hand-to-hand struggle

[2]**grapple** *vt* to seize (as if) with a grapple ~ *vi* to come to grips *with*; wrestle – **grappler** *n*

[1]**grasp** /grahsp‖grɑːsp/ *vi* to make the motion of seizing; clutch ~ *vt* **1** to take, seize, or clasp eagerly (as if) with the fingers or arms **2** to succeed in understanding; comprehend – **graspable** *adj*, **grasper** *n*

[2]**grasp** *n* **1** a firm hold **2** control, power <*he is in her* ~> **3** the power of seizing and holding or attaining <*success was just beyond his* ~> **4** comprehension <*showed a firm* ~ *of her subject*>

grasping /ˈgrahsping‖ˈgrɑːspɪŋ/ *adj* eager for material possessions; avaricious – **graspingly** *adv*, **graspingness** *n*

[1]**grass** /grahs‖grɑːs/ *n* **1a** herbage suitable or used for grazing animals **b** pasture, grazing **2** any of a large family of plants with slender leaves and (green) flowers in small spikes or clusters, that includes bamboo, wheat, rye, corn, etc **3** land on which grass is grown <*keep off the* ~> **4** grass leaves or plants **5** cannabis; *specif* marijuana – slang **6** *Br* a police informer – slang – **put/send out to grass** to cause (sby) to enter usu enforced retirement

[2]**grass** *vt* **1** to feed (livestock) on grass **2** to cover or seed with grass – often + *down* ~*vi, Br* to inform the police; *esp* to betray sby to the police – slang

ˈ**grassˌhopper** /-ˌhopə‖-ˌhɒpə/ *n* any of numerous plant-eating insects with hind legs adapted for leaping

ˈ**grassland** /-lənd, -ˌland‖-lənd, -ˌlænd/ *n* **1** farmland used for grazing **2** land on which the natural dominant plant forms are grasses

ˌ**grass** ˈ**roots** *n pl but sing or pl in constr* **1** society at the local level as distinguished from the centres of political leadership **2** the fundamental level or source – **grass-roots** *adj*

ˌ**grass** ˈ**widow** *n* a woman whose husband is temporarily away from her

grassy /ˈgrahsi‖ˈgrɑːsɪ/ *adj* **1** consisting of or covered with grass **2** (having a smell) like grass

[1]**grate** /grayt‖greɪt/ *n* **1** a frame or bed of metal bars to hold the fuel in a fireplace, stove, or furnace **2** a fireplace

[2]**grate** *vt* **1** to reduce to small particles by rubbing on sthg rough **2a** to gnash or grind noisily **b** to cause to make a rasping sound ~ *vi* **1** to rub or rasp noisily **2** to cause irritation; jar <*his manner of talking* ~s *on my nerves*> – **grater** *n*

grateful /ˈgraytf(ə)l‖ˈgreɪtf(ə)l/ *adj* **1** feeling or expressing thanks **2** pleasing, comforting – **gratefully** *adv*, **gratefulness** *n*

graticule /ˈgratikyoohl‖ˈgrætɪkjuːl/ *n* **1** a network or scale visible when using a telescope, microscope, etc and used in locating or measuring objects **2** the network of latitude and longitude lines on which a map is drawn

gratification /ˌgratifiˈkaysh(ə)n‖ˌgrætɪfɪˈkeɪʃ(ə)n/ *n* **1** gratifying or being gratified **2** a source of satisfaction or pleasure

gratify /ˈgratiˌfie‖ˈgrætɪˌfaɪ/ *vt* **1** to be a source of or give pleasure or satisfaction to **2** to give in to; satisfy < ~ *a whim*> – **gratifyingly** *adv*

grating /ˈgrayting‖ˈgreɪtɪŋ/ *n* **1** a partition, covering, or frame of parallel bars or crossbars **2** a lattice used to close or floor any of various openings **3** a set of close parallel lines or bars ruled on a polished surface to produce (optical) spectra by diffraction

gratis /ˈgratis, ˈgrah-, ˈgray-‖ˈgrætɪs, ˈgrɑː-, ˈgreɪ-/ *adv or adj* without charge or recompense; free

gratitude /ˈgratiˌtyoohd‖ˈgrætɪˌtjuːd/ *n* the state or feeling of being grateful; thankfulness

gratuitous /grəˈtyooh·itəs‖grəˈtjuːɪtəs/ *adj* **1a** costing nothing; free **b** not involving a return benefit or compensation **2** not called for by the circumstances; unwarranted – **gratuitously** *adv*, **gratuitousness** *n*

gratuity /grəˈtyooh·əti‖grəˈtjuːətɪ/ *n* sthg given voluntarily, usu in return for or in anticipation of some service; *esp* a tip

[1]**grave** /grayv‖greɪv/ *vt* **graven, graved** to engrave

[2]**grave** *n* an excavation for burial of a body; *broadly* a tomb

[3]**grave** *vt* to clean and then tar (e g a ship's bottom)

[4]**grave** /grayv‖greɪv/ *adj* **1a** requiring serious consideration; important < ~ *problems*> **b** likely to produce great harm or danger <*a* ~ *mistake*> **2** serious, dignified **3** drab in colour; sombre **4** *of a sound* low in pitch – **gravely** *adv*, **graveness** *n*

[5]**grave** /grahv‖grɑːv/ *adj or n* (being or marked with) an accent ˋ used to show that a vowel is pronounced with a fall of pitch (e g in ancient Greek) or has a certain quality (e g *è* in French)

[1]**gravel** /ˈgravl‖ˈgrævl/ *n* **1** (a stratum or surface of) loose rounded fragments of rock mixed with sand **2** a sandy deposit of small stones in the kidneys and urinary bladder

[2]**gravel** *adj* GRAVELLY 2

[3]**gravel** *vt* **-ll-** (*NAm* **-l-**, **-ll-**) **1** to cover or spread with gravel **2** to perplex, confound

gravelly /ˈgravl·i‖ˈgrævlɪ/ *adj* **1** of, containing, or covered with gravel **2** harsh, grating <*a* ~ *voice*>

ˈ**graveˌstone** /-ˌstohn‖-ˌstəʊn/ *n* a stone over or at one end of a grave, usu inscribed with the name and details of the dead person

ˈ**graveˌyard** /-ˌyahd‖-ˌjɑːd/ *n* **1** a cemetery **2** a condition of final disappointment or failure <*the* ~ *of their hopes*>

graving dock /ˈgrayving‖ˈgreɪvɪŋ/ *n* DRY DOCK

gravitate /ˈgravitayt‖ˈgrævɪteɪt/ *vb* to (cause to) move under the influence of gravitation – **gravitate towards** to move or be compulsively drawn towards

gravitation /ˌgraviˈtaysh(ə)n‖ˌgrævɪˈteɪʃ(ə)n/ *n* (movement resulting from) the natural force of mutual attraction between bodies or particles – **gravitational** *adj*, **gravitationally** *adv*, **gravitative** *adj*

gravity /ˈgravəti‖ˈgrævətɪ/ *n* **1a** dignity or sobriety of bearing **b** significance; *esp* seriousness **2** (the quality of having) weight **3** (the attraction of a celestial body for bodies at or near its surface resulting from) gravitation – **gravity** *adj*

gravy /ˈgrayvi‖ˈgreɪvɪ/ *n* the (thickened and seasoned) fat and juices from cooked meat used as a sauce

gray /gray‖greɪ/ *vb, n, or adj, chiefly NAm* (to) grey

[1]**graze** /grayz‖greɪz/ *vi* to feed on growing herbage ~ *vt* **1a** to crop and eat (growing herbage) **b** to feed on the herbage of (e g a pasture) **2** to put to graze < ~d *the cows on the meadow*> – **grazable** *adj*, **grazer** *n*

[2]**graze** *vt* **1** to touch lightly in passing **2** to abrade, scratch < ~d *her elbow*> ~ *vi* to touch or rub against sthg in passing <*our bumpers just* ~d>

[3]**graze** *n* (an abrasion, esp of the skin, made by) a scraping along a surface

[1]**grease** /grees‖griːs/ *n* **1a** melted down animal fat **b** oily matter **c** a thick lubricant **2** oily wool as it comes from the sheep **greaseproof** *adj* – **in the grease** *of wool or fur* in the natural uncleaned condition

[2]**grease** *vt* **1** to smear, lubricate, or soil with grease **2** to hasten or ease the process or progress of – **greaser** *n* – **grease the palm of** to bribe

ˈ**greaseˌpaint** /-ˌpaynt‖-ˌpeɪnt/ *n* theatrical make-up

greasy /ˈgreesi‖ˈgriːsɪ/ *adj* **1a** smeared or soiled with grease **b** oily in appearance, texture, or manner <*his* ~ *smile* – Jack London> **c** slippery **2** containing an unusual amount of grease < ~ *food*> – **greasily** *adv*, **greasiness** *n*

[1]**great** /grayt‖greɪt/ *adj* **1a** notably large in size or number **b** of a relatively large kind – in plant and animal names **c** elaborate, ample < ~ *detail*> **2a** extreme in amount, degree, or effectiveness < ~ *bloodshed*> **b** of importance; significant <*a* ~ *day in European history*> **3** full of emotion < ~ *with anger*> **4a** eminent, distinguished <*a* ~ *poet*> **b** aristocratic, grand < ~ *ladies*> **5** main, principal <*a reception in the* ~ *hall*> **6** removed in a family relationship by at least 3 stages directly or 2 stages indirectly – chiefly in combination <*great-grandfather*> **7** markedly superior in character or quality; *esp* noble **8a** remarkably skilled **b** enthusiastic, keen <*she was a* ~ *film-goer*> **9** *archaic* pregnant < ~ *with child*> **10** – used as a generalized term of approval <*had a* ~ *time*>; infml –

great *adv*, **greatly** *adv*, **greatness** *n* – **no great shakes** not very good, skilful, effective, etc

[2]**great** *n, pl* **great, greats** one who is great – usu pl <*the* ~s *of the stage*>

ˌ**Great** ˈ**Bear** *n* URSA MAJOR

great circle *n* a circle formed on the surface of a sphere, specif the earth, by the intersection of a plane that passes through the centre of the sphere

ˈ**great**ˌ**coat** /-ˌkoht‖-ˌkəʊt/ *n* a heavy overcoat

ˌ**Great** ˈ**Dane** /dayn‖deɪn/ *n* any of a breed of massive powerful smooth-coated dogs

greater /ˈgraytə‖ˈgreɪtə/ *adj, often cap* consisting of a central city together with adjacent areas that are geographically or administratively connected with it <Greater *London*>

grebe /greeb‖gri:b/ *n* any of a family of swimming and diving birds closely related to the loons but having lobed instead of webbed toes

Grecian /ˈgreesh(ə)n‖ˈgri:ʃ(ə)n/ *adj* Greek – **Grecian** *n*, **grecianize** *vt, often cap*

Greco- /greekoh-, grekoh-‖gri:kəʊ-, grekəʊ-/ *comb form, chiefly NAm* Graeco-

greed /greed‖gri:d/ *n* **1** excessive acquisitiveness; avarice **2** excessive desire for or consumption of food

greedy /ˈgreedi‖ˈgri:dɪ/ *adj* **1** having a usu excessive desire for sthg, esp food or money **2** having a great need *for* <*plants* ~ *for water*> – **greedily** *adv*, **greediness** *n*

ˈ**greedy-**ˌ**guts** *n, pl* **greedy-guts** *chiefly Br* one who eats too much; a glutton – infml

[1]**Greek** /greek‖gri:k/ *n* **1** a native or inhabitant of Greece **2** the Indo-European language used by the Greeks **3** *not cap* sthg unintelligible <*it's all* ~ *to me*> – infml

[2]**Greek** *adj* **1** of Greece, the Greeks, or Greek **2 Greek, Greek Orthodox 2a** ORTHODOX 2a **b** of an Eastern church, esp the established Orthodox church of Greece using the Byzantine rite in Greek

[1]**green** /green‖gri:n/ *adj* **1** of the colour green **2a** covered by green growth or foliage <~ *fields*> **b** consisting of green (edible) plants <*a* ~ *salad*> **3a** youthful, vigorous **b** not ripened or matured; immature <~ *apples*> **c** fresh, new **4** appearing pale, sickly, or nauseated **5** affected by intense envy or jealousy **6a** not aged <*a* ~ *ham*> **b** not dressed or tanned <~ *hides*> **c** *of wood* freshly sawn; unseasoned **7a** deficient in training, knowledge, or experience **b** lacking sophistication; naive **8** being an exchange unit that has a differential rate of exchange in relation to the specified currency and is used for paying agricultural producers in the European economic community <*the* ~ *pound*> **9** environmentalist – **greenly** *adv*, **greenness** *n*

[2]**green** *vi* to become green

[3]**green** *n* **1** a colour whose hue resembles that of growing fresh grass or the emerald and lies between blue and yellow in the spectrum **2** sthg of a green colour **3** *pl* green leafy vegetables (e g spinach and cabbage) the leaves and stems of which are often cooked **4a** a common or park in the centre of a town or village **b** a smooth area of grass for a special purpose (e g bowling or putting) **5** an environmentalist – **greeny** *adj*

ˈ**green**ˌ**back** /-ˌbak‖-ˌbæk/ *n, NAm* a legal-tender note issued by the US government – infml

green belt *n* a belt of parks, farmland, etc encircling an urban area and usu subject to restrictions on new building

greenery /ˈgreenəri‖ˈgri:nərɪ/ *n* green foliage or plants

ˌ**green** ˈ**fingers** *n pl* an unusual ability to make plants grow – **green-fingered** *adj*

ˈ**green**ˌ**fly** /-ˌflie‖-ˌflaɪ/ *n Br* (an infestation by) any of various green aphids that are destructive to plants

ˈ**green**ˌ**gage** /-ˌgayj‖-ˌgeɪdʒ/ *n* any of several small rounded greenish cultivated plums [*green* + Sir William *Gage* (*fl* 1725), English botanist]

ˈ**green**ˌ**grocer** /-ˌgrohsə‖-ˌgrəʊsə/ *n, chiefly Br* a retailer of fresh vegetables and fruit – **greengrocery** *n*

ˈ**green**ˌ**horn** /-ˌhawn‖-ˌhɔ:n/ *n* **1** an inexperienced or unsophisticated (easily cheated) person **2** *chiefly NAm* a newcomer (e g to a country) unacquainted with local manners and customs

ˈ**green**ˌ**house** /-ˌhows‖-ˌhaʊs/ *n* a glassed enclosure for the cultivation or protection of tender plants

ˈ**greenhouse ef**ˌ**fect** *n* the gradual warming of the air near the Earth's surface caused by carbon dioxide which accumulates in the upper atmosphere and keeps in the heat

greenish /ˈgreenish‖ˈgri:nɪʃ/ *adj* rather green – **greenishness** *n*

green light *n* authority or permission to undertake a project

green pepper *n* SWEET PEPPER

ˈ**greenroom** /-room, -ˌroohm‖-rʊm, -ˌru:m/ *n* a room in a theatre or concert hall where performers can relax when not on stage

ˌ**green** ˈ**tea** *n* tea that is light in colour from incomplete fermentation of the leaf before firing

Greenwich Mean Time /ˈgrenich, ˈgrinij, -nich‖ˈgrenɪtʃ, ˈgrɪnɪdʒ, -nɪtʃ/ *n* the mean solar time of the meridian of Greenwich used as the primary point of reference for standard time throughout the world

ˈ**green**ˌ**wood** /-ˌwood‖-ˌwʊd/ *n* a forest green with foliage

[1]**greet** /greet‖gri:t/ *vt* **1** to welcome with gestures or words **2** to meet or react to in a specified manner <*the candidate was* ~ed *with catcalls*> **3** to be perceived by <*a surprising sight* ~ed *her eyes*> – **greeter** *n*

[2]**greet** *vi* **grat** /grat‖græt/; **grutten** /ˈgrutn‖ˈgrʌtn/ *Scot* to weep, lament

greeting /ˈgreeting‖ˈgri:tɪŋ/ *n* **1** a salutation at meeting **2** an expression of good wishes; regards – usu pl with sing. meaning

gregarious /griˈgeəri·əs‖grɪˈgeərɪəs/ *adj* **1a** tending to associate with others of the same kind <*a* ~ *gull*> **b** marked by or indicating a liking for companionship; sociable **c** of a crowd, flock, or other group of people, animals, etc **2** *of a plant* growing in a cluster or a colony [Latin *gregarius* of a flock or herd, fr *greg-*, *grex* flock, herd] – **gregariously** *adv*, **gregariousness** *n*

Gregorian calendar /gri'gawri·ən‖grɪ'gɔːrɪən/ *n* a revision of the Julian Calendar now in general use, that was introduced in 1582 by Pope Gregory XIII and adopted in Britain and the American colonies in 1752 and that restricts leap years to every 4th year except for those centenary years not divisible by 400

Gregorian chant *n* a rhythmically free liturgical chant in unison practised in the Roman Catholic church

gremlin /'gremlin‖'gremlɪn/ *n* a mischievous creature said to cause malfunctioning of machinery or equipment

grenade /grə'nayd‖grə'neɪd/ *n* **1** a small missile that contains explosive, gas, incendiary chemicals, etc and is thrown by hand or launcher **2** a glass container of chemicals that bursts when thrown, releasing a fire extinguishing agent, tear gas, etc

grenadier /ˌgrenə'diə‖ˌgrenə'dɪə/ *n* a member of a regiment or corps formerly specially trained in the use of grenades

grenadine /ˌgrenə'deen, '---‖ˌgrenə'diːn, '---/ *n* a syrup flavoured with pomegranates and used in mixed drinks

grew /grooh‖gruː/ *past of* GROW

[1]**grey**, *NAm chiefly* **gray** /gray‖greɪ/ *adj* **1** of the colour grey **2a** dull in colour **b** having grey hair **3a** lacking cheer or brightness; dismal <*a ~ day*> **b** intermediate or unclear in position, condition, or character <*a ~ area*> **4** *of a textile* being in an unbleached undyed state as taken from the loom **5** *of a horse* having white hair but dark skin – **greyly** *adv*, **greyness** *n*

[2]**grey**, *NAm chiefly* **gray** *n* **1** any of a series of neutral colours ranging between black and white **2** sthg grey; *esp* grey clothes, paint, or horses

[3]**grey**, *NAm chiefly* **gray** *vb* to make or become grey

ˈgreyˌbeard /-ˌbiəd‖-ˌbɪəd/ *n* an old man

ˈgreyhound /-hownd‖-haʊnd/ *n* (any of) a tall slender smooth-coated breed of dogs characterized by swiftness and keen sight and used for coursing game and racing [Old English *grīghund*, fr *grīg-* (akin to Old Norse *grey* bitch) + *hund* hound]

grey matter *n* **1** brownish-grey nerve tissue, esp in the brain and spinal cord, containing nerve-cell bodies as well as nerve fibres **2** brains, intellect – infml

grid /grid‖grɪd/ *n* **1** a grating **2a** a network of conductors for distribution of electric power **b** (sthg resembling) a network of uniformly spaced horizontal and perpendicular lines for locating points on a map **3** the starting positions of vehicles on a racetrack **4** GRILL 1 – **gridded** *adj*

griddle /'gridl‖'grɪdl/ *n* a flat metal surface on which food is cooked by dry heat

ˈgridˌiron /-ˌie·ən‖-ˌaɪən/ *n* GRILL 1

grief /greef‖griːf/ *n* (a cause of) deep and poignant distress (e g due to bereavement) – **griefless** *adj*

grievance /'greev(ə)ns‖'griːv(ə)ns/ *n* **1** a cause of distress (e g unsatisfactory working conditions) felt to afford reason for complaint or resistance **2** the formal expression of a grievance; a complaint

grieve /greev‖griːv/ *vt* to cause to suffer grief ~*vi* to suffer from grief, esp over a bereavement – often + *for* [Old French *grever*, fr Latin *gravare* to burden, fr *gravis* heavy, grave] – **griever** *n*

grievous /'greevəs‖'griːvəs/ *adj* **1** causing or characterized by severe pain, suffering, or sorrow <*a ~ loss*> **2** serious, grave <*~ fault*> – **grievously** *adv*, **grievousness** *n*

griffin /'grifin‖'grɪfɪn/, **griffon, gryphon** /-fən‖-fən/ *n* a mythical animal with the head and wings of an eagle and the body and tail of a lion

[1]**grill** /gril‖grɪl/ *vt* **1** to cook on or under a grill by radiant heat **2a** to torture (as if) with great heat **b** to subject to intense and usu long periods of questioning – infml ~*vi* to become grilled – **griller** *n*

[2]**grill** *n* **1** a cooking utensil of parallel bars on which food is exposed to heat (e g from burning charcoal) **2** an article or dish of grilled food **3** **grill, grillroom** a usu informal restaurant or dining room, esp in a hotel **4** *Br* an apparatus on a cooker under which food is cooked or browned by radiant heat

grille, grill /gril‖grɪl/ *n* **1** a grating forming a barrier or screen; *specif* an ornamental metal one at the front end of a motor vehicle **2** an opening covered with a grille

grim /grim‖grɪm/ *adj* **-mm- 1** fierce or forbidding in disposition, action, or appearance **2** unflinching, unyielding <*~ determination*> **3** ghastly or sinister in character **4** unpleasant, nasty <*had a pretty ~ afternoon at the dentist's*> – infml – **grimly** *adv*, **grimness** *n*

grimace /'griməs, gri'mays‖'grɪməs, grɪ'meɪs/ *n* a distorted facial expression, usu of disgust, anger, or pain – **grimace** *vi*, **grimacer** *n* –

grime /griem‖graɪm/ *n* soot or dirt, esp when sticking to or embedded in a surface – **grime** *vt*, **grimy** *adj*, **griminess** *n*

grin /grin‖grɪn/ *vi* **-nn-** to smile so as to show the teeth – **grin** *n*, **grinner** *n*

[1]**grind** /griend‖graɪnd/ *vb* **ground** /grownd‖graʊnd/ *vt* **1** to reduce to powder or small fragments by crushing between hard surfaces **2** to wear down, polish, or sharpen by friction; whet <*~ an axe*> **3a** to rub, press, or twist harshly <ground *the cigarette out with a heel*> <ground *his fist into his opponent's stomach*> **b** to press together with a rotating motion <*~ the teeth*> **4** to operate or produce by turning a crank <*~ a hand organ*> ~ *vi* **1** to perform the operation of grinding **2** to become pulverized, polished, or sharpened by friction **3** to move with difficulty or friction, esp so as to make a grating noise <~ing *gears*> **4** to work monotonously; *esp* to study hard <*~ for an exam*> **5** to rotate the hips in an erotic manner – **grindingly** *adv* – **grind into** to instil (knowledge, facts, etc) into (sby) with great difficulty

[2]**grind** *n* **1** dreary monotonous labour or routine **2** the result of grinding; *esp* material obtained by grinding to a particular degree of fineness **3a** the act of rotating the hips in an erotic manner **b** *Br* an act of sexual intercourse – vulg **4** *chiefly NAm* a swot – infml

grind down *vt* to oppress, harass

grind out *vt* to produce in a mechanical way <grind out *best-sellers*> – derog

'**grind,stone** /-,stohn‖-,stəʊn/ *n* **1** MILLSTONE 1 **2** a flat circular stone that revolves on an axle and is used for grinding, shaping, etc

gringo /'gring·goh‖'grɪŋgəʊ/ *n, pl* **gringos** an (English-speaking) foreigner in Spain or Latin America

[1]**grip** /grip‖grɪp/ *vb* **-pp-** *vt* **1** to seize or hold firmly **2** to attract and hold the interest of <*a story that* ~s *the reader*> ~*vi* to take firm hold – **gripper** *n*, **grippingly** *adv*

[2]**grip** *n* **1a** a strong or tenacious grasp **b** manner or style of gripping **2a** control, mastery, power <*he kept a good* ~ *on his pupils*> **b** (power of) understanding or doing <*she has a good* ~ *of the situation*> **3** a part or device that grips <*a hair* ~> **4** a part by which sthg is grasped; *esp* a handle **5** one who handles scenery, properties, lighting, or camera equipment in a theatre or film or television studio **6** a travelling bag

[1]**gripe** /griep‖graɪp/ *vt* to cause intestinal gripes in ~ *vi* **1** to experience intestinal gripes **2** to complain persistently – infml – **griper** *n*

[2]**gripe** *n* **1** a stabbing spasmodic intestinal pain – usu pl **2** a grievance, complaint – infml

grippe /grip‖grɪp/ *n* influenza – **grippy** *adj*

grisly /'grizli‖'grɪzlɪ/ *adj* inspiring horror, intense fear, or disgust; forbidding – **grisliness** *n*

grist /grist‖grɪst/ *n* **1** (a batch of) grain for grinding **2** the product obtained from grinding grain – **grist to the mill** sthg that can be put to use or profit

gristle /'grisl‖'grɪsl/ *n* cartilage; *broadly* tough cartilaginous or fibrous matter, esp in cooked meat – **gristly** *adj*, **gristliness** *n*

[1]**grit** /grit‖grɪt/ *n* **1** a hard sharp granule (e g of sand or stone); *also* material composed of such granules **2** the structure or texture of a stone that adapts it to grinding **3** firmness of mind or spirit; unyielding courage – infml

[2]**grit** *vb* **-tt-** *vi* to give forth a grating sound ~ *vt* **1** to cover or spread with grit **2** to cause (esp one's teeth) to grind or grate

grits /grits‖grɪts/ *n pl but sing or pl in constr* grain, esp oats, husked and usu coarsely ground

grizzle /'grizl‖'grɪzl/ *vi Br* **1** *of a child* to cry quietly and fretfully **2** to complain in a self-pitying way – often + *about USE* infml

'**grizzled** *adj* sprinkled or streaked with grey <*a* ~ *beard*>

[1]'**grizzly** /-li‖-lɪ/ *adj* grizzled

[2]**grizzly**, **grizzly bear** *n* a very large typically brownish yellow bear that lives in the highlands of western N America

groan /grohn‖grəʊn/ *vi* **1** to utter a deep moan **2** to creak under strain ~*vt* to utter with groaning – **groan** *n*, **groaner** *n*

[1]**groat** /groht‖grəʊt/ *n* hulled grain (broken into fragments larger than grits) – usu pl with sing. meaning but sing. or pl in constr

[2]**groat** *n* a former British coin worth 4 old pence

grocer /'grohsə‖'grəʊsə/ *n* a dealer in (packaged or tinned) staple foodstuffs, household supplies, and usu fruit, vegetables, and dairy products [Middle French *grossier* wholesaler, fr *gros* coarse, wholesale, fr Latin *grossus* thick, coarse]

grocery /'grohs(ə)ri‖'grəʊs(ə)rɪ/ *n* **1** *pl* commodities sold by a grocer **2** a grocer's shop

grog /grog‖grɒg/ *n* alcoholic drink; *specif* spirits (e g rum) mixed with water [*Old Grog*, nickname of Edward Vernon (1684-1757), English admiral responsible for diluting the sailors' rum]

groggy /'grogi‖'grɒgɪ/ *adj* weak and dazed, esp owing to illness or tiredness – **groggily** *adv*, **grogginess** *n*

groin /groyn‖grɔɪn/ *n* **1a** the fold marking the join between the lower abdomen and the inner part of the thigh **b** the male genitals – euph **2** the line along which 2 intersecting vaults meet **3** *chiefly NAm* a groyne

[1]**groom** /groohm‖gru:m/ *n* **1** one who is in charge of the feeding, care, and stabling of horses **2** a bridegroom **3** *archaic* a manservant

[2]**groom** *vt* **1** to clean and care for (e g a horse) **2** to make neat or attractive <*an impeccably* ~ed *woman*> **3** to get into readiness for a specific objective; prepare <*was being* ~ed *as a Tory candidate*> ~*vi* to groom oneself – **groomer** *n*

[1]**groove** /groohv‖gru:v/ *n* **1a** a long narrow channel or depression **b** the continuous spiral track on a gramophone record whose irregularities correspond to the recorded sounds **2** a fixed routine; a rut **3** top form – infml <*a great talker when he is in the* ~> **4** an enjoyable or exciting experience – infml; no longer in vogue

[2]**groove** *vt* **1** to make a groove in **2** to excite pleasurably – infml; no longer in vogue ~ *vi* **1** to form a groove **2** to enjoy oneself intensely; *also* to get on well – infml; no longer in vogue – **groover** *n*

groovy /'groohvi‖'gru:vɪ/ *adj* fashionably attractive or exciting – infml; no longer in vogue

grope /grohp‖grəʊp/ *vi* **1** to feel about blindly or uncertainly *for* **2** to search blindly or uncertainly *for* or *after* <groping *for the right words*> ~ *vt* **1** to touch or fondle the body of (a person) for sexual pleasure **2** to find (e g one's way) by groping – **grope** *n*, **groper** *n*

[1]**gross** /grohs‖grəʊs/ *adj* **1** glaringly noticeable, usu because excessively bad or objectionable; flagrant <~ *error*> **2a** big, bulky; *esp* excessively fat **b** *of vegetation* dense, luxuriant **3** consisting of an overall total before deductions (e g for taxes) are made <~ *income*> **4** made up of material or perceptible elements; corporal <*the* ~er *part of human nature*> **5** coarse in nature or behaviour; *specif* crudely vulgar – **grossly** *adv*, **grossness** *n*

[2]**gross** *n* an overall total exclusive of deductions

[3]**gross** *vt* to earn or bring in (an overall total) exclusive of deductions – **grosser** *n*

[4]**gross** *n, pl* **gross** a group of 12 dozen things <*a* ~ *of pencils*>

[1]**grotesque** /groh'tesk‖grəʊ'tesk/ *n* **1** a style of decorative art in which incongruous or fantastic human and animal forms are interwoven with natural motifs (e g foliage) **2** sby grotesque **3** SANS SERIF [Middle French, fr Italian (*pittura*) *grottesca*, lit., cave painting]

[2]**grotesque** *adj* (having the characteristics) of the grotesque: e g **a** fanciful, bizarre **b** absurdly

incongruous **c** departing markedly from the natural, expected, or typical – **grotesquely** *adv*, **grotesqueness** *n*

grotto /ˈgrotoh‖ˈgrɒtəʊ/ *n, pl* **grottoes** *also* **grottos** **1** an esp picturesque cave **2** an excavation or structure made to resemble a natural cave [Italian, fr Latin *crypta* cavern, crypt - see CRYPT]

grotty /ˈgroti‖ˈgrɒtɪ/ *adj, Br* nasty, unpleasant – slang – **grottily** *adv*

grouch /growch‖graʊtʃ/ *n* **1** a bad-tempered complaint **2** a habitually irritable or complaining person; a grumbler – **grouch** *vi*, **grouchy** *adj*

[1]**ground** /grownd‖graʊnd/ *n* **1a** the bottom of a body of water **b** *pl* **b(1)** SEDIMENT 1 **b(2)** ground coffee beans after brewing **2** a basis for belief, action, or argument – often pl with sing. meaning <~s *for complaint*> **3a** a surrounding area; a background **b** (material that serves as) a substratum **4a** the surface of the earth **b** an area used for a particular purpose <*parade* ~> **c** *pl* the area round and belonging to a house or other building **d** an area to be won or defended (as if) in battle **e** an area of knowledge or special interest <*covered a lot of* ~ *in his lecture*> **5a** [3]SOIL 2b **b** *chiefly NAm* EARTH 8 – **off the ground** started and in progress <*the programme never got* off the ground> – **to ground** into hiding

[2]**ground** *vt* **1** to bring to or place on the ground **2a** to provide a reason or justification for **b** to instruct in fundamentals (e g of a subject) **3** to restrict (e g a pilot or aircraft) to the ground **4** *chiefly NAm* to earth ~*vi* to run aground

[3]**ground** *past of* GRIND

ˈ**groundˌbait** /-ˌbayt‖-ˌbeɪt/ *n* bait scattered on the water so as to attract fish

ˈ**ground ˌbass** /bays‖beɪs/ *n* a short bass passage continually repeated below constantly changing melody and harmony

ˌ**ground ˈfloor** *n* the floor of a house on a level with the ground

grounding /ˈgrownding‖ˈgraʊndɪŋ/ *n* fundamental training in a field of knowledge

ˈ**groundless** /-lis‖-lɪs/ *adj* having no foundation <~ *fears*> – **groundlessly** *adv*, **groundlessness** *n*

ˈ**groundˌnut** /-ˌnut‖-ˌnʌt/ *n* **1** (a N American leguminous plant with) an edible tuberous root **2** *chiefly Br* the peanut

ground plan *n* **1** a plan of the ground floor of a building **2** a first or basic plan

ground rent *n* the rent paid by a lessee for the use of land, esp for building

ground rule *n* a basic rule of procedure

groundsel /ˈgrown(d)zl, -sl‖ˈgraʊn(d)zl, -sl/ *n* a (plant related to a) European composite plant that is a common weed and has small yellow flower heads [Old English *grundeswelge*, fr *grund* ground + *swelgan* to swallow]

ˈ**groundˌsheet** /-ˌsheet‖-ˌʃiːt/ *n* a waterproof sheet placed on the ground (e g in a tent)

ˈ**groundsman** /-mən‖-mən/ *n* sby who tends a playing field, esp a cricket pitch

ˈ**groundˌstaff** /-ˌstahf‖-ˌstɑːf/ *n* the people who maintain a sports ground

ground swell *n* a sea swell caused by an often distant gale or ground tremor

ˈ**groundˌwork** /-ˌwuhk‖-ˌwɜːk/ *n* (work done to provide) a foundation or basis

[1]**group** /groohp‖gruːp/ *n* **1** two or more figures or objects forming a complete unit in a composition **2** *sing or pl in constr* **2a** a number of individuals or objects assembled together or having some unifying relationship **b** an operational and administrative unit belonging to a command of an air force **3a** an assemblage of atoms forming part of a molecule; a radical <*a methyl* ~> **b** all the (similar) chemical elements forming one of the vertical columns of the periodic table

[2]**group** *vt* **1** to combine in a group **2** to assign to a group; classify ~*vi* to form or belong to a group – **groupable** *adj*

group captain *n* an officer in the Royal Air Force ranking below air commodore

groupie /ˈgroohpi‖ˈgruːpɪ/ *n* an ardent (female) fan of a famous person, esp a rock star, who follows the object of admiration on tour

grouping /ˈgroohping‖ˈgruːpɪŋ/ *n* a set of individuals or objects combined in a group

group practice *n* a practice run by a group of associated medical general practitioners

group therapy *n* the treatment of several individuals (with similar psychological problems) simultaneously through group discussion and mutual aid

[1]**grouse** /grows‖graʊs/ *n, pl* **grouse** any of several (important game) birds with a plump body and strong feathered legs

[2]**grouse** *vi or n* (to) grumble – infml – **grouser** *n*

grove /grohv‖grəʊv/ *n* a small wood, group, or planting of trees

grovel /ˈgrovl‖ˈgrɒvl/ *vi* **-ll-** (*NAm* **-l-**, **-ll-**) **1** to lie or creep with the body prostrate in token of subservience or abasement **2** to abase or humble oneself – **groveller** *n*, **grovellingly** *adv*

grow /groh‖grəʊ/ *vb* **grew** /grooh‖gruː/; **grown** /grohn‖grəʊn/ *vi* **1a** to spring up and develop to maturity (in a specified place or situation) **b** to assume some relation (as if) through a process of natural growth <*2 tree trunks* grown *together*> **2a** to increase in size by addition of material (e g by assimilation into a living organism or by crystallization) **b** to increase, expand **3** to develop from a parent source <*the book* grew *out of a series of lectures*> **4** to become gradually <grew *pale*> ~ *vt* **1** to cause to grow; produce <~ *roses*> **2** DEVELOP 5 <~ *wings*> – **grower** *n*, **growingly** *adv* – **grow on** to have an increasing influence on; *esp* to become more pleasing to

ˈ**growing ˌpains** *n pl* **1** pains in the legs of growing children that have no known cause **2** the early problems attending a new project or development

[1]**growl** /growl‖graʊl/ *vi* **1a** to rumble **b** to utter a growl **2** to complain angrily

[2]**growl** *n* a deep guttural inarticulate sound

grown /grohn‖grəʊn/ *adj* **1** fully grown; mature <~ *men*> **2** overgrown or covered (*with*)

ˈ**grown-ˌup** *n or adj* (an) adult

growth /grohth‖grəʊθ/ *n* **1a** (a stage in the process of) growing **b** progressive development **c** an increase, expansion **2a** sthg that grows or has grown **b** a tumour or other abnormal growth of tissue **3** the result of growth; a product

grow up *vi* **1** *of a person* to develop towards or arrive at a mature state **2** to arise and develop <*the movement* grew up *in the 60s*>

groyne, *chiefly NAm* **groin** /groyn‖grɔɪn/ *n* a rigid structure built out from a shore, esp to check erosion of the beach

[1]**grub** /grub‖grʌb/ *vb* **-bb-** *vt* **1** to clear by digging up roots and stumps **2** to dig *up* or *out* (as if) by the roots ~ *vi* **1** to dig in the ground, esp for sthg that is difficult to find or extract **2** to search about; rummage – **grubber** *n*

[2]**grub** *n* **1** a soft thick wormlike larva of an insect **2** food – infml

grubby /ˈgrubi‖ˈgrʌbɪ/ *adj* dirty, grimy <~ *hands*> – **grubbily** *adv*, **grubbiness** *n*

ˈ**Grub ˌStreet** *n* the world or life-style of needy literary hacks [*Grub Street*, London, formerly inhabited by literary hacks]

[1]**grudge** /gruj‖grʌdʒ/ *vt* to be unwilling or reluctant to give or admit; begrudge <~d *the money to pay taxes*> – **grudger** *n*

[2]**grudge** *n* a feeling of deep-seated resentment or ill will

grudging /ˈgrujing‖ˈgrʌdʒɪŋ/ *adj* unwilling, reluctant – **grudgingly** *adv*

gruel /ˈgrooh·əl‖ˈgruːəl/ *n* a thin porridge

gruelling, *NAm chiefly* **grueling** /ˈgrooh·əling‖ˈgruːəlɪŋ/ *adj* trying or taxing to the point of causing exhaustion; punishing <*a* ~ *race*>

gruesome /ˈgroohs(ə)m‖ˈgruːs(ə)m/ *adj* inspiring horror or repulsion – **gruesomely** *adv*, **gruesomeness** *n*

gruff /gruf‖grʌf/ *adj* **1** brusque or stern in manner, speech, or aspect <*a* ~ *reply*> **2** deep and harsh <*a* ~ *voice*> – **gruffly** *adv*, **gruffness** *n*

grumble /ˈgrumbl‖ˈgrʌmbl/ *vi* **1** to mutter in discontent **2** to rumble ~*vt* to express in a moaning or discontented way – **grumble** *n*, **grumbler** *n*, **grumblingly** *adv*, **grumbly** *adj*

grumbling /ˈgrumbling‖ˈgrʌmblɪŋ/ *adj* causing intermittent pain or discomfort <*a* ~ *appendix*>

grumpy /ˈgrumpi‖ˈgrʌmpɪ/ *adj* moodily cross; surly – **grumpily** *adv*, **grumpiness** *n*

[1]**grunt** /grunt‖grʌnt/ *vb* to utter (with) a grunt – **grunter** *n*

[2]**grunt** *n* the deep short guttural sound of a pig; *also* a similar sound

Gruyère /ˈgrooh·yeə ‖ˈgruːjeə (*Fr* gryjɛːr)/ *n* a Swiss cheese with smaller holes and a slightly fuller flavour than Emmenthal

gryphon /ˈgrifən‖ˈgrɪfən/ *n* a griffin

ˈ**G-ˌstring** *n* a small piece of cloth, leather, etc covering the genitalia and held in place by thongs, elastic, etc that is passed round the hips and between the buttocks

guano /ˈgwahnoh‖ˈgwɑːnəʊ/ *n* (an artificial fertilizer similar to) a phosphate-rich substance consisting chiefly of the excrement of seabirds and used as a fertilizer

[1]**guarantee** /ˌgarənˈtee‖ˌgærənˈtiː/ *n* **1** one who guarantees **2** a written undertaking to answer for the payment of a debt or the performance of a duty of another in case of the other's default **3a** an agreement by which one person accepts responsibility for another's obligations, esp debts, in case of default **b** an assurance of the quality of or of the length of use to be expected from a product offered for sale, accompanied by a promise to replace it or pay the customer back **4** sthg given as security; a pledge

[2]**guarantee** *vt* **guaranteed; guaranteeing 1** to undertake to answer for the debt or default of **2a** to undertake to do or secure (sthg) <*she* ~d *delivery of the goods*> **b** to engage for the existence, permanence, or nature of **3** to give security to

guarantor /ˌgarənˈtaw‖ˌgærənˈtɔː/ *n* **1** one who guarantees **2** one who makes or gives a guarantee

guaranty /ˈgarənti‖ˈgærəntɪ/ *n* GUARANTEE 2

[1]**guard** /gahd‖gɑːd/ *n* **1** a defensive position in boxing, fencing, etc **2** the act or duty of protecting or defending **3** a person or a body of men on sentinel duty **4a** a person or group whose duty is to protect a place, people, etc **b** *pl* HOUSEHOLD TROOPS **5** a protective or safety device; *esp* a device on a machine for protecting against injury **6** *Br* the person in charge of a railway train

[2]**guard** *vt* **1** to protect from danger, esp by watchful attention; make secure <*policemen* ~ing *our cities*> **2** to watch over so as to prevent escape, entry, theft, etc; *also* to keep in check <~ *your tongue*> ~*vi* to watch by way of caution or defence; stand guard – **guarder** *n* – **guard against** to attempt to prevent (sthg) by taking precautions

guarded /ˈgahdid‖ˈgɑːdɪd/ *adj* marked by caution <*a* ~ *reply*> – **guardedly** *adv*, **guardedness** *n*

ˈ**guardˌhouse** /-ˌhows‖-ˌhaʊs/ *n* a building used by soldiers on guard duty or as a prison

guardian /ˈgahdi·ən, -dyən‖ˈgɑːdɪən, -djən/ *n* **1** one who or that which guards or protects **2** sby who has the care of the person or property of another; *specif* sby entrusted by law with the care of sby who is of unsound mind, not of age, etc – **guardianship** *n*

ˈ**guardˌrail** /-ˌrayl‖-ˌreɪl/ *n* a railing for guarding against danger or trespass

ˈ**guardroom** /-room, -ˌroohm‖-rʊm, -ˌruːm/ *n* a room serving as a guardhouse

ˈ**guardsman** /-mən‖-mən/ *n* a member of a military body called *guard* or *guards*

ˈ**guard's ˌvan** *n*, *Br* a railway wagon or carriage attached usu at the rear of a train for the use of the guard

guava /ˈgwahvə‖ˈgwɑːvə/ *n* (the sweet acid yellow edible fruit of) a shrubby tropical American tree

gubernatorial /ˌgyoohbənəˈtawri·əl‖ˌgjuːbənəˈtɔːrɪəl/ *adj* of a governor

[1]**gudgeon** /ˈguj(ə)n‖ˈgʌdʒ(ə)n/ *n* **1** a pivot or journal **2** a socket for a rudder pintle

[2]**gudgeon** *n* a small European freshwater fish used esp for food or bait

guelder rose /ˈgeldə‖ˈgeldə/ *n* a (cultivated) shrub of the honeysuckle family with clusters of white flowers

guerrilla, guerilla /gəˈrilə‖gəˈrɪlə/ *n* a member of a small independent fighting force which engages in sabotage, unexpected assaults, etc [Spanish *guerrilla*, fr diminutive of *guerra* war, of Germanic origin]

[1]**guess** /ges‖ges/ *vt* **1** to form an opinion of with little or no consideration of the facts **2** to arrive at a correct conclusion about by conjecture, chance, or intuition < ~ed *the answer*> **3** *chiefly NAm* to believe, suppose <*I* ~ *you're right*> – infml ~*vi* to make a guess – **guesser** *n*

[2]**guess** *n* a surmise, estimate

guesstimate /'gestimət‖'gestɪmət/ *n* an estimate made without adequate information – infml – **guesstimate** *vb*

'**guess,work** /-,wuhk‖-,wɜːk/ *n* (judgment based on) the act of guessing

[1]**guest** /gest‖gest/ *n* **1a** a person entertained in one's home **b** a person taken out, entertained, and paid for by another **c** a person who pays for the services of an establishment (e g a hotel) **2** one who is present by invitation <*a* ~ *star on a TV programme*>

[2]**guest** *vi* to appear as a guest

'**guest,house** /-,hows‖-,haʊs/ *n* a private house used to accommodate paying guests

guffaw /'gufaw, gə'faw‖'gʌfɔː, gə'fɔː/ *vi or n* (to utter) a loud or boisterous laugh

guidance /'gied(ə)ns‖'gaɪd(ə)ns/ *n* **1** help, advice **2** the process of controlling the course of a projectile by a built-in mechanism

[1]**guide** /gied‖gaɪd/ *n* **1a** one who leads or directs another **b** one who shows and explains places of interest to travellers, tourists, etc **c** sthg, esp a guidebook, that provides sby with information about a place, activity, etc **d** sthg or sby that directs a person in his/her conduct or course of life **2** a bar, rod, etc for steadying or directing the motion of sthg **3** *often cap, chiefly Br* a member of a worldwide movement of girls and young women comparable to the Scouts; *specif* a member of the intermediate section for girls aged from 10 to 15

[2]**guide** *vt* **1** to act as a guide to; direct in a way or course **2** to direct or supervise, usu to a particular end; *also* to supervise the training of ~*vi* to act or work as a guide; give guidance – **guider** *n*, **guidable** *adj*

'**guide,line** /-,lien‖-,laɪn/ *n* a line by which one is guided; *esp* an indication of policy or conduct

guild /gild‖gɪld/ *n sing or pl in constr* an association of people with similar interests or pursuits; *esp* a medieval association of merchants or craftsmen – **guildship** *n*

guilder /'gildə‖'gɪldə/ *n* a gulden

,**guild'hall** /-'hawl‖-'hɔːl/ *n* a hall where a guild or corporation usu assembles; *esp* TOWN HALL

guile /giel‖gaɪl/ *n* deceitful cunning; duplicity – **guileful** *adj*, **guilefully** *adv*, **guileless** *adj*, **guilelessly** *adv*

guillemot /'gili,mot‖'gɪlɪ,mɒt/ *n* any of several narrow-billed auks of northern seas

guillotine /'gilәteen‖'gɪlətiːn/ *n* **1** a machine for beheading consisting of a heavy blade that slides down between grooved posts **2** an instrument (e g a paper cutter) that works like a guillotine **3** limitation of the discussion of legislative business by the imposition of a time limit [Joseph *Guillotin* (1738-1814), French physician who advocated its adoption] – **guillotine** *vt*

guilt /gilt‖gɪlt/ *n* **1** the fact of having committed a breach of conduct, esp one that violates law **2a** responsibility for a criminal or other offence **b** feelings of being at fault or to blame, esp for imagined offences or from a sense of inadequacy

guilty /'gilti‖'gɪltɪ/ *adj* **1** justly answerable for an offence **2a** suggesting or involving guilt <*a* ~ *deed*> **b** feeling guilt <*their* ~ *consciences*> – **guiltily** *adv*, **guiltiness** *n*

guinea /'gini‖'gɪnɪ/ *n* **1** a former British gold coin worth 21 shillings **2** a money unit worth £1 and 5 new pence [*Guinea*, region of W Africa, supposed source of the gold from which it was made]

'**guinea ,fowl** /'gini‖'gɪnɪ/ *n* a W African bird with white-speckled slaty plumage that is related to the pheasants and is widely kept for food

'**guinea ,pig** *n* **1** a small stout-bodied short-eared nearly tailless rodent often kept as a pet **2** sby or sthg used as a subject of (scientific) research or experimentation

guise /giez‖gaɪz/ *n* **1** external appearance; aspect **2** assumed appearance; semblance – **in the guise of** masquerading as

guitar /gi'tah‖gɪ'tɑː/ *n* a flat-bodied stringed instrument with a long fretted neck, plucked with a plectrum or the fingers – **guitarist** *n*

gulch /gulch‖gʌltʃ/ *n, chiefly NAm* a ravine, esp with a torrent flowing through it

gulden /'goold(ə)n‖'gʊld(ə)n/ *n, pl* **guldens, gulden** the standard unit of money in the Netherlands

[1]**gulf** /gulf‖gʌlf/ *n* **1** a partially landlocked part of the sea, usu larger than a bay **2** a deep chasm; an abyss **3** an unbridgeable gap <*the* ~ *between theory and practice*>

[2]**gulf** *vt* to engulf

[1]**gull** /gul‖gʌl/ *n* any of numerous related long-winged web-footed largely white, grey, or black aquatic birds

[2]**gull** *vt* to trick, cheat, or deceive < ~ed *into a bad purchase*>

gullet /'gulit‖'gʌlɪt/ *n* the oesophagus; *broadly* the throat

gullible /'guləbl‖'gʌləbl/ *adj* easily deceived or cheated – **gullibility** *n*

[1]**gully** *also* **gulley** /'guli‖'gʌlɪ/ *n* **1** a trench worn in the earth by running water after rain **2** a deep gutter or drain **3** a fielding position in cricket close to the batsman on the off side and between point and the slips

[2]**gully** *vt* to make gullies in

gulp /gulp‖gʌlp/ *vt* to swallow hurriedly, greedily, or in 1 swallow – often + *down* ~*vi* to make a sudden swallowing movement as if surprised or nervous – **gulp** *n*, **gulper** *n*

[1]**gum** /gum‖gʌm/ *n* (the tissue that surrounds the teeth and covers) the parts of the jaws from which the teeth grow

[2]**gum** *n* **1a** any of numerous sugary plant substances that are gelatinous when moist but harden on drying **b** any of various substances (e g a mucilage or gum resin) that exude from plants **2** a substance or deposit resembling a plant gum (e g in adhesive quality) **3** *Austr* a eucalyptus – **gummy** *adj*

[3]**gum** *vb* **-mm-** *vt* to smear or stick (as if) with gum ~*vi* to exude or form gum – **gummer** *n*

[4]**gum** *n* God – esp in *by gum* as a mild oath

ˌ**gum ˈarabic** *n* a water-soluble gum obtained from several acacias and used esp in the manufacture of adhesives and in pharmacy

gumbo /ˈgumboh‖ˈgʌmbəʊ/ *n* **1** a (meat and vegetable) soup thickened with okra pods **2** *NAm* OKRA 1

gumboil /ˈgumˌboyl‖ˈgʌmˌbɔɪl/ *n* an abscess in the gum

ˈ**gumˌboot** /-ˌbooht‖-ˌbuːt/ *n* a strong waterproof rubber boot reaching usu to the knee

gumption /ˈgumpsh(ə)n‖ˈgʌmpʃ(ə)n/ *n* **1** shrewd practical common sense **2** initiative; *specif* boldness

gum up *vt* to prevent or impede the proper working or carrying out of – esp in *gum up the works*; infml

[1]**gun** /gun‖gʌn/ *n* **1a** a piece of ordnance, usu with a high muzzle velocity and a comparatively flat trajectory **b** a rifle, pistol, etc **c** a device that throws a projectile **2** a discharge of a gun **3a** sby who carries a gun in a shooting party **b** *NAm* one who is skilled with a gun; *esp* a gunman – **gunned** *adj*

[2]**gun** *vt* **-nn-** **1** to fire on **2** to shoot – often + *down* – **gun for** to search for in order to attack – infml

[1]ˈ**gunˌboat** /-ˌboht‖-ˌbəʊt/ *n* a relatively heavily armed ship of shallow draught

[2]**gunboat** *adj* of or employing the high-handed use of naval or military power < ~ *diplomacy*>

ˈ**gunˌcotton** /-ˌkot(ə)n‖-ˌkɒt(ə)n/ *n* (an explosive highly nitrated with) cellulose nitrate

ˈ**gunˌdog** /-ˌdog‖-ˌdɒg/ *n* a dog trained to locate or retrieve game for hunters

ˈ**gunˌfire** /-ˌfie·ə‖-ˌfaɪə/ *n* the (noise of) firing of guns

gunge /gunj‖gʌndʒ/ *n, Br* an unpleasant, dirty, or sticky substance – slang – **gungy** *adj*

ˈ**gunˌlock** /-ˌlok‖-ˌlɒk/ *n* the mechanism for igniting the charge of a firearm

ˈ**gunman** /-mən‖-mən/ *n* a man armed with a gun; *esp* a professional killer

ˈ**gunˌmetal** /-ˌmetl‖-ˌmetl/ *n* (a metal treated to imitate) a bronze formerly used for cannon – **gunmetal** *adj*

gunner /ˈgunə‖ˈgʌnə/ *n* **1** a soldier or airman who operates a gun; *specif* a private in the Royal Artillery **2** sby who hunts with a gun **3** a warrant officer who supervises naval ordnance and ordnance stores

gunnery /ˈgunəri‖ˈgʌnərɪ/ *n* the use of guns; *specif* the science of the flight of projectiles and of the effective use of guns

gunny /ˈguni‖ˈgʌnɪ/ *n* a coarse heavy material, usu of jute, used esp for sacking

gunpoint /ˈgunˌpoynt‖ˈgʌnˌpɔɪnt/ *n* – **at gunpoint** under threat of being shot

ˈ**gunˌpowder** /-ˌpowdə‖-ˌpaʊdə/ *n* an explosive mixture of potassium nitrate, charcoal, and sulphur used in gunnery and blasting

ˈ**gunˌrunner** /-ˌrunə‖-ˌrʌnə/ *n* one who carries or deals in contraband arms and ammunition – **gunrunning** *n*

ˈ**gunˌshot** /-ˌshot‖-ˌʃɒt/ *n* **1** a shot or projectile fired from a gun **2** the range of a gun <*out of* ~>

ˈ**gun-ˌshy** *adj, esp of a dog* afraid of the sound of a gun

ˈ**gunˌsmith** /-ˌsmith‖-ˌsmɪθ/ *n* sby who designs, makes, or repairs firearms

gunwale, gunnel /ˈgunl‖ˈgʌnl/ *n* the upper edge of a ship's or boat's side

guppy /ˈgupi‖ˈgʌpɪ/ *n* a small (aquarium) fish native to the W Indies and S America [R J L *Guppy* (died 1916), Trinidadian naturalist]

gurgle /ˈguhgl‖ˈgɜːgl/ *vi* to make the sound (as if) of unevenly flowing water; *also* to flow or move with such a sound ~*vt* to utter with a gurgling sound – **gurgle** *n*

guru /ˈgoohrooh, ˈgoo-‖ˈguːruː, ˈgʊ-/ *n, pl* **gurus** **1** a personal religious teacher and spiritual guide (e g in Hinduism) **2a** a spiritual and intellectual guide; a mentor **b** an acknowledged leader or chief proponent (e g of a cult or idea) – infml [Hindi *gurū*, fr Sanskrit *guru*, fr *guru*, heavy, venerable]

[1]**gush** /gush‖gʌʃ/ *vi* **1** to issue copiously or violently **2** to emit a sudden copious flow **3** to make an effusive often affected display of sentiment or enthusiasm <*women* ~ing *over the baby*> ~*vt* to emit in a copious free flow – **gushy** *adj*, **gushing** *adj*

[2]**gush** *n* **1** (sthg emitted in) a sudden outpouring **2** an effusive and usu affected display of sentiment or enthusiasm

gusher /ˈgushə‖ˈgʌʃə/ *n* an oil well with a copious natural flow

gusset /ˈgusit‖ˈgʌsɪt/ *n* **1** a piece of material inserted in a seam (e g the crotch of an undergarment) to provide expansion or reinforcement **2** a plate or bracket for strengthening an angle in framework – **gusset** *vt*

[1]**gust** /gust‖gʌst/ *n* **1** a sudden brief rush of (rain carried by the) wind **2** a sudden outburst; a surge <*a* ~ *of emotion*> – **gustily** *adv*, **gustiness** *n*, **gusty** *adj*

[2]**gust** *vi* to blow in gusts <*winds* ~ing *up to 40 mph*>

gustatory /ˈgustət(ə)ri‖ˈgʌstət(ə)rɪ/, **gustative** /-tiv‖-tɪv/ *adj* of, associated with, or being the sense of taste – **gustation** *n*

gusto /ˈgustoh‖ˈgʌstəʊ/ *n* enthusiastic and vigorous enjoyment or vitality [Spanish, fr Latin *gustus* taste, liking]

[1]**gut** /gut‖gʌt/ *n* **1a** the basic emotionally or instinctively responding part of a person **b** (a part of) the alimentary canal **c** the belly or abdomen **d** catgut **2** *pl* the inner essential parts <*the* ~s *of a car*> – infml **3** *pl* courage, determination – infml

[2]**gut** *vt* **-tt-** **1** to eviscerate, disembowel **2a** to destroy the inside of <*fire* ~ted *the building*> **b** to destroy the essential power or effectiveness of <*inflation* ~ting *the economy of a country*> **3** to extract the essentials of < ~ *a novel*>

ˈ**gutless** /-lis‖-lɪs/ *adj* lacking courage; cowardly – infml – **gutlessness** *n*

ˈ**gutsy** /-si‖-sɪ/ *adj* **1** courageous **2** expressing or appealing strongly to the physical passions; lusty *USE* infml – **gutsiness** *n*

gutta-percha /ˌgutə ˈpuhchə‖ˌgʌtə ˈpɜːtʃə/ *n* a tough plastic substance obtained from the latex of several Malaysian trees and used esp for electrical insulation

[1]**gutter** /ˈgutə‖ˈgʌtə/ *n* **1** a trough just below the eaves or at the side of a street to catch and carry off rainwater, surface water, etc **2** a white space between 2 pages of a book, 2 postage stamps on a sheet, etc **3** *the* lowest or most vulgar level or condition of human life

[2]**gutter** *vt* to cut or wear gutters in ~ *vi* **1** to flow in rivulets **2a** *of a candle* to burn unevenly so that melted wax runs down one side **b** *of a flame* to burn fitfully or feebly; be on the point of going out

[3]**gutter** *adj* (characteristic) of the gutter; *esp* marked by extreme vulgarity or cheapness <*the ~ press*>

ˈ**gutter,snipe** /-ˌsniep‖-ˌsnaɪp/ *n* a deprived child living in poverty and usu dressed in ragged clothes

guttural /ˈgut(ə)rəl‖ˈgʌt(ə)rəl/ *adj* **1** of the throat **2** formed or pronounced in the throat – **gutturally** *adv*, **gutturalize** *vt*, **gutturalization** *n*

guv /guv‖gʌv/ *n, Br* GOVERNOR 3 – slang

guvnor /ˈguvnə‖ˈgʌvnə/ *n, Br* GOVERNOR 3 – slang

[1]**guy** /gie‖gaɪ/ *vt or n* (to steady or reinforce with) a rope, chain, rod, etc attached to sthg as a brace or guide

[2]**guy** *n* **1** *often cap* a humorous effigy of a man burnt in Britain on Guy Fawkes Night **2** a man, fellow – infml [*Guy* Fawkes (1570-1606), English conspirator]

[3]**guy** *vt* to make fun of; ridicule

ˈ**Guy ˌFawkes ˌNight** /ˌgie ˈfawks‖ˌgaɪ ˈfɔːks/ *n* November 5 observed in Britain with fireworks and bonfires in commemoration of the arrest of Guy Fawkes in 1605 for attempting to blow up the Houses of Parliament

guzzle /ˈguzl‖ˈgʌzl/ *vb* to consume (sthg) greedily, continually, or habitually – **guzzler** *n*

gym /jim‖dʒɪm/ *n* **1** a gymnasium **2** development of the body by games, exercises, etc, esp in school

gymkhana /jimˈkahnə‖dʒɪmˈkɑːnə/ *n* a sporting event featuring competitions and displays; *specif* a meeting involving competition in horse riding and carriage driving [prob fr Hindi *gend-khāna* racket court]

gymnasium /jimˈnayzi·əm, -zyəm‖dʒɪmˈneɪzɪəm, -zjəm/ *n, pl* **gymnasiums, gymnasia** /-zi·ə‖-zɪə/ **1** a large room or separate building used for indoor sports and gymnastic activities **2** a German or Scandinavian secondary school that prepares pupils for university [Latin, exercise ground, school, fr Greek *gymnasion*, fr *gymnazein* to exercise naked, fr *gymnos* naked]

gymnast /ˈjimnast‖ˈdʒɪmnæst/ *n* sby trained in gymnastics – **gymnastic** *adj*

gymnastics /jimˈnastiks‖dʒɪmˈnæstɪks/ *n pl but sing or pl in constr* **1** physical exercises developing or displaying bodily strength and coordination, often performed in competition **2** an exercise in intellectual or physical dexterity

gymnosperm /ˈjimnoh,spuhm‖ˈdʒɪmnəʊˌspɜːm/ *n* any of a class of woody vascular seed plants (e g conifers) that produce naked seeds not enclosed in an ovary – **gymnospermy** *n*, **gymnospermous** *adj*

[1]**gymslip** /ˈjim,slip‖ˈdʒɪm,slɪp/ *n, chiefly Br* a girl's tunic or pinafore dress that is worn usu with a belt as part of a school uniform

[2]**gymslip** *adj, chiefly Br* of a schoolgirl or a girl of school age <*a ~ pregnancy*> – infml

gyn-, **gyno-** *comb form* **1** woman <gyno*cracy*> **2** female reproductive organ; ovary <gyno*phore*>; pistil <gyno*ecium*>

gynaecology /ˌgienəˈkoləji, ˌjie-‖ˌgaɪnəˈkɒlədʒɪ, ˌdʒaɪ-/ *n* a branch of medicine that deals with diseases and disorders (of the reproductive system) of women [deriv of Greek *gynaik-, gynē* woman + *logos* word] – **gynaecologist** *n*, **gynaecologic, gynaecological** *adj*

[1]**gyp** /jip‖dʒɪp/ *n* **1** *Br* a college servant at Cambridge university **2** *NAm* **2a** a cheat, swindler **b** a fraud, swindle *USE* (*2*) infml

[2]**gyp** *vb* **-pp-** *NAm* to cheat – infml

[3]**gyp** *n* sharp pain – chiefly in *give one gyp*; infml

gypsum /ˈjipsəm‖ˈdʒɪpsəm/ *n* hydrated calcium sulphate occurring as a mineral and used esp in plaster of paris – **gypseous** *adj*, **gypsiferous** *adj*

gypsy /ˈjipsi‖ˈdʒɪpsɪ/ *n, chiefly NAm* a gipsy

gyr-, **gyro-** *comb form* **1** ring; circle; spiral; rotation <gyro*magnetic*> **2** gyroscope <gyro*compass*>

gyrate /jieˈrayt‖dʒaɪˈreɪt/ *vb* **1** to revolve round a point or axis **2** to (cause to) move with a circular or spiral motion – **gyrator** *n*, **gyration** *n*, **gyrational** *adj*, **gyratory** *adj*

gyroscope /ˈjie·rə,skohp‖ˈdʒaɪrəˌskəʊp/ *n* a wheel that is mounted to spin rapidly about an axis and is free to turn in various directions but that maintains constant orientation while spinning in the absence of applied forces – **gyroscopic** *adj*, **gyroscopically** *adv*

h /aych‖eɪtʃ/ *n, pl* **h's, hs** *often cap* (a graphic representation of or device for reproducing) the 8th letter of the English alphabet

ha /hah‖hɑː/ *interj* – used esp to express surprise, joy, triumph, etc

habeas corpus /ˌhaybi·əs ˈkawpəs, -byəs‖ˌheɪbɪəs ˈkɔːpəs, -bjəs/ *n* a judicial writ requiring a detained person to be brought before a court so that the legality of his/her detention may be examined [Medieval Latin, lit., you should have the body (the opening words of the writ)]

haberdasher /ˈhabə,dashə‖ˈhæbəˌdæʃə/ *n* **1** *Br* a dealer in buttons, thread, ribbon, etc used in making clothes **2** *NAm* a dealer in shirts, ties, and other minor articles of menswear

ˈ**haber,dashery** /-ri‖-rɪ/ *n* **1** goods sold by a haberdasher **2** a haberdasher's shop

habiliment /həˈbilimənt‖həˈbɪlɪmənt/ *n* an article of clothing (characteristic of an occupation or occasion) – usu pl; fml

[1]**habit** /ˈhabit‖ˈhæbɪt/ *n* **1** a costume characteristic of a calling, rank, or function <*monk's ~*> **2** bodily or mental make-up <*a cheerful ~ of mind*> **3a** a settled tendency or usual manner of behaviour **b** an acquired pattern or mode

of behaviour **4** addiction <*a drug* ~> **5** characteristic mode of growth, occurrence, or appearance (e g of a plant or crystal) [Old French, fr Latin *habitus* condition, character, fr *habit-*, *habēre* to have, hold]

[2]**habit** *vt* to clothe, dress – fml

habitable /ˈhabitəbl‖ˈhæbɪtəbl/ *adj* capable of being lived in – **habitableness** *n*, **habitably** *adv*, **habitability** *n*

habitat /ˈhabitat‖ˈhæbɪtæt/ *n* **1** the (type of) place where a plant or animal naturally grows or lives **2** HABITATION 2

habitation /ˌhabiˈtaysh(ə)n‖ˌhæbɪˈteɪʃ(ə)n/ *n* **1** the act of inhabiting; occupancy **2** a dwelling place; a residence, home

habit-forming /ˈhabitˌfawming‖ˈhæbɪtˌfɔːmɪŋ/ *adj* tending to create an addiction

habitual /həˈbityooəl, -chooəl‖həˈbɪtjʊəl, -tʃʊəl/ *adj* **1** having the nature of a habit **2** by force of habit <~ *drunkard*> **3** in accordance with habit; customary – **habitually** *adv*, **habitualness** *n*

habituate /həˈbityooayt, -choo-‖həˈbɪtjʊeɪt, -tʃʊ-/ *vb* to make or become accustomed *to* – **habituation** *n*

habitué /həˈbityooˌay, -chooˌay‖həˈbɪtjʊˌeɪ, -tʃʊˌeɪ/ *n* one who frequents a specified place

hacienda /ˌhasiˈendə‖ˌhæsɪˈendə/ *n* (the main house of) a large estate or plantation, esp in a Spanish-speaking country

[1]**hack** /hak‖hæk/ *vt* **1a** to cut (as if) with repeated irregular or unskilful blows **b** to sever with repeated blows **2** to clear by cutting away vegetation <~ *a path*> **3** to kick (an opposing player or the ball in football) **1** to make cutting blows or rough cuts **2** to cough in a short dry manner – **hacker** *n*

[2]**hack** *n* **1** a mattock, pick, etc **2** (a wound from) a kick in football **3** a hacking blow

[3]**hack** *n* **1a** a riding horse let out for hire **b** [1]JADE 1 **c** a light easy saddle horse **2** an act of hacking; a ride **3** one who produces mediocre work for financial gain; *esp* a commercial writer **4** *NAm* a taxi

[4]**hack** *adj* **1** performed by, suited to, or characteristic of a hack <~ *writing*> **2** hackneyed, trite

[5]**hack** *vb* to ride (a horse) at an ordinary pace, esp over roads – **hacker** *n*

hacker /ˈhakə‖ˈhækə/ *n* **1** sby who studies and programs computers purely as a hobby **2** sby who gains unauthorized access to computer systems through a telephone connection

hackle /ˈhakl‖ˈhækl/ *n* **1** a steel comb with long teeth for dressing flax or hemp **2a** any of the long narrow feathers on the neck of a domestic cock or other bird **b** *pl* the erectile hairs along the neck and back of esp a dog **3** an artificial fishing fly made from a cock's hackles

[1]**hackney** /ˈhakni‖ˈhæknɪ/ *n* any of an English breed of rather compact English horses with a conspicuously high leg action

[2]**hackney** *adj* kept for public hire <*a* ~ *cab*>

hackneyed /ˈhaknid‖ˈhæknɪd/ *adj* lacking in freshness or originality; meaningless because used or done too often

hacksaw /ˈhakˌsaw‖ˈhækˌsɔː/ *n* a fine-toothed saw, esp for cutting metal – **hacksaw** *vt*

had /d, əd, həd‖d, əd, həd; *strong* had‖hæd/ *past of* HAVE

haddock /ˈhadək‖ˈhædək/ *n*, an important Atlantic food fish, usu smaller than the related common cod

Hades /ˈhaydeez‖ˈheɪdiːz/ *n* **1** the underground abode of the dead in Greek mythology **2** *often not cap* hell – euph

hadn't /ˈhadnt‖ˈhædnt/ had not

haem, *chiefly NAm* **heme** /heem‖hiːm/ *n* a deep red iron-containing compound that occurs esp as the oxygen-carrying part of haemoglobin

haem-, **haema-**, **haemo-**, *NAm* **hem-**, **hema-**, **hemo-** *comb form* blood <haemo*philia*>

haemoglobin /ˌheemohˈglohbin‖ˌhiːməʊˈgləʊbɪn/ *n* an iron-containing protein that occurs in the red blood cells of vertebrates and carries oxygen from the lungs to the body tissues

haemophilia /ˌheemohˈfili·ə, -mə-‖ˌhiːməʊˈfɪlɪə, -mə-/ *n* delayed clotting of the blood with consequent difficulty in controlling bleeding even after minor injuries, occurring as a hereditary defect, usu in males – **haemophilic** *adj*

ˌhaemoˈphiliac /-liak‖-lɪæk/ *n or adj* (sby) suffering from haemophilia

haemorrhage /ˈhemərij‖ˈhemərɪdʒ/ *n* a (copious) loss of blood from the blood vessels [Latin *haemorrhagia*, fr Greek *haimorrhagia*, fr *haima* blood + *-rrhagia* discharge, fr *rhēgnynai* to break, burst] – **haemorrhage** *vi*, **haemorrhagic** *adj*

haemorrhoid /ˈhemərody‖ˈhemərɔɪd/ *n* a mass of dilated veins in swollen tissue round or near the anus – usu pl with sing. meaning – **haemorrhoidal** *adj*

haft /hahft‖hɑːft/ *n* the handle of a weapon or tool

hag /hag‖hæg/ *n* **1** a witch **2** an ugly and usu ill-natured old woman – **haggish** *adj*

[1]**haggard** /ˈhagəd‖ˈhægəd/ *adj* **1** *of a hawk* not tamed **2** having a worn or emaciated appearance, esp through anxiety or lack of sleep – **haggardly** *adv*, **haggardness** *n*

[2]**haggard** *n* an adult hawk caught wild

haggis /ˈhagis‖ˈhægɪs/ *n* a traditionally Scottish dish made of the heart, liver, and lungs of a sheep, calf, etc minced with suet, oatmeal, and seasonings and traditionally boiled in the stomach of the animal

haggle /ˈhagl‖ˈhægl/ *vi* to bargain, wrangle – **haggler** *n*

hagiography /ˌhagiˈogrəfi‖ˌhægɪˈɒgrəfɪ/ *n* **1** biography of saints or venerated people **2** idealizing or idolizing biography [deriv of Greek *hagios* saint + *graphein* to write] – **hagiographer** *n*, **hagiographic** *adj*, **hagiographical** *adj*,

[1]**ha-ha** /hah ˈhah‖hɑː ˈhɑː/ *interj* – used to express or represent laughter or derision

[2]**ha-ha** /ˈhah ˌhah‖ˈhɑː ˌhɑː/ *n* a fence or retaining wall sunk into a ditch and used as a boundary (e g of a park or grounds) so as to give an uninterrupted view

haiku /ˈhieˌkooh‖ˈhaɪˌkuː/ *n*, *pl* **haiku** (a poem in) an unrhymed Japanese verse form of 3 lines containing 5, 7, and 5 syllables respectively

[1]**hail** /hayl‖heɪl/ *n* **1** (precipitation in the form of) small particles of clear ice or compacted snow **2** a group of things directed at sby or sthg and

intended to cause pain, damage, or distress <*a ~ of bullets*>

[2]**hail** *vi* **1** to precipitate hail **2** to pour down or strike like hail

[3]**hail** *interj* **1** – used to express acclamation <*~ to the chief*> **2** *archaic* – used as a salutation

[4]**hail** *vt* **1a** to salute, greet **b** to greet with enthusiastic approval; acclaim *as* **2** to greet or summon by calling <*~ a taxi*> *~vi* to call (a greeting to a passing ship) – **hailer** *n* – **hail from** to be or have been a native or resident of

[5]**hail** *n* **1** a call to attract attention **2** hearing distance <*stayed within ~*> **3** *archaic* an exclamation of greeting or acclamation

hail-fellow-well-met *adj* heartily and often excessively informal from the first moment of meeting

ˈhailˌstone /-ˌstohn‖-ˌstəʊn/ *n* a pellet of hail

hair /heə‖heə/ *n* **1a** (a structure resembling) a slender threadlike outgrowth on the surface of an animal; *esp* (any of) the many usu pigmented hairs that form the characteristic coat of a mammal **b** the coating of hairs, esp on the human head or other body part **2** HAIR'S BREADTH – **hairless** *adj*, **hairlessness** *n*, **hairlike** *adj*

ˈhairˌbrush /-ˌbrush‖-ˌbrʌʃ/ *n* a brush for the hair

ˈhairˌcut /-ˌkut‖-ˌkʌt/ *n* (the result of) cutting and shaping of the hair – **haircutter** *n*, **haircutting** *n*

ˈhairˌdo /-ˌdooh‖-ˌduː/ *n, pl* **hairdos** a hairstyle

ˈhairˌdresser /-ˌdresə‖-ˌdresə/ *n* sby whose occupation is cutting, dressing, and styling the hair – **hairdressing** *n*

haired /heəd‖heəd/ *adj* having hair (of a specified kind) <*fair*-haired>

ˈhairˌgrip /-ˌgrip‖-ˌgrɪp/ *n, Br* a flat hairpin with prongs that close together

ˈhairˌline /-ˌlien‖-ˌlaɪn/ *n* **1** a very slender line; *esp* a tiny line or crack on a surface **2** (a fabric with) a design consisting of lengthways or widthways lines usu 1 thread wide **3** the line above the forehead beyond which hair grows – **hairline** *adj*

ˈhairˌpiece /-ˌpees‖-ˌpiːs/ *n* a section of false hair worn to enhance a hairstyle or make a person's natural hair seem thicker or more plentiful

[1]**ˈhairˌpin** /-ˌpin‖-ˌpɪn/ *n* **1** a 2-pronged U-shaped pin of thin wire for holding the hair in place **2** a sharp bend in a road

[2]**hairpin** *adj* having the shape of a hairpin <*a ~ bend*>

ˈhair-ˌraising *adj* causing terror or astonishment – **hair-raisingly** *adv*

ˈhair's ˌbreadth *n* a very small distance or margin

ˈhair ˌshirt *n* a rough shirt worn next to the skin as a penance

ˈhair-ˌslide *n, Br* a (decorative) clip for the hair

ˈhairˌsplitting /-ˌspliting‖-ˌsplɪtɪŋ/ *n* argument over unimportant differences and points of detail; quibbling – **hairsplitting** *adj*, **hairsplitter** *n*

ˈhairˌspring /-ˌspring‖-ˌsprɪŋ/ *n* a slender spiral spring that regulates the motion of the balance wheel of a timepiece

ˈhair-ˌtrigger *adj* immediately responsive to or disrupted by the slightest stimulus <*a ~ temper*>

hair trigger *n* a trigger so adjusted that very slight pressure will fire the gun

hairy /ˈheəri‖ˈheərɪ/ *adj* **1** covered with (material like) hair **2** made of or resembling hair **3** frighteningly dangerous – infml – **hairiness** *n*

hake /hayk‖heɪk/ *n*, any of several marine food fishes related to the common Atlantic cod

halberd /ˈhalbəd‖ˈhælbəd/ *n* a long-handled weapon combining a spear and battle-axe, used esp in the 15th and 16th c – **halberdier** *n*

[1]**halcyon** /ˈhalsi·ən‖ˈhælsɪən/ *n*, a kingfisher – poetic

[2]**halcyon** *adj* calm, peaceful – esp in *halcyon days*

hale /hayl‖heɪl/ *adj* free from defect, disease, or infirmity; sound <*a ~ and hearty old man*>

[1]**half** /hahf‖hɑːf/ *n, pl* **halves** /hahvz‖hɑːvz/ **1a** either of 2 equal parts into which sthg is divisible **b** half an hour – used in designation of time **2** either of a pair: e g **2a** a partner <*my other ~*> **b** a school term – used esp at some British public schools **3** sthg of (approximately) half the value or quantity: e g **3a** half a pint **b** a child's ticket **c** HALFPENNY 1 – **by half** by a great deal – **by halves** halfheartedly – **in half** into 2 (nearly) equal parts

[2]**half** *adj* **1a** being one of 2 equal parts **b(1)** amounting to approximately half **b(2)** falling short of the full or complete thing <*~ measures*> **2** extending over or covering only half <*~ sleeves*> **3** *Br* half past <*~ seven*> – **halfness** *n*

[3]**half** *adv* **1** in an equal part or degree <*she was ~ crying, ~ laughing*> **2** nearly but not completely <*~ cooked*> – **half as much again** one-and-a-half times as much

ˌhalf-a-ˈcrown *n* HALF CROWN

ˌhalf a ˈdozen *n* a set of 6; *also* several

ˈhalfˌback /-ˌbak‖-ˌbæk/ *n* a player in rugby, soccer, hockey, etc positioned immediately behind the forward line – **halfback** *adj*

ˌhalf-ˈbaked *adj* marked by or showing a lack of forethought or judgment; foolish

ˈhalf-ˌbreed *n* the offspring of parents of different races – **half-breed** *adj*

half brother *n* a brother related through 1 parent only

ˈhalf-ˌcaste *n* a half-breed – **half-caste** *adj*

half cock *n* **1** the position of the hammer of a firearm when about half retracted and held by the safety catch so that it cannot be operated by a pull on the trigger **2** a state of inadequate preparation – esp in *go off at half cock*

ˌhalf-ˈcocked *adj* lacking adequate preparation or forethought

ˌhalf ˈcrown *n* (a former British silver coin worth) 2 shillings and sixpence

ˌhalf-ˈhardy *adj, of a plant* able to withstand a moderately low temperature but injured by severe frost

ˌhalfˈhearted /-ˈhahtid‖-ˈhɑːtɪd/ *adj* lacking enthusiasm or effort – **halfheartedly** *adv*, **halfheartedness** *n*

ˌhalf-ˈholiday *n* a holiday of half a day, esp an afternoon

ˈhalf-ˌlife *n* **1** the time required for half of

the the atoms of a radioactive substance to disintegrate **2** the time required for half the amount of a drug or other substance to be eliminated from an organism naturally

ˌhalf-ˈmast *n* the position of a flag lowered halfway down the staff as a mark of mourning

ˌhalf-ˈmoon *n* (sthg shaped like) the figure of the moon when half its disc is illuminated – **half-moon** *adj*

ˌhalf ˈnelson /ˈnels(ə)n‖ˈnels(ə)n/ *n* a wrestling hold in which one arm is thrust under the corresponding arm of an opponent and the hand placed on the back of the opponent's neck

ˈhalf ˌnote *n, NAm* a minim

halfpenny /ˈhaypni‖ˈheɪpnɪ/ *n* **1** (a British bronze coin representing) one half of a penny **2** a small amount – **halfpenny** *adj*

halfpennyworth /ˈhaypəth‖ˈheɪpəθ/ *n* as much as can be bought for 1 halfpenny; *broadly* a small amount

half sister *n* a sister related through 1 parent only

ˌhalf ˈterm *n, chiefly Br* (a short holiday taken at) a period about halfway through a school term

ˌhalf-ˈtimbered *adj* constructed of timber framework with spaces filled in by brickwork or plaster – **half-timbering** *n*

ˌhalfˈtime /-ˈtiem‖-ˈtaɪm/ *n* (an intermission marking) the completion of half of a game or contest

ˈhalfˌtone /-ˌtohn‖-ˌtəʊn/ *n* **1** any of the shades of grey between the darkest and the lightest parts of a photographic image **2** a photoengraving made from an image photographed through a screen and then etched so that the details of the image are reproduced in dots – **halftone** *adj*

ˈhalf-ˌtrack *n* (a vehicle with) a drive system of an endless chain or track at the back and wheels at the front – **half-track, half-tracked** *adj*

ˌhalf-ˈvolley *n* **1** a shot in tennis made at a ball just after it has bounced **2** an easily-hit delivery of the ball in cricket that bounces closer than intended to the batsman

ˌhalfˈway /-ˈway‖-ˈweɪ/ *adj or adv* **1** midway between 2 points **2** (done or formed) partially – **halfway** *adv*

ˈhalf-ˌwit *n* a foolish or mentally deficient person – derog – **half-witted** *adj*, **half-wittedness** *n*

halibut /ˈhalibət‖ˈhælɪbət/ *n*, a large marine food flatfish

halitosis /ˌhaliˈtohsis‖ˌhælɪˈtəʊsɪs/ *n* (a condition of having) offensively smelling breath [Latin *halitus* breath, fr *halare* to breathe] – **halitotic** *adj*

hall /hawl‖hɔːl/ *n* **1a** the house of a medieval king or noble **b** the chief living room in a medieval house or castle **2** the manor house of a landed proprietor **3a** a building used by a college or university for some special purpose <*a ~ of residence*> **b** (a division of) a college at some universities **c** (a meal served in) the common dining room of an English college **4** the entrance room or passage of a building **5** a large room for public assembly or entertainment **6** *NAm* a corridor or passage in a building

hallelujah /ˌhaliˈloohyə‖ˌhælɪˈluːjə/ *n or interj* (a shout, song, etc) used to express praise, joy, or thanks [Hebrew *halălūyāh* praise (ye) the Lord]

halliard /ˈhalyəd‖ˈhæljəd/ *n* a halyard

[1]hallmark /ˈhawlˌmahk‖ˈhɔːlˌmɑːk/ *n* **1** an official mark stamped on gold and silver articles in Britain after an assay test to testify to their purity **2** a distinguishing characteristic or object [Goldsmiths' *Hall*, London, where gold and silver articles were assayed and stamped]

[2]hallmark *vt* to stamp with a hallmark

[1]hallo /haˈloh, hə-‖hæˈləʊ, hə-/, **halloa** /-ˈloh(ə)‖-ˈləʊ(ə)/ *vb, interj, or n* **halloing; halloed; halloaing; halloaed;** *pl* **hallos; halloas** (to) hollo

[2]hallo *n or interj, pl* **hallos** *chiefly Br* (a) hello

hallow /ˈhaloh‖ˈhæləʊ/ *vt* **1** to make holy or set apart for holy use **2** to respect and honour greatly; venerate

Halloween, Hallowe'en /ˌhalohˈeen‖ˌhæləʊˈiːn/ *n* October 31, the eve of All Saints' Day, observed by dressing up in disguise, party turns, etc

hallstand /ˈhawlˌstand‖ˈhɔːlˌstænd/ *n* a piece of furniture with pegs for holding coats, hats, and umbrellas

hallucinate /həˈloohsinayt‖həˈluːsɪneɪt/ *vt* to perceive or experience as a hallucination ~*vi* to have hallucinations

hallucination /həˌloohsiˈnaysh(ə)n‖həˌluːsɪˈneɪʃ(ə)n/ *n* **1** the perception of sthg apparently real to the perceiver but which has no objective reality, *also* the image, object, etc perceived **2** a completely unfounded or mistaken impression or belief – **hallucinational** *adj*, **hallucinative** *adj*

hallucinatory /həˌloohsiˈnayt(ə)ri, həˈloohsinət(ə)ri‖həˌluːsɪˈneɪt(ə)rɪ, həˈluːsɪnət(ə)rɪ/ *adj* **1** tending to produce hallucination <~ *drugs*> **2** resembling or being a hallucination

hallucinogen /həˈloohsinəjən‖həˈluːsɪnədʒən/ *n* a substance (e g LSD) that induces hallucinations – **hallucinogenic** *adj*

hallway /ˈhawlˌway‖ˈhɔːlˌweɪ/ *n* an entrance hall or corridor

[1]halo /ˈhayloh‖ˈheɪləʊ/ *n, pl* **halos, haloes 1** a circle of light appearing to surround the sun or moon and resulting from refraction or reflection of light by ice particles in the earth's atmosphere **2a** NIMBUS 1, 2 **b** a differentiated zone surrounding a central object **3** the aura of glory or veneration surrounding an idealized person or thing

[2]halo *vt* **haloing; haloed** to form into or surround with a halo

halogen /ˈhaləjen‖ˈhælədʒen/ *n* any of the 5 elements fluorine, chlorine, bromine, iodine, and astatine that form part of group VII A of the periodic table – **halogenate** *vt*, **halogenation** *n*, **halogenous** *adj*

[1]halt /hawlt‖hɔːlt/ *adj, archaic* lame

[2]halt *vi* **1** to hesitate between alternative courses; waver **2** to display weakness or imperfection (e g in speech or reasoning); falter

[3]halt *n* **1** a (temporary) stop or interruption **2** *Br* a railway stopping place, without normal station facilities, for local trains

[4]halt *vi* to come to a halt ~ *vt* **1** to bring to a stop <*the strike has* ~*ed tubes and buses*> **2** to cause to stop; end <~ *the slaughter of seals*>

[1]**halter** /ˈhawltə‖ˈhɔːltə/ *n* **1a** a rope or strap for leading or tying an animal **b** a band round an animal's head to which a lead may be attached **2** a noose for hanging criminals

[2]**halter** *vt* to put a halter on or catch (as if) with a halter

ˈhalter ˌneck *n* (a garment having) a neckline formed by a strap passing from the front of a garment round the neck and leaving the shoulders and upper back bare

halting /ˈhawlting‖ˈhɔːltɪŋ/ *adj* hesitant, faltering <*the witness spoke in a ~ manner*> – **haltingly** *adv*

halve /hahv‖hɑːv/ *vt* **1a** to divide into 2 equal parts **b** to reduce to a half **2** to play (e g a hole or match in golf) in the same number of strokes as one's opponent

[1]**halves** /hahvz‖hɑːvz/ *pl of* HALF

[2]**halves** *adv* with equal half shares <*let's go ~*>

halyard, halliard /ˈhalyəd‖ˈhæljəd/ *n* a rope or tackle for hoisting or lowering

[1]**ham** /ham‖hæm/ *n* **1** a buttock with its associated thigh – usu pl **2** (the meat of) the rear end of a bacon pig, esp the thigh, when removed from the carcass before curing with salt **3a** an inexpert but showy performer; *also* an actor performing in an exaggerated theatrical style **b** an operator of an amateur radio station – **ham** *adj*

[2]**ham** *vb* **-mm-** *vt* to execute with exaggerated speech or gestures; overact ~*vi* to overplay a part

hamburger /ˈhambuhgə‖ˈhæmbɜːgə/ *n* a round flat cake of minced beef; *also* a sandwich of a fried hamburger in a bread roll [German *Hamburger* of Hamburg, fr *Hamburg*, city in Germany]

ˌham-ˈfisted *adj, chiefly Br* clumsy with the hands – infml

hamlet /ˈhamlit‖ˈhæmlɪt/ *n* a small village

[1]**hammer** /ˈhamə‖ˈhæmə/ *n* **1a** a hand tool that consists of a solid head set crosswise on a handle and is used to strike a blow (e g to drive in a nail) **b** a power tool that substitutes a metal block or a drill for the hammerhead **2a** a lever with a striking head for ringing a bell or striking a gong **b** the part of the mechanism of a modern gun whose action ignites the cartridge **c** the malleus **d** a gavel **e(1)** a padded mallet in a piano action for striking a string **e(2)** a hand mallet for playing various percussion instruments **3** (an athletic field event using) a metal sphere weighing 16lb (about 7.3kg) attached by a wire to a handle and thrown for distance – **under the hammer** for sale at auction

[2]**hammer** *vi* **1** to strike blows, esp repeatedly, (as if) with a hammer; pound **2** to make repeated efforts *at*; *esp* to reiterate an opinion or attitude <*the lectures all* ~ed *away at the same points*> ~ *vt* **1** to beat, drive, or shape (as if) with repeated blows of a hammer **2** to force as if by hitting repeatedly <*wanted to ~ him into submission*> **3** to declare formally that (a member of the Stock Exchange) is insolvent and is therefore forbidden to trade **4** to beat decisively – infml <*we* ~ed *them at football*> – **hammerer** *n* – **hammer into** to cause (sby) to learn or remember (sthg) by continual repetition

ˌhammer and ˈsickle *n* an emblem consisting of a crossed hammer and sickle used chiefly as a symbol of Communism

hammer out *vt* to produce or bring about through lengthy discussion <hammered out *a new policy*>

hammock /ˈhamək‖ˈhæmək/ *n* a hanging bed, usu made of netting or canvas and suspended by cords at each end [Spanish *hamaca*, fr Taino (an American Indian language)]

[1]**hamper** /ˈhampə‖ˈhæmpə/ *vt* **1** to restrict the movement or operation of by bonds or obstacles; hinder **2** to interfere with; encumber

[2]**hamper** *n* a large basket with a cover for packing, storing, or transporting crockery, food, etc <*picnic ~*>

hamster /ˈhamstə‖ˈhæmstə/ *n* any of numerous small Old World rodents with very large cheek pouches

[1]**hamstring** /ˈhamˌstring‖ˈhæmˌstrɪŋ/ *n* **1** either of 2 groups of tendons at the back of the human knee **2** a large tendon above and behind the hock of a quadruped

[2]**hamstring** *vt* **hamstrung** /-strung‖-strʌŋ/ **1** to cripple by cutting the leg tendons **2** to make ineffective or powerless; cripple

[1]**hand** /hand‖hænd/ *n* **1a** (the segment of the forelimb of vertebrate animals corresponding to) the end of the forelimb of human beings, monkeys, etc when modified as a grasping organ **b** sthg resembling a hand: e g **b(1)** a stylized figure of a hand used as a pointer or marker **b(2)** a group of usu large leaves (e g of tobacco) reaped or tied together or of bananas growing together **c** a forehock of pork **d** an indicator or pointer on a dial **2a** possession – usu pl with sing. meaning <*the documents fell into the* ~s *of the enemy*> **b** control, supervision – usu pl with sing. meaning <*I'll leave the matter in your capable* ~s> **3a** a side, direction <*men fighting on either ~*> **b** either of 2 sides or aspects of an issue or argument <*on the one ~ we can appeal for peace, on the other declare war*> **4** a pledge, esp of betrothal or marriage **5** handwriting **6a** skill, ability <*tried her ~ at sailing*> **b** an instrumental part <*had a ~ in the crime*> **7** a unit of measure equal to 4in (about 102mm) used esp for the height of a horse **8a** assistance or aid, esp when involving physical effort <*lend a ~*> **b** a round of applause **9a** (the cards or pieces held by) a player in a card or board game **b** a single round in a game **c** the force or solidity of one's position (e g in negotiations) **d** a turn to serve in a game (e g squash) in which only the server may score points **10a** one who performs or executes a particular work <*2 portraits by the same ~*> **b** a worker, employee <*employed over 100* ~s>; *esp* one employed at manual labour or general tasks <*a field ~*> **c** a member of a ship's crew <*all* ~s *on deck*> **d** one skilled in a particular action or pursuit <*she's an old ~ at this job*> **11a** handiwork **b** style of execution; workmanship <*the ~ of a master*> – **at hand** near in time or place – **at the hands of, at the hand of** by the act or instrumentality of – **by hand** with the hands, usu as opposed to mechanically – **in hand 1** not used up or lost and at one's disposal <*they have a game* in

hand> **2** *of a horse* being led rather than being ridden **3** UNDER WAY <*put the work* in hand> – **off one's hands** out of one's care or charge – **on hand 1** ready to use **2** in attendance; present – **on one's hands** in one's possession, care, or management – **out of hand 1** without delay; without reflection or consideration <*refused it* out of hand> **2** out of control <*that child has got quite* out of hand> – **to hand** available and ready for use; *esp* within reach

[2]**hand** *vt* **1** to lead or assist with the hand <*he* ~ed *her out of the car*> **2** to give or pass (as if) with the hand <~ *a letter to her*> – **hand it to** to give credit to

handbag /ˈhandˌbag‖ˈhændˌbæg/ *n* a bag designed for carrying small personal articles and money, carried usu by women

ˈhandˌball *n* **1** (the small rubber ball used in) a game resembling fives and played in a walled court or against a single wall **2** an indoor or outdoor game between 2 teams of 7 or 11 players whose object is to direct a soccer ball into the opponent's goal by throwing and catching

ˈhandˌbarrow *n* a flat rectangular frame with handles at both ends for carrying loads

ˈhandˌbill *n* a small printed sheet to be distributed (e g for advertising) by hand

ˈhandˌbook *n* a short reference book, esp on a particular subject

handcuff /ˈhandˌkuf‖ˈhændˌkʌf/ *vt* to apply handcuffs to; manacle

handcuffs *n pl* a pair of metal rings, usu connected by a chain or bar, for locking round prisoners' wrists

hand down *vt* **1** to transmit in succession (e g from father to son); bequeath **2** to give (an outgrown article of clothing) to a younger member of one's family **3** to deliver in court <hand down *a judgment*>

-handed /handid‖hændɪd/ *comb form* (*adj* → *adj*) having or using a specified (kind of) hand or (number of) hands <*right*-handed> – **-hander** *comb form* (*adj* → *n*)

handful /ˈhandf(ə)l‖ˈhændf(ə)l/ *n, pl* **handfuls** *also* **handsful** /ˈhandzf(ə)l‖ˈhændzf(ə)l/ **1** as much or as many as the hand will grasp **2** a small quantity or number **3** sby or sthg (e g a child or animal) that is difficult to control – infml

ˈhandˌgun *n* a firearm held and fired with 1 hand

ˈhandˌhold *n* sthg to hold on to for support (e g in mountain climbing)

[1]**handicap** /ˈhandiˌkap‖ˈhændɪˌkæp/ *n* **1** (a race or contest with) an artificial advantage or disadvantage given to contestants so that all have a more equal chance of winning **2** a (physical) disability or disadvantage that makes achievement unusually difficult

[2]**handicap** *vt* **-pp- 1** to assign handicaps to; impose handicaps on **2** to put at a disadvantage

handicraft /ˈhandiˌkrahft‖ˈhændɪˌkrɑːft/ *n* **1** (an occupation requiring) manual skill **2** articles fashioned by handicraft – **handicrafter** *n*

handiwork /ˈhandiˌwuhk‖ˈhændɪˌwɜːk/ *n* **1** (the product of) work done by the hands **2** work done personally

handkerchief /ˈhangkəˌcheef, -chif‖ˈhæŋkəˌtʃiːf, -tʃɪf/ *n, pl* **handkerchiefs** *also* **handkerchieves** /-ˌcheevz‖-ˌtʃiːvz/ a small piece of cloth used for various usu personal purposes (e g blowing the nose or wiping the eyes) or as a clothing accessory

[1]**handle** /ˈhandl‖ˈhændl/ *n* **1** a part that is designed to be grasped by the hand **2** the feel of a textile **3** a title; *also* an esp aristocratic or double-barrelled name – infml – **handled** *adj*

[2]**handle** *vt* **1a** to try or examine (e g by touching or moving) with the hand <~ *silk to judge its weight*> **b** to manage with the hands <~ *a horse*> **2a** to deal with (e g a subject or idea) in speech or writing, or as a work of art **b** to manage, direct <*a solicitor* ~s *all my affairs*> **3** to deal with, act on, or dispose of <~d *the clients very well*> **4** to engage in the buying, selling, or distributing of (a commodity) ~*vi* to respond to controlling movements in a specified way <*car that* ~s *well*> – **handleable** *adj*

ˈhandleˌbar *n* a bar, esp on a cycle or scooter, for steering – often pl with sing. meaning

handler /ˈhandlə‖ˈhændlə/ *n* one who is in immediate physical charge of an animal

ˌhandˈmade *adj* made by hand rather than by machine

ˈhandˌmaiden *n* a personal maid or female servant

ˈhand-me-ˌdown *n* a reach-me-down

hand on *vt* HAND DOWN

ˈhandˌout *n* **1** sthg (e g food, clothing, or money) distributed free, esp to people in need **2** a folder or circular of information for free distribution

hand out *vt* **1** to give freely or without charge **2** to administer <hand out *a severe punishment*>

hand over *vb* to yield control or possession (of)

ˌhandˈpick *vt* **1** to pick by hand rather than by machine **2** to select personally and carefully

ˈhandˌrail *n* a narrow rail for grasping with the hand as a support, esp near stairs

ˈhandˌshake *n* a clasping and shaking of each other's usu right hand by 2 people (e g in greeting or farewell)

handsome /ˈhansəm‖ˈhænsəm/ *adj* **1** considerable, sizable <*a painting that commanded a* ~ *price*> **2** marked by graciousness or generosity; liberal <~ *contributions to charity*> **3a** *of a man* having a pleasing appearance; good-looking **b** *of a woman* attractive in a dignified statuesque way – **handsomely** *adv*, **handsomeness** *n*

ˌhands-ˈon *adj* of, being, or having direct practical experience of an operation or activity

ˈhandˌstand *n* an act of supporting and balancing the body on only the hands with the legs in the air

ˌhand-to-ˈhand *adj* involving physical contact; very close <~ *fighting*> – **hand to hand** *adv*

ˌhand-to-ˈmouth *adj* having or providing only just enough to live on; precarious <*a* ~ *existence*>

ˈhandˌwork *n* work done with the hands and not by machine – **handworker** *n*

ˈhandˌwriting *n* writing done by hand; *esp*

the style of writing peculiar to a particular person

handy /'handi‖'hændɪ/ *adj* **1a** convenient for use; useful **b** *of a vessel or vehicle* easily handled **2** clever in using the hands, esp in a variety of practical ways **3** conveniently near – infml – **handily** *adv*, **handiness** *n*

'handyman /-mən, -ˌman‖-mən, -ˌmæn/ *n* **1** sby who does odd jobs **2** sby competent in a variety of skills or repair work

[1]**hang** /hang‖hæŋ/ *vb* **hung** /hung‖hʌŋ/, (*1b*) **hanged** *vt* **1a** to fasten to some elevated point by the top so that the lower part is free; suspend **b** to suspend by the neck until dead – often used as a mild oath <*I'll be* ~ed> **c** to fasten on a point of suspension so as to allow free motion within given limits <~ *a door*> **d** to suspend (meat, esp game) before cooking to make the flesh tender and develop the flavour **2** to decorate, furnish, or cover by hanging sthg up (e g flags or bunting) <*a room* hung *with tapestries*> **3** to hold or bear in a suspended or inclined position <hung *his head in shame*> **4** to fasten (sthg, esp wallpaper) to a wall (e g with paste) **5** to display (pictures) in a gallery ~ *vi* **1a** to remain fastened at the top so that the lower part is free; dangle **b** to die by hanging **2** to remain poised or stationary in the air **3** to stay on; persist <*the smell of the explosion* hung *in the afternoon air*> **4** to be imminent; impend <*doom* hung *over the nation*> **5** to fall or droop from a usu tense or taut position <*his mouth* hung *open*> **6** to depend <*election* ~s *on one vote*> **7** to lean, incline, or jut over or downwards **8** to fall in flowing lines <*the coat* ~s *well*> – **hang fire 1** to be slow in the explosion of a charge after its primer has been discharged **2** to be delayed or held up – **hang in the balance** to be uncertain or at stake – **hang on 1** to pay close attention to <hangs on *her every word*> **2** to depend on <*the success of the whole enterprise* hangs on *your cooperation*> **3** to be burdensome or oppressive <*time* hangs on *his hands*>

[2]**hang** *n* **1** the manner in which a thing hangs **2** a downward slope; *also* a droop **3** the special method of doing, using, or dealing with sthg; the knack – chiefly in *get the hang of*

hang about *vi, Br* **1** to wait or stay, usu without purpose or activity **2** to delay or move slowly *USE* infml

hangar /'hangə‖'hæŋə/ *n* a shed; *esp* a large shed for housing aircraft

hang around *vi* HANG ABOUT 1

hang back *vi* to be reluctant to move or act; hesitate

hangdog /'hangˌdog‖'hæŋˌdɒg/ *adj* ashamed; *also* abject

[1]**hanger** /'hangə‖'hæŋə/ *n* a wood growing on a steeply sloping hillside

[2]**hanger** *n* a device (e g a loop or strap) by which or to which sthg is hung or hangs; *esp* a hook and crosspiece to fit inside the shoulders of a dress, coat, etc to keep the shape of the garment when hung up

ˌhanger-'on *n, pl* **hangers-on** one who attempts to associate with a person, group, etc, esp for personal gain; a dependant

'hang-ˌglider *n* (sby who flies) a glider that resembles a kite and is controlled by the body movements of the harnessed person suspended beneath it – **hang-glide** *vi*

[1]**hanging** /'hang·ing‖'hæŋɪŋ/ *n* **1** (an) execution by suspension from a noose **2a** a curtain **b** a covering (e g a tapestry) for a wall

[2]**hanging** *adj* **1** situated or lying on steeply sloping ground <~ *gardens*> **2** jutting out; overhanging <*a* ~ *rock*> **3** adapted for sustaining a hanging object <*a* ~ *rail*> **4** deserving or liable to inflict hanging <*a* ~ *matter*> <*a* ~ *judge*>

'hangman /-mən‖-mən/ *n* one who hangs a condemned person; a public executioner

hangnail /'hangˌnayl‖'hæŋˌneɪl/ *n* a bit of skin hanging loose at the side or root of a fingernail

hang on *vi* **1** to keep hold; hold onto sthg **2** to persist tenaciously <*a cold that* hung on *all spring*> **3** to wait for a short time <hang on *a second*> **4** to remain on the telephone <*could you* hang on *please and I'll connect you*> – **hang on to** to hold or keep tenaciously <*learned to* hang on to *his money*>

'hangˌout *n* a place where one is often to be seen – slang

hang out *vi* **1** to protrude, esp downwards **2** to live or spend much time – slang <*the kids* hang out *on street corners*>

hangover /'hang·ohvə‖'hæŋəʊvə/ *n* **1** sthg (e g a custom) that remains from the past **2** the disagreeable physical effects following heavy consumption of alcohol or use of other drugs

'hang-ˌup *n* a source of mental or emotional difficulty – infml

hang up *vt* **1** to place on a hook or hanger <*told the child to* hang up *his coat*> **2** to delay, suspend <*the negotiations were* hung up *for a week*> ~*vi* to terminate a telephone conversation, often abruptly

hank /hangk‖hæŋk/ *n* **1** a coil, loop; *specif* a coiled or looped bundle (e g of yarn, rope, or wire) usu containing a definite length **2** a ring attaching a jib or staysail to a stay

hanker /'hangkə‖'hæŋkə/ *vi* to desire strongly or persistently – usu + *after* or *for* – **hankering** *n*

hankie, hanky /'hangki‖'hæŋkɪ/ *n* a handkerchief – infml

ˌhanky-'panky /'pangki‖'pæŋkɪ/ *n* mildly improper or deceitful behaviour – infml

Hansard /'hansahd‖'hænsɑːd/ *n* the official report of Parliamentary proceedings [Luke *Hansard* (1752-1828), English printer]

hansom /'hansəm‖'hænsəm/, **hansom cab** *n* a light 2-wheeled covered carriage with the driver's seat high up at the back [Joseph *Hansom* (1803-82), English architect & inventor]

haphazard /hap'hazəd‖hæp'hæzəd/ *adj* marked by lack of plan or order; aimless – **haphazard** *adv*, **haphazardly** *adv*, **haphazardness** *n*

hapless /'haplis‖'hæplɪs/ *adj* having no luck; unfortunate – **haplessly** *adv*, **haplessness** *n*

hap'orth, ha'porth, ha'p'orth /'haypəth‖'heɪpəθ/ *n* a halfpennyworth <*doesn't make a* ~ *of difference*>

happen /'hapn‖'hæpn/ *vi* **1** to occur by chance – often + *it* <*it so* ~s *I'm going your way*> **2** to come into being as an event; occur **3**

to have the luck or fortune *to*; chance <*he* ~ed *to overhear the plotters*> [Middle English *happenen*, fr *hap* event, chance, fortune, fr Old Norse *happ* good luck] – **happen on/upon** to see or meet (sthg or sby) by chance

happening /ˈhapn·ing, ˈhapning‖ˈhæpnɪŋ, ˈhæpnɪŋ/ *n* **1** sthg that happens; an occurrence **2a** the creation or presentation of a nonobjective work of art (e g an action painting) **b** a usu unscripted or improvised often multimedia public performance in which the audience participates

happily /ˈhapəli‖ˈhæpəlɪ/ *adv* **1** by good fortune; luckily <~, *he never knew*> **2** in a happy manner or state <*lived* ~ *ever after*> **3** in an adequate or fitting manner; successfully <*white wine goes* ~ *with fish*>

happy /ˈhapi‖ˈhæpɪ/ *adj* **1** favoured by luck or fortune; fortunate **2** well adapted or fitting; felicitous <*a* ~ *choice*> **3a** enjoying or expressing pleasure and contentment **b** glad, pleased <*I was very* ~ *to hear from you*> **4** characterized by a dazed irresponsible state – usu in combination <*a punch*-happy *boxer*> **5** impulsively quick or overinclined to use sthg – usu in combination <*trigger*-happy> **6** having or marked by an atmosphere of good fellowship; friendly **7** satisfied as to the fact; confident, sure <*we're now quite* ~ *that the murder occurred at about 5.30*> **8** tipsy – euph – **happiness** *n*

ˈ**happy-go-**ˈ**lucky** *adj* blithely unconcerned; carefree

hara-kiri /ˌharə ˈkiri‖ˌhærə ˈkɪrɪ/ *n* suicide by ritual disembowelment practised by the Japanese samurai, esp when disgraced or found guilty of a crime carrying the death penalty for commoners [Japanese *harakiri*, fr *hara* belly + *kiri* cutting]

[1]**harangue** /həˈrang‖həˈræŋ/ *n* **1** a speech addressed to a public assembly **2** a lengthy, ranting, and usu censorious speech or piece of writing

[2]**harangue** *vb* to make or address in a harangue

harass /ˈharəs‖ˈhærəs/ *vt* **1** to worry and impede by repeated raids <~ed *the enemy*> **2** to annoy or worry persistently – **harasser** *n*, **harassment** *n*

harbinger /ˈhahbinjə‖ˈhɑːbɪndʒə/ *n* **1** one who pioneers or initiates a major change; a precursor **2** sthg that presages or foreshadows what is to come – **harbinger** *vt*

[1]**harbour**, *NAm chiefly* **harbor** /ˈhahbə‖ˈhɑːbə/ *n* **1** a place of security and comfort; a refuge **2** a part of a body of water providing protection and anchorage for ships <*the ship came into* ~>

[2]**harbour**, *NAm chiefly* **harbor** *vt* **1** to give shelter or refuge to **2** to be the home or habitat of; contain <*these cracks can* ~ *dangerous bacteria*> **3** to have or keep (e g thoughts or feelings) in the mind <~ed *a grudge*> ~*vi* to take shelter (as if) in a harbour

[1]**hard** /hahd‖hɑːd/ *adj* **1** not easily penetrated or yielding to pressure; firm **2a** *of alcoholic drink* having a high percentage of alcohol **b** *of water* containing salts of calcium, magnesium, etc that inhibit lathering with soap **3a** metal as distinct from paper <~ *money*> **b** *of currency* stable in value; *also* soundly backed and readily convertible into foreign currencies without large discounts **c** being high and firm <~ *prices*> **4a(1)** firm, definite <*reached a* ~ *agreement*> **a(2)** not speculative or conjectural; factual <~ *evidence*> **b** close, searching <*gave a* ~ *look*> **5a(1)** difficult to endure <~ *times*> **a(2)** oppressive, inequitable <*indirect taxes are* ~ *on the poor*> **b** lacking consideration or compassion; <*a* ~ *heart*> **c(1)** harsh, severe <*said some* ~ *things*> **c(2)** resentful <~ *feelings*> **d** inclement <~ *winter*> **e(1)** forceful, violent <~ *blows*> **e(2)** demanding energy or stamina <~ *work*> **e(3)** using or performing with great energy or effort <*a* ~ *worker*> **6a** sharply defined; stark <*a* ~ *outline*> **b** *of c and g* pronounced /k/ and /g/ respectively – not used technically **7a** difficult to do, understand, or explain <~ *problems*> **b** having difficulty in doing sthg <~ *of hearing*> **8a** *of a drug* addictive and gravely detrimental to health **b** *of pornography* HARD-CORE 2 **9** PERSISTENT 2b – **hardness** *n*

[2]**hard** *adv* **1a** with great or maximum effort or energy; strenuously <*were* ~ *at work*> **b** in a violent manner; fiercely **c** to the full extent – used in nautical directions <*steer* ~ *aport*> **d** in a searching or concentrated manner <*stared* ~ *at him*> **2a** in such a manner as to cause hardship, difficulty, or pain; severely **b** with bitterness or grief <*took his defeat* ~> **3** in a firm manner; tightly **4** to the point of hardness <*the water froze* ~> **5** close in time or space <*the house stood* ~ *by the river*> – **hard done by** unfairly treated

[3]**hard** *n, chiefly Br* a firm usu artificial foreshore or landing place

ˌ**hard-and-**ˈ**fast** *adj* fixed, strict <*a* ~ *rule*>

ˈ**hard**ˌ**back** *n* a book bound in stiff covers – **hardback** *adj*

ˌ**hard-**ˈ**bitten** *adj* steeled by difficult experience; tough

ˈ**hard**ˌ**board** *n* (a) composition board made by compressing shredded wood chips

ˌ**hard-**ˈ**boiled** *adj* devoid of sentimentality; tough

ˌ**hard** ˈ**cash** *n* money in the form of coin or bank notes as opposed to cheques or credit

ˈ**hard**ˌ**core** *n, Br* compacted rubble or clinker used esp as a foundation for roads, paving, or floors

ˌ**hard-**ˈ**core** *adj* **1** of or constituting a hard core <~ *Conservative supporters*> **2** *of pornography* extremely explicit; *specif* showing real rather than simulated sexual acts

ˌ**hard** ˈ**core** *n sing or pl in constr* the unyielding or uncompromising members that form the nucleus of a group

harden /ˈhahdn‖ˈhɑːdn/ *vt* **1** to make hard or harder **2** to confirm in disposition, feelings, or action; *esp* to make callous <~ed *his heart*> **3a** to toughen, inure <~ *troops*> **b** to inure (e g plants) to cold or other unfavourable environmental conditions – often + *off* **4** to protect from blast or heat <~ *a missile emplacement*> ~ *vi* **1** to become hard or harder **2a** to become confirmed or strengthened <*opposition began to* ~> **b** to assume an appearance of harshness <*her face* ~ed *at the word*> **3** to become higher or less subject to fluctuations downwards <*prices* ~ed *quickly*> – **hardener** *n*

ˌhardˈheaded *adj* **1** stubborn **2** sober, realistic <~ *common sense*> – **hardheadedly** *adv*, **hardheadedness** *n*

ˌhardˈhearted *adj* lacking in sympathetic understanding; unfeeling – **hardheartedly** *adv*, **hardheartedness** *n*

ˌhard ˈlabour *n* compulsory labour as part of prison discipline

ˌhard-ˈline *adj* advocating or involving a persistently firm course of action; unyielding – **hard-liner** *n*

ˌhard ˈluck *n, chiefly Br* bad luck – often used as an interjection expressing mild sympathy

hardly /ˈhahdli‖ˈhɑːdlɪ/ *adv* **1** in a severe manner; harshly **2** with difficulty; painfully **3** only just; barely <*I* ~ *knew her*> **4** scarcely <*that news is* ~ *surprising*>

ˌhard-ˈnosed *adj* **1** hard-bitten, stubborn **2** HARDHEADED 2

ˌhard-of-ˈhearing *adj* partially deaf

hard palate *n* the bony front part of the palate forming the roof of the mouth

ˈhardˌpan *n* a hard compact soil layer

hard sell *n* aggressive high-pressure salesmanship

hardship /ˈhahdship‖ˈhɑːdʃɪp/ *n* (an instance of) suffering, privation

ˌhard ˈshoulder *n* either of 2 surfaced strips of land along a road, esp a motorway, on which stopping is allowed only in an emergency

ˈhardˌtack *n* SHIP'S BISCUIT

ˈhardˌtop *n* a motor car with a rigid top

ˌhard ˈup *adj* short of sthg, esp money <*I'm very* ~ *for summer clothes*> – infml

ˈhardˌware *n* **1** items sold by an ironmonger **2** the physical components (e g electronic and electrical devices) of a vehicle (e g a spacecraft) or an apparatus (e g a computer) **3** tape recorders, closed-circuit television, etc used as instructional equipment

ˌhardˈwearing *adj* durable

ˈhardˌwood *n* (the wood of) a broad-leaved as distinguished from a coniferous tree – **hardwood** *adj*

hardy /ˈhahdi‖ˈhɑːdɪ/ *adj* **1** bold, audacious **2a** inured to fatigue or hardships; robust **b** capable of withstanding adverse conditions; *esp* capable of living outdoors over winter without artificial protection <~ *plants*> – **hardiness** *n*

[1]hare /heə‖heə/ *n* **1** any of various swift timid long-eared mammals like large rabbits with long hind legs **2** – figure of a hare moved mechanically along a dog track for the dogs to chase

[2]hare *vi* to run fast – infml

ˌhare and ˈhounds *n* PAPER CHASE

ˈhareˌbell *n* a slender plant with blue bell-shaped flowers that grows esp on heaths and in open woodlands

ˈhareˌbrained *adj* flighty, foolish – infml

ˌhareˈlip *n* a split in the upper lip like that of a hare occurring as a congenital deformity – **harelipped** *adj*

harem /ˈheərəm, hahˈreem‖ˈheərəm, hɑːˈriːm/ *n* **1a** a usu secluded (part of a) house allotted to women in a Muslim household **b** *sing or pl in constr* the women occupying a harem **2** a group of females associated with 1 male [Arabic *ḥarīm*, lit., something forbidden & *ḥaram*, lit., sanctuary]

haricot /ˈharikoh‖ˈhærɪkəʊ/, **ˌharicot ˈbean** *n* FRENCH BEAN

hark /hahk‖hɑːk/ *vi* to listen closely

hark back *vi* to return *to* an earlier topic or circumstance

harlequin /ˈhahlikwin‖ˈhɑːlɪkwɪn/ *n* **1a** *cap* a stock character in comedy and pantomime **b** a buffoon **2** a variegated pattern (e g of a textile)

harlequinade /ˌhahlikwiˈnayd‖ˌhɑːlɪkwɪˈneɪd/ *n* a part of a play or pantomime in which Harlequin has a leading role

harlot /ˈhahlət‖ˈhɑːlət/ *n, archaic* a prostitute – **harlotry** *n*

[1]harm /hahm‖hɑːm/ *n* **1** physical or mental damage; injury **2** mischief, wrong – **harmful** *adj*, **harmfully** *adv*, **harmfulness** *n* – **out of harm's way** safe from danger

[2]harm *vt* to cause harm to

harmless /ˈhahmlis‖ˈhɑːmlɪs/ *adj* **1** free from harm, liability, or loss **2** lacking capacity or intent to injure – **harmlessly** *adv*, **harmlessness** *n*

[1]harmonic /hahˈmonik‖hɑːˈmɒnɪk/ *adj* **1** of musical harmony, a harmonic, or harmonics **2** pleasing to the ear; harmonious – **harmonically** *adv*, **harmonicalness** *n*

[2]harmonic *n* **1** a tone in a harmonic series **2** a flutelike tone produced on a stringed instrument by touching a vibrating string at a point (e g the midpoint) which divides it into halves, thirds, etc

harmonica /hahˈmonikə‖hɑːˈmɒnɪkə/ *n* a small rectangular wind instrument with free reeds recessed in air slots from which notes are sounded by breathing out and in

harmonious /hahˈmohnyəs, -ni·əs‖hɑːˈməʊnjəs, -nɪəs/ *adj* **1** musically concordant **2** having the parts arranged so as to produce a pleasing effect **3** marked by agreement – **harmoniously** *adv*, **harmoniousness** *n*

harmonium /hahˈmohni·əm, -nyəm‖hɑːˈməʊnɪəm, -njəm/ *n* a reed organ in which pedals operate a bellows that forces air through free reeds

harmon·ize, -ise /ˈhahməniez‖ˈhɑːmənaɪz/ *vi* **1** to be in harmony **2** to play or sing in harmony ~ *vt* **1** to bring into consonance or accord **2** to provide or accompany with harmony – **harmonizer** *n*, **harmonization** *n*

harmony /ˈhahməni‖ˈhɑːmənɪ/ *n* **1a** the (pleasant-sounding) combination of simultaneous musical notes in a chord **b** (the science of) the structure of music with respect to the composition and progression of chords **2a** pleasing or congruent arrangement of parts **b** agreement, accord <*lives in* ~ *with her neighbours*> [Middle French *armonie*, fr Latin *harmonia*, fr Greek, joint, harmony, fr *harmos* joint]

[1]harness /ˈhahnis‖ˈhɑːnɪs/ *n* **1a** the gear of a draught animal other than a yoke **b** (military) equipment (for a knight) **2** sthg that resembles a harness (e g in holding or fastening sthg) <*a safety* ~> – **in harness 1** in one's usual work, surroundings, or routine <*back* in harness *after* *a long illness*> 2 in close association <*working* in harness *with his colleagues*>

[2]**harness** *vt* **1a** to put a harness on (e g a horse) **b** to attach (e g a wagon) by means of a harness **2** to tie together; yoke **3** to utilize; *esp* to convert (a natural force) into energy

[1]**harp** /hahp‖hɑːp/ *n* a musical instrument that has strings stretched across an open triangular frame, plucked with the fingers – **harpist** *n*

[2]**harp** *vi* – **harp on** to dwell on or return to (a subject) tediously or monotonously

harpoon /hahˈpoohn‖hɑːˈpuːn/ *n* a barbed spear used esp in hunting large fish or whales – **harpoon** *vt*, **harpooner** *n*

harpsichord /ˈhahpsi,kawd‖ˈhɑːpsɪ,kɔːd/ *n* a chromatic keyboard instrument having a horizontal frame and strings and producing notes by the action of quills or leather points plucking the strings [Italian *arpicordo*, fr *arpa* harp + *corda* string] – **harpsichordist** *n*

harpy /ˈhahpi‖ˈhɑːpɪ/ *n* **1** *cap* a rapacious creature of Greek mythology with the head of a woman and the body of a bird **2** a predatory person; *esp* a rapacious woman – derog

harridan /ˈharid(ə)n‖ˈhærɪd(ə)n/ *n* an ill-tempered unpleasant woman

[1]**harrier** /ˈhari·ə‖ˈhærɪə/ *n* **1** a hunting dog resembling a small foxhound and used esp for hunting hares **2** a runner in a cross-country team

[2]**harrier** *n* any of various slender hawks with long angled wings

,Harris ˈtweed /ˈharis‖ˈhærɪs/ *trademark* – used for a loosely woven tweed made in the Outer Hebrides

[1]**harrow** /ˈharoh‖ˈhærəʊ/ *n* a cultivating implement set with spikes, spring teeth, or discs and drawn over the ground esp to pulverize and smooth the soil

[2]**harrow** *vt* **1** to cultivate (ground or land) with a harrow **2** to cause distress to; agonize – **harrower** *n*

harry /ˈhari‖ˈhærɪ/ *vt* **1** to make a destructive raid on; ravage **2** to torment (as if) by constant attack; harass

harsh /hahsh‖hɑːʃ/ *adj* **1** having a coarse uneven surface; rough **2** disagreeable or painful to the senses <*a ~ light*> **3** unduly exacting; severe **4** lacking in aesthetic appeal or refinement; crude – **harshen** *vb*, **harshly** *adv*, **harshness** *n*

hart /haht‖hɑːt/ *n, chiefly Br* the male of the (red) deer, esp when over 5 years old

hartebeest /ˈhahti,beest‖ˈhɑːtɪ,biːst/ *n* any of several large African antelopes with ridged horns that project upwards and outwards

harum-scarum /,heərəm ˈskeərəm‖,heərəm ˈskeərəm/ *adj* reckless, irresponsible – infml – **harum-scarum** *adv*

[1]**harvest** /ˈhahvist‖ˈhɑːvɪst/ *n* **1** (the season for) the gathering in of agricultural crops **2** (the yield of) a mature crop of grain, fruit, etc **3** the product or reward of exertion

[2]**harvest** *vt* **1** to gather in (a crop); reap **2** to gather (a natural product) as if by harvesting <*~ bacteria*> *~vi* to gather in a food crop – **harvestable** *adj*, **harvester** *n*

,Harvest ˈFestival *n* a festival of thanksgiving for the harvest celebrated on a Sunday in September or October in British churches

,harvest ˈhome *n* **1** the gathering or the time of harvest **2** a festival at the close of harvest

,harvest ˈmoon *n* the full moon nearest the time of the September equinox

has /haz‖hæz/ *pres 3rd sing of* HAVE

ˈhas-,been *n* sby or sthg that has passed the peak of effectiveness, success, or popularity – infml

[1]**hash** /hash‖hæʃ/ *vt* to chop (e g meat and potatoes) into small pieces

[2]**hash** *n* **1** (a dish consisting chiefly of reheated cooked) chopped food, esp meat **2** a rehash **3** a muddle, mess <*made a ~ of things*> *USE*(2 & 3) infml

[3]**hash** *n* hashish – infml

hashish /ˈhashish, -sheesh‖ˈhæʃɪʃ, -ʃiːʃ/ *n* the resin from the flowering tops of the female hemp plant that is smoked, chewed, etc for its intoxicating effect

hasn't /ˈhaznt‖ˈhæznt/ has not

hasp /hahsp‖hɑːsp/ *n* a device for fastening; *esp* a hinged metal strap that fits over a staple and is secured by a pin or padlock – **hasp** *vt*

[1]**hassle** /ˈhasl‖ˈhæsl/ *n* **1** a heated often protracted argument; a wrangle **2** a trying problem; a struggle <*it's such a ~ getting across London*> *USE* infml

[2]**hassle** *vi* to argue, fight <*~d with the referee*> *~vt* to subject to usu persistent harassment *USE* infml

hassock /ˈhasək‖ˈhæsək/ *n* **1** a tussock **2** a cushion for kneeling on, esp in church

hast /hast‖hæst/ *archaic pres 2 sing of* HAVE

[1]**haste** /hayst‖heɪst/ *n* **1** rapidity of motion; swiftness **2** rash or headlong action; precipitateness <*marry in ~, repent at leisure*> – **make haste** to act quickly; hasten

[2]**haste** *vi* to move or act swiftly – fml

hasten /ˈhays(ə)n‖ˈheɪs(ə)n/ *vt* **1** to cause to hurry **2** to accelerate <*~ the completion of the project*> *~vi* to move or act quickly; hurry – **hastener** *n*

hasty /ˈhaysti‖ˈheɪstɪ/ *adj* **1** done or made in a hurry **2** precipitate, rash **3** prone to or showing anger; irritable – **hastily** *adv*, **hastiness** *n*

hat /hat‖hæt/ *n* **1** a covering for the head usu having a shaped crown and brim **2** a role, position – infml <*wearing his ministerial ~*>

ˈhat,band *n* a fabric, leather, etc band round the crown of a hat just above the brim

[1]**hatch** /hach‖hætʃ/ *n* **1** a small door or opening (e g in a wall or aircraft) **2a** (the covering for) an opening in the deck of a ship or in the floor or roof of a building **b** a hatchway

[2]**hatch** *vi* **1** to emerge from an egg or pupa **2** to incubate eggs; brood **3** to give forth young <*the egg ~ed*> *~ vt* **1** to produce (young) from an egg by applying heat **2** to devise, esp secretly; originate – **hatchable** *adj*, **hatcher** *n*

[3]**hatch** *n* (a brood of young produced by) hatching

[4]**hatch** *vt* to mark (e g a drawing, map, or engraving) with fine closely spaced parallel lines – **hatching** *n*

ˈhatch,back *n* (a motor car with) an upward-opening hatch giving entry to the luggage and passenger compartment

hatchery /ˈhachəri‖ˈhætʃərɪ/ *n* a place for

hatching (esp fish) eggs

hatchet /ˈhachit‖ˈhætʃɪt/ *n* a short-handled axe

ˈ**hatchet ˌman** *n* one hired for murder, coercion, or attack – slang

ˈ**hatchˌway** *n* a passage giving access (e g to a lower deck in a ship); *also* [1]HATCH 2a

[1]**hate** /hayt‖heɪt/ *n* **1** intense hostility or dislike; loathing **2** an object of hatred – infml <*one of my pet* ~s>

[2]**hate** *vb* to feel extreme enmity or aversion (towards) – **hater** *n* – **hate someone's guts** to hate sby with great intensity

ˈ**hateful** /-f(ə)l‖-f(ə)l/ *adj* **1** full of hate; malicious **2** deserving of or arousing hate – **hatefully** *adv*, **hatefulness** *n*

hath /hath‖hæθ/ *archaic pres 3 sing of* HAVE

hatred /ˈhaytrid‖ˈheɪtrɪd/ *n* hate

ˈ**hat ˌtrick** *n* three successes by 1 person or side in a usu sporting activity; *specif* the dismissing of 3 batsmen with 3 consecutive balls by a bowler in cricket [prob fr a former practice of rewarding the feat by the gift of a hat]

hauberk /ˈhawˌbuhk‖ˈhɔːˌbɜːk/ *n* a tunic of chain mail worn as defensive armour, esp from the 12th to the 14th c

haughty /ˈhawti‖ˈhɔːtɪ/ *adj* disdainfully proud; arrogant [Middle English *haute*, fr Middle French *haut*, lit., high, fr Latin *altus*] – **haughtily** *adv*, **haughtiness** *n*

[1]**haul** /hawl‖hɔːl/ *vt* **1a** to pull with effort; drag **b** to transport in a vehicle, esp a cart **2** to bring *up* (e g before an authority for judgment) – infml <~ed *up before the magistrate for a traffic offence*> ~ *vi* **1** to pull, drag <~ed *on the rope*> **2** *of the wind* to shift – **haulage** *n*

[2]**haul** *n* **1** the act or process of hauling **2a** an amount gathered or acquired; a take <*the burglar's* ~> **b** the fish taken in a single draught of a net **3a** transport by hauling or the load transported **b** the distance or route over which a load is transported <*a long* ~>

haulier /ˈhawli·ə‖ˈhɔːlɪə/, *NAm* **hauler** /ˈhawlə‖ˈhɔːlə/ *n* a person or commercial establishment whose business is transport by lorry

haulm /hawm‖hɔːm/ *n* **1** the stems or tops of potatoes, peas, beans, etc (after the crop has been gathered) **2** *Br* an individual plant stem

haunch /hawnch‖hɔːntʃ/ *n* **1** [2]HIP 1a **2a** HINDQUARTER 2 – usu pl **b** HINDQUARTER 1 – **on one's haunches** in a squatting position

[1]**haunt** /hawnt‖hɔːnt/ *vt* **1a** to visit often; frequent **b** to continually seek the company of (a person) **2a** to recur constantly and spontaneously to <*the tune* ~ed *her all day*> **b** to reappear continually in; pervade <*a sense of tension that* ~s *his writing*> **3** to visit or inhabit as a ghost ~ *vi* **1** to stay around or persist; linger **2** to appear habitually as a ghost – **haunter** *n*, **hauntingly** *adv*

[2]**haunt** *n* a place habitually frequented <*the bar was a favourite* ~ *of criminals*>

hautboy, hautbois /ˈohboy‖ˈəʊbɔɪ/ *n, archaic* an oboe [Middle French *hautbois*, fr *haut* high + *bois* wood]

haute couture /ˌoht koohˈtyooə ‖ˌəʊt kuːˈtjʊə (*Fr* ot kutyːr)/ *n* (the houses or designers that create) exclusive and often trend-setting fashions for women [French, lit., high sewing]

hauteur /ohˈtuh ‖əʊˈtɜː (*Fr* otœːr)/ *n* arrogance, haughtiness

Havana /həˈvanə‖həˈvænə/ *n* (a cigar made in Cuba or from) tobacco (of the type) grown in Cuba

[1]**have** /v, əv, həv‖v, əv, həv; *strong* hav‖hæv/ *vb* **has** /s, z, əz, həz‖s, z, əz, həz; *strong* haz‖hæz/; **had** /d, əd, həd‖d, əd, həd; *strong* had‖hæd/ *vt* **1a** to hold in one's possession or at one's disposal <~ *a car*> **b** to contain as a constituent or be characterized by <~ *red hair*> <has *it in him to win*> **2** to own as an obligation or necessity – + *to* and an expressed or understood infinitive <~ *to go*> <*don't* ~ *to if you don't want to*> **3** to stand in relationship to <~ *2 sisters*> **4a** to get, obtain <*these shoes are the best to be* had> **b** to receive <had *news*> **c** to accept; *specif* to accept in marriage **d** to have sexual intercourse with (a woman or passive partner) **5** to display, show <~ *mercy on us*> **6a** to experience, esp by undergoing or suffering <~ *my watch stolen*> **b** to undertake and make or perform <~ *a bath*> **c** to entertain in the mind <~ *an opinion*> **d** to engage in; CARRY ON <~ *a meeting*> **7a** to cause to by persuasive or forceful means <*so he would* ~ *us believe*> **b** *chiefly Br* to bring into a specified condition by the action of another <~ *my shoes mended*> **c** to cause to be <*soon* ~ *it finished*> **d** to invite as a guest <~ *them over for drinks*> **8** to allow, permit <*I'm not* having *any more of that*> **9a** to hold in a position of disadvantage or certain defeat <*we* ~ *him now*> **b** to perplex, floor <*you* ~ *me there*> **10** to be able to exercise; be entitled to <*I* ~ *my rights*> **11a** to be pregnant with or be the prospective parents of <*they're* having *a baby in August*> **b** to give birth to <*the cat's just* had *kittens*> **12** to partake of; consume <~ *dinner*> **13** to take advantage of; fool <*been* had *by his partner*> – infml ~ *va* **1** – used with the past participle to form the present perfect <has *gone home*>, the past perfect <had *already eaten*>, the future perfect <*will* ~ *finished dinner by then*>, or nonfinite perfective forms <having *gone*> <*silly not to* ~ *gone*>; used with *got* to express obligation or necessity <~ *got to go*>; used in the past tense with the past participle as a rather literary expression of the conditional <had *I known*> **2** WOULD 1b <*I* had *as soon not*> – **have a lot/enough on one's plate** to be (fully) occupied, often with a variety of tasks, problems, etc – **have an ear to the ground** to be in receipt of information not generally known – **have a screw/slate loose** to be slightly cracked, feebleminded, or eccentric – **have a way with** to be good at dealing with <*he* has a way with *old ladies*> – **have a way with one** to be charming, esp persuasively – **have been around** to be sophisticated or well-informed – **have coming** to deserve or merit what one gets, benefits by, or suffers <*he* had *that* coming *to him*> – **have done with** to bring to an end; have no further concern with <*let us* have done with *name-calling*> – **have had it 1** to have had and missed one's chance – infml **2** to have passed one's prime; be obsolete, smashed, or dead – infml – **have it 1** to

maintain, affirm <*as rumour* has it> **2** to live in the specified conditions <*never* had it *so good*> – **have it both ways** to exploit or profit from each of a pair of contradictory positions, circumstances, etc; *also* to maintain 2 contradictory views simultaneously – **have it coming to one** to deserve what one is going to get – **have it in for** to intend to do harm to – **have it off/away** to copulate *with* – slang – **have it out** to settle a matter of contention by discussion or a fight – **have no time for** to be unable or reluctant to spend time on; dislike – infml – **have one's eye on 1** to watch, esp constantly and attentively **2** to have as an objective – **have one's hands full** to be fully occupied – **have one's head screwed on** to be sensible, practical, or provident – **have one's work cut out** to be hard put to it – **have taped** to have the measure of; be in command or control of <*soon have the problem* taped> – **have the advantage of** to have superiority over; *specif* to have personal unreciprocated knowledge of – **have the wind of** to be to windward of – **have to do with 1** to deal with **2** to have in the way of connection or relation with or effect on <*the lawyer would* have *nothing* to do with *the case*> – compare TO DO WITH – **have up one's sleeve** to have as an undeclared resource <*he*'s got *some new ideas* up his sleeve> – **not have a clue** to know nothing; not to know – **what have you** any of various other things that might also be mentioned <*paper clips, pins, and* what have you>

[2]**have** *n* a wealthy person – usu pl; esp in *the haves and have-nots*

haven /ˈhayv(ə)n‖ˈheɪv(ə)n/ *n* **1** a harbour, port **2** a place of safety or refuge

ˈhave-ˌnot *n* a poor person – usu pl; compare [2]HAVE

haven't /ˈhavnt‖ˈhævnt/ have not

ˌhave ˈon *vt* **1** to be wearing <have *a new suit* on> **2** to have plans for <*what do you* have on *for tomorrow?*> **3** *chiefly Br* to deceive, tease – infml

haver /ˈhayvə‖ˈheɪvə/ *vi, chiefly Br* to be indecisive; hesitate

haversack /ˈhavəˌsak‖ˈhævəˌsæk/ *n* a knapsack [French *havresac*, fr German *habersack* bag for oats, fr *haber* oats + *sack* bag]

ˌhave ˈup *vt* to bring before the authorities <*he was* had up *in court for dangerous driving*> – infml

havoc /ˈhavək‖ˈhævək/ *n* **1** widespread destruction; devastation **2** great confusion and disorder

[1]**haw** /haw‖hɔː/ *n* (a berry of) hawthorn

[2]**haw** *vi* to utter a sound resembling *haw*, esp in hesitation <*hummed and* ~ed *before answering*>

[3]**haw** *interj* – often used to indicate hesitation

[1]**hawk** /hawk‖hɔːk/ *n* **1** any of numerous medium-sized birds of prey that have (short) rounded wings and long tails and that hunt during the day **2** a small board with a handle on the underside for holding mortar or plaster **3** one who takes a militant attitude; a supporter of a warlike policy – usu contrasted with *dove* – **hawkish** *adj*, **hawkishly** *adv*, **hawkishness** *n*

[2]**hawk** *vi* **1** to hunt game with a trained hawk **2** to soar and strike like a hawk <*birds* ~ ing *after insects*> ~*vt* to hunt on the wing like a hawk

[3]**hawk** *vt* to offer for sale in the street <~ing *newspapers*>

[4]**hawk** *vi* to utter a harsh guttural sound (as if) in clearing the throat ~*vt* to raise by hawking <~ *up phlegm*>

[5]**hawk** *n* an audible effort to force up phlegm from the throat

[1]**hawker** /ˈhawkə‖ˈhɔːkə/ *n* a falconer

[2]**hawker** *n* sby who hawks wares

hawser /ˈhawzə‖ˈhɔːzə/ *n* a large rope

hawthorn /ˈhawˌthawn‖ˈhɔːˌθɔːn/ *n* any of a genus of spring-flowering spiny shrubs with white or pink flowers and small red fruits

[1]**hay** /hay‖heɪ/ *n* herbage, esp grass, mowed and cured for fodder

[2]**hay** *vi* to cut, cure, and store grass for hay

[3]**hay, hey** *n* a rustic dance featuring winding and interweaving dance figures

ˈhayˌcock *n* a small conical pile of hay in a field

ˈhay ˌfever *n* nasal catarrh and conjunctivitis occurring usu in the spring and summer through allergy to pollen

ˈhayˌmaker *n* **1** one who tosses and spreads hay to dry after cutting **2** *chiefly NAm* a powerful blow – **haymaking** *n*

ˈhayˌstack *n* a relatively large sometimes thatched outdoor pile of hay

ˈhayˌwire *adj* **1** out of order <*the radio went* ~> **2** emotionally or mentally upset; crazy <*went completely* ~ *after the accident*> *USE* infml

[1]**hazard** /ˈhazəd‖ˈhæzəd/ *n* **1** a game of chance played with 2 dice **2a** a risk, peril **b** a source of danger **3** a golf-course obstacle (e g a bunker) [Middle French *hasard*, fr Arabic *az-zahr* the dice]

[2]**hazard** *vt* **1** to expose to danger <*a captain guilty of* ~ing *his ship*> **2** to venture, risk <~ *a guess*>

hazardous /ˈhazədəs‖ˈhæzədəs/ *adj* **1** depending on hazard or chance **2** involving or exposing one to risk (e g of loss or harm) <*a* ~ *occupation*> – **hazardously** *adv*, **hazardousness** *n*

[1]**haze** /hayz‖heɪz/ *vb* to make or become hazy or cloudy

[2]**haze** *n* **1** vapour, dust, smoke, etc causing a slight decrease in the air's transparency **2** vagueness or confusion of mental perception

[3]**haze** *vt, chiefly NAm* to harass (a new student) with ridicule, criticism, etc – **hazer** *n*, **hazing** *n*

hazel /ˈhayzl‖ˈheɪzl/ *n* **1** (the wood or nut of) any of a genus of shrubs or small trees bearing nuts **2** a yellowish light to strong brown – **hazel** *adj*

hazy /ˈhayzi‖ˈheɪzɪ/ *adj* **1** obscured, cloudy <*a* ~ *view of the mountains*> **2** vague, indefinite <*had only a* ~ *recollection of what happened*> – **hazily** *adv*, **haziness** *n*

ˈH-ˌbomb *n* HYDROGEN BOMB

[1]**he** /(h)i, ee‖(h)ɪ, iː; *strong* hee‖hiː/ *pron* **1** that male person or creature who is neither speaker nor hearer – + cap in reference to God **2** – used in a generic sense or when the sex of the person is unspecified <~ *who laughs last laughs longest*>

²he *n* **1** a male person or creature <*a* he-*goat*> **2** ²IT 1

¹head /hed‖hed/ *n, pl* **heads,** (*4b*) **head** **1** the upper or foremost division of the body containing the brain, the chief sense organs, and the mouth **2a** the seat of the intellect; the mind <*2* ~s *are better than 1*> **b** natural aptitude or talent <*a good* ~ *for figures*> **c** mental or emotional control; composure <*a level* ~> **d** a headache **3** the obverse of a coin – usu pl with sing. meaning **4a** a person, individual <*a* ~ *count*> **b** a single individual (domestic animal) out of a number – usu pl <*500* ~ *of cattle*> **5a** the end that is upper, higher, or opposite the foot <*the* ~ *of the table*> **b** the source of a stream, river, etc **c** either end of sthg (e g a cask or drum) whose 2 ends need not be distinguished **d** DRIFT 5 **6** a director, leader: e g **6a** a school principal **b** one in charge of a department in an institution **7** the foliaged part of a plant, esp when consisting of a compact mass of leaves or fruits **8** the leading part of a military column, procession, etc **9a** the uppermost extremity or projecting part of an object; the top **b** the striking part of a weapon, tool, implement, etc **10a** a body of water kept in reserve at a height **b** a mass of water in motion **11a** (the pressure resulting from) the difference in height between 2 points in a body of liquid **b** the pressure of a fluid <*a good* ~ *of steam*> **12a** (parts adjacent to) the bow of a ship **b** a (ship's) toilet – usu pl with sing. meaning in British English **13** a measure of length equivalent to a head <*the horse won by a* ~> **14** the place of leadership, honour, or command <*at the* ~ *of his class*> **15a** a word often in larger letters placed above a passage in order to introduce or categorize **b** a separate part or topic **16** the foam or froth that rises on a fermenting or effervescing liquid **17a** the part of a boil, pimple, etc at which it is likely to break **b** a culminating point; a crisis – esp in *come to a head* **18a** a part of a machine or machine tool containing a device (e g a cutter or drill); *also* the part of an apparatus that performs the chief or a particular function **b** any of at least 2 electromagnetic components which bear on the magnetic tape in a tape recorder, such that one can erase recorded material if desired and another may either record or play back **19** one who uses LSD, cannabis, etc habitually or excessively – often in combination; slang – **headless** *adj*, **headlessness** *n* – **off one's head** crazy, mad – **over someone's head 1** beyond sby's comprehension **2** so as to pass over sby's superior standing or authority <*went* over his *supervisor's* head *to complain*>

²head *adj* **1** principal, chief <~ *cook*> **2** situated at the head

³head *vt* **1** to cut back or off the upper growth of (a plant) **2a** to provide with a head **b** to form the head or top of <*tower* ~ed *by a spire*> **3** to be at the head of; lead <~ *a revolt*> **4** to go round the head of (a stream) **5a** to put sthg at the head of (e g a list); *also* to provide with a heading **b** to stand as the first or leading member of <~s *the list of heroes*> **6** to set the course of <~ *a ship northwards*> **7** to drive (e g a soccer ball) with the head ~ *vi* **1** to form a head <*this cabbage* ~s *early*> **2** to point or proceed in a specified direction <~ing *for disaster*>

headache /ˈhedayk‖ˈhedeɪk/ *n* **1** pain in the head **2** a difficult situation or problem – **headachy** *adj*

ˈheadˌband *n* a band worn round the head, esp to keep hair out of the eyes

ˈheadˌboard *n* a board forming the head (e g of a bed)

ˈheadˌdress *n* an often elaborate covering for the head

headed /ˈhedid‖ˈhedɪd/ *adj* **1** having a head or a heading <~ *notepaper*> **2** having a head or heads of a specified kind or number – in combination <*a cool*headed *businessman*>

header /ˈhedə‖ˈhedə/ *n* **1** a brick or stone laid in a wall with its end towards the face of the wall **2** a headfirst fall or dive **3** a shot or pass in soccer made by heading the ball

ˌheadˈfirst *adv* with the head foremost; headlong – **headfirst** *adj*

ˈhead-ˌhunting *n* **1** decapitating and preserving the heads of enemies as trophies **2** searching for and recruitment of personnel, esp at executive level and often from other firms – **headhunter** *n*

heading /ˈheding‖ˈhedɪŋ/ *n* **1** the compass direction in which a ship or aircraft points **2a** an inscription, headline, or title standing at the top or beginning (e g of a letter or chapter) **b** a piece used in making either of the flat ends of a barrel **3** DRIFT 5

headland /ˈhedlənd‖ˈhedlənd/ *n* **1** unploughed land near an edge of a field **2** a point of usu high land jutting out into a body of water

ˈheadˌlight *n* (the beam cast by) the main light mounted on the front of a motor vehicle

ˈheadˌline *n* a title printed in large type above a newspaper story or article; *also, pl, Br* a summary given at the beginning or end of a news broadcast

ˈheadˌlong *adv or adj* **1** headfirst **2** without deliberation **3** without pause or delay

ˈheadman /-mən‖-mən/ *n* a chief of a primitive community

ˌheadˈmaster, *fem* **ˌheadˈmistress** *n* one who heads the staff of a school – **headmastership** *n*

head off *vt* to stop the progress of or turn aside by taking preventive action; block

ˌhead-ˈon *adv or adj* **1** with the head or front making the initial contact <*a* ~ *collision*> **2** in direct opposition <*a* ~ *confrontation*>

ˈheadˌphone *n* an earphone held over the ear by a band worn on the head – usu pl

ˈheadˌpiece *n* an ornamental printed device esp at the beginning of a chapter

ˌheadˈquarters *n, pl* **headquarters** **1** a place from which a commander exercises command **2** the administrative centre of an enterprise *USE* often pl with sing. meaning

ˈheadˌrest *n* a support for the head; *esp* a cushioned pad supporting the head in a vehicle

ˈheadroom /-room, -roohm‖-rʊm, -ru:m/ *n* vertical space (e g beneath a bridge) sufficient to allow passage or unrestricted movement

ˈheadˌset *n* an attachment for holding earphones and a microphone to one's head

ˈheadship /-ship‖-ʃɪp/ *n* the position or office of a head (e g a headmaster); leadership

ˈheadˌshrinker *n* **1** a headhunter who shrinks the heads of his/her victims **2** a psychoanalyst or psychiatrist – humor

ˈheadˌstall *n* the part of a bridle or halter that encircles the head

ˌhead ˈstart *n* **1** an advantage granted or achieved at the beginning of a race, competition, etc **2** an advantageous or favourable beginning

ˈheadˌstone *n* a memorial stone placed at the head of a grave

ˈheadˌstrong *adj* wilful, obstinate

ˈheadˌway *n* **1a** (rate of) motion in a forward direction **b** advance, progress **2** headroom **3** the time interval between 2 vehicles travelling in the same direction on the same route

ˈheadˌwind /-ˌwind‖-ˌwɪnd/ *n* a wind blowing in a direction opposite to a course, esp of a ship or aircraft

ˈheadˌword *n* a word or term placed at the beginning (e g of a chapter or encyclopedia entry)

heady /ˈhedi‖ˈhedɪ/ *adj* **1** violent, impetuous **2a** tending to make giddy or exhilarated; intoxicating **b** giddy, exhilarated <*~ with his success*> – **headily** *adv*, **headiness** *n*

heal /heel‖hiːl/ *vt* **1a** to make sound or whole <*~ a wound*> **b** to restore to health **2** to restore to a sound or normal state; mend <*~ a breach between friends*> ~*vi* to return to a sound or healthy state – **healer** *n*

health /helth‖helθ/ *n* **1a** soundness of body, mind, or spirit **b** the general condition of the body <*in poor ~*> **2** condition <*the economic ~ of the country is not good*>; *esp* a sound or flourishing condition; well-being **3** a toast to sby's health or prosperity

ˈhealthful /-f(ə)l‖-f(ə)l/ *adj* **1** beneficial to health of body or mind **2** HEALTHY 1

healthy /ˈhelthi‖ˈhelθɪ/ *adj* **1** enjoying or showing health and vigour of body, mind, or spirit **2** conducive to good health **3** prosperous, flourishing – **healthily** *adv*, **healthiness** *n*

[1]**heap** /heep‖hiːp/ *n* **1** a collection of things lying one on top of another; a pile **2** a great number or large quantity; a lot – infml; often pl with sing. meaning <*~s more to say*>

[2]**heap** *vt* **1a** to throw or lay in a heap; pile *up* <*his sole object was to ~ up riches*> **b** to form or round into a heap <*~ed the earth into a mound*> **2** to supply abundantly *with*; *also* to bestow lavishly or in large quantities *upon*

hear /hiə‖hɪə/ *vb* **heard** /huhd‖hɜːd/ *vt* **1** to perceive (sound) with the ear **2** to learn by hearing <*I ~d you were leaving*> **3a** to listen to with attention; heed <*~ me out*> **b** to attend <*~ mass*> **4** to give a legal hearing to ~ *vi* **1** to have the capacity of perceiving sound **2** to gain information; learn <*I've ~d about what you did*> **3** – often in the expression *Hear! Hear!* indicating approval (e g during a speech) – **hearer** *n* – **hear from** to receive a communication from – **hear of** to entertain the idea of – usu neg <*wouldn't* hear of *it*>

hearing /ˈhiəring‖ˈhɪərɪŋ/ *n* **1a** the one of the 5 basic physical senses by which waves received by the ear are interpreted by the brain as sounds varying in pitch, intensity, and timbre **b** earshot **2a** an opportunity to be heard **b** a trial in court

ˈhearing ˌaid *n* an electronic device worn by a deaf person for amplifying sound before it reaches the ears

hearken /ˈhahkən‖ˈhɑːkən/ *vi* to listen *to*; *also* to heed – poetic

hearsay /ˈhiəˌsay‖ˈhɪəˌseɪ/ *n* sthg heard from another; rumour

hearse /huhs‖hɜːs/ *n* a vehicle for transporting a dead body in its coffin

heart /haht‖hɑːt/ *n* **1a** a hollow muscular organ that by its rhythmic contraction acts as a force pump maintaining the circulation of the blood **b** the breast, bosom **c** sthg resembling a heart in shape; *specif* a conventionalized representation of a heart **2a** a playing card marked with 1 or more red heart-shaped figures **b** *pl but sing or pl in constr* the suit comprising cards identified by this figure **c** *pl but sing in constr* a card game in which the object is to avoid taking tricks containing a heart or the queen of spades **3a** humane disposition; compassion <*have you no ~?*> **b** love, affections <*lost his ~ to her*> **c** courage, spirit <*had no ~ for the task*> **4** one's innermost character or feelings <*a man after my own ~*> **5a** the central or innermost part (of a lettuce, cabbage, etc) **b** the essential or most vital part <*the ~ of the matter*> – **by heart** by rote or from memory

ˈheartˌache *n* mental anguish; sorrow

ˈheart atˌtack *n* an instance of abnormal functioning of the heart; *esp* CORONARY THROMBOSIS

ˈheartˌbeat *n* a single complete pulsation of the heart

ˈheartˌbreak *n* intense grief or distress

ˈheartˌbreaking *adj* **1** causing intense sorrow or distress **2** extremely trying or difficult <*a ~ task*> – **heartbreakingly** *adv*

ˈheartˌbroken *adj* overcome by sorrow

ˈheartˌburn *n* a burning pain behind the lower part of the breastbone usu resulting from spasm of the stomach or throat muscles

hearted /ˈhahtid‖ˈhɑːtɪd/ *adj* having a heart, esp of a specified kind – usu in combination <*a broken*hearted *lover*>

hearten /ˈhahtn‖ˈhɑːtn/ *vt* to cheer, encourage – **hearteningly** *adv*

ˈheart ˌfailure *n* (inability of the heart to perform adequately often leading to) cessation of the heartbeat and death

ˈheartˌfelt *adj* deeply felt; earnest

hearth /hahth‖hɑːθ/ *n* **1a** a brick, stone, or cement area in front of the floor of a fireplace **b** the lowest section of a metal-processing furnace **2** home, fireside <*the comforts of ~ and home*>

heartily /ˈhahtəli‖ˈhɑːtəlɪ/ *adv* **1a** with all sincerity; wholeheartedly <*I ~ recommend it*> **b** with zest; vigorously <*ate ~*> **2** quite, thoroughly <*~ sick of all this talk*>

ˈheartless /-lis‖-lɪs/ *adj* unfeeling, cruel – **heartlessly** *adv*, **heartlessness** *n*

ˈheartˌrending *adj* HEARTBREAKING 1 – **heartrendingly** *adv*

ˈheartsˌease *n* any of various violas; *esp* the wild pansy

ˈheartˌsick *adj* very despondent;

depressed – **heartsickness** *n*

'heartˌstrings *n pl* the deepest emotions or affections <*pulled at his* ~>

'heartˌthrob *n* one who is the object of or arouses infatuation

[1]**ˌheart-to-'heart** *adj* sincere and intimate <~ *confidences*>

[2]**heart-to-heart** *n* a frank or intimate talk – infml

'heartˌwarming *adj* inspiring sympathetic feeling; cheering

'heartˌwood *n* the older harder nonliving central wood in a tree, usu darker and denser than the surrounding sapwood

[1]**hearty** /'hahti‖'hɑːtɪ/ *adj* **1a** enthusiastically or exuberantly friendly; jovial **b** unrestrained, vigorous <*a* ~ *laugh*> **2a** robustly healthy <*hale and* ~> **b** substantial, abundant <*a* ~ *meal*> – **heartiness** *n*

[2]**hearty** *n* **1** a sailor **2** *chiefly Br* a sporty outgoing person <*rugger* hearties>

[1]**heat** /heet‖hiːt/ *vb* to make or become warm or hot – often + *up* – **heatable** *adj*, **heatedly** *adv*

[2]**heat** *n* **1a** the condition of being hot; warmth; *also* a marked degree of this **b** excessively high bodily temperature **c** the form of energy associated with the random motions of the molecules, atoms, etc of which matter is composed, transmitted by conduction, convection, or radiation **d** an esp high temperature <*at melting* ~> **e** any of a series of degrees of heating <*this iron has 4* ~s> **2a** intensity of feeling or reaction <*the* ~ *of passion*> **b** the height or stress of an action or condition <*in the* ~ *of battle*> **c** readiness for sexual intercourse in a female mammal; *specif* oestrus – usu in *on heat* or (*chiefly NAm*) *in heat* **3** pungency of flavour **4a** a single round of a contest that has 2 or more rounds for each contestant **b** any of several preliminary contests whose winners go into the final **5** pressure, coercion <*his enemies turned the* ~ *on him*> – slang – **heatless** *adj*, **heatproof** *adj*

heated /'heetid‖'hiːtɪd/ *adj* marked by anger <*a* ~ *argument*>

heater /'heetə‖'hiːtə/ *n* a device that gives off heat or holds sthg to be heated

heath /heeth‖hiːθ/ *n* **1** any of various related evergreen plants that thrive on barren usu acid soil, with whorls of needlelike leaves and clusters of small flowers **2a** a tract of wasteland **b** a large area of level uncultivated land usu with poor peaty soil and bad drainage

heathen /'heedh(ə)n‖'hiːð(ə)n/ *n, pl* **heathens, heathen 1** an unconverted member of a people or nation that does not acknowledge the God of the Bible – often pl + *the* <*the* ~ *say there is no God*> **2** an uncivilized or irreligious person – **heathen** *adj*, **heathenish** *adj*, **heathenism** *n*, **heathendom** *n*, **heathenize** *vt*

heather /'hedhə‖'heðə/ *n* a (common usu purplish-pink flowered northern) heath – **heather** *adj*

'heat ˌpump *n* an apparatus for transferring heat by mechanical means to a place of higher temperature (e g for heating or cooling a building)

'heat ˌrash *n* PRICKLY HEAT

'heat ˌsink *n* a means of absorbing or dissipating unwanted heat

'heatˌstroke *n* overheating of the body resulting from prolonged exposure to high temperature and leading to (fatal) collapse

'heat ˌwave *n* a period of unusually hot weather

[1]**heave** /heev‖hiːv/ *vb* **heaved, hove** /hohv‖həʊv/ *vt* **1** to lift upwards or forwards, esp with effort **2** to throw, cast **3** to utter with obvious effort <~d *a sigh*> **4** to cause to swell or rise **5** to haul, draw ~ *vi* **1** to rise or become thrown or raised up **2a** to rise and fall rhythmically <*his chest* ~ing *with sobs*> **b** to pant **3** to vomit **4** to pull – **heaver** *n* – **heave in/into sight** to come into view

[2]**heave** *n* **1a** an effort to heave or raise **b** a throw, cast **2** an upward motion; *esp* a rhythmical rising <*the* ~ *of the sea*> **3** *pl but sing or pl in constr* BROKEN WIND

heaven /'hev(ə)n‖'hev(ə)n/ *n* **1** (any of the spheres of) the expanse of space that surrounds the earth like a dome; the firmament – usu pl with sing. meaning **2** *often cap* the dwelling place of God, his angels, and the spirits of those who have received salvation; Paradise **3** *cap* GOD 1 **4** a place or condition of utmost happiness

'heavenly /-li‖-lɪ/ *adj* **1** of heaven or the heavens; celestial <*the* ~ *choirs*> **2a** suggesting the blessed state of heaven; divine <~ *peace*> **b** delightful <*what a* ~ *idea*> – infml – **heavenliness** *n*

ˌheaven-'sent *adj* providential

'heavenward /-wood‖-wʊd/ *adj* directed towards heaven or the heavens – **heavenwards,** *NAm chiefly* **heavenward** *adv*

ˌheave 'to *vb* to bring (a ship) to a stop with head to wind

heavily /'hevəli‖'hevəlɪ/ *adv* **1** slowly and laboriously; dully **2** to a great degree; severely

[1]**heavy** /'hevi‖'hevɪ/ *adj* **1a** having great weight **b** having great weight in proportion to size **c** *of an isotope or compound* having, being, or containing atoms of greater than normal mass <~ *hydrogen*> **2** hard to bear; *specif* grievous <*a* ~ *sorrow*> **3** of weighty import; serious <*a* ~ *book*> **4** emotionally intense; profound <*a* ~ *silence*> **5a** oppressed; burdened <*returned with* ~ *spirit from the meeting*> **b** pregnant; *esp* approaching parturition – often + *with* **6a** slow, sluggish <~ *movements*> **b** lacking sparkle or vivacity; dull <*the book made* ~ *reading*> **7** dulled with weariness; drowsy <*his eyelids felt* ~ *with sleep*> **8a** of an unusually large amount <~ *traffic*> **b** of great force <~ *seas*> **c** overcast <*a* ~ *sky*> **d** *of ground or soil* full of clay and inclined to hold water; impeding motion **e** loud and deep <*the* ~ *roll of thunder*> **f** laborious, difficult <*made* ~ *going of it*> **g** of large capacity or output **h** consuming in large quantities – usu + *on* <*this car is* ~ *on petrol*> **9a** digested with difficulty, usu because of excessive richness <~ *fruit cake*> **b** *esp of bread* not sufficiently raised or leavened **10** producing heavy usu large goods (e g coal, steel, or machinery) often used in the production of other goods <~ *industry*> **11a** of the larger variety <*a* ~ *howitzer*> **b** heavily armoured,

armed, or equipped <*the ~ cavalry*> **12** *of rock music* loud and strongly rhythmic – slang **13** *chiefly NAm* frighteningly serious; *specif* threatening – slang; often used as an interjection – **heaviness** *n* – **with a heavy hand 1** with little mercy; sternly **2** without grace; clumsily

[2]**heavy** *adv* in a heavy manner; heavily <*time hangs ~ on us*>

[3]**heavy** *n* **1** *pl* units (e g of bombers, artillery, or cavalry) of the heavy sort **2a** (an actor playing) a villain **b** sby of importance or significance – infml **3** a serious newspaper – usu pl; infml **4** one hired to compel or deter by means of threats or physical violence <*set a gang of* heavies *on him*> – slang

ˌheavy-ˈduty *adj* able or designed to withstand unusual strain or wear

ˌheavy-ˈhanded *adj* **1** clumsy, awkward **2** oppressive, harsh – **heavy-handedly** *adv*, **heavy-handedness** *n*

ˌheavyˈhearted *adj* despondent, melancholy – **heavyheartedly** *adv*, **heavyheartedness** *n*

ˈheavy ˌwater *n* water enriched esp with the hydrogen isotope deuterium

ˈheavyˌweight *n* **1** sby or sthg above average weight **2** one in the usu heaviest class of contestants: e g **2a** a boxer whose weight is not limited if he is professional or is more than 81kg (about 12st 10lb) if he is amateur **b** a wrestler weighing over 100kg (about 15st 10lb) **c** a weight-lifter weighing over 110kg (about 17st 4lb) **3** an important or influential person

hebdomadal /hebˈdomədl‖hebˈdɒmədl/ *adj* weekly – fml – **hebdomadally** *adv*

hebe /ˈheebi‖ˈhiːbɪ/ *n* any of a genus of evergreen shrubs, mostly native to New Zealand, often cultivated for their decorative leaves and usu white or purplish flowers

Hebraic /hiˈbrayik‖hɪˈbreɪɪk/, **Hebraistic** /ˌheebrayˈistik‖ˌhiːbreɪˈɪstɪk/ *adj* of the Hebrews, their culture, or Hebrew – **Hebraically** *adv*, **Hebraistically** *adv*

Hebrew /ˈheebrooh‖ˈhiːbruː/ *n* **1** a member or descendant of any of a group of N Semitic peoples including the Israelites; *esp* an Israelite **2** the Semitic language of the ancient Hebrews; *also* a later form of Hebrew – **Hebrew** *adj*

hecatomb /ˈhekətoohm, -tohm‖ˈhekətuːm, -təʊm/ *n* **1** an ancient Greek and Roman sacrifice of 100 oxen or cattle **2** the sacrifice or slaughter of many victims

heck /hek‖hek/ *n* HELL 2a – used as an interjection or intensive <*what the ~!*> <*a ~ of a lot of money*>

heckle /ˈhekl‖ˈhekl/ *vt* to harass and try to disconcert (e g a speaker) with questions, challenges, or gibes – **heckler** *n*

hectare /ˈhektah‖ˈhektɑː/ *n* a metric unit of area equal to 100 are (2.471 acres)

hectic /ˈhektik‖ˈhektɪk/ *adj* **1** of, being, or suffering from a fluctuating fever (e g in tuberculosis) **2** filled with excitement or feverish activity <*the ~ days before Christmas*> [Late Latin *hecticus*, fr Greek *hektikos* habitual, consumptive, fr *echein* to have] – **hectically** *adv*

hector /ˈhektə‖ˈhektə/ *vi* to play the bully; swagger ~*vt* to intimidate by bullying or blustering – **hectoringly** *adv*

he'd /eed, id, hid‖iːd, ɪd, hɪd; *strong* heed‖hiːd/ he had; he would

[1]**hedge** /hej‖hedʒ/ *n* **1a** a boundary formed by a dense row of shrubs or low trees **b** a barrier, limit **2** a means of protection or defence (e g against financial loss) **3** a calculatedly noncommittal or evasive statement

[2]**hedge** *vt* **1** to enclose or protect (as if) with a hedge **2** to hem in or obstruct (as if) with a barrier; hinder **3** to protect oneself against losing (e g a bet), esp by making counterbalancing transactions ~ *vi* **1** to plant, form, or trim a hedge **2** to avoid committing oneself to a definite course of action, esp by making evasive statements **3** to protect oneself financially: e g **3a** to buy or sell commodity futures as a protection against loss due to price fluctuation – often + *against* **b** to minimize the risk of a bet – **hedger** *n*, **hedgingly** *adv*

hedgehog /ˈhejˌhog‖ˈhedʒˌhɒg/ *n* any of a genus of small Old World spine-covered insect-eating mammals that are active at night

ˈhedgeˌhop *vi* **-pp-** to fly an aircraft close to the ground and rise over obstacles as they appear – **hedgehopper** *n*

ˈhedgeˌrow /-ˌroh‖-ˌrəʊ/ *n* a row of shrubs or trees surrounding a field

ˈhedge ˌsparrow *n* a dunnock

hedonism /ˈhedəˌniz(ə)m, ˈhee-‖ˈhedəˌnɪz(ə)m, ˈhiː-/ *n* (conduct based on) the doctrine that personal pleasure is the sole or chief good [Greek *hēdonē* pleasure] – **hedonist** *n*, **hedonistic** *adj*, **hedonistically** *adv*

heebie-jeebies /ˌheebi ˈjeebiz‖ˌhiːbɪ ˈdʒiːbɪz/ *n pl the* jitters, willies – infml

[1]**heed** /heed‖hiːd/ *vb* to pay attention (to)

[2]**heed** *n* attention, notice <*take ~*>

ˈheedful /-f(ə)l‖-f(ə)l/ *adj* attentive, mindful *of* – **heedfully** *adv*, **heedfulness** *n*

ˈheedless /-lis‖-lɪs/ *adj* inconsiderate, thoughtless – **heedlessly** *adv*, **heedlessness** *n*

hee-haw /ˈhee ˌhaw‖ˈhiː ˌhɔː/ *n* **1** the bray of a donkey **2** a loud rude laugh; a guffaw – **hee-haw** *vi*

[1]**heel** /heel‖hiːl/ *n* **1** (the back part of the hind limb of a vertebrate corresponding to) the back of the human foot below the ankle and behind the arch or an anatomical structure resembling this **2** either of the crusty ends of a loaf of bread **3** the part of a garment or an article of footwear that covers or supports the human heel **4a** the lower end of a mast **b** the base of a tuber or cutting of a plant used for propagation **5** a backward kick with the heel in rugby, esp from a set scrum **6** a contemptible person – slang – **heeled** *adj*, **heelless** *adj* – **down at (the) heel** in or into a run-down or shabby condition – **on the heels of** immediately following; closely behind – **to heel 1** close behind – usu used in training a dog **2** into agreement or line; under control

[2]**heel** *vt* **1** to supply with a heel; *esp* to renew the heel of <*~ a sock*> **2** to exert pressure on, propel, or strike (as if) with the heel; *specif* to kick (a rugby ball) with the heel, esp out of a scrum ~*vi* to move along at the heels of sby or close behind sthg <*a dog that ~s well*> – **heeler** *n*

[3]**heel** *vi* to tilt to one side ~ *vt* to cause

(a boat) to heel

[4]**heel** *n* (the extent of) a tilt to one side

ˈ**heel͵ball** *n* a mixture of wax and lampblack used to polish the heels of footwear and to take brass or stone rubbings

hefty /ˈhefti‖ˈheftɪ/ *adj* **1** large or bulky and usu heavy **2** powerful, mighty <*a* ~ *blow*> **3** impressively large <*a* ~ *price to pay*> – **heftily** *adv*, **heftiness** *n*

hegemony /hiˈgeməni‖hɪˈgemənɪ/ *n* domination by one nation, group, etc over others [Greek *hēgemonia*, fr *hēgemōn* leader, fr *hēgeisthai* to lead]

hegira *also* **hejira** /ˈhejirə‖ˈhedʒɪrə/ *n* a journey, esp when undertaken to escape from a dangerous or undesirable situation; *specif, cap* the flight of Muhammad from Mecca to Medina in 622 AD, the event marking the beginning of the Muhammadan era [Medieval Latin *hegira*, fr Arabic *hijrah*, lit., flight]

heifer /ˈhefə‖ˈhefə/ *n* a young cow (that has at most 1 calf)

heigh-ho /ˈhay ͵hoh‖ˈheɪ ͵həʊ/ *interj* – used to express boredom, weariness, or sadness

height /hiet‖haɪt/ *n* **1** the highest or most extreme point; the zenith <*at the* ~ *of his powers*> **2a** the distance from the bottom to the top of sthg standing upright **b** the elevation above a level **3** the condition of being tall or high **4a** a piece of land (e g a hill or plateau) rising to a considerable degree above the surrounding country – usu pl with sing. meaning **b** a high point or position

heighten /ˈhiet(ə)n‖ˈhaɪt(ə)n/ *vt* **1a** to increase the amount or degree of; augment <~ed *his awareness of the problem*> **b** to deepen, intensify <*her colour was* ~ed *by emotion*> **2** to raise high or higher; elevate <*the building was* ~ed *by another storey*> ~ *vi* **1** to become great or greater in amount, degree, or extent **2** to intensify

heinous /ˈhaynəs, ˈheenəs‖ˈheɪnəs, ˈhiːnəs/ *adj* hatefully or shockingly evil; abominable – **heinously** *adv*, **heinousness** *n*

heir /eə‖eə/ *n* **1** sby who inherits or is entitled to succeed to an estate or rank **2** sby who receives or is entitled to receive some position, role, or quality passed on from a parent or predecessor – **heirless** *adj*, **heirship** *n*

͵**heir apˈparent** *n, pl* **heirs apparent** **1** an heir who cannot be displaced so long as he/she outlives the person from whom he/she is to inherit **2** one whose succession, esp to a position or role, appears certain under existing circumstances

heiress /ˈeəris‖ˈeərɪs/ *n* a female heir, esp to great wealth

ˈ**heir͵loom** /-loohm‖-luːm/ *n* **1** a piece of valuable property handed down within a family for generations **2** sthg of special value handed on from one generation to another [Middle English *heirlome*, fr *heir* + *lome* implement]

͵**heir preˈsumptive** *n, pl* **heirs presumptive** an heir who can be displaced only by the birth of a child with a superior claim

hejira /ˈhejirə‖ˈhedʒɪrə/ *n* a hegira

held /held‖held/ *past of* HOLD

helicopter /ˈheli͵koptə‖ˈhelɪ͵kɒptə/ *n* an aircraft which derives both lift and propulsive power from a set of horizontally rotating rotors or vanes and is capable of vertical takeoff and landing [French *hélicoptère*, fr Greek *helik-*, *helix* spiral + *pteron* wing]

heliograph /ˈheeli·ə͵grahf, -͵graf‖ˈhiːlɪə-͵grɑːf, -͵græf/ *n* **1** a photoheliograph **2** an apparatus for signalling using the sun's rays reflected from a mirror [deriv of Greek *hēlios* sun + *graphein* to write]

heliotrope /ˈheeli·ə͵trohp‖ˈhiːlɪə͵trəʊp/ *n* **1** any of a genus of plants of the borage family **2** light purple

heliport /ˈheli͵pawt‖ˈhelɪ͵pɔːt/ *n* a place for helicopters to take off and land

helium /ˈheeli·əm, -lyəm‖ˈhiːlɪəm, -ljəm/ *n* a noble gaseous element found in natural gases and used esp for inflating balloons and in low-temperature research

helix /ˈheeliks‖ˈhiːlɪks/ *n, pl* **helices** /ˈheli͵seez‖ˈhelɪ͵siːz/ *also* **helixes** **1** sthg spiral in form (e g a coil formed by winding wire round a uniform tube) **2** the rim curved inwards of the external ear **3** a curve traced on a cylinder at a constant rate; *broadly* SPIRAL 1b – **helical** *adj*, **helically** *adj*

hell /hel‖hel/ *n* **1a** a nether world (e g Hades or Sheol) inhabited by the spirits of the dead **b** the nether realm of the devil in which the souls of those excluded from Paradise undergo perpetual torment **c** the home of the devil and demons in which the damned suffer punishment **2a** a place or state of torment, misery, or wickedness – often as an interjection, an intensive, or as a generalized term of abuse <*one* ~ *of a mess*> <*go to* ~> **b** a place or state of chaos or destruction <*all* ~ *broke loose*> **c** a severe scolding <*got* ~ *for coming in late*> – **for the hell of it** for the intrinsic amusement or satisfaction of an activity – **hell to pay** serious trouble <*if he's late there'll be* hell to pay> – **like hell 1** very hard or much <*worked* like hell *to get the job done on time*> **2** – used to intensify denial of a statement; slang <*'I did 4 hours overtime.'* 'Like hell *you did!*'> – **what the hell** it doesn't matter

he'll /hil, eel, il‖hɪl, iːl, ɪl; *strong* heel‖hiːl/ he will; he shall

͵**hell-ˈbent** *adj* stubbornly and often recklessly determined

Hellene /ˈheleen‖ˈheliːn/ *n* GREEK 1

Hellenic /heˈlenik, -ˈleenik, hə-‖heˈlenɪk, -ˈliːnɪk, hə-/ *adj* of Greece, its people, or its language

Hellenistic /͵heliˈnistik‖͵helɪˈnɪstɪk/ *adj* of Greek history, culture, or art after Alexander the Great

[1]**hellish** /ˈhelish‖ˈhelɪʃ/ *adj* of, resembling, or befitting hell; diabolical – **hellishly** *adv*, **hellishness** *n*

[2]**hellish** *adv* extremely, damnably <*a* ~ *cold day*>

hello /heˈloh, ˈheloh, hə-‖heˈləʊ, ˈheləʊ, hə-/ *n, pl* **hellos** an expression or gesture of greeting – used interjectionally in greeting, in answering the telephone, to express surprise, or to attract attention

[1]**helm** /helm‖helm/ *n* HELMET 1

[2]**helm** *n* **1** a tiller or wheel controlling the steering of a ship **2** the position of control; the head <*a new dean is at the* ~ *of the medical school*>

[3]**helm** *vt* to steer (as if) with a helm

helmet /ˈhelmit‖ˈhelmɪt/ *n* **1** a covering or enclosing headpiece of ancient or medieval armour **2** any of various protective head coverings, esp made of a hard material to resist impact **3** sthg, esp a hood-shaped petal or sepal, resembling a helmet – **helmeted** *adj*, **helmetlike** *adj*

helmsman /ˈhelmzmən‖ˈhelmzmən/ *n* the person at the helm – **helmsmanship** *n*

helot /ˈhelət‖ˈhelət/ *n* **1** *cap* a serf in ancient Sparta **2** a serf, slave – **helotry** *n*

[1]**help** /help‖help/ *vt* **1** to give assistance or support to <~ *a child to understand his lesson*> **2** to remedy, relieve <*took an aspirin to* ~ *her headache*> **3a** to be of use to; benefit **b** to further the advancement of; promote <~ing *industry with loans*> **4a** to refrain from <*couldn't* ~ *laughing*> **b** to keep from occurring; prevent <*they couldn't* ~ *the accident*> **c** to restrain (oneself) from taking action <*tried not to say anything, but couldn't* ~ *myself*> **5** to serve with food or drink, esp at a meal <*let me* ~ *you to some salad*> **6** to appropriate sthg for (oneself), esp dishonestly <~ed *himself to my pen*> ~ *vi* to be of use or benefit <*every little* ~s> – **helper** *n* – **help somebody on/off with** to help sby take off/put on (an article of clothing)

[2]**help** *n* **1** aid, assistance **2** remedy, relief <*there was no* ~ *for it*> **3a** sby, esp a woman, hired to do work, esp housework <*a mother's* ~> **b** the services of a paid worker; *also, chiefly NAm* the workers providing such services <~ *wanted*>

ˈ**helpful** /-f(ə)l‖-f(ə)l/ *adj* of service or assistance; useful – **helpfully** *adv*, **helpfulness** *n*

helping /ˈhelping‖ˈhelpɪŋ/ *n* a serving of food

ˈ**helpless** /-lis‖-lɪs/ *adj* **1** lacking protection or support; defenceless **2** lacking strength or effectiveness; powerless – **helplessly** *adv*, **helplessness** *n*

ˈ**help,mate** *n* one who is a companion and helper; *esp* a spouse

help out *vb* to give assistance or aid (to), esp when in great difficulty <*she* helped *me* out *when I was in hospital*>

[1]**helter-skelter** /ˌheltə ˈskeltə‖ˌheltə ˈskeltə/ *adj or adv* (done) in a hurried and disorderly manner

[2]ˌ**helter-ˈskelter** *n* a spiral slide at a fairground

helve /helv‖helv/ *n* a haft

[1]**hem** /hem‖hem/ *n* **1** the border of a cloth article when turned back and stitched down; *esp* the bottom edge of a garment finished in this manner **2** a similar border on an article of plastic, leather, etc

[2]**hem** *vb* **-mm-** *vt* **1a** to finish (e g a skirt) with a hem **b** to border, edge **2** to enclose, confine – usu + *in* or *about* <~med *in by enemy troops*> ~ *vi* to make a hem in sewing – **hemmer** *n*

[3]**hem** *interj* – often used to indicate a pause in speaking

hem-, hema-, hemo- *comb form, NAm* haem-

ˈ**he-,man** /ˈhee‖ˈhiː/ *n* a strong virile man – infml

hemisphere /ˈhemi,sfiə‖ˈhemɪ,sfɪə/ *n* **1a** a half of the celestial sphere when divided into 2 halves by the horizon, the celestial equator, or the ecliptic **b** the northern or southern half of the earth divided by the equator or the eastern or western half divided by a meridian **2** either of the 2 half spheres formed by a plane that passes through the sphere's centre – **hemispheric, hemispherical** *adj*

hemline /ˈhem,lien‖ˈhem,laɪn/ *n* the line formed by the lower hemmed edge of a garment, esp a dress

hemlock /ˈhemlok‖ˈhemlɒk/ *n* **1** (a poison obtained from) a very tall plant of the carrot family or a related very poisonous plant **2** (the soft light wood of) any of a genus of evergreen coniferous trees of the pine family

hemo- – see HAEM-

hemp /hemp‖hemp/ *n* **1** (marijuana, hashish, or a similar drug obtained from) a tall widely cultivated plant from which a tough fibre used esp for making rope is prepared **2** the fibre of hemp or (a plant yielding) a similar fibre (e g jute) – **hempen** *adj*

ˈ**hem,stitch** *vt or n* (to decorate with) drawnwork that consists of open spaces and embroidered groups of cross threads and is used esp on or next to the stitching line of hems

[1]**hen** /hen‖hen/ *n* **1a** a female bird, specif a domestic fowl (over a year old) **b** a female lobster, crab, fish, or other aquatic animal **2** an esp fussy woman – infml **3** *chiefly Scot* DEAR 1b – used to girls and women

[2]**hen** *adj* relating to or intended for women only <*a* ~ *party*>

ˈ**hen,bane** /-,bayn‖-,beɪn/ *n* a poisonous fetid Old World plant of the nightshade family

hence /hens‖hens/ *adv* **1** from this time; later than now **2** because of a preceding fact or premise <*born at Christmas;* ~ *the name Noel*> **3** from here; away – fml <*go* ~>; sometimes + *from* <*depart from* ~>

ˌ**henceˈforth** *adv* from this time or point on

henchman /ˈhenchmən‖ˈhentʃmən/ *n* **1** a trusted follower; a right-hand man **2** a follower whose support is chiefly for personal advantage [Middle English *hengestman* groom, fr *hengest* stallion + *man*]

[1]**henna** /ˈhenə‖ˈhenə/ *n* **1** an Old World tropical shrub or small tree with fragrant white flowers **2** a reddish brown dye obtained from the leaves of the henna plant and used esp on hair

[2]**henna** *vt* **hennaing; hennaed** to dye or tint (esp hair) with henna

henpecked /ˈhen,pekt‖ˈhen,pekt/ *adj* cowed by persistent nagging <~ *husband*>

hepatitis /ˌhepəˈtietəs‖ˌhepəˈtaɪtəs/ *n, pl* **hepatitides** /-ˈtitədeez‖-ˈtɪtədiːz/ (a condition marked by) inflammation of the liver: **a** INFECTIOUS HEPATITIS **b** SERUM HEPATITIS

heptagon /ˈheptəgən‖ˈheptəgən/ *n* a polygon of 7 angles and 7 sides [Greek *hepta* seven + *gōnia* angle] – **heptagonal** *adj*

[1]**her** /hə, ə‖hə, ə; *strong* huh‖hɜː/ *adj* of, belonging to, or done by or to her or herself

[2]**her** *pron, objective case of* SHE

herald /ˈherəld‖ˈherəld/ *n* **1a** an officer whose original duties of officiating at tournaments gave rise to other duties (e g recording names, pedigrees, and armorial bearings or tracing genealogies) **b** an official messenger between leaders, esp in war **c** an officer of arms ranking above a pursuivant and below a king of arms **2a** an official crier or messenger **b** sby or sthg that conveys news or proclaims **3** a harbinger, forerunner – **herald** *vt*

heraldic /hi'raldik‖hɪ'rældɪk/ *adj* of a herald or heraldry – **heraldically** *adv*

heraldry /'herəldri‖'herəldrɪ/ *n* **1** the system, originating in medieval times, of identifying individuals by hereditary insignia; *also* the practice of granting, classifying, and creating these **2** the study of the history, display, and description of heraldry and heraldic insignia **3** pageantry

herb /huhb‖hɜːb/ *n* **1** a seed plant that does not develop permanent woody tissue and dies down at the end of a growing season **2** a plant (part) valued for its medicinal, savoury, or aromatic qualities <*cultivated her ~ garden*> – **herbal** *adj*

herbaceous /huh'bayshəs‖hɜː'beɪʃəs/ *adj* of, being, or having the characteristics of a (part of a) herb

herbage /'huhbij‖'hɜːbɪdʒ/ *n* (the succulent parts of) herbaceous plants (e g grass), esp when used for grazing

herbal /'huhbl‖'hɜːbl/ *n* a book about (the medicinal properties of) plants

'**herbalist** /-ist‖-ɪst/ *n* sby who grows or sells herbs, esp for medicines

herbivore /'huhbivaw‖'hɜːbɪvɔː/ *n* a plant-eating animal – **herbivorous** *adj*

herculean /ˌhuhkyoo'lee·ən‖ˌhɜːkjʊ'liːən/ *adj* of extraordinary strength, size, or difficulty <*a ~ task*> [*Hercules*, Greco-Roman mythological hero]

[1]**herd** /huhd‖hɜːd/ *n* **1** a number of animals of 1 kind kept together or living as a group **2a** *sing or pl in constr* a group of people usu having a common bond – often derog <*the ~ instinct*> **b** *the* masses – derog <*the common ~*> – **herdlike** *adj*

[2]**herd** *vi* to assemble or move in a herd or group ~ *vt* **1** to keep or move (animals) together **2** to gather, lead, or drive as if in a herd <*~ed his pupils into the hall*>

'**herdsman** /-mən‖-mən/ *n* a manager, breeder, or tender of livestock

[1]**here** /hiə‖hɪə/ *adv* **1** in or at this place <*turn ~*> – often interjectional, esp in answering a roll call **2** at or in this point or particular <*~ we agree*> **3** to this place or position <*come ~*> **4** – used when introducing, offering, or drawing attention <*~ she comes*> <*~ is the news*> <*~, take it*> **5** – used interjectionally to attract attention <*~, what's all this?*> – **here goes** – used to express resolution at the outset of a bold act; infml – **here's to** – used when drinking a toast – **here, there, and everywhere** scattered lavishly about – **here we go again** the same distressing events are repeating themselves – **here you are 1** here is what you wanted **2** you have arrived – **neither here nor there** of no consequence; irrelevant

[2]**here** *adj* **1** – used for emphasis, esp after a demonstrative <*this book ~*> <*ask my son ~*> **2** – used for emphasis between a demonstrative and the following noun; substandard <*this ~ book*>

[3]**here** *n* this place or point <*full up to ~*>

'**herea,bouts** /-əˌbowts‖-əˌbaʊts/ *adv* in this vicinity

[1]**ˌhere'after** /-'ahftə‖-'ɑːftə/ *adv* **1** after this **2** in some future time or state

[2]**ˌhere'after** *n, often cap* **1** *the* future **2** an existence beyond earthly life

ˌhere and 'there *adv* **1** in one place and another **2** FROM TIME TO TIME

hereby /hiə'bie, 'hiə-‖hɪə'baɪ, 'hɪə-/ *adv* by this means or pronouncement <*I ~ declare her elected*>

hereditament /ˌheri'ditəmənt‖ˌherɪ'dɪtəmənt/ *n* (real) property that can be inherited

hereditary /hi'redit(ə)ri‖hɪ'redɪt(ə)rɪ/ *adj* **1a** genetically transmitted or transmissible from parent to offspring **b** characteristic of one's predecessors; ancestral <*~ pride*> **2a** received or passing by inheritance **b** having title through inheritance <*~ peer*> **3** traditional <*~ enemy*> **4** of inheritance or heredity – **hereditarily** *adv*

heredity /hi'rediti‖hɪ'redɪtɪ/ *n* **1** the sum of the qualities and potentialities genetically derived from one's ancestors **2** the transmission of qualities from ancestor to descendant through a mechanism lying primarily in the chromosomes

herein /hiə'rin‖hɪə'rɪn/ *adv* in this – fml

ˌherein'after /-'ahftə‖-'ɑːftə/ *adv* in the following part of this writing or document – fml

hereof /hiə'rov‖hɪə'rɒv/ *adv* of this – fml

heresy /'herəsi‖'herəsɪ/ *n* **1** (adherence to) a religious belief or doctrine contrary to or incompatible with an explicit church dogma **2** an opinion or doctrine contrary to generally accepted belief

heretic /'herətik‖'herətɪk/ *n* **1** a dissenter from established church dogma; *esp* a baptized member of the Roman Catholic church who disavows a revealed truth **2** one who dissents from an accepted belief or doctrine – **heretic, heretical** *adj*, **heretically** *adv*

hereto /hiə'tooh‖hɪə'tuː/ *adv* to this matter or document – fml

heretofore /ˌhiətooh'faw‖ˌhɪətuː'fɔː/ *adv* up to this time; hitherto – fml

hereunder /hiə'rundə‖hɪə'rʌndə/ *adv* under or in accordance with this writing or document – fml

hereupon /ˌhiərə'pon‖ˌhɪərə'pɒn/ *adv* **1** on this matter <*if all are agreed ~*> **2** immediately after this <*let us ~ adjourn*>

herewith /hiə'widh‖hɪə'wɪð/ *adv* **1** hereby **2** with this; enclosed in this – fml

heritable /'heritəbl‖'herɪtəbl/ *adj* **1** capable of being inherited **2** HEREDITARY 1a, 2a – **heritability** *n*

heritage /'heritij‖'herɪtɪdʒ/ *n* **1** sthg transmitted by or acquired from a predecessor; a legacy <*a rich ~ of folklore*> **2** a birthright <*the ~ of natural freedom*>

hermaphrodite /huh'mafrədiet‖hɜː'mæfrədaɪt/ *n* **1** an animal or plant having both male and female reproductive organs **2** sthg that is a combination of 2 usu opposing elements

[Latin *hermaphroditus*, fr Greek *hermaphroditos*, fr *Hermaphroditos*, mythological son of Hermes and Aphrodite who became joined in body with the nymph Salmacis] – **hermaphrodite** *adj*, **hermaphroditism** *n*, **hermaphroditic** *adj*, **hermaphroditically** *adv*

hermetic /huh'metik‖hɜː'metɪk/ *also* **hermetical** /-kl‖-kl/ *adj* **1a** airtight < ~ *seal*> **b** impervious to external influences **2** *often cap* abstruse, recondite – infml – **hermetically** *adv*

hermit /'huhmit‖'hɜːmɪt/ *n* **1** one who retires from society and lives in solitude, esp for religious reasons **2** a recluse [Middle French *eremite*, deriv of Greek *erēmitēs*, living in the desert, fr *erēmia* desert, fr *erēmos* lonely] – **hermitism** *n*, **hermitic** *adj*

'hermitage /-tij‖-tɪdʒ/ *n* **1** the habitation of one or more hermits **2** a secluded residence or private retreat; a hideaway

hernia /'huhni·ə, -nyə‖'hɜːnɪə, -njə/ *n, pl* **hernias, herniae** /-ni,ee‖-nɪ,iː/ a protrusion of (part of) an organ through a wall of its enclosing cavity (e g the abdomen) – **hernial** *adj*, **herniated** *adj*

hero /'hiəroh‖'hɪərəʊ/ *n, pl* **heroes** **1a** a mythological or legendary figure often of divine descent endowed with great strength or ability **b** an illustrious warrior **c** a person, esp a man, admired for noble achievements and qualities (e g courage) **2** the principal male character in a literary or dramatic work – **heroize** *vt*

heroic /hi'roh·ik‖hɪ'rəʊɪk/ *also* **heroical** /-kl‖-kl/ *adj* **1** of or befitting heroes **2a** showing or marked by courage **b** grand, noble **3** of impressive size, power, or effect; potent **4** of heroic verse – **heroically** *adv*

he,roic 'couplet *n* a rhyming couplet in iambic pentameter

heroics *n pl* **1** HEROIC VERSE **2** extravagantly grand behaviour or language

he,roic 'verse *n* the verse form employed in epic poetry (e g the heroic couplet in English)

heroin /'heroh·in‖'herəʊɪn/ *n* a strongly physiologically addictive narcotic made from, but more potent than, morphine – **heroinism** *n*

heroism /'heroh,iz(ə)m‖'herəʊ,ɪz(ə)m/ *n* heroic conduct or qualities; *esp* extreme courage

heron /'herən‖'herən/ *n* any of various long-necked long-legged wading birds with a long tapering bill, large wings, and soft plumage

'heronry /-ri‖-rɪ/ *n* a place where herons breed

herpes /'huhpeez‖'hɜːpiːz/ *n* any of several inflammatory virus diseases of the skin – **herpetic** *adj*

Herr /heə‖heə/ *n, pl* **Herren** /'heərən, 'herən‖'heərən, 'herən/ – used of a German-speaking man as a title equivalent to *Mr*

herring /'hering‖'herɪŋ/ *n* a N Atlantic food fish that is preserved in the adult state by smoking or salting

'herring,bone /-,bohn‖-,bəʊn/ *n* (sthg arranged in) a pattern made up of rows of parallel lines with any 2 adjacent rows slanting in opposite directions; *esp* a twilled fabric decorated with this pattern

hers /huhz‖hɜːz/ *pron, pl* **hers** that which or the one who belongs to her

herself /hə'self‖hə'self/ *pron* **1** that identical female person or creature – used reflexively <*she considers* ~ *lucky*>, for emphasis <*she* ~ *did it*>, or in absolute constructions < ~ *an orphan, she understood the situation*> **2** her normal self <*isn't quite* ~ >

hertz /huhts‖hɜːts/ *n, pl* **hertz** the SI unit of frequency equal to 1 cycle per second [Heinrich *Hertz* (1857-94), German physicist]

he's /hiz, eez, iz‖hɪz, iːz, ɪz; *strong* heez‖hiːz/ he is; he has

hesitant /'hezit(ə)nt‖'hezɪt(ə)nt/ *adj* tending to hesitate; irresolute – **hesitance, hesitancy** *n*, **hesitantly** *adv*

hesitate /'hezitayt‖'hezɪteɪt/ *vi* **1** to hold back, esp in doubt or indecision **2** to be reluctant or unwilling *to* – **hesitater** *n*, **hesitatingly** *adv*, **hesitative** *adj*, **hesitation** *n*

hessian /'hesi·ən‖'hesɪən/ *n* **1** a coarse heavy plain-weave fabric, usu of jute or hemp, used esp for sacking **2** a lightweight material resembling hessian and used chiefly in interior decoration [*Hesse*, region or state in SW Germany]

heter-, hetero- *comb form* other; different; abnormal <hetero*morphic*>

heterodox /'hetəroh,doks‖'hetərəʊ,dɒks/ *adj* contrary to or opposed to established doctrines or opinions, esp in matters of religion [Greek *heterodoxos*, fr *heteros* other + *doxa* opinion] – **heterodoxy** *n*

heterogeneous /,hetərə'jeeni·əs, -nyəs‖,hetərə'dʒiːnɪəs, -njəs/ *adj* consisting of dissimilar ingredients or constituents; disparate – **heterogeneously** *adv*, **heterogeneousness** *n*, **heterogeneity** *n*

heterosexism /,het(ə)rə'seksizm‖,het(ə)rə-'seksɪzm/ *n* discrimination against a person on the grounds of his/her homosexuality

,hetero'sexual /-'seksyoo(ə)l, -sh(ə)l‖-'seksjʊ(ə)l, -ʃ(ə)l/ *adj or n* (of or being) sby having a sexual preference for members of the opposite sex – **heterosexually** *adv*, **heterosexuality** *n*

,het 'up *adj* highly excited; upset – infml

heuristic /,hyooə'ristik, hoy-‖,hjʊə'rɪstɪk, hɔɪ-/ *adj* **1** furthering investigation but otherwise unproved or unjustified <*a* ~ *assumption*> **2** of problem-solving techniques that proceed by trial and error <*a* ~ *computer program*> – **heuristically** *adv*

hew /hyooh‖hjuː/ *vb* **hewed; hewed, hewn** /hyoohn‖hjuːn/ *vt* **1** to strike, chop, or esp fell with blows of a heavy cutting instrument **2** to give form or shape to (as if) with heavy cutting blows – often + *out* <*she* ~ed *out a career for herself*> ~*vi* to make cutting blows – **hewer** *n*

[1]hex /heks‖heks/ *vb, NAm vi* to practise witchcraft ~*vt* to affect as if by an evil spell; jinx [German *hexen*, fr *hexe* witch] – **hexer** *n*

[2]hex *n, NAm* **1** a spell, jinx **2** a witch

hexa-, hex- *comb form* **1** six <hexa*merous*> **2** containing 6 atoms, groups, or chemical equivalents in the molecular structure <hexa*valent*>

hexagon /'heksəgən‖'heksəgən/ *n* a polygon of 6 angles and 6 sides [Greek *hex* six + *gōnia* angle] – **hexagonal** *adj*, **hexagonally** *adv*

hexagram /'heksəgram‖'heksəgræm/ *n* a 6-pointed star drawn by extending the sides of a regular hexagon

hexameter /hek'samitə‖hek'sæmɪtə/ *n* a line of verse consisting of 6 metrical feet

[1]**hey** /hay‖heɪ/ *interj* – used esp to call attention or to express inquiry, surprise, or exultation

[2]**hey** *n* [3]HAY

heyday /ˈhay͵day‖ˈheɪ͵deɪ/ *n* the period of one's greatest vigour, prosperity, or fame

hey presto /͵hay ˈprestoh‖͵heɪ ˈprestəʊ/ *interj* – used as an expression of triumph or satisfaction on completing or demonstrating sthg; *esp* used by conjurers about to reveal the outcome of a trick

hi /hie‖haɪ/ *interj* – used esp to attract attention or, esp in the USA, as a greeting

[1]**hiatus** /hieˈaytəs‖haɪˈeɪtəs/ *n* **1a** a break, gap **b** an (abnormal) anatomical gap or passage **2a** a lapse in continuity **b** the occurrence of 2 vowel sounds together without pause or intervening consonantal sound

[2]**hiatus** *adj* **1** involving a hiatus **2** *of a hernia* having a part that protrudes through the oesophageal opening of the diaphragm

hibernate /ˈhiebənayt‖ˈhaɪbəneɪt/ *vi* **1** to pass the winter in a torpid or resting state **2** to be or become inactive or dormant – **hibernator** *n*, **hibernation** *n*

hibiscus /hieˈbiskəs, hi-‖haɪˈbɪskəs, hɪ-/ *n* any of a genus of herbaceous plants, shrubs, or small trees with large showy flowers

[1]**hiccup** *also* **hiccough** /ˈhikup‖ˈhɪkʌp/ *n* **1** a spasmodic involuntary inhalation with closure of the glottis accompanied by a characteristic sharp sound **2** an attack of hiccuping – usu pl but sing. or pl in constr **3** *chiefly Br* a brief interruption or breakdown; a hitch <*a mistake due to a ~ in the computer*> – infml

[2]**hiccup** *also* **hiccough** *vi* **-p-, -pp-** to make a hiccup or hiccups

hick /hik‖hɪk/ *n, chiefly NAm* an unsophisticated provincial person – **hick** *adj*

hickory /ˈhikəri‖ˈhɪkərɪ/ *n* (the usu tough pale wood of) any of a genus of N American hardwood trees that often have sweet edible nuts – **hickory** *adj*

[1]**hide** *vb* **hid** /hid‖hɪd/; **hidden** /hid(ə)n‖hɪd(ə)n/, **hid** *vt* **1** to put out of sight; conceal **2** to keep secret <hid *the news from his parents*> **3** to screen from view <*house* hidden *by trees*> ~ *vi* **1** to conceal oneself **2** to remain out of sight – often + *out* – **hider** *n*

[2]**hide** *n, chiefly Br* a camouflaged hut or other shelter used for observation, esp of wildlife or game

[3]**hide** *n* the raw or dressed skin of an animal – used esp with reference to large heavy skins – **hide or/nor hair** the least vestige or trace – infml <*hadn't seen* hide or hair *of his wife for 20 years*>

ˈ**hide-and-**͵**seek** *n* a children's game in which one player covers his/her eyes and then hunts for the other players who have hidden themselves

ˈ**hide**͵**away** /-ə͵way‖-ə͵weɪ/ *n* a retreat, hideout

ˈ**hide**͵**bound** /-͵bownd‖-͵baʊnd/ *adj* narrow or inflexible in character

hideous /ˈhidi·əs‖ˈhɪdɪəs/ *adj* **1** offensive to the senses, esp the sight; exceedingly ugly **2** morally offensive; shocking – **hideously** *adv*, **hideousness** *n*

[1]**hiding** /ˈhieding‖ˈhaɪdɪŋ/ *n* a state or place of concealment <*go into ~*>

[2]**hiding** *n* a beating, thrashing <*gave him a good ~*>; *also* a severe defeat – infml

hie /hie‖haɪ/ *vb* **hying, hieing** *archaic* to hurry

hierarchy /ˈhie·ərahki, ˈhiə-‖ˈhaɪərɑːkɪ, ˈhɪə-/ *n* **1** (church government by) a body of clergy organized according to rank, specif the bishops of a province or nation **2** a graded or ranked series

hieroglyph /ˈhie·ərə͵glif, ˈhiərə-‖ˈhaɪərə͵glɪf, ˈhɪərə-/ *n* a pictorial character used in hieroglyphics – **hieroglyphic** *adj*

hieroglyphics *n pl but sing or pl in constr* **1** a system of hieroglyphic writing; *specif* the picture script of various ancient peoples (e g the Egyptians) **2** sthg like hieroglyphics, esp in being difficult to decipher [deriv of Greek *hieros* sacred + *glyphein* to carve]

hi-fi /ˈhie ͵fie, ͵hie ˈfie‖ˈhaɪ ͵faɪ, ͵haɪ ˈfaɪ/ *n* **1** HIGH FIDELITY **2** equipment for the high-fidelity reproduction of sound *USE* infml

higgledy-piggledy /͵higldi ˈpigldi‖͵hɪgldɪ ˈpɪgldɪ/ *adv* in confusion; topsy-turvy – infml – **higgledy-piggledy** *adj*

[1]**high** /hie‖haɪ/ *adj* **1a** extending upwards for a considerable or above average distance <*rooms with ~ ceilings*> **b** situated at a considerable height above a base (e g the ground) <*a ~ plateau*> **c** *of physical activity* extending to or from, or taking place at a considerable height above, a base (e g the ground or water) <*~ diving*> **d** having a specified elevation; tall <*6 feet ~*> – often in combination <*sky*-high> **2** at the period of culmination or fullest development <*~ summer*> **3** elevated in pitch <*a ~ note*> **4** relatively far from the equator <*~ latitudes*> **5** *of meat, esp game* slightly decomposed or tainted **6a** exalted in character; noble <*~ principles*> **b** good, favourable <*has a very ~ opinion of her*> **7** of greater degree, amount, cost, value, or content than average <*~ prices*> <*food ~ in iron*> **8a** foremost in rank, dignity, or standing <*~ officials*> **b** critical, climactic <*the ~ point of the novel is the escape*> **c** marked by sublime or heroic events or subject matter <*~ tragedy*> **9** forcible, strong <*~ winds*> **10a** showing elation or excitement <*feelings ran ~*> **b** intoxicated by alcohol or a drug **11** advanced in complexity, development, or elaboration <*~er mathematics*> <*~ technology*> **12** *of a gear* designed for fast speed **13** *of words* expressive of anger **14** rigidly traditionalist <*a ~ Tory*>; *specif* HIGH CHURCH – **highly** *adv* – **on one's high horse** stubbornly or disdainfully proud <*gave up trying to reason with him when he got* on his high horse>

[2]**high** *adv* at or to a high place, altitude, or degree <*threw the ball ~ in the air*>

[3]**high** *n* **1** a region of high atmospheric pressure **2** a high point or level; a height <*sales have reached a new ~*> **3** *NAm* TOP 4 – **on high** in or to a high place, esp heaven

͵**high-and-**ˈ**mighty** *adj* arrogant, imperious

highball /ˈhie͵bawl‖ˈhaɪ͵bɔːl/ *n* a drink of

spirits (e g whisky) and water or a carbonated beverage, served with ice in a tall glass

ˌhighˈborn /-ˈbawn‖-ˈbɔːn/ *adj* of noble birth

ˈhighˌboy /-ˌboy‖-ˌbɔɪ/ *n, NAm* TALLBOY 1

ˈhighˌbrow /-ˌbrow‖-ˌbraʊ/ *adj* dealing with, possessing, or having pretensions to superior intellectual and cultural interests or activities – **highbrow** *n*, **highbrowed** *adj*, **highbrowism** *n*

ˈhigh ˌchair *n* a child's chair with long legs, a footrest, and usu a feeding tray

ˌHigh ˈChurch *adj* tending, in the Anglican church, towards Roman Catholicism in liturgy, ceremonial, and dogma – **High Churchman** *n*

ˌhigh-ˈclass *adj* superior, first-class

ˌhigh comˈmissioner *n* a principal commissioner; *esp* an ambassadorial representative of one Commonwealth country stationed in another

ˌHigh ˈCourt *n* the lower branch of the Supreme Court of Judicature of England and Wales

ˌhigher eduˈcation *n* education beyond the secondary level, at a college or university

high explosive *n* an explosive (e g TNT) that explodes with extreme rapidity and has a shattering effect

ˌhighfaˈlutin /-fəˈloohtin‖-fəˈluːtɪn/ *adj* pretentious, pompous – infml

high fidelity *n* the faithful reproduction of sound – **high-fidelity** *adj*

ˌhigh-ˈflier, high-flyer *n* a person who shows extreme ambition or outstanding promise

ˌhigh-ˈflown *adj* **1** excessively ambitious or extravagant **2** excessively elaborate or inflated; pretentious

ˌhigh-ˈflying *adj* **1** rising to considerable height **2** marked by extravagance, pretension, or excessive ambition

ˌHigh ˈGerman *n* German as used in S and central Germany

ˌhigh-ˈgrade *adj* **1** of superior grade or quality **2** being near the upper or most favourable extreme of a specified range

ˌhigh-ˈhanded *adj* overbearingly arbitrary – **high-handedly** *adv*, **high-handedness** *n*

ˌhigh ˈjinks /jingks‖dʒɪŋks/ *n pl* high-spirited fun and games

ˈhigh ˌjump *n* (an athletic field event consisting of) a jump for height over a bar suspended between uprights – **high jumper** *n*, **high jumping** *n* – **for the high jump** about to receive a severe reprimand or punishment

highland /ˈhieland‖ˈhaɪlənd/ *n* high or mountainous land – usu pl with sing. meaning – **highland** *adj*, **highlander** *n*

Highland *adj* **1** of the Highlands of Scotland **2** relating to or being a member of a shaggy long-haired breed of hardy beef cattle – **Highlander** *n*

ˌHighland ˈfling *n* a lively solo Scottish folk dance

ˈHighlands *n pl the* northwest mountainous part of Scotland

ˌhigh-ˈlevel *adj* **1** occurring, done, or placed at a high level **2** of high importance or rank <~ *diplomats*> **3** *of a computer language* having each word equal to several machine code instructions and being easily understandable to humans

ˈhigh ˌlife *n* luxurious living associated with the rich

[1]**ˈhighˌlight** /-ˌliet‖-ˌlaɪt/ *n* **1** the lightest spot or area (e g in a painting or photograph) **2** an event or detail of special significance or interest **3** a contrasting brighter part in the hair or on the face that reflects or gives the appearance of reflecting light

[2]**ˈhighˌlight** *vt* **1a** to focus attention on; emphasize **b** to emphasize (e g a figure) with light tones in painting, photography, etc **2** to give highlights to – **highlighter** *n*

highly /ˈhieli‖ˈhaɪlɪ/ *adv* **1** to a high degree; extremely **2** with approval; favourably <*speak ~ of someone*>

ˌhighly-ˈstrung, high-strung *adj* extremely nervous or sensitive

ˌhigh ˈmass *n, often cap H&M* an elaborate sung mass

ˌhigh-ˈminded *adj* having or marked by elevated principles and feelings – **high-mindedly** *adv*, **high-mindedness** *n*

Highness /ˈhienis‖ˈhaɪnɪs/ *n* – used as a title for a person of exalted rank (e g a king or prince)

ˌhigh-ˈoctane *adj* having a high octane number and hence good antiknock properties <~ *petrol*>

ˌhigh-ˈpitched *adj* **1** having a high pitch <*a ~ voice*> **2** marked by or exhibiting strong feeling; agitated <*a ~ election campaign*>

ˌhigh-ˈpowered *also* **high-power** *adj* having great drive, energy, or capacity; dynamic

ˌhigh-ˈpressure *adj* **1** having or involving a (comparatively) high pressure, esp greatly exceeding that of the atmosphere **2a** using, involving, or being aggressive and insistent sales techniques **b** imposing or involving severe strain or tension <~ *occupations*>

ˌhigh ˈpriest *n* **1** a chief priest, esp of the ancient Jewish Levitical priesthood **2** the head or chief exponent of a movement – **high priesthood** *n*

ˌhigh reˈlief *n* sculptural relief in which at least half of the circumference of the design stands out from the surrounding surface

ˌhigh-ˈrise *adj* (situated in a building) constructed with a large number of storeys <~ *flats*> – **high rise** *n*

ˈhighˌroad /-ˌrohd‖-ˌrəʊd/ *n* **1** *the* easiest course *to* <*the ~ to success*> **2** *chiefly Br* a main road

ˈhigh ˌschool *n* **1** *chiefly Br* secondary school; *esp* GRAMMAR SCHOOL 2 – now chiefly in names **2** *NAm* a school usu for pupils aged about 15-18

ˌhigh ˈsea *n* the part of a sea or ocean outside territorial waters – usu pl with sing. meaning

ˌhigh-ˈsounding *adj* pompous, but meaningless

ˌhigh-ˈspeed *adj* **1** (adapted to be) operated at high speed **2** relating to the production of photographs by very short exposures

ˌhigh-ˈspirited *adj* characterized by a bold or lively spirit; *also* highly-strung <*a ~ horse*> – **high-spiritedly** *adv*, **high-spiritedness** *n*

ˈhigh͵spot /-͵spot‖-͵spɒt/ *n* the most important or enjoyable feature of sthg

ˈhigh ͵street *n, Br* a main or principal street, esp containing shops

͵high-ˈstrung *adj* highly-strung

high table *n, often cap H&T* a dining-room table, usu on a platform, used by the masters and fellows of a British college, or at a formal dinner or reception (e g by distinguished guests)

͵high ˈtea *n, Br* a fairly substantial early evening meal (at which tea is served)

high technology *n* technology using or producing the most advanced processes and devices (e g in microelectronics)

͵high-ˈtension *adj* having a high voltage; *also* relating to apparatus to be used at high voltage

͵high ˈtide *n* **1** (the time of) the tide when the water reaches its highest level **2** the culminating point; the climax

͵high-ˈtoned *adj* high in social, moral, or intellectual quality; dignified

͵high ˈtreason *n* TREASON 2

͵high ˈwater *n* HIGH TIDE 1

͵high-ˈwater ͵mark *n* **1** a mark showing the highest level reached by the surface of a body of water **2** the highest point or stage

ˈhigh͵way /-͵way‖-͵weɪ/ *n* **1** a public way; *esp* a main direct road **2** a busbar

͵highway ˈcode *n, often cap H&C, Br* the official code of rules and advice for the safe use of roads

ˈhighwayman /-mən‖-mən/ *n* a (mounted) robber of travellers on a road, esp in former times

hijack, high-jack /ˈhiejak‖ˈhaɪdʒæk/ *vt* **1a** to stop and steal from (a vehicle in transit) **b** to seize control of, and often divert, (a means of transport) by force **2** to steal, rob, or kidnap as if by hijacking – **hijack** *n*, **hijacker** *n*

[1]hike /hiek‖haɪk/ *vi* to go on a hike – **hiker** *n*

[2]hike *n* **1** a long walk in the country, esp for pleasure or exercise **2** *chiefly NAm* an increase or rise <*a new wage* ~>

hike up *vt, chiefly NAm* to move, pull, or raise with a sudden movement <hiked *himself* up *on the wall*> – infml

hilarious /hiˈleəri·əs‖hɪˈleərɪəs/ *adj* marked by or causing hilarity – **hilariously** *adv*, **hilariousness** *n*

hilarity /hiˈlarəti‖hɪˈlærətɪ/ *n* mirth, merriment

hill /hil‖hɪl/ *n* **1** a usu rounded natural rise of land lower than a mountain **2** an artificial heap or mound (e g of earth) **3** an esp steep slope – **hilly** *adj* – **over the hill** past one's prime; too old

hillbilly /ˈhil͵bili‖ˈhɪl͵bɪlɪ/ *n, chiefly NAm* a person from a remote or culturally unsophisticated area

hillock /ˈhilək‖ˈhɪlək/ *n* a small hill – **hillocky** *adj*

hilt /hilt‖hɪlt/ *n* a handle, esp of a sword or dagger – **to the hilt** completely

him /him‖hɪm/ *pron, objective case of* HE

himself /himˈself‖hɪmˈself; *medially often* im-‖ɪm-/ *pron* **1a** that identical male person or creature – used reflexively <*he considers* ~ *lucky*>, for emphasis <*he* ~ *did it*>, or in absolute constructions <~ *unhappy, he understood the situation*> **b** – used reflexively when the sex of the antecedent is unspecified <*everyone must fend for* ~> **2** his normal self <*isn't quite* ~ *today*> **3** *chiefly NAm* oneself – used with *one* <*one should wash* ~>

[1]hind /hiend‖haɪnd/ *n, pl* **hinds** *also* **hind** a female (red) deer

[2]hind *adj* situated at the back or behind; rear

[1]hinder /ˈhində‖ˈhɪndə/ *vt* **1** to retard or obstruct the progress of; hamper **2** to restrain, prevent – often + *from* – **hinderer** *n*

[2]hinder /ˈhiendə‖ˈhaɪndə/ *adj* situated behind or at the rear; posterior

Hindi /ˈhindi‖ˈhɪndɪ/ *n* an official Indo-European language of India; *also* any of a group of dialects of N India

hindmost /ˈhiend͵mohst‖ˈhaɪnd͵məʊst/ *adj* furthest to the rear; last

hindquarter /͵heindˈkwawtə, ˈheind-͵kwawtə‖͵heɪndˈkwɔːtə, ˈheɪnd͵kwɔːtə/ *n* **1** the back half of a side (of the carcass) of a quadruped **2** *pl* the hind legs (and adjoining structures) of a quadruped

hindrance /ˈhindrəns‖ˈhɪndrəns/ *n* **1** the action of hindering **2** an impediment, obstacle

hindsight /ˈhiend͵siet‖ˈhaɪnd͵saɪt/ *n* the grasp or picture of a situation that one has after it has occurred

Hindu, *archaic* **Hindoo** /ˈhindooh, hinˈdooh‖ˈhɪnduː, hɪnˈduː/ *n* an adherent of Hinduism – **Hindu** *adj*

ˈHindu͵ism /-͵iz(ə)m‖-͵ɪz(ə)m/ *n* the dominant religion of India which involves belief in the illusory nature of the physical universe and in cycles of reincarnation, and is associated with a caste system of social organization

[1]hinge /hinj‖hɪndʒ/ *n* **1a** a jointed or flexible device on which a swinging part (e g a door or lid) turns **b** a flexible joint in which bones are held together by ligaments **c** a small piece of thin gummed paper used in fastening a postage stamp in an album **2** a point or principle on which sthg turns or depends

[2]hinge *vt* to attach by or provide with hinges ~ *vi* **1** to hang or turn (as if) on a hinge <*door* ~s *outwards*> **2** to depend or turn *on* a single consideration or point

[1]hint /hint‖hɪnt/ *n* **1** a brief practical suggestion or piece of advice <~s *for home decorators*> **2** an indirect or veiled statement; an insinuation **3** a slight indication or trace; a suggestion – usu + *of* <*a* ~ *of irony in her voice*>

[2]hint *vt* to indicate indirectly or by allusion <~ed *that something was up*> ~*vi* to give a hint – **hint at** to imply or allude to (sthg)

hinterland /ˈhintə͵land‖ˈhɪntə͵lænd/ *n* **1** a region lying inland from a coast **2** a region remote from urban or cultural centres [German, fr *hinter* hinder + *land*]

[1]hip /hip‖hɪp/ *n* the ripened fruit of a rose

[2]hip *n* **1a** the projecting region at each side of the lower or rear part of the mammalian trunk formed by the pelvis and upper part of the thigh **b** HIP JOINT **2** an external angle between 2 adjacent sloping sides of a roof

[3]hip *interj* – usu used to begin a cheer <~ ~ *hooray*>

[4]hip *adj* **-pp-** keenly aware of or interested in the newest developments; *broadly* trendy – infml – **hipness** *n*

'hip ,flask *n* a flat flask, usu for holding spirits, carried in a hip pocket

'hip ,joint *n* the joint between the femur and the hipbone

hippie, hippy /'hipi‖'hɪpɪ/ *n* a usu young person, esp during the 1960s, who rejected social conventions and, in many cases, used psychedelic drugs; *broadly* a long-haired unconventionally dressed young person – **hippiehood** *n*, **hippie** *adj*, **hippiedom** *n*

Hippocratic oath /,hipə'kratik‖,hɪpə'krætɪk/ *n* an oath embodying a code of medical ethics [*Hippocrates* (died about 377 BC), Greek physician]

hippodrome /'hipədrohm‖'hɪpədrəʊm/ *n* **1** an arena for equestrian performances or circuses **2** a music hall, theatre, etc – esp in names

hippopotamus /,hipə'potəməs‖,hɪpə'pɒtəməs/ *n, pl* **hippopotamuses, hippopotami** /-mie‖-maɪ/ any of several large plant-eating 4-toed chiefly aquatic mammals, with an extremely large head and mouth, very thick hairless skin, and short legs [Latin, fr Greek *hippopotamos*, fr *hippos* horse + *potamos* river]

hipster /'hipstə‖'hɪpstə/ *n* **1** sby who is unusually aware of and interested in new and unconventional patterns, esp in jazz **2** *pl* trousers that start from the hips rather than the waist

[1]hire /hie·ə‖haɪə/ *n* **1** payment for the temporary use of sthg **2** hiring or being hired

[2]hire *vt* **1a** to engage the services of for a set sum < ~ *a new crew*> **b** to engage the temporary use of for an agreed sum < ~ *a hall*> **2** to grant the services of or temporary use of for a fixed sum < ~ *themselves out*> – **hirer** *n*

'hireling /-ling‖-lɪŋ/ *n* a person who works for payment, esp for purely mercenary motives – derog

,hire 'purchase *n, chiefly Br* a system of paying for goods by instalments

hirsute /huh'syooht‖hɜː'sjuːt/ *adj* covered with (coarse stiff) hairs – **hirsuteness** *n*

[1]his /iz‖ɪz; *strong* hiz‖hɪz/ *adj* **1** of, belonging to, or done by or to him or himself **2** *chiefly NAm* one's – used with *one* <*one's duty to* ~ *public*>

[2]his /hiz‖hɪz/ *pron, pl* **his** that which or the one who belongs to him

Hispanic /hi'spanik‖hɪ'spænɪk/ *adj* (characteristic) of Spain, Portugal, or Latin America – **Hispanicism** *n*, **Hispanicist** *n*, **Hispanicize** *vt*

hiss /his‖hɪs/ *vi* to make a sharp voiceless sound like a prolonged *s*, esp in disapproval ~ *vt* **1** to show disapproval of by hissing **2** to utter with a hiss – **hiss** *n*

hist /hist‖hɪst/ *interj* – used to attract attention

histamine /'histəmin, -meen‖'hɪstəmɪn, -miːn/ *n* an amine that is a neurotransmitter in the autonomic nervous system and whose release under certain conditions causes an allergic reaction – **histaminic** *adj*

histology /his'toləji‖hɪs'tɒlədʒɪ/ *n* (anatomy that deals with) the organization and microscopic structure of animal and plant tissues – **histologist** *n*, **histological** *adj*, **histologic** *adj*, **histologically** *adv*

historian /hi'stawri·ən‖hɪ'stɔːrɪən/ *n* a student or writer of history

historic /hi'storik‖hɪ'stɒrɪk/ *adj* **1** (likely to be) famous or important in history **2** *of a tense* expressive of past time

hi'storical /-kl‖-kl/ *adj* **1a** of or based on history **b** used in the past **2** famous in history **3** dealing with or representing the events of history <*a* ~ *novel*> – **historically** *adv*

history /'histəri‖'hɪstərɪ/ *n* **1** (a chronological record of) significant past events **2a** a treatise presenting systematically related natural phenomena <*a* ~ *of British birds*> **b** an account of sby's medical, sociological, etc background **3** a branch of knowledge that records the past **4a** past events <*that's all* ~ *now*> **b** an unusual or interesting past <*this goblet has a* ~> **c** previous treatment, handling, or experience [Latin *historia*, fr Greek, inquiry, history, fr *histōr, istōr* knowing, learned]

histrionic /,histri'onik‖,hɪstrɪ'ɒnɪk/ *adj* **1** of actors, acting, or the theatre **2** deliberately affected, theatrical – **histrionically** *adv*

histrionics *n pl but sing or pl in constr* deliberate display of emotion for effect

[1]hit /hit‖hɪt/ *vb* **-tt-; hit** *vt* **1a** to reach (as if) with a blow; strike < ~ *the ball*> < ~ *by an attack of flu*> **b** to make sudden forceful contact with <*the car* ~ *the tree*> **2a** to bring into contact < ~ *the stick against the railings*> **b** to deliver, inflict < ~ *a severe blow*> **3** to have a usu detrimental effect or impact on < ~ *hard by the drought*> **4** to discover or meet, esp by chance <*I seem to have* ~ *a snag*> **5a** to reach, attain <*prices* ~ *a new high*> **b** to cause a propelled object to strike (e g a target), esp for a score in a contest **c** *of a batsman* to score (runs) in cricket; *also* to score runs off a ball bowled by (a bowler) **6** to indulge in, esp excessively < ~ *the bottle*> **7** to arrive at or in < ~ *town*> **8** to rob **9** *chiefly NAm* to kill ~ *vi* **1** to strike a blow **2a** to come into forceful contact with sthg **b** to attack <*wondered where the enemy would* ~ *next*> **c** to happen or arrive, esp with sudden or destructive force <*the epidemic* ~ *that summer*> **3** to come, esp by chance; arrive at or find sthg – + *on* or *upon* < ~ *on a solution*> *USE* (*vt 6 & 7*) infml; (*vt 8 & 9*) slang – **hit it off** to get along well – infml – **hit the jackpot** to be or become notably and unexpectedly successful – **hit the nail on the head** to be exactly right – **hit the road** to start on a journey – infml – **hit the roof** to give vent to a burst of anger or angry protest – infml

[2]hit *n* **1** a blow; *esp* one that strikes its target **2a** a stroke of luck **b** sthg (e g a popular tune) that enjoys great success <*the song was a big* ~> **3** a telling remark **4** a robbery **5** *chiefly NAm* an act of murder *USE* (*4 & 5*) slang

,hit-and-'run *adj* **1** being or involving a driver who does not stop after causing damage or injury **2** involving rapid action and immediate withdrawal < ~ *raids on coastal towns*>

[1]hitch /hich‖hɪtʃ/ *vt* **1** to move by jerks **2** to catch or fasten (as if) by a hook or knot < ~*ed his horse to the top rail of the fence*> – often + *up* **3** to solicit and obtain (a free lift) in a passing vehicle ~*vi* to hitchhike – infml – **hitcher** *n*

[2]hitch *n* **1** a sudden movement or pull; a jerk <*gave his trousers a* ~> **2** a sudden halt or obstruction; a stoppage *<a ~ in the proceedings>* **3** a knot used for a temporary fastening **4** *NAm* a period usu of military service – slang

ˈhitchˌhike /-ˌhiek‖-ˌhaɪk/ *vi* to travel by obtaining free lifts in passing vehicles – **hitchhiker** *n*

[1]**hither** /ˈhidhə‖ˈhɪðə/ *adv* to or towards this place – fml

[2]**hither** *adj* NEAR 3a *<the ~ side of the hill>* – fml

ˌhitherˈto /-ˈtooh‖-ˈtuː/ *adv* up to this time; until now – fml

hit off *vt* to represent or imitate accurately

ˌhit-or-ˈmiss *adj* showing a lack of planning or forethought; haphazard

hit out *vi* **1** to aim violent blows *at* **2** to aim angry verbal attacks *at*; speak violently *against*

ˈhit paˌrade *n* a group or listing of popular songs ranked in order of the number of records of each sold

[1]**hive** /hiev‖haɪv/ *n* **1** (a structure for housing) a colony of bees **2** a place full of busy occupants *<a ~ of industry>*

[2]**hive** *vt* to collect into a hive ~*vi, of bees* to enter and take possession of a hive

hive off *vt* to separate from a group or larger unit; *specif* to assign (e g assets or responsibilities) to a subsidiary company or agency ~ *vi* to become separated from a group; form a separate or subsidiary unit

hives /hievz‖haɪvz/ *n pl but sing or pl in constr* urticaria

ho /hoh‖həʊ/ *interj* **1** – used esp to attract attention to sthg specified *<land ~>* **2** – used to express surprise or triumph

[1]**hoard** /hawd‖hɔːd/ *n* **1** an often secret supply (e g of money or food) stored up for preservation or future use **2** a cache of valuable archaeological remains

[2]**hoard** *vb* to lay up a hoard (of)

hoarding /ˈhawding‖ˈhɔːdɪŋ/ *n* **1** a temporary fence put round a building site **2** *Br* a large board designed to carry outdoor advertising

ˈhoarˌfrost /-ˌfrost‖-ˌfrɒst/ *n* FROST 1b

hoarse /haws‖hɔːs/ *adj* **1** rough or harsh in sound; grating *<~ voice>* **2** having a hoarse voice *<~ with shouting>* – **hoarsely** *adv*, **hoarseness** *n*, **hoarsen** *vb*

hoary /ˈhawri‖ˈhɔːrɪ/ *adj* **1a** grey or white with age; *also* grey-haired **b** having greyish or whitish hair, down, or leaves **2** impressively or venerably old; ancient **3** hackneyed *<a ~ old joke>* – **hoariness** *n*

[1]**hoax** /hohks‖həʊks/ *vt* to play a trick on; deceive – **hoaxer** *n*

[2]**hoax** *n* an act of deception; a trick

[1]**hob** /hob‖hɒb/ *n, dial Br* a goblin, elf

[2]**hob** *n* **1** a ledge near a fireplace on which sthg may be kept warm **2** a horizontal surface either on a cooker or installed as a separate unit that contains heating areas on which pans are placed

[1]**hobble** /ˈhobl‖ˈhɒbl/ *vi* to move along unsteadily or with difficulty; *esp* to limp ~ *vt* **1** to cause to limp **2** to fasten together the legs of (e g a horse) to prevent straying; fetter

[2]**hobble** *n* **1** a hobbling movement **2** sthg (e g a rope) used to hobble an animal

hobbledehoy /ˌhobldiˈhoy‖ˌhɒbldɪˈhɔɪ/ *n* an awkward gawky youth

[1]**hobby** /ˈhobi‖ˈhɒbɪ/ *n* a leisure activity or pastime engaged in for interest or recreation [short for *hobbyhorse*] – **hobbyist** *n*

[2]**hobby** *n* a small Old World falcon that catches small birds while in flight

ˈhobbyˌhorse /-ˌhaws‖-ˌhɔːs/ *n* **1** a figure of a horse fastened round the waist of a performer in a morris dance **2a** a toy consisting of an imitation horse's head attached to one end of a stick on which a child can pretend to ride **b** a toy horse on a merry-go-round **c** ROCKING HORSE **3** a topic to which one constantly returns

hobgoblin /ˌhobˈgoblin‖ˌhɒbˈgɒblɪn/ *n* **1** a goblin **2** a bugbear; BOGEY 2

hobnail /ˈhobˌnayl‖ˈhɒbˌneɪl/ *n* a short large-headed nail for studding shoe soles – **hobnailed** *adj*

hobnob /ˈhobˌnob‖ˈhɒbˌnɒb/ *vi* **-bb-** **1** to associate familiarly **2** to talk informally *USE* usu + *with*; infml

hobo /ˈhohˌboh‖ˈhəʊˌbəʊ/ *n, pl* **hoboes** *also* **hobos** **1** *chiefly NAm* a migratory worker **2** *NAm* TRAMP 1

Hobson's choice /ˈhobs(ə)nz‖ˈhɒbs(ə)nz/ *n* an apparently free choice which offers no real alternative [prob fr Thomas *Hobson* (died 1631) English liveryman, who required every customer to take the horse nearest the door]

[1]**hock** /hok‖hɒk/ *n* the tarsal joint of the hind limb of a horse or related quadruped that corresponds to the ankle in human beings [Old English *hōh* heel]

[2]**hock** *n, often cap, chiefly Br* a dry to medium-dry or sometimes sweet white table wine produced in the Rhine valley [German *hochheimer*, fr *Hochheim*, town in Germany]

[3]**hock** *n* **1** [1]PAWN 2 *<got her watch out of ~>* **2** DEBT 1 *<in ~ to the bank>* USE infml [Dutch *hok* pen, prison]

[4]**hock** *vt* to pawn – infml

hockey /ˈhoki‖ˈhɒkɪ/ *n* **1** a game played on grass between 2 teams of usu 11 players whose object is to direct a ball into the opponents' goal with a stick that has a flat-faced blade **2** *NAm* ICE HOCKEY

hocus-pocus /ˈhohkəs ˈpohkəs‖ˌhəʊkəs ˈpəʊkəs/ *n* **1** SLEIGHT OF HAND **2** pointless activity or words, usu intended to obscure or deceive

hod /hod‖hɒd/ *n* **1** a trough mounted on a pole handle for carrying mortar, bricks, etc **2** a coal scuttle; *specif* a tall one used to shovel fuel directly onto a fire

hodgepodge /ˈhojˌpoj‖ˈhɒdʒˌpɒdʒ/ *n, chiefly NAm* a hotchpotch

[1]**hoe** /hoh‖həʊ/ *n* any of various implements, esp one with a long handle and flat blade, used for tilling, weeding, etc

[2]**hoe** *vi* to work with a hoe ~ *vt* **1** to weed or cultivate (land or a crop) with a hoe **2** to remove (weeds) by hoeing

[1]**hog** /hog‖hɒg/ *n* **1** a warthog or other wild pig **2** *Br* a castrated male pig raised for slaughter **3** *chiefly NAm* a domestic (fully grown) pig **4** a selfish, gluttonous, or filthy person – slang

[2]**hog** *vt* **-gg-** **1** to cut (a horse's mane) off or short **2** to appropriate a selfish or excessive share of; monopolize *<~ged the discussion>* – infml

hoggish /ˈhogish‖ˈhɒgɪʃ/ *adj* grossly selfish, gluttonous, or filthy

Hogmanay /ˈhogmənay, ˌhogməˈnay‖ˈhɒgməneɪ, ˌhɒgməˈneɪ/ *n, Scot* the eve of New Year's Day

ˈ**hogs,head** /-ˌhed‖-ˌhed/ *n* **1** a large cask or barrel **2** any of several measures of capacity; *esp* a measure of $52^1/_2$ imperial gallons (about 238l)

ˈ**hog,wash** /-ˌwosh‖-ˌwɒʃ/ *n* **1** SWILL 1, SLOP 3a **2** sthg worthless; *specif* meaningless talk – slang

hoi polloi /ˌhoy pəˈloy‖ˌhɔɪ pəˈlɔɪ/ *n pl the* common people; *the* masses [Greek, the many]

[1]**hoist** /hoyst‖hɔɪst/ *vt* to raise into position (as if) by means of tackle; *broadly* to raise

[2]**hoist** *n* **1** an apparatus for hoisting **2a** the distance a flag extends along its staff or support **b** the end of a flag next to the staff

[3]**hoist** *adj* – **hoist with one's own petard** made a victim of or hurt by one's own usu malicious scheme

hoity-toity /ˌhoyti ˈtoyti‖ˌhɔɪtɪ ˈtɔɪtɪ/ *adj* having an air of assumed importance; haughty – infml

[1]**hold** /hohld‖həʊld/ *vb* **held** /held‖held/ *vt* **1a** to have in one's keeping; possess < ~s *the title to the property*> **b** to retain by force <*troops* ~ing *the ridge*> **c** to keep by way of threat or coercion < ~ing *the child for ransom*> **2a** to keep under control; check <held *her tongue*> **b** to stop the action of temporarily; delay <held *the presses to insert a late story*> **c** to keep from advancing or from attacking successfully <held *their opponents to a draw*> **d** to restrict, limit < ~ *price increases to a minimum*> **e** to bind legally or morally < ~ *a man to his word*> **3a** to have, keep, or support in the hands or arms; grasp <held *her to him*> **b** to keep in a specified situation, position, or state < ~ *the ladder steady*> **c** to support, sustain <*the roof won't* ~ *much weight*> **d** to retain <*houses should* ~ *their value*> **e** to keep in custody **f** to set aside; reserve < ~ *a room*> **4** to bear, carry <*the soldierly way he* ~s *himself*> **5a** to keep up without interruption; continue <*ship* held *its course*> **b** to keep the uninterrupted interest or attention of <held *the audience in suspense*> **6a** to contain or be capable of containing <*the can* ~s *5 gallons*> **b** to have in store <*what the future* ~s> **7a** to consider to be true; believe **b** to have in regard <*she* held *the matter to be of little importance*> **8a** to engage in with sby else or with others < ~ *a conference*> **b** to cause to be conducted; convene < ~ *a meeting of the council*> **9a** to occupy as a result of appointment or election < ~s *a captaincy in the navy*> **b** to have earned or been awarded < ~s *a PhD*> ~ *vi* **1a** to maintain position <*the defensive line is* ~ing> **b** to continue unchanged; last <*hopes the weather will* ~ > **2** to withstand strain without breaking or giving way <*the anchor* held *in the rough sea*> **3** to bear or carry oneself <*asked her to* ~ *still*> **4** to be or remain valid; apply <*the rule* ~s *in most cases*> **5** to maintain a course; continue <held *south for several miles*> – **hold a brief for** to be retained as counsel for – **hold forth** to speak at great length – **hold good** to be true or valid – **hold one's own** to maintain one's ground, position, or strength in the face of competition or adversity – **hold the fort** to cope with problems for or look after the work of sby who is absent – **hold to 1** to remain steadfast or faithful to; ABIDE BY **2** to cause to hold to <held *him* to *his promise*> – **hold water** to stand up under criticism or analysis – **hold with** to agree with or approve of – **not hold a candle to** to be much inferior to; not qualify for comparison with

[2]**hold** *n* **1a** a manner of grasping an opponent in wrestling **b** influence, control <*his father had a strong* ~ *over him*> **c** possession <*tried to get* ~ *of a road map*> **2** sthg that may be grasped as a support **3** a temporary stoppage of a countdown (e g in launching a spacecraft)

[3]**hold** *n* **1** a space below a ship's deck in which cargo is stored **2** the cargo compartment of a plane

ˈ**hold,all** /-ˌawl‖-ˌɔːl/ *n* a bag or case for miscellaneous articles

hold back *vt* **1** to hinder the progress of; restrain **2** to retain in one's keeping ~*vi* to keep oneself in check

hold down *vt* **1** to keep within limits; *specif* to keep at a low level <*try to* hold *prices* down> **2** to hold and keep (a position of responsibility) <holding down *2 jobs*>

holder /ˈhohldə‖ˈhəʊldə/ *n* **1** a device that holds an often specified object <*cigarette* ~ > **2a** an owner **b** a tenant **c** a person in possession of and legally entitled to receive payment of a bill, note, or cheque

holding /ˈhohlding‖ˈhəʊldɪŋ/ *n* **1** land held **2** property (e g land or securities) owned – usu pl with sing. meaning

ˈ**holding ˌcompany** *n* a company whose primary business is holding a controlling interest in the shares of other companies

hold off *vt* **1** to keep at a distance <hold *the dogs* off> **2** to resist successfully; withstand <hold off *the enemy attack*> **3** to defer action on; postpone ~ *vi* **1** to keep off or at a distance <*hope the rain* holds off> **2** to defer action; delay

hold on *vi* **1** to persevere in difficult circumstances **2** to wait; HANG ON <hold on *a minute!*> – **hold on to** to keep possession of

hold out *vt* to present as likely or realizable; proffer <*the doctors* hold out *every hope of her recovery*> ~ *vi* **1** LAST 2 <*hope the car* holds out *till we get home*> **2** to refuse to yield or give way <*the garrison* held out *against the enemy attack*> – **hold out for** to insist on as the price for an agreement – **hold out on** to withhold sthg (e g information) from – infml

hold over *vt* **1** to postpone **2** to prolong the engagement or tenure of <*the show was* held over *for another week by popular demand*>

ˈ**hold,up** /-ˌup‖-ˌʌp/ *n* **1** an armed robbery **2** a delay

hold up *vt* **1** to delay, impede <*got* held up *in the traffic*> **2** to rob at gunpoint **3** to present, esp as an example <*her work was* held up *as a model*> ~*vi* to endure a test; HOLD OUT

[1]**hole** /hohl‖həʊl/ *n* **1** an opening into or through a thing **2a** a hollow place; *esp* a pit or cavity **b** a deep place in a body of water **c** a

place in the crystal structure of a semiconductor, equivalent to a positively charged particle, where an electron has left its normal position **3** an animal's burrow **4** a serious discrepancy or flaw <*picked* ~s *in his story*> **5a** the unit of play from the tee to the hole in golf **b** a cavity in a putting green into which the ball is to be played in golf **6** a dirty or dingy place <*lives in a dreadful* ~> **7** an awkward position; a fix *USE* (*6 & 7*) infml – **holey** *adj*

[2]**hole** *vt* **1** to make a hole in **2** to drive into a hole ~ *vi* **1** to make a hole in sthg **2** to play one's ball into the hole in golf – usu + *out*

ˌ**hole-and-ˈcorner** *adj* clandestine, underhand

hole up *vi* to take refuge or shelter *in* ~*vt* to place (as if) in a refuge or hiding place *USE* infml

[1]**holiday** /ˈholiday, -di‖ˈhɒlɪdeɪ, -dɪ/ *n* **1** a day, often in commemoration of some event, on which no paid employment is carried out **2** a period of relaxation or recreation spent away from home or work – often pl with sing. meaning [Old English *hāligdæg*, fr *hālig* holy + *dæg* day]

[2]**holiday** *vi* to take or spend a holiday

ˈ**holidayˌmaker** /-ˌmaykə‖-ˌmeɪkə/ *n* a person who is on holiday

holiness /ˈhohlinis‖ˈhəʊlɪnɪs/ *n* **1** *cap* – used as a title for various high religious dignitaries **2** sanctification

holistic /hohˈlistik/ *adj* based on the principle that a thing or being has a nature of its own and is more than simply the sum of its parts

holland /ˈholənd‖ˈhɒlənd/ *n, often cap* a cotton or linen fabric in plain weave, usu heavily sized or glazed

holler /ˈholə‖ˈhɒlə/ *vb, chiefly NAm* to call out or shout (sthg) – **holler** *n*

[1]**hollow** /ˈholoh‖ˈhɒləʊ/ *adj* **1a** having a recessed surface; sunken **b** curved inwards; concave **2** having a cavity within <*a* ~ *tree*> **3** echoing like a sound made in or by beating on an empty container; muffled **4a** deceptively lacking in real value <*a* ~ *victory*> **b** lacking in truth, deceitful < ~ *promises*> – **hollowly** *adv*, **hollowness** *n*

[2]**hollow** *vb* to make or become hollow

[3]**hollow** *n* **1** a depressed or hollow part of a surface; *esp* a small valley or basin **2** an unfilled space; a cavity

[4]**hollow** *adv* **1** in a hollow manner <*his laughter rang* ~> **2** completely, totally – infml <*she beat me* ~>

hollow out *vt* to form a cavity or hole in; *also* to make in this way

holly /ˈholi‖ˈhɒlɪ/ *n* (the foliage of) any of a genus of trees and shrubs with thick glossy spiny-edged leaves and usu bright red berries

hollyhock /ˈholiˌhok‖ˈhɒlɪˌhɒk/ *n* a tall orig Chinese plant of the mallow family with large coarse rounded leaves and tall spikes of showy flowers

holm oak /hohm‖həʊm/ *n* a S European evergreen oak

holocaust /ˈholəˌkawst‖ˈhɒləˌkɔːst/ *n* **1** a sacrificial offering consumed by fire **2** an instance of wholesale destruction or loss of life **3** *often cap the* genocidal persecution of European Jewry by Hitler and the Nazi party during WW II [deriv of Greek *holokaustos* burnt whole, fr *holos* whole + *kaustos* burnt, fr *kaiein* to burn]

hologram /ˈholəgram‖ˈhɒləgræm/ *n* a pattern produced by the interference between one part of a split beam of coherent light (e g from a laser) and the other part of the same beam reflected off an object; *also* a photographic reproduction of this pattern that when suitably illuminated produces a three-dimensional picture [deriv of Greek *holos* whole + *gramma* letter, writing]

holstein /ˈholstien‖ˈhɒlstaɪn/ *n, chiefly NAm* a Friesian

holster /ˈhohlstə, ˈhol-‖ˈhəʊlstə, ˈhɒl-/ *n* a usu leather holder for a pistol

holy /ˈhohli‖ˈhəʊlɪ/ *adj* **1** set apart to the service of God or a god; sacred **2a** characterized by perfection and transcendence; commanding absolute adoration and reverence <*the* ~ *Trinity*> **b** spiritually pure; godly **3** evoking or worthy of religious veneration or awe <*the* ~ *cross*> **4** terrible, awful – used as an intensive <*a* ~ *terror*>

ˌ**Holy Comˈmunion** *n* COMMUNION 1

ˌ**Holy ˈGrail** *n the* cup or platter that according to medieval legend was used by Christ at the Last Supper and became the object of knightly quests

ˌ**Holy ˈSee** *n the* papacy

ˌ**Holy ˈSpirit** *n the* 3rd person of the Trinity

ˈ**Holy ˌWeek** *n* the week before Easter during which the last days of Christ's life are commemorated

ˌ**holy ˈwrit** *n, often cap H&W* a writing or utterance of unquestionable authority

hom-, **homo-** *comb form* one and the same; similar; alike <homo*graph*> <homo*sexual*>

homage /ˈhomij‖ˈhɒmɪdʒ/ *n* **1a** a ceremony by which a man acknowledges himself the vassal of a lord **b** an act done or payment made by a vassal **2a** reverential regard; deference **b** flattering attention; tribute [Old French *hommage*, fr *homme* man, vassal, fr Latin *homin-*, *homo* man]

homburg /ˈhombuhg‖ˈhɒmbɜːg/ *n* a felt hat with a stiff curled brim and a high crown creased lengthways

[1]**home** /hohm‖həʊm/ *n* **1a** a family's place of residence; a domicile **b** a house **2** the social unit formed by a family living together <*comes from a broken* ~> **3a** a congenial environment <*the theatre is my spiritual* ~> **b** a habitat **4a** a place of origin; *also* one's native country **b** the place where sthg originates or is based <*Lord's,* ~ *of cricket*> **5** an establishment providing residence and often care for children, convalescents, etc – **homeless** *adj*, **homelessness** *n* – **at home 1** relaxed and comfortable; AT EASE 2 **2** on familiar ground; knowledgeable <*teachers* at home *in their subjects*>

[2]**home** *adv* **1** to or at home <*wrote* ~> **2** to a final, closed, or standard position <*drive a nail* ~> **3** to an ultimate objective (e g a finishing line) **4** to a vital sensitive core <*the truth struck* ~> **5** HOME AND DRY

3**home** *adj* **1** of or being a home, place of origin, or base of operations **2** prepared, carried out, or designed for use in the home < ~ *cooking*> **3** operating or occurring in a home area <*the* ~ *team*>

4**home** *vi* **1** to go or return home **2** *of an animal* to return accurately to one's home or birthplace from a distance – **home in on** to be directed at or head towards (a specified goal, target, etc)

ˌhome and ˈdry *adv* having safely or successfully achieved one's purpose

ˈhome ˌbrew *n* an alcoholic drink (e g beer) made at home

ˈhomeˌcoming /-ˌkuming‖-ˌkʌmɪŋ/ *n* a returning home

ˌhome ecoˈnomics *n pl but sing or pl in constr* DOMESTIC SCIENCE – **home economist** *n*

ˌhome from ˈhome *n*, *Br* a place as comfortable or congenial as one's own home

ˌhome ˈfront *n* the sphere of civilian activity in war

ˌhomeˈgrown /-ˈgrohn‖-ˈgrəʊn/ *adj* produced in, coming from, or characteristic of the home country or region

ˌhome ˈhelp *n*, *Br* a person employed by a local authority to carry out household chores for the sick, elderly, or disabled

ˈhomeland /-lənd‖-lənd/ *n* **1** one's native land **2** a Bantustan

ˈhomeˌlike /-ˌliek‖-ˌlaɪk/ *adj* characteristic of one's own home, esp in being cheerful or cosy

ˈhomely /-li‖-lɪ/ *adj* **1** commonplace, familiar <*explained the problem in* ~ *terms*> **2** of a sympathetic character; kindly **3** simple, unpretentious <*a* ~ *meal of bacon and eggs*> **4** *chiefly NAm* not good-looking; plain – **homeliness** *n*

ˌhomeˈmade /-ˈmayd‖-ˈmeɪd/ *adj* made in the home, on the premises, or by one's own efforts

ˈhome ˌoffice *n*, *often cap H&O the* government office concerned with internal affairs

ˈhome ˌplate *n* a rubber slab at which a baseball batter stands

Homeric /hohˈmerik‖həʊˈmerɪk/ *adj* **1** (characteristic) of Homer, his age, or his writings **2** of epic proportions; heroic <*a* ~ *feat of endurance*> [*Homer* (*fl* about 850 BC), Greek epic poet]

ˌhome ˈrule *n* limited self-government by the people of a dependent political unit

ˌhome ˈrun *n* a hit in baseball that enables the batter to make a complete circuit of the bases and score a run

ˈhomeˌsick /-ˌsik‖-ˌsɪk/ *adj* longing for home and family while absent from them – **homesickness** *n*

1**ˈhomeˌspun** /-ˌspun‖-ˌspʌn/ *adj* **1** made of homespun **2** lacking sophistication; simple < ~ *prose*>

2**homespun** *n* a loosely woven usu woollen or linen fabric orig made from yarn spun at home

ˈhomestead /-stid‖-stɪd/ *n* **1** a house and adjoining land occupied by a family **2** *Austr & NZ* the owner's living quarters on a sheep or cattle station – **homesteader** *n*

ˈhome ˌstraight *n the* straight final part of a racecourse usu opposite the grandstand

ˈhomeˌstretch /-ˌstrech‖-ˌstretʃ/ *n the* final stage (e g of a project)

ˌhome ˈtruth *n* an unpleasant but true fact about a person's character or situation – often pl

ˈhomeward /-wood‖-wʊd/ *adj* being or going towards home

ˈhomewards, *chiefly NAm* **homeward** *adv* towards home

ˈhomeˌwork /-ˌwuhk‖-ˌwɜːk/ *n* **1** work done in one's own home for pay **2** an assignment given to a pupil to be completed esp away from school **3** preparatory reading or research (e g for a discussion) <*she's done her* ~ *on the subject*> – **homeworker** *n*

homey /ˈhohmi‖ˈhəʊmɪ/ *adj* homy

homicide /ˈhomisied‖ˈhɒmɪsaɪd/ *n* (the act of) sby who kills another [Middle French fr Latin *homicida* & *homicidium*, fr *homo* man + *caedere* to cut, kill] – **homicidal** *adj*

homiletic /ˌhomiˈletik‖ˌhɒmɪˈletɪk/, **homiletical** /-kl‖-kl/ *adj* **1** of or resembling a homily **2** relating to homiletics

ˌhomiˈletics *n pl but sing in constr* the art of preaching

homily /ˈhomili‖ˈhɒmɪlɪ/ *n* **1** a sermon **2** a lecture on moral conduct [Late Latin *homilia*, fr Late Greek, fr Greek, conversation, discourse, fr *homilein* to consort with, address, fr *homilos* crowd, assembly]

ˈhoming ˌpigeon /ˈhohming‖ˈhəʊmɪŋ/ *n* a domesticated pigeon trained to return home

hominy /ˈhomini‖ˈhɒmɪnɪ/ *n* crushed or coarsely ground husked maize, esp when boiled with water or milk

1**homo** /hohmoh‖həʊməʊ/ *n*, *pl* **homos** any of a genus of primate mammals including recent man and various extinct ancestors

2**homo** *n*, *pl* **homos** a homosexual – chiefly derog

homoeopath /ˈhomi·əˌpath‖ˈhɒmɪəˌpæθ/ *n* a practitioner of a system of disease treatment relying on the administration of minute doses of a remedy that produces symptoms like those of the disease [deriv of Greek *homoios* similar + *pathos* suffering] – **homoeopathic** *adj*, **homoeopathy** *n*

homogeneous /ˌhoməˈjeenyəs, -ni·əs‖ˌhɒməˈdʒiːnjəs, -nɪəs/ *adj* **1** of the same or a similar kind or nature **2** of uniform structure or composition throughout <*a culturally* ~ *neighbourhood*> [Medieval Latin *homogeneus*, fr Greek *homogenēs*, fr *homos* same + *genos* kind] – **homogeneously** *adv*, **homogeneousness** *n*

homogen·ize, **-ise** /hoˈmojəniez, hə-‖hɒˈmɒdʒənaɪz, hə-/ *vt* **1** to make homogeneous **2** to reduce the particles of so that they are uniformly small and evenly distributed; *esp* to break up the fat globules of (milk) into very fine particles ~ *vi* to become homogenized – **homogenizer** *n*, **homogenization** *n*

homograph /ˈhomәgrahf, -ˌgraf, ˈhoh-‖ˈhɒməgrɑːf, -ˌgræf, ˈhəʊ-/ *n* any of 2 or more words spelt alike but different in meaning, derivation, or pronunciation – **homographic** *adj*

homonym /ˈhomənim‖ˈhɒmənɪm/ *n* **1a** a homophone **b** a homograph **c** any of 2 or more words that are both spelt and pronounced alike **2** a namesake – chiefly fml – **homonymic, homonymous** *adj*, **homonymously** *adv*, **homonymy** *n*

homophone /ˈhoməfohn‖ˈhɒməfəʊn/ *n* **1** any of 2 or more words pronounced alike but different in meaning, derivation, or spelling (e g *to, too*, and *two*) **2** a character or group of characters pronounced the same as another – **homophonous** *adj*

Homo sapiens /ˌhohmoh ˈsapi·enz, ˈhomoh-‖ˌhəʊməʊ ˈsæpɪenz, ˈhɒməʊ-/ *n* mankind

homosexual /ˌhomə'seksyoo(ə)l, -ˈseksh(ə)l‖ˌhɒməˈseksjʊ(ə)l, -ˈsekʃ(ə)l/ *adj or n* (of, for, or being) sby having a sexual preference for members of his/her own sex – **homosexually** *adj*, **homosexuality** *n*

homy, homey /ˈhoʰmi‖ˈhəʊmɪ/ *adj* homelike – chiefly infml

hone /hohn‖həʊn/ *vt or n* (to sharpen or make more keen or effective with or as if with) a stone for sharpening a cutting tool <*finely* ~d *sarcasm*>

honest /ˈonist‖ˈɒnɪst/ *adj* **1** free from fraud or deception; legitimate, truthful **2** respectable or worthy **3a** marked by integrity **b** frank, sincere <*an* ~ *answer*> [Old French *honeste*, fr Latin *honestus* honourable, fr *honos, honor* honour]

ˈ**honestly** /-li‖-lɪ/ *adv* to speak in an honest way <~, *I don't know why I bother*>

honesty /ˈonisti‖ˈɒnɪstɪ/ *n* **1a** upright and straightforward conduct; integrity **b** sincerity, truthfulness **2** any of a genus of European plants of the mustard family with large broad smooth semitransparent seed pods

honey /ˈhuni‖ˈhʌnɪ/ *n* **1a** (a pale golden colour like that typical of) a sweet viscous sticky liquid formed from the nectar of flowers in the honey sac of various bees **b** a sweet liquid resembling honey that is collected or produced by various insects **2** sthg sweet or agreeable; sweetness **3** *chiefly NAm* sweetheart, dear

ˈ**honeyˌbee** /-ˌbee‖-ˌbiː/ *n* (a social honey-producing bee related to) a European bee kept for its honey and wax

[1]ˈ**honeyˌcomb** /-ˌkohm‖-ˌkəʊm/ *n* **1** (sthg resembling in shape or structure) a mass of 6-sided wax cells built by honeybees in their nest to contain their brood and stores of honey **2** (tripe from) the second stomach of a cow or other ruminant mammal

[2]**honeycomb** *vt* **1** to cause to be chequered or full of cavities like a honeycomb **2** to penetrate into every part; riddle <*the government is* ~ed *with spies* – T H White>

ˈ**honeyˌdew** /-ˌdyooh‖-ˌdjuː/ *n* a sweet deposit secreted on the leaves of plants usu by aphids

ˌ**honeydew** ˈ**melon** *n* a pale smooth-skinned muskmelon with greenish sweet flesh

honeyed *also* **honied** /ˈhunid‖ˈhʌnɪd/ *adj* sweetened (as if) with honey <~ *words*>

ˈ**honeyˌmoon** /-ˌmoohn‖-ˌmuːn/ *n* **1** the period immediately following marriage, esp when taken as a holiday by the married couple **2** a period of unusual harmony following the establishment of a new relationship <*the government's* ~ *with the public*> – **honeymoon** *vi*, **honeymooner** *n*

ˈ**honeyˌsuckle** /-ˌsukl‖-ˌsʌkl/ *n* any of a genus of (climbing) shrubs usu with showy sweet-smelling flowers rich in nectar

[1]**honk** /hongk‖hɒŋk/ *n* (a sound made by a car's electric horn like) the short loud unmusical tone that is the characteristic cry of the goose

[2]**honk** *vb* to (cause to) make a honk <*the driver* ~ed *his horn*> – **honker** *n*

honkie, honky /ˈhongki‖ˈhɒŋkɪ/ *n, chiefly NAm* a white man – derog; used by Blacks

honky-tonk /ˈhongki ˌtongk‖ˈhɒŋkɪ ˌtɒŋk/ *n* **1** a form of ragtime piano playing **2** a cheap nightclub or dance hall – chiefly infml – **honky-tonk** *adj*

honorarium /ˌonəˈreəri·əm‖ˌɒnəˈreərɪəm/ *n, pl* **honorariums, honoraria** /-ri·ə‖-rɪə/ a payment in recognition of professional services on which no price is set

honorary /ˈon(ə)rəri‖ˈɒn(ə)rərɪ/ *adj* **1a** conferred or elected in recognition of achievement, without the usual obligations <*an* ~ *degree*> **b** unpaid, voluntary <*an* ~ *chairman*> **2** depending on honour for fulfilment <*an* ~ *obligation*> – **honorarily** *adv*

[1]**honorific** /ˌonəˈrifik‖ˌɒnəˈrɪfɪk/ *adj* conferring or conveying honour <~ *titles*> – **honorifically** *adv*

[2]**honorific** *n* an honorific expression

[1]**honour**, *NAm chiefly* **honor** /ˈonə‖ˈɒnə/ *n* **1a** good name or public esteem <*his* ~ *was at stake*> **b** outward respect; recognition **2** a privilege <*I have the* ~ *to welcome you*> **3** *cap* a person of superior social standing – now used esp as a title for a holder of high office (e g a judge in court) <*if Your* Honour *pleases*> **4** one who brings respect or fame <*was an* ~ *to his profession*> **5** a mark or symbol of distinction: e g **5a** an exalted title or rank **b** a ceremonial rite or observance – usu pl <*buried with full military* ~s> **6** *pl* a course of study for a university degree more exacting and specialized than that leading to a pass degree **7** (a woman's) chastity or purity **8a** a high standard of ethical conduct; integrity **b** one's word given as a pledge <~ *bound*> **9** *pl* social courtesies or civilities extended by a host <*did the* ~s *at the table*> **10a** an ace, king, queen, or jack of the trump suit in whist; *also* these cards and the 10 in bridge or the 4 aces when the contract is no trumps **b** the privilege of playing first from the tee in golf awarded to the player who won the previous hole

[2]**honour**, *NAm chiefly* **honor** *vt* **1a** to regard or treat with honour or respect **b** to confer honour on **2a** to live up to or fulfil the terms of <~ *a commitment*> **b** to accept and pay when due <~ *a cheque*> **3** to salute (e g one's partner) with a bow in a country dance

honourable, *NAm chiefly* **honorable** /ˈon(ə)rəbl‖ˈɒn(ə)rəbl/ *adj* **1** worthy of honour **2** performed or accompanied with marks of honour or respect **3** entitled to honour – used as a title for the children of certain British noblemen and for various government officials **4a** bringing credit to the possessor or doer <*an* ~ *performance*> **b** consistent with an untarnished reputation <*an* ~ *discharge from the army*> **5** characterized by (moral) integrity <*his intentions were* ~>

hooch /hoohch‖huːtʃ/ *n, NAm* spirits, esp when inferior or illicitly made or obtained – slang

¹**hood** /hood‖hʊd/ *n* **1a** a loose often protective covering for the top and back of the head and neck that is usu attached to the neckline of a garment **b** a usu leather covering for a hawk's head and eyes **2a** an ornamental scarf worn over an academic gown that indicates by its colour the wearer's university and degree **b** a hoodlike marking, crest, or expansion on the head of an animal (e g a cobra or seal) **3a** a folding waterproof top cover for an open car, pram, etc **b** a cover or canopy for carrying off fumes, smoke, etc **4** *NAm* BONNET 2 – **hood** *vt*

²**hood** *n* a hoodlum or gangster – infml

-hood /-hood‖-hʊd/ *suffix* (*adj or n → n*) **1** state or condition of <*man*hood> **2** quality or character of <*likeli*hood> **3** time or period of <*child*hood> **4** instance of (a specified quality or condition) <*a false*hood> **5** *sing or pl in constr* body or class of people sharing (a specified character or state) <*priest*hood>

ˈ**hooded** *adj* **1** covered (as if) by a hood <~ *eyes*> **2** shaped like a hood

hoodlum /ˈhoohdləm‖ˈhuːdləm/ *n* **1** a (violent) thug **2** a young rowdy – **hoodlumish** *adj*

¹**hoodoo** /ˈhooh,dooh‖ˈhuː,duː/ *n, pl* **hoodoos** *chiefly NAm* voodoo – **hoodooism** *n*

²**hoodoo** *vt, chiefly NAm* to cast an evil spell on; *broadly* to bring bad luck to

hoodwink /ˈhood,wingk‖ˈhʊd,wɪŋk/ *vt* to deceive, delude – chiefly infml – **hoodwinker** *n*

hooey /ˈhooh·i‖ˈhuːɪ/ *n* nonsense – slang

¹**hoof** /hoohf, hoof‖huːf, hʊf/ *n, pl* **hooves** /hoohvz‖huːvz/, **hoofs** (a foot with) a curved horny casing that protects the ends of the digits of a horse, cow, or similar mammal and that corresponds to a nail or claw – **hoofed** *adj* – **on the hoof** *of a meat animal* before being butchered; while still alive

²**hoof** *vt* to kick ~ *vi* to go on foot – usu + *it*

hoo-ha /ˈhooh ,hah‖ˈhuː ,hɑː/ *n* a fuss, to-do – chiefly infml

¹**hook** /hook‖hʊk/ *n* **1** (sthg shaped like) a curved or bent device for catching, holding, or pulling **2a** (a flight of) a ball in golf that deviates from a straight course in a direction opposite to the dominant hand of the player propelling it **b** an attacking stroke in cricket played with a horizontal bat aimed at a ball of higher than waist height and intended to send the ball on the leg side **3** a short blow delivered in boxing with a circular motion while the elbow remains bent and rigid – **by hook or by crook** by any possible means – **hook, line, and sinker** completely <*swallowed all the lies* hook, line, and sinker>

²**hook** *vt* **1** to form into a hook (shape) **2** to seize, make fast, or connect (as if) by a hook **3** to make (e g a rug) by drawing loops of yarn, thread, or cloth through a coarse fabric with a hook **4a** to hit or throw (a ball) so that a hook results **b** to play a hook in cricket at (a ball) or at the bowling of (a bowler) **5** to steal – infml ~ *vi* **1** to form a hook; curve **2** to become hooked **3** to play a hook in cricket or golf

hookah /ˈhookə, -kah‖ˈhʊkə, -kɑː/ *n* a water pipe (with a single flexible tube by which smoke is drawn through water and into the mouth) [Arabic *ḥuqqah* bottle of a water pipe]

hooked *adj* **1** (shaped) like or provided with a hook **2** made by hooking <*a* ~ *rug*> **3a** addicted to drugs – slang **b** very enthusiastic or compulsively attached (to sthg specified) <~ *on skiing*> – infml

hooker /ˈhookə‖ˈhʊkə/ *n* **1** (the position of) a player in rugby stationed in the middle of the front row of the scrum **2** *chiefly NAm* a woman prostitute – slang

ˈ**hook,up** /-,up‖-,ʌp/ *n* (the plan of) a combination (e g of electronic circuits) used for a specific often temporary purpose (e g radio transmission)

ˈ**hook,worm** /-,wuhm‖-,wɜːm/ *n* (infestation with or disease caused by) any of several parasitic nematode worms that have strong mouth hooks for attaching to the host's intestinal lining

hooky, hookey /ˈhooki‖ˈhʊkɪ/ *n, chiefly NAm* truant – chiefly in *play hooky*; infml

hooligan /ˈhoohligən‖ˈhuːlɪgən/ *n* a young ruffian or hoodlum [perhaps fr Patrick *Hooligan* (*fl* 1898), Irish criminal in London] – **hooliganism** *n*

¹**hoop** /hoohp‖huːp/ *n* **1** a large (rigid) circular strip used esp for holding together the staves of containers, as a child's toy, or to expand a woman's skirt **2** a circular figure or object **3** an arch through which balls must be hit in croquet

²**hoop** *vt* to bind or fasten (as if) with a hoop – **hooper** *n*

hoop-la /ˈhoohp ,lah‖ˈhuːp ,lɑː/ *n* a (fairground) game in which prizes are won by tossing rings over them

hooray /hooˈray‖hʊˈreɪ/ *interj* hurray

¹**hoot** /hooht‖huːt/ *vi* **1** to utter a loud shout, usu in contempt **2a** to make (a sound similar to) the long-drawn-out throat noise of an owl **b** to sound the horn, whistle, etc of a motor car or other vehicle <*the driver* ~ed *at me as he passed*> **3** to laugh loudly – infml ~ *vt* **1** to assail or drive out by hooting <~ed *down the speaker*> **2** to express in or by hooting <~ed *their disapproval*>

²**hoot** *n* **1** a sound of hooting **2** DAMN 2 <*I couldn't care 2* ~s> **3** a source of laughter or amusement <*the play was an absolute* ~> *USE* (*2, 3*) infml

hooter /ˈhoohtə‖ˈhuːtə/ *n, chiefly Br* **1** a device (e g the horn of a car) for producing a loud hooting noise **2** the nose – infml

hoover /ˈhoohvə‖ˈhuːvə/ *vb* to clean using a vacuum cleaner

Hoover *trademark* – used for a vacuum cleaner

¹**hop** /hop‖hɒp/ *vb* **-pp-** *vi* **1** to move by a quick springy leap or in a series of leaps; *esp* to jump on 1 foot **2** to make a quick trip, esp by air **3** to board or leave a vehicle <~ *onto a bus*> ~ *vt* **1** to jump over <~ *a fence*> **2** *NAm* to ride on, esp without authorization <~ *a train*> *USE* (*vi 2, 3*) infml – **hop it** *Br* go away! – infml

²**hop** *n* **1a** a short leap, esp on 1 leg **b** a bounce, a rebound **2** a short or long flight between 2 landings <*flew to Bangkok in 3* ~s> **3** DANCE 2 – infml

³**hop** *n* **1** a climbing plant of the hemp family with inconspicuous green flowers of which the

female ones are in cone-shaped catkins **2** *pl* the ripe dried catkins of a hop used esp to impart a bitter flavour to beer

[4]**hop** *vt* **-pp-** to impregnate (esp beer) with hops

[1]**hope** /hohp‖həʊp/ *vi* to wish with expectation of fulfilment ~ *vt* **1** to long for with expectation of obtainment **2** to expect with desire; trust – **hoper** *n* – **hope against hope** to hope without any basis for expecting fulfilment

[2]**hope** *n* **1** trust, reliance <*all my ~ is in the Lord*> **2a** desire accompanied by expectation of or belief in fulfilment <*has high ~s of an early recovery*> **b** sby or sthg on which hopes are centred **c** sthg hoped for

ˈ**hope ˌchest** *n, NAm* BOTTOM DRAWER

[1]ˈ**hopeful** /-f(ə)l‖-f(ə)l/ *adj* **1** full of hope <*I'm ~ he'll come*> **2** inspiring hope <*the situation looks ~*> – **hopefulness** *n*

[2]**hopeful** *n* a person who aspires to or is likely to succeed

ˈ**hopefully** /-f(ə)l·i‖-f(ə)lɪ/ *adv* **1** in a hopeful manner **2** it is hoped <~ *he will arrive in time*> – disapproved of by some speakers

ˈ**hopeless** /-lis‖-lɪs/ *adj* **1** having no expectation of success **2a** giving no grounds for hope <*a ~ case*> **b** incapable of solution, management, or accomplishment <*a ~ task*> **3** incompetent, useless – chiefly infml <*I'm ~ at sums*> – **hopelessly** *adv*, **hopelessness** *n*

hopper /ˈhopə‖ˈhɒpə/ *n* **1** a leaping insect; *specif* an immature hopping form of an insect **2a** a (funnel-shaped) receptacle for the discharging or temporary storage of grain, coal, etc **b** a goods wagon with a floor through which bulk materials may be discharged **c** a barge that can discharge dredged material through an opening bottom

ˈ**hopˌscotch** /-ˌskoch‖-ˌskɒtʃ/ *n* a children's game in which a player tosses an object (e g a stone) into areas of a figure outlined on the ground and hops through the figure and back to regain the object

ˌ**hop, ˌskip, and ˈjump** *n* a short distance – infml

horde /hawd‖hɔːd/ *n* **1** a (Mongolian) nomadic people or tribe **2** a crowd, swarm

horizon /həˈriez(ə)n‖həˈraɪz(ə)n/ *n* **1** the apparent junction of earth and sky **2a** the plane that is tangent to the earth's surface at an observer's position **b** (the great circle formed by the intersection with the celestial sphere of) the plane parallel to such a plane but passing through the earth's centre **c** range of perception [Late Latin, fr Greek *horizōn*, fr *horizein* to bound, define, fr *horos* boundary] – **horizonal** *adj*

horizontal /ˌhoriˈzontl‖ˌhɒrɪˈzɒntl/ *adj* **1a** near the horizon **b** in the plane of or (operating in a plane) parallel to the horizon or a base line; level <~ *distance*> <*a ~ engine*> **2** of or concerning relationships between people of the same rank in different hierarchies – **horizontally** *adv*

hormone /ˈhawmohn‖ˈhɔːməʊn/ *n* (a synthetic substance with the action of) a product of living cells that usu circulates in body liquids (e g the blood or sap) and produces a specific effect on the activity of cells remote from its point of origin [Greek *hormōn*, stirring up, fr *horman* to stir up, fr *hormē* impulse, assault] – **hormonal** *adj*, **hormonally** *adv*

horn /hawn‖hɔːn/ *n* **1a(1)** any of the usu paired bony projecting parts on the head of cattle, giraffes, deer, and similar hoofed mammals and some extinct mammals and reptiles **a(2)** a permanent solid pointed part consisting of keratin that is attached to the nasal bone of a rhinoceros **b** a natural projection from an animal (e g a snail or owl) resembling or suggestive of a horn **c** the tough fibrous material consisting chiefly of keratin that covers or forms the horns and hooves of cattle and related animals, or other hard parts (e g claws or nails) **d** a hollow horn used as a container **2** sthg resembling or suggestive of a horn: e g **2a** either of the curved ends of a crescent **b** a horn-shaped body of land or water **3a** an animal's horn used as a wind instrument **b(1)** HUNTING HORN **b(2)** FRENCH HORN **c** a wind instrument used in a jazz band; *esp* a trumpet **d** a device (e g on a motor car) for making loud warning noises <*a fog ~*> – **horn** *adj*, **horned** *adj*

hornbeam /ˈhawnˌbeem‖ˈhɔːnˌbiːm/ *n* any of a genus of trees of the hazel family with smooth grey bark and hard white wood

ˈ**hornˌbill** /-ˌbil‖-ˌbɪl/ *n* any of a family of large Old World birds with enormous bills

hornet /ˈhawnit‖ˈhɔːnɪt/ *n* a large wasp with a black and yellow banded abdomen and a powerful sting

ˈ**hornet's ˌnest** *n* an angry or hostile reaction – esp in *stir up a hornet's nest*

horn in *vi* to intrude – slang; often + *on*

ˈ**hornˌpipe** /-ˌpiep‖-ˌpaɪp/ *n* (a piece of music for) a lively British folk dance typically associated with sailors

ˈ**horn-ˌrims** *n pl* glasses with horn rims – **horn-rimmed** *adj*

horny /ˈhawni‖ˈhɔːnɪ/ *adj* **1** (made) of horn **2** sexually aroused – slang

horology /hoˈroləji‖hɒˈrɒlədʒɪ/ *n* **1** the science of measuring time **2** the art of constructing instruments for indicating time – **horologer** *n*, **horologist** *n*, **horologic, horological** *adj*

horoscope /ˈhorəˌskohp‖ˈhɒrəˌskəʊp/ *n* (an astrological forecast based on) a diagram of the relative positions of planets and signs of the zodiac at a specific time, esp sby's birth, used by astrologers to infer individual character and personality traits and to foretell events in a person's life [Middle French, fr Latin *horoscopus*, fr Greek *hōroskopos*, fr *hōra* hour + *skopein* to look at]

horrendous /həˈrendəs‖həˈrendəs/ *adj* dreadful, horrible – **horrendously** *adv*

horrible /ˈhorəbl‖ˈhɒrəbl/ *adj* **1** marked by or arousing horror <*a ~ accident*> **2** extremely unpleasant or disagreeable – chiefly infml <~ *weather*> – **horribleness** *n*, **horribly** *adv*

horrid /ˈhorid‖ˈhɒrɪd/ *adj* **1** horrible, shocking **2** repulsive, nasty <*a ~ little boy*> [Latin *horridus* rough, shaggy, bristling, fr *horrēre* to bristle, shudder] – **horridly** *adv*, **horridness** *n*

horrific /həˈrifik‖həˈrɪfɪk/ *adj* arousing horror; horrifying <*a ~ account of the tragedy*> – **horrifically** *adv*

horrify /ˈhorifie‖ˈhɒrɪfaɪ/ *vt* **1** to cause to feel

horror **2** to fill with distaste; shock – **horrifyingly** *adv*

horror /ˈhorə‖ˈhɒrə/ *n* **1a** intense fear, dread, or dismay **b** intense aversion or repugnance **2** (sby or sthg that has) the quality of inspiring horror **3** *pl* a state of horror, depression, or apprehension – chiefly infml

ˈhorror-ˌstruck, ˈhorror-ˌstricken *adj* filled with horror

hors de combat /ˌaw də ˈkombah ‖ˌɔː də ˈkɒmbɑː (*Fr* ɔːr də kɔ̃ba)/ *adv or adj* out of the fight; disabled

hors d'oeuvre /ˌaw ˈduhv ‖ˌɔː ˈdɜːv (*Fr* ɔːr dœvr)/ *n, pl* **hors d'oeuvres** *also* **hors d'oeuvre** /ˈduhv(z) ‖ˈdɜːv(z) (*Fr* ~)/ any of various savoury foods usu served as appetizers [French *hors-d'œuvre*, lit., outside of work]

[1]horse /haws‖hɔːs/ *n, pl* **horses,** (*3*) **horse** **1a(1)** a large solid-hoofed plant-eating quadruped mammal domesticated by humans since prehistoric times and used as a beast of burden, a draught animal, or for riding **a(2)** a racehorse <*play the* ~s> **b** a male horse; a stallion or gelding **2a** a usu 4-legged frame for supporting sthg (e g planks) **b(1)** POMMEL HORSE **b(2)** VAULTING HORSE **3** *sing or pl in constr* the cavalry **4** heroin – slang – **from the horse's mouth** from the original source

[2]horse *vi* to engage in horseplay <horsing *around*> ~ *vt* to provide (e g a person or vehicle) with a horse

[1]ˈhorseˌback /-bak‖-bæk/ *n* – **on horseback** mounted on a horse

[2]horseback *adv, chiefly NAm* ON HORSEBACK

ˈhorseˌbox /-ˌboks‖-ˌbɒks/ *n* a lorry or closed trailer for transporting horses

ˌhorse ˈchestnut *n* (the large glossy brown seed of) a large tree with 5-lobed leaves and erect conical clusters of showy flowers

ˈhorseˌfly /-ˌflie‖-ˌflaɪ/ *n* any of a family of swift usu large flies with bloodsucking females

ˈhorseˌhair /-ˌheə‖-ˌheə/ *n* hair (from the mane or tail) of a horse; *also* cloth made from this

ˈhorseˌlaugh /-ˌlahf‖-ˌlɑːf/ *n* a loud boisterous laugh

ˈhorseman /-mən‖-mən/, *fem* **ˈhorseˌwoman** *n* **1** a rider on horseback **2** a (skilled) breeder, tender, or manager of horses – **horsemanship** *n*

ˈhorseˌplay /-ˌplay‖-ˌpleɪ/ *n* rough or boisterous play

ˈhorseˌpower /-ˌpowə‖-ˌpaʊə/ *n* an imperial unit of power equal to about 746 watts

ˈhorseˌradish /-ˌradish‖-ˌrædɪʃ/ *n* **1** a tall coarse white-flowered plant of the mustard family **2** (a condiment prepared from) the pungent root of the horseradish

ˈhorse ˌsense *n* COMMON SENSE

ˈhorseˌshit /-ˌshit‖-ˌʃɪt/ *n, chiefly NAm* bullshit – vulg

ˈhorseˌshoe /-ˌshooh‖-ˌʃuː/ *n* (sthg with a shape resembling) a shoe for horses, usu consisting of a narrow U-shaped plate of iron fitting the rim of the hoof – **horseshoe** *vt*, **horseshoer** *n*

ˈhorse-ˌtrading *n* negotiation accompanied by hard bargaining and reciprocal concessions

ˈhorseˌwhip /-ˌwip‖-ˌwɪp/ *vt* to flog (as if) with a whip for horses

ˈhorseˌwoman /-ˌwoomən‖-ˌwʊmən/ *n* a female horseman

horsey, horsy /ˈhawsi‖ˈhɔːsɪ/ *adj* **1** of or resembling a horse **2** very interested in horses, horse riding, or horse racing **3** characteristic of horsemen – **horsily** *adv*, **horsiness** *n*

hortative /ˈhawtətiv‖ˈhɔːtətɪv/, **hortatory** /ˈhawtət(ə)ri‖ˈhɔːtət(ə)rɪ/ *adj* giving encouragement – fml – **hortatively** *adv*

horticulture /ˈhawtiˌkulchə‖ˈhɔːtɪˌkʌltʃə/ *n* the science and art of growing fruits, vegetables, and flowers [Latin *hortus* garden + *cultura* cultivation] – **horticultural** *adj*, **horticulturally** *adv*, **horticulturist** *n*

hosanna /hohˈzanə‖həʊˈzænə/ *interj or n* (used as) a cry of acclamation and adoration

[1]hose /hohz‖həʊz/ *n, pl* (*1*) **hose,** (*2*) **hoses** **1** a leg covering that sometimes covers the foot: e g **1a** short breeches reaching to the knee <*doublet and* ~> **b** *pl, chiefly NAm* stockings; *also* tights **2** a flexible tube for conveying fluids (e g from a tap or in a car engine)

[2]hose *vt* to spray, water, or wash with a hose

hosiery /ˈhohzyəri‖ˈhəʊzjərɪ/ *n* socks, stockings, and tights in general

hospice /ˈhospis‖ˈhɒspɪs/ *n* **1** a place of shelter for travellers or the destitute (run by a religious order) **2** *Br* a nursing home, esp for terminally ill patients

hospitable /hoˈspitəbl, ˈhos-‖hɒˈspɪtəbl, ˈhɒs-/ *adj* **1a** offering a generous and cordial welcome (to guests or strangers) **b** offering a pleasant or sustaining environment <*a* ~ *climate*> **2** readily receptive <~ *to new ideas*> – **hospitably** *adv*

hospital /ˈhospitl‖ˈhɒspɪtl/ *n* **1** an institution where the sick or injured are given medical care **2** a repair shop for specified small objects <*a doll's* ~> [Old French, fr Medieval Latin *hospitale*, deriv of Latin *hospitalis* of a guest, fr *hospit-, hospes* host, guest]

hospitality /ˌhospiˈtaləti‖ˌhɒspɪˈtælətɪ/ *n* hospitable treatment or reception

hospital·ize, -ise /ˈhospitl·iez‖ˈhɒspɪtlaɪz/ *vt* to place in a hospital as a patient – **hospitalization** *n*

[1]host /hohst‖həʊst/ *n* **1** a very large number; a multitude **2** an army – chiefly poetic or archaic

[2]host *n* **1a** an innkeeper <*mine* ~> **b** one who receives or entertains guests socially or officially **c** sby or sthg that provides facilities for an event or function <*our college served as* ~ *for the chess tournament*> **2a** a living animal or plant on or in which a parasite or smaller organism lives **b** an individual into which a tissue or part is transplanted from another **3** a compere on a radio or television programme

[3]host *vt* to act as host at or of <~ed *a series of TV programmes*>

[4]host *n, often cap* the bread consecrated in the Eucharist

hostage /ˈhostij‖ˈhɒstɪdʒ/ *n* a person held by one party as a pledge that promises will be kept or terms met by another party

hostel /ˈhostl‖ˈhɒstl/ *n* **1** *chiefly Br* a supervised residential home: e g **1a** an establishment providing accommodation for nurses, students, etc **b** an institution for junior offenders, ex-offenders, etc, encouraging social adaptation **2** YOUTH HOSTEL **3** an inn – chiefly poetic or archaic – **hosteller** *n*

'hostelry /-ri‖-rɪ/ *n* an inn, hotel

hostess /hoh'stes‖həʊ'stes/ *n* **1** a woman who entertains socially or acts as host **2a** a female employee on a ship, aeroplane, etc who manages the provisioning of food and attends to the needs of passengers **b** a woman who acts as a companion to male patrons, esp in a nightclub; *also* a prostitute

hostile /'hostiel‖'hɒstaɪl/ *adj* **1** of or constituting an enemy **2** antagonistic, unfriendly **3** not hospitable <*a ~ environment*> [Latin *hostilis*, fr *hostis* enemy] – **hostile** *n*, **hostilely** *adv*

hostility /ho'stiləti‖hɒ'stɪlətɪ/ *n* **1** *pl* overt acts of warfare **2** antagonism, opposition, or resistance

hostler /'oslə‖'ɒslə/ *n, chiefly NAm* an ostler

¹hot /hot‖hɒt/ *adj* **-tt- 1a** having a relatively high temperature **b** capable of giving a sensation of heat or of burning, searing, or scalding **c** having a temperature higher than normal body temperature **2a** vehement, fiery <*a ~ temper*> **b** sexually excited; *also* sexually arousing **c** eager, enthusiastic <*~ on the idea*> **d** of or being an exciting style of jazz with strong rhythms **3** severe, stringent – usu + *on* <*police are ~ on drunken drivers*> **4** having or causing the sensation of an uncomfortable degree of body heat <*felt too ~*> **5a** very recent; fresh <*~ off the press*> **b** close to sthg sought <*guess again, you're getting ~*> **6a** suggestive of heat or of burning objects <*~ colours*> **b** pungent, peppery <*a ~ curry*> **7a** of intense and immediate interest; sensational **b** performing well or strongly fancied to win (e g in a sport) <*~ favourite*> **c** currently popular; selling very well **d** very good – used as a generalized term of approval <*his English is not so ~*> **8** (of, being, or for material that is) radioactive **9a** recently and illegally obtained <*~ jewels*> **b** wanted by the police *USE* (*2b, 2c, & 7d*) infml, (*9*) slang – **hottish** *adj*, **hotness** *n*

²hot *adv* hotly

,hot 'air *n* empty talk – chiefly infml

'hot,bed /-,bed‖-,bed/ *n* **1** a bed of soil heated esp by fermenting manure and used for forcing or raising seedlings **2** an environment that favours rapid growth or development, esp of sthg specified <*a ~ of crime*>

,hot-'blooded *adj* excitable, ardent – **hot-bloodedness** *n*

hotchpotch /hoch,poch‖hɒtʃ,pɒtʃ/ *n* a mixture composed of many usu unrelated parts; a jumble

,hot ,cross 'bun *n* a yeast-leavened spicy bun marked with a cross and eaten esp on Good Friday

'hot ,dog *n* a frankfurter or other sausage (heated and served in a bread roll)

hotel /(h)oh'tel‖(h)əʊ'tel/ *n* a usu large establishment that provides meals and (temporary) accommodation for the public, esp for people travelling away from home

hotelier /(h)oh·telyə, -yay‖(h)əʊteljə, -jeɪ/ *n* a proprietor or manager of a hotel

,hot 'flush *n* a sudden brief flushing and sensation of heat, usu associated with an imbalance of endocrine hormones occurring esp at the menopause

'hot,foot /-,foot‖-,fʊt/ *vi or adv* (to go) in haste – **hotfoot it** to hotfoot

'hot,head /-,hed‖-,hed/ *n* a hotheaded person

hotheaded /-'hedid‖'hedɪd/ *adj* fiery, impetuous – **hotheadedly** *adv*, **hotheadedness** *n*

'hot,house /-,hows‖-,haʊs/ *n* a heated greenhouse, esp for tropical plants

'hot ,line *n* a direct telephone line kept in constant readiness for immediate communication (e g between heads of state)

'hotly /-li‖-lɪ/ *adv* in a hot or fiery manner <*a ~ debated issue*>

'hot ,plate *n* a metal plate or spiral, usu on an electric cooker, on which food can be heated and cooked

'hot ,pot *n* a (mutton, lamb, or beef and potato) stew cooked esp in a covered pot

,hot po'tato *n* a controversial or sensitive question or issue – infml

'hot ,rod *n* a motor vehicle rebuilt or modified for high speed and fast acceleration – **hot-rodder** *n*

'hot ,seat *n* **1** a position involving risk, embarrassment, or responsibility for decision-making <*in the ~ at the interview*> – infml **2** ELECTRIC CHAIR – slang

,hot 'spring *n* a spring of naturally hot water

,hot 'stuff *n* **1** sby or sthg of outstanding ability or quality **2** sby or sthg sexually exciting *USE* infml

Hottentot /'hot(ə)n,tot‖'hɒt(ə)n,tɒt/ *n* a member, or the language, of a people of southern Africa apparently of mixed Bushman and Bantu origin

hot up *vi* to become hot; increase in activity, intensity, liveliness, excitement, etc *~vt* to make hotter, livelier, or faster

,hot 'water *n* a distressing predicament (likely to lead to punishment); trouble – infml

,hot-'water ,bottle *n* a usu flat rubber container that is filled with hot water and used esp to warm a (person in) bed

¹hound /hownd‖haʊnd/ *n* **1** a dog; *esp* one of any of various hunting breeds typically with large drooping ears and a deep bark that track their prey by scent **2** a mean or despicable person **3** one who is devoted to the pursuit of sthg specified

²hound *vt* **1** to pursue (as if) with hounds **2** to harass persistently – **hounder** *n*

,hounds,tooth 'check /-,toohth‖-,tu:θ/, **hound's-tooth check** *n* a small broken-check textile pattern

hour /owə‖aʊə/ *n* **1** (any of the 7 times of day set aside for) a daily liturgical devotion **2** the 24th part of a day; a period of 60 minutes **3a** *the* time of day reckoned in hours and minutes by the clock; *esp* the beginning of each full hour measured by the clock <*the train leaves on the ~*> **b** *pl* the time reckoned in one 24-hour period from midnight to midnight <*attack at 0900 ~s*> **4a** a fixed or customary period of time set aside for a usu specified purpose <*the lunch ~*> – often pl <*during office ~s*> **b** a particular, usu momentous, period or point of time <*in his ~ of need*> **c** *the* present <*the story of the ~*> **5** *pl* one's regular time of getting up or going to bed <*kept late ~s*> **6** the work done or distance travelled at normal rate in an hour <*the city was 2 ~s away*>

[1]'**hour,glass** /-,glahs||-,glɑːs/ *n* a glass or perspex instrument for measuring time consisting of 2 bulbs joined by a narrow neck from the uppermost of which a quantity of sand, water, etc runs into the lower in the space of an hour

[2]**hourglass** *adj* shapely with a narrow waist <*an ~ figure*>

'**hour ,hand** *n* the short hand that marks the hours on the face of a watch or clock

houri /'hooəri||'huəri/ *n, pl* **houris** **1** any of the female virgin attendants of the blessed in the Muslim paradise **2** a voluptuously beautiful young woman

[1]**hourly** /'owəli||'auəli/ *adv* **1** at or during every hour; *also* continually <*we're expecting him ~*> **2** by the hour <*~ paid workers*>

[2]**hourly** *adj* **1** occurring or done every hour; *also* continual **2** reckoned by the hour

[1]**house** /hows||haus/ *n, pl* **houses** /'howziz||'hauziz/ **1** a building designed for people to live in **2a** an animal's shelter or refuge (e g a nest or den) **b** a building in which sthg is housed or stored <*a hen ~*> **c** a building used for a particular purpose, esp eating, drinking, or entertainment <*a public ~*> **3** any of the 12 equal sectors into which the celestial sphere is divided in astrology **4a** *sing or pl in constr* the occupants of a house <*you'll wake the whole ~*> **b** a family including ancestors, descendants, and kindred <*the ~ of Tudor*> **5a** (a residence of) a religious community **b** any of several groups into which a British school may be divided for social purposes or games **6** (the chamber of) a legislative or deliberative assembly; *esp* a division of a body consisting of 2 chambers **7a** a business organization or establishment <*a publishing ~*> **b** *cap* a large building used by a business or institution – used in names <*Transport* House> **c** (the audience in) a theatre or concert hall <*a full ~*> – **on the house** at the expense of an establishment or its management <*have a drink* on the house>

[2]**house** /howz||hauz/ *vt* **1** to provide with accommodation or storage space **2** to serve as shelter for; contain <*a library ~s thousands of books*>

'**house ar,rest** *n* confinement to one's place of residence instead of prison

'**house,boat** /-,boht||-,bəut/ *n* an often permanently moored boat that is fitted out as a home

'**house,bound** /-,bownd||-,baund/ *adj* confined to the house (e g because of illness)

'**house,breaking** /-,brayking||-,breikiŋ/ *n* an act of breaking into and entering the house of another with a criminal purpose – **housebreaker** *n*

'**house,broken** /-,brohkən||-,brəukən/ *adj, chiefly NAm* housetrained

'**house,coat** /-,koht||-,kəut/ *n* a woman's light dressing gown for wear round the house; *also* a short overall

'**house,craft** /-,krahft||-,krɑːft/ *n* **1** DOMESTIC SCIENCE **2** skill in running a household

'**house,father** /-,fahdhə||-,fɑːðə/, *fem* '**house,mother** /-,mudhə||-,mʌðə/ *n* sby in charge of a group of young people living in care (e g in a children's home)

'**house,fly** /-,flie||-,flai/ *n* a fly found in most parts of the world that frequents houses and carries disease

[1]'**house,hold** /-,hohld||-,həuld/ *n sing or pl in constr* all the people who live together in a dwelling

[2]**household** *adj* **1** domestic **2** familiar, common <*a ~ name*>

'**house,holder** /-,hohldə||-,həuldə/ *n* a person who occupies a dwelling as owner or tenant

household troops *n pl* troops appointed to guard a sovereign or his/her residence

'**house,keeper** /-,keepə||-,kiːpə/ *n* sby, esp a woman, employed to take charge of the running of a house

'**house,keeping** /-,keeping||-,kiːpiŋ/ *n* **1** (money used for) the day-to-day running of a house and household affairs **2** the general management of an organization which ensures its smooth running (e g the provision of equipment, keeping of records, etc) **3** the routine tasks that have to be done in order for sthg to function properly

'**house,lights** /-,liets||-,laits/ *n pl* the lights that illuminate the auditorium of a theatre

'**house,maid** /-,mayd||-,meid/ *n* a female servant employed to do housework

house,maid's knee *n* a swelling over the knee due to an enlargement of the bursa in the front of the kneecap

'**houseman** /-mən||-mən/ *n* (one holding) the most junior grade of British hospital doctor

'**house ,martin** *n* a European martin with blue-black plumage and white rump that nests on cliffs and under the eaves of houses

'**house,master** /-,mahstə||-,mɑːstə/, *fem* '**house,mistress** *n* a teacher in charge of a school house

'**house,mother** /-,mudhə||-,mʌðə/, *masc* '**house,father** *n* sby in charge of a group of young people living in care (e g in a children's home)

house of cards *n* a precarious structure or situation

,**House of 'Commons** *n* the lower house of the British and Canadian parliaments

,**House of 'Lords** *n* **1** the upper house of Parliament **2** the body of Law Lords that constitutes the highest British court of appeal

House of Representatives *n* the lower house of the US Congress or Australian Parliament

'**house ,party** *n* a party lasting for a day or more held at a large, usu country, house

'**house-,proud** *adj* (excessively) careful about the management and appearance of one's house

'**house ,sparrow** *n* a brown Eurasian sparrow that lives esp in or near human settlements

,**house-to-'house** *adj* DOOR-TO-DOOR 1

'**house,top** /-,top||-,tɒp/ *n* a roof – **from the housetops** for all to hear; IN PUBLIC <*shouting their grievances* from the housetops>

ˈhouseˌtrain /-ˌtrayn‖-ˌtreɪn/ *vt* **1** *chiefly Br* to train (e g a pet) to defecate and urinate outdoors **2** to teach (e g a person) to behave acceptably – humor

ˈhouseˌwarming /-ˌwawming‖-ˌwɔːmɪŋ/ *n* a party to celebrate moving into a new house or premises

housewife /ˈhowsˌwief‖ˈhaʊsˌwaɪf; *sense 2* ˈhuzif‖ˈhʌzɪf/ *n* **1** a usu married woman who runs a house **2** a small container for needlework articles (e g thread) – **housewifely** *adj*, **housewifery** *n*

ˈhouseˌwork /-ˌwuhk‖-ˌwɜːk/ *n* the work (e g cleaning) involved in maintaining a house

housing /ˈhowzing‖ˈhaʊzɪŋ/ *n* **1** (the provision of) houses or dwelling-places collectively **2** a protective cover for machinery, sensitive instruments, etc

housing association *n* a nonprofitmaking society that constructs, renovates, and helps tenants to rent or buy housing

hove /hohv‖həʊv/ *past of* HEAVE

hovel /ˈhovl‖ˈhɒvl/ *n* a small, wretched, and often dirty house or abode

hover /ˈhovə‖ˈhɒvə/ *vi* **1** to hang in the air or on the wing **2a** to linger or wait restlessly around a place **b** to be in a state of uncertainty, irresolution, or suspense – **hover** *n*, **hoverer** *n*

ˈhoverˌcraft /-ˌkrahft‖-ˌkrɑːft/ *n, pl* **hovercraft** a vehicle supported on a cushion of air provided by fans and designed to travel over both land and sea

[1]how /how‖haʊ/ *adv* **1a** in what manner or way <~ *do you spell it?*> <*know* ~ *it works*> **b** with what meaning; to what effect <~ *can you explain it?*> **c** for what reason; why <~ *could you do it?*> **2** by what measure or quantity <~ *much does it cost?*> – often used in an exclamation as an intensive <~ *nice of you to come!*> **3** in what state or condition (e g of health) <~ *are you?*> – **how about** what do you say to or think of <how about *going to London for the day?*> – **how come** how does it happen; why is it <how come *we never meet?*> – infml – **how do you do** – used as a formal greeting between people meeting for the first time – **how's that 1** – used to call attention to and invite comment on sthg <how's that *for enterprise?*> **2** please repeat **3** – used in cricket as an appeal to the umpire to give the batsman out

[2]how *conj* **1a** the way, manner, or state in which <*remember* ~ *they fought*> **b** that <*do you remember* ~ *he arrived right at the end*> **2** however, as <*do it* ~ *you like*>

howdah /ˈhowdə‖ˈhaʊdə/ *n* a usu canopied seat on the back of an elephant or camel

ˌhow-do-you-ˈdo, how d'ye do /dyə‖djə/ *n* a confused or embarrassing situation – infml

howdy /ˈhowdi‖ˈhaʊdɪ/ *n, chiefly NAm* hello – infml

[1]however /howˈevə‖haʊˈevə/ *conj* in whatever manner or way <*can go* ~ *he likes*>

[2]however *adv* **1** to whatever degree or extent; no matter how <~ *fast I eat*> **2** in spite of that; nevertheless <*would like to go,* ~, *I think I'd better not*> **3** how in the world <~ *did you manage it?*> – infml

howitzer /ˈhow·itzə‖ˈhaʊɪtzə/ *n* a short cannon usu with a medium muzzle velocity and a relatively high trajectory

howl /howl‖haʊl/ *vi* **1a** *esp of dogs, wolves, etc* to make a loud sustained doleful cry **b** *of wind* to make a sustained wailing sound **2** to cry loudly and without restraint (e g with pain or laughter) ~*vt* to utter with a loud sustained cry – **howl** *n*

howl down *vt* to express one's disapproval of (e g a speaker or his/her views), esp by shouting in order to prevent from being heard

howler /ˈhowlə‖ˈhaʊlə/ *n* a stupid and comic blunder – infml

howling /ˈhowling‖ˈhaʊlɪŋ/ *adj* very great, extreme, or severe <*a* ~ *success*> – infml

hoyden /ˈhoydn‖ˈhɔɪdn/ *n* a boisterous girl – **hoydenish** *adj*

hub /hub‖hʌb/ *n* **1** the central part of a wheel, propeller, or fan through which the axle passes **2** the centre of activity or importance

hubble-bubble /ˈhubl ˌbubl‖ˈhʌbl ˌbʌbl/ *n* **1** WATER PIPE 2 **2** a flurry of noise or activity; a commotion

hubbub /ˈhubub‖ˈhʌbʌb/ *n* a noisy confusion; uproar

hubby /ˈhubi‖ˈhʌbɪ/ *n* a husband – infml

hubcap /ˈhubˌkap‖ˈhʌbˌkæp/ *n* a removable metal cap placed over the hub of a wheel

hubris /ˈhyoohbris‖ˈhjuːbrɪs/ *n* overweening pride, usu leading to retribution – **hubristic** *adj*

huckaback /ˈhukəˌbak‖ˈhʌkəˌbæk/ *n* an absorbent durable fabric of cotton, linen, or both, used chiefly for towels

huckleberry /ˈhuklb(ə)ri, -ˌberi‖ˈhʌklb(ə)rɪ, -ˌberɪ/ *n* **1** (an edible dark blue or black berry of) any of a genus of American shrubs of the heath family **2** a blueberry

[1]huckster /ˈhukstə‖ˈhʌkstə/ *n* **1** a hawker, pedlar **2** *chiefly NAm* one who writes advertising material, esp for radio or television

[2]huckster *vi* to haggle ~ *vt* **1** to deal in or bargain over **2** to promote or advertise, esp in an aggressive or underhand manner

[1]huddle /ˈhudl‖ˈhʌdl/ *vt* **1** to crowd together **2** to draw or curl (oneself) up ~ *vi* **1** to gather in a closely-packed group **2** to curl up; crouch

[2]huddle *n* **1** a closely-packed group; a bunch **2** a secretive or conspiratorial meeting

hue /hyooh‖hjuː/ *n* **1** a complexion, aspect <*political factions of every* ~> **2** the attribute of colours that permits them to be classed as red, yellow, green, blue, or an intermediate between any adjacent pair of these colours; *also* a colour having this attribute

ˌhue and ˈcry *n* **1** a cry formerly used when in pursuit of a criminal **2** a clamour of alarm or protest

[1]huff /huf‖hʌf/ *vi* to emit loud puffs (e g of breath or steam)

[2]huff *n* – **huffily** *adv*, **huffiness** *n*, **huffish** *adj*, **huffy** *adj* – **in a huff** in a piqued and resentful mood

[1]hug /hug‖hʌg/ *vt* **-gg- 1** to hold or press tightly, esp in the arms **2a** to feel very pleased with (oneself) **b** to cling to; cherish <~ged *his miseries like a sulky child* – John Buchan> **3** to stay close to <*thick smoke* ~ged *the ground*> – **huggable** *adj*

[2]**hug** *n* a tight clasp or embrace

huge /hyoohj‖hju:dʒ/ *adj* great in size, scale, degree, or scope; enormous – **hugely** *adv*, **hugeness** *n*

ˈ**hugely** /-li‖-lɪ/ *adv* very much; enormously <*was ~ excited*>

hugger-mugger /ˈhugə ˌmugə‖ˈhʌgə ˌmʌgə/ *n* **1** secrecy **2** confusion, muddle – **hugger-mugger** *adj or adv*

huh /huh, hah‖hɜ:, hɑ:/ *interj* – used to express surprise, disapproval, or inquiry

hula *also* ˌ**hula-ˈhula** /ˈhoolə‖ˈhʊlə/ *n* a Polynesian dance involving swaying of the hips

hulk /hulk‖hʌlk/ *n* **1a** the hull of a ship that is no longer seaworthy and is used as a storehouse or, esp formerly, as a prison **b** an abandoned wreck or shell, esp of a vessel **2** a person, creature, or thing that is bulky or unwieldy <*a big ~ of a man*>

hulking /ˈhulking‖ˈhʌlkɪŋ/ *adj* bulky, massive

[1]**hull** /hul‖hʌl/ *n* **1a** the outer covering of a fruit or seed **b** the calyx that surrounds some fruits (e g the strawberry) **2** the main frame or body of a ship, flying boat, airship, etc **3** a covering, casing

[2]**hull** *vt* **1** to remove the hulls of **2** to hit or pierce the hull of (e g a ship) – **huller** *n*

hullabaloo /ˌhuləbəˈlooh‖ˌhʌləbəˈlu:/ *n, pl* **hullabaloos** a confused noise; uproar – infml

hullo /huˈloh‖hʌˈləʊ/ *interj or n, chiefly Br* hello

[1]**hum** /hum‖hʌm/ *vb* **-mm-** *vi* **1a** to utter a prolonged /m/ sound **b** to make the characteristic droning noise of an insect in motion or a similar sound **2** to be lively or active – infml **3** to have an offensive smell – slang ~ *vt* **1** to sing with the lips closed and without articulation **2** to affect or express by humming – **hum** *n* – **hum and ha** *also* **hum and haw** to equivocate

[2]**hum** *interj* – used to express hesitation, uncertainty, disagreement, etc

[1]**human** /ˈhyoohmən‖ˈhju:mən/ *adj* **1** (characteristic) of humans <*~ voice*> **2** consisting of men and women <*the ~ race*> **3a** having the esp good attributes (e g kindness and compassion) thought to be characteristic of humans <*is really very ~*> **b** having, showing, or concerned with qualities or feelings characteristic of mankind <*to err is ~*> – **humanness** *n*

[2]**human,** ˌ**human ˈbeing** *n* a man, woman, or child; a person

humane /hyoohˈmayn‖hju:ˈmeɪn/ *adj* **1a** marked by compassion or consideration for other human beings or animals **b** causing the minimum pain possible <*~ killing of animals*> **2** characterized by broad humanistic culture; liberal <*~ studies*> – **humanely** *adv*, **humaneness** *n*

humanism /ˈhyoohməˌniz(ə)m‖ˈhju:məˌnɪz(ə)m/ *n* **1** a cultural movement dominant during the Renaissance that was characterized by a revival of classical learning and a shift of emphasis from religious to secular concerns; *broadly* literary culture **2** humanitarianism **3** a doctrine, attitude, or way of life based on human interests or values; *esp* a philosophy that asserts the intrinsic worth of man and that usu rejects religious belief – **humanist** *n or adj*, **humanistic** *adj*, **humanistically** *adv*

humanitarian /hyoohˌmaniˈteəri·ən‖hju:ˌmænɪˈteərɪən/ *n* one who promotes human welfare and social reform; a philanthropist – **humanitarian** *adj*, **humanitarianism** *n*

humanity /hyoohˈmanəti‖hju:ˈmænətɪ/ *n* **1** the quality of being humane **2** the quality or state of being human **3** *pl the* cultural branches of learning **4** mankind

human·ize, -ise /ˈhyoomәˌniez‖ˈhjʊməˌnaɪz/ *vt* **1** to cause to be or seem human **2** to make humane – **humanization** *n*

ˌ**humanˈkind** /-ˈkiend‖-ˈkaɪnd/ *n sing or pl in constr* human beings collectively

ˈ**humanly** /-li‖-lɪ/ *adv* **1a** from a human viewpoint **b** within the range of human capacity <*as perfectly as is ~ possible*> **2a** in a manner characteristic of humans, esp in showing emotion or weakness **b** with humaneness

humanoid /ˈhyoohməˌnoyd‖ˈhju:məˌnɔɪd/ *adj* having human form or characteristics – **humanoid** *n*

[1]**humble** /ˈhumbl‖ˈhʌmbl/ *adj* **1** having a low opinion of oneself; unassertive **2** marked by deference or submission <*a ~ apology*> **3a** ranking low in a hierarchy or scale <*man of ~ origins*> **b** modest, unpretentious <*a ~ dwelling*> [Old French, fr Latin *humilis* low, humble, fr *humus* earth] – **humbleness** *n*, **humbly** *adv*

[2]**humble** *vt* **1** to make humble in spirit or manner; humiliate **2** to destroy the power, independence, or prestige of

[1]**humbug** /ˈhumˌbug‖ˈhʌmˌbʌg/ *n* **1a** sthg designed to deceive and mislead **b** an impostor, sham **2** pretence, deception **3** drivel, nonsense **4** a hard usu peppermint-flavoured striped sweet made from boiled sugar – **humbuggery** *n*

[2]**humbug** *vb* **-gg-** to deceive with a hoax

humdinger /ˈhumˌdingə‖ˈhʌmˌdɪŋə/ *n* an excellent or remarkable person or thing – infml

humdrum /ˈhumˌdrum‖ˈhʌmˌdrʌm/ *adj* monotonous, dull – **humdrum** *n*

humerus /ˈhyoohmərəs‖ˈhju:mərəs/ *n, pl* **humeri** /-ˌrie‖-ˌraɪ/ the long bone of the upper arm or forelimb extending from the shoulder to the elbow

humid /ˈhyoohmid‖ˈhju:mɪd/ *adj* containing or characterized by perceptible moisture <*a ~ climate*> – **humidly** *adv*

humidify /hyoohˈmidifie‖hju:ˈmɪdɪfaɪ/ *vt* to make humid – **humidification** *n*

humidity /hyoohˈmidəti‖hju:ˈmɪdətɪ/ *n* (the degree of) moisture or dampness, esp in the atmosphere

humidor /ˈhyoohmidaw‖ˈhju:mɪdɔ:/ *n* a case or room in which cigars or tobacco can be kept moist

humiliate /hyoohˈmiliayt‖hju:ˈmɪlɪeɪt/ *vt* to cause to feel humble; lower the dignity or self-respect of – **humiliation** *n*

humility /hyoohˈmiləti‖hju:ˈmɪlətɪ/ *n* the quality or state of being humble

hummingbird /ˈhumingˌbuhd‖ˈhʌmɪŋˌbɜ:d/ *n* any of numerous tiny brightly coloured usu tropical American birds related to the swifts, having a slender bill and narrow wings that beat rapidly making a humming sound

hummock /ˈhumək‖ˈhʌmək/ *n* **1** a hillock **2** a ridge of ice – **hummocky** *adj*

humorist /'hyoohmərist||'hju:mərɪst/ *n* a person specializing in or noted for humour in speech, writing, or acting – **humoristic** *adj*

humorous /'hyoohmərəs||'hju:mərəs/ *adj* full of, characterized by, or expressing humour – **humorously** *adv*, **humorousness** *n*

[1]**humour,** *NAm chiefly* **humor** /'hyoohmə||'hju:mə/ *n* **1** any of the 4 fluids of the body (blood, phlegm, and yellow and black bile) formerly held to determine, by their relative proportions, a person's health and temperament **2** characteristic or habitual disposition <*a man of cheerful* ~> **3** a state of mind; a mood **4** a sudden inclination; a caprice **5a** (sthg having) the quality of causing amusement **b** the faculty of expressing or appreciating what is comic or amusing – **humourless** *adj*, **humourlessness** *n* – **out of humour** in a bad temper

[2]**humour,** *NAm chiefly* **humor** *vt* to comply with the mood or wishes of; indulge

[1]**hump** /hump||hʌmp/ *n* **1** a rounded protuberance: e g **1a** a humped or crooked back **b** a fleshy protuberance on the back of a camel, bison, etc **c** a mound, knoll **2** a difficult, trying, or critical phase <*we're over the* ~ *now*> **3** *Br* a fit of depression or sulking – infml; + *the* <*he's got the* ~> – **humped** *adj*

[2]**hump** *vt* **1** to form or curve into a hump **2** *chiefly Br* to carry with difficulty <~ing *suitcases around*> **3** to have sexual intercourse with ~ *vi* **1** to rise in a hump **2** *Austr* to travel around or go on foot **3** to have sexual intercourse *USE* (*vt2; vi2*) infml; (*vt3; vi3*) slang

'**hump,back** /-,bak||-,bæk/ *n* **1** a hunchback **2** *also* **humpback whale** a large whale having very long flippers – **humpbacked** *adj*

humph /hum(p)f||hʌm(p)f/ *vi or interj* (to utter) a gruntlike sound used to express doubt or contempt

humus /'hyoohməs||'hju:məs/ *n* a brown or black organic soil material resulting from partial decomposition of plant or animal matter – **humic** *adj*

Hun /hun||hʌn/ *n* **1** a member of a nomadic Mongolian people who overran a large part of central and E Europe under Attila during the 4th and 5th c AD **2a** *often not cap* a person who is wantonly destructive **b** a German; *esp* a German soldier in WW I or II – derog – **Hunnish** *adj*

[1]**hunch** /hunch||hʌntʃ/ *vi* to assume a bent or crooked posture ~*vt* to bend into a hump or arch <~ed *his shoulders*>

[2]**hunch** *n* **1** HUMP 1 **2** a strong intuitive feeling

'**hunch,back** /-,bak||-,bæk/ *n* (sby with) a humped back – **hunchbacked** *adj*

hundred /'hundrəd||'hʌndrəd/ *n, pl* **hundreds, hundred 1** (the number) 100 **2** the number occupying the position 3 to the left of the decimal point in Arabic notation; *also, pl* this position **3** 100 units or digits; *specif* £100 <*must have cost* ~s> **4** *pl the* numbers 100 to 999 **5** a score of 100 or more runs made by a batsman in cricket **6** *pl the* 100 years of a specified century <*the 19* ~s> **7** a historical subdivision of a county **8** an indefinitely large number – infml; often pl with sing. meaning – **hundred** *adj*, **hundredth** *adj or n*

'**hundred,weight** /-,wayt||-,weɪt/ *n, pl* **hundredweight, hundredweights 1** a British unit of weight equal to 112lb (about 50.80kg) **2** *chiefly NAm* a US unit of weight equal to 100lb (about 4536kg)

hung /hung||hʌŋ/ *past of* HANG

Hungarian /hung'geəri·ən||hʌŋ'geərɪən/ *n or adj* (a native or inhabitant or the language) of Hungary

[1]**hunger** /'hung·gə||'hʌŋgə/ *n* **1** (a weakened condition or unpleasant sensation arising from) a craving or urgent need for food **2** a strong desire; a craving

[2]**hunger** *vi* **1** to feel or suffer hunger **2** to have an eager desire – usu + *for* or *after*

'**hunger ,strike** *n* refusal, as an act of protest, to eat enough to sustain life – **hunger striker** *n*

hungry /'hung·gri||'hʌŋgrɪ/ *adj* **1a** feeling hunger **b** characterized by or indicating hunger or appetite <*a* ~ *look*> **2** eager, avid <~ *for power*> **3** not rich or fertile; barren – **hungrily** *adv*, **hungriness** *n*

hunk /hungk||hʌŋk/ *n* **1** a large lump or piece **2** a usu muscular sexually attractive man – infml

hunkers /'hungkəz||'hʌŋkəz/ *n pl* the haunches – infml

[1]**hunt** /hunt||hʌnt/ *vt* **1a** to pursue for food or enjoyment <~ *foxes*> **b** to use (e g hounds) in the search for game **2a** to pursue with intent to capture <~ed *the escaped prisoner*> **b** to search out; seek **3** to persecute or chase, esp by harrying **4** to traverse in search of prey ~ *vi* **1** to take part in a hunt, esp regularly **2** to attempt to find sthg **3** *of a device, machine, etc* to run alternately fast and slowly

[2]**hunt** *n* **1** the act, the practice, or an instance of hunting **2a** *sing or pl in constr* a group of usu mounted hunters and their hounds **b** the area hunted

hunter /'huntə||'hʌntə/, *fem* (*1a&2*) **huntress** /-tris||-trɪs/ *n* **1a** sby who hunts game, esp with hounds **b** a usu fast strong horse used in hunting **2** a person who hunts or seeks sthg, esp over-eagerly <*a fortune* ~> **3** a watch with a hinged metal cover to protect it

hunting /'hunting||'hʌntɪŋ/ *n* the pursuit of game on horseback with hounds

'**hunting ,ground** *n* an area of usu fruitful search or exploitation

'**hunting ,horn** *n* a signal horn used in the chase, usu consisting of a long coiled tube with a flared bell

,**hunting 'pink** *adj or n* (of) the red colour of the coats worn by fox-hunters

'**huntsman** /-mən||-mən/ *n* **1** HUNTER 1a **2** sby who looks after the hounds of a hunt

[1]**hurdle** /'huhdl||'hɜ:dl/ *n* **1a** a portable framework, usu of interlaced branches and stakes, used esp for enclosing land or livestock **b** a frame formerly used for dragging traitors to execution **2a** a light barrier jumped by men, horses, dogs, etc in certain races **b** *pl* any of various races over hurdles **3** a barrier, obstacle

[2]**hurdle** *vt* **1** to jump over, esp while running **2** to overcome, surmount ~*vi* to run in hurdle races – **hurdler** *n*

hurdy-gurdy /ˌhuhdi ˈguhdi‖ˌhɜːdɪ ˈgɜːdɪ/ *n* a musical instrument in which the sound is produced by turning a crank; *esp* BARREL ORGAN

hurl /huhl‖hɜːl/ *vt* **1** to drive or thrust violently **2** to throw forcefully **3** to utter or shout violently < ~ed *insults at him*> ~*vi* to rush, hurtle – **hurl** *n*, **hurler** *n*

hurling /ˈhuhling‖ˈhɜːlɪŋ/ *n* an Irish game resembling hockey played between 2 teams of 15 players each

hurly-burly /ˌhuhli ˈbuhli‖ˌhɜːlɪ ˈbɜːlɪ/ *n* (an) uproar, commotion

hurray /hooˈray‖hʊˈreɪ/ *interj* – used to express joy, approval, or encouragement

hurricane /ˈhurikən‖ˈhʌrɪkən/ *n* (a usu tropical cyclone with) a wind of a velocity greater than 117km/h (73 to 136mph) [Spanish *huracán*, fr Taino (an American Indian language) *hurakán*]

ˈ**hurricane** ˌ**lamp** *n* a candlestick or oil lamp equipped with a glass chimney to protect the flame

hurried /ˈhurid‖ˈhʌrɪd/ *adj* done in a hurry – **hurriedly** *adv*

[1]**hurry** /ˈhuri‖ˈhʌrɪ/ *vt* **1a** to transport or cause to go with haste; rush < ~ *him to hospital*> **b** to cause to move or act with (greater) haste **2** to hasten the progress or completion of <*don't* ~ *this passage of the music*> ~*vi* to move or act with haste – often + *up*

[2]**hurry** *n* **1** flurried and often bustling haste **2** a need for haste; urgency <*there's no* ~ *for it*> – **in a hurry 1** without delay; hastily **2** eager <*never* in a hurry *to get up*> **3** without difficulty; easily <*won't manage that* in a hurry> – infml

[1]**hurt** /huht‖hɜːt/ *vb* **hurt** *vt* **1a** to afflict with physical pain; wound **b** to cause mental distress to; offend **2** to be detrimental to < ~ *his chances of success*> ~ *vi* **1** to feel pain; suffer **2** to cause damage, distress, or pain

[2]**hurt** *n* **1** a bodily injury or wound **2** (a cause of) mental distress **3** wrong, harm – **hurtful** *adj*, **hurtfully** *adv*, **hurtfulness** *n*

hurtle /hurtl‖hʌrtl/ *vi* to move rapidly or precipitately ~ *vt* to hurl, fling

[1]**husband** /ˈhuzbənd‖ˈhʌzbənd/ *n* a married man, esp in relation to his wife [Old English *hūsbonda* master of a house, fr Old Norse *hūsbōndi*, fr *hūs* house + *bōndi* householder] – **husbandly** *adj*

[2]**husband** *vt* to make the most economical use of; conserve < ~ *one's strength*>

husbandry /ˈhuzbəndri‖ˈhʌzbəndrɪ/ *n* **1** the judicious management of resources **2** farming, esp of domestic animals

[1]**hush** /hush‖hʌʃ/ *vb* to make or become quiet or calm

[2]**hush** *n* a silence or calm, esp following noise

ˌ**hush-**ˈ**hush** *adj* secret, confidential – infml

ˈ**hush** ˌ**money** *n* money paid secretly to prevent disclosure of damaging information

hush up *vt* to keep secret; suppress

[1]**husk** /husk‖hʌsk/ *n* **1** a dry or membranous outer covering (e g a shell or pod) of a seed or fruit **2** a useless outer layer of sthg

[2]**husk** *vt* to strip the husk from

[1]**husky** /ˈhuski‖ˈhʌskɪ/ *adj* of, resembling, or containing husks

[2]**husky** *adj* hoarse, breathy <*a* ~ *voice*> – **huskily** *adv*, **huskiness** *n*

[3]**husky** *adj* burly, hefty – infml

[4]**husky** *n* ESKIMO DOG

hussar /hooˈzah‖hʊˈzɑː/ *n* **1** a Hungarian horseman of the 15th c **2** *often cap* a member of any of various European cavalry regiments

hussy /ˈhusi‖ˈhʌsɪ/ *n* an impudent or promiscuous woman or girl

hustings /ˈhustingz‖ˈhʌstɪŋz/ *n pl but sing or pl in constr* **1** a raised platform used until 1872 for the nomination of candidates for Parliament and for election speeches **2** a place where election speeches are made **3** the proceedings of an election campaign [Old English *hūsting* deliberative assembly, fr Old Norse *hūsthing*, fr *hūs* house + *thing* assembly]

hustle /ˈhusl‖ˈhʌsl/ *vt* **1** to push or convey roughly, forcibly, or hurriedly **2** to swindle, cheat *out of* – infml ~ *vi* **1** to hasten, hurry **2** *chiefly NAm* to make strenuous, often dishonest, efforts to secure money or business **3** *chiefly NAm* to engage in prostitution; solicit – **hustle** *n*, **hustler** *n*

hut /hut‖hʌt/ *n* a small often temporary dwelling of simple construction

hutch /huch‖hʌtʃ/ *n* **1** a pen or cage for a small animal (e g a rabbit) **2** a shack, shanty – infml; derog

hutment /ˈhutmənt‖ˈhʌtmənt/ *n* an encampment of huts

hyacinth /ˈhie·əˌsinth‖ˈhaɪəˌsɪnθ/ *n* **1** a common garden plant with fragrant usu blue, pink, or white flowers that grow in spikes; *also* any of various related bulbous plants of the lily family **2** a colour varying from light violet to mid-purple

hyaena /hieˈeenə‖haɪˈiːnə/ *n* a hyena

hybrid /ˈhiebrid‖ˈhaɪbrɪd/ *n* **1** an offspring of 2 animals or plants of different races, breeds, varieties, etc **2** a person of mixed cultural background **3** sthg heterogeneous in origin or composition – **hybrid** *adj*, **hybridism** *n*, **hybridist** *n*, **hybridize** *vb*, **hybridization** *n*

hydr-, **hydro-** *comb form* **1a** water <hydro*electricity*> **b** liquid <hydro*meter*> **2** hydrogen; containing or combined with hydrogen <hydro*carbon*> [Greek, fr *hydōr* water; akin to Old English *wæter* water - see WATER]

hydra /ˈhiedrə‖ˈhaɪdrə/ *n* **1** a persistent evil that is not easily overcome **2** any of numerous small tubular freshwater polyps having a mouth surrounded by tentacles [*Hydra*, a serpent in Greek mythology with many heads which regrew when cut off]

hydrangea /hieˈdraynjə‖haɪˈdreɪndʒə/ *n* any of a genus of shrubs which produce large clusters of white, pink, or pale blue flowers

hydrant /ˈhiedrənt‖ˈhaɪdrənt/ *n* a discharge pipe with a valve and nozzle from which water may be drawn from a main

[1]**hydrate** /ˈhiedrayt‖ˈhaɪdreɪt/ *n* a compound or complex ion formed by the union of water with another substance

[2]**hydrate** /ˈhiedrayt, hieˈdrayt‖ˈhaɪdreɪt, haɪˈdreɪt/ *vt* to cause to take up or combine with (the elements of) water – **hydrator** *n*, **hydration** *n*

hydraulic /hieˈdrolik, -draw-‖haɪˈdrɒlɪk,

-drɔː-/ *adj* **1** operated, moved, or effected by means of liquid, esp liquid moving through pipes **2** of hydraulics <~ *engineer*> **3** hardening or setting under water <~ *cement*> – **hydraulically** *adv*

hy'draulics *n pl but sing in constr* a branch of physics that deals with the practical applications of liquid in motion

hydro- – see HYDR-

hydrocarbon /ˌhiedroh'kahb(ə)n‖ˌhaɪdrəʊ-'kɑːb(ə)n/ *n* an organic compound (e g benzene) containing only carbon and hydrogen – **hydrocarbonous, hydrocarbonaceous, hydrocarbonic** *adj*

ˌhydroˌchloric 'acid /ˌhiedrə'klorik‖ˌhaɪdrə'klɒrɪk/ *n* a solution of hydrogen chloride in water that is a strong corrosive acid and is naturally present in the gastric juice

ˌhydrocyˌanic 'acid /ˌhiedrohsie'anik‖ˌhaɪdrəʊsaɪ'ænɪk/ *n* a solution of hydrogen cyanide in water that is a highly poisonous weak acid

ˌhydroe'lectric /-i'lektrik‖-ɪ'lektrɪk/ *adj* of or being the production of electricity by waterpower – **hydroelectrically** *adv*, **hydroelectricity** *n*

hydrofoil /'hiedrəˌfoyl‖'haɪdrəˌfɔɪl/ *n* (a ship or boat fitted with) an aerofoil-like device that, when attached to a ship, lifts the hull out of the water at speed

hydrogen /'hiedrəj(ə)n‖'haɪdrədʒ(ə)n/ *n* the simplest and lightest of the elements that is normally a highly inflammable gas – **hydrogenous** *adj*

'hydrogen ˌbomb *n* a bomb whose violent explosive power is due to the sudden release of atomic energy resulting from the nuclear fusion of hydrogen initiated by the explosion of an atom bomb

ˌhydrogen pe'roxide *n* an unstable compound used esp as an oxidizing and bleaching agent, an antiseptic, and a rocket propellant

hydrophobia /ˌhiedrə'fohbi·ə‖ˌhaɪdrə-'fəʊbɪə/ *n* **1** abnormal dread of water **2** rabies

hydroplane /'hiedrohˌplayn, -drə-‖'haɪdrəʊˌpleɪn, -drə-/ *n* **1** a speedboat fitted with hydrofoils or a stepped bottom so that the hull is raised wholly or partly out of the water when moving at speed **2** a horizontal surface on a submarine's hull, used to control movement upwards or downwards

hydroponics /ˌhiedroh'poniks, -drə-‖ˌhaɪdrəʊ'pɒnɪks, -drə-/ *n pl but sing in constr* the growing of plants in (a mechanically supporting medium containing) nutrient solutions rather than soil – **hydroponic** *adj*, **hydroponically** *adv*

hydrotherapy /ˌhiedroh'therəpi‖ˌhaɪdrəʊ-'θerəpɪ/ *n* the use of water in the treatment of disease; *esp* treatment using exercise in heated water

hydroxide /hie'droksied‖haɪ'drɒksaɪd/ *n* a compound of hydroxyl with an element or radical

hydroxyl /hie'droksil, -siel‖haɪ'drɒksɪl, -saɪl/ *n* the univalent group or radical OH consisting of 1 hydrogen atom and 1 oxygen atom that is characteristic of hydroxides, alcohols, etc – **hydroxylate** *vt*, **hydroxylic** *adj*

hyena, hyaena /hie'eenə‖haɪ'iːnə/ *n* any of several large strong nocturnal flesh-eating Old World mammals that usu feed as scavengers

hygiene /'hieˌjeen‖'haɪˌdʒiːn/ *n* (conditions or practices, esp cleanliness, conducive to) the establishment and maintenance of health [deriv of Greek *hygieinos* healthful, fr *hygiēs* healthy] – **hygienist** *n*, **hygienic** *adj*, **hygenics** *n pl but sing in constr*, **hygienically** *adv*

hymen /'hiemen‖'haɪmen/ *n* a fold of mucous membrane partly closing the opening of the vagina in virgins – **hymenal** *adj*

hymeneal /ˌhieme'nee·əl‖ˌhaɪme'niːəl/ *adj* nuptial – poetic

¹hymn /him‖hɪm/ *n* **1** a song of praise to God; *esp* a metrical composition that can be included in a religious service **2** a song of praise or joy

²hymn *vt* to praise or worship in hymns ~ *vi* to sing a hymn

hymnal /'himnəl‖'hɪmnəl/ *n* (a book containing) a collection of church hymns

hype /hiep‖haɪp/ *n* **1** extravagant and usu false publicity **2** a fraudulent deception – slang – **hype** *vt*

hyper- *prefix* **1** above; beyond; super- <hyper*physical*> **2a** excessively <hyper*sensitive*> **b** excessive <hyper*tension*> **3** that exists in or is a space of more than 3 dimensions <hyper*space*>

hyperbola /hie'puhbələ‖haɪ'pɜːbələ/ *n, pl* **hyperbolas, hyperbolae** /-ˌlee‖-ˌliː/ a plane curve generated by a point so moving that the difference of its distances from 2 fixed points is a constant; the intersection of a double right circular cone with a plane that cuts both halves of the cone

hyperbole /hie'puhbəli‖haɪ'pɜːbəlɪ/ *n* a figure of speech based on extravagant exaggeration – **hyperbolist** *n*, **hyperbolize** *vb*

¹hyperbolic /ˌhiepə'bolik‖ˌhaɪpə'bɒlɪk/ *also* **hyperbolical** /-kl‖-kl/ *adj* of, characterized by, or given to hyperbole – **hyperbolically** *adv*

²hyperbolic *also* **hyperbolical** *adj* of or analogous to a hyperbola

'hyperˌmarket /-ˌmahkit‖-ˌmɑːkɪt/ *n* a very large self-service retail store, usu situated on the outskirts of a town

ˌhyperme'tropia /-me'trohpi·ə, -pyə‖-me-'trəʊpɪə, -pjə/ *n* a condition in which visual images come to a focus behind the retina of the eye and vision is better for distant than for near objects; longsightedness – **hypermetropic, hypermetropical** *adj*

hyperon /'hiepəron‖'haɪpərɒn/ *n* any of a group of unstable elementary particles that belong to the baryon group

ˌhyper'sensitive /-'sensətiv‖-'sensətɪv/ *adj* abnormally susceptible (e g to a drug or antigen) – **hypersensitiveness** *n*, **hypersensitivity** *n*

hypha /'hiefə‖'haɪfə/ *n, pl* **hyphae** /-ˌfee‖-ˌfiː/ any of the threads that make up the mycelium of a fungus – **hyphal** *adj*

hyphen /'hief(ə)n‖'haɪf(ə)n/ *n* a punctuation mark - used to divide or to join together words, word elements, or numbers

'hyphenˌate /-ayt‖-eɪt/ *vt* to join or separate with a hyphen – **hyphenation** *n*

hypnosis /hip'nohsis‖hɪp'nəʊsɪs/ *n, pl* **hypnoses** /-seez‖-siːz/ **1** any of various conditions that (superficially) resemble sleep; *specif* one induced by a person to whose suggestions the subject is then markedly susceptible **2** HYPNOTISM 1 [deriv of Greek *hypnos* sleep]

[1]**hypnotic** /hip'notik‖hɪp'nɒtɪk/ *adj* **1** tending to produce sleep; soporific **2** of hypnosis or hypnotism – **hypnotically** *adv*

[2]**hypnotic** *n* **1** something (e g a drug) that induces sleep **2** a person or animal that is or can be hypnotized

hypnotism /'hipnə,tiz(ə)m‖'hɪpnə,tɪz(ə)m/ *n* **1** the induction of hypnosis **2** HYPNOSIS 1 – **hypnotist** *n*

hypnot·ize, -ise /'hipnətiez‖'hɪpnətaɪz/ *vt* **1** to induce hypnosis in **2** to dazzle or overcome (as if) by suggestion; mesmerize – **hypnotizable** *adj*, **hypnotization** *n*

[1]**hypo** /'hiepoh‖'haɪpəʊ/ *n, pl* **hypos** sodium thiosulphate used as a fixing agent in photography

[2]**hypo** *n, pl* **hypos** a hypodermic

hypo-, hyp- *prefix* **1** under; beneath <hypo*dermic*> **2** less than normal or normally <hypo*tension*>

hypochondria /,hiepə'kondri·ə‖,haɪpə'kɒndrɪə/ *also* **hypochondriasis** /-kond'rie·əsis‖-kɒnd'raɪəsɪs/ *n* morbid concern about one's health

hypochondriac /,hiepə'kondriak‖,haɪpə'kɒndrɪæk/ *n or adj* (sby) affected by hypochondria

hypocrisy /hi'pokrəsi‖hɪ'pɒkrəsɪ/ *n* the feigning of virtues, beliefs, or standards, esp in matters of religion or morality

hypocrite /'hipəkrit‖'hɪpəkrɪt/ *n* one given to hypocrisy – **hypocritical** *adj*, **hypocritically** *adv*

[1]**hypodermic** /,hiepə'duhmik‖,haɪpə'dɜːmɪk/ *adj* **1** of the parts beneath the skin **2** adapted for use in or administered by injection beneath the skin – **hypodermically** *adv*

[2]**hypodermic** *n* **1** a hypodermic injection **2** HYPODERMIC SYRINGE

hypodermic syringe *n* a small syringe used with a hollow needle for injection or withdrawal of material beneath the skin

hypotenuse /hie'pot(ə)n,yoohz‖haɪ'pɒt(ə)n,juːz/ *n* the side of a right-angled triangle that is opposite the right angle

hypothermia /,hiepoh'thuhmi·ə‖,haɪpəʊ'θɜːmɪə/ *n* abnormally low body temperature – **hypothermic** *adj*

hypothesis /hie'pothəsis‖haɪ'pɒθəsɪs/ *n, pl* **hypotheses** /-seez‖-siːz/ **1** a provisional assumption made in order to investigate its logical or empirical consequences **2** a proposition assumed for the sake of argument [Greek, fr *hypotithenai* to put under, suppose, fr *hypo* under + *tithenai* to put] – **hypothesize** *vb*

hypothetical /,hiepə'thetikl‖,haɪpə'θetɪkl/ *adj* involving hypothesis; conjectural – **hypothetically** *adv*

hysterectomy /,histə'rektəmi‖,hɪstə'rektəmɪ/ *n* surgical removal of the uterus – **hysterectomize** *vt*

hysteria /hi'stiəri·ə‖hɪ'stɪərɪə/ *n* **1** a mental disorder marked by emotional excitability and disturbances (e g paralysis) of the normal bodily processes **2** unmanageable emotional excess [deriv of Greek *hystera* womb; fr the former notion that hysteric women were suffering from disturbances of the womb] – **hysteric** *n*, **hysteric, hysterical** *adj*, **hysterically** *adv*

hysterics /hi'steriks‖hɪ'sterɪks/ *n pl but sing or pl in constr* a fit of uncontrollable laughter or crying; hysteria

i /ie‖aɪ/ *n, pl* **i's, is** *often cap* **1** (a graphic representation of or device for reproducing) the 9th letter of the English alphabet **2** one

I /ie‖aɪ/ *pron* the one who is speaking or writing

-ial – see [1]-AL

iamb /'ie·am(b)‖'aɪæm(b)/ *n* a metrical foot consisting of 1 short or unstressed syllable followed by 1 long or stressed syllable – **iambic** *adj or n*

-ian – see -AN

Iberian *n* **1a** a member of any of the Caucasian peoples that in ancient times inhabited Spain and Portugal **b** a native or inhabitant of Spain or Portugal **2** any of the languages of the ancient Iberians – **Iberian** *adj*

ibex /'iebeks‖'aɪbeks/ *n*, any of several wild goats living chiefly in high mountain areas of the Old World and having large ridged backward-curving horns

ibidem /i'biedem‖ɪ'baɪdem/ *adv* in the same book, chapter, passage, etc as previously mentioned [Latin, in the same place]

-ibility /-ə'biləti‖-ə'bɪlətɪ/ – see -ABILITY

ibis /'iebis‖'aɪbɪs/ *n*, any of several wading birds related to the herons but distinguished by a long slender downward-curving bill

-ible /-ibl, -əbl‖-ɪbl, -əbl/ – see -ABLE

[1]**-ic** /-ik‖-ɪk/ *suffix* (*n* → *adj*) **1** having the character or form of; being <*panoram*ic> **2a** (characteristic) of or associated with <*Homer*ic> <*quixot*ic> **b** related to, derived from, or containing <*alcohol*ic> **3** utilizing <*atom*ic> **4** exhibiting <*nostalg*ic>; affected with <*allerg*ic> **5** characterized by; producing <*analges*ic>

[2]**-ic** *suffix* (→ *n*) **1** one having the character or nature of <*fanat*ic> **2** one belonging to or associated with <*ep*ic> **3** one affected by <*alcohol*ic> **4** one that produces <*emet*ic>

-ical /-ikl‖-ɪkl/ *suffix* (*n* → *adj*) -ic <*symmetr*ical>

ICBM *n, pl* **ICBM's, ICBMs** an intercontinental ballistic missile

[1]**ice** /ies‖aɪs/ *n* **1a** frozen water **b** a sheet or stretch of ice **2** a substance reduced to the solid state by cold **3** (a serving of) a frozen dessert: e g **3a** ICE CREAM **b** WATER ICE **4** *NAm* diamonds – slang – **iceless** *adj* – **on ice** in abeyance; in reserve for later use

[2]**ice** *vt* **1a** to coat with or convert into ice **b** to supply or chill with ice **2** to cover (as if) with icing ~ *vi* **1** to become ice-cold **2** to become covered or clogged with ice <*the carburettor* ~d *up*>

'ice ,age *n* **1** a time of widespread glaciation **2** *cap I&A* the Pleistocene glacial epoch

'ice ˌaxe *n* a combination pick and adze with a spiked handle used in climbing on snow or ice
'ice ˌbag *n* a bag of ice for application of cold to a part of the body
'iceˌberg /-ˌbuhg‖-ˌbɜːg/ *n* **1** a large floating mass of ice detached from a glacier **2** an emotionally cold person
'iceˌbox /-ˌboks‖-ˌbɒks/ *n* **1** *Br* the freezing compartment of a refrigerator **2** *NAm* a refrigerator
'iceˌbreaker /-ˌbraykə‖-ˌbreɪkə/ *n* a ship equipped to make and maintain a channel through ice
'ice ˌcap /-ˌkap‖-ˌkæp/ *n* a lasting (extensive) cover of ice
ice cream /ˌies 'kreem, 'ies ˌkreem‖ˌaɪs 'kriːm, 'aɪs ˌkriːm/ *n* a sweet flavoured frozen food containing cream (substitute) and often eggs
'ice ˌhockey *n* a game played on an ice rink by 2 teams of 6 players on skates whose object is to drive a puck into the opponent's goal with a hockey stick
[1]**Icelandic** /ies'landik‖aɪs'lændɪk/ *adj* (characteristic) of Iceland
[2]**Icelandic** *n* the N Germanic language of the Icelandic people
ice lolly /ˌies 'loli, 'ies ˌloli‖ˌaɪs 'lɒlɪ, 'aɪs ˌlɒlɪ/ *n* an ice cream or esp a flavoured piece of ice on a stick
'iceˌman /-ˌman‖-ˌmæn/ *n* one who sells or delivers ice, esp in the USA
'ice ˌpack *n* **1** an expanse of pack ice **2** ICE BAG
'ice ˌpick *n* a hand tool ending in a spike for chipping ice
'ice ˌskate *n* a shoe with a metal runner attached for skating on ice – **ice-skate** *vi*, **ice skater** *n*
ichneumon /ik'nyoohmən‖ɪk'njuːmən/ *n* **1** a mongoose **2** any of various related 4-winged insects whose larvae are usu internal parasites of other insect larvae, esp caterpillars
icicle /'iesikl‖'aɪsɪkl/ *n* a hanging tapering mass of ice formed by the freezing of dripping water
icing /'iesing‖'aɪsɪŋ/ *n* a sweet (creamy) coating for cakes or other baked goods
icon, ikon /'iekon‖'aɪkɒn/ *n* **1** a usu pictorial representation; an image **2** a conventional religious image typically painted on a small wooden panel and used in worship by the Eastern Christian Church – **iconic** *adj*, **iconically** *adv*, **iconicity** *n*
iconoclasm /ie'konəˌklazm‖aɪ'kɒnəˌklæzm/ *n* the doctrine, practice, or attitude of an iconoclast
i'conoˌclast /-ˌklast‖-ˌklæst/ *n* **1** a person who destroys religious images or opposes their veneration **2** one who attacks established beliefs or institutions [Medieval Latin *iconoclastes*, fr Middle Greek *eikonoklastēs*, lit., image destroyer, fr Greek *eikōn* image + *klan* to break] – **iconoclastic** *adj*, **iconoclastically** *adv*
-ics /-iks‖-ɪks/ *suffix* (→ *n pl but sing or pl in constr*) **1** study, knowledge, skill, or practice of <*linguistics*> **2** actions, activities, or mode of behaviour characteristic of (a specified person or thing) <*acrobatics*> **3** qualities, operations, or phenomena relating to <*mechanics*>
icy /'iesi‖'aɪsɪ/ *adj* **1a** covered with, full of, or consisting of ice **b** intensely cold **2** characterized by personal coldness <*an* ~ *stare*> – **icily** *adv*, **iciness** *n*
id /id‖ɪd/ *n* the one of the 3 divisions of the mind in psychoanalytic theory that is completely unconscious and is the source of psychic energy derived from instinctual needs and drives
I'd /ied‖aɪd/ I had; I should; I would
ID card /ˌie 'dee‖ˌaɪ 'diː/ *n* IDENTITY CARD
idea /ie'diə‖aɪ'dɪə/ *n* **1a** a transcendent entity of which existing things are imperfect representations **b** a plan of action **2a** an indefinite or vague impression **b** sthg (e g a thought, concept, or image) actually or potentially present in the mind **3** a formulated thought or opinion **4** whatever is known or supposed about sthg **5** an individual's conception of the perfect or typical example of sthg specified <*not my* ~ *of a good time*> **6** the central meaning or aim of a particular action or situation <*the* ~ *of the game is to score goals*>
[1]**ideal** /ie'deel‖aɪ'diːl/ *adj* **1a** existing only in the mind; *broadly* lacking practicality **b** relating to or constituting mental images, ideas, or conceptions **2** of or embodying an ideal; perfect
[2]**ideal** *n* **1** a standard of perfection, beauty, or excellence **2** one looked up to as embodying an ideal or as a model for imitation **3** an ultimate object or aim
idealism /ie'deeˌliz(ə)m‖aɪ'diːˌlɪz(ə)m/ *n* **1a** a theory that the essential nature of reality lies in consciousness or reason **b** a theory that only what is immediately perceived (e g sensations or ideas) is real **2** the practice of living according to one's ideals
i'dealist /-list‖-lɪst/ *n* sby guided by ideals; *esp* one who places ideals before practical considerations – **idealist, idealistic** *adj*, **idealistically** *adv*
ideal·ize, -ise /ie'deeliez‖aɪ'diːlaɪz/ *vt* **1** to attribute qualities of excellence or perfection to **2** to represent in an ideal form ~ *vi* to form ideals – **idealizer** *n*, **idealization** *n*
i'deally /-li‖-lɪ/ *adv* **1** in accordance with an ideal; perfectly **2** for best results <~, *we should eat less sugar*>
idem /'idem, 'iedem‖'ɪdem, 'aɪdem/ *pron* the same as previously mentioned
identical /ie'dentikl‖aɪ'dentɪkl/ *adj* **1** being the same **2** being very similar or exactly alike **3** *of twins, triplets, etc* derived from a single egg
identification /ieˌdentifi'kaysh(ə)n‖aɪˌdentɪfɪ'keɪʃ(ə)n/ *n* **1a** identifying or being identified **b** evidence of identity **2a** the putting of oneself mentally in the position of another **b** the (unconscious) attribution of the characteristics of another to oneself in order to attain gratification, emotional support, etc
identification parade *n, chiefly Br* a line-up of people arranged by the police to allow a witness to identify a suspect
identify /ie'dentifie‖aɪ'dentɪfaɪ/ *vt* **1a** to cause to be or become identical **b** to associate or link closely <*groups that are* identified *with conservation*> **2** to establish the identity of ~*vi* to experience psychological identification <~ *with the*

hero of a novel> – **identifiable** *adj*, **identifiably** *adv*, **identifier** *n*

[1]**identikit** /ie'dentikit‖aɪ'dentɪkɪt/ *n, often cap* a set of alternative facial characteristics used by the police to build up a likeness, esp of a suspect; *also* a likeness constructed in this way

[2]**identikit** *adj, often cap* **1** of or produced by identikit **2** like many others of the same type *<a middlebrow ~ novel>*

identity /ie'dentəti‖aɪ'dentətɪ/ *n* **1** the condition of being exactly alike **2** the distinguishing character or personality of an individual **3** the condition of being the same as sthg or sby known or supposed to exist *<establish the ~ of the stolen goods>* **4** an algebraic equation that remains true whatever values are substituted for the symbols

i'dentity ˌcard *n* a card bearing information that establishes the identity of the holder

ideogram /'idi·əˌgram‖'ɪdɪəˌgræm/ *n* **1** a stylized picture or symbol used instead of a word or sound to represent a thing or idea **2** a logogram – **ideogramic, ideogrammic** *adj*, **ideogrammatic** *adj*

ideology /ˌiedi'oləji‖ˌaɪdɪ'ɒlədʒɪ/ *n* **1** a systematic body of concepts **2** a manner of thinking characteristic of an individual, group, or culture **3** the ideas behind a social, political, or cultural programme – **ideologist** *n*, **ideological** *also* **ideologic** *adj*, **ideologically** *adv*

ides /iedz‖aɪdz/ *n pl but sing or pl in constr* (the week preceding) the 15th day of March, May, July, or October or the 13th day of any other month in the ancient Roman calendar

idiocy /'idi·əsi‖'ɪdɪəsɪ/ *n* **1** extreme mental deficiency **2** sthg notably stupid or foolish

idiom /'idi·əm‖'ɪdɪəm/ *n* **1a** the language peculiar to a people or to a district, community, or class **b** the syntactic, grammatical, or structural form peculiar to a language **2** an expression in the usage of a language that has a meaning that cannot be derived from the sum of the meanings of its elements **3** a characteristic style or form of artistic expression

idiomatic /ˌidi·ə'matik‖ˌɪdɪə'mætɪk/ *adj* of or conforming to idiom – **idiomatically** *adv*, **idiomaticity** *n*

idiosyncrasy /ˌidioh'singkrəsi‖ˌɪdɪəʊ'sɪŋkrəsɪ/ *n* **1** characteristic peculiarity of habit or structure **2** a characteristic of thought or behaviour peculiar to an individual or group; *esp* an eccentricity [Greek *idiosynkrasia*, fr *idios* one's own + *syn* with + *kerannynai* to mingle, mix] – **idiosyncratic** *adj*, **idiosyncratically** *adv*

idiot /'idi·ət‖'ɪdɪət/ *n* **1** an (ineducable) person afflicted with idiocy, esp from birth **2** a silly or foolish person – **idiot** *adj*, **idiotic** *adj*, **idiotically** *adv*

[1]**idle** /'iedl‖'aɪdl/ *adj* **1** having no particular purpose or value *<~ curiosity>* **2** groundless *<~ rumour>* **3** not occupied or employed: e g **3a** not in use or operation *<machines lying ~>* **b** not turned to appropriate use *<~ funds>* **4** lazy – **idleness** *n*, **idly** *adv*

[2]**idle** *vi* **1a** to spend time in idleness **b** to move idly **2** *esp of an engine* to run without being connected to the part (e g the wheels of a car) that is driven, so that no useful work is done ~ *vt* **1** to pass in idleness **2** to cause to idle – **idler** *n*

idol /'iedl‖'aɪdl/ *n* **1** an image or symbol used as an object of worship; *broadly* a false god **2** an object of passionate or excessive devotion

idolater /ie'dolətə‖aɪ'dɒlətə/ *n* **1** a worshipper of idols **2** a passionate and often uncritical admirer

idolatry /ie'dolətri‖aɪ'dɒlətrɪ/ *n* **1** the worship of a physical object as a god **2** excessive attachment or devotion to sthg – **idolatrous** *adj*, **idolatrously** *adv*, **idolatrousness** *n*

idol·ize, -ise /'ied(ə)lˌiez‖'aɪd(ə)lˌaɪz/ *vt* to worship idolatrously; *broadly* to love or admire to excess ~ *vi* to practise idolatry – **idolizer** *n*, **idolization** *n*

idyll, idyl /'idil‖'ɪdɪl/ *n* **1** a simple work in poetry or prose describing peaceful rustic life or pastoral scenes **2** an episode suitable for an idyll **3** a pastoral or romantic musical composition – **idyllic** *adj*, **idyllically** *adv*

-ie /-ee‖-iː/ *suffix* (*n* → *n*) [4]-Y

-ier /-iə‖-ɪə/ – see [2]-ER

[1]**if** /if‖ɪf/ *conj* **1a** in the event that *<~ she should telephone, let me know>* **b** supposing *<~ you'd listened, you'd know>* **c** on condition that **2** whether *<asked ~ the mail had come>* **3** – used to introduce an exclamation expressing a wish *<~ it would only rain>* **4** even if; although *<an interesting ~ irrelevant point>* **5** that – used after expressions of emotion *<I don't care ~ she's cross>* *<it's not surprising ~ you're annoyed>* **6** – used with a negative when an expletive introduces startling news *<blow me ~ he didn't hit her!>* – **if anything** on the contrary even; perhaps even <if anything, *you ought to apologize>*

[2]**if** *n* **1** a condition, stipulation *<the question depends on too many ~s>* **2** a supposition *<a theory full of ~s>*

iffy /'ifi‖'ɪfɪ/ *adj* uncertain or unreliable – infml

-iform /-ifawm‖-ɪfɔːm/ – see -FORM

-ify /-ifie, -əfie‖-ɪfaɪ, -əfaɪ/ – see -FY

igloo /'iglooh‖'ɪgluː/ *n, pl* **igloos** **1** an Eskimo dwelling, usu made of snow blocks and in the shape of a dome **2** a structure shaped like a dome [Eskimo *iglu, igdlu* house]

igneous /'igni·əs‖'ɪgnɪəs/ *adj* **1** fiery **2** relating to or formed by the flow or solidification of molten rock from the earth's core *<~ rocks>*

ignite /ig'niet‖ɪg'naɪt/ *vt* **1a** to set fire to; *also* to kindle **b** to cause (a fuel mixture) to burn **2** to spark off; excite, esp suddenly ~ *vi* **1** to catch fire **2** to begin to glow **3** to burst forth suddenly into violence or conflict – **ignitable** *also* **ignitible** *adj*, **igniter, ignitor** *n*

ignition /ig'nish(ə)n‖ɪg'nɪʃ(ə)n/ *n* **1** the act or action of igniting **2** the process or means (e g an electric spark) of igniting a fuel mixture

ignoble /ig'nohbl‖ɪg'nəʊbl/ *adj* **1** of low birth or humble origin **2** base, dishonourable – **ignobleness** *n*, **ignobly** *adv*, **ignobility** *n*

ignominious /ˌignə'mini·əs‖ˌɪgnə'mɪnɪəs/ *adj* **1** marked by or causing disgrace or discredit **2** humiliating, degrading – **ignominiously** *adv*, **ignominiousness** *n*

ignominy /'ignəmini‖'ɪgnəmɪnɪ/ *n* **1** deep personal humiliation and disgrace **2** disgraceful or dishonourable conduct or quality

ignoramus /ˌignəˈraymas‖ˌɪgnəˈreɪməs/ *n* an ignorant person

ignorance /ˈignərəns‖ˈɪgnərəns/ *n* the state of being ignorant

ignorant /ˈignərənt‖ˈɪgnərənt/ *adj* **1** lacking knowledge, education, or comprehension (of sthg specified) **2** caused by or showing lack of knowledge **3** lacking social training; impolite – chiefly infml – **ignorantly** *adv*

ignore /igˈnaw‖ɪgˈnɔː/ *vt* to refuse to take notice of; disregard – **ignorable** *adj*, **ignorer** *n*

iguana /ˌigyooˈahnə, iˈgwahnə‖ˌɪgjʊˈɑːnə, ɪˈgwɑːnə/ *n* any of various large lizards; *esp* a plant-eating (dark-coloured) tropical American lizard with a serrated crest on its back

ikon /ˈiekon‖ˈaɪkɒn/ *n* an icon

il- /il-‖ɪl-/ – see IN-

ileum /ˈili·əm‖ˈɪlɪəm/ *n, pl* **ilea** /ˈili·ə‖ˈɪlɪə/ the last division of the small intestine extending between the jejunum and the large intestine – **ileal** *adj*

ilex /ˈieleks‖ˈaɪleks/ *n* **1** HOLM OAK **2** the holly

[1]ilk /ilk‖ɪlk/ *pron, chiefly Scot* *that* same – esp in the names of landed families

[2]ilk *n* sort, kind <*politicians and others of that* ~>

[3]ilk *adj, chiefly Scot* each, every

[1]ill /il‖ɪl/ *adj* **worse** /wuhs‖wɜːs/; **worst** /wuhst‖wɜːst/ **1** bad: e g **1a** morally evil <~ *deeds*> **b** malevolent, hostile <~ *feeling*> **c** attributing evil or an objectionable quality <*held an* ~ *opinion of his neighbours*> **2a** causing discomfort or inconvenience; disagreeable <~ *effects*> **b(1)** not normal or sound <~ *health*> **b(2)** not in good health; *also* nauseated **b(3)** *chiefly Br* hurt, wounded <*still very* ~ *after the accident*> **3** unlucky, disadvantageous <*an* ~ *omen*> **4** socially improper <~ *breeding*> **5a** unfriendly, hostile <~ *feeling*> **b** harsh <~ *treatment*>

[2]ill *adv* **worse; worst** **1a** with displeasure or hostility **b** in a harsh manner <*used him* ~> **c** so as to reflect unfavourably <*spoke* ~ *of his neighbours*> **2** in a reprehensible, harsh, or deficient manner <*fared* ~> **3** hardly, scarcely <~ *at ease*> <*can* ~ *afford such extravagances*> **4a** in an unfortunate manner; badly, unluckily <ill-*fated*> **b** in a faulty, imperfect, or unpleasant manner <ill-*equipped*> *USE* often in combination

[3]ill *n* **1** the opposite of good; evil **2a** (a) misfortune, trouble <*hope no more* ~s *befall him*> **b(1)** an ailment **b(2)** sthg that disturbs or afflicts <*economic and social* ~s> **3** sthg that reflects unfavourably <*spoke no* ~ *of him*>

I'll /iel‖aɪl/ I will; I shall

ˌill-adˈvised *adj* showing lack of proper consideration or sound advice – **ill-advisedly** *adv*

ˌill at ˈease *adj* uneasy, uncomfortable

ˌill-ˈbred *adj* having or showing bad upbringing; impolite

illegal /iˈleegl‖ɪˈliːgl/ *adj* not authorized by law – **illegally** *adv*, **illegality** *n*

illegible /iˈlejəbl‖ɪˈledʒəbl/ *adj* not legible – **illegibly** *adv*, **illegibility** *n*

illegitimate /ˌiliˈjitimət‖ˌɪlɪˈdʒɪtɪmət/ *adj* **1** not recognized as lawful offspring; *specif* born out of wedlock **2** wrongly deduced or inferred **3** departing from the regular; abnormal **4** illegal – **illegitimately** *adv*, **illegitimacy** *n*

ˌill-ˈfavoured *adj* **1** unattractive in physical appearance **2** offensive, objectionable

ˌill-ˈgotten *adj* acquired by illicit or improper means – esp in *ill-gotten gains*

illiberal /ˌiˈlib(ə)rəl‖ˌɪˈlɪb(ə)rəl/ *adj* not liberal: e g **a** lacking culture and refinement **b** not broad-minded; bigoted **c** opposed to liberalism – **illiberalism** *n*, **illiberally** *adv*, **illiberalness, illiberality** *n*

illicit /iˈlisit‖ɪˈlɪsɪt/ *adj* not permitted; unlawful <~ *love affairs*> – **illicitly** *adv*

illiterate /iˈlit(ə)rət‖ɪˈlɪt(ə)rət/ *adj* **1** unable to read or write **2** showing lack of education – **illiterate** *n*, **illiterately** *adv*, **illiterateness, illiteracy** *n*

ˌill-ˈmannered *adj* having bad manners

ˌill-ˈnatured *adj* having a disagreeable disposition; surly – **ill-naturedly** *adv*

illness /ˈilnis‖ˈɪlnɪs/ *n* an unhealthy condition of body or mind

illogical /iˈlojikl‖ɪˈlɒdʒɪkl/ *adj* **1** contrary to the principles of logic **2** devoid of logic; senseless – **illogically** *adv*, **illogicalness, illogicality** *n*

ˌill-ˈtempered *adj* ill-natured – **ill-temperedly** *adv*

ˌill-ˈtimed *adj* badly timed; *esp* inopportune

ˌill-ˈtreat *vt* to treat cruelly or improperly – **ill-treatment** *n*

illuminate /iˈl(y)oohminayt‖ɪˈl(j)uːmɪneɪt/ *vt* **1a(1)** to cast light on; fill with light **a(2)** to brighten **b** to enlighten spiritually or intellectually **2** to elucidate **3** to decorate (a manuscript) with elaborate initial letters or marginal designs in gold, silver, and brilliant colours – **illuminatingly** *adv*, **illuminator** *n*, **illuminative** *adj*

illumination /iˌloohmiˈnaysh(ə)n, iˌlyooh-‖ɪˌluːmɪˈneɪʃ(ə)n, ɪˌljuː-/ *n* **1** illuminating or being illuminated: e g **1a** spiritual or intellectual enlightenment **b** decorative lighting or lighting effects **c** decoration of a manuscript by the art of illuminating **2** the amount of light per unit area of a surface on which it falls **3** any of the decorative features used in the art of illuminating or in decorative lighting

illusion /iˈl(y)oohzh(ə)n‖ɪˈl(j)uːʒ(ə)n/ *n* **1** a false impression or notion <*I have no* ~s *about my ability*> **2a(1)** a misleading image presented to the vision **a(2)** sthg that deceives or misleads intellectually **b(1)** perception of an object in such a way that it presents a misleading image <*an optical* ~> **b(2)** HALLUCINATION 1 – **illusional** *adj*, **illusionist** *n*

illusory /iˈl(y)oohsəri, -zəri‖ɪˈl(j)uːsərɪ, -zərɪ/ *adj* deceptive, unreal – **illusorily** *adv*, **illusoriness** *n*

illustrate /ˈiləstrayt‖ˈɪləstreɪt/ *vt* **1a** to clarify (by giving or serving as an example or instance) **b** to provide (e g a book) with visual material **2** to show clearly; demonstrate ~*vi* to give an example or instance – **illustrator** *n*

illustration /ˌiləˈstraysh(ə)n‖ˌɪləˈstreɪʃ(ə)n/ *n* **1** illustrating or being illustrated **2** sthg that serves to illustrate: e g **2a** an example that explains or clarifies sthg **b** a picture or diagram that helps to make sthg clear or attractive – **illustrational** *adj*

illustrative /ˈiləstrətiv, -stray-‖ˈɪləstrətɪv,

-streɪ-/ *adj* serving or intended to illustrate – **illustratively** *adv*

illustrious /iˈlustri·əs‖ɪˈlʌstrɪəs/ *adj* marked by distinction or renown – **illustriously** *adv*, **illustriousness** *n*

ˌill ˈwill *n* unfriendly feeling

im- /im-‖ɪm-/ – see IN-

I'm /iem‖aɪm/ I am

image /ˈimij‖ˈɪmɪdʒ/ *n* **1** a reproduction (e g a portrait or statue) of the form of a person or thing **2a** the optical counterpart of an object produced by a lens, mirror, etc or an electronic device **b** a likeness of an object produced on a photographic material **3a** exact likeness **b** a person who strikingly resembles another specified person <*he's the ~ of his father*> **4** a typical example or embodiment (e g of a quality) <*he's the ~ of goodness*> **5a** a mental picture of sthg (not actually present) **b** an idea, concept **6** a figure of speech, esp a metaphor or simile **7** a conception created in the minds of people, esp the general public <*worried about his public ~*>

imagery /ˈimij(ə)ri‖ˈɪmɪdʒ(ə)rɪ/ *n* **1** (the art of making) images **2** figurative language **3** mental images; *esp* the products of imagination

imaginable /iˈmajinəbl‖ɪˈmædʒɪnəbl/ *adj* capable of being imagined – **imaginableness** *n*, **imaginably** *adv*

imaginary /iˈmajin(ə)ri‖ɪˈmædʒɪn(ə)rɪ/ *adj* **1** existing only in imagination; lacking factual reality **2** containing or relating to (a multiple of) the positive square root of minus 1 – **imaginarily** *adv*, **imaginariness** *n*

imagination /iˌmajiˈnaysh(ə)n‖ɪˌmædʒɪˈneɪʃ(ə)n/ *n* **1** the act or power of forming a mental image of sthg not present to the senses or never before wholly perceived in reality **2** creative ability **3** a fanciful or empty notion

imaginative /iˈmaj(i)nətiv‖ɪˈmædʒ(ɪ)nətɪv/ *adj* **1** of or characterized by imagination **2** given to imagining; having a lively imagination **3** of images; *esp* showing a command of imagery – **imaginatively** *adv*, **imaginativeness** *n*

imagine /iˈmaj(ə)n‖ɪˈmædʒ(ə)n/ *vt* **1** to form a mental image of (sthg not present) **2** to suppose, think <*I ~ it will rain*> **3** to believe without sufficient basis <~s *himself to be indispensable*> ~*vi* to use the imagination

imam /iˈmahm, ˈ--‖ɪˈmɑːm, ˈ--/ *n* **1** the leader of prayer in a mosque **2** *cap* a Shiite leader held to be the divinely appointed successor of Muhammad **3** a caliph; *also* any of various Islamic doctors of law or theology – **imamate** *n*

imbalance /imˈbaləns‖ɪmˈbæləns/ *n* lack of balance: e g **a** lack of functional balance in a physiological system <*hormonal ~*> **b** lack of balance between segments of a country's economy **c** numerical disproportion

imbecile /ˈimbəseel, -siel‖ˈɪmbəsiːl, -saɪl/ *n* **1** MENTAL DEFECTIVE **2** a fool, idiot – **imbecile, imbecilic** *adj*

imbecility /ˌimbəˈsiləti‖ˌɪmbəˈsɪlətɪ/ *n* **1** being (an) imbecile **2** (an instance of) utter foolishness or nonsense

imbed /imˈbed‖ɪmˈbed/ *vb* **-dd-** to embed

imbibe /imˈbieb‖ɪmˈbaɪb/ *vt* **1** to drink **2** to take in or up; absorb, assimilate ~*vi* DRINK 2 – **imbiber** *n*

imbroglio /imˈbrohlioh‖ɪmˈbrəʊlɪəʊ/ *n, pl* **imbroglios 1** a confused mass **2a** an intricate or complicated situation (e g in a drama) **b** a confused or complicated misunderstanding or disagreement [Italian, fr *imbrogliare* to entangle]

imbue /imˈbyooh‖ɪmˈbjuː/ *vt* **1** to tinge or dye deeply **2** to cause to become permeated <*a man* ~d *with a strong sense of duty*>

imitate /ˈimitayt‖ˈɪmɪteɪt/ *vt* **1** to follow as a pattern, model, or example **2** to reproduce **3** to resemble **4** to mimic; TAKE OFF – **imitable** *adj*, **imitator** *n*

¹imitation /ˌimiˈtaysh(ə)n‖ˌɪmɪˈteɪʃ(ə)n/ *n* **1** an act or instance of imitating **2** sthg produced as a copy; a counterfeit **3** the repetition in one musical part of the melodic theme, phrase, or motive previously found in another musical part – **imitational** *adj*

²imitation *adj* made in imitation of sthg else that is usu genuine and of better quality

imitative /ˈimitətiv‖ˈɪmɪtətɪv/ *adj* **1a** marked by or given to imitation <*acting is an ~ art*> **b** onomatopoeic **2** imitating sthg superior – **imitatively** *adv*, **imitativeness** *n*

immaculate /iˈmakyoolət‖ɪˈmækjʊlət/ *adj* **1** without blemish; pure **2** free from flaw or error **3** perfectly clean – **immaculately** *adv*, **immaculateness, immaculacy** *n*

Immaculate Conception *n* the conception of the Virgin Mary held in Roman Catholic dogma to have freed her from original sin

immanent /ˈimənənt‖ˈɪmənənt/ *adj* **1** indwelling; *esp* having existence only in the mind **2** pervading nature or the souls of men <*belief in an ~ God*> – **immanence, immanency** *n*, **immanently** *adv*

immaterial /ˌiməˈtiəri·əl‖ˌɪməˈtɪərɪəl/ *adj* **1** not consisting of matter; incorporeal **2** unimportant – **immaterially** *adv*, **immaterialness, immateriality** *n*, **immaterialize** *vt*

immature /ˌiməˈtyooə‖ˌɪməˈtjʊə/ *adj* **1** lacking complete growth, differentiation, or development **2a** not having arrived at a definitive form or state <*a vigorous but ~ school of art*> **b** exhibiting less than an expected degree of maturity <*emotionally ~ adults*> – **immature** *n*, **immaturely** *adv*, **immatureness, immaturity** *n*

immeasurable /iˈmezh(ə)rəbl‖ɪˈmeʒ(ə)rəbl/ *adj* indefinitely extensive – **immeasurableness** *n*, **immeasurably** *adv*

immediacy /iˈmeedi·əsi‖ɪˈmiːdɪəsɪ/ *n* **1** the quality or state of being immediate **2** sthg requiring immediate attention – usu pl <*the* immediacies *of life*>

immediate /iˈmeedi·ət, -dyət‖ɪˈmiːdɪət, -djət/ *adj* **1a** acting or being without any intervening agency or factor <*the ~ cause of death*> **b** involving or derived from a single premise <*an ~ inference*> **2** next in line or relationship <*only the ~ family was present*> **3** occurring at once or very shortly **4** in close or direct physical proximity <*the ~ neighbourhood*> **5** directly touching or concerning a person or thing – **immediateness** *n*

¹imˈmediately /-li‖-lɪ/ *adv* **1** in direct relation or proximity; directly <*the parties ~ involved in the case*> **2** without delay

²immediately *conj* AS SOON AS

immemorial /ˌimiˈmawri·əl‖ˌɪmɪˈmɔːrɪəl/ *adj* extending beyond the reach of memory, record, or tradition <*existing from time* ~ > – **immemorially** *adv*

immense /iˈmens‖ɪˈmens/ *adj* very great, esp in size, degree, or extent – **immensely** *adv*, **immenseness, immensity** *n*

immerse /iˈmuhs‖ɪˈmɜːs/ *vt* **1** to plunge into sthg, esp a fluid, that surrounds or covers **2** to baptize by complete submergence **3** to engross, absorb <*completely* ~d *in his work*> – **immersible** *adj*, **immersion** *n*

imˈmersion ˌheater *n* an electrical apparatus for heating a liquid in which it is immersed; *esp* an electric water-heater fixed inside a domestic hot-water storage tank

immigrant /ˈimigrənt‖ˈɪmɪgrənt/ *n* **1** one who comes to a country to take up permanent residence **2** a plant or animal that becomes established in an area where it was previously unknown – **immigrant** *adj*

immigrate /ˈimigrayt‖ˈɪmɪgreɪt/ *vi* to come into a country of which one is not a native for permanent residence ~*vt* to bring in or send as immigrants – **immigration** *n*, **immigrational** *adj*

imminent /ˈiminənt‖ˈɪmɪnənt/ *adj* about to take place; *esp* impending, threatening – **imminently** *adv*, **imminentness, imminence** *n*

immobile /iˈmohbiel‖ɪˈməʊbaɪl/ *adj* **1** incapable of being moved **2** motionless <*keep the patient* ~> – **immobility** *n*

immobil·ize, -ise /iˈmohbiliez‖ɪˈməʊbɪlaɪz/ *vt* **1** to prevent freedom of movement or effective use of **2** to reduce or eliminate motion of (sby or a body part) by mechanical means or by strict bed rest – **immobilizer** *n*, **immobilization** *n*

immoderate /iˈmod(ə)rət‖ɪˈmɒd(ə)rət/ *adj* lacking in moderation; excessive – **immoderately** *adv*, **immoderacy, immoderateness, immoderation** *n*

immodest /iˈmodist‖ɪˈmɒdɪst/ *adj* not conforming to standards of sexual propriety – **immodestly** *adv*, **immodesty** *n*

immolate /ˈimohlayt‖ˈɪməʊleɪt/ *vt* **1** to kill as a sacrificial victim **2** to kill, destroy [Latin *immolare*, fr *in* in + *mola* meal; fr the custom of sprinkling victims with sacrificial meal] – **immolator** *n*, **immolation** *n*

immoral /iˈmorəl‖ɪˈmɒrəl/ *adj* not conforming to conventional moral standards, esp in sexual matters – **immorally** *adv*, **immorality** *n*

[1]**immortal** /iˈmawtl‖ɪˈmɔːtl/ *adj* **1** exempt from death <*the* ~ *gods*> **2** enduring forever; imperishable <~ *fame*> – **immortally** *adv*, **immortalize** *vt*, **immortality** *n*

[2]**immortal** *n* **1a** one exempt from death **b** *pl, often cap* the gods of classical antiquity **2** a person of lasting fame

immovable /iˈmoohvəbl‖ɪˈmuːvəbl/ *adj* **1** not moving or not intended to be moved **2a** steadfast, unyielding **b** incapable of being moved emotionally – **immovably** *adv*, **immovableness, immovability** *n*

immune /iˈmyoohn‖ɪˈmjuːn/ *adj* **1** free, exempt <~ *from prosecution*> **2** having a high degree of resistance to a disease <~ *to diphtheria*> **3a** having or producing antibodies to a corresponding antigen <*an* ~ *serum*> **b** concerned with or involving immunity <*an* ~ *response*> – **immune** *n*, **immunize** *vt*, **immunization** *n*

immunity /iˈmyoohnəti‖ɪˈmjuːnətɪ/ *n* being immune; *specif* the ability to resist the effects or development of a disease-causing parasite, esp a microorganism

immunology /ˌimyooˈnoləji‖ˌɪmjʊˈnɒlədʒɪ/ *n* a branch of biology that deals with the phenomena and causes of immunity – **immunologist** *n*, **immunologic, immunological** *adj*

immure /iˈmyooə‖ɪˈmjʊə/ *vt* **1** to enclose (as if) within walls; imprison **2** to build into, or esp entomb in, a wall – **immurement** *n*

immutable /iˈmyoohtəbl‖ɪˈmjuːtəbl/ *adj* not capable of or susceptible to change – **immutably** *adv*, **immutableness, immutability** *n*

imp /imp‖ɪmp/ *n* **1** a small demon **2** a mischievous child; a scamp

[1]**impact** /imˈpakt‖ɪmˈpækt/ *vt* to fix or press firmly (as if) by packing or wedging ~*vi* to impinge or make contact, esp forcefully – **impactive** *adj*

[2]**impact** /ˈimpakt‖ˈɪmpækt/ *n* **1a** an impinging or striking, esp of one body against another **b** (the impetus produced by or as if by) a violent contact or collision **2** a strong or powerful effect or impression <*the* ~ *of modern science on our society*>

imˈpacted *adj, of a tooth* not erupted as a result of lack of space in the jaw or of obstruction by bone or other teeth

impair /imˈpeə‖ɪmˈpeə/ *vt* to diminish in quality, strength, or amount – **impairer** *n*, **impairment** *n*

impala /imˈpahlə‖ɪmˈpɑːlə/ *n* a large brownish African antelope

impale /imˈpayl‖ɪmˈpeɪl/ *vt* **1** to pierce (as if) with sthg pointed; *esp* to torture or kill by fixing on a stake **2** to join (coats of arms) on a heraldic shield divided in half vertically – **impalement** *n*

impalpable /imˈpalpəbl‖ɪmˈpælpəbl/ *adj* **1** incapable of being sensed by the touch; intangible **2** not easily discerned or grasped by the mind – **impalpably** *adv*, **impalpability** *n*

impanel /imˈpanl‖ɪmˈpænl/ *vt* to empanel

impart /imˈpaht‖ɪmˈpɑːt/ *vt* **1** to convey, transmit <*the flavour* ~ed *by herbs*> **2** to make known; disclose – **impartable** *adj*, **impartment, impartation** *n*

impartial /imˈpahsh(ə)l‖ɪmˈpɑːʃ(ə)l/ *adj* not biased – **impartially** *adv*, **impartiality** *n*

impassable /imˈpahsəbl‖ɪmˈpɑːsəbl/ *adj* incapable of being passed, traversed, or surmounted – **impassably** *adv*, **impassableness, impassability** *n*

impasse /ˈamˌpas ‖ˈæmˌpæs (*Fr* ɛ̃pɑːs)/ *n* **1** a predicament from which there is no obvious escape **2** DEADLOCK 2

impassion /imˈpash(ə)n‖ɪmˈpæʃ(ə)n/ *vt* to arouse the feelings or passions of – **impassioned** *adj*

impassive /imˈpasiv‖ɪmˈpæsɪv/ *adj* **1** incapable of or not susceptible to emotion **2** showing no feeling or emotion – **impassively** *adv*, **impassiveness, impassivity** *n*

impatient /imˈpaysh(ə)nt‖ɪmˈpeɪʃ(ə)nt/ *adj*

1a restless or quickly roused to anger or exasperation **b** intolerant <~ *of delay*> **2** showing or caused by a lack of patience <*an* ~ *reply*> **3** eagerly desirous; anxious <~ *to see her boyfriend*> – **impatience** *n*, **impatiently** *adv*

impeach /im'peech‖ɪm'piːtʃ/ *vt* **1a** to bring an accusation against **b** to charge with a usu serious crime; *specif, chiefly NAm* to charge (a public official) with misconduct in office **2** to cast doubt on; *esp* to challenge the credibility or validity of <~ *the testimony of a witness*> – **impeachable** *adj*, **impeachment** *n*

impeccable /im'pekəbl‖ɪm'pekəbl/ *adj* **1** incapable of sinning **2** free from fault or blame; flawless – **impeccably** *adv*, **impeccability** *n*

impecunious /ˌimpi'kyoohnyəs, -ni·əs‖ˌɪmpɪ'kjuːnjəs, -nɪəs/ *adj* having very little or no money – chiefly fml – **impecuniously** *adv*, **impecuniousness, impecuniosity** *n*

impedance /im'peed(ə)ns‖ɪm'piːd(ə)ns/ *n* sthg that impedes; *esp* the opposition in an electrical circuit to the flow of an alternating current that is analogous to the opposition of an electrical resistance to the flow of a direct current

impede /im'peed‖ɪm'piːd/ *vt* to interfere with or retard the progress of – **impeder** *n*

impediment /im'pedimənt‖ɪm'pedɪmənt/ *n* **1** sthg that impedes; *esp* a physiological speech defect **2** a hindrance to lawful marriage

impedimenta /imˌpedi'mentə‖ɪmˌpedɪ'mentə/ *n pl* **1** unwieldy baggage or equipment **2** things that impede; encumbrances

impel /im'pel‖ɪm'pel/ *vt* **-ll-** **1** to urge forward or force into action **2** to propel

impend /im'pend‖ɪm'pend/ *vi* **1a** to hover threateningly; menace **b** to be about to happen **2** *archaic* to be suspended; hang

impenetrable /im'penitrəbl‖ɪm'penɪtrəbl/ *adj* **1a** incapable of being penetrated or pierced **b** inaccessible to intellectual influences or ideas **2** incapable of being comprehended – **impenetrableness** *n*, **impenetrably** *adv*, **impenetrability** *n*

[1]**imperative** /im'perətiv‖ɪm'perətɪv/ *adj* **1a** of or being the grammatical mood that expresses command **b** expressive of a command, entreaty, or exhortation **c** having power to restrain, control, and direct **2** urgent <*an* ~ *duty*> – **imperatively** *adv*, **imperativeness** *n*

[2]**imperative** *n* **1** (a verb form expressing) the imperative mood **2** sthg imperative: e g **2a** a command, order **b** an obligatory act or duty **c** an imperative judgment or proposition

imperceptible /impə'septəbl‖ɪmpə'septəbl/ *adj* **1** not perceptible by the mind or senses **2** extremely slight, gradual, or subtle <*an* ~ *change in attitude*> – **imperceptibly** *adv*, **imperceptibility** *n*

[1]**imperfect** /im'puhfikt‖ɪm'pɜːfɪkt/ *adj* **1** not perfect: e g **1a** defective **b** not having the stamens and carpels in the same flower **2** of or being a verb tense expressing a continuing state or an incomplete action, esp in the past **3** *of a cadence* passing to a dominant chord from a tonic chord – **imperfectly** *adv*, **imperfectness** *n*, **imperfection** *n*

[2]**imperfect** *n* (a verb form expressing) the imperfect tense

imperial /im'piəri·əl‖ɪm'pɪərɪəl/ *adj* **1a** of or befitting an empire, emperor, or empress **b** of the British Empire **2a** sovereign, royal **b** regal, imperious **3** belonging to an official nonmetric British series of weights and measures – **imperially** *adv*

imperialism /im'piəri·əˌliz(ə)m‖ɪm'pɪərɪəˌlɪz(ə)m/ *n* **1** government by an emperor **2** the policy, practice, or advocacy of extending the power and dominion of a nation, esp by territorial acquisition – **imperialist** *n or adj*, **imperialistic** *adj*, **imperialistically** *adv*

imperil /im'perəl‖ɪm'perəl/ *vt* **-ll-** (*NAm* **-l-**, **-ll-**) to endanger – **imperilment** *n*

imperious /im'piəri·əs‖ɪm'pɪərɪəs/ *adj* marked by arrogant assurance; domineering – **imperiously** *adv*, **imperiousness** *n*

imperishable /im'perishəbl‖ɪm'perɪʃəbl/ *adj* **1** not perishable or subject to decay **2** enduring permanently <~ *fame*> – **imperishable** *n*, **imperishably** *adv*, **imperishableness, imperishability** *n*

impermanent /im'puhmənənt‖ɪm'pɜːmənənt/ *adj* transient – **impermanence, impermanency** *n*, **impermanently** *adv*

impermeable /im'puhmi·əbl‖ɪm'pɜːmɪəbl/ *adj* not permitting passage, esp of a fluid – **impermeably** *adv*, **impermeability** *n*

impersonal /im'puhs(ə)nl‖ɪm'pɜːs(ə)nl/ *adj* **1a** denoting verbal action with no expressed subject (e g *methinks*) or with a merely formal subject (e g *rained* in *it rained*) **b** *of a pronoun* indefinite **2a** having no personal reference or connection; objective **b** not involving or reflecting the human personality or emotions <*spoke in a flat* ~ *tone*> **c** not having personality <*an* ~ *deity*> – **impersonalize** *vt*, **impersonally** *adv*, **impersonality** *n*

impersonate /im'puhsənayt‖ɪm'pɜːsəneɪt/ *vt* to assume or act the character of – **impersonator** *n*, **impersonation** *n*

impertinent /im'puhtinənt‖ɪm'pɜːtɪnənt/ *adj* **1** not restrained within due or proper bounds <~ *curiosity*>; *also* rude, insolent **2** irrelevant – chiefly fml – **impertinence** *n*, **impertinently** *adv*

imperturbable /ˌimpə'tuhbəbl, -puh-‖ˌɪmpə'tɜːbəbl, -pɜː-/ *adj* marked by extreme calm and composure – **imperturbably** *adv*, **imperturbability** *n*

impervious /im'puhvi·əs‖ɪm'pɜːvɪəs/ *adj* **1** impenetrable <*a coat* ~ *to rain*> **2** not capable of being affected or disturbed <~ *to criticism*> *USE* usu + *to* – **imperviously** *adv*, **imperviousness** *n*

impetigo /ˌimpə'tiegoh‖ˌɪmpə'taɪgəʊ/ *n* a contagious skin disease characterized by blisters and pustules – **impetiginous** *adj*

impetuous /im'petyoo·əs‖ɪm'petjʊəs/ *adj* **1** marked by impulsive vehemence <*an* ~ *temperament*> **2** marked by forceful and violent movement – chiefly poetic – **impetuousness** *n*, **impetuously** *adv*, **impetuosity** *n*

impetus /'impitəs‖'ɪmpɪtəs/ *n* **1a** a driving force **b** an incentive, stimulus <*gave a new* ~ *to the ailing economy*> **2** the energy possessed by a moving body

impiety /im'pie·əti‖ɪm'paɪətɪ/ *n* (an act showing) a lack of reverence

impinge /im'pinj‖ɪm'pɪndʒ/ *vi* **1** to strike,

dash **2** to make an impression **3** to encroach, infringe <~ *on other people's rights*> ***USE*** usu + *on* or *upon* – **impingement** *n*

impious /ˈimpi·əs‖ˈɪmpɪəs/ *adj* lacking in reverence or proper respect (e g for God); irreverent – **impiously** *adv*

impish /ˈimpish‖ˈɪmpɪʃ/ *adj* mischievous – **impishly** *adv*, **impishness** *n*

implacable /imˈplakəbl‖ɪmˈplækəbl/ *adj* not capable of being appeased or pacified <*an* ~ *enemy*> – **implacableness** *n*, **implacably** *adv*, **implacability** *n*

[1]implant /imˈplahnt‖ɪmˈplɑːnt/ *vt* **1a** to fix or set securely or deeply **b** to set permanently in the consciousness or habit patterns **2** to insert in the tissue of a living organism – **implantable** *adj*, **implanter** *n*, **implantation** *n*

[2]implant /ˈim,plahnt‖ˈɪm,plɑːnt/ *n* sthg (e g a graft or hormone pellet) implanted in tissue

[1]implement /ˈimplimənt‖ˈɪmplɪmənt/ *n* **1** an article serving to equip <*the* ~s *of religious worship*> **2** (sby or sthg that serves as) a utensil or tool

[2]implement /ˈimpliment, -mənt‖ˈɪmplɪment, -mənt/ *vt* CARRY OUT; *esp* to give practical effect to <*plans not yet* ~ed *due to lack of funds*> – **implementation** *n*

implicate /ˈimplikayt‖ˈɪmplɪkeɪt/ *vt* **1** to involve as a consequence, corollary, or inference; imply **2a** to bring into (incriminating) connection **b** to involve in the nature or operation of sthg; affect **3** *archaic* to entwine

implication /,impliˈkaysh(ə)n‖,ɪmplɪˈkeɪʃ(ə)n/ *n* **1a** implicating or being implicated **b** incriminating involvement **2a** implying or being implied **b** a logical relation between 2 propositions such that if the first is true the second must be true **3** sthg implied – **implicative** *adj*

implicit /imˈplisit‖ɪmˈplɪsɪt/ *adj* **1a** implied rather than directly stated <*an* ~ *assumption*> **b** potentially present though not realized or visible **2** unquestioning, absolute <~ *obedience*> – **implicitly** *adv*, **implicitness** *n*

implode /imˈplohd‖ɪmˈpləʊd/ *vb* to collapse inwards suddenly – **implosion** *n*, **implosive** *adj*

implore /imˈplaw‖ɪmˈplɔː/ *vt* **1** to call on in supplication; beseech **2** to call or beg for earnestly; entreat

imply /imˈplie‖ɪmˈplaɪ/ *vt* **1** to involve or indicate as a necessary or potential though not expressly stated consequence **2** to express indirectly; hint at <*his silence* implied *consent*>

impolite /,impəˈliet‖,ɪmpəˈlaɪt/ *adj* not polite; rude – **impolitely** *adv*, **impoliteness** *n*

impolitic /imˈpolətik‖ɪmˈpɒlətɪk/ *adj* unwise, ill-advised – chiefly fml – **impoliticly** *adv*

imponderable /imˈpond(ə)rəbl‖ɪmˈpɒnd(ə)rəbl/ *n or adj* (sthg) incapable of being precisely weighed or evaluated – **imponderably** *adv*, **imponderability** *n*

[1]import /imˈpawt‖ɪmˈpɔːt/ *vt* **1** to bring from a foreign or external source; *esp* to bring (e g merchandise) into a place or country from another country **2** to convey as meaning or portent; signify – chiefly fml – **importable** *adj*, **importer** *n*, **importation** *n*

[2]import /ˈimpawt‖ˈɪmpɔːt/ *n* **1** sthg imported **2** importing, esp of merchandise **3** purport, meaning **4** (relative) importance <*it is hard to determine the* ~ *of this decision*> ***USE*** (*3 & 4*) fml

importance /imˈpawt(ə)ns‖ɪmˈpɔːt(ə)ns/ *n* consequence, significance

important /imˈpawt(ə)nt‖ɪmˈpɔːt(ə)nt/ *adj* of considerable significance or consequence – **importantly** *adv*

importunate /imˈpawtyoonət, -chənət‖ɪmˈpɔːtjʊnət, -tʃənət/ *adj* troublesomely urgent; extremely persistent in request or demand – chiefly fml – **importunately** *adv*, **importunity** *n*

importune /imˈpawtyoohn, -choohn‖ɪmˈpɔːtjuːn, -tʃuːn/ *vt* **1** to press or urge with repeated requests; solicit with troublesome persistence **2** to solicit for purposes of prostitution ~*vi* to beg, urge, or solicit importunately ***USE*** chiefly fml – **importuner** *n*

impose /imˈpohz‖ɪmˈpəʊz/ *vt* **1a** to establish or apply as compulsory **b** to establish or make prevail by force **2** to arrange (typeset or plated pages) in order for printing **3** PALM OFF <~ *fake antiques on the public*> **4** to force into the company or on the attention of another <~ *oneself on others*> ~*vi* to take unwarranted advantage <~d *on his good nature*>; *also* to be an excessive requirement or burden ***USE*** (*except vt 1 & 2*) + *on* or *upon* – **imposer** *n*

imposing /imˈpohzing‖ɪmˈpəʊzɪŋ/ *adj* impressive because of size, bearing, dignity, or grandeur – **imposingly** *adv*

imposition /,impəˈzish(ə)n‖,ɪmpəˈzɪʃ(ə)n/ *n* **1** the act of imposing **2** sthg imposed: e g **2a** a levy, tax **b** an excessive or unwarranted requirement or burden

impossible /imˈposəbl‖ɪmˈpɒsəbl/ *adj* **1a** incapable of being or occurring; not possible **b** seemingly incapable of being done, attained, or fulfilled; insuperably difficult **c** difficult to believe <*an* ~ *story*> **2** extremely undesirable or difficult to put up with <*life became* ~ *because of lack of money*> – **impossibly** *adv*, **impossibility** *n*

impostor, imposter /imˈpostə‖ɪmˈpɒstə/ *n* one who assumes a false identity or title for fraudulent purposes

imposture /imˈposchə‖ɪmˈpɒstʃə/ *n* (an instance of) fraud, deception

impotent /ˈimpət(ə)nt‖ˈɪmpət(ə)nt/ *adj* **1** lacking in efficacy, strength, or vigour **2a** unable to copulate through an inability to maintain an erection of the penis **b** *of a male* STERILE 1 – not used technically – **impotence, impotency** *n*, **impotent** *n*, **impotently** *adv*

impound /imˈpownd‖ɪmˈpaʊnd/ *vt* **1a** to shut up (as if) in a pound; confine **b** to take and hold in legal custody **2** to collect and confine (water) (as if) in a reservoir – **impoundment** *n*

impoverish /imˈpov(ə)rish‖ɪmˈpɒv(ə)rɪʃ/ *vt* **1** to make poor **2** to deprive of strength, richness, or fertility – **impoverisher** *n*, **impoverishment** *n*

impracticable /imˈpraktikəbl‖ɪmˈpræktɪkəbl/ *adj* **1** incapable of being put into effect or carried out **2** impassable <*an* ~ *road*> – **impracticably** *adv*, **impracticableness, impracticability** *n*

impractical /imˈpraktikl‖ɪmˈpræktɪkl/ *adj*

not practical: e g **a** incapable of dealing sensibly with practical matters **b** impracticable <*economically* ~> – **impracticality** *n*, **impractically** *adv*

imprecate /'imprikayt‖'ɪmprɪkeɪt/ *vb* to invoke evil (on); curse – **imprecatory** *adj*, **imprecation** *n*

impregnable /im'pregnəbl‖ɪm'pregnəbl/ *adj* **1** incapable of being taken by assault <*an* ~ *fortress*> **2** beyond criticism or question <*an* ~ *social position*> – **impregnably** *adv*, **impregnability** *n*

[1]**impregnate** /'impregnayt‖'ɪmpregneɪt/ *adj* filled, saturated

[2]**impregnate** *vt* **1a** to introduce sperm cells into **b** to make pregnant; fertilize **2a** to cause to be imbued, permeated, or saturated **b** to permeate thoroughly – **impregnable** *adj*, **impregnation** *n*, **impregnator** *n*

impresario /ˌimpri'sahrioh‖ˌɪmprɪ'sɑːrɪəʊ/ *n*, *pl* **impresarios** one who organizes, puts on, or sponsors a public entertainment (e g a sports event); *esp* the manager or conductor of an opera or concert company [Italian, fr *impresa* undertaking, fr *imprendere* to undertake]

[1]**impress** /im'pres‖ɪm'pres/ *vt* **1a** to apply with pressure so as to imprint **b** to mark (as if) by pressure or stamping **2a** to fix strongly or deeply (e g in the mind or memory) **b** to produce a deep and usu favourable impression on **3** to transmit (force or motion) by pressure ~ *vi* to produce a (favourable) impression – **impressible** *adj*

[2]**impress** /'impres‖'ɪmpres/ *n* **1** the act of impressing **2** a mark made by pressure **3** an impression, effect

[3]**im'press** *vt* **1** to force into naval service **2** to procure or enlist by forcible persuasion – **impressment** *n*

impression /im'presh(ə)n‖ɪm'preʃ(ə)n/ *n* **1** the act or process of impressing **2** the effect produced by impressing: e g **2a** a stamp, form, or figure produced by physical contact **b** a (marked) influence or effect on the mind or senses; *esp* a favourable impression **3a** an effect of alteration or improvement <*the settlement left little* ~ *on the wilderness*> **b** a telling image impressed on the mind or senses <*first* ~s *of Greece*> **4a** the amount of pressure with which an inked printing surface deposits its ink on the paper **b** (a print or copy made from) the contact of a printing surface and the material being printed **c** all the copies of a publication (e g a book) printed in 1 continuous operation **5** a usu indistinct or imprecise notion or recollection **6** an imitation or representation of salient features in an artistic or theatrical medium; *esp* an imitation in caricature of a noted personality as a form of theatrical entertainment

im'pressionable /-əbl‖-əbl/ *adj* **1** easily influenced **2** easily moulded – **impressionability** *n*

impressionism /-iz(ə)m‖-ɪz(ə)m/ *n* **1** *often cap* an art movement, esp in late 19th-c France, that tries to convey the effects of actual reflected light on natural usu outdoor subjects **2** literary depiction that seeks to convey a general subjective impression rather than a detailed re-creation of reality – **impressionist** *n or adj, often cap*

imˌpression'istic /-'istik‖-'ɪstɪk/ *adj* **1** of or being impressionism **2** based on or involving subjective impression as distinct from knowledge, fact, or systematic thought – **impressionistically** *adv*

impressive /im'presiv‖ɪm'presɪv/ *adj* making a marked impression; stirring deep feelings, esp of awe or admiration – **impressively** *adv*, **impressiveness** *n*

imprimatur /ˌimpri'mahtə, -'maytə‖ˌɪmprɪ'mɑːtə, -'meɪtə/ *n* **1** a licence granted, esp by Roman Catholic episcopal authority, to print or publish **2** sanction, approval [Modern Latin, let it be printed, fr *imprimere* to print, fr Latin, to imprint, impress]

[1]**imprint** /im'print‖ɪm'prɪnt/ *vt* **1** to mark (as if) by pressure **2** to fix indelibly or permanently (e g on the memory)

[2]**imprint** /'imprint‖'ɪmprɪnt/ *n* **1** a mark or depression made by pressure <*the fossil* ~ *of a dinosaur's foot*> **2** a publisher's name printed at the foot of a title-page **3** an indelible distinguishing effect or influence

imprison /im'priz(ə)n‖ɪm'prɪz(ə)n/ *vt* to put (as if) in prison – **imprisonment** *n*

improbable /im'probəbl‖ɪm'prɒbəbl/ *adj* unlikely to be true or to occur – **improbably** *adv*, **improbability** *n*

[1]**impromptu** /im'promptyooh‖ɪm'prɒmptjuː/ *adj* made, done, composed, or uttered (as if) on the spur of the moment [French, fr *impromptu* extemporaneously, fr Latin *in promptu* in readiness] – **impromptu** *adv*

[2]**impromptu** *n* **1** sthg impromptu **2** a musical composition suggesting improvisation

improper /im'propə‖ɪm'prɒpə/ *adj* **1** not in accordance with fact, truth, or correct procedure <~ *inference*> **2** not suitable or appropriate **3** not in accordance with propriety or modesty; indecent – **improperly** *adv*

improper fraction *n* a fraction whose numerator is equal to, larger than, or of equal or higher degree than the denominator

impropriety /ˌimprə'prie·əti‖ˌɪmprə'praɪətɪ/ *n* **1** being improper **2** an improper act or remark; *esp* an unacceptable use of a word

improve /im'proohv‖ɪm'pruːv/ *vt* **1a** to enhance in value or quality; make better **b** to increase the value of (land or property) by making better (e g by cultivation or the erection of buildings) **2** to use to good purpose ~ *vi* **1** to advance or make progress in what is desirable **2** to make useful additions or amendments <*the new version* ~s *on the original*>

im'provement /-mənt‖-mənt/ *n* **1** improving or being improved **2** (sthg that gives) increased value or excellence <~s *to an old house*>

improvident /im'provid(ə)nt‖ɪm'prɒvɪd(ə)nt/ *adj* lacking foresight; not providing for the future – **improvidence** *n*, **improvidently** *adv*

improvise /'imprəviez‖'ɪmprəvaɪz/ *vb* **1** to compose, recite, or perform impromptu or without a set script, musical score, etc **2** to make, devise, or provide (sthg) without preparation (from what is conveniently to hand) – **improviser** *n*, **improvisation** *n*, **improvisatory** *adj*

imprudent /im'proohd(ə)nt‖ɪm'pruːd(ə)nt/

adj lacking discretion or caution – **imprudence** *n*, **imprudently** *adv*

impudent /ˈimpyood(ə)nt‖ˈɪmpjʊd(ə)nt/ *adj* marked by contemptuous or cocky boldness or disregard of others – **impudence** *n*, **impudently** *adv*

impugn /imˈpyoohn‖ɪmˈpjuːn/ *vt* to assail by words or arguments; call into question the validity or integrity of – **impugnable** *adj*, **impugner** *n*

impulse /ˈimpuls‖ˈɪmpʌls/ *n* **1a** (motion produced by) the act of driving onwards with sudden force **b** a wave of excitation transmitted through a nerve that results in physiological (e g muscular) activity or inhibition **2a** a force so communicated as to produce motion suddenly **b** inspiration, stimulus <*the creative* ~> **3a** a sudden spontaneous inclination or incitement to some usu unpremeditated action **b** a propensity or natural tendency, usu other than rational **4a** the change in momentum produced by a (large) force **b** PULSE 4a

impulsion /imˈpulsh(ə)n‖ɪmˈpʌlʃ(ə)n/ *n* **1a** impelling or being impelled **b** an impelling force **c** an impetus **2** IMPULSE 3

impulsive /imˈpulsiv‖ɪmˈpʌlsɪv/ *adj* **1** having the power of driving or impelling **2** actuated by or prone to act on impulse **3** acting momentarily – **impulsively** *adv*, **impulsiveness** *n*

impunity /imˈpyoohnəti‖ɪmˈpjuːnətɪ/ *n* exemption or freedom from punishment, harm, or loss

impure /imˈpyooə‖ɪmˈpjʊə/ *adj* not pure: e g **a** not chaste **b** containing sthg unclean <~ *water*> **c** ritually unclean **d** mixed; *esp* adulterated – **impurely** *adv*, **impurity** *n*

impute /imˈpyooht‖ɪmˈpjuːt/ *vt* **1** to lay the responsibility or blame for, often unjustly **2** to credit to a person or a cause; *esp* to attribute unjustly – **imputable** *adj*, **imputative** *adj*, **imputation** *n*

[1]**in** /in‖ɪn/ *prep* **1a(1)** – used to indicate location within or inside sthg three-dimensional <*swimming* ~ *the lake*> **a(2)** – used to indicate location within or not beyond limits <~ *reach*> <*wounded* ~ *the leg*> **a(3)** at – used with the names of cities, countries, and seas <~ *London*> **a(4)** during <~ *1959*> <*lost* ~ *transit*> **a(5)** by or before the end of <*wrote it* ~ *a week*> <*will come* ~ *an hour*> **b** INTO 1a <*went* ~ *the house*> **2a** – used to indicate means, instrumentality, or medium of expression <*drawn* ~ *pencil*> <*written* ~ *French*> **b** – used to describe costume <*a child* ~ *gumboots*> **3a** – used to indicate qualification, manner, circumstance, or condition <~ *fun*> <~ *public*> <~ *a hurry*> <~ *pain*> **b** so as to be <*broke* ~ *pieces*> **c** – used to indicate occupation or membership <*a job* ~ *insurance*> **4a** as regards <*equal* ~ *distance*> **b** by way of <*said* ~ *reply*> **5a** – used to indicate division, arrangement, or quantity <*standing* ~ *a circle*> **b** – used to indicate the larger member of a ratio <*one* ~ *six is eligible*> **6** *of an animal* pregnant with <~ *calf*> **7** – used to introduce indirect objects <*rejoice* ~> or to form adverbial phrases; compare IN FACT, IN RETURN – **in it** of advantage (e g between competitors or alternatives) <*there's not much* in it *between them*>

[2]**in** *adv* **1a** to or towards the inside or centre <*come* ~ *out of the rain*> **b** so as to incorporate <*mix* ~ *the flour*> **c** to or towards home, the shore, or one's destination <*3 ships came sailing* ~> **d** at a particular place, esp at one's home or business <*be* ~ *for lunch*> **e** into concealment <*the sun went* ~> **2a** so as to be added or included <*fit a piece* ~> **b** in or into political power <*voted them* ~> **c(1)** on good terms <~ *with the boss*> **c(2)** in a position of assured success **c(3)** into a state of efficiency or proficiency <*work a horse* ~> **d** in or into vogue or fashion **e** in or into a centre, esp a central point of control <*letters pouring* ~> <*went* ~ *to bat*> – **in for** certain to experience <in for *trouble*> – compare LET IN FOR – **in on** having a share in

[3]**in** *adj* **1a** located inside **b** being in operation or power <*the fire's still* ~> **c** shared by a select group <*an* ~ *joke*> **2** directed or serving to direct inwards <*the* ~ *tray*> **3** extremely fashionable <*the* ~ *place to go*>

[1]**in-** /in-‖ɪn-/, **il-** /il-‖ɪl-/, **im-** /im-‖ɪm-/, **ir-** /ir-‖ɪr-/ *prefix* not; non-; un- – usu *il-* before *l* <il*logical*>, *im-* before *b,m,* or *p* <im*balance*> <im*moral*> <im*practical*>, *ir-* before *r* <ir*reducible*>, and *in-* before other sounds <in*conclusive*>

[2]**in-, il-, im-, ir-** *prefix* **1** in; within; into; towards; on <in*flux*> <im*merse*> – usu *il-* before *l, im-* before *b,m,* or *p, ir-* before *r*, and *in-* before other sounds **2** [1]EN- <im*peril*>

inability /ˌinəˈbiləti‖ˌɪnəˈbɪlətɪ/ *n* lack of sufficient power, resources, or capacity <*his* ~ *to do maths*>

inaccessible *adj*

inaccurate /inˈakyoorət‖ɪnˈækjʊrət/ *adj* not accurate; faulty – **inaccurately** *adv*, **inaccuracy** *n*

inaction /inˈaksh(ə)n‖ɪnˈækʃ(ə)n/ *n* lack of action or activity

inactive /inˈaktiv‖ɪnˈæktɪv/ *adj* **1** not given to action or effort **2** out of use; not functioning **3** relating to members of the armed forces who are not performing or available for military duties **4** *of a disease* quiescent **5** chemically or biologically inert, esp because of the loss of some quality – **inactively** *adv*, **inactivate** *vt*, **inactivity** *n*

inadequate /inˈadikwət‖ɪnˈædɪkwət/ *adj* not adequate: e g **a** insufficient **b** characteristically unable to cope – **inadequacy** *n*, **inadequately** *adv*, **inadequateness** *n*

inadmissible *adj*

inadvertence /ˌinədˈvuht(ə)ns‖ˌɪnədˈvɜːt(ə)ns/, **inadvertency** /-si‖-sɪ/ *n* (a result of) inattention

inadvertent /ˌinədˈvuht(ə)nt‖ˌɪnədˈvɜːt(ə)nt/ *adj* **1** heedless, inattentive **2** unintentional – **inadvertently** *adv*

inalienable /inˈaylyənabl‖ɪnˈeɪljənəbl/ *adj* incapable of being alienated – **inalienably** *adv*, **inalienability** *n*

inamorata /ˌinaməˈrahtə, inˌamə-‖ˌɪnæməˈrɑːtə, ɪnˌæmə-/ *n* a woman with whom one is in love or is having a sexual relationship

inane /iˈnayn‖ɪˈneɪn/ *adj* lacking significance, meaning, or point – **inanely** *adv*, **inaneness, inanity** *n*

inanimate /in'animət‖ɪn'ænɪmət/ *adj* **1** not endowed with life or spirit **2** lacking consciousness or power of motion – **inanimately** *adv*, **inanimateness** *n*

inanition /ˌinə'nish(ə)n‖ˌɪnə'nɪʃ(ə)n/ *n* **1** the quality of being empty **2** the absence or loss of social, moral, or intellectual vitality or vigour *USE* fml

inapplicable *adj*

inappropriate *adj*

inapt /in'apt‖ɪn'æpt/ *adj* not suitable or appropriate – **inaptly** *adv*, **inaptness** *n*

inaptitude /in'aptityoohd‖ɪn'æptɪtjuːd/ *n* lack of aptitude

inarticulate /ˌinah'tikyoolət‖ˌɪnɑː'tɪkjʊlət/ *adj* **1a** not understandable as spoken words < ~ *cries*> **b** incapable of (being expressed by) speech, esp under stress of emotion **2a** not giving or not able to give coherent, clear, or effective expression to one's ideas or feelings **b** not coherently, clearly, or effectively expressed <*an ~ speech*> **3** not jointed or hinged – **inarticulately** *adv*, **inarticulateness** *n*

inartistic /ˌinah'tistik‖ˌɪnɑː'tɪstɪk/ *adj* **1** not conforming to the principles of art **2** not appreciative of art – **inartistically** *adv*

inasmuch as /inəz'much əz‖ɪnəz'mʌtʃ əz/ *conj* **1** INSOFAR AS **2** in view of the fact that; because

inattention /ˌinə'tensh(ə)n‖ˌɪnə'tenʃ(ə)n/ *n* failure to pay attention; disregard

inattentive *adj*

inaudible *adj*

[1]**inaugural** /in'awgyoorəl‖ɪn'ɔːgjʊrəl/ *adj* marking a beginning; first in a projected series

[2]**inaugural** *n* an address at inauguration

inaugurate /in'awgyoorayt‖ɪn'ɔːgjʊreɪt/ *vt* **1** to induct ceremonially into office **2** to observe formally, or bring about, the beginning of – **inaugurator** *n*, **inauguration** *n*

inauspicious *adj*

inboard /in'bawd‖ɪn'bɔːd/ *adv* **1** towards the centre line of a vessel **2** in a position closer or closest to the long axis of an aircraft – **inboard** *adj*

in'born /-'bawn‖-'bɔːn/ *adj* **1** born in or with one; forming part of one's natural make-up **2** hereditary, inherited

ˌin'bred /-'bred‖-'bred/ *adj* **1** rooted and deeply ingrained in one's nature **2** subjected to or produced by inbreeding

'inˌbreeding /-ˌbreeding‖-ˌbriːdɪŋ/ *n* **1** the interbreeding of closely related individuals, esp to preserve and fix desirable characters **2** confinement to a narrow range or a local or limited field of choice – **inbreed** *vt*, **inbreeder** *n*

Inca /'ingkə‖'ɪŋkə/ *n* **1** a king or member of the ruling family of an empire existing in Peru before the Spanish conquest **2** a member of the Indian peoples inhabiting the Inca empire – **Incan** *adj*

incalculable /in'kalkyooləbl‖ɪn'kælkjʊləbl/ *adj* **1** too large or numerous to be calculated **2** unpredictable, uncertain – **incalculably** *adv*, **incalculability** *n*

incandescent /ˌinkan'des(ə)nt‖ˌɪnkæn'des(ə)nt/ *adj* **1a** white, glowing, or luminous with intense heat **b** strikingly bright, radiant, or clear **2** of or being visible light produced by a (white) hot body – **incandesce** *vb*, **incandescence** *n*, **incandescently** *adv*

incandescent lamp *n* an electric lamp in which an electrically-heated filament gives off light

incantation /ˌinkan'taysh(ə)n‖ˌɪnkæn'teɪʃ(ə)n/ *n* the use of spoken or sung spells in magic ritual; *also* a formula so used – **incantatory** *adj*

incapable /in'kaypəbl‖ɪn'keɪpəbl/ *adj* lacking capacity, ability, or qualification for the purpose or end in view: e g **a** not in a state or of a kind to admit *of* **b** not able or fit for the doing or performance *of* – **incapableness** *n*, **incapably** *adv*, **incapability** *n*

incapacitate /ˌinkə'pasitayt‖ˌɪnkə'pæsɪteɪt/ *vt* **1** to deprive of capacity or natural power; disable **2** to disqualify legally – **incapacitation** *n*

incapacity /ˌinkə'pasəti‖ˌɪnkə'pæsətɪ/ *n* lack of ability or power or of natural or legal qualifications

incarcerate /in'kahsərayt‖ɪn'kɑːsəreɪt/ *vt* to imprison, confine – **incarceration** *n*

[1]**incarnate** /in'kahnət, -nayt‖ɪn'kɑːnət, -neɪt/ *adj* **1** invested with bodily, esp human, nature and form **2** that is the essence of; typified <*evil* ~>

[2]**incarnate** /'inkahˌnayt‖'ɪnkɑːˌneɪt/ *vt* to make incarnate

incarnation /ˌinkah'naysh(ə)n‖ˌɪnkɑː'neɪʃ(ə)n/ *n* **1** making or being incarnate **2a(1)** the embodiment of a deity or spirit in an earthly form **a(2)** *cap* Christ's human manifestation **b** a quality or concept typified or made concrete, esp in a person **3** any of several successive bodily manifestations or lives

[1]**incendiary** /in'sendyəri‖ɪn'sendjərɪ/ *n* **1a** one who deliberately sets fire to property **b** an incendiary agent (e g a bomb) **2** one who inflames or stirs up factions, quarrels, or sedition – **incendiarism** *n*

[2]**incendiary** *adj* **1** of the deliberate burning of property **2** tending to inflame or stir up trouble **3** (of, being, or involving the use of a missile containing a chemical) that ignites spontaneously on contact

[1]**incense** /'insens‖'ɪnsens/ *n* **1** material used to produce a fragrant smell when burned **2** the perfume given off by some spices and gums when burned; *broadly* a pleasing scent

[2]**incense** /in'sens‖ɪn'sens/ *vt* to arouse the extreme anger or indignation of

incentive /in'sentiv‖ɪn'sentɪv/ *n* sthg that motivates or spurs one on (e g to action or effort) – **incentive** *adj*

inception /in'sepsh(ə)n‖ɪn'sepʃ(ə)n/ *n* an act, process, or instance of beginning

incertitude /in'suhtityoohd‖ɪn'sɜːtɪtjuːd/ *n* uncertainty, doubt

incessant /in'ses(ə)nt‖ɪn'ses(ə)nt/ *adj* continuing without interruption – **incessancy** *n*, **incessantly** *adv*

incest /'insest‖'ɪnsest/ *n* sexual intercourse between people so closely related that they are forbidden by law to marry [Latin *incestum*, fr neut of *incestus* impure, fr *in-* not + *castus* pure]

incestuous /in'sestyoo·əs‖ɪn'sestjʊəs/ *adj* **1**

being, guilty of, or involving incest **2** unhealthily closed to outside influences – **incestuously** *adv*, **incestuousness** *n*

[1]**inch** /inch‖ɪntʃ/ *n* **1** a unit of length equal to $^1/_{36}$yd (about 25.4mm) **2** a small amount, distance, or degree **3** *pl* stature, height **4** a fall of rain, snow, etc enough to cover a surface to the depth of 1in – **every inch** to the utmost degree <*looks* every inch *a winner*> – **within an inch of one's life** very thoroughly; soundly <*thrashed him* within an inch of his life>

[2]**inch** *vb* to move by small degrees

inchoate /ˈinkoh·ayt‖ˈɪnkəʊeɪt/ *adj* only partly in existence or operation; *esp* imperfectly formed or formulated <*an* ~ *longing*> – fml – **inchoately** *adv*, **inchoateness** *n*

incidence /ˈinsid(ə)ns‖ˈɪnsɪd(ə)ns/ *n* **1a** an occurrence **b** the rate of occurrence or influence <*a high* ~ *of crime*> **2** the meeting of sthg (e g a projectile or a ray of light) with a surface

[1]**incident** /ˈinsid(ə)nt‖ˈɪnsɪd(ə)nt/ *n* **1** an occurrence of an action or situation that is a separate unit of experience **2** an occurrence that is a cause of conflict or disagreement <*a serious border* ~> **3** an event occurring as part of a series or as dependent on or subordinate to sthg else

[2]**incident** *adj* **1** that is a usual accompaniment or consequence <*the confusion* ~ *to moving house*> **2** dependent on another thing in law **3** falling or striking on sthg <~ *light rays*>

[1]**incidental** /ˌinsiˈdentl‖ˌɪnsɪˈdentl/ *adj* **1** occurring merely by chance **2** likely to ensue as a chance or minor consequence

[2]**incidental** *n* **1** sthg incidental **2** *pl* minor items (e g of expenses)

incidentally /ˌinsiˈdentl·i‖ˌɪnsɪˈdentlɪ/ *adv* **1** by chance **2** BY THE WAY

incidental music *n* descriptive music played during a play to project a mood or to accompany stage action

incinerate /inˈsinərayt‖ɪnˈsɪnəreɪt/ *vt* to cause to burn to ashes – **incineration** *n*

incinerator /inˈsinəraytə‖ɪnˈsɪnəreɪtə/ *n* a furnace or container for incinerating waste materials

incipient /inˈsipi·ənt‖ɪnˈsɪpɪənt/ *adj* beginning to come into being or to become apparent – **incipience, incipiency** *n*, **incipiently** *adv*

incise /inˈsiez‖ɪnˈsaɪz/ *vt* **1** to cut into **2a** to carve letters, figures, etc into; engrave **b** to carve (e g an inscription) into a surface

incision /inˈsizh(ə)n‖ɪnˈsɪʒ(ə)n/ *n* **1a** a (marginal) notch **b** a cut or gash; *specif* one made, esp in surgery, into the body **2** an incising

incisive /inˈsiesiv‖ɪnˈsaɪsɪv/ *adj* impressively direct and decisive (e g in manner or presentation) – **incisively** *adv*, **incisiveness** *n*

incisor /inˈsiezə‖ɪnˈsaɪzə/ *n* a cutting tooth; *specif* any of the cutting teeth in mammals in front of the canines

incite /inˈsiet‖ɪnˈsaɪt/ *vt* to move to action; stir up – **inciter** *n*, **incitement, incitation** *n*

incivility /ˌinsiˈviləti‖ˌɪnsɪˈvɪlətɪ/ *n* **1** being uncivil **2** a rude or discourteous act

inclement /inˈklemənt‖ɪnˈklemənt/ *adj* physically severe; stormy – **inclemency** *n*, **inclemently** *adv*

inclination /ˌinkliˈnaysh(ə)n‖ˌɪnklɪˈneɪʃ(ə)n/ *n* **1a** a bow, nod **b** a tilting of sthg **2** a particular tendency or propensity; *esp* a liking **3a** (the degree of) a deviation from the vertical or horizontal **b** a slope **c** the angle between 2 lines or planes <*the* ~ *of 2 rays of light*> – **inclinational** *adj*

[1]**incline** /inˈklien‖ɪnˈklaɪn/ *vb* **1** to (cause to) lean, tend, or become drawn towards an opinion or course of conduct **2** to (cause to) deviate or move from a line, direction, or course, esp from the vertical or horizontal

[2]**incline** /ˈinklien‖ˈɪnklaɪn/ *n* an inclined surface; a slope

inclined plane *n* a plane surface that makes an angle with the plane of the horizon

inclose /inˈklohz‖ɪnˈkləʊz/ *vt* to enclose – **inclosure** *n*

include /inˈkloohd‖ɪnˈkluːd/ *vt* **1** to contain, enclose **2** to take in or comprise as a part of a larger group, set, or principle – **includable, includible** *adj*

inclusion /inˈkloohzh(ə)n‖ɪnˈkluːʒ(ə)n/ *n* **1** including or being included **2** sthg included: e g **2a** a gaseous, liquid, or solid foreign body enclosed in a mass, esp a mineral **b** sthg (e g a starch grain) taken up by, or stored within, a living cell

inclusive /inˈkloohsiv, -ziv‖ɪnˈkluːsɪv, -zɪv/ *adj* **1a** broad in orientation or scope **b** covering or intended to cover all or the specified items, costs, or services <~ *of VAT*> **2** including the stated limits or extremes <*Monday to Friday* ~> – **inclusively** *adv*, **inclusiveness** *n*

[1]**incognito** /ˌinkogˈneetoh‖ˌɪnkɒgˈniːtəʊ/ *adv or adj* with one's identity concealed [Italian, fr Latin *incognitus* unknown, fr *in-* not + *cognitus*, past participle of *cognoscere* to know]

[2]**incognito** *n, pl* **incognitos** the state or disguise of one who is incognito

incoherent /ˌinkohˈhiərənt‖ˌɪnkəʊˈhɪərənt/ *adj* lacking in logical connection or clarity of expression; unintelligible – **incoherence, incoherency** *n*, **incoherently** *adv*

incombustible /ˌinkəmˈbustəbl‖ˌɪnkəmˈbʌstəbl/ *adj* incapable of being ignited or burned – **incombustibility** *n*

income /ˈinkum, ˈinkəm‖ˈɪnkʌm, ˈɪnkəm/ *n* **1** a coming in; an input, influx **2** (the amount of) a usu periodic gain or recurrent benefit usu measured in money that derives from one's work, property, or investment

ˈ**income ˌtax** *n* a tax on income

[1]**incoming** /ˈinˌkuming‖ˈɪnˌkʌmɪŋ/ *n* **1** a coming in, arrival **2** *pl* INCOME 2

[2]**incoming** *adj* **1** arriving or coming in <*an* ~ *ship*> **2** just starting, beginning, or succeeding <*the* ~ *president*>

incommensurable /ˌinkəˈmensh(ə)rəbl‖ˌɪnkəˈmenʃ(ə)rəbl/ *adj* lacking a common basis of comparison in respect to a quality normally subject to comparison; incapable of being compared – **incommensurably** *adv*, **incommensurability** *n*

incommensurate /ˌinkəˈmenshərət‖ˌɪnkəˈmenʃərət/ *adj* not adequate (in proportion) – **incommensurately** *adv*

incommode /ˌinkəˈmohd‖ˌɪnkəˈməʊd/ *vt* to inconvenience, trouble – fml

incommodious /ˌinkəˈmohdi·əs‖ˌɪnkə

'məʊdɪəs/ *adj* inconvenient or uncomfortable, esp because of being too small – fml – **incommodiously** *adv*, **incommodiousness** *n*

incommunicado /ˌinkəˌmyoohni'kahdoh‖ˌɪnkəˌmju:nɪ'kɑ:dəʊ/ *adv or adj* without means of communication; *also* in solitary confinement

incomparable /in'komp(ə)rəbl‖ɪn'kɒmp(ə)rəbl/ *adj* **1** matchless **2** not suitable for comparison – **incomparableness** *n*, **incomparably** *adv*, **incomparability** *n*

incompatible /ˌinkəm'patəbl‖ˌɪnkəm'pætəbl/ *adj* **1** (incapable of association because) incongruous, discordant, or disagreeing **2** unsuitable for use together because of undesirable chemical or physiological effects <~ *drugs*> – **incompatibly** *adv*, **incompatibility** *n*

incompetent /in'kompit(ə)nt‖ɪn'kɒmpɪt(ə)nt/ *adj* **1** lacking the qualities needed for effective action **2** not legally qualified <*an* ~ *witness*> **3** inadequate to or unsuitable for a particular purpose – **incompetence, incompetency** *n*, **incompetent** *n*, **incompetently** *adv*

incomplete /ˌinkəm'pleet‖ˌɪnkəm'pli:t/ *adj* **1** unfinished **2** lacking a part – **incompletely** *adv*, **incompleteness** *n*

incomprehensible /ˌinkompri'hensəbl, -ˌ- -'---‖ˌɪnkɒmprɪ'hensəbl,-ˌ--'---/ *adj* impossible to comprehend or understand – **incomprehensibleness** *n*, **incomprehensibly** *adv*, **incomprehensibility** *n*

incomprehension /ˌinkompri'hensh(ə)n‖ˌɪnkɒmprɪ'henʃ(ə)n/ *n* lack of comprehension or understanding

inconceivable /ˌinkən'seevəbl‖ˌɪnkən'si:vəbl/ *adj* **1** beyond comprehension; unimaginable **2** unbelievable – **inconceivableness** *n*, **inconceivably** *adv*, **inconceivability** *n*

inconclusive /ˌinkən'kloohsiv‖ˌɪnkən'klu:sɪv/ *adj* leading to no conclusion or definite result – **inconclusively** *adv*, **inconclusiveness** *n*

incongruous /in'kong·groo·əs‖ɪn'kɒŋgrʊəs/ *adj* out of place; discordant or disagreeing – **incongruously** *adv*, **incongruousness, incongruity** *n*

inconsequent /in'konsikwənt‖ɪn'kɒnsɪkwənt/ *adj* **1** lacking reasonable sequence; illogical **2** irrelevant – **inconsequence** *n*, **inconsequently** *adv*

inconsequential /ˌinkonsi'kwensh(ə)l‖ˌɪnkɒnsɪ'kwenʃ(ə)l/ *adj* **1** irrelevant **2** of no significance – **inconsequentially** *adv*, **inconsequentiality** *n*

inconsiderable /ˌinkən'sid(ə)rəbl‖ˌɪnkən'sɪd(ə)rəbl/ *adj* trivial <*exercised no* ~ *influence*> – **inconsiderableness** *n*, **inconsiderably** *adv*

inconsiderate /ˌinkən'sid(ə)rət‖ˌɪnkən'sɪd(ə)rət/ *adj* careless of the rights or feelings of others; thoughtless – **inconsiderately** *adv*, **inconsiderateness, inconsideration** *n*

inconsistent /ˌinkən'sist(ə)nt‖ˌɪnkən'sɪst(ə)nt/ *adj* **1** not compatible; containing incompatible elements <*an* ~ *argument*> **2** not consistent or logical in thought or actions – **inconsistency, inconsistence** *n*, **inconsistently** *adv*

inconsolable /ˌinkən'sohləbl‖ˌɪnkən'səʊləbl/ *adj* incapable of being consoled; brokenhearted – **inconsolably** *adv*

ˌincon'spicuous /ˌinkən'spikyoo·əs‖ˌɪnkən'spɪkjʊəs/ *adj* not readily noticeable – **inconspicuously** *adv*, **inconspicuousness** *n*

inconstant /in'konst(ə)nt‖ɪn'kɒnst(ə)nt/ *adj* **1** likely to change frequently without apparent reason **2** unfaithful <*an* ~ *lover*> – **inconstancy** *n*, **inconstantly** *adv*

incontestable /ˌinkən'testəbl‖ˌɪnkən'testəbl/ *adj* not contestable; unquestionable – **incontestably** *adv*, **incontestability** *n*

incontinent /in'kontinənt‖ɪn'kɒntɪnənt/ *adj* **1** lacking self-restraint (e g in sexual appetite) **2** suffering from lack of control of urination or defecation **3** not under control or restraint – **incontinence** *n*, **incontinently** *adv*

incontrovertible /ˌinkontrə'vuhtəbl, inˌkon-‖ˌɪnkɒntrə'vɜ:təbl, ɪnˌkɒn-/ *adj* indisputable – **incontrovertibly** *adv*

inconvenience /ˌinkən'veenyəns, -ni·əns‖ˌɪnkən'vi:njəns, -nɪəns/ *vt or n* (to subject to) difficulty or discomfort or sthg that is inconvenient

inconvenient /ˌinkən'veenyənt, -ni·ənt‖ˌɪnkən'vi:njənt, -nɪənt/ *adj* not convenient, esp in causing difficulty, discomfort, or annoyance – **inconveniently** *adv*

incorporate /in'kawpərayt‖ɪn'kɔ:pəreɪt/ *vt* **1a** to unite thoroughly with or work indistinguishably into sthg **b** to admit to membership in a corporate body **2a** to combine thoroughly to form a consistent whole **b** to form into a legal corporation ~ *vi* **1** to unite in or as 1 body **2** to form a legal corporation – **incorporator** *n*, **incorporable** *adj*, **incorporation** *n*

in'corporated *also* **incorporate** *adj* **1** united in 1 body **2** formed into a legal corporation

incorporeal /ˌinkaw'pawri·əl‖ˌɪnkɔ:'pɔ:rɪəl/ *adj* **1** having no material body or form **2** based upon property (e g bonds or patents) which has no intrinsic value – **incorporeally** *adv*, **incorporeity** *n*

incorrect /ˌinkə'rekt‖ˌɪnkə'rekt/ *adj* **1** inaccurate; factually wrong **2** not in accordance with an established norm; improper – **incorrectly** *adv*, **incorrectness** *n*

incorrigible /in'korijəbl‖ɪn'kɒrɪdʒəbl/ *adj* **1** incapable of being corrected or amended; *esp* incurably bad **2** unwilling or unlikely to change – **incorrigibly** *adv*, **incorrigibility** *also* **incorrigibleness** *n*

incorruptible /ˌinkə'ruptəbl‖ˌɪnkə'rʌptəbl/ *adj* **1** not subject to decay or dissolution **2** incapable of being bribed or morally corrupted – **incorruptibly** *adv*, **incorruptibility** *n*

[1]**increase** /in'krees‖ɪn'kri:s/ *vi* **1** to become progressively greater (e g in size, amount, quality, number, or intensity) **2** to multiply by the production of young ~*vt* to make greater – **increasable** *adj*, **increasingly** *adv*

[2]**increase** /'inkrees‖'ɪnkri:s/ *n* **1** (an) addition or enlargement in size, extent, quantity, etc **2** sthg (e g offspring, produce, or profit) added to an original stock by addition or growth

incredible /in'kredəbl‖ɪn'kredəbl/ *adj* **1** too extraordinary and improbable to be believed; *also* hard to believe **2** – used as a generalized term of approval – **incredibly** *adv*, **incredibility** *n*

incredulous /in'kredyooləs‖ɪn'kredjʊləs/ *adj* **1** unwilling to admit or accept what is offered as true **2** expressing disbelief –

incredulously *adv*, **incredulity** *n*

increment /'ingkrimənt, in-‖'ɪŋkrɪmənt, ɪn-/ *n* **1** (the amount of) an increase, esp in quantity or value **2a** any of a series of regular consecutive additions **b** a minute increase in the value of a variable (e g velocity) **3** a regular increase in pay resulting from an additional year's service – **incremental** *adj*, **incrementally** *adv*

incriminate /in'kriminayt‖ɪn'krɪmɪneɪt/ *vt* to involve in or demonstrate involvement in a crime or fault – **incriminatory** *adj*, **incrimination** *n*

incrust /in'krust‖ɪn'krʌst/ *vb* to encrust

incrustation /,inkru'staysh(ə)n‖,ɪnkrʌ'steɪʃ(ə)n/ *n* **1** encrusting or being encrusted **2** (a growth or accumulation resembling) a crust or hard coating

incubate /'ingkyoobayt, 'in-‖'ɪŋkjʊbeɪt, 'ɪn-/ *vt* **1** to sit on so as to hatch (eggs) by the warmth of the body; *also* to maintain (e g an embryo or a chemically active system) under conditions favourable for hatching, development, or reaction **2** to cause (e g an idea) to develop ~ *vi* **1** to sit on eggs **2** to undergo incubation – **incubative, incubatory** *adj*

incubation /,ingkyoo'baysh(ə)n, ,in-‖,ɪŋkjʊ'beɪʃ(ə)n, ,ɪn-/ *n* **1** incubating **2** the period between infection by a disease-causing agent and the manifestation of the disease

incubator /'ingkyoo,baytə, 'in-‖'ɪŋkjʊ,beɪtə, 'ɪn-/ *n* **1** an apparatus in which eggs are hatched artificially **2** an apparatus that maintains controlled conditions, esp for the housing of premature or sick babies or the cultivation of microorganisms

incubus /'ingkyoobəs, 'in-‖'ɪŋkjʊbəs, 'ɪn-/ *n*, *pl* **incubuses, incubi** /-,bie‖-,baɪ/ **1** a male demon believed to have sexual intercourse with women in their sleep **2** (one who or that which oppresses or burdens like) a nightmare

inculcate /'inkulkayt‖'ɪnkʌlkeɪt/ *vt* to teach or instil by frequent repetition or warning [Latin *inculcare*, lit., to tread on, fr *in-* in + *calcare* to trample, fr *calc-*, *calx* heel] – **inculcator** *n*, **inculcation** *n*

inculpate /'inkulpayt‖'ɪnkʌlpeɪt/ *vt* to incriminate – **inculpatory** *adj*, **inculpation** *n*

incumbency /in'kumb(ə)nsi‖ɪn'kʌmb(ə)nsɪ/ *n* the sphere of action or period of office of an incumbent

[1]incumbent /in'kumb(ə)nt‖ɪn'kʌmb(ə)nt/ *n* the holder of an office or Anglican benefice

[2]incumbent *adj* **1** imposed as a duty or obligation – usu + *on* or *upon* **2** occupying a specified office <*the* ~ *caretaker*>

incur /in'kuh‖ɪn'kɜː/ *vt* **-rr-** to become liable or subject to; bring upon oneself <*she* ~red *several debts*> – **incurrable** *adj*, **incurrence** *n*

incurable *adj*

incurious /in'kyooəri·əs‖ɪn'kjʊərɪəs/ *adj* lacking a normal or usual curiosity – **incuriously** *adv*, **incuriosity** *n*

incursion /in'kuhsh(ə)n‖ɪn'kɜːʃ(ə)n/ *n* an unexpected or sudden usu brief invasion or entrance, esp into another's territory – **incursive** *adj*

incus /'ingkəs‖'ɪŋkəs/ *n*, *pl* **incudes** /in'kyoohdeez‖ɪn'kjuːdiːz/ the middle bone of a chain of 3 small bones in the ear of a mammal; the anvil

Ind-, Indo- *comb form* Indian <Indo-*British*>; Indian and <Indo-*African*>

indebted /in'detid‖ɪn'detɪd/ *adj* **1** owing money **2** owing gratitude or recognition to another – **indebtedness** *n*

in'decent /in'dees(ə)nt‖ɪn'diːs(ə)nt/ *adj* **1** hardly suitable; unseemly **2** morally offensive – **indecency** *n*, **indecently** *adv*

indecent assault *n* a sexual assault exclusive of rape

indecent exposure *n* intentional public exposure of part of one's body (e g the genitals) in violation of generally accepted standards of decency

indecision /,indi'sizh(ə)n‖,ɪndɪ'sɪʒ(ə)n/ *n* a wavering between 2 or more possible courses of action

indecisive /,indi'siesiv‖,ɪndɪ'saɪsɪv/ *adj* **1** giving an uncertain result <*an* ~ *battle*> **2** marked by or prone to indecision – **indecisively** *adv*, **indecisiveness** *n*

indecorous *adj*

indecorum /,indi'kawrəm‖,ɪndɪ'kɔːrəm/ *n* impropriety

indeed /in'deed‖ɪn'diːd/ *adv* **1** without any question; truly <*it is* ~ *remarkable*> – often used in agreement <~ *I will*> **2** – used for emphasis after *very* and an adjective or adverb <*very cold* ~> **3** in point of fact; actually <*I don't mind;* ~, *I'm pleased*> **4** – expressing irony, disbelief, or surprise <*'she wants to marry him.'* 'Indeed?' *'Does she* ~*!'*>

indefatigable /,indi'fatigəbl‖,ɪndɪ'fætɪgəbl/ *adj* tireless – **indefatigably** *adv*, **indefatigability** *n*

,inde'fensible /-di'fensəbl‖-dɪ'fensəbl/ *adj* incapable of being defended or justified – **indefensibly** *adv*, **indefensibility** *n*

,inde'finable /-di'fienəbl‖-dɪ'faɪnəbl/ *adj* incapable of being precisely described or analysed – **indefinable** *n*, **indefinably** *adv*

in'definite /-'definət‖-'defɪnət/ *adj* **1** designating an unidentified or not immediately identifiable person or thing <*the* ~ *articles* a *and* an> **2** not precise; vague **3** having no exact limits – **indefinite** *n*, **indefinitely** *adv*, **indefiniteness** *n*

indelible /in'deləbl‖ɪn'deləbl/ *adj* (making marks difficult to remove or) incapable of being removed or erased [Latin *indelebilis*, fr *in-* not + *delēre* to destroy, delete] – **indelibly** *adv*, **indelibility** *n*

indelicate /in'delikət‖ɪn'delɪkət/ *adj* offensive to good manners or refined taste – **indelicacy** *n*, **indelicately** *adv*

indemnify /in'demnifie‖ɪn'demnɪfaɪ/ *vt* **1** to secure against harm, loss, or damage **2** to make compensation to for incurred harm, loss, or damage – **indemnification** *n*

indemnity /in'demnəti‖ɪn'demnətɪ/ *n* security against harm, loss, or damage

[1]indent /in'dent‖ɪn'dent/ *vt* **1a** to cut or divide (a document) to produce sections with edges that can be matched for authentication **b** to draw up (e g a deed) in 2 or more exact copies **2** to notch the edge of **3** to set (e g a line of a paragraph) in from the margin **4** *chiefly Br* to requisition officially ~ *vi* **1** to form an indentation **2** *chiefly Br* to make out an official requisition – **indenter** *n*

[2]**indent** /ˈindent‖ˈɪndent/ *n* **1** an indenture **2** an indention **3** *chiefly Br* an official requisition
[3]**indent** /-ˈ-/ *vt* (to force inwards so as) to form a depression in – **indenter** *n*
[4]**indent** /ˈ--/ *n* (an) indentation
indentation /ˌindenˈtaysh(ə)n‖ˌɪndenˈteɪʃ(ə)n/ *n* **1a** an angular cut in an edge **b** a usu deep recess (e g in a coastline) **2** indention
indention /inˈdensh(ə)n‖ɪnˈdenʃ(ə)n/ *n* **1** indenting or being indented **2** the blank space produced by indenting
[1]**indenture** /inˈdenchə‖ɪnˈdentʃə/ *n* **1a** an indented document **b** a contract binding sby to work for another – usu pl with sing. meaning **2a** a formal certificate (e g an inventory or voucher) prepared for purposes of control **b** a document stating the terms under which a security (e g a bond) is issued
[2]**indenture** *vt* to bind (e g an apprentice) by indentures
independence /ˌindiˈpend(ə)ns‖ˌɪndɪˈpend(ə)ns/ *n* being independent
Independence Day *n* a day set aside for public celebration of the achievement of national independence; *esp* the public holiday observed in the USA on July 4 commemorating the Declaration of Independence in 1776
[1]**independent** /ˌindiˈpend(ə)nt‖ˌɪndɪˈpend(ə)nt/ *adj* **1** not dependent: e g **1a(1)** self-governing **a(2)** not affiliated with a larger controlling unit **b(1)** not relying on sthg else *<an ~ conclusion>* **b(2)** not committed to a political party **c(1)** not requiring or relying on, or allowing oneself to be controlled by, others (e g for guidance or care) **c(2)** having or providing enough money to live on, esp without working *<a woman of ~ means>* **2a** MAIN 4 *<the ~ clause>* **b** neither deducible from nor incompatible with another statement *<~ postulates>* – **independently** *adv*
[2]**independent** *n, often cap* sby not bound by a political party
indescribable /ˌindiˈskriebəbl‖ˌɪndɪˈskraɪbəbl/ *adj* **1** that cannot be described *<an ~ sensation>* **2** surpassing description *<~ joy>* – **indescribably** *adv*
indestructible *adj*
indeterminable /ˌindiˈtuhminəbl‖ˌɪndɪˈtɜːmɪnəbl/ *adj* incapable of being definitely decided or ascertained
indeterminate /ˌindiˈtuhminət‖ˌɪndɪˈtɜːmɪnət/ *adj* **1** not definitely or precisely determined or fixed **2** having an infinite number of solutions *<a system of ~ equations>* – **indeterminacy** *n*, **indeterminately** *adv*, **indeterminateness, indetermination** *n*
[1]**index** /ˈindeks‖ˈɪndeks/ *n, pl* **indexes, indices** /ˈindiseez‖ˈɪndɪsiːz/, *(4) usu* **indices** **1** a guide or list to aid reference: e g **1a** an alphabetical list of items (e g topics or names) treated in a printed work that gives with each item the page number where it appears **b** CARD INDEX **2** sthg that points towards or demonstrates a particular state of affairs *<the fertility of the land is an ~ of the country's wealth>* **3** a list of restricted or prohibited material; *specif, cap the* list of books banned by the Roman Catholic church **4** a mathematical figure, letter, or expression; *esp* an exponent **5** a character **6** a number derived from a series of observations and used as an indicator or measure (e g of change in prices)
[2]**index** *vt* **1** to provide with or list in an index **2** to serve as an index of **3** to cause to be index-linked ~*vi* to prepare an index – **indexer** *n*
ˈ**index** ˌ**finger** *n* the forefinger
Indian /ˈindi·ən‖ˈɪndɪən/ *n* **1** a native or inhabitant of India **2a** a member of any of the indigenous peoples of N, Central, or S America excluding the Eskimos **b** any of the native languages of American Indians – **Indian** *adj*
Indian club *n* a club shaped like a large bottle that is swung for gymnastic exercise
Indian corn *n, chiefly NAm* maize
ˈ**Indian** ˌ**file** *n* SINGLE FILE
Indian hemp *n* HEMP 1
ˌ**indian** ˈ**ink** *n, often cap 1st I, Br* (an ink made from) a solid black pigment used in drawing and lettering
ˌ**Indian** ˈ**summer** *n* **1** a period of warm weather in late autumn or early winter **2** a happy or flourishing period occurring towards the end of sthg, esp of a person's life
ˌ**india** ˈ**rubber** *n, often cap I* [1]RUBBER 1b
indicate /ˈindikayt‖ˈɪndɪkeɪt/ *vt* **1a(1)** to point to; point out **a(2)** to show or demonstrate as or by means of a sign or pointer **b** to be a sign or symptom of **c** to demonstrate or suggest the necessity or advisability of – chiefly pass **2** to state or express briefly; suggest
indication /ˌindiˈkaysh(ə)n‖ˌɪndɪˈkeɪʃ(ə)n/ *n* **1** the action of indicating **2a** sthg (e g a sign or suggestion) that serves to indicate **b** sthg indicated as advisable or necessary **3** the degree indicated on a graduated instrument
[1]**indicative** /inˈdikətiv‖ɪnˈdɪkətɪv/ *adj* **1** of or constituting the grammatical mood that represents the denoted act or state as an objective fact **2** serving to indicate *<actions ~ of fear>* – **indicatively** *adv*
[2]**indicative** *n* the indicative mood; *also* a verb form expressing it
indicator /ˈindikaytə‖ˈɪndɪkeɪtə/ *n* **1a** a hand or needle on an instrument (e g a dial) **b** an instrument for giving visual readings attached to a machine or apparatus **c** a device (e g a flashing light) on a vehicle that indicates an intention to change direction **2a** a substance (e g litmus) that shows, esp by change of colour, the condition (e g acidity or alkalinity) of a solution **b** TRACER 2 **3** a statistic (e g the level of industrial production) that gives an indication of the state of a national economy – **indicatory** *adj*
indices /ˈindiseez‖ˈɪndɪsiːz/ *pl of* INDEX
indict /inˈdiet‖ɪnˈdaɪt/ *vt* **1** to charge with an offence **2** to charge with a crime – **indicter, indictor** *n*
indictable /inˈdietəbl‖ɪnˈdaɪtəbl/ *adj* (making one) liable to indictment
indictment /inˈdietmənt‖ɪnˈdaɪtmənt/ *n* **1** indicting **2** a formal written accusation by a prosecuting authority **3** grounds for severe censure; condemnation – usu + *of* *<a searing ~ of contemporary society>*
indifferent /inˈdifrənt‖ɪnˈdɪfrənt/ *adj* **1** that does not matter one way or the other **2** not

interested in or concerned about sthg <*completely ~ to the outcome*> **3a** neither good nor bad; mediocre <*does ~ work at the office*> **b** not very good; inferior <*a very ~ wine*> **4** chemically, magnetically, etc neutral – **indifferently** *adv*, **indifference** *n*

indigenous /in'dij(ə)nəs‖ɪn'dɪdʒ(ə)nəs/ *adj* **1** originating, growing, or living naturally in a particular region or environment **2** innate, inborn – **indigenously** *adv*, **indigenize** *vt*

indigent /'indij(ə)nt‖'ɪndɪdʒ(ə)nt/ *adj* needy, poor – fml – **indigence** *n*, **indigent** *n*

indigestible /ˌindi'jestəbl‖ˌɪndɪ'dʒestəbl/ *adj* not (easily) digested – **indigestibility** *n*

indigestion /ˌindi'jeschən‖ˌɪndɪ'dʒestʃən/ *n* (pain in the digestive system usu resulting from) difficulty in digesting sthg

indignant /in'dignənt‖ɪn'dɪgnənt/ *adj* filled with or marked by indignation – **indignantly** *adv*

indignation /ˌindig'naysh(ə)n‖ˌɪndɪg'neɪʃ(ə)n/ *n* anger aroused by sthg judged unjust, unworthy, or mean

indignity /in'dignəti‖ɪn'dɪgnətɪ/ *n* **1** an act that offends against a person's dignity or self-respect **2** humiliating treatment

indigo /'indigoh‖'ɪndɪgəʊ/ *n, pl* **indigos, indigoes** **1** (any of several dyes related to) a blue dye with a coppery lustre formerly obtained from a plant and now made artificially **2** a dark greyish blue colour whose hue lies between violet and blue in the spectrum **3** a (leguminous) plant that yields indigo [Italian dialect, fr Latin *indicum*, fr Greek *indikon*, fr *indikos* Indian]

indirect /ˌindi'rekt, -die-‖ˌɪndɪ'rekt, -daɪ-/ *adj* **1a** deviating from a direct line or course **b** not going straight to the point **2** not straightforward or open **3** not directly aimed at <*~ consequences*> **4** stating what a real or supposed original speaker said but with changes of tense, person, etc <*~ speech*> – **indirectly** *adv*, **indirectness** *n*

indirect object *n* a grammatical object representing the secondary goal of the action of its verb (e g *her* in *I gave her the book*)

indiscernible /ˌindi'suhnəbl‖ˌɪndɪ'sɜːnəbl/ *adj* **1** that cannot be perceived or recognized **2** not recognizable as separate or distinct

indiscipline /in'disiplin‖ɪn'dɪsɪplɪn/ *n* lack of discipline – **indisciplined** *adj*

indiscreet /ˌindi'skreet‖ˌɪndɪ'skriːt/ *adj* not discreet; imprudent – **indiscreetly** *adv*

ˌindiˈscretion /-di'skresh(ə)n‖-dɪ'skreʃ(ə)n/ *n* (an act or remark showing) lack of discretion

ˌindiˈscriminate /-di'skriminət‖-dɪ'skrɪmɪnət/ *adj* **1** not marked by careful distinction; lacking in discrimination and discernment **2** not differentiated; confused – **indiscriminately** *adv*, **indiscriminateness** *n*

ˌindiˈspensable /-di'spensəbl‖-dɪ'spensəbl/ *adj* that cannot be done without – **indispensable** *n*, **indispensableness** *n*, **indispensably** *adv*, **indispensability** *n*

ˌindiˈsposed *adj* **1** slightly ill **2** averse

ˌindispoˈsition /-dispə'zish(ə)n‖-dɪspə'zɪʃ(ə)n/ *n* **1** disinclination **2** (a) slight illness

ˌindiˈsputable /-di'spyoohtəbl‖-dɪ'spjuːtəbl/ *adj* incontestable – **indisputableness** *n*, **indisputably** *adv*

ˌindisˈsoluble /-di'solyoobl‖-dɪ'sɒljʊbl/ *adj* incapable of being dissolved, decomposed, undone, or annulled – **indissolubility** *n*, **indissolubly** *adv*

ˌindiˈstinct /-di'stingkt‖-dɪ'stɪŋkt/ *adj* not distinct: e g **a** not sharply outlined or separable; not clearly seen **b** not clearly recognizable or understandable – **indistinctly** *adv*, **indistinctness** *n*

ˌindiˈstinguishable /-di'sting·gwishəbl‖-dɪ'stɪŋgwɪʃəbl/ *adj* incapable of being **a** clearly perceived **b** discriminated – **indistinguishably** *adv*

[1]**individual** /ˌindi'vidyooəl, -jəl‖ˌɪndɪ'vɪdjʊəl, -dʒəl/ *adj* **1a** of or being an individual **b** intended for 1 person <*an ~ serving*> **2** existing as a distinct entity; separate **3** having marked individuality <*an ~ style*> – **individually** *adv*

[2]**individual** *n* **1** a particular person, being, or thing (as distinguished from a class, species, or collection) **2** a person <*an odd ~*>

individualism /ˌindi'vidyooəˌliz(ə)m, -jəliz(ə)m‖ˌɪndɪ'vɪdjʊəˌlɪz(ə)m, -dʒəlɪz(ə)m/ *n* (conduct guided by) **a** a doctrine that bases morality on the interests of the individual **b** a theory maintaining the independence of the individual and stressing individual initiative

individualist /ˌindi'vidyooəˌlist‖ˌɪndɪ'vɪdjʊəˌlɪst/ *n* one who shows great individuality or independence in thought or behaviour – **individualist, individualistic** *adj*

individuality /ˌindividyoo'aləti, -joo-‖ˌɪndɪvɪdjʊ'ælətɪ, -dʒʊ-/ *n* **1** the total character peculiar to and distinguishing an individual from others **2** the tendency to pursue one's course with marked independence or self-reliance

individual·ize, -ise /ˌindi'vidyooəˌliez, -jəliez‖ˌɪndɪ'vɪdjʊəˌlaɪz, -dʒəlaɪz/ *vt* **1** to make individual in character **2** to treat or notice individually **3** to adjust or adapt to suit a particular individual – **individualization** *n*

indivisible *adj*

Indo- – see IND-

indoctrinate /in'doktrinayt‖ɪn'dɒktrɪneɪt/ *vt* to imbue with a usu partisan or sectarian opinion, point of view, or ideology – **indoctrinator** *n*, **indoctrination** *n*

ˌIndo-Euroˈpean *adj or n* (of or belonging to) a family of languages spoken in most of Europe, Asia as far east as N India, and N and S America

indolent /'indələnt‖'ɪndələnt/ *adj* **1a** causing little or no pain **b** slow to develop or heal <*an ~ ulcer*> **2a** averse to activity, effort, or movement **b** conducive to or exhibiting laziness – **indolence** *n*, **indolently** *adv*

indomitable /in'domitəbl‖ɪn'dɒmɪtəbl/ *adj* incapable of being subdued – **indomitably** *adv*, **indomitability** *n*

Indonesian /ˌində'neezh(ə)n, -zyən‖ˌɪndə'niːʒ(ə)n, -zjən/ *n* **1** a native or inhabitant of Indonesia or the Malay archipelago **2** the official language of Indonesia – **Indonesian** *adj*

indoor /in'daw‖ɪn'dɔː/ *adj* **1** of the interior of a building **2** done, living, or belonging indoors <*an ~ sport*>

indoors /in'dawz‖ɪn'dɔːz/ *adv* in or into a building

indorse /in'daws‖ɪn'dɔːs/ *vt* to endorse

indrawn /in'drawn‖ɪn'drɔːn/ *adj* **1** drawn in

2 aloof, reserved

indubitable /in'dyoohbitəbl‖ɪn'dju:bɪtəbl/ *adj* too evident to be doubted – **indubitably** *adv*, **indubitability** *n*

induce /in'dyoohs‖ɪn'dju:s/ *vt* **1** to lead on to do sthg; move by persuasion or influence **2a** to cause to appear or to happen; BRING ON; *specif* to cause (labour) to begin by the use of drugs **b** to cause the formation of **c** to produce (e g an electric current) by induction **3** to establish by logical induction; *specif* to infer from particulars – **inducer** *n*, **inducible** *adj*

in'ducement /-mənt‖-mənt/ *n* sthg that induces; *esp* a motive or consideration that encourages one to do sthg

induct /in'dukt‖ɪn'dʌkt/ *vt* **1** to place formally in office **2a** to introduce, initiate **b** *NAm* to enrol for military training or service

induction /in'duksh(ə)n‖ɪn'dʌkʃ(ə)n/ *n* **1a** the act or process of inducting (e g into office) **b** an initial experience; an initiation **2** the act or an instance of reasoning from particular premises to a general conclusion; *also* a conclusion reached by such reasoning **3a** the act of causing or bringing on or about **b** the process by which an electrical conductor becomes electrified when near a charged body, by which a magnetizable body becomes magnetized when in a magnetic field or in the magnetic flux set up by a magnetomotive force, or by which an electromotive force is produced in a circuit by varying the magnetic field linked with the circuit **c** the drawing of the fuel-air mixture from the carburettor into the combustion chamber of an internal-combustion engine – **inductive** *adj*

indue /in'dyooh‖ɪn'dju:/ *vt* to endue

indulge /in'dulj‖ɪn'dʌldʒ/ *vt* **1a** to give free rein to (e g a taste) **b** to allow (oneself) to do sthg pleasurable or gratifying **2** to treat with great or excessive leniency, generosity, or consideration ~*vi* to indulge oneself – **indulger** *n*

indulgence /in'dulj(ə)ns‖ɪn'dʌldʒ(ə)ns/ *n* **1** a remission of (part of) the purgatorial atonement for confessed sin in the Roman Catholic church **2** indulging or being indulgent **3** an indulgent act **4** sthg indulged in

indulgent /in'dulj(ə)nt‖ɪn'dʌldʒ(ə)nt/ *adj* indulging or characterized by indulgence – **indulgently** *adv*

industrial /in'dustri·əl‖ɪn'dʌstrɪəl/ *adj* **1** of, involved in, or derived from industry **2** characterized by highly developed industries <*an ~ nation*> **3** used in industry <~ *diamonds*> – **industrially** *adv*

in'dustrial e,state *n* an area, usu at a distance from the centre of a city or town, designed esp for a community of industries and businesses

industrialism /in'dustri·ə,liz(ə)m‖ɪn'dʌstrɪə,lɪz(ə)m/ *n* social organization in which industries, esp large-scale industries, are dominant

industrialist /in'dustri·əlist‖ɪn'dʌstrɪəlɪst/ *n* one who is engaged in the management of an industry

industrial·ize, -ise /in'dustri·ə,liez‖ɪn'dʌstrɪə,laɪz/ *vb* to make or become industrial; introduce industry (to) – **industrialization** *n*

in,dustrial revo'lution *n* a rapid major development of an economy (e g in England in the late 18th c) marked by the general introduction of mechanized techniques and large-scale production

industrious /in'dustri·əs‖ɪn'dʌstrɪəs/ *adj* **1** persistently diligent **2** constantly, regularly, or habitually occupied – **industriously** *adv*, **industriousness** *n*

industry /'indəstri‖'ɪndəstrɪ/ *n* **1** diligence in an employment or pursuit **2a** systematic work, esp for the creation of value **b(1)** a usu specified group of productive or profit-making enterprises <*the car ~*> **b(2)** an organized field of activity regarded in its commercial aspects <*the Shakespeare ~*> **c** manufacturing activity as a whole <*the nation's ~*>

-ine /-ien, -een, -in‖-aɪn, -i:n, -ɪn/ *suffix* (→ *adj*) **1** of or resembling <*equ*ine> **2** made of; like <*crystall*ine>

inebriate /in'eebriayt‖ɪn'i:brɪeɪt/ *vt* to exhilarate or stupefy (as if) by liquor; intoxicate – **inebriant** *adj or n*, **inebriate** *adj or n*, **inebriation, inebriety** *n*

inedible /in'edəbl‖ɪn'edəbl/ *adj* not fit to be eaten

ineffable /in'efəbl‖ɪn'efəbl/ *adj* **1** unutterable **2** not to be uttered; taboo <*the ~ name of Jehovah*> – **ineffably** *adv*

ineffective /,ini'fektiv‖,ɪnɪ'fektɪv/ *adj* **1** not producing an intended effect **2** not capable of performing efficiently or achieving results – **ineffectively** *adv*, **ineffectiveness** *n*

ineffectual /,ini'fektyooəl, -chooəl‖,ɪnɪ'fektjʊəl, -tʃʊəl/ *adj* **1** not producing or not able to give the proper or intended effect **2** unable to get things done; weak in character <*a very ~ person*> – **ineffectually** *adv*, **ineffectualness** *n*

inefficient /,ini'fish(ə)nt‖,ɪnɪ'fɪʃ(ə)nt/ *adj* not producing the effect intended or desired, esp in a capable or economical way – **inefficiency** *n*, **inefficiently** *adv*

inelastic /,ini'lastik‖,ɪnɪ'læstɪk/ *adj* **1** slow to react or respond to changing conditions **2** inflexible, unyielding – **inelasticity** *n*

inelegant /in'eligənt‖ɪn'elɪgənt/ *adj* lacking in refinement, grace, or good taste – **inelegance** *n*, **inelegantly** *adv*

ineligible /in'elijəbl‖ɪn'elɪdʒəbl/ *adj* not qualified or not worthy to be chosen or preferred – **ineligibility** *n*

ineluctable /,ini'luktəbl‖,ɪnɪ'lʌktəbl/ *adj* not to be avoided, changed, or resisted – fml – **ineluctably** *adv*

inept /i'nept‖ɪ'nept/ *adj* **1** not suitable or apt to the time, place, or occasion **2** lacking sense or reason **3** generally incompetent – **ineptitude** *n*, **ineptly** *adv*, **ineptness** *n*

inequality /,ini'kwoləti‖,ɪnɪ'kwɒlətɪ/ *n* **1a** social disparity **b** disparity of distribution or opportunity **2** an instance of being unequal

inequitable /in'ekwitəbl‖ɪn'ekwɪtəbl/ *adj* unfair – **inequitably** *adv*

inequity /in'ekwiti‖ɪn'ekwɪtɪ/ *n* (an instance of) injustice or unfairness

ineradicable /,ini'radikəbl‖,ɪnɪ'rædɪkəbl/ *adj* incapable of being eradicated – **ineradicably** *adv*

inert /i'nuht‖ɪ'nɜ:t/ *adj* **1** lacking the power to move **2** deficient in active (chemical or biological) properties **3** not moving; inactive, indolent

[Latin *inert-, iners* unskilled, idle, fr *in-* not + *art-, ars* skill] – **inertly** *adv*, **inertness** *n*

inertia /i'nuhshə‖ɪ'nɜːʃə/ *n* **1** a property of matter by which it remains at rest or in uniform motion in the same straight line unless acted on by some external force **2** indisposition to motion, exertion, or change – **inertial** *adj*, **inertially** *adv*

inescapable /ˌini'skaypəbl‖ˌɪnɪ'skeɪpəbl/ *adj* unavoidable – **inescapably** *adv*

inessential /ˌini'sensh(ə)l‖ˌɪnɪ'senʃ(ə)l/ *n or adj* (sthg) that is not essential

inestimable /in'estiməbl‖ɪn'estɪməbl/ *adj* **1** too great to be estimated **2** too valuable or excellent to be measured – **inestimably** *adv*

inevitable /in'evitəbl‖ɪn'evɪtəbl/ *adj* incapable of being avoided or evaded; bound to happen or to confront one – **inevitableness** *n*, **inevitably** *adv*, **inevitability** *n*

inexact /ˌinig'zakt‖ˌɪnɪg'zækt/ *adj* not precisely correct or true – **inexactitude** *n*, **inexactly** *adv*, **inexactness** *n*

inexcusable /ˌiniks'kyoohzəbl‖ˌɪnɪks'kjuːzəbl/ *adj* without excuse or justification – **inexcusableness** *n*, **inexcusably** *adv*

inexhaustible /ˌinig'zawstəbl‖ˌɪnɪg'zɔːstəbl/ *adj* incapable of being used up or worn out – **inexhaustibly** *adv*, **inexhaustibility** *n*

inexorable /in'eks(ə)rəbl‖ɪn'eks(ə)rəbl/ *adj* **1** not to be persuaded or moved by entreaty **2** continuing inevitably; that cannot be averted – **inexorably** *adv*, **inexorability** *n*

inexpedient *adj*

inexpensive /ˌinik'spensiv‖ˌɪnɪk'spensɪv/ *adj* reasonable in price; cheap – **inexpensively** *adv*, **inexpensiveness** *n*

inexperience /ˌinik'spiəri·əns‖ˌɪnɪk'spɪərɪəns/ *n* **1** lack of (the skill gained from) experience **2** lack of knowledge of the ways of the world – **inexperienced** *adj*

inexpert /in'ekspuht‖ɪn'ekspɜːt/ *adj* unskilled – **inexpertly** *adv*, **inexpertness** *n*

inexplicable /ˌinik'splikəbl, in'eksplikəbl‖ˌɪnɪk'splɪkəbl, ɪn'eksplɪkəbl/ *adj* incapable of being explained, interpreted, or accounted for – **inexplicableness** *n*, **inexplicably** *adv*, **inexplicability** *n*

inexpressible /ˌinik'spresəbl‖ˌɪnɪk'spresəbl/ *adj* beyond one's power to express – **inexpressibly** *adv*, **inexpressibility** *n*

inextinguishable /ˌinik'sting·gwishəbl‖ˌɪnɪk'stɪŋgwɪʃəbl/ *adj* unquenchable – **inextinguishably** *adv*

in extremis /ˌin ik'streemis‖ˌɪn ɪk'striːmɪs/ *adv* in extreme circumstances; *esp* at the point of death

inextricable /in'ekstrikəbl‖ɪn'ekstrɪkəbl/ *adj* **1** from which one cannot extricate oneself **2** incapable of being disentangled or untied <*an* ~ *knot*> – **inextricably** *adv*

infallible /in'faləbl‖ɪn'fæləbl/ *adj* **1** incapable of error; *esp, of the Pope* incapable of error in defining dogma **2** not liable to fail – **infallibly** *adv*, **infallibility** *n*

infamous /'infəməs‖'ɪnfəməs/ *adj* **1** having a reputation of the worst kind; notorious **2** disgraceful – **infamously** *adv*

infamy /'infəmi‖'ɪnfəmɪ/ *n* **1** evil reputation brought about by sthg grossly criminal, shocking, or brutal **2** an extreme and publicly known criminal or evil act

infancy /'inf(ə)nsi‖'ɪnf(ə)nsɪ/ *n* **1** early childhood **2** a beginning or early period of existence <*when sociology was in its* ~> **3** the legal status of an infant

[1]**infant** /'inf(ə)nt‖'ɪnf(ə)nt/ *n* **1** a child in the first period of life **2** a minor [Latin *infant-, infans*, fr *infant-, infans* incapable of speech, young, fr *in-* not + *fari* to speak]

[2]**infant** *adj* **1** in an early stage of development **2** concerned with or intended for young children, esp those aged from 5 to 7 or 8 <*an* ~ *teacher*>

infanticide /in'fantisied‖ɪn'fæntɪsaɪd/ *n* (the act of) sby who kills an infant

infantile /'inf(ə)ntiel‖'ɪnf(ə)ntaɪl/ *adj* (suggestive) of infants or infancy <~ *behaviour*>

infantile paralysis *n* poliomyelitis

infantry /'inf(ə)ntri‖'ɪnf(ə)ntrɪ/ *n sing or pl in constr* (a branch of an army containing) soldiers trained, armed, and equipped to fight on foot [Middle French *infanterie*, fr Italian *infanteria*, fr *infante* boy, foot soldier, fr Latin *infant-, infans* infant]

'infantryman /-mən‖-mən/ *n* an infantry soldier

'infant ˌschool *n, Br* a kindergarten for children aged from 5 to 7 or 8

infatuate /in'fatyooayt‖ɪn'fætjʊeɪt/ *vt* **1** to affect with folly **2** to inspire with powerful but superficial or short-lived feelings of love and desire – **infatuated** *adj*, **infatuation** *n*

infect /in'fekt‖ɪn'fekt/ *vt* **1** to contaminate (e g air or food) with a disease-causing agent **2a** to pass on a disease or a disease-causing agent to **b** to invade (an individual or organ), usu by penetration – used with reference to a pathogenic organism **3** to transmit or pass on sthg (e g an emotion) to – **infector** *n*

infection /in'feksh(ə)n‖ɪn'fekʃ(ə)n/ *n* **1** infecting **2** (an agent that causes) a contagious or infectious disease **3** the communication of emotions or qualities through example or contact

infectious /in'fekshəs‖ɪn'fekʃəs/ *adj* **1a infectious, infective** capable of causing infection **b** communicable by infection **2** readily spread or communicated to others <~ *excitement*> – **infectiously** *adv*, **infectiousness** *n*

infectious hepatitis *n* a highly infectious liver inflammation caused by a virus

infectious mononucleosis *n* an acute infectious disease characterized by fever and swelling of lymph glands

infelicitous /ˌinfə'lisitəs‖ˌɪnfə'lɪsɪtəs/ *adj* not apt; not suitably chosen for the occasion – **infelicitously** *adv*

infer /in'fuh‖ɪn'fɜː/ *vb* **-rr-** *vt* **1** to derive as a conclusion from facts or premises **2** to suggest, imply – disapproved of by some speakers ~*vi* to draw inferences – **inferable** *adj*

inference /'inf(ə)rəns‖'ɪnf(ə)rəns/ *n* **1a** the act of inferring **b** the act of passing from statistical sample data to generalizations (e g of the value of population parameters), usu with calculated degrees of certainty **2** sthg inferred; *esp* a proposition arrived at by inference

inferential /ˌinfəˈrensh(ə)l‖ˌɪnfəˈrenʃ(ə)l/ *adj* deduced or deducible by inference

inferior /inˈfiəri·ə‖ɪnˈfɪərɪə/ *adj* **1** situated lower down **2** of low or lower degree or rank **3** of little or less importance, value, or merit **4** *of a planet* nearer the sun than the earth is – **inferior** *n*, **inferiorly** *adv*, **inferiority** *n*

inferiˈority ˌcomplex *n* a sense of personal inferiority often resulting either in timidity or, through overcompensation, in exaggerated aggressiveness

infernal /inˈfuhnl‖ɪnˈfɜːnl/ *adj* **1** of hell **2** hellish, diabolical **3** damned – infml <*an* ~ *nuisance*> – **infernally** *adv*

inferno /inˈfuhnoh‖ɪnˈfɜːnəʊ/ *n, pl* **infernos** a place or a state that resembles or suggests hell, esp in intense heat or raging fire

infertile /inˈfuhtiel‖ɪnˈfɜːtaɪl/ *adj* not fertile or productive – **infertility** *n*

infest /inˈfest‖ɪnˈfest/ *vt* **1** to spread or swarm in or over in a troublesome manner <*shark*-infested *waters*> **2** to live in or on as a parasite – **infestation** *n*

infidel /ˈinfidl‖ˈɪnfɪdl/ *n* **1a** an unbeliever in or opponent of a particular religion, esp of Christianity or Islam **b** sby who acknowledges no religious belief **2** a disbeliever in sthg specified or understood – **infidel** *adj*

infidelity /ˌinfiˈdeləti‖ˌɪnfɪˈdelətɪ/ *n* **1** lack of belief in a religion **2a** unfaithfulness, disloyalty **b** marital unfaithfulness

infield /ˈinfeeld‖ˈɪnfiːld/ *n* (the fielding positions in) the area of a cricket or baseball field relatively near the wickets or bounded by the bases – **infielder** *n*

infighting /ˈinˌfieting‖ˈɪnˌfaɪtɪŋ/ *n* **1** fighting or boxing at close quarters **2** prolonged and often bitter dissension among members of a group or organization – **infighter** *n*

infiltrate /ˈinfiltrayt‖ˈɪnfɪltreɪt/ *vt* **1** to cause (e g a liquid) to permeate sthg (e g by penetrating its pores or interstices) **2** to pass into or through (a substance) by filtering or permeating **3** to enter or become established in gradually or unobtrusively ~*vi* to enter, permeate, or pass through a substance or area by filtering or by insinuating gradually – **infiltrative** *adj*, **infiltrator** *n*, **infiltration** *n*

[1]**infinite** /ˈinfinət‖ˈɪnfɪnət/ *adj* **1** subject to no limitation or external determination **2** extending indefinitely **3** immeasurably or inconceivably great or extensive **4a** extending beyond, lying beyond, or being greater than any arbitrarily chosen finite value, however large <*there are an* ~ *number of positive integers*> **b** extending to infinity <~ *plane surface*> – **infinitely** *adv*, **infiniteness** *n*

[2]**infinite** *n* **1** divineness, sublimity – + *the* **2** an incalculable or very great number **3** an infinite quantity or magnitude

[1]**infinitesimal** /ˌinfiniˈtesiml‖ˌɪnfɪnɪˈtesɪml/ *n* an infinitesimal variable or quantity

[2]**infinitesimal** *adj* **1** taking on values arbitrarily close to zero **2** immeasurably or incalculably small – **infinitesimally** *adv*

infinitive /inˈfinətiv‖ɪnˈfɪnətɪv/ *adj or n* (using) a verb form that performs some functions of a noun and that in English is used with *to* (e g *go* in *I asked him to go*) except with auxiliary and various other verbs (e g *go* in *I must go*) – **infinitival** *adj or n*

infinitude /inˈfinityoohd‖ɪnˈfɪnɪtjuːd/ *n* **1** the quality or state of being infinite **2** sthg infinite, esp in extent **3** an infinite number or quantity

infinity /inˈfinəti‖ɪnˈfɪnətɪ/ *n* **1a** the quality of being infinite **b** unlimited extent of time, space, or quantity **2** an indefinitely great number or amount **3** a distance so great that the rays of light from a point source at that distance may be regarded as parallel

infirm /inˈfuhm‖ɪnˈfɜːm/ *adj* **1** physically feeble, esp from age **2** weak in mind, will, or character – **infirmly** *adv*

infirmary /inˈfuhməri‖ɪnˈfɜːmərɪ/ *n* HOSPITAL 1

infirmity /inˈfuhməti‖ɪnˈfɜːmətɪ/ *n* **1** being infirm or frail **2** a disease, malady

inflame /inˈflaym‖ɪnˈfleɪm/ *vt* **1** to set on fire **2a** to excite or arouse passion or excessive action or feeling in **b** to make more heated or violent **3** to cause to redden or grow hot **4** to cause inflammation in (bodily tissue) ~ *vi* **1** to burst into flame **2** to become excited or angered **3** to become affected with inflammation – **inflamer** *n*

inflammable /inˈflaməbl‖ɪnˈflæməbl/ *adj* **1** capable of being easily ignited and of burning rapidly **2** easily inflamed, excited, or angered – **inflammable** *n*, **inflammableness, inflammability** *n*

inflammation /ˌinfləˈmaysh(ə)n‖ˌɪnfləˈmeɪʃ(ə)n/ *n* **1** inflaming or being inflamed **2** a response to cellular injury marked by local redness, heat, and pain

inflammatory /inˈflamət(ə)ri‖ɪnˈflæmət(ə)rɪ/ *adj* **1** tending to inflame <~ *speeches*> **2** accompanied by or tending to cause inflammation

inflatable /inˈflaytəbl‖ɪnˈfleɪtəbl/ *n* an inflatable boat, toy, etc

inflate /inˈflayt‖ɪnˈfleɪt/ *vt* **1** to swell or distend (with air or gas) **2** to increase (a price level) or cause (a volume of credit or the economy) to expand ~*vi* to become inflated – **inflatable** *adj*, **inflator, inflater** *n*

inˈflated *adj* **1** bombastic, exaggerated **2** expanded to an abnormal or unjustifiable volume or level <~ *prices*> **3** swelled out; distended

inflation /inˈflaysh(ə)n‖ɪnˈfleɪʃ(ə)n/ *n* inflating or being inflated; *esp* a substantial and continuing rise in the general level of prices, caused by or causing an increase in the volume of money and credit or an expansion of the economy – **inflationary** *adj*

inflect /inˈflekt‖ɪnˈflekt/ *vt* **1** to vary (a word) by inflection **2** to change or vary the pitch of (a voice or note) ~*vi* to become modified by inflection – **inflective** *adj*

inflection, *Br also* **inflexion** /inˈfleksh(ə)n‖ɪnˈflekʃ(ə)n/ *n* **1** change in pitch or loudness of the voice **2a** the change in the form of a word showing its case, gender, number, tense, etc **b** an element (e g a suffix) showing such variation – **inflectional** *adj*

inflexible /inˈfleksəbl‖ɪnˈfleksəbl/ *adj* rigidly firm: e g **a** lacking or deficient in suppleness **b** UNYIELDING 2 **c** incapable of change – **inflexibly**

adv, **inflexibility** *n*
inflict /in'flikt‖ɪn'flɪkt/ *vt* to force or impose (sthg damaging or painful) on sby – **inflicter, inflictor** *n*, **infliction** *n*
inflow /'infloh‖'ɪnfləʊ/ *n* a flowing in
1**influence** /'infloo·əns‖'ɪnflʊəns/ *n* **1** the power to achieve sthg desired by using wealth or position **2** the act, power, or capacity of causing or producing an effect in indirect or intangible ways **3** sby or sthg that exerts influence; *esp* sby or sthg that tends to produce a moral or immoral effect on another
2**influence** *vt* to affect, alter, or modify by indirect or intangible means
influential /ˌinfloo'ensh(ə)l‖ˌɪnflʊ'enʃ(ə)l/ *adj* exerting or possessing influence – **influentially** *adv*
influenza /ˌinfloo'enzə‖ˌɪnflʊ'enzə/ *n* a highly infectious virus disease characterized by sudden onset, fever, severe aches and pains, and inflammation of the respiratory mucous membranes [Italian, lit., influence; fr the belief that epidemics were due to the influence of the stars]
influx /'influks‖'ɪnflʌks/ *n* a usu sudden increase in flowing in; the arrival of large amounts
info /'infoh‖'ɪnfəʊ/ *n* information – infml
inform /in'fawm‖ɪn'fɔːm/ *vt* **1** to impart an essential quality or character to **2** to communicate knowledge to ~ *vi* **1** to give information or knowledge **2** to act as an informer *against* or *on* – **informant** *n*
informal /in'fawml‖ɪn'fɔːml/ *adj* marked by an absence of formality or ceremony; everyday – **informally** *adv*, **informality** *n*
informatics /ˌinfə'matiks/ *n* the science of electronic data processing
information /ˌinfə'maysh(ə)n‖ˌɪnfə'meɪʃ(ə)n/ *n* **1** the communication or reception of facts or ideas **2a** knowledge obtained from investigation, study, or instruction **b** news **c** (significant) facts or data **d** a signal or character (e g in a radio transmission or computer) representing data **3** a formal accusation presented to a magistrate – **informational** *adj*
information technology *n* the gathering, processing, and circulation of information by a combination of computing and telecommunications
informative /in'fawmətiv‖ɪn'fɔːmətɪv/, **informatory** /in'fawmət(ə)ri‖ɪn'fɔːmət(ə)rɪ/ *adj* conveying facts or ideas; instructive – **informatively** *adv*, **informativeness** *n*
informed /in'fawmd‖ɪn'fɔːmd/ *adj* **1** possessing or based on possession of information **2** knowledgeable about matters of contemporary interest
informer /in'fawmə‖ɪn'fɔːmə/ *n* one who informs against another, esp to the police for a financial reward
infra /'infrə‖'ɪnfrə/ *adv* lower on the same or a following page
infra- /infrə-‖ɪnfrə-/ *prefix* **1** below <infra*structure*>; less than <infra*human*> **2** within <infra*territorial*> **3** below in a scale or series <infra*red*>
infraction /in'fraksh(ə)n‖ɪn'frækʃ(ə)n/ *n* a violation, infringement
ˌinfra 'dig *adj* beneath one's dignity – infml [short for Latin *infra dignitatem*]
infrared /ˌinfrə'red‖ˌɪnfrə'red/ *adj or n* (being, using, producing, or sensitive to) electromagnetic radiation with a wavelength between the red end of the visible spectrum and microwaves, that is commonly perceived as heat
'infraˌstructure /-ˌstrukchə‖-ˌstrʌktʃə/ *n* **1** an underlying foundation or basic framework **2** the permanent installations required for military purposes
infrequent /in'freekwənt‖ɪn'friːkwənt/ *adj* **1** rare **2** not habitual or persistent – **infrequency** *n*, **infrequently** *adv*
infringe /in'frinj‖ɪn'frɪndʒ/ *vt* to encroach on; violate ~*vi* to encroach, trespass – **infringement** *n*
infuriate /in'fyooəriayt‖ɪn'fjʊərɪeɪt/ *vt* to make furious – **infuriate** *adj*, **infuriatingly** *adv*
infuse /in'fyoohz‖ɪn'fjuːz/ *vt* **1** to inspire, imbue **2** to steep in liquid without boiling so as to extract the soluble properties or constituents – **infuser** *n*
infusion /in'fyoohzh(ə)n‖ɪn'fjuːʒ(ə)n/ *n* **1** infusing **2** the continuous slow introduction of a solution, esp into a vein **3** an extract obtained by infusing
1**-ing** /-ing‖-ɪŋ/ *suffix* (→ *vb or adj*) – used to form the present participle <*sail*ing> and sometimes to form an adjective resembling a present participle but not derived from a verb <*swashbuckl*ing>
2**-ing** *suffix* (→ *n*) **1** action or process of <*running*> <*sleep*ing>; *also* instance of (a specified action or process) <*a meet*ing> – sometimes used to form a noun resembling a gerund but not derived from a verb <*skydiv*ing> **2** product or result of (a specified action or process) <*an engrav*ing> – often pl with sing. meaning <*earn*ings> **3** activity or occupation connected with <*bank*ing> **4a** collection or aggregate of <*hous*ing> **b** sthg connected with, consisting of, or used in making <*scaffold*ing> **5** sthg related to (a specified concept) <*off*ing>
ingenious /in'jeeni·əs‖ɪn'dʒiːnɪəs/ *adj* marked by originality, resourcefulness, and cleverness [Latin *ingenium* natural disposition - see ENGINE] – **ingeniously** *adv*
ingenue, ingénue /ˌanzhay'nooh ‖ˌænʒeɪ'nuː (*Fr* ɛ̃ʒeny)/ *n* **1** a naive or artless young woman **2** (an actress playing) the stage role of an ingenue [French *ingénue*, feminine of *ingénu* ingenuous, fr Latin *ingenuus*]
ingenuity /ˌinji'nyooh·əti‖ˌɪndʒɪ'njuːətɪ/ *n* (resourceful) cleverness; inventiveness
ingenuous /in'jenyoo·əs‖ɪn'dʒenjʊəs/ *adj* showing innocent or childlike simplicity; frank, candid [Latin *ingenuus* native, free born, fr *in* in + *gignere* to beget] – **ingenuously** *adv*, **ingenuousness** *n*
ingest /in'jest‖ɪn'dʒest/ *vt* to take in (as if) for digestion; absorb – **ingestible** *adj*, **ingestion** *n*, **ingestive** *adj*
inglenook /'ing·glˌnook‖'ɪŋglˌnʊk/ *n* (a seat in) an alcove by a large open fireplace [Scottish Gaelic *aingeal* light, fire + English *nook*]
inglorious /in'glawri·əs‖ɪn'glɔːrɪəs/ *adj*

shameful, ignominious – **ingloriously** *adv*

ingoing /ˈingoh·ing‖ˈɪngəʊɪŋ/ *adj* entering

ingot /ˈing·gət‖ˈɪŋgət/ *n* a (bar-shaped) mass of cast metal

ˈinˌgrained *adj* firmly and deeply implanted; deep-rooted – **ingrainedly** *adv*

ingratiate /inˈgrayshiˌayt‖ɪnˈgreɪʃɪˌeɪt/ *vt* to gain favour for (e g oneself) by deliberate effort <~ *themselves with the public*> – **ingratiatingly** *adv*, **ingratiatory** *adj*, **ingratiation** *n*

ingratitude /inˈgratityoohd‖ɪnˈgrætɪtjuːd/ *n* forgetfulness or scant recognition of kindness received

ingredient /inˈgreedi·ənt‖ɪnˈgriːdɪənt/ *n* sthg that forms a component part of a compound, combination, or mixture

ingress /ˈin·gres‖ˈɪngres/ *n* **1** the act of entering **2** the right of entrance or access

ingrowing /ˈinˌgroh·ing‖ˈɪnˌgrəʊɪŋ/, *NAm chiefly* **ingrown** /-grohn‖-grəʊn/ *adj* growing inwards; *specif* having the free tip or edge embedded in the flesh <*an* ~ *toenail*>

inhabit /inˈhabit‖ɪnˈhæbɪt/ *vt* to occupy or be present in <*the hopes and fears that* ~ *the human mind*> – **inhabitable** *adj*, **inhabitancy** *n*, **inhabitant** *n*, **inhabitation** *n*

inhalation /ˌinhəˈlaysh(ə)n‖ˌɪnhəˈleɪʃ(ə)n/ *n* (material for) inhaling

inhale /inˈhayl‖ɪnˈheɪl/ *vb* to breathe in

inhaler /inˈhaylə‖ɪnˈheɪlə/ *n* a device used for inhaling a medication

inharmonious /ˌinhahˈmohnyəs, -ni·əs‖ˌɪnhɑːˈməʊnjəs, -nɪəs/ *adj* **1** not harmonious **2** not congenial or compatible – **inharmoniously** *adv*

inhere /inˈhiə‖ɪnˈhɪə/ *vi* to be inherent; belong <*power to make laws* ~s *in the state*>

inherent /inˈherənt, -ˈhiə-‖ɪnˈherənt, -ˈhɪə-/ *adj* intrinsic to the constitution or essence of sthg – **inherence** *n*, **inherently** *adv*

inherit /inˈherit‖ɪnˈherɪt/ *vt* **1** to receive **1a** by right **b** from an ancestor at his/her death **2** to receive by genetic transmission <~ *a strong constitution*> ~ *vi* to receive sthg by inheritance – **inheritor** *n*, **inheritress, inheritrix** *n*

inheritance /inˈherit(ə)ns‖ɪnˈherɪt(ə)ns/ *n* **1a** inheriting property **b** the transmission of genetic qualities from parent to offspring **c** the acquisition of a possession, condition, or trait from past generations **2a** sthg that is or may be inherited **b** sthg acquired or derived from the past

inhibit /inˈhibit‖ɪnˈhɪbɪt/ *vt* **1** to prohibit *from* doing sthg **2a** to restrain **b** to discourage from free or spontaneous activity, esp by psychological or social controls ~ *vi* to cause inhibition – **inhibitive** *adj*, **inhibitory** *adj*

inhibition /ˌinhiˈbish(ə)n‖ˌɪnhɪˈbɪʃ(ə)n/ *n* **1a** inhibiting or being inhibited **b** sthg that forbids, debars, or restricts **2a** a psychological restraint on another psychological or physical activity <*sexual* ~s> **b** a restraining of a function (e g of a bodily organ or enzyme)

inhospitable /ˌinhoˈspitəbl‖ˌɪnhɒˈspɪtəbl/ *adj* **1** not friendly or welcoming **2** providing no shelter or means of support – **inhospitableness** *n*, **inhospitably** *adv*

inhuman /inˈhyoohmən‖ɪnˈhjuːmən/ *adj* **1a** inhumane **b** failing to conform to basic human needs **2** being other than human – **inhumanly** *adv*

inhumane /ˌinhyoohˈmayn‖ˌɪnhjuːˈmeɪn/ *adj* lacking in kindness or compassion – **inhumanely** *adv*

inhumanity /ˌinhyoohˈmanəti‖ˌɪnhjuːˈmænətɪ/ *n* **1** being pitiless or cruel **2** a cruel or barbarous act

inimical /iˈnimik(ə)l‖ɪˈnɪmɪk(ə)l/ *adj* **1** hostile or indicating hostility **2** adverse in tendency, influence, or effects – **inimically** *adv*

inimitable /iˈnimitəbl‖ɪˈnɪmɪtəbl/ *adj* defying imitation – **inimitableness** *n*, **inimitably** *adv*

iniquity /iˈnikwəti‖ɪˈnɪkwətɪ/ *n* **1** gross injustice **2** a sin – **iniquitous** *adj*

¹initial /iˈnish(ə)l‖ɪˈnɪʃ(ə)l/ *adj* **1** of the beginning <*the* ~ *symptoms of a disease*> **2** first <*the* ~ *number of a code*> – **initially** *adv*

²initial *n* **1** the first letter of a name **2** *pl* the first letter of each word in a full name

³initial *vt* **-ll-** (*NAm* **-l-, -ll-**) to put initials (indicating ownership or authorization) on

¹initiate /iˈnishiayt‖ɪˈnɪʃɪeɪt/ *vt* **1** to cause or enable the beginning of; start **2** to instil with rudiments or principles (of sthg complex or obscure) **3** to induct into membership (as if) by formal rites – **initiator** *n*, **initiatory** *adj*

²initiate /iˈnishi·ət‖ɪˈnɪʃɪət/ *adj* **1** initiated or properly admitted (e g to membership or an office) **2** instructed in some secret knowledge

³iˈnitiate /-ət‖-ət/ *n* **1** sby who is undergoing or has undergone initiation **2** sby who is instructed or proficient in a complex or specialized field

initiation /iˌnishiˈaysh(ə)n‖ɪˌnɪʃɪˈeɪʃ(ə)n/ *n* **1** initiating or being initiated **2** the ceremony or formal procedure with which sby is made a member of a sect or society

¹initiative /iˈnish(y)ətiv‖ɪˈnɪʃ(j)ətɪv/ *adj* introductory, preliminary

²initiative *n* **1** a first step, esp in the attainment of an end or goal **2** energy or resourcefulness displayed in initiation of action **3** a procedure enabling voters to propose a law by petition – **on one's own initiative** without being prompted; independently of outside influence or control

inject /inˈjekt‖ɪnˈdʒekt/ *vt* **1a** to throw, drive, or force into sthg <~ *fuel into an engine*> **b** to force a fluid into **2** to introduce as an element or factor – **injector** *n*

injection /inˈjeksh(ə)n‖ɪnˈdʒekʃ(ə)n/ *n* **1a** injecting **b** the placing of an artificial satellite or a spacecraft into an orbit or on a trajectory **2** sthg (e g a medication) that is injected

injudicious /ˌinjoohˈdishəs‖ˌɪndʒuːˈdɪʃəs/ *adj* indiscreet, unwise – **injudiciously** *adv*, **injudiciousness** *n*

injunction /inˈjungksh(ə)n‖ɪnˈdʒʌŋkʃ(ə)n/ *n* **1** an order, warning **2** a writ requiring sby to do or refrain from doing a particular act – **injunctive** *adj*

injure /ˈinjə‖ˈɪndʒə/ *vt* **1** to do injustice to **2a** to inflict bodily hurt on **b** to impair the soundness of **c** to inflict damage or loss on

injurious /inˈjooəri·əs‖ɪnˈdʒʊərɪəs/ *adj* inflicting or tending to inflict injury – **injuriously** *adv*, **injuriousness** *n*

injury /ˈinjəri‖ˈɪndʒərɪ/ *n* **1** a wrong **2** hurt, damage, or loss sustained

injustice /in'justis‖ın'dʒʌstıs/ *n* (an act or state of) unfairness

[1]**ink** /ingk‖ıŋk/ *n* **1** a coloured liquid used for writing and printing **2** the black secretion of a squid or similar cephalopod mollusc that hides it from a predator or prey – **inky** *adj*

[2]**ink** *vt* to apply ink to

inkling /'ingkling‖'ıŋklıŋ/ *n* **1** a faint indication **2** a slight knowledge or vague idea

'ink,stand /-,stand‖-,stænd/ *n* a stand with fittings for holding ink and often pens

'ink,well /-,wel‖-,wel/ *n* a container for ink

inlaid /in'layd‖ın'leıd/ *adj* **1** set into a surface in a decorative design <*tables with ~ marble*> **2** decorated with a design or material set into a surface <*a table with an ~ top*>

[1]**inland** /'in,land, -lənd‖'ın,lænd, -lənd/ *adv or n* (into or towards) the interior part of a country

[2]**inland** /'inlənd‖'ınlənd/ *adj* **1** of the interior of a country **2** *chiefly Br* not foreign; domestic

,Inland 'Revenue *n* the government department responsible for collecting taxes in Britain

'in-,law *n* a relative by marriage – infml

[1]**inlay** /in'lay‖ın'leı/ *vt* **inlaid** /-'layd‖-'leıd/ **1** to set into a surface or ground material for decoration or reinforcement **2** to decorate with inlaid material

[2]**inlay** /'inlay‖'ınleı/ *n* **1** inlaid work or a decorative inlaid pattern **2** a dental filling shaped to fit a cavity

inlet /'inlet, -lit‖'ınlet, -lıt/ *n* **1** a (long and narrow) recess in a shoreline or a water passage between 2 land areas **2** a means of entry; *esp* an opening for intake <*a fuel ~*>

inmate /'inmayt‖'ınmeıt/ *n* any of a group occupying a place of residence, esp a prison or hospital

in memoriam /,in mi'mawri·əm, -am‖,ın mı'mɔːrıəm, -æm/ *prep* in memory of

inmost /'inmohst‖'ınməʊst/ *adj* **1** furthest within **2** most intimate

inn /in‖ın/ *n* **1a** an establishment (e g a small hotel) providing lodging and food, esp for travellers **b** PUBLIC HOUSE **2** a residence formerly provided for students in London

innards /'inədz‖'ınədz/ *n pl* **1** the internal organs of a human being or animal; *esp* the viscera **2** the internal parts of a structure or mechanism *USE* infml

innate /i'nayt‖ı'neıt/ *adj* **1a** existing in or belonging to an individual from birth **b** inherent **c** originating in the intellect **2** ENDOGENOUS 2 – **innately** *adv*, **innateness** *n*

inner /'inə‖'ınə/ *adj* **1a** situated within; internal <*an ~ chamber*> **b** situated near to a centre, esp of influence <*an ~ circle of government ministers*> **2** of the mind or soul <*the ~ life of man*> – **inner** *n*, **innermost** *adj*

,inner 'light *n*, *often cap I&L* a divine influence held, esp in Quaker doctrine, to enlighten and guide the soul

'inner ,tube *n* an inflatable tube inside the casing of a pneumatic tyre

inning /'ining‖'ınıŋ/ *n* a baseball team's turn at batting or a division of a baseball game consisting of a turn at batting for each team

'innings *n*, *pl* **innings** **1a** any of the alternating divisions of a cricket match during which one side bats and the other bowls **b** the (runs scored in or quality of the) turn of 1 player to bat **2a** a period in which sby has opportunity for action or achievements **b** *chiefly Br* the duration of sby's life <*he had a good ~*>

innkeeper /'in,keepə‖'ın,kiːpə/ *n* the landlord of an inn

innocent /'inəs(ə)nt‖'ınəs(ə)nt/ *adj* **1a** free from guilt or sin; pure **b** harmless in effect or intention <*an ~ conversation*> **c** free from legal guilt **2** lacking or deprived of sthg <*a face ~ of make-up*> **3a** artless, ingenuous **b** ignorant, unaware [Middle French, fr Latin *innocent-, innocens*, fr *in-* not + *nocēre* to harm] – **innocence, innocency** *n*, **innocent** *n*, **innocently** *adv*

innocuous /i'nokyoo·əs‖ı'nɒkjʊəs/ *adj* inoffensive – **innocuously** *adv*, **innocuousness** *n*

innovate /'inəvayt‖'ınəveıt/ *vi* to make changes; introduce sthg new – **innovative** *adj*, **innovator** *n*, **innovatory** *adj*, **innovation** *n*

,Inns of 'Court *n pl* (4 buildings housing) 4 societies of students and barristers in London which have the exclusive right of admission to the English Bar

innuendo /,inyoo'endoh‖,ınjʊ'endəʊ/ *n*, *pl* **innuendos, innuendoes** an oblique allusion; *esp* a veiled slight on sby's character or reputation [Latin, by hinting, fr *innuere* to hint, fr *in* in + *nuere* to nod]

innumerable /i'nyoohmərəbl‖ı'njuːmərəbl/ *adj* countless – **innumerably** *adv*

inoculate /i'nokyoolayt‖ı'nɒkjʊleıt/ *vt* **1a** to introduce a microorganism into <*~ mice with anthrax*> **b** to introduce (e g a microorganism) into a culture, animal, etc for growth **c** VACCINATE 2 **2** to imbue – **inoculative** *adj*, **inoculator** *n*, **inoculation** *n*

inoffensive /,inə'fensiv‖,ınə'fensıv/ *adj* **1** not causing any harm **2** not objectionable to the senses – **inoffensively** *adv*, **inoffensiveness** *n*

inoperable /in'op(ə)rəbl‖ın'ɒp(ə)rəbl/ *adj* **1** not suitable for surgery **2** impracticable

inoperative /in'op(ə)rətiv‖ın'ɒp(ə)rətıv/ *adj* not functioning; having no effect

inopportune /,inopə'tyoohn‖,ınɒpə'tjuːn/ *adj* inconvenient, unseasonable – **inopportunely** *adv*, **inopportuneness** *n*

inordinate /in'awdinət‖ın'ɔːdınət/ *adj* exceeding reasonable limits – **inordinately** *adv*

inorganic /,inaw'ganik‖,ınɔː'gænık/ *adj* **1a** being or composed of matter other than plant or animal; mineral **b** of, being, or dealt with by a branch of chemistry concerned with inorganic substances **2** not arising through natural growth – **inorganically** *adv*

inpatient /'in,paysh(ə)nt‖'ın,peıʃ(ə)nt/ *n* a hospital patient who receives lodging and food as well as treatment

[1]**input** /'inpoot‖'ınpʊt/ *n* **1a** an amount coming or put in **b** sthg (e g energy, material, or data) supplied to a machine or system **c** a component of production (e g land, labour, or raw materials) **2** the point at which an input (e g of energy, material, or data) is made

[2]**input** *vt* **-tt-** to enter (e g data) into a computer or data-processing system

inquest /ˈinkwest‖ˈɪnkwest/ *n* **1** a judicial inquiry, esp by a coroner, into the cause of a death **2** an inquiry or investigation, esp into sthg that has failed

inquietude /inˈkwie·ətyoohd‖ɪnˈkwaɪətjuːd/ *n* uneasiness, restlessness

inquire /inˈkwie·ə‖ɪnˈkwaɪə/ *vt* to ask about; ask to be told ~ *vi* **1** to seek information by questioning **2** to make a search or inquiry – **inquirer** *n*, **inquiringly** *adv* – **inquire after** to ask about the health of

inquiry /inˈkwie·əri‖ɪnˈkwaɪərɪ/ *n* **1** a request for information **2** a systematic investigation

inquisition /ˌinkwiˈzish(ə)n‖ˌɪnkwɪˈzɪʃ(ə)n/ *n* **1** the act of inquiring **2** a judicial or official inquiry **3a** *cap* a former Roman Catholic tribunal for the discovery and punishment of heresy **b** a ruthless investigation or examination – **inquisitional** *adj*

inquisitive /inˈkwizətiv‖ɪnˈkwɪzətɪv/ *adj* **1** eager for knowledge or understanding **2** fond of making inquiries; *esp* unduly curious about the affairs of others – **inquisitively** *adv*, **inquisitiveness** *n*

inquisitor /inˈkwizitə‖ɪnˈkwɪzɪtə/ *n* one who inquires or conducts an inquisition (harshly or with hostility)

inquisitorial /inˌkwiziˈtawri·əl‖ɪnˌkwɪzɪˈtɔːrɪəl/ *adj* of a system of criminal procedure in which the judge is also the prosecutor – **inquisitorially** *adv*

inroad /ˈinˌrohd‖ˈɪnˌrəʊd/ *n* **1** a raid **2** a serious or forcible encroachment or advance <*an illness made* ~s *on his savings*>

inrush /ˈinˌrush‖ˈɪnˌrʌʃ/ *n* a crowding or flooding in

insalubrious /ˌinsəˈl(y)oohbri·əs‖ˌɪnsəˈl(j)uːbrɪəs/ *adj* unhealthy – **insalubriously** *adv*, **insalubrity** *n*

insane /inˈsayn‖ɪnˈseɪn/ *adj* **1** mentally disordered; exhibiting insanity **2** typical of or intended for insane people <*an* ~ *asylum*> **3** utterly absurd – **insanely** *adv*, **insanity** *n*

insanitary /inˈsanit(ə)ri‖ɪnˈsænɪt(ə)rɪ/ *adj* unclean enough to endanger health; filthy, contaminated

insatiable /inˈsaysh(y)əbl‖ɪnˈseɪʃ(j)əbl/ *adj* incapable of being satisfied – **insatiably** *adv*, **insatiability** *n*

insatiate /inˈsayshi·ət‖ɪnˈseɪʃɪət/ *adj* insatiable

inscribe /inˈskrieb‖ɪnˈskraɪb/ *vt* **1a** to write, engrave, or print (as a lasting record) **b** to enter on a list; enrol **2** to address or dedicate to sby, esp by a handwritten note – **inscriber** *n*

inscription /inˈskripsh(ə)n‖ɪnˈskrɪpʃ(ə)n/ *n* **1a** a title, superscription **b** EPIGRAPH 2 **c** LEGEND 2a **2** a handwritten dedication in a book or on a work of art **3a** the act of inscribing **b** the enrolment of a name (as if) on a list – **inscriptional** *adj*, **inscriptive** *adj*

inscrutable /inˈskroohtəbl‖ɪnˈskruːtəbl/ *adj* hard to interpret or understand; enigmatic – **inscrutableness** *n*, **inscrutably** *adv*, **inscrutability** *n*

insect /ˈinsekt‖ˈɪnsekt/ *n* **1** any of a class of arthropods with a well-defined head, thorax, and abdomen, only 3 pairs of legs, and typically 1 or 2 pairs of wings **2** any of various small invertebrate animals (e g woodlice and spiders) – not used technically **3** a worthless or insignificant person [Latin *insectum*, fr *insect-*, *insecare* to cut into, fr *in* in + *secare* to cut]

insecticide /inˈsektisied‖ɪnˈsektɪsaɪd/ *n* sthg that destroys insects – **insecticidal** *adj*

insectivore /inˈsektiˌvaw‖ɪnˈsektɪˌvɔː/ *n* **1** any of an order of mammals including moles, shrews, and hedgehogs that are mostly small, nocturnal, and eat insects **2** an insect-eating plant or animal

insecure /ˌinsiˈkyooə‖ˌɪnsɪˈkjʊə/ *adj* **1** lacking adequate protection or guarantee <*an* ~ *job*> **2** not firmly fixed or supported <*the hinge is* ~> **3a** not stable or well-adjusted <*an* ~ *marriage*> **b** deficient in assurance; beset by fear and anxiety – **insecurely** *adv*, **insecurity** *n*

inseminate /inˈseminayt‖ɪnˈsemɪneɪt/ *vt* **1** sow 1b, 1c **2** to introduce semen into the genital tract of (a female) – **inseminator** *n*, **insemination** *n*

insensate /inˈsensayt, -sət‖ɪnˈsenseɪt, -sət/ *adj* **1** insentient **2** lacking in human feeling – **insensately** *adv*

insensible /inˈsensəbl‖ɪnˈsensəbl/ *adj* **1** incapable or bereft of feeling or sensation: e g **1a** having lost consciousness **b** lacking or deprived of sensory perception <~ *to pain*> **2** incapable of being felt or sensed **3** lacking concern or awareness – **insensibly** *adv*, **insensibility** *n*

insensitive /inˈsensətiv‖ɪnˈsensətɪv/ *adj* **1** lacking the ability to respond to or sympathize with the needs or feelings of others **2** not physically or chemically sensitive <~ *to light*> – **insensitively** *adv*, **insensitiveness, insensitivity** *n*

insentient /inˈsenshi·ənt‖ɪnˈsenʃɪənt/ *adj* not endowed with the capacity to perceive – **insentience** *n*

inseparable /inˈsep(ə)rəbl‖ɪnˈsep(ə)rəbl/ *adj* incapable of being separated – **inseparable** *n*, **inseparably** *adv*, **inseparability** *n*

[1]**insert** /inˈzuht, -ˈsuht‖ɪnˈzɜːt, -ˈsɜːt/ *vt* **1** to put or thrust in <~ *a coin in a slot machine*> **2** to put or introduce into the body of sthg <~ *an advertisement in a newspaper*> **3** to set in and make fast; *esp* to insert by sewing between 2 cut edges ~*vi*, *of a muscle* to be in attachment to a specified part <*muscles* ~ *on bone*> – **inserter** *n*

[2]**insert** /ˈ--/ *n* sthg (esp written or printed) inserted

insertion /inˈzuhsh(ə)n, -ˈsuh-‖ɪnˈzɜːʃ(ə)n, -ˈsɜː-/ *n* **1** the mode or place of attachment of an organ or part **2** embroidery or needlework inserted as ornament between 2 pieces of fabric **3** a single appearance of an advertisement (e g in a newspaper) – **insertional** *adj*

[1]**inset** /ˈinset‖ˈɪnset/ *n* sthg set in: e g **a** a small illustration set within a larger one **b** a piece of cloth set into a garment for decoration, shaping, etc

[2]**inˈset** *vt* **-tt-; inset, insetted** to insert as an inset

inshore /inˈshaw‖ɪnˈʃɔː/ *adj or adv* (near or moving) towards the shore

[1]**inside** /inˈsied‖ɪnˈsaɪd/ *n* **1** an inner side or surface **2a** an interior or internal part <*fire destroyed the* ~ *of the house*> **b** inward nature, thoughts, or feeling **c** the middle or main part of

a division of time <*the ~ of a week*> **d** viscera, entrails – usu pl with sing. meaning **3** a position of confidence or of access to confidential information **4** the middle portion of a playing area

[2]**inside** *adj* **1** of, on, near, or towards the inside <*an ~ toilet*> **2** of or being the inner side of a curve or being near the side of the road nearest the kerb or hard shoulder <*driving on the ~ lane*>

[3]**inside** *prep* **1a** in or into the interior of **b** on the inner side of **2** within <*~ an hour*>

[4]**inside** *adv* **1** to or on the inner side **2** in or into the interior **3** indoors **4** *chiefly Br* in or into prison – slang

in'side of *prep* **1** in less time than **2** *chiefly NAm* inside ***USE*** infml

,inside 'out *adv* **1** with the inner surface on the outside <*turned his socks ~*> **2** in a very thorough manner – infml <*knows his subject ~*>

insider /in'siedə‖ɪn'saɪdə/ *n* sby recognized or accepted as a member of a group, category, or organization; *esp* one who has access to confidential information or is in a position of power

insidious /in'sidi·əs‖ɪn'sɪdɪəs/ *adj* **1** harmful but enticing **2a** acting gradually and imperceptibly but with grave consequences **b** *of a disease* developing so gradually as to be well established before becoming apparent [Latin *insidiosus*, fr *insidiae* ambush, fr *insidēre* to sit in, sit on, fr *in* in + *sedēre* to sit] – **insidiously** *adv*, **insidiousness** *n*

insight /'in,siet‖'ɪn,saɪt/ *n* the power of or an act or result of discerning the true or underlying nature of sthg – **insightful** *adj*

insignia /in'signi·ə‖ɪn'sɪgnɪə/ *n pl in constr, pl* **insignia, insignias** badges of authority or honour – sometimes treated as sing. in American English

insignificant /,insig'nifikənt‖,ɪnsɪg'nɪfɪkənt/ *adj* **1** lacking meaning or import; inconsequential **2** very small in size, amount, or number – **insignificance, insignificancy** *n*, **insignificantly** *adv*

insincere /,insin'siə‖,ɪnsɪn'sɪə/ *adj* hypocritical – **insincerely** *adv*, **insincerity** *n*

insinuate /in'sinyoo,ayt‖ɪn'sɪnjʊ,eɪt/ *vt* **1** to introduce (an idea) or suggest (sthg unpleasant) in a subtle or oblique manner **2** to gain acceptance for (e g oneself) by craft or stealth – **insinuative** *adj*, **insinuator** *n*

insinuation /in,sinyoo'aysh(ə)n‖ɪn,sɪnjʊ'eɪʃ(ə)n/ *n* a sly and usu derogatory reference

insipid /in'sipid‖ɪn'sɪpɪd/ *adj* **1** devoid of any definite flavour **2** devoid of interesting or stimulating qualities – **insipidly** *adv*, **insipidity** *n*

insist /in'sist‖ɪn'sɪst/ *vi* **1** to take a resolute stand **2** to place great emphasis or importance *on* sthg *~vt* to maintain persistently

insistent /in'sist(ə)nt‖ɪn'sɪst(ə)nt/ *adj* **1** insisting forcefully or repeatedly; emphatic **2** demanding attention – **insistence** *n*, **insistently** *adv*

in situ /in 'sityooh‖ɪn 'sɪtjuː/ *adv or adj* in the natural or original position

,inso'far as /insə'fah, insoh'fah‖ɪnsə'fɑː, ɪnsəʊ'fɑː/ *conj* to the extent or degree that <*I'll help you ~ I can*>

insole /'in,sohl‖'ɪn,səʊl/ *n* **1** an inside sole of a shoe **2** a strip the shape of the sole that is placed inside a shoe for warmth or comfort

insolent /'insələnt‖'ɪnsələnt/ *adj* showing disrespectful rudeness; impudent – **insolence** *n*, **insolently** *adv*

insoluble /in'solyoobl‖ɪn'sɒljʊbl/ *adj* **1** having or admitting of no solution or explanation **2** (practically) incapable of being dissolved in liquid – **insoluble** *n*, **insolubleness** *n*, **insolubly** *adv*, **insolubility** *n*

insolvable /in'solvəbl‖ɪn'sɒlvəbl/ *adj, chiefly NAm* impossible to solve <*an apparently ~ problem*> – **insolvably** *adv*

insolvent /in'solvənt‖ɪn'sɒlvənt/ *adj* **1** unable to pay debts as they fall due; *specif* having liabilities in excess of the value of assets held **2** relating to or for the relief of insolvents – **insolvency** *n*, **insolvent** *n*

insomnia /in'somni·ə‖ɪn'sɒmnɪə/ *n* prolonged (abnormal) inability to obtain adequate sleep – **insomniac** *adj or n*

insouciance /in'soohsyəns ‖ɪn'suːsjəns (*Fr* ɛ̃suːsjɑ̃ːs)/ *n* lighthearted unconcern [French, fr *in-* not + *soucier* to trouble, disturb] – **insouciant** *adj*, **insouciantly** *adv*

inspect /in'spekt‖ɪn'spekt/ *vt* **1** to examine closely and critically; scrutinize **2** to view or examine officially – **inspection** *n*, **inspective** *adj*

inspector /in'spektə‖ɪn'spektə/ *n* a police officer ranking immediately above a sergeant – **inspectorate** *n*, **inspectorship** *n*

inspiration /,inspi'raysh(ə)n‖,ɪnspɪ'reɪʃ(ə)n/ *n* **1a** a divine influence or action on a person which qualifies him/her to receive and communicate sacred revelation **b** the action or power of stimulating the intellect or emotions **2** the drawing of air into the lungs **3a** being inspired **b** an inspired idea <*I've had an ~, let's go to the seaside*> **4** an inspiring agent or influence – **inspirational** *adj*, **inspirationally** *adv*, **inspiratory** *adj*

inspire /in'spie·ə‖ɪn'spaɪə/ *vt* **1** to inhale **2a** to influence or guide by divine inspiration **b** to exert an animating or exalting influence on <*inspiring music*> **c** to act as a stimulus for <*threats don't necessarily ~ people to work harder*> **d** to affect – usu + *with* <*seeing the old room again ~d him with nostalgia*> **3** to communicate to an agent supernaturally <*writings ~d by God*> *~vi* to breathe in – **inspirer** *n*

in'spired *adj* outstanding or brilliant in a way that suggests divine inspiration

instability /,instə'biləti‖,ɪnstə'bɪlətɪ/ *n* lack of (emotional or mental) stability

install /in'stawl‖ɪn'stɔːl/ *vt* **1** to induct into an office, rank, or order, esp with ceremonies or formalities <*~ed the new department chairman*> **2** to establish in a specified place, condition, or status **3** to place in usu permanent position for use or service <*had a shower ~ed in the bathroom*> – **installer** *n*

installation /,instə'laysh(ə)n‖,ɪnstə'leɪʃ(ə)n/ *n* **1** a device, apparatus, or piece of machinery fixed or fitted in place to perform some specified function **2** a military base or establishment

instalment, *NAm chiefly* **installment** /in 'stawlmənt‖ɪn'stɔːlmənt/ *n* **1** any of the parts into which a debt is divided when payment is made at intervals **2a** any of several parts (e g of a publication) presented at intervals **b** a single part of a serial story

1**instance** /'inst(ə)ns‖'ɪnst(ə)ns/ *n* **1** an example cited as an illustration or proof **2** the institution of a legal action <*a court of first* ~> **3** a situation viewed as 1 stage in a process or series of events <*prefers, in this* ~, *to go home*> **4** a solicitation, request – fml <*am writing to you at the* ~ *of my client*> – **for instance** as an example

2**instance** *vt* **1** to exemplify by an instance **2** to put forward as a case or example; cite

1**instant** /'inst(ə)nt‖'ɪnst(ə)nt/ *n* **1** an infinitesimal space of time; *esp* a point in time separating 2 states <*at the* ~ *of death*> **2** the present or current month

2**instant** *adj* **1a** present, current <*previous felonies not related to the* ~ *crime*> **b** of or occurring in the present month – used in commercial communications **2** immediate <*the play was an* ~ *success*> **3** *of food or drink* ready for easy final preparation **4** demanding, urgent – fml

instantaneous /,inst(ə)n'tayni·əs‖,ɪnst(ə)n'teɪnɪəs/ *adj* **1** done, occurring, or acting in an instant or instantly; IMMEDIATE 3 <*death was* ~> **2** occurring or present at a particular instant <~ *velocity*> – **instantaneously** *adv*, **instantaneousness, instantaneity** *n*

instantly /'inst(ə)ntli‖'ɪnst(ə)ntlɪ/ *adv* immediately; AT ONCE

instead /in'sted‖ɪn'sted/ *adv* as a substitute or alternative <*was going to write but called* ~>

in'stead of *prep* as a substitute for or alternative to

instep /'in,step‖'ɪn,step/ *n* **1** (the upper surface of) the arched middle portion of the human foot **2** the part of a shoe or stocking over the instep

instigate /'instigayt‖'ɪnstɪgeɪt/ *vt* **1** to goad or urge forwards; provoke, incite **2** to initiate (a course of action or procedure, e g a legal investigation) – **instigator** *n*, **instigation** *n*

instil, *NAm chiefly* **instill** /in'stil‖ɪn'stɪl/ *vt* **-ll-** **1** to cause to enter drop by drop <~ *medication into the infected eye*> **2** to impart gradually <~ling *in children a love of learning*> – + *in* or *into* – **instillment, instillation** *n*

1**instinct** /'instingkt‖'ɪnstɪŋkt/ *n* **1** a natural or inherent aptitude, impulse, or capacity <*had an* ~ *for the right word*> **2** (a largely inheritable tendency of an organism to make a complex and specific) response to environmental stimuli without involving reason – **instinctive** *adj*, **instinctively** *adv*, **instinctual** *adj*

2**instinct** *adj* imbued, infused – fml <~ *with patriotism*>

1**institute** /'instityooht‖'ɪnstɪtjuːt/ *vt* **1** to instate **2** to originate and establish; inaugurate <~d *many social reforms*>

2**institute** *n* sthg instituted: e g **a(1)** an elementary principle recognized as authoritative **a(2)** *pl* a (legal) compendium **b** (the premises used by) an organization for the promotion of a cause <*an* ~ *for the blind*> **c** an educational institution

institution /,insti'tyoohsh(ə)n‖,ɪnstɪ'tjuːʃ(ə)n/ *n* **1** an established practice in a culture <*the* ~ *of marriage*>; *also* a familiar object **2** an established organization or (public) body (e g a university or hospital) – **institutional** *adj*

instruct /in'strukt‖ɪn'strʌkt/ *vt* **1** to teach **2a** to direct authoritatively **b** COMMAND 1 **3** to engage (a lawyer, specif a barrister) for a case

instruction /in'struksh(ə)n‖ɪn'strʌkʃ(ə)n/ *n* **1a** ORDER 7b, COMMAND 1 – often pl with sing. meaning <*had* ~s *not to admit strangers*> **b** *pl* an outline or manual of technical procedure **c** a code that tells a computer to perform a particular operation **2** teaching – **instructional** *adj*

instructive /in'struktiv‖ɪn'strʌktɪv/ *adj* carrying a lesson; enlightening – **instructively** *adv*, **instructiveness** *n*

instructor /in'struktə‖ɪn'strʌktə/, *fem* **instructress** /-tris‖-trɪs/ *n* a teacher: e g **a** a teacher of a technical or practical subject <*a swimming* ~> **b** *NAm* a college teacher below professorial rank – **instructorship** *n*

1**instrument** /'instrəmənt‖'ɪnstrəmənt/ *n* **1a** a means whereby sthg is achieved, performed, or furthered **b** a dupe; TOOL 3 **2** an implement, tool, or device designed esp for delicate work or measurement <*scientific* ~s> **3** a device used to produce music **4** a formal legal document **5** an electrical or mechanical device used in navigating an aircraft

2**instrument** *vt* to orchestrate

1**instrumental** /,instrə'mentl‖,ɪnstrə'mentl/ *adj* **1a** serving as an instrument, means, agent, or tool <*was* ~ *in organizing the strike*> **b** of or done with an instrument or tool **2** relating to, composed for, or performed on a musical instrument **3** of or being a grammatical case or form expressing means or agency – **instrumentally** *adv*

2**instrumental** *n* a musical composition or passage for instruments but not voice

instrumentalist /,instrə'mentl,ist‖,ɪnstrə'mentl,ɪst/ *n* a player on a musical instrument

instrumentality /,instrəmen'taləti‖,ɪnstrəmen'tælətɪ/ *n* a means, agency

instrumentation /,instrəmən'taysh(ə)n, -men-‖,ɪnstrəmən'teɪʃ(ə)n, -men-/ *n* the arrangement or composition of music for instruments

insubordinate /,insə'bawdinət‖,ɪnsə'bɔːdɪnət/ *adj* unwilling to submit to authority – **insubordinately** *adv*, **insubordination** *n*

insubstantial /,insəb'stansh(ə)l‖,ɪnsəb'stænʃ(ə)l/ *adj* **1** lacking substance or material nature; unreal **2** lacking firmness or solidity; flimsy – **insubstantiality** *n*

insufferable /in'suf(ə)rəbl‖ɪn'sʌf(ə)rəbl/ *adj* intolerable – **insufferably** *adv*

insufficiency /,insə'fish(ə)nsi‖,ɪnsə'fɪʃ(ə)nsɪ/ *n* being insufficient; *specif* inability of an organ or body part (e g the heart or kidneys) to function normally

insufficient /,insə'fish(ə)nt‖,ɪnsə'fɪʃ(ə)nt/ *adj* deficient in power, capacity, or competence – **insufficiently** *adv*

insular /'insyoolə‖'ɪnsjʊlə/ *adj* **1** of or being an island **2a** of island people **b** that results (as if) from lack of contact with other peoples or cultures; narrow-minded **3** of an island of cells or tissue – **insularism** *n*, **insularly** *adv*, **insularity** *n*

insulate /'insyoolayt‖'ɪnsjʊleɪt/ *vt* to place in a detached situation; *esp* to separate from conducting bodies by means of nonconductors so as to prevent transfer of electricity, heat, or sound

insulation /,insyoo'laysh(ə)n‖,ɪnsjʊ'leɪʃ(ə)n/ *n* **1** insulating or being insulated **2** material used in insulating

insulator /ˈinsyoo,laytə‖ˈɪnsjʊ,leɪtə/ *n* (a device made from) a material that is a poor conductor of electricity and is used for separating or supporting conductors to prevent undesired flow of electricity

insulin /ˈinsyoo,lin‖ˈɪnsjʊ,lɪn/ *n* a protein pancreatic hormone secreted by the islets of Langerhans that is essential esp for the metabolism of carbohydrates and is used in the treatment of diabetes mellitus

[1]insult /inˈsult‖ɪnˈsʌlt/ *vt* to treat with insolence, indignity, or contempt – **insultingly** *adv*

[2]insult /ˈinsult‖ˈɪnsʌlt/ *n* **1** an act of insulting; sthg that insults **2** (sthg that causes) injury to the body or 1 of its parts

insuperable /inˈs(y)oohprəbl‖ɪnˈs(j)uːprəbl/ *adj* incapable of being surmounted, overcome, or passed over < ~ *difficulties*> – **insuperably** *adv*

insupportable /,insəˈpawtəbl‖,ɪnsəˈpɔːtəbl/ *adj* **1** unendurable < ~ *pain*> **2** incapable of being sustained < ~ *charges*> – **insupportably** *adv*

insurance /inˈshooərəns, -ˈshaw-‖ɪnˈʃʊərəns, -ˈʃɔː-/ *n* **1** insuring or being insured **2a** the business of insuring people or property **b** (the protection offered by) a contract whereby one party undertakes to indemnify or guarantee another against loss by a particular contingency or risk **c(1)** the premium demanded under such a contract **c(2)** the sum for which sthg is insured

insure /inˈshooə, inˈshaw‖ɪnˈʃʊə, ɪnˈʃɔː/ *vt* **1** to give, take, or procure insurance on or for **2** *chiefly NAm* to ensure ~*vi* to contract to give or take insurance; *specif* to underwrite – **insurable** *adj*, **insurer** *n*

inˈsured *n, pl* **insured** sby whose life or property is insured

insurgent /inˈsuhj(ə)nt‖ɪnˈsɜːdʒ(ə)nt/ *n* a rebel – **insurgence, insurgency** *n*, **insurgent** *adj*

insurmountable /,insəˈmowntəbl‖,ɪnsəˈmaʊntəbl/ *adj* insuperable – **insurmountably** *adv*

insurrection /,insəˈreksh(ə)n‖,ɪnsəˈrekʃ(ə)n/ *n* (a) revolt against civil authority or established government – **insurrectional** *adj*, **insurrectionary** *adj or n*, **insurrectionist** *n*

intact /inˈtakt‖ɪnˈtækt/ *adj* **1** untouched, esp by anything that harms or diminishes; whole, uninjured **2a** being a virgin **b** not castrated

intaglio /inˈtahlioh‖ɪnˈtɑːlɪəʊ/ *n, pl* **intaglios** **1a** (the act or process of producing) an incised or engraved design made in hard material, esp stone, and sunk below the surface of the material **b** printing done from a plate engraved in intaglio **2** sthg (e g a gem) carved in intaglio

intake /ˈin,tayk‖ˈɪn,teɪk/ *n* **1** an opening through which liquid or gas enters an enclosure or system **2a** a taking in **b(1)** *sing or pl in constr* an amount or number taken in **b(2)** sthg taken in

intangible /inˈtanjəbl‖ɪnˈtændʒəbl/ *n or adj* (sthg) not tangible – **intangibly** *adv*, **intangibility** *n*

integer /ˈintijə‖ˈɪntɪdʒə/ *n* the number 1 or any number (e g 6, 0, -23) obtainable by once or repeatedly adding 1 to or subtracting 1 from the number 1

[1]integral /ˈintigrəl‖ˈɪntɪgrəl; *esp in maths* inˈtegrəl‖ɪnˈtegrəl/ *adj* **1a** essential to completeness; constituent – chiefly in *integral part* **b** of a mathematical integer, integral, or integration **c** formed as a unit with another part **2** composed of integral parts **3** lacking nothing essential; whole – **integrally** *adv*, **integrality** *n*

[2]integral *n* **1** a mathematical expression denoting a definite integral or an indefinite integral **2** a solution of a differential equation

integral calculus *n* a branch of mathematics dealing with methods of finding indefinite integrals and with their applications (e g to the determination of lengths, areas, and volumes and to the solution of differential equations)

integrate /ˈintigrayt‖ˈɪntɪgreɪt/ *vt* **1** to form or blend into a whole **2a** to combine together or with sthg else **b** to incorporate into a larger unit – usu + *into* **3** to find the integral of (e g a function or differential equation) **4** to end the segregation of or in ~ *vi* **1** to become integrated **2** to calculate an integral – **integrative** *adj*, **integration** *n*

,integrated ˈcircuit *n* an electronic circuit formed in or on a single tiny slice of semiconductor material (e g silicon) – **integrated circuitry** *n*

integrity /inˈtegrəti‖ɪnˈtegrətɪ/ *n* **1** an unimpaired condition **2** uncompromising adherence to a code of esp moral or artistic values **3** the quality or state of being complete or undivided <*the* ~ *of the Empire was threatened*>

integument /inˈtegyoomənt‖ɪnˈtegjʊmənt/ *n* a skin, membrane, husk, or other covering or enclosure, esp of (part of) a living organism – **integumental** *adj*, **integumentary** *adj*

intellect /ˈint(ə)lekt‖ˈɪnt(ə)lekt/ *n* the capacity for intelligent thought, esp when highly developed

[1]intellectual /,int(ə)lˈektyoo·əl, -chəl‖,ɪnt(ə)lˈektjʊəl, -tʃəl/ *adj* **1a** of the intellect **b** developed or chiefly guided by the intellect rather than by emotion or experience <*a coldly* ~ *artist*> **2** given to or requiring the use of the intellect – **intellectualize** *vb*, **intellectually** *adv*, **intellectuality** *n*

[2]intellectual *n* an intellectual person

intelligence /inˈtelij(ə)ns‖ɪnˈtelɪdʒ(ə)ns/ *n* **1** the ability to learn, apply knowledge, or think abstractly, esp in allowing one to deal with new or trying situations; *also* the skilled use of intelligence or reason **2** the act of understanding **3a** news; INFORMATION 2a, c **b** (a group of people who gather) information concerning an enemy

intelligence quotient *n* a number expressing the ratio of sby's intelligence as determined by a test to the average for his/her age

intelligent /inˈtelij(ə)nt‖ɪnˈtelɪdʒ(ə)nt/ *adj* having or indicating esp high intelligence [Latin *intelligere, intellegere* to understand, fr *inter* between + *legere* to gather, select] – **intelligently** *adv*

intelligentsia /in,teliˈjentsi·ə‖ɪn,telɪˈdʒentsɪə/ *n sing or pl in constr* the intellectuals who form an artistic, social, or political vanguard

intelligible /inˈtelijəbl‖ɪnˈtelɪdʒəbl/ *adj* **1** capable of being understood **2** able to be apprehended by the intellect only – **intelligibly** *adv*, **intelligibility** *n*

intemperate /inˈtemp(ə)rət‖ɪnˈtemp(ə)rət/ *adj* not temperate; *esp* going beyond the bounds of reasonable behaviour – **intemperately** *adv*, **intemperateness** *n*

intend /inˈtend‖ɪnˈtend/ *vt* **1** to mean, signify **2a** to have in mind as a purpose or goal **b** to design for a specified use or future <*poems* ~ed *for reading aloud*>

inˈtended *n* one's future spouse – infml

intense /inˈtens‖ɪnˈtens/ *adj* **1a** existing or occurring in an extreme degree **b** having or showing a usual characteristic in extreme degree **2** INTENSIVE a **3a** feeling emotion deeply, esp by nature or temperament **b** deeply felt – **intensely** *adv*, **intenseness** *n*

intensify /inˈtensiˌfie‖ɪnˈtensɪˌfaɪ/ *vb* to make or become (more) intense – **intensification** *n*, **intensifier** *n*

intensity /inˈtensəti‖ɪnˈtensətɪ/ *n* **1** extreme degree of strength, force, or energy **2** the magnitude of force or energy per unit (e g of surface, charge, or mass) **3** SATURATION 1

intensive /inˈtensiv‖ɪnˈtensɪv/ *adj* of or marked by intensity or intensification: e g **a** highly concentrated **b** constituting or relating to a method designed to increase productivity by the expenditure of more capital and labour rather than by increase in the land or raw materials used <~ *farming*> – **intensively** *adv*

[1]**intent** /inˈtent‖ɪnˈtent/ *n* **1a** the act or fact of intending **b** the state of mind with which an act is done **2** criminal intention <*loitering with* ~> **3** meaning, significance – **to all intents and purposes** in every practical or important respect; virtually

[2]**intent** *adj* **1** directed with strained or eager attention; concentrated **2** having the mind, attention, or will concentrated *on* sthg or some end or purpose <~ *on his work*> – **intently** *adv*, **intentness** *n*

intention /inˈtensh(ə)n‖ɪnˈtenʃ(ə)n/ *n* **1** a determination to act in a certain way; a resolve **2** *pl* purpose with respect to proposal of marriage **3a** what one intends to do or bring about; an aim **b** the object for which religious devotion is offered **4** a concept

intentional /inˈtensh(ə)nl‖ɪnˈtenʃ(ə)nl/ *adj* done by intention or design – **intentionally** *adv*

inter /inˈtuh‖ɪnˈtɜː/ *vt* **-rr-** to deposit (a dead body) in the earth or a tomb [Old French *enterrer*, deriv of Latin *in* in + *terra* earth]

inter- /intə-‖ɪntə-/ *prefix* **1** between; among; in the midst <inter*city*> **2a** reciprocal <inter*relation*> **b** reciprocally <inter*marry*> **3** located between <inter*face*> **4** carried on between <inter*national*> **5** occurring between <inter*glacial*>

interact /ˌintəˈrakt‖ˌɪntəˈrækt/ *vi* to act upon each other – **interactant** *n*, **interaction** *n*

interactive /ˌintəˈraktiv‖ˌɪntəˈræktɪv/ *adj* involving interaction; *specif* involving the exchange of information between a computer and user while a program is being run

inter alia /ˌintə ˈrayli·ə‖ˌɪntə ˈreɪlɪə/ *adv* among other things

ˌinterˈbreed /-ˈbreed‖-ˈbriːd/ *vb* **interbred** /-ˈbred‖-ˈbred/ *vi* **1** to crossbreed **2** to breed within a closed population ~*vt* to cause to interbreed

intercalary /inˈtuhkəl(ə)ri‖ɪnˈtɜːkəl(ə)rɪ/ *adj* **1a** inserted in a calendar to resynchronize it with some objective time-measure (e g the solar year) **b** *of a year* containing an intercalary period **2** inserted between other elements or layers; interpolated

intercalate /inˈtuhkəˌlayt‖ɪnˈtɜːkəˌleɪt/ *vt* to insert between or among existing items, elements, or layers – **intercalation** *n*

intercede /ˌintəˈseed‖ˌɪntəˈsiːd/ *vi* to beg or plead on behalf of another with a view to reconciling differences

[1]**ˌinterˈcept** /-ˈsept‖-ˈsept/ *vt* **1** to stop, seize, or interrupt in progress, course, or movement, esp from one place to another **2** to intersect – **interception** *n*

[2]**ˈinterˌcept** *n* **1** the distance from the origin to a point where a graph crosses a coordinate axis **2** an interception

ˈinterˌceptor, intercepter /-ˌseptə‖-ˌseptə/ *n* a high-speed fast-climbing fighter plane or missile designed for defence against raiding bombers or missiles

ˌinterˈcession /-ˈsesh(ə)n‖-ˈseʃ(ə)n/ *n* the act of interceding, esp by prayer, petition, or entreaty – **intercessional** *adj*, **intercessor** *n*, **intercessory** *adj*

[1]**ˌinterˈchange** /-ˈchaynj‖-ˈtʃeɪndʒ/ *vt* **1** to put each of (2 things) in the place of the other **2** EXCHANGE 1 ~*vi* to change places reciprocally – **interchangeable** *adj*, **interchangeably** *adv*, **interchangeability** *n*

[2]**ˈinterˌchange** *n* **1** (an) interchanging **2** a junction of 2 or more roads having a system of separate levels that permit traffic to pass from one to another without the crossing of traffic streams

ˈinterˌcom /-ˌkom‖-ˌkɒm/ *n* a local communication system (e g in a ship or building) with a microphone and loudspeaker at each station

ˌinterˌcontiˈnental /-ˌkontiˈnentl‖-ˌkɒntɪˈnentl/ *adj* extending among continents; *also* carried on or (capable of) travelling between continents <~ *ballistic missile*>

ˈinterˌcourse /-ˌkaws‖-ˌkɔːs/ *n* **1** connection or dealings between people or groups **2** exchange, esp of thoughts or feelings **3** SEXUAL INTERCOURSE a

ˌinterdeˈpend /-diˈpend‖-dɪˈpend/ *vi* to depend on each other – **interdependence, interdependency** *n*, **interdependent** *adj*

[1]**ˈinterˌdict** /-ˌdikt‖-ˌdɪkt/ *n* **1** a Roman Catholic disciplinary measure withdrawing most sacraments and Christian burial from a person or district **2** a prohibition

[2]**ˌinterˈdict** *vt* to forbid in a usu formal or authoritative manner – **interdiction** *n*, **interdictory** *adj*

[1]**interest** /ˈint(ə)rest, -rəst‖ˈɪnt(ə)rest, -rəst/ *n* **1a(1)** right, title, or legal share in sthg **a(2)** participation in advantage and responsibility **b** a business in which one has an interest **2** benefit; ADVANTAGE 2; *specif* self-interest <*it is to your*

~ *to speak first*> **3a** a charge for borrowed money, generally a percentage of the amount borrowed **b** sthg added above what is due **4** a financially interested group **5a** readiness to be concerned with, moved by, or have one's attention attracted by sthg; curiosity **b** (the quality in) a thing that arouses interest <*sport doesn't hold much ~ for me*>

²**interest** *vt* **1** to induce or persuade to participate or engage, esp in an enterprise **2** to concern or engage (sby, esp oneself) *in* an activity or cause **3** to engage the attention or arouse the interest of

ˈ**interested** *adj* **1** having the interest aroused or attention engaged **2** affected or involved; not impartial – **interestedly** *adv*

interesting /ˈint(ə)resting‖ˈɪnt(ə)restɪŋ/ *adj* holding the attention – **interestingly** *adv*

¹ˈ**interˌface** /-ˌfays‖-ˌfeɪs/ *n* **1** a surface forming a common boundary of 2 bodies, regions, or phases <*an oil-water* ~> **2** the place at which (diverse) independent systems meet and act on or communicate with each other <*the man-machine* ~> – **interfacial** *adj*

²ˌ**interˈface** *vt* **1** to connect by means of an interface <~ *a machine with a computer*> **2** to serve as an interface for ~ *vi* **1** to become interfaced **2** to serve as an interface

ˌ**interˈfere** /-ˈfiə‖-ˈfɪə/ *vi* **1** to get in the way of, hinder, or impede another – + *with* <*noise* ~*s with my work*> **2** to enter into or take a part in matters that do not concern one **3** *of sound, light, etc waves* to act so as to augment, diminish, or otherwise affect one another **4** to claim priority for an invention **5** to hinder illegally an attempt of a player to catch or hit a ball or puck – usu + *with*

ˌ**interˈference** /-ˈfiərəns‖-ˈfɪərəns/ *n* **1** the phenomenon resulting from the meeting of 2 wave trains (e g of light or sound) with an increase in intensity at some points and a decrease at others **2** the illegal hindering of an opponent in hockey, ice hockey, etc **3** (sthg that produces) the confusion of received radio signals by unwanted signals or noise – **interferential** *adj*

¹**interim** /ˈintərim‖ˈɪntərɪm/ *n* an intervening time <*in the* ~>

²**interim** *adj* temporary, provisional

¹**interior** /inˈtiəri·ə‖ɪnˈtɪərɪə/ *adj* **1** lying, occurring, or functioning within the limits or interior **2** away from the border or shore **3** of the mind or soul – **interiorize** *vt*, **interiorly** *adv*, **interiority** *n*

²**interior** *n* **1** the internal or inner part of a thing; *also* the inland **2** internal affairs <*the minister of the* ~> **3** a representation of the interior of a building or room

interject /ˌintəˈjekt‖ˌɪntəˈdʒekt/ *vt* to throw in (e g a remark) abruptly among or between other things – **interjector** *n*, **interjectory** *adj*

ˌ**interˈjection** /-ˈjeksh(ə)n‖-ˈdʒekʃ(ə)n/ *n* an exclamation usu expressing emotion – **interjectional** *adj*, **interjectionally** *adv*

ˌ**interˈlace** /-ˈlays‖-ˈleɪs/ *vt* **1** to unite (as if) by lacing together **2** to mingle, blend, or intersperse <*narrative* ~*d with anecdotes*> ~*vi* to cross one another intricately – **interlacement** *n*

ˌ**interˈlard** /-ˈlahd‖-ˈlɑːd/ *vt* to intersperse, esp *with* sthg foreign or irrelevant

interleaf /-ˌleef‖-ˌliːf/ *n* a usu blank leaf inserted between two leaves of a book

interleave /-ˈleev‖-ˈliːv/ *vt* **1** to provide (a book) with interleaves **2** to arrange (as if) in alternate layers or leaves

ˌ**interˈlinear** /-ˈlini·ə‖-ˈlɪnɪə/ *adj* inserted between lines already written or printed

ˌ**interˈlock** /-ˈlok‖-ˈlɒk/ *vi* to become engaged, interrelated, or interlocked ~ *vt* **1** to lock together **2** to connect so that motion of any part is constrained by another – **interlock** *n or adj*

ˌ**interˈlocutor** /-ˈlokyootə‖-ˈlɒkjʊtə/, *fem* **interlocutress** /-tris‖-trɪs/ *n* one who takes part in dialogue or conversation – **interlocution** *n*

ˈ**interˌloper** /-ˌlohpə‖-ˌləʊpə/ *n* sby who interferes or encroaches; an intruder – **interlope** *vi*

ˈ**interˌlude** /-ˌloohd‖-ˌluːd/ *n* **1** an intervening or interruptive period, space, or event, esp of a contrasting character; an interval **2** a musical composition inserted between the parts of a longer composition, a drama, or a religious service

ˌ**interˈmarriage** /-ˈmarij‖-ˈmærɪdʒ/ *n* marriage between members of different families, tribes, etc

ˌ**interˈmarry** /-ˈmari‖-ˈmærɪ/ *vi* **1** to marry each other or sby from the the same group **2** to become connected by marriage with another group or with each other <*the different races* ~ *freely*>

ˌ**interˈmediary** /-ˈmeedi·əri‖-ˈmiːdɪərɪ/ *n or adj* (sby or sthg) acting as a mediator or go-between

¹ˌ**interˈmediate** /-ˈmeedi·ət‖-ˈmiːdɪət/ *adj* being or occurring at or near the middle place, stage, or degree or between 2 others or extremes – **intermediately** *adv*, **intermediacy** *n*

²**intermediate** *n* a chemical compound formed as an intermediate step in a reaction

interment /inˈtuhmənt‖ɪnˈtɜːmənt/ *n* burial

intermezzo /ˌintəˈmetsoh‖ˌɪntəˈmetsəʊ/ *n, pl* **intermezzi** /-see‖-siː/, **intermezzos** **1** a movement coming between the major sections of an extended musical work (e g an opera) **2** a short independent instrumental composition [Italian, deriv of Latin *intermedius* intermediate]

interminable /inˈtuhminəbl‖ɪnˈtɜːmɪnəbl/ *adj* having or seeming to have no end; *esp* wearisomely long – **interminableness** *n*, **interminably** *adv*, **interminability** *n*

ˌ**interˈmingle** /-ˈming·gl‖-ˈmɪŋgl/ *vb* to mix or mingle together or with sthg else

ˌ**interˈmission** /-ˈmish(ə)n‖-ˈmɪʃ(ə)n/ *n* **1** intermitting or being intermitted **2** an intervening period of time (e g between acts of a performance or attacks of a disease)

ˌ**interˈmittent** /-ˈmit(ə)nt‖-ˈmɪt(ə)nt/ *adj* coming and going at intervals; not continuous – **intermittence** *n*, **intermittently** *adv*

¹**intern** /inˈtuhn‖ɪnˈtɜːn/ *vt* to confine, esp during a war – **internee** *n*, **internment** *n*

²**intern**, **interne** /ˈintuhn‖ˈɪntɜːn/ *n*, *NAm* an advanced student or graduate in medicine, teaching, etc gaining supervised practical experience (e g in a hospital or classroom) – **intern** *vi*, **internship** *n*

internal /inˈtuhnl‖ɪnˈtɜːnl/ *adj* **1** existing or

situated within the limits or surface of sthg **2** applied through the stomach by swallowing <*an ~ medicine*> **3** of or existing within the mind **4** depending only on the properties of the thing under consideration without reference to things outside it <*~ evidence of forgery in a document*> **5** (present or arising) within (a part of) the body or an organism <*an ~ organ*> **6** within a state <*~ strife*> <*~ affairs*> – **internally** *adv*, **internality** *n*

in,ternal-com'bustion ,engine *n* a heat engine in which the combustion that generates the heat energy takes place inside the engine (e g in a cylinder)

internal·ize, -ise /in'tuhnl·,iez‖ɪn'tɜːnl,aɪz/ *vt* to make internal; *specif* to incorporate (e g learnt values) within the self as guiding principles – **internalization** *n*

[1]**,inter'national** /-'nash(ə)nl‖-'næʃ(ə)nl/ *adj* **1** affecting or involving 2 or more nations <*~ trade*> **2** known, recognized, or renowned in more than 1 country <*an ~ celebrity*> – **internationally** *adv*, **internationality** *n*

[2]**international** *n* **1** (sby who plays or has played in) a sports, games, etc match between 2 national teams **2** *also* **internationale** *often cap* any of several socialist or communist organizations of international scope

international date line *n, often cap I, D, & L* an arbitrary line approximately along the 180th meridian, east and west of which the date differs by 1 calendar day

,inter'national,ism /-,iz(ə)m‖-,ɪz(ə)m/ *n* **1** international character, interests, or outlook **2** (an attitude favouring) cooperation among nations – **internationalist** *n or adj*

,inter'national·,ize, -ise /-,iez‖-,aɪz/ *vb* to make or become international; *esp* to place under international control – **internationalization** *n*

internecine /,intə'neesien‖,ɪntə'niːsaɪn/ *adj* **1** mutually destructive **2** of or involving conflict within a group

interpellate /in'tuhpilayt‖ɪn'tɜːpɪleɪt/ *vt* to question (e g a minister) formally concerning an action or policy – **interpellator** *n*, **interpellation** *n*

interpenetrate /,intə'penitrayt‖,ɪntə'penɪtreɪt/ *vt* to penetrate thoroughly *~vi* to penetrate mutually – **interpenetration** *n*

,inter'planetary /-'planit(ə)ri‖-'plænɪt(ə)rɪ/ *adj* existing, carried on, or operating between planets

'inter,play /-,play‖-,pleɪ/ *n* interaction – **interplay** *vi*

'Inter,pol /-,pol‖-,pɒl/ *n* an international police organization for liaison between national police forces

interpolate /in'tuhpəlayt‖ɪn'tɜːpəleɪt/ *vt* **1** to alter or corrupt (e g a text) by inserting new or foreign matter **2** to insert between other things or parts; *esp* to insert (words) into a text or conversation **3** to estimate values of (a function) between 2 known values – **interpolative** *adj*, **interpolator** *n*, **interpolation** *n*

interpose /,intə'pohz‖,ɪntə'pəʊz/ *vt* **1** to place between 2 things or in an intervening position **2** to put forth by way of interference or intervention <*prevented a decision by* interposing *a veto*> **3** to interrupt with (words) during a conversation or argument *~ vi* **1** to be or come in an intervening position **2** INTERVENE 3 **3** to interrupt – **interposer** *n*, **interposition** *n*

interpret /in'tuhprit‖ɪn'tɜːprɪt/ *vt* **1** to expound the meaning of <*~ a dream*> **2** to conceive of in the light of one's beliefs, judgments, or circumstances; construe **3** to represent by means of art; bring to realization by performance <*~s a role*> *~vi* to act as an interpreter – **interpretable** *adj*, **interpretive, interpretative** *adj*, **interpretatively** *adv*

interpretation /in,tuhpri'taysh(ə)n‖ɪn,tɜːprɪ'teɪʃ(ə)n/ *n* an instance of artistic interpreting in performance or adaptation – **interpretational** *adj*

interpreter /in'tuhpritə‖ɪn'tɜːprɪtə/ *n* **1** one who translates orally for people speaking in different languages **2** a computer program that translates an instruction into machine language for immediate execution

interregnum /,intə'regnəm‖,ɪntə'regnəm/ *n, pl* **interregnums, interregna** /-'regnə‖-'regnə/ **1** the time during which **1a** a throne is vacant between reigns **b** the normal functions of government are suspended **2** a lapse or pause in a continuous series

,interre'late /-ri'layt‖-rɪ'leɪt/ *vb* to bring into or be in a relationship where each one depends upon or is acting upon the other – **interrelation, interrelationship** *n*

interrogate /in'terəgayt‖ɪn'terəgeɪt/ *vt* **1** to question formally **2** to give or send out a signal to (e g a computer) to trigger a response [Latin *interrogare*, fr *inter* between + *rogare* to ask] – **interrogator** *n*, **interrogation** *n*

[1]**interrogative** /,intə'rogətiv‖,ɪntə'rɒgətɪv/, **interrogatory** /-t(ə)ri‖-t(ə)rɪ/ *adj* **1a** of or being the grammatical mood that expresses a question **b** used in a question **2** questioning – **interrogatively** *adv*

[2]**interrogative** *n* **1** an interrogative utterance **2** a word, esp a pronoun, used in asking questions **3** the interrogative mood of a language

interrogatory /,intə'rogət(ə)ri‖,ɪntə'rɒgət(ə)rɪ/ *n* a formal question; *esp* a written question to be answered under direction of a court

interrupt /,intə'rupt‖,ɪntə'rʌpt/ *vt* **1** to break the flow or action of (a speaker or speech) **2** to break the uniformity or continuity of (sthg) *~vi* to interrupt an action; *esp* to interrupt another's utterance with one's own – **interrupter** *n*, **interruptible** *adj*, **interruption** *n*, **interruptive** *adj*

,inter'sect /-'sekt‖-'sekt/ *vt* to pierce or divide (e g a line or area) by passing through or across *~ vi* to meet and cross at a point

intersection /'intə,seksh(ə)n, ,--'--‖'ɪntə,sekʃ(ə)n, ,--'--/ *n* **1** a place where 2 or more things (e g streets) intersect **2** the set of elements common to 2 sets; *esp* the set of points common to 2 geometric configurations

,inter'sperse /-'spuhs‖-'spɜːs/ *vt* **1** to insert at intervals among other things <interspersing *drawings throughout the text*> **2** to diversify or vary with scattered things <interspersing *the text with drawings*> – **interspersion** *n*

[1]**,inter'state** /-'stayt‖-'steɪt/ *adj* between 2 or more states, esp of the USA or of Australia <*an ~ highway*>

[2]**interstate** *adv, Austr* to or in another state

<*went ~ to live*>
ˌinterˈstellar /-ˈstelə‖-ˈstelə/ *adj* located or taking place among the stars
interstice /inˈtuhstis‖ɪnˈtɜːstɪs/ *n* a small space between adjacent things – fml
ˌinterˈtwine /-ˈtwien‖-ˈtwaɪn/ *vt* to twine together ~ *vi* to twine about one another – **intertwinement** *n*
interval /ˈintəv(ə)l‖ˈɪntəv(ə)l/ *n* **1** an intervening space: e g **1a** a time between events or states; a pause **b** a distance or gap between objects, units, or states <*lamp posts placed at regular ~s*> **c** the difference in pitch between 2 notes **2** a set of real numbers between 2 numbers; *also* the set of real numbers greater or less than some number **3** *Br* a break in the presentation of an entertainment (e g a play)
ˌinterˈvene /-ˈveen‖-ˈviːn/ *vi* **1** to enter or appear as sthg irrelevant or extraneous **2** to occur or come between 2 things, esp points of time or events **3** to come in or between so as to hinder or modify **4a** to enter a lawsuit as a third party **b** to interfere in another nation's internal affairs – **intervenor** *n*, **intervention** *n*
ˈinterˌview /-vyooh‖-vjuː/ *n* **1** a formal consultation usu to evaluate qualifications (e g of a prospective student or employee) **2** (a report of) a meeting at which information is obtained (e g by a journalist) from sby – **interview** *vt*, **interviewer** *n*, **interviewee** *n*
ˌinterˈweave /-ˈweev‖-ˈwiːv/ *vb* **interwove** /-ˈwohv‖-ˈwəʊv/ *also* **interweaved; interwoven** /-ˈwohv(ə)n‖-ˈwəʊv(ə)n/ *also* **interweaved 1** to weave together **2** to intermingle, blend – **interwoven** *adj*, **interweave** *n*
[1]intestate /inˈtestayt, -tət‖ɪnˈtesteɪt, -tət/ *adj* having made no valid will – **intestacy** *n*
[2]intestate *n* sby who dies intestate
intestinal /inˈtestinl‖ɪnˈtestɪnl/ *adj* of, being, affecting, or occurring in the intestine – **intestinally** *adv*
[1]intestine /inˈtestin‖ɪnˈtestɪn/ *adj* of the internal affairs of a state or country
[2]intestine *n* the tubular part of the alimentary canal that extends from the stomach to the anus
intimacy /ˈintiməsi‖ˈɪntɪməsɪ/ *n* **1** familiarity **2** SEXUAL INTERCOURSE – euph
[1]intimate /ˈintimayt‖ˈɪntɪmeɪt/ *vt* to make known: e g **a** to announce **b** to hint; IMPLY 2 – **intimation** *n*
[2]intimate /ˈintimət‖ˈɪntɪmət/ *adj* **1a** intrinsic, essential **b** belonging to or characterizing one's deepest nature **2** marked by very close association, contact, or familiarity **3a** marked by a warm friendship developing through long association **b** suggesting informal warmth or privacy **4** of a very personal or private nature **5** involved in a sexual relationship; *specif* engaging in an act of sexual intercourse – euph – **intimately** *adv*
[3]intimate *n* a close friend or confidant
intimidate /inˈtimidayt‖ɪnˈtɪmɪdeɪt/ *vt* to frighten; *esp* to compel or deter (as if) by threats – **intimidator** *n*, **intimidatory** *adj*, **intimidation** *n*
into /ˈintə‖ˈɪntə *before consonants; otherwise* ˈintooh‖ˈɪntuː/ *prep* **1a** so as to be inside <*come ~ the house*> **b** so as to be <*grow ~ a woman*> <*divide it ~ sections*> **c** so as to be in (a state) <*get ~ trouble*> **d** so as to be expressed in <*translate it ~ French*>, dressed in <*changed ~ his uniform*>, engaged in <*go ~ farming*>, or a member of <*enter ~ an alliance*> **e** – used in division as the inverse of *by* or *divided by* <*divide 35 ~ 70*> **2** – used to indicate a partly elapsed period of time or a partly traversed extent of space <*far ~ the night*> <*deep ~ the jungle*> **3** in the direction of; *esp* towards the centre of <*look ~ the sun*> <*inquire ~ the matter*> **4** to a position of contact with; against <*ran ~ a wall*> **5** involved with <*they were ~ hard drugs*>; *esp* keen on <*are you ~ meditation?*> – infml
intolerable /inˈtol(ə)rəbl‖ɪnˈtɒl(ə)rəbl/ *adj* unbearable – **intolerableness** *n*, **intolerably** *adv*
inˈtolerant /-ˈtolərənt‖-ˈtɒlərənt/ *adj* **1** unable or unwilling to endure <*a plant ~ of direct sunlight*> **2** unwilling to grant or share social, professional, political, or religious rights; bigoted – **intolerance** *n*, **intolerantly** *adv*
intonation /ˌintəˈnaysh(ə)n‖ˌɪntəˈneɪʃ(ə)n/ *n* **1** sthg that is intoned; *specif* the opening notes of a Gregorian chant **2** performance of music with respect to correctness of pitch and harmony **3** the rise and fall in pitch of the voice in speech
intone /inˈtohn‖ɪnˈtəʊn/ *vb* to utter (sthg) in musical or prolonged tones; recite in singing tones or in a monotone – **intoner** *n*
in toto /in ˈtohtoh‖ɪn ˈtəʊtəʊ/ *adv* totally, entirely
intoxicate /inˈtoksikayt‖ɪnˈtɒksɪkeɪt/ *vt* **1** POISON 1a **2a** to excite or stupefy by alcohol or a drug, esp to the point where physical and mental control is markedly diminished **b** to cause to lose self-control through excitement or elation [Medieval Latin *intoxicare*, fr Latin *in* in + *toxicum* poison – see TOXIC] – **intoxicant** *n or adj*, **intoxicatedly** *adv*, **intoxication** *n*
intra- /intrə-‖ɪntrə-/ *prefix* **1** within; inside <intra*uterine*> **2** intro- <*an* intra*muscular injection*>
intractable /inˈtraktəbl‖ɪnˈtræktəbl/ *adj* **1** not easily managed or directed; OBSTINATE 1 **2** not easily manipulated, wrought, or solved **3** not easily relieved or cured <~ *pain*> – **intractableness** *n*, **intractably** *adv*, **intractability** *n*
intramural /ˌintrəˈmyooərəl‖ˌɪntrəˈmjʊərəl/ *adj* within the limits of a community or institution (e g a university) – **intramurally** *adv*
intransigent /inˈtransij(ə)nt, -ˈtranzi-‖ɪnˈtrænsɪdʒ(ə)nt, -ˈtrænzɪ-/ *adj* refusing to compromise or to abandon an extreme position or attitude, esp in politics; uncompromising – **intransigence** *n*, **intransigent** *n*, **intransigently** *adv*
inˈtransitive /-ˈtransitiv, -ˈtrahn-, -zitiv‖-ˈtrænsɪtɪv, -ˈtrɑːn-, -zɪtɪv/ *adj* characterized by not having a direct object <*an ~ verb*> – **intransitive** *n*, **intransitively** *adv*
intrapreneur /ˌintrəprəˈnuh‖ˌɪntrəprəˈnɜː/ *n* sby who initiates or manages a new business or division within an established company – **intrapreneurial** *adj*, **intrapreneurship** *n*
intrauterine /ˌintrəˈyoohtərin,-rien‖ɪntrəˈjuːtərɪn,-raɪn/ *adj* situated, used, or occurring in the uterus
intrauterine device, intrauterine contraceptive device *n* a device inserted and left in the

uterus to prevent conception

ˌintraˈvenous /-ˈveenəs‖-ˈviːnəs/ *adj* situated or occurring in, or entering by way of a vein; *also* used in intravenous procedures – **intravenously** *adv*

intrench /inˈtrench‖ɪnˈtrentʃ/ *vb* to entrench

intrepid /inˈtrepid‖ɪnˈtrepɪd/ *adj* fearless, bold, and resolute – **intrepidly** *adv*, **intrepidity** *n*

intricate /ˈintrikət‖ˈɪntrɪkət/ *adj* **1** having many complexly interrelating parts or elements **2** difficult to resolve or analyse [Latin *intricare* to entangle, fr *in* in + *tricae* trifles, impediments] – **intricacy** *n*, **intricately** *adv*

1intrigue /inˈtreeg‖ɪnˈtriːg/ *vt* **1** to arouse the interest or curiosity of **2** to captivate; FASCINATE 2 <*her beauty* ~s *me*> ~ *vi* to carry on an intrigue; *esp* to plot, scheme – **intriguer** *n*

2intrigue /ˈintreeg, -ˈ-‖ˈɪntriːg, -ˈ-/ *n* **1a** a secret scheme or plot **b** the practice of engaging in or using scheming or underhand plots **2** a clandestine love affair

intrinsic /inˈtrinzik‖ɪnˈtrɪnzɪk/ *adj* **1** belonging to the essential nature or constitution of sthg <*an ornament of no* ~ *worth but of great sentimental value*> **2** originating or situated within the body – **intrinsically** *adv*

intro /ˈintroh‖ˈɪntrəʊ/ *n, pl* **intros** INTRODUCTION 1 – infml

intro- *prefix* **1** in; into <intro*jection*> **2** inwards; within <intro*vert*>

introduce /ˌintrəˈdyoohs‖ˌɪntrəˈdjuːs/ *vt* **1** to lead or bring in, esp for the first time <~ *a rare plant species into the country*> **2a** to bring into play <~ *a new line of approach into the argument*> **b** to bring into practice or use; institute **3** to lead to or make known by a formal act, announcement, or recommendation: e g **3a** to cause to be acquainted; make (oneself or sby) known to another **b** to present formally (e g at court or into society) **c** to announce formally or by an official reading **d** to make preliminary explanatory or laudatory remarks about (e g a speaker) **4** PLACE 2a, INSERT 2 <*the risk of* introducing *harmful substances into the body*> **5** to bring to a knowledge or discovery of sthg <~ *her to the works of Byron*>

introduction /ˌintrəˈduksh(ə)n‖ˌɪntrəˈdʌkʃ(ə)n/ *n* **1a** a preliminary treatise or course of study **b** a short introductory musical passage **2** sthg introduced; *specif* a plant or animal new to an area

introductory /ˌintrəˈdukt(ə)ri‖ˌɪntrəˈdʌkt(ə)rɪ/ *adj* of or being a first step that sets sthg going or in proper perspective; preliminary – **introductorily** *adv*

introit /ˈintroyt‖ˈɪntrɔɪt/ *n* a piece of music sung or played at the beginning of a church service; *specif, often cap* the antiphon or psalm sung as the priest approaches the altar to celebrate the Eucharist

introspect /-ˈspekt‖-ˈspekt/ *vi* to examine one's own mind or its contents reflectively – **introspection** *n*, **introspective** *adj*

1ˌintroˈvert /-ˈvuht‖-ˈvɜːt/ *vt* to turn inwards or in on itself or oneself: e g **a** to draw in (a tubular part) **b** to concentrate or direct (the mind, thoughts, or emotions) on oneself – **introversion** *n*

2ˈintroˌvert *n* **1** sthg (e g the eyestalk of a snail) that is or can be drawn in **2** one whose attention and interests are directed towards his/her own mental life

intrude /inˈtroohd‖ɪnˈtruːd/ *vi* **1** to thrust oneself in without invitation, permission, or welcome **2** to enter as a geological intrusion ~ *vt* **1** to thrust or force in or on, esp without permission, welcome, or suitable reason **2** to cause (e g rock) to intrude – **intruder** *n*

intrusion /inˈtroohzh(ə)n‖ɪnˈtruːʒ(ə)n/ *n* **1** intruding or being intruded; *specif* wrongfully entering upon the property of another **2** (the forcible entry of) rock or magma forced while molten into or between other rock formations

intrusive /inˈtroohsiv, -ziv‖ɪnˈtruːsɪv, -zɪv/ *adj* **1** characterized by (a tendency to) intrusion **2** *of a rock* being an intrusion – **intrusively** *adv*

intrust /inˈtrust‖ɪnˈtrʌst/ *vt* to entrust

intuit /inˈtyooh·it‖ɪnˈtjuːɪt/ *vt* to apprehend by intuition – **intuitable** *adj*

intuition /ˌintyoohˈish(ə)n‖ˌɪntjuːˈɪʃ(ə)n/ *n* **1a** (knowledge gained by) immediate apprehension or cognition **b** the power of attaining direct knowledge without evident rational thought and the drawing of conclusions from evidence available **2** quick and ready insight – **intuitional** *adj*, **intuitive** *adj*, **intuitively** *adv*

intumesce /ˌintyooˈmes‖ˌɪntjʊˈmes/ *vi* ENLARGE 1, SWELL 1b – **intumescence** *n*, **intumescent** *adj*

inundate /ˈinundayt‖ˈɪnʌndeɪt/ *vt* to cover or overwhelm (as if) with a flood – **inundation** *n*

inure /iˈnyooə‖ɪˈnjʊə/ *vt* to accustom *to* sthg undesirable – **inurement** *n*

invade /inˈvayd‖ɪnˈveɪd/ *vt* **1** to enter (e g a country) for hostile purposes **2** to encroach on <*a noise* ~d *his privacy*> **3a** to spread over or into as if invading **b** to affect injuriously and progressively <*gangrene* ~s *healthy tissue*> – **invader** *n*

1invalid /inˈvalid‖ɪnˈvælɪd/ *adj* **1** without legal force **2** logically inconsistent – **invalidly** *adv*, **invalidity** *n*

2invalid /ˈinvəlid‖ˈɪnvəlɪd; *also* -ˌleed‖-ˌliːd/ *adj* **1** suffering from disease or disability **2** of or suited to an invalid

3invalid /ˈinvəlid‖ˈɪnvəlɪd/ *n* one who is sickly or disabled

4invalid /ˈinvəlid, ˌinvəˈleed‖ˈɪnvəlɪd, ˌɪnvəˈliːd/ *vt* to remove from active duty by reason of sickness or disability <*he was* ~ed *out of the army*>

invalidate /inˈvalidayt‖ɪnˈvælɪdeɪt/ *vt* to make invalid; *esp* to weaken or destroy the convincingness of (e g an argument or claim) – **invalidation** *n*

invaluable /inˈvalyooəbl‖ɪnˈvæljʊəbl/ *adj* valuable beyond estimation; priceless – **invaluably** *adv*

invariable /inˈveəri·əbl‖ɪnˈveərɪəbl/ *adj* not (capable of) changing; constant – **invariable** *n*, **invariableness** *n*, **invariably** *adv*, **invariability** *n*

invasion /inˈvayzh(ə)n‖ɪnˈveɪʒ(ə)n/ *n* **1** an invading, esp by an army **2** the incoming or spread of sthg usu harmful – **invasive** *adj*

invective /inˈvektiv‖ɪnˈvektɪv/ *n* abusive or insulting (use of) language; denunciation – **invective** *adj*, **invectively** *adv*

inveigh /in'vay‖ɪn'veɪ/ *vi* to speak or protest bitterly or vehemently *against*

inveigle /in'vaygl‖ɪn'veɪgl/ *vt* to win (sby or sthg) over by ingenuity or flattery [Middle French *aveugler* to blind, hoodwink, fr *avogle* blind, fr Medieval Latin *ab oculis*, lit., lacking eyes] – **inveiglement** *n*

invent /in'vent‖ɪn'vent/ *vt* **1** to think up <~ *an excuse*> **2** to produce (e g sthg useful) for the first time – **inventor** *n*, **inventress** *n*

invention /in'vensh(ə)n‖ɪn'venʃ(ə)n/ *n* **1** productive imagination; inventiveness **2a** sthg invented: e g **2a(1)** a (misleading) product of the imagination **a(2)** a contrivance or process devised after study and experiment **b** a short keyboard composition, usu in double counterpoint

inventive /in'ventiv‖ɪn'ventɪv/ *adj* **1** creative **2** characterized by invention – **inventively** *adv*, **inventiveness** *n*

[1]**inventory** /'invəntri‖'ɪnvəntrɪ/ *n* **1a** an itemized list (e g of the property of an individual or estate) **b** a list of traits, preferences, attitudes, etc used to evaluate personal characteristics or skills **2a** the items listed in an inventory **b** *NAm* the quantity of goods, components, or raw materials on hand; STOCK 5b **3** the taking of an inventory

[2]**inventory** *vt* to make an inventory of; catalogue

[1]**inverse** /in'vuhs, '--‖ɪn'vɜːs, '--/ *adj* **1** opposite in order, direction, nature, or effect **2** *of a mathematical function* expressing the same relationship as another function but from the opposite viewpoint **3** being or relating to an inverse function <~ *sine*> – **inversely** *adv*

[2]**inverse** *n* **1** a direct opposite **2** an inverse function or operation in mathematics <*addition is the* ~ *of subtraction*>

inversion /in'vuhsh(ə)n‖ɪn'vɜːʃ(ə)n/ *n* **1** the act or process of inverting **2** a reversal of position, order, form, or relationship: e g **2a(1)** a change in normal word order; *esp* the placement of a verb before its subject **a(2)** the process or result of changing, converting, or reversing the relative positions of the elements of a musical interval, chord, or phrase **b** being turned inwards or inside out **3** the operation of forming the inverse of a magnitude, operation, or element **4** homosexuality – **inversive** *adj*

[1]**invert** /in'vuht‖ɪn'vɜːt/ *vt* **1a** to turn inside out or upside down **b** to turn (e g a foot) inwards **2a** to reverse in position, order, or relationship **b** to subject to musical inversion **c** to express the mathematical inverse, esp the reciprocal, of – **invertible** *adj*

[2]**invert** /'invuht‖'ɪnvɜːt/ *n* sby or sthg characterized by inversion; *esp* a homosexual

invertebrate /in'vuhtibrət, -brayt‖ɪn'vɜːtɪbrət, -breɪt/ *adj* **1** (of animals) lacking a spinal column or notochord **2** lacking in strength or vitality of character – **invertebrate** *n*

in,verted 'comma *n* **1** a comma in type printed upside down at the top of the line **2** *chiefly Br* QUOTATION MARK

[1]**invest** /in'vest‖ɪn'vest/ *vt* **1** to confer (the symbols of) authority, office, or rank on **2** to clothe, endow, or cover (as if) *with* sthg <~ed *with an air of mystery*> **3** to surround with troops or ships so as to prevent escape or entry

[2]**invest** *vt* **1** to commit (money) to a particular use (e g buying shares or new capital outlay) in order to earn a financial return **2** to devote (e g time or effort) to sthg for future advantages ~*vi* to make an investment <~ *in a new car*> – **investable** *adj*, **investor** *n*

investigate /in'vestigayt‖ɪn'vestɪgeɪt/ *vb* **1** to make a systematic examination or study (of) **2** to conduct an official inquiry (into) – **investigational** *adj*, **investigative** *adj*, **investigator** *n*, **investigatory** *adj*, **investigation** *n*

investiture /in'vestichə‖ɪn'vestɪtʃə/ *n* a formal ceremony conferring an office or honour on sby

[1]**investment** /in'vestmənt‖ɪn'vestmənt/ *n* a siege or blockade

[2]**investment** *n* (a sum of) money invested for income or profit; *also* the asset (e g property) purchased

inveterate /in'vet(ə)rət‖ɪn'vet(ə)rət/ *adj* **1** firmly, obstinately, and persistently established **2** habitual <*an* ~ *liar*> – **inveteracy** *n*, **inveterately** *adv*

invidious /in'vidi·əs‖ɪn'vɪdɪəs/ *adj* **1** tending to cause discontent, ill will, or envy **2** of an unpleasant or objectionable nature; of a kind causing or likely to cause harm or resentment – **invidiously** *adv*, **invidiousness** *n*

invigilate /in'vijilayt‖ɪn'vɪdʒɪleɪt/ *vb* to keep watch (over); *specif, Br* to supervise (candidates) at (an examination) – **invigilator** *n*, **invigilation** *n*

invigorate /in'vigərayt‖ɪn'vɪgəreɪt/ *vt* to give fresh life and energy to – **invigoratingly** *adv*, **invigorator** *n*, **invigoration** *n*

invincible /in'vinsəbl‖ɪn'vɪnsəbl/ *adj* incapable of being conquered or subdued – **invincibleness** *n*, **invincibly** *adv*, **invincibility** *n*

inviolable /in'vie·ələbl‖ɪn'vaɪələbl/ *adj* (to be kept) secure from violation, profanation, or assault – **inviolably** *adv*, **inviolability** *n*

inviolate /in'vie·ələt, -,layt‖ɪn'vaɪələt, -,leɪt/ *adj* not violated or profaned – **inviolacy** *n*, **inviolately** *adv*, **inviolateness** *n*

invisible /in'vizəbl‖ɪn'vɪzəbl/ *adj* **1** incapable (by nature or circumstances) of being seen **2a** not appearing in published financial statements <~ *assets*> **b** not reflected in statistics <~ *earnings*> **c** of or being trade in services (e g insurance or tourism) rather than goods **3** too small or unobtrusive to be seen or noticed; inconspicuous – **invisible** *n*, **invisibleness** *n*, **invisibly** *adv*, **invisibility** *n*

invitation /,invi'taysh(ə)n‖,ɪnvɪ'teɪʃ(ə)n/ *n* **1** an often formal request to be present or participate **2** an incentive, inducement – **invitational** *adj*

[1]**invite** /in'viet‖ɪn'vaɪt/ *vt* **1a** to offer an incentive or inducement to **b** to (unintentionally) increase the likelihood of <*his actions* ~ *trouble*> **2** to request (the presence of) formally or politely – **invitatory** *adj*, **inviter** *n*, **invitee** *n*

[2]**invite** /'inviet‖'ɪnvaɪt/ *n* an invitation – infml

inviting /in'vieting‖ɪn'vaɪtɪŋ/ *adj* attractive, tempting – **invitingly** *adv*

invocation /,invə'kaysh(ə)n‖,ɪnvə'keɪʃ(ə)n/ *n* **1** the act or process of petitioning for help or support; *specif, often cap* an invocatory prayer, esp at the beginning of a church service **2** the performing of magical rites in order to summon spirits – **invocational** *adj*, **invocatory** *adj*

[1]**invoice** /'invoys||'ɪnvɔɪs/ *n* **1** [4]BILL 3a; *specif* an itemized list of goods shipped, usu specifying the price and the terms of sale **2** a consignment of merchandise

[2]**invoice** *vt* to submit an invoice for or to

invoke /in'vohk||ɪn'vəʊk/ *vt* **1a** to petition (e g a deity) for help or support **b** to appeal to or cite as an authority **2** to call forth (e g a spirit) by uttering a spell or magical formula **3** to make an earnest request for; SOLICIT 3 **4** to put into effect < ~ *economic sanctions*> – **invoker** *n*

involuntary /in'volənt(ə)ri||ɪn'vɒlənt(ə)rɪ/ *adj* **1** done contrary to or without choice **2** not subject to conscious control; reflex < ~ *muscle*> – **involuntarily** *adv*, **involuntariness** *n*

involve /in'volv||ɪn'vɒlv/ *vt* **1a** to cause to be associated or take part **b** to occupy (oneself) absorbingly; *esp* to commit (oneself) emotionally **2** to envelop **3** to relate closely **4a** to have within or as part of itself **b** to require as a necessary accompaniment – **involvement** *n*, **involver** *n*

in'volved *adj* **1** (needlessly or excessively) complex **2** taking part *in* <*workers* ~ *in building a dam*> – **involvedly** *adv*

invulnerable /in'vulnərəbl||ɪn'vʌlnərəbl/ *adj* **1** incapable of being injured or harmed **2** immune to or proof against attack – **invulnerableness** *n*, **invulnerably** *adv*, **invulnerability** *n*

inward /'inwood||'ɪnwʊd/ *adj* **1** situated within or directed towards the inside **2** of or relating to the mind or spirit <*struggled to achieve* ~ *peace*> – **inwardness** *n*

'**inwards**, *NAm chiefly* **inward** *adv* **1** towards the inside, centre, or interior **2** towards the inner being

iodine /'ie·ə,deen||'aɪə,di:n/ *n* a (solid blackish grey) halogen element – **iodinate** *vt*, **iodination** *n*

iod·ize, **-ise** /'ie·ə,diez||'aɪə,daɪz/ *vt* to treat with iodine or a compound of iodine < ~d *salt*>

ion /'ie·ən||'aɪən/ *n* **1** an atom or group of atoms that carries a positive or negative electric charge as a result of having lost or gained 1 or more electrons **2** a free electron or other charged subatomic particle

-ion /-i·ən||-ɪən/ *suffix* (*vb* → *n*) **1a** act or process of <*validation*> **b** result of (a specified act or process) <*regulation*> **2** quality or condition of <*hydration*>

ionic /ie'onik||aɪ'ɒnɪk/ *adj* **1** of, existing as, or characterized by ions < ~ *gases*> **2** functioning by means of ions < ~ *conduction*> – **ionicity** *n*

Ionic *adj* **1** (characteristic) of the ancient region of Ionia **2** of that 1 of the 3 Greek orders of architecture that is characterized esp by the scroll-shaped ornament of its capital

ion·ize, **-ise** /'ie·ə,niez||'aɪə,naɪz/ *vb* to convert or become converted wholly or partly into ions – **ionizable** *adj*, **ionizer** *n*, **ionization** *n*

ionosphere /ie'onə,sfiə||aɪ'ɒnə,sfɪə/ *n* the part of the earth's atmosphere that extends from an altitude above that of the stratosphere out to at least 480km (about 300mi) and consists of several distinct regions containing free ions; *also* a comparable region surrounding another planet – **ionospheric** *adj*, **ionospherically** *adv*

iota /ie'ohtə||aɪ'əʊtə/ *n* **1** the 9th letter of the Greek alphabet **2** an infinitesimal amount

IOU /,ie oh 'yooh||,aɪ əʊ 'ju:/ *n* (a written acknowledgment of) a debt

ipso facto /,ipsoh 'faktoh||,ɪpsəʊ 'fæktəʊ/ *adv* by the very nature of the case [Modern Latin, lit., by the fact itself]

IQ *n* INTELLIGENCE QUOTIENT

ir- – see IN-

Iranian /i'rayni·ən, i'rahni·ən||ɪ'reɪnɪən, ɪ-'rɑ:nɪən/ *n* **1** a native or inhabitant of Iran **2** a branch of the Indo-European family of languages that includes Persian – **Iranian** *adj*

irascible /i'rasibl||ɪ'ræsɪbl/ *adj* having an easily provoked temper – **irascibleness** *n*, **irascibly** *adv*, **irascibility** *n*

irate /ie'rayt||aɪ'reɪt/ *adj* roused to or arising from anger – **irately** *adv*, **irateness** *n*

ire /ie·ə||aɪə/ *n* intense and usu openly displayed anger – **ireful** *adj*

iridescence /iri'des(ə)ns||ɪrɪ'des(ə)ns/ *n* (a display or effect suggestive of) a play of changing colours in a soap bubble, bird's plumage, etc – **iridescent** *adj*, **iridescently** *adv*

iridium /i'ridi·əm||ɪ'rɪdɪəm/ *n* a silver-white hard brittle very heavy metallic element of the platinum group – **iridic** *adj*

iris /'ieris||'aɪrɪs/ *n*, *pl* (*1*) **irises**, **irides** /'ierideez||'aɪrɪdi:z/, (*2*) **irises**, **irides**, *esp collectively* **iris** **1a** the opaque contractile diaphragm perforated by the pupil that forms the coloured portion of the eye **b** **iris**, **iris diaphragm** an adjustable diaphragm of thin opaque plates that can be moved to control the size of an aperture **2** any of a large genus of plants with long straight leaves and large showy flowers

[1]**Irish** /'ierish||'aɪrɪʃ/ *adj* **1** of Ireland or the Irish (language) **2** amusingly illogical – **Irishman** *n*

[2]**Irish** *n* **1** *pl in constr* the people of Ireland **2** **Irish**, **Irish Gaelic** the Celtic language of Ireland, esp as used since the end of the medieval period

,**Irish** '**setter** *n* (any of) a breed of chestnut-brown or mahogany-red gundogs

irk /uhk||ɜ:k/ *vt* to make weary, irritated, or bored

'**irksome** /-s(ə)m||-s(ə)m/ *adj* troublesome, annoying – **irksomely** *adv*, **irksomeness** *n*

[1]**iron** /'ie·ən||'aɪən/ *n* **1** a heavy malleable ductile magnetic silver-white metallic element that readily rusts in moist air, occurs in most igneous rocks, and is vital to biological processes **2** sthg (orig) made of iron: e g **2a** sthg used to bind or restrain – usu pl **b** a heated metal implement used for branding or cauterizing **c** a metal implement with a smooth flat typically triangular base that is heated (e g by electricity) and used to smooth or press clothing **d** a stirrup **e** any of a numbered series of usu 9 golf clubs with metal heads of varying angles for hitting the ball to various heights and lengths **3** great strength or hardness – **iron in the fire** a prospective course of action; a plan not yet realized

[2]**iron** *adj* **1** (made) of iron **2** resembling iron (e g in appearance, strength, solidity, or durability) – **ironness** *n*

[3]**iron** *vt* **1** to smooth (as if) with a heated iron

< ~ed *his shirt*> **2** to remove (e g wrinkles) by ironing – often + *out* ~*vi* to be capable of being ironed <*this skirt* ~s *well*>

Iron Age *n* the period of human culture characterized by the widespread use of iron for making tools and weapons and dating from before 1000 BC

[1]ˌiron'clad /-'klad‖-'klæd/ *adj* sheathed in iron or steel armour

[2]'ironˌclad *n* an ironclad naval vessel, esp in the 19th c

ˌiron 'curtain *n, often cap I&C* an esp political and ideological barrier between the Communist countries of E Europe and the non-Communist countries of (and those friendly to) W Europe

ˌiron 'grey *adj or n* dark greenish grey

ironic /ie'ronik‖aɪ'rɒnɪk/, **ironical** /-kl‖-kl/ *adj* **1** of, containing, or constituting irony **2** given to irony – **ironically** *adv*, **ironicalness** *n*

ironing /'ie·əning‖'aɪənɪŋ/ *n* clothes and cloth articles (e g towels and tablecloths) that are (to be) ironed

'ironing ˌboard *n* a narrow flat board, on which clothes are ironed, mounted on collapsible and adjustable legs

ˌiron 'lung *n* a device for artificial respiration that fits over the patient's chest and forces air into and out of the lungs

'ironˌmonger /-ˌmung·gə‖-ˌmʌŋgə/ *n, Br* a dealer in esp household hardware – **ironmongery** *n*

iron out *vt* to put right or correct (e g a problem or defect); resolve (e g difficulties)

ˌiron 'pyrites *n* iron disulphide occurring as a lustrous pale brass-yellow mineral

'ironˌstone /-ˌstohn‖-ˌstəʊn/ *n* a hard sedimentary iron ore, esp a siderite

'ironˌware /-ˌweə‖-ˌweə/ *n* articles, esp vessels and implements for domestic use, made of iron

'ironˌworks /-ˌwuhks‖-ˌwɜːks/ *n, pl* **ironworks** a mill or building where iron or steel is smelted or heavy iron or steel products are made – often pl with sing. meaning

irony /'ierəni‖'aɪrənɪ/ *n* **1a** the use of words to express a meaning other than and esp the opposite of the literal meaning **b** an expression or utterance using irony **2a** (an event or situation showing) incongruity between actual circumstances and the normal, appropriate, or expected result **b** DRAMATIC IRONY **3** an attitude of detached awareness of incongruity [Latin *ironia*, fr Greek *eirōneia*, fr *eirōn* dissembler]

irradiate /i'raydiayt‖ɪ'reɪdɪeɪt/ *vt* **1a** to cast rays (of light) upon **b** to give intellectual or spiritual insight to **c** to affect or treat by (exposure to) radiant energy (e g heat) **2** to emit like rays (of light); RADIATE 2 – **irradiance** *n*, **irradiative** *adj*, **irradiator** *n*

[1]irrational /i'rash(ə)nl‖ɪ'ræʃ(ə)nl/ *adj* not rational: e g **a** not governed by or according to reason **b** being or having a value that is an irrational number <*an* ~ *root of an equation*> – **irrationalism** *n*, **irrationalist** *n*, **irrationally** *adv*, **irrationality** *n*

[2]irrational, irrational number *n* a number (e g π) that cannot be expressed as the result of dividing 1 integer by another

[1]irreconcilable /i'rekənˌsieləbl‖ɪ'rekənˌsaɪləbl/ *adj* impossible to reconcile: e g **a** resolutely opposed **b** INCOMPATIBLE 1 – **irreconcilableness** *n*, **irreconcilably** *adv*, **irreconcilability** *n*

[2]irreconcilable *n* an opponent of compromise or collaboration

irrecoverable /ˌiri'kuv(ə)rəbl‖ˌɪrɪ'kʌv(ə)rəbl/ *adj* not capable of being recovered or retrieved – **irrecoverably** *adv*

irredeemable /ˌiri'deeməbl‖ˌɪrɪ'diːməbl/ *adj* not redeemable; *esp* beyond remedy; hopeless – **irredeemably** *adv*

irreducible /ˌiri'dyoohsəbl‖ˌɪrɪ'djuːsəbl/ *adj* impossible to bring into a desired, normal, or simpler state – **irreducibly** *adv*, **irreducibility** *n*

irrefutable /ˌiri'fyoohtəbl, i'refyootəbl‖ˌɪrɪ'fjuːtəbl, ɪ'refjʊtəbl/ *adj* incontrovertible – **irrefutably** *adv*, **irrefutability** *n*

[1]irregular /i'regyoolə‖ɪ'regjʊlə/ *adj* **1a** contrary to rule, custom, or moral principles **b** not inflected in the normal manner; *specif* STRONG 14 **c** inadequate because of failure to conform **d** *of troops* not belonging to the regular army organization **2** lacking symmetry or evenness **3** lacking continuity or regularity, esp of occurrence or activity – **irregularly** *adv*

[2]irregular *n* an irregular soldier

irregularity /iˌregyoo'larəti‖ɪˌregjʊ'lærətɪ/ *n* sthg irregular (e g contrary to accepted professional or ethical standards)

irrelevant /i'reliv(ə)nt‖ɪ'relɪv(ə)nt/ *adj* not relevant; inapplicable – **irrelevance** *n*, **irrelevancy** *n*, **irrelevantly** *adv*

irreligion /ˌiri'lij(ə)n‖ˌɪrɪ'lɪdʒ(ə)n/ *n* hostility to or disregard of religion – **irreligionist** *n*, **irreligious** *adj*, **irreligiously** *adv*

irremediable /ˌiri'meedi·əbl, -dyəbl‖ˌɪrɪ'miːdɪəbl, -djəbl/ *adj* not remediable; *specif* incurable – **irremediableness** *n*, **irremediably** *adv*

irreparable /i'rep(ə)rəbl‖ɪ'rep(ə)rəbl/ *adj* not able to be restored to a previous condition – **irreparableness** *n*, **irreparably** *adv*

irreplaceable /ˌiri'playsəbl‖ˌɪrɪ'pleɪsəbl/ *adj* having no adequate substitute – **irreplaceably** *adv*

irrepressible /ˌiri'presəbl‖ˌɪrɪ'presəbl/ *adj* impossible to restrain or control – **irrepressibly** *adv*, **irrepressibility** *n*

irreproachable /ˌiri'prohchəbl‖ˌɪrɪ'prəʊtʃəbl/ *adj* offering no foundation for blame or criticism – **irreproachably** *adv*, **irreproachability** *n*

irresistible /ˌiri'zistəbl‖ˌɪrɪ'zɪstəbl/ *adj* impossible to resist successfully; highly attractive or enticing – **irresistibleness** *n*, **irresistibly** *adv*, **irresistibility** *n*

irresolute /i'rezəl(y)ooht‖ɪ'rezəl(j)uːt/ *adj* lacking decision or a firm aim and purpose – **irresolutely** *adv*, **irresoluteness** *n*, **irresolution** *n*

ˌirre'spective of /ˌiri'spektiv‖ˌɪrɪ'spektɪv/ *prep* without regard or reference to; IN SPITE OF

irresponsible /ˌiri'sponsəbl‖ˌɪrɪ'spɒnsəbl/ *adj* **1** showing no regard for the consequences of one's actions **2** unable to bear responsibility – **irresponsibly** *adv*, **irresponsibility** *n*

irreverence /i'rev(ə)rəns‖ɪ'rev(ə)rəns/ *n* (an

act or utterance showing) lack of reverence – **irreverent** *adj*, **irreverently** *adv*

irreversible /ˌiri'vuhsəbl‖ˌɪrɪ'vɜːsəbl/ *adj* unable to be changed back into a previous state or condition – **irreversibly** *adv*, **irreversibility** *n*

irrevocable /i'revəkəbl‖ɪ'revəkəbl/ *adj* incapable of being revoked or altered – **irrevocably** *adv*, **irrevocability** *n*

irrigate /'irigayt‖'ɪrɪgeɪt/ *vt* to wet, moisten: e g **a** to supply (e g land) with water by artificial means **b** to flush (e g an eye or wound) with a stream of liquid ~*vi* to practise irrigation – **irrigator** *n*, **irrigation** *n*

irritable /'iritəbl‖'ɪrɪtəbl/ *adj* capable of being irritated: e g **a** easily exasperated or excited **b** (excessively) responsive to stimuli – **irritableness** *n*, **irritably** *adv*, **irritability** *n*

irritant /'irit(ə)nt‖'ɪrɪt(ə)nt/ *n* sthg that irritates or excites – **irritant** *adj*

irritate /'iritayt‖'ɪrɪteɪt/ *vt* **1** to excite impatience, anger, or displeasure in **2** to induce a response to a stimulus in or of ~*vi* to cause or induce displeasure or anger – **irritatingly** *adv*, **irritative** *adj*, **irritation** *n*

irrupt /i'rupt‖ɪ'rʌpt/ *vi* to rush in forcibly or violently – **irruption** *n*, **irruptive** *adj*, **irruptively** *adv*

is /z‖z; *strong* iz‖ɪz/ *pres 3 sing of* BE, *dial pres 1&2 sing of* BE, *substandard pres pl of* BE

ischaemia /is'keemi·ə‖ɪs'kiːmɪə/ *n* local deficiency of blood due to decreased arterial flow

-ise /-iez‖-aɪz/ – see -IZE

-ish /-ish‖-ɪʃ/ *suffix* **1** (*n* → *adj*) of or belonging to (a specified country or ethnic group) <*Finn*ish> **2a(1)** (*adj, n* → *adj*) having a trace of <*summer*ish>; slightly <*purpl*ish> **a(2)** (*n* → *adj*) having the approximate age of <*forty*ish> **a(3)** (*n* → *adj*) being or occurring at the approximate time of <*eight*ish> **b** (*n* → *adj*) having the characteristics of <*boy*ish> – often derog <*child*ish>

isinglass /'iezing,glahs‖'aɪzɪŋˌglɑːs/ *n* a very pure gelatin prepared from the air bladders of sturgeons and other fishes and used esp in jellies and glue

Islam /'izlahm, -lam‖'ɪzlɑːm, -læm/ *n* **1** the religious faith of Muslims including belief in Allah as the sole deity and in Muhammad as his prophet **2a** the civilization or culture accompanying Islamic faith **b** the group of modern nations in which Islam is the dominant religion [Arabic *islām* submission (to the will of God)] – **Islamic** *n or adj*, **Islamize** *vt*, **Islamization** *n*

island /'ielənd‖'aɪlənd/ *n* **1** an area of land surrounded by water and smaller than a continent **2** sthg like an island (e g in being isolated or surrounded) **3** TRAFFIC ISLAND – **islander** *n*

isle /iel‖aɪl/ *n* a (small) island – used in some names

islet /'ielit‖'aɪlɪt/ *n* **1** a little island **2** a small isolated mass of 1 type of tissue

-ism /-iz(ə)m‖-ɪz(ə)m/ *suffix* (*n, adj* → *n*) **1a** act, practice, or process of <*plagiar*ism> **b** mode of behaviour characteristic of (sby or sthg specified) <*cannibal*ism> **2a** state, condition, or property of <*magnet*ism> **b** pathological state or condition resulting from excessive use of (a specified drug) <*alcohol*ism> or marked by resemblance to (a specified person or thing) <*gigant*ism> **3a** doctrine, theory, or cult of <*Buddh*ism> **b** adherence to (a specified doctrine or system) <*stoic*ism> **c** prejudice on grounds of <*sex*ism> **4** characteristic or peculiar feature of (a specified language or variety of language) <*colloquial*ism>

isn't /'iznt‖'ɪznt/ is not

isobar /'iesohbah, 'iesə-‖'aɪsəʊbɑː, 'aɪsə-/ *n* **1** a line on a chart connecting places where the atmospheric pressure is the same **2** any of 2 or more atoms or elements having the same atomic weights or mass numbers but different atomic numbers [deriv of Greek *isos* equal + *baros* weight] – **isobaric** *adj*

isolate /'ies(ə)layt‖'aɪs(ə)leɪt/ *vt* **1** to set apart from others; *also* to quarantine **2** to separate from another substance so as to obtain in a pure form **3** to insulate – **isolatable** *adj*, **isolator** *n*, **isolable** *adj*, **isolation** *n*

isolationism /ˌiesə'layshənˌiz(ə)m‖ˌaɪsə'leɪʃənˌɪz(ə)m/ *n* a policy of national isolation by refraining from engaging in international relations – **isolationist** *n or adj*

isometrics /ˌiesoh'metriks‖ˌaɪsəʊ'metrɪks/ *n pl but sing or pl in constr* (a system of) exercises aimed at improving the tone of muscles – **isometric** *adj*

isosceles /ie'sosəleez‖aɪ'sɒsəliːz/ *adj, of a triangle* having 2 equal sides [Greek *isoskelēs*, fr *isos* equal + *skelos* leg]

isotherm /'iesohˌthuhm, 'iesə-‖'aɪsəʊˌθɜːm, 'aɪsə-/ *n* **1** a line on a chart connecting points having the same temperature at a given time or the same mean temperature for a given period **2** a line on a chart representing changes of volume or pressure under conditions of constant temperature – **isothermal** *adj*

isotope /'iesəˌtohp‖'aɪsəˌtəʊp/ *n* any of 2 or more species of atoms of a chemical element that have the same atomic number and nearly identical chemical behaviour but differ in atomic mass or mass number and physical properties – **isotopic** *adj*, **isotopically** *adv*, **isotopy** *n*

Israeli /iz'rayli‖ɪz'reɪlɪ/ *adj* (characteristic) of modern Israel – **Israeli** *n*

Israelite /'izrəliet‖'ɪzrəlaɪt/ *n* any of the descendants of the Hebrew patriarch Jacob; *specif* a member of any of the 10 Hebrew tribes occupying northern Palestine in biblical times – **Israelite** *adj*

[1]**issue** /'ish(y)ooh, 'isyooh‖'ɪʃ(j)uː, 'ɪsjuː/ *n* **1** the action of going, coming, or flowing out **2** a means or place of going out **3** offspring <*died without* ~> **4** an outcome that usu resolves or decides a problem **5** a matter that is in dispute between 2 or more parties; a controversial topic **6** sthg coming out from a usu specified source **7a** the act of publishing, giving out, or making available **b** the thing or the whole quantity of things given out, published, or distributed at 1 time <*read the latest* ~> – **issueless** *adj* – **at issue** under discussion or consideration; in dispute – **join/take issue** to take an opposing or conflicting stand; disagree or engage in argument on a point of dispute

[2]**issue** *vi* **1a** to go, come, or flow out **b** to emerge **2** to descend from a specified parent or

ancestor **3** to be a consequence – + *in* **4** to appear or become available through being given out, published, or distributed ~ *vt* **1** to cause to come out **2a** to give out, distribute, or provide officially **b** to send out for sale or circulation – **issuer** *n*

[1]**-ist** /-ist‖-ɪst/ *suffix* (→ *n*) **1a** one who performs (a specified action) <*cycl*ist> **b** one who makes or produces (a specified thing) <*novel*ist> **c** one who plays (a specified musical instrument) <*harp*ist> **d** one who operates (a specified mechanical instrument or device) <*motor*ist> **2** one who specializes in or practises (a specified art, science, skill, or profession) <*geolog*ist> **3** one who adheres to or advocates (a specified doctrine, system, or code of behaviour) <*social*ist> **4** one who is prejudiced on grounds of <*sex*ist>

[2]**-ist** *suffix* (→ *adj*) **1** relating to, or characteristic of <*obscurant*ist> **2** showing prejudice on grounds of <*rac*ist>

isthmus /ˈisməs‖ˈɪsməs; *also* ˈisthməs‖ˈɪsθməs/ *n* **1** a narrow strip of land connecting 2 larger land areas **2** a narrow anatomical part connecting 2 larger parts

[1]**it** /it‖ɪt/ *pron* **1a** that thing, creature, or group – used as subject or object **b** the person in question <*who is ~? It's me*> **2** – used as subject of an impersonal verb <*~'s raining*> <*~'s not far to London*> **3a** – used as anticipatory subject or object of a verb <*~'s no fun being a secretary*> <*I take ~ that you refuse*> **b** – used to highlight part of a sentence <*~ was the President who arrived yesterday*> <*~ was yesterday that he arrived*> **c** – used with many verbs and prepositions as a meaningless object <*run for ~*> <*footed ~ back to camp*> **4a** this, that – used to refer to previous or following information <*She failed. It's a shame*> **b** – used to refer to an explicit or implicit state of affairs <*how's ~ going?*> **5** that which is available <*one boiled egg and that's ~*>, important <*yes, that's just ~*>, or appropriate <*a bit tighter; that's ~*>

[2]**it** *n* **1** the player in a usu children's game who performs a unique role (e g trying to catch others in a game of tag) **2** SEX APPEAL; *also* SEXUAL INTERCOURSE – infml

Italian /iˈtali·ən‖ɪˈtælɪən/ *n* **1** a native or inhabitant of Italy **2** the Romance language of the Italians – **Italian** *adj*, **Italianate** *adj*

[1]**italic** /iˈtalik‖ɪˈtælɪk/ *adj* **1** *cap* (characteristic) of ancient Italy or of Italic **2** of a type style with characters that slant upwards to the right (e g in '*these words are italic*')

[2]**italic** *n* **1** (a character in) an italic type style **2** *cap* the Italic branch of the Indo-European language family that includes Latin, ancient Italian languages, and the Romance languages descended from Latin

italic·ize, **-ise** /iˈtaliˌsiez‖ɪˈtælɪˌsaɪz/ *vt* to print in italics – **italicization** *n*

[1]**itch** /ich‖ɪtʃ/ *vi* **1** to have or produce an itch **2** to have a restless desire <*were ~ing to go outside*> ~ – infml ~*vt* to cause to itch

[2]**itch** *n* **1a** an irritating sensation in the upper surface of the skin that makes one want to scratch **b** a skin disorder characterized by such a sensation **2** a restless desire – infml – **itchiness** *n*, **itchy** *adj*

it'd /ˈitəd‖ˈɪtəd/ it had; it would

-ite /-iet‖-aɪt/ *suffix* (→ *n*) **1a** one who belongs to (a specified place, group, etc) <*Israel*ite> <*social*ite> **b** adherent or follower of (a specified doctrine or movement) <*Pre-Raphael*ite> **2a** product of <*metabol*ite> **b** commercially manufactured product <*ebon*ite> **3** fossil <*ammon*ite> **4** mineral <*baux*ite>

[1]**item** /ˈietəm‖ˈaɪtəm/ *adv* and in addition – used to introduce each article in a list or enumeration [Latin, fr *ita* thus]

[2]**item** *n* **1** a separate unit in an account or series **2** a separate piece of news or information

item·ize, **-ise** /ˈietəmiez‖ˈaɪtəmaɪz/ *vt* to list – **itemization** *n*

iterate /ˈitərayt‖ˈɪtəreɪt/ *vt* to say or do again or repetitively – **iteration** *n*

itinerant /ieˈtinərənt, iˈti-‖aɪˈtɪnərənt, ɪˈtɪ-/ *adj* travelling from place to place; *esp* covering a circuit <~ *preacher*> – **itinerant** *n*

iˈtinerary /ieˈtinərəri, iˈti-‖aɪˈtɪnərərɪ, ɪˈtɪ-/ *n* **1** the (proposed) route of a journey **2** a travel diary **3** a traveller's guidebook

-itis /-ietəs‖-aɪtəs/ *suffix pl* **-itises** *also* **-itides** /-ietədeez‖-aɪtədiːz/ (→ *n*), **1** disease or inflammation of <*bronch*itis> **2a** suffering caused by a surfeit or excess of <*election*itis> **b** infatuation or obsession with <*jazz*itis> *USE* (*2*) humor

it'll /ˈitl‖ˈɪtl/ it will; it shall

its /its‖ɪts/ *adj* of, belonging to, or done by or to it or itself

it's /its‖ɪts/ it is; it has

itself /itˈself‖ɪtˈself/ *pron* **1** that identical thing, creature, or group emphasis <*the letter ~ was missing*>; compare ONESELF **2** its normal self – **in itself** intrinsically considered <*not dangerous* in itself>

itsy-bitsy /ˌitsi ˈbitsi‖ˌɪtsɪ ˈbɪtsɪ/ *adj* tiny – infml

-ity /-əti‖-ətɪ/ *suffix* (→ *n*) **1** quality or state of <*theatrical*ity>; *also* instance of (a specified quality or state) <*an obscen*ity> **2** amount or degree of <*humid*ity>

IUD *n* INTRAUTERINE DEVICE

[1]**-ive** /-iv‖-ɪv/ *suffix* (→ *adj*) **1** tending to; disposed to <*correct*ive> **2** performing (a specified function) <*descript*ive>

[2]**-ive** *suffix* (→ *n*) **1** sby or sthg that performs or serves to accomplish (a specified action) <*detect*ive> **2** sby who is in or affected by (a specified state or condition) <*consumpt*ive>

I've /iev‖aɪv/ I have

ivied /ˈievid‖ˈaɪvɪd/ *adj* overgrown with ivy <~ *walls*>

ivory /ˈievəri‖ˈaɪvərɪ/ *n* **1** the hard creamy-white substance of which the tusks of elephants and other tusked mammals are made **2** a creamy slightly yellowish white colour **3** *pl* things (e g dice or piano keys) made of (sthg resembling) ivory – infml – **ivory** *adj*

ˌivory ˈtower *n* aloofness from practical concerns; *also* a place encouraging such an attitude

ivy /ˈievi‖ˈaɪvɪ/ *n* a very common Eurasian

woody climbing plant with evergreen leaves, small yellowish flowers, and black berries

-ize, **-ise** /-iez‖-aɪz/ *suffix* (→ *vb*) **1a(1)** cause to be, conform to, or resemble <*liquidize*> **a(2)** subject to (a specified action) <*criticize*> **a(3)** impregnate, treat, or combine with <*oxidize*> **b** treat like; make into <*lionize*> **c** treat according to the method of <*bowdlerize*> **2a** become; become like <*crystallize*> **b** engage in (a specified activity) <*philosophize*>

J

j /jay‖dʒeɪ/ *n, pl* **j's, js** *often cap* (a graphic representation of or device for reproducing) the 10th letter of the English alphabet

[1]**jab** /jab‖dʒæb/ *vb* **-bb-** *vt* **1a** to pierce (as if) with a sharp object **b** to poke quickly or abruptly **2** to strike with a short straight blow ~ *vi* **1** to make quick or abrupt thrusts (as if) with a sharp or pointed object **2** to strike sby with a short straight blow

[2]**jab** *n* **1** a short straight punch in boxing delivered with the leading hand **2** a hypodermic injection – infml

jabber /ˈjabə‖ˈdʒæbə/ *vi or n* (to engage in) rapid or unintelligible talk or chatter – **jabberer** *n*

[1]**jack** /jak‖dʒæk/ *n* **1a** MAN 1a(1), e, 3 – usu as an intensive in such phrases as *every man jack* **b** a labourer, lumberjack, or steeplejack **2** any of various portable mechanisms for exerting pressure or lifting a heavy object a short distance **3** a male donkey **4a** a small white target ball in lawn bowling **b(1)** *pl but sing in constr* a game in which players toss and pick up small bone or metal objects in between throws of a ball **b(2)** a small 6-pointed metal object used in the game of jacks **5** a playing card carrying the figure of a soldier or servant and ranking usu below the queen **6a** JACK PLUG **b** JACK SOCKET

[2]**jack** *vt* **1** to move or lift (as if) by a jack **2** to raise the level or quality of **3** GIVE UP – usu + *in*; infml <*I was fed up with my job so I* ~ed *it in*> *USE* (*1&2*) usu + *up*

jackal /ˈjakl‖ˈdʒækl/ *n* any of several Old World wild dogs smaller than the related wolves

jackanapes /ˈjakəˌnayps‖ˈdʒækəˌneɪps/ *n* **1** a monkey, ape **2a** an impudent or conceited person **b** a mischievous child

jackaroo, **jackeroo** /ˌjakəˈrooh‖ˌdʒækəˈruː/ *n, Austr* a young inexperienced worker on a cattle or sheep station

jackass /ˈjakˌas‖ˈdʒækˌæs/ *n* **1** a male ass **2** a stupid person

ˈ**jackˌboot** /-ˌbooht‖-ˌbuːt/ *n* **1** a heavy military leather boot extending above the knee and worn esp during the 17th and 18th c **2a** a laceless military boot reaching to the calf **b** political repression effected by military or paramilitary force – + *the* – **jackbooted** *adj*

jackdaw /ˈjakˌdaw‖ˈdʒækˌdɔː/ *n* a common black and grey Eurasian bird that is related to but smaller than the common crow

jacket /ˈjakit‖ˈdʒækɪt/ *n* **1** an outer garment for the upper body opening down the full length of the centre front **2a** the natural coat of an animal **b** the skin of a (baked) potato **3a** a thermally insulating cover (e g for a hot water tank) **b(1)** DUST JACKET **b(2)** the cover of a paperback book

ˌ**Jack ˈFrost** *n* frost or frosty weather personified

ˈ**jack-in-the-ˌbox** *n, pl* **jack-in-the-boxes, jacks-in-the-box** a toy consisting of a small box out of which a figure springs when the lid is raised

[1]ˈ**jackˌknife** /-ˌnief‖-ˌnaɪf/ *n* **1** a large clasp knife for the pocket **2** a dive in which the diver bends from the waist, touches the ankles, and straightens out before hitting the water

[2]**jackknife** *vt* to cause to double up like a jackknife ~ *vi* **1** to double up like a jackknife **2** *esp of an articulated lorry* to turn or rise and form an angle of 90 degrees or less

ˌ**jack-of-ˈall-ˌtrades** *n, pl* **jacks-of-all-trades** a handy versatile person – sometimes derog

ˈ**jack ˌplug** *n* a single-pronged electrical plug for insertion into a jack socket

ˈ**jackˌpot** /-ˌpot‖-ˌpɒt/ *n* **1** (a combination that wins) a top prize on a fruit machine **2** a large prize (e g in a lottery), often made up of several accumulated prizes that have not been previously won

ˈ**jack ˌsocket** *n* an electrical socket that is designed to receive a jack plug

ˌ**jack ˈtar** *n* a sailor – infml

Jacobean /ˌjakəˈbee·ən‖ˌdʒækəˈbiːən/ *adj* of (the age of) James I

Jacobite /ˈjakəbiet‖ˈdʒækəbaɪt/ *n* a supporter of James II or of the Stuarts after 1688 – **Jacobitism** *n*

Jacuzzi /jəˈkoohzi‖dʒəˈkuːzɪ/ *trademark* – used for a system of underwater jets to be fitted into a hot bath for massage

[1]**jade** /jayd‖dʒeɪd/ *n* **1** a vicious or worn-out old horse **2** *archaic* a flirtatious or disreputable woman

[2]**jade** *n* either of 2 typically green hard gemstones

ˈ**jaded** *adj* fatigued (as if) by overwork or dissipation

jaffa /ˈjafə‖ˈdʒæfə/ *n, often cap* a large type of orange grown esp in Israel [*Jaffa*, former port in Israel]

[1]**jag** /jag‖dʒæg/ *vt* **-gg-** **1** to cut or tear unevenly or raggedly **2** to cut indentations into

[2]**jag** *n* a sharp projecting part – **jaggy** *adj*

[3]**jag** *n* a spree – slang

jagged /ˈjagid‖ˈdʒægɪd/ *adj* having a sharply uneven edge or surface – **jaggedly** *adv*, **jaggedness** *n*

jaguar /ˈjagyoo·ə‖ˈdʒægjʊə/ *n* a big cat of tropical America that is typically brownish yellow or buff with black spots

jai alai /ˌkhay ahˈlay‖ˌxeɪ ɑːˈleɪ/ *n* a court game for 2 or 4 players who use a long curved wicker basket strapped to the wrist to catch and hurl a ball against a wall

[1]**jail**, *Br also* **gaol** /jayl‖dʒeɪl/ *n* a prison

[2]**jail**, *Br also* **gaol** *vt* to confine (as if) in a jail

ˈ**jailˌbird** /-ˌbuhd‖-ˌbɜːd/ *n* a person who has

been (habitually) confined in jail

ˈjailˌbreak /-ˌbrayk‖-ˌbreɪk/ *n* an escape from jail

jailer, jailor /ˈjaylə‖ˈdʒeɪlə/ *n* a keeper of a jail

jalopy /jəˈlopi‖dʒəˈlɒpɪ/ *n* a dilapidated old vehicle or aircraft – infml

[1]jam /jam‖dʒæm/ *vb* **-mm-** *vt* **1a** to press, squeeze, or crush into a close or tight position **b** to cause to become wedged so as to be unworkable **c** to block passage of or along <*crowds* ~ming *the streets*> **d** to fill (to excess) <*a book* ~med *with facts*> **2** CRUSH 1; *also* to bruise by crushing **3** to send out interfering signals or cause reflections so as to make **3a** (a radio signal) unintelligible **b** (a radio device) ineffective ~ *vi* **1a** to become blocked or wedged **b** to become unworkable through the jamming of a movable part **2** to crowd or squash tightly together **3** to take part in a jam session – slang

[2]jam *n* **1** a crowded mass that impedes or blocks **2** the pressure or congestion of a crowd **3** a difficult state of affairs – infml

[3]jam *n* a preserve made by boiling fruit and sugar to a thick consistency

jamb /jam‖dʒæm/ *n* a straight vertical member or surface forming the side of an opening for a door, window, etc

jamboree /ˌjambəˈree‖ˌdʒæmbəˈriː/ *n* **1** a large festive gathering **2** a large gathering of scouts or guides in a camp

jammy /ˈjami‖ˈdʒæmɪ/ *adj, Br* **1** lucky **2** easy *USE* infml

jam on *vt* to apply (brakes) suddenly and forcibly

ˌjam-ˈpacked *adj* full to overflowing

ˈjam ˌsession *n* an impromptu jazz performance that features group improvisation

jangle /ˈjang·gl‖ˈdʒæŋgl/ *vi* **1** *of the nerves* to be in a state of tense irritation **2** to make a harsh or discordant often ringing noise ~ *vt* **1** to utter or cause to sound in a jangling way **2** to excite (e g nerves) to tense irritation – **jangle** *n*, **jangly** *adj*

janissary /ˈjanisəri‖ˈdʒænɪsərɪ/ *n* **1** *often cap* a soldier of a former élite corps of Turkish troops **2** a loyal or subservient official or supporter

janitor /ˈjanitə‖ˈdʒænɪtə/, *fem* **janitress** /-tris‖-trɪs/ *n* **1** a doorkeeper; [1]PORTER **2** *NAm* a caretaker – **janitorial** *adj*

January /ˈjanyoo(ə)ri‖ˈdʒænjʊ(ə)rɪ/ *n* the 1st month of the Gregorian calendar [Latin *Januarius*, 1st month of the ancient Roman year, fr *Janus*, god of doors, gates, & beginnings, fr *janus* arch, gate]

[1]japan /jəˈpan‖dʒəˈpæn/ *n* **1** a varnish giving a hard brilliant finish **2** work (e g lacquer ware) finished and decorated in the Japanese manner

[2]japan *vt* **-nn- 1** to cover with a coat of japan **2** to give a high gloss to

Japanese /ˌjapəˈneez‖ˌdʒæpəˈniːz/ *n, pl* **Japanese 1** a native or inhabitant of Japan **2** the language of the Japanese – **Japanese** *adj*

jape /jayp‖dʒeɪp/ *vi or n* (to) jest, joke

japonica /jəˈponikə‖dʒəˈpɒnɪkə/ *n* a hardy ornamental shrub with clusters of scarlet, white, or pink flowers

[1]jar /jah‖dʒɑː/ *vb* **-rr-** *vi* **1a** to make a harsh or discordant noise **b** to be out of harmony *with* **c** to have a harshly disagreeable effect – + *on* or *upon* **2** to vibrate ~*vt* to cause to jar, esp by shaking or causing a shock to – **jarringly** *adv*

[2]jar *n* **1** a jarring noise **2a** a sudden or unexpected shake **b** an unsettling shock (e g to nerves or feelings)

[3]jar *n* **1a** a usu cylindrical short-necked and wide-mouthed container, made esp of glass **b** the contents of or quantity contained in a jar **2** a glass of an alcoholic drink, esp beer – infml – **jarful** *n*

jargon /ˈjahgən‖ˈdʒɑːgən/ *n* **1a** confused unintelligible language **b** outlandish or barbarous language **2** the terminology or idiom of a particular activity or group **3** obscure and often pretentious language – **jargonize** *vb*, **jargonistic** *adj*

jasmine /ˈjasmin, ˈjaz-‖ˈdʒæsmɪn, ˈdʒæz-/ *n* **1** any of numerous often climbing shrubs that usu have extremely fragrant flowers; *esp* a high-climbing half-evergreen Asian shrub with fragrant white flowers **2** a light yellow

jasper /ˈjaspə‖ˈdʒæspə/ *n* an opaque quartz which is usu red brown, yellow, or dark green – **jaspery** *adj*

jaundice /ˈjawndis‖ˈdʒɔːndɪs/ *n* **1** an abnormal condition marked by yellowish pigmentation of the skin, tissues, and body fluids caused by the deposition of bile pigments **2** a state of prejudice inspired by bitterness, envy, or disillusionment – **jaundiced** *adj*

jaunt /jawnt‖dʒɔːnt/ *vi or n* (to make) a short journey for pleasure

ˈjaunting ˌcar /ˈjawnting‖ˈdʒɔːntɪŋ/ *n* a light open 2-wheeled horse-drawn vehicle used formerly in Ireland

jaunty /ˈjawnti‖ˈdʒɔːntɪ/ *adj* having or showing airy self-confidence; sprightly – **jauntily** *adv*, **jauntiness** *n*

Javanese /ˈjahvəˈneez‖ˌdʒɑːvəˈniːz/ (an inhabitant or the language) of the island of Java

javelin /ˈjav(ə)lin‖ˈdʒæv(ə)lɪn/ *n* a light spear thrown as a weapon or in an athletic field event; *also* the sport of throwing the javelin

[1]jaw /jaw‖dʒɔː/ *n* **1a** either of 2 cartilaginous or bony structures that in most vertebrates form a framework above and below the mouth in which the teeth are set **b** any of various organs of invertebrates that perform the function of the vertebrate jaws **2** *pl* **2a** the entrance of a narrow pass or channel **b** the 2 parts of a machine, tool, etc between which sthg may be clamped or crushed **c** a position or situation of imminent danger <*stared into the* ~s *of death*> **3a** continual and esp impudent or offensive talk – infml **b** a friendly chat – infml

[2]jaw *vi* to talk or gossip for a long time or long-windedly – infml

ˈjawˌbone /-ˌbohn‖-ˌbəʊn/ *n* the bone of an esp lower jaw

ˈjawˌbreaker /-ˌbraykə‖-ˌbreɪkə/ *n* a word which is difficult to pronounce – infml

jay /jay‖dʒeɪ/ *n* an Old World bird of the crow family with a dull pink body, black, white, and blue wings, and a black-and-white crest

ˈjayˌwalk /-ˌwawk‖-ˌwɔːk/ *vi* to cross a street

carelessly so as to be endangered by traffic – **jaywalker** *n*

jazz /jaz‖dʒæz/ *n* **1** music developed esp from ragtime and blues and characterized by syncopated rhythms and individual or group improvisation around a basic theme or melody **2** empty pretentious talk – infml **3** similar but unspecified things <*parties and all that* ~> > – infml [prob fr NAm Negro slang *jazz* copulation, frenzy, prob of W African origin]

jazz up *vt* **1** to play (e g a piece of music) in the style of jazz **2** to enliven **3** to make bright, esp in a vivid or garish way *USE* infml

jazzy /ˈjazi‖ˈdʒæzɪ/ *adj* **1** having the characteristics of jazz **2** garish, gaudy – infml – **jazzily** *adv*, **jazziness** *n*

jealous /ˈjeləs‖ˈdʒeləs/ *adj* **1a** intolerant of rivalry or unfaithfulness **b** apprehensive of and hostile towards a (supposed) rival **2** resentful, envious *of* **3** vigilant in guarding a possession, right, etc **4** distrustfully watchful – **jealously** *adv*, **jealousness** *n*, **jealousy** *n*

jean /jeen‖dʒiːn/ *n* a durable twilled cotton cloth used esp for work clothes [short for *jean fustian*, fr Middle English *Gene* Genoa, city in Italy]

jeans /jeenz‖dʒiːnz/ *n pl* casual usu close-fitting trousers, made esp of blue denim

jeep /jeep‖dʒiːp/ *n* a small rugged general-purpose motor vehicle with 4-wheel drive, used esp by the armed forces [alteration of *gee pee*, fr *g*eneral-*p*urpose]

¹jeer /jiə‖dʒɪə/ *vb* to laugh mockingly or scoff (at) – **jeerer** *n*, **jeeringly** *adv*

²jeer *n* a jeering remark; a taunt

Jehovah /jiˈhohvə‖dʒɪˈhəʊvə/ *n* GOD 1

Je,hovah's ˈWitness *n* a member of a fundamentalist sect practising personal evangelism, rejecting the authority of the secular state, and preaching that the end of the present world is imminent

jejune /jiˈjoohn‖dʒɪˈdʒuːn/ *adj* **1** lacking nutritive value or substance; *also* barren **2** lacking interest or significance **3** lacking maturity; puerile – **jejunely** *adv*, **jejuneness** *n*

jejunum /jiˈjoohnəm‖dʒɪˈdʒuːnəm/ *n* the section of the small intestine between the duodenum and the ileum – **jejunal** *adj*

jell /jel‖dʒel/ *vb, chiefly NAm* to gel

¹jelly /ˈjeli‖ˈdʒelɪ/ *n* **1a** a soft fruit-flavoured transparent dessert set with gelatin **b** a savoury food product of similar consistency, made esp from meat stock and gelatin **2** a clear fruit preserve made by boiling sugar and the juice of fruit **3** a substance resembling jelly in consistency

²jelly *vi* to jell ~ *vt* **1** to bring to the consistency of jelly; cause to set **2** to set in a jelly <jellied *beef*>

ˈjelly,fish /-,fish‖-,fɪʃ/ *n* a free-swimming marine coelenterate that has a nearly transparent saucer-shaped body and extendable tentacles covered with stinging cells

jemmy /ˈjemi‖ˈdʒemɪ/ *vt or n, Br* (to force open with) a steel crowbar, used esp by burglars

jenny /ˈjeni‖ˈdʒenɪ/ *n* **1** a female donkey **2** SPINNING JENNY

jeopard·ize, -ise /ˈjepədiez‖ˈdʒepədaɪz/ *vt* to put in jeopardy

jeopardy /ˈjepədi‖ˈdʒepədɪ/ *n* **1** exposure to or risk of death, loss, injury, etc; danger **2** liability to conviction faced by a defendant in a criminal trial

jerboa /juhˈboh·ə‖dʒɜːˈbəʊə/ *n* any of several nocturnal Old World desert rodents with long legs adapted for jumping

jeremiad /,jerəˈmie·əd‖,dʒerəˈmaɪəd/ *n* a prolonged lamentation or complaint

¹jerk /juhk‖dʒɜːk/ *vt* **1** to give a quick suddenly arrested push, pull, twist, or jolt to **2** to propel with short abrupt motions **3** to utter in an abrupt or snappy manner ~ *vi* **1** to make a sudden spasmodic motion **2** to move in short abrupt motions – **jerker** *n*

²jerk *n* **1** a single quick motion (e g a pull, twist, or jolt) **2a** an involuntary spasmodic muscular movement due to reflex action **b** *pl* spasmodic movements due to nervous excitement **3** *chiefly NAm* a stupid, foolish, or naive person – infml

³jerk *vt* to preserve (e g beef or venison) by cutting into long slices or strips and drying in the sun

jerkin /ˈjuhkin‖ˈdʒɜːkɪn/ *n* **1** a close-fitting hip-length sleeveless jacket, made esp of leather and worn by men in the 16th and 17th c **2** a man's or woman's sleeveless jacket

jerk off *vb, chiefly NAm* to masturbate – vulg

jerky /ˈjuhki‖ˈdʒɜːkɪ/ *adj* **1** marked by irregular or spasmodic movements **2** marked by abrupt or awkward changes – **jerkily** *adv*, **jerkiness** *n*

jeroboam /,jerəˈboh·əm, -əm‖,dʒerəˈbəʊæm, -əm/ *n* a wine bottle holding 4 to 6 times the usual amount

Jerry /ˈjeri‖ˈdʒerɪ/ *n, chiefly Br* **1** a German; *esp* a German soldier in WW II **2** *sing or pl in constr* the German armed forces in WW II

ˈjerry-,build /ˈjeri-‖ˈdʒerɪ-/ *vt* **jerry-built** /bilt‖bɪlt/ to build (e g houses) cheaply and flimsily – **jerry-builder** *n*, **jerry-built** *adj*

jerry can, jerrican /ˈjeri kan‖ˈdʒerɪ kæn/a narrow flat-sided container for carrying petrol, water, or other liquids

jersey /ˈjuhzi‖ˈdʒɜːzɪ/ *n* **1** a plain weft-knitted fabric made of wool, nylon, etc and used esp for clothing **2** ²JUMPER 1 **3** *often cap* any of a breed of small short-horned cattle noted for their rich milk [*Jersey*, one of the Channel islands]

Jerusalem artichoke /jəˈroohsələm‖dʒəˈruːsələm/ *n* (an edible sweet-tasting tuber of) a perennial N American sunflower

¹jest /jest‖dʒest/ *n* **1** an amusing or mocking act or utterance; a joke **2** a frivolous mood or manner <*was just said in* ~>

²jest *vi* **1** to speak or act without seriousness **2** to make a witty remark

jester /ˈjestə‖ˈdʒestə/ *n* one who jests; *esp* a retainer formerly kept in great households to provide casual amusement and commonly dressed in a brightly coloured costume

Jesuit /ˈjezyoo·it‖ˈdʒezjʊɪt/ *n* **1** a member of the Society of Jesus, a Roman Catholic order founded in 1534 which is devoted to missionary and educational work **2** one given to intrigue or equivocation – **jesuitism, jesuitry** *n, often cap*, **jesuitize** *vb, often cap*, **jesuitic, jesuitical** *adj, often* *cap*, **jesuitically** *adv*, *often cap*

[1]**jet** /jet‖dʒet/ *n* **1** a hard velvet-black form of coal that is often polished and used for jewellery **2** an intense black

[2]**jet** *vb* **-tt-** *vi* to spout forth in a jet or jets ~ *vt* **1** to emit in a jet or jets **2** to direct a jet of liquid or gas at

[3]**jet** *n* **1a** a forceful stream of fluid discharged from a narrow opening or a nozzle **b** a nozzle or other narrow opening for emitting a jet of fluid **2** (an aircraft powered by) a jet engine

[4]**jet** *vi* -tt- to travel by jet aircraft

ˌ**jet-ˈblack** *adj* of a very dark black

ˈ**jet ˌengine** *n* an engine that produces motion in one direction as a result of the discharge of a jet of fluid in the opposite direction; *specif* an aircraft engine that discharges the hot air and gases produced by the combustion of a fuel to produce propulsion or lift

ˌ**jet-proˈpelled** *adj* moving (as if) by jet propulsion

jet propulsion *n* propulsion of a body produced by the forwardly directed forces resulting from the backward discharge of a jet of fluid; *specif* propulsion of an aeroplane by jet engines

jetsam /ˈjetsəm‖ˈdʒetsəm/ *n* **1** goods thrown overboard to lighten a ship in distress; *esp* such goods when washed ashore **2** FLOTSAM AND JETSAM

ˈ**jet ˌset** *n sing or pl in constr* an international wealthy elite who frequent fashionable resorts – **jet-set** *adj*, **jetsetter** *n*

[1]**jettison** /ˈjetis(ə)n‖ˈdʒetɪs(ə)n/ *n* **1** the act of jettisoning cargo **2** abandonment

[2]**jettison** *vt* **1** to throw (e g goods or cargo) overboard to lighten the load of a ship in distress **2** to cast off as superfluous or encumbering; abandon **3** to drop (e g unwanted material) from an aircraft or spacecraft in flight – **jettisonable** *adj*

jetty /ˈjeti‖ˈdʒetɪ/ *n* **1** a structure (e g a pier or breakwater) extending into a sea, lake, or river to influence the current or tide or to protect a harbour **2** a small landing pier

jew /jooh‖dʒuː/ *vt* to get the better of financially, esp by hard bargaining – often + *out of*; derog

Jew, *fem* **Jewess** /-ˈes, -is‖-ˈes, -ɪs/ *n* **1** a member of a Semitic people existing as a nation in Palestine from the 6th c BC to the 1st c AD, some of whom now live in Israel and others in various countries throughout the world **2** a person whose religion is Judaism **3** sby given to hard financial bargaining – derog – **Jewish** *adj*

jewel /ˈjooh·əl‖ˈdʒuːəl/ *n* **1** an ornament of precious metal often set with stones and worn as an accessory **2** sby or sthg highly esteemed **3** a precious stone **4** a bearing for a pivot (e g in a watch or compass) made of crystal, precious stone, or glass – **jewelled** *adj*

jeweller, *NAm chiefly* **jeweler** /ˈjooh·ələ‖ˈdʒuːələ/ *n* sby who deals in, makes, or repairs jewellery and often watches, silverware, etc

ˈ**jewellery**, *NAm chiefly* **jewelry** /-ri‖-rɪ/ *n* jewels, esp as worn for personal adornment

ˌ**Jew's ˈharp**, **Jews' harp** *n* a small lyre-shaped instrument that is placed between the teeth and sounded by striking a metal tongue with the finger

Jezebel /ˈjezəbel, -bl‖ˈdʒezəbel, -bl/ *n*, *often not cap* a shameless or immoral woman

[1]**jib** /jib‖dʒɪb/ *n* a triangular sail set on a stay extending from the top of the foremast to the bow or the bowsprit

[2]**jib** *n* the projecting arm of a crane

[3]**jib** *vi* **-bb-** *esp of a horse* to refuse to proceed further – **jibber** *n* – **jib at** to recoil or baulk at

jibe /jieb‖dʒaɪb/ *vb* to gibe

jiffy /ˈjifi‖ˈdʒɪfɪ/ *n* a moment, instant – infml

[1]**jig** /jig‖dʒɪg/ *n* **1** (a piece of music for) any of several lively springy dances in triple time **2a** any of several fishing lures that jerk up and down in the water **b** a device used to hold a piece of work in position (e g during machining or assembly) and to guide the tools working on it **c** a device in which crushed ore or coal is separated from waste by agitating in water

[2]**jig** *vb* **-gg-** *vt* **1** to dance in the rapid lively manner of a jig **2a** to cause to make a rapid jerky movement **b** to separate (a mineral from waste) with a jig **3** to catch (a fish) with a jig **4** to machine by using a jig ~ *vi* **1a** to dance a jig **b** to move with rapid jerky motions **2** to fish with a jig **3** to work with or operate a jig

jigger /ˈjigə‖ˈdʒɪgə/ *n* **1** (a glass container holding) a variable measure of spirits used esp in mixing drinks **2** *chiefly NAm* sthg, esp a gadget or small piece of apparatus, which one is (temporarily) unable to designate accurately – infml

jiggered /ˈjigəd‖ˈdʒɪgəd/ *adj* **1** blowed, damned <*well I'll be* ~> – infml **2** *N Eng* tired out; exhausted

jiggery-pokery /ˌjigəri ˈpohkəri‖ˌdʒɪgərɪ ˈpəʊkərɪ/ *n*, *Br* dishonest underhand dealings or scheming – infml [Scots *joukery-pawkery*, fr *jouk* to cheat + *pawk* trick]

jiggle /ˈjigl‖ˈdʒɪgl/ *vb* to (cause to) move with quick short jerks – infml – **jiggle** *n*

jigsaw /ˈjigˌsaw‖ˈdʒɪgˌsɔː/ *n* **1** a power-driven fretsaw **2** **jigsaw, jigsaw puzzle** a puzzle consisting of small irregularly cut pieces, esp of wood or card, that are fitted together to form a picture for amusement; *broadly* sthg composed of many disparate parts or elements

jihad /jiˈhad‖dʒɪˈhæd/ *n* **1** a holy war waged on behalf of Islam as a religious duty **2** a crusade for a principle or belief

jilt /jilt‖dʒɪlt/ *vt* to cast off (e g one's lover) capriciously or unfeelingly

ˌ**jim ˈcrow** /jim‖dʒɪm/ *n*, *often cap J&C*, *NAm* **1** racial discrimination, esp against black Americans <~ *laws*> **2** a Negro – derog

jimjams /ˈjimˌjamz‖ˈdʒɪmˌdʒæmz/ *n pl* **1** DELIRIUM TREMENS **2** JITTERS 1 *USE* infml; + *the*

[1]**jingle** /ˈjing·gl‖ˈdʒɪŋgl/ *vb* to (cause to) make a light clinking or tinkling sound

[2]**jingle** *n* **1** a light, esp metallic clinking or tinkling sound **2** a short catchy song or rhyme characterized by repetition of phrases and used esp in advertising – **jingly** *adj*

jingo /ˈjing·goh‖ˈdʒɪŋgəʊ/ *interj* – used as a mild oath in *by jingo*

ˈ**jingoˌism** /-ˌiz(ə)m‖-ˌɪz(ə)m/ *n* belligerent patriotism; chauvinism [fr the use of *by jingo* in the refrain of a 19th-c English chauvinistic song] – **jingoist** *n*, **jingoistic** *adj*, **jingoistically** *adv*

[1]**jink** /jingk‖dʒɪŋk/ *n* **1** a quick evasive turn **2** *pl* pranks, frolics – esp in *high jinks*

[2]**jink** *vi* to move quickly with sudden turns and shifts (e g in dodging)

jinn, djinn /jin‖dʒɪn/ *n, pl* **jinns, jinn 1** any of a class of spirits that according to Muslim demonology inhabit the earth, assume various forms, and exercise supernatural power **2** a spirit, often in human form, which serves whoever summons it

jinx /jingks‖dʒɪŋks/ *n* sby or sthg (e g a force or curse) which brings bad luck – infml – **jinx** *vt*

jitney /ˈjitni‖ˈdʒɪtnɪ/ *n, NAm* NICKEL 2 – slang

[1]**jitter** /ˈjitə‖ˈdʒɪtə/ *vi* **1** to be nervous or act in a nervous way **2** to make continuous fast repetitive movements

[2]**jitter** *n* **1** *pl* panic or extreme nervousness – usu + *the* **2** an irregular random movement – **jittery** *adj*

ˈ**jitter,bug** /-ˌbug‖-ˌbʌg/ *n* (one who dances) a jazz variation of the two-step in which couples swing, balance, and twirl

jiu-jitsu /ˌjooh ˈjitsooh‖ˌdʒu: ˈdʒɪtsu:/ *n* ju-jitsu

[1]**jive** /jiev‖dʒaɪv/ *n* **1** (dancing or *the* energetic dance performed to) swing music **2** *NAm* **2a** glib or deceptive talk **b** a type of jargon used esp by jazz musicians

[2]**jive** *vi* **1** to dance to or play jive **2** *NAm* to kid ~ *vt,NAm* to cajole; TEASE 2b

[1]**job** /job‖dʒɒb/ *n* **1a** a piece of work; *esp* a small piece of work undertaken at a stated rate **b** sthg produced by work **2a(1)** a task **a(2)** sthg requiring unusual exertion <*it was a real* ~ *to talk over that noise*> **b** a specific duty, role, or function **c** a regular paid position or occupation **d** *chiefly Br* a state of affairs – + *bad* or *good* <*make the best of a bad* ~> **3** an object of a usu specified type <*bought myself a brand-new V-8 sports* ~> **4a** a plan or scheme designed or carried out for private advantage <*suspected the whole incident was a put-up* ~> **b** a crime; *specif* a robbery *USE* (*3&4*) infml – **jobless** *adj* – **on the job 1** engaged in one's occupation; AT WORK 1 **2** in the act of copulation – vulg

[2]**job** *vb* **-bb-** *vi* **1** to do odd or occasional pieces of work, usu at a stated rate <*a* ~bing *gardener*> **2** to carry on public business for private gain **3a** to carry on the business of a middleman or wholesaler **b** to work as a stockjobber ~ *vt* **1** to buy and sell (e g shares) for profit **2** to hire or let for a definite job or period of service **3** to get, deal with, or effect by jobbery **4** to subcontract – usu + *out*

jobber /ˈjobə‖ˈdʒɒbə/ *n* a stockjobber

jobbery /ˈjobəri‖ˈdʒɒbərɪ/ *n* corruption in public office

ˈ**job ˌcentre** *n* a labour exchange

ˌ**job ˈlot** *n* a miscellaneous collection of goods sold as a lot; *broadly* any miscellaneous collection of articles

[1]**jockey** /ˈjoki‖ˈdʒɒkɪ/ *n* **1** sby who rides a horse, esp as a professional in races **2** *NAm* sby who operates a specified vehicle, device, or object <*a truck* ~>

[2]**jockey** *vt* **1** to ride (a horse) as a jockey **2** to manoeuvre or manipulate by adroit or devious means <~ed *me into handing over the money*> **3** *chiefly NAm* to drive or operate; *also* to manoeuvre ~ *vi* **1** to act as a jockey **2** to manoeuvre for advantage <~ed *for position*>

jockstrap /ˈjokˌstrap‖ˈdʒɒkˌstræp/ *n* a support for the genitals worn by men taking part in strenuous esp sporting activities

jocose /jəˈkohs‖dʒəˈkəʊs/ *adj* **1** given to joking **2** jocular *USE* fml or poetic – **jocosely** *adv*, **jocoseness** *n*, **jocosity** *n*

jocular /ˈjokyoolə‖ˈdʒɒkjʊlə/ *adj* **1** habitually jolly **2** characterized by joking – **jocularly** *adv*, **jocularity** *n*

jocund /ˈjokənd‖ˈdʒɒkənd/ *adj* marked by or suggestive of high spirits; merry – fml or poetic – **jocundly** *adv*, **jocundity** *n*

jodhpurs /ˈjodpəz‖ˈdʒɒdpəz/ *n pl in constr, pl* **jodhpurs** riding trousers cut full at the hips and close-fitting from knee to ankle [*Jodhpur*, city in India]

[1]**jog** /jog‖dʒɒg/ *vb* **-gg-** *vt* **1** to give a slight shake or push to; nudge **2** to rouse (the memory) ~ *vi* **1** to move up and down or about with a short heavy motion **2a** to run or ride at a slow trot **b** to go at a slow or monotonous pace

[2]**jog** *n* **1** a slight shake **2a** a jogging movement or pace **b** a slow trot

joggle /ˈjogl‖ˈdʒɒgl/ *vb* to (cause to) move or shake slightly – infml – **joggle** *n*

ˈ**jog ˌtrot** *n* a slow regular trot (e g of a horse)

john /jon‖dʒɒn/ *n* **1** *NAm* TOILET 2 – infml **2** *chiefly NAm* a prostitute's client – slang

ˌ**John ˈBarley,corn** /ˈbahliˌkawn‖ˈbɑ:lɪˌkɔ:n/ *n* alcoholic liquor personified

ˌ**John ˈBull** /bool‖bʊl/ *n* **1** the English nation personified **2** a typical Englishman, esp regarded as truculently insular – **John Bullish** *adj*, **John Bullishness** *n*, **John Bullism** *n*

johnny /ˈjoni‖ˈdʒɒnɪ/ *n, often cap* a fellow, guy – infml

joie de vivre /ˌzhwah də ˈveev‖ˌʒwɑ: də ˈvi:v (*Fr* ʒwa də vi:vr)/ *n* keen enjoyment of life [French, lit., joy of living]

[1]**join** /joyn‖dʒɔɪn/ *vt* **1a** to put or bring together so as to form a unit **b** to connect (e g points) by a line **c** to adjoin; MEET 1c <*where the river* ~s *the sea*> **2** to put or bring into close association or relationship <~ed *in marriage*> **3a** to come into the company of <~ed *us for lunch*> **b** to become a member of <~ed *the sports club*> ~ *vi* **1** to come together so as to be connected **2** to come into close association: e g **2a** to form an alliance **b** to become a member of a group **c** to take part in a collective activity – usu + *in* – **joinable** *adj* – **join battle** to engage in battle or conflict

[2]**join** *n* JOINT 2a

joiner /ˈjoynə‖ˈdʒɔɪnə/ *n* **1** one who constructs or repairs wooden articles, esp furniture or fittings **2** a gregarious person who joins many organizations – infml

joinery /ˈjoynəri‖ˈdʒɔɪnərɪ/ *n* **1** the craft or trade of a joiner **2** woodwork done or made by a joiner

[1]**joint** /joynt‖dʒɔɪnt/ *n* **1a(1)** a point of contact between 2 or more bones of an animal skeleton together with the parts that surround and support it **a(2)** NODE 3a **b** a part or space included

between 2 articulations, knots, or nodes **c** a large piece of meat (for roasting) cut from a carcass **2a** a place where 2 things or parts are joined **b** an area at which 2 ends, surfaces, or edges are attached **c** a crack in rock not accompanied by dislocation **d** the hinge of the binding of a book along the back edge of each cover **3** a shabby or disreputable place of entertainment – infml **4** a marijuana cigarette – slang – **jointed** *adj*, **jointedly** *adv*, **jointedness** *n* – **out of joint 1** *of a bone* dislocated **2** disordered, disorganized

[2]joint *adj* **1** united, combined <*a ~ effort*> **2** common to 2 or more: e g **2a** involving the united activity of 2 or more **b** held by, shared by, or affecting 2 or more **3** sharing with another <*~ heirs*>

[3]joint *vt* **1** to fit together **2** to provide with a joint **3** to prepare (e g a board) for joining by planing the edge **4** to separate the joints of (e g meat)

'jointly /-li‖-lɪ/ *adv* together

joint-stock company *n* a company consisting of individuals who own shares representing a joint stock of capital

join up *vi* to enlist in an armed service

joist /joyst‖dʒɔɪst/ *n* any of the parallel small timbers or metal beams that support a floor or ceiling

[1]joke /johk‖dʒəʊk/ *n* **1a** sthg said or done to provoke laughter; *esp* a brief oral narrative with a humorous twist **b** the humorous or ridiculous element in sthg **c** an instance of joking or making fun <*can't take a ~*> **d** a laughingstock **2** sthg of little difficulty or seriousness; a trifling matter – **jokey, joky** *adj*

[2]joke *vi* to make jokes – **jokingly** *adv*

joker /'johkə‖'dʒəʊkə/ *n* **1** sby given to joking **2** a playing card added to a pack usu as a wild card **3a** sthg (e g an expedient or stratagem) held in reserve to gain an end or escape from a predicament **b** *chiefly NAm* an unsuspected or misunderstood clause in a document that greatly alters it **c** *chiefly NAm* a not readily apparent factor or condition that nullifies a seeming advantage **4** a fellow; *esp* an insignificant, obnoxious, or incompetent person – infml

jollification /ˌjolifi'kaysh(ə)n‖ˌdʒɒlɪfɪ'keɪʃ(ə)n/ *n* (an instance of) merrymaking

[1]jolly /'joli‖'dʒɒlɪ/ *adj* **1a** full of high spirits **b** given to conviviality **c** expressing, suggesting, or inspiring gaiety **2** extremely pleasant or agreeable – infml **3** *Br* slightly drunk – euph – **jolliness** *n*, **jollity** *n*

[2]jolly *adv* very – infml <*~ cold for the time of year*>

[3]jolly *vt* **1** to (try to) put in good humour, esp to gain an end – usu + *along* **2** to make cheerful or bright – + *up*; infml

'jolly ˌboat *n* a ship's boat of medium size used for general work

ˌJolly 'Roger /'rojə‖'rɒdʒə/ *n* a pirate's black flag with a white skull and crossbones

[1]jolt /johlt‖dʒəʊlt/ *vt* **1** to cause to move with a sudden jerky motion **2** to give a (sudden) knock or blow to **3** to abruptly disturb the composure of ~ *vi* to move with a jerky motion

[2]jolt *n* an unsettling blow, movement, or shock – **jolty** *adj*

jonquil /'jongkwil‖'dʒɒŋkwɪl/ *n* a Mediterranean plant of the daffodil family that is widely cultivated for its yellow or white fragrant flowers

'joss ˌstick /jos‖dʒɒs/ *n* a slender stick of incense (e g for burning in front of an idol)

jostle /'josl‖'dʒɒsl/ *vb* **1a** to come in contact or into collision (with) **b** to make (one's way) by pushing **2** to vie (with) in gaining an objective – **jostle** *n*

[1]jot /jot‖dʒɒt/ *n* the least bit

[2]jot *vt* **-tt-** to write briefly or hurriedly – **jotting** *n*

jotter /'jotə‖'dʒɒtə/ *n* a small book or pad for notes or memoranda

joule /joohl‖'dʒu:l/ *n* the SI unit of work or energy equal to the work done when a force of 1 newton moves its point of application through a distance of 1m [James *Joule* (1818-89), English physicist]

journal /'juhnl‖'dʒɜ:nl/ *n* **1** a record of current transactions: e g **1a** an account of day-to-day events **b** a private record of experiences, ideas, or reflections kept regularly **c** a record of the transactions of a public body, learned society, etc **d** LOG 3, 4 **2a** a daily newspaper **b** a periodical dealing esp with matters of current interest or specialist subjects **3** the part of a rotating shaft, axle, roll, or spindle that turns in a bearing

ˌjournal'ese /-'eez‖-'i:z/ *n* a style of writing supposed to be characteristic of newspapers; *specif* loose or cliché-ridden writing

'journalˌism /-ˌiz(ə)m‖-ˌɪz(ə)m/ *n* **1** (the profession of) the collecting and editing of material of current interest for presentation through news media **2a** writing designed for publication in a newspaper or popular magazine **b** writing characterized by a direct presentation of facts or description of events without an attempt at interpretation

'journalist /-ist‖-ɪst/ *n* a person engaged in journalism, esp one working for a news medium – **journalistic** *adj*

journey /'juhni‖'dʒɜ:nɪ/ *n* **1** travel from one place to another, esp by land and over a considerable distance **2** the distance involved in a journey, or the time taken to cover it – **journey** *vi*, **journeyer** *n*

'journeyman /-mən‖-mən/ *n* **1** a worker who has learned a trade and is employed by another person, usu by the day **2** an experienced reliable worker or performer, as distinguished from one who is outstanding

[1]joust /jowst‖dʒaʊst/ *vi* to fight in a joust or tournament – **jouster** *n*

[2]joust *n* a combat on horseback between 2 knights or men-at-arms with lances

Jove /johv‖dʒəʊv/ *n* Jupiter, the chief Roman god – often used interjectionally to express surprise or agreement <*by ~!*>

jovial /'johvi·əl‖'dʒəʊvɪəl/ *adj* markedly good-humoured – **jovially** *adj*, **joviality** *n*

[1]jowl /jowl‖dʒaʊl/ *n* **1** the jaw; *esp* a mandible **2** CHEEK 1

[2]jowl *n* usu slack flesh associated with the lower jaw or throat – often pl with sing. meaning

joy /joy‖dʒɔɪ/ *n* **1** (the expression of) an emotion or state of great happiness, pleasure, or delight **2** a source or cause of delight **3** *Br* success, satisfaction <*had no ~ at the first shop he went into*> – infml – **joyless** *adj*, **joylessly** *adv*, **joylessness** *n*

ˈjoyful /-f(ə)l‖-f(ə)l/ *adj* filled with, causing, or expressing joy – **joyfully** *adv*, **joyfulness** *n*

ˈjoyous /-əs‖-əs/ *adj* joyful – **joyously** *adv*, **joyousness** *n*

ˈjoyˌride /-ˌried‖-ˌraɪd/ *n* **1** a ride in a motor car taken for pleasure and often without the owner's consent **2** a short pleasure flight in an aircraft – **joyrider** *n*, **joyriding** *n*

ˈjoyˌstick /-ˌstik‖-ˌstɪk/ *n* **1** a hand-operated lever that controls an aeroplane's elevators and ailerons **2** a control for any of various devices that resembles an aeroplane's joystick, esp in being capable of motion in 2 or more directions

jubilant /ˈjoohbilənt‖ˈdʒuːbɪlənt/ *adj* filled with or expressing great joy – **jubilance** *n*, **jubilantly** *adv*

jubilation /ˌjoohbiˈlaysh(ə)n‖ˌdʒuːbɪˈleɪʃ(ə)n/ *n* being jubilant; rejoicing

jubilee /ˌjoohbiˈlee, ˈ--ˌ-‖ˌdʒuːbɪˈliː, ˈ--ˌ-/ *n* **1** *often cap* a year of emancipation and restoration provided by ancient Hebrew law to be kept every 50 years **2** (a celebration of) a special anniversary (e g of a sovereign's accession) **3** a period of time, proclaimed by the Pope ordinarily every 25 years, during which a special plenary indulgence is granted to Catholics who perform certain works of repentance and piety **4** a season or occasion of celebration [Late Latin *jubilaeus*, fr Late Greek *iōbēlaios*, fr Hebrew *yōbhēl* ram's horn, jubilee]

Judaism /ˈjoohdayˌiz(ə)m‖ˈdʒuːdeɪˌɪz(ə)m/ *n* **1** a religion developed among the ancient Hebrews and characterized by belief in 1 transcendent God and by a religious life in accordance with Scriptures and rabbinic traditions **2** (conformity with) the cultural, social, and religious beliefs and practices of the Jews – **Judaize** *vt*, **Judaizer** *n*, **Judaic** *adj*

Judas /ˈjoohdəs‖ˈdʒuːdəs/ *n* **1** one who betrays, esp under the guise of friendship **2 judas, judas hole** a peephole in a door [*Judas* Iscariot, the apostle who betrayed Christ]

judder /ˈjudə‖ˈdʒʌdə/ *vi, chiefly Br* to vibrate jerkily – **judder** *n*

[1]judge /juj‖dʒʌdʒ/ *vt* **1** to form an opinion about through careful weighing of evidence **2** to sit in judgment on **3** to determine or pronounce after deliberation **4** to decide the result of (a competition or contest) **5** to form an estimate or evaluation of **6** to hold as an opinion ~ *vi* **1** to form a judgment or opinion **2** to act as a judge <*to ~ between us*>

[2]judge *n* sby who judges: e g **a** a public official authorized to decide questions brought before a court **b** *often cap* a Hebrew tribal leader in the period after the death of Joshua **c** sby appointed to decide in a competition or (sporting) contest (e g diving) **d** sby who gives an (authoritative) opinion <*a good ~ of character*> – **judgeship** *n*

judgment, judgement /ˈjujmənt‖ˈdʒʌdʒmənt/ *n* **1** (a formal utterance of) an authoritative opinion **2a** a formal decision by a court **b** an obligation (e g a debt) created by a court decision **3a Judgment, Last Judgment** *the* final judging of mankind by God **b** a calamity held to be sent by God as a punishment **4** (the process of forming) an opinion or evaluation based on discerning and comparing **5** the capacity for judging – **judgmental** *adj*

ˈJudgment ˌDay *n* the day of God's judgment of mankind at the end of the world, according to various theologies

judicature /ˈjoohdikəchə‖ˈdʒuːdɪkətʃə/ *n* **1** the administration of justice **2** a court of justice **3** JUDICIARY 1 **4** (the duration of) a judge's office

judicial /joohˈdish(ə)l‖dʒuːˈdɪʃ(ə)l/ *adj* **1** of a judgment, judging, justice, or the judiciary **2** ordered by a court <*~ separation*> **3** of, characterized by, or expressing judgment; CRITICAL 1c – **judicially** *adv*

judiciary /joohˈdishəri‖dʒuːˈdɪʃərɪ/ *n* **1a** a system of courts of law **b** the judges of these courts **2** a judicial branch of the US government – **judiciary** *adj*

judicious /joohˈdishəs‖dʒuːˈdɪʃəs/ *adj* having, exercising, or characterized by sound judgment – **judiciously** *adv*, **judiciousness** *n*

judo /ˈjoohdoh‖ˈdʒuːdəʊ/ *n* a martial art developed from ju-jitsu and emphasizing the use of quick movement and leverage to throw an opponent [Japanese *jūdō*, fr *jū* weakness, gentleness + *dō* art] – **judoist** *n*

[1]jug /jug‖dʒʌg/ *n* **1a(1)** *chiefly Br* a vessel for holding and pouring liquids that typically has a handle and a lip or spout **a(2)** *chiefly NAm* a large deep earthenware or glass vessel for liquids that usu has a handle and a narrow mouth often fitted with a cork; FLAGON 1b **b** the contents of or quantity contained in a jug; a jugful **2** prison – infml – **jugful** *n*

[2]jug *vt* **-gg- 1** to stew (e g a hare) in an earthenware vessel **2** to imprison – infml

juggernaut /ˈjugəˌnawt‖ˈdʒʌgəˌnɔːt/ *n* **1** an inexorable force or object that crushes anything in its path **2** *chiefly Br* a very large, usu articulated, lorry; *esp* one considered too large for safety [Hindi *Jagannāth*, title of the god Vishnu, lit., lord of the world; fr a former belief that devotees of Vishnu threw themselves beneath the wheels of a cart bearing his image in procession]

[1]juggle /ˈjugl‖ˈdʒʌgl/ *vi* **1** to perform the tricks of a juggler **2** to engage in manipulation, esp in order to achieve a desired end ~ *vt* **1** to manipulate, esp in order to achieve a desired end <~ *an account to hide a loss*> **2** to hold or balance precariously **3** to toss in the manner of a juggler

[2]juggle *n* an act or instance of juggling

juggler /ˈjuglə‖ˈdʒʌglə/ *n* one skilled in keeping several objects in motion in the air at the same time by alternately tossing and catching them – **jugglery** *n*

Jugoslavian /ˌyoohgohˈslavi·ən‖ˌjuːgəʊˈslaːvɪən/ *n or adj* (a) Yugoslavian

jugular vein /ˈjugyoolə‖ˈdʒʌgjʊlə/, **jugular** *n* any of several veins of each side of the neck that return blood from the head

juice /joohs‖dʒuːs/ *n* **1** the extractable fluid contents of cells or tissues **2a** *pl* the natural fluids of an animal body **b** the liquid or moisture contained in sthg **3** the inherent quality of sthg; *esp* the basic force or strength of sthg **4** a medium (e g electricity or petrol) that supplies power – infml – **juiceless** *adj*

juicy /'joohsi‖'dʒu:sɪ/ *adj* **1** succulent **2** financially rewarding or profitable – infml **3** rich in interest <*a ~ problem*>; *esp* interesting because of titillating content <*~ scandal*> – infml – **juicily** *adv*, **juiciness** *n*

ju-jitsu, jiu-jitsu /,jooh 'jitsooh‖,dʒu: 'dʒɪtsu:/ *n* a martial art employing holds, throws, and paralysing blows to subdue or disable an opponent [Japanese *jūjutsu*, fr *jū* weakness, gentleness + *jutsu* art]

juju /'jooh,jooh‖'dʒu:,dʒu:/ *n* (a magic attributed to) a fetish or charm of W African peoples

jujube /'jooh,joohb‖'dʒu:,dʒu:b/ *n* **1** (the edible fruit of) any of several trees of the buckthorn family **2** a fruit-flavoured gum or lozenge

jukebox /'joohk,boks‖'dʒu:k,bɒks/ *n* a coin-operated record player that automatically plays records chosen from a restricted list [fr earlier *juke-house* brothel, bar with music for dancing, fr Gullah (an American Negro dialect) *juke* disorderly, of W African origin]

julep /'joohlip‖'dʒu:lɪp/ *n, chiefly NAm* a drink consisting of a spirit and sugar poured over crushed ice and garnished with mint

Julian calendar /'joohlyən, -li·ən‖'dʒu:ljən, -lɪən/ *n* a calendar introduced in Rome in 46 BC establishing the 12-month year of 365 days with an extra day every fourth year

July /joo'lie‖dʒʊ'laɪ/ *n* the 7th month of the Gregorian calendar [Old English *Julius*, fr Latin, fr Gaius *Julius* Caesar (100-44 BC), Roman statesman]

[1]jumble /'jumbl‖'dʒʌmbl/ *vt* to mix *up* in a confused or disordered mass

[2]jumble *n* **1** a mass of things mingled together without order or plan **2** *Br* articles for a jumble sale

'jumble ,sale *n, Br* a sale of donated secondhand articles, usu conducted to raise money for some charitable purpose

jumbo /'jumboh‖'dʒʌmbəʊ/ *n, pl* **jumbos** a very large specimen of its kind – **jumbo** *adj*

[1]jump /jump‖dʒʌmp/ *vi* **1a** to spring into the air, esp using the muscular power of feet and legs **b** to move suddenly or involuntarily from shock, surprise, etc **c** to move quickly or energetically (as if) with a jump; *also* to act with alacrity **2** to pass rapidly, suddenly, or abruptly (as if) over some intervening thing: e g **2a** to skip <~ed *to the end of the book*> **b** to rise suddenly in rank or status **c** to make a mental leap **d** to come to or arrive at a position or judgment without due deliberation <~ *to conclusions*> **e** to undergo a sudden sharp increase <*prices* ~ed *sky-high*> **3** to move haphazardly or aimlessly **4** to make a sudden verbal or physical attack – usu + *on* or *upon* **5** *NAm* to bustle with activity <*by midnight the place was really* ~ing> ~ *vt* **1a** to (cause to) leap over <~ *a hurdle*> <~ed *his horse over the fence*> **b** to pass over, esp to a point beyond; skip, bypass **c** to act, move, or begin before (e g a signal) **2a** to escape or run away from **b** to leave hastily or in violation of an undertaking <~ed *bail*> **c** to depart from (a normal course) <*the train* ~ed *the rails*> **3a** to make a sudden or surprise attack on **b** to occupy without proper legal rights <~ *a mining claim*> **4** *chiefly NAm* to leap aboard, esp so as to travel illegally – **jump at** to accept eagerly <jump at *the chance*> – **jump the gun 1** to start in a race before the starting signal **2** to act, move, or begin sthg before the proper time – **jump the queue 1** to move in front of others in a queue **2** to obtain an unfair advantage over others who have been waiting longer – **jump to it 1** to make an enthusiastic start **2** to hurry

[2]jump *n* **1a(1)** an act of jumping; a leap **a(2)** a sports contest (e g the long jump) including a jump **a(3)** a space, height, or distance cleared by a jump **a(4)** an obstacle to be jumped over (e g in a horse race) **b** a sudden involuntary movement; a start **2a** a sharp sudden increase (e g in amount, price, or value) **b** a sudden change or transition; *esp* one that leaves a break in continuity **c** any of a series of moves from one place or position to another; a move **3** *pl the* fidgets – infml

,jumped-'up *adj* recently risen in wealth, rank, or status – derog

[1]jumper /'jumpə‖'dʒʌmpə/ *n* **1** a short wire used to close a break in or cut out part of a circuit **2** a jumping animal; *esp* a horse trained to jump obstacles

[2]jumper *n* **1** *Br* a knitted or crocheted garment worn on the upper body **2** *NAm* PINAFORE 2

jumpy /'jumpi‖'dʒʌmpɪ/ *adj* **1** having jumps or sudden variations **2** nervous, jittery – **jumpiness** *n*

junction /'jungksh(ə)n‖'dʒʌŋkʃ(ə)n/ *n* **1** joining or being joined **2a** a place of meeting **b** an intersection of roads, esp where 1 terminates **c** a point of contact or interface between dissimilar metals or semiconductor regions (e g in a transistor) **3** sthg that joins – **junctional** *adj*

juncture /'jungkchə‖'dʒʌŋktʃə/ *n* **1** an instance or place of joining; a connection or joining part **2** a point of time (made critical by a concurrence of circumstances)

June /joohn‖dʒu:n/ *n* the 6th month of the Gregorian calendar [Latin *Junius*, prob fr *Junius*, name of a Roman clan]

jungle /'jung·gl‖'dʒʌŋgl/ *n* **1** an area overgrown with thickets or masses of (tropical) trees and other vegetation **2a** a confused, disordered, or complex mass <*the* ~ *of tax laws*> **b** a place of ruthless struggle for survival <*the blackboard* ~> [Hindi *jaṅgal*] – **jungly** *adj*

[1]junior /'joohnyə‖'dʒu:njə/ *n* **1** a person who is younger than another **2a** a person holding a lower or subordinate position in a hierarchy of ranks **b** a member of a younger form in a school **3** *NAm* a student in the next-to-the-last year before graduating **4** *NAm* a male child; a son – infml

[2]junior *adj* **1** younger – used, esp in the USA, to distinguish a son with the same name as his father **2** lower in standing or rank **3** for children aged from 7 to 11 <*a* ~ *school*>

juniper /'joohnipə‖'dʒu:nɪpə/ *n* any of several evergreen shrubs or trees of the cypress family

[1]junk /jungk‖dʒʌŋk/ *n* **1** pieces of old cable or rope used for mats, swabs, or oakum **2a**

secondhand or discarded articles or material; *broadly* RUBBISH 1 **b** sthg of little value or inferior quality **3** narcotics; *esp* heroin – slang – **junky** *adj*

[2]**junk** *vt* to get rid of as worthless – infml

[3]**junk** *n* a sailing ship used in the Far East with a high poop and overhanging stem, little or no keel, and lugsails often stiffened with horizontal battens

[1]**junket** /'jungkit‖'dʒʌŋkɪt/ *n* **1** a dessert of sweetened flavoured milk curdled with rennet **2** a festive social affair (at public or a firm's expense) – chiefly infml

[2]**junket** *vi* to feast, banquet – infml – **junketer** *n*, **junketeer** *n*

junk food *n* food that has a high carbohydrate content but low nutritional value, and is often extensively processed

junkie, junky /'jungki‖'dʒʌŋkɪ/ *n* a drug peddler or addict – infml

Junoesque /ˌjoohnoh'esk‖ˌdʒu:nəʊ'esk/ *adj, of a woman* having stately beauty

junta /'juntə, 'hoontə‖'dʒʌntə, 'hʊntə/ *n sing or pl in constr* **1** a political council or committee; *esp* a group controlling a government after a revolution **2** a junto [Spanish, fr feminine of *junto* joined, fr Latin *junct-, jungere* to join]

junto /'juntoh‖'dʒʌntəʊ/ *n sing or pl in constr, pl* **juntos** a group of people joined for a common purpose

Jupiter /'joohpitə‖'dʒu:pɪtə/ *n* the largest of the planets and 5th in order from the sun

Jurassic /joo'rasik‖dʒʊ'ræsɪk/ *adj or n* (of or being) the middle period of the Mesozoic era

juridical /joo'ridikl‖dʒʊ'rɪdɪkl/ *also* **juridic** /joo'ridik‖dʒʊ'rɪdɪk/ *adj* **1** JUDICIAL 1 **2** of or being jurisprudence; legal <*~ terms*> – **juridically** *adv*

ˌjuris'diction /ˌjooəris'diksh(ə)n‖ˌdʒʊərɪs-'dɪkʃ(ə)n/ *n* **1** the power, right, or authority to apply the law **2** the authority of a sovereign power **3** the limits within which authority may be exercised – **jurisdictional** *adj*, **jurisdictionally** *adv*

ˌjuris'prudence /-'proohd(ə)ns‖-'pru:d-(ə)ns/ *n* (the science or philosophy of) a body or branch of law <*criminal ~*> – **jurisprudential** *adj*

jurist /'jooərist‖'dʒʊərɪst/ *n* **1** sby with a thorough knowledge of law **2** *NAm* a lawyer; *specif* a judge

juror /'jooərə‖'dʒʊərə/ *n* **1** a member of a jury **2** one who takes an oath

[1]**jury** /'jooəri‖'dʒʊərɪ/ *n* **1** a body of usu 12 people who hear evidence in court and are sworn to give an honest verdict, esp of guilty or not guilty, based on this evidence **2** a committee for judging a contest or exhibition

[2]**jury** *adj* improvised for temporary use (in an emergency) <*a ~ rig for a sailing boat*>

'juryman /-mən‖-mən/, *fem* **'juryˌwoman** *n* JUROR 1

[1]**just** /just‖dʒʌst/ *adj* **1a** conforming (rigidly) to fact or reason <*a ~ but not a generous decision*> **b** conforming to a standard of correctness; proper **2a(1)** acting or being in conformity with what is morally upright or equitable **a(2)** being what is merited; deserved **b** legally correct – **justly** *adv*, **justness** *n*

[2]**just** *adv* **1a** exactly, precisely <*~ the thing for your cold*> **b** at this moment and not sooner <*he's only ~ arrived*> – sometimes used with the past tense <*the bell ~ rang*> **c** only at this moment and not later <*I'm ~ coming*> **2a** by a very small margin; immediately, barely <*only ~ possible*> **b** only, simply <*~ a short note*> **3** quite <*not ~ yet*> <*~ as well I asked*> **4** perhaps, possibly **5** very, completely <*~ wonderful*> **6** indeed – sometimes expressing irony <*didn't he ~!*> *USE (5, 6)* infml – **just about 1** almost **2** not more than <just about *room to cook*> – **just in case** as a precaution – **just now 1** at this moment **2** a moment ago – **just on** almost exactly – used with reference to numbers and quantities – **just so 1** tidily arranged **2** – used to express agreement – **just the same** nevertheless; EVEN SO

justice /'justis‖'dʒʌstɪs/ *n* **1a** the maintenance or administration of what is just **b** the administration of law **c** JUSTICE OF THE PEACE **2a** the quality of being just, impartial, or fair **b** (conformity to) the principle or ideal of just dealing or right action **3** conformity to truth, fact, or reason **4** *Br* – used as a title for a judge <*Mr* Justice *Smith*>

ˌjustice of the 'peace *n* a lay magistrate empowered chiefly to administer summary justice in minor cases and to commit for trial

justify /'justifie‖'dʒʌstɪfaɪ/ *vt* **1** to prove or show to be just, right, or reasonable **2** to extend freedom from the consequences of sin to, by Christ's righteousness or by grace **3** to space out (e g a line of printed text) so as to be flush with a margin – **justifier** *n*, **justifiable** *adj*, **justifiably** *adv*, **justificatory** *adj*, **justification** *n*

[1]**jut** /jut‖dʒʌt/ *vi* **-tt-** to extend out, up, or forwards; project, protrude – often + *out*

[2]**jut** *n* sthg that juts (out)

jute /jooht‖dʒu:t/ *n* the glossy fibre of either of 2 E Indian plants used chiefly for sacking, burlap, and twine

Jute *n* a member of a Germanic people that invaded England and esp Kent along with the Angles and Saxons in the 5th c AD – **Jutish** *adj*

[1]**juvenile** /'joovəniel‖'dʒʊvənaɪl/ *adj* **1** physiologically immature or undeveloped **2** (characteristic) of or suitable for children or young people – **juvenilely** *adv*, **juvenility** *n*

[2]**juvenile** *n* **1a** a young person **b** a book for young people **2** a young individual resembling an adult of its kind except in size and reproductive activity **3** an actor who plays youthful parts

juxtapose /ˌjukstə'pohz‖ˌdʒʌkstə'pəʊz/ *vt* to place side by side – **juxtaposition** *n*, **juxtapositional** *adj*

k /kay‖keɪ/ *n, pl* **k's, ks,** *often cap* **1** (a graphic representation of or device for reproducing) the 11th letter of the English alphabet **2** a unit of computer storage capacity equal to

1024 bytes **3** thousand

Kaffir, Kafir /ˈkafə‖ˈkæfə/ *n* **1** a member of a group of southern African Bantu-speaking peoples **2** *often not cap, chiefly SAfr* a S African Black – derog

kaftan /ˈkaf,tan‖ˈkæf,tæn/ *n* a caftan

kaiser /ˈkiezə‖ˈkaɪzə/ *n* an emperor of Germany during the period 1871 to 1918 – **kaiserdom** *n*

kale, kail /kayl‖keɪl/ *n* a hardy cabbage with curled often finely cut leaves that do not form a dense head

kaleidoscope /kəˈliedə,skohp‖kəˈlaɪdə-,skəʊp/ *n* **1** a tubular instrument containing loose chips of coloured glass between mirrors so placed that an endless variety of symmetrical patterns is produced as the instrument is rotated and the chips of glass change position **2** sthg that is continually changing; *esp* a variegated changing pattern, scene, or succession of events [Greek *kalos* beautiful + *eidos* form + English *-scope*] – **kaleidoscopic, kaleidoscopical** *adj*, **kaleidoscopically** *adv*

kalends /ˈkaləndz‖ˈkæləndz/ *n pl but sing or pl in constr* calends

[1]**kamikaze** /,kamiˈkahzi‖,kæmɪˈkɑːzɪ/ *n* **1** a Japanese pilot in WWII who volunteered to crash an explosive - laden aircraft on a target **2** the aircraft used by a kamikaze pilot [Japanese, lit., divine wind; originally referring to a storm which destroyed a Mongol fleet attacking Japan in 1281]

[2]**kamikaze** *adj* suicidal – humor

kangaroo /,kang·gəˈrooh‖,kæŋgəˈruː/ *n, pl* **kangaroos** any of various plant-eating marsupial mammals of Australia, New Guinea, and adjacent islands that hop on their long powerful hind legs

kangaroo court *n* an unauthorized or irresponsible court in which justice is perverted

kaolin /ˈkayəlin‖ˈkeɪəlɪn/ *n* a fine usu white clay formed from decomposed feldspar and used esp in ceramics

kapok /ˈkaypok‖ˈkeɪpɒk/ *n* a mass of silky fibres that surround the seeds of a tropical tree and are used esp as a soft (insulating) filling for mattresses, cushions, sleeping bags, etc

kaput /kəˈpoot‖kəˈpʊt/ *adj* no longer able to function; broken, exhausted – infml

karat /ˈkarət‖ˈkærət/ *n, NAm* CARAT 2

karate /kəˈrahti‖kəˈrɑːtɪ/ *n* a martial art in which opponents use their hands and feet to deliver crippling blows [Japanese, lit., empty hand]

karma /ˈkahmə‖ˈkɑːmə/ *n, often cap* the force generated by a person's actions, held in Hinduism and Buddhism to determine his/her destiny in his/her next existence – **karmic** *adj, often cap*

kayak /ˈkie(y)ak‖ˈkaɪ(j)æk/ *n* an Eskimo canoe made of a frame covered with skins; *also* a similar canvas-covered or fibreglass canoe

kazoo /kəˈzooh‖kəˈzuː/ *n, pl* **kazoos** a musical instrument consisting of a tube into which one sings or hums to vibrate a membrane covering a side hole

kebab /kiˈbab‖kɪˈbæb/ *n* cubes of (marinated) meat cooked with onions, mushrooms, etc, usu on a skewer

kedgeree /,kejəˈree, ˈ---‖,kedʒəˈriː, ˈ---/ *n* a dish containing rice, flaked fish, and chopped hard-boiled eggs

[1]**keel** *n* **1a** a timber or plate which extends along the centre of the bottom of a vessel and usu projects somewhat from the bottom **b** the main load-bearing member (e g in an airship) **2** a projection (e g the breastbone of a bird) suggesting a keel **3** a ship – poetic – **keeled** *adj*, **keelless** *adj*

[2]**keel** *vt* to cause to turn over ~ *vi* **1** to turn over **2** to fall *over* (as if) in a faint

ˈ**keel,haul** /-,hawl‖-,hɔːl/ *vt* **1** to drag (a person) under the keel of a ship as punishment **2** to rebuke severely

[1]**keen** /keen‖kiːn/ *adj* **1a** having or being a fine edge or point; sharp **b** affecting one as if by cutting or piercing <*a ~ wind*> **2** enthusiastic, eager <*a ~ swimmer*> **3a** intellectually alert; *also* shrewdly astute <*a ~ awareness of the problem*> **b** sharply contested; competitive; *specif, Br, of prices* low in order to be competitive **c** extremely sensitive in perception <*~ eyesight*> **4** *chiefly NAm* wonderful, excellent – **keenly** *adv*, **keenness** *n* – **keen on** interested in; attracted to

[2]**keen** *vi or n* (to utter) a loud wailing lamentation for the dead, typically at Irish funerals – **keener** *n*

[1]**keep** /keep‖kiːp/ *vb* **kept** /kept‖kept/ *vt* **1a** to take notice of by appropriate conduct; fulfil (the obligations of) <*~ a promise*> <*~ the law*> **b** to act fittingly in relation to (a feast or ceremony) <*~ the Sabbath*> **c** to conform to in habits or conduct <*~ late hours*> **d** to stay in accord with (a beat) <*~ time*> **2a** to watch over and defend; guard <*~ us from harm*> <*~s goal for the local team*> **b(1)** to take care of, esp as an owner; tend <*~s a dog*> **b(2)** to support <*earns enough to ~ himself*> **b(3)** to maintain in a specified condition – often in combination <*a well-*kept *garden*> **c** to continue to maintain <*~ a lookout*> **d(1)** to cause to remain in a specified place, situation, or condition <*~ him waiting*> **d(2)** to store habitually for use <*where do you ~ the butter?*> **d(3)** to preserve (food) in an unspoilt condition **e** to have or maintain in one's service, employment, or possession or at one's disposal <*~ a car*> **f** to record by entries in a book <*~ accounts*> **g** to have customarily in stock for sale **3a** to delay, detain <*~ children in after school*> **b** to hold back; restrain <*~ him from going*> **c** to save, reserve <*~ some for later*> **d** to refrain from revealing or releasing <*~ a secret*> **4** to retain possession or control of <kept *the money he found*> <*~ a copy of the letter*> **5a** to continue to follow <*~ the path*> **b** to stay or remain on or in, often against opposition <*~ your seat*> **6** to manage, run <*~s a shop*> ~ *vi* **1a** to maintain a course <*~ right*> **b** to continue, usu without interruption <*~ talking*> **c** to persist in a practice <kept *bothering them*> **2a** to stay or remain in a specified desired place, situation, or condition <*~ warm*> <*~ off the grass*> **b** to remain in good condition <*meat will ~ in the freezer*> **c** to be or remain with regard to health <*how are you ~*ing*?*> **3** to act as wicketkeeper or goalkeeper – infml – **keep an/one's eye on** to

watch over – **keep at** to persist in doing or concerning oneself with – **keep company** to provide with companionship <*won't anyone stay and* keep *me* company?> – **keep from** to refrain from; help <*can't* keep from *laughing*> – **keep one's eye in** *chiefly Br* to keep in practice; *specif* to retain ability to judge the speed and direction of a moving ball – **keep one's eyes open/peeled,** *Br* **keep one's eyes skinned** to be on the alert; be watchful – **keep one's feet** to avoid overbalancing – **keep one's fingers crossed** to hope for the best – **keep one's hand in** to remain in practice – **keep one's head above water** to remain solvent; *broadly* to stay out of difficulty – **keep one's nose clean** to keep one's record untarnished by playing safe – **keep one's shirt on,** *Br* **keep one's hair on** to remain calm; keep one's temper – infml – **keep the ball rolling** to play one's part (e g in conversation) – **keep to 1** to stay in or on <keep to *the path*> **2** not to deviate from; ABIDE BY <keep to *the rules*> – **keep to oneself 1** to keep secret <kept *the facts* to himself> **2** *also* **keep oneself to oneself** to remain solitary or apart from other people – **keep warm** to occupy (a position) temporarily for another

²**keep** *n* **1** a castle, fortress, or fortified tower **2** the means (e g food) by which one is kept <*earned his* ~> – **for keeps 1** with the provision that one keeps as one's own what one wins or receives <*he gave it to me* for keeps> – infml **2** FOR GOOD <*came home* for keeps> – infml

keeper /ˈkeepə‖ˈkiːpə/ *n* **1a** a protector, guardian **b** a gamekeeper **c** a custodian **d** a curator **2** any of various devices (e g a latch or guard ring) for keeping sthg in position **3a** a goalkeeper **b** a wicketkeeper *USE* (*3*) chiefly infml

keeping /ˈkeeping‖ˈkiːpɪŋ/ *n* custody, care – **out of/in keeping** not/conforming or agreeing with sthg implied or specified – usu + *with*

keep on *vi* to talk continuously; *esp* to nag

ˈ**keep,sake** /-ˈsayk‖-ˈseɪk/ *n* sthg (given, to be) kept as a memento, esp of the giver

keep up *vt* **1** to persist or persevere in; continue <keep up *the good work*> **2** to preserve from decline <keep up *appearances*> ~ *vi* **1** to maintain an equal pace or level of activity, progress, or knowledge (e g with another) **2** to continue without interruption <*rain* kept up *all night*>

keg /keg‖keg/ *n, Br* **1** a small barrel having a capacity of (less than) 10gal (about 45.5l litres); *specif* a metal beer barrel from which beer is pumped by pressurized gas **2** beer from a keg

kelp /kelp‖kelp/ *n* **1** any of various large brown seaweeds **2** the ashes of seaweed used esp as a source of iodine

kelvin /ˈkelvin‖ˈkelvɪn/ *n* the SI unit of temperature defined by the Kelvin scale

Kelvin *adj* of, conforming to, or being a scale of temperature on which absolute zero is at 0 and water freezes at 273.16K under standard conditions [William Thomson, Lord *Kelvin* (1824-1907), Scottish physicist]

¹**ken** /ken‖ken/ *vb* **-nn-** *chiefly Scot* to have knowledge (of); know

²**ken** *n* the range of perception, understanding, or knowledge – usu + *beyond, outside*

kennel /ˈkenl‖ˈkenl/ *n* **1a** a shelter for a dog **b** an establishment for the breeding or boarding of dogs – often pl with sing. meaning but sing. or pl in constr <*runs a* ~s *in the country*> **2** a pack of dogs

kepi /ˈkaypee ‖ˈkeɪpiː (*Fr* kepi)/ *n* a round French military cap with a flat top and a horizontal peak

kept /kept‖kept/ *past of* KEEP

keratin /ˈkerətin‖ˈkerətɪn/ *n* any of various fibrous proteins that form the chemical basis of nails, claws, and other horny tissue and hair – **keratinous** *adj*, **keratinize** *vb*

kerb /kuhb‖kɜːb/ *n, Br* the edging, esp of stone, to a pavement, path, etc

kerb crawler *n* sby who drives slowly close to a pavement with the intention of enticing a potential sexual partner into the car – **kerb crawling** *n*

kerchief /ˈkuhchif‖ˈkɜːtʃɪf/ *n, pl* **kerchiefs** /-chivz‖-tʃɪvz/ *also* **kerchieves** /~, -cheevz‖~, -tʃiːvz/ **1** a square or triangle of cloth used as a head covering or worn as a scarf around the neck **2** a handkerchief [Old French *cuevrechief*, fr *covrir* to cover + *chief* head]

kerfuffle /kəˈfufl‖kəˈfʌfl/ *n, chiefly Br* a fuss, commotion – infml

kernel /ˈkuhnl‖ˈkɜːnl/ *n* **1** the inner softer often edible part of a seed, fruit stone, or nut **2** a whole seed of a cereal **3** a central or essential part; CORE 2

kerosine, kerosene /ˈkerəseen‖ˈkerəsiːn/ *n, chiefly NAm* PARAFFIN 3

kestrel /ˈkestrəl‖ˈkestrəl/ *n* a small common Eurasian and N African falcon that is noted for its habit of hovering in the air against a wind

ketch /kech‖ketʃ/ *n* a fore-and-aft rigged ship with the mizzenmast stepped forward of the rudder

ketchup /ˈkechəp, -up‖ˈketʃəp, -ʌp/, *NAm chiefly* **catchup** /~, ˈkachəp‖~, ˈkætʃəp/ *n* any of several sauces made with vinegar and seasonings and used as a relish; *esp* a sauce made from seasoned tomato puree [Malay *kĕchap* spiced fish sauce]

kettle /ˈketl‖ˈketl/ *n* a metal vessel, usu with a handle and spout, used for boiling liquids, esp water

ˈ**kettle,drum** /-,drum‖-,drʌm/ *n* a percussion instrument that consists of a hollow brass or copper hemisphere with a parchment head whose tension can be changed to vary the pitch

¹**key** /kee‖kiː/ *n* **1a** a usu metal instrument by which the bolt of a lock is turned **b** sthg having the form or function of such a key <*a* ~ *for a clock*> **2a** a means of gaining or preventing entrance, possession, or control **b** an instrumental or deciding factor **3a** sthg that gives an explanation or identification or provides a solution **b** a list of words or phrases explaining symbols or abbreviations **c** an arrangement of the important characteristics of a group of plants or animals used for identification **4** a small piece of wood or metal used as a wedge or for preventing motion between parts **5a** any of the levers of a keyboard musical instrument that is pressed by a finger or foot to actuate the mechanism and produce the notes **b** a lever that controls a vent in

the side of a woodwind instrument or a valve in a brass instrument **c** a small button or knob on a keyboard (e g of a typewriter) designed to be pushed down by the fingers **6** a (particular) system of 7 notes based on their relationship to a tonic **7** characteristic style or tone **8** a small switch for opening or closing an electric circuit **9** a dry usu single-seeded fruit (e g of an ash or elm tree) **10** the indentation, roughness, or roughening of a surface to improve adhesion of plaster, paint, etc – **keyed** *adj*, **keyless** *adj*

[2]**key** *vt* **1** to secure or fasten by a key **2** to roughen (a surface) to provide a key for plaster, paint, etc **3** to bring into harmony or conformity; make appropriate **4** to make nervous, tense, or excited – usu + *up* **5** to keyboard

[3]**key** *adj* of basic importance; fundamental

[4]**key** *n* a low island or reef, esp in the Caribbean area

[1]ˈ**keyˌboard** /-ˌbawd‖-ˌbɔːd/ *n* **1a** a bank of keys on a musical instrument (e g a piano) typically having 7 usu white and 5 raised usu black keys to the octave **b** any instrument having such a keyboard, esp when forming part of a pop or jazz ensemble **2** a set of systematically arranged keys by which a machine is operated

[2]**keyboard** *vi* to operate a machine (e g for typesetting) by means of a keyboard ~*vt* to capture or set (e g data or text) by means of a keyboard – **keyboarder** *n*

ˈ**keyˌhole** /-ˌhohl‖-ˌhəʊl/ *n* a hole in a lock into which the key is put

ˈ**key ˌmoney** *n* a payment made by a tenant to secure occupancy of a rented property

keynote /ˈkeeˌnoht‖ˈkiːˌnəʊt/ *n* **1** the first and harmonically fundamental note of a scale **2** the fundamental or central fact, principle, idea, or mood

ˈ**keyˌpunch** /-ˌpunch‖-ˌpʌntʃ/ *n* a machine with a keyboard used to cut holes or notches in punched cards – **keypunch** *vt*, **keypuncher** *n*

key signature *n* the sharps or flats placed on the musical staff to indicate the key

ˈ**keyˌstone** /-ˌstohn‖-ˌstəʊn/ *n* **1** the wedge-shaped piece at the apex of an arch that locks the other pieces in place **2** sthg on which associated things depend for support

khaki /ˈkahki‖ˈkɑːkɪ/ *n* **1** a dull yellowish brown **2** a khaki-coloured cloth made usu of cotton or wool and used esp for military uniforms [Hindi *khākī* dust-coloured, fr *khāk* dust, fr Persian] – **khaki** *adj*

khan /kahn‖kɑːn/ *n* a medieval supreme ruler over the Turkish, Tartar, and Mongol tribes – **khanate** *n*

kibbutz /kiˈboots‖kɪˈbʊts/ *n, pl* **kibbutzim** /-ˈt-seem‖-ˈtsiːm/ a collective farm or settlement in Israel

kibosh /ˈkieˌbosh‖ˈkaɪˌbɒʃ/ *n* sthg that serves as a check or stop <*put the* ~ *on that*> – infml – **kibosh** *vt*

[1]**kick** /kik‖kɪk/ *vi* **1a** to strike out with the foot or feet **b** to make a kick in football **2** to show opposition; rebel **3** *of a firearm* to recoil when fired ~ *vt* **1** to strike suddenly and forcefully (as if) with the foot **2** to score by kicking a ball **3** to free oneself of (a drug or drug habit) – infml – **kicker** *n* – **kick oneself** to reprove oneself for some stupidity or omission – **kick one's heels 1** to be kept waiting **2** to be idle – **kick over the traces** to cast off restraint, authority, or control – **kick the bucket** DIE 1 – infml, humor – **kick upstairs** to promote to a higher but less desirable position

[2]**kick** *n* **1a** a blow or sudden forceful thrust with the foot; *specif* one causing the propulsion of an object **b** the power to kick **c** a repeated motion of the legs used in swimming **d** a sudden burst of speed, esp in a footrace **2** the recoil of a gun **3** power or strength to resist; *broadly* resilience <*still has some* ~ *in him*> **4a** a stimulating effect or quality <*this drink has quite a* ~> **b** a stimulating or pleasurable experience or feeling – often pl <*he did it for* ~s> **c** an absorbing or obsessive new interest <*on a health food* ~ *at present*>

[3]**kick** *n* an indentation in the base of a glass vessel, esp a bottle

kick about *vb* KICK AROUND

kick around *vt* **1** to treat inconsiderately or high-handedly **2** to consider (a problem) from various angles, esp in an unsystematic or experimental way ~ *vi* **1** to wander aimlessly or idly **2** to lie unused or unwanted *USE* (*vt & vi*) infml

ˈ**kickˌback** /-ˌbak‖-ˌbæk/ *n* **1** a sharp violent reaction **2** a money return received usu because of help or favours given or sometimes because of confidential agreement or coercion

ˈ**kickˌoff** /-ˌof‖-ˌɒf/ *n* **1** a kick that puts the ball into play in soccer, rugby, etc **2** an act or instance of starting or beginning

kick off *vi* **1** to start or resume play with a kickoff **2** to start or begin proceedings – infml

kick out *vt* to dismiss or eject forcefully or summarily – infml

kick-starter *n* a foot-operated starter (e g for a motorcycle) – **kick-start** *vt*

kick up *vt* **1** to cause to rise upwards; raise <*clouds of dust* kicked up *by passing cars*> **2** to stir up (a row, a fuss, trouble, etc) – infml

[1]**kid** /kid‖kɪd/ *n* **1** the young of a goat or related animal **2** the flesh, fur, or skin of a kid **3** a child; *also* a young person (e g a teenager) – infml – **kiddish** *adj* – **with kid gloves** with special consideration

[2]**kid** *vi* **-dd-** *of a goat or antelope* to bring forth young

[3]**kid** *vb* **-dd-** *vt* **1a** to mislead as a joke to convince (oneself) of sthg untrue or improbable **2** to make fun of ~*vi* to engage in good-humoured fooling *USE* (*vt & vi*) infml – **kidder** *n*, **kiddingly** *adv*

kiddie, kiddy /kidi‖kɪdɪ/ *n* a small child – infml

kidnap /ˈkidnap‖ˈkɪdnæp/ *vt* **-pp-, -p-** to seize and detain (a person) by force and often for ransom – **kidnapper, kidnaper** *n*

kidney /ˈkidni‖ˈkɪdnɪ/ *n* **1a** either of a pair of organs situated in the body cavity near the spinal column that excrete waste products of metabolism in the form of urine **b** an excretory organ of an invertebrate **2** the kidney of an animal eaten as food **3** sort, kind, or type, esp with regard to temperament

ˈ**kidney ˌbean** *n* (any of the kidney-shaped seeds of) the French bean

[1]**kill** /kil‖kɪl/ *vt* **1** to deprive of life **2a** to put an

end to **b** to defeat, veto **3a** to destroy the vital, active, or essential quality of <~ed *the pain with drugs*> **b** to spoil, subdue, or neutralize the effect of <*that colour* ~s *the room*> **c(1)** to turn off (studio or stage lighting) **c(2)** to remove (a shadow) by adjusting lighting or moving a camera **4** to cause (time) to pass (e g while waiting) **5** to hit (a shot) so hard in a racket game that a return is impossible **6** to cause (e g an engine) to stop **7** to cause extreme pain to **8** to overwhelm with admiration or amusement **9** to discard or abandon further investigation of (a story) – journ ~*vi* to destroy life *USE* (*6, 7, 8*) infml – **killer** *n* – **to kill** TO THE NINES <*dressed* to kill>

[2]**kill** *n* **1** a killing or being killed **2** sthg killed: e g **2a** animals killed in a shoot, hunt, season, or particular period of time **b** an enemy aircraft, submarine, etc destroyed by military action

ˈ**killer ˌwhale** /ˈkilə‖ˈkɪlə/ *n* a flesh-eating gregarious black-and-white toothed whale found in most seas of the world

[1]**killing** /ˈkiling‖ˈkɪlɪŋ/ *n* a sudden notable gain or profit – infml

[2]**killing** *adj* **1** extremely exhausting or difficult to endure **2** highly amusing *USE* infml – **killingly** *adv*

ˈ**killˌjoy** /-ˌjoy‖-ˌdʒɔɪ/ *n* one who spoils the pleasure of others

kill off *vt* to destroy totally or in large numbers

kiln /kiln‖kɪln/ *n* an oven, furnace, or heated enclosure used for processing a substance by burning, firing, or drying – **kiln** *vt*

kilo /ˈkeeloh‖ˈkiːləʊ/ *n, pl* **kilos 1** a kilogram **2** a kilometre

kilo- *comb form* thousand <kilo*ton*>

ˈ**kiloˌcalorie** /-ˌkaləri‖-ˌkælərɪ/ *n* the quantity of heat required to raise the temperature of 1 kg of water 1°C under standard conditions

ˈ**kiloˌgram** /-ˌgram‖-ˌgræm/ *n* **1** the SI unit of mass and weight approximately equal to the weight of a litre of water (2.205lb) **2** a unit of force equal to the weight of a kilogram mass under the earth's gravitational attraction

ˈ**kiloˌhertz** /-ˌhuhts‖-ˌhɜːts/ *n* a unit of frequency equal to 1000 hertz

kilometre /ˈkiləˌmeetə, kiˈlomitə‖ˈkɪləˌmiːtə, kɪˈlɒmɪtə/ *n* 1000 metres

ˈ**kiloˌwatt** /-ˌwot‖-ˌwɒt/ *n* 1000 watts

kilt /kilt‖kɪlt/ *n* a skirt traditionally worn by Scotsmen that is formed usu from a length of tartan, is pleated at the back and sides, and is wrapped round the body and fastened at the front

kimono /kiˈmohnoh‖kɪˈməʊnəʊ/ *n, pl* **kimonos** a loose robe with wide sleeves and a broad sash traditionally worn by the Japanese

[1]**kin** /kin‖kɪn/ *n* **1** a group of people of common ancestry **2** *sing or pl in constr* one's relatives **3** *archaic* kinship

[2]**kin** *adj* kindred, related

-kin /-kin‖-kɪn/ *also* **-kins** *suffix* (→ *n*) small kind of <*cat*kin>

[1]**kind** /kiend‖kaɪnd/ *n* **1** fundamental nature or quality **2a** a group united by common traits or interests **b** a specific or recognized variety – often in combination **c** a doubtful or barely admissible member of a category <*a* ~ *of grey*> – **in kind 1** in goods, commodities, or natural produce as distinguished from money **2** in a similar way or with the equivalent of what has been offered or received

[2]**kind** *adj* **1** disposed to be helpful and benevolent **2** forbearing, considerate, or compassionate **3** showing sympathy, benevolence, or forbearance **4** cordial, friendly **5** not harmful; mild, gentle – **kindness** *n*

kindergarten /ˈkindəˌgahtn‖ˈkɪndəˌgɑːtn/ *n* a school or class for small children [German, fr *kinder* children + *garten* garden]

kindhearted /ˌkiendˈhahtid‖ˌkaɪndˈhɑːtɪd/ *adj* marked by a sympathetic nature – **kindheartedly** *adv*, **kindheartedness** *n*

kindle /ˈkindl‖ˈkɪndl/ *vt* **1** to set (a fire, wood, etc) burning **2** to stir up (e g emotion) ~ *vi* **1** to catch fire **2** to become animated or aroused

kindling /ˈkindling‖ˈkɪndlɪŋ/ *n* material (e g dry wood and leaves) for starting a fire

[1]**kindly** /ˈkiendli‖ˈkaɪndlɪ/ *adj* **1** agreeable, beneficial **2** sympathetic, generous – **kindliness** *n*

[2]**kindly** *adv* **1** in an appreciative or sincere manner <*I'd take it* ~ *if you'd put in a good word for the boy*> **2** – used (1) to add politeness or emphasis to a request <~ *fill in the attached questionnaire*> (2) to convey irritation or anger in a command <*will you* ~ *shut that door*>

ˈ**kind of** *adv* **1** to a moderate degree; somewhat <*it's* ~ *late to begin*> **2** in a manner of speaking <*all you can do is* ~ *nurse it*> **3** roughly, approximately *USE* infml

[1]**kindred** /ˈkindrid‖ˈkɪndrɪd/ *n* **1** *sing or pl in constr* (one's) relatives **2** family relationship

[2]**kindred** *adj* similar in nature or character

kine /kien‖kaɪn/ *archaic pl of* COW

kinetic /kiˈnetik‖kɪˈnetɪk/ *adj* of motion [Greek *kinētikos*, fr *kinein* to move]

kinetic art *n* art (e g sculpture) depending for its effect on the movement of surfaces or volumes – **kinetic artist** *n*

kinetic energy *n* energy that a body or system has by virtue of its motion

kiˈnetics *n pl but sing or pl in constr* **1** science that deals with the effects of forces on the motions of material bodies or with changes in a physical or chemical system **2** the mechanism by which a physical or chemical change is effected

king /king‖kɪŋ/ *n* **1** a male monarch of a major territorial unit; *esp* one who inherits his position and rules for life **2** the holder of a preeminent position **3** the principal piece of each colour in a set of chessmen that has the power to move 1 square in any direction and must be protected against check **4** a playing card marked with a stylized figure of a king and ranking usu below the ace **5** a draughtsman that has reached the opposite side of the board and is empowered to move both forwards and backwards – **kingship** *n*

ˈ**kingˌbolt** /-ˌbohlt‖-ˌbəʊlt/ *n* a large or major bolt

ˌ**king ˈcobra** *n* a large venomous cobra of southeastern Asia and the Philippines

ˈ**kingˌcup** /-ˌkup‖-ˌkʌp/ *n* MARSH MARIGOLD

ˈ**kingdom** /-d(ə)m‖-d(ə)m/ *n* **1** a territorial unit with a monarchical form of government **2** *often cap* the eternal kingship of God **3** an area or sphere in which sby or sthg holds a preeminent position **4** any of the 3 primary divisions into which natural objects are commonly classified

ˈking,fisher /-ˌfishə‖-ˌfɪʃə/ *n* any of numerous small brightly-coloured fish-eating birds with a short tail and a long stout sharp bill

ˌKing ˈJames ˌVersion /jaymz‖dʒeɪmz/ *n* AUTHORIZED VERSION

ˈking,maker /-ˌmaykə‖-ˌmeɪkə/ *n* sby having influence over the choice of candidates for office

ˈking,pin /-ˌpin‖-ˌpɪn; *also sense 1* ˌ-ˈ-/ *n* **1** the key person or thing in a group or undertaking **2** a kingbolt

Kings /kingz‖kɪŋz/ *n pl but sing in constr* any of 2 or, in the Roman Catholic canon, 4 narrative and historical books of the Old Testament

ˌKing's ˈBench *n* QUEEN'S BENCH – used when the British monarch is a man

ˌKing's ˈCounsel *n* QUEEN'S COUNSEL – used when the British monarch is a man

ˌKing's ˈEnglish *n* standard or correct S British English speech or usage – used when the monarch is a man

ˌking's ˈevil *n, often cap K&E* scrofula

kingship /ˈkingship‖ˈkɪŋʃɪp/ *n* the position, office, or dignity of a king

kink /kingk‖kɪŋk/ *n* **1** a short tight twist or curl caused by sthg doubling or winding on itself **2** an eccentricity or mental peculiarity; *esp* such eccentricity in sexual behaviour or preferences – **kink** *vb*

kinky /ˈkingki‖ˈkɪŋkɪ/ *adj* **1** closely twisted or curled **2a** offbeat **b** titillatingly unusual or bizarre; *esp* sexually perverted *USE* (*2*) infml – **kinkiness** *n*

kinsfolk /ˈkinzˌfohk‖ˈkɪnzˌfəʊk/ *n pl* relatives

kinship /ˈkinship‖ˈkɪnʃɪp/ *n* **1** blood relationship **2** similarity

kinsman /ˈkinzmən‖ˈkɪnzmən/, *fem* **ˈkinsˌwoman** *n* a (male) relative

kiosk /ˈkeeˌosk‖ˈkiːˌɒsk/ *n* **1** an open summerhouse or pavilion common in Turkey or Iran **2** a small stall or stand used esp for the sale of newspapers, cigarettes, and sweets **3** *Br* a public telephone box [Turkish *köşk*, fr Persian *kūshk* portico]

¹kip *n, chiefly Br* **1** a place to sleep **2** a period of sleep *USE* infml

²kip *vi* **-pp-** *chiefly Br* **1** to sleep **2** to lie down to sleep – often + *down USE* infml

¹kipper /ˈkipə‖ˈkɪpə/ *n* a kippered fish, esp a herring

²kipper *vt* to cure (split dressed fish) by salting and drying, usu by smoking

kirk /kuhk‖kɜːk/ *n* **1** *cap the* national Church of Scotland as distinguished from the Church of England or the Episcopal Church in Scotland **2** *chiefly Scot* a church

kirsch /kiəsh‖kɪəʃ/ *n* a dry colourless spirit distilled from the fermented juice of the black morello cherry

kismet /ˈkizmet, ˈkis-‖ˈkɪzmet, ˈkɪs-/ *n, often cap* FATE 1, 2a [Turkish, fr Arabic *qismah* portion, lot]

¹kiss /kis‖kɪs/ *vt* **1a** to touch with the lips, esp as a mark of affection or greeting **b** to express or effect by kissing < ~ed *her good night* > **2** to touch gently or lightly < *wind gently* ~ing *the trees* > ~ *vi* **1** to touch one another with the lips, esp as a mark of love or sexual desire **2** to come into gentle contact – **kissable** *adj*

²kiss *n* an act or instance of kissing

kisser /ˈkisə‖ˈkɪsə/ *n* the mouth or face – slang

kiss of life *n* **1** artificial respiration in which the rescuer blows air into the victim's lungs with mouth-to-mouth contact **2** an action that restores or revitalizes

¹kit /kit‖kɪt/ *n* **1** a set of tools or implements **2** a set of parts ready to be assembled **3** a set of clothes and equipment for use in a specified situation; *esp* the equipment carried by a member of the armed forces

²kit *vt* **-tt-** *chiefly Br* to equip, outfit; *esp* to clothe – usu + *out* or *up*

ˈkit,bag /-ˌbag‖-ˌbæg/ *n* a large cylindrical bag carried over the shoulder and used for holding the kit, esp of a member of the armed forces

kitchen /ˈkichin‖ˈkɪtʃɪn/ *n* a room where food is prepared and cooked [Old English *cycene*, deriv of Late Latin *coquina*, fr Latin *coquere* to cook]

kitchenette /ˌkichiˈnet‖ˌkɪtʃɪˈnet/ *n* a small kitchen or alcove containing cooking facilities

ˌkitchen ˈgarden *n* a garden in which vegetables are grown

kite /kiet‖kaɪt/ *n* **1** any of various hawks with long narrow wings, a deeply forked tail, and feet adapted for taking insects and small reptiles as prey **2** a light frame covered with thin material (e g paper or cloth), designed to be flown in the air at the end of a long string

kith /kith‖kɪθ/ *n* friends or neighbours < ~ *and kin* >

kitsch /kich‖kɪtʃ/ *n* artistic or literary material that is pretentious or inferior and is usu designed to appeal to popular or sentimental taste – **kitschy** *adj*

¹kitten /ˈkitn‖ˈkɪtn/ *n* the young of a cat or other small mammal

²kitten *vi* to give birth to kittens

kittenish /ˈkitn·ish‖ˈkɪtnɪʃ/ *adj* coyly playful or flirtatious

kittiwake /ˈkitiˌwayk‖ˈkɪtɪˌweɪk/ *n* any of various gulls that have a short or rudimentary hind toe

¹kitty /ˈkiti‖ˈkɪtɪ/ *n* CAT 1a; *esp* a kitten – used chiefly as a pet name or calling name

²kitty *n* a jointly held fund of money (e g for household expenses)

kiwi /ˈkeewi‖ˈkiːwɪ/ *n* **1** a flightless New Zealand bird with hairlike plumage **2** *cap* a New Zealander

kiwi fruit *n* an edible oval fruit, borne on an Asian climbing plant, that has a brown hairy skin, green flesh, and black seeds

Klaxon /ˈklaks(ə)n‖ˈklæks(ə)n/ *trademark* – used for a powerful electrically operated horn or warning signal

Kleenex /ˈkleeneks‖ˈkliːneks/ *trademark* – used for a paper handkerchief

kleptomania /ˌkleptəˈmaynyə‖ˌkleptəˈmeɪnjə/ *n* an irresistible desire to steal, esp when not accompanied by economic motives or desire for financial gain [Greek *kleptein* to steal + *mania* madness] – **kleptomaniac** *n*

knack /nak‖næk/ *n* a special ability, capacity, or skill that enables one to do sthg, esp of a difficult or unusual nature, with ease; *broadly* APTITUDE 1

[1]**knacker** /ˈnakə‖ˈnækə/ *n, Br* **1** sby who buys and slaughters worn-out horses for use esp as animal food or fertilizer **2** a buyer of old ships, houses, or other structures for their constituent materials – **knackery** *n*

[2]**knacker** *vt, chiefly Br* to exhaust – infml

knapsack /ˈnap,sak‖ˈnæp,sæk/ *n* a (soldier's) bag (e g of canvas or leather) strapped on the back and used for carrying supplies or personal belongings

knave /nayv‖neɪv/ *n* **1** an unprincipled deceitful fellow **2** JACK 5 – **knavery** *n*, **knavish** *adj*, **knavishly** *adv*

knead /need‖niːd/ *vt* **1** to work and press into a mass (as if) with the hands **2** to manipulate (as if) by kneading < ~ *the idea into shape*> – **kneadable** *adj*, **kneader** *n*

[1]**knee** /nee‖niː/ *n* **1a** (the part of the leg that includes) a joint in the middle part of the human leg that is the articulation between the femur, tibia, and kneecap **b** a corresponding joint in an animal, bird, or insect **2** sthg (e g a piece of wood or iron) shaped like the human knee – **kneed** *adj*

[2]**knee** *vt* to strike with the knee

[1]**kneecap** /ˈnee,kap‖ˈniː,kæp/ *n* a thick flat triangular movable bone that forms the front point of the knee and protects the front of the joint

[2]**kneecap** *vt* to smash the kneecap of, as a punishment or torture

,**knee-ˈdeep** *adj* **1** knee-high **2** immersed *in* (as if) up to the knees

,**knee-ˈhigh** *adj* high or deep enough to reach up to the knees

kneel /neel‖niːl/ *vi* **knelt** /nelt‖nelt/, **kneeled** to fall or rest on the knee or knees – **kneeler** *n*

[1]**knell** /nel‖nel/ *vi* **1** *of a bell* to ring, esp for a death, funeral, etc **2** to sound ominously ~ *vt* to summon, announce, or proclaim (as if) by a knell

[2]**knell** *n* **1** (the sound of) a bell rung slowly (e g for a funeral or disaster) **2** an indication of the end or failure of sthg

knew /nyooh‖njuː/ *past of* KNOW

knickerbockers /ˈnikə,bokəz‖ˈnɪkə,bɒkəz/ *n pl* short baggy trousers gathered on a band at the knee [Diedrich *Knickerbocker*, character in Washington Irving's *History of New York* who is depicted wearing knee-breeches]

knickers /ˈnikəz‖ˈnɪkəz/ *n pl* **1** *Br* women's pants **2** *NAm* knickerbockers

ˈ**knick-,knack** /ˈnik,nak‖ˈnɪk,næk/ *n* a small trivial ornament or trinket – infml

[1]**knife** /nief‖naɪf/ *n, pl* **knives** /nievz‖naɪvz/ **1a** a cutting implement consisting of a blade fastened to a handle **b** such an instrument used as a weapon **2** a sharp cutting blade or tool in a machine

[2]**knife** *vt* **1** to cut, slash, or wound with a knife **2** to cut, mark, or spread with a knife **3** *chiefly NAm* to try to defeat by underhand means – infml

ˈ**knife-,edge** *n* **1** a sharp wedge of hard material (e g steel) used as a fulcrum or pivot in a pair of scales, a pendulum, etc **2** sthg sharp and narrow (e g a ridge of rock) resembling the edge of a knife **3** an uncertain or precarious position or condition

[1]**knight** /niet‖naɪt/ *n* **1a(1)** a mounted man-at-arms serving a feudal superior; *esp* a man ceremonially inducted into special rank after service as page and squire **a(2)** a man honoured by a sovereign for merit, ranking below a baronet **b** a man devoted to the service of a lady (e g as her champion) **2** either of 2 pieces of each colour in a set of chessmen that move from 1 corner to the diagonally opposite corner of a rectangle of 3 by 2 squares over squares that may be occupied – **knightly** *adj or adv*, **knighthood** *n*

[2]**knight** *vt* to make a knight of

,**knight-ˈerrant** *n, pl* **knights-errant** **1** a knight travelling in search of chivalrous adventures **2** a quixotic or chivalrous person

[1]**knit** /nit‖nɪt/ *vb* **knit, knitted; -tt-** *vt* **1a** to link firmly or closely **b** to unite intimately **2a** to cause to grow together <*time and rest will* ~ *a fractured bone*> **b** to contract into wrinkles < ~ted *her brow in thought*> **3a** to form (e g a fabric, garment, or design) by working 1 or more yarns into a series of interlocking loops using 2 or more needles or a knitting machine **b** to work (e g a specified number of rows) using a knitting stitch, specif knit stitch < ~ *1, purl 1*> ~ *vi* **1a** to make knitted fabrics or articles **b** to work yarn or thread in a knitting stitch, specif knit stitch **2a** to become compact **b** to grow together **c** to become joined or drawn together – **knitter** *n*

[2]**knit, knit stitch** *n* a basic knitting stitch that produces a raised pattern on the front of the work

knitting /ˈniting‖ˈnɪtɪŋ/ *n* work that has been or is being knitted

knob /nob‖nɒb/ *n* **1a** a rounded protuberance **b** a small rounded ornament, handle, or control (for pushing, pulling, or turning) **2** a small piece or lump (e g of coal or butter) – **knobbed** *adj*, **knobby** *adj* – **with knobs on** to an even greater degree – infml

knobble /ˈnobl‖ˈnɒbl/ *n* a small rounded irregularity – **knobbly** *adj*

knobkerrie /ˈnob,keri‖ˈnɒb,kerɪ/ *n* a short wooden club with a knobbed head used esp by S African tribesmen [Afrikaans *knopkierie*, fr *knop* knob + *kierie* club]

[1]**knock** /nok‖nɒk/ *vi* **1** to strike sthg with a sharp (audible) blow; *esp* to strike a door seeking admittance **2** to collide with sthg **3** to be in a place, often without any clearly defined aim or purpose – usu + *about* or *around* **4a** to make a sharp pounding noise **b** *of an internal-combustion engine* to make a metallic rapping noise because of a mechanical defect; *also* [7]PINK 3 **5** to find fault ~ *vt* **1a(1)** to strike sharply **a(2)** to drive, force, make, or take (as if) by so striking < ~ed *a hole in the wall*> **b** to set forcibly in motion with a blow **2** to cause to collide (with each other) < ~ed *their heads together*> **3** to find fault with <*always* ~ing *those in authority*> *USE* (*vi 5; vt 3*) infml –

knock together to make or assemble, esp hurriedly or shoddily

[2]**knock** *n* **1a** (the sound of) a knocking or a sharp blow or rap <*the engine has a* ~> **b** a piece of bad luck or misfortune **2** a harsh and often petty criticism **3** INNINGS 1b – infml

knockabout /ˈnokəˌbowt‖ˈnɒkəˌbaʊt/ *adj* **1** suitable for rough use <~ *clothes*> **2** (characterized by antics that are) boisterous <*a* ~ *comedy*>

knock about *vt* to treat roughly or with physical violence

knock back *vt, chiefly Br* **1** to drink (an alcoholic beverage) rapidly **2** to cost; SET BACK 2 **3** to surprise, disconcert *USE* infml

[1]**ˈknockˌdown** /-ˌdown‖-ˌdaʊn/ *n* sthg (e g a piece of furniture) that can be easily assembled or dismantled

[2]**knockdown** *adj* **1** having such force as to strike down or overwhelm **2** easily assembled or dismantled <*a* ~ *table*> **3** *of a price* very low or substantially reduced; *esp* being the lowest acceptable to the seller

knock down *vt* **1** to strike to the ground (as if) with a sharp blow **2** to dispose of (an item for sale at an auction) *to* a bidder **3** to take apart; disassemble **4** to make a reduction in <knock *the price* down *to £4*>

knocker /ˈnokə‖ˈnɒkə/ *n* a metal ring, bar, or hammer hinged to a door for use in knocking

ˈknockers *n pl* a woman's breasts – vulg

ˌknock-ˈknee *n* a condition in which the legs curve inwards at the knees – often pl with sing. meaning but sing. or pl in constr – **knock-kneed** *adj*

knock off *vi* to stop doing sthg, esp one's work ~ *vt* **1** to do hurriedly or routinely <knocked off *one painting after another*> **2** to discontinue, stop <knocked off *work at 5*> **3** to deduct <knocked off *a pound to make the price more attractive*> **4** to kill; *esp* to murder **5** to steal **6** *Br* to have sexual intercourse with *USE* (*4&5*) infml, (*6*) slang

ˈknock-ˌon *n* (an instance of) the knocking of the ball forwards on the ground with the hand or arm in rugby in violation of the rules – **knock on** *vt*

knockout, knock-out /ˈnokˌowt‖ˈnɒkˌaʊt/ *n* **1a** knocking out or being knocked out **b** a blow that knocks out an opponent (or knocks him down for longer than a particular time, usu 10s, and results in the termination of a boxing match) **c** TECHNICAL KNOCKOUT **2** a competition or tournament with successive rounds in which losing competitors are eliminated until a winner emerges in the final **3** sby or sthg that is sensationally striking or attractive – infml – **knockout** *adj*

knock out *vt* **1** to empty (a tobacco pipe) by striking on or with sthg **2** KNOCK UP 1 **3a** to defeat (a boxing opponent) by a knockout **b** to make unconscious **4** to tire out; exhaust **5** to eliminate (an opponent) from a knockout competition **6** to overwhelm with amazement or pleasure – infml

knock up *vt* **1** to make, prepare, or arrange hastily **2** KNOCK OUT 4 **3** to achieve a total of <knocked up *300runs in the first day*> **4** *Br* to rouse, awaken **5** *chiefly NAm* to make pregnant – infml ~*vi* to practise informally before a tennis, squash, etc match

knoll /nol‖nɒl/ *n* a small round hill; a mound

[1]**knot** /not‖nɒt/ *n* **1a** an interlacing of (parts of) 1 or more strings, threads, etc that forms a lump or knob **b** a piece of ribbon, braid etc tied as an ornament **c** a (sense of) tight constriction <*his stomach was all in* ~s> **2** sthg hard to solve **3** a bond of union; *esp* the marriage bond **4a** a protuberant lump or swelling in tissue **b** (a rounded cross-section in timber of) the base of a woody branch enclosed in the stem from which it arises **5** a cluster of people or things **6a** a speed of 1 nautical mile per hour **b** 1 nautical mile – not used technically

[2]**knot** *vb* **-tt-** *vt* **1** to tie in or with a knot **2** to unite closely or intricately ~*vi* to form a knot or knots – **knotter** *n*

[3]**knot** *n* (a bird of) a species of migratory sandpiper

ˈknotˌhole /-ˌhohl‖-ˌhəʊl/ *n* a hole in a board or tree trunk where a knot or branch has come out

knotty /ˈnoti‖ˈnɒtɪ/ *adj* complicated or difficult (to solve) <*a* ~ *problem*> – **knottiness** *n*

knout /nowt‖naʊt/ *n* a whip formerly used in Russia for flogging criminals – **knout** *vt*

[1]**know** /noh‖nəʊ/ *vb* **knew** /nyooh‖njuː/; **known** /nohn‖nəʊn/ *vt* **1a(1)** to perceive directly; have direct cognition of **a(2)** to have understanding of **a(3)** to recognize or identify <*would* ~ *him again*> **b(1)** to be acquainted or familiar with **b(2)** to have experience of **2a** to be aware of the truth or factual nature of; be convinced or certain of **b** to have a practical understanding of <~s *how to write*> **3** *archaic* to have sexual intercourse with ~*vi* to (come to) have knowledge (of sthg) – **knowable** *adj*, **knower** *n* – **not know someone from Adam** have no idea who sby is – **you know** – used for adding emphasis to a statement <*you'll have to try harder,* you know, *if you want to succeed*>

[2]**know** *n* – **in the know** in possession of confidential or otherwise exclusive knowledge or information

ˈknow-ˌall *n* one who behaves as if he knows everything

ˈknow-ˌhow *n* (practical) expertise

knowing /ˈnoh·ing‖ˈnəʊɪŋ/ *adj* **1** having or reflecting knowledge, information, or intelligence **2** shrewd or astute; *esp* implying (that one has) knowledge of a secret **3** deliberate, conscious – **knowingly** *adv*

knowledge /ˈnolij‖ˈnɒlɪdʒ/ *n* **1a** the fact or condition of knowing sthg or sby through experience or association **b** acquaintance with, or understanding or awareness of, sthg **2a** the range of a person's information, perception, or understanding <*is it true? Not to my* ~> **b** the fact or condition of having information or of being learned <*a man of little* ~> **3** the sum of what is known; the body of truth, information, and principles acquired by mankind (on some subject)

knowledgeable /ˈnolijəbl‖ˈnɒlɪdʒəbl/ *adj* having or exhibiting knowledge or intelligence; well-informed – **knowledgeably** *adv*

known /nohn‖nəʊn/ *adj* generally recognized <*a ~ authority on this topic*>
knuckle /ˈnukl‖ˈnʌkl/ *n* **1** the rounded prominence formed by the ends of the 2 bones at a joint; *specif* any of the joints between the hand and the fingers or the finger joints closest to these **2** a cut of meat consisting of the lowest leg joint of a pig, sheep, etc with the adjoining flesh – **near the knuckle** almost improper or indecent
knuckle down *vi* to apply oneself earnestly
ˈ**knuckle-ˌduster** *n* a metal device worn over the front of the doubled fist for protection and use as a weapon
knuckle under *vi* to give in, submit
[1]**KO** /ˌkayˈoh‖ˌkeɪˈəʊ/ *n, pl* **KOs** KNOCKOUT 1 – infml
[2]**KO** *vt* **KO's; KO'ing; KO'd** to knock out – infml
koala /kohˈahlə‖kəʊˈɑːlə/, **koˌala ˈbear** *n* an Australian tree-dwelling marsupial mammal that has large hairy ears, grey fur, and sharp claws and feeds on eucalyptus leaves
kohl /kohl‖kəʊl/ *n* (a cosmetic preparation made with) a black powder used, orig chiefly by Asian women, to darken the eyelids
kohlrabi /ˈkohlˌrahbi‖ˈkəʊlˌrɑːbɪ/ *n, pl* **kohlrabies** a cabbage with a greatly enlarged fleshy turnip-shaped edible stem
kookaburra /ˈkookəˌburə‖ˈkʊkəˌbʌrə/ *n* a large Australian kingfisher that has a call resembling loud laughter
kopeck, **copeck** *also* **kopek** /ˈkohpek‖ˈkəʊpek/ *n* a coin in the USSR, worth 1/100 of a rouble
Koran, **Qur'an** /kawˈrahn‖kɔːˈrɑːn/ *n* the book composed of writings accepted by Muslims as revelations made to Muhammad by Allah through the angel Gabriel – **Koranic** *adj*
korfball /ˈkawfˌbawl‖ˈkɔːfˌbɔːl/ *n* a game resembling basketball played by 2 mixed teams of 12 players each [Dutch *korfbal*, fr *korf* basket + *bal* ball]
kosher /ˈkohshə‖ˈkəʊʃə/ *adj* **1a** *of food* prepared according to Jewish law **b** selling kosher food <*a ~ butcher*> **2** proper, legitimate – infml [Yiddish, fr Hebrew *kāshēr* fit, proper] – **kosher** *n*
[1]**kowtow** /ˈkowˌtow, ˈkoh-‖ˈkaʊˌtaʊ, ˈkəʊ-/ *n* a (Chinese) gesture of deep respect in which one kneels and touches the ground with one's forehead [Chinese (Peking dialect) *k'o*[1] *t'ou*[2], fr *k'o*[1] to bump + *t'ou*[2] head]
[2]**kowtow** /ˌ-ˈ-/ *vi* **1** to make a kowtow **2** to show obsequious deference
[1]**kraal** /krahl‖krɑːl/ *n* **1** a village of S African tribesmen **2** an enclosure for domestic animals in S Africa
[2]**kraal** *vt* to pen in a kraal
kremlin /ˈkremlin‖ˈkremlɪn/ *n* **1** a citadel within a Russian town or city **2** *cap the* government of the USSR
kris /krees‖kriːs/ *n* a Malay or Indonesian dagger with a wavy blade
Krugerrand /ˈkroohgəˌrahnt, -ˌrand‖ˈkruːgəˌrɑːnt, -ˌrænd/ *n* a 1-ounce (28.35g) gold coin of S Africa
kudos /ˈk(y)oohdos‖ˈk(j)uːdɒs/ *n* fame and renown, esp resulting from an act or achievement
Ku Klux Klan /ˌk(y)ooh ˌkluks ˈklan‖ˌk(j)uː ˌklʌks ˈklæn/ *n* a secret society in the USA that is hostile to blacks
kukri /ˈkookri‖ˈkʊkrɪ/ *n* a short curved knife used esp by Gurkhas
kumquat, **cumquat** /ˈkumkwot‖ˈkʌmkwɒt/ *n* (any of several trees that bear) any of several small citrus fruits that are used chiefly for preserves [Chinese (Cantonese dialect) *kam kwat*, fr *kam* gold + *kwat* orange]
kung fu /ˌkung ˈfooh, ˌkoong‖ˌkʌŋ ˈfuː, ˌkʊŋ/ *n* a Chinese martial art resembling karate
kyrie /ˈkiriˌay‖ˈkɪrɪˌeɪ/, **kyrie eleison** /e-ˈlay(i)son‖eˈleɪ(ɪ)sɒn/ *n, often cap* a short liturgical prayer, often set to music, that begins with or consists of the words "Lord, have mercy' [Late Latin *kyrie eleison*, transliteration of Greek *kyrie eleēson* Lord, have mercy]

L

l /el‖el/ *n, pl* **l's, ls** *often cap* **1a** (a graphic representation of or device for reproducing) the 12th letter of the English alphabet **b** sthg shaped like the letter L **2** fifty
la /lah‖lɑː/ *n* the 6th note of the diatonic scale in solmization
laager /ˈlahgə‖ˈlɑːgə/ *n* a camp; *esp* an encampment protected by a circle of wagons or armoured vehicles – **laager** *vi*
lab /lab‖læb/ *n* a laboratory
[1]**label** /ˈlaybl‖ˈleɪbl/ *n* **1** a slip (e g of paper or cloth), inscribed and fastened to sthg to give information (e g identification or directions) **2** a descriptive or identifying word or phrase **3** an adhesive stamp **4** TRADE NAME 1b, 2; *specif* a name used by a company producing commercial recordings
[2]**label** *vt* **-ll-** (*NAm* **-l-, -ll-**) **1a** to fasten a label to **b** to describe or categorize (as if) with a label **2** to make (e g an element) traceable, by substitution of a radioactive or other special isotope – **labellable** *adj*, **labeller** *n*
[1]**labial** /ˈlaybi·əl‖ˈleɪbɪəl/ *adj* **1** of the lips or labia **2** articulated using 1 or both lips – **labially** *adv*, **labialize** *vt*, **labialization** *n*
[2]**labial** *n* a labial consonant (e g /f/ and /p/)
labium /ˈlaybi·əm‖ˈleɪbɪəm/ *n, pl* **labia** /-bi·ə‖-bɪə/ **1** any of the folds at the margin of the vulva **2** the (lower) lip of a flower divided into 2 lip-like parts **3a** a lower mouthpart of an insect **b** a liplike part of various invertebrates
laboratory /ləˈborətri‖ləˈbɒrətrɪ/ *n* a place equipped for scientific experiment, testing, or analysis; *broadly* a place providing opportunity for research in a field of study
laborious /ləˈbawri·əs‖ləˈbɔːrɪəs/ *adj* involving or characterized by effort – **laboriously** *adv*, **laboriousness** *n*
[1]**labour**, *NAm chiefly* **labor** /laybə‖leɪbə/ *n* **1a** expenditure of effort, esp when difficult or compulsory; toil **b** human activity that provides the goods or services in an economy **c** (the period of) the physical activities involved in the birth of young **2** an act or process requiring labour; a task **3a** *sing or pl in constr* an economic group

comprising those who do manual work or work for wages **b** workers <*local* ~ *isn't suitable*> **4** *sing or pl in constr, cap* the Labour party

[2]**labour,** *NAm chiefly* **labor** *vi* **1** to exert one's powers of body or mind, esp with great effort; work, strive **2** to move with great effort **3** to be in labour when giving birth **4** to suffer from some disadvantage or distress <~ *under a delusion*> **5** *of a ship* to pitch or roll heavily ~ *vt* **1** to treat in laborious detail <~ *the obvious*> **2** *archaic* to spend labour on or produce by labour

Labour *adj* of or being a political party, specif one in the UK, advocating a planned socialist economy and associated with working-class interests

ˈ**Labour** ˌ**Day** *n* a day set aside for special recognition of working people: e g **a** the first Monday in September observed in the USA and Canada as a public holiday **b** MAY DAY

labourer /ˈlayb(ə)rə‖ˈleɪb(ə)rə/ *n* one who does unskilled manual work, esp outdoors

ˈ**labour ex**ˌ**change** *n, often cap L&E* a government office that seeks to match unemployed people and vacant jobs and that is responsible for paying out unemployment benefit

labourite /ˈlaybəriet‖ˈleɪbəraɪt/ *n, often cap* a member or supporter of the Labour party

ˌ**labour of** ˈ**love** *n* a task performed for the pleasure it yields rather than for personal gain

labrador /ˈlabrədaw‖ˈlæbrədɔː/ *n, often cap* LABRADOR RETRIEVER

ˌ**Labrador re**ˈ**triever** *n* a retriever characterized by a dense black or golden coat [*Labrador*, peninsula in Canada]

laburnum /ləˈbuhnəm‖ləˈbɜːnəm/ *n* any of a small genus of Eurasian leguminous shrubs and trees with bright yellow flowers and poisonous seeds

labyrinth /ˈlabərinth‖ˈlæbərɪnθ/ *n* **1** a place that is a network of intricate passageways, tunnels, blind alleys, etc **2** sthg perplexingly complex or tortuous in structure, arrangement, or character **3** (the tortuous anatomical structure in) the ear or its bony or membranous part – **labyrinthine** *adj*

lac /lak‖læk/ *n* a resinous substance secreted by a scale insect

[1]**lace** /lays‖leɪs/ *n* **1** a cord or string used for drawing together 2 edges (e g of a garment or shoe) **2** an ornamental braid for trimming coats or uniforms **3** an openwork usu figured fabric made of thread, yarn, etc, used for trimmings, household furnishings, garments, etc [Old French *laz*, fr Latin *laqueus* snare]

[2]**lace** *vt* **1** to draw together the edges of (as if) by means of a lace passed through eyelets **2** to draw or pass (e g a lace) through sthg **3** to confine or compress by tightening laces, esp of a corset **4** to adorn (as if) with lace **5** to beat, lash **6a** to add a dash of an alcoholic drink to **b** to give savour or variety to <*a mundane story line* ~d *with witty repartee*> ~*vi* to be fastened or tied *up* with a lace

lacerate /ˈlasəˌrayt‖ˈlæsəˌreɪt/ *vt* **1** to tear or rend roughly **2** to cause sharp mental or emotional pain to

laceration /ˌlasəˈraysh(ə)n‖ˌlæsəˈreɪʃ(ə)n/ *n* a torn and ragged wound

lachrymal, lacrimal /ˈlakriməl‖ˈlækrɪməl/ *adj* **1** of or constituting the glands that produce tears **2** of or marked by tears

lachrymose /ˈlakrimohs‖ˈlækrɪməʊs/ *adj* **1** given to weeping **2** tending to cause tears – **lachrymosely** *adv*

[1]**lack** /lak‖læk/ *vi* **1** to be deficient or missing **2** to be short or have need of sthg – usu + *for* <*she will not* ~ *for advisers*> ~*vt* to stand in need of; suffer from the absence or deficiency of

[2]**lack** *n* **1** the fact or state of being wanting or deficient **2** sthg lacking

lackadaisical /ˌlakəˈdayzikl‖ˌlækəˈdeɪzɪkl/ *adj* lacking life or zest; *also* (reprehensibly) casual or negligent – **lackadaisically** *adv*

lackey /ˈlaki‖ˈlækɪ/ *n* **1** a usu liveried retainer **2** a servile follower

ˈ**lack**ˌ**lustre** /-ˌlustə‖-ˌlʌstə/ *adj* lacking in sheen, radiance, or vitality; dull

laconic /ləˈkonik‖ləˈkɒnɪk/ *adj* using, or involving the use of, a minimum of words; terse [Latin *laconicus* Spartan, fr Greek *lakōnikos*; fr the Spartan reputation for terseness] – **laconically** *adv*, **laconicism** *n*

[1]**lacquer** /ˈlakə‖ˈlækə/ *n* **1** a clear or coloured varnish obtained by dissolving a substance (e g shellac) in a solvent (e g alcohol) **2** a durable natural varnish; *esp* one obtained from an Asian shrub of the sumach family

[2]**lacquer** *vt* to coat with lacquer – **lacquerer** *n*

lacrosse /ləˈkros‖ləˈkrɒs/ *n* a game played on grass by 2 teams of 10 players, whose object is to throw a ball into the opponents' goal, using a long-handled stick that has a triangular head with a loose mesh pouch for catching and carrying the ball

lactation /lakˈtaysh(ə)n‖lækˈteɪʃ(ə)n/ *n* (the period of time given to) the secretion of milk by a mammal – **lactational** *adj*, **lactationally** *adv*

lactic /ˈlaktik‖ˈlæktɪk/ *adj* of milk

ˌ**lactic** ˈ**acid** *n* an organic acid, normally present in living tissue, and used esp in food and medicine and in industry

lactose /ˈlaktohz, -tohs‖ˈlæktəʊz, -təʊs/ *n* a sugar that is present in milk

lacuna /ləˈkyoohnə‖ləˈkjuːnə/ *n, pl* **lacunae** /-ni‖-nɪ/, **lacunas** **1** a blank space or a missing part **2** a small cavity in an anatomical structure – **lacunal** *adj*, **lacunar** *adj*, **lacunary** *adj*, **lacunate** *adj*

lacy /ˈlaysi‖ˈleɪsɪ/ *adj* resembling or consisting of lace

lad /lad‖læd/ *n* **1** a male person between early boyhood and maturity **2** a fellow, chap **3** *Br* STABLE LAD

[1]**ladder** /ˈladə‖ˈlædə/ *n* **1** a structure for climbing up or down that has 2 long sidepieces of metal, wood, rope, etc joined at intervals by crosspieces on which one may step **2a** sthg that resembles or suggests a ladder in form or use **b** *chiefly Br* a vertical line in hosiery or knitting caused by stitches becoming unravelled **3** a series of ascending steps or stages **4** a means of rising or climbing (e g to a higher status or social position)

[2]**ladder** *vb, chiefly Br* to develop a ladder (in) <*she* ~ed *her tights*> <*her tights have* ~ed>

laddie /ˈladi‖ˈlædɪ/ *n* a (young) lad
lade /layd‖leɪd/ *vt* **laded, laden** /ˈlaydn‖ˈleɪdn/ **1** to put a load or burden on or in (e g a ship); load **2** to put or place as a load, esp for shipment **3** to weigh down with sthg
la-di-da, lah-di-dah /ˌlah di ˈdah‖ˌlɑː dɪ ˈdɑː/ *adj* affectedly refined, esp in voice and pronunciation – infml
ladies /ˈlaydiz‖ˈleɪdɪz/ *n pl but sing in constr, often cap, chiefly Br* a public lavatory for women – infml
ˈ**ladies'** ˌ**man, lady's man** *n* a man who likes to please or to be with women
lading /ˈlayding‖ˈleɪdɪŋ/ *n* cargo, freight
[1]**ladle** /ˈlaydl‖ˈleɪdl/ *n* **1** a deep-bowled long-handled spoon used esp for taking up and conveying liquids or semiliquid foods (e g soup) **2** a vessel for carrying molten metal
[2]**ladle** *vt* to take up and convey (as if) in a ladle
lady /ˈlaydi‖ˈleɪdɪ/ *n* **1a** a woman with authority, esp as a feudal superior **b** a woman receiving the homage or devotion of a knight or lover **2a** a woman of refinement or superior social position **b** a woman – often in courteous reference <*show the* ~ *to a seat*> or usu pl in address <ladies *and gentlemen*> **3** a wife <*the captain and his* ~> **4a** *cap* any of various titled women in Britain – used as a title **b** *cap* a female member of an order of knighthood [Old English *hlǣfdīge*, fr *hlāf* bread + *dǣge* kneader of bread]
ˈ**lady**ˌ**bird** /-ˌbuhd‖-ˌbɜːd/ *n* any of numerous small beetles of temperate and tropical regions; *esp* any of several ladybirds that have red wing cases with black spots
ˌ**lady-in-**ˈ**waiting** *n, pl* **ladies-in-waiting** a lady of a queen's or princess's household appointed to wait on her
ˈ**lady-**ˌ**killer** *n* a man who captivates women
ˈ**lady**ˌ**like** /-ˌliek‖-ˌlaɪk/ *adj* **1** resembling a lady, esp in manners; well-bred **2** becoming or suitable to a lady
ˈ**ladyship** /-ship‖-ʃɪp/ *n* – used as a title for a woman having the rank of lady
ˌ**laevo**ˈ**rotatory** /ˌleevoˈrohtət(ə)ri, -rohˈtayt(ə)ri‖ˌliːvəʊˈrəʊtət(ə)rɪ, -rəʊˈteɪt(ə)rɪ/ *adj* turning towards the left or anticlockwise; *esp* rotating the plane of polarization of light to the left – **laevorotation** *n*
[1]**lag** /lag‖læg/ *vi* **-gg- 1a** to stay or fall behind; fail to keep pace – often + *behind* **b** to become retarded in attaining maximum value **2** to slacken or weaken gradually
[2]**lag** *n* **1** the act or an instance of lagging **2** comparative slowness or retardation **3** an interval between related events; *specif* TIME LAG
[3]**lag** *vt* **-gg- 1** to send to prison **2** to arrest *USE* slang
[4]**lag** *n* **1** a convict **2** an ex-convict
[5]**lag** *n* lagging
[6]**lag** *vt* **-gg-** to cover or provide with lagging – **lagger** *n*
lager /ˈlahgə‖ˈlɑːgə/ *n* a light beer brewed by slow fermentation [German *lagerbier* beer made for storage, fr *lager* storehouse + *bier* beer]
laggard /ˈlagəd‖ˈlægəd/ *n* sby who or sthg that lags or lingers – **laggardly** *adv or adj*
lagging /ˈlaging‖ˈlægɪŋ/ *n* material for thermal insulation (e g wrapped round a boiler or laid in a roof)
lagoon /ləˈgoohn‖ləˈguːn/ *n* a shallow channel or pool usu separated from a larger body of water by a sand bank, reef, etc [French *lagune*, fr Italian *laguna*, fr Latin *lacuna* pit, pool, fr *lacus* lake]
lah-di-dah /ˌlah di ˈdah‖ˌlɑː dɪ ˈdɑː/ *adj* la-di-da
laid /layd‖leɪd/ *past of* LAY
ˌ**laid-**ˈ**back** *adj* relaxed, casual – infml
lain /layn‖leɪn/ *past part of* LIE
lair /leə‖leə/ *n* **1** the resting or living place of a wild animal **2** a refuge or place for hiding
laird /leəd‖leəd/ *n, Scot* a member of the landed gentry
laissez-faire, *Br also* **laisser-faire** /ˌlesay ˈfeə‖ˌleseɪ ˈfeə (*Fr* lese fɛːr)/ *n* a doctrine opposing government interference in economic affairs [French *laissez faire*, imperative of *laisser faire* to let (people) do (as they choose)] – **laissez-faire** *adj*
laity /ˈlayəti‖ˈleɪətɪ/ *n sing or pl in constr* **1** the people of a religion other than its clergy **2** the mass of the people as distinguished from those of a particular profession
[1]**lake** /layk‖leɪk/ *n* a large inland body of water; *also* a pool of oil, pitch, or other liquid
[2]**lake** *n* **1a** a deep purplish red pigment orig prepared from lac or cochineal **b** any of numerous usu bright pigments composed essentially of a soluble dye absorbed in or combined with an inorganic carrier **2** CARMINE 2
lam /lam‖læm/ *vt* **-mm-** to beat soundly – infml
lama /ˈlahmə‖ˈlɑːmə/ *n* a Lamaist monk
Lamaism /ˈlahməˌiz(ə)m‖ˈlɑːməˌɪz(ə)m/ *n* the Buddhism of Tibet, marked by a dominant monastic hierarchy headed by the Dalai Lama – **Lamaist** *n or adj*, **Lamaistic** *adj*
lamasery /ˈlahməsəri‖ˈlɑːməsərɪ/ *n* a monastery of lamas
[1]**lamb** /lam‖læm/ *n* **1a** a young sheep, esp one that is less than a year old or without permanent teeth **b** the young of various animals (e g the smaller antelopes) other than sheep **2a** a gentle, meek, or innocent person **b** a dear, pet **3** the flesh of a lamb used as food
[2]**lamb** *vi* to give birth to a lamb ~*vt* to tend (ewes) at lambing time – **lamber** *n*
lambaste, lambast /lamˈbast‖læmˈbæst/ *vt* **1** to beat, thrash **2** to attack verbally; censure
lambent /ˈlamb(ə)nt‖ˈlæmb(ə)nt/ *adj* **1** playing lightly on or over a surface; flickering <~ *flames*> **2** softly bright or radiant <*eyes* ~ *with love*> **3** marked by lightness or brilliance, esp of expression <*a* ~ *wit*> *USE* fml – **lambently** *adv*, **lambency** *n*
lambskin /ˈlamˌskin‖ˈlæmˌskɪn/ *n* **1** (leather made from) the skin of a lamb or small sheep **2** the skin of a lamb dressed with the wool on
[1]**lame** /laym‖leɪm/ *adj* **1** having a body part, esp a leg, so disabled as to impair freedom of movement; *esp* having a limp caused by a disabled leg **2** weak, unconvincing <*a* ~ *excuse*> – **lamely** *adv*, **lameness** *n*
[2]**lame** *vt* **1** to make lame **2** to make weak or ineffective
lamé /ˈlahmay‖ˈlɑːmeɪ/ *n* a brocaded clothing

fabric made from any of various fibres combined with tinsel weft threads often of gold or silver

ˌlame ˈduck *n* sby or sthg (e g a person or business) that is weak or incapable

[1]**lament** /lə'ment‖lə'ment/ *vi* to feel or express grief or deep regret; mourn aloud – often + *for* or *over* ~*vt* to lament or mourn (demonstratively) for – **lamentation** *n*

[2]**lament** *n* **1** an expression of grief **2** a dirge, elegy

lamentable /'laməntəbl‖'læməntəbl/ *adj* that is to be regretted; deplorable – **lamentableness** *n*, **lamentably** *adv*

lamina /'laminə‖'læmɪnə/ *n, pl* **laminae** /-ni‖-nɪ/, **laminas** a thin plate, scale, layer, or flake

[1]**laminate** /'lamiˌnayt‖'læmɪˌneɪt/ *vt* **1** to roll or compress (e g metal) into a thin plate or plates **2** ~*vi* to separate into laminae **3** to make by uniting superimposed layers of 1 or more materials **4** to overlay with a thin sheet or sheets of material (e g metal or plastic) ~ *vi* to separate into laminae

[2]**laminate** /'laminət, -nayt‖'læmɪnət, -neɪt/ *adj* covered with or consisting of laminae

[3]**laminate** /'laminət, -nayt‖'læmɪnət, -neɪt/ *n* a product made by laminating

lamp /lamp‖læmp/ *n* **1** any of various devices for producing visible light: e g **1a** a vessel containing an inflammable substance (e g oil or gas) that is burnt to give out artificial light **b** a usu portable electric device containing a light bulb **2** any of various light-emitting devices (e g a sunlamp) which produce electromagnetic radiation (e g heat radiation)

ˈlampˌblack /-ˌblak‖-ˌblæk/ *n* a pigment made from finely powdered black soot

lampoon /lam'poohn‖læm'puːn/ *vt or n* (to make the subject of) a harsh vitriolic satire – **lampooner, lampoonist** *n*, **lampoonery** *n*

ˈlamp ˌpost *n* a post, usu of metal or concrete, that supports a light which illuminates a street or other public area (e g a park)

lamprey /'lampri‖'læmprɪ/ *n* any of several eel-like aquatic vertebrates that have a large sucking mouth with no jaws

ˈlampˌshade /-ˌshayd‖-ˌʃeɪd/ *n* a decorative translucent cover placed round an electric light bulb to reduce glare

[1]**lance** /lahns‖lɑːns/ *n* **1** a weapon having a long shaft with a sharp steel head carried by horsemen for use when charging **2a** LANCET 1 **b** a spear or harpoon for killing whales **3** LANCER 1

[2]**lance** *vt* **1** to pierce (as if) with a lance **2** to open (as if) with a lancet

ˌlance ˈcorporal *n* a noncommissioned officer of the lowest rank in the British army or US marines

lancer /'lahnsə‖'lɑːnsə/ *n* **1** a member of a light-cavalry unit (formerly) armed with lances **2** *pl but sing in constr* (the music for) a set of 5 quadrilles each in a different metre

lancet /'lahnsit‖'lɑːnsɪt/ *n* **1** a sharp-pointed and usu 2-edged surgical instrument used to make small incisions **2a** *also* **lancet window** a high narrow window with an acutely pointed head **b** *also* **lancet arch** an acutely pointed arch

[1]**land** /land‖lænd/ *n* **1a** the solid part of the surface of a celestial body, esp the earth **b** ground or soil of a specified situation, nature, or quality <*wet* ~> **2** (*the* way of life in) *the* rural and esp agricultural regions of a country <*going back to the* ~> **3** (the people of) a country, region, etc **4** a realm, domain <*in the* ~ *of dreams*> **5** ground owned as property – often pl with sing. meaning – **landless** *adj*

[2]**land** *vt* **1** to set or put on shore from a ship **2a** to set down (e g passengers or goods) after conveying **b** to bring to or cause to reach a specified place, position, or condition <*his carelessness* ~ed *him in trouble*> **c** to bring (e g an aeroplane) to a surface from the air **3a** to catch and bring in (e g a fish) **b** to gain, secure <~ *a job*> – infml **4** to strike, hit <~ed *him one on the nose*> – infml **5** to present or burden *with* sthg unwanted – infml ~ *vi* **1a** to go ashore from a ship; disembark **b** *of a boat, ship, etc* to come to shore; *also* to arrive on shore in a boat, ship, etc **2a** to end up – usu + *up* <*took the wrong bus and* ~ed *up on the other side of town*> **b** to strike or come to rest on a surface (e g after a fall) <~ed *on his head*> **c** *of an aircraft, spacecraft, etc* to alight on a surface; *also* to arrive in an aircraft, spacecraft, etc which has alighted on a surface

ˈland ˌagent *n* ESTATE AGENT

landau /'landaw‖'lændɔː/ *n* a 4-wheeled carriage with a folding top divided into 2 sections

ˈland ˌbreeze *n* a breeze blowing seawards from the land, generally at night

ˈland ˌcrab *n* any of various crabs that live mostly on land and breed in the sea

landed /'landid‖'lændɪd/ *adj* **1** owning land <~ *proprietors*> **2** consisting of land <~ *property*>

ˈlandˌfall /-ˌfawl‖-ˌfɔːl/ *n* an act or instance of sighting or reaching land after a voyage or flight

landing /'landing‖'lændɪŋ/ *n* **1** the act of going or bringing to a surface from the air or to shore from the water **2** a place for discharging and taking on passengers and cargo **3** a level space at the end of a flight of stairs or between 2 flights of stairs

ˈlanding ˌcraft *n* any of numerous naval craft designed for putting troops and equipment ashore

ˈlanding ˌstage *n* a sometimes floating platform for landing passengers or cargo

ˈlanding ˌstrip *n* a runway without normal airfield or airport facilities

ˈlandˌlady /-ˌlaydi‖-ˌleɪdɪ/ *n* **1** a female landlord **2** the female proprietor of a guesthouse or lodging house

ˈlandˌlocked /-ˌlokt‖-ˌlɒkt/ *adj* (nearly) enclosed by land

ˈlandˌlord /-ˌlawd‖-ˌlɔːd/ *n* **1** sby who owns land, buildings, or accommodation for lease or rent **2** sby who owns or keeps an inn; an innkeeper

ˈlandˌlubber /-ˌlubə‖-ˌlʌbə/ *n* a person unacquainted with the sea or seamanship – **landlubberly** *adj*

ˈlandˌmark /-mahk‖-mɑːk/ *n* **1a** an object

(e g a stone) that marks a boundary **b** a conspicuous object that can be used to identify a locality **2** an event that marks a turning point or new development

[1]**ˈland,scape** /-ˌskayp‖-ˌskeɪp/ *n* **1** natural, esp inland scenery **2a** a picture, drawing, etc of landscape **b** the art of depicting landscape

[2]**landscape** *vt* to improve or modify the natural beauties of ~ *vi* to engage in the occupation of landscape gardening – **landscaper** *n*

ˌlandscape ˈgardener *n* one who designs and arranges the layout of gardens and grounds – **landscape gardening** *n*

ˈland,slide /-ˌslied‖-ˌslaɪd/ *n* **1** a usu rapid movement of rock, earth, etc down a slope; *also* the moving mass **2** an overwhelming victory, esp in an election

ˈland,slip /-ˌslip‖-ˌslɪp/ *n* a small landslide

lane /layn‖leɪn/ *n* **1** a narrow passageway, road, or street **2a** a fixed ocean route used by ships **b** a strip of road for a single line of vehicles **c** AIR LANE **d** any of several marked parallel courses to which a competitor must keep during a race (e g in running or swimming) **e** a narrow hardwood surface down which the ball is sent towards the pins in tenpin bowling

language /ˈlang·gwij‖ˈlæŋgwɪdʒ/ *n* **1a** those words, their pronunciation, and the methods of combining them used by a particular people, nation, etc <*the English* ~> **b(1)** (the faculty of making and using) audible articulate meaningful sound **b(2)** a systematic means of communicating using conventionalized signs, sounds, gestures, or marks **b(3)** the suggestion by objects, actions, or conditions of associated ideas or feelings <*body* ~> **b(4)** a formal system of signs and symbols (e g a logical calculus or one for use with a computer) together with rules for the formation and transformation of admissible expressions **2a** a particular style or manner of verbal expression **b** the specialized vocabulary and phraseology belonging to a particular group or profession [Old French, fr *langue* tongue, language, fr Latin *lingua*]

ˈlanguage laˌboratory *n* a room, usu divided into booths each equipped with a tape recorder, where foreign languages are learnt by listening and speaking

languid /ˈlang·gwid‖ˈlæŋgwɪd/ *adj* **1** drooping or flagging (as if) from exhaustion; weak **2a** spiritless or apathetic in character **b** *esp of literary style* lacking colour; uninteresting **3** lacking force or quickness, esp of movement; sluggish – **languidly** *adv*, **languidness** *n*

languish /ˈlang·gwish‖ˈlæŋgwɪʃ/ *vi* **1** to be or become feeble or enervated **2a** to become dispirited or depressed; pine – often + *for* **b** to lose intensity or urgency <*his interest* ~ed> **c** to suffer hardship or neglect < ~ed *in prison for 2 years*> **3** to assume an expression of emotion appealing for sympathy – **languishingly** *adv*, **languishment** *n*

languor /ˈlang·gə‖ˈlæŋgə/ *n* **1** weakness or weariness of body or mind **2** a feeling or mood of wistfulness or dreaminess **3** heavy or soporific stillness – **languorous** *adj*, **languorously** *adv*

lank /langk‖læŋk/ *adj* **1** lean, gaunt **2** straight, limp, and usu greasy < ~ *hair*> – **lankly** *adv*, **lankness** *n*

lanky /ˈlangki‖ˈlæŋkɪ/ *adj* ungracefully tall and thin – **lankily** *adv*, **lankiness** *n*

lanolin, **lanoline** /ˈlanəlin‖ˈlænəlɪn/ *n* wool grease, esp when refined for use in ointments and cosmetics

lantern /ˈlantən‖ˈlæntən/ *n* **1** a portable protective case with transparent windows that houses a light (e g a candle) **2a** the chamber in a lighthouse containing the light **b** a structure above an opening in a roof which has glazed or open sides for light or ventilation **3** MAGIC LANTERN

lanyard /ˈlanyəd‖ˈlænjəd/ *n* **1** a piece of rope or line for fastening sthg on board ship **2** a cord worn round the neck as a decoration or to hold sthg (e g a knife)

[1]**lap** /lap‖læp/ *n* (the clothing covering) the front part of the lower trunk and thighs of a seated person – **lapful** *n* – **drop/land (sthg) in someone's lap** to (cause to) become sby's responsibility – **in the lap of luxury** in an environment of great ease, comfort, and wealth – **in the lap of the gods** beyond human influence or control

[2]**lap** *vb* **-pp-** *vt* **1a** to fold or wrap over or round **b** to envelop entirely; swathe **2** to surround or hold protectively (as if) in the lap **3a** to place or lie so as to (partly) cover (one another) < ~ *tiles on a roof*> **b** to unite (e g beams or timbers) so as to preserve the same breadth and depth throughout **4a** to dress, smooth, or polish (e g a metal surface) to a high degree of refinement or accuracy **b** to work (2 surfaces) together with or without abrasives until a very close fit is produced **5a** to overtake and thereby lead or increase the lead over (another contestant) by a full circuit of a racetrack **b** to complete a circuit of (a racetrack) ~ *vi* **1** to overlap **2** to traverse or complete a circuit of a course

[3]**lap** *n* **1a** the amount by which one object overlaps another **b** the part of an object that overlaps another **2** a smoothing and polishing tool (e g for metal or precious stones), usu consisting of a rotating disc covered with abrasive **3** a layer of a flexible substance (e g fibres or paper) wound round sthg, esp a roller **4a** (the distance covered during) the act or an instance of moving once round a closed course or track **b** one stage or segment of a larger unit (e g a journey) **c** one complete turn (e g of a rope round a drum)

[4]**lap** *vb* **-pp-** *vi* **1** to take in liquid with the tongue **2** to move in little waves, usu making a gentle splashing sound <*the sea* ~ped *gently against the edge of the quay*> ~ *vt* **1a** to take in (liquid) with the tongue **b** to take in eagerly or quickly – usu + *up* <*the crowd* ~ped *up every word he said*> **2** to flow or splash against in little waves

[5]**lap** *n* **1** an act or instance of lapping **2** a thin or weak beverage or food **3** a gentle splashing sound

lapdog /ˈlap,dog‖ˈlæp,dɒg/ *n* a small dog that may be held in the lap

lapel /ləˈpel‖ləˈpel/ *n* a fold of the top front edge of a coat or jacket that is continuous with the collar

[1]**lapidary** /ˈlapidəri‖ˈlæpɪdərɪ/ *n* sby who cuts, polishes, or engraves precious stones

[2]**lapidary** *adj* **1a** sculptured in or engraved on

stone **b** of or relating to (the cutting of) gems **2** *of literary style* having the elegance and dignity associated with monumental inscriptions

lapis lazuli /ˌlapis 'lazyoolie, -li‖ˌlæpɪs 'læzjʊlaɪ, -lɪ/ *n* (the colour of) a rich blue semi-precious stone

[1]**lapse** /laps‖læps/ *n* **1** a slight error (e g of memory or in manners) **2a** a drop; *specif* a drop in temperature, humidity, or pressure with increasing height **b** an esp moral fall or decline <*a ~ from grace*> **3a(1)** the legal termination of a right or privilege through failure to exercise it **a(2)** the termination of insurance coverage for nonpayment of premiums **b** a decline into disuse **4** an abandonment of religious faith **5** a continuous passage or elapsed period <*returned after a ~ of several years*>

[2]**lapse** *vi* **1a** to fall or depart from an attained or accepted standard or level (e g of morals) – usu + *from* **b** to sink or slip gradually <*the guests ~* d *into silence*> **2** to go out of existence or use **3** to pass to another proprietor by omission or negligence **4** *of time* to pass

lap-top *n* a portable computer small enough to be operated on a person's lap – **lap-top** *adj*

lapwing /'lapˌwing‖'læpˌwɪŋ/ *n* a crested Old World plover noted for its shrill wailing cry

larceny /'lahsəni‖'lɑːsənɪ/ *n* theft [Middle French *larcin* theft, fr Latin *latrocinium* robbery, fr *latro* mercenary soldier]

larch /lahch‖lɑːtʃ/ *n* (the wood of) any of a genus of trees of the pine family with short deciduous leaves

[1]**lard** /lahd‖lɑːd/ *vt* **1a** to dress (e g meat) for cooking by inserting or covering with fat, bacon, etc **b** to cover with grease **2** to intersperse or embellish (e g speech or writing) *with* sthg

[2]**lard** *n* a soft white solid fat obtained by rendering the esp abdominal fat of a pig – **lardy** *adj*

larder /'lahdə‖'lɑːdə/ *n* a place where food is stored; a pantry

[1]**large** /lahj‖lɑːdʒ/ *adj* **1** having more than usual power, capacity, or scope **2** exceeding most other things of like kind (in quantity or size) **3** dealing in great numbers or quantities; operating on an extensive scale <*a ~ and highly profitable business*> – **largeness** *n*, **largish** *adj*

[2]**large** *n* – **at large 1** without restraint or confinement; AT LIBERTY <*the escaped prisoner is still* at large> **2** AS A WHOLE <*society* at large>

large intestine *n* the rear division of the vertebrate intestine that is divided into caecum, colon, and rectum, and concerned esp with the resorption of water and formation of faeces

largely /'lahjli‖'lɑːdʒlɪ/ *adv* to a large extent

largess, largesse /lah'jes‖lɑː'dʒes/ *n* **1** liberal giving, esp to an inferior **2** sthg (e g money) given generously as a gift

largo /'lahgoh‖'lɑːgəʊ/ *n, adv, or adj, pl* **largos** (a movement to be) played in a very slow and broad manner – used in music [Italian, slow, broad, fr Latin *largus* abundant]

lariat /'lari·ət‖'lærɪət/ *n, chiefly NAm* a lasso

[1]**lark** /lahk‖lɑːk/ *n* any of numerous brown singing birds mostly of Europe, Asia, and northern Africa; *esp* a skylark

[2]**lark** *vi* to have fun – usu + *about* or *around*

[3]**lark** *n* **1** a lighthearted adventure; *also* a prank **2** *Br* a type of activity; *esp* a business, job <*it's a good ~: 80 quid a week, own car, and no questions asked*> *USE* infml

larkspur /'lahkˌspuh‖'lɑːkˌspɜː/ *n* a delphinium; *esp* a cultivated annual delphinium grown for its bright irregular flowers

larrikin /'larikin‖'lærɪkɪn/ *n, Austr* a hooligan

larrup /'larəp‖'lærəp/ *vt, Br dial* to beat soundly – infml

larva /'lahvə‖'lɑːvə/ *n, pl* **larvae** /-vi‖-vɪ/ **1** the immature, wingless, and often wormlike feeding form that hatches from the egg of many insects and is transformed into a pupa or chrysalis from which the adult emerges **2** the early form (e g a tadpole) of an animal (e g a frog) that undergoes metamorphosis before becoming an adult – **larval** *adj*

laryngitis /ˌlarin'jietəs‖ˌlærɪn'dʒaɪtəs/ *n* inflammation of the larynx – **laryngitic** *adj*

larynx /'laringks‖'lærɪŋks/ *n, pl* **larynges** /lə'rinˌjeez‖lə'rɪnˌdʒiːz/, **larynxes** the modified upper part of the trachea of air-breathing vertebrates that contains the vocal cords in human beings, most other mammals, and a few lower forms – **laryngeal** *adj*

lasagne /lə'zanyə‖lə'zænjə/ *n* (a baked dish of minced meat, sauce, and) pasta in the form of broad flat sheets [Italian, pl of *lasagna*, fr Latin *lasanum* cooking-pot, fr Greek *lasanon* chamber pot]

lascivious /lə'sivi·əs‖lə'sɪvɪəs/ *adj* inclined or inciting to lechery or lewdness – **lasciviously** *adv*, **lasciviousness** *n*

laser /'layzə‖'leɪzə/ *n* a device that generates an intense beam of coherent light or other electromagnetic radiation of a single wavelength by using the natural oscillations of atoms or molecules [*l*ight *a*mplification by *s*timulated *e*mission of *r*adiation]

[1]**lash** /lash‖læʃ/ *vi* **1** to move violently or suddenly **2** to beat, pour <*rain ~*ed *down*> **3** to attack physically or verbally, (as if) with a whip – often + *at, against,* or *out* ~ *vt* **1** to strike quickly and forcibly (as if) with a lash **2a** to drive (as if) with a whip; rouse <~ed *the crowd into a frenzy*> **b** to cause to lash

[2]**lash** *n* **1a(1)** a stroke (as if) with a whip **a(2)** (the flexible part of) a whip **b** a sudden swinging movement or blow **2** violent beating <*the ~ of a north wind*> **3** an eyelash **4** *Austr & NZ* an attempt, go – infml

[3]**lash** *vt* to bind or fasten with a cord, rope, etc – **lasher** *n*

[1]**lashing** /'lashing‖'læʃɪŋ/ *n* a physical or verbal beating

[2]**lashing** *n* sthg used for binding, wrapping, or fastening

lashings *n pl* an abundance – usu + *of* <*~ of hot water*>; infml

lash out *vi* **1** to make a sudden violent physical or verbal attack – usu + *at* or *against* **2** *Br* to spend unrestrainedly – often + *on*; infml

lass /las‖læs/, **lassie** /'lasi‖'læsɪ/ *n* a young woman; a girl

Lassa fever /'lasə‖'læsə/ *n* an acute often fatal virus disease of tropical countries [*Lassa*, village in Nigeria]

[1]**lasso** /la'sooh, 'lasoh||læ'su:, 'læsəʊ/ *n, pl* **lassos, lassoes** a rope or long thong of leather with a running noose that is used esp for catching horses and cattle [Spanish *lazo*, fr Latin *laqueus* snare]

[2]**lasso** *vt* **lassos, lassoes; lassoed; lassoing** to catch (as if) with a lasso – **lassoer** *n*

[1]**last** /lahst||lɑ:st/ *vi* **1** to continue in time **2a** to remain in good or adequate condition, use, or effectiveness **b** to manage to continue (e g in a course of action) **c** to continue to live <*he won't ~ much longer*> ~ *vt* **1** to continue in existence or action as long as or longer than – often + *out* <*couldn't ~ out the training*> **2** to be enough for the needs of <*the supplies will ~ them a week*> – **laster** *n*

[2]**last** *adj* **1** following all the rest: e g **1a** final, latest **b** being the only remaining <*his ~ pound*> **2** of the final stage of life <*~ rites*> **3** next before the present; most recent <*~ week*> <*this is better than his ~ book*> **4a** lowest in rank or standing; *also* worst **b** least suitable or likely <*he'd be the ~ person to fall for flattery*> **5a** conclusive, definitive <*the ~ word on the subject*> **b** single – used as an intensive <*ate every ~ scrap*> – **lastly** *adv* – **last but one 1** second most recent **2** penultimate

[3]**last** *adv* **1** after all others; at the end <*came ~ and left first*> **2** on the most recent occasion <*when we ~ met*> **3** in conclusion; lastly <*and ~, the economic aspect*>

[4]**last** *n* sby or sthg last – **at last/at long last** after everything; finally; *esp* after much delay – **to the last** till the end

[5]**last** *n* a form (e g of metal) shaped like the human foot, over which a shoe is shaped or repaired

ˌlast-ˈditch *adj* made as a final effort, esp to avert disaster <*a ~ attempt*>

lasting /'lahsting||'lɑ:stɪŋ/ *adj* existing or continuing for a long while – **lastingly** *adv*, **lastingness** *n*

ˌlast ˈstraw *n* *the* last of a series (e g of events or indignities) stretching one's patience beyond its limit [fr the fable of the last straw that broke the camel's back when added to his burden]

ˌlast ˈword *n* **1** the final remark in a verbal exchange **2** the power of final decision **3** the most up-to-date or fashionable example of its kind <*the ~ in sports cars*>

[1]**latch** /lach||lætʃ/ *vi* **1** to attach oneself <*~ed onto a rich widow*> **2** to gain understanding or comprehension *USE* + *on* or *onto*

[2]**latch** *n* **1** a fastener (e g for a door) with a pivoted bar that falls into a notch on the door post **2** a fastener (e g for a door) in which a spring slides a bolt into a hole when the door is shut – **latch** *vt*

ˈlatchˌkey /-ˌkee||-ˌki:/ *n* a key to an outside (front) door

[1]**late** /layt||leɪt/ *adj* **1a** occurring or arriving after the expected time <*a ~ spring*> **b** of the end of a specified time span <*the ~ Middle Ages*> **2a** (recently) deceased – used with reference to names, positions or specified relationships <*the ~ James Scott*> <*his ~ wife*> <*the ~ chairman*> **b** just prior to the present, esp as the most recent of a succession <*the ~ government*> <*some ~ news has just arrived*> **3** far on in the day or night <*it's too ~ to go now*> – **lateness** *n*

[2]**late** *adv* **1a** after the usual or proper time <*stayed up ~*> **b** at or near the end of a period of time or of a process – often + *on* <*~ on in the experiment*> **2** until lately <*Dr Evans, ~ of Birmingham, now lectures at Durham*> – **of late** in the period shortly or immediately before; recently <*have not seen him* of late>

lateen /lə'teen||lə'ti:n/ *adj* of or being a rig characterized by a triangular sail hung from a long spar set obliquely on a low mast

lately /'laytli||'leɪtlɪ/ *adv* recently; OF LATE

latent /'layt(ə)nt||'leɪt(ə)nt/ *adj* present but not manifest <*a ~ infection*> – **latency** *n*, **latently** *adj*

ˌlatent ˈheat *n* heat given off or absorbed in a change of phase without a change in temperature

lateral /'lat(ə)rəl||'læt(ə)rəl/ *adj* of the side; situated on, directed towards, or coming from the side – **laterally** *adv*

latest /'laytist||'leɪtɪst/ *n* **1** *the* most recent or currently fashionable style or development **2** *the* latest acceptable time <*be home by one at the ~*>

latex /'layteks||'leɪteks/ *n, pl* **latices** /'latəˌseez||'lætəˌsi:z/, **latexes 1** a milky usu white fluid that is produced by various flowering plants (e g of the spurge and poppy families) and is the source of rubber, gutta-percha, chicle, and balata **2** a water emulsion of a synthetic rubber or plastic – **laticiferous** *adj*

[1]**lath** /lahth||lɑ:θ/ *n, pl* **laths**, /lahths, lahdhz||lɑ:θs, lɑ:ðz/ **lath** a thin narrow strip of wood, esp for nailing to woodwork (e g rafters or studding) as a support (e g for tiles or plaster)

[2]**lath** *vt* to cover or line with laths – **lathing** *n*

lathe *n* a machine in which work is rotated about a horizontal axis and shaped by a fixed tool

[1]**lather** /'lahdhə||'lɑ:ðə/ *n* **1a** a foam or froth formed when a detergent (e g soap) is agitated in water **b** foam or froth from profuse sweating (e g on a horse) **2** an agitated or overwrought state – **lathery** *adj*

[2]**lather** *vt* **1** to spread lather over **2** to beat severely – infml ~*vi* to form a (froth like) lather – **latherer** *n*

[1]**Latin** /'latin||'lætɪn/ *adj* **1** of Latium or the Latins **2a** of or composed in Latin **b** Romance **3** of the part of the Christian church using a Latin liturgy; *broadly* ROMAN CATHOLIC **4** of the peoples or countries using Romance languages **5** *chiefly NAm* of the peoples or countries of Latin America – **Latinize** *vb*

[2]**Latin** *n* **1** the Italic language of ancient Latium and of Rome **2** a member of the people of ancient Latium **3** a member of any of the Latin peoples **4** *chiefly NAm* a native or inhabitant of Latin America

latin·ize, -ise /'latiniez||'lætɪnaɪz/ *vt* **1** to give a Latin form or character to **2** ROMANIZE 2 – **latinization** *n*

latitude /'latityoohd||'lætɪtju:d/ *n* **1a** the angular distance of a point on the surface of a celestial body, esp the earth, measured N or S from the equator **b** the angular distance of a celestial body from the ecliptic **2** a region as marked by its latitude – often pl with sing. meaning **3** (permitted) freedom of action or choice – **latitudinal** *adj*, **latitudinally** *adv*

latitudinarian /ˌlatiˌtyoohdiˈneəri·ən‖ˌlætɪˌtjuːdɪˈneərɪən/ *n or adj* (a person) liberal in standards of religious belief and conduct; *specif* a member of the Church of England favouring freedom of doctrine and practice within it – **latitudinarianism** *n*

latrine /ləˈtreen‖ləˈtriːn/ *n* a small pit used as a toilet, esp in a military camp, barracks, etc; *broadly* a toilet

[1]latter /ˈlatə‖ˈlætə/ *adj* **1** of the end; later, final <*the ~ stages of a process*> **2** recent, present <*in ~ years*> **3** second of 2 things, or last of several things mentioned or understood

[2]latter *n, pl* **latter** the second or last mentioned

ˈlatter-ˌday *adj* of present or recent times

ˈlatterly /-li‖-lɪ/ *adv* **1** towards the end or latter part of a period **2** lately

lattice /ˈlatis‖ˈlætɪs/ *n* **1** (a window, door, etc having) a framework or structure of crossed wooden or metal strips with open spaces between **2** a network or design like a lattice **3a** a regular geometrical arrangement of points or objects over an area or in space **b** the geometrical arrangement of the atoms or ions in a crystal – **lattice** *vt*, **latticed** *adj*

[1]laud /lawd‖lɔːd/ *n* **1** *pl but sing or pl in constr, often cap* an office usu immediately following matins and forming with it the first of the canonical hours **2** praise – used esp in hymns

[2]laud *vt* to praise, esp with hymns

laudable /ˈlawdəbl‖ˈlɔːdəbl/ *adj* worthy of praise; commendable – **laudableness** *n*, **laudably** *adv*, **laudability** *n*

laudanum /ˈlawdənəm‖ˈlɔːdənəm/ *n* **1** any of various preparations of opium formerly used in medicine **2** a tincture of opium

laudatory /ˈlawdət(ə)ri‖ˈlɔːdət(ə)rɪ/, **laudative** /-dətiv‖-dətɪv/ *adj* of or expressing praise

[1]laugh /lahf‖lɑːf/ *vi* **1a** to make the explosive vocal sounds characteristically expressing amusement, mirth, joy, or derision **b** to experience amusement, mirth, joy, or derision <~ed *inwardly though her face remained grave*> **2** to produce a sound of or like laughter – chiefly poetic <*a* ~ing *brook*> ~ *vt* **1** to influence or bring to a specified state by laughter <~ed *him out of his fears*> **2** to utter (as if) with a laugh <~ed *her consent*> **3** to dismiss as trivial – + *off* or *away* – **laugher** *n*, **laughingly** *adv* – **laugh up one's sleeve** to be secretly amused

[2]laugh *n* **1** the act or sound of laughing **2** an expression of mirth or scorn **3** a means of entertainment; a diversion – often pl with sing. meaning **4** a cause for derision or merriment; a joke – infml

laughable /ˈlahfəbl‖ˈlɑːfəbl/ *adj* of a kind to provoke laughter or derision; ridiculous – **laughableness** *n*, **laughably** *adv*

ˈlaughing ˌgas *n* NITROUS OXIDE

ˌlaughing ˈjackˌass *n* the kookaburra

ˈlaughingˌstock /-ˌstok‖-ˌstɒk/ *n* an object of ridicule

laughter /ˈlahftə‖ˈlɑːftə/ *n* **1** a sound (as if) of laughing **2** the action of laughing

[1]launch /lawnch‖lɔːntʃ/ *vt* **1a** to throw forward; hurl **b** to release or send off (e g a self-propelled object) <~ *a rocket*> **2a** to set (an esp newly built boat or ship) afloat **b** to start or set in motion (e g on a course or career) **c** to introduce (a new product) onto the market <*a party to ~ a new book*> ~ *vi* **1** to throw oneself energetically – + *into* or *out into* <~ed *into a brilliant harangue*> **2** to make a start – usu + *out* or *forth* <~ed *forth on a long-winded explanation*>

[2]launch *n* an act or instance of launching

[3]launch *n* **1** the largest boat carried by a warship **2** a large open or half-decked motorboat

ˈlaunching ˌpad /ˈlawnching‖ˈlɔːntʃɪŋ/ *n* a noninflammable platform from which a rocket can be launched

launder /ˈlawndə‖ˈlɔːndə/ *vt* **1** to wash (e g clothes) in water **2** to make ready for use by washing, sometimes starching, and ironing **3** to give (sthg, esp money, obtained illegally) the appearance of being respectable or legal ~*vi* to become clean by washing, ironing, etc <*clothes that ~ well*> – **launderer** *n*, **laundress** *n*

launderette /ˌlawnd(ə)ˈret‖ˌlɔːnd(ə)ˈret/ *n* a self-service laundry

laundry /ˈlawndri‖ˈlɔːndrɪ/ *n* **1** clothes or cloth articles that have been or are to be laundered, esp by being sent to a laundry **2** a place where laundering is done; *esp* a commercial laundering establishment

laureate /ˈlawri·ət‖ˈlɔːrɪət/ *n* a person specially honoured for achievement in an art or science – **laureate** *adj*, **laureateship** *n*

laurel /ˈlorəl‖ˈlɒrəl/ *n* **1** any of a genus of trees or shrubs that have alternate entire leaves, small flowers, and fruits that are ovoid berries **2** a tree or shrub that resembles the true laurel **3** a crown of laurel awarded as a token of victory or preeminence; distinction, honour – usu pl with sing. meaning

lava /ˈlahvə‖ˈlɑːvə/ *n* (solidified) molten rock that issues from a volcano [Italian, fr Latin *labes* fall] – **lavalike** *adj*

lavatory /ˈlavətri‖ˈlævətrɪ/ *n* **1** a toilet **2** *NAm* a room with facilities for washing and usu with 1 or more toilets – **lavatory** *adj*

lave /layv‖leɪv/ *vt* to wash; BATHE 1 – poetic

lavender /ˈlavində‖ˈlævɪndə/ *n* **1** a Mediterranean plant widely cultivated for its narrow aromatic leaves and spikes of lilac-purple flowers which are dried and used in perfume sachets **2** pale purple

[1]lavish /ˈlavish‖ˈlævɪʃ/ *adj* **1** expending or bestowing profusely **2** expended, bestowed, or produced in abundance – **lavishly** *adj*, **lavishness** *n*

[2]lavish *vt* to expend or bestow with profusion

law /law‖lɔː/ *n* **1a(1)** a rule of conduct formally recognized as binding or enforced by authority **a(2)** the whole body of such rules <*the ~ of the land*> **a(3)** COMMON LAW **b** the control brought about by such law – esp in *law and order* **c** litigation <*ready to go to ~*> **2a** a rule one should observe **b** control, authority **3a** *often cap* the revelation of the will of God set out in the Old Testament **b** *cap* the first part of the Jewish scriptures; the Pentateuch **4** a rule of action, construction, or procedure <*the* ~s *of poetry*> **5** the law relating to one subject <*company* ~> **6** *often cap the* legal profession **7** jurisprudence **8a** a statement of an order or relation of natural phenomena <*the first* ~ *of thermodynamics*> **b** a necessary relation between mathematical or logical expressions **9** *sing or pl in constr, often cap the* police – infml – **in/at law** according to the law – **law unto him-/her-/itself** sby or sthg that does not follow accepted conventions

ˈlaw-aˌbiding *adj* abiding by or obedient to the law

ˈlawˌbreaker /-ˌbraykə‖-ˌbreɪkə/ *n* one who violates the law – **lawbreaking** *adj or n*

lawful /ˈlawf(ə)l‖ˈlɔːf(ə)l/ *adj* **1** allowed by law **2** rightful <*your* ~ *Queen*> – **lawfully** *adv*, **lawfulness** *n*

lawless /ˈlawlis‖ˈlɔːlɪs/ *adj* **1** not regulated by or based on law **2** not restrained or controlled by law – **lawlessly** *adv*, **lawlessness** *n*

[1]**lawn** /lawn‖lɔːn/ *n* a fine sheer linen or cotton fabric of plain weave that is thinner than cambric [*Laon*, town in France] – **lawny** *adj*

[2]**lawn** *n* an area of ground (e g around a house or in a garden or park) that is covered with grass and is kept mowed [Middle French *lande* heath, of Celtic origin]

ˌlawn ˈtennis *n* tennis played on a grass court

ˈlawˌsuit /-ˌs(y)ooht‖-ˌs(j)uːt/ *n* a noncriminal case in a court of law

lawyer /ˈlawyə, ˈloyə‖ˈlɔːjə, ˈlɔɪə/ *n* sby whose profession is to conduct lawsuits or to advise on legal matters

lax /laks‖læks/ *adj* **1** *of the bowels* loose, open **2** not strict or stringent; negligent <~ *morals*> <~ *in his duties*>; *also* deficient in firmness or precision <*his ideas are a bit* ~> **3a** not tense, firm, or rigid; slack <*a* ~ *rope*> **b** not compact or exhibiting close cohesion; loose <*a* ~ *flower cluster*> – **laxity, laxness** *n*, **laxly** *adv*, **laxation** *n*

laxative /ˈlaksətiv‖ˈlæksətɪv/ *n or adj* (a usu mild purgative) having a tendency to loosen or relax the bowels (to relieve constipation) – **laxativeness** *n*

[1]**lay** /lay‖leɪ/ *vb* **laid** /layd‖leɪd/ *vt* **1** to beat or strike down with force <*a blow that* laid *him to the ground*> **2a** to put or set down **b** to place for rest or sleep; *esp* to bury **3** *of a bird* to produce (an egg) **4** to calm, allay <~ *the dust*> <~ *a ghost*> **5** to bet, wager <~ *odds on the favourite*> **6** to press down giving a smooth and even surface <laid *tarmac on the road*> **7a** to dispose or spread over or on a surface <~ *a cloth on the table*> **b** to set in order or position <~ *bricks*> **c** to put (strands) in place and twist to form a rope, hawser, or cable **8a** to put or impose as a duty, burden, or punishment – esp + *on* or *upon* **b** to put as a burden of reproach <laid *the blame on him*> **c** to advance as an accusation; impute <laid *a charge of manslaughter*> **9** to place (sthg immaterial) on sthg <~ *stress on grammar*> **10** to prepare, contrive <*a well-*laid *plan*> **11a** to bring into position or against or into contact with sthg <laid *the watch to his ear*> **b** to prepare or position for action or operation <~ *a fire in the fireplace*> **c** to adjust (a gun) to the proper direction and elevation **12** to bring to a specified condition <~ *waste the land*> **13a** to assert, allege <~ *claim to an estate*> **b** to submit for examination and judgment <laid *his case before the tribunal*> **14** to place fictitiously; locate <*the scene is* laid *in wartime London*> **15** to put aside for future use; store, reserve – + *aside*, *by*, *in*, or *up* **16** to put out of use or consideration – + *aside* or *by* **17** to copulate with – slang ~ *vi* **1** *esp of a hen* to produce eggs **2** to wager, bet **3** to apply oneself vigorously <laid *to his oars*> **4** [1]LIE – nonstandard – **lay about one** to deal blows indiscriminately; lash out on all sides – **lay hands on 1** to seize forcibly **2** to find – **lay into** to attack with words or blows – **lay it on 1** to exaggerate, esp in order to flatter or impress <*that was really* laying it on *a bit thick*> **2** to charge an exorbitant price – **lay on the table** to make public; disclose – **lay low 1** to knock or bring down; *esp* destroy **2** to cause to be ill or physically weakened – **lay open** to expose: e g **a** to cut <*a blow that* laid *his head* open> **b** to explain or make known; UNCOVER 1 <*the facts of the case were* laid *wide* open> – **lay siege to 1** to besiege militarily **2** to attempt to conquer or persuade diligently or persistently

[2]**lay** *n* **1** (a partner in) sexual intercourse – slang **2** *chiefly NAm* the position or situation in which sthg lies, esp relative to sthg else <*the* ~ *of the land*> – **in lay** *esp of a hen* in condition to lay eggs

[3]**lay** *past of* LIE

[4]**lay** *n* a simple narrative poem intended to be sung; a ballad

[5]**lay** *adj* **1** of or performed by the laity **2** of domestic or manual workers in a religious community <*a* ~ *brother*> **3** not belonging to a particular profession

layabout /ˈlayəbowt‖ˈleɪəbaʊt/ *n, chiefly Br* a lazy shiftless person

ˈlay-ˌby *n, pl* **lay-bys** *Br* a branch from or widening of a road to permit vehicles to stop without obstructing traffic

lay down *vt* **1** to surrender; GIVE UP <laid down *her life for the cause*> **2a** to begin to construct (e g a ship or railway) **b** to establish, prescribe; *esp* to dictate <~ *the law*> **3** to store; *specif* to store (wine) in a cellar

[1]**layer** /ˈlayə‖ˈleɪə/ *n* **1a** a single thickness of some substance spread or lying over or under another (as part of a series)· **b** any of a series of gradations or depths <~s *of meaning*> **2a** a branch or shoot of a plant treated to induce rooting while still attached to the parent plant **b** a plant developed by layering

[2]**layer** *vt* **1** to propagate (a plant) by means of layers **2** to cut (hair) in layers **3** to arrange or form (as if) in layers <*potato slices* ~ed *with cheese*> **4** to form out of or with layers ~*vi, of a plant* to form roots where a stem comes in contact with the ground

layette /layˈet‖leɪˈet/ *n* a complete outfit of clothing and equipment for a newborn infant [French, fr Middle French, diminutive of *laye* box]

lay figure *n* **1** a jointed model of the human body used by artists, esp to show the arrangement of drapery **2** a person likened to a dummy or puppet

layman /ˈlaymən‖ˈleɪmən/, *fem* ˈ**layˌwoman** *n* **1** a person not of the clergy **2** a person without special (e g professional) knowledge of some field

ˈ**layˌoff** /-ˌof‖-ˌɒf/ *n* **1** the laying off of an employee or work force **2** a period of unemployment, inactivity, or idleness

lay off *vt* **1** to cease to employ (a worker), usu temporarily **2a** to let alone **b** to avoid ~*vi* to stop or desist, specif from an activity causing annoyance *USE* (*vt 2; vi*) infml

lay on *vt, chiefly Br* **1** to supply (e g water or gas) to a building **2** to supply; organize <*they* laid on *a good meal*>

ˈ**layˌout** /-ˌowt‖-ˌaʊt/ *n* **1** arranging or laying out **2** the plan, design, or arrangement of sthg (e g rooms in a building or matter to be printed) laid out **3** sthg laid out <*a model train* ~>

lay out *vt* **1** to prepare (a corpse) for a funeral **2** to arrange according to a plan <*flower beds and lawns were* laid out *in a formal pattern*> **3** to knock flat or unconscious **4** to spend **5** to exert (oneself) for a purpose *USE* (*except 1 & 2*) infml

lay reader *n* a lay person authorized to conduct parts of church services

lay up *vt* **1** to store up; have or keep for future use **2** to disable or confine with illness or injury **3** to take out of active service

laze /layz‖leɪz/ *vi* to act or rest lazily ~*vt* to pass (time) *away* in idleness or relaxation – **laze** *n*

lazy /ˈlayzi‖ˈleɪzɪ/ *adj* **1a** disinclined or averse to activity; indolent; *also* not energetic or vigorous <*a* ~ *manner*> **b** encouraging inactivity or indolence <*a* ~ *afternoon*> **2** moving slowly <*a* ~ *river*> – **lazily** *adv*, **laziness** *n*

lea /lee‖liː/ *n* (an area of) grassland, pasture – chiefly poetic

leach /leech‖liːtʃ/ *vt* to separate the soluble components from (a mixture) or remove (sthg soluble) by the action of a percolating liquid ~*vi* to pass out or through (as if) by percolation – **leach** *n*, **leacher** *n*

[1]**lead** /leed‖liːd/ *vb* **led** /led‖led/ *vt* **1a(1)** to guide on a way, esp by going in advance **a(2)** to cause to go with one (under duress) <led *the condemned man to the scaffold*> **b** to direct or guide on a course or to a state or condition; influence <*reflection* led *him to a better understanding of the problem*> **c** to serve as a channel or route for <*the road* led *her to a small village*> **2** to go through; live <~ *a quiet life*> **3a(1)** to direct the operations, activity, or performance of; have charge of <led *a safari into little known territory*> **a(2)** to act as or be a leader in or of <~ *an orchestra*> **b** to go or be at the head or ahead of **4** to begin play, esp at a card game, with ~ *vi* **1a(1)** to guide sby or sthg along a way **a(2)** to act as or be a leader **b(1)** to lie or run in a specified place or direction <*the path* ~s *uphill*> **b(2)** to serve as an entrance or passage <*this door* ~s *to the garden*> **2a** to be first or ahead **b(1)** to begin, open – usu + *off* <led *off with a speech by the chairman*> **b(2)** to play the first card of a trick, round, or game **3** to tend or be directed towards a specified result <*study* ~ing *to a degree*> **4** to direct the first of a series of blows at an opponent in boxing (*with* the right or left hand) – **lead up to** to prepare the way for, esp by using a gradual or indirect approach – **lead someone a dance** to cause sby a lot of trouble

[2]**lead** /leed‖liːd/ *n* **1a(1)** position at the front or ahead **a(2)** the act or privilege of leading in cards; *also* the card or suit led **b** guidance, direction; (an) example **c** a margin or position of advantage or superiority **2a** a channel of water **2a(1)** leading to a mill **a(2)** through an ice field **b** an indication, clue **c** (one who plays) a principal role in a dramatic production **d** a line or strap for leading or restraining an animal (e g a dog) **e** a news story of chief importance **3** an insulated electrical conductor

[3]**lead** /led‖led/ *n* **1** a heavy soft malleable bluish-white metallic element used esp in pipes, cable sheaths, batteries, solder, type metal, and shields against radioactivity **2a** the (lead) weight on a sounding line **b** *pl* lead framing for panes in windows **c** a thin strip of metal used to separate lines of type in printing **3a** a thin stick of graphite or crayon in or for a pencil **b** WHITE LEAD **4** bullets, projectiles <*the* ~ *was flying*> **5** *pl, Br* (a usu flat roof covered with) thin lead sheets

[4]**lead** /led‖led/ *vt* **1** to fix (window glass) in position with leads **2** to separate lines of (type) with leads **3** to treat or mix with (a compound of) lead <~ed *petrol*>

leaden /ˈled(ə)n‖ˈled(ə)n/ *adj* **1a** made of lead **b** dull grey **2a** oppressively heavy <~ *limbs*> **b** lacking spirit or animation; sluggish <~ *prose*> – **leadenly** *adv*, **leadenness** *n*

leader /ˈleedə‖ˈliːdə/ *n* **1a** a main or end shoot of a plant **b** *pl* dots or hyphens used to lead the eye horizontally **c** a blank section at the beginning or end of a reel of film or recorded tape **2a** sby or sthg that ranks first, precedes others, or holds a principal position **b** sby who has commanding authority or influence **c(1)** the principal officer of a political party <~ *of the opposition*> **c(2)** either of 2 government ministers in charge of government business in Parliament **c(3)** the principal member of the ruling party in a totalitarian system **3** a horse placed in advance of the other horse or horses of a pair or team **4** *chiefly Br* a newspaper editorial **5a** *Br* the principal first violinist and usu assistant conductor of an orchestra **b** *NAm* CONDUCTOR 2 – **leaderless** *adj*, **leadership** *n*

ˈ**lead-ˌin** /leed‖liːd/ *n* **1** introductory matter **2** the part of the groove on a record before the recording

[1]**leading** /ˈleeding‖ˈliːdɪŋ/ *adj* coming or ranking first; foremost, principal <*the* ~ *role*>

[2]**leading** /ˈleding‖ˈledɪŋ/ *n* [3]LEAD 2c; *also* a space between printed lines made (as if) with a lead

leading article *n, chiefly Br* LEADER 4

ˌ**leading** ˈ**light** *n* a prominent and influential person in a particular sphere

ˌ**leading** ˈ**question** *n* a question so phrased as to suggest the expected answer

[1]**leading ˌreins** *n pl* straps by which children are supported when beginning to walk

ˈ**leading ˌstrings** *n pl* **1** LEADING REINS **2** a state of unnecessary or prolonged dependence – chiefly in *in leading strings*

ˈ**lead-ˌoff** /leed‖liːd/ *n* a beginning or leading action; a start

lead on *vt* **1** to entice or induce to proceed in a (mistaken or unwise) course **2** to cause to believe sthg that is untrue

[1]**leaf** /leef‖liːf/ *n, pl* **leaves** /leevz‖liːvz/ **1a(1)** any of the usu green flat and typically broad-bladed outgrowths from the stem of a plant that function primarily in food manufacture by photosynthesis **a(2)** a modified leaf (e g a petal or sepal) **b(1)** (the state of having) foliage <*in* ~> **b(2)** the leaves of a plant (e g tobacco) as an article of commerce **2a** a part of a book or folded sheet of paper containing a page on each side **b(1)** a part (e g of a window shutter, folding door, or table) that slides or is hinged **b(2)** a section that can be inserted into a tabletop to extend it **c(1)** a thin sheet of metal, marble, etc **c(2)** metal (e g gold or silver) in sheets, usu thinner than foil – **leafless** *adj*, **leaflike** *adj*

[2]**leaf** *vi* to shoot out or produce leaves – **leaf through** to turn over the pages of (e g a book) quickly while only glancing at the contents

leafage /ˈleefij‖ˈliːfɪdʒ/ *n* FOLIAGE 1

-leafed *comb form* (*adj* → *adj*) -leaved

leaflet /ˈleeflit‖ˈliːflɪt/ *n* **1a** any of the divisions of a compound leaf **b** a small or young foliage leaf **2** a single sheet of paper or small loose-leaf pamphlet containing printed matter (e g advertising)

ˈ**leaf ˌmould** *n* a compost or soil layer composed chiefly of decayed vegetable matter

leafy /ˈleefi‖ˈliːfɪ/ *adj* **1** having or thick with leaves <~ *woodlands*> **2** consisting chiefly of leaves <*green* ~ *vegetables*> – **leafiness** *n*

[1]**league** /leeg‖liːg/ *n* any of various units of distance of about 3mi (5km)

[2]**league** *n* **1a** an association of nations, groups, or people for a common purpose or to promote a common interest **b** (a competition for an overall title, in which each person or team plays all the others at least once, held by) an association of people or sports clubs **2** a class, category <*the top* ~> – **leaguer** *n* – **in league** in alliance

[3]**league** *vb* to form into a league

[1]**leak** /leek‖liːk/ *vi* **1** to (let a substance) enter or escape through a crack or hole **2** to become known despite efforts at concealment – often + *out* ~ *vt* **1** to permit to enter or escape (as if) through a leak **2** to give out (information) surreptitiously <~ed *the story to the press*> – **leakage** *n*

[2]**leak** *n* **1a** a crack or hole through which sthg (e g a fluid) is admitted or escapes, usu by mistake **b** a means by which sthg (e g secret information) is admitted or escapes, usu with prejudicial effect **c** a loss of electricity due to faulty insulation **2** a leaking or that which is leaked; *esp* a disclosure **3** an act of urinating – slang

leaky /ˈleeki‖ˈliːkɪ/ *adj* permitting fluid, information, etc to leak in or out; *broadly* not watertight <*a* ~ *argument*> – **leakiness** *n*

[1]**lean** /leen‖liːn/ *vb* **leant** /lent‖lent/, **leaned** /leend, lent‖liːnd, lent/ *vi* **1a** to incline or bend from a vertical position <~t *forward to look*> **b** to rest supported *on/against* sthg **2** to rely for support or inspiration – + *on* or *upon* **3** to incline in opinion, taste, etc **4** to exert pressure; use coercion – + *on*; infml ~ *vt* to place *on/against* for support – **lean** *n*

[2]**lean** *adj* **1a** lacking or deficient in flesh or bulk **b** *of meat* containing little or no fat **2** lacking richness, sufficiency, or value **3a** deficient in an essential or important quality or ingredient **b** *esp of a fuel mixture* low in the combustible component – **leanly** *adv*, **leanness** *n*

[3]**lean** *n* the part of meat that consists principally of fat-free muscular tissue

leaning /ˈleening‖ˈliːnɪŋ/ *n* a definite but weak attraction, tendency, or partiality

ˈ**lean-ˌto** *n, pl* **lean-tos** a small building having a roof that rests on the side of a larger building or wall

[1]**leap** /leep‖liːp/ *vb* **leapt** /lept‖lept/, **leaped** /leept, lept‖liːpt, lept/ *vi* **1** to jump in or through the air **2a** to pass abruptly from one state or topic to another; *esp* to rise quickly <*the idea* ~t *into his mind*> **b** to seize eagerly *at* an opportunity, offer, etc ~ *vt* to pass over by leaping – **leaper** *n*

[2]**leap** *n* **1a** (the distance covered by) a jump **b** a place leapt over or from **2** a sudden transition, esp a rise or increase

[1]ˈ**leapˌfrog** /-ˌfrog‖-ˌfrɒg/ *n* a game in which one player bends down and another leaps over him/her

[2]**leapfrog** *vb* **-gg- 1** to leap (over) (as if) in leapfrog **2** to go ahead of (each other) in turn

ˈ**leap ˌyear** *n* a year with an extra day added to make it coincide with the solar year; *esp* a year in the Gregorian calendar with February 29 as the 366th day [prob fr the 'leap' made by any date after February in a leap year over the weekday on which it would normally fall]

learn /luhn‖lɜːn/ *vb* **learnt** /luhnt‖lɜːnt/, **learned** /luhnd, luhnt‖lɜːnd, lɜːnt/ *vt* **1a(1)** to gain knowledge of or skill in <~ *a trade*> **a(2)** to memorize <~ *the lines of a play*> **b** to come to be able – + infinitive <~ *to dance*> **c** to come to realize or know <*we* ~ed *that he was ill*> **2** to teach – substandard ~ *vi* to acquire knowledge or skill – **learnable** *adj*, **learner** *n*

learned /ˈluhnid‖ˈlɜːnɪd; *sense 2* luhnd‖lɜːnd/ *adj* **1** characterized by or associated with learning; erudite **2** acquired by learning – **learnedly** *adv*, **learnedness** *n*

learning /ˈluhning‖ˈlɜːnɪŋ/ *n* **1** acquired knowledge or skill **2** modification of a behavioural tendency by experience (e g exposure to conditioning)

[1]**lease** /lees‖liːs/ *n* **1** a contract putting the land or property of one party at the disposal of another, usu for a stated period and rent **2** a (prospect of) continuance – chiefly in *lease of life*

[2]**lease** *vt* to grant by or hold under lease

ˈ**leaseˌhold** /-ˌhohld‖-ˌhəʊld/ *n* tenure by or property held by lease – **leaseholder** *n*

leash /leesh‖liːʃ/ *n* **1a** [2]LEAD 2d **b** a restraint, check **2** a set of 3 animals (e g greyhounds, foxes, or hares) – **leash** *vt*

[1]**least** /leest||li:st/ *adj* **1** lowest in rank, degree, or importance **2a** smallest in quantity or extent **b** being (of) a kind distinguished by small size <~ *bittern*> **c** smallest possible; slightest <*haven't the ~ idea*> – **at least 1** as a minimum; if not more <*costs* at least *£5*> **2** if nothing else; IN ANY CASE <at least *it is legal*>

[2]**least** *n* the smallest quantity, number, or amount <*it's the ~ I can do*> <*to say the ~*> – **least of all** especially not <*no one,* least of all *the children paid attention*>

[3]**least** *adv* to the smallest degree or extent <least-*known*> <*when we ~ expected it*>

'**least,ways** /-,wayz||-,weɪz/, **leastwise** /-wiez||-waɪz/ *adv, chiefly dial* AT LEAST 2

[1]**leather** /'ledhə||'leðə/ *n* **1** animal skin dressed for use **2** sthg wholly or partly made of leather; *esp* a piece of chamois, used esp for polishing metal or glass

[2]**leather** *vt* to beat with a strap; thrash

Leatherette /,ledhə'ret||,leðə'ret/ *trademark* – used for an imitation leather

leathery /'ledhəri||'leðərɪ/ *adj* resembling leather in appearance or consistency; *esp* tough

[1]**leave** /leev||li:v/ *vb* **left** /left||left/ *vt* **1a(1)** to bequeath **a(2)** to have (esp members of one's family) remaining after one's death **b** to cause to remain as an aftereffect **2a** to cause or allow to be or remain in a specified or unaltered condition <*his manner* left *me cold*> <~ *the washing-up for tomorrow*> **b** to fail to include, use, or take along <left *his notes at home*> – sometimes + *off* or *out* <left *his name off the list*> **c** to have remaining or as a remainder <*10 from 12* ~s *2*> **d** to permit to be or remain subject to the action or control of a specified person or thing <*just ~ everything to me*> <*nothing* left *to chance*> **e** to allow to do or continue sthg without interference <~ *you to take care of things*> **3a** to go away from <*told him to ~ the room*> **b** to desert, abandon <left *his wife*> **c** to withdraw from <left *school at 15*> **4** to put, station, deposit, or deliver, esp before departing <*the postman* left *a package for you*> <~ *your name with the receptionist*> ~*vi* to depart; SET OUT – **leaver** *n* – **leave alone/be** LET ALONE/BE – **leave go** LET GO – **leave well alone** to avoid meddling

[2]**leave** *n* **1** permission to do sthg **2** authorized (extended) absence (e g from employment)

-leaved /-leevd||-li:vd/ *comb form* (*adj* → *adj*) having (such or so many) leaves <*palmate*-leaved>

[1]**leaven** /'lev(ə)n||'lev(ə)n/ *n* **1** a substance (e g yeast) used to produce fermentation or a gas in dough, batter, etc to lighten it; *esp* a mass of fermenting dough reserved for this purpose **2** sthg that modifies or lightens

[2]**leaven** *vt* to raise or make lighter (as if) with a leaven

leave off *vb* to stop, cease

leaves /leevs||li:vs/ *pl of* leaf

'**leave-,taking** *n* a departure, farewell

leavings /'leevingz||'li:vɪŋz/ *n pl* remains, residue

lecher /'lechə||'letʃə/ *n* a man who engages in lechery [Old French *lecheor*, fr *lechier* to lick, live in debauchery, of Germanic origin]

lechery /'lechəri||'letʃərɪ/ *n* inordinate indulgence in sexual activity; debauchery, lasciviousness – **lecherous** *adj*, **lecherously** *adv*

lecithin /'lesəthin||'lesəθɪn/ *n* any of several waxy compounds that are widely distributed in animals and plants and have emulsifying, wetting, and antioxidant properties

lectern /'lek,tuhn||'lek,tɜ:n/ *n* a reading desk; *esp* one from which the Bible is read in church

[1]**lecture** /'lekchə||'lektʃə/ *n* **1** a discourse given to an audience, esp for instruction **2** a reproof delivered at length; a reprimand

[2]**lecture** *vi* to deliver a lecture or series of lectures ~ *vt* **1** to deliver a lecture to **2** to reprove at length or severely – **lecturer** *n*

'**lectureship** /-ship||-ʃɪp/ *n* the office of an academic lecturer

led /led||led/ *past of* LEAD

LED /,el ,ee 'dee||,el ,i: 'di:; *also* led||led/ *n* a diode that emits light when an electric current is passed through it and that is used esp to display numbers, symbols, etc on a screen (e g in a pocket calculator) [*l*ight-*e*mitting *d*iode]

ledge /lej||ledʒ/ *n* **1** a (narrow) horizontal surface that projects from a vertical or steep surface (e g a wall or rock face) **2** an underwater ridge or reef **3** a mineral-bearing lode or vein – **ledgy** *adj*

ledger /'lejə||'ledʒə/ *n* **1** a book containing (the complete record of all) accounts **2** a horizontal piece of timber secured to the uprights of scaffolding

lee /lee||li:/ *n* **1** protecting shelter **2 lee, lee side** the side (e g of a ship) sheltered from the wind

[1]**leech** /leech||li:tʃ/ *n* **1** any of numerous flesh-eating or bloodsucking usu freshwater worms **2** one who gains or seeks to gain profit or advantage from another, esp by clinging persistently **3** *archaic* a physician, surgeon

[2]**leech** *vt* to bleed by the use of leeches

[3]**leech** *n* **1** either vertical edge of a square sail **2** the rear edge of a fore-and-aft sail

leek /leek||li:k/ *n* a biennial plant of the lily family grown for its mildly pungent leaves and esp for its thick edible stalk

leer /liə||lɪə/ *vi or n* (to give) a lascivious, knowing, or sly look

lees /leez||li:z/ *n pl* the sediment of a liquor (e g wine) during fermentation and aging

lee shore *n* a shore lying off a ship's lee side

[1]**leeward** /'leewood||'li:wʊd; *naut* 'looh·əd||'lu:əd/ *adj or adv* in or facing the direction towards which the wind is blowing

[2]**leeward** *n* LEE 2

'**lee,way** /-,way||-,weɪ/ *n* **1** off-course sideways movement of a ship in the direction of the wind **2a** an allowable margin of freedom or variation; tolerance **b** a margin of shortcoming in performance <*she has a lot of ~ to make up after her absence*>

[1]**left** /left||left/ *adj* **1a** of, situated on, or being the side of the body in which most of the heart is located **b(1)** located nearer to the left hand than to the right; *esp* located on the left hand when facing in the same direction as an observer <*the ~ wing of an army*> **b(2)** located on the left when facing downstream <*the ~ bank of a river*> **2** *often cap* of the Left

in politics – **left** *adv*

[2]left *n* **1a** (a blow struck with) the left hand **b** the location or direction of the left side **c** the part on the left side **2** *sing or pl in constr, often cap* the members of a European legislative body occupying the left of a legislative chamber as a result of holding more radical political views than other members **3** *sing or pl in constr* **3a** *cap* those professing socialist or radical political views **b** *often cap* LEFT WING 1

[3]left *past of* LEAVE

ˌleft-ˈhand *adj* **1** situated on the left **2** left-handed

ˌleft-ˈhanded *adj* **1** using the left hand habitually or more easily than the right; *also* swinging from left to right <*a ~ batsman*> **2** of, designed for, or done with the left hand **3** morganatic **4** clumsy, awkward **5** ambiguous, double-edged <*a ~ compliment*> **6** anticlockwise – used of a twist, rotary motion, or spiral curve as viewed from a given direction with respect to the axis of rotation – **left-handed, left-handedly** *adv*, **left-handedness** *n*

ˌleft-ˈhander *n* **1** a left-handed person **2** a blow struck with the left hand

leftism /ˈlefˌtiz(ə)m‖ˈlefˌtɪz(ə)m/ *n, often cap* (advocacy of) the principles and policy of the Left – **leftist** *n or adj*

ˌleft-ˈluggage *adj, Br* of or for the storing of luggage for safekeeping

ˈleftˌover /-ˌohvə‖-ˌəʊvə/ *n* an unused or unconsumed residue; *esp* leftover food – often pl – **leftover** *adj*

leftward /ˈleftwood‖ˈleftwʊd/ *adj* towards or on the left

ˈleftwards, *chiefly NAm* **leftward** *adv* towards the left

ˌleft ˈwing *n sing or pl in constr* **1** *often cap L&W* the more socialist division of a group or party **2** *cap L&W* LEFT 3a – **left-wing** *adj*, **left-winger** *n*

[1]leg /leg‖leg/ *n* **1** a limb of an animal used esp for supporting the body and for walking: e g **1a** (an artificial replacement for) either of the lower limbs of a human **b** a (hind) leg of a meat animal, esp above the hock **c** any of the appendages on each segment of an arthropod (e g an insect or spider) used in walking and crawling **2a** a pole or bar serving as a support or prop <*the ~s of a tripod*> <*a table ~*> **b** a branch of a forked or jointed object <*the ~s of a compass*> **3** the part of a garment that covers (part of) the leg **4** either side of a triangle as distinguished from the base or hypotenuse **5a** LEG SIDE **b** a fielding position in cricket on the leg side of the pitch – usu in combination <*fine ~*> <*short ~*> **6a** the course and distance sailed on a single tack **b** a portion of a trip; a stage **c** the part of a relay race run by 1 competitor **d** any of a set of events or games that must all be won to decide a competition – **a leg to stand on** the least support or basis for one's position, esp in a controversy – **on one's last legs** at or near the end of one's resources; on the verge of failure, exhaustion, or ruin

[2]leg *vi* **-gg-** – **leg it** to walk or run fast; *esp* to hurry

[3]leg *adj* **1** *esp of a ball bowled in cricket* moving or tending to move in the direction of the off side <*a ~ break*> **2** in, on, through, or towards the leg side of a cricket field <*the ~ stump*>

legacy /ˈlegəsi‖ˈlegəsɪ/ *n* **1** a gift by will; a bequest **2** sthg passed on or remaining from an ancestor or predecessor or from the past <*the bitter ~ of 2 world wars*>

legal /ˈleegl‖ˈliːgl/ *adj* **1** of law **2a** deriving authority from law **b** established by or having a formal status derived from law **3** permitted by law **4** recognized in common law as distinguished from equity – **legalize** *vt*, **legally** *adv*, **legalization** *n*

ˌlegal ˈaid *n* payments from public funds to those who cannot afford legal advice or representation

ˌlegal ˈfiction *n* an assertion recognized by the law as fictitious but accepted for convenience as true

legality /liˈgaləti‖lɪˈgæləti/ *n* **1** lawfulness **2** *pl* the requirements and procedures of the law

ˌlegal ˈtender *n* currency which a creditor is bound by law to accept as payment of a money debt

legate /ˈlegət‖ˈlegət/ *n* an official delegate or representative – **legateship** *n*, **legatine** *adj*

legatee /ˌlegəˈtee‖ˌlegəˈtiː/ *n* one to whom a legacy is bequeathed

legation /liˈgaysh(ə)n‖lɪˈgeɪʃ(ə)n/ *n* (the official residence of) a diplomatic mission in a foreign country headed by a minister

legato /liˈgahtoh‖lɪˈgɑːtəʊ/ *n, adv, or adj, pl* **legatos** (a manner of performing or passage of music performed) in a smooth and connected manner

ˈleg ˌbye *n* a run scored in cricket after the ball has touched a part of the batsman's body but not his bat or hands

legend /ˈlej(ə)nd‖ˈledʒ(ə)nd/ *n* **1a(1)** a story coming down from the past; *esp* one popularly regarded as historical **a(2)** a body of such stories <*a character in Celtic ~*> **b** a person, act, or thing that inspires legends <*a ~ in her own lifetime*> **2a** an inscription or title on an object (e g a coin) **b** CAPTION 2 **c** the key to a map, chart, etc – **legendry** *n*

legendary /ˈlejənd(ə)ri‖ˈledʒənd(ə)rɪ/ *adj* (characteristic) of (a) legend; *esp* told of in legend

legerdemain /ˌlejədəˈman, -ˈmayn‖ˌledʒədəˈmæn, -ˈmeɪn/ *n* **1** SLEIGHT OF HAND **2** a display of artful skill, trickery, or adroitness [Middle French *leger de main* light of hand]

-legged /-ˈlegid‖-ˈlegɪd; *also* -ˈlegd‖-ˈlegd/ *comb form* (*adj* → *adj*) having (such or so many) legs <*a 4-legged animal*>

legging /ˈleging‖ˈlegɪŋ/ *n* a closely fitting covering (e g of leather) that reaches from the ankle to the knee or thigh

leggy /ˈlegi‖ˈlegɪ/ *adj* **1** having disproportionately long legs <*a ~ colt*> **2** *esp of a woman* having attractively long legs **3** *of a plant* spindly

legible /ˈlejəbl‖ˈledʒəbl/ *adj* capable of being read or deciphered – **legibly** *adv*, **legibility** *n*

[1]legion /ˈleej(ə)n‖ˈliːdʒ(ə)n/ *n sing or pl in constr* **1** the principal unit of the ancient Roman army comprising 3000 to 6000 foot soldiers with cavalry **2** a very large number; a multitude **3** a national association of ex-servicemen

²legion *adj* many, numerous <*the problems are* ~>

¹legionary /'leejən(ə)ri‖'li:dʒən(ə)rɪ/ *adj* of or being a legion

²legionary *n* a legionnaire

legionnaire /ˌleejə'neə‖ˌli:dʒə'neə/ *n* a member of a (foreign) legion

legionnaire's disease *n* a serious infectious disease, with symptoms like those of pneumonia, caused by a bacterium

legislate /'lejiˌslayt‖'ledʒɪˌsleɪt/ *vi* to make or enact laws

legislation /ˌleji'slaysh(ə)n‖ˌledʒɪ'sleɪʃ(ə)n/ *n* **1** (the making of) laws **2** a prospective law – **legislative** *adj*, **legislatively** *adv*

legislator /'lejiˌslaytə‖'ledʒɪˌsleɪtə/ *n* a maker of laws – **legislatress, legislatrix** *n*, **legislatorial** *adj*

legislature /'lejislәchə‖'ledʒɪslәtʃə/ *n* a body of people having the power to legislate

legit /lə'jit‖lə'dʒɪt/ *adj* LEGITIMATE 2, 3a, 4, 5 – infml

¹legitimate /lə'jitimət‖lə'dʒɪtɪmət/ *adj* **1** lawfully begotten; *specif* born in wedlock **2** neither spurious nor false; genuine <~ *grievance*> **3a** in accordance with law <*a* ~ *government*> **b** ruling by or based on the strict principle of hereditary right <*a* ~ *king*> **4** conforming to recognized principles or accepted rules and standards **5** relating to plays acted by professional actors but not including revues, music hall, or some forms of musical comedy **6** in accord with reason or logic; following logically <*a* ~ *deduction*> – **legitimately** *adv*, **legitimacy** *n*

²legitimate /-ˌmayt‖-ˌmeɪt/, **legitimat·ize, -ise** /lə'jitiməˌteiz‖lə'dʒɪtɪməˌteɪz/ **legitim·ize, -ise** |/-ˌmeiz‖-ˌmeɪz/ *vt* **1a** to give legal status to **b** JUSTIFY 1 **2** to give (an illegitimate child) the legal status of one legitimately born – **legitimation, legitimatization, legitimization** *n*

legless /'leglis‖'leglɪs/ *adj* **1** without legs **2** *chiefly Br* drunk – infml

'leg-ˌpull *n* a playful trick or hoax intended to deceive sby

legroom /'legroohm, -ˌroom‖'legru:m, -ˌrʊm/ *n* space in which to extend the legs while seated

'leg ˌside, leg *n* the part of a cricket field on the side of a line joining the middle stumps in which the batsman stands when playing a ball

legume /'legyoohm‖'legju:m/ *n* **1** the (edible) pod or seed of a leguminous plant **2** any of a large family of plants, shrubs, and trees having pods containing 1 or many seeds and including important food and forage plants (e g peas, beans, or clovers) – **leguminous** *adj*

lei /lay‖leɪ/ *n* a wreath or necklace usu of flowers or leaves that is a symbol of affection in Polynesia

leisure /'lezhə‖'leʒə/ *n* **1** freedom provided by the cessation of activities; *esp* time free from work or duties **2** unhurried ease – **leisureless** *adj* – **at leisure, at one's leisure 1** at an unhurried pace **2** at one's convenience

'leisured *adj* **1** having plenty of free time, esp because of not needing to work **2** leisurely

¹'leisurely /-li‖-lɪ/ *adv* without haste; deliberately

²leisurely *adj* characterized by leisure; unhurried – **leisureliness** *n*

leitmotiv, leitmotif /'lietmohˌteef‖'laɪtməʊ-ˌti:f/ *n* **1** a musical phrase that accompanies the reappearance of an idea, person, or situation **2** a (dominant) recurring theme, esp in a literary work [German *leitmotiv*, fr *leiten* to lead + *motiv* motive]

lekker /'lekə‖'lekə/ *adj, SAfr* pleasant, nice – infml

lemming /'leming‖'lemɪŋ/ *n* any of several small short-tailed furry-footed northern voles; *esp* one of northern mountains that undergoes recurrent mass migrations

lemon /'lemən‖'lemən/ *n* **1** (a stout thorny tree that bears) an oval yellow acid citrus fruit **2** a pale yellow colour **3** one who or that which is unsatisfactory or worthless; a dud – infml [Middle French *limon*, fr Medieval Latin *limon-, limo*, fr Arabic *laymūn*] – **lemony** *adj*

lemonade /ˌlemə'nayd‖ˌlemə'neɪd/ *n* a (carbonated) soft drink made or flavoured with lemon

ˌlemon 'sole *n* a flatfish that is found in N Atlantic and European waters and is highly valued for food

lemur /'leemə‖'li:mə/ *n* any of numerous tree-dwelling chiefly nocturnal mammals, esp of Madagascar, typically having a muzzle like a fox, large eyes, very soft woolly fur, and a long furry tail

lend /lend‖lend/ *vb* **lent** /lent‖lent/ *vt* **1a** to give for temporary use on condition that the same or its equivalent be returned **b** to let out (money) for temporary use on condition of repayment with interest **2a** to give the assistance or support of; afford, contribute <~s *great force to his argument*> **b** to adapt or apply (oneself); accommodate <*a topic that* ~s *itself admirably to class discussion*> ~*vi* to make a loan – **lender** *n*

length /leng(k)th‖leŋ(k)θ/ *n* **1a(1)** the longer or longest dimension of an object **a(2)** the extent from end to end <*walked the* ~ *of the street*> **b** a measured distance or dimension <*a 2m* ~ *of tube*> **c** the quality or state of being long **2a** duration or extent in or with regard to time <*the* ~ *of a broadcast*> **b** relative duration or stress of a sound **3a** distance or extent in space <*an arm's* ~ *apart*> **b** the length of sthg taken as a unit of measure <*his horse led by a* ~> **4** the degree to which sthg (e g a course of action or a line of thought) is carried; a limit, extreme – often pl with sing. meaning <*went to great* ~s *to learn the truth*> **5a** a long expanse or stretch <~s *of hair*> **b** a piece, esp of a certain length (being or usable as part of a whole or of a connected series) <*a* ~ *of pipe*> **6** the (ideal) distance down a cricket pitch which the bowled ball travels before pitching **7** the vertical extent of sthg (e g an article of clothing), esp with reference to the position it reaches on the body – usu in combination <*shoulder*-length *hair*> – **at length 1** fully, comprehensively **2** for a long time **3** finally; AT LAST

lengthen /'length(ə)n, 'lengkth(ə)n‖'leŋθ(ə)n, 'leŋkθ(ə)n/ *vb* to make or become longer

'length,ways /-,wayz‖-,weɪz/, **lengthwise** /-,wiez‖-,waɪz/ *adv or adj* in the direction of the length <*bricks are generally laid* ~ >

lengthy /'leng(k)thi‖'leŋ(k)θɪ/ *adj* of great or unusual length; long; *also* excessively or tediously protracted – **lengthily** *adv*, **lengthiness** *n*

lenient /'leenyənt, 'leeni·ənt‖'liːnjənt, 'liːnɪənt/ *adj* **1** of a mild or merciful nature; not severe < ~ *laws*> **2** *archaic* exerting a soothing or easing influence – **lenience, leniency** *n*, **leniently** *adv*

lenity /'lenəti‖'lenətɪ/ *n* gentleness, mercy – fml

lens /lenz‖lenz/ *n* **1a** a piece of glass or other transparent material with 2 opposite regular surfaces, at least 1 of which is curved, that is used either singly or combined in an optical instrument to form an image by focussing rays of light **b** a combination of 2 or more simple lenses **2** a device for directing or focussing radiation other than light (e g sound waves or electrons) **3** sthg shaped like an optical lens with both sides convex **4** a transparent lens-shaped or nearly spherical body in the eye that focuses light rays (e g on the retina) – **lensed** *adj*, **lensless** *adj*

Lent /lent‖lent/ *n* the 40 weekdays from Ash Wednesday to Easter observed by Christians as a period of penitence and fasting – **Lenten** *adj*

lentil /'lentl‖'lentl/ *n* (the small round edible seed of) a widely cultivated Eurasian leguminous plant

lento /'lentoh‖'lentəʊ/ *adv or adj* in a slow manner – used in music [Italian, fr *lento* slow, fr Latin *lentus* pliant, sluggish, slow]

Leo /'lee·oh‖'liːəʊ/ *n* (sby born under) the 5th sign of the zodiac in astrology, pictured as a lion

leonine /'lee·ənien‖'liːənaɪn/ *adj* resembling a lion; having the characteristics (e g courage) popularly ascribed to a lion

leopard /'lepəd‖'lepəd/, *fem* **leopardess** /-'des‖-'des/ *n* **1** a big cat of southern Asia and Africa that is usu tawny or buff with black spots arranged in broken rings or rosettes **2** a heraldic charge that is a lion with the farther forepaw raised and its head turned towards the observer

leotard /'lee·ə,tahd‖'liːə,tɑːd/ *n* a close-fitting one-piece garment worn by dancers or others performing physical exercises [Jules *Léotard* (died 1870), French trapeze performer]

leper /'lepə‖'lepə/ *n* **1** sby suffering from leprosy **2** a person shunned for moral or social reasons; an outcast

leprechaun /'leprik(h)awn‖'leprɪk(h)ɔːn/ *n* a mischievous elf of Irish folklore [Irish Gaelic *leipreachān*, fr Middle Irish *lūchorpān*, fr *lū* small + *corpān* body]

leprosy /'leprəsi‖'leprəsɪ/ *n* a long-lasting bacterial disease characterized by loss of sensation with eventual paralysis, wasting of muscle, and production of deformities and mutilations – **leprotic** *adj*

lesbian /'lezbi·ən‖'lezbɪən/ *n, often cap* a female homosexual [*Lesbos*, island in the Aegean Sea, home of Sappho (*fl* about 600 BC), Greek poetess & reputed homosexual] – **lesbian** *adj*, **lesbianism** *n*

,lese 'majesty /leez, lez‖liːz, lez/, **lèse majesté** /(*Fr* lɛz maʒɛste)/ *n* **1a** a crime (e g treason) committed against a sovereign power **b** an offence violating the dignity of a ruler **2** an affront to dignity or importance [Middle French *lese majesté*, fr Latin *laesa majestas*, lit., injured majesty]

lesion /'leezh(ə)n‖'liːʒ(ə)n/ *n* **1** injury, harm **2** abnormal change in the structure of an organ or part due to injury or disease

1less /les‖les/ *adj* **1** fewer < ~ *than 3*> <*a call for* ~ *government controls*> – disapproved of by some speakers **2** lower in rank, degree, or importance <*no* ~ *a person than the president himself*> **3** smaller in quantity or extent <*of* ~ *importance*> <*in* ~ *time*>

2less *adv* to a lesser degree or extent <*sleeps* ~ *in summer*> <*much* ~ *angrily*> – **less and less** to a progressively smaller size or extent

3less *prep* diminished by; minus <*£100* ~ *tax*>

4less *n, pl* **less** a smaller portion or quantity – **less of 1** not so truly <*he's* less of *a fool than I thought*> **2** enough of <less of *your cheek!*> – infml

-less /-lis‖-lɪs/ *suffix* (→ *adj*) **1a** destitute of; not having <*brain*less> **b** free from <*pain*less> **2** unable to (so act or be acted on) <*tire*less>

lessee /le'see‖le'siː/ *n* sby who holds property under a lease

lessen /'les(ə)n‖'les(ə)n/ *vb* to reduce in size, extent, etc; diminish, decrease

lesser /'lesə‖'lesə/ *adj or adv* less in size, quality, or significance <lesser-*known*> <*the* ~ *of 2 evils*> – not used in comparatives

lesson /'les(ə)n‖'les(ə)n/ *n* **1** a passage from sacred writings read in a service of worship **2a** a reading or exercise to be studied **b** a period of instruction **3a** sthg, esp a piece of wisdom, learned by study or experience <*her years of travel had taught her valuable* ~s> **b** an instructive or warning example <*the* ~s *history holds for us*>

lessor /'lesaw, -'-‖'lesɔː, -'-/ *n* sby who conveys property by lease

lest /lest‖lest/ *conj* **1** so that not; IN CASE <*obeyed her* ~ *she should be angry*> **2** that – used after an expression of fear <*afraid* ~ *she be angry*>

1let /let‖let/ *n* **1** a serve or rally in tennis, squash, etc that does not count and must be replayed **2** sthg that impedes; an obstruction – fml <*without* ~ *or hindrance*>

2let *vt* **let; -tt- 1** to cause to; make < ~ *it be known*> **2a** to offer or grant for rent or lease < ~ *rooms*> **b** to assign, esp after bids < ~ *a contract*> **3a** to give opportunity to, whether by positive action or by failure to prevent; allow to <*please* ~ *me know*> < ~ *the prisoner go*> **b** to allow to escape, enter, or pass < ~ *the dogs loose*> <*she* ~ *out a scream*> **4** – used in the imperative to introduce a request or proposal < ~ *us pray*> < ~ *me see*>, a challenge <*just* ~ *him try*>, a command < ~ *it be known*>, or sthg to be supposed for the sake of argument < ~ *AB be equal to BC*> – **let alone/be** to stop or refrain from molesting, disturbing, or interrupting <*please* let *the cat* alone> – **let fall/drop** to mention casually as if by accident – **let fly** to aim a blow – **let go** to stop holding <let go *of the handle*> – **let in for** to involve (sby, esp oneself) in sthg undesirable <let *myself* in for *a lot of work*> – **let into** to insert into (a surface) <*a tablet* let into *the wall*> – **let loose on** to give freedom of access to or of action with respect to <*can't* let *him* loose on *the files just yet*> – **let oneself go 1** to behave with relaxed ease or abandonment **2** to allow one's appearance to deteriorate – **let rip** to proceed with abandon <*lost his temper and really* let rip> – infml – **let slip 1** LET FALL **2** to fail to take <let slip *a chance*> – **let up on** to become less severe towards

[3]**let** *n, Br* **1** an act or period of letting premises (e g a flat or bed-sitter) **2** premises rented or for rent

-let /-lit‖-lɪt/ *suffix* (→ *n*) **1** -ETTE 1 <*book*let> **2** article worn on (a specified part of the body) <*ank*let>

'let,down /-,down‖-,daʊn/ *n* a disappointment, disillusionment – infml

let down *vt* **1** to make (a garment) longer **2** to fail in loyalty or support; disappoint <let *her friend* down *badly*>

lethal /'leeth(ə)l‖'li:θ(ə)l/ *adj* relating to or (capable of) causing death – **lethally** *adv*, **lethality** *n*

lethargic /lə'thahjik‖lə'θɑ:dʒɪk/ *adj* **1** sluggish **2** indifferent, apathetic – **lethargically** *adv*

lethargy /'lethəji‖'leθədʒɪ/ *n* **1** abnormal drowsiness **2** lack of energy or interest [Late Latin *lethargia*, fr Greek *lēthargia*, fr *lēthargos* forgetful, lethargic, fr *lēthē* forgetfulness + *argos* lazy]

let off *vt* **1** to cause to explode <let *the fireworks* off> **2** to excuse from punishment **3** *chiefly Br* to offer (part of a building) for rent

let on *vi* **1** to reveal or admit sthg; *esp* to divulge secret information <*nobody* let on *about the surprise party*> **2** to pretend <*she* let on *that she was a stranger*> – infml

'let-,out *n* sthg (e g an exclusion clause in a contract) that provides an opportunity to escape or be released from an obligation – infml

let out *vt* **1** to make (a garment) wider (e g by inserting an inset) **2** to excuse from an obligation or responsibility **3** *chiefly Br* to express publicly; *esp* to blab **4** *chiefly Br* to rent out (e g property)

[1]**letter** /'letə‖'letə/ *n* **1** a symbol, usu written or printed, representing a speech sound and constituting a unit of an alphabet **2a** a written or printed message addressed to a person or organization and usu sent through the post **b** a formal written communication containing a grant or authorization – usu pl with sing. meaning **3** *pl but sing or pl in constr* **3a** literature; BELLES LETTRES **b** learning; *esp* scholarly knowledge of or achievement in literature <*a man of* ~s> **4** the precise wording; the strict or literal meaning <*obeyed the instructions to the* ~> **5a** a single piece of type **b** a style of type

[2]**letter** *vt* to set down in or mark with letters

'letter ,box *n, Br* a hole or box (e g in a door) to receive material delivered by post

'lettered *adj* learned, educated

'letter,head /-,hed‖-,hed/ *n* stationery printed with a heading; *also* the heading itself

lettering /'letəring‖'letərɪŋ/ *n* the letters used in an inscription, esp as regards their style or quality

'letter,press /-,pres‖-,pres/ *n* **1** (work produced by) printing from an inked raised surface **2** *chiefly Br* text (e g of a book) as distinct from pictorial illustrations

letters patent *n pl* a formal document (e g from a sovereign) conferring on sby the sole right to exploit his/her invention

letting /'leting‖'letɪŋ/ *n, chiefly Br* [3]LET

lettuce /'letis‖'letɪs/ *n* a common garden vegetable whose succulent edible leaves are used esp in salads

letup /'letup‖'letʌp/ *n* a cessation or lessening of effort, activity, or intensity

let up *vi* **1a** to diminish, slow down, or cease **b** to relax or cease one's efforts or activities **2** to become less severe – usu + *on*; infml

leucocyte /'l(y)oohkə,siet‖'l(j)u:kə,saɪt/ *n* WHITE BLOOD CELL

leucorrhoea /,l(y)oohkə'riə‖,l(j)u:kə'rɪə/ *n* a thick whitish discharge from the vagina resulting from inflammation or congestion of the mucous membrane

leucotomy /l(y)ooh'kotəmi‖l(j)u:'kɒtəmɪ/ *n* a lobotomy

leukaemia /l(y)ooh'keemyə, -mi·ə‖l(j)u:'ki:mjə, -mɪə/ *n* any of several usu fatal types of cancer that are characterized by an abnormal increase in the number of white blood cells in the body tissue, esp the blood, and occur in acute or chronic form [deriv of Greek *leukos* white + *haima* blood]

[1]**levee** /'levi‖'levɪ/ *n* **1** a reception of visitors formerly held by a person of rank on rising from bed **2** a reception, usu in honour of a particular person

[2]**levee** *n, NAm* **1** an embankment for preventing or confining flooding **2** a river landing place

[1]**level** /'levəl‖'levəl/ *n* **1** a device (e g a spirit level) for establishing a horizontal line or plane **2a** a horizontal state or condition **b** the equilibrium of a fluid marked by a horizontal surface of even altitude <*water seeks its own* ~> **c** an (approximately) horizontal line, plane, or surface **3a** a position of height in relation to the ground; height <*eye* ~> **b** a practically horizontal or flat area, esp of land **4** a position or place in a scale or rank (e g of value or importance) <*a high* ~ *of academic excellence*> **5** (a passage in) an interconnecting series of regularly worked horizontal mine passages **6** the (often measurable) size or amount of sthg specified <*noise* ~> – **on the level** honest; BONA FIDE

[2]**level** *vb* **-ll-** (*NAm* **-l-**, **-ll-**) *vt* **1a** to make (a line or surface) horizontal; make level, even, or uniform **b** to raise or lower to the same height – often + *up* <~ up *the picture with the one next to it*> **2a** to bring to a horizontal aiming position **b** to aim, direct – + *at* or *against* <~led *a charge of fraud at her*> **3** to bring to a common level, plane, or standard; equalize <*love* ~s *all ranks* – W S Gilbert> **4** to lay level with the ground; raze **5** to find the heights of different points in (a land area) ~ *vi* **1** to attain or come to a level – usu + *out* or *off* <*the plane* ~led *off at 10,000ft*> **2** to aim a gun or other weapon horizontally **3** to deal frankly and openly – infml

³**level** *adj* **1a** having no part higher than another **b** parallel with the plane of the horizon; conforming to the curvature of the liquid parts of the earth's surface **2a** even, unvarying <*a ~ temperature*> **b** equal in advantage, progression, or standing <*drew ~ with the leaders*> **c** steady, unwavering <*spoke in ~ tones*> **3** distributed evenly; uniform <*~ stress*> – **levelly** *adv*, **levelness** *n* – **level best** very best <*she did her* level best>

ˌ**level 'crossing** *n, Br* the crossing of railway and road or 2 railways on the same level

leveller, *NAm chiefly* **leveler** /ˈlevələ‖ˈlevələ/ *n* **1** *cap* a member of a radical group during the English Civil War who advocated legal equality and religious tolerance **2** an advocate of equality **3** sthg that tends to reduce human differences

¹**lever** /ˈleevə‖ˈliːvə/ *n* **1a** a bar used for prizing up or dislodging sthg **b** an inducing or compelling force; a tool **2a** a rigid bar used to exert a pressure or sustain a weight at one end by applying force at the other and turning it on a fulcrum **b** a projecting part by which a mechanism is operated or adjusted

²**lever** *vt* to prize, raise, or move (as if) with a lever

leverage /ˈleevərij‖ˈliːvərɪdʒ/ *n* **1** the action of a lever or the mechanical advantage gained by it **2** power, influence

leveret /ˈlev(ə)rit‖ˈlev(ə)rɪt/ *n* a hare in its first year

leviathan /ləˈvie·əthən‖ləˈvaɪəθən/ *n* **1** *often cap* a biblical sea monster **2** sthg large or formidable – **leviathan** *adj*

levitate /ˈleviˌtayt‖ˈlevɪˌteɪt/ *vb* to (cause to) rise or float in the air, esp in apparent defiance of gravity – **levitation** *n*, **levitational** *adj*

levity /ˈlevəti‖ˈlevətɪ/ *n* lack of seriousness; *esp* excessive or unseemly frivolity

¹**levy** /ˈlevi‖ˈlevɪ/ *n* **1a** the imposing or collection of a tax, fine, etc **b** an amount levied **2a** the enlistment or conscription of men for military service **b** *sing or pl in constr* troops raised by levy

²**levy** *vt* **1** to impose, collect, or demand by legal authority <*~ a tax*> **2** to enlist or conscript for military service **3** to prepare for and make (war) – usu + *on* or *upon* – **leviable** *adj*

lewd /l(y)oohd‖l(j)uːd/ *adj* **1** sexually coarse or suggestive **2** obscene, salacious – **lewdly** *adv*, **lewdness** *n*

lexical /ˈleksikl‖ˈleksɪkl/ *adj* **1** of words or the vocabulary of a language as distinguished from its grammar and construction **2** of a lexicon – **lexically** *adv*, **lexicality** *n*

lexicography /ˌleksiˈkogrəfi‖ˌleksɪˈkɒgrəfɪ/ *n* (the principles of) the editing or making of a dictionary – **lexicographer** *n*, **lexicographic, lexicographical** *adj*

lexicon /ˈleksikən‖ˈleksɪkən/ *n, pl* **lexica** /-kə‖-kə/, **lexicons 1** a dictionary, esp of Greek, Latin, or Hebrew **2** the vocabulary of a language, individual, or subject

lexis /ˈleksis‖ˈleksɪs/ *n, pl* **lexes** /-seez‖-siːz/ LEXICON 2

liability /ˌlie·əˈbiləti‖ˌlaɪəˈbɪlətɪ/ *n* **1** being liable **2** sthg for which one is liable; *esp, pl* debts **3** a hindrance, drawback – infml

liable /ˈlie·əbl‖ˈlaɪəbl/ *adj* **1** legally responsible **2** exposed or subject *to* **3** habitually likely *to* <*she's ~ to get annoyed*>

liaise /leeˈayz‖liːˈeɪz/ *vi* **1** to establish a connection and cooperate **2** to act as a liaison officer

liaison /leeˈayzon, -z(ə)n, -zonh‖liːˈeɪzɒn, -z(ə)n, -zɑ̃/ *n* **1a** a close bond or connection **b** an illicit sexual relationship; AFFAIR 3a **2** communication, esp between parts of an armed force

liana /liˈahnə‖lɪˈɑːnə/ *n* a climbing plant, esp of tropical rain forests, that roots in the ground – **lianoid** *adj*

liar /ˈlie·ə‖ˈlaɪə/ *n* one who (habitually) tells lies

lib /lib‖lɪb/ *n, often cap* LIBERATION 2 – infml – **libber** *n*

libation /lieˈbaysh(ə)n‖laɪˈbeɪʃ(ə)n/ *n* **1** (an act of pouring) a liquid used in a sacrifice to a god **2a** an act or instance of drinking **b** a beverage, esp alcoholic ***USE*** (*2*) fml or humor

¹**libel** /ˈliebl‖ˈlaɪbl/ *n* **1** (a) defamation of sby by published writing or pictorial representation as distinguished from spoken words or gestures **2** a false insulting statement [Latin *libellus* small book, defamatory publication, fr *liber* book] – **libellous** *adj*

²**libel** *vb* **-ll-** (*NAm* **-l-**, **-ll-**) to make or publish a libel (against) – **libeller** *n*, **libellist** *n*

¹**liberal** /ˈlib(ə)rəl‖ˈlɪb(ə)rəl/ *adj* **1** of or in liberal studies <*~ education*> **2a** generous, openhanded <*a ~ giver*> **b** abundant, ample <*a ~ helping*> **3** broad-minded, tolerant; *esp* not bound by authoritarianism, orthodoxy, or tradition **4** *cap* based on or advocating (political) liberalism; *specif* of a political party in the UK advocating economic freedom and moderate reform [Middle French, fr Latin *liberalis* suitable for a freeman, generous, fr *liber* free] – **liberally** *adv*, **liberalness, liberality** *n*

²**liberal** *n* **1** one who is not strict in the observance of orthodox ways (e g in politics or religion) **2** *cap* a supporter of a Liberal party **3** a champion of individual rights

liberalism /ˈlib(ə)rəliz(ə)m‖ˈlɪb(ə)rəlɪz(ə)m/ *n* **1** breadth of mind; tolerance, understanding **2a** a political philosophy based on belief in progress and the protection of political and civil liberties **b** *cap* Liberal principles and policies – **liberalist** *n or adj*, **liberalistic** *adj*

liberal·ize, -ise /ˈlib(ə)rəˌliez‖ˈlɪb(ə)rəˌlaɪz/ *vb* to make or become (more) liberal – **liberalization** *n*

liberate /ˈlibəˌrayt‖ˈlɪbəˌreɪt/ *vt* **1** to set free; *specif* to free (e g a country) from foreign domination **2** to free (a molecule, ion, etc) from combination **3** to steal – euph or humor – **liberator** *n*

liberation /ˌlibəˈraysh(ə)n‖ˌlɪbəˈreɪʃ(ə)n/ *n* **1** liberating or being liberated **2** the seeking of equal rights and status <*gay ~*> – **liberationist** *n*

libertarian /ˌlibəˈteəri·ən‖ˌlɪbəˈteərɪən/ *n* **1** a believer in free will **2** an advocate of liberty – **libertarian** *adj*, **libertarianism** *n*

libertine /ˈlibəteen‖ˈlɪbətiːn/ *n* a person who is unrestrained by convention or morality; *specif* one leading a dissolute life – **libertinage, libertinism** *n*

liberty /ˈlibəti‖ˈlɪbətɪ/ *n* **1a** the power to do as one pleases **b** freedom from physical restraint or dictatorial control **c** the enjoyment of various rights and privileges <*civil* ~> **d** the power of choice **2** a right or immunity awarded or granted; a privilege **3a** a breach of etiquette or propriety **b** a risk, chance <*took foolish* liberties *with her health*> – **at liberty 1** free **2** at leisure; unoccupied

libidinous /li'bidinəs‖lɪ'bɪdɪnəs/ *adj* having or marked by strong sexual desire; lascivious – **libidinously** *adv*, **libidinousness** *n*

libido /li'beedoh‖lɪ'bi:dəʊ/ *n, pl* **libidos 1** emotional or mental energy derived in psychoanalytic theory from primitive biological urges **2** sexual drive [Latin, desire, lust, fr *libēre* to please] – **libidinal** *adj*

Libra /'leebrə, 'lie-‖'li:brə, 'laɪ-/ *n* (sby born under) the 7th sign of the zodiac in astrology, pictured as a pair of scales – **Libran** *n or adj*

librarian /lie'breəri·ən‖laɪ'breərɪən/ *n* sby who manages or assists in a library – **librarianship** *n*

library /'liebrəri‖'laɪbrərɪ/ *n* **1a** a place in which books, recordings, films, etc are kept for reference or for borrowing by the public **b** a collection of such books, recordings, etc **2** a series of related books issued by a publisher

libretto /li'bretoh‖lɪ'bretəʊ/ *n, pl* **librettos, libretti** /-ti‖-tɪ/ (the book containing) the text of a work (e g an opera) that is both theatrical and musical [Italian, diminutive of *libro* book, fr Latin *liber*] – **librettist** *n*

lice /lies‖laɪs/ *pl of* LOUSE

licence, *NAm chiefly* **license** /'lies(ə)ns‖'laɪs(ə)ns/ *n* **1a** permission to act **b** freedom of action **2** (a certificate giving evidence of) permission granted by authority to engage in an otherwise unlawful activity, esp the sale of alcoholic drink **3a** freedom that allows or is used with irresponsibility **b** disregard for rules of propriety or personal conduct **4** freedom claimed by an artist or writer to alter facts or deviate from the rules of an art, esp for the sake of the effect gained

license, licence /'lies(ə)ns‖'laɪs(ə)ns/ *vt* to give official permission to or for (esp the sale of alcoholic drink)

ˌlicensed ˈvictualler *n, Br* a publican holding a licence to sell food and alcoholic drink on the premises

licensee /ˌlies(ə)n'see‖ˌlaɪs(ə)n'si:/ *n* the holder of a licence; *esp, Br* a publican

ˈlicense ˌplate *n, NAm* a renewable number plate showing that the vehicle to which it is attached is licensed

licentiate /lie'sens(h)i·ət, -ayt‖laɪ'sensɪət, -ɪeɪt, -enʃɪ-/ *n* **1** one licensed to practise a profession **2** an academic degree awarded by some European universities

licentious /lie'senshəs‖laɪ'senʃəs/ *adj* behaving in a sexually uncontrolled manner – **licentiously** *adv*, **licentiousness** *n*

lichen /'liekən, 'lichin‖'laɪkən, 'lɪtʃɪn/ *n* any of numerous complex plants made up of an alga and a fungus growing in symbiotic association on a solid surface (e g a rock or tree trunk) – **lichenous** *adj*, **lichenoid** *adj*

licit /'lisit‖'lɪsɪt/ *adj* not forbidden (by law); permissible – **licitly** *adv*

[1]**lick** /lik‖lɪk/ *vt* **1a(1)** to draw the tongue over, esp in order to taste, moisten, or clean <~ *a stamp*> **a(2)** to flicker or play over like a tongue **b** to take into the mouth with the tongue; lap – usu + *up* **2a** to strike repeatedly; thrash **b** to get the better of; overcome <*has* ~ed *every problem*> ~*vi* to lap (as if) with the tongue; *also* to dart like a tongue <*flames* ~ing *at the windows*> *USE* (*vt 2*) infml – **lick into shape** to put into proper form or condition

[2]**lick** *n* **1a** an act or instance of licking **b** a small amount; a touch <*a* ~ *of paint*> **2** [5]BLOW 1 **3** a place to which animals regularly go to lick a salt deposit **4** speed, pace <*the car was travelling at a good* ~> – infml – **a lick and a promise** sthg hastily and not thoroughly done; *esp* a quick wash

licking /'liking‖'lɪkɪŋ/ *n* **1** a sound thrashing; a beating **2** a severe setback; a defeat *USE* infml

licorice /'likərish, -ris‖'lɪkərɪʃ, -rɪs/ *n* liquorice

lid /lid‖lɪd/ *n* a hinged or detachable cover (for a receptacle) – **lidded** *adj*

lido /'liedoh, 'lee-‖'laɪdəʊ, 'li:-/ *n, pl* **lidos 1** a fashionable beach resort **2** a public open-air swimming pool [*Lido*, resort near Venice in Italy, fr Latin *litus* shore]

[1]**lie** /lie‖laɪ/ *vi* **lying; lay** /lay‖leɪ/; **lain** /layn‖leɪn/ **1a** to be or to stay at rest in a horizontal position; rest, recline <~ *motionless*> <~ *asleep*> **b** to assume a horizontal position – often + *down* **c** to be or remain in a specified state or condition <~ *in wait*> <*machinery* lying *idle*> **2a** *of sthg inanimate* to be or remain in a flat or horizontal position on a surface <*books* lying *on the table*> **b** *of snow* to remain on the ground without melting **3** to have as a direction; [1]LEAD 1b(1) <*the route* lay *to the west*> **4a** to occupy a specified place or position <*hills* ~ *behind us*> <*the responsibility* ~s *with us*> **b** to have an adverse or disheartening effect; weigh <*remorse* lay *heavily on her*> **c** *of an action, claim, etc in a court of law* to be sustainable or admissible **5** to remain at anchor or becalmed – **lie low 1** to stay in hiding; strive to avoid notice **2** to bide one's time

[2]**lie** *n* **1** the way, position, or situation in which sthg lies <*the* ~ *of the land*> **2** a haunt of an animal or fish

[3]**lie** *vi* **lying** /'lie·ing‖'laɪɪŋ/ **1** to make an untrue statement with intent to deceive; speak falsely **2** to create a false or misleading impression <*the camera never* ~s>

[4]**lie** *n* **1** an untrue or false statement, esp when made with intent to deceive **2** sthg that misleads or deceives

lied /leed ‖li:d (*Ger* li:t)/ *n, pl* **lieder** /'leedə ‖ 'li:də (*Ger* li:dər)/ a German song; *esp* a 19th-c setting of a lyrical poem

ˈlie deˌtector *n* an instrument for detecting physical evidence of the mental tension that accompanies telling lies

ˈlie-ˌdown *n, chiefly Br* a brief rest, esp on a bed – infml

lie down *vi* to submit meekly or abjectly to defeat, disappointment, or insult <*won't take that criticism* lying down>

lief /leef‖li:f/ *adv, archaic* soon, gladly <*I'd as* ~ *go as not*>

[1]liege /leej‖liːdʒ/ *adj* **1a** entitled to feudal allegiance **b** owing feudal allegiance **2** faithful, loyal

[2]liege *n* **1a** a feudal vassal **b** a loyal subject **2** a feudal superior

lie in *vi* **1** to be confined to give birth to a child **2** *chiefly Br* to stay in bed until later than usual in the morning – **lie-in** *n*

lien /ˈlee·ən, leen‖ˈliːən, liːn/ *n* the legal right to hold another's property until a claim is met

lie off *vi, of a ship* to keep a little distance away from the shore or another ship

lie over *vi* to await attention at a later time <*several jobs* lying over *from last week*>

lie to *vi, of a ship* to stay stationary with head to windward

lieu /l(y)ooh‖l(j)uː/ *n* – **in lieu** in substitution; instead <*I'm sending this message* in lieu *of a letter*>

lie up *vi* **1** to stay in bed, esp for a long period **2** *of a ship* to remain in dock or out of commission **3** to remain inactive or at rest

lieutenant /lefˈtenənt‖lefˈtenənt; *Royal Navy* ləˈtenənt‖ləˈtenənt; *NAm* loohˈtenənt‖luːˈtenənt/ *n* **1** an official empowered to act for a higher official; a deputy or representative **2** an officer of low rank in the navy, army, or US airforce **3** an officer with the rank next below the one named <lieutenant *colonel*> [Middle French, fr *lieu* place + *tenant* holding]

[1]life /lief‖laɪf/ *n, pl* **lives** /lievz‖laɪvz/ **1a** the quality that distinguishes a vital and functional being from a dead body **b** a principle or force considered to underlie the distinctive quality of animate beings **c** a state of matter (e g a cell or an organism) characterized by capacity for metabolism, growth, reaction to stimuli, and reproduction **2a** the sequence of physical and mental experiences that make up the existence of an individual **b** an aspect of the process of living <*the sex* ~ *of the frog*> **3** BIOGRAPHY 1 **4** a state or condition of existence <~ *after death*> **5a** the period from birth to death or to the present time <*I have lived here all my* ~> **b** a specific phase of earthly existence <*adult* ~> **c** the period from an event or the present time until death <*a member for* ~> **d** a sentence of imprisonment for life <*got* ~ *for the murder*> **6** a way or manner of living <*a holy* ~> **7** a person <*many* lives *were lost in the disaster*> **8** the source of pleasure, interest, or enjoyment in living; the reason for living <*his work was his whole* ~> **9** the living form considered as a model <*painted from* ~> **10** the period of usefulness, effectiveness, or functioning of sthg inanimate <*the expected* ~ *of torch batteries*> **11** a period of existence (e g of a subatomic particle) **12** living beings (e g of a specified kind or environment) <*forest* ~> **13a** the active part of human existence, esp in a wide range of circumstances or experiences <*left home to see* ~> **b** activity from living things; movement <*stirrings of* ~> **c** the activities of a specified sphere, area, or time <*the political* ~ *of the country*> **14** (one who provides) interest, animation, or vigour <*the* ~ *and soul of the party*> **15** any of several chances to participate given to a contestant in some games, 1 of which is forfeited each time he/she loses; *also* a failed chance to get a batsman out <*dropped a catch and gave the batsman a* ~>

[2]life *adj* **1** using a living model <*a* ~ *class*> **2** of, being, or provided by life insurance <*a* ~ *policy*>

ˈlife ˌbelt *n* a buoyant belt for keeping a person afloat

ˈlifeˌblood /-ˌblud, ˌ-ˈ-‖-ˌblʌd, ˌ-ˈ-/ *n* **1** the blood necessary to life **2** a vital or life-giving force

ˈlifeˌboat /-ˌboht‖-ˌbəʊt/ *n* a robust buoyant boat for use in saving lives at sea

ˈlife ˌbuoy /boy‖bɔɪ/ *n* a buoyant often ring-shaped float to which a person may cling in the water

ˈlife ˌcycle *n* the series of stages in form and functional activity through which an organism, group, culture, etc passes during its lifetime

ˈlifeˌguard /-ˌgahd‖-ˌgɑːd/ *n* a usu expert swimmer employed to safeguard other swimmers – **lifeguard** *vi*

ˌlife ˈhistory *n* the changes through which an organism passes in its development from the primary stage to its natural death

ˈlife ˌjacket *n* a buoyant device that is designed to keep a person afloat and can be worn continuously as a precaution against drowning

ˈlifeless /-lis‖-lɪs/ *adj* **1a** dead **b** inanimate **2** having no living beings <*a* ~ *planet*> **3** lacking qualities expressive of life and vigour; dull <*a* ~ *voice*> – **lifelessly** *adv*, **lifelessness** *n*

ˈlifeˌlike /-ˌliek‖-ˌlaɪk/ *adj* accurately representing or imitating (the appearance of objects in) real life

ˈlifeˌline /-ˌlien‖-ˌlaɪn/ *n* **1a** a rope for saving or safeguarding life: e g **1a(1)** one stretched along the deck of a ship in rough weather **a(2)** one fired to a ship in distress by means of a rocket **b** the line by which a diver is lowered and raised **2** sthg, esp the sole means of communication, regarded as indispensable for the maintenance or protection of life

ˈlifeˌlong /-ˌlong‖-ˌlɒŋ/ *adj* lasting or continuing throughout life

ˌlife ˈpeer, *fem* **life peeress** *n* a British peer whose title is not hereditary – **life peerage** *n*

ˈlife preˌserver *n* **1** *chiefly Br* a small weighted club **2** *chiefly NAm* a life jacket, life buoy, etc

lifer /ˈliefə‖ˈlaɪfə/ *n* one sentenced to life imprisonment – infml

ˈlife-ˌsize, life-sized *adj* of natural size; of the size of the original <*a* ~ *statue*>

ˈlifeˌtime /-ˌtiem‖-ˌtaɪm/ *n* the length of time for which a person, living thing, subatomic particle, etc exists

ˌlifeˈwork /-ˈwuhk‖-ˈwɜːk/ *n* the entire or principal work (filling the whole) of one's lifetime

[1]lift /lift‖lɪft/ *vt* **1a** to raise from a lower to a higher position; elevate **b** to raise in rank or condition **2** to put an end to (a blockade or siege) by withdrawing the surrounding forces **3** to revoke, rescind <~ *an embargo*> **4a** to plagiarize **b** to take out of normal setting <~ *a word out of context*> **5** to take up (e g a root crop) from the ground **6** to hit (e g a cricket ball) or to hit the bowling of (a bowler) into the air **7**

to steal <*had her purse* ~ed> – infml ~ *vi* **1** to ascend, rise **2a** to disperse upwards <*until the fog* ~s > **b** *of bad weather* to cease temporarily <*the rain finally* ~ed> **3** *of a bowled ball in cricket* to rise at a sharper angle than expected after pitching – **liftable** *adj*, **lifter** *n*

[2]lift *n* **1a** (a device for) lifting or (the amount) being lifted **b** the lifting up of a dancer or skater usu by her partner **2** a usu free ride as a passenger in a motor vehicle **3** a slight rise or elevation of ground **4** the distance or extent to which sthg (e g water in a canal lock) rises **5** a usu temporary feeling of cheerfulness, pleasure, or encouragement **6** the upward part of the aerodynamic force acting on an aircraft or aerofoil that opposes the pull of gravity **7** an organized transport of men, equipment, or supplies; *esp* an airlift **8** any of the ropes by which the yard is suspended from the mast on a square-rigged ship **9** *chiefly Br* a device for conveying people or objects from one level to another, esp in a building

ˈlift-ˌoff *n* a vertical takeoff by an aircraft, rocket vehicle, or missile – **lift off** *vi*

ligament /ˈligəmənt‖ˈlɪgəmənt/ *n* a tough band of connective tissue forming the capsule round a joint or supporting an organ (e g the womb) – **ligamentary, ligamentous** *adj*

ligature /ˈligəchə‖ˈlɪgətʃə/ *n* **1a** sthg that is used to bind; *specif* a thread used in surgery **b** sthg that unites or connects **2** the action of binding or tying **3** [2]SLUR 1 **4** a character consisting of 2 or more letters or characters joined together; *esp* one (e g) other than a diphthong

[1]light /liet‖laɪt/ *n* **1a** (the sensation aroused by) sthg that makes vision possible by stimulating the sense of sight **b** an electromagnetic radiation in the wavelength range including infrared, visible, ultraviolet, and X rays; *specif* the part of this range that is visible to the human eye **2** daylight **3** a source of light: e g **3a** a celestial body **b** a burning candle **c** an electric light **4a** spiritual illumination **b** INNER LIGHT **c** understanding, knowledge **d** *the* truth <*see the* ~> **5a** public knowledge <*facts brought to* ~> **b** a particular aspect or appearance in which sthg is viewed <*now saw the matter in a different* ~> **6** a particular illumination in a place <*studio with a north* ~> **7** (enlightening) information or explanation <*he shed some* ~ *on the problem*> **8** a medium (e g a window) through which light is admitted **9** *pl* a set of principles, standards, or opinions <*true by your* ~s> **10** LEADING LIGHT **11** a specified expression, perceived as being in sby's eyes <*the* ~ *of love in his eyes*> **12a** a lighthouse **b** TRAFFIC LIGHT **13** the representation in art of the effect of light on objects or scenes **14** a flame or spark for lighting sthg (e g a cigarette) **15** *Br* the answer to 1 of the clues of a crossword – **lightless** *adj*, **lightproof** *adj* – **in the light of** with the insight provided by

[2]light *adj* **1** having plenty of light; bright <*a* ~ *airy room*> **2a** pale in colour or colouring **b** *of colours* medium in saturation and high in lightness

[3]light *vb* **lit** /lit‖lɪt/, **lighted** /ˈlietid‖ˈlaɪtɪd/ *vi* **1** LIGHT UP 1 **2** to catch fire ~ *vt* **1** to set fire to **2a** to conduct (sby) with a light; guide **b** to illuminate <*a room* lit *by a bay window*>

[4]light *adj* **1a** having little weight; not heavy **b** designed to carry a comparatively small load <*a* ~ *van*> **c** of the smaller variety <*a* ~ *gun*> **d** (made of materials) having relatively little weight in proportion to bulk <*aluminium is a* ~ *metal*> **e** containing less than the legal, standard, or usual weight <*a* ~ *coin*> **2a** of little importance; trivial **b** not abundant <~ *rain*> <*a* ~ *crop of wheat*> **3a** *of sleep or a sleeper* easily disturbed **b** exerting a minimum of force or pressure; gentle, soft <*a* ~ *touch*> <*a* ~ *breeze*> <*a* ~ *voice*> **c** faint <~ *print*> **4a** easily endurable <~ *taxation*> **b** requiring little effort <~ *work*> **5** nimble <~ *on his feet*> **6** lacking seriousness; frivolous **7** free from care; cheerful <*a* ~ *heart*> **8** intending or intended chiefly to entertain <~ *reading*> **9** *of a drink* having a comparatively low alcoholic content or a mild flavour <*a* ~ *white wine*> **10a** easily digested <*a* ~ *dessert*> **b** well leavened <*a* ~ *cake*> **11** lightly armoured, armed, or equipped <~ *cavalry*> **12** easily pulverized; crumbly <~ *soil*> **13** dizzy, giddy <*felt* ~ *in the head*> **14a** carrying little or no cargo <*the ship returned* ~> **b** producing light usu small goods often for direct consumption <~ *industry*> – **lightish** *adj*, **lightly** *adv*, **lightness** *n*

[5]light *adv* **1** lightly **2** with the minimum of luggage <*travel* ~>

[6]light *vi* **lighted, lit** /lit‖lɪt/ **1** to settle, alight <*a bird* lit *on the lawn*> **2** to arrive by chance; happen <lit *upon a solution*>

ˈlight ˌbulb *n* INCANDESCENT LAMP

[1]lighten /ˈliet(ə)n‖ˈlaɪt(ə)n/ *vt* **1** to make (more) light or clear; illuminate **2** to make (e g a colour) lighter ~ *vi* **1** to grow lighter; brighten **2** to discharge flashes of lightning – **lightener** *n*

[2]lighten *vt* **1** to reduce the weight of **2** to relieve (partly) of a burden <*the news* ~ed *his mind*> **3** to make less wearisome; alleviate <~ed *his gloom*>; *broadly* to cheer, gladden ~ *vi* **1** to become lighter or less burdensome **2** to become more cheerful <*his mood* ~ed> – **lightener** *n*

[1]lighter /ˈlietə‖ˈlaɪtə/ *vt or n* (to convey by) a large usu flat-bottomed barge used esp in unloading or loading ships

[2]lighter *n* a device for lighting (a cigar, cigarette, etc)

lighterage /ˈlietərij‖ˈlaɪtərɪdʒ/ *n* (the charge for) the loading, unloading, or transport of goods by means of a lighter

ˌlight-ˈfingered *adj* **1** adroit in stealing, esp picking pockets **2** having a light and dexterous touch; nimble – **light-fingeredness** *n*

ˌlight-ˈheaded *adj* **1** mentally disoriented; dizzy **2** frivolous – **light-headedly** *adv*, **light-headedness** *n*

ˌlightˈhearted /-ˈhahtid‖-ˈhɑːtɪd/ *adj* free from care or worry; cheerful – **lightheartedly** *adv*, **lightheartedness** *n*

ˈlightˌhouse /-ˌhows‖-ˌhaʊs/ *n* a tower, mast, etc equipped with a powerful light to warn or guide shipping at sea

lighting /ˈlieting‖ˈlaɪtɪŋ/ *n* (the apparatus providing) an artificial supply of light

ˈlightness /-nis‖-nɪs/ *n* the attribute of object

colours by which more or less of the incident light is reflected or transmitted

[1]**lightning** /ˈlietning‖ˈlaɪtnɪŋ/ *n* (the brilliant light flash resulting from) an electric discharge between 2 clouds or between a cloud and the earth

[2]**lightning** *adj* very quick, short, or sudden

ˈlightning conˌductor *n* a metal rod fixed to the highest point of a building or mast and connected to the earth or water below as a protection against lightning

light out *vi, NAm* to leave in a hurry – infml <lit out *for home as soon as he could*>

light pen *n* a pen-shaped photoelectric device that is held or moved over a VDU screen to draw, modify, or delete information

lights /liets‖laɪts/ *n pl* the lungs, esp of a slaughtered sheep, pig, etc

ˈlightˌship /-ˌship‖-ˌʃɪp/ *n* a moored vessel equipped with a powerful light to warn or guide shipping at sea

ˈlights-ˌout *n* **1** a command or signal for putting out lights **2** a prescribed bedtime for people living in an institution (e g boarding school)

light up *vb* **1** to illuminate or become illuminated or lit (in a sudden or conspicuous manner) **2** to ignite (a cigarette, pipe, etc)

ˈlightˌweight /-ˌwayt‖-ˌweɪt/ *n or adj* **1** (a boxer) weighing not more than 9st 9lb (61.2kg) if professional or more than 57kg (about 8st 13lb) but not more than 60kg (about 9st 6lb) if amateur **2** (sby) of little ability or importance

ˈlight-ˌyear *n* a unit of length in astronomy equal to the distance that light travels in 1 year in a vacuum; 9,460 thousand million km (about 5,878 thousand million mi)

lignite /ˈligniet‖ˈlɪgnaɪt/ *n* a brownish black coal that is harder than peat but usu retains the texture of the original wood – **lignitic** *adj*

lignum vitae /ˌlignəm ˈvieti‖ˌlɪgnəm ˈvaɪtɪ/ *n, pl* **lignum vitaes** (the very hard heavy dark wood of) any of several tropical American trees

likable *also* **likeable** /ˈliekəbl‖ˈlaɪkəbl/ *adj* pleasant, agreeable – **likableness** *n*, **likability** *n*

[1]**like** /liek‖laɪk/ *vt* **1a** to find agreeable, acceptable, or pleasant; enjoy **b** to feel towards; regard <*how would you* ~ *a change?*> **2** to wish or choose to have, be, or do; want <~s *to help*> <~s *us to come early*> ~*vi* to feel inclined; choose <*you can leave any time you* ~> – **if you like** SO TO SPEAK

[2]**like** *n* a liking, preference <*one's* ~s *and dislikes*>

[3]**like** *adj* **1a** alike in appearance, character, or quantity <*suits of* ~ *design*> **b** bearing a close resemblance; *esp* faithful <*his portrait is very* ~> **2** likely

[4]**like** *prep* **1a** having the characteristics of; similar to <*his house is* ~ *a barn*> **b** typical of <*was* ~ *her to do that*> **2a** in the manner of; similarly to <*act* ~ *a fool*> **b** to the same degree as <*fits* ~ *a glove*> **c** close to <*cost something* ~ *£5*> **3** appearing to be, threaten, or promise <*you seem* ~ *a sensible man*> **4** – used to introduce an example <*a subject* ~ *physics*> – **like that 1** in that way <*don't eat* like that> **2** without demur or hesitation <*can't change jobs just* like that> – **like anything/crazy** – used to emphasize a verb; infml <*run* like anything>

[5]**like** *n* one who or that which is like another, esp in high value; a counterpart <*never saw the* ~ *of it*> <*had no use for the* ~s *of him*> <*her* ~ *will never be seen again*> – **the like** similar things <*football, tennis, and* the like>

[6]**like** *adv* **1** likely, probably <*he'll come as* ~ *as not*> **2** SO TO SPEAK <*went up to her casually,* ~> – nonstandard

[7]**like** *conj* **1** in the same way as <*if she can sing* ~ *she can dance*> **2** *chiefly NAm* as if <*acts* ~ *he knows what he's doing*>

-like /-liek‖-laɪk/ *comb form* (*n* → *adj*) resembling or characteristic of <*lady*like>

likelihood /ˈliekliˌhood‖ˈlaɪklɪˌhʊd/ *n* probability <*in all* ~ *it will rain*>

[1]**likely** /ˈliekli‖ˈlaɪklɪ/ *adj* **1** having a high probability of being or occurring <~ *to succeed*> <*the* ~ *result*> **2a** reliable, credible <*a* ~ *enough story*> **b** incredible – used ironically <*a* ~ *tale!*> **3** seeming appropriate; suitable <*a* ~ *spot*> **4** promising <~ *lads*>

[2]**likely** *adv* probably – often in *most/very/more/quite likely* <*he most* ~ *will give up*>

ˌlike-ˈminded *adj* having a similar outlook or disposition – **like-mindedly** *adv*, **like-mindedness** *n*

liken /ˈliekən‖ˈlaɪkən/ *vt* to find or point out similarities in; compare

ˈlikeness /-nis‖-nɪs/ *n* **1** resemblance **2** a copy, portrait <*a good* ~ *of her*> **3** *archaic* an appearance, semblance

ˈlikeˌwise /-ˌwiez‖-ˌwaɪz/ *adv* **1** in like manner; similarly <*go and do* ~> **2** moreover; IN ADDITION **3** similarly so with me <*answered '*~*' to 'Pleased to meet you'*>

liking /ˈlieking‖ˈlaɪkɪŋ/ *n* favourable regard; fondness, taste <*took a* ~ *to the newcomer*>

lilac /ˈlielək, -lak‖ˈlaɪlək, -læk/ *n* **1** a European shrub of the olive family with heart-shaped leaves and large clusters of fragrant white or (pale pinkish) purple flowers **2** pale pinkish purple

lilliputian /ˌliliˈpyoohsh(y)ən‖ˌlɪlɪˈpjuːʃ(j)ən/ *n or adj, often cap* (sby or sthg) remarkably tiny or diminutive [*Lilliput*, imaginary country of tiny people in *Gulliver's Travels* by Jonathan Swift (1667-1745), Irish satirist]

Li-Lo /ˈlie ˌloh‖ˈlaɪ ˌləʊ/ *trademark* – used for an airbed

[1]**lilt** /lilt‖lɪlt/ *vb* to sing or speak rhythmically and with varying pitch – **liltingly** *adv*

[2]**lilt** *n* **1** (a song or tune with) a rhythmic swing, flow, or rising and falling inflection **2** a light springy motion <*a* ~ *in her step*>

lily /ˈlili‖ˈlɪlɪ/ *n* **1** any of a genus of plants that grow from bulbs and are widely cultivated for their variously coloured showy flowers; *also* any of various other plants of the lily or the related daffodil or iris families **2** WATER LILY **3** FLEUR-DE-LIS 2 **4** one resembling a lily in fairness, purity, or fragility – poetic – **liliaceous** *adj*

ˌlily-ˈlivered /ˈlivəd‖ˈlɪvəd/ *adj* lacking courage; cowardly

ˌlily of the ˈvalley *n* a low perennial plant

of the lily family that has usu 2 large leaves and a stalk of fragrant drooping bell-shaped white flowers

ˌlily-ˈwhite *adj* **1** pure white **2** irreproachable, pure

ˈlima ˌbean /ˈliemə‖ˈlaɪmə/ *n* (the flat edible seed of) any of various widely cultivated bushy or tall-growing orig tropical American beans [*Lima*, capital city of Peru]

[1]**limb** /lim‖lɪm/ *n* **1** any of the projecting paired appendages of an animal body used esp for movement and grasping but sometimes modified into sensory or sexual organs; *esp* a leg or arm of a human being **2** a large primary branch of a tree **3** an active member or agent <~s *of the law*> **4** an extension, branch; *specif* any of the 4 branches or arms of a cross **5** *archaic* a mischievous child – **limbless** *adj* – **out on a limb** in an exposed and unsupported position

[2]**limb** *vt* to dismember; *esp* to cut off the limbs of (a felled tree)

[3]**limb** *n* **1** the graduated edge of a quadrant, levelling staff, etc **2** the outer edge of the apparent disc of a celestial body **3** the broad flat part of a petal or sepal furthest from its base

limbed /limd‖lɪmd/ *adj* having (a specified kind or number of) limbs – usu in combination <*strong*-limbed>

[1]**limber** /ˈlimbə‖ˈlɪmbə/ *n* a 2-wheeled (ammunition-carrying) vehicle to which a gun may be attached

[2]**limber** *adj* supple in mind or body; flexible – **limberly** *adv*, **limberness** *n*

limber up *vb* to (cause to) become supple, flexible, or prepared for physical action <limbered up *before the match*>

[1]**limbo** /ˈlimboh‖ˈlɪmbəʊ/ *n, pl* **limbos 1** *often cap* an abode of souls that are according to Roman Catholic theology barred from heaven because of not having received Christian baptism **2a** a place or state of restraint or confinement, or of neglect or oblivion **b** an intermediate or transitional place or state

[2]**limbo** *n,* a W Indian acrobatic dance that involves bending over backwards and passing under a low horizontal pole

[1]**lime** /liem‖laɪm/ *n* **1** birdlime **2a** a caustic solid consisting of calcium (and some magnesium) oxide, obtained by heating calcium carbonate (e g in the form of shells or limestone) to a high temperature, and used in building (e g in plaster) and in agriculture **b** calcium hydroxide (occurring as a dry white powder), made by treating caustic lime with water – **limy** *adj*

[2]**lime** *vt* to treat or cover with lime

[3]**lime** *n* (the light fine-grained wood of) any of a genus of widely planted (ornamental) trees that usu have heart-shaped leaves

[4]**lime** *n* a (spiny tropical citrus tree cultivated for its) small spherical greenish-yellow fruit

ˈlime-ˌjuicer /ˈjoohsə‖ˈdʒuːsə/ *n, NAm* a British ship or sailor – slang [fr the former use of lime juice on British ships as a drink to prevent scurvy]

ˈlimeˌlight /-ˌliet‖-ˌlaɪt/ *n* **1** (the white light produced by) a stage lighting instrument producing illumination by means of an intense flame directed on a cylinder of lime **2** *the* centre of public attention

limerick /ˈlimərik‖ˈlɪmərɪk/ *n* a humorous and often epigrammatic or indecent verse form of 5 lines with a rhyme scheme of aabba

ˈlimeˌstone /-ˌstohn‖-ˌstəʊn/ *n* a widely-occurring rock consisting mainly of calcium carbonate

limey /ˈliemi‖ˈlaɪmɪ/ *n, often cap, NAm* a British person, esp a sailor – slang

[1]**limit** /ˈlimit‖ˈlɪmɪt/ *n* **1a** a boundary **b** *pl* the place enclosed within a boundary <*must not go off* ~s> **2a** sthg that bounds, restrains, or confines <*worked within the* ~s *of his knowledge*> <*set a* ~ *on his spending*> **b** a line or point that cannot or should not be passed **3** a prescribed maximum or minimum amount, quantity, or number **4** sby or sthg exasperating or intolerable – + *the*; infml – **limitless** *adj*, **limitlessly** *adv*, **limitlessness** *n*

[2]**limit** *vt* **1** to restrict to specific bounds or limits **2** to curtail or reduce in quantity or extent; curb <*we must* ~ *the power of aggressors*> – **limitable** *adj*, **limiter** *n*, **limitative** *adj*

limitation /ˌlimiˈtaysh(ə)n‖ˌlɪmɪˈteɪʃ(ə)n/ *n* **1** (sthg that is) limiting; *esp* a limit of capability **2** a period defined by statute after which a claimant is barred from bringing a legal action – **limitational** *adj*

limited /ˈlimitid‖ˈlɪmɪtɪd/ *adj* **1** confined within limits; restricted **2** restricted as to the scope of powers <*a* ~ *monarchy*> **3** lacking the ability to grow or do better **4** *Br* being a limited company

limited company, *n* a company in which the responsibility of an individual shareholder for the company's debts is limited according to the amount of his/her personal interest

limousine /ˌliməˈzeen, ˈ---‖ˌlɪməˈziːn, ˈ---/ *n* a luxurious motor car

[1]**limp** /limp‖lɪmp/ *vi* **1** to walk in a manner that avoids putting the full weight of the body on 1 (injured) leg **2** to proceed slowly or with difficulty – **limper** *n*

[2]**limp** *n* a limping movement or gait

[3]**limp** *adj* **1a** lacking firmness and body; drooping or shapeless **b** not stiff or rigid <*a* ~ *cover for a book*> **2** lacking energy – **limply** *adv*, **limpness** *n*

limpet /ˈlimpit‖ˈlɪmpɪt/ *n* **1** a marine gastropod mollusc with a low conical shell broadly open beneath, that clings very tightly to rock when disturbed **2** sby or sthg that clings tenaciously **3** an explosive device designed to cling to the hull of a ship, tank, etc

limpid /ˈlimpid‖ˈlɪmpɪd/ *adj* **1** transparent, pellucid <~ *streams*> **2** clear and simple in style <~ *prose*> – **limpidly** *adv*, **limpidness, limpidity** *n*

linchpin, lynchpin /ˈlinchˌpin‖ˈlɪntʃˌpɪn/ *n* **1** a locking pin inserted crosswise (e g through the end of an axle or shaft) **2** sby or sthg regarded as a vital or coordinating factor <*the* ~ *of the organization*>

linctus /ˈlingktəs‖ˈlɪŋktəs/ *n* any of various syrupy usu medicated liquids used to relieve throat irritation and coughing

linden /ˈlind(ə)n‖ˈlɪnd(ə)n/ *n* [3]LIME

[1]**line** /lien‖laɪn/ *vt* **1** to cover the inner surface

of; provide with a lining <~ *a cloak with silk*> **2** to fill <lining *his pockets with other people's money*> **3** to serve as the lining of <*tapestries* ~d *the walls*>

²line *n* **1a(1)** a (comparatively strong slender) cord or rope **a(2)** a rope used on shipboard **b(1)** a device for catching fish consisting of a cord with hooks, floats, a reel, etc **b(2)** scope for activity **c** a length of material (e g cord) used in measuring and levelling <*a plumb* ~> **d** piping for conveying a fluid (e g steam or compressed air) **e(1)** (a connection for communication by means of) a set of wires connecting one telephone or telegraph (exchange) with another **e(2)** the principal circuits of an electric power distribution system **2a** a horizontal row of written or printed characters **b** a single row of words in a poem **c** a short letter; a note **d** a short sequence of words spoken by an actor playing a particular role; *also, pl* all of the sequences making up a particular role **3a** sthg (e g a ridge, seam, or crease) that is distinct, elongated, and narrow **b** a wrinkle (e g on the face) **c(1)** the course or direction of sthg in motion <*the* ~ *of march*> **c(2)** the trail of scent left by a hunted animal **d** a real or imaginary straight line <*lies on a* ~ *between London and Glasgow*> **e** a boundary or limit (of an area) **f** (a single set of rails forming) a railway track **4a** a course of conduct, action, or thought **b** a field of activity or interest <*what's your* ~*?*> **c** a specified way or theme of talking or writing **5a(1)** a related series of people or things coming one after the other in time; a family, lineage **a(2)** a strain produced and maintained by selective breeding **b** a linked series of trenches and fortifications, esp facing the enemy – usu pl with sing. meaning **c** a military formation in which men, companies, etc are abreast of each other **d** naval ships arranged in a regular order <*the fleet changed from* ~ *ahead to* ~ *abreast*> **e** the regular and numbered infantry regiments of the army as opposed to auxiliary forces or household troops **f** a rank of objects of 1 kind; a row **g** (the company owning or operating) a group of vehicles, ships, aeroplanes, etc carrying passengers or goods regularly over a route <*a shipping* ~> **h** an arrangement of operations in manufacturing allowing ordered occurrence of various stages of production **6** a narrow elongated mark drawn, projected, or imagined (e g on a map): e g **6a** a boundary, contour, circle of latitude or longitude, etc **b** *the* equator **c** any of the horizontal parallel strokes on a music staff on or between which notes are placed **d** a mark (e g in pencil) that forms part of the formal design of a picture; *also* an artist's use of such lines <*purity of* ~> **e** (a single passage of the scanning spot tracing) a horizontal line on a television screen **f** a narrow part of a spectrum (e g of light from the sun) distinguished by being noticeably more or less bright than neighbouring areas <*the sodium* ~s *occur in the yellow part of the spectrum*> **g** a demarcation of a limit with reference to which the playing of some game or sport is regulated – usu in combination <*a touch*line> **7** a straight or curved geometric element, generated by a moving point (continually satisfying a particular condition), that has length but no breadth **8a** a defining outline; a contour <*the* ~ *of a building*> <*the clean* ~s *of a ship*> **b** a general plan; a model – usu pl with sing. meaning <*writing sthg on the* ~s *of a guidebook*> **9** merchandise or services of the same general class for sale or regularly available **10** an indication (e g of intention) based on insight or investigation <*got a* ~ *on their plans*> **11** *pl, Br* a row of tents or huts in a military camp **12** *chiefly Br* a pica **13** *pl, Br* a (specified) number of lines of writing, esp to be copied as a school punishment – **liny** *also* **liney** *adj* – **between the lines 1** by concealed implication **2** by way of inference <*if you read* between the lines, *the meaning is different*> – **in line for** due or in a position to receive – **into line** into a state of agreement or obedience – **on the line** at risk <*put his job* on the line *because of his principles*>

³line *vt* **1** to mark or cover with a line or lines **2** to place or form a line along <*pedestrians* ~ *the streets*> **3** to form into a line or lines; LINE UP

lineage /'lini·ij||'lɪnɪɪdʒ/ *n* a (group of organisms belonging to the same) line of descent from a common ancestor or source

lineal /'lini·əl||'lɪnɪəl/ *adj* **1** composed of or arranged in lines **2** consisting of or being in a direct line of ancestry or descent – usu contrasted with *collateral* **3** of, being, or dealing with a lineage – **lineally** *adv*, **lineality** *n*

lineament /'lini·əmənt||'lɪnɪəmənt/ *n* a distinctive outline, feature, or contour of a body or figure, esp a face – usu pl – **lineamental** *adj*

linear /'lini·ə||'lɪnɪə/ *adj* **1a(1)** of, being, or resembling a line **a(2)** involving a single dimension **b** *of an equation, function, etc* containing any number of variables, all of the first degree, and represented graphically by a straight line **c(1)** characterized by an emphasis on line; *esp* having clearly defined outlines **c(2)** *esp of writing* composed of simply drawn lines with little attempt at pictorial representation **d** consisting of a straight chain of atoms **2** having or being a response or output that is directly proportional to the input <*a good amplifier is* ~> – **linearly** *adv*, **linearity** *n*

linear motor *n* an electric motor that produces thrust in a straight line by direct induction (e g between a track and a vehicle running on it)

linear perspective *n* representation in a drawing or painting of parallel lines as converging in order to give the illusion of depth and distance

linen /'linin||'lɪnɪn/ *n* **1** cloth or yarn made from flax **2** clothing or household articles (e g sheets and tablecloths) made of a usu washable cloth, esp linen

ˌline of ˈsight *n* a straight line from an observer's eye to a distant point towards which he/she is looking

ˈline-ˌout *n* (a method in Rugby Union of returning the ball to play after it has crossed a touchline which involves throwing it in between) a line of forwards from each team

ˈline ˌprinter *n* a high-speed printing device

(e g for a computer) that prints each line as a unit rather than character by character – **line printing** *n*

[1]**liner** /'lienə‖'laınə/ *n* a passenger ship belonging to a shipping company and usu sailing scheduled routes

[2]**liner** *n* a replaceable (metal) lining (for reducing the wear of a mechanism) – **linerless** *adj*

linesman /'lienzmən‖'laınzmən/ *n* an official who assists the referee or umpire in various games, esp in determining if a ball or player is out of the prescribed playing area

'line,up /-,up‖-,ʌp/ *n* (a list of) the players playing for usu 1 side in a game

'line-,up *n* **1** a line of people arranged esp for inspection or as a means of identifying a suspect **2** a group of people or items assembled for a particular purpose

line up *vi* to assume an orderly arrangement in a line ~ *vt* **1** to put into alignment **2** to assemble or organize

[1]**ling** /ling‖lıŋ/ *n* a large food fish of shallow seas off Greenland and Europe

[2]**ling** *n* the commonest British heather

-ling /-ling‖-lıŋ/ *suffix (adj or n → n)* **1** one connected with <*hire*ling> **2** young, small, or lesser kind of <*duck*ling> **3** one having (a specified quality or attribute) <*under*ling>

linger /'ling·gə‖'lıŋgə/ *vi* **1a** to delay going, esp because of reluctance to leave; tarry **b** to dwell on a subject – usu + *over, on,* or *upon* **2** to continue unduly or unhappily in a failing or moribund state – often + *on* **3** to be slow to act; procrastinate **4** to be protracted or slow in disappearing – **lingerer** *n*, **lingeringly** *adv*

lingerie /'lonh·zhəri, 'lan- ‖'lɑ̃ʒərı, 'læn- (*Fr* lɛ̃ʒri)/ *n* women's underwear and nightclothes

lingo /'ling·goh‖'lıŋgəʊ/ *n, pl* **lingoes 1** a foreign language **2** JARGON 2 *USE* infml

lingua franca /,ling·gwə 'frangkə‖,lıŋgwə 'fræŋkə/ *n, pl* **lingua francas, linguae francae** /,ling·gwie 'frangkie‖,lıŋgwaı 'fræŋkaı/ **1** a language spoken in Mediterranean ports that consists of a mixture of Italian with French, Spanish, Greek, and Arabic **2** a language used as a common or commercial tongue among people not speaking the same native language **3** sthg resembling a common language [Italian, lit., Frankish language]

lingual /'ling·gwəl‖'lıŋgwəl/ *adj* **1a** of or resembling the tongue **b** lying near or next to the tongue **2** linguistic – **lingually** *adv*

linguist /'ling·gwist‖'lıŋgwıst/ *n* **1** sby accomplished in languages; *esp* POLYGLOT 1 **2** sby who specializes in linguistics

linguistic /ling'gwistik‖lıŋ'gwıstık/ *adj* of language or linguistics – **linguistically** *adv*

linguistics /ling'gwistiks‖lıŋ'gwıstıks/ *n pl but sing in constr* the study of human language with regard to its nature, structure, and modification

liniment /'linimənt‖'lınımənt/ *n* a liquid preparation that is applied to the skin, esp to allay pain or irritation

lining /'liening‖'laınıŋ/ *n* **1** (a piece of) material used to line sthg (e g a garment) **2** providing sthg with a lining

[1]**link** /lingk‖lıŋk/ *n* **1** a connecting structure: e g **1a(1)** a single ring or division of a chain **a(2)** a unit of length formerly used in surveying equal to 7.92in (about 20.12cm) **b** the fusible part of an electrical fuse **2** sthg analogous to a link of chain: e g **2a** a connecting element <*sought a ~ between smoking and cancer*> **b** a unit in a communications system – **linker** *n*

[2]**link** *vt* to join, connect <*road that* ~s *2 towns*> ~*vi* to become connected by a link – often + *up*

linkage /'lingkij‖'lıŋkıdʒ/ *n* **1** the manner or style of being joined; *specif* BOND 3a **2** the relationship between genes on the same chromosome that causes them to be inherited together **3a** a system of links **b** the degree of electromagnetic interaction expressed as the product of the number of turns of a coil and the magnetic flux linked by the coil

linkman /'lingkmən‖'lıŋkmən/ *n* a broadcaster whose function is to link and introduce separate items, esp in a news programme

links /lingks‖lıŋks/ *n pl* **1** GOLF COURSE – often pl with sing. meaning **2** *Scot* sand hills, esp along the seashore

'link,up /-,up‖-,ʌp/ *n* **1** the establishment of contact; a meeting <*the ~ of 2 spacecraft*> **2a** sthg that serves as a linking device or factor **b** a functional whole that is the result of a linkup

linnet /'linit‖'lınıt/ *n* a common small Old World finch having variable reddish brown plumage

lino /'lienoh‖'laınəʊ/ *n, chiefly Br* linoleum

'lino,cut /-,kut‖-,kʌt/ *n* (a print made from) a design cut in relief on a piece of linoleum

linoleum /li'nohli·əm‖lı'nəʊlıəm/ *n* a floor covering with a canvas back and a coloured or patterned surface of hardened linseed oil and a filler (e g cork dust) [Latin *lin*um flax + *oleum* oil]

Linotype /'lienə,tiep, -noh-‖'laınə,taıp, -nəʊ-/ *trademark* – used for a keyboard-operated typesetting machine that produces each line of type in the form of a solid metal slug

linseed /'linseed‖'lınsi:d/ *n* the seed of flax used esp as a source of linseed oil

'linseed ,oil *n* a yellowish drying oil obtained from flaxseed and used esp in paint, varnish, printing ink, and linoleum and for conditioning cricket bats

lint /lint‖lınt/ *n* **1** a soft absorbent material with a fleecy surface that is made from linen and is used chiefly for surgical dressings **2** *chiefly NAm* FLUFF 1a – **linty** *adj*

lintel /'lintl‖'lıntl/ *n* a horizontal architectural member spanning and usu carrying the load above an opening

lion /'lie·ən‖'laıən/, *fem* **lioness** /'lie·ənes‖'laıənes/ *n* **1a** a flesh-eating big cat of open or rocky areas of Africa and formerly southern Asia that has a tawny body with a tufted tail and in the male a shaggy blackish or dark brown mane **b** *cap* Leo **2** a person of interest or importance

,lion'hearted /-'hahtid‖-'hɑ:tıd/ *adj* courageous, brave

lion·ize, -ise /'lie·ə,niez‖'laıə,naız/ *vt* to treat as an object of great interest or importance – **lionizer** *n*, **lionization** *n*

lip /lip‖lıp/ *n* **1** either of the 2 fleshy folds that surround the mouth **2a** a fleshy edge or margin (e g of a wound) **b** a labium **3** the edge of a hollow vessel or cavity; *esp* one shaped to make pouring easy **4** an embouchure **5** impudent or insolent talk, esp in reply – slang – **lipless** *adj*, **liplike** *adj*

lipid /'lipid, 'lie-‖'lɪpɪd, 'laɪ-/ *n* any of various substances that with proteins and carbohydrates form the principal structural components of living cells and that include fats, waxes, and related and derived compounds – **lipidic** *adj*

lipped /lipt‖lɪpt/ *adj* having a lip or lips, esp of a specified kind or number – often in combination <*tight*-lipped>

'lip,reading /-,reeding‖-,riːdɪŋ/ *n* the interpreting of a speaker's words (e g by the deaf) by watching the movements of the lips – **lip-read** *vb*, **lip-reader** *n*

'lip ,service *n* support in words but not in deeds

lipstick /'lip,stik‖'lɪp,stɪk/ *n* (a cased stick of) a waxy solid cosmetic for colouring the lips

liquefaction /,likwi'faksh(ə)n‖,lɪkwɪ'fækʃ(ə)n/ *n* **1** the process of making or becoming liquid **2** the state of being liquid

liquefy *also* **liquify** /'likwifie‖'lɪkwɪfaɪ/ *vt* to reduce to a liquid state ~*vi* to become liquid – **liquefiable** *adj*, **liquefier** *n*, **liquefiability** *n*

liquescent /li'kwes(ə)nt‖lɪ'kwes(ə)nt/ *adj* being or tending to become liquid

liqueur /li'kyooə‖lɪ'kjʊə/ *n* any of several usu sweetened alcoholic drinks variously flavoured

liquid /'likwid‖'lɪkwɪd/ *adj* **1** flowing freely like water **2** neither solid nor gaseous <~ *mercury*> **3a** shining and clear <*large* ~ *eyes*> **b** *of a sound* flowing, pure, and free of harshness **c** smooth and unconstrained in movement **4** consisting of or capable of ready conversion into cash <~ *assets*> – **liquid** *n*, **liquidly** *adv*, **liquidness** *n*, **liquidity** *n*

,liquid 'air *n* air in the liquid state that is intensely cold and used chiefly as a refrigerant

liquidate /'likwidayt‖'lɪkwɪdeɪt/ *vt* **1a** to settle (a debt), esp by payment **b** to settle the accounts of (e g a business) and use the assets towards paying off the debts **2** to get rid of; *specif* to kill **3** to convert (assets) into cash ~ *vi* **1** to liquidate debts, damages, or accounts **2** to be or become liquidated – **liquidation** *n*

liquidator /'likwi,daytə‖'lɪkwɪ,deɪtə/ *n* a person appointed by law to liquidate a company

liquid·ize, -ise /'likwidiez‖'lɪkwɪdaɪz/ *vt* to cause to be liquid; *esp* to pulverize (e g fruit or vegetables) into a liquid

liquid·izer, -iser /'likwidiezə‖'lɪkwɪdaɪzə/ *n*, *chiefly Br* a domestic electric appliance for grinding, puréeing, liquidizing, or blending foods

liquor /'likə‖'lɪkə/ *n* a liquid substance: e g **a** a solution of a drug in water **b** BATH 2c **c** a liquid, esp water, in which food has been cooked **d** *chiefly NAm* a usu distilled rather than fermented alcoholic drink

liquorice /'likərish, -ris‖'lɪkərɪʃ, -rɪs/ *n* **1** a European leguminous plant having spikes of blue flowers and grown for its roots **2** the dried root of liquorice; *also* an extract of this used esp in medicine, brewing, and confectionery [Old French *licorice*, deriv of Greek *glykyrrhiza*, fr *glykys* sweet + *rhiza* root]

lira /'liərə‖'lɪərə/ *n*, *pl (1)* **lire** *also* **liras**, *(2)* **liras** *also* **lire** **1** the standard unit of money in Italy **2** the standard unit of money in Turkey

lisle /liel‖laɪl/ *n* a smooth tightly twisted thread usu made of cotton [*Lisle*, former name of Lille, city in N France]

¹lisp /lisp‖lɪsp/ *vi* **1** to pronounce /s/ and /z/ imperfectly, esp by giving them the sounds of /th/ and /dh/ **2** to speak with a lisp – **lisper** *n*

²lisp *n* a speech defect or affectation characterized by lisping

lissom, lissome /'lis(ə)m‖'lɪs(ə)m/ *adj* easily flexed; lithe, nimble

¹list /list‖lɪst/ *n* **1** a band or strip of material; *esp* a selvage **2** *pl but sing or pl in constr* **2a** (the fence surrounding) a tiltyard **b** a scene of competition

²list *n* a roll or catalogue of words or numbers (e g representing people or objects belonging to a class), usu arranged in order so as to be easily found

³list *vt* **1** to make a list of **2** to include on a list; *specif, Br* to include (a building) in an official list as being of architectural or historical importance and hence protected from demolition

⁴list *vb* to (cause to) lean to one side – **list** *n*

¹listen /'lis(ə)n‖'lɪs(ə)n/ *vi* **1** to pay attention to sound <~ *to music*> **2** to hear or consider with thoughtful attention; heed **3** to be alert to catch an expected sound – **listener** *n*

²listen *n* an act of listening – infml

listen in *vi* to tune in to or monitor a broadcast – **listener-in** *n*

listless /'listlis‖'lɪstlɪs/ *adj* characterized by indifference, lack of energy, and disinclination for exertion; languid – **listlessly** *adv*, **listlessness** *n*

lit /lit‖lɪt/ *past of* LIGHT

litany /'lit(ə)n·i‖'lɪt(ə)nɪ/ *n* a prayer consisting of a series of petitions by the leader with alternate responses by the congregation

litchi, lichee /'liechee, -'-‖'laɪtʃiː, -'-/ *n* (a Chinese tree that bears) an oval fruit that has a hard scaly outer covering and a small hard seed surrounded by edible pulp

liter /'leetə‖'liːtə/ *n*, *NAm* a litre

literacy /'lit(ə)rəsi‖'lɪt(ə)rəsɪ/ *n* the quality or state of being literate

¹literal /'lit(ə)rəl‖'lɪt(ə)rəl/ *adj* **1a** according with the exact letter of a written text; *specif* according with the letter of the scriptures **b** having the factual or ordinary construction or primary meaning of a term or expression; actual **c** characterized by a lack of imagination; prosaic **2** of or expressed in letters **3** reproduced word for word; exact, verbatim – **literalness, literality** *n*, **literally** *adv*

²literal *n* a misprint involving a single letter

literary /'lit(ə)rəri‖'lɪt(ə)rərɪ/ *adj* **1a** of, being, or concerning literature **b** characteristic of or being in a formal, rather than colloquial, style **2a** well-read **b** producing, well versed in, or connected with literature – **literarily** *adv*, **literariness** *n*

¹literate /'lit(ə)rət‖'lɪt(ə)rət/ *adj* **1a** educated, cultured **b** able to read and write **2** versed in literature or creative writing – **literately** *adv*, **literateness** *n*

[2]**literate** *n* a literate person
literati /ˌlitəˈrahti‖ˌlɪtəˈrɑːtɪ/ *n pl* the educated class; the intelligentsia
literature /ˈlit(ə)rəchə‖ˈlɪt(ə)rətʃə/ *n* **1a** writings in prose or verse; *esp* writings having artistic value or expression and expressing ideas of permanent or universal interest **b** the body of writings on a particular subject <*scientific* ~> **c** printed matter (e g leaflets or circulars) **2** the body of musical compositions <*the piano* ~ *of Brahms*>
lithe /liedh‖laɪð/ *adj* flexible, supple – **lithely** *adv*, **litheness** *n*
lithium /ˈlithi·əm‖ˈlɪθɪəm/ *n* a soft silver-white element of the alkali metal group that is the lightest metal known
lithograph /ˈlithəˌgrahf, -ˌgraf‖ˈlɪθəˌgrɑːf, -ˌgræf/ *vt or n* (to produce or copy in the form of) a print made by lithography – **lithographic** *adj*, **lithographically** *adv*
lithography /liˈthogrəfi‖lɪˈθɒgrəfɪ/ *n* the process of printing from a surface (e g a stone or a metal plate) on which the image to be printed is ink-receptive and the blank area ink-repellent [deriv of Greek *lithos* stone + *graphein* to write]
litigate /ˈlitigayt‖ˈlɪtɪgeɪt/ *vi* to carry on a lawsuit ~*vt* to contest (an issue) at law – **litigable** *adj*, **litigant** *n or adj*, **litigation** *n*
litigious /liˈtijəs‖lɪˈtɪdʒəs/ *adj* **1** (excessively) inclined to engage in lawsuits **2** subject to litigation **3** tending to argue; disputatious – fml – **litigiously** *adv*, **litigiousness** *n*
litmus /ˈlitməs‖ˈlɪtməs/ *n* a colouring matter from lichens that turns red in acid solutions and blue in alkaline solutions and is used as an acid-alkali indicator
ˈlitmus ˌpaper *n* absorbent paper coloured with litmus and used as an indicator
litotes /ˈlietəˌteez, ˈli-, lieˈtohteez‖ˈlaɪtəˌtiːz, ˈlɪ-, laɪˈtəʊtiːz/ *n, pl* **litotes** /~‖~/ understatement in which an affirmative is expressed by the negative of its opposite (e g in 'not a bad singer')
litre, *NAm chiefly* **liter** /ˈleetə‖ˈliːtə/ *n* a metric unit of capacity equal to about 0.220gal
[1]**litter** /ˈlitə‖ˈlɪtə/ *n* **1a** a covered and curtained couch carried by people or animals **b** a stretcher or other device for carrying a sick or injured person **2a** material used as bedding for animals **b** the uppermost slightly decayed layer of organic matter on the forest floor **3** a group of offspring of an animal, born at 1 birth **4a** rubbish or waste products, esp in a public place **b** an untidy accumulation of objects (e g papers) – **littery** *adj*
[2]**litter** *vt* **1** to provide (e g a horse) with litter as a bed **2** to give birth to (young) **3a** to strew with litter, esp scattered articles <~ *the horse's stall*> <~ *the desk-top with papers*> **b** to scatter about in disorder ~ *vi* **1** to give birth to a litter **2** to strew litter
litterateur *also* **littérateur** /ˌlitərəˈtuh‖ˌlɪtərəˈtɜː (*Fr* literatœːr)/ *n* a literary man; *esp* a professional writer
ˈlitterˌlout /-ˌlowt‖-ˌlaʊt/ *n* one who carelessly drops rubbish in public places – infml
[1]**little** /ˈlitl‖ˈlɪtl/ *adj* **littler** /ˈlitlə‖ˈlɪtlə/, **less** /les‖les/, **lesser** /ˈlesə‖ˈlesə/; **littlest** /ˈlitlist‖ˈlɪtlɪst/, **least** /leest‖liːst/ **1a** amounting to only a small quantity <*had* ~ *or no time*> **b** *of a plant or animal* small in comparison with related forms – used in vernacular names **c** small in condition, distinction, or scope **d** narrow, mean <*the pettiness of* ~ *minds*> **2** not much: e g **2a** existing only in a small amount or to a slight degree <*unfortunately he has* ~ *money*> **b** short in duration; brief <*wait a* ~ *while*> **c** existing to an appreciable though not extensive degree or amount – + *a* <*fortunately she had a* ~ *money in the bank*> **3** small in importance or interest; trivial – **littleness** *n*
[2]**little** *adv* **less** /les‖les/; **least** /leest‖liːst/ **1** to no great degree or extent; not much <*little-known*> **2** not at all <*cared* ~ *for his neighbours*>
[3]**little** *n* **1a** only a small portion or quantity; not much <*understood* ~ *of his speech*> <*do what* ~ *I can*> **b** at least some, though not much – + *a* <*have a* ~ *of this cake*> **2** a short time or distance <*walk for a* ~> – **a little** somewhat, rather <a little *over 50 years*> <*found the play* a little *boring*>
ˌlittle ˈfinger *n* the fourth and smallest finger of the hand counting the index finger as the first
ˈlittle ˌpeople *n pl* imaginary beings (e g fairies, elves, etc) of folklore – + *the*
ˌlittle ˈtoe *n* the outermost and smallest digit of the foot
ˌlittle ˈwoman *n* one's wife – humor; often derog
[1]**littoral** /ˈlitərəl‖ˈlɪtərəl/ *adj* of or occurring on or near a (sea) shore
[2]**littoral** *n* a coastal region
liturgical /liˈtuhjikl‖lɪˈtɜːdʒɪkl/ *adj* **1** (having the characteristics) of liturgy **2** using or favouring the use of liturgy – **liturgically** *adv*
liturgy /ˈlitəji‖ˈlɪtədʒɪ/ *n* **1** *often cap* the form of service used in the celebration of Communion, esp in the Orthodox church **2** a prescribed form of public worship
livable *also* **liveable** /ˈlivəbl‖ˈlɪvəbl/ *adj* **1** suitable for living in or with **2** endurable – **livableness** *n*
[1]**live** /liv‖lɪv/ *vi* **1** to be alive; have the life of an animal or plant **2** to continue alive <*his illness is so serious, he is lucky to* ~> **3** to maintain oneself; subsist <*she* ~d *by writing*> <*he* ~d *by his wits*> **4** to conduct or pass one's life <~d *only for her work*> **5** to occupy a home; dwell <*they had always* ~d *in the country*> **6** to attain eternal life <*though he were dead, yet shall he* ~ – Jn 11:25 (AV)> **7** to have a life rich in experience <*the right to* ~, *not merely to exist*> **8** to cohabit – + *together* or *with* **9** *chiefly Br, of a thing* to be found in a specified place, esp normally or usually – infml ~ *vt* **1** to pass, spend, or experience **2** to enact, practise <~ *a lie*> <*really* ~s *her faith*> – **live in sin** to cohabit – **live it up** to enjoy an exciting or extravagant social life or social occasion – **live up to** to act or be in accordance with (esp a standard expected by sby)
[2]**live** /liev‖laɪv/ *adj* **1** having life **2** containing living organisms <~ *yoghourt*> **3** exerting force or containing energy: e g **3a** glowing <~ *coals*> **b** connected to electric power **c** *of ammunition, bombs, etc* unexploded, unfired **d**

driven by or imparting motion or power **e** *of a nuclear reactor or nuclear bomb* charged with material capable of undergoing fission **4** of continuing or current interest <*~ issues*> **5** *esp of a rock* not quarried or cut; native **6** in play in a game <*a ~ ball*> **7a** of or involving the presence or participation of real people <*a ~ audience*> <*~ music*> **b** broadcast while happening <*a ~ television programme*>

[3]**live** /liev‖laɪv/ *adv* during, from, or at a live production

live down /liv‖lɪv/ *vt* to cause (e g a crime or mistake) to be forgotten, esp by future good behaviour

live in /liv‖lɪv/ *vi* to live in one's place of work <*the housekeeper is required to* live in>

livelihood /ˈlievli͵hood‖ˈlaɪvlɪ͵hʊd/ *n* a means of support or sustenance [Middle English *livelode* course of life, fr Old English *līflād*, fr *līf* life + *lād* course]

livelong /ˈliv͵long‖ˈlɪv͵lɒŋ/ *adj* whole, entire – chiefly poetic <*the ~ day*> [Middle English *lef long*, fr *lef* dear + *long*]

lively /ˈlievli‖ˈlaɪvlɪ/ *adj* **1** briskly alert and energetic; vigorous, animated <*a ~ discussion*> <*~ children racing home from school*> **2** brilliant, vivid <*a ~ flashing wit*> <*a ~ colour*> **3** quick to rebound; resilient **4** responding readily to the helm <*a ~ boat*> **5** full of life, movement, or incident <*the crowded streets made a ~ scene*> **6** full of possibly disagreeable or dangerous action – humor <*given a ~ time by enemy artillery*> – **livelily** *adv*, **liveliness** *n*, **lively** *adv*

liven /ˈliev(ə)n‖ˈlaɪv(ə)n/ *vb* to make or become lively – often + *up*

live out /liv‖lɪv/ *vi* to live outside one's place of work ~*vt* to live till the end of <*will the sick man* live out *the month?*>

[1]**liver** /ˈlivə‖ˈlɪvə/ *n* **1a** a large vascular glandular organ of vertebrates that secretes bile and causes changes in the blood (e g by converting blood sugar into glycogen) **b** any of various large digestive glands of invertebrates **2** the liver of an animal (e g a calf or pig) eaten as food **3** a greyish reddish brown **4** *archaic* the seat of the emotions

[2]**liver** *n* one who lives, esp in a specified way <*a clean ~*>

liverish /ˈlivərish‖ˈlɪvərɪʃ/ *adj* **1** suffering from liver disorder; bilious **2** peevish, irascible; *also* glum – **liverishness** *n*

ˈ**liver** ͵**sausage** *n* a sausage consisting chiefly of cooked minced liver often with pork trimmings

[1]**livery** /ˈlivəri‖ˈlɪvərɪ/ *n* **1a** the distinctive clothing worn by a member of a livery company or guild **b** the uniform of servants employed by an individual or a single household **c** distinctive colouring or marking; *also* distinctive dress **d** a distinctive colour scheme (e g on aircraft) distinguishing an organization or group **2** the legal delivering of property **3** *chiefly NAm* LIVERY STABLE – **liveried** *adj*

[2]**livery** *adj* liverish

ˈ**livery** ͵**company** *n* any of various London craft or trade associations that are descended from medieval guilds

ˈ**liveryman** /-mən‖-mən/ *n* a freeman of the City of London who is a member of a livery company

ˈ**livery** ͵**stable** *n* an establishment where horses are stabled and fed for their owners

lives /lievz‖laɪvz/ *pl of* LIFE

ˈ**live**͵**stock** /-͵stok‖-͵stɒk/ *n* **1** animals kept or raised for use or pleasure; *esp* farm animals kept for use and profit **2** *Br* small verminous creatures (e g lice or fleas) – chiefly humor

͵**live** ˈ**wire** /ˈliev‖ˈlaɪv/ *n* an alert, active, or aggressive person

livid /ˈlivid‖ˈlɪvɪd/ *adj* **1** discoloured by bruising **2** ashen, pallid **3** reddish **4** very angry; enraged <*was ~ at his son's disobedience*> – **lividness** *n*, **lividity** *n*

[1]**living** /ˈliving‖ˈlɪvɪŋ/ *adj* **1a** having life; alive **b** existing in use <*a ~ language*> **2** [2]LIVE 3a **3a** true to life; exact – esp in *the living image of* **b** suited for living <*the ~ area*> **4** – used as an intensive <*scared the ~ daylights out of him*> **5** *of feelings, ideas, etc* full of power and force <*in ~ colour*> – **livingness** *n*

[2]**living** *n* **1** the condition of being alive **2** a manner of life **3a** means of subsistence; a livelihood <*earning a ~*> **b** *Br* a benefice

͵**living** ˈ**death** *n* a life so full of misery that death would be preferable

ˈ**living** ͵**room** *n* a room in a residence used for everyday activities

ˈ**living** ͵**standard** *n* STANDARD OF LIVING

͵**living** ˈ**wage** *n* **1** a subsistence wage **2** a wage sufficient to provide an acceptable standard of living

lizard /ˈlizəd‖ˈlɪzəd/ *n* any of a suborder of reptiles distinguished from the snakes by 2 pairs of well differentiated functional limbs (which may be lacking in burrowing forms), external ears, and eyes with movable lids

'll /-l‖-l/ *vb* will, shall <*you*'ll *be late*>

llama /ˈlahmə‖ˈlɑːmə/ *n* any of several wild and domesticated S American ruminant mammals related to the camels but smaller and without a hump

lo /loh‖ləʊ/ *interj, archaic* – used to call attention or to express wonder or surprise

[1]**load** /lohd‖ləʊd/ *n* **1a** an amount, esp large or heavy, that is (to be) carried, supported, or borne; a burden **b** the quantity that can be carried at 1 time by a specified means – often in combination <*a boat*load *of tourists*> **2** the forces to which a structure is subjected <*the ~ on the arch*> **3** a burden of responsibility, anxiety, etc <*took a ~ off her mind*> **4** external resistance overcome by a machine or other source of power **5a** power output (e g of a power plant) **b** a device to which power is delivered **6** the amount of work to be performed by a person, machine, etc **7** a large quantity or amount; a lot – usu pl with sing. meaning; infml <*there's ~s of room on the back seat*> – **get a load of** to pay attention to (sthg surprising) – slang

[2]**load** *vt* **1a** to put a load in or on <*~ a van with furniture*> **b** to place in or on a means of conveyance <*~ cargo*> **2** to encumber or oppress with sthg heavy, laborious, or disheartening; burden <*a company ~ed down with debts*> **3a** to weight or shape (dice) to fall unfairly **b** to

charge with one-sided or prejudicial influences; bias **c** to charge with emotional associations or hidden implications <*a* ~ed *statement*> **4a** to put a load or charge in (a device or piece of equipment) < ~ *a gun*> **b** to place or insert in a device or piece of equipment < ~ *a film in a camera*> **5** to affect, often adversely, (the output of a preceding stage of an electrical circuit) ~ *vi* **1** to receive a load **2** to put a load on or in a carrier, device, or container; *esp* to insert the charge in a firearm – **loader** *n*

ˈ**loaded** *adj* having a large amount of money – infml

ˈ**load,star** /-ˌstah‖-ˌstɑː/ *n* a lodestar

ˈ**load,stone** /-ˌstohn‖-ˌstəʊn/ *n* (a) lodestone

[1]**loaf** /lohf‖ləʊf/ *n, pl* **loaves** /lohvz‖ləʊvz/ **1** a mass of bread often having a regular shape and standard weight **2** a shaped or moulded often symmetrical mass of food (e g sugar or chopped cooked meat) **3** *Br* head, brains – slang; esp in *use one's loaf* [Old French *hlāf*; sense 3 fr rhyming slang *loaf (of bread)* head]

[2]**loaf** *vi* to spend time in idleness

loafer /ˈlohfə‖ˈləʊfə/ *n* **1** one who loafs **2** *chiefly NAm* a low leather shoe similar to a moccasin but with a broad flat heel

loam /lohm‖ləʊm/ *n* [3]SOIL 2a; *specif* crumbly soil consisting of a mixture of clay, silt, and sand – **loamy** *adj*

[1]**loan** /lohn‖ləʊn/ *n* **1a** money lent at interest **b** sthg lent, usu for the borrower's temporary use **2** the grant of temporary use

[2]**loan** *vt* to lend < ~ed *to the gallery by an unnamed owner*> – **loanable** *adj*

ˌ**lo and beˈhold** /loh‖ləʊ/ *interj* – used to express wonder or surprise

ˈ**loan,word** /-ˌwuhd‖-ˌwɜːd/ *n* a word taken from another language and at least partly naturalized

loath, **loth** /lohth‖ləʊθ/ *also* **loathe** /lohdh‖ləʊð/ *adj* unwilling *to* do sthg disliked; reluctant

loathe /lohdh‖ləʊð/ *vt* to dislike greatly, often with disgust or intolerance; detest – **loather** *n*

loathing /ˈlohdhing‖ˈləʊðɪŋ/ *n* extreme disgust; detestation

loathsome /ˈlohdhs(ə)m, ˈlohth-‖ˈləʊðs(ə)m, ˈləʊθ-/ *adj* giving rise to loathing; disgusting – **loathsomely** *adv*, **loathsomeness** *n*

loaves /lohvz‖ləʊvz/ *pl of* LOAF

[1]**lob** /lob‖lɒb/ *vb* **-bb-** *vt* **1** to throw, hit, or propel easily or in a high arc **2** to hit a lob against (an opponent, esp in tennis) ~ *vi* to hit a ball easily in a high arc, esp in tennis, squash, etc

[2]**lob** *n* a ball that is lobbed

[1]**lobby** /ˈlobi‖ˈlɒbɪ/ *n* **1** a porch or small entrance hall **2** an anteroom of a legislative chamber to which members go to vote during a division **3** *sing or pl in constr* a group of people engaged in lobbying

[2]**lobby** *vi* to try to influence members of a legislative body towards an action ~ *vt* **1** to secure the passage of (legislation) by influencing public officials **2** to try to influence (e g a member of a legislative body) towards an action – **lobbyer** *n*, **lobbyist** *n*

lobe /lohb‖ləʊb/ *n* a curved or rounded projection or division; *esp* such a projection or division of a bodily organ or part – **lobed** *adj*, **lobar** *adj*, **lobate, lobated** *adj*

lobotomy /ləˈbotəmi, loh-‖ləˈbɒtəmɪ, ləʊ-/ *n* a brain operation used, esp formerly, in the treatment of some mental disorders (e g violent psychoses) in which nerve fibres in the cerebral cortex are cut in order to change behaviour – **lobotomize** *vt*

lobster /ˈlobstə‖ˈlɒbstə/ *n* any of a family of large edible 10-legged marine crustaceans that have stalked eyes, a pair of large claws, and a long abdomen

ˈ**lobster ˌpot** *n* (a basket used as) a trap for catching lobsters

lobule /ˈlobyoohl‖ˈlɒbjuːl/ *n* (a subdivision of) a small lobe

[1]**local** /ˈlohk(ə)l‖ˈləʊk(ə)l/ *adj* **1** characterized by or relating to position in space **2** (characteristic) of or belonging to a particular place; not general or widespread < ~ *news*> **3a** primarily serving the needs of a particular limited district < ~ *government*> **b** *of a public conveyance* making all the stops on a route **4** involving or affecting only a restricted part of a living organism – **locally** *adv*

[2]**local** *n* a local person or thing <*spoke to the friendly* ~s>: e g **a** *Br the* neighbourhood pub **b** *NAm* a local public conveyance (e g a train or bus)

ˌ**local ˈcolour** *n* the description in a literary work of the features and peculiarities of a particular locality and its inhabitants

locale /lohˈkahl‖ləʊˈkɑːl/ *n* a place or locality, esp when viewed in relation to a particular event or characteristic; a scene

locality /lohˈkaləti‖ləʊˈkælətɪ/ *n* **1** the fact or condition of having a location in space or time **2** a particular place, situation, or location

local·ize, -ise /ˈlok(ə)lˌiez‖ˈlɒk(ə)lˌaɪz/ *vt* **1** to give local characteristics to **2** to assign to or keep within a definite locality ~ *vi* to collect in a specific or limited area – **localization** *n*

locate /lohˈkayt‖ləʊˈkeɪt/ *vt* **1** to determine or indicate the place, site, or limits of **2** to set or establish in a particular spot – **locatable** *adj*, **locater** *n*

location /lohˈkaysh(ə)n‖ləʊˈkeɪʃ(ə)n/ *n* **1** a particular place or position **2** a place outside a studio where a (part of a) picture is filmed – usu in *on location* – **locational** *adj*, **locationally** *adv*

loch /lokh‖lɒx/ *n* a lake or (nearly landlocked) arm of the sea in Scotland

loci /ˈlohsi‖ˈləʊsɪ; *also* lohki‖ləʊkɪ/ *pl of* LOCUS

[1]**lock** /lok‖lɒk/ *n* **1** a curl, tuft, etc of hair **2** *pl* the hair of the head

[2]**lock** *n* **1a** a fastening that can be opened and often closed only by means of a particular key or combination **b** a gunlock **2a** an enclosed section of waterway (e g a canal) which has gates at each end and in which the water level can be raised or lowered to move boats from one level to another **b** AIR LOCK **3a** a locking or fastening together **b** a hold in wrestling secured on a usu specified body part **4** *chiefly Br* the (maximum) extent to which the front wheels of a vehicle are turned to change the direction of travel

[3]**lock** *vt* **1a** to fasten the lock of **b** to make fast (as if) with a lock < ~ *up the house*> **2a** to shut in or out or make secure or inaccessible (as

if) by means of locks <~ed *himself away from the curious world*> **b** to hold fast or inactive; fix in a particular situation or method of operation **3a** to make fast by the interlacing or interlocking of parts **b** to hold in a close embrace **c** to grapple in combat; *also* to bind closely – often pass <*administration and students were* ~ed *in conflict*> **4** to move or permit (e g a ship) to pass by raising or lowering in a lock ~*vi* to become locked – **lockable** *adj*

locker /ˈlokə‖ˈlɒkə/ *n* **1** a cupboard or compartment that may be closed with a lock; *esp* one for individual storage use **2** a chest or compartment on board ship

locket /ˈlokit‖ˈlɒkɪt/ *n* a small case usu of precious metal that has space for a memento (e g a small picture) and is usu worn on a chain round the neck

lockjaw /ˈlok,jaw‖ˈlɒk,dʒɔː/ *n* an early symptom of tetanus characterized by spasm of the jaw muscles and inability to open the jaws; *also* tetanus

ˈlock,keeper /-,keepə‖-,kiːpə/ *n* sby who looks after a canal or river lock

ˈlock,nut /-,nut‖-,nʌt/ *n* **1** a nut screwed hard up against another to prevent either of them from moving **2** a nut so constructed that it locks itself when screwed up tight

ˈlock,out /-,owt‖-,aʊt/ *n* a whole or partial closing of a business by an employer in order to gain concessions from or resist demands of employees

lock out *vt* to subject (a body of employees) to a lockout

ˈlock,smith /-,smith‖-,smɪθ/ *n* sby who makes or mends locks as an occupation

ˈlock,stitch /-,stich‖-,stɪtʃ/ *n* a sewing machine stitch formed by the looping together of 2 threads, 1 on each side of the material being sewn – **lockstitch** *vb*

ˈlock,up /-,up‖-,ʌp/ *n* **1** (the time of) locking; the state of being locked **2** a (small local) prison **3** *Br* a lock-up shop or garage

ˈlock-,up *adj, Br, of a building* (able to be) locked up and left when not in use

[1]loco /ˈlohkoh‖ˈləʊkəʊ/ *n, pl* **locos** a locomotive

[2]loco *adj, chiefly NAm* out of one's mind – slang

locomotion /,lohkəˈmohsh(ə)n‖,ləʊkəˈməʊʃ(ə)n/ *n* **1** an act or the power of moving from place to place **2** TRAVEL 1, 2a [Latin *locus* place + English *motion*]

[1]locomotive /,lohkəˈmohtiv‖,ləʊkəˈməʊtɪv/ *adj* **1** of or functioning in locomotion **2** of travel **3** moving, or able to move, by self-propulsion

[2],locoˈmotive *n* an engine that moves under its own power; *esp* one that moves railway carriages and wagons

locum /ˈlohkəm‖ˈləʊkəm/ *n* sby filling an office for a time or temporarily taking the place of another – used esp with reference to a doctor or clergyman [short for *locum tenens*, fr Medieval Latin, lit., one holding a place]

locus /ˈlohkəs, ˈlokəs‖ˈləʊkəs, ˈlɒkəs/ *n, pl* **loci** /ˈlohsie, ˈlohsi‖ˈləʊsaɪ, ˈləʊsɪ; *also* ˈlohkie, ˈlohki‖ˈləʊkaɪ, ˈləʊkɪ/ *also* **locuses** **1** a place, locality **2** the set of all points whose location is determined by stated conditions **3** the position on a chromosome of a particular gene or allele

,locus ˈclassicus /ˈklasikəs‖ˈklæsɪkəs/ *n, pl* **loci classici** /ˈklasiki, -kie‖ˈklæsɪkɪ, -kaɪ/ the best-known and most authoritative passage or work on a particular subject

locust /ˈlohkəst‖ˈləʊkəst/ *n* **1** a migratory grasshopper that often travels in vast swarms stripping the areas passed of all vegetation **2** any of various hard-wooded leguminous trees; *esp* a carob

locution /lohˈkyoohsh(ə)n, lə-‖ləʊˈkjuːʃ(ə)n, lə-/ *n* **1** a word or expression characteristic of a region, group, or cultural level **2** phraseology

lode /lohd‖ləʊd/ *n* an ore deposit

lodestar, loadstar /ˈlohd,stah‖ˈləʊd,stɑː/ *n* **1** a star that guides; *esp* POLE STAR **2** sthg that serves as a guiding star

ˈlode,stone, loadstone /-,stohn‖-,stəʊn/ *n* **1** (a piece of) magnetized mineral iron oxide **2** sthg that strongly attracts; a magnet

[1]lodge /loj‖lɒdʒ/ *vt* **1a** to provide temporary, esp rented, accommodation for **b** to establish or settle in a place **2** to serve as a receptacle for; contain, house **3** to beat (e g a crop) flat to the ground **4** to fix in place **5** to deposit for safeguard or preservation <~ *your money in the nearest bank*> **6** to place or vest (e g power), esp in a source, means, or agent **7** to lay (e g a complaint) before authority ~ *vi* **1a** to occupy a place, esp temporarily **b** to be a lodger **2** to come to rest; settle <*the bullet* ~d *in his chest*> **3** *esp of hay or grain crops* to fall or lie down

[2]lodge *n* **1** the meeting place of a branch of an esp fraternal organization **2** a house set apart for residence in a particular season (e g the hunting season) **3a** a house orig for the use of a gamekeeper, caretaker, porter, etc **b** a porter's room (e g at the entrance to a college, block of flats, etc) **c** the house where the head of a university college lives, esp in Cambridge **4** a den or lair of an animal or a group of animals (e g beavers or otters) **5** a wigwam

lodger /ˈlojə‖ˈlɒdʒə/ *n* one who occupies a rented room in another's house

lodging /ˈlojing‖ˈlɒdʒɪŋ/ *n* **1** a place to live; a dwelling **2a** a temporary place to stay <*a* ~ *for the night*> **b** a rented room or rooms for residing in, usu in a private house rather than a hotel – usu pl with sing. meaning

ˈlodging ,house *n* a house where lodgings are provided and let

loess /ˈloh·is, les‖ˈləʊɪs, les/ *n* a usu yellowish brown loamy deposit found in Europe, Asia, and N America and believed to be chiefly deposited by the wind – **loessial**

[1]loft /loft‖lɒft/ *n* **1** an attic **2a** a gallery in a church or hall **b** an upper floor in a barn or warehouse used for storage – sometimes in combination <*a hay*loft> **c** a shed or coop for pigeons **3** the backward slant of the face of a golf-club head **4** *NAm* an upper room or floor

[2]loft *vt* to propel through the air or into space <~ed *the ball over midwicket*>

lofty /ˈlofti‖ˈlɒftɪ/ *adj* **1** having a haughty overbearing manner; supercilious **2a** elevated in character and spirit; noble **b** elevated in position; superior **3** rising to a great height; impressively high <~ *mountains*> – **loftily** *adv*, **loftiness** *n*

[1]**log** /log‖lɒg/ *n* **1** a usu bulky piece or length of unshaped timber (ready for sawing or for use as firewood) **2** an apparatus for measuring the rate of a ship's motion through the water **3a** the record of the rate of a ship's speed or of her daily progress; *also* the full nautical record of a ship's voyage **b** the full record of a flight by an aircraft **4** any of various records of performance <*a computer* ~>

[2]**log** *vb* **-gg-** *vt* **1** to cut (trees) for timber **2** to enter details of or about in a log **3a** to move or attain (e g an indicated distance, speed, or time) as noted in a log **b(1)** to sail a ship or fly an aircraft for (an indicated distance or period of time) **b(2)** to have (an indicated record) to one's credit; achieve <~ged *about 30,000 miles a year in his car*> ~*vi* to cut logs for timber

[3]**log** *n* a logarithm

loganberry /'lohgənb(ə)ri, -ˌberi‖'ləʊgən -b(ə)rɪ, -ˌberɪ/ *n* (the red sweet edible berry of) an upright-growing raspberry hybrid [James H *Logan* (1841-1928), US lawyer]

logarithm /'logəˌridh(ə)m‖'lɒgəˌrɪð(ə)m/ *n* the exponent that indicates the power to which a number is raised to produce a given number [deriv of Greek *logos* speech, reason + Greek *arithmos* number] – **logarithmic** *adj*, **logarithmically** *adv*

'**logˌbook** /-ˌbook‖-ˌbʊk/ *n* **1** LOG 3, 4 **2** *Br* a document held with a motor vehicle that gives the vehicle's registration number, make, engine size, etc and a list of its owners – not now used technically

logger /'logə‖'lɒgə/ *n*, *NAm* a lumberjack

loggerhead /'logəˌhed‖'lɒgəˌhed/ *n* any of various very large marine turtles – **at loggerheads** in or into a state of quarrelsome disagreement

loggia /'loj(i)ə‖'lɒdʒ(ɪ)ə/ *n*, *pl* **loggias** *also* **loggie** /'lojie‖'lɒdʒaɪ/ a roofed open gallery behind a colonnade or arcade

logic /'lojik‖'lɒdʒɪk/ *n* **1a(1)** a science that deals with the formal principles and structure of thought and reasoning **a(2)** a specified branch or system of logic **b** a particular mode of reasoning viewed as valid or faulty <*couldn't follow his* ~> **c** the interrelation or sequence of facts or events when seen as inevitable or predictable **d** the fundamental principles and the connection of circuit elements for performing Boolean operations (e g those needed for arithmetical computation) in a computer; *also* the circuits themselves **2** sthg that forces a decision apart from or in opposition to reason <*the* ~ *of war*> – **logician** *n*

logical /'lojikl‖'lɒdʒɪkl/ *adj* **1** of or conforming with logic <*a* ~ *argument*> **2** capable of reasoning or of using reason in an orderly fashion <*a* ~ *thinker*> – **logically** *adv*, **logicalness, logicality** *n*

logistics /lo'jistiks, lə-‖lɒ'dʒɪstɪks, lə-/ *n pl but sing or pl in constr* **1** the aspect of military science dealing with the transportation, quartering, and supplying of troops in military operations **2** the handling of the details of an operation – **logistic** *adj*, **logistically** *adv*

logjam /'logˌjam‖'lɒgˌdʒæm/ *n*, *chiefly NAm* a deadlock, impasse

logo /'logoh‖'lɒgəʊ/ *n*, *pl* **logos** an identifying symbol (e g for advertising)

logogram /'logəˌgram‖'lɒgəˌgræm/ *n* a character or sign used (e g in shorthand) to represent an entire word – **logogrammatic** *adj*

logrolling /'logˌrohling‖'lɒgˌrəʊlɪŋ/ *n*, *chiefly NAm* the trading of votes by members of a legislature to secure favourable action on projects of mutual interest

-logy /-ləji‖-lədʒɪ/ *comb form* (→ *n*) **1** oral or written expression <*phraseo*logy>; *esp* body of writings of (a specified kind) or on (a specified subject) <*hagio*logy> **2** doctrine; theory; science <*ethno*logy>

loin /loyn‖lɔɪn/ *n* **1a** the part of a human being or quadruped on each side of the spinal column between the hipbone and the lower ribs **b** a cut of meat comprising this part of one or both sides of a carcass with the adjoining half of the vertebrae included **2** *pl* **2a** the upper and lower abdominal regions and the region about the hips **b(1)** the pubic region **b(2)** the genitals

'**loinˌcloth** /-ˌkloth‖-ˌklɒθ/ *n* a cloth worn about the hips and covering the genitals

loiter /'loytə‖'lɔɪtə/ *vi* **1** to remain in an area for no obvious reason; HANG ABOUT **2** to make frequent pauses while travelling; dawdle – **loiterer** *n*

loll /lol‖lɒl/ *vi* **1** to hang down loosely <*his tongue* ~ed *out*> **2** to recline, lean, or move in a lazy or excessively relaxed manner; lounge

lollipop, lollypop /'loliˌpop‖'lɒlɪˌpɒp/ *n* a large often round flat sweet of boiled sugar on the end of a stick

'**lollipop ˌman**, *fem* '**lollipop ˌlady** *n*, *Br* sby controlling traffic to allow (school) children to cross busy roads

lollop /'loləp‖'lɒləp/ *vi* to move or proceed with an ungainly loping motion

lolly /'loli‖'lɒlɪ/ *n* **1** a lollipop or ice lolly **2** *Br* money – infml

lone /lohn‖ləʊn/ *adj* **1** only, sole **2** situated alone or separately; isolated **3** having no company; solitary – fml – **loneness** *n*

lonely /'lohnli‖'ləʊnlɪ/ *adj* **1** cut off from others; solitary **2** not frequented by people; desolate **3** sad from being alone or without friends – **lonelily** *adv*, **loneliness** *n*

ˌ**lonely** '**hearts** *adj* of or for lonely people seeking companions or spouses <*a* ~ *club*>

loner /'lohnə‖'ləʊnə/ *n* a person or animal that prefers solitude

[1]**lonesome** /'lohns(ə)m‖'ləʊns(ə)m/ *adj* **1** lonely **2** LONE 2 – **lonesomely** *adv*, **lonesomeness** *n*

[2]**lonesome** *n* self – infml <*sat all on his* ~>

ˌ**lone** '**wolf** *n* a person who prefers to work, act, or live alone

[1]**long** /long‖lɒŋ/ *adj* **1a** extending for a considerable distance **b** having greater length or height than usual **2a** having a specified length <*6ft* ~> **b** forming the chief linear dimension <*the* ~ *side of the room*> **3** extending over a

considerable or specified time <*a ~ friendship*> <*2 hours ~*> **4** containing a large or specified number of items or units <*a ~ list*> **5a** *of a speech sound or syllable* of relatively long duration **b** being one of a pair of similarly spelt vowel sounds that is longer in duration <~ a *in* fate> **c** bearing a stress or accent **6a** having the capacity to reach or extend a considerable distance <*a ~ left jab*> **b** hit for a considerable distance <*a ~ drive from the tee*> **7** *of betting odds* greatly differing in the amounts wagered on each side **8** subject to great odds <*a ~ chance*> **9** owning or accumulating securities or goods, esp in anticipation of an advance in prices <*they are now ~ on wheat*> – **longish** *adj*, **longness** *n* – **before long** in a short time; soon – **in the long run** in the course of sufficiently prolonged time, trial, or experience – compare IN THE SHORT RUN – **long in the tooth** past one's best days; old – **not by a long chalk** not at all

[2]**long** *adv* **1** for or during a long or specified time <*not ~ returned*> **2** at a point of time far before or after a specified moment or event <*was excited ~ before the big day*> **3** after or beyond a specified time <*said it was no ~er possible*> – **so long** goodbye – infml

[3]**long** *n* a long syllable – **the long and (the) short** the gist; the outline <the long and the short *of it was that we had to walk home*>

[4]**long** *vi* to feel a strong desire or craving, esp *for* sthg not likely to be attained

'long,boat /-,boht‖-,bəʊt/ *n* the largest boat carried by a sailing vessel

'long,bow /-,boh‖-,bəʊ/ *n* a long wooden bow for shooting arrows, specif that used in medieval England that was about 6ft (1.8m) long, was made of yew or ash, and was drawn by hand

[1]**,long-'distance** *adj* **1** covering or effective over a long distance **2** *of telephone communication* between points a long distance apart

[2]**long-distance** *adv* by long-distance telephone

,long di'vision *n* arithmetical division in which the calculations corresponding to the division of parts of the dividend by the divisor are written out

,long-,drawn-'out *adj* extended to a great length; protracted

longevity /lon'jevəti‖lɒn'dʒevətɪ; *also* long-'gevəti‖lɒŋ'gevətɪ/ *n* (great) length of life [Late Latin *longaevitas*, fr Latin *longaevus* long-lived, fr *longus* long + *aevum* age]

'long,hair /-,heə‖-,heə/ *n* a person with, or usu thought of as having, long hair; e g **a** a hippie **b** sby of an artistic, esp avant-garde, temperament **c** an unworldly intellectual – **long-hair, long-haired** *adj*

'long,hand /-,hand‖-,hænd/ *n* ordinary writing; handwriting

,long 'haul *n* **1** a lengthy usu difficult period of time **2** the transport of goods over long distances – **long-haul** *adj*

'long ,hop *n* an easily hit short-pitched delivery of a cricket ball

longing /'long·ing‖'lɒŋɪŋ/ *n* a strong desire, esp for sthg difficult to attain – **longingly** *adv*

longitude /'lonjityoohd‖'lɒndʒɪtju:d; *also* 'long·gi,tyoohd‖'lɒŋgɪ,tju:d/ *n* the (time difference corresponding to) angular distance of a point on the surface of a celestial body, esp the earth, measured E or W from a prime meridian (e g that of Greenwich)

,longi'tudinal /-'tyoohdinl‖-'tju:dɪnl/ *adj* **1** of length or the lengthways dimension **2** placed or running lengthways – **longitudinally** *adv*

'long ,johns /jonz‖dʒɒnz/ *n pl* underpants with legs extending usu down to the ankles – infml

'long ,jump *n* (an athletic field event consisting of) a jump for distance from a running start – **long jumper** *n*

,long-'lived /livd‖lɪvd/ *adj* **1** characterized by long life <*a ~ family*> **2** long-lasting, enduring – **long-livedness** *n*

,long-'range *adj* **1** involving or taking into account a long period of time <~ *planning*> **2** relating to or fit for long distances <~ *rockets*>

'long ,run *n* a relatively long period of time – usu in *in the long run* – **long-run** *adj*

'long,ship /-,ship‖-,ʃɪp/ *n* a long open ship propelled by oars and a sail and used by the Vikings principally to carry warriors

'long,shoreman /-,shawmən‖-,ʃɔ:mən/ *n, chiefly NAm* a docker

'long ,shot *n* **1** (a bet at long odds on) a competitor given little chance of winning **2** a venture that involves considerable risk and has little chance of success – **by a long shot** by a great deal

,long'sighted /-'sietid‖-'saɪtɪd/ *adj* hypermetropic – **longsightedness** *n*

,long-'standing *adj* of long duration

'long ,stop *n* a now little-used fielding position in cricket near the boundary and directly behind the wicketkeeper

,long-'suffering *n or adj* (the quality of) patiently enduring pain, difficulty, or provocation – **long-sufferingly** *adv*

,long-'term *adj* occurring over or involving a relatively long period of time

,long 'ton *n* a British unit of weight equal to 2240lb (about 1016.05kg)

longueur /long'guh ‖lɒŋ'gɜ: (*Fr* lɔ̃gœ:r)/ *n, pl* **longueurs** /long'guh(z) ‖lɒŋ'gɜ:(z) (*Fr* ~)/ a dull and tedious part or period [French, lit., length]

,long va'cation *n* the long summer holiday of British law courts and universities

'long ,wave *n* a band of radio waves typically used for sound broadcasting and covering wavelengths of 1000m or more

'long,ways /-,wayz, wiz‖-,weɪz, wɪz/ *adv* lengthways

,long-'winded /-'windid‖-'wɪndɪd/ *adj* tediously long in speaking or writing – **long-windedly** *adv*, **long-windedness** *n*

longwise /'long,wiez, -wiz‖'lɒŋ,waɪz, -wɪz/ *adv* lengthways

loo *n, chiefly Br* TOILET 2 – infml [perhaps from French *lieu (d'aisance)* toilet or *l'eau* the water]

loofah /'loohfə‖'lu:fə/ *n* a dried seed pod of any of several plants of the cucumber family that is used as a bath sponge

[1]**look** /look‖lʊk/ *vt* **1** to find out or learn by the use of one's eyes <~ *what time it starts*> <~

what you've done!> **2** to regard intensely; examine <~ *him in the eye*> <~ *a gift horse in the mouth*> **3** to express by the eyes or facial expression <~ed *daggers at him*> **4** to have an appearance that befits or accords with <*really* ~ed *the part*> ~ *vi* **1a** to use the power of sight; *esp* to make a visual search *for* **b** to direct one's attention <~ *into the matter*> **c** to direct the eyes <~ *at him!*> **2** to have the appearance of being; appear, seem <~s *very ill*> <~ed *to be crying* – Colin MacInnes> **3** to have a specified outlook <*the house* ~ed *east*> – **look after** to take care of – **look sharp** to be quick; hurry

[2]**look** *n* **1a** the act of looking **b** [2]GLANCE 3 **2a** a facial expression <*she had a funny* ~ *on her face*> **b** (attractive) physical appearance – usu pl with sing. meaning **3** the state or form in which sthg appears <*a new* ~ *in knitwear*> <*has the* ~ *of a loser about him*>

ˈlook-aˌlike *n* sby or sthg that looks like another; a double

look back *vi* **1** to remember – often + *to, on* **2** to fail to make successful progress – in *never look back* <*after his initial success, he never* looked back>

look down *vi* to have an attitude of superiority or contempt – usu + *on* or *upon* <*snobbishly* looks down *on the poor*>

looker /ˈlookə‖ˈlʊkə/ *n* **1** one having an appearance of a specified kind – often in combination <*a good*-looker> **2** an attractive person, esp a woman – infml

ˈlook-ˌin *n* a chance to take part; *also* a chance of success – infml

look in *vi, Br* to pay a short visit <*will* look in *on the party*>

ˈlooking ˌglass /ˈlooking‖ˈlʊkɪŋ/ *n* a mirror

look on *vi* to be a spectator

ˈlookˌout /-ˌowt‖-ˌaʊt/ *n* **1** one engaged in keeping watch **2** a place or structure affording a wide view for observation **3** a careful looking or watching **4** a matter of care or concern <*it's your* ~ *if you do such a silly thing*> **5** *chiefly Br* a future possibility; a prospect

look out *vi* **1** to take care – often imper **2** to keep watching <look out *for your parents*> ~*vt, chiefly Br* to choose by inspection; select <look out *a suit for the interview*>

look over *vt* to examine (quickly) – **lookover** *n*

look up *vi* to improve in prospects or conditions <*business is* looking up> ~ *vt* **1** to search for (as if) in a reference work <look up *a phone number in the directory*> **2** to pay a usu short visit to <looked up *my friend while I was there*> **3** to have an attitude of respect – + *to* <*always* looked up *to their parents*>

[1]**loom** /loohm‖lu:m/ *n* a frame or machine for weaving together yarns or threads into cloth

[2]**loom** *vi* **1** to come into sight indistinctly, in enlarged or distorted and menacing form, often as a result of atmospheric conditions **2a** to appear in an impressively great or exaggerated form **b** to take shape as an impending occurrence <*exams* ~ed *large*>

[1]**loon** /loohn‖lu:n/ *n* a mad or silly person

[2]**loon** *n* any of several large fish-eating diving birds that have the legs placed far back under the body

loony, looney /ˈloohni‖ˈlu:nɪ/ *adj* crazy, foolish – infml – **looniness** *n*, **loony** *n*

ˈloony ˌbin *n* MADHOUSE 1 – humor

[1]**loop** /loohp‖lu:p/ *n* **1** a (partially) closed figure that has a curved outline surrounding a central opening **2a** sthg shaped like a loop **b** a manoeuvre in which an aircraft passes successively through a climb, inverted flight, and a dive, and then returns to normal flight **c** a zigzag-shaped intrauterine contraceptive device **3** a ring or curved piece used to form a fastening or handle **4** a piece of film or magnetic tape whose ends are spliced together so as to reproduce the same material continuously **5** a series of instructions (e g for a computer) that is repeated until a terminating condition is reached

[2]**loop** *vi* **1** to make, form, or move in a loop or loops **2** to execute a loop in an aircraft ~ *vt* **1a** to make a loop in, on, or about **b** to fasten with a loop **2** to join (2 courses of loops) in knitting **3** to form a loop with <~ed *the wool round the knitting needle*> – **loop the loop** to perform a loop in an aircraft

[1]**loophole** /ˈloohpˌhohl‖ˈlu:pˌhəʊl/ *n* **1** a small opening through which missiles, firearms, etc may be discharged or light and air admitted **2** a means of escape; *esp* an ambiguity or omission in a text through which its intent may be evaded

[2]**loophole** *vt* to make loopholes in

[1]**loose** /loohs‖lu:s/ *adj* **1a** not rigidly fastened or securely attached **b** having worked partly free from attachments <*the masonry is* ~ *at the base of the wall*> **c** *of a cough* produced freely and accompanied by rising of mucus **d** not tight-fitting <*a* ~ *cardigan*> **2a** free from a state of confinement, restraint, or obligation <*a lion* ~ *in the streets*> **b** not brought together in a bundle, container, or binding <~ *hair*> **3** not dense, close, or compact in structure or arrangement **4a** lacking in (power of) restraint <*a* ~ *tongue*> <~ *bowels*> **b** dissolute, promiscuous <~ *living*> **5** not tightly drawn or stretched; slack **6a** lacking in precision, exactness, or care <*a* ~ *translation*> **b** permitting freedom of interpretation <*the wording of the document is very* ~> – **loosely** *adv*, **loosen** *vb*, **looseness** *n*

[2]**loose** *vt* **1a** to let loose; release **b** to free from restraint **2** to make loose; untie <~ *a knot*> **3** to cast loose; detach **4** to let fly; discharge (e g a bullet)

[3]**loose** *adv* in a loose manner; loosely <*the rope hung* ~>

ˈloose ˌbox *n, Br* an individual enclosure within a barn or stable in which an animal may move about freely

ˌloose-ˈleaf *adj* bound so that individual leaves can be detached or inserted <*a* ~ *photograph album*>

[1]**loot** /looht‖lu:t/ *n* **1** goods, usu of considerable value, taken in war; spoils **2** sthg taken illegally (e g by force or deception) <*the robbers'* ~> [Hindi *lūṭ*, fr Sanskrit *luṇṭati* he robs]

[2]**loot** *vb* **1** to plunder or sack (a place) in war **2** to seize and carry away (sthg) by force or illegally, esp in war or public disturbance – **looter** *n*

[1]**lop** /lop‖lɒp/ *n* small branches and twigs cut from a tree

[2]**lop** *vt* **-pp- 1a** to cut off branches or twigs from **b** to cut from a person **2** to remove or do away with as unnecessary or undesirable – usu + *off* or *away* <~ped *several thousand off the annual budget*> – **lopper** *n*

[1]**lope** /lohp‖ləʊp/ *n* an easy bounding gait capable of being sustained for a long time

[2]**lope** *vi* to go, move, or ride at a lope – **loper** *n*

ˌ**lop-ˈeared** *adj* having ears that droop

lopsided /ˌlopˈsiedid‖ˌlɒpˈsaɪdɪd/ *adj* **1** having one side heavier or lower than the other **2** lacking in balance, symmetry, or proportion – **lopsidedly** *adv*, **lopsidedness** *n*

loquacious /ləˈkwayshəs‖ləˈkweɪʃəs/ *adj* talkative – fml – **loquaciously** *adv*, **loquaciousness** *n*, **loquacity** *n*

loquat /ˈlohkwət, -kwot‖ˈləʊkwət, -kwɒt/ *n* (the yellow edible fruit of) an often cultivated Asiatic evergreen tree of the rose family

[1]**lord** /lawd‖lɔːd/ *n* **1** one having power and authority over others: e g **1a** a (hereditary) ruler **b** sby from whom a feudal fee or estate is held **c** BARON 3 **2** *cap* **2a** GOD 1 **b** Jesus – often + *Our* **3** a man of rank or high position: e g **3a** a feudal tenant holding land directly from the king **b** a British nobleman: e g **b(1)** BARON 2a **b(2)** a marquess, earl, or viscount **b(3)** the son of a duke or marquess or the eldest son of an earl **b(4)** a bishop of the Church of England **4** *pl, cap* HOUSE OF LORDS – often + *the* **5** – used as the title of a lord or as an official title <Lord *Advocate*> [Old English *hlāford*, fr *hlāf* loaf + *weard* keeper]

[2]**lord** *vi* to act like a lord; *esp* to put on airs – usu + *it* <~s *it over his friends*>

Lord *interj* – used to express surprise, amazement, or dismay; esp in *Oh Lord!*, *Good Lord!*, etc

ˌ**lord ˈchancellor** *n, often cap L&C* an officer of state who presides over the House of Lords, serves as head of the judiciary, and is usu a member of the cabinet

lordly /ˈlawdli‖ˈlɔːdlɪ/ *adj* **1a** (having the characteristics) of a lord; dignified **b** grand, noble **2** disdainful and arrogant – **lordliness** *n*, **lordly** *adv*

ˈ**lordship** /-ship‖-ʃɪp/ *n* **1** – used as a title for a lord **2** the authority of a lord

ˌ**Lord's ˈPrayer** *n the* prayer taught by Jesus beginning 'Our Father'

lore /law‖lɔː/ *n* a specified body of knowledge or tradition

lorgnette /lawˈnyet‖lɔːˈnjet (*Fr* lɔrɲɛt)/ *n* a pair of glasses or opera glasses with a handle [French, fr *lorgner* to take a sidelong look at, fr Middle French, fr *lorgne* cross-eyed]

lorry /ˈlori‖ˈlɒrɪ/ *n, Br* a large motor vehicle for carrying loads by road

lose /loohz‖luːz/ *vb* **lost** /lost‖lɒst/ *vt* **1a** to bring to destruction; perish – usu pass <*the ship was* lost *on the reef*> **b** to damn <lost *souls*> **2** to miss from one's possession or from a customary or supposed place; *also* to fail to find <lost *her glasses*> **3** to suffer deprivation of; part with, esp in an unforeseen or accidental manner <lost *his leg in an accident*> **4** to suffer loss through the death of or final separation from (sby) <lost *a son in the war*> **5a** to fail to use; let slip by <*he* lost *his chance of a place in the team*> **b(1)** to be defeated in (a contest for) <~ *a battle*> <~ *a prize*> **b(2)** to have less of <*the aircraft began to* ~ *height*> **c** to fail to catch with the senses or the mind <lost *part of what was said*> **6** to cause the loss of <*one careless statement* lost *her the election*> **7** to fail to keep or maintain <lost *her balance*> **8a** to cause to miss one's way <lost *themselves in the maze of streets*> **b** to withdraw (oneself) from immediate reality <lost *himself in a book*> **9** to fail to keep in sight or in mind <*I* lost *track of his reasoning*> **10** to free oneself from; get rid of <*dieting to* ~ *some weight*> **11** to run slow by the amount of – used with reference to a timepiece <*my watch* ~s *a minute each day*> ~ *vi* **1** to undergo deprivation of sthg of value **2** to undergo defeat **3** *of a timepiece* to run slow – **lose one's head** to lose self-control (e g in anger or panic)

lose out *vi* **1** to make a loss **2** to be the loser, esp unluckily *USE* often + *on*

loser /ˈloohzə‖ˈluːzə/ *n* **1** one who loses, esp consistently **2** one who does poorly; a failure

loss /los‖lɒs/ *n* **1a** the act or an instance of losing possession **b** the harm or privation resulting from loss or separation **2** a person, thing, or amount lost <*the woman who retired is a great* ~ *to her firm*>: e g **2a** *pl* killed, wounded, or captured soldiers **b** the power diminution of a circuit element corresponding to conversion of electric power into heat **3a** failure to gain, win, obtain, or use sthg **b** an amount by which cost exceeds revenue **4** decrease in amount, size, or degree **5** destruction, ruin <*the ship went down with the* ~ *of many lives*> – **at a loss** uncertain, puzzled

loss leader *n* an article sold at a loss in order to draw customers

lost /lost‖lɒst/ *adj* **1a** unable to find the way **b** no longer visible **c** bewildered, helpless **2** ruined or destroyed physically or morally **3a** no longer possessed <*one's* ~ *youth*> **b** no longer known <*the* ~ *art of letter-writing*> **4a** taken away or beyond reach or attainment; denied **b** insensible, hardened <~ *to shame*> **5** rapt, absorbed <~ *in reverie*>

ˌ**lost ˈcause** *n* a cause that has lost all prospect of success

[1]**lot** /lot‖lɒt/ *n* **1** an object used as a counter in deciding a question by chance <*they drew* ~s *for who was to go*> **2** (the use of lots as a means of making) a choice **3a** sthg that falls to sby by lot; a share **b** one's way of life or worldly fate; fortune <*it's my* ~ *to be misunderstood*> **4a** a portion of land; *esp* one with fixed boundaries designated on a plot or survey **b** a film studio and its adjoining property **5** an article or a number of articles offered as 1 item (e g in an auction sale) <*what am I bid for* ~ *16?*> **6a** *sing or pl in constr* a number of associated people; a set <*hello you* ~ – Margaret Drabble> **b** a kind, sort – chiefly in *a bad lot* **7** a considerable amount or number <*a* ~ *of illness*> <*has* ~s *of friends*> – often pl with sing. meaning **8** *chiefly Br* the whole amount or number <*ate up the whole* ~> *USE* (*6a&8*) infml – chiefly infml – chiefly infml – **a lot 1** lots <*drove* a lot *faster*> **2** often, frequently <*goes there* a lot>

[2]**lot** *vt* **-tt- 1** to form or divide into lots **2** to

allot, apportion

loth /lohth‖ləʊθ/ *adj* loath

lotion /ˈlohsh(ə)n‖ˈləʊʃ(ə)n/ *n* a medicinal or cosmetic liquid for external use

lottery /ˈlot(ə)ri‖ˈlɒt(ə)rɪ/ *n* **1** (a way of raising money by the sale or) the distribution of numbered tickets some of which are later randomly selected to entitle the holder to a prize **2** an event or affair whose outcome is (apparently) decided by chance <*buying a secondhand car is a* ~>

lotto /ˈlotoh‖ˈlɒtəʊ/ *n* bingo

lotus /ˈlohtəs‖ˈləʊtəs/ *n* **1** a fruit considered in Greek legend to cause indolence and dreamy contentment **2** any of various water lilies including several represented in ancient Egyptian and Hindu art and religious symbolism **3** any of a genus of widely distributed upright herbaceous plants (e g bird's-foot trefoil)

ˈlotus-ˌeater *n* sby who lives in dreamy indolence

loud /lowd‖laʊd/ *adj* **1** marked by or producing a high volume of sound **2** clamorous, noisy **3** obtrusive or offensive in appearance; flashy <*a* ~ *checked suit*> – **loud** *adv*, **louden** *vb*, **loudly** *adv*, **loudness** *n*

ˌloud-ˈhailer *n, chiefly Br* a megaphone

ˈloudˌmouth /-ˌmowth‖-ˌmaʊθ/ *n* a person given to much loud offensive talk – infml – **loudmouthed** *adj*

loudspeaker /ˌlowdˈspeekə‖ˌlaʊdˈspiːkə/ *n* (a cabinet that contains) an electromechanical device that converts electrical energy into acoustic energy and that is used to reproduce audible sounds in a room, hall, etc

lough /lokh‖lɒx/ *n* a loch in Ireland

[1]**lounge** /lownj‖laʊndʒ/ *vi* to act or move idly or lazily; loll – **lounger** *n*

[2]**lounge** *n* **1** a room in a private house for sitting in; SITTING ROOM **2** a room in a public building providing comfortable seating; *also* a waiting room (e g at an airport)

lounge bar *n, Br* SALOON BAR

ˈlounge ˌsuit *n* a man's suit for wear during the day and on informal occasions

lour /ˈlowə‖ˈlaʊə/ *vi or n, chiefly Br* [1, 2]LOWER – **loury** *adj*, **louring** *adj*

louse /lows‖laʊs/ *n, pl* **lice**, /lies‖laɪs/; *sense 2* **louses** **1a** any of various small wingless usu flattened insects parasitic on warm-blooded animals **b** any of several small arthropods that are not parasitic – usu in combination <*book* ~> **2** a contemptible person – infml

louse up /lows, lowz‖laʊs, laʊz/ *vt* to make a mess of; spoil – infml

lousy /ˈlowzi‖ˈlaʊzɪ/ *adj* **1** infested with lice **2a** very mean; despicable <*a* ~ *trick to play*> **b** very bad, unpleasant, useless, etc **c** amply or excessively supplied <~ *with money*> *USE* (*2*) infml – **lousily** *adv*, **lousiness** *n*

lout /lowt‖laʊt/ *n* a rough ill-mannered man or youth – **loutish** *adj*

louvre, louver /ˈloohvə‖ˈluːvə/ *n* **1** a roof lantern or turret with slatted apertures for the escape of smoke or admission of light **2** an opening provided with 1 or more slanted fixed or movable strips of metal, wood, glass, etc to allow flow of air or sound but to exclude rain or sun or to provide privacy – **louvered, louvred** *adj*

lovable *also* **loveable** /ˈluvəbl‖ˈlʌvəbl/ *adj* having qualities that deserve love; worthy of love – **lovableness** *n*, **lovably** *adv*

[1]**love** /luv‖lʌv/ *n* **1a(1)** strong affection for another <*maternal* ~ *for a child*> **a(2)** attraction based on sexual desire; strong affection and tenderness felt by lovers **b** an assurance of love <*give her my* ~> **2** warm interest in, enjoyment of, or attraction to sthg <~ *of music*> **3a** the object of interest and enjoyment <*music was his first* ~> **b** a person who is loved; DEAR 1a; *also* DEAR 1b **4a** unselfish loyal and benevolent concern for the good of another **b(1)** the fatherly concern of God for man **b(2)** a person's adoration of God **5** a god or personification of love **6** an amorous episode; LOVE AFFAIR <*My Life and* Loves – Frank Harris> **7** a score of zero in tennis, squash, etc **8** SEXUAL INTERCOURSE – euph – **for love or money** in any possible way – usu neg <*couldn't get a ticket for love or money*>

[2]**love** *vt* **1** to hold dear; cherish **2a** to feel a lover's passion, devotion, or tenderness for **b(1)** to caress **b(2)** to have sexual intercourse with **3** to like or desire actively; take pleasure in <~d *to play the violin*> **4** to thrive in <*the rose* ~s *sunlight*> ~*vi* to feel love or affection or experience desire

ˈlove afˌfair *n* **1** an often temporary romantic attachment between lovers, esp a man and a woman **2** a lively enthusiasm

ˈloveˌbird /-ˌbuhd‖-ˌbɜːd/ *n* any of various small usu grey or green parrots that show great affection for their mates

ˈlove ˌchild *n* an illegitimate child – euph

ˈlove ˌfeast *n* a meal eaten together by a Christian congregation in token of brotherly love

ˈloveless /-lis‖-lɪs/ *adj* **1** without love <*a* ~ *marriage*> **2** unloving **3** unloved – **lovelessly** *adv*, **lovelessness** *n*

ˈloveˌlorn /-ˌlawn‖-ˌlɔːn/ *adj* sad because of unrequited love – **lovelornness** *n*

[1]**lovely** /ˈluvli‖ˈlʌvlɪ/ *adj* **1** delicately or delightfully beautiful **2** very pleasing; fine <*a* ~ *view*> – **lovelily** *adv*, **loveliness** *n*, **lovely** *adv*

[2]**lovely** *n* a beautiful woman – infml <*hello, my* ~>

ˈloveˌmaking /-ˌmayking‖-ˌmeɪkɪŋ/ *n* **1** courtship **2** sexual activity; *esp* SEXUAL INTERCOURSE

lover /ˈluvə‖ˈlʌvə/ *n* **1a** a person in love **b** a man with whom a woman has sexual relations, esp outside marriage **c** *pl* 2 people in love with each other; *esp* 2 people who habitually have sexual relations **2** DEVOTEE 2 <*a* ~ *of the theatre*>

ˈloveˌsick /-ˌsik‖-ˌsɪk/ *adj* languishing with love – **lovesickness** *n*

lovey /ˈluvi‖ˈlʌvɪ/ *n, chiefly Br* LOVE 3b – infml

loving /ˈluving‖ˈlʌvɪŋ/ *adj* feeling or showing love; affectionate – **lovingly** *adv*

ˈloving ˌcup *n* a large ornamental drinking vessel with 2 or more handles that is passed among a group of people for all to drink from

[1]**low** /loh‖ləʊ/ *vi or n* (to make) the deep sustained throat sound characteristic of esp a cow

[2]**low** *adj* **1a** not measuring much from the base

to the top; not high <*a ~ wall*> **b** situated or passing little above a reference line, point, or plane <*~ bridges*> <*his work was ~ on his list of priorities*> **c** low-necked **2a** situated or passing below the normal level or below the base of measurement <*~ ground*> **b** marking a nadir or bottom <*the ~ point of her career*> **3a** *of sound* not shrill or loud; soft **b** depressed in pitch <*a ~ note*> **4** near the horizon <*it was evening, and the sun was ~*> **5** humble in character or status <*people of ~ birth*> **6a** lacking strength, health, or vitality; weak <*he's been very ~ with pneumonia*> **b** lacking spirit or vivacity; depressed <*~ spirits*> **7** of less than usual degree, size, amount, or value <*~ pressure*> <*prices are ~ at the moment*> **8a** lacking dignity or formality <*a ~ style of writing*> **b** morally reprehensible <*played a ~ trick on her*> **c** coarse, vulgar <*~ language*> **9** unfavourable, disparaging <*had a ~ opinion of him*> **10** *of a gear* designed for slow speed **11** *of a vowel* open – **lowness** *n*

[3]**low** *n* **1** sthg low: e g **1a** a depth, nadir <*sales have reached a new ~*> **b** a region of low atmospheric pressure **2** *NAm* BOTTOM 4c

[4]**low** *adv* at or to a low place, altitude, or degree

ˌlowˈborn /-ˈbawn‖-ˈbɔːn/ *adj* born to parents of low social rank

ˌlowˈbred /-ˈbred‖-ˈbred/ *adj* rude, vulgar

ˈlowˌbrow /-ˌbrow‖-ˌbraʊ/ *adj* dealing with, possessing, or having unsophisticated or unintellectual tastes, esp in the arts – often derog – **lowbrow** *n*

ˌLow ˈChurch *adj* tending, esp in the Anglican church, to minimize emphasis on the priesthood, sacraments, and ceremonial and often to emphasize evangelical principles – **Low Churchman** *n*

ˌlow ˈcomedy *n* comedy bordering on farce and depending on physical action and situation rather than wit and characterization

ˈlowˌdown /-ˌdown‖-ˌdaʊn/ *n* inside information – usu + *the*; infml

ˌlow-ˈdown *adj* contemptible, base – infml

[1]**lower**, *Br chiefly* **lour** /ˈlowə‖ˈlaʊə/ *vi* **1** to look sullen; frown **2** to become dark, gloomy, and threatening – **lowering** *adj*

[2]**lower**, *Br chiefly* **lour** *n* **1** a lowering look; a frown **2** a gloomy sky or aspect of weather – **lowery** *adj*

[3]**lower** /ˈloh·ə‖ˈləʊə/ *adj* **1** relatively low in position, rank, or order **2** less advanced in the scale of evolutionary development <*~ organisms*> **3** constituting the popular, more representative, and often (e g in Britain) more powerful branch of a legislative body consisting of 2 houses <*the ~ chamber*>

[4]**lower** /ˈloh·ə‖ˈləʊə/ *vi* to move down; drop; *also* to diminish ~ *vt* **1a** to cause to descend; let down in height <*~ed the boat over the side of the ship*> <*~ your aim*> **b** to reduce the height of <*~ed the ceiling*> **2a** to reduce in value, amount, degree, strength, or pitch <*~ the price*> <*~ your voice*> **b** to bring down; degrade; *also* to humble <*I wouldn't ~ myself to speak to them*> **c** to reduce the objective of <*~ed their sights and accepted less*>

ˌlower-ˈcase *adj, of a letter* of or conforming to the series (e g a, b, c rather than A, B, C) typically used elsewhere than at the beginning of sentences or proper names [fr the compositor's practice of keeping such letters in the lower of a pair of type cases]

lower case *n* **1** a type case containing lower-case letters and usu spaces and quads **2** lower-case letters

ˌlower ˈdeck *n* **1** a deck below the main deck of a ship **2** *sing or pl in constr, chiefly Br* the petty officers and men of a ship or navy as distinguished from the officers

ˈlowerˌmost /-ˌmohst, -məst‖-ˌməʊst, -məst/ *adj* lowest

ˌLow ˈGerman *n* a colloquial language of N Germany

ˌlow-ˈkey *also* **low-keyed** /keed‖kiːd/ *adj* of low intensity; restrained

Lowland /ˈlohlənd‖ˈləʊlənd/ *adj* of the Lowlands of Scotland – **Lowlander** *n*

[1]**lowly** /ˈlohli‖ˈləʊlɪ/ *adv* **1** in a humble or meek manner **2** in a low position, manner, or degree

[2]**lowly** *adj* **1** humble and modest in manner or spirit **2** low in the scale of biological or cultural evolution **3** ranking low in a social or economic hierarchy – **lowliness** *n*

ˌlow-ˈlying *adj* lying below the normal level or surface or below the base of measurement or mean elevation <*~ clouds*>

ˌlow-ˈnecked, **low-neck** *adj* having a low-cut neckline

ˌlow-ˈpitched *adj* **1** *of sound* not shrill; deep **2** *of a roof* sloping gently

ˌlow ˈprofile *n* an inconspicuous mode of operation or behaviour (intended to attract little attention)

ˌlow-ˈspirited *adj* dejected, depressed – **low-spiritedly** *adv*, **low-spiritedness** *n*

low technology *n* technology using old-established resources and devices, usu to produce staple items

ˌlow ˈtide *n* (the time of) the tide when the water reaches its lowest level

ˌlow ˈwater *n* LOW TIDE

loyal /ˈloyəl‖ˈlɔɪəl/ *adj* **1** unswerving in allegiance (e g to a person, country, or cause); faithful **2** showing such allegiance <*her ~ determination to help the party*> – **loyally** *adv*, **loyalty** *n*

loyalist /ˈloyəlist‖ˈlɔɪəlɪst/ *n* sby loyal to a government or sovereign, esp in time of revolt

lozenge /ˈlozinj‖ˈlɒzɪndʒ/ *n* **1** (sthg shaped like) a figure with 4 equal sides and 2 acute and 2 obtuse angles **2** a small often medicated sweet

LP /ˌel ˈpee‖ˌel ˈpiː/ *n* a gramophone record designed to be played at $33^1/_3$ revolutions per minute and typically having a diameter of 12in (30.5cm) and a playing time of 20–25min [*l*ong *p*laying]

LSD /ˌel es ˈdee‖ˌel es ˈdiː/ *n* a drug taken illegally for its potent action in producing hallucinations and altered perceptions [*ly*sergic acid *d*iethylamide]

lubber /ˈlubə‖ˈlʌbə/ *n* **1** a big clumsy fellow **2** a clumsy seaman – **lubberliness** *n*, **lubberly** *adj or adv*

lubricant /ˈloohbrikənt‖ˈluːbrɪkənt/ *n* **1** a substance (e g grease or oil) capable of reducing friction, heat, and wear when introduced as a film between solid surfaces **2** sthg that lessens or prevents difficulty – **lubricant** *adj*

lubricate /ˈloohbrikayt‖ˈluːbrɪkeɪt/ *vt* **1** to make smooth or slippery **2** to apply a lubricant to ~*vi* to act as a lubricant – **lubricator** *n*, **lubricative** *adj*, **lubrication** *n*

lubricious /loohˈbrishəs‖luːˈbrɪʃəs/ *adj* **1** lecherous, salacious **2** slippery, smooth *USE* fml – **lubriciously** *adv*, **lubricity** *n*

lucerne *also* **lucern** /loohˈsuhn‖luːˈsɜːn/ *n*, *chiefly Br* a deep-rooted European leguminous plant widely grown for fodder

lucid /ˈloohsid‖ˈluːsɪd/ *adj* **1** having full use of one's faculties; sane **2** clear to the understanding; plain – **lucidly** *adv*, **lucidness, lucidity** *n*

luck /luk‖lʌk/ *n* **1** whatever good or bad events happen to a person by chance **2** the tendency for a person to be consistently fortunate or unfortunate **3** success as a result of good fortune

lucky /ˈluki‖ˈlʌkɪ/ *adj* having, resulting from, or bringing good luck – **luckily** *adv*, **luckiness** *n*

ˌlucky ˈdip *n*, *Br* an attraction (e g at a fair) in which articles can be drawn unseen from a receptacle

lucrative /ˈloohkrətiv‖ˈluːkrətɪv/ *adj* profitable – **lucratively** *adv*, **lucrativeness** *n*

lucre /ˈloohkə‖ˈluːkə/ *n* financial gain; profit; *also* money – esp in *filthy lucre*

Luddite /ˈludiet‖ˈlʌdaɪt/ *n* **1** a member of a group of early 19th-c English workmen who destroyed machinery as a protest against unemployment **2** an opponent of industrial or technological innovation [Ned *Ludd* (*fl* 1779), English workman who destroyed knitting machines]

ludicrous /ˈloohdikrəs‖ˈluːdɪkrəs/ *adj* **1** amusing because of obvious absurdity or incongruity **2** meriting derision – **ludicrously** *adv*, **ludicrousness** *n*

ludo /ˈloohdoh‖ˈluːdəʊ/ *n* a simple game played on a square board with counters and dice [Latin, I play, fr *ludere* to play]

¹luff /luf‖lʌf/ *n* the forward edge of a fore-and-aft sail

²luff *vi* to sail nearer the wind – often + *up*

¹lug /lug‖lʌg/ *vt* **-gg-** to drag, pull, or carry with great effort – infml

²lug *n* a lugsail

³lug *n* **1** sthg (e g a handle) that projects like an ear **2** ¹EAR 1a – chiefly dial. or humor

luggage /ˈlugij‖ˈlʌgɪdʒ/ *n* (cases, bags, etc containing) the belongings that accompany a traveller

lugger /ˈlugə‖ˈlʌgə/ *n* a small fishing or coasting boat that carries 1 or more lugsails

lughole /ˈlugˌhohl‖ˈlʌgˌhəʊl/ *n*, *Br* ¹EAR 1a – chiefly dial or humor

lugsail /ˈlugˌsayl, -səl‖ˈlʌgˌseɪl, -səl/ *n* a 4-sided fore-and-aft sail attached to an obliquely hanging yard

lugubrious /loohˈgoohbri·əs, lə-‖luːˈguːbrɪəs, lə-/ *adj* (exaggeratedly or affectedly) mournful – **lugubriously** *adv*, **lugubriousness** *n*

lugworm /ˈlugˌwuhm‖ˈlʌgˌwɜːm/ *n* any of a genus of marine worms that are used for bait

lukewarm /ˌloohkˈwawm‖ˌluːkˈwɔːm/ *adj* **1** moderately warm; tepid **2** lacking conviction; indifferent – **lukewarmly** *adv*, **lukewarmness** *n*

¹lull /lul‖lʌl/ *vt* **1** to cause to sleep or rest; soothe **2** to cause to relax vigilance, esp by deception

²lull *n* a temporary pause or decline in activity

lullaby /ˈluləbie‖ˈlʌləbaɪ/ *n* a song to quieten children or lull them to sleep

lumbago /lumˈbaygoh‖lʌmˈbeɪgəʊ/ *n* muscular pain of the lumbar region of the back

lumbar /ˈlumbə‖ˈlʌmbə/ *adj* of or constituting the loins or the vertebrae between the thoracic vertebrae and sacrum

¹lumber /ˈlumbə‖ˈlʌmbə/ *vi* to move heavily or clumsily

²lumber *n* **1** surplus or disused articles (e g furniture) that are stored away **2** *NAm* timber or logs, esp when dressed for use – **lumber** *adj*

³lumber *vt* **1** to clutter (as if) with lumber; encumber, saddle **2** *NAm* to cut down and saw the timber of – **lumberer** *n*

ˈlumberˌjack /-ˌjak‖-ˌdʒæk/ *n* a person engaged in logging

luminary /ˈloohmin(ə)ri‖ˈluːmɪn(ə)rɪ/ *n* a source of light or illumination: e g **a** a natural body that gives light (e g the sun or moon) **b** a person brilliantly outstanding in some respect

luminescence /ˌloohmiˈnes(ə)ns‖ˌluːmɪˈnes(ə)ns/ *n* (an emission of) light that occurs at low temperatures and that is produced by physiological processes (e g in the firefly), by chemical action, by friction, or by electrical action – **luminescent** *adj*

luminosity /ˌloohmiˈnosəti‖ˌluːmɪˈnɒsətɪ/ *n* **1a** being luminous **b** sthg luminous **2a** the relative quantity of light **b** relative brightness of sthg

luminous /ˈloohminəs‖ˈluːmɪnəs/ *adj* **1** emitting or full of light; bright **2** easily understood; *also* explaining clearly – **luminously** *adv*, **luminousness** *n*

luminous paint *n* paint containing a phosphorescent compound causing it to glow in the dark

lumme /ˈlumi‖ˈlʌmɪ/ *interj*, *Br* – used to express surprise; infml

lummox /ˈluməks‖ˈlʌməks/ *n* a clumsy person – infml

¹lump /lump‖lʌmp/ *n* **1** a usu compact piece or mass of indefinite size and shape **2a** an abnormal swelling **b** BRUISE 1 **3** a heavy thickset person; *specif* one who is stupid or dull **4** *Br the* whole group of casual nonunion building workers

²lump *vt* **1** to group without discrimination **2** to make lumps on, in, or of ~*vi* to become formed into lumps

³lump *adj* not divided into parts; entire <*a ~ sum*>

⁴lump *vt* to put up with – chiefly in *like it or lump it*; infml

lumpish /ˈlumpish‖ˈlʌmpɪʃ/ *adj* **1** dull, sluggish **2** heavy, awkward – **lumpishly** *adv*, **lumpishness** *n*

lumpy /ˈlumpi‖ˈlʌmpɪ/ *adj* **1a** filled or covered with lumps **b** characterized by choppy waves **2** having a thickset clumsy appearance – **lumpily** *adv*, **lumpiness** *n*

lunacy /ˈloohnəsi‖ˈluːnəsɪ/ *n* **1** insanity **2** wild foolishness; extravagant folly **3** a foolish act

lunar /ˈloohnə‖ˈlu:nə/ *adj* **1a** of the moon **b** designed for use on the moon < ~ *vehicles*> **2** **lunar, lunate** shaped like a crescent **3** measured by the moon's revolution < ~ *month*>

lunar month *n* the period of time, averaging $29^1/_2$ days, between 2 successive new moons

lunatic /ˈloohnətik‖ˈlu:nətɪk/ *adj* **1a** insane **b** of or designed for the care of insane people **2** wildly foolish [Late Latin *lunaticus*, fr Latin *luna* moon; fr the belief that lunacy fluctuated with the phases of the moon] – **lunatic** *n*

lunatic fringe *n* the extremist or fanatical members of a political or social movement

¹lunch /lunch‖lʌntʃ/ *n* (the food prepared for) a light midday meal; *broadly, NAm* a light meal

²lunch *vi* to eat lunch

luncheon /ˈlunch(ə)n‖ˈlʌntʃ(ə)n/ *n* a (formal) lunch

ˈluncheon ˌmeat *n* a precooked mixture of meat (e g pork) and cereal shaped in a loaf

lung /lung‖lʌŋ/ *n* **1** either of the usu paired compound saclike organs in the chest that constitute the basic respiratory organ of air-breathing vertebrates **2** any of various respiratory organs of invertebrates

¹lunge /lunj‖lʌndʒ/ *vb* to make a lunge (with)

²lunge *n* **1** a sudden thrust or forceful forward movement **2** the act of plunging forward

ˈlungˌfish /-ˌfish‖-ˌfɪʃ/ *n* any of various fishes that breathe by a modified air bladder as well as gills

lupin *also* **lupine** /ˈloohpin‖ˈlu:pɪn/ *n* any of a genus of leguminous plants some of which are cultivated for fertiliser, fodder, their edible seeds, or their long spikes of variously coloured flowers

¹lurch /luhch‖lɜ:tʃ/ *n* – **in the lurch** in a vulnerable and unsupported position; deserted – infml

²lurch *vi* **1** to roll or tip abruptly; pitch **2** to stagger – **lurch** *n*

¹lure /lyooə, looə‖ljʊə, lʊə/ *n* **1** a bunch of feathers and often meat attached to a long cord and used by a falconer to recall his/her bird **2a** sby or sthg used to entice or decoy **b** the power to appeal or attract <*the* ~ *of success*> **3** a decoy for attracting animals to capture

²lure *vt* **1** to recall (a hawk) by means of a lure **2** to tempt with a promise of pleasure or gain

lurid /ˈl(y)ooərid‖ˈl(j)ʊərɪd/ *adj* **1** wan and ghastly pale in appearance **2a** causing horror or revulsion; gruesome **b** sensational < ~ *newspaper reports of the crime*> **c** highly coloured; gaudy – **luridly** *adv*, **luridness** *n*

lurk /luhk‖lɜ:k/ *vi* **1a** to lie hidden in wait, esp with evil intent **b** to move furtively or inconspicuously **2** to lie hidden; *esp* to be a hidden threat – **lurker** *n*

luscious /ˈlushəs‖ˈlʌʃəs/ *adj* **1** having a delicious taste or smell **2** having sensual appeal; seductive **3** richly luxurious or appealing to the senses; *also* excessively ornate – **lusciously** *adv*, **lusciousness** *n*

¹lush /lush‖lʌʃ/ *adj* **1** producing or covered by luxuriant growth < ~ *grass*> **2** opulent, sumptuous – **lushly** *adv*

²lush *n, chiefly NAm* a heavy drinker; an alcoholic

¹lust /lust‖lʌst/ *n* **1** strong sexual desire, esp as opposed to love **2** an intense longing; a craving – **lustful** *adj*

²lust *vi* to have an intense (sexual) desire or craving

¹lustre, *NAm chiefly* **luster** /ˈlustə‖ˈlʌstə/ *n* **1** (the quality of) the glow of reflected light from a surface (e g of a mineral) **2a** a glow of light (as if) from within **b** radiant beauty **3** glory, distinction **4** a glass pendant used esp to ornament a chandelier – **lustreless** *adj*

²lustre, *NAm chiefly* **luster** *vt* to give lustre or distinction to – **lustring** *n*

lustrous /ˈlustrəs‖ˈlʌstrəs/ *adj* evenly shining <*a* ~ *satin*> – **lustrously** *adv*

lusty /ˈlusti‖ˈlʌstɪ/ *adj* **1** full of vitality; healthy **2** full of strength; vigorous – **lustily** *adv*, **lustiness** *n*

lute /looht‖lu:t/ *n* a stringed instrument with a large pear-shaped body, a neck with a fretted fingerboard, and pairs of strings tuned in unison [Middle French *lut*, fr Old Provençal *laut*, fr Arabic *al-'ūd*, lit., the wood]

lutenist /ˈloohtinist‖ˈlu:tɪnɪst/, **lutanist** /-tən-‖-tən-/ *n* a lute player

luxuriant /lugˈzhooəri·ənt‖lʌgˈʒʊərɪənt/ *adj* **1** characterized by abundant growth **2a** exuberantly rich and varied; prolific **b** richly or excessively ornamented < ~ *prose*> – **luxuriance** *n*, **luxuriantly** *adv*

luxuriate /lugˈzhooəriayt‖lʌgˈʒʊərɪeɪt/ *vi* to enjoy oneself consciously; revel – often + *in*

luxurious /lugˈzhooəri·əs‖lʌgˈʒʊərɪəs/ *adj* **1** fond of luxury or self-indulgence; *also* voluptuous **2** characterized by opulence and rich abundance – **luxuriously** *adv*, **luxuriousness** *n*

luxury /ˈlukshəri‖ˈlʌkʃərɪ/ *n* **1** great ease or comfort based on habitual or liberal use of expensive items without regard to cost **2a** sthg desirable but costly or difficult to obtain **b** sthg relatively expensive adding to pleasure or comfort but not indispensable

¹-ly /-li‖-lɪ/ *suffix* (→ *adj*) **1** like in appearance, manner, or nature; having the characteristics of <*queen*ly> **2** recurring regularly at intervals of; every <*hour*ly>

²-ly *suffix* (→ *adv*) **1** in (such) a manner <*slow*ly>; like <*king*ly> **2** from (such) a point of view <*musical*ly *speaking*> **3** with respect to <*part*ly> **4** as is (specified); it is (specified) that <*natural*ly> **5** speaking (in a specified way) <*frank*ly>

lychee /ˈliechi‖ˈlaɪtʃɪ/ *n* a litchi

ˈlych-ˌgate /lich‖lɪtʃ/ *n* a roofed gate in a churchyard traditionally used as resting place for a coffin during part of a burial service [Middle English *lycheyate*, fr *lich* body, corpse + *gate*, *yate* gate]

lye /lie‖laɪ/ *n* a strong alkaline liquid rich in potassium carbonate, leached from wood ashes, and used esp in making soap; *broadly* a strong alkaline solution

ˌlying-ˈin /ˈlie·ing‖ˈlaɪɪŋ/ *n, pl* **lyings-in, lying-ins** confinement for childbirth

lymph /limf‖lɪmf/ *n* a pale fluid resembling blood plasma that contains white blood cells but normally no red blood cells, that circulates in the lymphatic vessels, and bathes the cells of the body

[1]**lymphatic** /lim'fatik‖lɪm'fætɪk/ *adj* **1** of, involving, or produced by lymph or lymphocytes **2** conveying lymph

[2]**lymphatic** *n* a vessel that contains or conveys lymph

lymphocyte /'limfəsiet‖'lɪmfəsaɪt/ *n* a white blood cell that is present in large numbers in lymph and blood and defends the body by immunological responses to invading or foreign matter (e g by producing antibodies) – **lymphocytic** *adj*

lynch /linch‖lɪntʃ/ *vt* to put to death illegally by mob action – **lyncher** *n*

'lynch ˌlaw *n* the punishment of presumed crimes or offences usu by death without due process of law [prob fr William *Lynch* (1742-1820), US citizen who organized extralegal tribunals in Virginia]

lynx /lingks‖lɪŋks/ *n, pl* **lynx, lynxes** any of various wildcats with relatively long legs, a short stubby tail, mottled coat, and often tufted ears

'lynx-ˌeyed *adj* having keen eyesight

lyre /'lie·ə‖'laɪə/ *n* a stringed instrument of the harp family used by the ancient Greeks esp to accompany song and recitation

'lyreˌbird /-ˌbuhd‖-ˌbɜːd/ *n* either of 2 Australian birds the male of which displays tail feathers in the shape of a lyre during courtship

[1]**lyric** /'lirik‖'lɪrɪk/ *adj* **1** suitable for being set to music and sung **2** expressing direct personal emotion <~ *poetry*>

[2]**lyric** *n* **1** a lyric poem **2** *pl* the words of a popular song – **lyricist, lyrist** *n*

lyrical /'lirikl‖'lɪrɪkl/ *adj* **1** lyric **2** full of admiration or enthusiasm – esp in *wax lyrical* – **lyrically** *adv*

lyricism /'lirisiz(ə)m‖'lɪrɪsɪz(ə)m/ *n* **1** a directly personal and intense style or quality in an art **2** great enthusiasm or exuberance

M

m /em‖em/ *n, pl* **m's, ms** *often cap* **1** (a graphic representation of or device for reproducing) the 13th letter of the English alphabet **2** one thousand **3** sthg shaped like the letter M **4** an em

'm /-m‖-m/ *vb* am <*I'm going*>

ma /mah‖mɑː/ *n* MOTHER 1a – chiefly as a term of address; infml

ma'am /mam, mahm‖mæm, mɑːm; *unstressed* məm‖məm/ *n* madam – used widely in the USA and in Britain, esp by servants and when addressing the Queen or a royal princess

mac, mack /mak‖mæk/ *n, Br* a raincoat – infml

Mac *n* – used informally to address **a** a Scotsman **b** *NAm* an unknown man

macabre /mə'kahb(r)ə‖mə'kɑːb(r)ə/ *adj* **1** having death as a subject **2** dwelling on the gruesome **3** tending to produce horror in an onlooker

macadam /mə'kadəm‖mə'kædəm/ *n* material used in making a macadamized road [John *McAdam* (1756-1836), Scottish engineer]

macadam·ize /mə'kadəmiez‖mə'kædəmaɪz/, **-ise** *vt* to construct or finish (a road) by compacting into a solid mass successive layers of small broken stones

macaroni /makə'rohni‖mækə'rəʊnɪ/ *n, pl* (2) **macaronis, macaronies 1** pasta made from durum wheat and shaped in hollow tubes that are wider in diameter than spaghetti **2** an English dandy of the late 18th and early 19th c who affected continental ways

macaroon /ˌmakə'roohn‖ˌmækə'ruːn/ *n* a small cake or biscuit composed chiefly of egg whites, sugar, and ground almonds or occasionally coconut

macaw /mə'kaw‖mə'kɔː/ *n* any of numerous parrots including some of the largest and showiest

[1]**mace** /mays‖meɪs/ *n* **1** a medieval heavy spiked staff or club **2** an ornamental staff used as a symbol of authority

[2]**mace** *n* an aromatic spice consisting of the dried external fibrous covering of a nutmeg

Mace *trademark* – used for a riot control agent containing tear gas

macerate /'masərayt‖'mæsəreɪt/ *vt* **1** to cause to waste away (as if) by excessive fasting **2** to cause to become soft or separated into constituent elements (as if) by steeping in fluid ~*vi* to soften and wear away, esp as a result of being wetted – **macerator** *n*, **maceration** *n*

Mach /mak, mahk‖mæk, mɑːk/ *n* MACH NUMBER

machete /mə'sheti, -'chayti‖mə'ʃetɪ, -'tʃeɪtɪ/ *n* a large heavy knife used for cutting vegetation and as a weapon

Machiavellian /ˌmaki·ə'veli·ən‖ˌmækɪə'velɪən/ *adj* cunning and deceitful [Niccolò *Machiavelli* (1469-1527), Italian statesman & political theorist]

machinate /'makinayt‖'mækɪneɪt/ *vi* to plan or plot, esp to do harm – **machinator** *n*

machination /ˌmaki'naysh(ə)n‖ˌmækɪ'neɪʃ(ə)n/ *n* a scheming or crafty action or plan intended to accomplish some usu evil end

[1]**machine** /mə'sheen‖mə'ʃiːn/ *n* **1a** a combination of parts that transmit forces, motion, and energy one to another in a predetermined manner <*a sewing* ~> **b** an instrument (e g a lever or pulley) designed to transmit or modify the application of power, force, or motion **c** a combination of mechanically, electrically, or electronically operated parts for performing a task **d** a coin-operated device **e** machinery – + *the* or in pl <*humanity must not become the servant of the* ~> **2a** a person or organization that acts like a machine **b** the (controlling or inner) organization (e g of a group or activity) <*the war* ~> **c** a highly organized political group

[2]**machine** *vt* **1** to shape, finish, or operate on by a machine **2** to act on, produce, or perform a particular operation or activity on, using a machine; *esp* to sew using a sewing machine <~ *the zip in place*> – **machinable** *also* **machineable** *adj*

ma'chine ˌgun *n* an automatic gun for rapid continuous fire – **machine-gun** *vb*, **machine gunner** *n*

machinery /mə'sheen(ə)ri‖mə'ʃiːn(ə)rɪ/ *n* **1a**

machines in general or as a functioning unit **b** the working parts of a machine **2** the means by which sthg is kept in action or a desired result is obtained **3** the system or organization by which an activity or process is controlled

ma'chine ˌtool *n* a usu power-driven machine designed for cutting or shaping wood, metal, etc

machinist /mə'sheenist‖mə'ʃi:nɪst/ *n* **1** a craftsman skilled in the use of machine tools **2** one who operates a machine, esp a sewing machine

machismo /mə'kizmoh‖mə'kɪzməʊ/ *n* an exaggerated awareness and assertion of masculinity

'Mach ˌnumber, **Mach** *n* a number representing the ratio of the speed of a body to the speed of sound in the surrounding atmosphere [Ernst *Mach* (1838-1916), Austrian physicist]

macho /'machoh, 'makoh‖'mætʃeʊ, 'mækəʊ/ *adj* aggressively virile [Spanish, male, fr Latin *masculus*]

mackerel /'mak(ə)rəl‖'mæk(ə)rəl/ *n* a fish of the N Atlantic that is green with dark blue bars above and silvery below and is one of the most important food fishes; *also* any of various usu small or medium-sized related fishes

mackintosh *also* **macintosh** /'makintosh‖'mækɪntɒʃ/ *n, chiefly Br* a raincoat [Charles *Macintosh* (1766-1843), Scottish chemist & inventor]

macrame, **macramé** /mə'krahmi‖mə'krɑ:mɪ/ *n* (the act of making) a coarse lace or fringe made by knotting threads or cords in a geometrical pattern

macro- *comb form* **1** long <macro*diagonal*> **2** large <macro*spore*>

macrobiotic /ˌmakrəbie'otik, -kroh-‖ˌmækrəbaɪ'ɒtɪk, -krəʊ-/ *adj* of or being a restricted diet, esp one consisting chiefly of whole grains or whole grains and vegetables, that is usu undertaken with the intention of promoting health and prolonging life [Greek *makrobiotos* long-lived, fr *makros* long + *bios* life]

macrocosm /'makrəˌkoz(ə)m‖'mækrəˌkɒz(ə)m/ *n* **1** the universe **2** a complex that is a large-scale reproduction of 1 of its constituents – **macrocosmic** *adj*, **macrocosmically** *adv*

mad /mad‖mæd/ *adj* **1** mentally disordered; insane – not now used technically **2** utterly foolish; senseless **3** carried away by intense anger **4** carried away by enthusiasm or desire **5** affected with rabies **6** intensely excited or distraught; frantic **7** marked by intense and often chaotic activity <*made a* ~ *dash for cover*> – **like mad** very hard, fast, loud, etc <*shouted* like mad>

madam /'madəm‖'mædəm/ *n, pl* **madams**, (1) **mesdames** /'mayˌdam‖'meɪˌdæm/ **1** a lady – used without a name as a form of respectful or polite address to a woman **2** a mistress – used as a title formerly with the Christian name but now with the surname or esp with a designation of rank or office <Madam *Chairman*> <Madam *President*> **3** a female brothel keeper **4** *Br* a conceited pert young lady or girl <*a little* ~>

madame /'madəm‖'mædəm (*Fr* madam)/ *n, pl* **mesdames** /'mayˌdam‖'meɪˌdæm/, (2) **madames** – used as a title equivalent to *Mrs* preceding the name of a married woman not of English-speaking nationality or used without a name as a generalized term of direct address

madcap /'madˌkap‖'mædˌkæp/ *adj* marked by impulsiveness or recklessness – **madcap** *n*

madden /'madn‖'mædn/ *vt* **1** to drive mad; craze **2** to exasperate, enrage

madder /'madə‖'mædə/ *n* **1** a Eurasian plant with whorled leaves and small yellowish flowers **2** (a dye prepared from) the root of the madder

made /mayd‖meɪd/ *adj* **1** assembled or prepared, esp by putting together various ingredients <~ *mustard*> **2** assured of success <*you've got it* ~> – infml

Madeira /mə'diərə‖mə'dɪərə/ *n* any of several fortified wines from Madeira

madeira cake *n, often cap, Br* a very rich sponge cake

mademoiselle /ˌmadmwə'zel ‖ˌmædmwə'zel (*Fr* madmwazɛl)/ *n, pl* **mademoiselles**, **mesdemoiselles** /ˌmaydmwə'zel ‖ˌmeɪdmwə'zel (*Fr* mɛdmwazɛl)/ **1** an unmarried French-speaking girl or woman – used as a title equivalent to *Miss* for an unmarried woman not of English-speaking nationality **2** a French governess or female language teacher

ˌmade-to-'measure *adj, of a garment* made according to an individual's measurements in order to achieve a good fit

madhouse /'madˌhows‖'mædˌhaʊs/ *n* **1** a lunatic asylum – not used technically **2** a place of uproar or confusion

'madly /-li‖-lɪ/ *adv* to a degree suggestive of madness: e g **a** with great energy; frantically **b** without restraint; passionately

'madman /-mən‖-mən/, *fem* **'madˌwoman** *n* a person who is or acts insane

'madness /-nis‖-nɪs/ *n* **1a** insanity **b** extreme folly **2** any of several ailments of animals marked by frenzied behaviour; *specif* rabies

Madonna /mə'donə‖mə'dɒnə/ *n* VIRGIN MARY

Ma'donna ˌlily *n* a white lily with trumpet-shaped flowers

madras /mə'dras, -'drahs‖mə'dræs, -'drɑ:s/ *n* a fine usu cotton plain-woven shirting and dress fabric, usu in brightly coloured checked or striped designs [*Madras*, city in India]

madrigal /'madrig(ə)l‖'mædrɪg(ə)l/ *n* **1** a short medieval love poem **2** an unaccompanied and often complex secular song for several voices – **madrigalian** *adj*

maelstrom /'maylstrohm‖'meɪlstrəʊm/ *n* **1** a powerful whirlpool **2** sthg resembling a maelstrom in turbulence and violence

maenad /'meenad‖'mi:næd/ *n* **1** a female participant in ritual orgies in honour of Dionysus **2** a distraught woman – **maenadic** *adj*

maestro /'miestroh‖'maɪstrəʊ/ *n, pl* **maestros**, **maestri** /-tri‖-trɪ/ a master in an art; *esp* an eminent composer, conductor, or teacher of music [Italian, lit., master, fr Latin *magister*]

Mafia /'mafi·ə‖'mæfɪə/ *n sing or pl in constr* **1** a secret society of Sicilian political terrorists **2** an organized secret body originating in Sicily and prevalent esp in the USA that controls illicit activities (e g vice and narcotics) **3** *often not cap* an excessively influential coterie of a usu specified kind <*the literary* ~> [Italian, fr Italian dial., boldness, bragging]

mag /mag‖mæg/ *n* a magazine – infml

magazine /ˌmagəˈzeen, ˈ---‖ˌmægəˈziːn, ˈ---/ *n* **1** a storeroom for arms, ammunition, or explosives (e g gunpowder) **2a** a usu illustrated periodical, bound in paper covers, containing miscellaneous pieces by different authors **b** a television or radio programme containing a number of usu topical items, often without a common theme **3** a supply chamber: e g **3a** a holder from which cartridges can be fed into a gun chamber automatically **b** a lightproof chamber for films or plates in a camera or for film in a film projector [Middle French, fr Old Provençal, fr Arabic *makhāzin*, pl of *makhzan* storehouse]

magenta /məˈjentə‖məˈdʒentə/ *n* **1** fuchsine **2a** a deep purplish red **b** a pinkish red – used in photography with reference to one of the primary colours [*Magenta*, town in Italy]

maggot /ˈmagət‖ˈmægət/ *n* a soft-bodied legless grub that is the larva of a 2-winged fly (e g the housefly) – **maggoty** *adj*

magi /ˈmayjie‖ˈmeɪdʒaɪ/ *pl of* MAGUS

[1]**magic** /ˈmajik‖ˈmædʒɪk/ *n* **1** (rites, incantations, etc used in) the art of invoking supernatural powers to control natural forces by means of charms, spells, etc **2a** an extraordinary power or influence producing results which defy explanation **b** sthg that seems to cast a spell <*the ~ of the voice*> **3** the art of producing illusions by sleight of hand

[2]**magic** *adj* **1** of, being, or used in magic **2** having seemingly supernatural qualities **3** – used as a general term of approval; infml <*this new record is really ~*> – **magical** *adj*, **magically** *adv*

[3]**magic** *vt* **-ck-** to affect, influence, or take *away* (as if) by magic

ˌ**magic ˈeye** *n* PHOTOELECTRIC CELL

magician /məˈjish(ə)n‖məˈdʒɪʃ(ə)n/ *n* **1** one skilled in magic **2** a conjurer

ˌ**magic ˈlantern** *n* an early device for the projection of still pictures from slides

magisterial /ˌmajiˈstiəri·əl‖ˌmædʒɪˈstɪərɪəl/ *adj* **1a** of, being, or having the characteristics of a master or teacher **b** having masterly skill **2** of a magistrate – **magisterially** *adv*

magistrate /ˈmajistrayt, -strət‖ˈmædʒɪstreɪt, -strət/ *n* a civil legislative or executive official: e g **a** a principal official exercising governmental powers **b** a paid or unpaid local judicial officer who presides in a magistrates' court – **magistracy** *n*, **magistrature** *n*, **magistratical** *adj*

magistrates' court *n* a court of summary jurisdiction for minor criminal cases and preliminary hearings

maglev /ˈmagˌlev‖ˈmægˌlev/ *n* a railway system in which an electrically-driven train is raised above the track by powerful magnets

magma /ˈmagmə‖ˈmægmə/ *n* **1** a thin pasty suspension (e g of a precipitate in water) **2** molten rock material within the earth from which an igneous rock results by cooling – **magmatic** *adj*

magnanimous /magˈnanimǝs‖mæg-ˈnænɪməs/ *adj* **1** showing or suggesting a lofty and courageous spirit **2** showing or suggesting nobility of feeling and generosity of mind; not subject to petty feelings – **magnanimously** *adv*, **magnanimity** *n*

magnate /ˈmagnayt‖ˈmægneɪt/ *n* a person of wealth or influence, often in a specified area of business or industry

magnesia /magˈneezh(y)ə, -zyə‖mægˈniːʒ(j)ə, -zjə/ *n* **1** a white oxide of magnesium used esp in making cements, insulation, fertilizers, and rubber, and in medicine as an antacid and mild laxative **2** magnesium – **magnesian** *adj*

magnesium /magˈneezyəm‖mægˈniːzjəm/ *n* a silver-white bivalent metallic element that burns with an intense white light, is lighter than aluminium, and is used in making light alloys

magnet /ˈmagnit‖ˈmægnɪt/ *n* **1a** LODESTONE 1 **b** a body (of iron, steel, etc) that has an (artificially imparted) magnetic field external to itself and attracts iron **2** sthg that attracts [Middle French *magnete*, fr Latin *magnet-*, *magnes*, fr Greek *magnēs* (*lithos*), lit., stone of Magnesia, ancient city in Asia Minor]

magnetic /magˈnetik‖mægˈnetɪk/ *adj* **1a** of magnetism or a magnet **b** (capable of being) magnetized **c** working by magnetic attraction **2** possessing an extraordinary power or ability to attract or charm – **magnetically** *adv*

magnetic field *n* a region of space (near a body possessing magnetism or carrying an electric current) in which magnetic forces can be detected

magnetic pole *n* either of 2 small nonstationary regions in the N and S geographical polar areas of the earth or another celestial body towards which a magnetic needle points from any direction

magnetic tape *n* a ribbon of thin paper or plastic with a magnetizable coating for use in recording sound, video, etc signals

magnetism /ˈmagniˌtiz(ə)m‖ˈmægnɪˌtɪz(ə)m/ *n* **1** (physics dealing with) a class of physical forces and interactions that includes the attraction for iron shown by a permanent magnet or an electromagnet and is believed to be produced by moving electric charges **2** an ability to attract or charm

ˈ**magnet·ize, -ise** /-tiez‖-taɪz/ *vt* **1** to attract like a magnet **2** to cause to be a magnet – **magnetizable** *adj*, **magnetizer** *n*, **magnetization** *n*

magneto /magˈneetoh‖mægˈniːtəʊ/ *n, pl* **magnetos** an alternator with permanent magnets (formerly) used to generate a high voltage for the ignition in an internal-combustion engine

Magnificat /magˈnifikat‖mægˈnɪfɪkæt/ *n* (a musical setting of) the canticle of the Virgin Mary in Luke 1:46–55

magnification /ˌmagnifiˈkaysh(ə)n‖ˌmægnɪfɪˈkeɪʃ(ə)n/ *n* **1** a magnifying or being magnified **2** the apparent enlargement of an object by a microscope, telescope, etc

magnificent /magˈnifis(ə)nt‖mægˈnɪfɪs(ə)nt/ *adj* **1** marked by stately grandeur and splendour **2a** sumptuous in structure and adornment **b** strikingly beautiful or impressive **3** sublime <*her ~ prose*> **4** exceptionally fine or excellent <*a ~ day*> – **magnificence** *n*, **magnificently** *adv*

magnify /ˈmagnifie‖ˈmægnɪfaɪ/ *vt* **1** to (falsely) increase in significance **2** to enlarge in fact or in appearance <*a telescope* magnifies *distant* *objects>* ~*vi* to have the power of causing objects to appear larger than they are – **magnifier** *n*

ˈ**magnifying** ˌ**glass** *n* a single optical lens for magnifying

magniloquent /magˈniləkwənt‖mægˈnɪləkwənt/ *adj* grandiloquent – **magniloquence** *n*, **magniloquently** *adv*

magnitude /ˈmagnityoohd‖ˈmægnɪtjuːd/ *n* **1a** (great) size or extent **b** a quantity, number **2** the importance or quality of sthg **3** the apparent brightness of a celestial body, esp a star, measured on a logarithmic scale in which a difference of 5 units corresponds to the multiplication or division of the brightness of light by 100

magnolia /magˈnohli·ə, -lyə‖mægˈnəʊlɪə, -ljə/ *n* any of a genus of shrubs and trees with evergreen or deciduous leaves and usu large white, yellow, rose, or purple flowers [Pierre *Magnol* (1638-1715), French botanist]

magnum /ˈmagnəm‖ˈmægnəm/ *n* a wine bottle holding twice the usual amount (about 1.5l)

ˌ**magnum** ˈ**opus** /ˈohpəs‖ˈəʊpəs/ *n* the greatest achievement of an artist, writer, etc [Latin, great work]

magpie /ˈmagpie‖ˈmægpaɪ/ *n* **1** any of numerous birds of the crow family with a very long tail and black-and-white plumage **2** one who chatters noisily **3** one who collects objects in a random fashion

maguey /ˈmagway‖ˈmægweɪ/ *n* (a hard fibre obtained from) any of various fleshy-leaved agave plants

magus /ˈmaygəs‖ˈmeɪgəs/ *n, pl* **magi** /-jie‖-dʒaɪ/ **1a** a member of a Zoroastrian hereditary priestly class in ancient Persia **b** *often cap* any of the traditionally 3 wise men from the East who paid homage to the infant Jesus **2** a magician, sorcerer

maharajah, **maharaja** /ˌmah·hahˈrahjə‖ˌmɑːhɑːˈrɑːdʒə/ *n* a Hindu prince ranking above a rajah [Sanskrit *mahārāja*, fr *mahat* great + *rājan* raja]

maharani, **maharanee** /ˌmah·hahˈrahnee‖ˌmɑːhɑːˈrɑːniː/ *n* **1** the wife of a maharaja **2** a Hindu princess ranking above a rani

mahatma /mahˈhatmə‖mɑːˈhætmə/ *n* a person revered for outstanding moral and spiritual qualities – used as a title of honour, esp by Hindus

mah-jong, **mah-jongg** /ˌmah ˈjong‖ˌmɑːˈdʒɒŋ/ *n* a game of Chinese origin usu played by 4 people with 144 tiles that are drawn and discarded until one player secures a winning hand

mahogany /məˈhog(ə)ni‖məˈhɒg(ə)nɪ/ *n* **1** (any of various tropical, esp W Indian, trees that yield) a durable usu reddish-brown moderately hard and heavy wood, widely used for fine cabinetwork **2** the reddish-brown colour of mahogany

mahout /məˈhowt‖məˈhaʊt/ *n* a keeper and driver of an elephant

maid /mayd‖meɪd/ *n* **1** an unmarried girl or woman; *also* a female virgin **2** a female servant

[1]**maiden** /ˈmayd(ə)n‖ˈmeɪd(ə)n/ *n* **1** an unmarried girl or woman **2** a former Scottish beheading device like a guillotine **3** a horse that has never won a race **4 maiden, maiden over** an over in cricket in which no runs are credited to the batsman – **maidenly** *adj*, **maidenliness** *n*, **maidenhood** *n*

[2]**maiden** *adj* **1a(1)** not married **a(2)** VIRGIN 2, 3 **b** *of a female animal* never having borne young or been mated **c** that has not been altered from its original state **2** being the first or earliest of its kind *<the ship's ~ voyage>*

ˈ**maidenˌhair** /-ˌheə‖-ˌheə/ *n* any of a genus of ferns with fronds that have delicate spreading branches

ˈ**maidenˌhead** /-ˌhed‖-ˌhed/ *n* **1** virginity **2** the hymen

ˈ**maiden** ˌ**name** *n* the surname of a woman prior to marriage

ˌ**maid of** ˈ**honour** *n, pl* **maids of honour** **1** a bride's principal unmarried wedding attendant **2** a puff pastry tartlet filled with custard

ˈ**maidˌservant** /-ˌsuhv(ə)nt‖-ˌsɜːv(ə)nt/ *n* a female servant

[1]**mail** /mayl‖meɪl/ *n* **1a** a bag of posted items conveyed from one post office to another **b** the postal matter that makes up 1 particular consignment **c** a conveyance that transports mail **2** a postal system

[2]**mail** *vt* [4]POST 1 – **mailable** *adj*

[3]**mail** *n* **1** armour made of interlocking metal rings, chains, or sometimes plates **2** a hard enclosing covering of an animal – **mailed** *adj*

[4]**mail** *vt* to clothe (as if) with mail

ˈ**mailˌbag** /-ˌbag‖-ˌbæg/ *n* a bag used to carry mail

ˈ**mailˌbox** /-ˌboks‖-ˌbɒks/ *n, NAm* a letter box

ˈ**mailing** ˌ**list** /ˈmayling‖ˈmeɪlɪŋ/ *n* an organization's list of the names and addresses to which it regularly sends information

ˈ**mail** ˌ**order** *n* an order for goods that is received and fulfilled by post – **mail-order** *adj*

mailshot /ˈmaylshot/ *n* a circular posted to many people at one time

maim /maym‖meɪm/ *vt* to mutilate, disfigure, or wound seriously; cripple – **maimer** *n*

[1]**main** /mayn‖meɪn/ *n* **1** physical strength – in *with might and main* **2** the chief or essential part – chiefly in *in the main* **3** the chief pipe, duct, or cable of a public service (e g gas, electricity, or water) – often pl with sing. meaning **4a** a mainland **b** the high sea

[2]**main** *adj* **1** chief, principal **2** fully exerted *<used ~ force>* **3** connected with or located near the mainmast or mainsail **4** *of a clause* able to stand alone (e g *he laughed* in *he laughed when he heard*)

main chance *n the* chance that promises most advantage or profit – esp in *have an eye for the main chance*

ˌ**main** ˈ**deck** *n* **1** the highest deck that extends the full width and length of a naval vessel **2** the upper deck of a merchant vessel between the poop and forecastle

ˈ**mainland** /-lənd‖-lənd/ *n* the largest land area of a continent, country, etc, considered in relation to smaller offshore islands – **mainlander** *n*

ˈ**mainˌline** /-ˌlien‖-ˌlaɪn/ *vb* to inject (a narcotic or other drug of abuse) into a vein – slang – **mainliner** *n*

ˌ**main** ˈ**line** *n* a principal railway line

ˈ**mainly** /-li‖-lɪ/ *adv* in most cases or for the

most part; chiefly

ˈmainˌmast /-ˌmahst‖-ˌmɑːst; *naut* -məst‖-məst/ *n* (the lowest section of) a sailing vessel's principal mast

mains /maynz‖meɪnz/ *adj* of or (suitable to be) powered by electricity from the mains <*a ~ razor*>

ˈmainˌsail /-ˌsayl‖-ˌseɪl; *naut* -s(ə)l‖-s(ə)l/ *n* **1** the lowest square sail on the mainmast of a square-rigged ship **2** the principal fore-and-aft sail on the mainmast of a fore-and-aft rigged ship

ˈmainˌspring /-ˌspring‖-ˌsprɪŋ/ *n* **1** the chief spring, esp of a watch or clock **2** the chief motive, agent, or cause

ˈmainˌstay /-ˌstay‖-ˌsteɪ/ *n* **1** a rope that stretches forwards from a sailing ship's maintop, usu to the foot of the foremast, and provides the chief support of the mainmast **2** a chief support

ˈmainˌstream /-ˌstreem‖-ˌstriːm/ *n* a prevailing current or direction of activity or influence – **mainstream** *adj*

maintain /maynˈtayn‖meɪnˈteɪn/ *vt* **1** to keep in an existing state (e g of operation, repair, efficiency, or validity) **2** to sustain against opposition or danger **3** to continue or persevere in **4** to support, sustain, or provide for <*has a family to ~*> **5** to affirm (as if) in argument – **maintainable** *adj*, **maintainer** *n*

maintenance /ˈmayntinəns‖ˈmeɪntɪnəns/ *n* **1** maintaining or being maintained **2** (payment for) the upkeep of property or equipment **3** *chiefly Br* payments for the support of one spouse by another, esp of a woman by a man, pending or following legal separation or divorce

maisonette /ˌmays(ə)nˈet‖ˌmeɪs(ə)nˈet/ *n* **1** a small house **2** a part of a house, usu on 2 floors, let or sold separately [French *maisonnette*, diminutive of *maison* house, fr Latin *mansion-, mansio* dwelling place]

maize /mayz‖meɪz/ *n* (the ears or edible seeds of) a tall widely cultivated cereal grass bearing seeds on elongated ears

majesty /ˈmajəsti‖ˈmædʒəstɪ/ *n* **1** sovereign power **2** – used in addressing or referring to a king or queen <*Your* Majesty> **3a** impressive bearing or aspect **b** greatness or splendour of quality or character – **majestic** *adj*, **majestically** *adv*

majolica /məˈjolikə, -ˈyol-‖məˈdʒɒlɪkə, -ˈjɒl-/ *n* a type of early Italian tin-glazed earthenware [Italian *maiolica*, fr Medieval Latin *Majolica* Majorca, largest of the Balearic Islands]

[1]**major** /ˈmayjə‖ˈmeɪdʒə/ *adj* **1a** greater in importance, size, rank, or degree <*one of our ~ poets*> **b** of considerable importance <*a ~ improvement*> **2** having attained the age of majority **3** notable or conspicuous in effect or scope **4** involving serious risk to life; serious <*a ~ operation*> **5a** *esp of a scale or mode* having semitones between the third and fourth and the seventh and eighth degrees **b** being or based on a (specified) major scale <*in a ~ key*> <*a piece in D ~*> **c** being an interval (equivalent to that) between the first and the second, third, sixth, or seventh degree of a major scale **d** *of a chord* having an interval of a major third between the root and the next note above it

[2]**major** *n* **1** one who has attained the age of majority **2** a major musical interval, scale, key, or mode **3** an officer in the army or US airforce ranking below lieutenant colonel

majordomo /ˌmayjəˈdohmoh‖ˌmeɪdʒəˈdəʊməʊ/ *n, pl* **majordomos** **1** a man having charge of a large household (e g a palace) **2** a butler or steward

majorette /ˌmayjəˈret‖ˌmeɪdʒəˈret/ *n* a girl or woman who twirls a baton and accompanies a marching band

ˌmajor ˈgeneral *n* an officer in the army or US airforce ranking below lieutenant general

majority /məˈjorəti‖məˈdʒɒrətɪ/ *n* **1** the (status of one who has attained the) age at which full legal rights and responsibilities are acquired **2a** a number greater than half of a total **b** the amount by which such a greater number exceeds the remaining smaller number **3** the greatest in number of 2 or more groups constituting a whole; *specif* (the excess of votes over its rival obtained by) a group having sufficient votes to obtain control **4** the military office, rank, or commission of a major

ˈmajor ˌsuit *n* either of the suits of hearts or spades that are of superior scoring value in bridge

[1]**make** /mayk‖meɪk/ *vb* **made** /mayd‖meɪd/ *vt* **1a** to create or produce (for someone) by work or action <*~ a dress*> <*she* made *herself a cup of coffee*> **b** to cause; BRING ABOUT <*~ a disturbance*> **2** to formulate in the mind <*~ plans*> **3** to put together from ingredients or components <*butter is* made *from milk*> – often + *up* **4** to compute or estimate to be <*what time do you ~ it?*> **5a** to assemble and set alight the materials for (a fire) **b** to renew or straighten the bedclothes on (a bed) **6a** to cause to be or become <made *him bishop*> <*couldn't ~ himself heard*> **b** to cause (sthg) to appear or seem to; represent as <*in the film they ~ the battle take place in winter*> **c(1)** to change, transform <*~ the material into a skirt*> **c(2)** to produce as an end product <*the navy will ~ a man of you*> **d** to carry on right through (a period) <*take sandwiches and ~ a day of it*> **7a** to enact, establish <*~ laws*> **b** to draft or produce a version of <*~ a will*> **8** to cause (an electric circuit) to be completed **9a** to perform; CARRY OUT <*~ a speech*> <*~ a sweeping gesture*> **b** to eat <*~ a good breakfast*> **c** to put forward for acceptance <*~ an offer*> **10** to cause to act in a specified way; compel <*rain* ~s *the flowers grow*> **11a** to amount to; count as <*4 and 4 ~ 8*> <~s *a great difference*> **b** to be integral or essential to the existence or success of <*it* made *my day*> **c** to combine to form <*hydrogen and oxygen ~ water*> **12** to be capable of becoming or of serving as <*you'll ~ a golfer yet*> **13** to reach, attain <*never ~ the airfield*> <*the story* made *the papers*> – often + *it* <*you'll never ~ it that far*> **14** to gain (e g money) by working, trading, dealing, etc **15a** to act so as to acquire <*~ enemies*> **b** to score (points, runs, etc) in a game or sport **16a** to fulfil (a contract) in bridge or another card game **b** to win a trick with (a card) **17** to persuade to consent to sexual intercourse – infml ~ *vi* **1a** to

behave so as to seem <made *as though he were angry*> **b** to behave as if beginning a specified action <made *as if to hand it over*> **c** to act so as to be <~ *ready to leave*> **2** to set out or go (in a specified direction) <*we're* making *for the coast*> **3** to undergo manufacture or processing – usu + *up* <*the silk* ~s *up beautifully*> – **maker** *n* – **as near as makes no difference** almost exactly – **make a book** to take bets *on* – **make a meal of** *Br* to make more of than is necessary or tactful – **make an exhibition of oneself** to behave foolishly in public – **make away with 1** MAKE OFF WITH <*the thief* made away with *her handbag*> **2** to destroy – **make believe** to pretend, feign – **make bold** to venture, dare <made *so* bold *as to ask for more*> – **make certain/sure 1** to ascertain by enquiry **2** to take measures to ensure <make certain *of a seat*> – **make do** to get along or manage with the means at hand – **make ends meet** to live within one's income – **make eyes** to ogle – + *at* – **make fast** to tie or attach firmly – **make for** to be conducive to <*courtesy* makes for *safer driving*> – **make free with** to take excessive or disrespectful liberties with – **make friends 1** to acquire friends **2** to become friendly <make friends *with a neighbour*> – **make fun of** to make an object of amusement or ridicule – **make good 1** MAKE UP *vt* 4 **2** to be successful in life **3** *chiefly Br* to repair <make good *the brickwork under the window*> – **make head or tail of** to understand in the least <*I can't make* head or tail of *it*> – **make it 1** to be successful <*actors trying to* make it *in the big time*> – infml **2** to achieve sexual intercourse – slang – **make like** to act the part of; imitate – slang – **make love 1** to woo, court; *also* to pet, neck **2** to engage in sexual intercourse – **make no bones** to have no hesitation or shame <makes no bones *about giving her opinion*> – **make of 1** to attribute a specified degree of significance to <*tends to* make *too much* of *his problems*> **2** to understand by; conclude as to the meaning of <*could* make *nothing* of *the play*> – **make oneself scarce** to hide or avoid sby or sthg unobtrusively – **make public** to disclose – **make the grade** MAKE IT 1 – **make tracks** to leave <*its getting late; we'll have to* make tracks> – infml – **make water** to urinate – euph – **make way** to give room <*the crowd* made way *for the ambulance*> – **make with** *chiefly NAm* to produce, perform – usu + *the*; slang

[2]**make** *n* **1a** the manner or style in which sthg is constructed **b** a place or origin of manufacture; BRAND 3a **2** the physical, mental, or moral constitution of a person **3** the type or process of making or manufacturing – **on the make 1** rising or attempting to rise to a higher social or financial status **2** *NAm* in search of a sexual partner or sexual adventure

'make-be,lieve *n or adj* (sthg) imaginary or pretended

make off *vi* to leave in haste – **make off with** to take away; steal

make out *vt* **1** to draw up in writing **2** to complete (e g a printed form or document) by writing information in appropriate spaces **3** to find or grasp the meaning of <*tried to* make out *what had happened*> **4** to claim or pretend to be true <made out *that he had never heard of me*> **5** to identify (e g by sight or hearing) with difficulty or effort ~ *vi* **1** to fare, manage <*how is he* making out *in his new job?*> **2** *chiefly NAm* to engage in sexual intercourse – slang

make over *vt* **1** to transfer the title of (property) <made over *the estate to his eldest son*> **2** *chiefly NAm* to remake, remodel <made *the whole house* over>

Maker /'maykə‖'meɪkə/ *n* GOD 1

'make,shift /-,shift‖-,ʃɪft/ *adj or n* (being) a crude and temporary expedient

'make-,up *n* **1a** the way in which the parts of sthg are put together **b** physical, mental, and moral constitution **2a** cosmetics (e g lipstick and mascara) applied, esp to the face, to give colour or emphasis **b** the effect achieved by the application of make-up **c** materials (e g wigs and cosmetics) used for special costuming (e g for a play)

make up *vt* **1a** to invent (e g a story), esp in order to deceive **b** to set (an account) in order **2a** to arrange typeset matter into (columns or pages) for printing **b** to produce (e g clothes) by cutting and sewing **c** PREPARE 3a <make up *a prescription*> **3** to wrap or fasten up <make *the books* up *into a parcel*> **4** to compensate for (a deficiency); *esp* to make (e g a required amount or number) complete **5** to settle, decide <made up *his mind to leave*> <made up *their differences*> **6a** to prepare in physical appearance for a role **b** to apply cosmetics to ~ *vi* **1** to become reconciled **2** to compensate *for* <*we* made up *for lost time*> **3** to put on costumes or make-up (e g for a play) **4** to assemble a finished article; *esp* to complete a garment by sewing together

making /'mayking‖'meɪkɪŋ/ *n* **1** a process or means of advancement or success **2a** the essential qualities for becoming – often pl with sing. meaning <*had the* ~s *of a great artist*> **b** *pl, chiefly NAm & Austr* paper and tobacco used for rolling one's own cigarettes – **in the making** in the process of becoming, forming, or developing

mal- *comb form* **1a** bad <mal*practice*>; faulty <mal*function*> **b** badly <mal*odorous*>; deficiently <mal*nourished*> **2a** abnormal <mal*formation*> **b** abnormally <mal*formed*> **3** not <mal*content*>

ma'lacca ,cane /mə'lakə‖mə'lækə/ *n* an often mottled cane from an Asiatic rattan palm used esp for walking sticks [*Malacca*, city & state in Malaya]

malachite /'malə,kiet‖'mælə,kaɪt/ *n* hydrated copper carbonate occurring as a green mineral and used esp for ornaments

maladjusted /,malə'justid‖,mælə'dʒʌstɪd/ *adj* poorly or inadequately adjusted, specif to one's social environment and conditions of life – **maladjustment** *n*

maladministration /,malədmini'straysh(ə)n‖,mælədmɪnɪ'streɪʃ(ə)n/ *n* incompetent or corrupt administration, esp in public office – **maladminister** *vt*

maladroit /malə'droyt‖mælə'drɔɪt/ *adj* clumsy, inept

malady /'malədi‖'mælədɪ/ *n* an animal disease or disorder

malaise /ma'lez, -'layz‖mæ'lez, -'leɪz/ *n* **1** an indeterminate feeling of debility or lack of health, often accompanying the start of an illness

2 a vague sense of mental or moral unease

malapropism /ˈmaləpro,piz(ə)m‖ˈmæləprɒ,pɪz(ə)m/ *n* (an instance of) an incongruous misapplication of a word (e g in 'dressed in neon stockings') [Mrs *Malaprop*, character often misusing words in *The Rivals*, comedy by R B Sheridan (1751-1816), Irish dramatist]

malaria /məˈleəri·ə‖məˈleərɪə/ *n* a disease caused by protozoan parasites in the red blood cells, transmitted by the bite of mosquitoes, and characterized by periodic attacks of chills and fever [Italian, fr *mala aria* bad air] – **malarious** *adj*, **malarial** *adj*, **malarian** *adj*

Malay /məˈlay‖məˈleɪ/ *n* (the language of) a member of a people of the Malay peninsula and adjacent islands – **Malay** *adj*, **Malayan** *n or adj*

[1]**malcontent** /,malkənˈtent‖,mælkənˈtent/ *n* a discontented person; *esp* sby violently opposed to a government or regime

[2]**malcontent, malcontented** *adj* dissatisfied with the existing state of affairs

[1]**male** /mayl‖meɪl/ *adj* **1a(1)** of or being the sex that produces relatively small sperms, spermatozoids, or spermatozoa by which the eggs of a female are made fertile **a(2)** *of a plant or flower* having stamens but no ovaries **b(1)** (characteristic) of the male sex **b(2)** made up of male individuals **2** designed for fitting into a corresponding hollow part – **maleness** *n*

[2]**male** *n* a male person, animal, or plant

malediction /,maləˈdiksh(ə)n‖,mæləˈdɪkʃ(ə)n/ *n* a curse – fml – **maledictory** *adj*

malefactor /ˈmali,faktə‖ˈmælɪ,fæktə/ *n* **1** a criminal; *esp* a felon **2** one who does evil – fml

malefic /məˈlefik‖məˈlefɪk/ *adj* **1** having malignant influence **2** harmful, malicious *USE* fml – **maleficence** *n*, **maleficent** *adj*

malevolent /məˈlevələnt‖məˈlevələnt/ *adj* having, showing, or arising from an often intense desire to do harm – **malevolence** *n*, **malevolently** *adv*

malfeasance /malˈfeez(ə)ns‖mælˈfi:z(ə)ns/ *n* (official) misconduct

malformation /,malfawˈmaysh(ə)n‖,mælfɔ:ˈmeɪʃ(ə)n/ *n* anomalous, abnormal, or faulty formation or structure – **malformed** *adj*

,malˈfunction /-ˈfungksh(ə)n‖-ˈfʌŋkʃ(ə)n/ *vi* to fail to operate in the normal manner – **malfunction** *n*

malice /ˈmalis‖ˈmælɪs/ *n* conscious desire to harm; *esp* a premeditated desire to commit a crime – **malicious** *adj*, **maliciously** *adv*, **maliciousness** *n*

[1]**malign** /məˈlien‖məˈlaɪn/ *adj* **1a** harmful in nature, influence, or effect **b** *of a disease* malignant, virulent **2** bearing or showing (vicious) ill will or hostility

[2]**malign** *vt* to utter injuriously (false) reports about; speak ill of

malignant /məˈlignənt‖məˈlɪgnənt/ *adj* **1a** harmful in nature, influence, or effect **b** passionately and relentlessly malevolent **2** *of a disease* very severe or deadly <~ *malaria*>; *specif, of a tumour* tending to infiltrate, spread, and cause death – **malignantly** *adv*, **malignancy** *n*

malinger /məˈling·gə‖məˈlɪŋgə/ *vi* to pretend illness or incapacity so as to avoid duty or work – **malingerer** *n*

mall /mawl, mal‖mɔ:l, mæl/ *n* **1** a public promenade, often bordered by trees **2** *NAm* a shopping precinct, usu with associated parking space

mallard /ˈmalahd, -ləd‖ˈmælɑ:d, -ləd/ *n* a common large wild duck that is the ancestor of the domestic ducks

malleable /ˈmali·əbl‖ˈmælɪəbl/ *adj* **1** *esp of metals* capable of being beaten or rolled into a desired shape **2** easily shaped by outside forces or influences – **malleableness** *n*, **malleability** *n*

mallet /ˈmalit‖ˈmælɪt/ *n* **1** a hammer with a usu large head of wood, plastic, etc **2** an implement with a large usu cylindrical wooden head for striking the ball in croquet, polo, etc **3** a light hammer with a small rounded or spherical usu padded head used in playing certain musical instruments (e g a vibraphone)

malleus /ˈmali·əs‖ˈmælɪəs/ *n, pl* **mallei** /-li,ie‖-lɪ,aɪ/ the outermost of the chain of 3 small bones that transmit sound to the inner ear of mammals

mallow /ˈmaloh‖ˈmæləʊ/ *n* any of various related plants with usu deeply cut lobed leaves and showy flowers

malmsey /ˈmahmzi‖ˈmɑ:mzɪ/ *n, often cap* the sweetest variety of Madeira [Medieval Latin *Malmasia* Monemvasia, village in Greece where it was originally produced]

malnutrition /,malnyoohˈtrish(ə)n‖,mælnju:ˈtrɪʃ(ə)n/ *n* faulty or inadequate nutrition

,malˈodorous /-ˈohd(ə)rəs‖-ˈəʊd(ə)rəs/ *adj* smelling bad – fml

malpractice /malˈpraktis‖mælˈpræktɪs/ *n* **1** failure to exercise due professional skill or care **2** an instance of improper conduct; malfeasance – **malpractitioner** *n*

[1]**malt** /mawlt‖mɔ:lt/ *n* **1** grain softened in water, allowed to germinate, then roasted and used esp in brewing and distilling **2** unblended malt whisky produced in a particular area <*the finest Highland* ~s> – **malty** *adj*

[2]**malt** *vt* **1** to convert into malt **2** to make or treat with malt or malt extract ~*vi* to become malt

Maltese /mawlˈteez‖mɔ:lˈti:z/ *n, pl* **Maltese** (the language of) a native or inhabitant of Malta – **Maltese** *adj*

,Maltese ˈcross *n* a cross consisting of 4 equal arms that widen out from the centre and have their outer ends indented by a V

maltreat /,malˈtreet‖,mælˈtri:t/ *vt* to treat cruelly or roughly – **maltreatment** *n*

[1]**mama, mamma** /məˈmah‖məˈmɑ:/ *n* [1]MOTHER 1a – formerly used in address

[2]**mama, mamma** /ˈmumə‖ˈmʌmə; *NAm* ˈmahmə‖ˈmɑ:mə/ *n* mummy – used informally and by children

mamba /ˈmambə‖ˈmæmbə/ *n* any of several (tropical) African venomous snakes related to the cobras but with no hood

mambo /ˈmamboh‖ˈmæmbəʊ/ *n, pl* **mambos** (the music for) a ballroom dance of Haitian origin that resembles the rumba – **mambo** *vi*

mammal /ˈmaməl‖ˈmæməl/ *n* any of a class of higher vertebrates comprising humans and all other animals that have mammary glands and nourish their young with milk [deriv of Late Latin *mammalis* of the breast, fr Latin *mamma* breast] – **mammalian** *adj or n*, **mammalology** *n*

mammary /'maməri‖'mæmərɪ/ *adj* of, lying near, or affecting the mammary glands

Mammon /'mamən‖'mæmən/ *n* material wealth or possessions, esp considered as an evil

[1]**mammoth** /'maməth‖'mæməθ/ *n* any of numerous large hairy long-tailed extinct Pleistocene elephants

[2]**mammoth** *adj* of very great size

mammy /'mami‖'mæmɪ/ *n* **1** mamma, mummy – used esp by children **2** *NAm* a Negro nanny of white children, esp formerly in the southern USA

[1]**man** /man‖mæn/ *n, pl* **men** /men‖men/ **1a(1)** a human being; *esp* an adult male as distinguished from a woman or child **a(2)** a man belonging to a usu specified category – usu in combination <*business*man> <*horse*man> **a(3)** a husband – esp in *man and wife* **a(4)** a male sexual partner **b** the human race **c** a member of a family of biped primate mammals anatomically related to the great apes but distinguished esp by greater brain development and a capacity for articulate speech and abstract reasoning; *broadly* any ancestor of modern man **d** one possessing the qualities associated with manhood (e g courage and strength) **e** a fellow, chap – used interjectionally **2a** a feudal vassal **b** *pl* the members of (the ranks of) a military force **c** *pl* the working force as distinguished from the employer and usu the management **d** *pl* the members of a team **3a** an individual, person <*what can a* ~ *do in this situation?*> **b** the most suitable man <*he's your* ~ *for the job*> **4** any of the pieces moved by each player in chess, draughts, etc **5** *often cap, NAm the* police **6** *often cap, NAm the* white establishment – used by Negroes **7** – used interjectionally to express intensity of feeling <~, *what a party!*> *USE* (*5, 6 & 7*) slang – **manless** *adj*, **manlike** *adj* – **to a man** without exception

[2]**man** *vt* **-nn- 1** to supply with the man or men necessary **2** to take up station by <~ *the pumps*> **3** to serve in the force or complement of

[1]**manacle** /'manəkl‖'mænəkl/ *n* **1** a shackle or handcuff **2** a restraint *USE* usu pl

[2]**manacle** *vt* **1** to confine (the hands) with manacles **2** to subject to a restraint

manage /'manij‖'mænɪdʒ/ *vt* **1a** to make and keep submissive **b** to use (e g money) economically **2** to succeed in handling (e g a difficult situation or person) **3** to succeed in accomplishing <*she could only* ~ *a smile*> <*always* ~s *to win*> **4** to conduct the running of (esp a business); *also* to have charge of (e g a sports team or athlete) ~*vi* to be able to cope with difficulties; *esp* to use one's finances to the best advantage [Italian *maneggiare*, fr *mano* hand, fr Latin *manus*] – **manageable** *adj*

'**management** /-mənt‖-mənt/ *n* **1** the act or art of managing **2** *sing or pl in constr* the collective body of those who manage or direct an enterprise

manager /'manijə‖'mænɪdʒə/, *fem* **manageress** /-jə,res‖-dʒə,res/ *n* **1** one who conducts business or household affairs **2** sby who directs a sports team, player, entertainer, etc – **managership** *n*, **managerial** *adj*

,**man-at-'arms** *n, pl* **men-at-arms** a (heavily armed and usu mounted) soldier

manatee /,manə'tee‖,mænə'tiː/ *n* any of several (tropical) aquatic plant-eating mammals with broad tails

mandarin /'mandərin, ,--'-‖'mændərɪn, ,--'-/ *n* **1a** a public official in the Chinese Empire ranked according to any of 9 grades **b** a person of position and influence, esp in literary or bureaucratic circles; *esp* an elder and often reactionary member of such a circle **2** *cap* **2a** the primarily northern dialect of Chinese used by the court and officials under the Empire **b** the chief dialect of Chinese that has a standard variety spoken in the Peking area **3 mandarin, mandarin orange** (a small spiny Chinese orange tree that bears) a yellow to reddish orange fruit

,**mandarin 'duck** *n* a brightly marked crested Asian duck, often found domesticated

[1]**mandate** /'mandayt, -dət‖'mændeɪt, -dət/ *n* **1** an authoritative command from a superior **2** an authorization to act on the behalf of another; *specif* the political authority given by electors to parliament <*the* ~ *of the people*> **3a** an order granted by the League of Nations to a member nation for the establishment of a responsible government over a conquered territory **b** a mandated territory

[2]**mandate** /'mandayt‖'mændeɪt/ *vt* to administer or assign under a mandate

[1]**mandatory** /'mandət(ə)ri‖'mændət(ə)rɪ/ *adj* **1** containing or constituting a command **2** compulsory, obligatory

[2]**mandatory** *n* a nation or person holding a mandate

mandible /'mandibl‖'mændɪbl/ *n* **1a** JAW 1a **b** a lower jaw together with its surrounding soft parts **c** the upper or lower part of a bird's bill **2** any of various mouth parts in insects or other invertebrates for holding or biting food – **mandibular** *adj*, **mandibulate** *adj or n*

mandolin *also* **mandoline** /,mandə'lin‖,mændə'lɪn/ *n* a musical instrument of the lute family with a fretted neck

mandrake /'mandrayk‖'mændreɪk/ *n* (the root of) a Mediterranean plant of the nightshade family with whitish or purple flowers and a large forked supposedly man-shaped root formerly used in medicine

mandrill /'mandril‖'mændrɪl/ *n* a large gregarious baboon found in W Africa, the male of which has red and blue striped cheeks

mane /mayn‖meɪn/ *n* **1** long thick hair growing about the neck of a horse, male lion, etc **2** long thick hair on a person's head

'**man-,eater** *n* a person or animal that eats human flesh – **man-eating** *adj*

maneuver /mə'noohvə‖mə'nuːvə/ *vb or n, NAm* (to) manoeuvre

manful /'manf(ə)l‖'mænf(ə)l/ *adj* having courage and resolution – **manfully** *adv*

manganese /,mang·gə'neez‖,mæŋgə'niːz/ *n* a greyish white hard divalent or hexavalent metallic element – **manganic** *adj*, **manganous** *adj*

mange /manj, maynj‖mændʒ, meɪndʒ/ *n* any

of various contagious skin diseases affecting domestic animals or sometimes human beings, marked by inflammation and loss of hair and caused by a minute parasitic mite

mangel-wurzel /'mang·gl ˌwuhzl‖'mæŋgl ˌwɜːzl/, **mangel** *n* a large yellow to orange type of beet grown as food for livestock [German *mangoldwurzel, mangelwurzel*, fr *mangold* beet + *wurzel* root]

manger /'maynjə‖'meɪndʒə/ *n* a trough or open box in a stable for holding feed

[1]**mangle** /'mang·gl‖'mæŋgl/ *vt* **1** to hack or crush (as if) by repeated blows **2** to spoil by poor work, errors, etc

[2]**mangle** *vt or n* (to pass through) a machine with rollers for squeezing water from and pressing laundry

mango /'mang·goh‖'mæŋgəʊ/ *n, pl* **mangoes, mangos** (a tropical evergreen tree that bears) a yellowish red fruit with a firm skin, large stone, and juicy edible slightly acid pulp

mangrove /'mang,grohv‖'mæŋ,grəʊv/ *n* any of a genus of tropical maritime trees or shrubs with aerial roots that form dense masses

mangy /'manji, 'maynji‖'mændʒɪ, 'meɪndʒɪ/ *adj* **1** suffering or resulting from mange **2** having many worn or bare spots

manhandle /man'handl, '-ˌ--‖mæn'hændl, ''-ˌ--/ *vt* **1** to move or manage by human force **2** to handle roughly

manhole /'manˌhohl‖'mænˌhəʊl/ *n* a covered opening through which a person may go, esp to gain access to an underground or enclosed structure (e g a sewer)

'**manhood** /-hood‖-hʊd/ *n* **1** manly qualities **2** the condition of being an adult male as distinguished from a child or female **3** *sing or pl in constr* adult males collectively

'**man-ˌhour** *n* a unit of 1 hour's work by 1 person, used esp as a basis for cost accounting and wage calculation

mania /'maynyə‖'meɪnjə/ *n* **1** abnormal excitement and euphoria marked by mental and physical hyperactivity and disorganization of behaviour **2** excessive or unreasonable enthusiasm – often in combination <*Beatle*mania>

maniac /'mayniak‖'meɪnɪæk/ *n* one who is or acts as if (violently) insane; a lunatic – not used technically

maniacal /mə'nie·əkl‖mə'naɪəkl/ *also* **maniac** /'mayniak‖'meɪnɪæk/ *adj* **1** affected with or suggestive of madness **2** characterized by ungovernable frenzy

manic /'manik‖'mænɪk/ *adj* affected by, relating to, or resembling mania – **manic** *n*, **manically** *adv*

ˌ**manic-de'pressive** *adj* of or affected by a mental disorder characterized by alternating mania and (extreme) depression – **manic-depressive** *n*

[1]**manicure** /'manikyooə‖'mænɪkjʊə/ *n* **1** (a) treatment for the care of the hands and fingernails **2** a manicurist

[2]**manicure** *vt* **1** to give a manicure to **2** to trim closely and evenly – **manicurist** *n*

[1]**manifest** /'manifest‖'mænɪfest/ *adj* readily perceived by the senses (e g sight) or mind; obvious – **manifestly** *adv*

[2]**manifest** *vt* to make evident or certain by showing or displaying ~*vi of a spirit, ghost, etc* to appear in visible form – **manifester** *n*, **manifestation** *n*

[3]**manifest** *n* a list of passengers or an invoice of cargo, esp for a ship

manifesto /ˌmani'festoh‖ˌmænɪ'festəʊ/ *n, pl* **manifestos, manifestoes** a public declaration of intentions, esp by a political party before an election

[1]**manifold** /'manifohld‖'mænɪfəʊld/ *adj* many and varied – **manifoldly** *adv*, **manifoldness** *n*

[2]**manifold** *n* **1** a whole that unites or consists of many diverse elements **2** a hollow fitting (e g connecting the cylinders of an internal combustion engine with the exhaust pipe) with several outlets or inlets for connecting 1 pipe with several other pipes

manikin, mannikin /'manikin‖'mænɪkɪn/ *n* **1** a mannequin **2** a little man

manila paper *n, often cap M* a strong paper of a brownish or buff colour with a smooth finish [*Manila*, city in the Philippine islands]

manipulate /mə'nipyoolayt‖mə'nɪpjʊleɪt/ *vt* **1** to handle or operate, esp skilfully **2a** to manage or use skilfully **b** to control or influence by artful, unfair, or insidious means, esp to one's own advantage **3** to examine and treat (a fracture, sprain, etc) by moving bones into the proper position manually [deriv of Latin *manipulus* handful, fr *manus* hand] – **manipulatable** *adj*, **manipulator** *n*, **manipulative** *adj*, **manipulatory** *adj*, **manipulation** *n*

ˌ**man 'jack** *n* individual man <*every* ~>

mankind /man'kiend‖mæn'kaɪnd/ *n sing but sing or pl in constr* the human race

manky /'manki‖'mænkɪ/ *adj, Br* nasty, messy – slang

manly /-li‖-lɪ/ *adj* (marked by the good qualities) befitting a man – **manliness** *n*

ˌ**man-'made** *adj* made or produced by human beings rather than nature; *also* synthetic

manna /'manə‖'mænə/ *n* **1** food miraculously supplied to the Israelites in their journey through the wilderness **2** a sudden source of benefit

manned /mand‖mænd/ *adj* **1** equipped with men **2** *of a spacecraft* carrying a human crew

mannequin /'manikin‖'mænɪkɪn/ *n* **1** an artist's, tailor's, or dressmaker's model of the human figure; *also* such a model used esp for displaying clothes **2** a woman who models clothing

manner /'manə‖'mænə/ *n* **1** a kind, sort; *also* sorts <*all* ~ *of information*> **2a** the mode or method in which sthg is done or happens **b** a method of artistic execution; a style **3** *pl* **3a** (rules of) social conduct **b** social behaviour evaluated as to politeness; *esp* conduct indicating good background **4** characteristic or distinctive bearing, air, or deportment – **mannerless** *adj*

mannered /'manəd‖'mænəd/ *adj* **1** having manners of a specified kind – usu in combination <*well*-mannered> **2** having an artificial or stilted character

mannerism /'manəˌriz(ə)m‖'mænəˌrɪz(ə)m/ *n* **1a** exaggerated or affected adherence to a particular style in art or literature **b** *often cap* a style of art in late 16th-c Europe characterized by distortion of the human figure **2** a characteristic (unconscious) gesture or trait; an idiosyncrasy – **mannerist** *n*, **manneristic** *adj*

ˈmannerly /-li‖-lɪ/ *adj* showing or having good manners – **mannerliness** *n*, **mannerly** *adv*

mannish /ˈmanish‖ˈmænɪʃ/ *adj* resembling, befitting, or typical of a man rather than a woman – **mannishly** *adv*, **mannishness** *n*

[1]**manoeuvre,** *NAm chiefly* **maneuver** /məˈnoohvə‖məˈnuːvə/ *n* **1a** a military or naval movement **b** a (large-scale) training exercise for the armed forces **2** an intended and controlled deviation from a straight and level flight path in the operation of an aircraft **3** a skilful or dexterous movement **4** an adroit and clever management of affairs, often using deception [French *manœuvre*, fr Old French *maneuvre* work done by hand, fr Medieval Latin *manuopera*, fr Latin *manu operare* to work by hand]

[2]**manoeuvre,** *NAm chiefly* **maneuver** *vi* **1** to perform a military or naval manoeuvre (to secure an advantage) **2** to perform a manoeuvre **3** to use stratagems ~ *vt* **1** to cause (e g troops) to execute manoeuvres **2** to manipulate with adroitness **3** to bring about or secure as a result of contriving – **manoeuvrable** *adj*, **manoeuvrer** *n*, **manoeuvrability** *n*

ˌman-of-ˈwar *n, pl* **men-of-war** /men‖men/ a warship (of the days of sail)

manometer /məˈnomitə‖məˈnɒmɪtə/ *n* an instrument for measuring the pressure of gases and vapours – **manometry** *n*, **manometric, manometrical** *adj*, **manometrically** *adv*

manor /ˈmanə‖ˈmænə/ *n* **1** a landed estate **2a** a medieval estate under a lord who held a variety of rights over land and tenants, including the right to hold court **b manor, manor house** the house of the lord of a manor **3** a district of police administration – slang – **manorial** *adj*, **manorialism** *n*

ˈmanˌpower *n* the total supply of people available for work or service

manqué /ˈmongˌkay‖ˈmɒŋˌkeɪ (*Fr* mɑ̃ke)/ *adj* that could have been but failed to be – used after the noun modified <*a poet* ~> [French, fr past participle of *manquer* to lack, fail]

mansard /ˈmansahd, -səd‖ˈmænsɑːd, -səd/, **mansard roof** *n* a roof with a lower steeper slope and a higher shallower one on all 4 sides [François *Mansart* (1598-1666), French architect]

manse /mans‖mæns/ *n* the residence of an esp Presbyterian or Baptist clergyman

manservant /ˈmanˌsuhv(ə)nt‖ˈmænˌsɜːv(ə)nt/ *n, pl* **manservants** a male servant, esp a valet

mansion /ˈmansh(ə)n‖ˈmænʃ(ə)n/ *n* **1a** the house of the lord of a manor **b** a large imposing residence **2** a separate apartment in a large structure **3** *archaic* a dwelling

manslaughter /ˈmanˌslawtə‖ˈmænˌslɔːtə/ *n* the unlawful killing of sby without malicious intent

mantelpiece /ˈmantlˌpees‖ˈmæntlˌpiːs/, **mantel** *n* an ornamental structure round a fireplace; *also* a mantelshelf

ˈmantelˌshelf /-ˌshelf‖-ˌʃelf/, **mantel** *n* a shelf forming part of or above a mantelpiece

mantilla /manˈtilə‖mænˈtɪlə/ *n* a light scarf worn over the head and shoulders esp by Spanish and Latin-American women

mantis /ˈmantis‖ˈmæntɪs/ *n, pl* **mantises, mantes** /-teez‖-tiːz/ any of several insects that feed on other insects; *esp* PRAYING MANTIS

[1]**mantle** /ˈmantl‖ˈmæntl/ *n* **1a** a loose sleeveless garment worn over other clothes; a cloak **b** a mantle regarded as a symbol of preeminence or authority **2** sthg that covers, envelops, or conceals **3** the feathers covering the back, shoulders,and wings of a bird **4** a lacelike sheath of some reflecting material that gives light by incandescence when placed over a flame **5** the part of the earth or a similar planet that lies between the crust and central core

[2]**mantle** *vt* to cover (as if) with a mantle

ˌman-to-ˈman *adj* **1** characterized by frankness and honesty **2** of or being a defensive system in soccer, basketball, etc in which each player marks 1 specific opponent

mantra /ˈmantrə‖ˈmæntrə/ *n* a devotional incantation (e g in Hinduism or Buddhism)

ˈmanˌtrap *n* a trap for catching people

[1]**manual** /ˈmanyooəl‖ˈmænjʊəl/ *adj* **1** of or involving the hands **2** requiring or using physical skill and energy **3** worked or done by hand and not by machine or automatically – **manually** *adv*

[2]**manual** *n* **1** a book of instructions; a handbook **2** the set movements in the handling of a weapon during a military drill or ceremony **3** a keyboard for the hands; *specif* any of the several keyboards of an organ that control separate divisions of the instrument

[1]**manufacture** /ˌmanyooˈfakchə‖ˌmænjʊˈfæktʃə/ *n* **1** the esp large-scale making of wares by hand or by machinery **2** an industry using mechanical power and machinery **3** the act or process of producing sthg

[2]**manufacture** *vt* **1** to make (materials) into a product suitable for use **2** to make (wares) from raw materials by hand or by machinery, esp on a large scale **3** to invent, fabricate **4** to produce as if by manufacturing <*writers who* ~ *stories for television*> – **manufacturing** *n*

manufacturer /ˌmanyooˈfakchərə‖ˌmænjʊˈfæktʃərə/ *n* an employer in a manufacturing industry

manumit /ˌmanyooˈmit‖ˌmænjʊˈmɪt/ *vt* **-tt-** to release from slavery – **manumission** *n*

[1]**manure** /məˈnyooə‖məˈnjʊə/ *vt* to enrich (land) by the application of manure – **manurer** *n*

[2]**manure** *n* material that fertilizes land; *esp* the faeces of domestic animals – **manurial** *adj*

manuscript /ˈmanyooˌskript‖ˈmænjʊˌskrɪpt/ *n or adj* (a composition or document) written by hand or typed as distinguished from a printed copy [Latin *manu scriptus* written by hand]

[1]**Manx** /mangks‖mæŋks/ *adj* (characteristic) of the Isle of Man

[2]**Manx** *n* **1** *pl in constr* the people of the Isle of Man **2** the almost extinct Celtic language of the Manx people

ˌManx ˈcat *n* (any of) a breed of short-haired domestic cats some of which have no external tail

[1]**many** /ˈmeni‖ˈmenɪ/ *adj* **more** /maw‖mɔː/; **most** /mohst‖məʊst/ **1** consisting of or amounting to a large but unspecified number <*worked for* ~

years> <many-*sided*> **2** being one of a large number <~ *a man*> <~ *is the time I've wondered*> – **as many** the same in number <*saw 3 plays in* as many *days*>

[2]**many** *pron pl in constr* a large number of people or things <~ *prefer to stay at home*> <*I haven't got as* ~ *as you*>

[3]**many** *n pl in constr* **1** a large but indefinite number <*a good* ~ *of them have already left*> **2** *the* great majority

[4]**many** *adv* to a considerable degree or amount; far – with plurals <~ *more cars than usual*>

ˌmany-ˈsided *adj* **1** having many sides or aspects **2** having many interests or aptitudes – **many-sidedness** *n*

Maori /ˈmowri, ˈmahri‖ˈmaʊrɪ, ˈmɑːrɪ/ *n* **1** a member of the indigenous people of New Zealand **2** the Austronesian language of the Maori

[1]**map** /map‖mæp/ *n* **1** a representation, usu on a flat surface, of (part of) the earth's surface, the celestial sphere, etc **2** sthg that represents with a clarity suggestive of a map

[2]**map** *vt* **-pp- 1a** to make a map of **b** to delineate as if on a map **c** to survey in order to make a map **2** to assign to every element of (a mathematical set) an element of the same or another set **3** to plan in detail – often + *out* <~ *out a programme*> – **mappable** *adj*, **mapper** *n*

maple /ˈmaypl‖ˈmeɪpl/ *n* (the hard light-coloured close-grained wood, used esp for furniture, of) any of a genus of widely planted trees or shrubs

maple sugar *n* sugar made by boiling maple syrup

maquis /ˈmaki‖ˈmækɪ/ *n, pl* **maquis** /~/ **1** (an area of) thick scrubby underbrush of Mediterranean shores **2a** *often cap* a member of the French Resistance during WW II **b** *sing or pl in constr* a band of maquis

mar /mah‖mɑː/ *vt* **-rr-** to detract from the perfection or wholeness of

maraschino /ˌmarəˈsheenoh, -ˈskeenoh‖ˌmærəˈʃiːnəʊ, -ˈskiːnəʊ/ *n, pl* **maraschinos** *often cap* **1** a sweet liqueur distilled from the fermented juice of a bitter wild cherry **2** a usu large cherry preserved in true or imitation maraschino

marathon /ˈmarəth(ə)n‖ˈmærəθ(ə)n/ *n* **1** a long-distance race; *specif* a foot race of 26mi 385yd (about 42.2km) that is contested on an open course in major athletics championships **2a** an endurance contest **b** an event or activity characterized by great length or concentrated effort [*Marathon*, Greece, site of a victory of Greeks over Persians in 490 BC, the news of which was reputedly carried to Athens by a long-distance runner]

maraud /məˈrawd‖məˈrɔːd/ *vi* to roam about in search of plunder ~*vt* to raid, pillage – **marauder** *n*

[1]**marble** /ˈmahbl‖ˈmɑːbl/ *n* **1a** (more or less) crystallized limestone that can be highly polished and is used esp in building and sculpture **b** a sculpture or carving made of marble **2a** a little ball made of a hard substance, esp glass, and used in children's games **b** *pl but sing in constr* any of several games played with marbles, the object of which is to hit a mark or hole, to hit another player's marble, or to knock as many marbles as possible out of a ring **3** marbling **4** *pl* elements of common sense; *esp* sanity – infml <*he's lost his* ~*!*>

[2]**marble** *vt* to give a veined or mottled appearance to (e g the edges of a book) – **marbling** *n*

ˈmarbled *adj* **1a** made of or veneered with marble **b** marked by an extensive use of marble as an architectural or decorative feature <*ancient* ~ *cities*> **2** *of meat* marked by a mixture of fat and lean

marcasite /ˌmahkəˈseet, ˈmahkəˌsiet‖ˌmɑːkəˈsiːt, ˈmɑːkəˌsaɪt/ *n* (a piece of) crystallized iron pyrites or a similar mineral, used esp for jewellery

[1]**march** /mahch‖mɑːtʃ/ *n, often cap* a border region; *esp* a tract of land between 2 countries whose ownership is disputed – usu pl <*the Welsh* ~es>

[2]**march** *vi* to have common borders or frontiers <*a region that* ~es *with Canada in the north*>

[3]**march** *vi* **1** to move along steadily, usu in step with others **2a** to move in a direct purposeful manner **b** to make steady progress <*time* ~es *on*> ~ *vt* **1** to cause to march <~ed *him off to the police station*> **2** to cover by marching <~ed *30 miles*>

[4]**march** *n* **1a** the action of marching **b** the distance covered within a specified period of time by marching **c** a regular measured stride or rhythmic step used in marching **d** steady forward movement **2** a musical composition, usu in duple or quadruple time, that has a strongly accentuated beat and is designed or suitable to accompany marching – **on the march** moving steadily; advancing

March *n* the 3rd month of the Gregorian calendar [Old French, fr Latin *martius*, fr *martius* of Mars, fr *Mars*, Roman god of war]

ˈmarching ˌorders /ˈmahching‖ˈmɑːtʃɪŋ/ *n pl* **1** official notice for troops to move **2** notice of dismissal <*the player was given his* ~ *after the brutal foul*>

marchioness /ˌmahshəˈnes, ˈmahshənis‖ˌmɑːʃəˈnes, ˈmɑːʃənɪs/ *n* **1** the wife or widow of a marquess **2** a woman having in her own right the rank of a marquess

Mardi Gras /ˌmahdi ˈgrah‖ˌmɑːdɪ ˈgrɑː/ *n* (a carnival period culminating on) Shrove Tuesday often observed (e g in New Orleans) with parades and festivities [French, lit., fat Tuesday]

[1]**mare** /meə‖meə/ *n* a female equine animal, esp when fully mature or of breeding age; *esp* a female horse

[2]**mare** /ˈmahray‖ˈmɑːreɪ/ *n, pl* **maria** /-ri·ə‖-rɪə/ any of several large dark areas on the surface of the moon or Mars

ˈmare's ˌnest /meəz‖meəz/ *n, pl* **mare's nests, mares' nests** a false discovery, illusion, or deliberate hoax

margarine /ˌmahjəˈreen‖ˌmɑːdʒəˈriːn; *also* ˌmahgəˈreen, ˈ---‖ˌmɑːgəˈriːn, ˈ---/ *n* a substitute for butter made usu from vegetable oils churned with ripened skimmed milk to a smooth emulsion [French, fr Greek *margaron* pearl]

[1]**margin** /ˈmahjin‖ˈmɑːdʒɪn/ *n* **1** the part of a page outside the main body of printed or written text **2** the outside limit and adjoining surface

of sthg **3a** a spare amount or measure or degree allowed (e g in case of error) **b(1)** a bare minimum below which or an extreme limit beyond which sthg becomes impossible or is no longer desirable **b(2)** the limit below which economic activity cannot be continued under normal conditions **4** the difference between net sales and the cost of merchandise sold **5** measure or degree of difference – **margined** *adj*

[2]**margin** *vt* to provide with a border

[1]**marginal** /ˈmahjinl‖ˈmɑːdʒɪnl/ *adj* **1** written or printed in the margin **2** of or situated at a margin or border **3** close to the lower limit of qualification, acceptability, or function **4** of or providing a nominal profit margin **5** being a constituency where the Member of Parliament was elected with only a small majority – **marginally** *adv*, **marginality** *n*

[2]**marginal** *n* a marginal constituency

marguerite /ˌmahgəˈreet‖ˌmɑːgəˈriːt/ *n* (a single-flowered chrysanthemum like) an oxeye daisy

marigold /ˈmarigohld‖ˈmærɪgəʊld/ *n* any of a genus of composite plants with showy yellow or red flower heads

marijuana, **marihuana** /ˌmarəˈ(h)wahnə, -yooˈahnə‖ˌmærəˈ(h)wɑːnə, -jʊˈɑːnə/ *n* **1** HEMP 1 **2** a usu mild form of cannabis

marimba /məˈrimbə‖məˈrɪmbə/ *n* a percussion instrument resembling a large xylophone

marina /məˈreenə‖məˈriːnə/ *n* a dock or basin providing secure moorings for motorboats, yachts, etc

marinade /ˌmariˈnayd‖ˌmærɪˈneɪd/ *vt or n* (to soak in) a blend of oil, wine or vinegar, herbs, and spices in which meat, fish, etc is soaked, esp to enrich its flavour

marinate /ˈmarinayt‖ˈmærɪneɪt/ *vt* to marinade

[1]**marine** /məˈreen‖məˈriːn/ *adj* **1** of or (living) in the sea **2** of or used in the navigation or commerce of the sea <*a ~ chart*> <*~ law*>

[2]**marine** *n* **1** seagoing ships (of a specified nationality or class) <*the mercantile ~*> **2a** any of a class of soldiers serving on shipboard or in close association with a naval force **b** a person holding the lowest rank in the Royal Marines **3** a seascape

mariner /ˈmarinə‖ˈmærɪnə/ *n* a seaman, sailor

marionette /ˌmari·əˈnet‖ˌmærɪəˈnet/ *n* a small-scale usu wooden figure with jointed limbs that is moved from above by attached strings or wires

marital /ˈmaritl‖ˈmærɪtl/ *adj* of marriage – **maritally** *adv*

maritime /ˈmariˌtiem‖ˈmærɪˌtaɪm/ *adj* **1** MARINE 2•**2** of or bordering on the sea

marjoram /ˈmahjəram, -rəm‖ˈmɑːdʒəræm, -rəm/ *n* any of various plants of the mint family used as herbs; *also* oregano

[1]**mark** /mahk‖mɑːk/ *n* **1a(1)** a conspicuous object serving as a guide for travellers **a(2)** sthg (e g a line, notch, or fixed object) designed to record position **b** any of the points on a sounding line that correspond to a depth in whole fathoms **c** TARGET 2a **d** the starting line or position in a track event **e** a goal or desired object **f** the point under discussion <*that comment was rather off the ~*> **g** an established or accepted standard of performance, quality, or condition <*his singing was hardly up to the ~*> **2a(1)** a sign or token <*a ~ of his esteem*> **a(2)** an impression on the surface of sthg; *esp* a scratch, stain, etc that spoils the appearance of a surface **a(3)** a distinguishing characteristic <*bears the ~ of an educated woman*> **b(1)** a symbol used for identification or indication of ownership **b(2)** a symbol, esp a cross, made in place of a signature **c** a written or printed symbol <*punctuation ~s*> **d** *cap* – used with a numeral to designate a particular model of a weapon or machine <Mark *II*> **e** a symbol representing a judgment of merit, esp one used by a teacher **f** a point or level (reached) <*passed the halfway ~*> **3a** attention, notice <*nothing worthy of ~ occurred*> **b** importance, distinction <*a person of little ~*> **c** a lasting or strong impression <*years of warfare have left their ~ on the country*> **d** an assessment of merits <*got high ~s for honesty*> **4** an object of attack; *specif* a victim of a swindle – infml

[2]**mark** *vt* **1a(1)** to fix or trace *out* the limits of **a(2)** to plot the course of **b** to set apart (as if) by a line or boundary – usu + *off* **2a(1)** to designate or identify (as if) by a mark <*~ed for greatness*> **a(2)** to make or leave a mark on **a(3)** to label (merchandise) so as to indicate price or quality **a(4)** to add appropriate symbols, characters, or other marks to or on <*~ the manuscript for the printer*> – usu + *up* **b(1)** to indicate by a mark <*X ~s the spot*> **b(2)** to register, record <*~ the date in your diary*> **b(3)** to evaluate by marks <*~ examination papers*> **c(1)** to characterize, distinguish <*the flamboyance that ~s her stage appearance*> **c(2)** to be the occasion of (sthg notable); to indicate as a particular time <*this year ~s the 50th anniversary of the organization*> **3** to take notice of <*~ what I say*> **4** *Br* to stay close to (an opposing player) in hockey, soccer, etc so as to hinder the getting or play of the ball ~ *vi* **1** to become or make sthg stained, scratched, etc <*it won't ~ will it?*> **2** to evaluate sthg by marks – **marker** *n* – **mark time 1** to keep the time of a marching step by moving the feet alternately without advancing **2** to function listlessly or unproductively while waiting to progress or advance

[3]**mark** *n* **1** *often cap* (a note or coin representing) the basic money unit of either East or West Germany **2** a markka

ˈ**markˌdown** *n* (the amount of) a reduction in price – **mark down** *vt*

marked /mahkt‖mɑːkt/ *adj* **1a** having natural marks (of a specified type) <*wings ~ with white*> **b** made identifiable by marking <*a ~ card*> **2** having a distinctive or emphasized character <*a ~ American accent*> **3** being an object of attack, suspicion, or vengeance <*a ~ man*> **4** distinguished from a basic form (e g the singular) by the presence of a particular linguistic feature (e g *s* indicating the plural form) – **markedly** *adv*

[1]**market** /ˈmahkit‖ˈmɑːkɪt/ *n* **1a** a meeting together of people for the purpose of trade, by private purchase and sale **b** an open space,

building, etc where a market (e g for trading in provisions or livestock) is held **2a** (a geographical area or section of the community in which there is) demand for commodities <*the foreign* ~> **b** commercial activity; extent of trading **c** an opportunity for selling <*create new* ~s *for our product*> **d** the area of economic activity in which the forces of supply and demand affect prices <~ *value*> – **in the market** interested in buying <in the market *for a house*> – **on the market** available for purchase

[2]**market** *vi* to deal in a market ~*vt* to sell – **marketable** *adj*, **marketability** *n*

ˌ**market 'garden** *n* a plot in which vegetables are grown for market – **market gardener** *n*, **market gardening** *n*

marketing /'mahkiting‖'mɑːkɪtɪŋ/ *n* the skills and functions, including packaging, promotion, and distribution, involved in selling goods

'**marketˌplace** *n* **1** an open place in a town where markets are held **2** MARKET 2c, d

ˌ**market 'research** *n* research (e g the collection and analysis of information about consumer preferences) dealing with the patterns or state of demand (for a particular product) in a market

marking /'mahking‖'mɑːkɪŋ/ *n* **1** (the giving of) a mark or marks **2** arrangement, pattern, or disposition of marks

'**marking ˌink** *n* indelible ink for marking fabric

marksman /'mahksmən‖'mɑːksmən/, *fem* '**marksˌwoman** *n, pl* **marksmen,** *fem* **markswomen** a person skilled in hitting a mark or target – **marksmanship** *n*

'**markˌup** *n* (the amount of) an increase in price – **mark up** *vt*

marl /mahl‖mɑːl/ *vt or n* (to fertilize with) a crumbly earthy deposit (e g of silt or clay) that contains calcium carbonate and is used esp as a fertilizer for lime-deficient soils – **marly** *adj*

marline, marlin /'mahlin‖'mɑːlɪn/ *n* a thin 2-stranded usu tarred rope used on board ship

'**marlineˌspike, marlinspike** /-ˌspiek‖-ˌspaɪk/ *n* a pointed steel tool used to separate strands of rope or wire

[1]**marmalade** /'mahməˌlayd‖'mɑːməˌleɪd/ *n* a clear sweetened preserve made from oranges, lemons, etc and usu containing pieces of fruit peel [Portuguese *marmelada* quince conserve, fr *marmelo* quince, fr Latin *melimelum*, a sweet apple, fr Greek *melimēlon*, fr *meli* honey + *mēlon* apple]

[2]**marmalade** *adj, esp of cats* brownish orange

marmoreal /mah'mawri·əl‖mɑː'mɔːrɪəl/, *also* **marmorean** /-ri·ən‖-rɪən/ *adj* of or like marble or a marble statue – chiefly poetic

marmoset /'mahməzet‖'mɑːməzet/ *n* any of numerous soft-furred S and Central American monkeys

marmot /'mahmət‖'mɑːmət/ *n* any of several stout-bodied short-legged small-eared burrowing rodents

[1]**maroon** /mə'roohn‖mə'ruːn/ *vt* **1** to abandon on a desolate island or coast **2** to isolate in a helpless state [*Maroon*, a fugitive Negro slave in the West Indies, deriv of American Spanish *cimarrón* wild, savage]

[2]**maroon** *n* **1** a dark brownish red **2** an explosive rocket used esp as a distress signal [French *marron* Spanish chestnut]

marquee /mah'kee‖mɑː'kiː/ *n* **1** a large tent (e g for an outdoor party or exhibition) **2** *NAm* a permanent canopy projecting over an entrance (e g of a hotel or theatre)

marquess, marquis /'mahkwis‖'mɑːkwɪs/ *n, pl* **marquesses, marquises, marquis** (a European nobleman equivalent in rank to) a member of the British peerage ranking below a duke and above an earl – **marquessate, marquisate** *n*

marquetry *also* **marqueterie** /'mahkətri‖'mɑːkətrɪ/ *n* decorative work of pieces of wood, ivory, etc inlaid in a wood veneer that is then applied to a surface (e g of a piece of furniture)

marriage /'marij‖'mærɪdʒ/ *n* **1a** the state of being or mutual relation of husband and wife **b** the institution whereby a man and a woman are joined in a special kind of social and legal dependence **2** an act or the rite of marrying; *esp* the wedding ceremony **3** an intimate or close union – **marriageable** *adj*

[1]**married** /'marid‖'mærɪd/ *adj* **1a** joined in marriage **b** of married people **2** united, joined

[2]**married** *n* a married person <*young* ~s>

marrow /'maroh‖'mærəʊ/ *n* **1a** a soft tissue that fills the cavities and porous part of most bones and contains many blood vessels **b** the substance of the spinal cord **2** the inmost, best, or essential part; the core **3** *chiefly Br* VEGETABLE MARROW – **marrowless** *adj*, **marrowy** *adj*

marrowbone /'marəˌbohn, -roh-‖'mærəˌbəʊn, -rəʊ-/ *n* a bone rich in marrow

marrowfat /'marəˌfat, -roh-‖'mærəˌfæt, -rəʊ-/ *n* any of several types of large pea

[1]**marry** /'mari‖'mærɪ/ *vt* **1a** to give in marriage **b** to take as spouse **c** to perform the ceremony of marriage for **d** to obtain by marriage <*she* married *money*> **2** to bring together closely, harmoniously, and usu permanently ~ *vi* **1a** to take a spouse **b** to become husband and wife **2** to join in a close or harmonious relationship – **marry into** to become a member of or obtain by marriage <married into *a prominent family*>

[2]**marry** *interj, archaic* – used for emphasis, esp to express amused or surprised agreement

Mars /mahz‖mɑːz/ *n* the planet 4th in order from the sun and conspicuous for its red colour

Marsala /mah'sahlə‖mɑː'sɑːlə/ *n* a (sweet) fortified wine from Sicily

marsh /mahsh‖mɑːʃ/ *n* (an area of) soft wet land usu covered with sedges, rushes, etc – **marshy** *adj*, **marshiness** *n*

[1]**marshal** /'mahsh(ə)l‖'mɑːʃ(ə)l/ *n* **1a** a high official in a medieval royal household **b** one who arranges and directs a ceremony **c** one who arranges the procedure at races **2a** FIELD MARSHAL **b** an officer of the highest military rank **3a** a chief officer in the USA responsible for court processes in a district **b** the head of a US police or fire department – **marshalcy, marshalship** *n*

[2]**marshal** *vb* **-ll-** (*NAm* **-l-, -ll-**) *vt* **1** to place in proper rank or position **2** to bring together and order in an effective way <~ *one's thoughts*> **3** to lead ceremoniously or solicitously; usher ~*vi* to form or collect together (in a proper order)

'**marshalling ˌyard** *n, chiefly Br* a place

where railway vehicles are shunted and assembled into trains

marshal of the Royal Air Force *n* an officer of the highest rank in the Royal Air Force

ˈmarsh ˌgas *n* methane

marshmallow /ˌmahshˈmaloh‖ˌmɑːʃˈmæləʊ/ *n* **1** a pink-flowered Eurasian marsh plant of the mallow family **2** a light spongy confection made from the root of the marshmallow or from sugar, albumen, and gelatin – **marshmallowy** *adj*

ˌmarsh ˈmariˌgold /ˈmariˌgohld‖ ˈmærɪˌgəʊld/ *n* a European and N American marsh plant of the buttercup family with large bright yellow flowers

[1]**marsupial** /mahˈsyoohpi·əl, -ˈsooh-‖mɑːˈsjuːpɪəl, -ˈsuː-/ *adj* **1** of or being a marsupial **2** of or forming a marsupium or pouch

[2]**marsupial** *n* any of an order of lower mammals including the kangaroos, wombats, and opossums that have a pouch on the abdomen of the female for carrying young, and do not develop a placenta

marˈsupium /-pi·əm‖-pɪəm/ *n, pl* **marsupia** /-pi·ə‖-pɪə/ the abdominal pouch of a marsupial, formed by a fold of the skin and enclosing the mammary glands

mart /maht‖mɑːt/ *n* a place of trade (e g an auction room or market)

marten /ˈmahtin‖ˈmɑːtɪn/ *n* any of several slender-bodied flesh-eating tree-dwelling mammals larger than the related weasels

martial /ˈmahsh(ə)l‖ˈmɑːʃ(ə)l/ *adj* of or suited to war or a warrior; *also* warlike [Latin *martialis* of (the god) Mars, fr *Mars* Roman god of war] – **martially** *adv*

ˌmartial ˈart *n* an Oriental art of combat (e g judo or karate) practised as a sport

ˌmartial ˈlaw *n* the law administered by military forces in occupied territory or in an emergency

Martian /ˈmahsh(ə)n‖ˈmɑːʃ(ə)n/ *adj* of or coming from the planet Mars – **Martian** *n*

martin /ˈmahtin‖ˈmɑːtɪn/ *n* any of various birds of the swallow family: e g **a** a house martin **b** a sand martin

martinet /ˌmahtiˈnet‖ˌmɑːtɪˈnet/ *n* a strict disciplinarian [Jean *Martinet* (died 1672), French army officer]

martini /mahˈteeni‖mɑːˈtiːnɪ/ *n* a cocktail made of gin and dry vermouth

Martinmas /ˈmahtinməs, -ˌmas‖ˈmɑːtɪnməs, -ˌmæs/ *n* November 11 celebrated as the feast of St Martin

[1]**martyr** /ˈmahtə‖ˈmɑːtə/ *n* **1** one who is put to death for adherence to a cause, esp a religion **2** a victim, esp of constant (self-inflicted) suffering – **martyrize** *vt*, **martyrdom** *n*, **martyrization** *n*

[2]**martyr** *vt* **1** to put to death as a martyr **2** to inflict agonizing pain on

[1]**marvel** /ˈmahv(ə)l‖ˈmɑːv(ə)l/ *n* one who or that which is marvellous

[2]**marvel** *vi* **-ll-** (*NAm* **-l-**, **-ll-**) to become filled with surprise, wonder, or amazed curiosity

marvellous, *NAm chiefly* **marvelous** /ˈmahv(ə)l·əs‖ˈmɑːv(ə)ləs/ *adj* **1** causing wonder **2** of the highest kind or quality – **marvellously** *adv*, **marvellousness** *n*

Marxism /ˈmahksiz(ə)m‖ˌmɑːksɪz(ə)m/ *n* the political and economic principles and policies advocated by Karl Marx, that stress the importance of human labour in determining economic value, the struggle between classes as an instrument of social change, and dictatorship of the proletariat [Karl *Marx* (1818-83), German political philosopher] – **Marxist** *n or adj*, **Marxian** *adj*

marzipan /ˈmahziˌpan‖ˈmɑːzɪˌpæn/ *n* a paste made from ground almonds, sugar, and egg whites, used for coating cakes or shaped into small sweets

mascara /maˈskahrə‖mæˈskɑːrə/ *n* a cosmetic for colouring, esp darkening, the eyelashes [Spanish *máscara* mask, disguise, fr Italian *maschera*]

mascot /ˈmaskot, -kət‖ˈmæskɒt, -kət/ *n* a person, animal, or object adopted as a (good luck) symbol

[1]**masculine** /ˈmaskyoolin‖ˈmæskjʊlɪn/ *adj* **1a** male **b** having qualities appropriate to a man <*her deep ~ voice*> **2** of, belonging to, or being the gender that normally includes most words or grammatical forms referring to males **3** having or occurring in a stressed final syllable – **masculinely** *adv*, **masculineness** *n*, **masculinize** *vt*, **masculinity** *n*

[2]**masculine** *n* (a word or morpheme of) the masculine gender

maser /ˈmayzə‖ˈmeɪzə/ *n* a device that works like a laser for amplifying or generating (microwave) radiation

[1]**mash** /mash‖mæʃ/ *n* **1** crushed malt or grain meal steeped and stirred in hot water to ferment **2** a mixture of bran or similar feeds and usu hot water for livestock **3** a soft pulpy mass **4** *Br* mashed potatoes – infml

[2]**mash** *vt* **1** to crush, pound, etc to a soft pulpy state **2** to heat and stir (e g crushed malt) in water to prepare wort – **masher** *n*

[1]**mask** /mahsk‖mɑːsk/ *n* **1a** a (partial) cover for the face used for disguise or protection **b(1)** a figure of a head worn on the stage in ancient times to identify the character **b(2)** a grotesque false face worn at carnivals or in rituals **c** a copy of a face made by sculpting or by means of a mould **2a** sthg that disguises or conceals; *esp* a pretence, facade **b** a translucent or opaque screen to cover part of the sensitive surface in taking or printing a photograph **3** a device covering the mouth and nose used **3a** to promote breathing (e g by connection to an oxygen supply) **b** to remove noxious gas from air **c** to prevent exhalation of infective material (e g during surgery) **4** a face-pack **5** the head or face of a fox, dog, etc

[2]**mask** *vt* **1** to provide, cover, or conceal (as if) with a mask: e g **1a** to make indistinct or imperceptible <*~s the strong flavour*> **b** to cover up <*~ed his real purpose*> **2** to cover for protection **3** to modify the shape of (e g a photograph) by means of a mask

masochism /ˈmasəˌkiz(ə)m‖ˈmæsəˌkɪz(ə)m/ *n* **1** a sexual perversion in which pleasure is experienced from being physically or mentally abused **2** pleasure from sthg tiresome or painful – not used technically [Leopold von

Sacher-*Masoch* (1836-95), Austrian novelist] – **masochist** *n*, **masochistic** *adj*, **masochistically** *adv*

mason /ˈmays(ə)n‖ˈmeɪs(ə)n/ *n* **1** a skilled worker with stone **2** *cap* a freemason

Masonic /məˈsonik‖məˈsɒnɪk/ *adj* (characteristic) of Freemasons or Freemasonry

masonry /ˈmays(ə)nri‖ˈmeɪs(ə)nrɪ/ *n* **1** work done with or sthg constructed of stone; *also* a brick construction **2** *cap* FREEMASONRY 1

masque /mahsk‖mɑːsk/ *n* **1** MASQUERADE 1 **2** a short allegorical dramatic entertainment of the 16th and 17th c performed by masked actors

[1]**masquerade** /ˌmaskəˈrayd‖ˌmæskəˈreɪd/ *n* **1** a social gathering of people wearing masks and often fantastic costumes **2** sthg that is merely show

[2]**masquerade** *vi* **1** to disguise oneself; *also* to wear a disguise **2** to assume the appearance of sthg that one is not – usu + *as* – **masquerader** *n*

[1]**mass** /mas‖mæs/ *n* **1** *cap* the liturgy or a celebration of the Eucharist, esp in Roman Catholic and Anglo-Catholic churches **2** a musical setting for the ordinary of the Mass

[2]**mass** *n* **1a** a quantity of matter or the form of matter that holds together in 1 body **b(1)** an (unbroken) expanse <*a mountain* ~> <*a* ~ *of colour*> **b(2)** the principal part or main body **b(3)** a total, whole – esp in *in the mass* **c** the property of a body that is a measure of its inertia, causes it to have weight in a gravitational field, and is commonly taken as a measure of the amount of material it contains **2** a large quantity, amount, or number – often pl with sing. meaning <*there was* ~es *of food left*> **3** *pl* the body of ordinary people as contrasted with the élite – **massless** *adj*

[3]**mass** *vb* to assemble in or collect into a mass

[4]**mass** *adj* **1a** of, designed for, or consisting of the mass of the people <*a* ~ *market*> **b** participated in by or affecting a large number of individuals <~ *murder*> **c** large scale **2** viewed as a whole; total

[1]**massacre** /ˈmasəkə‖ˈmæsəkə/ *vt* **1** to kill (as if) in a massacre **2** to defeat severely; *also* MANGLE 2 – infml – **massacrer** *n*

[2]**massacre** *n* **1** the ruthless and indiscriminate killing of large numbers **2** complete defeat or destruction

massage /ˈmasahj, -sahzh‖ˈmæsɑːdʒ, -sɑːʒ/ *n* (an act of) kneading, rubbing, etc of the body in order to relieve aches, tone muscles, give relaxation, etc – **massage** *vt*, **massager** *n*

masseur /maˈsuh‖mæˈsɜː/, *fem* **masseuse** /masˈsuhz‖mæsˈsɜːz/ *n* one who practises massage and physiotherapy

massif /ˈmaseef‖ˈmæsiːf/ *n* **1** a principal mountain mass **2** a mountainous block bounded by faults or folds and displaced as a unit

massive /ˈmasiv‖ˈmæsɪv/ *adj* **1a** large, solid, or heavy **b** impressively large or ponderous **c** *of a mineral* not obviously crystalline **2a** large or impressive in scope or degree **b** large in comparison to what is typical <*a* ~ *dose of penicillin*> **c** extensive and severe <~ *haemorrhage*> – **massively** *adv*, **massiveness** *n*

ˌmass ˈmedia *n pl* broadcasting, newspapers, and other means of communication designed to reach large numbers of people

ˌmass-proˈduce /prəˈdyoohs‖prəˈdjuːs/ *vt* to produce (goods) in large quantities by standardized mechanical processes – **mass production** *n*

massy /ˈmasi‖ˈmæsɪ/ *adj* massive, heavy – fml

[1]**mast** /mahst‖mɑːst/ *n* **1** a tall pole or structure rising from the keel or deck of a ship, esp for carrying sails **2** a vertical pole or lattice supporting a radio or television aerial – **before the mast** as an ordinary sailor, not an officer

[2]**mast** *vt* to give a mast to

[3]**mast** *n* beechnuts, acorns, etc accumulated on the forest floor and often serving as food for animals (e g pigs)

mastectomy /maˈstektəmi‖mæˈstektəmɪ/ *n* excision or amputation of a breast

[1]**master** /ˈmahstə‖ˈmɑːstə/ *n* **1a(1)** a male teacher **a(2)** a person holding an academic degree higher than a bachelor's but lower than a doctor's **b** *often cap* a revered religious leader **c** a workman qualified to teach apprentices <*a* ~ *carpenter*> **d** an artist, performer, player, etc of consummate skill **2a** one having control or authority over another **b** one who or that which conquers or masters; a victor **c** a person qualified to command a merchant ship **d(1)** an owner, esp of a slave or animal **d(2)** *often cap* one who directs a hunt and has overall control of the pack of hounds **e** an employer **f** the male head of a household **3** *cap* a youth or boy too young to be called *mister* – used as a title **4** a presiding officer in an institution or society (e g a Masonic lodge) or at a function **5a** a mechanism or device that controls the operation of another **b** an original from which copies (e g of film or gramophone records) can be made **6** *archaic* Mr – **mastership** *n*

[2]**master** *vt* **1** to become master of; overcome **2a** to become skilled or proficient in the use of **b** to gain a thorough understanding of

[3]**master** *adj* **1** having chief authority; controlling **2** principal, main <*the* ~ *bedroom*>

ˌmaster-at-ˈarms *n, pl* **masters-at-arms** a petty officer responsible for maintaining discipline aboard ship

ˈmasterful /-f(ə)l‖-f(ə)l/ *adj* **1** inclined to take control and dominate **2** having or showing the technical, artistic, or intellectual skill of a master – **masterfully** *adv*, **masterfulness** *n*

ˈmaster ˌkey *n* a key designed to open several different locks

ˈmasterly /-li‖-lɪ/ *adj* showing superior knowledge or skill – **masterliness** *n*

[1]**ˈmasterˌmind** *n* **1** one who masterminds a project **2** a person of outstanding intellect

[2]**ˈmasterˌmind** *vt* to be the intellectual force behind (a project)

ˌmaster of ˈarts *n, often cap M&A* the recipient of a master's degree, usu in an arts subject

ˌmaster of ˈceremonies, *fem* **ˌmistress of ˈceremonies** /ˈmistris‖ˈmɪstrɪs/ *n* **1** one who determines the procedure to be observed on a state or public occasion **2** one who acts as host, esp by introducing speakers, performers, etc, at an event

ˌmaster of ˈscience *n, often cap M&S* the recipient of a master's degree in a scientific subject

ˈmaster,piece *n* a work done with extraordinary skill; *esp* the supreme creation of a type, period, or person

ˈmaster,stroke *n* a masterly performance or move

mastery /ˈmahstəri‖ˈmɑːstərɪ/ *n* **1a** the authority of a master **b** the upper hand in a contest or competition **2a** possession or display of great skill or technique **b** skill or knowledge that makes one master of a subject

masthead /ˈmahst,hed‖ˈmɑːst,hed/ *n* **1** the top of a mast **2** the name of a newspaper displayed on the top of the first page

mastic /ˈmastik‖ˈmæstɪk/ *n* **1** an aromatic resin that exudes from a S European tree and is used esp in varnishes **2** a pasty substance used as a protective coating or cement

masticate /ˈmastikayt‖ˈmæstɪkeɪt/ *vt* **1** to grind or crush (food) before swallowing, (as if) with the teeth; to chew **2** to soften or reduce to pulp (e g by crushing) ~*vi* to chew – **masticator** *n*, **masticatory** *adj or n*, **mastication** *n*

mastiff /ˈmastif‖ˈmæstɪf/ *n* any of a breed of very large powerful deep-chested smooth-coated dogs used chiefly as guard dogs

mastitis /maˈstietəs‖mæˈstaɪtəs/ *n* inflammation of the breast or udder, usu caused by infection – **mastitic** *adj*

mastodon /ˈmastə,don‖ˈmæstə,dɒn/ *n* any of numerous extinct mammals similar to the related mammoths and elephants – **mastodont** *adj or n*, **mastodontic** *adj*

mastoid /ˈmastoyd‖ˈmæstɔɪd/ *adj or n* (of, near, or being) a somewhat conical part of the temporal bone lying behind the ear – **mastoiditis** *n*

masturbation /,mastəˈbaysh(ə)n‖,mæstəˈbeɪʃ(ə)n/ *n* stimulation of the genitals commonly resulting in orgasm and accomplished by any means except sexual intercourse – **masturbate** *vb*, **masturbatory** *adj*

[1]**mat** /mat‖mæt/ *n* **1a** a piece of coarse usu woven, felted, or plaited fabric (e g of rushes or rope) used esp as a floor covering; *also* RUG 1 **b** DOORMAT 1 **c** an often decorative piece of material used to protect a surface from heat, moisture, etc caused by an object placed on it **d** a large thick pad used as a protective surface for wrestling, tumbling, gymnastics, etc **2** sthg made up of many intertwined or tangled strands

[2]**mat** *vb* **-tt-** *vt* **1** to provide with a mat or matting **2** to form into a tangled or compact mass ~*vi* to become tangled or intertwined

[3]**mat** *vt, adj, or n* **-tt-** (to) matt

matador /ˈmatədaw‖ˈmætədɔː/ *n* one who has the principal role and who kills the bull in a bullfight [Spanish, fr *matar* to kill]

[1]**match** /mach‖mætʃ/ *n* **1a** one who or that which is equal to or able to contend with another **b** a person or thing exactly like another **2** two people, animals, or things that go well together **3** a contest between 2 or more teams or individuals **4a** a marriage union **b** a prospective partner in marriage

[2]**match** *vt* **1a** to be equal to (an opponent) **b** to set in competition, opposition, or comparison **2a** to cause to correspond <~ing *life-style to income*> **b(1)** to be, find, or provide the exact counterpart or equal of or for **b(2)** to harmonize with **c** to provide funds complementary to **3** *archaic* to join or give in marriage ~ *vi* **1** to be a counterpart or equal **2** to harmonize – **matcher** *n*

[3]**match** *n* **1** a chemically prepared wick or cord formerly used in firing firearms or powder **2** a short slender piece of wood, cardboard, etc tipped with a mixture that ignites when subjected to friction

ˈmatchless /-lis‖-lɪs/ *adj* having no equal – **matchlessly** *adv*

matchlock /ˈmach,lok‖ˈmætʃ,lɒk/ *n* (a musket with) a gunlock with a match for igniting the charge

matchmaker /ˈmach,maykə‖ˈmætʃ,meɪkə/ *n* one who arranges marriages; *also* one who derives vicarious pleasure from contriving to arrange marriages – **matchmaking** *n*

ˈmatch ,point *n* a situation in tennis, badminton, etc in which a player will win the match by winning the next point

matchstick /ˈmach,stik‖ˈmætʃ,stɪk/ *n* [3]MATCH 2; *specif* one made of wood

matchwood /ˈmach,wood‖ˈmætʃ,wʊd/ *n* wood suitable for matches; *also* wood splinters

[1]**mate** /mayt‖meɪt/ *vt* CHECKMATE 2

[2]**mate** *n* CHECKMATE 1

[3]**mate** *n* **1a** an associate, companion – usu in combination <*flat*mate> <*play*mate> **b** an assistant to a more skilled workman <*plumber's* ~> **c** a friend, chum – often used in familiar address, esp to a man by a man **2** a deck officer on a merchant ship ranking below the captain **3a** either of a pair: e g **3a(1)** either member of a breeding pair of animals **a(2)** either of 2 matched objects **b** a marriage partner

[4]**mate** *vt* **1** to join or fit together; couple **2a** to join together as mates **b** to provide a mate for ~ *vi* **1** to become mated <*gears that* ~ *well*> **2** to copulate

maté, mate /ˈmatay, ˈmahtay‖ˈmæteɪ, ˈmɑːteɪ/ *n* **1** a tealike aromatic beverage used chiefly in S America **2** (the leaves and shoots, used in making maté, of) a S American holly

matelot /ˈmat(ə)loh‖ˈmæt(ə)ləʊ/ *n, Br* SAILOR 1b – infml

[1]**material** /məˈtiəri·əl‖məˈtɪərɪəl/ *adj* **1a(1)** of, derived from, or consisting of matter; *esp* physical **a(2)** bodily **b** of matter rather than form <~ *cause*> **2** important, significant <*facts* ~ *to the investigation*> **3** of or concerned with physical rather than spiritual things – **materially** *adv*, **materiality** *n*

[2]**material** *n* **1a(1)** the elements, constituents, or substances of which sthg is composed or can be made **a(2)** matter that has usu specified qualities which give it individuality <*sticky* ~> **b(1)** data that may be worked into a more finished form **b(2)** a person considered with a view to his/her potential for successful training <*I don't think he's officer* ~> **c** cloth **2** *pl* apparatus necessary for doing or making sthg

maˈteria,lism /-,liz(ə)m‖-,lɪz(ə)m/ *n* **1a** a theory that only physical matter is real and that all processes and phenomena can be explained by reference to matter **b** a doctrine that the highest values lie in material well-being and material progress **2** a preoccupation with or stress on material rather than spiritual things – **materialist** *n or adj*, **materialistic** *adj*

materialize, **-ise** /mə'tiəri·ə,liez‖mə'tɪərɪə-,laɪz/ *vb* **1** to (cause to) have existence or tangibility <~ *an idea in words*> **2** to (cause to) appear in or assume bodily form – **materialization** *n*

maternal /mə'tuhnl‖mə'tɜ:nl/ *adj* **1** (characteristic) of a mother **2** related through a mother – **maternally** *adv*

[1]**maternity** /mə'tuhnəti‖mə'tɜ:nətɪ/ *n* **1a** motherhood **b** motherliness **2** a hospital department for the care of women before and during childbirth

[2]**maternity** *adj* designed for wear during pregnancy <*a* ~ *dress*>

[1]**matey** /'mayti‖'meɪtɪ/ *n, chiefly Br* [3]MATE 1c – chiefly in familiar address

[2]**matey** *adj, chiefly Br* friendly – infml – **mateyness, matiness** *n*

mathematical /,mathə'matikl‖,mæθə-'mætɪkl/ *also* **mathematic** /-tik‖-tɪk/ *adj* **1** of, used in, using, or according with mathematics **2** rigorously exact [Latin *mathematicus*, fr Greek *mathēmatikos*, fr *mathēmat-*, *mathēma* mathematics, fr *manthanein* to learn] – **mathematically** *adv*

mathematics /,mathə'matiks‖,mæθə-'mætɪks/ *n pl but sing or pl in constr* **1** the science of numbers and their operations, interrelations, and combinations and of space configurations and their structure, measurement, etc **2** the mathematics or mathematical operations involved in a particular problem, field of study, etc – **mathematician** *n*

matinée, **matinee** /'matinay‖'mætɪneɪ/ *n* a musical or dramatic performance during the day, esp the afternoon [French *matinée*, lit., morning, deriv of Latin *matutinus* of the morning, fr *Matuta*, goddess of the dawn]

'**matinee ,jacket** *n, Br* a cardigan worn by babies

matins /'matinz‖'mætɪnz/ *n pl but sing or pl in constr often cap* **1** the (night) office forming with lauds the first of the canonical hours **2** MORNING PRAYER

matriarch /'maytri,ahk‖'meɪtrɪ,ɑ:k/ *n* a woman who rules a family, group, or state; *specif* a mother who is the head of her family – **matriarchal** *adj*

'**matri,archy** /-ki‖-kɪ/ *n* a (system of) social organization in which the female is the head of the family, and descent and inheritance are traced through the female line

matricide /'maytri,sied‖'meɪtrɪ,saɪd/ *n* (the act of) one who kills his/her mother – **matricidal** *adj*

matriculate /mə'trikyoolayt‖mə'trɪkjʊleɪt/ *vt* to enrol as a member of a body, esp a college or university ~*vi* to become eligible) to be matriculated – **matriculation** *n*

matrimony /'matriməni‖'mætrɪmənɪ/ *n* MARRIAGE 1 – **matrimonial** *adj*, **matrimonially** *adv*

matrix /'maytriks‖'meɪtrɪks/ *n, pl* **matrices** /-,seez‖-,si:z/, **matrixes** **1** a substance, environment, etc within which sthg else originates or develops **2** a mould in which sthg is cast or from which a surface in relief (e g a piece of type) is made by pouring or pressing **3** the (natural) material in which sthg (e g a fossil, gem, or specimen for study) is embedded **4** the substance between the cells of a tissue that holds them together **5** a rectangular array of mathematical elements treated as a unit and subject to special algebraic laws

matron /'maytrən‖'meɪtrən/ *n* **1a** a (dignified mature) married woman **b** a woman in charge of living arrangements in a school, residential home, etc **2** *Br* a woman in charge of the nursing in a hospital – not now used technically – **matronly** *adj*

[1]**matt**, **mat**, **matte** /mat‖mæt/ *vt* to make (e g metal or colour) matt

[2]**matt**, **mat**, **matte** *adj* lacking lustre or gloss; *esp* having an even surface free from shine or highlights

[3]**matt**, **mat**, **matte** *n* **1** a border round a picture between the picture and frame or serving as the frame **2** a dull or roughened finish (e g on gilt or paint)

[1]**matter** /'matə‖'mætə/ *n* **1a** a subject of interest or concern or which merits attention **b** an affair, concern <*it's no laughing* ~> **c** material (for treatment) in thought, discourse, or writing **d** that part of a legal case which deals with facts rather than law **e** a condition (unfavourably) affecting a person or thing <*what's the* ~*?*> **2a** the substance of which a physical object is composed **b** material substance that occupies space and has mass **c** sth of a specified kind or for a specified purpose <*mineral* ~> <*reading* ~> **d(1)** material (e g faeces or urine) discharged from the living body **d(2)** material discharged by suppuration; pus **3** the formless substratum of all existing things **4** a more or less definite amount or quantity <*a* ~ *of 10 years*> – **as a matter of fact** as it happens; actually – often used in correcting a misapprehension – **for that matter** so far as that is concerned – **no matter** it does not matter; irrespective of <*would be calm* no matter *what the provocation*>

[2]**matter** *vi* **1** to be of importance **2** to form or discharge pus

,**matter of 'course** *n* sthg routine or to be expected as a natural consequence

,**matter-of-'fact** *adj* keeping to or concerned with fact; *esp* not fanciful or imaginative – **matter-of-factly** *adv*, **matter-of-factness** *n*

matting /'mating‖'mætɪŋ/ *n* material (e g hemp) for mats

mattock /'matək‖'mætək/ *n* a digging tool with a head like that of a pick and often a blade like that of an axe or adze

mattress /'matris‖'mætrɪs/ *n* a fabric casing filled with resilient material (e g foam rubber or an arrangement of coiled springs) used esp on a bed [Old French *materas*, fr Arabic *maṭraḥ* place where something is thrown]

[1]**mature** /mə'tyooə‖mə'tjʊə/ *adj* **1** based on careful consideration <*a* ~ *judgment*> **2a** having completed natural growth and development; ripe **b** having attained a final or desired state **3a**

(characteristic) of or having a condition of full or adult development **b** older or more experienced than others of his/her kind <*a ~ student*> **4** due for payment <*a ~ loan*> – **maturely** *adv*, **matureness, maturity** *n*

[2]**mature** *vt* to bring to full development or completion ~ *vi* **1** to become mature **2** to become due for payment – **maturation** *n*, **maturational** *adj*

maudlin /ˈmawdlin‖ˈmɔːdlɪn/ *adj* **1** weakly and effusively sentimental **2** drunk enough to be emotionally silly

[1]**maul** /mawl‖mɔːl/ *vt* **1** *esp of an animal* to attack and tear the flesh of **2** to handle roughly – **mauler** *n*

[2]**maul** *n* **1** a situation in Rugby Union in which 1 or more players from each team close round the player carrying the ball who tries to get the ball out to his own team **2** a confused and noisy struggle

maunder /ˈmawndə‖ˈmɔːndə/ *vi* **1** to act or wander idly **2** to speak in a rambling or indistinct manner; *also, Br* to grumble – **maunderer** *n*

ˌ**Maundy** ˈ**Thursday** /ˌmawndi‖ˌmɔːndɪ/ *n* the Thursday before Easter observed in commemoration of the Last Supper

mausoleum /ˌmawsəˈlee·əm‖ˌmɔːsəˈliːəm/ *n, pl* **mausoleums** *also* **mausolea** /-ˈlee·ə‖-ˈliːə/ a large and elaborate tomb [Latin, fr Greek *mausōleion*, fr *Mausōlos* Mausolus (died about 353 BC), ruler of Caria in Asia Minor]

mauve /mohv‖məʊv/ *n or adj* bluish purple

maverick /ˈmav(ə)rik‖ˈmæv(ə)rɪk/ *n* **1** an independent and nonconformist individual **2** *NAm* an unbranded range animal; *esp* a motherless calf [Samuel A *Maverick* (1803-70), US pioneer who did not brand his calves]

maw /maw‖mɔː/ *n* **1a** an animal's stomach or crop **b** the throat, gullet, or jaws, esp of a voracious flesh-eating animal **2** sthg resembling a maw, esp in gaping or tending to swallow things up

mawkish /ˈmawkish‖ˈmɔːkɪʃ/ *adj* **1** having an insipid often unpleasant taste **2** sickly or feebly sentimental – **mawkishly** *adv*, **mawkishness** *n*

maxi /ˈmaksi‖ˈmæksɪ/ *n, pl* **maxis** a floor-length woman's coat, skirt, etc

maxi- *comb form* **1** extra long <maxi-*skirt*> **2** extra large <maxi-*budget*>

maxim /ˈmaksim‖ˈmæksɪm/ *n* (a succinct expression of) a general truth, fundamental principle, or rule of conduct

maximal /ˈmaksiml‖ˈmæksɪml/ *adj* **1** greatest; most comprehensive **2** being an upper limit – **maximally** *adv*

maxim·ize, ise /ˈmaksiˌmiez‖ˈmæksɪˌmaɪz/ *vt* to increase to a maximum or to the highest possible degree – **maximization** *n*

maximum /ˈmaksimәm‖ˈmæksɪmәm/ *n, pl* **maxima** /-mә‖-mә/, **maximums** **1** the greatest quantity or value attainable or attained **2** the period of highest or most extreme development – **maximum** *adj*

may /may‖meɪ/ *verbal auxiliary, pres sing & pl* **may**; *past* **might** /miet‖maɪt/ *va* **1a** have permission to <*you ~ go now* >; have liberty to <*what's this, ~ I ask?*> **b** be in some degree likely to <*you ~ be right*> <*the road ~ well be closed*> **2** – used to express a wish or desire, esp in prayer, curse, or benediction <*long ~ he reign*> **3** – used to express purpose or expectation <*sit here so I ~ see you better*>, contingency <*he'll do his duty come what ~* >, or concession <*he ~ be slow but he is thorough*>; used in questions to emphasize ironic uncertainty <*and who ~ you be?*>

May *n* **1** the 5th month of the Gregorian calendar **2** *not cap* (the blossom of) hawthorn [Latin *Maius*, fr *Maia*, Roman goddess]

maybe /ˈmayˌbee‖ˈmeɪˌbiː/ *adv* perhaps

Mayday /ˈmayˌday‖ˈmeɪˌdeɪ/ – used for an international radiotelephone signal word used as a distress call [French *m'aider* help me]

ˈ**May** ˌ**Day** *n* May 1 celebrated as a springtime festival and in many countries as a public holiday in honour of working people

ˈ**mayˌfly** /-ˌflie‖-ˌflaɪ/ *n* any of an order of insects with an aquatic nymph and a short-lived fragile adult with membranous wings

mayhem /ˈmayhem‖ˈmeɪhem/ *n* **1** needless or wilful damage **2** a state of great confusion or disorder

mayn't /maynt‖meɪnt/ may not

mayonnaise /ˌmayəˈnayz‖ˌmeɪəˈneɪz/ *n* a thick dressing (e g for salad) made with egg yolks, vegetable oil, and vinegar or lemon juice

mayor /meə‖meə/ *n* the chief executive or nominal head of a city or borough – **mayoral** *adj*

mayoralty /ˈmeərəlti‖ˈmeərəltɪ/ *n* the (term of) office of a mayor

mayoress /ˈmeəris‖ˈmeərɪs/ *n* **1** the wife or hostess of a mayor **2** a female mayor

maypole /ˈmayˌpohl‖ˈmeɪˌpəʊl/ *n* a tall ribbon-wreathed pole forming a centre for dances, esp on May Day

maze *n* **1a** (a drawn representation of) a network of paths designed to confuse and puzzle those who attempt to walk through it **b** sthg intricately or confusingly complicated **2** *archaic* a state of bewilderment – **mazy** *adj*

mazurka *also* **mazourka** /məˈzuhkə‖məˈzɜːkə/ *n* (music for, or in the rhythm of) a Polish folk dance in moderate triple time

MC *n* MASTER OF CEREMONIES

[1]**me** /mee‖miː/ *pron, objective case of* I <*looked at ~*> <*fatter than ~*> <*it's ~*>

[2]**me** *n* sthg suitable for me <*that dress isn't really ~*>

[3]**me** *n* the 3rd note of the diatonic scale in solmization

[1]**mead** /meed‖miːd/ *n* a fermented alcoholic drink made of water, honey, malt, and yeast

[2]**mead** *n* a meadow – archaic or poetic

meadow /ˈmedoh‖ˈmedəʊ/ *n* (an area of moist low-lying usu level) grassland

ˈ**meadowˌsweet** *n* a tall Eurasian plant of the rose family with creamy-white fragrant flowers

meagre, *NAm chiefly* **meager** /ˈmeegə‖ˈmiːgə/ *adj* **1** having little flesh **2** deficient in quality or quantity – **meagrely** *adv*, **meagreness** *n*

[1]**meal** /meel, miəl‖miːl, mɪəl/ *n* **1** the portion of food taken or provided at 1 time to satisfy appetite **2** (the time of) eating a meal

[2]**meal** *n* (a product resembling, esp in texture) the usu coarsely ground seeds of a cereal

grass or pulse

mealie /ˈmeeli‖ˈmiːlɪ/ *n, SAfr* (an ear of) maize

ˈmealˌtime *n* the usual time for a meal

mealy /ˈmeeli‖ˈmiːlɪ/ *adj* **1** soft, dry, and crumbly **2** containing meal **3a** covered with meal or fine granules **b** *esp of a horse* flecked with another colour

ˈmealyˌbug /-ˌbug‖-ˌbʌg/ *n* any of numerous scale insects with a white powdery covering that are pests, esp of fruit trees

ˌmealy-ˈmouthed *adj* unwilling to speak plainly or directly, esp when this may offend

[1]**mean** /meen‖miːn/ *adj* **1** lacking distinction or eminence; merely ordinary or inferior <*a man of ~ estate*> <*no ~ feat*> **2** of poor shabby inferior quality or status **3** not honourable or worthy; base; *esp* small-minded **4a** not generous **b** characterized by petty malice; spiteful **c** *chiefly NAm* particularly bad-tempered, unpleasant, or disagreeable **d** excellent, impressive – infml <*blows a ~ trumpet – Globe & Mail* (Toronto)> – **meanly** *adv*, **meanness** *n*

[2]**mean** *vb* **meant** /ment‖ment/ *vt* **1** to have in mind as a purpose; intend <*she ~*t *no offence*> <*I ~ to leave soon*> **2** to serve or intend to convey, produce, or indicate; signify <*red ~*s *danger*> <*this action will ~ war*> **3** to intend for a particular use or purpose <*it is ~*t *to relieve pain*> <*I ~*t *it as a warning*> **4** to have significance or importance to the extent or degree of <*health ~*s *everything*> *~vi* to have an intended purpose – chiefly in *to mean well/ill* – **I mean** – used to introduce and emphasize a clause or sentence or when hesitating <*it wasn't too bad.* I mean *it didn't even hurt*> – **mean business** to be in earnest

[3]**mean** *n* **1a** a middle point between extremes **b** a value that lies within a range of values and is computed according to a prescribed law; *esp* ARITHMETIC MEAN **2** *pl but sing or pl in constr* that which enables a desired purpose to be achieved; *also* the method used to attain an end **3** *pl* resources available for disposal; *esp* wealth <*a man of ~*s>

[4]**mean** *adj* **1** occupying a middle position; intermediate in space, order, time, kind, or degree **2** being the mean of a set of values <*~ temperature*>

[1]**meander** /miˈandə‖mɪˈændə/ *n* a turn or winding of a stream – usu pl [Latin *maeander*, fr Greek *maiandros*, fr *Maiandros* (now *Menderes*), river in Asia Minor]

[2]**meander** *vi* **1** to follow a winding course **2** to wander aimlessly without urgent destination

[1]**meaning** /ˈmeening‖ˈmiːnɪŋ/ *n* **1** that which is conveyed or which one intends to convey, esp by language **2** significant quality; value <*this has no ~ in law*> **3** implication of a hidden or special significance <*a glance full of ~*> – **meaningful** *adj*, **meaningfully** *adv*, **meaningfulness** *n*, **meaningless** *adj*, **meaninglessly** *adv*, **meaninglessness** *n*

[2]**meaning** *adj* significant, expressive – **meaningly** *adv*

ˈmeans ˌtest *n* an examination into sby's financial state to determine his/her eligibility for public assistance, for a student grant, etc

meant /ment‖ment/ *adj, past of* MEAN *Br* expected, supposed <*you are ~ to stop when the lights are red*>

[1]**meantime** /ˈmeenˌtiem‖ˈmiːnˌtaɪm/ *n* the intervening time <*in the ~*>

[2]**meantime** *adv* meanwhile

[1]**meanwhile** /ˈmeenˌwiel‖ˈmiːnˌwaɪl/ *n* the meantime

[2]**meanwhile** *adv* **1** during the intervening time **2** during the same period <*~, down on the farm*>

measles /ˈmeezlz‖ˈmiːzlz/ *n pl but sing or pl in constr* **1** (German measles or another disease similar to) an infectious virus disease marked by a rash of distinct red circular spots **2** infestation with larval tapeworms, esp in pigs or pork

measly /ˈmeezli‖ˈmiːzlɪ/ *adj* **1** infected with measles **2** containing larval tapeworms <*~ pork*> **3** contemptibly small; *also* worthless – infml

[1]**measure** /ˈmezhə‖ˈmeʒə/ *n* **1a(1)** an appropriate or due portion <*had their ~ of luck*> **a(2)** a (moderate) extent, amount, or degree <*a ~ of respectability*> **a(3)** a fixed, suitable, or conceivable limit <*wisdom beyond ~*> **b(1)** the dimensions, capacity, or amount of sthg ascertained by measuring **b(2)** the character, nature, or capacity of sby or sthg ascertained by assessment – esp in *get the measure of* **b(3)** the width of a full line of type **c** a measured quantity <*a ~ of whisky*> <*short ~*> **2a** an instrument or utensil for measuring **b(1)** a standard or unit of measurement <*the metre is a ~ of length*> **b(2)** a system of standard units of measure <*metric ~*> <*liquid ~*> **3a** a (slow and stately) dance **b(1)** poetic rhythm measured by quantity or accent; *specif* [2]METRE 1 **b(2)** musical time **c(1)** the notes and rests that form a bar of music **c(2)** a metrical unit; FOOT 4 **4** an exact divisor or factor of a quantity **5** a basis or standard of comparison **6a** a step planned or taken to achieve an end <*we must take ~*s *to improve sales*> **b** a proposed legislative act <*~*s *to combat unemployment*>

[2]**measure** *vt* **1** to choose or control with cautious restraint; regulate <*~*d *his words to suit the occasion*> **2** to take or allot in measured amounts – usu + *out* <*~ out 60g of flour*> **3** to mark off by making measurements – often + *off* **4** to ascertain the measurements of **5** to estimate or appraise by a criterion – usu + *against* or *by* **6** to serve as a measure of <*a thermometer ~*s *temperature*> *~ vi* **1** to take or make a measurement **2** to have a specified measurement <*~*s *2ft from end to end*> – **measurable** *adj*, **measurably** *adv*

ˈmeasured *adj* **1** rhythmical; *esp* slow and regular **2** carefully thought out <*a ~ remark*> – **measuredly** *adv*

ˈmeasureless /-lis‖-lɪs/ *adj* having no observable limit; immeasurable

ˈmeasurement /-mənt‖-mənt/ *n* **1** measuring **2** a figure, extent, or amount obtained by measuring **3** MEASURE 2b

measure up *vi* to have necessary or fitting qualifications – often + *to*

meat /meet‖miːt/ *n* **1a** food; *esp* solid food as distinguished from drink **b** the edible part of sthg as distinguished from a husk, shell, or other covering **2** animal tissue used as food; *esp* FLESH 2 **3** the core or essence of sthg **4** *archaic* a meal; *esp* dinner

meaty /'meeti‖'mi:tɪ/ *adj* **1** full of meat; fleshy **2** rich in matter for thought **3** of or like meat – **meatiness** *n*

mecca /'mekə‖'mekə/ *n, often cap* a place regarded as a goal (by a specified group of people)

mechanic /mi'kanik‖mɪ'kænɪk/ *n* a skilled worker who repairs or maintains machinery

me'chanical /-kl‖-kl/ *adj* **1a** of or using machinery **b** made, operated by, or being a machine or machinery **2** done as if by machine; lacking in spontaneity **3** of, dealing with, or in accordance with (the principles of) mechanics <~ *energy*> <~ *engineering*> **4** caused by or being a physical as opposed to a chemical process – **mechanically** *adv*

mechanics /mi'kaniks‖mɪ'kænɪks/ *n pl but sing or pl in constr* **1** the physics and mathematics of (the effect on moving and stationary bodies of) energy and forces **2** the practical application of mechanics to the design, construction, or operation of machines or tools **3** mechanical or functional details

mechanism /'mekəniz(ə)m‖'mekənɪz(ə)m/ *n* **1a** a piece of machinery **b** a process or technique for achieving a result **2** mechanical operation or action **3** a theory that all natural processes are mechanically determined and can be explained by the laws of physics and chemistry **4** the physical or chemical processes involved in a natural phenomenon (e g an action, reaction, or biological evolution) – **mechanist** *n*, **mechanistic** *adj*, **mechanistically** *adv*

mechan·ize, -ise /'mekəniez‖'mekənaɪz/ *vt* **1** to make mechanical or automatic **2a** to equip with machinery, esp in order to replace human or animal labour **b** to equip with (armed and armoured) motor vehicles – **mechanization** *n*

medal /'medl‖'medl/ *n* a piece of metal with a (stamped) design, emblem, inscription, etc that commemorates a person or event or is awarded for excellence or achievement – **medallic** *adj*

medallion /mi'dalyən‖mɪ'dæljən/ *n* **1** a large medal **2** a decorative tablet, panel, etc, often bearing a figure or portrait in relief

'medallist, *NAm chiefly* **medalist** /-ist‖-ɪst/ *n* **1** a designer, engraver, or maker of medals **2** a recipient of a (specified) medal as an award

meddle /'medl‖'medl/ *vi* to interest oneself in what is not one's concern; interfere unduly – usu + *in* or *with* – **meddler** *n*, **meddlesome** *adj*

media *pl of* MEDIUM

mediaeval /,medi'eevl‖,medɪ'i:vl/ *adj* medieval

medial /'meedi·əl‖'mi:dɪəl/ *adj* being, occurring in, or extending towards the middle; median – **medially** *adv*

[1]median /'meedi·ən‖'mi:dɪən/ *n* **1** a median vein, nerve, etc **2** a value in a series above and below which there are an equal number of values **3** a line from a vertex of a triangle to the midpoint of the opposite side

[2]median *adj* **1** in the middle or in an intermediate position **2** lying in the plane that divides an animal into right and left halves

[1]mediate /'meedi·ət‖'mi:dɪət/ *adj* acting through an intervening agent or agency – **mediacy** *n*, **mediately** *adv*

[2]mediate /'meedi,ayt‖'mi:dɪ,eɪt/ *vi* to intervene between parties in order to reconcile them ~ *vt* **1** to bring about (a settlement) by mediation **2a** to act as intermediary agent in or between **b** to transmit or effect by acting as an intermediate mechanism or agency – **mediator** *n*, **mediatory** *adj*, **mediative** *adj*, **mediation** *n*

medic /'medik‖'medɪk/ *n* a medical doctor or student – infml

[1]medical /'medikl‖'medɪkl/ *adj* **1** of or concerned with physicians or the practice of medicine **2** requiring or devoted to medical treatment [Late Latin *medicalis*, fr Latin *medicus* physician, fr *mederi* to heal] – **medically** *adv*

[2]medical /'medikl‖'medɪkl/, **medical examination** *n* an examination to determine sby's physical fitness

medicament /mi'dikəmənt‖mɪ'dɪkəmənt/ *n* MEDICINE 1

medicare /'medi,keə‖'medɪ,keə/ *n* comprehensive medical insurance, esp for the aged, sponsored by the US and Canadian governments

medicate /'medikayt‖'medɪkeɪt/ *vt* **1** to treat medicinally **2** to impregnate with a medicinal substance <~d *soap*> – **medication** *n*

medicinal /mə'dis(ə)nl‖mə'dɪs(ə)nl/ *n or adj* (a substance) tending or used to cure disease or relieve pain – **medicinally** *adv*

medicine /'medəsin‖'medəsɪn/ *n* **1** a substance or preparation used (as if) in treating disease **2** the science and art of the maintenance of health and the prevention and treatment of disease (using nonsurgical methods)

'medicine ,ball *n* a heavy ball that is usu thrown between people for exercise

'medicine ,man *n* a healer or sorcerer, esp among the N American Indians

medico /'medikoh‖'medɪkəʊ/ *n, pl* **medicos** a medic – infml

medieval, mediaeval /,medi'eevl‖,medɪ'i:vl/ *adj* of or like the Middle Ages [Latin *medius* middle + *aevum* age] – **medievalism** *n*, **medievalist** *n*, **medievally** *adv*

mediocre /,meedi'ohkə‖,mi:dɪ'əʊkə/ *adj* **1** neither good nor bad; indifferent; *esp* conspicuously lacking distinction or imagination **2** not good enough; fairly bad [Middle French, fr Latin *mediocris*, lit., halfway up a mountain, fr *medius* middle + *ocris* stony mountain] – **mediocrity** *n*

meditate /'meditayt‖'medɪteɪt/ *vt* to focus one's thoughts on; consider or plan in the mind ~ *vi* **1** to engage in deep or serious reflection **2** to empty the mind of thoughts and fix the attention on 1 matter, esp as a religious exercise – **meditator** *n*, **meditative** *adj*, **meditatively** *adv*, **meditation** *n*

Mediterranean /,meditə'raynyən, -ni·ən‖,medɪtə'reɪnjən, -nɪən/ *adj* **1** of or characteristic of (the region round) the Mediterranean sea **2** of or resembling a physical type of the Caucasian race characterized by medium or short stature, slender build, and dark complexion

[1]medium /'meedi·əm‖'mi:dɪəm/ *n, pl* **mediums, media** /-di·ə‖-dɪə/, (*2b(2)*) **media,** (*2e*) **mediums,**

(*3b*) **media** *also* **mediums** **1** (sthg in) a middle position or state **2** a means of effecting or conveying sthg: e g **2a(1)** a substance regarded as the means of transmission of a force or effect <*air is the* ~ *that conveys sound*> **a(2)** a surrounding or enveloping substance; *esp* MATRIX 3 **b(1)** a channel of communication **b(2)** *pl but sing or pl in constr* MASS MEDIA **c** a mode of artistic expression or communication <*discovered his true* ~ *as a writer*> **d** an intermediary, go-between **e** one through whom others seek to communicate with the spirits of the dead **f** a material or technical means of artistic expression <*found watercolour a satisfying* ~> **3a** a condition or environment in which sthg may function or flourish **b** a nutrient for the artificial cultivation of bacteria and other (single-celled) organisms **c** a liquid with which dry pigment can be mixed

[2]**medium** *adj* intermediate in amount, quality, position, or degree

ˈ**medium ˌwave** *n* a band of radio waves, typically used for sound broadcasting, covering wavelengths between about 180m and 600m – sometimes pl with sing. meaning

medlar /ˈmedlə‖ˈmedlə/ *n* (a small Eurasian tree of the rose family that bears) a fruit like a crab apple used in preserves

medley /ˈmedli‖ˈmedlɪ/ *n* **1** a (confused) mixture **2** a musical composition made up of a series of songs or short musical pieces

meek /meek‖miːk/ *adj* **1** patient and without resentment **2** lacking spirit and courage; timid – **meekly** *adv*, **meekness** *n*

meerschaum /ˈmiəshəm‖ˈmɪəʃəm/ *n* **1** hydrated magnesium silicate occurring, chiefly in Asia Minor, as a white clayey mineral and used esp for tobacco pipes **2** a tobacco pipe with a bowl made of meerschaum [German, fr *meer* sea + *schaum* foam]

[1]**meet** /meet‖miːt/ *vb* **met** /met‖met/ *vt* **1a** to come into the presence of by accident or design **b** to be present to greet the arrival of <met *the London train*> **c** to come into contact or conjunction with <*where the river* ~s *the sea*> **d** to appear to the perception of <*hazy sunshine* ~s *the eye*> **2** to encounter as antagonist or foe **3** to answer, esp in opposition <*his speech was* met *by loud catcalls*> **4** to conform to, esp exactly and precisely; satisfy <*this should* ~ *your requirements*> **5** to pay fully <~ *the cost*> **6** to become acquainted with **7** to experience during the course of sthg <met *his death during the war*> ~ *vi* **1** to come together **1a** from different directions **b** for a common purpose **c** as contestants, opponents, or enemies **2** to join at a fastening <*the waistcoat won't* ~> **3** to become acquainted – **meet someone halfway** to make concessions to; compromise with

[2]**meet** *n* the assembling of participants for a hunt or for competitive sports

[3]**meet** *adj* suitable, proper – fml – **meetly** *adv*

meeting /ˈmeeting‖ˈmiːtɪŋ/ *n* **1** a coming together: e g **1a** an assembly of people for a common purpose **b** a session of horse or greyhound racing **2** a permanent organizational unit of the Quakers **3** an intersection, junction

ˈ**meeting ˌhouse** *n* a building used for Protestant worship

mega- /megə-‖megə-/, **meg-** *comb form* **1a** great; large <mega*lith*> **b** having (a specified part) of large size <mega*cephalic*> **2** million (10^6) <mega*watt*>

ˈ**megaˌdeath** /-ˌdeth‖-ˌdeθ/ *n* one million deaths – used as a unit esp in reference to atomic warfare

ˈ**megaˌhertz** /-ˌhuhts‖-ˌhɜːts/ *n* a unit of frequency equal to 1,000,000 hertz

megalith /ˈmegəlith‖ˈmegəlɪθ/ *n* a huge undressed block of stone used in prehistoric monuments [Greek *megas* large + *lithos* stone] – **megalithic** *adj*

megalomania /ˌmeg(ə)ləˈmaynyə‖ˌmeg(ə)ləˈmeɪnjə/ *n* **1** a mania for grandiose things **2** feelings of personal omnipotence and grandeur occurring as a delusional mental disorder – **megalomaniac** *adj or n*, **megalomaniacal** *adj*

megaphone /ˈmegəˌfohn‖ˈmegəˌfəʊn/ *n* a hand-held device used to amplify or direct the voice – **megaphonic** *adj*

ˈ**megaˌton** /-tun‖-tʌn/ *n* an explosive force (of an atom or hydrogen bomb) equivalent to that of 1,000,000 tons of TNT

[1]**megrim** /ˈmeegrəm‖ˈmiːgrəm/ *n* **1** migraine **2** vertigo, dizziness – usu pl with sing. meaning

[2]**megrim** *n* any of several small flounders or other flatfishes

meiosis /mieˈohsis‖maɪˈəʊsɪs/ *n, pl* **meioses** /-ˌseez‖-ˌsiːz/ **1** understatement **2** a specialized cellular process of division in gamete-producing cells by which 1 of each pair of chromosomes passes to each resulting gametic cell which thus has half the number of chromosomes of the original cell – **meiotic** *adj*, **meiotically** *adv*

melancholia /ˌmelənˈkohliə‖ˌmelənˈkəʊlɪə/ *n* feelings of extreme depression and worthlessness occurring as an abnormal mental condition – **melancholiac** *n*

[1]**melancholy** /ˈmelənkəli, -koli‖ˈmelənkəlɪ, -kɒlɪ/ *n* **1** (a tendency to) irascibility or depression; melancholia **2a** depression of mind or spirits **b** a sad pensive mood [Middle French *melancolie*, fr Late Latin *melancholia*, fr Greek, fr *melan-*, *melas* black + *cholē* bile] – **melancholic** *adj or n*, **melancholically** *adv*

[2]**melancholy** *adj* **1** depressed in spirits; dejected **2** causing, tending to cause, or expressing sadness or depression

mélange /ˈmaylonhzh ‖ˈmeɪlɑ̃ʒ (*Fr* melɑ̃ːʒ)/ *n* a mixture (of incongruous elements) [French, fr *mêler* to mix, deriv of Latin *miscēre*]

[1]**meld** /meld‖meld/ *vb* to declare (a card or combination of cards) for a score in a card game, esp by placing face up on the table

[2]**meld** *n* a card or combination of cards that is or can be melded

[3]**meld** *vb, chiefly NAm* to merge

mêlée, **melee** /ˈmelay‖ˈmeleɪ/ *n* a confused or riotous struggle; *esp* a general hand-to-hand fight

meliorate /ˈmeeliəˌrayt‖ˈmiːlɪəˌreɪt/ *vb* to ameliorate – **meliorative** *adj*, **melioration** *n*

mellifluous /məˈliflooəs‖məˈlɪflʊəs/, **mellifluent** /-ənt‖-ənt/ *adj* smoothly or sweetly flowing <*a* ~ *voice*> – **mellifluously**, **mellifluently** *adv*, **mellifluousness**, **mellifluence** *n*

mellow /ˈmeloh‖ˈmeləʊ/ *adj* **1a** *of a fruit* tender and sweet because ripe **b** *of a wine* well aged and pleasingly mild **2a** made gentle by age or experience **b** rich and full but free from harshness <~ *lighting*> **c** pleasantly intoxicated – **mellow** *vb*, **mellowly** *adv*, **mellowness** *n*

melodic /mə'lodik‖mə'lɒdɪk/ *adj* **1** of or forming melody **2** melodious – **melodically** *adv*

melodious /mə'lohdi·əs‖mə'ləʊdɪəs/ *adj* of or producing (a pleasing) melody – **melodiously** *adv*, **melodiousness** *n*

melodrama /'melə,drahmə‖'melə,drɑːmə/ *n* **1a** a work (e g a film or play) characterized by crude emotional appeal and by the predominance of plot and action over characterization **b** the dramatic genre comprising such works **2** sensational or sensationalized events or behaviour – **melodramatic** *adj*, **melodramatically** *adv*, **melodramatist** *n*, **melodramatize** *vt*

melody /'melədi‖'melədɪ/ *n* **1** an agreeable succession or arrangement of sounds **2a** a rhythmic succession of single notes organized as an aesthetic whole **b** the chief part in a harmonic composition

melon /'melən‖'melən/ *n* (any of various plants of the cucumber family having) a fruit (e g a watermelon) containing sweet edible flesh and usu eaten raw

[1]**melt** /melt‖melt/ *vi* **1** to become altered from a solid to a liquid state, usu by heating **2a** to dissolve, disintegrate <*food that* ~s *in the mouth*> **b** to disappear as if by dissolving <*his anger* ~ed> **3** to be or become mild, tender, or gentle **4** to lose distinct outline; blend <*tried to* ~ *into the background*> ~ *vt* **1** to reduce from a solid to a liquid state, usu by heating **2** to cause to disappear or disperse **3** to make tender or gentle – **meltable** *adj*, **meltingly** *adv*

[2]**melt** *n* **1a** molten material **b** the mass melted at a single operation **2** (the period of) melting or being melted <*the river overflowed during the Spring* ~>

[3]**melt** *n* the spleen, esp when used as food

'melting ,point /'melting‖'meltɪŋ/ *n* the temperature at which a solid melts

'melting ,pot *n* a place, a situation, or the result of mixing diverse ideas, peoples, traditions, etc

member /'membə‖'membə/ *n* **1** a part or organ of the body: e g **1a** a limb **b** the penis – euph **2a** an individual or unit belonging to or forming part of a group or organization **b** *often cap* one who is entitled to sit in a legislative body; *esp* a member of Parliament **3a** a constituent part of a whole **b** a beam or similar (load-bearing) structure, esp in a building **c** either of the expressions on either side of a mathematical equation or inequality

'membership /-ship‖-ʃɪp/ *n sing or pl in constr* the body of members <*an organization with a large* ~>

membrane /'membrayn‖'membreɪn/ *n* a thin pliable sheet or layer, esp in an animal or plant – **membranous** *adj*

memento /mə'mentoh‖mə'mentəʊ/ *n, pl* **mementos, mementoes** sthg (e g a souvenir) that serves as a reminder of past events, people, etc

memo /'memoh‖'meməʊ/ *n, pl* **memos** a memorandum

memoir /'memwah‖'memwɑː/ *n* **1a** a narrative written from personal experience **b** an autobiography – usu pl with sing. meaning **c** a biography **2** a learned essay on a particular topic *USE* (*1a&1c*) often pl with sing. meaning [French *mémoire*, lit., memory, fr Latin *memoria*] – **memoirist** *n*

memorabilia /,mem(ə)rə'bili·ə‖,mem(ə)rə'bɪlɪə/ *n pl* (records of) memorable events

memorable /'mem(ə)rəbl‖'mem(ə)rəbl/ *adj* worth remembering; notable – **memorability** *n*, **memorably** *adv*

memorandum /,memə'randəm‖,memə'rændəm/ *n, pl* **memorandums, memoranda** /-də‖-də/ **1** an often unsigned informal record or communication; *also* a written reminder **2** a document recording the terms of an agreement, the formation of a company, etc **3** a usu brief communication for internal circulation (e g within an office)

[1]**memorial** /mə'mawri·əl‖mə'mɔːrɪəl/ *adj* serving to commemorate a person or event – **memorially** *adv*, **memorialize** *vt*

[2]**memorial** *n* **1** sthg, esp a monument, that commemorates a person or event **2** a historical record – often pl

memor·ize, -ise /'meməriez‖'meməraɪz/ *vt* to commit to memory; learn by heart – **memorizable** *adj*, **memorization** *n*

memory /'mem(ə)ri‖'mem(ə)rɪ/ *n* **1** (the power or process of recalling or realizing) the store of things learned and retained from an organism's experience <*good visual* ~> **2** commemorative remembrance <*a statue in* ~ *of the hero*> **3a** (the object of) recall or recollection <*had no* ~ *of the incident*> <*left many happy* memories> **b** (posthumous) image or impression <*his* ~ *will stay with us*> **c** the time within which past events can be or are remembered **4** (the capacity of) a device in which information, esp for a computer, can be inserted and stored, and from which it may be extracted when wanted **5** a capacity of a metal, plastic, etc for retaining effects as the result of past treatment, or for returning to a former condition

memsahib /'mem,sah·hib‖'mem,sɑːhɪb/ *n* a white foreign woman of high social status living in India; *broadly* any woman of rank in India

men /men‖men/ *pl of* MAN

[1]**menace** /'menis‖'menɪs/ *n* **1** a show of intention to inflict harm; a threat **2a** a source of danger **b** a person who causes annoyance

[2]**menace** *vb* to threaten or show intent to harm – **menacingly** *adv*

ménage /me'nahzh, '--‖me'nɑːʒ, '--/ *n* a household

,ménage à 'trois /ah trwah‖ɑː trwɑː/ *n* a relationship in which 3 people, esp a married couple and the lover of 1, live together [French, lit., household for three]

menagerie /mə'najəri‖mə'nædʒərɪ/ *n* a place where animals are kept and trained, esp for exhibition; *also* a zoo

[1]**mend** /mend‖mend/ *vt* **1** to improve or rectify <~ *one's ways*> <*attempt to* ~ *matters*> **2a** to restore to sound condition or working order; repair **b** to restore to health; cure ~ *vi* **1** to undergo improvement **2** to improve in health;

also to heal – **mendable** *adj*, **mender** *n*

[2]**mend** *n* a mended place or part – **on the mend** improving, esp in health

mendacity /men'dasəti‖men'dæsətı/ *n* (sthg marked by) untruthfulness – fml – **mendacious** *adj*, **mendaciously** *adv*

Mendelian /men'deeli·ən‖men'di:lıən/ *adj* of or according with the genetic principle that genes occur in pairs, each gamete receives 1 member of each pair, and that an organism thus has 1 gene of each pair randomly selected from each of its parents – **Mendelian** *n*, **Mendelism** *n*

mendicant /'mendikənt‖'mendıkənt/ *n* **1** BEGGAR 1 **2** *often cap* a friar living off alms – **mendicant** *adj*, **mendicancy, mendicity** *n*

menfolk /'men,fohk‖'men,fəʊk/ *n pl in constr* **1** men in general **2** the men of a family or community

[1]**menial** /'meenyəl, -ni·əl‖'mi:njəl, -nıəl/ *adj* **1** of servants; lowly **2a** degrading; *also* servile **b** lacking in interest or status <*a boring* ~ *job*> – **menially** *adv*

[2]**menial** *n* a domestic servant or retainer

meningitis /,menin'jietəs‖,menın'dʒaıtəs/ *n* bacterial, fungal, or viral inflammation of the meninges – **meningitic** *adj*

meninx /'meningks, 'mee-‖'menıŋks, 'mi:-/ *n*, *pl* **meninges** /mə'ninjeez‖mə'nındʒi:z/ any of the 3 membranes (the dura mater, pia mater, and arachnoid) that envelop the brain and spinal cord – usu pl

meniscus /mə'niskəs‖mə'nıskəs/ *n*, *pl* **menisci** /-'nisie‖-'nısaı/ *also* **meniscuses** **1** a crescent-shaped body or figure **2** a lens that is concave on one side and convex on the other **3** the curved concave or convex upper surface of a column of liquid

menopause /'menə,pawz‖'menə,pɔ:z/ *n* (the time of) the natural cessation of menstruation occurring usu between the ages of 45 and 50 – **menopausal** *adj*

menses /'menseez‖'mensi:z/ *n pl but sing or pl in constr* the menstrual flow

'men's ,room *n*, *chiefly NAm* a men's toilet

menstruation /,menstroo'aysh(ə)n‖,menstrʊ'eıʃ(ə)n/ *n* the discharging of blood, secretions, and tissue debris from the uterus that recurs in nonpregnant primate females of breeding age at approximately monthly intervals; *also* a single occurrence of this – **menstruous** *adj*, **menstruate** *vi*, **menstrual** *adj*

mensuration /,menshə'raysh(ə)n‖,menʃə'reıʃ(ə)n/ *n* **1** measurement **2** geometry applied to the computation of lengths, areas, or volumes – **mensurable** *adj*, **mensural** *adj*

-ment /-mənt‖-mənt/ *suffix* (*vb* → *n*) **1a** concrete result, object, or agent of a (specified) action <*entangle*ment> **b** concrete means or instrument of a (specified) action <*entertain*ment> **2a** action; process <*develop*ment> **b** place of a (specified) action <*encamp*ment>

mental /'mentl‖'mentl/ *adj* **1a** of the mind or its activity <~ *health*> <~ *processes*> **b** of intellectual as contrasted with emotional or physical activity <~ *ability*> <*a* ~ *age of 3*> **c** (performed or experienced) in the mind <~ *arithmetic*> <~ *anguish*> **2** of, being, or (intended for the care of people) suffering from a psychiatric disorder <*a* ~ *patient*> <~ *illness*> **3** crazy; *also* stupid – infml – **mentally** *adv*

,mental de'fective *n* one who is mentally deficient

mentality /men'taləti‖men'tælətı/ *n* **1** mental power or capacity; intelligence **2** a mode of thought; mental disposition or outlook

menthol /'menthol‖'menθɒl/ *n* an alcohol that occurs esp in mint oils and has the smell and cooling properties of peppermint – **mentholated** *adj*

[1]**mention** /'mensh(ə)n‖'menʃ(ə)n/ *n* **1** a brief reference to sthg; a passing remark **2** a formal citation for outstanding achievement

[2]**mention** *vt* to make mention of; refer to; *also* to cite for outstanding achievement – **mentionable** *adj*

mentor /'mentaw‖'mentɔ:/ *n* a wise and trusted adviser [*Mentor*, tutor of Odysseus' son Telemachus in Homer's *Odyssey*]

menu /'menyooh‖'menju:/ *n*, *pl* **menus** (a list of) the dishes that may be ordered (e g in a restaurant) or that are to be served (e g at a banquet) [French, fr *menu* small, detailed, fr Latin *minutus* small]

meow /mee'ow‖mi:'aʊ/ *vi or n* (to) miaow

mercantile /'muhkəntiel‖'mɜ:kəntaıl/ *adj* **1** of or concerned with merchants or trading <~ *law*> **2** of mercantilism

mercantilism /'muhkəntl,iz(ə)m, -,tiel,iz(ə)m‖'mɜ:kəntl,ız(ə)m, -,taıl,ız(ə)m/ *n* an economic system first prominent in the 17th c that was intended to increase the power and wealth of a nation by strict governmental regulation of the national economy – **mercantilist** *n or adj*

Mercator's projection /muh'kaytəz‖mɜ:'keıtəz/ *n* a map projection showing the lines of longitude as parallel evenly-spaced straight lines and the lines of latitude as parallel straight lines whose distance from each other increases with their distance from the equator

[1]**mercenary** /'muhs(ə)nri‖'mɜ:s(ə)nrı/ *n* a hired soldier in foreign service

[2]**mercenary** *adj* **1** serving merely for (financial) reward **2** hired for service in the army of a foreign country – **mercenariness** *n*, **mercenarily** *adv*

mercer /'muhsə‖'mɜ:sə/ *n*, *Br* a dealer in (fine quality) textile fabrics – **mercery** *n*

[1]**merchandise** /'muhchən,dies‖'mɜ:tʃən,daıs/ *n* **1** the commodities that are bought and sold in commerce **2** wares for sale

[2]**merchandise** /'muhchən,diez‖'mɜ:tʃən,daız/ *vb* to buy and sell in business; trade (in) – **merchandiser** *n*

[1]**merchant** /'muhchənt‖'mɜ:tʃənt/ *n* **1** a wholesaler; *also, chiefly NAm* a shopkeeper **2** a person who is given to a specified activity – chiefly derog <*a speed* ~>

[2]**merchant** *adj* of or used in commerce; *esp* of a merchant navy

'merchantman /-mən‖-mən/ *n*, *pl* **merchantmen** /-mən‖-mən/ a ship used in commerce

,merchant 'navy *n*, *Br* (the personnel of) the privately or publicly owned commercial ships of a nation

[1]**mercurial** /muh'kyooəri·əl‖mɜ:'kjʊərıəl/ *adj*

1 of or born under the planet Mercury 2 having qualities of eloquence, ingenuity, or thievishness attributed to Mercury 3 characterized by rapid and unpredictable changes of mood 4 of, containing, or caused by mercury – **mercurially** *adv*

[2]**mercurial** *n* a drug or chemical containing mercury

mercury /ˈmuhkyoori‖ˈmɜːkjʊrɪ/ *n* 1 a heavy silver-white poisonous univalent or bivalent metallic element that is liquid at ordinary temperatures and used in thermometers, barometers, etc 2 *cap* the planet nearest the sun – **mercuric** *adj*, **mercurous** *adj*

mercy /ˈmuhsi‖ˈmɜːsɪ/ *n* 1 compassion or forbearance shown esp to an offender 2a an act of divine compassion; a blessing b a fortunate circumstance <*it was a ~ they found her before she froze*> 3 compassionate treatment of those in distress – **merciful** *adj*, **mercifully** *adv*, **mercifulness** *n*, **merciless** *adj*, **mercilessly** *adv*, **mercilessness** *n* – **at the mercy of** wholly in the power of; with no way to protect oneself against

ˈmercy ˌkilling *n* euthanasia

[1]**mere** /miə‖mɪə/ *n* a (small) lake

[2]**mere** *adj* being what is specified and nothing else; nothing more than <*a ~ child*> – **merely** *adv*

meretricious /ˌmerəˈtrishəs‖ˌmerəˈtrɪʃəs/ *adj* 1 tawdrily and falsely attractive 2 based on pretence or insincerity; specious [Latin *meretricius* of a prostitute, fr *meretrix* prostitute, fr *merēre* to earn] – **meretriciously** *adv*, **meretriciousness** *n*

merge /muhj‖mɜːdʒ/ *vb* 1 to (cause to) combine or unite 2 to blend or (cause to) come together gradually without abrupt change – **mergence** *n*

merger /ˈmuhjə‖ˈmɜːdʒə/ *n* 1 the absorption of an estate, contract, or interest in another – used in law 2 a combining or combination, esp of 2 organizations (e g business concerns)

meridian /məˈridi·ən‖məˈrɪdɪən/ *n* 1 a great circle passing through the poles of the celestial sphere and the zenith of a given place 2 a high point, esp of success or greatness 3 (a representation on a map or globe of) a circle on the surface of the earth or other celestial body passing through both poles – **meridian** *adj*

meridional /məˈridi·ənl‖məˈrɪdɪənl/ *adj* 1 of, characteristic of, or (being people) situated in the south, esp of France 2 of a meridian – **meridional** *n*, **meridionally** *adv*

meringue /məˈrang‖məˈræŋ/ *n* (a small cake, cream-filled shell, etc made with) a mixture of stiffly beaten egg whites and sugar baked until crisp

merino /məˈreenoh‖məˈriːnəʊ/ *n*, *pl* **merinos** 1 (any of) a breed of fine-woolled white orig Spanish sheep 2 a soft wool or wool and cotton clothing fabric resembling cashmere 3 a fine wool and cotton yarn used for hosiery and knitwear

[1]**merit** /ˈmerit‖ˈmerɪt/ *n* 1a the quality of deserving well or ill <*payment by ~*> b a praiseworthy quality; virtue c worth, excellence 2 spiritual credit held to be earned by performance of righteous acts and to ensure future benefits 3 *pl* the intrinsic rights and wrongs of a (legal) case

[2]**merit** *vt* to be worthy of or entitled to

meritocracy /ˌmeriˈtokrəsi‖ˌmerɪˈtɒkrəsɪ/ *n* (a social system based on) leadership by the talented – **meritocratic** *adj*

meritorious /ˌmeriˈtawri·əs‖ˌmerɪˈtɔːrɪəs/ *adj* deserving of reward or honour – **meritoriously** *adv*, **meritoriousness** *n*

mermaid /ˈmuhˌmayd‖ˈmɜːˌmeɪd/, *masc* **merman** /-ˌman‖-ˌmæn/ *n*, *pl masc* **mermen** /-ˌmen‖-ˌmen/ a mythical sea creature usu represented with a woman's body to the waist and a fish's tail

merriment /ˈmerimənt‖ˈmerɪmənt/ *n* lighthearted gaiety or fun

merry /ˈmeri‖ˈmerɪ/ *adj* 1 full of gaiety or high spirits 2 marked by festivity 3 slightly drunk; tipsy – infml – **merrily** *adv*, **merriness** *n*

ˈmerry-go-ˌround *n* a fairground machine with seats, often shaped like horses, that revolve about a fixed centre

ˈmerryˌmaking *n* gay or festive activity – **merrymaker** *n*

mesa /ˈmaysə‖ˈmeɪsə/ *n* a usu isolated hill, esp in SW USA, with steeply sloping sides and a level top

mescal /meˈskal‖meˈskæl/ *n* 1 a small cactus with rounded stems covered with mescaline-containing jointed protuberances used as a hallucinogen, esp among the Mexican Indians 2 (a usu colourless Mexican spirit made esp from) the maguey plant

meˈscal ˌbutton *n* any of the dried disc-shaped tops of the mescal

mescaline /ˈmeskəlin, -leen‖ˈmeskəlɪn, -liːn/ *n* a hallucinogenic alkaloid found in mescal buttons

mesdames /mayˈdam‖meɪˈdæm/ *pl of* MADAM *or of* MADAME *or of* MRS

mesdemoiselles /ˌmaydəmwahˈzel‖ˌmeɪdəmwɑːˈzel/ *pl of* MADEMOISELLE

[1]**mesh** /mesh‖meʃ/ *n* 1 an open space in a net, network, etc 2a the cords, wires, etc that make up a net; NETWORK 1 <*wire ~*> b a woven, knitted, or knotted fabric with evenly spaced small holes 3a an interlocking or intertwining arrangement or construction b a web, snare – usu pl with sing. meaning 4 working contact (e g of the teeth of gears) <*in ~*>

[2]**mesh** *vt* 1 to catch or entangle (as if) in the openings of a net 2 to cause to engage ~ *vi* 1 *esp of gears* to be in or come into mesh 2 to fit or work together properly or successfully

mesmerism /ˈmezməˌriz(ə)m‖ˈmezməˌrɪz(ə)m/ *n* hypnotism [F A *Mesmer* (1734-1815), Austrian physician & hypnotist] – **mesmerist** *n*, **mesmeric** *adj*

mesmer·ize, **-ise** /ˈmezməriez‖ˈmezməraɪz/ *vt* 1 to hypnotize 2 to fascinate, rivet – **mesmerizer** *n*

mesoderm /ˈmeezəˌduhm, ˈmesoh-‖ˈmiːzəˌdɜːm, ˈmesəʊ-/ *n* (tissue derived from) the middle of the 3 primary germ layers of an embryo that is the source of bone, muscle, connective tissue, and the inner layer of the skin in the adult – **mesodermal**, **mesodermic** *adj*

Mesozoic /ˌmezohˈzoh·ik‖ˌmezəʊˈzəʊɪk/ *adj or n* (of or being) an era of geological history that extends from about 230 million to 65 million years ago

[1]**mess** /mes‖mes/ *n* 1 a prepared dish of soft or

liquid food; *also* a usu unappetizing mixture of ingredients eaten together **2a(1)** *sing or pl in constr* a group of people (e g servicemen or servicewomen) who regularly take their meals together **a(2)** a meal so taken **b** a place where meals are regularly served to a group <*the officers'* ~> **3a** a confused, dirty, or offensive state or condition **b** a disordered situation resulting from misunderstanding, blundering, or misconduct

[2]**mess** *vi* **1** to take meals with a mess **2** to make a mess **3a** to dabble, potter **b** to handle or play *with* sthg, esp carelessly **c** to interfere, meddle ***USE*** (*3*) often + *about* or *around*

mess about *vb, chiefly Br vi* **1a** to waste time **b** to work according to one's whim or mood <messing about *in boats*> **2** to conduct an affair *with* <messing about *with someone else's husband*> ~*vt* to treat roughly or without due consideration <*he shouldn't* mess *the men* about *too much, they know their job – The Lorry Driver*>

message /'mesij‖'mesɪdʒ/ *n* **1** a communication in writing, in speech, or by signals **2** a messenger's errand or function **3** a central theme or idea intended to inspire, urge, warn, enlighten, advise, etc

messenger /'mesinjə‖'mesɪndʒə/ *n* one who bears a message or does an errand: e g **a** a dispatch bearer in government or military service **b** an employee who carries messages

messiah /mə'sie·ə‖mə'saɪə/ *n* **1** *often cap* **1a** *the* expected king and deliverer of the Jews **b** Jesus **2** a professed leader of some cause – **messiahship** *n*

messianic /ˌmesi'anik‖ˌmesɪ'ænɪk/ *adj* **1** of a messiah **2** marked by idealistic enthusiasm for a cherished cause **3** of a time of blessedness and peace associated with the Jewish and Christian concept of the end of the world – **messianism** *n*

messieurs /'mesyuh, 'mesəz ‖'mesjɜː, 'mesəz (*Fr* mesjø)/ *pl of* MONSIEUR

'mess,mate /-ˌmayt‖-ˌmeɪt/ *n* a member of a (ship's) mess

Messrs /'mesəz‖'mesəz/ *pl of* MR <~ *Jones, Brown, and Robinson*>

messuage /'meswij‖'meswɪdʒ/ *n* a dwelling house with its outbuildings and land

mess up *vt* to make a mess of; spoil – infml

messy /'mesi‖'mesɪ/ *adj* **1** marked by confusion, disorder, or dirt **2** lacking neatness or precision; slovenly **3** unpleasantly or tryingly difficult to conclude – **messily** *adv*, **messiness** *n*

[1]**met** /met‖met/ *past of* MEET

[2]**met** *adj* meteorological <*the* ~ *office forecast*>

meta- /metə-‖metə-/, **met-** *prefix* **1a** situated behind or beyond <meta*carpus*> **b** later or more highly organized or specialized form of <meta*xylem*> **2** change; transformation <meta*morphosis*> **3** more comprehensive; transcending; of a higher or second order <meta*psychology*> – used with the name of a discipline to designate a new but related discipline designed to deal critically with the original one <meta*language*>

metabolism /mə'tablˌiz(ə)m‖mə'tæblˌɪz(ə)m/ *n* all the processes (by which a specified substance is dealt with) in the building up and destruction of living tissue; *specif* the chemical changes in living cells by which energy is provided and new material is assimilated – **metabolize** *vb*, **metabolic** *adj*

metacarpal /ˌmetə'kahpl‖ˌmetə'kɑːpl/ *n* a metacarpal bone

ˌmeta'carpus /-'kahpəs‖-'kɑːpəs/ *n* the part of the hand or forefoot between the wrist and fingers or the ankle and toes – **metacarpal** *adj*

metal /'metl‖'metl/ *n* **1** any of various opaque, fusible, ductile, and typically lustrous substances (e g iron, copper, or mercury), esp chemical elements, that are good conductors of electricity and heat, form positive ions by loss of electrons, and yield basic oxides and hydroxides **2** glass in its molten state **3** either of the heraldic colours gold or silver **4** *chiefly Br* ROAD METAL – **metalliferous** *adj*

metallic /mi'talik‖mɪ'tælɪk/ *adj* **1** of, containing, like, or being (a) metal **2** yielding metal **3** having an acrid quality – **metallically** *adv*

[1]**metalloid** /'metl·oyd‖'metlɔɪd/ *n* an element (e g arsenic) having some properties of typical metals and some properties of typical nonmetals

[2]**metalloid** *also* **metalloidal** /ˌmetl'oydl‖ˌmetl'ɔɪdl/ *adj* **1** resembling a metal **2** of or being a metalloid

metallurgy /mə'taləji, 'metlˌuhji‖mə'tælədʒɪ, 'metlˌɜːdʒɪ/ *n* the science and technology of metals – **metallurgist** *n*, **metallurgical** *adj*, **metallurgically** *adv*

'metalˌwork /-ˌwuhk‖-ˌwɜːk/ *n* the craft or product of shaping things out of metal – **metalworker** *n*

metamorphic /ˌmetə'mawfik‖ˌmetə'mɔːfɪk/ *adj* **1** of or involving metamorphosis **2** *of a rock* of or produced by metamorphism – **metamorphically** *adv*

metamorphism /ˌmetə'mawfiz(ə)m‖ˌmetə'mɔːfɪz(ə)m/ *n* a change in rock effected esp by heat and pressure and resulting in a more compact and crystalline structure

metamorphose /metə'mawfohz, ˌ---'-‖metə'mɔːfəʊz, ˌ---'-/ *vt* **1a** to change into a different physical form **b** to change strikingly the appearance or character of; transform **2** to cause (rock) to undergo metamorphism ~*vi* to undergo metamorphosis

ˌmeta'morphosis /-'mawfəsis‖-'mɔːfəsɪs/ *n, pl* **metamorphoses** /-seez‖-siːz/ **1a** change of form, structure, or substance, esp by supernatural means **b** a striking alteration (e g in appearance or character) **2** a marked (abrupt) change in the form or structure of a butterfly, frog, etc occurring in the course of development [Latin, fr Greek *metamorphōsis*, fr *metamorphoun* to transform, fr *meta-* among, with, after, change + *morphē* form]

metaphor /'metəfə, -ˌfaw‖'metəfə, -ˌfɔː/ *n* (an instance of) a figure of speech in which a word or phrase literally denoting one kind of object or idea is applied to another to suggest a likeness or analogy between them (e g in *the ship ploughs the sea*) – **metaphoric, metaphorical** *adj*, **metaphorically** *adv*

ˌmeta'physical /-'fizikl‖-'fɪzɪkl/ *adj* **1** of

metaphysics **2** *often cap* of or being poetry, esp of the early 17th c, marked by elaborate subtleties of thought and expression – **metaphysically** *adv*

ˌmetaˈphysics *n pl but sing in constr* **1** a division of philosophy concerned with ultimate causes and the underlying nature of things; *esp* ontology **2** pure or speculative philosophy – **metaphysician** *n*

metatarsal /ˌmetəˈtahsl‖ˌmetəˈtɑːsl/ *n* a metatarsal bone

ˌmetaˈtarsus /-ˈtahsəs‖-ˈtɑːsəs/ *n* the part of the foot in human beings or of the hind foot in 4-legged animals between the ankle and toes – **metatarsal** *adj*

mete /meet‖miːt/ *vt* to assign by measure; allot – usu + *out*

metempsychosis /ˌmetem(p)sieˈkohsis‖ˌmetem(p)saɪˈkəʊsɪs/ *n* the passing of the soul at death into another body

meteor /ˈmeeti·ˌə, -ˌaw‖ˈmiːtɪˌə, -ˌɔː/ *n* a phenomenon in the atmosphere; *esp* (the streak of light produced by the passage of) any of many small particles of matter in the solar system observable only when heated by friction so that they glow as they fall into the earth's atmosphere

meteoric /ˌmeetiˈorik‖ˌmiːtɪˈɒrɪk/ *adj* **1** of a meteor **2** resembling a meteor in speed or in sudden and temporary brilliance <~ *rise to fame*> – **meteorically** *adv*

meteorite /ˈmeeti·əˌriet‖ˈmiːtɪəˌraɪt/ *n* a meteor that reaches the surface of the earth without being completely vaporized – **meteoritic, meteoritical** *adj*

meteoroid /ˈmeeti·əˌroyd‖ˈmiːtɪəˌrɔɪd/ *n* a particle in orbit round the sun that becomes a meteor when it meets the earth's atmosphere – **meteoroidal** *adj*

meteorology /ˌmeeti·əˈroləji‖ˌmiːtɪəˈrɒlədʒɪ/ *n* **1** the science of the atmosphere and its phenomena, esp weather and weather forecasting **2** the weather or atmospheric phenomena of a region – **meteorologist** *n*, **meteorologic, meteorological** *adj*, **meteorologically** *adv*

[1]**meter** /ˈmeetə‖ˈmiːtə/ *n*, *NAm* a metre

[2]**meter** *n* an instrument for measuring (and recording) the amount of sthg (e g gas, electricity, or parking time) used

[3]**meter** *vt* **1** to measure by means of a meter **2** to supply in a measured or regulated amount

[1]**-meter** /-mətə‖-mətə/ *comb form* (→ *n*) measure or unit of metrical verse <*penta*meter>

[2]**-meter** *comb form* (→ *n*) instrument or means for measuring <*baro*meter>

methane /ˈmeeˌthayn‖ˈmiːˌθeɪn/ *n* an inflammable gaseous hydrocarbon of the alkane series used as a fuel and as a raw material in chemical synthesis

methanol /ˈmethənol‖ˈmeθənɒl/ *n* a volatile inflammable poisonous liquid alcohol that is added to ethyl alcohol to make it unfit to drink and is used as a solvent and as a raw material in chemical synthesis

methinks /miˈthingks‖mɪˈθɪŋks/ *vb impersonal* **methought** /miˈthawt‖mɪˈθɔːt/ *archaic* it seems to me

method /ˈmethəd‖ˈmeθəd/ *n* **1a** a systematic procedure for doing sthg **b** a regular way of doing sthg **2a** an orderly arrangement or system **b** the habitual practice of orderliness and regularity **3** *cap* a dramatic technique by which an actor seeks to identify closely with the inner personality of the character being portrayed – usu + *the*

methodical /məˈthodikl‖məˈθɒdɪkl/, *NAm also* **methodic** *adj* **1** arranged, characterized by, or performed with method or order **2** habitually proceeding according to method; systematic – **methodically** *adv*, **methodicalness** *n*

Methodism /ˈmethədiz(ə)m‖ˈmeθədɪz(ə)m/ *n* (the doctrines and practice of) the Methodist churches

Methodist /ˈmethədist‖ˈmeθədɪst/ *n or adj* (a member) of any of the denominations deriving from the Wesleyan revival in the Church of England

methodology /ˌmethəˈdoləji‖ˌmeθəˈdɒlədʒɪ/ *n* (the analysis of) the body of methods and rules employed by a science or discipline – **methodologist** *n*, **methodological** *adj*

meths /meths‖meθs/ *n pl but sing in constr*, *Br* METHYLATED SPIRITS – infml

methyl alcohol /ˈmethil, ˈmeethil, -thiel‖ˈmeθɪl, ˈmiːθɪl, -θaɪl/ *n* methanol

ˌmethylated ˈspirits /ˌmethilaytid‖ˌmeθɪleɪtɪd/ *n pl but sing or pl in constr* alcohol mixed with an adulterant, esp methanol, to make it undrinkable and therefore exempt from duty

methylene /ˈmethəˌleen‖ˈmeθəˌliːn/ *n* a bivalent hydrocarbon radical CH_2 derived from methane

meticulous /məˈtikyooləs‖məˈtɪkjʊləs/ *adj* marked by extreme or excessive care over detail – **meticulously** *adv*, **meticulousness** *n*

métier /ˈmaytyay‖ˈmeɪtjeɪ/ *n* one's trade; *also* sthg (e g an activity) in which one is expert or successful [French, deriv of Latin *ministerium* work, ministry]

[1]**metre**, *NAm chiefly* **meter** /ˈmeetə‖ˈmiːtə/ *n* the SI unit of length equal to about 1.094yd [French *mètre*, fr Greek *metron* measure]

[2]**metre**, *NAm chiefly* **meter** *n* **1** systematically arranged and measured rhythm in verse <*iambic* ~> **2** a basic recurrent rhythmical pattern of accents and beats per bar in music – **metrist** *n*

metric /ˈmetrik‖ˈmetrɪk/ *adj* **1 metric, metrical** (using or being units) based on the metre, litre, and kilogram as standard of measurement **2** metrical – **metrically** *adv*

-metric /-ˈmetrik‖-ˈmetrɪk/, **-metrical** /-kl‖-kl/ *comb form* (→ *adj*) **1** of, employing, or obtained by (a specified meter) <*galvano*metric> **2** of or relating to the art, process, or science of measuring (sthg specified) <*chrono*metric>

metrical /ˈmetrikl‖ˈmetrɪkl/, **metric** *adj* **1** of or composed in metre **2** of measurement – **metrically** *adv*

metricate /ˈmetrikayt‖ˈmetrɪkeɪt/ *vt* to change into or express in the metric system ~*vi* to adopt the metric system – **metrication** *n*

metric ton *n* a tonne

metro /ˈmetroh‖ˈmetrəʊ/ *n*, *pl* **metros** an underground railway system in a city

metronome /ˈmetrəˌnohm‖ˈmetrəˌnəʊm/ *n* an instrument designed to mark exact time by a regularly repeated tick – **metronomic** *adj*

metropolis /miˈtropəlis‖mɪˈtrɒpəlɪs/ *n* **1** the chief city of a country, state, or region **2** a centre of a usu specified activity **3** a large or important city [Late Latin, fr Greek *mētropolis*, fr *mētr-*, *mētēr* mother + *polis* city]

[1]**metropolitan** /ˌmetrəˈpolit(ə)n‖ˌmetrəˈpɒlɪt(ə)n/ *n* **1** the primate of an ecclesiastical province **2** one who lives in a metropolis

[2]**metropolitan** *adj* **1** of or constituting a metropolitan or his see **2** (characteristic) of a metropolis **3** of or constituting a mother country

mettle /ˈmetl‖ˈmetl/ *n* **1** strength of spirit or temperament **2** staying quality; stamina – **on one's mettle** aroused to do one's best

ˈ**mettlesome** /-s(ə)m‖-s(ə)m/ *adj* spirited

[1]**mew** /myooh‖mjuː/ *vi* to utter a miaow or similar sound <*gulls* ~ed *over the bay*> ~*vt* to miaow – **mew** *n*

[2]**mew** *vt* to shut up; confine – often + *up*

mews /myoohz‖mjuːz/ *n pl but sing or pl in constr, pl* **mews** *chiefly Br* (living accommodation adapted from) stables built round an open courtyard

Mexican /ˈmeksik(ə)n‖ˈmeksɪk(ə)n/ *n or adj* (a native or inhabitant) of Mexico

mezzanine /ˈmezəneen‖ˈmezəniːn/ *n* a low-ceilinged storey between 2 main storeys, esp the ground and first floors, of a building

mezzo /ˈmetsoh‖ˈmetsəʊ/, **mezzo-soprano** *n, pl* **mezzos, mezzo-sopranos** (a singer with) a woman's voice with a range between that of the soprano and contralto

mezzotint /ˈmetsoh,tint‖ˈmetsəʊ,tɪnt/ *n* (a print produced by) a method of engraving on copper or steel by scraping or burnishing a roughened surface to produce light and shade

mi /mee‖miː/ *n* the 3rd note of the diatonic scale in solmization

miaow, meow /miˈow, myow‖mɪˈaʊ, mjaʊ/ *vi or n* (to make) the characteristic cry of a cat

miasma /miˈazmə‖mɪˈæzmə/ *n, pl* **miasmas** *also* **miasmata** /-mətə‖-mətə/ **1** a heavy vapour (e g from a swamp) formerly believed to cause disease; *broadly* any heavy or malodorous vapour **2** a pervasive influence that tends to weaken or corrupt – **miasmal** *adj*, **miasmatic** *adj*, **miasmic** *adj*

mica /ˈmiekə‖ˈmaɪkə/ *n* any of various coloured or transparent silicate materials occurring as crystals that readily separate into very thin flexible leaves – **micaceous** *adj*

mice /mies‖maɪs/ *pl of* MOUSE

Michaelmas /ˈmik(ə)lməs‖ˈmɪk(ə)lməs/ *n* September 29 celebrated as the feast of St Michael the Archangel

Michaelmas daisy *n* any of several (Autumn-blooming) asters widely grown as garden plants

mick /mik‖mɪk/ *n* an Irishman – chiefly derog

mickey /miki‖mɪkɪ/ *n* – **take the mickey** to make sby an object of amusement by humorous or playful ridicule – infml

micro- *comb form* **1a** small; minute <micro*cosm*> **b** used for or involving minute quantities or variations <micro*barograph*> **c** microscopic <micro*organism*> **2** one millionth (10^6) part of (a specified unit) <micro*second*> **3** enlarging; magnifying; amplifying <micro*phone*> **4a** used in or involving microscopy <micro*dissection*> **b** used in or connected with microphotography <micro*film*> **5** of a small or localized area <micro*climate*>

microbe /ˈmiekrohb‖ˈmaɪkrəʊb/ *n* a microorganism, germ – **microbial, microbic** *adj*

microbiology /ˌmiekrəbieˈoləji, -kroh-‖ˌmaɪkrəbaɪˈɒlədʒɪ, -krəʊ-/ *n* the biology of bacteria and other microscopic forms of life – **microbiologist** *n*, **microbiological, microbiologic** *adj*

microchip /ˈmiekrə, chip/ *n* a chip bearing an integrated circuit

ˈ**microcom,puter** /-kəm,pyoohtə‖-kəmˌpjuːtə/ *n* a small self-contained computer that is based on one or more microprocessors and that typically has a keyboard and a visual display unit

microcosm /ˈmiekrə,koz(ə)m‖ˈmaɪkrə,kɒz(ə)m/ *n* **1** a little world; *esp* an individual human being or human nature seen as an epitome of the world or universe **2** a whole (e g a community) that is an epitome of a larger whole – **microcosmic** *adj*

ˌ**microelecˈtronics** /-iˌlekˈtroniks, -ˌelek-‖-ɪˌlekˈtrɒnɪks, -ˌelek-/ *n pl but sing in constr* a branch of electronics that deals with or produces miniaturized electronic circuits and components – **microelectronic** *adj*

ˈ**micro,fiche** /-,feesh‖-,fiːʃ/ *n, pl* **microfiche, microfiches** /-shiz‖-ʃɪz/ a sheet of microfilm containing rows of very small images of pages of printed matter

microfilm /ˈmiekrə,film‖ˈmaɪkrə,fɪlm/ *n* a film bearing a photographic record on a reduced scale of graphic matter (e g printing) – **microfilm** *vb*, **microfilmable** *adj*

microlight /ˈmiekrəliet‖ˈmaɪkrəlaɪt/ *n* a single- or two-seat aeroplane with a weight not exceeding 150kg

micrometer /mieˈkromitə‖maɪˈkrɒmɪtə/ *n* **1** an instrument for measuring distances between objects seen through a microscope or telescope **2** a gauge for making precise measurements of length by means of a spindle moved by a finely threaded screw

micron /ˈmiekron‖ˈmaɪkrɒn/ *n, pl* **microns** *also* **micra** /-krə‖-krə/ one millionth (10^{-6}) part of a metre – not now recommended for technical use

ˌ**microˈorganism** /-ˈawgəniz(ə)m‖-ˈɔːgənɪz(ə)m/ *n* an organism of (smaller than) microscopic size

microphone /ˈmiekrə,fohn‖ˈmaɪkrə,fəʊn/ *n* a device that converts sounds into electrical signals, esp for transmission or recording – **microphonic** *adj*

ˌ**microˈprocessor** /-ˈprohsesə‖-ˈprəʊsesə/ *n* a very small computer composed of 1 or more integrated circuits functioning as a unit

microscope /ˈmiekrə,skohp‖ˈmaɪkrə,skəʊp/ *n* an instrument consisting of (a combination of) lenses for making enlarged images of minute objects using light or other radiations [deriv of Greek *mikros* small + *skopein* to look at]

ˌ**microˈscopic** /-ˈskopik‖-ˈskɒpɪk/ *also* **microscopical** /-kl‖-kl/ *adj* **1** of or conducted with the microscope or microscopy **2** resembling a microscope, esp in perception **3a** invisible or indistinguishable without the use of a microscope **b** very small, fine, or precise –

microscopically *adv*

microwave /ˈmiekrəˌwayv‖ˈmaɪkrəˌweɪv/ *n* a band of very short electromagnetic waves of between 1m and 0.1m in wavelength

[1]**mid** /mid‖mɪd/ *adj* **1** being the part in the middle or midst <*in* ~ *ocean*> – often in combination <mid-*August*> <*in* mid-*sentence*> **2** occupying a middle position – **mid** *adv*

[2]**mid** *prep* amid – poetic

ˌmidˈair /-ˈeə‖-ˈeə/ *n* a point or region in the air not immediately near the ground

ˌmidˈday /-ˈday‖-ˈdeɪ/ *n* the middle part of the day; noon

midden /ˈmid(ə)n‖ˈmɪd(ə)n/ *n* **1** a dunghill **2** a refuse heap; *esp* a heap or stratum of domestic rubbish found on the site of an ancient settlement

[1]**middle** /ˈmidl‖ˈmɪdl/ *adj* **1** equally distant from the extremes; central **2** at neither extreme **3** *cap* **3a** constituting a division intermediate between those prior and later or upper and lower <Middle *Palaeozoic*> **b** belonging to a period of a language intermediate between Old and New or Modern forms <Middle *Dutch*>

[2]**middle** *n* **1** a middle part, point, or position **2** the waist **3** the position of being among or in the midst of sthg **4** sthg intermediate between extremes; a mean

[3]**middle** *vt* to hit (a shot) correctly with the middle of the bat in cricket

ˌmiddle ˈage *n* the period of life from about 40 to about 60 – **middle-aged** *adj*

ˈMiddle ˌAges *n pl* the period of European history from about AD 500 to about 1500

ˈmiddleˌbrow /-ˌbrow‖-ˌbraʊ/ *adj* dealing with or having conventional and often bourgeois intellectual and cultural interests and activities – often derog – **middlebrow** *n*

ˌmiddle ˈclass *n* a class occupying a position between upper and lower; *esp* a fluid heterogeneous grouping of business and professional people, bureaucrats, and some farmers and skilled workers – often pl with sing. meaning – **middle-class** *adj*

ˌmiddle-ˈdistance *adj* of or being a foot-race over a distance between 400m and 1mi

middle distance *n* the part of a picture or view between the foreground and the background

middle ear *n* a cavity through which sound waves are transmitted by a chain of tiny bones from the eardrum to the inner ear

Middle English *n* English from about 1151 to 1500

ˈmiddleˌman /-ˌman‖-ˌmæn/ *n* an intermediary between 2 parties; *esp* a dealer intermediate between the producer of goods and the retailer or consumer

middle name *n* **1** a name between one's first name and surname **2** a quality of character for which sby is well known <*generosity is her* ~>

ˌmiddle-of-the-ˈroad *adj* conforming to the majority in taste, attitude, or conduct; *also* neither right-wing nor left-wing in political conviction – **middle-of-the-roader** *n*, **middle-of-the-roadism** *n*

middle school *n* (part of) a school for pupils aged 8–12 or 9–13

ˈmiddleˌweight /-ˌwayt‖-ˌweɪt/ *n* a boxer who weighs not more than 11st 6lb (72.6kg) if professional or more than 71kg (about 11st 2lb) but not more than 75kg (about 11st 11lb) if amateur

middling /ˈmidling‖ˈmɪdlɪŋ/ *adj* **1** of middle or moderate size, degree, or quality **2** mediocre, second-rate – **middling** *adv*, **middlingly** *adv*

midge /mij‖mɪdʒ/ *n* a tiny two-winged fly

midget /ˈmijit‖ˈmɪdʒɪt/ *n* **1** a very small person; a dwarf **2** sthg (e g an animal) much smaller than usual – **midget** *adj*

midi /ˈmidi‖ˈmɪdɪ/ *n* a woman's garment that extends to the mid-calf

midland /ˈmidlənd‖ˈmɪdlənd/ *n*, *often cap* the central region of a country – usu pl with sing. meaning – **midland** *adj*, *often cap*

ˈmidˌmost /-ˌmohst‖-ˌməʊst/ *adj* in or near the middle – **midmost** *adv or n*

midnight /ˈmidˌniet‖ˈmɪdˌnaɪt/ *n* the middle of the night; *specif* 12 o'clock at night – **midnight** *adj*, **midnightly** *adv or adj*

ˌmidnight ˈsun *n* the sun visible at midnight in the arctic or antarctic summer

ˌmid-ˈoff *n* a fielding position in cricket near the bowler on the off side of the pitch

ˌmid-ˈon *n* a fielding position in cricket near the bowler on the leg side of the pitch

ˈmidˌpoint /-ˌpoynt‖-ˌpɔɪnt/ *n* a point midway between the beginning and end of sthg

midriff /ˈmidrif‖ˈmɪdrɪf/ *n* **1** DIAPHRAGM 1 **2** the middle part of the human torso

midshipman /ˈmidˌshipmən‖ˈmɪdˌʃɪpmən/ *n* (the rank of) a young person training to become a naval officer

ˈmidˌships /-ˌships‖-ˌʃɪps/ *adv* amidships

midst /midst‖mɪdst/ *n* **1** the inner or central part or point; the middle **2** a position near to the members of a group <*a traitor in our* ~> **3** the condition of being surrounded or beset (e g by problems) **4** a period of time about the middle of a continuing act or state <*in the* ~ *of the celebrations*> – **midst** *prep*

ˌmidˈsummer /-ˈsumə‖-ˈsʌmə/ *n* the summer solstice

ˌMidsummer ˈDay *n* June 24 celebrated as the feast of the nativity of John the Baptist

ˌmidˈway /-ˈway‖-ˈweɪ/ *adv* halfway

ˌmidˈweek /-ˈweek‖-ˈwiːk/ *n* the middle of the week – **midweek** *adj*, **midweekly** *adj or adv*

ˌmid-ˈwicket *n* a fielding position in cricket on the leg side equidistant from each wicket

midwife /ˈmidˌwief‖ˈmɪdˌwaɪf/ *n* **1** a woman who assists other women in childbirth **2** sby or sthg that helps to produce or bring forth sthg [Middle English *midwif*, fr *mid* with + *wif* woman]

midwifery /ˈmidˌwifəri‖ˈmɪdˌwɪfərɪ/ *n* (the art of) assisting at childbirth; *also* obstetrics

mien /meen‖miːn/ *n* air or bearing, esp as expressive of mood or personality – fml

[1]**miff** /mif‖mɪf/ *n* **1** a brief outburst of bad temper **2** a trivial quarrel ***USE*** infml

[2]**miff** *vt* to make cross or peeved – infml

[1]**might** /miet‖maɪt/ *past of* MAY – used to express permission or liberty in the past <*asked whether he* ~ *come*> <*the king* ~ *do nothing without parliament's consent*>, a past or present

possibility contrary to fact <*I ~ well have been killed*> <*if he were older he ~ understand*>, purpose or expectation in the past <*wrote it down so that I ~ not forget it*>, less probability or possibility than *may* <*~ get there before it rains*>, a polite request <*you ~ post this letter for me*>, or as a polite or ironic alternative to *may* <*who ~ you be?*> or to *ought* or *should* <*you ~ at least apologize*> <*he ~ have offered to help*>

[2]**might** *n* **1** power, authority, or resources wielded individually or collectively **2a** physical strength **b** all the power or effort one is capable of

mightily /ˈmiet(ə)l·i‖ˈmaɪt(ə)lɪ/ *adv* very much <*it amused us ~* – Charles Dickens>

mightn't /ˈmietnt‖ˈmaɪtnt/ might not

[1]**mighty** /ˈmieti‖ˈmaɪtɪ/ *adj* **1** powerful **2** accomplished or characterized by might <*a ~ thrust*> **3** imposingly great <*the ~ mountains*> – **mightiness** *n*

[2]**mighty** *adv* to a great degree; extremely <*a ~ big man*>

mignonette /ˌminyəˈnet‖ˌmɪnjəˈnet/ *n* an annual garden plant with fragrant greenish yellow flowers or any of various related plants

migraine /ˈmeegrayn‖ˈmiːgreɪn/ *n* recurrent severe headache usu associated with disturbances of vision, sensation, and movement often on only 1 side of the body [French, fr Late Latin *hemicrania* pain in one side of the head, fr Greek *hēmikrania*, fr *hēmi-* half + *kranion* skull] – **migrainous** *adj*

migrant /ˈmiegrənt‖ˈmaɪgrənt/ *n* **1** a person who moves regularly in order to find work, esp in harvesting crops **2** an animal that moves from one habitat to another – **migrant** *adj*

migrate /mieˈgrayt‖maɪˈgreɪt/ *vi* **1** to move from one country or locality to another **2** *of an animal* to pass usu periodically from one region or climate to another for feeding or breeding – **migration** *n*, **migrational** *adj*, **migrator** *n*

migratory /ˈmiegrət(ə)ri‖ˈmaɪgrət(ə)rɪ/ *adj* wandering, roving

mikado /miˈkahdoh‖mɪˈkɑːdəʊ/ *n, pl* **mikados** – formerly used as a title for the emperor of Japan

mike /miek‖maɪk/ *n* a microphone – infml

milady /miˈlaydi‖mɪˈleɪdɪ/ *n* an Englishwoman of noble or gentle birth – often used as a term of address or reference

milch /milch‖mɪltʃ/ *adj, of a domestic animal* bred or used primarily for milk production

[1]**mild** /mield‖maɪld/ *adj* **1** gentle in nature or manner **2a** not strong in flavour or effect **b** not being or involving what is extreme **3** not severe; temperate <*a ~ climate*> **4** easily worked; malleable <*~ steel*> – **mildly** *adv*, **mildness** *n*

[2]**mild** *n, Br* a dark-coloured beer not flavoured with hops

[1]**mildew** /ˈmildyooh‖ˈmɪldjuː/ *n* (a fungus producing) a usu whitish growth on the surface of organic matter (e g paper or leather) or living plants – **mildewy** *adj*

[2]**mildew** *vb* to affect or become affected (as if) with mildew

mile /miel‖maɪl/ *n* **1** any of various units of distance: e g **1a** a unit equal to 1760yd (about 1.61km) **b** NAUTICAL MILE **2** a large distance or amount – often pl with sing. meaning [Old French *mil*, deriv of Latin *milia* miles, fr *milia passuum*, lit., thousands of paces, fr *milia*, pl of *mille* thousand] – **miles from nowhere** in an extremely remote place

mileage /ˈmielij‖ˈmaɪlɪdʒ/ *n* **1** an allowance for travelling expenses at a certain rate per mile **2** total length or distance in miles: e g **2a** the number of miles travelled over a period of time **b** the distance, or distance covered, in miles **c** the average distance in miles a vehicle will travel for an amount of fuel

ˈ**mileˌpost** /-ˌpohst‖-ˌpəʊst/ *n* a post indicating the distance in miles from or to a given point

miler /ˈmielə‖ˈmaɪlə/ *n* a person or horse that competes in mile races

milestone /ˈmielˌstohn‖ˈmaɪlˌstəʊn/ *n* **1** a stone serving as a milepost **2** a crucial stage in sthg's development

milieu /ˈmeelyuh ‖ˈmiːljɜː (*Fr* miljø)/ *n, pl* **milieus, milieux** /-lyuh(z) (‖-ljɜː(z) (*Fr* ~)‖~)/ an environment, setting

militant /ˈmilit(ə)nt‖ˈmɪlɪt(ə)nt/ *adj* **1** engaged in warfare or combat **2** aggressively active (e g in a cause); combative – **militancy** *n*, **militant** *n*, **militantly** *adv*, **militantness** *n*

militarism /ˈmilitəˌriz(ə)m‖ˈmɪlɪtəˌrɪz(ə)m/ *n* **1** exaltation of military virtues and ideals **2** a policy of aggressive military preparedness – **militarist** *n*, **militaristic** *adj*, **militaristically** *adv*

militar·ize, -ise /ˈmilitəˌriez‖ˈmɪlɪtəˌraɪz/ *vt* **1** to equip with military forces and defences **2** to give a military character to – **militarization** *n*

[1]**military** /ˈmilit(ə)ri‖ˈmɪlɪt(ə)rɪ/ *adj* **1** (characteristic) of soldiers, arms, or war **2** carried on or supported by armed force <*a ~ dictatorship*> **3** of the army or armed forces – **militarily** *adv*

[2]**military** *n* **1** *pl in constr* soldiers **2** *sing or pl in constr the* army (as opposed to civilians or police)

military police *n* a branch of an army that carries out police functions within the army

militate /ˈmilitayt‖ˈmɪlɪteɪt/ *vi* to have significant weight or effect – often + *against*

militia /miˈlish(y)ə‖mɪˈlɪʃ(j)ə/ *n sing or pl in constr* a body of citizens with some military training who are called on to fight only in an emergency – **militiaman** *n*

[1]**milk** /milk‖mɪlk/ *n* **1** a (white or creamy) liquid secreted by the mammary glands of females for the nourishment of their young (and used as a food by humans) **2** a milklike liquid: e g **2a** the latex of a plant **b** the juice of a coconut **c** a cosmetic lotion, esp a cleanser – **milky** *adj*, **milkiness** *n*

[2]**milk** *vt* **1** to draw milk from the breasts or udder of **2** to draw sthg from as if by milking: e g **2a** to induce (a snake) to eject venom **b** to compel or persuade to yield illicit or excessive profit or advantage <*opera stars who ~ their audience for applause*> – **milker** *n*

ˈ**milk ˌfloat** *n, Br* a light usu electrically-propelled vehicle for carrying esp milk for domestic delivery

ˈ**milkˌmaid** /-ˌmayd‖-ˌmeɪd/ *n* a female who works in a dairy

ˈmilkman /-mən‖-mən/ *n* one who sells or delivers milk
ˌmilk of magˈnesia *n* a white suspension of magnesium hydroxide in water, used as an antacid and mild laxative
ˌmilk ˈpudding *n* a pudding consisting of rice, tapioca, sago, etc boiled or baked in (sweetened) milk
ˈmilk ˌrun *n* a regular journey or course
milk shake *n* a thoroughly shaken or blended beverage made of milk and a flavouring syrup
ˈmilkˌsop /-ˌsop‖-ˌsɒp/ *n* a weak and unmanly male
milk tooth *n* a tooth of a mammal, esp a child, that is replaced later in life
ˈmilkˌweed /-ˌweed‖-ˌwiːd/ *n* any of various plants that secrete milky latex
ˌMilky ˈWay /ˈmilki‖ˈmɪlkɪ/ *n* a broad irregular band of faint light that stretches completely round the celestial sphere and is caused by the light of the many stars forming the galaxy of which the sun and the solar system are a part
[1]**mill** /mil‖mɪl/ *n* **1** a building provided with machinery for grinding grain into flour **2a** a machine or apparatus for grinding grain **b** a machine or hand-operated device for crushing or grinding a solid substance (e g coffee beans or peppercorns) **3** a building or collection of buildings with machinery for manufacturing **4** MILLING MACHINE **5** an experience that has a hardening effect on the character – usu in *through the mill*
[2]**mill** *vt* **1** to subject to an operation or process in a mill: e g **1a** to grind into flour, meal, or powder **b** to shape or dress by means of a rotary cutter **2** to give a raised rim or a ridged edge to (a coin) **3** to cut grooves in the metal surface of (e g a knob) ~ *vi* **1** to move in a confused swirling mass – usu + *about* or *around* **2** to undergo milling
ˈmillˌboard /-ˌbawd‖-ˌbɔːd/ *n* strong cardboard suitable for book covers and for panelling in furniture
ˈmillˌdam /-ˌdam‖-ˌdæm/ *n* a dam to make a millpond
millenarian /ˌmiliˈneəri·ən‖ˌmɪlɪˈneərɪən/ *adj* **1** of or relating to 1000 years **2** of or having belief in the millennium – **millenarian** *n*, **millenarianism** *n*
millennium /miˈleni·əm‖mɪˈlenɪəm/ *n, pl* **millennia** /-ni·ə‖-nɪə/, **millenniums** **1a** a period of 1000 years **b** (the celebration of) a 1000th anniversary **2a** *the* thousand years mentioned in Revelation 20 during which holiness is to prevail and Christ is to reign on earth **b** a (future) golden age – **millennial** *adj*
millepede /ˈmiliˌpeed‖ˈmɪlɪˌpiːd/ *n* a millipede
miller /ˈmilə‖ˈmɪlə/ *n* sby who owns or works a mill, esp for corn
millet /ˈmilit‖ˈmɪlɪt/ *n* (the seed of) any of various small-seeded annual cereal and forage grasses cultivated for their grain, used as food
milli- /mili-‖mɪlɪ-/ *comb form* one thousandth (10^{-3}) part of (a specified unit) <milli*ampere*>
millibar /ˌmiliˈbah‖ˌmɪlɪˈbɑː/ *n* a unit of pressure equal to $^{1}/_{1000}$ bar
milligram /ˈmiliˌgram‖ˈmɪlɪˌgræm/ *n* one thousandth of a gram (about 0.015 grain)
millilitre *n* a thousandth of a litre (.002pt)
millimetre /ˈmiliˌmeetə‖ˈmɪlɪˌmiːtə/ *n* one thousandth of a metre (about 0.039in)
milliner /ˈmilinə‖ˈmɪlɪnə/ *n* sby who designs, makes, trims, or sells women's hats [obs *Myllaner* person from Milan, fr *Milan*, city in Italy from which women's finery was imported in the 16th c] – **millinery** *n*
ˈmilling maˌchine /ˈmiling‖ˈmɪlɪŋ/ *n* a machine tool for shaping metal against rotating milling cutters
million /ˈmilyən‖ˈmɪljən/ *n, pl* **millions, million** **1** (the number) 1,000,000 **2** an indefinitely large number – infml; often pl with sing. meaning <~s *of cars in that traffic jam*> **3** *pl* ˈMASS 3 <*appealing to the* ~s> – **million** *adj*, **millionth** *adj or n*
millionaire /ˌmilyəˈneə‖ˌmɪljəˈneə/ *n* sby whose wealth is estimated at a million or more money units
millipede, millepede /ˈmiliˌpeed‖ˈmɪlɪˌpiːd/ *n* any of numerous myriopods usu with a cylindrical segmented body and 2 pairs of legs on each segment [Latin *millepeda*, a small crawling animal, fr *mille* thousand + *ped-*, *pes* foot]
millpond /ˈmilˌpond‖ˈmɪlˌpɒnd/ *n* a pond produced by damming a stream to produce a head of water for operating a mill
ˈmillˌrace /-ˌrays‖-ˌreɪs/ *n* (the current in) a channel in which water flows to and from a mill wheel
ˈmillˌstone /-ˌstohn‖-ˌstəʊn/ *n* **1** either of a pair of circular stones that rotate against each other and are used for grinding (grain) **2** a heavy or crushing burden
ˈmill ˌwheel *n* a waterwheel that drives a mill
ˈmillˌwright /-ˌriet‖-ˌraɪt/ *n* sby who plans, builds, or maintains mills
milometer /mieˈlomitə‖maɪˈlɒmɪtə/ *n* an odometer calibrated in miles
milord /miˈlawd‖mɪˈlɔːd/ *n* an Englishman of noble or gentle birth – often used in imitation of foreigners
milt /milt‖mɪlt/ *n* the male reproductive glands of fishes when filled with secretion; *also* the secretion of these glands – **milty** *adj*
[1]**mime** /miem‖maɪm/ *n* **1** an ancient dramatic entertainment representing scenes from life usu in a ridiculous manner **2** the art of portraying a character or telling a story by body movement
[2]**mime** *vi* to act a part with mimic gesture and action, usu without words ~ *vt* **1** to mimic **2** to act out in the manner of a mime – **mimer** *n*
mimetic /miˈmetik‖mɪˈmetɪk/ *adj* **1** imitative **2** relating to, characterized by, or exhibiting mimicry – **mimetically** *adv*
[1]**mimic** /ˈmimik‖ˈmɪmɪk/ *adj* **1a** IMITATIVE 1 **b** imitation, mock <*a* ~ *battle*> **2** of mime or mimicry – **mimical** *adj*
[2]**mimic** *vt* **-ck-** **1** to imitate slavishly; ape **2** to ridicule by imitation **3** to simulate **4** to resemble by biological mimicry – **mimic** *n*
mimicry /ˈmimikri‖ˈmɪmɪkrɪ/ *n* **1** the act or an instance of mimicking **2** resemblance of one organism to another that secures it an advantage (e g protection from predation)

mimosa /mi'mohzə, -sə||mɪ'məʊzə, -sə/ *n* any of a genus of leguminous trees, shrubs, and herbaceous plants of warm regions with globular heads of small white, pink, or esp yellow flowers

minaret /ˌminə'ret||ˌmɪnə'ret/ *n* a slender tower attached to a mosque and surrounded by 1 or more projecting balconies from which the summons to prayer is made

minatory /'minət(ə)ri||'mɪnət(ə)rɪ/ *adj* menacing, threatening – fml

[1]mince /mins||mɪns/ *vt* **1** to cut or chop into very small pieces **2** to keep (one's words) within the bounds of decorum <*doesn't* ~ *his words*> ~*vi* to walk with short affected steps – **mincer** *n*

[2]mince *n* minced meat

'minceˌmeat /-ˌmeet||-ˌmiːt/ *n* a finely chopped mixture of raisins, apples, suet, spices, etc (with brandy) which traditionally used to contain meat

ˌmince 'pie *n* a sweet usu small and round pie filled with mincemeat

mincing /'minsing||'mɪnsɪŋ/ *adj* affectedly dainty or delicate <*trying to speak in a small* ~ *treble* – George Eliot> – **mincingly** *adv*

[1]mind /miend||maɪnd/ *n* **1** the (capabilities of the) organized conscious and unconscious mental processes of an organism that result in reasoning, thinking, perceiving, etc **2a** recollection, memory <*keep that in* ~> **b** attention, concentration <*can't keep her* ~ *on her work*> **3** the normal condition of the mental faculties <*lost his* ~> **4a** an intention, desire <*he changed his* ~> <*doesn't know his own* ~> <*I've a good* ~ *to box his ears*> <*had half a* ~ *to leave early*> **b** an opinion, view <*unwilling to speak his* ~> <*they were of the same* ~> <*though she's just a child, she has a* ~ *of her own*> <*in two* ~s *about the problem*> **5** a disposition, mood <*her state of* ~ *was calm*> <*always has good peace of* ~> **6** the mental attributes of a usu specified group <*the scientific* ~> **7** a person considered as an intellectual being <*one of the finest* ~s *of the academic world*> **8a** the intellect and rational faculties as contrasted with the emotions **b** the human spirit and intellect as opposed to the body and the material world <~ *over matter*> – **bear/keep in mind** to think of, esp at the appropriate time; not forget – **on one's mind** as a preoccupation; troubling one's thoughts <*she can't work with the problem of the mortgage* on her mind>

[2]mind *vt* **1** to attend to closely <~ *how you behave*> <~ *your manners*> <~ *your own business*> **2** to pay attention to or follow (advice, instructions, or orders) **3a** to be concerned about; care <*I don't* ~ *what we do*> <*Never* ~ *the hole in your tights: no one will notice*> **b** to object to <*do you* ~ *going?*> <*I don't* ~ *the noise*> **4a** to be careful <~ *you finish your homework!*> **b** to be cautious about <~ *the step*> **5** to give protective care to; look after <~ed *the children while their parents were out*> ~ *vi* **1** to be attentive or wary – often + *out* **2** to be or become concerned; care <*would you prefer tea or coffee? I don't* ~> – **mind you** take this fact into account; notice this <mind you, *I don't blame him*>

'mindˌbending /-ˌbending||-ˌbendɪŋ/ *adj* at the limits of understanding or credibility – infml – **mindbendingly** *adv*, **mindbender** *n*

'mind-ˌblowing *adj* **1** of or causing a psychic state similar to that produced by a psychedelic drug **2** mentally or emotionally exhilarating *USE* infml – **mindblower** *n*

'mind-ˌboggling *adj* causing great surprise or wonder – infml

'minded *adj* **1** having a (specified kind of) mind – usu in combination <*narrow*-minded> **2** inclined, disposed <*was not* ~ *to report his losses*> – **mindedness** *n*

minder /'miendə||'maɪndə/ *n* **1** one who looks after – usu in combination <*child*minder> **2** *Br* one who acts as assistant and physical protector to someone, esp to someone operating outside or on the edge of the law

'mind-exˌpanding *adj* PSYCHEDELIC 1b – infml

'mindful /-f(ə)l||-f(ə)l/ *adj* keeping in mind; aware *of* – **mindfully** *adv*, **mindfulness** *n*

'mindless /-lis||-lɪs/ *adj* **1** devoid of thought or intelligence; senseless <~ *violence*> **2** involving or requiring little thought or concentration <*the work is routine and fairly* ~> **3** inattentive, heedless – usu + *of* <*dashed into the burning house* ~ *of the danger*> – **mindlessly** *adv*, **mindlessness** *n*

'mind ˌreader *n* sby who can, or is thought to be able to, perceive another's thought directly – **mind reading** *n*

ˌmind's 'eye *n* the faculty of visual memory or imagination

[1]mine /mien||maɪn/ *adj, archaic* my – used before a vowel or *h* <~ *host*> or sometimes to modify a preceding noun <*mistress* ~>

[2]mine *pron, pl* **mine** that which or the one who belongs to me

[3]mine *n* **1a** an excavation from which mineral substances are taken **b** an ore deposit **2** an underground passage beneath an enemy position **3** an encased explosive designed to destroy enemy personnel, vehicles, or ships **4** a rich source *of* <*a* ~ *of information*>

[4]mine *vt* **1a** to dig an underground passage to gain access to or cause the collapse of (an enemy position) **b** UNDERMINE 2 **2** to obtain from a mine **3** to place military mines in, on, or under <~ *a harbour*> **4** to dig into for ore, coal, etc **5** to seek valuable material in ~*vi* to dig a mine – **miner** *n*, **mining** *n*

'mineˌlayer /-ˌlayə||-ˌleɪə/ *n* a vessel or aircraft for laying mines

mineral /'min(ə)rəl||'mɪn(ə)rəl/ *n* **1** (a synthetic substance resembling) a solid homogeneous crystalline material that results from the inorganic processes of nature; *broadly* any of various naturally occurring substances (e g stone, coal, and petroleum) obtained by drilling, mining, etc **2** sthg neither animal nor vegetable **3** *Br* MINERAL WATER – usu pl – **mineral** *adj*

mineral kingdom *n* the one of the 3 basic groups of natural objects that includes inorganic objects

mineralogy /ˌminə'raləji||ˌmɪnə'rælədʒɪ/ *n* a science dealing with the structure, properties, and classification of minerals – **mineralogist** *n*, **mineralogical** *adj*

ˈ**mineral ˌoil** *n* an oil of mineral as opposed to vegetable origin

ˈ**mineral ˌwater** *n* water naturally or artificially impregnated with mineral salts or gases (e g carbon dioxide)

minestrone /ˌminiˈstrohni‖ˌmɪnɪˈstrəʊnɪ/ *n* a rich thick vegetable soup usu containing pasta (e g macaroni) [Italian, fr *minestrare* to serve, dish up, fr Latin *ministrare*, fr *minister* servant]

minesweeper /ˈmienˌsweepə‖ˈmaɪnˌswiːpə/ *n* a ship designed for removing or neutralizing mines – **minesweeping** *n*

mingle /ˈming·gl‖ˈmɪŋgl/ *vt* to bring or mix together or with sthg else ~ *vi* **1** to become mingled **2** to mix with or go among a group of people

mingy /ˈminji‖ˈmɪndʒɪ/ *adv* mean, stingy – infml

mini /ˈmini‖ˈmɪnɪ/ *n, pl* **minis** **1** sthg small of its kind (e g a motor car) **2** a woman's skirt or dress with the hemline several inches above the knee – **mini** *adj*

mini- /mini-‖mɪnɪ-/ *comb form* miniature; of small dimensions <mini*computer*>; *specif* having a hemline several inches above the knee <mini*skirt*>

[1]**miniature** /ˈminəchə‖ˈmɪnətʃə/ *n* **1a** a copy or representation on a much reduced scale **b** sthg small of its kind **2** a painting in an illuminated manuscript **3** the art of painting miniatures **4** a very small painting (e g a portrait on ivory or metal) [Italian *miniatura* art of illuminating a manuscript, deriv of Latin *miniatus* coloured with a red pigment, fr *minium* red pigment] – **miniaturist** *n*

[2]**miniature** *adj* **1** (represented) on a small or reduced scale **2** of still photography using film 35mm wide or smaller

minibus /ˈminiˌbus‖ˈmɪnɪˌbʌs/ *n* a small bus for carrying usu between 5 and 10 passengers

minicab /ˈminikab/ *n* a taxi that is hired by telephone and does not ply for hire

minim /ˈminim‖ˈmɪnɪm/ *n* **1** a musical note with the time value of 2 crotchets or $^1/_2$ of a semibreve **2** a unit of capacity equal to $^1/_{60}$ fluid drachm (about 59.19mm^3) – **minim** *adj*

minimal /ˈminiml‖ˈmɪnɪml/ *adj* of or being a minimum; constituting the least possible – **minimalize** *vt*, **minimally** *adv*

minim·ize, -ise /ˈminimiez‖ˈmɪnɪmaɪz/ *vt* **1** to reduce to a minimum **2** to represent (sby or sthg) at less than true value; PLAY DOWN – **minimizer** *n*, **minimization** *n*

minimum /ˈminimәm‖ˈmɪnɪmәm/ *n, pl* **minima** /-mə‖-mə/, **minimums** **1** the least quantity or value assignable, admissible, or possible **2** the lowest degree or amount reached or recorded – **minimum** *adj*

minimum wage *n* a wage fixed by legal authority or by contract as the least that may be paid either to employees generally or to a particular category of employees

minion /ˈminyən‖ˈmɪnjən/ *n* **1** a servile attendant **2** FAVOURITE 1 **3** a minor official – derog

[1]**minister** /ˈministə‖ˈmɪnɪstə/ *n* **1** AGENT 1a, 2 **2a** one officiating or assisting the officiant in Christian worship **b** a clergyman, esp of a Protestant or nonconformist church **c** the superior of any of several religious orders **3** a high officer of state managing a division of government **4** a diplomatic representative accredited to a foreign state – **ministerial** *adj*, **ministerially** *adv*

[2]**minister** *vi* **1** to perform the functions of a minister of religion **2** to give aid or service <~ *to the sick*> – **ministrant** *n or adj*

ministration /ˌminiˈstraysh(ə)n‖ˌmɪnɪˈstreɪʃ(ə)n/ *n* the act or process of ministering, esp in religious matters

ministry /ˈministri‖ˈmɪnɪstrɪ/ *n* **1** service, ministration **2** the office, duties, or functions of a minister **3** the body of ministers of religion or government **4** the period of service or office of a minister or ministry **5** a government department presided over by a minister

mink /mingk‖mɪŋk/ *n* **1** any of several semi-aquatic flesh-eating mammals that resemble weasels and have partially webbed feet and a soft thick coat **2** the soft fur or pelt of the mink

minnow /ˈminoh‖ˈmɪnəʊ/ *n* **1** a small dark-coloured freshwater fish or any of various small fishes **2** sthg small or insignificant of its kind

[1]**minor** /ˈmienə‖ˈmaɪnə/ *adj* **1a** inferior in importance, size, rank, or degree <*a* ~ *poet*> **b** comparatively unimportant <*a* ~ *alteration*> **2** not having attained majority **3a** *esp of a scale or mode* having semitones between the second and third, fifth and sixth, and sometimes seventh and eighth steps **b** being or based on a (specified) minor scale <*in a* ~ *key*> <*a piece in A* ~> **c** being an interval less by a semitone than a corresponding major interval **d** *of a chord* having an interval of a minor third between the root and the next note above it **4** not serious or involving risk to life <*a* ~ *illness*>

[2]**minor** *n* **1** sby who has not attained majority **2** a minor musical interval, scale, key, or mode

minority /mieˈnorəti, mi-‖maɪˈnɒrətɪ, mɪ-/ *n* **1a** the period before attainment of majority **b** the state of being a legal minor **2** the smaller of 2 groups constituting a whole; *specif* a group with less than the number of votes necessary for control **3** *sing or pl in constr* a group of people who share common characteristics or interests differing from those of the majority of a population

minor planet *n* an asteroid

minor suit *n* either of the suits of clubs or diamonds that in bridge are of inferior scoring value

Minotaur /ˈmienəˌtaw‖ˈmaɪnəˌtɔː/ *n* a mythological monster shaped half like a man and half like a bull and confined in the labyrinth at Crete

minster /ˈminstə‖ˈmɪnstə/ *n* a large or important church often having cathedral status

minstrel /ˈminstrəl‖ˈmɪnstrəl/ *n* **1** a medieval singer, poet, or musical entertainer **2** any of a troupe of performers usu with blackened faces giving a performance of supposedly Negro singing, jokes, dancing, etc

ˈ**minstrelsy** /-si‖-sɪ/ *n* **1** the singing and playing of a minstrel **2** *sing or pl in constr* a body of minstrels **3** songs or poems (composed or performed by minstrels)

[1]**mint** /mint‖mɪnt/ *n* **1** a place where money is made **2** a vast sum or amount – infml [Old English *mynet* coin, money, deriv of Latin *moneta* mint, coin, fr *Moneta*, epithet of Juno, Roman goddess in whose temple the Romans coined money]

[2]**mint** *vt* **1** to make (e g coins) by stamping metal **2** to fabricate, invent < ~ *a new word*> – **minter** *n*

[3]**mint** *adj* unspoilt as if fresh from a mint; pristine <*in* ~ *condition*>

[4]**mint** *n* **1** any of a genus of plants that have whorled leaves and foliage with a characteristic strong taste and smell, used esp as a flavouring **2** a sweet, chocolate, etc flavoured with mint

minuet /ˌminyooˈet‖ˌmɪnjʊˈet/ *n* (music for or in the rhythm of) a slow graceful dance in $^{3}_{4}$ time

[1]**minus** /ˈmienəs‖ˈmaɪnəs/ *prep* **1** diminished by <*seven* ~ *four is three*> **2** without < ~ *his hat*>

[2]**minus** *n* **1** a negative quantity **2** a deficiency, defect

[3]**minus** *adj* **1** negative <*a* ~ *quantity*> <*a temperature of* ~ *10°C*> **2** having negative qualities; *esp* involving a disadvantage <*a* ~ *factor*> **3** falling low in a specified range <*a mark of B* ~>

[1]**minuscule** /ˈminəˌskyoohl‖ˈmɪnəˌskjuːl/ *n* (a lower-case letter in) a style of small flowing handwriting [French, fr Latin *minusculus* rather small, fr *minor* smaller]

[2]**minuscule** *adj* **1** written in minuscules **2** very small

[1]**minute** /ˈminit‖ˈmɪnɪt/ *n* **1** the 60th part of an hour of time or of a degree **2** the distance one can cover in a minute <*lived 5* ~*s from the station*> **3** a short space of time; a moment **4a** MEMORANDUM 3 **b** *pl* the official record of the proceedings of a meeting [Middle French, fr Late Latin *minuta*, fr Latin *minutus* small, fr *minuere* to lessen]

[2]**minute** *vb* to make notes or a brief summary (of)

[3]**minute** /mieˈnyooht‖maɪˈnjuːt/ *adj* **1** extremely small **2** of minor importance; petty **3** marked by painstaking attention to detail – **minutely** *adv*, **minuteness** *n*

ˈminute ˌhand *n* the long hand that marks the minutes on the face of a watch or clock

ˈminuteˌman /-ˌman‖-ˌmæn/ *n* a member of a group of armed men pledged to take the field at a minute's notice during and immediately before the American Revolution

minutia /miˈnyoohshyə, mie-‖mɪˈnjuːʃjə, maɪ-/ *n, pl* **minutiae** /-shiˌee‖-ʃɪˌiː/ a minor detail – usu pl

minx /mingks‖mɪŋks/ *n* a flirtatious girl

miracle /ˈmirəkl‖ˈmɪrəkl/ *n* **1** an extraordinary event manifesting divine intervention in human affairs **2** an astonishing or unusual event, thing, or accomplishment **3** a person or thing that is a remarkable example or instance of sthg <*this watch is a* ~ *of precision*>

ˈmiracle ˌplay *n* a medieval drama based on episodes from the Bible or the life of a saint; *also* MYSTERY PLAY

miraculous /miˈrakyooləs‖mɪˈrækjʊləs/ *adj* **1** of the nature of a miracle; supernatural **2** evoking wonder like a miracle; marvellous **3** (capable of) working miracles – **miraculously** *adv*, **miraculousness** *n*

mirage /ˈmirahzh‖ˈmɪrɑːʒ/ *n* **1** an optical illusion appearing esp as a pool of water or as the reflection of distant objects caused by the reflection of rays of light by a layer of heated air (near the ground) **2** sthg illusory and unattainable [French, fr *mirer* to look at, fr Latin *mirari*]

[1]**mire** /ˈmie·ə‖ˈmaɪə/ *n* **1** a tract of soft waterlogged ground; a marsh, bog **2** (deep) mud or slush – **miry** *adj*

[2]**mire** *vt* to cause to stick fast (as if) in mire; BOG DOWN

[1]**mirror** /ˈmirə‖ˈmɪrə/ *n* **1** a smooth surface (e g of metal or silvered glass) that forms images by reflection **2** sthg that gives a true representation – **mirrorlike** *adj*

[2]**mirror** *vt* to reflect (as if) in a mirror

ˌmirror ˈimage *n* sthg that has its parts reversely arranged in comparison with another similar thing

mirth /muhth‖mɜːθ/ *n* happiness or amusement accompanied with laughter – **mirthful** *adj*, **mirthfully** *adv*, **mirthfulness** *n*, **mirthless** *adj*

mis- /mis-‖mɪs-/ *prefix* **1** badly; wrongly; unfavourably <mis*judge*> <mis*behave*> **2** suspicious; apprehensive <mis*giving*> **3** bad; wrong <mis*deed*> <mis*fit*> **4** opposite or lack of <mis*trust*> <mis*fortune*> **5** not <mis*understand*> badly; wrongly; unfavourably <mis*judge*> bad; wrong <mis*deed*> opposite or lack of <mis*trust*>

misadventure /ˌmisədˈvenchə‖ˌmɪsədˈventʃə/ *n* a misfortune, mishap

ˌmisalˈliance /-əˈlie·əns‖-əˈlaɪəns/ *n* an improper or unsuitable alliance; *esp* a mésalliance

misandry /miˈsandri‖mɪˈsændrɪ/ *n* a hatred of men

misanthrope /ˈmiz(ə)nˌthrohp‖ˈmɪz(ə)nˌθrəʊp/, **misanthropist** /miˈzanthrəpist‖mɪˈzænθrəpɪst/ *n* one who hates or distrusts people [Greek *misanthrōpos* hating mankind, fr *misein* to hate + *anthrōpos* person] – **misanthropic** *adj*, **misanthropy** *n*

misapply /ˌmisəˈplie‖ˌmɪsəˈplaɪ/ *vt* to apply wrongly – **misapplication** *n*

ˌmisappreˈhend /-apriˈhend‖-æprɪˈhend/ *vt* to misunderstand – **misapprehension** *n*

ˌmisapˈpropriate /-əˈprohpriayt‖-əˈprəʊprɪeɪt/ *vt* to appropriate wrongly (e g by theft or embezzlement) – **misappropriation** *n*

ˌmisbeˈgotten /-biˈgotn‖-bɪˈgɒtn/ *adj* **1** having a disreputable or improper origin **2** *archaic* illegitimate, bastard

ˌmisbeˈhave /-biˈhayv‖-bɪˈheɪv/ *vi* to behave badly – **misbehaviour** *n*

ˌmisˈcalculate /-ˈkalkyoolayt‖-ˈkælkjʊleɪt/ *vb* to calculate wrongly – **miscalculation** *n*

ˈmisˌcarriage /-ˌkarij‖-ˌkærɪdʒ/ *n* **1** a failure in administration **2** the expulsion of a human foetus before it is viable, esp after the 12th week of gestation

ˌmisˈcarry /-ˈkari‖-ˈkærɪ/ *vi* **1** to suffer miscarriage of a foetus **2** to fail to achieve an intended purpose

ˌ**misˈcast** /-ˈkahst‖-ˈkɑːst/ *vt* **miscast** to cast in an unsuitable role

miscegenation /ˌmisˌejiˈnaysh(ə)n, ˌmis-ijə-‖ˌmɪsˌedʒɪˈneɪʃ(ə)n, ˌmɪsɪdʒə-/ *n* interbreeding of races, esp between sby white and sby non-white [Latin *miscēre* to mix + *genus* race]

miscellaneous /ˌmisəˈlaynyəs, -ni·əs‖ˌmɪsəˈleɪnjəs, -nɪəs/ *adj* **1** consisting of diverse items or members **2** having various characteristics or capabilities – **miscellaneously** *adv*, **miscellaneousness** *n*

miscellany /miˈseləni‖mɪˈselənɪ/ *n* **1** a mixture of various things **2** a book containing miscellaneous literary pieces – **miscellanist** *n*

mischance /ˌmisˈchahns‖ˌmɪsˈtʃɑːns/ *n* (a piece of) bad luck

mischief /ˈmischif‖ˈmɪstʃɪf/ *n* **1** a specific injury or damage from a particular agent **2** sthg or esp sby that causes harm or annoyance **3** often playful action that annoys or irritates, usu without causing or intending serious harm **4** the quality or state of being mischievous

mischievous /ˈmischivəs‖ˈmɪstʃɪvəs/ *adj* **1** harmful, malicious **2** able or tending to cause annoyance, unrest, or minor injury **3a** playfully provocative; arch **b** disruptively playful – **mischievously** *adv*, **mischievousness** *n*

miscible /ˈmisibl‖ˈmɪsɪbl/ *adj, esp of a liquid* capable of being mixed (with another liquid in any proportion without separating) – **miscibility** *n*

misconceive /ˌmiskənˈseev‖ˌmɪskənˈsiːv/ *vt* to interpret wrongly; misunderstand – **misconception** *n*

misˈconduct /-ˈkondukt‖-ˈkɒndʌkt/ *n* **1** mismanagement of responsibilities **2** adultery – **misconduct** *vt*

ˌ**misconˈstrue** /-kənˈstrooh‖-kənˈstruː/ *vt* to misinterpret – **misconstruction** *n*

misˈcount /-ˈkownt‖-ˈkaʊnt/ *vt* to count wrongly ~*vi* to make a wrong count – **miscount** *n*

miscreant /ˈmiskri·ənt‖ˈmɪskrɪənt/ *adj or n* (of) one who behaves criminally or maliciously

ˌ**misˈcue** /-ˈkyooh‖-ˈkjuː/ *vi or n* (to make) a faulty stroke in billiards or snooker in which the cue slips

ˌ**misˈdate** /-ˈdayt‖-ˈdeɪt/ *vt* to date (e g a letter) wrongly

ˌ**misˈdeal** /-ˈdeel‖-ˈdiːl/ *vb* to deal (cards) incorrectly – **misdeal** *n*

ˌ**misˈdeed** /-ˈdeed‖-ˈdiːd/ *n* a wrong deed; an offence

ˌ**misdeˈmeanour** /-diˈmeenə‖-dɪˈmiːnə/ *n* **1** a minor crime formerly technically distinguished from a felony **2** a misdeed

ˌ**misdiˈrect** /-diˈrekt, -die-‖-dɪˈrekt, -daɪ-/ *vt* **1** to give a wrong direction to **2** to address (mail) wrongly – **misdirection** *n*

mise-en-scène /ˌmeez onh ˈsen ‖ˌmiːz ɑ̃ ˈsen (*Fr* miz ɑ̃ sɛn)/ *n, pl* **mise-en-scènes** /sen(z) ‖ sen(z) (*Fr* ~)/ **1** the arrangement of actors, props, and scenery on a stage in a theatrical production **2** the environment or setting in which sthg takes place

miser /ˈmiezə‖ˈmaɪzə/ *n* a mean grasping person; *esp* one who hoards wealth – **miserly** *adj*, **miserliness** *n*

miserable /ˈmiz(ə)rəbl‖ˈmɪz(ə)rəbl/ *adj* **1a** wretchedly inadequate or meagre **b** causing extreme discomfort or unhappiness **2** in a pitiable state of distress or unhappiness **3** shameful, contemptible – **miserableness** *n*, **miserably** *adv*

misery /ˈmizəri‖ˈmɪzərɪ/ *n* **1** (a cause of) physical or mental suffering or discomfort **2** great unhappiness and distress **3** *chiefly Br* a grumpy or querulous person; *esp* a killjoy – infml

ˌ**misˈfire** /-ˈfie·ə‖-ˈfaɪə/ *vi* **1** *of a motor vehicle, engine, etc* to have the explosive or propulsive charge fail to ignite at the proper time **2** *esp of a firearm* to fail to fire **3** to fail to have an intended effect – **misfire** *n*

ˈ**misˌfit** /-ˌfit‖-ˌfɪt/ *n* **1** sthg that fits badly **2** a person poorly adjusted to his/her environment

ˌ**misˈfortune** /-ˈfawchoohn, -chən‖-ˈfɔːtʃuːn, -tʃən/ *n* **1** bad luck **2** a distressing or unfortunate incident or event; *also* the resultant unhappy situation

ˌ**misˈgiving** /-ˈgiving‖-ˈgɪvɪŋ/ *n* a feeling of doubt, suspicion, or apprehension, esp concerning a future event

ˌ**misˈgovern** /-ˈguvən‖-ˈgʌvən/ *vt* to govern badly – **misgovernment** *n*

ˌ**misˈguide** /-ˈgied‖-ˈgaɪd/ *vt* to lead astray – **misguidance** *n*

ˌ**misˈguided** *adj* directed by mistaken ideas, principles, or motives – **misguidedly** *adv*, **misguidedness** *n*

ˌ**misˈhandle** /-ˈhandl‖-ˈhændl/ *vt* **1** to treat roughly, maltreat **2** to mismanage (a situation, crisis, etc)

mishap /ˈmisˌhap‖ˈmɪsˌhæp/ *n* an unfortunate accident

ˌ**misˈhear** /-ˈhiə‖-ˈhɪə/ *vb* **misheard** /-ˈhuhd‖-ˈhɜːd/ to hear wrongly

ˌ**misˈhit** /-ˈhit‖-ˈhɪt/ *vt* **mishit; -tt-** to hit (a ball or stroke) faultily – **mishit** *n*

mishmash /ˈmishˌmash‖ˈmɪʃˌmæʃ/ *n* a hotchpotch, jumble – infml

misinform /ˌmisinˈfawm‖ˌmɪsɪnˈfɔːm/ *vt* to give untrue or misleading information to – **misinformation** *n*

ˌ**misinˈterpret** /-inˈtuhprit‖-ɪnˈtɜːprɪt/ *vt* to understand or explain wrongly – **misinterpretation** *n*

ˌ**misˈjudge** /-ˈjuj‖-ˈdʒʌdʒ/ *vt* **1** to estimate wrongly **2** to have an unjust opinion of ~*vi* to make a mistaken judgment – **misjudgment** *n*

mislay /misˈlay‖mɪsˈleɪ/ *vt* **mislaid** /-ˈlayd‖-ˈleɪd/ to leave in an unremembered place

ˌ**misˈlead** /-ˈleed‖-ˈliːd/ *vt* **misled** /-ˈled‖-ˈled/ to lead in a wrong direction or into a mistaken action or belief – **misleadingly** *adv*

ˌ**misˈmanage** /-ˈmanij‖-ˈmænɪdʒ/ *vt* to manage wrongly or incompetently – **mismanagement** *n*

ˌ**misˈmatch** /-ˈmach‖-ˈmætʃ/ *vt* to match incorrectly or unsuitably, esp in marriage – **mismatch** *n*

ˌ**misˈname** /-ˈnaym‖-ˈneɪm/ *vt* to call by the wrong name

ˌ**misˈnomer** /-ˈnohmə‖-ˈnəʊmə/ *n* (a use of) a wrong name or designation

misogynist /miˈsoj(ə)n·ist, mie-‖mɪˈsɒdʒ(ə)nɪst, maɪ-/ *n* one who hates women [Greek *misogynēs*, fr *misein* to hate + *gynē* woman] – **misogynous** *adj*, **misogyny** *n*, **misogynistic** *adj*

misplace /mis'plays‖mɪs'pleɪs/ *vt* **1a** to put in the wrong place **b** to mislay **2** to direct towards a wrong object or outcome <~d *enthusiasm*> – **misplacement** *n*

ˌmis'print /-'print‖-'prɪnt/ *vt* to print wrongly – **misprint** *n*

ˌmispro'nounce /-prə'nowns‖-prə'naʊns/ *vt* to pronounce wrongly – **mispronunciation** *n*

ˌmis'quote /-'kwoht‖-'kwəʊt/ *vt* to quote incorrectly – **misquotation** *n*

ˌmis'read /-'reed‖-'ri:d/ *vt* **misread** /-'red‖-'red/ to read or interpret incorrectly

ˌmisre'port /-ri'pawt‖-rɪ'pɔ:t/ *vt* to report falsely – **misreport** *n*

ˌmisrepre'sent /-repri'zent‖-reprɪ'zent/ *vt* to represent falsely; give an untrue or misleading account of – **misrepresentation** *n*

[1]**ˌmis'rule** /-'roohl‖-'ru:l/ *vt* to rule incompetently

[2]**ˌmis'rule** *n* **1** misruling or being misruled **2** disorder, anarchy

[1]**miss** /mis‖mɪs/ *vt* **1** to fail to hit, reach, contact, or attain <~ed *the train*> **2** to discover or feel the absence of, esp with regret <~ed *his wife desperately*> **3** to escape, avoid <*narrowly* ~ed *being run over*> **4** to leave out; omit – often + *out* **5** to fail to understand, sense, or experience <*he* ~ed *the point of the speech*> **6** to fail to perform or attend <~ed *his appointment*> ~ *vi* **1** to fail to hit sthg **2** to misfire <*the engine* ~ed> – **miss out on** to lose or not to have had (a good opportunity) – **miss the boat** to fail to take advantage of an opportunity

[2]**miss** *n* **1** a failure to hit **2** a failure to attain a desired result **3** a deliberate avoidance or omission of sthg <*felt so full he gave the dessert a* ~>

[3]**miss** *n* **1** – used as a title preceding the name of an unmarried woman or girl **2** young lady – used without a name as a conventional term of address to a young woman **3** a young unmarried woman or girl – chiefly infml

missal /'misl‖'mɪsl/ *n* a book containing the order of service of the mass for the whole year

misshape /ˌmis'shayp‖ˌmɪs'ʃeɪp/ *vt* to shape badly; deform – **misshapen** *adj*, **misshapenly** *adv*

missile /'misiel‖'mɪsaɪl; *NAm* 'misl‖'mɪsl/ *n* an object thrown or projected, usu so as to strike sthg at a distance; *also* a self-propelled weapon that travels through the air

missing /'mising‖'mɪsɪŋ/ *adj* absent; *also* lost <~ *in action*>

ˌmissing 'link *n* **1** an item needed to complete a continuous series **2** a supposed intermediate form between man and his anthropoid ancestors

mission /'mish(ə)n‖'mɪʃ(ə)n/ *n* **1a** a ministry commissioned by a religious organization to propagate its faith or carry on humanitarian work, usu abroad **b** assignment to or work in a field of missionary enterprise **c** a mission establishment **d** *pl* organized missionary work **e** a campaign to increase church membership or strengthen Christian faith **2a** a group sent to a foreign country to negotiate, advise, etc **b** a permanent embassy or legation **3** a specific task with which a person or group is charged **4** a definite military, naval, or aerospace task or operation **5** a calling, vocation

[1]**missionary** /'mishən(ə)ri‖'mɪʃən(ə)rɪ/ *adj* **1** relating to, engaged in, or devoted to missions **2** characteristic of a missionary

[2]**missionary** *n* a person undertaking a mission; *esp* one in charge of a religious mission in some remote part of the world

missive /'misiv‖'mɪsɪv/ *n* a written communication; a letter – fml

misspell /ˌmis'spel‖ˌmɪs'spel/ *vt* **misspelt,** *Nam chiefly* **misspelled** to spell incorrectly

ˌmis'spend /-'spend‖-'spend/ *vt* **misspent** /-'spent‖-'spent/ to spend wrongly or foolishly; squander

ˌmis'state /-'stayt‖-'steɪt/ *vt* to state incorrectly; give a false account of – **misstatement** *n*

missus, missis /'misiz‖'mɪsɪz/ *n* **1** a wife – infml or humor <*have you met the* ~?> **2** *chiefly Br* – used to address a married woman; infml

missy /'misi‖'mɪsɪ/ *n* a young girl; miss – infml

[1]**mist** /mist‖mɪst/ *n* **1** water in the form of diffuse particles in the atmosphere, esp near the earth's surface **2** sthg that dims or obscures <*the* ~s *of time*> **3** a film, esp of tears, before the eyes **4a** a cloud of small particles suggestive of a mist **b** a suspension of a finely divided liquid in a gas

[2]**mist** *vi* to be or become misty ~*vt* to cover (as if) with mist

[1]**mistake** /mi'stayk‖mɪ'steɪk/ *vt* **mistook** /mi'stook‖mɪ'stʊk/; **mistaken** /mi'staykən‖mɪ'steɪkən/ **1** to choose wrongly <mistook *her way in the dark*> **2a** to misunderstand the meaning, intention, or significance of **b** to estimate wrongly **3** to identify wrongly; confuse with another <*I* mistook *him for his brother*>

[2]**mistake** *n* **1** a misunderstanding of the meaning or significance of sthg **2** a wrong action or statement arising from faulty judgment, inadequate knowledge, or carelessness

mistaken /mi'staykən‖mɪ'steɪkən/ *adj* **1** *of a person* wrong in opinion **2** *of an action, idea, etc* based on wrong thinking; incorrect – **mistakenly** *adv*

mister /'mistə‖'mɪstə/ *n* **1** – used sometimes in writing instead of the usual *Mr* **2** sir – used without a name as a generalized infml term of direct address to a male stranger **3** a man not entitled to a title of rank or an honorific or professional title

mistime /ˌmis'tiem‖ˌmɪs'taɪm/ *vt* to time badly

'mistle ˌthrush, missel thrush /'misl‖'mɪsl/ *n* a large Eurasian thrush with larger spots on its underparts than the song thrush

mistletoe /'misl,toh‖'mɪsl,təʊ/ *n* a European shrub that grows as a parasite on the branches of trees and has thick leaves and waxy white glutinous berries

mistral /'mistrəl, mi'strahl ‖'mɪstrəl, mɪ'strɑ:l (*Fr* mistral)/ *n* a strong cold dry northerly wind of S France

mistress /'mistris‖'mɪstrɪs/ *n* **1a** a woman in a position of power or authority **b** the female head of a household **2** a woman who has achieved mastery of a subject or skill **3** sthg personified as female that rules or directs **4** a woman with whom a man has a continuing sexual relationship outside marriage **5** *chiefly Br* a schoolmistress **6** – used archaically as a title preceding the name of a woman and now superseded by *Mrs*, *Miss*, and *Ms*

mistrial /ˌmis'trie·əl‖ˌmɪs'traɪəl/ *n* a trial declared void because of some error in the proceedings

ˌmis'trust /-'trust‖-'trʌst/ *vt* **1** to have little trust in; be suspicious of **2** to doubt the reliability or effectiveness of – **mistrust** *n*, **mistrustful** *adj*, **mistrustfully** *adv*

misty /'misti‖'mɪstɪ/ *adj* **1** obscured by mist **2** not clear to the mind or understanding; indistinct – **mistily** *adv*, **mistiness** *n*

misunderstand /ˌmisundə'stand‖ˌmɪsʌndə'stænd/ *vt* **1** to fail to understand **2** to interpret incorrectly

ˌmisunder'standing /-'standing‖-'stændɪŋ/ *n* **1** a failure to understand; a misinterpretation **2** a disagreement, dispute

ˌmis'use /-'yoohz‖-'juːz/ *vt* **1** to put to wrong or improper use **2** to abuse or maltreat – **misuse** *n*

mite /miet‖maɪt/ *n* **1** any of numerous (extremely) small arachnids that often infest animals, plants, and stored foods **2** a small coin or sum of money **3** a very small object or creature; *esp* a small child – **a mite** to a small extent – infml

mitigate /'mitigayt‖'mɪtɪgeɪt/ *vt* **1** to cause to become less harsh or hostile **2a** to make less severe or painful; alleviate **b** to extenuate <mitigating *circumstances*> – **mitigatory** *adj*, **mitigation** *n*

mitochondrion /ˌmietoh'kondri·ən‖ˌmaɪtəʊ'kɒndrɪən/ *n*, *pl* **mitochondria** /-dri·ə‖-drɪə/ any of several specialized parts in a cell that are rich in fats, proteins, and enzymes and produce energy – **mitochondrial** *adj*, **mitochondrially** *adv*

mitosis /mie'tohsis‖maɪ'təʊsɪs/ *n*, *pl* **mitoses** /-seez‖-siːz/ the formation of 2 new nuclei from an original nucleus, each having the same number of chromosomes as the original nucleus, during cell division; *also* cell division in which this occurs – **mitotic** *adj*

[1]**mitre,** *NAm chiefly* **miter** /'mietə‖'maɪtə/ *n* **1** a tall pointed divided headdress worn by bishops and abbots on ceremonial occasions **2** MITRE JOINT **3** a seam joining 2 parts of a sail whose fabric runs in different directions

[2]**mitre,** *NAm chiefly* **miter** *vt* **1** to bevel the ends of to make a mitre joint **2** to match or fit together in a mitre joint

'mitre ˌjoint *n* a joint made by cutting the ends of 2 pieces of wood at an oblique angle so that they form a right angle when fitted together

mitt /mit‖mɪt/ *n* **1a** a glove that leaves the (ends of the) fingers uncovered **b** MITTEN 1 **c** a baseball catcher's protective glove **2** a hand or paw; *specif* a person's hand – infml

mitten /'mit(ə)n‖'mɪt(ə)n/ *n* **1** a glove that is divided into one part covering the fingers and another part covering the thumb **2** MITT 1a

[1]**mix** /miks‖mɪks/ *vt* **1a** to combine or blend into a mass **b** to bring into close association <~ *business with pleasure*> **2** to prepare by mixing different components or ingredients **3** to control the balance of (various sounds), esp during the recording of a film, broadcast, record, etc ~ *vi* **1a** to become mixed **b** to be capable of mixing **2** to seek or enjoy the society of others **3** to crossbreed **4** to become actively involved <*decided not to* ~ *in politics*> – **mix it** to fight, brawl – infml

[2]**mix** *n* **1** an act or process of mixing **2** a product of mixing; *specif* a commercially prepared mixture of food ingredients **3** a combination **4** a combination in definite proportions of 2 or more recordings (e g of a singer and an accompaniment)

mixed /mikst‖mɪkst/ *adj* **1** combining diverse elements **2** made up of or involving people of different races, national origins, religions, classes, or sexes **3** including or accompanied by conflicting or dissimilar elements <~ *feelings*> **4** deriving from 2 or more races or breeds <*a person of* ~ *blood*>

ˌmixed 'bag *n* a miscellaneous collection; an assortment

mixed economy *n* an economic system in which free enterprise and nationalized industries coexist

ˌmixed 'farming *n* the growing of food crops and the rearing of livestock on the same farm

ˌmixed 'grill *n* a dish of several meats and vegetables grilled together

ˌmixed 'metaphor *n* a combination of incongruous metaphors (e g in *iron out bottlenecks*)

ˌmixed-'up *adj* marked by perplexity, uncertainty, or disorder; confused – infml

mixer /'miksə‖'mɪksə/ *n* **1a** a set of adjustable electrical resistances or attenuators used to combine signals, esp sound signals, from a number of sources in variable proportions for recording, broadcasting, etc; *also* one who operates such a device **b** a container, device, or machine for mixing sthg (e g food or concrete) **2a** a person considered with respect to his/her sociability <*was shy and a poor* ~> **b** a nonalcoholic beverage intended to be drunk mixed with spirits

mixture /'mikschə‖'mɪkstʃə/ *n* **1a** mixing or being mixed **b** the relative proportions of constituents; *specif* the proportion of fuel to air produced in a carburettor **2a** (a portion of) matter consisting of 2 or more components in varying proportions that retain their own properties **b** a combination of several different kinds; a blend

'mix-ˌup *n* a state or instance of confusion

mix up *vt* **1** to make untidy or disordered **2** to mistake or confuse <*it's easy to* mix *her* up *with her sister*>

mizzen, mizen /'miz(ə)n‖'mɪz(ə)n/ *n* (the principal fore-and-aft sail set on) a mizzenmast

'mizzenˌmast /-ˌmahst‖-ˌmaːst/ *n* the mast behind the mainmast in a sailing vessel

mizzle /'mizl‖'mɪzl/ *vi* to drizzle – **mizzle** *n*, **mizzly** *adj*

[1]**mnemonic** /ni'monik, nee-‖nɪ'mɒnɪk, niː-/ *adj* **1** assisting or intended to assist the memory **2** of memory – **mnemonically** *adv*

[2]**mnemonic** *n* a mnemonic device or code

mneˈmonics *n pl but sing in constr* the art of improving the memory

mo, mo' /moh‖məʊ/ *n, chiefly Br* a very short space of time; a moment – infml

moa /ˈmoh·ə‖ˈməʊə/ *n* a very large extinct flightless bird of New Zealand

[1]**moan** /mohn‖məʊn/ *n* **1** a complaint **2** a low prolonged sound of pain or grief

[2]**moan** *vt* **1** to lament **2** to utter with moans ~ *vi* **1** to produce (a sound like) a moan **2** to complain, grumble – **moaner** *n*

moat /moht‖məʊt/ *n* a deep wide trench round a castle, fortified home, etc that is usu filled with water

[1]**mob** /mob‖mɒb/ *n* **1** *the* masses, populace **2** a disorderly riotous crowd **3** a criminal gang **4** *chiefly Austr* a flock, drove, or herd of animals **5** *sing or pl in constr, chiefly Br* a crowd, bunch – infml [short for earlier *mobile*, fr Latin *mobile vulgus* fickle crowd]

[2]**mob** *vt* **-bb-** **1** to attack in a large crowd or group **2** to crowd round, esp out of curiosity or admiration

[1]**mobile** /ˈmohbiel‖ˈməʊbaɪl/ *adj* **1** capable of moving or being moved **2** changing quickly in expression or mood **3** (capable of) undergoing movement into a different social class **4** marked by movement < ~ *warfare*> – **mobility** *n*

[2]**mobile** *n* a structure (e g of cardboard or metal) with usu suspended parts that are moved by air currents or machinery

mobil·ize, -ise /ˈmohbiliez‖ˈməʊbɪlaɪz/ *vt* **1a** to put into movement or circulation **b** to release (sthg stored in the body) for use in an organism **2a** to assemble and make ready (e g troops) for active service **b** to marshal (e g resources) for action ~*vi* to undergo mobilization – **mobilization** *n*

mobster /ˈmobstə‖ˈmɒbstə/ *n, chiefly NAm* a member of a criminal gang

moccasin /ˈmokəsin‖ˈmɒkəsɪn/ *n* a soft leather heelless shoe

mocha /ˈmokə, ˈmohkə‖ˈmɒkə, ˈməʊkə/ *n* **1** a coffee of superior quality **2** a flavouring obtained from a (mixture of cocoa or chocolate with a) strong coffee infusion [*Mocha*, town in Arabia]

[1]**mock** /mok‖mɒk/ *vt* **1** to treat with contempt or ridicule **2** to disappoint the hopes of **3** to mimic in fun or derision ~*vi* to jeer, scoff – **mocker** *n*, **mockingly** *adv*

[2]**mock** *n* a school examination used as a rehearsal for an official one

[3]**mock** *adj* (having the character) of an imitation or simulation < ~ *cream*> <*a* ~ *battle*>

mockery /ˈmokəri‖ˈmɒkərɪ/ *n* **1** jeering or contemptuous behaviour or words **2** an object of laughter or derision **3** a deceitful or contemptible imitation; a travesty **4** sthg insultingly or ridiculously inappropriate

mockingbird /ˈmoking,buhd‖ˈmɒkɪŋ,bɜːd/ *n* a common bird of esp the southern USA that imitates the calls of other birds

mock turtle soup *n* a soup made from a calf's head in imitation of green turtle soup

ˈ**mock-ˌup** *n* a full-sized structural model built accurately to scale

modal /ˈmohdl‖ˈməʊdl/ *adj* **1** of modality in logic **2** of or being (in) a mode (e g in music); *specif* being in one of the church modes rather than a major or minor key **3** of general form or structure as opposed to particular substance or content **4** of or being a form or category indicating grammatical mood – **modally** *adv*

modal auxiliary *n* an auxiliary verb (e g *can, must, may*) expressing a distinction of mood

modality /mohˈdaləti‖məʊˈdælətɪ/ *n* **1** a modal quality or attribute; a form **2** the classification of logical propositions according to the possibility, impossibility, contingency, or necessity of their content **3** a procedure (e g massage) or apparatus used in (physical) therapy **4** MOOD

mod con /ˌmod ˈkon‖ˌmɒd ˈkɒn/ *n, Br* a modern convenience; *esp* a household fitting or device designed to increase comfort or save time – infml

[1]**mode** /mohd‖məʊd/ *n* **1** an arrangement of the 8 diatonic musical notes of an octave in any of several fixed schemes **2** [2]MOOD **3** MODALITY 2 **4a** a particular form or variety of sthg **b** a form or manner of expression; a style **5** a way of doing or carrying out sthg **6** a particular functional arrangement or condition <*a spacecraft in orbiting* ~> **7** the most frequently occurring value in a set of data

[2]**mode** *n* a prevailing fashion or style (e g of dress or behaviour) – fml

[1]**model** /ˈmodl‖ˈmɒdl/ *n* **1** structural design <*built his home on the* ~ *of an old farmhouse*> **2** a replica of sthg in relief or 3 dimensions; *also* a representation of sthg to be constructed **3** an example worthy of imitation or emulation <*this essay is a* ~ *of clarity*> **4** sby or sthg that serves as a pattern for an artist; *esp* one who poses for an artist **5** one who is employed to wear merchandise, esp clothing, in order to display it <*a fashion* ~> **6** a type or design of an article or product (e g a garment or car) **7** a (simplified) description or analogy used to help visualize sthg (e g an atom) that cannot be directly observed **8** a system of postulates, data, and inferences presented as a mathematical description of an entity or state of affairs **9** a prostitute – euph

[2]**model** *vb* **-ll-** (*NAm* **-l-**, **-ll-**) *vt* **1** to plan or form after a pattern **2** to shape in a mouldable material; *broadly* to produce a representation or simulation of <*using a computer to* ~ *a problem*> **3** to construct or fashion in imitation of a particular model **4** to display, esp by wearing < ~led *hats for a living*> ~ *vi* **1** to design or imitate forms **2** to work or act as a fashion model – **modeller** *n*

[3]**model** *adj* **1** (worthy of) being a pattern for others <*a* ~ *student*> **2** being a miniature representation of sthg <*a* ~ *aeroplane*>

modem /ˈmohdem‖ˈməʊdem/ *n* an electronic device that converts data from a form understandable by a computer into a form that can be transmitted via a telephone line, radio signal, etc and that reconverts data so received (e g to allow communication between distant computers) [*mo*dulator + *dem*odulator]

[1]**moderate** /ˈmod(ə)rət‖ˈmɒd(ə)rət/ *adj* **1a** avoiding extremes of behaviour or expression **b**

not violent; temperate **2a** being (somewhat less than) average in quality, amount, or degree **b** (done or kept) within reasonable limits < ~ *wage demands*> – **moderately** *adv*, **moderateness** *n*

[2]**moderate** /ˈmodərayt‖ˈmɒdəreɪt/ *vt* **1** to lessen the intensity or extremeness of **2** to preside over ~ *vi* **1** to act as a moderator **2** to decrease in violence, severity, intensity, or volume – **moderation** *n*

[3]**moderate** /ˈmod(ə)rət‖ˈmɒd(ə)rət/ *n* one who holds moderate views or favours a moderate course

moderato /ˌmodəˈrahtoh‖ˌmɒdəˈrɑːtəʊ/ *adv or adj* in a moderate tempo – used in music

moderator /ˈmodəraytə‖ˈmɒdəreɪtə/ *n* **1** a mediator **2** the presiding officer of a Presbyterian governing body **3** a substance (e g graphite) used for slowing down neutrons in a nuclear reactor – **moderatorship** *n*

modern /ˈmodən‖ˈmɒdən/ *adj* **1a** (characteristic) of a period extending from a particular point in the past to the present time **b** (characteristic) of the present or the immediate past; contemporary **2** involving recent techniques, styles, or ideas **3** *cap* constituting the present or most recent period of a language – **modernness, modernity** *n*

modernism /ˈmodəniz(ə)m‖ˈmɒdənɪz(ə)m/ *n* **1** a practice, usage, or expression characteristic of modern times **2** *often cap* a tendency in theology to adapt traditional doctrine to contemporary thought by minimizing the role of the supernatural **3** the theory and practices of modern art; *esp* a search for new forms of expression involving a deliberate break with the past – **modernist** *n or adj*, **modernistic** *adj*

modern·ize, -ise /ˈmodəniez‖ˈmɒdənaɪz/ *vt* to adapt to modern needs, style, or standards ~*vi* to adopt modern views, habits, or techniques – **modernization** *n*

modest /ˈmodist‖ˈmɒdɪst/ *adj* **1** having a moderate estimate of one's abilities or worth; not boastful or self-assertive **2** (characteristic) of a modest nature **3** carefully observant of proprieties of dress and behaviour **4** small or limited in size, amount, or aim – **modestly** *adv*, **modesty** *n*

modicum /ˈmodikəm‖ˈmɒdɪkəm/ *n* a small or limited amount

modification /ˌmodifiˈkaysh(ə)n‖ˌmɒdɪfɪˈkeɪʃ(ə)n/ *n* **1** the limiting of a statement **2** the making of a limited change to sthg

modify /ˈmodifie‖ˈmɒdɪfaɪ/ *vt* **1** to make less extreme **2** to limit in meaning; qualify **3a** to make minor changes in **b** to make basic changes in, often for a specific purpose ~*vi* to undergo change – **modifiable** *adj*, **modifier** *n*

modish /ˈmohdish‖ˈməʊdɪʃ/ *adj* fashionable, stylish – **modishly** *adv*, **modishness** *n*

modular /ˈmodyoolə‖ˈmɒdjʊlə/ *adj* of or based on a module or modulus – **modularly** *adv*, **modularity** *n*

modulate /ˈmodyoolayt‖ˈmɒdjʊleɪt/ *vt* **1** to vary in tone; make tuneful < ~ *one's voice*> **2** to adjust to or keep in proper measure or proportion **3** to vary the amplitude, frequency, or phase of (a carrier wave or signal) by combining with a wave of a different frequency, so as to transmit a radio, television, etc signal ~*vi* to pass by regular chord or melodic progression from one musical key or tonality into another – **modulator** *n*, **modulatory** *adj*, **modulation** *n*

module /ˈmodyoohl‖ˈmɒdjuːl/ *n* **1** a standard or unit of measure; *esp* one by which the proportions of an architectural composition are regulated **2** a standardized or independent unit used in construction (e g of buildings, electronic systems, or spacecraft)

modus operandi /ˌmohdəs opəˈrandi‖ˌməʊdəs ɒpəˈrændɪ/ *n, pl* **modi operandi** /ˈmohdie‖ˈməʊdaɪ/ a method of procedure

ˌ**modus viˈvendi** /viˈvendi‖vɪˈvendɪ/ *n, pl* **modi vivendi** **1** a practical compromise, esp between opposed or quarrelling parties **2** a manner of living; a way of life [Modern Latin, manner of living]

moggie, moggy /ˈmogi‖ˈmɒgɪ/ *n, Br* CAT 1a – infml

mogul /ˈmohg(ə)l‖ˈməʊg(ə)l/ *n* **1 Mogul, Moghul** a member of a Muslim dynasty of Turkish and Mongolian origin ruling India from the 16th to the 18th c **2** a great or prominent (business) person

mohair /ˈmohˌheə‖ˈməʊˌheə/ *n* a fabric or yarn made (partly) from the long silky hair of the Angora goat [obs Italian *mocaiarro*, fr Arabic *mukhayyar*, lit., choice]

Mohammedan /məˈhamid(ə)n‖məˈhæmɪd(ə)n/ *adj* Muhammadan

moiety /ˈmoyəti‖ˈmɔɪətɪ/ *n* **1** either of 2 (approximately) equal parts **2** any of the portions into which sthg is divided

moiré /ˈmwahray ‖ˈmwɑːreɪ (*Fr* mware)/, **moire** /ˈmwahray‖ˈmwɑːreɪ; *also* mwah‖mwɑː/ *n* an irregular wavy sheen on a fabric or metal – **moiré** *adj*

moist /moyst‖mɔɪst/ *adj* **1** slightly wet; damp **2** highly humid – **moistly** *adv*, **moistness** *n*, **moisten** *vb*

moisture /ˈmoyschə‖ˈmɔɪstʃə/ *n* liquid diffused, condensed, or absorbed in relatively small amounts

moistur·ize, -ise /ˈmoyschəˌriez‖ˈmɔɪstʃəˌraɪz/ *vt* to add or restore moisture to (e g the skin) – **moisturizer** *n*

moke /mohk‖məʊk/ *n* **1** *Br* a donkey **2** *Austr* a horse, esp of poor appearance *USE* slang

[1]**molar** /ˈmohlə‖ˈməʊlə/ *n* a grinding tooth with a rounded or flattened surface; *specif* one lying behind the incisors and canines of a mammal

[2]**molar** *adj* of or located near the molar teeth

[3]**molar** *adj* **1** of a mass of matter as distinguished from the properties of individual molecules or atoms **2** of or containing 1 gram molecule (of solute) in 1 litre of solution – **molarity** *n*

molasses /məˈlasiz‖məˈlæsɪz/ *n* the darkest most viscous syrup remaining after all sugar that can be separated by crystallization has been removed during the refining of raw sugar

mold /mohld‖məʊld/ *vt or n, NAm* (to) mould

[1]**mole** /mohl‖məʊl/ *n* a pigmented spot, mark, or lump on the human body; *esp* a naevus

[2]**mole** *n* **1** any of numerous small burrowing insect-eating mammals with minute eyes, concealed ears, and soft fur **2** one who works subversively within an organization, esp to secretly

further the interests of a rival organization or government

[3]**mole** *n* (a harbour formed by) a massive work of masonry, large stones, etc laid in the sea as a pier or breakwater

[4]**mole** *n* an abnormal mass in the womb, esp when containing foetal tissues

[5]**mole** *also* **mol** /mohl‖məʊl/ *n* the basic SI unit of substance; the amount of substance that contains the same number of atoms, molecules, ions, etc as there are atoms in 0.012kg of carbon-12

molecular /məˈlekyooləˈ‖məˈlekjʊlə/ *adj* of, produced by, or consisting of molecules <~ *oxygen*> – **molecularly** *adv*, **molecularity** *n*

molecule /ˈmolikyoohl‖ˈmɒlɪkjuːl/ *n* the smallest particle of a substance that retains its characteristic properties, consisting of 1 or more atoms

ˈ**moleˌhill** /-ˌhil‖-ˌhɪl/ *n* a mound of earth thrown up by a burrowing mole

molest /məˈlest‖məˈlest/ *vt* to annoy, disturb, or attack; *specif* to annoy or attack (esp a child or woman) sexually – **molester** *n*, **molestation** *n*

moll /mol‖mɒl/ *n* **1** a prostitute **2** a gangster's girl friend *USE* infml

mollify /ˈmolifie‖ˈmɒlɪfaɪ/ *vt* **1** to lessen the anger or hostility of **2** to reduce in intensity – **mollification** *n*

mollusc, *NAm chiefly* **mollusk** /ˈmoləsk‖ˈmɒləsk/ *n* any of a large phylum of invertebrate animals with soft bodies not divided into segments and usu enclosed in a shell, including the snails, shellfish, octopuses, and squids – **molluscan** *adj*

mollycoddle /ˈmoliˌkodl‖ˈmɒlɪˌkɒdl/ *vt* to treat with excessive indulgence and attention

ˌ**Molotov** ˈ**cocktail** /ˈmolətof‖ˈmɒlətɒf/ *n* a crude hand grenade made from a bottle filled with petrol or other inflammable liquid with usu a saturated rag for a wick [Vyacheslav M *Molotov* (born 1890), Russian statesman]

molt /mohlt‖məʊlt/ *vb or n, NAm* (to) moult

molten /ˈmohlt(ə)n‖ˈməʊlt(ə)n/ *adj* melted by heat

molto /ˈmoltoh‖ˈmɒltəʊ/ *adv* much, very – used in music <~ *sostenuto*> [Italian, fr Latin *multum*, fr *multus* much]

molybdenum /məˈlibd(ə)nəm‖məˈlɪbd(ə)nəm/ *n* a metallic element resembling chromium and tungsten and used esp in strengthening and hardening steel

mom /mom‖mɒm/ *n, NAm* [2]MUM

moment /ˈmohmənt‖ˈməʊmənt/ *n* **1** a very brief interval or point of time **2a** present time <*at the* ~> **b** a time of excellence or prominence <*she has her* ~*s*> **3** importance in influence or effect **4** a stage in historical or logical development **5** (a measure of) the tendency of a force to produce turning motion **6** the product of a force and the distance from its line of action to a particular axis

momentarily /ˈmohmənt(ə)rəli, ˌmohmənˈterəli‖ˈməʊmənt(ə)rəlɪ, ˌməʊmənˈterəlɪ/ *adv* **1** for a moment **2** *chiefly NAm* instantly

momentary /ˈmohmənt(ə)ri‖ˈməʊmənt(ə)rɪ/ *adj* lasting a very short time – **momentariness** *n*

ˌ**moment of** ˈ**truth** *n* **1** the moment of the final sword thrust in a bullfight **2** a moment of crisis on whose outcome everything depends

momentous /məˈmentəs, moh-‖məˈmentəs, məʊ-/ *adj* of great consequence or significance – **momentousness** *n*

momentum /məˈmentəm, moh-‖məˈmentəm, məʊ-/ *n, pl* **momenta** /-tə‖-tə/, **momentums** the product of the mass of a body and its velocity

momma /ˈmomə, ˈmumə‖ˈmɒmə, ˈmʌmə/ *n, NAm* [2]MUM

mon-, **mono-** *comb form* **1** one; single; alone <mono*plane*> **2a** containing 1 (specified) atom, radical, or group <mono*hydrate*> **b** monomolecular <mono*layer*>

monarch /ˈmonək‖ˈmɒnək/ *n* **1** sby who reigns over a kingdom or empire **2** sby or sthg occupying a commanding or preeminent position **3** a large American butterfly with orange-brown wings with black veins and borders [Late Latin *monarcha*, fr Greek *monarchos*, fr *monos* alone, single + *archos* ruler] – **monarchal**, **monarchial**, **monarchic**, **monarchical** *adj*

monarchism /ˈmonəˌkiz(ə)m‖ˈmɒnəˌkɪz(ə)m/ *n* government by or the principles of monarchy – **monarchist** *n or adj*, **monarchistic** *adj*

monarchy /ˈmonəki‖ˈmɒnəkɪ/ *n* (a government or state with) undivided rule by a monarch

monastery /ˈmonəst(ə)ri‖ˈmɒnəst(ə)rɪ/ *n* a residence occupied by a religious community, esp of monks

monastic /məˈnastik‖məˈnæstɪk/ *adj* of or being monasteries, monks, or nuns – **monastic** *n*, **monastically** *adv*, **monasticism** *n*

Monday /ˈmunday, -di‖ˈmʌndeɪ, -dɪ/ *n* the day of the week following Sunday [Old English *mōnandæg*, fr *mōna* moon + *dæg* day]

monetarism /ˈmunitəˌriz(ə)m‖ˈmʌnɪtəˌrɪz(ə)m/ *n* an economic theory that the most effective way of controlling the economy is by controlling the money supply – **monetarist** *n or adj*

monetary /ˈmunit(ə)ri‖ˈmʌnɪt(ə)rɪ/ *adj* of money or its behaviour in an economy – **monetarily** *adv*

money /ˈmuni‖ˈmʌnɪ/ *n, pl* **moneys, monies** **1** sthg generally accepted as a means of payment; *esp* officially printed, coined, or stamped currency **2** (one who has) wealth reckoned in terms of money **3** a form or denomination of coin or paper money [Middle French *moneie*, fr Latin *moneta* – see [1]MINT]

moneybags /ˈmuniˌbagz‖ˈmʌnɪˌbægz/ *n, pl* **moneybags** a wealthy person – derog

ˈ**money** ˌ**box** *n* a container for small personal savings, usu with a slot for the insertion of coins

ˈ**money** ˌ**changer** *n* one whose occupation is the exchanging of kinds or denominations of currency

moneyed, **monied** /ˈmunid‖ˈmʌnɪd/ *adj* **1** having much money **2** consisting of or derived from money

ˈ**money** ˌ**grubber** *n* a person sordidly bent on accumulating money – infml – **money-grubbing** *adj or n*

ˈ**moneyˌlender** /-ˌlendə‖-ˌlendə/ *n* one whose business is lending money and charging interest on it

ˈ**money-**ˌ**maker** *n* a product or enterprise that produces much profit – **moneymaking** *adj or n*

ˈ**money-ˌspinner** *n, chiefly Br* a money-maker – infml – **money-spinning** *adj or n*

monger /ˈmung·gə‖ˈmʌŋgə/ *n* **1** a trader or dealer <*ale*monger> **2** one who attempts to stir up or spread sthg petty or discreditable <*gossip*monger> *USE* usu in combination *n* **1** a member of any of the chiefly pastoral peoples of Mongolia **2** MONGOLIAN 2 **3** *often not cap* a sufferer from Down's syndrome – **Mongol** *adj*

Mongol /ˈmongˌgol, ˈmong·gl‖ˈmɒŋggɒl, ˈmɒŋgl/ *n* **1** a member of any of the chiefly pastoral peoples of Mongolia **2** MONGOLIAN 2 **3** *often not cap* a sufferer from Down's syndrome – **Mongol** *adj*

Mongolian /mongˈgohlyən, -li·ən‖mɒŋˈgəʊljən, -lɪən/ *n* **1a** MONGOL 1 **b** a native or inhabitant of Mongolia or of the Mongolian People's Republic **2** the language of the Mongol people – **Mongolian** *adj*

mongolism /ˈmong·g(ə)lˌiz(ə)m‖ˈmɒŋg(ə)lˌɪz(ə)m/ *n* DOWN'S SYNDROME

mongoose /ˈmongˌgoohs‖ˈmɒŋˌguːs/ *n, pl* **mongooses** *also* **mongeese** /-ˌgees‖-ˌgiːs/ an agile ferret-sized esp Indian mammal that feeds on snakes and rodents

mongrel /ˈmong·grəl, ˈmung-‖ˈmɒŋgrəl, ˈmʌŋ-/ *n* a dog or other individual (of unknown ancestry) resulting from the interbreeding of diverse breeds – **mongrel, mongrelly** *adj*, **mongrelize** *vt*, **mongrelization** *n*

[1]**monitor** /ˈmonitə‖ˈmɒnɪtə/, *fem* **monitress** /ˈmonitris‖ˈmɒnɪtrɪs/ *n* **1a** a pupil appointed to help a teacher **b** sby or sthg that monitors or is used in monitoring: e g **b(1)** a receiver used to view the picture being picked up by a television camera **b(2)** a device for observing a biological condition or function <*a heart* ~> **2** any of various large tropical Old World lizards closely related to the iguanas – **monitorship** *n*, **monitorial** *adj*

[2]**monitor** *vt* **1** to keep (a broadcast) under surveillance by means of a receiver, in order to check the quality or fidelity to a frequency or to investigate the content (e g for political significance) **2** to observe or inspect, esp for a special purpose **3** to regulate or control the operation of (e g a machine or process)

monk /mungk‖mʌŋk/ *n* a male member of a religious order, living apart from the world under vows of poverty, chastity, etc

[1]**monkey** /ˈmungki‖ˈmʌŋkɪ/ *n* **1** any (small long-tailed) primate mammal with the exception of the human beings and usu also the lemurs and tarsiers **2a** a mischievous child; a scamp **b** a ludicrous figure; a fool <*made a* ~ *of him*> **3** £500 or $500 – slang *USE* (2) infml

[2]**monkey** *vi* **1** to act in an absurd or mischievous manner **2** TAMPER 2 – usu + *with USE* infml; often + *about* or *around*

ˈ**monkey ˌbusiness** *n* mischievous or underhand activity – infml

ˈ**monkey ˌnut** *n* PEANUT 1

ˈ**monkey-ˌpuzzle** *n* a commonly planted S American evergreen gymnospermous tree with intertwined branches and stiff sharp leaves

ˈ**monkey ˌwrench** *n* a large spanner with one fixed and one adjustable jaw

monkshood /ˈmungksˌhood‖ˈmʌŋksˌhʊd/ *n* a very poisonous Eurasian plant with showy spikes of white or purplish flowers

mono /ˈmonoh‖ˈmɒnəʊ/ *adj or n* monophonic (sound reproduction)

mono- – see MON-

monochrome /ˈmonəˌkrohm‖ˈmɒnəˌkrəʊm/ *adj or n* (of, using, or being) reproduction or execution in 1 colour, black and white, or shades of grey – **monochromist** *n*, **monochromic** *adj*

monocle /ˈmonəkl‖ˈmɒnəkl/ *n* an eyeglass for 1 eye [French, fr Late Latin *monoculus* one-eyed, fr Latin *mon-* one + *oculus* eye] – **monocled** *adj*

monogamy /məˈnogəmi‖məˈnɒgəmɪ/ *n* the state or custom of being married to 1 person at a time – **monogamist** *n*, **monogamous** *adj*, **monogamously** *adv*, **monogamic** *adj*

monoglot /ˈmonəˌglot‖ˈmɒnəˌglɒt/ *adj* monolingual

monogram /ˈmonəˌgram‖ˈmɒnəˌgræm/ *vt or n* (to mark with) a character usu formed of the interwoven initials of a name – **monogrammatic** *adj*

monograph /ˈmonəˌgrahf, -ˌgraf‖ˈmɒnəˌgrɑːf, -ˌgræf/ *n* a treatise on a small area of learning – **monographic** *adj*

monolingual /ˌmonohˈling·gwəl‖ˌmɒnəʊˈlɪŋgwəl/ *adj* knowing or using only one language

monolith /ˈmonəˌlith‖ˈmɒnəˌlɪθ/ *n* **1** a single large block of stone, often in the form of an obelisk or column **2** a massive structure **3** an organized whole that acts as a single powerful force

monolithic /ˌmonəˈlithik‖ˌmɒnəˈlɪθɪk/ *adj* **1** formed from or produced in or on a single crystal <*a* ~ *silicon chip*> **2** constituting a massive uniform whole <*the* ~ *totalitarian state*> – **monolithically** *adv*

monologue, *NAm also* **monolog** /ˈmonəˌlog‖ˈmɒnəˌlɒg/ *n* **1** a dramatic or literary soliloquy; *also* a dramatic sketch performed by 1 speaker **2** a long speech monopolizing conversation – **monologuist, monologist** *n*

monomania /ˌmonohˈmaynyə‖ˌmɒnəʊˈmeɪnjə/ *n* obsessional concentration on a single object or idea – **monomaniac** *n or adj*

monomolecular /ˌmonohməˈlekyoolə‖ˌmɒnəʊməˈlekjʊlə/ *adj* (of a layer) only 1 molecule thick <*a* ~ *film*>

mononucleosis /ˌmonohˌnyoohkliˈohsis‖ˌmɒnəʊˌnjuːklɪˈəʊsɪs/ *n* INFECTIOUS MONONUCLEOSIS

monophonic /ˌmonohˈfonik‖ˌmɒnəʊˈfɒnɪk/ *adj* of or being a system for sound reproduction in which the sound signal is not split into 2 or more different channels between the source and the point of use – **monophonically** *adv*

monoplane /ˈmonəˌplayn‖ˈmɒnəˌpleɪn/ *n* an aeroplane with only 1 main pair of wings

monopolist /moˈnopəlist‖mɒˈnɒpəlɪst/ *n* one who has or favours a monopoly – **monopolistic** *adj*

monopol·ize, -ise /məˈnopəliez‖məˈnɒpəlaɪz/ *vt* to get a monopoly of; assume complete possession or control of – **monopolizer** *n*, **monopolization** *n*

monopoly /məˈnopəli‖məˈnɒpəlɪ/ *n* **1** (a person or group having) exclusive ownership or control (through legal privilege, command of the supply of a commodity, concerted action, etc) **2** sthg, esp a commodity, controlled by one party [Latin *monopolium*, fr Greek *monopōlion*, fr *monos* alone, single + *pōlein* to sell]

monorail /'monoh,rayl‖'mɒnəʊ,reɪl/ *n* (a vehicle running on) a single rail serving as a track for a wheeled vehicle

monosaccharide /,monoh'sakəried‖,mɒnəʊ'sækəraɪd/ *n* a sugar (e g glucose) not decomposable to simpler sugars

monosyllable /'monə,siləbl‖'mɒnə,sɪləbl/ *n* a word of 1 syllable; *specif* one used by sby intending to be pointedly brief in answering or commenting – **monosyllabic** *adj*, **monosyllabically** *adv*

monotheism /'monohthee,iz(ə)m‖'mɒnəʊθiː,ɪz(ə)m/ *n* the doctrine or belief that there is only 1 God – **monotheist** *n*, **monotheistic** *adj*

[1]**monotone** /'monə,tohn‖'mɒnə,təʊn/ *n* **1** a succession of speech sounds in 1 unvarying pitch **2** a single unvaried musical note **3** a tedious sameness or repetition

[2]**monotone** *adj* **1** having a uniform colour **2** MONOTONIC 2

monotonic /,monə'tonik‖,mɒnə'tɒnɪk/ *adj* **1** uttered in a monotone **2** *of a mathematical function* increasing continuously or decreasing continuously as the independent variable increases – **monotonically** *adv*

monotonous /mə'not(ə)nəs‖mə'nɒt(ə)nəs/ *adj* **1** uttered or sounded in 1 unvarying tone **2** tediously uniform or repetitive – **monotonously** *adv*, **monotonousness, monotony** *n*

Monotype *trademark* – used for a keyboard-operated typesetting machine that casts and sets metal type in separate characters

monsieur /mə'syuh‖mə'sjɜː/ *n, pl* **messieurs** /me'syuh, mə'syuhz‖me'sjɜː, mə'sjɜːz/ – used by or to a French-speaking man as a title equivalent to Mr or without a name as a term of direct address

monsignor /,monsin'yaw‖,mɒnsɪn'jɔː/ *n, pl* **monsignors, monsignori** /-ri‖-rɪ/ – used as a title for certain Roman Catholic prelates and officers of the papal court – **monsignorial** *adj*

monsoon /mon'soohn‖mɒn'suːn/ *n* **1** a seasonal wind of S Asia blowing from the SW in summer and the NE in winter **2** the season of the SW monsoon, marked by very heavy rains [obs Dutch *monssoen*, fr Portuguese *monção*, fr Arabic *mawsim* time, season] – **monsoonal** *adj*

monster /'monstə‖'mɒnstə/ *n* **1a** an animal or plant of (grotesquely) abnormal form or structure **b** an (imaginary) animal of incredible shape or form that is usu dangerous or horrifying **2** one exceptionally large for its kind <*~ tomatoes*> **3** sthg monstrous; *esp* a person of appalling ugliness, wickedness, or cruelty

monstrance /'monstrəns‖'mɒnstrəns/ *n* a vessel in which the consecrated Host is exposed for veneration, esp in a Catholic church

monstrosity /mon'strosəti‖mɒn'strɒsətɪ/ *n* **1** MONSTER 1a **2** (the quality or state of being) sthg monstrous

monstrous /'monstrəs‖'mɒnstrəs/ *adj* **1** having the qualities or appearance of a monster; extraordinarily large **2a** extraordinarily ugly or vicious **b** outrageously wrong or ridiculous – **monstrously** *adv*, **monstrousness** *n*

mons veneris /,monz 'venəris‖,mɒnz 'venərɪs/ *n, pl* **montes veneris** /'monteez‖'mɒntiːz/ a rounded raised mass of fatty tissue over the pubic bone and above the vulva of the human female

montage /mon'tahzh‖mɒn'tɑːʒ/ *n* **1a** a picture made by combining or overlapping several separate pictures **b** an artistic composition made from different materials combined or juxtaposed **2** (a film sequence using) a method of film editing in which the chronological sequence of events is interrupted by juxtaposed or rapidly succeeding shots

month /munth‖mʌnθ/ *n* **1a** any of the 12 divisions of the year in the Julian or Gregorian calendars corresponding roughly with the period of the moon's rotation; *also* any similar division of the year in other calendars **b** 28 days or 4 weeks; *also* the interval between the same date in adjacent months **2** *pl* an indefinite usu protracted period of time <*he's been gone for ~s*> **3** a ninth of the typical duration of human pregnancy <*in her 8th ~*> – **monthly** *adv or adj*

[1]**monthly** /-li‖-lɪ/ *n* **1** a monthly periodical **2** *pl* a menstrual period – infml

monument /'monyoomənt‖'mɒnjʊmənt/ *n* **1** a written record **2a** a lasting evidence or reminder of sby or sthg notable or influential **b** a memorial stone, sculpture, or structure erected to commemorate a person or event **3** a structure or site of historical or archaeological importance

monumental /,monyoo'mentl‖,mɒnjʊ'mentl/ *adj* **1a** of, serving as, or resembling a monument **b** occurring or used on a monument <*a ~ inscription*> **2** very great in degree; imposing, outstanding – **monumentally** *adv*

moo /mooh‖muː/ *vi or n* [1]LOW

mooch /moohch‖muːtʃ/ *vi* **1** to wander aimlessly or disconsolately – usu + *around, about,* or *along* **2** *NAm* to sponge, cadge ~*vt, NAm* **1** to steal; MAKE OFF WITH **2** to cadge, beg ***USE*** infml – **moocher** *n*

[1]**mood** /moohd‖muːd/ *n* **1a** (the evocation, esp in art or literature, of) a predominant emotion, feeling, or frame of mind **b** the right frame of mind <*you must be in the ~, or you'll fall asleep – The Listener*> **2** a fit of often silent anger or bad temper **3** a prevailing attitude

[2]**mood** *n* a distinct form or set of inflectional forms of a verb indicating whether the action or state it denotes is considered a fact, wish, possibility, etc <*the subjunctive ~*>

moody /'moohdi‖'muːdɪ/ *adj* **1** sullen or gloomy **2** temperamental – **moodily** *adv*, **moodiness** *n*

[1]**moon** /moohn‖muːn/ *n* **1a** (the appearance or visibility from the earth of) the earth's natural satellite that shines by reflecting the sun's light <*there is a ~ tonight*> **b** a satellite **2** LUNAR MONTH – poetic – **moonless** *adj*, **moonlet** *n*, **moonlike** *adj* – **over the moon** absolutely delighted

[2]**moon** *vi* **1** to move about listlessly **2** to spend time in idle gazing or daydreaming ***USE*** often + *around* or *about*; infml

[1]**moon,beam** /-,beem‖-,biːm/ *n* a ray of light

from the moon

ˈmoonˌcalf /-ˌkahf‖-ˌkɑːf/ *n* MONSTER 1a

ˈmoonˌlight /-ˌliet‖-ˌlaɪt/ *vi* **moonlighted** to hold a second job in addition to a regular one – **moonlighter** *n*

ˈmoonˌlit /-ˌlit‖-ˌlɪt/ *adj* lighted (as if) by the moon

ˈmoonˌshine /-ˌshien‖-ˌʃaɪn/ *n* **1** the light of the moon **2** empty talk; nonsense **3** (illegally distilled) spirits, esp whisky – infml

ˈmoonˌstone /-ˌstohn‖-ˌstəʊn/ *n* a transparent or translucent opalescent feldspar used as a gem

ˈmoonˌstruck /-ˌstruk‖-ˌstrʌk/ *adj* affected (as if) by the moon; *specif* mentally unbalanced

moony /ˈmoohni‖ˈmuːnɪ/ *adj* inanely dreamy; moonstruck – infml

[1]**moor** /maw, mooə‖mɔː, mʊə/ *n, chiefly Br* an expanse of open peaty infertile usu heath-covered upland

[2]**moor** *vt* to make (e g a boat or buoy) fast with cables, lines, or anchors ~ *vi* **1** to secure a vessel by mooring **2** to be made fast

Moor *n* a member of the mixed Arab and Berber people that conquered Spain in the 8th c AD – **Moorish** *adj*

moorhen /ˈmawˌhen, ˈmooə-‖ˈmɔːˌhen, ˈmʊə-/ *n* a common red-billed blackish bird of the rail family that nests near fresh water

mooring /ˈmawring, ˈmooəring‖ˈmɔːrɪŋ, ˈmʊərɪŋ/ *n* **1** a place where or an object to which a ship, boat, etc can be made fast **2** the lines, chains, anchors, etc used to make a ship, boat, etc fast <*she may have dragged her* ~s> *USE* usu pl with sing. meaning

moose /moohs‖muːs/ *n, pl* **moose** **1** a large N American ruminant mammal of the deer family with very large flattened antlers **2** the European elk

[1]**moot** /mooht‖muːt/ *n* **1** an early English assembly to decide points of community and political interest **2** a mock court in which law students argue hypothetical cases

[2]**moot** *vt* to put forward for discussion

[3]**moot** *adj* open to question; debatable – usu in *moot point*

[1]**mop** /mop‖mɒp/ *n* **1** an implement consisting of a head made of absorbent material fastened to a long handle and used esp for cleaning floors **2** (sthg like) a shock of untidy hair

[2]**mop** *vt* **-pp-** **1** to clean (a floor or other surface) with a mop **2** to wipe (as if) with a mop <~ped *his brow with a handkerchief*> – **mopper** *n*

mope /mohp‖məʊp/ *vi* to give oneself up to brooding; become listless or dejected – **moper** *n*

moped /ˈmohped‖ˈməʊped/ *n* a low-powered motorcycle whose engine can be pedal-assisted (e g for starting)

moppet /ˈmopit‖ˈmɒpɪt/ *n* a young child; *esp* a little girl – chiefly infml; apprec

mop up *vt* **1** to eliminate remaining resistance in (e g a previously occupied area in a war) **2** to absorb, take up, or deal with (esp a remnant or remainder) ~*vi* to complete a project or transaction – **mop-up** *n*

moquette /moˈket‖mɒˈket/ *n* a carpet or upholstery fabric with a velvety pile

moraine /moˈrayn‖mɒˈreɪn/ *n* an accumulation of earth and stones carried and deposited by a glacier – **morainal, morainic** *adj*

[1]**moral** /ˈmorəl‖ˈmɒrəl/ *adj* **1a** of or being principles of right and wrong in conduct; ethical **b** expressing or teaching a conception of right conduct <*a ~ poem*> **c** conforming to a standard of right conduct <*a ~ person*> **d** sanctioned by, resulting from, or operative on one's conscience or (correct) moral judgment <*a ~ obligation*> <*a ~ right*> **e** capable of distinguishing right and wrong <*man is a ~ being*> **2** very probable though not proved <*a ~ certainty*> **3** of, occurring in, or acting on the mind, emotions, or will <*a ~ victory*> <*~ support*> – **morally** *adv*

[2]**moral** *n* **1** (a concluding passage pointing out) the moral significance or practical lesson **2** *pl* **2a** moral practices or teachings; standards of esp sexual conduct <*a man of loose ~*s> **b** ethics

morale /məˈrahl‖məˈrɑːl/ *n* the mental and emotional condition (e g of enthusiasm or loyalty) of an individual or group with regard to the function or tasks at hand

moralist /ˈmorəlist‖ˈmɒrəlɪst/ *n* **1** one concerned with moral principles and problems **2** one concerned with regulating the morals of others – often derog – **moralistic** *adj*, **moralistically** *adv*

morality /məˈraləti‖məˈrælətɪ/ *n* **1** a system or sphere of moral conduct <*Christian ~*> **2** (degree of conformity to standards of) right conduct or moral correctness <*questioned the ~ of his act*>

moˈrality ˌplay *n* a form of allegorical drama popular esp in the 15th and 16th c in which the characters personify moral or abstract qualities (e g pride or youth)

moral·ize, -ise /ˈmorəliez‖ˈmɒrəlaɪz/ *vt* **1** to interpret morally; draw a moral from **2** to make moral or morally better ~*vi* to make moral reflections – **moralizer** *n*, **moralization** *n*

morass /məˈras‖məˈræs/ *n* **1** a marsh, swamp **2** sthg that ensnares, confuses, or impedes – **morassy** *adj*

moratorium /ˌmorəˈtawri·əm‖ˌmɒrəˈtɔːrɪəm/ *n, pl* **moratoriums, moratoria** /-ri·ə‖-rɪə/ **1** a legally authorized delay in the performance of an obligation or the payment of a debt **2** a suspension of (a specified) activity – usu + *on* [Late Latin *moratorius* dilatory, fr Latin *morari* to delay, fr *mora* delay]

morbid /ˈmawbid‖ˈmɔːbɪd/ *adj* **1** of, affected with, induced by, or characteristic of disease <*~ anatomy*> **2** abnormally susceptible to or characterized by gloomy feelings; *esp* having an unnatural preoccupation with death **3** grisly, gruesome <*~ curiosity*> – **morbidly** *adv*, **morbidness** *n*

morbidity /mawˈbidəti‖mɔːˈbɪdətɪ/ *n* the relative incidence of (a) disease

[1]**mordant** /ˈmawd(ə)nt‖ˈmɔːd(ə)nt/ *adj* **1** caustic or sharply critical in thought, manner, or style <*~ wit*> **2** acting as a mordant **3** burning, pungent – **mordancy** *n*, **mordantly** *adv*

[2]**mordant** *n* **1** a chemical that fixes a dye by

combining with it to form an insoluble compound **2** a corroding substance used in etching

[1]**more** /maw‖mɔː/ *adj* **1** greater in quantity or number <*something ~ than she expected*> <*7 is 2 ~ than 5*> **2** additional, further <*three ~ guests arrived*> <*have some ~ tea*> <*what ~ do you want?*> – **neither/nothing more or/nor less than** simply, plainly

[2]**more** *adv* **1a** as an additional amount <*not much ~ to do*> **b** moreover, again <*summer is here once ~*> **2** to a greater degree or extent <*you should practise ~*> <*~ sad than angry*> – often used with an adjective or adverb to form the comparative <*much ~ evenly matched*> – **more often than not** at most times; usually

[3]**more** *n, pl* **more** **1** a greater or additional quantity, amount, or part <*hope to see ~ of her*> <*tell me ~*> <*~ than meets the eye*> **2** *pl* additional ones <*many ~ were found as the search continued*> – **more of** nearer to being (sthg specified) <*it's* more of *a sofa than a bed*>

morello /məˈreloh‖məˈreləʊ/ *n, pl* **morellos** a cultivated red-skinned sour cherry used esp in jams

ˌ**more or ˈless** *adv* **1** to some extent or degree; somewhat **2** almost, nearly

moreover /mawˈrohvə‖mɔːˈrəʊvə/ *adv* in addition to what has been said – used to introduce new matter

mores /ˈmawreez‖ˈmɔːriːz/ *n pl* the (morally binding) customs or conventions of a particular group [Latin, pl of *mor-, mos* custom]

morganatic /ˌmawgəˈnatik‖ˌmɔːgəˈnætɪk/ *adj* of or being a marriage between people of different rank in which the rank of the inferior partner remains unchanged and the children do not succeed to the titles or property of the parent of higher rank – **morganatically** *adv*

morgue /mawg‖mɔːg/ *n* **1a** a mortuary **b** a gloomy dispiriting place **2** a collection of reference works and files in a newspaper office

moribund /ˈmoriˌbund‖ˈmɒrɪˌbʌnd/ *adj* dying – **moribundity** *n*

Mormon /ˈmawmən‖ˈmɔːmən/ *n* a member of the Church of Jesus Christ of Latter-Day Saints, founded in 1830 in the USA by Joseph Smith, and following precepts contained in the Book of Mormon, a sacred text that he discovered – **Mormonism** *n*

morn /mawn‖mɔːn/ *n* the morning – chiefly poetic

morning /ˈmawning‖ˈmɔːnɪŋ/ *n* **1a** the dawn **b** the time from midnight or sunrise to noon **2** an early period (e g of time or life); the beginning – **in the morning** tomorrow morning

ˈ**morning ˌcoat** *n* a man's tailcoat that is worn on formal occasions during the day

ˈ**morning ˌdress** *n* men's dress for formal occasions (e g a wedding) during the day

ˌ**morning ˈglory** *n* any of various usu twining plants of the bindweed family with showy trumpet-shaped flowers

ˌ**Morning ˈPrayer** *n* a daily morning office of the Anglican church

ˈ**mornings** *adv, chiefly NAm* in the morning; on any morning

ˈ**morning ˌsickness** *n* nausea and vomiting occurring esp in the morning during the earlier months of a woman's pregnancy

ˌ**morning ˈstar** *n* a bright planet, specif Venus, seen in the eastern sky before or at sunrise

morocco /məˈrokoh‖məˈrɒkəʊ/ *n* a fine leather made from goatskin tanned with sumach [*Morocco*, country in N Africa]

moron /ˈmawron‖ˈmɔːrɒn/ *n* **1** MENTAL DEFECTIVE **2** a very stupid person – infml [Greek *mōros* foolish, stupid] – **moronism** *n*, **moronic** *adj*

morose /məˈrohs‖məˈrəʊs/ *adj* (having a disposition) marked by or expressive of gloom – **morosely** *adv*, **moroseness** *n*

morpheme /ˈmawfeem‖ˈmɔːfiːm/ *n* a meaningful linguistic unit that contains no smaller meaningful parts – **morphemic** *adj*

morphia /ˈmawfi·ə‖ˈmɔːfɪə/ *n* morphine

morphine /ˈmawfeen‖ˈmɔːfiːn/ *n* the principal alkaloid of opium that is an addictive narcotic drug used esp as a powerful painkiller [French, fr *Morpheus*, Greco-Roman god of dreams] – **morphinism** *n*, **morphinic** *adj*

morphology /mawˈfoləji‖mɔːˈfɒlədʒɪ/ *n* **1** (the biology of) the form and structure of animals and plants **2a** a study and description of word formation in a language including inflection, derivation, and compounding **b** the system of word-forming elements and processes in a language **3** (a study of) the structure or form of sthg – **morphologist** *n*, **morphological** *adj*

ˈ**morris ˌdance** /ˈmoris‖ˈmɒrɪs/ *n* any of several traditional English dances that are performed by groups of people wearing costumes to which small bells are attached [Middle English *moreys daunce*, fr *moreys* Moorish + *daunce* dance] – **morris dancer** *n*

morrow /ˈmoroh‖ˈmɒrəʊ/ *n* **1** the next day – fml **2** *archaic* the morning

Morse /maws‖mɔːs/, ˌ**Morse ˈcode** *n* a signalling code consisting of dots and dashes used to send messages by light or by sound signals or esp by radio [Samuel *Morse* (1791-1872), US artist & inventor] – **morse** *vb*

morsel /ˈmawsl‖ˈmɔːsl/ *n* **1** a small piece of food **2** a small quantity; a scrap

[1]**mortal** /ˈmawtl‖ˈmɔːtl/ *adj* **1** causing or about to cause death; fatal **2a** not living forever; subject to death **b** humanly conceivable <*every ~ thing*> **3** marked by relentless hostility <*a ~ enemy*> **4** very great, intense, or severe **5** of or connected with death

[2]**mortal** *n* **1** a human being **2** a person of a specified kind

mortality /mawˈtaləti‖mɔːˈtælətɪ/ *n* **1** being mortal **2** the death of large numbers of people, animals, etc **3** the human race <*take these tears, ~'s relief* – Alexander Pope> **4a** the number of deaths in a given time or place **b** the ratio of deaths in a given time to population **c** the number lost, or the rate of loss or failure

mortally /ˈmawtl·i‖ˈmɔːtlɪ/ *adv* **1** in a deadly or fatal manner **2** to an extreme degree; intensely

ˌ**mortal ˈsin** *n* a sin (e g murder) of such gravity that it totally debars the soul from divine grace – **mortal sinner** *n*

[1]**mortar** /ˈmawtə‖ˈmɔːtə/ *n* **1** a strong usu

bowl-shaped vessel (e g of stone) in which substances are pounded or ground with a pestle **2** a usu muzzle-loading artillery gun having a tube short in relation to its calibre, a low muzzle velocity, and a high trajectory

[2]**mortar** *n* a mixture of cement, lime, gypsum plaster, etc with sand and water, that hardens and is used to join bricks, stones, etc or for plastering

[3]**mortar** *vt* to plaster or make fast with mortar

'mortarˌboard /-ˌbawd‖-ˌbɔːd/ *n* **1** [1]HAWK 2 **2** an academic cap consisting of a close-fitting crown with a stiff flat square attached on top

[1]**mortgage** /'mawgij‖'mɔːgɪdʒ/ *n* **1** a transfer of the ownership of property (e g for security on a loan) on condition that the transfer becomes void on payment **2** the state of the property whose ownership is transferred by a mortgage [Middle French *morgage*, fr *mort* dead + *gage* pledge]

[2]**mortgage** *vt* **1** to transfer the ownership of (property) by a mortgage **2** to make subject to a claim or obligation

mortgagee /ˌmawgi'jee‖ˌmɔːgɪ'dʒiː/ *n* sby to whom property is mortgaged

mortgagor /'mawgijə, ˌmawgi'jaw‖'mɔːgɪdʒə, ˌmɔːgɪ'dʒɔː/ *also* **mortgager** /'mawgijə‖'mɔːgɪdʒə/ *n* sby who mortgages his/her property

mortician /maw'tish(ə)n‖mɔː'tɪʃ(ə)n/ *n, chiefly NAm* an undertaker

mortify /'mawtifie‖'mɔːtɪfaɪ/ *vt* **1** to subdue (e g bodily needs and desires), esp by abstinence or self-inflicted suffering **2** to subject to feelings of shame or acute embarrassment ~*vi* to become necrotic or gangrenous – **mortification** *n*

[1]**mortise** *also* **mortice** /'mawtis‖'mɔːtɪs/ *n* a usu rectangular cavity cut into a piece of material (e g wood) to receive a protrusion, esp a tenon, of another piece

[2]**mortise** *also* **mortice** *vt* **1** to join or fasten securely, specif by a mortise and tenon joint **2** to cut or make a mortise in

'mortise ˌlock *n* a lock that is designed to be fitted into a mortise in the edge of a door

[1]**mortuary** /'mawtyooəri, -chəri‖'mɔːtjʊərɪ, -tʃərɪ/ *n* a room or building in which dead bodies are kept before burial or cremation

[2]**mortuary** *adj* of death or the burial of the dead

mosaic /mə'zayik, moh-‖mə'zeɪk, məʊ-/ *n* **1** (a piece of) decorative work made from small pieces of different coloured material (e g glass or stone) inlaid to form pictures or patterns **2** sthg like a mosaic **3a** (a part of) an organism composed of cells with different genetic make-up; CHIMERA 3 **b** a virus disease of plants (e g tobacco) characterized esp by diffuse yellow and green mottling of the foliage – **mosaic** *adj*, **mosaicism** *n*, **mosaicist** *n*

Mosaic *adj* of Moses or the institutions or writings attributed to him

Moselle, Mosel /moh'zel‖məʊ'zel/ *n* a typically light-bodied white table wine made in the valley of the Moselle

mosey /'mohzi‖'məʊzɪ/ *vi, NAm* to saunter – infml

Moslem /'moozlim‖'mʊzlɪm/ *n or adj* (a) Muslim

mosque /mosk‖mɒsk/ *n* a building used for public worship by Muslims [Middle French *mosquee*, deriv of Arabic *masjid* temple, fr *sajada* to prostrate oneself]

mosquito /mo'skeetoh‖mɒ'skiːtəʊ/ *n, pl* **mosquitoes** *also* **mosquitos** any of numerous 2-winged flies with females that suck the blood of animals and often transmit diseases (e g malaria) to them – **mosquitoey** *adj*

mo'squito ˌnet *n* a net or screen for keeping out mosquitoes

moss /mos‖mɒs/ *n* **1** (any of various plants resembling) any of a class of primitive plants with small leafy stems bearing sex organs at the tip; *also* many of these plants growing together and covering a surface **2** *chiefly Scot* a (peat) bog – **mosslike** *adj*, **mossy** *adj*

[1]**most** /mohst‖məʊst/ *adj* **1** the majority of *<~ men>* **2** greatest in quantity or extent *<the ~ ability>*

[2]**most** *adv* **1** to the greatest degree or extent *<what I like ~ about him>* – often used with an adjective or adverb to form the superlative *<the ~ challenging job he ever had>* **2** very *<shall ~ certainly come>* *<her argument was ~ persuasive>*

[3]**most** *n, pl* **most** the greatest quantity, number, or amount *<it's the ~ I can do>* *<spends ~ of her time in bed>* *<~ became discouraged and left>* *<she made the ~ of the fine weather>* – **at most, at the most 1** as a maximum limit *<took him an hour* at most *to finish the job>* **2** AT BEST

[4]**most** *adv, archaic, dial, or NAm* almost

-most /-mohst‖-məʊst/ *suffix* (→ *adj*) **1** most; to the highest possible degree *<inner*most*>* **2** most towards *<top*most*>*

mostly /'mohstli‖'məʊstlɪ/ *adv* for the greatest part; mainly; *also* in most cases; usually

MOT *also* **MoT** *n* a compulsory annual roadworthiness test in Britain for motor vehicles older than a certain age [*M*inistry *O*f *T*ransport]

mote /moht‖məʊt/ *n* a small particle; *esp* a particle of dust suspended in the air

motel /moh'tel‖məʊ'tel/ *n* an establishment which provides accommodation and parking and in which the rooms are usu accessible from an outdoor parking area [blend of *motor* and *hotel*]

motet /moh'tet‖məʊ'tet/ *n* a choral composition on a sacred text

moth /moth‖mɒθ/ *n* **1** CLOTHES MOTH **2** a usu night-flying insect with feathery antennae and a stouter body and duller colouring than the butterflies

'mothˌball /-ˌbawl‖-ˌbɔːl/ *n* **1** a naphthalene or (formerly) camphor ball used to keep moths from clothing **2** *pl* a state of indefinitely long protective storage; *also* a state of having been rejected as of no further use or interest – **mothball** *vt*

'moth-ˌeaten *adj* **1** eaten into by moth larvae *<~ clothes>* **2a** very worn-out or shabby in appearance **b** antiquated, outmoded

[1]**mother** /'mudhə‖'mʌðə/ *n* **1a** a female parent **b** an old or elderly woman **2** a source, origin *<necessity is the ~ of invention>* – **motherhood** *n*, **motherless** *adj*

[2]**mother** *adj* **1a** of or being a mother **b** bearing the relation of a mother **2** derived (as if) from one's mother **3** acting as or providing a parental stock – used without reference to sex

[3]**mother** *vt* **1a** to give birth to **b** to give rise to; initiate, produce **2** to care for or protect like a mother – often derog

ˌ**Mother** ˌ**Carey's** ˈ**chicken** /ˈkeəriz‖ˈkeərɪz/ *n* STORM PETREL

ˌ**Mother** ˈ**Goose** ˌ**rhyme** *n, chiefly NAm* NURSERY RHYME

ˈ**mother-in-**ˌ**law** *n, pl* **mothers-in-law** the mother of one's spouse

ˈ**motherly** /-li‖-lɪ/ *adj* **1** (characteristic) of a mother **2** like a mother; maternal – **motherliness** *n*

ˌ**mother-of-**ˈ**pearl** *n* the hard pearly iridescent substance forming the inner layer of a mollusc shell

ˌ**mother su**ˈ**perior** *n, often cap M&S* the head of a religious community of women

ˈ**mother** ˌ**tongue** *n* **1** one's native language **2** a language from which another language derives

mothproof /ˈmoth,proohf‖ˈmɒθ,pruːf/ *vt or adj* (to make) resistant to attack by the larvae of (clothes) moths

motif /mohˈteef‖məʊˈtiːf/ *n* **1** a recurring element forming a theme in a work of art or literature; *esp* a dominant idea or central theme **2** a single or repeated design or colour **3** a leitmotiv

[1]**motion** /ˈmohsh(ə)n‖ˈməʊʃ(ə)n/ *n* **1a** a formal proposal made in a deliberative assembly **b** an application to a court or judge for an order, ruling, or direction **2a** an act, process, or instance of changing position; movement **b** an active or functioning state or condition **3a** an act or instance of moving the body or its parts; a gesture **b** *pl* actions, movements; *esp* merely simulated or mechanical actions – often in *go through the motions* **4** melodic change of pitch **5a** an evacuation of the bowels – usu pl with sing. meaning **b** the matter evacuated – **motional** *adj*, **motionless** *adj*, **motionlessness** *n*

[2]**motion** *vt* to direct by a gesture < ~ed *me to a seat*>

ˈ**motion** ˌ**picture** *n, chiefly NAm* a film, movie

motivate /ˈmohtivayt‖ˈməʊtɪveɪt/ *vt* to provide with a motive or incentive; impel < ~d *by fear*> – **motivation** *n*

[1]**motive** /ˈmohtiv‖ˈməʊtɪv/ *n* **1** a need, desire, etc that causes sby to act **2** a recurrent phrase or figure that is developed through the course of a musical composition – **motiveless** *adj*

[2]**motive** *adj* **1** moving or tending to move to action **2** of (the causing of) motion < ~ *energy*>

mot juste /ˌmoh ˈzhoohst ‖ˌməʊ ˈʒuːst (*Fr* mo ʒyst)/ *n, pl* **mots justes** /~/ the exactly right word or phrasing

[1]**motley** /ˈmotli‖ˈmɒtlɪ/ *adj* **1** multicoloured **2** composed of varied (disreputable or unsightly) elements

[2]**motley** *n* **1** a woollen fabric of mixed colours made in England between the 14th and 17th c **2** a haphazard mixture (of incompatible elements)

moto-cross /ˈmohtoh ˌkros‖ˈməʊtəʊ ˌkrɒs/ *n* the sport of racing motorcycles across country on a rugged usu hilly closed course

[1]**motor** /ˈmohtə‖ˈməʊtə/ *n* **1** sthg or sby that imparts motion **2** any of various power units that develop energy or impart motion: e g **2a** a small compact engine **b** INTERNAL-COMBUSTION ENGINE **c** a rotating machine that transforms electrical energy into mechanical energy **3** MOTOR VEHICLE; *esp* MOTOR CAR [Latin, one who moves fr *mot-*, *movēre* to move] – **motorless** *adj*

[2]**motor** *adj* **1a** causing or imparting motion **b** of or being a nerve (fibre) that conducts an impulse causing the movement of a muscle **c** of or involving muscular movement **2a** equipped with or driven by a motor **b** of or involving motor vehicles <*the* ~ *trade*>

[3]**motor** *vi* to travel by motor car; *esp* DRIVE 2

ˈ**motor** ˌ**bike** *n* a motorcycle – infml

ˈ**motor**ˌ**boat** /-ˌboht‖-ˌbəʊt/ *n* a usu small boat propelled by a motor

ˈ**motor**ˌ**cade** /-ˌkayd‖-ˌkeɪd/ *n* a procession of motor vehicles

ˈ**motor** ˌ**car** *n* a usu 4-wheeled motor vehicle designed for transporting a small number of people and typically propelled by an internal-combustion engine

ˈ**motor**ˌ**cycle** /-ˌsiekl‖-ˌsaɪkl/ *n* a 2-wheeled motor vehicle that can carry 1 or sometimes 2 people astride the engine – **motorcycle** *vi*, **motorcyclist** *n*

motorist /ˈmohtərist‖ˈməʊtərɪst/ *n* sby who drives a car

motor·ize, **-ise** /ˈmohtəriez‖ˈməʊtəraɪz/ *vt* **1** to equip (e g a vehicle) with a motor **2** to provide with motor-driven equipment (e g for transport) – **motorization** *n*

ˈ**motorman** /-mən‖-mən/ *n* a driver of a motor-driven vehicle (e g a bus or underground train)

ˈ**motor** ˌ**scooter** *n* a usu 2-wheeled motor vehicle having a seat so that the driver sits in front of rather than astride the engine

ˈ**motor** ˌ**vehicle** *also* **motor** *n* an automotive vehicle not operated on rails; *esp* one with rubber tyres for use on roads

ˈ**motor**ˌ**way** /-ˌway‖-ˌweɪ/ *n, Br* a major road designed for high-speed traffic that has separate carriageways for different directions and certain restrictions on the types of vehicle and driver allowed on it

[1]**mottle** /ˈmotl‖ˈmɒtl/ *n* **1** a coloured spot or blotch **2** an irregular pattern of spots or blotches on a surface – **mottled** *adj*

[2]**mottle** *vt* to mark with mottles

motto /ˈmotoh‖ˈmɒtəʊ/ *n, pl* **mottoes** *also* **mottos** **1** a sentence, phrase, or word inscribed on sthg as appropriate to or indicative of its character or use **2** a short expression of a guiding principle; a maxim **3** (a piece of paper printed with) a usu humorous or sentimental saying [Italian, fr Latin *muttum* grunt, fr *muttire* to mutter]

[1]**mould**, *NAm chiefly* **mold** /mohld‖məʊld/ *n* crumbling soft (humus-rich) soil suited to plant growth

[2]**mould**, *NAm chiefly* **mold** *n* **1** distinctive character or type <*need to recruit more men of his* ~> **2** the frame on or round which an object is

constructed **3** a cavity or form in which a substance (e g a jelly or a metal casting) is shaped **4** a moulding **5** a fixed pattern or form

[3]**mould,** *NAm chiefly* **mold** *vt* **1** to give shape to **2** to form in a mould **3** to exert a steady formative influence on **4** to fit closely to the contours of **5** to ornament with moulding or carving < ~ed *picture frames*>

[4]**mould,** *NAm chiefly* **mold** *n* (a fungus producing) an often woolly growth on the surface of damp or decaying organic matter

moulder, *NAm chiefly* **molder** /ˈmohldə‖ˈməʊldə/ *vi* to crumble into dust or decayed fragments, esp gradually

moulding /ˈmohlding‖ˈməʊldɪŋ/ *n* **1** an article produced by moulding **2** a decorative recessed or embossed surface **3** a decorative band or strip used for ornamentation or finishing (e g on a cornice)

mouldy /ˈmohldi‖ˈməʊldɪ/ *adj* **1** of, resembling, or covered with a mould-producing fungus **2** old and mouldering; fusty, crumbling **3a** miserable, nasty **b** stingy *USE* (*3*) infml

[1]**moult,** *NAm chiefly* **molt** /mohlt‖məʊlt/ *vb* to shed or cast off (hair, feathers, shell, horns, or an outer layer) periodically

[2]**moult,** *NAm chiefly* **molt** *n* moulting; *specif* ecdysis

mound /mownd‖maʊnd/ *n* **1a(1)** an artificial bank of earth or stones **a(2)** the slightly elevated ground on which a baseball pitcher stands **b** a knoll, hill **2** a heap, pile

[1]**mount** /mownt‖maʊnt/ *n* a high hill; a mountain – usu before a name

[2]**mount** *vi* **1** to increase in amount, extent, or degree **2** to rise, ascend **3** to get up on or into sthg above ground level; *esp* to seat oneself (e g on a horse) for riding ~ *vt* **1a** to go up; climb **b(1)** to seat or place oneself on <*the speaker* ~ed *the platform*> **b(2)** COVER 6a **2a** to lift up; raise, erect **b** to place (e g artillery) in position **c** to initiate and carry out (e g an assault or strike) **3a** to set (sby) on a means of conveyance < ~ed *his little daughter on a donkey*> **b** to provide with animals for riding **4** to station for defence or observation or as an escort < ~ *guard over the palace*> **5a** to attach to a support **b** to arrange or assemble for use or display **6a** to prepare (e g a specimen) for examination or display **b** to organize and present for public viewing or performance; stage < ~ed *a sumptuous opera*>

[3]**mount** *n* **1** an opportunity to ride a horse, esp in a race **2** sthg on which sby or sthg is mounted: e g **2a** the material (e g cardboard) on which a picture is mounted **b** a jewellery setting **c** an attachment for an accessory **d** a hinge, card, etc for mounting a stamp in a stamp collection **3** a horse for riding

mountain /ˈmownt(ə)n, -tayn‖ˈmaʊnt(ə)n, -teɪn/ *n* **1** a landmass that projects conspicuously above its surroundings and is higher than a hill **2a** a vast amount or quantity – often pl with sing meaning **b** a supply, esp of a specified usu agricultural commodity, in excess of demand <*a butter* ~>

ˌ**mountain** ˈ**ash** *n* a rowan or related tree of the rose family usu with small red fruits

mountaineering /ˌmowntəˈniəring‖ˌmaʊntəˈnɪərɪŋ/ *n* the pastime or technique of climbing mountains and rock faces – **mountaineer** *n*

mountain lion *n* a puma

mountainous /ˈmownt(ə)nəs‖ˈmaʊnt(ə)nəs/ *adj* **1** containing many mountains **2** resembling a mountain; huge – **mountainously** *adv*

mountebank /ˈmowntiˌbangk‖ˈmaʊntɪˌbæŋk/ *n* **1** sby who sells quack medicines from a platform **2** a charlatan [Italian *montimbanco*, fr *montare* to mount + *in* in, on + *banco, banca* bench] – **mountebankery** *n*

Mountie /ˈmownti‖ˈmaʊntɪ/ *n* a member of the Royal Canadian Mounted Police

mourn /mawn‖mɔːn/ *vi* to feel or express (e g in a conventional manner) grief or sorrow, esp for a death ~ *vt* to feel or express grief or sorrow for – **mourner** *n*

ˈ**mournful** /-f(ə)l‖-f(ə)l/ *adj* expressing, causing, or filled with sorrow – **mournfully** *adv*, **mournfulness** *n*

mourning /ˈmawning‖ˈmɔːnɪŋ/ *n* **1** the act or state of one who mourns **2a** an outward sign (e g black clothes or an armband) of grief for a person's death <*is wearing* ~> **b** a period of time during which signs of grief are shown

[1]**mouse** /mows‖maʊs/ *n, pl* **mice** /mies‖maɪs/ **1** any of numerous small rodents with a pointed snout, rather small ears, and slender tail **2** a timid person **3** a small box connected to a computer which, when moved across a table or desk, causes a cursor to move across a VDU screen and enables the operator to execute commands or change data

[2]**mouse** *vi* to hunt for mice ~*vt, chiefly NAm* to search for carefully – usu + *out* – **mouser** *n*

ˈ**mouse**ˌ**trap** /-ˌtrap‖-ˌtræp/ *n* a trap for mice

moussaka, **mousaka** /moohˈsahkə‖muːˈsɑːkə/ *n* a Greek dish consisting of layers of minced meat (e g lamb), aubergine or potato, tomato, and cheese with cheese or savoury custard topping

mousse /moohs‖muːs/ *n* a light sweet or savoury cold dish usu containing cream, gelatin, and whipped egg whites

moustache, *NAm chiefly* **mustache** /məˈstahsh, məˈstash‖məˈstɑːʃ, məˈstæʃ/ *n* **1** the hair growing or allowed to grow on sby's upper lip **2** hair or bristles round the mouth of a mammal

mousy, **mousey** /ˈmowsi‖ˈmaʊsɪ/ *adj* **1** of or resembling a mouse: e g **1a** quiet, stealthy **b** timid; *also* colourless **2** *of hair* light greyish brown

[1]**mouth** /mowth‖maʊθ/ *n, pl* **mouths** /mowdhz‖maʊðz/ **1a** the opening through which food passes into an animal's body; *also* the cavity in the head of the typical vertebrate animal bounded externally by the lips that encloses the tongue, gums, and teeth **b** a grimace made with the lips **c** a horse's response to pressure on the bit **d** an individual, esp a child, requiring food <*too many* ~s *to feed*> **2a** utterance <*finally gave* ~ *to his feelings*> **b** MOUTHPIECE 3 **3** sthg like a mouth, esp in affording entrance or exit: e g **3a** the place where a river enters a sea, lake, etc **b** the opening of a cave, volcano, etc **c** the opening of a container **4a** a tendency to talk too

much **b** impertinent language *USE* (*4*) infml – **mouthed** *adj*, **mouthlike** *adj* – **down in the mouth** dejected, sulky

[2]**mouth** /mowdh‖maʊð/ *vt* **1** to utter pompously **2** to repeat without comprehension or sincerity **3** to form (words) soundlessly with the lips ~*vi* to talk pompously

mouthful /ˈmowthf(ə)l‖ˈmaʊθf(ə)l/ *n* **1a** a quantity that fills the mouth **b** the amount (of food) put into the mouth at 1 time **2** a small quantity **3a** a word or phrase that is very long or difficult to pronounce **b** *chiefly NAm* a very apt or significant comment or statement – chiefly in *say a mouthful USE* (*3*) infml

ˈ**mouth ˌorgan** *n* a harmonica

ˈ**mouthˌpiece** /-ˌpees‖-ˌpiːs/ *n* **1** sthg placed at or forming a mouth **2** a part (e g of a musical instrument or a telephone) that goes in the mouth or is put next to the mouth **3** sby or sthg that expresses or interprets another's views

ˈ**mouth-ˌwatering** *adj* stimulating or appealing to the appetite; appetizing – **mouth-wateringly** *adv*

movable, moveable /ˈmoohvəbl‖ˈmuːvəbl/ *n or adj* (property) able to be removed – often used to distinguish personal property from buildings, land, etc; usu pl

ˌ**movable** ˈ**feast** *n* an annual church festival (e g Easter) not celebrated on the same date each year

[1]**move** /moohv‖muːv/ *vi* **1a(1)** to go or pass with a continuous motion **a(2)** to proceed or progress towards a (specified) place or condition <moving *up the executive ladder*> – often + *on* <~ *on to the next item*> **b** to go away <*it's time we were* moving> **c(1)** to transfer a piece in a board game (e g in chess) from one position to another <*it's your turn to* ~> **c(2)** *of a piece in board games* to travel or be capable of travelling to another position <*the bishop* ~s *diagonally*> **d(1)** to change one's residence **d(2)** to change one's (official) location **2** to pass one's life in a specified environment <~s *in fashionable circles*> **3** to change position or posture **4** to take action; act **5** to make a formal request, application, or appeal **6** to change hands by being sold or rented – often + *quickly* or *slowly* **7** *of the bowels* to evacuate **8a** to operate or function, esp mechanically **b** to show marked activity or speed – infml <*after a brief lull things really began to* ~> ~ *vt* **1a** to change the place or position of **b** to transfer (e g a piece in chess) from one position to another **2a(1)** to cause to go or pass with a continuous motion **a(2)** to take (furniture and possessions) from one residence or location to another **b** to cause to operate or function <*this button* ~s *the whole machine*> **3** to cause (the body or part of the body) to change position or posture **4** to prompt to action **5** to affect in such a way as to lead to a show of emotion or of a specified emotion **6** to propose formally in a deliberative assembly **7** to cause (the bowels) to evacuate – **mover** *n*

[2]**move** *n* **1a** the act of moving a piece (e g in chess) **b** the turn of a player to move **2a** a step taken so as to gain an objective **b** a movement **c** a change of residence or official location – **on the move 1** in a state of moving about from place to place <*a salesman is constantly* on the move> **2** in a state of moving ahead or making progress <*said that civilization is always* on the move>

move in *vi* **1** to take up occupation of a dwelling or place of work **2** to advance aggressively in order to gain control – often + *on* <*police* moved in *on the criminals hiding in the house*>

ˈ**movement** /-mənt‖-mənt/ *n* **1a** the act or process of moving; *esp* change of place, position, or posture **b** a particular instance or manner of moving **c** an action, activity – usu pl with sing. meaning <*troop* ~s> **2a** a trend, specif in prices **b** an organized effort to promote an end <*the civil rights* ~> **3** the moving parts of a mechanism that transmit motion **4** a unit or division having its own key, rhythmic structure, and themes and forming a separate part of an extended musical composition **5a** the development of the action in a work of literature **b** the quality of a book, play, etc of having a quickly moving plot **6** MOTION 5

move on *vi* to change one's residence or location for another ~*vt* to cause to depart <*the squatters were* moved on *by the police*>

move out *vi* to leave a dwelling or place of work

move over *vi* to make room

movie /ˈmoohvi‖ˈmuːvɪ/ *n* FILM 3a, b

moving /ˈmoohving‖ˈmuːvɪŋ/ *adj* **1a** marked by or capable of movement **b** of a change of residence **2a** producing or transferring motion or action <*the* ~ *spirit behind the scheme*> **b** evoking a deep emotional response – **movingly** *adv*

ˌ**moving** ˈ**picture** *n*, *chiefly NAm* a film, movie

[1]**mow** /mow‖maʊ/ *n* **1** a stack of hay, grain, fodder, etc (in a barn) **2** the part of a barn where hay or straw is stored

[2]**mow** /moh‖məʊ/ *vb* **mowed; mowed, mown** /mohn‖məʊn/ *vt* **1** to cut down (a crop, esp grass) **2** to cut down the standing herbage, esp grass, of (e g a field) ~*vi* to cut down standing herbage, esp grass – **mower** *n*

mow down *vt* **1** to kill, destroy, or knock down, esp in great numbers or mercilessly **2** to overcome swiftly and decisively; rout

Mr /ˈmistə‖ˈmɪstə/ *n, pl* **Messrs** /ˈmesəz‖ˈmesəz/ **1** – used as a conventional title of courtesy before a man's surname, except when usage requires the substitution of a title of rank or an honorary or professional title **2** – used in direct address before a man's title of office <*may I ask one more question,* ~ *Chairman?*>

Mrs /ˈmisiz‖ˈmɪsɪz/ *n, pl* **Mesdames** /may ˈdahm‖meɪˈdɑːm/ **1** – used as a conventional title of courtesy before a married woman's surname, except when usage requires the substitution of a title of rank or an honorary or professional title <*spoke to* ~ *Smith*> **2** a wife <*took the* ~ *along to the pub*> – infml

Ms /məz, miz‖məz, mɪz/ *n* – used instead of Mrs or Miss, esp when marital status is unknown or irrelevant

[1]**much** /much‖mʌtʃ/ *adj* **more** /maw‖mɔː/; **most** /mohst‖məʊst/ **1** great in quantity or extent

<not ~ money> <nothing ~ to do> <how ~ milk is there?> **2** excessive, immoderate *<it's a bit ~ having to work so late>* – **too much 1** wonderful, exciting **2** terrible, awful

[2]**much** *adv* **more; most 1a(1)** to a great degree or extent; considerably *<~ happier> <don't ~ like it> <~ to my surprise> <how ~ did it cost?>* **a(2)** very – with verbal adjectives *<was ~ amused>* **b** frequently, often *<~ married>* **c** by far *<~ the fatter> <I'd ~ rather not> <~ the brightest student>* **2** nearly, approximately *<looks ~ the way his father did>* – **as much 1** the same quantity **2** that, so *<I thought* as much*>* – **much less** and certainly not *<can't even walk,* much less *run>*

[3]**much** *n* **1** a great quantity, amount, or part *<gave away ~> <~ of the night> <got too ~ to do>* **2** sthg considerable or impressive *<wasn't ~ to look at> <the film wasn't up to ~> <I don't think ~ of that idea>* **3** a relative quantity or part *<I'll say this ~ for him>* – **too much for 1** more than a match for **2** beyond the endurance of

muchness /ˈmuchnis‖ˈmʌtʃnɪs/ *n* – **much of a muchness** very much the same

mucilage /ˈmyoohsilij‖ˈmjuːsɪlɪdʒ/ *n* a gelatinous substance obtained esp from seaweeds and similar to plant gums

mucilaginous /ˌmyoohsiˈlajinəs‖ˌmjuːsɪˈlædʒɪnəs/ *adj* **1** sticky, viscid **2** of, full of, or secreting mucilage

muck /muk‖mʌk/ *n* **1** soft moist farmyard manure **2** slimy dirt or filth **3** mire, mud **4a** a worthless or useless thing; rubbish – infml **b** *Br* – used in *Lord Muck* and *Lady Muck* to designate an arrogantly patronizing person – **mucky** *adj*

muck about *vb, chiefly Br* MESS ABOUT – infml

muck in *vi, Br* to share or join in esp a task *<all* mucked in *together>*; *also* to share sleeping accommodation – infml

muck out *vi* to remove manure or filth, esp from an animal's quarters ~*vt* to clear (e g a stable) of manure

ˈ**muckˌrake** /-ˌrayk‖-ˌreɪk/ *vi* to search out and publicly expose real or apparent misconduct of prominent individuals – **muckraker** *n*

muck up *vt, chiefly Br* **1** to dirty (as if) with muck; soil **2** to bungle, spoil *USE* infml

mucous /ˈmyoohkəs‖ˈmjuːkəs/ *adj* of, like, secreting, or covered (as if) with mucus

ˌ**mucous** ˈ**membrane** /ˈmembrayn‖ˈmembreɪn/ *n* a membrane rich in mucous glands, specif lining body passages and cavities (e g the mouth) with openings to the exterior

mucus /ˈmyoohkəs‖ˈmjuːkəs/ *n* a thick slippery secretion produced by mucous membranes (e g in the nose) which it moistens and protects

mud /mud‖mʌd/ *n* **1** (a sticky mixture of a solid and a liquid resembling) soft wet earth **2** abusive and malicious remarks or charges

[1]**muddle** /ˈmudl‖ˈmʌdl/ *vt* **1** to stupefy, esp with alcohol **2** to mix confusedly in one's mind – often + *up* **3** to cause confusion to ~*vi* to proceed or get along in a confused aimless way – + *along* or *on* – **muddler** *n*

[2]**muddle** *n* **1** a state of (mental) confusion **2** a confused mess

ˌ**muddleˈheaded** /-ˈhedid‖-ˈhedɪd/ *adj* **1** mentally confused **2** inept, bungling – **muddleheadedness** *n*

muddle through *vi* to succeed in spite of incompetence or lack of method and planning

[1]**muddy** /ˈmudi‖ˈmʌdɪ/ *adj* **1** lacking in clarity or brightness **2** obscure in meaning; muddled, confused – **muddily** *adv*, **muddiness** *n*

[2]**muddy** *vt* to make cloudy, dull, or confused

ˈ**mudˌflat** /-ˌflat‖-ˌflæt/ *n* a muddy area of ground covered at high tide – often pl with sing. meaning

ˈ**mudˌguard** /-ˌgahd‖-ˌgɑːd/ *n* a metal or plastic guard over the wheel of a bicycle, motorcycle, etc to deflect or catch mud

ˈ**mudˌpack** /-ˌpak‖-ˌpæk/ *n* a face-pack containing fuller's earth

muesli /ˈm(y)oohzli, ˈmwayzli‖ˈm(j)uːzlɪ, ˈmweɪzlɪ/ *n* a (breakfast) dish of Swiss origin consisting of rolled oats, dried fruit, nuts, grated apple, etc

muezzin /moohˈezin‖muːˈezɪn/ *n* a mosque official who calls the faithful to prayer at fixed daily times, usu from a minaret

[1]**muff** /muf‖mʌf/ *n* a warm cylindrical wrap in which both hands are placed

[2]**muff** *n* **1** a failure to hold a ball in attempting a catch **2** a timid awkward person, esp in sports – infml

[3]**muff** *vt* **1** to handle awkwardly; bungle **2** to fail to hold (a ball) when attempting a catch

muffin /ˈmufin‖ˈmʌfɪn/ *n* a light round yeast-leavened bun usu served hot

[1]**muffle** /ˈmufl‖ˈmʌfl/ *vt* **1** to wrap up so as to conceal or protect **2a** to wrap or pad with sthg to dull the sound **b** to deaden the sound of **3** to keep down; suppress <~d *laughter*>

[2]**muffle** *n* a chamber in a furnace or kiln where articles can be heated without direct contact with flames or combustion products

muffler /ˈmuflə‖ˈmʌflə/ *n* **1** a warm scarf worn round the neck **2** *NAm* a silencer for a motor vehicle

[1]**mufti** /ˈmufti‖ˈmʌftɪ/ *n* a professional Muslim jurist

[2]**mufti** *n* civilian or ordinary clothes worn by one who is usually in uniform

[1]**mug** /mug‖mʌg/ *n* **1** a large usu cylindrical drinking cup **2** the face or mouth of sby **3** *Br* sby easily deceived; a sucker *USE* (*2 & 3*) infml

[2]**mug** *vt* **-gg-** to assault, esp in the street with intent to rob – **mugger** *n*

muggins /ˈmuginz‖ˈmʌgɪnz/ *n, pl* **mugginses, muggins** a fool, simpleton – slang

muggy /ˈmugi‖ˈmʌgɪ/ *adj, of weather* warm, damp, and close – **muggily** *adv*, **mugginess** *n*

ˈ**mug's** ˌ**game** *n, chiefly Br* a profitless activity – infml

mug up *vb, Br* to study hard – infml

ˈ**mugˌwump** /-ˌwump‖-ˌwʌmp/ *n, chiefly NAm* an independent in politics

Muhammadan /məˈhamid(ə)n‖məˈhæmɪd(ə)n/ *adj* of Muhammad or Islam – **Muhammadan** *n*, **Muhammadanism** *n*

mulatto /myoohˈlatoh‖mjuːˈlætəʊ/ *n, pl* **mulattoes, mulattos** the first-generation offspring of a Negro and a white person

mulberry /'mulb(ə)ri‖'mʌlb(ə)rɪ/ *n* (any of a genus of trees of the fig family bearing) an edible usu purple multiple fruit

mulch /mulch‖mʌltʃ/ *n* a protective covering (e g of compost) spread on the ground to control weeds, enrich the soil, etc – **mulch** *vt*

[1]**mulct** /mulkt‖mʌlkt/ *n* a fine, penalty

[2]**mulct** *vt* **1** to punish by a fine **2a** to swindle **b** to obtain by swindling

[1]**mule** /myoohl‖mjuːl/ *n* **1** the offspring of a mating between a (female) horse and an ass **2** a very stubborn person **3** a machine for simultaneously drawing and twisting fibre into yarn or thread and winding it onto spindles

[2]**mule** *n* a backless shoe or slipper

muleteer /ˌmyoohlə'tiə‖ˌmjuːlə'tɪə/ *n* sby who drives mules

mulish /'myoohlish‖'mjuːlɪʃ/ *adj* unreasonably and inflexibly obstinate – **mulishly** *adv*, **mulishness** *n*

[1]**mull** /mul‖mʌl/ *vt* to heat, sweeten, and flavour (e g wine or beer) with spices

[2]**mull** *n* crumbly soil humus forming a layer of mixed organic matter and mineral soil and merging into the underlying mineral soil

[3]**mull** *n* a headland or peninsula in Scotland

mullet /'mulit‖'mʌlɪt/ *n* any of a family of **a** food fishes with elongated bodies **b** red or golden fishes with 2 barbels on the chin

mulligatawny /ˌmuligə'tawni‖ˌmʌlɪgə'tɔːnɪ/ *n* a rich meat soup of Indian origin seasoned with curry [Tamil *miḷakutaṇṇi*, a strongly seasoned soup, fr *miḷaku* pepper + *taṇṇi* water]

mullion /'muli·ən‖'mʌlɪən/ *n* a slender vertical bar placed esp between panes or panels (e g of windows or doors) – **mullion** *vt*

mull over *vt* to consider at length

multi- /multi-‖mʌltɪ-/ *comb form* **1a** many; multiple; much <multi-*storey*> **b** more than 2 <multi*lateral*> **c** more than 1 <multi*parous*> **2** many times over <multi*millionaire*>

'multiˌcoloured /-ˌkuləd‖-ˌkʌləd/ *adj* of various colours

ˌmulti'farious /-'feəri·əs‖-'feərɪəs/ *adj* having or occurring in great variety; diverse – **multifariously** *adv*, **multifariousness** *n*

'multiˌform /-ˌfawm‖-ˌfɔːm/ *adj* having many forms or appearances – **multiformity** *n*

ˌmulti'lateral /-'lat(ə)rəl‖-'læt(ə)rəl/ *adj* **1** having many sides **2** participated in by more than 2 parties **3** *of a school* divided into more than 2 separately organized sides offering different curricula – **multilaterally** *adv*

ˌmulti'lingual /-'ling·gwəl‖-'lɪŋgwəl/ *adj* **1** POLYGLOT 2 **2** using or able to use several languages – **multilingualism** *n*, **multilingually** *adv*

ˌmultiˌmillio'naire /-ˌmilyə'neə‖-ˌmɪljə'neə/ *n* sby whose wealth is estimated at many millions of money units

multinational /-'nash(ə)nl‖-'næʃ(ə)nl/ *adj* **1** of or involving more than 2 nations **2** *of a company* having divisions in more than 2 countries – **multinational** *n*

[1]**multiple** /'multipl‖'mʌltɪpl/ *adj* **1** consisting of, including, or involving more than 1 **2** many, manifold <~ *achievements*> **3** shared by many <~ *ownership*> **4** *of a fruit* formed by coalescence of the ripening ovaries of several flowers

[2]**multiple** *n* **1** the product of a quantity by an integer <*35 is a ~ of 7*> **2 multiple, multiple store** *chiefly Br* CHAIN STORE

ˌmultiple scle'rosis *n* progressively developing partial or complete paralysis and jerking muscle tremor resulting from the formation of patches of hardened nerve tissue in nerves of the brain and spinal cord that have lost their myelin

[1]**multiplex** /'multiˌpleks‖'mʌltɪˌpleks/ *adj* **1** manifold, multiple **2** being or relating to a system allowing several messages to be transmitted simultaneously by the same circuit or channel

[2]**multiplex** *vb* to send (messages or signals) by a multiplex system – **multiplexer, multiplexor** *n*

multiplication /ˌmultipli'kaysh(ə)n‖ˌmʌltɪplɪ'keɪʃ(ə)n/ *n* **1** multiplying or being multiplied **2** a mathematical operation that at its simplest is an abbreviated process of adding an integer to itself a specified number of times and that is extended to other numbers in accordance with laws that are valid for integers – **multiplicative** *adj*, **multiplicatively** *adv*

multiplicity /ˌmulti'plisəti‖ˌmʌltɪ'plɪsətɪ/ *n* **1** the quality or state of being multiple or various **2** a great number <*a ~ of errors*>

multiply /'multiplie‖'mʌltɪplaɪ/ *vt* **1** to increase in number, esp greatly or in multiples; augment **2a** to combine by multiplication <~ *7 and 8*> **b** to combine with (another number) by multiplication – usu pass <*7* multiplied *by 8 is 56*> ~ *vi* **1a** to become greater in number; spread **b** to breed or propagate **2** to perform multiplication – **multipliable** *adj*

ˌmulti'racial /-'raysh(ə)l‖-'reɪʃ(ə)l/ *adj* composed of, involving, or representing various races – **multiracialism** *n*

ˌmulti-'storey /-'stawri‖-'stɔːrɪ/ *n or adj* (a building, esp a car park) having several storeys

multitude /'multityoohd‖'mʌltɪtjuːd/ *n* **1** the state of being many **2** a great number; a host **3** a crowd – chiefly fml **4** *the* populace, masses

multitudinous /ˌmulti'tyoohdinəs‖ˌmʌltɪ'tjuːdɪnəs/ *adj* **1** comprising a multitude of individuals; populous **2** existing in a great multitude **3** existing in or consisting of innumerable elements or aspects *USE* fml – **multitudinously** *adv*, **multitudinousness** *n*

[1]**mum** /mum‖mʌm/ *adj* silent <*keep* ~> – infml

[2]**mum** *n*, *chiefly Br* MOTHER 1a – infml

mumble /'mumbl‖'mʌmbl/ *vb* to say (words) in an inarticulate usu subdued voice – **mumble** *n*, **mumbler** *n*

mumbo jumbo /ˌmumboh 'jumboh‖ˌmʌmbəʊ 'dʒʌmbəʊ/ *n* **1** elaborate but meaningless ritual **2** involved activity or language that obscures and confuses

mummery /'muməri‖'mʌmərɪ/ *n* **1** a performance of mumming **2** an absurd or pretentious ceremony or performance

mummify /'mumifie‖'mʌmɪfaɪ/ *vt* **1** to embalm and dry (the body of an animal or human being) **2** to cause to dry up and shrivel ~*vi* to dry up and shrivel like a mummy – **mummification** *n*

mumming /ˈmuming‖ˈmʌmɪŋ/ *n* **1** the practice of performing in a traditional pantomime **2** the custom of going about merrymaking in disguise during festivals – **mummer** *n*

[1]**mummy** /ˈmumi‖ˈmʌmɪ/ *n* **1** a body embalmed for burial in the manner of the ancient Egyptians **2** an unusually well-preserved dead body [Middle French *momie* powdered parts of a mummified body used as a drug, deriv of Arabic *mūmiyah* bitumen, embalmed body, fr Persian *mūm* wax]

[2]**mummy** *n, chiefly Br* MOTHER 1a – used esp by or to children [baby talk, variant of *mama, mamma*]

mumps /mumps‖mʌmps/ *n pl but sing or pl in constr* an infectious virus disease marked by gross swelling of esp the parotid glands

munch /munch‖mʌntʃ/ *vb* to chew (food) with a crunching sound and visible movement of the jaws – **muncher** *n*

mundane /munˈdayn‖mʌnˈdeɪn/ *adj* **1** (characteristic) of this world in contrast to heaven **2** practical and ordinary, esp to the point of dull familiarity – **mundanely** *adv*, **mundaneness** *n*

municipal /myoohˈnisipl‖mjuːˈnɪsɪpl/ *adj* **1a** of a municipality **b** having local self-government **2** restricted to 1 locality – **municipally** *adv*

municipality /myooh͵nisiˈpaləti‖mjuː͵nɪsɪˈpæləti/ *n* (the governing body of) a primarily urban political unit having corporate status and some self-government

munificent /myoohˈnifis(ə)nt‖mjuːˈnɪfɪs(ə)nt/ *adj* **1** giving or bestowing with great generosity **2** characterized by great liberality *USE* fml – **munificence** *n*, **munificently** *adv*

muniment /ˈmyoohnimənt‖ˈmjuːnɪmənt/ *n* a document kept as evidence of title or privilege – usu pl

munition /myoohˈnish(ə)n‖mjuːˈnɪʃ(ə)n/ *n* armament, ammunition – usu pl with sing. meaning – **munition** *vt*

[1]**mural** /ˈmyooərəl‖ˈmjʊərəl/ *adj* of, resembling, or applied to a wall

[2]**mural** *n* a mural work of art (e g a painting) – **muralist** *n*

[1]**murder** /ˈmuhdə‖ˈmɜːdə/ *n* **1** the crime of unlawfully and intentionally killing sby **2** sthg very difficult, dangerous, or disagreeable – infml <*it was ~ trying to park*>

[2]**murder** *vt* **1** to kill (sby) unlawfully and intentionally **2** to slaughter brutally **3a** to put an end to **b** to mutilate, mangle <~ *a sonata*> ~*vi* to commit murder – **murderer,** *fem* **murderess** *n*

murderous /ˈmuhd(ə)rəs‖ˈmɜːd(ə)rəs/ *adj* **1a** having the purpose or capability of murder **b** characterized by or causing murder or bloodshed **2** capable of overwhelming <~ *heat*> – **murderously** *adv*, **murderousness** *n*

murk /muhk‖mɜːk/ *n* gloom, darkness; *also* fog

murky /ˈmuhki‖ˈmɜːkɪ/ *adj* dark and gloomy – **murkily** *adv*, **murkiness** *n*

[1]**murmur** /ˈmuhmə‖ˈmɜːmə/ *n* **1** a half-suppressed or muttered complaint **2a** a low indistinct (continuous) sound **b** a subdued or gentle utterance **3** an atypical sound of the heart indicating an abnormality

[2]**murmur** *vi* **1** to make a murmur **2** to complain, grumble ~*vt* to say in a murmur <~ed *an apology for being late*> – **murmurer** *n*

muscat /ˈmuskət, -kat‖ˈmʌskət, -kæt/ *n* any of several cultivated grapes used in making wine and raisins

muscatel /͵muskəˈtel‖͵mʌskəˈtel/ *n* **1** a sweet dessert wine made from muscat grapes **2** a raisin made from muscat grapes

muscle /ˈmusl‖ˈmʌsl/ *n* **1** (an organ that moves a body part, consisting of) a tissue made of modified elongated cells that contract when stimulated to produce motion **2** muscular strength; brawn [Middle French, fr Latin *musculus*, lit., small mouse, fr *mus* mouse] – **muscled** *adj*

ˈ**muscle-͵bound** /-͵bownd‖-͵baʊnd/ *adj* **1** having enlarged muscles with impaired elasticity, often as a result of excessive exercise **2** lacking flexibility; rigid

muscle in *vi* to interfere forcibly – infml; often + *on*

Muscovite /ˈmuskə͵viet‖ˈmʌskə͵vaɪt/ *n* a native or inhabitant of (the ancient principality of) Moscow – **Muscovite** *adj*

muscular /ˈmuskyoolə‖ˈmʌskjʊlə/ *adj* **1a** of, constituting, or performed by muscle or the muscles **b** having well-developed musculature **2** having strength of expression or character; vigorous – **muscularly** *adv*, **muscularity** *n*

͵**muscular** ˈ**dystrophy** *n* progressive wasting of muscles occurring as a hereditary disease

[1]**muse** /myoohz‖mjuːz/ *vi* to become absorbed in thought; *esp* to engage in daydreaming ~*vt* to think or say reflectively – **muser** *n*

[2]**muse** *n* **1** *cap* any of the 9 sister goddesses in Greek mythology who were the patrons of the arts and sciences **2** a source of inspiration; *esp* a woman who influences a creative artist

museum /myoohˈzee·əm‖mjuːˈziːəm/ *n* an institution devoted to the acquiring, care, study, and display of objects of interest or value; *also* a place exhibiting such objects

muˈseum ͵piece *n* **1** an object interesting enough for a museum to display **2** sthg absurdly old-fashioned

mush /mush‖mʌʃ/ *n* **1** a soft mass of semiliquid material **2** mawkish sentimentality

[1]**mushroom** /ˈmushroohm, -room‖ˈmʌʃruːm, -rʊm/ *n* **1** the enlarged, esp edible, fleshy fruiting body of a class of fungus, consisting typically of a stem bearing a flattened cap **2** a fungus

[2]**mushroom** *vi* **1** to spring up suddenly or multiply rapidly **2** to flatten at the end on impact **3** to pick wild mushrooms <*go* ~ing>

mushy /ˈmushi‖ˈmʌʃɪ/ *adj* **1** having the consistency of mush **2** mawkishly sentimental – **mushily** *adv*, **mushiness** *n*

music /ˈmyoohzik‖ˈmjuːzɪk/ *n* **1a** the science or art of ordering tones or sounds in succession and combination to produce a composition having unity and continuity **b** vocal, instrumental, or mechanical sounds having rhythm, melody, or harmony **2** an agreeable sound **3** the score of a musical composition set down on paper

[1]**musical** /ˈmyoohzikl‖ˈmjuːzɪkl/ *adj* **1** having the pleasing harmonious qualities of music **2**

having an interest in or talent for music **3** set to or accompanied by music **4** of music, musicians, or music lovers – **musically** *adv*, **musicality** *n*

[2]**musical** *n* a film or theatrical production that consists of songs, dances, and dialogue based on a unifying plot

'**musical ,box**, *chiefly NAm* **music box** *n* a container enclosing an apparatus that reproduces music mechanically when activated

,**musical 'chairs** *n pl but sing in constr* a game in which players march to music round a row of chairs numbering 1 less than the players and scramble for seats when the music stops

'**music ,hall** *n* (a theatre formerly presenting) entertainments consisting of a variety of unrelated acts (e g acrobats, comedians, or singers)

musician /myooh'zish(ə)n‖mju:'zɪʃ(ə)n/ *n* a composer, conductor, or performer of music; *esp* an instrumentalist – **musicianship** *n*

musk /musk‖mʌsk/ *n* **1a** (a synthetic substitute for) a substance with a penetrating persistent smell that is obtained from a gland of the male musk deer and used as a perfume fixative; *also* a similar substance from another animal **b** the odour of musk **2** any of various plants with musky smells – **musky** *adj*

'**musk ,deer** *n* a small heavy-limbed hornless deer of central Asia, the male of which produces musk

musket /'muskit‖'mʌskɪt/ *n* a heavy large-calibre shoulder firearm with a smooth bore

musketeer /,muskə'tiə‖,mʌskə'tɪə/ *n* a soldier armed with a musket

musketry /'muskitri‖'mʌskɪtrɪ/ *n* **1** (troops armed with) muskets **2** musket fire

muskmelon /'musk,melən‖'mʌsk,melən/ *n* (an Asiatic plant that bears) a usu sweet musky-smelling edible melon

'**musk,rat** /-,rat‖-,ræt/ *n* an aquatic rodent of N America with a long scaly tail and webbed hind feet

'**musk ,rose** *n* a rose of the Mediterranean region with musky flowers

Muslim /'moozlim, 'muz-‖'mʊzlɪm, 'mʌz-/ *n* an adherent of Islam [Arabic *muslim*, lit., one who surrenders (to God)] – **Muslim** *adj*

muslin /'muzlin‖'mʌzlɪn/ *n* a plain-woven sheer to coarse cotton fabric [French *mousseline*, fr Italian *mussolina*, fr Arabic *mawṣilīy* of Mosul, fr al-*Mawṣil* Mosul, city in Iraq]

musquash /'muskwosh‖'mʌskwɒʃ/ *n* (the dark glossy brown fur or pelt of) the muskrat

[1]**muss** /mus‖mʌs/ *n, NAm* a state of disorder; mess – infml – **mussy** *adj*

[2]**muss** *vt, NAm* to make untidy; disarrange, dishevel – infml

mussel /'musl‖'mʌsl/ *n* **1** a marine bivalve mollusc with a dark elongated shell **2** a freshwater bivalve mollusc whose shell has a lustrous mother-of-pearl lining

[1]**must** /məs(t)‖məs(t); *strong* must‖mʌst/ *verbal auxiliary, pres & past all persons* **must** **1a** be commanded or requested to <*you* ~ *stop*> **b** certainly should; ought by all means to <*I* ~ *read that book*> <*we* mustn't *despair*> **2** be compelled by physical, social, or legal necessity to <*man* ~ *eat to live*> <*I* ~ *say you're looking much better*>; be required by need or purpose to <*we* ~ *hurry if we want to catch the bus*> – past often replaced by *had to* except in reported speech; used in the negative to express the idea of prohibition <*we* ~ *not park here*> **3** [1]WILL 6 <*if you* ~ *go at least wait till morning*>; *esp* be unreasonably or perversely compelled to <*why* ~ *you be so stubborn?*> <*in spite of my advice, she* ~ *go and do the opposite*> **4** be logically inferred or supposed to <*it* ~ *be time*> <*they* mustn't *have arrived*> **5** was presumably certain to; was or were bound to <*if he really was there I* ~ *have seen him*>

[2]**must** /must‖mʌst/ *n* an essential or prerequisite

[3]**must** /must‖mʌst/ *n* grape juice before and during fermentation

mustache /mə'stahsh, mə'stash‖mə'stɑ:ʃ, mə'stæʃ/ *n, chiefly NAm* a moustache

mustachio /mə'stahshioh, mə'stashioh‖mə'stɑ:ʃɪəʊ, mə'stæʃɪəʊ/ *n, pl* **mustachios** a (large) moustache – **mustachioed** *adj*

mustang /'mustang‖'mʌstæŋ/ *n* the small hardy naturalized horse of the western plains of the USA

mustard /'mustəd‖'mʌstəd/ *n* (a pungent yellow powder used as a condiment or in medicine, esp as an emetic or counterirritant, and ground from the seeds of) any of several related plants with lobed leaves, yellow flowers, and straight seed pods – **mustardy** *adj*

'**mustard ,gas** *n* an irritant and blister-inducing oily liquid used as a poison gas

[1]**muster** /'mustə‖'mʌstə/ *vt* **1a** to assemble, convene **b** to call the roll of **2** to summon in response to a need <*all the courage he could* ~> ~*vi* to come together; congregate

[2]**muster** *n* **1a** assembling (for military inspection) **b** an assembled group; a collection **2** a critical examination <*slipshod work that would never pass* ~>

mustn't /'musnt‖'mʌsnt/ must not

musty /'musti‖'mʌstɪ/ *adj* **1** affected by mould, damp, or mildew **2** tasting or smelling of damp and decay – **mustily** *adv*, **mustiness** *n*

mutable /'myoohtəbl‖'mju:təbl/ *adj* **1** capable of or liable to change or alteration **2** capable of or subject to mutation – **mutableness** *n*, **mutably** *adv*, **mutability** *n*

mutation /myooh'taysh(ə)n‖mju:'teɪʃ(ə)n/ *n* **1** (a) significant and fundamental alteration **2** sandhi; *specif* umlaut **3** (an individual or strain differing from others of its type and resulting from) a relatively permanent change in an organism's hereditary material – **mutational** *adj*, **mutationally** *adv*, **mutant** *n*, **mutate** *vb*

mutatis mutandis /mooh,tahtis mooh'tandis‖mu:,tɑ:tɪs mu:'tændɪs/ *adv* with the necessary changes having been made or respective differences considered

[1]**mute** /myooht‖mju:t/ *adj* **1** unable to speak; dumb **2a** felt but not expressed <~ *sympathy*> **b** refusing to plead <*the prisoner stands* ~> **3** *of letters (e g the* b *in* plumb) not pronounced – **mutely** *adv*, **muteness** *n*

[2]**mute** *n* **1** one who cannot or does not speak **2** STOP 7 **3** a device attached to a musical instrument to reduce, soften, or muffle its tone

[3]**mute** *vt* **1** to muffle or reduce the sound of **2** to tone down (a colour)

ˈ**muted** *adj* **1** silent, subdued **2** provided with or produced or modified by the use of a mute – **mutedly** *adv*

mutilate /ˈmyoohtilayt‖ˈmjuːtɪleɪt/ *vt* **1** to cut off or permanently destroy or damage a limb or essential part of **2** to damage or deface <*the censors had* ~d *the script*> – **mutilator** *n*, **mutilation** *n*

mutineer /ˌmyoohtiˈniə‖ˌmjuːtɪˈnɪə/ *n* sby who mutinies

mutinous /ˈmyoohtinəs‖ˈmjuːtɪnəs/ *adj* **1** tending to mutiny; rebellious **2** of or constituting mutiny – **mutinously** *adv*, **mutinousness** *n*

mutiny /ˈmyoohtini‖ˈmjuːtɪnɪ/ *n* open resistance to lawful authority; *esp* concerted revolt (e g of a naval crew) against discipline or a superior officer – **mutiny** *vi*

mutt /mut‖mʌt/ *n* **1** a dull or stupid person **2** a (mongrel) dog

mutter /ˈmutə‖ˈmʌtə/ *vi* **1** to utter sounds or words in a low or indistinct voice **2** to utter muffled threats or complaints ~*vt* to utter, esp in a low or indistinct voice **mutter** *n*, **mutterer** *n*

mutton /ˈmutn‖ˈmʌtn/ *n* the flesh of a mature sheep used as food – **muttony** *adj*

ˈ**muttonˌchops** /-ˌchops‖-ˌtʃɒps/ *n pl* side-whiskers that are narrow at the temple and broad by the lower jaws

mutual /ˈmyoohtyooəl, -chəl‖ˈmjuːtjʊəl, -tʃəl/ *adj* **1a** directed by each towards the other <~ *affection*> **b** having the same specified feeling for each other <*they had long been* ~ *enemies*> **2** shared by 2 or more in common – **mutualize** *vb*, **mutually** *adv*, **mutuality** *n*

Muzak /ˈmyoohzak‖ˈmjuːzæk/ *trademark* – used for recorded background music played in public places

[1]**muzzle** /ˈmuzl‖ˈmʌzl/ *n* **1a** the projecting jaws and nose of a dog or other animal **b** a covering for the mouth of an animal used to prevent biting, barking, etc **2** the discharging end of a pistol, rifle, etc

[2]**muzzle** *vt* **1** to fit with a muzzle **2** to restrain from free expression; gag – **muzzler** *n*

ˈ**muzzle-ˌloader** *n* a firearm that is loaded through the muzzle

muzzy /ˈmuzi‖ˈmʌzɪ/ *adj* mentally confused; befuddled – **muzzily** *adv*, **muzziness** *n*

my /mie‖maɪ/ *adj* **1** of, belonging to, or done by or to me or myself **2** – used interjectionally to express surprise and sometimes reduplicated <~ *oh* ~!>, in certain fixed exclamations <~ *God!*>, and with names of certain parts of the body to express doubt or disapproval <~ *foot!*>

mycelium /mieˈseelyəm‖maɪˈsiːljəm/ *n, pl* **mycelia** /-lyə‖-ljə/ the mass of interwoven filamentous hyphae that forms the body of a fungus and is usu submerged in another body (e g of soil or the tissues of a host) – **mycelial** *adj*

mycology /mieˈkoləji‖maɪˈkɒlədʒɪ/ *n* (the biology of) fungal life or fungi – **mycologist** *n*, **mycological** *also* **mycologic** *adj*, **mycologically** *adv*

myelin /ˈmie·əlin‖ˈmaɪəlɪn/ *n* a soft white fatty material that forms a thick sheath about the cytoplasmic core of nerve cells adapted for fast conduction of nervous impulses – **myelinic** *adj*

myelitis /ˌmie·əˈlietəs‖ˌmaɪəˈlaɪtəs/ *n* inflammation of the bone marrow

myna, **mynah** *also* **mina** /ˈmienə‖ˈmaɪnə/ *n* any of various Asian starlings; *esp* a largely black one easily taught to pronounce words

myopia /mieˈohpi·ə‖maɪˈəʊpɪə/ *n* defective vision of distant objects resulting from the focussing of the visual images in front of the retina; shortsightedness [Greek *myōpia*, fr *myōps* shortsighted, fr *myein* to be closed + *ōps* eye, face] – **myopic** *adj*, **myopically** *adv*

[1]**myriad** /ˈmiri·əd‖ˈmɪrɪəd/ *n* **1** ten thousand **2** an indefinitely large number – often pl with sing. meaning

[2]**myriad** *adj* innumerable, countless

myrrh /muh‖mɜː/ *n* (a mixture of labdanum with) brown bitter aromatic gum resin obtained from any of several African and Asian trees

myrtle /ˈmuhtl‖ˈmɜːtl/ *n* **1** an evergreen S European bushy shrub with shiny leaves, fragrant white or rosy flowers, and black berries, or a related tropical shrub or tree **2** *NAm* [1]PERIWINKLE

myself /mieˈself‖maɪˈself/ *pron* **1** that identical one that is I – used reflexively <*I got* ~ *a new suit*>, for emphasis <*I* ~ *will go*>, or in absolute constructions <~ *a tourist, I nevertheless avoided other tourists*> **2** my normal self <*I'm not quite* ~ *today*>

mysterious /miˈstiəri·əs‖mɪˈstɪərɪəs/ *adj* **1** difficult to comprehend **2** containing, suggesting, or implying mystery – **mysteriously** *adv*, **mysteriousness** *n*

mystery /ˈmist(ə)ri‖ˈmɪst(ə)rɪ/ *n* **1a** a religious truth disclosed by revelation alone **b(1)** any of the 15 events (e g the Nativity, the Crucifixion, or the Assumption) serving as a subject for meditation during the saying of the rosary **b(2)** *cap* a Christian sacrament; *specif* the Eucharist **c** a secret religious rite (e g of Eleusinian or Mithraic cults) **2a** sthg not understood or beyond understanding <*his disappearance remains a* ~> <*a* ~ *illness*> **b** a fictional work dealing usu with the solution of a mysterious crime **3** an enigmatic or secretive quality

ˈ**mystery ˌplay**, **mystery** *n* a medieval religious drama based on episodes from the Scriptures

mystic /ˈmistik‖ˈmɪstɪk/ *n* a person who believes that God or ultimate reality can only be apprehended by direct personal experience (and who orders his/her life towards this goal)

mystical /ˈmistikl‖ˈmɪstɪkl/, **mystic** *adj* **1** having a sacred or spiritual meaning not given by normal modes of thought or feeling **2** of or resulting from a person's direct experience of communion with God or ultimate reality **3** of mysteries or esoteric rites **4** of mysticism or mystics **5a** mysterious, incomprehensible **b** obscure, esoteric **c** arousing awe and wonder – **mystically** *adv*, **mysticism** *n*

mystification /ˌmistifiˈkaysh(ə)n‖ˌmɪstɪfɪˈkeɪʃ(ə)n/ *n* mystifying or being mystified

mystify /ˈmistifie‖ˈmɪstɪfaɪ/ *vt* **1** to perplex, bewilder **2** to cause to appear mysterious or obscure – **mystifier** *n*, **mystifyingly** *adv*

mystique /miˈsteek‖mɪˈstiːk/ *n* **1** a mystical reverential atmosphere or quality associated with a person or thing **2** an esoteric skill peculiar to an occupation or activity

myth /mith‖mɪθ/ *n* **1** a traditional story that embodies popular beliefs or explains a practice, belief, or natural phenomenon **2** a parable, allegory **3** a fictitious person or thing

mythical /ˈmithikl‖ˈmɪθɪkl/ *also* **mythic** *adj* **1** based on or described in a myth **2** invented or imagined – **mythically** *adv*

mythological /ˌmithəˈlojikl‖ˌmɪθəˈlɒdʒɪkl/ *adj* **1** of or dealt with in mythology or myths **2** lacking factual or historical basis – **mythologically** *adv*

mythology /miˈtholəji‖mɪˈθɒlədʒɪ/ *n* **1** a body of myths, esp those dealing with the gods and heroes of a particular people **2** a branch of knowledge that deals with myths **3** a body of beliefs, usu with little factual foundation, lending glamour or mystique to sby or sthg – **mythologist** *n*

myxoma /mikˈsohmə‖mɪkˈsəʊmə/ *n, pl* **myxomas, myxomata** a soft tumour made up of gelatinous connective tissue – **myxomatous** *adj*

myxomatosis /ˌmiksəməˈtohsis‖ˌmɪksəməˈtəʊsɪs/ *n* a severe flea-transmitted virus disease of rabbits

N

n /en‖en/ *n, pl* **n's, ns** *often cap* **1** (a graphic representation of or device for reproducing) the 14th letter of the English alphabet **2** an indefinite number **3** an en

-n – see [1]-EN

'n' *also* **'n** /(ə)n‖(ə)n/ *conj* and <*fish ~ chips*>

Naafi /ˈnafi‖ˈnæfɪ/ *n* the organization which runs shops and canteens in British military establishments; *also* any of these shops or canteens [*N*avy, *A*rmy, and *A*ir *F*orce *I*nstitutes]

nab /nab‖næb/ *vt* **-bb- 1** to arrest; apprehend **2** to catch hold of; grab *USE* infml

nabob /ˈnaybob‖ˈneɪbɒb/ *n* **1** a provincial governor of the Mogul empire in India **2** a man of great wealth – used orig of an Englishman grown rich in India [Hindi & Urdu *nawwāb*, fr Arabic *nuwwāb*, pl of *nā'ib* governor]

nacelle /naˈsel‖næˈsel/ *n* a housing for an aircraft engine

nacre /ˈnaykə‖ˈneɪkə/ *n* mother-of-pearl – **nacreous** *adj*

nadir /ˈnaydiə, ˈnah-‖ˈneɪdɪə, ˈnɑː-/ *n* **1** the point of the celestial sphere that is directly opposite the zenith and vertically downwards from the observer **2** the lowest point

naevus /ˈneevəs‖ˈniːvəs/ *n* a birthmark

[1]**nag** /nag‖næg/ *n* a horse; *esp* one that is old or in poor condition

[2]**nag** *vb* **-gg-** *vi* **1** to find fault incessantly **2** to be a persistent source of annoyance or discomfort ~*vt* to subject to constant scolding or urging – **nagger** *n*, **nagging** *adj*, **naggingly** *adv*

[3]**nag** *n* a person, esp a woman, who nags habitually

Nahuatl /ˈnahˌwahtl, -ˌwo-‖ˈnɑːˌwɑːtl, -ˌwɒ-/ *n* (the language of) a group of American Indian peoples, including the Aztecs, of S Mexico and Central America

naiad /ˈniead‖ˈnaɪæd/ *n, pl* **naiads, naiades** /ˈnie·əˌdeez‖ˈnaɪəˌdiːz/ *often cap* a nymph in classical mythology living in lakes, rivers, etc

[1]**nail** /nayl‖neɪl/ *n* **1** (a claw or other structure corresponding to) a horny sheath protecting the upper end of each finger and toe of human beings and other primates **2** a slender usu pointed and headed spike designed to be driven in, esp with a hammer, to join materials, act as a support, etc

[2]**nail** *vt* **1** to fasten (as if) with a nail **2** to fix steadily **3** to catch, trap **4** to detect and expose (e g a lie or scandal) so as to discredit **5** *chiefly NAm* to hit, strike *USE* (*except 1*) infml – **nailer** *n*

nail down *vt* **1** to define or establish clearly **2** to secure a definite promise or decision from

naive, naïve /nahˈeev, nie-‖nɑːˈiːv, naɪ-/ *adj* **1** ingenuous, unsophisticated **2** lacking in worldly wisdom or informed judgment; *esp* credulous **3** PRIMITIVE 3d – **naively** *adv*, **naiveness** *n*

naivety *also* **naïvety** /nahˈeevəti, nie-‖nɑːˈiːvətɪ, naɪ-/ *n* **1** being naive **2** a naive remark or action

naked /ˈnaykid‖ˈneɪkɪd/ *adj* **1** having no clothes on **2a** *of a knife or sword* not enclosed in a sheath or scabbard **b** exposed to the air or to full view <*a ~ light*> **c** *of (part of) a plant or animal* lacking hairs or other covering or enveloping parts (e g a shell or feathers) **d** lacking foliage or vegetation **3** without furnishings or ornamentation **4** unarmed, defenceless **5** not concealed or disguised <*the ~ truth*> **6** unaided by any optical device <*visible to the ~ eye*> – **nakedly** *adv*, **nakedness** *n*

namby-pamby /ˌnambi ˈpambi‖ˌnæmbɪ ˈpæmbɪ/ *adj* **1** insipidly sentimental **2** lacking resolution or firmness [*Namby Pamby*, satirical nickname of Ambrose Philips (1675?-1749), English poet]

[1]**name** /naym‖neɪm/ *n* **1** a word or phrase designating an individual person or thing **2** a descriptive usu disparaging epithet **3a** reputation <*gave the town a bad ~*> **b** a famous or notorious person or thing **4** family, kindred <*was a disgrace to his ~*> **5** semblance as opposed to reality <*a friend in ~ only*> – **one's name is mud** one is in disgrace

[2]**name** *vt* **1** to give a name to; call **2** to identify by name **3** to nominate, appoint **4** to decide on; choose <*~ the day for the wedding*> **5** to mention explicitly; specify – **nameable** *adj*, **namer** *n*

ˈname ˌday *n* the feast day of the saint whose name one has taken at baptism

ˈname-ˌdropping *n* seeking to impress others by the apparently casual mention of prominent people as friends – **name-dropper** *n*

ˈnameless /-lis‖-lɪs/ *adj* **1** obscure, undistinguished **2** not known by name; anonymous **3** having no legal right to a name; illegitimate **3a** having no name **b** left purposely unnamed **4a** not capable of being described; indefinable <*~ fears*> **b** too terrible or distressing to describe <*a ~ horror*> – **namelessly** *adv*, **namelessness** *n*

ˈnamely /-li‖-lɪ/ *adv* that is to say

ˈnameˌplate /-ˌplayt‖-ˌpleɪt/ *n* a plate or

plaque bearing a name

ˈname,sake /-ˌsayk‖-ˌseɪk/ *n* sby or sthg that has the same name as another

nanny *also* **nannie** /ˈnani‖ˈnænɪ/ *n, chiefly Br* a child's nurse; a nursemaid

ˈnanny ˌgoat *n* a female domestic goat – infml

¹nap /nap‖næp/ *vi* **-pp-** **1** to take a short sleep, esp during the day **2** to be off one's guard <*caught his opponent* ~ping>

²nap *n* a short sleep, esp during the day

³nap *n* a hairy or downy surface (e g on a woven fabric); a pile – **napless** *adj*, **napped** *adj*

⁴nap *vt* **-pp-** to raise a nap on (fabric or leather)

⁵nap *n* NAPOLEON 2

⁶nap *vt* **-pp-** to recommend (a horse) as a possible winner – **nap** *n*

¹napalm /ˈnay,pahm‖ˈneɪ,pɑːm/ *n* **1** a thickener consisting of a mixture of aluminium soaps **2** petrol jellied with napalm and used esp in incendiary bombs and flamethrowers

²napalm *vt* to attack with napalm

nape /nayp‖neɪp/ *n* the back of the neck

naphtha /ˈnafthə‖ˈnæfθə/ *n* **1** petroleum **2** any of various liquid hydrocarbon mixtures used chiefly as solvents

naphthalene /ˈnafthəleen‖ˈnæfθəliːn/ *n* a hydrocarbon usu obtained by distillation of coal tar and used esp in the synthesis of organic chemicals – **naphthalenic** *adj*

napkin /ˈnapkin‖ˈnæpkɪn/ *n* **1** a usu square piece of material (e g linen or paper) used at table to wipe the lips or fingers and protect the clothes **2** *chiefly Br* a nappy – fml

napoleon /nəˈpohli·ən‖nəˈpəʊlɪən/ *n* **1** a French 20-franc gold coin **2** (a bid to win all 5 tricks at) a card game played with hands of 5 cards

nappy /ˈnapi‖ˈnæpɪ/ *n, chiefly Br* a square piece of cloth or paper worn by babies to absorb and retain excreta and usu drawn up between the legs and fastened at the waist

narcissism /ˈnahsi,siz(ə)m‖ˈnɑːsɪ,sɪz(ə)m/ *n* love of or sexual desire for one's own body [*Narcissus*, a youth in Greek mythology who died for love of his own reflection & was turned into a narcissus] – **narcissist** *n or adj*, **narcissistic** *adj*

narcissus /nahˈsisəs‖nɑːˈsɪsəs/ *n* a daffodil; *esp* one whose flowers are borne separately and have a short corona

¹narcotic /nahˈkotik‖nɑːˈkɒtɪk/ *n* a usu addictive drug, esp (a derivative of) morphine, that dulls the senses, induces prolonged sleep, and relieves pain – **narcotize** *vb*

²narcotic *adj* **1a** like, being, or yielding a narcotic **b** inducing mental lethargy; soporific **2** of (addiction to) narcotics – **narcotically** *adv*

¹nark /nahk‖nɑːk/ *n* **1** *Br* a police informer **2** *chiefly Austr* an annoying person or thing *USE* slang

²nark *vb, Br vi* to act as an informer – slang; often + *on* ~*vt* to offend, affront – infml

narrate /nəˈrayt‖nəˈreɪt/ *vt* to recite the details of (a story) – **narrator** *n*

narration /nəˈraysh(ə)n‖nəˈreɪʃ(ə)n/ *n* **1** (a) narrating **2** a story, narrative – **narrational** *adj*

narrative /ˈnarətiv‖ˈnærətɪv/ *n* **1** sthg (e g a story) that is narrated **2** the art or practice of narration – **narrative** *adj*, **narratively** *adv*

¹narrow /ˈnaroh‖ˈnærəʊ/ *adj* **1** of little width, esp in comparison with height or length **2** limited in size or scope; restricted **3** inflexible, hidebound **4** only just sufficient or successful <*a* ~ *escape*> – **narrowly** *adv*, **narrowness** *n*

²narrow *n* a narrow part or (water) passage; *specif* STRAIT 1 – usu pl with sing. meaning

³narrow *vt* **1** to make narrow or narrower **2** to restrict the scope or sphere of ~*vi* to become narrow or narrower

ˈnarrow ˌboat *n* a canal barge with a beam of 21m (7ft) or less

ˌnarrow ˈgauge /gayj‖geɪdʒ/ *n* a railway gauge narrower than standard gauge

ˌnarrow-ˈminded /-ˈmiendid‖-ˈmaɪndɪd/ *adj* lacking tolerance or breadth of vision; bigoted – **narrow-mindedly** *adv*, **narrow-mindedness** *n*

narwhal *also* **narwal** /ˈnahwəl‖ˈnɑːwəl/ *n* a small arctic whale, the male of which has a long twisted ivory tusk

¹nasal /ˈnayzl‖ˈneɪzl/ *n* a nasal speech sound

²nasal *adj* **1** of the nose **2a** uttered through the nose with the mouth passage closed (as in English /m, n, ng/) **b** uttered with both the mouth and nose passage open (as in French *en*) **c** characterized by resonance produced through the nose – **nasally** *adv*, **nasality** *n*

nasal,·ize, -ise /ˈnayzl,iez‖ˈneɪzl,aɪz/ *vb* to speak or say in a nasal manner – **nasalization** *n*

nascent /ˈnas(ə)nt, ˈnay-‖ˈnæs(ə)nt, ˈneɪ-/ *adj* in the process of being born; just beginning to develop – fml – **nascence** *n*, **nascency** *n*

nasturtium /nəˈstuhsh(ə)m‖nəˈstɜːʃ(ə)m/ *n* (any of a genus of plants related to) a widely cultivated plant with showy spurred flowers and pungent seeds

nasty /ˈnahsti‖ˈnɑːstɪ/ *adj* **1a** disgustingly filthy **b** repugnant, esp to smell or taste **2** obscene, indecent **3** mean, tawdry <*cheap and* ~ *furniture*> **4a** harmful, dangerous <*a* ~ *accident*> **b** disagreeable, dirty <~ *weather*> **5** giving cause for concern or anxiety <*a* ~ *suspicion*> **6** spiteful, vicious <*trespassers who turn* ~ *when challenged*> – **nastily** *adv*, **nastiness** *n*

natal /ˈnaytl‖ˈneɪtl/ *adj* of, present at, or associated with (one's) birth <*a* ~ *star*>

nation /ˈnaysh(ə)n‖ˈneɪʃ(ə)n/ *n* **1** *sing or pl in constr* **1a** a people with a common origin, tradition, and language (capable of) constituting a nation-state **b** a community of people possessing a more or less defined territory and government **2** a tribe or federation of tribes (e g of American Indians) [Middle French, fr Latin *nation-*, *natio* birth, race, nation, fr *nat-*, *nasci* to be born] – **nationhood** *n*

¹national /ˈnash(ə)nl‖ˈnæʃ(ə)nl/ *adj* **1** of a nation **2** belonging to or maintained by the central government **3** of or being a coalition government – **nationally** *adv*

²national *n* **1** a citizen of a specified nation **2** a competition that is national in scope – usu pl

ˌnational asˈsistance *n, Br, often cap N&A* SUPPLEMENTARY BENEFIT – not now used technically

ˌnational ˈdebt *n* the amount of money owed by the government of a country

ˌNational ˈGuard *n* a militia force recruited

by each state of the USA and equipped by the federal government that can be called up by either

ˌNational ˈHealth ˌService, National Health *n* the British system of medical care, started in 1948, by which every person receives free medical treatment paid for by taxation

ˌnational inˈsurance *n, often cap N&I* a compulsory social-security scheme in Britain funded by contributions from employers, employees, and the government which insures the individual against sickness, retirement, and unemployment

nationalism /ˈnash(ə)nlˌiz(ə)m‖ˈnæʃ(ə)nlˌɪz(ə)m/ *n* loyalty and devotion to a nation; *esp* the exalting of one nation above all others

ˈnationalˌist /-ˌist‖-ˌɪst/ *n* **1** an advocate of nationalism **2** *cap* a member of a political group advocating national independence or strong national government – **nationalist, nationalistic** *adj*, **nationalistically** *adv*

nationality /ˌnash(ə)nˈaləti‖ˌnæʃ(ə)nˈælətɪ/ *n* **1** national character **2** national status **3** citizenship of a particular nation **4** existence as a separate nation **5a** NATION 1a **b** an ethnic group within a larger unit

national·ize, -ise /ˈnash(ə)nlˌiez‖ˈnæʃ(ə)nlˌaɪz/ *vt* **1** to make national **2** to invest control or ownership of in the national government – **nationalizer** *n*, **nationalization** *n*

ˌnational ˈpark *n* an area of special scenic, historical, or scientific importance preserved and maintained by the government

ˌnational ˈservice *n* conscripted service in the British armed forces – **national serviceman** *n*

ˌnational ˈsocialism *n* Nazism – **national socialist** *adj*

[1]**native** /ˈnaytiv/ *adj* **1** inborn, innate <~ *talents*> **2** belonging to a particular place by birth <~ *to Yorkshire*> **3a** belonging to or being the place of one's birth <*my* ~ *language*> **b** of or being one's first language or sby using his/her first language <*a* ~ *speaker*> <~ *fluency*> **4** living (naturally), grown, or produced in a particular place; indigenous **5** found in nature, esp in a pure form <*mining* ~ *silver*> – **natively** *adv*, **nativeness** *n*

[2]**native** *n* **1** one born or reared in a particular place <*a* ~ *of London*> **2a** an original or indigenous (non-European) inhabitant **b** a plant, animal, etc indigenous to a particular locality **3** a local resident

nativity /nəˈtivəti‖nəˈtɪvətɪ/ *n* **1** birth; *specif, cap* the birth of Jesus **2** a horoscope

natter /ˈnatə‖ˈnætə/ *vi or n, chiefly Br* (to) chatter, gossip – infml

natty /ˈnati‖ˈnætɪ/ *adj* neat and trim; spruce – **nattily** *adv*, **nattiness** *n*

[1]**natural** /ˈnachərəl‖ˈnætʃərəl/ *adj* **1** based on an inherent moral sense <~ *justice*> <~ *law*> **2** in accordance with or determined by nature **3** related by blood rather than by adoption <*his* ~ *parents*> **4** innate, inherent <*a* ~ *talent for art*> **5** of nature as an object of study **6** having a specified character or attribute by nature <*a* ~ *athlete*> **7** happening in accordance with the ordinary course of nature <*death from* ~ *causes*> **8** normal or expected <*events followed their* ~ *course*> **9** existing in or produced by nature without human intervention <~ *scenery*> **10** (as if) in a state unenlightened by culture or morality <~ *man*> **11a** having a physical or real existence **b** of the physical as opposed to the spiritual world **12a** true to nature; lifelike **b** free from affectation or constraint **c** not disguised or altered in appearance or form **13a** (containing only notes that are) neither sharp nor flat **b** having the pitch modified by the natural sign – **naturalness** *n*

[2]**natural** *n* **1** one born mentally defective **2** (a note affected by) a sign placed on the musical staff to nullify the effect of a preceding sharp or flat **3** one having natural skills or talents <*as an actor, he was a* ~> **4** one who is likely to be particularly suitable or successful *USE* (*3 & 4*) infml

ˌnatural ˈgas *n* gas from the earth's crust; *specif* a combustible mixture of methane and other hydrocarbons used chiefly as a fuel and as raw material in industry

ˌnatural ˈhistory *n* **1** a treatise on some aspect of nature **2** the natural development of an organism, disease, etc over a period of time **3** the usu amateur study, esp in the field, of natural objects (e g plants and animals), often in a particular area

naturalism /ˈnachərəˌliz(ə)m‖ˈnætʃərəˌlɪz(ə)m/ *n* **1** action or thought based on natural desires and instincts **2** a theory discounting supernatural explanations of the origin and meaning of the universe **3** realism in art or literature, esp when emphasizing scientific observation of life without idealization of the ugly – **naturalist** *adj*, **naturalistic** *adj*, **naturalistically** *adv*

naturalist /ˈnachərəˌlist‖ˈnætʃərəˌlɪst/ *n* **1** a follower or advocate of naturalism **2** a student of natural history

natural·ize, -ise /ˈnachərəˌliez‖ˈnætʃərəˌlaɪz/ *vt* **1a** to introduce into common use or into the vernacular **b** to cause (e g a plant) to become established as if native **2** to make natural **3** to admit to citizenship ~*vi* to become naturalized – **naturalization** *n*

ˈnaturally /-li‖-lɪ/ *adv* **1** by nature <~ *timid*> **2** as might be expected <~, *we shall be there*> **3** in a natural manner

ˌnatural ˈnumber *n* the number 1 or any number (e g 3, 12, 432) obtained by repeatedly adding 1 to the number 1

ˌnatural reˈsources *n pl* industrial materials and capacities (e g mineral deposits and waterpower) supplied by nature

ˌnatural ˈscience *n* any of the sciences (e g physics or biology) that deal with objectively measurable phenomena – **natural scientist** *n*

ˌnatural seˈlection *n* a natural process that tends to result in the survival of organisms best adapted to their environment and the elimination of (mutant) organisms carrying undesirable traits

nature /ˈnaychə‖ˈneɪtʃə/ *n* **1a** the inherent character or constitution of a person or thing **b** disposition, temperament **2a** a creative and controlling force in the universe **b** the inner forces in an individual **3** a kind, class <*documents of a confidential* ~> **4** the physical constitution of an organism **5** the external world in its entirety **6** (a way of life resembling) mankind's original or natural condition **7** natural scenery

naturism /ˈnaychəˌriz(ə)m‖ˈneɪtʃəˌrɪz(ə)m/ *n* nudism – **naturist** *adj or n*

naturopathy /ˌnaychəˈropəthi‖ˌneɪtʃəˈrɒpəθɪ/ *n* treatment of disease emphasizing stimulation of the natural healing processes, including the use of herbal medicines – **naturopathic** *adj*

naught /nawt‖nɔːt/ *n* **1** nothing **2** NOUGHT 2

naughty /ˈnawti‖ˈnɔːtɪ/ *adj* **1** badly behaved; wicked <*you* ~ *boy!*> **2** slightly improper – euph or humor – **naughtily** *adv*, **naughtiness** *n*

nausea /ˈnawzi·ə‖ˈnɔːzɪə/ *n* **1** a feeling of discomfort in the stomach accompanied by a distaste for food and an urge to vomit **2** extreme disgust [Latin, seasickness, nausea, fr Greek *nautia, nausia*, fr *nautēs* sailor] – **nauseant** *n or adj*

nauseate /ˈnawziˌayt‖ˈnɔːzɪˌeɪt/ *vb* to (cause to) become affected with nausea or disgust – **nauseatingly** *adv*

nauseous /ˈnawzi·əs‖ˈnɔːzɪəs/ *adj* causing or affected with nausea or disgust – **nauseously** *adv*, **nauseousness** *n*

nautch /nawch‖nɔːtʃ/ *n* an entertainment in India performed by professional dancing girls

nautical /ˈnawtikl‖ˈnɔːtɪkl/ *adj* of or associated with seamen, navigation, or ships – **nautically** *adv*

ˌnautical ˈmile *n* any of various units of distance used for sea and air navigation based on the length of a minute of arc of a great circle of the earth: e g **a** a British unit equal to 6080ft (about 1853.18m) **b** an international unit equal to 1852m (about 6076.17ft)

nautilus /ˈnawtiləs‖ˈnɔːtɪləs/ *n, pl* **nautiluses, nautili** /-ˌlie‖-ˌlaɪ/ **1** any of a genus of molluscs related to the octopuses and squids that live in the Pacific and Indian oceans and have a spiral shell **2** PAPER NAUTILUS

naval /ˈnayvl‖ˈneɪvl/ *adj* **1** of a navy **2** consisting of or involving warships

[1]**nave** /nayv‖neɪv/ *n* the hub of a wheel

[2]**nave** *n* the main body of a church lying to the west of the chancel; *esp* the long central space flanked by aisles

navel /ˈnayvl‖ˈneɪvl/ *n* **1** a depression in the middle of the abdomen marking the point of former attachment of the umbilical cord **2** the central point

ˈnavel ˌorange *n* a seedless orange with a pit at the top enclosing a small secondary fruit

navigable /ˈnavigəbl‖ˈnævɪgəbl/ *adj* **1** suitable for ships to pass through or along **2** capable of being steered – **navigableness** *n*, **navigably** *adv*, **navigability** *n*

navigate /ˈnavigayt‖ˈnævɪgeɪt/ *vi* **1** to travel by water **2** to steer a course through a medium **3** to perform the activities (e g taking sightings and making calculations) involved in navigation ~ *vt* **1a** to sail over, on, or through **b** to make one's way over or through **2a** to steer or manage (a boat) in sailing **b** to operate or direct the course of (e g an aircraft) – **navigator** *n*

navigation /ˌnaviˈgaysh(ə)n‖ˌnævɪˈgeɪʃ(ə)n/ *n* **1** navigating **2** the science of determining position, course, and distance travelled during a journey and hence advising on the best course to be steered or taken **3** ship traffic or commerce – **navigational** *adj*, **navigationally** *adv*

navvy /ˈnavi‖ˈnævɪ/ *n, Br* an unskilled labourer

navy /ˈnayvi‖ˈneɪvɪ/ *n* **1** a nation's ships of war and support vessels together with the organization needed for maintenance **2** *sing or pl in constr* the personnel manning a navy **3** NAVY BLUE

ˌnavy ˈblue *adj or n* deep dark blue

[1]**nay** /nay‖neɪ/ *adv* **1** not merely this but also <*she was happy,* ~, *ecstatic*> **2** *N Eng or archaic* no

[2]**nay** *n* **1** denial, refusal **2** a vote or voter against

nazi /ˈnahtsi‖ˈnɑːtsɪ/ *n, often cap* a member of the German fascist party controlling Germany from 1933 to 1945 [German, by shortening & alteration fr *Nationalsozialist* National Socialist] – **nazi** *adj*, **nazify** *vt*, **nazification** *n*

Nazism /ˈnahtˌsiz(ə)m‖ˈnɑːtˌsɪz(ə)m/, **Naziism** /ˈnahtsiˌiz(ə)m‖ˈnɑːtsɪˌɪz(ə)m/ *n* the totalitarian and racialist doctrines of the fascist National Socialist German Workers' party in the 3rd German Reich

NCO *n* NONCOMMISSIONED OFFICER

-nd *suffix* (→ *adj*), *chiefly Br* – used after the figure 2 to indicate the ordinal number *second* <2nd>

ne-, neo- *comb form* **1a** new; recent <Ne*ocene*> **b** new, subsequent, or revived period or form of <Neo*platonism*> **c** in a new, subsequent, or revived form or manner <neo-*Georgian*> **2** New World <Neo*tropical*>

Neanderthal man *n* a Middle Palaeolithic man known from skeletal remains in Europe, N Africa, and W Asia – **Neanderthaloid** *adj or n*

Neapolitan /ˌnee·əˈpolitn‖ˌniːəˈpɒlɪtn/ *n or adj* (a native or inhabitant) of Naples

neap tide /neep‖niːp/ *n* a tide of minimum height occurring at the 1st and the 3rd quarters of the moon

[1]**near** /niə‖nɪə/ *adv* **1** in or into a near position or manner <*came* ~ *to tears*> **2** closely approximating; nearly <*a* near-*perfect performance*> <*isn't anywhere* ~ *clever enough*> – **near on** CLOSE ON

[2]**near** *prep* near to <*went too* ~ *the edge*> <*call me* ~er *the time*>

[3]**near** *adj* **1** intimately connected or associated <*he and I are* ~ *relations*> **2a** not far distant in time, space, or degree <*in the* ~ *future*> **b** close, narrow <*a* ~ *miss*> <*a* ~ *resemblance*> **3a** being the closer of 2 <*the* ~ *side*> **b** being the left-hand one of a pair <*the* ~ *wheel of a cart*> – **nearness** *n*

[4]**near** *vb* to approach

ˌnearˈby /-ˈbie‖-ˈbaɪ/ *adv or adj* close at hand <*live* ~> <*a* ~ *café*>

nearly /ˈniəli‖ˈnɪəlɪ/ *adv* **1** in a close manner or relationship <~ *related*> **2** almost but not quite <*very* ~ *identical*> <~ *a year later*>

ˌnearˈside /-ˈsied‖-ˈsaɪd/ *n, Br* the left-hand side (e g of a vehicle or road) <*hit a car parked on his* ~> – **nearside** *adj*

ˌnearˈsighted /-ˈsietid‖-ˈsaɪtɪd/ *adj* able to

see near things more clearly than distant ones; myopic – **nearsightedly** *adv*, **nearsightedness** *n*

[1]**neat** /neet‖ni:t/ *n, pl* **neat, neats** *archaic* the common domestic ox or cow

[2]**neat** *adj* **1a** without addition or dilution <~ *gin*> **b** free from irregularity; smooth **2** elegantly simple **3a** precise, well-defined <*a ~ solution to the problem*> **b** skilful, adroit **4** (habitually) tidy and orderly <*a ~ room*> <*a ~ little man*> **5** *chiefly NAm* fine, excellent – infml – **neatly** *adv*, **neatness** *n*

[3]**neat** *adv* without addition or dilution; straight <*drinks his whisky ~*>

neath /neeth‖ni:θ/ *prep* beneath – poetic

nebula /ˈnebyoolə‖ˈnebjʊlə/ *n, pl* **nebulas, nebulae** /-li‖-lɪ/ **1** a cloudy patch on the cornea **2a** any of many immense bodies of highly rarefied gas or dust in interstellar space **b** a galaxy – **nebular** *adj*

nebulous /ˈnebyooləs‖ˈnebjʊləs/ *adj* **1** indistinct, vague **2** of or resembling a nebula; nebular – **nebulously** *adv*, **nebulousness** *n*

necessarily /ˈnesəs(ə)rəli, ˌnesəˈserəli‖ˈnesəs(ə)rəlɪ, ˌnesəˈserəlɪ/ *adv* as a necessary consequence; inevitably

[1]**necessary** /ˈnesəs(ə)ri, ˈnesəˌseri‖ˈnesəs(ə)rɪ, ˈnesəˌserɪ/ *n* an indispensable item; an essential

[2]**necessary** *adj* **1a** inevitable, inescapable **b(1)** logically unavoidable <*a ~ conclusion*> **b(2)** that cannot be denied without contradiction of some other statement **c** determined by a previous state of affairs **d** acting under compulsion; not free <*a ~ agent*> **2** essential, indispensable

necessitate /nəˈsesitayt‖nəˈsesɪteɪt/ *vt* to make necessary or unavoidable – **necessitation** *n*

necessitous /nəˈsesitəs‖nəˈsesɪtəs/ *adj* needy, impoverished – fml – **necessitously** *adv*, **necessitousness** *n*

necessity /nəˈsesəti‖nəˈsesətɪ/ *n* **1** the quality of being necessary, indispensable, or unavoidable **2** impossibility of a contrary order or condition <*physical ~*> **3** poverty, want **4a** sthg necessary or indispensable <*the bare* necessities *of life*> **b** a pressing need or desire – **of necessity** necessarily

[1]**neck** /nek‖nek/ *n* **1a** the part of an animal that connects the head with the body; *also* a cut of beef, mutton, etc taken from this part **b** the part of a garment that covers the neck; *also* the neckline **2a** a narrow part, esp shaped like a neck <*~ of a bottle*> **b** the part of a stringed musical instrument extending from the body and supporting the fingerboard and strings **c** a narrow stretch of land **d** STRAIT 1 **e** a column of solidified magma of a volcanic pipe or laccolith **3** a narrow margin <*won by a ~*> – **neck of the woods** area or district in which one lives; locality

[2]**neck** *vt* to reduce the diameter of ~ *vi* **1** to become constricted **2** to kiss and caress in sexual play – infml

ˌneck and ˈneck *adv* evenly matched; running level

necked /nekt‖nekt/ *adj* having a (specified kind of) neck – often in combination <*long-necked*>

neckerchief /ˈnekəˌcheef, -ˌchif‖ˈnekəˌtʃi:f, -ˌtʃɪf/ *n, pl* **neckerchiefs** *also* **neckerchieves** /-cheevz‖-tʃi:vz/ a square of fabric folded and worn round the neck

necklace /ˈneklis‖ˈneklɪs/ *n* a string of jewels, beads, etc worn round the neck as an ornament

ˈneckˌline /-ˌlien‖-ˌlaɪn/ *n* the upper edge of a garment that forms the opening for the neck and head

ˈneckˌtie /-ˌtie‖-ˌtaɪ/ *n, chiefly NAm* TIE 5

necromancy /ˈnekrəˌmansi‖ˈnekrəˌmænsɪ/ *n* **1** the conjuring up of the spirits of the dead in order to predict or influence the future **2** magic, sorcery – **necromancer** *n*, **necromantic** *adj*, **necromantically** *adv*

necrophilia /ˌnekrəˈfili·ə‖ˌnekrəˈfɪlɪə/ *n* obsession with and usu erotic interest in corpses – **necrophile** *n*, **necrophiliac** *adj or n*, **necrophilic** *adj*, **necrophilism** *n*

necropolis /neˈkropəlis, ni-‖neˈkrɒpəlɪs, nɪ-/ *n, pl* **necropolises, necropoles** /-pəleez‖-pəli:z/, **necropoleis** /-lays‖-leɪs/, **necropoli** /-lie, -li‖-laɪ, -lɪ/ a cemetery; *esp* a large elaborate cemetery of an ancient city

necrosis /neˈkrohsis, ni-‖neˈkrəʊsɪs, nɪ-/ *n, pl* **necroses** /-seez‖-si:z/ (localized) death of living tissue – **necrotic** *adj*, **necrotize** *vb*

nectar /ˈnektə‖ˈnektə/ *n* **1** the drink of the gods in classical mythology; *broadly* a delicious drink **2** a sweet liquid secreted by the flowers of many plants that is the chief raw material of honey – **nectarous** *adj*

nectarine /ˈnektərin, -reen‖ˈnektərɪn, -ri:n/ *n* (a tree that bears) a smooth-skinned peach

née, nee /nay‖neɪ/ *adj* – used to identify a woman by her maiden name <*Mrs Thomson, ~ Wilkinson*> [French *née*, fem of *né*, lit., born, fr *naître* to be born, fr Latin *nasci*]

[1]**need** /need‖ni:d/ *n* **1a** a necessary duty; an obligation **b** reason or grounds for an action or condition **2a** a lack of sthg necessary, desirable, or useful <*socks in ~ of mending*> **b** a physiological or psychological requirement for the well-being of an organism **3** a condition requiring supply or relief <*help in time of ~*> **4** poverty, want – **needful** *adj*, **needfulness** *n*

[2]**need** *vt* **1** to be in need of; require <*the soup ~s salt*> <*my socks ~ mending*> **2** to be constrained <*I'll ~ to work hard*> *~vi* be under necessity or obligation to <*~ I go?*> <*he ~ not answer*>

ˈneedful /-f(ə)l‖-f(ə)l/ *adj* necessary, requisite <*do whatever is ~*>

[1]**needle** /ˈneedl‖ˈni:dl/ *n* **1a** a small slender usu steel instrument with an eye for thread at one end and a sharp point at the other, used for sewing **b** any of various similar larger instruments without an eye, used for carrying thread and making stitches (e g in crocheting or knitting) **c** the slender hollow pointed end of a hypodermic syringe for injecting or removing material **2** a slender, usu sharp-pointed, indicator on a dial; *esp* a magnetic needle **3a** a slender pointed object resembling a needle: e g **3a(1)** a pointed crystal **a(2)** a sharp pinnacle of rock **a(3)** an obelisk **b** a needle-shaped leaf, esp of a conifer **c** STYLUS b **d** a slender pointed rod controlling a fine inlet or outlet (e g in a valve) **4** a beam used to take the load of a wall while supported

at each end by shores **5** *Br* a feeling of enmity or ill will – infml <*a ~ match*> – **needlelike** *adj*

[2]**needle** *vt* **1** to sew or pierce (as if) with a needle **2** to provoke by persistent teasing or gibes – **needler** *n*, **needling** *n*

ˈneedleˌpoint /-ˌpoynt‖-ˌpɔɪnt/ *n* **1** lace worked over a paper or parchment pattern **2** embroidery worked on canvas usu in a simple even stitch (e g cross- or tent stitch) – **needlepoint** *adj*

needless /ˈneedlis‖ˈniːdlɪs/ *adj* not needed; unnecessary < ~ *to say*> – **needlessly** *adv*, **needlessness** *n*

ˈneedleˌwoman /-ˌwoomən‖-ˌwʊmən/ *n* a woman who does needlework

ˈneedleˌwork /-ˌwuhk‖-ˌwɜːk/ *n* sewing; *esp* fancy work (e g embroidery)

needn't /ˈneednt‖ˈniːdnt/ need not – **needn't have** was under no necessity to but did <*I* needn't have *worn this sweater*>

needs /needz‖niːdz/ *adv* necessarily <*must ~ be recognized*>

needy /ˈneedi‖ˈniːdɪ/ *adj* in want, impoverished – **neediness** *n*

neep /neep‖niːp/ *n, dial Scot* a turnip

ne'er /neə‖neə/ *adv* never – poetic

ˈne'er-do-ˌwell *n* an idle worthless person – **ne'er-do-well** *adj*

nefarious /niˈfeəri·əs‖nɪˈfeərɪəs/ *adj* iniquitous, evil – **nefariously** *adv*, **nefariousness** *n*

negate /niˈgayt‖nɪˈgeɪt/ *vt* **1** to deny the existence or truth of **2** to make ineffective or invalid – **negate** *n*, **negator, negater** *n*

negation /niˈgaysh(ə)n‖nɪˈgeɪʃ(ə)n/ *n* **1a** a denial or refusal **b** a negative statement; *esp* an assertion of the falsity of a given proposition **2a** sthg that is merely the absence of sthg actual or positive <*anarchy is the ~ of government*> **b** sthg opposite to sthg regarded as positive – **negational** *adj*

[1]**negative** /ˈnegətiv‖ˈnegətɪv/ *adj* **1a** marked by denial, prohibition, or refusal **b** expressing negation **2** lacking positive or agreeable features <*a ~ outlook on life*> **3a** less than zero and opposite in sign to a positive number that when added to the given number yields zero <*-2 is a ~ number*> **b** in a direction opposite to an arbitrarily chosen regular direction < ~ *angle*> **4a** being, relating to, or charged with electricity as a result of an excess of electrons **b** having lower electric potential and constituting the part towards which the current flows from the external circuit **5a** not showing the presence or existence of the organism, condition, etc in question **b** directed or moving away from a source of stimulation < ~ *tropism*> **6** having the light and dark parts in approximately inverse order to those of the original photographic subject – **negatively** *adv*, **negativeness** *n*, **negativity** *n*

[2]**negative** *n* **1a** a proposition by which sthg is denied or contradicted **b** a negative reply **2** sthg that is the negation or opposite of sthg else **3** an expression (e g the word *no*) of negation or denial **4** the side that upholds the contradictory proposition in a debate **5** the plate of a voltaic or electrolytic cell that is at the lower potential **6** a negative photographic image on transparent material used for printing positive pictures

[3]**negative** *vt* **1a** to refuse to accept or approve **b** to reject, veto **2** to demonstrate the falsity of; disprove

[1]**neglect** /niˈglekt‖nɪˈglekt/ *vt* **1** to pay insufficient attention to; disregard **2** to leave undone or unattended to – **neglecter** *n*

[2]**neglect** *n* neglecting or being neglected

neˈglectful /-f(ə)l‖-f(ə)l/ *adj* careless, forgetful – **neglectfully** *adv*, **neglectfulness** *n*

negligee, negligé /ˈneglizhay‖ˈneglɪʒeɪ/ *n* a woman's light decorative housecoat, often designed to be worn with a matching nightdress

negligence /ˈneglij(ə)ns‖ˈneglɪdʒ(ə)ns/ *n* **1** forgetfulness; carelessness **2** failure to exercise the proper care expected of a prudent person

negligent /ˈneglij(ə)nt‖ˈneglɪdʒ(ə)nt/ *adj* **1** (habitually or culpably) neglectful **2** pleasantly casual in manner – **negligently** *adv*

negligible /ˈneglijəbl‖ˈneglɪdʒəbl/ *adj* trifling, insignificant – **negligibly** *adv*, **negligibility** *n*

negotiable /niˈgohshyəbl‖nɪˈgəʊʃjəbl/ *adj* **1** transferable to another < ~ *securities*> **2** capable of being passed along or through <*a difficult but ~ road*> **3** capable of being dealt with or settled through discussion – **negotiability** *n*

negotiate /niˈgohshiayt‖nɪˈgəʊʃɪeɪt/ *vi* to confer with another in order to reach an agreement or settlement ~ *vt* **1** to arrange or bring about through discussion **2a** to transfer (e g a bill of exchange) to another by delivery or endorsement **b** to convert into cash or the equivalent value < ~ *a cheque*> **3a** to travel successfully along or over **b** to complete or deal with successfully [Latin *negotiari* to carry on business, fr *negotium* business, fr *neg-* not + *otium* leisure] – **negotiant** *n*, **negotiator** *n*, **negotiatory** *adj*

negotiation /niˌgohshiˈaysh(ə)n‖nɪˌgəʊʃɪˈeɪʃ(ə)n/ *n* negotiating or being negotiated; *esp* discussion of a disputed issue – often pl with sing. meaning

Negress /ˈneegris‖ˈniːgrɪs/ *n* a female Negro – chiefly derog and technical

Negro /ˈneegroh‖ˈniːgrəʊ/ *n, pl* **Negroes** **1** a member of the esp African branch of the black race of mankind **2** a person of Negro descent [Spanish or Portuguese, fr *negro* black, fr Latin *nigr-, niger*] – **Negro** *adj, often not cap*, **Negroid** *n or adj, often not cap*

neigh /nay‖neɪ/ *vi* to make the loud prolonged cry characteristic of a horse – **neigh** *n*

[1]**neighbour,** *NAm chiefly* **neighbor** /ˈnaybə‖ˈneɪbə/ *n* **1** one living or situated near another **2** a fellow human being <*love thy ~*>

[2]**neighbour,** *NAm chiefly* **neighbor** *vt* to adjoin or lie near to

ˈneighbourˌhood /-ˌhood‖-ˌhʊd/ *n* **1** an adjacent or surrounding region **2** an approximate amount, extent, or degree <*cost in the ~ of £300*> **3a** *sing or pl in constr* the neighbours **b** a district lived in by neighbours **c** (the inhabitants of) a district of a town, city etc, forming a distinct community **4** the set of all points whose distances from a given point are not greater than a given positive number

neighbouring /ˈnayb(ə)ring‖ˈneɪb(ə)rɪŋ/ *adj* nearby, adjacent

ˈneighbourly /-li‖-lɪ/ *adj* characteristic of congenial neighbours; *esp* friendly

[1]neither /ˈniedhə, ˈnee-‖ˈnaɪðə, ˈniː-/ *pron* not the one or the other <~ *of us*>
[2]neither *conj* **1** not either <~ *here nor there*> <~ *ate, drank, nor smoked*> **2** also not; nor <*he didn't go and* ~ *did I*>
[3]neither *adj* not either <~ *hand*>
[4]neither *adv* **1** similarly not; also not <*'I can't swim.' 'Neither can I.'*> **2** *chiefly dial* either
nelson /ˈnels(ə)n‖ˈnels(ə)n/ *n* FULL NELSON; *also* HALF NELSON
nematode /ˈneməˌtohd‖ˈneməˌtəʊd/ *n* any of a phylum of elongated cylindrical worms parasitic in animals or plants or free-living in soil or water
nemesis /ˈneməsis‖ˈneməsɪs/ *n, pl* **nemeses** /-seez‖-siːz/ **1a** (an agent of) retribution or vengeance **b** a formidable enemy or opponent **2** downfall, undoing
neo- – see NE-
neoclassic /ˌneeohˈklasik‖ˌniːəʊˈklæsɪk/, **neoclassical** /-kl‖-kl/ *adj* of or constituting a revival or adaptation of the classical, esp in literature, music, art, or architecture – **neoclassicism** *n*, **neoclassicist** *n or adj*
ˌneocoˈlonialism /-kəˈlohnyəliz(ə)m, -ni·əl-‖-kəˈləʊnjəlɪz(ə)m, -nɪəl-/ *n* the economic and political policies by which a great power indirectly extends its influence over other areas – **neocolonial** *adj*, **neocolonialist** *n or adj*
Neolithic /ˌnee·əˈlithik‖ˌniːəˈlɪθɪk/ *adj* of the last period of the Stone Age characterized by polished stone implements
neologism /niˈoləjiz(ə)m‖nɪˈɒlədʒɪz(ə)m/ *n* (the use of) a new word, usage, or expression – **neology** *n*, **neological** *adj*, **neologistic** *adj*
neon /ˈneeon‖ˈniːɒn/ *n* **1** a noble gaseous element used esp in electric lamps **2** a discharge lamp in which the gas contains a large proportion of neon – **neon** *adj*, **neoned** *adj*
neophyte /ˈnee·əˌfiet‖ˈniːəˌfaɪt/ *n* **1** a new convert **2** a beginner
neoplasm /ˈnee·əˌplaz(ə)m‖ˈniːəˌplæz(ə)m/ *n* an abnormal growth of tissue; a tumour – **neoplastic** *adj*
nephew /ˈnefyooh‖ˈnefjuː/ *n* a son of one's brother or sister or of one's brother-in-law or sister-in-law
nephritis /niˈfrietəs‖nɪˈfraɪtəs/ *n, pl* **nephritides** /niˈfritədeez‖nɪˈfrɪtədiːz/ inflammation of the kidneys
ne plus ultra /ˌnay ploos ˈooltrə‖ˌneɪ plʊs ˈʊltrə/ *n* **1** the highest point or stage **2** the greatest degree of a quality or state
nepotism /ˈnepəˌtiz(ə)m‖ˈnepəˌtɪz(ə)m/ *n* favouritism shown to a relative (e g by appointment to office) [French *népotisme*, fr Italian *nepotismo*, fr *nepote* nephew, fr Latin *nepot-*, *nepos* grandson, nephew] – **nepotist** *n*
Neptune /ˈneptyoohn‖ˈneptjuːn/ *n* **1** the ocean personified **2** the planet 8th in order from the sun – **Neptunian** *adj*
neptunium /nepˈtyoohni·əm‖nepˈtjuːnɪəm/ *n* a radioactive metallic element that is obtained in nuclear reactors as a by-product of the production of plutonium
nerd /nuhd‖nɜːd/ *n* an unpleasant or foolish person – infml
[1]nerve /nuhv‖nɜːv/ *n* **1** sinew, tendon <*strain every* ~> **2** any of the filaments of nervous tissue that conduct nervous impulses to and from the nervous system and are made up of axons and dendrites **3a** fortitude, tenacity **b** (disrespectful) assurance or boldness **4a** a sore or sensitive subject – esp in *hit/touch a nerve* **b** *pl* acute nervousness or anxiety **5** VEIN 3 **6** the sensitive pulp of a tooth
[2]nerve *vt* **1** to give strength and courage to **2** to prepare (oneself) psychologically *for* – often + *up* <~d *herself up for the confrontation*>
ˈnerve ˌcell *n* a neuron
ˈnerve ˌcentre *n* **1** CENTRE 3 **2** a source of leadership, control, or energy
ˈnerveless /-lis‖-lɪs/ *adj* **1** lacking strength or vigour **2** not agitated or afraid; cool – **nervelessly** *adv*, **nervelessness** *n*
ˈnerve-ˌracking, ˈnerve-ˌwracking *adj* placing a great strain on the nerves
nervous /ˈnuhvəs‖ˈnɜːvəs/ *adj* **1** of, affected by, or composed of (the) nerves or neurons **2a** easily excited or agitated **b** timid, apprehensive – **nervously** *adv*, **nervousness** *n*
ˌnervous ˈbreakˌdown *n* (an occurrence of) a disorder in which worrying, depression, severe tiredness, etc prevent one from coping with one's responsibilities
ˈnervous ˌsystem *n* the brain, spinal cord, or other nerves and nervous tissue together forming a system for interpreting stimuli from the sense organs and transmitting impulses to muscles, glands, etc
nervy /ˈnuhvi‖ˈnɜːvɪ/ *adj* **1** suffering from nervousness or anxiety **2** brash, imprudent – infml – **nerviness** *n*
ness /nes‖nes/ *n* a cape or headland
-ness /-nis‖-nɪs/ *suffix* (*adj* → *n*) **1** state or quality of <*good*ness>; *also* instance of (a specified state or quality) <*a kind*ness> **2** degree or amount of <*big*ness>
[1]nest /nest‖nest/ *n* **1a** a bed or receptacle prepared by a bird for its eggs and young **b** a place or structure in which animals live, esp in their immature stages <*an ants'* ~> **2a** a place of rest, retreat, or lodging **b** a den or haunt **3a** a group of similar things **b** a hotbed **4** a series of objects made to fit close together or one inside another
[2]nest *vi* **1** to build or occupy a nest **2** to fit compactly together ~ *vt* to pack or fit compactly together – **nester** *n*
ˈnest ˌegg *n* **1** a real or artificial egg left in a nest to induce a fowl to continue to lay there **2** an amount of money saved up as a reserve
nestle /ˈnesl‖ˈnesl/ *vi* **1** to settle snugly or comfortably **2** to lie in a sheltered position ~ *vt* **1** to shelter or enclose (as if) in a nest **2** to press closely and affectionately
nestling /ˈnes(t)ling‖ˈnes(t)lɪŋ/ *n* a young bird that has not abandoned the nest
[1]net /net‖net/ *n* **1a** an open meshed fabric twisted, knotted, or woven together at regular intervals **b** a device for catching fish, birds, or insects **c** a net barricade which divides a tennis, badminton, etc court in half and over which a ball or shuttlecock must be hit to be in play **d** the fabric that encloses the sides and back of a soccer, hockey, etc goal **e(1)** a practice cricket

pitch surrounded by nets – usu pl **e(2)** a period of practice in such a net **2** an entrapping situation **3** a network of lines, fibres, etc

[2]**net** *vt* **-tt- 1** to cover or enclose (as if) with a net **2** to catch (as if) in a net **3a** to hit (a ball) into the net for the loss of a point in a game **b** to hit or kick (a ball or puck) into the goal for a score in hockey, soccer, etc – **netter** *n*

[3]**net,** *chiefly Br* **nett** *adj* **1a** remaining after all deductions (e g for taxes, outlay, or loss) <~ *earnings*> **b** excluding all tare <~ *weight*> **2** final, ultimate <*the* ~ *result*>

[4]**net,** *chiefly Br* **nett** *vt* **-tt- 1** to make by way of profit **2** to get possession of

[5]**net** *n* a net amount, profit, weight, price, or score

ˈnetˌball /-ˌbawl‖-ˌbɔːl/ *n* a game, usu for women, between 2 sides of 7 players each who score goals by tossing a ball through a high horizontal ring on a post

nether /ˈnedhə‖ˈneðə/ *adj* **1** beneath the earth's surface <*the* ~ *regions*> **2** lower, under – fml – **nethermost** *adj*

netting /ˈneting‖ˈnetɪŋ/ *n* NETWORK 1

[1]**nettle** /ˈnetl‖ˈnetl/ *n* **1** any of a genus of widely distributed green-flowered plants covered with stinging hairs **2** any of various plants like the nettle – used in combination deadnettle

[2]**nettle** *vt* **1** to strike or sting (as if) with nettles **2** to arouse to annoyance or anger

ˈnettle ˌrash *n* urticaria

[1]**ˈnetˌwork** /-ˌwuhk‖-ˌwɜːk/ *n* **1** a fabric or structure of cords or wires that cross at regular intervals and are knotted or secured at the crossings **2** a system of crisscrossing lines or channels **3** an interconnected chain, group, or system **4** a group of radio or television stations linked together so that they can broadcast the same programmes if desired

[2]**network** *vt* to present on or integrate into a radio or television network

neur-, neuro- *comb form* **1** nerve; nervous system <neur*al*> <neuro*surgeon*> **2** neural; neural and <neuro*muscular*>

neural /ˈnyooərəl‖ˈnjʊərəl/ *adj* **1** of or affecting a nerve or the nervous system **2** dorsal – **neurally** *adv*

neuralgia /nyoo(ə)ˈraljə‖njʊ(ə)ˈrældʒə/ *n* intense paroxysms of pain radiating along the course of a nerve without apparent cause – **neuralgic** *adj*

neurasthenia /ˌnyooərəsˈtheenyə‖ˌnjʊərəsˈθiːnjə/ *n* severe fatigue, depression, etc occurring as a mental disorder; NERVOUS BREAKDOWN – not now used technically – **neurasthenic** *adj*, **neurasthenically** *adv*

neuritis /nyooəˈrietəs‖njʊəˈraɪtəs/ *n* inflammation or degeneration of a nerve, causing pain, sensory disturbances, etc – **neuritic** *adj or n*

neurology /nyoo(ə)ˈroləji‖njʊ(ə)ˈrɒlədʒɪ/ *n* the study of (diseases of) the nervous system – **neurologist** *n*, **neurologic, neurological** *adj*, **neurologically** *adv*

neuron /ˈnyooəron‖ˈnjʊərɒn/ *n* a specialized cell that conducts nerve impulses and is the basic functional unit of nerve tissue

neurosis /nyoo(ə)ˈrohsis‖njʊ(ə)ˈrəʊsɪs/ *n, pl* **neuroses** /-ˌseez‖-ˌsiːz/ a nervous disorder, unaccompanied by disease of the nervous system, in which phobias, compulsions, anxiety, and obsessions make normal life difficult

neurotic /nyoo(ə)ˈrotik‖njʊ(ə)ˈrɒtɪk/ *n* one who is emotionally unstable or is affected with a neurosis – **neurotic** *adj*, **neurotically** *adv*, **neuroticism** *n*

ˌneurotransˈmitter /ˌnyooəroh-‖ˌnjʊərəʊ-/ *n* a substance that is released at a nerve ending and transmits nerve impulses across the synapse – **neurotransmission** *n*

[1]**neuter** /ˈnyoohtə‖ˈnjuːtə/ *adj* **1** of or belonging to the gender that is neither masculine nor feminine **2** lacking generative organs or having nonfunctional ones

[2]**neuter** *n* **1** (a word or morpheme of) the neuter gender **2a** WORKER 2 **b** a castrated animal

[3]**neuter** *vt* CASTRATE 1

[1]**neutral** /ˈnyoohtrəl‖ˈnjuːtrəl/ *adj* **1** (of or being a country, person, etc) not engaged on either side of a war, dispute, etc **2a** indifferent, indefinite **b** without colour **c** NEUTER 2 **d** neither acid nor alkaline **e** not electrically charged or positive or negative; not live – **neutrally** *adv*, **neutralism** *n*, **neutralist** *n*, **neutrality** *n*

[2]**neutral** *n* **1** a neutral country, person, etc **2** a neutral colour **3** a position (of a gear lever) in which gears are disengaged **4** a neutral electrical conductor

neutral·ize, -ise /ˈnyoohtrəˌliez‖ˈnjuːtrəˌlaɪz/ *vt* **1** to make (chemically, politically, electrically, etc) neutral **2** to nullify or counteract (the effect of) with an opposing action, force, etc ~*vi* to become neutralized – **neutralization** *n*

neutron /ˈnyoohˌtron‖ˈnjuːˌtrɒn/ *n* an uncharged elementary particle with a mass about that of the proton, present in the nuclei of all atoms except those of normal hydrogen

never /ˈnevə‖ˈnevə/ *adv* **1** not ever; at no time **2** not in any degree; not under any condition <*this will* ~ *do*> **3** surely not <*you're* ~ *18!*> – chiefly infml – **I never 1** – used to express amazement <*well* I never>; chiefly infml **2** I didn't do it – nonstandard <*no she* never>

ˌneverˈmore *adv* never again

ˌnever-ˈnever *n, Br* HIRE PURCHASE – + *the*; infml

ˌnever-ˈnever ˌland *n* an ideal or imaginary place

nevertheless /ˌnevədhəˈles‖ˌnevəðəˈles/ *adv* in spite of that; yet <*true but* ~ *unkind*>

[1]**new** /nyooh‖njuː/ *adj* **1** not old; not used previously; recent <*a* ~ *book*> <*a* ~ *science*> **2a(1)** only recently discovered, recognized, or in use; novel <*the* ~ *morality*> **a(2)** fresh, unfamiliar <*visit* ~ *places*> **b** different from or replacing a former one of the same kind <*a* ~ *model*> **3** having been in the specified condition or relationship for only a short time; unaccustomed <~ *to the job*> <*a* ~ *member*> **4a** beginning as the repetition of a previous act or thing <*a* ~ *day*> **b** refreshed, regenerated <*awoke, a* ~ *man*> **5** *cap* MODERN 3; *esp* in use after medieval times – **newish** *adj*, **newness** *n* – **new lease of life** a renewed period of healthy activity, strength, or usefulness

[2]**new** *adv* newly, recently – usu in combination

<new-*mown grass*>

ˌnew'born /-'bawn‖-'bɔːn/ *n or adj, pl* **newborn, newborns** (an individual who is) recently born

'newˌcomer /-ˌkumə‖-ˌkʌmə/ *n* **1** a recent arrival **2** a beginner, novice

New Deal *n* the programme of economic and social reform in the USA during the 1930s

newel /'nyooh·əl‖'njuːəl/ *n* **1** an upright post about which the steps of a spiral staircase wind **2** *also* **newel post** a principal post supporting either end of a staircase handrail

ˌnew'fangled /-'fang·gld‖-'fæŋgld/ *adj* modern and unnecessarily complicated or gimmicky – derog or humor – **newfangledness** *n*

Newfoundland /nyooh'fowndlənd‖njuː-'faʊndlənd/ *n* (any of) a breed of large intelligent dogs with coarse dense usu black hair [*Newfoundland*, island of Canada]

newly /'nyoohli‖'njuːlɪ/ *adv* **1** lately, recently <*a ~ married couple*> **2** anew

'newlyˌwed /-ˌwed‖-ˌwed/ *n or adj* (one who is) recently married

ˌnew 'moon *n* the phase of the moon when its dark side is towards the earth; *also* the thin crescent moon seen a few days after this

ˌnew 'penny *n* PENNY 1a(2)

news /nyoohz‖njuːz/ *n pl but sing in constr* **1** (a report or series of reports of) recent (notable) events; new information about sthg <*have you heard the ~?*> <*there is no ~ of him*> **2a** news reported in a newspaper, a periodical, or a broadcast **b** material that is newsworthy **3** a radio or television broadcast of news – **newsless** *adj*

'newsˌagent /-ˌayjənt‖-ˌeɪdʒənt/ *n, chiefly Br* a retailer of newspapers and magazines

'newsˌboy /-ˌboy‖-ˌbɔɪ/, *fem* **'newsˌgirl** *n* a paperboy

'newsˌcast /-ˌkahst‖-ˌkɑːst/ *n* NEWS 3 – **newscaster** *n*, **newscasting** *n*

'newsˌletter /-ˌletə‖-ˌletə/ *n* a printed pamphlet containing news or information of interest chiefly to a special group

'newsˌmonger /-ˌmung·gə‖-ˌmʌŋgə/ *n* a gossip

newspaper /'nyoohsˌpaypə‖'njuːsˌpeɪpə/ *n* **1** (an organization that publishes) a paper printed and distributed usu daily or weekly and containing news, articles of opinion, features, and advertising **2** the paper on which a newspaper is printed

'newsˌprint /-ˌprint‖-ˌprɪnt/ *n* cheap paper made chiefly from wood pulp and used mostly for newspapers

'newsˌreel /-ˌreel‖-ˌriːl/ *n* a short film dealing with current events

'newsˌroom /-room, -ˌroohm‖-rʊm, -ˌruːm/ *n* a place (e g an office) where news is prepared for publication or broadcast

'newsˌstand /-ˌstand‖-ˌstænd/ *n* a stall where newspapers and periodicals are sold

'newsˌvendor /-ˌvendə‖-ˌvendə/ *n* one who sells newspapers, esp in the street at a regular place

'newsˌworthy /-ˌwuhdhi‖-ˌwɜːðɪ/ *adj* sufficiently interesting to warrant reporting

newsy /'nyoohzi‖'njuːzɪ/ *adj* full of (inconsequential) news – **newsiness** *n*

newt /nyooht‖njuːt/ *n* any of various small semiaquatic salamanders

ˌNew 'Testament *n* the second part of the Christian Bible comprising the canonical Gospels and Epistles, the books of Acts, and the book of Revelation

newton /'nyooht(ə)n‖'njuːt(ə)n/ *n* the SI unit of force equal to the force that when acting for 1s on a free mass of 1kg will give it a velocity of 1m/s [Sir Isaac *Newton* (1642-1727), English mathematician & scientist]

Newtonian /nyooh'tohnyən, -ni·ən‖njuː-'təʊnjən, -nɪən/ *adj* of, following, or agreeing with (the discoveries of) Isaac Newton <*~ mechanics*>

new town *n* any of several towns in Britain planned and built as a unit since 1946

ˌNew 'World *n* the W hemisphere; *esp* the continental landmass of N and S America

ˌNew 'Year *n* the first day or days of a year; *esp* NEW YEAR'S DAY

ˌNew ˌYear's 'Day *n* January 1 observed as a public holiday in many countries

¹next /nekst‖nekst/ *adj* **1** immediately adjacent or following (e g in place or order) <*the ~ house*> **2** immediately after the present or a specified time <*~ week*> <*he left the very ~ Monday*>

²next *adv* **1** in the time, place, or order nearest or immediately succeeding <*~ we drove home*> <*the ~ closest school*> **2** on the first occasion to come <*when ~ we meet*>

³next *prep* nearest or adjacent to <*wear wool ~ the skin*>

⁴next *n* the next occurrence, item, or issue of a kind <*to be contained in our ~*>

ˌnext-'door *adj* situated or living in the next building, room, etc

next door *adv* in or to the next building, room, etc

ˌnext of 'kin *n, pl* **next of kin** the person most closely related to another person

¹'next to *prep* immediately following or adjacent to <*sit ~ Mary*> <*~ gin I like sherry best*>

²next to *adv* very nearly; almost <*it was ~ impossible to see in the fog*> <*the article told me ~ nothing*>

nexus /'neksəs‖'neksəs/ *n, pl* **nexuses, nexus** **1** a connection or link **2** a connected group or series

niacin /'nie·əsin‖'naɪəsɪn/ *n* NICOTINIC ACID

¹nib /nib‖nɪb/ *n* **1** a bill or beak **2a** the sharpened point of a quill pen **b** (each of the 2 equal divisions of) a small thin (detachable) piece of metal at the end of a pen, that tapers to a split point which is placed in contact with the paper or other surface to be marked **3** a small pointed or projecting part or article <*roasted almond ~s*>

²nib *vt* **-bb-** to make into a nib or give a nib to

¹nibble /'nibl‖'nɪbl/ *vt* **1a** to bite cautiously, gently, or playfully **b** to eat or chew in small bites **2** to produce by repeated small bites ~ *vi* **1** to take gentle, small, or cautious bites **2** to show cautious or qualified interest ***USE*** (*vi*) usu + *at* – **nibbler** *n*

[2]**nibble** *n* **1** an act of nibbling **2** a very small amount (e g of food) ***USE*** infml

nibs /nibz‖nɪbz/ *n pl but sing in constr* an important or self-important person – infml; chiefly in *his nibs* or *His Nibs*

nice /nies‖naɪs/ *adj* **1** showing or requiring fine discrimination or treatment <*a ~ distinction*> **2a** pleasant, agreeable **b** well done; well-executed <*~ shot!*> **3** inappropriate or unpleasant – usu ironic <*he's a ~ one to talk*>; compare PRETTY 2 **4a** socially acceptable; well-bred **b** decent, proper [Old French, foolish, wanton, fr Latin *nescius* ignorant, fr *nescire* not to know, fr *ne-* not + *scire* to know] – **nicely** *adv*, **niceness** *n* – **nice and** to a satisfactory degree <*it's* nice and *cool*>

nicety /'niesəti‖'naɪsətɪ/ *n* **1** an elegant or refined feature **2** a fine point or distinction **3** (the showing or requiring of) delicacy, discernment, or careful attention to details – **to a nicety** to the point at which sthg is at its best <*roasted* to a nicety>

[1]**niche** /neesh, nich‖niːʃ, nɪtʃ/ *n* **1** a recess in a wall, esp for a statue **2a** a place or activity for which a person is best suited **b** the ecological role of an organism in a community, esp in regard to food consumption

[2]**niche** *vt* to place (as if) in a niche

[1]**nick** /nik‖nɪk/ *n* **1** a small notch or groove **2** the point at which the back or side wall of a squash court meets the floor **3** EDGE 4 **4** *Br* state of health or repair – infml; esp in *in good/bad nick* <*it's not in very good ~*> **5** *Br* a prison or police station – slang <*he's been in the ~ for the last 3 years*> – **in the nick of time** at the final critical moment; just before it would be too late

[2]**nick** *vt* **1a** to make a nick in **b** to cut into or wound slightly **2** *Br* **2a** STEAL 1a **b** ARREST 2 ~*vi esp of domestic animals* to complement one another genetically and produce superior offspring ***USE*** (*vt 2*) slang

nickel /'nik(ə)l‖'nɪk(ə)l/ *n* **1** a hard bivalent metallic transition element with magnetic properties like those of iron **2** (a US coin containing 1 part of nickel to 3 of copper and worth) the sum of 5 cents

[1]**nicker** /'nikə‖'nɪkə/ *n, pl* **nicker** *Br* the sum of £1 – slang

[2]**nicker** *vi* to whinny

nicknack /'nikˌnak‖'nɪkˌnæk/ *n* a knick-knack

nickname /'nikˌnaym‖'nɪkˌneɪm/ *n* **1** a name used in place of or in addition to a proper name **2** a familiar form of a proper name, esp of a person [Middle English *nekename* additional name, incorrect form of *ekename*, fr *eke* also + *name*] – **nickname** *vt*

nicotine /'nikəteen‖'nɪkətiːn/ *n* an alkaloid that is the chief drug in tobacco and has the actions of the neurotransmitter acetylcholine on some of its receptors, esp those in skeletal muscle [Jean *Nicot* (died 1600), French diplomat & scholar who introduced tobacco into France] – **nicotinic** *adj*

ˌnicoˌtinic 'acid /-'teenik, -'tinik‖-'tiːnɪk, -'tɪnɪk/ *n* a vitamin of the vitamin B complex that is found widely in animals and plants and whose lack results in pellagra

niece /nees‖niːs/ *n* a daughter of one's brother or sister or of one's brother-in-law or sister-in-law

niff /nif‖nɪf/ *n, Br* an unpleasant smell – slang – **niffy** *adj*

nifty /'nifti‖'nɪftɪ/ *adj* very good or effective; *esp* cleverly conceived or executed – infml – **nifty** *adv*

niggard /'nigəd‖'nɪgəd/ *n* a mean and stingy person – **niggard** *adj*

'niggardly /-li‖-lɪ/ *adj* **1** grudgingly mean; miserly **2** provided in meagre amounts <*~ praise*> – **niggardliness** *n*, **niggardly** *adv*

nigger /'nigə‖'nɪgə/ *n* a Negro; *broadly* a member of any dark-skinned race – derog

niggle /'nigl‖'nɪgl/ *vi* **1** to waste time or effort on minor details **2** to find fault constantly in a petty way ~*vt* to cause slight irritation to; bother – **niggle** *n*, **niggler** *n*, **niggly** *adj*

niggling /'nigling‖'nɪglɪŋ/ *adj* **1** petty **2** persistently annoying <*~ doubts*> – **nigglingly** *adv*

nigh /nie‖naɪ/ *adv, adj, or prep* near (in place, time, or relation) <*~ on 50 years*>

night /niet‖naɪt/ *n* **1** the period of darkness from dusk to dawn caused by the earth's daily rotation **2** an evening characterized by a specified event or activity <*Thursday is bingo ~*> <*opening ~*> **3a** darkness **b** a state of affliction, ignorance, or obscurity

night blindness *n* reduced vision in faint light (e g at night) – **night-blind** *adj*

'nightˌcap /-ˌkap‖-ˌkæp/ *n* **1** a cloth cap worn in bed **2** a drink taken at bedtime

'nightˌclub /-ˌklub‖-ˌklʌb/ *n* a place of entertainment open at night that has a floor show, provides music and space for dancing, and usu serves drinks and food

'nightˌdress /-ˌdres‖-ˌdres/ *n* a woman's or girl's nightgown

'nightˌfall /-ˌfawl‖-ˌfɔːl/ *n* dusk

'nightˌhawk /-ˌhawk‖-ˌhɔːk/ *n* a nightjar, owl, or similar bird that flies at night

nightingale /'nietingˌgayl‖'naɪtɪŋˌgeɪl/ *n* any of several Old World thrushes noted for the sweet usu nocturnal song of the male [Old English *nihtegale*, fr *niht* night + *galan* to sing]

'nightˌjar /-ˌjah‖-ˌdʒɑː/ *n* a Eurasian insect-eating bird that is active at night and has a characteristic churring call

'nightˌlife /-ˌlief‖-ˌlaɪf/ *n* late evening entertainment or social life

'night-ˌlight *n* a dim light kept burning all night long, esp in sby's bedroom

'nightly /-li‖-lɪ/ *adj or adv* (of, occurring, taken, or done) at or by night or every night

'nightˌmare /-ˌmeə‖-ˌmeə/ *n* **1** an evil spirit that causes frightening dreams **2** a frightening dream accompanied by a sense of oppression or suffocation that usu awakens the sleeper **3** an experience, situation, or object that causes acute anxiety or terror – **nightmare, nightmarish** *adj*, **nightmarishly** *adv*

nights *adv* in the night repeatedly; on any night

'night ˌschool *n* classes, often in subjects leading to a qualification, held in the evening

nightshade /'nietˌshayd‖'naɪtˌʃeɪd/ *n* any of

various related usu poisonous plants: e g **a** bittersweet **b** DEADLY NIGHTSHADE

ˈnight,shirt /-ˌshuht‖-ˌʃɜːt/ *n* a long loose shirt for sleeping in

ˈnight ˌsoil *n* human excrement collected for fertilizing the soil

ˈnight,stick /-ˌstik‖-ˌstɪk/ *n, NAm* a club carried by a policeman

ˌnight ˈwatchman *n* **1** sby who keeps watch (e g over a building) by night **2** a relatively inexpert batsman who is sent in to bat towards the end of a day's play so that a more expert batsman need not face the bowling until the following day

nihilism /ˈnie·əˌliz(ə)m, ˈni-‖ˈnaɪəˌlɪz(ə)m, ˈnɪ-/ *n* **1** a view that rejects all values and beliefs as meaningless or unfounded **2a** *often cap* the doctrine that social conditions are so bad as to make destruction desirable for its own sake, adhered to specif by a 19th-c Russian terrorist revolutionary party **b** terrorism – **nihilist** *n or adj*, **nihilistic** *adj*

nil /nil‖nɪl/ *n* nothing, zero *<a score of 2 points to ~>* – **nil** *adj*

Nilotic /nieˈlotik‖naɪˈlɒtɪk/ *adj* of (the inhabitants or languages of) the Nile or Nile region

nimble /ˈnimbl‖ˈnɪmbl/ *adj* **1** quick, light, and easy in movement **2** quick and clever in thought and understanding – **nimbleness** *n*, **nimbly** *adv*

nimbus /ˈnimbəs‖ˈnɪmbəs/ *n, pl* **nimbi** /-ˌbie, -bi‖-ˌbaɪ, -bɪ/, **nimbuses** **1** a luminous vapour, cloud, or atmosphere surrounding a god or goddess **2** a luminous circle about the head of a representation of a god, saint, or sovereign **3** a cloud from which rain is falling

nincompoop /ˈningkəmˌpoohp‖ˈnɪŋkəmˌpuːp/ *n* a silly or foolish person

nine /nien‖naɪn/ *n* **1** (the number) 9 **2** the ninth in a set or series **3** sthg having 9 parts or members or a denomination of 9 **4** the first or last 9 holes of an 18-hole golf course **5** *pl in constr, cap the* Common Market countries between 1973 and 1981 – **nine** *adj or pron*, **ninefold** *adj or adv* – **to the nines** elaborately in special, formal, or party clothes *<dressed up* to the nines*>*

ˌnine ˌdays' ˈwonder *n* sthg that creates a short-lived sensation

nineteen /nienˈteen‖naɪnˈtiːn/ *n* (the number) 19 – **nineteen** *adj or pron*, **nineteenth** *adj or n* – **nineteen to the dozen** very fast and volubly *<talking* nineteen to the dozen*>*

ninety /ˈnienti‖ˈnaɪntɪ/ *n* **1** (the number) 90 **2** *pl* (a range of temperatures, ages, or dates within a century characterized by) the numbers 90 to 99 – **ninety** *adj or pron*, **ninetyfold** *adj or adv*, **ninetieth** *adj or n*

ninny /ˈnini‖ˈnɪnɪ/ *n* a silly or foolish person – humor; infml

ninth /nienth‖naɪnθ/ *n* **1** number nine in a countable series **2a** (a chord containing) a musical interval of an octave and a second **b** the note separated by this interval from a lower note – **ninth** *adj or adv*

[1]**nip** /nip‖nɪp/ *vb* **-pp-** *vt* **1** to catch hold of and squeeze sharply; pinch **2a** to sever (as if) by pinching sharply – often + *off* **b** to prevent the growth or development of *<her plans were ~ped in the bud>* **3** to injure or make numb with cold *~vi chiefly Br* to go quickly or briefly; hurry – infml *<I'll just ~ out to the shops>*

[2]**nip** *n* **1** a sharp stinging cold *<a ~ in the air>* **2** (an instance of) nipping; a pinch **3** *chiefly NAm* a pungent flavour; a tang

[3]**nip** *n* a small measure or drink of spirits

[4]**nip** *vb* **-pp-** to take nips of (a drink)

Nip *n* a Japanese – derog

ˌnip and ˈtuck *adj or adv, chiefly NAm* NECK AND NECK

nipper /ˈnipə‖ˈnɪpə/ *n* **1** any of various devices (e g pincers) for gripping or cutting – usu pl with sing. meaning **2** *chiefly Br* a child; *esp* a small boy – infml

nipple /ˈnipl‖ˈnɪpl/ *n* **1** the small protuberance of a mammary gland (e g a breast) from which milk is drawn in the female **2a** an artificial teat through which a bottle-fed infant feeds **b** a device with a hole through which the discharge of a liquid can be regulated **3** a small projection through which oil or grease is injected into machinery

nippy /ˈnipi‖ˈnɪpɪ/ *adj* **1** nimble and lively; snappy **2** CHILLY 1 – **nippily** *adv*, **nippiness** *n*

nirvana /niəˈvahnə, nuh-‖nɪəˈvɑːnə, nɜː-/ *n, often cap* **1** a Hindu and Buddhist state of final bliss and freedom from the cycle of rebirth, attainable through the extinction of desire and individual consciousness **2** a place or state of relief from pain or anxiety

nisi /ˈniesie, ˈneezi‖ˈnaɪsaɪ, ˈniːzɪ/ *adj* taking effect at a specified time unless previously modified or avoided *<a decree ~>*

ˈNissen ˌhut /ˈnis(ə)n‖ˈnɪs(ə)n/ *n* a prefabricated shelter with a semicircular arching roof of corrugated iron and a concrete floor [Peter *Nissen* (1871-1930), British mining engineer]

[1]**nit** /nit‖nɪt/ *n* (the egg of) a parasitic insect (e g a louse)

[2]**nit** *n, chiefly Br* a nitwit – infml

ˈnit-ˌpicking *n* petty and usu unjustified criticism – **nitpick** *vi*

[1]**nitrate** /ˈnietrayt‖ˈnaɪtreɪt/ *n* **1** a salt or ester of nitric acid **2** sodium or potassium nitrate used as a fertilizer

[2]**nitrate** *vt* to treat or combine with nitric acid or a nitrate – **nitrator** *n*, **nitration** *n*

nitre, *NAm chiefly* **niter** /ˈnietə‖ˈnaɪtə/ *n* POTASSIUM NITRATE – not now used technically

nitric /ˈnietrik‖ˈnaɪtrɪk/ *adj* of or containing nitrogen (with a relatively high valency) *<~ oxide>*

ˌnitric ˈacid *n* a corrosive inorganic liquid acid used esp as an oxidizing agent and in making fertilizers, dyes, etc

nitrogen /ˈnietrəj(ə)n‖ˈnaɪtrədʒ(ə)n/ *n* a trivalent gaseous chemical element that constitutes about 78 per cent by volume of the atmosphere and is found in combined form as a constituent of all living things – **nitrogenous** *adj*

nitroglycerine /ˌnietrohˈglisəreen, -rin‖ˌnaɪtrəʊˈglɪsəriːn, -rɪn/ *n* an oily explosive liquid used chiefly in making dynamite and, as a weak solution in water, in medicine to dilate the blood vessels

nitrous /ˈnietrəs‖ˈnaɪtrəs/ *adj* of or containing

a potassium nitrate **b** nitrogen (with a relatively low valency)

ˌnitrous ˈoxide *n* a gas used as a general anaesthetic, esp in obstetrics and dentistry

nitty-gritty /ˌniti ˈgriti‖ˌnɪtɪ ˈgrɪtɪ/ *n the* important basic realities – infml – **nitty-gritty** *adj*

nitwit /ˈnitˌwit‖ˈnɪtˌwɪt/ *n* a scatterbrained or stupid person – infml – **nit-witted** *adj*

[1]nix /niks‖nɪks/, *fem* **nixie** /-si‖-sɪ/ *n* a water sprite of Germanic folklore

[2]nix *n* nothing – slang

[3]nix *adv, NAm* no – slang

[4]nix *vt, NAm* to veto, forbid – slang

[1]no /noh‖nəʊ/ *adv* **1** – used to negate an alternative choice <*whether you like it or* ~> **2** in no respect or degree – in comparisons <~ *better than before*> **3** – used in answers expressing negation, dissent, denial, or refusal; contrasted with *yes* <~, *I'm not going*> **4** – used like a question demanding assent to the preceding statement <*she's pretty,* ~*?*> **5** nay <*happy,* ~*, ecstatic*> **6** – used as an interjection to express incredulity <*'She's 17.'* 'No!'> **7** *chiefly Scot* not <*it's* ~ *canny*>

[2]no *adj* **1a** not any <~ *money*> <*there's* ~ *denying*> <~ *parking*> **b** hardly any; very little <*I'll be finished in* ~ *time*> **2a** not a; quite other than a <*he's* ~ *expert*> **b** – used before a noun phrase to give force to an opposite meaning <*in* ~ *uncertain terms*>; compare NOT 3

[3]no *n, pl* **noes, nos** a negative reply or vote

No, Noh /noh‖nəʊ/ *n, pl* **No, Noh** a classic Japanese (form of) dance-drama

[1]nob /nob‖nɒb/ *n* **1** a jack of the same suit as the card turned by the dealer in cribbage, that scores 1 point for the holder – chiefly in *his nob/nobs* <*one for his* ~> **2** a person's head – infml

[2]nob *n, chiefly Br* a wealthy or influential person – infml

[1]ˌno-ˈball *interj or n* – (used as a call by an umpire to indicate) an illegal delivery of the ball in cricket which cannot take a wicket and counts 1 run to the batsman's side if the batsman does not score a run off it

[2]no-ball *vt, of an umpire in cricket* to declare (a bowler) to have delivered or (a delivery) to be a no-ball ~*vi* to bowl a no-ball

nobble /ˈnobl‖ˈnɒbl/ *vt Br* **1** to incapacitate (esp a racehorse), esp by drugging **2a** to win over to one's side, esp by dishonest means **b** to get hold of, esp dishonestly **c** to swindle, cheat *USE* (*1*) infml; (*2*) slang – **nobbler** *n*

ˌNobel ˈprize /nohˈbel‖nəʊˈbel/ *n* any of various annual prizes for the encouragement of people who work for the interests of humanity (e g in the fields of peace, literature, medicine, and physics) [Alfred *Nobel* (1833-96), Swedish manufacturer, inventor, & philanthropist]

nobility /nohˈbiləti‖nəʊˈbɪlətɪ/ *n* **1** being noble **2** *sing or pl in constr* the people making up a noble class

[1]noble /ˈnohbl‖ˈnəʊbl/ *adj* **1a** gracious and dignified in character or bearing **b** famous, notable <*a* ~ *victory*> **2** of or being high birth or exalted rank **3** of fine quality; excellent <*a* ~ *vintage*> **4** imposing, stately **5** having or showing a magnanimous character or high ideals <*a* ~ *deed*> – **nobleness** *n*, **nobly** *adv*

[2]noble *n* **1** a person of noble rank or birth **2** a former English gold coin worth £$^1/_3$

ˈnobleman /-mən‖-mən/, *fem* **ˈnobleˌwoman** *n* a man of noble rank

noblesse oblige /ˌnohbles oˈbleezh, no-‖ˌnəʊbles ɒˈbliːʒ, nɒ-/ *n* the obligation of honourable and responsible behaviour associated with high rank [French, lit., nobility obligates]

[1]nobody /ˈnohbədi, -ˌbodi‖ˈnəʊbədɪ, -ˌbɒdɪ/ *pron* not anybody <~ *likes me*>

[2]nobody *n* a person of no influence or consequence

nocturnal /nokˈtuhnl‖nɒkˈtɜːnl/ *adj* **1** of or occurring in the night **2** active at night <*a* ~ *predator*> – **nocturnally** *adv*

nocturne /ˈnoktuhn‖ˈnɒktɜːn/ *n* a work of art dealing with evening or night; *esp* a dreamy pensive composition for the piano

[1]nod /nod‖nɒd/ *vb* **-dd-** *vi* **1** to make a short downward movement of the head (e g in assent or greeting) **2** to bend or sway gently downwards or forwards **3a** to become drowsy or sleepy <~ *in front of the fire*> **b** to make a slip or error in a moment of inattention <*even Homer sometimes* ~s> ~ *vt* **1** to incline (e g the head) in a quick downward movement **2** to express by a nod <~ded *their approval*> – **nodder** *n*

[2]nod *n* **1** (an instance of) nodding **2** an unconsidered indication of agreement, approval, etc – infml <*the motion went through on the* ~>

nodding /ˈnoding‖ˈnɒdɪŋ/ *adj* **1** pendulous or drooping <*a plant with* ~ *flowers*> **2** casual, superficial <*a* ~ *acquaintance with French*>

noddle /ˈnodl‖ˈnɒdl/ *n* a person's head – infml

node /nohd‖nəʊd/ *n* **1** a thickening or swelling (e g of a rheumatic joint) **2** either of the 2 points where the orbit of **2a** a planet or comet intersects the ecliptic **b** an earth satellite crosses the plane of the equator **3a** a point on a stem at which 1 or more leaves are attached **b** a point at which a curve intersects itself **4** a point, line, etc of a vibrating body at which vibration is at a minimum – **nodal** *adj*, **nodally** *adv*

nodule /ˈnodyoohl‖ˈnɒdjuːl/ *n* a small rounded mass: e g **a** a small rounded lump of a mineral or mineral aggregate **b** a swelling on the root of a leguminous plant (e g clover) containing symbiotic bacteria that convert atmospheric nitrogen into a form in which it can be used by the plant – **nodular** *adj*, **nodulated** *adj*, **nodulation** *n*

Noel, Noël /nohˈel‖nəʊˈel/ *n* the Christmas season

noes /nohz‖nəʊz/ *pl of* NO

nog /nog‖nɒg/ *n* (an) eggnog

noggin /ˈnogin‖ˈnɒgɪn/ *n* **1** a small mug or cup **2** a small measure of spirits, usu 0.142 litres ($^1/_4$pt) **3** a person's head – infml

no-go /ˌnoh ˈgoh‖ˌnəʊ ˈgəʊ/ *adj* having prohibited or restricted access <*a* ~ *military zone*>

nohow /ˈnohˌhow‖ˈnəʊˌhaʊ/ *adv* in no way; not at all – chiefly dial or humor

[1]noise /noyz‖nɔɪz/ *n* **1** loud confused shouting or outcry **2a** a (harsh or unwanted) sound **b** unwanted signals or fluctuations in an electrical circuit **c** irrelevant or meaningless information occurring with desired information in the output of a computer **3** a usu trite remark of a specified type – usu pl <*made sympathetic* ~s> [Old French, strife, quarrel, noise, fr Latin *nausea* nausea] – **noiseless** *adj*, **noiselessly** *adv*

[2]**noise** *vt* to spread by gossip or hearsay – usu + *about* or *abroad*

noisome /'noys(ə)m‖'nɔɪs(ə)m/ *adj* repellent, offensive – fml – **noisomely** *adv*, **noisomeness** *n*

noisy /'noyzi‖'nɔɪzɪ/ *adj* **1** making noise **2** full of or characterized by noise – **noisily** *adv*, **noisiness** *n*

nomad /'nohmad‖'nəʊmæd/ *n* **1** a member of a people that wanders from place to place, usu seasonally and within a well-defined territory **2** one who wanders aimlessly from place to place – **nomad** *adj*, **nomadism** *n*, **nomadic** *adj*

'no-ˌman's-ˌland *n* **1a** an area of waste or unclaimed land **b** an unoccupied area between opposing armies **2** an area of anomalous, ambiguous, or indefinite character

nom de plume /ˌnom de 'ploohm‖ˌnɒm de 'plu:m/ *n, pl* **noms de plume** /~/ a pseudonym under which an author writes [French *nom* name + *de* of + *plume* pen]

nomenclature /no'menklәchә‖nɒ-'menklәtʃә/ *n* **1** a name, designation **2** (an instance of) naming, esp within a particular system **3** a system of terms used in a particular science, discipline, or art – **nomenclatural** *adj*

[1]**nominal** /'nominl‖'nɒmɪnl/ *adj* **1** of or being a nominal **2** of or constituting a name **3a** being sthg in name only **b** assigned as a convenient approximation (e g to an actual weight or size) **c** negligible, insignificant <*a ~ rent*> – **nominally** *adv*

[2]**nominal** *n* a word (group) functioning as a noun

nominate /'nominayt‖'nɒmɪneɪt/ *vt* **1** to designate, specify **2a** to appoint or recommend for appointment **b** to propose for an honour, award, or candidature – **nominator** *n*, **nominee** *n*, **nomination** *n*

nominative /'nominәtiv‖'nɒmɪnәtɪv/ *adj* **1** of or being the grammatical case expressing the subject of a verb **2** nominated – **nominative** *n*

-nomy /-nәmi‖-nәmɪ/ *comb form* (→ *n*) **1** system of laws or principles governing a (specified) field; science of <*astro*nomy> **2** management <*eco*nomy> **3** government, rule <*auto*nomy>

non- /non-‖nɒn-/ *prefix* **1** not; reverse of; absence of <non*conformity*> <non*alcoholic*> **2** failure to be; refraining from <non*smoker*> <non*violent*> **3** lacking the usual characteristics of the thing specified <non*event*> **4** proof against; designed to avoid <non*stick*>

nonage /'nohnij, 'nonij‖'nәʊnɪdʒ, 'nɒnɪdʒ/ *n* a period or state of youth or immaturity

nonagenarian /ˌnohnәji'neәri·әn, ˌnonә-‖ˌnәʊnәdʒɪ'neәrɪәn, ˌnɒnә-/ *n* a person between 90 and 99 years old – **nonagenarian** *adj*

nonaligned /ˌnonә'liend‖ˌnɒnә'laɪnd/ *adj* not allied with other nations, esp any of the great powers – **nonalignment** *n*

nonce /nons‖nɒns/ *n* the present occasion, time, or purpose <*for the ~*> <*a ~ word*>

nonchalant /'nonshәlәnt‖'nɒnʃәlәnt/ *adj* giving an impression of easy unconcern or indifference – **nonchalance** *n*, **nonchalantly** *adv*

noncombatant /non'kombәt(ә)nt, -kәm'bat(ә)nt‖nɒn'kɒmbәt(ә)nt, -kәm'bæt(ә)nt/ *n* a civilian, army chaplain, etc who does not engage in combat – **noncombatant** *adj*

ˌnoncomˌmissioned 'officer /nonkә-'mish(ә)nd‖nɒnkә'mɪʃ(ә)nd/ *n* a subordinate officer (e g a sergeant) in the armed forces appointed from among the personnel who do not hold a commission

ˌnoncom'mittal /-kә'mitl‖-kә'mɪtl/ *adj* giving no clear indication of attitude or feeling – **noncommittally** *adv*

non compos mentis /ˌnon ˌkompәs 'mentis‖ˌnɒn ˌkɒmpәs 'mentɪs/ *adj* not of sound mind [Latin, lit., not having mastery of one's mind]

ˌnoncon'ductor /-kәn'duktә‖-kәn'dʌktә/ *n* a substance that conducts heat, electricity, etc only very slightly under normal conditions

ˌnoncon'formist /-kәn'fawmist‖-kәn'fɔ:mɪst/ *n* **1** *often cap* a person who does not conform to an established church; *specif* a member of a Protestant body separated from the Church of England **2** one who does not conform to a generally accepted pattern of thought or behaviour – **nonconformism** *n, often cap*, **nonconformist** *adj, often cap*

ˌnoncon'formity /-kәn'fawmәti‖-kәn'fɔ:mәtɪ/ *n* **1** refusal to conform to an established creed, rule, or practice **2** absence of correspondence or agreement

nondescript /'nondiskript‖'nɒndɪskrɪpt/ *adj* **1** (apparently) belonging to no particular class or kind **2** lacking distinctive or interesting qualities; dull – **nondescript** *n*

[1]**none** /nun‖nʌn/ *pron, pl* **none** **1** not any; no part or thing <*~ of the money is missing*> <*~ of the telephones are working*> **2** not one person; nobody <*it's ~ other than Tom*> <*~ but a fool*> **3** not any such thing or person <*a bad film is better than ~ at all*>

[2]**none** *adv* **1** by no means; not at all <*~ too soon to begin*> **2** in no way; to no extent <*~ the worse for wear*>

[3]**none** /nohn‖nәʊn/ *n, often cap* the fifth of the canonical hours that was orig fixed for 3 pm

nonentity /no'nentiti‖nɒ'nentɪtɪ/ *n* **1** sthg that does not exist or exists only in the imagination **2** nonexistence **3** sby or sthg of little importance or interest

nonesuch *also* **nonsuch** /'nunˌsuch‖'nʌnˌsʌtʃ/ *n* a person or thing without an equal; a paragon – **nonesuch** *adj*

nonetheless /ˌnundhә'les‖ˌnʌnðә'les/ *adv* nevertheless

nonevent /ˌnoni'vent‖ˌnɒnɪ'vent/ *n* an event that is (unexpectedly) dull or inconsequential

ˌnon'flammable /-'flamәbl‖-'flæmәbl/ *adj* difficult or impossible to set alight – **nonflammability** *n*

ˌnoninter'vention /-intә'vensh(ә)n‖-ɪntә-'venʃ(ә)n/ *n* the state or policy of not intervening – **noninterventionist** *n or adj*

nonpareil /'nonpәrel, ˌnonpә'rayl‖'nɒnpәrel, ˌnɒnpә'reɪl/ *n or adj* (sby or sthg) having no equal

nonplus /ˌnonˈplus‖ˌnɒnˈplʌs/ *vt* **-ss-** (*NAm* **-s-, -ss-**) to perplex or disconcert

ˌnonproˌlifeˈration /-prəˌlifəˈraysh(ə)n‖-prəˌlɪfəˈreɪʃ(ə)n/ *adj or n* (providing for) the stoppage of proliferation (e g of nuclear weapons)

ˌnonˈresident /-ˈrezid(ə)nt‖-ˈrezɪd(ə)nt/ *adj* not residing in a particular place (e g a hotel) – **nonresident** *n*, **nonresidence, nonresidency** *n*

nonsense /ˈnonsəns‖ˈnɒnsəns/ *n* **1a** meaningless words or language **b** (an instance of) foolish or absurd language, conduct, or thought **2** frivolous or insolent behaviour **3** – used interjectionally to express forceful disagreement – **nonsensical** *adj*, **nonsensically** *adv*, **nonsensicalness** *n*

non sequitur /ˌnon ˈsekwitə‖ˌnɒn ˈsekwɪtə/ *n* **1** a conclusion that does not follow from the premises **2** a statement that does not follow logically from anything previously said [Latin, it does not follow]

ˌnonˈskid /-ˈskid‖-ˈskɪd/ *adj, of a tyre or road* designed or equipped to prevent skidding

ˌnonˈstandard /ˈstandəd‖ˈstændəd/ *adj* not conforming in pronunciation, grammatical construction, idiom, or word choice to accepted usage

ˌnonˈstarter /-ˈstahtə‖-ˈstɑːtə/ *n* sby or sthg that is sure to fail or prove impracticable

ˌnonˈstick /-ˈstik‖-ˈstɪk/ *adj* having or being a surface that prevents adherence of food during cooking

ˌnonˈstop /-ˈstop‖-ˈstɒp/ *adj* done or made without a stop – **nonstop** *adv*

ˌnon-ˈU /ˈyooh‖ˈjuː/ *adj* not characteristic of the upper classes

ˌnonˈunion /-ˈyoohnyən‖-ˈjuːnjən/ *adj* not belonging to or connected with a trade union <~ *plumbers*> <*a* ~ *job*>

ˌnonˈviolence /-ˈvie·ələns‖-ˈvaɪələns/ *n* **1** refraining from violence on moral grounds **2** passive resistance or peaceful demonstration for political ends – **nonviolent** *adj*, **nonviolently** *adv*

ˌnonˈwhite /-ˈwiet‖-ˈwaɪt/ *n or adj* (one who is) not Caucasian

[1]**noodle** /ˈnoohdl‖ˈnuːdl/ *n* a silly or foolish person – humor

[2]**noodle** *n* a narrow flat ribbon of pasta made with egg

nook /nook‖nʊk/ *n* a small secluded or sheltered place or part

noon /noohn‖nuːn/ *n* **1 noon, noonday** the middle of the day; midday **2** the highest or culminating point

ˈno ˌone *pron* nobody

[1]**noose** /noohs‖nuːs/ *n* a loop with a running knot that tightens as the rope is pulled

[2]**noose** *vt* **1** to secure by a noose **2** to make a noose in or of

nope /nohp‖nəʊp/ *adv, chiefly NAm* no – infml

nor /naw‖nɔː/ *conj* **1** – used to join 2 sentence elements of the same class or function <*neither here* ~ *there*> <*not done by you* ~ *me* ~ *anyone*> **2** also not; neither <*it didn't seem hard,* ~ *was it*>

nor' /naw, nə-‖nɔː, nə-/ *n* north – often in combination <~*-easter*>

Nordic /ˈnawdik‖ˈnɔːdɪk/ *adj* **1** of a tall, fair, longheaded, blue-eyed physical type characteristic of the Germanic peoples of N Europe, esp Scandinavia **2** of competitive ski events consisting of ski jumping and cross-country racing

Norfolk jacket /ˈnawfək‖ˈnɔːfək/ *n* a man's semifitted belted single-breasted jacket with box pleats

norm /nawm‖nɔːm/ *n* **1** an authoritative standard; a model **2** a principle of correctness that is binding upon the members of a group, and serves to regulate action and judgment **3** the average: e g **3a** a set standard of development or achievement, usu derived from the average achievement of a large group **b** a pattern typical of a social group

[1]**normal** /ˈnawml‖ˈnɔːml/ *adj* **1** PERPENDICULAR 1 **2** conforming to or constituting a norm, rule, or principle **3** occurring naturally <~ *immunity*> **4a** having average intelligence or development **b** free from mental disorder **5** *of a solution* having a concentration of 1 gram equivalent weight of a solute in 1l **6** of, involving, or being a normal curve or normal distribution – **normally** *adv*, **normalcy, normality** *n*

[2]**normal** *n* **1** a line that is normal **2** sby or sthg that is normal

normal·ize, -ise /ˈnawmlˌiez‖ˈnɔːmlˌaɪz/ *vt* to make normal – **normalizable** *adj*, **normalization** *n*

Norman /ˈnawmən‖ˈnɔːmən/ *n* **1** a native or inhabitant of Normandy: e g **1a** any of the Scandinavian conquerors of Normandy in the 10th c **b** any of the Norman-French conquerors of England in 1066 **2 Norman, Norman-French** the French language of the medieval Normans **3** a style of architecture characterized, esp in its English form, by semicircular arches and heavy pillars – **Norman** *adj*

normative /ˈnawmətiv‖ˈnɔːmətɪv/ *adj* serving as or prescribing a norm – **normatively** *adv*, **normativeness** *n*

[1]**Norse** /naws‖nɔːs/ *n* **1** *pl in constr* Scandinavians; *specif* Norwegians **2a** the (older forms of the) language of Norway **b** NORTH GERMANIC

[2]**Norse** *adj* Scandinavian; *esp* of ancient Scandinavia or Norway

[1]**north** /nawth‖nɔːθ/ *adj or adv* towards, at, belonging to, or coming from the north

[2]**north** *n* **1** (the compass point corresponding to) the direction of the north terrestrial pole **2** *often cap* regions or countries lying to the north of a specified or implied point of orientation – **northward** *adv, adj, or n*, **northwards** *adv*

[1]**ˌnorthˈeast** /-ˈeest‖-ˈiːst/ *adj or adv* towards, at, belonging to, or coming from the northeast

[2]**ˌnorthˈeast** *n* **1** (the general direction corresponding to) the compass point midway between north and east **2** *often cap* regions or countries lying to the northeast of a specified or implied point of orientation – **northeastward** *adv, adj, or n*, **northeastwards** *adv*

[1]**northeasterly** /-ˈeestəli‖-ˈiːstəlɪ/ *adj or adv* northeast

[2]**northeasterly, ˌnorthˈeaster** /-ˈeestə‖-ˈiːstə/ *n* a wind from the northeast

ˌnorthˈeastern /-ˈeest(ə)n‖-ˈiːst(ə)n/ *adj* **1**

often cap (characteristic) of a region conventionally designated Northeast **2** northeast – **northeasternmost** *adj*

[1]**northerly** /ˈnawdhəli‖ˈnɔːðəlɪ/ *adj or adv* north

[2]**northerly** *n* a wind from the north

northern /ˈnawdhən‖ˈnɔːðən/ *adj* **1** *often cap* (characteristic) of a region conventionally designated North **2** north – **northernmost** *adj*

Northerner /ˈnawdhənə‖ˈnɔːðənə/ *n* a native or inhabitant of the North

ˌnorthern ˈlights *n pl* AURORA BOREALIS

ˌNorth Gerˈmanic *n* a group of Germanic languages comprising the Scandinavian languages including Icelandic and Faroese

ˌnorth ˈpole *n* **1a** *often cap N&P* the northernmost point of the rotational axis of the earth or another celestial body **b** the northernmost point on the celestial sphere, about which the stars seem to revolve **2** the northward-pointing pole of a magnet

[1]**ˌnorthˈwest** /-ˈwest‖-ˈwest/ *adj or adv* towards, at, belonging to, or coming from the northwest

[2]**ˌnorthˈwest** *n* **1** (the general direction corresponding to) the compass point midway between north and west **2** *often cap* regions or countries lying to the northwest of a specified or implied point of orientation – **northwestward** *adv, adj, or n,* **northwestwards** *adv*

[1]**ˌnorthˈwesterly** /-ˈwestəli‖-ˈwestəlɪ/ *adj or adv* northwest

[2]**northˈwesterly, northwester** /-ˈwestə‖-ˌwestə/ *n* a wind from the northwest

ˌnorthˈwestern /-ˈwest(ə)n‖-ˈwest(ə)n/ *adj* **1** *often cap* (characteristic) of a region conventionally designated Northwest **2** northwest

Norwegian /nawˈweej(ə)n‖nɔːˈwiːdʒ(ə)n/ *n or adj* (a native or inhabitant or the North Germanic language) of Norway

[1]**nose** /nohz‖nəʊz/ *n* **1a** the part of the face that bears the nostrils and covers the front part of the nasal cavity (together with the nasal cavity itself) **b** the front part of the head above or projecting beyond the mouth; a snout, muzzle **2a** the sense or (vertebrate) organ of smell **b** aroma, bouquet **3** the projecting part or front end of sthg **4a** the nose as a symbol of undue curiosity or interference **b** a knack for detecting what is latent or concealed – **through the nose** at an exorbitant rate <*had to pay* through the nose>

[2]**nose** *vt* **1** to detect (as if) by smell; scent **2** to push (as if) with the nose **3** to touch or rub with the nose; nuzzle ~ *vi* **1** to use the nose in examining, smelling, etc; to sniff or nuzzle **2a** to pry – often + *into* **b** to search or look inquisitively – usu + *about* or *around* **3** to move ahead slowly or cautiously

ˈnose ˌbag *n* a bag for feeding a horse or other animal, that covers the muzzle and is fastened on top of the head

ˈnoseˌbleed /-ˌbleed‖-ˌbliːd/ *n* an attack of bleeding from the nose

nosed /nohzd‖nəʊzd/ *adj* having a (specified kind of) nose – usu in combination <*snub*-nosed>

ˈnose ˌdive *n* **1** a downward nose-first plunge of an aircraft or other flying object **2** a sudden dramatic drop – **nose-dive** *vb*

ˈnoseˌgay /-ˌgay‖-ˌgeɪ/ *n* a small bunch of flowers; a posy

[1]**nosh** /nosh‖nɒʃ/ *vt* to chew, munch ~*vi* to eat – infml – **nosher** *n*

[2]**nosh** *n* food (in sufficient quantities for a meal); a meal – infml

ˈnosh-ˌup *n, Br* a large meal – infml

nostalgia /noˈstaljə‖nɒˈstældʒə/ *n* **1** homesickness **2** a wistful or excessively sentimental yearning for sthg past or irrecoverable [deriv of Greek *nostos* return home + *algos* pain] – **nostalgic** *adj or n,* **nostalgically** *adv*

nostril /ˈnostril, nostrəl‖ˈnɒstrɪl, nɒstrəl/ *n* the opening of the nose to the outside (together with the adjoining nasal passage) [Old English *nosthyrl*, fr *nosu* nose + *thyrel* hole]

nostrum /ˈnostrəm‖ˈnɒstrəm/ *n* **1** a quack medicine **2** a facile or questionable remedy

nosy, nosey /ˈnohzi‖ˈnəʊzɪ/ *adj* inquisitive, prying – infml – **nosily** *adv,* **nosiness** *n*

ˌnosy ˈparker /ˈpahkə‖ˈpɑːkə/ *n, Br* a busybody – infml

not /not‖nɒt/ *adv* **1** – used to negate a word or word group <~ *thirsty*> <~ *to complain*>; often *n't* after auxiliary verbs <*can't go*> **2** – used to negate a preceding word or word group <*will it rain? I hope* ~> <*are you ready? If* ~, *hurry up*> **3** – used to give force to an opposite meaning <~ *without reason*> <~ *a few of us*> – compare [2]NO 2b – **not a** not even one – **not at all** – used in answer to thanks or to an apology <*'Sorry to trouble you.'* 'Not at all!'> – **not half 1** *chiefly Br* not nearly <not half *long enough*> **2** very much; totally <*did*n't half *scold us*> <*'Are you busy?'* 'Not half!'> – slang

notability /ˌnohtəˈbiləti‖ˌnəʊtəˈbɪlətɪ/ *n* **1** a notable **2** being notable

[1]**notable** /ˈnohtəbl‖ˈnəʊtəbl/ *adj* **1** worthy of note; remarkable **2** distinguished, prominent – **notableness** *n,* **notably** *adv*

[2]**notable** *n* **1** a prominent person **2** *pl, often cap* a group of people summoned, esp in France when it was a monarchy, to act as a deliberative body

notar·ize, -ise /ˈnohtəˌriez‖ˈnəʊtəˌraɪz/ *vt, chiefly NAm* to validate as a notary public

notary /ˈnohtəri‖ˈnəʊtərɪ/, **notary public** *n, pl* **notaries, notaries public, notary publics** a public officer appointed to administer oaths and draw up and authenticate documents

notation /nohˈtaysh(ə)n‖nəʊˈteɪʃ(ə)n/ *n* **1** (a representation of sthg by) a system or set of marks, signs, symbols, figures, characters, or abbreviated expressions (e g to express technical facts or quantities) **2** *chiefly NAm* an annotation, note – **notational** *adj*

[1]**notch** /noch‖nɒtʃ/ *n* **1a** a V-shaped indentation **b** a slit or cut used as a record **2** a degree, step **3** *NAm* a deep narrow pass; a gap – **notched** *adj*

[2]**notch** *vt* **1** to make a notch in **2a** to mark or record (as if) by a notch – often + *up* **b** to score or achieve – usu + *up*

[1]**note** /noht‖nəʊt/ *vt* **1a** to take due or special notice of **b** to notice, observe **c** to record in writing **2** to make special mention of;

remark – **noter** *n*

[2]**note** *n* **1a(1)** a sound having a definite pitch **a(2)** a call, esp of a bird **b** a written symbol used to indicate duration and pitch of a tone by its shape and position on the staff **2a** a characteristic feature of smell, flavour, etc **b** a mood or quality **3a** a memorandum **b(1)** a brief comment or explanation **b(2)** a printed comment or reference set apart from the text **c** a piece of paper money **d(1)** a short informal letter **d(2)** a formal diplomatic communication **e** a short essay **4a** distinction, reputation **b** observation, notice

ˈ**noteˌbook** /-ˌbook‖-ˌbʊk/ *n* a book for notes or memoranda

noted /ˈnohtid‖ˈnəʊtɪd/ *adj* well-known, famous – **notedly** *adv*, **notedness** *n*

ˈ**noteˌworthy** /-ˌwuhdhi‖-ˌwɜːðɪ/ *adj* worthy of or attracting attention; notable – **noteworthily** *adv*, **noteworthiness** *n*

[1]**nothing** /ˈnuthing‖ˈnʌθɪŋ/ *pron* **1** not any thing; no thing <*~ greasy*> <*~ much to eat*> <*eats next to ~*> **2** sthg of no consequence <*it means ~ to me*> <*thinks ~ of walking 20 miles*> <*would be ~ without his title*> **3** no truth or value <*there's ~ in this rumour*> – **like nothing on earth 1** severely indisposed or embarrassed **2** grotesque, outlandish

[2]**nothing** *adv* not at all; in no degree <*~ like as cold*>

[3]**nothing** *n* **1a** sthg that does not exist **b** NOTHINGNESS 2b **2** sby or sthg of no or slight value or size <*whisper sweet ~s*>

[4]**nothing** *adj* of no account; worthless

ˈ**nothingness** /-nis‖-nɪs/ *n* **1a** nonexistence **b** utter insignificance **2a** a void, emptiness **b** a metaphysical entity opposed to and devoid of being

[1]**notice** /ˈnohtis‖ˈnəʊtɪs/ *n* **1a** warning of a future occurrence **b** notification of intention of terminating an agreement at a particular time **2** attention, heed **3** a written or printed announcement **4** a review (e g of a play)

[2]**notice** *vt* **1** to comment upon; refer to **2** to take notice of; mark **3** *chiefly NAm* to give a formal notice to

noticeable /ˈnohtisəbl‖ˈnəʊtɪsəbl/ *adj* **1** worthy of notice **2** capable of being noticed; perceptible – **noticeably** *adv*

ˈ**notice-ˌboard** *n, chiefly Br* a board on which notices may be (temporarily) displayed

notifiable /ˈnohtiˌfie·əbl‖ˈnəʊtɪˌfaɪəbl/ *adj, of a disease* required by law to be reported to official health authorities

notification /ˌnohtifiˈkaysh(ə)n‖ˌnəʊtɪfɪˈkeɪʃ(ə)n/ *n* **1** (an instance of) notifying **2** sthg written that gives notice

notify /ˈnohtiˌfie‖ˈnəʊtɪˌfaɪ/ *vt* **1** to give (official) notice to **2** to make known – **notifier** *n*

notion /ˈnohsh(ə)n‖ˈnəʊʃ(ə)n/ *n* **1a(1)** a broad general concept **a(2)** a conception, impression <*had no ~ of the poem's meaning*> **b** a whim or fancy **2** *pl, chiefly NAm* small articles of merchandise (e g haberdashery)

notional /ˈnohsh(ə)nl‖ˈnəʊʃ(ə)nl/ *adj* **1** theoretical, speculative **2** existing only in the mind; imaginary – **notionally** *adv*, **notionality** *n*

notochord /ˈnohtəˌkawd‖ˈnəʊtəˌkɔːd/ *n* a longitudinal rod that forms the supporting axis of the body in the lancelet, lamprey, etc and in the embryos of higher vertebrates – **notochordal** *adj*

notoriety /ˌnohtəˈrie·əti‖ˌnəʊtəˈraɪətɪ/ *n* the quality or state of being notorious

notorious /nohˈtawri·əs‖nəʊˈtɔːrɪəs/ *adj* well-known, esp for a specified (unfavourable) quality or trait – **notoriously** *adv*, **notoriousness** *n*

[1]**notwithstanding** /ˌnotwidhˈstanding, -with-‖ˌnɒtwɪðˈstændɪŋ, -wɪθ-/ *prep* in spite of

[2]**notwithstanding** *adv* nevertheless

[3]**notwithstanding** *conj* although

nougat /ˈnugət, ˈnoohˌgah‖ˈnʌgət, ˈnuːˌgɑː/ *n* a sweetmeat of nuts or fruit pieces in a semisolid sugar paste

nought /nawt‖nɔːt/ *n* **1** NAUGHT 1 **2** the arithmetical symbol 0; zero

ˌ**noughts and ˈcrosses** *n pl but sing in constr* a game in which 2 players alternately put noughts and crosses in usu 9 square spaces arranged in a square in an attempt to get a row of 3 noughts or 3 crosses

noun /nown‖naʊn/ *n* a word that is the name of a person, place, thing, substance, or state and that belongs to 1 of the major form classes in grammar

nourish /ˈnurish‖ˈnʌrɪʃ/ *vt* **1** to nurture, rear **2** to encourage the growth of; foster **3a** to provide or sustain with nutriment; feed **b** to cherish, entertain – **nourisher** *n*, **nourishing** *adj*

ˈ**nourishment** /-mənt‖-mənt/ *n* **1** food, nutriment **2** nourishing or being nourished

nous /nows‖naʊs/ *n* **1** mind, reason **2** *chiefly Br* gumption, common sense

nouveau riche /ˌnoohvoh ˈreesh ‖ˌnuːvəʊ ˈriːʃ (*Fr* nuvo riʃ)/ *n, pl* **nouveaux riches** /~/ sby who has recently become rich (and shows it) [French, lit., new rich]

nova /ˈnohvə‖ˈnəʊvə/ *n, pl* **novas, novae** /-vi, -vay‖-vɪ, -veɪ/ a previously faint star that becomes suddenly very bright and then fades away to its former obscurity over months or years – **novalike** *adj*

[1]**novel** /ˈnovl‖ˈnɒvl/ *adj* **1** new and unlike anything previously known **2** original and striking, esp in conception or style

[2]**novel** *n* an invented prose narrative that is usu long and complex and deals esp with human experience and social behaviour – **novelist** *n*, **novelistic** *adj*

novelette /ˌnovlˈet‖ˌnɒvlˈet/ *n* a short novel or long short story, often of a sentimental nature – **novelettish** *adj*

novella /noˈvelə‖nɒˈvelə/ *n, pl* **novellas** *also* **novelle** /-li‖-lɪ/ a short novel, usu more complex than a short story

novelty /ˈnov(ə)lti‖ˈnɒv(ə)ltɪ/ *n* **1** sthg new and unusual **2** the quality or state of being novel **3** a small manufactured often cheap article for personal or household adornment

November /nohˈvembə‖nəʊˈvembə/ *n* the 11th month of the Gregorian calendar [Latin *November* (ninth month of the early Roman calendar), fr *novem* nine]

novice /ˈnovis‖ˈnɒvɪs/ *n* **1** a person admitted to probationary membership of a religious community **2** a beginner

novitiate /nohˈvishi·ət, -ayt, nə-‖nəʊˈvɪʃɪət, -eɪt, nə-/ *n* **1** (the duration of) the state of being a novice **2** a house where novices are trained

[1]**now** /now‖naʊ/ *adv* **1a** at the present time **b** in the immediate past **c** in the time immediately to follow; forthwith <*come in* ~> <~ *for tea*> **2** – used with the sense of present time weakened or lost **2a** to introduce an important point or indicate a transition <~ *if we turn to the next aspect of the problem*> **b** to express command, request, or warning <*oh, come* ~> <~, ~, *don't squabble*> <~ *then, what's the matter?*> **3** sometimes – linking 2 or more coordinate words or phrases <~ *one and* ~ *another*> **4** under the changed or unchanged circumstances <*he'll never believe me* ~, *after what happened*> **5** at the time referred to <~ *the trouble began*> **6** up to the present or to the time referred to <*haven't been for years* ~>

[2]**now** *conj* in view of the fact that; since <~ *that we are here*>

[3]**now** *n* **1** the present time <*been ill up to* ~> <*goodbye for* ~> **2** the time referred to <*by* ~ *the rain was falling*>

nowadays /ˈnowəˌdayz‖ˈnaʊəˌdeɪz/ *adv* in these modern times; today

ˌnow and aˈgain *adv* at occasional intervals; from time to time

noway /ˈnohˌway‖ˈnəʊˌweɪ/, **noways** *adv* in no way whatever; not at all – fml

ˌno ˈway *interj, chiefly NAm* – used to express forceful refusal; infml

[1]**nowhere** /ˈnohˌweə‖ˈnəʊˌweə/ *adv* **1** not anywhere **2** to no purpose or result <*this will get us* ~>

[2]**nowhere** *n* a nonexistent place

ˈnoˌwise /-ˌwiez‖-ˌwaɪz/ *adv* noway

noxious /ˈnokshəs‖ˈnɒkʃəs/ *adj* **1** harmful to living things <~ *industrial wastes*> **2** having a harmful moral influence; unwholesome – **noxiously** *adv*, **noxiousness** *n*

nozzle /ˈnozl‖ˈnɒzl/ *n* a projecting part with an opening that usu serves as an outlet; *esp* a short tube with a taper or constriction used on a hose, pipe, etc to speed up or direct a flow of fluid

-n't /-nt‖-nt/ *comb form* not <*isn't*>

nth /enth‖enθ/ *adj* **1** of or having an unspecified or indefinitely large number **2** extreme, utmost <*to the* ~ *degree*>

nuance /ˈnyoohˌonhs ‖ˈnjuːˌɑ̃s (*Fr* nɥɑ̃ːs)/ *n* a subtle distinction or gradation; a shade [French, lit., shade of colour, fr *nuer* to make shades of colour, fr *nue* cloud, fr Latin *nubes*] – **nuanced** *adj*

nub /nub‖nʌb/ *n* **1** a knob, lump <*a* ~ *of coal*> **2** *the* gist or crux

nubile /ˈn(y)oohˌbiel‖ˈn(j)uːˌbaɪl/ *adj, of a girl* of marriageable age; *esp* young and sexually attractive – often humor – **nubility** *n*

nuclear /ˈnyoohkli·ə‖ˈnjuːklɪə/ *adj* **1** of or constituting a nucleus **2** of, using, or being the atomic nucleus, atomic energy, the atom bomb, or atomic power

ˌnuclear disˈarmament *n* the reduction or giving up of a country's nuclear weapons

nuclear winter *n* a state of extreme coldness on earth, caused by clouds of smoke blocking sunlight, which some scientists consider a likely consequence of a nuclear war

nuˌcleic ˈacid /nyoohˈklayik, -ˈklee-‖njuː-ˈkleɪɪk, -ˈkliː-/ *n* RNA, DNA, or another acid composed of a chain of nucleotide molecules linked to each other

nucleotide /ˈnyoohkli·əˌtied‖ˈnjuːklɪəˌtaɪd/ *n* any of several compounds that form the structural units of RNA and DNA

nucleus /ˈnyoohkli·əs‖ˈnjuːklɪəs/ *n, pl* **nuclei** /-kliˌie, -kli·i‖-klɪˌaɪ, -klɪɪ/ *also* **nucleuses** **1** a small bright and dense part of a galaxy or head of a comet **2** a central point, mass, etc about which gathering, concentration, etc takes place: e g **2a** a usu round membrane-surrounded cellular organelle containing the chromosomes **b** a (discrete) mass of nerve cells in the brain or spinal cord **c** the positively charged central part of an atom that accounts for nearly all of the atomic mass and consists of protons and usu neutrons [Latin, kernel, central part, diminutive of *nuc-, nux* nut]

[1]**nude** /n(y)oohd‖n(j)uːd/ *adj* **1** lacking sthg essential to legal validity <*a* ~ *contract*> **2a** without clothing; naked **b** without natural covering or adornment; bare – **nudely** *adv*, **nudeness, nudity** *n*

[2]**nude** *n* **1a** a representation of a nude human figure **b** a nude person **2** the state of being nude <*in the* ~>

nudge /nuj‖nʌdʒ/ *vt* **1** to touch or push gently; *esp* to catch the attention of by a push of the elbow **2** to move (as if) by pushing gently or slowly – **nudge** *n*

nudism /ˈnoohˌdiz(ə)m, ˈnyooh-‖ˈnuːˌdɪz(ə)m, ˈnjuː-/ *n* the cult or practice of going nude as much as possible – **nudist** *adj or n*

nugatory /ˈnyoohgət(ə)ri‖ˈnjuːgət(ə)rɪ/ *adj* **1** trifling, inconsequential **2** inoperative *USE* fml

nugget /ˈnugət‖ˈnʌgət/ *n* a solid lump, esp of a precious metal in its natural state

nuisance /ˈnyoohs(ə)ns‖ˈnjuːs(ə)ns/ *n* **1** (legally actionable) harm or injury **2** an annoying or troublesome person or thing

nuke /nyoohk‖njuːk/ *vt or n* (to destroy with) a nuclear weapon – slang

[1]**null** /nul‖nʌl/ *adj* **1** having no force in law – esp in *null and void* **2** amounting to nothing; nil **3** without character or distinction **4** *of an instrument* indicating (e g by a zero reading on a scale) when current or voltage is zero **5** of or being a method of measurement that uses a null instrument

[2]**null** *n* **1** ZERO 3 **2** a minimum or zero value of an electric current or of a radio signal

ˌnull and ˈvoid *adj* completely invalid

nullify /ˈnulifie‖ˈnʌlɪfaɪ/ *vt* **1** to make (legally) null **2** to make worthless, unimportant, or ineffective

nullity /ˈnuləti‖ˈnʌlətɪ/ *n* **1** (an act or document characterized by) legal invalidity **2** sthg null

numb /num‖nʌm/ *adj* **1** devoid of sensation, esp as a result of cold or anaesthesia **2** devoid of emotion – **numb** *vt*, **numbingly** *adv*, **numbly** *adv*, **numbness** *n*

[1]**number** /ˈnumbə‖ˈnʌmbə/ *n* **1a(1)** a total **a(2)** *sing or pl in constr* an indefinite, usu large, total <*a ~ of members were absent*> **a(3)** *pl* a numerous group; many; *also* an instance of numerical superiority <*there is safety in ~*s> **b(1)** any of an ordered set of standard names or symbols (e g 2, 5, 27th) used in counting or in assigning a position in an order; *esp* NATURAL NUMBER **b(2)** an element (e g 6, -3, $^5/_8$, $\sqrt{7}$) belonging to an arithmetical system based on or analogous to the numbers used in counting and subject to specific rules of addition, subtraction, and multiplication **c** *pl* arithmetic <*teach children their ~*s> **2** a distinction of word form denoting reference to singular or plural *also* a set of forms so distinguished **3a** a word, symbol, letter, or combination of symbols representing a number **b** one or more numerals or digits used to identify or designate <*a car ~*> <*a telephone ~*> **4a** a member of a sequence or collection designated by esp consecutive numbers; *also* an individual or item (e g a single act in a variety show or an issue of a periodical) singled out from a group **b** a position in a numbered sequence **5** a group of individuals <*he is not of our ~*> **6** *pl but sing or pl in constr* a form of US lottery in which bets are made on the appearance of a certain combination of 3 digits in sets of numbers regularly published in newspapers (e g the stock-market receipts) **7a** sthg viewed in terms of the advantage or enjoyment obtained from it <*her job is a really cushy ~*> <*drives round in a fast little ~*> **b** an article of esp women's clothing <*wearing a chic little black ~*> **c** a person or individual, esp an attractive girl <*who's the blonde ~ over there?*> **8** insight into a person's motives or character <*soon had his ~*> *USE* (*7&8*) infml – **without number** innumerable

[2]**number** *vt* **1** to count **2** to include as part of a whole or total <*proud to ~ her among my friends*> **3** to restrict to a definite number; limit – usu pass <*knew his days were ~*ed> **4** to assign a number to <~ed *the team members 1 to 10*> <*a ~*ed *road*> **5** to comprise in number; total <*the inhabitants ~*ed *150,000*> ~ *vi* **1** to be part of a total number <~s *among my closest friends*> **2** to call *off* numbers in sequence – **numberable** *adj*

ˈ**numberless** /-lis‖-lɪs/ *adj* innumerable, countless

ˌ**number ˈone** *n* **1** sthg that is first in rank, order, or importance <*~ in her list of priorities*> **2** one's own interests or welfare – infml <*always thinking of ~*> **3** an act of urinating – euph; used by or to children

ˈ**numberˌplate** /-ˌplayt‖-ˌpleɪt/ *n, chiefly Br* a rectangular identifying plate fastened to a vehicle and bearing the vehicle's registration number

numeracy /ˈnyoohm(ə)rəsi‖ˈnjuːm(ə)rəsɪ/ *n, Br* the quality or state of being numerate

[1]**numeral** /ˈnyoohm(ə)rəl‖ˈnjuːm(ə)rəl/ *adj* of or expressing numbers – **numerally** *adv*

[2]**numeral** *n* a conventional symbol that represents a natural number or zero

numerate /ˈnyoohm(ə)rət‖ˈnjuːm(ə)rət/ *adj* understanding basic mathematics; able to use numbers in calculation

numeration /ˌnyoohməˈraysh(ə)n‖ˌnjuːməˈreɪʃ(ə)n/ *n* **1a** counting **b** designating by a number **2** expressing in words numbers written as numerals **3** a system of numbering or counting – **numerate** *vt*

numerator /ˈnyoohməˌraytə‖ˈnjuːməˌreɪtə/ *n* the part of a fraction that is above the line and signifies the number of parts of the denominator that is shown by the fraction

numerical /nyoohˈmerikl‖njuːˈmerɪkl/, **numeric** *adj* of, expressed in, or involving numbers or a number system <*the ~ superiority of the enemy*> <*~ standing in a class*> <*a ~ code*> – **numerically** *adv*

numerology /ˌnyoohməˈroləji‖ˌnjuːməˈrɒlədʒɪ/ *n* the study of the occult significance of numbers – **numerologist** *n*, **numerological** *adj*

numerous /ˈnyoohm(ə)rəs‖ˈnjuːm(ə)rəs/ *adj* consisting of many units or individuals – **numerously** *adv*, **numerousness** *n*

numinous /ˈnyoohminəs‖ˈnjuːmɪnəs/ *adj* **1** awe-inspiring, mysterious **2** filled with a sense of the presence of divinity

numismatics /ˌnyoohmizˈmatiks‖ˌnjuːmɪzˈmætɪks/ *n pl but sing in constr* the study or collection of coinage, coins, paper money, medals, tokens, etc [French *numismatique*, fr Latin *nomismat-*, *nomisma* coin, fr Greek, custom, coin] – **numismatic** *adj*, **numismatically** *adv*, **numismatist** *n*

numskull, numbskull /ˈnumˌskul‖ˈnʌmˌskʌl/ *n* a dull or stupid person

nun /nun‖nʌn/ *n* a female member of a religious order living in a convent under vows of chastity, poverty, etc and often engaged in educational or nursing work

nuncio /ˈnuns(h)ioh‖ˈnʌnsɪəʊ,-ʃɪəʊ/ *n, pl* **nuncios** a papal ambassador to a civil government

nunnery /ˈnunəri‖ˈnʌnərɪ/ *n* a convent of nuns

[1]**nuptial** /ˈnupsh(ə)l‖ˈnʌpʃ(ə)l/ *adj* **1** of marriage **2** characteristic of or occurring in the breeding season <*a ~ flight*>

[2]**nuptial** *n* a wedding – usu pl

[1]**nurse** /nuhs‖nɜːs/ *n* **1a** WET NURSE **b** a woman employed to take care of a young child **2** sby skilled or trained in caring for the sick or infirm, esp under the supervision of a physician <*she and her brother are both ~*s> **3** a member of the worker caste in an ant, bee, etc society, that cares for the young

[2]**nurse** *vt* **1** to suckle **2a** to rear, nurture **b** to encourage the development of; foster <*carefully ~*d *his tomatoes*> **3a** to attempt to cure (e g an illness or injury) by appropriate treatment **b** to care for and wait on (e g a sick person) **4** to hold in one's mind; harbour <*~ a grievance*> **5** to handle carefully in order to conserve or prolong **6** to hold (e g a baby) lovingly or caressingly ~ *vi* **1a** to suckle an offspring **b** to suck at the breast **2** to act or serve as a nurse

ˈ**nurseˌmaid** /-ˌmayd‖-ˌmeɪd/ *n* a girl or woman employed to look after children

nursery /ˈnuhs(ə)ri‖ˈnɜːs(ə)rɪ/ *n* **1** a child's bedroom or playroom **2a** a place where small children are looked after in their parents' absence **b** NURSERY SCHOOL **3** a place where young animals (e g fish) grow or are cared for **4** an area where plants, trees, etc are grown for propagation, sale, or transplanting

'nurseryman /-mən, -ˌman‖-mən, -ˌmæn/ *n* one whose occupation is the cultivation of plants, usu for sale

'nursery ˌrhyme *n* a short traditional story in rhyme for children

'nursery ˌschool *n* a school for children aged usu from 2 to 5

'nursing ˌhome /'nuhsing‖'nɜːsɪŋ/ *n* a usu private hospital or home (where care is provided for the aged, chronically ill, etc)

nursling /'nuhsling‖'nɜːslɪŋ/ *n* a child under the care of a nurse, esp in former times

[1]**nurture** /'nuhchə‖'nɜːtʃə/ *n* **1** training, upbringing **2** food, nourishment **3** all the environmental influences that affect the innate genetic potentialities of an organism

[2]**nurture** *vt* **1** to give care and nourishment to **2** to educate or develop

[1]**nut** /nut‖nʌt/ *n* **1** (the often edible kernel of) a dry fruit or seed with a hard separable rind or shell **2** a difficult person, problem, or undertaking <*a tough* ~> **3** a typically hexagonal usu metal block that has a central hole with an internal screw thread cut on it, and can be screwed onto a piece, esp a bolt, with an external thread to tighten or secure sthg **4** the ridge in a stringed instrument (e g a violin) over which the strings pass on the upper end of the fingerboard **5** a small piece or lump <*a* ~ *of butter*> **6** *pl* nonsense – often used interjectionally **7** a person's head **8a** an insane or wildly eccentric person **b** an ardent enthusiast *USE* (*6, 7, & 8*) infml – **nutlike** *adj*

[2]**nut** *vi* **-tt-** to gather or seek nuts – chiefly in *go nutting*

ˌnut-'brown *adj or n* (of) the colour of a ripe hazelnut

'nutˌcase /-ˌkays‖-ˌkeɪs/ *n* a nut, lunatic – infml

'nutˌcracker /-ˌkrakə‖-ˌkrækə/ *n* an implement for cracking nuts, usu consisting of 2 hinged metal arms between which the nut is held and compressed – often pl with sing. meaning

'nutˌhouse /-ˌhows‖-ˌhaʊs/ *n* a madhouse – slang; humor

nutmeg /'nutmeg‖'nʌtmeg/ *n* (an Indonesian tree that produces) an aromatic seed used as a spice

nutria /'nyoohtri·ə‖'njuːtrɪə/ *n* **1** a coypu **2** the fur of the coypu

nutrient /'nyoohtri·ənt‖'njuːtrɪənt/ *n or adj* (sthg) that provides nourishment

nutriment /'nyoohtrimənt‖'njuːtrɪmənt/ *n* sthg that nourishes or promotes growth

nutrition /nyooh'trish(ə)n‖njuː'trɪʃ(ə)n/ *n* nourishing or being nourished; *specif* all the processes by which an organism takes in and uses food – **nutritional** *adj*, **nutritionally** *adv*, **nutritionist** *n*

nutritious /nyooh'trishəs‖njuː'trɪʃəs/ *adj* nourishing – **nutritiously** *adv*, **nutritiousness** *n*

nutritive /'nyoohtritiv‖'njuːtrɪtɪv/ *adj* **1** of nutrition **2** nourishing – **nutritively** *adv*

nuts /nuts‖nʌts/ *adj* **1** passionately keen or enthusiastic <*he's* ~ *on ice-hockey*> **2** crazy, mad *USE* infml

'nutˌshell /-ˌshel‖-ˌʃel/ *n* the hard outside covering enclosing the kernel of a nut – **in a nutshell** in a brief accurate account

nutty /'nuti‖'nʌtɪ/ *adj* **1** having or producing nuts **2** having a flavour like that of nuts **3** eccentric, silly; *also* NUTS 2 – infml – **nuttiness** *n*

nuzzle /'nuzl‖'nʌzl/ *vi* **1** to push or rub sthg with the nose **2** to lie close or snug; nestle ~*vt* to root or rub (as if) with the nose

nylon /'nielon‖'naɪlɒn/ *n* **1** any of numerous strong tough elastic synthetic polyamide materials fashioned into fibres, sheets, etc and used esp in textiles and plastics **2** *pl* stockings made of nylon

nymph /nimf‖nɪmf/ *n* **1** any of the minor female divinities of nature in classical mythology **2** any of various immature insects; *esp* a larva of a dragonfly or other insect with incomplete metamorphosis **3** a girl – poetic – **nymphal** *adj*

nymphet /'nimfit‖'nɪmfɪt/ *n* a sexually desirable girl in early adolescence

nymphomania /ˌnimfə'maynyə‖ˌnɪmfə'meɪnjə/ *n* excessive sexual desire in a female – **nymphomaniac** *n or adj*, **nymphomaniacal** *adj*

o /oh‖əʊ/ *n, pl* **o's, os** *often cap* **1** (a graphic representation of or device for reproducing) the 15th letter of the English alphabet **2** sthg shaped like the letter O; *esp* zero

O /oh‖əʊ/ *interj or n* oh

o' *also* **o** /ə‖ə/ *prep* **1** of <*one o'clock*> **2** *chiefly dial* on

oaf /ohf‖əʊf/ *n* a clumsy slow-witted person – **oafish** *adj*, **oafishly** *adv*, **oafishness** *n*

oak /ohk‖əʊk/ *n*, (the tough hard durable wood of) any of various trees or shrubs of the beech family, usu having lobed leaves and producing acorns as fruits – **oaken** *adj*

'oak ˌapple *n* a large round gall produced on oak stems or leaves by a gall wasp

oakum /'ohkəm‖'əʊkəm/ *n* hemp or jute fibre impregnated with tar or a tar derivative and used in packing joints and stopping up gaps between the planks of a ship

[1]**oar** /aw‖ɔː/ *n* **1** a long usu wooden shaft with a broad blade at one end used for propelling or steering a boat **2** an oarsman – **oared** *adj*

[2]**oar** *vb* [1]ROW – poetic

'oarˌlock /-ˌlok‖-ˌlɒk/ *n, chiefly NAm* a rowlock

oarsman /'awzmən‖'ɔːzmən/ *n* one who rows a boat, esp in a racing crew – **oarsmanship** *n*

oasis /oh'aysis‖əʊ'eɪsɪs/ *n, pl* **oases** /-seez‖-siːz/ **1** a fertile or green area in a dry region **2** sthg providing relaxation or relief

'oast ˌhouse /ohst‖əʊst/ *n* a usu circular building housing a kiln for drying hops or malting barley

oat /oht‖əʊt/ *n* **1a** (any of various wild grasses related to) a widely cultivated cereal grass – usu pl **b** *pl* a crop or plot of oats **2** an oat seed – **oaten** *adj*

'oat,cake *n* a usu crisp unleavened biscuit or bread made of oatmeal

oath /ohth‖əʊθ/ *n, pl* **oaths** /ohdhz‖əʊðz/ **1a** a solemn calling upon God or a revered person or thing to witness to the true or binding nature of one's declaration **b** sthg (e g a promise) formally confirmed by an oath **c** a form of expression used in taking an oath **2** an irreverent use of a sacred name; *broadly* a swearword – **on/under oath** bound by a solemn promise to tell the truth

'oat,meal /-,meel, -,miəl‖-,miːl, -,mɪəl/ *n* **1** meal made from oats, used esp in porridge **2** a greyish beige colour

ob-, oc-, of-, op- *prefix* **1** out; forth <ob*trude*> **2** so as to involve compliance <ob*serve*> **3** against; in opposition to <op*ponent*>; resisting <ob*stinate*> **4** in the way of; hindering <ob*stacle*> **5** hidden; concealed <oc*cult*> **6** inversely <ob*ovate*>

[1]obbligato /,obli'gahtoh‖,ɒblɪ'gɑːtəʊ/ *adj* not to be omitted – used in music

[2]obbligato *n, pl* **obbligatos** *also* **obbligati** /-ti‖-tɪ/ an elaborate, esp melodic, accompaniment, usu played by a single instrument

obdurate /'obdyoorət, -joo-‖'ɒbdjʊrət, -dʒʊ-/ *adj* **1** stubbornly persistent in wrong doing **2** inflexible, unyielding – **obdurately** *adv*, **obdurateness, obduracy** *n*

obeah /'ohbi·ə‖'əʊbɪə/ *n, often cap* sorcery and magic ritual as practised among Negroes, esp of the British W Indies

obedient /ə'beedi·ənt, oh-‖ə'biːdɪənt, əʊ-/ *adj* submissive to the will or authority of a superior; willing to obey – **obediently** *adv*, **obedience** *n*

obeisance /oh'bay(i)səns, -'bee-‖əʊ-'beɪ(ɪ)səns, -'biː-/ *n* **1** a movement or gesture made as a sign of respect or submission **2** deference, homage – **obeisant** *adj*, **obeisantly** *adv*

obelisk /'obəlisk‖'ɒbəlɪsk/ *n* **1** an upright 4-sided usu monolithic pillar that gradually tapers towards the top and terminates in a pyramid **2** DAGGER 2

obese /oh'bees‖əʊ'biːs/ *adj* excessively fat [Latin *obesus*, fr *ob-* against + *es-*, *edere* to eat] – **obesity** *n*

obey /ə'bay, oh'bay‖ə'beɪ, əʊ'beɪ/ *vt* **1** to submit to the commands or guidance of **2** to comply with; execute ~*vi* to act obediently

obfuscate /'obfus,kayt‖'ɒbfʌs,keɪt/ *vt* **1** to make obscure or difficult to understand **2** to confuse, bewilder – **obfuscation** *n*, **obfuscatory** *adj*

obiter dictum /,obitə 'diktəm‖,ɒbɪtə 'dɪktəm/ *n, pl* **obiter dicta** /'diktə‖'dɪktə/ **1** an incidental observation made by a judge which is not material to his judgment and therefore not binding **2** an incidental remark or observation [Late Latin, lit., something said in passing]

obituary /ə'bityoo(ə)ri‖ə'bɪtjʊ(ə)rɪ/ *n* a notice of a person's death, usu with a short biography [Medieval Latin *obituarium*, fr Latin *obitus* death, fr *obit-*, *obire* to go to meet, die, fr *ob-* in the way + *ire* to go] – **obituary** *adj*

[1]object /'objekt, -ikt‖'ɒbdʒekt, -ɪkt/ *n* **1** sthg that is (capable of) being sensed physically or examined mentally <*an* ~ *of study*> **2a** sthg or sby that arouses an emotion or provokes a reaction or response <*an* ~ *of derision*> **b** sby or sthg that is ridiculous, outlandish, or pathetic in appearance <*looked a real* ~> **3** an end towards which effort, action, etc is directed; a goal <*what's the* ~ *of the exercise?*> **4** a noun or noun equivalent appearing in a prepositional phrase or representing the goal or the result of the action of its verb (e g *house* in *we built a house*) **5** sthg of paramount concern <*if money's no* ~ *then buy it*> – **objectless** *adj*

[2]object /əb'jekt‖əb'dʒekt/ *vb* **1** to oppose sthg with words or arguments **2** to feel dislike or disapproval <*I* ~ *to his condescending manner*> ~*vt* to offer in opposition or objection – **objector** *n*

objection /əb'jeksh(ə)n‖əb'dʒekʃ(ə)n/ *n* **1** a reason or argument presented in opposition **2** a feeling or statement of dislike, disapproval, or opposition

objectionable /əb'jeksh(ə)nəbl‖əb'dʒekʃ-(ə)nəbl/ *adj* unpleasant or offensive – **objectionableness** *n*, **objectionably** *adv*

[1]objective /əb'jektiv‖əb'dʒektɪv/ *adj* **1a** constituting an object: e g **1a(1)** existing independently of the mind **a(2)** belonging to the external world and observable or verifiable **a(3)** *of a symptom of disease* perceptible to other people as well as the affected individual **b** concerned with or expressing the nature of external reality rather than personal feelings or beliefs **c** dealing with facts without distortion by personal feelings or prejudices **2** of or in the case that follows a preposition or a transitive verb – **objectively** *adv*, **objectiveness, objectivity** *n*

[2]objective *n* **1** sthg towards which efforts are directed; a goal **2** sthg to be attained or achieved by a military operation **3** (a word in) the objective case **4** a lens or system of lenses that forms an image of an object

'object ,lesson *n* **1** a lesson that takes a material object as its basis **2** sthg that serves as a concrete illustration of a principle

objet d'art /,obzhay 'dah ‖,ɒbʒeɪ 'dɑː (*Fr* ɔbʒɛ dar)/ *n, pl* **objets d'art** /~/ a usu small article of some artistic value [French, lit., art object]

[1]oblate /'oblayt‖'ɒbleɪt/ *adj* flattened or depressed at the poles <*an* ~ *spheroid*> – **oblateness** *n*

[2]oblate *n* a (lay) member of any of several Roman Catholic communities

oblation /ə'blaysh(ə)n‖ə'bleɪʃ(ə)n/ *n* **1** *cap* the act of offering to God the bread and wine used at Communion **2** an offering made for religious purposes

obligate /'obligayt‖'ɒblɪgeɪt/ *vt* to constrain legally or morally

obligation /,obli'gaysh(ə)n‖,ɒblɪ'geɪʃ(ə)n/ *n* **1** sthg (e g a contract or promise) that binds one to a course of action **2** (the amount of) a financial commitment <*the company was unable to meet its financial* ~s> **3** sthg one is bound to do; a duty **4** (indebtedness for) a service or favour <*her kindness has put me under an* ~ *to her*>

obligatory /ə'bligət(ə)ri‖ə'blɪgət(ə)rɪ/ *adj* **1** binding in law or conscience **2** relating to or enforcing an obligation <*a writ* ~> **3** mandatory, compulsory – **obligatorily** *adv*

oblige /ə'bliej‖ə'blaɪdʒ/ *vt* **1** to constrain by

force or circumstance **2a** to put in one's debt by a favour or service – usu pass <*we're much* ~d *to you for all your help*> **b** to do a favour for <~d *the assembled company with a song*> ~*vi* to do sthg as a favour; be of service <*always ready to* ~>

obliging /ə'bliejing‖ə'blaɪdʒɪŋ/ *adj* eager to help; accommodating – **obligingly** *adv*, **obligingness** *n*

oblique /ə'bleek‖ə'bli:k/ *adj* **1a** neither perpendicular nor parallel; inclined **b** having the axis not perpendicular to the base <*an* ~ *cone*> **c** having no right angle <*an* ~ *triangle*> **d** *of an angle* greater than but not a multiple of 90° **2** not straightforward or explicit; indirect <~ *references to financial difficulties*> **3** *of a muscle* situated obliquely with 1 end not attached to bone – **oblique** *n*, **obliquely** *adv*, **obliqueness** *n*

obliterate /ə'blitərayt‖ə'blɪtəreɪt/ *vt* **1** to make illegible or imperceptible **2** to destroy all trace or indication of **3** to cause (e g a blood vessel or other body part) to collapse or disappear **4** CANCEL 5 – **obliterative** *adj*, **obliterator** *n*, **obliteration** *n*

oblivion /ə'blivi·ən‖ə'blɪvɪən/ *n* **1** the state of forgetting or being oblivious **2** the state of being forgotten **3** official disregarding of offences

oblivious /ə'blivi·əs‖ə'blɪvɪəs/ *adj* lacking conscious knowledge; completely unaware – usu + *of* or *to* – **obliviously** *adv*, **obliviousness** *n*

oblong /'oblong‖'ɒblɒŋ/ *adj* deviating from a square by being longer; *esp* rectangular with adjacent sides unequal – **oblong** *n*

obloquy /'obləkwi‖'ɒbləkwɪ/ *n* **1** strongly-worded condemnation **2** discredit, disgrace

obnoxious /əb'nokshəs‖əb'nɒkʃəs/ *adj* highly offensive or repugnant – **obnoxiously** *adv*, **obnoxiousness** *n*

oboe /'oh,boh‖'əʊ,bəʊ/ *n* a double-reed woodwind instrument with a conical tube and a usual range from B flat below middle C upwards for about 2½ octaves [Italian, fr French *hautbois* – see HAUTBOY] – **oboist** *n*

obscene /əb'seen‖əb'si:n/ *adj* **1** offending standards of esp sexual propriety or decency; *specif* inciting sexual depravity <*confiscated various* ~ *publications*> **2** (morally) repugnant – **obscenely** *adv*

obscenity /əb'senəti‖əb'senətɪ/ *n* **1** the quality or state of being obscene **2** an obscene act or utterance

obscurantism /,obskyoo'rantiz(ə)m‖,ɒbskjʊ'ræntɪz(ə)m/ *n* opposition to the advance of knowledge – **obscurantist** *n or adj*

¹obscure /əb'skyooə‖əb'skjʊə/ *adj* **1** hard to understand; abstruse **2** not well-known or widely acclaimed **3** faint, indistinct **4** constituting or representing the unstressed vowel /M/ – **obscurely** *adv*, **obscureness** *n*

²obscure *vt* **1** to conceal (as if) by covering **2** to make indistinct or unintelligible – **obscuration** *n*

obscurity /əb'skyooərəti‖əb'skjʊərətɪ/ *n* **1** the quality or state of being obscure **2** an obscure person or thing

obsequious /əb'seekwi·əs‖əb'si:kwɪəs/ *adj* showing a servile willingness to oblige – **obsequiously** *adv*, **obsequiousness** *n*

obsequy /'obsikwi‖'ɒbsɪkwɪ/ *n* a funeral ceremony – usu pl with sing. meaning

observable /əb'zuhvəbl‖əb'zɜ:vəbl/ *adj* capable of being observed; discernible – **observable** *n*, **observably** *adv*

observance /əb'zuhv(ə)ns‖əb'zɜ:v(ə)ns/ *n* **1a** a customary practice, rite, or ceremony – often pl **b** a rule governing members of a religious order **2** an act of complying with a custom, rule, or law

observant /əb'zuhv(ə)nt‖əb'zɜ:v(ə)nt/ *adj* **1** paying close attention; watchful **2** careful to observe; mindful – + *of* **3** quick to notice; alert – **observantly** *adv*

observation /,obzə'vaysh(ə)n‖,ɒbzə'veɪʃ(ə)n/ *n* **1** an act or the faculty of observing **2** the gathering of information by noting facts or occurrences <*weather* ~s> **3** a remark, comment **4** the condition of sby or sthg that is observed <*under* ~ *at the hospital*> – **observational** *adj*

,obser'vation ,car *n*, *NAm* a railway carriage with large windows and often a partly transparent roof that affords passengers a broad view

observatory /əb'zuhvət(ə)ri‖əb'zɜ:vət(ə)rɪ/ *n* a building or institution for the observation and interpretation of natural phenomena, esp in astronomy

observe /əb'zuhv‖əb'zɜ:v/ *vt* **1a** to act in due conformity with <*always* ~d *the law*> <*careful to* ~ *local customs*> **b** to celebrate or perform (e g a ceremony or festival) according to a prescribed or traditional form <~d *the fast of Ramadan*> **2** to perceive or take note of, esp by concentrated attention **3** to utter as a comment <~d *that things weren't what they used to be*> **4** to make a scientific observation on or of

observer /əb'zuhvə‖əb'zɜ:və/ *n* **1** sby sent to observe but not participate officially in a gathering **2** sby who accompanies the pilot of an aircraft to make observations

obsess /əb'ses‖əb'ses/ *vt* to preoccupy intensely or abnormally – **obsessive** *adj or n*, **obsessively** *adv*, **obsessiveness** *n*

obsession /əb'sesh(ə)n‖əb'seʃ(ə)n/ *n* a persistent (disturbing) preoccupation with an often unreasonable idea; *also* an idea causing such a preoccupation – **obsessional** *adj*, **obsessionally** *adv*

obsidian /əb'sidi·ən‖əb'sɪdɪən/ *n* a usu black volcanic glass which splits to give a convex surface

obsolescent /,obsə'les(ə)nt‖,ɒbsə'les(ə)nt/ *adj* going out of use; becoming obsolete – **obsolescence** *n*

obsolete /'obsəleet‖'ɒbsəli:t/ *adj* **1** no longer in use **2** outdated, outmoded – **obsoleteness** *n*

obstacle /'obstəkl‖'ɒbstəkl/ *n* sthg that hinders or obstructs

obstetrics /əb'stetriks, ob-‖əb'stetrɪks, ɒb-/ *n pl but sing or pl in constr* a branch of medicine dealing with the care and treatment of women before, during, and after childbirth – **obstetrician** *n*

obstinate /'obstinət‖'ɒbstɪnət/ *adj* **1** clinging stubbornly to an opinion or course of action; not yielding to arguments or persuasion **2** not easily subdued, remedied, or removed <*an* ~

fever> – **obstinately** *adv*, **obstinacy** *n*

obstreperous /əbˈstrep(ə)rəs‖əbˈstrep(ə)rəs/ *adj* **1** aggressively noisy; clamorous **2** vociferously defiant; unruly [Latin *obstreperus*, fr *obstrepere* to clamour against, fr *ob-* against + *strepere* to make a noise] – **obstreperously** *adv*, **obstreperousness** *n*

obstruct /əbˈstrukt‖əbˈstrʌkt/ *vt* **1** to block or close up by an obstacle <*the road is* ~ed *by a landslide*> <*the fence* ~s *the view*> **2** to hinder, impede – **obstructive** *adj or n*, **obstructiveness** *n*, **obstructively** *adv*, **obstructor** *n*

obstruction /əbˈstruksh(ə)n‖əbˈstrʌkʃ(ə)n/ *n* **1** a condition of being clogged or blocked **2** an attempted delay of business in a deliberative body (e g Parliament) **3** sthg that obstructs

obˈstructionˌism /-ˌiz(ə)m‖-ˌɪz(ə)m/ *n* deliberate interference with (legislative) business – **obstructionist** *n*, **obstructionistic** *adj*

obtain /əbˈtayn‖əbˈteɪn/ *vt* to acquire or attain ~*vi* to be generally accepted or practised – fml – **obtainable** *adj*, **obtainer** *n*, **obtainment** *n*, **obtainability** *n*

obtrude /əbˈtroohd‖əbˈtruːd/ *vt* **1** to thrust out **2** to assert without warrant or request ~*vi* to thrust oneself forward with unwarranted assertiveness – **obtruder** *n*, **obtrusion** *n*

obtrusive /əbˈtroohsiv, -ziv‖əbˈtruːsɪv, -zɪv/ *adj* **1** forward in manner; pushing **2** unduly noticeable – **obtrusively** *adv*, **obtrusiveness** *n*

obtuse /əbˈtyoohs‖əbˈtjuːs/ *adj* **1** lacking sensitivity or mental alertness **2a** being or forming an angle greater than 90° but less than 180° **b** having an obtuse angle <*an* ~ *triangle*> **c** not pointed or acute **3** *of a leaf* rounded at the end furthest from the stalk – **obtusely** *adv*, **obtuseness** *n*

[1]**obverse** /ˈobvuhs‖ˈɒbvɜːs/ *adj* **1** facing the observer or opponent **2** with the base narrower than the top <*an* ~ *leaf*> **3** constituting a counterpart or complement – **obversely** *adv*

[2]**obverse** *n* **1a** the side of a coin, medal, or currency note that bears the principal device and lettering; *broadly* a front or principal surface **b** the more conspicuous of 2 possible sides or aspects **2** a counterpart to a fact or truth

obviate /ˈobviayt‖ˈɒbvɪeɪt/ *vt* **1** to anticipate and dispose of in advance **2** to make unnecessary – **obviation** *n*

obvious /ˈobvi·əs‖ˈɒbvɪəs/ *adj* **1** evident to the senses or understanding **2** unsubtle <*the symbolism of the novel was rather* ~> [Latin *obvius*, fr *obviam* in the way, fr *ob* in the way of + *via* way] – **obviously** *adv*, **obviousness** *n*

ocarina /ˌokəˈreenə‖ˌɒkəˈriːnə/ *n* a simple wind instrument with an oval body

[1]**occasion** /əˈkayzh(ə)n‖əˈkeɪʒ(ə)n/ *n* **1** a suitable opportunity or circumstance <*this is hardly the* ~ *for laughter*> **2** a state of affairs that provides a reason or grounds <*you have no* ~ *to be annoyed*> **3** the immediate or incidental cause **4** a time at which sthg occurs <*on the* ~ *of his daughter's marriage*> **5** a special event or ceremony <*the wedding was a real* ~> – **on occasion** from time to time

[2]**occasion** *vt* to bring about; cause – fml

occasional /əˈkayzh(ə)nl‖əˈkeɪʒ(ə)nl/ *adj* **1** of a particular occasion **2** composed for a particular occasion <~ *verse*> **3** occurring at irregular or infrequent intervals **4** acting in a specified capacity from time to time <*an* ~ *golfer*> **5** designed for use as the occasion demands <*an* ~ *table*> – **occasionally** *adv*

Occident /ˈoksid(ə)nt‖ˈɒksɪd(ə)nt/ *n* WEST 2a

occidental /ˌoksiˈdentl‖ˌɒksɪˈdentl/ *adj, often cap* of or situated in the Occident; western – **occidentalism** *n, often cap*, **occidentalize** *vt, often cap*, **occidentally** *adv, often cap*

Occidental *n* a member of any of the indigenous peoples of the Occident

[1]**occult** /ˈokult, -ˈ-‖ˈɒkʌlt, -ˈ-/ *vt* to conceal by occultation

[2]**occult** *adj* **1** secret; *esp* esoteric **2** not easily understood; abstruse **3** involving (secret knowledge of) supernatural powers **4** not present, manifest, or detectable by the unaided eye <~ *blood loss*> – **occult** *n*, **occultly** *adv*

occultation /ˌokulˈtaysh(ə)n‖ˌɒkʌlˈteɪʃ(ə)n/ *n* the eclipsing of one celestial body by another, usu much larger, one

occupancy /ˈokyoopənsi‖ˈɒkjʊpənsɪ/ *n* **1** the act of taking and holding possession of land, a property, etc **2** becoming or being an occupant; *also* being occupied

occupant /ˈokyoopənt‖ˈɒkjʊpənt/ *n* **1** one who acquires title by occupancy **2** a resident

occupation /ˌokyooˈpaysh(ə)n‖ˌɒkjʊˈpeɪʃ(ə)n/ *n* **1a** an activity in which one engages **b** an activity by which one earns a living **2a** the occupancy of land **b** tenure **3a** the act of taking possession or the holding and control of a place or area, esp by a foreign military force **b** *sing or pl in constr* a military force occupying a country **c** the period of time for which a place or area is occupied

occupational /ˌokyooˈpaysh(ə)nl‖ˌɒkjʊˈpeɪʃ(ə)nl/ *adj* of or resulting from a particular occupation <~ *hazards*> – **occupationally** *adv*

ˌoccuˌpational ˈtherapy *n* creative activity used as therapy for promoting recovery or rehabilitation – **occupational therapist** *n*

occupy /ˈokyoopie‖ˈɒkjʊpaɪ/ *vt* **1** to engage the attention or energies of **2** to fill up (a portion of space or time) **3** to take or maintain possession of **4** to reside in or use as an owner or tenant – **occupier** *n*

occur /əˈkuh‖əˈkɜː/ *vi* **-rr-** **1** to be found; exist **2** to become the case; happen **3** to come to mind <*it* ~s *to me that I haven't posted the letter*>

occurrence /əˈkurəns‖əˈkʌrəns/ *n* **1** sthg that takes place; an event **2** the action or process of occurring

ocean /ˈohsh(ə)n‖ˈəʊʃ(ə)n/ *n* **1** (any of the large expanses that together constitute) the whole body of salt water that covers nearly $^3/_4$ of the surface of the globe **2** *pl* a huge amount – infml <*no need to hurry, we've got* ~s *of time*> – **oceanic** *adj*

ˈoceanˌgoing /-ˌgoh·ing‖-ˌgəʊɪŋ/ *adj* of or designed for travel on the ocean

oceanography /ˌohsh(ə)nˈogrəfi‖ˌəʊʃ(ə)nˈɒgrəfɪ/ *n* the science dealing with oceans and their form, biology, and resources – **oceanographer** *n*, **oceanographic** *also* **oceanographical**

adj, **oceanographically** *adv*

ocelot /ˈosə͵lot‖ˈɒsə͵lɒt/ *n* a medium-sized American wildcat with a yellow or greyish coat dotted and striped with black [French, fr Nahuatl *ocelotl* jaguar]

oche /ˈoki‖ˈɒkɪ/ *n* the line behind which a player must stand when throwing darts at a dartboard; *broadly* the place where a dart player stands when throwing

ochre, *NAm chiefly* **ocher** /ˈohkə‖ˈəʊkə/ *n* **1** the colour of esp yellow ochre **2** an earthy usu red or yellow (impure) iron ore used as a pigment – **ochreous** *adj*

ocker /ˈokə‖ˈɒkə/ *n, often cap, Austr & NZ* an Australian; *specif* one who boorishly asserts Australian nationality

o'clock /əˈklok‖əˈklɒk/ *adv* **1** according to the clock – used in specifying the exact hour <*the time is 3* ~> **2** – used for indicating position or direction as if on a clock dial that is oriented vertically or horizontally <*an aircraft approaching at 6* ~>

octagon /ˈoktəgon, -gən‖ˈɒktəgɒn, -gən/ *n* a polygon of 8 angles and 8 sides – **octagonal** *adj*, **octagonally** *adv*

octane /ˈoktayn‖ˈɒkteɪn/ *n* a liquid hydrocarbon that occurs esp in petroleum

octave /ˈoktiv, ˈoktayv‖ˈɒktɪv, ˈɒkteɪv/ *n* **1** a group of 8 lines of verse, esp the first 8 of a sonnet **2a** (the combination of 2 notes at) a musical interval of 8 diatonic degrees **b** a note separated from a lower note by this interval **c** the whole series of notes or piano, organ, etc keys within this interval that form the unit of the modern scale **3** a group of 8

octavo /okˈtayvoh‖ɒkˈteɪvəʊ/ *n, pl* **octavos** (a book or page in) the size of a piece of paper cut 8 from a sheet

octet /okˈtet‖ɒkˈtet/ *n* **1** (a musical composition for) 8 instruments, voices, or performers **2** OCTAVE 1

October /okˈtohbə‖ɒkˈtəʊbə/ *n* the 10th month of the Gregorian calendar [Latin *October* (8th month of the early Roman calendar), fr *octo* eight]

octogenarian /͵oktəjəˈneəri·ən‖͵ɒktədʒəˈneərɪən/ *n* a person between 80 and 89 years old – **octogenarian** *adj*

octopus /ˈoktəpəs‖ˈɒktəpəs/ *n, pl* **octopuses, octopi** /-pie‖-paɪ/ **1** any of a genus of molluscs related to the squids and cuttlefishes with 8 muscular arms equipped with 2 rows of suckers **2** sthg having many radiating branches or far-reaching controlling influence [deriv of Greek *oktō* eight + *pod-, pous* foot]

octosyllable /ˈoktoh͵siləbl, -tə-‖ˈɒktəʊ͵sɪləbl, -tə-/ *n* a word or line of 8 syllables – **octosyllabic** *adj*

¹ocular /ˈokyoolə‖ˈɒkjʊlə/ *adj* **1** performed or perceived with the eyes **2** of the eye

²ocular *n* an eyepiece

oculist /ˈokyoolist‖ˈɒkjʊlɪst/ *n* an ophthalmologist or optician

odalisque /ˈohd(ə)l·isk‖ˈəʊd(ə)lɪsk/ *n* a female slave or concubine in a harem

odd /od‖ɒd/ *adj* **1a** left over when others are paired or grouped **b** not matching <~ *socks*> **2** not divisible by 2 without leaving a remainder **3** somewhat more than the specified number – usu in combination <*300-odd pages*> **4** not regular or planned; casual, occasional <~ *jobs*> **5** different from the usual or conventional; strange – **oddly** *adv*, **oddness** *n*

ˈodd͵ball /-͵bawl‖-͵bɔːl/ *n* an eccentric or peculiar person – infml – **oddball** *adj*

oddity /ˈodəti‖ˈɒdətɪ/ *n* **1** an odd person, thing, event, or trait **2** oddness, strangeness

͵odd man ˈout *n* sby or sthg that differs in some respect from all the others in a set or group

oddment /ˈodmənt‖ˈɒdmənt/ *n* **1** sthg left over; a remnant **2** *pl* ODDS AND ENDS

odds /odz‖ɒdz/ *n pl but sing or pl in constr* **1a** an amount by which one thing exceeds or falls short of another <*won the election against considerable* ~> **b** a difference in terms of advantage or disadvantage <*it makes no* ~> **2** the probability (expressed as a ratio) that one thing will happen rather than another <*the* ~ *are 50 to 1 against the newcomer*> **3** disagreement, variance <*was at* ~ *with management*> **4** the ratio between the amount to be paid off for a winning bet and the amount of the bet <*gave* ~ *of 3 to 1*>

͵odds and ˈends *n pl* miscellaneous items or remnants

͵odds-ˈon *adj* (viewed as) having a better than even chance to win <*the* ~ *favourite*>

ode /ohd‖əʊd/ *n* a lyric poem, often addressed to a particular subject, marked by a usu exalted tone and varying meter and length of line

odious /ˈohdi·əs‖ˈəʊdɪəs/ *adj* arousing hatred or revulsion – **odiously** *adv*, **odiousness** *n*

odium /ˈohdi·əm‖ˈəʊdɪəm/ *n* general condemnation or disgrace associated with a despicable act – fml

odometer /ohˈdomitə‖əʊˈdɒmɪtə/ *n* an instrument for measuring the distance travelled (e g by a vehicle)

odoriferous /͵ohdəˈrif(ə)rəs‖͵əʊdəˈrɪf(ə)rəs/ *adj* yielding a scent or odour – **odoriferously** *adv*

odorous /ˈohd(ə)rəs‖ˈəʊd(ə)rəs/ *adj* having a scent or odour – **odorously** *adv*

odour, *NAm chiefly* **odor** /ˈohdə‖ˈəʊdə/ *n* **1** (the sensation resulting from) a quality of sthg that stimulates the sense of smell **2** repute, favour <*in bad* ~> – fml **3** a characteristic quality; a savour – chiefly derog – **odourless** *adj*

odyssey /ˈodəsi‖ˈɒdəsɪ/ *n* a long wandering or quest [the *Odyssey*, epic poem by Homer recounting the long wanderings of Odysseus]

oecumenical /͵ekyooˈmenikl, ͵eekyoo-‖͵ekjʊˈmenɪkl, ͵iːkjʊ-/ *adj* ecumenical

oedema, *NAm chiefly* **edema** /iˈdeemə‖ɪˈdiːmə/ *n* abnormal accumulation of liquid derived from serum causing abnormal swelling of the tissues

Oedipus complex /ˈeedipəs‖ˈiːdɪpəs/ *n* (an adult personality disorder resulting from) the sexual attraction developed by a child towards the parent of the opposite sex with accompanying jealousy of the parent of the same sex [*Oedipus*, figure in Greek mythology who unknowingly killed his father and married his mother] – **Oedipal** *adj*

o'er /aw, ˈoh·ə‖ɔː, ˈəʊə/ *adv or prep* over – poetic

oesophagus /ee'sofəgəs‖iː'sɒfəgəs/ *n, pl* **oesophagi** /-ˌgie‖-ˌgaɪ/ the muscular tube leading from the back of the mouth to the stomach [Greek *oisophagos*, fr *oisein* to be going to carry + *phagein* to eat] – **oesophageal**

oestrogen /'eestrəj(ə)n, 'estrə-‖'iːstrədʒ(ə)n, 'estrə-/ *n* a substance, esp a sex hormone, that stimulates the development of secondary sex characteristics in female vertebrates and promotes oestrus in lower mammals – **oestrogenic** *adj*, **oestrogenically** *adv*

oestrus /'eestrəs, 'estrəs‖'iːstrəs, 'estrəs/ *n* a regularly recurrent state of sexual excitability in the female of most lower mammals when she will copulate with the male – **oestral, oestrous** *adj*

'oestrus ˌcycle *n* the series of changes in a female mammal occurring from one period of oestrus to the next

of /əv‖əv; *strong* ov‖ɒv/ *prep* **1a** – used to indicate origin or derivation <*a man ~ noble birth*> <*they expect it ~ me*> **b** – used to indicate cause, motive, or reason <*died ~ pneumonia*> <*did it ~ her own free will*> **c** proceeding from; on the part of <*the approval ~ the minister*> <*the buzzing ~ the bees*> <*very kind ~ him*> **d** BY 4a(2) <*the plays ~ Shaw*> **2a(1)** composed or made from <*a crown ~ gold*> <*a staff ~ teachers*> <*a family ~ 5*> **a(2)** using as a material <*what did he make the crown ~?*> <*made the dress ~ silk rather than cotton*> **b** containing <*cup ~ water*> **c** – used to indicate the mass noun or class that includes the part denoted by the previous word <*an inch ~ rain*> <*a blade ~ grass*> **d** from among <*most ~ the army*> <*one ~ his last poems*> <*the fattest ~ the girls*> <*members ~ the team*> <*she, ~ all people!*> <*the elder ~ the two*> **3a** belonging to; related to <*the leg ~ the chair*> <*the colour ~ her dress*> <*the relatives ~ those who were killed*> <*the wife ~ the managing director*> <*the hat ~ the old gentleman*> **b** that is or are – used before possessive forms <*a friend ~ John's*> <*that nose ~ his*> **c** characterized by; with, having <*a man ~ courage*> <*an area ~ hills*> <*a woman ~ no importance*> <*suitcases ~ a suitable size*> **d** connected with <*the king ~ England*> <*a teacher ~ French*> <*a smell ~ mice*> <*the time ~ arrival*> **e** existing or happening in or on <*the battle ~ Blenheim*> <*my letter ~ the 19th*> **4a** relating to (a topic); concerning <*stories ~ his travels*> <*dreamed ~ home*> <*what ~ it?*> **b** in respect to <*slow ~ speech*> <*north ~ the lake*> <*have hopes ~ him*> <*fond ~ chocolate*> <*guilty ~ murder*> **c** directed towards <*love ~ nature*> <*care ~ guinea pigs*> <*the shooting ~ seals*> <*ask a question ~ him*> **d** – used to show separation or removal <*eased ~ pain*> <*cured him ~ mumps*> <*cheated him ~ his rights*> **e** – used as a function word to indicate a whole or quantity from which a part is removed or expended <*gave ~ his time*> **5** – used to indicate apposition <*the city ~ Rome*> <*the age ~ 8*> <*the art ~ painting*> **6** *NAm* to (a specified hour) <*a quarter ~ four*> **7** in, during <*died ~ a Monday*> <*go there ~ an evening*> – infml – **of a** -like <*that palace* of a *house*> <*that brute* of a *dog*> – used after expressions of strong feeling

¹off /of‖ɒf/ *adv* **1a(1)** from a place or position <*march ~*> <*frighten them ~*>; *specif* away from land <*ship stood ~ to sea*> **a(2)** away in space or ahead in time <*stood 10 paces ~*> <*Christmas is a week ~*> **b** from a course; aside <*turned ~ into a lay-by*>; *specif* away from the wind **c** into sleep or unconsciousness <*dozed ~*> **2a** so as to be not supported <*rolled to the edge of the table and ~*>, not in close contact <*took his coat ~*>, or not attached <*handle came ~*> **b** so as to be divided <*surface marked ~ into squares*> <*a corner screened ~*> **3a** to or in a state of discontinuance or suspension <*shut ~ an engine*> <*game was rained ~*> <*the radio is ~*> **b** so as to be completely finished or no longer existent <*finish it ~*> <*kill them ~*> <*walk it ~*> <*sleep it ~*> **c** in or into a state of putrefaction <*cream's gone ~*> **d** (as if) by heart <*know it ~ pat*> **4** away from an activity or function <*the night shift went ~*> <*take time ~ for lunch*> **5** offstage <*noises ~*> **6** to a sexual climax <*brought him ~*> – slang

²off *prep* **1a** – used to indicate physical separation or distance from <*take it ~ the table*> <*jumped ~ his bicycle*> <*wear it ~ the shoulder*> **b** to seaward of <*2 miles ~ shore*> **c** lying or turning aside from; adjacent to <*a shop just ~ the high street*> **d** (slightly) away from – often in combination <*a week ~ work*> <*completely ~ the point*> <*off-target*> <*off-centre*> **2** – used to indicate the source from which sthg derives or is obtained <*dined ~ oysters*> <*bought it ~ a friend*> <*claim it ~ tax*> **3a** not occupied in <*~ duty*> **b** tired of; no longer interested in or using <*he's ~ drugs*> <*I've gone ~ science fiction*> **c** below the usual standard or level of <*~ his game*>

³off *adj* **1a** FAR 3 **b** seaward **c** being the right-hand one of a pair <*the ~ wheel of a cart*> **d** situated to one side; adjoining <*bedroom with dressing room ~*> **2a** started on the way <*~ on a spree*> **b** not taking place or staying in effect; cancelled <*the match is ~*> **c** *of a dish on a menu* no longer being served **3a** not up to standard; unsatisfactory in terms of achievement <*an ~ day*> **b** slack <*~ season*> **4** affected (as if) with putrefaction <*this fish is ~*> **5** provided <*well ~*> <*how are you ~ for socks?*> **6a** in, on, through, or towards the off side of a cricket field **b** *esp of a ball bowled in cricket* moving or tending to move in the direction of the leg side <*~ break*> **7** *of behaviour* not what one has a right to expect; *esp* rather unkind or dishonest <*it was a bit ~ to leave without a word of thanks!*> – infml

⁴off *vi* to go away; leave

⁵off *n* the start or outset; *also* a starting signal <*ready for the ~*>

offal /'ofl‖'ɒfl/ *n* **1** the by-products of milling used esp for animal feeds **2** the liver, heart, kidney, etc of a butchered animal used as food

3 refuse

ˌoffˈbeat /-ˈbeet‖-ˈbiːt/ *adj* unusual; *esp* unconventional – infml

ˌoff-ˈcolour *adj* **1** unwell <*feeling a bit* ~> **2** *chiefly NAm* somewhat indecent; risqué

offence, *NAm chiefly* **offense** /əˈfens‖əˈfens/ *n* **1** sthg that occasions a sense of outrage **2** (an) attack, assault **3** displeasure, resentment **4a** a sin or misdeed **b** an illegal act; a crime **5** *chiefly NAm* ATTACK 6 – **offenceless** *adj*

offend /əˈfend‖əˈfend/ *vi* **1** to break a moral or divine law – often + *against* **2** to cause displeasure, difficulty, or discomfort ~ *vt* **1** to cause pain or displeasure to; hurt <*colours that* ~ *the eye*> **2** to cause to feel indignation or disgust – **offender** *n*

[1]**offensive** /əˈfensiv‖əˈfensɪv/ *adj* **1a** aggressive, attacking **b** of or designed for attack <~ *weapons*> **2** arousing physical disgust; repellent **3** causing indignation or outrage – **offensively** *adv*, **offensiveness** *n*

[2]**offensive** *n* **1** *the* position or attitude of an attacking party <*took the* ~> **2** an esp military attack on a large scale

[1]**offer** /ˈofə‖ˈɒfə/ *vt* **1** to present (e g a prayer or sacrifice) in an act of worship or devotion – often + *up* **2a** to present for acceptance, rejection, or consideration **b** to present in order to satisfy a requirement <*candidates may* ~ *Welsh as one of their foreign languages*> **3** to declare one's willingness <~ed *to help me*> **4** to put up <~ed *stubborn resistance*> **5a** to make available; afford <*the hotel* ~s *a full range of facilities*> **b** to present (goods) for sale **6** to present in performance or exhibition **7** to tender as payment; bid ~ *vi* **1** to make an offer for consideration, acceptance, etc **2** to present itself; occur

[2]**offer** *n* **1a** a proposal; *specif* a proposal of marriage **b** an undertaking to do or give sthg on a specific condition **2** a price named by a prospective buyer – **on offer** being offered; *specif* for sale, esp at a reduced price – **under offer** sold subject to the signing of contracts – used in connection with sales of real estate

offering /ˈof(ə)ring‖ˈɒf(ə)rɪŋ/ *n* **1** the act of one who offers **2** sthg offered; *esp* a sacrifice ceremonially offered as a part of worship **3** a contribution to the support of a church or other religious organization

offertory /ˈofət(ə)ri‖ˈɒfət(ə)rɪ/ *n* **1** *often cap* (a text said or sung during) the offering of the Communion bread and wine to God before consecration **2** (the collection and presentation of) the offerings of the congregation at public worship

offhand /ˌofˈhand‖ˌɒfˈhænd/ *adv or adj* **1** without forethought or preparation **2** without proper attention or respect – **offhanded** *adj*, **offhandedly** *adv*, **offhandedness** *n*

office /ˈofis‖ˈɒfɪs/ *n* **1** an esp beneficial service or action carried out for another <*through her good* ~s *I recovered my belongings*> **2a** a position giving authority to exercise a public function <*the* ~ *of Prime Minister*> **b** a position with special duties or responsibilities **3** a prescribed form or service of worship; *esp, cap* DIVINE OFFICE **4a** a place, esp a large building, where the business of a particular organization is carried out **b** (a group of people sharing) a room in which the administrative, clerical, or professional work of an organization is performed **c** a place, esp a small room, where a particular service is provided <*the lost property* ~> **5a** *cap* a major administrative unit in some governments <*the Foreign* Office> **b** a subdivision of some government departments [Old French, fr Latin *officium* service, duty, office, fr *opus* work + *facere* to make, do]

ˈoffice ˌboy, *fem* **ˈoffice ˌgirl** *n* a young person employed to run errands in an office

[1]**officer** /ˈofisə‖ˈɒfɪsə/ *n* **1** a policeman **2** one who holds a position with special duties or responsibilities (e g in a government or business) **3a** one who holds a position of authority or command in the armed forces; *specif* a commissioned officer **b** a master or any of the mates of a merchant or passenger ship

[2]**officer** *vt* **1** to supply with officers **2** to command or direct as an officer

[1]**official** /əˈfish(ə)l‖əˈfɪʃ(ə)l/ *n* one who holds an esp public office <*government* ~s> – **officialdom** *n*, **officialese** *n*

[2]**official** *adj* **1** of an office and its duties **2** holding an office **3a** authoritative, authorized **b** prescribed or recognized as authorized, esp by a pharmacopoeia **4** suitable for or characteristic of a person in office; formal – **officially** *adv*

Ofˌficial Reˈceiver *n* a public official appointed to administer a bankrupt's property

officiate /əˈfishiayt‖əˈfɪʃɪeɪt/ *vi* **1** to perform an esp religious ceremony, function, or duty <~ *at a wedding*> **2** to act as an official or in an official capacity – **officiant** *n*, **officiation** *n*

officious /əˈfishəs‖əˈfɪʃəs/ *adj* **1** given to or marked by overzealousness in exercising authority or carrying out duties **2** *esp of a diplomatic agreement* informal, unofficial – **officiously** *adv*, **officiousness** *n*

offing /ˈofing‖ˈɒfɪŋ/ *n* the part of the deep sea visible from the shore – **in the offing** likely to happen in the near future <*thought more unemployment was* in the offing>

offish /ˈofish‖ˈɒfɪʃ/ *adj* inclined to be aloof or distant – infml – **offishly** *adv*, **offishness** *n*

ˈoff-ˌlicence *n*, *Br* a shop, part of a public house, etc licensed to sell alcoholic drinks to be consumed off the premises; *also* the licence permitting such sale – **off-licensee** *n*

ˈoff-ˌline *adj* not controlled directly by a computer

ˌoff-ˈload *vt* UNLOAD 1, 2

ˌoff-ˈpeak *adj* (used) at a time of less than the maximum demand or activity <~ *electricity*> <~ *travel*>

ˈoffˌprint /-ˌprint‖-ˌprɪnt/ *n* a separately printed excerpt (e g an article from a magazine) – **offprint** *vt*

ˌoff-ˈputting *adj, chiefly Br* disagreeable, disconcerting – infml

[1]**ˈoffˌset** /-ˌset‖-ˌset/ *n* **1** a short shoot or bulb growing out to the side from the base of a plant **2a** an offshoot, esp of a family or race **b** a spur in a range of hills **3** an abrupt bend in an object by which one part is turned aside out of line **4** sthg that serves to compensate for sthg else **5** a printing process in which an inked impression

from a plate is first made on a rubber surface and then transferred to paper

2**ˌoffˈset** *vt* **-tt-; offset 1a** to balance <*credits* ~ *debits*> **b** to compensate or make up for **2** to print (e g a book) by using the offset process

ˈoffˌshoot /-ˌshooht‖-ˌʃuːt/ *n* **1** a branch of a plant's main stem **2a** a lateral branch (e g of a mountain range) **b** a subsidiary branch, descendant, or member

ˌoffˈshore /-ˈshaw‖-ˈʃɔː/ *adj or adv* **1** (coming or moving) away from the shore **2** at a distance from the shore

ˌoffˈside /-ˈsied‖-ˈsaɪd/ *adv or adj* illegally in advance of the ball or puck in a team game

ˈoff ˌside *n* **1** the part of a cricket field on the opposite side of a line joining the middle stumps to that in which the batsman stands when playing a ball **2** *chiefly Br* the right side of a horse, vehicle, etc

ˈoffˌspring /-ˌspring‖-ˌsprɪŋ/ *n, pl* **offspring** the progeny of a person, animal, or plant; young

ˌoffˈstage /-ˈstayj‖-ˈsteɪdʒ/ *adv or adj* **1** on a part of the stage not visible to the audience **2** behind the scenes; away from the public gaze

ˌoff-the-ˈrecord *adj or adv* (given or made) unofficially or in confidence

ˌoff-ˈwhite *n or adj* (a) yellowish or greyish white

oft /oft‖ɒft/ *adv* often – poetic

often /ˈof(t)ən‖ˈɒf(t)ən/ *adv* **1** (at) many times **2** in many cases <*they* ~ *die young*>

ogle /ˈohgl‖ˈəʊgl/ *vb* to glance or stare with esp sexual interest (at) – **ogle** *n*, **ogler** *n*

ogre /ˈohgə‖ˈəʊgə/, *fem* **ogress** /ˈohgris‖ˈəʊgrɪs/ *n* **1** a hideous giant of folklore believed to feed on human beings **2** a dreaded person or thing – **ogreish** *adj*

1**oh, O** /oh‖əʊ/ *interj* – used to express surprise, pain, disappointment, etc

2**oh, O** *n* nought

ohm /ohm‖əʊm/ *n* the derived SI unit of electrical resistance equal to the resistance between 2 points of a conductor when a constant potential difference of 1 volt applied to these points produces a current of 1 ampere [Georg Simon *Ohm* (1787-1854), German physicist] – **ohmic** *adj*, **ohmically** *adv*

oho /ohˈhoh‖əʊˈhəʊ/ *interj* – used to express amused surprise, exultation, etc

1**-oid** /-oyd‖-ɔɪd/ *suffix* (→ *n*) sthg resembling (a specified object) or having (a specified quality) <*asteroid*>

2**-oid** *suffix* (→ *n, adj*) **1** resembling; having the form or appearance of <*petal*oid> **2** bearing an imperfect resemblance to <*human*oid>

1**oil** /oyl‖ɔɪl/ *n* **1** any of numerous smooth greasy combustible liquids or low melting-point solids that are insoluble in water but dissolve in organic solvents **2** a substance (e g a cosmetic preparation) of oily consistency **3a** OIL PAINT <*a portrait done in* ~s> **b** OIL PAINTING **4** petroleum [Old French *oile*, fr Latin *oleum* olive oil, fr Greek *elaion*, fr *elaia* olive] – **oil** *adj*

2**oil** *vt* to treat or lubricate with oil ~ *vi* to change from a solid fat into an oil by melting – **oiler** *n* – **oil the wheels** to help things run smoothly

ˈoil ˌcake *n* the solid residue left after extracting the oil from seeds (e g of cotton)

ˈoilˌcan /-ˌkan‖-ˌkæn/ *n* a vessel with a nozzle designed to release oil in a controlled flow (e g for lubricating machinery)

ˈoilˌcloth /-ˌkloth‖-ˌklɒθ/ *n* cloth treated with oil or paint and used for table and shelf coverings

ˈoil ˌcolour *n* OIL PAINT

ˈoil ˌfield *n* a region rich in petroleum deposits; *esp* one producing petroleum in commercial quantities

ˈoil ˌpaint *n* paint consisting of ground pigment mixed with oil

ˈoil ˌpainting *n* (a product of) the art of painting with oil paints

ˈoilˌskin /-ˌskin‖-ˌskɪn/ *n* **1** an oiled waterproof cloth used for coverings and garments **2** an oilskin or plastic raincoat **3** *pl* an oilskin or plastic suit of coat and trousers

ˈoil ˌslick *n* a film of oil floating on water

ˈoil ˌwell *n* a well drilled in the earth from which petroleum is obtained

oily /ˈoyli‖ˈɔɪlɪ/ *adj* **1** of, resembling, containing, or covered with oil **2** unctuous, ingratiating – **oilily** *adv*, **oiliness** *n*

oink /oyngk‖ɔɪŋk/ *n* the grunt of a pig – humor – **oink** *vi*

ointment /ˈoyntmənt‖ˈɔɪntmənt/ *n* a soothing or healing salve for application to the skin

1**OK, okay** /ohˈkay, ˈ-ˌ-‖əʊˈkeɪ, ˈ-ˌ-/ *adv, adj, or interj* ALL RIGHT [prob abbreviation of *oll korrect*, facetious spelling of *all correct*]

2**OK, okay** /ohˈkay‖əʊˈkeɪ/ *vt or n* **OK's; OK'ing; OK'd** (to give) approval or authorization (of); sanction

okapi /ohˈkahpi‖əʊˈkɑːpɪ/ *n* an African mammal closely related to the giraffe but with a shorter neck and black and cream rings on the upper parts of the legs

okra /ˈohkrə, ˈokrə‖ˈəʊkrə, ˈɒkrə/ *n* **1** a tall annual plant of the mallow family cultivated for its green pods used as a vegetable; *also* the pods of this plant **2** GUMBO 1

1**old** /ohld‖əʊld/ *adj* **1a** dating from the esp remote past <~ *traditions*> **b** persisting from an earlier time <*an* ~ *ailment*> **c** of long standing <*an* ~ *friend*> **2** *cap* constituting an early period in the development of a language <Old *Irish*> **3** having existed for a specified period of time <*3 years* ~> **4** advanced in years or age **5** experienced <*an* ~ *hand*> **6** former **7a** made long ago; *esp* worn with time or use **b** no longer in use; discarded **8a** long familiar <*the same* ~ *story*> **b** – used as an intensive <*a high* ~ *time*> <*any* ~ *time*> – **oldish** *adj*, **oldness** *n*

2**old** *n* **1** old or earlier time <*men of* ~> **2** one of a specified age – usu in combination <*a 3-year*-old>

ˌold ˈage *n* the final stage of the normal life span

ˌold age ˈpension *n* a state pension paid to retired people – **old age pensioner** *n*

ˌold ˈboy, *fem* **ˌold ˈgirl** *n, chiefly Br* **1** a former pupil of a particular, esp public, school **2** a fellow or friend – often used as an informal term of address

ˌold ˈboy ˌnetwork *n, chiefly Br* the system

of favouritism operating among people of a similar privileged background, esp among former pupils of public schools

ˈold ˌcountry *n* an immigrant's country of origin

olden /ˈohldn‖ˈəʊldn/ *adj* of a bygone era – poetic

Old English *n* English before 1150 or thereabouts

olde-worlde /ˌohld ˈwuhld‖ˌəʊld ˈwɜːld; *often* ˌohldi ˈwuhldi‖ˌəʊldɪ ˈwɜːldɪ/ *adj* (excessively or falsely) old-world

ˌold-ˈfashioned *adj* **1** (characteristic) of a past era; outdated **2** clinging to customs of a past era – **old-fashionedly** *adv*

ˌold ˈguard *n sing or pl in constr, often cap O&G* the (original) conservative members of a group or party

ˌold ˈhand *n* VETERAN 1

ˌold ˈhat *adj* **1** old-fashioned **2** hackneyed, trite

ˌold ˈlady *n* one's wife or mother – infml

ˌold ˈmaid *n* **1** SPINSTER 2 **2** a prim fussy person – infml – **old-maidish** *adj*

ˌold ˈman *n* **1** one's husband or father **2** one in authority (e g one's employer, manager, or commander) – + *the USE* infml

ˌold ˈmaster *n* (a work by) a distinguished European painter of the 16th to early 18th c

ˌOld ˈNick /nik‖nɪk/ *n* – used as an informal or humorous name for the devil

ˌold ˈschool *n* adherents of traditional ideas and practices

ˌold ˌschool ˈtie *n* **1** a tie displaying the colours of an English public school, worn by former pupils **2** the conservatism and upper-class solidarity traditionally attributed to former members of British public schools

ˌold ˈstager /ˈstayjə‖ˈsteɪdʒə/ *n* VETERAN 1

oldster /ˈohldstə‖ˈəʊldstə/ *n, chiefly NAm* an old or elderly person – infml

ˌOld ˈTestament *n* a collection of writings forming the Jewish canon of Scripture and the first part of the Christian Bible

ˌold-ˈtimer *n* **1** VETERAN 1 **2** *chiefly NAm* an old man

ˌold ˈwives' ˌtale *n* a traditional superstitious notion

ˌold ˈwoman *n* **1** one's wife or mother **2** a timid, prim, or fussy person, esp a man – derog *USE* infml

ˌold-ˈworld *adj* **1** of the E hemisphere **2** reminiscent of a past age; *esp* quaintly charming

ˌOld ˈWorld *n* the E Hemisphere; *specif* Europe, Asia, and Africa

oleaginous /ˌohliˈajinəs‖ˌəʊlɪˈædʒɪnəs/ *adj* resembling, containing, or producing oil; oily – **oleaginously** *adv*, **oleaginousness** *n*

oleander /ˌohliˈandə‖ˌəʊlɪˈændə/ *n* a poisonous evergreen shrub of the periwinkle family with fragrant white, pink, or red flowers

oleoresin /ˌohliohˈrezin‖ˌəʊlɪəʊˈrezɪn/ *n* a solution of resin in oil, occurring naturally as a plant product (e g turpentine) or made synthetically

ˈO ˌlevel *n* ORDINARY LEVEL

olfaction /olˈfaksh(ə)n‖ɒlˈfækʃ(ə)n/ *n* smelling or the sense of smell – **olfactive, olfactory** *adj*

oligarch /ˈoligahk‖ˈɒlɪgɑːk/ *n* a member of an oligarchy [Greek *oligarchēs*, fr *oligos* few + *archos* ruler]

oligarchy /ˈoligahki‖ˈɒlɪgɑːkɪ/ *n* **1** government by a small group **2** a state or organization in which a small group exercises control, esp for its own interests **3** a small group exercising such control – **oligarchic, oligarchical** *adj*

oligopoly /ˌoliˈgopəli‖ˌɒlɪˈgɒpəlɪ/ domination of a market by a small number of producers

[1]**olive** /ˈoliv‖ˈɒlɪv/ *n* **1** (an Old World evergreen tree that grows esp around the Mediterranean and bears) a small stone fruit used as a food and a source of oil **2 olive, olive green** a dull yellowish green colour resembling that of an unripe olive

[2]**olive**, **ˌolive ˈgreen** *adj* of the colour olive

ˈolive ˌbranch *n* an offer or gesture of conciliation or goodwill

olympiad /əˈlimpiˌad‖əˈlɪmpɪˌæd/ *n, often cap* **1** any of the 4-year intervals between Olympian games by which time was reckoned in ancient Greece **2** OLYMPIC GAMES

[1]**Olympian** /əˈlimpi·ən‖əˈlɪmpɪən/ *adj* of the ancient Greek region of Olympia

[2]**Olympian** *n, chiefly NAm* a participant in the Olympic Games

[3]**Olympian** *adj* **1** of Mount Olympus in Thessaly **2** lofty, detached

[4]**Olympian** *n* **1** an inhabitant of the ancient Greek region of Olympia **2** any of the ancient Greek deities dwelling on Olympus **3** a loftily detached or superior person

OˌIympian ˈGames *n pl* a festival held every 4th year by the ancient Greek states and consisting of contests in sport, music, and literature

Olympic /əˈlimpik‖əˈlɪmpɪk/ *adj* **1** [3]OLYMPIAN **2** of or executed in the Olympic Games

OˌIympic ˈGames *n pl but sing or pl in constr, pl* **Olympic Games** an international sports meeting that is a modified revival of the and is held once every 4 years in a different host country

ombre /ˈombə‖ˈɒmbə/ *n* a 3-handed card game popular in Europe in the 17th and 18th c

ombudsman /ˈomboodzmən‖ˈɒmbʊdzmən/ *n* a government official appointed to investigate complaints made by individuals against government or public bodies [Swedish, lit., representative, fr Old Norse *umbothsmathr*, fr *umboth* commission + *mathr* man]

omega /ˈohmigə‖ˈəʊmɪgə/ *n* **1** the 24th and last letter of the Greek alphabet **2** the last one in a series, order, etc

omelette, *NAm chiefly* **omelet** /ˈomlit‖ˈɒmlɪt/ *n* a mixture of beaten eggs cooked until set in a shallow pan and often served folded in half over a filling

omen /ˈohmen, ˈohmən‖ˈəʊmen, ˈəʊmən/ *n* an event or phenomenon believed to be a sign of some future occurrence

ominous /ˈominəs‖ˈɒmɪnəs/ *adj* portentous; *esp* foreboding evil or disaster – **ominously** *adv*, **ominousness** *n*

omission /ohˈmish(ə)n, ə-‖əʊˈmɪʃ(ə)n, ə-/ *n* **1** omitting or being omitted **2** sthg neglected or left undone

omit /ohˈmit, ə-‖əʊˈmɪt, ə-/ *vt* **-tt-** **1** to leave out or unmentioned **2** to fail to do or perform – **omissible** *adj*

omni- /omni-‖ɒmnɪ-/ *comb form* all; universally <omni*directional*>

[1]**omnibus** /ˈomnibəs‖ˈɒmnɪbəs/ *n* **1** a book containing reprints of a number of works, usu by 1 author **2** BUS 1 – fml [French, bus, fr Latin, for all, fr *omnis* all]

[2]**omnibus** *adj* of, containing, or providing for many things at once

omnipotent /omˈnipət(ə)nt‖ɒmˈnɪpət(ə)nt/ *adj* having unlimited or very great power or influence; *specif, often cap* ALMIGHTY 1 – **omnipotence** *n*, **omnipotently** *adv*

Omnipotent *n* GOD 1

omnipresent /ˌomniˈprez(ə)nt‖ˌɒmnɪˈprez(ə)nt/ *adj* present in all places at all times – **omnipresence** *n*

omniscient /omˈnisi·ənt, omˈnish(ə)nt‖ɒmˈnɪsɪənt, ɒmˈnɪʃ(ə)nt/ *adj* **1** having infinite awareness or understanding **2** possessed of complete knowledge; all-knowing – **omniscience** *n*, **omnisciently** *adv*

omnivorous /omˈnivərəs‖ɒmˈnɪvərəs/ *adj* **1** feeding on both animal and vegetable substances **2** avidly taking in, and esp reading, everything – **omnivorously** *adv*, **omnivorousness** *n*, **omnivore** *n*

[1]**on** /on‖ɒn/ *prep* **1a(1)** in contact with or supported from below by <*a fly ~ the ceiling*> <*stand ~ 1 foot*> <*a book ~ the table*> **a(2)** attached or fastened to <*a dog ~ a lead*> **a(3)** carried on the person of <*have you a match ~ you?*> **a(4)** very near to, esp along an edge or border <*towns ~ the frontier*> <*Walton-~-Thames*> **a(5)** within the limits of a usu specified area <*~ the steppes*> <*~ page 17*> **b** at the usual standard or level of <*~ form*> **c(1)** in the direction of <*~ the right*> <*crept up ~ him*> **c(2)** into contact with <*jumped ~ the horse*> **c(3)** with regard to; concerning <*keen ~ sports*> <*unfair ~ me*> <*evidence ~ the matter*> **c(4)** with a specified person or thing as object <*try it out ~ her*> **c(5)** having as a topic; about <*a book ~ India*> **c(6)** staked on the success of <*put £5 ~ a horse*> **c(7)** doing or carrying out a specified action or activity <*here ~ business*> <*went ~ an errand*> **c(8)** working for, supporting, or belonging to <*~ a committee*> <*~ their side*> **c(9)** working at; in charge of <*the man ~ the gate*> **2a** having as a basis or source (e g of knowledge or comparison) <*have it ~ good authority*> <*swear ~ the Bible*> <*prices are down ~ last year*> **b** at the expense of <*got it ~ the National Health*> <*drinks are ~ the house*> **3a** in the state or process of <*~ fire*> <*~ strike*> <*~ holiday*> <*~ offer*> <*~ the increase*> **b** in the specified manner <*~ the cheap*> **c** using as a medium <*played it ~ the clarinet*>; *esp* OVER 4b <*talking ~ the telephone*> **d** using by way of transport <*arrived ~ foot*> <*left ~ the early train*> **e** sustained or powered by <*live ~ vegetables*> <*car runs ~ petrol*> <*people ~ low incomes*> <*dined out ~ the story*> **f** regularly taking <*~ Valium*> **4** through contact with <*cut himself ~ a piece of glass*> **5a** at the time of <*came ~ Monday*> <*every hour ~ the hour*> <*cash ~ delivery*> **b** on the occasion of or immediately after and usu in consequence of <*shot ~ sight*> <*fainted ~ hearing the news*> **c** in the course of <*~ a journey*> <*~ tour*> <*~ my way*> **d** AFTER 2b <*blow ~ blow*>

[2]**on** *adv* **1** so as to be supported from below <*put the top ~*>, in close contact <*has new shoes ~*>, or attached <*sew the buttons ~*> **2a** ahead or forwards in space or time <*went ~ home*> <*do it later ~*> <*40 years ~*> <*getting ~ for 5*> **b** with the specified part forward <*cars crashed head ~*> **c** without interruption <*chattered ~ and ~*> **d** in continuance or succession <*and so ~*> **3a** in or into (a state permitting) operation <*switch the light ~*> <*get the potatoes ~*> <*put a record ~*> **b** in or into an activity or function <*the night shift came ~*>

[3]**on** *adj* **1a** LEG 2 <*~ drive*> **b** taking place <*the game is ~*> **c** performing or broadcasting <*we're ~ in 10 minutes*> **d** intended, planned <*has nothing ~ for tonight*> **e** worn as clothing <*went out with just a cardigan ~*> **2a** committed to a bet **b** in favour of a win <*the odds are 2 to 1 ~*> **3** *chiefly Br* possible, practicable – usu neg <*you can't refuse, it's just not ~*> **4a** *chiefly Br* nagging <*she's always ~ at him about his hair*> **b** talking dully, excessively, or incomprehensibly <*what's he ~ about?*> ***USE*** *(3&4)* infml

[1]**once** /wuns‖wʌns/ *adv* **1** one time and no more <*met only ~*> <*shaves ~ a week*> **2** even 1 time; ever <*if ~ we lose the key*> **3** at some indefinite time in the past; formerly <*there ~ lived a king*> **4** by 1 degree of relationship <*2nd cousin ~ removed*> – **once again/more 1** now again as before <*back home* once again> **2** for 1 more time

[2]**once** *n* one single time <*~ is enough*> <*just this ~*> – **all at once 1** all at the same time **2** ALL OF A SUDDEN – **at once 1** at the same time; simultaneously <*both spoke* at once> **2** IMMEDIATELY 2 – **once and for all, once for all** for the final or only time; conclusively

[3]**once** *conj* from the moment when; as soon as <*~ he arrives we can start*> <*~ over the wall we're safe*>

ˈ**once-ˌover** *n* a swift appraising glance – infml <*gave him the ~*>

oncoming /ˈonˌkuming‖ˈɒnˌkʌmɪŋ/ *adj* coming nearer in time or space; advancing

[1]**one** /wun‖wʌn/ *adj* **1a** being a single unit or thing <*~ day at a time*> **b** being the first – used after the noun modified <*on page ~*> **2** being a particular but unspecified instance <*saw her early ~ morning*> **3a(1)** the same; identical <*both of ~ mind*> <*it's all ~ to me where we go*> **a(2)** constituting a unified entity <*all shouted with ~ voice*> <*the combined elements form ~ substance*> **b** being in a state of agreement; united <*I am ~ with the rest of you in this matter*> **4** being some unspecified instance – used esp of future time <*will see you ~ day soon*> <*we might try it ~ weekend*> **5a** being a particular object or person <*close first ~ eye*

then the other> **b** being the only individual of an indicated or implied kind <*the ~ and only person she wanted to marry*> – **one and the same** the very same

[2]**one** *pron, pl* **ones** **1** a single member or specimen of a usu specified class or group <*saw ~ of his friends*> **2** an indefinitely indicated person; anybody at all <*~ has a duty to ~'s public*> <*~ never knows*> **3** – used to refer to a noun or noun phrase previously mentioned or understood <*2 grey shirts and 3 red ~s*> <*if you want a book about bees, try this ~*> <*the question is ~ of great importance*> *USE* used as a subject or object; no pl for senses 2 and 3

[3]**one** *n* **1** (the number) 1 **2** the number denoting unity **3** the first in a set or series <*takes a ~ in shoes*> **4a** a single person or thing **b** a unified entity <*is secretary and treasurer in ~*> <*they all rose up as ~ and clamoured for more pay*> **c** a particular example or instance <*~ of the coldest nights this year*> **d** a certain specified person <*~ George Hopkins*> **5a** a person with a liking or interest for a specified thing; an enthusiast <*he's rather a ~ for baroque music*> **b** a bold, amusing, or remarkable character <*oh! you are a ~*> **6a** a blow, stroke <*socked him ~ on the jaw*> **b** a drink <*just time for a quick ~*> **c** a remark; *esp* a joke <*have you heard this ~?*> **7** sthg having a denomination of 1 <*I'll take the money in ~s*> – **at one** in harmony; in a state of agreement – **for one** even if alone; not to mention others – **one by one** singly, successively

ˌone aˈnother *pron* each other

ˌone-armed ˈbandit *n* FRUIT MACHINE

ˌone-ˈman *adj* **1** consisting of only 1 person **2** done or produced by only 1 person

ˌone-night ˈstand *n* **1** a performance given only once in any particular locality **2** (a person with whom one has) a sexual relationship lasting only 1 night

ˌone-ˈpiece *adj* consisting of or made in a single undivided piece

onerous /ˈohnərəs, ˈon-‖ˈəunərəs, ˈɒn-/ *adj* burdensome, troublesome – **onerously** *adv*, **onerousness** *n*

oneself /wunˈself‖wʌnˈself/ *pron* **1** a person's self; one's own self – used reflexively <*one should wash ~*> or for emphasis <*to do it ~*> **2** one's normal self <*not feeling quite ~*> – **be oneself** to behave in a normal, unconstrained, or unpretentious manner – **by oneself** ON ONE'S OWN – **to oneself** for one's exclusive use or knowledge

ˌone-ˈsided *adj* **1a** having or occurring on 1 side only **b** having 1 side prominent or more developed **2** partial, biased – **one-sidedly** *adv*, **one-sidedness** *n*

ˈoneˌtime /-ˌtiem‖-ˌtaɪm/ *adj* former, sometime

ˌone-ˈtrack *adj* interested or absorbed in 1 thing only <*a ~ mind*>

ˌone-ˈupmanship /ˈupmənship‖ˈʌpmənʃɪp/ *n* the art of gaining a psychological advantage over others by professing social or professional superiority

ˌone-ˈway *adj* **1** that moves in or allows movement in only 1 direction <*~ traffic*> **2** one-sided, unilateral

ongoing /ˈonˌgoh·ing‖ˈɒnˌgəuɪŋ/ *adj* **1** actually in progress **2** growing, developing

onion /ˈunyən‖ˈʌnjən/ *n* (the pungent edible bulb, eaten as a vegetable, of) an Asian plant of the lily family or any of various related plants

ˌon-ˈline *adj* controlled directly by or in direct communicaion with a computer

onlooker /ˈonˌlookə‖ˈɒnˌlʊkə/ *n* a passive spectator – **onlooking** *adj*

[1]**only** /ˈohnli‖ˈəunlɪ/ *adj* **1** unquestionably the best <*flying is the ~ way to travel*> **2** alone in its class or kind; sole <*an ~ child*> <*the ~ detergent that contains fabric softener*>

[2]**only** *adv* **1a** nothing more than; merely <*~ a little one*> <*if it would ~ rain!*> **b** solely, exclusively <*known ~ to him*> **2** nothing other than <*it was ~ too true*> **3a** in the final outcome <*will ~ make you sick*> **b** with nevertheless the final result <*won the battle, ~ to lose the war*> **4** no earlier than <*~ last week*> <*has ~ just left*>

[3]**only** *conj* **1** but, however <*they look very nice, ~ we can't use them*> **2** were it not for the fact that <*I'd tell you, ~ you'll just spread it around*> *USE* infml

onomatopoeia /ˌonəˌmatəˈpee·ə‖ˌɒnəˌmætəˈpiːə/ *n* the formation or use of words intended to be a vocal imitation of the sound associated with the thing or action designated (e g in *buzz, cuckoo*) [Late Latin, fr Greek *onomatopoiia*, fr *onomat-, onoma* name + *poiein* to make] – **onomatopoeic** *adj*, **onomatopoeically** *adv*

onrush /ˈonˌrush‖ˈɒnˌrʌʃ/ *n* a forceful rushing forwards

onset /ˈonˌset‖ˈɒnˌset/ *n* **1** an attack, assault **2** a beginning, commencement

ˌonˈshore /-ˈshaw‖-ˈʃɔː/ *adj or adv* **1** (moving) towards the shore **2** on or near the shore

ˌonˈside /-ˈsied‖-ˈsaɪd/ *adv or adj* not offside

onslaught /ˈonˌslawt‖ˈɒnˌslɔːt/ *n* a fierce attack

onstream /ˈonstreem/ *adj or adv* in operation or ready to go into operation – used of an industrial process

onto, on to /ˈontə‖ˈɒntə; *strong* ˈontooh‖ˈɒntuː/ *prep* **1** to a position on **2** in or into a state of awareness about <*put the police ~ him*> **3** – used as a function word to indicate a mathematical set, each element of which is the image of at least 1 element of another set <*a function mapping the set* S *~ the set* T> **4** *chiefly Br* in or into contact with <*been ~ him about the drains*>; *esp* on at; nagging

ontology /onˈtoləji‖ɒnˈtɒlədʒɪ/ *n* a branch of philosophy concerned with the nature of being – **ontologist** *n*, **ontological** *adj*

onus /ˈohnəs‖ˈəunəs/ *n* **1a** duty, responsibility **b** blame **2** BURDEN OF PROOF

onward /ˈonwood‖ˈɒnwʊd/ *adj* directed or moving onwards; forward

ˈonwards, onward *adv* towards or at a point lying ahead in space or time; forwards <*from his childhood ~*>

onyx /ˈoniks‖ˈɒnɪks/ *n* **1** a translucent variety of quartz with layers of different colours, typically green and white or black or brown and white **2 onyx, onyx marble** a translucent or semitranslucent calcium carbonate mineral, usu calcite, with marble-like bands of colour

oodles /ˈoohdlz‖ˈuːdlz/ *n pl but sing or pl in constr* a great quantity; a lot – infml

oomph /oom(p)f‖ʊm(p)f/ *n* vitality, enthusiasm – humor

oops /oops, oohps‖ʊps, uːps/ *interj* – used to express apology or surprise

[1]**ooze** /oohz‖uːz/ *n* **1** a soft deposit of mud, slime, debris, etc on the bottom of a body of water **2** (the muddy ground of) a marsh or bog – **oozy** *adj*

[2]**ooze** *n* **1** an infusion of vegetable material (e g bark) used for tanning leather **2** sthg that oozes – **oozy** *adj*

[3]**ooze** *vi* **1a** to pass or flow slowly through small openings **b** to diminish gradually; dwindle *away* **2** to exude moisture ~ *vt* **1** to emit or give out slowly **2** to display in abundance <*positively* ~d *vitality*>

op /op‖ɒp/ *n* OPERATION 3, 5 – infml

opacity /ohˈpasəti‖əʊˈpæsətɪ/ *n* **1** opaqueness **2** obscurity of meaning; unintelligibility **3** an opaque spot on a normally transparent structure (e g the lens of the eye)

opal /ˈohp(ə)l‖ˈəʊp(ə)l/ *n* a transparent to translucent mineral consisting of a hydrated silica and used in its opalescent forms as a gem

opalescent /ˌohplˈes(ə)nt, ˌohpəˈles(ə)nt‖ˌəʊplˈes(ə)nt, ˌəʊpəˈles(ə)nt/ *adj* reflecting a milky iridescent light – **opalescence** *n*

opaque /ohˈpayk‖əʊˈpeɪk/ *adj* **1** not transmitting radiant energy, esp light; not transparent **2** hard to understand; unintelligible – **opaquely** *adv*, **opaqueness** *n*

ˌ**op ˈart** /op‖ɒp/ *n* OPTICAL ART – **op artist** *n*

[1]**open** /ˈohp(ə)n‖ˈəʊp(ə)n/ *adj* **1** having no enclosing or confining barrier <*the* ~ *hillside*> **2** allowing passage; not shut or locked **3a** exposed to general view or knowledge; public <*regarded him with* ~ *hatred*> **b** vulnerable to attack or question; liable <~ *to doubt*> **4a** not covered or protected <*an* ~ *boat*> <*an* ~ *wound*> **b** not fastened or sealed **5** not restricted to a particular category of participants; *specif* contested by both amateurs and professionals **6** presenting no obstacle to passage or view **7** having the parts or surfaces spread out or unfolded **8** articulated with the tongue low in the mouth <*an* ~ *vowel*> **9a** available <*the only course* ~ *to us*> **b** not taken up with duties or engagements <*keep an hour* ~ *on Friday*> **c** not finally decided or settled <*an* ~ *question*> **d** available for a qualified applicant; vacant **e** remaining available for use or filling until cancelled <*an* ~ *order for more items*> **10a(1)** willing to consider new ideas; unprejudiced <*an* ~ *mind*> **a(2)** willing to receive and consider <*always* ~ *to suggestions*> **b** candid, frank **11a** containing many small openings or spaces; *specif* porous **b** having relatively wide spacing between words or lines <~ *type*> **c** *of a compound word* elements separated by a space in writing or printing (e g in *ski lift*) **12a** *of a string on a musical instrument* not stopped by the finger **b** *of a note* produced on a musical instrument without fingering the strings, valves, slides, or keys **13** in operation; *esp* ready for business or use <*the shop is* ~ *from 9 to 5*> <*the new motorway will be* ~ *next week*> **14** free from checks or restraints <*an* ~ *economy*> **15** *of a mathematical set* containing a neighbourhood of every element <*the interior of a sphere is an* ~ *set*> **16** *Br, of a cheque* payable in cash to the person, organization, etc named on it; not crossed – **open** *adv*, **openness** *n*

[2]**open** *vt* **1a** to change or move from a closed position **b** to permit entry into or passage through **c** to gain access to the contents of <~ *a parcel*> **2a** to make available for or active in a particular use or function; *specif* to establish <~ed *a new shop*> **b** to declare available for use, esp ceremonially **c** to make the necessary arrangements for (e g a bank account), esp by depositing money **3a** to disclose, reveal – often + *up* **b** to make more responsive or enlightened **4a** to make 1 or more openings in **b** to loosen and make less compact <~ *the soil*> **5** to spread out; unfold **6** to begin, commence <~ed *the meeting*> **7** to begin (e g the bidding, betting, or play) in a card game **8a** to initiate (a side's innings) as one of the 2 first batsmen **b** to initiate (a side's bowling attack) by bowling one of the first 2 overs of an innings ~ *vi* **1** to become open **2** to commence, start <~ed *with a prayer*> **3** to give access – usu + *into* or *onto* **4** to extend, unfold – usu + *out* <*the view* ~ed *out in front of us*> – **openable** *adj*, **openability** *n*

[3]**open** *n* **1** OUTDOORS 2 **2** *often cap* an open contest, competition, or tournament – **bring into/be in the open** to (cause to) be generally known

ˌ**open-ˈair** *adj* outdoor

ˌ**open ˈair** *n* OUTDOORS 2

ˌ**open-and-ˈshut** *adj* easily settled <*an* ~ *case*>

ˌ**openˈcast** /-ˈkahst‖-ˈkɑːst/ *adj, of a mine or mining* worked from or carried out on the earth's surface by removing material covering the mineral mined for

ˌ**open ˈdoor** *n* a policy of equal commercial relations with all nations – **open-door** *adj*

ˌ**open-ˈended** *adj* without any definite limits or restrictions (e g of time or purpose) set in advance – **open-endedness** *n*

opener /ˈohp(ə)nə‖ˈəʊp(ə)nə/ *n* **1a** an instrument that opens sthg – usu in combination <*a bottle* ~> **b** one who opens; *specif* an opening batsman **2** *pl* cards of sufficient value for a player to open the betting in a poker game **3** the first item or event in a series

ˌ**openˈhanded** /-ˈhandid‖-ˈhændɪd/ *adj* generous in giving – **openhandedly** *adv*, **openhandedness** *n*

ˌ**open-ˈheart** *adj* of or performed on a heart surgically opened whilst its function is temporarily taken over by a heart-lung machine <~ *surgery*>

ˌ**openˈhearted** /-ˈhahtid‖-ˈhɑːtɪd/ *adj* **1** candidly straightforward **2** kind, generous – **openheartedly** *adv*, **openheartedness** *n*

opening /ˈohp(ə)ning‖ˈəʊp(ə)nɪŋ/ *n* **1** an act of making or becoming open **2** a breach, aperture **3a** an often standard series of moves made at the beginning of a game of chess or draughts

b a first performance **4a** a favourable opportunity; a chance **b** an opportunity for employment; a vacancy

ˈopening ˌtime *n* the time at which a business, shop, etc opens; *specif* the statutory time at which a public house may open for the sale of alcohol

ˌopen ˈletter *n* a letter, esp of protest, appeal, or explanation, usu addressed to an individual but intended for the general public, and published in a newspaper, periodical, etc

ˈopenly /-li‖-lɪ/ *adv* in an open and frank manner

ˌopen-ˈminded *adj* receptive to new arguments or ideas – **open-mindedly** *adv*, **open-mindedness** *n*

ˌopenˈmouthed /-ˈmowdhd‖-ˈmaʊðd/ *adj* having the mouth open, esp in surprise

open out *vi* to speak more freely and confidently

ˌopen ˈsandwich *n* a sandwich without a top slice of bread

ˈopen ˌseason *n* a period during which it is legal to kill or catch game or fish protected at other times by law

ˌopen ˈsecret *n* a supposed secret that is in fact widely known

ˌopen ˈsesame /ˈsezəmi, ˈsesəmi‖ˈsezəmɪ, ˈsesəmɪ/ *n* a means of gaining access to sthg otherwise inaccessible [*open sesame*, the magical command used by Ali Baba to open the door of the robbers' den in the Arabian folktale *Ali Baba and the Forty Thieves*]

ˌopen ˈshop *n* an establishment in which eligibility for employment is not dependent on membership of a trade union

ˌOpen Uniˈversity *n* the nonresidential British university that caters mainly for adults studying part-time, has no formal entrance requirements, and operates mainly through correspondence and broadcasting

open up *vi* **1** to commence firing **2** OPEN OUT **3** to open a door <open up, *it's the police!*> **4** *of a game, competition, etc* to become more interesting, esp because more closely contested ~ *vt* to make available or accessible <*the deal* opened up *important new possibilities for trade*>

ˌopen ˈverdict *n* a verdict at an inquest that records a death but does not state its cause

ˈopenˌwork /-ˌwuhk‖-ˌwɜːk/ *n* work (e g in fabric or metal) that is perforated or pierced – **open-worked** *adj*

[1]opera /ˈop(ə)rə‖ˈɒp(ə)rə/ *pl of* OPUS

[2]opera /ˈoprə‖ˈɒprə/ *n* **1** (the performance of or score for) a drama set to music and made up of vocal pieces with orchestral accompaniment and usu other orchestral music (e g an overture) **2** the branch of the arts concerned with such works **3** a company performing operas – **operatic** *adj*, **operatically** *adv*

operable /ˈop(ə)rəbl‖ˈɒp(ə)rəbl/ *adj* suitable for surgical treatment <*an* ~ *cancer*> – **operably** *adv*, **operability** *n*

ˈopera ˌglass *n* small binoculars suitable for use at the opera or theatre – often pl with sing. meaning

ˈopera ˌhat *n* a man's collapsible top hat

ˈopera ˌhouse *n* a theatre designed for the performance of opera

operate /ˈopərayt‖ˈɒpəreɪt/ *vi* **1** to exert power or influence; act <*factors* operating *against our success*> **2** to produce a desired effect **3a** to work, function **b** to perform surgery – usu + *on* **c** to carry on a military or naval action or mission **4** to be in action; *specif* to carry out trade or business ~ *vt* **1** to effect; BRING ABOUT **2a** to cause to function; work **b** to put or keep in operation; manage [Latin *operari* to work, fr *oper-, opus* work]

ˈoperating ˌtheatre *n*, *Br* a room, usu in a hospital, where surgical operations are carried out

operation /ˌopəˈraysh(ə)n‖ˌɒpəˈreɪʃ(ə)n/ *n* **1a** the act, method, or process of operating **b** sthg (to be) done; an activity **2** the state of being functional or operative <*the plant is now in* ~> **3** a procedure carried out on a living body with special instruments, usu for the repair of damage or the restoration of health **4** any of various mathematical or logical processes (e g addition) carried out to derive one expression from others according to a rule **5** a usu military action, mission, or manoeuvre and its planning **6** a business or financial transaction **7** a single step performed by a computer in the execution of a program – **operational** *adj*

[1]operative /ˈop(ə)rətiv‖ˈɒp(ə)rətɪv/ *adj* **1a** producing an appropriate effect; efficacious **b** significant, relevant **2** in force or operation **3** based on, consisting of, or using an esp surgical operation – **operatively** *adv*, **operativeness** *n*

[2]operative *n* an operator: e g **a** a workman **b** *NAm* PRIVATE DETECTIVE

operator /ˈopəˌraytə‖ˈɒpəˌreɪtə/ *n* **1a** one who operates a machine or device **b** one who owns or runs a business, organization, etc <*a tour* ~> **c** one who is in charge of a telephone switchboard **2** a mathematical or logical symbol denoting an operation to be performed **3** a shrewd and skilful manipulator – infml

operetta /ˌopəˈretə‖ˌɒpəˈretə/ *n* a usu romantic comic opera that includes dancing – **operettist** *n*

ophthalmia /ofˈthalmi·ə‖ɒfˈθælmɪə; *also* op-‖ɒp-/ *n* inflammation of the conjunctiva or the eyeball

ophthalmic /ofˈthalmɪk‖ɒfˈθælmɪk; *also* op-‖ɒp-/ *adj* of or situated near the eye

ophthalmology /ˌofthalˈmoləji‖ˌɒfθælˈmɒlədʒɪ; *also* op-‖ɒp-/ *n* the branch of medical science dealing with the structure, functions, and diseases of the eye – **ophthalmological** *also* **ophthalmologic** *adj*, **ophthalmologically** *adv*

ophthalmoscope /ofˈthalməˌskohp‖ɒfˈθælməˌskəʊp; *also* op-‖ɒp-/ *n* an instrument used to view the retina and other structures inside the eye – **ophthalmoscopic** *adj*, **ophthalmoscopy** *n*

[1]opiate /ˈohpi·ət, -ˌayt‖ˈəʊpɪət, -ˌeɪt/ *adj* **1** containing or mixed with opium **2** inducing sleep; narcotic

[2]opiate *n* **1** a preparation or derivative of opium; *broadly* a narcotic **2** sthg that induces inaction or calm

opine /ohˈpien‖əʊˈpaɪn/ *vt* to state as an opinion – fml

opinion /ə'pinyən‖ə'pɪnjən/ *n* **1a** a view or judgment formed about a particular matter **b** an esp favourable estimation **2a** a belief unsupported by positive knowledge **b** a generally held view **3a** a formal expression by an expert of his/her professional judgment or advice; *esp* a barrister's written advice to a client **b** *chiefly NAm* a formal expression of the principles on which a legal decision is based

opinionated /ə'pinyə,naytid‖ə'pɪnjə,neɪtɪd/ *adj* stubbornly sticking to one's own opinions

opium /'ohpi·əm‖'əʊpɪəm/ *n* the dried juice of the unripe seed capsules of the opium poppy, containing morphine and other addictive narcotic alkaloids

'opium ,poppy *n* an annual Eurasian poppy cultivated as the source of opium or for its edible seeds or showy flowers

opossum /ə'posəm‖ə'pɒsəm/ *n*, any of various American (tree-dwelling) marsupial mammals; *also* any of several Australian marsupial mammals resembling this

oppo /'opoh‖'ɒpəʊ/ *n*, *Br* a colleague or companion – infml

opponent /ə'pohnənt‖ə'pəʊnənt/ *n* one who takes the opposite side in a contest, conflict, etc

opportune /,opə'tyoohn, '--,-‖,ɒpə'tju:n, '--,-/ *adj* **1** suitable or convenient for a particular occurrence **2** occurring at an appropriate time – **opportunely** *adv*, **opportuneness** *n*

opportunism /,opə'tyooh,niz(ə)m‖,ɒpə'tju:-,nɪz(ə)m/ *n* the taking advantage of opportunities or circumstances, esp with little regard for principles or consequences – **opportunist** *n or adj*, **opportunistic** *adj*

opportunity /,opə'tyoohnəti‖,ɒpə'tju:nətɪ/ *n* **1** a favourable set of circumstances **2** a chance for advancement or progress

oppose /ə'pohz‖ə'pəʊz/ *vt* **1** to place opposite or against sthg so as to provide counterbalance, contrast, etc **2** to offer resistance to – **opposer** *n*

[1]**opposite** /'opəzit‖'ɒpəzɪt/ *n* **1** sthg or sby opposed or contrary **2** an antonym

[2]**opposite** *adj* **1a** set over against sthg that is at the other end or side of an intervening line or space < ~ *ends of a diameter*> **b** *of plant parts* situated in pairs at the same level on opposite sides of an axis < ~ *leaves*> **2a** occupying an opposing position < ~ *sides of the question*> **b** diametrically different; contrary **3** being the other of a matching or contrasting pair <*the ~ sex*> – **oppositely** *adv*, **oppositeness** *n*

[3]**opposite** *adv* on or to an opposite side

[4]**opposite** *prep* **1** across from and usu facing <*sat ~ each other*> **2** in a role complementary to <*played ~ the leading lady*>

,opposite 'number *n* a counterpart

opposition /,opə'zish(ə)n‖,ɒpə'zɪʃ(ə)n/ *n* **1** an opposite position of 2 celestial bodies in which their longitude differs by 180 degrees **2** the relation between 2 propositions having the same subject and predicate but differing in quantity or quality or both **3** placing opposite or being so placed **4** hostile or contrary action **5** *sing or pl in constr* **5a** the body of people opposing sthg **b** *often cap* a political party opposing the party in power – **oppositional** *adj*

oppress /ə'pres‖ə'pres/ *vt* **1** to crush by harsh or authoritarian rule **2** to weigh heavily on the mind or spirit of – **oppressor** *n*

oppression /ə'presh(ə)n‖ə'preʃ(ə)n/ *n* **1** unjust or harsh exercise of authority or power **2** a sense of being weighed down in body or mind

oppressive /ə'presiv‖ə'presɪv/ *adj* **1** unreasonably harsh or severe **2** tyrannical **3** physically or mentally depressing or overpowering – **oppressively** *adv*, **oppressiveness** *n*

opprobrious /ə'prohbri·əs‖ə'prəʊbrɪəs/ *adj* scurrilous and abusive < ~ *language*> – fml – **opprobriously** *adv*

opprobrium /ə'prohbri·əm‖ə'prəʊbrɪəm/ *n* (a cause of) public infamy or disgrace – fml

opt /opt‖ɒpt/ *vi* to decide in favour of sthg ***USE*** – usu + *for*

[1]**optic** /'optik‖'ɒptɪk/ *adj* of vision or the eye

[2]**optic** *n* **1** the eye **2** any of the lenses, prisms, or mirrors of an optical instrument

optical /'optikl‖'ɒptɪkl/ *adj* **1** of optics **2a** visual <*an ~ illusion*> **b** visible <*an ~ galaxy*> **c** designed to aid vision <*an ~ instrument*> **3** of or using light < ~ *microscopy*> – **optically** *adv*

,optical 'art *n* abstract art that uses linear or geometric patterns to create an optical illusion

optical disk *n* a disk on which data (e g sounds or images) are stored in digital form in microscopic pits and are read by a laser scanner

,optical il'lusion *n* ILLUSION 2a(1)

optician /op'tish(ə)n‖ɒp'tɪʃ(ə)n/ *n* one who prescribes correctional lenses for eye defects or supplies (lenses for) spectacles on prescription

optics /'optiks‖'ɒptɪks/ *n pl but sing or pl in constr* **1** the science of the nature, properties, and uses of (radiation or particles that behave like) light **2** optical properties or components

optimism /'opti,miz(ə)m‖'ɒptɪ,mɪz(ə)m/ *n* **1** the doctrine that this world is the best possible world **2** a tendency to emphasize favourable aspects of situations or events or to expect the best possible outcome [French *optimisme*, fr Latin *optimus* best] – **optimist** *n*, **optimistic** *adj*, **optimistically** *adv*

optimum /'optiməm‖'ɒptɪməm/ *n*, *pl* **optima** /-mə‖-mə/ *also* **optimums** (the amount or degree of) sthg that is most favourable to a particular end – **optimum** *adj*, **optimize** *vt*

[1]**option** /'opsh(ə)n‖'ɒpʃ(ə)n/ *n* **1** an act of choosing **2a** the power or right to choose **b** (a contract conveying) a right to buy or sell designated securities or commodities at a specified price during a stipulated period **3a** an alternative course of action **b** an item offered in addition to or in place of standard equipment

[2]**option** *vt* to grant or take an option on

optional /'opsh(ə)nl‖'ɒpʃ(ə)nl/ *adj* not compulsory; available as a choice – **optionally** *adv*

opt out *vi* to choose not to participate in sthg – often + *of*

opulent /'opyoolənt‖'ɒpjʊlənt/ *adj* **1** wealthy, rich **2** abundant, profuse – **opulence** *n*, **opulently** *adv*

opus /'ohpəs‖'əʊpəs/ *n*, *pl* **opera** /'op(ə)rə‖'ɒp(ə)rə/ *also* **opuses** WORK 7; *specif* a musical composition or set of compositions, usu numbered in the order of issue

[1]**or** /ə‖ə; *strong* aw‖ɔː/ *conj* **1a** – used to join 2 sentence elements of the same class or function and often introduced by *either* to indicate that what immediately follows is another or a final alternative <*either sink ~ swim*> <*red, blue, ~ green*> <*coffee ~ tea ~ whisky*> <*whether you like it ~ not*> **b** – used before the second and later of several suggestions to indicate approximation or uncertainty <*five ~ six days*> <*a place such as Venice ~ Florence ~ somewhere like that – SEU S*> **2** and not – used after a neg <*never drinks ~ smokes*> **3** that is – used to indicate equivalence or elucidate meaning <*lessen ~ abate*> <*a heifer ~ young cow*> **4** – used to indicate the result of rejecting a preceding choice <*hurry ~ you'll be late*> **5** – used to introduce an afterthought <*$e=mc^2$– ~ am I boring you?*> – **or so** – used to indicate an approximation or conjecture <*I've known him 20 years* or so>

[2]**or** /aw‖ɔː/ *n* a gold colour; *also* yellow – used in heraldry

[1]**-or** /-ə‖-ə/ *suffix* (→ *n*) one that performs (a specified action) <*vendor*>

[2]**-or** /-ə‖-ə/ *suffix* (→ *n*) quality, condition, or state of <*horror*>; *also* instance of (a specified quality or state) <*an error*>

oracle /ˈorəkl‖ˈɒrəkl/ *n* **1a** an often cryptic answer to some question, usu regarding the future, purporting to come from a deity **b** (a shrine housing) a priest or priestess who delivers oracles **2** (a statement by) a person giving wise or authoritative decisions

Oracle *trademark* – used for a service provided by ITV which transmits information (e g the weather or sports results) on usu special channels

oracular /oˈrakyoolə‖ɒˈrækjʊlə/ *adj* **1** of or being an oracle **2** resembling an oracle (e g in solemnity or obscurity of expression) – **oracularly** *adv*

[1]**oral** /ˈawrəl, ˈo-‖ˈɔːrəl, ˈɒ-/ *adj* **1a** uttered in words; spoken **b** using speech **2a** of, given through, or affecting the mouth <*~ contraceptive*> **b** of or characterized by (passive dependency, aggressiveness, or other personality traits typical of) the first stage of sexual development in which gratification is derived from eating, sucking, and later by biting – **orally** *adv*, **orality** *n*

[2]**oral** *n* an oral examination

[1]**orange** /ˈorinj‖ˈɒrɪndʒ/ *n* **1a** (a small evergreen tree of the rue family with hard yellow wood and fragrant white flowers that bears) a spherical fruit with a reddish yellow leathery aromatic rind and sweet juicy edible pulp **2** any of several trees or fruits resembling the orange **3** a colour whose hue resembles that of the orange and lies between red and yellow in the spectrum

[2]**orange** *adj* of the colour orange

Orange *adj* of Orangemen <*an ~ lodge*> – **Orangeism** *n*

ˈ**Orangeman** /-mən‖-mən/ *n, pl* **Orangemen** /~/ **1** a member of a Protestant loyalist society in the north of Ireland **2** a Protestant Irishman, esp of Ulster [William III of England, Prince of *Orange* (1650-1702), Protestant ruler who deposed the Roman Catholic James II]

orangutan, orangoutan /awˌrang·(y)oohˈtan‖ɔːˌræŋ(j)uːˈtæn/ *n* a largely plant-eating tree-dwelling anthropoid ape of Borneo and Sumatra with brown skin and hair and very long arms [Malay *orang hutan*, fr *orang* man + *hutan* forest]

oration /awˈraysh(ə)n, oˈr-‖ɔːˈreɪʃ(ə)n, ɒˈr-/ *n* a speech delivered in a formal and dignified manner

orator /ˈorətə‖ˈɒrətə/ *n* **1** one who delivers an oration **2** a skilled public speaker

oratorio /ˌorəˈtawrioh‖ˌɒrəˈtɔːrɪəʊ/ *n, pl* **oratorios** a choral work based usu on a religious subject and composed chiefly of recitatives, arias, and choruses without action or scenery

[1]**oratory** /ˈorət(ə)ri‖ˈɒrət(ə)rɪ/ *n* **1** a place of prayer; *esp* a private or institutional chapel **2** *cap* an Oratorian congregation, house, or church

[2]**oratory** *n* **1** the art of public speaking **2** public speaking characterized by (excessive) eloquence

orb /awb‖ɔːb/ *n* **1** a spherical body; *esp* a celestial sphere **2** a sphere surmounted by a cross symbolizing royal power and justice

[1]**orbit** /ˈawbit‖ˈɔːbɪt/ *n* **1** the bony socket of the eye **2** (1 complete passage of) a path described by one body in its revolution round another (e g that of the earth round the sun) **3** a sphere of influence **4** the eye – poetic – **orbital** *adj*

[2]**orbit** *vt* **1** to revolve in an orbit round **2** to send up and make revolve in an orbit ~ *vi* to travel in circles

orchard /ˈawchəd‖ˈɔːtʃəd/ *n* a usu enclosed area in which fruit trees are planted

orchestra /ˈawkistrə‖ˈɔːkɪstrə/ *n* **1** the circular space used by the chorus in front of the stage in an ancient Greek theatre **2** the space in front of the stage in a modern theatre that is used by an orchestra **3** a group of musicians including esp string players organized to perform ensemble music

orchestral /awˈkestrəl‖ɔːˈkestrəl/ *adj* of or composed for an orchestra – **orchestrally** *adv*

orchestrate /ˈawkiˌstrayt‖ˈɔːkɪˌstreɪt/ *vt* **1** to compose or arrange (music) for an orchestra **2** to provide with orchestration <*~ a ballet*> – **orchestrator** *n*

orchid /ˈawkid‖ˈɔːkɪd/ *n* a plant or flower of a large family of plants related to the grasses and lilies and usu having striking 3-petalled flowers with an enlarged liplike middle petal

ordain /awˈdayn‖ɔːˈdeɪn/ *vt* **1** to invest officially with priestly authority (e g by the laying on of hands) **2a** to order by appointment, decree, or law; enact **b** to destine, foreordain – **ordainment** *n*

ordeal /awˈdeel‖ɔːˈdiːl/ *n* **1** a method formerly used to determine guilt or innocence by submitting the accused to dangerous or painful tests whose outcome was believed to depend on divine or supernatural intervention <*~ by fire*> **2** a severe or testing experience

[1]**order** /ˈawdə‖ˈɔːdə/ *n* **1a** a religious body or community living under a specific rule and often required to take vows of renunciation of earthly things **b** a military decoration **2a** any of the several grades of the Christian ministry **b** *pl* the office of a person in the Christian ministry **3a** a rank or group in a community **b** a category in the classification of living things ranking above

the family and below the class **4a(1)** a rank or level **a(2)** a category or kind **b** arrangement of objects or events according to sequence in space, time, value, importance, etc **c** DEGREE 7a **d** the number of times mathematical differentiation is applied successively *<derivatives of higher* ~ *>* **e** the number of columns or rows in a square matrix **f** the number of elements in a finite mathematical group **5a** (a sphere of) a sociopolitical system *<the present economic* ~ *>* **b** regular or harmonious arrangement **6a** customary procedure, esp in debate *<point of* ~ *>* **b** a prescribed form of a religious service **7a** the rule of law or proper authority *<law and* ~ *>* **b** a specific rule, regulation, or authoritative direction **8a** a style of building; *esp* any of the classical styles of building *<the Doric* ~ *>* **b** a column and entablature proportioned and decorated according to one of the classical styles **9** a proper, orderly, or functioning condition *<telephone is out of* ~ *>* **10a** a written direction to pay money to sby **b** a direction to purchase, sell, or supply goods or to carry out work **c** goods bought or sold **d** an assigned undertaking – chiefly in *a tall order* **11** the style of dress and equipment for a specified purpose *<troops in full marching* ~ *>* – **in order that** THAT 2a(1) – **in order to** for the purpose of – **in the order of** about as much or as many as; approximately – **on order** having been ordered – **to order** according to the specifications of an order *<furniture made* to order*>*

[2]**order** *vt* **1** to put in order; arrange **2a** to give an order to; command **b** to command to go or come to a specified place **c** to place an order for *<~ a meal>* ~*vi* to give or place an order

ˈ**ordered** *adj* **1** well regulated or ordered **2a** having elements succeeding or arranged according to rule **b** having a specified first element *<a set of* ~ *pairs>*

[1]**orderly** /ˈawdəli‖ˈɔːdəlɪ/ *adj* **1a** arranged in order; neat, tidy **b** liking or exhibiting order; methodical **2** well behaved; peaceful – **orderliness** *n*

[2]**orderly** *n* **1** a soldier assigned to carry messages, relay orders, etc for a superior officer **2** a hospital attendant who does routine or heavy work (e g carrying supplies or moving patients)

ˌ**order of the** ˈ**day** *n* **1** an agenda **2** the characteristic or dominant feature or activity

ˈ**order** ˌ**paper** *n* a programme of the day's business in a legislative assembly

[1]**ordinal** /ˈawdinl‖ˈɔːdɪnl/ *n* **1a** *cap* (a book containing) the forms of service for ordination **b** a book containing the Roman Catholic services proper to every day of the year **2** ORDINAL NUMBER

[2]**ordinal** *adj* of a specified order or rank in a series

ordinal number *n* a number designating the place (e g first, second, or third) occupied by an item in an ordered set

ordinance /ˈawdinəns‖ˈɔːdɪnəns/ *n* **1** an authoritative decree; *esp* a municipal regulation **2** a prescribed usage, practice, or ceremony

ordinand /ˈawdiˌnand‖ˈɔːdɪˌnænd/ *n* a candidate for ordination

[1]**ordinary** /ˈawdn(ə)ri, ˈawd(ə)nri‖ˈɔːdn(ə)rɪ, ˈɔːd(ə)nrɪ/ *n* **1** *often cap* the invariable parts of the Mass **2** the regular or customary state of affairs – chiefly in *out of the ordinary* **3** any of the simplest heraldic charges bounded by straight lines (e g a chevron)

[2]**ordinary** *adj* **1** routine, usual **2** not exceptional; commonplace – **ordinarily** *adv*, **ordinariness** *n*

Ordinary level *n, often cap L* an examination that is the lowest of the 3 levels of the British General Certificate of Education

ˌ**ordinary** ˈ**seaman** *n* a person holding the lowest rank in the British navy

ordinate /ˈawdinət‖ˈɔːdɪnət/ *n* the coordinate of a point in a plane Cartesian coordinate system obtained by measuring parallel to the y-axis

ordination /ˌawdiˈnaysh(ə)n‖ˌɔːdɪˈneɪʃ(ə)n/ *n* (an) ordaining; being ordained

ordnance /ˈawdnəns‖ˈɔːdnəns/ *n* **1** (a branch of government service dealing with) military supplies **2** cannon, artillery

ˌ**Ordnance** ˈ**Survey** *n* (a British or Irish government organization that produces) a survey of Great Britain or Ireland published as a series of detailed maps

ordure /ˈawdyooə‖ˈɔːdjʊə/ *n* excrement [Middle French, fr *ord* filthy, fr Latin *horridus* horrid]

ore /aw‖ɔː/ *n* a mineral containing a metal or other valuable constituent for which it is mined

oregano /oriˈgahnoh, əˈregənoh‖ɒrɪˈgɑːnəʊ, əˈregənəʊ/ *n* a bushy plant of the mint family whose leaves are used as a herb in cooking

organ /ˈawgən‖ˈɔːgən/ *n* **1a** a wind instrument consisting of sets of pipes made to sound by compressed air and controlled by keyboards; *also* an electronic keyboard instrument producing a sound approximating to that of an organ **b** REED ORGAN **c** any of various similar cruder instruments **2** a differentiated structure (e g the heart or a leaf) consisting of cells and tissues and performing some specific function in an organism **3** a subordinate organization that performs specialized functions *<the various* ~s *of government>* **4** a periodical – **organist** *n*

organdie, organdy /ˈawgəndi‖ˈɔːgəndɪ/ *n* a very fine transparent muslin with a stiff finish

organelle /ˌawgəˈnel‖ˌɔːgəˈnel/ *n* a part of a cell (e g a mitochondrion) that has a specialized structure and usu a specific function

ˈ**organ-**ˌ**grinder** *n* an itinerant street musician who operates a barrel organ

organic /awˈganik‖ɔːˈgænɪk/ *adj* **1a** of or arising in a bodily organ **b** affecting the structure of the organism *<an* ~ *disease>* **2a** of or derived from living organisms **b** of or being food produced using fertilizer solely of plant or animal origin without the aid of chemical fertilizers, pesticides, etc *<~ farming>* **3a** forming an integral element of a whole **b** having systematic coordination of parts **c** containing carbon compounds, esp those occurring in living organisms; *also* of or being the branch of chemistry dealing with these **d** resembling or developing in the manner of an organism **4** of or constituting the law by which a government exists – **organically** *adv*

organism /ˈawgəˌniz(ə)m‖ˈɔːgəˌnɪz(ə)m/ *n* **1**

a complex structure of interdependent and subordinate elements **2** a living being – **organismic** *adj*, **organismal** *adj*

organ·ization, -isation /ˌawgənieˈzaysh(ə)n‖ˌɔːgənaɪˈzeɪʃ(ə)n/ *n* **1a** organizing or being organized **b** the condition or manner of being organized **2a** an association, society **b** an administrative and functional body – **organizational** *adj*

organ·ize, -ise /ˈawgəˌniez‖ˈɔːgəˌnaɪz/ *vt* **1** to cause to develop an organic structure **2** to arrange or form into a complete or functioning whole **3a** to set up an administrative structure for **b** to persuade to associate in an organization; *esp* to unionize <~d *labour*> **4** to arrange by systematic planning and effort ~ *vi* **1** to arrange elements into a whole **2** to form an organization, esp a trade union – **organizer** *n*

orgasm /ˈawˌgaz(ə)m‖ˈɔːˌgæz(ə)m/ *n* intense or paroxysmal emotional excitement; *esp* (an instance of) the climax of sexual excitement, occurring typically as the culmination of sexual intercourse – **orgasmic** *adj*, **orgastic** *adj*

orgy /ˈawji‖ˈɔːdʒɪ/ *n* **1** the secret rites of an ancient Greek or Roman deity, often accompanied by ecstatic singing and dancing **2a** drunken revelry **b** a wild party characterized by sexual promiscuity **3** an excessive or frantic indulgence in a specified activity <*an ~ of destruction*> – **orgiastic** *adj*

oriel window /ˈawri·əl‖ˈɔːrɪəl/ *n* a bay window projecting from an upper storey and supported by a corbel or bracket

[1]**orient** /ˈawri·ənt, ˈo-‖ˈɔːrɪənt, ˈɒ-/ *n* **1** *cap* EAST 2 **2** a pearl of great lustre

[2]**orient** *adj* **1** lustrous, sparkling <~ *gems*> **2** *archaic* ORIENTAL 1

[3]**orient** /ˈawriˌent, ˈo-‖ˈɔːrɪˌent, ˈɒ-/ *vt* **1a** to cause to face or point towards the east; *specif* to build (a church or temple) with the longitudinal axis pointing eastwards **b** to set in a definite position, esp in relation to the points of the compass **c** to ascertain the bearings of **2a** to adjust to an environment or a situation **b** to acquaint (oneself) with the existing situation or environment

oriental /ˌawriˈentl, ˌo-‖ˌɔːrɪˈentl, ˌɒ-/ *adj, often cap* relating to or characteristic of the Orient or its peoples

Oriental *n* a member of any of the indigenous peoples of the Orient

orientalist /ˌawriˈentl·ist, ˌo-‖ˌɔːrɪˈentlɪst, ˌɒ-/ *n, often cap* a specialist in oriental subjects

orientate /ˈawri·ənˌtayt, ˈo-‖ˈɔːrɪənˌteɪt, ˈɒ-/ *vt, chiefly Br* to orient ~*vi* to face east

orientation /ˌawri·ənˈtaysh(ə)n, ˌo-‖ˌɔːrɪən-ˈteɪʃ(ə)n, ˌɒ-/ *n* **1a** orienting or being oriented **b** an arrangement or alignment **2** a lasting tendency of thought, inclination, or interest **3** change of position by (a part of) an organism in response to an external stimulus – **orientational** *adj*

orienteering /ˌawri·ənˈtiəring, o-‖ˌɔːrɪən-ˈtɪərɪŋ, ɒ-/ a sport in which contestants race on foot over an unfamiliar course, using a map and compass

orifice /ˈorifis‖ˈɒrɪfɪs/ *n* an opening (e g a vent or mouth) through which sthg may pass – **orificial** *adj*

origin /ˈorijin‖ˈɒrɪdʒɪn/ *n* **1** ancestry, parentage **2** a source or starting-point **3** the more fixed, central, or large attachment or part of a muscle

[1]**original** /əˈrijənl‖əˈrɪdʒənl/ *n* **1** that from which a copy, reproduction, or translation is made **2** an eccentric person

[2]**original** *adj* **1** initial, earliest **2a** not secondary, derivative, or imitative **b** being the first instance or source of a copy, reproduction, or translation **3** inventive, creative – **originally** *adv*

originality /əˌrijəˈnaləti‖əˌrɪdʒəˈnælətɪ/ *n* **1** freshness, novelty **2** the power of imaginative and independent thought or creation

oˌriginal ˈsin *n* (the doctrine of) man's innate sinfulness resulting from Adam's fall

originate /əˈrijəˌnayt‖əˈrɪdʒəˌneɪt/ *vb* to (cause to) begin or come into existence – **originator** *n*, **origination** *n*

oriole /ˈawriˌohl, -əl‖ˈɔːrɪˌəʊl, -əl/ *n* any of a family of birds with black and either orange or yellow plumage

orison /ˈoriz(ə)n‖ˈɒrɪz(ə)n/ *n, archaic* a prayer

Orlon /ˈawlon‖ˈɔːlɒn/ *trademark* – used for an acrylic fibre

ormolu /ˈawməˌlooh‖ˈɔːməˌluː/ *n* gilded brass or bronze used to decorate furniture, ornaments, etc [French *or moulu*, lit., ground gold]

[1]**ornament** /ˈawnəmənt‖ˈɔːnəmənt/ *n* **1** sthg that lends grace or beauty; (a) decoration or embellishment **2** a person who adds honour or importance to sthg **3** an embellishing note not belonging to the essential harmony or melody

[2]**ornament** /ˈawnəˌment‖ˈɔːnəˌment/ *vt* to add ornament to; embellish

ornamental /ˌawnəˈmentl‖ˌɔːnəˈmentl/ *adj or n* (of or being) a decorative object, esp a plant cultivated for its beauty – **ornamentally** *adv*

ornamentation /ˌawnəmenˈtaysh(ə)n‖ˌɔːnəmenˈteɪʃ(ə)n/ *n* **1** ornamenting or being ornamented **2** sthg that ornaments; an embellishment

ornate /awˈnayt‖ɔːˈneɪt/ *adj* **1** rhetorical or florid in style **2** elaborately or excessively decorated – **ornately** *adv*, **ornateness** *n*

ornery /ˈawnəri‖ˈɔːnərɪ/ *adj, NAm* cantankerous – infml – **orneriness** *n*

ornithology /ˌawnəˈtholəji‖ˌɔːnəˈθɒlədʒɪ/ *n* a branch of zoology dealing with birds [deriv of Greek *ornith-, ornis* bird + *logos* word] – **ornithologist** *n*, **ornithological** *adj*

orotund /ˈorətund, ˈoroh-‖ˈɒrətʌnd, ˈɒrəʊ-/ *adj* **1** marked by fullness of sound; sonorous **2** pompous, bombastic [Latin *ore rotundo*, lit., with round mouth] – **orotundity** *n*

[1]**orphan** /ˈawf(ə)n‖ˈɔːf(ə)n/ *n* **1** a child 1 or both of whose parents are dead **2** a young animal that has lost its mother – **orphanhood** *n*

[2]**orphan** *vt* to cause to be an orphan

orphanage /ˈawf(ə)n·ij‖ˈɔːf(ə)nɪdʒ/ *n* an institution for the care of orphans

orris /ˈoris‖ˈɒrɪs/ *n* (a European iris with) a fragrant rootstock used esp in perfume and perfumed sachets

ˈorrisˌroot /-ˌrooht‖-ˌruːt/ *n* the fragrant rootstock of orris or another iris

orth-, ortho- *comb form* **1** straight; upright; vertical <ortho*rhombic*> **2** correct;

corrective <ortho*dontics*>

orthodontics /ˌawthə'dontiks‖ˌɔːθə'dɒntɪks/ *n pl but sing in constr* dentistry dealing with (the correction of) irregularities of the teeth – **orthodontic** *adj*, **orthodontist** *n*

orthodox /'awthəˌdoks‖'ɔːθəˌdɒks/ *adj* **1a** conforming to established, dominant, or official doctrine (e g in religion) **b** conventional **2a** *cap* (consisting) of the Eastern churches headed by the patriarch of Constantinople which separated from the Western church in the 9th c **b** *cap* relating to Judaism that keeps to strict and conservative interpretation of scripture and tradition [Late Greek *orthodoxos*, fr Greek *orthos* straight, correct + *doxa* opinion] – **orthodoxly** *adv*

orthodoxy /'awthədoksi‖'ɔːθədɒksɪ/ *n* **1** being orthodox **2** an orthodox belief or practice

orthography /aw'thogrəfi‖ɔː'θɒgrəfɪ/ *n* **1** correct spelling **2** the manner of spelling – **orthographic** *adj*, **orthographically** *adv*

orthopaedics, *NAm chiefly* **orthopedics** /ˌawthə'peediks‖ˌɔːθə'piːdɪks/ *n pl but sing or pl in constr* the correction or prevention of skeletal and muscular deformities, esp by surgery – **orthopaedic** *adj*, **orthopaedist** *n*

ortolan /'awtələn‖'ɔːtələn/ *n* a brown and greyish-green European bunting

[1]**-ory** /-(ə)ri‖-(ə)rɪ/ *suffix* (→ *n*) **1** place of or for <*observat*ory> **2** sthg that serves for <*direct*ory>

[2]**-ory** *suffix* (→ *adj*) **1** of or involving <*compuls*ory> **2** serving for or producing <*justificat*ory>

oryx /'oriks‖'ɒrɪks/ *n* any of a genus of large straight-horned African antelopes

Oscar /'oskə‖'ɒskə/ *n* a statuette awarded annually by a US professional organization for outstanding achievement in the cinema [*Oscar* Pierce, 20th-c US wheat and fruit grower]

oscillate /'osiˌlayt‖'ɒsɪˌleɪt/ *vi* **1a** to swing backwards and forwards like a pendulum **b** to move or travel back and forth between 2 points **2** to vary between opposing beliefs, feelings, or courses of action – **oscillatory** *adj*

oscillation /ˌosi'laysh(ə)n‖ˌɒsɪ'leɪʃ(ə)n/ *n* **1** oscillating **2** a variation, fluctuation **3** a flow of electricity periodically changing direction **4** a single swing (e g of sthg oscillating) from one extreme limit to the other

oscillator /'osiˌlaytə‖'ɒsɪˌleɪtə/ *n* **1** sby or sthg that oscillates **2** a device for producing alternating current; *esp* a radio-frequency or audio-frequency signal generator

oscillograph /ə'siləˌgrahf, -ˌgraf‖ə'sɪləˌgrɑːf, -ˌgræf/ *n* an instrument for recording (electrical) oscillations – **oscillographic** *adj*, **oscillography** *n*

oscilloscope /ə'siləˌskohp‖ə'sɪləˌskəʊp/ *n* an instrument in which electrical oscillations register as a temporary visible wave form on the fluorescent screen of a cathode-ray tube – **oscilloscopic** *adj*

osculate /'oskyooˌlayt‖'ɒskjʊˌleɪt/ *vt* to kiss – humor or fml – **osculation** *n*

osier /'ohzhə‖'əʊʒə/ *n* **1** any of various willows whose pliable twigs are used for furniture and basketry **2** a willow rod used in basketry

-osis /-'ohsis‖-'əʊsɪs/ *suffix, pl* **-oses** /-'ohseez‖-'əʊsiːz/, **-osises** /-ohsiseez‖-əʊsɪsiːz/ (→ *n*) **1a** action, process, or condition of <*hypn*osis> **b** abnormal or pathological condition of <*thromb*osis> **2** increase or formation of <*leucocyt*osis> – **-otic** *adj*, **-otically** *adv*

osmosis /oz'mohsis, os-‖ɒz'məʊsɪs, ɒs-/ *n* **1** movement of a solvent through a semipermeable membrane (e g of a living cell) into a solution of higher concentration that tends to equalize the concentrations on the 2 sides of the membrane **2** a process of absorption or diffusion suggestive of osmosis – **osmotic** *adj*

osprey /'ospray, -pri‖'ɒspreɪ, -prɪ/ *n* **1** a large fish-eating hawk with dark brown and white plumage **2** a feather trimming used for millinery

osseous /'osi·əs‖'ɒsɪəs/ *adj* BONY 1

ossify /'osiˌfie‖'ɒsɪˌfaɪ/ *vi* **1** to become bone **2** to become unfeeling, unimaginative, or rigid ~ *vt* to change (e g cartilage) into bone – **ossification** *n*

ostensible /o'stensəbl‖ɒ'stensəbl/ *adj* being such in appearance rather than reality; professed, declared – **ostensibly** *adv*

ostentation /ˌosten'taysh(ə)n‖ˌɒsten'teɪʃ(ə)n/ *n* unnecessary display of wealth, knowledge, etc designed to impress or attract attention – **ostentatious** *adj*, **ostentatiously** *adv*, **ostentatiousness** *n*

osteoarthritis /ˌostiohah'thrietəs‖ˌɒstɪəʊɑː'θraɪtəs/ *n* degenerative arthritis – **osteoarthritic** *adj*

osteopathy /ˌosti'opəthi‖ˌɒstɪ'ɒpəθɪ/ *n* a system of treatment of diseases based on the theory that they can be cured by manipulation of bones – **osteopath** *n*, **osteopathic** *adj*

ostler, *chiefly NAm* **hostler** /'oslə‖'ɒslə/ *n* a groom or stableman at an inn

ostracism /'ostrəˌsiz(ə)m‖'ɒstrəˌsɪz(ə)m/ *n* **1** temporary banishment by popular vote as practised in ancient Greece **2** exclusion by general consent from common privileges or social acceptance

ostrac·ize, **-ise** /'ostrəˌsiez‖'ɒstrəˌsaɪz/ *vt* to exile or exclude by ostracism [Greek *ostrakizein* to banish by voting with potsherds, fr *ostrakon* shell, potsherd]

ostrich /'ostrich, ‖'ɒstrɪtʃ, *also* 'ostrij‖'ɒstrɪdʒ/ *n* **1** a swift-footed 2-toed flightless bird that has valuable wing and tail plumes and is the largest of existing birds **2** one who refuses to face up to unpleasant realities

[1]**other** /'udhə‖'ʌðə/ *adj* **1a** being the 1 left of 2 or more <*held on with 1 hand and waved with the ~ one*> **b** being the ones distinct from that or those first mentioned <*taller than the ~ boys*> **c** SECOND 2 <*every ~ day*> **2a** not the same; different <*schools ~ than her own*> **b** far, opposite <*lives the ~ side of town*> **3** additional, further <*John and 2 ~ boys*> **4** recently past <*the ~ evening*>

[2]**other** *pron, pl* **others** *also* **other** **1** the remaining or opposite one <*went from one side to the ~*> <*the ~s came later*> **2** a different or additional one <*some film or ~*> <*some left, but many ~s stayed*>

[3]**other** *adv* otherwise – + *than* <*can't get there ~ than by swimming*>

[1]**ˈotherˌwise** /-ˌwiez‖-ˌwaɪz/ *adv* **1** in a different way **2** in different circumstances <*might ~ have left*> **3** in other respects <*an ~ excellent dinner*> **4** if not; or else <*do what I say, ~ you'll be sorry*> **5** not – used to express the opposite <*mothers, whether married or ~*> <*guilty unless proved ~*> **6** alias <*Chee Soo, ~ Cliff Gibbs – Sportsworld*>

[2]**otherwise** *adj* of a different kind <*how can I be ~ than grateful*>

ˌotherˈworldly *adj* concerned with spiritual or intellectual matters rather than the material world – **otherworldliness** *n*

otic /ˈohtik‖ˈəʊtɪk/ *adj* of or located in the region of the ear

otiose /ˈohshiˌohs, ˈohti-‖ˈəʊʃɪˌəʊs, ˈəʊtɪ-/ *adj* **1** at leisure; idle **2** futile, pointless *USE* fml – **otiosely** *adv*, **otioseness** *n*

otter /ˈotə‖ˈɒtə/ *n* (the dark brown fur or pelt of) any of several aquatic fish-eating mammals with webbed and clawed feet, related to the weasels [Old English *otor*; akin to Old English *wæter* water – more at WATER]

ottoman /ˈotəmən‖ˈɒtəmən/ *n* **1** *cap* a Turk **2a** a usu heavily upholstered box or seat without a back or arms **b** a cushioned stool for the feet

Ottoman *adj* TURKISH 1

ouch *interj* – used esp to express sudden sharp pain

[1]**ought** /awt‖ɔːt/ *verbal auxiliary* – used to express moral obligation <*~ to pay our debts*>, advisability <*~ to be boiled for 10 minutes*>, enthusiastic recommendation <*you ~ to hear her sing*>, natural expectation <*~ to have arrived by now*>, or logical consequence <*the result ~ to be infinity*>; used in the negative to express moral condemnation of an action <*you ~ not to treat him like that*>; often used with the perfect infinitive to express unfulfilled obligation <*~ never to have been allowed*>

[2]**ought** *n or adj* (a) zero

Ouija /ˈweejə, -ji‖ˈwiːdʒə, -dʒɪ/ *trademark* – used for a board with the alphabet and other signs on it that is used to produce automatic writing in spiritualistic seances

[1]**ounce** /owns‖aʊns/ *n* **1a** a unit of weight equal to 16 drams (28.35g) **b** a small amount <*an ~ of common sense*> **2** FLUID OUNCE [Middle French, *unce*, fr Latin *uncia* twelfth part, ounce, fr *unus* one]

[2]**ounce** *n* SNOW LEOPARD [Old French *once*, alteration of *lonce*, fr Latin *lync-, lynx* lynx]

our /ˈowə, ah‖ˈaʊə, ɑː/ *adj* of, belonging to, or done by or to us or ourselves

ˌOur ˈFather *n* LORD'S PRAYER

ˌOur ˈLady *n* VIRGIN MARY

ours /ˈowəz, ahz‖ˈaʊəz, ɑːz/ *pron, pl* **ours** that which or the one who belongs to us

ourˈselves /-ˈselvz‖-ˈselvz/ *pron, pl in constr* **1** those identical people that are we – used reflexively <*we're doing it solely for ~*> or for emphasis <*we ~ will never go*>; compare ONESELF **2** our normal selves <*not feeling quite ~*>

-ous /-əs‖-əs/ *suffix* (→ *adj*) **1** full of; characterized by; possessing the quality of <*clamorous*> <*envious*> **2** having a valency relatively lower than in (specified compounds or ions named with an adjective ending in *-ic*) <*ferrous*> <*mercurous*> – **-ously** *suffix* (→ *adv*)

ousel /ˈoohzl‖ˈuːzl/ *n* an ouzel

oust /owst‖aʊst/ *vt* **1** to remove from or dispossess of property or position **2** to take the place of; supplant

[1]**out** /owt‖aʊt/ *adv* **1a** away from the inside or centre <*went ~ into the garden*> **b** from among other things <*separate ~ the bad apples*> **c** away from the shore, the city, or one's homeland <*~ at sea*> <*go ~ to Africa*> <*live ~ in the country*> **d** away from a particular place, esp of one's home or business <*~ for lunch*> <*~ on strike*> <*move ~ into lodgings*> **e(1)** clearly in or into view <*when the sun's ~*> **e(2)** *of a flower* in or into full bloom **2a(1)** out of the proper place <*left a word ~*> <*put his shoulder ~*> **a(2)** amiss in reckoning <*more than 4 lb ~ – Punch*> **b** in all directions from a central point of control <*lent ~ money*> **c** from political power <*voted them ~*> **d** into shares or portions <*parcelled ~ the farm*> **e** out of vogue or fashion **3a** to or in a state of extinction or exhaustion <*burn ~*> <*before the year is ~*> **b** to the fullest extent or degree; completely <*all decked ~*> <*hear me ~*> <*clean ~ the attic*> **c** in or into a state of determined effort <*~ to fight pollution*> **4a** aloud <*cried ~*> <*~ with it!*> **b** in existence; ever – with a superlative; infml <*the funniest thing ~*> **5** so as to be put out of a game <*bowled ~*> **6** – used on a 2-way radio circuit to indicate that a message is complete and no reply is expected

[2]**out** *vi* to become publicly known

[3]**out** *adj* **1** located outside; external **2** located at a distance; outlying <*the ~ islands*> **3** not being in operation or power <*the fire's ~*> **4** directed or serving to direct outwards <*the ~ tray*> **5** not allowed to continue batting **6** out of the question <*your suggestion's definitely ~*>

[4]**out** *prep* OUT OF 1a(1)

[5]**out** *n* a way of escaping from an embarrassing or difficult situation

out- *prefix* **1** forth <out*cry*> <out*burst*> <out*rush*> **2** result; product <out*put*> <out*come*> **3** in a manner that goes beyond, surpasses, or excels <out*manoeuvre*> <out*strip*>

ˈoutˌback /-ˌbak‖-ˌbæk/ *n* isolated rural (Australian) country

ˌoutˈbalance /-ˈbaləns‖-ˈbæləns/ *vt* to outweigh in value or importance

ˌoutˈbid /-ˈbid‖-ˈbɪd/ *vt* **outbid; -dd-** to make a higher bid than

[1]**ˈoutˌboard** /-ˌbawd‖-ˌbɔːd/ *adj* **1** situated outboard **2** having, using, or limited to the use of an outboard motor

[2]**outboard** *adv* **1** in a lateral direction from the hull of a ship or the fuselage of an aircraft **2** in a position closer or closest to either of the wing tips of an aeroplane or of the sides of a motor vehicle

[3]**outboard** *n* **1 outboard, outboard motor** a motor, propeller, and rudder attached as a unit to the stern of a small boat **2** a boat with an outboard

'**out,break** /-,brayk‖-,breɪk/ *n* **1a** a sudden or violent breaking out <*the ~ of war*> **b** a sudden increase in numbers of a harmful organism or in sufferers from a disease within a particular area <*an ~ of locusts*> <*an ~ of measles*> **2** an insurrection, revolt

'**out,building** /-,bilding‖-,bɪldɪŋ/ *n* a smaller building (e g a stable or a woodshed) separate from but belonging to a main building

'**out,burst** /-,buhst‖-,bɜːst/ *n* **1** a violent expression of feeling **2** a surge of activity or growth

'**out,cast** /-,kahst‖-,kɑːst/ *n* one who is cast out by society – **outcast** *adj*

'**out,caste** /-,kahst‖-,kɑːst/ *n* **1** a Hindu who has been ejected from his/her caste **2** one who has no caste

,**out'class** /-'klahs‖-'klɑːs/ *vt* to excel, surpass

'**out,come** /-,kum‖-,kʌm/ *n* a result, consequence

1'**out,crop** /-,krop‖-,krɒp/ *n* **1** (the emergence of) the part of a rock formation that appears at the surface of the ground **2** an outbreak

2,**out'crop** *vi* **-pp-** to project as an outcrop

'**out,cry** /-,krie‖-,kraɪ/ *n* **1** a loud cry; a clamour **2** a public expression of anger or disapproval

,**out'dated** /-'daytid‖-'deɪtɪd/ *adj* outmoded

,**out'distance** /-'dist(ə)ns‖-'dɪst(ə)ns/ *vt* to go far ahead of (e g in a race)

,**out'do** /-'dooh‖-'duː/ *vt* **outdoes** /-'duz‖-'dʌz/; **outdid** /-'did‖-'dɪd/; **outdone** /-'dun‖-'dʌn/ to surpass in action or performance

'**out,door** /-,daw‖-,dɔː/ *also* ,**out'doors** *adj* **1** of or performed outdoors **2** not enclosed; without a roof <*an ~ restaurant*>

1,**out'doors** *adv* outside a building; in or into the open air

2,**out'doors** *n pl but sing in constr* **1** *the* open air **2** *the* world remote from human habitation <*the great ~*>

outer /'owtə‖'aʊtə/ *adj* **1** existing independently of the mind; objective **2a** situated farther out <*the ~ limits*> **b** away from a centre <*the ~ planets*> **c** situated or belonging on the outside <*the ~ covering*> – **outermost** *adj*

,**outer 'space** *n* space outside the earth's atmosphere

,**out'face** /-'fays‖-'feɪs/ *vt* **1** to cause to waver or submit (as if) by staring **2** to confront unflinchingly; defy

'**out,fall** /-,fawl‖-,fɔːl/ *n* the outlet for a river, lake, drain, sewer, etc

'**out,field** /-,feeld‖-,fiːld/ *n* the part of a cricket field beyond the prepared section on which wickets are laid out or of a baseball field furthest from the bases – **outfielder** *n*

1'**out,fit** /-,fit‖-,fɪt/ *n* **1a** a complete set of equipment needed for a particular purpose **b** a set of garments worn together, often for a specified occasion or activity **2** *sing or pl in constr* a group that works as a team – infml

2**outfit** *vt* **-tt-** to equip with an outfit

,**out'flank** /-'flangk‖-'flæŋk/ *vt* **1** to go round or extend beyond the flank of (an opposing force) **2** to gain an advantage over by doing sthg unexpected

'**out,flow** /-,floh‖-,fləʊ/ *n* **1** a flowing out **2** sthg that flows out – **outflow** *vi*

,**out'general** /-'jen(ə)rəl‖-'dʒen(ə)rəl/ *vt* **-ll-** (*NAm* **-l-**) to surpass in generalship

'**out,going** /-,goh·ing‖-,gəʊɪŋ/ *adj* **1a** going away; departing **b** retiring or withdrawing from a position <*the ~ president*> **2** friendly, sociable – **outgoingness** *n*

'**out,goings** *n pl* expenditures; *esp* overheads

,**out'grow** /-'groh‖-'grəʊ/ *vt* **outgrew** /-'grooh‖-'gruː/; **outgrown** /-'grohn‖-'grəʊn/ **1** to grow or increase faster than **2** to grow too large or too old for

'**out,growth** /-,grohth‖-,grəʊθ/ *n* **1** a process or product of growing out <*an ~ of hair*> **2** a consequence, by-product

'**out,house** /-,hows‖-,haʊs/ *n* an outbuilding; *esp, chiefly NAm* PRIVY 1

outing /'owting‖'aʊtɪŋ/ *n* a short pleasure trip

outlandish /owt'landish‖aʊt'lændɪʃ/ *adj* strikingly unusual; bizarre – **outlandishly** *adv*

,**out'last** /-'lahst‖-'lɑːst/ *vt* to last longer than

1'**out,law** /-,law‖-,lɔː/ *n* **1** sby excluded from the protection of the law **2** a fugitive from the law – **outlaw** *adj*

2**outlaw** *vt* **1** to deprive of the protection of law **2** to make illegal – **outlawry** *n*

'**out,lay** /-,lay‖-,leɪ/ *n* expenditure, payment

outlet /'owtlit, -,let‖'aʊtlɪt, -,let/ *n* **1a** an exit or vent **b** a means of release or satisfaction for an emotion or drive **2** an agency (e g a shop or dealer) through which a product is marketed **3** *chiefly NAm* POWER POINT

1'**out,line** /-,lien‖-,laɪn/ *n* **1a** a line bounding the outer limits of sthg **b** SHAPE 1,2 **2** (a) drawing with no shading **3a** a condensed treatment of a subject **b** a summary of a written work **4** a preliminary account of a project

2**outline** /'-,-, ,-'-/ *vt* **1** to draw the outline of **2** to indicate the principal features of

,**out'live** /-'liv‖-'lɪv/ *vt* **1** to live longer than **2** to survive the effects of

'**out,look** /-,look‖-,lʊk/ *n* **1** a view from a particular place <*house with a pleasant ~*> **2** an attitude; POINT OF VIEW **3** a prospect for the future

'**out,lying** /-,lie·ing‖-,laɪɪŋ/ *adj* remote from a centre or main point

,**outma'noeuvre**, *NAm* **outmaneuver** /-mə'noohvə‖-mə'nuːvə/ *vt* to defeat by more skilful manoeuvring

,**out'match** /-'mach‖-'mætʃ/ *vt* to surpass, outdo

,**out'moded** /-'mohdid‖-'məʊdɪd/ *adj* **1** no longer in fashion **2** no longer acceptable or usable; obsolete

,**out'number** /-'numbə‖-'nʌmbə/ *vt* to exceed in number

'**out of** *prep* **1a(1)** from within to the outside of <*walked ~ the room*> **a(2)** – used to indicate a change in quality, state, or form <*woke up ~ a deep sleep*> **b(1)** beyond the range or limits of <*~ sight*> <*lived a mile ~ the town*> **b(2)** – used to indicate a position or state away from a qualification or circumstance <*~ practice*> <*~ perspective*> **2a** – used to indicate origin or cause <*came ~ fear*> <*did well ~ the war*> <*what do I get ~ it?*> **b** using as a material <*built ~ old timber*> **c** having as a mother – used esp of horses <*a colt ~ an ordinary mare*>; compare BY 4b(1) **3** – used to indicate exclusion from or deprivation of <*~ breath*> <*we're right ~ soap*> <*cheated him ~ his savings*> **4** from among; *also* IN 5 <*one ~ 4 survived*> – **out of it 1** not part of a group, activity, or fashion **2** hence, away <*get off* out of it>

ˌout-of-ˈdate *adj* outmoded, obsolete

ˌout-of-ˈpocket *adj* **1** requiring an outlay of cash <*~ expenses*> **2** having spent or lost more money than one can afford <*that shopping spree has left me ~*>

ˌout-of-the-ˈway *adj* **1** off the beaten track; remote **2** unusual

ˈoutˌpatient /-ˌpaysh(ə)nt‖-ˌpeɪʃ(ə)nt/ *n* a patient who is not an inmate of a hospital but visits it for diagnosis or treatment

ˌoutˈplay /-ˈplay‖-ˈpleɪ/ *vt* to defeat or play better than in a game <*~ed his rival*>

ˌoutˈpoint /-ˈpoynt‖-ˈpɔɪnt/ *vt* to score more points than (and so defeat)

ˈoutˌpost /-ˌpohst‖-ˌpəʊst/ *n* **1** a post or detachment established at a distance from a main body of troops, esp to protect it from surprise attack **2a** an outlying or frontier settlement **b** an outlying branch of a main organization or body

ˈoutˌpouring /-ˌpawring‖-ˌpɔːrɪŋ/ *n* an effusive expression (e g of emotion) – usu pl with sing. meaning

[1]**output** /-ˌpoot‖-ˌpʊt/ *n* **1** mineral, agricultural, or industrial production <*steel ~*> **2** mental or artistic production **3** the amount produced by sby in a given time **4a** sthg (e g energy, material, or data) produced by a machine or system **b** the terminal for the output on an electrical device

[2]**ˈoutˌput** *vt* **-tt-; output** to produce as output

[1]**outrage** /-ˌrayj‖-ˌreɪdʒ/ *n* **1** an act of violence or brutality **2** an act that violates accepted standards of behaviour or taste [Old French, excess, outrage, fr *outre* beyond, in excess, fr Latin *ultra*]

[2]**ˌoutˈrage** *vt* **1** to violate the standards or principles of **2** to rape – euph

outrageous /owtˈrayjəs‖aʊtˈreɪdʒəs/ *adj* **1** not conventional or moderate; extravagant **2** going beyond all standards of propriety, decency, or taste; shocking, offensive – **outrageously** *adv*, **outrageousness** *n*

ˌoutˈrank /-ˈrangk‖-ˈræŋk/ *vt* to rank higher than

outré /ˈoohtray ‖ˈuːtreɪ (*Fr* utre)/ *adj* violating convention or propriety; bizarre [French, fr past participle of *outrer* to carry to excess]

ˌoutˈride /-ˈried‖-ˈraɪd/ *vt* **outrode** /-ˈrohd‖-ˈrəʊd/; **outridden** /-ˈrid(ə)n‖-ˈrɪd(ə)n/ to ride out (a storm)

ˈoutˌrider /-ˌriedə‖-ˌraɪdə/ *n* a mounted attendant or motorcyclist who rides ahead of or beside a carriage or car as an escort

ˈoutˌrigger /-ˌrigə‖-ˌrɪgə/ *n* **1** a spar, beam, or framework run out or projecting from a ship's side (e g to help secure a mast or support a float or rowlock) **2** a member projecting from a main structure to provide additional stability or support sthg

[1]**ˌoutˈright** /-ˈriet‖-ˈraɪt/ *adv* **1** completely **2** instantaneously; ON THE SPOT 2

[2]**ˈoutˌright** *adj* being completely or exactly what is stated <*an ~ lie*>

ˌoutˈrun /-ˈrun‖-ˈrʌn/ *vt* **outran** /-ˈran‖-ˈræn/; **outrun; -nn- 1** to run faster than **2** to exceed, surpass

ˌoutˈsell /-ˈsel‖-ˈsel/ *vt* **outsold** /-ˈsohld‖-ˈsəʊld/ to surpass in selling, salesmanship, or numbers sold

outset /-ˌset‖-ˌset/ *n the* beginning, start

ˌoutˈshine /-ˈshien‖-ˈʃaɪn/ *vt* **outshone** /-ˈshon‖-ˈʃɒn/, **outshined 1** to shine brighter than **2** to outdo or excel (in splendour)

[1]**outside** /ˌowtˈsied, ˈ-ˌ-‖ˌaʊtˈsaɪd, ˈ-ˌ-/ *n* **1a** an external part; the region beyond a boundary **b** the area farthest from a point of reference: e g **b(1)** the section of a playing area towards the sidelines; *also* a corner **b(2)** the side of a pavement nearer the traffic **2** an outer side or surface **3** an outer manifestation; an appearance **4** the extreme limit of an estimation or guess; a maximum <*the crowd numbered 10,000 at the ~*>

[2]**ˈoutˌside** *adj* **1a** of or being on, near, or towards the outside <*an ~ lavatory*> <*an ~ telephone line*> **b** of or being the outer side of a curve or near the middle of the road <*driving on the ~ lane*> **2** maximum **3a** originating elsewhere <*an ~ broadcast*> <*~ agitators*> **b** not belonging to one's regular occupation or duties <*~ interests*> **4** barely possible; remote <*an ~ chance*>

[3]**ˌoutˈside** *adv* **1** on or to the outside <*wait ~ in the passage*> **2** outdoors **3** *chiefly Br* not in prison – slang

[4]**outside** /ˈ-ˌ-, ˌ-ˈ-/ *prep* **1** on or to the outside of <*live a mile ~ Cambridge*> **2** beyond the limits of <*~ my experience*> **3** except, besides <*few interests ~ her children*>

ˌoutˈside of *prep, chiefly NAm* outside

outsider /owtˈsiedə‖aʊtˈsaɪdə/ *n* **1** sby who does not belong to a particular group **2** a competitor who has only an outside chance of winning

outsize /ˈowtˌsiez‖ˈaʊtˌsaɪz/ *adj or n* (of) an unusual or above standard size

ˈoutˌskirt /-ˌskuht‖-ˌskɜːt/ *n* an outer area, esp of a town or city – usu pl with sing. meaning

ˌoutˈsmart /-ˈsmaht‖-ˈsmɑːt/ *vt* to get the better of; outwit

ˌoutˈspoken /-ˈspohkən‖-ˈspəʊkən/ *adj* direct and open in speech or expression; frank – **outspokenly** *adv*, **outspokenness** *n*

ˌoutˈstanding /-ˈstanding‖-ˈstændɪŋ/ *adj* **1a** unpaid <*left several bills ~*> **b** continuing, unresolved **2a** standing out from a group; conspicuous **b** marked by eminence and distinction – **outstandingly** *adv*

ˌoutˈstay /-ˈstay‖-ˈsteɪ/ *vt* **1** to overstay <*~ed his welcome*> **2** to surpass in staying power

ˌoutˈstretch /-ˈstrech‖-ˈstretʃ/ *vt* to stretch out; extend

ˌoutˈstrip /-ˈstrip‖-ˈstrɪp/ *vt* **-pp- 1** to go faster or farther than **2** to get ahead of; leave behind

ˌ**outˈvote** /-ˈvoht‖-ˈvəʊt/ *vt* to defeat by a majority of votes

[1]ˈ**outward** /-wood‖-wʊd/ *adj* **1a** situated at or directed towards the outside **b** being or going away from home <*the ~ voyage*> **2** of the body or external appearances <*~ calm*>

[2]**outward** *n* external form, appearance, or reality

ˈ**outwardly** /-li‖-lɪ/ *adv* in outward appearance; superficially

ˈ**outwards** *adv* towards the outside

ˌ**outˈwear** /-ˈweə‖-ˈweə/ *vt* **outwore** /-ˈwaw‖-ˈwɔː/; **outworn** /-ˈwawn‖-ˈwɔːn/ to last longer than

ˌ**outˈweigh** /-ˈway‖-ˈweɪ/ *vt* to exceed in weight, value, or importance

ˌ**outˈwit** /-ˈwit‖-ˈwɪt/ *vt* **-tt-** to get the better of by superior cleverness

ˈ**outˌwork** /-ˌwuhk‖-ˌwɜːk/ *n* **1** a minor defensive position constructed outside a fortified area **2** work done for a business or organization off its premises usu by employees based at home – **outworker** *n*

ˌ**outˈworn** /-ˈwawn‖-ˈwɔːn/ *adj* no longer useful or acceptable; outmoded

ouzel, ousel /ˈoohzl‖ˈuːzl/ *n* **1** RING OUZEL **2** a dipper

ouzo /ˈoohzoh‖ˈuːzəʊ/ *n* an unsweetened Greek spirit flavoured with aniseed that is usu drunk with water

ova /ˈohvə‖ˈəʊvə/ *pl of* OVUM

[1]**oval** /ˈohvl‖ˈəʊvl/ *adj* having the shape of an egg; *also* exactly or approximately elliptical – **ovally** *adv*, **ovalness** *n*

[2]**oval** *n* an oval figure or object

ovary /ˈohvəri‖ˈəʊvərɪ/ *n* **1** the typically paired female reproductive organ that produces eggs and female sex hormones **2** the enlarged rounded usu basal female part of a flowering plant that bears the ovules and consists of 1 or more carpels – **ovarian** *adj*, **ovaritis** *n*

ovation /ohˈvaysh(ə)n‖əʊˈveɪʃ(ə)n/ *n* an expression of popular acclaim

oven /ˈuv(ə)n‖ˈʌv(ə)n/ *n* a chamber used for baking, heating, or drying

ˈ**ovenˌware** /-ˌweə‖-ˌweə/ *n* heat-resistant dishes (e g casseroles) in which food can be cooked in an oven

[1]**over** /ˈohvə‖ˈəʊvə/ *adv* **1a** across a barrier <*climb ~*> **b** across an intervening space <*went ~ to the States*>; *also* ROUND 5 <*ask them ~ for drinks*> **c** downwards from an upright position <*fell ~*> <*knocked him ~*> **d** across the brim or brink <*soup boiled ~*> **e** so as to bring the underside up <*turned his cards ~*> <*rolled ~ and ~*> **f** so as to be reversed or folded <*change the 2 pictures ~*> <*bend it ~*> **g** from one person or side to another <*hand it ~*> <*won them ~*> <*went ~ to the enemy*> **h** ACROSS 3 <*got his point ~*> **2a(1)** beyond some quantity or limit <*£10 or ~*> <*show ran a minute ~*> **a(2)** excessively, inordinately – often in combination <over-*optimistic*> <over*value*> **a(3)** in excess; remaining <*there wasn't much ~*> <*3 into 7 goes twice and 1 ~*> **b** till a later time <*stay ~ till Monday*> **3** so as to cover the whole surface <*windows boarded ~*> **4a** at an end <*the day is ~*> **b** – used on a two-way radio circuit to indicate that a message is complete and a reply is expected **5a** – used to show repetition <*10 times ~*> <*told you ~ and ~ again*> **b** *chiefly NAm* once more <*do one's sums ~*>

[2]**over** *prep* **1a** higher than; above <*towered ~ his mother*> **b** vertically above but not touching <*lamp hung ~ the table*> **c** – used to indicate movement down upon <*hit him ~ the head*> or down across the edge of <*fell ~ the cliff*> **d** ACROSS 1 <*climbed ~ the gate*> <*flew ~ the lake*> **e** so as to cover <*laid a blanket ~ the child*> <*curtains drawn ~ the windows*> **f** divided by <*6 ~ 2 is 3*> **2a** with authority, power, or jurisdiction in relation to <*respected those ~ him*> **b** – used to indicate superiority, advantage, or preference <*a big lead ~ the others*> **3** more than <*cost ~ £5*> **4a** all through or throughout <*showed me all ~ the house*> <*went ~ his notes*> **b** by means of (a medium or channel of communication) <*~ the radio*> <*~ the phone*> **5a** in the course of; during <*~ the past 25 years*> <*wrote it ~ the weekend*> **b** until the end of <*stay ~ Sunday*> **c** past, beyond <*we're ~ the worst*> **6a** – used to indicate an object of solicitude or reference <*the Lord watches ~ them*> <*laughed ~ the incident*> **b** – used to indicate an object of occupation or activity <*sitting ~ their wine*> <*spent an hour ~ cards*>

[3]**over** *adj* **1** upper, higher <over*lord*> **2** outer, covering <over*coat*> **3** excessive <over*imagination*> <over*confidence*> *USE* often in combination

[4]**over** *n* any of the divisions of an innings in cricket during which 1 bowler bowls 6 or 8 balls from the same end of the pitch

ˌ**overˈact** /-ˈakt‖-ˈækt/ *vb* to perform (a part) with undue exaggeration

[1]**overall** /ˌohvəˈrawl‖ˌəʊvəˈrɔːl/ *adv* **1** as a whole; IN TOTO **2** from end to end, esp of a ship

[2]**overall** /ˈohvəˌrawl‖ˈəʊvəˌrɔːl/ *n* **1** *pl* a protective garment resembling a boiler suit or dungarees **2** *chiefly Br* a usu loose-fitting protective coat worn over other clothing

[3]**overall** *adj* including everything

overarm /ˈohvəˌrahm‖ˈəʊvəˌrɑːm/ *adj or adv* overhand

ˌ**overˈawe** /-ˈaw‖-ˈɔː/ *vt* to fill with respect or fear

ˌ**overˈbalance** /-ˈbaləns‖-ˈbæləns/ *vt* to cause to lose balance *~vi chiefly Br* to lose one's balance

ˌ**overˈbear** /-ˈbeə‖-ˈbeə/ *vt* **overbore** /-ˈbaw‖-ˈbɔː/; **overborne** *also* **overborn** /-ˈbawn‖-ˈbɔːn/ **1** to bring down by superior weight or force **2a** to domineer over **b** to surpass in importance or cogency; outweigh

ˌ**overˈbearing** /-ˈbeəring‖-ˈbeərɪŋ/ *adj* harshly masterful or domineering – **overbearingly** *adv*

ˌ**overˈbid** /-ˈbid‖-ˈbɪd/ *vb* **overbid; -dd-** *vi* **1** to bid in excess of value **2** to bid more than the scoring capacity of a hand at cards *~vt* to bid in excess of; *esp* to bid more than the value of (one's hand at cards) – **overbid** *n*

[1]ˌ**overˈblown** /-ˈblohn‖-ˈbləʊn/ *adj*

inflated, pretentious

[2]**overblown** *adj* past the prime of bloom <~ *roses*>

'**over,board** /-,bawd‖-,bɔːd/ *adv* **1** over the side of a ship or boat into the water **2** to extremes of enthusiasm <*went ~ for the plan*> **3** aside <*threw the plan ~*>

[1]**,over'burden** /-'buhd(ə)n‖-'bɜːd(ə)n/ *vt* to place an excessive burden on

[2]**'over,burden** *n* soil, rock, etc overlying a useful deposit (e g of coal)

,over'call /-'kawl‖-'kɔːl/ *vb* to make a higher bid than (the previous bid or player) in a card game – **overcall** *n*

overcast /'ohvə,kahst, ,--'-‖'əʊvə,kɑːst, ,--'-/ *adj* being, having, or characterized by a cloudy sky

,over'charge /-'chahj‖-'tʃɑːdʒ/ *vt* **1** to charge too much or too fully **2** to fill too full **3** to exaggerate ~*vi* to make an excessive charge – **overcharge** *n*

,over'cloud /-'klowd‖-'klaʊd/ *vt* to cover with clouds

'**over,coat** /-,koht‖-,kəʊt/ *n* **1** a warm usu thick coat for wearing outdoors over other clothing **2** a protective coat (e g of paint)

,over'come /-'kum‖-'kʌm/ *vb* **overcame** /-'kaym‖-'keɪm/; **overcome** *vt* **1** to get the better of; surmount <~ *difficulties*> **2** to overpower, overwhelm ~*vi* to gain superiority; win

,over,compen'sation /-,kompen'saysh-(ə)n, -pən-‖-,kɒmpen'seɪʃ(ə)n, -pən-/ *n* excessive reaction to feelings of inferiority, guilt, inadequacy, etc

,over'crowd /-'krowd‖-'kraʊd/ *vb* to (cause to) be too crowded

,over'do /-'dooh‖-'duː/ *vt* **overdoes** /-'duz‖-'dʌz/; **overdid** /-'did‖-'dɪd/; **overdone** /-'dun‖-'dʌn/ **1a** to do or use in excess **b** to exaggerate **2** to cook too much

overdose /'ohvə,dohs‖'əʊvə,dəʊs/ *vb or n* (to give or take) too great a dose of drugs, medicine, etc

'**over,draft** /-,drahft‖-,drɑːft/ *n* an act of overdrawing at a bank; the state of being overdrawn; *also* the sum overdrawn

,over'draw /-'draw‖-'drɔː/ *vb* **overdrew** / -'drooh‖-'druː/; **overdrawn** /-'drawn‖-'drɔːn/ *vt* **1** to draw cheques on (a bank account) for more than the balance <*his account was* overdrawn> **2** to exaggerate, overstate ~*vi* to make an overdraft

,over'drawn /-'drawn‖-'drɔːn/ *adj* having an overdrawn account

[1]**,over'dress** /-'dres‖-'dres/ *vb* to dress (oneself) too elaborately or formally

[2]**'over,dress** *n* a dress worn over another, or over a jumper, blouse, etc

'**over,drive** /-,driev‖-,draɪv/ *n* a transmission gear in a motor vehicle that provides a ratio higher than the normal top gear and that drives the propeller shaft at a speed greater than the engine speed

,over'due /-'dyooh‖-'djuː/ *adj* **1a** unpaid when due **b** delayed beyond an appointed time **2** more than ready or ripe

,over'estimate /-'estimayt‖-'estɪmeɪt/ *vt* **1** to estimate as being more than the actual amount or size **2** to place too high a value on; overrate – **overestimate** *n*, **overestimation** *n*

[1]**,over'flow** /-'floh‖-'fləʊ/ *vt* **1** to cover (as if) with water; inundate **2** to flow over the brim, edge, or limit of ~*vi* to flow over or beyond a brim, edge, or limit

[2]**'over,flow** *n* **1** a flowing over; an inundation **2** sthg that flows over; *also, sing or pl in constr* the excess members of a group **3** an outlet or receptacle for surplus liquid

,over'fly /-'flie‖-'flaɪ/ *vt* **overflew** /-'flooh‖-'fluː/; **overflown** /-'flohn‖-'fləʊn/ to fly over, esp in an aircraft

,over'grow /-'groh‖-'grəʊ/ *vb* **overgrew** / -'grooh‖-'gruː/; **overgrown** /-'grohn‖-'grəʊn/ *vt* **1** to grow over so as to cover with vegetation **2** to grow beyond; to outgrow ~*vi* ~ *vi* **1** to grow excessively **2** to become overgrown – **overgrowth** *n*

,over'grown /-'grohn‖-'grəʊn/ *adj* **1** grown over or choked with vegetation **2** grown too large

'**over,hand** /-,hand‖-,hænd/ *adj or adv* with the hand brought forwards and down from above shoulder level

[1]**,over'hang** /-'hang‖-'hæŋ/ *vb* **overhung** /-'hung‖-'hʌŋ/ *vt* **1** to project over **2** to threaten ~*vi* to project so as to be over sthg

[2]**'over,hang** *n* **1** sthg that overhangs; *also* the extent by which sthg overhangs **2** a projection of the roof or upper storey of a building beyond the wall of the lower part

,over'haul /-'hawl‖-'hɔːl/ *vt* **1** to examine thoroughly and carry out necessary repairs **2** to overtake – **overhaul** *n*

[1]**,over'head** /-'hed‖-'hed/ *adv* above one's head

[2]**'over,head** *adj* **1** operating, lying, or coming from above **2** of overhead expenses

[3]**'over,head** *n* **1** a business expense (e g rent, insurance, or heating) not chargeable to a particular part of the work or product – often pl with sing. meaning **2** a stroke in squash, tennis, etc made above head height; a smash

,over'hear /-'hiə‖-'hɪə/ *vb* **overheard** /-'huhd‖-'hɜːd/ to hear (sby or sthg) without the speaker's knowledge or intention

,over'joyed /-'joyd‖-'dʒɔɪd/ *adj* extremely pleased; elated

[1]**,over'kill** /-'kil‖-'kɪl/ *vt* to obliterate (a target) with more nuclear force than required

[2]**'over,kill** *n* **1** the capability of destroying an enemy or target with a force, esp nuclear, larger than is required **2** an excess of sthg beyond what is required or suitable for a particular purpose

[1]**'over,land** /-,land‖-,lænd/ *adv or adj* by, upon, or across land rather than sea or air

[2]**overland** *vb, Austr* to drive (stock) overland for long distances – **overlander** *n*

,over'lap /-'lap‖-'læp/ *vb* **-pp-** *vt* to extend over and cover a part of ~*vi* to coincide partly; have sthg in common – **overlap** *n*

[1]**,over'lay** /-'lay‖-'leɪ/ *vt* **overlaid** /-'layd‖-'leɪd/ to lay or spread over or across

[2]**'over,lay** *n* sthg (designed to be) laid over sthg else; *esp* a transparent sheet containing graphic matter to be superimposed on another sheet

,over'leaf /-'leef‖-'liːf/ *adv* on the other side

of the page <*continued* ~>

ˌoverˈload /-ˈlohd‖-ˈləʊd/ *vt* **overloaded, overladen** /-ˈlaydn‖-ˈleɪdn/ to load to excess – **overload** *n*

ˌoverˈlong /-ˈlong‖-ˈlɒŋ/ *adj or adv* too long

ˌoverˈlook /-ˈlook‖-ˈlʊk/ *vt* **1** to have or provide a view of from above **2a** to fail to notice; miss **b** to ignore **c** to excuse

ˈoverˌlord /-ˌlawd‖-ˌlɔːd/ *n* **1** a lord who is superior to other lords **2** an absolute or supreme ruler – **overlordship** *n*

ˈoverly /-li‖-lɪ/ *adv, chiefly NAm & Scot* to an excessive degree

ˌoverˈman /-ˈman‖-ˈmæn/ *vt* **-nn-** to have or provide too many workers for <~ *a ship*>

ˌoverˈmaster /-ˈmahstə‖-ˈmɑːstə/ *vt* to overpower, subdue

ˌoverˈmuch /-ˈmuch‖-ˈmʌtʃ/ *adj or adv* too much

ˌoverˈnight /-ˈniet‖-ˈnaɪt/ *adv* **1** during or throughout the evening or night **2** suddenly – **overnight** *adj*

ˈoverˌpass /-ˌpahs‖-ˌpɑːs/ *n* a flyover; *also* the crossing of 2 roads, paths, railways, or combinations of these

ˌoverˈpay /-ˈpay‖-ˈpeɪ/ *vt* to give excessively high payment to or for

ˌoverˈplay /-ˈplay‖-ˈpleɪ/ *vt* **1** to exaggerate (e g a dramatic role) **2** to give too much emphasis to – **overplay one's hand** to overestimate one's capacities

ˌoverˌpopuˈlation /-ˌpopyooˈlaysh(ə)n‖-ˌpɒpjʊˈleɪʃ(ə)n/ *n* the condition of having too dense a population, so that the quality of life is impaired – **overpopulated** *adj*

ˌoverˈpower /-ˈpowə‖-ˈpaʊə/ *vt* **1** to overcome by superior force **2** to overwhelm – **overpoweringly** *adv*

ˈoverˌprint /-ˌprint‖-ˌprɪnt/ *n* a printed marking added to a postage stamp to alter the original or to commemorate a special event – **overprint** *vt*

ˌoverˈrate /-ˈrayt‖-ˈreɪt/ *vt* to rate too highly

ˌoverˈreach /-ˈreech‖-ˈriːtʃ/ *vt* to defeat (oneself) by trying to do or gain too much ~*vi, of a horse* to strike the hind foot against the forefoot

[1]**ˌoverˈride** /-ˈried‖-ˈraɪd/ *vt* **overrode** /-ˈrohd‖-ˈrəʊd/; **overridden** /-ˈrid(ə)n‖-ˈrɪd(ə)n/ **1a** to prevail over; dominate <*an* overriding *consideration*> **b** to set aside or annul; *esp* to neutralize the action of (e g an automatic control) **2** to overlap

[2]**ˈoverˌride** *n* a device or system used to override a control

ˌoverˈrule /-ˈroohl‖-ˈruːl/ *vt* to rule against or set aside, esp by virtue of superior authority

ˌoverˈrun /-ˈrun‖-ˈrʌn/ *vt* **overran** /-ˈran‖-ˈræn/; **-nn- 1a** to defeat decisively and occupy the positions of **b** to swarm over; infest **2a** to run or go beyond or past **b** to readjust (set type) by shifting letters or words from one line into another **3** to flow over – **overrun** *n*

[1]**ˌoverˈseas** /-ˈseez‖-ˈsiːz/, **oversea** /-ˈsee‖-ˈsiː/ *adv* beyond or across the seas

[2]**ˈoverˌseas, oversea** *adj* **1** of transport across the seas **2** of, from, or in (foreign) places across the seas

ˌoverˈsee /-ˈsee‖-ˈsiː/ *vt* **oversaw** /-ˈsaw‖-ˈsɔː/; **overseen** /-ˈseen‖-ˈsiːn/ to supervise

ˈoverˌseer /-ˌsee·ə‖-ˌsiːə/ *n* a supervisor

ˌoverˈsell /-ˈsel‖-ˈsel/ *vt* **oversold** /-ˈsohld‖-ˈsəʊld/ **1** to sell too much of **2** to make excessive claims for – **oversell** *n*

ˌoverˈsexed /-ˈsekst‖-ˈsekst/ *adj* with an abnormally strong sexual drive

ˌoverˈshadow /-ˈshadoh‖-ˈʃædəʊ/ *vt* **1** to cast a shadow over **2** to exceed in importance; outweigh

ˈoverˌshoe /-ˌshooh‖-ˌʃuː/ *n* a usu rubber shoe worn over another as protection (e g from rain or snow)

ˌoverˈshoot /-ˈshooht‖-ˈʃuːt/ *vt* **overshot** /-ˈshot‖-ˈʃɒt/ to shoot or pass over or beyond, esp so as to miss – **overshoot** *n*

ˈoverˌsight /-ˌsiet‖-ˌsaɪt/ *n* **1** supervision **2** an inadvertent omission or error

ˌoverˈsimpliˌfy /-ˈsimpliˌfie‖-ˈsɪmplɪˌfaɪ/ *vb* to simplify (sthg) to such an extent as to cause distortion or error – **oversimplification** *n*

ˌoverˈsleep /-ˈsleep‖-ˈsliːp/ *vi* **overslept** /-ˈslept‖-ˈslept/ to sleep beyond the intended time

ˈoverˌspill /-ˌspil‖-ˌspɪl/ *n, chiefly Br* people who have moved away from crowded urban areas; *also* the movement of such people

ˌoverˈstate /-ˈstayt‖-ˈsteɪt/ *vt* to state in too strong terms; exaggerate – **overstatement** *n*

ˌoverˈstay /-ˈstay‖-ˈsteɪ/ *vt* to stay beyond the time or the limits of

ˈoverˌsteer /-ˌstiə‖-ˌstɪə/ *n* the tendency of a motor vehicle to steer into a sharper turn than the driver intends – **oversteer** *vb*

ˌoverˈstep /-ˈstep‖-ˈstep/ *vt* **-pp-** to exceed, transgress – esp in *overstep the mark*

ˌoverˈstrung /-ˈstrung‖-ˈstrʌŋ/ *adj* too highly strung; too sensitive

ˌoverˈstuff /-ˈstuf‖-ˈstʌf/ *vt* to cover (e g a chair) thickly with upholstery

ˌoversubˈscribe /-səbˈskrieb‖-səbˈskraɪb/ *vt* to subscribe for more of than is offered for sale – **oversubscription** *n*

overt /ˈohvuht, ˌ-ˈ-‖ˈəʊvɜːt, ˌ-ˈ-/ *adj* public, manifest – **overtly** *adv*

ˌoverˈtake /-ˈtayk‖-ˈteɪk/ *vb* **overtook** /-ˈtook‖-ˈtʊk/; **overtaken** /-ˈtaykən‖-ˈteɪkən/ *vt* **1a** to catch up with **b** to catch up with and pass beyond **2** to come upon suddenly ~*vi, chiefly Br* to catch up with and pass by another vehicle going in the same direction

ˌoverˈtax /-ˈtaks‖-ˈtæks/ *vt* **1** to tax too heavily **2** to put too great a burden or strain on

[1]**ˌoverˈthrow** /-ˈthroh‖-ˈθrəʊ/ *vt* **overthrew** /-ˈthrooh‖-ˈθruː/; **overthrown** /-ˈthrohn‖-ˈθrəʊn/ **1** to overturn, upset **2** to cause the downfall of; defeat

ˈoverˌtime /-ˌtiem‖-ˌtaɪm/ *n* **1** time in excess of a set limit; *esp* working time in excess of a standard working day or week **2** the wage paid for overtime – **overtime** *adv*

ˈoverˌtone /-ˌtohn‖-ˌtəʊn/ *n* **1a** any of the higher harmonics produced simultaneously with the fundamental in a complex musical note **b** HARMONIC 2 **2** a secondary effect, quality, or meaning; a suggestion – often pl with sing. meaning

ˌoverˈtop /-ˈtop‖-ˈtɒp/ *vt* **-pp- 1** to rise above the top of **2** to surpass

overture /ˈohvətyooə, -chə‖ˈəʊvətjʊə, -tʃə/ *n* **1a** an initiative towards agreement or action – often pl with sing. meaning **b** sthg introductory; a prelude **2a** the orchestral introduction to a musical dramatic work **b** an orchestral concert piece written esp as a single movement

ˌoverˈturn /-ˈtuhn‖-ˈtɜːn/ *vt* **1** to cause to turn over; upset **2** to overthrow; BRING DOWN 1 ~*vi* TURN OVER 1 – **overturn** *n*

ˌoverˈweening /-ˈweening‖-ˈwiːnɪŋ/ *adj* **1** arrogant, presumptuous **2** immoderate, exaggerated

[1]**ˈoverˌweight** /-ˌwayt‖-ˌweɪt/ *n* weight above what is normal, average, or required

[2]**ˌoverˈweight** *vt* **1** to give too much weight or consideration to **2** to weight excessively

[3]**ˌoverˈweight** *adj* exceeding the expected, normal, or proper (bodily) weight

ˌoverˈwhelm /-ˈwelm‖-ˈwelm/ *vt* **1** to cover over completely; submerge **2** to overcome by superior force or numbers **3** to overpower with emotion – **overwhelmingly** *adv*

ˌoverˈwork /-ˈwuhk‖-ˈwɜːk/ *vt* **1** to cause to work too hard or too long **2** to make excessive use of ~*vi* to work too much or too long – **overwork** *n*

ˌoverˈwrought /-ˈrawt‖-ˈrɔːt/ *adj* extremely excited; agitated

oviduct /ˈohviˌdukt‖ˈəʊvɪˌdʌkt/ *n* the tube that serves for the passage of eggs from an ovary, esp before laying – **oviductal** *adj*

oviparous /ohˈvipərəs‖əʊˈvɪpərəs/ *adj* involving or producing eggs that develop and hatch outside the mother's body – **oviparously** *adv*, **oviparousness** *n*, **oviparity** *n*

ovoid /ˈohvoyd‖ˈəʊvɔɪd/, **ovoidal** /ohˈvoydl‖əʊˈvɔɪdl/ *adj* shaped like an egg – **ovoid** *n*

ovulate /ˈovyooˌlayt‖ˈɒvjʊˌleɪt/ *vi* to produce eggs or discharge them from an ovary – **ovulation** *n*, **ovulatory** *adj*

ovule /ˈovyoohl, ˈoh-‖ˈɒvjuːl, ˈəʊ-/ *n* **1** an outgrowth of the ovary of a seed plant that develops into a seed after fertilization of the egg cell it contains **2** a small egg, esp one in an early stage of growth – **ovular** *adj*

ovum /ˈohvəm‖ˈəʊvəm/ *n, pl* **ova** /ˈohvə‖ˈəʊvə/ an animal's female gamete that when fertilized can develop into a new individual

ow /ow‖aʊ/ *interj* – used esp to express sudden mild pain

owe /oh‖əʊ/ *vt* **1a** to be under obligation to pay or render **b** to be indebted to **2** to have or enjoy as a result of the action or existence of sthg or sby else <~s *his fame to luck*> ~*vi* to be in debt

ˈowing to /ˈoh·ing‖ˈəʊɪŋ/ *prep* BECAUSE OF 1

owl /owl‖aʊl/ *n* any of an order of chiefly nocturnal birds of prey with large head and eyes and a short hooked bill

owlet /ˈowlit‖ˈaʊlɪt/ *n* a small or young owl

owlish /ˈowlish‖ˈaʊlɪʃ/ *adj* having a round face or a wide-eyed stare – **owlishly** *adv*

[1]**own** /ohn‖əʊn/ *adj* belonging to, for, or relating to oneself or itself – usu after a possessive pronoun <*cooked his ~ dinner*>

[2]**own** *vt* **1** to have or hold as property; possess **2** to acknowledge, admit ~*vi* to acknowledge sthg to be true or valid – + *to* – **owner** *n*, **ownership** *n*

[3]**own** *pron, pl* **own** one belonging to oneself or itself – usu after a possessive pronoun <*a country with oil of its ~*> – **on one's own 1** in solitude; alone **2** without assistance or control

ˌowner-ˈoccupier *n* sby who owns the house he/she lives in

own up *vi* to confess a fault frankly

ox /oks‖ɒks/ *n, pl* **oxen** /ˈoks(ə)n‖ˈɒks(ə)n/ *also* **ox 1** a (domestic species of) bovine mammal **2** an adult castrated male domestic ox

Oxbridge /ˈoksˌbrij‖ˈɒksˌbrɪdʒ/ *adj or n* (of) the universities of Oxford and Cambridge

ˌoxˌeye ˈdaisy /oksie‖ˈɒksaɪ/ *n* a leafy-stemmed European composite plant with long white ray florets

ˈOxford ˌmovement /ˈoksfəd‖ˈɒksfəd/ *n* a Victorian High Church movement within the Church of England

oxide /ˈoksied‖ˈɒksaɪd/ *n* a compound of oxygen with an element or radical – **oxidic** *adj*

oxid·ize, -ise /ˈoksiˌdiez‖ˈɒksɪˌdaɪz/ *vt* **1** to combine with oxygen **2** to remove hydrogen or 1 or more electrons from (e g an atom, ion, or molecule) ~*vi* to become oxidized – **oxidizable** *adj*, **oxidizer** *n*, **oxidation** *n*, **oxidative** *adj*

Oxonian /okˈsohnyən, -ni·ən‖ɒkˈsəʊnjən, -nɪən/ *n* a student or graduate of Oxford University – **Oxonian** *adj*

oxtail /ˈoksˌtayl‖ˈɒksˌteɪl/ *n* the tail of cattle (skinned and used for food, esp in soup)

oxyacetylene /ˌoksi·əˈset(ə)lin, -leen‖ˌɒksɪəˈset(ə)lɪn, -liːn/ *adj* of or using a mixture of oxygen and acetylene, esp for producing a hot flame

oxygen /ˈoksij(ə)n‖ˈɒksɪdʒ(ə)n/ *n* a gaseous chemical element that forms about 21 per cent by volume of the atmosphere, is found combined in water, most minerals, and many organic compounds, is required for most burning processes, and is essential for the life of all plants and animals [French *oxygène*, fr Greek *oxys* sharp, acid + *genos* birth] – **oxygenic** *adj*

oxygenate /okˈsijənayt‖ɒkˈsɪdʒəneɪt/ *vt* to impregnate, combine, or supply (e g blood) with oxygen – **oxygenator** *n*, **oxygenation** *n*

ˈoxygen ˌmask *n* a device worn over the nose and mouth through which oxygen is supplied from a storage tank

ˈoxygen ˌtent *n* a canopy placed over sby in bed to maintain a flow of oxygen-enriched air

oxymoron /ˌoksiˈmawron‖ˌɒksɪˈmɔːrɒn/ *n, pl* **oxymora** /-rə‖-rə/ a combination of contradictory or incongruous words (e g *cruel kindness*) [Late Greek *oxymōron*, fr *oxymōros* pointedly foolish, fr Greek *oxys* sharp, keen + *mōros* foolish]

oyez /ohˈyay, -yes‖əʊˈjeɪ, -jes/ *vb imper* – uttered by a court official or public crier to gain attention [Anglo French, hear ye, imperative pl of *oir* to hear, fr Latin *audire*]

oyster /ˈoystə‖ˈɔɪstə/ *n* any of various (edible) marine bivalve molluscs with a rough irregular shell

ˈoyster ˌbed *n* a place where oysters grow or are cultivated

ˈoysterˌcatcher /-ˌkachə‖-ˌkætʃə/ *n* any of a genus of usu black-and-white stout-legged wading birds

ozone /ˈohˌzohn‖ˈəʊˌzəʊn/ *n* **1** a form of

oxygen with 3 atoms in each molecule that is a bluish irritating gas with a pungent smell and occurs naturally in the upper atmosphere **2** pure and refreshing air – **ozonous** *adj*, **ozonize** *vt*, **ozonic** *adj*, **ozoniferous** *adj*

p /pee‖piː/ *n, pl* **p's, ps** *often cap* (a graphic representation of or device for reproducing) the 16th letter of the English alphabet

pa /pah‖pɑː/ *n* father – infml

pabulum /ˈpabyooləm‖ˈpæbjʊləm/ *n* **1** food **2** intellectual sustenance

[1]**pace** /pays‖peɪs/ *n* **1a** rate of movement **b** parallel rate of growth or development <*wages do not keep* ~ *with inflation*> **c** rate or manner of doing sthg **2** a manner of walking **3a** STEP 2a(1) **b** the distance covered by a single step in walking, usu taken to be about 0.75m (about 30in) **4a** GAIT 2; *esp* a fast 2-beat gait of a horse in which the legs move in lateral pairs **b** *pl* an exhibition of skills or abilities <*put him through his* ~s>

[2]**pace** *vi* **1** to walk with a slow or measured tread **2** *esp of a horse* to go at a pace ~ *vt* **1a** to measure by pacing – often + *out* or *off* **b** to traverse at a walk **2** *of a horse* to cover (a course) by pacing **3** to set or regulate the pace of; *specif* to go ahead of (e g a runner) as a pacemaker – **pacer** *n*

[3]**pace** /ˈpaysi‖ˈpeɪsɪ/ *prep* with due respect to

ˈ**paceˌmaker** /-ˌmaykə‖-ˌmeɪkə/ *n* **1** sby or sthg that sets the pace for another (e g in a race) **2** (a device for applying regular electric shocks to the heart that reproduces the function of) a part of the heart that maintains rhythmic (coordinated) contractions – **pacemaking** *n*

ˈ**paceˌsetter** /-ˌsetə‖-ˌsetə/ *n* PACEMAKER 1

pachyderm /ˈpakiduhm‖ˈpækɪdɜːm/ *n* an elephant, rhinoceros, pig, or other usu thick-skinned (hoofed) nonruminant mammal [French *pachyderme*, fr Greek *pachydermos* thick-skinned, fr *pachys* thick + *derma* skin] – **pachydermal** *adj*, **pachydermatous** *adj*

pacific /pəˈsifik‖pəˈsɪfɪk/ *adj* **1** tending to bring about peace; conciliatory **2** having a mild peaceable nature **3** *cap* of (the region round) the Pacific ocean – **pacifically** *adv*

pacifism /ˈpasifiz(ə)m‖ˈpæsɪfɪz(ə)m/ *n* opposition to war as a means of settling disputes; *specif* refusal to bear arms on moral or religious grounds – **pacifist** *n*

pacify /ˈpasifie‖ˈpæsɪfaɪ/ *vt* **1** to allay the anger or agitation of **2a** to restore to a peaceful state; subdue **b** to reduce to submission – **pacifiable** *adj*, **pacifier** *n*, **pacification** *n*

[1]**pack** /pak‖pæk/ *n* **1** a bundle or bag of things carried on the shoulders or back; *specif* a knapsack **2a** a large amount or number <*a* ~ *of lies*> **b** a full set of playing cards **3** a method of packing <*vacuum* ~> **4** *sing or pl in constr* **4a** a group of people with a common characteristic <*a* ~ *of thieves*> **b** an organized troop (e g of cub scouts) **5** *sing or pl in constr the* forwards in a rugby team, esp when acting together **6** *sing or pl in constr* **6a** a group of domesticated animals trained to hunt or run together <*a* ~ *of hounds*> **b** a group of (predatory) animals of the same kind <*a wolf* ~> **7** a concentrated mass; *specif* PACK ICE **8** wet absorbent material for application to the body as treatment (e g for a bruise) **9** *chiefly NAm* a packet

[2]**pack** *vt* **1a** to stow (as if) in a container, esp for transport or storage **b** to cover, fill, or surround with protective material **2a** to crowd together so as to fill; cram **b** to force into a smaller volume; compress **3** to bring to an end; finish – + *up* or *in* <*he's* ~ing *up his job next year*> **4** to gather into a pack **5** to cover or surround with a pack **6** to cause or be capable of making (an impact) <*a book that* ~s *quite a punch*> ~ *vi* **1** to stow goods or equipment for transporting – often + *up* **2** to crowd together **3** to become compacted in a layer or mass – **packable** *adj*, **packer** *n*, **packability** *n* – **pack it in** to stop doing it; give it up – infml

[3]**pack** *vt* to influence the composition of (e g a jury) so as to bring about a desired result

[1]**package** /ˈpakij‖ˈpækɪdʒ/ *n* **1a** a small or medium-sized pack; a parcel **b** sthg wrapped or sealed **2** a wrapper or container in which sthg is packed **3** PACKAGE DEAL

[2]**package** *vt* to make into or enclose in a package – **packager** *n*

ˈ**package ˌdeal** *n* an offer or agreement involving a number of related items and making acceptance of one item dependent on the acceptance of all; *also* the items so offered

packed /pakt‖pækt/ *adj* **1a** that is crowded or stuffed – often in combination <*an action*-packed *story*> **b** compressed <*hard*-packed *snow*> **2** filled to capacity <*played to a* ~ *house*>

packet /ˈpakit‖ˈpækɪt/ *n* **1** a small pack or parcel <*a* ~ *of biscuits*> **2** a passenger boat carrying mail and cargo on a regular schedule **3** *Br* a large sum of money <*cost a* ~> – infml

ˈ**pack ˌice** *n* sea ice crushed together into a large floating mass

packing /ˈpaking‖ˈpækɪŋ/ *n* **1** the action, process, or method of packing sthg **2** material used to pack

ˈ**packing ˌcase** *n* a usu wooden crate in which goods are packed for storage or transport

pack off *vt* to send away, esp abruptly or unceremoniously – infml <pack *the kids* off *to school*>

ˈ**packˌsaddle** /-ˌsadl‖-ˌsædl/ *n* a saddle designed to support a pack on an animal's back

pack up *vi* **1** to finish work **2** to cease to function <*the engine* packed up> *USE* infml

pact /pakt‖pækt/ *n* an agreement, treaty

[1]**pad** /pad‖pæd/ *n* **1** a thin flat mat or cushion: e g **1a** padding used to shape an article of clothing **b** a padded guard worn to shield body parts, esp the legs of a batsman, against impact **c** a piece of absorbent material used as a surgical dressing or protective covering **2a** the foot of an animal **b** the cushioned thickening of the underside of the toes of cats, dogs, etc **3** a large floating leaf of a water plant **4** a number of sheets of

paper (e g for writing or drawing on) fastened together at 1 edge **5a** a flat surface for a vertical takeoff or landing **b** LAUNCHING PAD **6** living quarters – infml

[2]**pad** *vt* **-dd- 1** to provide with a pad or padding **2** to expand or fill out (speech or writing) with superfluous matter – often + *out*

[3]**pad** *vb* **-dd-** *vt* to go along on foot ~*vi* to walk with a muffled step

padding /ˈpading‖ˈpædɪŋ/ *n* material used to pad

[1]**paddle** /ˈpadl‖ˈpædl/ *n* **1a** a usu wooden implement similar to but smaller than an oar, used to propel and steer a small craft (e g a canoe) **b** an implement with a short handle and broad flat blade used for stirring, mixing, hitting, etc **2** any of the broad boards at the circumference of a paddle wheel or waterwheel

[2]**paddle** *vi* to go on or through water (as if) by means of paddling a craft ~*vt* to propel (as if) by a paddle – **paddler** *n*

[3]**paddle** *vi* to walk, play, or wade in shallow water – **paddle** *n*, **paddler** *n*

ˈ**paddle ˌsteamer** *n* a vessel propelled by a pair of paddle wheels mounted amidships or by a single paddle wheel at the stern

ˈ**paddle ˌwheel** *n* a power-driven wheel with paddles, floats, or boards round its circumference used to propel a boat

paddock /ˈpadək‖ˈpædək/ *n* **1** a small usu enclosed field, esp for pasturing or exercising animals; *esp* one where racehorses are saddled and paraded before a race **2** an area at a motor-racing track where cars, motorcycles, etc are parked and worked on before a race

paddy /ˈpadi‖ˈpædɪ/ *n* **1** (threshed unmilled) rice **2** a paddyfield [Malay *padi*]

Paddy *n* an Irishman – chiefly derog [*Paddy*, common Irish nickname for *Patrick*]

padlock /ˈpadlok‖ˈpædlɒk/ *n* a portable lock with a shackle that can be passed through a staple or link and then secured – **padlock** *vt*

padre /ˈpahdri‖ˈpɑːdrɪ/ *n* **1** a Christian priest **2** a military chaplain

paean /ˈpee·ən‖ˈpiːən/ *n* a joyously exultant song or hymn of praise, tribute, thanksgiving, or triumph

paediatrics /ˌpeediˈatriks‖ˌpiːdɪˈætrɪks/ *n pl but sing or pl in constr* medicine dealing with the development, care, and diseases of children [deriv of Greek *paid-*, *pais* child + *iatros* physician] – **paediatric** *adj*, **paediatrician** *n*

paella /pieˈelə‖paɪˈelə/ *n* a saffron-flavoured Spanish dish containing rice, meat, seafood, and vegetables

paeony /ˈpee·əni‖ˈpiːənɪ/ *n* a peony

pagan /ˈpaygən‖ˈpeɪgən/ *n* **1** a follower of a polytheistic religion **2** an irreligious person [Late Latin *paganus*, fr Latin, country dweller, fr *pagus* country district] – **pagan** *adj*, **paganish** *adj*, **paganism** *n*, **paganize** *vt*

[1]**page** /payj‖peɪdʒ/ *n* **1a(1)** a youth being trained for the medieval rank of knight and in the personal service of a knight **a(2)** a youth attending on a person of rank **b** a boy serving as an honorary attendant at a formal function (e g a wedding) **2** sby employed to deliver messages or run errands

[2]**page** *vt* **1** to summon by repeatedly calling out the name of (e g over a public-address system) **2** to summon by a coded signal emitted esp by a short-range radio transmitter

[3]**page** *n* **1** (a single side of) a leaf of a book, magazine, etc **2** sthg worth being recorded in writing <*the brightest ~ of her career*> **3** a sizable subdivision of computer memory used chiefly for convenience of reference in programming

[4]**page** *vt* to paginate

pageant /ˈpaj(ə)nt‖ˈpædʒ(ə)nt/ *n* **1** an ostentatious display **2** a show, exhibition; *esp* a series of scenes in which people express a common theme **3** PAGEANTRY 1

pageantry /ˈpaj(ə)ntri‖ˈpædʒ(ə)ntrɪ/ *n* **1** pageants and the presentation of pageants **2** colourful or splendid display; spectacle

pager /ˈpayjə/ *n* a receiver for a paging system, esp one that is small and portable

paginate /ˈpajinayt‖ˈpædʒɪneɪt/ *vt* to number the sides of the leaves of (e g a book) in a sequence – **pagination** *n*

pagoda /pəˈgohdə‖pəˈgəʊdə/ *n* a many-storied usu polygonal tower with upturned projecting roofs at the division of each storey and erected esp as a temple or memorial in the Far East

paid /payd‖peɪd/ *past of* PAY

ˌ**paid-ˈup** *adj* having paid the necessary fees to be a full member of a group or organization; *broadly* showing the characteristic attitudes and behaviour of a specified group to a marked degree <*a ~ member of the awkward squad*>

pail /payl‖peɪl/ *n* (the contents of or quantity contained in) an esp wooden or metal bucket – **pailful** *n*

paillasse /ˈpalias, palˈyas‖ˈpælɪæs, pælˈjæs/ *n* a palliasse

[1]**pain** /payn‖peɪn/ *n* **1a** a basic bodily sensation induced by a noxious stimulus or physical disorder and characterized by physical discomfort (e g pricking, throbbing, or aching) **b** acute mental or emotional distress **2** *pl* the throes of childbirth **3** *pl* trouble or care taken **4** sby or sthg that annoys or is a nuisance – infml <*she's a real ~*> – **painless** *adj*, **painlessly** *adv*, **painlessness** *n* – **on/under pain of** subject to penalty or punishment of <*ordered to leave the country* on pain of *death*>

[2]**pain** *vt* to make suffer or cause distress to; hurt ~*vi* to give or have a sensation of pain

painful /ˈpaynf(ə)l‖ˈpeɪnf(ə)l/ *adj* **-ll- 1a** feeling or giving pain **b** irksome, annoying **2** requiring effort or exertion <*a long ~ trip*> – **painfully** *adv*, **painfulness** *n*

ˈ**painˌkiller** /-ˌkilə‖-ˌkɪlə/ *n* sthg, esp a drug (e g morphine or aspirin), that relieves pain – **painkilling** *adj*

painstaking /ˈpaynˌstayking‖ˈpeɪnˌsteɪkɪŋ/ *adj* showing diligent care and effort – **painstakingly** *adv*

[1]**paint** /paynt‖peɪnt/ *vt* **1a** to apply colour, pigment, paint, or cosmetics to **b** to apply with a movement resembling that used in painting **2a** to represent in colours on a surface by applying pigments **b** to decorate by painting **c** to produce or evoke as if by painting <*her novel ~s*

glowing pictures of rural life> **3** to depict as having specified or implied characteristics <*not as black as he's* ~ed> ~*vi* to practise the art of painting

[2]**paint** *n* **1a(1)** a mixture of a pigment and a suitable liquid which forms a closely adherent coating when spread on a surface **a(2)** pigment, esp in compressed form **b** an applied coat of paint <*wet* ~> **2** (coloured) make-up – infml – **painty** *adj*

ˈpaintˌbrush /-ˌbrush‖-ˌbrʌʃ/ *n* a brush for applying paint

[1]**painter** /ˈpayntə‖ˈpeɪntə/ *n* **1** an artist who paints **2** sby who applies paint (e g to a building), esp as an occupation

[2]**painter** *n* a line used for securing or towing a boat

painting /ˈpaynting‖ˈpeɪntɪŋ/ *n* **1** a product of painting; *esp* a painted work of art **2** the art or occupation of painting

ˈpaintˌwork /-ˌwuhk‖-ˌwɜːk/ *n* paint that has been applied to a surface; *also* a painted surface <*damaged the* ~ *of the car*>

[1]**pair** /peə‖peə/ *n sing or pl in constr, pl* **pairs** *also* **pair** **1a(1)** two corresponding things usu used together <*a* ~ *of shoes*> **a(2)** two corresponding bodily parts <*a beautiful* ~ *of legs*> **b** a single thing made up of 2 connected corresponding pieces <*a* ~ *of trousers*> **2a** two similar or associated things: e g **2a(1)** a couple in love, engaged, or married <*were a devoted* ~> **a(2)** two playing cards of the same value in a hand **a(3)** two horses harnessed side by side **a(4)** two mated animals **b** a partnership between 2 people, esp in a contest against another partnership **c** two members from opposite sides of a deliberative body who agree not to vote on a specific issue during a time agreed on **d** a failure to score runs in either innings of a match by a batsman in cricket

[2]**pair** *vt* **1** to arrange a voting pair between **2** to arrange in pairs <*she succeeded in* ~ing *the socks*>

pair off *vb* to (cause to) form pairs, esp male and female

paisley /ˈpayzli‖ˈpeɪzlɪ/ *adj, often cap* of a fabric or garment made usu of soft wool and woven or printed with colourful abstract teardrop-shaped figures – **paisley** *n*

pajamas /pəˈjahməz‖pəˈdʒɑːməz/ *n pl in constr, pl* **pajamas** *chiefly NAm* pyjamas – **pajama** *adj*

Pakistani /ˌpakiˈstahni, ˌpah-‖ˌpækɪˈstɑːnɪ, ˌpɑː-/ *n* **1** a native or inhabitant of Pakistan **2** a descendant of Pakistanis – **Pakistani** *adj*

pal /pal‖pæl/ *n* **1** a close friend **2** – used as a familiar form of address, esp to a stranger *USE* infml [Romany *phral, phal* brother, friend, fr Sanskrit *bhrātṛ* brother]

palace /ˈpalis‖ˈpælɪs/ *n* **1** the official residence of a ruler (e g a sovereign or bishop) **2a** a large stately house **b** a large public building **c** a large and often ornate place of public entertainment <*a picture* ~>

paladin /ˈpalədin‖ˈpælədɪn/ *n* a champion of a medieval prince

palaeography /ˌpaliˈogrəfi‖ˌpælɪˈɒgrəfɪ/ *n* the study of ancient writings and inscriptions [deriv of Greek *palaios* ancient + *graphein* to write] – **palaeographer** *n*

Palaeolithic /ˌpali·əˈlithik‖ˌpælɪəˈlɪθɪk/ *adj or n* (of or being) the 2nd era of the Stone Age characterized by rough or chipped stone implements

palaeontology /ˌpalionˈtoləji‖ˌpælɪɒnˈtɒlədʒɪ/ *n* a science dealing with the life of past geological periods as inferred from fossil remains – **palaeontologist** *n*, **palaeontological** *adj*

ˌPalaeoˈzoic /ˌpali·əˈzohik‖ˌpælɪəˈzəʊɪk/ *adj or n* (of or being) an era of geological history that extends from about 570 million to 230 million years ago

palais /ˈpalay, ˈpali‖ˈpæleɪ, ˈpælɪ/, **palais de dance** /~ də ˈdonhs‖~ də ˈdɑ̃s/ *n* a public dance hall – chiefly infml

palanquin /ˈpalənkeen‖ˈpælənkiːn/ *n* a litter formerly used in eastern Asia, esp for 1 person, and usu hung from poles borne on the bearers' shoulders

palatable /ˈpalətəbl‖ˈpælətəbl/ *adj* **1** pleasant to the taste **2** acceptable to the mind – **palatableness** *n*, **palatably** *adv*, **palatability** *n*

palate /ˈpalət‖ˈpælət/ *n* **1** the roof of the mouth, separating it from the nasal cavity **2a** the sense of taste **b** a usu intellectual taste or liking – **palatal** *adj*

palatial /pəˈlaysh(ə)l‖pəˈleɪʃ(ə)l/ *adj* **1** of or being a palace **2** suitable to a palace; magnificent – **palatially** *adv*, **palatialness** *n*

palatinate /pəˈlatinət‖pəˈlætɪnət/ *n* the territory of a palatine

[1]**palatine** /ˈpalətien‖ˈpælətaɪn/ *n* a feudal lord (e g a count or bishop) with sovereign power

[2]**palatine** *adj* of or lying near the palate

palaver /pəˈlahvə‖pəˈlɑːvə/ *n* **1** a long parley or discussion **2** idle talk – **palaver** *vi*

[1]**pale** /payl‖peɪl/ *adj* **1** deficient in (intensity of) colour **2** not bright or brilliant; dim <*a* ~ *sun shining through the fog*> **3** feeble, faint <*a* ~ *imitation*> **4** *of a colour* not intense <*a* ~ *pink*> – **pale** *vb*, **palish** *adj*, **palely** *adv*, **paleness** *n*

[2]**pale** *n* **1** PICKET 1 **2** a territory under a particular jurisdiction – **beyond the pale** in violation of good manners, social convention etc

paleface /ˈpaylˌfays‖ˈpeɪlˌfeɪs/ *n* a white person, esp as distinguished from an American Indian

palette /ˈpalit‖ˈpælɪt/ *n* **1** a thin board held in the hand on which an artist mixes pigments **2** a particular range, quality, or use of colour; *esp* that of an individual artist

ˈpalette ˌknife *n* a knife with a flexible steel blade and no cutting edge, used esp in cooking or by artists for mixing and applying paints

palfrey /ˈpawlfri‖ˈpɔːlfrɪ/ *n, archaic* a saddle horse other than a war-horse, esp for a woman

palimony /ˌpaliməni‖ˈpælɪmənɪ/ *n, chiefly NAm* payments ordered by a court to be paid by one member of an unmarried couple formerly living together to the other [blend of *pal* and *alimony*]

palimpsest /ˈpalimpsest‖ˈpælɪmpsest/ *n* writing material (e g a parchment or tablet) reused after earlier writing has been erased [Latin *palimpsestus*, fr Greek *palimpsēstos* scraped again, fr *palin* back, again + *psēn* to rub, scrape]

palindrome /'palindrohm‖'pælɪndrəʊm/ *n* a word, sentence, etc that reads the same backwards or forwards [Greek *palindromos* running back again, fr *palin* back, again + *dramein* to run] – **palindromic** *adj*

paling /'payling‖'peɪlɪŋ/ *n* (a fence of) stakes or pickets

[1]**palisade** /ˌpali'sayd‖ˌpælɪ'seɪd/ *n* **1** a fence of stakes, esp for defence **2** a long strong stake pointed at the top and set close with others as a defence

[2]**palisade** *vt* to surround or fortify with palisades

[1]**pall** /pawl‖pɔːl/ *n* **1a** a square of linen used to cover the chalice containing the wine used at Communion **b** a heavy cloth draped over a coffin or tomb **2** sthg heavy or dark that covers or conceals <*a* ~ *of thick black smoke*>

[2]**pall** *vi* to cease to be interesting or attractive

pallbearer /'pawlˌbeərə‖'pɔːlˌbeərə/ *n* a person who helps to carry the coffin at a funeral or is part of its immediate escort

[1]**pallet** /'palit‖'pælɪt/ *n* **1** a straw-filled mattress **2** a small hard often makeshift bed

[2]**pallet** *n* **1** a flat-bladed wooden tool used esp by potters for shaping clay **2** a lever or surface in a timepiece that receives an impulse from the escapement wheel and imparts motion to a balance or pendulum **3** a portable platform intended for handling, storing, or moving materials and packages

palliasse, paillasse /'palias, pal'yas‖'pælɪæs, pæl'jæs/ *n* a thin straw mattress

palliate /'paliayt‖'pælɪeɪt/ *vt* **1** to lessen the unpleasantness of (e g a disease) without removing the cause **2** to disguise the gravity of (a fault or offence) by excuses or apologies; extenuate **3** to moderate the intensity of <*trying to* ~ *the boredom*> – **palliator** *n*, **palliative** *n or adj*, **palliation** *n*

pallid /'palid‖'pælɪd/ *adj* **1** lacking colour; wan **2** lacking sparkle or liveliness; dull – **pallidly** *adv*, **pallidness** *n*

pallor /'palə‖'pælə/ *n* deficiency of (facial) colour; paleness

pally /'pali‖'pælɪ/ *adj* friendly – infml

[1]**palm** /pahm‖pɑːm; *NAm* pah(l)m‖pɑː(l)m/ *n* **1** any of a family of tropical or subtropical trees, shrubs, or climbing plants related to the lilies, grasses, and orchids and usu having a simple stem and a crown of large leaves **2** a leaf of the palm as a symbol of victory, distinction, or rejoicing; *also* a branch (e g of laurel) similarly used **3** a symbol of triumph or distinction; *also* a victory, triumph – **palmlike** *adj*, **palmaceous** *adj*

[2]**palm** *n* **1** the concave part of the human hand between the bases of the fingers and the wrist **2** a unit of measurement based on the length (e g about 200mm or 8in) or breadth (e g about 100mm or 4in) of the human hand

[3]**palm** *vt* **1a** to conceal in or with the hand **b** to pick up stealthily **2** to impose by fraud

palmer /'palmə, 'pahmə‖'pælmə, 'pɑːmə/ *n* a pilgrim wearing 2 crossed palm leaves as a sign of a visit to the Holy Land

palmetto /pal'metoh‖pæl'metəʊ/ *n, pl* **palmettos, palmettoes** any of several usu low-growing fan-leaved palms

palmistry /'pahmistri‖'pɑːmɪstrɪ/ *n* reading a person's character or future from the markings on his/her palms – **palmist** *n*

palm off *vt* to get rid of (sthg unwanted or inferior) by deceiving sby into taking it – often + *on*

'**palm ˌoil** *n* an edible fat obtained from the fruit of several palms and used esp in soap and candles

ˌ**Palm 'Sunday** *n* the Sunday before Easter celebrated in commemoration of Christ's triumphal entry into Jerusalem

palmy /'pahmi, 'pahlmi‖'pɑːmɪ, 'pɑːlmɪ/ *adj* marked by prosperity; flourishing <~ *days*>

palomino /ˌpalə'meenoh‖ˌpælə'miːnəʊ/ *n, pl* **palominos** a light tan or cream usu slender-legged horse

palpable /'palpəbl‖'pælpəbl/ *adj* **1** capable of being touched or felt; tangible **2** easily perceptible by the mind; manifest – **palpably** *adv*, **palpability** *n*

palpate /'palpayt‖'pælpeɪt/ *vt* to examine, esp medically, by touch – **palpation** *n*

palpitate /'palpitayt‖'pælpɪteɪt/ *vi* to beat rapidly and strongly; throb – **palpitation** *n*

[1]**palsy** /'pawlzi, 'polzi‖'pɔːlzɪ, 'pɒlzɪ/ *n* paralysis or uncontrollable tremor of (a part of) the body

[2]**palsy** *vt* to affect (as if) with palsy

palter /'pawltə, 'poltə‖'pɔːltə, 'pɒltə/ *vi* **1** to act insincerely or deceitfully; equivocate **2** to haggle – + *with* – **palterer** *n*

paltry /'pawltri‖'pɔːltrɪ/ *adj* **1** mean, despicable <*a* ~ *trick*> **2** trivial <*a* ~ *sum*> – **paltriness** *n*

pampa /'pampə‖'pæmpə/ *n* an extensive (grass-covered) plain of temperate S America east of the Andes – usu pl with sing. meaning but sing. or pl in constr

pampas grass /'pampəs‖'pæmpəs/ *n* a tall S American grass with large silky flower heads frequently cultivated as an ornamental plant

pamper /'pampə‖'pæmpə/ *vt* to treat with extreme or excessive care and attention <~ed *their guests*>

pamphlet /'pamflit‖'pæmflɪt/ *n* a usu small unbound printed publication with a paper cover, often dealing with topical matters

pamphleteer /ˌpamfli'tiə‖ˌpæmflɪ'tɪə/ *n* a writer of (political) pamphlets attacking sthg or urging a cause

[1]**pan** /pan‖pæn/ *n* **1a** any of various usu broad shallow open receptacles: e g **1a(1)** WARMING PAN **a(2)** a dustpan **a(3)** a bedpan **a(4)** a metal or plastic dish in a pair of scales **a(5)** a round metal container or vessel usu with a long handle, used to heat or cook food **b** any of various similar usu metal receptacles: e g **b(1)** the hollow part of the gunlock in old guns or pistols for receiving the priming **b(2)** a vessel in which gold or a similar metal is separated from waste by washing **2** a hollow or depression in land <*a salt* ~> **3** hardpan **4a** *chiefly Br* the bowl of a toilet **b** *chiefly NAm* TIN 2b

[2]**pan** *vb* **-nn-** *vi* **1** to wash earth, gravel, etc in a pan in search of metal (e g gold) **2** to yield precious metal in panning ~ *vt* **1a** to wash (earth, gravel, etc) in a pan **b** to separate (e g gold) by panning **2** to criticize severely – infml

[3]**pan** /pahn‖pɑːn/ *n* (a substance for chewing consisting of betel nut and various spices etc wrapped in) a betel leaf

[4]**pan** /pan‖pæn/ *vb* **-nn-** *vi* **1** to rotate a film or television camera horizontally so as to keep a moving object in view or obtain a panoramic effect **2** *of a camera* to undergo panning ~*vt* to cause (a camera) to pan

[5]**pan** /pan‖pæn/ *n* the act or process of panning a camera; the movement of the camera in a panning shot

pan- /pan-‖pæn-/ *comb form* **1** all; completely <pan*chromatic*> **2a** of all of (a specified group) <Pan-*American*> **b** advocating or involving the union of (a specified group) <Pan-*Asian*> **3** whole; general <pan*demic*>

panacea /ˌpanəˈsee·ə‖ˌpænəˈsiːə/ *n* a remedy for all ills or difficulties [Latin, fr Greek *panakeia*, fr *pan-* all + *akeisthai* to heal, fr *akos* remedy] – **panacean** *adj*

panache /pəˈnash, pa-‖pəˈnæʃ, pæ-/ *n* **1** an ornamental tuft (e g of feathers), esp on a helmet **2** dash or flamboyance in style and action; verve

panama /ˌpanəˈmah‖ˌpænəˈmɑː/ *n, often cap* a lightweight hat of plaited straw

panatela, panatella /ˌpanəˈtelə‖ˌpænəˈtelə/ *n* a long slender straight-sided cigar rounded off at the sealed mouth end

pancake /ˈpanˌkayk‖ˈpænˌkeɪk/ *n* **1** a flat cake made from thin batter and cooked on both sides usu in a frying pan **2** make-up compressed into a flat cake or stick form

ˈ**Pancake ˌDay** *n* Shrove Tuesday as marked by the eating of pancakes

pancake landing *n* a landing in which an aircraft descends in an approximately horizontal position with little forward motion

panchromatic /ˌpankrohˈmatik, -krə-‖ˌpænkrəʊˈmætɪk, -krə-/ *adj* sensitive to light of all colours in the visible spectrum

pancreas /ˈpangkri·əs‖ˈpæŋkrɪəs/ *n* a large compound gland in vertebrates that secretes digestive enzymes into the intestines and the hormones insulin and glucagon into the blood – **pancreatic** *adj*

panda /ˈpandə‖ˈpændə/ *n* **1** a long-tailed Himalayan flesh-eating mammal resembling the American raccoon and having long chestnut fur spotted with black **2** a large black-and-white plant-eating mammal of western China resembling a bear

ˈ**panda ˌcar** *n, Br* a small car used by police patrols, esp in urban areas

pandemic /panˈdemik‖pænˈdemɪk/ *n or adj* (a disease) occurring over a wide area and affecting an exceptionally high proportion of the population

pandemonium /ˌpandiˈmohnyəm, -ni·əm‖ˌpændɪˈməʊnjəm, -nɪəm/ *n* a wild uproar; a tumult [*Pandaemonium*, capital city of Hell in John Milton's poem *Paradise Lost*, fr Greek *pan-* all + *daimōn* evil spirit]

[1]**pander** /ˈpandə‖ˈpændə/ *n* **1** a pimp **2** sby who encourages or exploits the weaknesses or vices of others [*Pandarus*, mythical Greek procurer]

[2]**pander** *vi* to act as a pander; *esp* to provide gratification for others' desires – usu + *to*

pandit /ˈpundit‖ˈpʌndɪt/ *n* a wise or learned man in India – often used as an honorary title

pane /payn‖peɪn/ *n* **1** a piece, section, or side of sthg; *esp* a framed sheet of glass in a window or door **2** any of the sections into which a sheet of postage stamps is cut for distribution

panegyric /ˌpaniˈjirik‖ˌpænɪˈdʒɪrɪk/ *n* a eulogistic oration or piece of writing; *also* formal or elaborate praise – **panegyrical** *adj*, **panegyrically** *adv*, **panegyrist** *n*

[1]**panel** /ˈpanl‖ˈpænl/ *n* **1a(1)** a list of people summoned for jury service **a(2)** the jury so summoned **b(1)** a group of people selected to perform some service (e g investigation or arbitration) **b(2)** a group of people who discuss before an audience topics of usu political or social interest **b(3)** a group of entertainers who appear as contestants in a quiz or guessing game on radio or television **2** a separate or distinct part of a surface: e g **2a(1)** a thin usu rectangular board set in a frame (e g in a door) **a(2)** a usu sunken or raised section of a surface set off by a margin **b** a vertical section of fabric <*skirt made with 8 ~s*> **3** a thin flat piece of wood on which a picture is painted **4a** a flat often insulated support (e g for parts of an electrical device) usu with controls on 1 face **b** a usu vertical mount for controls or dials (e g in a car or aircraft) *USE* (*1a(2) & 1b*) sing. or pl in constr

[2]**panel** *vt* **-ll-** (*NAm* **-l-, -ll-**) to furnish or decorate with panels

panellist /ˈpanl·ist‖ˈpænlɪst/ *n* a member of a discussion or advisory panel or of a radio or television panel

pang /pang‖pæŋ/ *n* **1** a brief piercing spasm of pain **2** a sharp attack of mental anguish <~*s of remorse*>

panhandle /ˈpanˌhandl‖ˈpænˌhændl/ *vb, NAm* to beg (from) in the street *USE* – infml – **panhandler** *n*

[1]**panic** /ˈpanik‖ˈpænɪk/ *n* **1** a sudden overpowering fright; *esp* a sudden unreasoning terror that spreads rapidly through a group **2** a sudden widespread fright concerning financial affairs and resulting in a depression in values [French *panique*, fr Greek *panikos*, lit., of Pan, fr *Pan* Greek god of woods & shepherds] – **panic** *adj*, **panicky** *adj*

[2]**panic** *vb* **-ck-** to (cause to) be affected with panic

ˈ**panic-ˌstricken** *adj* overcome with panic

Panjabi /poonˈjahbi‖pʊnˈdʒɑːbɪ/ *n or adj* (a) Punjabi

panjandrum /panˈjandrəm‖pænˈdʒændrəm/ *n, pl* **panjandrums** *also* **panjandra** /-drə‖-drə/ a powerful personage or self-important official – humor

pannier, panier /ˈpanyə, ˈpani·ə‖ˈpænjə, ˈpænɪə/ *n* **1** a large basket; *esp* either of a pair carried on the back of an animal **2** a hoop petticoat or overskirt that gives extra width to the sides of a skirt at hip level **3** *chiefly Br* either of a pair of bags or boxes fixed on either side of the rear wheel of a bicycle or motorcycle

panoply /ˈpanəpli‖ˈpænəplɪ/ *n* **1a** a full suit of armour **b** ceremonial dress **2** a magnificent or impressive array <*the full ~ of a military* *funeral*> – **panoplied** *adj*

panorama /ˌpanəˈrahmə‖ˌpænəˈrɑːmə/ *n* **1a** a large pictorial representation encircling the spectator **b** a picture exhibited by being unrolled before the spectator **2a** an unobstructed or complete view of a landscape or area **b** a comprehensive presentation or survey of a series of events [Greek *pan-* all + *horama* sight, fr *horan* to see] – **panoramic** *adj*, **panoramically** *adv*

pan out *vi* to turn out as specified; *esp* to succeed

ˈ**panˌpipe** /ˈpanˌpiep, ˌ-ˈ-‖ˈpænˌpaɪp, ˌ-ˈ-/ *n* a primitive wind instrument consisting of a graduated series of short vertical pipes bound together with the mouthpieces in an even row – often pl with sing. meaning

pansy /ˈpanzi‖ˈpænzɪ/ *n* **1** (a flower of) a garden plant derived from wild violets **2** an effeminate male or male homosexual – derog

[1]**pant** /pant‖pænt/ *vi* **1a** to breathe quickly, spasmodically, or in a laboured manner **b** to run panting <~ing *along beside the bicycle*> **c** to make a puffing sound **2** to long eagerly; yearn **3** to throb, pulsate ~*vt* to utter with panting; gasp <~ed *his apologies for arriving so late*>

[2]**pant** *n* **1** a panting breath **2** a puffing sound

pantaloon /ˌpantəˈloohn‖ˌpæntəˈluːn/ *n* **1** a stock character in the commedia dell'arte who is usu a skinny old dotard wearing pantaloons **2** *pl* any of several kinds of men's breeches or trousers; *esp* close-fitting trousers fastened under the calf or instep and worn in the 18th and 19th c

pantechnicon /panˈteknikən‖pænˈteknɪkən/ *n*, *Br* a large van, esp for transporting household possessions, furniture, etc

pantheism /ˈpantheeˑiz(ə)m‖ˈpænθiːɪz(ə)m/ *n* **1** a doctrine that equates God with the forces and laws of nature **2** the indiscriminate worship of all the gods of different religions and cults; *also* toleration of such worship (e g at certain periods of the Roman empire) – **pantheist** *n*, **pantheistic, pantheistical** *adj*, **pantheistically** *adv*

pantheon /ˈpanthiˑən, panˈtheeˑən‖ˈpænθɪən, pænˈθiːən/ *n* **1** a building serving as the burial place of or containing memorials to famous dead **2** the gods of a people; *esp* the officially recognized gods

panther /ˈpanthə‖ˈpænθə/ *n* **1** a leopard, esp of the black colour phase **2** *NAm* a puma

panties /ˈpantiz‖ˈpæntɪz/ *n pl* pants for women or children; *also* knickers

pantile /ˈpanˌtiel‖ˈpænˌtaɪl/ *n* a roofing tile whose transverse section is a flattened S-shape – **pantiled** *adj*

panto /ˈpantoh‖ˈpæntəʊ/ *n*, *Br* PANTOMIME 1b – infml

pantograph /ˈpantəˌgrahf, -ˌgraf‖ˈpæntəˌgrɑːf, -ˌgræf/ *n* **1** an instrument for copying sthg (e g a map) on a predetermined scale **2** a framework mounted on an electric vehicle (e g a railway locomotive) for collecting current from an overhead wire – **pantographic** *adj*

pantomime /ˈpantəˌmiem‖ˈpæntəˌmaɪm/ *n* **1a** any of various dramatic or dancing performances in which a story is told by bodily or facial movements **b** a British theatrical and musical entertainment of the Christmas season based on a nursery tale with stock roles and topical jokes **2** conveyance of a story by bodily or facial movements, esp in drama or dance – **pantomimic** *adj*

pantry /ˈpantri‖ˈpæntrɪ/ *n* **1** a room or cupboard used for storing provisions or tableware **2** a room (e g in a hotel or hospital) for preparation of cold foods to order

pants /pants‖pænts/ *n pl* **1** *chiefly Br* an undergarment that covers the crotch and hips and that may extend to the waist and partly down each leg **2** *chiefly NAm* trousers

ˈ**panty ˌhose** /ˈpanti‖ˈpæntɪ/ *n pl*, *chiefly NAm* tights

[1]**pap** /pap‖pæp/ *n*, *chiefly dial* a nipple, teat

[2]**pap** *n* **1** a soft food for infants or invalids **2** sthg lacking solid value or substance

[1]**papa** /pəˈpah‖pəˈpɑː/ *n*, *chiefly Br* father – formerly used formally, esp in address

[2]**papa** /ˈpapə‖ˈpæpə/ *n* daddy – used informally and by children

papacy /ˈpaypəsi‖ˈpeɪpəsɪ/ *n* **1** the (term of) office of pope **2** *cap* the system of government of the Roman Catholic church of which the pope is the supreme head

papal /ˈpaypl‖ˈpeɪpl/ *adj* of a pope or the Roman Catholic church – **papally** *adv*

papaw /*1* pəˈpaw‖pəˈpɔː; *2* ˈpawpaw, ˈpah-‖ˈpɔːpɔː, ˈpɑː-/ *n* **1** papaya **2** (a N American tree that bears purple flowers and) a yellow edible fruit

papaya /pəˈpieˑə‖pəˈpaɪə/ *n* (a tropical American tree that bears) a large oblong yellow edible fruit

[1]**paper** /ˈpaypə‖ˈpeɪpə/ *n* **1** a sheet of closely compacted vegetable fibres (e g of wood or cloth) **2a** a piece of paper containing a written or printed statement; a document; *specif* a document carried as proof of identity or status – often pl **b** a piece of paper containing writing or print **c** a formal written composition **d** the question set or answers written in an examination in 1 subject **3** a paper container or wrapper **4** a newspaper **5** the negotiable notes or instruments of commerce **6** wallpaper [Middle French *papier*, fr Latin *papyrus* papyrus, paper, fr Greek *papyros* papyrus] – **on paper** in theory; hypothetically

[2]**paper** *vt* to cover or line with paper; *esp* to apply wallpaper to ~*vi* to hang wallpaper – **paperer** *n*

[3]**paper** *adj* **1a** made of paper, thin cardboard, or papier-mâché **b** papery **2** of clerical work or written communication **3** existing only in theory; nominal **4** issued as paper money

ˈ**paperˌback** /-ˌbak‖-ˌbæk/ *n* a book with a flexible paper binding – **paperback** *adj*

ˈ**paperˌboy** /-ˌboy‖-ˌbɔɪ/, *fem* ˈ**paperˌgirl** *n* a boy who delivers or sells newspapers

paper chase *n* a game in which some of the players scatter bits of paper as a trail which others follow to find and catch them

paper clip *n* a small clip made from 2 loops of wire, used for holding sheets of paper together

ˈ**paperˌhanger** /-ˌhangˑə‖-ˌhæŋə/ *n* sby who applies wallpaper to walls

paper knife *n* a knife for slitting envelopes or

unopened pages

paper money *n* bank notes

paper nautilus *n* a mollusc related to the octopuses and squids, the female of which has a delicate papery shell

paper over *vt* **1** to gloss over, explain away, or patch up (e g major differences), esp in order to maintain a semblance of unity **2** to hide, conceal

ˈ**paper**ˌ**weight** /-ˌwayt‖-ˌweɪt/ *n* a usu small heavy object used to hold down loose papers (e g on a desk)

ˈ**paper**ˌ**work** /-ˌwuhk‖-ˌwɜːk/ *n* routine clerical or record-keeping work, often incidental to a more important task

papery /ˈpayp(ə)ri‖ˈpeɪp(ə)rɪ/ *adj* resembling paper in thinness or consistency – **paperiness** *n*

papier-mâché /ˌpapyay ˈmashay, məˈshay, ˈpaypə‖ˌpæpjeɪ ˈmæʃeɪ, məˈʃeɪ, ˈpeɪpə/ *n* a light strong moulding material, made of paper pulped with glue, that is used for making boxes, trays, etc [French, lit., chewed paper] – **papier-mâché** *adj*

papist /ˈpaypist‖ˈpeɪpɪst/ *n, often cap* a Roman Catholic – chiefly derog – **papist** *adj*, **papistry** *n*

papoose /pəˈpoohs‖pəˈpuːs/ *n* a young N American Indian child

paprika /ˈpaprikə, paˈpreekə‖ˈpæprɪkə, pæˈpriːkə/ *n* (a mild to hot red condiment consisting of the finely ground dried pods of) any of various cultivated sweet peppers [Hungarian, fr Serbian, fr *papar* pepper, fr Greek *peperi*]

papyrus /pəˈpie·ərəs‖pəˈpaɪərəs/ *n, pl* **papyruses, papyri** /-rie‖-raɪ/ **1** a tall sedge of the Nile valley **2** the pith of the papyrus plant, esp when made into a material for writing on **3** a usu ancient manuscript written on papyrus

par /pah‖pɑː/ *n* **1a** the established value of the monetary unit of one country expressed in terms of the monetary unit of another country **b** the money value assigned to each share of stock in the charter of a company **2** a common level; equality – esp in *on a par with* **3a** an amount taken as an average or norm **b** an accepted standard; *specif* a usual standard of physical condition or health **4** the standard score (of a good player) for each hole of a golf course – **par** *adj*

para /ˈparə‖ˈpærə/ *n, pl* **paras** a paratrooper

[1]**para-** /parə-‖pærə-/, **par-** *prefix* **1a** beside; alongside <para*thyroid*> **b** beyond <para*normal*> **2** faulty; abnormal <par*aesthesia*> <para*noia*> **3** associated in a subsidiary or auxiliary capacity <para*medical*> **4** closely resembling or related to <para*typhoid*>

[2]**para-** *comb form* parachute <para*trooper*>

parable /ˈparəbl‖ˈpærəbl/ *n* a usu short allegorical story illustrating a moral or religious principle [Middle French, fr Late Latin *parabola*, fr Greek *parabolē*, fr *paraballein* to compare, fr *para* beside + *ballein* to throw]

parabola /pəˈrabələ‖pəˈræbələ/ *n* a plane curve generated by a point moving so that its distance from a fixed point is equal to its distance from a fixed line; the intersection of a right circular cone with a plane parallel to a straight line in the surface of the cone

[1]**parachute** /ˈparəˌshooht‖ˈpærəˌʃuːt/ *n* a folding device of light fabric used esp for ensuring a safe descent of a person or object from a great height (e g from a aeroplane) – **parachutist** *n*

[2]**parachute** *vi* to descend by means of a parachute

Paraclete /ˈparəkleet‖ˈpærəkliːt/ *n* HOLY SPIRIT

[1]**parade** /pəˈrayd‖pəˈreɪd/ *n* **1** an ostentatious show; an exhibition <*made a ~ of his superior knowledge*> **2** the (ceremonial) ordered assembly of a body of troops before a superior officer **3** a public procession **4** *chiefly Br* a row of shops, esp with a service road

[2]**parade** *vt* **1** to cause to manoeuvre or march **2** to exhibit ostentatiously ~ *vi* **1** to march in a procession **2** to promenade **3a** SHOW OFF **b** to masquerade <*myths which ~ as modern science* – M R Cohen> – **parader** *n*

paradigm /ˈparədiem‖ˈpærədaɪm/ *n* **1** an example or pattern **2** an example of a conjugation or declension showing a word in all its inflectional forms – **paradigmatic** *adj*

paradise /ˈparədies‖ˈpærədaɪs/ *n* **1** *often cap* **1a** the garden of Eden **b** Heaven **2** a place of bliss, felicity, or delight – **paradisiacal** *adj*

paradox /ˈparəˌdoks‖ˈpærəˌdɒks/ *n* **1** a tenet contrary to received opinion **2a** a statement that is apparently contradictory or absurd and yet might be true **b** a self-contradictory statement that at first seems true **3** sthg (e g a person, condition, or act) with seemingly contradictory qualities or phases [Latin *paradoxum*, fr Greek *paradoxon*, fr *paradoxos* contrary to expectation, fr *para* beside, beyond + *doxa* opinion]

paraffin /ˈparəfin, ˌ--ˈ-‖ˈpærəfɪn, ˌ--ˈ-/ *n* **1** a usu waxy inflammable mixture of hydrocarbons obtained from distillates of wood, coal, petroleum, etc and used chiefly in candles, chemical synthesis, and cosmetics **2** an alkane **3** an inflammable liquid hydrocarbon obtained by distillation of petroleum and used esp as a fuel – **paraffinic** *adj*

paragon /ˈparəgən‖ˈpærəgən/ *n* a model of excellence or perfection

paragraph /ˈparəˌgrahf, -ˌgraf‖ˈpærəˌgrɑːf, -ˌgræf/ *n* **1a** a usu indented division of a written composition that develops a single point or idea **b** a composition or news item that is complete in 1 paragraph **2** a sign (e g ¶) used as a reference mark or to indicate the beginning of a paragraph – **paragraph** *vt*, **paragraphic** *adj*

parakeet, *NAm also* **parrakeet** /ˌparəˈkeet, ˈ- -ˌ-‖ˌpærəˈkiːt, ˈ--ˌ-/ *n* any of numerous usu small slender long-tailed parrots

[1]**parallel** /ˈparəlel‖ˈpærəlel/ *adj* **1a** extending in the same direction, everywhere equidistant, and not meeting <*~ rows of trees*> **b** everywhere equally distant <*concentric spheres are ~*> **2** being or relating to an electrical circuit having a number of conductors in parallel **3** analogous, comparable

[2]**parallel** *n* **1a** a parallel line, curve, or surface **b** a circle or line of latitude on (a globe or map of) the earth **c** a sign ‖ used as a reference mark – often pl with sing. meaning **2** sby or sthg equal or similar in all essential particulars; a

counterpart, analogue **3** a comparison to show resemblance <*drew a* ~ *between the 2 states*> **4a** the state of being physically parallel **b** the arrangement of 2-terminal electrical devices in which one terminal of each device is joined to one conductor and the others are joined to another conductor

[3]**parallel** *vt* **1** to compare **2a** to equal, match <*no one has* ~ed *my success in business*> **b** to correspond to

[4]**parallel** *adv* in a parallel manner

,parallel 'bars *n pl but sing or pl in constr* (a men's gymnastic event using) a pair of bars supported horizontally 1.7m (5ft 7in) above the floor usu by a common base

parallelism /'parəleliz(ə)m‖'pærəlelɪz(ə)m/ *n* **1** the quality or state of being parallel **2** a resemblance, correspondence

parallelogram /,parə'leləgram‖,pærə'leləgræm/ *n* a quadrilateral with opposite sides parallel and equal

paralysis /pə'raləsis‖pə'ræləsɪs/ *n, pl* **paralyses** /-seez‖-siːz/ **1** (partial) loss of function, esp when involving motion or sensation in a part of the body **2** loss of the ability to move **3** a state of powerlessness or incapacity to act – **paralyse**, *NAm* **paralyze** *vt*, **paralysation** *n*

[1]**paralytic** /,parə'litik‖,pærə'lɪtɪk/ *adj* **1** of, resembling, or affected with paralysis **2** *chiefly Br* very drunk – infml

[2]**paralytic** *n* one suffering from paralysis

parameter /pə'ramitə‖pə'ræmɪtə/ *n* **1** an arbitrary constant whose value characterizes a member of a system (e g a family of curves) **2** a characteristic, factor <*political dissent as a* ~ *of modern life*> – **parametric** *also* **parametrical** *adj*, *parametrically adv*

paramilitary /,parə'milit(ə)ri‖,pærə'mɪlɪt(ə)rɪ/ *adj* formed on a military pattern (as a potential auxiliary military force) <*a* ~ *border patrol*>

paramount /'parəmownt‖'pærəmaʊnt/ *adj* superior to all others; supreme

paramour /'parəmooə‖'pærəmʊə/ *n* an illicit lover; *esp* a mistress

paranoia /,parə'noyə‖,pærə'nɔɪə/ *n* **1** a mental disorder characterized by delusions of persecution or grandeur **2** a tendency towards excessive or irrational suspiciousness and distrustfulness of others – **paranoiac** *adj or n*, **paranoid** *adj or n*

paranormal /parə'nawml‖pærə'nɔːml/ *adj* not scientifically explainable; supernatural – **paranormally** *adv*, **paranormality** *n*

parapet /'parəpit, -pet‖'pærəpɪt, -pet/ *n* **1** a wall, rampart, or elevation of earth or stone to protect soldiers **2** a low wall or balustrade to protect the edge of a platform, roof, or bridge – **parapeted** *adj*

paraphernalia /,parəfə'naylyə‖,pærəfə'neɪljə/ *n pl but sing or pl in constr* **1** personal belongings **2a** articles of equipment **b** accessory items [Medieval Latin, personal property of a married woman, deriv of Greek *parapherna* goods a bride brings in addition to the dowry, fr *para* beside, beyond + *phernē* dowry, fr *pherein* to bear]

[1]**paraphrase** /'parə,frayz‖'pærə,freɪz/ *n* a restatement of a text, passage, or work giving the meaning in another form

[2]**paraphrase** *vb* to make a paraphrase (of) – **paraphrasable** *adj*, **paraphraser** *n*

paraplegia /,parə'pleejə‖,pærə'pliːdʒə/ *n* paralysis of the lower half of the body including the legs – **paraplegic** *adj or n*

paraquat /'parəkwot, -kwat‖'pærəkwɒt, -kwæt/ *n* a very poisonous herbicide used esp as a weedkiller

parasite /'parəsiet‖'pærəsaɪt/ *n* **1** an organism living in or on another organism in parasitism **2** sthg resembling a biological parasite in dependence on sthg else for existence or support without making a useful or adequate return – **parasitic** *also* **parasitical** *adj*, **parasitically** *adv*, **parasitology** *n*, **parasitologist** *n*

parasitism /'parəsie,tiz(ə)m‖'pærəsaɪ,tɪz(ə)m/ *n* an intimate association between organisms of 2 or more kinds in which a parasite benefits at the expense of a host – **parasitize** *vt*

parasol /'parəsol‖'pærəsɒl/ *n* a lightweight umbrella used, esp by women, as a protection from the sun

parathyroid /,parə'thie·əroyd‖,pærə'θaɪərɔɪd/, **parathyroid gland** *n* any of 4 small endocrine glands near the thyroid gland that produce a hormone – **parathyroid** *adj*

paratroops /'parə,troohps‖'pærə,truːps/ *n pl* troops trained and equipped to parachute from an aeroplane – **paratrooper** *n*

paratyphoid /,parə'tiefoyd‖,pærə'taɪfɔɪd/ *n* a disease caused by salmonella that resembles typhoid fever and is commonly contracted by eating contaminated food – **paratyphoid** *adj*

parboil /'pah,boyl‖'pɑː,bɔɪl/ *vt* to boil briefly as a preliminary or incomplete cooking procedure

[1]**parcel** /'pahsl‖'pɑːsl/ *n* **1** a plot of land **2** PACK 2a **3** a wrapped bundle; a package

[2]**parcel** *vt* **-ll-** (*NAm* **-l-, -ll-**) **1** to divide into parts; distribute – often + *out* **2** to make up into a parcel; wrap – often + *up* **3** to cover (e g a rope) with strips of canvas

parch /pahch‖pɑːtʃ/ *vt* **1** to roast (e g peas) slightly in a dry heat **2** to make dry or scorched ~*vi* to become dry or scorched

parchment /'pahchmənt‖'pɑːtʃmənt/ *n* **1** the skin of an animal, esp of a sheep or goat, prepared for writing on **2** strong paper made to resemble parchment **3** a parchment manuscript [Old French *parchemin*, fr Latin *pergamena*, fr Greek *pergamēnē*, fr *Pergamēnos* of Pergamum, fr *Pergamon* Pergamum, ancient city in Asia Minor]

pard /pahd‖pɑːd/ *n, archaic* a leopard

[1]**pardon** /'pahdn‖'pɑːdn/ *n* **1** INDULGENCE 1 **2** a release from legal penalties **3** excuse or forgiveness for a fault, offence, or discourtesy

[2]**pardon** *vt* **1** to absolve from the consequences of a fault or crime **2** to allow (an offence) to pass without punishment – **pardonable** *adj*, **pardonably** *adv*

pardoner /'pahd(ə)nə‖'pɑːd(ə)nə/ *n* a medieval preacher delegated to raise money by granting indulgences

pare /peə‖peə/ *vt* **1** to cut or shave off **1a** (an outer surface) < ~ *the skin from an apple*> **b** the outer surface of < ~ *an apple*> **2** to diminish gradually (as if) by paring < ~ *expenses*> – **parer** *n*

parent /'peərənt‖'peərənt/ *n* **1** sby who begets or brings forth offspring; a father or mother **2a** an animal or plant regarded in relation to its offspring **b** the material or source from which sthg is derived – **parent** *adj*, **parenthood** *n*, **parental** *adj*, **parentally** *adv*

parentage /'peərəntij‖'peərəntɪdʒ/ *n* descent from parents or ancestors; lineage <*a woman of noble* ~>

parenthesis /pə'renthəsis‖pə'renθəsɪs/ *n, pl* **parentheses** /-,seez‖-,si:z/ **1a** an amplifying or explanatory word or phrase inserted in a passage from which, in writing, it is usu set off by punctuation **b** either or both of the curved marks (or) used in writing and printing to enclose a parenthesis or to group a symbolic unit in a logical or mathematical expression **2** an interlude, interval – **parenthetic, parenthetical** *adj*, **parenthetically** *adv*

parent-teacher association *n sing or pl in constr* an organization of teachers at a school and the parents of their pupils, that works for the improvement of the school

par excellence /pah'reks(ə)ləns ‖pɑ:'reks-(ə)ləns (*Fr* par ɛksɛlɑ̃:s)/ *adj* being the best example of a kind; without equal – used postpositively <*the dictionary* ~> [French, lit., by excellence]

pariah /pə'rie·ə, 'pari·ə‖pə'raɪə, 'pærɪə/ *n* **1** a member of a low caste of S India and Burma **2** an outcast

parietal /pə'rie·ətl‖pə'raɪətl/ *adj* **1** of the walls of an anatomical part or cavity **2** of or forming the upper rear wall of the skull

pari-mutuel /,pari 'myoohtyooəl‖,pærɪ-'mju:tjʊəl/ *n* **1** a betting pool in which those who bet on the winners of the first 3 places share the total amount bet, minus a percentage for the management **2** *NAm* a totalizator

paring /'peəring‖'peərɪŋ/ *n* **1** the act of cutting away an edge or surface **2** sthg pared off <*apple* ~s>

parish /'parish‖'pærɪʃ/ *n* **1** the subdivision of a diocese served by a single church or clergyman **2** a unit of local government in rural England, often coinciding with an original ecclesiastical parish

parishioner /pə'rish(ə)nə‖pə'rɪʃ(ə)nə/ *n* a member or inhabitant of a parish

[1]**parity** /'parəti‖'pærətɪ/ *n* **1** the quality or state of being equal or equivalent **2** equivalence of a commodity price expressed in one currency to its price expressed in another **3a** the property of an integer with respect to being odd or even <*3 and 7 have the same* ~> **b** the state of being odd or even that is the basis of a method of detecting errors in binary-coded data **4** the property whereby a quantity (e g the charge of an elementary particle) changes from positive to negative or vice versa or remains unaltered during a particular interaction or reaction

[2]**parity** *n* the state or fact of having borne offspring; *also* the number of children previously borne

[1]**park** /pahk‖pɑ:k/ *n* **1** an enclosed area of lawns, woodland, pasture, etc attached to a country house and used as a game reserve or for recreation **2a** an area of land for recreation in or near a city or town **b** an area maintained in its natural state as a public property **3** an assigned space for military animals, vehicles, or materials **4a** *Br* a pitch where professional soccer is played **b** *NAm* an arena or stadium used for ball games

[2]**park** *vt* **1a** to leave or place (a vehicle) for a time, esp at the roadside or in a car park or garage **b** to land or leave (e g an aeroplane) **c** to establish (e g a satellite) in orbit **2** to assemble (e g equipment or stores) in a military dump or park **3** to set and leave temporarily – infml < ~ed *her boyfriend at the bar*> to park a vehicle – **parker** *n*

parka /'pahkə‖'pɑ:kə/ *n* **1** a hooded fur garment for wearing in the arctic **2** an anorak

parkin /'pahkin‖'pɑ:kɪn/ *n* a thick heavy ginger cake made with oatmeal and treacle

parking ,lot *n, NAm* an outdoor car park

parking ,meter *n* a coin-operated device which registers the payment and displays the time allowed for parking a motor vehicle

Parkinson's di,sease /'pahkins(ə)nz‖pɑ:kɪns(ə)nz/ *n* tremor, weakness of resting muscles, and a peculiar gait occurring in later life as a progressive nervous disease [James *Parkinson* (1755-1824), English physician] – **parkinsonian** *adj*

Parkinson's Law *n* an observation in office organization: work expands so as to fill the time available for its completion [C Northcote *Parkinson* (born 1909), English historian]

parkland /'pahk,land‖'pɑ:k,lænd/ *n* land with clumps of trees and shrubs in cultivated condition suitable for use as a park

parky /'pahki‖'pɑ:kɪ/ *adj, Br* CHILLY 1 – infml

parlance /'pahləns‖'pɑ:ləns/ *n* manner of speech and esp choice of words <*in legal* ~>

[1]**parley** /'pahli‖'pɑ:lɪ/ *vi* to speak with another; confer; *specif* to discuss terms with an enemy

[2]**parley** *n* a conference for discussion of points in dispute; *specif* a conference under truce to discuss terms with an enemy

parliament /'pahləmənt, ‖'pɑ:ləmənt,*also* -lyə-‖-ljə-/ *n* **1** a formal conference for the discussion of public affairs **2** *often cap* the supreme legislative body of the UK that consists of the House of Commons and the House of Lords and is called together and dissolved by the sovereign; *also* a similar body in another nation or state [Old French *parlement*, fr *parler* to speak, deriv of Late Latin *parabola* parable, speech –see PARABLE]

parliamentarian /,pahləmən'teəri·ən, -men-, ‖,pɑ:ləmən'teərɪən, -men-,*also* -lyə-‖-ljə-/ *n* **1** *often cap* an adherent of the parliament during the Civil War **2** an expert in parliamentary rules and practice **3** *Br* a Member of Parliament

,parlia'mentary /,pahlə'ment(ə)ri, ‖,pɑ:lə-'ment(ə)rɪ,*also* -lyə-‖-ljə-/ *adj* **1** of, appropriate to, or enacted by a parliament **2** of or supporting the parliament during the Civil War

[1]**parlour**, *NAm* **parlor** /'pahlə‖'pɑ:lə/ *n* **1a** a

room in a private house for the entertainment of guests **b** a room in an inn, hotel, or club for conversation or semiprivate uses **2** any of various business places <*a funeral* ~> <*a beauty* ~> **3** a place for milking cows

[2]**parlour** *adj* fostered or advocated in comfortable seclusion without consequent action or application to affairs

ˈ**parlour ˌgame** *n* an indoor word game, board game, etc

parlous /ˈpahləs‖ˈpɑːləs/ *adj* full of uncertainty and danger – fml or humor

Parmesan /ˌpahmiˈzan, ˈ---‖ˌpɑːmɪˈzæn, ˈ---/ *n* a very hard dry strongly flavoured cheese that is often used grated [French *parmesan* of Parma, fr *Parma*, city in Italy]

parochial /pəˈrohki·əl‖pəˈrəʊkɪəl/ *adj* **1** of a (church) parish **2** limited in range or scope (e g to a narrow area or region); provincial, narrow – **parochially** *adv*

[1]**parody** /ˈparədi‖ˈpærədɪ/ *n* **1** a literary or musical work in which the style of an author is imitated for comic or satirical effect **2** a feeble or ridiculous imitation – **parodic** *adj*, **parodist** *n*

[2]**parody** *vt* to compose a parody on <~ *a poem*>

[1]**parole** /pəˈrohl‖pəˈrəʊl/ *n* **1** a pledge of one's honour; *esp* the promise of a prisoner of war to fulfil stated conditions in consideration of release or the granting of privileges **2** a password given only to officers of the guard and of the day **3** a conditional release of a prisoner **4** linguistic behaviour

[2]**parole** *vt* to put on parole – **parolee** *n*

paroxysm /ˈparəkˌsiz(ə)m‖ˈpærəkˌsɪz(ə)m/ *n* **1** a fit, attack, or sudden increase or recurrence of (disease) symptoms; a convulsion <*a* ~ *of coughing*> **2** a sudden violent emotion or action <*a* ~ *of rage*> – **paroxysmal** *adj*

[1]**parquet** /ˈpahkay, -ki‖ˈpɑːkeɪ, -kɪ/ *vt* **parqueted** /ˈpahkayd‖ˈpɑːkeɪd/; **parqueting** /ˈpahkaying‖ˈpɑːkeɪɪŋ/ to furnish with a floor of parquetry

[2]**parquet** *n* parquetry

parquetry /ˈpahkitri‖ˈpɑːkɪtrɪ/ *n* work in the form of usu geometrically patterned wood laid or inlaid esp for floors

parr /pah‖pɑː/ *n, pl* **parr** *also* **parrs** a young salmon actively feeding in fresh water

parricide /ˈparisied‖ˈpærɪsaɪd/ *n* (the act of) sby who murders his/her father, mother, or a close relative – **parricidal** *adj*

[1]**parrot** /ˈparət‖ˈpærət/ *n* **1** any of numerous chiefly tropical birds that have a distinctive stout hooked bill, are often crested and brightly variegated, and are excellent mimics **2** a person who parrots another's words

[2]**parrot** *vt* to repeat or imitate (e g another's words) without understanding or thought

parry /ˈpari‖ˈpærɪ/ *vi* to ward off a weapon or blow ~ *vt* **1** to ward off (e g a blow) **2** to evade, esp by an adroit answer <~ *an embarrassing question*> – **parry** *n*

parse /pahz‖pɑːz/ *vt* **1** to resolve (e g a sentence) into component parts of speech and describe them grammatically **2** to describe grammatically by stating the part of speech and the inflectional and syntactic relationships

Parsi, **Parsee** /ˌpahˈsee, ˈ-ˌ-‖ˌpɑːˈsiː, ˈ-ˌ-/ *n* a Zoroastrian descended from Persian refugees settled principally in Bombay

parsimonious /ˌpahsiˈmohnyəs‖ˌpɑːsɪˈməʊnjəs/ *adj* frugal to the point of stinginess; niggardly – **parsimoniously** *adv*

parsimony /ˈpahsiməni‖ˈpɑːsɪmənɪ/ *n* **1** the quality of being careful with money or resources; thrift **2** the quality or state of being niggardly; stinginess

parsley /ˈpahsli‖ˈpɑːslɪ/ *n* an orig S European plant of the carrot family widely cultivated for its leaves used as a herb or garnish in cooking [Old English *petersilie*, deriv of Latin *petroselinum*, fr Greek *petroselinon*, fr *petros* stone + *selinon* celery]

parsnip /ˈpahsnip‖ˈpɑːsnɪp/ *n* (the long edible tapering root of) a European plant of the carrot family with large leaves and yellow flowers

parson /ˈpahs(ə)n‖ˈpɑːs(ə)n/ *n* **1** the incumbent of a parish **2** a clergyman

parsonage /ˈpahsənij‖ˈpɑːsənɪdʒ/ *n* the house provided by a church for its parson

ˌ**parson's ˈnose** /ˈpahs(ə)nz‖ˈpɑːs(ə)nz/ *n* the fatty extension of the rump of a cooked fowl

[1]**part** /paht‖pɑːt/ *n* **1a(1)** any of the often indefinite or unequal subdivisions into which sthg is (regarded as) divided and which together constitute the whole **a(2)** an essential portion or integral element **b** an amount equal to another amount <*mix 1* ~ *of the powder with 3* ~s *of water*> **c(1)** an organ, member, or other constituent element of a plant or animal body **c(2)** *pl* PRIVATE PARTS **d** a division of a literary work **e(1)** a vocal or instrumental line or melody in concerted music or in harmony **e(2)** (the score for) a particular voice or instrument in concerted music **f** a constituent member of an apparatus (e g a machine); *also* SPARE PART **2** sthg falling to one in a division or apportionment; a share **3** any of the opposing sides in a conflict or dispute <*took his son's* ~ *in the argument*> **4** a portion of an unspecified territorial area <*took off for unknown* ~s> **5** a function or course of action performed <*the government's* ~ *in the strike*> <*did you take* ~ *in the fighting?*> **6a** an actor's lines in a play **b** ROLE 1b **7** a constituent of character or capacity; a talent <*a man of many* ~s> **8** *NAm* [1]PARTING 2 – **for the most part** in most cases or respects; mainly – **in part** in some degree; partly – **on the part of** with regard to the one specified

[2]**part** *vi* **1a** to separate from or take leave of sby **b** to take leave of one another **2** to become separated into parts <*the clouds* ~ed *and the sun appeared*> **3** to become separated, detached, or broken <*the strands of the rope* ~ed> **4** to relinquish possession or control, esp reluctantly <*hated to* ~ *with her money*> ~ *vt* **1a** to divide into parts **b** to separate (the hair) by combing on each side of a line **2a** to remove from contact or association; separate <*till death do us* ~> **b** to hold (e g combatants) apart

[3]**part** *adv* partly <*a centaur is* ~ *man* ~ *horse*>

[4]**part** *adj* PARTIAL 3

partake /pahˈtayk‖pɑːˈteɪk/ *vi* **partook** /-ˈtook‖-ˈtʊk/; **partaken** /-ˈtaykən‖-ˈteɪkən/ to take a part or share; participate – usu + *in* or *of*;

fml – **partaker** *n*

parterre /pahˈteə‖pɑːˈteə/ *n* an ornamental garden with paths between the beds

ˌparthenogenesis /ˌpahthinohˈjenəsis‖ˌpɑːθɪnəʊˈdʒenəsɪs/ *n* reproduction by development of an unfertilized gamete that occurs esp among lower plants and invertebrate animals – **parthenogenetic** *adj*

[1]**partial** /ˈpahsh(ə)l‖ˈpɑːʃ(ə)l/ *adj* **1** inclined to favour one party more than the other; biased **2** markedly fond of sby or sthg – + *to* <*~ to beans*> **3** of a part rather than the whole; not general or total <*a ~ solution*> – **partially** *adv*

[2]**partial** *n* OVERTONE 1a

partiality /ˌpahshiˈaləti‖ˌpɑːʃɪˈælətɪ/ *n* **1** the quality or state of being partial; a bias **2** a special taste or liking

participate /pahˈtisipayt‖pɑːˈtɪsɪpeɪt/ *vi* **1** TAKE PART **2** to have a part or share in sthg – **participator** *n*, **participant** *n*, **participation** *n*, **participatory** *adj*

participle /ˈpahtiˌsipl, pahˈtisipl‖ˈpɑːtɪˌsɪpl, pɑːˈtɪsɪpl/ *n* a verbal form (e g *singing* or *sung*) that has the function of an adjective and at the same time can be used in compound verb forms – **participial** *adj*

particle /ˈpahtikl‖ˈpɑːtɪkl/ *n* **1** a minute subdivision of matter (e g an electron, atom or molecule) **2** a minute quantity or fragment **3a** a minor unit of speech including all uninflected words or all words except nouns and verbs; *esp* FUNCTION WORD **b** AFFIX 1

parti-coloured /ˈpahti‖ˈpɑːtɪ/ *adj* showing different colours or tints <*~ threads*>

[1]**particular** /pəˈtikyoolə‖pəˈtɪkjʊlə/ *adj* **1** of or being a single person or thing; specific <*the ~ person I had in mind*> **2** detailed, exact **3** worthy of notice; special, unusual <*there was nothing in the letter of ~ importance*> **4** *of a proposition in logic* predicating a term of some but not all members of a specified class **5a** concerned over or attentive to details; meticulous **b** hard to please; exacting – **particularity** *n*

[2]**particular** *n* an individual fact, point, circumstance, or detail <*complete in every ~*> – **in particular** particularly, especially

particular·ize, -ise /pəˈtikyooləriez‖pəˈtɪkjʊləraɪz/ *vt* to state in detail; specify ~ *vi* to go into details – **particularization** *n*

particularly /pəˈtikyooləli‖pəˈtɪkjʊləlɪ/ *adv* **1** in a particular manner; IN DETAIL **2** to an unusual degree

[1]**parting** /ˈpahting‖ˈpɑːtɪŋ/ *n* **1** a place or point where a division or separation occurs **2 parting**, *NAm* **part** the line where the hair is parted

[2]**parting** *adj* given, taken, or performed at parting <*a ~ kiss*>

[1]**partisan, partizan** /ˌpahtiˈzan‖ˌpɑːtɪˈzæn/ *n* **1** a firm adherent to a party, faction, cause, or person; *esp* one exhibiting blind, prejudiced, and unreasoning allegiance **2** a guerrilla – **partisan** *adj*, **partisanship** *n*

[2]**partisan, partizan** *n* a weapon of the 16th and 17th c consisting of a broad blade mounted on a long shaft

[1]**partition** /pahˈtish(ə)n‖pɑːˈtɪʃ(ə)n/ *n* **1a** division into parts **b** separation of a class or whole into constituent elements **2** sthg that divides; *esp* a light interior dividing wall **3** a part or section of a whole – **partitionist** *n*

[2]**partition** *vt* **1** to divide into parts or shares **2** to divide or separate *off* by a partition <*can we ~ off part of the room to use as an office?*>

partitive /ˈpahtətiv‖ˈpɑːtətɪv/ *adj* of or denoting a part of a whole – **partitively** *adv*

partly /ˈpahtli‖ˈpɑːtlɪ/ *adv* in some measure or degree; partially

[1]**partner** /ˈpahtnə‖ˈpɑːtnə/ *n* **1a** either of a couple who dance together **b** sby who plays with 1 or more others in a game against an opposing side **c** a person with whom one is having a sexual relationship; a spouse, lover, etc **2** a member of a partnership

[2]**partner** *vt* **1** to act as a partner to **2** to provide with a partner

ˈpartnership /-ship‖-ʃɪp/ *n* **1** the state of being a partner; association **2** (a legal relation between) 2 or more joint principals in a business **3** an association involving close cooperation

ˌpart of ˈspeech *n* a class of words distinguished according to the kind of idea denoted and the function performed in a sentence

partridge /ˈpahtrij‖ˈpɑːtrɪdʒ/ *n* any of various typically medium-sized stout-bodied Old World game birds with variegated plumage

ˈpart-ˌsong *n* a usu unaccompanied song consisting of 2 or more voice parts with 1 part carrying the melody

ˌpart-ˈtime *adj* involving or working less than customary or standard hours <*a ~ job*> <*~ students*> – **part-time** *adv*, **part-timer** *n*

parturition /ˌpahtyooˈrish(ə)n‖ˌpɑːtjʊˈrɪʃ(ə)n/ *n* the action or process of giving birth to offspring

party /ˈpahti‖ˈpɑːtɪ/ *n* **1a** a person or group taking 1 side of a question, dispute, or contest **b** *sing or pl constr* a group of people organized to carry out an activity or fulfil a function together <*sent out a search ~*> **2** *sing or pl in constr* a group organized for political involvement **3** one who is involved; a participant – usu + *to* <*a ~ to the transaction*> **4** a (festive) social gathering **5** sby who is concerned in an action or activity – chiefly fml <*a third ~ was involved*> <*is this the guilty ~?*> **6** a particular individual – infml <*a shameless old ~*>

party line *n* **1** a single telephone line connecting 2 or more subscribers with an exchange **2** the official principles of a political party

party wall *n* a wall which divides 2 adjoining properties and in which each owner has a joint interest

parvenu /ˈpahvənyooh‖ˈpɑːvənjuː/ *n* a person of low social position who has recently or suddenly acquired wealth or power; an upstart [French, fr past participle of *parvenir* to arrive, fr Latin *pervenire*, fr *per* through + *venire* to come] – **parvenu, parvenue** *adj*

paschal /ˈpaskl‖ˈpæskl/ *adj* **1** of the Passover **2** of or appropriate to Easter

pasha /ˈpahshə, ˈpashə‖ˈpɑːʃə, ˈpæʃə/ *n* a man of high rank or office (e g in Turkey or N Africa) <*Glubb* Pasha>

[1]**pass** /pahs‖pɑːs/ *vi* **1** to move, proceed **2a** to go away <*the panic* ~ed *very quickly*> – often

+ *off* <*his headache had* ~ed *off by lunchtime*> **b** to die – often + *on* or *away*; euph **3a** to go by; move past <*waved from the car window as she* ~ed> **b** *of time* to elapse <*4 years* ~ed *before we met again*> **c** to overtake another vehicle <*we can* ~ *once we're round this bend*> **4a** to go across, over, or through <*allow no one to* ~> **b** to go uncensured or unchallenged <*let her remark* ~> **5** to go from one quality, state, or form to another <~es *from a liquid to a gaseous state*> **6a** to pronounce a judgment **b** to be legally pronounced **7** to go from the control or possession of one person or group to that of another <*the throne* ~ed *to the king's daughter*> **8** to take place as a mutual exchange or transaction <*angry words* ~ed *between them*> **9a** to become approved by a body (e g a legislature) <*the proposal* ~ed> **b** to undergo an inspection, test, or examination successfully **10a** to be accepted or regarded as adequate or fitting <*it's only a quick repair but it will* ~> **b** to resemble or act the part of so well as to be accepted – usu + *for* **11** to kick, throw, or hit a ball or puck to a teammate **12** to decline to bid, bet, or play in a card game ~ *vt* **1** to go beyond: e g **1a** to surpass, exceed <~es *all expectations*> **b** to advance or develop beyond <*societies that have* ~ed *the feudal stage*> **c** to go by; move past **2a** to go across, over, or through <~ *a barrier*> **b** to spend (time) <~ed *the holidays at her sister's home*> **3a** to secure the approval of (e g a legislative body) **b** to succeed in satisfying the requirements of (a test, inspection, or examination) **4a** to cause or permit to win approval or sanction <~ *a law*> **b** to accept (sby or sthg) after examination <*I can't* ~ *this bad piece of work!*> **5a** to put in circulation <~ *bad cheques*> **b** to transfer from one person to another <*please* ~ *the salt*> **c** to move or place, esp in or for a short time <~ed *his hand across his brow*> <~ *a rope round a tree*> **d** to throw, hit, or kick (a ball or puck), esp to a teammate **6a** to pronounce judicially <~ *sentence*> **b** to utter – esp in *pass a comment, pass a remark* **7a** to cause or permit to go past or through a barrier **b** to cause to march or go by in order <~ *the troops in review*> **8** to emit or discharge from a bodily part, esp the bowels or bladder **9** to hit a ball past (an opponent), esp in tennis – **in passing** as a relevant digression; parenthetically – **pass muster** to be found adequate, esp in passing an inspection or examination – **pass the buck** to shift a responsibility to sby else – **past the time of day** to give or exchange friendly greetings – **pass water** to urinate – euph

²pass *n* a narrow passage over low ground in a mountain range

³pass *n* **1** a usu distressing or bad state of affairs – often in *come to a pretty pass* **2a** a written permission to move about freely in a place or to leave or enter it **b** a written leave of absence from a military post or station for a brief period **c** a permit or ticket allowing free transport or free admission **3** a movement of the hands over or along sthg **4** the passing of an examination <*2 A-level* ~es> **5** a single complete mechanical operation (e g in manufacturing or data processing) **6a** an act of passing in cards, soccer, rugby, etc; *also* a ball or puck passed **b** a ball hit to the side and out of reach of an opponent, esp in tennis **7** a single passage or movement of a man-made object (e g an aircraft) over a place or towards a target **8** a sexually inviting gesture or approach – usu in *make a pass at*

passable /'pahsəbl‖'pɑːsəbl/ *adj* **1** capable of being passed, crossed, or travelled on <~ *roads*> **2** barely good enough; tolerable – **passably** *adv*

passage /'pasij‖'pæsɪdʒ/ *n* **1** the action or process of passing from one place or condition to another **2a** a way of exit or entrance; a road, path, channel, or course by which sthg passes **b** a corridor or lobby giving access to the different rooms or parts of a building or apartment **3a(1)** a specified act of travelling or passing, esp by sea or air <*a rough* ~> **a(2)** a right to be conveyed as a passenger <*secured a* ~ *to France*> **b** the passing of a legislative measure **4** a right, liberty, or permission to pass **5a** a brief noteworthy portion of a written work or speech **b** a phrase or short section of a musical composition **6** passing sthg or undergoing a passing **7** incubation of a pathogen (e g a virus) in culture, a living organism, or a developing egg

'passage,way /-,way‖-,weɪ/ *n* a corridor

pass away *vi* **1** to go out of existence **2** to die – euph

'pass,book /-,book‖-,bʊk/ *n* a (building society) account-holder's book in which deposits and withdrawals are recorded

passé /'pahsay, 'pasay‖'pɑːseɪ, 'pæseɪ/ *adj* **1** outmoded **2** behind the times

passenger /'pasinjə, -s(ə)n-‖'pæsɪndʒə, -sɪ(ə)n-/ *n* **1** sby who travels in, but does not operate, a public or private conveyance **2** *chiefly Br* a member of a group who contributes little or nothing to the functioning or productivity of the group

passe-partout /,pahs pah'tooh‖,pɑːs pɑː'tuː/ *n* **1** MASTER KEY **2** a strong paper gummed on 1 side and used esp for mounting pictures [French, fr *passe partout* pass everywhere]

passerby /,pahsə'bie‖,pɑːsə'baɪ/ *n, pl* **passersby** /,pahsəz-‖,pɑːsəz-/ a person who happens by chance to pass by a particular place

passim /'pasim‖'pæsɪm/ *adv* HERE AND THERE 1 [Latin, fr *passus* scattered, fr past participle of *pandere* to spread]

passing /'pahsing‖'pɑːsɪŋ/ *adj* **1** going by or past <*a* ~ *pedestrian*> **2** having a brief duration <*a* ~ *whim*> **3** superficial **4** of or used in or for passing <*a* ~ *place in a road*>

passion /'pash(ə)n‖'pæʃ(ə)n/ *n* **1** *often cap* **1a** the sufferings of Christ between the night of the Last Supper and his death **b** a musical setting of a gospel account of the Passion story **2a** intense, driving, or uncontrollable feeling **b** an outbreak of anger **3a** ardent affection; love **b** (the object of) a strong liking, devotion, or interest **c** strong sexual desire – **passional** *adj*

passionate /'pash(ə)nət‖'pæʃ(ə)nət/ *adj* **1** easily aroused to anger **2a** capable of, affected by, or expressing intense feeling, esp love, hatred, or anger **b** extremely enthusiastic; keen <*a* ~

interest in sport> – **passionately** *adv*, **passionateness** *n*

'passion,flower /-,flowə‖-,flaʊə/ *n* any of a genus of chiefly tropical plants with usu showy flowers and pulpy often edible berries

'passion ,play *n, often cap 1st P* a dramatic representation of the passion and crucifixion of Christ

,Passion 'Sunday *n* the fifth Sunday in Lent

'Passion ,Week *n* the second week before Easter

[1]passive /'pasiv‖'pæsɪv/ *adj* **1a** acted on, receptive to, or influenced by external forces or impressions **b** *of a verb form or voice* expressing an action that is done to the grammatical subject of a sentence (e g *was hit* in 'the ball was hit') **c** *esp of an animal* placid **d** *of a person* lacking in energy, will, or initiative; meekly accepting **2a** not active or operative; inert **b** of or characterized by chemical inactivity; *esp* resistant to corrosion **c** not involving expenditure of chemical energy <~ *transport across a cell membrane*> **d** relating to or being an electronic component (e g a capacitor or resistor) or network of components whose characteristics cannot be controlled electronically and which show no gain **e** operating solely by means of the power of an input signal <*a* ~ *communication satellite that reflects radio waves*> **f** operating by intercepting signals emitted from a target <*a* ~ *homing missile*> **3** offering no resistance; submissive <~ *surrender to fate*> – **passively** *adv*, **passiveness** *n*, **passivity** *n*

[2]passive *n* the passive voice of a verb

passive resistance *n* resistance characterized by nonviolent noncooperation

passkey /'pahs,kee‖'pɑːs,kiː/ *n* MASTER KEY

pass off *vt* **1** to present with intent to deceive **2** to give a false identity or character to <passed *herself* off *as a millionairess*> ~*vi* to take place and be completed <*his stay in France* passed off *smoothly* – *TLS*>

pass out *vi* **1** to lose consciousness **2** *chiefly Br* to finish a period of (military) training

Passover /'pahsohvə‖'pɑːsəʊvə/ *n* the Jewish celebration of the liberation of the Hebrews from slavery in Egypt

pass over *vt* **1** to ignore in passing <*I will* pass over *this aspect of the book in silence*> **2** to pay no attention to the claims of; disregard <*was* passed over *for the chairmanship*>

passport /'pahs,pawt‖'pɑːs,pɔːt/ *n* **1** an official document issued by a government **1a** as proof of identity and nationality to one of its citizens for use when leaving or reentering the country and affording some protection when abroad **b** as a safe-conduct to a foreign citizen passing through its territory **2a** a permission or authorization to go somewhere **b** sthg that secures admission or acceptance <*education as a* ~ *to success*>

pass up *vt* to decline, reject

'pass,word /-,wuhd‖-,wɜːd/ *n* **1** a word or phrase that must be spoken by a person before being allowed to pass a guard **2** WATCHWORD 1

[1]past /pahst‖pɑːst/ *adj* **1a** just gone or elapsed <*for the* ~ *few months*> **b** having gone by; earlier <~ *generations*> <*in years* ~> **2** finished, ended <*winter is* ~> **3** of or constituting the past tense expressing elapsed time **4** preceding, former <~ *president*>

[2]past *prep* **1a** beyond the age of or for <*he's* ~ *80*> <~ *playing with dolls*> **b** subsequent to in time <*half* ~ *2*> **2a** at the farther side of; beyond **b** up to and then beyond <*drove* ~ *the house*> **3** beyond the capacity, range, or sphere of <~ *belief*> <*wouldn't put it* ~ *her to cheat*> – **past it** no longer effective or in one's prime – infml

[3]past *n* **1a** time gone by **b** sthg that happened or was done in the past <*regret the* ~> **2** the past tense of a language **3** a past life, history, or course of action; *esp* one that is kept secret <*she has a* ~, *you know*>

[4]past *adv* so as to pass by the speaker <*children ran* ~> <*days crawled* ~>

pasta /'pastə‖'pæstə/ *n* any of several (egg or oil enriched) flour and water doughs that are usu shaped and used fresh or dried (e g as spaghetti)

[1]paste /payst‖peɪst/ *n* **1a** a fat-enriched dough used esp for pastry **b** a usu sweet doughy confection <*almond* ~> **c** a smooth preparation of meat, fish, etc used as a spread **2** a soft plastic mixture or composition: e g **2a** a preparation of flour or starch and water used as an adhesive **b** clay or a clay mixture used in making pottery or porcelain **3** a brilliant glass used in making imitation gems

[2]paste *vt* **1** to stick with paste **2** to cover with sthg pasted on

[1]'paste,board /-,bawd‖-,bɔːd/ *n* board made by pasting together sheets of paper

[2]pasteboard *adj* **1** made of pasteboard **2** sham, insubstantial

[1]pastel /'pastl‖'pæstl; *NAm* pas'tel‖pæs'tel/ *n* **1** (a crayon made of) a paste of powdered pigment mixed with gum **2** a drawing in pastel **3** any of various pale or light colours – **pastellist** *n*

[2]pastel *adj* pale and light in colour

pastern /'pastuhn‖'pæstɜːn/ *n* (a part of an animal's leg corresponding to) a part of a horse's foot extending from the fetlock to the hoof

'paste-,up *n* **1** a piece of copy for photographic reproduction consisting of text and artwork in the proper positions **2** DUMMY 4

pasteur·ization, -isation /,pahstyoorie'zaysh(ə)n, pa-, -stərie-‖,pɑːstjʊraɪ'zeɪʃ(ə)n, pæ-, -stəraɪ-/ *n* partial sterilization of a substance, esp a liquid (e g milk), by heating for a short period [Louis *Pasteur* (1822-95), French chemist] – **pasteurize** *vt*

pastiche /pa'steesh‖pæ'stiːʃ/ *n* **1** a literary, artistic, or musical work that imitates the style of a previous work **2** a musical, literary, or artistic composition made up of elements borrowed from various sources

pastille *also* **pastil** /'past(ə)l, -stil, -steel‖'pæst(ə)l, -stɪl, -stiːl/ *n* **1** a small cone of aromatic paste, burned to fumigate or scent a room **2** an aromatic or medicated lozenge

pastime /'pahs,tiem‖'pɑːs,taɪm/ *n* sthg (e g a hobby, game, etc) that amuses and serves to make time pass agreeably

pasting /'paysting‖'peɪstɪŋ/ *n* a beating,

trouncing – infml

ˌpast ˈmaster *n* one who is expert or experienced (in a particular activity)

pastor /ˈpahstə‖ˈpɑːstə/ *n* one having responsibility for the spiritual welfare of a group (e g a congregation) – **pastorate** *n*, **pastorship** *n*

[1]**pastoral** /ˈpahst(ə)rəl‖ˈpɑːst(ə)rəl/ *adj* **1a(1)** (composed) of shepherds or herdsmen **a(2)** used for or based on livestock rearing **b** of the countryside; not urban **c** portraying rural life, esp in an idealized and conventionalized manner <~ *poetry*> **d** pleasingly peaceful and innocent; idyllic **2a** of or providing spiritual care or guidance, esp of a church congregation **b** of the pastor of a church – **pastoralism** *n*, **pastorally** *adv*

[2]**pastoral** *n* **1 pastoral, pastoral letter** a letter addressed by a bishop to his diocese **2a** a pastoral literary work **b** an (idealized) depiction of country life **c** a pastorale

past participle *n* a participle with past, perfect, or passive meaning

past perfect *adj* of or constituting a verb tense (e g *had finished*) that expresses completion of an action at or before a past time – **past perfect** *n*

pastrami /pəˈstrahmi‖pæˈstrɑːmɪ/ *n* a highly seasoned smoked beef

pastry /ˈpaystri‖ˈpeɪstrɪ/ *n* **1** PASTE 1a; *esp* paste when baked (e g for piecrust) **2** (an article of) usu sweet food made with pastry

pasturage /ˈpastyoorij, ˈpahschərij‖ˈpæstjʊrɪdʒ, ˈpɑːstʃərɪdʒ/ *n* pasture

[1]**pasture** /ˈpahschə‖ˈpɑːstʃə/ *n* **1** plants (e g grass) grown for feeding (grazing) animals **2** (a plot of) land used for grazing **3** the feeding of livestock; grazing

[2]**pasture** *vi* to graze on pasture ~ *vt* to feed (e g cattle) on pasture

[1]**pasty** /ˈpasti‖ˈpæstɪ/ *n* a small filled usu savoury pie or pastry case baked without a container

[2]**pasty** /ˈpaysti‖ˈpeɪstɪ/ *adj* resembling paste; *esp* pallid and unhealthy in appearance – **pastiness** *n*

[1]**pat** /pat‖pæt/ *n* **1** a light tap, esp with the hand or a flat instrument **2** a light tapping sound **3** a small mass of sthg (e g butter) shaped (as if) by patting

[2]**pat** *vt* **-tt- 1** to strike lightly with the open hand or some other flat surface **2** to flatten, smooth, or put into place or shape with light blows <*he* ~ted *his hair into place*> **3** to tap or stroke gently with the hand to soothe, caress, or show approval

[3]**pat** *adv* in a pat manner; aptly, promptly

[4]**pat** *adj* **1** prompt, immediate **2** suspiciously appropriate; contrived <*a* ~ *answer*> **3** learned, mastered, or memorized exactly

ˈpat-ˌball *n* slow or feeble play (e g in cricket or tennis)

[1]**patch** /pach‖pætʃ/ *n* **1** a piece of material used to mend or cover a hole or reinforce a weak spot **2** a tiny piece of black silk worn on the face, esp by women in the 17th and 18th c, to set off the complexion **3a** a cover (e g a piece of adhesive plaster) applied to a wound **b** a shield worn over the socket of an injured or missing eye **4a** a small piece; a scrap **b** a small area distinct from its surroundings <*damp* ~es *on the wall*> **c** a small piece of land usu used for growing vegetables <*a cabbage* ~> **5** a piece of cloth sewn on a garment as an ornament or insignia **6** a temporary connection in a communications system **7** a temporary correction in a faulty computer program **8** *chiefly Br* a usu specified period <*poetry is going through a bad* ~ – Cyril Connolly> **9** *chiefly Br* an area for which a particular individual or unit (e g of police) has responsibility – **not a patch on** not nearly as good as

[2]**patch** *vt* **1** to mend or cover (a hole) with a patch **2** to provide with a patch <*a* ~ed *pair of trousers*> **3a** to make from patchwork **b** to mend or put together, esp in a hasty or shabby fashion – usu + *up* **c** to make a patch in (a computer program); *also* to make a change in (data stored on a computer) without following the standard routine for this procedure **4** to connect (e g circuits) by a patch cord

patchouli, patchouly /ˈpachooli, pəˈchoohli‖ˈpætʃʊlɪ, pəˈtʃuːlɪ/ *n* **1** an E Indian shrubby plant of the mint family that yields a fragrant essential oil **2** a heavy perfume made from patchouli

ˈpatch ˌpocket *n* a flat pocket attached to the outside of a garment

patch up *vt* to bring (a quarrel, dispute, etc) to an end

ˈpatchˌwork /-ˌwuhk‖-ˌwɜːk/ *n* **1** sthg composed of miscellaneous or incongruous parts **2** work consisting of pieces of cloth of various colours and shapes sewn together

patchy /ˈpachi‖ˈpætʃɪ/ *adj* **1** uneven in quality; incomplete <*my knowledge of French is* ~> **2** *of certain types of weather* appearing in patches <~ *fog*> – **patchily** *adv*, **patchiness** *n*

pate /payt‖peɪt/ *n* (the crown of) the head – **pated** *adj*

pâté /ˈpatay‖ˈpæteɪ/ *n* a rich savoury paste of seasoned and spiced meat, fish, etc

patella /pəˈtelə‖pəˈtelə/ *n, pl* **patellae** /-li‖-lɪ/, **patellas** the kneecap – **patellar** *adj*

[1]**patent** /ˈpayt(ə)nt, ˈpat(ə)nt‖ˈpeɪt(ə)nt, ˈpæt(ə)nt; *sense 5* ˈpayt(ə)nt‖ˈpeɪt(ə)nt/ *adj* **1a** secured by or made under a patent <~ *locks*> **b** proprietary <~ *drugs*> **2a** of patents <*a* ~ *lawyer*> **b** made of patent leather <~ *shoes*> **3** original and ingenious as if protected by patent <*a* ~ *way of pickling onions*> **4** affording free passage; unobstructed <*a* ~ *opening*> **5** readily visible or intelligible; not hidden or obscure – **patency** *n*, **patently** *adv*

[2]**patent** /ˈpayt(ə)nt, ˈpat(ə)nt‖ˈpeɪt(ə)nt, ˈpæt(ə)nt/ *n* **1** LETTERS PATENT **2a** (a formal document securing to an inventor) the exclusive right to make or sell an invention **b** a patented invention **3** a privilege, licence

[3]**patent** *vt* to obtain a patent for (an invention) – **patentable** *adj*

patentee /ˌpayt(ə)nˈtee, ˌpa-‖ˌpeɪt(ə)nˈtiː, ˌpæ-/ *n* sby to whom a grant is made or a privilege secured by patent

ˌpatent ˈleather /ˈpayt(ə)nt‖ˈpeɪt(ə)nt/ *n* a leather with a hard smooth glossy surface

patent medicine /ˈpayt(ə)nt‖ˈpeɪt(ə)nt/ *n* a medicine that is made and marketed under a patent, trademark, etc

pater /ˈpaytə‖ˈpeɪtə/ *n, chiefly Br* a father – now usu humor

paterfamilias /ˌpaytəfəˈmiliˌas‖ˌpeɪtəfəˈmɪlɪˌæs/ *n, pl* **patresfamilias** /ˌpahtrayz-‖ˌpɑːtreɪz-/ the male head of a household

paternal /pəˈtuhnl‖pəˈtɜːnl/ *adj* **1** fatherly <~ *benevolence*> **2** received or inherited from one's male parent **3** related through one's father <~ *grandfather*> – **paternally** *adv*

paˈternalˌism /-ˌiz(ə)m‖-ˌɪz(ə)m/ *n* a system under which a government or organization deals with its subjects or employees in an authoritarian but benevolent way, esp by supplying all their needs and regulating their conduct – **paternalist** *n or adj*, **paternalistic** *adj*

paternity /pəˈtuhnəti‖pəˈtɜːnətɪ/ *n* **1** being a father **2** origin or descent from a father

paternoster /ˌpatəˈnostə, ˌpah-‖ˌpætəˈnɒstə, ˌpɑː-/ *n, often cap* LORD'S PRAYER

path /pahth‖pɑːθ/ *n, pl* **paths** /pahdhz‖pɑːðz/ **1** a track formed by the frequent passage of people or animals **2** a track specially constructed for a particular use <*garden* ~*s*> **3a** a course, route <*the* ~ *of a planet*> **b** a way of life, conduct, or thought <*his* ~ *through life was difficult*> **4** the continuous series of positions or configurations that can be assumed in any motion or process of change by a moving or varying system

pathetic /pəˈthetik‖pəˈθetɪk/ *adj* **1a** PITIFUL 1 <*a* ~ *lost child*> **b** PITIFUL 2 <*a* ~ *performance*> <~ *attempts to learn German*> **2** marked by sorrow or melancholy; sad – **pathetically** *adv*

pathetic fallacy *n* the attribution of human characteristics or feelings to inanimate nature (e g in *cruel sea*)

pathfinder /ˈpahthˌfiendə‖ˈpɑːθˌfaɪndə/ *n* **1** sby or sthg that explores unexplored regions to mark out a new route **2** sby who discovers new ways of doing things – **pathfinding** *n or adj*

pathogen /ˈpathəj(ə)n, -jen‖ˈpæθədʒ(ə)n, -dʒen/ *n* a bacterium, virus, or other disease-causing agent – **pathogenic** *adj*, **pathogenically** *adv*, **pathogenicity** *n*

pathologist /pəˈtholəjist‖pəˈθɒlədʒɪst/ *n* one who studies pathology; *specif* one who conducts postmortems to determine the cause of death

pathology /pəˈtholəji‖pəˈθɒlədʒɪ/ *n* **1** the study of (the structure and functional changes produced by) diseases **2** sthg abnormal: **2a** the anatomical and physiological abnormalities that constitute or characterize (a particular) disease **b** deviation from an assumed normal state of mentality or morality – **pathological, pathologic** *adj*, **pathologically** *adv*

pathos /ˈpaythos‖ˈpeɪθɒs/ *n* **1** a quality in experience or in artistic representation evoking pity or compassion **2** an emotion of sympathetic pity [Greek, suffering, experience, emotion, fr *paschein* to experience, suffer]

pathway /ˈpahthˌway‖ˈpɑːθˌweɪ/ *n* **1** a path, course **2** the sequence of enzyme-catalysed reactions by which a substance is synthesized or an energy-yielding substance is used by living tissue <*metabolic* ~*s*>

patience /ˈpaysh(ə)ns‖ˈpeɪʃ(ə)ns/ *n* **1** the capacity, habit, or fact of being patient **2** *chiefly Br* any of various card games that can be played by 1 person and usu involve the arranging of cards into a prescribed pattern

[1]**patient** /ˈpaysh(ə)nt‖ˈpeɪʃ(ə)nt/ *adj* **1** bearing pains or trials calmly or without complaint **2** manifesting forbearance under provocation or strain **3** not hasty or impetuous **4** steadfast despite opposition, difficulty, or adversity – **patiently** *adv*

[2]**patient** *n* an individual awaiting or under medical care

patina /ˈpatinə‖ˈpætɪnə/ *n, pl* **patinas, patinae** /-ni‖-nɪ/ **1** a (decorative) usu green film formed on copper and bronze by (simulated) weathering and valued as aesthetically pleasing **2** a surface appearance of sthg (e g polished wood) that has grown more beautiful esp with age or use

patio /ˈpatiˑoh‖ˈpætɪəʊ/ *n, pl* **patios** a usu paved area adjoining a dwelling

patisserie /pəˈteesəri, -ˈti-‖pəˈtiːsərɪ, -ˈtɪ-/ *n* **1** PASTRY 2 **2** an establishment where patisserie is made and sold

patois /ˈpatwah‖ˈpætwɑː/ *n, pl* **patois** /ˈpatwahz‖ˈpætwɑːz/ **1** a provincial dialect other than the standard or literary dialect **2** JARGON 2

patrial /ˈpaytriˑəl‖ˈpeɪtrɪəl/ *n* sby who has a legal right to reside in the UK because one of his/her parents or grandparents was born there – **patrial** *adj*, **patriality** *n*

patriarch /ˈpaytriˌahk, ˈpat-‖ˈpeɪtrɪˌɑːk, ˈpæt-/ *n* **1a** any of the biblical fathers of the human race or of the Hebrew people **b** a man who is father or founder (e g of a race, science, religion, or class of people) **c(1)** the oldest member or representative of a group **c(2)** a venerable old man **d** a man who is head of a patriarchy **2a** any of the bishops of the ancient or Orthodox sees of Constantinople, Alexandria, Antioch, and Jerusalem **b** the head of any of various Eastern churches – **patriarchal** *adj*

patriarchate /ˌpaytriˈahkət, -kayt, ˌpatri‖ˌpeɪtrɪˈɑːkət, -keɪt, ˌpætrɪ/ *n* the (duration of) office or jurisdiction of a patriarch

patriarchy /ˈpaytriˌahki, ˈpatri-‖ˈpeɪtrɪˌɑːkɪ, ˈpætrɪ-/ *n* a system or an instance of social organization marked by the supremacy of the father in the clan or family, the legal dependence of wives and children, and the reckoning of descent and inheritance in the male line

patrician /pəˈtrish(ə)n‖pəˈtrɪʃ(ə)n/ *n* **1** a member of any of the original citizen families of ancient Rome **2a** sby of high birth; an aristocrat **b** sby of breeding and cultivation – **patrician** *adj*

patricide /ˈpatriˌsied‖ˈpætrɪˌsaɪd/ *n* (the act of) sby who kills his/her father – **patricidal** *adj*

patrimony /ˈpatriməni‖ˈpætrɪmənɪ/ *n* **1a** property inherited from one's father or ancestor **b** sthg derived from one's father or ancestors; a heritage **2** an estate or endowment belonging to a church – **patrimonial** *adj*

patriot /ˈpaytriˑət, ˈpatri-‖ˈpeɪtrɪət, ˈpætrɪ-/ *n* one who loves and zealously supports his/her country [Middle French *patriote*, fr Late Latin *patriota*, fr Greek *patriōtēs*, fr *patrios* of one's father, fr *patr-*, *patēr* father] – **patriotism** *n*, **patriotic** *adj*, **patriotically** *adv*

[1]**patrol** /pəˈtrohl‖pəˈtrəʊl/ *n* **1a** traversing a district or beat or going the rounds of a garrison

or camp for observation or the maintenance of security **b** *sing or pl in constr* a detachment of men employed for reconnaissance, security, or combat **2** *sing or pl in constr* a subdivision of a scout troop or guide company that has 6 to 8 members

[2]**patrol** *vb* **-ll-** to carry out a patrol (of) – **patroller** *n*

pa'trol ˌcar *n* a usu high-performance car used by police to patrol esp motorways

pa'trolman /-mən‖-mən/ *n, NAm* a policeman assigned to a beat

pa'trol ˌwagon *n, NAm* an enclosed van used by police to carry prisoners

patron /'paytrən‖'peɪtrən; *sense 6* pa'tronh‖pæ'trɑ̃/, *fem* **patroness** /'paytrənəs, -'nes‖'peɪtrənəs, -'nes/ *n* **1a** sby chosen, named, or honoured as a special guardian, protector, or supporter **b** a wealthy or influential supporter of an artist or writer **2** sby who uses his/her wealth or influence to help an individual, institution, or cause **3** CUSTOMER 1 **4** the holder of the right of presentation to an English ecclesiastical benefice **5** a master in ancient times who freed his slave but retained some rights over him/her **6** the proprietor of an establishment (e g an inn), esp in France

patronage /'patrənij‖'pætrənɪdʒ/ *n* **1** advowson **2** the support or influence of a patron **3** the granting of favours in a condescending way **4** business or activity provided by patrons **5** the power to appoint to government jobs

patron·ize, -ise /'patrəniez‖'pætrənaɪz/ *vt* **1** to act as patron of **2** to adopt an air of condescension towards **3** to be a patron of – **patronizingly** *adv*

ˌpatron 'saint *n* a saint regarded as having a particular person, group, church, etc under his/her special care and protection

patronymic /ˌpatrə'nimik‖ˌpætrə'nɪmɪk/ *n* a name derived from that of the father or a paternal ancestor, usu by the addition of an affix – **patronymic** *adj*

patten /'patn‖'pætn/ *n* a sandal or overshoe set on a wooden sole or metal device to elevate the foot

[1]**patter** /'patə‖'pætə/ *vb* to say or talk glibly and volubly – **patterer** *n*

[2]**patter** *n* **1** cant **2** the sales talk of a street hawker **3** empty chattering talk **4a** the rapid-fire talk of a comedian **b** the talk with which an entertainer accompanies his/her routine

[3]**patter** *vi* **1** to strike or tap rapidly and repeatedly <*rain* ~ed *against the window pane*> **2** to run with quick light-sounding steps ~ *vt* to cause to patter – **patter** *n*

[1]**pattern** /'pat(ə)n‖'pæt(ə)n/ *n* **1** a form or model proposed for imitation; an example **2** a design, model, or set of instructions for making things <*a dress* ~> **3** a model for making a mould into which molten metal is poured to form a casting **4** a specimen, sample **5** a usu repeated decorative design (e g on fabric) **6** a natural or chance configuration <*a frost* ~> <*the* ~ *of events*> **7** the grouping on a target by bullets, bombs, etc **8** the flight path prescribed for an aircraft coming in for a landing

[2]**pattern** *vt* **1** to make or model according to a pattern **2** to decorate with a design

patty /'pati‖'pætɪ/ *n* **1** a little pie or pasty **2** *NAm* a small flat cake of chopped food <*a hamburger* ~>

paucity /'pawsəti‖'pɔːsətɪ/ *n* **1** smallness of number **2** smallness of quantity; scarcity *USE* fml

paunch /pawnch‖pɔːntʃ/ *n* **1** the belly **2** a potbelly

paunchy /'pawnchi‖'pɔːntʃɪ/ *adj* having a potbelly

pauper /'pawpə‖'pɔːpə/ *n* a very poor person; *specif* sby supported by charity or from public funds – **pauperism** *n*

pauper·ize, -ise /'pawpəˌriez‖'pɔːpəˌraɪz/ *vt* to reduce to poverty or destitution

[1]**pause** /pawz‖pɔːz/ *n* **1** a temporary stop **2** a caesura **3** temporary inaction, esp as caused by uncertainty; hesitation **4** the sign denoting a fermata

[2]**pause** *vi* **1** to stop temporarily **2** to linger for a time

pavane *also* **pavan** /pə'van, pə'vahn, 'pavən‖pə'væn, pə'vɑːn, 'pævən/ *n* (music for or having the slow duple rhythm of) a stately court dance by couples

pave /payv‖peɪv/ *vt* **1** to lay or cover with material (e g stone or concrete) to form a firm level surface for walking or travelling on **2** to serve as a covering or pavement of <*palaces* ~d *with marble*> – **paver** *n* – **pave the way** to prepare a smooth easy way; facilitate development

paved /payvd‖peɪvd/ *adj* covered with a pavement

pavement /'payvmənt‖'peɪvmənt/ *n* a paved surface: e g **a** *chiefly Br* a surfaced walk for pedestrians at the side of a road **b** *NAm* the artificially covered surface of a road

'pavement ˌartist *n* sby who draws coloured pictures on the pavement in the hope that passersby will give him/her money

[1]**pavilion** /pə'vilyən, -li·ən‖pə'vɪljən, -lɪən/ *n* **1** a large often sumptuous tent **2** a part of a building projecting from the rest **3a** a light sometimes ornamental structure in a garden, park, etc **b** a temporary structure erected at an exhibition by an individual exhibitor **4** the lower faceted part of a cut gem below the girdle **5** *chiefly Br* a permanent building on a sports ground, specif a cricket ground, containing changing rooms and often also seats for spectators [Old French *paveillon*, fr Latin *papilion-, papilio* butterfly]

[2]**pavilion** *vt* to provide with or put in a pavilion

'paving ˌstone /'payving‖'peɪvɪŋ/ *n* a thin rectangular stone or concrete block used for paving

[1]**paw** /paw‖pɔː/ *n* **1** the (clawed) foot of a lion, dog, or other (quadruped) animal **2** a human hand – infml; chiefly humor

[2]**paw** *vt* **1** to feel or touch clumsily, rudely, or indecently **2** to touch or strike at with a paw **3** to scrape or strike (as if) with a hoof ~ *vi* **1** to beat or scrape sthg (as if) with a hoof **2** to touch or strike with a paw

pawky /'pawki‖'pɔːkɪ/ *adj, chiefly Br* artfully shrewd, esp in a humorous way; canny

pawl /pawl‖pɔːl/ *n* a pivoted tongue or sliding

bolt on one part of a machine that is adapted to fall into notches on another part (e g a ratchet wheel) so as to permit motion in only 1 direction

[1]**pawn** /pawn‖pɔːn/ *n* **1** sthg delivered to or deposited with another as a pledge or security (e g for a loan) **2** the state of being pledged – usu + *in*

[2]**pawn** *vt* to deposit in pledge or as security

[3]**pawn** *n* **1** any of the 8 chessmen of each colour of least value that have the power to move only forwards usu 1 square at a time and to capture only diagonally forwards, and that may be promoted to any piece except a king upon reaching the opposite side of the board **2** sby or sthg that can be used to further the purposes of another

'pawn,broker /-ˌbrohkə‖-ˌbrəʊkə/ *n* one who lends money on the security of personal property pledged in his/her keeping – **pawnbroking** *n*

'pawn,shop /-ˌshop‖-ˌʃɒp/ *n* a pawnbroker's shop

pawpaw /'paw,paw‖'pɔːˌpɔː/ *n* PAPAW 2

[1]**pay** /pay‖peɪ/ *vb* **paid,** (*7*) **paid** *also* **payed** /payd‖peɪd/ *vt* **1a** to make due return to for services done or property received **b** to engage for money; hire <*you couldn't* ~ *me to do that*> **2a** to give in return for goods or service <~ *wages*> **b** to discharge indebtedness for; settle <~ *a bill*> **c** to make a disposal or transfer of (money) <~ *money into the bank*> **3** to give or forfeit in reparation or retribution <~ *the penalty*> **4a** to make compensation for **b** to requite according to what is deserved <~ *him back*> <~ *her out*> **5** to give, offer, or make willingly or as fitting <~ *attention*> <~ *heed*> **6a** to be profitable to; be worth the expense or effort to <*it* ~s *shopkeepers to stay open late*> **b** to bring in as a return <*an investment* ~ing *5 per cent*> **7** to slacken (e g a rope) and allow to run out – usu + *out* ~ *vi* **1** to discharge a debt or obligation **2** to be worth the expense or effort <*it* ~s *to advertise*> – **payer** *n*, **payee** *n*, **payable** *adj*

[2]**pay** *n* **1** the status of being paid by an employer; employ <*was in the* ~ *of the enemy*> **2** sthg paid as a salary or wage

[3]**pay** *adj* **1** containing or leading to sthg valuable **2** equipped with a coin slot for receiving a fee for use <*a* ~ *phone*> **3** requiring payment

[4]**pay** *vt* **payed** *also* **paid** to coat with a waterproof composition

'pay,day /-ˌday‖-ˌdeɪ/ *n* a regular day on which wages are paid

'pay,load /-ˌlohd‖-ˌləʊd/ *n* **1** the revenue-producing load that a vehicle of transport can carry **2** the explosive charge carried in the warhead of a missile **3** the load (e g instruments) carried in a spacecraft relating directly to the purpose of the flight as opposed to the load (e g fuel) necessary for operation

'pay,master /-ˌmahstə‖-ˌmɑːstə/ *n* an officer or agent whose duty it is to pay salaries or wages

,paymaster 'general *n, often cap P&G* a British government minister who is often made a member of the cabinet and entrusted with special functions

'payment /-mənt‖-mənt/ *n* **1** the act of paying **2** sthg that is paid **3** a recompense (e g a reward or punishment)

'pay,off /-ˌof‖-ˌɒf/ *n* **1** a profit or reward, esp received by a player in a game **2** a decisive fact or factor resolving a situation or bringing about a definitive conclusion **3** the climax of an incident or chain of events; *specif, chiefly NAm* the denouement of a narrative – infml

pay off *vt* **1** to give all due wages to; *esp* to pay in full and discharge (an employee) **2** to pay (a debt or a creditor) in full ~*vi* to yield returns <*it was a risk but it* paid off>

payola /pay'ohlə‖peɪ'əʊlə/ *n* an undercover or indirect payment for unofficial promotion of a commercial product

'pay-,out *n* (the act of making) a usu large payment of money – infml

'pay-,packet *n, Br* (an envelope containing) sby's wages

'pay,roll /-ˌrohl‖-ˌrəʊl/ *n* **1** a list of those entitled to be paid and of the amounts due to each **2** the sum necessary to pay those on a payroll **3** *sing or pl in constr* the people on a payroll

pay up *vb* to pay in full

pea /pee‖piː/ *n, pl* **peas** *also* **pease** /peez‖piːz; *also* pees‖piːs/ **1a** (a leguminous climbing plant that bears) an edible rounded protein-rich green seed **b** *pl* the immature pods of the pea with their seeds **2** any of various leguminous plants related to or resembling the pea – usu with a qualifying term <*chick*-pea>

peace /pees‖piːs/ *n* **1** a state of tranquillity or quiet: e g **1a** freedom from civil disturbance **b** public order and security maintained by law or custom <*a breach of the* ~> **2** freedom from disquieting or oppressive thoughts or emotions <~ *of mind*> **3** harmony in personal relations **4a** mutual concord between countries **b** an agreement to end hostilities **5** – used interjectionally as a command or request for silence or calm or as a greeting or farewell – **at peace** in a state of concord or tranquillity

peaceable /'peesəbl‖'piːsəbl/ *adj* **1a** disposed to peace; not inclined to dispute or quarrel **b** quietly behaved **2** free from strife or disorder – **peaceableness** *n*, **peaceably** *adv*

'peace ,corps *n* a body of trained volunteer personnel sent by the US government to assist developing nations

'peaceful /-f(ə)l‖-f(ə)l/ *adj* **1** PEACEABLE 1 **2** untroubled by conflict, agitation, or commotion; quiet, tranquil **3** of a state or time of peace – **peacefully** *adv*, **peacefulness** *n*

'peace ,offering *n* sthg given or done to produce peace or reconciliation

'peace ,pipe *n* a calumet

'peace,time /-ˌtiem‖-ˌtaɪm/ *n* a time when a nation is not at war

[1]**peach** /peech‖piːtʃ/ *n* **1** (a low spreading tree of the rose family that grows in temperate areas, has stalkless usu pink spring flowers, and bears) an edible fruit with a large stone, thin downy skin, and sweet white or yellow flesh **2** light yellowish pink **3** a particularly excellent person or thing; *specif* an unusually attractive girl or young woman – infml

[2]**peach** *vi* to turn informer <~ed

on his accomplices>

peacock /ˈpeekok‖ˈpi:kɒk/ *n* a male peafowl with very large tail feathers that are usu tipped with eyelike spots and can be erected and spread in a fan shimmering with iridescent colour; *broadly* a peafowl

ˌpeacock ˈblue *n* lustrous greenish blue

ˈpeaˌfowl /-ˌfowl‖-ˌfaʊl/ *n* a very large ornamental ground-living pheasant of SE Asia and the E Indies

ˌpea ˈgreen *n* light yellowish green

ˈpeaˌhen /-ˌhen‖-ˌhen/ *n* a female peafowl

[1]**peak** /peek‖pi:k/ *vi* to grow thin or sickly

[2]**peak** *n* **1** a projecting part on the front of a cap or hood **2** a sharp or pointed end **3a** (the top of) a hill or mountain ending in a point **b** sthg resembling a mountain peak **4a** the upper aftermost corner of a 4-cornered fore-and-aft sail **b** the narrow part of a ship's bow or stern **5a** the highest level or greatest degree **b** a high point in a course of development, esp as represented on a graph

[3]**peak** *vi* to reach a maximum

[4]**peak** *adj* at or reaching the maximum of capacity, value, or activity < ~ *traffic hours*>

[1]**peaked** /peekt‖pi:kt/ *adj* having a peak; pointed – **peakedness** *n*

[2]**peaked** *adj* peaky

peaky /ˈpeeki‖ˈpi:kɪ/ *adj* looking pale and wan; sickly

[1]**peal** /peel‖pi:l/ *n* **1a** a complete set of changes on a given number of bells **b** a set of bells tuned to the notes of the major scale for change ringing **2** a loud prolonged sound < ~s *of laughter*>

[2]**peal** *vi* to give out peals ~*vt* to utter or give forth loudly

peanut /ˈpeenut‖ˈpi:nʌt/ *n* **1** (the pod or oily edible seed of) a low-branching widely cultivated leguminous plant with showy yellow flowers and pods containing 1 to 3 seeds that ripen in the earth **2** *pl* a trifling amount – infml

pear /peə‖peə/ *n* (a tree of the rose family that bears) a large fleshy edible fruit wider at the end furthest from the stalk

[1]**pearl** /puhl‖pɜ:l/ *n* **1a** a dense usu milky white lustrous mass of mother-of-pearl layers, formed as an abnormal growth in the shell of some molluscs, esp oysters, and used as a gem **b** mother-of-pearl **2** sby or sthg very rare or precious

[2]**pearl** *vt* **1** to set or adorn (as if) with pearls **2** to form into small round grains ~ *vi* **1** to form drops or beads like pearls **2** to fish or search for pearls – **pearler** *n*

[3]**pearl** *adj* **1a** of or resembling pearl **b** made of or adorned with pearls **2** having medium-sized grains < ~ *barley*>

[1]**pearly** /ˈpuhli‖ˈpɜ:lɪ/ *adj* resembling, containing, or decorated with pearls or mother-of-pearl

[2]**pearly** *n, Br* **1** a button made of mother-of-pearl **2** a member of certain cockney families who are traditionally costermongers and entitled to wear a special costume covered with pearlies

peasant /ˈpez(ə)nt‖ˈpez(ə)nt/ *n* **1** a small landowner or farm labourer **2** a usu uneducated person of low social status [Middle French *paisant*, fr *païs* country, fr Late Latin *pagensis* inhabitant of a district, fr Latin *pagus* district] – **peasantry** *n sing or pl in constr*

pease /peez‖pi:z; *also* pees‖pi:s/ *n, chiefly Br* PEA 1a – archaic except in attributive use < ~ *pudding*>

ˈpeaˌshooter /-ˌshoohtə‖-ˌʃu:tə/ *n* a toy blowpipe for shooting peas

ˌpea-ˈsouper /ˈsoohpə‖ˈsu:pə/ *also* **pea soup** *n* a heavy fog

peat /peet‖pi:t/ *n* (a piece of) partially carbonized vegetable tissue formed by partial decomposition in water of various plants (e g mosses), found in large bogs, and used esp as a fuel for domestic heating and as a fertilizer – **peaty** *adj*

[1]**pebble** /ˈpebl‖ˈpebl/ *n* a small usu rounded stone, often worn smooth by the action of water – **pebbly** *adj*

[2]**pebble** *vt* to pave or cover with (sthg resembling) pebbles

ˈpebbleˌdash /-ˌdash‖-ˌdæʃ/ *n* a finish for exterior walls consisting of small pebbles embedded in a stucco base

pecan /piˈkan, ˈpeekan‖pɪˈkæn, ˈpi:kæn/ *n* (the smooth oblong thin-shelled edible nut of) a large hickory tree

peccadillo /ˌpekəˈdiloh‖ˌpekəˈdɪləʊ/ *n, pl* **peccadilloes, peccadillos** a slight or trifling offence

peccary /ˈpekəri‖ˈpekərɪ/ *n* either of 2 largely nocturnal social American mammals resembling the related pigs

[1]**peck** /pek‖pek/ *n* a unit of volume or capacity equal to 2gall (about 9.1l)

[2]**peck** *vt* **1a** to strike or pierce (repeatedly) with the beak or a pointed tool **b** to make by pecking < ~ *a hole*> **c** to kiss perfunctorily **2** to pick up with the beak ~ *vi* **1** to strike, pierce, or pick up sthg (as if) with the beak **2** to eat reluctantly and in small bites

[3]**peck** *n* **1** an impression or hole made by pecking **2** a quick sharp stroke **3** a quick perfunctory kiss

pecker /ˈpekə‖ˈpekə/ *n* **1** *chiefly Br* courage – in *keep one's pecker up*; infml **2** *NAm* a penis – vulg

ˈpecking ˌorder /ˈpeking‖ˈpekɪŋ/, **peck order** *n* **1** the natural hierarchy within a flock of birds, esp poultry, in which each bird pecks another lower in the scale without fear of retaliation **2** a social hierarchy

peckish /ˈpekish‖ˈpekɪʃ/ *adj, chiefly Br* agreeably hungry – infml

pectin /ˈpektin‖ˈpektɪn/ *n* any of various water-soluble substances that bind adjacent cell walls in plant tissues and yield a gel which acts as a setting agent in jams and fruit jellies – **pectic** *adj*

pectoral /ˈpekt(ə)rəl‖ˈpekt(ə)rəl/ *adj* of, situated in or on, or worn on the chest

peculate /ˈpekyoolayt‖ˈpekjʊleɪt/ *vt* to embezzle – **peculator** *n*, **peculation** *n*

[1]**peculiar** /piˈkyoohli·ə, -lyə‖pɪˈkju:lɪə, -ljə/ *adj* **1** belonging exclusively to 1 person or group **2** distinctive **3** different from the usual or normal; strange, curious – **peculiarly** *adv*

[2]**peculiar** *n* sthg exempt from ordinary jurisdiction; *esp* a church or parish independent of the diocese in which it is situated

peculiarity /piˌkyoohliˈarəti‖pɪˌkju:lɪˈærətɪ/ *n* a distinguishing characteristic

pecuniary /pi'kyoohnyəri||pɪ'kju:njərɪ/ *adj* of or measured in money – fml – **pecuniarily** *adv*

pedagogue /'pedəgog||'pedəgɒg/ *n* a teacher, schoolmaster – now chiefly derog

pedagogy /'pedəgoji, -gogi, -goh-||'pedəgɒdʒɪ, -gɒgɪ, -gəʊ-/ *n* the science of teaching

[1]**pedal** /'pedl||'pedl/ *n* **1** a lever pressed by the foot in playing a musical instrument **2** a foot lever or treadle by which a part is activated in a mechanism

[2]**pedal** *adj* of the foot

[3]**pedal** *vb* **-ll-** (*NAm* **-l-** *also* **-ll-**) *vi* **1** to use or work a pedal or pedals **2** to ride a bicycle ~*vt* to work the pedals of

pedant /'ped(ə)nt||'ped(ə)nt/ *n* one who is unimaginative or unnecessarily concerned with detail, esp in academic matters – **pedantic** *adj*, **pedantry** *n*

peddle /'pedl||'pedl/ *vi* to sell goods as a pedlar ~ *vt* **1** to sell as a pedlar **2** to deal out or seek to disseminate (e g ideas or opinions)

peddler /'pedlə||'pedlə/ *n* **1** one who peddles dangerous or illicit drugs; a pusher **2** *NAm* a pedlar

pederast, paederast /'pedə,rast, 'pee-||'pedə,ræst, 'pi:-/ *n* one who practises anal intercourse, esp with a boy – **pederasty** *n*, **pederastic** *adj*

pedestal /'pedistl||'pedɪstl/ *n* **1a** a base supporting a late classic or neoclassic column **b** the base of an upright structure (e g a statue) **2** a base, foundation **3** a position of esteem or idealized respect

[1]**pedestrian** /pi'destri·ən||pɪ'destrɪən/ *adj* **1** commonplace, unimaginative **2a** going or performed on foot **b** of or designed for walking <*a ~ precinct*> – **pedestrianism** *n*

[2]**pedestrian** *n* sby going on foot; a walker

pe,destrian 'crossing *n* a usu marked stretch of road on which pedestrians crossing the road have priority over the traffic in certain circumstances

pedicel /'pedisel||'pedɪsel/ *n* **1** a plant stalk that supports a fruiting or spore-bearing organ **2** a narrow basal attachment of an animal organ or part – **pedicellate** *adj*

pedicure /'pedikyooə||'pedɪkjʊə/ *n* **1** one who practises chiropody **2** (a) treatment for the care of the feet and toenails

[1]**pedigree** /'pedigree||'pedɪgri:/ *n* **1** a register recording a line of ancestors **2a** an esp distinguished ancestral line; a lineage **b** the origin and history of sthg **3** the recorded purity of breed of an individual or strain [Middle French *pie de grue* crane's foot; so called fr the shape made by the lines of a genealogical chart] – **pedigreed** *adj*

[2]**pedigree** *adj* of, being, or producing pedigree animals

pediment /'pedimənt||'pedɪmənt/ *n* the triangular gable of a 2-pitched roof in classic architecture – **pedimental** *adj*

pedlar, *NAm chiefly* **peddler** /'pedlə||'pedlə/ *n* **1** one who travels about offering small wares for sale **2** one who deals in or promotes sthg intangible – **pedlary** *n*

pedometer /pi'domitə||pɪ'dɒmɪtə/ *n* an instrument that records the distance a walker covers

[1]**pee** /pee||pi:/ *vi* to urinate – euph

[2]**pee** *n* **1** an act of urinating **2** urine *USE* euph

[3]**pee** *n, pl* **pee** *Br* PENNY 1a(2) – infml

peek /peek||pi:k/ *vi* **1** to look furtively – often + *in* or *out* **2** to take a brief look; glance – **peek** *n*

[1]**peekaboo** /'peekə,booh||'pi:kə,bu:/ *n* a game for amusing a baby in which one repeatedly hides and comes back into view, typically exclaiming 'Peekaboo!'

[2]**peekaboo** *adj* trimmed with eyelet embroidery <*a ~ blouse*>

[1]**peel** /peel||pi:l/ *vt* **1** to strip off an outer layer of <*~ an orange*> **2** to remove by stripping <*~ the label off the can*> ~ *vi* **1a** to come off in sheets or scales **b** to lose an outer layer (e g of skin) <*his face is ~ing*> **2** to take off one's clothes – usu + *off*; infml <*they ~ed off and dived into the water*> – **peeler** *n*

[2]**peel** *n* the skin or rind of a fruit

peeler /'peelə||'pi:lə/ *n, archaic Br* a policeman [Sir Robert *Peel* (1788-1850), English statesman who founded the Irish constabulary]

peeling /'peeling||'pi:lɪŋ/ *n* a strip of skin, rind, etc that has been stripped off

peel off *vi* **1** to veer away from an aircraft formation, esp when diving or landing **2** to break away from a group or formation (e g of marchers or ships in a convoy)

[1]**peep** /peep||pi:p/ *vi* **1** to utter a feeble shrill sound characteristic of a newly hatched bird; cheep **2** to utter a slight sound

[2]**peep** *n* **1** a cheep **2** a slight sound, esp spoken – infml <*don't let me hear another ~ out of you*>

[3]**peep** *vi* **1** to look cautiously or slyly, esp through an aperture; peek **2** to begin to emerge (as if) from concealment; show slightly

[4]**peep** *n* **1** the first faint appearance <*at the ~ of dawn*> **2** a brief or furtive look; a glance

peeper /'peepə||'pi:pə/ *n* **1** a voyeur **2** an eye – infml

'peep,hole /-,hohl||-,həʊl/ *n* a hole or crevice to peep through

Peeping Tom /,peeping 'tom||,pi:pɪŋ 'tɒm/ *n, often not cap P* a voyeur

'peep ,show *n* an entertainment (e g a film) or object (e g a small painting) viewed through a small opening or a magnifying glass

[1]**peer** /piə||pɪə/ *n* **1** sby who is of equal standing with another **2** a duke, marquess, earl, viscount, or baron of the British peerage

[2]**peer** *adj* belonging to the same age, grade, or status group <*a ~ group of adolescents*>

[3]**peer** *vi* to look narrowly or curiously; *esp* to look searchingly at sthg difficult to discern

peerage /'piərij||'pɪərɪdʒ/ *n* **1** *sing or pl in constr* the body of peers **2** the rank or dignity of a peer

peeress /'piəris||'pɪərɪs/ *n* **1** the wife or widow of a peer **2** a woman having in her own right the rank of a peer

'peerless /-lis||-lɪs/ *adj* matchless, incomparable – **peerlessly** *adv*, **peerlessness** *n*

peeve /peev||pi:v/ *vt* to make peevish or resentful; annoy – infml

peevish /'peevish||'pi:vɪʃ/ *adj* querulous in temperament or mood; fretful –

peevishly *adv*, **peevishness** *n*

peewit, pewit /ˈpeewit‖ˈpiːwɪt/ *n* a lapwing

[1]**peg** /peg‖peg/ *n* **1** a small usu cylindrical pointed or tapered piece of wood, metal, or plastic used to pin down or fasten things or to fit into or close holes; a pin <*they secured the guy ropes with tent* ~s> **2a** a projecting piece used to hold or support <*he hung his hat on the* ~ *in the hall*> **b** sthg (e g a fact or opinion) used as a support, pretext, or reason <*the strike was simply a* ~ *for their prejudices*> **3a** any of the wooden pins set in the head of a stringed instrument and turned to regulate the pitch of the strings **b** a step or degree, esp in estimation – esp in *take sby down a peg (or two)* **4** *Br* a clothes peg **5** *Br* a drink, esp of spirits <*poured himself out a stiff* ~ – Dorothy Sayers> – **off the peg** mass-produced; READY-MADE 1 <*men over 7 feet have difficulty in finding clothes* off the peg *to fit*>

[2]**peg** *vt* **-gg- 1** to put a peg into **2** to pin down; restrict **3** to fix or hold (e g prices) at a predetermined level **4** *Br* to fasten (e g washing) to a clothesline with a clothes peg – often + *out*

peg away *vi, chiefly Br* to work hard and steadily – often + *at*

ˌ**peg ˈleg** *n* (one who wears) an artificial leg

peg out *vi* **1** to finish a game in croquet by hitting the peg with the ball **2** *chiefly Br* DIE 1 – infml ~*vt* to mark by pegs <peg out *the boundaries of an estate*>

pejorative /pəˈjorətiv, ‖pəˈdʒɒrətɪv,*also* ˈpeej(ə)rətiv‖ˈpiːdʒ(ə)rətɪv/ *adj* depreciatory, disparaging – **pejorative** *n*, **pejoratively** *adv*

Pekingese, Pekinese /ˌpekiˈneez, ˌpee-‖ˌpekɪˈniːz, ˌpiː-/ *n, pl* **Pekingese, Pekinese 1a** a native or inhabitant of Peking **b** Mandarin **2** (any of) a Chinese breed of small short-legged dogs with a broad flat face and a long thick soft coat

pekoe /ˈpeekoh‖ˈpiːkəʊ/ *n* a black tea of superior quality

pelagic /peˈlajik‖peˈlædʒɪk/ *adj* of, occurring, or living (at or above moderate depths) in the open sea

pelargonium /ˌpeləˈgohnyəm, -ni·əm‖ˌpeləˈgəʊnjəm, -nɪəm/ *n* any of a genus of plants of the geranium family with showy red, pink, or white flowers

pelf /pelf‖pelf/ *n* money, riches

pelican /ˈpelikən‖ˈpelɪkən/ *n* any of a genus of large web-footed birds with a very large bill containing a pouch in which fish are kept

pellagra /pəˈlaygrə, -ˈla-‖pəˈleɪgrə, -ˈlæ-/ *n* dermatitis and nervous symptoms associated with a deficiency of nicotinic acid and protein in the diet – **pellagrous** *adj*

pellet /ˈpelit‖ˈpelɪt/ *n* **1** a usu small rounded or spherical body (e g of food or medicine) **2** a piece of small shot – **pelletal** *adj*, **pelletize** *vt*

pell-mell /ˌpel ˈmel‖ˌpel ˈmel/ *adv* **1** in confusion or disorder **2** in confused haste – **pell-mell** *adj or n*

pellucid /piˈl(y)oohsid‖pɪˈl(j)uːsɪd/ *adj* **1** transparent **2** easy to understand *USE* fml or poetic – **pellucidly** *adv*, **pellucidity** *n*

pelmet /ˈpelmit‖ˈpelmɪt/ *n, chiefly Br* a length of board or fabric placed above a window to conceal curtain fixtures [prob fr French *palmette* palm-leaf design, fr *palme* palm, fr Latin *palma*]

pelota /pəˈlotə‖pəˈlɒtə/ *n* any of various Spanish or Latin-American court games; *specif* JAI ALAI

[1]**pelt** /pelt‖pelt/ *n* **1** a usu undressed skin with its hair, wool, or fur **2** a skin stripped of hair or wool before tanning

[2]**pelt** *vt* **1** to strike with a succession of blows or missiles <~ed *him with stones*> **2** to hurl, throw **3** to beat or dash repeatedly against <*rain* ~ing *the windows*> ~ *vi* **1** *of rain* to fall heavily and continuously **2** to move rapidly and vigorously; hurry <*the children* ~ed *down the road*>

[3]**pelt** *n* – **at full pelt** as fast as possible

pelvis /ˈpelvis‖ˈpelvɪs/ *n, pl* **pelvises, pelves** /-veez‖-viːz/ **1** (the cavity of) a basin-shaped structure in the skeleton of many vertebrates that is formed by the pelvic girdle and adjoining bones of the spine **2** the funnel-shaped cavity of the kidney into which urine is discharged – **pelvic** *adj*

pemmican *also* **pemican** /ˈpemikən‖ˈpemɪkən/ *n* a concentrated food of lean dried pounded meat mixed with melted fat traditionally made by N American Indians; *also* a similar preparation usu of beef and dried fruits used for emergency rations

[1]**pen** /pen‖pen/ *n* **1** a small enclosure for animals **2** a small place of confinement or storage **3** a (heavily fortified) dock or slip for a submarine

[2]**pen** *vt* **-nn-** to shut in a pen

[3]**pen** *n* **1** an implement for writing or drawing with fluid (e g ink): e g **1a** a quill **b** a penholder fitted with a nib **c** FOUNTAIN PEN **d** a ballpoint **2a** a writing instrument as a means of expression <*the* ~ *is mightier than the sword*> **b** a writer – fml

[4]**pen** *vt* **-nn-** to write – fml <~ *a letter*>

[5]**pen** *n* a female swan

penal /ˈpeenl‖ˈpiːnl/ *adj* **1** of punishment **2** liable to punishment <*a* ~ *offence*> **3** used as a place of punishment <*a* ~ *colony*> – **penally** *adv*

penal·ize, -ise /ˈpeenl·iez‖ˈpiːnlaɪz/ *vt* **1** to inflict a penalty on **2** to put at a serious disadvantage – **penalization** *n*

penalty /ˈpen(ə)lti‖ˈpen(ə)ltɪ/ *n* **1** a punishment legally imposed or incurred **2** a forfeiture to which a person agrees to be subject if conditions are not fulfilled **3a** disadvantage, loss, or suffering due to some action <*paid the* ~ *for his heavy drinking*> **b** a disadvantage imposed for violation of the rules of a sport **4** PENALTY KICK

ˈ**penalty ˌarea** *n* a rectangular area 44yd (about 40m) wide and 18yd (about 16m) deep in front of each goal on a soccer pitch

ˈ**penalty ˌbox** *n* **1** PENALTY AREA **2** an area alongside an ice hockey rink to which penalized players are confined

ˈ**penalty ˌkick** *n* **1** a free kick in rugby **2** a free kick at the goal in soccer awarded for a serious offence committed in the penalty area and taken from a point 12yd (about 11m) in front of the goal with only the goalkeeper to defend it

penance /ˈpenəns‖ˈpenəns/ *n* an act of

self-abasement or devotion performed to show repentance for sin; *also* a sacramental rite of the Roman, Orthodox, and some Anglican churches involving confession and a penance directed by the confessor

pence /pens‖pens/ *pl of* PENNY

penchant /ˈpenchənt, ˈpon(h)shonh ‖ ˈpentʃənt, ˈpɒnʃɑ̃, ˈpɑ̃- (*Fr* pɑ̃ʃɑ̃)/ *n* a strong leaning; a liking

¹pencil /ˈpensl‖ˈpensl/ *n* **1a** an implement for writing, drawing, or marking consisting of or containing a slender cylinder or strip of a solid marking substance (e g graphite) **b** a small medicated or cosmetic roll or stick for local applications **2** a set of light rays, esp when diverging from or converging to a point **3** sthg long and thin like a pencil [Middle French *pincel* paintbrush, deriv of Latin *penicillus*, lit., little tail, fr *penis* tail, penis]

²pencil *vt* **-ll-** (*NAm* **-l-, -ll-**) to draw, write, or mark with a pencil – **penciller** *n*

pendant *also* **pendent** /ˈpend(ə)nt‖ˈpend(ə)nt/ *n* **1** sthg suspended (e g an ornament allowed to hang free) **2** a companion piece or supplement **3** *chiefly Br* a pennant

pendent, pendant /ˈpend(ə)nt‖ˈpend(ə)nt/ *adj* **1** suspended **2** jutting or leaning over; overhanging <*a ~ cliff*> **3** remaining undetermined; pending

¹pending /ˈpending‖ˈpendɪŋ/ *prep* until – fml

²pending *adj* **1** not yet decided or dealt with **2** imminent, impending – **pendency** *n*

pendulous /ˈpendyooləs‖ˈpendjʊləs/ *adj* suspended, inclined, or hanging downwards <*~ jowls*> – **pendulously** *adv*

pendulum /ˈpendyooləm‖ˈpendjʊləm/ *n* a body suspended from a fixed point so as to swing freely periodically under the action of gravity and commonly used to regulate movements (e g of clockwork)

penetrate /ˈpenitrayt‖ˈpenɪtreɪt/ *vt* **1a** to pass into or through **b** to enter, esp by overcoming resistance; pierce **2** to see into or through; discern **3** to diffuse through or into ~*vi* to be absorbed by the mind; be understood <*I heard what he said, but it didn't ~*> – **penetrable** *adj*, **penetrability** *n*, **penetrative** *adj*

penetrating /ˈpenitrayting‖ˈpenɪtreɪtɪŋ/ *adj* **1** having the power of entering, piercing, or pervading <*a ~ shriek*> <*the cold is ~*> **2** acute, discerning <*~ insights into life*> – **penetratingly** *adv*

penetration /ˌpeniˈtraysh(ə)n‖ˌpenɪˈtreɪʃ(ə)n/ *n* **1a** the entering of a country so that influence is established **b** the process of successfully introducing or increasing sales of a product in an existing market **2a** the depth to which sthg penetrates **b** the ability to discern deeply and acutely <*a critic gifted with great powers of ~*>

ˈpen-ˌfriend *n* a person, esp one in another country, with whom a friendship is made through correspondence

penguin /ˈpeng·gwin‖ˈpeŋgwɪn/ *n* any of various erect short-legged flightless aquatic birds of the southern hemisphere

penicillin /ˌpeniˈsilin‖ˌpenɪˈsɪlɪn/ *n* (a salt, ester, or mixture of salts and esters of) any of several antibiotics or antibacterial drugs orig obtained from moulds, that act by interfering with the synthesis of bacterial cell walls and are active against a wide range of bacteria

peninsula /pəˈninsyoolə‖pəˈnɪnsjʊlə/ *n* a piece of land jutting out into or almost surrounded by water; *esp* one connected to the mainland by an isthmus [Latin *paeninsula*, fr *paene* almost + *insula* island]

penis /ˈpeenis‖ˈpiːnɪs/ *n, pl* **penes** /-neez‖-niːz/, **penises** the male organ of copulation by which semen is introduced into the female during coitus

¹penitent /ˈpenit(ə)nt‖ˈpenɪt(ə)nt/ *adj* feeling or expressing sorrow for sins or offences – **penitence** *n*, **penitently** *adv*

²penitent *n* **1** sby who repents of sin **2** sby under church censure but admitted to penance, esp under the direction of a confessor

penitential /ˌpeniˈtensh(ə)l‖ˌpenɪˈtenʃ(ə)l/ *adj* of penitence or penance – **penitentially** *adv*

¹penitentiary /ˌpeniˈtensh(ə)ri‖ˌpenɪˈtenʃ(ə)rɪ/ *n* a prison in the USA

²penitentiary *adj, NAm* of or incurring confinement in a penitentiary

penknife /ˈpenˌnief‖ˈpenˌnaɪf/ *n* a small pocketknife

ˈpenmanship *n* **1** the art or practice of writing with the pen **2** quality or style of handwriting

ˈpen ˌname *n* an author's pseudonym

pennant /ˈpenənt‖ˈpenənt/ *n* **1** any of various nautical flags used for identification or signalling **2** a flag that tapers to a point or has a swallowtail

penniless /ˈpenilis‖ˈpenɪlɪs/ *adj* lacking money; poor

pennon /ˈpenən‖ˈpenən/ *n* a long usu triangular or swallow-tailed streamer typically attached to the head of a lance as a knight's personal flag

penny /ˈpeni‖ˈpenɪ/ *n, pl* **pennies, pence** /pens‖pens/, (3) **pennies** **1a** (a usu bronze coin representing) (1) a former British money unit worth £$^{1}/_{240}$ (2) a British money unit in use since 1971 that is worth £$^{1}/_{100}$ **b** (a coin representing) 1/100 of various other units (e g the Irish punt) **2** a denarius **3** *NAm* a cent – **the penny drops** the true meaning finally dawns

-penny /-p(ə)ni‖-p(ə)nɪ; *since decimalization also* -peni‖-penɪ/ *comb form* (→ *adj*) costing (so many) pence <*nine*penny>

ˌpenny-ˈfarthing *n, Br* an early type of bicycle having 1 small and 1 large wheel

ˈpenny-ˌpinching *adj* mean, niggardly, stingy – **penny pincher** *n*, **penny- pinching** *n*

ˈpennyˌweight /-ˌwayt‖-ˌweɪt/ *n* a unit of troy weight equal to 24grains (about 1.56g)

ˈpennyˌwort /-wuht‖-wɜːt/ *n* any of various round-leaved plants

penology /peeˈnoləji‖piːˈnɒlədʒɪ/ *n* criminology dealing with prison management and the treatment of offenders – **penologist** *n*, **penological** *adj*

ˈpen ˌpal *n* a pen-friend – infml

ˈpen ˌpusher *n* one whose work involves usu boring or repetitive writing at a desk; *specif* CLERK 2a

[1]**pension** /ˈpensh(ə)n‖ˈpenʃ(ə)n; *sense 2* ˈponhsyonh ‖ˈpãsjã (*Fr* pãsjɔ̃)/ *n* **1** a fixed sum paid regularly to a person (e g following retirement or as compensation for a wage-earner's death) <*a widow's* ~> **2** (bed and board provided by) a hotel or boardinghouse, esp in continental Europe – **pensionless** *adj*

[2]**pension** /ˈpensh(ə)n‖ˈpenʃ(ə)n/ *vt* to grant or pay a pension to

pensionable /ˈpensh(ə)nəbl‖ˈpenʃ(ə)nəbl/ *adj* (that makes sby) entitled to receive a pension

pensioner /ˈpensh(ə)nə‖ˈpenʃ(ə)nə/ *n* one who receives or lives on an esp old-age pension

pension off *vt* **1** to dismiss or retire from service with a pension <pensioned off *his faithful old servant*> **2** to set aside or dispense with after long use – infml <pensioned off *his old trousers*>

pensive /ˈpensiv‖ˈpensɪv/ *adj* sadly or dreamily thoughtful – **pensively** *adv*, **pensiveness** *n*

pentagon /ˈpentəgən, -ˌgon‖ˈpentəgən, -ˌgɒn/ *n* a polygon of 5 angles and 5 sides – **pentagonal** *adj*, **pentagonally** *adv*

Pentagon *n sing or pl in constr* *the* US military establishment

pentagram /ˈpentəˌgram‖ˈpentəˌgræm/ *n* a 5-pointed star used as a magical symbol

pentameter /penˈtamitə‖penˈtæmɪtə/ *n* a line of verse consisting of 5 metrical feet

Pentateuch /ˈpentəˌtyoohk‖ˈpentəˌtjuːk/ *n* *the* first 5 books of the Old Testament – **pentateuchal** *adj*

pentathlon /penˈtathlon‖penˈtæθlɒn/ *n* an athletic contest in which all contestants compete in 5 events [Greek, fr *pente* five + *athlon* contest] – **pentathlete** *n*

Pentecost /ˈpentikost‖ˈpentɪkɒst/ *n* (a Christian festival on the 7th Sunday after Easter commemorating the descent of the Holy Spirit on the apostles at) the Jewish festival of Shabuoth [Old English *pentecosten*, fr Late Latin *pentecoste*, fr Greek *pentēkostē*, lit., fiftieth (day), fr *pentēkonta* fifty]

penthouse /ˈpentˌhows‖ˈpentˌhaʊs/ *n* **1** a structure (e g a shed or roof) attached to and sloping from a wall or building **2** a structure or dwelling built on the roof of a (tall) building <*a* ~ *flat*>

ˌ**pent-**ˈ**up** /pent‖pent/ *adj* confined, held in check <~ *emotions*>

penultimate /piˈnultimət, pe-‖pɪˈnʌltɪmət, pe-/ *adj* next to the last <*the* ~ *chapter of a book*> [Latin *paenultimus*, fr *paene* almost + *ultimus* last] – **penultimately** *adv*

penumbra /piˈnumbrə‖pɪˈnʌmbrə/ *n, pl* **penumbrae** /-bri‖-brɪ/, **penumbras** **1** a region of partial darkness (e g in an eclipse) in a shadow surrounding the umbra **2** a less dark region surrounding the dark centre of a sunspot – **penumbral** *adj*

penurious /piˈnyooəri·əs‖pɪˈnjʊərɪəs/ *adj* marked by or suffering from penury – fml – **penuriously** *adv*, **penuriousness** *n*

penury /ˈpenyoori‖ˈpenjʊrɪ/ *n* a cramping and oppressive lack of resources, esp money; *esp* severe poverty – fml

peon /ˈpee·ən‖ˈpiːən/ *n, pl* **peons, peones** /payˈohneez‖peɪˈəʊniːz/, (3) **peons** **1** an Indian or Sri Lankan infantryman, orderly, or other worker **2** an agricultural labourer in Spanish America **3** a drudge, menial

peony, paeony /ˈpee·əni‖ˈpiːənɪ/ *n* any of a genus of plants with very large usu double showy red, pink, or white flowers

[1]**people** /ˈpeepl‖ˈpiːpl/ *n pl in constr*, (5) *sing or pl in constr* **1** human beings in general **2** a group of persons considered collectively <*poor* ~> **3** the members of a family or kinship <*his* ~ *have been farmers for generations*> **4** the mass of a community <*disputes between the* ~ *and the nobles*> **5** a body of persons that are united by a common culture and that often constitute a politically organized group <*the Jewish* ~> **6** the citizens of a state who are qualified to vote – **of all people** – used to show surprise <*the Archbishop* of all people *said that?*>

[2]**people** *vt* **1** to supply or fill with people **2** to dwell in; inhabit

pep /pep‖pep/ *vt or n* **-pp-** (to liven up or instil with) brisk energy or initiative and high spirits – **peppy** *adj*, **peppiness** *n*

[1]**pepper** /ˈpepə‖ˈpepə/ *n* **1a(1)** BLACK PEPPER **a(2)** WHITE PEPPER **b** any of a genus of tropical mostly climbing shrubs with aromatic leaves; *esp* one with red berries from which black pepper and white pepper are prepared **2** any of various products similar to pepper; *esp* a pungent condiment obtained from capsicums – used with a qualifying term <*cayenne* ~> **3** (the usu red or green fruit of) a capsicum whose fruits are hot peppers or sweet peppers – **pepper** *adj*

[2]**pepper** *vt* **1a** to sprinkle, season, or cover (as if) with pepper **b** to shower with shot or other missiles **2** to sprinkle <~ed *his report with statistics*>

ˌ**pepper-and-**ˈ**salt** *adj, of a fabric or garment* having black and white or dark and light colour intermingled in small flecks

ˈ**pepper**ˌ**corn** /-ˌkawn‖-ˌkɔːn/ *n* a dried berry of the pepper plant

ˈ**pepper**ˌ**mint** /-ˌmint‖-ˌmɪnt/ *n* **1** (an aromatic essential oil obtained from) a mint with dark green tapering leaves and whorls of small pink flowers **2** a sweet flavoured with peppermint oil – **pepperminty** *adj*

ˈ**pepper** ˌ**pot** *n, Br* a small usu cylindrical container with a perforated top used for sprinkling ground pepper on food

peppery /ˈpep(ə)ri‖ˈpep(ə)rɪ/ *adj* **1** hot, pungent **2** hot-tempered, touchy <*a* ~ *old man*> **3** fiery, stinging <*a* ~ *speech*>

ˈ**pep** ˌ**pill** *n* a tablet of a stimulant drug

pepsin /ˈpepsin‖ˈpepsɪn/ *n* an enzyme of the stomach that breaks down most proteins in an acid environment

ˈ**pep** ˌ**talk** *n* a usu brief, high-pressure, and emotional talk designed esp to encourage an audience (e g a sports team)

peptic /ˈpeptik‖ˈpeptɪk/ *adj* **1** of or promoting digestion **2** connected with or resulting from the action of digestive juices <*a* ~ *ulcer*>

peptide /ˈpeptied‖ˈpeptaɪd/ *n* a short chain of 2 or more amino acids joined by peptide bonds – **peptidic** *adj*

peptide bond *n* the chemical bond between the carbon of one amino acid and the nitrogen of another that links amino acids in peptides and proteins

per /pə‖pə; *strong* puh‖pɜː/ *prep* **1** by the means or agency of; through <*send it* ~ *rail*> **2** with respect to every; for each <*£30* ~ *head* ~ *week*> **3** ACCORDING TO 1 <~ *list price*>

per- *prefix* **1a** through; throughout <per*ambulate*> **b** thoroughly; very <per*fervid*> **2** to the bad; to destruction <per*jure*>

peradventure /pərəd'venchə, ˌpuh-‖pərəd-'ventʃə, ˌpɜː-/ *adv, archaic* perhaps, possibly

perambulate /pə'rambyoolayt‖pə-'ræmbjʊleɪt/ *vt* to travel over or through on foot; traverse ~*vi* to stroll *USE* fml – **perambulation** *n*, **perambulatory** *adj*

perambulator /pə'rambyoolaytə‖pə-'ræmbjʊleɪtə/ *n, chiefly Br* a pram

per 'annum /pər 'anəm‖pər 'ænəm/ *adv* in or for each year

per 'capita /'kapitə‖'kæpɪtə/ *adv or adj* per unit of population; by or for each person <*the highest income* ~ *of any European country*>

perceive /pə'seev‖pə'siːv/ *vt* **1** to understand, realize **2** to become aware of through the senses; *esp* to see, observe – **perceivable** *adj*, **perceivably** *adv*, **perceiver** *n*

[1]**per cent** /pə 'sent‖pə 'sent/ *adv* in or for each 100 <*50* ~ *of our workers are married*>

[2]**per cent** *n, pl* **per cent** **1** one part in a 100 <*gave half a* ~ *of her income to charity*> **2** a percentage <*a large* ~ *of the total*>

[3]**per cent** *adj* **1** reckoned on the basis of a whole divided into 100 parts <*a 10* ~ *increase*> **2** *of bonds, securities, etc* paying interest at a specified per cent

percentage /pə'sentij‖pə'sentɪdʒ/ *n* **1** a proportion (expressed as per cent of a whole) <*what* ~ *of the population own their own houses?*> <*the* ~ *of car owners has increased to 50*> **2** a share of winnings or profits <*they did him out of his* ~> **3** an advantage, profit – infml

percentile /pə'sentiel‖pə'sentaɪl/ *n* a statistical measure (e g used in educational and psychological testing) that expresses a value as a percentage of all the values that are lower than or equal to it

perceptible /pə'septəbl‖pə'septəbl/ *adj* capable of being perceived, esp by the senses – **perceptibly** *adv*, **perceptibility** *n*

perception /pə'sepsh(ə)n‖pə'sepʃ(ə)n/ *n* **1a** a result of perceiving; an observation **b** a mental image; a concept **2** the mental interpretation of physical sensations produced by stimuli from the external world **3** intuitive discernment; insight, understanding <*has little* ~ *of what is required*> – **perceptional** *adj*, **perceptual** *adj*

perceptive /pə'septiv‖pə'septɪv/ *adj* **1** capable of or exhibiting (keen) perception; observant, discerning <*a* ~ *scholar*> **2** characterized by sympathetic understanding or insight – **perceptively** *adv*, **perceptiveness** *n*, **perceptivity** *n*

[1]**perch** /puhch‖pɜːtʃ/ *n* **1** a roost for a bird **2** *chiefly Br* ROD 2 **3a** a resting place or vantage point; a seat **b** a prominent position <*his new* ~ *as president*> *USE* (*3*) infml

[2]**perch** *vt* to place on a perch, height, or precarious spot ~*vi* to alight, settle, or rest, esp briefly or precariously

[3]**perch** *n* a small European freshwater spiny-finned fish

perchance /pə'chahns‖pə'tʃɑːns/ *adv* perhaps, possibly – usu poetic or humor

percipient /pə'sipi·ənt‖pə'sɪpɪənt/ *adj* perceptive, discerning – fml – **percipience** *n*

percolate /'puhkəlayt‖'pɜːkəleɪt/ *vt* **1a** to cause (esp a liquid) to pass through a permeable substance, esp for extracting a soluble constituent **b** to prepare (coffee) in a percolator **2** to be diffused through; permeate ~ *vi* **1** to ooze or filter through a permeable substance; seep **2** to become percolated **3** to become diffused <*sunlight* ~d *into the room*> – **percolation** *n*

percolator /'puhkəlaytə‖'pɜːkəleɪtə/ *n* a coffee pot in which boiling water rising through a tube is repeatedly deflected downwards through a perforated basket containing ground coffee beans

percussion /pə'kush(ə)n‖pə'kʌʃ(ə)n/ *n* **1a** the beating or striking of a musical instrument **b** the tapping of the surface of a body part (e g the chest) to learn the condition of the parts beneath (e g the lungs) by the resultant sound **2** the striking of sound on the ear **3** *sing or pl in constr* percussion instruments that form a section of a band or orchestra – **percussion** *adj*, **percussive** *adj*

per'cussion ˌcap *n* CAP 6

percussionist /pə'kush(ə)nist‖pə'kʌʃ(ə)nɪst/ *n* one who plays percussion instruments

[1]**per 'diem** /'dee·em, 'die·em‖'diːem, 'daɪem/ *adj or adv* (paid) by the day or for each day

[2]**per diem** *n, pl* **per diems** a daily allowance or fee

perdition /pə'dish(ə)n‖pə'dɪʃ(ə)n/ *n* eternal damnation; Hell

peregrination /ˌperigri'naysh(ə)n‖ˌperɪgrɪ-'neɪʃ(ə)n/ *n* a long and wandering journey, esp in a foreign country – humor – **peregrinate** *vb*

peregrine /'perigrin‖'perɪgrɪn/, **peregrine falcon** *n* a smallish swift widely occurring falcon formerly much used in falconry

peremptory /pə'rempt(ə)ri‖pə'rempt(ə)rɪ/ *adj* **1** admitting no contradiction or refusal <*a* ~ *conclusion*> <*a* ~ *command*> **2** expressive of urgency or command <*a* ~ *call*> **3** (having an attitude or nature) characterized by imperious or arrogant self-assurance <*a* ~ *disregard for safety measures*> <*a* ~ *tone*> – **peremptorily** *adv*, **peremptoriness** *n*

perennial /pə'renyəl, -ni·əl‖pə'renjəl, -nɪəl/ *adj* **1** present at all seasons of the year **2** *of a plant* living for several years, usu with new herbaceous growth each year **3** lasting for a long time or forever; constant <*politics provide a* ~ *topic of argument*> – **perennial** *n*, **perennially** *adv*

[1]**perfect** /'puhfikt‖'pɜːfɪkt/ *adj* **1** expert, proficient <*practice makes* ~> **2a** entirely without fault or defect; flawless <*a* ~ *gemstone*> **b** satisfactory in every respect <*the holiday was* ~> **c** corresponding to an ideal standard or abstract concept <*a* ~ *gentleman*> **3a** accurate, exact <~ *pitch*> <*a* ~ *circle*> **b** lacking in no essential detail; complete **c** absolute, utter <*I felt a* ~ *fool*> **4** of or constituting a verb tense or form that expresses an action or state completed at the time of speaking or at a time spoken of

5a *of the musical intervals fourth, fifth, and octave* having a character that is retained when inverted; not augmented or diminished **b** *of a cadence* passing from a dominant or subdominant to a tonic chord **6** having the stamens and carpels in the same flower – **perfectness** *n*, **perfectly** *adv*

[2]**perfect** /pə'fekt‖pə'fekt/ *vt* **1** to make perfect; improve, refine **2** to bring to final form – **perfecter** *n*, **perfectible** *adj*, **perfectibility** *n*

perfection /pə'feksh(ə)n‖pə'fekʃ(ə)n/ *n* **1a** making or being perfect **b** freedom from (moral) fault or defect **c** full development; maturity <*Greek civilization slowly flowered to* ~> **2** (an example of) unsurpassable accuracy or excellence

perfectionism /pə'fekshə,niz(ə)m‖pə'fekʃə,nɪz(ə)m/ *n* **1** the theological doctrine that a state of freedom from sin is attainable on earth **2** a disposition to regard anything short of perfection, esp in one's own work, as unacceptable – **perfectionist** *adj or n*

perfidy /'puhfidi‖'pɜːfɪdɪ/ *n* being faithless or disloyal; treachery – **perfidious** *adj*, **perfidiously** *adv*, **perfidiousness** *n*

perforate /'puhfə,rayt‖'pɜːfə,reɪt/ *vt* **1** to make a hole through; *specif* to make a line of holes in or between (e g rows of postage stamps in a sheet) to make separation easier **2** to pass through or into (as if) by making a hole ~ *vi* to penetrate or make a hole in a surface [Latin *perforare* to bore through, fr *per* through + *forare* to bore] – **perforator** *n*, **perforate** *adj*, **perforation** *n*

perforce /pə'faws‖pə'fɔːs/ *adv* by force of circumstances – fml

perform /pə'fawm‖pə'fɔːm/ *vt* **1** to do; CARRY OUT <~ed *a small service*> **2a** to do in a formal manner or according to prescribed ritual <~ *a marriage ceremony*> **b** to give a rendering of; present <*they* ~ed *a new play*> ~ *vi* **1** to carry out an action or pattern of behaviour; act, function **2** to give a performance – **performable** *adj*, **performer** *n*

performance /pə'fawməns‖pə'fɔːməns/ *n* **1a** the execution of an action **b** sthg accomplished; a deed, feat **2** the fulfilment of a claim, promise, etc **3** a presentation to an audience of a (character in a) play, a piece of music, etc <*3* ~s *a night*> <*gave a brilliant* ~ *in the title rôle*> **4** the ability to perform or work (efficiently or well) <*good engine* ~ *requires good tuning*> **5** manner of reacting to stimuli; behaviour <*the* ~ *of the stock market*> **6** language as manifested in actual speech and writing **7a** a lengthy or troublesome process or activity <*going through the customs was such a* ~*!*> **b** a display of bad behaviour *USE* (7) infml

[1]**perfume** /'puhfyoohm‖'pɜːfjuːm/ *n* **1** a sweet or pleasant smell; a fragrance **2** a pleasant-smelling (liquid) preparation (e g of floral essences)

[2]**perfume** /pə'fyoohm, 'puhfyoohm‖pə'fjuːm, 'pɜːfjuːm/ *vt* to fill or imbue with a sweet smell

perfumery /pə'fyoohm(ə)ri‖pə'fjuːm(ə)rɪ/ *n* **1** (the manufacture of) perfumes **2** a place where perfumes are made or sold – **perfumer** *n*

perfunctory /pə'fungkt(ə)ri‖pə'fʌŋkt(ə)rɪ/ *adj* characterized by routine or superficiality; mechanical, cursory <*a* ~ *smile*> – **perfunctorily** *adv*, **perfunctoriness** *n*

pergola /'puhgələ‖'pɜːgələ/ *n* (an arbour made by training plants over) a support for climbing plants

perhaps /pə'haps, p(ə)raps‖pə'hæps, p(ə)ræps/ *adv* possibly but not certainly; maybe <~ *I'm mistaken*> <~ *you would open it?*>

peri- /peri-‖perɪ-/ *prefix* **1** all; round; about <peri*scope*> **2** near <peri*helion*> **3** enclosing; surrounding <peri*meter*>

pericarp /'peri,kahp‖'perɪ,kɑːp/ *n* the structure that surrounds the seed(s) of a fruit and consists of the ripened wall of a plant ovary

'**peri,gee** /-,jee‖-,dʒiː/ *n* the point in an orbit round the earth that is nearest the centre of the earth – **perigean** *adj*

perihelion /,peri'heeli·ən, -lyən‖,perɪ'hiːlɪən, -ljən/ *n, pl* **perihelia** /-li·ə‖-lɪə/ the point in the path of a planet, comet, etc that is nearest to the sun – **perihelic** *adj*

peril /'perəl, -ril‖'perəl, -rɪl/ *n* **1** exposure to the risk of being injured, destroyed, or lost; danger <*fire put the city in* ~> **2** sthg that imperils; a risk – **perilous** *adj*, **perilously** *adv*, **perilousness** *n*

perimeter /pə'rimitə‖pə'rɪmɪtə/ *n* **1** (the length of) the boundary of a closed plane figure **2** a line, strip, fence, etc bounding or protecting an area <*a* ~ *fence*> **3** the outer edge or limits of sthg [French *périmètre*, fr Latin *perimetros*, fr Greek, fr *peri* around + *metron* measure]

[1]**period** /'piəri·əd‖'pɪərɪəd/ *n* **1** a well-proportioned sentence of several clauses **2a** the full pause at the end of a sentence; *also, chiefly NAm* FULL STOP **b** a stop, end **3a** a portion of time **b** the (interval of) time that elapses before a cyclic motion or phenomenon begins to repeat itself; the reciprocal of the frequency **c** (a single cyclic occurrence of) menstruation **4a** a chronological division; a stage (of history) **b** a division of geological time longer than an epoch and included in an era **5** any of the divisions of **5a** the school day **b** the playing time of a game

[2]**period** *adj* of, representing, or typical of a particular historical period <~ *furniture*>

periodic /,piəri'odik‖,pɪərɪ'ɒdɪk/ *adj* **1** recurring at regular intervals **2** consisting of or containing a series of repeated stages <~ *decimals*> <*a* ~ *vibration*> – **periodicity** *n*

[1]**periodical** /,piəri'odikl‖,pɪərɪ'ɒdɪkl/ *adj* **1** PERIODIC 1 **2** *of a magazine or journal* published at fixed intervals (e g weekly or quarterly) – **periodically** *adv*

[2]**periodical** *n* a periodical publication

periodic table *n* an arrangement of chemical elements in the order of their atomic numbers, that shows a periodic variation in their properties

'**period ,piece** *n* a piece (e g of fiction, art, furniture, or music) whose special value lies in its evocation of a historical period

[1]**peripatetic** /,peripə'tetik‖,perɪpə'tetɪk/ *n* sby, esp a teacher unattached to a particular school, or sthg that travels about from place to place (on business)

[2]**peripatetic** *adj* itinerant – **peripatetically** *adv*

[1]**peripheral** /pəˈrif(ə)rəl‖pəˈrɪf(ə)rəl/ *adj* **1** of, involving, or forming a periphery <~ *nerves*>; *also* of minor significance **2** located away from a centre or central portion; external **3** of, using, or being the outer part of the field of vision <*good* ~ *vision*> **4** auxiliary or supplementary <~ *equipment*> – **peripherally** *adv*

[2]**peripheral** *n* a device (e g a VDU) connected to a computer to provide communication (e g input and output) or auxiliary functions (e g additional storage)

periphery /pəˈrif(ə)ri‖pəˈrɪf(ə)rɪ/ *n* **1** the perimeter of a closed curve (e g a circle or polygon) **2** the external boundary or surface of a (person's) body, esp as distinguished from its internal regions or centre

periphrasis /pəˈrifrəsis‖pəˈrɪfrəsɪs/ *n, pl* **periphrases** /-seez‖-siːz/ (a) circumlocution

periphrastic /ˌperiˈfrastik‖ˌperɪˈfræstɪk/ *adj* of or characterized by periphrasis – **periphrastically** *adv*

periscope /ˈperiˌskohp‖ˈperɪˌskəʊp/ *n* a tubular optical instrument containing lenses, mirrors, or prisms for seeing objects not in the direct line of sight [deriv of Greek *peri* around + *skopein* to look at]

perish /ˈperish‖ˈperɪʃ/ *vi* **1a** to be destroyed or ruined <~ *the thought!*> **b** to die, esp in a terrible or sudden way – poetic or journ **2** *chiefly Br* to deteriorate, spoil <*the rubber had begun to* ~> ~*vt, of cold or exposure* to weaken, numb <*we were* ~ed *with cold*>

perishable /ˈperishəbl‖ˈperɪʃəbl/ *n or adj* (sthg, esp food) liable to spoil or decay – **perishability** *n*

perisher /ˈperishə‖ˈperɪʃə/ *n, Br* an annoying or troublesome person or thing; *esp* a mischievous child – infml

perishing /ˈperishing‖ˈperɪʃɪŋ/ *adj* **1** freezingly cold **2** damnable, confounded – **perishingly** *adv*

ˈ**periˌstyle** /-ˌstiel‖-ˌstaɪl/ *n* a colonnade surrounding a building or court

peritoneum /ˌperitohˈnee·əm‖ˌperɪtəʊˈniːəm/ *n, pl* **peritoneums, peritonea** /-ˈnee·ə‖-ˈniːə/ the smooth transparent membrane that lines the cavity of the mammalian abdomen – **peritoneal** *adj*, **peritoneally** *adv*

peritonitis /ˌperitəˈnietəs‖ˌperɪtəˈnaɪtəs/ *n* inflammation of the peritoneum

periwig /ˈperiˌwig‖ˈperɪˌwɪg/ *n* a peruke – **periwigged** *adj*

[1]**periwinkle** /ˈperiˌwingkl‖ˈperɪˌwɪŋkl/ *n* any of several trailing evergreen plants with blue or white flowers

[2]**periwinkle** *n* any of various (related) edible marine snails

perjure /ˈpuhjə‖ˈpɜːdʒə/ *vt* to make (oneself) guilty of perjury – **perjurer** *n*

perjury /ˈpuhj(ə)ri‖ˈpɜːdʒ(ə)rɪ/ *n* the voluntary violation of an oath, esp by a witness

[1]**perk** /puhk‖pɜːk/ *n, chiefly Br* a privilege, gain, or profit incidental to regular salary or wages

[2]**perk** *vi, of coffee* to percolate

perk up *vb* to (cause to) recover one's vigour or cheerfulness, esp after a period of weakness or depression

perky /ˈpuhki‖ˈpɜːkɪ/ *adj* **1** briskly self-assured; cocky <*a* ~ *salesman*> **2** jaunty – **perkily** *adv*, **perkiness** *n*

[1]**perm** /puhm‖pɜːm/ *n* a long-lasting wave set in the hair by chemicals

[2]**perm** *vt, Br* to give a perm to

[3]**perm** *vt, Br* to permute; *specif* to pick out and combine (a specified number of teams in a football pool) in all the possible permutations – **perm** *n*

permafrost /ˈpuhməˌfrost‖ˈpɜːməˌfrɒst/ *n* a layer of permanently frozen ground in frigid regions

[1]ˈ**permanent** /ˈpuhmənənt‖ˈpɜːmənənt/ *adj* **1** continuing or enduring without fundamental or marked change; lasting, stable **2** not subject to replacement according to political circumstances <~ *undersecretary at the Home Office*> – **permanence, permanency** *n*, **permanently** *adv*

[2]**permanent** *n, NAm* ¹PERM

permanent way *n, Br* the rails, sleepers, and ballast that make up the track of a railway system

permanganate /pəˈmang·gənət, -ˌnayt‖pəˈmæŋgənət, -ˌneɪt/ *n* a usu dark purple salt containing manganese

permeable /ˈpuhmi·əbl‖ˈpɜːmɪəbl/ *adj* capable of being permeated; *esp* having pores or openings that permit liquids or gases to pass through – **permeableness** *n*, **permeably** *adv*

permeate /ˈpuhmiˌayt‖ˈpɜːmɪˌeɪt/ *vi* to diffuse through or penetrate sthg ~ *vt* **1** to spread or diffuse through **2** to pass through the pores, gaps, cracks, etc of – **permeance** *n*, **permeant** *adj or n*, **permeation** *n*

permissible /pəˈmisəbl‖pəˈmɪsəbl/ *adj* allowable – **permissibly** *adv*, **permissibility** *n*

permission /pəˈmish(ə)n‖pəˈmɪʃ(ə)n/ *n* formal consent; authorization

permissive /pəˈmisiv‖pəˈmɪsɪv/ *adj* **1** tolerant; *esp* accepting a relaxed social or sexual morality <*the* ~ *age*> **2** allowing (but not enforcing) <~ *legislation*> – **permissively** *adv*, **permissiveness** *n*

[1]**permit** /pəˈmit‖pəˈmɪt/ *vb* **-tt-** *vt* **1** to consent to, usu expressly or formally <~ *access to records*> **2** to give leave; authorize **3** to make possible ~*vi* to give an opportunity; allow <*if time* ~s> <*weather* ~ting> – **permitter** *n*

[2]**permit** /ˈpuhmit‖ˈpɜːmɪt/ *n* a written warrant allowing the holder to do or keep sthg

permutation /ˌpuhmyooˈtaysh(ə)n‖ˌpɜːmjʊˈteɪʃ(ə)n/ *n* **1** a variation or change (e g in character or condition) brought about by rearrangement of existing elements **2** (the changing from one to another of) any of the various possible ordered arrangements of a set of objects, numbers, letters, etc – **permutational** *adj*

permute /pəˈmyooht‖pəˈmjuːt/ *vt* to change the order or arrangement of; *esp* to arrange successively in all possible ways

pernicious /pəˈnishəs, puh-‖pəˈnɪʃəs, pɜː-/ *adj* highly injurious or destructive; deadly – **perniciously** *adv*, **perniciousness** *n*

pernicious anaemia *n* anaemia marked by a decrease in the number of red blood cells which is caused by a reduced ability to absorb vitamin B_{12}

pernickety /pəˈnikəti‖pəˈnɪkətɪ/ *adj* **1** fussy

about small details; fastidious <*a* ~ *teacher*> **2** requiring precision and care <*a* ~ *job*>

peroration /ˌperəˈraysh(ə)n‖ˌperəˈreɪʃ(ə)n/ *n* **1** the concluding part of a discourse, in which the main points are summed up **2** a highly rhetorical speech – **perorational** *adj*, **perorate** *vi*

[1]**peroxide** /pəˈroksied‖pəˈrɒksaɪd/ *n* **1** an oxide containing a high proportion of oxygen; *esp* a compound containing the peroxy radical **2** HYDROGEN PEROXIDE – **peroxidic** *adj*

[2]**peroxide** *vt* to bleach (hair) with hydrogen peroxide – **peroxidation** *n*

[1]**perpendicular** /ˌpuhpənˈdikyoolə‖ˌpɜːpənˈdɪkjʊlə/ *adj* **1** being or standing at right angles to the plane of the horizon or a given line or plane **2** extremely steep; precipitous **3** *cap* of, being, or built in a late Gothic style of architecture prevalent in England from the 15th to the 16th c characterized by large windows, fan vaults, and an emphasis on vertical lines – **perpendicularly** *adv*, **perpendicularity** *n*

[2]**perpendicular** *n* a line, plane, or surface at right angles to the plane of the horizon or to another line or surface

perpetrate /ˈpuhpiˌtrayt‖ˈpɜːpɪˌtreɪt/ *vt* to be guilty of performing or doing; commit <~ *a fraud*> <~ *a blunder*> – **perpetrator** *n*, **perpetration** *n*

perpetual /pəˈpetyoo(ə)l, -choo(ə)l‖pəˈpetjʊ(ə)l, -tʃʊ(ə)l/ *adj* **1a** continuing or valid forever; everlasting **b** holding sthg (e g an office) for life or for an unlimited time **2** occurring continually; constant <*a* ~ *complaint*> **3** *of a plant* blooming continuously throughout the season – **perpetually** *adv*

perpetuate /pəˈpetyooˌayt, -chooˌayt‖pəˈpetjʊˌeɪt, -tʃʊˌeɪt/ *vt* to make perpetual; cause to last indefinitely <~ *the species*> – **perpetuator** *n*, **perpetuation** *n*

perpetuity /ˌpuhpiˈtyooh·əti‖ˌpɜːpɪˈtjuːətɪ/ *n* (the quality or state of) sthg that is perpetual; eternity <*bequeathed to them in* ~>

perplex /pəˈpleks‖pəˈpleks/ *vt* **1** to puzzle, confuse <*her attitude* ~es *me*> <*a* ~ing *problem*> **2** to complicate – **perplexedly** *adv*, **perplexingly** *adv*

perplexity /pəˈpleksəti‖pəˈpleksətɪ/ *n* (sthg that causes) the state of being perplexed or bewildered

perquisite /ˈpuhkwizit‖ˈpɜːkwɪzɪt/ *n* **1** sthg held or claimed as an exclusive right or possession **2** a perk – fml

perry /ˈperi‖ˈperɪ/ *n* an alcoholic drink made from fermented pear juice [Middle French *peré*, deriv of Latin *pirum* pear]

per se /pə ˈsay‖pə ˈseɪ/ *adv* by, of, or in itself; intrinsically

persecute /ˈpuhsiˌkyooht‖ˈpɜːsɪˌkjuːt/ *vt* **1** to harass in a manner designed to injure or afflict; *specif* to cause to suffer because of race, religion, political beliefs, etc **2** to annoy with persistent or urgent approaches, attacks, pleas, etc; pester – **persecutor** *n*, **persecution** *n*, **persecutory** *adj*

perseverance /ˌpuhsiˈviərəns‖ˌpɜːsɪˈvɪərəns/ *n* **1** persevering, steadfastness **2** continuance in a state of grace

persevere /ˌpuhsiˈviə‖ˌpɜːsɪˈvɪə/ *vi* to persist in a state, enterprise, or undertaking in spite of adverse influences, opposition, or discouragement

Persian /ˈpuhsh(ə)n, ‖ˈpɜːʃ(ə)n,*also* -zh(ə)n‖-ʒ(ə)n/ *n or adj* (a native, inhabitant, or language) of ancient Persia or modern Iran

persiflage /ˈpuhsiˌflahzh‖ˈpɜːsɪˌflɑːʒ/ *n* frivolous bantering talk

persimmon /puhˈsimən‖pɜːˈsɪmən/ *n* (the orange several-seeded globular fruit of) any of a genus of American and Asian trees of the ebony family with hard fine wood

persist /pəˈsist‖pəˈsɪst/ *vi* **1** to go on resolutely or stubbornly in spite of opposition or warning **2** to be insistent in the repetition or pressing of an utterance (e g a question or opinion) **3** to continue to exist, esp past a usual, expected, or normal time – **persister** *n*

persistent /pəˈsist(ə)nt‖pəˈsɪst(ə)nt/ *adj* **1** continuing to exist in spite of interference or treatment <*a* ~ *cough*> **2a** remaining **2a(1)** beyond the usual period <*a* ~ *leaf*> **a(2)** without change in function or structure <~ *gills*> **b** *of a chemical substance* broken down only slowly in the environment <~ *pesticides*> – **persistence, persistency** *n*, **persistently** *adv*

persnickety /pəˈsnikəti‖pəˈsnɪkətɪ/ *adj, NAm* **1** pernickety **2** snobbish

person /ˈpuhs(ə)n‖ˈpɜːs(ə)n/ *n* **1** a human being (considered as having a character of his/her own, or as being different from all others) <*you're just the* ~ *I wanted to see*> **2** any of the 3 modes of being in the Trinity as understood by Christians **3** a living human body or its outward appearance <*she was small and neat of* ~> <*insured against damage to* ~ *and property*> **4** an individual, corporation, etc with recognized legal rights and duties **5** any of 3 forms of verb or pronoun that indicate reference to the speaker, to one spoken to, or to sby or sthg spoken of – **in person** in one's own bodily presence <*he appeared* in person *last time*>

persona /puhˈsohnə‖pɜːˈsəʊnə/ *n, pl* (*1*) **personae** /-ni‖-nɪ/, (*2*) **personas** **1** *pl* the characters in a fictional work **2** an individual's social facade that, esp in Jungian psychology, reflects the role that the individual is playing in life

personable /ˈpuhs(ə)nəbl‖ˈpɜːs(ə)nəbl/ *adj* pleasing in person; attractive – **personableness** *n*

personage /ˈpuhs(ə)nij‖ˈpɜːs(ə)nɪdʒ/ *n* **1** a person of rank, note, or distinction; *esp* one distinguished in presence and personal power **2** a dramatic, fictional, or historical character **3** a human individual; a person – fml

personal /ˈpuhs(ə)nl‖ˈpɜːs(ə)nl/ *adj* **1** of or affecting a person; private <*done purely for* ~ *financial gain*> **2a** done in person without the intervention of another; *also* proceeding from a single person **b** carried on between individuals directly <*a* ~ *interview*> **3** of the person or body **4** of or referring to (the character, conduct, motives, or private affairs of) an individual, often in an offensive manner <*don't make* ~ *remarks*> **5** of personal property <*a* ~ *estate*> **6** denoting grammatical person

personality /ˈpuhs(ə)nˈaləti‖ˈpɜːs(ə)nˈælətɪ/

n **1** *pl* reference, esp critical, to a particular person <*let's keep* personalities *out of this debate*> **2** the totality of an individual's behavioural and emotional tendencies; *broadly* a distinguishing complex of individual or group characteristics **3a** (sby having) distinction or excellence of personal and social traits **b** a person of importance, prominence, renown, or notoriety <*a well-known stage* ~>

person'ality ˌcult *n* the officially encouraged slavish admiration of a leader

personal·ize, -ise /ˈpuhs(ə)nlˌiez‖ˈpɜːs(ə)nl-ˌaɪz/ *vt* **1** PERSONIFY 1 **2** to make personal or individual; *specif* to mark as the property of a particular person <~d *stationery*> – **personalization** *n*

personally /ˈpuhs(ə)nli‖ˈpɜːs(ə)nlɪ/ *adv* **1** IN PERSON <*attend to the matter* ~> **2** as a person; in personality <~ *attractive but not very trustworthy*> **3** for oneself; as far as oneself is concerned <~, *I don't think much of it*> **4** as directed against oneself in a personal way <*don't take my remarks about your plan* ~>

personal pronoun *n* a pronoun (e g *I, you,* or *they*) that expresses a distinction of person

personal property *n* all property other than freehold estates and interests in land

persona non grata /puhˌsohnə non ˈgrahtə‖pɜːˌsəʊnə nɒn ˈgrɑːtə/ *adj* personally unacceptable or unwelcome

personification /pəˌsonifiˈkaysh(ə)n‖pəˌsɒnɪfɪˈkeɪʃ(ə)n/ *n* **1** the personifying of an abstract quality or thing **2** an embodiment, incarnation

personify /pəˈsonifie‖pəˈsɒnɪfaɪ/ *vt* **1** to conceive of or represent as having human qualities or form **2** to be the embodiment of in human form; incarnate <*he was kindness* personified> – **personifier** *n*

personnel /ˌpuhsəˈnel‖ˌpɜːsəˈnel/ *n* **1** *sing or pl in constr* a body of people employed (e g in a factory, office, or organization) or engaged on a project **2** a division of an organization concerned with the employees and their welfare at work

[1]**perspective** /pəˈspektiv‖pəˈspektɪv/ *adj* of, using, or seen in perspective <*a* ~ *drawing*> – **perspectively** *adv*

[2]**perspective** *n* **1a** (the technique of accurately representing on a flat or curved surface) the visual appearance of solid objects with respect to their relative distance and position **b** LINEAR PERSPECTIVE **2a** the aspect of an object of thought from a particular standpoint <*try to get a different* ~ *on your problem*> **b** (the capacity to discern) the true relationship or relative importance of things <*get things in* ~> **3** a picture or view giving a distinctive impression of distance; a vista

Perspex /ˈpuhˌspeks‖ˈpɜːˌspeks/ *trademark* – used for a transparent acrylic plastic

perspicacious /ˌpuhspiˈkayshəs‖ˌpɜːspɪˈkeɪʃəs/ *adj* of acute mental vision or discernment; KEEN 3a – fml – **perspicaciously** *adv*, **perspicaciousness** *n*, **perspicacity** *n*

perspiration /ˌpuhspiˈraysh(ə)n‖ˌpɜːspɪˈreɪʃ(ə)n/ *n* **1** sweating **2** [2]SWEAT 1 – **perspiratory** *adj*

perspire /pəˈspie·ə‖pəˈspaɪə/ *vi* [1]SWEAT 1

persuade /pəˈswayd‖pəˈsweɪd/ *vt* **1** to move by argument, reasoning, or entreaty to a belief, position, or course of action **2** to cause to feel certain; convince <*the icy roads* ~d *him of the need to drive carefully*> **3** to get (sthg) with difficulty *out of* or *from* <*finally* ~d *an answer out of her*> – **persuadable** *adj*, **persuader** *n*

persuasion /pəˈswayzh(ə)n‖pəˈsweɪʒ(ə)n/ *n* **1a** persuading or being persuaded **b** persuasiveness <*she has great powers of* ~> **2a** an opinion held with complete assurance **b** (a group adhering to) a particular system of religious beliefs **3** a kind, sort <*people of the same* ~>

persuasive /pəˈswaysiv, -ziv‖pəˈsweɪsɪv, -zɪv/ *adj* tending or able to persuade – **persuasively** *adv*, **persuasiveness** *n*

pert /puht‖pɜːt/ *adj* **1** impudent and forward; saucy **2** trim and chic; jaunty <*a* ~ *little hat*> – **pertly** *adv*, **pertness** *n*

pertain /pəˈtayn‖pəˈteɪn/ *vi* **1a** to belong *to* as a part, attribute, feature, function, or right <*the destruction and havoc* ~ing *to war*> **b** to be appropriate to sthg <*the criteria that* ~ *elsewhere do not apply here*> **2** to have reference *to* <*books* ~ing *to birds*>

pertinacious /ˌpuhtiˈnayshəs‖ˌpɜːtɪˈneɪʃəs/ *adj* clinging resolutely to an opinion, purpose, or design, often to the point of stubbornness – fml – **pertinaciously** *adv*, **pertinaciousness** *n*, **pertinacity** *n*

pertinent /ˈpuhtinənt‖ˈpɜːtɪnənt/ *adj* clearly relevant (to the matter in hand) <~ *details*> – **pertinence, pertinency** *n*, **pertinently** *adv*

perturb /pəˈtuhb, puh-‖pəˈtɜːb, pɜː-/ *vt* **1** to disturb greatly in mind; disquiet **2** to throw into confusion; disorder **3** to cause (a moving object, celestial body, etc) to deviate from a theoretically regular (orbital) motion – **perturbable** *adj*, **perturbation** *n*, **perturbational** *adj*

peruke /pəˈroohk‖pəˈruːk/ *n* a long curly wig worn by men in the 17th and 18th c

peruse /pəˈroohz‖pəˈruːz/ *vt* **1** to examine or consider with attention and in detail; study – fml **2** to look over the contents of (e g a book) – often humor – **perusal** *n*, **peruser** *n*

pervade /pəˈvayd, puh-‖pəˈveɪd, pɜː-/ *vt* to become diffused throughout every part of – **pervasion** *n*, **pervasive** *adj*, **pervasively** *adv*, **pervasiveness** *n*

perverse /pəˈvuhs, puh-‖pəˈvɜːs, pɜː-/ *adj* **1a** obstinate in opposing what is right, reasonable, or accepted; wrongheaded **b** arising from or indicative of stubbornness or obstinacy **2** unreasonably opposed to the wishes of others; uncooperative, contrary – **perversely** *adv*, **perversity, perverseness** *n*

perversion /pəˈvuhsh(ə)n, puh-‖pəˈvɜːʃ(ə)n, pɜː-/ *n* **1** perverting or being perverted **2** sthg perverted; *esp* abnormal sexual behaviour – **perversive** *adj*

[1]**pervert** /pəˈvuht‖pəˈvɜːt/ *vt* **1** to cause to turn aside or away from what is good, true, or morally right; corrupt **2a** to divert to a wrong end or purpose; misuse **b** to twist the meaning or sense of; misinterpret [Middle French *pervertir*, fr Latin *pervertere* to overturn, corrupt, fr *per-* thoroughly + *vertere* to turn] – **perverter** *n*

[2]**pervert** /'puhvuht‖'pɜ:vɜ:t/ *n* a perverted person; *specif* one given to some form of sexual perversion

peseta /pə'seetə, pə'saytə‖pə'si:tə, pə'seɪtə/ *n* the standard unit of money in Spain

pesky /'peski‖'peskɪ/ *adj, NAm* troublesome, vexatious – infml

peso /'paysoh‖'peɪsəʊ/ *n, pl* **pesos** **1** a former silver coin of Spain and Spanish America **2** (a note or coin representing) the basic money unit of certain Spanish-speaking South and Latin American countries (e g Argentina, Chile, Mexico, Uruguay) and the Philippines

pessary /'pesəri‖'pesərɪ/ *n* **1** a vaginal suppository **2** a device worn in the vagina to support the uterus or prevent conception

pessimism /'pesi,miz(ə)m‖'pesɪ,mɪz(ə)m/ *n* **1** a tendency to stress the adverse aspects of a situation or event or to expect the worst possible outcome **2** the doctrine that this is the worst of all possible worlds [French *pessimisme*, fr Latin *pessimus* worst] – **pessimist** *n*, **pessimistic** *adj*, **pessimistically** *adv*

pest /pest‖pest/ *n* **1** a pestilence **2** a plant or animal capable of causing damage or carrying disease **3** sby or sthg that pesters or annoys; a nuisance

pester /'pestə‖'pestə/ *vt* to harass with petty irritations; annoy

pesticide /'pestisied‖'pestɪsaɪd/ *n* a chemical used to destroy insects and other pests

pestiferous /pe'stif(ə)rəs‖pe'stɪf(ə)rəs/ *adj* **1** dangerous to society; pernicious **2** carrying or propagating infection – **pestiferously** *adv*

pestilence /'pestiləns‖'pestɪləns/ *n* a virulent and devastating epidemic disease; *specif* BUBONIC PLAGUE

pestilent /'pestilənt‖'pestɪlənt/ *adj* **1** destructive of life; deadly **2** morally harmful; pernicious **3** causing displeasure or annoyance; irritating – **pestilently** *adv*

[1]**pestle** /'pesl‖'pesl/ *n* **1** a usu club-shaped implement for pounding substances in a mortar **2** any of various devices for pounding, stamping, or pressing

[2]**pestle** *vb* to pound or pulverize (as if) with a pestle

[1]**pet** /pet‖pet/ *n* **1** a domesticated animal kept for companionship rather than work or food **2** sby who is treated with unusual kindness or consideration; a favourite **3** *chiefly Br* DARLING 1 – used chiefly by women as an affectionate form of address

[2]**pet** *adj* **1a** kept or treated as a pet **b** for pet animals <*a ~ shop*> **2** expressing fondness or endearment <*a ~ name*> **3** favourite <*his ~ project*>

[3]**pet** *vb* **-tt-** *vt* **1** to stroke in a gentle or loving manner **2** to treat with unusual kindness and consideration; pamper *~vi* to engage in amorous embracing, caressing, etc – **petter** *n*

[4]**pet** *n* a fit of peevishness, sulkiness, or anger

petal /'petl‖'petl/ *n* any of the modified often brightly coloured leaves of the corolla of a flower – **petaled, petalled** *adj*, **petallike** *adj*, **petaloid** *adj*

petard /pe'tahd, pi-‖pe'tɑ:d, pɪ-/ *n* **1** a case containing an explosive for military demolitions **2** a firework that explodes with a loud report

peter /'peetə‖'pi:tə/ *vi* to diminish gradually and come to an end; give out – usu + *out*

petiole /'peti·ohl‖'petɪəʊl/ *n* the usu slender stalk by which a leaf is attached to a stem – **petiolated** *adj*, **petioled, petiolate** *adj*, **petiolar** *adj*

petit bourgeois /,peti 'booəzh·wah ‖,petɪ 'bʊəʒwɑ: (*Fr* pəti burʒwa)/ *n, pl* **petits bourgeois** /~/ a member of the petite bourgeoisie – **petit bourgeois** *adj*

petite /pə'teet‖pə'ti:t/ *adj, esp of a woman* having a small trim figure

petit four /,peti 'faw ‖,petɪ 'fɔ: (*Fr* pəti fur)/ *n, pl* **petits fours, petit fours** /fawz ‖fɔ:z (*Fr* ~)/ a small fancy cake or biscuit [French, lit., small oven]

[1]**petition** /pi'tish(ə)n‖pɪ'tɪʃ(ə)n/ *n* **1** an earnest request; an entreaty **2** (a document embodying) a formal written request to a superior **3** sthg asked or requested – **petitionary** *adj*

[2]**petition** *vb* to make an esp formal written request (to or for) – **petitioner** *n*

petit mal /,peti 'mal‖,petɪ 'mæl/ *n* (an attack of) mild epilepsy [French, lit., small illness]

petrel /'petrəl‖'petrəl/ *n* any of numerous seabirds; *esp* any of the smaller long-winged birds (e g a storm petrel) that fly far from land

petrifaction /,petri'faksh(ə)n‖,petrɪ'fækʃ(ə)n/ *n* **1** the process of petrifying; being petrified **2** sthg petrified

petrify /'petrifie‖'petrɪfaɪ/ *vt* **1** to convert (as if) into stone or a stony substance **2a** to make lifeless or inactive; deaden **b** to confound with fear, amazement, or awe; paralyse <*is* petrified *of talking in public* – Alan Frank> *~vi* to become stone or of stony hardness or rigidity

petrochemical /,petroh'kemikl, -trə-‖,petrəʊ'kemɪkl, -trə-/ *n* a chemical obtained from petroleum or natural gas – **petrochemical** *adj*, **petrochemistry** *n*

petrol /'petrəl‖'petrəl/ *n, chiefly Br* a volatile inflammable liquid hydrocarbon mixture refined from petroleum and used as a fuel for internal-combustion engines

petroleum /pə'trohli·əm, -lyəm‖pə'trəʊlɪəm, -ljəm/ *n* an oily inflammable usu dark liquid composed of a mixture of hydrocarbons, widely occurring in the upper strata of the earth, and refined for use as petrol, naphtha, etc [Medieval Latin, fr Latin *petra* rock + *oleum* oil – see OIL]

pe,troleum 'jelly *n* a semisolid mixture of hydrocarbons obtained from petroleum and used esp as the basis of ointments

petrology /pe'troləji‖pe'trɒlədʒɪ/ *n* a science that deals with the origin, structure, composition, etc of rocks – **petrologist** *n*, **petrologic, petrological** *adj*, **petrologically** *adv*

'petrol ,station *n, Br* FILLING STATION

[1]**petticoat** /'peti,koht‖'petɪ,kəʊt/ *n* **1** an outer skirt formerly worn by women and small children **2** a skirt designed to be worn as an undergarment – **petticoated** *adj*

[2]**petticoat** *adj* of or exercised by women; female <*~ government*> – chiefly humor or derog

pettifog /'peti,fog‖'petɪ,fɒg/ *vi* **-gg-** **1** to engage in legal chicanery **2** to quibble over insignificant details **pettifogger** *n*, **pettifoggery** *n*

petty /ˈpeti‖ˈpetɪ/ *adj* **1** having secondary rank or importance; *also* trivial **2** small-minded – **pettiness** *n*, **pettily** *adv*

petty bourgeois *n* PETIT BOURGEOIS

ˌ**petty** ˈ**cash** *n* cash kept on hand for payment of minor items

ˌ**petty** ˈ**larceny** *n*, *NAm* larceny involving property below a value specified by law – no longer used technically in the UK

petty officer *n* a noncommissioned officer in the navy

petulant /ˈpetyooləntǁˈpetjʊlənt/ *adj* characterized by temporary or capricious ill humour; peevish – **petulance** *n*, **petulantly** *adv*

petunia /piˈtyoohnyə, -ni·ə‖pɪˈtju:njə, -nɪə/ *n* any of a genus of plants of the nightshade family with large brightly coloured funnel-shaped flowers

pew /pyooh‖pju:/ *n* **1** a bench fixed in a row for the use of the congregation in a church; *also* a high compartment with such benches for the accommodation of a group (e g a family) **2** *Br* a seat <*take a* ~> – infml

pewit /ˈpeeˌwit‖ˈpi:ˌwɪt/ *n* a peewit

pewter /ˈpyoohtə‖ˈpju:tə/ *n* (utensils, vessels, etc made of) any of various tin-containing alloys; *esp* one of tin and lead – **pewter** *adj*

peyote /payˈohti, pi-‖peɪˈəʊtɪ, pɪ-/ *n* **1** any of several American cacti; *esp* MESCAL 1 **2** MESCAL BUTTON; *also* mescaline

pfennig /ˈ(p)fenig, -nikh ‖ˈ(p)fenɪg, -nɪx (*Ger* ˈpfɛnɪç)/ *n*, *pl* **pfennigs, pfennige** /-nigə ‖-nɪgə (*Ger* -nigə)/ *often cap* a German coin worth 1/100 of a mark

PG /pee ˈjee‖pi: ˈdʒi:/ *n or adj* (a film that is) certified in Britain as suitable for all ages but for which parental guidance is recommended for children under 15 [*P*arental *G*uidance]

pH /ˌpee ˈaych‖ˌpi: ˈeɪtʃ/ *n* the negative logarithm of the hydrogen-ion concentration in moles per litre, used to express the acidity or alkalinity of a solution on a scale of 0 to 14 with 7 representing neutrality

phagocyte /ˈfagəˌsiet‖ˈfægəˌsaɪt/ *n* a cell (e g a white blood cell) that characteristically engulfs foreign material (e g bacteria) and consumes debris (e g from tissue injury) – **phagocyte** *adj*, **phagocytic** *adj*, **phagocytically** *adv*

phalanx /ˈfalangks‖ˈfælæŋks/ *n*, *pl* **phalanges** /fəˈlanjeez‖fəˈlændʒi:z/, **phalanxes** **1** *sing or pl in constr* a body of troops, esp those of ancient Greece, in close array **2** any of the digital bones of the hand or foot of a vertebrate **3** *sing or pl in constr* a massed arrangement of people, animals, or things; *esp* a body of people organized for a common purpose

phallus /ˈfaləs‖ˈfæləs/ *n*, *pl* **phalli** /-lie‖-laɪ/ **phalluses** (a symbol or representation of) the penis – **phallic** *adj*

phantasm /ˈfanˌtaz(ə)m‖ˈfænˌtæz(ə)m/ *n* **1** an illusion **2a** a ghost, spectre **b** a figment of the imagination; a fantasy – **phantasmal** *adj*, **phantasmic** *adj*

phantasmagoria /ˌfantazməˈgawri·ə‖ˌfæntæzməˈgɔ:rɪə/ *n* **1** an optical effect by which figures on a screen appear to dwindle into the distance or to rush towards the observer with enormous increase of size **2** a constantly shifting, confused succession of things seen or imagined (e g in a dreaming or feverish state) – **phantasmagoric** *adj*

phantasy /ˈfantəsi‖ˈfæntəsɪ/ *vb or n* (to) fantasy

[1]**phantom** /ˈfantəm‖ˈfæntəm/ *n* **1a** sthg (e g a ghost) apparent to the senses but with no substantial existence **b** sthg elusive or unreal; a will-o'-the-wisp **c** sthg existing only in the imagination <*his dreams troubled by* ~s *of the past*> **2** sthg existing in appearance only; a form without substance – **phantomlike** *adv or adj*

[2]**phantom** *adj* **1** of the nature of, suggesting, or being a phantom **2** fictitious, dummy <~ *voters*>

pharaoh /ˈfeəroh‖ˈfeərəʊ/ *n*, *often cap* a ruler of ancient Egypt – **pharaonic** *adj*, *often cap*

pharisaic /ˌfariˈsay·ik‖ˌfærɪˈseɪɪk/, **pharisaical** /-kl‖-kl/ *adj* **1** *cap* of the Pharisees **2** marked by hypocritical self-righteousness – **pharisaism** *n*

pharisee /ˈfarisee‖ˈfærɪsi:/ *n* **1** *cap* a member of a Jewish party noted for strict adherence to (their own oral traditions interpreting) the Torah **2** a pharisaic person

[1]**pharmaceutical** /ˌfahməˈsyoohtikl‖ˌfɑ:məˈsju:tɪkl/ *also* **pharmaceutic** *adj* of or engaged in pharmacy or in the manufacture of medicinal substances [Late Latin *pharmaceuticus*, fr Greek *pharmakeutikos*, fr *pharmakeuein* to administer drugs, fr *pharmakon* drug] – **pharmaceutically** *adv*

[2]**pharmaceutical** *n* a medicinal drug

pharmacology /ˌfahməˈkoləji‖ˌfɑ:məˈkɒlədʒɪ/ *n* **1** the science of drugs and their effect on living things **2** the properties and effects of a usu specified drug – **pharmacologist** *n*, **pharmacologic, pharmacological** *adj*, **pharmacologically** *adv*

pharmacopoeia /ˌfahməkəˈpee·ə‖ˌfɑ:məkəˈpi:ə/ *n* **1** an (official) book describing drugs, chemicals, and medicinal preparations **2** a stock of drugs – **pharmacopoeial** *adj*

pharmacy /ˈfahməsi‖ˈfɑ:məsɪ/ *n* **1** the preparation, compounding, and dispensing of drugs **2a** a place where medicines are compounded or dispensed **b** CHEMIST 2 – **pharmacist** *n*

pharynx /ˈfaringks‖ˈfærɪŋks/ *n*, *pl* **pharynges** /faˈrinjeez‖fæˈrɪndʒi:z/ *also* **pharynxes** the part of the vertebrate alimentary canal between the mouth cavity and the oesophagus – **pharyngeal** *adj*, **pharyngitis** *n*

[1]**phase** /fayz‖feɪz/ *n* **1** a particular appearance or state in a regularly recurring cycle of changes <~s *of the moon*> **2a** a discernable part or stage in a course, development, or cycle <*the early* ~s *of his career*> **b** an aspect or part (e g of a problem) under consideration **3** a stage of progress in a regularly recurring motion or cyclic process (e g an alternating electric current) with respect to a starting point or standard position **4** a homogeneous and mechanically separable portion of matter present in a complex mixture – **phasic** *adj*

[2]**phase** *vt* **1** to conduct or carry out by planned phases **2** to schedule (e g operations) or contract for (e g goods or services) to be performed or supplied as required <~ *a development programme*>

phase in *vt* to introduce the practice, production, or use of in gradual stages <phase in *a new model*>

phase out *vt* to discontinue the practice, production, or use of in gradual stages <phase out *the old machinery*> – **phaseout** *n*

pheasant /ˈfez(ə)nt‖ˈfez(ə)nt/ *n* any of numerous large often long-tailed and brightly coloured Old World (game) birds [Old French *fesan*, fr Latin *phasianus*, fr Greek *phasianos*, fr *Phasis*, river in Asia]

phenobarbitone /ˌfeenohˈbahbiˌtohn‖ˌfiːnəʊˈbɑːbɪˌtəʊn/ *NAm chiefly* **phenobarbital** /-bit(ə)l‖-bɪt(ə)l/ *n, chiefly Br* a barbiturate used esp as a sedative and anticonvulsant in the treatment of epilepsy

phenol /ˈfeenol‖ˈfiːnɒl/ *n* (any of various derivatives of benzene containing a hydroxyl group and analogous to) a caustic poisonous hydroxy benzene used in dilute solution as a disinfectant – **phenolic** *adj*

phenomenal /fiˈnominl‖fɪˈnɒmɪnl/ *adj* relating to or being a phenomenon: e g **a** known through the senses rather than through thought or intuition **b** concerned with phenomena rather than with hypotheses **c** extraordinary, remarkable <*a ~ success*> – **phenomenally** *adv*

phenomenon /fiˈnominən‖fɪˈnɒmɪnən/ *n, pl* **phenomena** /-nə‖-nə/ *also* **phenomenons** **1** an observable fact or event **2a** an object of sense perception rather than of thought or intuition **b** a fact or event that can be scientifically described and explained **3a** a rare or significant fact or event <*vandalism is a social ~*> **b** an exceptional, unusual, or abnormal person, thing, or event; a prodigy

phew /fyooh‖fjuː/ *interj* – used to express shock, relief, or exhaustion

phial /ˈfie·əl‖ˈfaɪəl/ *n* a small closed or closable vessel, esp for holding liquid medicine

philander /fiˈlandə‖fɪˈlændə/ *vi* **1** *of a man* to flirt **2** to have many casual love affairs – **philanderer** *n*

philanthropic /ˌfilənˈthropik‖ˌfɪlənˈθrɒpɪk/ *also* **philanthropical** /-kl‖-kl/ *adj* **1** of or characterized by philanthropy; humanitarian **2** dispensing or receiving aid from funds set aside for humanitarian purposes <*a ~ institution*> – **philanthropically** *adv*

philanthropy /fiˈlanthrəpi‖fɪˈlænθrəpɪ/ *n* **1** goodwill to one's fellow men; *esp* active effort to promote the welfare of others **2** a philanthropic act or gift – **philanthropist** *n*

philately /fiˈlatəli‖fɪˈlætəlɪ/ *n* the study and collection of (postage) stamps [French *philatélie*, deriv of Greek *phil-* loving + *ateleia* tax exemption, fr *a-* not + *telos* tax] – **philatelist** *n*, **philatelic** *adj*, **philatelically** *adv*

Philharmonic /ˌfiləˈmonik, ˌfil(h)ah-‖ˌfɪləˈmɒnɪk, ˌfɪl(h)ɑː-/ *n* SYMPHONY ORCHESTRA

philippic /fiˈlipik‖fɪˈlɪpɪk/ *n* a speech or declamation full of bitter invective

philistine /ˈfilistien‖ˈfɪlɪstaɪn/ *n* **1** *cap* a native or inhabitant of ancient Philistia **2** *often cap* a person who professes indifference or opposition to intellectual or aesthetic values – **philistine** *adj*, **philistinism** *n*

philology /fiˈloləji‖fɪˈlɒlədʒɪ/ *n* (historical and comparative) linguistics – **philologist** *n*, **philological** *adj*, **philologically** *adv*

philosopher /fiˈlosəfə‖fɪˈlɒsəfə/ *n* **1a** a scholar, thinker **b** a specialist in philosophy **2** a person whose philosophical viewpoint enables him/her to meet trouble with equanimity [Middle French *philosophe*, fr Latin *philosophus*, fr Greek *philosophos*, fr *phil-* loving + *sophia* wisdom, fr *sophos* wise]

philosophers' stone *n* a substance believed by alchemists to have the power of transmuting base metals into gold

philosophical /ˌfiləˈsofikl‖ˌfɪləˈsɒfɪkl/ *adj* **1** of philosophers or philosophy **2** calm in the face of trouble

philosoph·ize, -ise /fiˈlosəfiez‖fɪˈlɒsəfaɪz/ *vi* **1** to engage in philosophical reasoning **2** to expand a trite or superficial philosophy

philosophy /fiˈlosəfi‖fɪˈlɒsəfɪ/ *n* **1a** the pursuit of wisdom **b** the study of the nature of knowledge and existence and the principles of moral and aesthetic value **2** the philosophical principles or teachings of a specified individual, group, or period **3a** the sum of beliefs and attitudes of a specified individual, group, or period <*the vegetarian ~*> **b** equanimity in the face of trouble or stress

philtre, *NAm chiefly* **philter** /ˈfiltə‖ˈfɪltə/ *n* a potion or drug reputed to have the power to arouse sexual passion

phizog /ˈfizog‖ˈfɪzɒg/ *n* FACE 1 –infml or humor

phlebitis /fliˈbietəs‖flɪˈbaɪtəs/ *n* inflammation of a vein

phlebotomy /fliˈbotəmi‖flɪˈbɒtəmɪ/ *n* the letting or taking of blood in the treatment or diagnosis of disease – **phlebotomize** *vb*, **phlebotomist** *n*

phlegm /flem‖flem/ *n* **1** thick mucus secreted in abnormal quantities in the respiratory passages **2** dull or apathetic coldness or indifference **3** intrepid coolness; composure – **phlegmy** *adj*

phlegmatic /flegˈmatik‖flegˈmætɪk/ *adj* **1** resembling, consisting of, or producing phlegm **2** having or showing a slow and stolid temperament – **phlegmatically** *adv*

phloem /ˈfloh·em‖ˈfləʊem/ *n* a complex vascular tissue of higher plants that functions chiefly in the conduction of soluble food substances (e g sugars)

phlox /floks‖flɒks/ *n* any of a genus of American plants with red, purple, white, or variegated flowers

phobia /ˈfohbi·ə, -byə‖ˈfəʊbɪə, -bjə/ *n* an exaggerated and illogical fear of sthg

phobic /ˈfohbik‖ˈfəʊbɪk/ *adj* **1** of or being a phobia **2** motivated by or based on withdrawal from an unpleasant stimulus <*a ~ response to light*>

Phoenician /fəˈneesh(ə)n, -shyən, -ˈni-‖fəˈniːʃ(ə)n, -ʃjən, -ˈnɪ-/ *n* (the language of) a native or inhabitant of ancient Phoenicia – **Phoenician** *adj*

phoenix /ˈfeeniks‖ˈfiːnɪks/ *n* a mythical bird believed to live for 500 years, burn itself on a pyre, and rise alive from the ashes to live another cycle – **phoenixlike** *adj*

[1]**phone** /fohn‖fəʊn/ *n* **1** an earphone

2 a telephone

[2]**phone** *vb* to telephone – often + *up*

[3]**phone** *n* a simple speech sound

-phone /-fohn‖-fəʊn/ *comb form* (→ *n*) **1** sound <*homo*phone> – often in names of musical instruments and sound-transmitting devices <*xylo*phone> **2** speaker of (a specified language) <*Anglo*phone>

'**phone-,in** *n* a broadcast programme in which viewers or listeners can participate by telephone

phoneme /'fohneem‖'fəʊniːm/ *n* the smallest unit of speech that can be used to differentiate the meanings of words

phonemic /fə'neemik‖fə'niːmɪk/ *adj* **1** of phonemes **2** linguistically distinctive

phone-tapping *n* listening to or recording telephone conversations with hidden electronic equipment

phonetic /fə'netik‖fə'netɪk/, **phonetical** /-kl‖-kl/ *adj* **1a** of spoken language or speech sounds **b** of the study of phonetics **2** representing speech sounds by symbols that each have 1 value only [Greek *phōnētikos*, fr *phōnein* to sound with the voice, fr *phōnē* voice] – **phonetically** *adv*

pho'netics *n pl* **1** *sing in constr* the study and classification of speech sounds **2** *sing or pl in constr* the system of speech sounds of a language – **phonetician** *n*

phoney, *NAm chiefly* **phony** /'fohni‖'fəʊnɪ/ *adj* not genuine or real: e g **a** intended to deceive, mislead, or defraud; counterfeit **b** false, sham <*a ~ name*> **c** *of a person* pretentious – **phoney** *n*

phonic /'fonik‖'fɒnɪk/ *adj* **1** of or producing sound; acoustic **2a** of speech sounds **b** of phonics – **phonically** *adv*

'**phonics** *n pl but sing in constr* a method of teaching reading and pronunciation through the phonetic value of letters, syllables, etc

phonograph /'fohnə,grahf, -,graf‖'fəʊnə-,grɑːf, -,græf/ *n* **1** an early device for recording or reproducing sound in which a stylus cuts or follows a groove on a cylinder **2** a gramophone – now chiefly NAm or humor

phonology /fə'noləji‖fə'nɒlədʒɪ/ *n* **1** the science of speech sounds **2** the phonetics and phonemics of a language at a particular time – **phonologist** *n*, **phonological** *also* **phonologic** *adj*

phooey /'fooh·i‖'fuːɪ/ *interj* – used to express scorn or incredulity; infml

phosphate /'fosfayt‖'fɒsfeɪt/ *n* **1** a salt or ester of a phosphoric acid **2** any of several phosphates used as fertilizers – **phosphatic** *adj*

phosphor *also* **phosphore** /'fosfə‖'fɒsfə/ *n* a substance showing phosphorescence [Latin *phosphorus*, fr Greek *phōsphoros*, lit., light bringer, fr *phōs* light + *pherein* to carry, bring]

phosphorescence /,fosfə'res(ə)ns‖,fɒsfə-'res(ə)ns/ *n* **1** light emission that is caused by the absorption of radiations and continues for a noticeable time after these radiations have stopped **2** lasting emission of light without noticeable heat – **phosphorescent** *adj*, **phosphoresce** *vi*

phosphoric /fos'forik‖fɒs'fɒrɪk/ *adj* of or containing (high valency) phosphorus

phosphorus /'fosf(ə)rəs‖'fɒsf(ə)rəs/ *n* **1** a nonmetallic trivalent or pentavalent element of the nitrogen family that occurs widely, esp as phosphates, 1 form of which ignites readily in warm moist air **2** a phosphorescent substance or body; *esp* one that shines or glows in the dark

phot-, **photo-** *comb form* **1** light; radiant energy <photo*graphy*> **2** photograph; photographic <photo*engraving*> **3** photoelectric <photo*cell*>

[1]**photo** /'fohtoh‖'fəʊtəʊ/ *vb or n* **photos; photoing; photoed;** *pl* **photos** (to) photograph

[2]**photo** *adj* PHOTOGRAPHIC 1

[1]**photocopy** /'fohtə,kopi, -toh-‖'fəʊtə,kɒpɪ, -təʊ-/ *n* a photographic reproduction of graphic matter

[2]**photocopy** *vb* to make a photocopy (of) – **photocopier** *n*

photoelectric /,fohtoh·i'lektrik‖,fəʊtəʊɪ-'lektrɪk/ *adj* involving, relating to, or using any of various electrical effects due to the interaction of radiation (e g light) with matter – **photoelectrically** *adv*

photoelectric cell *n* a cell whose electrical properties are modified by the action of light

photo finish *n* **1** a race finish so close that the winner is only revealed (as if) by a photograph of the contestants as they cross the finishing line **2** a close contest

photogenic /,fohtə'jenik, -'jeenik‖,fəʊtə-'dʒenɪk, -'dʒiːnɪk/ *adj* **1** producing or generating light; luminescent **2** suitable for being photographed – **photogenically** *adv*

[1]**photograph** /'fohtə,grahf, -,graf‖'fəʊtə-,grɑːf, -,græf/ *n* a picture or likeness obtained by photography [deriv of Greek *phōt*, *phōs* light + *graphein* to write]

[2]**photograph** *vt* to take a photograph of ~ *vi* **1** to take a photograph **2** to undergo being photographed – **photographer** *n*

photographic /,fohtə'grafik‖,fəʊtə'græfɪk/ *adj* **1** relating to, obtained by, or used in photography **2** capable of retaining vivid impressions <*~ memory*> – **photographically** *adv*

photography /fə'tografi‖fə'tɒgrəfɪ/ *n* the art or process of producing images on a sensitized surface (e g a film) by the action of radiant energy, esp light

photoheliograph /,fohtoh'heeli·ə,grahf, -,graf‖,fəʊtəʊ'hiːlɪə,grɑːf, -,græf/ *n* a telescope adapted for photographing the sun

photon /'fohton‖'fəʊtɒn/ *n* a quantum of electromagnetic radiation – **photonic** *adj*

,**photo'sensitive** /-'sensətiv‖-'sensətɪv/ *adj* sensitive or sensitized to radiant energy, esp light – **photosensitivity** *n*

,**photo'sensit·ize**, **-ise** /-'sensitiez‖-'sensɪtaɪz/ *vt* to make (abnormally) sensitive to the influence of radiant energy, esp light – **photosensitive** *adj*, **photosensitization** *n*

photostat /'fohtə,stat‖'fəʊtə,stæt/ *vt* to copy on a Photostat device; *broadly* to photocopy – **photostat** *n*, **photostatic** *adj*

Photostat *trademark* – used for a device for making a photographic copy of graphic matter

photosynthesis /,fohtoh'sinthəsis‖,fəʊtəʊ-'sɪnθəsɪs/ *n* the synthesis of organic chemical compounds from carbon dioxide using radiant energy, esp light; *esp* the formation of carbohydrates in the chlorophyll-containing tissues of plants exposed to light – **photosynthesize** *vi*, **photosynthetic** *adj*, **photosynthetically** *adv*

phrasal /ˈfrayzl‖ˈfreɪzl/ *adj* (consisting) of a phrase – **phrasally** *adv*

[1]**phrase** /frayz‖freɪz/ *n* **1** a mode or form of speech; diction **2** a brief usu idiomatic or pithy expression; *esp* a catchphrase **3** a group of musical notes forming a natural unit of melody that is usu 3 or 4 bars in length **4** a group of 2 or more grammatically related words that do not form a clause; *esp* a preposition with the words it governs

[2]**phrase** *vt* **1** to express in words or in appropriate or telling terms **2** to divide into melodic phrases

ˈ**phrase ˌbook** *n* a book containing words and idiomatic expressions of a foreign language and their translation

phraseology /ˌfrayziˈoləji‖ˌfreɪzɪˈɒlədʒɪ/ *n* **1** a mode of organization of words and phrases into longer elements; a style **2** choice of words – **phraseological** *adj*, **phraseologically** *adv*

phrenetic /friˈnetik‖frɪˈnetɪk/ *adj* frenetic

phrenology /friˈnoləji‖frɪˈnɒlədʒɪ/ *n* the study of the conformation of the skull as a supposed indicator of mental faculties and character – **phrenologist** *n*, **phrenological** *adj*, **phrenologically** *adv*

phthisis /ˈthiesis‖ˈθaɪsɪs/ *n, pl* **phthises** /-ˌseez‖-ˌsiːz/ a progressive wasting condition; *esp* lung tuberculosis

[1]**phut** /fut‖fʌt/ *n* a dull sound as of sthg bursting

[2]**phut** *adv, chiefly Br* WRONG 4 – chiefly in *go phut*; infml

phylloxera /ˌfilokˈsiərə‖ˌfɪlɒkˈsɪərə/ *n* any of various plant lice that are destructive to many plants (e g grapevines) – **phylloxeran** *adj or n*

phylum /ˈfieləm‖ˈfaɪləm/ *n, pl* **phyla** /-lə‖-lə/ a major group of related species in the classification of plants and animals

physi-, **physio-** *comb form* **1** nature <physi*ography*> **2** physical <physio*therapy*>

physic /ˈfizik‖ˈfɪzɪk/ *n* a medicinal preparation (e g a drug); *esp* a purgative

physical /ˈfizikl‖ˈfɪzɪkl/ *adj* **1a** having material existence; perceptible, esp through the senses, and subject to the laws of nature **b** of material things **2a** of natural science **b** of or involving physics <~ *chemistry*> **3a** of the body <~ *education*> **b** concerned or preoccupied with the body and its needs, as opposed to spiritual matters – **physically** *adv*

ˌ**physical geˈography** *n* geography that deals with the exterior physical features and changes of the earth

ˌ**physical ˈjerks** *n* bodily exercises – infml

physician /fiˈzish(ə)n‖fɪˈzɪʃ(ə)n/ *n* a person skilled in the art of healing; *specif* a doctor of medicine

physics /ˈfiziks‖ˈfɪzɪks/ *n pl but sing or pl in constr* **1** a science that deals with (the properties and interactions of) matter and energy in such fields as mechanics, heat, electricity, magnetism, atomic structure, etc **2** the physical properties and phenomena of a particular system – **physicist** *n*

physiognomy /ˌfiziˈonəmi‖ˌfɪzɪˈɒnəmɪ/ *n* **1** the art of judging character from outward appearance **2** the facial features, esp when revealing qualities of mind or character – **physiognomic, physiognomical** *adj*, **physiognomically** *adv*

physiological /ˌfizi·əˈlojikl‖ˌfɪzɪəˈlɒdʒɪkl/, **physiologic** *adj* **1** of physiology **2** characteristic of or appropriate to an organism's healthy or normal functioning <*the ~ level of a substance in the blood*> – **physiologically** *adv*

physiology /ˌfiziˈoləji‖ˌfɪzɪˈɒlədʒɪ/ *n* **1** biology that deals with the functions and activities of life or of living matter (e g organs, tissues, or cells) and the physical and chemical phenomena involved **2** the physiological activities of (part of) an organism or a particular bodily function <*the ~ of sex*> – **physiologist** *n*

physiotherapy /ˌfizi·ohˈtherəpi‖ˌfɪzɪəʊˈθerəpɪ/ *n* the treatment of disease by physical and mechanical means (e g massage and regulated exercise) – **physiotherapist** *n*

physique /fiˈzeek‖fɪˈziːk/ *n* the form or structure of a person's body

[1]**pi** /pie‖paɪ/ *n, pl* **pis** /piez‖paɪz/ **1** the 16th letter of the Greek alphabet **2** (the symbol π denoting) the ratio of the circumference of a circle to its diameter with a value, to 8 decimal places, of 3.14159265

[2]**pi** *vt* **pies; piing, pieing; pied** *chiefly NAm* [3]PIE

[3]**pi** *adj, Br* pious – derog

pianissimo /ˌpee·əˈnisimoh‖ˌpiːəˈnɪsɪməʊ/ *adv or adj* very soft – used in music

pianist /ˈpee·ənist‖ˈpiːənɪst/ *n* a performer on the piano

[1]**piano** /piˈahnoh, ˈpyah-‖pɪˈɑːnəʊ, ˈpjɑː-/ *adv or adj* in a soft or quiet manner – used in music [Italian, fr Late Latin *planus* smooth, fr Latin, level]

[2]**piano** /piˈanoh‖pɪˈænəʊ/ *n, pl* **pianos** a stringed instrument having steel wire strings that sound when struck by felt-covered hammers operated from a keyboard [Italian, short for *pianoforte*, fr *piano e forte* soft and loud]

Pianola /ˌpee·əˈnohlə‖ˌpiːəˈnəʊlə/ *trademark* – used for a mechanical piano operated by the pressure of air through perforations in a paper roll

piazza /piˈatsə, piˈadzə‖pɪˈætsə, pɪˈædzə/ *n, pl* **piazzas, piazze** /-si‖-sɪ/ **1** an open square, esp in an Italian town **2** *NAm* a veranda

pibroch /ˈpeebrok(h)‖ˈpiːbrɒk(h)/ *n* a set of martial or mournful variations for the Scottish Highland bagpipe

[1]**pica** /ˈpiekə‖ˈpaɪkə/ *n* **1** a unit of 4.23 mm (about 1/6 in) used in measuring typographical material **2** a typewriter type providing 10 characters to the linear inch

[2]**pica** *n* the pathological craving for and eating of inappropriate substances (e g chalk or ashes)

picador /ˈpikəˌdaw‖ˈpɪkəˌdɔː/ *n, pl* **picadors, picadores** /-dawˌrayz‖-dɔːˌreɪz/ a horseman who in a bullfight prods the bull with a lance to weaken its neck and shoulder muscles

picaresque /ˌpikəˈresk‖ˌpɪkəˈresk/ *adj* of or being fiction narrating in loosely linked episodes the adventures of a rogue

piccalilli /ˌpikəˈlili‖ˌpɪkəˈlɪlɪ/ *n* a hot relish of chopped vegetables, mustard, and spices

piccaninny, *chiefly NAm* **picaninny, pickaninny** /ˈpikəˌnini, ˌ--ˈ--‖ˈpɪkəˌnɪnɪ, ˌ--ˈ--/ *n* a small Negro child – chiefly derog [prob fr Portuguese *pequenino* very little, fr *pequeno* small]

piccolo /ˈpikəˌloh‖ˈpɪkəˌləʊ/ *n, pl* **piccolos** a small shrill flute whose range is an octave higher than that of an ordinary flute [Italian, short for *piccolo flauto* small flute] – **piccoloist** *n*

[1]**pick** /pik‖pɪk/ *vt* **1** to pierce, penetrate, or break up with a pointed instrument < ~ed *the hard clay*> **2a** to remove bit by bit < ~ *meat from bones*> **b** to remove covering or clinging matter from < ~ed *the bones clean*> **3a** to gather by plucking < ~ed *flowers*> **b** to choose, select <*tried to* ~ *the shortest route*> <*she* ~ed *out the most expensive dress*> **4** to pilfer from; rob < ~ *pockets*> **5** to provoke < ~ *a quarrel*> **6a** to dig into, esp in order to remove unwanted matter; probe < ~ *his teeth*> < ~ *his nose*> **b** to pluck with a plectrum or with the fingers < ~ *a guitar*> **c** to loosen or pull apart with a sharp point < ~ *wool*> **7** to unlock with a device (e g a wire) other than the key < ~ *a lock*> **8** to make (one's way) carefully on foot ~*vi* to gather or harvest sthg by plucking – **pick and choose** to select with care and deliberation – **pick at 1** to find fault with, esp in a petty way **2** to eat sparingly and with little interest; toy with – **pick on 1** to single out for unpleasant treatment or an unpleasant task **2** to single out for a particular purpose or for special attention – **pick someone's brains** to obtain ideas or information from sby – **pick someone/something to pieces** to subject to systematic adverse criticism

[2]**pick** *n* **1** the act or privilege of choosing or selecting; a choice <*take your* ~> **2** *sing or pl in constr* the best or choicest <*the* ~ *of the herd*> **3** the portion of a crop gathered at 1 time <*the first* ~ *of grapes*>

[3]**pick** *vt* to throw (a shuttle) across the loom

[4]**pick** *n* **1** a throw of the shuttle across a loom **2** one weft thread taken as a unit of fineness of fabric

[5]**pick** *n* **1** a heavy wooden-handled iron or steel tool with a head that is pointed at one or both ends **2** a toothpick **3** a plectrum

pickaback /ˈpikəˌbak‖ˈpɪkəˌbæk/ *n, adv, or adj* (a) piggyback

pickaxe /ˈpikˌaks‖ˈpɪkˌæks/ *n* [5]PICK 1

picked *adj* choice, prime

picker /ˈpikə‖ˈpɪkə/ *n* **1** a person or machine that picks sthg, esp crops **2** a person or the part of the loom that threads the shuttle

pickerel /ˈpik(ə)rəl‖ˈpɪk(ə)rəl/ *n dial chiefly Br* a young or small pike

[1]**picket** /ˈpikit‖ˈpɪkɪt/ *n* **1** a pointed or sharpened stake, post, or pale **2** *sing or pl in constr* **2a** a small body of troops detached to guard an army from surprise attack **b** a detachment kept ready in camp for such duty **3** a person posted by a trade union at a place of work affected by a strike; *also* a person posted for a demonstration or protest

[2]**picket** *vt* **1** to enclose, fence, or fortify with pickets **2** to tether **3** to guard with or post as a picket **4a** to post pickets at **b** to walk or stand in front of as a picket ~*vi* to serve as a picket – **picketer** *n*

ˈ**picket ˌline** *n* a line of people picketing a business, organization, etc

pickings /ˈpikingz‖ˈpɪkɪŋz/ *n pl* sthg picked (up): e g **a** gleanable or eatable fragments; scraps **b** yield or return for effort expended; *esp* rewards obtained by dishonest or dubious means

[1]**pickle** /ˈpikl‖ˈpɪkl/ *n* **1** a solution or bath for preserving or cleaning: e g **1a** a brine or vinegar solution in which meat, fish, vegetables, etc are preserved **b** an acidic solution for cleaning metal **2** (an article of) food preserved in a pickle; *also* chutney – often pl **3** a difficult situation – infml **4** *Br* a mischievous or troublesome child – infml

[2]**pickle** *vt* to treat, preserve, or clean in or with a pickle

ˈ**pickled** *adj* DRUNK 1 – infml

ˈ**pick-me-ˌup** *n* sthg that stimulates or restores; a tonic

pick off *vt* to shoot or bring down one by one <*the sniper* picked off *the enemy troops*>

pick out *vt* **1** to make clearly visible, esp as distinguished from a background <*the fences were* picked out *in red*> **2** to play the notes of by ear or one by one <*learned to* pick out *tunes on the piano*>

pick over *vt* to examine in order to select the best or discard the unwanted <picked over *the berries*>

ˈ**pickˌpocket** /-ˌpokit‖-ˌpɒkɪt/ *n* one who steals from pockets or bags

pickup /-ˌup‖-ˌʌp/ *n* **1** the act or process of picking up **2** sby or sthg picked up: e g **2a** a hitchhiker who is given a lift **b** a temporary casual acquaintance; *esp* one made with the intention of having sex **3** a device (e g on a record player) that converts mechanical movements into electrical signals **4** a device (e g a microphone or a television camera) for converting sound or an image into electrical signals **5** interference (e g to reception) from an adjacent electrical circuit or system **6** a light motor truck having an open body with low sides and tailboard

pick up *vt* **1a** to take hold of and lift up <picked up *the pencil*> **b** to gather together; collect <picked up *all the pieces*> **2** to take (passengers or freight) into a vehicle **3a** to acquire casually or by chance <picked up *a valuable antique at a jumble sale*> <picked up *some money doing odd jobs*> **b** to acquire by study or experience; learn <picking up *a great deal of information in the process*> **c** to collect <picked up *his clothes at the cleaners*> **d** to accept for the purpose of paying <*the government should* pick up *the bill for the damaged ship*> **4** to enter informally into conversation or companionship with (a previously unknown person), usu with the intention of having sex **5a** to take into custody **b** to discover and follow <picked up *the outlaw's trail*> **c** to bring within range of sight, hearing, or a sensor <picked up *the planes on the radar*> **6** to revive **7** to resume after a break; continue **8** *chiefly NAm* to clean up; tidy ~*vi*

picky /ˈpiki‖ˈpɪkɪ/ *adj, chiefly NAm* fussy, choosy <*a* ~ *eater*>

[1]**picnic** /ˈpiknik‖ˈpɪknɪk/ *n* **1** (the food eaten

at) an outing that includes an informal meal, usu lunch, eaten in the open **2** a pleasant or amusingly carefree experience <*don't expect marriage to be a* ~>; *also* an easily accomplished task or feat – infml – **picnicky** *adj*

[2]**picnic** *vi* **-ck-** to go on a picnic – **picnicker** *n*

ˌ**picric ˈacid** /ˈpikrik‖ˈpɪkrɪk/ *n* an explosive yellow strong acid used esp in powerful explosives and as an antiseptic

pictorial /pikˈtawri·əl‖pɪkˈtɔːrɪəl/ *adj* **1** of (a) painting or drawing <~ *perspective*> **2** consisting of or illustrated by pictures <~ *records*> **3** suggesting or conveying visual images – **pictorially** *adv*, **pictorialness** *n*

[1]**picture** /ˈpikchə‖ˈpɪktʃə/ *n* **1** a design or representation made by painting, drawing, etc **2a** a description so vivid or graphic as to suggest a mental image or give an accurate idea of sthg <*painted a vivid* ~ *of life in Victorian England*> **b** a presentation of the relevant or characteristic facts concerning a problem or situation <*drew an alarming* ~ *of the economic future*> **3a** an image, copy <*he was the* ~ *of his father*> **b** the perfect example <*he looked the* ~ *of health*> **c** a striking or picturesque sight <*his face was a* ~ *when he heard the news*> **4a** a transitory visible image or reproduction <*adjusted the television for a brighter* ~> **b** FILM 3a, b **c** *pl, chiefly Br* CINEMA 1b, 2 – infml <*what's on at the* ~s?> **5** a situation <*a look at the overall political* ~> [Latin *pictura*, fr *pict-*, *pingere* to paint] – **in the picture** fully informed and up to date

[2]**picture** *vt* **1** to paint or draw a representation, image, or visual conception of; depict **2** to describe graphically in words **3** to form a mental image of; imagine

ˌ**picture-ˈpostcard** *adj* picturesque <~ *villages*>

picturesque /ˌpikchəˈresk‖ˌpɪktʃəˈresk/ *adj* **1** quaint, charming **2** evoking striking mental images; vivid <~ *language*> – **picturesquely** *adv*, **picturesqueness** *n*

[1]**piddle** /ˈpidl‖ˈpɪdl/ *vi* **1** to act or work in an idle or trifling manner **2** to urinate *USE* infml

[2]**piddle** *n* **1** urine **2** an act of urinating *USE* infml

piddling /ˈpidling‖ˈpɪdlɪŋ/ *adj* trivial, paltry – infml

pidgin /ˈpijin‖ˈpɪdʒɪn/ *n* a language based on 2 or more languages and used esp for trade between people with different native languages [*Pidgin English*, oriental form of *business English*] – **pidginize** *vt*

[1]**pie** /pie‖paɪ/ *n* **1** MAGPIE 1 **2** a variegated animal

[2]**pie** *n* a dish consisting of a sweet or savoury filling covered or encased by pastry and baked in a container

[3]**pie,** *chiefly NAm* **pi** *vt* to spill or throw (type or typeset matter) into disorder – **pie** *n*

[1]**piebald** /ˈpieˌbawld‖ˈpaɪˌbɔːld/ *adj* **1** *esp of a horse* of different colours; *specif* spotted or blotched with different colours, esp black and white **2** composed of incongruous parts; heterogeneous

[2]**piebald** *n* a piebald horse or other animal

[1]**piece** /pees‖piːs/ *n* **1a** a part of a whole; *esp* a part detached, cut, or broken from a whole **b** a portion marked off <*bought a* ~ *of land*> **2** an object or individual regarded as a unit of a kind or class; an example <*fine teak tables copied from antique* ~s> **3** a standard quantity (e g of length, weight, or size) in which sthg is made or sold **4a** a literary, artistic, dramatic, or musical work **b** a passage to be recited **5** a coin, esp of a specified value – **of a piece** alike, consistent – **to pieces 1** into fragments **2** out of control < *went* to pieces *from shock*>

[2]**piece** *vt* **1** to repair, renew, or complete by adding pieces; patch – often + *up* **2** to join into a whole – often + *together* – **piecer** *n*

pièce de résistance /ˌpyes də rəzisˈtahns ‖ˌpjes də rəzɪsˈtɑːns (*Fr* pjɛs də rezistɑ̃ːs)/ *n, pl* **pièces de résistance** /~ **1** the chief dish of a meal **2** an outstanding item; a showpiece [French, lit., piece of resistance]

[1]ˈ**pieceˌmeal** /-meel‖-miːl/ *adv* **1** one piece at a time; gradually **2** in pieces or fragments; apart

[2]**piecemeal** *adj* done, made, or accomplished piece by piece or in a fragmentary way

ˈ**pieceˌwork** /-ˌwuhk‖-ˌwɜːk/ *n* work that is paid for at a set rate per unit – **pieceworker** *n*

ˈ**pie ˌchart** *n* a diagram in which the size of a sector of a circle corresponds to the frequency of the set represented

piecrust /ˈpieˌkrust‖ˈpaɪˌkrʌst/ *n* the baked pastry covering of a pie

pied /pied‖paɪd/ *adj* having patches of 2 or more colours

pied-à-terre /ˌpyay ah ˈteə ‖ˌpjeɪ ɑː ˈteə (*Fr* pje a tɛːr)/ *n, pl* **pieds-à-terre** /~/ a temporary or second lodging (e g a flat in a city kept by sby who lives in the country) [French, lit., foot to the ground]

ˌ**pie-ˈeyed** *adj* DRUNK 1 – infml

pier /piə‖pɪə/ *n* **1** an intermediate support for the adjacent ends of 2 bridge spans **2** a structure extending into water for use as a landing place, promenade, etc **3** a vertical structural support (e g for a wall)

pierce /ˈpiəs‖ˈpɪəs/ *vt* **1** to enter or thrust into sharply or painfully; stab <*the thorn* ~d *his finger*> **2** to make a hole in or through; perforate **3** to force or make a way into or through <*a light* ~d *the darkness*> **4** to penetrate with the eye or mind; discern **5** to move or affect the emotions of, esp sharply or painfully **6** *of cold* to penetrate <*the cold* ~d *them to the bone*> ~*vi* to force a way into or through sthg

piercing /ˈpiəsing‖ˈpɪəsɪŋ/ *adj* penetrating: e g **a** loud, shrill <~ *cries*> **b** perceptive <~ *eyes*> **c** penetratingly cold; biting <*a* ~ *winter wind*> **d** cutting, incisive <~ *sarcasm*> – **piercingly** *adv*

Pierrot /ˈpiəˌroh‖ˈpɪəˌrəʊ/ *n* a stock comic character of old French pantomime usu having a whitened face

pietà /ˌpee·ayˈtah, ˌpyay-‖ˌpiːeɪˈtɑː, ˌpjeɪ-/ *n, often cap* a representation of the Virgin Mary mourning over the dead body of Christ

piety /ˈpie·əti‖ˈpaɪətɪ/ *n* **1** the quality or state of being pious; devoutness **2** dutifulness, esp to parents **3** an act inspired by piety

piezoelectricity /pieˌeezohiˌlekˈtrisəti,

-ˌeelek-‖paɪˌiːzəʊɪˌlek'trɪsətɪ, -ˌiːlek-/ *n* electricity or electric polarity due to pressure, esp in a crystalline substance (e g quartz) [deriv of Greek *piezein* to press] – **piezoelectric** *adj*

piffle /'pifl‖'pɪfl/ *n* trivial nonsense – infml

piffling /'pifling‖'pɪflɪŋ/ *adj* trivial, derisory – infml

[1]**pig** /pig‖pɪg/ *n* **1a** *chiefly Br* any of various (domesticated) stout-bodied short-legged mammals with a thick bristly skin and a long mobile snout **b** *NAm* a young pig **2** pork **3** sby like or suggestive of a pig in habits or behaviour (e g in dirtiness, greed, or selfishness) **4** an animal related to or resembling the pig – usu in combination <*guinea* ~> **5** a shaped mass of cast crude metal, esp iron **6** a policeman – slang; derog – **piglet** *n*

[2]**pig** *vb* **-gg-** *vi* **1** to farrow **2** to live like a pig – + *it* ~ *vt* **1** to farrow (piglets) **2a** to eat (food) greedily **b** to overindulge (oneself) *USE* (*vt 2*) infml

pigeon /'pij(ə)n‖'pɪdʒ(ə)n/ *n* **1** any of a family of birds with a stout body and smooth and compact plumage, many of which are domesticated or live in urban areas **2** a matter of special concern; business – infml <*that's not my* ~>

[1]**'pigeonˌhole** /-ˌhohl‖-ˌhəʊl/ *n* **1** a small open compartment (e g in a desk or cabinet) for letters or documents **2** a neat category which usu fails to reflect actual complexities

[2]**pigeonhole** *vt* **1a** to place (as if) in the pigeonhole of a desk **b** to lay aside; shelve **2** to assign to a category; classify

ˌpigeon-'toed *adj* having the toes turned in

piggery /'pig(ə)ri‖'pɪg(ə)rɪ/ *n* **1** a place where pigs are kept **2** dirty or nasty behaviour

piggish /'pigish‖'pɪgɪʃ/, **piggy** /'pigi‖'pɪgɪ/ *adj* of or resembling a pig, esp in being dirty, greedy, or ill-mannered – **piggishly** *adv*, **piggishness** *n*

piggy /'pigi‖'pɪgɪ/ *n* a pig; *esp* a little pig – used esp by or to children

[1]**'piggyˌback** /-ˌbak‖-ˌbæk/ *adv* up on the back and shoulders <*carried the child* ~ *up the stairs*>

[2]**piggyback** *n* a ride on the back and shoulders of another

[3]**piggyback** *adj* **1** being up on the shoulders and back **2** being or relating to sthg carried as an extra load on the back of a vehicle (e g an aircraft)

'piggy ˌbank *n* a coin bank often in the shape of a pig

pigheaded /pig'hedid‖pɪg'hedɪd/ *adj* obstinate, stubborn – **pigheadedness** *n*

'pig ˌiron *n* crude iron from the blast furnace before refining

[1]**pigment** /'pigmənt‖'pɪgmənt/ *n* **1** a substance that colours other materials; *esp* a powdered substance that is mixed with a liquid in which it is relatively insoluble and is used to colour paints, inks, plastics, etc **2** (a colourless substance related to) any of various colouring matters in animals and plants – **pigmentary** *adj*

[2]**pigment** /pig'ment‖pɪg'ment/ *vt* to colour (as if) with pigment

pigmentation /ˌpigmen'taysh(ə)n‖ˌpɪgmen'teɪʃ(ə)n/ *n* (excessive) coloration with, or deposition of, (bodily) pigment

pigmy /'pigmi‖'pɪgmɪ/ *n* a pygmy

pignut /'pigˌnut‖'pɪgˌnʌt/ *n* a common plant of the carrot family

'pigˌskin /-ˌskin‖-ˌskɪn/ *n* (leather made from) the skin of a pig

'pigˌsticking /-ˌstiking‖-ˌstɪkɪŋ/ *n* the hunting of wild boar on horseback with a spear

'pigˌsty /-ˌstie‖-ˌstaɪ/ *n* **1** an enclosure with a covered shed for pigs **2** a dirty, untidy, or neglected place

'pigˌtail /-ˌtayl‖-ˌteɪl/ *n* **1** a tight plait of hair, esp when worn singly at the back of the head **2** either of 2 bunches of hair worn loose or plaited at either side of the head by young girls – **pigtailed** *adj*

[1]**pike** /piek‖paɪk/ *n, Br* a mountain or hill, esp in the Lake District, with a peaked summit

[2]**pike** *n* (any of various fishes related to or resembling) a large long-snouted fish-eating bony fish widely distributed in cooler parts of the N hemisphere

[3]**pike** *n* a weapon consisting of a long wooden shaft with a pointed steel head that was used by foot soldiers until superseded by the bayonet – **pike** *vt*

[4]**pike** *n* a body position (e g in diving) in which the hands touch the toes or clasp the legs at the knees, the hips are bent forwards, and the knees are straight

pikestaff /-ˌstahf‖-ˌstɑːf/ *n* **1** a spiked staff for use on slippery ground **2** the staff of a foot soldier's pike

pilaf, pilaff /'peeˌlaf, 'pi-‖'piːˌlæf, 'pɪ-/ *n* a dish of seasoned rice and often meat

pilaster /pi'lastə‖pɪ'læstə/ *n* an upright rectangular column that is usu embedded in a wall

pilau /'pilow, 'peeˌlow‖'pɪlaʊ, 'piːˌlaʊ/ *n* (a) pilaf

pilchard /'pilchəd‖'pɪltʃəd/ *n* (any of several sardines related to) a fish of the herring family that occurs in great schools along the coasts of Europe

[1]**pile** /piel‖paɪl/ *n* a beam of timber, steel, reinforced concrete, etc driven into the ground to carry a vertical load

[2]**pile** *vt* to drive piles into

[3]**pile** *n* **1a** a quantity of things heaped together **b** a heap of wood for burning a corpse or a sacrifice **c** a large quantity, number, or amount <*a* ~ *of stuff still to be read*> <~*s of friends*> **2** a large building or group of buildings **3** a great amount of money; a fortune <*now that he has made his* ~, *he can live in luxury*> **4** a vertical series of alternate discs of 2 dissimilar metals (e g copper and zinc) separated by discs of cloth or paper moistened with an electrolyte for producing an electric current **5** REACTOR 2

[4]**pile** *vt* **1** to lay or place in a pile; stack – often + *up* **2** to heap in abundance; load <~d *potatoes on his plate*> ~ *vi* to move or press forwards (as if) in a mass; crowd <~d *into the car*> – **pile it on** to exaggerate

[5]**pile** *n* **1** soft hair, down, fur, or wool **2** a soft raised surface on a fabric or carpet consisting of cut threads or loops – **piled** *adj*

[6]**pile** *n* a haemorrhoid – usu pl

ˈ**pile ˌdriver** *n* a machine for driving piles into the ground

ˈ**pileˌup** /-ˌup‖-ˌʌp/ *n* a collision involving usu several motor vehicles and causing damage or injury

pile up *vi* **1** to accumulate <*his work* piled up *over the holidays*> **2** to become involved in a pileup of vehicles

pileus /ˈpieli·əs‖ˈpaɪlɪəs/ *n, pl* **pilei** /-liˌie‖-lɪˌaɪ/ the (umbrella-shaped) fruiting body of many fungi (e g mushrooms) – **pileate** *adj*

pilfer /ˈpilfə‖ˈpɪlfə/ *vb* to steal stealthily in small amounts or to small value – **pilferage** *n*, **pilferer** *n*

pilgrim /ˈpilgrim‖ˈpɪlgrɪm/ *n* a person making a pilgrimage

pilgrimage /ˈpilgrimij‖ˈpɪlgrɪmɪdʒ/ *n* **1** a journey to a shrine or sacred place as an act of devotion, in order to acquire spiritual merit, or as a penance **2** the course of life on earth

ˌ**Pilgrim ˈFathers** *n pl* the English colonists who settled at Plymouth, Massachusetts, in 1620

pill /pil‖pɪl/ *n* **1a** a small rounded solid mass of medicine to be swallowed whole **b** an oral contraceptive in the form of a pill taken daily by a woman over a monthly cycle – + *the* **2** sthg repugnant or unpleasant that must be accepted or endured <*the loss of salary was a bitter* ~ *to swallow*> **3** sthg resembling a pill in size or shape **4** a disagreeable or tiresome person – infml

[1]**pillage** /ˈpilij‖ˈpɪlɪdʒ/ *n* **1** the act of looting or plundering, esp in war **2** sthg taken as booty

[2]**pillage** *vb* to plunder ruthlessly; loot – **pillager** *n*

[1]**pillar** /ˈpilə‖ˈpɪlə/ *n* **1a** a firm upright support for a superstructure **b** a usu ornamental column or shaft **2** a chief supporter; a prop <*a* ~ *of the Establishment*> **3** a solid mass of coal, ore, etc left standing to support a mine roof – **from pillar to post** from one place or one situation to another

[2]**pillar** *vt* to support or decorate (as if) with pillars

ˈ**pillar ˌbox** *n* a red pillar-shaped public letter box

pillbox /ˈpilˌboks‖ˈpɪlˌbɒks/ *n* **1** a box for pills; *esp* a shallow round box made of pasteboard **2** a small low concrete weapon emplacement **3** a small round brimless hat with a flat crown and straight sides, worn esp by women

pillion /ˈpilyən‖ˈpɪljən/ *n* a saddle or seat for a passenger on a motorcycle or motor scooter [Scottish Gaelic *pillean* or Irish Gaelic *pillīn* light saddle, fr *peall* covering, couch]

[1]**pillory** /ˈpiləri‖ˈpɪlərɪ/ *n* **1** a device for publicly punishing offenders consisting of a wooden frame with holes for the head and hands **2** a means for exposing one to public scorn or ridicule

[2]**pillory** *vt* **1** to put in a pillory **2** to expose to public contempt, ridicule, or scorn

[1]**pillow** /ˈpiloh‖ˈpɪləʊ/ *n* a usu rectangular cloth bag (e g of cotton) filled with soft material (e g down) and used to support the head of a reclining person

[2]**pillow** *vt* **1** to rest or lay (as if) on a pillow **2** to serve as a pillow for

ˈ**pillowˌcase** /-ˌkays‖-ˌkeɪs/ *n* a removable washable cover, esp of cotton or nylon, for a pillow

ˈ**pillow ˌlace** *n* lace worked with bobbins over a padded support

[1]**pilot** /ˈpielət‖ˈpaɪlət/ *n* **1** sby qualified and usu licensed to conduct a ship into and out of a port or in specified waters **2** a guide, leader **3** sby who handles or is qualified to handle the controls of an aircraft or spacecraft **4** a piece that guides a tool or machine part – **pilotage** *n*, **pilotless** *adj*

[2]**pilot** *vt* **1** to act as a guide to; lead or conduct over a usu difficult course **2a** to direct the course of <~ *a ship*> **b** to act as pilot of <~ *a plane*>

[3]**pilot** *adj* serving as a guide, activator, or trial <*a* ~ *scheme*>

ˈ**pilot ˌfish** *n* an oceanic fish that often swims in company with a shark

ˈ**pilot ˌlight** *n* **1** an indicator light showing whether power is on or where a switch or circuit breaker is located **2** a small permanent flame used to ignite gas at a burner

pilot officer *n* an officer of the lowest rank in the Royal Air Force

pimento /piˈmentoh‖pɪˈmentəʊ/ *n* **1** a sweet pepper with a mild sweet flavour **2** allspice

pimp /pimp‖pɪmp/ *n* a man who solicits clients for a prostitute or brothel – **pimp** *vi*

pimpernel /ˈpimpəˌnel‖ˈpɪmpəˌnel/ *n* any of several plants of the primrose family: e g **a** SCARLET PIMPERNEL **b** YELLOW PIMPERNEL

pimple /ˈpimpl‖ˈpɪmpl/ *n* (a swelling or protuberance like) a small solid inflamed (pus-containing) elevation of the skin – **pimpled** *adj*, **pimply** *adj*

[1]**pin** /pin‖pɪn/ *n* **1a** a piece of solid material (e g wood or metal) used esp for fastening separate articles together or as a support **b** sthg resembling a pin, esp in slender elongated form **2a** a small thin pointed piece of metal with a head used esp for fastening cloth, paper, etc **b** sthg of small value; a trifle <*doesn't care a* ~ *for anyone*> **c** an ornament or badge fastened to clothing with a pin **d** SAFETY PIN **3a** any of the wooden pieces constituting the target in various games (e g skittles and tenpin bowling) **b** the peg at which a quoit is pitched **c** the staff of the flag marking a hole on a golf course **4** a projecting metal bar on a plug which is inserted into a socket **5** PEG 3a **6** a leg – infml; usu pl <*wobbly on his* ~s> – **pinned** *adj*

[2]**pin** *vt* **-nn-** **1a** to fasten, join, or secure with a pin **b** to hold fast or immobile <~ned *him against the wall*> **2a** to attach, hang <~ned *his hopes on a miracle*> **b** to assign the blame or responsibility for <~ *the robbery on a night watchman*> **3** to make (a chess opponent's piece) unable to move without exposing the king to check or a valuable piece to capture

pinafore /ˈpinəˌfaw‖ˈpɪnəˌfɔː/ *n* **1** an apron, usu with a bib **2** *also* **pinafore dress** a sleeveless usu low-necked dress designed to be worn over another garment (e g a blouse)

ˈ**pinball maˌchine** *n* an amusement device for playing pinball and automatically recording the score

pince-nez /ˈpans ˌnay, ˈpins- ‖ˈpæns ˌneɪ, ˈpɪns- (*Fr* pɛ̃s ne)/ *n, pl* **pince-nez** /~/ glasses clipped to the nose by a spring [French, fr *pincer* to pinch + *nez* nose, fr Latin *nasus*]

pincer /ˈpinsə‖ˈpɪnsə/ *n* **1a** *pl* an instrument having 2 short handles and 2 grasping jaws working on a pivot and used for gripping things **b** a claw (e g of a lobster) resembling a pair of pincers **2** either part of a double military envelopment of an enemy position – **pincerlike** *adj*

[1]**pinch** /pinch‖pɪntʃ/ *vt* **1a** to squeeze or compress painfully (e g between the finger and thumb or between the jaws of an instrument) **b** to prune the tip of (a plant or shoot), usu to induce branching – + *out* or *back* **c** to cause to appear thin or shrunken <*faces* ~ed *with hunger and fatigue*> **2** to subject to strict economy or want; straiten **3** to sail (a ship) too close to the wind **4a** STEAL 1 – slang **b** ARREST 2 – slang ~ *vi* **1** to compress, squeeze **2** to press painfully <*my new shoes* ~> **3** *of a ship* to sail too close to the wind – **pincher** *n*

[2]**pinch** *n* **1a** a critical juncture; an emergency <*when it comes to the* ~*, he'll let you down*> **b(1)** pressure, stress <*when the* ~ *of foreign competition came at last* – G M Trevelyan> **b(2)** hardship, privation <*after a year of sanctions, they began to feel the* ~> **2a** an act of pinching; a squeeze **b** as much as may be taken between the finger and thumb <*a* ~ *of snuff*> – **at a pinch** in an emergency – **with a pinch of salt** with reservations as to the validity of sthg

pinchbeck /ˈpinchˌbek‖ˈpɪntʃˌbek/ *n* an alloy of copper and zinc used esp to imitate gold in jewellery [Christopher *Pinchbeck* (1670?-1732), English watchmaker] – **pinchbeck** *adj*

pincushion /ˈpinˌkoosh(ə)n‖ˈpɪnˌkʊʃ(ə)n/ *n* a small cushion in which pins are stuck ready for use, esp in sewing

pin down *vt* **1** to force (sby) to state his/her position or make a decision **2** to define precisely <*a vague feeling of unease that she couldn't quite* pin down> **3** to fasten down; prevent from moving

[1]**pine** /pien‖paɪn/ *vi* **1** to lose vigour or health (e g through grief); languish – often + *away* **2** to yearn intensely and persistently, esp for sthg unattainable; long <pining *for her lost youth*>

[2]**pine** *n* **1** (any of various trees related to) any of a genus of coniferous evergreen trees which have slender elongated needles **2** the straight-grained white or yellow usu durable and resinous wood of a pine – **piny, piney** *adj*

pineal gland /ˈpini·əl, pieˈnee·əl‖ˈpɪnɪəl, paɪˈniːəl/ *n* a small appendage of the brain of most vertebrates that has the structure of an eye in a few reptiles, and that secretes melatonin and other hormones – **pineal** *adj*

pineapple /ˈpienapl‖ˈpaɪnæpl/ *n* **1** (the large oval edible succulent yellow-fleshed fruit of) a tropical plant related to the grasses, lilies, and orchids, with rigid spiny leaves and a dense head of small flowers **2** a hand grenade – slang

ˈpineˌcone /ˈpienˌkohn‖ˈpaɪnˌkəʊn/ *n* a cone of a pine tree

ˈpine ˌmarten *n* a slender Eurasian marten with a yellow patch on the chest and throat

ping /ping‖pɪŋ/ *vi or n* (to make) a sharp ringing sound

Ping-Pong /ˈping ˌpong‖ˈpɪŋ ˌpɒŋ/ *trademark* – used for table tennis

pinhead /ˈpinˌhed‖ˈpɪnˌhed/ *n* **1** sthg very small or insignificant **2** a very dull or stupid person; a fool – infml

[1]**pinion** /ˈpinyən‖ˈpɪnjən/ *n* **1** (the end section of) a bird's wing **2** a bird's feather; a quill – **pinioned** *adj*

[2]**pinion** *vt* **1** to restrain (a bird) from flight, esp by cutting off the pinion of a wing **2a** to disable or restrain by binding the arms **b** to bind fast; shackle

[3]**pinion** *n* a gear with a small number of teeth designed to mesh with a larger gear wheel or rack

[1]**pink** /pingk‖pɪŋk/ *vt* **1** to pierce slightly; stab **2a** to perforate in an ornamental pattern **b** to cut a zigzag or saw-toothed edge on

[2]**pink** *n* a sailing vessel with a narrow overhanging stern

[3]**pink** *n* any of a genus of plants related to the carnation and widely grown for their white, pink, red, or variegated flowers – **in the pink** in the best of health – infml

[4]**pink** *adj* **1** of the colour pink **2** holding moderately radical political views – **pinkish** *adj*, **pinkness** *n*

[5]**pink** *n* **1** any of various shades of pale red **2** (the scarlet colour of) a fox hunter's coat

[6]**pink** *adv* to a high degree; enormously – in *tickled pink*; infml

[7]**pink** *vi, Br, of an internal-combustion engine* to make a series of sharp popping noises because of faulty combustion of the fuel-air mixture

ˌpink ˈelephants *n pl* any of various hallucinations arising esp from heavy drinking or use of drugs – infml

ˈpinkˌeye /-ˌie‖-ˌaɪ/ *n* a highly contagious conjunctivitis of human beings and various domestic animals

ˌpink ˈgin *n* a drink consisting of gin flavoured with angostura bitters

pinkie, pinky /ˈpingki‖ˈpɪŋkɪ/ *n, NAm & dial Br* LITTLE FINGER

ˈpinking ˌshears /ˈpingking‖ˈpɪŋkɪŋ/ *n pl* shears with a saw-toothed inner edge on the blades, used in sewing for making a zigzag cut in cloth to prevent fraying

pinko /ˈpingkoh‖ˈpɪŋkəʊ/ *n, pl* **pinkos, pinkoes** sby who holds moderately radical political views – chiefly derog

ˈpin ˌmoney *n* **1a** extra money earned by sby, esp a married woman (e g in a part-time job) **b** money set aside for the purchase of incidentals **2** a trivial amount of money

pinna /ˈpinə‖ˈpɪnə/ *n, pl* **pinnae** /-ni‖-nɪ/, **pinnas** **1** a leaflet or primary division of a pinnate leaf or frond **2** a largely cartilaginous projecting portion of the outer ear – **pinnal** *adj*

pinnace /ˈpinəs‖ˈpɪnəs/ *n* any of various ship's boats

[1]**pinnacle** /ˈpinəkl‖ˈpɪnəkl/ *n* **1** an architectural ornament resembling a small spire and used esp to crown a buttress **2** a structure or formation suggesting a pinnacle; *specif* a lofty mountain **3** the highest point of

development or achievement

[2]**pinnacle** *vt* to raise (as if) on a pinnacle

pinnate /'pinayt, -nət‖'pɪneɪt, -nət/ *adj* resembling a feather, esp in having similar parts arranged on opposite sides of an axis like the barbs on the shaft of a feather <*a* ~ *leaf*> – **pinnately** *adv*, **pinnation** *n*

pinny /'pini‖'pɪnɪ/ *n* PINAFORE 1 – infml

piñon /'pinyohn, 'pinyən, pin'yohn‖'pɪnjəʊn, 'pɪnjən, pɪn'jəʊn/ *n* (the edible nut-like seed of) any of various low-growing pines

[1]**pinpoint** /'pin,poynt‖'pɪn,pɔɪnt/ *vt* **1** to fix, determine, or identify with precision **2** to cause to stand out conspicuously; highlight

[2]**pinpoint** *adj* **1** extremely small, fine, or precise <*a* ~ *target*> **2** located, fixed, or directed with extreme precision

[3]**pinpoint** *n* a very small point or area <*saw a* ~ *of light at the end of the tube*>

'pin,prick /-,prik‖-,prɪk/ *n* **1** a small puncture made (as if) by a pin **2** a petty irritation or annoyance

,pins and 'needles *n pl* a pricking tingling sensation in a limb recovering from numbness

'pin,stripe /-,striep‖-,straɪp/ *n* **1** a very thin stripe, esp on a fabric **2** a suit or trousers with pinstripes – often pl with sing. meaning – **pin-striped** *adj*

pint /pient‖paɪnt/ *n* **1** either of 2 units of liquid capacity equal to $^1/_8$gal: **1a** a British unit of about 0.568l **b** a US unit of about 0.473l **2** a pint of liquid, esp milk or beer

'pin,table /-,taybl‖-,teɪbl/ *n* PINBALL MACHINE

'pint-,size, 'pint-,sized *adj* small – chiefly derog

pinup /'pin,up‖'pɪn,ʌp/ *n* (a person whose glamorous qualities make him/her a suitable subject of) a photograph pinned up on an admirer's wall – **pinup** *adj*

'pin,wheel /-,weel‖-,wi:l/ *n* **1** CATHERINE WHEEL **2** *NAm* WINDMILL 2

[1]**pioneer** /,pie·ə'niə‖,paɪə'nɪə/ *n* **1** a member of a military unit (e g engineers) engaging in light construction and defensive works **2a** a person or group that originates or helps open up a new line of thought or activity or a new method or technical development **b** any of the first people to settle in a territory

[2]**pioneer** *adj* **1** original, earliest **2** (characteristic) of early settlers or their time

[3]**pioneer** *vi* to act as a pioneer ~ *vt* **1** to open or prepare for others to follow; *esp* to settle **2** to originate or take part in the development of

pious /'pie·əs‖'paɪəs/ *adj* **1** devout **2** sacred or devotional as distinct from the profane or secular **3** dutiful **4** marked by sham or hypocritical virtue; sanctimonious – **piously** *adv*, **piousness** *n*

[1]**pip** /pip‖pɪp/ *n* **1** (a disorder marked by formation of) a scale or crust on a bird's tongue **2** a fit of irritation, low spirits, or disgust – chiefly infml; esp in *to give one the pip*

[2]**pip** *n* **1a** any of the dots on dice and dominoes that indicate numerical value **b** SPOT 2c **2** a star worn, esp on the shoulder, to indicate an army officer's rank

[3]**pip** *vt* **-pp-** to beat by a narrow margin – infml – **pip at the post** to beat at the very last minute (e g in a race or competition)

[4]**pip** *n* a small fruit seed of an apple, orange, etc

[5]**pip** *vt* **-pp-** to remove the pips from (a fruit)

[6]**pip** *n* a short high-pitched tone, esp broadcast in a series as a time signal

pipal /'peepl‖'pi:pl/ *n* a large long-lived Indian fig tree

[1]**pipe** /piep‖paɪp/ *n* **1a** a tubular wind instrument; *specif* a small fipple flute held in and played with one hand, esp while a tabor is played with the other **b(1)** FLUE PIPE **b(2)** REED PIPE **c** a bagpipe – usu pl with sing. meaning **2** a long tube or hollow body for conducting a liquid, gas, etc **3a** a tubular or cylindrical object, part, or passage **b** a roughly cylindrical body of ore **4** a large cask used esp for wine (e g port) and oil **5** (tobacco or other plant material held by the bowl of) a wood, clay, etc tube with a mouthpiece at one end, and at the other a small bowl in which plant material, esp tobacco, is burned for smoking <*he lit his* ~>

[2]**pipe** *vi* **1a** to play on a pipe **b** to convey orders or direct by signals on a boatswain's pipe **2a** to speak in a high or shrill voice **b** to make a shrill sound ~ *vt* **1a** to play (a tune) on a pipe **b** to utter in the shrill tone of a pipe **2** to lead, accompany, or announce ceremonially **3a** to trim with piping **b** to force (e g cream or icing) through a piping tube or nozzle in order to achieve a decorative effect **4** to supply or equip with pipes **5** to convey (as if) by pipes; *specif* to transmit by wire or coaxial cable

'pipe-,clay *vt* to whiten or clean with pipe clay

'pipe ,clay *n* a fine white clay used esp for making tobacco pipes and for whitening leather

'pipe ,cleaner *n* a piece of flexible wire covered with tufted fabric which is used to clean the stem of a tobacco pipe

,piped 'music /piept‖paɪpt/ *n* recorded background music in public places

pipe down *vi* to stop talking or making noise – infml

'pipe ,dream *n* an illusory or fantastic plan, hope, or story

'pipe,line /-,lien‖-,laɪn/ *n* **1** a line of pipe with pumps, valves, and control devices for conveying liquids, gases, etc **2a** the processes through which supplies pass from source to user **b** sthg considered as a continuous set of processes which the individual must go through or be subjected to **3** *NAm* a direct channel for information

,pipe of 'peace *n* a calumet

piper /'piepə‖'paɪpə/ *n* **1** one who or that which plays on a pipe **2** a maker, layer, or repairer of pipes

pipette, *NAm* **pipet** /pi'pet‖pɪ'pet/ *n* a narrow tube into which fluid is drawn (e g for dispensing or measuring) by suction and retained by closing the upper end

pipe up *vi* to begin to play or to sing or speak, esp unexpectedly

piping /'pieping‖'paɪpɪŋ/ *n* **1a** the music of a pipe **b** a sound, note, or call like that of a pipe **2** a quantity or system of pipes **3a** a narrow trimming consisting of a folded strip of cloth often enclosing a cord, used to decorate upholstery, garments, etc **b** a thin cordlike line of icing piped onto a cake

pipit /ˈpipit‖ˈpɪpɪt/ *n* any of various small birds resembling larks

pippin /ˈpipin‖ˈpɪpɪn/ *n* any of numerous apples with usu yellow skins strongly flushed with red

ˈ**pip-ˌsqueak** *n* a small or insignificant person – infml

piquant /ˈpeekənt‖ˈpiːkənt/ *adj* **1** agreeably stimulating to the palate; savoury **2** pleasantly stimulating to the mind – **piquancy** *n*, **piquantly** *adv*, **piquantness** *n*

[1]**pique** /peek‖piːk/ *n* (a fit of) resentment resulting from wounded vanity

[2]**pique** *vt* **1** to arouse anger or resentment in; *specif* to offend by slighting **2a** to excite or arouse by a provocation, challenge, or rebuff **b** to pride or congratulate (oneself), esp in respect of a particular accomplishment <*he* ~s *himself on his skill as a cook*>

piqué, pique /ˈpeekay‖ˈpiːkeɪ/ *n* a durable ribbed fabric of cotton, rayon, or silk

piquet /piˈket‖pɪˈket/ *n* **1** a 2-handed card game played with a 32-card pack with no cards below the 7 **2** PICKET 2

piracy /ˈpie·ərəsi‖ˈpaɪərəsɪ/ *n* **1** robbery or illegal violence on the high seas; *also* a similar act (e g hijacking) against an aircraft in flight **2** the infringement of a copyright, patent, etc **3** an act (as if) of piracy

piranha /piˈrahn(y)ə‖pɪˈrɑːn(j)ə/ *n* a small S American fish capable of attacking and (fatally) wounding human beings and large animals

[1]**pirate** /ˈpie·ərət‖ˈpaɪərət/ *n* **1** (a ship used by) sby who commits piracy **2** an unauthorized radio station; *esp* one located on a ship in international waters [Middle French, fr Latin *pirata*, fr Greek *peiratēs*, fr *peiran* to attempt, attack] – **piratical** *adj*, **piratically** *adv*

[2]**pirate** *vt* **1** to commit piracy on **2** to take or appropriate by piracy **3** to reproduce without authorization ~*vi* to commit or practise piracy

pirouette /ˌpirooˈet‖ˌpɪrʊˈet/ *n* a rapid whirling about of the body; *specif* a full turn on the toe or ball of one foot in ballet – **pirouette** *vi*

piscatory /ˈpiskət(ə)ri‖ˈpɪskət(ə)rɪ/, **piscatorial** /ˌpiskəˈtawri·əl‖ˌpɪskəˈtɔːrɪəl/ *adj* of or dependent on fishermen or fishing

Pisces /ˈpieseez‖ˈpaɪsiːz/ *n pl but sing in constr* (sby born under) the 12th sign of the zodiac in astrology, which is pictured as 2 fishes – **Piscean** *adj or n*

pish /pish‖pɪʃ/ *interj* – used to express disdain or contempt

[1]**piss** /pis‖pɪs/ *vi* **1** to urinate **2** to rain heavily – often with *down* ~ *vt* **1** to urinate in or on <~ *the bed*> **2** to discharge (as if) as urine <*to* ~ *blood*> *USE* vulg

[2]**piss** *n* **1** urine **2** an act of urinating *USE* vulg

pissed *adj, Br* drunk – slang

piss off *vb, Br vi* to go away ~*vt* to cause to be annoyed or fed up *USE* vulg

pistachio /piˈstahshi·oh‖pɪˈstɑːʃɪəʊ/ *n, pl* **pistachios 1** (the green edible nut of) a small tree of the sumach family **2** the vivid green colour of the pistachio nut

pistil /ˈpistil‖ˈpɪstɪl/ *n* a carpel

pistol /ˈpistl‖ˈpɪstl/ *n* a short firearm intended to be aimed and fired with 1 hand [Middle French *pistole*, fr German, fr Czech *pištal*, lit., pipe]

piston /ˈpist(ə)n‖ˈpɪst(ə)n/ *n* **1** a sliding disc or short cylinder fitting within a cylindrical vessel along which it moves back and forth by or against fluid pressure **2a** a sliding valve in a cylinder in a brass instrument that is used to lower its pitch **b** a button on an organ console for bringing in a preselected registration

ˈ**piston ˌring** *n* a springy split metal ring for sealing the gap between a piston and a cylinder wall

[1]**pit** /pit‖pɪt/ *n* **1a(1)** a hole, shaft, or cavity in the ground **a(2)** a mine **b(1)** an area often sunken or depressed below the adjacent floor area **b(2)** ORCHESTRA 2 **2** Hell – + *the* **3** a hollow or indentation, esp in the surface of a living plant or animal: e g **3a** a natural hollow in the surface of the body **b** any of the indented scars left in the skin by a pustular disease (e g smallpox) **4** any of the areas alongside a motor-racing track used for refuelling and repairing the vehicles during a race – usu pl with sing. meaning; + *the* **5** *chiefly Br* the floor of a theatre auditorium; *esp* the area between the stalls and the stage

[2]**pit** *vb* **-tt-** *vt* **1** to make pits in; *esp* to scar or mark with pits **2a** to set (e g fighting cocks) to fight (as if) in a cockpit – often + *against* **b** to set into opposition or rivalry; oppose ~*vi* to become marked with pits; *esp* to preserve for a time an indentation made by pressure

[3]**pit** *n, NAm* STONE 2

[4]**pit** *vt* **-tt-** *chiefly NAm* to remove the pit from (a fruit)

ˌ**pit-a-ˈpat** *n* pitter-patter – **pit-a-pat** *adv or adj*

[1]**pitch** /pich‖pɪtʃ/ *n* **1** (any of various bituminous substances similar to) a black or dark viscous substance obtained as a residue in the distillation of organic materials, esp tars **2** resin obtained from various conifers

[2]**pitch** *vt* to cover, smear, or treat (as if) with pitch

[3]**pitch** *vt* **1** to erect and fix firmly in place <~ *a tent*> **2** to throw, fling <~ *hay onto a wagon*> <~ed *a couple of drunks out of the party*>: e g **2a** to throw (a baseball) to a batter **b** to toss (e g coins) so as to fall at or near a mark **3a(1)** to cause to be at a particular level or of a particular quality **a(2)** to set in a particular musical pitch or key **b** to cause to be set at a particular angle; slope <*a* ~ed *roof*> **4** to hit (a golf ball) in a high arc with backspin **5** to bowl (a ball) in cricket to a specified place or in a specified manner ~ *vi* **1a** to fall precipitately or headlong **b(1)** *of a ship* to move so that the bow is alternately rising and falling **b(2)** *of an aircraft* to turn about a lateral axis so that the nose rises or falls in relation to the tail **c** BUCK 1 **2** to encamp **3** to incline downwards; slope **4** to pitch a baseball or golf ball **5** *of a ball, esp a bowled cricket ball* to bounce

[4]**pitch** *n* **1** pitching; *esp* an up-and-down movement **2a** a slope; *also* the degree of slope **b(1)** distance between one point on a gear tooth and the corresponding point on the next tooth **b(2)**

distance from any point on the thread of a screw to the corresponding point on an adjacent thread measured parallel to the axis **c** the distance advanced by a propeller in 1 revolution **d** the number of teeth on a gear or of threads on a screw per unit distance **e** the degree to which a blade of a propeller is slanted in relation to the axis of rotation **3a** the relative level, intensity, or extent of some quality or state <*were at a high ~ of excitement*> **b(1)** the property of a sound, esp a musical note, that is determined by the frequency of the waves producing it; highness or lowness of sound **b(2)** a standard frequency for tuning instruments **4** an often high-pressure sales talk or advertisement **5** WICKET 4b **6** *chiefly Br* **6a** a usu specially marked area used for playing soccer, rugby, hockey, etc **b** an area or place, esp in a street, to which a person lays unofficial claim for carrying out business or activities – **pitched** *adj*

,pitch-'black *adj* intensely dark or black

pitchblende /'pich,blend‖'pɪtʃ,blend/ *n* a radium-containing uranium oxide occurring as a brown to black lustrous mineral

,pitched 'battle *n* an intense battle; *specif* one fought on previously chosen ground

[1]**pitcher** /'pichə‖'pɪtʃə/ *n* a large deep usu earthenware vessel with a wide lip and a handle or 2 ear-shaped handles, for holding and pouring liquids; *broadly* a large jug

[2]**pitcher** *n* the player who pitches in a baseball game

[1]**pitchfork** /'pich,fawk‖'pɪtʃ,fɔ:k/ *n* a long-handled fork with 2 or 3 long curved prongs used esp for pitching hay

[2]**pitchfork** *vt* **1** to lift and toss (as if) with a pitchfork <*~ed the hay into the wagon*> **2** to thrust (sby) into a position, office, etc suddenly or without preparation

pitch in *vi* **1** to begin to work **2** to contribute to a common endeavour

piteous /'piti·əs‖'pɪtɪəs/ *adj* causing or deserving pity or compassion – **piteously** *adv*, **piteousness** *n*

pitfall /'pit,fawl‖'pɪt,fɔ:l/ *n* **1** a trap or snare; *specif* a camouflaged pit used to capture animals **2** a hidden or not easily recognized danger or difficulty

pith /pith‖pɪθ/ *n* **1a** a (continuous) central area of spongy tissue in the stems of most vascular plants **b** the white tissue surrounding the flesh and directly below the skin of a citrus fruit **2a** the essential part; the core **b** substantial quality (e g of meaning) <*made a speech that lacked ~*>

pithead /'pit,hed‖'pɪt,hed; *in mining communities usu* ,pit'hed‖,pɪt'hed/ *n* (the ground and buildings adjacent to) the top of a mining pit

pithy /'pithi‖'pɪθɪ/ *adj* **1** consisting of or having much pith **2** tersely cogent – **pithily** *adv*, **pithiness** *n*

pitiable /'piti·əbl‖'pɪtɪəbl/ *adj* deserving or exciting pity or contempt, esp because of inadequacy <*a ~ excuse*> – **pitiableness** *n*, **pitiably** *adv*

pitiful /'pitif(ə)l‖'pɪtɪf(ə)l/ *adj* **1** deserving or arousing pity or commiseration **2** exciting pitying contempt (e g by meanness or inadequacy) – **pitifully** *adv*, **pitifulness** *n*

pitiless /'pitilis‖'pɪtɪlɪs/ *adj* devoid of pity; merciless – **pitilessly** *adv*, **pitilessness** *n*

'pitman /-mən‖-mən/ *n, pl* (*1*) **pitmen** /-mən‖-mən/, (*2*) **pitmans** **1** a male mine worker **2** *NAm* CONNECTING ROD

piton /pi'ton(h) ‖pɪ'tɒn, pɪ'tɑ̃ (*Fr* pitɔ̃)/ *n* a spike or peg that is driven into a rock or ice surface as a support, esp for a rope, in mountaineering

pittance /'pit(ə)ns‖'pɪt(ə)ns/ *n* a small amount or allowance; *specif* a meagre wage or remuneration

'pitter-,patter /'pitə‖'pɪtə/ *n* a rapid succession of light sounds – **pitter-patter** *adv or adj*, **pitter-patter** *vi*

pituitary /pi'tyooh·it(ə)ri‖pɪ'tju:ɪt(ə)rɪ/ *adj or n* (of) the pituitary gland

pituitary gland *n* a small endocrine organ, attached to the brain, that consists of two lobes secreting many important hormones

[1]**pity** /'piti‖'pɪtɪ/ *n* **1a** (the capacity to feel) sympathetic sorrow for one suffering, distressed, or unhappy **b** a contemptuous feeling of regret aroused by the inferiority or inadequacy of another **2** sthg to be regretted <*it's a ~ you can't go*>

[2]**pity** *vb* to feel pity (for) – **pitier** *n*, **pityingly** *adv*

[1]**pivot** /'pivət‖'pɪvət/ *n* **1** a shaft or pin on which sthg turns **2a** a person, thing, or factor having a major or central role, function, or effect <*as if the ~ and pole of his life . . . was his Mother* – D H Lawrence> **b** a key player or position; *specif* [6]POST 2b

[2]**pivot** *vi* to turn (as if) on a pivot ~ *vt* **1** to provide with, mount on, or attach by a pivot **2** to cause to pivot – **pivotable** *adj*

[3]**pivot** *adj* **1** turning (as if) on a pivot **2** pivotal

'pivotal /-tl‖-tl/ *adj* **1** of or constituting a pivot **2** vitally important; crucial – **pivotally** *adv*

pixel /'piksəl‖'pɪksəl/ *n* any of the small separate elements that together form an image on a television or VDU screen

pixie, pixy /'piksi‖'pɪksɪ/ *n* a (mischievous) fairy – **pixieish** *adj*

pixilated /'piksi,laytid‖'pɪksɪ,leɪtɪd/ *adj, chiefly NAm* **1** somewhat unbalanced mentally; *also* bemused **2** drunk – **pixilation** *n*

pizza /'peetsə‖'pi:tsə/ *n* a round thin cake of baked bread dough spread with a mixture of tomatoes, cheese, herbs, etc

pizzazz, pizazz /pi'zaz‖pɪ'zæz/ *n, chiefly NAm* the quality of being exciting, glamorous, or lively – infml

pizzicato /,pitsi'kahtoh‖,pɪtsɪ'kɑ:təʊ/ *n, adv, or adj, pl* **pizzicati** /-ti‖-tɪ/ (a note or passage played) by means of plucking instead of bowing – used in music [Italian, past participle of *pizzicare* to pinch, pluck]

[1]**placard** /'plakahd‖'plækɑ:d/ *n* a notice for display or advertising purposes, usu printed on or fixed to a stiff backing material

[2]**placard** *vt* **1** to cover (as if) with placards **2** to give public notice of by means of placards

placate /plə'kayt‖plə'keɪt/ *vt* to soothe or mollify, esp by concessions; appease – **placation** *n*, **placative** *adj*, **placatory** *adj*

[1]**place** /plays‖pleɪs/ *n* **1a** physical environment;

a space **b** physical surroundings; atmosphere **2a** an indefinite region or expanse; an area **b** a building or locality used for a usu specified purpose *<a ~ of worship>* **3a** a particular region or centre of population **b** a house, dwelling *<invited them to his ~ for the evening>* **4** a particular part of a surface or body; a spot **5** relative position in a scale or series: e g **5a** a particular part in a piece of writing; *esp* the point at which a reader has temporarily stopped **b** an important or valued position *<there was never much of a ~ in his life for women>* **c** degree of prestige *<put her in her ~>* **d** a (numbered) point in an argument, explanation, etc *<in the first ~, you're wrong>* **6** a leading place, esp second or third, in a competition **7a** a proper or designated niche *<put it back in its ~>* **b** an appropriate moment or point *<this is not the ~ to discuss legal liability>* **8a** an available seat or accommodation **b** PLACE SETTING *<lay another ~ for our guest>* **9** the position of a figure in relation to others of a row or series; *esp* the position of a digit within a numeral *<in 316 the figure 1 is in the tens ~>* **10a** remunerative employment; a job; *esp* public office **b** prestige accorded to one of high rank; status **c** a duty accompanying a position of responsibility *<it was not his ~ to sack the employee>* **11** a public square **12** *chiefly Br* an available vacancy *<got a university ~>* – **in place of** so as to replace

[2]**place** *vt* **1** to distribute in an orderly manner; arrange *<~ these documents in their correct order>* **2a** to put in, direct to, or assign to a particular place *<~d her on the right of the host>* **b** to put in a particular state *<~ a performer under contract>* **3** to appoint to a position *<~d him in charge of the class>* **4** to find employment or a home for **5a** to assign to a position in a series or category **b** to estimate *<~d the value of the estate too high>* **c** to identify by connecting with an associated context *<couldn't quite ~ her face>* **d** to put, lay *<the teacher ~s a great deal of stress on correct spelling>* **6a** to give (an order) to a supplier **b** to give an order for *<~ a bet>* – **placeable** *adj*, **placement** *n*

placebo /plə'seeboh||plə'siːbəʊ/ *n, pl* **placebos** **1** the Roman Catholic vespers for the dead **2a(1)** a medication that has no physiological effect and is prescribed more for the mental relief of the patient **a(2)** an inert substance against which an active substance (e g a drug) is tested in a controlled trial **b** sthg tending to soothe or gratify [Latin, I shall please, fr *placēre* to please]

'place ˌcard *n* a card indicating the place a guest is to occupy at table during a formal dinner

placed *adj, chiefly Br* in a leading place, esp second or third, at the end of a competition, horse race, etc

'placeˌkick /-ˌkik||-ˌkɪk/ *vt or n* (to kick or score by means of) a kick at a ball (e g in rugby) placed or held in a stationary position on the ground – **placekicker** *n*

placenta /plə'sentə||plə'sentə/ *n, pl* **placentas, placentae** /-ti||-tɪ/ **1** the organ in all higher mammals that unites the foetus to the maternal uterus and provides for the nourishment of the foetus and the elimination of waste **2** the part of a flowering plant to which the ovules are attached – **placental** *adj or n*

'place ˌsetting *n* a table service for 1 person

placid /'plasid||'plæsɪd/ *adj* serenely free of interruption or disturbance *<~ summer skies>* *<a ~ disposition>* – **placidly** *adv*, **placidness, placidity** *n*

placket /'plakit||'plækɪt/ *n* a slit in a garment, esp a skirt, for a fastening or pocket

plagiarism /'playj(y)əˌriz(ə)m||'pleɪdʒ(j)əˌrɪz(ə)m/ *n* **1** plagiarizing **2** sthg plagiarized – **plagiarist** *n*, **plagiaristic** *adj*

plagiar·ize, -ise /'playj(y)əˌriez||'pleɪdʒ(j)əˌraɪz/ *vb* to appropriate and pass off (the ideas or words of another) as one's own [Latin *plagiarius*, kidnapper, plagiarist, fr *plagium* netting game, kidnapping, fr *plaga* net] – **plagiarizer** *n*

[1]**plague** /playg||pleɪg/ *n* **1a** a disastrous evil or affliction; a calamity **b** a large destructive influx *<a ~ of locusts>* **2** any of several epidemic virulent diseases that cause many deaths; *esp* a fever caused by a bacterium that occurs in several forms **3a** a cause of irritation; a nuisance **b** a sudden unwelcome outbreak *<a ~ of burglaries>*

[2]**plague** *vt* **1** to infest or afflict (as if) with disease, calamity, etc **2a** to cause worry or distress to **b** to disturb or annoy persistently – **plaguer** *n*

plaguey, plaguy /'playgi||'pleɪgɪ/ *adj* causing irritation or annoyance; troublesome – infml

plaice /plays||pleɪs/ *n, pl* **plaice** any of various flatfishes; *esp* a large European flounder

plaid /plad||plæd/ *n* **1** a rectangular length of tartan worn over the left shoulder as part of Highland dress **2** a usu twilled woollen fabric with a tartan pattern **3** a tartan – **plaid** *adj*, **plaided** *adj*

[1]**plain** /playn||pleɪn/ *n* **1a** an extensive area of level or rolling treeless country **b** a broad unbroken expanse **2** [2]KNIT

[2]**plain** *adj* **1** lacking ornament; undecorated **2** free of added substances; pure **3** free of impediments to view; unobstructed **4a** evident to the mind or senses; obvious *<it's perfectly ~ that they will resist>* **b** clear *<made his intentions ~>* **5** free from deceitfulness or subtlety; candid **6** lacking special distinction or affectation; ordinary **7a** characterized by simplicity; not complicated *<~ home cooking>* **b** not rich or elaborately prepared or decorated **8** unremarkable either for physical beauty or for ugliness **9** *of flour* not containing a raising agent – **plainly** *adv*, **plainness** *n*

[3]**plain** *adv* in a plain manner; clearly, simply; *also* totally, utterly *<it's just ~ daft>*

ˌplain 'clothes *n* ordinary civilian dress as opposed to (police) uniform – often attrib in *plain-clothes man*

ˌplain 'dealing *n* straightforward honesty

ˌplain 'sailing *n* easy progress along an unobstructed course (e g of action)

'plainˌsong /-ˌsong||-ˌsɒŋ/ *n* **1** the nonmetrical monophonic music of the medieval church; *esp* GREGORIAN CHANT **2** a liturgical chant of any of various Christian rites

ˌplain'spoken /-'spohkən||-'spəʊkən/ *adj* candid, frank – **plainspokenness** *n*

plaint /playnt||pleɪnt/ *n* a protest

plaintext /-ˌtekst‖-tekst/ *n* the intelligible form (e g the original form) of a text in code

plaintiff /ˈplayntif‖ˈpleɪntɪf/ *n* sby who commences a civil legal action

plaintive /ˈplayntiv‖ˈpleɪntɪv/ *adj* expressive of suffering or woe; melancholy, mournful – **plaintively** *adv*, **plaintiveness** *n*

[1]**plait** *also* **plat** /plat‖plæt/ *n* **1** a pleat **2** a length of plaited material, esp hair

[2]**plait,** *also* **plat** *vt* **1** to pleat **2a** to interweave the strands of **b** to make by plaiting – **plaiter** *n*

[1]**plan** /plan‖plæn/ *n* **1** a drawing or diagram drawn on a plane: e g **1a** a top or horizontal view of an object **b** a large-scale map of a small area **2a** a method for achieving an end **b** an often customary method of doing sthg; a procedure *<the usual ~ is to both arrive and leave early>* **c** a detailed formulation of a programme of action **d** a goal, aim *<his ~ was to get a degree in engineering>* – **planless** *adj*, **planlessly** *adv*

[2]**plan** *vb* **-nn-** *vt* **1** to design **2** to arrange in advance **3** to have in mind; intend *~vi* to make plans – **planner** *n*

[1]**plane** /playn‖pleɪn/ *vt* **1** to make flat or even with a plane *<~d the sides of the door>* **2** to remove by planing – often + *away* or *down* – **planer** *n*

[2]**plane,** ˈ**plane** ˌ**tree** *n* any of a genus of trees with large deeply cut lobed leaves and flowers in spherical heads

[3]**plane** *n* a tool with a sharp blade protruding from the base of a flat metal or wooden stock for smoothing or shaping a wood surface

[4]**plane** *n* **1a** a surface such that any 2 included points can be joined by a straight line lying wholly within the surface **b** a flat or level physical surface **2** a level of existence, consciousness, or development *<on the intellectual ~>* **3a** any of the main supporting surfaces of an aeroplane **b** an aeroplane

[5]**plane** *adj* **1** having no elevations or depressions; flat **2a** of or dealing with geometric planes **b** lying in a plane *<a ~ curve>*

[6]**plane** *vi* **1** to fly keeping the wings motionless **2** to skim across the surface of the water

planet /ˈplanit‖ˈplænɪt/ *n* **1** any of the bodies, except a comet, meteor, or satellite, that revolve round a star, esp the sun in our solar system; *specif* Mercury, Venus, Earth, Mars, Jupiter, Saturn, Uranus, Neptune, or Pluto **2** STAR 2a(1) [Old French *planete*, fr Latin *planeta*, fr Greek *planēt-, planēs*, lit., wanderer, fr *planasthai* to wander]

planetarium /ˌplaniˈteəri·əm‖ˌplænɪˈteərɪəm/ *n, pl* **planetariums, planetaria** /-ri·ə‖-rɪə/ **1** a model of the solar system **2** (a building or room housing) an optical projector for projecting images of celestial bodies and effects as seen in the night sky

planetary /ˈplanit(ə)ri‖ˈplænɪt(ə)rɪ/ *adj* **1a** of or being a planet **b** having a motion like that of a planet *<~ electrons>* **2** of or belonging to the earth; terrestrial **3** erratic, wandering – poetic

plangent /ˈplanj(ə)nt‖ˈplændʒ(ə)nt/ *adj* **1** loudly reverberating **2** having an expressive, esp plaintive, quality – **plangency** *n*, **plangently** *adv*

[1]**plank** /plangk‖plæŋk/ *n* **1a** a long thick piece of wood; *specif* one 2 to 4in (about 50 to 100mm) thick and at least 8in (about 200mm) wide **2a** an article in a political platform **b** a (principal) item of a policy or programme

[2]**plank** *vt* to cover or floor with planks

plankton /ˈplangktən‖ˈplæŋktən/ *n* the floating or weakly swimming minute animal and plant organisms of a body of water – **planktonic** *adj*

planning /ˈplaning‖ˈplænɪŋ/ *n* the establishment of goals, policies, and procedures for a social or economic unit

[1]**plant** /plahnt‖plɑːnt/ *vt* **1a** to put in the ground, soil, etc for growth *<~ seeds>* **b** to set or sow (land) with seeds or plants **c** to implant **2a** to establish, institute **b** to place (animals) in a new locality **c** to stock with animals **3** to place firmly or forcibly *<~ed a hard blow on his chin>* **4** to position secretly; *specif* to conceal in order to observe or deceive *<the spy ~ed a microphone in the hotel room>* *~vi* to plant sthg – **plantable** *adj*

[2]**plant** *n* **1a** a tree, vine, etc that is or can be planted; *esp* a small herbaceous plant **b** any of a kingdom of living things (e g a green alga, moss, fern, conifer, or flowering plant) typically lacking locomotive movement or obvious nervous or sensory organs **2a** the buildings, machinery, etc employed in carrying on a trade or an industrial business **b** a factory or workshop for the manufacture of a particular product **3** an act of planting **4** sthg or sby planted *<left muddy footprints as a ~ to confuse the police>* – **plantlike** *adj*

[1]**plantain** /ˈplantayn, -tin‖ˈplæntеɪn, -tɪn/ *n* any of a genus of short-stemmed plants bearing dense spikes of minute greenish or brownish flowers

[2]**plantain** *n* (the angular greenish starchy fruit of) a type of banana plant

plantation /plahnˈtaysh(ə)n, plan-‖plɑːnˈteɪʃ(ə)n, plæn-/ *n* **1** (a place with) a usu large group of plants, esp trees, under cultivation **2** a settlement in a new country or region; a colony **3** an agricultural estate, usu worked by resident labour

planter /ˈplahntə‖ˈplɑːntə/ *n* **1** one who owns or operates a plantation *<a tea ~>* **2** one who settles or founds a new colony **3** a container in which ornamental plants are grown **4** a planting machine

plant out *vb* to transplant (e g seedlings or a house plant) from a pot, seed tray, etc to open ground

plaque /plak, plahk‖plæk, plɑːk/ *n* **1a** an ornamental brooch; *esp* the badge of an honorary order **b** a commemorative or decorative inscribed tablet of ceramic, wood, metal, etc **2a** a localized abnormal patch on a body part or surface **b** a film of mucus on a tooth that harbours bacteria

[1]**plash** /plash‖plæʃ/ *n* a shallow or muddy pool

[2]**plash** *vt* to interweave (branches and twigs) to form a hedge; *also* to form (a hedge) thus

[3]**plash** *vt* to break the surface of (water); splash *~vi* to cause a splashing or spattering effect – **plash** *n*

plasma /ˈplazmə‖ˈplæzmə/ *n* **1** the fluid part of blood, lymph, or milk as distinguished from suspended material **2** protoplasm **3** a highly ionized gas (e g in the atmospheres of stars) containing approximately equal numbers of positive ions and electrons – **plasmatic** *adj*

[1]plaster /ˈplahstə‖ˈplɑːstə/ *n* **1** a medicated or protective dressing consisting of a film of cloth, plastic, etc often spread with a medicated substance; STICKING PLASTER **2** a pastelike mixture (e g of lime, water, and sand) that hardens on drying and is used esp for coating walls, ceilings, and partitions **3 plaster, plaster cast** a rigid dressing of gauze impregnated with plaster of paris for immobilizing a diseased or broken body part – **plastery** *adj*

[2]plaster *vt* **1** to overlay or cover with plaster **2** to apply a plaster to **3a** to cover over or conceal as if with a coat of plaster **b** to smear (sthg) thickly (on); coat <*he* ~ed *butter on his bread*> <*she* ~ed *her face with make-up*> **c** to cause to lie flat or stick to another surface <~ed *his hair down*> <*the rain* ~ed *his shirt to his body*> **4** to fasten (sthg) (to) or place (sthg) (on), esp conspicuously or in quantity <*walls* ~ed *with posters*> <~ed *posters all over the walls*> **5** to inflict heavy damage, injury, or casualties on, esp by a concentrated or unremitting attack – infml ~*vi* to apply plaster – **plasterer** *n*

ˈplasterˌboard /-ˌbawd‖-ˌbɔːd/ *n* a board with a plaster core used esp as a substitute for plaster on walls

ˈplastered *adj* drunk – infml

plastering /ˈplahst(ə)ring‖ˈplɑːst(ə)rɪŋ/ *n* **1** a coating (as if) of plaster **2** a decisive defeat – infml

ˌplaster of ˈparis /ˈparis‖ˈpærɪs/ *n, often cap 2nd P* a white powdery plaster made from gypsum that when mixed with water forms a quicksetting paste used chiefly for casts and moulds [*Paris*, capital city of France]

[1]plastic /ˈplastik‖ˈplæstɪk; *also* ˈplahstik‖ˈplɑːstɪk/ *adj* **1** formative, creative <~ *forces in nature*> **2a** capable of being moulded or modelled <~ *clay*> **b** supple, pliant **3** sculptural **4** made or consisting of a plastic **5** capable of being bent or stretched continuously and permanently in any direction without breaking **6** of, involving, or being plastic surgery **7** formed by or adapted to an artificial or conventional standard; synthetic – chiefly derog [Latin *plasticus* of modelling, fr Greek *plastikos*, fr *plassein* to mould, form] – **plastically** *adv*, **plasticize** *vt*, **plasticization** *n*

[2]plastic *n* any of numerous (synthetic) organic polymers that can be moulded, cast, extruded, etc into objects, films, or filaments

Plasticine /ˈplastiˌseen‖ˈplæstɪˌsiːn; *also* ˈplahs-‖ˈplɑːs-/ *trademark* – used for a modelling substance that remains plastic for a long period

plasticity /plasˈtisəti, plahs-‖plæsˈtɪsətɪ, plɑːs-/ *n* **1** being plastic; *esp* capacity for being moulded or altered **2** the ability to retain a shape produced by pressure deformation

ˌplastic ˈsurgery *n* surgery concerned with the repair, restoration, or cosmetic improvement of parts of the body chiefly by the grafting of tissue – **plastic surgeon** *n*

[1]plate /playt‖pleɪt/ *n* **1a** a smooth flat thin usu rigid piece of material **b** a very thin layer of metal deposited on a surface of a base metal by plating **c** (armour of) broad metal plates **d** an (external) scale or rigid layer of bone, horn, etc forming part of an animal body **e** any of the huge movable segments into which the earth's crust is divided **2a** domestic utensils and tableware made of or plated with gold, silver, or base metals **b** a shallow usu circular vessel, made esp of china, from which food is eaten or served **c** a plateful **3a** a prepared surface from which printing is done **b** a sheet of material (e g glass) coated with a light-sensitive photographic emulsion **c** an electrode in an accumulator **4** a flat piece or surface bearing letters or a design **5** a horizontal structural member (e g a timber) that provides bearing and anchorage, esp for rafters or joists **6** the part of a denture that fits to the mouth; *broadly* a denture **7** a full-page book illustration, often on different paper from the text pages **8** *NAm* **8a** a complete main course served on a plate **b** food and service supplied to 1 person <*a dinner at £5 a* ~> **9** *NAm* the anode of an electron tube – **platelike** *adj* – **on a plate** so as not to require effort – infml

[2]plate *vt* **1** to cover or equip with plate: e g **1a** to arm with armour plate **b** to cover permanently with an adherent layer, esp of metal; *also* to deposit (e g a layer) on a surface **2** to fix or secure with a plate – **plater** *n*

plateau /ˈplatoh‖ˈplætəʊ/ *n, pl* **plateaus, plateaux** /-tohz‖-təʊz/ **1** a usu extensive relatively flat land area raised sharply above adjacent land on at least 1 side **2** a relatively stable level, period, or condition <*a price* ~ *interrupting an inflationary spiral*>

ˌplate ˈglass *n* rolled, ground, and polished sheet glass

ˈplateˌlayer /-ˌlayə‖-ˌleɪə/ *n, Br* a person who lays and maintains railway track

platform /ˈplatfawm‖ˈplætfɔːm/ *n* **1** a declaration of (political) principles and policies **2a** a horizontal flat surface, usu higher than the adjoining area; *esp, Br* a raised surface at a railway station to facilitate access to trains **b** a raised flooring (e g for speakers) **c** a raised metal structure secured to the sea bed by posts and serving as a base for the extraction of oil **3** a place or opportunity for public discussion **4** (a shoe with) a thick sole **5** *chiefly Br* the area next to the entrance or exit of a bus

plating /ˈplayting‖ˈpleɪtɪŋ/ *n* **1** a coating of metal plates **2** a thin coating of metal

platinum /ˈplatinəm‖ˈplætɪnəm/ *n* a heavy precious greyish white noncorroding metallic element used esp as a catalyst and for jewellery

ˌplatinum ˈblonde *n* (sby having hair of) a pale silvery blond colour usu produced in human hair by bleach and bluish rinse

platitude /ˈplatityoohd‖ˈplætɪtjuːd/ *n* a banal, trite, or stale remark, esp when presented as if it were original and significant

platonic /pləˈtonik‖pləˈtɒnɪk/ *adj* **1** *cap* (characteristic) of Plato or Platonism **2a** of or being a close relationship between 2 people in which sexual desire is absent or has been repressed or sublimated **b** nominal, theoretical [Latin *platonicus*, fr Greek *platōnikos*, fr *Platōn* Plato (427? -347 BC), Greek philosopher] – **platonically** *adv*

platoon /plə'toohn‖plə'tuːn/ *n sing or pl in constr* **1** a subdivision of a military company normally consisting of 2 or more sections or squads **2** a group of people sharing a common characteristic or activity <*a* ~ *of waiters*>

platter /'platə‖'plætə/ *n* **1** a large often oval plate used esp for serving meat **2** *NAm* a gramophone record – **platterful** *n*

platypus /'platipəs‖'plætɪpəs/ *n, pl* **platypuses** *also* **platypi** /-pie‖-paɪ/ a small aquatic Australian and Tasmanian primitive mammal that lays eggs and has a fleshy bill resembling that of a duck, webbed feet, and a broad flattened tail [Greek *platypous* flat-footed, fr *platys* broad, flat + *pous* foot]

plaudit /'plawdit‖'plɔːdɪt/ *n* enthusiastic approval – usu pl with sing. meaning <*received the* ~*s of the critics*>

plausible /'plawzəbl‖'plɔːzəbl/ *adj* **1** apparently fair, reasonable, or valid but often specious <*a* ~ *pretext*> **2** *of a person* persuasive but deceptive – **plausibleness** *n*, **plausibly** *adv*, **plausibility** *n*

[1]**play** /play‖pleɪ/ *n* **1** the conduct, course, or (a particular) action in or of a game **2a** (children's spontaneous) recreational activity **b** the absence of serious or harmful intent; jest <*said it in* ~> **c** a playing on words or speech sounds **d** gaming, gambling **3a** operation, activity <*bringing other forces into* ~> **b** light, quick, transitory, or fitful movement <*the* ~ *of sunlight and shadows through the trees*> **c** free or unimpeded motion (e g of a part of a machine) **d** scope or opportunity for action **4a** the dramatized representation of an action or story on stage **b** a dramatic composition (for presentation in a theatre) **5** *chiefly NAm* **5a** an act or manoeuvre, esp in a game **b** a move or series of moves calculated to arouse friendly feelings – usu + *make* <*made a big* ~ *for the blonde*> – **in/into play 1** in/into condition or position to be legitimately played **2** in/into operation or consideration – **out of play** not in play

[2]**play** *vi* **1a** to engage in sport or recreation **b(1)** to behave aimlessly; toy, trifle <*don't* ~ *with your food*> **b(2)** to deal or behave frivolously, mockingly, or playfully – often + *around* or *about* **b(3)** to deal in a light speculative manner <*liked to* ~ *with ideas*> **b(4)** to make use of double meaning or of the similarity of sound of 2 words for stylistic or humorous effect – usu in *play on words* **2a** to take advantage <~ing *on fears*> **b** to move or operate in a lively, irregular, or intermittent manner <*a faint smile* ~s *on her lips*> **c** to move or function freely within prescribed limits <*a piston rod* ~s *within cylinders*> **d** to discharge repeatedly or in a stream <*hoses* ~ing *on a fire*> **3a(1)** to perform music **a(2)** to sound in performance <*the organ is* ~ing> **a(3)** to reproduce or emit sounds <*his radio is* ~ing> **b(1)** to act in a dramatic production **b(2)** to be presented at a place of entertainment (e g a theatre) **c** to act with special consideration so as to gain favour, approval, or sympathy – usu + *up to* **4a** to engage, take part, or make a move in a game **b** to perform (e g in a sport) in a specified position or manner <*the fullbacks are* ~ing *deep*> **c** to gamble **d(1)** to behave (or conduct oneself) in a specified way <~ *safe*> **d(2)** to feign a specified state or quality <~ *dead*> **d(3)** to take part in or assent to some activity; cooperate <~ *along with his scheme*> **5** to have (promiscuous or illicit) sexual relations – euph; usu in *play around* ~ *vt* **1a(1)** to engage in or occupy oneself with <~ *football*> **a(2)** to deal with, handle, or manage – often + *it* <*trying to* ~ *it cool*> **a(3)** to exploit, manipulate <~ *the stock market*> **b** to pretend to engage in <*children* ~ing *cops and robbers*> **c(1)** to perform or execute for amusement or to deceive or mock <~ *a trick*> **c(2)** to wreak <~ *havoc*> **2a(1)** to put on a performance of (a play) **a(2)** to act in the character or part of **a(3)** to act or perform in <~ed *leading theatres*> **b** to perform or act the part of <~ *the fool*> **3a(1)** to contend against in a game **a(2)** to use as a contestant in a game <*the selectors did not* ~ *him*> **a(3)** to perform the duties associated with (a certain position) <~ed *fullback*> **b(1)** to make bets on <~ *the horses*> **b(2)** to operate on the basis of <~ *a hunch*> **c** to put into action in a game <~ *the ace*> **d** to direct the course of (e g a ball); hit **4a** to perform (music) on an instrument <~ *a waltz*> **b** to perform music on <~ *the violin*> **c** to perform music of (a specified composer) **d** to reproduce sounds, esp music, on (an apparatus) <~s *her radio all day long*> <~ *us your favourite record*> **5a** to aim and fire or set off with continuous effect <~ed *the hose on the burning building*> **b** to cause to move or operate lightly and irregularly or intermittently <~ed *his torch along the fence*> **c** to allow (a hooked fish) to become exhausted by pulling against a line – **playable** *adj*, **player** *n*, **playability** *n* – **play ball** to cooperate – **play by ear** to deal with from moment to moment rather than making plans in advance – **play fast and loose** to act in a reckless, irresponsible, or craftily deceitful way – **play into the hands of** to act so as to prove advantageous to (an opponent) – **play second fiddle** to take a subordinate position – **play the game** to act according to a code or set of standards – **play with oneself** to masturbate – **to play with** at one's disposal <*a lot of funds* to play with>

playact /'play,akt‖'pleɪ,ækt/ *vi* **1** to make believe **2** to behave in a misleading or insincere manner ~*vt* ACT OUT 1a

'play,back /-,bak‖-,bæk/ *n* (a device that provides for) the reproduction of recorded sound or pictures

play back *vt* to listen to or look at material on (a usu recently recorded disc or tape)

'play,boy /-,boy‖-,bɔɪ/ *n* a man who lives a life devoted chiefly to the pursuit of pleasure

'play ,down *n* to cause to seem less important; minimize

,played 'out *adj* worn or tired out

player piano /'playə‖'pleɪə/ *n* a piano containing a mechanical device that operates the keys automatically

ˈplayful /-f(ə)l‖-f(ə)l/ *adj* **1** full of fun; frolicsome <*a* ~ *kitten*> **2** humorous, lighthearted <*the* ~ *tone of her voice*> – **playfully** *adv*, **playfulness** *n*

ˈplayˌground /-ˌgrownd‖-ˌgraʊnd/ *n* **1** a piece of land for children to play on **2** an area favoured for recreation or amusement <*that town was a gambler's* ~>

ˈplayˌgroup /-ˌgroohp‖-ˌgruːp/ *n, chiefly Br* a supervised group of children below school age who play together regularly

ˈplayˌhouse /-ˌhows‖-ˌhaʊs/ *n* **1** a theatre **2** *chiefly NAm* WENDY HOUSE

ˈplaying ˌcard /ˈplaying‖ˈpleɪɪŋ/ *n* any of a set of usu 52 thin rectangular pieces, usu of cardboard, marked on one side to show one of 13 ranks in one of 4 suits and used in playing any of numerous games

ˈplaying ˌfield *n* a field used for playing organized games and often divided into several separate pitches – often pl with sing. meaning

ˈplayˌmate /-ˌmayt‖-ˌmeɪt/ *n* a companion in play

ˈplay-ˌoff *n* a final contest to determine a winner

play off *vt* **1** to decide the winner of (a competition) or break (a tie) by a play-off **2** to set in opposition for one's own gain <*survived by* playing *his enemies* off *against each other*>

ˌplay on ˈwords *n* a pun

play out *vt* **1** to finish; USE UP **2** to unreel, unfold

ˈplayˌpen /-ˌpen‖-ˌpen/ *n* a portable usu collapsible enclosure in which a baby or young child may play

ˈplayˌsuit /-ˌs(y)ooht‖-ˌs(j)uːt/ *n* a garment, esp dungarees, for children to play in

ˈplayˌthing /-ˌthing‖-ˌθɪŋ/ *n* a toy

play up *vt* **1** to give special emphasis or prominence to <*the press* played up *the divorce story*> **2** *Br* to cause pain or distress to <*my corns have been* playing *me* up *again*> ~*vi* to behave in a disobedient or annoying manner; ACT UP

ˈplayˌwright /-ˌriet‖-ˌraɪt/ *n* one who writes plays

plaza /ˈplahzə‖ˈplɑːzə/ *n* a public square in a city or town

plea /plee‖pliː/ *n* **1** an allegation made by a party in support of his/her case **2** an accused person's answer to an indictment <*a* ~ *of guilty*> **3** sthg offered by way of excuse or justification **4** an earnest entreaty; an appeal

pleach /pleech‖pliːtʃ/ *vt* to interlace, plash

plead /pleed‖pliːd/ *vb* **pleaded, pled** /pled‖pled/ *vi* **1** to argue a case as an advocate in a court **2** to make or answer an allegation in a legal proceeding **3** to make a specified plea <~ *not guilty*> **4a** to urge reasons for or against sthg **b** to entreat or appeal earnestly; implore ~ *vt* **1** to maintain (e g a case) in a court **2** to offer as a (legal) plea <*to* ~ *ignorance*> – **pleadable** *adj*, **pleader** *n*, **pleadingly** *adv*

pleading /ˈpleeding‖ˈpliːdɪŋ/ *n* **1** advocacy of a case in a court **2** any of the formal usu written allegations made alternately by the parties in a legal action

pleasant /ˈplez(ə)nt‖ˈplez(ə)nt/ *adj* **1** having qualities that tend to give pleasure; agreeable <*a* ~ *day*> **2** *of a person* likable, friendly – **pleasantly** *adv*, **pleasantness** *n*

pleasantry /ˈplez(ə)ntri‖ˈplez(ə)ntrɪ/ *n* **1** an agreeable remark (made in order to be polite) **2** a humorous act or remark; a joke

please /pleez‖pliːz/ *vi* **1** to afford or give pleasure or satisfaction **2** to like, wish <*do as you* ~> **3** to be willing – usu used in the imperative (1) to express a polite request <*coffee,* ~> <~ *come in*> (2) to make polite a request for attention <~*, Sir, I don't understand*> (3) to express polite acceptance <*Coffee?* Please*!*> (4) to turn an apparent question into a request <*can you shut it,* ~*?*> ~ *vt* **1** to give pleasure to; gratify **2** to be the will or pleasure of <*may it* ~ *your Majesty*> – fml – **pleasing** *adj*, **pleasingly** *adv*

pleasurable /ˈplezh(ə)rəbl‖ˈpleʒ(ə)rəbl/ *adj* pleasant, enjoyable – **pleasurableness** *n*, **pleasurably** *adv*, **pleasurability** *n*

[1]**pleasure** /ˈplezh·ə‖ˈpleʒə/ *n* **1** a state of gratification **2a** sensual gratification <*he abandoned the monastery for a life of* ~> **b** enjoyment, recreation <*are you here on business or for* ~*?*> **3** a source of delight or joy <*it's always a* ~ *to talk to her*> **4** a wish, desire – fml

[2]**pleasure** *vt, archaic* to give (sexual) pleasure to

[1]**pleat** /pleet‖pliːt/ *vt* to fold; *esp* to arrange in pleats <~ *a skirt*> – **pleater** *n*

[2]**pleat** *n* a fold in cloth made by doubling material over on itself; *also* sthg resembling such a fold – **pleated** *adj*, **pleatless** *adj*

pleb /pleb‖pleb/ *n* a plebeian – chiefly derog

[1]**plebeian** /pliˈbee·ən‖plɪˈbiːən/ *n* a member of the (Roman) common people [Latin *plebeius* of the common people, fr *plebs* common people] – **plebeianism** *n*

[2]**plebeian** *adj* **1** of plebeians **2** crude or coarse in manner or style; common – **plebeianly** *adv*

plebiscite /ˈplebiˌsiet‖ˈplebɪˌsaɪt/ *n* a vote by the people of an entire country or district for or against a proposal, esp on a choice of government or ruler – **plebiscitary** *adj*

plectrum /ˈplektrəm‖ˈplektrəm/ *n, pl* **plectra** /-trə‖-trə/, **plectrums** a small thin piece of plastic, metal, etc used to pluck the strings of a stringed instrument

pled /pled‖pled/ *past of* PLEAD

[1]**pledge** /plej‖pledʒ/ *n* **1** a chattel delivered as security for an obligation (e g a debt) or for the performance of an act **2** the state of being held as a security <*his watch is in* ~> **3** a token, sign, or earnest of sthg else **4** TOAST 3 **5** a binding promise to do or forbear

[2]**pledge** *vt* **1** to make a pledge of; *specif* to deposit as security for fulfilment of a contract or obligation **2** to drink the health of **3** to bind by a pledge **4** to give a promise of <~ *allegiance to the flag*> – **pledger, pledgor** *n*

Pleistocene /ˈpliestəˌseen, -stoh-‖ˈplaɪstəˌsiːn, -stəʊ-/ *adj or n* (of or being) the earlier epoch of the Quaternary

plenary /ˈpleenəri‖ˈpliːnərɪ/ *adj* **1** absolute, unqualified <~ *power*> **2** attended by all entitled to be present <*a* ~ *session*>

plenipotentiary /ˌplenipəˈtensh(ə)ri‖ˌplenɪpəˈtenʃ(ə)rɪ/ *n or adj* (sby, esp a diplomatic agent) invested with full power to transact business

plenitude /ˈplenityoohd‖ˈplenɪtjuːd/ *n* **1** fullness, completeness **2** abundance *USE* fml

plenteous /ˈplentyəs‖ˈplentjəs/ *adj* plentiful – fml or poetic – **plenteously** *adv*, **plenteousness** *n*

plentiful /ˈplentif(ə)l‖ˈplentɪf(ə)l/ *adj* **1** containing or yielding plenty *<a ~ land>* **2** characterized by, constituting, or existing in plenty – **plentifully** *adv*, **plentifulness** *n*

[1]**plenty** /ˈplenti‖ˈplentɪ/ *n* **1a** *sing or pl in constr* a full or more than adequate amount or supply *<had ~ of time to finish the job>* *<there's ~ more>* **b** a large number or amount *<he's in ~ of trouble>* **2** copiousness, plentifulness *<years of ~>*

[2]**plenty** *adj, chiefly NAm* ample *<~ work to be done – Time>*

[3]**plenty** *adv* **1** quite, abundantly *<~ warm enough>* **2** *chiefly NAm* to a considerable or extreme degree; very *<~ hungry>* *USE* infml

pleonasm /ˈplee·əˌnaz(ə)m‖ˈpliːəˌnæz(ə)m/ *n* the use of more words than are necessary to convey the intended sense – **pleonastic** *adj*, **pleonastically** *adv*

plethora /ˈplethərə‖ˈpleθərə/ *n* **1** an abnormal excess of blood in the body – not now used technically **2** a superfluity, excess *<a ~ of regulations>* – **plethoric** *adj*

pleurisy /ˈplooərəsi‖ˈpluərəsɪ/ *n* inflammation of the pleura, usu with fever, painful breathing, and oozing of liquid into the pleural cavity – **pleuritic** *adj*

plexus /ˈpleksəs‖ˈpleksəs/ *n* **1** a network of interlacing blood vessels or nerves **2** a network of parts or elements in a structure or system – **plexiform** *adj*

pliable /ˈplie·əbl‖ˈplaɪəbl/ *adj* **1** easily bent without breaking; flexible **2** yielding readily to others; compliant – **pliableness** *n*, **pliably** *adv*, **pliability** *n*

pliant /ˈplie·ənt‖ˈplaɪənt/ *adj* PLIABLE 1 – **pliantly** *adv*, **pliantness, pliancy** *n*

pliers /ˈplie·əz‖ˈplaɪəz/ *n pl, pl* **pliers** a pair of pincers with long jaws for holding small objects or for bending and cutting wire

[1]**plight** /pliet‖plaɪt/ *vt* to put or give in pledge; engage *<~ one's troth>*

[2]**plight** *n* an (unpleasant or difficult) state; a predicament

plimsoll /ˈplims(ə)l, -sol, -sohl‖ˈplɪms(ə)l, -sɒl, -səʊl/ *n, Br* a shoe with a rubber sole and canvas top worn esp for sports

Plimsoll line *n* a set of markings indicating the draught levels to which a vessel may legally be loaded in various seasons and waters [Samuel *Plimsoll* (1824-98), English leader of shipping reform]

plinth /plinth‖plɪnθ/ *n* **1** a usu square block serving as a base (e g of a pedestal) **2** a part of a structure forming a continuous foundation or base

Pliocene /ˈplie·ohˌseen‖ˈplaɪəʊˌsiːn/ *adj or n* (of or being) the latest epoch of the Tertiary

plod /plod‖plɒd/ *vb* **-dd-** *vi* **1a** to walk heavily or slowly; trudge **b** to proceed slowly or tediously *<the film just ~s along>* **2** to work laboriously and monotonously *<~ding through stacks of unanswered letters>* *~vt* to tread slowly or heavily along or over *<~ded the streets all day, looking for work>* – **plod** *n*, **plodder** *n*, **ploddingly** *adv*

[1]**plonk** /plongk‖plɒŋk/ *vt* PLUNK 2

[2]**plonk** *n, chiefly Br* cheap or inferior wine – infml

plop /plop‖plɒp/ *vb* **-pp-** *vi* **1** to drop or move suddenly with a sound suggestive of sthg dropping into water **2** to allow the body to drop heavily *<~ped into a chair>* *~vt* to set, drop, or throw heavily – **plop** *n*

[1]**plot** /plot‖plɒt/ *n* **1** a small piece of land, esp one used or designated for a specific purpose *<a vegetable ~>* **2** the plan or main story of a literary work **3** a secret plan for accomplishing a usu evil or unlawful end; an intrigue **4** a chart or other graphic representation **5** *NAm* GROUND PLAN – **plotless** *adj*, **plotlessness** *n*

[2]**plot** *vb* **-tt-** *vt* **1a** to make a plot, map, or plan of **b** to mark or note (as if) on a map or chart **2** to lay out in plots **3a** to assign a position to (a point) by means of coordinates **b** to draw (a curve) by means of plotted points **c** to represent (an equation) by means of a curve so constructed **4** to plan or contrive, esp secretly *<~ted his revenge>* **5** to invent or devise the plot of (a literary work) *~vi* to form a plot; scheme – **plotter** *n*

[1]**plough,** *NAm* **plow** /plow‖plaʊ/ *n* **1** (any of various devices operating like) an implement used to cut, lift, and turn over soil, esp in preparing ground for sowing **2** ploughed land **3** *cap* URSA MAJOR – + *the*

[2]**plough,** *NAm* **plow** *vi* **1a** to use a plough **b** to bear or undergo ploughing **2** to force a way, esp violently *<the car ~ed into a group of spectators>* **3** to proceed steadily and laboriously; plod *<had to ~ through a summer reading list>* *~ vt* **1a** to turn, break up, or work (as if) with a plough **b** to make (e g a furrow) with a plough **2** to cut into, open, or make furrows or ridges in (as if) with a plough – often + *up* – **ploughable** *adj*, **plougher** *n*

plough back *vt* to reinvest (profits) in an industry

ˈ**ploughman** /-mən‖-mən/ *n* one who guides a plough; *broadly* a farm labourer

ˌ**ploughman's** ˈ**lunch** /-mənz‖-mənz/ *n* a cold lunch of bread, cheese, and usu pickled onions often served in a public house

ˈ**ploughˌshare** /-ˌsheə‖-ˌʃeə/ *n* the part of a mouldboard plough that cuts the furrow

plover /ˈpluvə‖ˈplʌvə/ *n* any of numerous wading birds with a short beak and usu a stout compact build

ploy /ploy‖plɔɪ/ *n* sthg devised or contrived, esp to embarrass or frustrate an opponent

[1]**pluck** /pluk‖plʌk/ *vt* **1** to pull or pick off or out *<she ~ed out a grey hair>* **2** to remove sthg from (as if) by plucking; *esp* to remove the feathers from (e g a chicken) **3** to pick, pull, or grasp at; *also* to play (an instrument) in this manner *~vi* to tug *at* *<~ed at the folds of her skirt>* – **plucker** *n*

[2]**pluck** *n* **1** an act or instance of plucking or pulling **2** the heart, liver, and lungs of a slaughtered animal, esp as food **3** courage and determination

plucky /'pluki‖'plʌkɪ/ *adj* marked by courage; spirited – **pluckily** *adv*, **pluckiness** *n*

[1]**plug** /plug‖plʌg/ *n* **1a** a piece used to fill a hole; a stopper **b** an obtruding or obstructing mass of material resembling a stopper <*a volcanic* ~> **2** a flat compressed cake of (chewing) tobacco; *also* a piece cut from this for chewing **3** a small core or segment removed from a larger object **4** a fire hydrant **5a** any of various devices resembling or functioning like an electrical plug **b** a device having usu 3 pins projecting from an insulated case for making electrical connection with a suitable socket; *also* the electrical socket **6** a piece of favourable publicity (e g for a commercial product) usu incorporated in general matter – infml

[2]**plug** *vb* **-gg-** *vt* **1** to block, close, or secure (as if) by inserting a plug **2** to hit with a bullet; SHOOT 2a **3** to advertise or publicize insistently ~*vi* to work doggedly and persistently <~ged *away at his homework*> – **plugger** *n*

plug in *vi* to establish an electric circuit by inserting a plug ~*vt* to attach or connect to a power point

plum /plum‖plʌm/ *n* **1** (any of numerous trees and shrubs of the rose family, that bear) an edible globular to oval smooth-skinned fruit with an oblong seed **2** a raisin when used in a pudding, cake, etc <~ *cake*> **3** sthg excellent or superior; *esp* an opportunity or position offering exceptional advantages <*a* ~ *job*> **4** a dark reddish purple – **plum** *adj*, **plumlike** *adj*

plumage /'ploohmij‖'plu:mɪdʒ/ *n* the entire covering of feathers of a bird – **plumaged** *adj*

[1]**plumb** /plum‖plʌm/ *n* **1** a lead weight attached to a cord and used to indicate a vertical line **2** any of various weights (e g a sinker for a fishing line or a lead for sounding)

[2]**plumb** *adv* **1** straight down or up; vertically **2** exactly, precisely <*his house is* ~ *in the middle of the island*> **3** *chiefly dial NAm* completely, absolutely USE (2&3) chiefly infml

[3]**plumb** *vt* **1** to measure the depth of with a plumb **2** to examine minutely and critically, esp so as to achieve complete understanding <~ing *the book's complexities*> **3** to adjust or test by a plumb line **4** to supply with or install as plumbing – often + *in*

[4]**plumb** *adj* **1** exactly vertical or true **2** *of a cricket wicket* flat and allowing little or no horizontal or vertical deviation of the bowled ball **3** downright, complete – infml

plumbago /plum'baygoh‖plʌm'beɪgəʊ/ *n, pl* **plumbagos** **1** graphite **2** any of a genus of plants of the thrift family with spikes of showy flowers

plumber /'plumə‖'plʌmə/ *n* sby who installs, repairs, and maintains water piping and fittings [Middle French *plombier* dealer or worker in lead, fr Latin *plumbarius*, fr *plumbum* lead]

plumbing /'pluming‖'plʌmɪŋ/ *n* **1** a plumber's occupation or trade **2** the apparatus (e g pipes and fixtures) concerned in the distribution and use of water in a building

[1]**plume** /ploohm‖plu:m/ *n* **1a** a (large showy) bird's feather **b** a cluster of distinctive feathers **2** a usu large feather or cluster of feathers worn esp as an ornament **3** sthg resembling a feather (e g in shape, appearance, or lightness): e g **3a** a feathery or feather-like animal or plant part; *esp* a full bushy tail **b** a trail of smoke, blowing snow, etc – **plumed** *adj*

[2]**plume** *vt* **1** to provide or deck with plumes **2** to pride or congratulate (oneself) *on* or *upon* **3a** *of a bird* to preen and arrange the feathers of (itself) **b** to preen and arrange (feathers)

[1]**plummet** /'plumit‖'plʌmɪt/ *n* a plumb (line)

[2]**plummet** *vi* to fall sharply and abruptly

plummy /'plumi‖'plʌmɪ/ *adj* **1** *of the voice* rich and mellow, often to the point of affectation **2** choice, desirable – infml

[1]**plump** /plump‖plʌmp/ *vi* to drop or sink suddenly or heavily <~ed *down in the chair*> ~*vt* to drop, cast, or place suddenly or heavily – **plump for** to decide on out of several choices or courses of action <plumped for *beer rather than wine*>

[2]**plump** *adv* **1** with a sudden or heavy drop **2** without qualification; directly

[3]**plump** *n* (the sound of) a sudden plunge, fall, or blow

[4]**plump** *adj* having a full rounded form; slightly fat – **plumpish** *adj*, **plumply** *adv*, **plumpness** *n*

[5]**plump** *vb* to make or become plump – often + *up* or *out*

ˌ**plum** ˈ**pudding** *n* a rich boiled or steamed pudding containing dried fruits (e g raisins) and spices

[1]**plunder** /'plundə‖'plʌndə/ *vt* **1** to pillage, sack **2** to take, esp by force (e g in war); steal ~*vi* to commit robbery or looting – **plunderer** *n*

[2]**plunder** *n* **1** an act of plundering; pillaging **2** sthg taken by force, theft, or fraud; loot

[1]**plunge** /plunj‖plʌndʒ/ *vt* **1a** to cause to penetrate quickly and forcibly **b** to sink (a potted plant) in the ground **2** to cause to enter a thing, state, or course of action, usu suddenly, unexpectedly, or violently ~ *vi* **1** to thrust or cast oneself (as if) into water **2a** to be thrown headlong or violently forwards and downwards; *also* to move oneself in such a manner **b** to act with reckless haste; enter suddenly or unexpectedly <*the firm* ~d *into debt*> **3** to descend or dip suddenly **4** to bet or gamble heavily and recklessly – infml

[2]**plunge** *n* a dive; *also* a swim

plunger /'plunjə‖'plʌndʒə/ *n* **1a** a device (e g a piston in a pump) that acts with a plunging or thrusting motion **b** a rubber suction cup on a handle used to free plumbing from blockages **2** a reckless gambler or speculator – chiefly infml

plunk /plungk‖plʌŋk/ *vt* **1** to pluck so as to produce a hollow, metallic, or harsh sound **2** to set down suddenly; plump – chiefly infml – **plunk** *n*, **plunker** *n*

plunk down *vi* to drop abruptly; settle into position ~ *vt* **1** to put down usu firmly or abruptly **2** to settle (oneself) into position *USE* chiefly infml

pluperfect /plooh'puhfikt‖plu:'pɜ:fɪkt/ *adj* PAST PERFECT – **pluperfect** *n*

plural /'plooərəl‖'plʊərəl/ *adj* **1** of or being a

word form (e g *we, houses, cattle*) denoting more than 1, or in some languages more than 2 or 3, persons, things, or instances **2** consisting of or containing more than 1 (kind or class) <*a* ~ *society*> – **plural** *n*, **plurally** *adv*, **pluralize** *vt*

pluralism /ˈplooərə,liz(ə)m‖ˈplʊərə,lɪz(ə)m/ *n* **1** the holding of 2 or more offices or positions (e g benefices) at the same time **2** a state of society in which members of diverse social groups develop their traditional cultures or special interests within a common civilization – **pluralist** *adj or n*, **pluralistic** *adj*, **pluralistically** *adv*

plurality /plooəˈraləti‖plʊəˈrælətɪ/ *n* **1a** the state of being plural or numerous **b** a large number or quantity **2** (a benefice held by) pluralism

[1]**plus** /plus‖plʌs/ *prep* **1** increased by; with the addition of <*4* ~ *5*> **2** and also <*the job needs experience* ~ *patience*>

[2]**plus** *n, pl* **-s-** *also* **-ss-** **1** an added quantity **2** a positive factor, quantity, or quality **3** a surplus

[3]**plus** *adj* **1** algebraically or electrically positive **2** additional and welcome <*a* ~ *factor is its nearness to the shops*>

[4]**plus** *conj* and moreover

,plus ˈfours *n pl* loose wide trousers gathered on a band and finishing just below the knee

[1]**plush** /plush‖plʌʃ/ *n* a fabric with an even pile longer and less dense than that of velvet

[2]**plush** *adj* **1** (made) of or resembling plush **2** PLUSHY 2 – **plushly** *adv*, **plushness** *n*

plushy /ˈplushi‖ˈplʌʃɪ/ *adj* **1** having the texture of or covered with plush **2** luxurious, showy – **plushiness** *n*

Pluto /ˈploohtoh‖ˈplu:təʊ/ *n* the planet furthest from the sun

plutocracy /ploohˈtokrəsi‖plu:ˈtɒkrəsɪ/ *n* (government by) a controlling class of wealthy people [Greek *ploutokratia*, fr *ploutos* wealth + *kratos* strength, power] – **plutocrat** *n*, **plutocratic** *adj*, **plutocratically** *adv*

plutonium /ploohˈtonyəm, -ni·əm‖plu:ˈtɒnjəm, -nɪəm/ *n* a radioactive metallic element similar to uranium that is formed in atomic reactors and is used in weapons and as a fuel for atomic reactors

[1]**ply** /plie‖plaɪ/ *vt* to twist together

[2]**ply** *n* **1a** a strand in a yarn, wool, etc **b** any of several layers (e g of cloth) usu sewn or laminated together **2a** (any of the veneer sheets forming) plywood **b** a layer of paper or paperboard

[3]**ply** *vt* **1a** to use or wield diligently <*busily* ~ing *his axe*> **b** to practise or perform diligently <~ing *his trade*> **2** to keep furnishing or supplying sthg to <plied *them with drinks*> **3** to go or travel over or on regularly ~ *vi* **1** to apply oneself steadily **2** *of a boatman, taxi driver, etc* to wait regularly in a particular place for custom – esp in *ply for hire* **3** to go or travel regularly

plywood /ˈplie,wood‖ˈplaɪ,wʊd/ *n* a light structural material of thin sheets of wood glued or cemented together with the grains of adjacent layers arranged crosswise usu at right angles

pneumatic /nyoohˈmatik‖nju:ˈmætɪk/ *adj* of or using gas (e g air or wind): **a** moved or worked by air pressure **b** adapted for holding or inflated with compressed air **c** having air-filled cavities [Latin *pneumaticus*, fr Greek *pneumatikos*, fr *pneumat-*, *pneuma* air, breath, spirit, fr *pnein* to breathe] – **pneumatically** *adv*

pneumoconiosis /,nyoohmoh,koniˈohsis‖,nju:məʊ,kɒnɪˈəʊsɪs/ *n, pl* **pneumoconioses** /-seez‖-si:z/ a crippling disease of the lungs, esp of miners, caused by the habitual inhalation of irritant mineral or metallic particles

pneumonia /nyoohˈmohnyə, -ni·ə‖nju:ˈməʊnjə, -nɪə/ *n* localized or widespread inflammation of the lungs with change from an air-filled to a solid consistency, caused by infection or irritants

po /poh‖pəʊ/ *n, pl* **pos** *Br* CHAMBER POT – infml

[1]**poach** /pohch‖pəʊtʃ/ *vt* to cook (e g fish or an egg) in simmering liquid

[2]**poach** *vt* **1** to trample or cut up (e g turf) (as if) with hoofs **2a** to trespass on **b** to take (game or fish) illegally **c** to take or acquire by unfair or underhand means ~ *vi* **1** *of land* to become soft or muddy when trampled on **2a** to (trespass while attempting to) take game or fish illegally **b** to trespass *on* or *upon* – **poacher** *n*

pock /pok‖pɒk/ *n* (a spot resembling) a pustule in an eruptive disease (e g smallpox) – **pock** *vt*, **pocky** *adj*

[1]**pocket** /ˈpokit‖ˈpɒkɪt/ *n* **1** a small bag that is sewn or inserted in a garment so that it is open at the top or side **2** a supply of money; means <*has houses to suit all* ~s> **3a** a receptacle, container **b** any of several openings at the corners or sides of a billiard table into which balls are propelled **4a** a small isolated area or group <~s *of unemployment*> **b** a cavity (e g in the earth) containing a deposit (e g of gold or water) **c** AIR POCKET **5** *chiefly SAfr* (the amount contained in) a bag – **pocketful** *n* – **in pocket** in the position of having made a profit – **out of pocket** having suffered a financial loss

[2]**pocket** *vt* **1a** to put or enclose (as if) in one's pocket **b** to appropriate to one's own use; steal **2** to accept; PUT UP WITH <~ *an insult*> **3** to set aside, suppress <~ed *his pride*> **4** to drive (a ball) into a pocket of a billiard table

[3]**pocket** *adj* **1** small enough to be carried in the pocket <*a* ~ *camera*> **2** small, miniature <*a* ~ *submarine*>

ˈpocket,book /-,book‖-,bʊk/ *n* **1** a pocket-size container for (paper) money and personal papers **2** *NAm* **2a** a small, esp paperback, book that can be carried in the pocket **b** a purse **c** a strapless handbag

ˈpocket,knife /-,nief‖-,naɪf/ *n* a knife that has 1 or more blades that fold into the handle so that it can be carried in the pocket

ˈpocket ,money *n* money for small personal expenses, esp as given to a child

pockmark /ˈpok,mahk‖ˈpɒk,mɑ:k/ *n* a mark or pit (like that) caused by smallpox – **pockmarked** *adj*

[1]**pod** /pod‖pɒd/ *n* **1** a long seed vessel or fruit, esp of the pea, bean, or other leguminous plant **2** an egg case of a locust or similar insect **3** a streamlined compartment under the wings or fuselage of an aircraft used as a container (e g for fuel) **4** a detachable compartment on a spacecraft or aircraft

[2]**pod** *vb* **-dd-** *vi* to produce pods ~ *vt* to remove (e g peas) from the pod

[3]**pod** *n* a small group of animals (e g

seals) close together

podgy /'poji||'pɒdʒɪ/ *adj* short and plump; chubby

podiatry /po'die·ətri||pɒ'daɪətrɪ/ *n, NAm* chiropody – **podiatrist** *n*, **podiatric** *adj*

podium /'pohdi·əm||'pəʊdɪəm/ *n, pl* **podiums, podia** /-di·ə||-dɪə/ **1** a low wall serving as a foundation or terrace wall: e g **1a** one round the arena of an ancient amphitheatre **b** the stone base supporting the columns of a classical structure **2** a small raised platform (for an orchestral conductor)

poem /'poh·im||'pəʊɪm/ *n* **1** an individual work of poetry **2** a creation, experience, or object suggesting a poem

poesy /'poh·izi, -si||'pəʊɪzɪ, -sɪ/ *n*, **1** a poem or body of poems **2** the art or composition of poetry

poet /'poh·it||'pəʊɪt/, *fem* **poetess** /'poh·ites, ˌpoh·i'tes||'pəʊɪtes, ˌpəʊɪ'tes/ *n* **1** one who writes poetry **2** a creative artist with special sensitivity to his/her medium <*a* ~ *of the piano*> [Old French *poete*, fr Latin *poeta*, fr Greek *poiētēs* maker, poet, fr *poiein* to make, create]

poetaster /ˌpoh·i'tastə||ˌpəʊɪ'tæstə/ *n* an inferior poet

poetic /poh'etik||pəʊ'etɪk/, **poetical** /-kl||-kl/ *adj* **1a** (characteristic) of poets or poetry **b** having the qualities associated with poetry **2** written in verse – **poetically** *adv*, **poeticism** *n*

poetic justice *n* an outcome in which vice is punished and virtue rewarded in an (ironically) appropriate manner

ˌpoet 'laureate *n, pl* **poets laureate, poet laureates** a poet appointed for life by the sovereign as a member of the British royal household and expected to compose poems for state occasions

poetry /'poh·itri||'pəʊɪtrɪ/ *n* **1a** metrical writing; verse **b** a poet's compositions; poems **2** writing that is arranged to formulate a concentrated imaginative awareness of experience through meaning, sound, and rhythm **3** a quality of beauty, grace, and great feeling <~ *in motion*>

ˌpo-'faced /poh||pəʊ/ *adj, Br* having a foolishly solemn or humourless expression – chiefly infml

'pogo ˌstick /'pohgoh||'pəʊgəʊ/ *n* a pole with a spring at the bottom and 2 footrests on which sby stands and can move along with a series of jumps

pogrom /'pogrəm||'pɒgrəm/ *n* an organized massacre, esp of Jews [Yiddish, fr Russian, lit., devastation]

poignant /'poynyənt||'pɔɪnjənt/ *adj* **1a** painfully affecting the feelings; distressing **b** deeply affecting; touching **2** designed to make an impression; cutting <~ *satire*> – **poignancy** *n*, **poignantly** *adv*

poinsettia /poyn'seti·ə||pɔɪn'setɪə/ *n* any of various spurges bearing flower clusters opposite brightly coloured bracts [Joel R *Poinsett* (1799-1851), US diplomat]

[1]**point** /poynt||pɔɪnt/ *n* **1a(1)** an individual detail; an item **a(2)** a distinguishing detail <*tact is one of her strong* ~*s*> **b** the most important essential in a discussion or matter <*missed the whole* ~ *of the joke*> **2** an end or object to be achieved; a purpose <*there is no* ~ *in going on*] **3a(1)** a geometric element that has a position but no extent or magnitude **a(2)** a geometric element determined by an ordered set of coordinates **b** (a narrowly localized place having) a precisely indicated position <*walked to a* ~ *50 yards north of the building*> **c(1)** an exact moment <*at this* ~ *he was interrupted*> **c(2)** a time interval immediately before sthg indicated; *the* verge <*at the* ~ *of death*> **d(1)** a particular step, stage, or degree in development <*had reached the* ~ *where nothing seemed to matter*> **d(2)** a definite position in a scale <*boiling* ~> **4a** the sharp or narrowly rounded end of sthg; a tip **b** the tip of the toes – used in ballet; usu pl **c** *pl* a contact breaker **5a** a projecting usu tapering piece of land **b(1)** the tip of a projecting body part **b(2)** TINE 2 **b(3)** *pl* (the markings of) the extremities of an animal, esp when of a different colour from the rest of the body **6a** a very small mark **b(1)** PUNCTUATION MARK; *esp* FULL STOP **b(2)** DECIMAL POINT **7** any of the 32 evenly spaced compass directions; *also* the 11° 15′ interval between 2 successive points **8a** lace worked with a needle; NEEDLEPOINT 1 **b** lace imitating needlepoint worked with bobbins; PILLOW LACE **9a** a unit of counting in the scoring of a game or contest **b** a unit used in evaluating the strength of a bridge hand **c** a unit used in quoting prices (e g of shares, bonds, and commodities) **d** a unit of 0.351mm (about $^1/_{72}$in) used to measure the body size of printing type **10a** the action of pointing **b** the rigidly intent attitude of a gundog when marking game for a hunter **11** (the position of) a defensive player in lacrosse **12** a fielding position in cricket near to the batsman and on a direct line with the popping crease on the off side **13** *pl, Br* a device made of usu 2 movable rails and necessary connections and designed to turn a locomotive or train from one track to another – **beside the point** irrelevant – **to the point** relevant, pertinent <*a suggestion that was* to the point>

[2]**point** *vt* **1a** to provide with a point; sharpen <~ing *a pencil with a knife*> **b** to give added force, emphasis, or piquancy to <~ *up a remark*> **2** to scratch out the old mortar from the joints of (e g a brick wall) and fill in with new material **3a** to punctuate **b** to mark signs or points in (e g psalms or Hebrew words) **4** *of a gundog* to indicate the presence and place of (game) for a hunter by a point **5** to cause to be turned in a particular direction <~ *a gun*> <~ed *the boat upstream*> ~ *vi* **1a** to indicate the fact or probability of sthg specified <*everything* ~s *to a bright future*> **b** to indicate the position or direction of sthg, esp by extending a finger <~ *at the map*> **c** to point game <*a dog that* ~s *well*> **2** to lie extended, aimed, or turned in a particular direction <*the signpost* ~ed *north*>

ˌpoint-'blank *adj* **1** so close to a target that a missile fired will travel in a straight line to the mark **2** direct, blunt <*a* ~ *refusal*> – **point-blank** *adv*

'point-ˌduty *n* traffic regulation carried out usu by a policeman stationed at a particular point

pointed /ˈpoyntid‖ˈpɔɪntɪd/ *adj* **1** having a point **2a** pertinent; TO THE POINT **b** aimed at a particular person or group **3** conspicuous, marked <~ *indifference*> – **pointedly** *adv*, **pointedness** *n*

pointer /ˈpoyntə‖ˈpɔɪntə/ *n* **1** a rod used to direct attention **2** a large strong slender smooth-haired gundog that hunts by scent and indicates the presence of game by pointing **3** a useful suggestion or hint; a tip

pointillism /ˈpwantiˌliz(ə)m, ˈpoyn-, -tiˌyiz-(ə)m‖ˈpwæntɪˌlɪz(ə)m, ˈpɔɪn-, -tɪˌjɪz(ə)m/ *n* the technique in art of applying small strokes or dots of pure colour to a surface so that from a distance they blend together – **pointillist** *also* **pointilliste** *n or adj*

ˈ**pointless** /-lis‖-lɪs/ *adj* devoid of meaning, relevance, or purpose; senseless – **pointlessly** *adv*, **pointlessness** *n*

point of no return *n* **1** the point in a long-distance journey after which return to the starting point is impossible **2** a critical point (e g in a course of action) at which turning back or reversal is not possible

ˌ**point of ˈorder** *n* a question relating to procedure in an official meeting

ˌ**point of ˈview** *n* a position from which sthg is considered or evaluated

point out *vt* to direct sby's attention to <point out *a mistake*>

pointsman /ˈpoyntsmən‖ˈpɔɪntsmən/ *n* **1** a policeman on point-duty **2** *Br* a person in charge of railway points

ˌ**point-to-ˈpoint** *n* a usu cross-country steeplechase for amateur riders – **point-to-pointer** *n*

[1]**poise** /poyz‖pɔɪz/ *vt* **1a** to balance; *esp* to hold or carry in equilibrium <*walked along gracefully with a water jar* ~d *on her head*> **b** to hold supported or suspended without motion in a steady position **2** to hold or carry in a particular way **3** to put into readiness; brace ~*vi* to hang (as if) suspended; hover

[2]**poise** *n* **1** a stably balanced state <*a* ~ *between widely divergent impulses* – F R Leavis> **2a** easy self-possessed assurance of manner **b** a particular way of carrying oneself

poised /poyzd‖pɔɪzd/ *adj* **1** marked by balance or equilibrium or by easy composure of manner **2** in readiness <~ *for flight*>

[1]**poison** /ˈpoyz(ə)n‖ˈpɔɪz(ə)n/ *n* **1** a substance that through its chemical action kills, injures, or impairs an organism **2** sthg destructive or harmful [Old French, drink, poisonous drink, poison, fr Latin *potion-, potio* drink – see POTION] – **poison** *adj*

[2]**poison** *vt* **1a** to injure or kill with poison **b** to treat, taint, or impregnate with poison **2** to exert a harmful influence on; corrupt <~ed *their minds*> – **poisoner** *n*

poison gas *n* a poisonous gas or a liquid or solid giving off poisonous vapours designed to kill, injure, or disable by inhalation or contact

ˌ**poison ˈivy** *n* (any of several plants related to) a N American climbing plant of the sumach family that has greenish flowers and white berries and produces an oil that causes an intensely itching skin rash

poisonous /ˈpoyz(ə)nəs‖ˈpɔɪz(ə)nəs/ *adj* having the properties or effects of poison – **poisonously** *adv*

ˌ**poison-ˈpen** *adj* written with malice and spite and usu anonymously <~ *letter*>

[1]**poke** /pohk‖pəʊk/ *n, chiefly dial NAm* a bag, sack

[2]**poke** *vt* **1a(1)** to prod, jab <~d *him in the ribs and grinned broadly*> **a(2)** to stir the coals or logs of (a fire) so as to promote burning **b** to produce by piercing, stabbing, or jabbing <~ *a hole*> **2** to cause to project <~d *her head out of the window*> **3** to hit, punch <~d *him in the nose*> – infml **4** *of a man* to have sexual intercourse with –vulg ~ *vi* **1** to make a prodding, jabbing, or thrusting movement, esp repeatedly **2a** to look about or through sthg without system; rummage <*found it while* poking *around in the attic*> **b** to meddle **3** to move or act slowly or aimlessly; potter <*just* ~d *about at home and didn't accomplish much*> **4** to become stuck out or forwards; protrude **5** *of a man* to have sexual intercourse – vulg – **poke fun at** to mock – **poke one's nose into** to meddle in or interfere with (esp sthg that does not concern one)

[3]**poke** *n* **1** a quick thrust; a jab **2** a punch – infml **3** an act of sexual intercourse – vulg

[1]**poker** /ˈpohkə‖ˈpəʊkə/ *n* a metal rod for poking a fire

[2]**poker** *n* any of several card games in which a player bets that the value of his/her hand is greater than that of the hands held by others and in which each subsequent player must either equal or raise the last bet or drop out

ˈ**poker ˌface** *n* an inscrutable face that reveals no hint of a person's thoughts or feelings – **poker-faced** *adj*

ˈ**pokerˌwork** /-ˌwuhk‖-ˌwɜːk/ *n* (the art of doing) decorative work burnt into a material by a heated instrument

poky *also* **pokey** /ˈpohki‖ˈpəʊkɪ/ *adj* small and cramped – infml – **pokily** *adv*, **pokiness** *n*

Polack /ˈpohlak‖ˈpəʊlæk/ *n, archaic or NAm* a Pole – now derog

polar /ˈpohlə‖ˈpəʊlə/ *adj* **1a** of, coming from, or characteristic of (the region round) a geographical pole **b** *esp of an orbit* passing over a planet's N and S poles **2** of 1 or more poles (e g of a magnet) **3** diametrically opposite **4** exhibiting polarity; *esp* having (molecules with) groups with opposing properties at opposite ends <*a* ~ *molecule*> <*a* ~ *solvent*> **5** resembling a pole or axis round which all else revolves; pivotal **6** of or expressed in polar coordinates <~ *equations*>; *also* of a polar coordinate system

ˌ**polar ˈbear** *n* a large creamy-white bear that inhabits arctic regions

polarity /pəˈlarəti, poh-‖pəˈlærətɪ, pəʊ-/ *n* **1** the quality or condition of a body that has opposite or contrasted properties or powers in opposite directions **2** attraction towards a particular object or in a specific direction **3** the particular electrical state of being either positive or negative **4** (an instance of) diametric opposition

polar·ize, -ise /ˈpohləriez‖ˈpəʊləraɪz/ *vt* **1a** to

affect (radiation, esp light) so that the vibrations of the wave assume a definite form (e g restriction to vibration in 1 plane) **b** to give electrical or magnetic polarity to **2** to divide into opposing factions or groupings ~*vi* to become polarized – **polarizable** *adj*, **polarizability** *n*, **polarization** *n*

Polaroid /ˈpohlərоyd‖ˈpəʊlərɔɪd/ *trademark* – used esp for a light-polarizing material used esp in glasses to prevent glare and in various optical devices

[1]**pole** /pohl‖pəʊl/ *n* **1a** a long slender usu cylindrical object (e g a length of wood) **b** a shaft which extends from the front axle of a wagon between the draught animals **2** ROD 2 **3** the most favourable front-row position on the starting line of a (motor) race

[2]**pole** *vb* to push or propel (oneself or sthg) with poles

[3]**pole** *n* **1** either extremity of an axis of (a body, esp the earth, resembling) a sphere **2a** either of 2 related opposites **b** a point of guidance or attraction **3a** either of the 2 terminals of an electric cell, battery, or dynamo **b** any of 2 or more regions in a magnetized body at which the magnetic flux density is concentrated **4** either of the anatomically or physiologically differentiated areas at opposite ends of an axis in an organism or cell

Pole *n* a native or inhabitant of Poland

[1]**poleaxe** /ˈpohl,aks‖ˈpəʊl,æks/ *n* **1** a battle-axe with a short handle and often a hook or spike opposite the blade **2** an axe used, esp formerly, in slaughtering cattle

[2]**poleaxe** *vt* to attack, strike, or fell (as if) with a poleaxe

polecat /ˈpohl,kat‖ˈpəʊl,kæt/ *n* **1** a European flesh-eating mammal of which the ferret is considered a domesticated variety **2** *NAm* SKUNK 1

polemic /pəˈlemik, po-, poh-, -ˈlee-‖pəˈlemɪk, pɒ-, pəʊ-, -ˈliː-/ *n* **1** an aggressive attack on or refutation of the opinions or principles of another **2** the art or practice of disputation or controversy – usu pl with sing. meaning but sing. or pl in constr [French *polémique*, deriv of Greek *polemikos* warlike, hostile, fr *polemos* war] – **polemic, polemical** *adj*, **polemicist** *n*

polestar /ˈpohl,stah‖ˈpəʊl,stɑː/ *n* **1** a directing principle; a guide **2** a centre of attraction

Pole Star *n* the star in the constellation Ursa Minor that lies very close to the N celestial pole

ˈpole ,vault *n* (an athletic field event consisting of) a jump for height over a crossbar with the aid of a pole – **pole-vault** *vi*, **pole-vaulter** *n*

[1]**police** /pəˈlees‖pəˈliːs/ *n* **1** the department of government concerned with maintenance of public order and enforcement of laws **2a** *sing or pl in constr* POLICE FORCE **b** *pl in constr* policemen **3** *sing or pl in constr* an organized body having similar functions to a police force within a more restricted sphere <*railway* ~> [Middle French, government, fr Late Latin *politia*, fr Greek *politeia*, fr *politēs* citizen, fr *polis* city, state]

[2]**police** *vt* **1** to control by use of police **2** to put in order **3** to supervise the operation of

poˈlice ,force *n sing or pl in constr* a body of trained people entrusted by a government with maintenance of public order and enforcement of laws

poˈliceman /-mən‖-mən/, *fem* **poˈlice,woman** *n* a member of a police force

police state *n* a political unit characterized by repressive governmental control of political, economic, and social life, usu enforced by (secret) police

poˈlice ,station *n* the headquarters of a local police force

[1]**policy** /ˈpolisi‖ˈpɒlɪsɪ/ *n* **1** procedure based primarily on material interest; wisdom <*it's bad ~ to smoke*> **2a** a definite course of action selected from among alternatives to guide and determine present and future decisions **b** an overall plan embracing general goals and procedures, esp of a governmental body

[2]**policy** *n* (a document embodying) a contract of insurance

polio /ˈpohli·oh‖ˈpəʊlɪəʊ/ *n* poliomyelitis

poliomyelitis /,pohli·oh,mie·əˈlietis‖,pəʊlɪəʊ,maɪəˈlaɪtɪs/ *n* an infectious virus disease, esp of children, characterized by inflammation of the nerve cells of the spinal cord, paralysis of the motor nerves, and atrophy of skeletal muscles often with permanent disability and deformity [Greek *polios* grey + *myelos* marrow] – **poliomyelitic** *adj*

[1]**polish** /ˈpolish‖ˈpɒlɪʃ/ *vt* **1** to make smooth and glossy, usu by friction **2** to refine in manners or condition **3** to bring to a highly developed, finished, or refined state; perfect – often + *up* ~*vi* to become smooth or glossy (as if) by friction – **polisher** *n*

[2]**polish** *n* **1a** a smooth glossy surface **b** freedom from rudeness or coarseness **2** the action or process of polishing <*give the table a* ~> **3** a preparation used to produce a gloss and often a colour for the protection and decoration of a surface <*furniture* ~>

[1]**Polish** /ˈpohlish‖ˈpəʊlɪʃ/ *adj* (characteristic) of Poland

[2]**Polish** *n* the language of the Poles

polish off *vt* to dispose of rapidly or completely

politburo /ˈpolit,byooəroh, -ˈ-,--‖ˈpɒlɪt,bjʊərəʊ, -ˈ-,--/ *n* the principal committee of a Communist party

polite /pəˈliet‖pəˈlaɪt/ *adj* **1** showing or characterized by correct social usage; refined **2** marked by an appearance of consideration and deference; courteous – **politely** *adv*, **politeness** *n*

politic /ˈpolitik‖ˈpɒlɪtɪk/ *adj* **1** *of a person* shrewd and sagacious in managing, contriving, or dealing **2** *of a policy* expedient

political /pəˈlitikl‖pəˈlɪtɪkl/ *adj* **1** of government **2a** of (party) politics **b** sensitive to politics <*highly* ~ *students*> **3** involving or charged with acts against a government <~ *criminals*> – **politically** *adv*

political economy *n* a social science dealing with the interrelationship of political and economic processes – **political economist** *n*

political science *n* a social science concerned chiefly with political institutions and processes – **political scientist** *n*

politician /,poliˈtish(ə)n‖,pɒlɪˈtɪʃ(ə)n/ *n* a person experienced or engaged in politics

politic·ize, **-ise** /pəˈlitisiez‖pəˈlɪtɪsaɪz/ *vi* to discuss politics ~*vt* to give a political tone to – **politicization** *n*
politico /pəˈlitikoh‖pəˈlɪtɪkəʊ/ *n, pl* **politicos** *also* **politicoes** a politician – infml
politics /ˈpolitiks‖ˈpɒlɪtɪks/ *n pl but sing or pl in constr* **1a** the art or science of government **b** POLITICAL SCIENCE **2a** political affairs; *specif* competition between interest groups in a government **b** political life as a profession **3** sby's political sympathies **4** the total complex of relations between human beings in society
polity /ˈpoləti‖ˈpɒlətɪ/ *n* (the form of) a politically organized unit
polka /ˈpolkə‖ˈpɒlkə/ *n* (music for or in the rhythm of) a vivacious dance of Bohemian origin in duple time – **polka** *vi*
ˈpolka ˌdot *n* any of many regularly distributed dots in a textile design – **polka-dot, polka-dotted** *adj*
[1]poll /pohl‖pəʊl/ *n* **1** (the hairy top or back of) the head **2** the broad or flat end of the head of a striking tool (e g a hammer) **3a** the casting of votes **b** the place where votes are cast – usu pl with sing. meaning <*at the* ~s> **c** the number of votes recorded <*a heavy* ~> **4** a survey conducted by the questioning of people selected at random or by quota
[2]poll *vt* **1** to cut off or cut short **1a** the hair or wool of **b** the horns of (a cow) **c** (e g wool) **2** to remove the top of (e g a tree); *specif* to pollard **3** to receive and record the votes of **4** to receive (votes) **5** to question in a poll ~*vi* to cast one's vote – **pollee** *n*, **poller** *n*
[3]poll *n* a polled animal
[1]pollard /ˈpoləd‖ˈpɒləd/ *n* **1** a hornless animal of a usu horned kind **2** a tree cut back to the main stem to promote the growth of a dense head of foliage
[2]pollard *vt* to make a pollard of (a tree)
pollen /ˈpolən‖ˈpɒlən/ *n* (a fine dust of) the minute granular spores discharged from the anther of the flower of a flowering plant that serve to fertilize the ovules – **pollinic** *adj*
ˈpollen ˌcount *n* a figure representing the amount of pollen in the air, available as a warning to people allergic to pollen
pollinate /ˈpoləˌnayt‖ˈpɒləˌneɪt/ *vt* to place pollen on the stigma of and so fertilize – **pollinator** *n*, **pollination** *n*
pollster /ˈpohlstə‖ˈpəʊlstə/ *n* one who conducts a poll or compiles data obtained by a poll
ˈpoll ˌtax *n* a tax of a fixed amount per person levied on adults
pollute /pəˈl(y)ooht‖pəˈl(j)uːt/ *vt* **1** to make morally impure; defile **2** to make physically impure or unclean; *esp* to contaminate (an environment), esp with man-made waste – **pollutant** *n*, **polluter** *n*, **pollutive** *adj*
pollution /pəˈl(y)oohsh(ə)n‖pəˈl(j)uːʃ(ə)n/ *n* **1** polluting or being polluted **2** material that pollutes
polo /ˈpohloh‖ˈpəʊləʊ/ *n* a game of oriental origin played by teams of usu 4 players on ponies or canoes, bicycles, etc using mallets with long flexible handles to drive a wooden ball into the opponent's goal [Balti (a language of N Kashmir), ball]
polonaise /ˌpoləˈnayz‖ˌpɒləˈneɪz/ *n* **1** a short-sleeved elaborate dress with a fitted waist and panniers at the sides and back drawn up on cords **2** (music in moderate $\frac{3}{4}$ time for) a stately Polish processional dance
polo neck *n, chiefly Br* (a jumper with) a very high closely fitting collar worn folded over
polony /pəˈlohni‖pəˈləʊnɪ/ *n* a dry sausage of partly cooked meat, esp pork; *also* a cooked sausage made from soya and meat and eaten cold
poltergeist /ˈpoltəˌgiest‖ˈpɒltəˌgaɪst/ *n* a noisy mischievous ghost believed to be responsible for unexplained noises and physical damage [German, fr *poltern* to knock + *geist* spirit]
poltroon /polˈtroohn‖pɒlˈtruːn/ *n* a spiritless coward
poly /ˈpoli‖ˈpɒlɪ/ *n, pl* **polys** *Br* a polytechnic – infml
poly- *comb form* many; several; much; multi- <poly*phonic*>
ˌpolyˈandrous /-ˈandrəs‖-ˈændrəs/ *adj* **1** having many usu free stamens **2** of or practising polyandry
polyandry /ˈpoliˌandri‖ˈpɒlɪˌændrɪ/ *n* **1** having more than 1 husband at a time **2** the state of being polyandrous
ˌpolyˈanthus /-ˈanthəs‖-ˈænθəs/ *n, pl* **polyanthuses, polyanthi** /-thie‖-θaɪ/ any of various cultivated hybrid primroses
ˌpolyˈester /-ˈestə‖-ˈestə/ *n* a polymer containing ester groups used esp in making fibres, resins, or plastics – **polyesterification** *n*
ˌpolyˈethylene /-ˈethiˌleen‖-ˈeθɪˌliːn/ *n* polythene
polygamous /pəˈligəməs‖pəˈlɪgəməs/, **polygamic** /ˌpoliˈgamik‖ˌpɒlɪˈgæmɪk/ *adj* **1a** of or practising polygamy **b** having more than 1 mate at a time <*baboons are* ~> **2** bearing both hermaphrodite and unisexual flowers on the same plant – **polygamously** *adv*
polygamy /pəˈligəmi‖pəˈlɪgəmɪ/ *n* **1** being married to more than 1 person at a time; *esp* marriage to more than 1 wife **2** the state of being polygamous – **polygamist** *n*, **polygamize** *vi*
[1]ˈpolyˌglot /-ˌglot‖-ˌglɒt/ *n* **1** one who is polyglot **2** *cap* a book, esp a bible, containing versions of the same text in several languages **3** a mixture or confusion of languages – **polyglottal** *adj*
[2]polyglot *adj* **1** MULTILINGUAL 2 **2** containing matter in several languages <*a* ~ *sign*>
polygon /ˈpoligən, -gon‖ˈpɒlɪgən, -gɒn/ *n* a closed plane figure bounded by straight lines – **polygonal** *adj*, **polygonally** *adv*
polyhedron /ˌpoliˈheedrən‖ˌpɒlɪˈhiːdrən/ *n, pl* **polyhedrons, polyhedra** /-drə‖-drə/ a solid formed by plane faces – **polyhedral** *adj*
ˈpolyˌmath /-ˌmath‖-ˌmæθ/ *n* one who has a wide range of learning or accomplishments [Greek *polymathēs* very learned, fr *polys* many, much + *manthanein* to learn] – **polymath** *adj*, **polymathic** *adj*, **polymathy** *n*
polymer /ˈpolimə‖ˈpɒlɪmə/ *n* a chemical compound or mixture of compounds containing repeating structural units and formed by chemical combination of many small molecules – **polymerize** *vb*, **polymerization** *n*, **polymeric** *adj*, **polymerically** *adv*

ˌ**polyˈmorphic** /-ˈmawfik‖-ˈmɔːfɪk/, **polymorphous** /-fəs‖-fəs/ *adj* having, assuming, or occurring in various forms, characters, or styles – **polymorphically, polymorphously** *adv*, **polymorphism** *n*

polyp /ˈpolip‖ˈpɒlɪp/ *n* **1** a coelenterate with a hollow cylindrical body attached at one end and having a central mouth surrounded by tentacles at the other **2** a projecting mass of tissue (e g a tumour) – **polypoid** *adj*, **polypous** *adj*

polyphony /pəˈlifəni‖pəˈlɪfənɪ/ *n* a style of musical composition in which 2 or more independent but organically related voice parts sound against one another

ˌ**polyˈstyrene** /-ˈstie·əreen‖-ˈstaɪəriːn/ *n* a rigid transparent polymer of styrene used esp in moulded products, foams, and sheet materials

ˌ**polysylˈlabic** /-siˈlabik‖-sɪˈlæbɪk/, **polysyllabical** /-kl‖-kl/ *adj* **1** having more than 3 syllables **2** characterized by polysyllables – **polysyllabically** *adv*

ˈ**polyˌsyllable** /-ˌsiləbl‖-ˌsɪləbl/ *n* a polysyllabic word

1ˌ**polyˈtechnic** /-ˈteknik‖-ˈteknɪk/ *adj* relating to or devoted to instruction in many technical arts or applied sciences

2**polytechnic** *n* a polytechnic school; *specif* any of a number of British institutions offering courses in various subjects but with a bias towards the vocational

ˈ**polytheˌism** /-thiˌiz(ə)m‖-θɪˌɪz(ə)m/ *n* belief in or worship of 2 or more gods – **polytheist** *adj or n*, **polytheistic** *adj*

ˈ**polythene** /-theen‖-θiːn/ *n* any of various lightweight ethylene polymers used esp for packaging and bowls, buckets, etc

ˌ**polyˈurethane** /-ˈyooəriˌthayn‖-ˈjʊərɪˌθeɪn/ *n* any of various polymers used esp in foams and paints

ˌ**polyˈvalent** /-ˈvaylənt‖-ˈveɪlənt/ *adj* **1** having a valency greater usu than 2 **2** having more than 1 valency – **polyvalence** *n*

ˌ**polyvinyl ˈchloride** /-ˈvienl‖-ˈvaɪnl/ *n* a plastic used esp as a rubber substitute (e g for raincoats and insulation for wires)

pomade /pəˈmahd, po-‖pəˈmɑːd, pɒ-/ *n* a perfumed ointment for the hair or scalp – **pomade** *vt*

pomander /poˈmandə, pə-‖pɒˈmændə, pə-/ *n* a mixture of aromatic substances enclosed in a perforated bag or box and used to scent clothes or linen or formerly carried as a guard against infection [Middle French *pome d'ambre*, lit., apple or ball of amber]

pomegranate /ˈpomiˌgranət‖ˈpɒmɪˌgrænət/ *n* (an Old World tree that bears) a thick-skinned reddish fruit about the size of an orange that contains many seeds each surrounded by a tart edible crimson pulp

Pomeranian /ˌpoməˈraynyən, -ni·ən‖ˌpɒməˈreɪnjən, -nɪən/ *n* (any of) a breed of very small compact long-haired dogs [*Pomerania*, region of N Europe]

1**pommel** /ˈpuməl, ˈpo-‖ˈpʌməl, ˈpɒ-/ *n* **1** the knob on the hilt of a sword **2** the protuberance at the front and top of a saddle **3** either of the pair of removable handles on the top of a pommel horse

2**pommel** /ˈpuməl‖ˈpʌməl/ *vt* **-ll-** (*NAm* **-l-, -ll-**) to pummel

ˈ**pommel ˌhorse** *n* (a men's gymnastic event using) a leather-covered horizontal rectangular or cylindrical form with 2 handles on the top that is supported above the ground and is used for swinging and balancing feats

Pommy, Pommie /ˈpomi‖ˈpɒmɪ/ *n, often not cap, Austr & NZ* a British person; *esp* a British immigrant [prob short for *pomegranate*, prob alteration (referring to the redness of the fruit and British complexions) of rhyming slang *Jimmy Grant* immigrant] – **Pommy, Pommie** *adj*

pomp /pomp‖pɒmp/ *n* **1** a show of magnificence; splendour **2** ostentatious or specious display

1**pom-pom** /ˈpom ˌpom‖ˈpɒm ˌpɒm/ *n* an automatic gun mounted on ships in pairs, fours, or eights

2**pom-pom** *n* an ornamental ball or tuft used esp on clothing, hats, etc

pompon /ˈpompon(h)‖ˈpɒmpɒn, -pɔ̃/ *n* a chrysanthemum or dahlia with small rounded flower heads

pomposity /pomˈposəti‖pɒmˈpɒsətɪ/ *n* **1** pompous demeanour, speech, or behaviour **2** a pompous gesture, habit, or act

pompous /ˈpompəs‖ˈpɒmpəs/ *adj* **1** self-important, pretentious **2** excessively elevated or ornate – **pompously** *adv*, **pompousness** *n*

1**ponce** /pons‖pɒns/ *n, Br* **1** a pimp **2** a man who behaves in an effeminate manner – infml

2**ponce** *vi, Br* **1** to pimp **2** to act in a frivolous, showy, or effeminate manner – usu + *around* or *about*; infml

poncho /ˈponchoh‖ˈpɒntʃəʊ/ *n, pl* **ponchos** a cloak resembling a blanket with a slit in the middle for the head

poncy, poncey /ˈponsi‖ˈpɒnsɪ/ *adj, Br* (characteristic) of a ponce – infml

pond /pond‖pɒnd/ *n* a body of (fresh) water usu smaller than a lake

ponder /ˈpondə‖ˈpɒndə/ *vt* **1** to weigh in the mind; assess **2** to review mentally; think over ~ *vi* to think or consider, esp quietly, soberly, and deeply – **ponderer** *n*

ponderous /ˈpond(ə)rəs‖ˈpɒnd(ə)rəs/ *adj* **1** unwieldy or clumsy because of weight and size **2** oppressively or unpleasantly dull; pedestrian – **ponderously** *adv*, **ponderousness** *n*

pong /pong‖pɒŋ/ *vi or n, Br* (to emit) an unpleasant smell; stink – infml

poniard /ˈponyəd‖ˈpɒnjəd/ *n* a small dagger

pontiff /ˈpontif‖ˈpɒntɪf/ *n* a bishop; *specif* the pope

1**pontifical** /ponˈtifikl‖pɒnˈtɪfɪkl/ *adj* **1** of a pontiff **2** pretentiously dogmatic – **pontifically** *adv*

2**pontifical** *n* episcopal dress – usu pl with sing. meaning

1**pontificate** /ponˈtifikət‖pɒnˈtɪfɪkət/ *n* the state, office, or term of office of the pope

2**pontificate** /ponˈtifikayt‖pɒnˈtɪfɪkeɪt/ *vi* **1** to officiate as a pontiff **2** to deliver oracular utterances or dogmatic opinions – **pontificator** *n*, **pontification** *n*

1**pontoon** /ponˈtoohn‖pɒnˈtuːn/ *n* a flat-bottomed boat or portable float (used in building a floating temporary bridge) [French *ponton* floating bridge, punt, fr Latin *ponton-, ponto*, fr *pont-, pons* bridge]

[2]**pontoon** *n* a gambling card game in which the object is to be dealt cards scoring more than those of the dealer up to but not exceeding 21 [prob alteration of *vingt-et-un*, fr French, lit., 21]

pony /ˈpohni‖ˈpəʊnɪ/ *n* **1** a small horse; *esp* a member of any of several breeds of very small stocky horses under 142 hands in height **2** a racehorse – usu pl; slang **3** *Br* the sum of £25 – slang

ˈpony,tail /-ˌtayl‖-ˌteɪl/ *n* a hairstyle in which the hair is drawn back tightly and tied high at the back of the head

ˈpony ˌtrekking *n* the pastime of riding ponies long distances across country in a group

pooch /poohch‖puːtʃ/ *n* DOG 1a – slang

poodle /ˈpoohdl‖ˈpuːdl/ *n* (any of) a breed of active intelligent dogs with a thick curly coat which is of 1 colour only [German *pudel*, short for *pudelhund*, fr *pudeln* to splash + *hund* dog]

poof, pouf /poohf, poof‖puːf, pʊf/ *n, Br* an effeminate man or male homosexual – chiefly derog

poofter /ˈpooftə‖ˈpʊftə/ *n, Br* a poof – chiefly derog

pooh /pooh‖puː/ *interj* – used to express contempt, disapproval, or distaste at an unpleasant smell

ˌpooh-ˈpooh *vb* to express contempt (for)

[1]**pool** /poohl‖puːl/ *n* **1a** a small and relatively deep body of usu fresh water (e g a still place in a stream or river) **b** sthg resembling a pool (e g in depth or shape) <~s *of light*> **2** a small body of standing liquid; a puddle <*lay in a* ~ *of blood*> **3** SWIMMING POOL

[2]**pool** *n* **1** an aggregate stake to which each player of a game has contributed **2** any of various games played on a billiard table with 6 pockets and often 15 numbered balls **3** a combination of the interests or property of different parties that subjects each party to the same controls and a common liability **4** a readily available supply; *esp* the whole quantity of a particular material present in the body and available for metabolism **5** a facility, service, or group of people providing a service for a number of people (e g the members of a business organization) <*a typing* ~> **6** *pl* FOOTBALL POOLS

[3]**pool** *vt* to contribute to a common stock (e g of resources or effort)

[1]**poop** /poohp‖puːp/ *n* an enclosed superstructure at the stern of a ship above the main deck

[2]**poop** *vt* **1** to break over the stern of **2** to receive (a sea or wave) over the stern

[3]**poop** *vb, chiefly NAm vt* to put out of breath; *also* to tire out ~*vi* to become exhausted *USE* (*vt & vi*) usu + *out*; infml

poor /pooə, paw‖pʊə, pɔː/ *adj* **1a** lacking material possessions **b** of or characterized by poverty **2** less than adequate; meagre <*a* ~ *harvest*> **3** exciting pity <~ *old soul!*> **4** inferior in quality, value, or workmanship <*in* ~ *health*> <*a* ~ *essay*> **5** humble, unpretentious <*in my* ~ *opinion*> **6** *of land* barren, unproductive – **poorish** *adj*, **poorly** *adv*, **poorness** *n*

ˈpoor ˌbox *n* a box (e g in a church) into which money for the poor can be put

ˈpoor,house /-ˌhows‖-ˌhaʊs/ *n* WORKHOUSE 1

ˈpoor ˌlaw *n* a law that in former times provided for the relief of the poor

poorly /ˈpooəli‖ˈpʊəlɪ/ *adj* somewhat ill

ˌpoor-ˈspirited *adj* lacking zest, confidence, or courage – **poor-spiritedly** *adv*, **poor-spiritedness** *n*

poor white *n* a member of an inferior or underprivileged white social group – chiefly derog

poove /poohv‖puːv/ *n, Br* a poof – chiefly derog

[1]**pop** /pop‖pɒp/ *vb* **-pp-** *vt* **1** to strike or knock sharply; hit <~ped *him one on the jaw*> **2** to push, put, or thrust suddenly <~ped *a sweet into his mouth*> **3** to cause to explode or burst open **4** to shoot at **5** to take (drugs) orally or by injection <*he* ~ped *pills*> **6** *Br* to pawn ~ *vi* **1a** to go, come, or enter suddenly or quickly <*just* ~ped *out to do some shopping*> **b** to escape or break away from sthg (e g a point of attachment) usu suddenly or unexpectedly **2** to make or burst with a sharp explosive sound **3** to protrude from the sockets <*eyes* ~ping *in amazement*> *USE* (*vt & vi*) infml – **pop the question** to propose marriage – infml

[2]**pop** *n* **1** a popping sound **2** a flavoured carbonated beverage **3** *Br* PAWN 2 *USE* (*1 & 3*) infml

[3]**pop** *adv* like or with a pop; suddenly – infml

[4]**pop** *n, chiefly NAm* a father – infml

[5]**pop** *adj* popular: e g **a** of pop music <~ *singer*> **b** of or constituting a mass culture widely disseminated through the mass media <~ *society*>

[6]**pop** *n* POP MUSIC

pop art *n, often cap P&A* art that incorporates everyday objects from popular culture and the mass media (e g comic strips) – **pop artist** *n*

ˈpop,corn /-ˌkawn‖-ˌkɔːn/ *n* (the popped kernels of) a maize whose kernels burst open when heated to form a white starchy mass

pope /pohp‖pəʊp/ *n* **1** *often cap* the prelate who as bishop of Rome is the head of the Roman Catholic church **2** a priest of an Eastern church **3** [1]RUFF

popery /ˈpohp(ə)ri‖ˈpəʊp(ə)rɪ/ *n* ROMAN CATHOLICISM – chiefly derog

ˈpop-ˌeyed *adj* having staring or bulging eyes (e g as a result of surprise or excitement)

ˈpop,gun /-ˌgun‖-ˌgʌn/ *n* a toy gun that shoots a cork or pellet and produces a popping sound; *also* an inadequate or inefficient firearm

popinjay /ˈpopin,jay‖ˈpɒpɪnˌdʒeɪ/ *n* a strutting supercilious person

popish /ˈpohpish‖ˈpəʊpɪʃ/ *adj* of popery – chiefly derog – **popishly** *adv*

poplar /ˈpoplə‖ˈpɒplə/ *n* **1** (the wood of) any of a genus of slender quick-growing trees (e g an aspen) of the willow family **2** TULIP TREE

poplin /ˈpoplin‖ˈpɒplɪn/ *n* a strong usu cotton fabric in plain weave with crosswise ribs

pop music *n* modern commercially promoted popular music that is usu short and simple and has a strong beat

pop off *vi* **1** to leave suddenly **2** to die unexpectedly **USE** infml

poppa /ˈpopə‖ˈpɒpə/ *n, NAm* a father – infml

poppadom /ˈpopədom‖ˈpɒpədɒm/ *n* a crisp wafer-thin pancake of deep-fried dough eaten with Indian food

popper /ˈpopə‖ˈpɒpə/ *n, chiefly Br* PRESS-STUD

poppet /ˈpopit‖ˈpɒpɪt/ *n* **1** a valve that rises up and down from its seat **2** *chiefly Br* a lovable or enchanting person or animal – infml

ˈpopping ˌcrease /ˈpoping‖ˈpɒpɪŋ/ *n* either of the lines drawn perpendicularly across a cricket pitch 4ft (about 1.22m) in front of each wicket and behind which the batsman must have a foot or his/her bat on the ground to avoid being run out or stumped

poppy /ˈpopi‖ˈpɒpɪ/ *n* any of several genera of plants with showy flowers and capsular fruits including the opium poppy and several other plants cultivated for their ornamental value

ˈpoppyˌcock /-ˌkok‖-ˌkɒk/ *n* empty talk; nonsense – infml [Dutch dial. *pappekak*, lit., soft dung, fr Dutch *pap* pap + *kak* dung]

popsy /ˈpopsi‖ˈpɒpsɪ/ *n, Br* GIRLFRIEND – infml; often derog

populace /ˈpopyooləs‖ˈpɒpjʊləs/ *n sing or pl in constr* the (common) people; the masses

popular /ˈpopyoolə‖ˈpɒpjʊlə/ *adj* **1** of the general public **2** suited to the needs, means, tastes, or understanding of the general public <*a ~ history of the war*> **3** having general currency **4** commonly liked or approved <*a very ~ girl*> – **popularly** *adv*, **popularity** *n*

popular·ize, -ise /ˈpopyooləˌriez‖ˈpɒpjʊləˌraɪz/ *vt* **1** to cause to be liked or esteemed **2** to present in a generally understandable or interesting form – **popularizer** *n*, **popularization** *n*

populate /ˈpopyoolayt‖ˈpɒpjʊleɪt/ *vt* **1** to have a place in; occupy, inhabit **2** to supply or provide with inhabitants; people

population /ˌpopyooˈlaysh(ə)n‖ˌpɒpjʊˈleɪʃ(ə)n/ *n* **1** *sing or pl in constr* the whole number of people or inhabitants in a country or region **2** *sing or pl in constr* a body of people or individuals having a quality or characteristic in common <*a floating ~ of drifters*> **3** the group of organisms inhabiting a particular area **4** a set (e g of individual people or items) from which samples are taken for statistical measurement

populist /ˈpopyoolist‖ˈpɒpjʊlɪst/ *n* **1** a member of a political party claiming to represent the common people **2** a believer in the rights, wisdom, or virtues of the common people – **populism** *n*, **populist** *also* **populistic** *adj*

populous /ˈpopyooləs‖ˈpɒpjʊləs/ *adj* densely populated – **populously** *adv*, **populousness** *n*

ˈpop-ˌup *adj* of or having a device that causes its contents to spring up or stand out in relief <*a ~ toaster*>

pop up *vi* to arise suddenly or unexpectedly; CROP UP – infml

porcelain /ˈpaws(ə)lin‖ˈpɔːs(ə)lɪn/ *n* **1a** a type of hard nonporous translucent white ceramic ware made from a mixture of kaolin, quartz, and feldspar fired at a high temperature **b** a type of translucent ceramic ware made from a mixture of refined clay and ground glass fired at a low temperature **2** porcelain ware – **porcelaneous, porcellaneous** *adj*

porch /pawch‖pɔːtʃ/ *n* **1** a covered usu projecting entrance to a building **2** *NAm* a veranda

porcine /ˈpawsien‖ˈpɔːsaɪn/ *adj* of or like pigs; *esp* obese

porcupine /ˈpawkyoopien‖ˈpɔːkjʊpaɪn/ *n* any of various ground-living or tree-dwelling relatively large rodents with stiff sharp erectile bristles mingled with the hair [Middle French *porc espin*, fr Italian *porcospino*, fr Latin *porcus* pig + *spina* spine, prickle]

[1]**pore** /paw‖pɔː/ *vi* **1** to study closely or attentively **2** to reflect or meditate steadily *USE* usu + *on, over*, or *upon*

[2]**pore** *n* a minute opening; *esp* one (e g in a membrane, esp the skin, or between soil particles) through which fluids pass or are absorbed – **pored** *adj*

pork /pawk‖pɔːk/ *n* the flesh of a pig used as food

porker /ˈpawkə‖ˈpɔːkə/ *n* PIG 1a; *esp* a young pig fattened for food

ˌporkpie ˈhat /ˌpawkˈpie‖ˌpɔːkˈpaɪ/ a man's hat with a low crown, flat top, and usu a turned-up brim

porky /ˈpawki‖ˈpɔːkɪ/ *adj* fat, fleshy <*a ~ young man*> – infml

porn /pawn‖pɔːn/ *n* pornography – infml

pornography /pawˈnogrəfi‖pɔːˈnɒgrəfɪ/ *n* (books, photographs, films, etc containing) the depiction of erotic behaviour intended to cause sexual excitement [Greek *pornographos* (adj) writing of prostitutes, fr *pornē* prostitute + *graphein* to write] – **pornographic** *adj*, **pornographically** *adv*

porous /ˈpawrəs‖ˈpɔːrəs/ *adj* **1** having or full of pores or spaces **2** permeable to liquids – **porously** *adv*, **porousness** *n*, **porosity** *n*

porphyry /ˈpawfiri‖ˈpɔːfɪrɪ/ *n* an igneous rock consisting of crystals (e g of feldspar) embedded in a compact mass of surrounding rock – **porphyritic** *adj*

porpoise /ˈpawpəs‖ˈpɔːpəs/ *n* (any of several small gregarious toothed whales related to) a blunt-snouted usu largely black whale about 2m (6ft) long [Middle French *porpois*, fr Medieval Latin *porcopiscis*, fr Latin *porcus* pig + *piscis* fish]

porridge /ˈporij‖ˈpɒrɪdʒ/ *n* **1** (sthg with the consistency of) a soft food made by boiling a cereal product, esp oatmeal, in milk or water until thick **2** *Br* time spent in prison – slang

porringer /ˈporinjə‖ˈpɒrɪndʒə/ *n* a small bowl from which esp soft or liquid foods (e g porridge) are eaten

[1]**port** /pawt‖pɔːt/ *n* **1** a town or city with a harbour where ships, hovercraft, etc may take on or discharge cargo or passengers **2** a place where goods and people may be permitted to pass into or out of a country [Old English & Old French, fr Latin *portus*]

[2]**port** *n* **1** an opening (e g in machinery) for intake or exhaust of a fluid **2** an opening in a ship's side to admit light or air or to load cargo **3** a hole in an armoured vehicle or fortification through which guns may be fired [Middle French *porte* gate, door, fr Latin *porta* passage, gate]

[3]**port** *n* the position in which a military weapon is carried at the command *port arms*

[4]**port** *adj or n* (of or at) the left side of a ship or aircraft looking forwards

[5]**port** *vt* to turn or put (a helm) to the left – used chiefly as a command

[6]**port** *n* a fortified sweet wine of rich taste and aroma made in Portugal [*Oporto*, seaport in Portugal]

portable /'portəbl‖'pɒrtəbl/ *n or adj* (sthg) capable of being carried or moved about – **portably** *adv*, **portability** *n*

[1]**portage** /'pawtij‖'pɔːtɪdʒ/ *n* **1** the carrying of boats or goods overland from one body of water to another **2** the route followed in portage; *also* a place where such a transfer is necessary

[2]**portage** *vt* to carry over a portage ~*vi* to move gear over a portage

[1]**portal** /'pawtl‖'pɔːtl/ *n* **1** a (grand or imposing) door or entrance **2** the point at which sthg (e g a disease-causing agent) enters the body

[2]**portal** *adj* **1** of the transverse fissure on the underside of the liver where most of the vessels enter **2** of or being a portal vein

portcullis /pawt'kulis‖pɔːt'kʌlɪs/ *n* a usu iron or wood grating that can prevent entry through the gateway of a fortified place by sliding down between grooves [Middle French *porte coleïce*, lit., sliding door]

portend /paw'tend‖pɔː'tend/ *vt* **1** to give an omen or anticipatory sign of; bode **2** to indicate, signify

portent /'pawt(ə)nt, -tent‖'pɔːt(ə)nt, -tent/ *n* **1** sthg foreshadowing a coming event; an omen **2** prophetic indication or significance

portentous /paw'tentəs‖pɔː'tentəs/ *adj* **1** eliciting amazement or wonder; prodigious **2** self-consciously weighty; pompous – **portentously** *adv*, **portentousness** *n*

[1]**porter** /'pawtə‖'pɔːtə/, *fem* **portress** /-tris‖-trɪs/ *n, chiefly Br* a gatekeeper or doorkeeper, esp of a large building, who usu regulates entry and answers enquiries

[2]**porter** *n* **1** sby who carries burdens; *specif* sby employed to carry luggage (e g in a hotel or railway station) **2** a heavy dark brown beer **3** *NAm* a sleeping car attendant

porterage /'pawt(ə)rij‖'pɔːt(ə)rɪdʒ/ *n* (the charge made for) the work performed by a porter

'porter,house /-,hows‖-,haʊs/ *n* a large steak cut from the back end of the sirloin above the ribs and containing part of the fillet

portfolio /pawt'fohli·oh‖pɔːt'fəʊlɪəʊ/ *n, pl* **portfolios** **1** a hinged cover or flexible case for carrying loose papers, pictures, etc **2** the office of a government minister or member of a cabinet <*the defence* ~> **3** the securities held by an investor [Italian *portafoglio*, fr *portare* to carry + *foglio* leaf, sheet]

porthole /'pawt,hohl‖'pɔːt,həʊl/ *n* **1** a usu glazed opening, esp in the side of a ship or aircraft **2** [2]PORT 2

portico /'pawtikoh‖'pɔːtɪkəʊ/ *n, pl* **porticoes, porticos** a colonnade or covered veranda, usu at the entrance of a building and characteristic of classical architecture

[1]**portion** /'pawsh(ə)n‖'pɔːʃ(ə)n/ *n* **1** a part or share of sthg: e g **1a** a helping of food **b** *archaic* a dowry **2** an individual's lot or fate

[2]**portion** *vt* to divide into portions; distribute – often + *out*

portland cement /'pawtlənd‖'pɔːtlənd/ *n* a hydraulic cement made from lime and clay

portland stone *n* a limestone much used in building [Isle of *Portland*, peninsula in Dorset, England, where the limestone is found]

portly /'pawtli‖'pɔːtlɪ/ *adj* rotund, stout – **portliness** *n*

[1]**portmanteau** /pawt'mantoh‖pɔːt'mæntəʊ/ *n, pl* **portmanteaus, portmanteaux** /-tohz‖-təʊz/ a trunk for a traveller's belongings that opens into 2 equal parts

[2]**portmanteau** *adj* combining more than 1 use or quality

portmanteau word *n* BLEND 2

,port of 'call *n* **1** a port where ships customarily stop during a voyage **2** a stop included in an itinerary

portrait /'pawtrit, -trayt‖'pɔːtrɪt, -treɪt/ *n* **1** a pictorial likeness of a person **2** a verbal portrayal or representation – **portraitist** *n*

portraiture /'pawtrichə‖'pɔːtrɪtʃə/ *n* the art of making portraits

portray /paw'tray‖pɔː'treɪ/ *vt* **1** to make a picture of; depict **2a** to describe in words **b** to play the role of – **portrayer** *n*

portrayal /paw'tray(ə)l‖pɔː'treɪ(ə)l/ *n* **1** the act or process of portraying; representation **2** a portrait

Portuguese /,pawchoo'geez, ,pawtyoo-'geez‖,pɔːtʃʊ'giːz, ,pɔːtjʊ'giːz/ *n, pl* **Portuguese** **1** a native or inhabitant of Portugal **2** the language of esp Portugal and Brazil – **Portuguese** *adj*

Portuguese man-of-war *n* any of several large floating jellyfishes with very long stinging tentacles

[1]**pose** /pohz‖pəʊz/ *vt* **1** to place (e g a model) in a studied attitude **2** to put or set forth; offer <*this attitude* ~s *a threat to our hopes for peace*> **3** to present for attention or consideration <*let me* ~ *a question*> ~ *vi* **1** to assume a posture or attitude, usu for artistic purposes **2** to affect an attitude or character; posture <~d *as an honest man*>

[2]**pose** *n* **1** a sustained posture; *esp* one assumed for artistic purposes **2** an assumed attitude of mind or mode of behaviour

[1]**poser** /'pohzə‖'pəʊzə/ *n* a puzzling or baffling question

[2]**poser** *n* a poseur

poseur /poh'zuh‖pəʊ'zɜː/ *n* an affected or insincere person

[1]**posh** /posh‖pɒʃ/ *adj* **1** very fine; splendid <*a* ~ *new car*> **2** socially exclusive or fashionable; *broadly* upper-class – often derog *USE* infml [perhaps fr earlier slang *posh* money, dandy]

[2]**posh** *adv* in a posh accent – infml <*talk* ~>

posit /'pozit‖'pɒzɪt/ *vt* to assume or affirm the existence of; postulate

[1]**position** /pə'zish(ə)n‖pə'zɪʃ(ə)n/ *n* **1** the statement of a proposition or thesis **2** an opinion; POINT OF VIEW <*made her* ~ *on the issue clear*> **3** a market commitment in securities or commodities; *also* the inventory of a market trader **4a** the place occupied by sby or sthg <*house in an attractive* ~ *overlooking the sea*>; *also* the proper place <*the cars are now in the starting* ~> **b** a disposition or attitude of (a part of) the body <*rose to a standing* ~> **5a** a

condition, situation <*is now in a ~ to make important decisions on his own*> **b** social or official rank or status **c** a situation that confers advantage or preference <*jockeying for ~*> **6** the disposition of the notes of a chord **7** a post, job – fml

[2]**position** *vt* to put in a proper or specified position

positional /pə'zish(ə)nl‖pə'zɪʃ(ə)nl/ *adj* of or fixed by position <~ *astronomy*>

[1]**positive** /'pozətiv‖'pɒzətɪv/ *adj* **1a** expressed clearly or peremptorily <*her answer was a ~ no*> **b** fully assured; confident <~ *that he is right*> **2** of or constituting the simple form of an adjective or adverb that expresses no degree of comparison **3** incontestable <~ *proof*> **4** utter <*a ~ disgrace*> **5** real, active <*a ~ influence for good in the community*> **6a** capable of being constructively applied; helpful <~ *advice*> **b** concentrating on what is good or beneficial; optimistic <*has a ~ attitude towards his illness*> **7a** having or expressing actual existence or quality as distinguished from deficiency **b** not speculative; empirical **8** having the light and dark parts similar in tone to those of the original photographic subject **9a** in a direction arbitrarily or customarily taken as that of increase or progression <~ *angles*> **b** directed or moving towards a source of stimulation <*a ~ response to light*> **10** numerically greater than zero <*+2 is a ~ integer*> **11a** of being, or charged with electricity as a result of a deficiency of electrons **b** having higher electric potential and constituting the part from which the current flows to the external circuit **12a** marked by or indicating acceptance, approval, or affirmation **b** showing the presence of sthg sought or suspected to be present <*a ~ test for blood*> **13** *of a lens* converging light rays and forming a real inverted image – **positively** *adv*, **positiveness** *n*

[2]**positive** *n* sthg positive: e g **a** the positive degree or form of an adjective or adverb **b** sthg about which an affirmation can be made; reality **c** a positive photograph or a print from a negative

positivism /'pozitiviz(ə)m‖'pɒzɪtɪvɪz(ə)m/ *n* a theory rejecting theology and metaphysics in favour of knowledge based on the scientific observation of natural phenomena – **positivist** *adj or n*, **positivistic** *adj*

positron /'pozitron‖'pɒzɪtrɒn/ *n* a positively charged elementary particle that has the same mass and magnitude of charge as the electron and is the antiparticle of the electron

posse /'posi‖'pɒsɪ/ *n sing or pl in constr* **1** a body of people summoned by a sheriff, esp in N America, to assist in preserving the public peace, usu in an emergency **2** a large group, often with a common interest [Medieval Latin *posse comitatus*, lit., power or authority of the county]

possess /pə'zes‖pə'zes/ *vt* **1a** to make the owner or holder – + *of* or *with* **b** to have possession of **2a** to have and hold as property; own **b** to have as an attribute, knowledge, or skill **3a** to take into one's possession **b** to influence so strongly as to direct the actions <*whatever ~ed her to act like that?*>; *also, of a demon, evil spirit, etc* to enter into and control – **possessor** *n*

pos'sessed *adj* **1** influenced or controlled by sthg (e g an evil spirit or a passion) **2** mad, crazed – **possessedly** *adv*, **possessedness** *n*

possession /pə'zesh(ə)n‖pə'zeʃ(ə)n/ *n* **1a** the act of having or taking into control **b** ownership; *also* control or occupancy (e g of property) without regard to ownership **2a** sthg owned, occupied, or controlled **b** *pl* wealth, property **3** domination by sthg (e g an evil spirit or passion) – **possessional** *adj*

[1]**possessive** /pə'zesiv‖pə'zesɪv/ *adj* **1** manifesting possession or the desire to own or dominate <*a ~ mother*> **2** of or being the grammatical possessive – **possessively** *adv*, **possessiveness** *n*

[2]**possessive** *n* (a form in) a grammatical case expressing ownership or a similar relation

posset /'posit‖'pɒsɪt/ *n* a comforting hot beverage of sweetened and spiced milk curdled with ale or wine; *also* a dessert made with cream, eggs, sugar and usu lemon

possibility /,posə'biləti‖,pɒsə'bɪlətɪ/ *n* **1** the condition or fact of being possible **2** sthg possible **3** potential or prospective value – usu pl with sing. meaning <*the house had great possibilities*>

[1]**possible** /'posəbl‖'pɒsəbl/ *adj* **1** within the limits of ability, capacity, or realization **2** capable of being done or occurring according to nature, custom, or manners **3** that may or may not occur <*it is ~ but not probable that he will win*> **4** having a specified potential use, quality, etc <*a ~ housing site*>

[2]**possible** *n* **1** sthg possible <*politics is the art of the ~*> **2** sby or sthg that may be selected for a specified role, task, etc <*a ~ for the post of Chancellor*>

possibly /'posəbli‖'pɒsəblɪ/ *adv* **1** it is possible that; maybe <~ *there is life on Mars*> <*he may ~ have caught a later train*> **2** – used as an intensifier with *can* or *could* <*you can't ~ eat all that cake*> <*I'll do all I ~ can to have it ready on time*>

possum /'pos(ə)m‖'pɒs(ə)m/ *n* an opossum – not used technically

[1]**post** /pohst‖pəʊst/ *n* **1** a piece of timber, metal, etc fixed firmly in an upright position, esp as a stay or support **2** a pole marking the starting or finishing point of a horse race **3** a goalpost

[2]**post** *vt* **1** to fasten to a wall, board, etc in order to make public – often + *up* **2** to publish, announce, or advertise (as if) by use of a placard

[3]**post** *n* **1** (a single despatch or delivery of) the mail handled by a postal system **2** *chiefly Br* a postal system or means of posting **3** *archaic* (the distance between) any of a series of stations for keeping horses for relays

[4]**post** *vt* **1** to send by post <~ *a letter*> **2a** to transfer or carry from a book of original entry to a ledger **b** to make transfer entries in **3** to provide with the latest news; inform <*kept her ~ed on the latest gossip*>

[5]**post** *adv* with post-horses; express

[6]**post** *n* **1a** the place at which a soldier is stationed **b** a station or task to which one is assigned **c** the place at which a body of troops is

stationed **2a** an office or position to which a person is appointed **b** (the position of) a player in basketball who provides the focal point of the attack **3** a trading post, settlement **4** *Br* either of 2 bugle calls giving notice of the hour for retiring at night

[7]**post** *vt* **1** to station **2** *chiefly Br* to assign to a unit or location

post- *prefix* **1a** after; subsequent; later <post*date*> **b** posterior; following after <post*script*> **2a** subsequent to; later than <post*operative*> **b** situated behind <post*orbital*>

postage /'pohstij‖'pəʊstɪdʒ/ *n* (markings or stamps representing) the fee for a postal service

'postage ,stamp *n* an adhesive or imprinted stamp used as evidence of prepayment of postage

postal /'pohstl‖'pəʊstl/ *adj* **1** of or being a system for the conveyance of written material, parcels, etc between a large number of users **2** conducted by post <~ *chess*> – **postally** *adv*

'postal ,order *n, Br* an order issued by a post office for payment of a specified sum of money usu at another post office

'post,bag /-,bag‖-,bæg/ *n, Br* **1** a mailbag **2** a single batch of mail usu delivered to 1 address

'post,box /-,boks‖-,bɒks/ *n* a secure receptacle for the posting of outgoing mail

'post,card /-,kahd‖-,kɑːd/ *n* a card that can be posted without an enclosing envelope

,post 'chaise /shayz‖ʃeɪz/ *n* a usu closed 4-wheeled carriage seating 2 to 4 people

'post,code /-,kohd‖-,kəʊd/ *n* a combination of letters and numbers that is used in the postal address of a place in the UK to assist sorting

,post'date /-'dayt‖-'deɪt/ *vt* **1a** to date with a date later than that of execution <~ *a cheque*> **b** to assign (an event) to a date subsequent to that of actual occurrence **2** to follow in time

poster /'pohstə‖'pəʊstə/ *n* a (decorative) bill or placard for display often in a public place

poste restante /,pohst 'restont‖,pəʊst 'restɒnt/ *n, chiefly Br* mail that is intended for collection from a post office [French, lit., waiting mail] – **poste restante** *adv*

[1]**posterior** /po'stiəri·ə‖pɒ'stɪərɪə/ *adj* **1** later in time; subsequent **2** situated behind or towards the back: e g **2a** *of an animal part* near the tail; caudal **b** *of the human body or its parts* dorsal **3** *of a plant part* (on the side) facing towards the stem or axis; *also* SUPERIOR

[2]**posterior** *n* the buttocks

posterity /po'sterəti‖pɒ'sterətɪ/ *n* **1** *sing or pl in constr* all the descendants of 1 ancestor **2** all future generations

postern /'postuhn, 'poh-‖'pɒstɜːn, 'pəʊ-/ *n* a back door or gate – **postern** *adj*

'poster ,paint *n* an opaque watercolour paint containing gum

,post-'free *adv, chiefly Br* postpaid

,post'graduate /-'gradyoo·ət‖-'grædjʊət/ *n* a student continuing higher education after completing a first degree – **postgraduate** *adj*

,post'haste /-'hayst‖-'heɪst/ *adv* with all possible speed

'post ,horn *n* a simple wind instrument with cupped mouthpiece used esp by postilions in the 18th and 19th c

posthumous /'postyooməs‖'pɒstjʊməs/ *adj* **1** born after the death of the father **2** published after the death of the author or composer **3** following or occurring after death <~ *fame*> – **posthumously** *adv*, **posthumousness** *n*

postilion, postillion /po'stilyən‖pɒ'stɪljən/ *n* sby who rides as a guide on the near horse of one of the pairs attached to a coach or post chaise, esp without a coachman

[1]**posting** /'pohsting‖'pəʊstɪŋ/ *n* the act of transferring an entry to the proper account in a ledger; *also* the resultant entry

[2]**posting** *n* an appointment to a post or a command

'postman /-mən‖-mən/, *fem* **'post,woman** *n* sby who delivers the post

,postman's 'knock *n* a children's game in which a kiss is the reward for the pretended delivery of a letter

'post,mark /-,mahk‖-,mɑːk/ *vt or n* (to mark with) a cancellation mark showing the post office and date of posting of a piece of mail

'post,master /-,mahstə‖-,mɑːstə/, *fem* **'post ,mistress** *n* sby who has charge of a post office – **postmastership** *n*

,postmaster 'general *n, pl* **postmasters general** an official in charge of a national post office

,post me'ridiem /mə'ridi·əm‖mə'rɪdɪəm/ *adj* being after noon – abbr **pm**

[1]**,post'mortem** /-'mawtəm‖-'mɔːtəm/ *adj* **1** occurring after death **2** following the event <*a ~ appraisal of the game*> [Latin *post mortem* after death]

[2]**postmortem** *n* **1** *also* **postmortem examination** an examination of a body after death for determining the cause of death or the character and extent of changes produced by disease **2** an examination of a plan or event that failed, in order to discover the cause of failure

'post ,office *n* **1** a national usu governmental organization that runs a postal system; *specif, cap P&O* the corporation that fulfils this function in the UK **2** a local branch of a national post office **3** *NAm* POSTMAN'S KNOCK

,post'paid /-'payd‖-'peɪd/ *adv* with the postage paid by the sender and not chargeable to the receiver

postpone /pə'spohn, ,pohs(t)'pohn‖pə'spəʊn, ,pəʊs(t)'pəʊn/ *vt* to hold back to a later time; defer – **postponable** *adj*, **postponement** *n*, **postponer** *n*

,post'prandial /-'prandi·əl‖-'prændɪəl/ *adj* following a meal – fml or humor

postscript /'pohs(t),skript‖'pəʊs(t),skrɪpt/ *n* **1** a note or series of notes appended to a completed article, a book, or esp a letter **2** a subordinate or supplementary part

postulant /'postyoolənt‖'pɒstjʊlənt/ *n* a person seeking admission to a religious order – **postulancy** *n*

[1]**postulate** /'postyoo,layt‖'pɒstjʊ,leɪt/ *vt* **1** to assume or claim as true **2** to assume as a postulate or axiom – **postulation** *n*, **postulational** *adj*

[2]**postulate** /'postyoolət‖'pɒstjʊlət/ *n* **1** a hypothesis advanced as a premise in a train of reasoning **2** AXIOM 2a

[1]**posture** /ˈposchə‖ˈpɒstʃə/ *n* **1** the position or bearing of (relative parts of) the body **2** a state or condition, esp in relation to other people or things <*put the country in a ~ of defence*> **3** a frame of mind; an attitude <*his ~ of moral superiority*> – **postural** *adj*

[2]**posture** *vi* **1** to assume a posture; *esp* to strike a pose for effect **2** to assume an artificial or insincere attitude; attitudinize – **posturer** *n*

postwar /ˌpohstˈwaw‖ˌpəʊstˈwɔː/ *adj* of or being the period after a war, esp WW I or II

posy /ˈpohzi‖ˈpəʊzɪ/ *n* a small bouquet of flowers; a nosegay

[1]**pot** /pot‖pɒt/ *n* **1a** any of various usu rounded vessels (e g of metal or earthenware) used for holding liquids or solids, esp in cooking **b** a potful <*a ~ of coffee*> **2** an enclosed framework for catching fish or lobsters **3** a drinking vessel (e g of pewter) used esp for beer **4** the total of the bets at stake at 1 time **5** *Br* a shot in billiards or snooker in which an object ball is pocketed **6** *NAm* the common fund of a group **7** a large amount (of money) – usu pl with sing. meaning; infml **8** a potbelly – infml **9** cannabis; *specif* marijuana – slang

[2]**pot** *vb* **-tt-** *vt* **1a** to place in a pot **b** to preserve in a sealed pot, jar, or can <~ted *chicken*> **2** to shoot (e g an animal) for food **3** to make or shape (earthenware) as a potter **4** to embed (e g electronic components) in a container with an insulating or protective material (e g plastic) **5** to sit (a young child) on a potty ~*vi* to take a potshot

potable /ˈpohtəbl‖ˈpəʊtəbl/ *adj* suitable for drinking – **potableness** *n*, **potability** *n*

potash /ˈpotash‖ˈpɒtæʃ/ *n* **1a** potassium carbonate, esp from wood ashes **b** potassium hydroxide **2** potassium or a potassium compound, esp as used in agriculture or industry

potassium /pəˈtasyəm, -si·əm‖pəˈtæsjəm, -sɪəm/ *n* a soft light univalent metallic element of the alkali metal group that occurs abundantly in nature, esp combined in minerals – **potassic** *adj*

poˌtassium ˈnitrate *n* a salt that occurs as a product of nitrification in arable soils, is a strong oxidizer, and is used esp in making gunpowder and in preserving meat

potation /pohˈtaysh(ə)n‖pəʊˈteɪʃ(ə)n/ *n* an act or instance of drinking; *also* a usu alcoholic drink – fml or humor

potato /pəˈtaytoh‖pəˈteɪtəʊ/ *n, pl* **potatoes 1** SWEET POTATO **2** a plant of the nightshade family widely cultivated in temperate regions for its edible starchy tubers; *also* a potato tuber eaten as a vegetable [Spanish *batata*, fr Taino (a S American Indian language)]

potato chip *n* **1** *chiefly Br* CHIP 6a **2** *NAm* a crisp

ˌ**potˈbelly** /-ˈbeli‖-ˈbelɪ/ *n* an enlarged, swollen, or protruding abdomen – **potbellied** *adj*

ˈ**potˌboiler** /-ˌboylə‖-ˌbɔɪlə/ *n* a usu inferior work (e g of art or literature) produced chiefly to make money

ˈ**pot-ˌbound** *adj, of a potted plant* having roots so densely matted as to allow little or no space for further growth

poteen, potheen /poˈcheen, poˈteen‖pɒˈtʃiːn, pɒˈtiːn/ *n* Irish whiskey illicitly distilled; *broadly* any distilled alcoholic drink made at home [Irish Gaelic *poitīn*, diminutive of *pota* pot]

potent /ˈpoht(ə)nt‖ˈpəʊt(ə)nt/ *adj* **1** having or wielding force, authority, or influence; powerful < ~ *arguments*> **2** achieving or bringing about a particular result; effective **3** chemically or medicinally effective <*a ~ vaccine*> **4** producing an esp unexpectedly powerful reaction; strong <*this whisky is ~ stuff*> **5** *esp of a male* able to have sexual intercourse – **potently** *adv*, **potence** *n*, **potency** *n*

potentate /ˈpoht(ə)nˌtayt‖ˈpəʊt(ə)nˌteɪt/ *n* one who wields controlling power

[1]**potential** /pəˈtensh(ə)l‖pəˈtenʃ(ə)l/ *adj* **1** existing in possibility; capable of being made real < ~ *benefits*> **2** of or constituting a verb phrase expressing possibility – **potentially** *adv*

[2]**potential** *n* **1** sthg that can develop or become actual; possible capacity or value <*a ~ for violence*> **2 potential, potential difference** the difference between the voltages at 2 points (e g in an electrical circuit or in an electrical field)

potentiality /pəˌtenshiˈaləti‖pəˌtenʃɪˈælətɪ/ *n* POTENTIAL 1

[1]**pother** /ˈpodhə‖ˈpɒðə/ *n* **1** a noisy disturbance; a commotion **2** needless agitation over a trivial matter; fuss

[2]**pother** *vb* to put into or be in a pother

potherb /ˈpotˌhuhb‖ˈpɒtˌhɜːb/ *n* a herb whose leaves or stems are cooked for use as greens; *also* one (e g parsley) used to season food

[1]ˈ**potˌhole** /-ˌhohl‖-ˌhəʊl/ *n* **1** a circular hole worn in the rocky bed of a river by stones or gravel whirled round by the water **2** a natural vertically descending hole in the ground or in the floor of a cave; *also* a system of these usu linked by caves **3** an unwanted hole in a road surface – **potholed** *adj*

[2]**pothole** *vi* to explore pothole systems – **potholer** *n*

ˈ**potˌhunter** /-ˌhuntə‖-ˌhʌntə/ *n* sby who shoots animals indiscriminately rather than as a sport – **pothunting** *n*

potion /ˈpohsh(ə)n‖ˈpəʊʃ(ə)n/ *n* a mixed drink, esp of medicine, often intended to produce a specified effect <*a love* ~> [Middle French, fr Latin *potion-, potio* drink, potion, fr *potare* to drink]

ˌ**potˈluck** /-ˈluk‖-ˈlʌk/ *n* **1** food that is available without special preparations being made **2** whatever luck or chance brings – esp in *take potluck*

potpourri /ˌpohpəˈree, pohˈpooəri‖ˌpəʊpəˈriː, pəʊˈpʊərɪ/ *n* **1** a mixture of dried flowers, herbs, and spices, usu kept in a jar for its fragrance **2** a miscellaneous collection; a medley [French *pot pourri*, lit., rotten pot]

ˈ**pot ˌroast** *n* a joint of meat cooked by braising, usu on the top of a cooker – **pot-roast** *vt*

ˈ**potˌsherd** /-ˌshuhd‖-ˌʃɜːd/ *n* a pottery fragment

ˈ**potˌshot** /-ˌshot‖-ˌʃɒt/ *n* **1** a shot taken in a casual manner or at an easy target **2** a critical remark made in a careless manner

pottage /ˈpotij‖ˈpɒtɪdʒ/ *n* a thick soup of vegetables (and meat)

potted /ˈpotid‖ˈpɒtɪd/ *adj* **1** planted or grown in a pot **2** *chiefly Br* abridged or summarized, usu in a simplified or popular form <~ *biographies*>

[1]**potter** /ˈpotə‖ˈpɒtə/ *n* one who makes pottery

[2]**potter** *vi* **1** to spend time in aimless or unproductive activity – often + *around* or *about* <*loves to* ~ *around at home*> **2** to move or travel in a leisurely or random fashion <*avoided the motorways and* ~ed *along country lanes*>

potter's wheel *n* a horizontal disc revolving on a vertical spindle, on which clay is shaped by a potter

pottery /ˈpot(ə)ri‖ˈpɒt(ə)rɪ/ *n* **1** a place where ceramic ware is made and fired **2a** the art or craft of the potter **b** the manufacture of pottery **3** articles of fired clay; *esp* coarse or hand-made ceramic ware

[1]**potty** /ˈpoti‖ˈpɒtɪ/ *adj, chiefly Br* **1** slightly crazy <*that noise is driving me* ~> **2** foolish, silly <*a* ~ *idea*> **3** having a great interest or liking <~ *about her new boyfriend*> *USE* infml – **pottiness** *n*

[2]**potty** *n* a chamber pot, esp for a small child

[1]**pouch** /powch‖paʊtʃ/ *n* **1** a small drawstring bag carried on the person **2** a bag of small or moderate size for storing or transporting goods; *specif* a lockable bag for mail or diplomatic dispatches **3** an anatomical structure resembling a pouch: e g **3a** a pocket of skin in the abdomen of marsupials for carrying their young **b** a pocket of skin in the cheeks of some rodents used for storing food **c** a loose fold of skin under the eyes **4** an arrangement of cloth (e g a pocket) resembling a pouch – **pouched** *adj*

[2]**pouch** *vt* **1** to put (as if) into a pouch **2** to form (as if) into a pouch <*his face was* ~ed *and lined from fatigue*> ~*vi* to form a pouch

pouf /poof, poohf‖pʊf, pu:f/ *n* a poof

poulterer /ˈpohlt(ə)rə‖ˈpəʊlt(ə)rə/ *n* one who deals in poultry, poultry products, or game

[1]**poultice** /ˈpohltis‖ˈpəʊltɪs/ *n* a soft usu heated and sometimes medicated mass spread on cloth and applied to inflamed or injured parts (e g sores)

[2]**poultice** *vt* to apply a poultice to

poultry /ˈpohltri‖ˈpəʊltrɪ/ *n* domesticated birds (e g chickens) kept for eggs or meat

[1]**pounce** /powns‖paʊns/ *vi* **1** to swoop on and seize sthg (as if) with talons **2** to make a sudden assault or approach

[2]**pounce** *n* the act of pouncing

[3]**pounce** *n* **1** a fine powder formerly used to prevent ink from blotting **2** a fine powder for making stencilled patterns

[1]**pound** /pownd‖paʊnd/ *n, pl* **pounds** *also* **pound** **1** a unit of mass and weight equal to 16oz avoirdupois (about 0.453kg) **2** the basic money unit of the UK and many other countries

[2]**pound** *vt* **1** to reduce to powder or pulp by beating or crushing <~ *the meat to a paste*> **2** to strike heavily or repeatedly <~ed *the door with his fists*> **3** to move or run along with heavy steps <*the policeman* ~s *his beat*> ~ *vi* **1** to strike heavy repeated blows <~ing *angrily on the table*> **2** to move with or make a dull repetitive sound <*his heart was* ~ing *with fear*>

[3]**pound** *n* an act or sound of pounding

[4]**pound** *n* **1** an enclosure for animals; *esp* a public enclosure for stray or unlicensed animals **2** a place for holding personal property until redeemed by the owner

[1]**poundage** /ˈpowndij‖ˈpaʊndɪdʒ/ *n* **1** a charge per pound of weight **2** weight in pounds

[2]**poundage** *n* impounding or being impounded

pounder /ˈpowndə‖ˈpaʊndə/ *n* **1** one having a usu specified weight or value in pounds – usu in combination <*caught a 9*-pounder *with his new fly rod*> **2** a gun firing a projectile of a specified weight – in combination <*the artillery were using 25*-pounders>

pound out *vt* to produce (as if) by striking repeated heavy blows <pounded out *a story on the typewriter*>

[1]**pour** /paw‖pɔ:/ *vt* **1** to cause to flow in a stream <~ *the dirty water down the sink*> **2** to dispense (a drink) into a container <~ *me a whisky*> **3** to supply or produce freely or copiously <*she* ~ed *money into the firm*> ~ *vi* **1** to move or issue with a continuous flow and in large quantities; stream <*people* ~ed *out of the offices at the end of the day*> **2** to rain hard – often + *down* – **pourable** *adj*, **pourer** *n*, **pouringly** *adv* – **pour cold water on** to be critical or unenthusiastic about <*he* poured cold water on *all their proposals*> – **pour oil on troubled waters** to calm or defuse a heated situation

[2]**pour** *n* sthg that is poured <*a* ~ *of concrete*>

pour out *vt* to speak or express volubly or at length <poured out *his woes*>

[1]**pout** /powt‖paʊt/ *n* any of several large-headed fishes (e g a bullhead or eelpout)

[2]**pout** *vi* **1a** to show displeasure by thrusting out the lips or wearing a sullen expression **b** to sulk **2** *of lips* to protrude ~*vt* to cause to protrude, usu in displeasure <~ed *her lips*>

[3]**pout** *n* **1** an act of pouting **2** *pl* a fit of pique – usu + *the*

poverty /ˈpovəti‖ˈpɒvətɪ/ *n* **1a** the lack of sufficient money or material possessions **b** the renunciation of individual property by a person entering a religious order **2a** a scarcity, dearth <*a* ~ *of ideas and images*> **b** the condition of lacking desirable elements; deficiency <*the* ~ *of our critical vocabulary*> *USE* (2) fml

ˈ**poverty-ˌstricken** *adj* very poor; destitute

[1]**powder** /ˈpowdə‖ˈpaʊdə/ *n* **1** matter reduced to a state of dry loose particles (e g by crushing or grinding) **2a** a preparation in the form of fine particles, esp for medicinal or cosmetic use **b** fine dry light snow **3** any of various solid explosives used chiefly in gunnery and blasting – **powdery** *adj*

[2]**powder** *vt* **1** to sprinkle or cover (as if) with powder **2** to reduce or convert to powder ~*vi* to become powder – **powderer** *n*

ˈ**powder ˌkeg** *n* an explosive place or situation

ˈ**powder ˌpuff** *n* a small (fluffy) pad for applying powder to the skin

ˈ**powder ˌroom** *n* a public toilet for women in a hotel, department store, etc

[1]**power** /ˈpow·ə‖ˈpaʊə/ *n* **1a** possession of control, authority, or influence over others **b** a sovereign state **c** a controlling group – often in *the powers that be* **2a** ability to act or produce or undergo an effect **b** legal or official authority or capacity <*the police had no* ~ *to intervene*>

3a physical might **b** mental or moral efficacy; vigour <*the ~ and insight of his analysis*> **c** political control or influence <*the balance of ~*> **4a** the number of times, as indicated by an exponent, that a number has to be multiplied by itself <*2 to the ~ 3 is* 2^3 *= 2x2x2*> **b** EXPONENT 1 **5a** a source or means of supplying energy; *specif* electricity **b** the rate at which work is done or energy emitted or transferred **6** MAGNIFICATION 2 **7** a large amount *of* – infml <*the walk did him a ~ of good*>

2**power** *vt* **1** to supply with esp motive power **2** to make (one's way) in a powerful and vigorous manner <~ed *her way to the top*> ~*vi* to move in a powerful and rigorous manner <~ing *down the back straight*>

3**power** *adj* driven by a motor <*a ~ saw*> <*a ~ mower*>

'**powerful** /-f(ə)l‖-f(ə)l/ *adj* having great power, prestige, or influence – **powerfully** *adv*

'**power,house** /-,hows‖-,haʊs/ *n* **1** POWER STATION **2** a dynamic individual of great physical or mental force

'**powerless** /-lis‖-lɪs/ *adj* **1** devoid of strength or resources; helpless **2** lacking the authority or capacity to act <*the police were ~ to intervene*> – **powerlessly** *adv*, **powerlessness** *n*

power of attorney *n* a legal document authorizing one to act as the agent of the grantor

'**power ,plant** *n* **1** POWER STATION **2** an engine and related parts supplying the motive power of a self-propelled object

'**power ,point** *n, Br* a set of terminals that are connected to the electric mains and to which an electrical device may be connected

power politics *n pl but sing or pl in constr* international politics characterized by attempts to advance national interests by force

'**power ,station** *n* an electricity generating station

1**powwow** /'pow,wow‖'paʊ,waʊ/ *n* **1** a N American Indian medicine man **2** a N American Indian ceremony **3** a meeting for discussion – infml

2**powwow** *vi* to hold a powwow

pox /poks‖pɒks/ *n, pl* **pox, poxes** **1** a virus disease (e g chicken pox) characterized by eruptive spots **2** syphilis – infml **3** *archaic* smallpox **4** *archaic* a disastrous evil; a plague <*a ~ on him*>

practicable /'praktikəbl‖'præktɪkəbl/ *adj* **1** capable of being carried out; feasible **2** usable <*the road was ~ despite the weather conditions*> – **practicableness** *n*, **practicably** *adv*, **practicability** *n*

1**practical** /'praktikl‖'præktɪkl/ *adj* **1a** of or manifested in practice or action <*for all ~ purposes*> **b** being such in practice or effect; virtual <*a ~ failure*> **2** capable of being put to use or account; useful <*he had a ~ knowledge of French*> **3** suitable for use <*a table of ~ design*> **4a** disposed to or capable of positive action as opposed to speculation; *also* prosaic **b** qualified by practice or practical training <*a good ~ mechanic*> – **practicalness** *n*, **practicality** *n*

2**practical** *n* a practical examination or lesson

,**practical 'joke** *n* a trick or prank played on sby to derive amusement from his/her discomfiture – **practical joker** *n*

practically /'praktikli‖'præktɪklɪ/ *adv* almost, nearly <*~ everyone went to the party*>

practice, *NAm also* **practise** /'praktis‖'præktɪs/ *n* **1a** actual performance or application <*ready to carry out in ~ what she advocated in principle*> **b** a repeated or customary action; a habit <*he made a ~ of going to bed early*> **c** the usual way of doing sthg <*it's wise to conform to local ~s*> **d** the established method of conducting legal proceedings **e** dealings, conduct – esp in *sharp practice* **2** (an instance of) regular or repeated exercise in order to acquire proficiency; *also* proficiency or experience gained in this way <*must get back into ~*> **3a** the continuous exercise of a profession, esp law or medicine **b** a professional business

practise, *NAm chiefly* **practice** /'praktis‖'præktɪs/ *vt* **1** to perform or work at repeatedly so as to become proficient <~d *the drums every day*> **2a** to apply; CARRY OUT 1 <*~ what he preaches*> **b** to make a habit or practice of **c** to be professionally engaged in <*~ medicine*> ~ *vi* **1** to exercise repeatedly so as to achieve proficiency **2** to pursue a profession actively <~s *as a lawyer*> – **practiser** *n*

'**practised**, *NAm chiefly* **practiced** *adj* **1** experienced, skilled **2** learned by practice – often derog <*a ~ smile*>

practitioner /prak'tish(ə)nə‖præk'tɪʃ(ə)nə/ *n* **1** one who practises a profession, esp law or medicine <*a legal ~*> **2** one who practises a skill or art – sometimes derog <*a ~ of fiction*>

praesidium /pri'sidi·əm, -'zidi-‖prɪ'sɪdɪəm, -'zɪdɪ-/ *n* a presidium

praetor, *chiefly NAm* **pretor** /'preetə‖'priːtə/ *n* an ancient Roman magistrate ranking below a consul – **praetorship** *n*, **praetorial** *adj*

praetorian /pree'tawri·ən‖priː'tɔːrɪən/ *adj, often cap* of the Roman imperial bodyguard – **praetorian** *n, often cap*

pragmatic /prag'matik‖præg'mætɪk/ *adj* concerned with practicalities or expediency rather than theory or dogma; realistic – **pragmatically** *adv*

pragmatism /'pragmə,tiz(ə)m‖'prægmə,tɪz(ə)m/ *n* **1** a practical approach to problems and affairs **2** an American philosophical movement asserting that the meaning or truth of a concept depends on its practical consequences – **pragmatist** *adj or n*, **pragmatistic** *adj*

prairie /'preəri‖'preərɪ/ *n* an extensive area of level or rolling (practically) treeless grassland, esp in N America

1**praise** /prayz‖preɪz/ *vt* **1** to express a favourable judgment of; commend **2** to glorify or extol (e g God or a god) – **praiser** *n*

2**praise** *n* **1** expression of approval; commendation <*won high ~ for her efforts*> **2** worship

'**praise,worthy** /-,wuhdhi‖-,wɜːðɪ/ *adj* laudable, commendable – **praiseworthily** *adv*, **praiseworthiness** *n*

praline /'prahleen‖'prɑːliːn/ *n* (sthg, esp a powder or paste, made from) a confection of nuts, esp almonds, caramelized in boiling sugar [French, fr Count Plessis-*Praslin* (1598-1675), French soldier whose cook invented it]

[1]**pram** /pram, prahm‖præm, prɑːm/ *n* a small lightweight nearly flat-bottomed boat with a broad transom and usu squared-off bow

[2]**pram** /pram‖præm/ *n, chiefly Br* a usu 4-wheeled carriage for 1 or 2 babies that is pushed by a person on foot

[1]**prance** /prahns‖prɑːns/ *vi* **1** *esp of a horse* to spring from the hind legs or move by so doing **2** to walk or move in a gay, lively, or haughty manner – **prancer** *n*, **prancingly** *adv*

[2]**prance** *n* a prancing movement

prank /prangk‖præŋk/ *n* a mildly mischievous act; a trick

prankster /ˈprangkstə‖ˈpræŋkstə/ *n* one who plays pranks

prat /prat‖præt/ *n, Br* a foolish or contemptible person – slang

prate /prayt‖preɪt/ *vi* to talk foolishly and excessively *about*; chatter <*he* ~d *on about his new car*> – **prater** *n*, **pratingly** *adv*

[1]**prattle** /ˈpratl‖ˈprætl/ *vi* to chatter in an artless or childish manner – **prattler** *n*, **prattlingly** *adv*

[2]**prattle** *n* idle or childish talk

prawn /prawn‖prɔːn/ *n* any of numerous widely distributed edible 10-legged crustaceans that resemble large shrimps

praxis /ˈpraksis‖ˈpræksɪs/ *n, pl* **praxes** /-seez‖-siːz/ **1** exercise or practice of an art, science, or skill, as opposed to theory **2** customary practice or conduct – fml

pray /pray‖preɪ/ *vt* to entreat, implore – often used to introduce a question, request, or plea; fml <~ *tell me*> ~ *vi* **1** to request earnestly or humbly **2** to address prayers to God or a god – **prayer** *n*

prayer /preə‖preə/ *n* **1a(1)** an address to God or a god in word or thought, with a petition, confession, thanksgiving, etc **a(2)** a set order of words used in praying **b** an earnest request **2** the act or practice of praying **3** a religious service consisting chiefly of prayers – often pl with sing. meaning **4** sthg prayed for **5** a slight chance <*tried hard but didn't have a* ~> – infml – **prayerful** *adj*

prayer book *n* a book containing directions for worship; *specif, often cap P&B* the official service book of the Anglican church

prayer wheel *n* a revolving cylinder to which written prayers may be attached, used by Tibetan Buddhists

ˌ**praying** ˈ**mantis** /ˈpraying‖ˈpreɪɪŋ/ *n* a (large green) mantis

pre- /ˌpree-, pri-‖ˌpriː-, prɪ-/ *prefix* **1a(1)** earlier than; prior to <pre*historic*> **a(2)** preparatory or prerequisite to <pre*medical*> **b** in advance; beforehand <pre*fabricate*> **2** situated in front of; anterior to <pre*molar*>

preach /preech‖priːtʃ/ *vi* **1** to deliver a sermon **2** to urge acceptance or abandonment of an idea or course of action, esp in an officious manner ~ *vt* **1** to set forth in a sermon **2** to advocate earnestly <~ed *revolution*> **3** to deliver (e g a sermon) publicly – **preacher** *n*, **preachingly** *adv*

preamble /ˈpreeˌambl‖ˈpriːˌæmbl/ *n* **1** an introductory statement; *specif* that of a constitution or statute **2** an introductory or preliminary fact or circumstance

ˌ**prearˈrange** /-əˈraynj‖-əˈreɪndʒ/ *vt* to arrange beforehand <*at a* ~d *signal*> – **prearrangement** *n*

prebend /ˈprebənd‖ˈprebənd/ *n* (a clergyman receiving) a stipend furnished by a cathedral or collegiate church to a member of its chapter – **prebendal** *adj*

prebendary /ˈprebənd(ə)ri‖ˈprebənd(ə)rɪ/ *n* a canon in a cathedral chapter, often in receipt of a prebend

Precambrian /ˌpreeˈkambri·ən‖ˌpriː-ˈkæmbrɪən/ *adj or n* (of or being) the earliest era of geological history, extending from about 4600 million to 570 million years ago

precarious /priˈkeəri·əs‖prɪˈkeərɪəs/ *adj* **1** dependent on chance or uncertain circumstances; doubtful **2** characterized by a lack of security or stability; dangerous [Latin *precarius* given as a favour, uncertain, fr *prec-, prex* entreaty, prayer] – **precariously** *adv*, **precariousness** *n*

precast /ˌpreeˈkahst‖ˌpriːˈkɑːst/ *adj* being concrete that is cast in the form of a panel, beam, etc before being placed in final position

precaution /priˈkawsh(ə)n‖prɪˈkɔːʃ(ə)n/ *n* **1** care taken in advance; foresight <*warned of the need for* ~> **2** a measure taken beforehand to avoid possible harmful or undesirable consequences; a safeguard – **precautionary** *adj*

precede /priˈseed‖prɪˈsiːd/ *vt* **1** to surpass in rank, dignity, or importance **2** to be, go, or come ahead or in front of **3** to be earlier than **4** to cause to be preceded; preface <*he* ~d *his address with a welcome to the visitors*> ~*vi* to go or come before – **preceding** *adj*

precedence /ˈpresid(ə)ns‖ˈpresɪd(ə)ns/ *also* **precedency** /-d(ə)nsi‖-d(ə)nsɪ/ *n* **1** the fact of preceding in time **2** the right to superior honour on a ceremonial or formal occasion **3** priority of importance; preference

[1]**precedent** /priˈseed(ə)nt, ˈpresid(ə)nt‖prɪˈsiːd(ə)nt, ˈpresɪd(ə)nt/ *adj* prior in time, order, arrangement, or significance

[2]**precedent** /ˈpresid(ə)nt‖ˈpresɪd(ə)nt/ *n* **1** an earlier occurrence of sthg similar **2** sthg done or said that may serve as an example or rule to justify a similar subsequent act or statement; *specif* a judicial decision that serves as a rule for subsequent similar cases

precentor /priˈsentə‖prɪˈsentə/ *n* **1** a leader of the singing of a choir or congregation **2** the officer of a church, esp a cathedral, who directs choral services – **precentorship** *n*, **precentorial** *adj*

precept /ˈpreesept‖ˈpriːsept/ *n* a command or principle intended as a general rule of conduct – **preceptive** *adj*

preceptor /priˈseptə‖prɪˈseptə/, *fem* **preceptress** /-tris‖-trɪs/ *n* a teacher, tutor – **preceptorial** *adj*

precession /priˈsesh(ə)n‖prɪˈseʃ(ə)n/ *n* a slow movement of the axis of rotation of a spinning body about another line intersecting it caused by the application of a turning force tending to change the direction of the axis of rotation – **precessional** *adj*

precinct /ˈpreesingkt‖ˈpriːsɪŋkt/ *n* **1a** an enclosure bounded by the walls of a building –

often pl with sing. meaning **b** *pl* the region immediately surrounding a place; environs **2** an area of a town or city containing a shopping centre and not allowing access to traffic <*a shopping* ~> **3** *NAm* an administrative district for election purposes or police control

preciosity /ˌpres(h)iˈosəti‖ˌpresɪˈɒsətɪ,ˌpreʃɪ-/ *n* (an instance of) fastidious or excessive refinement (e g in language)

[1]**precious** /ˈpreshəs‖ˈpreʃəs/ *adj* **1** of great value or high price <~ *stone*> **2** highly esteemed or cherished; dear <*his friendship was* ~ *to her*> **3** excessively refined; affected – **preciously** *adv*, **preciousness** *n*

[2]**precious** *adv* very, extremely <*has* ~ *little to say*>

[3]**precious** *n* a dear one; darling <*my* ~>

precipice /ˈpresipis‖ˈpresɪpɪs/ *n* **1** a very steep, perpendicular, or overhanging surface (e g of a rock or mountain) **2** the brink of disaster

[1]**precipitate** /priˈsipitayt‖prɪˈsɪpɪteɪt/ *vt* **1** to throw violently; hurl **2** to bring about suddenly, unexpectedly, or too soon <*the failure of government policy* ~d *a general election*> **3a** to cause to separate from solution or suspension **b** to cause (vapour) to condense and fall as rain, snow, etc ~ *vi* **1** to separate from solution or suspension **2** to fall as rain, snow, etc – **precipitable** *adj*, **precipitator** *n*, **precipitative** *adj*

[2]**precipitate** /priˈsipitət‖prɪˈsɪpɪtət/ *n* a substance separated from a solution or suspension by chemical or physical change, usu as an insoluble amorphous or crystalline solid

[3]**precipitate** /priˈsipitət‖prɪˈsɪpɪtət/ *adj* **1** exhibiting violent or undue haste <*a* ~ *departure*> **2** lacking due care or consideration; rash – **precipitately** *adv*, **precipitateness** *n*

precipitation /priˌsipiˈtaysh(ə)n‖prɪˌsɪpɪˈteɪʃ(ə)n/ *n* **1** a precipitating or the forming of a precipitate **2** (the amount of) a deposit of rain, snow, hail, etc on the earth **3** a precipitate

precipitous /priˈsipitəs‖prɪˈsɪpɪtəs/ *adj* **1** PRECIPITATE 1 **2** resembling a precipice, esp in being dangerously steep or perpendicular – **precipitously** *adv*, **precipitousness** *n*

[1]**précis** /ˈpraysee‖ˈpreɪsiː/ *n, pl* **précis** a concise summary of essential points, facts, etc [French, fr *précis* precise]

[2]**précis** *vt* **précising** /ˈpraysi·ing‖ˈpreɪsiːɪŋ/; **précised** /ˈpraysid‖ˈpreɪsɪd/ to make a précis of; summarize

precise /priˈsies‖prɪˈsaɪs/ *adj* **1** exactly or sharply defined or stated <~ *images*> **2** highly exact <~ *timing*> **3** strictly conforming to a rule, convention, etc; punctilious **4** distinguished from every other; very <*at that* ~ *moment*> – **precisely** *adv*, **preciseness** *n*

[1]**precision** /priˈsizh(ə)n‖prɪˈsɪʒ(ə)n/ *n* **1** being precise; exactness **2** the degree of refinement with which an operation is performed or a measurement stated – **precisionist** *n*

[2]**precision** *adj* **1** adapted for extremely accurate measurement or operation <~ *instruments*> **2** marked by precision of execution <~ *bombing*>

preclude /priˈkloohd‖prɪˈkluːd/ *vt* **1** to make ineffectual or impracticable; exclude **2** to make impossible; prevent – **preclusion** *n*, **preclusive** *adj*, **preclusively** *adv*

precocious /priˈkohshəs‖prɪˈkəʊʃəs/ *adj* **1** exceptionally early in development or occurrence **2** exhibiting mature qualities at an unusually early age – **precociously** *adv*, **precociousness** *n*, **precocity** *n*

precognition /ˌpreekogˈnish(ə)n‖ˌpriːkɒgˈnɪʃ(ə)n/ *n* clairvoyance relating to a future event – **precognitive** *adj*

ˌpreˈconceive /-kənˈseev‖-kənˈsiːv/ *vt* to form (e g an opinion) prior to actual knowledge or experience

ˌpreconˈception /-kənˈsepsh(ə)n‖-kənˈsepʃ(ə)n/ *n* **1** a preconceived idea **2** a prejudice

ˌpreconˈdition /-kənˈdish(ə)n‖-kənˈdɪʃ(ə)n/ *n* a prerequisite

precursor /priˈkuhsə‖prɪˈkɜːsə/ *n* **1a** sby or sthg that precedes and signals the approach of sby or sthg else; a forerunner **b** a predecessor **2** a substance from which another substance is formed

predacious, **predaceous** /priˈdayshəs‖prɪˈdeɪʃəs/ *adj* living by preying on other animals; predatory

predation /priˈdaysh(ə)n‖prɪˈdeɪʃ(ə)n/ *n* **1** the act of preying or plundering; depredation **2** a mode of life of certain animals in which food is primarily obtained by the killing and consuming of other animals – **predator** *n*

predatory /ˈpredət(ə)ri‖ˈpredət(ə)rɪ/ *adj* **1a** of or carrying out plunder or robbery **b** showing a disposition to injure or exploit others for one's own gain **2** living by predation; predacious; *also* adapted to predation – **predatorily** *adv*

predecease /ˌpreediˈsees‖ˌpriːdɪˈsiːs/ *vt* to die before (another person) – **predecease** *n*

predecessor /ˈpreediˌsesə‖ˈpriːdɪˌsesə/ *n* **1** the previous occupant of a position or office to which another has succeeded **2** an ancestor

[1]**ˌpreˈdestinate** /-ˈdestinət‖-ˈdestɪnət/ *adj* destined or determined beforehand

[2]**ˌpreˈdestinate** /-ˈdestinayt‖-ˈdestɪneɪt/ *vt* to predestine – **predestinator** *n*

ˌpredestiˈnation /-destiˈnaysh(ə)n‖-destɪˈneɪʃ(ə)n/ *n* the doctrine of God's foreknowledge of all events; *esp* the doctrine that salvation or damnation is foreordained

ˌpreˈdestine /-ˈdestin‖-ˈdestɪn/ *vt* to destine or determine (e g damnation or salvation) beforehand

ˌpredeˈtermine /-diˈtuhmin‖-dɪˈtɜːmɪn/ *vt* **1** to determine or arrange beforehand <*at a* ~d *signal*> **2** to impose a direction or tendency on beforehand – **predetermination** *n*

predicament /priˈdikəmənt‖prɪˈdɪkəmənt/ *n* a (difficult, perplexing, or trying) situation

[1]**predicate** /ˈpredikət‖ˈpredɪkət/ *n* **1** sthg that is stated or denied of the subject in a logical proposition **2** the part of a sentence or clause that expresses what is said of the subject

[2]**predicate** /ˈpredikayt‖ˈpredɪkeɪt/ *vt* **1** to affirm, declare **2** to assert to be a quality or property <~s *intelligence of man*> **3** to imply **4** *chiefly NAm* BASE 2 – usu + *on* or *upon* <*his theory is* ~d *on recent findings*> *USE* chiefly fml

predicative /priˈdikətiv‖prɪˈdɪkətɪv/ *adj* **1** of a predicate **2** joined to a modified noun by a copula (e g *red* in *the dress is red*) –

predicatively *adv*
predict /pri'dikt‖prɪ'dɪkt/ *vt* to declare in advance; *esp* to foretell (sthg) on the basis of observation, experience, or scientific reason – **predictable** *adj*, **predictably** *adv*, **predictor** *n*, **predictability** *n*
prediction /pri'diksh(ə)n‖prɪ'dɪkʃ(ə)n/ *n* sthg that is predicted; a forecast – **predictive** *adj*, **predictively** *adv*
predigest /ˌpreedi'jest, -die-‖ˌpri:dɪ'dʒest, -daɪ-/ *vt* to prepare (e g food or a book) in an easier form (for consumption) – **predigestion** *n*
predilection /preedi'leksh(ə)n‖pri:dɪ'lekʃ(ə)n/ *n* a liking, preference
ˌpredi'spose /-di'spohz‖-dɪ'spəʊz/ *vt* **1** to incline, esp in advance <*a good teacher* ~s *children to learn*> **2** to make susceptible *to* – **predisposition** *n*
predominant /pri'dominənt‖prɪ'dɒmɪnənt/ *adj* having superior strength, influence, or authority; prevailing – **predominance** *n*, **predominantly** *adv*
predominate /pri'dominayt‖prɪ'dɒmɪneɪt/ *vi* **1** to exert controlling power or influence; prevail **2** to hold advantage in numbers or quantity – **predomination** *n*
preeminent /pri'eminənt‖prɪ'emɪnənt/ *adj* excelling all others; paramount – **preeminence** *n*, **preeminently** *adj*
preempt /pri'empt‖prɪ'empt/ *vt* **1** to acquire by preemption **2** to seize on to the exclusion of others; appropriate <*the movement was then* ~ed *by a lunatic fringe*> **3** to take the place of; replace **4** to invalidate or render useless by taking action or appearing in advance <*the government decision to build an airport* ~ed *the council's plans*> ~*vi* to make a preemptive bid in bridge – **preemptor** *n*
preemption /pri'empsh(ə)n‖prɪ'empʃ(ə)n/ *n* **1a** the right of purchasing before others **b** a purchase under this right **2** a prior seizure or appropriation
preemptive /pri'emptiv‖prɪ'emptɪv/ *adj* **1** (capable) of preemption **2** of or being a bid in bridge high enough to shut out bids by the opponents **3** carried out in order to forestall intended action by others <*a* ~ *attack that disabled the enemy*> – **preemptively** *adv*
preen /preen‖pri:n/ *vt* **1** to trim or dress (as if) with a beak **2** to dress or smarten (oneself) up **3** to pride or congratulate (oneself) *on* ~ *vi* **1** to smarten oneself, esp in a vain way <~ing *in front of the mirror*> **2** to appear to be congratulating oneself; gloat <*couldn't help* ~ing *after his campaign victory*> **3** *of a bird* to trim and arrange the feathers – **preener** *n*
preexistence /ˌpree·ig'zist(ə)ns‖ˌpri:ɪg'zɪst(ə)ns/ *n* existence in a former state or previous to sthg else; *esp* existence of the soul before incarnation – **preexist** *vi*, **preexistent** *adj*
prefab /'preefab‖'pri:fæb/ *n* a prefabricated structure or building – **prefab** *adj*
prefabricate /pri'fabrikayt‖prɪ'fæbrɪkeɪt/ *vt* **1** to fabricate the parts of (e g a building) at a factory ready for assembly elsewhere **2** to produce artificially – **prefabricator** *n*, **prefabrication** *n*
[1]**preface** /'prefəs‖'prefəs/ *n* **1** an introduction to a book, speech, etc **2** sthg that precedes or heralds; a preliminary
[2]**preface** *vt* **1** to introduce *by* or provide *with* a preface **2** to be a preliminary or preface to – **prefacer** *n*
prefatory /'prefət(ə)ri‖'prefət(ə)rɪ/ *adj* of or constituting a preface; introductory – **prefatorily** *adv*
prefect /'preefekt‖'pri:fekt/ *n* **1** any of various high officials or magistrates in ancient Rome **2** a chief officer or chief magistrate (e g in France or Italy) **3** a monitor in a secondary school, usu with some authority over other pupils
prefecture /'preefekchə‖'pri:fektʃə/ *n* the office or official residence of a prefect – **prefectural** *adj*
prefer /pri'fuh‖prɪ'fɜ:/ *vt* **-rr- 1** to choose or esteem above another; like better <~s *sports to reading*> **2** to give (a creditor) priority **3** to bring against sby <*won't* ~ *charges*> **4** to bring forward or submit for consideration – **preferrer** *n*, **preferable** *adj*, **preferably** *adv*
preference /'pref(ə)rəns‖'pref(ə)rəns/ *n* **1** the power or opportunity of choosing <*gave him first* ~> **2** sby or sthg preferred; a choice <*which is your* ~?> **3** special favour or consideration <*give* ~ *to those with qualifications*> **4** priority in the settlement of an obligation – **preferential** *adj*, **preferentially** *adv* – **for preference** as being the more desirable; preferably <*use red wine* for preference>
'preference ˌshare *n* a share guaranteed priority over ordinary shares in the payment of dividends and usu in the distribution of assets
preferment /pri'fuhmənt‖prɪ'fɜ:mənt/ *n* (an esp ecclesiastical appointment affording) advancement or promotion in rank, station, etc
prefigure /ˌpree'figə‖ˌpri:'fɪgə/ *vt* **1** to represent or suggest in advance; foreshadow **2** to picture or imagine beforehand; foresee – **prefigurement** *n*, **prefigurative** *adj*, **prefiguration** *n*
[1]**prefix** /'preefiks‖'pri:fɪks/ *vt* **1** to attach as a prefix **2** to add to the beginning <~ed *a brief introduction to the article*>
[2]**prefix** *n* **1** an affix (e g *un* in *unhappy*) placed at the beginning of a word or before a root **2** a title used before a person's name – **prefixal** *adj*, **prefixally** *adv*
pregnancy /'pregnənsi‖'pregnənsɪ/ *n* **1** the condition or quality of being pregnant **2** fertility of mind; inventiveness
pregnant /'pregnənt‖'pregnənt/ *adj* **1** full of ideas or resourcefulness; inventive **2** rich in significance or implication; meaningful <*a* ~ *pause*> **3** containing unborn young within the body **4** showing signs of the future; portentous <*the* ~ *years of the prewar era*> **5** full, teeming – usu + *with* <*nature* ~ *with life*> – **pregnantly** *adv*
prehensile /pri'hensiel, ˌpree-‖prɪ'hensaɪl, ˌpri:-/ *adj* adapted for seizing or grasping, esp by wrapping round <*a* ~ *tail*> – **prehensility** *n*
prehistoric /ˌpreehi'storik‖ˌpri:hɪ'stɒrɪk/, **prehistorical** /-kl‖-kl/ *adj* of or existing in times antedating written history – **prehistorically** *adv*
ˌpre'history /-'histəri‖-'hɪstərɪ/ *n* (the study of) the prehistoric period of human beings' evolution – **prehistorian** *n*

ˌpreˈjudge /-ˈjuj‖-ˈdʒʌdʒ/ *vt* to pass judgment on prematurely or before a full and proper examination – **prejudger** *n*, **prejudgment** *n*

[1]**prejudice** /ˈprejoodis, -jə-‖ˈpredʒʊdɪs, -dʒə-/ *n* **1** disadvantage resulting from disregard of one's (legal) rights **2a** (an instance of) a preconceived judgment or opinion; *esp* a biased and unfavourable one formed without sufficient reason or knowledge **b** an irrational attitude of hostility directed against an individual, group, or race

[2]**prejudice** *vt* **1** to injure by some judgment or action **2** to cause (sby) to have an unreasonable bias

ˈ**prejudiced** *adj* having a prejudice or bias in favour of or esp against

prejudicial /prejəˈdish(ə)l‖predʒəˈdɪʃ(ə)l/, **prejudicious** /-ˈdishəs‖-ˈdɪʃəs/ *adj* **1** detrimental **2** leading to prejudiced judgments – **prejudicially** *adv*, **prejudicialness** *n*, **prejudiciously** *adv*

prelacy /ˈpreləsi‖ˈpreləsɪ/ *n* **1** the office of a prelate **2** episcopal church government

prelate /ˈprelət‖ˈprelət/ *n* an ecclesiastic (e g a bishop or abbot) of high rank

prelim /ˈpreelim‖ˈpriːlɪm/ *n* a preliminary

[1]**preliminary** /priˈlimin(ə)ri‖prɪˈlɪmɪn(ə)rɪ/ *n* sthg that precedes or is introductory or preparatory: e g **a** a preliminary scholastic examination **b** *pl, Br* matter (e g a list of contents) preceding the main text of a book

[2]**preliminary** *adj* preceding and preparing for what is to follow; introductory – **preliminarily** *adv*

preliterate /ˌpreeˈlitərət‖ˌpriːˈlɪtərət/ *adj* not yet employing writing – **preliterate** *n*

[1]**prelude** /ˈprelyoohd‖ˈpreljuːd/ *n* **1** an introductory or preliminary performance, action, or event; an introduction **2a** a musical section or movement introducing the theme or chief subject or serving as an introduction (e g to an opera) **b** a short separate concert piece, usu for piano or orchestra – **preludial** *adj*

[2]**prelude** *vt* to serve as prelude to; foreshadow – **preluder** *n*

premature /ˈpreməchə, ˌpreməˈtyooə, ˈpreməˌtyooə‖ˈpremətʃə, ˌpreməˈtjʊə, ˈpreməˌtjʊə/ *adj* happening, arriving, existing, or performed before the proper or usual time; *esp, of a human* born after a gestation period of less than 37 weeks – **prematureness** *n*, **prematurely** *adv*, **prematurity** *n*

premeditate /priˈmeditayt, ˌpree-‖prɪˈmedɪteɪt, ˌpriː-/ *vt* to think over and plan beforehand <~d *murder*> – **premeditator** *n*, **premeditative** *adj*, **premeditation** *n*

[1]**premier** /ˈpremyə, ˈpremi·ə‖ˈpremjə, ˈpremɪə/ *adj* **1** first in position, rank, or importance; principal **2** first in time; earliest

[2]**premier** *n* PRIME MINISTER – **premiership** *n*

premiere /ˈpremiˌeə, ˈpremi·ə‖ˈpremɪˌeə, ˈpremɪə/ *n* a first public performance or showing <*the ~ of a play*> [French *première*, fr *premier* first] – **premiere** *vt*

[1]**premise** /ˈpremis‖ˈpremɪs/ *n* **1** *Br also* **premiss** a proposition taken as a basis of argument or inference; *specif* either of the first 2 propositions of a syllogism **2** *pl, Br also* **premiss** matters previously stated; *specif* the preliminary and explanatory part of a deed **3** *pl* **3a** a piece of land with the buildings on it **b** (part of) a building

[2]**premise** *vt* **1** to state as a premise or introduction **2** to presuppose, postulate

[1]**premium** /ˈpreemyəm, -mi·əm‖ˈpriːmjəm, -mɪəm/ *n* **1a** a reward or recompense for a particular act **b** a sum above a fixed price or remuneration, paid chiefly as an incentive; a bonus <*willing to pay a ~ for immediate delivery*> **c** a sum in advance of or in addition to the nominal value of sthg **2** the sum paid for a contract of insurance **3** a high value or a value in excess of that normally expected <*put a ~ on accuracy*> [Latin *praemium* booty, payment, reward, fr *prae* in front of, before + *emere* to take, buy] – **at a premium** valuable because rare or difficult to obtain

[2]**premium** *adj, chiefly NAm* of exceptional quality or amount <*wine made from ~ grapes*>

premium bond *n* a government bond that is issued in units of £1 and which instead of earning interest is entered into a monthly draw for money prizes

premonition /ˌpreməˈnish(ə)n, ˌpree-‖ˌpreməˈnɪʃ(ə)n, ˌpriː-/ *n* **1** a previous notice or warning; a forewarning <*a ~ of the troubles that lay in store*> **2** an anticipation of an event without conscious reason; a presentiment <*felt a ~ of danger*> – **premonitory** *adj*

prenatal /ˌpreeˈnaytl‖ˌpriːˈneɪtl/ *adj* occurring or being in a stage before birth – **prenatally** *adv*

preoccupation /priˌokyooˈpaysh(ə)n, ˌpree-‖prɪˌɒkjʊˈpeɪʃ(ə)n, ˌpriː-/ *n* (sthg that causes) complete mental absorption

ˌ**preˈoccupied** /-ˈokyoopied‖-ˈɒkjʊpaɪd/ *adj* lost in thought; engrossed

ˌ**preˈoccupy** /-ˈokyoopie‖-ˈɒkjʊpaɪ/ *vt* **1** to engage or engross the attention of to the exclusion of other things **2** to take possession of or occupy in advance or before another

ˌ**preorˈdain** /-awˈdayn‖-ɔːˈdeɪn/ *vt* to decree or determine in advance – **preordainment** *n*, **preordination** *n*

ˌ**pre-ˈowned** *adj* secondhand – chiefly euph

prep /prep‖prep/ *n, Br* homework done at or away from school

preparation /ˌprepəˈraysh(ə)n‖ˌprepəˈreɪʃ(ə)n/ *n* **1** preparing **2** a state of being prepared; readiness **3** a preparatory act or measure – usu pl <*made his* ~s *for the journey*> **4** sthg prepared; *esp* a medicine <*a ~ for colds*>

[1]**preparatory** /priˈparət(ə)ri‖prɪˈpærət(ə)rɪ/, **preparative** /-tiv‖-tɪv/ *adj* preparing or serving to prepare for sthg; introductory – **preparatorily** *adv*

[2]**preparatory** *adv* by way of preparation; in a preparatory manner – usu + *to*

preˈparatory ˌschool *n* a private school preparing pupils **a** *Br* for public schools **b** *NAm* for college

prepare /priˈpeə‖prɪˈpeə/ *vt* **1a** to make ready beforehand for some purpose, use, or activity <*~ food for dinner*> **b** to put into a suitable frame of mind for sthg <~d *her gradually for the shocking news*> **2** to work out the details of; plan in advance <preparing *his strategy for*

the coming campaign> **3a** to put together < ~ *a prescription*> **b** to draw up in written form < ~ *a report*> ~*vi* to get ready; make preparations <preparing *for a career in teaching*> – **preparer** *n*

preˈpared *adj* subjected to a special process or treatment

preparedness /priˈpeə(ri)dnis‖prɪˈpeə(rɪ)dnɪs/ *n* adequate preparation (in case of war)

prepay /ˌpreeˈpay‖ˌpriːˈpeɪ/ *vt* **prepaid** to pay or pay the charge on in advance <*carriage* prepaid> – **prepayment** *n*

preponderant /priˈpond(ə)rənt‖prɪˈpɒnd(ə)rənt/ *also* **preponderate** /-rət‖-rət/ *adj* **1** having superior weight, force, or influence; predominant **2** occurring in greater number or quantity – **preponderance** *n*, **preponderantly** *adv*

preponderate /priˈpondərayt‖prɪˈpɒndəreɪt/ *vi* **1** to predominate in influence, power, or importance **2** to predominate in number or frequency – **preponderation** *n*

preposition /ˌprepəˈzish(ə)n‖ˌprepəˈzɪʃ(ə)n/ *n* a linguistic form (e g *by, of, for*) that combines with a noun, pronoun, or noun equivalent to form a phrase with a relation to some other word – **prepositional** *adj*, **prepositionally** *adv*

prepossess /ˌpreepəˈzes‖ˌpriːpəˈzes/ *vt* to prejudice, esp in favour of sby or sthg

ˌpreposˈsessing /-pəˈzesing‖-pəˈzesɪŋ/ *adj* tending to create a favourable impression; attractive – **prepossessingly** *adv*, **prepossessingness** *n*

ˌpreposˈsession /-pəˈzesh(ə)n‖-pəˈzeʃ(ə)n/ *n* **1** an opinion or impression formed beforehand; a prejudice **2** an exclusive concern with 1 idea or object; a preoccupation

preposterous /priˈpost(ə)rəs‖prɪˈpɒst(ə)rəs/ *adj* contrary to nature or reason; absurd; *also* ridiculous <*look at that* ~ *outfit*> [Latin *praeposterus*, lit., with the hindside in front, fr *prae* in front of, before + *posterus* coming after] – **preposterously** *adv*, **preposterousness** *n*

ˈprep ˌschool /prep‖prep/ *n* PREPARATORY SCHOOL

prepuce /ˈpreeˌpyoohs‖ˈpriːˌpjuːs/ *n* the foreskin; *also* a similar fold surrounding the clitoris – **preputial** *adj*

Pre-Raphaelite /ˌpree ˈrafəliet, -fyə-‖ˌpriːˈræfəlaɪt, -fjə-/ *adj or n* (of or relating to) a member of the Pre-Raphaelite Brotherhood, a group of English artists formed in 1848 which aimed to restore the artistic principles and practices of the early Renaissance – **Pre-Raphaelitism** *n*

prerecord /ˌpreeriˈkawd‖ˌpriːrɪˈkɔːd/ *vt* to record (e g a radio or television programme) in advance of presentation or use

prerequisite /priˈrekwizit‖prɪˈrekwɪzɪt/ *n* a requirement that must be satisfied in advance – **prerequisite** *adj*

prerogative /priˈrogətiv‖prɪˈrɒgətɪv/ *n* **1** an exclusive or special right or privilege belonging esp to a person or group of people by virtue of rank or status **2** the discretionary power inhering in the Crown – **prerogatived** *adj*

[1]presage /ˈpresij‖ˈpresɪdʒ/ *n* **1** sthg that foreshadows or portends a future event; an omen **2** an intuition of what is going to happen in the future; a presentiment – **presageful** *adj*

[2]presage /ˈpresij, priˈsayj‖ˈpresɪdʒ, prɪˈseɪdʒ/ *vt* **1** to give an omen or warning of; portend **2** to forecast, predict **3** to have a presentiment of ~*vi* to make or utter a prediction

presbyter /ˈprezbitə‖ˈprezbɪtə/ *n* **1** a member of the governing body of an early Christian church **2** [3]ELDER 3 – **presbyterate** *n*

[1]Presbyterian /ˌprezbiˈtiəri·ən‖ˌprezbɪˈtɪərɪən/ *adj* of or constituting a Christian church governed by elected representative bodies and traditionally Calvinistic in doctrine – **Presbyterianism** *n*

[2]Presbyterian *n* a member of a Presbyterian church

presbytery /ˈprezbit(ə)ri‖ˈprezbɪt(ə)rɪ/ *n* **1** the part of a church (e g the E end of the chancel) reserved for the officiating clergy **2** a local ruling body in Presbyterian churches **3** the house of a Roman Catholic parish priest

preschool /ˌpreeˈskoohl‖ˌpriːˈskuːl/ *adj* of the period from infancy to first attendance at primary school

prescience /ˈpresi·əns, -sh(ə)ns, -shi·əns‖ˈpresɪəns, -ʃ(ə)ns, -ʃɪəns/ *n* foreknowledge of events; *also* foresight – **prescient** *adj*, **presciently** *adv*

prescribe /priˈskrieb‖prɪˈskraɪb/ *vi* **1** to claim a title to sthg by right of prescription **2** to lay down a rule; dictate **3** to write or give medical prescriptions ~ *vt* **1a** to ordain; LAY DOWN 2b **b** to specify with authority **2** to designate or order the use of as a remedy – **prescriber** *n*

prescript /priˈskript, ˈpreeˌskript‖prɪˈskrɪpt, ˈpriːˌskrɪpt/ *n or adj* (sthg) prescribed as a rule

prescription /priˈskripsh(ə)n‖prɪˈskrɪpʃ(ə)n/ *n* **1** the establishment of a claim to sthg by use and enjoyment of it over a long period **2** the action of laying down authoritative rules or directions **3** a written direction or order for the preparation and use of a medicine; *also* the medicine prescribed **4** (a claim founded on) ancient or long-standing custom

prescriptive /priˈskriptiv‖prɪˈskrɪptɪv/ *adj* **1** serving to prescribe **2** established by, founded on, or arising from prescription or long-standing custom **3** authoritarian as regards language use – **prescriptively** *adv*

presence /ˈprez(ə)ns‖ˈprez(ə)ns/ *n* **1** the fact or condition of being present <*requested his* ~ *at the meeting*> **2a** the immediate vicinity of a specified person <*never looked at ease in my* ~> **b** the vicinity of one of superior, esp royal, rank <*bowed before withdrawing from the* ~> **3a** sby or sthg present; *also* a spirit felt to be present **b** a body of people from a specified place (e g a country), present and playing an influential role in another organization or nation <*the withdrawal of the American* ~ *in Vietnam*> **4a** a personal magnetism that attracts and holds the attention of others **b** a usu dignified or stately bearing or appearance **5** a quality of poise or distinction that enables a person, esp a performer, to impress, or have a strong effect on, others <*she had great stage* ~>

presence of mind *n* the ability to retain one's self-possession and act calmly in emergencies or difficult situations

[1]present /ˈprez(ə)nt‖ˈprez(ə)nt/ *n* sthg

presented; a gift

[2]**present** /pri'zent‖prɪ'zent/ *vt* **1a** to introduce (sby) esp to another of higher rank **b** to bring (e g a play) before the public **2** to make a gift to **3** to give or bestow formally **4** to lay (e g a charge) before a court **5** to nominate (a clergyman) to a benefice **6a** to offer for show; exhibit <~ *a bedraggled appearance*> **b** to offer for approval or consideration <~ *this report again next week in greater detail*> **7** to act as a presenter of (e g a television or radio programme) **8** to act the part of **9** to level or aim (e g a weapon) ~*vi* to come to notice or into view <*the patient* ~ed *with abdominal pain*>

[3]**present** /pri'zent‖prɪ'zent/ *n* PRESENT ARMS <*his gun held at the* ~>

[4]**present** /'prez(ə)nt‖'prez(ə)nt/ *adj* **1** now existing or in progress <*under the* ~ *system of government*> **2a** in or at a usu specified place <*he wasn't* ~ *at the meeting*> **b** existing in sthg mentioned or understood <*methane and air had to be* ~ *in the right quantities for combustion to take place*> **c** vividly felt, remembered, or imagined – usu + *to* or *in* <*the events of a decade ago are still* ~ *to our minds*> **3** being discussed, dealt with, or considered <*as far as the* ~ *writer is concerned*> **4** of or being a verb tense that expresses present time or the time of speaking – **presentness** *n*

[5]**present** /'prez(ə)nt‖'prez(ə)nt/ *n* **1** (a verb form in) the present tense of a language **2** the present time **3** *pl* the present words or statements – fml

presentable /pri'zentəbl‖prɪ'zentəbl/ *adj* **1** fit to be seen or inspected **2** fit (e g in dress or manners) to appear in company <*must make myself* ~ *for dinner*> – **presentableness** *n*, **presentably** *adv*, **presentability** *n*

present arms /pri'zent‖prɪ'zent/ *n* a saluting position in which the firearm is held vertically in front of the body

presentation /,prezən'taysh(ə)n‖,prezən'teɪʃ(ə)n/ *n* **1a** sthg offered or given; a gift **b** sthg put forward for consideration or notice **c** a descriptive or persuasive account (e g by a salesman of a product) **2a** the manner in which sthg is set forth, laid out, or presented <*his* ~ *of the argument was masterly*> **b** the position in which the foetus lies in the uterus in labour with respect to the mouth of the uterus **3** an immediate object of perception, cognition, or memory – **presentational** *adj*

,present-'day /'prez(ə)nt‖'prez(ə)nt/ *adj* now existing or occurring

presenter /pri'zentə‖prɪ'zentə/ *n* one who presents; *specif* a broadcaster who introduces and provides comments on broadcast material during a programme

presentiment /pri'zentimənt‖prɪ'zentɪmənt/ *n* a feeling that sthg will or is about to happen; a premonition – **presentimental** *adj*

presently /'prez(ə)ntli‖'prez(ə)ntlɪ/ *adv* **1** before long; soon **2** *chiefly NAm & Scot* at the present time; now

present participle /'prez(ə)nt‖'prez(ə)nt/ *n* a participle (e g *dancing, being*) with present or active meaning

present perfect *adj or n* (of or being) a verb tense (e g *have finished*) that expresses completion of an action at or before the time of speaking

preservative /pri'zuhvətiv‖prɪ'zɜːvətɪv/ *n or adj* (sthg) that preserves or has the power to preserve; *specif* (sthg) used to protect against decay, discoloration, or spoilage

[1]**preserve** /pri'zuhv‖prɪ'zɜːv/ *vt* **1** to keep safe from harm or destruction; protect **2a** to keep alive, intact, or free from decay **b** to maintain <~s *her habitual calm at all times*> **3a** to keep or save from decomposition **b** to can, pickle, or similarly prepare (a perishable food) for future use **c** to make a preserve of (fruit) **4** to keep and protect (e g land or game) for private, esp sporting, use ~ *vi* **1** to make preserves **2** to withstand preserving (e g by canning) <*some fruits do not* ~ *well*> – **preservable** *adj*, **preserver** *n*, **preservation** *n*

[2]**preserve** *n* **1** a preparation (e g a jam or jelly) consisting of fruit preserved by cooking whole or in pieces with sugar **2** an area restricted for the preservation of natural resources (e g animals or trees); *esp* one used for regulated hunting or fishing **3** sthg (e g a sphere of activity) reserved for certain people

preset /,pree'set‖,priː'set/ *vt* **-tt-**; **preset** to set beforehand – **preset** *adj*, **presettable** *adj*

,pre'shrunk /-'shrungk‖-'ʃrʌŋk/ *adj* of or being material subjected to a process during manufacture designed to reduce later shrinking

preside /pri'zied‖prɪ'zaɪd/ *vi* **1** to occupy the place of authority **2** to exercise guidance, authority, or control *over* **3** to perform as featured or chief instrumentalist – usu + *at* <~d *at the organ*> **4** to be prominent <*the* presiding *genius of the company*> – **presider** *n*

presidency /'prezid(ə)nsi‖'prezɪd(ə)nsɪ/ *n* **1** the office of president **2** the term during which a president holds office **3** the action or function of one who presides; superintendence

president /'prezid(ə)nt‖'prezɪd(ə)nt/ *n* **1** an official chosen to preside over a meeting or assembly **2** an elected head of state in a republic **3** *chiefly NAm* the chief officer of an organization (e g a business corporation or university) – **presidential** *adj*, **presidentially** *adv*

presidium /pri'sidi·əm, -'zi-‖prɪ'sɪdɪəm, -'zɪ-/ *n, pl* **presidia** /-di·ə‖-dɪə/, **presidiums** a permanent executive committee in a Communist country

[1]**press** /pres‖pres/ *n* **1** a crowd of people; a throng; *also* crowding **2** an apparatus or machine by which pressure is applied (e g for shaping material, extracting liquid, or compressing sthg) **3** a cupboard; *esp* one for books or clothes **4** an action of pressing or pushing; pressure **5a** PRINTING PRESS **b** the act or process of printing **c** (a building containing) a publishing house or printing firm **6a** *sing or pl in constr, often cap* **6a(1)** *the* newspapers and magazines collectively **a(2)** *the* journalists collectively **b** comment or notice in newspapers and magazines

[2]**press** *vt* **1** to push firmly and steadily against **2** to assail, harass – esp in *hard-pressed* **3a** to squeeze out the juice or contents of (e g citrus fruits) **b** to squeeze with apparatus or instruments to a desired density, smoothness, or shape

<~ed *flowers*> **c** IRON 1 <~ed *his trousers*> **4a** to exert influence on; constrain **b** to try hard to persuade; entreat **5** to move by means of pressure <~ *this button*> **6** to lay emphasis or insist on <*continued to* ~ *his point*> **7** to follow through (a course of action) <~ed *his claim*> **8** to clasp in affection or courtesy <~ed *his hand*> **9** to make (a gramophone record) from a matrix ~ *vi* **1** to crowd closely; mass **2** to force or push one's way <~ing *through the crowd*> **3** to seek urgently; contend <~ing *for salary increases*> **4** to require haste or speed in action <*time is* ~ing> **5** to exert pressure **6** to come to a desired condition, esp of smoothness, by being pressed – **presser** *n*

[3]**press** *vt* **1** to force into military service, esp in an army or navy **2a** to take by authority, esp for public use; commandeer **b** to take and force into any, usu temporary, service

[4]**press** *n* impressment into service, esp in a navy

ˈ**press ˌagent** *n* an agent employed to establish and maintain good public relations through publicity

ˈ**press ˌconference** *n* an interview given by a public figure to journalists by appointment

ˈ**press ˌcutting** *n, Br* a paragraph or article cut from a newspaper or magazine

ˈ**press-ˌgang** *n sing or pl in constr* a detachment empowered to press men into military or naval service

press gang *vt* to force into service (as if) by a press-gang

[1]**pressing** /ˈpresing‖ˈpresɪŋ/ *adj* **1** very important; critical **2** earnest, insistent <*a* ~ *invitation*> – **pressingly** *adv*

[2]**pressing** *n* one or more gramophone records produced from a single matrix

ˈ**pressman** /-mən‖-mən; *sense 2 or* -ˌman‖-ˌmæn/, *fem* ˈ**pressˌwoman** *n* **1** the operator of a printing press **2** *Br* a newspaper reporter

ˈ**pressˌmark** /-ˌmahk‖-ˌmɑːk/ *n, chiefly Br* a combination of characters assigned to a book to indicate its place in a library

press on *vi* **1** to continue on one's way <press on *along the Blackpool road*> **2** to proceed in an urgent or resolute manner <*the firm is* pressing on *with its plans for expansion*>

ˈ**press-ˌstud** *n, Br* a metal fastener consisting of 2 parts joined by pressing

ˈ**press-ˌup** *n* an exercise performed in a prone position by raising and lowering the body with the arms while supporting it only on the hands and toes

[1]**pressure** /ˈpreshə‖ˈpreʃə/ *n* **1a** the burden of physical or mental distress <*the* ~ *of family anxieties*> **b** trouble or difficulty resulting from social or economic constraints <*under severe financial* ~> **2** the application of force to sthg by sthg else in direct contact with it; compression **3a** the action of a force against an opposing force **b** the force or thrust exerted over a surface divided by its area **4** the stress of urgent matters <*people who work well under* ~> **5a** influence or compulsion directed towards achieving a particular end <*the unions put* ~ *on the government to increase wages*> **b** repeated persistent attack; harassment <*the English batsmen were under* ~ *from the Australian bowlers*> **6** the atmospheric pressure

[2]**pressure** *vt* **1** to apply pressure to **2** *chiefly NAm* to pressurize

ˈ**pressure ˌcooker** *n* a metal vessel with an airtight lid in which superheated steam under pressure produces a very high temperature, used for cooking food quickly – **pressure-cook** *vb*

ˈ**pressure ˌgauge** *n* a gauge for indicating the pressure of a fluid

ˈ**pressure ˌgroup** *n* an interest group organized to influence public, esp governmental, policy

pressur·ize, -ise /ˈpreshəriez‖ˈpreʃəraɪz/ *vt* **1** to maintain near-normal atmospheric pressure in (e g an aircraft cabin) **2** to apply pressure to <*the team* ~d *the opponents' goal and eventually scored*>; *specif* to coerce <*the prisoner's hunger strike* ~d *the authorities into action*> **3** to design to withstand pressure – **pressurizer** *n*, **pressurization** *n*

prestidigitation /ˌprestiˌdijiˈtaysh(ə)n‖ˌprestɪˌdɪdʒɪˈteɪʃ(ə)n/ *n* conjuring; SLEIGHT OF HAND – **prestidigitator** *n*

prestige /preˈsteezh, -ˈsteej‖preˈstiːʒ, -ˈstiːdʒ/ *n* **1** high standing or esteem in the eyes of others **2** superiority or desirability in the eyes of society resulting from associations of social rank or material success <*a* ~ *executive suite*> [French, fr Middle French, conjuror's trick, illusion, fr Latin *praestigia*, fr *praestringere* to tie up, blindfold, fr *prae* in front of + *stringere* to bind tight]

prestigious /preˈstijəs‖preˈstɪdʒəs/ *adj* having or conferring prestige – **prestigiously** *adv*, **prestigiousness** *n*

[1]**presto** /ˈprestoh‖ˈprestəʊ/ *n, adv, or adj, pl* **prestos** (a musical passage or movement played) at a rapid tempo – used in music [Italian, quick, quickly, fr Latin *praesto* ready on hand]

[2]**presto** *interj* HEY PRESTO

prestress /ˌpreeˈstres‖ˌpriːˈstres/ *vt* to introduce internal stresses into (e g a structural beam) to counteract stresses that will result from an applied load – **prestress** *n*

presume /priˈzyoohm‖prɪˈzjuːm/ *vt* **1** to undertake without leave or justification; dare <*I wouldn't* ~ *to tell you how to do your job*> **2** to suppose or assume, esp with some degree of certainty **3** to take for granted; imply ~ *vi* **1** to act or proceed on a presumption; take sthg for granted **2** to take liberties **3** to take advantage, esp in an unscrupulous manner – usu + *on* or *upon* <*don't* ~ *on his kindness*> – **presumable** *adj*, **presumably** *adv*, **presumer** *n*

presumption /priˈzumpsh(ə)n, priˈzumsh(ə)n‖prɪˈzʌmpʃ(ə)n, prɪˈzʌmʃ(ə)n/ *n* **1** presumptuous attitude or conduct; effrontery **2a** an attitude or belief based on reasonable evidence or grounds; an assumption **b** a ground or reason for presuming sthg **3** a legal inference as to the existence or truth of a fact

presumptive /priˈzum(p)tiv‖prɪˈzʌm(p)tɪv/ *adj* **1** giving grounds for reasonable opinion or belief <~ *evidence*> **2** based on probability or presumption <*heir* ~> – **presumptively** *adv*

presumptuous /priˈzum(p)choo·əs, -tyoo·əs‖prɪˈzʌm(p)tʃʊəs, -tjʊəs/ *adj* overstepping due bounds; forward – **presumptuously** *adv*, **presumptuousness** *n*

presuppose /,preesə'pohz‖,pri:sə'pəʊz/ *vt* **1** to suppose beforehand **2** to require as an antecedent in logic or fact – **presupposition** *n*

pretence, *NAm chiefly* **pretense** /pri'tens‖prɪ'tens/ *n* **1** a claim made or implied; *esp* one not supported by fact <*made no* ~ *to learning*> **2a** mere ostentation; pretentiousness <*a man entirely free of pomp and* ~> **b** a false or feigning act or assertion **3** an outward and often insincere or inadequate show; a semblance <*struggling to maintain some* ~ *of order in the meeting*> **4** a professed rather than a real intention or purpose; a pretext – esp in *false pretences*

[1]**pretend** /pri'tend‖prɪ'tend/ *vt* **1** to give a false appearance of; feign <*he* ~ed *deafness*> **2** to claim or assert falsely; profess <~ing *an emotion he could not really feel*> <~ed *affection*> ~ *vi* **1** to feign an action, part, or role (as if) in play **2** to lay claim <*did not* ~ *to high office*> – **pretended** *adj*, **pretendedly** *adv*

[2]**pretend** *adj* make-believe – used esp by children

pretender /pri'tendə‖prɪ'tendə/ *n* **1** sby who lays claim to sthg; *specif* a (false) claimant to a throne **2** sby who makes a false or hypocritical show <*a* ~ *to spirituality*>

pretension /pri'tensh(ə)n‖prɪ'tenʃ(ə)n/ *n* **1** (an effort to establish) an esp unjustified claim <*have no* ~ *to be a great writer*> **2** vanity, pretentiousness – **pretensionless** *adj*

pretentious /pri'tenshəs‖prɪ'tenʃəs/ *adj* making usu unjustified or excessive claims (e g of value or standing) – **pretentiously** *adv*, **pretentiousness** *n*

preterite, *chiefly NAm* **preterit** /'pretərit‖'pretərɪt/ *adj* of or constituting a verb tense that expresses action in the past without reference to duration, continuance, or repetition – **preterite** *n*

preternatural /,preetə'nachərəl‖,pri:tə'nætʃərəl/ *adj* **1** exceeding what is natural or regular; extraordinary **2** lying beyond or outside normal experience ***USE*** fml – **preternaturally** *adv*, **preternaturalness** *n*

pretext /'preetekst‖'pri:tekst/ *n* a false reason given to disguise the real one; an excuse

pretor /'preetə‖'pri:tə/ *n, chiefly NAm* a praetor – **pretorian** *adj*

prettify /'pritifie‖'prɪtɪfaɪ/ *vt* to make pretty or depict prettily, esp in an inappropriate way; *also* to palliate <*attempts to* ~ *criminal violence*> – **prettification** *n*

[1]**pretty** /'priti‖'prɪtɪ/ *adj* **1a** attractive or aesthetically pleasing, esp because of delicacy or grace, but less than beautiful <*a* ~ *girl*> **b** outwardly pleasant but lacking strength, purpose, or intensity **2** miserable, terrible <*a* ~ *mess you've got us into*> **3** moderately large; considerable <*a very* ~ *profit*> **4** *of a man* having delicate features; *specif* effeminate – derog – **prettily** *adv*, **prettiness** *n*, **prettyish** *adj*

[2]**pretty** *adv* **1a** in some degree; moderately <~ *comfortable*>; *esp* somewhat excessively <*felt* ~ *sick*> **b** very – used to emphasize *much* or *nearly* <~ *nearly ready*> **2** in a pretty manner; prettily – infml

[3]**pretty** *n, archaic* a dear or pretty child or young woman – in *my pretty*

,pretty-'pretty *adj* excessively pretty, esp in an insipid or inappropriate way

pretzel /'pretsl‖'pretsl/ *n* a brittle glazed and salted biscuit typically having the form of a loose knot

prevail /pri'vayl‖prɪ'veɪl/ *vi* **1** to gain ascendancy through strength or superiority; triumph – often + *against* or *over* **2** to persuade successfully – + *on, upon,* or *with* <~ed *on him to sing*> **3** to be frequent; predominate <*the west winds that* ~ *in the mountains*> **4** to be or continue in use or fashion; persist <*a custom that still* ~s> – **prevailing** *adj*, **prevailingly** *adj*

prevalent /'prevələnt‖'prevələnt/ *adj* generally or widely occurring or existing; widespread – **prevalently** *adv*, **prevalence** *n*

prevaricate /pri'varikayt‖prɪ'værɪkeɪt/ *vi* to speak or act evasively so as to hide the truth; equivocate – **prevaricator** *n*, **prevarication** *n*

prevent /pri'vent‖prɪ'vent/ *vt* **1** to keep from happening or existing <*steps to* ~ *war*> **2** to hold or keep back; stop – often + *from* – **preventable** *also* **preventible** *adj*, **preventer** *n*, **prevention** *n*, **preventability***n*

[1]**preventive** /pri'ventiv‖prɪ'ventɪv/, **preventative** /-tətiv‖-tətɪv/ *n* sthg that prevents (disease)

[2]**preventive, preventative** *adj* **1** intended or serving to prevent; precautionary **2** undertaken to forestall anticipated hostile action <~ *war*> – **preventively** *adv*, **preventiveness** *n*

preventive detention *n, Br* a term of imprisonment for habitual criminals over 30

[1]**preview** /'pree,vyooh‖'pri:,vju:/ *vt* to see beforehand; *specif* to view or show in advance of public presentation

[2]**preview** *n* **1** an advance showing or performance (e g of a film or play) **2** a brief view or foretaste of sthg that is to come **3** *also* **prevue** *chiefly NAm* a film or television trailer

previous /'preevyəs, -vi·əs‖'pri:vjəs, -vɪəs/ *adj* **1** going before in time or order **2** acting too soon; premature <*she was a bit* ~ *when she said she'd got the job*> – infml – **previously** *adv*, **previousness** *n*

'previous to *prep* before; PRIOR TO

prevision /,pree'vizh(ə)n‖,pri:'vɪʒ(ə)n/ *n* **1** foreknowledge, prescience **2** a forecast, prognostication – **previsional** *adj*, **previsionary** *adj*

,pre'war /-'waw‖-'wɔ:/ *adj* of or being the period preceding a war, esp WW I or II

[1]**prey** /pray‖preɪ/ *n* **1a** an animal taken by a predator as food **b** sby or sthg helpless or unable to resist attack; a victim **2** the act or habit of preying

[2]**prey** *vi* **1** to make raids for booty <*pirates* ~ed *on the coast*> **2a** to seize and devour prey – often + *on* or *upon* <*kestrels* ~ *upon mice*> **b** to live by extortion, deceit, or exerting undue influence <*confidence tricksters* ~ing *on elderly women*> **3** to have continuously oppressive or distressing effect <*problems that* ~ *on one's mind*> – **preyer** *n*

[1]**price** /pries‖praɪs/ *n* **1** the money, or amount of goods or services, that is exchanged or demanded in barter or sale **2** the terms for the sake of which sthg is done or undertaken: e g **2a** an amount sufficient to bribe sby <*believed every*

man had his ~> **b** a reward for the catching or killing of sby <*a man with a ~ on his head*> **3** the cost at which sthg is done or obtained <*the ~ of his carelessness was a broken window*> **4** *archaic* value, worth

[2]**price** *vt* **1** to set a price on **2** to find out the price of – **pricer** *n*

ˈ**priceless** /-lis‖-lɪs/ *adj* **1** having a worth beyond any price; invaluable **2** particularly amusing or absurd – infml

ˈ**price ˌtag** *n* a label on merchandise showing the price at which it is offered for sale

pricey *also* **pricy** /ˈpriesi‖ˈpraɪsɪ/ *adj, chiefly Br* expensive – infml

[1]**prick** /prik‖prɪk/ *n* **1** a mark or shallow hole made by a pointed instrument **2** a pointed instrument, weapon, etc **3** an instance of pricking or the sensation of being pricked: e g **3a** a nagging or sharp feeling of sorrow or remorse **b** a sharp localized pain <*the ~ of a needle*> **4** the penis – vulg **5** a disagreeable person – chiefly vulg

[2]**prick** *vt* **1** to pierce slightly with a sharp point **2** to affect with sorrow or remorse <*his conscience began to ~ him*> **3** to mark, distinguish, or note by means of a small mark **4** to trace or outline with punctures **5** to cause to be or stand erect <*a dog ~*ing *his ears*> – often + *up* ~ *vi* **1** to prick sthg or cause a pricking sensation **2** to feel discomfort as if from being pricked – **pricker** *n* – **prick up one's ears** to start to listen intently

[1]**prickle** /ˈprikl‖ˈprɪkl/ *n* **1** a sharp pointed spike arising from the skin or bark of a plant **2** a prickling sensation

[2]**prickle** *vt* to prick slightly ~*vi* to cause or feel a prickling or stinging sensation; tingle

prickly /ˈprik(ə)li‖ˈprɪk(ə)lɪ/ *adj* **1** full of or covered with prickles **2** marked by prickling; stinging <*a ~ sensation*> **3a** troublesome, vexatious <*~ issues*> **b** easily irritated <*had a ~ disposition*> – **prickliness** *n*

ˌ**prickly ˈheat** *n* a skin eruption of red spots with intense itching and tingling caused by inflammation round the sweat ducts

prickly pear *n* (the pulpy pearshaped edible fruit of) any of a genus of cacti having yellow flowers and bearing spines or prickly hairs

prick out *vt* to transplant (seedlings) from the place of germination to a more permanent position (e g in a flower bed)

[1]**pride** /pried‖praɪd/ *n* **1a** inordinate self-esteem; conceit **b** a reasonable or justifiable self-respect **c** delight or satisfaction arising from some act, possession, or relationship <*parental ~*> **2** a source of pride; *esp, sing or pl in constr* the best in a group or class <*this pup is the ~ of the litter*> **3** *sing or pl in constr* a group of lions

[2]**pride** *vt* to be proud of (oneself) – + *on* or *upon* <*he ~*d *himself on his generosity*>

prie-dieu /ˈpree ˌdyuh‖ˈpriː ˌdjɜː/ *n, pl* **prie-dieux** /~/ **1** a kneeling bench with a raised shelf, designed for use by a person at prayer **2** a low armless upholstered chair with a high straight back [French, lit., pray God]

priest /preest‖priːst/ *n* a person authorized to perform the sacred rites of a religion; *specif* a clergyman ranking below a bishop and above a deacon (e g in the Anglican and Roman Catholic churches) [Old English *prēost*, fr Late Latin *presbyter*, fr Greek *presbyteros* elder, priest, comparative of *presbys* old man] – **priestly** *adj*, **priestliness** *n*, **priesthood** *n*

prig /prig‖prɪg/ *n* one who is excessively self-righteous or affectedly precise about the observance of proprieties (e g of speech or manners) – **priggish** *adj*, **priggishly** *adv*, **priggishness** *n*, **priggery** *n*

prim /prim‖prɪm/ *adj* **-mm- 1** stiffly formal and proper; decorous **2** prudish – **primly** *adv*, **primness** *n*

prima ballerina /ˈpreemə‖ˈpriːmə/ *n* the principal female dancer in a ballet company

primacy /ˈpriemәsi‖ˈpraɪmәsɪ/ *n* **1** the office or rank of an ecclesiastical primate **2** the state of being first (e g in importance, order, or rank); preeminence – fml

prima donna /ˌpreemə ˈdonə‖ˌpriːmə ˈdɒnə/ *n, pl* **prima donnas 1** a principal female singer (e g in an opera company) **2** an extremely sensitive or temperamental person [Italian, lit., first lady]

primaeval /prieˈmeevl‖praɪˈmiːvl/ *adj, chiefly Br* primeval

[1]**prima facie** /ˌpriemə ˈfayshi‖ˌpraɪmə ˈfeɪʃɪ/ *adv* at first view; on the first appearance <*his arguments appear ~ true*>

[2]**prima facie** *adj* true, valid, or sufficient at first impression; apparent <*the theory offers a ~ solution*>

primal /ˈpriem(ə)l‖ˈpraɪm(ə)l/ *adj* **1** original, primitive **2** first in importance; fundamental <*our ~ concern*> – **primality** *n*

primarily /ˈpriem(ə)rəli, ‖ˈpraɪm(ə)rəlɪ,*also* prieˈmerəli‖praɪˈmerəlɪ/ *adv* **1** for the most part, chiefly **2** in the first place; originally

[1]**primary** /ˈpriem(ə)ri‖ˈpraɪm(ə)rɪ/ *adj* **1a** first in order of time or development; primitive **b** of or being formations of the Palaeozoic and earlier periods **2a** of first rank, importance, or value; principal **b** basic, fundamental **3a** direct, firsthand <*~ sources of information*> **b** not derivable from other colours, odours, or tastes **c** preparatory to sthg else in a continuing process; elementary <*~ instruction*> **d** of or at a primary school <*~ education*> **e** belonging to the first group or order in successive divisions, combinations, or ramifications <*~ nerves*> **f** of or being the inducing current or its circuit in an induction coil or transformer **4** of, involving, or derived directly from plant-forming tissue, specif meristem, at a growing point <*~ growth*> **5** of or being an industry (e g mining) that produces raw materials

[2]**primary** *n* **1** sthg that stands first in rank, importance, or value; a fundamental – usu pl **2** any of the usu 9 or 10 strong feathers on the joint of a bird's wing furthest from the body **3** PRIMARY COLOUR **4** a caucus **5** PRIMARY SCHOOL

primary colour *n* **1** any of the 3 spectral bands red, green, and bluish violet from which all other colours can be obtained by suitable combinations **2** any of the 3 coloured pigments red, yellow, and blue that cannot be matched by mixing other pigments

ˈ**primary ˌschool** *n* a school usu for pupils from 5 to 11, but sometimes also including nursery school

primate /ˈpriemayt‖ˈpraɪmeɪt *or* (*esp in sense 1*) -mət‖ -mət/ *n* **1** *often cap* a bishop having precedence (e g in a nation) **2** any of an order of mammals including human beings, the apes, monkeys, and related forms (e g lemurs and tarsiers) – **primateship** *n*, **primatial** *adj*, **primatology** *n*, **primatologist** *n*, **primatological** *adj*

[1]**prime** /priem‖praɪm/ *n* **1** *often cap* the second of the canonical hours, orig fixed for 6 am **2** the most active, thriving, or successful stage or period <*in the* ~ *of his life*> **3 prime, prime number** a positive integer that has no factor except itself and 1 **4** the symbol ′ used in mathematics as a distinguishing mark (e g in denoting derivatives of a function)

[2]**prime** *adj* **1** first in time; original **2** having no factor except itself and 1 <*3 is a* ~ *number*> **3a** first in rank, authority, or significance; principal **b** *of meat, esp beef* of the highest grade or best quality regularly marketed **4** not deriving from sthg else; primary – **primely** *adv*, **primeness** *n*

[3]**prime** *vt* **1** to fill, load; *esp* to fill or ply (a person) *with* liquor **2** to prepare (a firearm or charge) for firing by supplying with priming or a primer **3** to apply a first coat (e g of paint or oil) to (a surface), esp in preparation for painting **4** to put into working order by filling or charging with sthg, esp a liquid <~ *a pump with water*> **5** to instruct beforehand; prepare <~d *the witness*>

prime meridian *n the* meridian (at Greenwich) of 0° longitude from which other longitudes E and W are reckoned

ˌ**prime ˈminister** *n* **1** the chief minister of a ruler or state **2** the chief executive of a parliamentary government – **prime ministership** *n*, **prime ministry** *n*

prime mover *n* **1** God as the creator of (motion in) the physical universe **2a** an initial source of motive power (e g a windmill, water wheel, turbine, or internal-combustion engine) **b** a powerful tractor or lorry **3** the original or most influential force in a development or undertaking

[1]**primer** /ˈpriemə‖ˈpraɪmə/ *n* a small book for teaching children to read

[2]**primer** *n* **1** a device (e g a percussion cap) used for igniting a charge **2** material used in priming a surface

prime time *n* the peak television viewing time, for which the highest rates are charged to advertisers

primeval, *Br also* **primaeval** /prieˈmeevl‖praɪˈmiːvl/ *adj* **1** of the earliest age or ages **2** existing in or persisting from the beginning (e g of a universe) – **primevally** *adv*

priming /ˈprieming‖ˈpraɪmɪŋ/ *n* the explosive used for igniting a charge

[1]**primitive** /ˈprimətiv‖ˈprɪmətɪv/ *adj* **1** original, primary **2a** of the earliest age or period; primeval **b** belonging to or characteristic of an early stage of development or evolution <~ *technology*> **3a** elemental, natural **b** of or produced by a relatively simple people or culture <~ *art*> **c** lacking in sophistication or subtlety; crude; *also* uncivilized **d(1)** self-taught, untutored **d(2)** produced by a self-taught artist – **primitively** *adv*, **primitiveness** *n*, **primitivism** *n*, **primitivist** *n*, **primitivistic** *adj*, **primitivity** *n*

[2]**primitive** *n* **1a** a primitive concept, term, or proposition **b** a root word **2a(1)** an artist of an early, esp pre-Renaissance, period **a(2)** a later imitator of such an artist **b** an artist, esp self-taught, whose work is marked by directness and naiveté **c** a primitive work of art **3a** a member of a primitive people **b** an unsophisticated person

primogeniture /ˌpriemohˈjenichə‖ˌpraɪməʊˈdʒenɪtʃə/ *n* **1** the state or fact of being the firstborn of the children of the same parents **2** the principle by which right of inheritance belongs to the eldest son

primordial /prieˈmawdyəl‖praɪˈmɔːdjəl/ *adj* **1a** existing from or at the beginning; primeval **b** earliest formed in the development of an individual or structure **2** fundamental, primary – **primordially** *adv*

primp /primp‖prɪmp/ *vt* to dress, adorn, or arrange in a careful or fastidious manner ~*vi* to dress or groom oneself carefully

primrose /ˈprimrohz‖ˈprɪmrəʊz/ *n* **1** any of a genus of perennial plants with showy, esp yellow, flowers **2** pale yellow

primula /ˈprimyoolə‖ˈprɪmjʊlə/ *n* PRIMROSE 1

Primus /ˈpriemas‖ˈpraɪməs/ *trademark* – used for a portable oil-burning stove used chiefly for cooking (e g when camping)

primus inter pares /ˌpriemas intə ˈpeərˌeez‖ˌpraɪməs ɪntə ˈpeəriːz/ *n* first among equals

prince /prins‖prɪns/ *n* **1** a sovereign ruler, esp of a principality **2** a foreign nobleman of varying rank and status **3** a person of high rank or standing in his class or profession <*a* ~ *among poets*> – **princedom** *n*, **princeship** *n*

ˌ**prince ˈcharming** *n* an ideal suitor [*Prince Charming*, hero of the fairy tale *Cinderella*]

ˌ**prince ˈconsort** *n*, *pl* **princes consort** the husband of a reigning female sovereign – used only after the title has been specif conferred by the sovereign

ˈ**princely** /-li‖-lɪ/ *adj* **1** of a prince **2** befitting a prince; noble <~ *manners*> **3** magnificent, lavish <*a* ~ *sum*> – **princely** *adv*, **princeliness** *n*

princess /ˌprinˈses‖ˌprɪnˈses *as an ordinary word, usu* ˈprinses, ˈprinsəs ‖ˈprɪnses, ˈprɪnsəs *before a name*/ *n* **1** a female member of a royal family; *esp* a daughter of a sovereign **2** the wife or widow of a prince **3** a woman having in her own right the rank of a prince **4** a woman, or sthg personified as female, that is outstanding in a specified respect

[1]**principal** /ˈprinsipl‖ˈprɪnsɪpl/ *adj* most important, consequential, or influential; chief – **principally** *adv*

[2]**principal** *n* **1** a person who has controlling authority or is in a leading position: e g **1a** the head of an educational institution **b** one who employs another to act for him/her **c** the chief or an actual participant in a crime – no longer used technically **d** the person ultimately liable on a legal obligation **e** a leading performer **2** a matter or thing of primary importance: e g **2a** a

capital sum placed at interest, due as a debt, or used as a fund **b** a main rafter of a roof – **principalship** *n*

principal boy *n* the role of the hero in British pantomime traditionally played by a girl

principality /ˌprinsiˈpaləti‖ˌprɪnsɪˈpælətɪ/ *n* the office or territory of a prince

ˌprincipal ˈparts *n pl* that series of verb forms from which all the other forms of a verb can be derived

principle /ˈprinsipl‖ˈprɪnsɪpl/ *n* **1a** a universal and fundamental law, doctrine, or assumption **b(1)** a rule or code of conduct **b(2)** habitual devotion to right principles <*a man of* ~> **b(3)** a fundamental implication <*he objects to the* ~ *of the thing, not the method*> **c** the laws or facts of nature underlying the working of an artificial device **2** a primary source; a fundamental element <*the ancients emphasized the opposing* ~s *of heat and cold*> **3** an underlying faculty or endowment <*such* ~s *of human nature as greed and curiosity*> **4** an ingredient (e g a chemical) that exhibits or imparts a characteristic quality – **in principle** with respect to fundamentals <*prepared to accept the proposition* in principle>

ˈprincipled *adj* exhibiting, based on, or characterized by principle – often used in combination <*high*-principled>

prink /pringk‖prɪŋk/ *vb* to primp – **prinker** *n*

[1]**print** /print‖prɪnt/ *n* **1a** a mark made by pressure; an impression **b** sthg impressed with a print or formed in a mould **2** printed state or form **3** printed matter or letters **4a(1)** a copy made by printing (e g from a photographic negative) **a(2)** a reproduction of an original work of art (e g a painting) **a(3)** an original work of art (e g a woodcut or lithograph) intended for graphic reproduction **b** (an article made from) cloth with a pattern applied by printing **c** a photographic copy, esp from a negative – **in print** obtainable from the publisher – **out of print** not obtainable from the publisher

[2]**print** *vt* **1** to stamp (e g a mark or design) in or on sthg **2a** to make a copy of by impressing paper against an inked printing surface **b** to impress with a design or pattern **c** to publish in print **3** to write each letter of separately, not joined together **4** to make (a positive picture) on sensitized photographic surface from a negative or a positive ~ *vi* **1** to form a printed image **2a** to work as a printer **b** to produce printed matter **3** to produce sthg by printing **4** to use unjoined letters like those of roman type

printable /ˈprintəbl‖ˈprɪntəbl/ *adj* **1** capable of being printed or of being printed from or on **2** considered fit to publish – **printability** *n*

ˌprinted ˈcircuit *n* a circuit for electronic apparatus consisting of conductive material in thin continuous paths from terminal to terminal on an insulating surface

printer /ˈprintə‖ˈprɪntə/ *n* **1** a person engaged in printing **2** a machine for printing from photographic negatives **3** a device (e g a line printer) that produces printout

printing /ˈprinting‖ˈprɪntɪŋ/ *n* **1** reproduction in printed form **2** the art, practice, or business of a printer **3** IMPRESSION 4c

ˈprinting ˌpress *n* a machine that produces printed copies

ˈprintˌout /-ˌowt‖-ˌaʊt/ *n* a printed record produced automatically (e g by a computer) – **print out** *vt*

[1]**prior** /ˈprie·ə‖ˈpraɪə/ *n* **1** the deputy head of a monastery ranking next below the abbot **2** the head (of a house) of any of various religious communities – **priorate** *n*, **priorship** *n*

[2]**prior** *adj* **1** earlier in time or order **2** taking precedence (e g in importance) – **priorly** *adv*

prioritize, -ise /prieˈorətiez/ *vt* **1** to give priority to **2** to arrange in order of priority – **prioritization** *n*

priority /prieˈorəti‖praɪˈɒrətɪ/ *n* **1a** being prior **b(1)** superiority in rank **b(2)** legal precedence in exercise of rights **2** sthg meriting prior attention

ˈprior to *prep* before in time; in advance of – fml

priory /ˈprie·əri‖ˈpraɪərɪ/ *n* (the church of) a religious house under a prior or prioress

prise /priez‖praɪz/ *vt, chiefly Br* [5]PRIZE

prism /ˈpriz(ə)m‖ˈprɪz(ə)m/ *n* **1** a polyhedron whose ends are similar, equal, and parallel polygons and whose faces are parallelograms **2** a transparent body that is bounded in part by 2 nonparallel plane faces and is used to deviate or disperse a beam of light

prismatic /prizˈmatik‖prɪzˈmætɪk/ *adj* **1** of, like, or being a prism **2** formed, dispersed, or refracted (as if) by a prism <~ *effects*> <~ *colours*> – **prismatically** *adv*

prison /ˈpriz(ə)n‖ˈprɪz(ə)n/ *n* **1** a state of confinement or captivity **2** a place of enforced confinement; *specif* a building in which people are confined for safe custody while on trial or for punishment after conviction – **prison** *vt*

prisoner /ˈpriz(ə)nə‖ˈprɪz(ə)nə/ *n* sby kept under involuntary confinement; *esp* sby on trial or in prison

ˌprisoner of ˈwar *n* a person captured in war

prissy /ˈprisi‖ˈprɪsɪ/ *adj* prim and over-precise; finicky – **prissily** *adv*, **prissiness** *n*

pristine /ˈpristeen, -tien‖ˈprɪstiːn, -taɪn/ *adj* **1** belonging to the earliest period or state **2** free from impurity or decay; fresh and clean as if new

privacy /ˈprievəsi, pri-‖ˈpraɪvəsɪ, prɪ-/ *n* **1** being apart from the company or observation of others; seclusion **2** freedom from undesirable intrusions and esp publicity

[1]**private** /ˈprievit‖ˈpraɪvɪt/ *adj* **1a** intended for or restricted to the use of a particular person, group, etc <*a* ~ *park*> **b** belonging to or concerning an individual person, company, or interest <*a* ~ *house*> **c(1)** restricted to the individual or arising independently of others <*my* ~ *opinion is that the whole scheme's ridiculous*> **c(2)** independent of the usual institutions <~ *study*> **d** not general in effect <*a* ~ *statute*> **e** of or receiving medical treatment in Britain for which fees are charged and in which the patient has more privileges than a patient being treated under the National Health Service **f** of or administered by a private individual or organization as opposed to a governmental institution

or agency <*a ~ pension scheme*> **2a(1)** not holding public office or employment <*a ~ citizen*> **a(2)** not related to one's official position; personal <*~ correspondence*> **b** having the rank of a private <*a ~ soldier*> **3a(1)** withdrawn from company or observation; sequestered **a(2)** not seeking or having the companionship of others <*she was a very ~ person*> **b** not (intended to be) known publicly; secret – **privately** *adv*, **privateness** *n*

[2]**private** *n* a soldier of the lowest rank – **in private** not openly or in public

ˌprivate deˈtective *n* a person concerned with the maintenance of legal conduct or the investigation of crime either as a regular employee of a private interest (e g a hotel) or as a contractor for fees

private enterprise *n* FREE ENTERPRISE

privateer /ˌprievəˈtiə‖ˌpraɪvəˈtɪə/ *n* **1** an armed private ship commissioned to cruise against the commerce or warships of an enemy **2** the commander or any of the crew of a privateer – **privateer** *vi*

ˌprivate ˈeye *n* PRIVATE DETECTIVE

private parts *n pl* the external genital and excretory organs

private school *n* an independent school that is not a British public school

privation /prieˈvaysh(ə)n‖praɪˈveɪʃ(ə)n/ *n* **1** an act or instance of depriving; deprivation **2** being deprived; *esp* lack of the usual necessities of life

privatize /ˈprievəˌtiez‖ˈpraɪvəˌtaɪz/ to restore (a nationalized body) to private ownership – **privatization** *n*

privet /ˈprivit‖ˈprɪvɪt/ *n* an ornamental shrub with half-evergreen leaves widely planted for hedges

[1]**privilege** /ˈpriv(i)lij‖ˈprɪv(ɪ)lɪdʒ/ *n* a right, immunity, or advantage granted exclusively to a particular person, class, or group; a prerogative; *esp* such an advantage attached to a position or office

[2]**privilege** *vt* to grant a privilege to

ˈprivileged *adj* **1** having or enjoying 1 or more privileges <*~ classes*> **2** not subject to disclosure in court <*a ~ communication*>

[1]**privy** /ˈprivi‖ˈprɪvɪ/ *adj* **1** sharing in a secret – + *to* <*~ to the conspiracy*> **2** *archaic* secret, private – **privily** *adv*

[2]**privy** *n* **1** a small building containing a bench with a hole in it used as a toilet **2** *NAm* TOILET 2b

Privy Council *n* an advisory council nominally chosen by the British monarch and usu functioning through its committees – **Privy Councillor** *n*

privy purse *n, often cap both Ps* an allowance for the monarch's private expenses

[1]**prize** /priez‖praɪz/ *n* **1** sthg offered or striven for in competition or in a contest of chance **2** sthg exceptionally desirable or precious

[2]**prize** *adj* **1a** awarded or worthy of a prize <*a ~ pupil*> **b** awarded as a prize <*a ~ medal*> **2** outstanding of a kind <*a ~ idiot*>

[3]**prize** *vt* **1** to estimate the value of; rate **2** to value highly; esteem

[4]**prize** *n* property or shipping lawfully captured at sea in time of war

[5]**prize,** *Br also* **prise** /priez‖praɪz/ *vt* **1** to press, force, or move with a lever **2** to open, obtain, or remove with difficulty <*tried to ~ information out of him*>

[1]**pro** /proh‖prəʊ/ *n, pl* **pros** **1** an argument or piece of evidence in favour of a particular proposition or view <*an appraisal of the ~s and cons*> **2** one who favours or supports a particular proposition or view

[2]**pro** *adv* in favour or affirmation <*much has been written ~ and con*>

[3]**pro** *prep* for; IN FAVOUR OF 1

[4]**pro** *n or adj, pl* **pros** (a) professional – infml

[5]**pro** *n, pl* **pros** a prostitute – slang

[1]**pro-** *prefix* **1a** earlier than; prior to; before <pro*logue*> **b** rudimentary; prot- <pro*nucleus*> **2** projecting <pro*gnathous*>

[2]**pro-** /proh-‖prəʊ-/ *prefix* **1** taking the place of; substituting for <pro*cathedral*> **2** favouring; supporting; championing <pro-*American*> **3** onwards; forwards <pro*gress*>

pro-am /ˌproh ˈam‖ˌprəʊ ˈæm/ *n* an esp golf competition in which amateurs play professionals

probability /ˌprobəˈbiləti‖ˌprɒbəˈbɪlətɪ/ *n* **1** being probable **2** sthg (e g an occurrence or circumstance) probable **3** a measure of the likelihood that a given event will occur, usu expressed as the ratio of the number of times it occurs in a test series to the total number of trials in the series

[1]**probable** /ˈprobəbl‖ˈprɒbəbl/ *adj* **1** supported by evidence strong enough to establish likelihood but not proof **2** likely to be or become true or real <*~ events*> [Middle French, fr Latin *probabilis*, fr *probare* to test, approve, prove, fr *probus* good, honest] – **probably** *adv*

[2]**probable** *n* sby or sthg probable; *esp* sby who will probably be selected <*she's a ~ for the new post*>

[1]**probate** /ˈprohbayt, -bət‖ˈprəʊbeɪt, -bət/ *n* the judicial determination of the validity of a will; *also* an official copy of a will certified as valid

[2]**probate** *vt, NAm* to establish (a will) by probate

probation /prəˈbaysh(ə)n, proh-‖prəˈbeɪʃ(ə)n, prəʊ-/ *n* **1a** subjection of an individual to a period of testing to ascertain fitness **b** a method of dealing with (young) offenders by which sentence is suspended subject to regular supervision by a probation officer **2** the state or a period of being subject to probation – **probational** *adj*, **probationally** *adv*, **probationary** *adj*

probationer /prəˈbaysh(ə)nə‖prəˈbeɪʃ(ə)nə/ *n* **1** one (e g a newly admitted student nurse) whose fitness for a post is being tested during a trial period **2** an offender on probation

proˈbation ˌofficer *n* an officer appointed to supervise the conduct of offenders on probation

[1]**probe** /prohb‖prəʊb/ *n* **1** a slender surgical instrument for examining a cavity **2a** a slender pointed metal conductor (e g of electricity or sound) that is temporarily connected to or inserted in the monitored device or quantity **b** a device used to investigate or send back information, esp from interplanetary space **3a** the action

of probing **b** a tentative exploratory survey **c** a penetrating or critical investigation; an inquiry – journ

[2]**probe** *vt* **1** to examine (as if) with a probe **2** to investigate thoroughly – journ ~*vi* to make an exploratory investigation – **prober** *n*

probity /ˈprohbəti‖ˈprəʊbətɪ/ *n* adherence to the highest principles and ideals; uprightness – fml

[1]**problem** /ˈprobləm‖ˈprɒbləm/ *n* **1a** a question raised for inquiry, consideration, or solution **b** a proposition in mathematics or physics stating sthg to be done **2a** a situation or question that is difficult to understand or resolve **b** sby who is difficult to deal with or understand [Middle French *probleme*, fr Latin *problema*, fr Greek *problēma*, lit., something thrown forwards, fr *proballein* to throw forwards, fr *pro-* forwards + *ballein* to throw]

[2]**problem** *adj* **1** dealing with a social or human problem <*a ~ play*> **2** difficult to deal with; presenting a problem <*a ~ child*>

problematic /ˌprobləˈmatik‖ˌprɒbləˈmætɪk/, **problematical** /-kl‖-kl/ *adj* **1** difficult to solve or decide; puzzling **2** open to question or debate; questionable **3** *of a proposition in logic* asserted as possible – **problematically** *adv*

proboscis /prəˈbosis‖prəˈbɒsɪs/ *n, pl* **proboscises** *also* **proboscides** /-ˌdeez‖-ˌdiːz/ **1** a long flexible snout (e g the trunk of an elephant) **2** any of various elongated or extendable tubular parts (e g the sucking organ of a mosquito) of an invertebrate **3** the human nose – infml; humor

procedural /prəˈseej(ə)rəl, -dyoorəl, -dyə-‖prəˈsiːdʒ(ə)rəl, -djʊrəl, -djə-/ *adj* of procedure – **procedurally** *adv*

procedure /prəˈseejə, proh-‖prəˈsiːdʒə, prəʊ-/ *n* **1** a particular way of acting or accomplishing sthg **2** a series of ordered steps <*legal ~*> **3** an established method of doing things <*a stickler for ~*>

proceed /prəˈseed, proh-‖prəˈsiːd, prəʊ-/ *vi* **1** to arise from a source; originate <*this trouble* ~ed *from a misunderstanding*> **2** to continue after a pause or interruption **3** to begin and carry on an action, process, or movement **4** to move along a course; advance

proceeding /prəˈseeding, proh-‖prəˈsiːdɪŋ, prəʊ-/ *n* **1** a procedure **2** *pl* events, goings-on **3** *pl* legal action <*divorce* ~s> **4** *pl* an official record of things said or done **5** (an) affair, transaction – fml in sing.; usu pl with sing. meaning

proceeds /ˈprohseedz‖ˈprəʊsiːdz/ *n pl* **1** the total amount brought in <*the ~ of a sale*> **2** the net amount received

[1]**process** /ˈprohses‖ˈprəʊses/ *n* **1a** a moving forwards, esp as part of a progression or development <*the historical ~*> **b** sthg going on; a proceeding **2a** a natural phenomenon marked by gradual changes that lead towards a particular result <*the ~ of growth*> **b** a series of actions or operations designed to achieve an end; *esp* a continuous operation or treatment (e g in manufacture) **3a** a whole course of legal proceedings **b** a summons, writ **4** a prominent or projecting part of a living organism or an anatomical structure <*a bone ~*>

[2]**process** *vt* **1** to subject to a special process or treatment (e g in the course of manufacture) **2** to take appropriate action on <*~ an insurance claim*> – **processible, processable** *adj*

[3]**process** *vi, chiefly Br* to move in a procession

procession /prəˈsesh(ə)n‖prəˈseʃ(ə)n/ *n* **1** a group of individuals moving along in an orderly way, esp as part of a ceremony or demonstration **2** a succession, sequence

[1]**processional** /prəˈsesh(ə)nl‖prəˈseʃ(ə)nl/ *n* a musical composition (e g a hymn) designed for a procession

[2]**processional** *adj* of or moving in a procession – **processionally** *adv*

proclaim /prəˈklaym, proh-‖prəˈkleɪm, prəʊ-/ *vt* **1** to declare publicly and usu officially; announce **2** to give outward indication of; show – **proclaimer** *n*

proclamation /ˌprokləˈmaysh(ə)n‖ˌprɒkləˈmeɪʃ(ə)n/ *n* **1** proclaiming or being proclaimed **2** an official public announcement

proclivity /prəˈklivəti, proh-‖prəˈklɪvətɪ, prəʊ-/ *n* an inclination or predisposition towards sthg, esp sthg reprehensible – often pl with sing. meaning

proconsul /ˌprohˈkonsl‖ˌprəʊˈkɒnsl/ *n* **1** a governor or military commander of an ancient Roman province **2** an administrator in a modern dependency or occupied area – **proconsulship** *n*, **proconsular** *adj*, **proconsulate** *n*

procrastinate /prohˈkrastinayt, prə-‖prəʊˈkræstɪneɪt, prə-/ *vi* to delay intentionally and reprehensibly in doing sthg necessary – fml – **procrastinator** *n*, **procrastination** *n*

procreate /ˌprohkriˈayt‖ˌprəʊkrɪˈeɪt/ *vb* to beget or bring forth (young) – **procreative** *adj*, **procreator** *n*, **procreation** *n*

proctor /ˈproktə‖ˈprɒktə/ *n* a supervisor, monitor; *specif* one appointed to maintain student discipline at Oxford or Cambridge – **proctorship** *n*, **proctorial** *adj*

ˌprocurator-ˈfiscal /ˈprokyooˌraytə‖ˈprɒkjʊˌreɪtə/ *n, often cap P&F* a local public prosecutor in Scotland

procure /prəˈkyooə‖prəˈkjʊə/ *vt* **1** to get and provide (esp women) to act as prostitutes **2** to obtain, esp by particular care and effort **3** to achieve; BRING ABOUT ~*vi* to procure women *USE* (*vt 2&3*) fml – **procurable** *adj*, **procurance** *n*, **procurement** *n*

procurer /prəˈkyooərə‖prəˈkjʊərə/, *fem* **procuress** /-ris‖-rɪs/ *n* sby who procures women for prostitution

[1]**prod** /prod‖prɒd/ *vb* **-dd-** *vt* **1** to poke or jab (as if) with a pointed instrument **2** to incite to action; stir ~*vi* to make a prodding or jabbing movement, esp repeatedly – **prodder** *n*

[2]**prod** *n* **1** a pointed instrument **2** a prodding action; a jab **3** an incitement to act

[1]**prodigal** /ˈprodigl‖ˈprɒdɪgl/ *adj* **1** recklessly extravagant or wasteful **2** yielding abundantly; lavish <*~ of new ideas*> – fml [Latin *prodigus*, fr *prodigere* to drive away, squander, fr *pro-*, *prod-* forth + *agere* to drive] – **prodigally** *adv*, **prodigality** *n*

[2]**prodigal** *n* **1** a repentant sinner or reformed wastrel **2** one who spends or gives lavishly and foolishly

prodigious /prə'dijəs‖prə'dɪdʒəs/ *adj* **1** exciting amazement or wonder **2** extraordinary in bulk, quantity, or degree; enormous – **prodigiously** *adv*, **prodigiousness** *n*

prodigy /'prodiji‖'prɒdɪdʒɪ/ *n* **1a** sthg extraordinary, inexplicable, or marvellous **b** an exceptional and wonderful example <*a ~ of patience*> **2** a person, esp a child, with extraordinary talents

[1]**produce** /prə'dyoohs‖prə'dju:s/ *vt* **1** to offer to view or notice; exhibit **2** to give birth or rise to **3** to extend in length, area, or volume <*~ a side of a triangle*> **4** to act as a producer of **5** to give being, form, or shape to; make; *esp* to manufacture **6** to (cause to) accumulate *~vi* to bear, make, or yield sthg – **producible** *adj*

[2]**produce** /'prodyoohs‖'prɒdju:s/ *n* agricultural products; *esp* fresh fruits and vegetables as distinguished from grain and other staple crops

producer /prə'dyoohsə‖prə'dju:sə/ *n* **1** an individual or entity that grows agricultural products or manufactures articles **2a** sby who has responsibility for the administrative aspects of the production of a film (e g casting, schedules, and esp finance) **b** *Br* DIRECTOR 3

product /'prodəkt, -dukt‖'prɒdəkt, -dʌkt/ *n* **1** the result of the multiplying together of 2 or more numbers or expressions **2** sthg produced by a natural or artificial process; *specif* a result of a combination of incidental causes or conditions <*a typical ~ of an arts education*> **3** a salable or marketable commodity <*tourism should be regarded as a ~*>

production /prə'duksh(ə)n‖prə'dʌkʃ(ə)n/ *n* **1a** sthg produced; a product **b(1)** a literary or artistic work **b(2)** a work presented on the stage or screen or over the air **2a** the act or process of producing **b** the creation of utility; *esp* the making of goods available for human wants **3** total output, esp of a commodity or an industry – **productional** *adj*

production line *n* LINE 5h

productive /prə'duktiv‖prə'dʌktɪv/ *adj* **1** having the quality or power of producing, esp in abundance <*~ fishing waters*> **2** effective in bringing about; being the cause *of* **3a** yielding or furnishing results or benefits <*a ~ programme of education*> **b** yielding or devoted to the satisfaction of wants or the creation of utilities – **productively** *adv*, **productiveness** *n*, **productivity** *n*

proem /'proh·em‖'prəʊem/ *n* **1** a preface or introduction, esp to a book or speech **2** a prelude – **proemial** *adj*

prof /prof‖prɒf/ *n* a professor – slang

profanation /,profə'naysh(ə)n‖,prɒfə'neɪʃ(ə)n/ *n* (a) profaning

[1]**profane** /prə'fayn‖prə'feɪn/ *vt* **1** to treat (sthg sacred) with abuse, irreverence, or contempt; desecrate **2** to debase by an unworthy or improper use – **profaner** *n*

[2]**profane** *adj* **1** not concerned with religion or religious purposes **2** debasing or defiling what is holy; irreverent **3a** not among the initiated **b** not possessing esoteric or expert knowledge [Latin *profanus*, fr *pro* before + *fanum* temple] – **profanely** *adv*, **profaneness** *n*

profanity /prə'fanəti‖prə'fænətɪ/ *n* **1a** being profane **b** (the use of) profane language **2** a profane utterance

profess /prə'fes‖prə'fes/ *vt* **1** to receive formally into a religious community **2a** to declare or admit openly or freely; affirm **b** to declare falsely; pretend **3** to confess one's faith in or allegiance to **4** to be a professor of (an academic discipline) *~vi* to make a profession or avowal

pro'fessed *adj* **1** openly and freely admitted or declared <*a ~ atheist*> **2** professing to be qualified <*a ~ solicitor*> **3** pretended, feigned <*~ misery*> – **professedly** *adv*

profession /prə'fesh(ə)n‖prə'feʃ(ə)n/ *n* **1** the act of taking the vows of a religious community **2** an act of openly declaring or claiming a faith, opinion, etc; a protestation **3** an avowed religious faith **4a** a calling requiring specialized knowledge and often long and intensive academic preparation **b** a principal calling, vocation, or employment **c** *sing or pl in constr* the whole body of people engaged in a particular calling

[1]**professional** /prə'fesh(ə)nl‖prə'feʃ(ə)nl/ *adj* **1a** (characteristic) of a profession **b** engaged in 1 of the learned professions **c(1)** characterized by or conforming to the technical or ethical standards of a profession <*~ conduct*> **c(2)** characterized by conscientious workmanship <*did a really ~ job on the garden*> **2a** engaging for gain or livelihood in an activity or field of endeavour often engaged in by amateurs **b** engaged in by professionals <*~ football*> **3** following a line of conduct as though it were a profession <*a ~ agitator*> – derog **4** *of a breaking of rules, esp in sport* intentional – euph – **professionalize** *vt*, **professionally** *adv*

[2]**professional** *n* **1** one who engages in a pursuit or activity professionally **2** one with sufficient experience or skill in an occupation or activity to resemble a professional – infml

pro'fessionalism /-iz(ə)m‖-ɪz(ə)m/ *n* **1** the esp high and consistent conduct, aims, or qualities that characterize a profession or a professional person **2** the following for gain or livelihood of an activity often engaged in by amateurs

professor /prə'fesə‖prə'fesə/ *n* **1** sby who professes or declares sthg (e g a faith or opinion) **2a** a staff member of the highest academic rank at a university; *esp* the head of a university department **b** sby who teaches or professes special knowledge of an art, sport, or occupation requiring skill **c** *NAm* a teacher at a university, college, or sometimes secondary school – **professorship** *n*, **professorate** *n*, **professorial** *adj*

proffer /'profə‖'prɒfə/ *vt* to present for acceptance; tender

proficient /prə'fish(ə)nt‖prə'fɪʃ(ə)nt/ *adj* well advanced or expert in an art, skill, branch of knowledge, etc – **proficiency** *n*, **proficient** *n*, **proficiently** *adv*

[1]**profile** /'prohfiel‖'prəʊfaɪl/ *n* **1** a side view, esp of the human face **2** an outline seen or represented in sharp relief; a contour **3** a side or sectional elevation: e g **3a** a drawing showing a vertical section of the ground **b** a vertical section of a soil from the ground surface to the underlying material **4** a concise written or spoken biographical sketch

[2]**profile** *vt* **1** to represent in profile or by a

profile; produce a profile of (e g by drawing or writing) **2** to shape the outline of by passing a cutter round – **profiler** *n*

[1]**profit** /ˈprofit‖ˈprɒfɪt/ *n* **1** a valuable return; a gain **2** the excess of returns over expenditure **3** compensation for the assumption of risk in business enterprise, as distinguished from wages or rent – **profitless** *adj*

[2]**profit** *vi* to derive benefit; gain – usu + *from* or *by* <~ed *greatly from these lessons*> ~*vt* to be of service to; benefit <*it will not* ~ *you to start an argument*>

profitable /ˈprofitəbl‖ˈprɒfɪtəbl/ *adj* affording financial or other gains or profits – **profitableness** *n*, **profitably** *adv*, **profitability** *n*

profiteer /ˌprofiˈtiə‖ˌprɒfɪˈtɪə/ *n* one who makes an unreasonable profit, esp on the sale of scarce and essential goods – **profiteer** *vi*

profit sharing *n* a system or process under which employees receive a part of the profits of an industrial or commercial enterprise

[1]**profligate** /ˈprofligət‖ˈprɒflɪgət/ *adj* **1** utterly dissolute; immoral **2** wildly extravagant; prodigal – **profligacy** *n*, **profligately** *adv*

[2]**profligate** *n* a person given to wildly extravagant and usu grossly self-indulgent expenditure

profound /prəˈfownd‖prəˈfaʊnd/ *adj* **1a** having intellectual depth and insight **b** difficult to fathom or understand **2a** extending far below the surface **b** coming from, reaching to, or situated at a depth; deep-seated <*a* ~ *sigh*> **3a** characterized by intensity of feeling or quality **b** all encompassing; complete <~ *sleep*> – **profoundly** *adv*, **profoundness** *n*

profundity /prəˈfundəti‖prəˈfʌndətɪ/ *n* **1a** intellectual depth **b** sthg profound or abstruse **2** being profound or deep

profuse /prəˈfyoohs‖prəˈfjuːs/ *adj* **1** liberal, extravagant <~ *in their thanks*> **2** greatly abundant; bountiful <*a* ~ *harvest*> – **profusely** *adv*, **profuseness** *n*

profusion /prəˈfyoohzh(ə)n‖prəˈfjuːʒ(ə)n/ *n* **1** being profuse **2** a large or lavish amount

progenitor /ˌprohˈjenitə‖ˌprəʊˈdʒenɪtə/ *n* **1a** a direct ancestor; a forefather **b** a biologically ancestral form **2** a precursor, originator

progeny /ˈprojini‖ˈprɒdʒɪnɪ/ *n* **1** *sing or pl in constr* **1a** descendants, children **b** offspring of animals or plants **2** an outcome, product – fml

progesterone /prohˈjestəˌrohn‖prəʊˈdʒestəˌrəʊn/ *n* a steroid hormone that affects the ovulatory system

prognathous /progˈnaythəs‖prɒgˈneɪθəs/ *adj* having the jaws projecting beyond the upper part of the face

prognosis /progˈnohsis‖prɒgˈnəʊsɪs/ *n, pl* **prognoses** /-seez‖-siːz/ **1** the prospect of recovery as anticipated from the usual course of disease or peculiarities of a particular case **2** a forecast, prognostication – fml

prognostic /progˈnostik‖prɒgˈnɒstɪk/ *n* **1** sthg that foretells; a portent **2** prognostication, prophecy *USE* fml – **prognostic** *adj*

prognosticate /progˈnostiˌkayt‖prɒgˈnɒstɪˌkeɪt/ *vt* **1** to foretell from signs or symptoms; predict **2** to indicate in advance; presage *USE* fml – **prognosticator** *n*, **prognosticative** *adj*, **prognostication** *n*

[1]**program** /ˈprohgram‖ˈprəʊgræm/ *n* **1a** a plan for the programming of a mechanism (e g a computer) **b** a sequence of coded instructions that can be inserted into a mechanism (e g a computer) or that is part of an organism **2** *chiefly NAm* a programme

[2]**program** *vt* **-mm-** (*NAm* **-mm-, -m-**) **1** to work out a sequence of operations to be performed by (a computer or similar mechanism); provide with a program **2** *chiefly NAm* to programme – **programmable** *adj*, **programmability** *n*

[1]**programme,** *NAm chiefly* **program** /ˈprohgram‖ˈprəʊgræm/ *n* **1a** a brief usu printed (pamphlet containing a) list of the features to be presented, the people participating, etc (e g in a public performance or entertainment) **b** the performance of a programme **c** a radio or television broadcast characterized by some feature (e g a presenter, a purpose, or a theme) giving it coherence and continuity **2** a systematic plan of action <*a rehousing* ~> **3** a curriculum **4** a prospectus, syllabus **5** matter for programmed instruction [French *programme* agenda, public notice, fr Greek *programma*, fr *prographein* to write before, fr *pro* before + *graphein* to write]

[2]**programme,** *NAm chiefly* **program** *vt* **1a** to arrange or provide a programme of or for **b** to enter in a programme **2** to cause to conform to a pattern (e g of thought or behaviour); condition <*our visions of marriage have been* ~d *by Hollywood*> – **programmable** *adj*, **programming** *n*, **programmability** *n*

programme music *n* music intended to suggest a sequence of images or incidents

programmer, *NAm also* **programer** /ˈprohgramə‖ˈprəʊgræmə/ *n* **1** a person or device that prepares and tests programs for mechanisms **2** a person or device that programs a mechanism (e g a computer) **3** one who prepares educational programmes

[1]**progress** /ˈprohgres‖ˈprəʊgres/ *n* **1a** a ceremonial journey; *esp* a monarch's tour of his/her dominions **b** an expedition, journey, or march **2** a forward or onward movement (e g to an objective or goal); an advance **3** gradual improvement; *esp* the progressive development of mankind – **in progress** occurring; going on

[2]**progress** /prəˈgres‖prəˈgres/ *vi* **1** to move forwards; proceed **2** to develop to a higher, better, or more advanced stage ~ *vt* **1** to oversee and ensure the satisfactory progress or running of (e g a project) <*the editor must* ~ *articles from conception to publication*> **2** to ascertain and attempt to bring forward the delivery or completion date of <~ *these orders*>

progression /prəˈgresh(ə)n‖prəˈgreʃ(ə)n/ *n* **1** a sequence of numbers in which each term is related to its predecessor by a uniform law **2a** progressing, advance **b** a continuous and connected series; a sequence **3** succession of musical notes or chords – **progressional** *adj*

[1]**progressive** /prəˈgresiv‖prəˈgresɪv/ *adj* **1a** of or characterized by progress or progression **b** making use of or interested in new ideas, findings, or opportunities **c** of or being an educational theory marked by emphasis on the individual, informality, and self-expression **2** moving forwards continuously or in stages; advancing **3**

increasing in extent or severity <*a ~ disease*> **4** of or constituting a verb form (e g *am working*) that expresses action in progress **5** increasing in rate as the base increases <*a ~ tax*> – **progressively** *adv*, **progressiveness** *n*, **progressivism** *n*, **progressivist** *n or adj*, **progressivistic** *adj*

[2]**progressive** *n* **1** sby or sthg progressive **2** sby believing in moderate political change, esp social improvement; *esp, cap* a member of a political party that advocates these beliefs

prohibit /prəˈhibit, proh-‖prəˈhɪbɪt, prəʊ-/ *vt* **1** to forbid by authority **2a** to prevent from doing sthg **b** to preclude

prohibition /ˌproh·hiˈbish(ə)n‖ˌprəʊhɪˈbɪʃ(ə)n/ *n* **1** the act of prohibiting by authority **2** an order to restrain or stop **3** *often cap* the forbidding by law of the manufacture and sale of alcohol **4** a judicial writ prohibiting a lower court from proceeding in a case beyond its jurisdiction – **prohibitionist** *n*

prohibitive /prəˈhibətiv, proh-‖prəˈhɪbətɪv, prəʊ-/, **prohibitory** /-t(ə)ri‖-t(ə)rɪ/ *adj* **1** tending to prohibit or restrain **2** tending to preclude the use or acquisition of sthg <*the running expenses seemed* ~> – **prohibitively** *adv*, **prohibitiveness** *n*

[1]**project** /ˈprojekt‖ˈprɒdʒekt; *also* proh-‖prəʊ-/ *n* **1** a specific plan or design; a scheme **2** a planned undertaking: e g **2a** a definitely formulated piece of research **b** a large undertaking, esp a public works scheme **c** a task or problem engaged in usu by a group of pupils, esp to supplement and apply classroom studies

[2]**project** /prəˈjekt‖prəˈdʒekt/ *vt* **1a** to devise in the mind; design **b** to plan, figure, or estimate for the future **2** to throw forwards or upwards, esp by mechanical means **3** to present or transport in imagination <*a book that tries to ~ how the world will look in 2100*> **4** to cause to protrude **5** to cause (light or an image) to fall into space or on a surface **6** to reproduce (e g a point, line, or area) on a surface by motion in a prescribed direction **7a** to cause (one's voice) to be heard at a distance **b** to communicate vividly, esp to an audience **c** to present or express (oneself) in a manner that wins approval <*must learn to ~ yourself better if you want the job*> **8** to attribute (sthg in one's own mind) to a person, group, or object ~ *vi* **1** to jut out; protrude **2** to attribute sthg in one's own mind to a person, group, or object – **projectable** *adj*

[1]**projectile** /prəˈjektiel‖prəˈdʒektaɪl/ *n* **1** a body projected by external force and continuing in motion by its own inertia; *esp* a missile (e g a bullet, shell, or grenade) fired from a weapon **2** a self-propelling weapon (e g a rocket)

[2]**projectile** *adj* **1** projecting or impelling **2** capable of being thrust forwards

projection /prəˈjeksh(ə)n‖prəˈdʒekʃ(ə)n/ *n* **1a** a systematic representation on a flat surface of latitude and longitude from the curved surface of the earth, celestial sphere, etc **b** (a graphic reproduction formed by) the process of reproducing a spatial object on a surface by projecting its points **2** the act of throwing or shooting forward; ejection **3a** a jutting out **b** a part that juts out **4** the act of perceiving a subjective mental image as objective **5** the attribution of one's own ideas, feelings, or attitudes to other people or to objects, esp as a defence against feelings of guilt or inadequacy **6** the display of films or slides by projecting an image from them onto a screen **7** an estimate of future possibilities based on a current trend – **projectional** *adj*

projectionist /prəˈjekch(ə)nist‖prəˈdʒekʃ(ə)nɪst/ *n* the operator of a film projector or television equipment

projector /prəˈjektə‖prəˈdʒektə/ *n* an apparatus for projecting films or pictures onto a surface

prolapse /ˈprohˌlaps‖ˈprəʊˌlæps/ *n* the falling down or slipping of a body part (e g the uterus) from its usual position or relations – **prolapse** *vi*

prole /prohl‖prəʊl/ *n or adj* (a) proletarian – derog

prolegomenon /ˌprohleˈgominən, ˌpro-‖ˌprəʊleˈgɒmɪnən, ˌprɒ-/ *n, pl* **prolegomena** /-minə‖-mɪnə/ an introductory section, esp to a learned work – **prolegomenous** *adj*

proletarian /ˌprohliˈteəri·ən‖ˌprəʊlɪˈteərɪən/ *n or adj* (a member) of the proletariat [Latin *proletarius*, member of the lowest social class who served the state by producing offspring, fr *proles* progeny] – **proletarianize** *vt*, **proletarianization** *n*

proletariat /ˌprohliˈteəri·ət‖ˌprəʊlɪˈteərɪət/ *n sing or pl in constr* **1** the lowest class of a community **2** WORKING CLASS; *esp* those workers who lack their own means of production and hence sell their labour to live

[1]**proliferate** /prəˈlifərayt‖prəˈlɪfəreɪt/ *vi* to grow or increase (as if) by rapid production of new parts, cells, buds, etc – **proliferative** *adj*, **proliferatively** *adv*, **proliferation** *n*

[2]**proliferate** /prəˈlif(ə)rət‖prəˈlɪf(ə)rət/ *adj* increased in number or quantity

prolific /prəˈlifik‖prəˈlɪfɪk/ *adj* **1** producing young or fruit (freely) **2** marked by abundant inventiveness or productivity <*a ~ writer*> – **prolificacy** *n*, **prolifically** *adv*, **prolificness** *n*, **prolificity** *n*

prolix /ˈprohˌliks‖ˈprəʊˌlɪks/ *adj* **1** unduly prolonged or repetitious <*a ~ speech*> **2** given to verbosity in speaking or writing; long-winded – **prolixity** *n*, **prolixly** *adv*

prologue, *NAm also* **prolog** /ˈprohlog‖ˈprəʊlɒg/ *n* **1** the preface or introduction to a literary work **2** (the actor delivering) a speech, often in verse, addressed to the audience at the beginning of a play **3** an introductory or preceding event or development

prolong /prəˈlong‖prəˈlɒŋ/ *vt* **1** to lengthen in time; continue **2** to lengthen in space <*to ~ a line*> – **prolonger** *n*, **prolongation** *n*

prom /prom‖prɒm/ *n* **1** PROMENADE CONCERT **2** *Br* PROMENADE 2

[1]**promenade** /ˈpromәˌnahd, ˌ--ˈ-‖ˈprɒməˌnɑːd, ˌ--ˈ-/ *n* **1** a leisurely stroll or ride taken for pleasure, usu in a public place and often as a social custom **2** a place for strolling; *esp, Br* a paved walk along the seafront at a resort

[2]**promenade** *vi* to take or go on a promenade ~ *vt* **1** to walk about in or on **2** to display (as if) by promenading around <~d *his new bicycle in front of his friends*>

promenade concert *n* a concert at which some of the audience stand or can walk about

promenade deck *n* an upper deck or an area on a deck of a passenger ship where passengers may stroll

promenader /promə'nahdə‖prɒmə'nɑːdə/ *n* sby attending a promenade concert

prominence /'prominəns‖'prɒmɪnəns/ *n* **1** being prominent or conspicuous **2** sthg prominent; a projection <*a rocky* ~> **3** a large mass of gas arising from the lower solar atmosphere

prominent /'prominənt‖'prɒmɪnənt/ *adj* **1** projecting beyond a surface or line; protuberant **2a** readily noticeable; conspicuous **b** widely and popularly known; leading – **prominently** *adv*

promiscuity /ˌpromi'skyooh·əti‖ˌprɒmɪ'skjuːətɪ/ *n* **1** a miscellaneous mixture or mingling of people or things **2** promiscuous sexual behaviour

promiscuous /prə'miskyoo·əs‖prə'mɪskjʊəs/ *adj* **1** composed of a mixture of people or things **2** not restricted to 1 class or person; indiscriminate; *esp* not restricted to 1 sexual partner **3** casual, irregular <~ *eating habits*> – **promiscuously** *adv*, **promiscuousness** *n*

[1]**promise** /'promis‖'prɒmɪs/ *n* **1a** a declaration that one will do or refrain from doing sthg specified **b** a legally binding declaration **2** grounds for expectation usu of success, improvement, or excellence <*show* ~> **3** sthg promised

[2]**promise** *vt* **1** to pledge oneself to do, bring about, or provide (sthg for) <~ *aid*> <*but you* ~d *me*> **2** to assure <*it can be done, I* ~ *you*> **3** to betroth **4** to suggest beforehand; indicate <*dark clouds* ~ *rain*> ~ *vi* **1** to make a promise **2** to give grounds for expectation, esp of sthg good

promised land *n* a place or condition believed to promise final satisfaction or realization of hopes

promising /'promising‖'prɒmɪsɪŋ/ *adj* full of promise; likely to succeed or to yield good results – **promisingly** *adv*

promissory note /'promis(ə)ri‖'prɒmɪs(ə)rɪ/ *n* a written promise to pay, either on demand or at a fixed or determinable future time, a sum of money to a specified individual or to the bearer

promontory /'promənt(ə)ri‖'prɒmənt(ə)rɪ/ *n* **1** HEADLAND 2 **2** a bodily prominence

promote /prə'moht‖prə'məʊt/ *vt* **1a** to advance in station, rank, or honour; raise **b** to change (a pawn) into a more valuable piece in chess by moving to the 8th rank **c** to assign to a higher division of a sporting competition (e g a football league) **2a** to contribute to the growth or prosperity of; further <~ *international understanding*> **b** to help bring (e g an enterprise) into being; launch **c** to present (e g merchandise) for public acceptance through advertising and publicity – **promoter** *n*, **promotive** *adj*

promotion /prə'mohsh(ə)n‖prə'məʊʃ(ə)n/ *n* **1** the act or fact of being raised in position or rank; preferment **2a** the act of furthering the growth or development of sthg, esp sales or public awareness **b** sthg (e g a price reduction or free sample) intended to promote esp sales of merchandise – **promotional** *adj*

[1]**prompt** /'prompt‖'prɒmpt/ *vt* **1** to move to action; incite **2** to assist (sby acting or reciting) by saying the next words of sthg forgotten or imperfectly learnt **3** to serve as the inciting cause of; urge – **prompter** *n*

[2]**prompt** *adj* of or for prompting actors

[3]**prompt** *adj* **1a** ready and quick to act as occasion demands **b** PUNCTUAL 2 **2** performed readily or immediately – **promptly** *adv*, **promptness** *n*

[4]**prompt** *n* **1** the act or an instance of prompting; a reminder **2** (the contract fixing) a limit of time given for payment of an account for goods purchased

promulgate /'prom(ə)lˌgayt‖'prɒm(ə)lˌgeɪt/ *vt* to make known by open declaration; proclaim – fml – **promulgator** *n*, **promulgation** *n*

prone /prohn‖prəʊn/ *adj* **1** having a tendency or inclination; disposed *to* **2** having the front or ventral surface downwards; prostrate – **prone** *adv*, **pronely** *adv*, **proneness** *n*

[1]**prong** /prong‖prɒŋ/ *n* **1** any of the slender sharp-pointed parts of a fork **2** a subdivision of an argument, attacking force, etc

[2]**prong** *vt* to stab, pierce, or break up (as if) with a prong

pronged *adj* having or divided into prongs; *esp* having more than 1 attacking force, each coming from a different direction – usu in combination <*a 3*-pronged *attack*>

pronominal /ˌproh'nominl, prə-‖ˌprəʊ'nɒmɪnl, prə-/ *adj* of, resembling, or constituting a pronoun – **pronominally** *adv*

pronoun /'prohnown‖'prəʊnaʊn/ *n* a word used as a substitute for a noun or noun equivalent and referring to a previously named or understood person or thing

pronounce /prə'nowns‖prə'naʊns/ *vt* **1** to declare officially or ceremoniously <*the priest* ~d *them man and wife*> **2** to declare authoritatively or as an opinion <*doctors* ~d *him fit to resume duties*> **3** to utter the sounds of; *esp* to say correctly ~ *vi* **1** to pass judgment; declare one's opinion definitely or authoritatively – often + *on* or *upon* **2** to produce speech sounds <*she* ~s *abominably*> – **pronounceable** *adj*, **pronouncer** *n*

pro'nounced *adj* strongly marked; decided – **pronouncedly** *adv*

pro'nouncement /-mənt‖-mənt/ *n* **1** a usu formal declaration of opinion **2** an authoritative announcement

pronto /'prontoh‖'prɒntəʊ/ *adv* without delay; quickly – infml [Spanish, fr Latin *promptus* prompt]

pronunciation /prəˌnunsi'aysh(ə)n‖prəˌnʌnsɪ'eɪʃ(ə)n/ *n* the act or manner of pronouncing sthg – **pronunciational** *adj*

[1]**proof** /proohf‖pruːf/ *n* **1** the cogency of evidence that compels acceptance of a truth or a fact **2** an act, effort, or operation designed to establish or discover a fact or the truth; a test **3** legal evidence **4a** an impression (e g from type) taken for examination or correction **b** a proof impression of an engraving, lithograph, etc **c** a test photographic print **5** a test of the quality of an article or substance **6** the alcoholic content of a beverage compared with the standard for

proof spirit

[2]**proof** *adj* **1** designed for or successful in resisting or repelling; impervious – often in combination <*water*proof> **2** used in proving or testing or as a standard of comparison **3** of standard strength or quality or alcoholic content

[3]**proof** *vt* **1** to make or take a proof of **2** to give a resistant quality to; make (sthg) proof *against* – **proofer** *n*

'**proof,read** /-,reed‖-,ri:d/ *vt* to read and mark corrections on (a proof) – **proofreader** *n*

proof spirit *n* a mixture of alcohol and water containing a standard amount of alcohol, in Britain 57.1% by volume

[1]**prop** /prop‖prɒp/ *n* **1** a rigid usu auxiliary vertical support (e g a pole) **2** a source of strength or support **3** PROP FORWARD

[2]**prop** *vt* **-pp- 1** to support by placing sthg under or against **2** to support by placing against sthg *USE* often + *up*; compare PROP UP

[3]**prop** /prop‖prɒp/ *n* any article or object used in a play or film other than painted scenery or costumes

[4]**prop** /prop‖prɒp/ *n* a propeller

propaganda /,propə'gandə‖,prɒpə'gændə/ *n* **1** *cap* a division of the Roman curia having jurisdiction over missionary territories and related institutions **2** (the usu organized spreading of) ideas, information, or rumour designed to promote or damage an institution, movement, person, etc [Modern Latin, fr *Congregatio de Propaganda fide* Congregation for propagating the Faith, a missionary organization established by Pope Gregory XV in 1622]

propagand·ize, -ise /,propə'gandiez‖,prɒpə'gændaɪz/ *vb* to subject to or carry on propaganda – **propagandism** *n*, **propagandist** *n or adj*, **propagandistic** *adj*, **propagandistically** *adv*

propagate /'propə,gayt‖'prɒpə,geɪt/ *vt* **1** to reproduce or increase by sexual or asexual reproduction **2** to pass down (e g a characteristic) to offspring **3a** to cause to spread out and affect a greater number or area; disseminate **b** to publicize <~ *the Gospel*> **c** to transmit ~ *vi* **1** to multiply sexually or asexually **2** to increase, extend – **propagator** *n*, **propagable** *adj*, **propagative** *adj*

propagation /,propə'gaysh(ə)n‖,prɒpə'geɪʃ(ə)n/ *n* **1** an increase (e g of a type of organism) in numbers **2** the spreading of sthg (e g a belief) abroad or into new regions **3** an enlargement or extension (e g of a crack) in a solid body – **propagational** *adj*

propane /'prohpayn‖'prəʊpeɪn/ *n* a hydrocarbon of the alkane series used as a fuel

propel /prə'pel‖prə'pel/ *vt* **-ll- 1** to drive forwards by means of a force that imparts motion **2** to urge on; motivate

propellant *also* **propellent** /prə'pelənt‖prə'pelənt/ *n* sthg that propels: e g **a** a fuel for propelling projectiles **b** fuel plus oxidizer used by a rocket engine **c** a gas in a pressurized container for expelling the contents when the pressure is released

pro'peller *also* **propellor** /prə'pelə‖prə'pelə/ *n* SCREW PROPELLER

propelling pencil /prə'peling‖prə'pelɪŋ/ *n*, *Br* a usu metal or plastic pencil whose lead can be extended by a screw device

propensity /prə'pensəti‖prə'pensətɪ/ *n* a natural inclination or tendency – fml

[1]**proper** /'propə‖'prɒpə/ *adj* **1** suitable, appropriate **2** appointed for the liturgy of a particular day **3** belonging to one; own **4** represented heraldically in natural colour **5** belonging characteristically *to* a species or individual; peculiar **6** being strictly so-called <*the borough is not part of the city* ~> **7a** strictly accurate; correct **b** strictly decorous; genteel <*a very prim and* ~ *gentleman*> **8** *chiefly Br* thorough, complete <*I felt a* ~ *fool!*> – **properness** *n*

[2]**proper** *n* the parts of the mass that vary according to the liturgical calendar

[3]**proper** *adv*, *chiefly dial* in a thorough manner; completely

proper fraction *n* a fraction in which the numerator is less or of lower degree than the denominator

'**properly** /-li‖-lɪ/ *adv* **1** in a fit manner; suitably **2** strictly in accordance with fact; correctly <~ *speaking*> **3** *chiefly Br* to the full extent; completely

proper noun *n* a noun that designates a particular being or thing and is usu capitalized (e g *Janet, London*)

propertied /'propətid‖'prɒpətɪd/ *adj* possessing property, esp land

property /'propəti‖'prɒpətɪ/ *n* **1a** a quality, attribute, or power inherent in sthg **b** an attribute common to all members of a class **2a** sthg owned or possessed; *specif* a piece of real estate **b** ownership **c** sthg to which a person has a legal title **3** [3]PROP – **propertyless** *adj*

prop forward *n* (the position of) either of the 2 players in rugby on either side of the hooker in the front row of the scrum

prophecy /'profisi‖'prɒfɪsɪ/ *n* **1** the function or vocation of a prophet; (the capacity to utter) an inspired declaration of divine will and purpose **2** a prediction of an event

prophesy /'profisie‖'prɒfɪsaɪ/ *vt* **1** to utter (as if) by divine inspiration **2** to predict with assurance or on the basis of mystic knowledge ~ *vi* **1** to speak as if divinely inspired **2** to make a prediction – **prophesier** *n*

prophet /'profit‖'prɒfɪt/, *fem* **prophetess** /-tes, -'tes‖-tes, -'tes/ *n* **1** a person who utters divinely inspired revelations; *specif, often cap* the writer of any of the prophetic books of the Old Testament **2** one gifted with more than ordinary spiritual and moral insight **3** one who foretells future events; a predictor **4** a spokesman for a doctrine, movement, etc <*a* ~ *of socialism*> [Old French *prophete*, fr Latin *propheta*, fr Greek *prophētēs*, fr *pro* for + *phanai* to speak]

prophetic /prə'fetik‖prə'fetɪk/, **prophetical** /-kl‖-kl/ *adj* **1** (characteristic) of a prophet or prophecy **2** foretelling events; predictive – **prophetically** *adv*

Prophets /'profits‖'prɒfɪts/ *n pl* the second part of the Jewish scriptures

prophylactic /,profi'laktik‖,prɒfɪ'læktɪk/ *adj* **1** guarding or protecting from or preventing disease **2** tending to prevent or ward off; preventive – fml – **prophylactic** *n*, **prophylactically** *adv*

prophylaxis /ˌprofiˈlaksis‖ˌprɒfiˈlæksɪs/ *n, pl* **prophylaxes** /-ˈlakˌseez‖-ˈlækˌsiːz/ measures designed to preserve health and prevent the spread of disease

propinquity /prəˈpingkwəti‖prəˈpɪŋkwətɪ/ *n* **1** nearness of blood; kinship **2** nearness in place or time; proximity ***USE*** fml

propitiate /prəˈpishiˌayt‖prəˈpɪʃɪˌeɪt/ *vt* to gain or regain the favour or goodwill of; appease – **propitiator** *n*, **propitiable** *adj*, **propitiatory** *adj*, **propitiation** *n*

propitious /prəˈpishəs‖prəˈpɪʃəs/ *adj* **1** favourably disposed; benevolent **2** boding well; auspicious **3** tending to favour; opportune <*a ~ moment for the revolt to break out*> – **propitiously** *adv*, **propitiousness** *n*

propjet /ˈpropˌjet‖ˈprɒpˌdʒet/ *n* a turboprop

proponent /prəˈpohnənt‖prəˈpəʊnənt/ *n* one who argues in favour of sthg; an advocate

[1]**proportion** /prəˈpawsh(ə)n‖prəˈpɔːʃ(ə)n/ *n* **1** the relation of one part to another or to the whole with respect to magnitude, quantity, or degree **2** harmonious relation of parts to each other or to the whole; balance **3** a statement of equality of 2 ratios (e g in 4/2=10/5) **4a** proper or equal share <*each did his ~ of the work*> **b** a quota, percentage **5** *pl* size, dimension

[2]**proportion** *vt* **1** to adjust (a part or thing) in proportion to other parts or things **2** to make the parts of harmonious or symmetrical

[1]**proportional** /prəˈpawsh(ə)nl‖prəˈpɔːʃ(ə)nl/ *adj* **1a** proportionate – usu + *to* <a *is ~ to* b> **b** having the same or a constant ratio **2** regulated or determined in proportionate amount or degree – **proportionally** *adv*, **proportionality** *n*

[2]**proportional** *n* a number or quantity in a proportion

proportional representation *n* an electoral system designed to represent in a legislative body each political group in proportion to its voting strength in the electorate

[1]**proportionate** /prəˈpawsh(ə)nət‖prəˈpɔːʃ(ə)nət/ *adj* being in due proportion – **proportionately** *adv*

[2]**proportionate** /prəˈpawsh(ə)ˌnayt‖prəˈpɔːʃ(ə)ˌneɪt/ *vt* to make proportionate; proportion

proposal /prəˈpohzl‖prəˈpəʊzl/ *n* **1** an act of putting forward or stating sthg for consideration **2a** a proposed idea or plan of action; a suggestion **b** an offer of marriage **3** an application for insurance

propose /prəˈpohz‖prəˈpəʊz/ *vi* **1** to form or put forward a plan or intention <*man ~s, but God disposes*> **2** to make an offer of marriage ~ *vt* **1a** to present for consideration or adoption <*~d terms for peace*> **b** to establish as an aim; intend <*~d to spend the summer in study*> **2a** to recommend to fill a place or vacancy; nominate **b** to nominate (oneself) for an insurance policy **c** to offer as a toast <*~ the health of the bridesmaids*> – **proposer** *n*

[1]**proposition** /ˌpropəˈzish(ə)n‖ˌprɒpəˈzɪʃ(ə)n/ *n* **1a** sthg offered for consideration or acceptance; *specif* a proposal of sexual intercourse **b** a formal mathematical statement to be proved **2** an expression, in language or signs, of sthg that can be either true or false **3** a project, situation, or individual requiring to be dealt with <*the firm is not a paying ~*> – **propositional** *adj*

[2]**proposition** *vt* to make a proposal to; *specif* to propose sexual intercourse to

propound /prəˈpownd‖prəˈpaʊnd/ *vt* to offer for discussion or consideration – fml – **propounder** *n*

[1]**proprietary** /prəˈprie·ət(ə)ri‖prəˈpraɪət(ə)rɪ/ *n* a body of proprietors

[2]**proprietary** *adj* **1** (characteristic) of a proprietor <*~ rights*> **2** made and marketed under a patent, trademark, etc <*a ~ process*> **3** privately owned and managed <*a ~ clinic*>

proprietor /prəˈprie·ətə‖prəˈpraɪətə/, *fem* **proprietress** /-tris‖-trɪs/ *n* **1** an owner **2** sby having an interest less than absolute right – **proprietorship** *n*, **proprietorial** *adj*

propriety /prəˈprie·əti‖prəˈpraɪətɪ/ *n* **1** the quality or state of being proper; fitness **2** the standard of what is socially or morally acceptable in conduct or speech, esp between the sexes; decorum **3** *pl* the conventions and manners of polite society ***USE*** fml

propulsion /prəˈpulsh(ə)n‖prəˈpʌlʃ(ə)n/ *n* **1** the action or process of propelling **2** sthg that propels

propulsive /prəˈpulsiv‖prəˈpʌlsɪv/ *adj* having power to or tending to propel

prop up *vt* to give nonmaterial (e g moral or financial) support to

propylene /ˈpropileen‖ˈprɒpɪliːn/ *n* a hydrocarbon of the alkene series used chiefly in organic synthesis

pro rata /ˌproh ˈrahtə‖ˌprəʊ ˈrɑːtə/ *adv* proportionately according to an exactly calculable factor – **pro rata** *adj*

prorogue /prəˈrohg, ˌproh-‖prəˈrəʊg, ˌprəʊ-/ *vt* to terminate a session of (e g a parliament) by royal prerogative ~*vi* to suspend a legislative session – **prorogation** *n*

prosaic /prohˈzayik, prə-‖prəʊˈzeɪɪk, prə-/ *adj* **1a** characteristic of prose as distinguished from poetry **b** dull, unimaginative **2** belonging to the everyday world; commonplace – **prosaically** *adv*

proscenium /prohˈseenyəm, prə-, -ni·əm‖prəʊˈsiːnjəm, prə-, -nɪəm/ *n* the stage of an ancient Greek or Roman theatre

proscribe /prohˈskrieb‖prəʊˈskraɪb/ *vt* **1a** to put outside the protection of the law **b** to outlaw, exile; *specif, in ancient Rome* to outlaw by publishing the name of (a person) **2** to condemn or forbid as harmful; prohibit – **proscriber** *n*

proscription /prəˈskripsh(ə)n, proh-‖prəˈskrɪpʃ(ə)n, prəʊ-/ *n* **1** proscribing or being proscribed **2** an imposed restraint or restriction; a prohibition – **proscriptive** *adj*, **proscriptively** *adv*

prose /prohz‖prəʊz/ *n* **1a** ordinary nonmetrical language **b** a literary medium distinguished from poetry esp by its closer correspondence to the patterns of everyday speech **2** a commonplace quality or character; ordinariness [Middle French, fr Latin *prosa* (*oratio*), lit., straight forward (speech), *prorsus, prosus* straightforward, fr *provertere* to turn forwards, fr *pro-* forwards + *vertere* to turn] – **prose** *adj*

prosecute /ˈprosikyooht‖ˈprɒsɪkjuːt/ *vt* **1a** to institute and pursue criminal proceedings against **b** to institute legal proceedings with reference to < ~ *a claim*> **2** to follow through, pursue <*determined to ~ the investigation*> **3** CARRY OUT 1 ~*vi* to institute and carry on a prosecution *USE* (*2&3*) fml

prosecution /prosi'kyoohsh(ə)n‖prɒsɪ'kjuːʃ(ə)n/ *n* **1** prosecuting; *specif* the formal institution of a criminal charge **2** *sing or pl in constr* the party by whom criminal proceedings are instituted or conducted

prosecutor /'prosikyoohtə‖'prɒsɪkjuːtə/ *n* sby who institutes or conducts an official prosecution

[1]**proselyte** /'prosiliet‖'prɒsɪlaɪt/ *n* a new convert, esp to Judaism

[2]**proselyte** *vb, chiefly NAm* to proselytize

proselyt·ize, **-ise** /'prosili,tiez‖'prɒsɪlɪ,taɪz/ *vt* to convert (sby), esp to a new religion ~*vi* to (try to) make converts, esp to a new religion – **proselytizer** *n*, **proselytization** *n*

'**prose ,poem** *n* a work in prose that has some of the qualities of a poem – **prose poet** *n*

prosody /'prosədi‖'prɒsədɪ/ *n* the study of versification and esp of metrical structure – **prosodist** *n*, **prosodic** *adj*

[1]**prospect** /'prospekt‖'prɒspekt/ *n* **1** an extensive view; a scene **2a** a mental picture of sthg to come <*doesn't like the ~ of more examinations*> **b** expectation, possibility <*has a fine career in ~*> **c** *pl* **c(1)** financial and social expectations **c(2)** chances, esp of success **3a** a place showing signs of containing a mineral deposit **b** a partly developed mine **c** the mineral yield of a tested sample of ore or gravel **4** a potential client, candidate, etc

[2]**prospect** /prə'spekt‖prə'spekt/ *vb* to explore (an area), esp for mineral deposits – **prospector** *n*

prospective /prə'spektiv‖prə'spektɪv/ *adj* **1** likely to come about; expected **2** likely to be or become <*a ~ mother*> – **prospectively** *adv*

prospectus /prə'spektəs‖prə'spektəs/ *n* a printed statement, brochure, etc describing an organization or enterprise and distributed to prospective buyers, investors, or participants

prosper /prospə‖prɒspə/ *vi* to succeed, thrive; *specif* to achieve economic success ~*vt* to cause to succeed or thrive <*may the gods ~ our city*>

prosperity /pro'sperəti, prə-‖prɒ'sperətɪ, prə-/ *n* the condition of being successful or thriving; *esp* economic well-being

prosperous /'prosp(ə)rəs‖'prɒsp(ə)rəs/ *adj* marked by esp financial success – **prosperously** *adv*

[1]**prostate** /'prostayt‖'prɒsteɪt/, **prostate gland** *n* a partly muscular, partly glandular body situated around the base of the male mammalian urethra that secretes a major constituent of the ejaculatory fluid

[2]**prostate** *also* **prostatic** /pro'statik, prə-‖prɒ'stætɪk, prə-/ *adj* of or being the prostate gland

prosthesis /'prosthəsis, -'thee-‖'prɒsθəsɪs, -'θiː-/ *n, pl* **prostheses** /-,seez‖-,siːz/ an artificial device to replace a missing part of the body

[1]**prostitute** /'prosti,tyooht‖'prɒstɪ,tjuːt/ *vt* **1** to make a prostitute of **2** to devote to corrupt or unworthy purposes; debase < ~ *one's talents*> – **prostitution** *n*

[2]**prostitute** *n* a person, esp a woman, who engages in sexual practices for money

[1]**prostrate** /'prostrayt‖'prɒstreɪt/ *adj* **1** lying full-length face downwards, esp in adoration or submission **2a** physically and emotionally weak; overcome < ~ *with grief*> **b** physically exhausted **3** *of a plant* trailing on the ground

[2]**prostrate** /pro'strayt‖prɒ'streɪt/ *vt* **1** to throw or put into a prostrate position **2** to put (oneself) in a humble and submissive posture or state **3** to reduce to submission, helplessness, or exhaustion; overcome – **prostration** *n*

prosy /'prohzi‖'prəʊzɪ/ *adj* dull, commonplace; *esp* tedious in speech or manner – **prosily** *adv*

prot-, **proto-** *comb form* first in time; earliest; original <proto*type*>

protagonist /proh'tagənist, prə-‖prəʊ'tægənɪst, prə-/ *n* **1** one who takes the leading part in a drama, novel, or story **2** a leader or notable supporter of a cause [Greek *prōtagōnistēs*, fr *prōtos* first + *agōnistēs* competitor at games, actor, fr *agōn* contest, competition at games]

protean /proh'tee·ən‖prəʊ'tiːən/ *adj* **1** readily assuming different shapes or roles **2** displaying great diversity or variety [*Proteus*, mythological sea god with the power of assuming different shapes]

protect /prə'tekt‖prə'tekt/ *vt* **1** to cover or shield *from* injury or destruction; guard *against* **2** to shield or foster (a home industry) by a protective tariff – **protectant** *n*, **protective** *adj*, **protectively** *adv*, **protectiveness** *n*

protection /prə'teksh(ə)n‖prə'tekʃ(ə)n/ *n* **1** protecting or being protected **2** sthg that protects **3** the shielding of the producers of a country from foreign competition by import tariffs **4a** immunity from threatened violence, often purchased under duress **b** money extorted by racketeers posing as a protective association **5** COVERAGE 3a

pro'tectionist /-ist‖-ɪst/ *n* an advocate of government economic protection – **protectionism** *n*, **protectionist** *adj*

pro,tective 'custody *n* detention of sby (allegedly) for his/her own safety

pro'tector /prə'tektə‖prə'tektə/, *fem* **protectress** /-tris‖-trɪs/ *n* **1a** a guardian **b** a device used to prevent injury; a guard **2** *often cap* the executive head of the Commonwealth from 1653 to 1659 – **protectorship** *n*

protectorate /prə'tekt(ə)rət‖prə'tekt(ə)rət/ *n* **1a** government by a protector **b** *often cap* the government of the Commonwealth from 1653 to 1659 **c** the rank or (period of) rule of a protector **2a** the relationship of one state over another dependent state which it partly controls but has not annexed **b** the dependent political unit in such a relationship

protégé, *fem* **protégée** /'protə,zhay, 'proh-, -tay-‖'prɒtə,ʒeɪ, 'prəʊ-, -teɪ- (*Fr* prɔteʒe)/ *n* a person under the protection, guidance, or patronage of sby influential [French, fr past participle of *protéger* to protect, fr Latin *protegere*]

protein /'prohteen‖'prəʊtiːn/ *n* any of numerous genetically specified naturally occurring extremely complex combinations of amino acids linked by peptide bonds that are essential constituents of all living cells and are an essential part of the diet of animals and humans [French *protéine*, fr Late Greek *prōteios* primary, fr Greek *prōtos* first] – **proteinaceous** *adj*

pro tem /ˌproh 'tem‖ˌprəʊ 'tem/ *adv* for the time being [short for *pro tempore*, fr Latin]

[1]**protest** /'prohtest‖'prəʊtest/ *n* **1a** a sworn declaration that a note or bill has been duly presented and that payment has been refused **b** a formal declaration of dissent from an act of esp a legislature **c** a formal declaration of disapproval <*reprieved in response to international* ~s> **2** protesting; *esp* an organized public demonstration of disapproval **3** an objection or display of unwillingness <*went to the dentist under* ~>

[2]**protest** /prə'test‖prə'test/ *vt* **1** to make formal or solemn declaration or affirmation of **2** to execute or have executed a formal protest against (e g a bill or note) **3** *NAm* to make a formal protest against **4** *NAm* to remonstrate against <*unwilling to* ~ *the cost of her ticket*> ~ *vi* **1** to make a protestation **2** to enter a protest – **protester, protestor** *n*

protestant /'protistənt‖'prɒtɪstənt/ *n* **1** *cap* **1a** any of a group who protested against an edict of the Diet of Spires in 1529 intended to suppress the Lutheran movement **b** a Christian who denies the universal authority of the pope and affirms the principles of the Reformation **2** one who makes or enters a protest – **Protestantism** *n*

Protestant *adj* of Protestants, their churches, or their religion

protestation /ˌprote'staysh(ə)n, proh-, -ti-‖ˌprɒte'steɪʃ(ə)n, prəʊ-, -tɪ-/ *n* **1** an act of protesting **2** a solemn declaration or avowal

proto- – see PROT-

protocol /'prohtəkol‖'prəʊtəkɒl/ *n* **1** an original draft or record of a document or transaction **2** a preliminary memorandum often formulated and signed by diplomatic negotiators as a basis for a final treaty **3** a code of correct etiquette and precedence **4** *NAm* the plan of a scientific experiment or treatment

proton /'prohton‖'prəʊtɒn/ *n* an elementary particle that is identical with the nucleus of the hydrogen atom, that along with neutrons is a constituent of all other atomic nuclei, that carries a positive charge numerically equal to the charge of an electron, and that has a mass of 1.672×10^{-27}kg – **protonic** *adj*

protoplasm /'prohtəˌplaz(ə)m‖'prəʊtəˌplæz(ə)m/ *n* **1** the organized complex of organic and inorganic substances (e g proteins and salts in solution) that constitutes the living nucleus, cytoplasm, plastids, and mitochondria of the cell **2** cytoplasm – **protoplasmic** *adj*

prototype /'prohtəˌtiep, -toh-‖'prəʊtəˌtaɪp, -təʊ-/ *n* **1** an original model on which sthg is based; an archetype **2** sby or sthg that has the essential features of a later type <*the battle chariot is the* ~ *of the modern tank*> **3** sby or sthg that exemplifies the essential or typical features of a type <*mathematics is the* ~ *of logical thinking*> **4** a first full-scale and usu operational form of a new type or design of a construction (e g an aeroplane) – **prototypal** *adj*

protozoan /ˌprohtə'zoh·ən‖ˌprəʊtə'zəʊən/ *n* any of a phylum or subkingdom of minute single-celled animals which have varied structure and physiology and often complex life cycles – **protozoal** *adj*, **protozoan** *adj*, **protozoic** *adj*

protozoon /ˌprohtə'zoh·on‖ˌprəʊtə'zəʊɒn/ *n*, *pl* **protozoa** /-'zoh·ə‖-'zəʊə/ a protozoan

protract /prə'trakt‖prə'trækt/ *vt* **1** to prolong in time or space **2** to lay down the lines and angles of with scale and protractor **3** to extend forwards or outwards – **protraction** *n*, **protractive** *adj*

protractor /prə'traktə‖prə'træktə/ *n* **1** a muscle that extends a body part **2** an instrument that is used for marking out or measuring angles in drawing

protrude /prə'troohd‖prə'tru:d/ *vb* to (cause to) jut out from the surrounding surface or place – **protrusion** *n*, **protrusive** *adj*

protuberant /prə'tyoohb(ə)rənt‖prə'tju:b(ə)rənt/ *adj* thrusting or projecting out from a surrounding or adjacent surface – **protuberance** *n*

proud /prowd‖praʊd/ *adj* **1a** having or displaying excessive self-esteem **b** much pleased; exultant **c** having proper self-respect **2a** stately, magnificent **b** giving reason for pride; glorious <*the* ~est *moment of her life*> **3** projecting slightly from a surrounding surface – **proudly** *adv*

prove /proohv‖pru:v/ *vb* **proved, proven** /'proohv(ə)n‖'pru:v(ə)n/ *vt* **1a** to test the quality of; try out <*the exception* ~s *the rule*> **b** to subject to a testing process **2a** to establish the truth or validity of by evidence or demonstration **b** to check the correctness of (e g an arithmetical operation) **3a** to verify the genuineness of; *specif* to obtain probate of **b** PROOF 1 **4** to allow (bread dough) to rise and become light before baking ~ *vi* **1** to turn out, esp after trial <*the new drug* ~d *to be effective*> **2** *of bread dough* to rise and become aerated through the action of yeast

provenance /'provənəns‖'prɒvənəns/ *n* an origin, source – used esp with reference to works of art or literature

Provençal /ˌprovonh'sahl ‖ˌprɒvɑ̃'sɑ:l (*Fr* prɔvɑ̃sal)/ *n* **1** a native or inhabitant of Provence **2** a Romance language of SE France – **Provençal** *adj*

provender /'provində‖'prɒvɪndə/ *n* **1** dry food for domestic animals **2** food, provisions – humor

proverb /'provuhb‖'prɒvɜ:b/ *n* a brief popular epigram or maxim; an adage

proverbial /prə'vuhbyəl, -bi·əl‖prə'vɜ:bjəl, -bɪəl/ *adj* **1** of or like a proverb **2** that has become a proverb or byword; commonly spoken of – **proverbially** *adv*

provide /prə'vied‖prə'vaɪd/ *vi* **1** to take precautionary measures <~d *against future loss*> **2** to make a proviso or stipulation <*the regulations* ~ *for 2 directors*> **3** to supply what is needed for sustenance or support <~s *for a large family*> ~ *vt* **1a** to furnish, equip *with* <~ *the children with new shoes*> **b** to supply, afford <*curtains* ~ *privacy*> **2** to stipulate

pro'vided *conj* providing

providence /'provid(ə)ns‖'prɒvɪd(ə)ns/ *n* **1**

cap God conceived as the power sustaining and guiding human destiny **2** being provident

provident /ˈprovid(ə)nt||ˈprɒvɪd(ə)nt/ *adj* making provision for the future, esp by saving – **providently** *adv*

providential /ˌproviˈdensh(ə)l||ˌprɒvɪˈdenʃ(ə)l/ *adj* of or determined (as if) by Providence; lucky – **providentially** *adv*

provider /prəˈviedə||prəˈvaɪdə/ *n* one who provides for his/her family

providing /prəˈvieding||prəˈvaɪdɪŋ/ *conj* on condition; if and only if <*may come ~ that you pay for yourself*>

province /ˈprovins||ˈprɒvɪns/ *n* **1a** an administrative district of a country **b** *pl* all of a country except the metropolis – usu + *the* **2** a territorial unit of religious administration **3a** proper or appropriate function or scope; sphere **b** a field of knowledge or activity

[1]**provincial** /prəˈvinsh(ə)l||prəˈvɪnʃ(ə)l/ *n* **1** the head of a province of a Roman Catholic religious order **2** one living in or coming from a province **3a** a person with a narrow outlook **b** a person lacking polish or refinement

[2]**provincial** *adj* **1** of or coming from a province **2a** limited in outlook; narrow **b** lacking polish; unsophisticated – **provincialism** *n*, **provincialize** *vt*

ˈ**proving ˌground** /ˈproohving||ˈpruːvɪŋ/ *n* **1** a place designed for or used in scientific experimentation or testing; *esp* a place for testing vehicles **2** a place where sthg new is tried out

[1]**provision** /prəˈvizh(ə)n||prəˈvɪʒ(ə)n/ *n* **1a** providing **b** a measure taken beforehand; a preparation <*no ~ made for replacements*> **2** *pl* a stock of food or other necessary goods **3** a proviso, stipulation

[2]**provision** *vt* to supply with provisions

provisional /prəˈvizh(ə)nl||prəˈvɪʒ(ə)nl/ *adj* serving for the time being; temporary; *specif* requiring later confirmation <*gave her ~ consent*> – **provisionally** *adv*

Provisional *adj* of or being the secret terrorist wing of the IRA – **Provisional** *n*

proviso /prəˈviezoh||prəˈvaɪzəʊ/ *n, pl* **provisos, provisoes** **1** a clause that introduces a condition **2** a conditional stipulation

provocation /ˌprovəˈkaysh(ə)n||ˌprɒvəˈkeɪʃ(ə)n/ *n* **1** an act of provoking; incitement **2** sthg that provokes or arouses

provocative /prəˈvokətiv||prəˈvɒkətɪv/ *adj* serving or tending to provoke or arouse to indignation, sexual desire, etc – **provocatively** *adv*, **provocativeness** *n*

provoke /prəˈvohk||prəˈvəʊk/ *vt* **1** to incite to anger; incense **2a** to call forth; evoke **b** to stir up on purpose; induce <*always trying to ~ an argument*>

provoking /prəˈvohking||prəˈvəʊkɪŋ/ *adj* causing mild anger; annoying – **provokingly** *adv*

provost /ˈprovəst||ˈprɒvəst/ *n* **1** the head of a collegiate or cathedral chapter; *specif* one who is also the incumbent of a parish of which the cathedral is the church **2** the chief magistrate of a Scottish burgh **3** the head of certain colleges at Oxford, Cambridge, etc

proˌvost ˈmarshal /prəˈvoh||prəˈvəʊ/ *n* an officer who supervises the military police of a command

prow /prow||praʊ/ *n* **1** the bow of a ship **2** a pointed projecting front part

prowess /ˈprowis||ˈpraʊɪs/ *n* **1** outstanding (military) valour and skill **2** outstanding ability

[1]**prowl** /prowl||praʊl/ *vb* to move about (in) or roam (over) in a stealthy or predatory manner – **prowler** *n*

[2]**prowl** *n* an act or instance of prowling

proximal /ˈproksim(ə)l||ˈprɒksɪm(ə)l/ *adj, esp of an anatomical part* next to or nearest the point of attachment or origin – **proximally** *adv*

proximate /ˈproksimət||ˈprɒksɪmət/ *adj* **1a** very near; close **b** forthcoming; imminent **2** next preceding or following; *specif* next in a chain of cause and effect *USE* fml – **proximately** *adv*, **proximateness** *n*

proximity /prokˈsiməti||prɒkˈsɪmətɪ/ *n* being close in space, time, or association; *esp* nearness – fml

proximo /ˈproksimoh||ˈprɒksɪməʊ/ *adj* of or occurring in the next month after the present [Latin *proximo mense* in the next month]

proxy /ˈproksi||ˈprɒksɪ/ *n* **1** (the agency, function, or office of) a deputy authorized to act as a substitute for another <*marriage by ~*> **2** (a document giving) authority to act or vote for another – **proxy** *adj*

prude /proohd||pruːd/ *n* one who shows or affects extreme modesty or propriety, esp in sexual matters

prudence /ˈproohd(ə)ns||ˈpruːd(ə)ns/ *n* **1** discretion or shrewdness in the management of affairs **2** skill and good judgment in the use of resources; frugality **3** caution or circumspection with regard to danger or risk

prudent /ˈproohd(ə)nt||ˈpruːd(ə)nt/ *adj* characterized by, arising from, or showing prudence – **prudently** *adv*

prudential /proohˈdensh(ə)l||pruːˈdenʃ(ə)l/ *adj* **1** of or proceeding from prudence **2** exercising prudence, esp in business matters – **prudentially** *adv*

prudery /ˈproohd(ə)ri||ˈpruːd(ə)rɪ/ *n* **1** the quality of being a prude **2** a prudish act or remark

prudish /ˈproohdish||ˈpruːdɪʃ/ *adj* marked by prudery; priggish – **prudishly** *adv*, **prudishness** *n*

[1]**prune** /proohn||pruːn/ *n* a plum dried or capable of drying without fermentation

[2]**prune** *vt* **1** to cut off the dead or unwanted parts of (a usu woody plant or shrub) **2a** to reduce by eliminating superfluous matter <~d *the text*> **b** to remove as superfluous <*~ away all ornamentation*> *~vi* to cut away what is unwanted

prurient /ˈprooəri·ənt||ˈprʊərɪənt/ *adj* inclined to, having, or arousing an excessive or unhealthy interest in sexual matters – **prurience** *n*

pruritus /proo(ə)ˈrietəs||prʊ(ə)ˈraɪtəs/ *n* ITCH 1

ˌ**Prussian ˈblue** /ˈprush(ə)n||ˈprʌʃ(ə)n/ *n* **1** any of numerous blue iron pigments **2** a dark blue hydrated salt of iron and cyanide used as a test for ferric iron **3** a strong greenish blue colour

ˌ**prussic ˈacid** /ˈprusik||ˈprʌsɪk/ *n* HYDROCYANIC ACID

1**pry** /prie‖praɪ/ *vi* **1** to inquire in an overinquisitive or impertinent manner *into* **2** to look closely or inquisitively at sby's possessions, actions, etc < ~ing *neighbours*>

2**pry** *vt, chiefly NAm* 5PRIZE

psalm /sahm‖sɑːm/ *n, often cap* any of the sacred songs attributed to King David and collected in the Book of Psalms [Old English *psealm*, fr Late Latin *psalmus*, fr Greek *psalmos*, lit., twanging of a harp, fr *psallein* to pluck, play a stringed instrument]

psalmody /ˈsahmədi, ˈsalmədi‖ˈsɑːmədɪ, ˈsælmədɪ/ *n* **1** (the practice or art of) singing psalms in worship **2** a collection of psalms

Psalter /ˈsawltə‖ˈsɔːltə/ *n* a book containing a collection of Psalms for liturgical or devotional use

psaltery *also* **psaltry** /ˈsawlt(ə)ri‖ˈsɔːlt(ə)rɪ/ *n* an ancient stringed musical instrument similar to the dulcimer but plucked

psephology /seˈfoləji‖seˈfɒlədʒɪ/ *n* the scientific study of elections [Greek *psēphos* pebble, ballot, vote; fr the use of pebbles by the ancient Greeks in voting] – **psephologist** *n*, **psephological** *adj*

pseud /s(y)oohd‖s(j)uːd/ *n, chiefly Br* an intellectually or socially pretentious person – infml – **pseud** *adj*, **pseudy** *adj*

pseudo /ˈs(y)oohdoh‖ˈs(j)uːdəʊ/ *adj* apparent rather than actual; spurious <*distinction between true and ~ freedom*>

pseudo-, **pseud-** *comb form* false; sham; spurious <pseudo*science*> <pseud*axis*> <pseudo-*intellectual*>

pseudonym /ˈs(y)oohdəˌnim‖ˈs(j)uːdəˌnɪm/ *n* a fictitious name; *esp* one used by an author

pseudonymous /s(y)oohˈdoniməs‖s(j)uːˈdɒnɪməs/ *adj* bearing, using, or being a pseudonym [Greek *pseudōnymos*, fr *pseudēs* false + *onoma, onyma* name] – **pseudonymously** *adv*

pseudopodium /ˌs(y)oohdəˈpohdi·əm‖ˌs(j)uːdəˈpəʊdɪəm/ *n, pl* **pseudopodia** /-di·ə‖-dɪə/ a temporary protrusion of a cell (e g an amoeba) that serves to take in food, move the cell, etc

pshaw /(p)shaw‖(p)ʃɔː/ *interj* – used to express irritation, disapproval, or disbelief

psittacosis /ˌ(p)sitəˈkohsis‖ˌ(p)sɪtəˈkəʊsɪs/ *n* a severe infectious disease of birds caused by a rickettsia that causes a serious pneumonia when transmitted to human beings – **psittacotic** *adj*

psoriasis /(p)soˈrie·əsis, (p)sə-‖(p)sɒˈraɪəsɪs, (p)sə-/ *n* a chronic skin condition characterized by distinct red patches covered by white scales – **psoriatic** *adj or n*

psych, **psyche** /siek‖saɪk/ *vt* **1** *NAm* to psychoanalyse **2** *chiefly NAm* **2a** to anticipate correctly the intentions or actions of; outguess **b** to analyse or work out (e g a problem or course of action) <*I* ~ed *it all out by myself*> **3** *chiefly NAm* **3a** to make psychologically uneasy; intimidate – often + *out* **b** to make (oneself) psychologically ready for some action, test, etc – usu + *up* < ~ed *herself up for the race*> *USE* infml

psych- /siek-‖saɪk-/, **psycho-** *comb form* **1** psyche <psycho*gnosis*> **2a** mind; mental processes <psycho*active*> <psycho*logy*> **b** using psychoanalytical methods <psycho*therapy*> **c** brain <psycho*surgery*> **d** mental and <psycho*somatic*>

psyche /ˈsieki‖ˈsaɪkɪ/ *n* **1** the soul, self **2** the mind

psychedelic /ˌsiekəˈdelik‖ˌsaɪkəˈdelɪk/ *adj* **1a** *of drugs* capable of producing altered states of consciousness that involve changed mental and sensory awareness, hallucinations, etc **b** produced by or associated with the use of psychedelic drugs **2a** imitating or reproducing effects (e g distorted or bizarre images or sounds) resembling those produced by psychedelic drugs <*a ~ light show*> **b** *of colours* fluorescent [Greek *psychē* soul + *dēloun* to show]

psychiatry /sieˈkie·ətri‖saɪˈkaɪətrɪ/ *n* a branch of medicine that deals with mental, emotional, or behavioural disorders [deriv of Greek *psychē* soul + *iatros* physician] – **psychiatrist** *n*, **psychiatric** *adj*, **psychiatrically** *adv*

1**psychic** /ˈsiekik‖ˈsaɪkɪk/ *also* **psychical** /-kl‖-kl/ *adj* **1** of or originating in the psyche **2** lying outside the sphere of physical science or knowledge **3** *of a person* sensitive to nonphysical or supernatural forces and influences – **psychically** *adv*

2**psychic** *n* **1** a psychic person **2** MEDIUM 2e

psycho /ˈsiekoh‖ˈsaɪkəʊ/ *n, pl* **psychos** a psychopath, psychotic – infml – **psycho** *adj*

ˌpsychoˈanalyse /-ˈanəliez‖-ˈænəlaɪz/ *vt* to treat by means of psychoanalysis

ˌpsychoaˈnalysis /-əˈnaləsis‖-əˈnæləsɪs/ *n* a method of analysing unconscious mental processes and treating mental disorders, esp by allowing the patient to talk freely about early childhood experiences, dreams, etc – **psychoanalyst** *n*, **psychoanalytic, psychoanalytical** *adj*

psychokinesis /ˌsiekohkiˈneesis‖ˌsaɪkəʊkɪˈniːsɪs/ *n* apparent movement in physical objects produced by the power of the mind without physical contact – **psychokinetic** *adj*

psychological /ˌsiekəˈlojikl‖ˌsaɪkəˈlɒdʒɪkl/ *adj* **1a** of psychology **b** mental **2** directed towards or intended to affect the will or mind < ~ *warfare*> – **psychologically** *adv*

psychology /sieˈkoləji‖saɪˈkɒlədʒɪ/ *n* **1** the science or study of mind and behaviour **2** the mental or behavioural characteristics of an individual or group – **psychologist** *n*

psychopath /ˈsiekəpath‖ˈsaɪkəpæθ/ *n* a person suffering from a severe emotional and behavioural disorder characterized by antisocial tendencies and usu the pursuit of immediate gratification through often violent acts; *broadly* a dangerously violent mentally ill person – **psychopathic** *adj*, **psychopathy** *n*

psychosis /sieˈkohsis‖saɪˈkəʊsɪs/ *n, pl* **psychoses** /-ˌseez‖-ˌsiːz/ severe mental derangement (e g schizophrenia) that results in the impairment or loss of contact with reality – **psychotic** *adj or n*, **psychotically** *adv*

ˌpsychosoˈmatic /-səˈmatik‖-səˈmætɪk/ *adj* of or resulting from the interaction of psychological and somatic factors, esp the production of physical symptoms by mental processes < ~ *medicine*> [deriv of Greek *psychē* soul + *sōmat-*, *sōma* body]

ˌpsychoˈtherapy /-ˈtherəpi‖-ˈθerəpɪ/ *n*

treatment by psychological methods for mental, emotional, or psychosomatic disorders – **psychotherapist** *n*

ptarmigan /'tahmigən||'tɑːmɪgən/ *n* any of various grouse of northern regions whose plumage turns white in winter [Scottish Gaelic *tārmachan*]

pterodactyl /ˌterə'daktil||ˌterə'dæktɪl/ *n* any of an order of extinct flying reptiles without feathers [deriv of Greek *pteron* wing + *daktylos* finger]

Ptolemaic system /ˌtolə'mayik||ˌtɒlə'meɪɪk/ *n* the system of planetary motions according to which the sun, moon, and planets revolve round a stationary earth [*Ptolemy* (Claudius *Ptolemaeus*) (died about 168), Egyptian astronomer & geographer] – **Ptolemaist** *n*

ptomaine /'tohmayn||'təʊmeɪn/ *n* any of various often very poisonous organic compounds formed by the action of putrefactive bacteria on nitrogen-containing matter

pub /pub||pʌb/ *n* an establishment where alcoholic beverages are sold and consumed; *esp, chiefly Br* PUBLIC HOUSE

'pub ˌcrawl *n, chiefly Br* a visit to a series of pubs, usu involving at least 1 drink at each – infml

puberty /'pyoohbəti||'pjuːbətɪ/ *n* **1** the condition of being or the period of becoming capable of reproducing sexually **2** the age at which puberty occurs – **pubertal** *adj*

pubescent /pyooh'bes(ə)nt||pjuː'bes(ə)nt/ *adj* **1** arriving at or having reached puberty **2** covered with fine soft short hairs

pubic /'pyoohbik||'pjuːbɪk/ *adj* of or situated in or near the region of the pubis or the pubic hair

ˌpubic 'hair *n* the hair that appears at puberty round the genitals

pubis /'pyoohbis||'pjuːbɪs/ *n, pl* **pubes** /-beez||-biːz/ the bottom front of the 3 principal bones that form either half of the pelvis

[1]public /'publik||'pʌblɪk/ *adj* **1a** of or affecting all the people or the whole area of a nation or state <~ *law*> **b** of or being in the service of the community <~ *affairs*> **2** general, popular <*increasing ~ awareness*> **3** of national or community concerns as opposed to private affairs; social **4a** accessible to or shared by all members of the community <*a ~ park*> **b** capitalized in shares that can be freely traded on the open market <*the company has gone ~*> **5a** exposed to general view; open <*a ~ quarrel*> **b** well-known, prominent <~ *figures*>

[2]public *n* **1** *the* people as a whole; *the* populace **2** a group or section of people having common interests or characteristics <*the motoring ~*> – **in public** in the presence, sight, or hearing of strangers

ˌpublic-ad'dress ˌsystem *n* an apparatus including a microphone and loudspeakers used to address a large audience

publican /'publikən||'pʌblɪkən/ *n* **1** a Jewish tax collector for the ancient Romans **2** *chiefly Br* the licensee of a public house

publication /ˌpubli'kaysh(ə)n||ˌpʌblɪ'keɪʃ(ə)n/ *n* **1** the act or process of publishing **2** a published work

ˌpublic 'bar *n, Br* a plainly furnished and often relatively cheap bar in a public house

ˌpublic 'company *n* a company whose shares are offered to the general public

ˌpublic con'venience *n, Br* public toilet facilities provided by local government

ˌpublic corpo'ration *n* a corporation responsible for running a nationalized service or industry

ˌpublic 'house *n, chiefly Br* an establishment where alcoholic beverages are sold to be drunk on the premises

publicist /'publisist||'pʌblɪsɪst/ *n* an expert or commentator on public affairs

publicity /pu'blisəti||pʌ'blɪsətɪ/ *n* **1a** information with news value issued as a means of gaining public attention or support **b** paid advertising **c** the dissemination of information or promotional material **2** public attention or acclaim **3** being public <*the ~ of an open court*> – fml

public·ize, -ise /'publisiez||'pʌblɪsaɪz/ *vt* to give publicity to

publicly /'publikli||'pʌblɪklɪ/ *adv* **1** in a manner observable by or in a place accessible to the public; openly **2a** by the people generally; communally **b** by a government <~ *provided medical care*>

ˌpublic 'prosecutor *n* an official who conducts criminal prosecutions on behalf of the state

ˌpublic re'lations *n pl but usu sing in constr* the business of inducing the public to have understanding for and goodwill towards a person, organization, or institution; *also* the degree of understanding and goodwill achieved

ˌpublic 'school *n* **1** an endowed independent usu single-sex school in Britain, typically a large boarding school preparing pupils for higher education **2** *NAm & Scot* STATE SCHOOL

ˌpublic 'servant *n* a government employee

ˌpublic-'spirited *adj* motivated by concern for the general welfare

ˌpublic 'works *n pl* schools, roads, etc constructed for public use, esp by the government

publish /'publish||'pʌblɪʃ/ *vt* **1a** to make generally known **b** to announce publicly **2a** to produce or release for publication; *specif* to print **b** to issue the work of (an author) ~*vi* to put out an edition (e g of a newspaper) – **publishing** *n*

publisher /'publishə||'pʌblɪʃə/ *n* a person or company whose business is publishing

puce /pyoohs||pjuːs/ *adj or n* brownish purple

[1]puck /puk||pʌk/ *n* a mischievous sprite

[2]puck *n* a vulcanized rubber disc used in ice hockey

[1]pucker /'pukə||'pʌkə/ *vb* to (cause to) become wrinkled or irregularly creased

[2]pucker *n* a crease or wrinkle in a normally even surface

puckish /'pukish||'pʌkɪʃ/ *adj* impish, whimsical

pud /pood||pʊd/ *n, Br* a pudding – infml

pudding /'pooding||'pʊdɪŋ/ *n* **1** BLACK PUDDING **2** WHITE PUDDING **3a** any of various sweet or savoury dishes of a soft to spongy or fairly firm consistency that are made from rice, tapioca, flour, etc and are cooked by boiling, steaming, or baking <*sponge ~*> <*steak and kidney*

~> **b** dessert **4** a small podgy person – infml

ˈ**pudding ˌstone** *n* (a) conglomerate rock

puddle /ˈpudl‖ˈpʌdl/ *n* **1** a small pool of liquid; *esp* one of usu muddy rainwater **2** a mixture (e g of clay, sand, and gravel) used as a waterproof covering

pudendum /pyoohˈdendəm‖pjuːˈdendəm/ *n, pl* **pudenda** /-də‖-də/ the external genital organs of a (female) human being – usu pl with sing. meaning – **pudendal** *adj*

pudgy /ˈpuji‖ˈpʌdʒɪ/ *adj* podgy – **pudginess** *n*

puerile /ˈpyooəriel‖ˈpjʊəraɪl/ *adj* **1** juvenile **2** not befitting an adult; childish < ~ *remarks*> – **puerilism** *n*, **puerility** *n*

puerperal /pyoohˈuhp(ə)rəl‖pjuːˈɜːp(ə)rəl/ *adj* of or occurring during (the period immediately following) childbirth

[1]**puff** /puf‖pʌf/ *vi* **1a(1)** to blow in short gusts **a(2)** to exhale or blow forcibly < ~ed *into a blowpipe to shape the molten glass*> **b** to breathe hard and quickly; pant **c** to emit small whiffs or clouds (e g of smoke or steam) **2** to become distended; swell – usu + *up* ~ *vt* **1a** to emit, propel, or blow (as if) by puffs; waft **b** to draw on (a pipe, cigarette, etc) with intermittent exhalations of smoke **2a** to distend (as if) with air or gas; inflate **b** to make proud or conceited <*extravagant praise* ~ed *up his ego*> **c** to praise extravagantly and usu exaggeratedly; *also* to advertise by this means **3** to make (one's way) emitting puffs of breath or smoke < ~ed *her way up the hill*> *USE (2a&b)* usu + *up*

[2]**puff** *n* **1a** an act or instance of puffing **b** a slight explosive sound accompanying a puff **c** a small cloud (e g of smoke) emitted in a puff **d** DRAW 1a **2** a light round hollow pastry made of puff paste **3** a highly favourable notice or review, esp one that publicizes sthg or sby **4** *chiefly Br* BREATH 2a <*sat down until she got her* ~ *back*> – infml **5** *NAm* a quilted bed cover; an eiderdown **6** a poof – slang – **puffy** *adj*, **puffiness** *n*

ˈ**puff ˌadder** *n* a large venomous African viper that inflates its body and hisses loudly when disturbed

ˈ**puffˌball** /-ˌbawl‖-ˌbɔːl/ *n* any of various spherical and often edible fungi

puffed /puft‖pʌft/ *adj, chiefly Br* out of breath – infml

puffer /ˈpufə‖ˈpʌfə/ *n* a globefish

puffin /ˈpufin‖ˈpʌfɪn/ *n* any of several seabirds that have a short neck and a deep grooved multicoloured bill

puff out *vt* **1** to extinguish by blowing **2** to cause to enlarge, esp by filling or inflating with air ~ *vi* to be enlarged with air

puff pastry *n* a light flaky pastry made with a rich dough containing a large quantity of butter

[1]**pug** /pug‖pʌg/ *n* a small sturdy compact dog with a tightly curled tail and broad wrinkled face

[2]**pug** *vt* **-gg-** to work and mix (e g clay) when wet

pugilism /ˈpyoohjiˌliz(ə)m‖ˈpjuːdʒɪˌlɪz(ə)m/ *n* boxing – fml – **pugilist** *n*, **pugilistic** *adj*

pugnacious /pugˈnayshəs‖pʌgˈneɪʃəs/ *adj* inclined to fight or quarrel; belligerent – **pugnaciousness** *n*, **pugnacity** *n*

pug nose *n* a nose having a slightly concave bridge and flattened nostrils – **pug-nosed** *adj*

puissance /ˈpyooh·is(ə)ns, ˈpwis(ə)ns, pyoo(h)ˈis(ə)ns‖ˈpjuːɪs(ə)ns, ˈpwɪs(ə)ns, pjʊ(h)ˈɪs(ə)ns; *in showjumping* ˈpweesahnhs ‖ˈpwiːsɑːɑ̃s/ *n* **1** a showjumping competition which tests the horse's power to jump high obstacles **2** strength, power – fml or poetic – **puissant** *adj*

puke /pyoohk‖pjuːk/ *vb* to vomit – slang – **puke** *n*

pukka /ˈpukə‖ˈpʌkə/ *adj* **1** genuine, authentic; *also* first-class **2** *chiefly Br* stiffly formal or proper [Hindi *pakkā* cooked, ripe, solid, fr Sanskrit *pakva*]

pulchritude /ˈpulkriˌtyoohd‖ˈpʌlkrɪˌtjuːd/ *n* physical beauty – fml – **pulchritudinous** *adj*

pule /pyoohl‖pjuːl/ *vi* to whine, whimper

[1]**pull** /pool‖pʊl/ *vt* **1a** to draw out from the skin < ~ *feathers from a cock's tail*> **b** to pick from a plant or pluck by the roots < ~ *flowers*> < ~ *turnips*> **c** to extract < ~ *a tooth*> **2a** to exert force upon so as to (tend to) cause motion towards the force; tug at **b** STRAIN 2b < ~ed *a tendon*> **c** to hold back (a horse) from winning a race **d** to work (an oar) **3** to hit (e g a ball in cricket or golf) towards the left from a right-handed swing or towards the right from a left-handed swing **4** to draw apart; tear **5** to print (e g a proof) by impression **6** to bring out (a weapon) ready for use < ~ed *a knife on him*> **7** to draw from the barrel, esp by pulling a pump handle < ~ *a pint*> **8a** to carry out, esp with daring and imagination < ~ *a robbery*> < ~ed *another financial coup*> **b** to do, perform, or say with a deceptive intent <*been* ~ing *these tricks for years*> **9** to (attempt to) seduce or attract <*spends his weekends* ~ing *the birds*> < ~ *votes*> ~ *vi* **1a** to use force in drawing, dragging, or tugging **b** to move, esp through the exercise of mechanical energy <*the car* ~ed *out of the driveway*> **c** to draw or inhale hard in smoking **d** *of a horse* to strain against the bit **2** to be capable of being pulled *USE* (*vt 8a, 8b, & 9*) infml – **pull a fast one** to perpetrate a trick or fraud – infml – **pull oneself together** to regain one's self-possession or self-control – **pull one's punches** to refrain from using all the force at one's disposal – **pull one's weight** to do one's full share of the work – **pull out all the stops** to do everything possible to achieve an effect or action – **pull rank on somebody** to assert one's authority in order to get sthg pleasant – **pull someone's leg** to deceive sby playfully; hoax – **pull strings** to exert (secret) personal influence – **pull the wool over someone's eyes** to blind sby to the true situation; hoodwink sby – **pull together** to work in harmony towards a common goal; cooperate

[2]**pull** *n* **1a** the act or an instance of pulling **b(1)** a draught of liquid **b(2)** an inhalation of smoke (e g from a cigarette) **c** the effort expended in moving <*a long* ~ *uphill*> **d** an attacking stroke in cricket made by hitting the ball to the leg side with a horizontal bat **e** force required to overcome resistance to pulling **2** (special influence exerted to obtain) an advantage **3** PROOF 4a **4** a force that attracts, compels, or influences

pull away *vi* **1** to draw oneself back or away;

withdraw **2** to move off or ahead <pulled away *from the leaders on the last lap*>

pull down *vt* to demolish, destroy

pullet /'poolit‖'pʊlɪt/ *n* a young female domestic fowl less than a year old

pulley /'pooli‖'pʊlɪ/ *n* **1** a wheel with a grooved rim that is used with a rope or chain to change the direction and point of application of a pulling force; *also* such a wheel together with a block in which it runs **2** a wheel used to transmit power or motion by means of a belt, rope, or chain passing over its rim

'pull-,in *n, chiefly Br* a place where vehicles may pull in and stop; *also* a roadside café

pull in *vt* **1** to arrest **2** to acquire as payment or profit <pulls in *£10,000 a year*> – infml ~ *vi* **1** *esp of a train or road vehicle* to arrive at a destination or stopping place **2** *of a vehicle or driver* to move to the side of or off the road in order to stop

Pullman /'poolmən‖'pʊlmən/ *n* a railway passenger carriage with extra-comfortable furnishings, esp for night travel [George M *Pullman* (1831-97), US inventor]

pull off *vt* to carry out or accomplish despite difficulties

'pull-,on *n* a garment (e g a hat) that has no fastenings and is pulled onto the head or body – **pull-on** *adj*

'pull,out /-,owt‖-,aʊt/ *n* **1** a larger leaf in a book or magazine that when folded is the same size as the ordinary pages **2** a removable section of a magazine, newspaper, or book

pull out *vi* **1** *esp of a train or road vehicle* to leave, depart **2a** to withdraw from a military position **b** to withdraw from a joint enterprise or agreement **3** *of an aircraft* to resume horizontal flight after a dive <pulled out *at 400 feet*> **4** *of a motor vehicle* **4a** to move into a stream of traffic **b** to move out from behind a vehicle (e g when preparing to overtake)

'pull,over /-,ohvə‖-,əʊvə/ *n* a garment for the upper body, esp a jumper, put on by being pulled over the head

pull over *vi, of a driver or vehicle* to move towards the side of the road, esp in order to stop

'pull,through /-,throoh‖-,θruː/ *n* a weighted cord with a piece of cloth attached that is passed through a tube (e g the barrel of a rifle or a woodwind instrument) to clean it

pull through *vb* to (cause to) survive a dangerous or difficult situation (e g illness)

pullulate /'pulyoo,layt‖'pʌljʊ,leɪt/ *vi* **1a** to germinate, sprout **b** to breed or produce rapidly and abundantly **2** to swarm, teem – fml – **pullulation** *n*

'pull-,up *n* **1** an exercise performed by drawing oneself up while hanging by the hands until the chin is level with the support **2** *chiefly Br* a pull-in

pull up *vt* **1** to bring to a stop; halt **2** to reprimand, rebuke <*her manager* pulled *her* up *for her carelessness*> – infml ~ *vi* **1** to come to a halt; stop **2** to draw even with or gain on others (e g in a race) – **pull one's socks up** *or* **pull up one's socks** to make an effort to show greater application or improve one's performance

pulmonary /'poolmən(ə)ri, 'pul-‖'pʊlmən(ə)rɪ, 'pʌl-/, **pulmonic** /-'monik‖-'mɒnɪk/ *adj* of, associated with, or carried on by the lungs

¹pulp /pulp‖pʌlp/ *n* **1a** the soft juicy or fleshy part of a fruit or vegetable **b** a soft mass of vegetable matter from which most of the water has been pressed **c** the soft sensitive tissue that fills the central cavity of a tooth **d** a material prepared by chemical or mechanical means from rags, wood, etc that is used in making paper **2** pulverized ore mixed with water **3** a soft shapeless mass, esp produced by crushing or beating <*smashed his face to a* ~> **4** a magazine or book cheaply produced on rough paper and containing sensational material – **pulpiness** *n*, **pulpy** *adj*

²pulp *vt* **1** to reduce to pulp **2** to remove the pulp from **3** to produce or reproduce (written matter) in pulp form ~*vi* to become pulp or pulpy

pulpit /'pool,pit‖'pʊl,pɪt/ *n* **1** a raised platform or high reading desk in church from which a sermon is preached **2** *the* clergy as a profession

pulsar /'pul,sah‖'pʌl,sɑː/ *n* a celestial source, prob a rotating neutron star, of uniformly pulsating radio waves

pulsate /pul'sayt‖pʌl'seɪt/ *vi* **1** to beat with a pulse **2** to throb or move rhythmically; vibrate – **pulsatory** *adj*

pulsation /pul'saysh(ə)n‖pʌl'seɪʃ(ə)n/ *n* rhythmic throbbing or vibrating (e g of an artery); *also* a single beat or throb – **pulsatile** *adj*

¹pulse /puls‖pʌls/ *n* the edible seeds of any of various leguminous crops (e g peas, beans, or lentils); *also* the plant yielding these

²pulse /puls‖pʌls/ *n* **1a** a regular throbbing caused in the arteries by the contractions of the heart; *also* a single movement of such throbbing **b** the number of beats of a pulse in a specific period of time **2a** (an indication of) underlying sentiment or opinion <*felt the political* ~ *of the nation at Westminster*> **b** a feeling of liveliness; vitality **3a** rhythmical vibrating or sounding **b** a single beat or throb **4a** a short-lived variation of electrical current, voltage, etc whose value is normally constant **b** an electromagnetic wave or sound wave of brief duration

³pulse *vi* to pulsate, throb ~ *vt* **1** to drive (as if) by a pulsation **2** to cause to pulsate **3** to produce or modulate (e g electromagnetic waves) in the form of pulses <~d *waves*> – **pulser** *n*

pulver·ize, -ise /'pulvəriez‖'pʌlvəraɪz/ *vt* **1** to reduce (e g by crushing or grinding) to very small particles **2** to annihilate, demolish ~*vi* to become pulverized – **pulverizable** *adj*, **pulverizer** *n*, **pulverization** *n*

puma /'pyoohmə‖'pjuːmə/ *n* a powerful tawny big cat formerly widespread in the Americas but now extinct in many areas

pumice /'pumis‖'pʌmɪs/ *n* a light porous volcanic rock used esp as an abrasive and for polishing – **pumiceous** *adj*

pummel /'puml‖'pʌml/ *vb* **-ll-** (*NAm* **-l-, -ll-**) to pound or strike repeatedly, esp with the fists

¹pump /pump‖pʌmp/ *n* **1a** a device that raises, transfers, or compresses fluids or that reduces the density of gases, esp by suction or pressure or both **b** a mechanism (e g the sodium pump) for pumping atoms, ions, or molecules **2** the heart **3** an act or the process of pumping

[2]**pump** *vt* **1a** to raise (e g water) with a pump **b** to draw fluid from with a pump – often + *out* **2** to pour out or inject (as if) with a pump <~ed *money into the economy*> **3** to question persistently <~ed *her for information*> **4** to move (sthg) rapidly up and down as if working a pump handle <~ed *her hand warmly*> **5a** to inflate by means of a pump or bellows – usu + *up* **b** to supply with air by means of a pump or bellows <~ *an organ*> ~ *vi* **1** to work a pump; raise or move a fluid with a pump **2** to move in a manner resembling the action of a pump handle **3** to spurt out intermittently

[3]**pump** *n* **1** a low shoe without fastenings that grips the foot chiefly at the toe and heel **2** *Br* a plimsoll

pumpernickel /ˈpumpəˌnikl, ˈpoom-‖ˈpʌmpəˌnɪkl, ˈpʊm-/ *n* a dark coarse slightly sour-tasting bread made from wholemeal rye

pumpkin /ˈpum(p)kin‖ˈpʌm(p)kɪn/ *n* (a usu hairy prickly plant that bears) a very large usu round fruit with a deep yellow to orange rind and edible flesh

ˈ**pump** ˌ**room** *n* a room at a spa in which the water is distributed and drunk

[1]**pun** /pun‖pʌn/ *vt* to consolidate (e g earth, concrete, or hardcore) by repeated ramming or pounding

[2]**pun** *n* a humorous use of a word with more than 1 meaning or of words with (nearly) the same sound but different meanings

[3]**pun** *vi* **-nn-** to make puns

[1]**punch** /punch‖pʌntʃ/ *vt* **1** to strike, esp with a hard and quick thrust of the fist **2** to drive or push forcibly (as if) by a punch **3** to hit (a ball) with less than a full swing of a bat, racket, etc **4** to emboss, cut, or make (as if) with a punch ~*vi* to punch sthg [Middle French *poinçonner* to prick, stamp, fr *poinçon* puncheon (pointed tool), deriv of Latin *punctus*, past participle of *pungere* to prick] – **puncher** *n*

[2]**punch** *n* **1** a blow (as if) with the fist **2** effective energy or forcefulness <*an opening paragraph that packs a lot of* ~>

[3]**punch** *n* **1** a tool, usu in the form of a short steel rod, used esp for perforating, embossing, cutting, or driving the heads of nails below a surface **2** a device for cutting holes or notches in paper or cardboard

[4]**punch** *n* a hot or cold drink usu made from wine or spirits mixed with fruit, spices, water, and occas tea [perhaps fr Hindi *pā̃c* five, fr Sanskrit *pañca*; fr the number of ingredients]

ˈ**punch-**ˌ**bag** *n* an inflated or stuffed bag punched with the fists as a form of exercise or training

ˈ**punch** ˌ**ball** *n*, *Br* a punch-bag

ˈ**punch** ˌ**bowl** *n* a large bowl in which a beverage, esp punch, is mixed and served

ˈ**punch-**ˌ**drunk** *adj* **1** suffering brain damage as a result of repeated punches or blows to the head **2** behaving as if punch-drunk; dazed

ˌ**punched** ˈ**card**, ˈ**punch** ˌ**card** *n* a card used in data processing in which a pattern of holes or notches has been cut to represent information or instructions

ˈ**punch** ˌ**line** *n* a sentence or phrase, esp a joke, that forms the climax to a speech or dialogue

ˈ**punch-**ˌ**up** *n*, *chiefly Br* a usu spontaneous fight, esp with the bare fists – infml

punchy /ˈpunchi‖ˈpʌntʃɪ/ *adj* having punch; forceful

punctilio /pung(k)ˈtilioh‖pʌŋ(k)ˈtɪlɪəʊ/ *n*, *pl* **punctilios** **1** a minute detail of ceremony or observance **2** careful observance of forms (e g in social conduct) [Italian *puntiglio* point of honour, scruple, fr Spanish *puntillo*, lit., little point, fr *punto* point, fr Latin *punctum*]

punctilious /pung(k)ˈtili·əs‖pʌŋ(k)ˈtɪlɪəs/ *adj* strict or precise in observing codes of conduct or conventions – **punctiliously** *adv*, **punctiliousness** *n*

punctual /ˈpung(k)chooəl, -tyoo-‖ˈpʌŋ(k)tʃʊəl, -tjʊ-/ *adj* **1** relating to or having the nature of a point **2** (habitually) arriving, happening, performing, etc at the exact or agreed time – **punctually** *adv*, **punctuality** *n*

punctuate /ˈpung(k)chooˌayt, -tyoo-‖ˈpʌŋ(k)tʃʊˌeɪt, -tjʊ-/ *vt* **1** to mark or divide with punctuation marks **2** to break into or interrupt at intervals ~*vi* to use punctuation marks – **punctuator** *n*

punctuation /ˌpung(k)chooˈaysh(ə)n, -tyoo-‖ˌpʌŋ(k)tʃʊˈeɪʃ(ə)n, -tjʊ-/ *n* the dividing of writing with marks to clarify meaning; *also* a system of punctuation

punctuˈation ˌ**mark** *n* a standardized mark or sign used in punctuation

[1]**puncture** /ˈpung(k)chə‖ˈpʌŋ(k)tʃə/ *n* a perforation (e g a hole or narrow wound) made by puncturing; *esp* a small hole made accidentally in a pneumatic tyre

[2]**puncture** *vt* **1** to pierce with a pointed instrument or object **2** to cause a puncture in **3** to make useless or deflate as if by a puncture <*failures* ~d *her confidence*> ~*vi* to become punctured

pundit /ˈpundit‖ˈpʌndɪt/ *n* **1** a learned man or teacher; *specif* a pandit **2** one who gives opinions in an authoritative manner; an authority [Hindi *paṇḍit*, fr Sanskrit *paṇḍita*, fr *paṇḍita* learned] – **punditry** *n*

pungent /ˈpunj(ə)nt‖ˈpʌndʒ(ə)nt/ *adj* **1** having a stiff and sharp point <~ *leaves*> **2a** marked by a sharp incisive quality; caustic **b** to the point; highly expressive <~ *prose*> **3** having a strong sharp smell or taste; *esp* acrid – **pungency** *n*

Punic /ˈpyoohnik‖ˈpjuːnɪk/ *n or adj* (the dialect) of Carthage or the Carthaginians

punish /ˈpunish‖ˈpʌnɪʃ/ *vt* **1** to impose a penalty on (an offender) or for (an offence) **2** to treat roughly or damagingly <~ *an engine*> – infml ~*vi* to inflict punishment – **punishable** *adj*, **punisher** *n*

ˈ**punishment** /-mənt‖-mənt/ *n* **1a** punishing or being punished **b** a judicial penalty **2** rough or damaging treatment – infml <*the contender took plenty of* ~ *in the last round*>

punitive /ˈpyoohnətiv‖ˈpjuːnətɪv/ *adj* inflicting or intended to inflict punishment <*a* ~ *blow*> <*a* ~ *schedule*>

Punjabi /punˈjahbi, poon-‖pʌnˈdʒɑːbɪ, pʊn-/ *n* (the language spoken by) a native or inhabitant of the Punjab of NW India and Pakistan – **Punjabi** *adj*

[1]**punk** /pungk‖pʌŋk/ *n* **1** sby following punk styles in music, dress, etc **2** *chiefly NAm* sby considered worthless or inferior; *esp* a petty criminal

[2]**punk** *adj* **1** of or being a movement among young people of the 1970s and 1980s in Britain characterized by a violent rejection of established society and expressed through punk rock and the wearing of aggressively outlandish clothes and hairstyles **2** *chiefly NAm* of very poor quality; inferior – slang

[3]**punk** *n* a dry spongy substance prepared from fungi and used to ignite fuses

punnet /ˈpunit‖ˈpʌnɪt/ *n, chiefly Br* a small basket of wood, plastic, etc, esp for soft fruit or vegetables

punster /ˈpunstə‖ˈpʌnstə/ *n* one who is given to punning

[1]**punt** /punt‖pʌnt/ *n* a long narrow flat-bottomed boat with square ends, usu propelled with a pole

[2]**punt** *vt* to propel (e g a punt) with a pole; *also* to transport by punt ~*vi* to propel a punt; go punting

[3]**punt** *vi* **1** to play against the banker at a gambling game **2** *Br* to gamble

[4]**punt** *vb* to kick (a football) by means of a punt

[5]**punt** *n* the act of kicking a football with the top or tip of the foot after it is dropped from the hands and before it hits the ground

[6]**punt** /poont‖pʊnt/ *n* the standard unit of money in the Irish Republic

punter /puntə/ *n* **1** sby who punts **2** a gambler **3** a customer or client – infml **4** a prostitute's client – infml

puny /ˈpyoohni‖ˈpjuːnɪ/ *adj* slight or inferior in power, size, or importance; weak [Middle French *puisné* younger, lit., born afterwards, fr *puis* afterwards + *né* born] – **puniness** *n*

[1]**pup** /pup‖pʌp/ *n* a young dog; *also* a young seal, rat, etc

[2]**pup** *vi* **-pp-** to give birth to pups

pupa /ˈpyoohpə‖ˈpjuːpə/ *n, pl* **pupae** /-pi‖-pɪ/, **pupas** the intermediate usu inactive form of an insect that undergoes metamorphism (e g a bee, moth, or beetle) that occurs between the larva and the imago stages – **pupal** *adj*

pupate /pyoohˈpayt‖pjuːˈpeɪt/ *vi* to become a pupa – **pupation** *n*

[1]**pupil** /ˈpyoohpl‖ˈpjuːpl/ *n* **1** a child or young person at school or receiving tuition **2** one who has been taught or influenced by a distinguished person

[2]**pupil** *n* the contractile usu round dark opening in the iris of the eye – **pupilar** *adj*, **pupillary** *adj*

puppet /ˈpupit‖ˈpʌpɪt/ *n* **1a** a small-scale toy figure (e g of a person or animal) usu with a cloth body and hollow head that fits over and is moved by the hand **b** a marionette **2** one whose acts are controlled by an outside force or influence <*a ~ government*> – **puppetry** *n*, **puppeteer** *n*

puppy /ˈpupi‖ˈpʌpɪ/ *n* **1** a young dog (less than a year old) **2** a conceited or ill-mannered young man

ˈ**puppy** ˌ**fat** *n* temporary plumpness in children and adolescents

ˈ**puppy** ˌ**love** *n* short-lived romantic affection felt by an adolescent for sby of the opposite sex

purblind /ˈpuhˌbliend‖ˈpɜːˌblaɪnd/ *adj* **1** partly blind **2** lacking in vision or insight; obtuse – fml – **purblindness** *n*

[1]**purchase** /ˈpuhchəs‖ˈpɜːtʃəs/ *vt* **1a** to acquire (real estate) by means other than inheritance **b** to obtain by paying money or its equivalent; buy **c** to obtain by labour, danger, or sacrifice <~d *life at the expense of honour*> **2** to move or raise by a device (e g a lever or pulley) **3** to constitute the means for buying <*a pound seems to ~ less each year*> – **purchasable** *adj*, **purchaser** *n*

[2]**purchase** *n* **1** sthg obtained by payment of money or its equivalent **2a** a mechanical hold or advantage (e g that applied through a pulley or lever); *broadly* an advantage used in applying power or influence **b** a means, esp a mechanical device, by which one gains such an advantage

ˈ**purchase** ˌ**tax** *n* a tax levied on the sale of goods and services that is usu calculated as a percentage of the purchase price

purdah /ˈpuhdah, -də‖ˈpɜːdɑː, -də/ *n* the seclusion of women from public view among Muslims and some Hindus, esp in India; *also* a screen used for this purpose [Hindi *parda*, lit., screen, veil]

pure /pyooə‖pjʊə/ *adj* **1a(1)** unmixed with any other matter <~ *gold*> **a(2)** free from contamination <~ *food*> **a(3)** spotless; *specif* free from moral fault **b** *of a musical sound* being in tune and free from harshness **c** *of a vowel* monophthongal **2a** sheer, unmitigated <~ *folly*> **b** abstract, theoretical <~ *science*> **3a** free from anything that vitiates or weakens <*the ~ religion of our fathers*> **b** containing nothing that does not properly belong <*the ~ text*> **c** of unmixed ancestry **4a** chaste **b** ritually clean – **pureness** *n*

ˈ**pureˌblood** /-ˌblud‖-ˌblʌd/, **pure-blooded** /-ˈbludid‖-ˈblʌdɪd/ *adj* PURE 3c – **pureblood** *n*

ˈ**pureˌbred** /-ˌbred‖-ˌbred/ *adj* bred over many generations from members of a recognized breed, strain, or kind without mixture of other blood – **purebred** *n*

[1]**puree**, **purée** /ˈpyooəray‖ˈpjʊəreɪ/ *n* a thick pulp (e g of fruit or vegetable) usu produced by rubbing cooked food through a sieve or blending in a liquidizer; *also* a thick soup made from pureed vegetables

[2]**puree**, **purée** *vt* to reduce to a puree

purely /ˈpyooəli‖ˈpjʊəlɪ/ *adv* **1** without addition, esp of anything harmful **2** simply, merely <*read ~ for relaxation*> **3** in a chaste or innocent manner **4** wholly, completely <*a selection based ~ on merit*>

purgation /puhˈgaysh(ə)n‖pɜːˈgeɪʃ(ə)n/ *n* the act or result of purging

purgative /ˈpuhgətiv‖ˈpɜːgətɪv/ *n or adj* (a medicine) causing evacuation of the bowels

purgatory /ˈpuhgət(ə)ri‖ˈpɜːgət(ə)rɪ/ *n* **1** a place or state of punishment in which, according to Roman Catholic doctrine, the souls of those who die in God's grace may make amends for past sins and so become fit for heaven **2** a place or state of temporary suffering or misery – infml <*the return trip was absolute* ~> – **purgatorial** *adj*

[1]**purge** /puhj‖pɜːdʒ/ *vt* **1a** to clear of guilt **b** to free from moral or physical impurity **2a** to cause evacuation from (e g the bowels) **b(1)** to rid (e g a nation or party) of unwanted or undesirable members, often summarily or by force **b(2)** to get rid of (e g undesirable people) by means of a purge

[2]**purge** *n* **1** an (esp political) act of purging **2** a purgative

purify /ˈpyooərifie‖ˈpjʊərɪfaɪ/ *vt* **1** to free of physical or moral impurity or imperfection **2** to free from undesirable elements ~*vi* to grow or become pure or clean – **purifier** *n*, **purificator** *n*, **purification** *n*

purist /ˈpyooərist‖ˈpjʊərɪst/ *n* one who keeps strictly and often excessively to established or traditional usage, esp in language – **purism** *n*

puritan /ˈpyooərit(ə)n‖ˈpjʊərɪt(ə)n/ *n* **1** *cap* a member of a 16th- and 17th-c mainly calvinist Protestant group in England and New England which wished to purify the Church of England of all very ceremonial worship **2** one who practises or preaches a rigorous or severe moral code – **puritan** *adj, often cap*

puritanical /ˌpyooəriˈtanikl‖ˌpjʊərɪˈtænɪkl/ *adj* **1** puritan **2** of or characterized by a rigid morality; strict

purity /ˈpyooərəti‖ˈpjʊərətɪ/ *n* **1** pureness **2** SATURATION 1

[1]**purl** /puhl‖pɜːl/ *n* **1** a thread of twisted gold or silver wire used for embroidering or edging **2** **purl, purl stitch** a basic knitting stitch made by inserting the needle into the back of a stitch that produces a raised pattern on the back of the work **3** *Br* an ornamental edging of small loops or picots on lace, ribbon, or braid

[2]**purl** *vt* **1a** to decorate, edge, or border with gold or silver thread **b** to edge with loops; picot **2** to knit in purl stitch ~*vi* to do knitting in purl stitch

[3]**purl** *n* a gentle murmur or movement (e g of water)

[4]**purl** *vi, of a stream, brook, etc* to flow in eddies with a soft murmuring sound

purler /ˈpuhlə‖ˈpɜːlə/ *n, chiefly Br* a heavy headlong fall – infml

purlieus /ˈpuhlyoohz‖ˈpɜːljuːz/ *n pl* **1** environs, neighbourhood **2** confines, bounds – fml

purloin /puhˈloyn, pə-‖pɜːˈlɔɪn, pə-/ *vt* to take dishonestly; steal – fml

[1]**purple** /ˈpuhpl‖ˈpɜːpl/ *adj* **1** of the colour purple **2** highly rhetorical; ornate <~ *prose*>

[2]**purple** *n* **1a** a colour falling about midway between red and blue in hue **b** cloth dyed purple; *also* a purple robe worn as an emblem of rank or authority **c(1)** a mollusc yielding a purple dye, esp the Tyrian purple of ancient times **c(2)** a pigment or dye that colours purple **2** imperial, regal, or very high rank <*born to the* ~>

[3]**purple** *vb* to make or become purple

ˌpurple ˈheart *n* a light blue tablet containing the drug phenobarbitone and formerly prescribed as a hypnotic or sedative

ˌpurple ˈpassage *n* a piece of obtrusively ornate writing

purplish /ˈpuhplish‖ˈpɜːplɪʃ/ *adj* rather purple

[1]**purport** /ˈpuhpawt, -pɔt‖ˈpɜːpɔːt, -pɔt/ *n* professed or implied meaning; import; *also* substance – fml

[2]**purport** /pəˈpawt, puhˈpawt, ˈpuhpɔt‖pəˈpɔːt, pɜːˈpɔːt, ˈpɜːpɔt/ *vt* to (be intended to) seem; profess <*a book that* ~s *to be an objective analysis*>

[1]**purpose** /ˈpuhpəs‖ˈpɜːpəs/ *n* **1** the object for which sthg exists or is done; the intention **2** resolution, determination – **purposeless** *adj* – **on purpose** with intent; intentionally

[2]**purpose** *vt* to have as one's intention – fml

ˌpurpose-ˈbuilt *n, chiefly Br* designed to meet a specific need <*a* ~ *conference centre*>

ˈpurposeful /-f(ə)l‖-f(ə)l/ *adj* **1** full of determination **2** having a purpose or aim – **purposefully** *adv*, **purposefulness** *n*

ˈpurposely /-li‖-lɪ/ *adv* with a deliberate or express purpose

purposive /ˈpuhpəsiv‖ˈpɜːpəsɪv/ *adj* **1** serving or effecting a useful function though not necessarily as a result of deliberate intention **2** having or tending to fulfil a conscious purpose; purposeful *USE* fml – **purposively** *adv*, **purposiveness** *n*

purr /puh‖pɜː/ *vi* **1** to make the low vibratory murmur of a contented cat **2** to make a sound resembling a purr – **purr** *n*

[1]**purse** /puhs‖pɜːs/ *n* **1** a small flattish bag for money; *esp* a wallet with a compartment for holding change **2a** resources, funds **b** a sum of money offered as a prize or present; *also* the total amount of money offered in prizes for a given event **3** *NAm* a handbag

[2]**purse** *vt* to pucker, knit

purser /ˈpuhsə‖ˈpɜːsə/ *n* an officer on a ship responsible for documents and accounts and on a passenger ship also for the comfort and welfare of passengers

ˈpurse ˌstrings *n pl* control over expenditure <*she holds the* ~>

pursuance /pəˈsyooh·əns‖pəˈsjuːəns/ *n* a carrying out or into effect (e g of a plan or order); prosecution <*in* ~ *of her duties*> – fml

pursue /pəˈsyooh‖pəˈsjuː/ *vt* **1** to follow in order to overtake, capture, kill, or defeat **2** to find or employ measures to obtain or accomplish <~ *a goal*> **3** to proceed along <~s *a northern course*> **4a** to engage in <~ *a hobby*> **b** to follow up <~ *an argument*> **5** to continue to afflict; haunt <*was* ~d *by horrible memories*> ~*vi* to go in pursuit

pursuer /pəˈsyooh·ə‖pəˈsjuːə/ *n, Scot* **1** a plaintiff **2** a prosecutor

pursuit /pəˈsyooht‖pəˈsjuːt/ *n* **1** an act of pursuing **2** an activity that one regularly engages in (e g as a pastime or profession)

purulent /ˈpyooərələnt‖ˈpjʊərələnt/ *adj* **1** containing, consisting of, or being pus <*a* ~ *discharge*> **2** accompanied by suppuration – **purulence** *n*

purvey /pəˈvay, puh-‖pəˈveɪ, pɜː-/ *vt* to supply (e g provisions), esp in the course of business – **purveyance** *n*

purveyor /pəˈvayə, puh-‖pəˈveɪə, pɜː-/ *n* a victualler or caterer

purview /ˈpuhˌvyooh‖ˈpɜːˌvjuː/ *n* **1** the body

or enacting part of a statute **2** the range or limit of authority, responsibility, or concern **3** the range of vision or understanding *USE* (*2&3*) fml

pus /pus‖pʌs/ *n* thick opaque usu yellowish white fluid matter formed by suppuration (e g in an abscess)

[1]**push** /poosh‖pʊʃ/ *vt* **1a** to apply a force to (sthg) in order to cause movement away from the person or thing applying the force **b** to move (sthg) away or forwards by applying such a force <*to* ~ *a car uphill*> **2** to cause (sthg) to change in quantity or extent as if under pressure <*scarcity of labour* ~ed *up wages*> **3a** to develop (e g an idea or argument), esp to an extreme degree **b** to urge or press the advancement, adoption, or practice of; *specif* to make aggressive efforts to sell <*a drive to* ~ *tinned foods*> **c** to press or urge (sby) to sthg; pressurize <*keeps* ~ing *me to give her a rise*> **4** to force towards or beyond the limits of capacity or endurance <*poverty* ~ed *them to breaking point*> **5** to hit (a ball) towards the right from a right-handed swing or towards the left from a left-handed swing **6** to approach in age or number <*the old man was* ~ing *75*> – infml **7** to engage in the illicit sale of (drugs) – slang ~ *vi* **1** to press against sthg with steady force (as if) in order to move it away **2** to press forwards energetically against obstacles or opposition <*explorers* ~ed *out into the Antarctic*> **3** to exert oneself continuously or vigorously to achieve an end <*unions* ~ing *for higher wages*> – **push one's luck** to take an increasing risk

[2]**push** *n* **1a** a vigorous effort to attain an end; a drive **b** a military assault or offensive **c** an advance that overcomes obstacles **2a** an act or action of pushing **b** a nonphysical pressure; an urge <*the* ~ *and pull of conflicting emotions*> **c** vigorous enterprise or energy <*she'll need a lot of* ~ *to get to the top*> **3a** an exertion of influence to promote another's interests <*his father's* ~ *took him to the top*> **b** stimulation to activity; an impetus **4** a time for action; an emergency <*when it came to the* ~ *I forgot my lines*> **5** *Br* dismissal – esp in *get/give the push* <*he'll get the* ~ *if he's late again*> *USE* (*4&5*) infml – **at a push** *chiefly Br* if really necessary; if forced by special conditions

push around *vt* to order about; bully

ˈ**push-ˌbike** *n, Br* a pedal bicycle

ˈ**push-ˌbutton** *adj* **1** operated by means of a push button **2** characterized by the use of long-range weapons rather than physical combat <~ *warfare*>

ˈ**push ˌbutton** *n* a small button or knob that when pushed operates or triggers sthg, esp by closing an electric circuit

ˈ**pushˌchair** /-ˌcheə‖-ˌtʃeə/ *n, Br* a light folding chair on wheels in which young children may be pushed

pushed /poosht‖pʊʃt/ *adj* having difficulty in finding enough time, money, etc <*you'll be* ~ *to finish that by tonight*> – infml

pusher /ˈpooshə‖ˈpʊʃə/ *n* **1** a utensil used by a child for pushing food onto a spoon or fork **2** one who sells drugs illegally – slang

push in *vi* to join a queue at a point in front of others already waiting, esp by pushing or jostling

push off *vi* to go away, esp hastily or abruptly – infml

push on *vi* to continue on one's way, esp despite obstacles or difficulties

ˈ**pushˌover** /-ˌohvə‖-ˌəʊvə/ *n* **1** an opponent who is easy to defeat or a victim who is incapable of effective resistance **2** sby unable to resist a usu specified attraction; a sucker <*he's a* ~ *for blondes*> **3** sthg accomplished without difficulty; a cinch *USE* infml

pushy /ˈpooshi‖ˈpʊʃɪ/ *adj* self-assertive often to an objectionable degree; forward – infml – **pushily** *adv*, **pushiness** *n*

pusillanimous /ˌpyoohsiˈlaniməs‖ˌpju:sɪˈlænɪməs/ *adj* lacking courage and resolution; contemptibly timid – fml [Late Latin *pusillanimis*, fr Latin *pusillus* very small + *animus* spirit] – **pusillanimity** *n*

puss /poos‖pʊs/ *n* **1** a cat – used chiefly as a pet name or calling name **2** a girl <*a saucy little* ~> *USE* infml

[1]**pussy** /ˈpoosi‖ˈpʊsɪ/ *n* **1** a catkin of the pussy willow **2** a cat – infml; used chiefly as a pet name

[2]**pussy** *n* the vulva – vulg

ˈ**pussyˌcat** /-ˌkat‖-ˌkæt/ *n* a cat – used chiefly by or to children

ˈ**pussyˌfoot** /-ˌfoot‖-ˌfʊt/ *vi* **1** to tread or move warily or stealthily **2** to avoid committing oneself (e g to a course of action)

ˌ**pussy** ˈ**willow** *n* any of various willows having grey silky catkins

pustule /ˈpustyoohl‖ˈpʌstju:l/ *n* **1** a small raised spot on the skin having an inflamed base and containing pus **2** a small raised area like a blister or pimple – **pustular** *adj*

[1]**put** /poot‖pʊt/ *vb* **put; -tt-** *vt* **1a** to place in or move into a specified position or relationship <~ *the book on the table*> <~ *a child to bed*> **b** to thrust (e g a weapon) into or through sthg **c** to throw (a shot, weight, etc) with a put, esp in the shot put **d** to bring into a specified condition <~ *a rule into effect*> <~ *the matter right*> **2a** to cause to endure or undergo; subject <~ *me to a lot of expense*> **b** to impose, establish <~ *a tax on luxuries*> **3a** to formulate for judgment or decision <~ *the question*> <~ *the motion*> **b** to express, state <~ting *it mildly*> **4a** to turn into language or literary form <~ *her feelings into words*> **b** to adapt, set <*lyrics* ~ *to music*> **5a** to devote, apply <~ *his mind to the problem*> **b** to cause to perform an action; urge <~ *the horse at the fence*> **c** to impel, incite <~ *them into a frenzy*> **6a** to repose, rest <~s *his faith in reason*> **b** to invest <~ *his money into steel*> **7** to give as an estimate <~ *her age at about 40*>; *also* to imagine as being <~ *yourself in my place*> **8** to write, inscribe <~ *their names to what they wrote* – Virginia Woolf> **9** to bet, wager <~ *£5 on the favourite*> ~*vi, of a ship* to take a specified course <~ *back to port*> – **put a foot wrong** to make the slightest mistake – **put a good/bold face on** to represent (a matter) or confront (an ordeal) as if all were well – **put a sock in it** *Br* to stop talking; SHUT UP – slang – **put a spoke in someone's wheel** to thwart sby's plans –

put forth 1a to assert, propose **b** to make public; issue **2** to bring into action; exert **3** to produce or send out by growth <put forth *leaves*> – **put in mind** to remind – often + of – **put it across someone** *Br* to deceive sby into believing or doing sthg – compare PUT ACROSS – **put it past someone** to think sby at all incapable or unlikely <*wouldn't* put it past him *to cheat*> – **put it there** – used as an invitation to shake hands – **put one's best foot forward** to make every effort – **put one's finger on** to identify <put his finger on *the cause of the trouble*> – **put one's foot down** to take a firm stand – **put one's foot in it** to make an embarrassing blunder – **put one's shirt on** to risk all one's money on – **put one's shoulder to the wheel** to make an effort, esp a cooperative effort – **put on the map** to cause to be considered important – **put paid to** *Br* to ruin; FINISH 1a – **put someone's nose out of joint** to supplant sby distressingly – **put the lid on** *chiefly Br* to be the culminating misfortune of (a series) – **put the wind up** *Br* to scare, frighten – infml – **put to bed** to make the final preparations for printing (e g a newspaper) – **put together** to create as a united whole; construct – **put to it** to give difficulty to; press hard <*had been* put to it *to keep up*> – **put to shame** to disgrace by comparison <*their garden* puts *ours* to shame> – **put two and two together** to draw the proper conclusion from given premises – **put wise** to inform, enlighten – infml

[2]put *n* a throw made with an overhand pushing motion; *specif* the act or an instance of putting the shot

[3]put *adj* in the same position, condition, or situation – in *stay put*

put about *vi, of a ship* to change direction ~*vt* to cause (a ship) to put about

put across *vt* to convey (the meaning or significance of sthg) effectively

putative /ˈpyoohtətiv‖ˈpjuːtətɪv/ *adj* **1** commonly accepted or supposed **2** assumed to exist or to have existed *USE* fml – **putatively** *adv*

put away *vt* **1** to discard, renounce **2a** to place for storage when not in use <put *the knives* away *in the drawer*> **b** to save (money) for future use **3a** to confine, esp in an asylum **b** to kill; *esp* PUT DOWN 2 **4** to eat or drink up; consume <*used to* put away *a bottle without blinking*> – infml

put by *vt* PUT AWAY 2

[1]ˈput-ˌdown *n* a humiliating remark; a snub – infml

put down *vt* **1** to bring to an end; suppress <put down *a riot*> **2** to kill (e g a sick or injured animal) painlessly **3a** to put in writing <put *it* down *on paper*> **b** to enter in a list (e g of subscribers) <put *me* down *for £5*> **4** to pay as a deposit **5a** to place in a category <*I* put *him* down *as an eccentric*> **b** to attribute <put *it* down *to inexperience*> **6** to store or set aside (e g bottles of wine) for future use **7a** to disparage, belittle **b** to humiliate, snub ~*vi, of an aircraft or pilot* to land *USE* (7) infml

put forward *vt* **1** to propose (e g a theory) **2** to bring into prominence <*have no wish to* put *myself* forward>

put in *vt* **1** to make a formal offer or declaration of <put in *a plea of guilty*> **2** to come in with; interpose <put in *a word for her brother*> **3** to spend (time) at an occupation or job <put in *6 hours at the office*> ~ *vi* **1** to call at or enter a place, harbour, etc **2** to make an application, request, or offer *for* <*decided to* put in *for a pension*>

put off *vt* **1** to disconcert, distract **2a** to postpone <*decided to* put off *their departure*> **b** to get rid of or persuade to wait, esp by means of excuses or evasions <put *his creditors* off *for another few days*> **3a** to repel, discourage **b** to dissuade <*so keen it was impossible to* put *her* off> **4** to take off; rid oneself of

[1]ˈput-ˌon *adj* pretended, assumed

[2]put-on *n* an instance of deliberately misleading sby; *also, chiefly NAm* a parody, spoof

put on *vt* **1a** to dress oneself in; don **b** to make part of one's appearance or behaviour **c** to feign, assume <put on *a saintly manner*> **2** to cause to act or operate; apply <put on *more speed*> **3** to come to have an increased amount of <put on *weight*> **4** to stage, produce (e g a play) **5** to bet (a sum of money) **6** to bring to or cause to speak on the telephone <*is your father there*? Put *him* on, *then*> **7** to mislead deliberately, esp for amusement – infml

put out *vt* **1** to extinguish <put *the fire* out> **2** to publish, issue **3** to produce for sale **4a** to disconcert, confuse **b** to annoy, irritate **c** to inconvenience <*don't* put *yourself* out *for us*> **5** to cause to be out (in baseball, cricket, etc) **6** to give or offer (a job of work) to be done by another outside the premises ~ *vi* **1** to set out from shore **2** to make an effort

put over *vt* PUT ACROSS

putrefaction /ˌpyoohtriˈfaksh(ə)n‖ˌpjuːtrɪˈfækʃ(ə)n/ *n* **1** the decomposition of organic matter; *esp* the breakdown of proteins by bacteria and fungi, typically in the absence of oxygen, with the formation of foul-smelling incompletely oxidized products **2** being putrefied; corruption – **putrefactive** *adj*

putrefy /ˈpyoohtrifie‖ˈpjuːtrɪfaɪ/ *vb* to make or become putrid

putrescent /ˌpyoohˈtres(ə)nt‖ˌpjuːˈtres(ə)nt/ *adj* of or undergoing putrefaction – **putrescence** *n*

putrid /ˈpyoohtrid‖ˈpjuːtrɪd/ *adj* **1a** in a state of putrefaction **b** (characteristic) of putrefaction; *esp* foul-smelling **2** very unpleasant – slang – **putridness** *n*, **putridity** *n*

putsch /pooch‖pʊtʃ/ *n* a secretly plotted and suddenly executed attempt to overthrow a government

putt /put‖pʌt/ *n* a gentle golf stroke made to roll the ball towards or into the hole on a putting green – **putt** *vb*

puttee /ˈputi, puˈtee‖ˈpʌtɪ, pʌˈtiː/ *n* **1** a long cloth strip wrapped spirally round the leg from ankle to knee, esp as part of an army uniform **2** *NAm* a usu leather legging secured by a strap or catch or by laces [Hindi *paṭṭī* strip of cloth, fr Sanskrit *paṭṭikā*]

[1]putter /ˈputə‖ˈpʌtə/ *n* a golf club used for putting

[2]putter /ˈputə‖ˈpʌtə/ *vi, NAm* to potter

put through *vt* **1** to carry into effect or to a successful conclusion **2a** to make a telephone connection for **b** to obtain a connection for (a telephone call)

ˈputting ˌgreen /ˈputing‖ˈpʌtɪŋ/ *n* a smooth grassy area at the end of a golf fairway containing the hole into which the ball must be played

putto /ˈpootoh‖ˈpʊtəʊ/ *n, pl* **putti** /-ti‖-tɪ/ a figure of a Cupid-like boy, esp in Renaissance painting

[1]**putty** /ˈputi‖ˈpʌtɪ/ *n* **1** a pasty substance consisting of hydrated lime and water **2** a dough-like cement, usu made of whiting and boiled linseed oil, used esp in fixing glass in sashes and stopping crevices in woodwork

[2]**putty** *vt* to use putty on or apply putty to

ˈput-ˌup *adj* contrived secretly beforehand <*the vote was obviously a* ~ *job*> – infml

put up *vt* **1** to sheathe (a sword) **2** to flush (game) from cover **3** to nominate for election **4** to offer up (e g a prayer) **5** to offer for public sale <put *her possessions* up *for auction*> **6** to give food and shelter to; accommodate **7** to build, erect **8a** to make a display of; show <*desperate as she was, she* put up *a brave front*> **b** CARRY ON 2 <put up *a struggle against considerable odds*> **9a** to contribute, pay **b** to offer as a prize or stake **10** to increase the amount of; raise ~ *vi* **1** to shelter, lodge <*we'll* put up *here for the night*> **2** to present oneself as a candidate in an election – usu + *for* – **put someone's back up** to annoy or irritate sby – **put up to** to urge on, instigate <*they* put *him* up to *playing the prank*> – **put up with** to endure or tolerate without complaint or protest

ˈput-uˌpon *adj* imposed upon; taken advantage of

[1]**puzzle** /ˈpuzl‖ˈpʌzl/ *vt* to offer or represent a problem difficult to solve or a situation difficult to resolve; perplex; *also* to exert (e g oneself) over such a problem or situation <*they* ~d *their brains to find a solution*> ~*vi* to be uncertain as to action, choice, or meaning – usu + *over* or *about* – **puzzlement** *n*, **puzzler** *n*

[2]**puzzle** *n* **1** being puzzled; perplexity **2a** sthg that puzzles **b** a problem, contrivance, etc designed for testing one's ingenuity

puzzle out *vt* to find (a solution or meaning) by means of mental effort

PVC *n* POLYVINYL CHLORIDE

pygmy /ˈpigmi‖ˈpɪgmɪ/ *n* **1** *cap* a member of a people of equatorial Africa under 1.5m (about 5ft) in height **2** a very short person; a dwarf **3** one who is insignificant or inferior in a specified sphere or manner <*a political* ~> [Latin *Pygmaeus*, a member of a legendary race of dwarfs fr Greek *Pygmaios*, fr *pygmē* fist, measure of length] – **pygmoid** *adj*

pyjamas, *NAm chiefly* **pajamas** /pəˈjahməz‖pəˈdʒɑːməz/ *n pl, chiefly Br* **1** loose lightweight trousers traditionally worn in the East **2** a suit of loose lightweight jacket and trousers for sleeping in [Hindi *pājāma*, fr Persian *pā* leg + *jāma* garment] – **pyjama** *adj*

pylon /ˈpielon, -lən‖ˈpaɪlɒn, -lən/ *n* **1** either of 2 towers with sloping sides flanking the entrance to an ancient Egyptian temple **2** a tower for supporting either end of a wire, esp electricity power cables, over a long span **3** a rigid structure on the outside of an aircraft for supporting sthg

pyorrhoea /ˌpie·əˈriə‖ˌpaɪəˈrɪə/ *n* an inflammation of the sockets of the teeth

pyramid /ˈpirəmid‖ˈpɪrəmɪd/ *n* **1a** an ancient massive structure having typically a square base and tapering walls that meet at the top **b** a structure or object of similar form **2** a polyhedron having for its base a polygon and for faces triangles with a common vertex **3** a nonphysical structure or system (e g a social or organizational hierarchy) having a broad supporting base and narrowing gradually to an apex – **pyramidal** *adj*

ˈpyramid ˌselling *n* a fraudulent financial system whereby agents for the sale of a product are induced to recruit further agents on ever-dwindling commissions

pyre /ˈpie·ə‖ˈpaɪə/ *n* a heap of combustible material for burning a dead body as part of a funeral rite; *broadly* a pile of material to be burned

Pyrex /ˈpiereks‖ˈpaɪreks/ *trademark* – used for glass and glassware that is resistant to heat, chemicals, and electricity

pyrexia /pieˈreksi·ə‖paɪˈreksɪə/ *n* abnormal elevation of body temperature – **pyrexial** *adj*, **pyrexic** *adj*

pyrites /pieˈrieteez, pi-‖paɪˈraɪtiːz, pɪ-/ *n, pl* **pyrites** any of various metallic-looking sulphide minerals; *esp* IRON PYRITES – **pyritic** *adj*

pyromania /ˌpierəˈmaynyə, -ni·ə‖ˌpaɪrəˈmeɪnjə, -nɪə/ *n* a compulsive urge to start fires – **pyromaniac** *n*, **pyromaniacal** *adj*

pyrotechnic /ˌpierəˈteknik‖ˌpaɪrəˈteknɪk/ *n* **1** a firework **2** *pl* a brilliant or spectacular display (e g of oratory or extreme virtuosity) [deriv of Greek *pyr* fire + *technē* art] – **pyrotechnic** *adj*, **pyrotechnist** *n*

ˌPyrrhic ˈvictory /pirik‖pɪrɪk/ *n* a victory won at excessive cost [*Pyrrhus* (319-272 BC), King of Epirus who sustained heavy losses in defeating the Romans]

python /ˈpieth(ə)n‖ˈpaɪθ(ə)n/ *n* a large boa or other constrictor; *esp* any of a genus that includes the largest living snakes – **pythonine** *adj*

pyx /piks‖pɪks/ *n* **1** a container in which the bread used at Communion is kept; *esp* one used for carrying the Eucharist to the sick **2** a box in a mint for deposit of sample coins reserved for testing

q /kyooh‖kjuː/ *n, pl* **q's, qs** *often cap* (a graphic representation of or device for reproducing) the 17th letter of the English alphabet

qua /kway, kwah‖kweɪ, kwɑː/ *prep* in the capacity or character of; as

[1]**quack** /kwak‖kwæk/ *vi or n* (to make) the characteristic cry of a duck

[2]**quack** *n* **1** one who has or pretends to have medical skill **2** CHARLATAN 2 *USE* infml – **quackery** *n*, **quackish** *adj*

[3]**quack** *adj* (characteristic) of a quack <~ *medicines*>

[1]**quad** /kwod‖kwɒd/ *n* a quadrangle

[2]**quad** *n* a type-metal space that is 1 or

more ems in width

[3]**quad** *n* a quadruplet

[4]**quad** *adj* quadraphonic

Quadragesima /ˌkwodrəˈjesimə‖ˌkwɒdrəˈdʒesɪmə/ *n* the first Sunday in Lent

quadrangle /ˈkwodrang·gl‖ˈkwɒdræŋgl/ *n* **1** a quadrilateral **2** a 4-sided enclosure surrounded by buildings – **quadrangular** *adj*

quadrant /ˈkwodrənt‖ˈkwɒdrənt/ *n* **1a** an instrument for measuring angles, consisting commonly of a graduated arc of 90° **b** a device or mechanical part shaped like or suggestive of the quadrant of a circle **2** (the area of 1 quarter of a circle that is bounded by) an arc of a circle containing an angle of 90° **3** any of the 4 quarters into which sthg is divided by 2 lines that intersect each other at right angles

quadraphonic /ˌkwodrəˈfonik‖ˌkwɒdrəˈfɒnɪk/ *adj* of or being an audio system that uses 4 signal channels by which the signal is conveyed from its source to its final point of use – **quadraphonics** *n*, **quadraphony** *n*

quadratic /kwoˈdratik‖kwɒˈdrætɪk/ *n or adj* (an equation or expression) of or involving (terms of) the second power or order – **quadratically** *adv*

quadri-, **quadr-**, **quadru-** *comb form* **1** four <quadri*lateral*> **2** square <quadr*ic*> **3** fourth <quadri*centennial*>

quadrilateral /ˌkwodriˈlat(ə)rəl‖ˌkwɒdrɪˈlæt(ə)rəl/ *n or adj* (a polygon) having 4 sides

quadrille /kwəˈdril‖kwəˈdrɪl/ *n* **1** a 4-handed variant of ombre played with a pack of 40 cards and popular esp in the 18th c **2** (the music for) a square dance for 4 couples made up of 5 or 6 figures

quadrillion /kwoˈdrilyən‖kwɒˈdrɪljən/ *n* **1** *Br* a million million million millions (10^{24}) **2** *chiefly NAm* a thousand million millions (10^{15}) – **quadrillion** *adj*, **quadrillionth** *adj or n*

quadroon /kwoˈdroohn‖kwɒˈdru:n/ *n* sby of one-quarter Negro ancestry

quadruped /ˈkwodrooˌped‖ˈkwɒdrʊˌped/ *n* an animal having 4 feet – **quadruped, quadrupedal** *adj*

[1]**quadruple** /ˈkwodroopl, kwoˈdroohpl‖ˈkwɒdrʊpl, kwɒˈdru:pl/ *vb* to make or become 4 times as great or as many

[2]**quadruple** *n* a sum 4 times as great as another

[3]**quadruple** *adj* **1** having 4 units or members **2** being 4 times as great or as many **3** marked by 4 beats per bar <~ *time*> – **quadruply** *adv*

quadruplet /ˈkwodrooplit, kwoˈdroohplit‖ˈkwɒdrʊplɪt, kwɒˈdru:plɪt/ *n* **1** any of 4 offspring born at 1 birth **2** a combination of 4 of a kind **3** a group of 4 musical notes performed in the time of 3 notes of the same value

[1]**quadruplicate** /kwoˈdroohplikət‖kwɒˈdru:plɪkət/ *adj* **1** consisting of or existing in 4 corresponding or identical parts or examples <~ *invoices*> **2** being the fourth of 4 things exactly alike

[2]**quadruplicate** /kwoˈdroohplikayt‖kwɒˈdru:plɪkeɪt/ *vt* **1** to make quadruple or fourfold **2** to prepare in quadruplicate – **quadruplication** *n*

[3]**quadruplicate** /kwoˈdroohplikət‖kwɒˈdru:plɪkət/ *n* **1** any of 4 identical copies **2** 4 copies all alike – + *in* <*typed in* ~>

quaff /kwof, kwahf‖kwɒf, kwɑ:f/ *vb* to drink (a beverage) deeply in long draughts – **quaffer** *n*

quagga /ˈkwagə‖ˈkwægə/ *n* a recently extinct wild zebra of southern Africa

quagmire /ˈkwagˌmie·ə, ˈkwog-‖ˈkwægˌmaɪə, ˈkwɒg-/ *n* **1** soft miry land that shakes or yields under the foot **2** a predicament from which it is difficult to extricate oneself

[1]**quail** /kwayl‖kweɪl/ *n*, **1** a migratory Old World game bird **2** any of various small American game birds

[2]**quail** *vi* to shrink back in fear; cower

quaint /kwaynt‖kweɪnt/ *adj* **1** unusual or different in character or appearance; odd **2** pleasingly or strikingly old-fashioned or unfamiliar – **quaintly** *adv*, **quaintness** *n*

[1]**quake** /kwayk‖kweɪk/ *vi* **1** to shake or vibrate, usu from shock or instability **2** to tremble or shudder, esp inwardly from fear

[2]**quake** *n* **1** a quaking **2** an earthquake – infml

Quaker /ˈkwaykə‖ˈkweɪkə/ *n* a member of a pacifist Christian sect that stresses Inner Light and rejects sacraments and an ordained ministry – **Quakerish** *adj*, **Quakerism** *n*, **Quakerly** *adj*

qualification /ˌkwolifiˈkaysh(ə)n‖ˌkwɒlɪfɪˈkeɪʃ(ə)n/ *n* **1** a restriction in meaning or application; a limiting modification **2a** a quality or skill that fits a person (e g for a particular task or appointment) **b** a condition that must be complied with (e g for the attainment of a privilege)

qualified /ˈkwolified‖ˈkwɒlɪfaɪd/ *adj* **1a** fitted (e g by training or experience) for a usu specified purpose; competent **b** complying with the specific requirements or conditions (e g for appointment to an office); eligible **2** limited or modified in some way <~ *approval*>

qualifier /ˈkwoliˌfie·ə‖ˈkwɒlɪˌfaɪə/ *n* one who or that which qualifies: e g **a** sby or sthg that satisfies requirements or meets a specified standard **b** a preliminary heat or contest

qualify /ˈkwolifie‖ˈkwɒlɪfaɪ/ *vt* **1a** to reduce from a general to a particular or restricted form; modify **b** to make less harsh or strict; moderate **c** MODIFY 2 **2** to characterize or describe *as* <*cannot* ~ *it as either glad or sad*> **3a** to fit by training, skill, or ability for a special purpose **b** to render legally capable or entitled ~ *vi* **1** to be fit (e g for an office) <qualifies *for the job by virtue of his greater experience*> **2** to reach an accredited level of competence <*has just* qualified *as a lawyer*> **3** to exhibit a required degree of ability or achievement in a preliminary contest

qualitative /ˈkwolitətiv‖ˈkwɒlɪtətɪv/ *adj* of or involving quality or kind – **qualitatively** *adv*

[1]**quality** /ˈkwoləti‖ˈkwɒlətɪ/ *n* **1a** peculiar and essential character; nature **b** an inherent feature; a property **2a** degree of excellence; grade <*a decline in the* ~ *of applicants*> **b** superiority in kind <*proclaimed the* ~ *of his wife* – Compton Mackenzie> **3** high social position <*a man of* ~> **4** a distinguishing attribute; a characteristic <*listed all her good* qualities> **5** the identifying character of a vowel sound **6** *archaic* a capacity, role <*in the* ~ *of reader and companion* – Joseph Conrad>

[2]**quality** *adj* **1** concerned with or displaying excellence <~ *goods*> **2** *of a newspaper* aiming to appeal to an educated readership <*the ~ Sundays*>

qualm /kwahm, kwawm‖kwɑːm, kwɔːm/ *n* **1** a sudden and brief attack of illness, faintness, or nausea **2** a sudden feeling of anxiety or apprehension **3** a scruple or feeling of uneasiness, esp about a point of conscience or honour – **qualmish** *adj*

quandary /ˈkwond(ə)ri‖ˈkwɒnd(ə)rɪ/ *n* a state of perplexity or doubt

quango /ˈkwang·goh‖ˈkwæŋgəʊ/ *n* a self-governing body set up by a government and having statutory powers in a specific field [*qua*si-*a*utonomous *n*on-*g*overnmental (or *n*ational *g*overnmental) *o*rganization

quantify /ˈkwontifie‖ˈkwɒntɪfaɪ/ *vt* **1** to specify the logical quantity of **2** to determine, express, or measure the quantity of – **quantifier** *n*, **quantifiable** *adj*, **quantification** *n*

quantitative /ˈkwontitətiv‖ˈkwɒntɪtətɪv/ *adj* **1** (expressible in terms) of quantity **2** of or involving the measurement of quantity or amount **3** *of classical verse* based on the relative duration of sequences of sounds – **quantitatively** *adv*, **quantitativeness** *n*

quantity /ˈkwontəti‖ˈkwɒntətɪ/ *n* **1a** an indefinite amount or number **b** a known, measured or estimated amount <*precise* quantities *of 4 ingredients*> **c** the total amount or number **d** a considerable amount or number – often pl with sing. meaning <*wept like anything to see such* quantities *of sand* – Lewis Carroll> **2a** the aspect in which a thing is measurable in terms of degree of magnitude **b** the number, value, etc subjected to a mathematical operation **c** sby or sthg to take into account or be reckoned with <*an unknown ~ as military leader*> **3** the relative duration of a speech sound or sound sequence, specif a prosodic syllable

quantity surveyor *n* sby who estimates or measures quantities (e g for builders) – **quantity surveying** *n*

quantum /ˈkwontəm‖ˈkwɒntəm/ *n, pl* **quanta** /-tə‖-tə/ **1a** a quantity, amount **b** a portion, part **2** any of the very small parcels or parts into which many forms of energy are subdivided and which cannot be further subdivided *USE* (*1*) fml [Latin, neuter of *quantus* how much]

quantum leap *n* a sudden change, increase, or dramatic advance

ˈ**quantum** ˌ**theory** *n* a theory in physics based on the acceptance of the idea that all energy can be divided into quanta

[1]**quarantine** /ˈkworənˌteen‖ˈkwɒrənˌtiːn/ *n* **1** (the period of) a restraint on the activities or communication of people or the transport of goods or animals, designed to prevent the spread of disease or pests **2** a place in which people, animals, vehicles, etc under quarantine are kept **3** a state of enforced isolation [Italian *quarantina* period of forty days, fr Middle French *quarantaine*, fr *quarante* forty, fr Latin *quadraginta*]

[2]**quarantine** *vt* **1** to detain in or exclude by quarantine **2** to isolate from normal relations or communication

quark /kwahk, kwawk‖kwɑːk, kwɔːk/ *n* a hypothetical particle that carries a fractional electric charge and is held to be a constituent of known elementary particles

[1]**quarrel** /ˈkworəl‖ˈkwɒrəl/ *n* a short heavy square-headed arrow or bolt, esp for a crossbow

[2]**quarrel** *n* **1** a reason for dispute or complaint <*have no ~ with his reasoning*> **2** a usu verbal conflict between antagonists; a dispute

[3]**quarrel** *vi* **-ll-** (*NAm* **-l-**, **-ll-**) **1** to find fault *with* **2** to contend or dispute actively; argue – **quarreller** *n*

ˈ**quarrelsome** /-səm‖-səm/ *adj* inclined or quick to quarrel, esp in a petty manner – **quarrelsomely** *adv*, **quarrelsomeness** *n*

[1]**quarry** /ˈkwori‖ˈkwɒrɪ/ *n* the prey or game of a predator, esp a hawk, or of a hunter

[2]**quarry** *n* **1** an open excavation from which building materials (e g stone, slate, and sand) are obtained **2** a source from which useful material, esp information, may be extracted

[3]**quarry** *vt* **1** to obtain (as if) from a quarry **2** to make a quarry in ~ *vi* to dig (as if) in a quarry – **quarrier** *n*

quart /kwawt‖kwɔːt/ *n* either of 2 units of liquid capacity equal to 2pt: **a** a British unit equal to about 1.136l **b** a US unit equal to about 0.946l

[1]**quarter** /ˈkwawtə‖ˈkwɔːtə/ *n* **1** any of 4 equal parts into which sthg is divisible **2** any of various units equal to or derived from a fourth of some larger unit; *specif* a quarter of either an American or British hundredweight **3** a fourth of a measure of time: e g **3a** any of 4 3-month divisions of a year **b** a quarter of an hour – used in designation of time <~ *past four*> **4** (a coin worth) a quarter of a (US) dollar **5** a limb of a 4-limbed animal or carcass together with the adjacent parts; *esp* a hindquarter **6a** (the direction of or region round) a (cardinal) compass point **b** a person, group, direction, or place not specifically identified <*had financial help from many* ~s> **7** a division or district of a town or city <*the Chinese* ~> **8a** an assigned station or post – usu pl <*battle* ~s> **b** *pl* living accommodation; lodgings; *esp* accommodation for military personnel or their families **9** merciful consideration of an opponent; *specif* the clemency of not killing a defeated enemy <*gave him no* ~> **10** a fourth part of the moon's periodic cycle **11** any of the 4 or more parts of a heraldic shield that are marked off by horizontal and vertical lines **12** the part of a ship's side towards the stern; *also* any direction to the rear of abeam and from a specified side <*light on the port* ~> **13** any of the 4 equal periods into which the playing time of some games is divided

[2]**quarter** *vt* **1** to divide into 4 (almost) equal parts; *broadly* to divide into parts **2** to provide with lodgings or shelter; *esp* to assign (a member of the armed forces) to accommodation <~ed *his men on the villagers*> **3** *esp of a gun dog* to crisscross (an area) in many directions in search of game, or in order to pick up an animal's scent **4a** to arrange or bear (e g different coats of arms) in heraldic quarters on 1 shield **b** to add (a coat of arms) to others on 1 heraldic shield **c** to divide (a heraldic shield)

into 4 or more sections **5** *archaic* to divide (esp a traitor's body) into 4 parts, usu after hanging ~ *vi* **1** to lodge, dwell **2** to strike on a ship's quarter <*the wind was* ~ing>

[3]**quarter** *adj* consisting of or equal to a quarter

ˈ**quarter ˌday** *n* a day which begins a quarter of the year and on which a quarterly payment often falls due

ˈ**quarterˌdeck** /-ˌdek‖-ˌdek/ *n* **1** the stern area of a ship's upper deck **2** *sing or pl in constr, chiefly Br* the officers of a ship or navy

ˈ**quarterˌfinal** /-ˌfienl‖-ˌfaɪnl/ *n* a match whose winner goes through to the semifinals of a knockout tournament; *also, pl* a round made up of such matches – **quarterfinal** *adj*, **quarterfinalist** *n*

quartering /ˈkwawt(ə)ring‖ˈkwɔːt(ə)rɪŋ/ *n* the division of a heraldic shield into 4 or more heraldic quarters; *also* any of the heraldic quarters so formed or the coat of arms it bears

[1]**quarterly** /ˈkwawtəli‖ˈkwɔːtəlɪ/ *n* a periodical published at 3-monthly intervals

[2]**quarterly** *adj* **1** computed for or payable at 3-monthly intervals <*a* ~ *premium*> **2** recurring, issued, or spaced at 3-monthly intervals – **quarterly** *adv*

ˈ**quarterˌmaster** /-ˌmahstə‖-ˌmɑːstə/ *n* **1** a petty officer or seaman who attends to a ship's compass, tiller or wheel, and signals **2** an army officer who provides clothing, subsistence, and quarters for a body of troops

ˈ**quarter ˌnote** *n, NAm* a crotchet

ˈ**quarter ˌsessions** *n pl, often cap Q&S* a former English local court with limited criminal and civil jurisdiction, held quarterly

ˈ**quarterˌstaff** /-ˌstahf‖-ˌstɑːf/ *n, pl* **quarterstaves** /-ˌstayvz, -ˌstahvz‖-ˌsteɪvz, -ˌstɑːvz/ a long stout staff formerly used as a weapon

quartet *also* **quartette** /kwawˈtet‖kwɔːˈtet/ *n* **1** (a musical composition for) a group of 4 instruments, voices, or performers **2** *sing or pl in constr* a group or set of 4

quarto /ˈkwawtoh‖ˈkwɔːtəʊ/ *n, pl* **quartos** **1** (a book or page of) the size of a piece of paper cut 4 from a sheet **2** *Br* a size of paper usu 10 × 8in (about 25 × 20cm) – not used technically

[1]**quartz** /kwawts‖kwɔːts/ *n* a mineral consisting of a silicon dioxide occurring in colourless and transparent or coloured hexagonal crystals or in crystalline masses – **quartzose** *adj*

[2]**quartz** *adj* controlled by the oscillations of a quartz crystal <*a* ~ *watch*>

quasar /ˈkwaysah‖ˈkweɪsɑː/ *n* any of various unusually bright very distant star-like celestial objects that have spectra with large red shifts [*quas*i-stell*ar* radio source]

quash /kwosh‖kwɒʃ/ *vt* **1a** to nullify (by judicial action) **b** to reject (a legal document) as invalid **2** to suppress or extinguish summarily and completely; subdue

quasi- *comb form* to some degree; partly; seemingly <quasi-*officially*>

quatercentenary /ˌkwatəsenˈteenəri, -ˈtenəri‖ˌkwætəsenˈtiːnərɪ, -ˈtenərɪ/ *n* (the celebration of) a 400th anniversary

Quaternary /kwəˈtuhnəri‖kwəˈtɜːnərɪ/ *adj or n* (of or being) the geological period that extends from about 1.8 million years ago to the present

quatrain /ˈkwotrayn‖ˈkwɒtreɪn/ *n* a stanza of 4 lines

[1]**quaver** /ˈkwayvə‖ˈkweɪvə/ *vi* **1** *esp of the voice* to tremble, shake **2** to speak or sing in a trembling voice ~*vt* to utter in a quavering voice – **quaveringly** *adv*, **quavery** *adj*

[2]**quaver** *n* **1** a musical note with the time value of $^1/_2$ that of a crotchet **2** a tremulous sound

quay /kee‖kiː/ *n* an artificial landing place beside navigable water for loading and unloading ships – **quayage** *n*

quean /kween‖kwiːn/ *n, chiefly Scot* a woman; *esp* one who is young or unmarried

queasy *also* **queazy** /ˈkweezi‖ˈkwiːzɪ/ *adj* **1** causing or suffering from nausea **2** causing or feeling anxiety or uneasiness – **queasily** *adv*, **queasiness** *n*

[1]**queen** /kween‖kwiːn/ *n* **1** the wife or widow of a king **2** a female monarch **3** (sthg personified as) a woman who is preeminent in a specified respect <*a beauty* ~> <*Paris,* ~ *of cities*> **4** the most powerful piece of each colour in a set of chessmen, which has the power to move any number of squares in any direction **5** a playing card marked with a stylized figure of a queen and ranking usu below the king **6** the fertile fully developed female in a colony of bees, ants, or termites **7** a mature female cat **8** an aging male homosexual – used esp by male homosexuals

[2]**queen** *vi, of a pawn* to become a queen in chess ~*vt* to promote (a pawn) to a queen in chess – **queen it** to put on airs

ˌ**queen ˈconsort** *n, pl* **queens consort** the wife of a reigning king

ˌ**queen ˈmother** *n* a woman who is the widow of a king and the mother of the reigning sovereign

ˌ**Queen's ˈBench, Queen's Bench Division** *n* a division of the High Court hearing both civil and criminal cases – used when the British monarch is a queen

ˌ**Queen's ˈCounsel** *n* a barrister who has been appointed by the Crown to a senior rank with special privileges – used when the British monarch is a queen

[1]**queer** /kwiə‖kwɪə/ *adj* **1a** eccentric, unconventional **b** mildly insane **2** questionable, suspicious <~ *goings-on*> **3** not quite well; queasy – infml **4** homosexual – derog – **queerish** *adj*, **queerly** *adv*, **queerness** *n*

[2]**queer** *vt* to spoil the effect or success of <~ *one's plans*> – **queer someone's pitch** to prejudice or ruin sby's chances in advance

[3]**queer** *n* a usu male homosexual – derog

quell /kwel‖kwel/ *vt* **1** to overwhelm thoroughly and reduce to submission or passivity **2** to quiet, pacify <~ *fears*> – **queller** *n*

quench /kwench‖kwentʃ/ *vt* **1a** to put out (the light or fire of) <~ed *the fire by throwing on sand*> <~ed *the glowing coals*> **b** to cool (e g hot metal) suddenly by immersion in oil, water, etc; *broadly* to cause to lose heat or warmth **2a** to bring (sthg immaterial) to an end, esp by satisfying, damping, or decreasing <*the praise that* ~es *all desire to read the book* – T S Eliot> **b** to terminate (as if) by destroying; eliminate <~ *a rebellion*> **c** to relieve or satisfy with liquid

< ~ed *his thirst at a wayside spring*> – **quenchable** *adj*, **quencher** *n*, **quenchless** *adj*

querulous /'kwer(y)oolǝs‖'kwer(j)ʊlǝs/ *adj* habitually complaining; fretful, peevish – **querulously** *adv*, **querulousness** *n*

[1]query /'kwiǝri‖'kwɪǝrɪ/ *n* **1** a question, esp expressing doubt or uncertainty **2** QUESTION MARK; *esp* one used to question the accuracy of a text

[2]query *vt* **1** to put as a question <*'what's wrong?' she* queried> **2** to question the accuracy of (e g a statement) **3** to mark with a query **4** *chiefly NAm* to ask questions of – **querier** *n*

[1]quest /kwest‖kwest/ *n* **1** (the object of) a pursuit or search <*went in* ~ *of gold*> **2** an adventurous journey undertaken by a knight in medieval romance

[2]quest *vi* **1** *of a dog* to search for a trail or game **2** to go on a quest < ~ing *after gold*> ~*vt* to search for – chiefly poetic

[1]question /'kwesch(ǝ)n‖'kwestʃ(ǝ)n/ *n* **1a** a command or an interrogative expression used to elicit information or test knowledge <*unable to answer the exam* ~> **b** an interrogative sentence or clause **2** an act or instance of asking; an inquiry **3a** a subject or concern that is uncertain or in dispute; an issue <*the abortion* ~>; *broadly* a problem, matter <*it's only a* ~ *of time*> **b** a subject or point of debate or a proposition to be voted on in a meeting <*the* ~ *before the House*> **c** the specific point at issue **4a** (room for) doubt or objection <*her integrity is beyond* ~> **b** chance, possibility <*no* ~ *of escape*> – **in question** under discussion – **out of the question** preposterous, impossible

[2]question *vt* **1a** to ask a question of **b** to interrogate < ~ed *her as to her whereabouts*> **2** to doubt, dispute < ~ed *the wisdom of his decision*> **3** to subject (facts or phenomena) to analysis; examine ~ *vi* to ask questions; inquire – **questioner** *n*

questionable /'kweschǝnǝbl‖'kwestʃǝnǝbl/ *adj* **1** open to doubt or challenge; not certain or exact **2** of doubtful morality or propriety; shady – **questionableness** *n*, **questionably** *adv*

'question ˌmark *n* a punctuation mark ? used at the end of a sentence to indicate a direct question

'question-ˌmaster *n* one who puts questions during a quiz

questionnaire /ˌkweschǝ'neǝ‖ˌkwestʃǝ'neǝ; *also* ˌkes-‖ˌkes-/ *n* (a form having) a set of questions to be asked of a number of people to obtain statistically useful information

'question ˌtime *n* a period during which members of a parliamentary body may put questions to a minister

[1]queue /kyooh‖kjuː/ *n* **1** a pigtail **2a** a waiting line, esp of people or vehicles **b** WAITING LIST <*a housing* ~> [French, lit., tail, fr Latin *cauda, coda*]

[2]queue *vi* **queuing, queueing** to line up or wait in a queue – **queuer** *n*

[1]quibble /'kwibl‖'kwɪbl/ *n* a minor objection or criticism, esp used as an equivocation

[2]quibble *vi* **1** to equivocate **2** to bicker – **quibbler** *n*

quiche /keesh‖kiːʃ/ *n* a pastry shell filled with a rich savoury custard and other ingredients (e g ham or vegetables)

[1]quick /kwik‖kwɪk/ *adj* **1a** fast in understanding, thinking, or learning; mentally agile **b** reacting with speed and keen sensitivity **2a** fast in development or occurrence <*a* ~ *succession of events*> **b** done or taking place with rapidity <*gave them a* ~ *look*> **c** marked by speed, readiness, or promptness of physical movement <*walked with* ~ *steps*> **d** inclined to hastiness (e g in action or response) < ~ *to find fault*> **3** *archaic* alive – **quickly** *adv*, **quickness** *n*

[2]quick *adv* in a quick manner

[3]quick *n* **1** painfully sensitive flesh, esp under a fingernail, toenail, etc **2** the inmost sensibilities <*cut to the* ~ *by the remark*>

quicken /'kwikǝn‖'kwɪkǝn/ *vt* **1** to enliven, stimulate **2** to make more rapid; accelerate ~ *vi* **1** to come to life **2** to reach the stage of gestation at which foetal motion is felt **3** to become more rapid – **quickener** *n*

ˌquick-'freeze *vt* **quick-froze; quick-frozen** to freeze (food) for preservation so rapidly that the natural juices and flavour are preserved intact

quickie /'kwiki‖'kwɪkɪ/ *n* sthg done or made in a hurry – infml

'quickˌlime /-ˌliem‖-ˌlaɪm/ *n* LIME 2a

'quickˌsand /-ˌsand‖-ˌsænd/ *n* (a deep mass of) loose sand, esp mixed with water, into which heavy objects readily sink

'quickˌset /-ˌset‖-ˌset/ *n, chiefly Br* plant cuttings, esp hawthorn, set in the ground to grow into a hedgerow; *also* a hedge formed in this way

'quickˌsilver /-ˌsilvǝ‖-ˌsɪlvǝ/ *n* MERCURY 1 – **quicksilver** *adj*

'quickˌstep /-ˌstep‖-ˌstep/ *n* (a piece of music composed for) a fast fox-trot characterized by a combination of short rapid steps

'quick ˌtime *n* a rate of marching of about 120 steps in a minute

ˌquick-'witted *adj* quick in understanding; mentally alert – **quick-wittedly** *adv*, **quick-wittedness** *n*

[1]quid /kwid‖kwɪd/ *n, pl* **quid** *also* **quids** *Br* the sum of £1 – infml – **quids in** in the state of having made a usu large profit – infml

[2]quid *n* a wad of sthg, esp tobacco, for chewing

quid pro quo /ˌkwid proh 'kwoh‖ˌkwɪd prǝʊ 'kwǝʊ/ *n* sthg given or received in exchange for sthg else [Latin, something for something]

quiescent /kwi'es(ǝ)nt‖kwɪ'es(ǝ)nt/ *adj* **1** causing no trouble **2** at rest; inactive – fml – **quiescence** *n*, **quiescently** *adv*

[1]quiet /'kwie·ǝt‖'kwaɪǝt/ *n* being quiet; tranquillity – **on the quiet** without telling anyone; discreetly, secretly

[2]quiet *adj* **1a** marked by little or no motion or activity; calm <*a* ~ *day at the office*> **b** free from noise or uproar; still <*a* ~ *little village in the Cotswolds*> **c** secluded <*a* ~ *nook*> **d** enjoyed in peace and relaxation; undisturbed <*a* ~ *cup of tea*> **2a** gentle, reserved <*a* ~ *temperament*> **b** unobtrusive, conservative < ~ *clothes*> – **quietly** *adv*, **quietness** *n*

[3]quiet *adv* in a quiet manner

[4]quiet *vt* to calm, soothe ~ *vi, chiefly NAm* to become quiet – usu + *down* – **quieter** *n*

quieten /'kwie·ətn||'kwaɪətn/ *vb, chiefly Br* to make or become quiet – often + *down*
quietism /'kwie·ə,tiz(ə)m||'kwaɪə,tɪz(ə)m/ *n* (a system of religious mysticism teaching) a passive withdrawn attitude or policy towards the world or worldly affairs – **quietist** *adj or n*
quietude /'kwie·ətyoohd||'kwaɪətju:d/ *n* being quiet; repose – fml
quietus /kwie'eetəs, -'aytəs||kwaɪ'i:təs, -'eɪtəs/ *n* removal from activity; *esp* death
quiff /kwif||kwɪf/ *n, Br* a lock of hair brushed so as to stand up over the forehead
quill /kwil||kwɪl/ *n* **1a** a bobbin, spool, or spindle on which yarn is wound **b** a hollow shaft often surrounding another shaft and used in various mechanical devices **2a** the hollow horny barrel of a feather **b** any of the large stiff feathers of a bird's wing or tail **c** any of the hollow sharp spines of a porcupine, hedgehog, etc **3** sthg made from or resembling the quill of a feather; *esp* a pen for writing
[1]**quilt** /kwilt||kwɪlt/ *n* **1** a thick warm top cover for a bed consisting of padding held in place between 2 layers of cloth by lines of stitching **2** a usu thinnish cover for a bed; a bedspread
[2]**quilt** *vt* **1a** to fill, pad, or line like a quilt **b** to fasten between 2 pieces of material **2** to stitch or sew together in layers with padding in between to make quilts or quilted work – **quilter** *n*, **quilting** *n*
quin /kwin||kwɪn/ *n, Br* a quintuplet
quince /kwins||kwɪns/ *n* (a central Asian tree that bears) a fruit resembling a hard-fleshed yellow apple, used for jelly and preserves
quinine /'kwineen, -'-||'kwɪni:n, -'-/ *n* an alkaloid with a bitter taste that is obtained from cinchona bark, is used as a tonic, and was formerly the major drug in the treatment of malaria
Quinquagesima /,kwingkwə'jesimə||,kwɪŋkwə'dʒesɪmə/ *n* the Sunday before Lent
quinsy /'kwinzi||'kwɪnzɪ/ *n* a severe inflammation of the throat or adjacent parts with swelling and fever
quintal /'kwintl||'kwɪntl/ *n* **1** a hundredweight **2** a metric unit of weight equal to 100kg (about 220.5lb)
quintessence /kwin'tes(ə)ns||kwɪn'tes(ə)ns/ *n* **1** the pure and concentrated essence of sthg **2** the most typical example or representative (e g of a quality or class) [Middle French *quinte essence*, fr Medieval Latin *quinta essentia*, lit., fifth essence] – **quintessential** *adj*, **quintessentially** *adv*
quintet *also* **quintette** /kwin'tet||kwɪn'tet/ *n* **1** (a musical composition for) a group of 5 instruments, voices, or performers **2** *sing or pl in constr* a group or set of 5
quintuplet /'kwintyooplit, kwin'tyoohplit||'kwɪntjʊplɪt, kwɪn'tju:plɪt/ *n* **1** a combination of 5 of a kind **2** any of 5 offspring born at 1 birth **3** a group of 5 equal musical notes performed in the time given to 3, 4, etc of the same value
quip /kwip||kwɪp/ *vi or n* (to make) a clever, witty, or remark – **quipster** *n*
[1]**quire** /kwie·ə||kwaɪə/ *n* **1** twenty-four sheets of paper of the same size and quality **2** a set of folded sheets (e g of a book) fitting one within another
[2]**quire** *n, archaic* a choir
quirk /kwuhk||kwɜ:k/ *n* **1** an odd or peculiar trait; an idiosyncrasy **2** an accident, vagary *<by some ~ of fate>* – **quirky** *adj*
quisling /'kwizling||'kwɪzlɪŋ/ *n* a traitor who collaborates with invaders [Vidkun *Quisling* (1887-1945), Norwegian politician who collaborated with the Germans in WW II]
[1]**quit** /kwit||kwɪt/ *adj* released from obligation, charge, or penalty – + *of*
[2]**quit** *vb* **-tt-; quitted** (*NAm chiefly* **quit**) *vt* **1** to leave, depart from (a person or place) **2** to relinquish (e g a way of thinking or acting); stop **3** to give up (e g an activity or employment) **4** *archaic* to conduct (oneself) in a usu specified way ~ *vi* **1** to cease doing sthg; *specif* to give up one's job **2** *of a tenant* to vacate occupied premises **3** to admit defeat; GIVE UP – infml
quite /kwiet||kwaɪt/ *adv or adj* **1a** wholly, completely **b** positively, certainly **2** more than usually; rather **3** *chiefly Br* to only a moderate degree *<~ good but not perfect>* – **quite so** JUST SO 2
quits /kwits||kwɪts/ *adj* on even terms as a result of repaying a debt or retaliating for an injury
quittance /'kwit(ə)ns||'kwɪt(ə)ns/ *n* (a document giving proof of) discharge from a debt
quitter /'kwitə||'kwɪtə/ *n* one who gives up too easily; a defeatist
[1]**quiver** /'kwivə||'kwɪvə/ *n* a case for carrying or holding arrows
[2]**quiver** *vi* to shake or move with a slight trembling motion – **quiver** *n*
qui vive /,kee 'veev||,ki: 'vi:v/ *n the* alert, lookout – in *on the qui vive* [French *qui-vive*, fr *qui vive?* long live who?, challenge of a French sentry]
quixotic /kwik'sotik||kwɪk'sɒtɪk/, **quixotical** /-kl||-kl/ *adj* idealistic or chivalrous in a rash or impractical way [Don *Quixote*, hero of the novel *Don Quixote de la Mancha* by Miguel de Cervantes Saavedra (1547-1616), Spanish novelist] – **quixotically** *adv*
[1]**quiz** /kwiz||kwɪz/ *n* **-zz-** **1** a public test of (general) knowledge, esp as a television or radio entertainment **2** *NAm* an informal test given by a teacher to a student or class
[2]**quiz** *vt* **-zz-** **1** to question closely – journ **2** *NAm* to test (a student or class) informally – **quizzer** *n*
quizzical /'kwizikl||'kwɪzɪkl/ *adj* **1** gently mocking; teasing **2** indicating a state of puzzlement; questioning – **quizzically** *adv*, **quizzicality** *n*
quoit /koyt||kɔɪt; *also* kwoyt||kwɔɪt/ *n* **1** a ring (e g of rubber or iron) used in a throwing game **2** *pl but sing in constr* a game in which quoits are thrown at an upright pin in an attempt to ring the pin
quondam /'kwondam, -dəm||'kwɒndæm, -dəm/ *adj* former, sometime – fml
quorum /'kwawrəm||'kwɔ:rəm/ *n* the number of members of a body that when duly assembled is constitutionally competent to transact business
quota /'kwohtə||'kwəʊtə/ *n* **1** a proportional part or share; *esp* the share or proportion to be either contributed or received by an individual or body **2** the number or amount constituting a

proportional share **3** a numerical limit set on some class of people or things

quotable /'kwohtəbl‖'kwəʊtəbl/ *adj* fit for or worth quoting

quotation /kwoh'taysh(ə)n‖kwəʊ'teɪʃ(ə)n/ *n* **1** sthg quoted; *esp* a passage or phrase quoted from printed literature **2** quoting **3a** (the naming or publishing of) current bids and offers for or prices of shares, securities, commodities, etc **b** ESTIMATE 4

quo'tation ˌmark *n* either of a pair of punctuation marks " " or ' ' used to indicate the beginning and end of a direct quotation

[1]**quote** /kwoht‖kwəʊt/ *vt* **1a** to repeat (a passage or phrase previously said or written, esp by another) in writing or speech, usu with an acknowledgment **b** to repeat a passage or phrase from, esp in substantiation or illustration <*to ~ the Scriptures*> **2** to cite in illustration <*~ cases*> **3a** to name (the current or recent buying or selling price) of a commodity, stock, share, etc **b** to make an estimate of or give exact information on (e g the price of a commodity or service) **4** to set off by quotation marks ~ *vi* **1** to repeat sthg previously said or written **2** to name one's price

[2]**quote** *n* **1** a quotation **2** QUOTATION MARK – often used orally to indicate the beginning of a direct quotation

quoth /kwohth‖kwəʊθ/ *vb past, archaic* said – chiefly in the 1st and 3rd persons with a subject following <*~ he*>

quotidian /kwo'tidi·ən‖kwɒ'tɪdɪən/ *adj* **1** occurring or recurring every day <*~ fever*> **2** commonplace, ordinary – fml

quotient /'kwohsh(ə)nt‖'kwəʊʃ(ə)nt/ *n* **1** the result of the division of one number or expression by another **2** the ratio, usu multiplied by 100, between a test score and a measurement on which that score might be expected largely to depend

R

r /ah‖ɑː/ *n, pl* **r's, rs** *often cap* (a graphic representation of or device for reproducing) the 18th letter of the English alphabet

[1]**-r** *suffix* – used to form the comparative degree of adjectives and adverbs of 1 syllable, and of some adjectives and adverbs of 2 or more syllables, that end in *e* <*truer*>; compare [1]-ER

[2]**-r** *suffix* [2]-ER – used with nouns that end in *e* <*diner*>

rabbi /'rabie‖'ræbaɪ/ *n* **1** a Jew qualified to expound and apply Jewish law **2** a Jew trained and ordained for professional religious leadership; *specif* the official leader of a Jewish congregation – **rabbinic, rabbinical** *adj*

[1]**rabbit** /'rabit‖'ræbɪt/ *n,* **1** (the fur of) a small long-eared mammal that is related to the hares but differs from them in producing naked young and in its burrowing habits **2** *Br* an unskilful player (e g in golf, cricket, or tennis)

[2]**rabbit** *vi* **1** to hunt rabbits **2** *Br* to talk aimlessly or inconsequentially – infml; often + *on* – **rabbiter** *n*

'rabbit ˌpunch *n* a short chopping blow delivered to the back of the neck

rabble /'rabl‖'ræbl/ *n* **1** a disorganized or disorderly crowd of people; a mob **2** *the* common people; *the* lowest class of society – derog

'rabble-ˌrouser *n* one who stirs up the common people (e g to hatred or violence); a demagogue

Rabelaisian /ˌrabi'layzyən, -zh(y)ən‖ˌræbɪ'leɪzjən, -ʒ(j)ən/ *adj* marked by the robust humour, extravagant caricature, or bold naturalism characteristic of Rabelais or his works [François *Rabelais* (1494?-1553), French humorist]

rabid /'rabid‖'ræbɪd; *sense 2 also* 'raybid‖'reɪbɪd/ *adj* **1** unreasoning or fanatical in an opinion or feeling **2** affected with rabies – **rabidly** *adv*, **rabidness, rabidity** *n*

rabies /'raybeez, -biz‖'reɪbiːz, -bɪz/ *n,* a fatal short-lasting virus disease of the nervous system of warm-blooded animals, transmitted esp through the bite of an affected animal, and characterized by extreme fear of water and convulsions

raccoon, racoon /rə'koohn‖rə'kuːn/ *n,* (the fur of) a small flesh-eating mammal of N America that has a bushy ringed tail and lives chiefly in trees

[1]**race** /rays‖reɪs/ *n* **1a** a strong or rapid current of water in the sea, a river, etc **b** (the current flowing in) a watercourse used industrially (e g to turn the wheel of a mill) **2a** a contest of speed (e g in running or riding) **b** *pl* a meeting in which several races (e g for horses) are run **c** a contest or rivalry for an ultimate prize or position **3** a track or channel in which sthg rolls or slides; *specif* a groove for the balls in a ball bearing

[2]**race** *vi* **1** to compete in a race **2** to go or move at top speed or out of control **3** *of a motor, engine, etc* to revolve too fast under a diminished load ~ *vt* **1** to have a race with <~d *her brother to the garden gate*> **2a** to enter in a race <*always* ~s *his horses at Chepstow*> **b** to drive at high speed **c** to transport or propel at maximum speed **3** to accelerate (e g an engine) without a working load or with the transmission disengaged – **racer** *n*

[3]**race** *n* **1** a family, tribe, people, or nation belonging to the same stock **2** an actually or potentially interbreeding group within a species; *also* a category (e g a subspecies) in classification representing such a group **3a** a division of mankind having traits that are transmissible by descent and sufficient to characterize it as a distinct human type **b** human beings collectively <*the human ~*> **4** the division of mankind into races

'raceˌcourse /-ˌkaws‖-ˌkɔːs/ *n* a place where or the track on which races, esp horse races, are held

raceme /ray'seem, rə-‖reɪ'siːm, rə-/ *n* a simple stalk of flowers (e g that of the lily of the valley) in which the flowers are borne on short side-stalks of about equal length along an elongated main stem

racial /'raysh(ə)l‖'reɪʃ(ə)l/ *adj* **1** of or based on a race **2** existing or occurring between (human) races – **racially** *adv*

racialism /ˈrayshəˌliz(ə)m‖ˈreɪʃəˌlɪz(ə)m/ *n* **1** racial prejudice or discrimination **2** RACISM 1 – **racialist** *n or adj*, **racialistic** *adj*

racism /ˈraysiz(ə)m‖ˈreɪsɪz(ə)m/ *n* **1** a belief that racial differences produce an inherent superiority of a particular race **2** RACIALISM 1 – **racist** *n or adj*

[1]rack /rak‖ræk/ *n* a wind-driven mass of high often broken clouds

[2]rack *vi, of clouds* to fly or scud in high wind

[3]rack *n* **1** a framework for holding fodder for livestock **2** an instrument of torture on which the victim's body is stretched – usu + *the* **3** a framework, stand, or grating on or in which articles are placed **4** a bar with teeth on 1 face for meshing with a pinion or worm gear <~ *and pinion*> – **on the rack** under great mental or emotional stress

[4]rack *vt* **1** to torture on the rack **2** to cause to suffer torture, pain, or anguish <~ed *by headaches*> **3a** to stretch or strain considerably <~ed *his brains*> **b** to raise (rents) oppressively **4** to place in a rack

[5]rack *vt* to draw off (e g wine) from the lees

[6]rack *n* the front rib section of lamb used for chops or as a roast

[7]rack *n* destruction – chiefly in *rack and ruin*

[1]racket *also* **racquet** /ˈrakit‖ˈrækɪt/ *n* **1** a lightweight implement that consists of a netting stretched in an open frame with a handle attached and that is used for striking the ball or shuttle in any of various games (e g tennis, squash, or badminton) **2** *pl but sing in constr* a game for 2 or 4 players played with a ball and rackets on a 4-walled court [Middle French *raquette*, fr Italian *racchetta*, fr Arabic *rāḥah* palm of the hand]

[2]racket *n* **1** a loud and confused noise; a din **2a** a fraudulent enterprise made workable esp by bribery or intimidation **b** an easy and lucrative means of livelihood – infml **c** a usu specified occupation or business – slang <*he's in the publicity* ~>

[3]racket *vi* **1** to engage in an active, esp a dissipated, social life – usu + *about* or *round* **2** to move with or make a racket

racketeer /ˌrakiˈtiə‖ˌrækɪˈtɪə/ *n* one who extorts money or advantages by threats, blackmail, etc – **racketeer** *vi*

rack railway *n* a railway having between its running rails a rack that meshes with a gear wheel or pinion on a locomotive

ˈrack ˌrent *vt or n* (to subject to) an excessive or unreasonably high rent

raconteur /ˌrakonˈtuh‖ˌrækɒnˈtɜː/ *n* one who excels in telling anecdotes

racoon /rəˈkoohn‖rəˈkuːn/ *n* a raccoon

racy /ˈraysi‖ˈreɪsɪ/ *adj* **1** full of zest or vigour **2** having a strongly marked quality; piquant <*a ~ flavour*> **3** risqué, suggestive – **racily** *adv*, **raciness** *n*

radar /ˈraydah‖ˈreɪdɑː/ *n* an electronic device that generates high-frequency radio waves and locates objects in the vicinity by analysis of the radio waves reflected back from them [*ra*dio *de*tection *a*nd *r*anging]

raddled /ˈradld‖ˈrædld/ *adj* dilapidated; *esp* haggard with age or dissipation

[1]radial /ˈraydyəl‖ˈreɪdjəl/ *adj* **1** (having parts) arranged like rays or radii from a central point or axis **2a** relating to, placed like, or moving along a radius **b** characterized by divergence from a centre **3** of or situated near a radius bone (e g in the human forearm) – **radially** *adv*

[2]radial *n* **1** any line in a system of radial lines **2** a radial body part (e g an artery) **3 radial, radial tyre** a pneumatic tyre in which the ply cords are laid at a right angle to the centre line of the tread

[1]radiant /ˈraydyənt‖ˈreɪdjənt/ *adj* **1a** radiating rays or reflecting beams of light **b** vividly bright and shining; glowing **2** marked by or expressive of love, confidence, or happiness <*a ~ smile*> **3a** emitted or transmitted by radiation <~ *energy*> **b** of or emitting radiant heat – **radiance, radiancy** *n*, **radiantly** *adv*

[2]radiant *n* **1** the apparent point of origin of a meteor shower **2** a point or object from which light or heat emanates; *specif* the part of a gas or electric heater that becomes incandescent

[1]radiate /ˈraydiˌayt‖ˈreɪdɪˌeɪt/ *vi* **1** to send out rays of light, heat, or any other form of radiation **2** to issue in rays **3** to proceed in a direct line from or towards a centre ~ *vt* **1a** to send out in rays **b** to show or display clearly <~s *health and vitality*> **2** to disseminate (as if) from a centre

[2]radiate /-ət‖-ət/ *adj* having rays or radial parts; *specif* having radial symmetry – **radiately** *adv*

radiation /ˌraydiˈaysh(ə)n‖ˌreɪdɪˈeɪʃ(ə)n/ *n* **1** the action or process of radiating; *esp* the process of emitting radiant energy in the form of waves or particles **2** energy radiated in the form of waves or particles; *esp* electromagnetic radiation (e g light) or emission from radioactive sources (e g alpha rays) **3** a radial arrangement – **radiational** *adj*

radiˈation ˌsickness *n* sickness that results from overexposure to ionizing radiation (e g X-rays), commonly marked by fatigue, nausea, vomiting, loss of teeth and hair, and, in more severe cases, leukaemia

radiator /ˈraydiˌaytə‖ˈreɪdɪˌeɪtə/ *n* **1** a room heater (with a large surface area for radiating heat); *specif* one through which hot water or steam circulates as part of a central-heating system **2** a device with a large surface area used for cooling an internal-combustion engine by means of water circulating through it

[1]radical /ˈradikl‖ˈrædɪkl/ *adj* **1a** of or growing from the root or the base of a stem **b** of or constituting a linguistic root **c** of or involving a mathematical root **d** designed to remove the root of a disease or all diseased tissue <~ *surgery*> **2** essential, fundamental **3a** departing from the usual or traditional; extreme **b** affecting or involving the basic composition or nature of sthg; thoroughgoing <~ *changes*> **c** tending or disposed to make extreme changes in existing views, conditions, institutions, etc **d** of or constituting a political group advocating extreme measures <*the ~ right*> – **radicalism** *n*, **radicalize** *vt*, **radically** *adv*, **radicalness** *n*, **radicalization** *n*

[2]**radical** *n* **1** ROOT 6 **2** sby who is a member of a radical party or who holds radical views **3** a group of atoms that is replaceable in a molecule by a single atom and is capable of remaining unchanged during a series of reactions

radicle /ˈradikl‖ˈrædɪkl/ *n* **1** the lower part of the axis of a plant embryo or seedling, including the embryonic root **2** the rootlike beginning of an anatomical vessel or part **3** a radical – **radicular** *adj*

radii /ˈraydiˌie‖ˈreɪdɪˌaɪ/ *pl of* RADIUS

[1]**radio** /ˈraydiˌoh‖ˈreɪdɪˌəʊ/ *n, pl* **radios** **1** (the use of) the system of wireless transmission and reception of signals by means of electromagnetic waves **2** a radio receiver **3a** a radio transmitter (e g in an aircraft) **b** a radio broadcasting organization or station <Radio *London*> **c** the radio broadcasting industry **d** the medium of radio communication

[2]**radio** *adj* **1** of electric currents or phenomena of frequencies between about 15,000 and 10^{11}Hz **2a** of, used in, or transmitted or received by a radio **b** making or participating in radio broadcasts **c** controlled or directed by or using radio

[3]**radio** *vb* **radios; radioing; radioed** *vt* **1** to send or communicate by radio **2** to send a radio message to ~*vi* to send or communicate sthg by radio

radio-, **radi-** *comb form* **1** radial <radio*symmetrical*> **2a** radiant energy; radiation <radi*odermatitis*> **b** radioactive <radio*element*> **c** using ionizing radiation <radio*therapy*> **d** radioactive isotopes of (a specified element) <radi*ocarbon*> **e** radio <radio*telegraphy*>

ˌ**radioacˈtivity** /ˌraydioh·akˈtivəti‖ˌreɪdɪəʊækˈtɪvətɪ/ *n* the property possessed by some elements (e g uranium) of spontaneously emitting alpha or beta rays and sometimes also gamma rays by the disintegration of the nuclei of atoms – **radioactive** *adj*, **radioactively** *adv*

ˈ**radio** ˌ**frequency** *n* a frequency (e g of electromagnetic waves) intermediate between audio frequencies and infrared frequencies and used esp in radio and television transmission

radiogram /ˈraydi·əˌgram, -dioh-‖ˈreɪdɪəˌgræm, -dɪəʊ-/ *n* **1** a radiograph **2** *Br* a combined radio receiver and record player

radiograph /ˈraydi·əˌgrahf, -ˌgraf, -dioh-‖ˈreɪdɪəˌgrɑːf, -ˌgræf, -dɪəʊ-/ *n* a picture produced on a sensitive surface by a form of radiation other than light; *specif* an X-ray or gamma-ray photograph – **radiograph** *vt*, **radiographic** *adj*, **radiographically** *adv*, **radiographer** *n*

radioisotope /ˌraydiohˈiesətohp‖ˌreɪdɪəʊˈaɪsətəʊp/ *n* a radioactive isotope – **radioisotopic** *adj*, **radioisotopically** *adv*

radiology /ˌraydiˈoləji‖ˌreɪdɪˈɒlədʒɪ/ *n* the study and use of radioactive substances and high-energy radiations; *esp* the use of radiant energy (e g X rays and gamma rays) in the diagnosis and treatment of disease – **radiologist** *n*, **radiological** *adj*

radiotelegraphy /ˌraydiohtəˈlegrəfi‖ˌreɪdɪəʊtəˈlegrəfɪ/ *n* telegraphy carried out by means of radio waves – **radiotelegraphic** *adj*

ˌ**radioˈtelephone** /-ˈtelifohn‖-ˈtelɪfəʊn/ *n* an apparatus for enabling telephone messages to be sent via radio (e g from a moving vehicle) – **radiotelephony** *n*

ˌ**radio ˈtelescope** *n* a radio receiver connected to a large often dish-shaped aerial for recording and measuring radio waves from celestial bodies

ˌ**radioˈtherapy** /-ˈtherəpi‖-ˈθerəpɪ/ *n* the treatment of disease (e g cancer) by means of X rays or radiation from radioactive substances – **radiotherapist** *n*

radish /ˈradish‖ˈrædɪʃ/ *n* (a plant of the mustard family with) a pungent fleshy typically dark red root, eaten raw as a salad vegetable

radium /ˈraydyəm‖ˈreɪdjəm/ *n* an intensely radioactive metallic element that occurs in minute quantities in pitchblende and some other minerals and is used chiefly in luminous materials and in the treatment of cancer

radius /ˈraydi·əs‖ˈreɪdɪəs/ *n, pl* **radii** /-diˌie‖-dɪˌaɪ/ *also* **radiuses** **1** the bone on the thumb side of the human forearm; *also* a corresponding part in forms of vertebrate animals higher than fishes **2** (the length of) a straight line extending from the centre of a circle or sphere to the circumference or surface **3a** the circular area defined by a stated radius **b** a bounded or circumscribed area **4** a radial part (e g a spoke of a wheel)

raffia, **raphia** /ˈrafi·ə‖ˈræfɪə/ *n* the fibre of a palm used esp for making baskets, hats, and table mats

raffish /ˈrafish‖ˈræfɪʃ/ *adj* marked by careless unconventionality; rakish – **raffishly** *adv*, **raffishness** *n*

raffle /ˈrafl‖ˈræfl/ *vt or n* (to dispose of by means of) a lottery in which the prizes are usually goods

[1]**raft** /rahft‖rɑːft/ *n* **1a** a collection of logs or timber fastened together for transport by water **b** a flat usu wooden structure designed to float on water and used as a platform or vessel **2** a foundation slab for a building, usu made of reinforced concrete

[2]**raft** *vt* **1a** to transport in the form of or by means of a raft **b** to cross (e g a lake or river) by raft **2** to make into a raft ~*vi* to travel by raft

[3]**raft** *n, chiefly NAm* a large collection or quantity

[1]**rafter** /ˈrahftə‖ˈrɑːftə/ *n* any of the parallel beams that form the framework of a roof

[2]**rafter** *n* one who manoeuvres logs into position and binds them into rafts

[1]**rag** /rag‖ræg/ *n* **1a** (a waste piece of) worn cloth **b** *pl* clothes, esp when in poor or ragged condition **2** a usu sensational or poorly written newspaper

[2]**rag** *n* any of various hard rocks used in building

[3]**rag** *vb* **-gg-** *vt* to torment, tease ~*vi* to engage in horseplay

[4]**rag** *n, chiefly Br* **1** an outburst of boisterous fun; a prank **2** a series of processions and stunts organized by students to raise money for charity

[5]**rag** *n* (a composition or dance in) ragtime

raga /ˈrahgə‖ˈrɑːgə/ *n* (an improvisation based on) any of the ancient traditional melodic patterns or modes in Indian music

ragamuffin /ˈragəˌmufin‖ˈrægəˌmʌfɪn/ *n* a ragged often disreputable person, esp a child

ragbag /ˈragˌbag‖ˈrægˌbæg/ *n* **1** a dishevelled or slovenly person **2** a miscellaneous collection *USE* infml

[1]**rage** /rayj||reɪdʒ/ *n* **1** (a fit or bout of) violent and uncontrolled anger **2** violent action (e g of the wind or sea) **3** an intense feeling; passion **4** (an object of) fashionable and temporary enthusiasm – infml [Middle French, fr Late Latin *rabia*, fr Latin *rabies* rage, madness, fr *rabere* to be mad]

[2]**rage** *vi* **1** to be in a rage **2** to be violently stirred up or in tumult **3** to be unchecked in violence or effect

ragged /ˈragid||ˈrægɪd/ *adj* **1** having an irregular edge or outline **2** torn or worn to tatters **3** wearing tattered clothes **4a** straggly **b** showing irregularities; uneven – **raggedly** *adv*, **raggedness** *n*

raglan /ˈraglən||ˈræglən/ *n* a loose overcoat with raglan sleeves [F J H Somerset, Baron *Raglan* (1788-1855), English field-marshal]

raglan sleeve *n* a sleeve that extends to the neckline with slanted seams from under the arm to the neck

ragout /ˈragooh, -ˈ-||ˈrægu:, -ˈ-/ *n* a well-seasoned stew, esp of meat and vegetables, cooked in a thick sauce

ragtime /ˈrag,tiem||ˈræg,taɪm/ *n* (music having) rhythm characterized by strong syncopation in the melody with a regularly accented accompaniment

ˈ**rag ,trade** *n the* clothing trade – infml

[1]**raid** /rayd||reɪd/ *n* **1a** a usu hostile incursion made in order to seize sby or sthg <*a cattle* ~> **b** a surprise attack by a small force **2** a sudden invasion by the police (e g in search of criminals or stolen goods) **3** an attempt to depress share prices by concerted selling **4** an act of robbery

[2]**raid** *vt* to make a raid on ~*vi* to take part in a raid – **raider** *n*

[1]**rail** /rayl||reɪl/ *n* **1a** an esp horizontal bar, usu supported by posts, which may serve as a barrier (e g across a balcony) or as a support on or from which sthg (e g a curtain) may be hung **b** a horizontal structural support (e g in a door) **2a** RAILING 1 **b** either of the fences on each side of a horse-racing track – usu pl with sing. meaning **3a** either of a pair of lengths of rolled steel forming a guide and running surface (e g a railway) for wheeled vehicles **b** the railway <*always travels by* ~> – **off the rails 1** away from the proper or normal course; awry **2** mad, crazy

[2]**rail** *vt* to enclose or separate with a rail or rails – often + *off*

[3]**rail** *n* any of numerous wading birds of small or medium size, usu having very long toes which enable them to run on soft wet ground

[4]**rail** *vi* to utter angry complaints or abuse – often + *against* or *at* – **railer** *n*

railcar /ˈrayl,kah||ˈreɪl,kɑ:/ *n* a self-propelled railway carriage

railhead /ˈrayl,hed||ˈreɪl,hed/ *n* the farthest point reached by a railway; *also* the point at which goods are transferred to or from road transport

railing /ˈrayling||ˈreɪlɪŋ/ *n* **1** a usu vertical rail in a fence or similar barrier **2** (material for making) rails

raillery /ˈrayl(ə)ri||ˈreɪl(ə)rɪ/ *n* (a piece of) good-humoured teasing

[1]**railroad** /ˈrayl,rohd||ˈreɪl,rəʊd/ *n, NAm* a railway

[2]**railroad** *vt* **1a** to push through hastily or without due consideration **b** to hustle into taking action or making a decision **2** *NAm* to transport by rail **3** *NAm* to convict with undue haste or by unjust means – **railroader** *n*

railway /ˈrayl,way||ˈreɪl,weɪ/ *n, chiefly Br* **1** a line of track usu having 2 parallel lines or rails fixed to sleepers on which vehicles run to transport goods and passengers; *also* such a track and its assets (e g rolling stock and buildings) constituting a single property **2** an organization which runs a railway network

raiment /ˈraymənt||ˈreɪmənt/ *n* garments, clothing – poetic

[1]**rain** /rayn||reɪn/ *n* **1a** (a descent of) water falling in drops condensed from vapour in the atmosphere **b** rainwater **2** *pl* the rainy season **3** rainy weather **4** a dense flow or fall of sthg <*a steady* ~ *of fire from the helicopters*>

[2]**rain** *vi* **1** *of rain* to fall in drops from the clouds **2** to fall in profusion ~ *vt* **1** to cause to fall; pour or send down **2** to bestow abundantly – **rain cats and dogs** to rain heavily

rainbow /ˈraynboh||ˈreɪnbəʊ/ *n* **1** an arch in the sky consisting of a series of concentric arcs of the colours red, orange, yellow, green, blue, indigo, and violet, formed esp opposite the sun by the refraction, reflection, and interference of light rays in raindrops, spray, etc **2** an array of bright colours

,**rainbow ˈtrout** *n* a large stout-bodied trout of Europe and western N America

ˈ**rain,coat** /-,koht||-,kəʊt/ *n* a coat made from waterproof or water-resistant material

ˈ**rain,fall** /-,fawl||-,fɔ:l/ *n* **1** a fall of rain; a shower **2** the amount of rain that has fallen in a given area during a given time, usu measured by depth

ˈ**rain ,forest** *n* a dense tropical woodland with an annual rainfall of at least 2500mm (about 100in) and containing lofty broad-leaved evergreen trees forming a continuous canopy

ˈ**rain ,gauge** *n* an instrument for measuring rainfall

rain off *vt, chiefly Br* to interrupt or prevent (e g a sporting fixture) by rain – usu pass

ˈ**rain,proof** /-,proohf||-,pru:f/ *vt or adj* (to make) impervious to rain

ˈ**rain,water** /-,wawtə||-,wɔ:tə/ *n* water that has fallen as rain and is therefore usu soft

rainy /ˈrayni||ˈreɪnɪ/ *adj* **1** having or characterized by heavy rainfall **2** wet with rain <~ *streets*>

[1]**raise** /rayz||reɪz/ *vt* **1** to cause or help to rise to an upright or standing position **2a** to awaken, arouse **b** to stir up; incite **c** to recall (as if) from death **d** to establish radio communication with **3a** to build, erect **b** to lift up **c** to place higher in rank or dignity **d** to invigorate <~ *the spirits*> **e** to end the operation of <~ *a siege*> **4a** to levy, obtain <~ *funds*> **b** to assemble, collect <~ *an army*> **5a** to grow, cultivate **b** to rear (e g a child) **6a** to give rise to; provoke <~ *a laugh*> **b** to give voice or expression to <~ *a cheer*> **7** to bring up for consideration

or debate <~ *an issue*> **8a** to increase the strength, intensity, degree, or pitch of <~ *the temperature*> **b** to cause to rise in level or amount <~ *the rent*> **c(1)** to increase the amount of (a poker bet) **c(2)** to bet more than (a previous better) **9** to make light and porous, esp by adding yeast <~ *dough*> **10** to multiply (a quantity) by the same quantity a number of times so as to produce a specified power <*2* ~d *to the power 3 equals 8*> **11** to bring in sight on the horizon by approaching <~ *land*> **12a** to bring up the nap of (cloth), esp by brushing **b** to bring (e g a design) into relief **c** to cause (e g a blister) to form on the skin – **raiser** *n* – **raise Cain/hell/the roof** to create a usu angry and noisy disturbance; *esp* to complain vehemently – infml – **raise an eyebrow/eyebrows** to cause surprise, doubt, or disapproval <*his ideas would* raise eyebrows *in political circles*>

[2]**raise** *n* **1** an act of raising or lifting **2a** an increase of a bet or bid **b** *chiefly NAm* RISE 4b

raisin /'rayz(ə)n‖'reɪz(ə)n/ *n* a dried grape

raison d'être /ˌrayzon(h) 'detrə ‖ˌreɪzɒn 'detrə, ˌreɪzɑ̃ (*Fr* rezɔ̃ dɛtr)/ *n* a reason or justification for existence

raj /rahj‖rɑːdʒ/ *n* RULE 3; *specif, cap* British rule in India

rajah, raja /'rahjə‖'rɑːdʒə/ *n* **1** an Indian or Malay prince or chief **2** a person bearing a Hindu title of nobility

[1]**rake** /rayk‖reɪk/ *n* **1** a long-handled implement with a head on which a row of projecting prongs is fixed for gathering hay, grass, etc or for loosening or levelling the surface of the ground; *also* any of several implements similar in shape or use (e g a tool used to draw together the money or chips on a gaming table) **2** a mechanical implement, usu with rotating pronged wheels, used for gathering hay

[2]**rake** *vt* **1** to gather, loosen, or level (as if) with a rake **2** to search through, esp in a haphazard manner – often + *through* or *among* **3** to sweep the length of, esp with gunfire – **raker** *n*

[3]**rake** *vb* to (cause to) incline from the perpendicular

[4]**rake** *n* **1** inclination from the perpendicular; *esp* the overhang of a ship's bow or stern **2** the angle of inclination or slope, esp of a stage in a theatre

[5]**rake** *n* a dissolute man, esp in fashionable society

rake in *vt* to earn or gain (money) rapidly or in abundance – infml

'rake-ˌoff *n* a share of usu dishonestly gained profits – infml

rake up *vt* **1** to uncover, revive <raked up *an old grievance*> **2** to find or collect, esp with difficulty <*managed to* rake up *enough money for the rent*>

[1]**rakish** /'raykish‖'reɪkɪʃ/ *adj* dissolute, licentious

[2]**rakish** *adj* **1** *of a ship, boat, etc* having a smart stylish appearance suggestive of speed **2** dashing, jaunty <*with her hat at a* ~ *angle*> – **rakishly** *adv*, **rakishness** *n*

rallentando /ˌralən'tandoh‖ˌrælən'tændəʊ/ *n, adj, or adv, pl* **rallentandos, rallentandi** /-di‖-dɪ/ (a passage performed) with a gradual decrease in tempo – used in music [Italian, lit., slowing down, fr *rallentare* to slow down again]

[1]**rally** /'rali‖'rælɪ/ *vt* **1** to bring together for a common cause **2a** to arouse for or recall to order or action <rallied *his wits to face the problem*> **b** to rouse from depression or weakness <rallied *his strength*> ~ *vi* **1** to join in a common cause <*thousands will* ~ *to the new party*> **2** to come together again to renew an effort <*the troops* rallied *and drove back the enemy*> **3** to recover, revive <*began to* ~ *after his long illness*>

[2]**rally** *n* **1a** a mustering of scattered forces to renew an effort **b** a recovery of strength or courage after weakness or dejection **c** an increase in price after a decline **2** a mass meeting of people sharing a common interest or supporting a common, usu political, cause **3** a series of strokes interchanged between players (e g in tennis) before a point is won **4** *also* **rallye** a motor race, usu over public roads, designed to test both speed and navigational skills

[1]**ram** /ram‖ræm/ *n* **1** an uncastrated male sheep **2a** BATTERING RAM **b** a heavy beak on the prow of a warship for piercing enemy vessels; *also* a warship equipped with a ram **3a** the plunger of a hydrostatic press or force pump **b** the weight that strikes the blow in a pile driver

[2]**ram** *vb* **-mm-** *vi* to strike with violence <*her car* ~med *into a tree*> ~ *vt* **1** to force down or in by driving, pressing, or pushing <~med *his hat down over his ears*> **2** to force passage or acceptance of <~ *home an idea*> **3** to strike against violently and usu head-on – **rammer** *n* – **ram something down someone's throat** to force sby to accept or listen to sthg, esp by constant repetition

Ramadan, Ramadhan /'ramədan, -dahn, ˌ--'-‖'ræmədæn, -dɑːn, ˌ--'-/ *n* the 9th month of the Muslim year, during which fasting is practised daily from dawn to sunset

[1]**ramble** /'rambl‖'ræmbl/ *vi* **1** to walk for pleasure, esp without a planned route **2** to talk or write in a disconnected long-winded fashion **3** to grow or extend irregularly <*a* rambling *old house*> – **ramblingly** *adv*

[2]**ramble** *n* a leisurely walk taken for pleasure and often without a planned route

rambler /'ramblə‖'ræmblə/ *n* any of various climbing roses with small, often double, flowers in large clusters

rambunctious /ram'bungkshəs‖ræm'bʌŋkʃəs/ *adj, NAm* rumbustious, unruly – infml – **rambunctiously** *adv*, **rambunctiousness** *n*

ramification /ˌramifi'kaysh(ə)n‖ˌræmɪfɪ'keɪʃ(ə)n/ *n* **1a** the act or process of branching out **b** the arrangement of branches (e g on a plant) **2a** a branch, subdivision **b** a branched structure **3** a usu extended or complicated consequence <*the* ~s *of a problem*>

ramify /'ramifie‖'ræmɪfaɪ/ *vb* to (cause to) separate or split up into branches, divisions, or constituent parts

ramjet /'ramˌjet‖'ræmˌdʒet/ *n* a jet engine that uses the flow of compressed air produced by the forward movement of the aeroplane, rocket, etc to burn the fuel

ramp /ramp‖ræmp/ *n* **1** a sloping floor, walk,

or roadway leading from one level to another **2** a stairway for entering or leaving an aircraft

[1]**rampage** /ram'payj||ræm'peɪdʒ/ *vi* to rush about wildly or violently

[2]**rampage** /ram'payj, '--||ræm'peɪdʒ, '--/ *n* – **on the rampage** engaged in violent or uncontrolled behaviour

rampant /'rampənt||'ræmpənt/ *adj* **1** *of a heraldic animal* rearing upon the hind legs with forelegs extended – used postpositively **2a** characterized by wildness or absence of restraint (e g of opinion or action) <*a ~ militarist*> **b** spreading or growing unchecked <*a ~ crime wave*> – **rampancy** *n*, **rampantly** *adv*

rampart /'rampaht||'ræmpɑːt/ *n* **1** a broad embankment raised as a fortification (e g around a fort or city) and usu surmounted by a parapet **2** a protective barrier; a bulwark

ramrod /'ram,rod||'ræm,rɒd/ *n* **1** a rod for ramming home the charge in a muzzle-loading firearm **2** a rod for cleaning the barrels of rifles and other small arms

ramshackle /'ramshakl||'ræmʃækl/ *adj* badly constructed or needing repair; rickety

ran /ran||ræn/ *past of* RUN

[1]**ranch** /rahnch||rɑːntʃ/ *n* **1** a large farm for raising livestock esp in N America and Australia **2** *chiefly NAm* a farm or area devoted to raising a particular crop or animal <*a poultry ~*>

[2]**ranch** *vi* to own, work, or live on a ranch – **rancher** *n*

rancid /'ransid||'rænsɪd/ *adj* (smelling or tasting) rank – **rancidness, rancidity** *n*

rancour, *NAm* **rancor** /'rangkə||'ræŋkə/ *n* bitter and deep-seated ill will or hatred – **rancorous** *adj*

rand /rand||rænd/ *n, pl* **rand** the standard unit of money in the Republic of South Africa

[1]**random** /'randəm||'rændəm/ *n* – **at random** without definite aim, direction, rule, or method

[2]**random** *adj* **1** lacking a definite plan, purpose, or pattern **2** (of, consisting of, or being events, parts, etc) having or relating to a probability of occurring equal to that of all similar parts, events, etc – **randomly** *adv*, **randomness** *n*

random-access memory *n* a computer memory permitting access to stored data in any order and additions or changes to the data

randomize, -ise /'randəmiez/ *vt* to arrange so as to simulate a chance distribution, reduce interference by irrelevant variables, and yield unbiased statistical data

randy /'randi||'rændɪ/ *adj* sexually aroused; lustful – infml

rang /rang||ræŋ/ *past of* RING

[1]**range** /raynj||reɪndʒ/ *n* **1a** a series of mountains **b** a number of objects or products forming a distinct class or series **c** a variety, cross-section <*a good ~ of people here*> **2** a usu solid-fuel fired cooking stove with 1 or more ovens, a flat metal top, and 1 or more areas for heating pans **3a** an open region over which livestock may roam and feed, esp in N America **b** the region throughout which a kind of living organism or ecological community naturally lives or occurs **4a(1)** the distance to which a projectile can be propelled **a(2)** the distance between a weapon and the target **b** the maximum distance a vehicle can travel without refuelling **c** a place where shooting (e g with guns or missiles) is practised **5a** the space or extent included, covered, or used **b** the extent of pitch within a melody or within the capacity of a voice or instrument **6a** a sequence, series, or scale between limits <*a wide ~ of patterns*> **b** (the difference between) the least and greatest values of an attribute or series **7** the set of values a function may take; *esp* the values that a dependent variable may have **8** LINE 9

[2]**range** *vt* **1a** to set in a row or in the proper order <*troops were ~*d *on either side*> **b** to place among others in a specified position or situation <*~*d *himself with the radicals in the party*> **2** to roam over or through **3** to determine or give the elevation necessary for (a gun) to propel a projectile to a given distance ~ *vi* **1** to roam at large or freely <*the talk ~*d *over current topics*> **2** *esp of printing type* to align **3** to extend in a usu specified direction **4** *of a gun or projectile* to have a usu specified range **5** to change or differ within limits <*their ages ~*d *from 5 to 65*>

'range ,finder *n* a device for indicating or measuring the distance between a gun and a target or a camera and an object

ranger /'raynjə||'reɪndʒə/ *n* **1a** the keeper of a British royal park or forest **b** an officer who patrols a N American national park or forest **2a** a member of any of several bodies of armed men in N America who range over a usu specified region, esp to enforce the law **b** a soldier in the US army specially trained in close-range fighting and raiding tactics **3** *often cap* a private in an Irish line regiment **4** *cap* a senior member of the British Guide movement aged from 14 to 19

rani, ranee /rah'nee, '--||rɑː'niː, '--/ *n* a Hindu queen or princess; *esp* the wife of a rajah

[1]**rank** /rangk||ræŋk/ *adj* **1** (covered with vegetation which is) excessively vigorous and often coarse in growth **2** offensively gross or coarse **3a** shockingly conspicuous; flagrant <*lecture him on his ~ disloyalty*> **b** complete – used as an intensive <*a ~ outsider*> **4** offensive in odour or flavour – **rankly** *adv*, **rankness** *n*

[2]**rank** *n* **1a** a row, line, or series of people or things **b(1)** *sing or pl in constr* a line of soldiers ranged side by side in close order **b(2)** *pl* RANK AND FILE **c** any of the 8 rows of squares that extend across a chessboard perpendicular to the files **2** an esp military formation – often pl with sing. meaning <*to break ~*s> **3a** a degree or position in a hierarchy or order; *specif* an official position in the armed forces **b** (high) social position <*the privileges of ~*> **4** the number of rows in a mathematical matrix **5** *Br* a place where taxis wait to pick up passengers

[3]**rank** *vt* **1** to arrange in lines or in a regular formation **2** to determine the relative position of; rate **3** *NAm* to outrank ~*vi* to take or have a position in relation to others

,rank and 'file *n sing or pl in constr* **1** the body of members of an armed force as distinguished from the officers **2** the individuals constituting the body of an organization,

ranker /ˈrangkə‖ˈræŋkə/ *n* one who serves or has served in the ranks; *esp* a commissioned officer promoted from the ranks

ranking /ˈrangking‖ˈræŋkɪŋ/ *adj, chiefly NAm* having a high or the highest position

rankle /ˈrangkl‖ˈræŋkl/ *vi* to cause continuing anger, irritation, or bitterness

ransack /ˈransak‖ˈrænsæk/ *vt* **1** to search in a disordered but thorough manner **2** to rob, plunder – **ransacker** *n*

[1]**ransom** /ˈransəm‖ˈrænsəm/ *n* **1** a price paid or demanded for the release of a captured or kidnapped person **2** the act of ransoming [Old French *rançon*, fr Latin *redemptio* purchase, act of ransoming, fr *redimere* to buy back, ransom-see REDEEM]

[2]**ransom** *vt* **1** to deliver or redeem, esp from sin or its consequences **2** to free from captivity or punishment by paying a ransom – **ransomer** *n*

[1]**rant** /rant‖rænt/ *vi* to talk in a noisy, excited, or declamatory manner ~*vt* to declaim bombastically – **ranter** *n*, **rantingly** *adv*

[2]**rant** *n* (a) bombastic extravagant speech

[1]**rap** /rap‖ræp/ *n* **1** (the sound made by) a sharp blow or knock **2** blame, punishment – infml <*I ended up taking the* ~>

[2]**rap** *vb* **-pp-** *vt* **1** to strike with a sharp blow **2** to utter (e g a command) abruptly and forcibly – usu + *out* **3** to express or communicate (e g a message) by means of raps – usu + *out* **4** to criticize sharply – journ <*judge* ~s *police*> ~*vi* to strike a quick sharp blow – **(a) rap over the knuckles** (to give) a scolding

[3]**rap** *n* the least bit (e g of care or consideration) – infml <*doesn't care a* ~>

[4]**rap** *n, chiefly NAm* talk, conversation – slang

[5]**rap** *vi* **-pp-** *chiefly NAm* to talk freely and frankly – slang

rapacious /rəˈpayshəs‖rəˈpeɪʃəs/ *adj* **1** excessively grasping or covetous **2** *of an animal* living on prey – **rapaciously** *adv*, **rapaciousness, rapacity** *n*

[1]**rape** /rayp‖reɪp/ *n* a European plant of the mustard family grown as a forage crop and for its seeds which yield rapeseed oil [Latin *rapa*, *rapum* turnip, rape]

[2]**rape** *vt* **1** to despoil **2** to commit rape on [Latin *rapere* to seize by force, carry off, ravish] – **rapist** *n*

[3]**rape** *n* **1** an act or instance of robbing or despoiling <*the* ~ *of the countryside*> **2** (an instance of) the crime of forcing sby, esp a woman, to have sexual intercourse against his/her will **3** an outrageous violation <*a* ~ *of Justice*>

[1]**rapid** /ˈrapid‖ˈræpɪd/ *adj* moving, acting, or occurring with speed; swift – **rapidly** *adv*, **rapidness, rapidity** *n*

[2]**rapid** *n* a part of a river where the water flows swiftly over a steep usu rocky slope in the river bed – usu pl with sing. meaning

rapier /ˈraypi·ə‖ˈreɪpɪə/ *n* a straight 2-edged sword with a narrow pointed blade

rapine /ˈrapien‖ˈræpaɪn/ *n* pillage, plunder

rapport /raˈpaw‖ræˈpɔː/ *n* a sympathetic or harmonious relationship

rapprochement /raˈproshmonh‖ræˈprɒʃmɑ̃/ *n* the reestablishment of cordial relations, esp between nations [French, fr *rapprocher* to bring together, fr *re-* again + *approcher* to approach]

rapscallion /rapˈskalyən‖ræpˈskæljən/ *n* a rascal

rapt /rapt‖ræpt/ *adj* **1** enraptured **2** wholly absorbed – **raptly** *adv*, **raptness** *n*

rapture /ˈrapchə‖ˈræptʃə/ *n* **1a** a state or experience of being carried away by overwhelming emotion **b** a mystical experience in which the spirit is exalted to a knowledge of divine things **2** an expression or manifestation of ecstasy or extreme delight <*went into* ~s *over the new car*> – **rapturous** *adj*, **rapturously** *adv*, **rapturousness** *n*

[1]**rare** /reə‖reə/ *adj, of meat* cooked so that the inside is still red [alteration of earlier *rere*, fr Old English *hrēre* boiled lightly]

[2]**rare** *adj* **1** lacking in density; thin <*a* ~ *atmosphere*> **2** marked by unusual quality, merit, or appeal <*to show* ~ *tact*> **3** seldom occurring or found <*a* ~ *moth*> **4** superlative or extreme – infml <*gave her a* ~ *fright*> [Latin *rarus* sparse, scarce] – **rarely** *adv*, **rareness** *n*

ˌrare ˈearth *n* (an oxide of) any of a series of metallic elements that includes the elements with atomic numbers from 58 to 71, usu lanthanum, and sometimes yttrium and scandium – **rare-earth** *adj*

rarefied *also* **rarified** /ˈreərified‖ˈreərɪfaɪd/ *adj* **1** esoteric, abstruse **2** very high or exalted (e g in rank) <*moved in* ~ *political circles*>

rarefy *also* **rarify** /ˈreərifie‖ˈreərɪfaɪ/ *vt* **1** to make rare, porous, or less dense **2** to make more spiritual, refined, or abstruse ~*vi* to become less dense

raring /ˈreəring‖ˈreərɪŋ/ *adj* full of enthusiasm or eagerness <~ *to go*>

rarity /ˈreərəti‖ˈreərətɪ/ *n* **1** the quality, state, or fact of being rare **2** sby or sthg rare

rascal /ˈrahsk(ə)l‖ˈrɑːsk(ə)l/ *n* **1** an unprincipled or dishonest person **2** a mischievous person or animal – usu humor or affectionate – **rascally** *adj or adv*

[1]**rash** /rash‖ræʃ/ *adj* acting with, characterized by, or proceeding from undue haste or impetuosity – **rashly** *adv*, **rashness** *n*

[2]**rash** *n* **1** an outbreak of spots on the body **2** a large number of instances of a specified thing during a short period <*a* ~ *of arrests*>

rasher /ˈrashə‖ˈræʃə/ *n* a thin slice of bacon or ham

[1]**rasp** /rahsp‖rɑːsp/ *vt* **1** to rub with sthg rough; *specif* to abrade with a rasp **2** to grate upon; irritate **3** to utter in a grating tone ~*vi* to produce a grating sound – **rasper** *n*, **raspingly** *adv*

[2]**rasp** *n* a coarse file with rows of cutting teeth

raspberry /ˈrahzb(ə)ri‖ˈrɑːzb(ə)rɪ/ *n* **1** (a widely grown shrub that bears) any of various usu red edible berries **2** a rude sound made by sticking the tongue out and blowing noisily – slang

Rastafarian /ˌrastəˈfeəri·ən, ˌrastəfəˈrie·ən‖ˌræstəˈfeərɪən, ˈræstəfəˈraɪən/ *n* a follower of a movement among black W Indians which looks for the deliverance of the black race and the establishment of a homeland in Ethiopia, and venerates Haile Selassie [*Ras Tafari*, name of

Haile Selassie (1892-1975), Emperor of Ethiopia] – **Rastafarian** *adj,* **Rastafarianism** *n*

[1]**rat** /rat‖ræt/ *n* **1** any of numerous rodents that are considerably larger than the related mice **2a** a contemptible or wretched person; *specif* one who betrays or deserts his party, friends, or associates **b** a blackleg *USE* (*2*) infml – **ratlike** *adj*

[2]**rat** *vi* **-tt- 1** to betray, desert, or inform on one's associates – usu + *on* **2** to catch or hunt rats **3** to work as a blackleg

rat-a-tat /ˌrat ə ˈtat‖ˌræt ə ˈtæt/, **rat-a-tat-tat** /ˌrat ə tat ˈtat‖ˌræt ə tæt ˈtæt/ *n* a sharp repeated knocking or tapping sound

ratchet /ˈrachit‖ˈrætʃɪt/ *n* **1** a mechanism that consists of a bar or wheel having inclined teeth into which a pawl drops so that motion is allowed in 1 direction only **2** *also* **ratchet wheel** a toothed wheel held in position or turned by a pawl

[1]**rate** /rayt‖reɪt/ *vt, archaic* to scold angrily

[2]**rate** *n* **1** valuation <*appraised him at a low* ~> **2a** a fixed ratio between 2 things **b** a charge, payment, or price fixed according to a ratio, scale, or standard <~ *of exchange*> <~ *of interest*> **c** *Br* a tax levied by a local authority – usu pl with sing. meaning **3** a quantity, amount, or degree of sthg measured per unit of sthg else – **at any rate** in any case; anyway

[3]**rate** *vt* **1** to consider to be; value as <*was* ~d *an excellent pianist*> **2** to determine or assign the relative rank or class of **3** to assign a rate to **4** to be worthy of; deserve <*now* ~s *his own show*> **5** to think highly of; consider to be good – infml <*doesn't* ~ *Spurs' chances of avoiding relegation*> ~*vi* to be estimated at a specified level <~s *as the best show ever staged in London*>

-rate /-rayt‖-reɪt/ *comb form* of the specified level of quality <*fifth*-rate>

rateable, ratable /ˈraytəbl‖ˈreɪtəbl/ *adj* capable of or susceptible to being rated, estimated, or apportioned

rate-capping *n, Br* restriction by central government legislation of the level of rates which a local authority can levy – **rate-cap** *vb*

ratepayer /ˈraytˌpayə‖ˈreɪtˌpeɪə/ *n* a taxpayer; *also, Br* a person liable to pay rates

rate support grant *n, Br* a grant paid by central government to a local authority to finance a proportion of its expenditure

rather /ˈrahdhə‖ˈrɑːðə/ *adv or adj* **1** more readily or willingly; sooner <*left* ~ *than cause trouble*> <*I'd* ~ *not go*> – often used interjectionally, esp by British speakers, to express enthusiastic affirmation <*'will you come?'* 'Rather!'> **2** more properly, reasonably, or truly <*my father, or* ~ *my stepfather*> **3** to some degree; somewhat <*it's* ~ *warm*> <*I* ~ *thought so*>; *esp* somewhat excessively <*it's* ~ *far for me*> **4** on the contrary <*they did not go;* ~, *they stayed all night*>

ratify /ˈratifie‖ˈrætɪfaɪ/ *vt* to approve or confirm formally – **ratification** *n*

rating /ˈrayting‖ˈreɪtɪŋ/ *n* **1** a classification according to grade **2** relative estimate or evaluation **3** *pl* any of various indexes which list television programmes, new records, etc in order of popularity – usu + *the* **4** *chiefly Br* ORDINARY SEAMAN

ratio /ˈrayshioh‖ˈreɪʃɪəʊ/ *n, pl* **ratios 1** the indicated division of one mathematical expression by another **2** the relationship in quantity, number, or degree between things or between one thing and another thing

ratiocinate /ˌratiˈosinayt‖ˌrætɪˈɒsɪneɪt/ *vi* to reason logically or formally – fml – **ratiocinator** *n,* **ratiocinative** *adj,* **ratiocination** *n*

[1]**ration** /ˈrash(ə)n‖ˈræʃ(ə)n/ *n* a share or amount (e g of food) which one permits oneself or which one is permitted <*the petrol* ~>

[2]**ration** *vt* **1** to distribute or divide (e g commodities in short supply) in fixed quantities – often + *out* **2a** to limit (a person or commodity) to a fixed ration <*sugar was strictly* ~ed> **b** to use sparingly

[1]**rational** /ˈrash(ə)nl‖ˈræʃ(ə)nl/ *adj* **1** having, based on, or compatible with reason; reasonable <~ *behaviour*> **2** of, involving, or being (a mathematical expression containing) 1 or more rational numbers – **rationally** *adv,* **rationalness, rationality** *n*

[2]**rational** *n* sthg rational; *specif* RATIONAL NUMBER

rationale /ˌrashəˈnahl‖ˌræʃəˈnɑːl/ *n* **1** an explanation of controlling principles of opinion, belief, practice, or phenomena **2** an underlying reason; basis

rationalism /ˈrash(ə)nəˌliz(ə)m‖ˈræʃ(ə)nəˌlɪz(ə)m/ *n* **1** reliance on reason for the establishment of religious truth **2** a theory that reason is a source of knowledge superior to and independent of sense perception – **rationalist** *n,* **rationalist, rationalistic** *adj,* **rationalistically** *adv*

rational·ize, -ise /ˈrash(ə)nəliez‖ˈræʃ(ə)nəlaɪz/ *vt* **1** to free (a mathematical expression) from irrational parts <~ *a denominator*> **2** to bring into accord with reason or cause to seem reasonable; *specif* to attribute (e g one's actions) to rational and creditable motives without analysis of true, esp unconscious, motives in order to provide plausible but untrue reasons for conduct **3** to increase the efficiency of (e g an industry) by more effective organization ~*vi* to provide plausible but untrue reasons for one's actions, opinions, etc – **rationalizer** *n,* **rationalization** *n*

ˌrational ˈnumber *n* a number (e g 2, 5/2, –1/2) that can be expressed as the result of dividing one integer by another

ratline /ˈratlin‖ˈrætlɪn/ *n* any of the short transverse ropes attached to the shrouds of a ship to form rungs

ˈrat ˌrace *n* a fiercely competitive and wearisome activity; *specif* the struggle to maintain one's position in a career or survive the pressures of modern urban life

rattan /rəˈtan‖rəˈtæn/ *n* **1** a climbing palm with very long tough stems **2** a part of the stem of a rattan used esp for walking sticks and wickerwork

[1]**rattle** /ˈratl‖ˈrætl/ *vb* **1** to make a rapid succession of short sharp sounds **2** to chatter incessantly and aimlessly – often + *on* **3** to move with a clatter or rattle ~ *vt* **1** to say or perform in a brisk lively fashion – often + *off* <~d *off a*

long list of examples> **2** to cause to make a rattling sound **3** to upset to the point of loss of poise and composure <*he looked severely* ~d> – infml

[2]**rattle** *n* **1** a rattling sound **2a** a child's toy consisting of loose pellets in a hollow container that rattles when shaken **b** a device that consists of a springy tongue in contact with a revolving ratchet wheel which is rotated or shaken to produce a loud noise **3** the sound-producing organ on a rattlesnake's tail **4** a throat noise caused by air passing through mucus and heard esp at the approach of death

'rattle,snake /-,snayk‖-,sneɪk/ *n* any of various American poisonous snakes with horny interlocking joints at the end of the tail that rattle when shaken

[1]**rattling** /'ratling‖'rætlɪŋ/ *adj* lively, brisk <*moved at a* ~ *pace*> – not now in vogue – **rattlingly** *adv*

[2]**rattling** *adv* to an extreme degree; very – chiefly in *rattling good*; infml

ratty /'rati‖'rætɪ/ *adj* irritable – infml

raucous /'rawkəs‖'rɔːkəs/ *adj* disagreeably harsh or strident; noisy – **raucously** *adv*, **raucousness** *n*

raunchy /'rawnchi‖'rɔːntʃɪ/ *adj* earthy, gutsy <*a group with a confident* ~ *sound*> – infml – **raunchily** *adv*, **raunchiness** *n*

[1]**ravage** /'ravij‖'rævɪdʒ/ *n* damage resulting from ravaging – usu pl with sing. meaning <*the* ~s *of time*>

[2]**ravage** *vb* to wreak havoc (on); cause (violent) destruction (to) – **ravagement** *n*, **ravager** *n*

[1]**rave** /rayv‖reɪv/ *vi* **1** to talk irrationally (as if) in delirium; *broadly* to rage, storm **2** to talk with extreme or passionate enthusiasm <~d *about her beauty*>

[2]**rave** *n* **1** a raving **2** an extravagantly favourable review <*the play opened to* ~ *notices*> **3** a wild exciting period, experience, or event – slang <*the party was a real* ~>

[1]**ravel** /'ravl‖'rævl/ *vb* **-ll-** (*NAm* **-l-**, **-ll-**) *vt* **1** to unravel, disentangle – usu + *out* **2** to entangle, confuse ~ *vi* to fray

[2]**ravel** *n* **1** a tangle or tangled mass **2** a loose thread

[1]**raven** /'rayv(ə)n‖'reɪv(ə)n/ *n* a very large glossy black bird of the crow family

[2]**raven** *adj* glossy black <~ *hair*>

[3]**raven** /'rav(ə)n‖'ræv(ə)n/ *vt* **1** to devour greedily **2** to despoil <*men* ~ *the earth's resources*> ~ *vi* **1** to (seek after) prey **2** to plunder – **ravener** *n*

ravenous /'rav(ə)nəs‖'ræv(ə)nəs/ *adj* **1** urgently seeking satisfaction, gratification, etc; grasping, insatiable **2** fiercely eager for food; famished – **ravenously** *adv*, **ravenousness** *n*

raver /'rayvə‖'reɪvə/ *n*, *chiefly Br* an energetic and uninhibited person who enjoys a hectic social life; *also* a sexually uninhibited or promiscuous person – slang

'rave-,up *n*, *chiefly Br* a wild party – slang

ravine /rə'veen‖rə'viːn/ *n* a narrow steep-sided valley smaller than a canyon and usu worn by running water

[1]**raving** /'rayving‖'reɪvɪŋ/ *n* irrational, incoherent, wild, or extravagant utterance or declamation – usu pl with sing. meaning

[2]**raving** *adj* extreme, marked <*a* ~ *beauty*> – infml

ravioli /,ravi'ohli‖,rævɪ'əʊlɪ/ *n* little cases of pasta containing meat, cheese, etc [Italian, fr Italian dial., lit., little turnips, deriv of Latin *rava* turnip]

ravish /'ravish‖'rævɪʃ/ *vt* **1** to overcome with joy, delight, etc <~ed *by the beauty of the scene*> **2** to rape, violate – **ravisher** *n*, **ravishment** *n*

ravishing /'ravishing‖'rævɪʃɪŋ/ *adj* unusually attractive or pleasing – **ravishingly** *adv*

[1]**raw** /raw‖rɔː/ *adj* **1** not cooked **2a(1)** not processed or purified; in the natural state <~ *fibres*> <~ *sewage*> **a(2)** not diluted or blended <~ *spirits*> **b** not in a polished, finished, or processed form <~ *data*> <*hem this* ~ *edge to stop it fraying*> **3** having the surface abraded or chafed <~ *skin*> **4** lacking experience, training, etc; new <*a* ~ *recruit*> **5** disagreeably damp or cold – **rawly** *adv*, **rawness** *n*

[2]**raw** *n* a sensitive place or state <*touched her on the* ~> – **in the raw 1** in the natural or crude state <*life* in the raw> **2** naked <*slept* in the raw>

,raw'boned /-'bohnd‖-'bəʊnd/ *adj* having a heavy or clumsy frame that seems inadequately covered with flesh

,raw 'deal *n* an instance of unfair treatment

'raw,hide /-,hied‖-,haɪd/ *n* (a whip of) untanned hide

,raw ma'terial *n* material that can be converted by manufacture, treatment, etc into a new and useful product

[1]**ray** /ray‖reɪ/ *n* any of numerous fishes having the eyes on the upper surface of a flattened body and a long narrow tail

[2]**ray** *n* **1a** any of the lines of light that appear to radiate from a bright object **b** a narrow beam of radiant energy (e g light or X rays) **c** a stream of (radioactive) particles travelling in the same line **2a** a thin line suggesting a ray **b** any of a group of lines diverging from a common centre **3a** any of the bony rods that support the fin of a fish **b** any of the radiating parts of the body of a radially symmetrical animal (e g a starfish) **4** RAY FLOWER **5** a slight manifestation or trace (e g of intelligence or hope) – **rayed** *adj*, **rayless** *adj*

[3]**ray** *vi* **1** to shine (as if) in rays **2** to radiate from a centre ~ *vt* to emit in rays; radiate

'ray ,flower *n* any of the strap-shaped florets forming **a** the outer ring of the head of a composite plant (e g an aster or daisy) having central disc florets **b** the entire flower head of a composite plant (e g a dandelion) lacking disc florets

rayon /'rayon, -ən‖'reɪɒn, -ən/ *n* (a fabric made from) a yarn or fibre produced by forcing and drawing cellulose through minute holes

raze, rase /rayz‖reɪz/ *vt* to destroy or erase completely; *specif* to lay (e g a town or building) level with the ground

razor /'rayzə‖'reɪzə/ *n* a sharp-edged cutting implement for shaving or cutting (facial) hair – **razor** *vt*

ˌ**razor-ˈbacked,** ˈ**razorˌback** *adj* having a sharp narrow back <*a* ~ *whale*>

razzle /ˈrazl‖ˈræzl/ *n, chiefly Br* a spree, binge – usu in *on the razzle*; slang

[1]**re** /ray, ree‖reɪ, riː/ *n* the 2nd note of the diatonic scale in solmization

[2]**re** /ree‖riː/ *prep* WITH REGARD TO; concerning

re- *prefix* **1a** again; anew <re*born*> **b(1)** again in a new, altered, or improved way <re*write*> **b(2)** repeated, new, or improved version of <re*tread*> **2** back; backwards <re*call*>

're /ə‖ə/ *vb* are <*you*'re *right*>

[1]**reach** /reech‖riːtʃ/ *vt* **1** to stretch out <~ *out your hand to her*> **2a** to touch or grasp by extending a part of the body (e g a hand) or an object <*couldn't* ~ *the apple*> **b** to pick up and draw towards one; pass <~ *me my hat, will you?*> **c(1)** to extend to <*the shadow* ~ed *the wall*> **c(2)** to get up to or as far as; arrive at <*took 2 days to* ~ *the mountains*> <*they hoped to* ~ *an agreement*> **d** to contact or communicate with <~ed *her by phone at the office*> ~ *vi* **1a** to make a stretch (as if) with one's hand <~ed *towards the book on the top shelf*> **b** to strain after sthg <~ing *for the unattainable*> **2a** to project, extend <*her land* ~es *to the river*> **b** to arrive at or come to sthg <*as far as the eye could* ~> **3** to sail on a reach – **reachable** *adj*

[2]**reach** *n* **1a** the action or an act of reaching **b** the distance or extent of reaching or of ability to reach **c** a range; *specif* comprehension <*an idea well beyond his* ~> **2** a continuous stretch or expanse; *esp* a straight uninterrupted portion of a river or canal **3** the tack sailed by a vessel with the wind blowing more or less from the side **4** *pl* groups or levels in a usu specified activity or occupation; echelons <*the higher* ~es *of academic life*>

ˈ**reach-me-ˌdown** *n or adj, chiefly Br* (sthg) passed on from another <~ *clothes*> – infml

react /riˈakt‖rɪˈækt/ *vt* to cause to react chemically ~ *vi* **1** to exert a reciprocal or counteracting force or influence – often + *on* or *upon* **2** to respond to a stimulus **3** to act in opposition to a force or influence – usu + *against* **4** to undergo chemical reaction

reaction /riˈaksh(ə)n‖rɪˈækʃ(ə)n/ *n* **1a** a reacting **b** tendency towards a former and usu outmoded (political or social) order or policy **2** bodily response to or activity aroused by a stimulus: e g **2a** the response of tissues to a foreign substance (e g an antigen or infective agent) **b** a mental or emotional response to circumstances **3** the force that sthg subjected to the action of a force exerts equally in the opposite direction **4a** a chemical transformation or change; an action between atoms, molecules, etc to form 1 or more new substances **b** a process involving change in atomic nuclei resulting from interaction with a particle or another nucleus

reactionary /riˈakshən(ə)ri‖rɪˈækʃən(ə)rɪ/ *also* **reactionist** *n or adj* (a person) opposing radical social change or favouring a return to a former (political) order

reactivate /riˈaktivayt‖rɪˈæktɪveɪt/ *vb* to make or become active again – **reactivation** *n*

reactive /riˈaktiv‖rɪˈæktɪv/ *adj* **1** of or marked by reaction or reactance **2** tending to or liable to react <*highly* ~ *chemicals*> – **reactively** *adv*, **reactiveness, reactivity** *n*

reactor /riˈaktə‖rɪˈæktə/ *n* **1** a vat for an industrial chemical reaction **2** an apparatus in which a chain reaction of fissile material (e g uranium or plutonium) is started and controlled, esp for the production of nuclear power or elementary particles

[1]**read** /reed‖riːd/ *vb* **read** /red‖red/ *vt* **1a(1)** to look at or otherwise sense (e g letters, symbols, or words) with mental assimilation of the communication represented <*can't* ~ *his handwriting*> <*to* ~ *a book*> **a(2)** to look at, interpret, and understand (signs, communicative movements, etc) <~ *lips*> <~ *semaphore*> **a(3)** to utter aloud (interpretatively) the printed or written words of <~ *them a story*> – often + *out* **b** to learn or get to know by reading <~ *that he had died*> **c(1)** to study (a subject), esp for a degree <~ *law*> **c(2)** to read (the) works of (an author or type of literature) <~s *science fiction mainly*> **d** to receive and understand (a message) by radio **2a** to understand, comprehend <~ *his thoughts*> **b** to interpret the meaning or significance of <~s *dreams*> **c** to interpret the action of or in so as to anticipate what will happen or what needs doing <*in football the sweeper must be able to* ~ *the game*> **d** to attribute (a meaning) to sthg read or considered <~ *a nonexistent meaning into her words*> **3** to use as a substitute for or in preference to another written or printed word, character, etc <~ hurry *for* harry> **4** to indicate <*the thermometer* ~s *zero*> **5a** to sense the meaning of (information stored or recorded on punched cards, in a computer memory, etc) **b** *esp of a computer* to take (information) from storage ~ *vi* **1a** to perform the act of reading; read sthg **b(1)** to learn about sthg by reading – usu + *up* <~ing *up on astronomy*> **b(2)** to study a subject in order to qualify *for* <*to* ~ *for the Bar*> **2** to yield a (particular) meaning or impression when read <*the poem* ~s *rather badly*>

[2]**read** /reed‖riːd/ *n* **1** sthg to read with reference to the interest, enjoyment, etc it provides <*the book is a terrific* ~> **2** *chiefly Br* a period of reading <*had a* ~ *and went to bed early*>

[3]**read** /red‖red/ *adj* instructed by or informed through reading <*well*-read>

readable /ˈreedəbl‖ˈriːdəbl/ *adj* **1** legible **2** pleasurable or interesting to read – **readably** *adv*, **readability, readableness** *n*

reader /ˈreedə‖ˈriːdə/ *n* **1a** one appointed to read to others; *esp* LAY READER **b(1)** one who reads and corrects proofs **b(2)** one who evaluates manuscripts **2** a member of a British university staff between the ranks of lecturer and professor **3** a device that reads or displays coded information on a tape, microfilm, punched cards, etc **4** a usu instructive (introductory) book or anthology

readership /ˈreedəˌship‖ˈriːdəˌʃɪp/ *n* **1** the office, duties, or position of a (university) reader **2** *sing or pl in constr* a collective body of readers; *esp* the readers of a particular publication or author

readily /'redəli‖'redəlɪ/ *adv* **1** without hesitating **2** without much difficulty

reading /'reeding‖'riːdɪŋ/ *n* **1a** material read or for reading **b** the extent to which a person has read <*a man of wide* ~> **c** an event at which a play, poetry, etc is read to an audience **d** an act of formally reading a bill that constitutes any of 3 successive stages of approval by a legislature, specif Parliament **2a** a form or version of a particular (passage in a) text <*the generally accepted* ~> **b** the value indicated or data produced by an instrument <*examined the thermometer* ~> **3a** a particular interpretation <*what is your* ~ *of the situation?*> **b** a particular performance of sthg (e g a musical work)

'reading ,desk *n* a desk designed to support a book in a convenient position for a (standing) reader

read-only memory *n* a computer memory holding data in a permanent form which cannot be changed

'read,out /-,owt‖-,aʊt/ *n* (a device used for) the removal of information from storage (e g in a computer memory or on magnetic tape) for display in an understandable form (e g as a printout); *also* the information displayed

[1]**ready** /'redi‖'redɪ/ *adj* **1a** prepared mentally or physically for some experience or action **b** prepared or available for immediate use <*dinner is* ~> <*had little* ~ *cash*> **2a(1)** willingly disposed <~ *to agree to his proposal*> **a(2)** likely or about to do the specified thing <~ *to cry with vexation*> **b** spontaneously prompt <*always has a* ~ *answer*> <*a* ~ *wit*> **c** (presumptuously) eager <*he is very* ~ *with his criticism*> <~ *acceptance*> – **readiness** *n*

[2]**ready** *vt* to make ready

[3]**ready** *n* (ready) money – sometimes pl with sing. meaning; infml – **at/to the ready 1** *of a gun* prepared and in the position for immediate aiming and firing **2** [1]READY 1b

[4]**ready** *adv* in advance <*food that is bought* ~ *cooked*>

,ready-'made *adj* **1** made beforehand, esp for general sale or use rather than to individual specifications <~ *suits*> **2** lacking originality or individuality <~ *opinions*> **3** readily available <*her illness provided a* ~ *excuse*>

,ready 'reckoner *n, Br* an arithmetical table (e g a list of numbers multiplied by a fixed per cent) or set of tables for aid in calculating

,ready-to-'wear *adj, of a garment* off-the-peg

reafforest /,ree·ə'forəst‖,riːə'fɒrəst/ *vt, chiefly Br* to renew the forest cover of by seeding or planting – **reafforestation** *n*

reagent /ri'ayj(ə)nt‖rɪ'eɪdʒ(ə)nt/ *n* a substance that takes part in or brings about a particular chemical reaction, used esp to detect sthg

[1]**real** /reel, riəl‖riːl, rɪəl/ *adj* **1** of or being fixed or immovable property (e g land or buildings) **2a** not artificial, fraudulent, illusory, fictional, etc; *also* being precisely what the name implies; genuine **b** of practical or everyday concerns or activities <*left university to live in the* ~ *world*> **c** belonging to or concerned with the set of real numbers <*the* ~ *roots of an equation*> **d** formed by light rays converging at a point <*a* ~ *image*> **e** measured by purchasing power rather than the paper value of money <~ *income*> **f** complete, great – used chiefly for emphasis <*a* ~ *surprise*> – **realness** *n*

[2]**real** *n* – **for real** in earnest; seriously <*they were fighting* for real>

[3]**real** *adv, chiefly NAm & Scot* very

[4]**real** /ray'ahl‖reɪ'ɑːl/ *n, pl* **reals, reales** /-lays‖-leɪs/ (a coin representing) a former money unit of Spain and Spanish colonies

'real e,state *n* property in buildings and land

realign /,ree·ə'lien‖,riːə'laɪn/ *vt* to reorganize or make new groupings of – **realignment** *n*

realism /'ree,liz(ə)m, 'riə-‖'riː,lɪz(ə)m, 'rɪə-/ *n* **1** concern for fact or reality and rejection of the impractical and visionary **2** the belief that objects of sense perception have real existence independent of the mind **3** fidelity in art, literature, etc to nature and to accurate representation without idealization – **realist** *adj or n*, **realistic** *adj*, **realistically** *adv*

reality /ri'aləti‖rɪ'ælətɪ/ *n* **1** being real **2a** a real event, entity, or state of affairs <*his dream became a* ~> **b** the totality of real things and events <*trying to escape from* ~> – **in reality** AS A MATTER OF FACT

real·ize, -ise /'reeliez, 'riə-‖'riːlaɪz, 'rɪə-/ *vt* **1a** to convert into actual fact; accomplish <*finally* ~d *his goal*> **b** to cause to seem real <*a book in which the characters are carefully* ~d> **2a** to convert into actual money <~ *his assets*> **b** to bring or get by sale, investment, or effort <*the painting will* ~ *several thousand pounds*> **3** to be fully aware of <*she did not* ~ *the risk he was taking*> **4** to play or write (music) in full (e g from a figured bass) – **realizable** *adj*, **realization** *n*

really /'reeli, 'riəli‖'riːlɪ, 'rɪəlɪ/ *adv* **1a** in reality, actually <*did he* ~ *say that?*> <*not very difficult* ~> **b** without question; thoroughly <~ *cold weather*> <~ *hates him*> **2** more correctly – used to give force to an injunction <*you should* ~ *have asked me first*> **3** – expressing surprise or indignation <*'she wants to marry him.'* 'Really?'> <~, *you're being ridiculous*>

realm /relm‖relm/ *n* **1** a kingdom **2** a sphere, domain – often pl with sing. meaning <*within the* ~s *of possibility*>

,real 'number *n* a number (e g a square root of a positive number, an integer, or pi) that does not include a part that is a multiple of the square root of minus one

realpolitik /ray'ahlpoliteek, ray'al-‖reɪ-'ɑːlpɒlɪtiːk, reɪ'æl-/ *n* politics based on practical factors rather than on moral objectives [German, fr *real* practical + *politik* politics]

,real 'tennis *n* a game played with a racket and a ball in an irregularly-shaped indoor court divided by a net

,real-'time *adj* being or involving the almost instantaneous processing, presentation, or use of data by a computer

realtor /'reeltə, -taw, 'riəl-‖'riːltə, -tɔː, 'rɪəl-/ *n, NAm* a real estate agent, esp a member of the National Association of Real Estate Boards

realty /'reelti, 'riəl-‖'riːltɪ, 'rɪəl-/ *n* REAL ESTATE

[1]**ream** /reem‖riːm/ *n* **1** a quantity of paper

equal to 20 quires or variously 480, 500, or 516 sheets **2** a great amount (e g of sthg written or printed) – usu pl with sing. meaning <*composed* ~s *of poetry*> [Middle French *raime*, fr Arabic *rizmah*, lit., bundle]

[2]**ream** *vt* **1** to enlarge or widen (a hole) with a reamer **2** *NAm* to press the juice from (a citrus fruit)

reap /reep‖riːp/ *vt* **1a** to cut (a crop) with a sickle, scythe, or reaping machine; *also* to harvest thus **b** to clear (e g a field) of a crop by reaping **2** to obtain or win, esp as the reward for effort <*to* ~ *lasting benefits from study*> ~ *vi* to reap sthg – **reaper** *n*

[1]**rear** /riə‖rɪə/ *vt* **1** to build or construct **2** to raise upright **3a** to breed and tend (an animal) or grow (e g a crop) for use or sale **b** BRING UP 1 ~ *vi* **1** to rise to a height **2** *of a horse* to rise up on the hind legs – **rearer** *n*

[2]**rear** *n* **1** the back part of sthg: e g **1a** the part (e g of an army) away from the enemy **b** the part of sthg located opposite its front <*the* ~ *of a house*> **c** the buttocks **2** the space or position at the back <*moved to the* ~>

[3]**rear** *adj* at the back <*a* ~ *window*> – **rearmost** *adj*

ˌ**rear ˈadmiral** *n* an officer in the navy ranking below vice admiral

ˈ**rearˌguard** /-ˌgahd‖-ˌgɑːd/ *adj* of vigorous resistance in the face of defeat <*a* ~ *action*>

ˈ**rear ˌguard** *n* a military detachment for guarding the rear of a main body or force, esp during a retreat

rearm /ˌreeˈahm‖ˌriːˈɑːm/ *vt* to arm (e g a nation or military force) again, esp with new or better weapons ~*vi* to become armed again – **rearmament** *n*

[1]ˈ**rearˌward** /-ˌwood‖-ˌwʊd/ *n* the rear; *esp* the rear division (e g of an army) <*to* ~ *of the main column*>

[2]ˈ**rearward** /-wood‖-wʊd/ *adj* located at or directed towards the rear

ˈ**rearwards** /-woodz‖-wʊdz/ *also* **rearward** *adv* at or towards the rear; backwards

[1]**reason** /ˈreez(ə)n‖ˈriːz(ə)n/ *n* **1a** (a statement offered as) an explanation or justification **b** a rational ground or motive <*a good* ~ *to act soon*> **c** that which makes some phenomenon intelligible; cause <*wanted to know the* ~ *for earthquakes*> **2a(1)** the power of comprehending, inferring, or thinking, esp in orderly rational ways; intelligence **a(2)** proper exercise of the mind **b** sanity <*lost his* ~> – **within reason** within reasonable limits – **with reason** with good cause

[2]**reason** *vi* **1** to use the faculty of reason so as to arrive at conclusions **2** to talk or argue *with* another so as to influence his/her actions or opinions <*can't* ~ *with them*> ~ *vt* **1** to persuade or influence by the use of reason <~ed *myself out of such fears*> **2** to formulate, assume, analyse, or conclude by the use of reason – often + *out* <*to* ~ *out a plan*> – **reasoner** *n*

reasonable /ˈreez(ə)nəbl‖ˈriːz(ə)nəbl/ *adj* **1a** in accord with reason <*a* ~ *theory*> **b** not extreme or excessive <~ *requests*> **c** moderate, fair <*a* ~ *boss*> <~ *weather*> **d** inexpensive **2a** having the faculty of reason; rational **b** sensible – **reasonableness** *n*, **reasonably** *adv*

reasoning /ˈreez(ə)ning‖ˈriːz(ə)nɪŋ/ *n* the drawing of inferences or conclusions through the use of reason

reassure /ˌree·əˈshooə, -ˈshaw‖ˌriːəˈʃʊə, -ˈʃɔː/ *vt* **1** to assure anew <~d *him that the work was satisfactory*> **2** to restore confidence to <*I was* ~d *by his promise*> – **reassurance** *n*, **reassuringly** *adv*

rebarbative /riˈbahbətiv‖rɪˈbɑːbətɪv/ *adj* repellent, unattractive – fml

rebate /ˈreebayt‖ˈriːbeɪt/ *n* **1** a return of part of a payment <*tax* ~> **2** a deduction from a sum before payment; a discount <*10%* ~>

[1]**rebel** /ˈrebl‖ˈrebl/ *adj* **1** in rebellion **2** of rebels <*the* ~ *camp*> [Old French *rebelle*, fr Latin *rebellis*, fr *re-* back, again + *bellum* war]

[2]**rebel** *n* one who rebels against a government, authority, convention, etc

[3]**rebel** /riˈbel‖rɪˈbel/ *vi* **-ll-** **1a** to oppose or disobey (one in) authority or control **b** to resist by force the authority of one's government **2a** to act in or show opposition <~led *against the conventions of polite society*> **b** to feel or exhibit anger or revulsion <~led *at the injustice of life*>

rebellion /riˈbelyən‖rɪˈbeljən/ *n* **1** opposition to (one in) authority or dominance **2** (an instance of) open armed resistance to an established government

rebellious /riˈbelyəs‖rɪˈbeljəs/ *adj* **1a** in rebellion <~ *troops*> **b** (characteristic) of or inclined towards rebellion <*a* ~ *speech*> <*a* ~ *people*> **2** REFRACTORY 1 – **rebelliously** *adv*, **rebelliousness** *n*

rebirth /ˌreeˈbuhth‖ˌriːˈbɜːθ/ *n* **1a** a new or second birth **b** spiritual regeneration **2** a renaissance, revival <*a* ~ *of nationalism*>

reborn /ˌreeˈbawn‖ˌriːˈbɔːn/ *adj* born again; regenerated; *specif* spiritually renewed

[1]**rebound** /riˈbownd‖rɪˈbaʊnd/ *vi* **1** to spring back (as if) on collision or impact with another body **2** to return with an adverse effect to a source or starting point <*their hatred* ~ed *on themselves*>

[2]**rebound** /ˈreeˌbownd‖ˈriːˌbaʊnd; *also* riˈbownd‖rɪˈbaʊnd/ *n* **1a** a rebounding, recoil **b** a recovery <*a sharp* ~ *in prices*> **2** a shot (e g in basketball or soccer) that rebounds – **on the rebound** (whilst) in an unsettled or emotional state resulting from setback, frustration, or crisis <on the rebound *from an unhappy love affair*>

rebuff /riˈbuf‖rɪˈbʌf/ *vt or n* (to) snub

rebuke /riˈbyoohk‖rɪˈbjuːk/ *vt or n* (to) reprimand

rebus /ˈreebəs‖ˈriːbəs/ *n* (a riddle using) a representation of words or syllables by pictures that suggest the same sound

rebut /riˈbut‖rɪˈbʌt/ *vt* **-tt-** **1** to drive back; repel **2** to disprove or expose the falsity of; refute – **rebuttable** *adj*, **rebuttal** *n*

recalcitrant /riˈkalsitrənt‖rɪˈkælsɪtrənt/ *adj* **1** obstinately defiant of authority or restraint **2** difficult to handle or control [Latin *recalcitrare* to kick back, fr *re-* back, again + *calcitrare* to kick, fr *calc-, calx* heel] – **recalcitrance** *n*, **recalcitrant** *n*

[1]**recall** /ri'kawl‖rɪ'kɔːl/ *vt* **1a** to call or summon back <~ed *their ambassador*> **b** to bring back to mind <~s *his early years*> **2** to cancel, revoke – **recallable** *adj*

[2]**recall** /ri'kawl, 'ree,kawl‖rɪ'kɔːl, 'riː,kɔːl/ *n* **1** a call or summons to return <*a ~ of workers after a layoff*> **2** remembrance of what has been learned or experienced <*had almost perfect visual ~*> **3** the act of revoking or the possibility of being revoked **4** the ability (e g of an information retrieval system) to retrieve stored material

recant /ri'kant‖rɪ'kænt/ *vt* to withdraw or repudiate (a statement or belief) formally and publicly; renounce ~*vi* to make an open confession of error; *esp* to disavow a religious or political opinion or belief – **recantation** *n*

[1]**recap** /'ree,kap‖'riː,kæp/ *vt* **-pp-** *NAm* to partially retread (a worn pneumatic tyre) – **recappable** *adj*

[2]**recap** /'ree,kap, ri'kap‖'riː,kæp, rɪ'kæp/ *vb* **-pp-** to recapitulate – **recap** *n*

recapitulate /,reekə'pityoolayt‖,riːkə'pɪtjʊleɪt/ *vb* to repeat the principal points or stages of (e g an argument or discourse) in summing up

recapitulation /,reekəpityoo'laysh(ə)n‖,riːkəpɪtjʊ'leɪʃ(ə)n/ *n* **1** recapping; a concise summary **2** a modified repetition of the main themes forming the third section of a musical movement written in sonata form

recapture /,ree'kapchə‖,riː'kæptʃə/ *vt* **1a** to capture again **b** to experience again <*to ~ the atmosphere of the past*> **2** *NAm* to take (excess earnings or profits) by law – **recapture** *n*

recast /,ree'kahst‖,riː'kɑːst/ *vt* **recast** to cast again <~ *a gun*> <~ *a play*>; *also* to remodel, refashion <~s *his political image to fit the times*> – **recast** *n*

[1]**recce** /'reki‖'rekɪ/ *n* a reconnaissance – infml

[2]**recce** *vb* **recceing; recced, recceed** to reconnoitre – infml

[1]**recede** /ri'seed‖rɪ'siːd/ *vi* **1a** to move back or away; withdraw **b** to slant backwards <*a receding chin*> **2** to grow less, smaller, or more distant; diminish <*fears that demand will ~*> <*hope* ~d>

[2]**recede** /,ree'seed‖,riː'siːd/ *vt* to cede (e g land) back to a former possessor

[1]**receipt** /ri'seet‖rɪ'siːt/ *n* **1** the act or process of receiving <*please acknowledge ~ of the goods*> **2** sthg (e g goods or money) received – usu pl with sing. meaning <*took the days's* ~s *to the bank*> **3** a written acknowledgment of having received goods or money

[2]**receipt** *vt* to give a receipt for or acknowledge, esp in writing, the receiving of

receive /ri'seev‖rɪ'siːv/ *vt* **1a** to (willingly) come into possession of or be provided with **b** to accept for consideration; give attention to <*had to ~ their unwanted attentions*> <~ *a petition*> **2a** to act as a receptacle or container for; *also* to take (an impression, mark, etc) **b** to assimilate through the mind or senses <~ *new ideas*> **3a** to permit to enter; admit <~d *into the priesthood*> **b** to welcome, greet; *also* to entertain **c** to act in response to <*how did she ~ the offer?*> <*well* ~d *on his tour*> **4** to accept as authoritative or true <~d *wisdom*> **5a** to take the force or pressure of <*these pillars ~ the weight of the roof*> **b** to suffer the hurt or injury of <~ *a broken nose*> **6** to be the player who returns (the service of his/her opponent) in tennis, squash, etc **7** to convert (an incoming signal, esp radio waves) into a form suitable for human perception ~*vi* to be a recipient: e g **a** to be at home to visitors **b** to accept stolen goods – **receivable** *adj*

re'ceiver /ri'seevə‖rɪ'siːvə/ *n* **1** a person appointed to hold in trust and administer property of a bankrupt or insane person or property under litigation **2** one who receives stolen goods **3a** a radio, television, or other part of a communications system that receives the signal **b** the part of a telephone that contains the mouthpiece and earpiece – **receivership** *n*

recent /'rees(ə)nt‖'riːs(ə)nt/ *adj* **1** of a time not long past <*the ~ election*> **2** having lately come into existence <*the ~ snow*>

receptacle /ri'septəkl‖rɪ'septəkl/ *n* **1** an object that receives and contains sthg **2** the end of the flower stalk of a flowering plant upon which the floral organs are borne

reception /ri'sepsh(ə)n‖rɪ'sepʃ(ə)n/ *n* **1** receiving or being received: e g **1a** an admission <*his ~ into the church*> **b** a response, reaction <*the play met with a mixed ~*> **c** the receiving of a radio or television broadcast **2** a formal social gathering during which guests are received **3** *Br* an office or desk where visitors or clients (e g to an office, factory, or hotel) are received on arrival

receptionist /ri'sepshənist‖rɪ'sepʃənɪst/ *n* one employed to greet and assist callers or clients

re'ception ,room *n* **1** a waiting room for dental or medical patients **2** a room used primarily for the reception of guests or visitors

receptive /ri'septiv‖rɪ'septɪv/ *adj* **1** open and responsive to ideas, impressions, or suggestions **2** able to receive and transmit stimuli; sensory – **receptively** *adv*, **receptiveness** *n*, **receptivity** *n*

receptor /ri'septə‖rɪ'septə/ *n* **1** a cell or group of cells that receives stimuli; SENSE ORGAN **2** a molecule or group of molecules, esp on the surface of a cell, that have an affinity for a particular chemical (e g a neurotransmitter)

[1]**recess** /ri'ses, 'reeses‖rɪ'ses, 'riːses/ *n* **1** a hidden, secret, or secluded place – usu pl <*illuminating the* ~es *of American politics – TLS*> **2a** an indentation or cleft (e g in an anatomical or geological structure) **b** an alcove <*a pleasant ~ lined with books*> **3** a suspension of business or activity, usu for a period of rest or relaxation <*Parliament is in ~*>; *specif, NAm* a break between school classes

[2]**recess** /ri'ses‖rɪ'ses/ *vt* **1** to put in a recess <~ed *lighting*> **2** to make a recess in **3** *chiefly NAm* to interrupt for a recess ~*vi, chiefly NAm* to take a recess

recession /ri'sesh(ə)n‖rɪ'seʃ(ə)n/ *n* **1** a withdrawal **2** the withdrawal of clergy and choir at the end of a church service **3** a period of reduced economic activity – **recessional, recessionary** *adj*

recessional /ri'sesh(ə)nl‖rɪ'seʃ(ə)nl/ *n* a hymn or musical piece at the conclusion of a church service

recessive /ri'sesiv‖rɪ'sesɪv/ *adj* **1** receding or tending to recede **2** being the one of a pair of (genes determining) contrasting inherited characteristics that is suppressed if a dominant gene is present – **recessively** *adv*

recharge /ˌree'chahj‖ˌriː'tʃɑːdʒ/ *vi* to charge again; *esp* to renew the active materials in (a storage battery) – **recharge** *n*, **rechargeable** *adj*

recherché /rə'sheəshay ‖rə'ʃeəʃeɪ (*Fr* rəʃɛrʃe)/ *adj* **1** exotic, rare **2** precious, affected <*his* ~ *highbrow talk*>

recidivist /ri'sidivist‖rɪ'sɪdɪvɪst/ *n* one who relapses, specif into criminal behaviour – **recidivism** *n*, **recidivist, recidivistic** *adj*

recipe /'resipi‖'resɪpɪ/ *n* **1** PRESCRIPTION 3 **2** a list of ingredients and instructions for making sthg, specif a food dish **3** a procedure for doing or attaining sthg <*a* ~ *for success*> [Latin, take, imperative of *recipere* to take, receive, fr *re-* back, again + *capere* to take]

recipient /ri'sipi·ənt‖rɪ'sɪpɪənt/ *n* sby who or sthg that receives – **recipient** *adj*

[1]**reciprocal** /ri'siprəkl‖rɪ'sɪprəkl/ *adj* **1** *esp of mathematical functions* inversely related **2** shared, felt, or shown by both sides <~ *love*> **3** consisting of or functioning as a return in kind <*did not expect* ~ *benefit*> **4** mutually corresponding; equivalent <~ *trade agreements*> – **reciprocally** *adv*

[2]**reciprocal** *n* **1** either of a pair of numbers (e g $^2/_3$, $^3/_2$) that when multiplied together equal 1 <*the* ~ *of 2 is 0.5*> **2** the inverse of a number under multiplication

reciprocate /ri'siprəˌkayt‖rɪ'sɪprəˌkeɪt/ *vt* **1** to give and take mutually **2** to return in kind or degree <~ *a compliment gracefully*> ~ *vi* **1** to make a return for sthg <*we hope to* ~ *for your kindness*> **2** to move forwards and backwards alternately <*a* reciprocating *valve*> – **reciprocator** *n*, **reciprocative** *adj*, **reciprocation** *adj*

reciprocity /ˌresi'prosəti‖ˌresɪ'prɒsətɪ/ *n* **1** mutual dependence, action, or influence **2** a mutual exchange of privileges, specif between countries or institutions

recital /ri'sietl‖rɪ'saɪtl/ *n* **1a** a reciting **b** a detailed account <*a* ~ *of her troubles*> **c** a discourse, narration **2** a concert or public performance given by a musician, small group of musicians, or dancer – **recitalist** *n*

recitative /ˌresitə'teev‖ˌresɪtə'tiːv/ *n* (a passage delivered in) a rhythmically free declamatory style for singing a narrative text – **recitative** *adj*

recite /ri'siet‖rɪ'saɪt/ *vt* **1** to repeat from memory or read aloud, esp before an audience **2** to relate in detail; enumerate <~d *a catalogue of offences*> ~ *vi* to repeat or read aloud sthg memorized or prepared – **reciter** *n*, **recitation** *n*

reck /rek‖rek/ *vt* **1** to take account of <*he little* ~ed *what the outcome might be*> **2** to matter to; concern <*what* ~s *it me that I shall die tomorrow?*> *USE* archaic or poetic

reckless /'reklis‖'reklɪs/ *adj* marked by lack of proper caution; careless of consequences – **recklessly** *adv*, **recklessness** *n*

reckon /'rekən‖'rekən/ *vt* **1a** to count – usu + *up* **b** to estimate, compute <~ *the height of a building*> **c** to determine by reference to a fixed basis <*the Gregorian calendar is* ~ed *from the birth of Christ*> **2** to consider or think of in a specified way <*she is* ~ed *the leading expert*> **3** to suppose, think <*I* ~ *they're not coming*> **4** to esteem highly <*the boys* ~ *him because he's one of the lads*> – infml ~ *vi* **1** to settle accounts **2** to make a calculation **3** to place reliance <*I'm* ~ing *on your support*> – **reckon with** to take into account, esp because formidable – **reckon without** to fail to consider; ignore

reckoning /'rekəning‖'rekənɪŋ/ *n* **1a** a calculation or counting **b** an account, bill **2** a settling of accounts <*day of* ~> **3** an appraisal

reclaim /ri'klaym‖rɪ'kleɪm/ *vt* **1** to rescue or convert from an undesirable state; reform **2** to make available for human use by changing natural conditions <~ed *marshland*> **3** to obtain from a waste product – **reclaimable** *adj*, **reclamation** *n*, **reclamator** *n*

recline /ri'klien‖rɪ'klaɪn/ *vb* **1** (to cause or permit) to incline backwards <~d *the seat a little*> **2** to place or be in a recumbent position; lean, repose <~s *her head on the pillow*>

recluse /ri'kloohs‖rɪ'kluːs/ *n or adj* (sby) leading a secluded or solitary life – **reclusive** *adj*, **reclusion** *n*

recognition /ˌrekəg'nish(ə)n‖ˌrekəg'nɪʃ(ə)n/ *n* **1** recognizing or being recognized: e g **1a** (formal) acknowledgment (e g of a government or claim) **b** perception of sthg as identical with sthg already known in fact or by description <~ *of a former friend*> **2** special notice or attention <*a writer who has received much* ~> **3** the sensing and coding of printed or written data by a machine <*optical character* ~>

recognizance /ri'kogniz(ə)ns‖rɪ'kɒgnɪz(ə)ns/ *n* (the sum pledged as a guarantee for) a bond entered into before a court or magistrate that requires a person to do sthg (e g pay a debt or appear in court at a later date)

recogn·ize, -ise /'rekəgniez‖'rekəgnaɪz/ *vt* **1a** to perceive to be sthg or sby previously known or encountered <~d *the word*> **b** to perceive clearly <~d *his own inadequacy*> **2a** to show appreciation of (e g by praise or reward) **b** to acknowledge acquaintance with <~ *an old crony with a nod*> **c** to admit the fact of <~s *his obligation*> **3a** to admit as being of a particular status or having validity <~d *her as legitimate representative*> **b** to allow to speak in a meeting – **recognizable** *adj*, **recognizably** *adv*, **recognizability** *n*

[1]**recoil** /ri'koyl‖rɪ'kɔɪl/ *vi* **1** to shrink back physically or emotionally (e g in horror, fear, or disgust) **2** to spring back; rebound: e g **2a** to fly back into an uncompressed position <*the spring* ~ed> **b** *esp of a firearm* to move backwards sharply when fired **3** REBOUND 2

[2]**recoil** /'reeˌkoyl, ri'koyl‖'riːˌkɔɪl, rɪ'kɔɪl/ *n* recoiling; *esp* the backwards movement of a gun on firing

recollect /ˌrekə'lekt‖ˌrekə'lekt/ *vt* **1** to bring back to the level of conscious awareness; remember, recall **2** to bring (oneself) back to a state of composure or conventration ~ *vi* to call sthg to mind – **recollection** *n*, **recollective** *adj*

recommend /ˌrekə'mend‖ˌrekə'mend/ *vt* **1a**

to declare to be worthy of acceptance or trial <~ed *the restaurant*> **b** to endorse as fit, worthy, or competent <~s *her for the position*> **2** to make acceptable <*has other points to* ~ *it*> **3** to advise <~ *that the matter be dropped*> **4** *archaic* to entrust, commit <~ed *his soul to God*> – **recommendable** *adj*, **recommendation** *n*, **recommendatory** *adj*

[1]**recompense** /'rekəmpens‖'rekəmpens/ *vt* **1** to give sthg to by way of compensation <~d *him for his losses*> **2** to make or amount to an equivalent or compensation for <*a pleasure that* ~s *our trouble*>

[2]**recompense** *n* an equivalent or a return for sthg done, suffered, or given <*offered in* ~ *for injuries*>

reconcile /'rekənsiel‖'rekənsaɪl/ *vt* **1a** to restore to friendship or harmony **b** to settle, resolve <~ *differences*> **2** to make consistent or congruous <~ *an ideal with reality*> **3** to cause to submit to or accept <*was* ~d *to hardship*> – **reconcilable** *adj*, **reconciler, reconcilement** *n*, **reconciliation** *n*, **reconciliatory** *adj*

recondite /ri'kondiet, 'rekən-‖rɪ'kɒndaɪt, 'rekən-/ *adj* (of or dealing with sthg) little known, abstruse, or obscure – **reconditely** *adv*, **reconditeness** *n*

recondition /ˌreekən'dish(ə)n‖ˌri:kən'dɪʃ(ə)n/ *vt* to restore to good (working) condition (e g by replacing parts)

reconnaissance /ri'konəs(ə)ns‖rɪ'kɒnəs(ə)ns/ *n* a preliminary survey to gain information; *esp* an exploratory military survey of enemy territory or positions

reconnoitre, *NAm* **reconnoiter** /ˌrekə'noytə‖ˌrekə'nɔɪtə/ *vb* to make a reconnaissance (of)

reconsider /ˌreekən'sidə‖ˌri:kən'sɪdə/ *vb* to consider (sthg) again with a view to change, revision, or revocation – **reconsideration** *n*

reconstitute /ree'konstityooht, -chooht‖ri:'kɒnstɪtju:t, -tʃu:t/ *vt* to constitute again or anew; *esp* to restore to a former condition by adding water <~ *powdered milk*> – **reconstitution** *n*

reconstruct /ˌreekən'strukt‖ˌri:kən'strʌkt/ *vt* **1a** to restore to a previous condition **b** RECREATE a <~ing *a dinosaur from its bones*> **2** to reorganize, reestablish <~ing *society during the postwar period*> **3** to build up a mental image or physical representation of (e g a crime or a battle) from the available evidence – **reconstructible** *adj*, **reconstruction** *n*

[1]**record** /ri'kawd‖rɪ'kɔ:d/ *vt* **1a** to commit to writing so as to supply written evidence **b** to state or indicate (as if) for a record <*said he wanted to* ~ *certain reservations*> **c(1)** to register permanently by mechanical or other means <*earthquake shocks* ~ed *by a seismograph*> **c(2)** to indicate, read **2** to give evidence of; show **3** to convert (e g sound) into a permanent form fit for reproduction ~*vi* to record sthg – **recordable** *adj*

[2]**record** /'rekawd, 'rekəd‖'rekɔ:d, 'rekəd/ *n* **1** the state or fact of being recorded **2a** sthg recorded or on which information, evidence, etc has been registered **b** sthg that recalls, relates, or commemorates past events or feats **c** an authentic official document **d** the official copy of the papers used in a law case **3a(1)** a body of known or recorded facts regarding sthg or sby **a(2)** a list of previous criminal convictions **b** a performance, occurrence, or condition that goes beyond or is extraordinary among others of its kind; *specif* the best recorded performance in a competitive sport **4** (the sound recorded on) a flat usu plastic disc with a spiral groove whose undulations represent recorded sound for reproduction on a gramophone – **off the record** not for publication <*remarks that were* off the record> – **on record** in or into the status of being known, published, or documented <*he is* on record *as saying this*>

'**record ˌdeck** *n* the apparatus including a turntable and stylus on which a gramophone record is played

reˌcorded de'livery *adv or n* (by) a postal service available in the UK in which the delivery of a posted item is recorded

recorder /ri'kawdə‖rɪ'kɔ:də/ *n* **1** *often cap* a magistrate formerly presiding over the court of quarter sessions **2** any of a group of wind instruments consisting of a slightly tapering tube with usu 8 finger holes and a mouthpiece like a whistle

recording /ri'kawding‖rɪ'kɔ:dɪŋ/ *n* sthg (e g sound or a television programme) that has been recorded electronically

'**record ˌplayer** /'rekawd, -kəd‖'rekɔ:d, -kəd/ *n* an electronically-operated system for playing records; a gramophone

[1]**recount** /ri'kownt‖rɪ'kaʊnt/ *vt* to relate in detail

[2]**recount** /ˌree'kownt‖ˌri:'kaʊnt/ *vt* to count again

[3]**recount** /'reeˌkownt‖'ri:ˌkaʊnt/ *n* a recounting, esp of votes

recoup /ri'koohp‖rɪ'ku:p/ *vt* **1** to rightfully withhold part of (a sum due) **2a** to get an equivalent for (e g losses) **b** to pay (a person, organization, etc) back; compensate **3** to regain <*an attempt to* ~ *his fortune*> ~*vi* to make up for sthg lost – **recoupable** *adj*

recourse /ri'kaws‖rɪ'kɔ:s/ *n* **1** (a turning or resorting to) a source of help, strength, or protection <*to have* ~ *to the law*> **2** the right to demand payment

recover /ri'kuvə‖rɪ'kʌvə/ *vt* **1** to get back: e g **1a** to regain possession or use of <*quickly* ~ed *his senses*> **b** RECLAIM 2 **2** to bring back to a normal position or condition <*stumbled, then* ~ed *himself*> **3a** to make up for <~ *one's costs*> **b** to obtain by legal action <~ *damages*> **4** to obtain from an ore, waste product, or by-product ~*vi* to regain a normal or stable position or condition (e g of health) <~ing *from a cold*> – **recoverable** *adj*, **recoverability** *n*

recovery /ri'kuv(ə)ri‖rɪ'kʌv(ə)rɪ/ *n* a recovering: e g **a** a return to normal health **b** a regaining of balance or control (e g after a stumble or mistake) **c** an economic upturn (e g after a depression)

recreant /'rekri·ənt‖'rekrɪənt/ *adj* **1** cowardly **2** unfaithful to duty or allegiance *USE* fml or poetic – **recreant** *n*

recreate /ˌreekri'ayt‖ˌri:krɪ'eɪt/ *vt* to create again: e g **a** to reproduce so as to resemble exactly <~d *an old frontier town for the film*> **b**

to visualize or create again in the imagination – **recreatable** *adj*, **recreation** *n*

recreation /ˌrekriˈaysh(ə)n‖ˌrekrɪˈeɪʃ(ə)n/ *n* (a means of) pleasurable activity, diversion, etc <*his favourite ~ was spying on his neighbours*> – **recreational** *adj*

recriminate /riˈkrimiˌnayt‖rɪˈkrɪmɪˌneɪt/ *vi* to indulge in bitter mutual accusations – **recriminative, recriminatory** *adj*, **recrimination** *n*

recrudesce /ˌreekroohˈdes‖ˌriːkruːˈdes/ *vi, of sthg undesirable, esp a disease* to break out or become active again – fml – **recrudescence** *n*, **recrudescent** *adj*

[1]**recruit** /riˈkrooht‖rɪˈkruːt/ *n* a newcomer to a field or activity; *specif* a newly enlisted member of the armed forces [French *recrute, recrue* fresh growth, new levy of soldiers, fr Middle French fr *recroistre* to grow up again, fr Latin *recrescere*, fr *re-* back, again + *crescere* to grow]

[2]**recruit** *vt* **1a(1)** to enlist recruits for (e g an army, regiment, or society) **a(2)** to enlist (a person) as a recruit **b** to secure the services of; hire **2** to replenish, renew ~*vi* to enlist new members – **recruiter** *n*, **recruitment** *n*

rectal /ˈrekt(ə)l‖ˈrekt(ə)l/ *adj* of, affecting, or near the rectum – **rectally** *adv*

rectangle /ˈrektang·gl‖ˈrektæŋgl/ *n* a parallelogram all of whose angles are right angles; *esp* one that is not a square

rectangular /rekˈtang·gyoolə‖rekˈtæŋgjʊlə/ *adj* **1** shaped like a rectangle **2a** crossing, lying, or meeting at a right angle **b** having faces or surfaces shaped like rectangles – **rectangularly** *adv*, **rectangularity** *n*

rectify /ˈrektiˌfie‖ˈrektɪˌfaɪ/ *vt* **1** to set right; remedy <*to ~ mistakes*> **2** to purify (e g alcohol), esp by repeated or fractional distillation **3** to correct by removing errors **4** to convert (alternating current) to direct current – **rectifiable** *adj*, **rectification** *n*, **rectifier** *n*

rectilinear /ˌrektiˈlini·ə‖ˌrektɪˈlɪnɪə/ *adj* **1** (moving) in or forming a straight line **2** characterized by straight lines – **rectilinearly** *adv*

rectitude /ˈrektiˌtyoohd‖ˈrektɪˌtjuːd/ *n* **1** moral integrity **2** correctness in judgment or procedure

recto /ˈrektoh‖ˈrektəʊ/ *n, pl* **rectos** a right-hand page

rector /ˈrektə‖ˈrektə/ *n* **1a** a clergyman in charge of a parish; *specif* one in a Church of England parish where the tithes were formerly paid to the incumbent **b** a Roman Catholic priest directing a church with no pastor or one whose pastor has other duties **2** the head of a university or college – **rectorship** *n*, **rectorate, rectorial** *adj*

rectory /ˈrekt(ə)ri‖ˈrekt(ə)rɪ/ *n* a rector's residence or benefice

rectum /ˈrektəm‖ˈrektəm/ *n, pl* **rectums, recta** /-tə‖-tə/ the last part of the intestine of a vertebrate, ending at the anus

recumbent /riˈkumbənt‖rɪˈkʌmbənt/ *adj* **1** in an attitude suggestive of repose **2** lying down – **recumbency** *n*, **recumbently** *adv*

recuperate /riˈk(y)oohpəˌrayt‖rɪˈk(j)uːpəˌreɪt/ *vt* to regain <~ *financial losses*> ~*vi* to regain a former (healthy) state or condition – **recuperation** *n*, **recuperative** *adj*

recur /riˈkuh‖rɪˈkɜː/ *vi* **-rr-** to occur again, esp repeatedly or after an interval: e g **a** to come up again for consideration **b** to come again to mind – **recurrence** *n*

recurrent /riˈkurənt‖rɪˈkʌrənt/ *adj* **1** *esp of nerves and anatomical vessels* running or turning back in a direction opposite to a former course **2** returning or happening repeatedly or periodically – **recurrently** *adv*

recurved /riˈkuhvd‖rɪˈkɜːvd/ *adj* curved backwards or inwards

recusancy /ˈrekyooz(ə)nsi‖ˈrekjʊz(ə)nsɪ/, **recusance** *n* refusal to accept or obey established authority; *specif* the refusal of Roman Catholics to attend services of the Church of England, a statutory offence from about 1570 until 1791 – **recusant** *n or adj*

recycle /ˌreeˈsiekl‖ˌriːˈsaɪkl/ *vt* to pass through a series of changes or treatments so as to return to a previous stage in a cyclic process; *specif* to process (sewage, waste paper, glass, etc) for conversion back into a useful product ~*vi esp of an electronic device* to return to an original condition so that operation can begin again – **recyclable** *adj*, **recycler** *n*

[1]**red** /red‖red/ *adj* **-dd- 1** of the colour red **2a** flushed, esp with anger or embarrassment **b** bloodshot **c** *of hair or the coat of an animal* in the colour range between a medium orange and russet or bay **3** *cap* of a communist country, esp the Soviet Union **4** failing to show a profit <*a ~ financial statement*> **5a** inciting or endorsing radical social or political change, esp by force **b** *often cap* communist *USE* (*5*) infml or derog – **reddish** *adj*, **reddishness** *n*, **redly** *adv*, **redness** *n*

[2]**red** *n* **1** a colour whose hue resembles that of blood or of the ruby or is that of the long-wave extreme of the visible spectrum **2** sthg that is of or gives a red or reddish colour **3** the condition of being financially in debt or of showing a loss – usu in *in/out of the red*; compare BLACK 6 **4** a red traffic light meaning 'stop' **5a** a revolutionary radical **b** *cap* a communist *USE* (*5*) chiefly derog

ˌred ˈadmiral *n* a common N American and European butterfly that has broad orange-red bands on the fore wings and feeds on nettles in the larval stage

ˌred ˈblood ˌcell, red cell *n* any of the haemoglobin-containing cells that carry oxygen to the tissues and are responsible for the red colour of vertebrate blood

ˌred-ˈblooded *adj* full of vigour; virile

ˈredˌbreast /-ˌbrest‖-ˌbrest/ *n* a robin

ˈredˌbrick /-ˌbrik‖-ˌbrɪk/ *n or adj* (an English university) founded between 1800 and WW II

ˈredˌcap /-ˌkap‖-ˌkæp/ *n* **1** *Br* a military policeman **2** *NAm* a (railway) porter

ˌred ˈcarpet *n* a greeting or reception marked by ceremonial courtesy – usu in *roll out the red carpet* – **red-carpet** *adj*

ˈredˌcoat /-ˌkoht‖-ˌkəʊt/ *n* a British soldier, esp formerly when scarlet jackets were worn

ˌredˈcurrant /-ˈkurənt‖-ˈkʌrənt/ *n* (the small red edible fruit of) a widely cultivated European currant bush

redden /ˈred(ə)n‖ˈred(ə)n/ *vt* to make red or reddish ~*vi* to become red; *esp* to blush

redeem /riˈdeem‖rɪˈdiːm/ *vt* **1a** to repurchase (e g sthg pledged or lodged as security against a sum of money) <*to* ~ *a pawned ring*> **b** to get or win back **2** to free from what distresses or harms: e g **2a** to free from captivity by payment of ransom **b** to release from blame or debt <*hoped to* ~ *himself by these heroics*> **c** to free from the consequences of sin **3a** to eliminate another's right to (sthg) by payment of a debt **b(1)** to remove the obligation of (e g a bond) by making a stipulated payment <*the government* ~ *savings bonds on demand*>; *specif* to convert (paper money) into money in coin **b(2)** to convert (trading stamps, tokens, etc) into money or goods **c** to make good; fulfil <~ed *his promise*> **4a** to atone for <*to* ~ *an error*> **b(1)** to offset the bad effect of <*flashes of wit* ~ed *a dreary speech*> **b(2)** to make worthwhile; retrieve <*no efforts of hers could* ~ *such a hopeless undertaking*> [Middle French *redimer*, fr Latin *redimere*, fr *re-* back, again + *emere* to take, buy]

Redeemer /riˈdeemə‖rɪˈdiːmə/ *n* Jesus

redemption /riˈdempsh(ə)n, -ˈdemsh(ə)n‖rɪˈdempʃ(ə)n, -ˈdemʃ(ə)n/ *n* redeeming or being redeemed; *also* sthg that redeems – **redemptive** *adj*

redeploy /ˌreediˈploy‖ˌriːdɪˈplɔɪ/ *vb* to transfer (e g troops or workers) from one area or activity to another – **redeployment** *n*

ˌred ˈgiant *n* a star that has a low surface temperature and a large diameter relative to the sun

ˌred-ˈhanded *adv or adj* in the act of committing a crime or misdeed <*caught* ~>

ˈredˌhead /-ˌhed‖-ˌhed/ *n* a person with red hair – **redheaded** *adj*

red herring *n* **1** a herring cured by salting and slow smoking to a dark brown colour **2** sthg irrelevant that distracts attention from the real issue

ˌred-ˈhot *adj* **1** glowing with heat; extremely hot **2a** ardent, passionate <~ *anger*> **b** sensational; *specif* salacious <*this* ~ *story of a Regency love affair*> **c** full of energy, vigour, or enterprise <*a* ~ *band*> **d** arousing enthusiasm; currently extolled <*a* ~ *favourite for the National*> **3** new, topical <~ *news*>

ˌRed ˈIndian *n* a N American Indian

redirect /ˌreediˈrekt, -dieˈrekt‖ˌriːdɪˈrekt, -daɪˈrekt/ *vt* to change the course or direction of – **redirection** *n*

ˌred ˈlead /led‖led/ *n* an orange-red to brick-red lead oxide used in storage battery plates, in glass and ceramics, and as a paint pigment

ˌred-ˈletter *adj* of special (happy) significance [fr the practice of marking holy days in red letters in church calendars]

ˌred ˈlight *n* **1** a red warning light, esp on a road or railway, commanding traffic to stop **2** a cautionary sign <*saw her warning as a* ~ *to potential troublemakers*>

ˌred-ˈlight ˌdistrict *n* a district having many brothels

ˌred ˈmeat *n* dark-coloured meat (e g beef or lamb)

redo /ˌreeˈdooh‖ˌriːˈduː/ *vt* **redoes; redoing; redid; redone** **1** to do over again **2** to decorate (a room or interior of a building) anew

redolent /ˈredələnt‖ˈredələnt/ *adj* **1** full of a specified fragrance <*air* ~ *of seaweed*> **2** evocative, suggestive <*a city* ~ *of antiquity*> – **redolence** *n*, **redolently** *adv*

redouble /riˈdubl‖rɪˈdʌbl; *sense 2* ˌree-‖ˌriː-/ *vb* **1** to make or become greater, more numerous, or more intense <*to* ~ *our efforts*> **2** to double (an opponent's double) in bridge – **redouble** *n*

redoubt /riˈdowt‖rɪˈdaʊt/ *n* **1** a small usu temporary enclosed defensive fortified structure **2** a secure place; a stronghold

redoubtable /riˈdowtəbl‖rɪˈdaʊtəbl/ *adj* **1** formidable <*a* ~ *adversary*> **2** inspiring or worthy of awe or reverence – **redoubtably** *adv*

redound /riˈdownd‖rɪˈdaʊnd/ *vi* **1** to have a direct effect; lead or contribute *to* <*can only* ~ *to our advantage*> **2** to rebound *on* or *upon* <*the President's behaviour* ~s *on his Party*> *USE* fml

ˌred ˈpepper *n* CAYENNE PEPPER

[1]redress /riˈdres‖rɪˈdres/ *vt* **1a** to set right <*to* ~ *social wrongs*> **b** to make or exact reparation for **2** to adjust evenly; make stable or equal again <*to* ~ *the balance of power*>

[2]redress *n* **1** compensation for wrong or loss **2** the (means or possibility of) putting right what is wrong

ˈredˌskin /-ˌskin‖-ˌskɪn/ *n* a N American Indian – chiefly derog

ˌred ˈsquirrel *n* a reddish brown Eurasian squirrel native to British woodlands that is gradually being replaced by the grey squirrel

ˌred ˈtape *n* excessively complex bureaucratic routine that results in delay

reduce /riˈdyoohs‖rɪˈdjuːs/ *vt* **1** to diminish in size, amount, extent, or number; make less <~ *taxes*> <~ *the likelihood of war*> **2** to bring or force to a specified state or condition <*was* ~d *to tears of frustration*> **3** to force to capitulate <~d *the city after a lengthy siege*> **4** to bring to a systematic form or character <~ *natural events to laws*> **5** to correct (e g a fracture) by bringing displaced or broken parts back into normal position **6** to lower in grade, rank, status, or condition <~d *to the ranks*> <*living in* ~d *circumstances*> **7a** to diminish in strength, density, or value **b** to lower the price of <*shoes* ~d *in the sale*> **8** to change the denominations or form of without changing the value <~ *fractions to a common denominator*> **9** to break down by crushing, grinding, etc **10a** to convert (e g an ore) to a metal by removing nonmetallic elements **b** to combine with or subject to the action of hydrogen **c** to change (an atom, molecule, ion, etc) from a higher to a lower oxidation state, esp by adding electrons ~ *vi* **1** to become diminished or lessened; *esp* to lose weight by dieting **2** to become reduced <*ferric iron* ~s *to ferrous iron*> – **reducer** *n*, **reducible** *adj*, **reducibility** *n*

reductio ad absurdum /riˌduktiˑoh ad abˈsuhdəm‖rɪˌdʌktɪəʊ æd æbˈsɜːdəm/ *n* proof of the falsity of a proposition by revealing the absurdity of its logical consequences [Late Latin, lit., reduction to the absurd]

reduction /riˈduksh(ə)n‖rɪˈdʌkʃ(ə)n/ *n* **1** a

reducing or being reduced **2a** sthg made by reducing; *esp* a reproduction (e g of a picture) in a smaller size **b** the amount by which sthg is reduced – **reductive** *adj*

redundancy /ri'dundənsi‖rɪ'dʌndənsɪ/ *n* **1** being redundant **2** the part of a message that can be eliminated without loss of essential information **3** *chiefly Br* dismissal from a job

redundant /ri'dundənt‖rɪ'dʌndənt/ *adj* **1a** superfluous **b** characterized by or containing an excess; *specif* excessively verbose <*a ~ literary style*> **2** *chiefly Br* unnecessary, unfit, or no longer required for a job [Latin *redundare* to overflow, be excessive, fr *re-* back, again + *unda* wave, flow] – **redundantly** *adv*

reduplication /ˌreeˌdyoohpli'kaysh(ə)n‖ˌriː-ˌdjuːplɪ'keɪʃ(ə)n/ *n* a doubling or reiterating – **reduplicate** *vt or adj*, **reduplicative** *adj*

'redˌwing /-ˌwing‖-ˌwɪŋ/ *n* a Eurasian thrush with red patches beneath its wings

'redˌwood /-ˌwood‖-ˌwʊd/ *n* (the wood of) a commercially important Californian timber tree of the pine family that often reaches a height of 100m (about 300ft)

reecho /ˌree'ekoh‖ˌriː'ekəʊ/ *vb* **reechoes; reechoing; reechoed** *vi* to repeat or return an echo ~ *vt* to echo back; repeat

reed /reed‖riːd/ *n* **1a** (the slender, often prominently jointed, stem of) any of various tall grasses that grow esp in wet areas **b** a person or thing too weak to rely on **2** a growth or mass of reeds; *specif* reeds for thatching **3a** a thin elastic tongue or flattened tube (e g of cane or plastic) fastened over an air opening in a musical instrument (e g an organ or clarinet) and set in vibration by an air current **b** a woodwind instrument having a reed <*the* ~s *of an orchestra*> **4** a device on a loom resembling a comb, used to space warp yarns evenly **5** a semicircular convex moulding that is usu 1 of several set parallel

'reed ˌorgan *n* a keyboard wind instrument in which the wind acts on a set of reeds

'reed ˌpipe *n* an organ pipe producing its tone by vibration of a beating reed in an air current

reeducate /ˌree'edyookayt, -'ejoo-‖ˌriː-'edjʊkeɪt, -'edʒʊ-/ *vt* to rehabilitate through education – **reeducative** *adj*, **reeducation** *n*

reedy /'reedi‖'riːdɪ/ *adj* **1** full of, covered with, or made of reeds **2** slender, frail **3** having the tonal quality of a reed instrument; *esp* thin and high

[1]**reef** /reef‖riːf/ *n* a part of a sail taken in or let out to regulate the area exposed to the wind

[2]**reef** *vt* to reduce the area of (a sail) exposed to the wind by rolling up or taking in a portion

[3]**reef** *n* **1** a ridge of rocks or sand at or near the surface of water **2** a lode – **reefy** *adj*

[1]**reefer** /'reefə‖'riːfə/, **'reefer ˌjacket** *n* a close-fitting usu double-breasted jacket of thick cloth

[2]**reefer** *n* JOINT 4

'reef ˌknot *n* a symmetrical knot made of 2 half-knots tied in opposite directions and commonly used for joining 2 pieces of material

[1]**reek** /reek‖riːk/ *n* **1** a strong or disagreeable smell **2** *chiefly Scot & N Eng* smoke, vapour – **reeky** *adj*

[2]**reek** *vi* **1** to emit smoke or vapour **2a** to give off or become permeated with a strong or offensive smell **b** to give a strong impression (of some usu undesirable quality or feature) – + *of* or *with* <*an area that* ~s *of poverty*> <*man who* ~s *of charm*>

[1]**reel** /reel, riəl‖riːl, rɪəl/ *n* a revolvable device on which sthg flexible is wound: e g **a** a small wheel at the butt of a fishing rod for winding the line **b** a flanged spool for photographic film, magnetic tape, etc **c** *chiefly Br* a small spool for sewing thread

[2]**reel** *vt* **1** to wind (as if) on a reel **2** to draw by reeling a line <~ *a fish in*>

[3]**reel** *vi* **1** to be giddy; be in a whirl <*his mind was* ~ing> **2** to waver or fall back (e g from a blow) <~ed *back in horror*> **3** to walk or (appear to) move unsteadily (e g from dizziness or intoxication)

[4]**reel** *n* a reeling motion

[5]**reel** *n* (the music for) a lively esp Scottish-Highland or Irish dance in which 2 or more couples perform a series of circular figures and winding movements

reel off *vt* **1** to tell or repeat readily and without pause <reeled off *all the facts and figures*> **2** to chalk up, usu as a series <*to* reel off *6 wins in succession*>

reentry /ˌree'entri‖ˌriː'entrɪ/ *n* **1** the retaking of possession **2** a second or new entry <*a* ~ *visa*>; *esp* the return to and entry of the earth's atmosphere by a space vehicle – **reenter** *vb*

[1]**reeve** /reev‖riːv/ *n* a medieval English manor officer

[2]**reeve** *vt* **rove** /rohv‖rəʊv/, **reeved 1** to pass (e g a rope) through a hole or opening **2** to fasten by passing through a hole or round sthg **3** to pass a rope through (e g a block)

[3]**reeve** *n* the female of the ruff

ref /ref‖ref/ *n* REFEREE 2 – infml

refectory /ri'fekt(ə)ri‖rɪ'fekt(ə)rɪ/ *n* a dining hall in an institution (e g a monastery or college) [Late Latin *refectorium*, fr Latin *refect-*, *reficere* to restore, fr *re-* back, again + *facere* to make, do]

refer /ri'fuh‖rɪ'fɜː/ *vb* **-rr-** *vt* **1a** to explain in terms of a general cause <~s *their depression to the weather*> **b** to allot to a specified place, stage, period, or category <*to* ~ *the fall of Rome to 410* AD> **c** to experience (e g pain) as coming from or located in a different area from its source <*the pain in appendicitis may be* ~red *to any area of the abdomen*> **2** to send or direct for treatment, aid, information, testimony, or decision <*to* ~ *a patient to a specialist*> ~ *vi* **1a** to relate *to* sthg **b** to direct attention (by clear and specific mention); allude <*the numbers* ~ *to footnotes*> <*no one* ~red *to yesterday's quarrel*> **2** to have recourse; glance briefly for information <~red *frequently to his notes while speaking*> – **referable** *adj*, **referral** *n*

[1]**referee** /ˌrefə'ree‖ˌrefə'riː/ *n* **1** a person to whom sthg is referred: e g **1a** one to whom a legal matter is referred for investigation or settlement **b** one who reviews a (technical) paper before publication **c** REFERENCE 4a **2** an official who supervises the play and enforces the laws in any of several sports (e g football and boxing)

[2]**referee** *vb* to act as a referee (in or for)

[1]**reference** /ˈref(ə)rəns‖ˈref(ə)rəns/ *n* **1** referring or consulting <*a manual designed for ready* ~> **2** (a) bearing on or connection with a matter – often in *in/with reference to* **3** sthg that refers: e g **3a** an allusion, mention **b** sthg that refers a reader or consulter to another source of information (e g a book or passage) **4** one referred to or consulted: e g **4a** a person to whom inquiries as to character or ability can be made **b** a statement of the qualifications of a person seeking employment or appointment given by sby familiar with him/her **c** a source of information (e g a book or passage) to which a reader or inquirer is referred **d** a standard for measuring, evaluating, etc – **referential** *adj*

[2]**reference** *vt* to provide (e g a book) with references to authorities and sources of information

ˈ**reference** ˌ**book** *n* a book (e g a dictionary, encyclopedia, or atlas) intended primarily for consultation rather than for consecutive reading

ˈ**reference** ˌ**mark** *n* a conventional sign (e g * or †) to direct the reader's attention, esp to a footnote

referendum /ˌrefəˈrendəm‖ˌrefəˈrendəm/ *n, pl* **referendums** *also* **referenda** /-də‖-də/ the submitting to popular vote of a measure proposed by a legislative body or by popular initiative; *also* a vote on a measure so submitted

referent /ˈref(ə)rənt‖ˈref(ə)rənt/ *n* the thing that a symbol (e g a word or sign) stands for

refill /ˈreeˌfil‖ˈriːˌfɪl/ *n* a fresh or replacement supply (for a device) – **refill** *vb*, **refillable** *adj*

refine /riˈfien‖rɪˈfaɪn/ *vt* **1** to free from impurities <~ *sugar*> **2** to improve or perfect by pruning or polishing <~ *a poetic style*> **3** to free from imperfection, esp from what is coarse, vulgar, or uncouth ~ *vi* **1** to become pure or perfected **2** to make improvement by introducing subtleties or distinctions – **refiner** *n*

reˈfined *adj* **1** fastidious, cultivated **2** *esp of food* processed to the extent that desirable ingredients may be lost in addition to impurities or imperfections

reˈfinement /-mənt‖-mənt/ *n* **1** refining or being refined **2a** a (highly) refined feature, method, or distinction **b** a contrivance or device intended to improve or perfect <*a new model of car with many* ~s>

refinery /riˈfien(ə)ri‖rɪˈfaɪn(ə)rɪ/ *n* a plant where raw materials (e g metals, oil or sugar) are refined or purified

refit /ˌreeˈfit‖ˌriːˈfɪt/ *vt* **-tt-** to fit out or supply again; *esp* to renovate and modernize (e g a ship) – **refit** *n*

reflation /ˌreeˈflaysh(ə)n‖ˌriːˈfleɪʃ(ə)n/ *n* an expansion in the volume of available money and credit or in the economy, esp as a result of government policy – **reflationary** *adj*, **reflate** *vb*

reflect /riˈflekt‖rɪˈflekt/ *vt* **1** to send or throw (light, sound, etc) back or at an angle <*a mirror* ~s *light*> **2** to show as an image or likeness; mirror <*the clouds were* ~ed *in the water*> **3** to make manifest or apparent; give an idea of <*the pulse* ~s *the condition of the heart*> **4** to consider ~ *vi* **1** to throw back light or sound **2** to think quietly and calmly **3a** to tend to bring reproach or discredit – usu + *on* or *upon* <*an investigation that* ~s *on all the members of the department*> **b** to tend to bring about a specified appearance or impression – usu + *on* <*an act which* ~s *favourably on her*>

reflecting telescope /riˈflekting‖rɪˈflektɪŋ/ *n* REFLECTOR 2

reflection, *Br also* **reflexion** /riˈfleksh(ə)n‖rɪˈflekʃ(ə)n/ *n* **1** a reflecting of light, sound, etc **2** sthg produced by reflecting: e g **2a** an image given back (as if) by a reflecting surface **b** an effect produced by or related to a specified influence or cause <*a high crime rate is a* ~ *of an unstable society*> **3** an often obscure or indirect criticism **4** (a thought, opinion, etc formed by) consideration of some subject matter, idea, or purpose <*on* ~ *it didn't seem such a good plan*> **5** a transformation of a figure with respect to a reference line producing a mirror image of the figure – **reflectional** *adj*

reflective /riˈflektiv‖rɪˈflektɪv/ *adj* **1** capable of reflecting light, images, or sound waves **2** thoughtful, deliberative **3** of or caused by reflection <*the* ~ *glare of the snow*> – **reflectively** *adv*, **reflectiveness, reflectivity** *n*

reflector /riˈflektə‖rɪˈflektə/ *n* **1** a polished surface for reflecting radiation, esp light **2** a telescope in which the principal focussing element is a mirror

[1]**reflex** /ˈreefleks‖ˈriːfleks/ *n* **1a** reflected heat, light, or colour **b** a mirrored image **c** a reproduction or reflection that corresponds to some usu specified original; *specif* a word (element) in a form determined by development from an earlier stage of the language **2a** an automatic response to a stimulus that does not reach the level of consciousness **b** *pl* the power of acting or responding with adequate speed **c** an (automatic) way of behaving or responding <*lying became a natural* ~ *for him*>

[2]**reflex** *adj* **1** bent, turned, or directed back <*a stem with* ~ *leaves*> **2** directed back upon the mind or its operations; introspective **3** occurring as an (automatic) response **4** *of an angle* greater than 180° but less than 360° **5** of, being, or produced by a reflex without intervention of consciousness – **reflexly** *adv*

ˌ**reflex** ˈ**camera** *n* a camera in which the image formed by the lens is reflected onto a ground-glass screen or is seen through the viewfinder for focussing and composition

[1]**reflexive** /riˈfleksiv‖rɪˈfleksɪv/ *adj* **1** directed or turned back on itself **2** of, denoting, or being an action (e g in *he perjured himself*) directed back upon the agent or the grammatical subject – **reflexively** *adv*

[2]**reflexive** *n* a reflexive verb or pronoun

[1]**reform** /riˈfawm‖rɪˈfɔːm/ *vt* **1** to amend or alter for the better **2** to put an end to (an evil) by enforcing or introducing a better method or course of action **3** to induce or cause to abandon evil ways <~ *a drunkard*> ~*vi* to become changed for the better – **reformable** *adj*, **reformative, reformatory** *adj*

[2]**reform** *n* **1** amendment of what is defective or corrupt <*educational* ~> **2** (a measure intended to effect) a removal or correction of an

abuse, a wrong, or errors

reformation /ˌrefəˈmaysh(ə)n‖ˌrefəˈmeɪʃ(ə)n/ *n* **1** reforming or being reformed **2** *cap the* 16th-c religious movement marked ultimately by the rejection of papal authority and some Roman Catholic doctrines and practices, and the establishment of the Protestant churches – **reformational** *adj*

reformatory /riˈfawmət(ə)ri‖rɪˈfɔːmət(ə)rɪ/ *n, chiefly NAm* a penal institution to which young or first offenders or women are sent for reform – no longer used technically in Br

refract /riˈfrakt‖rɪˈfrækt/ *vt* **1** to deflect (light or another wave motion) from one straight path to another when passing from one medium (e g glass) to another (e g air) in which the velocity is different **2** to determine the refracting power of – **refraction** *n*, **refractive** *adj*, **refractivity** *n*

refracting telescope /riˈfrakting‖rɪˈfræktɪŋ/ *n* a refractor

refractor /riˈfraktə‖riˈfræktə/ *n* a telescope whose principal focussing element is a lens that refracts light rays

[1]**refractory** /riˈfrakt(ə)ri‖rɪˈfrækt(ə)rɪ/ *adj* **1** resisting control or authority; stubborn, unmanageable **2a** resistant to treatment or cure <*a* ~ *cough*> **b** immune <*after recovery they were* ~ *to infection*> **3** difficult to fuse, corrode, or draw out; *esp* capable of enduring high temperatures – **refractorily** *adv*, **refractoriness** *n*

[2]**refractory** *n* a heat-resisting ceramic material

[1]**refrain** /riˈfrayn‖rɪˈfreɪn/ *vi* to keep oneself from doing, feeling, or indulging in sthg, esp from following a passing impulse – usu + *from*

[2]**refrain** *n* (the musical setting of) a regularly recurring phrase or verse, esp at the end of each stanza or division of a poem or song; a chorus

refresh /riˈfresh‖rɪˈfreʃ/ *vt* **1** to restore strength or vigour to; revive (e g by food or rest) **2** to restore or maintain by renewing supply; replenish <*the waiter* ~ed *our glasses*> **3** to arouse, stimulate (e g the memory)

refresher /riˈfreshə‖rɪˈfreʃə/ *n* **1** sthg (e g a drink) that refreshes **2 refresher, refresher course** a course of instruction designed to keep one abreast of developments in one's professional field

refreshing /riˈfreshing‖rɪˈfreʃɪŋ/ *adj* agreeably stimulating because of freshness or newness – **refreshingly** *adv*

reˈfreshment /-mənt‖-mənt/ *n* **1** refreshing or being refreshed **2a** sthg (e g food or drink) that refreshes **b** assorted foods, esp for a light meal – usu pl with sing. meaning

refrigerate /riˈfrijərayt‖rɪˈfrɪdʒəreɪt/ *vb* to make or keep cold or cool; *specif* to freeze or chill (e g food) or remain frozen for preservation [Latin *refrigerare*, fr *re-* back, again + *frigerare* to cool, fr *frigor-*, *frigus* cold] – **refrigerant** *n or adj*, **refrigeration** *n*

refrigerator /riˈfrijəraytə‖rɪˈfrɪdʒəreɪtə/ *n* an insulated cabinet or room for keeping food, drink, etc cool

refuel /ˌreeˈfyooh·əl‖ˌriːˈfjuːəl/ *vb* **-ll-** (*NAm* **-l-**, **-ll-**) to provide with or take on additional fuel

refuge /ˈrefyoohj‖ˈrefjuːdʒ/ *n* **1** (a place that provides) shelter or protection from danger or distress <*to seek* ~ *in flight*> <*a mountain* ~> **2** a person, thing, or course of action that offers protection or is resorted to in difficulties <*patriotism is the last* ~ *of a scoundrel* – Samuel Johnson>

refugee /ˌrefyooˈjee‖ˌrefjʊˈdʒiː/ *n* one who flees for safety, esp to a foreign country to escape danger or avoid political, religious, or racial persecution

refulgence /riˈfulj(ə)ns‖rɪˈfʌldʒ(ə)ns/ *n* radiance, brilliance – fml – **refulgent** *adj*, **refulgently** *adv*

[1]**refund** /riˈfund‖rɪˈfʌnd/ *vt* **1** to return (money) in restitution, repayment, or balancing of accounts **2** to pay (sby) back – **refundable** *adj*

[2]**refund** /ˈreeˌfund‖ˈriːˌfʌnd/ *n* **1** a refunding **2** a sum refunded

[3]**refund** /ˌreeˈfund‖ˌriːˈfʌnd/ *vt* to fund (a debt) again

refurbish /ˌreeˈfuhbish‖ˌriːˈfɜːbɪʃ/ *vt* to renovate – **refurbishment** *n*

refusal /riˈfyoohzl‖rɪˈfjuːzl/ *n* **1** a refusing, denying, or being refused **2** the right or option of refusing or accepting sthg before others

[1]**refuse** /riˈfyoohz‖rɪˈfjuːz/ *vt* **1** to express oneself as unwilling to accept **2a** to show or express unwillingness to do or comply with <*the engine* ~d *to start*> **b** to deny <*they were* ~d *admittance to the game*> **3** to decline to jump over – used esp of a horse <~d *the water jump*> ~ *vi* **1** to withhold acceptance, compliance, or permission **2** *of a horse* to decline to jump a fence, wall, etc <~d *at the third fence*> – **refusable** *adj*, **refuser** *n*

[2]**refuse** /ˈrefyoohs‖ˈrefjuːs/ *n* worthless or useless stuff; rubbish, garbage

refute /riˈfyooht‖rɪˈfjuːt/ *vt* **1** to prove wrong by argument or evidence **2** to deny the truth or accuracy of – **refutable** *adj*, **refutably** *adv*, **refutation** *n*

regain /riˈgayn, ˌree-‖rɪˈgeɪn, ˌriː-/ *vt* to gain or reach again; recover

regal /ˈreegl‖ˈriːgl/ *adj* **1** of or suitable for a king or queen **2** stately, splendid – **regally** *adv*, **regality** *n*

regale /riˈgayl‖rɪˈgeɪl/ *vt* **1** to entertain sumptuously **2** to give pleasure or amusement to <~d *us with stories of her exploits*>

regalia /riˈgaylyə‖rɪˈgeɪljə/ *n pl but sing or pl in constr* **1** (the) ceremonial emblems or symbols indicative of royalty **2** special dress; *esp* official finery

[1]**regard** /riˈgahd‖rɪˈgɑːd/ *n* **1** a gaze, look **2a** attention, consideration <*due* ~ *should be given to all facets of the question*> **b** a protective interest <*ought to have more* ~ *for his health*> **3a** a feeling of respect and affection <*her hard work won her the* ~ *of her colleagues*> **b** *pl* friendly greetings <*give him my* ~s> **4** an aspect to be taken into consideration <*is a small school, and is fortunate in this* ~> – **regardful** *adj* – **in/with regard to** with reference to; on the subject of

[2]**regard** *vt* **1** to pay attention to; take into consideration or account **2** to look steadily at **3** to relate to; concern **4** to consider and appraise in a specified way or from a specified point of view <*he is highly* ~ed *as a mechanic*> – **as regards** WITH REGARD TO

regarding /riˈgahding‖rɪˈgɑːdɪŋ/ *prep* WITH REGARD TO

[1]**reˈgardless** /-lis‖-lɪs/ *adj* heedless, careless – **regardlessly** *adv*, **regardlessness** *n*

[2]**regardless** *adv* despite everything

reˈgardless of *prep* IN SPITE OF <regardless of *our mistakes*>

regatta /riˈgatə‖rɪˈgætə/ *n* a series of rowing, speedboat, or sailing races

regency /ˈreej(ə)nsi‖ˈriːdʒ(ə)nsɪ/ *n* **1** the office, period of rule, or government of a regent or regents **2** *sing or pl in constr* a body of regents

Regency *adj* of or resembling the styles (e g of furniture or dress) prevalent during the time of the Prince Regent

[1]**regenerate** /riˈjenərət‖rɪˈdʒenərət/ *adj* **1** formed or created again **2** spiritually reborn or converted **3** restored to a better, higher, or more worthy state – **regenerate** *n*, **regeneracy** *n*

[2]**regenerate** /riˈjenərayt‖rɪˈdʒenəreɪt/ *vi* **1** to become regenerate or regenerated **2** *of a body or body part* to undergo renewal or regrowth (e g after injury) ~ *vt* **1a** to subject to spiritual or moral renewal or revival **b** to change radically and for the better **2a** to generate or produce anew; *esp* to replace (a body part) by a new growth of tissue **b** to produce from a derivative or modified form, esp by chemical treatment <~d *cellulose*> **3** to restore to original strength or properties – **regenerator** *n*, **regenerable** *adj*, **regenerative** *adj*, **regeneration** *n*

regent /ˈreej(ə)nt‖ˈriːdʒ(ə)nt/ *n* one who governs a kingdom in the minority, absence, or disability of the sovereign – **regent** *adj*

reggae /ˈregay‖ˈregeɪ/ *n* popular music of West Indian origin that is characterized by a strongly accented subsidiary beat

regicide /ˈrejiˌsied‖ˈredʒɪˌsaɪd/ *n* (the act of) one who kills a king – **regicidal** *adj*

regime *also* **régime** /rayˈzheem‖reɪˈʒiːm/ *n* **1a** a regimen **b** a regular pattern of occurrence or action (e g of seasonal rainfall) **2a** a form of management or government **b** a government in power [French *régime*, fr Latin *regimen* rule, fr *regere* to rule]

regimen /ˈrejimən‖ˈredʒɪmən/ *n* a systematic plan (e g of diet, exercise, or medical treatment) adopted esp to achieve some end

[1]**regiment** /ˈrejimənt‖ˈredʒɪmənt/ *n sing or pl in constr* **1** a permanent military unit consisting usu of a number of companies, troops, batteries, or sometimes battalions **2** a large number or group – **regimental** *adj*, **regimentally** *adv*

[2]**regiment** /ˈrejiˌment‖ˈredʒɪˌment/ *vt* **1** to form into a regiment **2** to subject to strict and stultifying organization or control – **regimentation** *n*

regimentals /ˌrejiˈmentlz‖ˌredʒɪˈmentlz/ *n pl* **1** the uniform of a regiment **2** military dress

Regina /riˈjienə‖rɪˈdʒaɪnə/ *n* CROWN 5a – used when a queen is ruling [Latin, queen, fem of *reg-, rex* king]

region /ˈreej(ə)n‖ˈriːdʒ(ə)n/ *n* **1** an administrative area **2a** an indefinite area of the world or universe **b** a broadly uniform geographical or ecological area <*desert* ~s> **3** an indefinite area surrounding a specified body part <*the abdominal* ~> **4** a sphere of activity or interest <*the abstract* ~ *of higher mathematics*> **5** any of the zones into which the atmosphere is divided according to height or the sea according to depth – **in the region of** approximating to; MORE OR LESS

regional /ˈreejənl‖ˈriːdʒənl/ *adj* **1** (characteristic) of a region **2** affecting a particular region; localized – **regionally** *adv*

[1]**register** /ˈrejistə‖ˈredʒɪstə/ *n* **1** a written record containing (official) entries of items, names, transactions, etc **2a** a roster of qualified or available individuals <*the electoral* ~> **b** a school attendance record **3a** an organ stop **b** (a part of) the range of a human voice or a musical instrument **4** the language style and vocabulary appropriate to a particular subject matter **5** a device regulating admission of air, esp to solid fuel **6** REGISTRATION 1 **7** an automatic device registering a number or a quantity **8** a condition of correct alignment or proper relative position (e g of the plates used in colour printing) – often in *in/out of register*

[2]**register** *vt* **1a** to make or secure official entry of in a register <~ed *the birth of their daughter*> **b** to enrol formally **c** to record automatically; indicate <*this dial* ~s *speed*> **d** to make a (mental) record of; note **2** to secure special protection for (a piece of mail) by prepayment of a fee **3** to convey an impression of <~ed *surprise at the telegram*> **4** to achieve, win <~ed *an impressive victory*> ~ *vi* **1a** to put one's name in a register <~ed *at the hotel*> **b** to enrol formally (as a student) **2** to make or convey an impression <*the name didn't* ~> – **registrable** *adj*

ˈregistered *adj* qualified formally or officially

ˈregister ˌoffice *n* REGISTRY OFFICE

ˈregister ˌton *n* a unit of internal capacity for ships equal to $100ft^3$ (about $2.83m^3$)

registrar /ˌrejiˈstrah, ˈ--ˌ-‖ˌredʒɪˈstrɑː, ˈ--ˌ-/ *n* **1** an official recorder or keeper of records: e g **1a** a senior administrative officer of a university **b** a court official who deals with administrative and interlocutory matters and acts as a subordinate judge **2** (the post, senior to that of a senior house officer, of) a British hospital doctor in training

registration /ˌrejiˈstraysh(ə)n‖ˌredʒɪˈstreɪʃ(ə)n/ *n* **1** registering or being registered **2** an entry in a register

registry /ˈrejistri‖ˈredʒɪstrɪ/ *n* **1** REGISTRATION 1 **2** a place of registration; *specif* a registry office

ˈregistry ˌoffice *n, Br* a place where births, marriages, and deaths are recorded and civil marriages conducted

ˌregius proˈfessor /ˈreejəs‖ˈriːdʒəs/ *n* a holder of a professorship founded by royal subsidy at a British university

regnal /ˈregnəl‖ˈregnəl/ *adj* of a reign; *specif* calculated from a monarch's accession <*in his 8th* ~ *year*>

regnant /ˈregnənt‖ˈregnənt/ *adj* reigning <*a queen* ~>

[1]**regress** /ˈreeˌgres‖ˈriːˌgres/ *n* **1** REGRESSION 2a **2** an act of going or coming back – fml

[2]**regress** /riˈgres‖rɪˈgres/ *vi* **1** to undergo or exhibit backwards movement, esp to an earlier

state **2** to tend to approach or revert to a mean ~*vt* to induce, esp by hypnosis, a state of psychological regression in

regression /riˈgresh(ə)n‖rɪˈgreʃ(ə)n/ *n* **1** the act or an instance of regressing; *esp* (a) retrograde movement **2a** a trend or shift towards a lower, less perfect, or earlier state or condition **b** reversion to an earlier mental or behavioural level **3** the statistical analysis of the association between 2 or more variables, esp so that predictions (e g of sales over a future period of time) can be made – **regressive** *adj*, **regressively** *adv*

[1]**regret** /riˈgret‖rɪˈgret/ *vt* **-tt- 1** to mourn the loss or death of **2** to be very sorry about < ~s *his mistakes*> – **regrettable** *adj*

[2]**regret** *n* **1** (an expression of) the emotion arising from a wish that some matter or situation could be other than what it is; *esp* grief or sorrow tinged esp with disappointment, longing, or remorse **2** *pl* a conventional expression of disappointment, esp on declining an invitation <*couldn't come to tea, and sent her* ~s> – **regretful** *adj*, **regretfully** *adv*, **regretfulness** *n*

regrettably /riˈgretəbli‖rɪˈgretəblɪ/ *adv* **1** in a regrettable manner; to a regrettable extent <*a* ~ *steep decline in wages*> **2** it is regrettable that <~, *we had failed to consider alternatives*>

[1]**regular** /ˈregyoolə‖ˈregjʊlə/ *adj* **1** belonging to a religious order **2a** formed, built, arranged, or ordered according to some rule, principle, or type <*a* ~ *curve*> **b(1)** both equilateral and equiangular <*a* ~ *polygon*> **b(2)** having faces that are identical regular polygons with identical angles between them <*a* ~ *polyhedron*> <*a* ~ *solid*> **c** perfectly (radially) symmetrical or even **3a** steady or uniform in course, practice, or occurrence; habitual, usual, or constant <~ *habits*> **b** recurring or functioning at fixed or uniform intervals <*a* ~ *income*> **c** defecating or having menstrual periods at normal intervals **4a** constituted, conducted, or done in conformity with established or prescribed usages, rules, or discipline **b** real, absolute <*the office seemed like a* ~ *madhouse*> **c** inflecting normally; *specif* WEAK 7 **5** of or being a permanent standing army **6** *chiefly NAm* thinking or behaving in an acceptable manner <*wanted to prove he was a* ~ *guy*> – infml – **regularly** *adv*, **regularize** *vt*, **regularization** *n*, **regularity** *n*

[2]**regular** *n* **1a** a member of the regular clergy **b** a soldier in a regular army **2** one who is usu present or participating; *esp* one who habitually visits a particular place

regulate /ˈregyooˌlayt‖ˈregjʊˌleɪt/ *vt* **1** to govern or direct according to rule **2** to bring order, method, or uniformity to <~ *one's habits*> **3** to fix or adjust the time, amount, degree, or rate of <~ *the pressure of a tyre*> – **regulative, regulatory** *adj*, **regulator** *n*

[1]**regulation** /ˌregyooˈlaysh(ə)n‖ˌregjʊˈleɪʃ(ə)n/ *n* **1** regulating or being regulated **2a** an authoritative rule dealing with details or procedure <*safety* ~s *in a factory*> **b** a rule or order having the force of law

[2]**regulation** *adj* conforming to regulations; official <~ *uniform*>

regulo /ˈregyooloh‖ˈregjʊləʊ/ *n*, *chiefly Br* the temperature in a gas oven expressed as a specified number

regurgitate /riˈguhjiˌtayt‖rɪˈgɜːdʒɪˌteɪt/ *vb* to vomit or pour back or out (as if) from a cavity – **regurgitation** *n*

rehabilitate /ˌree(h)əˈbilitayt‖ˌriː(h)əˈbɪlɪteɪt/ *vt* **1** to reestablish the good name of **2a** to restore to a former capacity or state (e g of efficiency, sound condition, or solvency) <~ *slum areas*> **b** to restore to a condition of health or useful and constructive activity (e g after illness or imprisonment) – **rehabilitative** *adj*, **rehabilitation** *n*

[1]**rehash** /ˌreeˈhash‖ˌriːˈhæʃ/ *vt* to present or use again in another form without substantial change or improvement

[2]**rehash** /ˈreeˌhash, ˌ-ˈ-‖ˈriːˌhæʃ, ˌ-ˈ-/ *n* sthg presented in a new form without change of substance

ˌreˈhear /-ˈhiə‖-ˈhɪə/ *vt* **reheard** /-ˈhuhd‖-ˈhɜːd/ to hear (a trial or lawsuit) over again – **rehearing** *n*

rehearsal /riˈhuhsl‖rɪˈhɜːsl/ *n* **1** a rehearsing **2** a practice session, esp of a play, concert, etc preparatory to a public appearance

rehearse /riˈhuhs‖rɪˈhɜːs/ *vt* **1** to present an account of (again) <~ *a familiar story*> **2** to recount in order <*had* ~d *their grievances in a letter to the governor*> **3a** to give a rehearsal of; practice **b** to train or make proficient by rehearsal ~*vi* to engage in a rehearsal of a play, concert, etc [Middle French *rehercier*, lit., to harrow again, fr *re-* back, again + *hercier* to harrow, fr *herce* harrow, fr Latin *hirpex*] – **rehearser** *n*

rehouse /ˌreeˈhowz, -ˈhows‖ˌriːˈhaʊz, -ˈhaʊs/ *vt* to establish in new or better-quality housing

reify /ˈree·ifie‖ˈriːɪfaɪ/ *vt* to regard (sthg abstract) as a material thing – **reification** *n*

[1]**reign** /rayn‖reɪn/ *n* **1a** royal authority; sovereignty **b** the dominion, sway, or influence of one resembling or likened to a monarch <*the* ~ *of the military dictators*> **2** the time during which sby or sthg reigns

[2]**reign** *vi* **1a** RULE 1a **b** to hold office as head of state although possessing little governing power <*the queen* ~s *but does not rule*> **2** to be predominant or prevalent <*chaos* ~ed *in the classroom*>

ˌreign of ˈterror *n* a period of ruthless violence committed by those in power

reimburse /ˌree·imˈbuhs‖ˌriːɪmˈbɜːs/ *vt* **1** to pay back to sby <~ *travel expenses*> **2** to make restoration or payment to <~ *you*> – **reimbursable** *adj*, **reimbursement** *n*

[1]**rein** /rayn‖reɪn/ *n* **1** a long line fastened usu to both sides of a bit, by which a rider or driver controls an animal **2a** a restraining influence **b** controlling or guiding power <*the* ~s *of government*> **c** opportunity for unhampered activity or use <*gave free* ~ *to his emotions*> *USE* (*1 & 2b*) usu pl with sing. meaning

[2]**rein** *vt* to check or stop (as if) by pulling on reins – often + *in* <~ed *in his horse*> <*couldn't* ~ *his impatience*>

reincarnate /ˌreeˈinkahnayt, ˌ--ˈ--‖ˌriːˈɪnkɑːneɪt, ˌ--ˈ--/ *vt* **1** to incarnate again; give a new form or fresh embodiment to **2** to cause (a person or his/her soul) to be reborn in another (human) body after death – usu in pass; compare TRANSMIGRATE – **reincarnate** *adj*, **reincarnation** *n*, **reincarnationist** *n*

reindeer /ˈrayn,diə‖ˈreɪn,dɪə/ *n* any of several deer that inhabit N Europe, Asia, and America, have antlers in both sexes, and are often domesticated

reinforce /,ree·inˈfaws‖,riːɪnˈfɔːs/ *vt* **1** to strengthen by additional assistance, material, or support; make stronger or more pronounced **2** to strengthen or increase (e g an army) by fresh additions **3** to stimulate (an experimental subject) with a reward following a correct or desired performance; *also* to encourage (a response) with a reward – **reinforceable** *adj*, **reinforcement** *n*, **reinforcer** *n*

,reinforced ˈconcrete /,ree·inˈfawst, ˈ- -,-‖,riːɪnˈfɔːst, ˈ--,-/ *n* concrete in which metal is embedded for strengthening

reinstate /,ree·inˈstayt‖,riːɪnˈsteɪt/ *vt* **1** to place again (e g in possession or in a former position) **2** to restore to a previous effective state or condition – **reinstatement** *n*

reinsure /,ree·inˈshooə, -ˈshaw-‖,riːɪnˈʃʊə, -ˈʃɔː-/ *vt* to insure (a risk or person) by reinsurance – **reinsurer** *n*

reissue /,reeˈish(y)ooh, -ˈisyooh‖,riːˈɪʃ(j)uː, -ˈɪsjuː/ *vt* to issue again; *esp* to cause to become available again – **reissue** *n*

reiterate /,reeˈitərayt‖,riːˈɪtəreɪt/ *vt* to say or do over again or repeatedly, sometimes with wearying effect – **reiteration** *n*, **reiterative** *adj*, **reiteratively** *adv*

[1]**reject** /riˈjekt‖rɪˈdʒekt/ *vt* **1a** to refuse to accept, consider, submit to, or use **b** to refuse to accept or admit <*the underprivileged feel* ~ed *by society*> **2** to eject; *esp* VOMIT 1 **3** to fail to accept (e g a skin graft or transplanted organ) as part of the organism because of immunological differences – **rejecter, rejector** *n*, **rejection** *n*

[2]**reject** /ˈreejekt‖ˈriːdʒekt/ *n* a rejected person or thing; *esp* a substandard article of merchandise

rejoice /riˈjoys‖rɪˈdʒɔɪs/ *vt* to give joy to; gladden ~ *vi* to feel or express joy or great delight – **rejoicer** *n*, **rejoicingly** *adv*

rejoin /riˈjoyn‖rɪˈdʒɔɪn/ *vt* to say (sharply or critically) in response

rejoinder /riˈjoyndə‖rɪˈdʒɔɪndə/ *n* (an answer to) a reply

rejuvenate /,reeˈjoohvə,nayt, ri-‖,riːˈdʒuːvə-,neɪt, rɪ-/ *vt* **1** to make young or youthful again **2** to restore to an original or new state < ~ *old cars*> ~ *vi* to cause or undergo rejuvenation – **rejuvenator** *n*, **rejuvenation** *n*

[1]**relapse** /riˈlaps, ˈree,laps‖rɪˈlæps, ˈriː,læps/ *n* a relapsing or backsliding; *esp* a recurrence of symptoms of a disease after a period of improvement

[2]**relapse** /riˈlaps‖rɪˈlæps/ *vi* **1** to slip or fall back into a former worse state **2** to sink, subside < ~ *into deep thought*>

relate /riˈlayt‖rɪˈleɪt/ *vt* **1** to give an account of; tell **2** to show or establish logical or causal connection between ~ *vi* **1** to have relationship or connection **2** to respond, esp favourably <*can't* ~ *to that kind of music*> *USE* (*vi*) often + *to* – **relatable** *adj*, **relater** *n*

reˈlated *adj* **1** connected by reason of an established or discoverable relation **2** connected by common ancestry or sometimes by marriage – **relatedness** *n*

relation /riˈlaysh(ə)n‖rɪˈleɪʃ(ə)n/ *n* **1** the act of telling or recounting **2** an aspect or quality (e g resemblance) that connects 2 or more things as belonging or working together or as being of the same kind **3a** RELATIVE 3a **b** kinship **4** reference, respect, or connection <*in* ~ *to*> **5** the interaction between 2 or more people or groups – usu pl with sing. meaning <*race* ~s> **6** *pl* **6a** dealings, affairs <*foreign* ~s> **b** communication, contact <*broke off all* ~ *with her family*> **c** sexual intercourse – euph – **relational** *adj*

reˈlationship /-ship‖-ʃɪp/ *n* **1** the state or character of being related or interrelated <*show the* ~ *between 2 things*> **2** (a specific instance or type of) kinship **3** a state of affairs existing between those having relations or dealings <*had a good* ~ *with his family*>

[1]**relative** /ˈrelətiv‖ˈrelətɪv/ *n* **1** a word referring grammatically to an antecedent **2** sthg having or a term expressing a relation to, connection with, or necessary dependence on another thing **3a** a person connected with another by blood relationship or marriage **b** an animal or plant related to another by common descent

[2]**relative** *adj* **1** introducing a subordinate clause qualifying an expressed or implied antecedent <*a* ~ *pronoun*>; *also* introduced by such a connective <*a* ~ *clause*> **2** relevant, pertinent <*matters* ~ *to world peace*> **3a** not absolute or independent; comparative <*the* ~ *isolation of life in the country*> **b** expressing, having, or existing in connection with or reference to sthg else (e g a standard) < ~ *density*> <*supply is* ~ *to demand*> **4** *of major and minor keys and scales* having the same key signature – **relatively** *adv*, **relativeness** *n*

relativism /ˈreləti,viz(ə)m‖ˈrelətɪ,vɪz(ə)m/ *n* a theory that knowledge and moral principles are relative and have no objective standard – **relativist** *n*

relativistic /,relətiˈvistik‖,relətɪˈvɪstɪk/ *adj* **1** of or characterized by relativity or relativism **2** moving at or being a velocity that causes a significant change in properties (e g mass) in accordance with the theory of relativity <*a* ~ *electron*> – **relativistically** *adv*

relativity /,reləˈtivəti‖,reləˈtɪvətɪ/ *n* **1** being relative **2a** *also* **special theory of relativity** a theory (based on the 2 postulates (1) that the speed of light in a vacuum is constant and independent of the source or observer and (2) that all motion is relative) that leads to the assertion that mass and energy are equivalent and that mass, dimension, and time will change with increased velocity **b** *also* **general theory of relativity** an extension of this theory to include gravitation and related acceleration phenomena

relax /riˈlaks‖rɪˈlæks/ *vt* **1** to make less tense or rigid < ~ed *her muscles*> **2** to make less severe or stringent < ~ *immigration laws*> **3** to lessen the force, intensity, or strength of < ~ing *his concentration*> **4** to relieve from nervous tension ~ *vi* **1** to become lax, weak, or loose **2** to become less intense or severe **3** to cast off inhibition, nervous tension, or anxiety <*couldn't* ~ *in crowds*> **4** to seek rest or recreation – **relaxant** *adj or n*, **relaxer** *n*

relaxation /ˌreelak'saysh(ə)n‖ˌriːlæk'seɪʃ(ə)n/ *n* **1** relaxing or being relaxed **2** a relaxing or recreational state, activity, or pastime **3** the attainment of an equilibrium state following the abrupt removal of some influence (e g light, high temperature, or stress)

[1]**relay** /'reeˌlay‖'riːˌleɪ/ *n* **1a** a fresh supply (e g of horses) arranged beforehand for successive use **b** a number of people who relieve others in some work <*worked in* ~s *around the clock*> **2** a race between teams in which each team member successively covers a specified portion of the course **3** a device set in operation by variation in an electric circuit and operating other devices in turn **4** the act of passing sthg along by stages; *also* such a stage **5** sthg, esp a message, relayed

[2]**relay** /'reeˌlay, ri'lay‖'riːˌleɪ, rɪ'leɪ/ *vt* **1** to provide with relays **2** to pass along by relays <*news was* ~ed *to distant points*>

[1]**release** /ri'lees‖rɪ'liːs/ *vt* **1** to set free from restraint, confinement, or servitude **2** to relieve from sthg that confines, burdens, or oppresses <*was* ~d *from her promise*> **3** to relinquish (e g a claim or right) in favour of another **4** to give permission for publication, performance, exhibition, or sale of, on but not before a specified date; *also* to publish, issue <*the commission* ~d *its findings*>

[2]**release** *n* **1** relief or deliverance from sorrow, suffering, or trouble **2a** discharge from obligation or responsibility **b** (a document effecting) relinquishment or conveyance of a (legal) right or claim **3** freeing or being freed; liberation (e g from jail) **4** a device adapted to release a mechanism as required **5a** (the act of permitting) performance or publication **b** the matter released: e g **b(1)** a statement prepared for the press **b(2)** a (newly issued) gramophone record – **releaser** *n*

relegate /'reləˌgayt‖'reləˌgeɪt/ *vt* **1** to assign to a place of insignificance or oblivion; put out of sight or mind; *specif* to demote to a lower division of a sporting competition (e g a football league) **2a** to assign to an appropriate place or situation on the basis of classification or appraisal **b** to submit or refer to sby or sthg for appropriate action – **relegation** *n*

relent /ri'lent‖rɪ'lent/ *vi* **1** to become less severe, harsh, or strict, usu from reasons of humanity **2** to slacken; LET UP

re'lentless /-lis‖-lɪs/ *adj* persistent, unrelenting – **relentlessly** *adv*, **relentlessness** *n*

relevant /'reliv(ə)nt‖'relɪv(ə)nt/ *adj* **1** having significant and demonstrable bearing on the matter at hand **2** having practical application, esp to the real world – **relevance, relevancy** *n*, **relevantly** *adv*

reliable /ri'lie·əbl‖rɪ'laɪəbl/ *adj* suitable or fit to be relied on; dependable – **reliableness** *n*, **reliably** *adv*, **reliability** *n*

reliance /ri'lie·əns‖rɪ'laɪəns/ *n* **1** the act of relying; the condition or attitude of one who relies <~ *on military power to achieve political ends*> **2** sthg or sby relied on – **reliant** *adj*, **reliantly** *adv*

relic /'relik‖'relɪk/ *n* **1** a part of the body of or some object associated with a saint or martyr, that is preserved as an object of reverence **2** sthg left behind after decay, disintegration, or disappearance <~s *of ancient cities*> **3** a trace of sthg past, esp an outmoded custom, belief, or practice **4** *pl, archaic* remains, corpse

relict /'relikt‖'relɪkt/ *n* **1** a (type of) plant or animal that is a remnant of an otherwise extinct flora, fauna, or kind of organism **2** a geological or geographical feature (e g a lake or mountain) or a rock remaining after other parts have disappeared or substantially altered **3** *archaic* a widow

relief /ri'leef‖rɪ'liːf/ *n* **1a** removal or lightening of sthg oppressive, painful, or distressing <*sought* ~ *from asthma by moving to the coast*> **b** aid in the form of money or necessities, esp for the poor <*a* ~ *organization*> **c** military assistance to an endangered or surrounded post or force **d** a means of breaking or avoiding monotony or boredom <*studied medieval theology for light* ~> **2** (release from a post or duty by) one who takes over the post or duty of another <*a* ~ *teacher*> **3** legal compensation or amends **4** (a method of) sculpture in which the design stands out from the surrounding surface **5** sharpness of outline due to contrast <*a roof in bold* ~ *against the sky*> **6** the differences in elevation of a land surface

relief map *n* a map representing topographical relief **a** graphically by shading, hachures, etc **b** by means of a three-dimensional scale model

relieve /ri'leev‖rɪ'liːv/ *vt* **1a** to free from a burden; give aid or help to **b** to set free from an obligation, condition, or restriction – often + *of* **2** to bring about the removal or alleviation of **3** to release from a post, station, or duty **4** to remove or lessen the monotony of **5** to raise in relief **6** to give relief to (oneself) by urinating or defecating ~ *vi* to bring or give relief – **relievable** *adj*

re'lieved *adj* experiencing or showing relief, esp from anxiety or pent-up emotions – **relievedly** *adv*

religion /ri'lij(ə)n‖rɪ'lɪdʒ(ə)n/ *n* **1a(1)** the (organized) service and worship of a god, gods, or the supernatural **a(2)** personal commitment or devotion to religious faith or observance **b** the state of a member of a religious order **2** a cause, principle, or system of beliefs held to with ardour and faith; sthg considered to be of supreme importance

[1]**religious** /ri'lijəs‖rɪ'lɪdʒəs/ *adj* **1** of or manifesting faithful devotion to an acknowledged ultimate reality or deity **2** of, being, or devoted to the beliefs or observances of a religion **3** scrupulously and conscientiously faithful <~ *in his observance of rules of health*> – **religiously** *adv*, **religiousness** *n*

[2]**religious** *n, pl* **religious** a member of a religious order under monastic vows

relinquish /ri'lingkwish‖rɪ'lɪŋkwɪʃ/ *vt* **1** to renounce or abandon; GIVE UP 3b **2a** to stop holding physically <~ed *his grip*> **b** to give over possession or control of <*few leaders willingly* ~ *power*> – **relinquishment** *n*

reliquary /ˈrelikwəri‖ˈrelɪkwərɪ/ *n* a container or shrine in which sacred relics are kept

[1]**relish** /ˈrelish‖ˈrelɪʃ/ *n* **1** characteristic, pleasing, or piquant flavour or quality **2** enjoyment of or delight in sthg (that satisfies one's tastes, inclinations, or desires) <*eat with* ~> <*little* ~ *for sports*> **3** sthg that adds an appetizing or savoury flavour; *esp* a highly seasoned sauce (e g of pickles or mustard) eaten with plainer food

[2]**relish** *vt* **1** to add relish to **2** to enjoy; have pleasure from – **relishable** *adj*

relive /ˌreeˈliv‖ˌriːˈlɪv/ *vt* to live over again; *esp* to experience again in the imagination

reluctance /riˈluktəns‖rɪˈlʌktəns/ *n* **1** being reluctant **2** the opposition offered by a magnetic substance to magnetic flux; *specif* the ratio of the magnetic potential difference to the corresponding flux

reluctant /riˈluktənt‖rɪˈlʌktənt/ *adj* holding back; unwilling <~ *to condemn him*> – **reluctantly** *adv*

rely /riˈlie‖rɪˈlaɪ/ *vi* **1** to have confidence based on experience <*her husband was a man she could* ~ *on*> **2** to be dependent <*they* ~ *on a spring for their water*> *USE* + *on* or *upon*

remain /riˈmayn‖rɪˈmeɪn/ *vi* **1a** to be sthg or a part not destroyed, taken, or used up <*only a few ruins* ~> **b** to be sthg yet to be shown, done, or treated <*it* ~s *to be seen*> **2** to stay in the same place or with the same person or group; *specif* to stay behind **3** to continue to be <~ *faithful*>

[1]**remainder** /riˈmayndə‖rɪˈmeɪndə/ *n* **1** a future interest in property that is dependent upon the termination of a previous interest created at the same time **2a** a remaining group, part, or trace **b(1)** the number left after a subtraction **b(2)** the final undivided part after division, that is less than the divisor **3** a book sold at a reduced price by the publisher after sales have fallen off

[2]**remainder** *vt* to dispose of (copies of a book) as remainders

remains /riˈmaynz‖rɪˈmeɪnz/ *n* **1** a remaining part or trace <*threw away the* ~ *of the meal*> **2** writings left unpublished at a writer's death <*literary* ~> **3** a dead body

[1]**remake** /ˌreeˈmayk‖ˌriːˈmeɪk/ *vt* **remade** to make anew or in a different form

[2]**ˈreˌmake** *n* a new version of a film

remand /riˈmahnd‖rɪˈmɑːnd/ *vt* **1** to adjourn (a case) for further enquiries **2** to return to custody – **remand** *n*

reˈmand ˌhome *n, Br* a temporary centre for (juvenile) offenders – not now in technical use

[1]**remark** /riˈmahk‖rɪˈmɑːk/ *vt* **1** to express as an observation or comment **2** to take notice of; observe – chiefly fml ~*vi* to notice sthg and make a comment or observation *on* or *upon*

[2]**remark** *n* **1** mention or notice of that which deserves attention **2** a casual expression of an opinion or judgment

remarkable /riˈmahkəbl‖rɪˈmɑːkəbl/ *adj* worthy of being or likely to be noticed, esp as being uncommon or extraordinary – **remarkableness** *n*, **remarkably** *adv*

remedial /riˈmeedi·əl, -dyəl‖rɪˈmiːdɪəl, -djəl/ *adj* **1** intended as a remedy <~ *treatment*> **2** concerned with the correction of faulty study habits <~ *reading courses*> – **remedially** *adv*

[1]**remedy** /ˈremədi‖ˈremədɪ/ *n* **1** a medicine, application, or treatment that relieves or cures a disease **2** sthg that corrects or counteracts an evil or deficiency <*the firing squad made a simple* ~ *for discontent*> **3** (legal) compensation or amends

[2]**remedy** *vt* to provide or serve as a remedy for – **remediable** *adj*

remember /riˈmembə‖rɪˈmembə/ *vt* **1** to bring to mind or think of again (for attention or consideration) <~s *the old days*> <~ *me in your prayers*> **2** to give or leave (sby) a present, tip, etc <*was* ~ed *in the will*> **3** to retain in the memory <~ *the facts until the test is over*> **4** to convey greetings from <~ *me to your mother*> **5** to commemorate ~ *vi* **1** to exercise or have the power of memory **2** to have a recollection or remembrance

remembrance /riˈmembrəns‖rɪˈmembrəns/ *n* **1** the state of bearing in mind **2** the period over which one's memory extends **3** an act of recalling to mind <~ *of the offence angered him all over again*> **4** a memory of a person, thing, or event <*had only a dim* ~ *of that night*> **5a** sthg that serves to keep in or bring to mind **b** a commemoration, memorial **c** a greeting or gift recalling or expressing friendship or affection

Reˌmembrance ˈSunday *n* the Sunday closest to November 11, set aside in commemoration of fallen Allied servicemen and of the end of hostilities in 1918 and 1945

remind /riˈmiend‖rɪˈmaɪnd/ *vt* to put in mind of sthg; cause to remember – **reminder** *n*

reminisce /ˌremiˈnis‖ˌremɪˈnɪs/ *vi* to indulge in reminiscence

reminiscence /ˌremiˈnis(ə)ns‖ˌremɪˈnɪs(ə)ns/ *n* **1** the process or practice of thinking or telling about past experiences **2a** a remembered experience **b** an account of a memorable experience – often pl <*published the* ~s *of the old settler*> **3** sthg that recalls or is suggestive of sthg else

reminiscent /ˌremiˈnis(ə)nt‖ˌremɪˈnɪs(ə)nt/ *adj* **1** of (the character of) reminiscence **2** marked by or given to reminiscence **3** tending to remind one (e g of sthg seen or known before) <*a technology* ~ *of the Stone Age*>

remiss /riˈmis‖rɪˈmɪs/ *adj* **1** negligent in the performance of work or duty **2** showing neglect or inattention <*service was* ~ *in most of the hotels*> – **remissly** *adv*, **remissness** *n*

remission /riˈmish(ə)n‖rɪˈmɪʃ(ə)n/ *n* **1** the act or process of remitting **2** a state or period during which sthg (e g the symptoms of a disease) is remitted **3** reduction of a prison sentence

[1]**remit** /riˈmit‖rɪˈmɪt/ *vb* **-tt-** *vt* **1a** to release sby from the guilt or penalty of (sin) **b** to refrain from inflicting or exacting <~ *a tax*> <~ *the penalty of loss of pay*> **c** to give relief from (suffering) **2a** to desist from (an activity) **b** to let (e g attention or diligence) slacken **3** to refer for consideration; *specif* to return (a case) to a lower court **4** to put back **5** to postpone, defer

6 to send (money) to a person or place ~ *vi* **1a** to moderate **b** *of a disease or abnormality* to become less severe for a period **2** to send money (e g in payment) – **remitment** *n*, **remittable** *adj*, **remitter** *n*

[2]**remit** *n* **1** an act of remitting **2** sthg remitted to another person or authority for consideration or judgment

remittance /ri'mit(ə)ns‖rɪ'mɪt(ə)ns/ *n* **1a** a sum of money remitted **b** a document by which money is remitted **2** transmittal of money

remittent /ri'mit(ə)nt‖rɪ'mɪt(ə)nt/ *adj, of a disease* marked by alternating periods of abatement and increase of symptoms – **remittently** *adv*

remnant /'remnənt‖'remnənt/ *n* **1a** a usu small part or trace remaining **b** a small surviving group – often pl **2** an unsold or unused end of fabric

remodel /ˌree'modl‖ˌri:'mɒdl/ *vt* to reconstruct

remonstrance /ri'monstrəns‖rɪ'mɒnstrəns/ *n* an act or instance of remonstrating

remonstrate /'remənˌstrayt, ri'mon-‖'remənˌstreɪt, rɪ'mɒn-/ *vt* to say or plead in protest, reproof, or opposition ~*vi* to present and urge reasons in opposition – often + *with* – **remonstration** *n*, **remonstrative** *adj*, **remonstratively** *adv*, **remonstrator** *n*

remorse /ri'maws‖rɪ'mɔ:s/ *n* a deep and bitter distress arising from a sense of guilt for past wrongs – **remorseful** *adj*, **remorsefully** *adv*

remote /ri'moht‖rɪ'məʊt/ *adj* **1** far removed in space, time, or relation <*the ~ past*> <*comments ~ from the truth*> **2** out-of-the-way, secluded **3** acting on or controlling indirectly or from a distance <*~ computer operation*> **4** small in degree <*a ~ possibility*> **5** distant in manner – **remotely** *adv*, **remoteness** *n*

reˌmote conˈtrol *n* control over an operation (e g of a machine or weapon) exercised from a distance usu by means of an electrical circuit or radio waves

[1]**remould** /ˌree'mohld‖ˌri:'məʊld/ *vt* to refashion the tread of (a worn tyre)

[2]**remould** /'reeˌmohld‖'ri:ˌməʊld/ *n* a remoulded tyre

[1]**remount** /ˌree'mownt‖ˌri:'maʊnt/ *vt* **1** to mount again <*~ a picture*> **2** to provide (e g a unit of cavalry) with remounts ~*vi* to mount again

[2]**remount** /'reeˌmownt, ˌ-'-‖'ri:ˌmaʊnt, ˌ-'-/ *n* a fresh riding horse; *esp* one used as a replacement for one which is exhausted

removal /ri'moohvl‖rɪ'mu:vl/ *n* **1** *Br* the moving of household goods from one residence to another **2** removing or being removed; *specif* MOVE 2c – fml

[1]**remove** /ri'moohv‖rɪ'mu:v/ *vt* **1** to change the location, position, station, or residence of <*~ soldiers to the front*> **2** to move by lifting, pushing aside, or taking away or off <~s *his hat in church*> **3** to get rid of <*~ a tumour surgically*> ~*vi* to change location, station, or residence – fml <removing *from the city to the suburbs*> – **remover** *n*, **removable** *adj*, **removably** *adv*

[2]**remove** *n* **1a** a distance or interval separating one person or thing from another **b** a degree or stage of separation **2** a form intermediate between 2 others in some British schools

remunerate /ri'myoohnəˌrayt‖rɪ'mju:nəˌreɪt/ *vt* **1** to pay an equivalent for **2** to recompense – **remunerator** *n*, **remuneration** *n*, **remunerative** *adj*

renaissance /ri'nays(ə)ns, ri'nesonhs‖rɪ'neɪs(ə)ns, rɪ'nesɑ̃s/ *n* **1** *cap the* (period of the) humanistic revival of classical influence in Europe from the 14th c to the 17th c, expressed in a flowering of the arts and literature and by the beginnings of modern science **2** *often cap* a movement or period of vigorous artistic and intellectual activity **3** a rebirth, revival [French, fr Middle French, rebirth, fr *renaistre* to be born again, fr Latin *renasci*, fr *re-* back, again + *nasci* to be born]

renal /'reenl‖'ri:nl/ *adj* relating to, involving, or located in the region of the kidneys

reˈnascent /ri'nays(ə)nt‖rɪ'neɪs(ə)nt/ *adj* rising again into being or vigour – fml

rend /rend‖rend/ *vb* **rent** /rent‖rent/ *vt* **1** to wrest, split, or tear apart or in pieces (as if) by violence **2** to tear (the hair or clothing) as a sign of anger, grief, or despair **3a** to lacerate mentally or emotionally **b** to pierce with sound ~*vi* to become torn or split

render /'rendə‖'rendə/ *vt* **1a** to melt down; extract by melting <*~ lard*> **b** to treat so as to convert into industrial fats and oils or fertilizer **2a** to yield; GIVE UP 1 **b** to deliver for consideration, approval, or information **3a** to give in return or retribution **b** to restore; give back **c** to give in acknowledgment of dependence or obligation **d** to do (a service) for another **4a** to cause to be or become <*enough rain to ~ irrigation unnecessary*> **b(1)** to reproduce or represent by artistic or verbal means **b(2)** to give a performance of **c** to translate **5** to direct the execution of; administer <*~ justice*> **6** to apply a coat of plaster or cement directly to

rendering /'rend(ə)ring‖'rend(ə)rɪŋ/ *n* a covering material, usu of cement, sand, and a small percentage of lime, applied to exterior walls

rendezvous /'rondiˌvooh, -day-, 'ronh-‖'rɒndɪˌvu:, -deɪ-, 'rɑ̃-/ *n, pl* **rendezvous** **1** a place (appointed) for assembling or meeting **2** a meeting at an appointed place and time [Middle French, fr *rendez vous* present yourselves] – **rendezvous** *vi*

rendition /ren'dish(ə)n‖ren'dɪʃ(ə)n/ *n* the act or result of rendering: e g **a** a translation **b** a performance, interpretation

renegade /'reniˌgayd‖'renɪˌgeɪd/ *n* **1** a deserter from one faith, cause, or allegiance to another **2** an individual who rejects lawful or conventional behaviour – **renegade** *adj*

renege /ri'neeg, ri'nayg‖rɪ'ni:g, rɪ'neɪg/ *vi* to go back on a promise or commitment <~d *on her contract*> – **reneger** *n*

renew /ri'nyooh‖rɪ'nju:/ *vt* **1** to restore to freshness, vigour, or perfection <*as we ~ our strength in sleep*> **2** to make new spiritually; regenerate **3a** to revive **b** to make changes in; rebuild **4** to make or do again **5** to begin again; resume **6** to replace, replenish <*~ water in a tank*> **7a** to grant or obtain an extension of or on (e g a subscription, lease, or licence) **b** to grant or obtain a further loan of < ~ *a library book*> ~*vi* to make a renewal (e g of a lease) – **renewable** *adj*, **renewably** *adv*, **renewal** *n*, **renewer** *n*, **renewability** *n*

rennet /ˈrenit‖ˈrenɪt/ *n* **1a** the contents of the stomach of an unweaned animal, esp a calf **b** (a preparation from) the lining membrane of a stomach (e g the fourth of a ruminant) used for curdling milk **2** (a substitute for) rennin

rennin /ˈrenin‖ˈrenɪn/ *n* an enzyme, occurring in the digestive juice of a young calf or related mammal, that coagulates milk and is used in making cheese and junket

renounce /riˈnowns‖rɪˈnaʊns/ *vt* **1** to give up, refuse, or resign, usu by formal declaration < ~ *his errors*> **2** to refuse to follow, obey, or recognize any further **3** to fail to follow with a card from (the suit led) in a card game – **renouncement** *n*, **renouncer** *n*

renovate /ˈrenəˌvayt‖ˈrenəˌveɪt/ *vt* **1** to restore to life, vigour, or activity **2** to restore to a former or improved state (e g by cleaning, repairing, or rebuilding) – **renovator** *n*, **renovation** *n*

renown /riˈnown‖rɪˈnaʊn/ *n* a state of being widely acclaimed; fame

reˈnowned *adj* celebrated, famous

1**rent** /rent‖rent/ *n* **1a** a usu fixed periodical return made by a tenant or occupant of property or user of goods to the owner for the possession and use thereof **b** an amount paid or collected as rent **2** the portion of the income of an economy (e g of a nation) attributable to land as a factor of production in addition to capital and labour

2**rent** *vt* **1** to take and hold under an agreement to pay rent **2** to grant the possession and use of for rent ~ *vi* **1** to obtain the possession and use of a place or article for rent **2** to allow the possession and use of property for rent – **rentable** *adj*, **rentability** *n*

3**rent** *past of* REND

4**rent** *n* **1** an opening or split made (as if) by rending **2** an act or instance of rending

1**rental** /ˈrentl‖ˈrentl/ *n* **1** an amount paid or collected as rent **2** an act of renting **3** *NAm* sthg (e g a house) that is rented

2**rental** *adj* of or relating to rent or renting

renter /ˈrentə‖ˈrentə/ *n* the lessee or tenant of property

rentier /ˈrontiˌay, ˈronh- ‖ˈrɒntɪˌeɪ, ˈrɑ̃- (*Fr* rɑ̃tje)/ *n* one who receives a fixed income (e g from land or shares)

ˈ**rent** ˌ**strike** *n* a refusal by a group of tenants to pay rent

renunciation /riˌnunsiˈaysh(ə)n‖rɪˌnʌnsɪˈeɪʃ(ə)n/ *n* the act or practice of renouncing; *specif* self-denial practised for religious reasons – **renunciative** *adj*, **renunciatory** *adj*

reopen /ˌreeˈohp(ə)n‖ˌriːˈəʊp(ə)n/ *vt* **1** to open again **2** to resume (discussion or consideration of) < ~ *a contract*> **3** to begin again ~*vi* to open again <*school* ~s *in September*>

1**rep, repp** /rep‖rep/ *n* a plain-weave fabric with raised crosswise ribs

2**rep** *n* a representative; *specif, chiefly Br* SALES REPRESENTATIVE – infml

3**rep** *n* REPERTORY 2b, c – infml

1**repair** /riˈpeə‖rɪˈpeə/ *vi* to betake oneself; go < ~ed *to his home*> – fml

2**repair** *vt* **1** to restore by replacing a part or putting together what is torn or broken **2** to restore to a sound or healthy state **3** to remedy – **repairer** *n*, **repairable** *adj*, **repairability** *n*

3**repair** *n* **1** an instance or the act or process of repairing **2** relative condition with respect to soundness or need of repairing <*the car is in reasonably good* ~>

reparable /ˈrep(ə)rəbl‖ˈrep(ə)rəbl/ *adj* capable of being repaired

reparation /ˌrepəˈraysh(ə)n‖ˌrepəˈreɪʃ(ə)n/ *n* **1a** the act of making amends, offering expiation, or giving satisfaction for a wrong or injury **b** sthg done or given as amends or satisfaction **2** damages; *specif* compensation payable by a defeated nation for war damages – usu pl with sing. meaning – **reparative** *adj*

repartee /ˌrepahˈtee‖ˌrepɑːˈtiː/ *n* **1** a quick and witty reply **2** (skill in) amusing and usu light sparring with words

repast /riˈpahst‖rɪˈpɑːst/ *n* 1MEAL – fml

repatriate /ˌreeˈpatriˌayt, ri-, -ˈpay-‖ˌriːˈpætrɪˌeɪt, rɪ-, -ˈpeɪ-/ *vt* to restore to the country of origin – **repatriate** *n*, **repatriation** *n*

repay /riˈpay, ˌree-‖rɪˈpeɪ, ˌriː-/ *vt* **repaid** /-ˈpayd‖-ˈpeɪd/ **1a** to pay back < ~ *a loan*> **b** to give or inflict in return or requital < ~ *evil for evil*> **2** to compensate, requite **3** to recompense <*a company which* ~s *hard work*> – **repayable** *adj*, **repayment** *n*

repeal /riˈpeel‖rɪˈpiːl/ *vt* to revoke (a law) – **repeal** *n*, **repealable** *adj*

1**repeat** /riˈpeet‖rɪˈpiːt/ *vt* **1a** to say or state again **b** to say through from memory **c** to say after another < ~ *these words after me*> **2a** to make, do, perform, present, or broadcast again < ~ *an experiment*> **b** to experience again **3** to express or present (oneself or itself) again in the same words, terms, or form ~ *vi* **1** to say, do, or accomplish sthg again **2** *of food* to continue to be tasted intermittently after being swallowed – often + *on* – **repeatable** *adj*, **repeatability** *n*

2**repeat** *n* **1** the act of repeating **2a** sthg repeated; *specif* a television or radio programme that has previously been broadcast at least once **b** (a sign placed before or after) a musical passage to be repeated in performance

reˈpeated *adj* **1** renewed or recurring again and again < ~ *changes of plan*> **2** said, done, or presented again

repeatedly /riˈpeetidli‖rɪˈpiːtɪdlɪ/ *adv* again and again

repeater /riˈpeetə‖rɪˈpiːtə/ *n* **1** a watch that strikes the time when a catch is pressed **2** a firearm that fires several times without having to be reloaded

repel /riˈpel‖rɪˈpel/ *vt* **-ll- 1** to drive back; repulse **2a** to drive away **b** to be incapable of sticking to, mixing with, taking up, or holding <*a fabric that* ~s *moisture*> **c** to (tend to) force away or apart by mutual action at a distance <*2 like electric charges* ~ *one another*> **3** to cause aversion in; disgust

1**repellent** *also* **repellant** /riˈpelənt‖rɪˈpelənt/ *adj* **1** serving or tending to drive away or ward off **2** repulsive – **repellently** *adv*

[2]**repellent** *also* **repellant** *n* sthg that repels; *esp* a substance used to prevent insect attacks

[1]**repent** /ri'pent‖rɪ'pent/ *vi* **1** to turn from sin and amend one's life **2** to feel regret or contrition ~*vt* to feel sorrow, regret, or contrition for – **repentance** *n*, **repentant** *adj*, **repenter** *n*

[2]**repent** /'reepənt‖'riːpənt/ *adj, of a plant part* creeping, prostrate

repercussion /ˌreepə'kush(ə)n‖ˌriːpə'kʌʃ(ə)n/ *n* **1** an echo, reverberation **2a** an action or effect given or exerted in return **b** a widespread, indirect, or unforeseen effect of an act, action, or event – **repercussive** *adj*

repertoire /'repəˌtwah‖'repəˌtwɑː/ *n* **1a** a list or supply of dramas, operas, pieces, or parts that a company or person is prepared to perform **b** a range of skills, techniques, or expedients **2a** the complete list or range of skills, techniques, or ingredients used in a particular field, occupation, or practice **b** a list or stock of capabilities <*the instruction* ~ *of a computer*>

repertory /'repət(ə)ri‖'repət(ə)rɪ/ *n* **1** a repository **2a** a repertoire **b** (a theatre housing) a company that presents several different plays in the course of a season at one theatre **c** the production and presentation of plays by a repertory company <*acting in* ~>

repetition /ˌrepi'tish(ə)n‖ˌrepɪ'tɪʃ(ə)n/ *n* **1** repeating or being repeated **2** a reproduction, copy – **repetitional** *adj*

repetitious /ˌrepi'tishəs‖ˌrepɪ'tɪʃəs/ *adj* characterized or marked by repetition; *esp* tediously repeating – **repetitiously** *adv*, **repetitiousness** *n*

repetitive /ri'petətiv‖rɪ'petətɪv/ *adj* repetitious – **repetitively** *adv*, **repetitiveness** *n*

repine /ri'pien‖rɪ'paɪn/ *vi* to feel or express dejection or discontent –fml – **repiner** *n*

replace /ri'plays‖rɪ'pleɪs/ *vt* **1** to restore to a former place or position <~ *cards in a file*> **2** to take the place of, esp as a substitute or successor **3** to put sthg new in the place of <~ *a worn carpet*> – **replaceable** *adj*, **replacer** *n*

re'placement /-mənt‖-mənt/ *n* **1** replacing or being replaced **2** sthg or sby that replaces another

[1]**replay** /ˌree'play‖ˌriː'pleɪ/ *vt* to play again

[2]**replay** /'reeplay‖'riːpleɪ/ *n* **1a** an act or instance of replaying **b** the playing of a tape (e g a videotape) **2** a repetition, reenactment <*don't want a* ~ *of our old mistakes*> **3** a match played to resolve a tie in an earlier match

replenish /ri'plenish‖rɪ'plenɪʃ/ *vt* to stock or fill up again <~ed *his glass*> – **replenishment** *n*

replete /ri'pleet‖rɪ'pliːt/ *adj* **1** fully or abundantly provided or filled **2** abundantly fed; sated – **repleteness** *n*, **repletion** *n*

replica /'replikə‖'replɪkə/ *n* **1** a close reproduction or facsimile, esp by the maker of the original **2** a copy, duplicate

replicate /'repliˌkayt‖'replɪˌkeɪt/ *vt* **1** to duplicate, repeat <~ *a statistical experiment*> **2** to fold or bend back ~*vi* to produce a replica of itself <replicating *virus particles*> – **replicable** *adj*, **replicative** *adj*, **replicability** *n*

[1]**reply** /ri'plie‖rɪ'plaɪ/ *vi* **1a** to respond in words or writing **b** to make a legal replication **2** to do sthg in response ~*vt* to give as an answer

[2]**reply** *n* sthg said, written, or done in answer or response

[1]**report** /ri'pawt‖rɪ'pɔːt/ *n* **1a** (an account spread by) common talk **b** character or reputation <*a man of good* ~> **2a** a usu detailed account or statement <*a news* ~> **b** an account of a judicial opinion or decision **c** a usu formal record of the proceedings of a meeting or inquiry **d** a statement of a pupil's performance at school usu issued every term to the pupil's parents or guardian **3** a loud explosive noise

[2]**report** *vt* **1** to give information about; relate **2a** to convey news of **b** to relate the words or sense of (sthg said) **c** to make a written record or summary of **d** to present the newsworthy aspects or developments of in writing or for broadcasting **3a** to announce or relate (as the result of examination or investigation) <~ed *no sign of disease*> **b** to make known to the relevant authorities <~ *a fire*> **c** to make a charge of misconduct against ~ *vi* **1a** to give an account **b** to present oneself <~ *at the main entrance*> **c** to account for oneself as specified <~ed *sick on Friday*> **2** to make, issue, or submit a report **3** to act in the capacity of a news reporter – **reportable** *adj*

reportage /ˌrepaw'tahzh, ri'pawtij‖ˌrepɔː'tɑːʒ, rɪ'pɔːtɪdʒ/ *n* **1** the act or process of reporting news **2** writing intended to give a usu factual account of events

reportedly /ri'pawtidli‖rɪ'pɔːtɪdlɪ/ *adv* reputedly

reˌported 'speech /ri'pawtid‖rɪ'pɔːtɪd/ *n* the report of one utterance grammatically adapted for inclusion in another

reporter /ri'pawtə‖rɪ'pɔːtə/ *n* sby who or sthg that reports: e g **a** one who makes a shorthand record of a proceeding **b** a journalist who writes news stories **c** one who gathers and broadcasts news

[1]**repose** /ri'pohz‖rɪ'pəʊz/ *vt* to lay at rest <~ *her head on the cushion*> ~ *vi* **1a** to lie resting **b** to lie dead <reposing *in state*> **2** to take rest **3** to rest for support – chiefly fml <*a bowl* reposing *on the table*>

[2]**repose** *n* **1** a place or state of rest or resting; *esp* rest in sleep **2a** calm, tranquillity **b** a restful effect (e g of a painting or colour scheme) **3** cessation or absence of activity, movement, or animation <*the appearance of his face in* ~> **4** composure of manner – **reposeful** *adj*

repository /ri'pozət(ə)ri‖rɪ'pɒzət(ə)rɪ/ *n* **1** a place, room, or container where sthg is deposited or stored **2** sby who or sthg that holds or stores sthg nonmaterial (e g knowledge) **3** sby to whom sthg is confided or entrusted

repossess /ˌreepə'zes‖ˌriːpə'zes/ *vt* **1** to regain possession of **2** to resume possession of in default of the payment of instalments due – **repossession** *n*

reprehend /ˌrepri'hend‖ˌreprɪ'hend/ *vt* to voice disapproval of; censure

reprehensible /ˌrepri'hensəbl‖ˌreprɪ'hensəbl/ *adj* deserving censure; culpable – **reprehensibleness** *n*, **reprehensibly** *adv*, **reprehensibility** *n*

represent /ˌrepri'zent‖ˌreprɪ'zent/ *vt* **1** to convey a mental impression of <*a book which*

~s *the character of Tudor England*> **2** to serve as a sign or symbol of <*the snake* ~s *Satan*> **3** to portray or exhibit in art; depict **4a(1)** to take the place of in some respect; stand in for **a(2)** to act in the place of **b** to serve, esp in a legislative body, by delegated authority **5** to attribute a specified character or identity to <~s *himself as a friend of the workingman*> **6** to serve as a specimen, exemplar, or instance of **7** to form a mental impression of – **representable** *adj*, **representer** *n*

representation /ˌreprizen'taysh(ə)n‖ˌreprɪzen'teɪʃ(ə)n/ *n* **1** sby who or sthg that represents: e g **1a** an artistic likeness or image **b** a statement made to influence opinion – usu pl with sing. meaning **c** a usu formal protest <*a* ~ *in parliament*> **2** representing or being represented: e g **2a** the action or fact of one person standing in place of another so as to have the rights and obligations of the person represented **b** representing or being represented on or in some formal, esp legislative, body **3** the people representing a constituency – **representational** *adj*

representational /ˌreprizen'taysh(ə)nl‖ˌreprɪzen'teɪʃ(ə)nl/ *adj* **1** of representation **2** of realistic depiction of esp physical objects or appearances in the graphic or plastic arts

[1]**representative** /ˌrepri'zentətiv‖ˌreprɪ'zentətɪv/ *adj* **1** serving to represent <*a painting* ~ *of strife*> **2a** standing or acting for another, esp through delegated authority **b** of or based on representation of the people in government by election **3** serving as a typical or characteristic example <*a* ~ *area*> **4** of representation – **representatively** *adv*, **representativeness** *n*

[2]**representative** *n* **1** a typical example of a group, class, or quality **2** one who represents another or others: e g **2a(1)** one who represents a constituency **a(2)** a member of a House of Representatives or of a US state legislature **b** a deputy, delegate **c** one who represents a business organization; *esp* SALES REPRESENTATIVE **d** one who represents another as successor or heir

repress /ri'pres‖rɪ'pres/ *vt* **1a** to curb <*injustice was* ~ed> **b** to put down by force <~ *an insurrection*> **2a** to hold in or prevent the expression of, by self-control <~ed *a laugh*> **b** to exclude (e g a feeling) from consciousness by psychological repression – **repressible** *adj*, **repressive** *adj*, **repressor** *n*

repression /ri'presh(ə)n‖rɪ'preʃ(ə)n/ *n* **1a** repressing or being repressed <~ *of unpopular opinions*> **b** an instance of repressing <*racial* ~s> **2** a psychological process by which unacceptable desires or impulses are excluded from conscious awareness

[1]**reprieve** /ri'preev‖rɪ'priːv/ *vt* **1** to delay or remit the punishment of (e g a condemned prisoner) **2** to give temporary relief or rest to

[2]**reprieve** *n* **1a** reprieving or being reprieved **b** (a warrant for) a suspension or remission of a (death) sentence **2** a temporary remission (e g from pain or trouble)

[1]**reprimand** /'repriˌmahnd‖'reprɪˌmɑːnd/ *n* a severe (and formal) reproof

[2]**reprimand** /'--ˌ-, ˌ--'-/ *vt* to criticize sharply or formally censure, usu from a position of authority

reprint /'reeˌprint‖'riːˌprɪnt/ *n* **1** a subsequent impression of a book previously published in the same form **2** matter (e g an article) that has appeared in print before – **reprint** *vt*

reprisal /ri'priezl‖rɪ'praɪzl/ *n* **1** (a) retaliation by force short of war **2** the usu forcible retaking of sthg (e g territory) **3** a retaliatory act

reprise /ri'preez‖rɪ'priːz; *sense 1 also* ri'priez‖rɪ'praɪz/ *n* **1** a deduction or charge made yearly out of a manor or estate – usu pl **2** a repetition of a musical passage, theme, or performance

[1]**reproach** /ri'prohch‖rɪ'prəʊtʃ/ *n* **1** (a cause or occasion of) discredit or disgrace <*the poverty of millions is a constant* ~> **2** the act or action of reproaching or disapproving <*was beyond* ~> **3** an expression of rebuke or disapproval – **reproachful** *adj*, **reproachfully** *adv*, **reproachfulness** *n*

[2]**reproach** *vt* to rebuke – **reproachable** *adj*, **reproacher** *n*, **reproachingly** *adv*

[1]**reprobate** /'reprəˌbayt‖'reprəˌbeɪt/ *vt* **1** to condemn strongly as unworthy, unacceptable, or evil **2** to predestine to damnation – **reprobation** *n*, **reprobative** *adj*, **reprobatory** *adj*

[2]**reprobate** /'reprəbayt‖'reprəbeɪt/ *adj* **1** predestined to damnation **2** morally dissolute; unprincipled – **reprobate** *n*

reproduce /ˌreeprə'dyoohs‖ˌriːprə'djuːs/ *vt* **1** to produce (new living things of the same kind) by a sexual or asexual process **2** to cause to exist again or anew **3** to imitate closely <*sound-effects that* ~ *the sound of thunder*> **4** to make an image or copy of **5** to translate (a recording) into sound or an image ~ *vi* **1** to undergo reproduction in a usu specified manner <*the picture* ~s *well*> **2** to produce offspring – **reproducer** *n*, **reproducible** *adj*, **reproducibility** *n*

reproduction /ˌreeprə'duksh(ə)n‖ˌriːprə'dʌkʃ(ə)n/ *n* **1** the act or process of reproducing; *specif* the sexual or asexual process by which plants and animals give rise to offspring **2** sthg (e g a painting) that is reproduced – **reproductive** *adj*

reproof /ri'proohf‖rɪ'pruːf/ *n* criticism for a fault

reprove /ri'proohv‖rɪ'pruːv/ *vt* **1** to call attention to the remissness of <~ *a child's bad manners*> **2** to express disapproval of; censure <~ *a child for her bad manners*> – **reprover** *n*, **reprovingly** *adv*

reptile /'reptiel‖'reptaɪl/ *n* **1** any of a class of air-breathing vertebrates that include the alligators and crocodiles, lizards, snakes, turtles, and extinct related forms (e g the dinosaurs) and have a bony skeleton and a body usu covered with scales or bony plates **2** a grovelling or despicable person [Late Latin, fr *reptilis* creeping, fr Latin *rept-*, *repere* to creep]

[1]**reptilian** /rep'tilyən‖rep'tɪljən/ *adj* **1** resembling or having the characteristics of a reptile **2** of the reptiles

[2]**reptilian** *n* REPTILE 1

republic /ri'publik‖rɪ'pʌblɪk/ *n* **1a** a state whose head is not a monarch **b** a state in which supreme power resides in the people and is exercised by their elected representatives governing according to law **c** a (specified) republican government *<the French Fourth* Republic> **2** a body of people freely and equally engaged in a common activity *<the ~ of letters>* **3** a constituent political and territorial unit of the USSR or Yugoslavia [French *république*, fr Latin *respublica*, lit., public thing, commonwealth]

[1]**republican** /ri'publikən‖rɪ'pʌblɪkən/ *adj* **1a** of or like a republic **b** advocating a republic **2** *cap* of or constituting a political party of the USA that is usu primarily associated with business, financial, and some agricultural interests and is held to favour a restricted governmental role in social and economic life – **republicanism** *n*

[2]**republican** *n* **1** one who favours republican government **2** *cap* a member of the US Republican party

repudiate /ri'pyoohdi,ayt‖rɪ'pju:dɪ,eɪt/ *vt* **1** to refuse to have anything to do with; disown **2a** to refuse to accept; *esp* to reject as unauthorized or as having no binding force **b** to reject as untrue or unjust <~ *a charge*> **3** to refuse to acknowledge or pay <~ *a debt*> – **repudiation** *n*

repugnance /ri'pugnəns‖rɪ'pʌgnəns/ *n* **1** the quality or fact or an instance of being contradictory or incompatible **2** strong dislike, aversion, or antipathy

repugnant /ri'pugnənt‖rɪ'pʌgnənt/ *adj* **1** incompatible, inconsistent **2** arousing strong dislike or aversion – **repugnantly** *adv*

[1]**repulse** /ri'puls‖rɪ'pʌls/ *vt* **1** to drive or beat back <~ *the invading army*> **2** to repel by discourtesy, coldness, or denial **3** to cause repulsion in

[2]**repulse** *n* **1** a rebuff, rejection **2** repelling an assailant or being repelled

repulsion /ri'pulsh(ə)n‖rɪ'pʌlʃ(ə)n/ *n* **1** repulsing or being repulsed **2** a force (e g between like electric charges or like magnetic poles) tending to produce separation **3** a feeling of strong aversion

repulsive /ri'pulsiv‖rɪ'pʌlsɪv/ *adj* **1** tending to repel or reject; forbidding **2** serving or able to repulse **3** arousing strong aversion or disgust – **repulsively** *adv*, **repulsiveness** *n*

reputable /'repyootəbl‖'repjʊtəbl/ *adj* held in good repute; well regarded – **reputably** *adv*, **reputability** *n*

reputation /,repyoo'taysh(ə)n‖,repjʊ'teɪʃ(ə)n/ *n* **1a** overall quality or character as seen or judged by others **b** recognition by other people of some characteristic or ability *<has the ~ of being clever>* **2** a place in public esteem or regard; good name

[1]**repute** /ri'pyooht‖rɪ'pju:t/ *vt* to believe, consider <~d *to be the oldest specimen*>

[2]**repute** *n* **1** the character, quality, or status commonly ascribed **2** the state of being favourably known or spoken of

re'puted *adj* being such according to general or popular belief – **reputedly** *adv*

[1]**request** /ri'kwest‖rɪ'kwest/ *n* **1** the act or an instance of asking for sthg **2** sthg asked for **3** the condition or fact of being requested *<available on ~>* **4** the state of being sought after *<a book in great ~>*

[2]**request** *vt* **1** to make a request to or of <~ed *her to write a paper*> **2** to ask as a favour or privilege *<he* ~s *to be excused>* **3** to ask for <~ed *a brief delay*>

requiem /'rekwi·əm, -,em‖'rekwɪəm, -,em/ *n* **1** a mass for the dead **2** sthg that resembles a solemn funeral chant in tone or function **3** *often cap* **3a** a musical setting of the mass for the dead **b** a musical composition in honour of the dead [Latin (first word of the introit of the requiem mass), accusative of *requies* rest]

require /ri'kwie·ə‖rɪ'kwaɪə/ *vt* **1** to claim or demand by right and authority **2a** to call for as suitable or appropriate *<the occasion* ~s *formal dress>* **b** to call for as necessary or essential; have a compelling need for *<all living beings ~ food>* **3** to impose an obligation or command on; compel – **requirement** *n*

requisite /'rekwizit‖'rekwɪzɪt/ *adj* necessary, required *<make the ~ payment>* – **requisite** *n*, **requisiteness** *n*

requisition /,rekwi'zish(ə)n‖,rekwɪ'zɪʃ(ə)n/ *n* **1** the act of formally requesting sby to perform an action **2a** the act of requiring sthg to be supplied **b** a formal and authoritative (written) demand or application <~ *for army supplies*> – **requisition** *vt*

requite /ri'kwiet‖rɪ'kwaɪt/ *vt* **1** to make retaliation for **2a** to make suitable return to (for a benefit or service) **b** to compensate sufficiently for (an injury) – **requital** *n*

reredos /'riə,dos, 'riəri,dos, 'reərə-‖'rɪə,dɒs, 'rɪərɪ,dɒs, 'reərə-/ *n* a usu ornamental wood or stone screen or partition wall behind an altar

rerun /'ree,run‖'ri:,rʌn/ *n* a presentation of a film or television programme after its first run – **rerun** *vt*

rescind /ri'sind‖rɪ'sɪnd/ *vt* **1** to annul; TAKE BACK *<refused to ~ her harsh order>* **2** to repeal, revoke (e g a law, custom, etc) – **rescinder** *n*, **rescindment** *n*, **rescission** *n*

rescript /'ree,skript‖'ri:,skrɪpt/ *n* **1** a written answer (e g of a pope) to a legal inquiry or petition **2** an act or instance of rewriting

rescue /'reskyooh‖'reskju:/ *vt* to free from confinement, danger, or evil – **rescue** *n*, **rescuer** *n*

[1]**research** /ri'suhch, 'reesuhch‖rɪ'sɜ:tʃ, 'ri:sɜ:tʃ/ *n* **1** careful or diligent search **2** scientific or scholarly inquiry; *esp* study or experiment aimed at the discovery, interpretation, reinterpretation, or application of (new) facts, theories, or laws

[2]**research** *vt* **1** to search or investigate thoroughly <~ *a problem*> **2** to engage in research on or for <~ *a book*> ~*vi* to perform research – **researchable** *adj*, **researcher** *n*

resemble /ri'zembl‖rɪ'zembl/ *vt* to be like or similar to – **resemblance** *n*

resent /ri'zent‖rɪ'zent/ *vt* to harbour or express ill will or bitterness at – **resentful** *adj*, **resentfully** *adv*, **resentfulness** *n*, **resentment** *n*

reservation /,rezə'vaysh(ə)n‖,rezə'veɪʃ(ə)n/ *n* **1** an act of reserving sthg; *esp* (a promise, guarantee, or record of) an arrangement to have sthg (e g a hotel room) held for one's use **2** a tract of land set aside; *specif* one designated for the use of American Indians by treaty **3a** (the specifying of) a limiting condition *<agreed, but with* ~s> **b** a specific doubt or objection

<*had* ~s *about the results*> **4** a strip of land separating carriageways **5** *chiefly NAm* an area in which hunting is not permitted; *esp* one set aside as a secure breeding place

[1]**reserve** /ri'zuhv||rɪ'zɜːv/ *vt* **1** to hold in reserve; keep back <~ *grain for seed*> **2** to set aside (part of the consecrated elements) at the Eucharist for future use **3** to defer <~ *one's judgment on a plan*>

[2]**reserve** *n* **1** sthg retained for future use or need **2** sthg reserved or set aside for a particular use or reason: e g **2a(1)** a military force withheld from action for later use – usu pl with sing. meaning **a(2)** the military forces of a country not part of the regular services; *also* a reservist **b** *chiefly Br* a tract (e g of public land) set apart for the conservation of natural resources or (rare) flora and fauna <*a nature* ~>; *also* one used for regulated hunting or fishing <*a game* ~> **3** an act of reserving <*accepted without* ~> **4** restraint, closeness, or caution in one's words and actions **5** money, gold, foreign exchange, etc kept in hand or set apart usu to meet liabilities – often pl with sing. meaning **6** a player or participant who has been selected to substitute for another if the need should arise – **in reserve** held back ready for use if needed

re'served *adj* **1** restrained in speech and behaviour **2** kept or set apart or aside for future or special use – **reservedly** *adv*, **reservedness** *n*

reservist /ri'zuhvist||rɪ'zɜːvɪst/ *n* a member of a military reserve

reservoir /'rezə,vwah||'rezə,vwɑː/ *n* **1** a place where sthg is kept in store: e g **1a** an artificial lake where water is collected and kept in quantity for use **b** a part of an apparatus in which a liquid is held **2** an available but unused extra source or supply <*an untapped* ~ *of ideas*>

reset /,ree'set||,riː'set/ *vt* **-tt-; reset 1** to set again or anew <~ *type*> **2** to change the reading of <~ *a meter*> – **resettable** *adj*

reshuffle /,ree'shufl||,riː'ʃʌfl/ *vt* to reorganize by the redistribution of (existing) elements <*the cabinet was* ~d *by the Prime Minister*> – **reshuffle** *n*

reside /ri'zied||rɪ'zaɪd/ *vi* **1a** to dwell permanently or continuously; occupy a place as one's legal domicile **b** to make one's home for a time <*the King* ~d *at Lincoln*> **2a** to be present as an element or quality **b** to be vested as a right

residence /'rezid(ə)ns||'rezɪd(ə)ns/ *n* **1a** the act or fact of dwelling in a place **b** the act or fact of living in or regularly attending some place for the discharge of a duty or the enjoyment of a benefit **2** a (large or impressive) dwelling **3a** the period of abode in a place <*after a* ~ *of 30 years*> **b** a period of study, teaching, etc at a college or university **4** *chiefly NAm* housing or a unit of housing provided for students – **residency** *n* – **in residence 1** serving in a regular capacity **2** actually living in a usu specified place <*the Queen is* in residence *at Windsor*>

[1]**resident** /'rezid(ə)nt||'rezɪd(ə)nt/ *adj* **1a** living in a place, esp for some length of time **b** serving in a regular or full-time capacity <*the* ~ *engineer for a highway department*>; *also* being in residence **2** present, inherent **3** *of an animal* not migratory

[2]**resident** *n* one who resides in a place

residential /,rezi'densh(ə)l||,rezɪ'denʃ(ə)l/ *adj* **1a** used as a residence or by residents <~ *accommodation*> **b** entailing residence <*a* ~ *course*> **2** given over to private housing as distinct from industry or commerce <*a* ~ *neighbourhood*> **3** of residence or residences – **residentially** *adv*

[1]**residual** /ri'zidyooəl||rɪ'zɪdjʊəl/ *adj* of or constituting a residue – **residually** *adv*

[2]**residual** *n* sthg left over; a remainder, residue

re,siduary lega'tee /ri'zidyooəri||rɪ'zɪdjʊərɪ/ *n* sby who inherits a residue

residue /'rezidyooh||'rezɪdjuː/ *n* sthg that remains after a part is taken, separated, or designated; a remnant, remainder: e g **a** that part of a testator's estate remaining after the satisfaction of all debts and the payment of all bequests **b** a constituent structural unit of a usu complex molecule (e g a protein or nucleic acid)

resign /ri'zien||rɪ'zaɪn/ *vt* **1** to renounce voluntarily; *esp* to relinquish (e g a right or position) by a formal act **2** to reconcile, consign; *esp* to give (oneself) over without resistance <~ed *herself to her fate*> ~ *vi* to give up one's office or position – **resigner** *n*

resignation /,rezig'naysh(ə)n||,rezɪg'neɪʃ(ə)n/ *n* **1a** an act or instance of resigning sthg **b** a formal notification of resigning <*handed in her* ~> **2** the quality or state of being resigned

re'signed *adj* marked by or expressing submission to sthg regarded as inevitable <*a* ~ *look on his face*> – **resignedly** *adv*, **resignedness** *n*

resilience /ri'zilyəns||rɪ'zɪljəns/, **resiliency** /-si||-sɪ/ *n* **1** the ability of a body to recover its original form after deformation (e g due to stretching or applying pressure) **2** an ability to recover quickly from or adjust easily to misfortune, change, or disturbance

resilient /ri'zilyənt||rɪ'zɪljənt/ *adj* characterized or marked by resilience; *esp* capable of withstanding shock without permanent deformation or rupture – **resiliently** *adv*

resin /'rezin||'rezɪn/ *n* (a synthetic polymer or plastic with some of the characteristics of) any of various solid or semisolid yellowish to brown inflammable natural plant secretions (e g amber) that are insoluble in water and are used esp in varnishes, sizes, inks, and plastics – **resinoid** *adj or n*, **resinous** *adj*

resist /ri'zist||rɪ'zɪst/ *vt* **1** to withstand the force or effect of **2** to strive against <~ed *the enemy valiantly*> **3** to refrain from <*could never* ~ *a joke*> ~ *vi* to exert force in opposition – **resistible** *adj*, **resistibility** *n*

resistance /ri'zist(ə)ns||rɪ'zɪst(ə)ns/ *n* **1** an act or instance of resisting **2** the ability to resist **3** an opposing or retarding force **4a** the opposition offered to the passage of a steady electric current through a substance, usu measured in ohms **b** a resistor **5** *often cap* an underground organization of a conquered country engaging in sabotage

resistant /ri'zist(ə)nt||rɪ'zɪst(ə)nt/ *adj* capable of or offering resistance – often in combination <*heat-*resistant *paint*>

resistor /ri'zistə||rɪ'zɪstə/ *n* a component included in an electrical circuit to provide resistance

resolute /'rezəl(y)ooht‖'rezəl(j)u:t/ *adj* **1** firmly resolved; determined **2** bold, unwavering – **resolutely** *adv*, **resoluteness** *n*

resolution /ˌrezə'loohsh(ə)n, -'lyoohsh(ə)n‖ ˌrezə'lu:ʃ(ə)n, -'lju:ʃ(ə)n/ *n* **1** the act or process of reducing to simpler form: e g **1a** the act of making a firm decision **b** the act of finding out sthg (e g the answer to a problem); solving **c** the passing of a voice part from a dissonant to a consonant note or the progression of a chord from dissonance to consonance **d** the separating of a chemical compound or mixture into its constituents **e** the analysis of a vector into 2 or more vectors of which it is the sum **f** the process or capability (e g of a microscope) of making individual parts or closely adjacent images distinguishable **2** the subsidence of inflammation, esp in a lung **3a** sthg that is resolved **b** firmness of resolve **4** a formal expression of opinion, will, or intent voted by a body or group

¹resolve /ri'zolv‖rɪ'zɒlv/ *vt* **1a** to break up or separate into constituent parts **b** to reduce by analysis <~ *the problem into simple elements*> **2** to cause or produce the resolution of **3a** to deal with successfully <~ *doubts*> <~ *a dispute*> **b** to find an answer to **c** to find a mathematical solution of **d** to express (e g a vector) as the sum of 2 or more components **4** to reach a firm decision about <~ *disputed points in a text*> **5** to declare or decide by a formal resolution and vote **6** to make (e g voice parts) progress from dissonance to consonance ~ *vi* **1** to become separated into constituent parts; *also* to become reduced by dissolving or analysis **2** to form a resolution; determine <*he* ~d *against overeating at Christmas*> **3** to progress from dissonance to consonance – **resolvable** *adj*, **resolver** *n*

²resolve *n* **1** sthg that is resolved **2** fixity of purpose **3** a legal or official decision; *esp* a formal resolution

resonance /'rezənəns‖'rezənəns/ *n* **1a** the quality or state of being resonant **b** (the state of adjustment that produces) strong vibration in a mechanical or electrical system caused by the stimulus of a relatively small vibration of (nearly) the same frequency as that of the natural vibration of the system **2a** the intensification and enrichment of a musical tone by supplementary vibration **b** a quality imparted to voiced sounds by a buildup esp of vibrations in the vocal tract **3** the possession by a molecule, radical, etc of 2 or more possible structures differing only in the distribution of electrons

resonant /'rezənənt‖'rezənənt/ *adj* **1** continuing to sound **2a** capable of inducing resonance **b** relating to or exhibiting resonance **3** intensified and enriched by resonance – **resonant** *n*, **resonantly** *adv*

resonate /'rezəˌnayt‖'rezəˌneɪt/ *vi* to produce or exhibit resonance ~*vt* to make resonant

resonator /'rezənaytə‖'rezəneɪtə/ *n* sthg that resounds or resonates: e g **a** a device that responds to and can be used to detect a particular frequency **b** a device for increasing the resonance or amplifying the sound of a musical instrument

¹resort /ri'zawt‖rɪ'zɔ:t/ *n* **1a** sby who or sthg that is looked to for help; a refuge <*saw her as a last* ~> **b** recourse <*have* ~ *to force*> **2a** frequent, habitual, or general visiting <*a place of popular* ~> **b** a frequently visited place (e g a village or town), esp providing accommodation and recreation for holidaymakers

²resort *vi* **1** to go, esp frequently or in large numbers **2** to have recourse <~ *to force*>

resound /ri'zownd‖rɪ'zaʊnd/ *vi* **1** to become filled with sound **2** to produce a sonorous or echoing sound **3** to become renowned ~*vt* to extol loudly or widely

resounding /ri'zownding‖rɪ'zaʊndɪŋ/ *adj* **1a** resonating **b** impressively sonorous **2** vigorously emphatic; unequivocal <*a* ~ *success*> – **resoundingly** *adv*

resource /ri'zaws, ri'saws‖rɪ'zɔ:s, rɪ'sɔ:s/ *n* **1a** an available means of support or provision **b** a natural source of wealth or revenue **c** computable wealth **d** a source of information or expertise **2** a means of occupying one's spare time **3** the ability to deal with a difficult situation; resourcefulness *USE* (*1a, b, c*) usu pl

re'sourceful /-f(ə)l‖-f(ə)l/ *adj* skilful in handling situations; capable of devising expedients – **resourcefully** *adv*, **resourcefulness** *n*

¹respect /ri'spekt‖rɪ'spekt/ *n* **1** a relation to or concern with sthg usu specified; reference – in *with/in respect to* <*with* ~ *to your last letter*> **2a** high or special regard; esteem **b** the quality or state of being esteemed <*achieving* ~ *among connoisseurs*> **c** *pl* expressions of respect or deference <*paid his* ~s> **3** an aspect; detail <*a good plan in some* ~s> – **in respect of 1** from the point of view of **2** in payment of

²respect *vt* **1a** to consider worthy of high regard **b** to refrain from interfering with <~ *the sovereignty of a state*> **c** to show consideration for <~ *a person's privacy*> **2** to have reference to – **respecter** *n*

respectability /riˌspektə'biləti‖rɪˌspektə'bɪlətɪ/ *n* the quality or state of being socially respectable

respectable /ri'spektəbl‖rɪ'spektəbl/ *adj* **1** worthy of respect **2** decent or conventional in character or conduct **3a** acceptable in size or quantity <~ *amount*> **b** fairly good; tolerable **4** presentable <~ *clothes*> – **respectability** *n*, **respectably** *adv*

re'spectful /-f(ə)l‖-f(ə)l/ *adj* marked by or showing respect or deference – **respectfully** *adv*, **respectfulness** *n*

respecting /ri'spekting‖rɪ'spektɪŋ/ *prep* with regard to; concerning

respective /ri'spektiv‖rɪ'spektɪv/ *adj* of or relating to each; particular, separate <*their* ~ *homes*> – **respectiveness** *n*

re'spectively /-li‖-lɪ/ *adv* **1** in particular; separately **2** in the order given <*Mary and Anne were 12 and 16 years old* ~>

respiration /ˌrespi'raysh(ə)n‖ˌrespɪ'reɪʃ(ə)n/ *n* **1a** the process by which air or dissolved gases are brought into intimate contact with the circulating medium of a multicellular organism (e g by breathing) **b** (a single complete act of) breathing **2** the processes by which an organism supplies its cells with the oxygen needed for metabolism and removes the carbon dioxide formed in energy-producing reactions **3** any of various energy-yielding reactions involving oxidation that occur in living cells – **respirational** *adj*, **respiratory** *adj*

respirator /ˈrespi͵raytə‖ˈrespɪ͵reɪtə/ *n* **1** a device worn over the mouth or nose to prevent the breathing of poisonous gases, harmful dusts, etc **2** a device for maintaining artificial respiration

respire /riˈspie·ə‖rɪˈspaɪə/ *vi* **1** to breathe **2** *of a cell or tissue* to take up oxygen and produce carbon dioxide during respiration ~*vt* to breathe

respite /ˈrespiet, ˈrespit‖ˈrespaɪt, ˈrespɪt/ *n* **1** a period of temporary delay; *esp* REPRIEVE 1B **2** an interval of rest or relief

resplendent /riˈsplend(ə)nt‖rɪˈsplend(ə)nt/ *adj* characterized by splendour – **resplendently** *adv*, **resplendence** *n*

respond /riˈspond‖rɪˈspɒnd/ *vi* **1** to write or speak in reply; make an answer <~ *to the appeal for aid*> **2a** to react in response <~ *to a stimulus*> **b** to show favourable reaction <~ *to surgery*> ~*vt* to reply – **responder** *n*

[1]**respondent** /riˈspond(ə)nt‖rɪˈspɒnd(ə)nt/ *n* one who responds: e g **a** a defendant, esp in an appeal or divorce case **b** a person who replies to a poll

[2]**respondent** *adj* making response

response /riˈspons‖rɪˈspɒns/ *n* **1** an act of responding **2** sthg constituting a reply or reaction: e g **2a** sthg (e g a verse) sung or said by the people or choir after or in reply to the officiant in a liturgical service **b** a change in the behaviour of an organism resulting from stimulation **c** the output of a transducer or detecting device that results from a given input and is often considered as a function of some variable (e g frequency)

responsibility /ri͵sponsəˈbiləti‖rɪ͵spɒnsəˈbɪlətɪ/ *n* **1** the quality or state of being responsible: e g **1a** moral or legal obligation **b** reliability, trustworthiness **2** sthg or sby that one is responsible for

responsible /riˈsponsəbl‖rɪˈspɒnsəbl/ *adj* **1a** liable to be required to justify **b(1)** liable to be called to account as the agent or primary cause <*the woman* ~ *for the job*> **b(2)** being the reason or cause <*mechanical defects were* ~ *for the accident*> **2a** able to answer for one's own conduct **b** able to discriminate between right and wrong **3** marked by or involving responsibility or liability <*a* ~ *job*> – **responsibleness** *n*, **responsibly** *adv*

responsive /riˈsponsiv‖rɪˈspɒnsɪv/ *adj* **1** giving response; constituting a response <*a* ~ *glance*> <~ *aggression*> **2** quick to respond or react appropriately or sympathetically – **responsively** *adv*, **responsiveness** *n*

[1]**rest** /rest‖rest/ *n* **1** repose, sleep **2a** freedom or a break from activity or labour **b** a state of motionlessness or inactivity **c** the repose of death **3** a place for resting, lodging, or taking refreshment <*sailor's* ~> **4** peace of mind or spirit **5a** (a character representing) a silence in music of a specified duration **b** a brief pause in reading **6** sthg (e g an armrest) used for support – **at rest** resting or reposing, esp in sleep or death

[2]**rest** *vi* **1a** to relax by lying down; *esp* to sleep **b** to lie dead <~ *in peace*> **2** to cease from action or motion; desist from labour or exertion **3** to be free from anxiety or disturbance **4** to be set or lie fixed or supported <*a column* ~s *on its pedestal*> **5** to be based or founded <*the verdict* ~ed *on several sound precedents*> **6** to depend for action or accomplishment <*the answer* ~s *with him*> **7** *of farmland* to remain idle or uncropped **8** to stop introducing evidence in a law case ~ *vt* **1** to give rest to **2** to set at rest **3** to place on or against a support **4a** to cause to be firmly based or founded <~ed *all hope in his son*> **b** to stop presenting evidence pertinent to (a case at law) – **rester** *n*

[3]**rest** *n* a collection or quantity that remains over <*ate the* ~ *of the chocolate*>

restate /͵reeˈstayt‖͵riːˈsteɪt/ *vt* to state again or in a different way (e g more emphatically) – **restatement** *n*

restaurant /ˈrest(ə)ronh, -ront, -rənt‖ˈrest(ə)rɑ̃, -rɒnt, -rənt/ *n* a place where refreshments, esp meals, are sold usu to be eaten on the premises [French, fr *restaurer* to restore, fr Latin *restaurare*]

ˈ**restaurant** ͵**car** *n* DINING CAR

restaurateur /͵rest(ə)rəˈtuh, ͵resto-‖͵rest(ə)rəˈtɜː, ͵restɒ-/ *n* the manager or proprietor of a restaurant

restful /ˈrestf(ə)l‖ˈrestf(ə)l/ *adj* **1** marked by, affording, or suggesting rest and repose <*a* ~ *colour scheme*> **2** quiet, tranquil – **restfully** *adv*, **restfulness** *n*

restitution /͵restiˈtyoohsh(ə)n‖͵restɪˈtjuːʃ(ə)n/ *n* **1** restoration: e g **1a** the returning of sthg (e g property) to its rightful owner **b** the making good of or giving a compensation for an injury **2** a legal action serving to cause restoration of a previous state

restive /ˈrestiv‖ˈrestɪv/ *adj* **1** stubbornly resisting control **2** restless, uneasy – **restively** *adv*, **restiveness** *n*

ˈ**restless** /-lis‖-lɪs/ *adj* **1** affording no rest <*a* ~ *night*> **2** continuously agitated <*the* ~ *ocean*> **3** characterized by or manifesting unrest, esp of mind <~ *pacing*>; *also* changeful, discontented – **restlessly** *adv*, **restlessness** *n*

restoration /͵restəˈraysh(ə)n‖͵restəˈreɪʃ(ə)n/ *n* **1** restoring or being restored: e g **1a** a reinstatement **b** a handing back of sthg **2** a representation or reconstruction of the original form (e g of a fossil or building) **3** *cap* the reestablishment of the monarchy in England in 1660 under Charles II; *also* the reign of Charles II <Restoration *drama*>

restorative /riˈstawrətiv, -ˈsto-‖rɪˈstɔːrətɪv, -ˈstɒ-/ *n or adj* (sthg capable of) restoring esp health or vigour – **restoratively** *adv*

restore /riˈstaw‖rɪˈstɔː/ *vt* **1** to give back <~ *the book to its owner*> **2** to bring back into existence or use **3** to bring back to or put back into a former or original (unimpaired) state <*to* ~ *a painting*> **4** to put again in possession of sthg <*newly* ~d *to health*> – **restorable** *adj*, **restorer** *n*

restrain /riˈstrayn‖rɪˈstreɪn/ *vt* **1a** to prevent

from doing sthg < ~ed *the boy from jumping*> **b** to limit, repress, or keep under control <*she found it hard to ~ her anger*> **2** to deprive of liberty; *esp* to place under arrest – **restrainable** *adj*, **restrainer** *n*

re'strained *adj* characterized by restraint; being without excess or extravagance – **restrainedly** *adv*

restraint /ri'straynt‖rɪ'streɪnt/ *n* **1a** restraining or being restrained **b** a means of restraining; a restraining force or influence **2** moderation of one's behaviour; self-restraint

restrict /ri'strikt‖rɪ'strɪkt/ *vt* **1** to confine within bounds **2** to regulate or limit as to use or distribution

re'stricted *adj* **1a** not general; limited **b** available only to particular groups or for a particular purpose **c** subject to control, esp by law **d** not intended for general circulation <*a ~ document*> **2** narrow, confined – **restrictedly** *adv*

restriction /ri'striksh(ə)n‖rɪ'strɪkʃ(ə)n/ *n* **1** a regulation that restricts or restrains <~s *for motorists*> **2** restricting or being restricted

restrictive /ri'striktiv‖rɪ'strɪktɪv/ *adj* **1** restricting or tending to restrict <~ *regulations*> **2** identifying rather than describing a modified word or phrase <*a ~ clause*> – **restrictively** *adv*, **restrictiveness** *n*

'rest ˌroom *n, NAm* public toilet facilities in a public building (e g a restaurant)

restructure /ˌree'strukchə‖ˌriː'strʌktʃə/ *vt* to change the make-up, organization, or pattern of <~ *local government*>

1**result** /ri'zult‖rɪ'zʌlt/ *vi* **1** to proceed or arise as a consequence, effect, or conclusion, usu from sthg specified <*injuries* ~ing *from skiing*> **2** to have a usu specified outcome or end <*errors that ~ in tragedy*> [Medieval Latin *resultare*, fr Latin, to rebound, fr *re-* + *saltare* to leap]

2**result** *n* **1** sthg that results as a (hoped for or required) consequence, outcome, or conclusion **2** sthg obtained by calculation or investigation <*showed us the ~ of the calculations*> **3a** a win or tie as the conclusion of a cricket match **b** a win (e g in soccer)

resultant /ri'zult(ə)nt‖rɪ'zʌlt(ə)nt/ *adj* derived or resulting from sthg else, esp as the total effect of many causes – **resultantly** *adv*

resume /ri'zyoohm‖rɪ'zjuːm/ *vt* **1** to take or assume again <~d *his seat by the fire* – Thomas Hardy> **2** to return to or begin again after interruption ~*vi* to begin again after an interruption <*the meeting will ~ after lunch*> – **resumption** *n*

résumé, **resumé** *also* **resume** /'rezyooˌmay‖'rezjʊˌmeɪ/ *n* a summary: e g **a** a summing up of sthg (e g a speech or narrative) **b** *NAm* CURRICULUM VITAE

resurgence /ri'suhj(ə)ns‖rɪ'sɜːdʒ(ə)ns/ *n* a rising again into life, activity, or influence – **resurge** *vi*, **resurgent** *adj*

resurrect /ˌrezə'rekt‖ˌrezə'rekt/ *vt* **1** to bring back to life from the dead **2** to bring back into use or view

resurrection /ˌrezə'reksh(ə)n‖ˌrezə'rekʃ(ə)n/ *n* **1a** *cap* the rising of Christ from the dead **b** *often cap* the rising again to life of all the human dead before the last judgment **2** a resurgence, revival, or restoration – **resurrectional** *adj*

resuscitate /ri'susəˌtayt‖rɪ'sʌsəˌteɪt/ *vt* to revive from apparent death or from unconsciousness; *also* to revitalize ~*vi* to revive; COME TO – **resuscitation** *n*, **resuscitative** *adj*, **resuscitator** *n*

1**retail** /'reeˌtayl‖'riːˌteɪl; *sense 2 often* ri'tayl‖rɪ'teɪl/ *vt* **1** to sell (goods) in carrying on a retail business **2** 1RECOUNT ~*vi* to be sold at retail <*tomatoes ~ at a higher price*> – **retailer** *n*

2**retail** /'reetayl‖'riːteɪl/ *adj, adv, or n* (of, being, or concerned with) the sale of commodities or goods in small quantities to final consumers who will not resell them

retail price index *n* a monthly index of the cost of living in Britain, based on the retail prices of selected essential commodities

retain /ri'tayn‖rɪ'teɪn/ *vt* **1a** to keep in possession or use **b** to engage by paying a retainer <~ *a lawyer*> **c** to keep in mind or memory **2** to hold secure or intact; contain in place <*lead* ~s *heat*> – **retainable** *adj*

1**retainer** /ri'taynə‖rɪ'teɪnə/ *n* a fee paid to a lawyer or professional adviser for services

2**retainer** *n* an old and trusted domestic servant

re'taining ˌwall /ri'tayning‖rɪ'teɪnɪŋ/ *n* a wall built to withstand a mass of earth, water, etc

1**retake** /ˌree'tayk‖ˌriː'teɪk/ *vt* **retook** /ˌree'took‖ˌriː'tʊk/; **retaken** /ˌree'tayk(ə)n‖ˌriː'teɪk(ə)n/ **1** to recapture **2** to photograph again

2**retake** /'reetayk‖'riːteɪk/ *n* a second photographing or photograph

retaliate /ri'taliˌayt‖rɪ'tælɪˌeɪt/ *vi* to return like for like; *esp* to get revenge – **retaliation** *n*, **retaliative, retaliatory** *adj*

retard /ri'tahd‖rɪ'tɑːd/ *vt* to slow down or delay, esp by preventing or hindering advance or accomplishment – **retardant** *adj or n*, **retardation** *n*

retarded /ri'tahdid‖rɪ'tɑːdɪd/ *adj* slow in intellectual or emotional development or academic progress

retch /rech‖retʃ/ *vb* to (make an effort to) vomit – **retch** *n*

retention /ri'tensh(ə)n‖rɪ'tenʃ(ə)n/ *n* **1a** retaining or being retained **b** abnormal retaining of a fluid (e g urine) in a body cavity **2** retentiveness

retentive /ri'tentiv‖rɪ'tentɪv/ *adj* able or tending to retain; *esp* retaining knowledge easily – **retentively** *adv*, **retentiveness** *n*

rethink /ˌree'thingk‖ˌriː'θɪŋk/ *vb* **rethought** /ˌree'thawt‖ˌriː'θɔːt/ to think (about) again; *esp* to reconsider (a plan, attitude, etc) with a view to changing – **rethinker** *n*, **rethink** *n*

reticent /'retis(ə)nt‖'retɪs(ə)nt/ *adj* **1** inclined to be silent or reluctant to speak **2** restrained in expression, presentation, or appearance – **reticence** *n*, **reticently** *adv*

reticle /'retikl‖'retɪkl/ *n* a graticule visible in the eyepiece of an optical instrument

1**reticulate** /ri'tikyoolət‖rɪ'tɪkjʊlət/, **reticular** /-lə‖-lə/ *also* **reticulose** /-lohs, -lohz‖-ləʊs, -ləʊz/ *adj* resembling a net; *esp* having veins, fibres, or lines crossing

2**reticulate** /ri'tikyooˌlayt‖rɪ'tɪkjʊˌleɪt/ *vb* to divide, mark, or arrange (sthg) so as to form a network – **reticulation** *n*

reticule /'retikyoohl‖'retɪkjuːl/ *n* **1** a reticle **2**

a decorative drawstring bag used as a handbag by women in the 18th and 19th c

retina /ˈretinə‖ˈretɪnə/ *n, pl* **retinas, retinae** /-ni‖-nɪ/ the sensory membrane at the back of the eye that receives the image formed by the lens and is connected with the brain by the optic nerve – **retinal** *adj*

retinue /ˈretiˌnyooh‖ˈretɪˌnjuː/ *n* a group of retainers or attendants accompanying an important personage (e g a head of state)

retire /riˈtie·ə‖rɪˈtaɪə/ *vi* **1** to withdraw **1a** from action or danger **b** for rest or seclusion; go to bed **2** to recede; FALL BACK **3** to give up one's position or occupation; conclude one's working or professional career ~ *vt* **1a** to order (a military force) to withdraw **b** to withdraw (e g currency or shares) from circulation **2** to cause to retire from a position or occupation – **retirement** *n*

reˈtired *adj* **1** remote from the world; secluded **2** having concluded one's career

retiring /riˈtie·əring‖rɪˈtaɪərɪŋ/ *adj* reserved, shy – **retiringly** *adv*

[1]**retort** /riˈtawt‖rɪˈtɔːt/ *vt* **1** to fling back or return aggressively **2** to say or exclaim in reply or as a counter argument **3** to answer (e g an argument) by a counter argument ~*vi* to answer back sharply or tersely; retaliate

[2]**retort** *n* a terse, witty, or cutting reply; *esp* one that turns the first speaker's words against him/her

[3]**retort** *vt or n* (to treat by heating in) a vessel in which substances are distilled or decomposed by heat

retouch /ˌreeˈtuch‖ˌriːˈtʌtʃ/ *vt* **1** TOUCH UP 1 **2** to alter (e g a photographic negative) to produce a more acceptable appearance ~*vi* to retouch sthg – **retouch** *n*, **retoucher** *n*

retrace /ˌreeˈtrays‖ˌriːˈtreɪs/ *vt* to trace again or back

retract /riˈtrakt‖rɪˈtrækt/ *vt* **1** to draw back or in **2a** to withdraw; TAKE BACK **b** to refuse to admit or abide by ~ *vi* **1** to draw back **2** to recant or disavow sthg – **retractable** *adj*

retractile /riˈtraktiel‖rɪˈtræktaɪl/ *adj* capable of being retracted – **retractility** *n*

retraction /riˈtraksh(ə)n‖rɪˈtrækʃ(ə)n/ *n* an act of recanting; *specif* a statement made by one retracting

[1]**retread** /ˌreeˈtred‖ˌriːˈtred/ *vt* to replace and vulcanize the tread of (a worn tyre)

[2]**retread** /ˈreeˌtred‖ˈriːˌtred/ *n* (a tyre with) a new tread

[1]**retreat** /riˈtreet‖rɪˈtriːt/ *n* **1a** an act or process of withdrawing, esp from what is difficult, dangerous, or disagreeable; *specif* (a signal for) the forced withdrawal of troops from an enemy or position **b** the process of receding from a position or state attained <*the ~ of a glacier*> **c** a bugle call sounded at about sunset **2** a place of privacy or safety; a refuge **3** a period of usu group withdrawal for prayer, meditation, and study

[2]**retreat** *vi* **1** to make a retreat; withdraw **2** RECEDE 1b ~*vt* to draw or lead back; *specif* to move (a piece) back in chess – **retreater** *n*

retrench /riˈtrench‖rɪˈtrentʃ/ *vt* **1** to reduce <*~ company expenditure*> **2a** to cut out; excise <*~ offending paragraphs from an article*> **b** *Austr & WI* to make (a worker) redundant ~*vi* to make reductions, esp in expenses; economize – **retrenchment** *n*

retribution /ˌretriˈbyoohsh(ə)n‖ˌretrɪˈbjuːʃ(ə)n/ *n* **1** requital for an insult or injury **2** (the dispensing or receiving of reward or) punishment – used esp with reference to divine judgment – **retributively** *adv*, **retributive, retributory** *adj*

retrieval /riˈtreevl‖rɪˈtriːvl/ *n* a retrieving

retrieve /riˈtreev‖rɪˈtriːv/ *vt* **1** to discover and bring in (killed or wounded game) **2** to call to mind again **3a** to get back again; recover (and bring back) <~d *the keys he left on the bus*> **b** to rescue, save <*~ him from moral ruin*> **4** to return (e g a ball that is difficult to reach) successfully **5** to remedy the ill effects of <*~ the situation*> **6** to recover (e g information) from storage, esp in a computer memory ~*vi, esp of a dog* to retrieve game; *also* to bring back an object thrown by a person – **retrievable** *adj*, **retrievability** *n*, **retrievably** *adv*

retriever /riˈtreevə‖rɪˈtriːvə/ *n* a medium-sized dog with water-resistant coat used esp for retrieving game

retro- *prefix* **1a** back towards the past <retro*spect*> **b** backwards <retro*cede*> **2** situated behind <retro*choir*>

ˌretroˈactive /ˌretrohˈaktiv‖ˌretrəʊˈæktɪv/ *adj* extending in scope or effect to a prior time <*a ~ tax*> – **retroactively** *adv*, **retroactivity** *n*

[1]**retrograde** /ˈretrəgrayd‖ˈretrəgreɪd/ *adj* **1a** *of orbital or rotational movement* in a direction contrary to neighbouring celestial bodies **b** moving or directed backwards **c** ordered in a manner that is opposite to normal <*a ~ alphabet*> **2** tending towards or resulting in a worse or less advanced or specialized state – **retrogradely** *adv*

[2]**retrograde** *vi* **1** to move back; recede <*a glacier* ~s> **2** to undergo retrogression – **retrogradation** *n*

retrogress /ˌretrəˈgres‖ˌretrəˈgres/ *vi* to revert, regress. or decline from a better to a worse state – **retrogressive** *adj*, **retrogressively** *adv*

retrogression /ˌretrəˈgresh(ə)n‖ˌretrəˈgreʃ(ə)n/ *n* **1** REGRESSION 3 **2** a reversal in development or condition; *esp* a return to a less advanced or specialized state during the development of an organism

ˈretro-ˌrocket /ˈretroh‖ˈretrəʊ/ *n* a rocket on an aircraft, spacecraft, etc that produces thrust in a direction opposite to or at an angle to its motion for slowing it down or changing its direction

retrospect /ˈretrəspekt‖ˈretrəspekt/ *n* a survey or consideration of past events – **in retrospect** in considering the past or a past event

retrospection /ˌretrəˈspeksh(ə)n‖ˌretrəˈspekʃ(ə)n/ *n* the act or process or an instance of surveying the past

[1]**retrospective** /ˌretrəˈspektiv‖ˌretrəˈspektɪv/ *adj* **1a** of, being, or given to retrospection **b** based on memory <*a ~ report*> **2** relating to or affecting things past; retroactive – **retrospectively** *adv*

[2]**retrospective** *n* an exhibition showing the evolution of an artist's work over a period of years

retroussé /rə'troohsay‖rə'tru:seɪ/ *adj, esp of a nose* turned up (at the end) [French, fr past participle of *retrousser* to tuck up]

retroversion /ˌretroh'vuhsh(ə)n‖ˌretrəʊ'vɜ:ʃ(ə)n/ *n* the act or process of turning back or regressing

retsina /ret'seenə‖ret'si:nə/ *n* a usu white resin-flavoured Greek wine

[1]**return** /ri'tuhn‖rɪ'tɜ:n/ *vi* **1a** to go back or come back again <~ed *home*> **b** to go back *to* in thought, conversation, or practice <*soon* ~ed *to her old habits*> **2** to pass back to an earlier possessor <*the estate* ~ed *to a distant branch of the family*> **3** to reply, retort – fml ~ *vt* **1a** to state officially, esp in answer to a formal demand <~ed *details of her income*> **b** to elect (a candidate) **c** to bring in (a verdict) **2** to restore to a former or proper place, position, or state <~ *the book to the shelf*> **3** to retort <*she* ~ed *a pretty sharp answer*> **4** to bring in (e g a profit) **5a** to repay <*I cannot* ~ *the compliment*> **b** to give or send back, esp to an owner **6** to lead (a card) or a card of (a suit) in response to one's partner's earlier action, esp in bridge **7** to play (a ball or shuttlecock) hit, esp served, by an opponent – **returnable** *adj*, **returner** *n*

[2]**return** *n* **1** the act or process of coming back to or from a place or condition **2a** a (financial) account or formal report **b** a report or declaration of the results of an election – usu pl with sing. meaning **3a** the continuation, usu at a right angle, of the facade of a building or of a moulding **b** a means for conveying sthg (e g water) back to its starting point **4** the profit from labour, investment, or business – often pl with sing. meaning **5a** the act of returning sthg, esp to a former place, condition, or owner **b** sthg returned; *esp, pl* unsold newspapers, magazines, etc returned to the publisher for a refund **6** the returning of a ball (e g in tennis) or shuttlecock **7** *Br* a ticket bought for a trip to a place and back again – **by return (of post)** by the next returning post – **in return** in compensation or repayment

[3]**return** *adj* **1** doubled back on itself <*a* ~ *flue*> **2** played, delivered, or given in return; taking place for the second time <*a* ~ *match*> **3** used or followed on returning <*the* ~ *road*> **4** permitting return <*a* ~ *valve*> **5** of or causing a return to a place or condition

returning officer /ri'tuhning‖rɪ'tɜ:nɪŋ/ *n, Br* an official who presides over an election count and declares the result

reunion /ree'yoohnyən‖ri:'ju:njən/ *n* **1** reuniting or being reunited **2** a gathering of people (e g relatives or associates) after a period of separation

reunite /ˌreeyoo'niet‖ˌri:jʊ'naɪt/ *vb* to come or bring together again

reuse /ˌree'yoohz‖ˌri:'ju:z/ *vt* to use again, esp after reclaiming or reprocessing <*the need to* ~ *scarce resources*> – **reusable** *adj*, **reuser** *n*

[1]**rev** /rev‖rev/ *n* a revolution of a motor

[2]**rev** *vb* **-vv-** *vt* to increase the number of revolutions per minute of (esp an engine) – often + *up* ~*vi* to operate at an increased speed of revolution – usu + *up*

revalue /ˌree'valyooh‖ˌri:'vælju:/ *vt* **1** to change, specif to increase, the exchange rate of (a currency) **2** to reappraise

revamp /ˌree'vamp‖ˌri:'væmp/ *vt* **1** to renovate, reconstruct **2** to revise without fundamental alteration – **revamp** *n*

[1]**reveal** /ri'veel‖rɪ'vi:l/ *vt* **1** to make known through divine inspiration **2** to make known (sthg secret or hidden) <~ *a secret*> **3** to open up to view <*the uncurtained window* ~ed *a gloomy room*> – **revealable** *adj*, **revealer** *n*, **revealment** *n*

[2]**reveal** *n* the side of an opening (e g for a window) between a frame and the outer surface of a wall; *also* a jamb

revealing /ri'veeling‖rɪ'vi:lɪŋ/ *adj* exposing sthg usu intended to be concealed <*a* ~ *dress*> <*the answer was* ~>

reveille /ri'vali, -'ve-‖rɪ'vælɪ, -'ve-/ *n* a call or signal to get up in the morning; *specif* a military bugle call [French *réveillez*, imperative pl of *réveiller* to awaken, fr *re-* again + *eveiller* to awaken]

[1]**revel** /'revl‖'revl/ *vi* **-ll-** (*NAm* **-l-**, **-ll-**) **1** to take part in a revel **2** to take intense satisfaction *in* <~led *in his discomfiture*> – **reveller** *n*

[2]**revel** *n* a usu riotous party or celebration – often pl with sing. meaning

revelation /ˌrevə'laysh(ə)n‖ˌrevə'leɪʃ(ə)n/ *n* **1** (the communicating of) a divine truth revealed by God to man **2** *cap* a prophetic book of the New Testament – often pl with sing. meaning but sing. in constr **3** a revealing or sthg revealed; *esp* a sudden and illuminating disclosure

revelatory /'revələt(ə)ri, ˌrevə'layt(ə)ri‖'revələt(ə)rɪ, ˌrevə'leɪt(ə)rɪ/ *adj* serving to reveal sthg

revelry /'revlri‖'revlrɪ/ *n* exuberant festivity or merrymaking

[1]**revenge** /ri'venj‖rɪ'vendʒ/ *vt* **1** to inflict injury in return for (an insult, slight, etc) **2** to avenge (e g oneself) usu by retaliating in kind or degree – **revenger** *n*

[2]**revenge** *n* **1** (a desire for) retaliating in order to get even **2** an opportunity for getting satisfaction or requital

revenue /'revənyooh‖'revənju:/ *n* **1** the total yield of income; *esp* the income of a national treasury **2** a government department concerned with the collection of revenue

reverberate /ri'vuhbəˌrayt‖rɪ'vɜ:bəˌreɪt/ *vi* **1a** to be reflected **b** to continue (as if) in a series of echoes **2** to produce a continuing strong effect <*the scandal* ~d *round Whitehall*> ~*vt* to reflect or return (light, heat, sound, etc) – **reverberator** *n*, **reverberant, reverberative, reverberatory** *adj*, **reverberation** *n*

revere /ri'viə‖rɪ'vɪə/ *vt* to regard with deep and devoted or esp religious respect

[1]**reverence** /'rev(ə)rəns‖'rev(ə)rəns/ *n* **1** honour or respect felt or shown; *esp* profound respect accorded to sthg sacred **2** a gesture (e g a bow) denoting respect **3** being revered <*we*

hold her in ~> **4** – used as a title for a clergyman – **reverential** *adj*, **reverentially** *adv*

[2]**reverence** *vt* to regard or treat with reverence – **reverencer** *n*

[1]**reverend** /ˈrev(ə)rənd‖ˈrev(ə)rənd/ *adj* **1** revered **2** *cap* being a member of the clergy – used as a title, usu preceded by *the <the* Reverend *David Brown>*

[2]**reverend** *n* a member of the clergy – infml

reverent /ˈrev(ə)rənt‖ˈrev(ə)rənt/ *adj* expressing or characterized by reverence – **reverently** *adv*

reverie, revery /ˈrevəri‖ˈrevərɪ/ *n* **1** a daydream **2** the condition of being lost in thought or dreamlike fantasy

revers /riˈviə‖rɪˈvɪə/ *n, pl* **revers** /riˈviəz‖rɪˈvɪəz/ a wide turned-back or applied facing along each of the front edges of a garment; *specif* a lapel, esp on a woman's garment

reversal /riˈvuhsl‖rɪˈvɜːsl/ *n* **1** reversing **2** a conversion of a photographic positive into a negative or vice versa **3** a change for the worse *<his condition suffered a ~>*

[1]**reverse** /riˈvuhs‖rɪˈvɜːs/ *adj* **1a** (acting, operating, or arranged in a manner) opposite or contrary to a previous, normal, or usual condition *<put them in ~ order>* **b** having the front turned away from an observer or opponent **2** effecting reverse movement *<the ~ gear>* – **reversely** *adv*

[2]**reverse** *vt* **1a** to turn or change completely about in position or direction *<~ the order of the words>* **b** to turn upside down **2a** to overthrow (a legal decision) **b** to change (e g a policy) to the contrary **3** to cause (e g a motor car) to go backwards or in the opposite direction ~ *vi* **1** to turn or move in the opposite direction **2** to go or drive in reverse – **reverser** *n* – **reverse the charges** *Br* to arrange for the recipient of a telephone call to pay for it

[3]**reverse** *n* **1** the opposite of sthg **2** reversing or being reversed **3** a misfortune; REVERSAL 3 **4a** the side of a coin, medal, or currency note that does not bear the principal device **b** the back part of sthg; *esp* the back cover of a book **5** a gear that reverses sthg – **in reverse** backwards

reversion /riˈvuhsh(ə)n‖rɪˈvɜːʃ(ə)n/ *n* **1** (an owner's future interest in) property temporarily granted to another **2** the right of future possession or enjoyment **3a** the process of reverting **b** (an organism showing) a return to an ancestral type or reappearance of an ancestral character – **reversionary** *adj*

revert /riˈvuht‖rɪˈvɜːt/ *vi* **1a** to return, esp to a lower, worse, or more primitive condition or to an ancestral type **b** to go back in thought or conversation *<~ed to the subject of finance>* **2** *esp of property* to return to (the heirs of) the original owner after an interest granted away has expired – **reverter** *n*, **revertible** *adj*

[1]**review** /riˈvyooh‖rɪˈvjuː/ *n* **1** REVISION 1 *<prices are subject to ~>* **2** a formal military or naval inspection **3a** a general survey (e g of current affairs) **b** a retrospective view or survey (e g of one's life) **4** an act of inspecting or examining **5** judicial reexamination of a case **6a** a critical evaluation of a book, play, etc **b** (a part of) a magazine or newspaper devoted chiefly to reviews and essays

[2]**review** *vt* **1** to take a retrospective view of *<~ the past year>* **2a** to go over (again) or examine critically or thoughtfully *<~ed the results of the study>* **b** to give a review of (a book, play, etc) **3** to hold a review of (troops, ships, etc)

reviewer /riˈvyooh·ə‖rɪˈvjuːə/ *n* a writer of critical reviews

revile /riˈviel‖rɪˈvaɪl/ *vt* to subject to harsh verbal abuse – **revilement** *n*, **reviler** *n*

revise /riˈviez‖rɪˈvaɪz/ *vt* **1** to look over again in order to correct or improve **2** to make an amended, improved, or up-to-date version of *<~ a dictionary>* **3** *Br* to refresh knowledge of (e g a subject), esp before an exam *<busy* revising *her physics>* ~*vi*, *Br* to refresh one's knowledge of a subject, esp in preparation for an exam – **revisable** *adj*, **reviser, revisor** *n*

Reˌvised ˈVersion *n* a British revision of the Authorized Version of the Bible published in 1881 and 1885

revision /riˈvizh(ə)n‖rɪˈvɪʒ(ə)n/ *n* **1** the action or an act of revising **2** a revised version – **revisionary** *adj*

revisionism /riˈvizhəˌniz(ə)m‖rɪˈvɪʒəˌnɪz(ə)m/ *n* **1** advocacy of revision (e g of a doctrine) **2** a movement in Marxist socialism favouring an evolutionary rather than a revolutionary transition to socialism – chiefly derog – **revisionist** *adj or n*

revital·ize, -ise /ˌreeˈvietlˌiez‖ˌriːˈvaɪtlˌaɪz/ *vt* to impart new life or vigour to – **revitalization** *n*

revival /riˈvievl‖rɪˈvaɪvl/ *n* reviving or being revived: e g **a** renewed attention to or interest in sthg **b** a new presentation or production (e g of a play) **c** a period of renewed religious fervour **d** an often emotional evangelistic meeting or series of meetings **e** restoration of an earlier fashion, style, or practice

reˈvivalˌism /-ˌiz(ə)m‖-ˌɪz(ə)m/ *n* the spirit or evangelistic methods characteristic of religious revivals – **revivalist** *n or adj*, **revivalistic** *adj*

revive /riˈviev‖rɪˈvaɪv/ *vb* to return to consciousness, life, health, (vigorous) activity, or current use, esp from a depressed, inactive, or unused state – **revivable** *adj*, **reviver** *n*

revivify /ˌreeˈvivifie‖ˌriːˈvɪvɪfaɪ/ *vt* to revive – **revivification** *n*

[1]**revoke** /riˈvohk‖rɪˈvəʊk/ *vt* to annul, rescind, or withdraw *<~ a will>* ~*vi* to fail to follow suit when able in a card game, in violation of the rules – **revoker** *n*, **revocable** *also* **revokable** *adj*, **revocation** *n*

[2]**revoke** *n* an act or instance of revoking in a card game

[1]**revolt** /riˈvohlt‖rɪˈvəʊlt/ *vi* **1** to renounce allegiance or subjection to a government, employer, etc; rebel **2** to experience or recoil from disgust or abhorrence *<~ at their behaviour>* ~*vt* to cause to recoil with disgust or loathing; nauseate – **revolter** *n*

[2]**revolt** *n* **1** a (determined armed) rebellion **2** a movement or expression of vigorous opposition

revolting /riˈvohlting‖rɪˈvəʊltɪŋ/ *adj* extremely offensive; nauseating

revolution /ˌrevəˈloohsh(ə)n‖ˌrevəˈluːʃ(ə)n/ *n*

1a the action of or time taken by a celestial body in going round in an orbit **b** (a single recurrence of) a cyclic process or succession of related events **c** the motion of a figure or object about a centre or axis; ROTATION 1a, b **2a** a sudden or far-reaching change **b** a fundamental (political) change; *esp* (activity supporting) the overthrow of one government and the substitution of another by the governed

[1]**revolutionary** /ˌrevəˈloohshən(ə)ri‖ˌrevəˈluːʃən(ə)rɪ/ *adj* **1a** of or being a revolution <~ *war*> **b** promoting or engaging in revolution <*a ~ speech*>; *also* extremist <*a ~ outlook*> **2** completely new and different – **revolutionarily** *adv*, **revolutionariness** *n*

[2]**revolutionary** *n* sby who advocates or is engaged in a revolution

ˌ**revoˈlution·ize, -ise** /-iez‖-aɪz/ *vt* to cause a revolution in; change fundamentally or completely

[1]**revolve** /riˈvolv‖rɪˈvɒlv/ *vt* **1** to ponder <~d *a scheme in his mind*> **2** to cause to turn round (as if) on an axis ~ *vi* **1** to recur <*the seasons* ~d> **2** to be considered in turn <*all sorts of ideas* ~d *in her head*> **3** to move in a curved path round (and round) a centre or axis; turn round (as if) on an axis **4** to be centred on a specified theme or main point <*the dispute* ~d *around wages*> – **revolvable** *adj*

[2]**revolve** *n, Br* a device used on a stage to allow a piece of scenery to be rotated

revolver /riˈvolvə‖rɪˈvɒlvə/ *n* a handgun with a revolving cylinder of several chambers each holding 1 cartridge and allowing several shots to be fired without reloading

revue /riˈvyooh‖rɪˈvjuː/ *n* a theatrical production consisting typically of brief loosely connected often satirical sketches, songs, and dances

revulsion /riˈvulsh(ə)n‖rɪˈvʌlʃ(ə)n/ *n* **1** a sudden or violent reaction or change **2** a feeling of utter distaste or repugnance – **revulsive** *adj*

[1]**reward** /riˈwawd‖rɪˈwɔːd/ *vt* **1** to give a reward to or for **2** to recompense – **rewardable** *adj*, **rewarder** *n*, **rewardless** *adj*

[2]**reward** *n* sthg that is given in return for good or evil done or received; *esp* sthg offered or given for some service, effort, or achievement

rewarding /riˈwawding‖rɪˈwɔːdɪŋ/ *adj* yielding a reward; personally satisfying <*a very ~ experience*>

rewire /ˌreeˈwie·ə‖ˌriːˈwaɪə/ *vt* to provide (e g a house) with new electric wiring

reword /ˌreeˈwuhd‖ˌriːˈwɜːd/ *vt* to alter the wording of; *also* to restate in different words

[1]**rewrite** /ˌreeˈriet‖ˌriːˈraɪt/ *vb* **rewrote** /ˌreeˈroht‖ˌriːˈrəʊt/; **rewritten** /ˌreeˈritn‖ˌriːˈrɪtn/ to revise (sthg previously written) – **rewriter** *n*

[2]**rewrite** /ˈreeˌriet‖ˈriːˌraɪt/ *n* (the result, esp a rewritten news story, of) rewriting

rhapsod·ize, -ise /ˈrapsədiez‖ˈræpsədaɪz/ *vi* to speak or write rhapsodically or emotionally – **rhapsodist** *n*

rhapsody /ˈrapsədi‖ˈræpsədɪ/ *n* **1a** a highly rapturous or emotional utterance or literary composition **b** rapture, ecstasy **2** a musical composition of irregular form suggesting improvisation [Latin *rhapsodia* part of an epic poem suitable for recitation, fr Greek *rhapsōidia* fr *rhaptein* to sew, stitch together + *aidein* to sing] – **rhapsodic, rhapsodical** *adj*, **rhapsodically** *adv*

rhea /ˈriə‖ˈrɪə/ *n* any of several large tall flightless S American birds like but smaller than the ostrich

rheostat /ˈriəstat‖ˈrɪəstæt/ *n* an adjustable resistor for regulating an electric current [deriv of Greek *rhein* to flow + *-states* that which stops, fr *histanai* to cause to stand] – **rheostatic** *adj*

ˈ**rhesus ˌfactor** /ˈreesəs‖ˈriːsəs/ *n* any of several antigens in red blood cells that can induce intense allergic reactions

rhesus monkey *n* a pale brown E Indian monkey

rhetoric /ˈretərik‖ˈretərɪk/ *n* **1** the art of speaking or writing effectively; *specif* (the study of) the principles and rules of composition **2a** skill in the effective use of speech **b** insincere or exaggerated language (that is calculated to produce an effect)

rhetorical /riˈtorikl‖rɪˈtɒrɪkl/ *adj* **1** employed (merely) for rhetorical effect **2** given to rhetoric; grandiloquent – **rhetorically** *adv*

rheˌtorical ˈquestion *n* a question asked merely for effect with no answer expected

rhetorician /ˌretəˈrish(ə)n‖ˌretəˈrɪʃ(ə)n/ *n* **1** **rhetorician, rhetor** **1a** a master or teacher of rhetoric **b** an orator **2** an eloquent or grandiloquent writer or speaker

rheum /roohm‖ruːm/ *n* a watery discharge from the mucous membranes of the eyes, nose, etc – **rheumy** *adj*

[1]**rheumatic** /roohˈmatik, roo-‖ruːˈmætɪk, rʊ-/ *adj* of, being, characteristic of, or suffering from rheumatism – **rheumatically** *adv*

[2]**rheumatic** *n* sby suffering from rheumatism

rheuˌmatic ˈfever *n* inflammation and pain in the joints, pericardium, and heart valves, occurring together with fever as a short-lasting disease, esp in children

rheumaticky /roohˈmatiki, roo-‖ruːˈmætɪkɪ, rʊ-/ *adj* rheumatic – not used technically

rheumatics *n pl* rheumatism – not used technically

rheumatism /ˈroohməˌtiz(ə)m‖ˈruːməˌtɪz(ə)m/ *n* **1** any of various conditions characterized by inflammation and pain in muscles, joints, or fibrous tissue **2** RHEUMATOID ARTHRITIS

rheumatoid /ˈroohməˌtoyd‖ˈruːməˌtɔɪd/ *adj* characteristic of or affected with rheumatism or rheumatoid arthritis

ˌ**rheumatoid arthˈritis** *n* painful inflammation and swelling of joint structures occurring as a progressively worsening disease of unknown cause

ˈ**rhineˌstone** /ˈrienˌstohn‖ˈraɪnˌstəʊn/ *n* a lustrous imitation gem made of glass, paste, quartz, etc

rhinoceros /rieˈnos(ə)rəs‖raɪˈnɒs(ə)rəs/ *n* any of various large plant-eating very thick-skinned hoofed African or Asian mammals with 1 or 2 horns on the snout [Latin , fr Greek *rhinokerōs*, fr *rhin-, rhis* nose + *keras* horn]

rhizome /ˈriezohm‖ˈraɪzəʊm/ *n* an elongated (thickened and horizontal) underground plant stem distinguished from a true root in having buds and usu scalelike leaves – **rhizomic, rhizomatous** *adj*

rhododendron /ˌrohdəˈdendrən‖ˌrəʊdə-ˈdendrən/ *n* any of a genus of showy-flowered shrubs and trees of the heath family; *esp* one with leathery evergreen leaves [deriv of Greek *rhodon* rose + *dendron* tree]

[1]**rhomboid** /ˈromboyd‖ˈrɒmbɔɪd/ *n* a parallelogram that is neither a rhombus nor a square

[2]**rhomboid, rhomboidal** /romˈboydl‖rɒmˈbɔɪdl/ *adj* shaped like a rhombus or rhomboid

rhombus /ˈrombəs‖ˈrɒmbəs/ *n, pl* **rhombuses, rhombi** /-bie‖-baɪ/ a parallelogram with equal sides but unequal angles; a diamond-shaped figure

rhubarb /ˈroohbahb‖ˈruːbɑːb/ *n* **1** (the thick succulent stems, edible when cooked, of) any of several plants of the dock family **2** *chiefly Br* – used by actors to suggest the sound of (many) people talking in the background **3** *chiefly Br* nonsense, rubbish – slang or humor **4** *chiefly NAm* a heated or noisy dispute – slang [Middle French *reubarbe*, fr Medieval Latin *reubarbarum*, alteration of *rha barbarum*, lit., foreign rhubarb]

[1]**rhyme** /riem‖raɪm/ *n* **1a** correspondence in the sound of (the last syllable of) words, esp those at the end of lines of verse **b** a word that provides a rhyme for another **2** (a) rhyming verse – **rhymeless** *adj*

[2]**rhyme** *vi* **1** to make rhymes; *also* to compose rhyming verse **2a** *of a word or (line of) verse* to end in syllables that rhyme **b** to constitute a rhyme <date ~s *with* fate> ~ *vt* **1** to put into rhyme **2** to cause to rhyme; use as (a) rhyme – **rhymer** *n*

rhymester /ˈriemstə‖ˈraɪmstə/ *n* a poetaster

rhyming slang *n* slang in which the word actually meant is replaced by a rhyming phrase of which only the first element is usu pronounced (e g 'head' becomes 'loaf of bread' and then 'loaf')

rhythm /ˈridh(ə)m‖ˈrɪð(ə)m/ *n* **1a** the pattern of recurrent alternation of strong and weak elements in the flow of sound and silence in speech **b** [2]METRE 1 **2a** (the aspect of music concerning) the regular recurrence of a pattern of stress and length of notes **b** a characteristic rhythmic pattern <*music in rumba* ~>; *also* [2]METRE 2 **c rhythm, rhythm section** *sing or pl in constr* the group of instruments in a band (e g the drums, piano, and bass) supplying the rhythm **3** movement or fluctuation marked by a regular recurrence of elements (e g pauses or emphases) **4** a regularly recurrent change in a biological process or state (e g with night and day) **5** the effect created by the interaction of the elements in a play, film, or novel that relate to the development of the action **6 rhythm, rhythm method** birth control by abstinence from sexual intercourse during the period when ovulation is most likely to occur

rhythmic /ˈridhmik‖ˈrɪðmɪk/, **rhythmical** /-kl‖-kl/ *adj* **1** of or involving rhythm **2** moving or progressing with a pronounced or flowing rhythm **3** regularly recurring – **rhythmically** *adv*, **rhythmicity** *n*

[1]**rib** /rib‖rɪb/ *n* **1a** any of the paired curved rods of bone or cartilage that stiffen the body walls of most vertebrates and protect the heart, lungs, etc **b** a cut of meat including a rib **2** sthg resembling a rib in shape or function: e g **2a** a transverse member of the frame of a ship that runs from keel to deck **b** any of the stiff strips supporting an umbrella's fabric **c** an arched support or ornamental band in Romanesque and Gothic vaulting **3** an elongated ridge: e g **3a** a vein of a leaf or insect's wing **b** any of the ridges in a knitted or woven fabric; *also* ribbing

[2]**rib** *vt* **-bb- 1** to provide or enclose with ribs <~bed *vaulting*> **2** to form a pattern of vertical ridges in by alternating knit stitches and purl stitches

[3]**rib** *vt* **-bb-** to tease – infml

ribald /ˈrib(ə)ld, ˈrieˌbawld‖ˈrɪb(ə)ld, ˈraɪˌbɔːld/ *adj* **1** crude, offensive <~ *language*> **2** characterized by coarse or indecent humour <*a* ~ *youth*> – **ribaldry** *n*

ribbing /ˈribing‖ˈrɪbɪŋ/ *n* an arrangement of ribs; *esp* a knitted pattern of ribs

ribbon /ˈribən‖ˈrɪbən/ *n* **1a** a (length of a) narrow band of decorative fabric used for ornamentation (e g of hair), fastening, tying parcels, etc **b** a piece of usu multicoloured ribbon worn as a military decoration or in place of a medal **2** a long narrow ribbonlike strip; *esp* a strip of inked fabric or plastic used in a typewriter **3** *pl* tatters, shreds <*her coat was in* ~s> – **ribbonlike** *adj*

ˌribbon deˈvelopment *n* haphazard development of buildings and settlements along main roads

ˈrib ˌcage *n* the enclosing wall of the chest consisting chiefly of the ribs and their connections

riboflavin, riboflavine /ˌrieboh'flayvin‖ˌraɪbəʊˈfleɪvɪn/ *n* a yellow vitamin of the vitamin B complex occurring esp in milk and liver

ribosome /ˈriebəsohm‖ˈraɪbəsəʊm/ *n* any of the minute granules containing RNA and protein that occur in cells and are the sites where proteins are synthesized – **ribosomal** *adj*

rice /ries‖raɪs/ *n* (the seed, important as a food, of) a cereal grass widely cultivated in warm climates

ˈrice ˌpaper *n* a very thin edible paper made from the pith of an oriental tree

rich /rich‖rɪtʃ/ *adj* **1** having abundant possessions, esp material and financial wealth **2a** having high worth, value, or quality <*a* ~ *crop*> **b** well supplied or endowed – often + *in* <~ *in natural talent*> **3** sumptuous **4a** vivid and deep in colour <*a* ~ *red*> **b** full and mellow in tone and quality <*a* ~ *voice*> **c** pungent <~ *odours*> **5** highly productive or remunerative; giving a high yield <~ *farmland*> **6a** *of soil* having abundant plant nutrients **b** (of food that is) highly seasoned, fatty, oily, or sweet <*a* ~ *diet*> **c** *esp of mixtures of fuel with air* high in the combustible component; containing more petrol than normal **7a** highly amusing; *also* laughable – infml **b** full of import <~ *allusions*> – **richen** *vt*, **richness** *n*

riches /ˈrichiz‖ˈrɪtʃɪz/ *n pl* (great) wealth

richly /ˈrichli‖ˈrɪtʃlɪ/ *adv* in full measure; amply <*praise* ~ *deserved*>

[1]**rick** /rik‖rɪk/ *n* a stack (e g of hay) in the open air

[2]**rick** *vt, chiefly Br* to wrench or sprain (e g one's neck)

rickets /'rikits||'rɪkɪts/ *n pl but sing in constr* soft and deformed bones in children caused by failure to assimilate and use calcium and phosphorus, normally due to a lack of sunlight or vitamin D

rickettsia /ri'ketsi·ə||rɪ'ketsɪə/ *n, pl* **rickettsias, rickettsiae** /-si,ee||-sɪ,iː/ any of a family of microorganisms similar to bacteria that cause various diseases (e g typhus) [Howard T *Ricketts* (1871-1910), US pathologist] – **rickettsial** *adj*

rickety /'rikiti||'rɪkɪtɪ/ *adj* **1** suffering from rickets **2a** feeble in the joints <*a ~ old man*> **b** shaky, unsound <~ *stairs*>

rickshaw, ricksha /'rik,shaw||'rɪk,ʃɔː/ *n* a small covered 2-wheeled vehicle pulled by 1 or more people [Japanese *jinrikisha*, fr *jin* man + *riki* strength + *sha* vehicle]

ricochet /'rikəshay||'rɪkəʃeɪ; *also* -shet||-ʃet/ *n* the glancing rebound of a projectile (e g a bullet) off a hard or flat surface – **ricochet** *vi*

rid /rid||rɪd/ *vt* **-dd-; rid** *also* **ridded** to relieve, disencumber

riddance /'rid(ə)ns||'rɪd(ə)ns/ *n* deliverance, relief – often in *good riddance*

-ridden /,rid(ə)n||,rɪd(ə)n/ *comb form* (→ *adj*) **1** afflicted or excessively concerned with <*conscience*-ridden> **2** excessively full of or supplied with <*slum*-ridden>

[1]**riddle** /'ridl||'rɪdl/ *n* **1** a short and esp humorous verbal puzzle **2** a mystifying problem or fact <*the ~ of her disappearance*> **3** sthg or sby difficult to understand

[2]**riddle** *vi* to speak in or propound riddles – **riddler** *n*

[3]**riddle** *n* a coarse sieve (e g for sifting grain or gravel)

[4]**riddle** *vt* **1** to separate (e g grain from chaff) with a riddle; sift **2** to cover with holes <~d *with bullets*> **3** to spread through, esp as an affliction <*the management was ~d with corruption*>

[1]**ride** /ried||raɪd/ *vb* **rode** /rohd||rəʊd/; **ridden** /'rid(ə)n||'rɪd(ə)n/ *vi* **1a** to sit and travel mounted on and usu controlling an animal **b** to travel on or in a vehicle **2** to be sustained <rode *on a wave of popularity*> **3a** to lie moored or anchored **b** to appear to float <*the moon* rode *in the sky*> **4** to become supported on a point or surface **5** to continue without interference <*let it ~*> **6** to be contingent; depend <*everything ~s on her initial success*> **7** to work up the body <*shorts that ~ up*> **8** to be bet <*his money is* riding *on the favourite*> **9** to move from a correct or usual position <*the screwdriver tends to ~ out of the slot*> **10** *of a racetrack* to be in a usu specified condition for horse riding ~ *vt* **1a** to travel mounted on and in control of <~ *a bike*> **b** to move with or float on <~ *the waves*> **2a** to traverse by car, horse, etc **b** to ride a horse in <~ *a race*> **3** to survive without great damage or loss; last *out* <*rode out the gale*> **4** *esp of a male animal* to mount in copulation **5** to obsess, oppress <ridden *by anxiety*> **6** to give with (a punch) to soften the impact **7** *NAm* to harass persistently – **ride high** to experience success – **ride roughshod over** to disregard in a high-handed or arrogant way

[2]**ride** *n* **1** a trip on horseback or by vehicle **2** a usu straight road or path in a wood, forest, etc **3** any of various mechanical devices (e g at a funfair) for riding on

rider /'riedə||'raɪdə/ *n* **1** sby who rides; *specif* sby who rides a horse **2** sthg added by way of qualification or amendment **3** sthg used to overlie another or to move along on another piece

ridge /rij||rɪdʒ/ *n* **1a** a range of hills or mountains **b** an elongated elevation of land **2** the line along which 2 upward-sloping surfaces meet; *specif* the top of a roof at the intersection of 2 opposite slopes **3** an elongated part that is raised above a surrounding surface (e g the raised part between furrows on ploughed ground) – **ridge** *vt*, **ridged** *adj*, **ridger** *n*

ridgepiece /-,pees||-,piːs/ *n* a horizontal beam in a roof, supporting the upper ends of the rafters

'**ridge,pole** /-,pohl||-,pəʊl/ *n* the horizontal pole at the top of a tent

[1]**ridicule** /'ridikyoohl||'rɪdɪkjuːl/ *n* exposure to laughter

[2]**ridicule** *vt* to mock; MAKE FUN OF

ridiculous /ri'dikyooləs||rɪ'dɪkjʊləs/ *adj* arousing or deserving ridicule – **ridiculously** *adv*, **ridiculousness** *n*

riding /'rieding||'raɪdɪŋ/ *n* **1** any of the 3 former administrative jurisdictions of Yorkshire **2** an administrative or electoral district of a Commonwealth dominion [deriv of Old Norse *thrithjungr* third part, fr *thrithi* third]

Riesling /'reezling||'riːzlɪŋ/ *n* a typically medium-dry white table wine; *also* the grape variety from which this is made

rife /rief||raɪf/ *adj* **1** prevalent, esp to a rapidly increasing degree <*fear was ~ in the city*> **2** abundant, common **3** abundantly supplied – usu + *with* <~ *with rumours*>

riff /rif||rɪf/ *n* (a piece based on) a constantly repeated phrase in jazz or rock music, typically played as a background to a solo improvisation – **riff** *vi*

[1]**riffle** /'rifl||'rɪfl/ *n* **1** (the sound made while) shuffling sthg (e g cards) **2** *NAm* a shallow stretch of rough water in a stream **3** *NAm* RIPPLE 1

[2]**riffle** *vb* **1** to ruffle slightly **2a** to leaf through (e g a pile of papers) rapidly **b** to shuffle (playing cards) by separating the pack into 2 parts and riffling with the thumbs so the cards become mixed together

riffraff /'rif,raf||'rɪf,ræf/ *n sing or pl in constr* **1** disreputable people **2** rabble

[1]**rifle** /'riefl||'raɪfl/ *vt* to search through, esp in order to steal and carry away sthg – **rifler** *n*

[2]**rifle** *vt* to cut spiral grooves into the bore of (a rifle, cannon, etc)

[3]**rifle** *n* **1** a shoulder weapon with a rifled bore **2** *pl* a body of soldiers armed with rifles – **rifleman** *n*

[4]**rifle** *vt* to propel (e g a ball) with great force or speed

[1]**rift** /rift||rɪft/ *n* **1** a fissure or crack, esp in the earth **2** an opening made by tearing or splitting

apart **3** an estrangement

[2]**rift** *vt* to tear apart; split

rift valley *n* a valley formed by the subsidence of the earth's crust between at least 2 faults

[1]**rig** /rig‖rɪg/ *vt* **-gg- 1** to fit out (e g a ship) with rigging **2** to clothe, dress up – usu + *out* **3** to supply with special gear **4** to put together, esp for temporary use – usu + *up*

[2]**rig** *n* **1** the distinctive shape, number, and arrangement of sails and masts of a ship **2** an outfit of clothing worn for an often specified occasion or activity **3** tackle, equipment, or machinery fitted for a specified purpose

[3]**rig** *vt* **-gg-** to manipulate, influence, or control for dishonest purposes <~ *the election*>

rigging /ˈriging‖ˈrɪgɪŋ/ *n* **1** lines and chains used aboard a ship, esp for controlling sails and supporting masts and spars **2** a network similar to a ship's rigging used (e g in theatrical scenery) for support and manipulation

[1]**right** /riet‖raɪt/ *adj* **1** in accordance with what is morally good, just, or proper **2** conforming to facts or truth **3** suitable, appropriate <*the* ~ *woman for the job*> **4** straight <*a* ~ *line*> **5a** of, situated on, or being the side of the body that is away from the heart **b** located nearer to the right hand than to the left; *esp* located on the right hand when facing in the same direction as an observer <*stage* ~> **c** located on the right when facing downstream <*the* ~ *bank of a river*> **d** being the side of a fabric that should show or be seen when made up **6** having its axis perpendicular to the base <~ *cone*> **7** of or being the principal or more prominent side of an object **8** acting or judging in accordance with truth or fact; not mistaken **9** in a correct, proper, or healthy state <*not in his* ~ *mind*> **10** conforming to or influencing what is socially favoured or acceptable **11** *often cap* of the Right, esp in politics **12** *chiefly Br* real, utter – infml – **rightness** *n*

[2]**right** *n* **1** qualities (e g adherence to duty) that together constitute the ideal of moral conduct or merit moral approval **2a** a power, privilege, interest, etc to which one has a just claim **b** a property interest in sthg – often pl with sing. meaning <*mineral* ~s> **3** sthg one may legitimately claim as due **4** the cause of truth or justice <*trust that* ~ *may prevail*> **5a** (a blow struck with) the right hand **b** the location or direction of the right side **c** the part on the right side **6** the quality or state of being factually or morally correct **7** *sing or pl in constr, often cap* the members of a European legislative body occupying the right of a legislative chamber as a result of holding more conservative political views than other members **8a** *sing or pl in constr, cap* those professing conservative political views **b** *often cap* a conservative position – **by rights** with reason or justice; properly – **in one's own right** by virtue of one's own qualifications or properties – **to rights** into proper order

[3]**right** *adv* **1** in a right, proper, or correct manner <*guessed* ~> <*knew he wasn't doing it* ~> **2** in the exact location or position <~ *in the middle of the floor*> **3** in a direct line or course; straight <*go* ~ *home*> **4** all the way; completely <*blew* ~ *out of the window*> **5a** without delay; straight <~ *after lunch*> **b** immediately <~ *now*> **6** to the full <*entertained* ~ *royally*> – often in British titles **7** on or to the right <*looked left and* ~>

[4]**right** *vt* **1** to avenge **2a** to adjust or restore to the proper state or condition; correct **b** to bring or restore (e g a boat) to an upright position – **righter** *n*

ˈ**right ˌangle** *n* the angle bounded by 2 lines perpendicular to each other; an angle of 90° – **right-angled, right-angle** *adj*

ˌ**right aˈway** *adv* without delay or hesitation

righteous /ˈriechəs‖ˈraɪtʃəs/ *adj* **1** acting in accord with divine or moral law; free from guilt or sin **2a** morally right or justified **b** arising from an outraged sense of justice – **righteously** *adv*, **righteousness** *n*

rightful /ˈrietf(ə)l‖ˈraɪtf(ə)l/ *adj* **1** just, equitable **2a** having a just claim <*the* ~ *owner*> **b** held by right <~ *authority*> – **rightfully** *adv*, **rightfulness** *n*

ˌ**right-ˈhand** *adj* **1** situated on the right **2** right-handed **3** chiefly or constantly relied on

ˌ**right ˈhand** *n* **1a** the hand on the right-hand side of the body **b** a reliable or indispensable person **2a** the right side **b** a place of honour

ˌ**right-ˈhanded** *adj* **1** using the right hand habitually or more easily than the left; *also* swinging from right to left <*a* ~ *batsman*> **2** relating to, designed for, or done with the right hand **3** clockwise – used of a twist, rotary motion, or spiral curve as viewed from a given direction with respect to the axis of rotation – **right-handed** *adv*, **right-handedly** *adv*, **right-handedness** *n*

ˌ**right-ˈhander** /ˈhandə‖ˈhændə/ *n* **1** a blow struck with the right hand **2** a right-handed person

rightism /ˈrieˌtiz(ə)m‖ˈraɪˌtɪz(ə)m/ *n, often cap* (advocacy of) the doctrines of the Right – **rightist** *n or adj, often cap*

rightly /ˈrietli‖ˈraɪtlɪ/ *adv* **1** in accordance with right conduct; fairly **2** in the right manner; properly **3** according to truth or fact **4** with certainty <*I can't* ~ *say*>

ˌ**right-ˈminded** *adj* thinking and acting by just or honest principles – **right-mindedness** *n*

ˌ**right ˈoff** *adv* RIGHT AWAY, AT ONCE – infml

ˌ**right of ˈway** *n, pl* **rights of way 1** a legal right of passage over another person's property **2a** the course along which a right of way exists **b** the strip of land over which a public road is built **c** the land occupied by a railway for its tracks **3** a precedence in passing accorded to one vehicle over another by custom, decision, or statute

rightward /ˈrietwood‖ˈraɪtwʊd/ *adj* being towards or on the right

ˈ**rightwards** /-woodz‖-wʊdz/, *chiefly NAm* **rightward** *adv* towards or on the right

ˌ**right ˈwing** *n sing or pl in constr, often cap R&W* the more conservative division of a group or party – **right-wing** *adv*, **rightwinger** *n*

rigid /ˈrijid‖ˈrɪdʒɪd/ *adj* **1a** deficient in or devoid of flexibility **b** fixed in appearance <*her face* ~ *with pain*> **2a** inflexibly set in opinions or habits **b** strictly maintained <*a* ~

schedule> **3** firmly inflexible rather than lax or indulgent **4** precise and accurate in procedure **5a** having the gas containers enclosed within compartments of a fixed fabric-covered framework <*a ~ airship*> **b** having the outer shape maintained by a fixed framework – **rigidly** *adv*, **rigidness** *n*, **rigidify** *vb*, **rigidity** *n*

rigmarole /ˈrigmə,rohl‖ˈrɪgmə,rəʊl/ *n* **1** confused or nonsensical talk **2** an absurd and complex procedure

,rigor ˈmortis /ˈmawtis‖ˈmɔːtɪs/ *n* the temporary rigidity of muscles that occurs after death [Modern Latin, stiffness of death]

rigorous /ˈrigərəs‖ˈrɪgərəs/ *adj* **1** manifesting, exercising, or favouring rigour; very strict <~ *standards of hygiene*> **2** harsh, severe **3** scrupulously accurate – **rigorously** *adv*

rigour /ˈrigə‖ˈrɪgə/ *n* **1a(1)** harsh inflexibility in opinion, temper, or judgment **a(2)** the quality of being unyielding or inflexible **a(3)** severity of life; austerity **b** an act or instance of strictness or severity – often pl **2** a condition that makes life difficult, challenging, or painful; *esp* extremity of cold – often pl **3** strict precision <*logical* ~>

rigout /ˈrigowt‖ˈrɪgaʊt/ *n* a complete outfit of clothing – infml

rile /riel‖raɪl/ *vt* **1** to make angry or resentful **2** *NAm* ROIL 1

[1]rill /ril‖rɪl/ *n* a small brook – chiefly poetic

[2]rill, rille /ril‖rɪl/ *n* any of several long narrow valleys on the moon's surface

[1]rim /rim‖rɪm/ *n* **1** an outer usu curved edge or border **2** the outer ring of a wheel not including the tyre

[2]rim *vt* **-mm-** to serve as a rim for; border

[1]rime /riem‖raɪm/ *n* **1** FROST 1b **2** an accumulation of granular ice tufts on the windward sides of exposed objects at low temperatures – **rimy** *adj*

[2]rime *vt* to cover (as if) with rime

rimmed /rimd‖rɪmd/ *adj* having a rim – usu in combination <*dark*-rimmed *glasses*>

[1]rind /riend‖raɪnd/ *n* **1** the bark of a tree **2** a usu hard or tough outer layer of fruit, cheese, bacon, etc

[2]rind *vt* to remove the rind or bark from

rinderpest /ˈrində,pest‖ˈrɪndə,pest/ *n* an infectious fever, esp of cattle

[1]ring /ring‖rɪŋ/ *n* **1** a circular band for holding, connecting, hanging, moving, fastening, etc or for identification **2** a circlet usu of precious metal, worn on the finger **3a** a circular line, figure, or object **b** an encircling arrangement **c** a circular or spiral course **4a** an often circular space, esp for exhibitions or competitions; *esp* such a space at a circus **b** a square enclosure in which boxers or wrestlers contest **5** any of the concentric bands that revolve round some planets (e g Saturn or Uranus) **6** ANNUAL RING **7** *sing or pl in constr* an exclusive association of people for a selfish and often corrupt purpose <*a drug* ~> **8** a closed chain of atoms in a molecule **9** boxing as a profession <*retired after 9 years in the* ~> **10** an electric element or gas burner in the shape of a circle, set into the top of a cooker, stove, etc, which provides a source of heat for cooking – **ringlike** *adj*

[2]ring *vt* **ringed** **1** to place or form a ring round; encircle **2** to attach a ring to <~ *migrating geese*> **3** GIRDLE 3 **4** to throw a ring over (the peg) in a game (e g quoits)

[3]ring *vb* **rang** /rang‖ræŋ/; **rung** /rung‖rʌŋ/ *vi* **1** to sound resonantly <*the doorbell* rang> <*cheers* rang *out*> **2a** to be filled with resonant sound; resound **b** to have the sensation of a continuous humming sound **3** to sound a bell as a summons **4a** to be filled with talk or report **b** to sound repeatedly <*praise* rang *in her ears*> **5** *chiefly Br* to telephone – often + *up* ~ *vt* **1** to cause to ring, esp by striking **2** to sound (as if) by ringing a bell **3** to announce (as if) by ringing – often + *in* or *out* **4** *chiefly Br* to telephone – usu + *up* – **ring a bell** to sound familiar – **ring the changes** to run through the range of possible variations – **ring true** to appear to be true or authentic

[4]ring *n* **1** a set of bells **2** a clear resonant sound made by vibrating metal; *also* a similar sound **3** resonant tone **4** a loud sound continued, repeated, or reverberated **5** a sound or character suggestive of a particular quality or feeling **6a** an act or instance of ringing **b** a telephone call – usu in *give somebody a ring*

ring binder *n* a loose-leaf binder in which split metal rings attached to a metal back hold perforated sheets of paper in place

ringer /ˈring·ə‖ˈrɪŋə/ *n* **1** sby who rings bells **2** *NAm* sby or sthg that strongly resembles another – often + *dead* <*she's a dead* ~ *for the senator*> **3** a horse entered in a race under false representations; *broadly* an impostor – infml

ˈring ,finger *n* the third finger, esp of the left hand, counting the index finger as the first

ˈring,leader /-,leedə‖-,liːdə/ *n* a leader of a group that engages in objectionable activities

ringlet /ˈringlit‖ˈrɪŋlɪt/ *n* **1** a small ring or circle **2** a long lock of hair curled in a spiral

ˈring,master /-,mahstə‖-,mɑːstə/ *n* one in charge of performances in a ring (e g of a circus)

ring off *vi, chiefly Br* to terminate a telephone conversation

ˈring ,ouzel /ˈoohz(ə)l‖ˈuːz(ə)l/ *n* an Old World thrush, the male of which is black with a broad white bar across the breast

ˈring ,road *n, Br* a road round a town or town centre designed to relieve traffic congestion

[1]ˈring,side /-,sied‖-,saɪd/ *n* **1** the area surrounding a ring, esp providing a close view of a contest **2** a place that gives a close view

[2]ringside *adj or adv* at the ringside

ring up *vt* **1** to record by means of a cash register **2** to record, achieve

ringworm /ˈring,wuhm‖ˈrɪŋ,wɜːm/ *n* any of several contagious fungous diseases of the skin, hair, or nails in which ring-shaped discoloured blister-covered patches form on the skin

rink /ringk‖rɪŋk/ *n* **1a** (a building containing) a surface of ice for ice-skating **b** an enclosure for roller-skating **2** part of a bowling green being used for a match

[1]rinse /rins‖rɪns/ *vt* **1** to cleanse (e g from soap) with liquid (e g clean water) – often + *out* **2** to remove (dirt or impurities) by washing lightly – **rinser** *n*

[2]rinse *n* **1** (a) rinsing **2a** liquid used for rinsing

b a solution that temporarily tints the hair

riot /ˈrie·ət‖ˈraɪət/ *n* **1** unrestrained revelry **2** (a) violent public disorder; *specif* a disturbance of the peace by 3 or more people **3** a profuse and random display <*the woods were a* ~ *of colour*> **4** sby or sthg wildly funny – **riot** *vi*, **rioter** *n*

riotous /ˈrie·ətəs‖ˈraɪətəs/ *adj* **1** participating in a riot **2a** wild and disorderly **b** exciting, exuberant <*the party was a* ~ *success*> – **riotously** *adv*, **riotousness** *n*

[1]**rip** /rip‖rɪp/ *vb* **-pp-** *vi* **1** to become ripped; rend **2** to rush along <~ped *past the finishing post*> **3** to start or proceed without restraint <*let it* ~> ~ *vt* **1a** to tear or split apart, esp in a violent manner **b** to saw or split (wood) along the grain **2** to slit roughly (as if) with a sharp blade **3** to remove by force – + *out* or *off* – **ripper** *n*

[2]**rip** *n* a rough or violent tear

[3]**rip** *n* a body of rough water formed **a** by the meeting of opposing currents, winds, etc **b** by passing over ridges

[4]**rip** *n* **1** a worn-out worthless horse **2** a mischievous usu young person

riparian /rieˈpeəri·ən‖raɪˈpeərɪən/ *adj* of or occurring on the bank of a body of water, esp a river

ˈ**rip** ˌ**cord** *n* a cord or wire for releasing a parachute from its pack

ripe /riep‖raɪp/ *adj* **1** fully grown and developed; mature **2** mature in knowledge, understanding, or judgment **3** of advanced years **4a** fully arrived; propitious <*the time seemed* ~ *for the experiment*> **b** fully prepared; ready *for* **5** brought by aging to full flavour or the best state; mellow <~ *cheese*> **6** ruddy, plump, or full like ripened fruit **7** smutty, indecent – euph – **ripely** *adv*, **ripen** *vb*, **ripener** *n*, **ripeness** *n*

ˈ**rip-**ˌ**off** *n* **1** an act or instance of stealing **2** an instance of financial exploitation; *esp* the charging of an exorbitant price *USE* infml

rip off *vt* **1** to rob; *also* to steal **2** to defraud *USE* infml

riposte /riˈpohst, -post‖rɪˈpəʊst, -pɒst/ *n* **1** a fencer's quick return thrust following a parry **2** a piece of retaliatory banter **3** a usu rapid retaliatory manoeuvre or measure – **riposte** *vi*

[1]**ripple** /ˈripl‖ˈrɪpl/ *vi* **1a** to become covered with small waves **b** to flow in small waves or undulations **2** to flow with a light rise and fall of sound or inflection **3** to proceed with an undulating motion (so as to cause ripples) **4** to spread irregularly outwards, esp from a central point ~ *vt* **1** to stir up small waves on **2** to impart a wavy motion or appearance to <rippling *his muscles*> – **rippler** *n*

[2]**ripple** *n* **1** a small wave or succession of small waves **2a** RIPPLE MARK **b** a sound like that of rippling water <*a* ~ *of laughter*> **3** *NAm* RIFFLE 1

ˈ**ripple** ˌ**mark** *n* any of a series of small ridges produced, esp on sand, by wind or water

ˈ**rip-**ˌ**roaring** *adj* noisily excited or exciting; exuberant

ripsaw /ˈripˌsaw‖ˈrɪpˌsɔː/ *n* a coarse-toothed saw having teeth only slightly bent to alternate sides that is designed to cut wood in the direction of the grain

riptide /ˈripˌtied‖ˈrɪpˌtaɪd/ *n* a strong surface current flowing outwards from a shore

[1]**rise** /riez‖raɪz/ *vi* **rose** /rohz‖rəʊz/; **risen** /ˈriz(ə)n‖ˈrɪz(ə)n/ **1a** to assume an upright position, esp from lying, kneeling, or sitting **b** to get up from sleep or from one's bed **2** to return from death **3** to take up arms **4a** to respond warmly or readily; applaud – usu + *to* **b** to respond to nasty words or behaviour, esp by annoyance or anger <*despite the innuendos, he didn't* ~> **5** to end a session; adjourn **6** to appear above the horizon **7a** to move upwards; ascend **b** to increase in height or volume **8** to extend above other objects or people **9a** to become cheered or encouraged **b** to increase in fervour or intensity **10a** to attain a higher office or rank **b** to increase in amount or number **11a** to occur; TAKE PLACE **b** to come into being; originate **12** to show oneself equal to a challenge

[2]**rise** *n* **1** rising or being risen: e g **1a** a movement upwards **b** emergence (e g of the sun) above the horizon **c** the upward movement of a fish to seize food or bait **2** origin <*behaviour that gave* ~ *to much speculation*> **3** the vertical height of sthg; *specif* the vertical height of a step **4a** an increase, esp in amount, number, or intensity **b** an increase in price, value, rate, or sum; *specif, chiefly Br* an increase in pay **5a** an upward slope or gradient **b** a spot higher than surrounding ground – **get/take a rise out of** to provoke to annoyance by teasing

riser /ˈriezə‖ˈraɪzə/ *n* the upright part between 2 consecutive stair treads

risible /ˈrizəbl‖ˈrɪzəbl/ *adj* **1** inclined or susceptible to laughter **2** arousing or provoking laughter **3** associated with or used in laughter – **risibility** *n*

[1]**rising** /ˈriezing‖ˈraɪzɪŋ/ *n* an insurrection, uprising

[2]**rising** *adv* approaching a specified age

[1]**risk** /risk‖rɪsk/ *n* **1** possibility of loss, injury, or damage **2** a dangerous element or factor; hazard **3a** the chance of loss or the dangers to that which is insured in an insurance contract **b** sby who or sthg that is a specified hazard to an insurer <*a poor* ~ *for insurance*> **c** an insurance hazard from a specified cause <*war* ~> – **risky** *adj*, **riskily** *adv*, **riskiness** *n* – **at risk** in danger (e g of infection or of behaving in ways which are considered antisocial) – **on risk** *of an insurer* having assumed and accepting liability for a risk

[2]**risk** *vt* **1** to expose to hazard or danger **2** to incur the risk or danger of

risotto /riˈzotoh, -ˈso-‖rɪˈzɒtəʊ, -ˈsɒ-/ *n, pl* **risottos** an Italian dish of rice cooked in meat stock with onion, green pepper, etc

risqué /ˈreeskay, ˈri-‖ˈriːskeɪ, ˈrɪ-/ *adj* verging on impropriety or indecency [French, fr past participle of *risquer* to risk, fr *risque* risk]

rissole /ˈrisohl‖ˈrɪsəʊl/ *n* a small fried cake or ball of cooked minced food, esp meat

rite /riet‖raɪt/ *n* **1** (a prescribed form of words or actions for) a ceremonial act or action **2** the characteristic liturgy of a church or group of churches

[1]**ritual** /ˈrichooəl, -tyoo-‖ˈrɪtʃʊəl, -tjʊ-/ *adj* **1** of

rites or a ritual; ceremonial **2** according to religious law or social custom – **ritually** *adv*

[2]**ritual** *n* **1** the form or order of words prescribed for a religious ceremony **2** (a) ritual observance; *broadly* any formal and customary act or series of acts

ritualism /ˈrichooəˌliz(ə)m, -tyoo-‖ˈrɪtʃʊəˌlɪz(ə)m, -tjʊ-/ *n* (excessive devotion to) the use of ritual – **ritualist** *n*, **ritualistic** *adj*

ritzy /ˈritsi‖ˈrɪtsɪ/ *adj* ostentatiously smart – infml [*Ritz* hotels, noted for their opulence] – **ritziness** *n*

[1]**rival** /ˈrievl‖ˈraɪvl/ *n* **1a** any of 2 or more competing for a single goal **b** sby who tries to compete with and be superior to another **2** sby who or sthg that equals another in desirable qualities [Middle French fr Latin *rivalis* one using the same stream as another, rival in love, fr *rivalis* of a stream, fr *rivus* stream] – **rivalry** *n*

[2]**rival** *adj* having comparable pretensions or claims

[3]**rival** *vt* **-ll-** (*NAm* **-l, -ll-**) **1** to be in competition with; contend with **2** to strive to equal or excel **3** to possess qualities that approach or equal (those of another)

rive /riev‖raɪv/ *vb* **rived; riven** /ˈriv(ə)n‖ˈrɪv(ə)n/ *also* **rived** *vt* **1a** to wrench open or tear apart or to pieces **b** to split with force or violence; cleave **2** to rend with distress or dispute ~*vi* to become split

river /ˈrivə‖ˈrɪvə/ *n* **1** a natural stream of water of considerable volume **2a** a flow that matches a river in volume <*a ~ of lava*> **b** *pl* a copious or overwhelming quality

[1]**rivet** /ˈrivit‖ˈrɪvɪt/ *n* a headed metal pin used to unite 2 or more pieces by passing the shank through a hole in each piece and then beating or pressing down the plain end so as to make a second head

[2]**rivet** *vt* **1** to fasten (as if) with rivets **2** to hammer or flatten the end or point of (e g a metal pin, rod, or bolt) so as to form a head **3** to fix firmly **4** to attract and hold (e g the attention) completely – **riveter** *n*

riviera /ˌriviˈeərə‖ˌrɪvɪˈeərə/ *n, often cap* a coastal region, usu with a mild climate, frequented as a resort

rivulet /ˈrivyoolit‖ˈrɪvjʊlɪt/ *n* a small stream

RNA *n* any of various nucleic acids similar to DNA that contain ribose and uracil as structural components instead of deoxyribose and thymine, and are associated with the control of cellular chemical activities [*r*ibo*n*ucleic *a*cid]

[1]**roach** /rohch‖rəʊtʃ/ *n, pl* **roach** *also* **roaches** a silver-white European freshwater fish of the carp family

[2]**roach** *n* a concave or convex curvature in the edge of a sail

[3]**roach** *n, NAm* **1** a cockroach **2** the butt of a marijuana cigarette – slang

road /rohd‖rəʊd/ *n* **1** a relatively sheltered stretch of water near the shore where ships may ride at anchor – often pl with sing. meaning **2a** an open usu paved way for the passage of vehicles, people, and animals **b** the part of a paved surface used by vehicles **3** a route or path – **off the road** *of a vehicle* not roadworthy – **on the road** travelling or touring on business

ˈ**roadˌbed** /-ˌbed‖-ˌbed/ *n* **1** the bed on which the sleepers, rails, and ballast of a railway rest **2a** the earth foundation of a road prepared for surfacing **b** *NAm* ROAD 2b

ˈ**roadˌblock** /-ˌblok‖-ˌblɒk/ *n* **1** a road barricade set up by an army, the police, etc **2** an obstruction in a road **3** *chiefly NAm* an obstacle to progress or success

ˈ**road ˌhog** *n* a driver of a motor vehicle who obstructs or intimidates others

ˈ**roadˌhouse** /-ˌhows‖-ˌhaʊs/ *n* an inn situated usu on a main road in a country area

roadman /ˈrohdmən, -ˌman‖ˈrəʊdmən, -ˌmæn/ *n* one who mends or builds roads

ˈ**road ˌmetal** *n* broken stone used in making and repairing roads or ballasting railways

ˈ**roadˌside** /-ˌsied‖-ˌsaɪd/ *n* the strip of land beside a road; the side of a road

roadster /ˈrohdstə‖ˈrəʊdstə/ *n* **1** a horse for riding or driving on roads **2a** an open sports car that seats usu 2 people **b** *Br* a sturdy bicycle for ordinary use on common roads

ˈ**roadˌway** /-ˌway‖-ˌweɪ/ *n* a road

ˈ**roadˌwork** /-ˌwuhk‖-ˌwɜːk/ *n* **1** conditioning for an athletic contest (e g a boxing match) consisting mainly of long runs **2** *pl, Br* (the site of) the repair or construction of roads

ˈ**roadˌworthy** /-ˌwuhdhi‖-ˌwɜːðɪ/ *adj, of a vehicle* in a fit condition to be used on the roads; in proper working order – **roadworthiness** *n*

roam /rohm‖rəʊm/ *vi* **1** to go aimlessly from place to place; wander **2** to travel unhindered through a wide area ~*vt* to range or wander over – **roam** *n*, **roamer** *n*

[1]**roan** /rohn‖rəʊn/ *adj, esp of horses and cattle* having a coat of a usu reddish brown base colour that is muted and lightened by some white hairs

[2]**roan** *n* (the colour of) an animal (e g a horse) with a roan, specif a bay roan, coat

[1]**roar** /ˈraw‖ˈrɔː/ *vi* **1a** to give a roar **b** to sing or shout with full force **2a** to make or emit loud reverberations **b** to laugh loudly and deeply **3** to be boisterous or disorderly – usu + *about* **4** *of a horse suffering from roaring* to make a loud noise in breathing ~*vt* to utter with a roar

[2]**roar** *n* **1** the deep prolonged cry characteristic of a wild animal **2** a loud cry, call, etc (e g of pain, anger, or laughter) **3** a loud continuous confused sound <*the ~ of the waves*>

[1]**roaring** *adj* **1** making or characterized by a sound resembling a roar **2** marked by energetic or successful activity <*did a ~ trade*>

[2]**roaring** *adv* extremely, thoroughly – infml <*went and got ~ drunk*>

ˌ**roaring** ˈ**forties** *n pl* either of 2 areas of stormy westerly winds between latitudes 40° and 50° N and S

[1]**roast** /rohst‖rəʊst/ *vt* **1a** to cook by exposing to dry heat (e g in an oven) or by surrounding with hot embers **b** to dry and brown slightly by exposure to heat <*~ coffee*> **2** to heat (ore or other inorganic material) with air to cause the removal of volatile material, oxidation, etc **3** to heat to excess **4** *chiefly NAm* to criticize severely ~ *vi* **1** to cook food by roasting **2** to be subject to roasting

[2]**roast** *n* **1** a piece of meat roasted or suitable for roasting **2** *NAm* a party at which food is

roasted, esp in the open air

[3]**roast** *adj* roasted < ~ *beef*>

roaster /'rohstə‖'rəʊstə/ *n* **1** a device for roasting **2** a pig, fowl, vegetable, etc suitable for roasting

rob /rob‖rɒb/ *vb* **-bb-** *vt* **1** to steal sthg from (a person or place), esp by violence or threat **2** to deprive of sthg due, expected, or desired ~*vi* to commit robbery – **robber** *n*

robbery /'robəri‖'rɒbərɪ/ *n* the act of robbing; *specif* theft accompanied by violence or threat

[1]**robe** /rohb‖rəʊb/ *n* **1** a long flowing outer garment; *esp* one used for ceremonial occasions or as a symbol of office or profession – sometimes pl with sing. meaning **2** *NAm* a woman's dressing gown

[2]**robe** *vt* to clothe or cover (as if) with a robe ~*vi* to put on a robe; *broadly* DRESS 1a

robin /'robin‖'rɒbɪn/, **robin 'red,breast** /'red ,brest‖'red,brest/ *n* **1** a small brownish European thrush resembling a warbler and having an orange-red throat and breast **2** a large N American thrush with a dull reddish breast and underparts

robot /'rohbot‖'rəʊbɒt/ *n* **1a** a (fictional) humanoid machine that walks and talks **b** sby efficient or clever who lacks human warmth or sensitivity **2** an automatic apparatus or device that performs functions ordinarily ascribed to human beings or operates with what appears to be almost human intelligence [Czech, fr *robota* work]

robotics /roh'botiks, rə-‖rəʊ'bɒtɪks, rə-/ *n pl but sing or pl in constr* **1** the science concerned with the construcion, maintenance, and behaviour of robots **2** a form of dancing in which the dancers make jerky motions of their limbs

robust /roh'bust, '--‖rəʊ'bʌst, '--/ *adj* **1a** having or exhibiting vigorous health or stamina **b** firm in purpose or outlook **c** strongly formed or constructed **2** earthy, rude **3** requiring strenuous exertion **4** full-bodied <*a* ~ *red wine*> – **robustly** *adv*, **robustness** *n*

[1]**rock** /rok‖rɒk/ *vt* **1** to move gently back and forth (as if) in a cradle **2a** to cause to sway back and forth **b(1)** to daze or stun **b(2)** to disturb, upset ~ *vi* **1** to become moved rapidly or violently backwards and forwards (e g under impact) **2** to move rhythmically back and forth – **rock the boat** to disturb the equilibrium of a situation

[2]**rock**, **rock and roll**, **rock 'n' roll** /,rok (ə)n 'rohl‖,rɒk (ə)n 'rəʊl/ *n* popular music, usu played on electronically amplified instruments and characterized by a persistent heavily accented beat, much repetition of simple phrases, and often country, folk, and blues elements

[3]**rock** *n* **1** a large mass of stone forming a cliff, promontory, or peak **2** a large concreted mass of stony material **3** consolidated or unconsolidated solid mineral matter **4a** sthg like a rock in firmness; a firm or solid foundation or support **b** sthg that threatens or causes disaster – often pl with sing. meaning **5** a coloured and flavoured sweet produced in the form of a usu cylindrical stick **6** ROCK SALMON – used esp by fishmongers **7** *NAm* a small stone **8** a gem; *esp* a diamond – slang – **rock** *adj*, **rocklike** *adj* – **on the rocks 1** in or into a state of destruction or wreckage <*their marriage was* on the rocks> **2** on ice cubes <*Scotch* on the rocks>

,rock-'bottom *adj* being the lowest possible

,rock 'bottom *n* the lowest or most fundamental part or level

rock crystal *n* transparent colourless quartz

rocker /'rokə‖'rɒkə/ *n* **1a** either of the 2 curved pieces of wood or metal on which an object (e g a cradle) rocks **b** sthg mounted on rockers; *specif* ROCKING CHAIR **c** any object (with parts) resembling a rocker (e g a skate with a curved blade) **2** a device that works with a rocking motion **3** a member of a group of aggressive leather-jacketed young British motorcyclists in the 1960s – **off one's rocker** crazy, mad – infml

rockery /'rokəri‖'rɒkərɪ/ *n* a bank of rocks and earth where rock plants are grown

[1]**rocket** /'rokit‖'rɒkɪt/ *n* any of numerous plants of the mustard family

[2]**rocket** *n* **1a** a firework consisting of a long case filled with a combustible material fastened to a guiding stick and projected through the air by the rearward discharge of gases released in combustion **b** such a device used as an incendiary weapon or as a propelling unit (e g for a lifesaving line or whaling harpoon) **2** a jet engine that carries with it everything necessary for its operation and is thus independent of the oxygen in the air **3** a rocket-propelled bomb, missile, or projectile **4** *chiefly Br* a sharp reprimand – infml

[3]**rocket** *vi* **1** to rise or increase rapidly or spectacularly **2** to travel with the speed of a rocket

rocketry /'rockitri‖'rɒckɪtrɪ/ *n* the study of, experimentation with, or use of rockets

'rocking ,chair /'roking‖'rɒkɪŋ/ *n* a chair mounted on rockers

'rocking ,horse *n* a toy horse mounted on rockers

rock 'n' roll /,rok (ə)n 'rohl‖,rɒk (ə)n 'rəʊl/ *n* [2]ROCK

'rock ,plant *n* a small esp alpine plant that grows among rocks or in rockeries

,rock 'salmon *n* a dogfish – not now used technically

'rock ,salt *n* common salt occurring as a solid mineral

[1]**rocky** /'roki‖'rɒkɪ/ *adj* **1** full of or consisting of rocks **2** filled with obstacles; difficult – **rockiness** *n*

[2]**rocky** *adj* unsteady, tottering – **rockiness** *n*

[1]**rococo** /ro'kohkoh, rə-‖rɒ'kəʊkəʊ, rə-/ *adj* **1a** (typical) of a style of architecture and decoration in 18th-c Europe characterized by elaborate curved forms and shell motifs **b** of an 18th-c musical style marked by light gay ornamentation **2** excessively ornate or florid

[2]**rococo** *n* rococo work or style

rod /rod‖rɒd/ *n* **1a(1)** a straight slender stick **a(2)** (a stick or bundle of twigs used for) punishment **a(3)** a pole with a line for fishing **b(1)** a slender bar (e g of wood or metal) **b(2)** a wand or staff carried as a sign of office, power, or authority **2** a unit of length equal to $5^1/_2$yd (about 5m) **3** any of the relatively long rod-shaped light receptors in the retina that are sensitive to faint light **4** an angler

rode /rohd‖rəʊd/ *past of* RIDE

rodent /'rohd(ə)nt‖'rəʊd(ə)nt/ *n* any of an order of relatively small gnawing mammals including the mice, rats, squirrels, and beavers

rodeo /roh'dayoh, 'rohdi,oh‖rəʊ'deɪəʊ, 'rəʊdɪ,əʊ/ *n, pl* **rodeos** **1** a roundup **2** a public performance featuring the riding skills of cowboys [Spanish, fr *rodear* to surround, fr *rueda* wheel, fr Latin *rota*]

rodomontade /,rodəmon'tayd, -'tahd‖,rɒdəmɒn'teɪd, -'tɑːd/ *n* **1** a bragging speech **2** vain boasting or bluster; bombast – **rodomontade** *adj*

roe /roh‖rəʊ/ *n* **1** the eggs of a female fish, esp when still enclosed in a membrane, or the corresponding part of a male fish **2** the eggs or ovaries of an invertebrate (e g a lobster)

roebuck /'roh,buk‖'rəʊ,bʌk/ *n* a (male) roe deer

'roe ,deer *n* a small Eurasian deer with erect cylindrical antlers that is noted for its nimbleness and grace

roentgen /'rontgən, 'rentgən, -jən ‖'rɒntgən, 'rentgən, -dʒən (*Ger* rœntgən)/ *n* a röntgen

Ro'gation ,Day /roh'gaysh(ə)n‖rəʊ'geɪʃ(ə)n/ *n* any of the days of prayer, esp for the harvest, observed on the 3 days before Ascension Day and by Roman Catholics also on April 25

¹roger /'rojə‖'rɒdʒə/ *vt* to have sexual intercourse with – slang

¹rogue /rohg‖rəʊg/ *n* **1** a wilfully dishonest or corrupt person **2** a mischievous person; a scamp **3** sby or sthg that displays a chance variation making it inferior to others – **roguish** *adj*, **roguishly** *adv*, **roguishness** *n*

²rogue *adj, of an animal* (roaming alone and) vicious and destructive <*a* ~ *elephant*>

roguery /'rohg(ə)ri‖'rəʊg(ə)rɪ/ *n* an act characteristic of a rogue

roil /royl‖rɔɪl/ *vt* **1a** to make muddy or opaque by stirring up the sediment of **b** to stir up **2** to annoy, rile

role, rôle /rohl‖rəʊl/ *n* **1a(1)** a character assigned or assumed **a(2)** a socially expected behaviour pattern, usu determined by an individual's status in a particular society **b** a part played by an actor or singer **2** a function

¹roll /rohl‖rəʊl/ *n* **1a** a written document that may be rolled up; *specif* one bearing an official or formal record **b** a list of names or related items; a catalogue **c** an official list of people (e g members of a school or of a legislative body) **2** sthg rolled up to resemble a cylinder or ball; e g **2a** a quantity (e g of fabric or paper) rolled up to form a single package **b** any of various food preparations rolled up for cooking or serving; *esp* a small piece of baked yeast dough **3** ROLLER 1a(1) **4** *NAm* paper money folded or rolled into a wad

²roll *vt* **1a** to propel forwards by causing to turn over and over on a surface **b** to cause (sthg fixed) to revolve (as if) on an axis **c** to cause to move in a circular manner **d** to form into a mass by revolving and compressing **e** to carry forwards with an easy continuous motion <*the river* ~s *its waters to the sea*> **2a** to put a wrapping round **b** to wrap round on itself; shape into a ball or roll – often + *up* **3a** to press, spread, or level with a roller; make thin, even, or compact **b** to spread out <~ *out the red carpet*> **4** to move as specified on rollers or wheels **5a** to sound with a full reverberating tone **b** to make a continuous beating sound on <~ed *their drums*> **c** to utter with a trill **6** *NAm* to rob (sby sleeping or unconscious) – infml <~ *a drunk*> ~ *vi* **1a** to travel along a surface with a rotary motion **b(1)** to turn over and over **b(2)** to luxuriate *in* an abundant supply; wallow **2a** to move onwards in a regular cycle or succession **b** to shift the gaze continually and erratically <*eyes* ~ing *in terror*> **c** to revolve on an axis **3a** to flow with an undulating motion **b** to flow in an abundant stream; pour **c** to extend in broad undulations <~ing *hills*> **4a** to become carried on a stream **b** to move on wheels **5** to make a deep reverberating sound <*the thunder* ~s> **6a** to rock from side to side **b** to walk with a swinging gait **c** to move so as to reduce the impact of a blow – + *with* <~ed *with the punch*> **7** to take the form of a cylinder or ball – often + *up* **8a** to begin to move or operate <*let the cameras* ~> **b** to move forwards; develop and maintain impetus

³roll *n* **1a** a sound produced by rapid strokes on a drum **b** a rhythmic sonorous flow (of speech) **c** a reverberating sound **2** (an action or process involving) a rolling movement: e g **2a** a swaying movement of the body (e g in walking or dancing> **b** a side-to-side movement (e g of a ship) **c** a flight manoeuvre in which a complete revolution about the longitudinal axis of an aircraft is made with the horizontal direction of flight being approximately maintained

roll back *vt* to cause to retreat or withdraw; push back

'roll ,call *n* the calling out of a list of names (e g for checking attendance)

¹roller /'rohlə‖'rəʊlə/ *n* **1a(1)** a revolving cylinder over or on which sthg is moved or which is used to press, shape, or apply sthg **a(2)** a hair curler **b** a cylinder or rod on which sthg (e g a blind) is rolled up **2** a long heavy wave

²roller *n* **1** any of a group of mostly brightly coloured Old World birds noted for performing aerial rolls in their nuptial display **2** a canary that has a song in which the notes are soft and run together

'roller ,coaster *n* an elevated railway (e g in a funfair) constructed with curves and inclines on which the cars roll

'roller ,skate *n* (a shoe fitted with) a metal frame holding usu 4 small wheels that allows the wearer to glide over hard surfaces – **roller-skate** *vi*, **roller-skater** *n*

'roller ,towel *n* a continuous towel hung from a roller

¹rollicking /'roliking‖'rɒlɪkɪŋ/ *adj* boisterously carefree

²rollicking *n, Br* a severe scolding – infml

roll in *vi* to come or arrive in large quantities

'rolling ,mill /'rohling‖'rəʊlɪŋ/ *n* an establishment or machine in which metal is rolled into plates and bars

'rolling ,pin *n* a long usu wooden cylinder for rolling out dough

'rolling ,stock *n* **1** the vehicles owned and used by a railway **2** *NAm* the road vehicles owned and used by a company

ˌrolling ˈstone *n* one who leads a wandering or unsettled life

ˈroll-ˌon *n* **1** a woman's elasticated girdle without fastenings **2** a liquid preparation (e g deodorant) applied to the skin by means of a rolling ball in the neck of the container

ˌroll ˈon *interj, Br* – used to urge on a desired event <~ *summer!*>

ˌrolltop ˈdesk /ˈrohlˌtop‖ˈrəʊlˌtɒp/ *n* a writing desk with a sliding cover often of parallel slats fastened to a flexible backing

ˈroll-ˌup *n, Br* a hand-rolled cigarette – infml

roll up *vi* **1** to arrive in a vehicle **2** to turn up at a destination, esp unhurriedly

¹roly-poly /ˌrohli ˈpohli‖ˌrəʊlɪ ˈpəʊlɪ/ *n* a dish, esp a pudding, consisting of pastry spread with a filling (e g jam), rolled, and baked or steamed

²ˌroly-ˈpoly *adj* short and plump – infml

¹Roman /ˈrohmən‖ˈrəʊmən/ *n* **1** a native or inhabitant of (ancient) Rome **2** ROMAN CATHOLIC **3** *not cap* roman letters or type

²Roman *adj* **1** (characteristic) of Rome or the (ancient) Romans **2** *not cap, of numbers and letters* not slanted; perpendicular **3** of the see of Rome or the Roman Catholic church

¹ˌRoman ˈCatholic *n* a member of the Roman Catholic church

²Roman Catholic *adj* of the body of Christians headed by the pope, with a hierarchy of priests and bishops under the pope, a liturgy centred on the Mass, and a body of dogma formulated by the church as the infallible interpreter of revealed truth; *specif* of the Western rite of this church marked by a formerly Latin liturgy – **Roman Catholicism** *n*

¹romance /rohˈmans, rə-‖rəʊˈmæns, rə-/ *n* **1a(1)** a medieval usu verse tale dealing with chivalric love and adventure **a(2)** a prose narrative dealing with imaginary characters involved in usu heroic, adventurous, or mysterious events that are remote in time or place **a(3)** a love story **b** such literature as a class **2** sthg lacking any basis in fact **3** an emotional aura attaching to an enthralling era, adventure, or pursuit **4** LOVE AFFAIR

²romance *vi* **1** to exaggerate or invent detail or incident **2** to entertain romantic thoughts or ideas

³romance *n* a short instrumental piece of music in ballad style

Romance *adj* of or constituting the languages developed from Latin

Romanesque /ˌrohməˈnesk‖ˌrəʊməˈnesk/ *adj* of a style of architecture developed in Italy and western Europe and characterized after 1000 AD by the use of the round arch and vault, decorative arcading, and elaborate mouldings – **Romanesque** *n*

Romanian, Rumanian /rooˈmayni·ən, roh-‖ruː-ˈmeɪnɪən, reʊ-/ (a native or inhabitant or the Romance language) of Romania

roman·ize, -ise /ˈrohməniez‖ˈrəʊmənaɪz/ *vt* **1** *often cap* to make Roman; Latinize **2** to write or print (e g a language) in the roman alphabet – **romanization** *n, often cap*

ˌroman ˈlaw *n, often cap R* the legal system of the ancient Romans which forms the basis of many modern legal codes

ˌRoman ˈnumeral *n* a numeral in a system of notation based on the ancient Roman system using the symblos i, v, x, l, c, d, m

¹romantic /rəˈmantik, roh-‖rəˈmæntɪk, rəʊ-/ *adj* **1** consisting of or like a romance **2** having no basis in real life **3** impractical or fantastic in conception or plan **4a** marked by the imaginative appeal of the heroic, remote, or mysterious **b** *often cap* (having the characteristics) of romanticism **c** of or being (a composer of) 19th-c music characterized by an emphasis on subjective emotional qualities and freedom of form **5a** having an inclination for romance **b** marked by or constituting strong feeling, esp love – **romantically** *adv*

²romantic *n* **1** a romantic person **2** *cap* a romantic writer, artist, or composer

romanticism /rohˈmantiˌsiz(ə)m, rə-‖rəʊ-ˈmæntɪˌsɪz(ə)m, rə-/ *n, often cap* (adherence to) a chiefly late 18th- and early 19th-c literary, artistic, and philosophical movement that reacted against neoclassicism by emphasizing individual aspirations, nature, the emotions, and the remote and exotic – **romanticist** *n, often cap*

romantic·ize, -ise /rohˈmantiˌsiez, rə-‖rəʊ-ˈmæntɪˌsaɪz, rə-/ *vt* to give a romantic character to ~ *vi* **1** to hold romantic ideas **2** to present incidents or people in a (misleadingly) romantic way – **romanticization** *n*

Romany /ˈrohməni‖ˈrəʊmənɪ/ *n* **1** GIPSY 1 **2** the Indic language of the Gipsies – **Romany** *adj*

Romish /ˈrohmish‖ˈrəʊmɪʃ/ *adj* ROMAN CATHOLIC – chiefly derog

¹romp /romp‖rɒmp/ *n* **1** boisterous or bawdy entertainment or play **2** an effortless winning pace

²romp *vi* **1** to play in a boisterous manner **2** to win easily

romper /ˈrompə‖ˈrɒmpə/, **ˈromper ˌsuit** *n* a 1-piece child's garment combining a top or bib and short trousers – usu pl with sing. meaning

rondeau /ˈrondoh‖ˈrɒndəʊ/ *n, pl* **rondeaux** /ˈrondoh(z)‖ˈrɒndəʊ(z)/ (a poem in) a form of verse using only 2 rhymes, in which the opening words of the first line are used as a refrain

rondo /ˈrondoh‖ˈrɒndəʊ/ *n, pl* **rondos** an instrumental composition, esp a movement in a concerto or sonata, typically having a refrain or recurring theme

röntgen, roentgen, rontgen /ˈrontgən, ˈrentgən, -jən ‖ˈrɒntgən, ˈrentgən, -dʒən (*Ger* rœntgən)/ *n* a unit of ionizing radiation equal to the amount that produces ions of 1 sign carrying a charge of 2.58×10^{-4} coulomb in 1kg of air [Wilhelm Conrad *Röntgen* (1845-1923), German chemist]

rood /roohd‖ruːd/ *n* **1** a cross, crucifix; *specif* a large crucifix on a beam or screen at the entrance to the chancel of a medieval church **2** a British unit of land area equal to $^1/_4$ acre (about $1011m^2$)

¹roof /roohf‖ruːf/ *n, pl* **roofs** *also* **rooves** /roohvz‖ruːvz/ **1a** the upper usu rigid cover of a building **b** a dwelling, home <*couples sharing the same* ~> **2a** the highest point or level **b** sthg resembling a roof in form or function **3** the vaulted or covering part of the mouth, skull, etc

– **roofed** *adj*, **roofless** *adj*, **rooflike** *adj*, **roofing** *n*

[2]**roof** *vt* **1** to cover (as if) with a roof **2** to serve as a roof over

ˈ**roofˌtree** /-ˌtree‖-ˌtriː/ *n* a ridgepiece

[1]**rook** /rook‖rʊk/ *n* a common Old World social bird similar to the related carrion crow but having a bare grey face

[2]**rook** *vt* to defraud by cheating (e g at cards) – infml

[3]**rook** *n* either of 2 pieces of each colour in a set of chessmen having the power to move along the ranks or files across any number of consecutive unoccupied squares [Middle French *roc*, fr Arabic *rukhkh*, fr Persian]

rookery /ˈrookəri‖ˈrʊkərɪ/ *n* **1a** (the nests, usu built in the upper branches of trees, of) a colony of rooks **b** (a breeding ground or haunt of) a colony of penguins, seals, etc **2** a crowded dilapidated tenement or maze of dwellings

rookie /ˈrooki‖ˈrʊkɪ/ *n* a recruit; *also, chiefly NAm* a novice

[1]**room** /roohm, room‖ruːm, rʊm/ *n* **1** an extent of space occupied by, or sufficient or available for, sthg **2a** a partitioned part of the inside of a building **b** such a part used as a separate lodging – often pl **3** suitable or fit occasion; opportunity + *for* <~ *for improvement*>

[2]**room** /roohm‖ruːm/ *vt* to accommodate with lodgings ~*vi, NAm* to occupy a room; lodge

roomed /roohmd, roomd‖ruːmd, rʊmd/ *adj* containing rooms – usu in combination <*a 6-*roomed *house*>

roomer /ˈroohmə‖ˈruːmə/ *n, NAm* a lodger

roommate /ˈroohmˌmayt, ˈroom-‖ˈruːmˌmeɪt, ˈrʊm-/ *n* any of 2 or more people sharing the same room (e g in a university hall)

ˈ**room ˌservice** *n* the facility by which a hotel guest can have food, drinks, etc brought to his/her room

roomy /ˈroohmi‖ˈruːmɪ/ *adj* spacious – **roominess** *n*

[1]**roost** /roohst‖ruːst/ *n* **1** a support or place where birds roost **2** a group of birds roosting together

[2]**roost** *vi, esp of a bird* to settle down for rest or sleep; perch

rooster /ˈroohstə‖ˈruːstə/ *n, chiefly NAm* COCK 1a

[1]**root** /rooht‖ruːt/ *n* **1a** the (underground) part of a flowering plant that usu anchors and supports it and absorbs and stores food **b** a (fleshy and edible) root, bulb, tuber, or other underground plant part **2a** the end of a nerve nearest the brain and spinal cord **b** the part of a tooth, hair, the tongue, etc by which it is attached to the body **3a** sthg that is an underlying cause or basis (e g of a condition or quality) **b** one or more progenitors of a group of descendants **c** the essential core, the heart **d** *pl* a feeling of belonging established through close familiarity or family ties with a particular place **4a** a number which produces a given number when taken an indicated number of times as a factor <*2 is a fourth ~ of 16*> **b** a number that reduces an equation to an identity when it is substituted for 1 variable **5a** the lower part; the base **b** the part by which an object is attached to or embedded in sthg else **6** the basis from which a word is derived **7** the tone from whose overtones a chord is composed; the lowest note of a chord in normal position – **rooted** *adj*, **rootedness** *n*, **rootless** *adj*, **rootlet** *n*, **rootlike** *adj*, **rooty** *adj*

[2]**root** *vt* **1** to give or enable to develop roots **2** to fix or implant (as if) by roots ~ *vi* **1** to grow roots or take root **2** to have an origin or base

[3]**root** *vi* **1** *esp of a pig* to dig with the snout **2** to poke or dig about *in*; search (unsystematically) for sthg

[4]**root** *vi, chiefly NAm* to lend vociferous or enthusiastic support to sby or sthg – + *for* – **rooter** *n*

ˈ**root ˌcrop** *n* a crop (e g turnips or sugar beet) grown for its enlarged roots

root out *vt* **1** to discover or cause to emerge by rooting **2** to get rid of or destroy completely

ˈ**rootˌstock** /-ˌstok‖-ˌstɒk/ *n* **1** an underground plant part formed from several stems **2** a stock for grafting consisting of (a piece of) root; *broadly* STOCK 2b, 4

[1]**rope** /rohp‖rəʊp/ *n* **1a** a strong thick cord composed of strands of fibres or wire twisted or braided together **b** a long slender strip of material (used) like rope **c** a hangman's noose **2** a row or string consisting of things united (as if) by braiding, twining, or threading **3** *pl* special methods or procedures

[2]**rope** *vt* **1a** to bind, fasten, or tie with a rope **b** to enclose, separate, or divide by a rope **c** to connect (a party of climbers) with a rope **2** to enlist (sby reluctant) *in* a group or activity **3** *NAm* to lasso ~*vi* to put on a rope for climbing; *also* to climb *down* or *up* – **roper** *n*

ˈ**ropeˌdancer** /-ˌdahnsə‖-ˌdɑːnsə/ *n* one who dances, walks, or performs acrobatic feats on a rope high in the air – **ropedancing** *n*

rope ladder *n* a ladder having rope sides and rope, wood, or metal rungs

ˈ**ropeˌwalk** /-ˌwawk‖-ˌwɔːk/ *n* a long covered area where ropes are made

ˈ**ropeˌway** /-ˌway‖-ˌweɪ/ *n* an endless aerial cable moved by a stationary engine and used to transport goods (e g logs and ore)

ropy, ropey /ˈrohpi‖ˈrəʊpɪ/ *adj* **1a** capable of being drawn out into a thread **b** gelatinous or slimy from bacterial or fungal contamination <~ *milk*> **2** like rope in texture or appearance **3** *Br* **3a** of poor quality; shoddy **b** somewhat unwell *USE* (*3*) infml – **ropiness** *n*

Roquefort /ˈrok(ə)ˌfaw ‖ˈrɒk(ə)ˌfɔː (*Fr* rɔkfɔːr)/ *trademark* – used for a strong-flavoured crumbly French cheese with bluish green veins, made from the curds of ewes' milk

rosary /ˈrohz(ə)ri‖ˈrəʊz(ə)rɪ/ *n* a string of beads used in counting prayers [Medieval Latin *rosarium*, fr Latin, rose garden, fr *rosa* rose]

[1]**rose** /rohz‖rəʊz/ *past of* RISE

[2]**rose** *n* **1** (the showy often double flower of) any of a genus of widely cultivated usu prickly shrubs **2a** COMPASS CARD **b** (the form of) a gem, esp a diamond, with a flat base and triangular facets rising to a point **c** a perforated outlet for water (e g from a shower or watering can) **d** an electrical fitting that anchors the flex of a suspended light bulb to a ceiling **3** a pale to dark pinkish colour – **roselike** *adj*

[3]**rose** *adj* **1a** of, containing, or used for roses **b**

flavoured, sweetly scented, or coloured with or like roses **2** of the colour rose

rosé /roh'zay, '--‖rəʊ'zeɪ, '--/ *n* a light pink table wine made from red grapes by removing the skins after fermentation has begun [French, fr *rosé* pink, fr *rose* rose, fr Latin *rosa*]

roseate /'rohzi·ət‖'rəʊzɪət/ *adj* **1** resembling a rose, esp in colour **2** marked by unrealistic optimism – **roseately** *adv*

rosebud /'rohz,bud‖'rəʊz,bʌd/ *n* the bud of a rose

rosemary /'rohzməri‖'rəʊzmərɪ/ *n* a fragrant shrubby Eurasian plant used as a cooking herb [Latin *rosmarinus*, fr *ros* dew + *marinus* of the sea]

rosette /roh'zet, rə-‖rəʊ'zet, rə-/ *n* **1** an ornament usu made of material gathered so as to resemble a rose and worn as a badge, trophy, or trimming **2** a stylized carved or moulded rose used as a decorative motif in architecture **3** a rosette-shaped structure or marking on an animal **4** a cluster of leaves in crowded circles or spirals (e g in the dandelion)

rose window *n* a circular window filled with tracery radiating from its centre

'rose,wood /-,wood‖-,wʊd/ *n* (any of various esp leguminous tropical trees yielding) a valuable dark red or purplish wood, streaked and variegated with black

[1]**rosin** /'rozin‖'rɒzɪn/ *n* a translucent resin that is the residue from the distillation of turpentine and is used esp in making varnish and soldering flux and for rubbing on violin bows

[2]**rosin** *vt* to rub or treat (e g the bow of a violin) with rosin

roster /'rostə‖'rɒstə/ *n* **1** a list or register giving the order in which personnel are to perform a duty, go on leave, etc **2** an itemized list [Dutch *rooster*, lit., gridiron]

rostrum /'rostrəm‖'rɒstrəm/ *n, pl* **rostrums, rostra** /'rostrə‖'rɒstrə/ **1a** a stage for public speaking **b** a raised platform (on a stage) **2** a body part (e g an insect's snout or beak) shaped like a bird's bill [Latin, beak, ship's beak, fr *rodere* to gnaw; sense 1 fr Latin *Rostra* (pl), a stage in Rome ornamented with beaks of captured ships] – **rostral** *adj*

rosy /'rohzi‖'rəʊzɪ/ *adj* **1a** ROSE 2 **b** having a rosy complexion – often in combination <rosy-*cheeked youngsters*> **2** characterized by or encouraging optimism – **rosily** *adv*, **rosiness** *n*

[1]**rot** /rot‖rɒt/ *vb* **-tt-** *vi* **1a** to undergo decomposition, esp from the action of bacteria or fungi – often + *down* **b** to become unsound or weak (e g from chemical or water action) **2a** to go to ruin **b** to become morally corrupt ~*vt* to cause to decompose or deteriorate

[2]**rot** *n* **1** (sthg) rotting or being rotten; decay **2** any of several plant or animal diseases, esp of sheep, with breakdown and death of tissues **3** nonsense, rubbish – often used interjectionally

rota /'rohtə‖'rəʊtə/ *n, chiefly Br* **1** a list specifying a fixed order of rotation (e g of people or duties) **2** an ordered succession

[1]**rotary** /'roht(ə)ri‖'rəʊt(ə)rɪ/ *adj* **1a** turning on an axis like a wheel **b** proceeding about an axis <~ *motion*> **2** having a principal part that turns on an axis **3** characterized by rotation **4** of or being a printing press using a rotating curved printing surface

[2]**rotary** *n* **1** a rotary machine **2** *NAm* a roundabout

rotate /roh'tayt‖rəʊ'teɪt/ *vi* **1** to turn about an axis or a centre; revolve **2a** to take turns at performing an act or operation **b** to perform an ordered series of actions or functions ~ *vt* **1** to cause to turn about an axis or centre **2** to order in a recurring sequence – **rotatable** *adj*, **rotative** *adj*, **rotatory** *adj*

rotation /roh'taysh(ə)n‖rəʊ'teɪʃ(ə)n/ *n* **1a(1)** a rotating or being rotated (as if) on an axis or centre **a(2)** the act or an instance of rotating sthg **b** one complete turn; the angular displacement required to return a rotating body or figure to its original orientation **2a** recurrence in a regular series **b** the growing of different crops in succession in 1 field, usu in a regular sequence **3** the turning of a limb about its long axis – **rotational** *adj*

rote /roht‖rəʊt/ *n* the mechanical use of the memory

rotgut /'rot,gut‖'rɒt,gʌt/ *n* spirits of low quality – infml

rotisserie /roh'tisəri, -'tee-‖rəʊ'tɪsərɪ, -'tiː-/ *n* **1** a restaurant specializing in roast and barbecued meats **2** an appliance fitted with a spit on which food is cooked

rotor /'rohtə‖'rəʊtə/ *n* **1** a part that revolves in a machine; *esp* the rotating member of an electrical machine **2** a complete system of more or less horizontal blades that supplies (nearly) all the force supporting an aircraft (e g a helicopter) in flight

rotten /'rot(ə)n‖'rɒt(ə)n/ *adj* **1** having rotted; putrid **2** morally or politically corrupt **3** extremely unpleasant or inferior **4** marked by illness, discomfort, or unsoundness *USE* (*3, 4*) infml – **rottenly** *adv*, **rottenness** *n*

rotten borough *n* an election district with very few voters – used esp of certain English constituencies before 1832

rotter /'rotə‖'rɒtə/ *n* a thoroughly objectionable person – often humor

rotund /roh'tund‖rəʊ'tʌnd/ *adj* **1** rounded **2** high-flown or sonorous **3** markedly plump – **rotundity** *n*, **rotundly** *adv*, **rotundness** *n*

rotunda /roh'tundə‖rəʊ'tʌndə/ *n* a round building; *esp* one covered by a dome

rouble, ruble /'roohbl‖'ruːbl/ *n* the standard unit of money in the USSR

roué /'rooh·ay‖'ruːeɪ/ *n* a debauched man; *esp* one past his prime [French, lit., broken on the wheel, fr *rouer* to break on the wheel,fr *roue* wheel]

[1]**rouge** /roohzh‖ruːʒ/ *n* **1** a red cosmetic, esp for the cheeks **2** ferric oxide as a red powder, used as a pigment and in polishing glass, metal, or gems

[2]**rouge** *vt* to apply rouge to

[1]**rough** /ruf‖rʌf/ *adj* **1** having an irregular or uneven surface: e g **1a** not smooth **b** covered with or made up of coarse hair **c** covered with boulders, bushes, etc **2a** turbulent, stormy **b(1)** harsh, violent **b(2)** requiring strenuous effort <*had a* ~ *day*> **b(3)** unfortunate and hard to bear – often + *on* <*it's rather* ~ *on his wife*>

3 coarse or rugged in character or appearance: e g **3a** harsh to the ear **b** crude in style or expression **c** ill-mannered, uncouth **4a** crude, unfinished **b** executed hastily or approximately <*a ~ draft*> **5** *Br* poorly or exhausted, esp through lack of sleep or heavy drinking – infml – **roughish** *adj*, **roughness** *n*

[2]**rough** *n* **1** uneven ground covered with high grass, brush, and stones; *specif* such ground bordering a golf fairway **2** the rugged or disagreeable side or aspect **3a** sthg, esp written or illustrated, in a crude or preliminary state **b** broad outline **c** a quick preliminary drawing or layout **4** a hooligan, ruffian

[3]**rough** *adv, chiefly Br* in want of material comforts; without proper lodging – esp in *live/sleep rough*

[4]**rough** *vt* to roughen – **rough it** to live in uncomfortable or primitive conditions

roughage /'rufij||'rʌfɪdʒ/ *n* coarse bulky food (e g bran) that is relatively high in fibre and low in digestible nutrients and that by its bulk stimulates intestinal action

ˌ**rough-and-'tumble** *n* disorderly unrestrained fighting or struggling – **rough-and-tumble** *adj*

[1]**roughcast** /'rufˌkahst||'rʌfˌkɑːst/ *n* a plaster of lime mixed with shells or pebbles used for covering buildings

[2]**roughcast** *vt* **roughcast** to plaster with roughcast

roughen /'ruf(ə)n||'rʌf(ə)n/ *vb* to make or become (more) rough

ˌ**rough-'hewn** *adj* **1** in a rough or unfinished state **2** lacking refinement

roughhouse /'rufˌhows||'rʌfˌhaʊs/ *n* an instance of brawling or excessively boisterous play – infml – **roughhouse** *vi*

roughly /'rufli||'rʌflɪ/ *adv* **1a** with insolence or violence **b** in primitive fashion; crudely **2** without claim to completeness or exactness

roughneck /'rufˌnek||'rʌfˌnek/ *n* **1** a worker who handles the heavy drilling equipment of an oil rig **2** *NAm* a ruffian, tough

rough out *vt* **1** to shape or plan in a preliminary way **2** to outline

roughshod /'rufˌshod, ˌ-'-||'rʌfˌʃɒd, ˌ-'-/ *adv* forcefully and without justice or consideration

'**rough** ˌ**stuff** *n* violent behaviour; violence – infml

rough up *vt* to beat up – infml

roulette /rooh'let, roo-||ruː'let, rʊ-/ *n* **1** a gambling game in which players bet on which compartment of a revolving wheel a small ball will come to rest in **2** any of various toothed wheels or discs (e g for producing rows of dots on engraved plates or for perforating paper) [French, lit., small wheel, fr *roue* wheel]

[1]**round** /rownd||raʊnd/ *adj* **1a(1)** having every part of the surface or circumference equidistant from the centre **a(2)** cylindrical <*a ~ peg*> **b** approximately round <*a ~ face*> **2** well filled out; plump <*~ cheeks*> **3a** complete, full <*a ~ dozen*> **b** approximately correct; *esp* exact only to a specific decimal **c** substantial in amount <*a good ~ sum*> **4** direct in expression <*a ~ oath*> **5a** moving in or forming a ring or circle **b** following a roughly circular route <*a ~ tour of the Cotswolds*> **6** presented with lifelike fullness **7** having full resonance or tone – **roundness** *n*

[2]**round** *adv* **1a** in a circular or curved path **b** with revolving or rotating motion <*wheels go ~*> **c** in circumference <*a tree 5 feet ~*> **d** in, along, or through a circuitous or indirect route <*the road goes ~ by the lake*> **e** in an encircling position <*a field with a fence all ~*> **2a** in close from all sides so as to surround <*the children crowded ~*> **b** near, about **c** here and there in various places **3a** in rotation or recurrence <*your birthday will soon be ~ again*> **b** from beginning to end; through <*all the year ~*> **c(1)** in or to the other or a specified direction <*turn ~*> <*talk her ~*> **c(2)** TO 4 **c(3)** in the specified order or relationship <*got the story the wrong way ~*> **4** about, approximately <*~ 1900*> **5** to a particular person or place <*invite them ~ for drinks*> – **round about 1** approximately; MORE OR LESS **2** in a ring round; on all sides of

[3]**round** *prep* **1a** so as to revolve or progress about (a centre) **b** so as to encircle or enclose <*seated ~ the table*> **c** so as to avoid or get past; beyond the obstacle of <*got ~ his objections*> <*lives just ~ the corner*> **d** near to; about **2a** in all directions outwards from <*looked ~ her*> **b** here and there in or throughout <*travel ~ Europe*> **3** so as to have a centre or basis in <*a movement organized ~ the idea of service*> **4** continuously during; throughout

[4]**round** *n* **1a** sthg round (e g a circle, curve, or ring) **b** a circle of people or things **2** a musical canon sung in unison in which each part is continuously repeated **3** a rung of a ladder or chair **4a** a circling or circuitous path or course **b** motion in a circle or a curving path **5a** a route or assigned territory habitually traversed (e g by a milkman or policeman) **b** a series of visits made by **b(1)** a general practitioner to patients in their homes **b(2)** a hospital doctor to the patients under his/her care **c** a series of customary social calls <*doing the ~*s *of her friends*> **6** a set of usu alcoholic drinks served at 1 time to each person in a group **7** a recurring sequence of actions or events <*a ~ of talks*> **8** a period of time that recurs in fixed succession <*the daily ~*> **9** a unit of ammunition consisting of the parts necessary to fire 1 shot **10a** any of a series of units of action in a game or sport (e g covering a prescribed time) **b** a division of a tournament in which each contestant plays 1 other **11** a prolonged burst (e g of applause) **12a** a cut of beef between the rump and the lower leg **b** a single slice of bread or toast; *also* a sandwich made with 2 whole slices of bread **13** a rounded or curved part *USE* (*5b, c*) usu pl with sing. meaning – **in the round 1** in full sculptured form unattached to a background **2** with a centre stage surrounded by an audience <*theatre* in the round>

[5]**round** *vt* **1a** to make round or rounded **b(1)** to make (the lips) round and protruded **b(2)** to produce (e g the vowel /ooh/) with rounded lips; labialize **2** to go round (e g a bend, corner)

<*the ship* ~ed *the headland*> **3** to encircle, encompass **4** to bring to completion or perfection – often + *off* or *out* **5** to express as a round number – often + *off, up,* or *down* <*11.3572* ~ed *off to 3 decimal places becomes 11.357*> ~ *vi* **1a** to become round, plump, or smooth in outline **b** to reach fullness or completion – usu + *off* or *out* **2** to follow a winding or circular course < ~ing *into the home stretch*> – **round on** to turn against and attack; *esp* to suddenly scold

[1]**roundabout** /'rowndə,bowt||'raʊndə,baʊt/ *n, Br* **1** a merry-go-round; *also* a rotatable platform that is an amusement in a children's playground **2** a road junction formed round a central island about which traffic moves in 1 direction only; *also* a paved or planted circle in the middle of this

[2]**roundabout** *adj* circuitous, indirect – **roundaboutness** *n*

round bracket *n, chiefly Br* PARENTHESIS 1b

roundel /'rowndl||'raʊndl/ *n* **1** a round figure or object: e g **1a** a circular panel, window, etc **b** a circular mark identifying the nationality of an aircraft, esp a warplane **2** (an English modification of) the rondeau

roundelay /'rowndi,lay||'raʊndɪ,leɪ/ *n* **1** a simple song with a refrain **2** a poem with a refrain recurring frequently or at fixed intervals

rounder /'rowndə||'raʊndə/ *n* **1** *pl but sing in constr* a game with bat and ball that resembles baseball **2** a boxing or wrestling match lasting a specified number of rounds <*a 10*-rounder>

Roundhead /'rownd,hed||'raʊnd,hed/ *n* an adherent of Parliament in its contest with Charles I

roundhouse /'rownd,hows||'raʊnd,haʊs/ *n* **1** a cabin or apartment on the after part of a quarterdeck **2** *chiefly NAm* a circular building for housing and repairing locomotives

roundly /'rowndli||'raʊndlɪ/ *adv* **1** in a round or circular form or manner **2** in a blunt or severe manner < ~ *rebuked him*>

,round 'robin *n* **1** a written petition or protest; *esp* one on which the signatures are arranged in a circle so that no name heads the list **2** a tournament in which every contestant plays every other contestant in turn

,round-'shouldered *adj* having stooping or rounded shoulders

roundsman /'rowndzmən||'raʊndzmən/ *n* sby (e g a milkman) who takes, orders, sells, or delivers goods on an assigned route

,round 'table *n* a meeting or conference of several people on equal terms – **round-table** *adj*

,round-the-'clock *adj* lasting or continuing 24 hours a day; constant

,round 'trip *n* a trip to a place and back, usu over the same route

'round,up /-,up||-,ʌp/ *n* **1a** the collecting in of cattle by riding round them and driving them **b** a gathering in of scattered people or things **2** a summary of information (e g from news bulletins)

round up *vt* **1** to collect (cattle) by a roundup **2** to gather in or bring together from various quarters

rouse /rowz||raʊz/ *vi* **1** to become aroused **2** to become stirred ~ *vt* **1** to stir up; provoke **2** to arouse from sleep or apathy

rousing /'rowzing||'raʊzɪŋ/ *adj* giving rise to enthusiasm; stirring

roustabout /'rowstə,bowt||'raʊstə,baʊt/ *n, Br* **1** a deck hand or docker **2** an unskilled or semiskilled labourer, esp in an oil field or refinery

[1]**rout** /rowt||raʊt/ *n* **1** a disorderly crowd of people; a mob **2** *archaic* a fashionable social gathering

[2]**rout** *vi* [3]ROOT 1 ~ *vt* to gouge out or make a furrow in

[3]**rout** *n* **1** a state of wild confusion; *specif* a confused retreat; headlong flight **2** a disastrous defeat

[4]**rout** *vt* **1** to disorganize completely; wreak havoc among **2** to put to headlong flight **3** to defeat decisively or disastrously

[1]**route** /rooht||ru:t/ *n* **1a** a regularly travelled way <*the trunk* ~ *north*> **b** a means of access **2** a line of travel **3** an itinerary

[2]**route** *vt* **1** to send by a selected route; direct **2** to divert in a specified direction

'route ,march *n* a usu long and tiring march, esp as military training

[1]**routine** /rooh'teen||ru:'ti:n/ *n* **1a** a regular course of procedure **b** habitual or mechanical performance of an established procedure **2** a fixed piece of entertainment often repeated <*a dance* ~> **3** a particular sequence of computer instructions for carrying out a given task

[2]**routine** *adj* **1** commonplace or repetitious in character **2** of or in accordance with established procedure – **routinely** *adv*

rout out /rowt||raʊt/ *vt* ROOT OUT

roux /rooh||ru:/ *n, pl* **roux** /rooh(z)||ru:(z)/ a cooked mixture of fat and flour used as a thickening agent in a sauce

[1]**rove** /rohv||rəʊv/ *vb* to wander aimlessly or idly (through or over)

[2]**rove** *past of* REEVE

[3]**rove** *vt* to join (textile fibres) with a slight twist and draw out into roving

[4]**rove** *n* roving

[1]**rover** /'rohvə||'rəʊvə/ *n* a pirate

[2]**rover** *n* a wanderer

[1]**roving** /'rohving||'rəʊvɪŋ/ *adj* **1** not restricted as to location or area of concern **2** inclined to ramble or stray <*a* ~ *fancy*>

[2]**roving** *n* a slightly twisted roll or strand of textile fibres

,roving 'eye *n* promiscuous sexual interests

[1]**row** /roh||rəʊ/ *vi* **1** to propel a boat by means of oars **2** to move (as if) by the propulsion of oars ~ *vt* **1a** to propel (as if) with oars **b** to compete against in rowing **2** to transport in a boat propelled by oars **3** to occupy a specified position in a rowing crew – **rower** *n*

[2]**row** /roh||rəʊ/ *n* an act of rowing a boat

[3]**row** /roh||rəʊ/ *n* **1** a number of objects arranged in a (straight) line; *also* the line along which such objects are arranged **2** a way, street – **in a row** one after another; successively

[4]**row** /row||raʊ/ *n* **1** a noisy quarrel or stormy dispute **2** excessive or unpleasant noise

[5]**row** /row||raʊ/ *vi* to engage in quarrelling

rowan /'roh·ən||'rəʊən/ *n* (the red berry of) a small Eurasian tree that bears flat clusters of white flowers

rowdy /'rowdi‖'raʊdɪ/ *n or adj* (sby) coarse or boisterous – **rowdily** *adv*, **rowdiness** *n*, **rowdyism** *n*

rowel /'rowəl‖'raʊəl/ *n* a revolving disc with sharp marginal points at the end of a spur

'rowing ˌboat /'roh·ing‖'rəʊɪŋ/ *n*, *Br* a small boat designed to be rowed

rowlock /'rolək‖'rɒlək; *also (not tech)* 'roh-ˌlok‖'rəʊˌlɒk/ *n*, *chiefly Br* a device for holding an oar in place and providing a fulcrum for its action

[1]**royal** /'roy(ə)l‖'rɔɪ(ə)l/ *adj* **1a** of monarchical ancestry <*the ~ family*> **b** of the crown <*the ~ estates*> **c** in the crown's service <Royal *Air Force*> **2** suitable for royalty; regal, magnificent **3** of superior size, magnitude, or quality **4** of or being a part of the rigging of a sailing ship next above the topgallant – **royally** *adv*

[2]**royal** *n* **1** a stag of 8 years or more having antlers with at least 12 points **2** a royal sail or mast **3** a size of paper usu 25 x 20in (635 × 508mm) **4** sby of royal blood – infml

ˌroyal 'flush *n* a straight flush having an ace as the highest card

royalist /'royəlist‖'rɔɪəlɪst/ *n*, *often cap* a supporter of a king or of monarchical government (e g a Cavalier) – **royalism** *n*, **royalist** *adj*

ˌroyal 'jelly *n* a highly nutritious secretion of the honeybee that is fed to the very young larvae and to all larvae that will develop into queens

ˌroyal pre'rogative *n* the constitutional rights of the monarch

royalty /'royəlti‖'rɔɪəltɪ/ *n* **1a** royal sovereignty **b** a monetary benefit received by a sovereign (e g a percentage of minerals) **2** regal character or bearing **3a** people of royal blood **b** a privileged class of a specified type **4** a right of jurisdiction granted by a sovereign **5a** a share of the product or profit reserved by one who grants esp an oil or mining lease **b** a payment made to an author, composer, or inventor for each copy or example of his/her work sold

[1]**rub** /rub‖rʌb/ *vb* **-bb-** *vi* to move along a surface with pressure and friction ~ *vt* **1** to subject to pressure and friction, esp with a back-and-forth motion **2a** to cause (a body) to move with pressure and friction along a surface **b** to treat in any of various ways by rubbing **3** to bring into reciprocal back-and-forth or rotary contact – **rub shoulders** to associate closely; mingle socially – **rub the wrong way** to arouse the antagonism or displeasure of; irritate

[2]**rub** *n* **1a** an obstacle, difficulty – usu + *the* **b** sthg grating to the feelings (e g a gibe or harsh criticism) **2** the application of friction and pressure

rub along *vi* **1** to continue coping in a trying situation **2** to remain on friendly terms

[1]**rubber** /'rubə‖'rʌbə/ *n* **1a** an instrument or object used in rubbing, polishing, or cleaning **b** *Br* a small piece of rubber or plastic used for rubbing out esp pencil marks on paper, card, etc **2** (any of various synthetic substances like) an elastic substance, obtained by coagulating the milky juice of the rubber tree or other plant, that is used, esp when toughened by chemical treatment, in car tyres, waterproof materials, etc **3** sthg like or made of rubber: e g **3a** *NAm* a galosh **b** *NAm* a condom – **rubber** *adj*, **rubbery** *adj*

[2]**rubber** *n* a contest consisting of an odd number of games won by the side that takes a majority

ˌrubber 'band *n* a continuous band of rubber used for holding small objects together

rubber·ize, -ise /'rubəriez‖'rʌbəraɪz/ *vt* to coat or impregnate with (a solution of) rubber

[1]**rubberneck** /'rubəˌnek‖'rʌbəˌnek/ *also* **rubbernecker** /-ˌnekə‖-ˌnekə/ *n*, *NAm* **1** an overinquisitive person **2** a tourist, sightseer; *esp* one on a guided tour *USE* derog

[2]**rubberneck** *vi*, *NAm* **1** to show exaggerated curiosity – infml **2** to engage in sightseeing – derog

'rubber ˌplant *n* a tall Asian tree of the fig family frequently dwarfed and grown as an ornamental plant

ˌrubber-'stamp *vt* **1** to imprint with a rubber stamp **2** to approve, endorse, or dispose of as a matter of routine or at the dictate of another

ˌrubber 'stamp *n* **1** a stamp of rubber for making imprints **2** sby who unthinkingly assents to the actions or policies of others **3** a routine endorsement or approval

'rubber ˌtree *n* a S American tree of the spurge family that is cultivated in plantations and is the chief source of rubber

rubbing /'rubing‖'rʌbɪŋ/ *n* an image of a raised surface obtained by placing paper over it and rubbing the paper with charcoal, chalk, etc

[1]**rubbish** /'rubish‖'rʌbɪʃ/ *n* **1** worthless or rejected articles; trash **2** sthg worthless; NONSENSE 1a, b – often used interjectionally – **rubbishy** *adj*

[2]**rubbish** *vt* **1** to condemn as rubbish **2** to litter with rubbish

rubble /'rubl‖'rʌbl/ *n* **1** broken fragments of building material (e g brick, stone, etc) **2** rough broken stones or bricks used in coarse masonry or in filling courses of walls **3** rough stone from the quarry

rubdown /'rubˌdown‖'rʌbˌdaʊn/ *n* a brisk rubbing of the body

rubella /rooh'belə‖ru:'belə/ *n* GERMAN MEASLES

Rubicon /'roohbikən‖'ru:bɪkən/ *n* a bounding or limiting line; *esp* one that when crossed commits sby irrevocably [*Rubicon*, river of N Italy, whose crossing by Julius Caesar in 49 BC began a civil war]

rubicund /'roohbikənd‖'ru:bɪkənd/ *adj* ruddy – **rubicundity** *n*

rub in *vt* to harp on (e g sthg unpleasant or embarrassing)

ruble /'roohbl‖'ru:bl/ *n* a rouble

rub off *vi* **1** to disappear as the result of rubbing **2** to exert an influence through contact or example

rub out *vt* **1** to remove (e g pencil marks) with a rubber; *broadly* to obliterate **2** *chiefly NAm* to kill, murder – slang

rubric /'roohbrik‖'ru:brɪk/ *n* **1** a heading (e g in a book or manuscript) written or printed in a distinctive colour (e g red) or style **2a** a heading under which sthg is classed **b** an authoritative rule; *esp* a rule for the conduct of church ceremonial **c** an explanatory or introductory commentary – **rubric, rubrical** *adj*

rub up *vt* to revive or refresh knowledge of; revise

[1]**ruby** /ˈroohbi‖ˈruːbɪ/ *n* **1** a red corundum used as a gem **2a** the dark red colour of the ruby **b** sthg like a ruby in colour

[2]**ruby** *adj* of or marking a 40th anniversary <~ *wedding*>

[1]**ruck** /ruk‖rʌk/ *n* **1a** an indistinguishable mass **b** *the* usual run of people or things **2** a situation in Rugby Union in which 1 or more players from each team close round the ball when it is on the ground and try to kick the ball out to their own team

[2]**ruck** *vb* to wrinkle, crease – often + *up*

rucksack /ˈruk,sak‖ˈrʌk,sæk/ *n* a lightweight bag carried on the back and fastened by straps over the shoulders, used esp by walkers and climbers

ruckus /ˈrukəs‖ˈrʌkəs/ *n, chiefly NAm* a row or disturbance – infml

ruction /ˈruksh(ə)n‖ˈrʌkʃ(ə)n/ *n* **1** a violent dispute **2** a disturbance, uproar *USE* infml

rudder /ˈrudə‖ˈrʌdə/ *n* **1** a flat piece or structure of wood or metal hinged vertically to a ship's stern for changing course with **2** a movable auxiliary aerofoil, usu attached to the fin, that serves to control direction of flight of an aircraft in the horizontal plane – **rudderless** *adj*

ruddy /ˈrudi‖ˈrʌdɪ/ *adj* **1** having a healthy reddish colour **2** red, reddish **3** *Br* BLOODY 4 – euph – **ruddily** *adv*, **ruddiness** *n*

rude /roohd‖ruːd/ *adj* **1a** in a rough or unfinished state **b** primitive, undeveloped **c** simple, elemental **2** lacking refinement or propriety: e g **2a** discourteous **b** vulgar, indecent **c** uncivilized **d** ignorant, unlearned **3** showing or suggesting lack of training or skill **4** robust, vigorous – esp in *rude health* **5** sudden and unpleasant; abrupt <*a* ~ *awakening*> – **rudely** *adv*, **rudeness** *n*, **rudery** *n*

rudiment /ˈroohdimənt‖ˈruːdɪmənt/ *n* **1** a basic principle or element or a fundamental skill **2a** sthg as yet unformed or undeveloped **b(1)** a deficiently developed body part or organ; VESTIGE 2 **b(2)** a primordium *USE* usu pl with sing. meaning [Latin *rudimentum* beginning, early training, fr *rudis* raw, rude] – **rudimental** *adj*

rudimentary /,roohdiˈment(ə)ri‖,ruːdɪˈment(ə)rɪ/ *adj* **1** basic, fundamental **2** of a primitive kind; crude **3** very poorly developed or represented only by a vestige <*the* ~ *tail of a hyrax*> – **rudimentarily** *adv*

[1]**rue** /rooh‖ruː/ *vt* to feel penitence or bitter regret for

[2]**rue** *n* a strong-scented woody plant with bitter leaves formerly used in medicine

rueful /ˈroohf(ə)l‖ˈruːf(ə)l/ *adj* **1** arousing pity or compassion **2** mournful, regretful; *also* feigning sorrow – **ruefully** *adv*, **ruefulness** *n*

[1]**ruff, ruffe** /ruf‖rʌf/ *n* a small freshwater European perch

[2]**ruff** *n* **1** a broad starched collar of fluted linen or muslin worn in the late 16th and early 17th c **2** a fringe or frill of long hairs or feathers growing round the neck **3** *fem* **reeve** a Eurasian sandpiper the male of which has a large ruff of erectable feathers during the breeding season – **ruffed** *adj*

[3]**ruff** *vt* TRUMP 1 – **ruff** *n*

ruffian /ˈrufi·ən‖ˈrʌfɪən/ *n* a brutal and lawless person – **ruffianism** *n*, **ruffianly** *adj*

[1]**ruffle** /ˈrufl‖ˈrʌfl/ *vt* **1a** to disturb the smoothness of **b** to trouble, vex <~d *his composure*> **2** to erect (e g feathers) (as if) in a ruff **3** to make into a ruffle ~*vi* to become ruffled

[2]**ruffle** *n* **1** a disturbance of surface evenness (e g a ripple or crumple) **2a** a strip of fabric gathered or pleated on 1 edge **b** [2]RUFF 2

rug /rug‖rʌg/ *n* **1** a heavy mat, usu smaller than a carpet and with a thick pile, which is used as a floor covering **2a** a woollen blanket, often with fringes on 2 opposite edges, used as a wrap esp when travelling **b** a blanket for an animal (e g a horse)

rugby /ˈrugbi‖ˈrʌgbɪ/ *n, often cap* a football game that is played with an oval football, that features kicking, lateral hand-to-hand passing, and tackling, and in which forward passing is prohibited [*Rugby* School, in Warwickshire, England]

rugged /ˈrugid‖ˈrʌgɪd/ *adj* **1** having a rough uneven surface or outline <~ *mountains*> **2** seamed with wrinkles and furrows <*a* ~ *face*> **3** austere, stern; *also* uncompromising <~ *individualism*> **4a** strongly built or constituted; sturdy **b** presenting a severe test of ability or stamina – **ruggedly** *adv*, **ruggedness** *n*

[1]**ruin** /ˈrooh·in‖ˈruːɪn/ *n* **1** physical, moral, economic, or social collapse **2a** the state of being wrecked or decayed <*the city lay in* ~s> **b** the remains of sthg destroyed – usu pl with sing. meaning **3** (a cause of) destruction or downfall **4** a ruined person or structure – **ruination** *n*

[2]**ruin** *vt* **1** to reduce to ruins **2a** to damage irreparably; spoil **b** to reduce to financial ruin – **ruiner** *n*

ruinous /ˈrooh·inəs‖ˈruːɪnəs/ *adj* **1** dilapidated, ruined **2** causing (the likelihood of) ruin <~ *sales performance*> – **ruinously** *adv*, **ruinousness** *n*

[1]**rule** /roohl‖ruːl/ *n* **1a** a prescriptive specification of conduct or action **b** the laws or regulations prescribed by the founder of a religious order for observance by its members **c** an established procedure, custom, or habit **d** a legal precept or doctrine **2a(1)** a usu valid generalization **a(2)** a generally prevailing quality, state, or form **b** a standard of judgment **c** a regulating principle, esp of a system <*the* ~s *of grammar*> **3** the exercise or a period of dominion **4** a strip or set of jointed strips of material marked off in units and used for measuring or marking off lengths – **as a rule** generally; FOR THE MOST PART

[2]**rule** *vt* **1a** to exert control, direction, or influence on **b** to exercise control over, esp by restraining <~d *her appetites firmly*> **2a** to exercise power or firm authority over **b** to be preeminent in; dominate <*an actor who* ~s *the stage*> **3** to lay down authoritatively, esp judicially **4a** to mark with lines drawn (as if) along the straight edge of a ruler **b** to mark (a line) on

sthg with a ruler ~ *vi* **1** to exercise supreme authority **2** to make a judicial decision

rule out *vt* **1a** to exclude, eliminate **b** to deny the possibility of <rule out *further discussion*> **2** to make impossible; prevent

ruler /'roohlə‖'ru:lə/ *n* **1** sby, specif a sovereign, who rules **2** a smooth-edged strip of material that is usu marked off in units (e g centimetres) and is used for guiding a pen or pencil in drawing lines, for measuring, or for marking off lengths – **rulership** *n*

[1]**ruling** /'roohling‖'ru:lɪŋ/ *n* an official or authoritative decision

[2]**ruling** *adj* **1** exerting power or authority **2** chief, predominant

[1]**rum** /rum‖rʌm/ *adj* **-mm-** *chiefly Br* queer, strange – infml

[2]**rum** *n* a spirit distilled from a fermented cane product (e g molasses)

rumba, rhumba /'rumbə‖'rʌmbə/ *n* (the music for) a ballroom dance of Cuban Negro origin marked by steps with a delayed transfer of weight and pronounced hip movements

[1]**rumble** /'rumbl‖'rʌmbl/ *vi* **1** to make a low heavy rolling sound **2** *NAm* to engage in a street fight – infml ~ *vt* **1** to utter or emit with a low rolling sound **2** to reveal or discover the true character of – infml – **rumbler** *n*

[2]**rumble** *n* **1a** a rumbling sound **b** low-frequency noise from a record deck caused by the vibrations of the turntable **2** *NAm* a street fight, esp between gangs – infml

rumbustious /rum'buschəs‖rʌm'bʌstʃəs/ *adj, chiefly Br* irrepressibly or coarsely exuberant – **rumbustiousness** *n*

[1]**ruminant** /'roohminənt‖'ru:mɪnənt/ *n* a ruminant mammal

[2]**ruminant** *adj* **1a** that chews the cud **b** of or being (a member of) a group of hoofed mammals including the cattle, sheep, giraffes, and camels that chew the cud and have a complex 3- or 4-chambered stomach **2** meditative

ruminate /'roohmi,nayt‖'ru:mɪ,neɪt/ *vb* **1** to chew again (what has been chewed slightly and swallowed) **2** to engage in contemplation (of) [Latin *ruminari* to chew the cud, muse upon, fr *rumin-, rumen* gullet] – **ruminator** *n*, **ruminative** *adj*, **ruminatively** *adv*, **rumination** *n*

[1]**rummage** /'rumij‖'rʌmɪdʒ/ *n* **1** a thorough search, esp among a jumbled assortment of objects **2a** *chiefly NAm* JUMBLE 2 **b** *NAm* a miscellaneous or confused accumulation

[2]**rummage** *vt* **1** to make a thorough search of (an untidy or congested place) **2** to uncover by searching – usu + *out* ~*vi* to engage in a haphazard search – **rummager** *n*

rummy /'rumi‖'rʌmɪ/ *n* any of several card games for 2 or more players in which each player tries to assemble combinations of 3 or more related cards and to be the first to turn all his/her cards into such combinations

[1]**rumour,** *NAm chiefly* **rumor** /'roohmə‖'ru:mə/ *n* **1** a statement or report circulated without confirmation of its truth **2** talk or opinion widely disseminated but with no identifiable source

[2]**rumour,** *NAm chiefly* **rumor** *vt* to tell or spread by rumour

rump /rump‖rʌmp/ *n* **1** the rear part of a quadruped mammal, bird, etc; the buttocks **2** a cut of beef between the loin and round **3** a small or inferior remnant of a larger group (e g a parliament)

[1]**rumple** /'rumpl‖'rʌmpl/ *n* a fold, wrinkle

[2]**rumple** *vb* **1** to wrinkle, crumple **2** to make unkempt; tousle ~*vi* to become rumpled

rumpus /'rumpəs‖'rʌmpəs/ *n* a usu noisy commotion

[1]**run** /run‖rʌn/ *vb* **-nn-; ran** /ran‖ræn/; **run** *vi* **1a** to go faster than a walk; *specif* to go steadily by springing steps so that both feet leave the ground for an instant in each step **b** *of a horse* to move at a fast gallop **c** to flee, escape <*dropped his gun and* ran> **2a** to go without restraint <*let his chickens* ~ *loose*> **b** to sail before the wind as distinct from reaching or sailing close-hauled **3a** to hasten with a specified often distressing purpose <~ *and fetch the doctor*> **b** to make a quick, easy, or casual trip or visit <~ *up to town for the day*> **4** to contend in a race; *also* to finish a race in the specified place <ran *third*> **5a** to move (as if) on wheels <*a chair that* ~s *on castors*> **b** to pass or slide freely or cursorily <*a thought* ran *through my mind*> **6** to sing or play quickly <~ *up the scale*> **7a** to go back and forth; ply <*made the trains* ~ *on time*> **b** *of fish* to migrate or move in schools; *esp* to ascend a river to spawn **8** to function, operate <*the engine* ~s *on petrol*> **9a** to continue in force <*the lease has 2 more years to* ~> **b** to continue to accumulate or become payable <*interest on the loan* ~s *from July 1st*> **10** to pass, esp by negligence or indulgence, into a specified state <*money* ran *low*> **11a(1)** to flow, course <~ning *water*> **a(2)** to become by flowing <*the water* ran *cold*> **a(3)** to discharge liquid <*left the tap* ~ning> **a(4)** to reach a specified state by discharging liquid <*the well* ran *dry*> **b** MELT 1 <*butter started to* ~> **c** to spread, dissolve <*colours guaranteed not to* ~> **d** to discharge pus or serum <*a* ~ning *sore*> **12a** to develop rapidly in some specific direction; *esp* to throw out an elongated shoot **b** to have a tendency; be prone <*they* ~ *to big noses in that family*> **13a** to lie or extend in a specified position, direction, or relation to sthg <*the road* ~s *through a tunnel*> **b** to extend in a continuous range <*shades* ~ *from white to dark grey*> **c** to be in a certain form or expression <*the letter* ~s *as follows*> **14a** to occur persistently <*a note of despair* ~s *through the narrative*> **b** to continue to be as specified <*profits were* ~ning *high*> **c** to play or be featured continuously (e g in a theatre or newspaper) <*the musical* ran *for 6 months*> **15** to spread quickly from point to point <*chills* ran *up his spine*> **16** to ladder **17** *chiefly NAm* STAND 10 <~ *for President*> ~ *vt* **1a** to bring to a specified condition (as if) by running <ran *himself to death*> **b** to go in pursuit of; hunt <*dogs that* ~ *deer*> <ran *the rumour to its source*> **c** to drive, chase <~ *him out of town*> **d** to enter, register, or enrol as a contestant in a race **e** to put forward as a candidate for office **2a** to drive (livestock), esp to a grazing place **b** to provide pasturage for (livestock) **3a** to cover, accomplish, or perform (as if) by

running <ran *10 miles*> <~ *errands for his mother*> **b** to slip through or past <~ *a blockade*> **4a** to cause or allow to penetrate or enter <ran *a splinter into his toe*> **b** to stitch **c** to cause to lie or extend in a specified position or direction <~ *a wire in from the aerial*> **d** to cause to collide <ran *his head into a post*> **e** to smuggle <~ *guns*> **5** to cause to pass lightly, freely, or cursorily <ran *a comb through her hair*> **6a(1)** to cause or allow (a vehicle or vessel) to go <~ *his car off the road*> **a(2)** to cause to ply or travel along a regular route <~ *an extra train on Saturdays*> **a(3)** to own and drive <*she* ~s *an old banger*> **a(4)** to convey in a vehicle <*can I* ~ *you home?*> **b** to operate <~ *your razor off the mains*> **c** to carry on, manage, or control <~ *a factory*> **7** to be full of; flow with <*streets* ran *blood*> **8a** to cause to move or flow in a specified way or into a specified position **b(1)** to cause to pour out liquid <~ *the hot tap*> **b(2)** to fill from a tap <~ *a hot bath*> **9a** to melt and cast in a mould **b** to subject to a treatment or process <~ *a problem through a computer*> **10** to make oneself liable to <~ *risks*> **11** to permit (e g charges) to accumulate before settling <~ *an account at the grocer's*> **12a** RUN OFF 1b <*a book to be* ~ *on lightweight paper*> **b** to carry in a printed medium; print – **run across** to meet with or discover by chance – **run after** to pursue, chase; *esp* to seek the company of – **run a temperature** to be feverish – **run foul of 1** to collide with <run foul of *a hidden reef*> **2** to come into conflict with <run foul of *the law*> – **run into 1a** to merge with **b** to mount up to <*income often* runs into *five figures*> **2a** to collide with **b** to encounter, meet <ran into *an old friend the other day*> – **run into the ground** to tire out or use up with heavy work – **run it fine** to leave only the irreducible margin – **run on** to be concerned with; dwell on <*her mind keeps* running on *the past*> – **run rings round** to show marked superiority over; defeat decisively – **run riot 1** to act or function wildly or without restraint <*let one's imagination* run riot> **2** to grow or occur in profusion – **run short 1** to become insufficient **2** to come near the end of available supplies <*we* ran short *of tea*> – **run somebody off his/her feet 1** to tire sby out with running **2** to keep sby very busy – **run through 1** to squander **2a** RUN THROUGH *vt* 2 <ran through *it quickly*> **b** to deal with rapidly and usu perfunctorily – **run to 1** to extend to <*the book* runs to *500 pages*> **2a** to afford **b** *of money* to be enough for <*his salary won't* run to *a car*> – **run to earth/ground** to find after protracted search

[2]**run** *n* **1a** an act or the activity of running; continued rapid movement **b** a quickened gallop; *broadly* the gait of a runner **c** (a school of fish) migrating or ascending a river to spawn **d** a running race <*a mile* ~> **2a** the direction in which sthg (e g a vein of ore or the grain of wood) lies **b** general tendency or direction <*watching the* ~ *of the stock market*> **3** a continuous series or unbroken course, esp of identical or similar things <*a* ~ *of bad luck*>: e g **3a** a rapid passage up or down a musical scale **b** a number of rapid small dance steps executed in even tempo **c** an unbroken course of performances or showings **d** a set of consecutive measurements, readings, or observations **e** a persistent and heavy commercial or financial demand <*a* ~ *on gilt-edged securities*> **f** three or more playing cards usu of the same suit in consecutive order of rank **4** the quantity of work turned out in a continuous operation **5** the average or prevailing kind or class <*the general* ~ *of students*> **6a** the distance covered in a period of continuous journeying **b(1)** a regularly travelled course or route <*ships on the Far East* ~> **b(2)** a short excursion in a car <*went for a Sunday* ~> **c** the distance a golf ball travels after touching the ground **d** freedom of movement in or access to a place <*has the* ~ *of the house*> **7a** a way, track, etc frequented by animals **b** an enclosure for domestic animals where they may feed or exercise **c** an inclined passageway **8a** an inclined course (e g for skiing) **b** a support or channel (e g a track, pipe, or trough) along which sthg runs **9** a unit of scoring in cricket made typically by each batsman running the full length of the wicket **10** LADDER 2b – **runless** *adj* – **on the run 1** in haste; without pausing **2** in hiding or running away, esp from lawful authority – **run for one's money** the profit or enjoyment to which one is legitimately entitled

runabout /ˈrunə,bowt||ˈrʌnə,baʊt/ *n* a light motor car, aeroplane, or motorboat

run along *vi* to go away; depart – often used as an order or request

runaround /ˈrunə,rownd||ˈrʌnə,raʊnd/ *n, chiefly NAm* delaying action, esp in response to a request

[1]**runaway** /ˈrunə,way||ˈrʌnə,weɪ/ *n* **1** a fugitive **2** sthg (e g a horse) that is running out of control

[2]**runaway** *adj* **1** fugitive **2** accomplished as a result of running away <*a* ~ *marriage*> **3** won by a long lead; decisive <*a* ~ *victory*> **4** out of control <~ *inflation*>

run away *vi* **1a** to take to flight **b** to flee from home; *esp* to elope **2** to run out of control; stampede, bolt – **run away with 1** to take away in haste or secretly; *esp* to steal **2** to believe too easily <*don't* run away with *the idea that you needn't go*> **3** to carry beyond reasonable limits <*his imagination* ran away with *him*>

rundown /ˈrun,down||ˈrʌn,daʊn/ *n* **1** the running down of sthg <*the* ~ *of the steel industry*> **2** an item-by-item report; a résumé

,run-ˈdown *adj* **1** in a state of disrepair **2** in poor health **3** *NAm* completely unwound <*a* ~ *clock*>

run down *vt* **1a** to knock down, esp with a motor vehicle **b** to run against and cause to sink **2a** to chase to exhaustion or until captured **b** to find by searching <run down *a book in the library*> **3** to disparage <*don't* run *him* down*; he's an honest fellow*> **4** to allow the gradual decline or closure of <*the lead mines are being gradually* run down> ~ *vi* **1** to cease to operate because of the exhaustion of motive power <*that battery* ran down *weeks ago*> **2** to decline in physical condition

rune /roohn||ruːn/ *n* **1** any of the characters of an alphabet prob derived from Latin and Greek and used in medieval times, esp in carved inscriptions, by the Germanic peoples **2** a magical or cryptic utterance or inscription – **runic** *adj*

[1]**rung** /rung‖rʌŋ/ *past part of* RING

[2]**rung** *n* **1a** a rounded part placed as a crosspiece between the legs of a chair **b** any of the crosspieces of a ladder **2** a level or stage in sthg that can be ascended <*the bottom* ~ *of the social scale*>

ˈ**run-ˌin** *n* **1** the final part of a race(track) **2** *NAm* a quarrel

run in *vt* **1** to make (typeset matter) continuous without a paragraph or other break **2** to use (e g a motor car) cautiously for an initial period **3** to arrest, esp for a minor offence – infml

runnel /ˈrunl‖ˈrʌnl/ *n* a small stream; a brook

runner /ˈrunə‖ˈrʌnə/ *n* **1** an entrant for a race who actually competes in it **2a** a bank or stockbroker's messenger **b** sby who smuggles or distributes illicit or contraband goods – usu in combination <*a dope*-runner> **3** a straight piece on which sthg slides: e g **3a** a longitudinal piece on which a sledge or ice skate slides **b** a groove or bar along which sthg (e g a drawer or sliding door) slides **4** a stolon **5a** a long narrow carpet (e g for a hall or staircase) **b** a narrow decorative cloth for a table or dresser top **6** RUNNER BEAN **7** a player who runs in place of an injured batsman in cricket

ˌ**runner ˈbean** *n, chiefly Br* (the long green edible pod of) a widely cultivated orig tropical American high-climbing bean with large usu bright red flowers

ˌ**runner-ˈup** *n, pl* **runners-up** *also* **runner-ups** a competitor in a contest who finishes in second place

[1]**running** /ˈruning‖ˈrʌnɪŋ/ *n* **1** the state of competing, esp with a good chance of winning – in *in/out of the running* **2** management, operation <*the* ~ *of a small business*>

[2]**running** *adj* **1** runny **2a** having stages that follow in rapid succession <*a* ~ *battle*> **b** made during the course of a process or activity <~ *repairs*> **3** cursive, flowing **4** designed or used for races on foot <*a* ~ *track*>

[3]**running** *adv* in succession <*for 3 days* ~>

ˈ**running ˌboard** *n* a footboard, esp at the side of a motor car

running knot *n* a knot that slips along the rope or line round which it is tied

ˈ**running ˌmate** *n* a candidate standing for a subordinate place in a US election

runny /ˈruni‖ˈrʌnɪ/ *adj* tending to run

runoff /ˈrunˌof‖ˈrʌnˌɒf/ *n* a final decisive race, contest, or election

run off *vt* **1a** to compose rapidly or glibly **b** to produce with a printing press or copier **c** to decide (e g a race) by a runoff **2** to drain off (a liquid) **3** *NAm* to steal (e g cattle) by driving away ~*vi* RUN AWAY 1 – **run off with** RUN AWAY WITH 1

ˌ**run-of-the-ˈmill** *adj* average, commonplace

run on *vi* **1** to keep going without interruption **2** to talk or narrate at length ~ *vt* to continue (written material) without a break or a new paragraph

run out *vi* **1a** to come to an end <*time* ran out> **b** to become exhausted or used up <*the petrol* ran out> **2** to finish a course or contest in the specified position <ran out *the winner*> **3** *of a horse* to evade a fence by turning aside ~ *vt* **1** to dismiss (a batsman who is outside his crease and attempting a run) by breaking the wicket with the ball **2** *chiefly NAm* to compel to leave <run *him* out *of town*> – **run out of** to use up the available supply of – **run out on** [3]DESERT

run over *vi* **1** to overflow **2** to exceed a limit ~ *vt* **1** to glance over, repeat, or rehearse quickly **2** to injure or kill with a motor vehicle

runt /runt‖rʌnt/ *n* **1** an animal unusually small of its kind; *esp* the smallest of a litter of pigs **2** a puny person – **runty** *adj*

ˈ**run-ˌthrough** *n* **1** a cursory reading, summary, or rehearsal **2** a sequence of actions performed for practice

run through *vt* **1** to pierce with a weapon (e g a sword) **2** to perform, esp for practice or instruction

ˈ**run-ˌup** *n* **1** (the track or area provided for) an approach run to provide momentum (e g for a jump or throw) **2** *Br* a period that immediately precedes an action or event

run up *vt* **1** to make (esp a garment) quickly **2a** to erect hastily **b** to hoist (a flag) **3** to accumulate or incur (debts) – **run up against** to encounter (e g a difficulty)

runway /ˈrunˌway‖ˈrʌnˌweɪ/ *n* **1** a (beaten) path made by or for animals **2** an artificially surfaced strip of ground on an airfield for the landing and takeoff of aeroplanes

rupee /roohˈpee‖ruːˈpiː/ *n* (a note or coin representing) the basic money unit of various countries of the Indian subcontinent and the Indian Ocean (e g India, Pakistan, Seychelles, and Sri Lanka)

[1]**rupture** /ˈrupchə‖ˈrʌptʃə/ *n* **1** breach of peace or concord; *specif* open hostility between nations **2a** the tearing apart of a tissue, esp muscle **b** a hernia **3a** a breaking apart or bursting **b** the state of being broken apart or burst [Middle French, fr Latin *ruptura* fracture, fr *rupt-*, *rumpere* to break]

[2]**rupture** *vt* **1a** to part by violence; break, burst **b** to create a breach of **2** to produce a rupture in ~*vi* to have or undergo a rupture

rural /ˈrooərəl‖ˈrʊərəl/ *adj* of the country, country people or life, or agriculture – **rurally** *adv*

ˌ**rural ˈdean** *n* a priest supervising 1 district of a diocese

ruse /roohz‖ruːz/ *n* a wily subterfuge

[1]**rush** /rush‖rʌʃ/ *n* any of various often tufted marsh plants with cylindrical (hollow) leaves, used for the seats of chairs and for plaiting mats – **rushy** *adj*

[2]**rush** *vi* to move forwards, progress, or act quickly or eagerly or without preparation ~ *vt* **1** to push or impel forwards with speed or violence **2** to perform or finish in a short time or at high speed <~ed *his breakfast*> **3** to urge to an excessive speed **4** to run against in attack, often with an element of surprise; charge – **rusher** *n*

[3]**rush** *n* **1a** a rapid and violent forward motion **b** a sudden onset of emotion <*a quick* ~ *of sympathy*> **2a** a surge of activity; *also* busy or

hurried activity **b** a burst of productivity or speed **3** a great movement of people, esp in search of wealth **4** the unedited print of a film scene processed directly after shooting – usu pl

[4]**rush** *adj* requiring or marked by special speed or urgency

ˈ**rush ˌhour** *n* a period of the day when traffic is at a peak

rusk /rusk‖rʌsk/ *n* (a light dry biscuit similar to) a piece of sliced bread baked again until dry and crisp

russet /ˈrusit‖ˈrʌsɪt/ *n* **1** a reddish to yellowish brown **2** any of various russet-coloured winter eating apples – **russet** *adj*

Russian /ˈrush(ə)n‖ˈrʌʃ(ə)n/ *n* **1** a native or inhabitant of Russia; *broadly* a native or inhabitant of the USSR **2** a Slavonic language of the Russians – **Russian** *adj*

ˌ**Russian rouˈlette** *n* an act of bravado consisting of spinning the cylinder of a revolver loaded with 1 cartridge, pointing the muzzle at one's own head, and pulling the trigger

[1]**rust** /rust‖rʌst/ *n* **1a** brittle reddish hydrated ferric oxide that forms as a coating on iron, esp iron chemically attacked by moist air **b** a comparable coating produced on another metal **c** sthg like rust **2** corrosive or injurious influence or effect **3** (a fungus causing) any of numerous destructive diseases of plants in which reddish brown pustular lesions form **4** a reddish brown to orange colour

[2]**rust** *vi* **1** to form rust; become oxidized **2** to degenerate, esp through lack of use or advancing age **3** to become reddish brown as if with rust **4** to be affected with a rust fungus ~*vt* to cause (a metal) to form rust

[1]**rustic** /ˈrustik‖ˈrʌstɪk/ *adj* **1** of or suitable for the country **2a** made of the rough limbs of trees <~ *furniture*> **b** finished by rusticating **3** characteristic of country people [Latin *rusticus*, fr *rus* country, land] – **rustically** *adv*, **rusticity** *n*

[2]**rustic** *n* an unsophisticated rural person

rusticate /ˈrustiˌkayt‖ˈrʌstɪˌkeɪt/ *vt* **1** to suspend (a student) from college or university **2** to bevel or cut a groove, channel etc in (e g the edges of stone blocks) to make the joints conspicuous **3** to impart a rustic character to – **rustication** *n*, **rustication** *n*

[1]**rustle** /ˈrusl‖ˈrʌsl/ *vi* **1a** to make or cause a rustle **b** to move with a rustling sound **2** *chiefly NAm* to steal cattle or horses ~*vt*, *chiefly NAm* to steal (e g cattle) – **rustler** *n*

[2]**rustle** *n* a quick succession or confusion of faint sounds

rusty /ˈrusti‖ˈrʌstɪ/ *adj* **1** affected (as if) by rust; *esp* stiff (as if) with rust <*the creaking of* ~ *hinges*> **2** inept and slow through lack of practice or advanced age **3a** of the colour rust **b** dulled in colour by age and use; shabby <*a* ~ *old suit of clothes*> – **rustily** *adv*, **rustiness** *n*

[1]**rut** /rut‖rʌt/ *n* **1** an annually recurrent state of readiness to copulate, in the male deer or other mammal; *also* oestrus, heat **2** the period during which rut normally occurs – often + *the*

[2]**rut** *n* **1** a track worn by habitual passage, esp of wheels on soft or uneven ground **2** an established practice; *esp* a tedious routine <*get into a* ~> – **rutted** *adj*

ruthless /ˈroohthlis‖ˈruːθlɪs/ *adj* pitiless – **ruthlessly** *adv*, **ruthlessness** *n*

-ry /-ri‖-rɪ/ – see -ERY

rye /rie‖raɪ/ *n* (the seeds, from which a wholemeal flour is made, of) a hardy grass widely grown for grain

ˌ**rye ˈwhisky** *n* a whisky distilled from rye or from rye and malt

S

s /es‖es/ *n, pl* **s's, ss** /ˈesiz‖ˈesɪz/ *often cap* (a graphic representation of or device for reproducing) the 19th letter of the English alphabet

[1]**-s** /-s, -z‖-s, -z/ *suffix* (→ *n pl*) **1a** – used to form the plural of most nouns that do not end in *s, z, sh, ch*, or postconsonantal *y* <*cats*> <*heads*> **b** – used with or without a preceding apostrophe to form the plural of abbreviations, numbers, letters, and symbols used as nouns <*MCs*> <*the 1940's*> **2** *chiefly NAm* – used to form adverbs denoting usual or repeated action or state <*always at home Sundays*>

[2]**-s** *suffix* (→ *vb*) – used to form the third person singular present of most verbs that do not end in *s, z, sh, ch*, or postconsonantal *y* <*falls*> <*takes*> <*plays*>

[1]**'s** *vb* **1** is <*she's here*> **2** has <*he's seen them*> **3** does – in questions <*what's he want?*>

[2]**'s** *pron* us – + *let* <*let's*>

-'s *suffix* (→ *n* or *pron*) – used to form the possessive of singular nouns <*boy's*>, of plural nouns not ending in *s* <*children's*>, of some pronouns <*anyone's*>, and of word groups functioning as nouns <*the man in the corner's hat*> or pronouns <*someone else's*>

Sabbatarian /sabəˈteəri·ən‖sæbəˈteərɪən/ *n* **1** a person who observes the Sabbath on Saturday in strict conformity with the 4th commandment **2** an adherent of Sabbatarianism – **Sabbatarian** *adj*

sabbath /ˈsabəth‖ˈsæbəθ/ *n* **1** *often cap* the 7th day of the week observed from Friday evening to Saturday evening as a day of rest and worship by Jews **2** *often cap* Sunday observed among Christians as a day of rest and worship **3** a midnight assembly of witches [Lattin *sabbatum*, fr Greek *sabbaton*, fr Hebrew *shabbāth*, lit., rest]

[1]**sabbatical** /səˈbatikl‖səˈbætɪkl/, **sabbatic** *adj* **1** of the sabbath <~ *laws*> **2** of or being a sabbatical

[2]**sabbatical** *n* a leave, often with pay, granted usu every 7th year (e g to a university teacher)

[1]**sable** /ˈsaybl‖ˈseɪbl/ *n* **1** (the valuable dark brown fur of) a N Asian and European flesh-eating mammal related to the martens **2** BLACK 2 – poetic or used technically in heraldry

[2]**sable** *adj* of the colour sable

sabot /ˈsaboh‖ˈsæbəʊ/ *n* a wooden shoe worn in various European countries

[1]**sabotage** /ˈsabəˌtahzh‖ˈsæbəˌtɑːʒ/ *n* **1** destructive or obstructive action carried on by a

civilian or enemy agent, intended to hinder military activity **2** deliberate subversion (e g of a plan or project) [French, fr *saboter* to clatter with sabots, botch, sabotage, fr *sabot*]

[2]**sabotage** *vt* to practise sabotage on

saboteur /ˌsabəˈtuh‖ˌsæbəˈtɜː/ *n* one who commits sabotage

[1]**sabre,** *NAm chiefly* **saber** /ˈsaybə‖ˈseɪbə/ *n* **1** a cavalry sword with a curved blade, thick back, and guard **2** a light fencing or duelling sword having an arched guard that covers the back of the hand and a tapering flexible blade with a full cutting edge along one side

[2]**sabre,** *NAm chiefly* **saber** *vt* to strike or kill with a sabre

ˈ**sabre** ˌ**rattling** *n* blustering display of military power

ˌ**sabre-toothed** ˈ**tiger** *n* an extinct big cat with long curved upper canines

sac /sak‖sæk/ *n* a (fluid-filled) pouch within an animal or plant – **saclike** *adj*

saccharin /ˈsak(ə)rin‖ˈsæk(ə)rɪn/ *n* a compound containing no calories that is several hundred times sweeter than cane sugar and is used as a sugar substitute (e g in low-calorie diets)

saccharine /ˈsak(ə)rin, -reen‖ˈsæk(ə)rɪn, -riːn/ *adj* **1** of, like, or containing sugar **2** excessively sweet; mawkish – **saccharinity** *n*

sacerdotal /ˌsasəˈdohtl‖ˌsæsəˈdəʊtl/ *adj* of priests or a priesthood – **sacerdotally** *adv*

ˌ**sacer**ˈ**dotal**ˌ**ism** /-ˌiz(ə)m‖-ˌɪz(ə)m/ *n* religious belief emphasizing the role of priests as essential mediators between God and human beings – **sacerdotalist** *n*

sachet /ˈsashay‖ˈsæʃeɪ/ *n* **1** a small usu plastic bag or packet; *esp* one holding just enough of sthg (e g shampoo or sugar) for use at 1 time **2** a small bag containing a perfumed powder used to scent clothes and linens

[1]**sack** /sak‖sæk/ *n* **1** a usu rectangular large bag (e g of paper or canvas) **2** the amount contained in a sack **3** a garment without shaping: e g **3a** a loosely fitting dress **b** a loose coat or jacket; *esp* one worn by men in the 19th c **4** dismissal from employment – usu + *get* or *give* + *the*; infml [Old English *sacc* bag, sackcloth, fr Latin *saccus* bag & Late Latin *saccus* sackcloth, both fr Greek *sakkos* bag, sackcloth] – **sackful** *n*

[2]**sack** *vt* **1** to place in a sack **2** to dismiss from a job – infml – **sacker** *n*

[3]**sack** *n* any of various dry white wines formerly imported to England from S Europe [Middle French *sec* dry, fr Latin *siccus*]

[4]**sack** *n* the plundering of a place captured in war [Middle French *sac*, fr Italian *sacco*, lit., bag, fr Latin *saccus*]

[5]**sack** *vt* **1** to plunder (e g a town) after capture **2** to strip (a place) of valuables – **sacker** *n*

sackcloth /ˈsakˌkloth‖ˈsækˌklɒθ/ *n* **1** sacking **2** a garment of sackcloth worn as a sign of mourning or penitence

[1]**sacral** /ˈsaykrəl‖ˈseɪkrəl/ *adj* of or lying near the sacrum

[2]**sacral** *adj* holy, sacred

sacrament /ˈsakrəmənt‖ˈsækrəmənt/ *n* **1** a formal religious act (e g baptism) functioning as a sign or symbol of a spiritual reality **2** *cap* the bread and wine used at Communion; *specif* the consecrated Host

sacramental /ˌsakrəˈmentl‖ˌsækrəˈmentl/ *adj* (having the character) of a sacrament – **sacramentally** *adv*

sacred /ˈsaykrid‖ˈseɪkrɪd/ *adj* **1a** dedicated or set apart for the service or worship of a god or gods **b** dedicated as a memorial <~ *to his memory*> **2a** worthy of religious veneration **b** commanding reverence and respect **3** of religion; not secular or profane – **sacredly** *adv*, **sacredness** *n*

ˌ**sacred** ˈ**cow** *n* sby or sthg granted unreasonable immunity from criticism

[1]**sacrifice** /ˈsakrifies‖ˈsækrɪfaɪs/ *n* **1** an act of offering to a deity; *esp* the killing of a victim on an altar **2** sthg offered in sacrifice **3a** destruction or surrender of one thing for the sake of another of greater worth or importance **b** sthg given up or lost <*the* ~s *made by parents*>

[2]**sacrifice** *vt* **1** to offer as a sacrifice **2** to give up or lose for the sake of an ideal or end ~ *vi* to offer up or perform rites of a sacrifice – **sacrificer** *n*

sacrificial /ˌsakriˈfish(ə)l‖ˌsækrɪˈfɪʃ(ə)l/ *adj* of or involving sacrifice – **sacrificially** *adv*

sacrilege /ˈsakrilij‖ˈsækrɪlɪdʒ/ *n* **1** a technical violation of what is sacred **2** gross irreverence toward sby or sthg sacred – **sacrilegious** *adj*, **sacrilegiously** *adv*, **sacrilegiousness** *n*

sacristan /ˈsakristən‖ˈsækrɪstən/ *n* a person in charge of the sacristy and ceremonial equipment; *also* a sexton

sacristy /ˈsakristi‖ˈsækrɪstɪ/ *n* a room in a church where sacred vessels and vestments are kept and where the clergy put on their vestments

sacrosanct /ˈsakrəsangkt‖ˈsækrəsæŋkt/ *adj* accorded the highest reverence and respect; *also* regarded with unwarranted reverence – **sacrosanctity** *n*

sacrum /ˈsaykrəm‖ˈseɪkrəm/ *n, pl* **sacra** /ˈsaykrə‖ˈseɪkrə/ the part of the vertebral column that is directly connected with or forms part of the pelvis and in humans consists of 5 united vertebrae

sad /sad‖sæd/ *adj* **-dd- 1a** affected with or expressing unhappiness **b(1)** causing or associated with unhappiness **b(2)** deplorable, regrettable <*a* ~ *decline in standards*> **2** of a dull sombre colour **3** *of baked goods* [1]HEAVY 9b – **sadly** *adv*, **sadness** *n*

sadden /ˈsadn‖ˈsædn/ *vb* to make or become sad

[1]**saddle** /ˈsadl‖ˈsædl/ *n* **1a(1)** a usu padded and leather-covered seat secured to the back of a horse, donkey, etc for the rider to sit on **a(2)** a part of a harness for a draught animal (e g a horse pulling a carriage) comparable to a saddle that is used to keep in place the strap that passes under the animal's tail **b** a seat in certain types of vehicles (e g a bicycle or agricultural tractor) **2** sthg like a saddle in shape, position, or function **3** a ridge connecting 2 peaks **4a** a large cut of meat from a sheep, hare, rabbit, deer, etc consisting of both sides of the unsplit back including both loins **b** the rear part of a male fowl's back extending to the tail **5** a saddle-shaped marking on the back of an animal – **saddleless** *adj* – **in the saddle** in control

[2]**saddle** *vt* **1** to put a saddle on **2** to encumber <*got* ~d *with the paperwork*>

ˈsaddleˌbag /-ˌbag‖-ˌbæg/ *n* a pouch or bag on the back of a horse behind the saddle, or either of a pair laid across behind the saddle or hanging over the rear wheel of a bicycle or motorcycle

saddler /ˈsadlə‖ˈsædlə/ *n* one who makes, repairs, or sells furnishings (e g saddles) for horses

saddlery /ˈsadləri‖ˈsædlərɪ/ *n* **1** the trade, articles of trade, or shop of a saddler **2** a set of the equipment used for sitting on and controlling a riding horse

sadism /ˈsaydiz(ə)m‖ˈseɪdɪz(ə)m/ *n* **1** a sexual perversion in which pleasure is obtained by inflicting physical or mental pain on others **2** delight in inflicting pain [Marquis (really Count) de *Sade* (1740-1814), French writer] – **sadist** *adj or n*, **sadistic** *adj*, **sadistically** *adv*

sadomasochism /ˌsaydohˈmasəkiz(ə)m‖ˌseɪdəʊˈmæsəkɪz(ə)m/ *n* sadism and masochism occurring together in the same person – **sadomasochist** *n*, **sadomasochistic** *adj*

sae /ˌesˌayˈee‖ˌesˌeɪˈiː/ *n* a stamped addressed envelope

[1]**safari** /səˈfahri‖səˈfɑːrɪ/ *n* (the caravan and equipment of) a hunting or scientific expedition, esp in E Africa [Arabic *safarīy* of a trip] – **safari** *vi*

[2]**safari** *adj* made of lightweight material, esp cotton, and typically having 2 breast pockets and a belt

saˈfari ˌpark *n* a park stocked with usu big game animals (e g lions) so that visitors can observe them in natural-appearing surroundings

[1]**safe** /sayf‖seɪf/ *adj* **1** freed from harm or risk **2** secure from threat of danger, harm, or loss **3** affording safety from danger **4a** not threatening or entailing danger <*is your dog* ~?> **b** unlikely to cause controversy <*keeping to* ~ *subjects*> **5a** not liable to take risks **b** trustworthy, reliable **6** being a constituency where the MP was elected with a large majority – **safe** *adv*, **safely** *adv*, **safeness** *n*

[2]**safe** *n* **1** a room or receptacle for the safe storage of valuables **2** a receptacle, esp a cupboard, for the temporary storage of fresh and cooked foods that typically has at least 1 side of wire mesh to allow ventilation while preventing flies from entering

ˌsafe-ˈconduct *n* (a document authorizing) protection given to a person passing through a military zone or occupied area

[1]**ˈsafeˌguard** /-ˌgahd‖-ˌgɑːd/ *n* **1** a pass, safe-conduct **2** a precautionary measure or stipulation

[2]**safeguard** *vt* **1** to provide a safeguard for **2** to make safe; protect

ˌsafeˈkeeping /-ˈkeeping‖-ˈkiːpɪŋ/ *n* keeping safe or being kept safe

safety /ˈsayfti‖ˈseɪftɪ/ *n* **1** the condition of being safe from causing or suffering hurt, injury, or loss **2** SAFETY CATCH **3** a billiard shot made with no attempt to score or so as to leave the balls in an unfavourable position for the opponent

ˈsafety ˌbelt *n* a belt fastening a person to an object to prevent falling or injury

ˈsafety ˌcatch *n* a device (e g on a gun or machine) designed to prevent accidental use

ˈsafety ˌcurtain *n* a fireproof curtain which can isolate the stage from the auditorium in case of fire

ˈsafety ˌglass *n* glass strengthened by tempering so that when broken, it shatters into relatively safe rounded granules

ˈsafety ˌlamp *n* a miner's lamp constructed to avoid ignition of inflammable gas, usu by enclosing the flame in wire gauze

ˈsafety ˌmatch *n* a match capable of being ignited only on a specially prepared surface

ˈsafety ˌpin *n* a pin in the form of a clasp with a guard covering its point when fastened

ˈsafety ˌrazor *n* a razor with a guard for the blade

ˈsafety ˌvalve *n* **1** an automatic escape or relief valve (e g for a steam boiler) **2** an outlet for pent-up energy or emotion <*a* ~ *for life's frustrations*>

saffron /ˈsafron, ˈsafrən‖ˈsæfrɒn, ˈsæfrən/ *n* **1** (the deep orange aromatic pungent dried stigmas, used to colour and flavour foods, of) a purple-flowered crocus **2** orange-yellow

[1]**sag** /sag‖sæg/ *vi* **-gg- 1** to droop, sink, or settle (as if) from weight, pressure, or loss of tautness **2** to lose firmness or vigour <*spirits* ~ging *from overwork*> **3** to fail to stimulate or retain interest <~ged *a bit in the last act*>

[2]**sag** *n* **1** a sagging part <*the* ~ *in a rope*> **2** an instance or amount of sagging <~ *is inevitable in a heavy unsupported span*>

saga /ˈsahgə‖ˈsɑːgə/ *n* **1** (a modern heroic narrative resembling) a medieval Icelandic narrative dealing with historic or legendary figures and events **2** a long detailed account **3** a roman-fleuve

sagacious /səˈgayshəs‖səˈgeɪʃəs/ *adj* **1** of keen and farsighted judgment <~ *judge of character*> **2** prompted by or indicating acute discernment <~ *purchase of stock*> – **sagaciously** *adv*, **sagaciousness, sagacity** *n*

[1]**sage** /sayj‖seɪdʒ/ *adj* **1** wise on account of reflection and experience **2** proceeding from or indicating wisdom and sound judgment <~ *counsel*> [Old French, deriv of Latin *sapere* to taste, have good taste, be wise] – **sagely** *adv*, **sageness** *n*

[2]**sage** *n* **1** sby (e g a great philosopher) renowned for wise teachings **2** a venerable man of sound judgment

[3]**sage** *n* **1** a plant of the mint family whose greyish green aromatic leaves are used esp in flavouring meat **2** sagebrush [Middle French *sauge*, fr Latin *salvia*, fr *salvus* healthy]

ˈsageˌbrush /-ˌbrush‖-ˌbrʌʃ/ *n* any of several composite undershrubs that cover large areas of plains in the W USA

Sagittarius /ˌsajiˈteəri·əs‖ˌsædʒɪˈteərɪəs/ *n* (sby born under) the 9th sign of the zodiac in astrology, pictured as a centaur shooting an arrow – **Sagittarian** *adj or n*

sago /ˈsaygoh‖ˈseɪgəʊ/ *n, pl* **sagos** a dry powdered starch prepared from the pith of a sago palm and used esp as a food (e g in a milk pudding)

sahib /ˈsah·(h)ib‖ˈsɑː(h)ɪb/ *n* sir, master – used,

esp among Hindus and Muslims in colonial India, when addressing or speaking of a European of some social or official status

said /sed‖sed/ *adj* aforementioned

[1]**sail** /sayl‖seɪl/ *n, pl* **sails,** (*1b*) **sail** *also* **sails 1a** an expanse of fabric which is spread to catch or deflect the wind as a means of propelling a ship, sand yacht, etc **b** (a ship equipped with) sails **2** sthg like a sail in function or form <*the* ~s *of a windmill*> **3** a voyage by ship <*a 5-day* ~ *from the nearest port*> – **sailed** *adj* – **under sail** in motion with sails set

[2]**sail** *vi* **1a** to travel in a boat or ship **b** to make journeys in or manage a sailing boat for pleasure **2a** to travel on water, esp by the action of wind on sails **b** to move without visible effort or in a stately manner **3** to begin a journey by water <~ *with the tide*> ~ *vt* **1** to travel over (a body of water) in a ship <~ *the 7 seas*> **2** to direct or manage the operation of (a ship or boat) – **sailable** *adj* – **sail into** to attack vigorously or sharply – **sail close to the wind 1** to sail as nearly as possible against the main force of the wind **2** to be near to dishonesty or improper behaviour

ˈ**sail,board** /-ˌbawd‖-ˌbɔːd/ *n* a flat buoyant board that is equipped with a sail, centreboard, and rudder and is used in the sport of wind-surfing

ˈ**sail,cloth** /-ˌkloth‖-ˌklɒθ/ *n* a heavy canvas used for sails, tents, or upholstery; *also* a lightweight canvas used for clothing

ˈ**sailing ˌboat** /ˈsayling‖ˈseɪlɪŋ/ *n* a boat fitted with sails for propulsion

sailor /ˈsaylə‖ˈseɪlə/ *n* **1a** a seaman, mariner **b** a member of a ship's crew other than an officer **2** a traveller by water; *esp* one considered with reference to any tendency to seasickness <*a bad* ~>

sailplane /ˈsaylˌplayn‖ˈseɪlˌpleɪn/ *n* a glider designed to rise in an upward air current – **sailplane** *vi*, **sailplaner** *n*

saint /saynt‖seɪnt; *before a name usu* s(ə)nt‖s(ə)nt/ *n* **1** a person officially recognized through canonization as being outstandingly holy and so worthy of veneration **2a** any of the spirits of the departed in heaven **b** ANGEL 1 <Saint *Michael the Archangel*> **3** any (of various Christian groups regarding themselves as) of God's chosen people **4** a person of outstanding piety or virtue – **sainthood** *n*, **saintlike** *adj*, **saintly** *adj*, **saintliness** *n*

ˈ**saint's ˌday** /ˈsaynts‖ˈseɪnts/ *n* a day in a church calendar on which a saint is commemorated

saith /seth, sayth‖seθ, seɪθ/ *archaic pres 3 sing of* SAY

[1]**sake** /sayk‖seɪk/ *n* – **for the sake of, for someone's/something's sake 1** for the purpose of <for the sake of *argument*> **2** so as to get, keep, or improve <for *conscience* sake> <*study Latin* for *its own* sake> **3** so as to help, please, or honour <*to go to the sea* for the sake of *the children*> <for *old times'* sake> **–for God's/goodness/Heaven's/pity's sake** – used in protest or supplication

[2]**sake, saki** /ˈsahki‖ˈsɑːkɪ/ *n* a Japanese alcoholic drink of fermented rice

[1]**salaam** /səˈlahm‖səˈlɑːm/ *n* **1** a ceremonial greeting in E countries **2** an obeisance made by bowing low and placing the right palm on the forehead [Arabic *salām*, lit., peace]

[2]**salaam** *vb* to perform a salaam (to)

salable, saleable /ˈsayləbl‖ˈseɪləbl/ *adj* capable of being or fit to be sold – **salability** *n*

salacious /səˈlayshəs‖səˈleɪʃəs/ *adj* **1** arousing or appealing to sexual desire **2** lecherous, lustful – **salaciously** *adv*, **salaciousness** *n*

salad /ˈsaləd‖ˈsæləd/ *n* **1a** (mixed) raw vegetables (e g lettuce, watercress, or tomato) often served with a dressing **b** a dish of raw or (cold) cooked foods often cut into small pieces and combined with a dressing <*fruit* ~> **2** a vegetable or herb eaten raw (in salad); *esp* lettuce [Middle French *salade*, fr Old Provençal *salada*, fr *salar* to salt, fr *sal* salt, fr Latin]

ˈ**salad ˌdays** *n pl* time of youthful inexperience or indiscretion

ˈ**salad ˌoil** *n* an edible vegetable oil (e g olive oil) used in salad dressings

salamander /ˈsaləˌmandə, ˌ--ˈ--‖ˈsæləˌmændə, ˌ--ˈ--/ *n* **1** a mythical animal with the power to endure fire without harm **2** any of numerous scaleless amphibians superficially resembling lizards – **salamandrine** *adj*

salami /səˈlahmi‖səˈlɑːmɪ/ *n, pl* **salamis** a highly seasoned, esp pork, sausage often containing garlic

salary /ˈsaləri‖ˈsælərɪ/ *n* a fixed usu monthly payment for regular services, esp of a nonmanual kind [Latin *salarium* salt money, salary, fr *sal* salt] – **salaried** *adj*

sale /sayl‖seɪl/ *n* **1** the act or an instance of selling; *specif* the transfer of ownership of and title to property or goods from one person to another for a price **2a** opportunity of selling or being sold <*counting on a large* ~ *for the new product*> **b** quantity sold – often pl with sing. meaning <*total* ~s *rose last year*> **3** an event at which goods are offered for sale <*an antiques* ~> **4** public disposal to the highest bidder **5** a selling of goods at bargain prices **6a** *pl* operations and activities involved in promoting and selling goods or services <*manager in charge of* ~s> **b** gross receipts obtained from selling – **on/for sale** available for purchase

saleable /ˈsayləbl‖ˈseɪləbl/ *adj* salable

saleroom /ˈsaylroohm, -room‖ˈseɪlruːm, -rʊm/ *n, chiefly Br* a place where goods are displayed for sale, esp by auction

sales /saylz‖seɪlz/ *adj* of, engaged in, or used in selling

ˈ**sales,clerk** /-ˌklahk‖-ˌklɑːk; *NAm* -ˌkluhk‖-ˌklɜːk/ *n* SHOP ASSISTANT

ˈ**sales,girl** /-ˌguhl‖-ˌgɜːl/ *n* a female shop assistant

ˈ**sales,lady** /-ˌlaydi‖-ˌleɪdɪ/ *n* a female shop assistant

ˈ**salesman** /-mən‖-mən/, *fem* ˈ**sales,woman** *n, pl* **salesmen** /~/, *fem* ˈ**sales,women** a salesperson – **salesmanship** *n*

ˈ**sales,person** /-ˌpuhs(ə)n‖-ˌpɜːs(ə)n/ *n* sby employed to sell goods or a service (e g in a shop or within an assigned territory)

ˈ**sales repre,sentative** *n* a person who

travels, usu in an assigned territory, to win orders for his/her firm's goods

[1]**salient** /'saylyənt, -li·ənt||'seɪljənt, -lɪənt/ *adj* **1** pointing upwards or outwards <*a ~ angle*> **2a** projecting beyond a line or level **b** standing out conspicuously <*~ characteristics*> – **saliently** *adv*, **salience, saliency** *n*

[2]**salient** *n* an outwardly projecting part of a fortification, trench system, or line of defence

[1]**saline** /'say,lien||'seɪ,laɪn/ *adj* **1** (consisting) of, containing, or resembling salt <*a ~ solution*> **2** *esp of a purgative* containing salts of potassium, sodium, or magnesium – **salinity** *n*

[2]**saline** *n* **1** a purgative salt of potassium, sodium, or magnesium **2** a saline solution (similar in concentration to body fluids)

saliva /sə'lievə||sə'laɪvə/ *n* a slightly alkaline mixture of water, protein, salts, and often enzymes that is secreted into the mouth by glands, and that lubricates ingested food and often begins the breakdown of starches – **salivary** *adj*

salivate /'salivayt||'sælɪveɪt/ *vi* to have an (excessive) flow of saliva – **salivation** *n*

[1]**sallow** /'saloh||'sæləʊ/ *n* any of various Old World broad-leaved willows some of which are important sources of charcoal

[2]**sallow** *adj* of a sickly yellowish colour – **sallowish** *adj*, **sallowness** *n*

[1]**sally** /'sali||'sælɪ/ *adj, chiefly dial* sallow

[2]**sally** *n* **1** a rushing forth; *esp* a sortie of troops from a besieged position **2a** a brief outbreak <*a ~ of rage*> **b** a witty or penetrating remark **3** a short excursion; a jaunt

[3]**sally** *vi* **1** to rush out or issue forth suddenly **2** to set out (e g on a journey) – usu + *forth*

salmon /'samən||'sæmən/ *n* **1** (any of various fishes related to) a large soft-finned game and food fish of the N Atlantic that is highly valued for its pink flesh **2** orangy-pink – **salmonoid** *adj*

salmonella /,salmə'nelə||,sælmə'nelə/ *n, pl* **salmonellae** /-li||-lɪ/, **salmonellas, salmonella** any of a genus of bacteria that cause diseases, esp food poisoning, in warm-blooded animals [Daniel E *Salmon* (1850-1914), US veterinarian] – **salmonellosis** *n*

salon /'salonh||'sælɑ̃/ *n* **1** an elegant reception room or living room **2** a gathering of literary figures, statesmen, etc held at the home of a prominent person and common in the 17th and 18th c **3** *cap* an exhibition, esp in France, of works of art by living artists **4** a stylish business establishment or shop <*a beauty ~*>

saloon /sə'loohn||sə'lu:n/ *n* **1** a public apartment or hall (e g a ballroom, exhibition room, or shipboard social area) **2** a railway carriage with no compartments **3** *Br* an enclosed motor car having no partition between the driver and passengers **4a** *Br* SALOON BAR **b** *NAm* a room or establishment in which alcoholic beverages are sold and consumed

sa'loon ,bar *n, Br* a comfortable, well-furnished, and often relatively expensive bar in a public house

salsify /'salsifie, -fi||'sælsɪfaɪ, -fɪ/ *n* (the long tapering edible root of) a European composite plant

[1]**salt** /sawlt, solt||sɔ:lt, sɒlt/ *n* **1a** sodium chloride, occurring naturally esp as a mineral deposit and dissolved in sea water, and used esp for seasoning or preserving **b** any of numerous compounds resulting from replacement of (part of) the hydrogen ion of an acid by a (radical acting like a) metal **c** *pl* **c(1)** a mixture of the salts of alkali metals or magnesium (e g Epsom salts) used as a purgative **c(2)** SMELLING SALTS **2a** an ingredient that imparts savour, piquancy, or zest **b** sharpness of wit **3** an experienced sailor <*a tale worthy of an old ~*> **4** a saltcellar – **above/below the salt** placed, esp seated, in a socially advantageous/disadvantageous position – **worth one's salt** worthy of respect; competent, effective

[2]**salt** *vt* **1** to treat, provide, season, or preserve with common salt or brine **2** to give flavour or piquancy to (e g a story) **3** to enrich (e g a mine) fraudulently by adding valuable matter, esp mineral ores **4** to sprinkle (as if) with a salt <*~ing clouds with silver iodide*> – **salter** *n*

[3]**salt** *adj* **1a** saline, salty **b** being or inducing a taste similar to that of common salt that is one of the 4 basic taste sensations **2** cured or seasoned with salt; salted <*~ pork*> **3** containing, overflowed by, or growing in salt water <*a ~ marsh*> **4** sharp, pungent <*a ~ wit* – John Buchan> – **saltness** *n*

salt away *vt* to put by in reserve; save <salted *his money* away>

'salt,cellar /-,selə||-,selə/ *n* a cruet for salt

saltire /'saltie·ə||'sæltaɪə/ *n* a diagonal heraldic cross

'salt ,lick *n* LICK 3

'salt,pan /-,pan||-,pæn/ *n* a depression (e g made in rock) or vessel for evaporating brine

,salt'petre, *NAm* **saltpeter** /-'peetə||-'pi:tə/ *n* POTASSIUM NITRATE [Middle French *salpetre*, fr Medieval Latin *sal petrae*, lit., salt of the rock]

,salt'water /-'wawtə||-'wɔ:tə/ *adj* of, living in, or being salt water

salty /'sawlti, 'solti||'sɔ:ltɪ, 'sɒltɪ/ *adj* **1** of, seasoned with, or containing salt **2** having a taste of (too much) salt **3a** piquant, witty **b** earthy, coarse – **saltily** *adv*, **saltiness** *n*

salubrious /sə'l(y)oohbri·əs||sə'l(j)u:brɪəs/ *adj* **1** favourable to health or well-being <*a ~ climate*> **2** RESPECTABLE 2 <*not a very ~ district*> – **salubriously** *adv*, **salubriousness, salubrity** *n*

salutary /'salyoot(ə)ri||'sæljʊt(ə)rɪ/ *adj* having a beneficial or edifying effect – **salutariness** *n*, **salutarily** *adv*

salutation /,salyoo'taysh(ə)n||,sæljʊ'teɪʃ(ə)n/ *n* **1a** an expression of greeting or courtesy by word or gesture **b** *pl* regards **2** the word or phrase of greeting (e g *Dear Sir*) that conventionally comes immediately before the body of a letter or speech – **salutational, salutatory** *adj*

[1]**salute** /sə'l(y)ooht||sə'l(j)u:t/ *vt* **1** to address with expressions of greeting, goodwill, or respect **2a** to honour by a conventional military or naval ceremony **b** to show respect and recognition to (a military superior) by assuming a prescribed position **c** to praise <*~d her courage*> **3** *archaic* to become apparent to (one of the senses) ~*vi* to make a salute – **saluter** *n*

[2]**salute** *n* **1** a greeting, salutation **2a** a sign or ceremony expressing goodwill or respect <*the festival was a ~ to the arts*> **b** an act of saluting a military superior; *also* the position (e g of the hand or weapon) or the entire attitude of a person saluting a superior

[1]**salvage** /'salvij‖'sælvɪdʒ/ *n* **1a** compensation paid to those who save property from loss or damage; *esp* compensation paid for saving a ship from wreckage or capture **b** the act of saving or rescuing a ship or its cargo **c** the act of saving or rescuing property in danger (e g from fire) **2a** property saved from a calamity (e g a wreck or fire) **b** sthg of use or value extracted from waste material

[2]**salvage** *vt* to rescue or save (e g from wreckage or ruin) – **salvager** *n*, **salvageable** *adj*, **salvageability** *n*

salvation /sal'vaysh(ə)n‖sæl'veɪʃ(ə)n/ *n* **1** (an agent or means which effects) deliverance from the power and effects of sin **2** deliverance from danger, difficulty, or destruction – **salvational** *adj*

Sal,vation 'Army *n* an international Christian group organized on military lines and founded in 1865 by William Booth for evangelizing and performing social work among the poor

Salvationist /sal'vayshənist‖sæl'veɪʃənɪst/ *n* a member of the Salvation Army – **salvationist** *adj, often cap*

[1]**salve** /salv, sahv‖sælv, sɑːv/ *n* **1** an ointment for application to wounds or sores **2** a soothing influence or agency <*a ~ to their hurt feelings*>

[2]**salve** *vt* **1** to remedy (as if) with a salve **2** to ease <*~ a troubled conscience*>

salver /'salvə‖'sælvə/ *n* a tray; *esp* an ornamental tray (e g of silver) on which food or beverages are served or letters and visiting cards are presented [French *salve*, fr Spanish *salva* sampling of food to detect poison, tray, fr *salvar* to save, sample food to detect poison]

salvia /'salvi·ə‖'sælvɪə/ *n* any of a genus of herbs or shrubs of the mint family; *esp* one grown for its scarlet or purple flowers

salvo /'salvoh‖'sælvəʊ/ *n, pl* **salvos, salvoes** **1a** a simultaneous discharge of 2 or more guns or missiles in military or naval action or as a salute **b** the release at one moment of several bombs or missiles from an aircraft **2** a sudden or emphatic burst (e g of cheering or approbation)

sal volatile /,sal və'latili‖,sæl və'lætɪlɪ/ *n* an aromatic solution of ammonium carbonate in alcohol or ammonia water used as smelling salts

Samaritan /sə'marit(ə)n‖sə'mærɪt(ə)n/ *n* **1** a native or inhabitant of ancient Samaria **2a** *often not cap* one who selflessly gives aid to those in distress **b** a member of an organization that offers help to those in despair [Late Latin *samaritanus*, fr Greek *samaritēs*, fr *Samaria*, district & city of ancient Palestine; sense 2 fr the parable of the good Samaritan, Luke 10:30–37] – **samaritan** *adj, often cap*

samba /'sambə‖'sæmbə/ *n* (the music for) a Brazilian dance of African origin characterized by a dip and spring upwards at each beat of the music – **samba** *vi*

[1]**same** /saym‖seɪm/ *adj* **1** being 1 single thing, person, or group; identical <*wear the ~ shoes for a week*> – often as an intensive <*born in this very ~ house*> **2** being the specified one or ones – + *as* or *that* <*made the ~ mistake as last time*> **3** corresponding so closely as to be indistinguishable <*2 brothers have the ~ nose*> – **at the same time** for all that; nevertheless

[2]**same** *pron, pl* **same** **1** *the* same thing, person, or group <*do the ~ for you*> **2** sthg previously mentioned <*ordered a drink and refused to pay for ~*>

[3]**same** *adv* in the same manner – + *the*

sameness /'saymnis‖'seɪmnɪs/ *n* **1** identity, similarity **2** monotony, uniformity

samovar /'samәvah, ,--'-‖'sæmәvɑː, ,--'-/ *n* a metal urn with a tap at its base and an interior heating tube, that is used, esp in Russia, to boil water for tea [Russian, fr *samo-* self + *varit'* to boil]

sampan /'sam,pan‖'sæm,pæn/ *n* a small flat-bottomed boat used in rivers and harbours in the Far East

[1]**sample** /'sahmpl‖'sɑːmpl/ *n* **1** an item serving to show the character or quality of a larger whole or group **2** a part of a statistical population whose properties are studied to gain information about the whole

[2]**sample** *vt* to take a sample of or from; *esp* to test the quality of by a sample

[3]**sample** *adj* intended as an example

[1]**sampler** /'sahmplə‖'sɑːmplə/ *n* a decorative piece of needlework typically having letters or verses embroidered on it in various stitches as an example of skill

[2]**sampler** *n* **1** sby or sthg that collects, prepares, or examines samples **2** *NAm* a collection of representative specimens <*a ~ of 18 poets*>

samurai /'sam(y)oo,rie‖'sæm(j)ʊ,raɪ/ *n, pl* **samurai** **1** a military retainer of a Japanese feudal baron **2** the warrior aristocracy of Japan

sanatorium /,sanə'tawri·əm‖,sænə'tɔːrɪəm/ *n, pl* **sanatoriums, sanatoria** /-ri·ə‖-rɪə/ an establishment that provides therapy, rest, or recuperation for convalescents, the chronically ill, etc

sanctify /'sangkti,fie‖'sæŋktɪ,faɪ/ *vt* **1** to set apart for a sacred purpose or for religious use **2** to free from sin **3** to give moral or social sanction to – **sanctification** *n*

sanctimonious /,sangkti'mohnyəs, -ni·əs‖,sæŋktɪ'məʊnjəs, -nɪəs/ *adj* self-righteous – **sanctimoniously** *adv*, **sanctimoniousness** *n*

[1]**sanction** /'sangksh(ə)n‖'sæŋkʃ(ə)n/ *n* **1** a formal ecclesiastical decree **2** sthg that makes an oath or moral precept binding **3** a penalty annexed to an offence **4a** a consideration that determines moral action or judgment **b** a mechanism of social control (e g shame) for enforcing a society's standards **c** official permission or authoritative ratification **5** an economic or military coercive measure adopted to force a nation to conform to international law

[2]**sanction** *vt* **1** to make valid; ratify **2** to give authoritative consent to

sanctity /'sangktəti‖'sæŋktətɪ/ *n* **1** holiness of life and character **2** the quality or state of being holy or sacred

sanctuary /'sangktyoo(ə)ri, -chəri‖'sæŋktjʊ-

(ə)rɪ, -tʃərɪ/ *n* **1** a consecrated place: e g **1a** the ancient temple at Jerusalem or its holy of holies **b** the most sacred part of a religious building; *esp* the part of a Christian church in which the altar is placed **c** a place (e g a church or a temple) for worship **2a(1)** a place of refuge and protection **a(2)** a refuge for (endangered) wildlife where predators are controlled and hunting is illegal <*a bird* ~> **b** the immunity from law attached to a sanctuary

sanctum /'sangktəm‖'sæŋktəm/ *n, pl* **sanctums** *also* **sancta** /-tə‖-tə/ a place of total privacy and security (e g a study)

Sanctus /'sangktəs‖'sæŋktəs/ *n* a hymn of adoration sung or said before the prayer of consecration in the celebration of the Eucharist

[1]**sand** /sand‖sænd/ *n* **1** loose granular particles smaller than gravel and coarser than silt that result from the disintegration of (silica-rich) rocks **2** an area of sand; a beach – usu pl with sing. meaning **3** moments of time measured (as if) with an hourglass – usu pl with sing. meaning **4** yellowish grey

[2]**sand** *vt* **1** to sprinkle (as if) with sand **2** to cover or choke with sand – usu + *up* **3** to smooth or dress by grinding or rubbing with an abrasive (e g sandpaper) – often + *down* – **sander** *n*

sandal /'sandl‖'sændl/ *n* a shoe consisting of a sole held on to the foot by straps or thongs

'sandalˌwood /-ˌwood‖-ˌwʊd/ *n* **1** (the compact close-grained fragrant yellowish heartwood, used in ornamental carving and cabinetwork, of) an Indo-Malayan tree **2** (any of various trees yielding) fragrant wood similar to true sandalwood

[1]**sandbag** /'sandˌbag‖'sændˌbæg/ *n* a bag filled with sand and used in usu temporary fortifications or constructions, as ballast, or as a weapon

[2]**sandbag** *vt* **-gg-** to barricade, stop up, or weight with sandbags

'sandˌbank /-ˌbangk‖-ˌbæŋk/ *n* a large deposit of sand, esp in a river or coastal waters

'sandˌbar /-ˌbah‖-ˌbɑː/ *n* a sandbank

'sandˌblast /-ˌblahst‖-ˌblɑːst/ *vt or n* (to treat with) a high-speed jet of sand propelled by air or steam (e g for cutting or cleaning glass or stone) – **sandblaster** *n*

'sandˌboy /-ˌboy‖-ˌbɔɪ/ *n* sby who is cheerfully absorbed or engrossed – chiefly in *happy as a sandboy*

'sandˌcastle /-ˌkahsl‖-ˌkɑːsl/ *n* a model of a castle made in damp sand, esp at the seaside

'sand ˌfly *n* any of various small biting two-winged flies

[1]**'sandˌpaper** /-ˌpaypə‖-ˌpeɪpə/ *n* paper to which a thin layer of sand has been glued for use as an abrasive; *broadly* any abrasive paper (e g glasspaper) – **sandpapery** *adj*

[2]**sandpaper** *vt* to rub (as if) with sandpaper

'sandˌpiper /-ˌpiepə‖-ˌpaɪpə/ *n* any of numerous small wading birds with longer bills than the plovers

'sandˌpit /-ˌpit‖-ˌpɪt/ *n* an enclosure containing sand for children to play in

'sandˌshoe /-ˌshooh‖-ˌʃuː/ *n, chiefly Br* a plimsoll

'sandˌstone /-ˌstohn‖-ˌstəʊn/ *n* a sedimentary rock consisting of cemented (quartz) sand

'sandˌstorm /-ˌstawm‖-ˌstɔːm/ *n* a storm driving clouds of sand, esp in a desert

[1]**sandwich** /'san(d)wij, -wich‖'sæn(d)wɪdʒ, -wɪtʃ/ *n* **1a** two slices of usu buttered bread containing a layer of any of various sweet or savoury foods **b** a sponge cake containing a filling **2** sthg like a sandwich in having a layered or banded arrangement [John Montagu, 4th Earl of *Sandwich* (1718-92), English diplomat]

[2]**sandwich** *vt* **1** to insert *between* 2 things of a different quality or character **2** to create room or time for – often + *in* or *between*

'sandwich ˌboard *n* either of 2 boards hung at the front of and behind the body by straps from the shoulders and used esp for advertising

'sandwich ˌcourse *n* a British vocational course consisting of alternate periods of some months' duration in college and in employment

sandy /'sandi‖'sændɪ/ *adj* **1** consisting of, containing, or sprinkled with sand **2** resembling sand in colour or texture – **sandiness** *n*

sane /sayn‖seɪn/ *adj* (produced by a mind that is) mentally sound; able to anticipate and appraise the effect of one's actions – **sanely** *adv*, **saneness** *n*

sang /sang‖sæŋ/ *past of* SING

sangfroid /ˌsong'frwah‖ˌsɒŋ'frwɑː/ *n* imperturbability, esp under strain [French *sang-froid*, lit., cold blood]

sangria /sang'gree·ə‖sæŋ'griːə/, **sangria** /'sang·gri·ə, ~‖'sæŋgrɪə, ~/ *n* a usu cold punch made of red wine, fruit juice, and soda water

sanguinary /'sang·gwin(ə)ri‖'sæŋgwɪn(ə)rɪ/ *adj* **1** bloodthirsty, murderous **2** accompanied by bloodshed **3** readily punishing with death *USE* fml – **sanguinarily** *adv*

sanguine /'sang·gwin‖'sæŋgwɪn/ *adj* **1** (having the bodily conformation and temperament marked by sturdiness, high colour, and cheerfulness held to be characteristic of sby) having blood as the predominating bodily humour – used in medieval physiology **2** confident, optimistic **3a** SANGUINARY 1 **b** ruddy *USE* (*3*) fml – **sanguinity** *n*

sanitary /'sanit(ə)ri‖'sænɪt(ə)rɪ/ *adj* **1** of or promoting health <~ *measures*> **2** free from danger to health

'sanitary ˌtowel *n* a disposable absorbent pad worn after childbirth or during menstruation to absorb the flow from the womb

sanitation /ˌsani'taysh(ə)n‖ˌsænɪ'teɪʃ(ə)n/ *n* (the promotion of hygiene and prevention of disease by) maintenance or improvement of sanitary conditions – **sanitate** *vt*

sanity /'sanəti‖'sænətɪ/ *n* being sane; *esp* soundness or health of mind

sank /sangk‖sæŋk/ *past of* SINK

sans /sanz‖sænz/ *prep, archaic* without

Sanskrit /'sanskrit‖'sænskrɪt/ *n* an ancient sacred Indic language of India and of Hinduism – **Sanskrit** *adj*

sans serif, sanserif /ˌsan 'serif‖ˌsæn 'serɪf/ *n* a letter or typeface with no serifs

Santa Claus /'santə ˌklawz, ˌ-- '-‖'sæntə

ˌklɔːz, ˌ-- ˈ-/ *n* FATHER CHRISTMAS [Dutch *Sinterklaas*, alteration of *Sint Nikolaas* Saint Nicholas (*fl* 4th c), bishop of Myra in Asia Minor and patron saint of children]

[1]**sap** /sap‖sæp/ *n* **1a** a watery solution that circulates through a plant's vascular system **b** (a fluid essential to life or) bodily health and vigour **2** a foolish gullible person – infml

[2]**sap** *vt* **-pp-** to drain or deprive of sap

[3]**sap** *n* the extension of a trench from within the trench itself to a point near an enemy's fortifications

[4]**sap** *vb* **-pp-** *vi* to proceed by or dig a sap ~ *vt* **1** to destroy (as if) by undermining < ~ped *the morale of their troops*> **2** to weaken or exhaust gradually **3** to operate against or pierce by a sap

sapient /ˈsaypyənt‖ˈseɪpjənt/ *adj* possessing or expressing great wisdom or discernment – fml – **sapience** *n*, **sapiently** *adv*

sapless /ˈsaplis‖ˈsæplɪs/ *adj* feeble, lacking vigour – **saplessness** *n*

sapling /ˈsapling‖ˈsæplɪŋ/ *n* **1** a young tree **2** YOUTH 2a

sapper /ˈsapə‖ˈsæpə/ *n* a (private) soldier of the Royal Engineers

sapphic /ˈsafik‖ˈsæfɪk/ *adj* **1** (consisting) of a 4-line stanza made up of chiefly trochaic and dactylic feet **2** lesbian [*Sappho* (*fl* about 600 BC), Greek poetess & reputed homosexual]

sapphire /ˈsafie·ə‖ˈsæfaɪə/ *n* **1** a semitransparent corundum of a colour other than red, used as a gem; *esp* a transparent rich blue sapphire **2** deep purplish blue – **sapphire** *adj*

sappy /ˈsapi‖ˈsæpɪ/ *adj* **1** resembling or consisting largely of sapwood **2** *NAm* SOPPY 2 – **sappiness** *n*

sapwood /ˈsapˌwood‖ˈsæpˌwʊd/ *n* the younger softer usu lighter-coloured living outer part of wood that lies between the bark and the heartwood

saraband, sarabande /ˈsarəband, ˌ--ˈ-‖ˈsærəbænd, ˌ--ˈ-/ *n* **1** a stately court dance resembling the minuet **2** a musical composition or movement in slow triple time with the accent on the second beat

sarcasm /ˈsahkaz(ə)m‖ˈsɑːkæz(ə)m/ *n* (the use of) caustic and often ironic language to express contempt or bitterness, esp towards an individual [French *sarcasme*, fr Late Latin *sarcasmos*, fr Greek *sarkasmos*, fr *sarkazein* to tear flesh, bite the lips in rage, sneer, fr *sark-*, *sarx* flesh] – **sarcastic** *adj*, **sarcastically** *adv*

sarcophagus /sahˈkofəgəs‖sɑːˈkɒfəgəs/ *n, pl* **sarcophagi** /-gie‖-gaɪ/ *also* **sarcophaguses** a stone coffin [L *sarcophagus* (*lapis*) limestone used for coffins, fr Gk (*lithos*) *sarkophagos*, lit., flesh-eating stone, fr *sark*, *sarx* flesh + *phagein* to eat]

sardine /sahˈdeen‖sɑːˈdiːn/ *n* the young of the European pilchard, or another small or immature fish, when of a size suitable for preserving for food

sardonic /sahˈdonik‖sɑːˈdɒnɪk/ *adj* disdainfully or cynically humorous; derisively mocking – **sardonically** *adv*

sarge /sahj‖sɑːdʒ/ *n* a sergeant – infml

sari *also* **saree** /ˈsahri‖ˈsɑːrɪ/ *n* a garment worn by Hindu women that consists of a length of lightweight cloth draped so that one end forms a skirt and the other a head or shoulder covering

sarky /ˈsahki‖ˈsɑːkɪ/ *adj, Br* sarcastic – infml

sarong /səˈrong, ˈsahrong‖səˈrɒŋ, ˈsɑːrɒŋ/ *n* **1** a loose skirt made of a long strip of cloth wrapped round the body and traditionally worn by men and women in Malaysia and the Pacific islands **2** cloth for sarongs

sarsaparilla /ˌsahs(ə)pəˈrilə‖ˌsɑːs(ə)pəˈrɪlə/ *n* **1** (the dried roots, used esp as a flavouring, of) any of various tropical American trailing plants of the lily family **2** *chiefly NAm* a sweetened fizzy drink flavoured with birch oil and sassafras

sartorial /sahˈtawri·əl‖sɑːˈtɔːrɪəl/ *adj* with regard to clothing < ~ *elegance*> – fml; humor; used esp with reference to men – **sartorially** *adv*

[1]**sash** /sash‖sæʃ/ *n* a band of cloth worn round the waist or over 1 shoulder as a dress accessory or as the emblem of an honorary or military order [Arabic *shāsh* muslin] – **sashed** *adj*

[2]**sash** *n, pl* **sash** *also* **sashes** the framework in which panes of glass are set in a window or door; *also* such a framework together with its panes forming a usu sliding part of a window [prob fr French *châssis* chassis (taken as pl)]

ˌ**sash** ˈ**window** *n* a window having 2 sashes that slide vertically in a frame

sassafras /ˈsasəfras‖ˈsæsəfræs/ *n* (the dried root bark, used esp as a flavouring, of) a tall N American tree of the laurel family with mucilage-containing twigs and leaves

sat /sat‖sæt/ *past of* SIT

Satan /ˈsayt(ə)n‖ˈseɪt(ə)n/ *n* the adversary of God and lord of evil in Judaism and Christianity [Old English, fr Late Latin, fr Greek, fr Hebrew *śāṭān* adversary, plotter]

satanic /səˈtanik‖səˈtænɪk/ *adj* **1** (characteristic) of Satan or satanism **2** extremely cruel or malevolent – **satanically** *adv*

satanism /ˈsayt(ə)niz(ə)m‖ˈseɪt(ə)nɪz(ə)m/ *n, often cap* **1** diabolism **2** obsession with or affinity to evil; *specif* the worship of Satan marked by the travesty of Christian rites – **satanist** *n, often cap*

satchel /ˈsachəl‖ˈsætʃəl/ *n* a usu stiff bag often with a shoulder strap; *esp* one carried by schoolchildren – **satchelful** *n*

sate /sayt‖seɪt/ *vt* **1** to surfeit with sthg **2** to satisfy (e g a thirst) by indulging to the full

sateen /saˈteen‖sæˈtiːn/ *n* a smooth durable lustrous fabric in which the weft predominates on the face

satellite /ˈsatəliet‖ˈsætəlaɪt/ *n* **1** an obsequious follower **2a** a celestial body orbiting another of larger size **b** a man-made object or vehicle intended to orbit a celestial body **3** sby or sthg attendant or dependent; *esp* a country subject to another more powerful country **4** an urban community that is physically separate from an adjacent city but dependent on it [Middle French, fr Latin *satellit-*, *satelles* attendant] – **satellite** *adj*

satiable /ˈsaysh(y)əbl‖ˈseɪʃ(j)əbl/ *adj* capable of being satisfied – fml

satiate /ˈsayshiˌayt‖ˈseɪʃɪˌeɪt/ *vt* to satisfy (e g a need or desire) to the point of excess – **satiation** *n*

satiety /sə'tie·əti, 'sayshyəti‖sə'taɪətɪ, 'seɪʃjətɪ/ *n* **1** being fed or gratified to or beyond capacity **2** the aversion caused by overindulgence

[1]**satin** /'satin‖'sætɪn/ *n* a fabric (e g of silk) in satin weave with lustrous face and dull back

[2]**satin** *adj* **1** made of satin **2** like satin, esp in lustrous appearance or smoothness – **satiny** *adj*

satinwood /'satin,wood‖'sætɪn,wʊd/ *n* (the lustrous yellowish brown wood of) an E Indian tree of the mahogany family or any of various trees with similar wood

satire /'satie·ə‖'sætaɪə/ *n* **1** a literary work holding up human vices and follies to ridicule or scorn; *also* the genre of such literature **2** biting wit, irony, or sarcasm intended to expose foolishness or vice [Middle French, fr Latin *satura, satira*, fr (*lanx*) *satura* full plate, medley, fr *satur* sated] – **satirical** *adj*

satir·ize, -ise /'sati,riez‖'sætɪ,raɪz/ *vi* to utter or write satire ~*vt* to censure or ridicule by means of satire

satisfaction /,satis'faksh(ə)n‖,sætɪs'fækʃ(ə)n/ *n* **1a** the payment through penance of the temporal punishment incurred by a sin **b** reparation for sin and fulfilment of the demands of divine justice, achieved for mankind by the death of Christ **2a** fulfilment of a need or want **b** being satisfied **c** a source of pleasure or fulfilment **3a** compensation for a loss, insult, or injury **b** the discharge of a legal claim **c** vindication of one's honour, esp through a duel **4** full assurance or certainty

satisfactory /,satis'fakt(ə)ri‖,sætɪs'fækt(ə)rɪ/ *adj* satisfying needs or requirements; adequate – **satisfactorily** *adv*, **satisfactoriness** *n*

satisfy /'satis,fie‖'sætɪs,faɪ/ *vt* **1a** to discharge; CARRY OUT **b** to meet a financial obligation to **2a** to make content **b** to gratify to the full **c** to meet the requirements of <~ *the examiners*> **3a** to convince **b** to put an end to <~ *every objection*> **4a** to conform to (e g criteria) **b** to make valid by fulfilling a condition ~*vi* to be adequate; suffice; *also* to please <*a taste that* satisfies> – **satisfyingly** *adv*, **satisfiable** *adj*

satsuma /sat'soohmə‖sæt'suːmə/ *n* a sweet seedless type of mandarin orange [*Satsuma*, former province of Japan]

saturate /'sachoorayt‖'sætʃʊreɪt/ *vt* **1** to treat or provide with sthg to the point where no more can be absorbed, dissolved, or retained <*water* ~d *with salt*> **2a** to fill completely with sthg that permeates or pervades **b** to fill to capacity **3** to cause to combine chemically until there is no further tendency to combine – **saturant** *adj or n*, **saturator** *n*

saturation /,sachoo'raysh(ə)n‖,sætʃʊ'reɪʃ(ə)n/ *n* **1** the chromatic purity of a colour; freedom from dilution with white **2** the point at which a market is supplied with all the goods it will absorb **3** an overwhelming concentration of military forces or firepower

Saturday /'satəday, -di‖'sætədeɪ, -dɪ/ *n* the day of the week following Friday [Old English *sæterndæg*, fr Latin *Saturnus* Saturn + Old English *dæg* day]

Saturn /'satən, 'sa,tuhn‖'sætən, 'sæ,tɜːn/ *n* the planet 6th in order from the sun and conspicuous for its rings

saturnalia /,satə'naylyə‖,sætə'neɪljə/ *n, pl* **saturnalias** *also* **saturnalia** **1** *pl but sing or pl in constr* the festival of Saturn in ancient Rome, observed as a time of unrestrained merrymaking **2** an unrestrained (licentious) celebration – **saturnalian** *adj*

saturnine /'satə,nien‖'sætə,naɪn/ *adj* **1** gloomy **2** sullen – **saturninely** *adv*

satyr /'satə‖'sætə/ *n* **1** *often cap* a Greek minor woodland deity having certain characteristics of a horse or goat **2** a lecherous man – **satyric** *adj*

[1]**sauce** /saws‖sɔːs/ *n* **1a** a liquid or soft preparation used as a relish, dressing, or accompaniment to food **b** *NAm* stewed or tinned fruit eaten as a dessert **2** sthg adding zest or piquancy **3** CHEEK 3 – infml [Middle French, fr Latin *salsa*, fem of *salsus* salted, fr *sal* salt]

[2]**sauce** *vt* **1** to dress or prepare with a sauce or seasoning **2** to be impudent to – infml

saucepan /'sawspən‖'sɔːspən/ *n* a deep usu cylindrical cooking pan typically having a long handle and a lid

saucer /'sawsə‖'sɔːsə/ *n* **1** a small usu circular shallow dish with a central depression in which a cup is set **2** sthg like a saucer; *esp* FLYING SAUCER

saucy /'sawsi‖'sɔːsɪ/ *adj* **1a** cheeky **b** engagingly forward and flippant **2** smart, trim <*a* ~ *ship*> – **saucily** *adv*, **sauciness** *n*

sauerkraut /'sowə,krowt‖'saʊə,kraʊt/ *n* finely cut cabbage fermented in a brine made from its juice [German, fr *sauer* sour + *kraut* cabbage]

sauna /'sawnə‖'sɔːnə/ *n* (a room or building for) a Finnish steam bath in which water is thrown on hot stones

saunter /'sawntə‖'sɔːntə/ *vi* to walk about in a casual manner – **saunter** *n*, **saunterer** *n*

saurian /'sawri·ən‖'sɔːrɪən/ *n* any of a group of reptiles including the lizards and formerly the crocodiles and dinosaurs – **saurian** *adj*

sausage /'sosij‖'sɒsɪdʒ/ *n* (sthg shaped like) a cylindrical mass of seasoned minced meat in a casing usu of prepared animal intestine

,**sausage 'roll** *n* a small pastry-encased roll or oblong of sausage meat

sauté /'sawtay, 'soh-‖'sɔːteɪ, 'səʊ-/ *vt* **sautéing; sautéed, sautéd** /-tayd‖-teɪd/ to fry in a small amount of fat – **sauté** *n or adj*

Sauternes, *NAm* **Sauterne** /soh'tuhn, '--‖səʊ'tɜːn, '--/ *n* a usu sweet golden-coloured Bordeaux made in the commune of Sauternes in France

[1]**savage** /'savij‖'sævɪdʒ/ *adj* **1a** not domesticated or under human control; untamed **b** lacking in social or moral restraints **2** rugged, rough **3** boorish, rude **4** lacking a developed culture – now usu taken to be offensive – **savagely** *adv*, **savageness, savagery** *n*

[2]**savage** *n* **1** a member of a primitive society **2** a brutal, rude, or unmannerly person

[3]**savage** *vt* to attack or treat brutally; *esp* to maul

savanna, savannah /sə'vanə‖sə'vænə/ *n* a tropical or subtropical grassland with scattered trees

savant /ˈsav(ə)nt‖ˈsæv(ə)nt/ *n* one who has exceptional knowledge of a particular field (e g science or literature) [French, fr present participle of *savoir* to know, fr Latin *sapere* to be wise]

[1]**save** /sayv‖seɪv/ *vt* **1a** to deliver from sin **b** to rescue from danger or harm **c** to preserve from injury, destruction, or loss **2a** to put aside as a store **b** to put aside for a particular use **c** to keep from being spent, wasted, or lost <~d *time by taking a short cut*> **d** to economize in the use of; conserve **3a** to make unnecessary <~s *me going into town*> **b** to prevent an opponent from scoring, winning, or scoring with <~d *the shot*> **4** to maintain <~ *appearances*> ~ *vi* **1** to rescue sby (e g from danger) **2a** to put aside money – often + *up* **b** to be economical in use or expenditure **3** to make a save – **savable, saveable** *adj*, **saver** *n*

[2]**save** *n* an action (e g by a goalkeeper) that prevents an opponent from scoring

[3]**save** *prep* BUT 1a – chiefly fml

[4]**save** *conj* were it not; only <*would have protested* ~ *that he was a friend*> – chiefly fml

saveloy /ˈsaviloy‖ˈsævɪlɔɪ/ *n* a precooked highly seasoned dry sausage

[1]**saving** /ˈsayving‖ˈseɪvɪŋ/ *n* **1** preservation from danger or destruction **2** sthg saved <*a* ~ *of 40 per cent*> **3a** *pl* money put by over a period of time **b** the excess of income over expenditures – often pl

[2]**saving** *prep* **1** except, save **2** without disrespect to

ˌ**saving ˈgrace** *n* a redeeming quality or feature

saviour, *NAm chiefly* **savior** /ˈsayvyə‖ˈseɪvjə/ *n* **1** one who brings salvation; *specif, cap* Jesus **2** one who saves sby or sthg from danger or destruction

savoir faire /ˌsavwah ˈfeə‖ˌsævwɑː ˈfeə/ *n* polished self-assurance in social behaviour [French *savoir-faire*, lit., knowing how to do]

savory /ˈsayv(ə)ri‖ˈseɪv(ə)rɪ/ *n* any of several aromatic plants of the mint family used as herbs in cooking

[1]**savour,** *NAm chiefly* **savor** /ˈsayvə‖ˈseɪvə/ *n* **1** the characteristic taste or smell of sthg **2** a particular flavour or smell **3** a (pleasantly stimulating) distinctive quality <*felt that argument added* ~ *to conversation*>

[2]**savour,** *NAm chiefly* **savor** *vi* to have a specified smell or quality; smack <*arguments that* ~ *of cynicism*> ~ *vt* **1** to taste or smell with pleasure; relish **2a** to have (pleasurable) experience of, esp at length **b** to delight in; enjoy

[1]**savoury,** *NAm chiefly* **savory** /ˈsayv(ə)ri‖ˈseɪv(ə)rɪ/ *adj* **1** piquantly pleasant to the mind **2** morally wholesome **3a** pleasing to the palate **b** salty, spicy, meaty, etc, rather than sweet

[2]**savoury,** *NAm chiefly* **savory** *n* a dish of piquant or stimulating flavour served usu at the end of a main meal but sometimes as an appetizer

savoy, savoy cabbage /səˈvoy‖səˈvɔɪ/ *n* a hardy cabbage with compact heads of wrinkled and curled leaves [*Savoy*, region of SE France]

[1]**savvy** /ˈsavi‖ˈsævɪ/ *vb* to know, understand – slang [Spanish *sabe* he knows, fr *saber* to know, fr Latin *sapere* to be wise]

[2]**savvy** *n* practical know-how; shrewd judgment – slang – **savvy** *adj*

[1]**saw** /saw‖sɔː/ *past of* SEE

[2]**saw** *n* a hand or power tool with a toothed part (e g a blade or disc) used to cut wood, metal, bone, etc – **sawlike** *adj*

[3]**saw** *vb* **sawed, sawn** /sawn‖sɔːn/ *vt* **1** to cut with a saw **2** to shape by cutting with a saw **3** to cut through as though with a saw ~ *vi* **1a** to use a saw **b** to cut (as if) with a saw **2** to make motions as though using a saw – **sawer** *n*

[4]**saw** *n* a maxim, proverb

ˈ**sawˌbones** /-ˌbohnz‖-ˌbəʊnz/ *n* a doctor; *specif* a surgeon – humor

ˈ**sawˌdust** /-ˌdust‖-ˌdʌst/ *n* fine particles of wood produced in sawing

ˈ**sawˌhorse** /-ˌhaws‖-ˌhɔːs/ *n* a rack on which wood is laid for sawing

ˈ**sawˌmill** /-ˌmil‖-ˌmɪl/ *n* a factory or machine that cuts wood

ˌ**sawn-ˈoff** *adj* having the end removed by sawing; *specif, of a shotgun* having the end of the barrel sawn off

sawyer /ˈsawyə‖ˈsɔːjə/ *n* sby employed to saw timber

saxifrage /ˈsaksifrij, -ˌfrayj‖ˈsæksɪfrɪdʒ, -ˌfreɪdʒ/ *n* any of a genus of usu showy-flowered plants often with tufted leaves

Saxon /ˈsaks(ə)n‖ˈsæks(ə)n/ *n* **1a(1)** a member of a Germanic people that invaded England along with the Angles and Jutes in the 5th c AD and merged with them to form the Anglo-Saxon people **a(2)** an Englishman or Lowlander as distinguished from a Welshman, Irishman, or Highlander **b** a native or inhabitant of Saxony **2** the Germanic language or dialect of any of the Saxon peoples – **Saxon** *adj*

saxophone /ˈsaksəˌfohn‖ˈsæksəˌfəʊn/ *n* any of a group of single-reed woodwind instruments having a conical metal tube and finger keys and used esp in jazz and popular music [Adolphe *Sax* (1814-94), Belgian maker of musical instruments] – **saxophonist** *n*

[1]**say** /say‖seɪ/ *vb* **says** /sez‖sez/; **said** /sed‖sed/ *vt* **1a** to state in spoken words **b** to form an opinion as to <*can't* ~ *when I met him*> **2a** to utter, pronounce <*can't* ~ *her 'h''s*> **b** to recite, repeat <said *his prayers*> **3a** to indicate, show <*the clock* ~s *12*> **b** to give expression to; communicate <*I* said *to myself 'That's funny'*> <*it* ~s *press button A*> **4a** to suppose, assume **b** to allege – usu pass <*the house is* said *to be 300 years old*> ~ *vi* **1** to speak, declare <*I'd rather not* ~> **2** *NAm* I SAY – used interjectionally – **sayer** *n* – **I say** *chiefly Br* – used as a weak expression of surprise or to attract attention – **not to say** and indeed; or perhaps even <*impolite*, not to say *rude*> – **say fairer** *Br* to express oneself any more generously <*you can't* say fairer *than that*> – **say when** to tell sby when to stop, esp when pouring a drink – **that is to say 1** in other words; IN EFFECT **2** or at least <*he's coming*, that is to say *he promised to*> – **to say nothing of** without even considering; not to mention

[2]**say** *n* **1** an expression of opinion – esp in *have one's say* **2** a right or power to influence action or decisions; *esp* the authority to

make final decisions

[3]**say** *adv* **1** at a rough estimate <*the picture is worth,* ~, *£200*> **2** FOR EXAMPLE <*we could leave next week,* ~ *on Monday*>

saying *n* a maxim, proverb

ˈ**say-ˌso** *n* **1** one's unsupported assertion **2** the right of final decision

[1]**scab** /skab‖skæb/ *n* **1** scabies of domestic animals **2** a crust of hardened blood and serum over a wound **3a** a contemptible person **b** BLACKLEG 3 **4** any of various plant diseases characterized by crusted spots; *also* any of these spots – **scabby** *adj*

[2]**scab** *vi* **-bb- 1** to become covered with a scab **2** to act as a scab

scabbard /ˈskabəd‖ˈskæbəd/ *n* a sheath for a sword, dagger, or bayonet

scabies /ˈskaybiz‖ˈskeɪbɪz/ *n, pl* **scabies** a skin disease, esp contagious itch or mange, caused by a parasitic mite and usu characterized by oozing scabs – **scabietic** *adj*

[1]**scabious** /ˈskaybi·əs‖ˈskeɪbɪəs/ *n* any of a genus of plants with flowers in dense heads at the end of usu long stalks

[2]**scabious** *adj* **1** scabby **2** of or resembling scabies

scabrous /ˈskaybrəs‖ˈskeɪbrəs/ *adj* **1** rough to the touch with scales, scabs, raised patches, etc **2** dealing with indecent or offensive themes **3** intractable, knotty *USE* (*2 & 3*) fml – **scabrously** *adv*, **scabrousness** *n*

scaffold /ˈskafohld, -f(ə)ld‖ˈskæfəʊld, -f(ə)ld/ *n* **1a** a temporary platform for workmen to stand or sit on when working at a height above the floor or ground **b** a platform on which a criminal is executed **c** a platform above ground or floor level **2** a supporting framework

scaffolding /ˈskafəlding‖ˈskæfəldɪŋ/ *n* **1** material used in scaffolds **2** SCAFFOLD 1a, 2

scag /skag‖skæg/ *n* heroin –slang

[1]**scalar** /ˈskaylə‖ˈskeɪlə/ *adj* **1** having a continuous series of steps <~ *chain of authority*> **2a** capable of being represented by a point on a scale <*a* ~ *quantity*> **b** of a scalar or scalar product <~ *multiplication*>

[2]**scalar** *n* **1** a real number rather than a vector **2** a quantity (e g mass or time) that has a magnitude describable by a real number, and no direction

scalawag /ˈskaləwag‖ˈskæləwæg/ *n, NAm* a scallywag

[1]**scald** /skawld‖skɔːld/ *vt* **1** to burn (as if) with hot liquid or steam **2a** to subject to boiling water or steam **b** to heat to just short of boiling <~ *milk*>

[2]**scald** *n* an injury to the body caused by scalding

scalding /ˈskawlding‖ˈskɔːldɪŋ/ *adj* **1** boiling hot **2** biting, scathing

[1]**scale** /skayl‖skeɪl/ *n* **1a** either pan of a balance **b** a beam that is supported freely in the centre and has 2 pans of equal weight suspended from its ends **2** an instrument or machine for weighing *USE* (*1b, 2*) usu pl with sing. meaning

[2]**scale** *vi* to have a specified weight on scales

[3]**scale** *n* **1** (a small thin plate resembling) a small flattened rigid plate forming part of the external body covering of a fish, reptile, etc **2** a small thin dry flake shed from the skin **3** a thin coating, layer, or incrustation: **3a** a (black scaly) coating of oxide forming on the surface of metals, esp iron when heated **b** a hard incrustation usu of calcium sulphate or carbonate that is deposited on the inside of a kettle, boiler, etc by the evaporation or constant passage of hard water **4** a usu thin, membranous, chaffy, or woody modified leaf **5** infestation with or disease caused by scale insects – **scaled** *adj*, **scaleless** *adj*

[4]**scale** *vt* **1** to remove scale or scales from (e g by scraping) **2** to remove in thin layers or scales <~ *paint from a wall*> **3** to cover with scale <*hard water* ~s *a boiler*> ~ *vi* **1** to shed or separate or come off in scales; flake **2** to become encrusted with scale – **scaler** *n*

[5]**scale** *n* **1** a graduated series of musical notes ascending or descending in order of pitch according to a specified scheme of their intervals **2** sthg graduated, esp when used as a measure or rule: e g **2a** a linear region divided by lines into a series of spaces and used to register or record sthg (e g the height of mercury in a barometer) **b** a graduated line on a map or chart indicating the length used to represent a larger unit of measure **c** an instrument having a scale for measuring or marking off distances or dimensions **3** a graduated system <*a* ~ *of taxation*> **4** a proportion between 2 sets of dimensions (e g between those of a drawing and its original) **5** a graded series of tests – **scale** *adj* – **to scale** according to the proportions of an established scale of measurement <*floor plans drawn* to scale>

[6]**scale** *vt* **1** to climb up or reach (as if) by means of a ladder **2a** to change the scale of **b** to pattern, make, regulate, set, or estimate according to some rate or standard <*a production schedule* ~d *to actual need*> <~ *down imports*> *USE* (*2*) often + *up* or *down* – **scaler** *n*

scalene /ˈskayleen‖ˈskeɪliːn/ *adj, of a triangle* having the 3 sides of unequal length

scallion /ˈskalyən‖ˈskæljən/ *n* **1** a leek **2** an onion forming a thick basal part without a bulb; *also* SPRING ONION **3** *chiefly NAm* a shallot

[1]**scallop** /ˈskoləp‖ˈskɒləp/ *n* **1** (a large muscle, used as food, of) any of various marine bivalve molluscs that have a shell consisting of 2 wavy-edged halves each with a fan-shaped pattern of ridges and that swim by opening and closing the halves of the shell **2** a scallop shell or a similarly shaped dish used for baking esp seafood **3** any of a continuous series of circle segments or angular projections forming a border

[2]**scallop** *vt* **1** to bake in a scallop shell or shallow baking dish, usu with a sauce covered with breadcrumbs **2a** to shape, cut, or finish (e g an edge or border) in scallops **b** to form scallops in

scallywag /ˈskaliˌwag‖ˈskælɪˌwæg/, *NAm chiefly* **scalawag** /ˈskaləwag‖ˈskæləwæg/ *n* a troublemaking or dishonest person; a rascal

[1]**scalp** /skalp‖skælp/ *n* **1** (the part of a lower mammal corresponding to) the skin of the human head, usu covered with hair in both sexes **2a** a part of the human scalp with attached hair cut or torn from an enemy as a trophy, esp formerly by N American Indian warriors **b** a trophy of victory **3** *chiefly Scot* a projecting

rocky mound

[2]**scalp** *vt* **1** to remove the scalp of **2** *NAm* **2a** to buy and sell to make small quick profits **b** to obtain speculatively and resell at greatly increased prices USE (*2*) infml

scalpel /ˈskalpl‖ˈskælpl/ *n* a small very sharp straight thin-bladed knife used esp in surgery

scaly /ˈskayli‖ˈskeɪlɪ/ *adj* **1** covered with or composed of scale or scales **2** flaky – **scaliness** *n*

scam /skam/ *n* a swindle – infml

[1]**scamp** /skamp‖skæmp/ *n* an impish or playful young person – **scampish** *adj*

[2]**scamp** *vt* to perform in a hasty, careless, or haphazard manner

[1]**scamper** /ˈskampə‖ˈskæmpə/ *vi* to run about nimbly and playfully

[2]**scamper** *n* a playful scurry

scampi /ˈskampi‖ˈskæmpɪ/ *n, pl* **scampi** a (large) prawn (often prepared with a batter coating)

[1]**scan** /skan‖skæn/ *vb* **-nn-** *vt* **1** to read or mark (a piece of text) so as to show metrical structure **2a** to subject to critical examination **b** to examine all parts of in a systematic order **c** to check or read hastily or casually <~ned *the small ads*> **3a** to traverse (a region) with a controlled beam: e g **3a(1)** to observe (a region) using a radar scanner **a(2)** to translate (an image) into an electrical signal by moving an electron beam across it according to a predetermined pattern (e g for television transmission); *also* to reproduce (an image) from such a signal **a(3)** to make a detailed examination of (e g the human body) using any of a variety of sensing devices (e g ones using ultrasonics, thermal radiation, X-rays, or radiation from radioactive materials) **b** to examine (a computer data source; e g a punched card) for the presence of recorded data ~*vi, of verse* to conform to a metrical pattern

[2]**scan** *n* **1** a scanning **2** a radar or television trace

scandal /ˈskandl‖ˈskændl/ *n* **1** loss of reputation caused by (alleged) breach of moral or social propriety **2** a circumstance or action that causes general offence or indignation or that disgraces those associated with it **3** malicious or defamatory gossip **4** indignation, chagrin, or bewilderment brought about by a flagrant violation of propriety or religious opinion [Late Latin *scandalum* stumbling block, offence, fr Greek *skandalon*]

scandal·ize, -ise /ˈskandlˌiez‖ˈskændlˌaɪz/ *vt* to offend the moral sense of – **scandalizer** *n*, **scandalization** *n*

ˈ**scandalˌmonger** /-ˌmung·gə‖-ˌmʌŋgə/ *n* sby who circulates scandal

scandalous /ˈskand(ə)ləs‖ˈskænd(ə)ləs/ *adj* **1** libellous, defamatory **2** offensive to propriety – **scandalously** *adv*, **scandalousness** *n*

Scandinavian /ˌskandiˈnayvyən, -vi·ən‖ˌskændɪˈneɪvjən, -vɪən/ *n* **1** a native or inhabitant of Scandinavia **2** NORTH GERMANIC – **Scandinavian** *adj*

scanner /ˈskanə‖ˈskænə/ *n* **1** a device that automatically monitors a system or process **2** a device for sensing recorded data **3** the rotating aerial of a radar set

scansion /ˈskansh(ə)n‖ˈskænʃ(ə)n/ *n* (the analysis of) the way in which a piece of verse scans

[1]**scant** /skant‖skænt/ *adj* **1a** barely sufficient; inadequate **b** lacking in quantity **2** having a small or insufficient supply – **scantly** *adv*, **scantness** *n*

[2]**scant** *vt* to restrict or withhold the supply of

scanty /ˈskanti‖ˈskæntɪ/ *adj* scant; *esp* deficient in coverage – **scantily** *adv*, **scantiness** *n*

scape /skayp‖skeɪp/ *n* **1** a leafless flower stalk arising directly from the root of a plant (e g in the dandelion) **2** the shaft of an animal part (e g an antenna or feather)

ˈ**scapeˌgoat** /-ˌgoht‖-ˌgəʊt/ *n* **1** a goat on whose head are symbolically placed the sins of the people after which he is sent into the wilderness in the biblical ceremony for Yom Kippur **2** sby or sthg made to bear the blame for others' faults – **scapegoat** *vt*

ˈ**scapeˌgrace** /-ˌgrays‖-ˌgreɪs/ *n* an incorrigible rascal

scapula /ˈskapyoolə‖ˈskæpjʊlə/ *n, pl* **scapulae** /-lı‖-lɪ/, **scapulas** a large flat triangular bone at the upper part of each side of the back forming most of each half of the shoulder girdle; SHOULDER BLADE

[1]**scar** /skah‖skɑː/ *n* a steep rocky place on a mountainside

[2]**scar** *n* **1** a mark left (e g on the skin) by the healing of injured tissue **2** CICATRIX 2 **3** a mark of damage or wear **4** a lasting moral or emotional injury – **scarless** *adj*

[3]**scar** *vb* **-rr-** *vt* **1** to mark with a scar **2** to do lasting injury to ~ *vi* **1** to form a scar **2** to become scarred

scarab /ˈskarəb‖ˈskærəb/ *n* **1** a scarabaeus or other scarabaeid beetle **2** a representation of a beetle, usu made of stone or glazed earthenware, used in ancient Egypt esp as a talisman

[1]**scarce** /skeəs‖skeəs/ *adj* **1** not plentiful or abundant **2** few in number; rare – **scarceness** *n*, **scarcity** *n*

[2]**scarce** *adv, archaic* scarcely, hardly

ˈ**scarcely** /-li‖-lɪ/ *adv* **1a** by a narrow margin; only just <*had ~ finished eating*> **b** almost not <*~ ever went to parties*> <*could ~ have been better qualified*> **2** not without unpleasantness or discourtesy <*could ~ interfere in a private dispute*>

[1]**scare** /skeə‖skeə/ *vt* **1** to frighten suddenly **2** to drive off by frightening ~*vi* to become scared – **scarer** *n*

[2]**scare** *n* **1** a sudden or unwarranted fright **2** a widespread state of alarm or panic <*a bomb ~*> – **scare** *adj*

ˈ**scareˌcrow** /-ˌkroh‖-ˌkrəʊ/ *n* **1** an object usu suggesting a human figure, set up to frighten birds away from crops **2** a skinny or ragged person – infml

ˈ**scareˌmonger** /-ˌmung·gə‖-ˌmʌŋgə/ *n* sby who (needlessly) encourages panic – **scaremongering** *n*

[1]**scarf** /skahf‖skɑːf/ *n, pl* **scarves** /skahvz‖skɑːvz/, **scarfs** a strip or square of cloth worn round the shoulders or neck or over the head for decoration or warmth

[2]**scarf** *n, pl* **scarfs** **1** either of the chamfered or cut away ends that fit together to form a scarf

joint **2 scarf, scarf joint** a joint made by chamfering, halving, or notching 2 pieces to correspond and lapping and bolting them

³**scarf, scarph** /skahf‖skɑːf/ *vt* **1** to unite by a scarf joint **2** to form a scarf on

scarify /ˈskeərifie, ˈskari-‖ˈskeərɪfaɪ, ˈskærɪ-/ *vt* **1** to make scratches or small cuts in (e g the skin) **2** to wound the feelings of (e g by harsh criticism) **3** to break up and loosen the surface of (e g a field or road) – **scarifier** *n*, **scarification** *n*

scarlet /ˈskahlət‖ˈskɑːlət/ *adj or n* (of) a vivid red colour tinged with orange

scarlet fever *n* an infectious fever caused by a streptococcus in which there is a red rash and inflammation of the nose, throat, and mouth

scarlet pimpernel *n* a common pimpernel with usu red flowers that close in cloudy weather

scarlet runner *n* RUNNER BEAN

scarlet woman *n* a prostitute – euph

¹**scarp** /skahp‖skɑːp/ *n* **1** the inner side of a ditch below the parapet of a fortification **2** a steep slope, esp a cliff face, produced by faulting or erosion

²**scarp** *vt* to cut down to form a vertical or steep slope

scarper /ˈskahpə‖ˈskɑːpə/ *vi, Br* to run away (e g from creditors) – infml

scary, scarey /ˈskeəri‖ˈskeərɪ/ *adj* **1** causing fright; alarming **2** easily scared; timid *USE* infml

¹**scat** /skat‖skæt/ *vi* **-tt-** to depart rapidly – infml

²**scat** *n* jazz singing with nonsense syllables – **scat** *vi*

scathing /ˈskaydhing‖ˈskeɪðɪŋ/ *adj* bitterly severe <*a* ~ *condemnation*> – **scathingly** *adv*

scatology /skaˈtoləji‖skæˈtɒlədʒɪ/ *n* **1** the biologically oriented study of excrement (e g for the determination of diet) **2** (literature characterized by) interest in or treatment of obscene matters – **scatological** *adj*

¹**scatter** /ˈskatə‖ˈskætə/ *vt* **1** to cause (a group or collection) to separate widely **2a** to distribute at irregular intervals **b** to distribute recklessly and at random **3** to sow (seed) by casting in all directions **4** to reflect or disperse (e g a beam of radiation or particles) irregularly and diffusely ~*vi* to separate and go in various directions – **scatterer** *n*, **scatteringly** *adv*

²**scatter** *n* **1** the act of scattering **2** a small supply or number irregularly distributed **3** the state or extent of being scattered

ˈ**scatter,brain** /-ˌbrayn‖-ˌbreɪn/ *n* sby incapable of concentration – **scatterbrained** *adj*

scatty /ˈskati‖ˈskætɪ/ *adj, Br* scatterbrained – infml

scavenge /ˈskavinj‖ˈskævɪndʒ/ *vt* **1** to salvage from discarded or refuse material; *also* to salvage usable material from **2** to feed on (carrion or refuse) ~ *vi* **1** to search for reusable material **2** to obtain food by scavenging <*dogs* scavenging *on kitchen waste*>

scavenger /ˈskavinjə‖ˈskævɪndʒə/ *n* **1** a refuse collector **2** a chemical used to remove or make innocuous an undesirable substance **3** an organism that feeds on refuse or carrion

scenario /siˈnahri·oh, -ˈneə-‖sɪˈnɑːrɪəʊ, -ˈneə-/ *n, pl* **scenarios** **1** an outline or synopsis of a dramatic work **2a** a screenplay **b** a shooting script **3** an account or synopsis of a projected course of action [Italian, scenary, fr Latin *scaenarius* of the stage, fr *scaena* stage]

¹**scend** /send‖send/ *vi* to rise upwards on a wave

²**scend** *n* the lifting motion of a wave

scene /seen‖siːn/ *n* **1** any of the smaller subdivisions of a dramatic work: e g **1a** a division of an act presenting continuous action in 1 place **b** an episode, sequence, or unit of dialogue in a play, film, or television programme **2** a vista suggesting a stage setting **3** the place of an occurrence or action <~ *of the crime*> **4** an exhibition of unrestrained feeling <*make a* ~> **5** a sphere of activity or interest – slang <*philosophy is not my* ~> – **behind the scenes** out of the public view; IN SECRET

scenery /ˈseen(ə)ri‖ˈsiːn(ə)rɪ/ *n* **1** the painted scenes or hangings and accessories used on a theatre stage **2** landscape, esp when considered attractive

ˈ**scene,shifter** /-ˌshiftə‖-ˌʃɪftə/ *n* a worker who moves the scenery in a theatre

scenic /ˈseenik‖ˈsiːnɪk/ *also* **scenical** /-kl‖-kl/ *adj* **1** of the stage, a stage setting, or stage representation **2** of or displaying (fine) natural scenery **3** representing graphically an action or event – **scenically** *adv*

¹**scent** /sent‖sent/ *vt* **1a** to perceive by the sense of smell **b** to get or have an inkling of **2** to fill with a usu pleasant smell ~*vi* to use the nose in seeking or tracking prey

²**scent** *n* **1** odour: e g **1a** a smell left by an animal on a surface it passes over <*hounds followed the* ~ *of the fox*> **b** a characteristic or particular, esp agreeable, smell **c** PERFUME 2 **2a** power of smelling; the sense of smell <*a keen* ~> **b** power of detection; a nose <*a* ~ *for heresy*> **3** a course of pursuit or discovery <*threw him off the* ~> **4** a hint, suggestion <*a* ~ *of trouble*> – **scentless** *adj*

sceptic /ˈskeptik‖ˈskeptɪk/ *n* a person disposed to scepticism, esp regarding religion or religious principles [Greek *skeptikos*, fr *skeptikos* thoughtful, fr *skeptesthai* to look, consider]

sceptical /ˈskeptikl‖ˈskeptɪkl/ *adj* relating to, characteristic of, or marked by scepticism

scepticism /ˈskeptiˌsiz(ə)m‖ˈskeptɪˌsɪz(ə)m/ *n* **1** doubt concerning basic religious principles (e g immortality, providence, or revelation) **2** the doctrine that certain knowledge is unattainable either generally or in a particular sphere **3** an attitude of doubt, esp associated with implied criticism

sceptre, *NAm chiefly* **scepter** /ˈseptə‖ˈseptə/ *n* **1** a staff borne by a ruler as an emblem of sovereignty **2** royal or imperial authority

¹**schedule** /ˈshedyool, -jəl‖ˈʃedjʊl, -dʒəl; *also, esp NAm* ˈskedyool, -jəl‖ˈskedjʊl, -dʒəl/ *n* **1** a statement of supplementary details appended to a document **2** a list, catalogue, or inventory **3** (the times fixed in) a timetable **4** a programme, proposal **5** a body of items to be dealt with

²**schedule** *vt* **1a** to place on a schedule **b** to make a schedule of **2** to appoint or designate for a fixed time **3** *Br* to place on a list of buildings or historical remains protected by state legislation – **scheduler** *n*

schema /'skeemə‖'ski:mə/ *n, pl* **schemata** /-mətə‖-mətə/ a diagrammatic representation; a plan
schematic /ski'matik‖skɪ'mætɪk/ *adj* of a scheme or schema; diagrammatic – **schematically** *adv*
schemat·ize, -ise /'skeemə,tiez‖'ski:mə,taɪz/ *vt* **1** to form into a systematic arrangement **2** to express or depict schematically – **schematization** *n*
[1]**scheme** /skeem‖ski:m/ *n* **1** a concise statement or table **2** a plan or programme of action; a project <*a hydroelectric* ~> **3** a crafty or secret strategy **4** a systematic arrangement of parts or elements [Latin *schemat-, schema* arrangement, figure, fr Greek *schēmat-, schēma*, fr *echein* to have, hold, be in (such) a condition]
[2]**scheme** *vt* to form a scheme for ~*vi* to make plans; *also* to plot, intrigue – **schemer** *n*
scherzo /'skeətsoh‖'skeətsəʊ/ *n, pl* **scherzos, scherzi** /-tsi‖-tsɪ/ a lively instrumental musical composition or movement in quick usu triple time [Italian, lit., joke, fr *scherzare* to joke, of Germanic origin]
schism /'siz(ə)m, 'skiz(ə)m‖'sɪz(ə)m, 'skɪz-(ə)m/ *n* **1** separation into opposed factions **2a** formal division in or separation from a religious body **b** the offence of promoting schism
[1]**schismatic** /siz'matik, skiz-‖sɪz'mætɪk, skɪz-/ *n* a person who creates or takes part in schism
[2]**schismatic** *also* **schismatical** /-kl‖-kl/ *adj* **1** (having the character) of schism **2** guilty of schism – **schismatically** *adv*
schist /shist‖ʃɪst/ *n* a metamorphic crystalline rock composed of thin layers of minerals and splitting along approx parallel planes – **schistose** *adj*
schizoid /'skitsoyd‖'skɪtsɔɪd/ *adj* characterized by, resulting from, tending towards, or suggestive of schizophrenia – **schizoid** *n*
schizophrenia /,skitsə'freenyə‖,skɪtsə-'fri:njə/ *n* a mental disorder characterized by loss of contact with reality and disintegration of personality, usu with hallucinations and disorder of feeling, behaviour, etc [deriv of Greek *schizein* to split + *phrēn* mind] – **schizophrenic** *adj or n*, **schizophrenically** *adv*
schmaltz, schmalz /shmalts‖ʃmælts/ *n* excessive sentimentalism, esp in music or art – **schmaltzy** *adj*
schnapps /shnaps‖ʃnæps/ *n, pl* **schnapps** strong gin as orig made in the Netherlands
schnitzel /'shnits(ə)l‖'ʃnɪts(ə)l/ *n* a veal escalope
schnorkel /'s(h)nawkl‖'snɔ:kl,ʃn-/ *vi or n* (to) snorkel
scholar /'skolə‖'skɒlə/ *n* **1** one who attends a school or studies under a teacher **2** one who has done advanced study **3** the holder of a scholarship
'**scholarly** /-li‖-lɪ/ *adj* learned, academic
'**scholarship** /-ship‖-ʃɪp/ *n* **1** a grant of money to a student **2** the character, methods, or attainments of a scholar; learning **3** a fund of knowledge and learning
scholastic /skə'lastik‖skə'læstɪk/ *adj* **1a** *often cap* of Scholasticism **b** suggestive or characteristic of a scholar or pedant, esp in specious subtlety or dryness **2** of schools or scholars – **scholastically** *adv*
scholasticism /skə'lasti,siz(ə)m‖skə'læstɪ-,sɪz(ə)m/ *n* **1** *cap* a chiefly late medieval philosophical movement that applied Aristotelian concepts and principles to the interpretation of religious dogma **2** pedantic adherence to the traditional teachings or methods of a school
[1]**school** /skoohl‖sku:l/ *n* **1a** an institution for the teaching of children **b(1)** any of the 4 faculties of a medieval university **b(2)** a part of a university <*the* ~ *of engineering*> **c** an establishment offering specialized instruction <*driving* ~s> **d** *pl, cap* the final honours examination for the Oxford BA **e** *NAm* a college, university **2a(1)** the process of teaching or learning, esp at a school **a(2)** a session of a school **b** a school building **3a** people with a common doctrine or teacher (e g in philosophy or theology) **b** a group of artists under a common stylistic influence **4** a body of people with similar opinions <*a* ~ *of thought*>
[2]**school** *vt* **1** to educate in an institution of learning **2a** to teach or drill in a specific knowledge or skill <~ *a horse*> **b** to discipline or habituate to sthg
[3]**school** *n* a large number of fish or aquatic animals of 1 kind swimming together
[4]**school** *vi* to swim or feed in a school
'**school,boy** /-,boy‖-,bɔɪ/, *fem* '**school,girl** *n* a schoolchild
'**school,child** /-,chield‖-,tʃaɪld/ *n* a child attending school
'**school,house** /-,hows‖-,haʊs/ *n* a building used as a school; *esp* a country primary school
schooling /'skoohling‖'sku:lɪŋ/ *n* **1a** instruction in school **b** training or guidance from practical experience **2** the cost of instruction and maintenance at school **3** the training of a horse to service; *esp* the teaching and exercising of horse and rider in the formal techniques of horse riding
'**school,marm, schoolma'am** /-,mahm‖-,mɑ:m/ *n* **1** a prim censorious woman **2** *chiefly NAm* a female schoolteacher; *esp* a rural or small-town schoolmistress
'**school,master** /-,mahstə‖-,mɑ:stə/, *fem* '**school,mistress** *n* a schoolteacher
schooner /'skoohnə‖'sku:nə/ *n* **1** a fore-and-aft rigged sailing vessel having 2 or more masts **2a** *Br* **2a(1)** a relatively tall narrow glass used esp for a large measure of sherry or port **a(2)** the capacity of a schooner used as a measure (e g for sherry) **b** *chiefly NAm & Austr* a large tall drinking glass, esp for beer
schwa /shwah‖ʃwɑ:/ *n* (the symbol / ə / used for) an unstressed vowel that is the usual sound of the first and last vowels of *banana*
sciatic /sie'atik‖saɪ'ætɪk/ *adj* **1** of or situated near the hip **2** of or caused by sciatica <~ *pains*>
sciatica /sie'atikə‖saɪ'ætɪkə/ *n* pain in the back of the thigh, buttocks, and lower back caused esp by pressure on the sciatic nerve
science /'sie·əns‖'saɪəns/ *n* **1a** a department of systematized knowledge <*the* ~ *of theology*> **b** sthg (e g a skill) that may be learned systematically <*the* ~ *of boxing*> **c** any of the

natural sciences **2a** coordinated knowledge of the operation of general laws, esp as obtained and tested through scientific method **b** such knowledge of the physical world and its phenomena; NATURAL SCIENCE **3** a system or method (purporting to be) based on scientific principles [Middle French, fr Latin *scientia*, fr *scient-, sciens* having knowledge, fr *scire* to know]

ˌscience ˈfiction *n* fiction of a type orig set in the future and dealing principally with the impact of science on society or individuals, but now including also works of literary fantasy

scientific /ˌsie·ənˈtifik‖ˌsaɪənˈtɪfɪk/ *adj* of or exhibiting the methods of science – **scientifically** *adv*

scientist /ˈsie·əntist‖ˈsaɪəntɪst/ *n* an expert in a science, esp natural science; a scientific investigator

Scientology /ˌsie·ənˈtoləji‖ˌsaɪənˈtɒlədʒɪ/ *trademark* – used for a religious and psychotherapeutic movement begun in 1952 by L Ron Hubbard

scimitar /ˈsimitə, -tah‖ˈsɪmɪtə, -tɑː/ *n* a chiefly Middle Eastern sword having a curved blade which narrows towards the hilt and is sharpened on the convex side

scintilla /sinˈtilə‖sɪnˈtɪlə/ *n* an iota, trace

scintillate /ˈsintiˌlayt‖ˈsɪntɪˌleɪt/ *vi* **1** to emit sparks **2** to emit flashes as if throwing off sparks; *also* to sparkle, twinkle **3** to be brilliant or animated <scintillating *wit*> – **scintillant** *adj*

scion /ˈsie·ən‖ˈsaɪən/ *n* **1** a detached living part of a plant joined to a stock in grafting and usu supplying parts above ground of the resulting graft **2** a (male) descendant or offspring

scissor /ˈsizə‖ˈsɪzə/ *vt* to cut (out) (as if) with scissors

scissors /ˈsizəz‖ˈsɪzəz/ *n pl* **1** a cutting instrument with 2 blades pivoted so that their cutting edges slide past each other **2** *sing or pl in constr* a gymnastic feat in which the leg movements suggest the opening and closing of scissors – **scissor** *adj*

sclera /ˈskliərə‖ˈsklɪərə/ *n pl* **scleras, sclera** /-rie‖-raɪ/ the opaque white outer coat enclosing the eyeball except the part covered by the cornea

sclerosis /skləˈrohsis‖skləˈrəʊsɪs/ *n* **1** (a disease characterized by) abnormal hardening of tissue, esp from overgrowth of fibrous tissue **2** the natural hardening of plant cell walls usu by the formation of lignin – **sclerose** *vb*

sclerotium /skləˈrohshyəm‖skləˈrəʊʃjəm/ *n, pl* **sclerotia** /-tyə‖-tjə/ a compact mass of hardened fungal mycelium that becomes detached and remains dormant until a favourable opportunity for growth occurs – **sclerotial** *adj*

[1]**scoff** /skof‖skɒf/ *n* an expression of scorn, derision, or contempt

[2]**scoff** *vi* to show contempt by derisive acts or language – often + *at* <~ *at conventional wisdom*> – **scoffer** *n*

[3]**scoff** *vt, chiefly Br* to eat, esp greedily, rapidly, or in an ill-mannered way – infml

[1]**scold** /skohld‖skəʊld/ *n* a woman who habitually nags or quarrels

[2]**scold** *vi* to find fault noisily and at length ~*vt* to reprove sharply – **scolder** *n*

scollop /ˈskoləp‖ˈskɒləp/ *n* a scallop

[1]**sconce** /skons‖skɒns/ *n* a bracket candlestick or group of candlesticks; *also* an electric light fixture patterned on a candle sconce

[2]**sconce** *n* a detached defensive work (e g a fort or mound)

scone /skon, skohn‖skɒn, skəʊn;/ *n* any of several small light cakes made from a dough or batter containing a raising agent and baked in a hot oven or on a griddle

[1]**scoop** /skoohp‖skuːp/ *n* **1a** a large ladle for taking up or skimming liquids **b** a deep shovel for lifting and moving granular material (e g corn or sand) **c** a handled utensil of shovel shape or with a hemispherical bowl for spooning out soft food (e g ice cream) **d** a small spoon-shaped utensil for cutting or gouging (e g in surgical operations) **2a** an act or the action of scooping **b** the amount held by a scoop <*a* ~ *of sugar*> **3** a cavity **4** material for publication or broadcast, esp when obtained ahead or to the exclusion of competitors – **scoopful** *n*

[2]**scoop** *vt* **1** to take out or up (as if) with a scoop **2** to empty by scooping **3** to make hollow; dig out **4** to obtain a news story in advance or to the exclusion of (a competitor) **5** to obtain by swift action or sudden good fortune – chiefly infml <~ *the lion's share of an aid programme*>

scoot /skooht‖skuːt/ *vi* to go suddenly and swiftly – infml – **scoot** *n*

scooter /ˈskoohtə‖ˈskuːtə/ *n* **1** a child's foot-operated vehicle consisting of a narrow board with usu 1 wheel at each end and an upright steering handle **2** MOTOR SCOOTER

[1]**scope** /skohp‖skəʊp/ *n* **1** space or opportunity for unhampered action, thought, or development **2a** extent of treatment, activity, or influence **b** extent of understanding or perception

[2]**scope** *n* a periscope, telescope, or other optical instrument – infml

-scope /-skohp‖-skəʊp/ *comb form* (→ *n*) instrument for viewing or observing <*micro*scope>

scorbutic /skawˈbyoohtik‖skɔːˈbjuːtɪk/ *adj* of, resembling, or diseased with scurvy – **scorbutically** *adv*

[1]**scorch** /skawch‖skɔːtʃ/ *vt* **1** to burn so as to produce a change in colour and texture **2a** to parch (as if) with intense heat **b** to criticize or deride bitterly **3** to devastate completely, esp before abandoning – used in *scorched earth*, of property of possible use to an enemy ~ *vi* **1** to become scorched **2** to travel at (excessive) speed – **scorchingly** *adv*

[2]**scorch** *n* a mark resulting from scorching

scorcher /ˈskawchə‖ˈskɔːtʃə/ *n* a very hot day – infml

[1]**score** /skaw‖skɔː/ *n, pl* **scores,** (*1a, b*) **scores, score** **1a** twenty **b** a group of 20 things – used in combination with a cardinal number <*fives*core> **c** *pl* an indefinite large number **2a** a line (e g a scratch or incision) made (as if) with a sharp instrument **b** a notch used for keeping a tally **3a** an account or reckoning kept by making incisions **b** an account of debts **c** an amount due **4** a grudge <*settle an old* ~> **5a** a reason, ground <*complain on the* ~ *of maltreatment*> **b** a subject, topic <*have no doubts on*

that ~> **6a** the copy of a musical composition in written or printed notation **b** the music for a film or theatrical production **c** a complete description of a dance composition in choreographic notation **7a** a number that expresses accomplishment (e g in a game or test) **b** an act (e g a goal, run, or try) in any of various games or contests that increases such a number **8** the inescapable facts of a situation <*knows the* ~>

2**score** *vt* **1a** to record (as if) by notches on a tally **b** to enter (a debt) in an account – usu + *to* or *against* **c** to cancel or strike out (e g record of a debt) with a line or notch – often + *out* **2** to mark with grooves, scratches, or notches **3a(1)** to gain (e g points) in a game or contest <~d *8 runs*> **a(2)** to have as a value in a game or contest <*a try* ~s *4 points*> **b** to gain, win <~d *a success with his latest novel*> **4a** to write or arrange (music) for specific voice or instrumental parts **b** to orchestrate **c** to compose a score for (e g a film) ~ *vi* **1** to record the scores or make a score in a game or contest **2** to obtain a rating or grade <~ *high in intelligence tests*> **3a** to gain or have an advantage or a success **b** to obtain illicit drugs – slang **c** to achieve a sexual success – slang – **scorer** *n* – **score off someone** *Br* to get the better of sby in debate or argument

'**score,board** /-,bawd||-,bɔːd/ *n* a usu large board for displaying the state of play (e g the score) in a game or match

1**scorn** /skawn||skɔːn/ *n* **1** vigorous contempt; disdain **2** an expression of extreme contempt **3** an object of extreme disdain or derision – **scornful** *adj*

2**scorn** *vt* to reject with outspoken contempt – **scorner** *n*

Scorpio /'skawpioh||'skɔːpɪəʊ/ *n* (sby born under) the 8th sign of the zodiac in astrology, which is pictured as a scorpion – **Scorpian** *adj or n*

scorpion /'skawpyən||'skɔːpjən/ *n* any of an order of arachnids having an elongated body and a narrow tail bearing a venomous sting at the tip

Scot /skot||skɒt/ *n* **1** a member of a Gaelic people orig of N Ireland that settled in Scotland about AD 500 **2** a native or inhabitant of Scotland

1**scotch** /skoch||skɒtʃ/ *vt* **1a** to stamp out; crush **b** to hinder, thwart <~ *schemes for sponsorship*> **2** to repudiate by exhibiting as false <~ *rumours*>

2**scotch** *n* a slight cut

1**Scotch** *adj* Scottish

2**Scotch** *n* **1** Scots **2** *pl in constr the* Scots **3** *often not cap* SCOTCH WHISKY; *broadly* (a) whisky

,**Scotch 'broth** *n* soup made from beef or mutton, vegetables, and barley

,**Scotch 'egg** *n* a hard-boiled egg covered with sausage meat, coated with breadcrumbs, and deep-fried

Scotch tape *trademark* – used for any of numerous adhesive tapes

,**Scotch 'whisky** *n* whisky distilled in Scotland, esp from malted barley

,**scot-'free** *adj* without any penalty, payment, or injury

,**Scotland 'Yard** /'skotlənd||'skɒtlənd/ *n sing or pl in constr* the criminal investigation department of the London metropolitan police force

1**Scots** /skots||skɒts/ *adj* Scottish

2**Scots** *n* the English language of Scotland

1**Scottish** /'skotish||'skɒtɪʃ/ *adj* (characteristic) of Scotland – **Scottishness** *n*

2**Scottish** *n* Scots

,**Scottish 'terrier** *n* (any of) a Scottish breed of terrier with short legs and a very wiry coat of usu black hair

scoundrel /'skowndrəl||'skaʊndrəl/ *n* a wicked or dishonest fellow – **scoundrelly** *adj*

1**scour** /'skowə||'skaʊə/ *vt* **1** to move through or range over usu swiftly **2** to make a rapid but thorough search of

2**scour** *vt* **1a** to rub vigorously in order to cleanse **b** to remove by rubbing, esp with rough or abrasive material **2** to clean out by purging **3** to free from impurities (as if) by washing **4** to clear, excavate, or remove (as if) by a powerful current of water ~ *vi* **1** to undertake scouring **2** *esp of cattle* to suffer from diarrhoea or dysentery **3** to become clean and bright by being rubbed – **scourer** *n*

3**scour** *n* **1** scouring action (e g of a glacier) **2** diarrhoea or dysentery, esp in cattle – usu pl with sing. meaning but sing. or pl in constr

1**scourge** /skuhj||skɜːdʒ/ *n* **1** a whip used to inflict punishment **2a** a means of vengeance or criticism **b** a cause of affliction

2**scourge** *vt* **1** to flog **2a** to punish severely **b** to subject to affliction; devastate **c** to subject to scathing criticism – **scourger** *n*

Scouse /skows||skaʊs/ *n or adj* (a native or inhabitant or the dialect) of Merseyside – chiefly infml [short for *lobscouse*, a type of stew popular on Merseyside]

1**scout** /skowt||skaʊt/ *vi* to make an advance survey (e g to obtain military information) ~ *vt* **1** to observe or explore in order to obtain information **2** to find by making a search – often + *out* or *up*

2**scout** *n* **1** the act or an instance of scouting **2a** sby or sthg sent to obtain (military) information **b** TALENT SCOUT **3** an Oxford university college servant **4** *often cap* a member of a worldwide movement of boys and young men that was founded with the aim of developing leadership and comradeship and that lays stress on outdoor activities; *specif* a British boy member aged from 11 to 15

'**scout,master** /-,mahstə||-,mɑːstə/ *n* the adult leader of a troop of scouts – no longer used technically

scow /skow||skaʊ/ *n* a large flat-bottomed usu unpowered boat used chiefly for transporting ore, sand, refuse, etc

1**scowl** /skowl||skaʊl/ *vi* **1** to frown or wrinkle the brows in expression of displeasure **2** to exhibit a gloomy or threatening aspect – **scowler** *n*

2**scowl** *n* an angry frown

1**scrabble** /'skrabl||'skræbl/ *vi* **1** to scratch or scrape about **2a** to scramble, clamber **b** to struggle frantically <*urchins* scrabbling *for leftovers*> *USE* infml – **scrabbler** *n*

[2]**scrabble** *n* **1** a persistent scratching or clawing **2** a scramble *USE* infml

Scrabble *trademark* – used for a board game of word-building from individual letters

[1]**scrag** /skrag||skræg/ *n* **1** a scraggy person or animal **2** (the bony end nearest the head of) a neck of mutton or veal

[2]**scrag** *vt* **-gg- 1** to kill or execute by hanging, garrotting, or wringing the neck of **2** to attack in anger – infml

scraggly /ˈskragli||ˈskræglı/ *adj, NAm* irregular; *also* ragged, unkempt – infml

scraggy /ˈskragi||ˈskrægı/ *adj* lean and lanky in growth or build

scram /skram||skræm/ *vi* **-mm-** to go away at once – infml

[1]**scramble** /ˈskrambl||ˈskræmbl/ *vi* **1a** to move or climb using hands and feet, esp hastily **b** to move with urgency or panic **2** to struggle eagerly or chaotically for possession of sthg **3a** to spread or grow irregularly **b** *of a plant* to climb over a support **4** *esp of an aircraft or its crew* to take off quickly in response to an alert ~ *vt* **1** to collect by scrambling – + *up* or *together* <~d *up a hasty supper*> **2a** to toss or mix together **b** to prepare (eggs) in a pan by stirring during cooking **3** to cause or order (an aircraft) to scramble **4** to encode (the elements of a telecommunications transmission) in order to make unintelligible on unmodified receivers

[2]**scramble** *n* **1** a scrambling movement or struggle **2** a disordered mess; a jumble **3** a rapid emergency takeoff of aircraft **4** a motorcycle race over very rough ground

[1]**scrap** /skrap||skræp/ *n* **1** *pl* fragments of discarded or leftover food **2a** a small detached fragment **b** an excerpt from sthg written or printed **c** the smallest piece **3** *pl* the remains of animal fat after rendering; cracklings **4a** the residue from a manufacturing process **b** manufactured articles or parts, esp of metal, rejected or discarded and useful only for reprocessing

[2]**scrap** *vt* **-pp- 1** to convert into scrap <~ *a battleship*> **2** to abandon or get rid of, as without further use <~ *outworn methods*>

[3]**scrap** *vi or n* **-pp-** (to engage in) a minor fight or dispute – infml

ˈ**scrap**ˌ**book** /-ˌbook||-ˌbʊk/ *n* a blank book in which miscellaneous items (e g newspaper cuttings or postcards) may be pasted

[1]**scrape** /skrayp||skreıp/ *vt* **1a** to remove (clinging matter) from a surface by usu repeated strokes of an edged instrument **b** to make (a surface) smooth or clean with strokes of an edged or rough instrument **2a** to grate harshly over or against **b** to damage or injure by contact with a rough surface **c** to draw roughly or noisily over a surface **3** to collect or procure (as if) by scraping – often + *up* or *together* <~ *up the price of a pint*> ~ *vi* **1** to move in sliding contact with a rough or abrasive surface **2** to accumulate money by small but difficult economies <scraping *and saving to educate their children*> **3** to draw back the foot along the ground in making a bow – chiefly in *bow and scrape* **4** to get by with difficulty or succeed by a narrow margin – often + *in, through*, or *by* <*the candidate* ~d *through with a majority of 6*> – **scraper** *n*

[2]**scrape** *n* **1a** an act, process, or result of scraping **b** the sound of scraping **2** a disagreeable predicament, esp as a result of foolish behaviour – infml

ˈ**scrap** ˌ**heap** *n* **1** a pile of discarded materials, esp metal **2** the place to which useless things are consigned

scrappy /ˈskrapi||ˈskræpı/ *adj* consisting of scraps

[1]**scratch** /skrach||skrætʃ/ *vt* **1** to scrape or dig with the claws or nails **2** to tear, mark, or cut the surface of with sthg sharp or jagged **3** to scrape or rub lightly (e g to relieve itching) **4** to scrape together <~ *a precarious living – Punch*> **5** to write or draw on a surface <~ed *his initials on the desk*> **6a** to cancel or erase (as if) by drawing a line through **b** to withdraw (an entry) from competition ~ *vi* **1** to use the claws or nails in digging, tearing, or wounding **2** to scrape or rub oneself (e g to relieve itching) **3** to acquire money by hard work and saving **4** to make a thin grating sound <*this pen* ~es> – **scratcher** *n*

[2]**scratch** *n* **1** a mark, injury, or slight wound (produced by scratching) **2** the sound of scratching **3** the most rudimentary beginning – in *from scratch* **4** standard or satisfactory condition or performance <*not up to* ~>

[3]**scratch** *adj* **1** made or done by chance and not as intended <*a* ~ *shot*> **2** arranged or put together haphazardly or hastily <*a* ~ *team*> **3** without handicap or allowance <*a* ~ *golfer*>

scratchy /ˈskrachi||ˈskrætʃı/ *adj* **1** tending to scratch or irritate <~ *wool*> **2** making a scratching noise <*a* ~ *pen*> **3** made (as if) with scratches <~ *drawing*> **4** uneven in quality **5** irritable, fractious – **scratchiness** *n*

scrawl /skrawl||skrɔːl/ *vb* to write or draw awkwardly, hastily, or carelessly – **scrawl** *n*, **scrawler** *n*, **scrawly** *adj*

scrawny /ˈskrawni||ˈskrɔːnı/ *adj* exceptionally thin and slight – **scrawniness** *n*

[1]**scream** /skreem||skriːm/ *vi* **1a(1)** to voice a sudden piercing cry, esp in alarm or pain **a(2)** to produce harsh high tones **b** to move with or make a shrill noise like a scream **2** to speak or write violently or hysterically <*a* ~ing *headline*> **3** to produce a vivid or startling effect <*a* ~ing *red*> ~ *vt* **1** to utter (as if) with a scream or screams **2** to bring to a specified state by screaming <~ *oneself hoarse*> – **screamer** *n*

[2]**scream** *n* **1** a shrill penetrating cry or noise **2** sby or sthg that provokes screams of laughter – infml

scree /skree||skriː/ *n* (a mountain slope covered with) loose stones or rocky debris

[1]**screech** /skreech||skriːtʃ/ *vi* **1** to utter a shrill piercing cry; cry out, esp in terror or pain [illegible] o make a sound like a screech <*the car* ~ed [illegible] *a halt*> – **screecher** *n*

[2]**screech** *n* a shrill sound or cry

ˈ**screech** ˌ**owl** *n* a barn owl or other owl with a harsh shrill cry

screed /skreed||skriːd/ *n* **1** an overlong usu dull piece of writing **2** a strip (e g of plaster) serving as a guide to the thickness of a subsequent coat **3** a levelling device drawn over freshly poured concrete

[1]**screen** /skreen||skri:n/ *n* **1a** a usu movable piece of furniture that gives protection from heat or draughts or is used as an ornament <*fire ~*> **b** an ornamental partition **2a** sthg that shelters, protects, or conceals <*a ~ of light infantry*> **b** a shield for secret usu illicit practices **3a** a sieve or perforated material set in a frame used to separate coarser from finer parts **b** a device that shields from interference (e g by electrical or magnetic fields) **c** a frame holding a netting used esp in a window or door to exclude mosquitoes and other pests **4a** a surface on which images are projected or reflected **b** the surface on which the image appears in a television or radar receiver **c** a ruled glass plate through which an image is photographed in making a halftone **5a** *the* film industry; films <*a star of stage and ~*> **b** *the* medium of television

[2]**screen** *vt* **1** to guard from injury, danger, or punishment **2a** to separate (as if) with a screen **b** to provide with a screen to keep out pests (e g insects) **3a** to pass (e g coal, gravel, or ashes) through a screen to separate the fine part from the coarse; *also* to remove (as if) by a screen **b(1)** to examine systematically so as to separate into different groups <*~ visa applications*> **b(2)** to test or check by a screening process **4a** to show or broadcast (a film or television programme) **b** to present in a film or on television – **screenable** *adj*, **screener** *n*

screening /'skreening||'skri:nɪŋ/ *n* **1** *pl but sing or pl in constr* material (e g waste or fine coal) separated out by a screen **2** metal or plastic mesh (e g for window screens) **3** a showing of a film or television programme

'screen,play /-,play||-,pleɪ/ *n* the script of a film including description of characters, details of scenes and settings, dialogue, and stage directions

[1]**screw** /skrooh||skru:/ *n* **1** a simple machine of the inclined plane type in which the applied force acts along a spiral path about a cylinder while the resisting force acts along the axis of the cylinder **2a** a usu pointed tapering metal rod having a raised thread along all or part of its length and a usu slotted head which may be driven into a body by rotating (e g with a screwdriver) **b** a screw-bolt that can be turned by a screwdriver **3a** sthg like a screw in form or function; a spiral **b** a turn of a screw; *also* a twist resembling such a turn **4** SCREW PROPELLER **5** a thumbscrew **6** backspin, esp when given to a cue ball in billiards, snooker, etc **7** *chiefly Br* a small twisted paper packet (e g of tobacco) **8** sby who drives a hard bargain – slang **9** a prison guard – slang **10** an act of sexual intercourse – vulg – **screwlike** *adj*

[2]**screw** *vt* **1a(1)** to attach, close, operate, adjust, etc by means of a screw **a(2)** to unite or separate by means of a screw or a twisting motion <*~ the 2 pieces together*> **b** to cause to rotate spirally about an axis **2a(1)** to contort (the face) or narrow (the eyes) (e g with effort or an emotion) – often + *up* **a(2)** to crush into irregular folds **b** to make a spiral groove or ridge in **3** to increase the intensity, quantity, or effectiveness of <*~ up one's courage*> **4** to give backwards spin to (a ball) **5a** to make oppressive demands on <*~ed him for every penny he'd got*> **b** to extract by pressure or threat – usu + *from* or *out of* **6** to copulate with ~ *vi* **1a** to rotate like or as a screw **b** to become secured (as if) by screwing – usu + *on* or *up* <*panels that ~ on*> **2** to turn or move with a twisting motion **3** to copulate *USE* (*vt 2a(2), 3*) usu + *up*; (*vt 5*) slang; (*vt 6; vi 3*) vulg – **screwer** *n*

'screw,ball /-,bawl||-,bɔ:l/ *n or adj, chiefly NAm* (sby) crazily eccentric or whimsical – infml

'screw,driver /-,drievə||-,draɪvə/ *n* a tool for turning screws

screw propeller *n* a device that consists of a central hub with radiating blades and is used to propel a vehicle (e g a ship or aeroplane)

screw top *n* (an opening designed to take) a cover secured by twisting

screw up *vt* **1** to fasten or lock (as if) by a screw **2** to bungle, botch **3** to cause to become anxious or neurotic *USE* (*2, 3*) slang

screwy /'skrooh·i||'skru:ɪ/ *adj* crazily absurd, eccentric, or unusual; *also* mad – infml – **screwiness** *n*

scribble /'skribl||'skrɪbl/ *vb* to write or draw without regard for legibility or coherence – **scribble** *n*

scribbler /'skriblə||'skrɪblə/ *n* a minor or worthless author

[1]**scribe** /skrieb||skraɪb/ *n* **1** a member of a learned class of lay jurists in ancient Israel up to New Testament times **2** a copier of manuscripts **3** an author; *specif* a journalist – chiefly humor – **scribal** *adj*

[2]**scribe** *vt* **1** to mark a line on by scoring with a pointed instrument **2** to make (e g a line) by scratching or gouging

scrimmage /'skrimij||'skrɪmɪdʒ/ *vi or n* (to take part in) **a** a confused fight or minor battle; a mêlée **b** the interplay between 2 American football teams that begins with the passing back of the ball from the ground and continues until the ball is dead

scrimp /skrimp||skrɪmp/ *vi* to be frugal or niggardly – esp in *scrimp and save* ~*vt* to be niggardly in providing (for) – **scrimpy** *adj*

scrimshank /'skrim,shangk||'skrɪm,ʃæŋk/ *vi, Br* to avoid duties or obligations – infml – **scrimshanker** *n*

scrimshaw /'skrim,shaw||'skrɪm,ʃɔ:/ *n* carved or coloured work made esp by sailors from ivory or whalebone – **scrimshaw** *vb*

scrip /skrip||skrɪp/ *n* any of various documents used as evidence that the holder or bearer is entitled to receive sthg

[1]**script** /skript||skrɪpt/ *n* **1a** sthg written; text <*handed him several pages of ~*> **b** an original document **c** the written text of a stage play, film, or broadcast (used in production or performance) **d** an examination candidate's written answers <*a pile of ~s to mark*> **2a** (printed lettering resembling) handwriting **b** the characters used in the alphabet of a particular language <*unable to decipher Cyrillic ~*> [Latin *scriptum* thing written, fr *script-*, *scribere* to write]

[2]**script** *vt* to prepare a script for or from

scriptural /'skripchərəl||'skrɪptʃərəl/ *adj* of,

contained in, or according to a sacred writing; *esp* biblical – **scripturally** *adv*

scripture /'skripchə‖'skrɪptʃə/ *n* **1a** *often cap* the sacred writings of a religion; *esp* the Bible – often pl with sing. meaning **b** a passage from the Bible **2** an authoritative body of writings

scriptwriter /'skript,rietə‖'skrɪpt,raɪtə/ *n* one who writes screenplays or radio or television programmes

scrivener /'skrivn·ə‖'skrɪvnə/ *n* a notary

scrofula /'skrofyoolə‖'skrɒfjʊlə/ *n* tuberculosis of lymph glands, esp in the neck – **scrofulous** *adj*

scroll /skrohl‖skrəʊl/ *n* **1** a written document in the form of a roll **2** a stylized ornamental design imitating the spiral curves of a scroll – **scrolled** *adj*

scrooge /skroohj‖skru:dʒ/ *n, often cap* a miserly person – infml [Ebenezer *Scrooge*, character in *A Christmas Carol*, story by Charles Dickens (1812-70), English writer]

scrotum /'skrohtəm‖'skrəʊtəm/ *n, pl* **scrota** /-tə‖-tə/, **scrotums** the external pouch of most male mammals that contains the testes – **scrotal** *adj*

[1]**scrounge** /skrownj‖skraʊndʒ/ *vt* to beg, wheedle <*can I ~ a cigarette off you?*> ~ *vi* **1** to hunt *around* **2** to wheedle – **scrounger** *n*

[2]**scrounge** *n* – **on the scrounge** attempting to obtain sthg by wheedling or cajoling

[1]**scrub** /skrub‖skrʌb/ *n* **1** (an area covered with) vegetation consisting chiefly of stunted trees or shrubs <~ *land*> <~ *vegetation*> **2a** a usu inferior type of domestic animal of mixed or unknown parentage; a mongrel **b** a small or insignificant person; a runt

[2]**scrub** *vb* **-bb-** *vt* **1a** to clean by rubbing, esp with a stiff brush **b** to remove by scrubbing **2** WASH 6b **3** to abolish; DO AWAY WITH <*let's ~ that idea*> – infml ~*vi* to use hard rubbing in cleaning

scrubber /'skrubə‖'skrʌbə/ *n* **1** an apparatus for removing impurities, esp from gases **2** *Br* a girl who is readily available for casual sex; *also* a prostitute **3** *Br* a coarse or unattractive person *USE* (*2, 3*) slang

'scrubbing ,brush /'skrubing‖'skrʌbɪŋ/, *NAm* **scrub brush** *n* a brush with hard bristles used for heavy cleaning, esp washing floors

scrubby /'skrubi‖'skrʌbɪ/ *adj* **1** inferior in size or quality; stunted <~ *cattle*> **2** covered with or consisting of scrub **3** lacking distinction; trashy – infml

[1]**scruff** /skruf‖skrʌf/ *n* the back of the neck; the nape

[2]**scruff** *n* an untidily dressed or grubby person – infml

scruffy /'skrufi‖'skrʌfɪ/ *adj* **1** seedy, disreputable <*a ~ neighbourhood*> **2** slovenly and untidy, esp in appearance – **scruffiness** *n*

scrum /skrum‖skrʌm/ *n* **1** a set piece in rugby in which the forwards of each side crouch in a tight formation with the 2 front rows of each team meeting shoulder to shoulder so that the ball can be put in play between them **2** a disorderly struggle – chiefly humor <*the morning ~ to board the bus*>

,scrum-'half *n* the player in rugby who puts the ball into the scrum

scrummage /'skrumij‖'skrʌmɪdʒ/ *vi or n* (to take part in) a scrum

scrumptious /'skrum(p)shəs‖'skrʌm(p)ʃəs/ *adj, esp of food* delicious – infml – **scrumptiously** *adv*, **scrumptiousness** *n*

scrumpy /'skrumpi‖'skrʌmpɪ/ *n, Br* dry rough cider

scrunch /skrunch‖skrʌntʃ/ *vt* **1** to crunch, crush **2** to crumple – often + *up* <~ *up a sheet of cardboard*> ~ *vi* **1** to move making a crunching sound <*her boots* ~ed *in the snow*> **2** *NAm* to hunch up – **scrunch** *n*

[1]**scruple** /'skroohpl‖'skru:pl/ *n* **1** a unit of weight equal to 1/24oz apothecary (about 1.296g) **2** *archaic* a minute part or quantity

[2]**scruple** *n* a moral consideration that inhibits action

[3]**scruple** *vi* to be reluctant on grounds of conscience

scrupulous /'skroohpyooləs‖'skru:pjʊləs/ *adj* **1** inclined to have moral scruples **2** painstakingly exact – **scrupulously** *adv*, **scrupulousness** *n*, **scrupulosity** *n*

scrutineer /,skroohti'niə‖,skru:tɪ'nɪə/ *n, Br* sby who examines or observes sthg, esp the counting of votes at an election

scrutin·ize, -ise /'skroohti,niez‖'skru:tɪ,naɪz/ *vt* to examine painstakingly – **scrutinizer** *n*

scrutiny /'skroohtini‖'skru:tɪnɪ/ *n* **1** a searching study, inquiry, or inspection **2** a searching or critical look

scuba /'sk(y)oohbə‖'sk(j)u:bə/ *n* an aqualung [*s*elf-*c*ontained *u*nderwater *b*reathing *a*pparatus]

[1]**scud** /skud‖skʌd/ *vi* **-dd-** **1** to move or run swiftly, esp as if swept along **2** *of a ship* to run before a gale

[2]**scud** *n* **1a** a sudden slight shower **b** ocean spray or loose vaporizing clouds driven swiftly by the wind **2** a gust of wind

[1]**scuff** /skuf‖skʌf/ *vi* **1** to slouch along without lifting the feet **2** to become scratched or roughened by wear ~ *vt* **1** to shuffle (the feet) along while walking or back and forth while standing **2** to scratch, chip, or abrade the surface of

[2]**scuff** *n* **1** (a blemish or injury caused by) scuffing **2** *NAm* a noise (as if) of scuffing

[1]**scuffle** /'skufl‖'skʌfl/ *vi* **1** to struggle confusedly and at close quarters **2** to move (hurriedly) about with a shuffling gait

[2]**scuffle** *n* a confused impromptu usu brief fight

[1]**scull** /skul‖skʌl/ *n* **1** an oar worked to and fro over the stern of a boat as a means of propulsion **2** either of a pair of light oars used by a single rower

[2]**scull** *vb* to propel (a boat) by sculls or by a large oar worked to and fro over the stern – **sculler** *n*

scullery /'skul(ə)ri‖'skʌl(ə)rɪ/ *n* a room for menial kitchen work (e g washing dishes and preparing vegetables)

scullion /'skulyən‖'skʌljən/ *n, archaic* a kitchen servant

sculpt /skulpt‖skʌlpt/ *vt* to sculpture

sculptor /'skulptə‖'skʌlptə/, *fem* **sculptress** /-tris‖-trɪs/ *n* an artist who sculptures

[1]**sculpture** /'skulpchə‖'skʌlptʃə/ *n* **1** the art of

creating three-dimensional works of art out of mouldable or hard materials by carving, modelling, casting, etc **2** (a piece of) work produced by sculpture – **sculptural** *adj*, **sculpturally** *adv*

[2]**sculpture** *vt* **1a** to represent in sculpture **b** to form (e g wood or stone) into a sculpture **2** to shape by erosion or other natural processes **3** to shape (as if) by carving or moulding

[1]**scum** /skum‖skʌm/ *n* **1** pollutants or impurities risen to or collected on the surface of a liquid **2** *pl in constr* the lowest class; the dregs <*the ~ of the earth*> – **scummy** *adj*

[2]**scum** *vi* **-mm-** to become covered (as if) with scum

[1]**scupper** /ˈskupə‖ˈskʌpə/ *n* an opening in a ship's side for draining water from the deck

[2]**scupper** *vt, Br* to wreck; PUT PAID TO – infml

scurf /skuhf‖skɜːf/ *n* thin dry scales detached from the skin; *specif* dandruff – **scurfy** *adj*

scurrilous /ˈskuriləs‖ˈskʌrɪləs/ *adj* **1a** using or given to coarse language **b** wicked and unscrupulous in behaviour **2** containing obscenities or coarse abuse – **scurrilously** *adv*, **scurrilousness** *n*, **scurrility** *n*

scurry /ˈskuri‖ˈskʌrɪ/ *vi* to move briskly, esp with short hurried steps, and often in some agitation – **scurry** *n*

[1]**scurvy** /ˈskuhvi‖ˈskɜːvɪ/ *adj* disgustingly mean or contemptible <*a ~ trick*> – **scurvily** *adv*, **scurviness** *n*

[2]**scurvy** *n* a deficiency disease caused by a lack of vitamin C

scut /skut‖skʌt/ *n* a short erect tail (e g of a hare)

[1]**scuttle** /ˈskutl‖ˈskʌtl/ *n* a vessel that resembles a bucket and is used for storing, carrying, and dispensing coal indoors

[2]**scuttle** *n* **1** a small opening or hatchway with a movable lid in the deck of a ship **2** *Br* the top part of a motor-car body forward of the 2 front doors, to which the windscreen and instrument panel are attached

[3]**scuttle** *vt* **1** to sink (a ship) by making holes in the hull or opening the sea-cocks **2** to scupper

[4]**scuttle** *vi* to scurry, scamper

[5]**scuttle** *n* **1** a quick shuffling pace **2** a short swift dash; *esp* a swift departure

[1]**scythe** /siedh‖saɪð/ *n* a long curving blade fastened at an angle to a long handle for cutting standing plants, esp grass

[2]**scythe** *vt* to cut (as if) with a scythe

sea /see‖siː/ *n* **1a** OCEAN 1; *broadly* the waters of the earth as distinguished from the land and air – often pl with sing. meaning **b** a large (partially) landlocked or inland body of salt water **c** a freshwater lake **2** (the direction of) surface motion caused by the wind on a large body of water; *also* a heavy swell or wave **3** sthg vast or overwhelming likened to the sea <*a ~ of faces*> **4** the seafaring life <*to run away to ~*> **5** [2]MARE – **at sea 1** on the sea; *specif* on a sea voyage **2** unable to understand; bewildered <*he was all* at sea, *having never done such work before*>

ˈ**sea ˌanchor** *n* a device, typically of canvas, thrown overboard to slow the drifting of a ship or seaplane and to keep its head to the wind

ˈ**sea aˌnemone** *n* any of numerous usu solitary and brightly coloured polyps with a cluster of tentacles superficially resembling a flower

ˈ**seaˌbird** /-ˌbuhd‖-ˌbɜːd/ *n* a bird (e g a gull or albatross) frequenting the open sea

ˈ**seaˌboard** /-ˌbawd‖-ˌbɔːd/ *n, chiefly NAm* (the land near) a seashore – **seaboard** *adj*

ˈ**seaˌborne** /-ˌbawn‖-ˌbɔːn/ *adj* conveyed on or over the sea <*~ trade*>

sea breeze *n* a cool breeze blowing usu during the day inland from the sea

ˈ**sea ˌcaptain** *n* the master of a (merchant) vessel

ˈ**sea ˌchange** *n* a complete transformation

ˈ**seaˌfaring** /-ˌfeəring‖-ˌfeərɪŋ/ *n* travel by sea; *esp* the occupation of a sailor – **seafaring** *adj*

ˈ**seaˌfood** /-ˌfoohd‖-ˌfuːd/ *n* edible marine fish, shellfish, crustaceans, etc

ˈ**seaˌfront** /-ˌfrunt‖-ˌfrʌnt/ *n* the waterfront of a seaside town

ˈ**seaˌgoing** /-ˌgoh·ing‖-ˌgəʊɪŋ/ *adj* of or designed for travel on the sea

ˈ**sea ˌgull** *n* [1]GULL

ˈ**sea ˌhorse** *n* **1** a mythical creature half horse and half fish **2** any of numerous small fishes whose head and body are shaped like the head and neck of a horse

ˈ**seaˌkale** /-ˌkayl‖-ˌkeɪl/ *n* **1** a fleshy European plant of the mustard family used as a herb in cooking **2** *also* **seakale beet** chard

[1]**seal** /seel‖siːl/ *n* **1** any of numerous marine flesh-eating mammals chiefly of cold regions with limbs modified into webbed flippers for swimming **2** sealskin

[2]**seal** *vi* to hunt seal

[3]**seal** *n* **1a** sthg that confirms, ratifies, or makes secure **b(1)** an emblem or word impressed or stamped on a document as a mark of authenticity **b(2)** an article used to impress such a word or emblem (e g on wax); *also* a disc, esp of wax, bearing such an impression **2a** a closure (e g a wax seal on a document or a strip of paper over the cork of a bottle) that must be broken in order to give access, and so guarantees that the item so closed has not been tampered with **b** a tight and effective closure (e g against gas or liquid) – **under seal** with an authenticating seal attached

[4]**seal** *vt* **1** to confirm or make secure (as if) by a seal <*~ed the agreement with a handshake*> **2a** to attach an authenticating seal to; *also* to authenticate, ratify **b** to mark with a stamp or seal (e g as evidence of size, accuracy, or quality) **3a** to fasten (as if) with a seal, esp to prevent or disclose interference **b** to close or make secure against access, leakage, or passage by a fastening or coating; *esp* to make airtight **c** to fix in position or close breaks in with a filling (e g of plaster) **4** to determine irrevocably <*that answer ~ed our fate*>

ˈ**sea ˌlegs** *n pl* bodily adjustment to the motion of a ship, indicated esp by ability to walk steadily and by freedom from seasickness

[1]**sealer** /ˈseelə‖ˈsiːlə/ *n* **1** a coat (e g of size) applied to prevent subsequent coats of paint or varnish from being too readily absorbed **2** *chiefly NAm* an official who certifies conformity to a standard of correctness

[2]**sealer** *n* a person or ship engaged in hunting seals

ˈ**sea ˌlevel** *n* the mean level of the surface of the sea midway between high and low tide

ˈ**sealing ˌwax** /ˈseeling‖ˈsiːlɪŋ/ *n* a resinous composition that becomes soft when heated and is used for sealing letters, parcels, etc

ˈ**sea ˌlion** *n* any of several large Pacific seals

seal off *vt* to close securely, esp in order to prevent passage <*troops* sealed off *the airport*>

ˈ**sealˌskin** /ˌskin‖ˌskɪn/ *n* **1** (leather made from) the skin of a seal **2** a garment of sealskin – **sealskin** *adj*

ˌ**Sealyham** ˈ**terrier** /ˈseeli·əm‖ˈsiːlɪəm/ *n* (any of) a breed of short-legged wirehaired chiefly white Welsh terriers [*Sealyham*, estate in Pembrokeshire, Wales]

[1]**seam** /seem‖siːm/ *n* **1** a line of stitching joining 2 separate pieces of fabric, esp along their edges **2** the space between adjacent planks or strakes of a ship **3a** a line, groove, or ridge formed at the meeting of 2 edges **b** a layer or stratum of coal, rock, etc **c** a line left by a cut or wound; *also* a wrinkle – **seamless** *adj*

[2]**seam** *vt* **1** to join (as if) by sewing **2** to mark with a seam, furrow, or scar

seaman /ˈseemən‖ˈsiːmən/ *n* **1** a sailor, mariner **2** a trained person holding a rank below that of a noncommissioned officer in the US navy – **seamanlike** *adj*, **seamanly** *adj*, **seamanship** *n*

sea mile *n* NAUTICAL MILE

seamstress /ˈseemstris‖ˈsiːmstrɪs/ *n* a woman whose occupation is sewing

seamy /ˈseemi‖ˈsiːmɪ/ *adj* unpleasant, sordid <*the* ~ *side of the building trade*> – **seaminess** *n*

séance /ˈsay·on(h)s‖ˈseɪɒns, ˈseɪɑ̃s/ *n* a meeting at which spiritualists attempt to communicate with the dead [French, fr *seoir* to sit, fr Latin *sedēre*]

ˈ**seaˌplane** /-ˌplayn‖-ˌpleɪn/ *n* an aeroplane designed to take off from and land on the water

ˈ**seaˌport** /-ˌpawt‖-ˌpɔːt/ *n* a port, harbour, or town accessible to seagoing ships

ˈ**sea ˌpower** *n* (a nation that commands) naval strength

[1]**sear** /siə‖sɪə/ *adj* sere

[2]**sear** *vt* **1** to make withered and dried up **2** to burn, scorch, or injure (as if) with a sudden application of intense heat **3** to mark (as if) with a branding iron <*a sight which was* ~ed *on my memory*> – **searingly** *adv*

[3]**sear** *n* a mark or scar left by searing

[1]**search** /suhch‖sɜːtʃ/ *vt* **1a** to look through or over carefully or thoroughly in order to find or discover sthg <~ed *the horizon*> <~ed *the house for clues*> **b** to examine (a person) for concealed articles (e g weapons or drugs) **c** to scrutinize, esp in order to discover intention or nature <~ed *her heart*> **2** to uncover or ascertain by investigation – usu + *out* <~ *out the relevant facts*> **3** to cover (an area) with gunfire ~ *vi* **1** to look or inquire carefully or thoroughly <~ed *for the papers*> **2** to make painstaking investigation or examination <~ed *into the matter very thoroughly*> – **searchable** *adj*, **searcher** *n* – **search me** – used to express ignorance of an answer

[2]**search** *n* **1** an act or process of searching; *esp* an organized act of searching <*the* ~ *for the escaped convicts is still in progress*> <*a* ~ *party*> **2** an exercise of the right of search

searching /ˈsuhching‖ˈsɜːtʃɪŋ/ *adj* piercing, penetrating <*a* ~ *gaze*> – **searchingly** *adv*

ˈ**searchˌlight** /-ˌliet‖-ˌlaɪt/ *n* (an apparatus for projecting) a movable beam of light

ˈ**search ˌwarrant** *n* a warrant authorizing a search of premises for unlawful possessions

ˈ**seaˌscape** /-ˌskayp‖-ˌskeɪp/ *n* (a picture representing) a view of the sea

ˈ**seaˌshell** /-ˌshel‖-ˌʃel/ *n* the shell of a sea animal, esp a mollusc

ˌ**seaˈshore** /-ˈshaw‖-ˈʃɔː/ *n* land (between high and low water marks) next to the sea

ˈ**seaˌsick** /-ˌsik‖-ˌsɪk/ *adj* suffering from the motion sickness associated with travelling by boat or hovercraft – **seasickness** *n*

ˈ**seaˌside** /-ˌsied‖-ˌsaɪd/ *n* (a holiday resort or beach on) land bordering the sea

[1]**season** /ˈseez(ə)n‖ˈsiːz(ə)n/ *n* **1a** any of the 4 quarters into which the year is commonly divided **b** a period characterized by a particular kind of weather <*the dry* ~> **c** a period of the year characterized by or associated with a particular activity or phenomenon <*the holiday* ~> <*the hunting* ~> <*an animal's mating* ~> **d** the time of year when a place is most frequented <*difficult to find accommodation there at the height of the* ~> **e** the time of a major holiday; *specif* the Christmas season <*send the* ~*'s greetings*> **2** *archaic* an indefinite length of time – **in season 1** *of food* readily available and in the best condition for eating **2** *of game* legally available to be hunted or caught **3** *of an animal* on heat **4** *esp of advice* given when most needed or most welcome – **out of season** not in season

[2]**season** *vt* **1a** to give (food) more flavour by adding seasoning or savoury ingredients **b** to make less harsh or unpleasant; relieve **c** to enliven <*conversation* ~ed *with wit*> **2a** to treat or expose (e g timber) over a period so as to prepare for use **b** to make fit or expert by experience <*a* ~ed *veteran*> – **seasoner** *n*

seasonable /ˈseez(ə)nəbl‖ˈsiːz(ə)nəbl/ *adj* **1** occurring in good or proper time; opportune **2** suitable to the season or circumstances – **seasonableness** *n*, **seasonably** *adv*

seasonal /ˈseez(ə)nl‖ˈsiːz(ə)nl/ *adj* **1** of, occurring, or produced at a particular season <~ *rainfall*> **2** determined by seasonal need or availability <~ *employment*> – **seasonally** *adv*

seasoning /ˈseez(ə)ning‖ˈsiːz(ə)nɪŋ/ *n* a condiment, spice, herb, etc added to food primarily for the savour that it imparts

ˈ**season ˌticket** *n, Br* a ticket sold, usu at a reduced price, for an unlimited number of trips over the same route during a limited period

[1]**seat** /seet‖siːt/ *n* **1a** a piece of furniture (e g a chair, stool, or bench) for sitting in or on **b** the part of sthg on which one rests when sitting <*the* ~ *of a chair*> <*trouser* ~>; *also* the buttocks **c** a place for sitting <*took his* ~ *next to her*> **d** a unit of seating accommodation <*a* ~ *for the game*> **2a** a special chair (e g a throne) of sby in authority; *also* the status symbolized by it **b** a right of sitting <*lost her* ~ *in the Commons*> **c** a large country mansion **3a** a place

where sthg is established or practised <*an ancient ~ of learning*> **b** a place from which authority is exercised <*the ~ of government*> **4** a bodily part in which a particular function, disease, etc is centred **5** posture in or a way of sitting on horseback **6a** a part at or forming the base of sthg **b** a part or surface on or in which another part or surface rests <*a valve ~*>

[2]**seat** *vt* **1a** to cause to sit or assist in finding a seat <~ed *her next to the door*> **b** to provide seats for <*a theatre* ~ing *1000 people*> **c** to put (e g oneself) in a sitting position **2** to fit correctly on a seat **3** to fit to or with a seat <~ *a valve*> ~*vi, of a garment* to become baggy in the area covering the buttocks – **seater** *n*

'seat ˌbelt *n* an arrangement of straps designed to secure a person in a seat in an aeroplane, vehicle, etc

seating /'seeting‖'siːtɪŋ/ *n* **1a** the act of providing with seats **b** the arrangement of seats (e g in a theatre) **2a** material for upholstering seats **b** a base on or in which sthg rests <*a valve ~*>

'sea ˌurchin *n* any of a class of echinoderms usu with a thin shell covered with movable spines

ˌsea'wall /-'wawl‖-'wɔːl/ *n* a wall or embankment to protect the shore from erosion or to act as a breakwater

'seaˌway /-ˌway‖-ˌweɪ/ *n* **1** a ship's headway **2** the sea as a route for travel **3** a deep inland waterway that admits ocean shipping

'seaˌweed /-ˌweed‖-ˌwiːd/ *n* (an abundant growth of) a plant, specif an alga, growing in the sea, typically having thick slimy fronds

'seaˌworthy /-ˌwuhdhi‖-ˌwɜːðɪ/ *adj* fit or safe for a sea voyage <*a ~ ship*> – **seaworthiness** *n*

sebaceous /si'bayshəs‖sɪ'beɪʃəs/ *adj* of, secreting, or being sebum or other fatty material

sebum /'seebəm‖'siːbəm/ *n* fatty lubricant matter secreted by sebaceous glands of the skin

[1]**sec** /sek‖sek/ *n, Br* a second, moment – infml <*hang on a ~!*>

[2]**sec** *adj, of wine* not sweet; dry

secateur /'sekəˌtuh, ˌ--'-‖'sekəˌtɜː, ˌ--'-/ *n, chiefly Br* a pair of pruning shears –usu pl with sing. meaning [French *sécateur*, fr Latin *secare* to cut]

secede /si'seed‖sɪ'siːd/ *vi* to withdraw from an organization (e g a church or federation) – **seceder** *n*

secession /si'sesh(ə)n‖sɪ'seʃ(ə)n/ *n* an act of seceding – **secessionism** *n*, **secessionist** *n*

seclude /si'kloohd‖sɪ'kluːd/ *vt* to remove or separate from contact with others

se'cluded *adj* **1** screened or hidden from view **2** living in seclusion – **secludedly** *adv*, **secludedness** *n*

seclusion /si'kloohzh(ə)n‖sɪ'kluːʒ(ə)n/ *n* **1** secluding or being secluded **2** a secluded or isolated place – **seclusive** *adj*, **seclusively** *adv*, **seclusiveness** *n*

[1]**second** /'sekənd‖'sekənd/ *adj* **1a** next to the first in place or time <*was ~ in line*> **b(1)** next to the first in value, quality, or degree **b(2)** inferior, subordinate <*was ~ to none*> **c** standing next below the top in authority or importance <~ *mate*> **2** alternate, other <*elects a mayor every ~ year*> **3** resembling or suggesting a prototype <*a ~ Napoleon*> **4** being the forward gear or speed 1 higher than first in a motor vehicle **5** relating to or having a part typically subordinate to or lower in pitch than the first part in concerted or ensemble music [Old French, fr Latin *secundus* second, following, favourable, fr *sequi* to follow] – **second, secondly** *adv* – **at second hand** from or through an intermediary <*heard the news* at second hand>

[2]**second** *n* **1a** number two in a countable series **b** sthg that is next after the first in rank, position, authority, or precedence <*the ~ in line*> **2** sby who aids, supports, or stands in for another; *esp* the assistant of a duellist or boxer **3a** (the combination of 2 notes at) a musical interval of 2 diatonic degrees **b** the supertonic **4** a slightly flawed or inferior article (e g of merchandise) **5a** a place next below the first in a contest **b** *also* **second class** *often cap* the second level of British honours degree **6** the second forward gear or speed of a motor vehicle **7** *pl* a second helping of food – infml

[3]**second** *n* **1a** a 60th part of a minute of time or of a minute of angular measure **b** the SI unit of time equal to the duration of a certain number of periods of vibration of a specific radiation of a particular caesium isotope **2** a moment

[4]**second** *vt* **1** to give support or encouragement to **2** to endorse (a motion or nomination) – **seconder** *n*

[5]**second** /si'kond‖sɪ'kɒnd/ *vt, chiefly Br* to release (e g a teacher, businessman, or military officer) from a regularly assigned position for temporary duty with another organization – **secondment** *n*

[1]**secondary** /'sekənd(ə)ri‖'sekənd(ə)rɪ/ *adj* **1** of second rank or importance **2a** immediately derived from sthg primary or basic; derivative <~ *sources*> **b** of or being the induced current or its circuit in an induction coil or transformer <*a ~ coil*> **3a** not first in order of occurrence or development **b** of the second order or stage in a series or sequence **c** produced away from a growing point by the activity of plant formative tissue, esp cambium <~ *growth*> **d** of or being the (feathers growing on the) second segment of the wing of a bird **e** of a secondary school **4** of or being a manufacturing industry – **secondarily** *adv*, **secondariness** *n*

[2]**secondary** *n* **1** a secondary electrical circuit or coil **2** a secondary feather **3** SECONDARY SCHOOL

secondary modern, secondary modern school *n* a secondary school formerly providing a practical rather than academic type of education

secondary picketing *n, chiefly Br* picketing by members of a trade union not directly involved in the original industrial dispute

secondary school *n* a school intermediate between primary school and higher education

ˌsecond-'best *adj* next after the best

second best *n* sby or sthg that comes after the best in quality or worth

ˌsecond 'childhood *n* dotage

[1]**ˌsecond-'class** *adj* **1** of a second class <*a ~ honours degree*> **2** inferior, mediocre; *also* socially, politically, or economically deprived

<~ *citizens*>

[2]**second-class** *adv* **1** in accommodation next below the best <*travel* ~> **2** by second-class mail <*send the letters* ~>

second class *n* the second and usu next to highest group in a classification

Second Coming *n* the return of Christ to judge the world on the last day

second-guess, *chiefly NAm vt* **1** to outguess **2** to predict ~ *vi* to be wise with the benefit of hindsight

[1]**ˌsecondˈhand** /-ˈhand‖-ˈhænd/ *adj* **1a** received from or through an intermediary <~ *information*> **b** not original; derivative **2a** acquired after being owned by another <*a* ~ *car*> **b** dealing in secondhand goods <*a* ~ *bookshop*>

[2]**secondhand** *adv* indirectly; AT SECOND HAND

ˌsecond-in-comˈmand *n* one who is immediately subordinate to a commander; a deputy commander

second lieutenant *n* an officer of the lowest rank in the army or US airforce

ˌsecond ˈnature *n* an action or ability that practice has made instinctive

second person *n* (any of) a set of linguistic forms referring to the person or thing addressed (e g 'you')

ˌsecond-ˈrate *adj* of inferior quality or value – **second-rateness** *n*, **second-rater** *n*

ˌsecond ˈsight *n* clairvoyance, precognition

secrecy /ˈseekrəsi‖ˈsiːkrəsɪ/ *n* **1** the habit or practice of keeping secrets or maintaining privacy or concealment **2** the condition of being hidden or concealed <*complete* ~ *surrounded the conference*>

[1]**secret** /ˈseekrit‖ˈsiːkrɪt/ *adj* **1a** kept or hidden from knowledge or view <*determined to keep his mission* ~> **b** marked by the practice of discretion; secretive **c** conducted in secret <~ *negotiations*> **2** retired, secluded **3** revealed only to the initiated; esoteric <~ *rites*> **4** containing information whose unauthorized disclosure could endanger national security [Middle French, fr Latin *secretus*, fr past participle of *secernere* to separate, distinguish, fr *se-* apart + *cernere* to sift] – **secretly** *adv*

[2]**secret** *n* **1a** sthg kept hidden or unexplained **b** a fact concealed from others or shared confidentially with a few <*a trade* ~> **2** sthg taken to be the means of attaining a desired end <*the* ~ *of longevity*> – **in secret** in a private place or manner; in secrecy

secret agent *n* a spy

secretariat /ˌsekrəˈteəri·ət‖ˌsekrəˈteərɪət/ *n* **1** the office of secretary **2** the clerical staff of an organization **3** a government administrative department

secretary /ˈsekrətri, -ˌteri‖ˈsekrətrɪ, -ˌterɪ/ *n* **1** sby employed to handle correspondence and manage routine work for a superior **2a** COMPANY SECRETARY **b** an officer of an organization or society responsible for its records and correspondence **3** an officer of state who superintends a government administrative department [Medieval Latin *secretarius* confidential employee, fr Latin *secretus* secret] – **secretaryship** *n*, **secretarial** *adj*

ˌsecretary-ˈgeneral *n, pl* **secretaries-general** a principal administrative officer (e g of the United Nations)

[1]**secrete** /siˈkreet‖sɪˈkriːt/ *vt* to form and give off (a secretion) – **secretory** *adj*

[2]**secrete** *vt* to deposit in a hidden place <~ *opium about his person*>

secretion /siˈkreesh(ə)n‖sɪˈkriːʃ(ə)n/ *n* **1** (a product formed by) the bodily process of making and releasing some material either functionally specialized (e g a hormone, saliva, latex, or resin) or isolated for excretion (e g urine) **2** the act of hiding sthg – **secretionary** *adj*

secretive /ˈseekrətiv‖ˈsiːkrətɪv/ *adj* inclined to secrecy; not open or outgoing in speech or behaviour – **secretively** *adv*, **secretiveness** *n*

secret service *n* a (secret) governmental agency concerned with national security; *esp, cap both Ss* a British government intelligence department

sect /sekt‖sekt/ *n* **1** a (heretical) dissenting or schismatic religious body **2a** a group maintaining strict allegiance to a doctrine or leader **b** a party; *esp* a faction **3** a denomination – chiefly derog

[1]**sectarian** /sekˈteəri·ən‖sekˈteərɪən/ *n* **1** a (fanatical) adherent of a sect **2** a bigoted person

[2]**sectarian** *adj* **1** (characteristic) of a sect or sectarian **2** limited in character or scope; parochial – **sectarianism** *n*, **sectarianize** *vb*

[1]**section** /ˈseksh(ə)n‖ˈsekʃ(ə)n/ *n* **1a** the action or an instance of (separating by) cutting; *esp* the action of dividing sthg (e g tissues) surgically <*caesarean* ~> **b** a part separated (as if) by cutting **2** a distinct part or portion of sthg written; *esp* a subdivision of a chapter **3** the profile of sthg as it would appear if cut through by an intersecting plane **4** a sign § used in printing as a mark for the beginning of a section **5** a distinct part of an area, community, or group **6** a part when considered in isolation <*the northern* ~ *of the route*> **7** *sing or pl in constr* a subdivision of a platoon, troop, or battery that is the smallest tactical military unit **8** a very thin slice (e g of tissue) suitable for microscopic examination **9** any of several component parts that may be separated and reassembled <*a bookcase in* ~s> **10** a division of an orchestra composed of 1 class of instruments **11** a printed sheet that is folded to form part (e g 8 leaves) of a book

[2]**section** *vt* **1** to cut or separate into sections **2** to represent in sections (e g by a drawing)

sectional /ˈseksh(ə)nl‖ˈsekʃ(ə)nl/ *adj* **1** restricted to a particular group or locality <~ *interests*> **2** composed of or divided into sections <~ *furniture*> – **sectionalize** *vt*, **sectionally** *adv*

sectionalism /ˈseksh(ə)nlˌiz(ə)m‖ˈsekʃ(ə)nl-ˌɪz(ə)m/ *n* an excessive concern for the interests of a region or group

sector /ˈsektə‖ˈsektə/ *n* **1** a part of a circle consisting of 2 radii and the portion of the circumference between them **2a** a portion of a military area of operation **b** a part of a field of activity, esp of business, trade, etc <*employment in the public and private* ~s>

[1]**secular** /ˈsekyoolə‖ˈsekjʊlə/ *adj* **1a** of this world rather than the heavenly or spiritual **b** not overtly or specifically religious **2** not bound by

monastic vows or rules; *specif* of or being clergy not belonging to a particular religious order **3a** taking place once in an age or a century **b** surviving or recurring through ages or centuries – **secularly** *adv*, **secularity** *n*

[2]**secular** *n, pl* **seculars, secular** a layman

secularism /ˈsekyooləˌriz(ə)m‖ˈsekjʊləˌrɪz(ə)m/ *n* disregard for or rejection of religious beliefs and practices – **secularist** *n or adj*, **secularistic** *adj*

secular·ize, -ise /ˈsekyooləˌriez‖ˈsekjʊləˌraɪz/ *vt* **1** to transfer (e g property) from ecclesiastical to civil use **2** to release from monastic vows **3** to convert to or imbue with secularism – **secularizer** *n*, **secularization** *n*

[1]**secure** /siˈkyooə‖sɪˈkjʊə/ *adj* **1a** calm in mind **b** confident in opinion or hope **2a** free from danger **b** free from risk of loss <~ *employment*> **c** affording safety <*a* ~ *hideaway*> **d** firm, dependable; *esp* firmly fastened <~ *foundation*> **3** assured, certain <*when the reinforcements arrived, victory was* ~> **4** *archaic* overconfident [Latin *securus* safe, secure, fr *se* without + *cura* care] – **securely** *adv*, **secureness** *n*

[2]**secure** *vt* **1a** to make safe from risk or danger <~d *the lid with a padlock*> **b** to guarantee against loss or denial <*a bill to* ~ *the rights of strikers*> **c** to give pledge of payment to (a creditor) or of (an obligation) <~ *a note by a pledge of collateral*> **2** to make fast; shut tightly <~ *a door*> **3** to obtain or bring about, esp as the result of effort <*spared no effort to* ~ *his ends*> – **securement** *n*, **securer** *n*

security /siˈkyooərəti‖sɪˈkjʊərətɪ/ *n* **1** being secure: e g **1a** freedom from danger, fear, or anxiety **b** stability, dependability **2a** sthg pledged to guarantee the fulfilment of an obligation **b** a surety **3** an evidence of debt or of ownership (e g a stock certificate) **4a** protection **b(1)** measures taken to protect against esp espionage or sabotage **b(2)** *sing or pl in constr* an organization whose task is to maintain security

Security Council *n* a permanent council of the United Nations responsible for the maintenance of peace and security

sedan /siˈdan‖sɪˈdæn/ *n, NAm & Austr* SALOON 3

sedan chair *n* a portable often enclosed chair, esp of the 17th and 18th c, designed to seat 1 person and be carried on poles by 2 people

[1]**sedate** /siˈdayt‖sɪˈdeɪt/ *adj* calm and even in temper or pace – **sedately** *adv*, **sedateness** *n*

[2]**sedate** *vt* to give a sedative to

sedation /siˈdaysh(ə)n‖sɪˈdeɪʃ(ə)n/ *n* (the induction, esp with a sedative, of) a relaxed easy state

sedative /ˈsedətiv‖ˈsedətɪv/ *n or adj* (sthg, esp a drug) tending to calm or to tranquillize nervousness or excitement

sedentary /ˈsed(ə)ntri‖ˈsed(ə)ntrɪ/ *adj* **1** *esp of birds* not migratory **2** doing or involving much sitting <*a* ~ *occupation*> **3** permanently attached <~ *barnacles*>

sedge /sej‖sedʒ/ *n* any of a family of usu tufted marsh plants differing from the related grasses esp in having solid stems – **sedgy** *adj*

sediment /ˈsedimənt‖ˈsedɪmənt/ *n* **1** the matter that settles to the bottom of a liquid **2** material deposited by water, wind, or glaciers – **sediment** *vb*

sedimentary /ˌsediˈment(ə)ri‖ˌsedɪˈment(ə)rɪ/ *adj* **1** of or containing sediment <~ *deposits*> **2** formed by or from deposits of sediment <~ *rock*>

sedimentation /ˌsedimenˈtaysh(ə)n‖ˌsedɪmenˈteɪʃ(ə)n/ *n* the forming or depositing of sediment

sedition /siˈdish(ə)n‖sɪˈdɪʃ(ə)n/ *n* incitement to defy or rise up against lawful authority – **seditionary** *adj*

seditious /siˈdishəs‖sɪˈdɪʃəs/ *adj* **1** tending to arouse or take part in sedition; guilty of sedition **2** of or constituting sedition – **seditiously** *adv*, **seditiousness** *n*

seduce /siˈdyoohs‖sɪˈdjuːs/ *vt* **1** to incite to disobedience or disloyalty **2** to lead astray, esp by false promises **3** to effect the physical seduction of – **seducer** *n*

seduction /siˈduksh(ə)n‖sɪˈdʌkʃ(ə)n/ *n* **1** the act of seducing to wrong; *specif* enticement to sexual intercourse **2** a thing or quality that attracts by its charm <*the* ~ *of riches*>

seductive /siˈduktiv‖sɪˈdʌktɪv/ *adj* tending to seduce; alluring – **seductively** *adv*, **seductiveness** *n*

sedulous /ˈsedyooləs‖ˈsedjʊləs/ *adj* **1** involving or accomplished with steady perseverance <~ *craftsmanship*> **2** diligent in application or pursuit <*a* ~ *student*> *USE* fml – **sedulously** *adv*, **sedulousness** *n*

[1]**see** /see‖siː/ *vb* **saw** /saw‖sɔː/; **seen** /seen‖siːn/ *vt* **1a** to perceive by the eye <*looked for her but couldn't* ~ *her in the crowd*> **b** to look at; inspect <*can I* ~ *your ticket please?*> **2a** to have experience of; undergo <*a coat that has* ~n *better days*> **b** to (try to) find out or determine <~ *if you can mend it*> **3a** to form a mental picture of; imagine, envisage <*can't* ~ *him objecting*> **b** to regard <*couldn't* ~ *him as a crook*> **4** to perceive the meaning or importance of; understand <*couldn't* ~ *the point of it*> **5a** to observe, watch <*want to* ~ *how he handles the problem*> **b** to be a witness of <*can't* ~ *her neglected*> **c(1)** to read <~ *page 17*> **c(2)** to read of <saw *it in the paper*> **d** to attend as a spectator <~ *a play*> **6** to ensure; MAKE CERTAIN 2 <~ *that order is kept*> **7a** to prefer to have <*I'll* ~ *him hanged first*> **b** to find acceptable or attractive <*can't understand what he* ~s *in her*> **8** *of a period of time* to be marked by <*the 5th century* saw *the collapse of the Western Roman Empire*> **9a** to call on; visit <~ *the dentist*> **b(1)** to keep company with <*they've been* ~ing *each other regularly for some time*> **b(2)** to meet to a specified extent <*haven't* ~n *much of her lately*> **c** to grant an interview to <*the president will* ~ *you*> **d** to accompany, escort <~ *the girls home*> **10** to meet (a bet) in poker or equal the bet of (a player) ~ *vi* **1a** to have the power of sight **b** to apprehend objects by sight <*too dark to* ~> **2a** to give or pay attention <~ *here!*> **b** to look about <*come to the window and* ~> **3** to have knowledge <~ *into the future*> **4** to

make investigation or inquiry; consider, deliberate <*let me* ~> – **see about 1** to deal with **2** to consider further <*we'll* see about *that*> – **see eye to eye** to have a common viewpoint; agree – **see fit** to consider proper or advisable <saw fit *to warn him of his impending dismissal*> – **see one's way to** to feel capable of – **see red** to become suddenly enraged – **see someone right** to protect and reward (a protégé) – **see someone through** to provide for, support, or help sby until the end of (a time of difficulty) <*enough supplies to* see *us* through *the winter*> <saw *him* through *his divorce*> – **see the light 1a** to be born **b** to be published **2** to undergo conversion – **see the wood for the trees** to grasp the total picture without being confused by detail – **see through** to grasp the true nature of; penetrate <saw through *his deceptions*> – **see to** to attend to; care for

[2]**see** *n* a bishopric

[1]**seed** /seed‖siːd/ *n* **1a(1)** the grains or ripened ovules of plants used for sowing **a(2)** the fertilized ripened ovule of a (flowering) plant that contains an embryo and is capable of germination to produce a new plant **b** semen or milt **c** SPAT 2 **d** the condition or stage of bearing seed <*in* ~> **2** a source of development or growth <*sowed the* ~s *of discord*> **3** sthg (e g a tiny particle) that resembles a seed in shape or size **4** a competitor who has been seeded in a tournament **5** *archaic* progeny – **seed** *adj*, **seeded** *adj*, **seedless** *adj*, **seedlike** *adj* – **go/run to seed 1** to develop seed **2** to decay; *also* to become unattractive by being shabby or careless about appearance

[2]**seed** *vi* **1** to sow seed **2** *of a plant* to produce or shed seeds ~ *vt* **1a** to plant seeds in; sow 1 <~ *land to grass*> **b** PLANT 1a **2** to treat with solid particles to stimulate crystallization, condensation, etc; *esp* to treat (a cloud) in this way to produce rain, snow, etc **3** to extract the seeds from (e g raisins) **4** to schedule (tournament players or teams) so that superior ones will not meet in early rounds

ˈ**seedˌbed** /-ˌbed‖-ˌbed/ *n* a place where sthg specified develops <*the* ~ *of revolution*>

ˈ**seedˌcake** /-ˌkayk‖-ˌkeɪk/ *n* a sweet cake containing aromatic seeds (e g caraway seeds)

seedling /ˈseedling‖ˈsiːdlɪŋ/ *n* **1** a plant grown from seed rather than from a cutting **2** a young plant; *esp* a nursery plant before permanent transplantation – **seedling** *adj*

seedsman /ˈseedzmən‖ˈsiːdzmən/ *n* sby who sows or deals in seeds

seedy /ˈseedi‖ˈsiːdɪ/ *adj* **1** containing or full of seeds **2a** shabby, grubby **b** somewhat disreputable; run-down **c** slightly unwell – infml – **seedily** *adv*, **seediness** *n*

seeing /ˈsee·ing‖ˈsiːɪŋ/ *conj* in view of the fact; since – often + *that* or, in nonstandard use, *as how*

seek /seek‖siːk/ *vb* **sought** /sawt‖sɔːt/ *vt* **1** to resort to; go to <~ *the shade on a hot day*> **2a** to go in search of – often + *out* **b** to try to discover <~ *a solution to the problem*> **3** to ask for <~s *advice*> **4** to try to acquire or gain <~ *fame*> **5** to make an effort; aim – + infinitive <~ *to cater for every taste*> ~*vi* to make a search or inquiry – **seeker** *n*

seem /seem‖siːm/ *vi* **1** to give the impression of being <*he* ~s *unhappy*> <*she* ~s *a bore*> **2** to appear to the observation or understanding <*I* ~ *to have caught a cold*> <*it* ~s *he lost his passport*> **3** to give evidence of existing <*there* ~s *no reason*> – **not seem** somehow not <*I don't* seem *to feel hungry*> – **would seem** to seem to one <*it* would seem *to be raining*>

seeming /ˈseeming‖ˈsiːmɪŋ/ *adj* apparent rather than real

ˈ**seemingly** /-li‖-lɪ/ *adv* **1** so far as can be seen or judged **2** to outward appearance only

seemly /ˈseemli‖ˈsiːmlɪ/ *adj* in accord with good taste or propriety – **seemliness** *n*

see off *vt* **1** to be present at the departure of <saw *his parents* off *on holiday*> **2** to avert, repel

see out *vt* **1** to escort to the outside (e g of a room, office, or house) **2** to last until the end of <*enough fuel to* see *the winter* out>

seep /seep‖siːp/ *vi* to pass slowly (as if) through fine pores or small openings <*water* ~ed *in through a crack*> – **seepage** *n*

seer /siə‖sɪə/ *n* **1a** sby who predicts future events **b** sby credited with exceptional moral and spiritual insight **2** sby who practises divination

seersucker /ˈsiəˌsukə‖ˈsɪəˌsʌkə/ *n* a light slightly puckered fabric of linen, cotton, or rayon [Hindi *śīrśakar*, fr Persian *shīr-o-shakar*, lit., milk and sugar]

[1]**seesaw** /ˈseeˌsaw‖ˈsiːˌsɔː/ *n* **1** an alternating up-and-down or backwards-and-forwards movement; *also* anything (e g a process or movement) that alternates <*a* ~ *of shame and defiance*> **2** (a game in which 2 or more children ride on opposite ends of) a plank balanced in the middle so that one end goes up as the other goes down – **seesaw** *adj or adv*

[2]**seesaw** *vi* **1a** to move backwards and forwards or up and down **b** to play at seesaw **2a** to alternate **b** to vacillate ~*vt* to cause to move with a seesaw motion

seethe /seedh‖siːð/ *vi* **1a** to be in a state of agitated usu confused movement **b** to churn or foam as if boiling **2** to feel or express violent emotion

ˈ**see-ˌthrough** *adj* transparent

see through *vt* to undergo or endure to the end <*bravely* saw *the fight* through>

[1]**segment** /ˈsegmənt‖ˈsegmənt/ *n* **1a** a separated piece of sthg <*chop the stalks into short* ~s> **b** any of the constituent parts into which a body, entity, or quantity is divided or marked off <*all* ~s *of the population agree*> **2** a portion cut off from a geometrical figure by 1 or more points, lines, or planes: e g **2a** a part of a circular area bounded by a chord of that circle and the arc subtended by it **b** a part of a sphere cut off by a plane or included between 2 parallel planes **c** the part of a line between 2 points in the line – **segmentary** *adj*, **segmental** *adj*

[2]**segment** /segˈment‖segˈment/ *vt* to separate into segments – **segmentation** *n*

segregate /ˈsegriˌgayt‖ˈsegrɪˌgeɪt/ *vt* **1** to separate or set apart **2** to cause or force separation of (e g criminals from society) or in (e g a community) ~ *vi* **1** to withdraw **2** to undergo (genetic) segregation – **segregative** *adj*

ˈsegreˌgated *adj* **1** set apart from others of the same kind **2** administered separately for different groups or races <~ *education*>

segregation /ˌsegriˈgaysh(ə)n‖ˌsegrɪˈgeɪʃ(ə)n/ *n* **1a** the separation or isolation of a race, class, or ethnic group **b** the separation for special treatment or observation of individuals or items from a larger group **2** the separation of pairs of genes controlling the same hereditary characteristic, that occurs during meiotic cell division – **segregationist** *n*

seigneur /sayˈnyuh‖seɪˈnjɜː/ *n* a feudal lord

seine /sayn‖seɪn/ *vb or n* (to catch with, fish in with, or use) a large fishing net with weights on one edge and floats on the other that hangs vertically in the water

seismic /ˈsiezmik‖ˈsaɪzmɪk/, **seismal** /-ml‖-ml/ *adj* **1** of or caused by an earth vibration, specif an earthquake **2** of a vibration on the moon or other celestial body comparable to a seismic event on earth [Greek *seismos* shock, earthquake, fr *seiein* to shake] – **seismicity** *n*

seismograph /ˈsiezməˌgrahf, -ˌgraf‖ˈsaɪzməˌgrɑːf, -ˌgræf/ *n* an apparatus to measure and record earth tremors – **seismographer** *n*, **seismography** *n*, **seismographic** *adj*

seismology /siezˈmoləji‖seɪzˈmɒlədʒɪ/ *n* a science that deals with earth vibrations, esp earthquakes – **seismologist** *n*, **seismological** *adj*

seize /seez‖siːz/ *vt* **1** *also* **seise** /~/ to put in possession of **2** to confiscate, esp by legal authority **3a** to take possession of by force **b** to take prisoner **4** to take hold of abruptly or eagerly <~d *his arm and pulled him clear of the fire*> **5a** to attack or afflict physically <~d *with an attack of arthritis*> **b** to possess (the mind) completely or overwhelmingly **6** to bind or fasten together with a lashing of cord or twine ~ *vi* **1** to lay hold of sthg suddenly, forcibly, or eagerly – usu + *on* or *upon* <~d *on her idea for a new TV series*> **2a** *of brakes, pistons, etc* to become jammed through excessive pressure, temperature, or friction – often + *up* **b** *of an engine* to fail to operate owing to the seizing of a part

seizure /ˈseezhə‖ˈsiːʒə/ *n* **1** the taking possession of sby or sthg by legal process **2** a sudden attack (e g of disease)

[1]**seldom** /ˈseldəm‖ˈseldəm/ *adv* in few instances; rarely, infrequently

[2]**seldom** *adj* rare, infrequent

[1]**select** /siˈlekt‖sɪˈlekt/ *adj* **1** picked out in preference to others **2a** of special value or quality **b** exclusively or fastidiously chosen, esp on the basis of social characteristics <*a* ~ *membership*> **3** judicious in choice <~ *appreciation*> – **selectness** *n*

[2]**select** *vt* to take according to preference from among a number; pick out ~ *vi* to make a selection or choice – **selector** *n*

select committee *n* a temporary committee of a legislative body, established to examine 1 particular matter

selection /siˈleksh(ə)n‖sɪˈlekʃ(ə)n/ *n* **1** sby or sthg selected; *also* a collection of selected items **2** a range of things from which to choose **3** a natural or artificially imposed process that results in the survival and propagation only of organisms with desired or suitable attributes so that their heritable characteristics only are perpetuated in succeeding generations

selective /siˈlektiv‖sɪˈlektɪv/ *adj* of or characterized by selection; selecting or tending to select – **selectively** *adv*, **selectiveness** *n*, **selectivity** *n*

selenium /siˈleeni·əm‖sɪˈliːnɪəm/ *n* a nonmetallic solid element, 1 form of which varies in electrical conductivity under the influence of light and is used in electronic devices (e g solar cells) – **selenic** *adj*

[1]**self** /self‖self/ *pron* myself, himself, herself

[2]**self** *adj* identical throughout, esp in colour

[3]**self** *n, pl* **selves** /selvz‖selvz/ **1** the entire being of an individual **2** a (part or aspect of a) person's individual character <*his true* ~ *was revealed*> **3** the body, emotions, thoughts, sensations, etc that constitute the individuality and identity of a person **4** personal interest, advantage, or welfare

self- *comb form* **1a** oneself; itself <self-*supporting*> **b** of oneself or itself <self-*abasement*> **c** by oneself or itself <self-*propelled*> **2** to, with, for, or in oneself or itself <self-*confident*> <self-*addressed*> <self-*love*>

ˌself-abˈsorbed *adj* preoccupied with one's own thoughts, activities, or welfare – **self-absorption** *n*

ˌself-aˈbuse *n* masturbation

ˌself-adˈdressed *adj* addressed for return to the sender <*a* ~ *envelope*>

ˌself-asˈsertion *n* the act of asserting oneself or one's own rights, claims, or opinions, esp aggressively or conceitedly – **self-assertive** *adj*

ˌself-asˈsurance *n* self-confidence

ˌself-ˈcentred *adj* concerned excessively with one's own desires or needs

ˌself-comˈmand *n* self-control

ˌself-conˈfessed *adj* openly acknowledged

ˌself-ˈconfidence *n* confidence in oneself and one's powers and abilities – **self-confident** *adj*

ˌself-ˈconscious *adj* **1a** conscious of oneself as a possessor of mental states and originator of actions **b** intensely aware of oneself **2** uncomfortably conscious of oneself as an object of notice; ill at ease – **self-consciously** *adv*, **self-consciousness** *n*

ˌself-conˈtained *adj* **1** complete in itself <*a* ~ *flat*> **2a** showing self-possession **b** formal and reserved in manner – **self-containedly** *adv*

ˌself-contraˈdiction *n* **1** contradiction of oneself **2** a statement that contains 2 contradictory elements or ideas – **self-contradictory** *adj*

ˌself-conˈtrol *n* restraint of one's own impulses or emotions – **self-controlled** *adj*

ˌself-deˈfeating *adj* having the effect of preventing its own success

ˌself-deˈfence *n* **1** the act of defending or justifying oneself **2** the legal right to defend oneself with reasonable force – **self-defensive** *adj*

ˌself-deˈnial *n* the restraint or limitation of one's desires or their gratification

ˌself-deˈnying *adj* showing self-denial

ˌself-determiˈnation *n* **1** free choice of

one's own actions or states without outside influence **2** determination by a territorial unit of its own political status – **self-determined** *adj*, **self-determining** *adj*

ˌself-ˈdiscipline *n* the act of disciplining or power to discipline one's thoughts and actions, usu for the sake of improvement – **self-disciplined** *adj*

self-drive *adj, chiefly Br, of a hired vehicle* intended to be driven by the hirer

ˌself-efˈfacement *n* the act of making oneself inconspicuous, esp because of modesty; humility – **self-effacing** *adj*, **self-effacingly** *adv*

ˌself-emˈployed *adj* earning income directly from one's own business, trade, or profession rather than as salary or wages from an employer – **self-employment** *n*

ˌself-eˈsteem *n* **1** confidence and satisfaction in oneself; self-respect **2** vanity

ˌself-ˈevident *adj* requiring no proof; obvious – **self-evidence** *n*, **self-evidently** *adv*

ˌself-examiˈnation *n* the analysis of one's conduct, motives, etc

ˌself-exˈplanatory *adj* capable of being understood without explanation

ˌself-ˈgoverning *adj* having control over oneself; *specif* having self-government

ˌself-ˈgovernment *n* control of one's own (political) affairs

ˌself-ˈhelp *n* the bettering or helping of oneself without dependence on others

ˌself-imˈportance *n* **1** an exaggerated sense of one's own importance **2** arrogant or pompous behaviour – **self-important** *adj*

ˌself-inˈdulgence *n* excessive or unrestrained gratification of one's own appetites, desires, or whims – **self-indulgent** *adj*

ˌself-ˈinterest *n* (a concern for) one's own advantage and well-being – **self-interested** *adj*

selfish /ˈselfish‖ˈselfɪʃ/ *adj* concerned with or directed towards one's own advantage, pleasure, or well-being without regard for others – **selfishly** *adv*, **selfishness** *n*

ˈselfless /-lis‖-lɪs/ *adj* having no concern for self; unselfish – **selflessly** *adv*, **selflessness** *n*

ˌself-ˈmade *adj* raised from poverty or obscurity by one's own efforts

ˌself-oˈpinionated *adj* **1** conceited **2** stubbornly holding to one's own opinion

ˌself-ˈpity *n* a self-indulgent dwelling on one's own sorrows or misfortunes – **self-pitying** *adj*

ˌself-posˈsessed *adj* having or showing self-possession – **self-possessedly** *adv*

ˌself-posˈsession *n* control of one's emotions or behaviour, esp when under stress; composure

ˌself-preserˈvation *n* an instinctive tendency to act so as to safeguard one's own existence

ˌself-ˈraising ˌflour *n* a commercially prepared mixture of flour containing a raising agent

ˌself-reˈliance *n* reliance on one's own efforts and abilities; independence – **self-reliant** *adj*

ˌself-reˈspect *n* a proper respect for one's human dignity

ˌself-reˈspecting *adj* having or characterized by self-respect or integrity

ˌself-ˈrighteous *adj* assured of one's own righteousness, esp in contrast with the actions and beliefs of others; narrow-mindedly moralistic – **self-righteously** *adv*, **self-righteousness** *n*

ˌself-ˈsacrifice *n* sacrifice of oneself or one's well-being for the sake of an ideal or for the benefit of others – **self-sacrificing** *adj*

ˈselfˌsame *adj* precisely the same; identical <*he left the ~ day*>

ˌself-satisˈfaction *n* a smug satisfaction with oneself or one's position or achievements

ˌself-ˈsatisfied *adj* feeling or showing self-satisfaction

ˌself-ˈseeker *n* sby self-seeking

ˌself-ˈseeking *adj* seeking only to safeguard or further one's own interests; selfish – **self-seeking** *n*

ˌself-ˈservice *n* the serving of oneself (e g in a cafeteria or supermarket) with things to be paid for at a cashier's desk, usu upon leaving – **self-service** *adj*

ˌself-ˈsow /soh‖səʊ/ *vi* **self-sown** /sohn‖səʊn/, **self-sowed** /sohd‖səʊd/ *of a plant* to grow from seeds spread naturally (e g by wind or water)

ˌself-ˈstarter *n* an electric motor used to start an internal-combustion engine

ˌself-ˈstyled *adj* called by oneself, esp without justification <*~ experts*>

ˌself-sufˈficient *adj* **1** able to maintain oneself or itself without outside aid; capable of providing for one's own needs <*a community ~ in dairy products*> **2** having unwarranted assurance of one's own ability or worth – **self-sufficiency** *n*

ˌself-supˈporting *adj* **1** meeting one's needs by one's own labour or income **2** supporting itself or its own weight <*a ~ wall*>

ˌself-ˈwill *n* stubborn or wilful adherence to one's own desires or ideas; obstinacy – **self-willed** *adj*

ˌself-ˈwinding /ˈwiending‖ˈwaɪndɪŋ/ *adj* not needing to be wound by hand <*a ~ watch*>

¹sell /sel‖sel/ *vb* **sold** /sohld‖səʊld/ *vt* **1** to deliver or give up in violation of duty, trust, or loyalty; betray – often + *out* **2a(1)** to give up (property) in exchange, esp for money **a(2)** to offer for sale <*~s insurance*> **b** to give up or dispose of foolishly or dishonourably (in return for sthg else) <*juries who* sold *the verdicts*> **3** to cause or promote the sale of <*advertising ~s newspapers*> **4** to achieve a sale of <*a book which* sold *a million copies*> **5a** to make acceptable, believable, or desirable by persuasion <*~ an idea*> **b** to persuade to accept or enjoy sthg – usu + *on*; infml <*~ children on reading*> **6** to deceive, cheat – usu pass; infml <*we've been sold!*> ~ *vi* **1** to transfer sthg to another's ownership by sale **2** to achieve a sale; *also* to achieve satisfactory sales <*hoped that the new line would ~*> **3** to have a specified price – + *at* or *for* – **sellable** *adj* – **sell down the river** to betray the faith of

²sell *n* **1** the act or an instance of selling **2** a deliberate deception; a hoax – infml

seller /ˈselə‖ˈselə/ *n* a product offered for sale and selling well, to a specified extent, or in a specified manner <*a million-copy ~*>

<*a poor* ~>

seller's market *n* a market in which demand exceeds supply

sell off *vt* to dispose of completely by selling, esp at a reduced price

sellotape /ˈseləˌtayp‖ˈseləˌteɪp/ *vt* to fix (as if) with Sellotape

Sellotape *trademark* – used for a usu transparent adhesive tape

ˈ**sell-ˌout** *n* **1** a performance, exhibition, or contest for which all tickets or seats are sold **2** a betrayal – infml

sell out *vt* **1** to dispose of entirely by sale **2** to betray or be unfaithful to (e g one's cause or associates), esp for the sake of money ~ *vi* **1** SELL UP **2** to betray one's cause or associates – usu + *on*

sell up *vb, chiefly Br* to sell (e g one's house or business) in a conclusive or forced transaction <sold up *and emigrated to Australia*>

selvage, selvedge /ˈselvij‖ˈselvɪdʒ/ *n* **1a** the edge on either side of a (woven) fabric, so finished as to prevent unravelling; *specif* a narrow border often of different or heavier threads than the fabric and sometimes in a different weave **b** an edge (e g of wallpaper) meant to be cut off and discarded **2** a border, edge

selves /selvz‖selvz/ *pl of* SELF

semantic /siˈmantik‖sɪˈmæntɪk/ *adj* of meaning in language – **semantically** *adv*

seˈmantics *n pl but sing or pl in constr* **1** the branch of linguistics concerned with meaning **2** a branch of semiotics dealing with the relation between signs and the objects they refer to – **semanticist** *n*

1**semaphore** /ˈseməˌfaw‖ˈseməˌfɔː/ *n* **1** an apparatus for conveying information by visual signals (e g by the position of 1 or more pivoted arms) **2** a system of visual signalling by 2 flags held 1 in each hand [Greek *sēma* sign, signal + *-phoros* carrying, fr *pherein* to carry]

2**semaphore** *vt* to convey (information) (as if) by semaphore ~*vi* to send signals (as if) by semaphore

semblance /ˈsembləns‖ˈsembləns/ *n* outward and often deceptive appearance; a show <*wrapped in a* ~ *of euphoria*>

semen /ˈseemən‖ˈsiːmən/ *n* a suspension of spermatozoa produced by the male reproductive glands that is conveyed to the female reproductive tract during coitus

semester /siˈmestə‖sɪˈmestə/ *n* an academic term lasting half a year, esp in America and Germany

semi /ˈsemi‖ˈsemɪ/ *n, Br* a semidetached house – infml

semi- /semi-‖semɪ-/ *prefix* **1a** precisely half of **b** forming a bisection of <semi*ellipse*> <semi*oval*> **c** occurring halfway through (a specified period of time) <semi*annual*> **2** to some extent; partly; incompletely <semi*civilized*> **3a** partial; incomplete <semi*consciousness*> **b** having some of the characteristics of <semi*metal*>

ˈ**semiˌbreve** /-ˌbreev‖-ˌbriːv/ *n* a musical note with the time value of 2 minims or 4 crotchets

ˈ**semiˌcircle** /-ˌsuhkl‖-ˌsɜːkl/ *n* (an object or arrangement in the form of) a half circle – **semicircular** *adj*

ˌ**semiˈcolon** /-ˈkohlon‖-ˈkəʊlɒn/ *n* a punctuation mark ; used chiefly to coordinate major sentence elements where there is no conjunction

ˌ**semiconˈductor** /-kənˈduktə‖-kənˈdʌktə/ *n* a substance (e g silicon) whose electrical conductivity at room temperature is between that of a conductor and that of an insulator

ˌ**semideˈtached** /-diˈtacht‖-dɪˈtætʃt/ *adj* forming 1 of a pair of residences joined into 1 building by a common wall – **semidetached** *n*

1ˌ**semiˈfinal** /-ˈfienl‖-ˈfaɪnl/ *adj* **1** next to the last in a knockout competition **2** of or participating in a semifinal

2**semifinal** /ˌ--ˈ--, ˈ--ˌ--/ *n* a semifinal match or round – often pl with sing. meaning – **semifinalist** *n*

seminal /ˈseminl‖ˈsemɪnl/ *adj* **1** (consisting) of, storing, or conveying seed or semen <~ *duct*> **2** containing or contributing the seeds of future development; original and influential <*a* ~ *book*> – **seminally** *adv*

seminar /ˈsemiˌnah‖ˈsemɪˌnɑː/ *n* **1** an advanced or graduate class often featuring informality and discussion **2** a meeting for exchanging and discussing information

seminarist /ˈseminərist‖ˈsemɪnərɪst/ *n* a seminarian

seminary /ˈsemin(ə)ri‖ˈsemɪn(ə)rɪ/ *n* **1** an institution of education **2** an institution for the training of candidates for the (Roman Catholic) priesthood

semiology, semeiology /ˌsemiˈoləji, ˌsee-‖ˌsemɪˈɒlədʒɪ, ˌsiː-/ *n* the study of signs; *esp* semiotics – **semiological** *adj*

semiotics /ˌsemiˈotiks, ˌsee-‖ˌsemɪˈɒtɪks, ˌsiː-/ *n pl but sing or pl in constr* a general philosophical theory of signs and symbols that includes syntactics and semantics – **semiotic** *adj*

ˌ**semiˈprecious** /-ˈpreshəs‖-ˈpreʃəs/ *adj, of a gemstone* of less commercial value than a precious stone

ˈ**semiˌquaver** /-ˌkwayvə‖-ˌkweɪvə/ *n* a musical note with time value of $\frac{1}{2}$ of a quaver

1**Semitic** /siˈmitik‖sɪˈmɪtɪk/ *adj* **1** of or characteristic of the Semites; *specif* Jewish **2** of a branch of the Afro-Asiatic language family that includes Hebrew, Aramaic, Arabic, and Ethiopic

2**Semitic** *n* (any of) the Semitic languages

ˈ**semiˌtone** /-ˌtohn‖-ˌtəʊn/ *n* the musical interval (e g E–F or F–F #) equal to the interval between 2 adjacent keys on a keyboard instrument – **semitonic** *adj*

ˌ**semiˈtropical** /-ˈtropikl‖-ˈtrɒpɪkl/ *adj* subtropical

ˌ**semiˈweekly** /-ˈweekli‖-ˈwiːklɪ/ *adj or adv* appearing or taking place twice a week <*a* ~ *news bulletin*>

semolina /ˌseməˈleenə‖ˌseməˈliːnə/ *n* the purified hard parts left after milling of (hard) wheat, used for pasta and in milk puddings [Italian *semolino*, diminutive of *semola* bran, fr Latin *simila* wheat flour]

sempstress /ˈsem(p)stris‖ˈsem(p)strɪs/ *n* a seamstress

senate /ˈsenit‖ˈsenɪt/ *n sing or pl in constr* **1a**

the supreme council of the ancient Roman republic and empire **b** the 2nd chamber in some legislatures that consist of 2 houses **2** the governing body of some universities [Old French *senat*, fr Latin *senatus*, lit., council of elders, fr *sen-, senex* old, old man]

senator /ˈsenətə‖ˈsenətə/ *n* a member of a senate – **senatorial** *adj*, **senatorship** *n*

[1]**send** /send‖send/ *vb* **sent** /sent‖sent/ *vt* **1** to direct or cause to go in a specified direction, esp violently <*the crash* sent *them scuttling out of their houses*> **2** *of God, fate, etc* to cause to be; grant; BRING ABOUT <~ *her victorious*> **3** to dispatch by a means of communication <~ *a telegram*> **4a** to cause, direct, order, or request to go <sent *her to buy some milk*> **b** to dismiss <*was* sent *home*> **5** to cause to assume a specified state <sent *him into a rage*> **6** to cause to issue: e g **6a** to pour out; discharge <*clouds* ~ing *forth rain*> **b** to utter <~ *forth a cry*> **c** to emit <sent *out waves of perfume*> **d** to grow out (parts) in the course of development <*a plant* ~ing *forth shoots*> **7** to consign to a destination (e g death or a place of imprisonment) **8** to delight, thrill – infml <*that music really* ~s *me*> ~ *vi* **1a** to dispatch sby to convey a message or do an errand <~ *out for coffee*> **b** to dispatch a request or order <*have to* ~ *to Germany for spares*> **2** to scend **3** to transmit – **sender** *n* – **send for** to request by message to come; summon – **send packing** to dismiss roughly or in disgrace

[2]**send** *n* a scend

send down *vt, Br* **1** to suspend or expel from a university **2** to send to jail – infml

send in *vt* **1** to cause to be delivered to an authority, group, or organization <send in *a letter of complaint*> **2** to assign with a view to tackling a crisis or difficulty <send *a receiver* in *to deal with the bankruptcy*>

ˈ**send-ˌoff** *n* a usu enthusiastic demonstration of goodwill at the beginning of a venture (e g a trip)

send off *vt* **1** to dispatch **2** to attend to the departure of

send on *vt* **1** to dispatch (e g luggage) in advance **2** to forward (readdressed mail)

send out *vt* **1** to issue for circulation <*had* sent *the invitations* out> **2** to dispatch (e g an order) from a shop or place of storage

ˈ**send-ˌup** *n, Br* a satirical imitation, esp on stage or television; a parody

send up *vt* **1** *chiefly Br* to make an object of mockery or laughter; ridicule **2** *chiefly NAm* SEND DOWN 2

senescence /siˈnes(ə)ns‖sɪˈnes(ə)ns/ *n* being or becoming old or withered – **senesce** *vi*, **senescent** *adj*

seneschal /ˈsenish(ə)l‖ˈsenɪʃ(ə)l/ *n* the agent or bailiff of a feudal lord's estate

senile /ˈseeniel‖ˈsiːnaɪl/ *adj* of, exhibiting, or characteristic of (the mental or physical weakness associated with) old age – **senility** *n*

[1]**senior** /ˈseenyə, ˈseeni·ə‖ˈsiːnjə, ˈsiːnɪə/ *n* **1** sby who is older than another <*5 years his* ~> **2a** sby of higher standing or rank **b** *NAm* a student in the final year before graduation from school, university, etc

[2]**senior** *adj* **1** elder – used, chiefly in the USA, to distinguish a father with the same name as his son **2** higher in standing or rank <~ *officers*>

ˌ**senior** ˈ**citizen** *n* sby beyond the usual age of retirement – euph

seniority /ˌseeniˈorəti‖ˌsiːnɪˈɒrətɪ/ *n* a privileged status attained by length of continuous service (e g in a company)

senna /ˈsenə‖ˈsenə/ *n* (the dried leaflets or pods, used as a purgative, of) any of a genus of leguminous plants, shrubs, and trees of warm regions

senor, señor /seˈnyaw‖seˈnjɔː/ *n, pl* **senors, señores** /-rays‖-reɪs/ a Spanish-speaking man – used as a title equivalent to *Mr* or as a generalized term of direct address

senora, señora /seˈnyawrə‖seˈnjɔːrə/ *n* a married Spanish-speaking woman – used as a title equivalent to *Mrs* or as a generalized term of direct address

senorita, señorita /ˌsenyəˈreetə‖ˌsenjəˈriːtə/ *n* an unmarried Spanish-speaking girl or woman – used as a title equivalent to *Miss*

sensation /senˈsaysh(ə)n‖senˈseɪʃ(ə)n/ *n* **1a** a mental process (e g seeing or hearing) resulting from stimulation of a sense organ **b** a state of awareness of a usu specified type resulting from internal bodily conditions or external factors; a feeling or sense <~s *of fatigue*> **2a** a surge of intense interest or excitement <*their elopement caused a* ~> **b** a cause of such excitement; *esp* sby or sthg in some respect remarkable or outstanding

sensational /senˈsaysh(ə)nl‖senˈseɪʃ(ə)nl/ *adj* **1** arousing an immediate, intense, and usu superficial interest or emotional reaction **2** exceptionally or unexpectedly excellent or impressive – infml – **sensationalize** *vt*, **sensationally** *adv*

senˈsationalˌism /-ˌiz(ə)m‖-ˌɪz(ə)m/ *n* the use of sensational subject matter or style – **sensationalist** *n*

[1]**sense** /sens‖sens/ *n* **1** a meaning conveyed or intended; *esp* any of a range of meanings a word or phrase may bear, esp as isolated in a dictionary entry **2** (the faculty of perceiving the external world or internal bodily conditions by means of) any of the senses of feeling, hearing, sight, smell, taste, etc **3** soundness of mind or judgment – usu pl with sing. meaning <*when he came to his* ~s *he was shocked to hear what he had done*> **4a** an ability to use the senses for a specified purpose <*a good* ~ *of balance*> **b** a definite but often vague awareness or impression <*felt a* ~ *of insecurity*> **c** an awareness that motivates action or judgment <*done out of a* ~ *of justice*> **d** a capacity for discernment and appreciation <*her* ~ *of humour*> **5** the prevailing view; a consensus <*the* ~ *of the meeting*> **6** an ability to put the mind to effective use; practical intelligence **7** either of 2 opposite directions (of motion)

[2]**sense** *vt* **1a** to perceive by the senses **b** to be or become conscious of <~ *danger*> **2** to grasp, comprehend <~ *the import of a remark*> **3** to detect (e g a symbol or radiation) automatically

ˈ**senseless** /-lis‖-lɪs/ *adj* deprived of, deficient in, or contrary to sense: e g **a** unconscious **b** foolish, stupid **c** meaningless, purposeless – **senselessly** *adv*, **senselessness** *n*

'sense ˌorgan *n* a bodily structure that responds to a stimulus (e g heat or sound waves) by initiating impulses in nerves that convey them to the central nervous system where they are interpreted as sensations

sensibility /ˌsensəˈbiləti‖ˌsensəˈbɪlətɪ/ *n* **1** ability to have sensations **2** heightened susceptibility to feelings of pleasure or pain (e g in response to praise or blame) – often pl with sing. meaning <*a man of strong* sensibilities> **3** the ability to discern and respond freely to sthg (e g emotion in another) **4** (exaggerated) sensitiveness in feelings and tastes

sensible /ˈsensəbl‖ˈsensəbl/ *adj* **1** capable of sensing <~ *to pain*> **2** having, containing, or indicative of good sense or sound reason <*made a* ~ *answer*> **3a** perceptible to the senses or to understanding <*his distress was* ~ *from his manner*> **b** large enough to be observed or noticed; considerable <*a* ~ *decrease*> **4** aware, conscious *of* **USE** (*3 & 4*) fml – **sensibleness** *n*, **sensibly** *adv*

sensitive /ˈsensətiv‖ˈsensətɪv/ *adj* **1** capable of being stimulated or excited by external agents (e g light, gravity, or contact) <*a photographic emulsion* ~ *to red light*> **2** highly responsive or susceptible: e g **2a(1)** easily provoked or hurt emotionally **a(2)** finely aware of the attitudes and feelings of others or of the subtleties of a work of art **b** hypersensitive <~ *to egg protein*> **c** capable of registering minute differences; delicate <~ *scales*> **d** readily affected or changed by external agents (e g light or chemical stimulation) **e** *of a radio receiving set* highly responsive to incoming waves **3** concerned with highly classified information <*a* ~ *document*> – **sensitively** *adv*, **sensitiveness** *n*, **sensitivity** *n*

sensit·ize, **-ise** /ˈsensətiez‖ˈsensətaɪz/ *vb* to make or become sensitive or hypersensitive – **sensitizer** *n*, **sensitization** *n*

sensor /ˈsensə, -saw‖ˈsensə, -sɔː/ *n* a device that responds to heat, light, sound, pressure, magnetism, etc and transmits a resulting impulse (e g for measurement or operating a control)

sensory /ˈsens(ə)ri‖ˈsens(ə)rɪ/ *adj* of sensation or the senses

sensual /ˈsensyoo·əl, -shoo-‖ˈsensjʊəl, -ʃʊ-/ *adj* **1** sensory **2** relating to or consisting in the gratification of the senses or the indulgence of appetites **3a** devoted to or preoccupied with the senses or appetites, rather than the intellect or spirit **b** voluptuous – **sensualism** *n*, **sensualist** *n*, **sensualize** *vt*, **sensually** *adv*, **sensuality** *n*

sensuous /ˈsensyoo·əs, -shoo·əs‖ˈsensjʊəs, -ʃʊəs/ *adj* **1a** of (objects perceived by) the senses **b** providing or characterized by gratification of the senses; appealing strongly to the senses <~ *pleasure*> **2** suggesting or producing rich imagery or sense impressions <~ *verse*> **3** readily influenced by sense perception – **sensuously** *adv*, **sensuousness** *n*, **sensuosity** *n*

sent /sent‖sent/ *past of* SEND

[1]sentence /ˈsentəns‖ˈsentəns/ *n* **1a** a judgment formally pronounced by a court and specifying a punishment **b** the punishment so imposed <*serve a* ~> **2** a grammatically self-contained speech unit that expresses an assertion, a question, a command, a wish, or an exclamation – **sentential** *adj*

[2]sentence *vt* **1** to impose a judicial sentence on **2** to consign to a usu unpleasant fate <*development that* ~s *rural industries to extinction*>

sententious /senˈtenshəs‖senˈtenʃəs/ *adj* **1** terse, pithy **2** given to or full of **2a** terse or pithy sayings **b** pompous moralizing – **sententiously** *adv*, **sententiousness** *n*

sentient /ˈsensh(ə)nt‖ˈsenʃ(ə)nt/ *adj* **1** capable of perceiving through the senses; conscious **2** keenly sensitive in perception or feeling **USE** chiefly fml – **sentiently** *adv*

sentiment /ˈsentimənt‖ˈsentɪmənt/ *n* **1a** (an attitude, thought, or judgment prompted or coloured by) feeling or emotion **b** a specific view or attitude; an opinion – usu pl with sing. meaning <*held similar* ~s *on the matter*> **2a** sensitive feeling; refined sensibility, esp as expressed in a work of art **b** indulgently romantic or nostalgic feeling **3** the emotional significance of a communication as distinguished from its overt meaning

sentimental /ˌsentiˈmentl‖ˌsentɪˈmentl/ *adj* **1** resulting from feeling rather than reason <*kept the gift for its* ~ *value*> **2** having an excess of superficial sentiment – **sentimentalism** *n*, **sentimentalist** *n*, **sentimentalize** *vb*, **sentimentally** *adv*, **sentimentality** *n*

[1]sentinel /ˈsentinl‖ˈsentɪnl/ *n* sby who or sthg that keeps guard

[2]sentinel *vt* **-ll-** (*NAm* **-l-**, **-ll-**) **1** to watch over as a sentinel **2** to post as a sentinel

sentry /ˈsentri‖ˈsentrɪ/ *n* a guard, watch; *esp* a soldier standing guard at a gate, door, etc

'sentry ˌbox *n* a shelter for a standing sentry

sepal /ˈsepl‖ˈsepl/ *n* any of the modified leaves comprising the calyx of a flower – **sepaloid** *adj*

separable /ˌsep(ə)rəbl‖ˌsep(ə)rəbl/ *adj* capable of being separated or dissociated – **separableness** *n*, **separably** *adv*, **separability** *n*

[1]separate /ˈsepərayt‖ˈsepəreɪt/ *vt* **1a** to set or keep apart; detach, divide **b** to make a distinction between; distinguish <~ *religion from magic*> **c** to disperse in space or time; scatter <*widely* ~d *hamlets*> **2** to part (a married couple) by separation **3** to isolate, segregate **4a** to isolate from a mixture or compound <~ *cream from milk*> **b** to divide into constituent parts or types **5** *NAm* to discharge <*was* ~d *from the army*> ~ *vi* **1** to become divided or detached; draw or come apart **2a** to sever an association; withdraw <~ *from a federation*> **b** to cease to live together as man and wife, esp by formal arrangement **3** to go in different directions **4** to become isolated from a mixture **USE** (*vt 4*; *vi 4*) often + *out* – **separative** *adj*, **separator** *n*

[2]separate /ˈsep(ə)rət‖ˈsep(ə)rət/ *adj* **1** set or kept apart; detached, separated **2** not shared with another; individual <~ *rooms*> **3a** existing independently; autonomous **b** different in kind; distinct <*6* ~ *ways of cooking an egg*> – **separately** *adv*, **separateness** *n*

separation /ˌsepəˈraysh(ə)n‖ˌsepəˈreɪʃ(ə)n/ *n* **1a** a point, line, or means of division **b** an intervening space; a gap, break **2** cessation of cohabitation between husband and wife by mutual agreement or judicial decree

separatism /ˈsep(ə)rəˌtiz(ə)m‖ˈsep(ə)rəˌtɪz(ə)m/ *n* a belief or movement advocating separation (e g schism, secession, or segregation) – **separatist** *adj or n*

[1]**sepia** /ˈseepyə‖ˈsiːpjə/ *n* **1** (a brown melanin-containing pigment from) the inky secretion of cuttlefishes **2** rich dark brown

[2]**sepia** *adj* **1** of the colour sepia **2** made of or done in sepia <*a* ~ *print*>

sepoy /ˈseepoy‖ˈsiːpɔɪ/ *n* an Indian soldier employed by a European power, esp Britain

sepsis /ˈsepsis‖ˈsepsɪs/ *n, pl* **sepses** /-seez‖-siːz/ the spread of bacteria from a focus of infection; *esp* septicaemia

September /sepˈtembə, səp-‖sepˈtembə, səp-/ *n* the 9th month of the Gregorian calendar [Latin *September* (seventh month of the early Roman calendar), fr *septem* seven]

septet /sepˈtet‖sepˈtet/ *n* **1** a musical composition for 7 instruments, voices, or performers **2** *sing or pl in constr* a group or set of 7; *esp* the performers of a septet

septic /ˈseptik‖ˈseptɪk/ *adj* **1** putrefactive **2** relating to, involving, or characteristic of sepsis

septicaemia /ˌseptiˈseemyə, -mi·ə‖ˌseptɪˈsiːmjə, -mɪə/ *n* invasion of the bloodstream by microorganisms from a focus of infection with chills, fever, etc

ˌseptic ˈtank *n* a tank in which the solid matter of continuously flowing sewage is disintegrated by bacteria

septuagenarian /ˌsepchooəjiˈneəri·ən, ˌseptwə-‖ˌseptʃʊədʒɪˈneərɪən, ˌseptwə-/ *n* sby between 70 and 79 years old – **septuagenarian** *adj*

Septuagesima /ˌsepchooəˈjesimə, ˌseptwə-‖ˌseptʃʊəˈdʒesɪmə, ˌseptwə-/ *n* the third Sunday before Lent

Septuagint /ˈsepchooəˌjint, ˈseptwə-‖ˈseptʃʊəˌdʒɪnt, ˈseptwə-/ *n* a pre-Christian Greek version of the Jewish Scriptures arranged and edited by Jewish scholars about 300 BC

septum /ˈseptəm‖ˈseptəm/ *n, pl* **septa** /-tə‖-tə/ a dividing wall or membrane, esp between bodily spaces or masses of soft tissue – **septal** *adj*

sepulchral /siˈpulkrəl‖sɪˈpʌlkrəl/ *adj* **1** of the burial of the dead **2** suited to or suggestive of a tomb; funereal <*a* ~ *whisper*> – **sepulchrally** *adv*

sepulchre, *NAm chiefly* **sepulcher** /ˈsep(ə)lkə‖ˈsep(ə)lkə/ *n* **1** a place of burial; a tomb **2** a receptacle (in an altar) for religious relics

sequel /ˈseekwəl‖ˈsiːkwəl/ *n* **1** a consequence, result **2a** subsequent development or course of events **b** a play, film, or literary work continuing the course of a narrative begun in a preceding one [Middle French *sequelle*, fr Latin *sequela*, fr *sequi* to follow]

sequence /ˈseekwəns‖ˈsiːkwəns/ *n* **1** a continuous or connected series: e g **1a** an extended series of poems united by theme **b** RUN 3f **c** a succession of repetitions of a melodic phrase or harmonic pattern each in a new position **d** a set of elements following the same order as the natural numbers **e** an episode, esp in a film **2a** order of succession **b** the order of amino acids in a protein, nucleotide bases in DNA or RNA, etc **3** a subsequent but not resultant occurrence or course **4** a continuous progression

sequential /siˈkwensh(ə)l‖sɪˈkwenʃ(ə)l/ *adj* **1** of or arranged in a sequence; serial **2** following in sequence – **sequentially** *adv*

sequester /siˈkwestə‖sɪˈkwestə/ *vt* **1a** to set apart; segregate **b** to seclude, withdraw <*a quiet* ~ed *spot*> **2** to seize (e g a debtor's property) judicially

sequestrate /siˈkwestrayt‖sɪˈkwestreɪt/ *vt* SEQUESTER 2 – **sequestration** *n*, **sequestrator** *n*

sequin /ˈseekwin‖ˈsiːkwɪn/ *n* a very small disc of shining metal or plastic used for ornamentation, esp on clothing

sequoia /siˈkwoyə‖sɪˈkwɔɪə/ *n* either of 2 huge coniferous Californian trees: **a** BIG TREE **b** a redwood

seraglio /seˈrahli·oh, -lyoh‖seˈrɑːlɪəʊ, -ljəʊ/ *n, pl* **seraglios** HAREM 1a

seraph /ˈserəf‖ˈserəf/ *n, pl* **seraphim** /-fim‖-fɪm/, **seraphs** any of the 6-winged angels standing in the presence of God – **seraphic** *adj*

Serbo-Croatian /ˌsuhboh krohˈaysh(ə)n‖ˌsɜːbəʊ krəʊˈeɪʃ(ə)n/ *n* the Slavonic language spoken by the natives or inhabitants of Serbia and Croatia in the Balkans

[1]**sere, sear** /siə‖sɪə/ *adj* shrivelled, withered – chiefly poetic

[2]**sere** *n* a series of successive ecological communities established in 1 area – **seral** *adj*

[1]**serenade** /ˌserəˈnayd‖ˌserəˈneɪd/ *n* **1** a complimentary vocal or instrumental performance (given outdoors at night for a woman) **2** an instrumental composition in several movements written for a small ensemble

[2]**serenade** *vb* to perform a serenade (in honour of) – **serenader** *n*

serendipity /ˌserənˈdipəti‖ˌserənˈdɪpətɪ/ *n* the faculty of discovering pleasing or valuable things by chance [fr its possession by the heroes of the Persian fairy tale *The Three Princes of Serendip*] – **serendipitous** *adj*

serene /səˈreen‖səˈriːn/ *adj* **1** free of storms or adverse changes; clear, fine <~ *skies*> **2** having or showing tranquillity and peace of mind <*a* ~ *smile*> – **serenely** *adv*, **sereneness** *n*, **serenity** *n*

serf /suhf‖sɜːf/ *n* a member of a class of agricultural labourers in a feudal society, bound in service to a lord, and esp transferred with the land they worked if its ownership changed hands – **serfage** *n*, **serfdom** *n*

serge /suhj‖sɜːdʒ/ *n* a durable twilled fabric having a smooth clear face and a pronounced diagonal rib on the front and the back

sergeant /ˈsahj(ə)nt‖ˈsɑːdʒ(ə)nt/ *n* **1** a police officer ranking in Britain between constable and inspector **2** a high-ranking noncommissioned officer in the army, airforce, or marines

ˌsergeant-at-ˈarms *n, pl* **sergeants-at-arms** *often cap S&A* an officer attending the British Speaker or Lord Chancellor; *also* a similar officer in other legislatures

ˌsergeant ˈmajor *n, pl* **sergeant majors, sergeants major** **1** a noncommissioned officer of the highest rank in the US army or marine corps **2** a warrant officer in the British army or Royal Marines

[1]serial /ˈsiəri·əl‖ˈsɪərɪəl/ *adj* **1** of or constituting a series, rank, or row < ~ *order*> **2** appearing in successive instalments <*a* ~ *story*> **3** of or being music based on a series of notes in an arbitrary but fixed order without regard for traditional tonality – **serially** *adv*

[2]serial *n* **1** a work appearing (e g in a magazine or on television) in parts at usu regular intervals **2** a publication issued as 1 of a consecutively numbered continuing series

ˈ**serial·ize, -ise** /-liez‖-laɪz/ *vt* to arrange or publish in serial form – **serialization** *n*

ˈ**serial** ˌ**number** *n* a number used as a means of identification that indicates position in a series

series /ˈsiəriz, -reez‖ˈsɪərɪz, -riːz/ *n, pl* **series 1** a number of things or events of the same kind following one another; *broadly* any group of systematically related items **2** a division of rock formations that is smaller than a system and comprises rocks deposited during an epoch **3** an arrangement of devices in an electrical circuit in which the whole current passes through each device **4** a number of games (e g of cricket) played between 2 teams

serif /ˈserif‖ˈserɪf/ *n* a short line stemming from the stroke of a letter – **seriffed** *adj*

seriocomic /ˌsiərioh'komik‖ˌsɪərɪəʊ'kɒmɪk/ *adj* having a mixture of the serious and the comic – **seriocomically** *adv*

serious /ˈsiəri·əs‖ˈsɪərɪəs/ *adj* **1** grave or thoughtful in appearance or manner; sober **2a** requiring careful attention and concentration < ~ *study*> **b** of or relating to a weighty or important matter <*a* ~ *play*> **3a** not jesting or deceiving; in earnest **b** deeply interested or committed < ~ *fishermen*> **4** having important or dangerous consequences; critical <*a* ~ *injury*> – **seriousness** *n*

ˈ**seriously** /-li‖-lɪ/ *adv* **1a** in a sincere manner; earnestly **b** to speak in a serious way < ~, *you should be more careful*> **2** to a serious extent; severely < ~ *injured*>

sermon /ˈsuhmən‖ˈsɜːmən/ *n* **1** a religious discourse delivered in public, usu by a clergyman as a part of a religious service **2** a speech on conduct or duty; *esp* one that is unduly long or tedious

sermon·ize, -ise /ˈsuhməˌniez‖ˈsɜːməˌnaɪz/ *vi* to give moral advice in an officious or dogmatic manner – **sermonizer** *n*

serpent /ˈsuhpənt‖ˈsɜːpənt/ *n* **1** a (large) snake **2** *the* Devil **3** a wily treacherous person **4** an old-fashioned bass woodwind instrument of serpentine form

[1]serpentine /ˈsuhpənˌtien‖ˈsɜːpənˌtaɪn/ *adj* **1** of or like a serpent (e g in form or movement) **2** subtly tempting; wily, artful **3** winding or turning one way and another

[2]serpentine *n* sthg wavy or winding; *specif* a serpentine movement in dressage

[3]serpentine *n* a usu dull green mottled mineral consisting mainly of hydrated magnesium silicate

[1]serrate /seˈrayt, sə-‖seˈreɪt, sə-/ *vt* to mark or provide with serrations

[2]serrate /ˈserət, -rayt‖ˈserət, -reɪt/ *adj* notched or having (forwards-pointing) teeth on the edge <*a* ~ *leaf*>

serration /seˈraysh(ə)n, sə-‖seˈreɪʃ(ə)n, sə-/ *n* **1** a formation resembling the teeth of a saw **2** any of the teeth of a serrated edge

serried /ˈserid‖ˈserɪd/ *adj* crowded or pressed together; compact

serum /ˈsiərəm‖ˈsɪərəm/ *n, pl* **serums, sera** /ˈsiərə‖ˈsɪərə/ the watery part of an animal liquid (remaining after coagulation): **a** blood serum, esp when containing specific antibodies **b** whey – **serous** *adj*

serum hepatitis *n* an often fatal inflammation of the liver caused by a virus that is contracted esp by contact with an infected person's blood

serval /ˈsuhv(ə)l‖ˈsɜːv(ə)l/ *n* a long-legged long-eared African wildcat with a tawny black-spotted coat

servant /ˈsuhv(ə)nt‖ˈsɜːv(ə)nt/ *n* sby who or sthg that serves others; *specif* sby employed to perform personal or domestic duties for another

[1]serve /suhv‖sɜːv/ *vi* **1a** to act as a servant **b** to do military or naval service **2** to act as server at Mass **3a** to be of use; fulfil a specified purpose – often + *as* **b** to be favourable, opportune, or convenient <*told the story whenever occasion* ~d> **c** to prove reliable or trustworthy <*it was last year, if memory* ~s> **d** to hold a post or office; discharge a duty < ~ *on a jury*> **4** to prove adequate or satisfactory; suffice <*dress that* ~s *for all occasions*> **5** to distribute drinks or helpings of food **6** to attend to customers in a shop **7** to put the ball or shuttle in play in any of various games (e g tennis or volleyball) ~ *vt* **1a** to act as a servant to **b** to give military or naval service to < ~d *France in the last war*> **c** to perform the duties of < ~d *his presidency*> **2** to act as server at (Mass) **3a** to work through or perform (a term of service) < ~d *his time as a mate*> **b** to undergo (a term of imprisonment) **4** to supply (food or drink) to (guests or diners) **5a(1)** to provide with sthg needed or desired <*3 schools* ~ *the area*> **a(2)** to attend to (a customer) in a shop **b** to supply (sthg needed or desired) <*garages refused to* ~ *petrol*> **6** to prove adequate for; suffice <*this sharp stone will* ~ *my purposes*> **7** to treat or act towards in a specified way <*he* ~d *me ill*> **8** to make legal service of (e g a writ or summons) or upon (a person there named) **9** *of a male animal* to copulate with **10** to wind yarn or wire tightly round (a rope or stay) for protection **11** to act so as to help or benefit <*the citizen's duty to* ~ *society*> **12** to put (the ball or shuttle) in play – **serve someone right** to be a deserved punishment for sby

[2]serve *n* the act of putting the ball or shuttle in play in any of various games (e g volleyball, badminton, or tennis); *also* a turn to serve

server /ˈsuhvə‖ˈsɜːvə/ *n* **1** sby who serves food or drink **2** the player who serves (e g in tennis) **3** sthg (e g tongs) used in serving food or drink **4** an assistant to the celebrant of a low mass

servery /ˈsuhv(ə)ri‖ˈsɜːv(ə)rɪ/ *n* a room, counter, or hatch (e g in a public house) from which food is served

[1]**service** /'suhvis‖'sɜːvɪs/ *n* **1a** work or duty performed for sby <*on active* ~> **b** employment as a servant <*entered* ~ *when she was 14*> **2a** the function performed by sby who or sthg that serves <*these shoes have given me good* ~> **b** help, use, benefit <*be of* ~ *to them*> **c** disposal for use or assistance <*I'm always at your* ~> **3a** a form followed in a religious ceremony **b** a meeting for worship **4** the act of serving: e g **4a** a helpful act; a favour <*did him a* ~> **b** a piece of useful work that does not produce a tangible commodity – usu pl with sing. meaning <*charge for professional* ~s> **c** a serve **5** a set of articles for a particular use; *specif* a set of matching tableware <*a 24-piece dinner* ~> **6a** an administrative division <*the consular* ~> **b** any of a nation's military forces (e g the army or navy) **7a(1)** a facility supplying some public demand <*bus* ~> **a(2)** *pl* utilities (e g gas, water sewage, or electricity) available or connected to a building **b(1)** a facility providing maintenance and repair <*television* ~> **b(2)** the usu routine repair and maintenance of a machine or motor vehicle <*the car is due for its 6000 mile* ~> **c** a facility providing broadcast programmes <*East European* Service> **8** the bringing of a legal writ, process, or summons to notice as prescribed **9** the act of copulating with a female animal

[2]**service** *adj* **1** of the armed services **2** used in serving or delivering <*tradesmen use the* ~ *entrance*> **3** providing services <*the* ~ *industries*>

[3]**service** *vt* to perform services for: e g **a** to repair or provide maintenance for **b** to meet interest and sinking fund payments on (e g government debt) **c** to perform any of the business functions auxiliary to production or distribution of **d** *of a male animal* SERVE 9 – **servicer** *n*

[4]**service**, 'service ˌtree *n* an Old World tree of the rose family resembling the related mountain ashes but with larger flowers and larger edible fruits

serviceable /'suhvisəbl‖'sɜːvɪsəbl/ *adj* **1** fit to use; suited for a purpose **2** wearing well in use; durable – **serviceableness** *n*, **serviceably** *adv*, **serviceability** *n*

'service ˌcharge *n* a proportion of a bill added onto the total bill to pay for service, usu instead of tips

'service ˌflat *n, Br* a flat of which the rent includes a charge for certain services (e g cleaning)

'serviceman /-mən‖-mən/, *fem* **'service ˌwoman** *n* **1** a member of the armed forces **2** *chiefly NAm* sby employed to repair or maintain equipment

'service ˌroad *n* a road that provides access for local traffic only

'service ˌstation *n* a retail station for servicing motor vehicles, esp with oil and petrol

serviette /ˌsuhvi'et‖ˌsɜːvɪ'et/ *n, chiefly Br* a table napkin

servile /'suhviel‖'sɜːvaɪl/ *adj* **1** of or befitting a slave or a menial position <*a* ~ *task*> **2** slavishly or unctuously submissive; abject, obsequious – **servilely** *adv*, **servility** *n*

serving /'suhving‖'sɜːvɪŋ/ *n* a single portion of food or drink; a helping

servitude /'suhvityoohd‖'sɜːvɪtjuːd/ *n* **1** lack of liberty; bondage <*penal* ~> **2** a right by which sthg owned by one person is subject to a specified use or enjoyment by another

servomechanism /'suhvohˌmekəniz(ə)m‖'sɜːvəʊˌmekənɪz(ə)m/ *n* an automatic device for controlling large amounts of power by means of very small amounts of power and automatically correcting performance of a mechanism

servomotor /'suhvohˌmohtə‖'sɜːvəʊˌməʊtə/ *n* a power-driven mechanism that supplements a primary control operated by a comparatively feeble force (e g in a servomechanism)

sesame /'sesəmi‖'sesəmɪ/ *n* (an E Indian plant with) small flattish seeds used as a source of oil and as a flavouring agent

sesquicentennial /ˌseskwisen'teni·əl‖ˌseskwɪsen'tenɪəl/ *adj or n* (of) a 150th anniversary

sesquipedalian /ˌseskwipə'daylyən‖ˌseskwɪpə'deɪljən/ *adj* **1** containing many syllables **2** using long words, esp to excess

session /'sesh(ə)n‖'seʃ(ə)n/ *n* **1** a meeting or series of meetings of a body (e g a court or council) for the transaction of business; a sitting **2** the period between the meeting of a legislative or judicial body and the final adjournment of that meeting **3** the period in which a school conducts classes **4** a period devoted to a particular activity, esp by a group of people <*a recording* ~> – **sessional** *adj*

sestet /ses'tet‖ses'tet/ *n* a stanza or poem of 6 lines

[1]**set** /set‖set/ *vb* **-tt-; set,** (*vt 10*) **setted** *vt* **1** to cause to sit; place in or on a seat **2a** to place with care or deliberate purpose and with relative stability <~ *a ladder against the wall*> **b** TRANSPLANT 1 <~ *seedlings*> **c** to make (e g a trap) ready to catch prey **3** to cause to assume a specified condition <~ *the room to rights*> **4a** to appoint or assign to an office or duty <~ *him over them as foreman*> **b** to post, station <~ *sentries*> **5a** to place in a specified relation or position <*a dish to* ~ *before a king*> **b** to place in a specified setting <*the story is* ~ *in 17th-c Spain*> **6a** to fasten **b** to apply <~ *pen to paper*> **7** to fix or decide on as a time, limit, or regulation; prescribe <~ *a wedding day*> **8a** to establish as the most extreme, esp the highest, level <~ *a new record*> **b** to provide as a pattern or model <~ *an example*> **c** to allot as or compose for a task <~ *the children some homework*> **9a** to adjust (a device, esp a measuring device) to a desired position <~ *the alarm for 7:00*> **b** to restore to normal position or connection after dislocation or fracturing <~ *a broken bone*>; *also* REDUCE 5 <~ *a fracture*> **c** to spread to the wind <~ *the sails*> **10a** to divide (an age-group of pupils) into sets **b** to teach (a school subject) by dividing the pupils into sets <*maths and science are* ~ted> **11a** to make ready for use <~ *another place for dinner*> **b** to provide music or instrumentation for (a text) **c(1)** to arrange (type) for printing **c(2)** to put into type or its equivalent (e g on film) **12a** to put a fine edge on by grinding or

honing <~ *a razor*> **b** to bend slightly the alternate teeth of (a saw) in opposite directions **c** to sink (the head of a nail) below the surface **13** to fix in a desired position **14** to fix (the hair) in a desired style by waving, curling, or arranging, usu while wet **15a** to adorn or surround with sthg attached or embedded; stud, dot <*river all ~ about with fever trees* – Rudyard Kipling> **b** to fix (e g a gem) in a metal setting **16a** to fix at a specified amount <~ *bail at £500*> **b** to value, rate <*his promises were ~ at naught*> **c** to place as an estimate of worth <~ *a high value on life*> **17** to place in relation for comparison <~ *her beside Michelangelo*>; *also* to offset <~ *our gains against our losses*> **18a** to direct to action <~ *her to write a report*> **b** to put into activity or motion <~ *the clock going*> <*it ~ me wondering*> **c** to incite to attack or antagonism <*war ~s brother against brother*> **19** *of a gundog* to point out the position of (game) by holding a fixed attitude **20** to defeat (an opponent or his/her contract) in bridge **21** to fix firmly; give rigid form to <~ *his jaw in determination*> **22** to cause to become firm or solid <~ *jelly by adding gelatin*> **23** to cause (e g fruit) to develop ~ *vi* **1** – used as an interjection to command runners to put themselves into the starting position before a race **2** *of a plant part* to undergo development, usu as a result of pollination **3** to pass below the horizon; go down <*the sun ~s*> **4** to make an attack – + *on* or *upon* **5** to have a specified direction in motion; flow, tend <*the wind was ~ting south*> **6** to apply oneself to some activity <~ *to work*> **7** *of a gundog* to indicate the position of game by crouching or pointing **8** to dance face to face with another in a square dance <~ *to your partner*> **9a** to become solid or thickened by chemical or physical attention <*the cement ~s rapidly*> **b** *of a broken bone* to become whole by knitting together **c** *of metal* to acquire a permanent twist or bend from strain **10** *chiefly dial* to sit – **set about 1** to begin to do <*how to* set about *losing weight*> **2** to attack <set about *the intruder with a rolling pin*> – **set foot** to pass over the threshold; enter – + *in, on,* or *inside* – **set in motion** to get (sthg) started; initiate <set *an inquiry* in motion> – **set on** to cause to attack or pursue <set *the dog* on *the trespassers*> – **set one's face against** to oppose staunchly – **set one's hand to** to become engaged in – **set one's heart** to resolve; *also* to want (sthg) very much – + *on* or *upon* <*she* set her heart *on succeeding*> – **set one's house in order** to introduce necessary reforms – **set one's sights** to focus one's concentration or intentions; aim – **set one's teeth on edge** to give one an unpleasant sensation (e g that caused by an acid flavour or squeaky noise) – **set sail** to begin a voyage – **set store by** to consider valuable, trustworthy, or worthwhile, esp to the specified degree – **set the scene** to provide necessary background information – **set to work** to apply oneself; begin <*he* set to work *to undermine their confidence*>

[2]**set** *adj* **1** intent, determined <~ *on going*> **2** fixed by authority or binding decision; prescribed, specified <*there are 3 ~ books for the examination*> **3** *of a meal* consisting of a specified combination of dishes available at a fixed price **4** reluctant to change; fixed by habit <~ *in his ways*> **5** immovable, rigid <*a ~ frown*> **6** ready, prepared <*all ~ for an early morning start*> **7** conventional, stereotyped <*her speech was full of ~ phrases*>

[3]**set** *n* **1** setting or being set **2a** a mental inclination, tendency, or habit **b** predisposition to act in a certain way in response to an anticipated stimulus or situation **3** a number of things, usu of the same kind, that belong or are used together or that form a unit <*a chess ~*> <*a good ~ of teeth*> **4** direction of flow <*the ~ of the wind*> **5** the form or carriage of the body or of its parts <*the graceful ~ of his head*> **6** the amount of deviation from a straight line; *specif* the degree to which the teeth of a saw have been set **7** permanent change of form due to repeated or excessive stress **8** the arrangement of the hair by curling or waving **9a** a young plant or rooted cutting ready for transplanting **b** a small bulb, corm, or (piece of) tuber used for propagation <*onion ~s*> **10** an artificial setting for a scene of a theatrical or film production **11** a division of a tennis match won by the side that wins at least 6 games beating the opponent by 2 games or that wins a tie breaker **12** the basic formation in a country dance or square dance **13** (the music played at) a session of music (e g jazz or rock music), usu followed by an intermission **14** *sing or pl in constr* a group of people associated by common interests <*the smart ~*> **15** a collection of mathematical elements (e g numbers or points) **16** an apparatus of electronic components assembled so as to function as a unit <*a radio ~*> **17** *sing or pl in constr* a group of pupils of roughly equal ability in a particular subject who are taught together **18** a sett

seta /ˈseetə‖ˈsiːtə/ *n, pl* **setae** /-ti‖-tɪ/ a slender bristle or similar part of an animal or plant – **setaceous** *adj*, **setaceously** *adv*, **setal** *adj*

set aside *vt* **1** to put to one side; discard **2** to reserve for a particular purpose; save **3** to reject from consideration **4** to annul or overrule (a sentence, verdict, etc)

ˈ**setˌback** /-ˌbak‖-ˌbæk/ *n* **1** an arresting of or hindrance in progress **2** a defeat, reverse

set back *vt* **1** to prevent or hinder the progress of; impede, delay **2** to cost <*a new suit* set *him* back *a full week's wages*> – infml

set down *vt* **1** to place at rest on a surface or on the ground; deposit **2** to cause or allow (a passenger) to alight from a vehicle **3** to land (an aircraft) on the ground or water **4** to put in writing **5a** to regard, consider <set *him* down *as a liar*> **b** to attribute, ascribe <set *her success* down *to sheer perseverance*>

set in *vt* to insert; *esp* to stitch (a small part) into a larger article <set in *a sleeve of a dress*> ~ *vi* **1** to become established <*the rot has* set in> **2** to blow or flow towards the shore <*the wind was beginning to* set in>

ˈ**set-ˌoff** *n* **1** sthg set off against another thing: **1a** a decoration, adornment **b** a counterbalance, compensation **2** the discharge of a debt by setting against it a sum owed by the creditor to the debtor

set off *vt* **1a** to put in relief; show up by contrast **b** to adorn, embellish **c** to make distinct or outstanding; enhance **2** to treat as a compensating item <set off *the 3 totals against one another*> **3a** to set in motion; cause to begin **b** to cause to explode; detonate **4** *chiefly NAm* to compensate for; offset ~*vi* to start out on a course or journey <set off *for home*>

set out *vt* **1** to state or describe at length; expound <*a pamphlet* setting out *his ideas in full*> **2a** to arrange and present graphically or systematically **b** to mark out (e g a design) **c** to create or construct according to a plan or design <set *gardens* out *on waste ground*> **3** to begin with a definite purpose or goal; intend, undertake <*you* set out *deliberately to annoy me*> ~*vi* to start out on a course, journey, or career

set piece *n* **1** (a part of) a work of art, literature, etc with a formal pattern or style **2** an arrangement of fireworks that forms a pattern while burning **3** any of various moves in soccer or rugby (e g a corner kick or free kick) by which the ball is put back into play after a stoppage

ˈ**setˌscrew** /-ˌskrooh‖-ˌskruː/ *n* **1** a screw that is tightened to prevent relative movement between parts (e g of a machine) and keep them in a set position **2** a screw that serves to adjust a machine

set square *n, chiefly Br* a flat triangular instrument with 1 right angle and 2 other precisely known angles, used to mark out or test angles

sett, **set** /set‖set/ *n* **1** the burrow of a badger **2** a usu rectangular block of stone or wood formerly used for paving streets

settee /seˈtee‖seˈtiː/ *n* a long often upholstered seat with a back and usu arms for seating more than 1 person; *broadly* a sofa

setter /ˈsetə‖ˈsetə/ *n* a large gundog trained to point on finding game; *specif* IRISH SETTER

set theory *n* a branch of mathematics or of symbolic logic that deals with the nature and relations of sets

setting /ˈseting‖ˈsetɪŋ/ *n* **1** the manner, position, or direction in which sthg (e g a dial) is set **2** the (style of) frame in which a gem is mounted **3a** the background, surroundings **b** the time and place of the action of a literary, dramatic, or cinematic work **c** the scenery used in a theatrical or film production **4** the music composed for a text (e g a poem) **5** PLACE SETTING

[1]**settle** /ˈsetl‖ˈsetl/ *n* a wooden bench with arms, a high solid back, and an enclosed base which can be used as a chest

[2]**settle** *vt* **1** to place firmly or comfortably <~d *herself in an armchair*> **2a** to establish in residence <~ *refugees on farmland*> **b** to supply with inhabitants; colonize **3a** to cause to sink and become compacted <*rain* ~d *the dust*> **b** to clarify by causing the sediment to sink <*put eggshells in the coffee to* ~ *it*> **4a** to free from pain, discomfort, disorder, or disturbance <*took a drink to* ~ *his nerves*> **b** to make subdued or well-behaved <*one word from the referee* ~d *him*> **5** to fix or resolve conclusively <~ *the question*> **6a** to bestow legally for life – usu + *on* <~d *her estate on her son*> **b** to arrange for or make a final disposition of <~d *her affairs*> **7** to pay (a bill or money claimed) ~ *vi* **1** to come to rest <*a sparrow* ~d *on the windowsill*> **2a** to sink gradually to the bottom; subside <*let the dust* ~ *before applying paint*> **b** to become clearer by the deposit of sediment or scum **c** *of a building, the ground, etc* to sink slowly to a lower level; subside **3a** to become fixed or permanent <*his mood* ~d *into apathy*> **b** to establish a residence or colony <~d *in Canada for a few years*> **4a** to become calm or orderly – often + *down* **b** to adopt an ordered or stable life-style – usu + *down* <*marry and* ~ *down*> **5a** to adjust differences or accounts – often + *with* or *up* **b** to end a legal dispute by the agreement of both parties, without court action <~d *out of court*> – **settle for** to be content with; accept

settle in *vi* to become comfortably established <*children quickly* settle in *at a new school*> ~*vt* to assist in becoming comfortably established

ˈ**settlement** /-mənt‖-mənt/ *n* **1** settling **2a** an act of bestowing possession under legal sanction **b** an estate, income, etc legally bestowed on sby **3a** a newly settled place or region **b** a small, esp isolated, village **4** an organization providing various community services in an underprivileged area **5** an agreement resolving differences <*reached a* ~ *on the strike*>

settler /ˈsetlə‖ˈsetlə/ *n* one who settles sthg (e g a new region)

ˈ**set-ˌto** *n, pl* **set-tos** a usu brief and vigorous conflict – chiefly infml

set to *vi* **1** to make an eager or determined start on a job or activity **2** to begin fighting

ˈ**set-ˌup** *n* **1** an arrangement; *also* an organization **2** *chiefly NAm* carriage of the body; bearing **3** *chiefly NAm* a task or contest with a prearranged or artificially easy course – chiefly infml

set up *vt* **1a** to raise into position; erect <set up *a statue*> <set up *road blocks*> **b** to put forward (e g a theory) for acceptance; propound **2a** to assemble and prepare for use or operation <set up *a printing press*> **b** to put (a machine) in readiness or adjustment for operation **3a** to give voice to, esp loudly; raise <set up *a din*> **b** to create; BRING ABOUT <*issues that* set up *personal tensions*> **4** to place in a high office or powerful position <set up *the general as dictator*> **5** to claim (oneself) to be a specified thing <sets *herself* up *as an authority*> **6a** to found, institute <set up *a fund for orphans*> **b** to install oneself in <set up *house together*> **7a** to provide with an independent livelihood <set *her* up *in business*> **b** to provide with what is necessary or useful – usu + *with* or *for* <*we're well* set up *with logs for the winter*> **8** to bring or restore to health or success <*a drink will* set *you* up> **9** to prepare detailed plans for <set up *a bank robbery*> ~*vi* to start business <set up *as a house agent*> – **set up shop** to establish one's business

seven /ˈsev(ə)n‖ˈsev(ə)n/ *n* **1** (the number) 7 **2** the seventh in a set or series <*the* ~ *of diamonds*> **3** sthg having 7 parts or members or a denomination of 7 **4** *pl but sing or pl in constr* a rugby game played with teams of 7 players each – **seven** *adj or pron*, **sevenfold** *adj or adv*

seventeen /ˌsev(ə)nˈteen‖ˌsev(ə)nˈtiːn/ *n* (the number) 17 – **seventeen** *adj or pron*, **seventeenth** *adj or n*

seventh /ˈsev(ə)nth‖ˈsev(ə)nθ/ *adj or n* (of or being) number seven in a countable series

ˌseventh ˈheaven *n* a state of supreme rapture or bliss

seventy /ˈsev(ə)nti‖ˈsev(ə)ntɪ/ *n* **1** (the number) 70 **2** *pl* the numbers 70 to 79; *specif* a range of temperatures, ages, or dates within a century characterized by those numbers – **seventieth** *adj or n*, **seventy** *adj or pron*

ˌseven-year ˈitch *n* marital discontent allegedly leading to infidelity after about 7 years of marriage

sever /ˈsevə‖ˈsevə/ *vt* **1** to put or keep apart; separate; *esp* to remove (a major part or portion) (as if) by cutting **2** to break off; terminate <~ *economic links*> ~*vi* to become separated – **severable** *adj*, **severance** *n*

[1]**several** /ˈsev(ə)rəl‖ˈsev(ə)rəl/ *adj* **1** more than 2 but fewer than many <~ *hundred times*> **2** separate or distinct from one another; respective <*specialists in their* ~ *fields*> – chiefly fml

[2]**several** *pron, pl in constr* an indefinite number more than 2 and fewer than many <~ *of the guests*> – **severalfold** *adj or adv*

severally /ˈsev(ə)rəli‖ˈsev(ə)rəlɪ/ *adv* each by itself or him-/herself; separately – chiefly fml

ˈseverance ˌpay /ˈsev(ə)rəns‖ˈsev(ə)rəns/ *n* an amount payable to an employee on termination of employment

severe /siˈviə‖sɪˈvɪə/ *adj* **1** having a stern expression or character; austere **2** rigorous in judgment, requirements, or punishment; stringent <~ *penalties*> <~ *legislation*> **3** strongly critical or condemnatory; censorious <*a* ~ *critic*> **4** sober or restrained in decoration or manner; plain **5** marked by harsh or extreme conditions <~ *winters*> **6** requiring much effort; arduous <*a* ~ *test*> **7** serious, grave <*a* ~ *illness*> – **severely** *adv*, **severity** *n*

sew /soh‖səʊ/ *vb* **sewed** /sohd‖səʊd/; **sewn** /sohn‖səʊn/, **sewed** *vt* **1** to unite, fasten, or attach by stitches made with a needle and thread **2** to close or enclose by sewing <~ *the money in a bag*> **3** to make or mend by sewing ~*vi* to practise or engage in sewing – **sewer** *n*

sewage /ˈs(y)ooh·ij, ˈs(y)oo·ij‖ˈs(j)uːɪdʒ, ˈs(j)ʊɪdʒ/ *n* waste matter carried off by sewers

sewer /ˈs(y)ooə‖ˈs(j)ʊə/ *n* an artificial usu underground conduit used to carry off waste matter, esp excrement, from houses, schools, towns, etc and surface water from roads and paved areas [Middle French *esseweur, seweur*, fr *essewer* to drain, deriv of Latin *ex* out of + *aqua* water]

sewerage /ˈs(y)ooərij‖ˈs(j)ʊərɪdʒ/ *n* **1** sewage **2** the removal and disposal of surface water by sewers **3** a system of sewers

sewing /ˈsoh·ing‖ˈsəʊɪŋ/ *n* **1** the act, action, or work of one who sews **2** work that has been or is to be sewn

sew up *vt* **1** to mend, close (e g a hole), or enclose by sewing **2** to bring to a successful or satisfactory conclusion – chiefly infml

[1]**sex** /seks‖seks/ *n* **1** either of 2 divisions of organisms distinguished as male or female **2** the structural, functional, and behavioural characteristics that are involved in reproduction and that distinguish males and females **3** SEXUAL INTERCOURSE

[2]**sex** *vt* to identify the sex of <~ *chicks*>

sexagenarian /ˌseksəjiˈneəri·ən‖ˌseksədʒɪˈneərɪən/ *n* a person between 60 and 69 years old – **sexagenarian** *adj*

Sexagesima /ˌseksəˈjesimə‖ˌseksəˈdʒesɪmə/ *n* the second Sunday before Lent

ˈsex apˌpeal *n* physical attractiveness for members of the opposite sex

sexed /sekst‖sekst/ *adj* having sex, sex appeal, or sexual instincts, esp to a specified degree <*highly* ~>

sexism /ˈsekˌsiz(ə)m‖ˈsekˌsɪz(ə)m/ *n* **1** a belief that sex determines intrinsic capacities and role in society and that sexual differences produce an inherent superiority of one sex, usu the male **2** discrimination on the basis of sex; *esp* prejudice against women on the part of men – **sexist** *adj or n*

ˈsexless /-lis‖-lɪs/ *adj* **1** lacking sexuality or sexual intercourse **2** lacking sex appeal

sexology /sekˈsoləji‖sekˈsɒlədʒɪ/ the study of sexual behaviour – **sexologist** *n*

sextant /ˈsekstənt‖ˈsekstənt/ *n* an instrument for measuring angles that is used, esp in navigation, to observe the altitudes of celestial bodies and so determine the observer's position on the earth's surface

sextet /sekˈstet‖sekˈstet/ *n* **1** (a musical composition for) a group of 6 instruments, voices, or performers **2** *sing or pl in constr* a group or set of 6

sexton /ˈsekstən‖ˈsekstən/ *n* a church officer who takes care of the church property and is often also the gravedigger

[1]**sextuple** /ˈsekstyoopl‖ˈsekstjʊpl/ *adj* **1** having 6 units or members **2** being 6 times as great or as many

[2]**sextuple** *vb* to make or become 6 times as much or as many

sextuplet /ˈsekstyooplit‖ˈsekstjʊplɪt/ *n* **1** a combination of 6 of a kind **2** any of 6 offspring born at 1 birth **3** a group of 6 equal musical notes performed in the time ordinarily given to 4 of the same value

sexual /ˈseksyoo(ə)l, -sh(ə)l‖ˈseksjʊ(ə)l, -ʃ(ə)l/ *adj* **1** of or associated with sex or the sexes <~ *conflict*> **2** having or involving sex <~ *reproduction*> – **sexually** *adv*, **sexuality** *n*

sexual intercourse *n* intercourse with genital contact **a** involving penetration of the vagina by the penis; coitus **b** other than penetration of the vagina by the penis

sexy /ˈseksi‖ˈseksɪ/ *adj* sexually suggestive or stimulating; erotic – **sexily** *adv*, **sexiness** *n*

sforzando /sfawtˈsandoh‖sfɔːtˈsændəʊ/ *n, adj, or adv, pl* **sforzandos, sforzandi** /-di‖-dɪ/ (a note or chord played) with prominent stress or accent – used in music

sh /sh‖ʃ/ *interj* – used often in prolonged or reduplicated form to urge or command silence

shabby /ˈshabi‖ˈʃæbɪ/ *adj* **1a** threadbare or faded from wear <*a* ~ *sofa*> **b** dilapidated, run-down <*a* ~ *district*> **2** dressed in worn or grubby clothes; seedy <*a ~ tramp*> **3** shameful, despicable <*what a ~ trick, driving off and leaving me to walk home!*> – **shabbily** *adv*, **shabbiness** *n*

shack /shak‖ʃæk/ *n* a small crudely built dwelling or shelter

[1]**shackle** /'shakl‖'ʃækl/ *n* **1** (a metal ring like) a manacle or handcuff **2** sthg that restricts or prevents free action or expression – usu pl with sing. meaning **3** a U-shaped piece of metal with a pin or bolt to close the opening

[2]**shackle** *vt* **1a** to bind with shackles; fetter **b** to make fast with shackles **2** to deprive of freedom of thought or action by means of restrictions or handicaps; impede

shack up *vi* to live with and have a sexual relationship with sby; *also* to spend the night as a partner in sexual intercourse – usu + *together* or *with*; infml

shad /shad‖ʃæd/ *n, pl* **shad** any of several fishes of the herring family that have a relatively deep body and are important food fishes of Europe and N America

[1]**shade** /shayd‖ʃeɪd/ *n* **1a** partial darkness caused by the interception of rays of light **b** relative obscurity or insignificance **2** a place sheltered (e g by foliage) from the direct heat and glare of the sun **3** a transitory or illusory appearance **4** *pl* the shadows that gather as night falls **5** GHOST 2 **6** sthg that intercepts or diffuses light or heat: e g **6a** a lampshade **b** *chiefly NAm* **b(1)** *pl* sunglasses – infml **b(2)** a window blind **7** the reproduction of shade in a picture **8a** a colour produced by a pigment mixed with some black **b** a particular level of depth or brightness of a colour <*a ~ of pink*> **9** a minute difference or amount <*the ~s of meaning in a poem*> – **a shade** a tiny bit; somewhat <a shade *too much salt*> – **shades of** – used interjectionally to indicate that one is reminded of or struck by a resemblance to a specified person or thing

[2]**shade** *vt* **1a** to shelter or screen by intercepting radiated light or heat **b** to cover with a shade **2** to darken or obscure (as if) with a shadow **3a** to represent the effect of shade on **b** to mark with shading or gradations of colour **4** to change by gradual transition ~*vi* to pass by slight changes or imperceptible degrees – usu + *into* or *off into*

shading /'shayding‖'ʃeɪdɪŋ/ *n* an area of filled-in outlines to suggest three-dimensionality, shadow, or degrees of light and dark in a picture

[1]**shadow** /'shadoh‖'ʃædəʊ/ *n* **1a** partial darkness caused by an opaque body interposed so as to cut off rays from a light source <*the thieves lurked in the ~ of the house*> **b** a dark area resembling shadow <~s *under his eyes from fatigue*> **2a** a faint representation or suggestion <~s *of future difficulties*> **b** a mere semblance or imitation of sthg <*she wore herself to a ~ by studying too hard*> **3** a dark figure cast on a surface by a body intercepting light rays <*the trees cast their ~*s *on the wall*> **4** a phantom **5** *pl* darkness **6** a shaded or darker portion of a picture **7** an attenuated form; a vestige <*after his illness he was only a ~ of his former self*> **8a** an inseparable companion or follower **b** one (e g a spy or detective) who shadows **9** a small degree or portion; a trace <*without a ~ of doubt*> **10** a source of gloom or disquiet <*her death cast a ~ on the festivities*> **11** a pervasive and often disabling influence <*governed under the ~ of his predecessor*>

[2]**shadow** *vt* **1** to cast a shadow over **2** to follow (a person) secretly; keep under surveillance **3** to shade

[3]**shadow** *adj* **1** identical with another in form but without the other's power or status <*a ~ government in exile*>; *specif* of or constituting the probable cabinet when the opposition party is returned to power <*the ~ spokesman on employment*> **2a** having an indistinct pattern <~ *plaid*> **b** having darker sections of design <~ *lace*> **3** shown by throwing the shadows of performers or puppets on a screen <*a ~ dance*>

'**shadow-ˌbox** *vi* to box with an imaginary opponent, esp as a form of training – **shadow-boxing** *n*

shadowy /'shadoh·i‖'ʃædəʊɪ/ *adj* **1a** of the nature of or resembling a shadow; insubstantial **b** scarcely perceptible; indistinct **2** lying in or obscured by shadow <*deep ~ interiors*> – **shadowiness** *n*

shady /'shaydi‖'ʃeɪdɪ/ *adj* **1** producing or affording shade <*a ~ tree*> **2** sheltered from the direct heat or light of the sun <*a ~ spot*> **3a** of questionable merit; uncertain, unreliable <*a ~ deal*> **b** of doubtful integrity; disreputable <*she's a ~ character*> – chiefly infml – **shadily** *adv*, **shadiness** *n*

shaft /shahft‖ʃɑːft/ *n* **1a** (the long handle of) a spear, lance, or similar weapon **b** a pole; *specif* either of 2 poles between which a horse is hitched to a vehicle **c** an arrow, esp for a longbow **2** a sharply delineated beam of light shining from an opening **3** sthg resembling the shaft of a spear, lance, etc, esp in having a long slender cylindrical form: e g **3a** the trunk of a tree **b** the cylindrical pillar between the capital and the base of a column **c** the handle of a tool or implement (e g a hammer or golf club) **d** a usu cylindrical bar used to support rotating pieces or to transmit power or motion by rotation **e** a man-made vertical or inclined opening leading underground to a mine, well, etc **f** a vertical opening or passage through the floors of a building <*a lift ~*> **g** the central stem of a feather **4** a scornful, satirical, or pithily critical remark; a barb

[1]**shag** /shag‖ʃæg/ *n* **1a** an unkempt or uneven tangled mass or covering (e g of hair) **b** long coarse or matted fibre or nap **2** a strong coarse tobacco cut into fine shreds **3** a European bird smaller than the closely related cormorant – **shaggy** *adj*, **shaggily** *adv*

[2]**shag** *vt* **-gg-** **1** to fuck, screw – vulg **2** *Br* to make utterly exhausted – usu + *out*; slang

[3]**shag** *n* an act of sexual intercourse – vulg

shaggy-dog story /'shagi‖'ʃægɪ/ *n* a protracted and inconsequential funny story whose humour lies in the pointlessness or irrelevance of the conclusion

shagreen /sha'green‖ʃæ'griːn/ *n* **1** an untanned leather covered with small round granulations and usu dyed green **2** the rough skin of various sharks and rays – **shagreen** *adj*

shah /shah‖ʃɑː/ *n, often cap* a sovereign of Iran – **shahdom** *n*

[1]**shake** /shayk‖ʃeɪk/ *vb* **shook** /shook‖ʃʊk/; **shaken** /ˈshaykən‖ˈʃeɪkən/ *vi* **1** to move to and fro with rapid usu irregular motion **2** to vibrate, esp from the impact of a blow or shock **3** to tremble as a result of physical or emotional disturbance **4** to shake hands <*if you've agreed then ~ on it*> ~ *vt* **1** to brandish, wave, or flourish, esp in a threatening manner **2** to cause to move with a rapidly alternating motion **3** to cause to quake, quiver, or tremble **4** to cause to waver; weaken <*~ one's faith*> **5** to put in a specified state by repeated quick jerky movements <shook *himself free from the woman's grasp*> **6** to dislodge or eject by quick jerky movements of the support or container <shook *the dust from the cloth*> **7** to clasp (hands) in greeting or farewell or to convey goodwill or agreement **8** to agitate the feelings of; upset <*the news* shook *him*> – **shakable, shakeable** *adj* – **shake a leg** to hurry up; hasten – infml – **shake one's head** to move one's head from side to side to indicate disagreement, denial, disapproval, etc

[2]**shake** *n* **1** an act of shaking <*indicated her disapproval with a ~ of the head*> **2** *pl* a condition of trembling (e g from chill or fever); *specif* DELIRIUM TREMENS **3** a wavering, vibrating, or alternating motion caused by a blow or shock **4** TRILL 1 **5** *chiefly NAm* MILK SHAKE **6** *chiefly NAm* an earthquake **7** a moment <*I'll be round in 2 ~*s> *USE* (*6&7*) infml

[1]**ˈshakeˌdown** /-ˌdown‖-ˌdaʊn/ *n* **1** a makeshift bed (e g one made up on the floor) **2** *NAm* an act or instance of shaking sby down; *esp* extortion **3** *NAm* a thorough search *USE* (*2&3*) infml

[2]**shakedown** *adj* designed to test a new ship, aircraft, etc and allow the crew to become familiar with it <*a ~ cruise*>

shake down *vi* **1** to stay the night or sleep, esp in a makeshift bed **2** to become comfortably established, esp in a new place or occupation ~ *vt* **1** to settle (as if) by shaking **2** to give a shakedown test to **3** *NAm* to obtain money from in a dishonest or illegal manner **4** *NAm* to make a thorough search of (a person); frisk *USE* (*3&4*) infml

shake off *vt* to free oneself from <shook off *a heavy cold*>

shaker /ˈshaykə‖ˈʃeɪkə/ *n* **1** a container or utensil used to sprinkle or mix a substance by shaking <*a flour ~*> <*a cocktail ~*> **2** *cap* a member of an American sect practising celibacy and a self-denying communal life, and looking forward to the millennium – **Shaker** *adj*, **Shakerism** *n*

ˈshake-ˌup *n* an act or instance of shaking up; *specif* an extensive and often drastic reorganization (e g of a company) – infml

shake up *vt* **1** to jar (as if) by a physical shock <*the collision* shook up *both drivers*> **2** to reorganize by extensive and often drastic measures – infml

shako /ˈshahkoh, ˈshakoh‖ˈʃɑːkəʊ, ˈʃækəʊ/ *n, pl* **shakos, shakoes** a stiff military hat with a high crown and plume

shaky /ˈshayki‖ˈʃeɪkɪ/ *adj* **1a** lacking stability; precarious <*a ~ coalition*> **b** lacking in firmness (e g of beliefs or principles) **2a** unsound in health; poorly **b** characterized by or affected with shaking **3** likely to give way or break down; rickety <*a ~ chair*> – **shakily** *adv*, **shakiness** *n*

shale /shayl‖ʃeɪl/ *n* a finely stratified or laminated rock formed by the consolidation of clay, mud, or silt

shale oil *n* a crude dark oil obtained from oil shale by heating

shall /shəl‖ʃəl; *strong* shal‖ʃæl/ *verbal auxiliary, pres sing & pl* **shall;** *past* **should** /shəd‖ʃəd; *strong* shood‖ʃʊd/ **1** – used to urge or command <*you ~ go*> or denote what is legally mandatory <*it ~ be unlawful to carry firearms*> **2a** – used to express what is inevitable or seems likely to happen in the future <*we ~ have to be ready*> <*we ~ see*> **b** – used in the question form to express simple futurity <*when ~ we expect you?*> or with the force of an offer or suggestion <*~ I open the window?*> **3** – used to express determination <*they ~ not pass*>

shallot /shəˈlot‖ʃəˈlɒt/ *n* (any of the small clusters of bulbs, used esp for pickling and in seasoning, produced by) a perennial plant that resembles the related onion

[1]**shallow** /ˈshaloh‖ˈʃæləʊ/ *adj* **1** having little depth <*~ water*> **2** superficial in knowledge, thought, or feeling **3** not marked or accentuated <*the plane went into a ~ dive*> <*a ~ curve*> – **shallowly** *adv*, **shallowness** *n*

[2]**shallow** *vi* to become shallow

[3]**shallow** *n* a shallow place in a body of water – usu pl with sing. meaning but sing. or pl in constr

shalom /shəˈlohm, shəˈlom‖ʃəˈləʊm, ʃəˈlɒm/ *interj* – used as a Jewish greeting and farewell [Hebrew *shālōm* peace]

shalt /shalt‖ʃælt/ *archaic pres 2 sing of* SHALL

[1]**sham** /sham‖ʃæm/ *n* **1** cheap falseness; hypocrisy <*the ~ . . . of the empty pageant* – Oscar Wilde> **2** an imitation or counterfeit purporting to be genuine **3** a person who shams – **sham** *adj*

[2]**sham** *vb* **-mm-** *vt* to act so as to counterfeit <*I ~*med *a headache to get away*> ~*vi* to create a deliberately false impression

shaman /ˈshamən, ˈshay-‖ˈʃæmən, ˈʃeɪ-/ *n* a priest believed to exercise magic power (e g for healing and divination), esp through ecstatic trances – **shamanism** *n*, **shamanist** *n*

[1]**shamble** /ˈshambl‖ˈʃæmbl/ *vi* to walk awkwardly with dragging feet; shuffle

[2]**shamble** *n* a shambling gait

shambles /ˈshamblz‖ˈʃæmblz/ *n, pl* **shambles** **1** a slaughterhouse **2a** a place of carnage **b** a scene or a state of great destruction, chaos, or confusion; a mess

[1]**shame** /shaym‖ʃeɪm/ *n* **1a** a painful emotion caused by consciousness of guilt, shortcomings, impropriety, or disgrace **b** susceptibility to such emotion <*was not upset because she had no ~*> **2** humiliating disgrace or disrepute; ignominy **3** sthg bringing regret or disgrace <*it's a ~ you weren't there*>

[2]**shame** *vt* **1** to bring shame to; disgrace **2** to put to shame by outdoing **3** to fill with a sense of shame **4** to compel by causing to feel guilty

< ~d *into confessing*>

ˌ**shameˈfaced** /-ˈfayst‖-ˈfeɪst/ *adj* **1** showing modesty; bashful **2** showing shame; ashamed – **shamefacedly** *adv*, **shamefacedness** *n*

ˈ**shameful** /-f(ə)l‖-f(ə)l/ *adj* **1** bringing disrepute or ignominy; disgraceful **2** arousing the feeling of shame – **shamefully** *adv*, **shamefulness** *n*

ˈ**shameless** /-lis‖-lɪs/ *adj* **1** insensible to disgrace **2** showing lack of shame; disgraceful – **shamelessly** *adv*

shammy /ˈshami‖ˈʃæmɪ/ *n* CHAMOIS 2

[1]**shampoo** /shamˈpooh‖ʃæmˈpuː/ *vt* **shampoos; shampooing; shampooed** **1** to clean (esp the hair or a carpet) with shampoo **2** to wash the hair of [Hindi *cāpo*, imperative of *cāpnā* to press, shampoo] – **shampooist** *n*

[2]**shampoo** *n, pl* **shampoos** **1** a washing of the hair esp by a hairdresser **2** a soap, detergent, etc used for shampooing

shamrock /ˈshamˌrok‖ˈʃæmˌrɒk/ *n* any of several plants (e g a wood sorrel or some clovers) whose leaves have 3 leaflets and are used as a floral emblem by the Irish [Irish Gaelic *seamrōg*]

shandy /ˈshandi‖ˈʃændɪ/ *n* a drink consisting of beer mixed with lemonade or ginger beer

shanghai /ˌshangˈhie‖ˌʃæŋˈhaɪ/ *vt* **shanghais; shanghaiing; shanghaied** /-hied‖-haɪd/ **1** to compel to join a ship's crew, esp by the help of drink or drugs **2** to put into an awkward or unpleasant position by trickery [*Shanghai*, seaport in E China; fr the former use of this method to procure sailors for voyages to the Orient]

Shangri-la /ˌshang·gri ˈlah‖ˌʃæŋgrɪ ˈlɑː/ *n* a remote imaginary place where life approaches perfection [*Shangri-La*, imaginary land depicted in the novel *Lost Horizon* by James Hilton (1900-54), English novelist]

shank /shangk‖ʃæŋk/ *n* **1a** a leg; *specif* the part of the leg between the knee and the ankle in human beings or the corresponding part in various other vertebrates **b** a cut of beef, veal, mutton, or lamb from the upper or the lower part of the leg **2** a straight narrow usu vital part of an object: e g **2a** the straight part of a nail or pin **b** the stem or stalk of a plant **c** the part of an anchor between the ring and the crown **d** the part of a fishhook between the eye and the bend **e** the part of a key between the handle and the bit **f** the narrow part of the sole of a shoe beneath the instep **3** a part of an object by which it can be attached to sthg else: e g **3a(1)** a projection on the back of a solid button **a(2)** a short stem of thread that holds a sewn button away from the cloth **b** the end (e g of a drill bit) that is gripped in a chuck

ˌ**shanks's** ˈ**pony** *n* one's own feet or legs considered as a means of transport – humor

shan't /shahnt‖ʃɑːnt/ shall not

shantung /ˌshanˈtung‖ˌʃænˈtʌŋ/ *n* a silk fabric in plain weave with a slightly irregular surface [*Shantung*, province in NE China]

[1]**shanty** /ˈshanti‖ˈʃæntɪ/ *n* a small crudely built or dilapidated dwelling or shelter; a shack [Canadian French *chantier*, fr French, gantry, fr Latin *cantherius* trellis]

[2]**shanty** *n* a song sung by sailors in rhythm with their work [French *chanter* to sing, fr Latin *cantare*]

ˈ**shantyˌtown** /-ˌtown‖-ˌtaʊn/ *n* (part of) a town consisting mainly of shanties

[1]**shape** /shayp‖ʃeɪp/ *vt* **1** to form, create; *esp* to give a particular form or shape to < ~d *the clay into a cube*> **2** to adapt in shape so as to fit neatly and closely <*a dress* ~d *to fit*> **3** to guide or mould into a particular state or condition <shaping *her plans for the future*> **4a** to determine or direct the course of (e g a person's life) **b** to cause to take a particular form or course < ~ *the course of history*> – **shapable, shapeable** *adj*, **shaper** *n*

[2]**shape** *n* **1a** the visible or tactile form of a particular (kind of) item **b(1)** spatial form <*all solids have* ~> **b(2)** a circle, square, or other standard geometrical form **2** the contour of the body, esp of the trunk; the figure **3a** a phantom, apparition **b** an assumed appearance; a guise <*the devil in the* ~ *of a serpent*> **4** definite form (e g in thought or words) <*the plan slowly took* ~> **5** a general structure or plan <*the final* ~ *of society*> **6** sthg made in a particular form <*a* ~ *for moulding jellies*> **7a** the condition of a person or thing, esp at a particular time <*in excellent* ~ *for his age*> **b** a fit or ordered condition <*got the car into* ~> – **shaped** *adj*

ˈ**shapely** /-li‖-lɪ/ *adj* having a pleasing shape; well-proportioned – **shapeliness** *n*

shape up *vi* to (begin to) behave or perform satisfactorily

shard /shahd‖ʃɑːd/ *n* **1** a piece or fragment of sthg brittle (e g earthenware) **2** SHERD 2

[1]**share** /sheə‖ʃeə/ *n* **1a** a portion belonging to, due to, or contributed by an individual **b** a full or fair portion <*she's had her* ~ *of fun*> **2a** the part allotted or belonging to any of a number owning property or interest together **b** any of the equal portions into which property or invested capital is divided **c** *pl, chiefly Br* the proprietorship element in a company, usu represented by transferable certificates

[2]**share** *vt* **1** to divide and distribute in shares; apportion – usu + *out* **2** to partake of, use, experience, or enjoy with others ~*vi* to have a share or part – often + *in* – **shareable, sharable** *adj*, **sharer** *n*

[3]**share** *n* a ploughshare

ˈ**shareˌcropper** /-ˌkropə‖-ˌkrɒpə/ *n, NAm* a tenant farmer, esp in the southern USA, who lives on credit provided by the landlord and receives an agreed share of the value of the crop – **sharecrop** *vb*

ˈ**shareˌholder** /-ˌhohldə‖-ˌhəʊldə/ *n* the holder or owner of a share in property

[1]**shark** /shahk‖ʃɑːk/ *n* any of numerous mostly large typically grey marine fishes that are mostly active, voracious, and predators and have gill slits at the sides and a mouth on the under part of the body

[2]**shark** *n* **1** a greedy unscrupulous person who exploits others by usury, extortion, or trickery **2** *NAm* one who excels greatly, esp in a specified field – infml

ˈ**sharkˌskin** /-ˌskin‖-ˌskɪn/ *n* **1** (leather from) the hide of a shark **2** a smooth stiff durable fabric in twill or basket weave with small woven designs

[1]**sharp** /shahp‖ʃɑːp/ *adj* **1** (adapted to) cutting

or piercing: e g **1a** having a thin keen edge or fine point **b** bitingly cold; icy <*a ~ wind*> **2a** keen in intellect, perception, attention, etc <*~ sight*> **b** paying shrewd usu selfish attention to personal gain <*a ~ trader*> **3a** brisk, vigorous <*a ~ trot*> **b** capable of acting or reacting strongly; *esp* caustic <*a ~ soap*> **4** severe, harsh: e g **4a** marked by irritability or anger; fiery <*a ~ temper*> **b** causing intense usu sudden anguish <*a ~ pain*> **c** cutting in language or implication <*a ~ rebuke*> **5** affecting the senses or sense organs intensely: e g **5a(1)** pungent, tart, or acid, esp in flavour **a(2)** acrid **b** shrill, piercing **c** issuing in a brilliant burst of light <*a ~ flash*> **6a** characterized by hard lines and angles <*~ features*> **b** involving an abrupt change in direction <*a ~ turn*> **c** clear in outline or detail; distinct <*a ~ image*> **d** conspicuously clear <*~ contrast*> **7** *of a musical note* raised a semitone in pitch **8** stylish, dressy – infml – **sharply** *adv*, **sharpness** *n*

[2]**sharp** *adv* **1** in an abrupt manner <*the car pulled up ~*> **2** exactly, precisely <*4 o'clock ~*> **3** above the proper musical pitch <*they're playing ~*>

[3]**sharp** *n* **1a** a musical note 1 semitone higher than another indicated or previously specified note **b** a character on the musical staff indicating a raising in pitch of a semitone **2** a relatively long needle with a sharp point and a small rounded eye for use in general sewing **3** *chiefly NAm* a swindler, sharper

sharpen /'shahpən‖'ʃɑ:pən/ *vb* to make or become sharp or sharper – **sharpener** *n*

sharper /'shahpə‖'ʃɑ:pə/ *n* a cheat, swindler; *esp* a gambler who habitually cheats

'sharp,shooter /-,shoohtə‖-,ʃu:tə/ *n* a good marksman – **sharpshooting** *n*

shatter /'shatə‖'ʃætə/ *vt* **1a** to break into pieces (e g by a sudden blow) **b** to cause to break down; impair, disable <*his nerves were ~ed*> **2** to have a forceful or violent effect on the feelings of <*she was absolutely ~ed by the news*> **3** to cause to be utterly exhausted <*felt ~ed by the long train journey*> *~vi* to break suddenly apart; disintegrate ***USE*** (*vt 2&3*) infml – **shatteringly** *adv*

[1]**shave** /shayv‖ʃeɪv/ *vb* **shaved, shaven** /'shayv(ə)n‖'ʃeɪv(ə)n/ *vt* **1a** to remove in thin layers or shreds – often + *off* <*~ off a thin slice of cheese*> **b** to cut off thin layers or slices from **c** to cut or trim closely <*a closely ~d lawn*> **2a** to remove the hair from by cutting close to the roots **b** to cut off (hair or beard) close to the skin **3** to come very close to or brush against in passing *~vi* to cut off hair or beard close to the skin

[2]**shave** *n* **1** a tool or machine for shaving **2** an act or process of shaving

shaver /'shayvə‖'ʃeɪvə/ *n* **1** an electric-powered razor **2** a boy, youngster – infml

shaving /'shayving‖'ʃeɪvɪŋ/ *n* sthg shaved off – usu pl <*wood ~s*>

shawl /shawl‖ʃɔ:l/ *n* a usu decorative square, oblong, or triangular piece of fabric that is worn to cover the head or shoulders

[1]**she** /shi‖ʃɪ; *strong* shee‖ʃi:/ *pron* **1** that female person or creature who is neither speaker nor hearer <*~ is my mother*> **2** – used to refer to sthg regarded as feminine (e g by personification) <*~ was a fine ship*>

[2]**she** /shee‖ʃi:/ *n* a female person or creature <*is the baby a he or a ~*> – often in combination <*she-cat*>

sheaf /sheef‖ʃi:f/ *n, pl* **sheaves** /sheevz‖ʃi:vz/ **1** a quantity of plant material, esp the stalks and ears of a cereal grass, bound together **2** a collection of items laid or tied together <*a ~ of papers*>

[1]**shear** /shiə‖ʃɪə/ *vb* **sheared, shorn** /shawn‖ʃɔ:n/ *vt* **1a** to cut off the hair from <*with* shorn *scalp*> **b** to cut or clip (hair, wool, a fleece, etc) from sby or sthg; *also* to cut sthg from <*~ a lawn*> **c** to cut (as if) with shears <*~ a metal sheet in 2*> **2** to cut with sthg sharp **3** to deprive of sthg as if by cutting off – usu passive + *of* <*has been* shorn *of her authority*> **4** to subject to a shear force *~ vi* **1** to become divided or separated under the action of a shear force <*the bolt may ~ off*> **2** *chiefly Scot* to reap crops with a sickle – **shearer** *n*, **shearing** *n*

[2]**shear** *n* **1a** a cutting implement similar to a pair of scissors but typically larger **b** any of various cutting tools or machines operating by the action of opposed cutting edges of metal **2** an action or force that causes or tends to cause 2 parts of a body to slide on each other in a direction parallel to their plane of contact ***USE*** (*1a, b*) usu pl with sing. meaning

sheath /sheeth‖ʃi:θ/ *n, pl* **sheaths** /sheedhz‖ʃi:ðz/ **1** a case or cover for a blade (e g of a knife or sword) **2** a cover or case of a (part of a) plant or animal body <*the leaves of grasses form a ~ round the main stalk*> **3** a cover or support (applied) like the sheath of a blade **4** a condom

sheathe /sheedh‖ʃi:ð/ *vt* **1** to put into or provide with a sheath <*~d her dagger*> **2** to withdraw (a claw) into a sheath **3** to encase or cover with sthg protective (e g thin boards or sheets of metal)

sheath knife *n* a knife that has a fixed blade and is carried in a sheath

shebang /shi'bang‖ʃɪ'bæŋ/ *n, chiefly NAm* an affair, business <*she's head of the whole ~*> – infml

shebeen /shi'been‖ʃɪ'bi:n/ *n, chiefly Irish* an unlicensed or illegally operated drinking establishment [Irish Gaelic *sībīn* little mug, bad ale]

[1]**shed** /shed‖ʃed/ *vb* **-dd-; shed** *vt* **1** to be incapable of holding or absorbing; repel <*a duck's plumage ~s water*> **2a** to cause (blood) to flow by wounding or killing **b** to pour forth; let flow <*~ tears*> **c** to give off or out; cast <*the book ~s some light on this subject*> **3** to cast off or let fall (a natural covering) *~vi* to cast off hairs, threads etc; moult <*the dog is ~ding*>

[2]**shed** *n* WATERSHED 1

[3]**shed** *n* a usu single-storied building for shelter, storage, etc, esp with 1 or more sides open

she'd /shid‖ʃɪd; *strong* sheed‖ʃi:d/ she had; she would

sheen /sheen‖ʃi:n/ *n* **1** a bright or shining quality or condition; brightness, lustre **2** a subdued shininess or glitter of a surface **3** a lustrous surface imparted to textiles through finishing processes or use of shiny yarns – **sheeny** *adj*

sheep /sheep‖ʃiːp/ *n, pl* **sheep** **1** any of numerous ruminant mammals related to the goats but stockier and lacking a beard in the male; *specif* one domesticated, esp for its flesh and wool **2** an inane or docile person; *esp* one easily influenced or led

'sheep-ˌdip *n* a liquid preparation into which sheep are plunged, esp to destroy parasites

'sheepˌdog /-ˌdog‖-ˌdɒg/ *n* a dog used to tend, drive, or guard sheep; *esp* BORDER COLLIE

'sheepˌfold /-ˌfohld‖-ˌfəʊld/ *n* a pen or shelter for sheep

sheepish /'sheepish‖'ʃiːpɪʃ/ *adj* embarrassed by consciousness of a fault <*a ~ look*> – **sheepishly** *adv*, **sheepishness** *n*

'sheepˌskin /-ˌskin‖-ˌskɪn/ *n* **1** (leather from) the skin of a sheep **2** the skin of a sheep dressed with the wool on <*a ~ coat*>

[1]**sheer** /shiə‖ʃɪə/ *adj* **1** transparently fine; diaphanous <*~ tights*> **2a** unqualified, utter <*~ ignorance*> **b** not mixed or mingled with anything else; pure, unadulterated **3** marked by great and unbroken steepness; precipitous <*a ~ cliff*>

[2]**sheer** *adv* **1** altogether, completely <*his name went ~ out of my head*> **2** straight up or down without a break <*rugged cliffs rose ~ out of the sea*>

[3]**sheer** *vb* to (cause to) deviate from a course

[4]**sheer** *n* a turn, deviation, or change in a course (e g of a ship)

[1]**sheet** /sheet‖ʃiːt/ *n* **1** a broad piece of cloth; *specif* a rectangle of cloth (e g of linen or cotton) used as an article of bed linen **2a** a usu rectangular piece of paper **b** a printed section for a book, esp before it has been folded, cut, or bound – usu pl **c** the unseparated postage stamps printed by 1 impression of a plate on a single piece of paper **3** a broad usu flat expanse <*a ~ of ice*> **4** a suspended or moving expanse <*a ~ of flame*> <*~s of rain*> **5a** a piece of sthg that is thin in comparison to its length and breadth **b** a flat metal baking utensil

[2]**sheet** *vt* to form into, provide with, or cover with a sheet or sheets ~ *vi* to come down in sheets <*the rain ~ed against the windows*>

[3]**sheet** *adj* rolled into or spread out in a sheet <*~ steel*>

[4]**sheet** *n* **1** a rope that regulates the angle at which a sail is set in relation to the wind **2** *pl* the spaces at either end of an open boat

sheet anchor *n* **1** an emergency anchor formerly carried in the broadest part of a ship **2** a principal support or dependence, esp in danger; a mainstay

sheeting /'sheeting‖'ʃiːtɪŋ/ *n* (material suitable for making into) sheets

sheet lightning *n* lightning in diffused or sheet form due to reflection and diffusion by clouds

sheet music *n* music printed on large unbound sheets of paper

sheikh, sheik /shayk, sheek‖ʃeɪk, ʃiːk/ *n* **1** an Arab chief **2 sheik, sheikh** a romantically attractive or dashing man – **sheikhdom** *n*

sheila, sheilah /'sheelə‖'ʃiːlə/ *n, Austr, NZ, & SAfr* a young woman; a girl – infml

shekel /'shekl‖'ʃekl/ *n* **1** an ancient Hebrew gold or silver coin **2** the standard unit of money in Israel **3** *pl* money – infml

sheldrake /'sheldrayk‖'ʃeldreɪk/ *n* a shelduck

shelduck /'shelduk‖'ʃeldʌk/ *n* any of various Old World ducks; *esp* a common mostly black and white duck slightly larger than the mallard

shelf /shelf‖ʃelf/ *n, pl* **shelves** /shelvz‖ʃelvz/ **1** a thin flat usu long and narrow piece of material (e g wood) fastened horizontally (e g on a wall or in a cupboard, bookcase, etc) at a distance from the floor to hold objects **2** sthg resembling a shelf in form or position: e g **2a** a (partially submerged) sandbank or ledge of rocks **b** a flat projecting layer of rock **c** CONTINENTAL SHELF – **off the shelf 1** available from stock **2** OFF THE PEG – **on the shelf 1** in a state of inactivity or uselessness **2** *of a single woman* considered as unlikely to marry, esp because too old

[1]**shell** /shel‖ʃel/ *n* **1a** a hard rigid often largely calcium-containing covering of an animal (e g a turtle, oyster, or beetle) **b** a seashell **c** the hard or tough outer covering of an egg, esp a bird's egg **2** the covering or outside part of a fruit or seed, esp when hard or fibrous **3** shell material or shells <*an ornament made of ~*> **4** sthg like a shell: e g **4a** a framework or exterior structure; *esp* the outer frame of a building that is unfinished or has been destroyed (e g by fire) **b** a hollow form devoid of substance <*mere effigies and ~s of men* – Thomas Carlyle> **c** an edible case for holding a filling <*a pastry ~*> **5** a cold and reserved attitude that conceals the presence or absence of feeling <*wish she'd come out of her ~*> **6** a narrow light racing rowing boat propelled by 1 or more rowers **7** any of various spherical regions surrounding the nucleus of an atom at various distances from it and each occupied by a group of electrons of approximately equal energy **8a** a projectile for a cannon containing an explosive bursting charge **b** a metal or paper case which holds the charge in cartridges, fireworks, etc – **shelly** *adj*

[2]**shell** *vt* **1** to take out of a natural enclosing cover (e g a shell, husk, pod, or capsule) <*~ peanuts*> **2** to fire shells at, on, or into ~ *vi* **1** to fall or scale off in thin pieces **2** to fall out of the pod or husk <*nuts which ~ on falling from the tree*>

she'll /shil‖ʃɪl; *strong* sheel‖ʃiːl/ she will; she shall

[1]**shellac** /'shelak‖'ʃelæk/ *n* the purified form of a resin produced by various insects, usu obtained as yellow or orange flakes; *also* a solution of this in alcohol used esp in making varnish

[2]**shellac** *vt* **-ck-** to treat, esp by coating, with shellac

'shellˌfish /-ˌfish‖-ˌfɪʃ/ *n* an aquatic invertebrate animal with a shell; *esp* an edible mollusc or crustacean

shell out *vb* to pay (money) – infml

'shell ˌshock *n* a mental disorder characterized by neurotic and often hysterical symptoms that occurs under conditions (e g wartime combat) that cause intense stress – **shell-shock** *vt*

[1]**shelter** /'sheltə‖'ʃeltə/ *n* **1** sthg, esp a structure, affording cover or protection <*an air-raid ~*> **2** the state of being covered and protected; refuge <*took ~*>

²shelter *vt* **1** to serve as a shelter for; protect <*a thick hedge* ~ed *the orchard*> **2** to keep concealed or protected <~ed *her family in a mountain cave*> ~*vi* to take shelter

shelve /shelv‖ʃelv/ *vt* **1** to provide with shelves **2** to place on a shelf **3a** to remove from active service; dismiss **b** to put off or aside <~ *a project*> ~*vi* to slope gently

shelving /ˈshelving‖ˈʃelvɪŋ/ *n* (material for constructing) shelves

shenanigan /shiˈnanigən‖ʃɪˈnænɪgən/ *n* **1** deliberate deception; trickery **2** boisterous mischief; high jinks – usu pl with sing. meaning *USE* infml

¹shepherd /ˈshepəd‖ˈʃepəd/ *n* **1** *fem* **shepherdess** /-des/ one who tends sheep **2** a pastor

²shepherd *vt* **1** to tend as a shepherd **2** to guide, marshal, or conduct (people) like sheep <~ed *the children onto the train*>

ˌshepherd's ˈpie *n* a hot dish of minced meat, esp lamb, with a mashed potato topping

sherbet /ˈshuhbət‖ˈʃɜːbət/ *n* **1** (a drink made with) a sweet powder that effervesces in liquid and is eaten dry or used to make fizzy drinks **2** a water ice with egg white, gelatin, or sometimes milk added [Turkish *şerbet*, fr Persian *sharbat*, fr Arabic *sharbah* drink]

sherd /shuhd, shahd‖ʃɜːd, ʃɑːd/ *n* **1** SHARD 1 **2** fragments of pottery vessels

sheriff /ˈsherif‖ˈʃerɪf/ *n* **1** the honorary chief executive officer of the Crown in each English county who has mainly judicial and ceremonial duties **2** the chief judge of a Scottish county or district **3** a county law enforcement officer in the USA – **sheriffdom** *n*

Sherpa /ˈshuhpə‖ˈʃɜːpə/ *n* a member of a Tibetan people living on the high southern slopes of the Himalayas

sherry /ˈsheri‖ˈʃerɪ/ *n* a blended fortified wine from S Spain that varies in colour from very light to dark brown [alteration of earlier *sherris* (taken as pl), fr *Xeres* (now *Jerez*), city in Spain]

she's /shiz‖ʃɪz; *strong* sheez‖ʃiːz/ she is; she has

ˌShetland ˈpony /shetlənd‖ʃetlənd/ *n* (any of) a breed of small stocky shaggy hardy ponies that originated in the Shetland islands

Shetland wool *n* (yarn spun from) fine wool from sheep raised in the Shetland islands

shew /show‖ʃəʊ/ *vb, archaic Br* to show

shibboleth /ˈshibəˌleth‖ˈʃɪbəˌleθ/ *n* **1a** a catchword, slogan **b** a use of language that distinguishes a group of people **c** a commonplace belief or saying <*the* ~ *that crime does not pay*> **2** a custom that characterizes members of a particular group [Hebrew *shibbōleth* stream; fr the use of this word as a test to distinguish two peoples who pronounced it differently (Judges 12:5-6)]

shickered /ˈshikəd‖ˈʃɪkəd/ *adj, Austr & NZ* drunk – infml

¹shield /sheeld‖ʃiːld/ *n* **1** a piece of armour (e g of wood, metal, or leather) carried on the arm or in the hand and used esp for warding off blows **2** sby or sthg that protects or defends; a defence **3** sthg designed to protect people from injury from moving parts of machinery, live electrical conductors, etc **4** a defined area, the surface of which constitutes a heraldic field, on which heraldic arms are displayed; *esp* one that is wide at the top and rounds to a point at the bottom **5** sthg resembling a shield: e g **5a** a trophy awarded in recognition of achievement (e g in a sporting event) **b** a decorative or identifying emblem

²shield *vt* **1** to protect (as if) with a shield; provide with a protective cover or shelter **2** to cut off from observation; hide <*accomplices who* ~ *a thief*>

¹shift /shift‖ʃɪft/ *vt* **1** to exchange for or replace by another; change <*the traitor* ~ed *his allegiance*> **2** to change the place, position, or direction of; move <*I can't* ~ *the grand piano*> **3** to get rid of; dispose of – infml ~ *vi* **1** to change place, position, or direction <~ing *uneasily in his chair*> <*the wind* ~ed> **2a** to assume responsibility <*had to* ~ *for herself*> **b** to resort to expedients; GET BY **3** *NAm* to change gear in a motor vehicle

²shift *n* **1a** a deceitful or underhand scheme or method; a subterfuge, dodge **b** an expedient tried in difficult circumstances – usu pl **2** a loose unfitted slip or dress **3a** a change in direction <*a* ~ *in the wind*> **b** a change in emphasis, judgment, or attitude **4a** *sing or pl in constr* a group who work (e g in a factory) in alternation with other groups **b** a scheduled period of work or duty <*on the night* ~> **5** a change in place or position: e g **5a** the relative displacement of rock masses on opposite sides of a fault **b** a change in position of a line or band in a spectrum **6** systematic sound change as a language evolves **7** *NAm* the gear change in a motor vehicle

ˈshift ˌkey *n* a key on a keyboard (e g of a typewriter) that when held down permits a different set of characters, esp the capitals, to be printed

ˈshiftless /-lis‖-lɪs/ *adj* **1** lacking resourcefulness; inefficient **2** lacking ambition or motivation; lazy – **shiftlessly** *adv*, **shiftlessness** *n*

ˈshifty /-ti‖-tɪ/ *adj* **1** given to deception, evasion, or fraud; slippery **2** indicative of a fickle or devious nature <~ *eyes*> – **shiftily** *adv*, **shiftiness** *n*

shillelagh /shiˈlayli‖ʃɪˈleɪlɪ/ *n* an Irish cudgel [*Shillelagh*, town in SE Ireland famed for its oak trees]

shilling /ˈshiling‖ˈʃɪlɪŋ/ *n* **1a** (a coin representing) a former money unit of the UK worth 12 old pence or £$^1/_{20}$ **b** a money unit equal to £$^1/_{20}$ of any of various other countries (formerly) in the Commonwealth **2** (a coin or note representing) the basic money unit of certain E African countries

shilly-shally /ˈshili ˌshali‖ˈʃɪlɪ ˌʃælɪ/ *vi* to show hesitation or lack of decisiveness – **shilly-shally** *n*

¹shimmer /ˈshimə‖ˈʃɪmə/ *vi* **1** to shine with a softly tremulous or wavering light; glimmer **2** to (cause sthg to) appear in a fluctuating wavy form <*the* ~ing *heat from the pavement*>

²shimmer *n* **1** a shimmering light **2** a wavering and distortion of the visual image of a far object usu resulting from heat-induced changes in atmospheric refraction – **shimmery** *adj*

[1]**shin** /shin‖ʃɪn/ *n* the front part of the leg of a vertebrate animal below the knee; *also* a cut of meat from this part, esp from the front leg of a quadruped <*a* ~ *of beef*>

[2]**shin** *vb* **-nn-** *vi* to climb by gripping with the hands or arms and the legs and hauling oneself up or lowering oneself down <~ned *up the tree*> ~ *vt* **1** to kick on the shins **2** to climb by shinning

ˈ**shin͵bone** /-͵bohn‖-͵bəʊn/ *n* TIBIA 1

shindig /ˈshindig‖ˈʃɪndɪg/ *n* a usu boisterous social gathering – infml

shindy /ˈshindi‖ˈʃɪndɪ/ *n, pl* **shindys, shindies** a quarrel, brawl – infml

[1]**shine** /shien‖ʃaɪn/ *vb* **shone** /shon‖ʃɒn/, (*vt 2*) **shined** *vi* **1** to emit light **2** to be bright with reflected light **3** to be outstanding or distinguished <*she always* ~s *in mathematics*> **4** to have a radiant or lively appearance <*his face* shone *with enthusiasm*> ~ *vt* **1a** to cause to emit light **b** to direct the light of <shone *her torch into the corner*> **2** to make bright by polishing <~d *his shoes*>

[2]**shine** *n* **1** brightness caused by the emission or reflection of light **2** brilliance, splendour <*pageantry that has kept its* ~ *over the centuries*> **3** fine weather; sunshine <*come rain, come* ~> **4** an act of polishing shoes **5** *chiefly NAm* a fancy, crush – esp in *take a shine to*; infml

shiner /ˈshienə‖ˈʃaɪnə/ *n* BLACK EYE – slang

[1]**shingle** /ˈshing·gl‖ˈʃɪŋgl/ *n* **1** a small thin piece of building material for laying in overlapping rows as a covering for the roof or sides of a building **2** a woman's short haircut in which the hair is shaped into the nape of the neck

[2]**shingle** *vt* **1** to cover (as if) with shingles **2** to cut (hair) in a shingle

[3]**shingle** *n* (a place, esp a seashore, strewn with) small rounded pebbles – **shingly** *adj*

shingles /ˈshing·glz‖ˈʃɪŋglz/ *n pl but sing in constr* severe short-lasting inflammation of certain ganglia of the nerves that leave the brain and spinal cord, caused by a virus and associated with a rash of blisters and often intense neuralgic pain [Medieval Latin *cingulus*, fr Latin *cingulum* girdle, fr *cingere* to gird]

shining /ˈshiening‖ˈʃaɪnɪŋ/ *adj* **1** emitting or reflecting light; bright **2** possessing a distinguished quality; outstanding <*a* ~ *example of bravery*>

Shinto /ˈshintoh‖ˈʃɪntəʊ/ *n* the indigenous animistic religion of Japan, including the veneration of the Emperor as a descendant of the sun-goddess – **Shinto** *adj*, **Shintoism** *n*, **Shintoist** *n or adj*, **Shintoistic** *adj*

shiny /ˈshieni‖ˈʃaɪnɪ/ *adj* **1** bright or glossy in appearance; lustrous, polished <~ *new shoes*> **2** *of material, clothes, etc* rubbed or worn to a smooth surface that reflects light – **shininess** *n*

[1]**ship** /ship‖ʃɪp/ *n* **1a** a large seagoing vessel **b** a square-rigged sailing vessel having a bowsprit and usu 3 masts **2** a boat (propelled by power or sail) **3** *sing or pl in constr* a ship's crew **4** an airship, aircraft, or spacecraft – **when one's ship comes in** when one becomes rich

[2]**ship** *vb* **-pp-** *vt* **1** to place or receive on board a ship for transportation **2** to put in place for use <~ *the tiller*> **3** to take into a ship or boat <~ *the gangplank*> **4** to engage for service on a ship **5** to cause to be transported or sent away <~ped *him off to boarding school*> – infml ~ *vi* **1** to embark on a ship **2** to go or travel by ship **3** to engage to serve on shipboard – **shippable** *adj*

-ship /-ship‖-ʃɪp/ *suffix* (*n* → *n*) **1** state, condition, or quality of <*friend*ship> **2a** office, status, or profession of <*professor*ship> **b** period during which (a specified office or position) is held <*during his dictator*ship> **3** art or skill of <*horseman*ship> **4** *sing or pl in constr* whole group or body sharing (a specified clan or state) <*member*ship> **5** one entitled to (a specified rank, title, or appellation) <*his Lord*ship>

[1]ˈ**ship͵board** /-͵bawd‖-͵bɔːd/ *n* – **on shipboard** on board ship

[2]**shipboard** *adj* existing or taking place on board a ship

ˈ**ship͵builder** /-͵bildə‖-͵bɪldə/ *n* a person or company that designs or constructs ships – **shipbuilding** *n*

ship canal *n* a canal large enough to allow the passage of sea-going vessels

ˈ**ship͵mate** /-͵mayt‖-͵meɪt/ *n* a fellow sailor

ˈ**shipment** /-mənt‖-mənt/ *n* **1** the act or process of shipping **2** the quantity of goods shipped <*a* ~ *of oranges*>

shipper /ˈshipə‖ˈʃɪpə/ *n* a person or company that ships goods

shipping /ˈshiping‖ˈʃɪpɪŋ/ *n* **1** ships (in 1 place or belonging to 1 port or country) **2** the act or business of a shipper

ship's biscuit *n, chiefly Br* a type of hard biscuit orig for eating on board ship

ˈ**ship͵shape** /-͵shayp‖-͵ʃeɪp/ *adj* trim, tidy

[1]ˈ**ship͵wreck** /-͵rek‖-͵rek/ *n* **1** a wrecked ship or its remains **2** the destruction or loss of a ship **3** an irrevocable collapse or destruction <*suffered the* ~ *of his fortune*>

[2]**shipwreck** *vt* **1** to cause to undergo shipwreck **2** to ruin

ˈ**ship͵wright** /-͵riet‖-͵raɪt/ *n* a carpenter skilled in ship construction and repair

shire /shie·ə‖ʃaɪə/ *n* **1a** an administrative subdivision; *specif* an English county, esp one with a name ending in *-shire* **b** *pl the* English fox-hunting district consisting chiefly of Leicestershire and Northamptonshire **2** any of a British breed of large heavy draught horses

shirk /shuhk‖ʃɜːk/ *vt* to evade or dodge (a duty, responsibility, etc) – **shirker** *n*

shirring /ˈshuhring‖ˈʃɜːrɪŋ/ *n* a decorative gathering, esp in cloth, made by drawing up the material along 2 or more parallel lines of stitching or by stitching in rows of elastic thread or an elastic webbing

shirt /shuht‖ʃɜːt/ *n* an (esp man's) garment for the upper body; *esp* one that opens the full length of the centre front and has sleeves and a collar

shirting /ˈshuhting‖ˈʃɜːtɪŋ/ *n* fabric suitable for shirts

ˈ**shirt-͵sleeve** *also* **shirt-sleeves, shirt-sleeved** *adj* **1** (having members) without a jacket <*a* ~ *audience*> **2** marked by informality and directness <~ *diplomacy*>

ˈ**shirt͵waister** /-͵waystə‖-͵weɪstə/ *n, chiefly Br* a fitted dress that fastens down the centre front to just below the waist or to the hem

shirty /'shuhti||'ʃɜːtɪ/ *adj* bad-tempered, fractious – infml

shish kebab /ˌshish ki'bab||ˌʃɪʃ kɪ'bæb/ *n* kebab cooked on skewers

[1]**shit** /shit||ʃɪt/ *vb* **-tt-; shitted, shit, shat** /shat||ʃæt/ *vb* to defecate (in) – vulg

[2]**shit** *n* **1** faeces **2** an act of defecation **3a** nonsense, foolishness **b** a despicable person *USE* vulg

shitty /'shiti||'ʃɪtɪ/ *adj* nasty, unpleasant – vulg

[1]**shiver** /'shivə||'ʃɪvə/ *n* any of the small pieces that result from the shattering of sthg brittle

[2]**shiver** *vb* to break into many small fragments; shatter

[3]**shiver** *vi* to tremble, esp with cold or fever

[4]**shiver** *n* an instance of shivering; a tremor – **shivery** *adj*

[1]**shoal** /shohl||ʃəʊl/ *n* **1** a shallow **2** an underwater sandbank; *esp* one exposed at low tide

[2]**shoal** *vi* to become shallow or less deep ~*vt* to come to a shallow or less deep part of

[3]**shoal** *n* a large group (e g of fish)

[1]**shock** /shok||ʃɒk/ *n* a pile of sheaves of grain or stalks of maize set upright in a field – **shock** *vt*

[2]**shock** *n* **1** a violent shaking or jarring <*an earthquake* ~> **2a(1)** a disturbance in the equilibrium or permanence of sthg (e g a system) **a(2)** a sudden or violent disturbance of thoughts or emotions **b** sthg causing such disturbance <*the news came as a terrible* ~> **3** a state of serious depression of most bodily functions associated with reduced blood volume and pressure and caused usu by severe injuries, bleeding, or burns **4** sudden stimulation of the nerves and convulsive contraction of the muscles caused by the passage of electricity through the body

[3]**shock** *vt* **1a** to cause to feel sudden surprise, terror, horror, or offence **b** to cause to undergo a physical or nervous shock **2** to cause (e g an animal) to experience an electric shock **3** to impel (as if) by a shock <~ed *her into realizing her selfishness*>

[4]**shock** *n* a thick bushy mass, usu of hair

'shock abˌsorber *n* any of various devices for absorbing the energy of sudden impulses or shocks in machinery, vehicles, etc

shocker /'shokə||'ʃɒkə/ *n* **1** sthg horrifying or offensive (e g a sensational work of fiction or drama) **2** an incorrigible or naughty person (e g a child) – infml

ˌshock-'headed *adj* having a thick bushy mass of hair

shocking /'shoking||'ʃɒkɪŋ/ *adj* **1** giving cause for indignation or offence **2** very bad <*had a* ~ *cold*> – infml – **shockingly** *adv*

'shockˌproof /-ˌproohf||-ˌpruːf/ *adj* resistant to shock

'shock ˌtroops *n pl* troops trained and selected for assault

shod /shod||ʃɒd/ *adj* **1a** wearing shoes, boots, etc **b** equipped with (a specified type of) tyres **2** furnished or equipped with a shoe – often in combination

[1]**shoddy** /'shodi||'ʃɒdɪ/ *n* **1** a wool of better quality and longer fibre length than mungo, reclaimed from materials that are not felted **2** a fabric often of inferior quality manufactured wholly or partly from reclaimed wool

[2]**shoddy** *adj* **1** made wholly or partly of shoddy **2a** cheaply imitative; vulgarly pretentious **b** hastily or poorly done; inferior **c** shabby – **shoddily** *adv*, **shoddiness** *n*

[1]**shoe** /shooh||ʃuː/ *n* **1a** an outer covering for the human foot that does not extend above the ankle and has a thick or stiff sole and often an attached heel **b** a metal plate or rim for the hoof of an animal **2** sthg resembling a shoe in shape or function **3** *pl* a situation, position; *also* a predicament <*I wouldn't be in the president's* ~s *for anything*> **4** the part of a vehicle braking system that presses on the brake drum

[2]**shoe** *vt* **shoeing; shod** /shod||ʃɒd/ *also* **shoed** /shoohd||ʃuːd/ **1** to fit (e g a horse) with a shoe **2** to protect or reinforce with a usu metal shoe

'shoeˌhorn /-ˌhawn||-ˌhɔːn/ *n* a curved piece of metal, plastic, etc used to ease the heel into the back of a shoe

'shoeˌlace /-ˌlays||-ˌleɪs/ *n* a lace or string for fastening a shoe

'shoeˌmaker /-ˌmaykə||-ˌmeɪkə/ *n* sby whose occupation is making or repairing footwear

'shoeˌstring /-ˌstring||-ˌstrɪŋ/ *n* **1** a shoelace **2** an amount of money inadequate or barely adequate to meet one's needs <*run a business on a* ~>

shogun /'shohgən||'ʃəʊgən/ *n* a military governor of Japan before the revolution of 1867-68 [Japanese *shōgun* general]

shone /shon||ʃɒn/ *past of* SHINE

[1]**shoo** /shooh||ʃuː/ *interj* – used in frightening away an (esp domestic) animal

[2]**shoo** *vt* to drive away (as if) by crying 'Shoo!'

[1]**shook** /shook||ʃʊk/ *past & chiefly dial past part of* SHAKE

[2]**shook** *n* **1** [1]SHOCK **2** *NAm* a set of wooden staves and end pieces for making a hogshead, cask, or barrel

[1]**shoot** /shooht||ʃuːt/ *vb* **shot** /shot||ʃɒt/ *vt* **1a** to eject or impel or cause to be ejected or impelled by a sudden release of tension (e g of a bowstring or by a flick of a finger) <~ *an arrow*> **b** to drive forth or cause to be driven forth **b(1)** by an explosion (e g of a powder charge in a firearm or of ignited fuel in a rocket) **b(2)** by a sudden release of gas or air <~ *darts from a blowpipe*> **c** to drive (e g a ball) forth or away by striking or pushing with the arm, hand, or foot or with an implement **d(1)** to utter (e g words or sounds) rapidly, suddenly, or violently <~ *out a stream of invective*> **d(2)** to emit (e g light or flame) suddenly and rapidly **d(3)** to send forth with suddenness or intensity <shot *a look of anger at her*> **e** to discharge or empty (e g rubbish) from a container **2a** to strike and esp wound or kill with a bullet, arrow, shell, etc shot from a gun, bow, etc **b** to remove or destroy by use of firearms; *also* to wreck, explode **3a** to push or slide (a bolt) in order to fasten or unfasten a door **b** to pass (a shuttle) through the warp threads in weaving **c** to push or thrust forwards; stick out – usu + *out* <*toads* ~ing *out their tongues*> **d** to put forth in growing –

usu + *out* **4a** to engage in (a sport, game, or part of a game that involves shooting); play <~ *pool*> **b** to score by shooting <~ *a basket*> **5** to hunt over with a firearm or bow <~ *a tract of woodland*> **6a** to cause to move suddenly or swiftly forwards <shot *the car onto the highway*> **b** to send or carry quickly; dispatch **7** to pass swiftly by, over, or along <~ing *rapids*> **8** to plane (e g the edge of a board) straight or true **9** to take a picture or series of pictures or television images of; film; *also* to make (a film, videotape, etc) **10** to pass through (a road junction or traffic lights) without slowing down or stopping – infml **11** to take (a drug) by hypodermic needle – slang ~ *vi* **1a** to go or pass rapidly or violently <*sparks* ~ing *up*> **b** to move ahead by superior speed, force, momentum, etc **c** to stream out suddenly; spurt <*blood* shot *from the wound*> **d** to dart (as if) in rays from a source of light **e** to dart with a piercing sensation <*pain* shot *up his arm*> **2a** to cause a weapon or other device to discharge a missile **b** to use a firearm or bow, esp for sport **3** to propel a missile <*guns that* ~ *many miles*> **4** to protrude, project – often + *out* <*a mountain-range* ~ing *out into the sea*> **5** to grow or sprout (as if) by putting forth shoots **6a** to propel an object (e g a ball) in a particular way **b** to drive the ball or puck in football, hockey, etc towards a goal **7** to slide into or out of a fastening <*a bolt that* ~s *in either direction*> **8a** to record a series of visual images (e g on cinefilm or videotape); make a film or videotape **b** to operate a camera or set cameras in operation – **shoot a line** to invent romantic or boastful detail – infml – **shoot one's bolt** to exhaust one's capabilities and resources – **shoot one's mouth off** to talk foolishly or indiscreetly

[2]**shoot** *n* **1a** a stem or branch with its leaves, buds, etc, esp when not yet mature **b** an offshoot **2a** a shooting trip or party **b** (land over which is held) the right to shoot game **c** a shooting match **3** a sudden or rapid advance **4** (a rush of water down) a descent in a stream **5** *chiefly NAm* a momentary darting sensation; a twinge

shoot down *vt* to assert or show the invalidity of; *also* to veto – infml

shooter /ˈshoohtə‖ˈʃuːtə/ *n* a repeating pistol – usu in combination <*six*-shooter>

ˈshooting ˌbrake *n, Br* ESTATE CAR

ˈshooting ˌgallery *n* a usu covered range equipped with targets for practice in shooting with firearms

ˈshooting ˌmatch *n* an affair, matter – chiefly in *the whole shooting match*; infml

ˌshooting ˈstar *n* a meteor appearing as a temporary streak of light in the night sky

ˈshooting ˌstick *n* a spiked stick with a handle that opens out into a seat

ˈshoot-ˌout *n* a usu decisive battle fought with handguns or rifles

shoot up *vi* **1** to grow or increase rapidly <*house prices have* shot up *in recent months*> **2** to inject a narcotic drug into a vein – slang

[1]**shop** /shop‖ʃɒp/ *n* **1** a building or room for the retail sale of merchandise or for the sale of services **2** a place or part of a factory where a particular manufacturing or repair process takes place **3** the jargon or subject matter peculiar to an occupation or sphere of interest – chiefly in *talk shop*

[2]**shop** *vb* **-pp-** *vi* **1** to visit a shop with intent to purchase goods **2** to make a search; hunt <~ *for winning designs*> ~*vt* to inform on; betray – slang – **shopper** *n*

shop around *vi* to investigate a market or situation in search of the best buy or alternative

ˈshop ˌassistant *n, Br* one employed to sell goods in a retail shop

ˌshopˈfloor /-ˈflaw‖-ˈflɔː/ *n* the area in which machinery or workbenches are located in a factory or mill, esp considered as a place of work; *also, sing or pl in constr* the workers in an establishment as distinct from the management

ˈshopˌkeeper /-ˌkeepə‖-ˌkiːpə/ *n* one who runs a retail shop

ˈshopˌlift /-ˌlift‖-ˌlɪft/ *vb* to steal from a shop – **shoplifter** *n*, **shoplifting** *n*

ˈshopping ˌcentre *n* a group of retail shops and service establishments of different types, often designed to serve a community or neighbourhood

ˈshopˌsoiled /-ˌsoyld‖-ˌsɔɪld/ *adj, chiefly Br* **1** deteriorated (e g soiled or faded) through excessive handling or display in a shop **2** no longer fresh or effective; clichéd <~ *slogans*>

ˌshop ˈsteward *n* a union member elected to represent usu manual workers

ˈshopˌworn /-ˌwawn‖-ˌwɔːn/ *adj, chiefly NAm* shopsoiled

[1]**shore** /shaw‖ʃɔː/ *n* **1** the land bordering the sea or another (large) body of water **2** land as distinguished from the sea

[2]**shore** *vt* **1** to support with shores; prop **2** to give support to; brace, sustain – usu + *up* <~ *up farm prices*>

[3]**shore** *n* a prop for preventing sinking or sagging

ˈshore ˌleave *n* time granted to members of a ship's crew to go ashore

shorn /shawn‖ʃɔːn/ *past part of* SHEAR

[1]**short** /shawt‖ʃɔːt/ *adj* **1** having little or insufficient length or height **2a** not extended in time; brief <*a* ~ *vacation*> **b** *of the memory* not retentive **c** quick, expeditious <*made* ~ *work of the problem*> **d** seeming to pass quickly <*made great progress in just a few* ~ *years*> **3a** *of a speech sound* having a relatively short duration **b** *of a syllable in prosody* **b(1)** of relatively brief duration **b(2)** unstressed **4** limited in distance <*a* ~ *walk*> **5a** not coming up to a measure or requirement <*in* ~ *supply*> <*the throw was* ~ *by 5 metres*> **b** insufficiently supplied <~ *of cash*> **6a** abrupt, curt **b** quickly provoked <*a* ~ *temper*> **7** SHORT-TERM 2 **8a** *of pastry, biscuits, etc* crisp and easily broken owing to the presence of fat **b** *of metal* brittle **9** made briefer; abbreviated <*Sue is* ~ *for Susan*> **10** being or relating to a sale of securities or commodities that the seller does not possess at the time of the sale <~ *sale*> **11a** of or occupying a fielding position in cricket near the batsman **b** *of a bowled ball* bouncing relatively far from the batsman – **shortness** *n* – **in the short run** for the immediate future

[2]**short** *adv* **1** curtly <*tends to talk ~ with people when he's busy*> **2** for or during a brief time <short-*lasting*> **3** in an abrupt manner; suddenly <*the car stopped ~*> **4** at a point or degree before a specified or intended goal or limit <*the shells fell ~*> – **be taken/caught short** *Br* to feel a sudden embarrassing need to defecate or urinate

[3]**short** *n* **1** a short sound or signal **2** *pl* a by-product of wheat milling that includes the germ, bran, and some flour **3** *pl* knee-length or less than knee-length trousers **4** *pl* short-term bonds **5** SHORT CIRCUIT **6** a brief often documentary or educational film **7** *Br* a drink of spirits – **for short** as an abbreviation – **in short** by way of summary; briefly

[4]**short** *vt* to short-circuit

shortage /ˈshawtij‖ˈʃɔːtɪdʒ/ *n* a lack, deficit

ˈshortˌbread /-ˌbred‖-ˌbred/ *n* a thick biscuit made from flour, sugar, and fat

ˈshortˌcake /-ˌkayk‖-ˌkeɪk/ *n* **1** shortbread **2** a thick short cake resembling biscuit that is usu sandwiched with a layer of fruit and cream and eaten as a dessert

ˌshortˈchange /-ˈchaynj‖-ˈtʃeɪndʒ/ *vt* **1** to give less than the correct amount of change to **2** to cheat – infml

ˌshort-ˈcircuit *vt* **1** to apply a short circuit to or cause a short circuit in (so as to render inoperative) **2** to bypass, circumvent

ˌshort ˈcircuit *n* the accidental or deliberate joining by a conductor of 2 parts of an electric circuit

ˈshortˌcoming /-ˌkuming‖-ˌkʌmɪŋ/ *n* a deficiency, defect

ˈshortˌcut /-ˌkut‖-ˌkʌt/ *n* a route or procedure quicker and more direct than one customarily followed

shorten /ˈshawt(ə)n‖ˈʃɔːt(ə)n/ *vt* **1** to make short or shorter **2** to add fat to (e g pastry dough) **3** to reduce the area or amount of (sail that is set)

shortening /ˈshawt(ə)n·ing‖ˈʃɔːt(ə)nɪŋ/ *n* an edible fat (e g butter or lard) used to shorten pastry, biscuits, etc

ˈshortˌfall /-ˌfawl‖-ˌfɔːl/ *n* (the degree or amount of) a deficit

ˈshortˌhand /-ˌhand‖-ˌhænd/ *n* **1** a method of rapid writing that substitutes symbols and abbreviations for letters, words, or phrases **2** a system or instance of rapid or abbreviated communication <*verbal ~*> – **shorthand** *adj*

ˌshortˈhanded /-ˈhandid‖-ˈhændɪd/ *adj* undermanned

ˌshorthand ˈtypist *n* sby who takes shorthand notes, esp from dictation, then transcribes them using a typewriter

ˈshortˌhorn /-ˌhawn‖-ˌhɔːn/ *n, often cap* any of a breed of beef cattle originating in the N of England and including good milk-producing strains

shortie /ˈshawti‖ˈʃɔːtɪ/ *n or adj* (a) shorty – infml

ˈshort-ˌlist *vt, Br* to place on a short list

ˈshort ˌlist *n, Br* a list of selected candidates (e g for a job) from whom a final choice must be made

ˌshort-ˈlived *adj* not living or lasting long

ˈshortly /-li‖-lɪ/ *adv* **1a** in a few words; briefly **b** in an abrupt manner **2a** in a short time <*we will be there ~*> **b** at a short interval <*~ after sunset*>

short order *n, NAm* an order for food that can be quickly cooked – **in short order** quickly

ˌshort-ˈrange *adj* **1** SHORT-TERM 1 **2** relating to, suitable for, or capable of travelling (only) short distances <*a ~ missile*>

short shrift *n* **1** a brief respite for confession before execution **2** summary or inconsiderate treatment

ˌshortˈsighted /-ˈsietid‖-ˈsaɪtɪd/ *adj* **1** able to see near objects more clearly than distant objects; myopic **2** lacking foresight – **shortsightedly** *adv*, **shortsightedness** *n*

ˌshort ˈstory *n* a piece of prose fiction usu dealing with a few characters and often concentrating on mood rather than plot

ˌshort-ˈterm *adj* **1** involving a relatively short period of time <*~ plans*> **2** of or constituting a financial operation or obligation based on a brief term, esp one of less than a year

short time *n* reduced working hours because of a lack of work

short ton /tun‖tʌn/ *n* a US unit of weight that is equal to 2000lb (about 746.48kg)

ˈshortˌwave /-ˌwayv‖-ˌweɪv/ *n* a band of radio waves having wavelengths between about 120m and 20m and typically used for amateur transmissions or long-range broadcasting – often pl with sing. meaning

ˌshort-ˈwinded *adj* **1** affected with or characterized by shortness of breath **2** brief or concise in speaking or writing

shorty, shortie /ˈshawti‖ˈʃɔːtɪ/ *n or adj* (sby or sthg) short – infml

[1]**shot** /shot‖ʃɒt/ *n* **1a** an action of shooting **b** a directed propelling of a missile; *specif* a directed discharge of a firearm **c** a stroke or throw in a game (e g tennis, cricket, or basketball); *also* an attempt to kick the ball into the goal in soccer **d** a hypodermic injection **2a(1)** small lead or steel pellets (for a shotgun) **a(2)** a single (nonexplosive) projectile for a gun or cannon **b(1)** a metal sphere that is thrown for distance as an athletic field event **b(2)** this event **3** the distance that a missile is or can be projected **4** one who shoots; *esp* a marksman **5a** an attempt, try <*had a ~ at mending the puncture*> **b** a guess, conjecture **6a** a single photographic exposure **b** an image or series of images in a film or a television programme shot by 1 camera from 1 angle without interruption **7** a charge of explosives **8** a small amount applied at one time; a dose – infml – **like a shot** very rapidly – **shot in the arm** a stimulus, boost – **shot in the dark** a wild guess

[2]**shot** *adj* **1a** *of a fabric* having contrasting and changeable colour effects; iridescent <*~ silk*> **b** suffused or streaked with (a different) colour <*hair ~ with grey*> **c** infused or permeated *with* a quality or element <*~ through with wit*> **2** utterly exhausted or ruined <*her nerves are ~*> – infml – **be/get shot of** *chiefly Br* GET RID OF – infml

[1]'**shot,gun** /-,gun‖-,gʌn/ *n* an often double-barrelled smoothbore shoulder weapon for firing quantities of metal shot at short ranges

[2]**shotgun** *adj* enforced <*a ~ wedding*>

'**shot ,put** /poot‖pʊt/ *n* SHOT 2b – **shot-putter** *n*, **shot-putting** *n*

should /shəd‖ʃəd; *strong* shood‖ʃʊd/ *past of* SHALL **1** – used (e g in the main clause of a conditional sentence) to introduce a contingent fact, possibility, or presumption <*I ~ be surprised if he wrote*> <*it's odd that you ~ mention that*> **2** ought to <*you ~ brush your teeth after every meal*> **3** – used in reported speech to represent *shall* or *will* <*she said we ~ be late – Punch*> **4** will probably <*with an early start, they ~ be here by noon*> **5** – used to soften direct statement <*I ~ have thought it was colder than that*>

[1]**shoulder** /'shohldə‖'ʃəʊldə/ *n* **1a** the part of the human body formed of bones, joints, and muscles that connects the arm to the trunk **b** a corresponding part of a lower vertebrate **2** *pl* **2a** the 2 shoulders and the upper part of the back <*shrugged his ~s*> **b** capacity for bearing a burden (e g of blame or responsibility) <*placed the guilt squarely on his ~s*> **3** a cut of meat including the upper joint of the foreleg and adjacent parts **4** an area adjacent to a higher, more prominent, or more important part: e g **4a(1)** the slope of a mountain near the top **a(2)** a lateral protrusion of a mountain **b** that part of a road to the side of the surface on which vehicles travel **5** a rounded or sloping part (e g of a stringed instrument or a bottle) where the neck joins the body – **shouldered** *adj*

[2]**shoulder** *vt* **1** to push or thrust (as if) with the shoulder **2a** to place or carry on the shoulder **b** to assume the burden or responsibility of ~*vi* to push aggressively with the shoulders; jostle

'**shoulder ,blade** *n* the scapula

'**shoulder ,strap** *n* a strap that passes across the shoulder and holds up a garment

shouldest /shoodist‖ʃʊdɪst/, **shouldst** /shoodst‖ʃʊdst/ *archaic past 2 sing of* SHALL

shouldn't /'shoodnt‖'ʃʊdnt/ should not

[1]**shout** /showt‖ʃaʊt/ *vi* **1** to utter a sudden loud cry **2** *Austr & NZ* to buy a round of drinks ~ *vt* **1** to utter in a loud voice **2** *Austr & NZ* **2a** to buy sthg, esp a drink, for (another person) **b** to buy (sthg, esp a drink) for sby *USE* (*vi 2, vt 2*) infml – **shouter** *n*

[2]**shout** *n* **1** a loud cry or call **2** [4]ROUND 6 – infml

shout down *vt* to drown the words of (a speaker) by shouting

shove /shuv‖ʃʌv/ *vt* **1** to push along with steady force **2** to push in a rough, careless, or hasty manner; thrust <~d *the book into his coat pocket*> ~ *vi* **1** to force a way forwards <*bargain hunters* shoving *up to the counter*> **2** to move sthg by pushing <*you pull and I'll* ~> – **shove** *n*, **shover** *n*

,**shove-'halfpenny** *n* a game played on a special flat board on which players shove discs (e g coins) into marked scoring areas

[1]**shovel** /'shuvl‖'ʃʌvl/ *n* **1a(1)** an implement consisting of a broad scoop or a dished blade with a handle, used to lift and throw loose material **a(2)** (a similar part on) a digging or earth-moving machine **b** sthg like a shovel **2** a shovelful

[2]**shovel** *vb* **-ll-** (*NAm* **-l-, -ll-**) *vt* **1** to dig, clear, or shift with a shovel **2** to convey clumsily or in a mass as if with a shovel <~led *his food into his mouth*> ~*vi* to use a shovel

shove off *vi* to go away; leave – infml

[1]**show** /shoh‖ʃəʊ/ *vb* **shown** /shohn‖ʃəʊn/, **showed** *vt* **1** to cause or permit to be seen; exhibit **2** to present as a public spectacle **3** to reveal by one's condition, nature, or behaviour <*was reluctant to ~ his feelings*> **4** to demonstrate by one's achievements <~ed *herself to be a fine pianist*> **5a** to point out to sby <~ed *him where she lived*> **b** to conduct, usher <~ed *me to an aisle seat*> **6** to accord, grant <~ *respect to one's elders*> **7a** to make evident; indicate <*a letter that* ~ed *his true feelings*> **b** to have as an attribute; manifest <*trade figures* ~ed *a large deficit*> <*the patient is* ~ing *some improvement*> **8a** to establish or make clear by argument or reasoning <~ *a plan to be faulty*> **b** to inform, instruct <~ed *me how to solve the problem*> **9** to present (an animal) for judging in a show ~ *vi* **1** to be or come in view; be noticeable <*he has a tear in his coat but it doesn't* ~> **2** to appear in a specified way <~ *to good advantage*> **3** to be staged or presented **4** *chiefly NAm* SHOW UP 2 <*failed to ~ for the award*> – **shower** *n* – **show one's hand** to declare one's intentions or reveal one's resources – **show one's true colours** to show one's real nature or opinions – **show over** *chiefly Br* to take on a tour or inspection of <*prospective buyers were* shown over *the new house*> – **show someone the door** to tell sby to get out

[2]**show** *n* **1** a display <*a ~ of hands*> – often + *on* <*all antiques on ~ are genuine*> **2a** a false semblance; a pretence <*he made a ~ of friendship*> **b** a more or less true appearance of sthg; a sign <*a ~ of reason*> **c** an impressive display <*a ~ of strength*> **d** ostentation **3** sthg exhibited, esp for wonder or ridicule; a spectacle **4a** a large display or exhibition arranged to arouse interest or stimulate sales **b** a competitive exhibition of animals, plants, etc to demonstrate quality in breeding, growing, etc **5** a public presentation: e g **5a** a theatrical presentation **b** a radio or television programme **6** an enterprise, affair <*he ran the whole* ~> **7** *chiefly NAm* a chance – esp in *give someone a show USE* (*6&7*) infml

'**show ,business** *n* the arts, occupations, and businesses (e g theatre, films, and television) that comprise the entertainment industry

'**show,case** /-,kays‖-,keɪs/ *n* **1** a case, box, or cabinet with a transparent usu glass front or top used for displaying and protecting articles in a shop or museum **2** a setting or surround for exhibiting sthg to best advantage

'**show,down** /-,down‖-,daʊn/ *n* the final settlement of a contested issue or the confrontation by which it is settled

[1]**shower** /'showə‖'ʃaʊə/ *n* **1** a fall of rain, snow, etc of short duration **2** sthg like a rain shower <*a ~ of tears*> <~s *of sparks from a*

bonfire> **3** an apparatus that provides a stream of water for spraying on the body; *also* an act of washing oneself using such an apparatus **4** *sing or pl in constr, Br* a motley or inferior collection of people – infml – **showery** *adj*

[2]**shower** *vi* **1** to descend (as if) in a shower <*letters* ~ed *on him in praise and protest*> **2** to take a shower ~ *vt* **1a** to wet copiously (e g with water) in a spray, fine stream, or drops **b** to cause to fall in a shower <*factory chimneys* ~ed *soot on the neighbourhood*>; *also* to cover (as if) with a shower **2** to bestow or present in abundance <~ed *him with honours*>

showgirl /ˈshohˌguhl‖ˈʃəʊˌgɜːl/ *n* a young woman who dances or sings in the chorus of a theatrical production; *broadly* a female stage performer whose presence is purely decorative

showing /ˈshoh·ing‖ˈʃəʊɪŋ/ *n* **1** an act of putting sthg on view; a display, exhibition **2** performance in competition <*made a good* ~ *in the finals*> **3** a statement or presentation of a case; evidence

ˈshowˌjumping /-ˌjumping‖-ˌdʒʌmpɪŋ/ *n* the competitive riding of horses 1 at a time over a set course of obstacles in which the winner is judged according to ability and speed – **showjumper** *n*

ˈshowman /-mən‖-mən/ *n* **1** one who presents a theatrical show; *also* the manager of a circus or fairground **2** a person with a flair for dramatically effective presentation – **showmanship** *n*

ˈshow-ˌoff *n* one who shows off; an exhibitionist

show off *vt* to exhibit proudly <*wanted to* show *his new car* off> ~*vi* to seek attention or admiration by conspicuous behaviour <*boys* showing off *on their bicycles*>

ˈshowˌpiece /-ˌpees‖-ˌpiːs/ *n* a prime or outstanding example used for exhibition

ˈshowˌplace /-ˌplays‖-ˌpleɪs/ *n* a place (e g an estate or building) regarded as an example of beauty or excellence

ˈshowˌroom /-ˌroohm‖-ˌruːm/ *n* a room where (samples of) goods for sale are displayed

show up *vt* **1** to expose (e g a defect, deception, or impostor) **2** to embarrass ~ *vi* **1a** to be plainly evident; STAND OUT **b** to appear in a specified light or manner **2** to arrive *USE* (*vt 2; vi 2*) infml

showy /ˈshoh·i‖ˈʃəʊɪ/ *adj* **1** making an attractive show; striking **2** given to or marked by pretentious display; gaudy – **showily** *adv*, **showiness** *n*

shrank /shrangk‖ʃræŋk/ *past of* SHRINK

shrapnel /ˈshrapnəl‖ˈʃræpnəl/ *n, pl* **shrapnel** **1** a hollow projectile that contains bullets or pieces of metal and that is exploded by a bursting charge to produce a shower of fragments **2** bomb, mine, or shell fragments thrown out during explosion [Henry *Shrapnel* (1761-1842), English artillery officer]

[1]**shred** /shred‖ʃred/ *n* a narrow strip cut or torn off; *also* a fragment, scrap

[2]**shred** *vb* **-dd-** *vt* to cut or tear into shreds ~*vi* to come apart in or be reduced to shreds – **shredder** *n*

shrew /shrooh‖ʃruː/ *n* **1** any of numerous small chiefly nocturnal mammals having a long pointed snout, very small eyes, and velvety fur **2** an ill-tempered nagging woman; a scold

shrewd /shroohd‖ʃruːd/ *adj* **1** marked by keen discernment and hardheaded practicality **2** wily, artful – **shrewdly** *adv*, **shrewdness** *n*

shrewish /ˈshrooh·ish‖ˈʃruːɪʃ/ *adj* ill-tempered, intractable – **shrewishly** *adv*, **shrewishness** *n*

[1]**shriek** /shreek‖ʃriːk/ *vi* to utter or make a shrill piercing cry; screech ~*vt* to utter with a shriek or sharply and shrilly – often + *out*

[2]**shriek** *n* (a sound similar to) a shrill usu wild cry

shrift /shrift‖ʃrɪft/ *n, archaic* **1** CONFESSION 1 **2** remission of sins pronounced by a priest in the sacrament of confession

shrike /shriek‖ʃraɪk/ *n* any of numerous usu largely grey or brownish birds that often impale their (insect) prey on thorns

[1]**shrill** /shril‖ʃrɪl/ *vi* to utter or emit a high-pitched piercing sound ~*vt* to scream

[2]**shrill** *adj* having, making, or being a sharp high-pitched sound – **shrillness** *n*, **shrilly** *adv*

[1]**shrimp** /shrimp‖ʃrɪmp/ *n*, **1** any of numerous mostly small marine 10-legged crustacean animals with a long slender body, compressed abdomen, and long legs **2** a very small or puny person – infml; humor – **shrimpy** *adj*

[2]**shrimp** *vi* to fish for or catch shrimps – usu in *go shrimping*

shrine /shrien‖ʃraɪn/ *n* **1a** a receptacle for sacred relics **b** a place in which devotion is paid to a saint or deity **2** a receptacle (e g a tomb) for the dead **3** a place or object hallowed by its history or associations – **shrine** *vt*

[1]**shrink** /shringk‖ʃrɪŋk/ *vb* **shrank** /shrangk‖ʃræŋk/ *also* **shrunk** /shrungk‖ʃrʌŋk/; **shrunk, shrunken** /ˈshrungkən‖ˈʃrʌŋkən/ *vi* **1** to draw back or cower away (e g from sthg painful or horrible) **2** to contract to a smaller volume or extent (e g as a result of heat or moisture) **3** to show reluctance (e g before a difficult or unpleasant duty); recoil ~*vt* to cause to contract; *specif* to compact (cloth) by a treatment (e g with water or steam) that results in contraction – **shrinkable** *adj*, **shrinkage** *n*, **shrinker** *n*

[2]**shrink** *n* **1** shrinkage **2** a psychoanalyst or psychiatrist – humor

shrive /shriev‖ʃraɪv/ *vt* **shrived, shrove** /shrohv‖ʃrəʊv/; **shriven** /ˈshriv(ə)n‖ˈʃrɪv(ə)n/, **shrived** *archaic* to hear the confession of and absolve

shrivel /ˈshrivl‖ˈʃrɪvl/ *vb* **-ll-** (*NAm* **-l-**, **-ll-**) to (cause to) contract into wrinkles, esp through loss of moisture

[1]**shroud** /shrowd‖ʃraʊd/ *n* **1** a burial garment (e g a winding-sheet) **2** sthg that covers, conceals, or guards **3** any of the ropes or wires giving support, usu in pairs, to a ship's mast

[2]**shroud** *vt* **1a** to envelop and conceal **b** to obscure, disguise **2** to dress for burial

ˌShrove ˈTuesday /shrohv‖ʃrəʊv/ *n* the Tuesday before Ash Wednesday; PANCAKE DAY

shrub /shrub‖ʃrʌb/ *n* a low-growing usu several-stemmed woody plant – **shrubby** *adj*

shrubbery /ˈshrub(ə)ri‖ˈʃrʌb(ə)rɪ/ *n* a planting or growth of shrubs

shrug /shrug‖ʃrʌg/ *vb* **-gg-** to lift and contract

(the shoulders), esp to express aloofness, aversion, or doubt – **shrug** *n*

shrug off *vt* to brush aside; disregard, belittle

[1]**shuck** /shuk‖ʃʌk/ *n* **1** a pod, husk **2** *NAm* sthg of no value – usu pl with sing. meaning **3** *pl* – used interjectionally to express mild annoyance or disappointment; infml

[2]**shuck** *vt, NAm* **1** to strip of shucks **2** to remove or dispose of like a shuck – often + *off* – **shucker** *n*

shudder /ˈshudə‖ˈʃʌdə/ *vi* **1** to tremble with a sudden brief convulsive movement **2** to quiver, vibrate – **shudder** *n*

[1]**shuffle** /ˈshufl‖ˈʃʌfl/ *vb* **1** to mix together in a confused mass; jumble **2** to rearrange (e g playing cards or dominoes) to produce a random order **3** to move (the feet) by sliding clumsily along or back and forth without lifting ~ *vi* **1** to act or speak in a shifty or evasive manner **2a** to move or walk by sliding or dragging the feet **b** to dance in a lazy nonchalant manner with scraping and tapping motions of the feet **3** to mix playing cards by shuffling – **shuffler** *n*

[2]**shuffle** *n* **1a** shuffling (e g of cards) **b** a right or turn to shuffle <*it's your* ~> **2** (a dance characterized by) a dragging sliding movement

ˈ**shuffle,board** /-ˌbawd‖-ˌbɔːd/ *n* a game in which players use long-handled cues to shove wooden discs into scoring areas of a diagram marked on a smooth surface

shufti /ˈshufti‖ˈʃʊftɪ/ *n, Br* a look, glance <*have a* ~ *at the radar screen*> – infml

shun /shun‖ʃʌn/ *vt* **-nn-** to avoid deliberately, esp habitually <*actors who* ~ *publicity*> – **shunner** *n*

[1]**shunt** /shunt‖ʃʌnt/ *vt* **1a** to move (e g a train) from one track to another **b** *Br* to move (railway vehicles) to different positions on the same track within terminal areas **2** to provide with or divert by means of an electrical shunt **3** to divert (blood) by means of a surgical shunt ~ *vi* **1** to move into a side track **2** to travel back and forth <~ed *between the 2 towns*> – **shunter** *n*

[2]**shunt** *n* **1** a means or mechanism for turning or thrusting aside: e g **1a** a conductor joining 2 points in an electrical circuit so as to form a parallel path through which a portion of the current may pass **b** a surgical passage created between 2 blood vessels to divert blood from one part to another **c** *chiefly Br* a siding **2** a usu minor collision of motor vehicles – infml

[1]**shush** /sh, shush‖ʃ, ʃʌʃ/ *n* – used interjectionally to demand silence

[2]**shush** *vt* to tell to be quiet, esp by saying 'Shush!' – infml

shut /shut‖ʃʌt/ *vb* **-tt-; shut** *vt* **1** to place in position to close an opening <~ *the lid*> <~ *the door*> **2** to confine (as if) by enclosure <~ *him in the cupboard*> **3** to fasten with a lock or bolt **4** to close by bringing enclosing or covering parts together <~ *the eyes*> **5** to cause to cease or suspend operation <~ *up shop*> ~ *vi* **1** to become closed <*flowers that* ~ *at night*> **2** to cease or suspend operation *USE* (*vt 5; vi 2*) often + *up* or *down*

shut away *vt* to remove or isolate from others <*governments that* shut *dissidents* away>

ˈ**shut,down** /-ˌdown‖-ˌdaʊn/ *n* the cessation or suspension of an activity (e g work in a mine or factory)

ˈ**shut-,eye** *n* sleep – infml

ˈ**shut,off** /-ˌof‖-ˌɒf/ *n, chiefly NAm* a stoppage, interruption

shut off *vt* **1a** to cut off, stop <shut *the water* off> **b** to stop the operation of (e g a machine) <shut *the motor* off> **2** to isolate, separate – usu + *from* <*a village* shut off *from the rest of the world*> ~*vi* to cease operating; stop <*the heater* shuts off *automatically*>

[1]**shutter** /ˈshutə‖ˈʃʌtə/ *n* **1a** a usu hinged outside cover for a window, often fitted as one of a pair **b** a usu movable cover or screen (e g over a door or as part of stage scenery) **2** a device that opens and closes the lens aperture of a camera **3** the movable slots in the box enclosing the swell organ part of a pipe organ, which are opened to increase the volume of the sound – **shutterless** *adj*

[2]**shutter** *vt* to provide or close with shutters

[1]**shuttle** /ˈshutl‖ˈʃʌtl/ *n* **1a** a usu spindle-shaped device that holds a bobbin and is used in weaving for passing the thread of the weft between the threads of the warp **b** a spindle-shaped device holding the thread in tatting, knotting, or netting **c** a sliding thread holder that carries the lower thread in a sewing machine through a loop of the upper thread to make a stitch **2** a lightweight conical object with a rounded nose that is hit as the object of play in badminton and consists of (a moulded plastic imitation of) a cork with feathers stuck in it **3a** (a route or vehicle for) a regular going back and forth over a usu short route **b** a reusable space vehicle for use esp between earth and outer space

[2]**shuttle** *vb* **1** to (cause to) move to and fro rapidly **2** to transport or be transported (as if) in or by a shuttle – **shuttler** *n*

ˈ**shuttle,cock** /-ˌkok‖-ˌkɒk/ *n* SHUTTLE 2

shut up *vt* to cause (sby) to be silent; *esp* to force (a speaker) to stop talking ~*vi* to become silent; *esp* to stop talking *USE* infml

[1]**shy** /shie‖ʃaɪ/ *adj* **shier, shyer; shiest, shyest 1** easily alarmed; timid, distrustful – often in combination <*camera-shy*> **2** wary *of* <~ *of disclosing his age*> **3** sensitively reserved or retiring; bashful; *also* expressive of such a state or nature <*spoke in a* ~ *voice*> **4** *chiefly NAm* lacking, short <*we're 3 points* ~ *of what we need to win*> – infml – **shyly** *adv*, **shyness** *n*

[2]**shy** *vi* **1** to start suddenly aside in fright or alarm; recoil **2** to move or dodge to evade a person or thing – usu + *away* or *from* <*they* shied *away from buying the flat when they learnt the full price*> – **shy** *n*

[3]**shy** *vt* to throw (e g a stone) with a jerking movement; fling ~*vi* to make a sudden throw *USE* infml

[4]**shy** *n* **1** a toss, throw **2** a verbal sally <*took a few* shies *at the integrity of his opponent*> **3** a stall (e g at a fairground) in which people throw balls at targets (e g coconuts) in order to knock them down **4** an attempt *USE* (*1, 2, & 4*) infml

shyster /ˈshiestə‖ˈʃaɪstə/ *n, chiefly NAm* sby (esp a lawyer) who is professionally unscrupulous

si /see‖siː/ *n* ti

SI *n* a system of units whose basic units are the metre, kilogram, second, ampere, kelvin, candela, and mole and which uses prefixes (e g micro-, kilo-, and mega-) to indicate multiples or fractions of 10 [French *Système International d'Unités* international system of units]

[1]Siamese /ˌsie·əˈmeez‖ˌsaɪəˈmiːz/ *adj* Thai

[2]Siamese *n, pl* **Siamese** **1** Thai **2** *also* **Siamese cat** any of a breed of slender blue-eyed short-haired domestic cats of oriental origin with pale fawn or grey body and darker ears, paws, tail, and face

ˌSiamese ˈtwin *n* either of a pair of congenitally joined twins [fr Chang and Eng (1811-74), congenitally joined twins born in Siam]

[1]sib /sib‖sɪb/ *adj* related by blood

[2]sib *n* **1** a blood relation **2** a brother or sister; *broadly* any plant or animal of a group sharing a degree of genetic relationship comparable to that of human sibs

[1]sibilant /ˈsibilənt‖ˈsɪbɪlənt/ *adj* having, containing, or producing a hissing sound – **sibilance, sibilancy** *n*, **sibilantly** *adv*

[2]sibilant *n* a sibilant speech sound

sibling /ˈsibling‖ˈsɪblɪŋ/ *n* SIB 2; *also* any of 2 or more individuals having 1 parent in common

sibyl /ˈsibil‖ˈsɪbɪl/ *n, often cap* any of several female prophets credited to widely separate parts of the ancient world; *broadly* any female prophet – **sibylline, sibylic, sibyllic** *adj*

sic /sik‖sɪk/ *adv* intentionally so written – used after a printed word or passage to indicate that it is intended exactly as printed or that it exactly reproduces an original <*said he seed [~] it all*> [Latin, so, thus]

[1]sick /sik‖sɪk/ *adj* **1a(1)** ill, ailing <*a ~ child*> **a(2)** of or intended for use in illness <*~ pay*> **b** queasy, nauseated; likely to vomit <*felt ~ in the car*> – often in combination <*carsick*> **2a** sickened by intense emotion (e g shame or fear) <*~ with fear*> **b** disgusted or weary, esp because of surfeit <*~ of flattery*> **c** distressed and longing for sthg that one has lost or been parted from **3a** mentally or emotionally disturbed; morbid **b** macabre, sadistic <*~ jokes*> **4a** lacking vigour; sickly **b** badly outclassed <*looked ~ in the contest*> – infml – **sickish** *adj*, **sickly** *adv* – **be sick** *chiefly Br* to vomit <was sick *on the rug*>

[2]sick *n, Br* vomit

ˈsick ˌbay *n* a compartment or room (e g in a ship) used as a dispensary and hospital

ˈsickˌbed /-ˌbed‖-ˌbed/ *n* the bed on which one lies sick

ˈsick ˌcall *n* a usu daily (army) parade at which individuals report as sick to the medical officer

sicken /ˈsikən‖ˈsɪkən/ *vt* **1** to cause to feel ill or nauseous **2** to drive to the point of despair or loathing *~vi* to become ill; show signs of illness <*looked as if she was ~*ing *for a cold*>

sickening /ˈsikəning‖ˈsɪkənɪŋ/ *adj* **1** causing sickness <*a ~ smell*> **2** very horrible or repugnant <*fell to the floor with a ~ thud*> – **sickeningly** *adv*

sick headache *n, chiefly NAm* migraine

[1]sickle /ˈsikl‖ˈsɪkl/ *n* **1** an agricultural implement for cutting plants or hedges, consisting of a curved metal blade with a short handle **2** a cutting mechanism (e g of a combine harvester) consisting of a bar with a series of cutting parts

[2]sickle *adj* having a curve resembling that of a sickle blade <*the ~ moon*>

[3]sickle *vt* **1** to mow, reap, or cut with a sickle **2** to form (a red blood cell) into a crescent shape *~vi* to become crescent-shaped <*the ability of red blood cells to ~*>

ˈsick ˌleave *n* absence from work because of illness

sickle-cell anaemia *n* a hereditary anaemia occurring primarily in Negroes, in which the sickling of most of the red blood cells causes recurrent short periods of fever and pain

sickly /ˈsikli‖ˈsɪklɪ/ *adj* **1** somewhat unwell; *also* habitually ailing **2** associated with sickness <*a ~ complexion*> **3** producing or tending to produce disease <*a ~ climate*> **4** suggesting sickness: **4a** strained, uneasy <*a ~ smile*> **b** feeble, weak <*a ~ plant*> **5a** tending to produce nausea <*a ~ taste*> **b** mawkish, saccharine <*~ sentiment*> – **sickliness** *n*

ˈsickness /-nis‖-nɪs/ *n* **1** ill health **2** a specific disease **3** nausea, queasiness

ˈsick ˌpay *n* salary or wages paid to an employee while on sick leave

ˈsickˌroom /-ˌroohm, -ˌroom‖-ˌruːm, -ˌrʊm/ *n* a room set aside for or occupied by sick people

sick up *vt, Br* to vomit – infml

[1]side /sied‖saɪd/ *n* **1a** the right or left part of the wall or trunk of the body <*a pain in the ~*> **b** the right or left half of the animal body or of a meat carcass **2** a location, region, or direction considered in relation to a centre or line of division <*the south ~ of the city*> <*surrounded on all ~*s> **3** a surface forming a border or face of an object **4** a slope of a hill, ridge, etc **5a** a bounding line of a geometrical figure <*each ~ of a square*> **b** FACE 5a(5) **c** either surface of a thin object <*one ~ of a record*> <*the right ~ of the cloth*> **6** company <*he never left her ~*> **7a** *sing or pl in constr* a person or group in competition or dispute with another **b** the attitude or activity of such a person or group; a part <*took my ~ of the argument*> **8** a line of descent traced through a parent <*the grandfather on his mother's ~*> **9** an aspect or part of sthg viewed in contrast with some other aspect or part <*the better ~ of his nature*> **10** a position viewed as opposite to or contrasted with another <*2 ~s to every question*> **11** *the* direction of a specified tendency – + *on* <*she was somewhat on the short ~*> **12** *Br* a television channel **13** *Br* sideways spin imparted to a billiard ball – **on the side 1** in addition to a principal occupation; *specif* as a dishonest or illegal secondary activity **2** *NAm* in addition to the main portion

[2]side *adj* **1** at, from, towards, etc the side **2a** incidental, subordinate <*a ~ issue*> **b** made on the side, esp in secret <*a ~ payment*> **c** additional to the main part or portion <*a ~ order for more rolls*>

[3]side *vi* to take sides; join or form sides <*~*d *with the rebels*>

'side ,arm *n* a weapon (e g a sword, revolver, or bayonet) worn at the side or in the belt

'side,board /-,bawd‖-,bɔːd/ *n* **1** a usu flat-topped piece of dining-room furniture having compartments and shelves for holding articles of table service **2** *pl, Br* whiskers on the side of the face that extend from the hairline to below the ears

sideburns /-,buhnz‖-,bɜːnz/ SIDEBOARDS 2 [alteration of *burnsides*, fr Ambrose E *Burnside* (1824-81), US general]

'side,car /-,kah‖-,kɑː/ *n* a car attached to the side of a motorcycle or motor scooter for 1 or more passengers

sided /'siedid‖'saɪdɪd/ *adj* having sides, usu of a specified number or kind <*one*-sided> – **sidedness** *n*

'side ef,fect *n* a secondary and usu adverse effect (e g of a drug)

'side,kick /-,kik‖-,kɪk/ *n, chiefly NAm* sby closely associated with another, esp as a subordinate – infml

'side,light /-,liet‖-,laɪt/ *n* **1** incidental or additional information **2a** the red port light or the green starboard light carried by ships travelling at night **b** a light at the side of a (motor) vehicle

'side,line /-,lien‖-,laɪn/ *n* **1** a line at right angles to a goal line or end line and marking a side of a court or field of play **2a** a line of goods manufactured or esp sold in addition to one's principal line **b** a business or activity pursued in addition to a full-time occupation **3** *pl* the standpoint of people not immediately participating – chiefly in *on the sidelines*

[1]'side,long /-,long‖-,lɒŋ/ *adv* towards the side; obliquely

[2]sidelong *adj* **1** inclining or directed to one side <~ *glances*> **2** indirect rather than straightforward

sidereal /sie'diəri·əl‖saɪ'dɪərɪəl/ *adj* of or expressed in relation to stars or constellations

sidesaddle /'sied,sadl‖'saɪd,sædl/ *n* a saddle for women in which the rider sits with both legs on the same side of the horse – **sidesaddle** *adv*

'side,show /-,shoh‖-,ʃəʊ/ *n* **1a** a minor show offered in addition to a main exhibition (e g of a circus) **b** a fairground booth or counter offering a game of luck or skill **2** an incidental diversion

'side,slip /-,slip‖-,slɪp/ *vi* **-pp-** to move sideways through the air in a downward direction – **sideslip** *n*

sidesman /'siedzmən‖'saɪdzmən/ *n* any of a group of people in an Anglican church who assist the churchwardens, esp in taking the collection in services

'side,splitting /-,spliting‖-,splɪtɪŋ/ *adj* causing raucous laughter

'side,step /-,step‖-,step/ *vb* **-pp-** *vi* **1** to step sideways or to one side **2** to evade an issue or decision ~ *vt* **1** to move quickly out of the way of <~ *a blow*> **2** to bypass, evade <*adept at* ~ping *awkward questions*>

'side ,step *n* **1** a step aside (e g in boxing to avoid a punch) **2** a step taken sideways (e g when climbing on skis)

'side ,street *n* a minor street branching off a main thoroughfare

'side,stroke /-,strohk‖-,strəʊk/ *n* a swimming stroke executed while lying on one's side

sideswipe /-,swiep‖-,swaɪp/ *n* an incidental deprecatory remark, allusion, or reference – infml

[1]'side,track /-,trak‖-,træk/ *n* **1** an unimportant line of thinking that is followed instead of a more important one **2** *NAm* a siding

[2]sidetrack *vt* to divert from a course or purpose; distract

'side,walk /-,wawk‖-,wɔːk/ *n, NAm* a pavement

'sidewards /-woodz‖-wʊdz/, *NAm chiefly* **sideward** *adv* towards one side

'side,ways /-,wayz‖-,weɪz/, *NAm also* **sideway** /-,way‖-,weɪ/ *adv or adj* **1** to or from the side <*a* ~ *movement*>; *also* askance **2** with 1 side forward <*turn it* ~> **3** to a position of equivalent rank <*he was promoted* ~>

siding /'sieding‖'saɪdɪŋ/ *n* a short railway track connected with the main track

sidle /'siedl‖'saɪdl/ *vi* **1** to move obliquely **2** to walk timidly or hesitantly; edge along – usu + *up* – **sidle** *n*

siege /seej‖siːdʒ/ *n* a military blockade of a city or fortified place to compel it to surrender; *also* the duration of or operations carried out in a siege – **lay siege to 1** to besiege militarily **2** to pursue diligently or persistently

sienna /si'enə‖sɪ'enə/ *n* an earthy substance containing oxides of iron and usu of manganese that is brownish yellow when raw and orange red or reddish brown when burnt and is used as a pigment [Italian *terra di Siena*, lit., Siena earth, fr *Siena, Sienna*, town in Italy]

sierra /si'eərə‖sɪ'eərə/ *n* a range of mountains, esp with a serrated or irregular outline

siesta /si'estə‖sɪ'estə/ *n* an afternoon nap or rest [Spanish, fr Latin *sexta* (*hora*) noon, lit., sixth hour]

'sieva ,bean /'seevə‖'siːvə/ *n* any of several small-seeded beans closely related to and sometimes classed as lima beans; *also* the seed of a lima bean

[1]sieve /siv‖sɪv/ *n* a device with a meshed or perforated bottom that will allow the passage of liquids or fine solids while retaining coarser material or solids

[2]sieve *vt* to sift

sift /sift‖sɪft/ *vt* **1a** to put through a sieve <~ *flour*> **b** to separate (out) (as if) by passing through a sieve **2** to scatter (as if) with a sieve <~ *sugar on a cake*> – **sift through** to make a close examination of (things in a mass or group)

sifter /'siftə‖'sɪftə/ *n* [2]CASTOR 2

[1]sigh /sie‖saɪ/ *vi* **1** to take a long deep audible breath (e g in weariness or grief) **2** *esp of the wind* to make a sound like sighing **3** to grieve, yearn – usu + *for* <~ing *for the days of his youth*> ~*vt* to express by or with sighs – **sigher** *n*

[2]sigh *n* **1** an act of sighing, esp when expressing an emotion or feeling (e g weariness or relief) **2** a sound of or resembling sighing <~s *of the summer breeze*>

[1]sight /siet‖saɪt/ *n* **1** sthg seen; *esp* a spectacle <*the familiar* ~ *of the postman coming along* *the street*> **2a** a thing (e g an impressive or historic building) regarded as worth seeing – often pl <*see the* ~s *of Paris*> **b** sthg ridiculous or displeasing in appearance <*you must get some sleep, you look a* ~> **3a** the process, power, or function of seeing; *specif* the one of the 5 basic physical senses by which light received by the eye is interpreted by the brain as a representation of the forms, brightness, and colour of the objects of the real world **b** a manner of regarding; an opinion **4a** the act of looking at or beholding sthg <*fainted at the* ~ *of blood*> **b** a view, glimpse <*got a* ~ *of the Queen*> **c** an observation (e g by a navigator) to determine direction or position **5a** a perception of an object by the eye **b** the range of vision **6a** a device for guiding the eye (e g in aiming a firearm or bomb) **b** a device with a small aperture through which objects are to be seen and by which their direction is ascertained **7** a great deal; a lot <*earned a* ~ *more as a freelance*> – infml – **sightless** *adj*, **sightlessness** *n* – **at first sight** when viewed without proper investigation – **at/on sight** as soon as presented to view – **out of sight 1** beyond all expectation or reason <*wages have risen* out of sight *during the past year*> **2** *chiefly NAm* marvellous, wonderful – infml; no longer in vogue – **sight for sore eyes** sby or sthg whose appearance or arrival is an occasion for joy or relief

[2]**sight** *vt* **1** to get or catch sight of <*several whales were* ~ed> **2** to aim (e g a weapon) by means of sights **3a** to equip (e g a gun) with sights **b** to adjust the sights of ~*vi* to take aim (e g in shooting) – **sighting** *n*

ˈ**sighted** *adj* having sight, esp of a specified kind – often in combination <*clear*-sighted>

ˈ**sightly** /-li‖-lɪ/ *adj* **1** pleasing to the eye; attractive **2** *chiefly NAm* affording a fine view <*homes in a* ~ *location*> – **sightliness** *n*

ˈ**sight-ˌread** /reed‖riːd/ *vb* **sight-read** /red‖red/ *vt* to read (e g a foreign language) or perform (music) without previous preparation or study ~*vi* to read at sight; *esp* to perform music at sight – **sight reader** *n*

sight screen *n* a screen placed on the boundary of a cricket field behind the bowler to improve the batsman's view of the ball

ˈ**sightˌseeing** /-ˌsee·ing‖-ˌsiːɪŋ/ *n* the act or pastime of touring interesting or attractive sights – often in *go sightseeing* – **sightseer** *n*

[1]**sign** /sien‖saɪn/ *n* **1a** a motion or gesture by which a thought, command, or wish is made known **b** SIGNAL 1 **2** a mark with a conventional meaning, used to replace or supplement words **3** any of the 12 divisions of the zodiac **4a(1)** a character (e g a flat or sharp) used in musical notation **a(2)** a segno **b** a character (e g ÷) indicating a mathematical operation; *also* either of 2 characters + and – that form part of the symbol of a number and characterize it as positive or negative **5** a board or notice bearing information or advertising matter or giving warning, command, or identification **6a** sthg material or external that stands for or signifies sthg spiritual **b** sthg serving to indicate the presence or existence of sby or sthg <*saw no* ~ *of him anywhere*> **c** a presage, portent <~s *of an early spring*> **d** objective evidence of plant or animal disease **7** a remarkable event indicating the will of a deity [Old French *signe*, fr Latin *signum* mark, token, sign, image, seal]

[2]**sign** *vt* **1a** to place a sign on **b** to indicate, represent, or express by a sign **2a** to put a signature to **b** to assign formally <~ed *over his property*> **c(1)** to write down (one's name) **c(2)** to write as the name of (oneself) <~ed *herself 'R E Swan'*> **3** to warn, order, or request by a sign <~ed *him to enter*> **4** to engage by securing the signature of on a contract of employment <~ed *a new striker from Arsenal*> – often + *on* or *up* ~ *vi* **1** to write one's signature, esp in token of assent, responsibility, or obligation **2** to make a sign or signal – **signer** *n*

[1]**signal** /ˈsignəl‖ˈsɪgnəl/ *n* **1** an act, event, or watchword agreed on as the occasion of concerted action <*waited for the* ~ *to begin the attack*> **2** sthg that occasions action <*his scolding was a* ~ *for the little girl to start crying*> **3** a conventional sign (e g a siren or flashing light) made to give warning or command <*a* ~ *that warns of an air raid*> **4a** an object used to transmit or convey information beyond the range of human voice **b** the sound or image conveyed in telegraphy, telephony, radio, radar, or television **c** the variations of a physical quantity (e g pressure or voltage) by which information may be transmitted: e g **c(1)** the wave that is used to modulate a carrier <*the video* ~> **c(2)** the wave produced by the modulation of a carrier by a signal <*a radio* ~>

[2]**signal** *vb* **-ll-** (*NAm* **-l-**, **-ll-**) *vt* **1** to warn, order, or request by a signal <~led *the fleet to turn back*> **2** to communicate by signals <~led *their refusal*> **3** to be a sign of; mark <*his resignation* ~led *the end of a long career*> ~*vi* to make or send a signal – **signaller**, *NAm chiefly* **signaler** *n*

[3]**signal** *adj* **1** used in signalling <*a* ~ *beacon*> **2** distinguished from the ordinary; conspicuous <*a* ~ *achievement*> – chiefly fml

ˈ**signalˌbox** /-ˌboks‖-ˌbɒks/ *n*, *Br* a raised building above a railway line from which signals and points are worked

signal·ize, **-ise** /ˈsignəliez‖ˈsɪgnəlaɪz/ *vt* **1** *chiefly NAm* to point out carefully or distinctly; draw attention to **2** to make noteworthy; distinguish <*a performance* ~d *by consummate artistry*> – fml – **signalization** *n*

signally /ˈsignəli‖ˈsɪgnəlɪ/ *adv* in a signal manner; remarkably – chiefly fml

ˈ**signalman** /-mən‖-mən/ *n*, *pl* **signalmen** /-mən‖-mən/ sby employed to operate signals (e g for a railway)

signatory /ˈsignət(ə)ri‖ˈsɪgnət(ə)rɪ/ *n* a signer with another or others; *esp* a government bound with others by a signed convention – **signatory** *adj*

signature /ˈsignəchə‖ˈsɪgnətʃə/ *n* **1a** the name of a person written with his/her own hand **b** the act of signing one's name **2** a letter or figure placed usu at the bottom of the first page on each sheet of printed pages (e g of a book) as a direction to the binder in gathering the sheets; *also* the sheet itself

ˈ**signature ˌtune** *n* a melody, passage, or

song used to identify a programme, entertainer, etc

signet /'signit‖'sɪgnɪt/ *n* **1** a personal seal used officially in lieu of signature **2** the impression made (as if) by a signet **3** a small intaglio seal (e g in a finger ring)

significance /sig'nifikəns‖sɪg'nɪfɪkəns/ *n* **1a** sthg conveyed as a meaning, often latently or indirectly **b** the quality of conveying or implying **2a** the quality of being important; consequence **b** the quality of being statistically significant

significant /sig'nifikənt‖sɪg'nɪfɪkənt/ *adj* **1** having meaning; *esp* expressive <*the painter's task to pick out the ~ details* – Herbert Read> **2** suggesting or containing a veiled or special meaning <*perhaps her glance was ~*> **3a** having or likely to have influence or effect; important <*the budget brought no ~ changes*> **b** probably caused by sthg other than chance <*statistically ~ correlation between vitamin deficiency and disease*> **c** being any of the figures that comes before or after the decimal point of a number and is not zero or is the first figure after the decimal point that is an exact zero – **significantly** *adv*

signification /,signifi'kaysh(ə)n‖,sɪgnɪfɪ'keɪʃ(ə)n/ *n* **1** signifying by symbolic means (e g signs) **2** the meaning that a term, symbol, or character normally conveys or is intended to convey

signify /'signifie‖'sɪgnɪfaɪ/ *vt* **1** to mean, denote **2** to show, esp by a conventional token (e g a word, signal, or gesture) *~vi* to have significance; matter – **signifiable** *adj*, **signifier** *n*

sign in *vi* to record one's arrival by signing a register or punching a card *~vt* to record the arrival of (a person) or receipt of (an article) by signing <*all deliveries must be* signed in *at the main gate*>

'sign ,language *n* **1** a system of hand gestures used for communication (e g by the deaf) **2** unsystematic communication chiefly by gesture between people speaking different languages

sign off *vi* **1** to announce the end of a message, programme, or broadcast and finish broadcasting **2** to end a letter (e g with a signature) – **sign-off** *n*

sign on *vi* **1** to commit oneself to a job by signature or agreement <sign on *as a member of the crew*> **2** *Br* to register as unemployed, esp at an employment exchange

signor /'seen,yaw, ,-'-‖'siːn,jɔː, ,-'-/ *n, pl* **signors, signori** /-ri‖-rɪ/ an Italian man – used as a title equivalent to *Mr*

signora /seen'yawrə‖siːn'jɔːrə/ *n, pl* **signoras, signore** /-ray‖-reɪ/ an Italian married woman – used as a title equivalent to *Mrs* or as a generalized term of direct address

signorina /,seenyaw'reenə‖,siːnjɔː'riːnə/ *n, pl* **signorinas, signorine** /-nay‖-neɪ/ an unmarried Italian girl or woman – used as a title equivalent to *Miss*

sign out *vi* to indicate one's departure by signing in a register <signed out *of the hospital*> *~vt* to record or approve the release or withdrawal of <sign *books* out *of a library*>

[1]**'sign,post** /-,pohst‖-,pəʊst/ *n* a post (e g at a road junction) with signs on it to direct travellers

[2]**signpost** *vt* **1** to provide with signposts or guides **2** to indicate, mark

sign up *vi* to join an organization or accept an obligation by signing a contract; *esp* to enlist in the armed services *~vt* to cause to sign a contract

Sikh /seek‖siːk/ *n or adj* (an adherent) of a monotheistic religion of India marked by rejection of idolatry and caste [Hindi, lit., disciple] – **Sikhism** *n*

silage /'sielij‖'saɪlɪdʒ/ *n* fodder converted, esp in a silo, into succulent feed for livestock

[1]**silence** /'sieləns‖'saɪləns/ *n* **1** forbearance from speech or noise; muteness – often interjectional **2** absence of sound or noise; stillness **3** failure to mention a particular thing <*can't understand the government's ~ on such an important topic*> **4a** oblivion, obscurity <*promising writers who vanish into ~*> **b** secrecy

[2]**silence** *vt* **1** to put or reduce to silence; still **2** to restrain from expression; suppress **3** to cause (a gun, mortar, etc) to cease firing by return fire, bombing, etc

silencer /'sielənsə‖'saɪlənsə/ *n* **1** a silencing device for a small firearm **2** *chiefly Br* a device for deadening the noise of the exhaust gas release of an internal-combustion engine

silent /'sielənt‖'saɪlənt/ *adj* **1a** making no utterance; mute, speechless **b** disinclined to speak; not talkative **2** free from sound or noise; still **3a** endured without utterance <*~ grief*> **b** conveyed by refraining from reaction or comment; tacit <*~ assent*> **4** making no mention; uninformative <*history is ~ about this man*> **5** MUTE 3 <*~* b *in* doubt> **6** lacking spoken dialogue <*a ~ film*> – **silently** *adv*, **silentness** *n*

silent partner *n, chiefly NAm* SLEEPING PARTNER

[1]**silhouette** /,silooh'et‖,sɪluː'et/ *n* **1** a portrait in profile cut from dark material and mounted on a light background **2** the shape of a body as it appears against a lighter background [Etienne de *Silhouette* (1709-67), French controller-general of finances; prob so called fr his petty economies]

[2]**silhouette** *vt* to represent by a silhouette; *also* to project on a background like a silhouette

silica /'silikə‖'sɪlɪkə/ *n* silicon dioxide occurring in many rocks and minerals (e g quartz, opal, and sand)

silicate /'silikət, -kayt‖'sɪlɪkət, -keɪt/ *n* any of numerous insoluble often complex compounds that contain silicon and oxygen, constitute the largest class of minerals, and are used in building materials (e g cement, bricks, and glass)

silicon /'silikən‖'sɪlɪkən/ *n* a nonmetallic element that occurs, in combination with other elements, as the most abundant element next to oxygen in the earth's crust and is used esp in alloys

silicone /'silikohn‖'sɪlɪkəʊn/ *n* any of various polymeric organic silicon compounds obtained as oils, greases, or plastics and used esp for water-resistant and heat-resistant lubricants, varnishes, and electrical insulators

silicosis /sili'kohsis‖sɪlɪ'kəʊsɪs/ *n* a disease of

the lungs marked by hardening of the tissue and shortness of breath and caused by prolonged inhalation of silica dusts – **silicotic** *adj or n*

silk /silk‖sɪlk/ *n* **1** a fine continuous protein fibre produced by various insect larvae, usu for cocoons; *esp* a lustrous tough elastic fibre produced by silkworms and used for textiles **2** thread, yarn, or fabric made from silk filaments **3** a King's or Queen's Counsel **4** *pl* the cap and shirt of a jockey made in the registered racing colour of his/her stable **5** a silky material or filament (e g that produced by a spider)

silken /ˈsilkən‖ˈsɪlkən/ *adj* **1** made of silk **2** resembling silk, esp in softness or lustre

silk screen, silk-screen printing *n* a stencil process in which paint or ink is forced onto the material to be printed, through the meshes of a prepared silk or organdie screen – **silk-screen** *vt*

ˈsilkˌworm /-ˌwuhm‖-ˌwɜːm/ *n* a moth whose larva spins a large amount of strong silk in constructing its cocoon

silky /ˈsilki‖ˈsɪlkɪ/ *adj* **1** silken **2** having or covered with fine soft hairs, plumes, or scales – **silkily** *adv*, **silkiness** *n*

sill /sil‖sɪl/ *n* **1** a horizontal piece (e g a timber) that forms the lowest member or one of the lowest members of a framework or supporting structure (e g a window frame or door frame) **2** a horizontal sheet of intrusive igneous rock running between strata of other rocks

sillabub /ˈsiləˌbub‖ˈsɪləˌbʌb/ *n* (a) syllabub

silly /ˈsili‖ˈsɪlɪ/ *adj* **1a** showing a lack of common sense or sound judgment <*a very ~ mistake*> **b** trifling, frivolous <*a ~ remark*> **2** stunned, dazed <*knocked me ~*> **3** of or occupying a fielding position in cricket in front of and dangerously near the batsman <*~ mid-off*> – **sillily** *adv*, **silliness** *n*, **silly** *n or adv*

silo /ˈsieloh‖ˈsaɪləʊ/ *n, pl* **silos** **1** a trench, pit, or esp a tall cylinder (e g of wood or concrete) usu sealed to exclude air and used for making and storing silage **2** an underground structure for housing a guided missile

[1]**silt** /silt‖sɪlt/ *n* a deposit of sediment (e g at the bottom of a river) – **silty** *adj*

[2]**silt** *vb* to make or become choked or obstructed with silt – often + *up* – **siltation** *n*

silvan /ˈsilvən‖ˈsɪlvən/ *adj* sylvan

[1]**silver** /ˈsilvə‖ˈsɪlvə/ *n* **1** a white ductile and malleable metallic element that takes a very high degree of polish and has the highest thermal and electrical conductivity of any substance **2** silver as a commodity **3** coins made of silver or cupro-nickel **4** articles, esp tableware, made of or plated with silver; *also* cutlery made of other metals **5** a whitish grey colour **6** SILVER MEDAL

[2]**silver** *adj* **1** made of silver **2a** resembling silver, esp in having a white lustrous sheen **b** giving a soft, clear, ringing sound **c** eloquently persuasive <*a ~ tongue*> **3** consisting of or yielding silver <*~ ore*> **4** relating to or characteristic of silver **5** of or marking a 25th anniversary <*~ wedding*>

[3]**silver** *vt* **1** to cover with (a substance resembling) silver **2** to impart a silvery lustre or whiteness to – **silverer** *n*

ˌsilver ˈbirch *n* a common Eurasian birch with a silvery-white trunk

ˈsilverˌfish /-ˌfish‖-ˌfɪʃ/ *n* **1** any of various silvery fishes **2** any of various small wingless insects; *esp* one found in houses and sometimes injurious to sized paper (e g wallpaper) or starched fabrics

ˌsilver ˈmedal *n* a medal of silver awarded to one who comes second in a competition – **silver medallist** *n*

ˌsilver ˈpaper *n* paper with a coating or lamination resembling silver

ˌsilver ˈplate *n* **1** a plating of silver **2** tableware and cutlery of silver or a silver-plated metal

ˈsilverˌside /-ˌsied‖-ˌsaɪd/ *n, Br* a cut of beef from the outer part of the top of the leg below the aitchbone, that is boned and often salted

ˈsilverˌsmith /-ˌsmith‖-ˌsmɪθ/ *n* sby who works in silver

ˈsilverˌware /-ˌweə‖-ˌweə/ *n* SILVER PLATE 2

silvery /ˈsilv(ə)ri‖ˈsɪlv(ə)rɪ/ *adj* **1** having a soft clear musical tone **2** having the lustre or whiteness of silver **3** containing or consisting of silver – **silveriness** *n*

simian /ˈsimi·ən‖ˈsɪmɪən/ *adj or n* (of or resembling) a monkey or ape

similar /ˈsimilə‖ˈsɪmɪlə/ *adj* **1** marked by correspondence or resemblance, esp of a general kind <*~ but not identical*> **2** alike in 1 or more essential aspects <*no 2 signatures are exactly ~*> **3** differing in size but not in shape <*~ triangles*> – **similarly** *adv*, **similarity** *n*

simile /ˈsimili‖ˈsɪmɪlɪ/ *n* a figure of speech explicitly comparing 2 unlike things (e g in *cheeks like roses*)

similitude /siˈmilityoohd‖sɪˈmɪlɪtjuːd/ *n* (an instance of) correspondence in kind, quality, or appearance – fml

simmer /ˈsimə‖ˈsɪmə/ *vi* **1a** *of a liquid* to bubble gently below or just at the boiling point **b** *of food* to cook in a simmering liquid **2a** to develop, ferment <*ideas ~ing in the back of his mind*> **b** to be agitated by suppressed emotion <*~ with anger*> *~vt* to cook (food) in a simmering liquid

simmer down *vi* to become calm or less excited

simony /ˈsiməni, ˈsie-‖ˈsɪmənɪ, ˈsaɪ-/ *n* the buying or selling of a church office or ecclesiastical promotion [Late Latin *simonia*, fr *Simon* Magus, Samaritan sorcerer (Acts 8:9–24)] – **simoniac** *adj or n*, **simoniacal** *adj*

[1]**simper** /ˈsimpə‖ˈsɪmpə/ *vi* to smile in a foolish self-conscious manner *~vt* to say with a simper <*~ed her apologies*> – **simperer** *n*

[2]**simper** *n* a foolish self-conscious smile

[1]**simple** /ˈsimpl‖ˈsɪmpl/ *adj* **1a** free from guile or vanity; unassuming **b** free from elaboration or showiness; unpretentious <*wrote in a ~ style*> **2** of humble birth or lowly position <*a ~ farmer*> **3a** lacking intelligence; *esp* mentally retarded **b** lacking sophistication; naive **4a** sheer, unqualified <*the ~ truth of the matter*> **b** free of secondary complications <*a ~ fracture*> **c** *of a sentence* consisting of only 1 main clause and no subordinate clauses **d** composed essentially of 1 substance **e** not made up of many like units <*a ~ eye*> **5a** not subdivided into branches or leaflets **b** consisting of a single

carpel **c** *of a fruit* developing from a single ovary **6** not limited; unconditional <*a ~ obligation*> **7** readily understood or performed; straightforward <*a ~ task*> – **simpleness** *n*

[2]**simple** *n, archaic* a medicinal plant

ˌ**simple-ˈhearted** *adj* having a sincere and unassuming nature; artless

simple interest *n* interest paid or calculated on only the original capital sum of a loan

ˌ**simpleˈminded** /-ˈmiendid‖-ˈmaɪndɪd/ *adj* devoid of subtlety; unsophisticated; *also* mentally retarded – **simplemindedly** *adv*, **simplemindedness** *n*

simpleton /ˈsimplt(ə)n‖ˈsɪmplt(ə)n/ *n* sby lacking common sense or intelligence

simplicity /simˈplisəti‖sɪmˈplɪsətɪ/ *n* **1** the state or quality of being simple **2** lack of subtlety or penetration; naivety **3** freedom from affectation or guile; sincerity, straightforwardness **4a** directness of expression; clarity **b** restraint in ornamentation; austerity, plainness

simplify /ˈsimplifie‖ˈsɪmplɪfaɪ/ *vt* to make simple or simpler: e g **a** to reduce to basic essentials **b** to diminish in scope or complexity; streamline <*~ a manufacturing process*> **c** to make more intelligible; clarify ~*vi* to become simple or simpler – **simplifier** *n*, **simplification** *n*

simply /ˈsimpli‖ˈsɪmplɪ/ *adv* **1a** without ambiguity; clearly <*a ~ worded reply*> **b** without ornamentation or show <*~ furnished*> **c** without affectation or subterfuge; candidly **2a** solely, merely <*eats ~ to keep alive*> **b** without any question <*the concert was ~ marvellous*>

simulacrum /ˌsimyooˈlaykrəm‖ˌsɪmjʊˈleɪkrəm/ *n, pl* **simulacra** /-krə‖-krə/ *also* **simulacrums** an often superficial or misleading likeness of sthg; a semblance – fml

simulate /ˈsimyooˌlayt‖ˈsɪmjʊˌleɪt/ *vt* **1** to assume the outward qualities or appearance of, usu with the intent to deceive **2** to make a functioning model of (a system, device, or process) (e g by using a computer) – **simulator** *n*, **simulation** *n*

simultaneous /ˌsiməlˈtaynyəs, -ni·əs‖ˌsɪməlˈteɪnjəs, -nɪəs/ *adj* **1** existing, occurring, or functioning at the same time **2** satisfied by the same values of the variables <*~ equations*> – **simultaneously** *adv*, **simultaneousness, simultaneity** *n*

[1]**sin** /sin‖sɪn/ *n* **1a** an offence against moral or religious law or divine commandments **b** an action considered highly reprehensible <*it's a ~ to waste food*> **2** a state of estrangement from God – **sinless** *adj*, **sinlessly** *adv*, **sinlessness** *n*

[2]**sin** *vi* **-nn- 1** to commit a sin **2** to commit an offence – often + *against* <*writers who ~ against good taste*> – **sinner** *n*

[1]**since** /sins‖sɪns/ *adv* **1** continuously from then until now <*has stayed there ever ~*> **2** before now; ago <*should have done it long ~*> **3** between then and now; subsequently <*has ~ become rich*> ***USE*** + tenses formed with *to have*

[2]**since** *prep* in the period between (a specified past time) and now <*haven't met ~ 1973*>; from (a specified past time) until now <*it's a long time ~ breakfast*> – + present tenses and tenses formed with *to have*

[3]**since** *conj* **1** between now and the past time when <*has held 2 jobs ~ he left school*>; continuously from the past time when <*ever ~ he was a child*> **2** in view of the fact that; because <*more interesting, ~ rarer*>

sincere /sinˈsiə‖sɪnˈsɪə/ *adj* free from deceit or hypocrisy; honest, genuine <*~ interest*> – **sincerely** *adv*, **sincereness, sincerity** *n*

sine /sien‖saɪn/ *n* the trigonometric function that for an acute angle in a right-angled triangle is the ratio between the side opposite the angle and the hypotenuse

sinecure /ˈsinikyooə, ˈsie-‖ˈsɪnɪkjʊə, ˈsaɪ-/ *n* an office or position that provides an income while requiring little or no work

sine die /ˌsieni ˈdee·ay, ˈdie·ee, ˌsini‖ˌsaɪnɪ ˈdiːeɪ, ˈdaɪiː, ˌsɪnɪ/ *adv* without any future date being designated (e g for resumption) <*the meeting adjourned ~*> [Latin, without day]

sine qua non /ˌsini kway ˈnon, kwah ˈnohn, ˌsieni‖ˌsɪnɪ kweɪ ˈnɒn, kwɑː ˈnəʊn, ˌsaɪnɪ/ *n* an absolutely indispensable or essential thing [Late Latin, without which not]

sinew /ˈsinyooh‖ˈsɪnjuː/ *n* **1** a tendon; *also* one prepared for use as a cord or thread **2a** solid resilient strength; vigour **b** the chief means of support; mainstay – usu pl <*the ~s of political stability*> – **sinewy** *adj*

sinful /ˈsinf(ə)l‖ˈsɪnf(ə)l/ *adj* tainted with, marked by, or full of sin; wicked – **sinfully** *adv*, **sinfulness** *n*

sing /sing‖sɪŋ/ *vb* **sang** /sang‖sæŋ/, **sung** /sung‖sʌŋ/; **sung** *vi* **1a** to produce musical sounds by means of the voice **b** to utter words in musical notes and with musical inflections and modulations (as a trained or professional singer) **2** to make a shrill whining or whistling sound **3** to produce musical or melodious sounds **4** to buzz, ring <*a punch that made his ears ~*> **5** to make a loud clear utterance **6** to give information or evidence – slang ~ *vt* **1** to utter with musical inflections; *esp* to interpret in musical notes produced by the voice **2a** to relate or celebrate in verse **b** to express vividly or enthusiastically <*~ his praises*> **3** to chant, intone <*~ a requiem mass*> **4** to bring to a specified state by singing <*~s the child to sleep*> – **singable** *adj*, **singer** *n*

singe /sinj‖sɪndʒ/ *vt* **singeing; singed** to burn superficially or slightly; scorch; *esp* to remove the hair, down, or nap from, usu by brief exposure to a flame – **singe** *n*

Singhalese /ˌsing·gəˈleez‖ˌsɪŋgəˈliːz/ *n or adj, pl* **Singhalese** (a) Sinhalese

[1]**single** /ˈsing·gl‖ˈsɪŋgl/ *adj* **1a** not married **b** of the unmarried state **2** not accompanied by others; sole <*the ~ survivor of the disaster*> **3a** consisting of or having only 1 part or feature <*use double, not ~ thread*> **b** *of a plant or flower* having the normal number of petals or ray flowers **4** consisting of a separate unique whole; individual <*food is our most important ~ need*> **5** *of combat* involving only 2 people **6** of, suitable for, or involving only 1 person <*a ~ portion of food*> – **singleness** *n*, **singly** *adv*

[2]**single** *n* **1a** a single thing or amount; *esp* a single measure of spirits **b** a (young) unmarried adult <*a ~s club*> **2** a flower having the number of petals or ray flowers typical of the species

3 a single run scored in cricket **4** a gramophone record, esp of popular music, with a single short track on each side **5** *Br* a ticket bought for a trip to a place but not back again

[3]**single** *vt* to select or distinguish from a number or group – usu + *out*

ˌ**single-ˈbreasted** *adj* having a centre fastening with 1 row of buttons <*a ~ coat*>

ˌ**single ˈfile** *n* a line (e g of people) moving one behind the other

ˌ**single-ˈhanded** *adj* **1** performed or achieved by 1 person or with 1 on a side **2** working or managing alone or unassisted by others – **single-handed, single-handedly** *adv*, **single-handedness** *n*

ˌ**single-ˈminded** *adj* having a single overriding purpose – **single-mindedly** *adv*, **single-mindedness** *n*

ˈ**singles** *n, pl* **singles** a game (e g of tennis) with 1 player on each side

ˈ**singleˌstick** /-ˌstik‖-ˌstɪk/ *n* one-handed fighting or fencing with a wooden stick; *also* the stick used

singlet /ˈsing·glit‖ˈsɪŋglɪt/ *n, chiefly Br* VEST 1; *also* a similar garment worn by athletes

singleton /ˈsing·glt(ə)n‖ˈsɪŋglt(ə)n/ *n* **1** a card that is the only one of its suit in a dealt hand **2** an individual as opposed to a pair or group; *specif* an offspring born singly

singsong /ˈsingˌsong‖ˈsɪŋˌsɒŋ/ *n* **1** a voice delivery characterized by a monotonous cadence or rhythm or rising and falling inflection **2** *Br* a session of group singing

[1]**singular** /ˈsing·gyoolə‖ˈsɪŋgjʊlə/ *adj* **1a** of a separate person or thing; individual **b** of or being a word form denoting 1 person, thing, or instance **2** distinguished by superiority; exceptional <*a man of ~ attainments*> **3** not general <*a ~ proposition in logic*> **4** very unusual or strange; peculiar <*the ~ events leading up to the murder*> – **singularize** *vt*, **singularly** *adv*

[2]**singular** *n* the singular number, the inflectional form denoting it, or a word in that form

Sinhalese /ˌsinhəˈleez‖ˌsɪnhəˈliːz/ *n, pl* **Sinhalese 1** a member of the predominant people that inhabit Sri Lanka **2** the Indic language of the Sinhalese – **Sinhalese** *adj*

sinister /ˈsinistə‖ˈsɪnɪstə/ *adj* **1** (darkly or insidiously) evil or productive of vice **2** threatening evil or ill fortune; ominous **3** of or situated on the left side or to the left of sthg, esp in heraldry [Latin *sinistr-, sinister* on the left side, inauspicious] – **sinisterly** *adv*, **sinisterness** *n*

[1]**sink** /sink‖sɪnk/ *vb* **sank** /sangk‖sæŋk/, **sunk** /sungk‖sʌŋk/; **sunk** *vi* **1a** to go down below a surface (e g of water or a soft substance) **2a** to fall or drop to a lower place or level <sank *to his knees*> **b** to disappear from view <*a red sun* ~ing *slowly in the west*> **c** to take on a hollow appearance <*my cakes always ~ in the middle*> **3** to become deeply absorbed <sank *into a reverie*> **4** to go downwards in quality, state, condition, amount, or worth <sank *into apathy*> <~ing *spirits*> **5** to deteriorate physically <*the patient was* ~ing *fast and hadn't long to live*> ~ *vt* **1a** to cause to sink <*~ a battleship*> **b** to force down, esp into the ground **c** to cause (sthg) to penetrate <sank *the dagger into his chest*> **2** to engage (oneself) completely *in* <sank *himself in his work*> **3** to dig or bore (a well or shaft) in the earth **4** to overwhelm, defeat <*if we don't reach the frontier by midnight we're* sunk> **5** to pay no heed to; ignore, suppress <sank *their differences*> **6** to invest **7** *Br* to drink down <sank *a couple of pints*> – infml – **sinkable** *adj*

[2]**sink** *n* **1a** a cesspool **b** a sewer **c** a basin, esp in a kitchen, connected to a drain and usu a water supply for washing up **2** a place of vice or corruption **3a** a depression in which water (e g from a river) collects and becomes absorbed or evaporated **b** SINKHOLE 2 **4** a body or process that stores or dissipates sthg (e g energy); *specif* HEAT SINK

sinker /ˈsingkə‖ˈsɪŋkə/ *n* a weight for sinking a fishing line, seine, or sounding line

ˈ**sink ˌhole** /-ˌhohl‖-ˌhəʊl/ *n* **1** SINK 3a **2** a hollow, esp in a limestone region, that communicates with an underground cavern or passage

sink in *vi* **1** to enter a solid through the surface <*don't leave the ink to* sink in> **2** to become understood

ˈ**sinking ˌfund** /ˈsingking‖ˈsɪŋkɪŋ/ *n* a fund set up and added to for paying off the original capital sum of a debt when it falls due

Sino- /sienoh-‖saɪnəʊ-/ *comb form* **1** Chinese nation, people, or culture <Sino*phile*> **2** Chinese and <Sino-*Tibetan*>

sinology /sieˈnoləji, si-‖saɪˈnɒlədʒɪ, sɪ-/ *n* the study of the Chinese and esp of their language, literature, history, and culture – **sinologist** *n*, **sinological** *adj*

sinuous /ˈsinyoo·əs‖ˈsɪnjʊəs/ *adj* **1a** of or having a serpentine or wavy form; winding **b** lithe, supple <*dancers with a ~ grace*> **2** intricate, tortuous <*~ argumentation*> – **sinuously** *adv*, **sinuousness, sinuosity** *n*

sinus /ˈsienəs‖ˈsaɪnəs/ *n* a cavity, hollow: e g **a** a narrow passage by which pus is discharged from a deep abscess or boil **b(1)** any of several cavities in the skull that usu communicate with the nostrils and contain air **b(2)** a channel for blood from the veins **b(3)** a wider part in a body duct or tube (e g a blood vessel) **c** a cleft or indentation between adjoining lobes (e g of a leaf)

[1]**sip** /sip‖sɪp/ *vb* **-pp-** to drink (sthg) delicately or a little at a time – **sipper** *n*

[2]**sip** *n* (a small quantity imbibed by) sipping

[1]**siphon, syphon** /ˈsiefən‖ˈsaɪfən/ *n* **1a** a tube by which a liquid can be transferred up over the wall of a container to a lower level by using atmospheric pressure **b** a bottle for holding carbonated water that is driven out through a tube by the pressure of the carbon dioxide in the bottle, when a valve in the tube is opened **2** any of various tubular organs in animals, esp molluscs or arthropods

[2]**siphon, syphon** *vt* to convey, draw off, or empty (as if) by a siphon ~*vi* to pass or become conveyed (as if) by a siphon

sir /sə‖sə; *strong* suh‖sɜː/ *n* **1a** a man of rank or position **b** a man entitled to be addressed as *sir* – used as a title before the Christian name of a knight or baronet **2a** – used as a usu respectful form of address to a male **b** *cap* – used as a conventional form of address at the beginning of a letter

[1]**sire** /sie·ə‖saɪə/ *n* **1** the male parent of a (domestic) animal **2** *archaic* **2a** a father **b** a male ancestor **3** a man of rank or authority; *esp* a lord – used formerly as a title and form of address

[2]**sire** *vt* **1** to beget – esp with reference to a male domestic animal **2** to bring into being; originate

siren /ˈsierən‖ˈsaɪrən/ *n* **1** *often cap* any of a group of mythological partly human female creatures that lured sailors to destruction by their singing **2** a dangerously alluring or seductive woman; a temptress **3a** an apparatus producing musical tones by the rapid interruption of a current of air, steam, etc by a perforated rotating disc **b** a usu electrically operated device for producing a penetrating warning sound

sirloin /ˈsuhˌloyn‖ˈsɜːˌlɔɪn/ *n* a cut of beef from the upper part of the hind loin just in front of the rump [alteration of earlier *surloin*, fr Middle French *surlonge*, fr *sur* over + *loigne, longe* loin]

sirocco /siˈrokoh‖sɪˈrɒkəʊ/ *n, pl* **siroccos** **1** a hot dust-laden wind from the Libyan deserts that blows onto the N Mediterranean coast **2** a warm moist oppressive southeasterly wind in the same regions [Italian *scirocco, sirocco*, fr Arabic *sharq* east]

sirrah *also* **sirra** /ˈsirə‖ˈsɪrə/ *n, obs* – used as a form of address implying inferiority in the person addressed

sis /sis‖sɪs/ *n, chiefly NAm* SISTER 1, 5 – infml; used esp in direct address

sisal /ˈsiesl‖ˈsaɪsl/ *n* (a widely cultivated W Indian agave plant whose leaves yield) a strong white fibre used esp for ropes and twine

sissy /ˈsissi‖ˈsɪsɪ/ *n or adj* (a) cissy – **sissy** *adj*

[1]**sister** /ˈsistə‖ˈsɪstə/ *n* **1a** a female having the same parents as another person **b** HALF SISTER **2** *often cap* **2a** a member of a women's religious order; *specif* (the title given to) a Roman Catholic nun **b** a female fellow member of a Christian church **3** a woman related to another person by a common tie or interest (e g adherence to feminist principles) **4** *chiefly Br* a female nurse; *esp* one who is next in rank below a nursing officer and is in charge of a ward or a small department **5** a girl, woman – used esp in direct address; infml – **sisterly** *adj*

[2]**sister** *adj* related (as if) by sisterhood; essentially similar < ~ *ships*>

ˈ**sisterhood** /-hood‖-hʊd/ *n* **1** the relationship between sisters **2** a society of women bound by religious vows

ˈ**sister-in-ˌlaw** *n, pl* **sisters-in-law** **1** the sister of one's spouse **2** the wife of one's brother

[1]**sit** /sit‖sɪt/ *vb* **-tt-; sat** /sat‖sæt/ *vi* **1a** to rest on the buttocks or haunches < ~ *in a chair*> **b** to perch, roost **2** to occupy a place as a member of an official body < ~ *on the parish council*> **3** to be in session for official business <*visited London when Parliament was* ~ting> **4** to cover eggs for hatching **5a** to take up a position for being photographed or painted **b** to act as a model **6** to lie or hang relative to a wearer <*the collar* ~s *awkwardly*> **7** to lie, rest <*a kettle* ~ting *on the stove*> **8** to be situated <*the house* ~s *well back from the road*> **9** to remain inactive or unused <*the car just* ~s *in the garage all day*> **10** to take an examination **11** to baby-sit ~ *vt* **1** to cause to be seated; place on or in a seat **2** to sit on (eggs) **3** to keep one's seat on < ~ *a horse*> **4** *Br* to take part in (an examination) as a candidate – **sit on 1** to repress, squash **2** to delay action or decision concerning – **sit on one's hands** to fail to take action – **sit on the fence** to adopt a position of neutrality or indecision

[2]**sit** *n* an act or period of sitting

sitar /siˈtah‖sɪˈtɑː/ *n* an Indian lute with a long neck and a varying number of strings – **sitarist** *n*

sit back *vi* to relinquish one's efforts or responsibility

sitcom /ˈsitˌkom‖ˈsɪtˌkɒm/ SITUATION COMEDY

[1]**site** /siet‖saɪt/ *n* **1a** an area of ground that was, is, or will be occupied by a structure or set of structures (e g a building, town, or monument) <*an archaeological* ~> **b** an area of ground or scene of some specified activity <*caravan* ~> <*battle* ~> <*building* ~> **2** the place, scene, or point of sthg <*the* ~ *of the wound*>

[2]**site** *vt* to place on a site or in position; locate

ˈ**sit-ˌin** *n* a continuous occupation of a building by a body of people as a protest and means towards forcing compliance with demands

sit in *vi* **1** to participate as a visitor or observer – usu + *on* <sit in *on a group discussion*> **2** to stage a sit-in

sit out *vt* **1** to remain until the end of or the departure of <sit *the film* out> **2** to refrain from participating in

sitter /ˈsitə‖ˈsɪtə/ *n* **1** sby who sits (e g as an artist's model) **2** a baby-sitter

[1]**sitting** /ˈsiting‖ˈsɪtɪŋ/ *n* **1** a single occasion of continuous sitting (e g for a portrait or meal) **2** a batch of eggs for incubation **3** a session

[2]**sitting** *adj* **1** that is sitting <*a* ~ *hen*> **2** in office or actual possession <*the* ~ *member for Leeds East*> – **sitting pretty** in a highly favourable or satisfying position

ˌ**sitting** ˈ**duck** *n* an easy or defenceless target for attack, criticism, or exploitation

ˈ**sitting ˌroom** *n* a room, esp in a private house, used for recreation and relaxation

[1]**situate** /ˈsityooˌayt, ˈsichoo-, -ət‖ˈsɪtjʊˌeɪt, ˈsɪtʃʊ-, -ət/ *adj* having a site; located – fml

[2]**situate** /ˈsityooˌayt, ˈsichoo-‖ˈsɪtjʊˌeɪt, ˈsɪtʃʊ-/ *vt* to place in a site, situation, or category; locate

situated /ˈsityooˌaytid, ˈsichoo-‖ˈsɪtjʊˌeɪtɪd, ˈsɪtʃʊ-/ *adj* **1** located **2** supplied to the specified extent with money or possessions <*comfortably* ~> **3** being in the specified situation <*rather awkwardly* ~>

ˌ**situˈation** /ˌsityooˈaysh(ə)n, ˌsichoo-‖ˌsɪtjʊˈeɪʃ(ə)n, ˌsɪtʃʊ-/ *n* **1a** the way in which sthg is placed in relation to its surroundings **b** a locality <*a house in a windswept* ~> **2** position with respect to conditions and circumstances <*the military* ~ *remains obscure*> **3a** the circumstances at a particular moment; *esp* a critical or problematic state of affairs <*the* ~ *called for swift action*> **b** a particular (complicated) state of affairs at a stage in the action of a narrative or drama **4** a position of employment; a post –

chiefly fml *<found a ~ as a gardener>* – **situational** *adj*

situation comedy *n* a radio or television comedy series that involves the same basic cast of characters in a succession of connected or unconnected episodes

sit up *vi* **1a** to rise from a reclining to a sitting position **b** to sit with the back straight **2** to show interest, alertness, or surprise <*news that made him* sit up> **3** to stay up after the usual time for going to bed <sat up *to watch the late film*>

six /siks||sɪks/ *n* **1** (the number) 6 **2** the sixth in a set or series *<the ~ of spades>* **3** sthg having 6 parts or members or a denomination of 6: e g **3a** a shot in cricket that crosses the boundary before it bounces and so scores 6 runs **b** the smallest unit in a cub-scout or brownie- guide pack **c** *pl in constr, cap the* Common Market countries before 1973 – **six** *adj or pron*, **sixfold** *adj or adv* – **at sixes and sevens** in disorder, confused, or in a muddle

ˈsix-ˌshooter *n* a 6-chambered revolver

sixteen /ˌsikˈsteen||ˌsɪkˈstiːn/ *n* **1** (the number) 16 **2** *pl but sing in constr* a book format in which a folded sheet forms 16 leaves – **sixteen** *adj or pron*, **sixteenth** *adj or n*

sixteenth note /siksˈteenth||sɪksˈtiːnθ/ *n, NAm* a semiquaver

sixth /siksth||sɪksθ/ *adj or n* (of or being) number six in a countable series

ˈsixth ˌform *n* the highest section of a British secondary school – **sixth-former** *n*

ˌsixth ˈsense *n* a keen intuitive power viewed as analogous to the 5 physical senses

sixty /ˈsiksti||ˈsɪkstɪ/ *n* **1** (the number) 60 **2** *pl* the numbers 60-69; *specif* a range of temperatures, ages, or dates in a century characterized by those numbers – **sixtieth** *adj or n*, **sixty** *adj or pron*, **sixtyfold** *adj or adv*

sizable, sizeable /ˈsiezəbl||ˈsaɪzəbl/ *adj* fairly large; considerable – **sizableness** *n*, **sizably** *adv*

[1]**size** /siez||saɪz/ *n* **1a** physical magnitude, extent, or bulk; relative or proportionate dimensions **b** relative amount or number **c** bigness *<you should have seen the ~ of him>* **2** any of a series of graduated measures, esp of manufactured articles (e g of clothing), conventionally identified by numbers or letters *<a ~ 7 hat>* **3** *the* actual state of affairs – infml *<that's about the ~ of it>*

[2]**size** *vt* **1** to make in a particular size <*systems* ~d *to fit anyone's living room*> **2** to arrange or grade according to size or bulk

[3]**size** *n* any of various thick and sticky materials (e g preparations of glue, flour, varnish, or resins) used for filling the pores in surfaces (e g of paper, textiles, leather, or plaster) or for applying colour or metal leaf (e g to book edges or covers)

[4]**size** *vt* to cover, stiffen, or glaze (as if) with size

[5]**size** *adj* SIZED 1 – usu in combination <*a bite*-size *biscuit*>

sized /siezd||saɪzd/ *adj* **1** having a specified size or bulk – usu in combination <*a small*-sized *house*> **2** arranged or graded according to size

size up *vt* to form a judgment of

sizzle /ˈsizl||ˈsɪzl/ *vi* to make a hissing sound (as if) in frying – **sizzle** *n*, **sizzler** *n*

sjambok /ˈshambok||ˈʃæmbɒk/ *n* a whip of rhinoceros hide used esp in S Africa

[1]**skate** /skayt||skeɪt/ *n*, any of numerous rays that have greatly developed pectoral fins and many of which are important food fishes

[2]**skate** *n* **1a** ROLLER SKATE **b** ICE SKATE **2** a period of skating

[3]**skate** *vi* **1** to glide along on skates propelled by the alternate action of the legs **2** to glide or slide as if on skates **3** to proceed in a superficial manner ~*vt* to go along or through (a place) or perform (an action) by skating – **skater** *n*

ˈskateˌboard /-ˌbawd||-ˌbɔːd/ *n* a narrow board about 60cm (2ft) long mounted on roller-skate wheels – **skateboarder** *n*, **skateboarding** *n*

skedaddle /skiˈdadl||skɪˈdædl/ *vi* to run away; *specif* to disperse rapidly – often imper; infml

skeet /skeet||skiːt/ *n* trapshooting in which clay targets are hurled across the shooting range from traps on either side

skein /skayn||skeɪn/ *n* **1** a loosely coiled length of yarn or thread; HANK 1 **2** sthg suggesting the twists or coils of a skein; a tangle *<unravel the ~ of evidence>* **3** a flock of wildfowl (e g geese) in flight

skeleton /ˈskelitn||ˈskelɪtn/ *n* **1** a supportive or protective usu rigid structure or framework of an organism; *esp* the bony or more or less cartilaginous framework supporting the soft tissues and protecting the internal organs of a vertebrate (e g a fish or mammal) **2** sthg reduced to its bare essentials **3** an emaciated person or animal **4** a basic structural framework **5** a secret cause of shame, esp in a family – often in *skeleton in the cupboard* [Greek, neuter of *skeletos* dried up] – **skeleton** *adj*, **skeletonize** *vt*, **skeletonic** *adj*, **skeletal** *adj*

skeleton key *n* a key, esp one with most or all of the serrations absent, that is able to open many simple locks

skep /skep||skep/ *n* **1** a farm basket used esp in mucking out stables **2** a beehive (of twisted straw)

skeptic /ˈskeptik||ˈskeptɪk/ *n, chiefly NAm* a sceptic – **skeptical** *adj*, **skeptically** *adv*, **skepticism** *n*

[1]**sketch** /skech||sketʃ/ *n* **1** a preliminary study or draft; *esp* a rough often preliminary drawing representing the chief features of an object or scene **2** a brief description or outline *<gave a ~ of his personality>* **3a** a short discursive literary composition **b** a short musical composition, usu for piano **c** a short theatrical piece having a single scene; *esp* a comic variety act [Dutch *schets*, fr Italian *schizzo*, fr *schizzare* to splash]

[2]**sketch** *vt* to make a sketch, rough draft, or outline of ~*vi* to draw or paint a sketch – **sketcher** *n*

sketchy /ˈskechi||ˈsketʃɪ/ *adj* lacking completeness, clarity, or substance; superficial, scanty – **sketchily** *adv*, **sketchiness** *n*

[1]**skew** /skyooh||skjuː/ *vi* to take an oblique course; twist ~ *vt* **1** to cause to skew **2** to distort from a true value or symmetrical curve <~ed *statistical data*>

[2]**skew** *adj* **1** set, placed, or running obliquely **2**

more developed on one side or in one direction than another; not symmetrical – **skewness** *n*

3**skew** *n* a deviation from a straight line or symmetrical curve

'**skew,bald** /-,bawld||-,bɔːld/ *n or adj* (an animal) marked with spots and patches of white and another colour, esp not black

1**skewer** /'skyooh·ə||'skjuːə/ *n* **1** a long pin of wood or metal used chiefly to fasten a piece of meat together while roasting or to hold small pieces of food for grilling (e g for a kebab) **2** sthg like a meat skewer in form or function

2**skewer** *vt* to fasten or pierce (as if) with a skewer

,**skew-'whiff** /'wif||'wɪf/ *adj, Br* askew – infml

1**ski** /skee||skiː/ *n, pl* **skis** **1a** a long narrow strip usu of wood, metal, or plastic that curves upwards in front and is typically one of a pair used esp for gliding over snow **b** WATER SKI **2** a runner on a vehicle [Norwegian, fr Old Norse *skīth* stick of wood, ski]

2**ski** *vb* **skiing; skied** to glide (over) on skis as a way of travelling or as a recreation or sport – **skiable** *adj*, **skier** *n*

skibob /'skee,bob||'skiː,bɒb/ *n* a bicycle-like vehicle with short skis in place of wheels that is used for gliding downhill over snow by a rider wearing miniature skis for balance – **skibobber** *n*, **skibobbing** *n*

1**skid** /skid||skɪd/ *n* **1** a plank or log used to support or elevate a structure or object **2** a ship's fender **3** a device placed under a wheel to prevent its turning or used as a drag **4** the act of skidding; a slide **5** a runner used as part of the undercarriage of an aircraft **6** *pl* a road to defeat or downfall – in *hit the skids, on the skids*; infml – **skiddy** *adj*

2**skid** *vb* **-dd-** *vt* **1** to apply a brake or skid to **2** to haul along, slide, hoist, or store on skids ~*vi* *of a vehicle, wheel, driver, etc* to slip or slide, esp out of control – **skidder** *n*

'**skid-,lid** *n, Br* a motorcyclist's crash helmet – infml

'**skid,pan** /-,pan||-,pæn/ *n, chiefly Br* a slippery surface on which vehicle drivers may practise the control of skids

,**skid 'row** /roh||rəʊ/ *n, chiefly NAm* a district frequented by down-and-outs and alcoholics

skiff /skif||skɪf/ *n* a light rowing or sailing boat

skiffle /'skifl||'skɪfl/ *n* jazz or folk music played by a group and using nonstandard instruments or noisemakers (e g washboards or Jew's harps)

skilful, *NAm chiefly* **skillful** /'skilf(ə)l||'skɪlf(ə)l/ *adj* possessing or displaying skill; expert – **skilfully** *adv*

'**ski ,lift** *n* a power-driven conveyer consisting usu of a series of bars or seats suspended from an endless overhead moving cable and used for transporting skiers or sightseers up and down a long slope or mountainside

skill /skil||skɪl/ *n* **1** the ability to utilize one's knowledge effectively and readily **2** a developed aptitude or ability in a particular field [Old Norse *skil* distinction, knowledge]

skilled *adj* **1** having mastery of or proficiency in sthg (e g a technique or trade) **2** of, being, or requiring workers with skill and training in a particular occupation or craft

skillet /'skilit||'skɪlɪt/ *n* **1** *chiefly Br* a small saucepan usu having 3 or 4 legs and used for cooking on the hearth **2** *chiefly NAm* FRYING PAN

1**skim** /skim||skɪm/ *vb* **-mm-** *vt* **1a** to clear (a liquid) of floating matter < ~ *boiling syrup*> **b** to remove (e g film or scum) from the surface of a liquid **c** to remove cream from by skimming **d(1)** to remove the best or most accessible contents from **d(2)** to remove (the choicest part or members) from sthg; cream **2** to read, study, or examine cursorily and rapidly; *specif* to glance through (e g a book) for the chief ideas or the plot **3** to throw so as to ricochet along the surface of water **4** to pass swiftly or lightly over ~ *vi* **1** to glide lightly or smoothly along or just above a surface **2** to give a cursory glance or consideration *USE* (*vt 1b & 1d(2)*) often + *off*

2**skim** *n* **1** a thin layer, coating, or film **2** the act of skimming

3**skim** *adj* having the cream removed by skimming < ~ *milk*>

skimmer /'skimə||'skɪmə/ *n* **1** a flat perforated scoop or spoon used for skimming **2** any of several long-winged sea birds that feed by flying with the elongated lower part of the beak immersed in the sea

skimp /skimp||skɪmp/ *vt* to give insufficient or barely sufficient attention or effort to or money for ~*vi* to save (as if) by skimping sthg

skimpy /'skimpi||'skɪmpɪ/ *adj* inadequate in quality, size, etc; scanty <*a* ~ *meal*> – **skimpily** *adv*, **skimpiness** *n*

1**skin** /skin||skɪn/ *n* **1a** the external covering of an animal (e g a fur-bearing mammal or a bird) separated from the body, usu with its hair or feathers; pelt **b(1)** the pelt of an animal prepared for use as a trimming or in a garment <*it took 40* ~s *to make the coat*> **b(2)** a container (e g for wine or water) made of animal skin **2a** the external limiting layer of an animal body, esp when forming a tough but flexible cover **b** any of various outer or surface layers (e g a rind, husk, or film) <*a sausage* ~> **3** the life or welfare of a person – esp in *save one's skin* **4** a sheathing or casing forming the outside surface of a ship, aircraft, etc – **by the skin of one's teeth** by a very narrow margin – **under the skin** beneath apparent or surface differences; fundamentally

2**skin** *vb* **-nn-** *vt* **1a** to cover (as if) with skin **b** to heal over with skin **2a** to strip, scrape, or rub away an outer covering (e g the skin or rind) of **b** to strip or peel off like skin < ~ *the insulation from the wire*> **c** to cut, graze, or damage the surface of <*fell and* ~ned *his knee*> **3** to strip of money or property; fleece – infml ~*vi* to become covered (as if) with skin – usu + *over* <*the wound had* ~ned *over within a*

,**skin-'deep** *adj* **1** as deep as the skin **2** superficial <*beauty is only* ~>

'**skin ,flick** *n* a film characterized by nudity and explicit sexual situations – infml

'**skin,flint** /-,flint||-,flɪnt/ *n* a miser, niggard

'**skin,ful** /-,f(ə)l||-,f(ə)l/ *n* an ample or satisfying quantity, esp of alcoholic drink – infml

'skin ˌgame *n, NAm* a swindling game or trick

'skin ˌgraft *n* a piece of skin that is taken from one area to replace skin in a defective or damaged area – **skin grafting** *n*

'skinˌhead /-ˌhed‖-ˌhed/ *n* **1** a person whose hair is cut very short **2** any of a group of young British people with very short hair and a distinctive way of dressing

skinned /skind‖skɪnd/ *adj* having skin, esp of a specified kind – usu in combination <*dark*-skinned>

skinny /'skini‖'skɪnɪ/ *adj* very thin; lean, emaciated – infml – **skinniness** *n*

skint /skint‖skɪnt/ *adj, Br* penniless – infml [alteration of *skinned*, past participle of [2]*skin*]

ˌskin'tight /-'tiet‖-'taɪt/ *adj* extremely closely fitted to the body <~ *jeans*>

[1]**skip** /skip‖skɪp/ *vb* **-pp-** *vi* **1a(1)** to move or proceed with light leaps and bounds; gambol **a(2)** to swing a rope round the body from head to toe, making a small jump each time it passes beneath the feet **b** to rebound from one point or thing after another; ricochet **2** to leave hurriedly or secretly; abscond <~ped *out without paying his bill*> **3** to pass over or omit an interval, section, or step <*the story* ~s *to the present day*> ~ *vt* **1** to leave out (a step in a progression or series); omit **2** to cause to ricochet across a surface; skim <~ *a stone over a pond*> **3** to fail to attend <*decided to* ~ *church that Sunday*> **4** *chiefly NAm* to depart from quickly and secretly <~ped *town*> – infml

[2]**skip** *n* **1** a light bounding step or gait **2** an act of omission (e g in reading)

[3]**skip** *n* the captain of a side in some games (e g curling or bowls)

[4]**skip** *n* **1** SKEP 1 **2** a bucket or cage for carrying men and materials (e g in mining or quarrying) **3** a large open container for waste or rubble

[1]**skipper** *n* **1** the master of a fishing, small trading, or pleasure boat **2** the captain or first pilot of an aircraft **3** *Br* the captain of a sports team *USE* (*2&3*) infml [Dutch *schipper*, fr *schip* ship]

[2]**skipper** *vt* to act as skipper of (e g a boat)

skirl /skuhl‖skɜːl/ *vi or n* (to emit) the high shrill sound of a bagpipe

[1]**skirmish** /'skuhmish‖'skɜːmɪʃ/ *n* **1** a minor or irregular fight in war, usu between small outlying detachments **2** a brief preliminary conflict; *broadly* any minor or petty dispute

[2]**skirmish** *vi* to engage in a skirmish – **skirmisher** *n*

[1]**skirt** /skuht‖skɜːt/ *n* **1a(1)** a free-hanging part of a garment (e g a coat) extending from the waist down **a(2)** a garment or undergarment worn by women and girls that hangs from and fits closely round the waist **b** either of 2 usu leather flaps on a saddle covering the bars on which the stirrups are hung **c** a flexible wall containing the air cushion of a hovercraft **2** the borders or outer edge of an area or group – often pl with sing. meaning **3** a part or attachment serving as a rim, border, or edging **4** *Br* any of various usu membranous and gristly cuts of beef from the flank **5** a girl, woman – slang – **skirted** *adj*

[2]**skirt** *vt* **1** to extend along or form the border or edge of; border **2** to provide a skirt for **3** to go or pass round; *specif* to avoid through fear of difficulty, danger, or dispute <~ed *the minefield*> ~*vi* to be, lie, or move along an edge, border, or margin <~ *round the coast*> – **skirter** *n*

'skirting ˌboard *n, Br* a board, esp with decorative moulding, that is fixed to the base of a wall and that covers the joint of the wall and floor

skit /skit‖skɪt/ *n* a satirical or humorous story or sketch

skitter /'skitə‖'skɪtə/ *vi* **1a** to glide or skip lightly or swiftly **b** to skim along a surface **2** to twitch a fishing lure or baited hook through or along the surface of water ~*vt* to cause to skitter – **skitter** *n*

skittish /'skitish‖'skɪtɪʃ/ *adj* **1a** lively or frisky in behaviour; capricious **b** variable, fickle **2** easily frightened; restive <*a* ~ *horse*> – **skittishly** *adv*, **skittishness** *n*

skittle /'skitl‖'skɪtl/ *n* **1** *pl but sing in constr* any of various bowling games played with 9 pins and wooden balls or discs **2** a pin used in skittles

skittle out *vt* to dismiss (a batting side in cricket) for a low score

skive /skiev‖skaɪv/ *vt* to cut off (e g leather or rubber) in thin layers or pieces; pare ~*vi, Br* to evade one's work or duty, esp out of laziness; shirk – often + *off*; infml

[1]**skivvy** /'skivi‖'skɪvɪ/ *n, Br* a female domestic servant

[2]**skivvy** *vi, Br* to perform menial domestic tasks; act as a skivvy

skua /'skyooh·ə‖'skjuːə/ *n* any of several large dark-coloured seabirds of northern and southern seas that tend to harass weaker birds until they drop or disgorge the fish they have caught

skulduggery, skullduggery /skul'dugəri‖skʌl'dʌgərɪ/ *n* devious trickery; *esp* underhand or unscrupulous behaviour

skulk /skulk‖skʌlk/ *vi* **1** to move in a stealthy or furtive manner; slink **2** to hide or conceal oneself, esp out of cowardice or fear or for a sinister purpose; lurk – **skulker** *n*

skull /skul‖skʌl/ *n* **1** the skeleton of the head of a vertebrate animal forming a bony or cartilaginous case that encloses and protects the brain and chief sense organs and supports the jaws **2** the seat of understanding or intelligence; the brain – usu derog <*get that fact into your thick* ~!> – **skulled** *adj*

ˌskull and 'crossbones /'krosˌbohnz‖'krɒsˌbəʊnz/ *n, pl* **skulls and crossbones** a representation of a human skull over crossbones, usu used as a warning of danger to life

'skullˌcap /-ˌkap‖-ˌkæp/ *n* a closely fitting cap; *esp* a light brimless cap for indoor wear

skunk /skungk‖skʌŋk/ *n* **1a** any of various common black-and-white New World mammals that have a pair of anal glands from which a foul-smelling secretion is ejected **b** the fur of a skunk **2** a thoroughly obnoxious person – infml

[1]**sky** /skie‖skaɪ/ *n* **1** the upper atmosphere when seen as an apparent great vault over the earth; the firmament, heavens **2** HEAVEN 2 **3a** weather

as manifested by the condition of the sky <*a clear* ~> **b** climate

[2]**sky** *vt* **skied, skyed** *chiefly Br* to throw, toss, or hit (e g a ball) high in the air

ˌ**sky ˈblue** *adj or n* (of) the light blue colour of the sky on a clear day

ˈ**skyˌdiving** /-ˌdieving‖-ˌdaɪvɪŋ/ *n* jumping from an aeroplane and executing body manoeuvres while in free-fall before pulling the rip cord of a parachute – **sky diver** *n*

ˌ**sky-ˈhigh** *adv or adj* **1a** very high **b** to a high level or degree <*prices rose* ~> **2** to bits; apart – in *blow sthg sky-high*

ˈ**skyˌjack** /-ˌjak‖-ˌdʒæk/ *vt* to hijack (an aircraft) – **skyjacker** *n*

[1]ˈ**skyˌlark** /-ˌlahk‖-ˌlɑːk/ *n* a common largely brown Old World lark noted for its song, esp as uttered in vertical flight or while hovering

[2]**skylark** *vi* to act in a high-spirited or mischievous manner; frolic – **skylarker** *n*

ˈ**skyˌlight** /-ˌliet‖-ˌlaɪt/ *n* **1** the diffused and reflected light of the sky **2** a window or group of windows in a roof or ceiling

ˈ**skyˌline** /-ˌlien‖-ˌlaɪn/ *n* **1** the apparent juncture of earth and sky; the horizon **2** an outline (e g of buildings or a mountain range) against the background of the sky

[1]ˈ**skyˌrocket** /-ˌrokit‖-ˌrɒkɪt/ *n* [2]ROCKET 1a

[2]**skyrocket** *vi* to shoot up abruptly <*shares in copper are* ~ing>

ˈ**skyˌscraper** /-ˌskraypə‖-ˌskreɪpə/ *n* a many-storeyed building; *esp* one containing offices

ˈ**skyˌwriting** /-ˌrieting‖-ˌraɪtɪŋ/ *n* (the formation of) writing in the sky by means of a visible substance (e g smoke) emitted from an aircraft

slab /slab‖slæb/ *n* a thick flat usu large plate or slice (e g of stone, wood, or bread)

[1]**slack** /slak‖slæk/ *adj* **1** insufficiently prompt, diligent, or careful; negligent **2a** characterized by slowness, indolence, or languor <*a* ~ *pace*> **b** *of tide* flowing slowly; sluggish **3a** not taut; relaxed <*a* ~ *rope*> **b** lacking in usual or normal firmness and steadiness; lax <~ *muscles*> <~ *supervision*> **4** wanting in activity <*a* ~ *market*> – **slackly** *adv*, **slackness** *n*

[2]**slack** *vt* **1a** to be sluggish or negligent in performing or doing **b** to lessen, moderate <~ed *his pace as the sun grew hot*> **2** to release tension in; loosen **3a** to cause to abate or moderate **b** SLAKE 2 ~ *vi* **1** to be or become slack <*our enthusiasm* ~ed *off*> **2** to shirk or evade work or duty – **slacker** *n*

[3]**slack** *n* **1** cessation in movement or flow; *specif* SLACK WATER **2** a part of sthg (e g a sail or a rope) that hangs loose without strain **3** *pl* trousers, esp for casual wear **4** a lull or decrease in activity; a dull season or period

[4]**slack** *n* the finest particles of coal produced at a mine

slacken /ˈslakən‖ˈslækən/ *vb* **1** to make or become less active, rapid, or intense – often + *off* **2** to make or become slack

slack water *n* the period at the turn of the tide when there is no apparent tidal motion

slag /slag‖slæg/ *n* **1** waste matter from the smelting of metal ores; dross **2** the rough cindery lava from a volcano **3** *Br* a dirty slovenly (immoral) woman – slang

slain /slayn‖sleɪn/ *past part of* SLAY

slake /slayk‖sleɪk/ *vt* **1** to satisfy, quench <~ *your thirst*> **2** to cause (e g lime) to heat and crumble by treatment with water

slalom /ˈslahləm‖ˈslɑːləm/ *n* a skiing or canoeing race against time on a zigzag or wavy course between obstacles [Norwegian, lit., sloping track]

[1]**slam** /slam‖slæm/ *n* GRAND SLAM

[2]**slam** *n* a banging noise; *esp* one made by a door

[3]**slam** *vb* **-mm-** *vt* **1** to strike or beat vigorously; knock <~med *him about the head with a book*> **2** to shut forcibly and noisily; bang **3a** to put or throw down noisily and violently <~med *his books on the table and stomped out*> **b** to force into sudden and violent action <~ *on the brakes*> **4** to criticize harshly – infml ~ *vi* **1** to make a banging noise <*the door* ~med *to behind him*> **2** to move violently or angrily <*he* ~med *out of his office*> – infml

[1]**slander** /ˈslahndə‖ˈslɑːndə/ *n* **1** the utterance of false charges which do damage to another's reputation **2** a false defamatory oral statement [Old French *esclandre*, fr Late Latin *scandalum* stumbling block, offence – see SCANDAL] – **slanderous** *adj*, **slanderously** *adv*, **slanderousness** *n*

[2]**slander** *vt* to utter slander against – **slanderer** *n*

[1]**slang** /slang‖slæŋ/ *n* **1** language peculiar to a particular group: e g **1a** argot **b** JARGON 2 **2** informal usu spoken vocabulary that is composed typically of coinages, novel senses of words, and picturesque figures of speech – **slang** *adj*, **slangy** *adj*

[2]**slang** *vt* to abuse with harsh or coarse language ~ *vi* to use harsh or vulgar abuse

[1]**slant** /slahnt‖slɑːnt/ *vi* **1** to turn or incline from a horizontal or vertical line or a level **2** to take a diagonal course, direction, or path ~ *vt* **1** to give an oblique or sloping direction to **2** to interpret or present in accord with a particular interest; bias <*stories* ~ed *towards youth*> – **slantingly** *adv*

[2]**slant** *n* **1** a slanting direction, line, or plane; a slope <*placed the mirror at a* ~> **2** SOLIDUS 2 **3a** a particular or personal point of view, attitude, or opinion **b** an unfair bias or distortion (e g in a piece of writing) – **slant** *adj*, **slantways** *adv*, **slantwise** *adv or adj*

[1]**slap** /slap‖slæp/ *n* a quick sharp blow, esp with the open hand – **slap in the face** a rebuff, insult

[2]**slap** *vt* **-pp-** **1** to strike sharply (as if) with the open hand **2** to put, place, or throw with careless haste or force <~ *paint on a wall*>

[3]**slap** *adv* directly, smack <*landed* ~ *on top of a holly bush*>

ˌ**slap and ˈtickle** *n* playful lovemaking – infml; humor

ˌ**slap-ˈbang** *adv* **1** in a highly abrupt or forceful manner **2** precisely <~ *in the middle*> *USE* infml

ˈ**slapˌdash** /-ˌdash‖-ˌdæʃ/ *adj* haphazard, slipshod

slap down *vt* to restrain or quash the initiative of rudely or forcefully

ˈ**slapˌhappy** /-ˌhapi‖-ˌhæpɪ/ *adj* **1**

punch-drunk **2** irresponsibly casual <*the ~ state of our democracies* – Alistair Cooke> **3** buoyantly carefree; happy-go-lucky

ˈslapˌstick /-ˌstik‖-ˌstɪk/ *n* **1** a wooden device that makes a loud noise when used by an actor to strike sby **2** comedy stressing farce and horseplay; knockabout comedy – **slapstick** *adj*

ˈslap-ˌup *adj, chiefly Br* marked by lavish consumption or luxury – infml

[1]slash /slash‖slæʃ/ *vt* **1a** to cut with violent usu random sweeping strokes **b** to make (one's way) (as if) by cutting down obstacles **2** LASH 1 **3** to cut slits in (e g a garment) so as to reveal an underlying fabric or colour **4** to criticize cuttingly **5** to reduce drastically; cut ~ *vi* **1** to cut or hit recklessly or savagely **2** *esp of rain* to fall hard and slantingly – **slasher** *n*

[2]slash *n* **1** the act of slashing; *also* a long cut or stroke made (as if) by slashing **2** an ornamental slit in a garment **3** *chiefly Br* an act of urinating – vulg

[1]slat /slat‖slæt/ *n* **1** a thin narrow flat strip, esp of wood or metal (e g a lath, louvre, or stave) **2** [1]SLOT 1a – **slat** *adj*

[2]slat *vt* **-tt-** to make or equip with slats

[1]slate /slayt‖sleɪt/ *n* **1** a piece of slate rock used as roofing material **2** a fine-grained metamorphic rock consisting of compressed clay, shale, etc and easily split into (thin) layers **3** a tablet of material, esp slate, used for writing on **4** dark bluish or greenish grey **5** *NAm* a list of candidates for nomination or election – **slate** *adj*, **slatelike** *adj*, **slaty** *adj*

[2]slate *vt* **1** to cover with slate **2** *NAm* to designate for action or appointment

[3]slate *vt, chiefly Br* to criticize or censure severely – infml

slattern /ˈslatən‖ˈslætən/ *n* an untidy slovenly woman; a slut

[1]slaughter /ˈslawtə‖ˈslɔːtə/ *n* **1** the act of killing; *specif* the butchering of livestock for market **2** killing of many people (e g in battle); carnage

[2]slaughter *vt* **1** to kill (animals) for food **2** to kill violently or in large numbers – **slaughterer** *n*

ˈslaughterˌhouse /-ˌhows‖-ˌhaʊs/ *n* an establishment where animals are killed for food

[1]slave /slayv‖sleɪv/ *n* **1** sby held in servitude as the property of another **2** sby who is dominated by a specified thing or person <*a ~ to drink*> **3** a device whose actions are controlled by and often mimic those of another **4** a drudge <*women who are merely kitchen ~s*> [Old French *esclave*, fr Medieval Latin *sclavus*, fr *Sclavus* Slav; fr the reduction to slavery of many Slavonic peoples] – **slave** *adj*

[2]slave *vi* **1** to work like a slave; toil **2** to traffic in slaves

ˈslave ˌdriver *n* **1** an overseer of slaves **2** a harsh taskmaster

[1]slaver /ˈslavə‖ˈslævə/ *vi* to drool, slobber

[2]slaver /ˈslayvə‖ˈsleɪvə/ *n* **1** sby engaged in the slave trade **2** a ship used in the slave trade

slavery /ˈslayv(ə)ri‖ˈsleɪv(ə)rɪ/ *n* **1** drudgery, toil **2a** the state of being a slave **b** the practice of owning slaves

ˈslave ˌtrade *n* traffic in slaves; *esp* the transportation of Negroes to America for profit

Slavic /ˈslahvik, ˈslavik‖ˈslɑːvɪk, ˈslævɪk/ *adj* *or n* Slavonic – **Slavicist** *n*, **Slavist** *n*

slavish /ˈslayvish‖ˈsleɪvɪʃ/ *adj* **1** (characteristic) of a slave; *esp* abjectly servile **2** obsequiously imitative; devoid of originality **3** *archaic* despicable, base – **slavishly** *adv*, **slavishness** *n*

[1]Slavonic /sləˈvonik‖sləˈvɒnɪk/ *adj* (characteristic) of the Slavs

[2]Slavonic *n* a branch of the Indo-European language family containing Bulgarian, Czech, Polish, Russian, etc

slay /slay‖sleɪ/ *vt* **slew** /slooh‖sluː/; **slain** /slayn‖sleɪn/ **1** to kill violently or with great bloodshed; slaughter **2** to affect overpoweringly (e g with awe or delight); overwhelm – infml – **slayer** *n*

sleazy /ˈsleezi‖ˈsliːzɪ/ *adj* squalid and disreputable – **sleaziness** *n*

[1]sled /sled‖sled/ *n, chiefly NAm* [2]SLEDGE

[2]sled *vb* **-dd-** *chiefly NAm* to sledge – **sledder** *n*

[1]sledge /slej‖sledʒ/ *n* a sledgehammer

[2]sledge *n* **1** a vehicle with runners that is pulled by reindeer, horses, dogs, etc and is used esp over snow or ice **2** *Br* a toboggan

[3]sledge *vb, chiefly Br vi* to ride or be conveyed in a sledge ~*vt* to transport on a sledge

ˈsledgeˌhammer /-ˌhamə‖-ˌhæmə/ *n* a large heavy hammer that is wielded with both hands

[1]sleek /sleek‖sliːk/ *vt* to slick

[2]sleek *adj* **1a** smooth and glossy as if polished <~ *dark hair*> **b** having a smooth well-groomed look <*a ~ cat*> **c** having a well fed or flourishing appearance **2** excessively or artfully suave; ingratiating **3** elegant, stylish – **sleeken** *vt*, **sleekly** *adv*, **sleekness** *n*

[1]sleep /sleep‖sliːp/ *n* **1** the natural periodic suspension of consciousness that is essential for the physical and mental well-being of higher animals **2** a sleeplike state: e g **2a** torpor **b** a state marked by a diminution of feeling followed by tingling <*his foot went to ~*> **c** the state of an animal during hibernation **d** death – euph <*put a cat to ~*> **3** a period spent sleeping <*need a good long ~*> – **sleeplike** *adj*

[2]sleep *vb* **slept** /slept‖slept/ *vi* **1** to rest in a state of sleep **2** to be in a state (e g of quiescence or death) resembling sleep **3** to have sexual relations – + *with* or *together*; infml ~ *vt* **1** to get rid of or spend in sleep <~ *away the hours*> <~ *off a headache*> **2** to provide sleeping accommodation for <*the boat ~s 6*> **3** to be slumbering in <slept *the sleep of the dead*> – poetic – **sleep on** to consider (sthg) fully before discussing again the next day – **sleep rough** SLEEP OUT 1

sleep around *vi* to be sexually promiscuous – infml

sleeper /ˈsleepə‖ˈsliːpə/ *n* **1** a timber, concrete, or steel transverse support to which railway rails are fixed **2** SLEEPING CAR **3** a ring or stud worn in a pierced ear to keep the hole open **4** *chiefly NAm* sby or sthg unpromising or unnoticed that suddenly attains prominence or value – infml

sleep in *vi* **1** LIVE IN **2** to sleep late, either intentionally or accidentally

ˈsleeping ˌbag /ˈsleeping‖ˈsliːpɪŋ/ *n* a large thick envelope or bag of warm material for sleeping in esp when camping

ˈsleeping ˌcar *n* a railway carriage divided

into compartments having berths for sleeping
ˌsleeping ˈpartner *n* a partner who takes no active part or an unknown part in the running of a firm's business
ˈsleeping ˌpill *n* a drug in the form of a tablet or capsule that is taken to induce sleep
sleeping policeman *n* a hump or ramp in a road, intended to slow vehicles to a low speed
ˈsleeping ˌsickness *n* a serious disease that is prevalent in much of tropical Africa, is marked by fever and protracted lethargy, and is caused by either of 2 trypanosomes and transmitted by tsetse flies
ˈsleepless /-lis||-lɪs/ *adj* **1** not able to sleep **2** unceasingly active – **sleeplessly** *adv*, **sleeplessness** *n*
sleep out *vi* **1** to sleep out of doors **2** LIVE OUT
ˈsleepˌwalker /-ˌwawkə||-ˌwɔːkə/ *n* a somnambulist – **sleepwalk** *vi*
sleepy /ˈsleepi||ˈsliːpɪ/ *adj* **1a** ready to fall asleep **b** (characteristic) of sleep **2** lacking alertness; sluggish, lethargic **3** sleep-inducing – **sleepily** *adv*, **sleepiness** *n*
ˈsleepyˌhead /-ˌhed||-ˌhed/ *n* a sleepy person – humor
[1]**sleet** /sleet||sliːt/ *n* precipitation in the form of partly frozen rain, or snow and rain falling together – **sleety** *adj*
[2]**sleet** *vi* to send down sleet
sleeve /sleev||sliːv/ *n* **1** a part of a garment covering the arm **2** a tubular machine part designed to fit over another part **3** a paper or often highly distinctive cardboard covering that protects a gramophone record when not in use – **sleeved** *adj*, **sleeveless** *adj* – **up one's sleeve** held secretly in reserve
[1]**sleigh** /slay||sleɪ/ *n* [2]SLEDGE 1
[2]**sleigh** *vi* to drive or travel in a sleigh
ˌsleight of ˈhand *n* **1** manual skill and dexterity in conjuring or juggling **2** adroitness in deception
slender /ˈslendə||ˈslendə/ *adj* **1a** gracefully slim **b** small or narrow in circumference or width in proportion to length or height **2a** flimsy, tenuous <*a ~ hope*> **b** limited or inadequate in amount; meagre <*a man of ~ means*> – **slenderly** *adv*, **slenderness** *n*
sleuth /sloohth||sluːθ/ *vi or n* (to act as) a detective – infml [short for *sleuthhound* bloodhound, fr Middle English, fr *sleuth* track (fr Old Norse *slōth*) + *hound*]
[1]**slew** /slooh||sluː/ *past of* SLAY
[2]**slew** *vt* to turn or twist (sthg) about a fixed point that is usu the axis ~ *vi* **1** to turn, twist, or swing about **2** to skid – **slew** *n*
[3]**slew** *n*, *NAm* a large number or quantity – infml
[1]**slice** /slies||slaɪs/ *n* **1a** a thin broad flat piece cut from a usu larger whole <*a ~ of ham*> **b** a wedge-shaped piece (e g of pie or cake) **2** an implement with a broad blade used for lifting, turning, or serving food <*a fish ~*> **3** (a flight of) a ball that deviates from a straight course in the direction of the dominant hand of the player propelling it **4a** a portion, share <*a ~ of the profits*> **b** a part or section detached from a larger whole
[2]**slice** *vt* **1** to cut through (as if) with a knife <*~ a melon in 2*> **2** to cut into slices <*~d bread*> **3** to hit (a ball) so that a slice results ~ *vi* to slice sthg – **sliceable** *adj*, **slicer** *n*
[1]**slick** /slik||slɪk/ *vt* to make sleek or smooth
[2]**slick** *adj* **1** superficially plausible; glib **2a** characterized by suave or wily cleverness **b** deft, skilful **3** *of a tyre* having no tread **4** *chiefly NAm* smooth, slippery – **slickly** *adv*, **slickness** *n*
[3]**slick** *n* (a patch of water covered with) a smooth film of crude oil
slicker /ˈslikə||ˈslɪkə/ *n*, *NAm* an artful crook; a swindler – infml
[1]**slide** /slied||slaɪd/ *vb* **slid** /slid||slɪd/ *vi* **1a** to move in continuous contact with a smooth surface **b** to glide over snow or ice (e g on a toboggan) **2** to slip or fall by loss of grip or footing **3** to pass quietly and unobtrusively; steal **4** to take an undirected course; drift <*let his affairs ~*> **5** to pass by smooth or imperceptible gradations <*the economy* slid *from recession to depression*> ~ *vt* **1** to cause to glide or slip **2** to place or introduce unobtrusively or stealthily <slid *the bill into his hand*> – **slider** *n*
[2]**slide** *n* **1a** an act or instance of sliding **b** a portamento **2** a sliding part or mechanism: e g **2a** a U-shaped section of tube in the trombone that is pushed out and in to produce notes of different pitch **b** a moving piece of a mechanism that is guided by a part along which it slides **3** a landslide, avalanche **4a(1)** a track or slope suitable for sliding or tobogganing **a(2)** a chute with a slippery surface down which children slide in play **b** a channel or track down or along which sthg is slid **5a** a flat piece of glass on which an object is mounted for examination using a light microscope **b** a photographic transparency on a small plate or film suitably mounted for projection **6** *Br* a hair-slide
ˈslide ˌrule *n* an instrument consisting in its simple form of a ruler with a central slide both of which are graduated in such a way that the addition of lengths corresponds to the multiplication of numbers
sliding scale /ˈslieding||ˈslaɪdɪŋ/ *n* a flexible scale (e g of fees or subsidies) adjusted to the needs or income of individuals
[1]**slight** /sliet||slaɪt/ *adj* **1a** having a slim or frail build **b** lacking strength or bulk; flimsy **c** trivial **d** not serious or involving risk; minor <*caught a ~ chill*> **2** small of its kind or in amount; scanty, meagre – **slightly** *adv*, **slightness** *n*
[2]**slight** *vt* **1** to treat as slight or unimportant <*~ed my efforts at reform*> **2** to treat with disdain or pointed indifference; snub **3** *NAm* to perform or attend to carelessly or inadequately
[3]**slight** *n* **1** an act of slighting **2** a humiliating affront
[1]**slim** /slim||slɪm/ *adj* **-mm- 1** of small or narrow circumference or width, esp in proportion to length or height **2** slender in build **3** scanty, slight <*a ~ chance of success*> – **slimly** *adv*, **slimness** *n*
[2]**slim** *vb* **-mm-** *vt* to cause to be or appear slender <*a style that ~s the waist*> ~*vi* to become thinner (e g by dieting)
[1]**slime** /sliem||slaɪm/ *n* **1** soft moist soil or clay;

esp viscous mud **2** a viscous or glutinous substance; *esp* mucus or a mucus-like substance secreted by slugs, catfish, etc

[2]**slime** *vt* to smear or cover with slime

slimy /ˈsliemi‖ˈslaımı/ *adj* **1** of or resembling slime; viscous; *also* covered with or yielding slime **2** characterized by obsequious flattery; offensively ingratiating **3** *chiefly NAm* vile, offensive *USE* (*2&3*) infml – **slimily** *adv*, **sliminess** *n*

[1]**sling** /sling‖slıŋ/ *vt* **slung** /slung‖slʌŋ/ **1** to cast with a careless and usu sweeping or swirling motion; fling <slung *the coat over her shoulder*> **2** to throw (e g a stone) with a sling **3** *Br* to cast forcibly and usu abruptly <*was* slung *out of the team for misconduct*> – infml – **slinger** *n*

[2]**sling** *n* an act of slinging or hurling a stone or other missile

[3]**sling** *n* **1** a device that gives extra force to a stone or other missile thrown by hand and usu consists of a short strap that is looped round the missile, whirled round, and then released at 1 end **2a** a usu looped line used to hoist, lower, or carry sthg (e g a rifle); *esp* a bandage suspended from the neck to support an arm or hand **b** a rope attached to a mast which supports a yard **c** a device (e g a rope net) for enclosing material to be hoisted by a tackle or crane

[4]**sling** *vt* **slung** /slung‖slʌŋ/ to place in a sling for hoisting or lowering

[5]**sling** *n* a drink made of whisky, brandy, or esp gin with water and sugar

ˈ**sling,shot** /-ˌshot‖-ˌʃɒt/ *n*, *NAm* a catapult

[1]**slink** /slingk‖slıŋk/ *vi* **slunk** /slungk‖slʌŋk/ *also* **slinked** **1** to go or move stealthily or furtively (e g in fear or shame); steal *vi* **2** to move in a graceful provocative manner

[2]**slink** *n* (the flesh or skin of) the prematurely born young (e g a calf) of an animal

[1]**slip** /slip‖slıp/ *vb* **-pp-** *vi* **1a** to move with a smooth sliding motion **b** to move quietly and cautiously; steal **2** *of time* to elapse, pass **3a** to slide out of place or away from a support or one's grasp <*I didn't break the vase, it just* ~ped*!*> **b** to slide on or down a slippery surface <~ *on the stairs*> **4** to get speedily *into* or *out of* clothing <~ *into his coat*> **5** to fall off from a standard or accustomed level by degrees; decline ~ *vt* **1** to cause to move easily and smoothly; slide **2a** to free oneself from <*the dog* ~ped *his collar*> **b** to escape from (one's memory or notice) **3** to put (a garment) on hurriedly **4a** to let loose from a restraining leash or grasp **b** to cause to slip open; release, undo <~ *a knot*> **c** to let go of **d** to detach (an anchor) instead of bringing it on board **5a** to insert, place, or pass quietly or secretly **b** to give or pay on the sly <~ped *him a fiver*> **6** to give birth to prematurely; abort – used with reference to an animal **7** to dislocate <~ped *his shoulder*> **8** to transfer (a stitch) from one needle to another in knitting without working a stitch – **slippage** *n*

[2]**slip** *n* **1** a sloping ramp extending out into the water to serve as a place for landing, repairing, or building ships **2** *the* act or an instance of eluding or evading <*gave his pursuer the* ~> **3a** a mistake in judgment, policy, or procedure; a blunder **b** an inadvertent and trivial fault or error <*a* ~ *of the tongue*> **4** a leash so made that it can be quickly unfastened **5a** the act or an instance of slipping <*a* ~ *on the ice*> **b** (a movement producing) a small geological fault **c** a fall from some level or standard **6a** a women's sleeveless undergarment with shoulder straps that resembles a light dress **b** a case into which sthg is slipped; *specif* a pillowcase **7** a disposition or tendency to slip easily **8** any of several fielding positions in cricket that are close to the batsman and just to the (off) side of the wicketkeeper

[3]**slip** *n* **1** a small shoot or twig cut for planting or grafting; a scion **2a** a long narrow strip of material (e g paper or wood) **b** a small piece of paper; *specif* a printed form **3** a young and slim person <*a mere* ~ *of a girl*>

[4]**slip** *vt* **-pp-** to take cuttings from (a plant); divide into slips

[5]**slip** *n* a semifluid mixture of clay and water used by potters (e g for coating or decorating ware)

ˈ**slip,knot** /-ˌnot‖-ˌnɒt/ *n* **1** RUNNING KNOT **2** a knot that can be untied by pulling

[1]ˈ**slip-,on** *n* a slip-on shoe

[2]**slip-on** *adj*, *esp of a garment* easily slipped on or off

ˌ**slipped** ˈ**disc** /slipt‖slıpt/ *n* a protrusion of 1 of the cartilage discs that normally separate the spinal vertebrae, producing pressure on spinal nerves and usu resulting in intense pain, esp in the region of the lower back

slipper /ˈslipə‖ˈslıpə/ *n* a light shoe that is easily slipped on the foot; *esp* a flat-heeled shoe that is worn while resting at home

slippery /ˈslip(ə)ri‖ˈslıp(ə)rı/ *adj* **1a** causing or tending to cause sthg to slide or fall <~ *roads*> **b** tending to slip from the grasp **2** not to be trusted; shifty – **slipperiness** *n*

slippy /ˈslipi‖ˈslıpı/ *adj* slippery – **be/look slippy** *chiefly Br* to be quick; hurry up – infml

slipshod /ˈslip,shod‖ˈslıp,ʃɒd/ *adj* careless, slovenly <~ *reasoning*>

[1]ˈ**slip,stream** /-ˌstreem‖-ˌstriːm/ *n* **1** a stream of fluid (e g air or water) driven backwards by a propeller **2** an area of reduced air pressure and forward suction immediately behind a rapidly moving vehicle **3** sthg that sweeps one along in its course

[2]**slipstream** *vi* to drive or ride in a slipstream and so gain the advantage of reduced air resistance (e g in a bicycle race)

ˈ**slip-,up** *n* a mistake, oversight

slip up *vi* to make a mistake; blunder

ˈ**slip,way** /-ˌway‖-ˌweı/ *n* a slip (on which ships are built)

[1]**slit** /slit‖slıt/ *vt* **-tt-; slit** **1** to make a slit in **2** to cut or tear into long narrow strips – **slitter** *n*

[2]**slit** *n* a long narrow cut or opening – **slit** *adj*, **slitless** *adj*

slither /ˈslidhə‖ˈslıðə/ *vi* **1** to slide unsteadily, esp (as if) on a slippery surface **2** to slip or slide like a snake ~*vt* to cause to slide – **slithery** *adj*

[1]**sliver** /ˈslivə‖ˈslıvə/ *n* a small slender piece cut, torn, or broken; a splinter

[2]**sliver** *vt* to cut or break into slivers ~*vi* to become split into slivers; splinter

slivovitz /ˈslivəvits, ˈslee-, -vich‖ˈslıvəvıts, ˈsliː-, -vıtʃ/ *n* a dry usu colourless plum brandy

[Serbo-Croatian *šljivovica*, fr *šljiva, sliva* plum]

slob /slob‖slɒb/ *n* a slovenly or uncouth person – infml – **slobbish** *adj*

[1]**slobber** /ˈslobə‖ˈslɒbə/ *vi* **1** to let saliva dribble from the mouth; drool **2** to express emotion effusively and esp oversentimentally – often + *over* ~*vt* to smear (as if) with food or saliva dribbling from the mouth <*the baby* ~ed *his bib*> – **slobberer** *n*

[2]**slobber** *n* **1** saliva drooled from the mouth **2** oversentimental language or conduct – **slobbery** *adj*

sloe /sloh‖sləʊ/ *n* (the small dark spherical astringent fruit of) the blackthorn

sloe gin *n* a liqueur consisting of gin in which sloes have been steeped

[1]**slog** /slog‖slɒg/ *vb* **-gg-** *vt* **1** to hit (e g a cricket ball or an opponent in boxing) hard and often wildly **2** to plod (one's way) with determination, esp in the face of difficulty ~ *vi* **1** to walk, move, or travel slowly and laboriously <~ged *through the snow*> **2** to work laboriously; toil – **slogger** *n*

[2]**slog** *n* **1** a hard and often wild blow **2** persistent hard work **3** an arduous march or tramp

slogan /ˈslohgən‖ˈsləʊgən/ *n* **1** a phrase used to express and esp make public a particular view, position, or aim **2** a brief catchy phrase used in advertising or promotion [alteration of earlier *slogorn*, fr Scottish Gaelic *sluagh-ghairm* army cry]

sloop /sloohp‖slu:p/ *n* a fore-and-aft rigged sailing vessel with 1 mast and a single foresail

[1]**slop** /slop‖slɒp/ *n* **1** thin tasteless drink or liquid food **2** liquid spilt or splashed **3a** waste food or a thin gruel fed to animals **b** liquid household refuse (e g dirty water or urine) **4** mawkish sentiment in speech or writing; gush *USE* (*1&3*) usu pl with sing. meaning

[2]**slop** *vb* **-pp-** *vt* **1a** to cause (a liquid) to spill over the side of a container **b** to splash or spill liquid on **2** to serve messily <~ *soup into a bowl*> **3** to feed slops to <~ *the pigs*> ~ *vi* **1** to tramp through mud or slush **2** to become spilled or splashed **3** to show mawkish sentiment; gush **4** to slouch, flop <*spends his whole day* ~ping *around the house*>

ˈ**slop ˌbasin** *n, Br* a bowl for receiving the dregs left in tea or coffee cups at table

[1]**slope** /slohp‖sləʊp/ *vi* **1** to take an oblique course **2** to lie at a slant; incline ~*vt* to cause to incline or slant

[2]**slope** *n* **1** a piece of inclined ground **2** upward or downward inclination or (degree of) slant **3** GRADIENT 1

slope off *vi* to go away, esp furtively; sneak off – infml

slop out *vi, of a prisoner* to empty slops from a chamber pot

sloppy /ˈslopi‖ˈslɒpɪ/ *adj* **1a** wet so as to splash; slushy <*a* ~ *racetrack*> **b** wet or smeared (as if) with sthg slopped over **2** slovenly, careless <*she's a* ~ *dresser*> **3** disagreeably effusive <~ *sentimentalism*> – **sloppily** *adv*, **sloppiness** *n*

[1]**slosh** /slosh‖slɒʃ/ *n* **1** slush **2** the slap or splash of liquid **3** *chiefly Br* a heavy blow; a bash – infml

[2]**slosh** *vi* **1** to flounder or splash through water, mud, etc **2** to flow with a splashing motion <*water* ~ed *all round him*> ~ *vt* **1** to splash (sthg) about in liquid **2** to splash (a liquid) about, on, or into sthg **3** to make wet by splashing **4** *chiefly Br* to hit, beat <~ed *him on the head with a bucket*> – infml

sloshed /slosht‖slɒʃt/ *adj* drunk – infml

[1]**slot** /slot‖slɒt/ *n* **1a** a narrow opening, groove, or passage; a slit **b** a passage through an aerofoil directing air rearwards from the lower to the upper surface so as to increase lift and delay stalling **2** a place or position in an organization or sequence; a niche

[2]**slot** *vb* **-tt-** *vt* **1** to cut a slot in **2** to place in or assign to a slot – often + *in* or *into* <~ted *some reading in as he waited*> ~*vi* to be fitted (as if) by means of a slot or slots <*a do-it-yourself bookcase that* ~s *together in seconds*>

sloth /slohth‖sləʊθ/ *n* **1** disinclination to action or work; indolence **2** any of several slow-moving tree-dwelling mammals that inhabit tropical forests of S and Central America, hang face upwards from the branches, and feed on leaves, shoots, and fruits – **slothful** *adj*, **slothfully** *adv*, **slothfulness** *n*

ˈ**slot maˌchine** *n* **1** a machine (e g for selling cigarettes, chocolate, etc or for gambling) whose operation is begun by dropping a coin or disc into a slot **2** *chiefly NAm* FRUIT MACHINE

[1]**slouch** /slowch‖slaʊtʃ/ *n* **1** a lazy, incompetent, or awkward person **2** a gait or posture characterized by stooping or excessive relaxation of body muscles – **slouchy** *adj*

[2]**slouch** *vi* **1** to sit, stand, or walk with a slouch <~ed *behind the wheel*> **2** to hang down limply; droop ~*vt* to cause to droop <~ed *his shoulders*>; *specif* to turn down one side of (a hat brim) – **sloucher** *n*

slouch hat *n* a soft usu felt hat with a wide flexible brim

[1]**slough** /slow‖slaʊ/ *n* **1a** a place of deep mud or mire **b** a swamp **2** a state of dejection <*a* ~ *of self-pity*>

[2]**slough** *also* **sluff** /sluf‖slʌf/ *n* **1** the cast-off skin of a snake **2** a mass of dead tissue separating from an ulcer

[3]**slough** *also* **sluff** /sluf‖slʌf/ *vi* **1** to become shed or cast off **2** to cast off a skin **3** to separate in the form of dead tissue from living tissue ~ *vt* **1** to cast off (e g a skin or shell) **2** to get rid of or discard as irksome or objectionable – usu + *off*

sloven /ˈsluvn‖ˈslʌvn/ *n* one habitually negligent of neatness or cleanliness, esp in personal appearance

slovenly /ˈsluvnli, ˈslo-‖ˈslʌvnlɪ, ˈslɒ-/ *adj* **1** untidy, esp in personal appearance or habits **2** lazily slipshod; careless – **slovenliness** *n*

[1]**slow** /sloh‖sləʊ/ *adj* **1a** lacking in intelligence; dull **b** naturally inert or sluggish <*a* ~ *imagination*> **2a** lacking in readiness, promptness, or willingness <*a shop with* ~ *service*> **b** not quickly aroused or excited <*was* ~ *to anger*> **3a** flowing or proceeding with little or less than usual speed <*traffic was* ~> **b** exhibiting or marked by retarded speed <*he moved with* ~ *deliberation*> **c** low, feeble <~ *fire*>

4 requiring a long time; gradual <*a ~ convalescence*> **5a** having qualities that hinder or prevent rapid movement <*a ~ putting green*> **b** (designed) for slow movement <*learner drivers should keep to the ~ lane*> **6** registering a time earlier than the correct one <*his clock is ~*> **7** lacking in liveliness or variety; boring – **slowish** *adj*, **slowly** *adv*, **slowness** *n*

[2]**slow** *adv* in a slow manner; slowly

[3]**slow** *vb* to make or become slow or slower – often + *down* or *up*

slowcoach /'sloh,kohch‖'sləʊ,kəʊtʃ/ *n* one who thinks or acts slowly

,slow 'motion *n* a technique in filming which allows an action to be shown as if it is taking place unnaturally slowly, which usu involves increasing the number of frames exposed in a given time and then projecting the film at the standard speed – **slow-motion** *adj*

'slow,worm /-,wuhm‖-,wɜːm/ *n* a legless European lizard popularly believed to be blind

sludge /sluj‖slʌdʒ/ *n* **1** (a deposit of) mud or ooze **2** a slimy or slushy mass, deposit, or sediment – **sludgy** *adj*

[1]**slue** /slooh‖sluː/ *vb, chiefly NAm* [2]SLEW

[2]**slue** *n, chiefly NAm* a slew

[1]**slug** /slug‖slʌg/ *n* any of numerous slimy elongated chiefly ground-living gastropod molluscs that are found in most damp parts of the world and have no shell or only a rudimentary one [Middle English *slugge* sluggard, of Scandinavian origin]

[2]**slug** *n* **1** a lump, disc, or cylinder of material (e g plastic or metal): e g **1a** a bullet – slang **b** *NAm* a disc for insertion in a slot machine; *esp* one used illegally instead of a coin **2a** a strip of metal thicker than a printer's lead **b** a line of type cast as 1 piece **3** *chiefly NAm* a quantity of spirits that can be swallowed at a single gulp – slang

[3]**slug** *n* a heavy blow, esp with the fist – infml

[4]**slug** *vt* **-gg-** to hit hard (as if) with the fist or a bat – infml – **slugger** *n*

sluggard /'slugəd‖'slʌgəd/ *n* a lazy person or animal – **sluggard** *adj*, **sluggardly** *adj*

sluggish /'slugish‖'slʌgɪʃ/ *adj* **1** averse to activity or exertion; indolent; *also* torpid **2** slow to respond (e g to stimulation or treatment) <*a ~ engine*> **3** markedly slow in movement, flow, or growth – **sluggishly** *adv*, **sluggishness** *n*

[1]**sluice** /sloohs‖sluːs/ *n* **1a** an artificial passage for water (e g in a millstream) fitted with a valve or gate for stopping or regulating flow **b** a body of water pent up behind a floodgate **2** a dock gate **3** a stream flowing through a floodgate **4** a long inclined trough (e g for washing ores or gold-bearing earth)

[2]**sluice** *vt* **1** to draw off by or through a sluice **2a** to wash with or in water running through or from a sluice **b** to drench with a sudden vigorous flow; flush ~ *vi* to pour (as if) from a sluice

'sluice,way /-,way‖-,weɪ/ *n* an artificial channel into which water is let by a sluice

[1]**slum** /slum‖slʌm/ *n* **1** a poor overcrowded run-down area, esp in a city – often pl with sing. meaning **2** a squalid disagreeable place to live – **slummy** *adj*

[2]**slum** *vi* **-mm-** **1** to live in squalor or on very slender means – often + *it* **2** to amuse oneself by visiting a place on a much lower social level; *also* to affect the characteristics of a lower social class – **slummer** *n*

[1]**slumber** /'slumbə‖'slʌmbə/ *vi* **1** to sleep **2** to lie dormant or latent <*a ~ing volcano*> – **slumberer** *n*

[2]**slumber** *n* sleep – often pl with sing. meaning

slumbrous, slumberous /'slumbrəs‖'slʌmbrəs/ *adj* **1** heavy with sleep; sleepy <*~ eyelids*> **2** inducing sleep; soporific **3** marked by or suggestive of a state of sleep or lethargy; drowsy

[1]**slump** /slump‖slʌmp/ *vi* **1a** to fall or sink abruptly <*morale ~ed with news of the defeat*> **b** to drop down suddenly and heavily; collapse <*~ed to the floor*> **2** to assume a drooping posture or carriage; slouch **3** to go into a slump <*sales ~ed*>

[2]**slump** *n* a marked or sustained decline, esp in economic activity or prices

slung /slung‖slʌŋ/ *past of* SLING

slunk /slungk‖slʌŋk/ *past of* SLINK

[1]**slur** /sluh‖slɜː/ *vb* **-rr-** *vi* to pass *over* without due mention, consideration, or emphasis <*~red over certain facts*> ~ *vt* **1** to perform (successive notes of different pitch) in a smooth or connected manner **2** to run together, omit, or pronounce unclearly (words, sounds, etc)

[2]**slur** *n* **1** (a curved line connecting) notes to be sung to the same syllable or performed without a break **2** a slurring manner of speech

[3]**slur** *vb* **-rr-** *vt* **1** to cast aspersions on; disparage **2** to make indistinct; obscure ~ *vi of a sheet being printed* to slip so as to cause a slur

[4]**slur** *n* **1a** an insulting or disparaging remark; a slight **b** a shaming or degrading effect; a stigma **2** a blurred spot in printed matter

slurp /sluhp‖slɜːp/ *vb* to eat or drink noisily or with a sucking sound – **slurp** *n*

slurry /'sluri‖'slʌri/ *n* a watery mixture of insoluble matter (e g mud, manure, or lime)

slush /slush‖slʌʃ/ *n* **1** partly melted or watery snow **2** liquid mud; mire **3** worthless and usu oversentimental material (e g literature) – **slushy** *adj*

'slush ,fund *n, chiefly NAm* a fund for bribing (public) officials or carrying on corrupting propaganda

slut /slut‖slʌt/ *n* **1** a dirty slovenly woman **2** an immoral woman; *esp* a prostitute – **sluttish** *adj*, **sluttishly** *adv*, **sluttishness** *n*

sly /slie‖slaɪ/ *adj* **slier** *also* **slyer; sliest** *also* **slyest** **1a** clever in concealing one's ends or intentions; furtive **b** lacking in integrity and candour; crafty **2** humorously mischievous; roguish <*gave me a ~ glance*> – **slyly** *adv*, **slyness** *n* – **on the sly** in a manner intended to avoid notice; secretly

[1]**smack** /smak‖smæk/ *n* (a slight hint of) a characteristic taste, flavour, or aura

[2]**smack** *vi* – **smack of** to have a trace or suggestion of <*a proposal that* smacks of *treason*>

[3]**smack** *vt* **1** to slap smartly, esp in punishment **2** to strike or put down with the sound of a smack **3** to open (the lips) with a sudden sharp sound, esp in anticipation of food or drink ~ *vi* to make or give a smack

[4]**smack** *n* **1** a sharp blow, esp from sthg flat; a

slap **2** a noisy parting of the lips **3** a loud kiss **4** *chiefly NAm* heroin – slang

5**smack** *adv* squarely and with force; directly – infml <*drove ~ into the car parked opposite*>

6**smack** *n* a small inshore fishing vessel

smacker /ˈsmakə‖ˈsmækə/ *n, Br* **1** 1POUND 2 **2** 4SMACK 3 *USE* infml

1**small** /smawl‖smɔːl/ *adj* **1a** having relatively little size or dimensions **b** immature, young <~ *children*> **2a** little in quantity, value, amount, etc **b** made up of few individuals or units <*a ~ audience*> **3** lower-case **4** lacking in strength <*a ~ voice*> **5a** operating on a limited scale <*a ~ farmer*> **b** minor in power, influence, etc <*only has a ~ say in the matter*> **c** limited in degree <*paid ~ heed to his warning*> **d** humble, modest <*a ~ beginning*> **6** of little consequence; trivial <*a ~ matter*> **7a** mean, petty **b** reduced to a humiliating position – **smallish** *adj*, **smallness** *n*

2**small** *adv* **1** in or into small pieces **2** in a small manner or size <*write ~*>

3**small** *n* **1** a part smaller and esp narrower than the remainder; *specif* the narrowest part of the back **2** *pl, Br* small articles of underwear – infml; used with reference to laundry

ˈ**small** ˌ**ad** /ad‖æd/ *n, Br* a classified advertisement

ˈ**small** ˌ**arm** *n* a firearm fired while held in the hands – usu pl

ˌ**small** ˈ**change** *n* coins of low denomination

ˈ**small** ˌ**fry** *n pl in constr* young or insignificant people or things; *specif* children – **small-fry** *adj*

ˈ**small**ˌ**holding** /-ˌhohlding‖-ˌhəʊldɪŋ/ *n, chiefly Br* a small agricultural farm – **smallholder** *n*

small hours *n pl* the hours immediately following midnight

ˌ**small in**ˈ**testine** *n* the part of the intestine that lies between the stomach and colon, consists of duodenum, jejunum, and ileum, secretes digestive enzymes, and is the chief site of the absorption of digested nutrients

ˌ**small-**ˈ**minded** *adj* **1** having narrow interests or outlook; narrow-minded **2** characterized by petty meanness – **small-mindedly** *adv*, **small-mindedness** *n*

smallpox /ˈsmawlˌpoks‖ˈsmɔːlˌpɒks/ *n* an acute infectious feverish virus disease characterized by skin eruption with pustules, sloughing, and scar formation

ˈ**small** ˌ**talk** *n* light or casual conversation; chitchat

ˌ**small-**ˈ**time** *adj* insignificant in operation and status; petty – **small-timer** *n*

smarm /smahm‖smɑːm/ *vt* **1** to plaster, smear <~ *on a thick layer of make-up*> **2** to make (one's way) by obsequiousness or fawning *USE* infml

smarmy /ˈsmahmi‖ˈsmɑːmɪ/ *adj* marked by flattery or smugness; unctuous – infml

1**smart** /smaht‖smɑːt/ *vi* **1** to be (the cause or seat of) a sharp pain; *also* to feel or have such a pain **2** to feel or endure mental distress <~*ing from a rebuke*> **3** to pay a heavy penalty <*would have to ~ for this foolishness*>

2**smart** *adj* **1** making one smart; causing a sharp stinging <*gave him a ~ blow with the ruler*> **2** forceful, vigorous **3** brisk, spirited <*walking at a ~ pace*> **4a** mentally alert; bright **b** clever, shrewd <*a ~ investment*> **5** witty, persuasive <*a ~ talker*> **6a** neat or stylish in dress or appearance <*a ~ new coat of paint*> **b** characteristic of or frequented by fashionable society <*a ~ restaurant*> – **smartly** *adv*, **smartness** *n*

3**smart** *adv* in a smart manner; smartly

4**smart** *n* **1** a smarting pain; *esp* a stinging local pain **2** poignant grief or remorse <*was not the sort to get over ~*s – Sir Winston Churchill>

ˈ**smart** ˌ**alec**, **smart aleck** /ˈalik‖ˈælɪk/ *n* an arrogant person with pretensions to knowledge or cleverness – derog – **smart-alecky, smart-alec** *adj*

smarten /ˈsmaht(ə)n‖ˈsmɑːt(ə)n/ *vt* to make smart or smarter; *esp* to spruce ~*vi* to smarten oneself *USE* usu + *up*

1**smash** /smash‖smæʃ/ *vt* **1** to break in pieces by violence; shatter **2a** to drive, throw, or hit violently, esp causing breaking or shattering; crash **b** to hit (e g a ball) with a forceful stroke, specif a smash **3** to destroy utterly; wreck – often + *up* ~ *vi* **1** to crash *into*; collide <~ed *into a tree*> **2** to become wrecked **3** to go to pieces suddenly under collision or pressure **4** to execute a smash (e g in tennis)

2**smash** *n* **1a(1)** a smashing blow, attack, or collision <*a 5-car ~*> **a(2)** the result of smashing; *esp* a wreck due to collision **b** a forceful overhand stroke (e g in tennis or badminton) **2** the condition of being smashed or shattered **3a** the action or sound of smashing **b** utter collapse; ruin; *esp* bankruptcy **4** SMASH HIT – infml

3**smash** *adv* with a resounding crash

ˌ**smash-and-**ˈ**grab** *n or adj, chiefly Br* (a robbery) committed by smashing a shop window and snatching the goods on display

smashed *adj* extremely drunk – infml

smasher /ˈsmashə‖ˈsmæʃə/ *n, chiefly Br* sby or sthg very fine or attractive – infml

ˌ**smash** ˈ**hit** *n* an outstanding success <*his latest play is a ~*>

smashing /ˈsmashing‖ˈsmæʃɪŋ/ *adj* extremely good; excellent – infml – **smashingly** *adv*

ˈ**smash-**ˌ**up** *n* a serious accident; a crash <*a 10-car ~ on the M1*>

smattering /ˈsmat(ə)ring‖ˈsmæt(ə)rɪŋ/ *n* a piecemeal or superficial knowledge *of*

1**smear** /smiə‖smɪə/ *n* **1** a mark or blemish made (as if) by smearing a substance **2** material smeared on a surface; *also* material taken or prepared for microscopic examination by smearing on a slide **3** a usu unsubstantiated accusation <*took the article as a personal ~*>

2**smear** *vt* **1a** to spread with sthg sticky, greasy, or viscous; daub **b** to spread esp thickly over a surface **2a** to stain or dirty (as if) by smearing **b** to sully, besmirch; *specif* to blacken the reputation of **3** to obscure or blur (as if) by smearing ~*vi* to become smeared – **smearer** *n*, **smeary** *adj*

1**smell** /smel‖smel/ *vb* **smelled, smelt** /smelt‖smelt/ *vt* **1** to perceive the odour of (as if) by use of the sense of smell **2** to detect or become aware of by instinct <*I could ~ trouble*> ~ *vi* **1** to exercise the sense of smell **2a(1)** to have a usu specified smell <*these clothes* ~ *damp*> **a(2)** to have a characteristic aura; be suggestive *of* <*reports of survivors seemed to* ~ *of truth*> **b** to have an offensive smell; stink – **smeller** *n* – **smell a rat** to have a suspicion of sthg wrong

[2]**smell** *n* **1a** the process, function, or power of smelling **b** the one of the 5 basic physical senses by which the qualities of gaseous or volatile substances in contact with certain sensitive areas in the nose are interpreted by the brain as characteristic odours **2** an odour **3** a pervading quality; an aura **4** an act or instance of smelling

'smelling ,salts /'smeling||'smelɪŋ/ *n pl but sing or pl in constr* a usu scented preparation of ammonium carbonate and ammonia water sniffed as a stimulant to relieve faintness

smell out *vt* **1** to detect or discover (as if) by smelling <*the dog* smelt out *the criminal*> **2** to fill with an esp offensive smell <*the cigarettes* smelt out *the room*>

smelly /'smeli||'smelɪ/ *adj* having an esp unpleasant smell

[1]**smelt** /smelt||smelt/ *n* any of various small fishes that closely resemble the trouts and have delicate oily flesh

[2]**smelt** *vt* **1** to melt (ore) to separate the metal **2** to separate (metal) by smelting – **smelter** *n*, **smeltery** *n*

[1]**smile** /smiel||smaɪl/ *vi* **1** to have or assume a smile **2a** to look with amusement or scorn <~d *at his own weakness*> **b** to bestow approval <*Heaven seemed to* ~ *on her labours*> **c** to appear pleasant or agreeable <*a green and* smiling *landscape*> ~ *vt* **1** to affect with or change by smiling <~d *away his embarrassment*> **2** to utter or express with a smile <~d *her thanks*> – **smiler** *n*, **smilingly** *adv*

[2]**smile** *n* **1** a change of facial expression in which the corners of the mouth curve slightly upwards and which expresses esp amusement, pleasure, approval, or sometimes scorn **2** a pleasant or encouraging appearance – **smiley** *adj*

smirch /smuhch||smɜːtʃ/ *vt* **1** to make dirty or stained, esp by smearing **2** to bring discredit or disgrace on – **smirch** *n*

smirk /smuhk||smɜːk/ *vi* to smile in a fatuous or scornful manner – **smirk** *n*, **smirkingly** *adv*

smite /smiet||smaɪt/ *vb* **smote** /smoht||sməʊt/; **smitten** /'smit(ə)n||'smɪt(ə)n/, **smote** *vt* **1** to strike sharply or heavily, esp with (an implement held in) the hand **2** to kill, injure, or damage by smiting **3a** to attack or afflict suddenly and injuriously <smitten *by disease*> **b** to have a sudden powerful effect on; afflict <smitten *with grief*>; *specif* to attract strongly <smitten *by her beauty*> **4** to cause to strike <smote *his hand against his side*> ~*vi* to beat down or come forcibly *on* or *upon* – **smiter** *n*

smith /smith||smɪθ/ *n* **1** a worker in metals; *specif* a blacksmith **2** a maker – often in combination <*gun*smith>

smithereens /,smidhə'reenz, '--,-||,smɪðə'riːnz, '--,-/ *n pl* fragments, bits <*the house was blown to* ~ *by the explosion*> [Irish Gaelic *smidirīn*, diminutive of *smiodar* fragment]

smithy /'smidhi||'smɪðɪ/ *n* the workshop of a smith

[1]**smock** /smok||smɒk/ *n* a light loose garment resembling a smock frock, esp in being gathered into a yoke; *also* SMOCK FROCK

[2]**smock** *vt* to ornament (e g a garment) with smocking

smock frock *n* an outer garment worn chiefly by farm labourers, esp in the 18th and 19th c, and resembling a long loose shirt gathered into a yoke

smocking /'smoking||'smɒkɪŋ/ *n* a decorative embroidery or shirring made by gathering cloth in regularly spaced round or diamond-shaped tucks held in place with ornamental stitching

smog /smog||smɒg/ *n* a fog made heavier and darker by smoke and chemical fumes [blend of *smoke* and *fog*] – **smoggy** *adj*, **smogless** *adj*

[1]**smoke** /smohk||sməʊk/ *n* **1a** the gaseous products of burning carbon-containing materials made visible by the presence of small particles of carbon **b** a suspension of particles in a gas **2** fumes or vapour resembling smoke **3** sthg of little substance, permanence, or value **4** sthg that obscures **5a** sthg (e g a cigarette) that is smoked **b** an act or spell of smoking esp tobacco – **smokelike** *adj*

[2]**smoke** *vi* **1** to emit smoke **2** to (habitually) inhale and exhale the fumes of burning plant material, esp tobacco ~ *vt* **1a** to fumigate **b** to drive out or away by smoke <~ *a fox from its den*> **2** to colour or darken (as if) with smoke <~d *glasses*> **3** to cure (e g meat or fish) by exposure to smoke, traditionally from green wood or peat **4** to inhale and exhale the smoke of (e g cigarettes)

smoke out *vt* **1** SMOKE 1b **2** to bring to public view or knowledge

smoker /'smohkə||'sməʊkə/ *n* **1** sby who regularly or habitually smokes tobacco **2** a carriage or compartment in which smoking is allowed

'smoke ,screen *n* **1** a screen of smoke to hinder observation **2** sthg designed to conceal, confuse, or deceive

'smoke,stack /-,stak||-,stæk/ *n* a chimney or funnel through which smoke and gases are discharged, esp from a locomotive or steamship

'smoking ,jacket /'smohking||'sməʊkɪŋ/ *n* a loosely fitting jacket formerly worn by men while smoking

smoky *also* **smokey** /'smohki||'sməʊkɪ/ *adj* **1** emitting smoke, esp in large quantities <*a* ~ *fire*> **2a** having the characteristics or appearance of smoke **b** suggestive of smoke, esp in flavour, smell, or colour **3a** filled with smoke **b** made black or grimy by smoke – **smokily** *adv*, **smokiness** *n*

smolder /'smohldə||'sməʊldə/ *vi, NAm* to smoulder

smooch /smoohch||smuːtʃ/ *vi* to kiss, caress – infml – **smoocher** *n*, **smoochy** *adj*

[1]**smooth** /smoohdh||smuːð/ *adj* **1a** having a continuous even surface **b** free from hair or hairlike projections **c** *of liquid* of an even consistency; free from lumps **d** giving no resistance to sliding; frictionless **2** free from difficulties or obstructions **3** even and uninterrupted in movement or flow **4a** equable, composed <*a* ~ *disposition*> **b** urbane, courteous **c** excessively

and often artfully suave; ingratiating <*a* ~ *salesman*> **5** not sharp or acid <*a* ~ *sherry*> – **smooth** *adv*, **smoothly** *adv*, **smoothness** *n*

[2]smooth *vt* **1** to make smooth **2** to free from what is harsh or disagreeable **3** to dispel or alleviate (e g enmity or perplexity) – often + *away* or *over* **4** to free from obstruction or difficulty **5** to press flat – often + *out* **6** to cause to lie evenly and in order – often + *down* <~ed *down his hair*> ~*vi* to become smooth – **smoother** *n*

[3]smooth *n* a smooth or agreeable side or aspect <*take the rough with the* ~>

smoothie, smoothy /ˈsmoohdhi‖ˈsmuːðɪ/ *n* a person, esp a man, who behaves with suave and often excessive self-assurance – infml

smorgasbord /ˈsmawgəsˌbawd, ˈsmuh-‖ˈsmɔːgəsˌbɔːd, ˈsmɜː-/ *n* a luncheon or supper buffet offering a variety of foods and dishes (e g hors d'oeuvres, hot and cold meats, smoked and pickled fish, cheeses, salads, and relishes) [Swedish *smörgåsbord*, fr *smörgås* open sandwich + *bord* table]

smote /smoht‖sməʊt/ *past of* SMITE

[1]smother /ˈsmudhə‖ˈsmʌðə/ *n* **1** a dense cloud of gas, smoke, dust, etc **2** a confused mass of things; a welter – **smothery** *adj*

[2]smother *vt* **1** to overcome or kill with smoke or fumes **2a** to kill by depriving of air **b** to overcome or discomfort (as if) through lack of air **c** to suppress (a fire) by excluding oxygen **3a** to suppress expression or knowledge of; conceal <~ *a yawn*> **b** to prevent the growth or development of; suppress **4a** to cover thickly; blanket <*snow* ~ed *the trees and hedgerows*> **b** to overwhelm <*aunts who always* ~ed *him with kisses*> ~*vi* to become smothered

[1]smoulder, *NAm chiefly* **smolder** /ˈsmohldə‖ˈsməʊldə/ *n* a smouldering fire

[2]smoulder, *NAm chiefly* **smolder** *vi* **1** to burn feebly with little flame and often much smoke **2** to exist in a state of suppressed ferment <*resentment* ~ed *in her*> **3** to show suppressed anger, hate, jealousy, etc <*eyes* ~ing *with hate*>

[1]smudge /smuj‖smʌdʒ/ *vt* **1** to soil (as if) with a smudge **2a** to smear, daub **b** to make indistinct; blur <*couldn't read the* ~d *address*> **3** *NAm* to disinfect or protect by means of smoke ~ *vi* **1** to make a smudge **2** to become smudged

[2]smudge *n* **1** a blurry spot or streak **2** an indistinct mass; a blur – **smudgily** *adv*, **smudginess** *n*, **smudgy** *adj*

smug /smug‖smʌg/ *adj* **-gg-** highly self-satisfied and complacent – **smugly** *adv*, **smugness** *n*

smuggle /ˈsmugl‖ˈsmʌgl/ *vt* **1** to import or export secretly contrary to the law, esp without paying duties **2** to convey or introduce surreptitiously <~d *his notes into the examination*> ~*vi* to import or export sthg in violation of customs laws – **smuggler** *n*

[1]smut /smut‖smʌt/ *vb* **-tt-** *vt* **1** to stain or taint with smut **2** to affect (a crop or plant) with smut ~*vi* to become affected by smut

[2]smut *n* **1** matter, esp a particle of soot, that soils or blackens; *also* a mark made by this **2** any of various destructive fungous diseases, esp of cereal grasses, marked by transformation of plant organs into dark masses of spores **3** obscene language or matter – **smuttily** *adv*, **smuttiness** *n*, **smutty** *adj*

[1]snack /snak‖snæk/ *vi, chiefly NAm* to eat a snack

[2]snack *n* a light meal; food eaten between regular meals – **snack** *adj*

[1]snaffle /ˈsnafl‖ˈsnæfl/ *n* a simple usu jointed bit for a bridle

[2]snaffle *vt* to appropriate, esp by devious means; pinch – infml

[1]snag /snag‖snæg/ *n* **1a** a stub or stump remaining after a branch has been lopped **b** a tree or branch embedded in a lake or stream bed and constituting a hazard to navigation **2a** a sharp or jagged projecting part **b** any of the secondary branches of an antler **3** a concealed or unexpected difficulty or obstacle <*the* ~ *is, there's no train on Sundays*> **4** an irregular tear or flaw made (as if) by catching on a snag <*a* ~ *in her stocking*> – **snaggy** *adj*

[2]snag *vb* **-gg-** *vt* **1** to catch (as if) on a snag **2** to clear (e g a river) of snags **3** *chiefly NAm* to halt or impede as if by catching on a snag **4** *chiefly NAm* to catch or obtain by quick action <~ged *a taxi*> ~*vi* to become snagged

snail /snayl‖sneɪl/ *n* **1** a gastropod mollusc; *esp* one that has an external enclosing spiral shell **2** a slow-moving or sluggish person or thing – **snaillike** *adj*

[1]snake /snayk‖sneɪk/ *n* **1** any of numerous limbless scaly reptiles with a long tapering body and with salivary glands often modified to produce venom which is injected through grooved or tubular fangs **2** a sly treacherous person **3** sthg long, slender, and flexible; *specif* a flexible rod for freeing clogged pipes **4** *often cap* a system in which the values of the currencies of countries in the European Economic Community are allowed to vary against each other within narrow limits – **snakelike** *adj*

[2]snake *vt* to wind (e g one's way) in the manner of a snake ~*vi* to crawl, move, or extend silently, secretly, or windingly

ˈsnake ˌcharmer *n* an entertainer who exhibits the power to control venomous snakes supposedly by magic

snaky /ˈsnayki‖ˈsneɪkɪ/ *adj* **1** (formed) of or entwined with snakes **2** serpentine, snakelike <*the* ~ *arms of an octopus*> **3** slyly venomous or treacherous **4** full of snakes – **snakily** *adv*

[1]snap /snap‖snæp/ *vb* **-pp-** *vi* **1a** to make a sudden closing of the jaws; seize sthg sharply with the mouth <*fish* ~ping *at the bait*> **b** to grasp or snatch at sthg eagerly <~ *at any chance*> **2** to utter sharp biting words; give an irritable retort <~ped *at his pupil when she apologized for being late*> **3a** to make a sharp or cracking sound **b** to break suddenly, esp with a sharp cracking sound <*the twig* ~ped> **c** to close or fit in place with an abrupt movement or sharp sound <*the catch* ~ped *shut*> ~ *vt* **1** to seize (as if) with a snap of the jaws <~ped *the food right out of his hand*> **2** to take possession or advantage of suddenly or eagerly – usu + *up* <*shoppers* ~ping *up bargains*> **3** to utter curtly or abruptly <~ped *out an answer*> **4a** to cause to make a snapping sound <~ped *her* *fingers*> **b** to cause to break suddenly, esp with a sharp cracking sound <~ped *the end off the twig*> **c** to put into or remove from a particular position with a sudden movement or sharp sound <~ *the lid shut*> **5a** to take photographically <~ *a picture*> **b** to photograph –**snap out of it** to free oneself from sthg (e g a mood) by an effort of will – infml

[2]**snap** *n* **1** an abrupt closing (e g of the mouth in biting or of scissors in cutting) **2** an act or instance of seizing abruptly; a sudden snatch or bite **3** a brief usu curt retort **4a** a sound made by snapping **b** a sudden sharp breaking of sthg thin or brittle **5** a sudden spell of harsh weather <*a cold* ~> **6** a thin brittle biscuit <*ginger* ~> **7** a snapshot **8** vigour, energy **9** a card game in which each player tries to be the first to shout '*snap*' when 2 cards of identical value are laid successively **10** *dial NEng* **10a** a small meal or snack; *esp* elevenses **b** food; *esp* the food taken by a workman to eat at work **11** *NAm* sthg that is easy and presents no problems; a cinch – infml

[3]**snap** *interj, Br* – used to draw attention to an identity or similarity <~! *You're reading the same book as me*>

[4]**snap** *adv* with (the sound of) a snap

[5]**snap** *adj* **1** performed suddenly, unexpectedly, or without deliberation <*a* ~ *judgment*> **2** *NAm* very easy or simple <*a* ~ *course*>

snapdragon /ˈsnap,drag(ə)n‖ˈsnæp,dræg(ə)n/ *n* any of several garden plants having showy white, red, or yellow 2-lipped flowers

snappish /ˈsnapish‖ˈsnæpɪʃ/ *adj* **1a** given to curt irritable speech **b** bad-tempered, testy **2** inclined to snap or bite <*a* ~ *dog*> – **snappishly** *adv*, **snappishness** *n*

snappy /ˈsnapi‖ˈsnæpɪ/ *adj* **1** SNAPPISH 1 **2a** brisk, quick <*make it* ~> **b** lively, animated <~ *repartee*> **c** stylish, smart <*a* ~ *dresser*> – **snappily** *adv*, **snappiness** *n*

snapshot /ˈsnap,shot‖ˈsnæp,ʃɒt/ *n* a casual photograph made typically by an amateur with a small hand-held camera and without regard to technique

[1]**snare** /sneə‖sneə/ *n* **1a** a trap often consisting of a noose for catching animals **b** sthg by which one is trapped or deceived **2** any of the catgut strings or metal spirals of a snare drum which produce a rattling sound

[2]**snare** *vt* **1a** to capture (as if) by use of a snare **b** to procure by artful or skilful actions <~ *a top job*> **2** to entangle or hold as if in a snare – **snarer** *n*

ˈ**snare ,drum** *n* a small double-headed drum with 1 or more snares stretched across its lower head

[1]**snarl** /snahl‖snɑːl/ *n* **1** a tangle, esp of hair or thread; a knot **2** a confused or complicated situation; *also, chiefly NAm* a snarl-up – **snarly** *adj*

[2]**snarl** *vt* **1** to cause to become knotted and intertwined; tangle **2** to make excessively confused or complicated ~*vi* to become snarled *USE* (*vt2; vi*) often + *up* – **snarler** *n*

[3]**snarl** *vi* **1** to growl with bared teeth **2** to speak in a vicious or bad-tempered manner ~*vt* to utter or express viciously or in a snarling manner – **snarl** *n*, **snarler** *n*

ˈ**snarl-,up** *n* an instance of confusion, disorder, or obstruction; *specif* a traffic jam

[1]**snatch** /snach‖snætʃ/ *vi* to attempt to seize sthg suddenly – often + *at* <~ *at a rope*> ~ *vt* **1** to take or grasp abruptly or hastily <~ *a quick glance*> **2** to seize or grab suddenly and usu forcibly, wrongfully, or with difficulty – **snatcher** *n*

[2]**snatch** *n* **1** a snatching at or of sthg **2a** a brief period of time or activity <*sleep came in* ~es> **b** sthg fragmentary or hurried <*caught a brief* ~ *of their conversation*> **3** a robbery – infml

snazzy /ˈsnazi‖ˈsnæzɪ/ *adj* stylishly or flashily attractive – infml

[1]**sneak** /sneek‖sniːk/ *vb* **sneaked**, *NAm also* **snuck** /snuk‖snʌk/ *vi* **1** to go or leave stealthily or furtively; slink <*boys* ~ing *over the orchard wall*> **2** to behave in a furtive or servile manner **3** *Br* to tell tales <*pupils never* ~ *on their classmates*> – infml ~*vt* to put, bring, or take in a furtive or artful manner <~ed *a glance at the report*> – **sneak up on** to approach or act on stealthily

[2]**sneak** *n* **1** a person who acts in a stealthy or furtive manner **2** the act or an instance of sneaking **3** *Br* a person, esp a schoolchild, who tells tales against others – infml – **sneaky** *adj*

sneaker /ˈsneekə‖ˈsniːkə/ *n, chiefly NAm* a plimsoll – usu pl

sneaking /ˈsneeking‖ˈsniːkɪŋ/ *adj* **1** furtive, underhand **2** mean, contemptible **3a** not openly expressed; secret <*a* ~ *desire for publicity*> **b** instinctively felt but unverified <*a* ~ *suspicion*> – **sneakingly** *adv*

ˈ**sneak ,thief** *n* a thief who steals without using violence or breaking into buildings

[1]**sneer** /sniə‖snɪə/ *vi* **1** to smile or laugh with a curl of the lips to express scorn or contempt **2** to speak or write in a scornfully jeering manner ~*vt* to utter with a sneer – **sneerer** *n*

[2]**sneer** *n* a sneering expression or remark

sneeze /sneez‖sniːz/ *vi or n* (to make) a sudden violent involuntary audible expiration of breath – **sneezer** *n*, **sneezy** *adj* – **sneeze at** to make light of

[1]**snick** /snik‖snɪk/ *vt* **1** to cut slightly; nick **2** EDGE 4

[2]**snick** *n* EDGE 4

snicker /ˈsnikə‖ˈsnɪkə/ *vi or n* (to) snigger – **snickerer** *n*, **snickery** *adj*

snide /snied‖snaɪd/ *adj* **1** slyly disparaging; insinuating <~ *remarks*> **2** *chiefly NAm* mean, low <*a* ~ *trick*> – **snidely** *adv*, **snideness** *n*

[1]**sniff** /snif‖snɪf/ *vi* **1** to draw air audibly up the nose, esp for smelling <~ed *at the flowers*> **2** to show or express disdain or scorn *at* <*not to be* ~ed *at*> ~ *vt* **1** to smell or take by inhalation through the nose **2** to utter in a haughty manner **3** to detect or become aware of (as if) by smelling

[2]**sniff** *n* **1** an act or sound of sniffing **2** a quantity that is sniffed <*a good* ~ *of sea air*>

[1]**sniffle** /ˈsnifl‖ˈsnɪfl/ *vi* to sniff repeatedly – **sniffler** *n*

[2]**sniffle** *n* **1** an act or sound of sniffling **2** *often pl* a head cold marked by nasal discharge <*he's got the* ~s>

sniffy /ˈsnifi‖ˈsnɪfɪ/ *adj* having or expressing a

haughty attitude; supercilious – infml – **sniffily** *adv*, **sniffiness** *n*

snifter /ˈsniftə‖ˈsnɪftə/ *n* a small drink of spirits – infml

snigger /ˈsnigə‖ˈsnɪgə/ *vi* to laugh in a partly suppressed often derisive manner – **snigger** *n*, **sniggerer** *n*

1**snip** /snip‖snɪp/ *n* **1a** a small piece snipped off; *also* a fragment, bit **b** a cut or notch made by snipping **c** an act or sound of snipping **2** *pl but sing or pl in constr* shears used esp for cutting sheet metal by hand **3** *Br* a bargain **4** *Br* CINCH 2a – infml

2**snip** *vb* **-pp-** *vt* to cut (as if) with shears or scissors, esp with short rapid strokes ~*vi* to make a short rapid cut (as if) with shears or scissors – **snipper** *n*

1**snipe** /sniep‖snaɪp/ *n* any of various birds that usu have long slender straight bills; *esp* any of several game birds that occur esp in marshy areas and resemble the related woodcocks

2**snipe** *vi* **1** to shoot *at* exposed individuals usu from in hiding at long range **2** to aim a snide or obliquely critical attack *at* – **sniper** *n*

snippet /ˈsnipit‖ˈsnɪpɪt/ *n* a small part, piece, or item; *esp* a fragment of writing or conversation – **snippety** *adj*

1**snitch** /snich‖snɪtʃ/ *vi* to turn informer; squeal on sby – infml ~*vt* to pilfer, pinch – infml – **snitcher** *n*

2**snitch** *n* an esp petty theft – infml

snivel /ˈsnivl‖ˈsnɪvl/ *vi* **-ll-** (*NAm* **-l-**, **-ll-**) **1** to run at the nose **2** to sniff mucus up the nose audibly **3** to whine, snuffle **4** to speak or act in a whining, tearful, cringing, or weakly emotional manner – **snivel** *n*, **sniveller** *n*

snob /snob‖snɒb/ *n* **1** one who blatantly attempts to cultivate or imitate those he/she admires as social superiors **2a** one who tends to patronize or avoid those he/she regards as inferior **b** one who has an air of smug superiority in matters of knowledge or taste <*a cultural* ~> [obs *snob* member of the lower classes, vulgar or ostentatious person, fr English dial., shoemaker] – **snobbish, snobby** *adj*, **snobbishly** *adv*, **snobbishness** *n*, **snobbism** *n*

snobbery /ˈsnob(ə)ri‖ˈsnɒb(ə)rɪ/ *n* (an instance of) snobbishness

snog /snog‖snɒg/ *vi* **-gg-** *Br* to kiss and cuddle – slang – **snog** *n*

snood /snoohd‖snuːd/ *n* **1** a net or fabric bag, formerly worn at the back of the head by women, to hold the hair **2** *Scot* a ribbon or band for a woman's hair – **snood** *vt*

snook /snoohk‖snuːk/ *n* a gesture of derision made by putting the thumb to the nose and spreading the fingers out

1**snooker** /ˈsnoohkə‖ˈsnuːkə/ *n* **1** a variation of pool played with 15 red balls and 6 variously coloured balls **2** a position of the balls in snooker in which a direct shot would lose points [prob fr earlier slang *snooker* new military cadet (the game being devised by army officers in India in the 1870s)]

2**snooker** *vt* **1** to prevent (an opponent) from making a direct shot in snooker by playing the cue ball so that another ball rests between it and the object ball **2** to present an obstacle to; thwart – infml – **snookered** *adj*

snoop /snoohp‖snuːp/ *vi* to look or pry in a sneaking or interfering manner – **snoop** *n*, **snooper** *n*

snooty /ˈsnoohti‖ˈsnuːtɪ/ *adj* **1** haughty, disdainful **2** characterized by snobbish attitudes *USE* infml – **snootily** *adv*, **snootiness** *n*

snooze /snoohz‖snuːz/ *vi or n* (to take) a nap – infml – **snoozer** *n*

snore /snaw‖snɔː/ *vi or n* (to breathe with) a rough hoarse noise due to vibration of the soft palate during sleep – **snorer** *n*

1**snorkel** /ˈsnawkl‖ˈsnɔːkl/ *n* **1** a tube housing an air intake and exhaust pipes that can be extended above the surface of the water from a submerged submarine **2** a J-shaped tube allowing a skin diver to breathe while face down in the water

2**snorkel** *vi* to operate or swim submerged using a snorkel – **snorkeler** *n*

1**snort** /snawt‖snɔːt/ *vb* **1** to force air violently through the nose with a rough harsh sound **2** to express scorn, anger, or surprise by a snort ~ *vt* **1** to utter with or express by a snort <~ed *his contempt*> **2** to take in (a drug) by inhalation <~ *coke*> – infml

2**snort** *n* **1** an act or sound of snorting **2** a snifter – infml

snorter /ˈsnawtə‖ˈsnɔːtə/ *n* sthg extremely powerful, difficult, or impressive – infml

snot /snot‖snɒt/ *n* **1** nasal mucus **2** a snotty person – slang

snotty /ˈsnoti‖ˈsnɒtɪ/ *adj* **1** soiled with nasal mucus – infml **2** arrogantly or snobbishly unpleasant **3** contemptible, despicable *USE* (*2&3*) slang

snout /snowt‖snaʊt/ *n* **1a(1)** a long projecting nose (e g of a pig) **a(2)** a forward prolongation of the head of various animals **b** the human nose, esp when large or grotesque **2** tobacco – slang – **snouted** *adj*, **snoutish** *adj*, **snouty** *adj*

1**snow** /snoh‖snəʊ/ *n* **1a** (a descent of) water falling in the form of white flakes consisting of small ice crystals formed directly from vapour in the atmosphere **b** fallen snow **2a** any of various congealed or crystallized substances resembling snow in appearance **b** cocaine – slang – **snowless** *adj*

2**snow** *vi* to fall in or as snow ~ *vt* **1** to cause to fall like or as snow **2** to cover, shut in, or block (as if) with snow – usu + *in* or *up* <*found themselves* ~ed *in after the blizzard*> **3** *chiefly NAm* to deceive, persuade, or charm glibly

1**ˈsnowˌball** /-ˌbawl‖-ˌbɔːl/ *n* a round mass of snow pressed or rolled together for throwing

2**snowball** *vt* to throw snowballs at **1** to throw snowballs **2** to increase or expand at a rapidly accelerating rate

ˈsnowberry /-b(ə)ri‖-b(ə)rɪ/ *n* any of several white-berried (garden) shrubs

ˈsnow ˌblindness *n* inflammation and painful sensitiveness to light caused by exposure of the eyes to ultraviolet rays reflected from snow or ice – **snow-blind, snow-blinded** *adj*

ˈsnowˌbound /-ˌbownd‖-ˌbaʊnd/ *adj* confined or surrounded by snow

ˈsnowˌcap /-ˌkap‖-ˌkæp/ *n* a covering cap of

snow (e g on a mountain top) – **snowcapped** *adj*

ˈsnowˌdrift /-ˌdrift‖-ˌdrɪft/ *n* a bank of drifted snow

ˈsnowˌdrop /-ˌdrop‖-ˌdrɒp/ *n* a bulbous European plant of the daffodil family bearing nodding white flowers in spring

ˈsnowˌfall /-ˌfawl‖-ˌfɔːl/ *n* the amount of snow falling at one time or in a given period

ˈsnowˌflake /-ˌflayk‖-ˌfleɪk/ *n* a flake or crystal of snow

snow leopard *n* a big cat of upland central Asia with long heavy fur that is irregularly blotched with brownish black in summer and almost pure white in winter

snow line *n* the lower margin of a permanent expanse of snow

ˈsnowˌman /-ˌman‖-ˌmæn/ *n* a pile of snow shaped to resemble a human figure

[1]**ˈsnowˌplough** /-ˌplow‖-ˌplaʊ/ *n* **1** any of various vehicles or devices used for clearing snow **2** a turn in skiing with the skis in the snowploughing position

[2]**snowplough** *vi* to force the heels of one's ski's outwards, keeping the tips together, in order to descend slowly or to stop

ˈsnowˌshoe /-ˌshooh‖-ˌʃuː/ *n* a light oval wooden frame that is strung with thongs and attached to the foot to enable a person to walk on soft snow without sinking

ˈsnowˌstorm /-ˌstawm‖-ˌstɔːm/ *n* a storm of or with snow

snow under *vt* **1** to overwhelm, esp in excess of capacity to handle or absorb sthg <snowed under *with applications for the job*> **2** *NAm* to defeat by a large margin

ˌsnow-ˈwhite *adj* spotlessly white

snowy /ˈsnoh·i‖ˈsnəʊɪ/ *adj* **1a** composed of (melted) snow **b** characterized by or covered with snow **2a** whitened (as if) by snow <*ground* ~ *with fallen blossom*> **b** snow-white – **snowily** *adv*, **snowiness** *n*

[1]**snub** /snub‖snʌb/ *vt* **-bb-** **1** to check or interrupt with a cutting retort; rebuke **2** to restrain (e g a rope) suddenly while running out, esp by wrapping round a fixed object; *also* to halt the motion of by snubbing a line **3** to treat with contempt, esp by deliberately ignoring

[2]**snub** *n* an act or an instance of snubbing; *esp* a slight

[3]**snub** *adj* short and stubby <*a* ~ *nose*> – **snubness** *n*

ˌsnub-ˈnosed /nohzd‖nəʊzd/ *adj* **1** having a short and slightly turned-up nose **2** having a very short barrel <*a* ~ *revolver*>

[1]**snuff** /snuf‖snʌf/ *n* the charred part of a candle wick

[2]**snuff** *vt* **1** to trim the snuff of (a candle) by pinching or by the use of snuffers **2a** to extinguish (a flame) by the use of snuffers **b** to make extinct; put an end to – usu + *out* <*an accident that* ~ed *out a life*> – **snuff it** to die – infml

[3]**snuff** *vb or n* (to) sniff

[4]**snuff** *n* a preparation of pulverized often scented tobacco inhaled usu through the nostrils

snuffer /ˈsnufə‖ˈsnʌfə/ *n* **1** an instrument resembling a pair of scissors for trimming the wick of a candle – usu pl but sing. or pl in constr **2** an instrument consisting of a small hollow cone attached to a handle, used to extinguish candles

snuffle /ˈsnufl‖ˈsnʌfl/ *vi* **1a** to sniff, usu audibly and repeatedly **b** to draw air through an obstructed nose with a sniffing sound **2** to speak (as if) through the nose ~*vt* to utter with much snuffling – **snuffle** *n*, **snuffler** *n*

[1]**snug** /snug‖snʌg/ *adj* **-gg-** **1** fitting closely and comfortably <*a* ~ *coat*> **2a** enjoying or affording warm secure comfortable shelter **b** marked by relaxation and cordiality <*a* ~ *evening among friends*> **3** affording a degree of comfort and ease <*a* ~ *income*> – **snug** *adv*, **snugly** *adv*, **snugness** *n*

[2]**snug** *vi* **-gg-** to snuggle

[3]**snug** *n*, *Br* a small private room or compartment in a pub; *also* a snuggery

snuggle /ˈsnugl‖ˈsnʌgl/ *vi* to curl up comfortably or cosily; nestle – infml ~*vt* to draw close, esp for comfort or in affection <*the dog* ~d *his muzzle under his master's arm*> – infml

[1]**so** /soh‖səʊ/ *adv* **1a(1)** in this way; thus <*since he was* ~ *high*> – often used as a substitute for a preceding word or word group <*do you really think* ~*?*> **a(2)** most certainly; indeed <*I hope to win and* ~ *I shall*> **b(1)** in the same way; also <*worked hard and* ~ *did she*> **b(2)** as an accompaniment – after *as* <*as the wind increased,* ~ *the sea grew rougher*> **c** in such a way – used esp before *as* or *that*, to introduce a result <*the book is* ~ *written that a child could understand it*> or to introduce the idea of purpose <*hid* ~ *as not to get caught*> **2a** to such an extreme degree <*had never been* ~ *happy*> – used before *as* to introduce a comparison, esp in the negative <*not* ~ *fast as mine*>, or, esp before *as* or *that*, to introduce a result <*was* ~ *tired I went to bed*> **b** very <*I'm* ~ *glad you could come*> **c** to a definite but unspecified extent or degree <*can only do* ~ *much in a day*> **3** therefore, consequently <*the witness is biased and* ~ *unreliable*> **4** then, subsequently <*and* ~ *home and to bed*> **5** *chiefly dial & NAm* – used, esp by children, to counter a negative charge <*you did* ~*!*>

[2]**so** *conj* **1** with the result that <*her diction is good,* ~ *every word is clear*> **2** in order that; THAT 2(1) <*be quiet* ~ *he can sleep*> **3a** for that reason; therefore <*don't want to go,* ~ *I won't*> **b(1)** – used as an introductory particle <~ *here we are*> often to belittle a point under discussion <~ *what?*> **b(2)** – used interjectionally to indicate awareness of a discovery <~, *that's who did it*> or surprised dissent

[3]**so** *adj* **1** conforming with actual facts; true <*said things that were not* ~> **2** disposed in a definite order <*his books are always exactly* ~>

[4]**so** *pron* such as has been specified or suggested; the same <*became chairman and remained* ~> – **or so** – used to indicate an approximation or conjecture <*I've known him 20 years* or so>

[5]**so, soh** *n* [1]SOL

[1]**soak** /sohk‖səʊk/ *vi* **1** to lie immersed in liquid (e g water), esp so as to become saturated or softened <*put the clothes to* ~> **2a** to enter or

pass through sthg (as if) by pores or small openings; permeate **b** to become fully felt or appreciated – usu + *in* or *into* ~ *vt* **1** to permeate so as to wet, soften, or fill thoroughly **2** to place in a surrounding element, esp liquid, to wet or permeate thoroughly **3** to extract (as if) by steeping <~ *the dirt out*> **4a** to draw in (as if) by absorption <~ed *up the sunshine*> **b** to intoxicate (oneself) with alcohol – infml **5** to charge an excessive amount of money – infml <~ed *the taxpayers*> – **soakage** *n*, **soaker** *n*

[2]**soak** *n* **1a** soaking or being soaked **b** that (e g liquid) in which sthg is soaked **2** a drunkard – infml

ˈ**so-and-ˌso** *n, pl* **so-and-sos, so-and-so's** **1** an unnamed or unspecified person or thing <*Miss* So-and-so> **2** a disliked or unpleasant person – euph <*the cheeky* ~!>

[1]**soap** /sohp‖səʊp/ *n* **1** a cleansing and emulsifying agent that lathers when rubbed in water and consists essentially of sodium or potassium salts of fatty acids **2** a salt of a fatty acid

[2]**soap** *vt* **1** to rub soap over or into **2** to flatter – often + *up*; infml

ˈ**soapˌbox** /-ˌboks‖-ˌbɒks/ *n* an improvised platform used by an informal orator – **soapbox** *adj*

ˈ**soap ˌopera** *n* a radio or television drama characterized by stock domestic situations and melodramatic or sentimental treatment [fr its frequently being sponsored in the USA by soap manufacturers]

ˈ**soapˌstone** /-ˌstohn‖-ˌstəʊn/ *n* a soft greyish green or brown stone having a soapy feel and composed mainly of magnesium silicate

soapy /ˈsohpi‖ˈsəʊpɪ/ *adj* **1** containing or combined with soap or saponin **2a** smooth and slippery **b** suave, ingratiating – **soapily** *adv*, **soapiness** *n*

soar /saw‖sɔː/ *vi* **1a** to fly high in the air **b(1)** to sail or hover in the air, often at a great height **b(2)** *of a glider* to fly without engine power and without loss of altitude **2** to rise rapidly or to a very high level <*temperatures* ~ed *into the upper 30s*> **3** to rise upwards in position or status <*a* ~ing *reputation*> **4** to be of imposing height or stature; tower <*mountains* ~ed *above us*> – **soarer** *n*

[1]**sob** /sob‖sɒb/ *vb* **-bb-** *vi* **1** to weep with convulsive catching of the breath **2** to make a sound like that of a sob or sobbing ~ *vt* to express or utter with sobs <~bed *out her grief*>

[2]**sob** *n* an act or sound of sobbing; *also* a similar sound

[1]**sober** /ˈsohbə‖ˈsəʊbə/ *adj* **1** not drunk or addicted to drink **2** gravely or earnestly thoughtful **3** calmly self-controlled; sedate **4a** well balanced; realistic <*a* ~ *estimate*> **b** sane, rational **5** subdued in tone or colour – **soberly** *adv*, **soberness** *n*

[2]**sober** *vb* to make or become sober – usu + *up*

sobriety /səˈbrie·əti‖səˈbraɪətɪ/ *n* being sober – fml

sobriquet /ˈsohbriˌkay‖ˈsəʊbrɪˌkeɪ/ *n* a nickname

ˈ**sob ˌstory** *n* a sentimental story or account intended chiefly to elicit sympathy – infml

ˌ**so-ˈcalled** *adj* **1** commonly named; popularly so termed <*involved in* ~ *campus politics*> **2** falsely or improperly so named <*deceived by his* ~ *friend*>

soccer /ˈsokə‖ˈsɒkə/ *n* a football game played with a round ball between teams of 11 players each, that features the kicking and heading of the ball [by shortening & alteration fr *association (football)*]

sociable /ˈsohsh(i)əbl‖ˈsəʊʃ(ɪ)əbl/ *adj* **1** inclined to seek or enjoy companionship; companionable **2** conducive to friendliness or cordial social relations <*spent a* ~ *evening at the club*> – **sociableness** *n*, **sociably** *adv*, **sociability** *n*

[1]**social** /ˈsohsh(ə)l‖ˈsəʊʃ(ə)l/ *adj* **1a** sociable **b** of or promoting companionship or friendly relations <*a* ~ *club*> **2a** tending to form cooperative relationships; gregarious <*man is a* ~ *being*> **b** living and breeding in more or less organized communities <~ *insects*> **3** of human society <~ *institutions*> [Latin *socialis*, fr *socius* companion, ally, associate] – **socially** *adv*

[2]**social** *n* a social gathering, usu connected with a church or club

ˌ**social ˈclimber** *n* one who strives to gain a higher social position or acceptance in fashionable society – derog – **social climbing** *n*

ˌ**social deˈmocracy** *n* a political movement advocating a gradual and democratic transition to socialism – **social democrat** *n*, **social democratic** *adj*

socialism /ˈsohsh(ə)lˌiz(ə)m‖ˈsəʊʃ(ə)lˌɪz(ə)m/ *n* **1** an economic and political theory advocating, or a system based on, collective or state ownership and administration of the means of production and distribution of goods **2** a transitional stage of society in Marxist theory distinguished by unequal distribution of goods according to work done

[1]ˈ**socialist** /-ist‖-ɪst/ *n* **1** one who advocates or practises socialism **2** *cap* a member of a socialist party or group

[2]**socialist** *adj* **1** of socialism **2** *cap* of or constituting a party advocating socialism

socialite /ˈsohsh(ə)liet‖ˈsəʊʃ(ə)laɪt/ *n* a socially active or prominent person

social·ize, -ise /ˈsohsh(ə)lˌiez‖ˈsəʊʃ(ə)lˌaɪz/ *vt* **1** to make social; *esp* to fit or train for life in society **2** to adapt to social needs or uses <~ *science*> **3** to constitute on a socialist basis <~ *industry*> ~*vi* to act in a sociable manner <*likes to* ~ *with his students*> – **socializer** *n*, **socialization** *n*

socialized medicine *n*, *NAm* medical services administered by an organized group (e g a state agency) and paid for by assessments, philanthropy, or taxation

ˌ**social ˈscience** *n* **1** the scientific study of human society and the relationships between its members **2** a science (e g economics or politics) dealing with a particular aspect of human society – **social scientist** *n*

ˌ**social seˈcurity** *n* **1** provision by the state through pensions, unemployment benefit, sickness benefit, etc for its citizens' economic security and social welfare **2** SUPPLEMENTARY BENEFIT

ˌsocial ˈservice *n* activity designed to promote social welfare; *esp* an organized service (e g education or housing) provided by the state

ˈsocial ˌwork *n* any of various professional activities concerned with the aid of the economically underprivileged and socially maladjusted – **social worker** *n*

[1]**society** /səˈsie·əti‖səˈsaɪətɪ/ *n* **1** companionship or association with others; company **2** *often cap* **a** the human race considered in terms of its structure of social institutions <~ *cannot tolerate lawlessness*> **b(1)** a community having common traditions, institutions, and collective interests <*the* Society *of Friends*> **b(2)** an organized group working together or periodically meeting because of common interests, beliefs, or profession <*the Royal* Society> **3a** a clearly identifiable social circle <*literary* ~> **b** a fashionable leisure class <*not seen in the best* ~>

[2]**society** *adj* (characteristic) of fashionable society <*a* ~ *wedding*>

sociology /ˌsohs(h)iˈoləji‖ˌsəʊsɪˈɒlədʒɪ,-əʊʃɪ-/ *n* the science of social institutions and relationships; *specif* the study of the behaviour of organized human groups – **sociologist** *n*, **sociological** *adj*

[1]**sock** /sok‖sɒk/ *n, pl* **socks**, *NAm also* **sox** a knitted or woven covering for the foot usu extending above the ankle and sometimes to the knee [Old English *socc* light shoe, fr Latin *soccus*]

[2]**sock** *vt* to hit or apply forcefully – infml – **sock it to** to subject to vigorous or powerful attack – infml

[3]**sock** *n* a vigorous or forceful blow; a punch – infml

[1]**socket** /ˈsokit‖ˈsɒkɪt/ *n* an opening or hollow that forms a holder for sthg <*the eye* ~> <*put the plug in the* ~>; *also* an electrical plug

[2]**socket** *vt* to provide with or place in a socket

[1]**sod** /sod‖sɒd/ *n* **1** TURF 1; *also* the grass-covered surface of the ground **2** one's native land – infml

[2]**sod** *n, Br* **1** an objectionable person, esp male **2** a fellow <*he's not a bad little* ~ – Noel Coward> *USE* slang

[3]**sod** *vt* **-dd-** *Br* to damn – usu used as an oath <~ *you!*> or in the present participle as a meaningless intensive; slang

soda /ˈsohdə‖ˈsəʊdə/ *n* (*2b*) *pl* **sodas** **1a** SODIUM CARBONATE **b** SODIUM BICARBONATE **c** SODIUM HYDROXIDE **2a** SODA WATER **b** *chiefly NAm* a sweet drink consisting of soda water, flavouring, and often ice cream

ˈsoda ˌfountain *n* **1** *chiefly NAm* an apparatus with a delivery tube and taps for drawing soda water **2** *NAm* a counter where sodas, sundaes, and ice cream are prepared and served

ˈsoda ˌwater *n* a beverage consisting of water highly charged with carbonic acid gas

sodden /ˈsod(ə)n‖ˈsɒd(ə)n/ *adj* **1** full of moisture or water; saturated <*the* ~ *ground*> **2** heavy, damp, or doughy because of imperfect cooking <~ *bread*> **3** dull or expressionless, esp from habitual drunkenness <*his* ~ *features*> – **soddenly** *adv*, **soddenness** *n*

sodium /ˈsohdi·əm, ˈsohdyəm‖ˈsəʊdɪəm, ˈsəʊdjəm/ *n* a silver white soft ductile element of the alkali metal group that occurs abundantly in nature in combined form and is very active chemically

ˌsodium biˈcarbonate *n* a white weakly alkaline salt used esp in baking powders, fire extinguishers, and medicine as an antacid

ˌsodium ˈcarbonate *n* a sodium salt of carbonic acid used esp in making soaps and chemicals, in water softening, in cleaning and bleaching, and in photography; *also* WASHING SODA

ˌsodium ˈchloride *n* SALT 1a

ˌsodium hyˈdroxide *n* a white brittle solid that is a strong caustic alkali used esp in making soap, rayon, and paper

ˌsod ˈoff /sod‖sɒd/ *vi, Br* to go away – slang

sodomite /ˈsodəmiet‖ˈsɒdəmaɪt/ *n* one who practises sodomy

sodomy /ˈsodəmi‖ˈsɒdəmɪ/ *n* a sexual act, resembling copulation, other than normal coitus: e g **a** the penetration of the penis into the mouth or esp the anus of another, esp another male **b** sexual relations between a human being and an animal [*Sodom*, city of ancient Palestine notorious for vice (Genesis 19:1–11)]

soever /sohˈevə‖səʊˈevə/ *adv* to any possible or known extent – used after an adjective preceded by *how* <*how fair* ~ *she may be*>; poetic

sofa /ˈsohfə‖ˈsəʊfə/ *n* a long upholstered seat with a back and 2 arms or raised ends that typically seats 2 to 4 people [Arabic *ṣuffah* long bench]

[1]**soft** /soft‖sɒft/ *adj* **1a** yielding to physical pressure <*a* ~ *mattress*> **b** of a consistency that may be shaped, moulded, spread, or easily cut <~ *cheese*> **c** relatively lacking in hardness <~ *wood*> **d** easily magnetized and demagnetized **e** deficient in or free from salts (e g of calcium or magnesium) that prevent lathering of soap <~ *water*> **f** having relatively low energy <~ *X rays*> **g** intended to avoid or prevent damage on impact <~ *landing of a spacecraft on the moon*> **2a** pleasing or agreeable to the senses; bringing ease or quiet **b** having a bland or mellow taste **c** not bright or glaring; subdued <*a* ~ *glow*> **d(1)** quiet in pitch or volume; not harsh **d(2)** *of c and g* pronounced /s/ and /j/ respectively (e g in *acid* and *age*) – not used technically **e(1)** *of the eyes* having a liquid or gentle appearance **e(2)** having a gently curved outline <~ *hills against the horizon*> **f** smooth or delicate in texture <~ *cashmere*> **g(1)** balmy or mild in weather or temperature **g(2)** falling or blowing with slight force or impact <~ *breezes*> **3** marked by a kindness, lenience, or moderation: e g **3a(1)** not being or involving harsh or onerous terms <~ *option*> **a(2)** demanding little effort; easy <*a* ~ *job*> **a(3)** based on negotiation and conciliation rather than on a show of power or on threats <*took a* ~ *line towards the enemy*> **b(1)** mild, low-key; *specif* not of the most extreme or harmful kind <~ *porn*> **b(2)** *of a drug* considered less detrimental than a hard drug; not (strongly) addictive **4a** lacking resilience or strength, esp as a result of having led a life of ease **b** not protected against enemy attack; vulnerable <*a*

~ *aboveground landing site*> **c** mentally deficient; feebleminded <~ *in the head*> **5a** impressionable **b** readily influenced or imposed upon; compliant **c(1)** lacking firmness or strength of character; feeble **c(2)** marked by a gradually declining trend; not firm <*wool prices are increasingly* ~> **d** amorously attracted, esp covertly – + *on* <*has been* ~ *on her for years*> **6** dealing with ideas, opinions, etc, rather than facts and figures <*the* ~ *sciences*> – **softish** *adj*, **softly** *adv*, **softness** *n*

[2]**soft** *adv* in a soft or gentle manner; softly

ˈ**softˌball** /-ˌbawl‖-ˌbɔːl/ *n* a game similar to baseball played on a smaller field with a ball larger than a baseball

ˌ**soft-ˈboil** *vt* to boil (an egg in its shell) to the point at which the white solidifies but the yolk remains unset

soften /ˈsof(ə)n‖ˈsɒf(ə)n/ *vt* **1** to make soft or softer **2a** to weaken the military resistance or the morale of **b** to impair the strength or resistance of <~ *him up with compliments*> ~*vi* to become soft or softer *USE* (*2*) often + *up* – **softener** *n*

ˌ**soft ˈfurnishing** *n, chiefly Br* (the practice of furnishing with) a cloth article (e g a curtain or chair cover) that increases the comfort, utility, or decorativeness of a room or piece of furniture – usu pl

ˌ**softˈhearted** /-ˈhahtid‖-ˈhɑːtɪd/ *adj* kind, compassionate – **softheartedly** *adv*, **softheartedness** *n*

softie /ˈsofti‖ˈsɒftɪ/ *n* a softy

ˌ**soft-ˈland** *vb* to (cause to) make a soft landing on a celestial body (e g the moon) – **soft-lander** *n*

soft palate *n* the fold at the back of the hard palate that partially separates the mouth and pharynx

ˌ**soft-ˈpedal** *vb* **-ll-** (*NAm* **-l-, -ll-**) to attempt to minimize the importance of (sthg), esp by talking cleverly or evasively <~ *the issue of arms sales*>

soft pedal *n* a foot pedal on a piano that reduces the volume of sound

soft sell *n* the use of suggestion or gentle persuasion in selling rather than aggressive pressure

ˌ**soft-ˈsoap** *vt* to persuade or mollify with flattery or smooth talk – infml – **soft-soaper** *n*

soft soap *n* **1** a semifluid soap **2** flattery – infml

ˌ**soft-ˈspoken** *adj* having a mild or gentle voice; *also* suave

soft spot *n* a sentimental weakness

ˈ**softˌware** /-ˌweə‖-ˌweə/ *n* **1** the entire set of programs, procedures, and related documentation associated with a system, esp a computer system; *specif* computer programs **2** sthg contrasted with hardware; *esp* materials for use with audiovisual equipment

ˈ**softˌwood** /-ˌwood‖-ˌwʊd/ *n* the wood of a coniferous tree – **softwood** *adj*

softy, softie /ˈsofti‖ˈsɒftɪ/ *n* **1** an excessively sentimental or susceptible person **2** a feeble, effeminate, or foolish person *USE* infml

soggy /ˈsogi‖ˈsɒgɪ/ *adj* **1a** waterlogged, soaked <*a* ~ *lawn*> **b** SODDEN 2 **2** heavily dull <~ *prose*> – **soggily** *adv*, **sogginess** *n*

soigné /ˈswahnyay, -ˈ-‖ˈswɑːnjeɪ, -ˈ-/, *fem* **soignée** /~/ *adj* well-groomed; *also* elegant [French, fr past participle of *soigner* to take care of]

[1]**soil** /soyl‖sɔɪl/ *vt* **1** to stain or make unclean, esp superficially; dirty **2** to defile morally; corrupt **3** to blacken or tarnish (e g a person's reputation) ~*vi* to become soiled or dirty

[2]**soil** *n* **1** stain, defilement **2** sthg (e g refuse or sewage) that spoils or pollutes

[3]**soil** *n* **1** firm land; earth **2a** the upper layer of earth that may be dug or ploughed and in which plants grow **b** the superficial unconsolidated and usu weathered part of the mantle of a planet, esp the earth **3** country, land <*his native* ~> **4** a medium in which sthg takes hold and develops – **soily** *adj*

soiree, soirée /ˈswahray‖ˈswɑːreɪ/ *n* a party or reception held in the evening [French *soirée* evening period, evening party, fr *soir* evening, fr Latin *sero* at a late hour, fr *serus* late]

sojourn /ˈsojən, ˈsu-‖ˈsɒdʒən, ˈsʌ-/ *vi or n* (to make) a temporary stay – fml – **sojourner** *n*

[1]**sol** /sol‖sɒl/ *n* the 5th note of the diatonic scale in solmization

[2]**sol** /sol‖sɒl/ *n* a fluid colloidal system; *esp* one in which the continuous phase is a liquid

[1]**solace** /ˈsoləs‖ˈsɒləs/ *n* (a source of) consolation or comfort in grief or anxiety

[2]**solace** *vt* **1** to give solace to; console **2** to alleviate, relieve <~ *grief*> – **solacement** *n*, **solacer** *n*

[1]**solar** /ˈsohlə‖ˈsəʊlə/ *adj* **1** of or derived from the sun, esp as affecting the earth **2** (of or reckoned by time) measured by the earth's course in relation to the sun **3** produced or operated by the action of the sun's light or heat; *also* using the sun's rays

[2]**solar** *n* an upper room in a medieval house

solar cell *n* a photovoltaic cell or thermopile that is able to convert the energy of sunlight into electrical energy and is used as a power source

solarium /səˈleəri·əm‖səˈleərɪəm/ *n, pl* **solaria** /-ri·ə‖-rɪə/ *also* **solariums** a room exposed to the sun (e g for relaxation or treatment of illness)

ˌ**solar ˈplexus** /ˈpleksəs‖ˈpleksəs/ *n* **1** an interlacing network of nerves in the abdomen behind the stomach **2** the pit of the stomach

ˈ**solar ˌsystem** *n* the sun together with the group of celestial bodies that are held by its attraction and revolve round it

sold /sohld‖səʊld/ *past of* SELL

[1]**solder** /ˈsohldə, ˈsoldə‖ˈsəʊldə, ˈsɒldə/ *n* an alloy, esp of tin and lead, used when melted to join metallic surfaces

[2]**solder** *vt* **1** to unite or make whole (as if) by solder **2** to hold or join together; unite <*a friendship* ~ed *by common interests*> ~*vi* to become united or repaired (as if) by solder – **solderer** *n*, **solderability** *n*

ˈ**soldering ˌiron** /ˈsohld(ə)ring, ˈsol-‖ˈsəʊld(ə)rɪŋ, ˈsɒl-/ *n* a usu electrically heated device that is used for melting and applying solder

[1]**soldier** /ˈsohljə‖ˈsəʊldʒə/ *n* **1a** sby engaged in military service, esp in the army **b** an enlisted man or woman **c** a person of usu specified military skill <*a good* ~> **2** any of a caste of ants or wingless termites having a large head and jaws

[Old French *soudier*, fr *soulde* pay, fr Late Latin *solidus* solidus] – **soldierly** *adj or adv*, **soldiership** *n*

[2]**soldier** *vi* **1** to serve as a soldier **2** to press doggedly forward – usu + *on*

soldier of fortune *n* sby who seeks an adventurous, esp military, life wherever chance allows

soldiery /'sohljəri‖'səʊldʒərɪ/ *n sing or pl in constr* **1** a body of soldiers **2** a set of soldiers of a specified sort <*a drunken* ~>

[1]**sole** /sohl‖səʊl/ *n* **1a** the undersurface of a foot **b** the part of a garment or article of footwear on which the sole rests **2** the usu flat bottom or lower part of sthg or the base on which sthg rests – **soled** *adj*

[2]**sole** *vt* to provide with a sole <~ *a shoe*>

[3]**sole** *n* any of several flatfish including some valued as superior food fishes

[4]**sole** *adj* **1** being the only one; only <*she was her mother's* ~ *confidante*> **2** belonging or relating exclusively to 1 individual or group <~ *rights of publication*> **3** *esp of a woman* not married – used in law – **soleness** *n*

solecism /'soli,siz(ə)m‖'sɒlɪ,sɪz(ə)m/ *n* **1** a minor blunder in speech or writing **2** a deviation from what is proper or normal; *esp* a breach of etiquette or decorum [Latin *soloecismus*, fr Greek *soloikismos*, fr *soloikos* speaking incorrectly, lit., inhabitant of Soloi, fr *Soloi*, city in ancient Cilicia where a substandard form of Attic was spoken] – **solecistic** *adj*

solely /'sohl(l)i‖'səʊl(l)ɪ/ *adv* **1** without another; singly <*was* ~ *responsible*> **2** to the exclusion of all else <*done* ~ *for money*>

solemn /'soləm‖'sɒləm/ *adj* **1** performed so as to be legally binding <*a* ~ *oath*> **2** marked by the observance of established form or ceremony; *specif* celebrated with full liturgical ceremony **3a** conveying a deep sense of reverence or exaltation; sublime <*was stirred by the* ~ *music*> **b** marked by seriousness and sobriety **c** sombre, gloomy – **solemnly** *adv*, **solemnness** *n*, **solemnify** *vt*

solemnity /sə'lemnəti‖sə'lemnətɪ/ *n* **1** formal or ceremonious observance of an occasion or event **2** a solemn event or occasion **3** solemn character or state <*the* ~ *of his words*>

solemn·ize, -ise /'soləmniez‖'sɒləmnaɪz/ *vt* **1** to observe or honour with solemnity **2** to perform with pomp or ceremony; *esp* to celebrate (a marriage) with religious rites **3** to make solemn or serious; dignify – **solemnization** *n*

sol-fa /'sol ,fah‖'sɒl ,fɑː/ *n* **1** *also* **sol-fa syllables** the syllables *do, re, mi*, etc used in singing the notes of the scale **2** solmization **3** TONIC SOL-FA

solicit /sə'lisit‖sə'lɪsɪt/ *vt* **1** to make a formal or earnest appeal or request to; entreat **2a** to attempt to lure or entice, esp into evil **b** *of a prostitute* to proposition publicly **3** to try to obtain by usu urgent requests or pleas <~ *military aid*> **4** to require; CALL FOR <*the situation* ~*s the closest attention*> – fml ~ *vi* **1** to ask earnestly *for*; importune **2** *of a prostitute* to proposition sby publicly – **solicitant** *n*, **solicitation** *n*

solicitor /sə'lisitə‖sə'lɪsɪtə/ *n* **1** a qualified lawyer who advises clients, represents them in the lower courts, and prepares cases for barristers to try in higher courts **2** the chief law officer of a US municipality, county, etc – **solicitorship** *n*

so,licitor 'general *n, pl* **solicitors general** **1** *often cap S&G* a Crown law officer ranking after the attorney general in England **2** a federally appointed assistant to the US attorney general

solicitous /sə'lisitəs‖sə'lɪsɪtəs/ *adj* **1** showing consideration or anxiety; concerned <~ *about the future*> **2** desirous *of*; eager *to* – fml – **solicitously** *adv*, **solicitousness** *n*

solicitude /sə'lisityoohd‖sə'lɪsɪtjuːd/ *n* **1** being solicitous; concern; *also* excessive care or attention **2** a cause of care or concern – usu pl with sing. meaning

[1]**solid** /'solid‖'sɒlɪd/ *adj* **1a** without an internal cavity <*a* ~ *ball of rubber*> **b** having no opening or division <*a* ~ *wall*> **c(1)** set in type or printed with minimum spacing (e g without leads) between lines **c(2)** joined without a hyphen <*a* ~ *compound*> **2** of uniformly close and coherent texture; compact **3** of good substantial quality or kind <~ *comfort*>: e g **3a** well constructed from durable materials <~ *furniture*> **b** sound, cogent <~ *reasons*> **4a** having, involving, or dealing with 3 dimensions or with solids **b** neither gaseous nor liquid **5a** without interruption; full <*waited 3* ~ *hours*> **b** unanimous <*had the* ~ *support of his party*> **6** of a single substance or character <~ *rock*>: e g **6a** (almost) entirely of 1 metal <~ *gold*> **b** of uniform colour or tone **7** reliable, reputable, or acceptable <*are his opinions* ~*?*> **8** *chiefly NAm* in staunch or intimate association <~ *with his boss*> – infml – **solidly** *adv*, **solidness** *n*, **solidify** *vb*, **solidifier** *n*, **solidity** *n*, **solidification** *n*

[2]**solid** *adv* in a solid manner <*the grease had set* ~>; *also* unanimously

[3]**solid** *n* **1** a substance that does not flow perceptibly under moderate stress **2** the part of a solution or suspension that when freed from solvent or suspending medium has the qualities of a solid – usu pl with sing. meaning <*milk* ~*s*> **3** a geometrical figure (e g a cube or sphere) having 3 dimensions **4** sthg solid; *esp* a solid colour

solidarity /,soli'darəti‖,sɒlɪ'dærətɪ/ *n* unity based on shared interests and standards

,solid-'state *adj* **1** relating to the properties, structure, or reactivity of solid material; *esp* relating to the arrangement or behaviour of ions, molecules, nucleons, electrons, and holes in the crystals of a substance (e g a semiconductor) or to the effect of crystal imperfections on the properties of a solid substance <~ *physics*> **2** using the electric, magnetic, or photic properties of solid materials; not using thermionic valves <*a* ~ *stereo system*>

solidus /'solidəs‖'sɒlɪdəs/ *n, pl* **solidi** /-die, -di‖-daɪ, -dɪ/ **1** an ancient Roman gold coin introduced by Constantine and used until the fall of the Byzantine Empire **2** a punctuation mark / used esp to denote 'per' (e g in *feet/second*), 'or' (e g in *straggler/deserter*), or 'cum' (e g in *restaurant/bar*) or to separate shillings and pence (e g in *2/6* and *7/-*), the terms of a fraction, or esp numbers in a list

soliloquy /sə'liləkwi‖sə'lɪləkwɪ/ *n* **1** the act of

talking to oneself **2** a dramatic monologue that gives the illusion of being a series of unspoken reflections [Late Latin *soliloquium*, fr Latin *solus* alone + *loqui* to speak] – **soliloquist** *n*, **soliloquize** *vi*

solipsism /'solip,siz(ə)m‖'sɒlɪp,sɪz(ə)m/ *n* a theory holding that only the self exists and that the external world is merely an idea generated by the self – **solipsist** *n*, **solipsistic** *adj*

solitaire /'soli,teə, ,--'-‖'sɒlɪ,teə, ,--'-/ *n* **1** a gem, esp a diamond, set by itself **2** a game played by 1 person in which a number of pieces are removed from a cross-shaped pattern according to certain rules **3** *chiefly NAm* PATIENCE 2

[1]**solitary** /'solit(ə)ri‖'sɒlɪt(ə)rɪ/ *adj* **1a** (fond of) being or living alone or without companions <*a ~ disposition*> **b** dispirited by isolation; lonely <*left ~ by his wife's death*> **2** taken, spent, or performed without companions <*a ~ weekend*> **3** growing or living alone; not gregarious, colonial, social, or compound **4** being the only one; sole <*the ~ example*> **5** unfrequented, remote <*lived in a ~ place*> – **solitariness** *n*, **solitarily** *adv*

[2]**solitary** *n* one who habitually seeks solitude

solitude /'solityoohd‖'sɒlɪtjuːd/ *n* **1** being alone or remote from society; seclusion **2** a lonely place; a fastness

solmization /,solmie'zaysh(ə)n‖,sɒlmaɪ'zeɪʃ(ə)n/ *n* the act, practice, or system of using syllables to denote musical notes or the degrees of a musical scale

[1]**solo** /'sohloh‖'səʊləʊ/ *n, pl* **solos** **1** a (musical composition for) performance by a single voice or instrument with or without accompaniment **2** a flight by 1 person alone in an aircraft; *esp* a person's first solo flight [Italian, fr *solo* alone, fr Latin *solus*] – **solo** *adj*, **soloist** *n*

[2]**solo** *adv* without a companion; alone

so 'long as *conj* **1** during and up to the end of the time that; while **2** provided that

solstice /'solstis‖'sɒlstɪs/ *n* (the time when the sun passes) either of the 2 points on the ecliptic at which the distance from the celestial equator is greatest and which is reached by the sun each year about June 22nd and December 22nd

soluble /'solyoobl‖'sɒljʊbl/ *adj* **1a** capable of being dissolved (as if) in a liquid **b** capable of being emulsified **2** capable of being solved or explained <*~ questions*> – **solubilize** *vt*, **solubleness** *n*, **solubly** *adv*, **solubility** *n*

solution /sə'loohsh(ə)n‖sə'luːʃ(ə)n/ *n* **1a** an act or the process by which a solid, liquid, or gaseous substance is uniformly mixed with a liquid or sometimes a gas or solid **b** a typically liquid uniform mixture formed by this process **c** a liquid containing a dissolved substance **d** the condition of being dissolved **2a** an action or process of solving a problem **b** an answer to a problem

solve /solv‖sɒlv/ *vt* to find a solution for <*~ a problem*> ~*vi* to solve sthg <*substitute the known values of the constants and ~ for* x> – **solver** *n*

[1]**solvent** /'solvənt‖'sɒlvənt/ *adj* **1** able to pay all legal debts; *also* in credit **2** that dissolves or can dissolve <*~ fluids*> <*~ action of water*> – **solvency** *n*, **solvently** *adv*

[2]**solvent** *n* a usu liquid substance capable of dissolving or dispersing 1 or more other substances

somatic /soh'matik, sə-‖səʊ'mætɪk, sə-/ *adj* **1** of or affecting the body, esp as distinguished from the germ cells or the mind **2** of the wall of the body; parietal – **somatically** *adv*

sombre, *NAm chiefly* **somber** /'sombə‖'sɒmbə/ *adj* **1** dark, gloomy **2** of a dull, dark, or heavy shade or colour **3a** serious, grave **b** depressing, melancholy <*~ thoughts*> – **sombrely** *adv*

sombrero /som'breəroh‖sɒm'breərəʊ/ *n, pl* **sombreros** a high-crowned hat of felt or straw with a very wide brim, worn esp in Mexico [Spanish, fr *sombra* shade]

[1]**some** /sum‖sʌm; *senses 1c and 1d* səm‖səm; *strong* sum‖sʌm/ *adj* **1a** being an unknown, undetermined, or unspecified unit or thing <*~ film or other*> **b** being an unspecified member of a group or part of a class <*~ gems are hard*> **c** being an appreciable number, part, or amount of <*have ~ consideration for others*> **d** being of an unspecified amount or number <*give me ~ water*> – used as an indefinite pl of A <*have ~ apples*> **2a** important, striking, or excellent <*that was ~ party*> – chiefly infml **b** no kind of <*~ friend you are!*> – chiefly infml

[2]**some** /sum‖sʌm/ *pron* **1** *sing or pl in constr* some part, quantity, or number but not all <*~ of my friends*> **2** *chiefly NAm* an indefinite additional amount <*ran a mile and then ~*>

[3]**some** /sum‖sʌm/ *adv* **1** ABOUT 3 <*~ 80 houses*> **2** somewhat – used in Br English in *some more* and more widely in NAm – **some little** a fair amount of – **some few** quite a number of

[1]**-some** /-s(ə)m‖-s(ə)m/ *suffix* (→ *adj*) characterized by a (specified) thing, quality, state, or action <*awe*some>

[2]**-some** *suffix* (→ *n*) group of (so many) members, esp people <*four*some>

[1]**somebody** /'sumbədi‖'sʌmbədɪ/ *pron* some indefinite or unspecified person

[2]**somebody** *n* a person of position or importance

somehow /'sum,how‖'sʌm,haʊ/ *adv* **1a** by some means not known or designated **b** no matter how <*got to get across ~*> **2** for some mysterious reason

someone /'sumwən, -,wun‖'sʌmwən, -,wʌn/ *pron* somebody

somersault /'sumə,sawlt‖'sʌmə,sɔːlt/ *n* a leaping or rolling movement in which a person turns forwards or backwards in a complete revolution bringing the feet over the head and finally landing on the feet [Middle French *sombresaut* leap, deriv of Latin *super* over + *saltus* leap, fr *salire* to leap] – **somersault** *vi*

[1]**something** /'sumthing‖'sʌmθɪŋ/ *pron* **1a** some indeterminate or unspecified thing <*look for ~ cheaper*> – used to replace forgotten matter or to express vagueness <*he's ~ or other in the Foreign Office*> **b** some part; a certain amount <*seen ~ of her work*> **2a** a person or thing of consequence <*their daughter is quite ~*> **b** some truth or value <*there's ~ in what you say*> – **something of a** a fairly notable <*is*

something of a *raconteur*>

[2]**something** *adv* **1** in some degree; somewhat <~ *over £5*> <*shaped* ~ *like a funnel*> – also used to suggest approximation <*there were* ~ *like 1,000 people there*> **2** to an extreme degree <*swears* ~ *awful*> – infml

[1]**sometime** /ˈsum,tiem‖ˈsʌm,taɪm/ *adv* **1** at some unspecified future time <*I'll do it* ~> **2** at some point of time in a specified period <~ *last night*> <~ *next week*>

[2]**sometime** *adj* having been formerly; LATE 2b <*the* ~ *chairman*>

[1]ˈ**some,times** *adv* at intervals; occasionally; NOW AND AGAIN

[2]**sometimes** *adj, archaic* sometime, former

somewhat /ˈsumwot‖ˈsʌmwɒt/ *adv* to some degree; slightly

[1]**somewhere** /ˈsum,weə‖ˈsʌm,weə/ *adv* **1** in, at, or to some unknown or unspecified place **2** to a place or state symbolizing positive accomplishment or progress <*at last we're getting* ~> **3** in the vicinity of; approximately <~ *about 9 o'clock*>

[2]**somewhere** *n* an undetermined or unnamed place

somnambulist /somˈnambyoolist‖sɒmˈnæmbjʊlɪst/ *n* sby who walks in his/her sleep [deriv of Latin *somnus* sleep + *ambulare* to walk] – **somnambulant** *adj*, **somnambulism** *n*, **somnambulate** *vi*, **somnambulistic** *adj*, **somnambulistically** *adv*

somnolent /ˈsomnələnt‖ˈsɒmnələnt/ *adj* **1** inclined to or heavy with sleep **2** tending to induce sleep <*a* ~ *sermon*> – **somnolence** *n*, **somnolently** *adv*

son /sun‖sʌn/ *n* **1a** a male offspring, esp of human beings **b** a male adopted child **c** a male descendant – often pl **2** *cap* the second person of the Trinity; Christ **3** a person closely associated with or deriving from a specified background, place, etc <*a* ~ *of the welfare state*> – **sonless** *adj*, **sonship** *n*

sonar /ˈsohnə‖ˈsəʊnə/ *n* an apparatus that detects the presence and location of a submerged object (by reflected sound waves) [*so*und *na*vigation *r*anging]

sonata /səˈnahtə‖səˈnɑːtə/ *n* an instrumental musical composition typically for 1 or 2 players and of 3 or 4 movements in contrasting forms and keys

son et lumière /,son ay loohˈmyeə‖,sɒn eɪ luːˈmjeə/ *n* an entertainment held at night at a historical site (e g a cathedral or stately home) that uses lighting and recorded sound to present the place's history [French, lit., sound and light]

song /song‖sɒŋ/ *n* **1** the act, art, or product of singing **2** poetry <*famous in* ~ *and story*> **3** (the melody of) a short musical composition usu with words **4** a very small sum <*sold for a* ~> **-on song** in form

ˈ**song,bird** /-,buhd‖-,bɜːd/ *n* **1** a bird that utters a succession of musical tones **2** a passerine bird

songster /ˈsongstə‖ˈsɒŋstə/, *fem* **songstress** /-stris‖-strɪs/ *n* a skilled singer

ˈ**song ,thrush** *n* a common Old World thrush that is largely brown above and white below

sonic /ˈsonik‖ˈsɒnɪk/ *adj* **1** *of waves and vibrations* having a frequency within the audibility range of the human ear **2** using, produced by, or relating to sound waves <~ *altimeter*> **3** of or being the speed of sound in air at sea level (about 340 m/s or 741 mph) – **sonically** *adv*

,**sonic** ˈ**boom** *n* a sound resembling an explosion produced when a shock wave formed at the nose of an aircraft travelling at supersonic speed reaches the ground

ˈ**son-in-,law** *n, pl* **sons-in-law** the husband of one's daughter

sonnet /ˈsonit‖ˈsɒnɪt/ *n* (a poem in) a fixed verse form with any of various rhyming schemes, consisting typically of 14 lines of 10 syllables each [Italian *sonetto*, fr Old Provençal *sonet* little song, fr *son* sound, song, fr Latin *sonus* sound]

sonny /ˈsuni‖ˈsʌnɪ/ *n* a young boy – usu used in address; infml

son of a bitch *n, pl* **sons of bitches** BASTARD 3 – slang

sonorous /ˈsonərəs, ˈsoh-‖ˈsɒnərəs, ˈsəʊ-/ *adj* **1** giving out sound (e g when struck) **2** pleasantly loud **3** impressive in effect or style <*made a* ~ *speech to the assembly*> – **sonorously** *adv*, **sonorousness** *n*, **sonority** *n*

sonsy, sonsie /ˈsunzi‖ˈsʌnzɪ/ *adj, chiefly Scot* buxom, comely

[1]**soon** /soohn‖suːn/ *adv* **1** before long; without undue time lapse <~ *after sunrise*> **2** in a prompt manner; speedily <*as* ~ *as possible*> **3** in agreement with one's preference; willingly – in comparisons ~er *walk than drive*> – **no sooner ... than** at the very moment that <no sooner *built* than *knocked down again*>

[2]**soon** *adj* advanced in time; early <*the* ~est *date that can be arranged – The Times*>

[1]**soot** /soot‖sʊt/ *n* a fine black powder that consists chiefly of carbon and is formed by combustion, or separated from fuel during combustion

[2]**soot** *vt* to coat or cover with soot

soothe /soohdh‖suːð/ *vt* **1** to calm (as if) by showing attention or concern; placate **2** to relieve, alleviate **3** to bring comfort or reassurance to ~*vi* to bring peace or ease – **soother** *n*, **soothingly** *adv*

soothsay /ˈsoohth,say‖ˈsuːθ,seɪ/ *vi* to predict the future; prophesy – **soothsayer** *n*

[1]**sop** /sop‖sɒp/ *n* **1** a piece of food, esp bread, dipped, steeped, or for dipping in a liquid (e g soup) **2** sthg offered as a concession, appeasement, or bribe

[2]**sop** *vt* **-pp-** to soak or dip (as if) in liquid <~ *bread in gravy*>

sophism /ˈsofiz(ə)m‖ˈsɒfɪz(ə)m/ *n* **1** an argument apparently correct but actually fallacious; *esp* such an argument used to deceive **2** use of sophisms; sophistry – **sophistic, sophistical** *adj*, **sophistically** *adv*

sophist /ˈsofist‖ˈsɒfɪst/ *n* a faultfinding or fallacious reasoner

sophisticate /səˈfistikət‖səˈfɪstɪkət/ *n* a sophisticated person

sophisticated /səˈfisti,kaytid‖səˈfɪstɪ,keɪtɪd/ *adj* **1a** highly complicated or developed; complex <~ *electronic devices*> **b** worldly-wise, knowing <*a* ~ *adolescent*> **2** intellectually subtle or refined <*a ~ novel*> **3** not in a natural, pure, or original state; adulterated <*a ~ oil*> – **sophisticatedly** *adv*, **sophistication** *n*

sophistry /ˈsofistri‖ˈsɒfɪstrɪ/ *n* speciously subtle reasoning or argument

sophomore /ˈsofə,maw‖ˈsɒfə,mɔː/ *n, NAm* a student in his/her second year at college or secondary school – **sophomoric** *adj*

[1]**soporific** /,sopəˈrifik‖,sɒpəˈrɪfɪk/ *adj* **1** causing or tending to cause sleep **2** of or marked by sleepiness or lethargy

[2]**soporific** *n* a soporific agent; *specif* HYPNOTIC 1

sopping /ˈsoping‖ˈsɒpɪŋ/ *adj* wet through; soaking

soppy /ˈsopi‖ˈsɒpɪ/ *adj* **1** weakly sentimental; mawkish **2** *chiefly Br* silly, inane *USE* infml – **soppily** *adv*, **soppiness** *n*

soprano /səˈprahnoh‖səˈprɑːnəʊ/ *n, pl* **sopranos** **1** the highest part in 4-part harmony **2** (a person with) the highest singing voice of women, boys, or castrati **3** a member of a family of instruments having the highest range [Italian, fr *sopra* above, fr Latin *supra*] – **soprano** *adj*

sop up /sop‖sɒp/ *vt* to mop up (e g water) so as to leave a dry surface

sorbet /ˈsawbit‖ˈsɔːbɪt/ *n* WATER ICE; *also* SHERBET 2

sorcerer /ˈsaws(ə)rə‖ˈsɔːs(ə)rə/, *fem* **sorceress** /-ris‖-rɪs/ *n* a person who uses magical power, esp with the aid of evil spirits; a wizard

sorcery /ˈsaws(ə)ri‖ˈsɔːs(ə)rɪ/ *n* the arts and practices of a sorcerer [Old French *sorcerie*, fr *sorcier* sorcerer, fr Latin *sort-, sors* chance, lot]

sordid /ˈsawdid‖ˈsɔːdɪd/ *adj* **1a** dirty, filthy **b** wretched, squalid **2** base, vile <*~ motives*> **3** meanly avaricious; niggardly **4** of a dull or muddy colour – **sordidly** *adv*, **sordidness** *n*

[1]**sore** /saw‖sɔː/ *adj* **1a** causing pain or distress **b** painfully sensitive <*~ muscles*> **c** hurt or inflamed so as to be or seem painful <*~ runny eyes*> **2a** causing irritation or offence <*overtime is a ~ point with him*> **b** causing great difficulty or anxiety; desperate <*in ~ straits*> **3** *chiefly NAm* angry, vexed – **soreness** *n*

[2]**sore** *n* **1** a localized sore spot on the body; *esp* one (e g an ulcer) with the tissues ruptured or abraded and usu infected **2** a source of pain or vexation; an affliction

[3]**sore** *adv, archaic* sorely

ˈ**sore,head** /-,hed‖-,hed/ *n, NAm* a person easily angered or disgruntled – infml – **sorehead, soreheaded** *adj*

sorely /ˈsawli‖ˈsɔːlɪ/ *adv* **1** painfully, grievously **2** much, extremely <*~ needed changes*>

sorghum /ˈsawgəm‖ˈsɔːgəm/ *n* any of an economically important genus of Old World tropical grasses similar to maize in habit but with the spikelets in pairs on a hairy stalk

sorority /səˈrorəti‖səˈrɒrətɪ/ *n* a club of women students usu living in the same house in some American universities

[1]**sorrel** /ˈsorəl‖ˈsɒrəl/ *n* **1** brownish orange to light brown **2** a sorrel-coloured animal; *esp* a sorrel-coloured horse

[2]**sorrel** *n* **1** [1]DOCK **2** WOOD SORREL

[1]**sorrow** /ˈsoroh‖ˈsɒrəʊ/ *n* **1** deep distress and regret (e g over the loss of sthg precious) **2** a cause or display of grief or sadness

[2]**sorrow** *vi* to feel or express sorrow – **sorrower** *n*

sorry /ˈsori‖ˈsɒrɪ/ *adj* **1** feeling regret, penitence, or pity <*felt ~ for the poor wretch*> **2** inspiring sorrow, pity, or scorn <*looked a ~ sight in his torn clothes*> – **sorriness** *n*

[1]**sort** /sawt‖sɔːt/ *n* **1a** a group constituted on the basis of any common characteristic; a class, kind **b** an instance of a kind <*a ~ of herbal medicine*> **2** nature, disposition <*people of an evil ~*> **3** a letter or piece of type in a fount **4** a person, individual – infml <*he's not a bad ~*> – **of sorts/of a sort** of an inconsequential or mediocre quality – **out of sorts 1** somewhat ill **2** grouchy, irritable

[2]**sort** *vt* **1** to put in a rank or particular place according to kind, class, or quality <*~ the good apples from the bad*> – often + *through* **2** *chiefly Scot* to put in working order; mend <*~ a vacuum cleaner*> – **sortable** *adj*, **sorter** *n* – **sort with** to correspond to; agree with – fml

sortie /ˈsawti‖ˈsɔːtɪ/ *n* **1** a sudden issuing of troops from a defensive position **2** a single mission or attack by 1 aircraft **3** a brief trip to a hostile or unfamiliar place – **sortie** *vi*

ˈ**sort of** *adv* **1** to a moderate degree; rather **2** KIND OF *USE* infml

ˈ**sort-,out** *n, chiefly Br* an act of putting things in order <*my study needs a good ~*>

sort out *vt* **1** to clarify or resolve, esp by thoughtful consideration <sorting out *his problems*> **2a** to separate from a mass or group <sort out *the important papers and throw the rest away*> **b** to clear up; tidy <*will take ages to* sort out *this mess*> **3** to make (e g a person) less confused or unsettled <*hoped the doctor would* sort *him* out> **4** *chiefly Br* to punish, esp by violent means – infml

SOS /,es oh ˈes‖,es əʊ ˈes/ *n* **1** an internationally recognized signal of distress which is rendered in Morse code as ··· – – – ··· **2** a call or request for help or rescue [letters chosen purely for being simple to transmit & recognize in Morse code]

[1]**so-so** /ˈsoh ,soh‖ˈsəʊ ,səʊ/ *adv* moderately well; tolerably

[2]**so-so** *adj* neither very good nor very bad; middling

sot /sot‖sɒt/ *n* a habitual drunkard – **sottish** *adj*

sotto voce /,sotoh ˈvohchi‖,sɒtəʊ ˈvəʊtʃɪ/ *adv or adj* **1** under the breath; in an undertone; *also* in a private manner **2** at a very low volume – used in music [Italian *sottovoce*, lit., under the voice]

sou /sooh‖suː/ *n, pl* **sous** /sooh(z)‖suː(z)/ **1** any of various former French coins of low value **2** the smallest amount of money <*hadn't a ~ to his name*>

soubrette /soohˈbret‖suːˈbret/ *n* (an actress who plays) a coquettish maid or frivolous young woman in comedies

soubriquet /ˈsoohbri,kay‖ˈsuːbrɪ,keɪ/ *n* a sobriquet

[1]**soufflé** /ˈsoohflay‖ˈsuːfleɪ/ *n* a light fluffy baked or chilled dish made with a thick sauce into which egg yolks, stiffly beaten egg whites, and sometimes gelatin are incorporated

[French, fr *soufflé*, past participle of *souffler* to blow, puff up, fr Latin *sufflare*, fr *sub-* up + *flare* to blow]

[2]**soufflé**, **souffléed** /'soohflayd‖'su:fleɪd/ *adj* puffed or made light by or in cooking

sough /sow‖saʊ/ *vi* to make a sound like that of wind in the trees – **sough** *n*

sought /sawt‖sɔ:t/ *past of* SEEK

'**sought-ˌafter** *adj* greatly desired or courted

[1]**soul** /sohl‖səʊl/ *n* **1** the immaterial essence or animating principle of an individual life **2** the spiritual principle embodied in human beings, all rational and spiritual beings, or the universe **3** all that constitutes a person's self **4a** an active or essential part <*minorities are the very* ~ *of democracy*> **b** a moving spirit; a leader <*the* ~ *of the rebellion*> **5** spiritual vitality; fervour **6** a person <*she's a kind old* ~> **7** exemplification, personification <*he's the* ~ *of integrity*> **8a** a strong positive feeling esp of intense sensitivity and emotional fervour conveyed esp by American Negro performers **b** negritude **c** music that originated in American Negro gospel singing, is closely related to rhythm and blues, and is characterized by intensity of feeling and earthiness – **souled** *adj*

[2]**soul** *adj* (characteristic) of American Negroes or their culture

'**soul ˌbrother** *n* a male Negro – used esp by other Negroes

'**soul-deˌstroying** *adj* giving no chance for the mind to work; very uninteresting

'**soulful** /-f(ə)l‖-f(ə)l/ *adj* full of or expressing esp intense or excessive feeling <*a* ~ *song*> – **soulfully** *adv*, **soulfulness** *n*

'**soulless** /-lis‖-lɪs/ *adj* **1** having no soul or no warmth of feeling **2** bleak, uninviting <*a* ~ *room*> – **soullessly** *adv*, **soullessness** *n*

'**soul-ˌsearching** *n* scrutiny of one's mind and conscience, esp with regard to aims and motives

[1]**sound** /sownd‖saʊnd/ *adj* **1a** healthy **b** free from defect or decay <~ *timber*> **2** solid, firm; *also* stable **3a** free from error, fallacy, or misapprehension <~ *reasoning*> **b** exhibiting or grounded in thorough knowledge and experience <~ *scholarship*> **c** conforming to accepted views; orthodox **4a** deep and undisturbed <*a* ~ *sleep*> **b** thorough, severe <*a* ~ *whipping*> **5** showing integrity and good judgment – **soundly** *adv*, **soundness** *n*

[2]**sound** *adv* fully, thoroughly <~ *asleep*>

[3]**sound** *n* **1a** the sensation perceived by the sense of hearing **b** a particular auditory impression or quality <*the* ~ *of children playing*> **c** mechanical radiant energy that is transmitted by longitudinal pressure waves in a material medium (e g air) and is the objective cause of hearing **2** a speech sound <-cher *of 'teacher' and* -ture *of 'creature' have the same* ~> **3** the impression conveyed by sthg <*he's having a rough time by the* ~ *of it*> **4** hearing distance; earshot **5** a characteristic musical style <*the Liverpool* ~ *of the 1960s*> **6** radio broadcasting as opposed to television – **soundless** *adj*, **soundlessly** *adv*

[4]**sound** *vi* **1a** to make a sound **b** to resound **c** to give a summons by sound <*the bugle* ~s *to battle*> **2** to have a specified import when heard; seem <*his story* ~s *incredible*> ~ *vt* **1a** to cause to emit sound <~ *a trumpet*> **b** to give out (a sound) <~ *an A*> **2** to put into words; voice **3a** to make known; proclaim <~ *his praises far and wide*> **b** to order, signal, or indicate by a sound <~ *the alarm*> **4** to examine by causing to emit sounds – **soundable** *adj*

[5]**sound** *n* **1a** a long broad sea inlet **b** a long passage of water connecting 2 larger bodies or separating a mainland and an island **2** the air bladder of a fish

[6]**sound** *vt* **1** to measure the depth of <~ *a well*> **2** to explore or examine (a body cavity) with sound ~ *vi* **1** to determine the depth of water, esp with a sounding line **2** *of a fish or whale* to dive down suddenly

[7]**sound** *n* a probe for exploring or sounding body cavities

'**sound ˌbarrier** *n* a sudden large increase in aerodynamic drag that occurs as an aircraft nears the speed of sound

'**soundˌboard** /-ˌbawd‖-ˌbɔ:d/ *n* **1** a thin resonant board so placed in a musical instrument as to reinforce its sound by sympathetic vibration **2** SOUNDING BOARD 1a(1)

[1]**sounding** /'sownding‖'saʊndɪŋ/ *n* **1a** measurement by sounding **b** the depth so determined **2** the measurement of atmospheric conditions **3** a probe, test, or sampling of opinion or intention – often pl

[2]**sounding** *adj* **1** sonorous, resounding **2** making a usu specified sound or impression – usu in combination <*odd* ~> – **soundingly** *adv*

'**sounding ˌboard** *n* **1a(1)** a structure behind or over a pulpit, rostrum, or platform to direct sound forwards **a(2)** SOUNDBOARD 1 **b** a device or agency that helps disseminate opinions or ideas **2** sby or sthg used to test reaction to new ideas, plans, etc

sound off *vi* **1** to voice opinions freely and vigorously **2** *chiefly NAm* to speak loudly *USE* infml

sound out *vt* to attempt to find out the views or intentions of <sound *him* out *about the new proposals*>

[1]'**soundˌproof** /-ˌproohf‖-ˌpru:f/ *adj* impervious to sound <~ *glass*>

[2]**soundproof** *vt* to insulate so as to obstruct the passage of sound

'**sound ˌtrack** *n* the area on a film that carries the sound recording; *also* the recorded music accompanying a film

soup /soohp‖su:p/ *n* **1** a liquid food typically having a meat, fish, or vegetable stock as a base and often thickened and containing pieces of solid food **2** an awkward or embarrassing predicament – infml <*he's really in the* ~ *over that business last night*> – **soupy** *adj*

soupçon /'sooh(p)son, -sonh‖'su:(p)sɒn, -sɑ̃/ *n* a little bit; a dash [French, lit., suspicion, fr Latin *suspect-*, *suspicere* to suspect, fr *sub-* up + *specere* to look at]

'**soup ˌkitchen** *n* an establishment dispensing minimum food (e g soup and bread) to the needy

soup up *vt* **1** to increase the power of (an

engine or car) **2** to make more attractive, interesting, etc *USE* infml

[1]**sour** /sowə‖saʊə/ *adj* **1** being or inducing the one of the 4 basic taste sensations that is produced chiefly by acids <~ *pickles*> **2a(1)** having the acid taste or smell (as if) of fermentation <~ *cream*> **a(2)** of or relating to fermentation **b** smelling or tasting of decay; rotten <~ *breath*> **c** wrong, awry <*a project gone* ~> **3a** unpleasant, distasteful **b** morose, bitter **4** *esp of soil* acid in reaction – **sourish** *adj*, **sourly** *adv*, **sourness** *n*

[2]**sour** *n* **1** the primary taste sensation produced by sthg sour **2** *chiefly NAm* a cocktail made with a usu specified spirit, lemon or lime juice, sugar, and sometimes soda water <*a whisky* ~>

[3]**sour** *vb* to make or become sour

source /saws‖sɔːs/ *n* **1** the point of origin of a stream of water **2a(1)** a generative force; a cause **a(2)** a means of supply <*a secret* ~ *of wealth*> **b(1)** a place of origin; a beginning **b(2)** sby or sthg that initiates **b(3)** a person, publication, etc that supplies information, esp at firsthand **3** *archaic* a spring, fountain – **sourceless** *adj*

sourdough /ˈsowəˌdoh‖ˈsaʊəˌdəʊ/ *n*, *NAm* an old-timer, esp a prospector, of Alaska or NW Canada

ˈ**sourˌpuss** /-ˌpoos‖-ˌpʊs/ *n* a habitually gloomy or bitter person – infml

sousaphone /ˈsoohzəˌfohn‖ˈsuːzəˌfəʊn/ *n* a large tuba that has a flared adjustable bell and is designed to encircle the player and rest on the left shoulder [John Philip *Sousa* (1854-1932), US bandmaster & composer]

[1]**souse** /sows‖saʊs/ *vt* **1** to pickle <~d *herring*> **2a** to plunge in liquid; immerse **b** to drench, saturate **3** to make drunk; inebriate – infml ~*vi* to become immersed or drenched

[2]**souse** *n* **1** an act of sousing; a wetting **2** *chiefly NAm* sthg pickled; *esp* seasoned and chopped pork trimmings, fish, or shellfish

[1]**south** /sowth‖saʊθ *adj or adv* towards, at, belonging to, or coming from the south

[2]**south** *n* **1** (the compass point corresponding to) the direction of the south terrestrial pole **2** *often cap* regions or countries lying to the south of a specified or implied point of orientation – **southward** *adv, adj, or n*, **southwards** *adv*

[1]ˌ**southˈeast** /-ˈeest‖-ˈiːst/ *adj or adv* towards, at, belonging to, or coming from the southeast

[2]**southeast** *n* **1** (the general direction corresponding to) the compass point midway between south and east **2** *often cap* regions or countries lying to the southeast of a specified or implied point of orientation – **southeastward** *adv, adj, or n*, **southeastwards** *adv*

[1]ˌ**southˈeasterly** /-ˈeestəli‖-ˈiːstəlɪ/ *adj or adv* southeast

[2]**southeasterly**, **southeaster** *n* a wind from the SE

ˌ**southˈeastern** /-ˈeestən‖-ˈiːstən/ *adj* **1** *often cap* (characteristic) of a region conventionally designated Southeast **2** southeast – **southeasternmost** *adj*

[1]**southerly** /ˈsudhəli‖ˈsʌðəlɪ/ *adj or adv* south

[2]**southerly** *n* a wind from the S

southern /ˈsudhən‖ˈsʌðən/ *adj* **1** *often cap* (characteristic) of a region conventionally designated South **2** south – **southernmost** *adj*

Southerner /ˈsudhənə‖ˈsʌðənə/ *n* a native or inhabitant of the South

ˌ**southern ˈlights** *n pl* AURORA AUSTRALIS

ˈ**southˌpaw** /-ˌpaw‖-ˌpɔː/ *n* a left-hander; *specif* a boxer who leads with the right hand and guards with the left – **southpaw** *adj*

ˌ**south ˈpole** *n* **1a** *often cap S&P* the southernmost point of the rotational axis of the earth or another celestial body **b** the southernmost point on the celestial sphere, about which the stars seem to revolve **2** the southward-pointing pole of a magnet

[1]**southwest** /ˌsowthˈwest‖ˌsaʊθˈwest; *esp tech* ˌsowˈwest‖ˌsaʊˈwest/ *adj or adv* towards, at, belonging to, or coming from the southwest

[2]**southwest** *n* **1** (the general direction corresponding to) the compass point midway between south and west **2** *often cap* regions or countries lying to the southwest of a specified or implied point of orientation – **southwestward** *adv, adj, or n*, **southwestwards** *adv*

southwester /ˌsowthˈwestə‖ˌsaʊθˈwestə; *esp tech* ˌsowˈwestə‖ˌsaʊˈwestə/ *n* a southwesterly

[1]ˌ**southˈwesterly** /-li‖-lɪ/ *adj or adv* southwest

[2]**southwesterly**, **southwester** *n* a wind from the SW

ˌ**southˈwestern** /-ˈwestən‖-ˈwestən/ *adj* **1** *often cap* (characteristic) of a region conventionally designated Southwest **2** southwest – **southwesternmost** *adj*

[1]**souvenir** /ˌsoohvəˈniə‖ˌsuːvəˈnɪə/ *n* sthg that serves as a reminder (e g of a place or past event); a memento [French, lit., act of remembering, fr (*se*) *souvenir* to remember, fr Latin *subvenire* to come up, come to mind, fr *sub*-up + *venire* to come] – **souvenir** *adj*

[2]**souvenir** *vt*, *chiefly Austr* to steal, pilfer – infml

sou'wester /ˌsowˈwestə‖ˌsaʊˈwestə/ *n* **1** a southwesterly **2a** a long usu oilskin waterproof coat worn esp at sea during stormy weather **b** a waterproof hat with a wide slanting brim longer at the back than in front

[1]**sovereign** /ˈsovrin‖ˈsɒvrɪn/ *n* **1a** one possessing sovereignty **b** an acknowledged leader <*the rose,* ~ *among flowers*> **2** a former British gold coin worth 1 pound

[2]**sovereign** *adj* **1a** possessing supreme (political) power <~ *ruler*> **b** unlimited in extent; absolute <~ *power*> **c** enjoying political autonomy <*a* ~ *state*> **2a** of outstanding excellence or importance <*their* ~ *sense of humour* – Sir Winston Churchill> **b** of an unqualified nature; utmost <~ *contempt*> **3** (characteristic) of or befitting a sovereign – **sovereignly** *adv*, **sovereignty** *n*

soviet /ˈsohvyət, ˈso-‖ˈsəʊvjət, ˈsɒ-/ *n* **1** an elected council in a Communist country **2** *pl, cap* the people, esp the leaders, of the USSR – **soviet** *adj, often cap*, **sovietism** *n, often cap*

[1]**sow** /sow‖saʊ/ *n* an adult female pig; *also* the adult female of various other animals (e g the grizzly bear)

[2]**sow** /soh‖səʊ/ *vb* **sowed; sown** /sohn‖səʊn/,

sowed *vi* to plant seed for growth, esp by scattering ~ *vt* **1a** to scatter (e g seed) on the earth for growth; *broadly* PLANT 1a **b** to strew (as if) with seed **c** to introduce into a selected environment **2** to implant, initiate <~ *suspicion*> **3** to disperse, disseminate – **sower** *n* – **sow one's wild oats** to indulge in youthful wildness and dissipation, usu before settling down to a steady way of life

soy /soy‖sɔɪ/ *n* **1** an oriental brown liquid sauce made by subjecting soya beans to long fermentation and to digestion in brine **2** SOYA BEAN

soya /ˈsoyə‖ˈsɔɪə/ *n* soy

soya bean *n* (the edible oil-rich and protein-rich seeds of) an annual Asiatic leguminous plant widely grown for its seed and soil improvement

ˈsoy,bean /-ˌbeen‖-ˌbiːn/ *n* SOYA BEAN

sozzled /ˈsoz(ə)ld‖ˈsɒz(ə)ld/ *adj, chiefly Br* drunk – slang; often humor

spa /spah‖spɑː/ *n* **1** a usu fashionable resort with mineral springs **2** a spring of mineral water [*Spa*, watering place in Belgium]

[1]space /spays‖speɪs/ *n* **1** (the duration of) a period of time **2a** a limited extent in 1, 2, or 3 dimensions; distance, area, or volume **b** an amount of room set apart or available <*parking* ~> **3** any of the degrees between or above or below the lines of a musical staff **4a** a boundless 3-dimensional extent in which objects and events occur and have relative position and direction **b** physical space independent of what occupies it **5** the region beyond the earth's atmosphere **6** (a piece of type giving) a blank area separating words or lines (e g on a page) **7** a set of mathematical points, each defined by a set of coordinates

[2]space *vt* to place at intervals or arrange with space between – **spacer** *n*

ˈspace,craft /-ˌkrahft‖-ˌkrɑːft/ *n* a device designed to travel beyond the earth's atmosphere

,spaced-ˈout *adj* dazed or stupefied (as if) by a narcotic substance – slang

ˈspace,ship /-ˌship‖-ʃɪp/ *n* a manned spacecraft

ˈspace ,suit *n* a suit equipped with life-supporting provisions to make life in space possible for its wearer

ˈspace ,walk *n* a trip outside a spacecraft made by an astronaut in space – **space walk** *vi*, **spacewalker** *n*, **spacewalking** *n*

spacing /ˈspaysing‖ˈspeɪsɪŋ/ *n* **1a** the act of providing with spaces or placing at intervals **b** an arrangement in space <*alter the* ~ *of the chairs*> **2** the distance between any 2 objects in a usu regularly arranged series

spacious /ˈspayshəs‖ˈspeɪʃəs/ *adj* **1** containing ample space; roomy **2a** broad or vast in area <*a country of* ~ *plains*> **b** large in scale or space; expansive – **spaciously** *adv*, **spaciousness** *n*

[1]spade /spayd‖speɪd/ *n* a digging implement that can be pushed into the ground with the foot – **spadeful** *n*

[2]spade *vt* to dig up, shape, or work (as if) with a spade

[3]spade *n* **1a** a playing card marked with 1 or more black figures shaped like a spearhead **b** *pl but sing or pl in constr* the suit comprising cards identified by these figures **2** a Negro – derog

ˈspade,work /-ˌwuhk‖-ˌwɜːk/ *n* the routine preparatory work for an undertaking

spaghetti /spəˈgeti‖spəˈgetɪ/ *n* pasta in the form of thin often solid strings of varying widths smaller in diameter than macaroni [Italian, lit., little strings, fr *spago* cord, string]

spake /spayk‖speɪk/ *archaic past of* SPEAK

Spam /spam‖spæm/ *trademark* – used for a tinned pork luncheon meat

[1]span /span‖spæn/ *archaic past of* SPIN

[2]span *n* **1** the distance from the end of the thumb to the end of the little finger of a spread hand; *also* a former English unit of length equal to 9in (about 0.23m) **2** an extent, distance, or spread between 2 limits: e g **2a** a limited stretch (e g of time); *esp* an individual's lifetime **b** the full reach or extent <*the remarkable* ~ *of his memory*> **c** the distance or extent between abutments or supports (e g of a bridge); *also* a part of a bridge between supports **d** a wingspan

[3]span *vt* **-nn- 1** to measure (as if) by the hand with fingers and thumb extended **2a** to extend across <*his career* ~ned *4 decades*> **b** to form an arch over <*a small bridge* ~ned *the pond*> **c** to place or construct a span over

[1]spangle /ˈspang·gl‖ˈspæŋgl/ *n* **1** a sequin **2** a small glittering object or particle <*gold* ~s *of dew* – Edith Sitwell>

[2]spangle *vt* to set or sprinkle (as if) with spangles ~ *vi* to glitter as if covered with spangles; sparkle

spaniel /ˈspanyəl‖ˈspænjəl/ *n* **1** any of several breeds of small or medium-sized mostly short-legged dogs usu having long wavy hair, feathered legs and tail, and large drooping ears **2** a fawning servile person [Middle French *espaignol*, lit., Spaniard]

Spanish /ˈspanish‖ˈspænɪʃ/ *n* **1** the official Romance language of Spain and of the countries colonized by Spaniards **2** *pl in constr* the people of Spain – **Spanish** *adj*

Spanish chestnut *n* a large widely cultivated edible chestnut

[1]spank /spangk‖spæŋk/ *vt* to strike, esp on the buttocks, (as if) with the open hand – **spank** *n*

[2]spank *vi* to move quickly or spiritedly <~ing *along in his new car*>

[1]spanking /ˈspangking‖ˈspæŋkɪŋ/ *adj* **1** remarkable of its kind; striking **2** vigorous, brisk <*rode off at a* ~ *pace*> – **spankingly** *adv*

[2]spanking *adv* completely and impressively <*a* ~ *new car*>

spanner /ˈspanə‖ˈspænə/ *n, chiefly Br* a tool with 1 or 2 ends shaped for holding or turning nuts or bolts with nut-shaped heads – **(put) a spanner in the works** (to cause) obstruction or hindrance (e g to a plan or operation) – infml

[1]spar /spah‖spɑː/ *n* **1** a stout pole **2a** a mast, boom, gaff, yard, etc used to support or control a sail **b** any of the main longitudinal members of the wing or fuselage of an aircraft

[2]spar *vi* **-rr- 1a** [5]BOX; *esp* to gesture without landing a blow to draw one's opponent or create an opening **b** to engage in a practice bout of boxing **2** to skirmish, wrangle **3** FENCE 1b(2)

[3]spar *n* any of various nonmetallic minerals

which usu split easily

[1]**spare** /speə‖speə/ *vt* **1** to refrain from destroying, punishing, or harming **2** to refrain from using <~ *the rod, and spoil the child*> **3** to relieve of the necessity of doing, undergoing, or learning sthg <~ *yourself the trouble*> **4** to refrain from; avoid <~d *no expense*> **5** to use or dispense frugally – chiefly neg <*don't* ~ *the butter*> **6a** to give up as surplus to requirements <*do you have any cash to* ~?> **b** to have left over, unused, or unoccupied <*time to* ~> ~ *vi* to be frugal <*some will spend and some will* ~ – Robert Burns>

[2]**spare** *adj* **1** not in use; *esp* reserved for use in emergency <*a* ~ *tyre*> **2a** in excess of what is required; surplus **b** not taken up with work or duties; free <~ *time*> **3** sparing, concise <*a* ~ *prose style*> **4** healthily lean; wiry **5** not abundant; meagre – infml **6** *Br* extremely angry or distraught – infml <*nearly went* ~ *with worry*> – **sparely** *adv*, **spareness** *n*

[3]**spare** *n* **1** a spare or duplicate item or part; *specif* a spare part for a motor vehicle **2** the knocking down of all 10 pins with the first 2 balls in a frame in tenpin bowling

ˌ**spare ˈpart** *n* a replacement for a component that may cease or has ceased to function

ˌ**spareˈrib** /-ˈrib‖-ˈrɪb/ *n* a pork rib with most of the surrounding meat removed for use as bacon [by folk etymology fr Low German *ribbesper* pickled pork ribs roasted on a spit, fr *ribbe* rib + *sper* spear, spit]

ˌ**spare ˈtyre** *n* a roll of fat at the waist – infml

sparing /ˈspeəring‖ˈspeərɪŋ/ *adj* **1** not wasteful; frugal **2** meagre, scant – **sparingly** *adv*

[1]**spark** /spahk‖spɑːk/ *n* **1a** a small particle of a burning substance thrown out by a body in combustion or remaining when combustion is nearly completed **b** a hot glowing particle struck from a larger mass <~s *flying from under a hammer*> **2** a luminous disruptive electrical discharge of very short duration between 2 conductors of opposite high potential separated by a gas (e g air) **3** a sparkle, flash **4** sthg that sets off or stimulates an event, development, etc **5** a trace, esp one which may develop; a germ <*still retains a* ~ *of decency*> **6** *pl but sing in constr* a radio operator on a ship – infml

[2]**spark** *vi* to produce or give off sparks ~ *vt* **1** to cause to be suddenly active; precipitate – usu + *off* <*the question* ~ed *off a lively discussion*> **2** to stir to activity; incite <*a player can* ~ *his team to victory*> – **sparker** *n*

[3]**spark** *n* a lively and usu witty person – esp in *bright spark* – **sparkish** *adj*

ˈ**sparking ˌplug** /ˈspahking‖ˈspɑːkɪŋ/ *n*, *chiefly Br* a part that fits into the cylinder head of an internal-combustion engine and produces the spark which ignites the explosive mixture

[1]**sparkle** /ˈspahkl‖ˈspɑːkl/ *vi* **1a** to give off sparks **b** to give off or reflect glittering points of light; scintillate **2** to effervesce <*wine that* ~s> **3** to show brilliance or animation <*the dialogue* ~s *with wit*> ~ *vt* to cause to glitter or shine

[2]**sparkle** *n* **1** a little spark; a scintillation **2** sparkling **3a** vivacity, gaiety **b** effervescence <*a wine full of* ~>

sparkler /ˈspahklə‖ˈspɑːklə/ *n* **1** a firework that throws off brilliant sparks on burning **2** a (cut and polished) diamond – infml

sparrow /ˈsparoh‖ˈspærəʊ/ *n* any of several small dull-coloured songbirds related to the finches; *esp* HOUSE SPARROW

sparse /spahs‖spɑːs/ *adj* of few and scattered elements; *esp* not thickly grown or settled – **sparsely** *adv*, **sparseness** *n*, **sparsity** *n*

[1]**Spartan** /ˈspaht(ə)n‖ˈspɑːt(ə)n/ *n* **1** a native or inhabitant of ancient Sparta **2** a person of great courage and endurance – **Spartanism** *n*

[2]**Spartan** *adj* **1** of Sparta in ancient Greece **2a** rigorously strict; austere **b** having or showing courage and endurance

spasm /ˈspaz(ə)m‖ˈspæz(ə)m/ *n* **1** an involuntary and abnormal muscular contraction **2** a sudden violent and brief effort or emotion <~s *of helpless mirth – Punch*> [Middle French *spasme*, fr Latin *spasmus*, fr Greek *spasmos*, fr *span* to draw, pull]

spasmodic /spazˈmodik‖spæzˈmɒdɪk/ *adj* **1a** relating to, being, or affected or characterized by spasm **b** resembling a spasm, esp in sudden violence <*a* ~ *jerk*> **2** acting or proceeding fitfully; intermittent <~ *attempts at studying*> – **spasmodical** *adj*, **spasmodically** *adv*

[1]**spastic** /ˈspastik‖ˈspæstɪk/ *adj* **1** of or characterized by spasm <*a* ~ *colon*> **2** suffering from spastic paralysis <*a* ~ *child*> – **spastically** *adv*, **spasticity** *n*

[2]**spastic** *n* **1** one who is suffering from spastic paralysis **2** an ineffectual person – used esp by children

spastic paralysis *n* paralysis with involuntary contraction or uncontrolled movements of the affected muscles

[1]**spat** /spat‖spæt/ *past of* SPIT

[2]**spat** *n* a young oyster or other bivalve mollusc

[3]**spat** *n* a cloth or leather gaiter covering the instep and ankle

[4]**spat** *n* **1** *NAm* a light splash **2** a petty argument – infml

spatchcock /ˈspachˌkok‖ˈspætʃˌkɒk/ *vt* **1** to cook (a fowl or small game bird) by splitting along the backbone and frying or grilling **2** to insert or put together in a forced or incongruous way

spate /spayt‖speɪt/ *n* **1** flood <*a river in full* ~> **2a** a large number or amount, esp occurring in a short space of time **b** a sudden or strong outburst; a rush

spatial /ˈspaysh(ə)l‖ˈspeɪʃ(ə)l/ *adj* relating to, occupying, or occurring in space – **spatially** *adv*, **spatiality** *n*

[1]**spatter** /ˈspatə‖ˈspætə/ *vt* **1** to splash or sprinkle (as if) with drops of liquid; *also* to soil in this way <*his coat was* ~ed *with mud*> **2** to scatter (as if) by splashing or sprinkling <~ *water*> ~ *vi* to spurt out in scattered drops <*blood* ~ing *everywhere*>

[2]**spatter** *n* **1** (the sound of) spattering **2** a drop spattered on sthg or a stain due to spattering

spatula /ˈspatyoolə, -chələ‖ˈspætjʊlə, -tʃələ/ *n* a flat thin usu metal implement used esp for spreading, mixing, etc soft substances or powders

spavin /ˈspavin‖ˈspævɪn/ *n* a bony enlargement or soft swelling of the hock of a horse associated with strain – **spavined** *adj*

[1]**spawn** /spawn‖spɔːn/ *vt* **1** *of an aquatic animal* to produce or deposit (eggs) **2** to bring forth, esp abundantly ~ *vi* **1** to deposit spawn **2** to produce young, esp in large numbers – **spawner** *n*

[2]**spawn** *n* **1** the large number of eggs of frogs, oysters, fish, etc **2** *sing or pl in constr* (numerous) offspring **3** mycelium, esp for propagating mushrooms

spay /spay‖speɪ/ *vt* to remove the ovaries of

speak /speek‖spiːk/ *vb* **spoke** /spohk‖spəʊk/; **spoken** /ˈspohkən‖ˈspəʊkən/ *vi* **1a** to utter words or articulate sounds with the ordinary voice; talk **b(1)** to give voice to thoughts or feelings **b(2)** to be on speaking terms <*still were not* ~ing *after the dispute*> **c** to address a group <*the professor* spoke *on his latest discoveries*> **2a** to express thoughts or feelings in writing <*diaries that* ~ *of his ambition*> **b** to act as spokesman *for* **3** to communicate by other than verbal means <*actions* ~ *louder than words*> **4** to make a claim *for*; reserve <*5 of the 10 new houses are already* spoken *for*> **5** to make a characteristic or natural sound <*the thunder* spoke> **6** to be indicative or suggestive <*his battered shoes* spoke *of a long journey*> ~ *vt* **1a** to utter with the speaking voice; pronounce **b** to express orally; declare <*free to* ~ *their minds*> **2** to make known in writing **3** to (be able to) use in oral communication <~s *Spanish*> – **speakable** *adj* – **so to speak** – used as an apologetic qualification for an imprecise, unusual, ambiguous, or unclear phrase <*this bus service has gone downhill,* so to speak> – **to speak of** worth mentioning – usu neg

speakeasy /ˈspeek,eezi‖ˈspiːk,iːzɪ/ *n* a place where alcoholic drinks were illegally sold during Prohibition in the USA in the 1920's and 30's

speaker /ˈspeekə‖ˈspiːkə/ *n* **1a** one who speaks, esp at public functions **b** one who speaks a specified language <*an Italian*-speaker> **2** the presiding officer of a deliberative or legislative assembly **3** a loudspeaker – **speakership** *n*

ˈspeaking ˌtube *n* a pipe through which conversation may be conducted (e g between different parts of a building)

speak out *vi* **1** to speak loudly enough to be heard **2** to speak boldly; express an opinion frankly <spoke out *on the issues*>

speak up *vi* **1** to speak more loudly – often imper **2** to express an opinion boldly <speak up *for justice*>

[1]**spear** /spiə‖spɪə/ *n* **1** a thrusting or throwing weapon with long shaft and sharp head or blade used esp by hunters or foot soldiers **2** a sharp-pointed instrument with barbs used in spearing fish

[2]**spear** *vt* to pierce, strike, or take hold of (as if) with a spear <~ed *a sausage from the dish*>

[3]**spear** *n* a usu young blade, shoot, or sprout (e g of asparagus or grass)

[1]**ˈspear,head** /-,hed‖-,hed/ *n* **1** the sharp-pointed head of a spear **2** a leading element or force in a development, course of action, etc

[2]**spearhead** *vt* to serve as leader or leading force of

ˈspear,mint /-,mint‖-,mɪnt/ *n* a common mint grown esp for its aromatic oil

spec /spek‖spek/ *n* a speculation – infml – **on spec** *Br* as a risk or speculation <*houses built* on spec>; *also* as a risk in the hope of finding or obtaining sthg desired <*the play may be sold out, but it would be worth going to the theatre* on spec> – infml

[1]**special** /ˈspesh(ə)l‖ˈspeʃ(ə)l/ *adj* **1** distinguished from others of the same category, esp because in some way superior **2** held in particular esteem <*a* ~ *friend*> **3** SPECIFIC 4 **4** other than or in addition to the usual <*a* ~ *day of thanksgiving*> **5** designed, undertaken, or used for a particular purpose or need <*devised a* ~ *method of restoring paintings*> **6** established or designed for the use or education of the handicapped <*a* ~ *school*> – **specially** *adv*, **specialness** *n*

[2]**special** *n* **1** sthg that is not part of a series **2** sby or sthg reserved or produced for a particular use or occasion <*caught the commuter* ~ *to work*>

specialist /ˈspesh(ə)list‖ˈspeʃ(ə)lɪst/ *n* **1a** one who devotes him-/herself to a special occupation or branch of knowledge **b** a medical practitioner limiting his/her practice to a specific group of complaints <*an ear, nose, and throat* ~> **2** a rank in the US Army enabling an enlisted man/woman to draw extra pay because of technical qualifications – **specialist, specialistic** *adj*

speciality /,speshiˈaləti‖,speʃɪˈælətɪ/ *n* **1** (the state of having) a distinctive mark or quality **2** a product or object of particular quality <*bread pudding was mother's* ~> **3a** a special aptitude or skill **b** a particular occupation or branch of knowledge

special·ize, -ise /ˈspesh(ə)liez‖ˈspeʃ(ə)laɪz/ *vt* to apply or direct to a specific end or use ~ *vi* **1** to concentrate one's efforts in a special or limited activity or field **2** to undergo structural adaptation of a body part to a particular function or of an organism for life in a particular environment – **specialization** *n*

special licence *n* a British form of marriage license permitting marriage without the publication of banns or at a time and place other than those prescribed by law

special pleading *n* **1** the allegation of special or new matter in a legal action, as distinguished from a direct denial of the matter pleaded by the opposite side **2** an argument that ignores the damaging or unfavourable aspects of a case

specialty /ˈspesh(ə)lti‖ˈspeʃ(ə)ltɪ/ *n, chiefly NAm* a speciality

specie /ˈspeeshi‖ˈspiːʃɪ/ *n* money in coin – **in specie** in the same or similar form or kind <*ready to return insult* in specie>

species /ˈspeeshiz‖ˈspiːʃɪz/ *n, pl* **species** **1a** a class of individuals having common attributes and designated by a common name **b(1)** a category in the biological classification of living things that ranks immediately below a genus and comprises related organisms or populations potentially capable of interbreeding **b(2)** an individual or kind belonging to a biological species

c a particular kind of atomic nucleus, atom, molecule, or ion **2** the consecrated bread and wine of the Roman Catholic or Eastern Orthodox eucharist **3** a kind, sort – chiefly derog *<a dangerous ~ of criminal>*

[1]**specific** /spəˈsifik‖spəˈsɪfɪk/ *adj* **1a** constituting or falling into a specifiable category **b** being or relating to those properties of sthg that allow it to be assigned to a particular category *<the ~ qualities of a drug>* **2a** confined to a particular individual, group, or circumstance *<a disease ~ to horses>* **b** having a specific rather than a general influence (e g on a body part or a disease) *<antibodies ~ for the smallpox virus>* **3** free from ambiguity; explicit *<~ instructions>* **4** of or constituting a (biological) species **5a** being any of various arbitrary physical constants, esp one relating a quantitative attribute to unit mass, volume, or area **b** imposed at a fixed rate per unit (e g of weight or amount) *<~ import duties>* – **specifically** *adv*, **specificity** *n*

[2]**specific** *n* **1** a drug or remedy having a specific effect on a disease **2a** a characteristic quality or trait **b** *pl, chiefly NAm* particulars

specification /ˌspesifiˈkaysh(ə)n‖ˌspesɪfɪˈkeɪʃ(ə)n/ *n* **1** specifying **2a** a detailed description of sthg (e g a building or car), esp in the form of a plan – usu pl with sing. meaning **b** a written description of an invention for which a patent is sought

speˌcific ˈgravity *n* the ratio of the density of a substance to the density of a substance (e g pure water or hydrogen) taken as a standard when both densities are obtained by weighing in air

specify /ˈspesifie‖ˈspesɪfaɪ/ *vt* **1** to name or state explicitly or in detail **2** to include as an item in a specification *<~ oak flooring>* – **specifiable** *adj*, **specifier** *n*

specimen /ˈspesimin‖ˈspesɪmɪn/ *n* **1** an item, part, or individual typical of a group or category; an example **2** a person, individual – chiefly derog [Latin, fr *specere* to look at, look]

specious /ˈspeesh(y)əs‖ˈspiːʃ(j)əs/ *adj* **1** having deceptive attraction or fascination **2** superficially sound or genuine but fallacious *<~ reasoning>* – **speciously** *adv*, **speciousness** *n*

[1]**speck** /spek‖spek/ *n* **1** a small spot or blemish, esp from stain or decay **2** a small particle *<a ~ of sawdust>*

[2]**speck** *vt* to mark with specks

[1]**speckle** /ˈspekl‖ˈspekl/ *n* a little speck (e g of colour)

[2]**speckle** *vt* to mark (as if) with speckles

spectacle /ˈspektəkl‖ˈspektəkl/ *n* **1a** sthg exhibited as unusual, noteworthy, or entertaining; *esp* a striking or dramatic public display or show **b** an object of scorn or ridicule, esp due to odd appearance or behaviour *<made a ~ of himself>* **2** *pl* GLASSES 2b(2)

ˈ**spectacled** *adj* having (markings suggesting) a pair of spectacles *<the ~ salamander>*

[1]**spectacular** /spekˈtakyoolə‖spekˈtækjʊlə/ *adj* of or being a spectacle; sensational – **spectacularly** *adv*

[2]**spectacular** *n* sthg (e g a stage show) that is spectacular

spectator /spekˈtaytə‖spekˈteɪtə/ *n* **1** one who attends an event or activity in order to watch **2** one who looks on without participating; an onlooker *<rescuers were hampered by ~s>* – **spectator** *adj*

spectral /ˈspektrəl‖ˈspektrəl/ *adj* **1** of or suggesting a spectre **2** of or made by a spectrum – **spectrally** *adv*, **spectralness** *n*, **spectrality** *n*

spectre, *NAm chiefly* **specter** /ˈspektə‖ˈspektə/ *n* **1** a visible ghost **2** sthg that haunts or perturbs the mind; a phantasm *<the ~ of hunger>*

spectroscope /ˈspektrəˌskohp‖ˈspektrəˌskəʊp/ *n* an instrument for forming and examining optical spectra – **spectroscopic, spectroscopical** *adj*, **spectroscopically** *adv*, **spectroscopist** *n*, **spectroscopy** *n*

spectrum /ˈspektrəm‖ˈspektrəm/ *n, pl* **spectra** /-trə‖-trə/, **spectrums** **1** an array of the components of an emission or wave separated and arranged in the order of some varying characteristic (e g wavelength, mass, or energy): e g **1a** a series of images formed when a beam of radiant energy is subjected to dispersion and brought to focus so that the component waves are arranged in the order of their wavelengths (e g when a beam of sunlight that is refracted and dispersed by a prism forms a display of colours) **b** ELECTROMAGNETIC SPECTRUM **c** the range of frequencies of sound waves **2** a sequence, range *<a wide ~ of interests>*

speculate /ˈspekyoolayt‖ˈspekjʊleɪt/ *vi* **1** to meditate *on* or ponder *about* sthg; reflect **2** to assume a business risk in the hope of gain; *esp* to buy or sell in expectation of profiting from market fluctuations – **speculator** *n*, **speculation** *n*

speculative /ˈspekyoolətiv‖ˈspekjʊlətɪv/ *adj* **1** involving, based on, or constituting speculation; *also* theoretical rather than demonstrable **2** questioning, inquiring *<a ~ glance>* – **speculatively** *adv*

speech /speech‖spiːtʃ/ *n* **1a** the communication or expression of thoughts in spoken words **b** conversation **2** a public discourse; an address **3a** a language, dialect **b** an individual manner of speaking **4** the power of expressing or communicating thoughts by speaking

speechify /ˈspeechifie‖ˈspiːtʃɪfaɪ/ *vi* to speak or make a speech in a pompous manner

ˈ**speechless** /-lis‖-lɪs/ *adj* **1a** unable to speak; dumb **b** deprived of speech (e g through horror or rage) **2** refraining from speech; silent – **speechlessly** *adv*, **speechlessness** *n*

[1]**speed** /speed‖spiːd/ *n* **1a** moving swiftly; swiftness **b** rate of motion; *specif* the magnitude of a velocity irrespective of direction **2** rate of performance or execution *<tried to increase his reading ~>* **3a** the sensitivity of a photographic film, plate, or paper expressed numerically **b** the light-gathering power of a lens or optical system **c** the duration of a photographic exposure **4** *chiefly NAm* a transmission gear in motor vehicles **5** (a drug related to) amphetamine – slang – **at speed** at a fast speed; while travelling rapidly

[2]**speed** *vb* **sped** /sped‖sped/, **speeded** *vi* **1** to move or go quickly *<*sped *to her bedside>* **2** to travel at excessive or illegal speed *<drivers who*

are fined for ~ing> ~ *vt* **1** to promote the success or development of **2** to cause to move quickly; hasten – **speeder** *n*, **speedster** *n*

'speed ,limit *n* the maximum speed permitted by law in a given area or under specified circumstances

speedometer /spee'domitə, spi-‖spi:'dɒmɪtə, spɪ-/ *n* **1** an instrument for indicating speed **2** an instrument for indicating distance travelled as well as speed; *also* an odometer

'speed ,trap *n* a stretch of road along which police officers, radar devices, etc are stationed so as to catch vehicles exceeding the speed limit

'speed-,up *n* an acceleration

speed up *vb* to (cause to) move, work, or take place faster; accelerate

'speed,way /-,way‖-,weɪ/ *n* **1** a usu oval racecourse for motorcycles **2** the sport of racing motorcycles usu belonging to professional teams on closed cinder or dirt tracks

'speed,well /-,wel‖-,wel/ *n* any of a genus of plants that mostly have slender stems and small blue or whitish flowers

speedy /'speedi‖'spi:dɪ/ *adj* swift, quick – **speedily** *adv*, **speediness** *n*

speleology /,speeli'oləji‖,spi:lɪ'ɒlədʒɪ/ *n* the scientific study of caves – **speleologist** *n*, **speleological** *adj*

1**spell** /spel‖spel/ *n* **1a** a spoken word or form of words held to have magic power **b** a state of enchantment **2** a compelling influence or attraction

2**spell** *vb* **spelt** /spelt‖spelt/, *NAm chiefly* **spelled** *vt* **1** to name or write the letters of (e g a word) in order; *also, of letters* to form (e g a word) **2** to amount to; mean <*crop failure would* ~ *famine for the whole region*> – chiefly journ ~*vi* to form words using the correct combination of letters <*managers who still can't* ~>

3**spell** *vb* **spelled** *vt* **1** to give a brief rest to **2** *chiefly NAm* to relieve for a time; stand in for <*the 2 guards* ~ed *each other*> ~*vi, chiefly Austr* to rest from work or activity for a time

4**spell** *n* **1** a period spent in a job or occupation <*did a* ~ *in catering*> **2** a short or indefinite period or phase <*there will be cold* ~s *throughout April*> **3** 2FIT 1b **4** *chiefly Austr* a period of rest from work, activity, or use

'spell,binder /-,biendə‖-,baɪndə/ *n* sby or sthg that holds one spellbound; *esp* a speaker of compelling eloquence – **spellbinding** *adj*

spelling /'speling‖'spelɪŋ/ *n* **1** the forming of or ability to form words from letters **2** the sequence of letters that make up a particular word

spell out *vt* **1** to read slowly and haltingly **2** to come to understand; discern <*tried in vain to* spell out *his meaning*> **3** to explain clearly and in detail

spend /spend‖spend/ *vb* **spent** /spent‖spent/ *vt* **1** to use up or pay out; expend <spent *£90 on a new suit*> **2** to wear out, exhaust <*the storm gradually* spent *itself*> **3** to cause or permit to elapse; pass <spent *the summer at the beach*> ~*vi* to pay out resources, esp money – **spendable** *adj*, **spender** *n* – **spend a penny** *Br* to urinate – euph

'spending ,money *n* POCKET MONEY

'spend,thrift /-,thrift‖-,θrɪft/ *n* one who spends carelessly or wastefully – **spendthrift** *adj*

spent /spent‖spent/ *adj* **1a** used up; consumed **b** exhausted of useful components or qualities <~ *grain*> <~ *matches*> **2** drained of energy; exhausted <~ *after his nightlong vigil*> **3** exhausted of spawn or sperm <*a* ~ *salmon*>

sperm /spuhm‖spɜ:m/ *n* **1a** the male fertilizing fluid; semen **b** a male gamete **2** spermaceti, oil, etc from the sperm whale

spermaceti /,spuhmə'seeti, -'seti‖,spɜ:mə'si:tɪ, -'setɪ/ *n* a waxy solid obtained from the oil of whales, esp sperm whales, and used in ointments, cosmetics, and candles [Medieval Latin *sperma ceti* whale sperm]

spermatozoon /,spuhmətə'zoh·ən‖,spɜ:mətə'zəʊən/ *n, pl* **spermatozoa** /-'zoh·ə‖-'zəʊə/ a motile male gamete of an animal, usu with rounded or elongated head and a long tail-like flagellum – **spermatozoal** *adj*

spermicide /'spuhmisied‖'spɜ:mɪsaɪd/ *n* a substance that kills sperm, esp as a contraceptive – **spermicidal** *adj*

'sperm ,whale *n* a large toothed whale that has a vast blunt head in the front part of which is a cavity containing a fluid mixture of spermaceti and oil

1**spew** /spyooh‖spju:/ *vi* **1** to vomit **2** to come forth in a flood or gush ~*vt* to propel or eject with violence or in great quantity <*a volcano* ~ing *ash and lava*> – **spewer** *n*

2**spew** *n* **1** vomit **2** material that gushes or is ejected from a source

sphagnum /'sfagnəm, 'spagnəm‖'sfægnəm, 'spægnəm/ *n* any of a large genus of atypical mosses that grow only in wet acid areas (e g bogs) where their remains become compacted with other plant debris to form peat

1**sphere** /sfiə‖sfɪə/ *n* **1a** (a globe depicting) the apparent surface of the heavens of which half forms the dome of the visible sky **b** any of the revolving spherical transparent shells in which, according to ancient astronomy, the celestial bodies are set **2a** a globular body; a ball **b** a planet, star **c** (a space or solid enclosed by) a surface, all points of which are equidistant from the centre **3** natural or proper place; *esp* social position or class **4** a field of action, existence, or influence – **spheral** *adj*, **spheric** *adj*, **sphericity** *n*

2**sphere** *vt* **1** to place or enclose in a sphere **2** to form into a sphere

spherical /'sferikl‖'sferɪkl/ *adj* **1** having the form of (a segment of) a sphere **2** relating to or dealing with (the properties of) a sphere – **spherically** *adv*

spheroid /'sfiəroyd‖'sfɪərɔɪd/ *n* a figure resembling a sphere – **spheroidal** *adj*, **spheroidally** *adv*

sphincter /'sfingktə‖'sfɪŋktə/ *n* a muscular ring, surrounding and able to contract or close a bodily opening – **sphincteral** *adj*

sphinx /sfinks‖sfɪnks/ *n, pl* **sphinxes, sphinges** /-jeez‖-dʒi:z/ **1a** *cap* a female monster in Greek mythology, with a lion's body and a human head, that killed those who failed to answer a riddle she asked **b** an enigmatic or mysterious person **2** an ancient Egyptian image in the form of a recumbent lion, usu with a human head

[1]**spice** /spies‖spaɪs/ *n* **1a** any of various aromatic vegetable products (e g pepper, ginger, or nutmeg) used to season or flavour foods **b** such products collectively **2** sthg that adds zest or relish <*variety's the very* ~ *of life* – William Cowper> **3** a pungent or aromatic smell

[2]**spice** *vt* **1** to season with spice **2** to add zest or relish to <*cynicism* ~d *with wit*>

spick-and-span, **spic-and-span** /ˌspik ənd ˈspan‖ˌspɪk ənd ˈspæn/ *adj* spotlessly clean and tidy; spruce

spicy /ˈspiesi‖ˈspaɪsɪ/ *adj* **1** lively, spirited <*a* ~ *temper*> **2** piquant, zestful **3** somewhat scandalous; risqué <~ *gossip*> – **spicily** *adv*, **spiciness** *n*

spider /ˈspiedə‖ˈspaɪdə/ *n* any of an order of arachnids having a body with 2 main divisions, 4 pairs of walking legs, and 2 or more pairs of abdominal organs for spinning threads of silk used for cocoons, nests, or webs

spider's web *n* the (geometrically patterned) silken web spun by most spiders and used as a resting place and a trap for small prey

spidery /ˈspied(ə)ri‖ˈspaɪd(ə)rɪ/ *adj* **1a** resembling a spider in form or manner; *specif* long, thin, and sharply angular like the legs of a spider **b** resembling a spider's web; *esp* composed of fine threads or lines in a weblike arrangement <~ *handwriting*> **2** infested with spiders

[1]**spiel** /s(h)peel‖spiːl,ʃp-/ *vb, chiefly NAm vi* to talk volubly or extravagantly ~ *vt* to utter or express volubly or extravagantly – usu + *off* *USE* infml [German *spielen* to play] – **spieler** *n*

[2]**spiel** *n, chiefly NAm* a voluble talk designed to influence or persuade; patter – infml

spigot /ˈspigət‖ˈspɪgət/ *n* **1** a small plug used to stop up the vent of a cask **2** the part of a tap, esp on a barrel, which controls the flow **3** a plain end of a piece of piping or guttering that fits into an adjoining piece

[1]**spike** /spiek‖spaɪk/ *n* **1** a very large nail **2a** any of a row of pointed iron pieces (e g on the top of a wall or fence) **b(1)** any of several metal projections set in the sole and heel of a shoe to improve traction **b(2)** *pl* a pair of (athletics) shoes having spikes attached **3** the act or an instance of spiking in volleyball **4a** a pointed element in a graph or tracing **b** an unusually high and sharply defined maximum (e g of amplitude in a wave train)

[2]**spike** *vt* **1** to fasten or provide with spikes <~ *the soles of climbing boots*> **2** to disable (a muzzle-loading cannon) by driving a spike into the vent **3** to pierce with or impale on a spike; *specif* to reject (newspaper copy), orig by impaling on a spike **4** to add spirits to (a nonalcoholic drink) **5** to drive (a volleyball) sharply downwards into an opponent's court **6** *chiefly NAm* to suppress or thwart completely <~d *the rumour*> – **spiker** *n* – **spike someone's guns** to frustrate sby's opposition; foil an opponent

[3]**spike** *n* **1** an ear of grain **2** an elongated plant inflorescence with the flowers stalkless on a single main axis

spiky /ˈspieki‖ˈspaɪkɪ/ *adj* **1** having a sharp projecting point or points **2** caustic, aggressive <*a* ~ *retort*>

[1]**spill** /spil‖spɪl/ *vb* **spilt** /spilt‖spɪlt/, *NAm chiefly* **spilled** *vt* **1** to cause (blood) to be shed **2a** to cause or allow to fall or flow out so as to be lost or wasted, esp accidentally **b** to empty, discharge <*train* spilt *its occupants onto the platform*> **3** to empty (a sail) of wind **4** to throw off or out <*his horse* spilt *him*> **5** to let out; divulge <~ *a secret*> – infml ~ *vi* **1a** to fall or flow out or over and become wasted, scattered, or lost **b** to cause or allow sthg to spill **2** to spread profusely or beyond limits <*crowds* spilt *into the streets*> – **spillable** *adj*, **spiller** *n* – **spill the beans** to divulge information indiscreetly – infml

[2]**spill** *n* **1** a fall from a horse or vehicle **2** a quantity spilt

[3]**spill** *n* a thin twist of paper or sliver of wood used esp for lighting a fire

spillway /ˈspilˌway‖ˈspɪlˌweɪ/ *n* a passage for surplus water from a dam

[1]**spin** /spin‖spɪn/ *vb* **-nn-;** **spun** /spun‖spʌn/ *vi* **1** to draw out and twist fibre into yarn or thread **2** *esp of a spider or insect* to form a thread by forcing out a sticky rapidly hardening fluid **3a** to revolve rapidly; whirl **b** to have the sensation of spinning; reel <*my head is* ~ning> **4** to move swiftly, esp on wheels or in a vehicle **5** to fish with a spinning lure **6** *of an aircraft* to fall in a spin ~ *vt* **1a** to draw out and twist into yarns or threads **b** to produce (yarn or thread) by drawing out and twisting a fibrous material **2** to form (e g a web or cocoon) by spinning **3** to compose and tell (a usu involved or fictitious story) <*is always* ~ning *yarns*> **4** to cause to revolve rapidly <~ *a top*>; *also* to cause (a cricket ball) to revolve in the manner characteristic of spin bowling **5** to shape into threadlike form in manufacture; *also* to manufacture by a whirling process

[2]**spin** *n* **1a** the act or an instance of spinning sthg **b** the whirling motion imparted (e g to a cricket ball) by spinning **c** a short excursion, esp in or on a motor vehicle **2** an aerial manoeuvre or flight condition consisting of a combination of roll and yaw with the longitudinal axis of the aircraft inclined steeply downwards and its wings in a state of (partial) stall **3** the property of an elementary particle that corresponds to intrinsic angular momentum, that can be thought of as rotation of the particle about its axis, and that is mainly responsible for magnetic properties **4** a state of mental confusion; a panic <*in a* ~> – infml – **spinless** *adj*

spina bifida /ˌspienə ˈbifidə‖ˌspaɪnə ˈbɪfɪdə/ *n* a congenital condition in which there is a defect in the formation of the spine allowing the meninges to protrude [Modern Latin, cleft spine]

spinach /ˈspinij, -nich‖ˈspɪnɪdʒ, -nɪtʃ/ *n* (the leaves, eaten as food, of) a plant of the goosefoot family cultivated for its edible leaves [Middle French *espinache*, fr Spanish *espinaca*, fr Arabic *isfānkh*, fr Persian]

spinal /ˈspienəl‖ˈspaɪnəl/ *adj* **1** of or situated near the backbone **2** of or affecting the spinal cord <~ *reflexes*> **3** of or resembling a spine – **spinally** *adv*

spinal column *n* the skeleton running the length of the trunk and tail of a vertebrate that consists of a jointed series of vertebrae and protects the spinal cord

spinal cord *n* the cord of nervous tissue that extends from the brain lengthways along the back in the spinal canal, carries impulses to and from the brain, and serves as a centre for initiating and coordinating many reflex actions

[1]**spindle** /ˈspindl‖ˈspɪndl/ *n* **1a** a round stick with tapered ends used to form and twist the yarn in hand spinning **b** the long slender pin by which the thread is twisted in a spinning wheel **c** any of various rods or pins holding a bobbin in a textile machine (e g a spinning frame) **d** the pin in a loom shuttle **e** the bar or shaft, usu of square section, that carries the knobs and actuates the latch or bolt of a lock **2** a spindle-shaped figure seen in microscopic sections of dividing cells along which the chromosomes are distributed **3a** a turned often decorative piece (e g in a baluster) **b** a newel **c** a pin or axis about which sthg turns

[2]**spindle** *vi* to grow into or have a long slender stalk – **spindler** *n*

ˈ**spindle** ˌ**tree** *n* any of a genus of often evergreen shrubs, small trees, or climbing plants typically having red fruits and a hard wood formerly used for spindle making

spindly /ˈspindli‖ˈspɪndlɪ/ *adj* having an unnaturally tall or slender appearance, esp suggestive of physical weakness <~ *legs*>

ˌ**spin-ˈdry** *vt* to remove water from (wet laundry) by placing in a rapidly rotating drum – **spin-drier** *n*

spine /spien‖spaɪn/ *n* **1a** SPINAL COLUMN **b** sthg like a spinal column or constituting a central axis or chief support **c** the back of a book, usu lettered with the title and author's name **2** a stiff pointed plant part; *esp* one that is a modified leaf or leaf part **3** a sharp rigid part of an animal or fish; *also* a pointed prominence on a bone – **spined** *adj*

spineless /ˈspienlis‖ˈspaɪnlɪs/ *adj* **1** free from spines, thorns, or prickles **2a** having no spinal column; invertebrate **b** lacking strength of character – **spinelessly** *adv*, **spinelessness** *n*

spinet /ˈspinit, spiˈnet‖ˈspɪnɪt, spɪˈnet/ *n* a small harpsichord having the strings at an angle to the keyboard [Italian *spinetta*, prob fr Giovanni *Spinetti* (*fl* 1503), its reputed inventor]

spinnaker /ˈspinəkə‖ˈspɪnəkə/ *n* a large triangular sail set forward of a yacht's mast on a long light pole and used when running before the wind

spinner /ˈspinə‖ˈspɪnə/ *n* **1** a fisherman's lure consisting of a spoon, blade, or set of wings that revolves when drawn through the water **2** a conical fairing attached to an aircraft propeller hub and revolving with it **3** (a delivery bowled by) a bowler of spin bowling

spinney /ˈspini‖ˈspɪnɪ/ *n*, *Br* a small wood with undergrowth [Middle French *espinaye* thorny thicket, fr *espine* thorn, fr Latin *spina*]

ˌ**spinning ˈjenny** /ˈjeni‖ˈdʒenɪ/ *n* an early multiple-spindle machine for spinning wool or cotton

ˈ**spinning** ˌ**wheel** *n* a small domestic machine for spinning yarn or thread by means of a spindle driven by a hand- or foot-operated wheel

ˈ**spin-**ˌ**off** *n* a by-product <*household products that are* ~s *of space research*>; *also* sthg which is a further development of some idea or product <*a* ~ *from a successful TV series*>

spin out *vt* **1** to cause to last longer, esp by thrift <spinning out *their meagre rations*> **2** to extend, prolong <spin out *a repair job*> **3** to dismiss (a batsman in cricket) by spin bowling

spinster /ˈspinstə‖ˈspɪnstə/ *n* an unmarried woman [Middle English *spinnestere* woman engaged in spinning, fr *spinnen* to spin] – **spinsterhood** *n*, **spinsterish** *adj*

spiny /ˈspieni‖ˈspaɪnɪ/ *adj* **1** covered or armed with spines; *broadly* bearing spines, prickles, or thorns **2** full of difficulties or annoyances; thorny <~ *problems*> **3** slender and pointed like a spine – **spininess** *n*

spiny lobster *n* any of several edible crustaceans distinguished from the true lobster by the simple unenlarged first pair of legs and the spiny carapace

[1]**spiral** /ˈspie·ərəl‖ˈspaɪərəl/ *adj* **1a** winding round a centre or pole and gradually approaching or receding from it <*the* ~ *curve of a watch spring*> **b** helical **2** of the advancement to higher levels through a series of cyclical movements <*a* ~ *theory of social development*> – **spirally** *adv*

[2]**spiral** *n* **1a** the path of a point in a plane moving round a central point while continuously receding from or approaching it **b** a 3-dimensional curve (e g a helix) with 1 or more turns about an axis **2** a single turn or coil in a spiral object **3a** sthg with a spiral form **b** a spiral flight **4** a continuously expanding and accelerating increase or decrease <*wage* ~s>

[3]**spiral** *vb* **-ll-** (*NAm* **-l-**, **-ll-**) *vi* to go, esp to rise, in a spiral course <*prices* ~led> ~*vt* to cause to take a spiral form or course

[1]**spire** /spie·ə‖spaɪə/ *n* **1** a slender tapering blade or stalk (e g of grass) **2** the upper tapering part of sthg (e g a tree or antler) **3** a tall tapering roof or other construction on top of a tower – **spired** *adj*, **spiry** *adj*

[2]**spire** *vi* to taper up to a point like a spire

[3]**spire** *n* **1** a spiral, coil **2** the inner or upper part of a spiral gastropod shell – **spired** *adj*

[4]**spire** *vi* to spiral

[1]**spirit** /ˈspirit‖ˈspɪrɪt/ *n* **1** an animating or vital principle of living organisms **2** a supernatural being or essence: e g **2a** *cap* HOLY SPIRIT **b** SOUL 2 **c** a being that has no body but can become visible; *specif* GHOST 2 **d** a malevolent being that enters and possesses a human being **3** temper or state of mind – often pl with sing. meaning <*in high* ~s> **4** the immaterial intelligent or conscious part of a person **5** the attitude or intention characterizing or influencing sthg <*undertaken in a* ~ *of fun*> **6** liveliness, energy; *also* courage **7** devotion, loyalty <*team* ~> **8** a person of a specified kind or character <*she's such a kind* ~> **9a** distilled liquor of high alcoholic content – usu pl with sing. meaning <*a glass of* ~s> **b** any of various volatile liquids obtained by distillation or cracking (e g of petroleum, shale, or wood) – often pl with sing.

meaning **c** ALCOHOL 1 **10a** prevailing characteristic < ~ *of the age*> **b** the true meaning of sthg (e g a rule or instruction) in contrast to its verbal expression **11** an alcoholic solution of a volatile substance < ~ *of camphor*> – **in spirits** in a cheerful or lively frame of mind – **out of spirits** in a gloomy or depressed frame of mind

[2]**spirit** *vt* to carry off, esp secretly or mysteriously – usu + *away* or *off*

ˈ**spirited** *adj* **1** full of energy, animation, or courage <*a* ~ *discussion*> **2** having a specified frame of mind – often in combination <*low*-spirited> – **spiritedly** *adv*, **spiritedness** *n*

ˈ**spirit ˌlevel** *n* a level that uses the position of a bubble in a curved transparent tube of liquid to indicate whether a surface is level

[1]**spiritual** /ˈspirichooəl‖ˈspɪrɪtʃʊəl/ *adj* **1** (consisting) of spirit; incorporeal <*man's* ~ *needs*> **2a** of sacred matters **b** ecclesiastical rather than lay or temporal **3** concerned with religious values **4** based on or related through sympathy of thought or feeling **5** of supernatural beings or phenomena – **spiritualize** *vt*, **spiritually** *adv*, **spiritualness** *n*

[2]**spiritual** *n* a usu emotional religious song of a kind developed esp among Negroes in the southern USA

spiritualism /ˈspirichooəˌliz(ə)m‖ˈspɪrɪtʃʊəˌlɪz(ə)m/ *n* **1** the doctrine that spirit is the ultimate reality **2** a belief that spirits of the dead communicate with the living, esp through a medium or at a séance – **spiritualist** *n, often cap*, **spiritualistic** *adj*

spirituality /ˌspirichooˈaləti‖ˌspɪrɪtʃʊˈælətɪ/ *n* **1** sensitivity or attachment to religious values **2** a practice of personal devotion and prayer

spirituous /ˈspirichooəs‖ˈspɪrɪtʃʊəs/ *adj* containing or impregnated with alcohol obtained by distillation < ~ *liquors*>

spirochaete, *NAm chiefly* **spirochete** /ˈspie·ərohkeet‖ˈspaɪərəʊkiːt/ *n* any of an order of slender spirally undulating bacteria including those causing syphilis and relapsing fever [deriv of Greek *speira* coil + *chaitē* long hair] – **spirochaetal** *adj*

spirt /spuht‖spɜːt/ *vb or n* [2, 3]SPURT

[1]**spit** /spit‖spɪt/ *n* **1** a slender pointed rod for holding meat over a source of heat (e g an open fire) **2** a small point of land, esp of sand or gravel, running into a river mouth, bay, etc

[2]**spit** *vt* **-tt-** to fix (as if) on a spit; impale

[3]**spit** *vb* **-tt-; spat** /spat‖spæt/, **spit** *vt* **1** to eject (e g saliva) from the mouth **2a** to express (hostile or malicious feelings) (as if) by spitting <spat *his contempt*> **b** to utter vehemently or with a spitting sound <spat *out his words*> **3** to emit as if by spitting <*the guns* spat *fire*> ~ *vi* **1a** to eject saliva from the mouth (as an expression of aversion or contempt) **b** to exhibit contempt **2** to rain or snow slightly or in flurries **3** to sputter – **spit it out** to utter promptly what is in the mind

[4]**spit** *n* **1a(1)** spittle, saliva **a(2)** the act or an instance of spitting **b** a frothy secretion exuded by some insects **2** perfect likeness – often in *spit and image* <*he's the very* ~ *and image of his father*>

ˌ**spit and ˈpolish** *n* extreme attention to cleanliness, orderliness, and ceremonial

[1]**spite** /spiet‖spaɪt/ *n* petty ill will or malice – **spiteful** *adj*, **spitefully** *adv* – **in spite of** in defiance or contempt of <*sorry* in spite of *himself*>

[2]**spite** *vt* to treat vindictively or annoy out of spite

spitfire /ˈspitˌfie·ə‖ˈspɪtˌfaɪə/ *n* a quick-tempered or volatile person

spitting image *n* [4]SPIT 2

spittle /ˈspitl‖ˈspɪtl/ *n* **1** saliva (ejected from the mouth) **2** [4]SPIT 1b

spittoon /spiˈtoohn‖spɪˈtuːn/ *n* a receptacle for spit

spiv /spiv‖spɪv/ *n, Br* a slick individual who lives by sharp practice or petty fraud; *specif* a black marketeer operating esp after WW II – **spivvery** *n*

[1]**splash** /splash‖splæʃ/ *vi* **1a** to strike and move about a liquid < ~ed *about in the bath*> **b** to move through or into a liquid and cause it to spatter < ~ *through a puddle*> **2a(1)** to become spattered about **a(2)** to spread or scatter in the manner of splashed liquid <*sunlight* ~ed *over the lawn*> **b** to flow, fall, or strike with a splashing sound <*a brook* ~ing *over rocks*> **3** *chiefly Br* to spend money liberally; splurge – usu + *out* < ~ed *out on a bottle of champagne*> ~ *vt* **1a** to dash a liquid or semiliquid substance on or against **b** to soil or stain with splashed liquid; spatter **c** to display very conspicuously <*the affair was* ~ed *all over the papers*> **2a** to cause (a liquid or semiliquid substance) to spatter about, esp with force **b** to spread or scatter in the manner of a splashed liquid <*sunset* ~ed *its colours across the sky*> – **splasher** *n*

[2]**splash** *n* **1a** a spot or daub (as if) from splashed liquid <*a mud* ~ *on the wing*> **b** a usu vivid patch of colour or of sthg coloured < ~es *of yellow tulips*> **2a** (the sound of) splashing **b** a short plunge **3** (a vivid impression created esp by) an ostentatious display **4** a small amount, esp of a mixer added to an alcoholic drink; a dash – **splashy** *n*

ˈ**splashˌdown** /-ˌdown‖-ˌdaʊn/ *n* the landing of a spacecraft in the ocean – **splash down** *vi*

splatter /ˈsplatə‖ˈsplætə/ *vt* to spatter ~ *vi* to scatter or fall (as if) in heavy drops <*rain* ~ed *against the windscreen*> – **splatter** *n*

[1]**splay** /splay‖spleɪ/ *vt* **1** to spread out **2** to make (e g the edges of an opening) slanting ~ *vi* **1** to become splayed **2** to slope, slant

[2]**splay** *adj* turned outwards < ~ *knees*>

ˈ**splayˌfoot** /-ˌfoot‖-ˌfʊt/ *n* a foot abnormally flattened and spread out – **splayfoot, splayfooted** *adj*

spleen /spleen‖spliːn/ *n* **1** a highly vascular ductless organ near the stomach or intestine of most vertebrates that is concerned with final destruction of blood cells, storage of blood, and production of lymphocytes **2** bad temper; spite **3** *archaic* melancholy – **spleeny** *adj*, **spleenful** *adj*

splendid /ˈsplendid‖ˈsplendɪd/ *adj* **1a** shining, brilliant **b** magnificent, sumptuous **2** illustrious, distinguished **3** of the best or most enjoyable kind; excellent <*a* ~ *picnic*> – **splendidly** *adv*, **splendidness** *n*

splendiferous /splenˈdif(ə)rəs‖splenˈdɪf

(ə)rəs/ *adj* splendid – infml – **splendiferously** *adv*, **splendiferousness** *n*

splendour, *NAm chiefly* **splendor** /ˈsplendə‖ˈsplendə/ *n* **1a** great brightness or lustre; brilliance **b** grandeur, pomp **2** sthg splendid – **splendorous, splendrous** *adj*

splenetic /spliˈnetik‖splɪˈnetɪk/ *adj* **1** bad tempered, spiteful **2** *archaic* given to melancholy – **splenetic** *n*, **splenetically** *adv*

[1]**splice** /splies‖splaɪs/ *vt* **1a** to join (e g ropes) by interweaving the strands **b** to unite (e g film, magnetic tape, or timber) by overlapping the ends or binding with adhesive tape **2** *Br* to unite in marriage; marry – infml – **splicer** *n*

[2]**splice** *n* a joining or joint made by splicing

[1]**splint** /splint‖splɪnt/ *n* **1** a thin strip of wood suitable for interweaving (e g into baskets) **2** material or a device used to protect and immobilize a body part (e g a broken arm)

[2]**splint** *vt* to support and immobilize (as if) with a splint

[1]**splinter** /ˈsplintə‖ˈsplɪntə/ *n* **1** a sharp thin piece, esp of wood or glass, split or broken off lengthways **2** a small group or faction broken away from a parent body – **splinter** *adj*, **splintery** *adj*

[2]**splinter** *vt* **1** to split or rend into long thin pieces; shatter **2** to split into fragments, parts, or factions ~*vi* to become splintered

[1]**split** /split‖splɪt/ *vb* **-tt-; split** *vt* **1** to divide, esp lengthways **2a(1)** to tear or rend apart; burst **a(2)** to subject (an atom or atomic nucleus) to artificial disintegration, esp by fission **b** to affect as if by shattering or tearing apart <*a roar that* ~ *the air*> **3** to divide into parts or portions: e g **3a** to divide between people; share <~ *a bottle of wine at dinner*> **b** to divide into opposing factions, parties, etc <*the bill* ~ *the opposition*> **c** to break down (a chemical compound) into constituents *also* to remove by such separation **d** *NAm* to mark (a ballot) or cast (a vote) so as to vote for opposed candidates **4** to separate (constituent parts) by interposing sthg <~ *an infinitive*> ~ *vi* **1a** to become split lengthways or into layers **b** to break apart; burst **2a** to become divided up or separated off <~ *into factions*> **b** to sever relations or connections – often + *up* <~ *up after 6 months' marriage*> **3** to share sthg (e g loot or profits) with others – often + *with*; infml **4** to let out a secret; act as an informer – often + *on*; slang **5** to leave, esp hurriedly; depart – slang – **splitter** *n* – **split hairs** to make oversubtle or trivial distinctions – **split one's sides** to laugh heartily – **split the difference** to compromise by taking the average of 2 amounts

[2]**split** *n* **1** a narrow break made (as if) by splitting **2** a piece broken off by splitting **3** a division into divergent groups or elements; a breach <*a* ~ *in party ranks*> **4a** splitting **b** *pl but sing in constr* the act of lowering oneself to the floor or leaping into the air with legs extended at right angles to the trunk **5** a wine bottle holding a quarter of the usual amount; *also* a small bottle of mineral water, tonic water, etc **6** a sweet dish composed of sliced fruit, esp a banana, ice cream, syrup, and often nuts and whipped cream

[3]**split** *adj* **1** divided, fractured **2** prepared for use by splitting <~ *bamboo*> <~ *hides*>

ˌ**split-ˈlevel** *adj* divided so that the floor level in one part is less than a full storey higher than an adjoining part <*a* ~ *house*> – **split-level** *n*

split pea *n* a dried pea in which the cotyledons are usu split apart

split personality *n* a personality composed of 2 or more internally consistent groups of behaviour tendencies and attitudes each acting more or less independently of the other

split ring *n* a metal ring of 2 flat turns on which keys may be kept

ˌ**split ˈsecond** *n* a fractional part of a second; a flash – **split-second** *adj*

splitting /ˈspliting‖ˈsplɪtɪŋ/ *adj* causing a piercing sensation <*a* ~ *headache*>

[1]**splotch** /sploch‖splɒtʃ/ *n* a large irregular spot or smear; a blotch – **splotchy** *adj*

[2]**splotch** *vt* to mark with a splotch or splotches

[1]**splurge** /spluhj‖splɜːdʒ/ *n* **1** an ostentatious display or enterprise **2** an extravagant spending spree *USE* infml

[2]**splurge** *vi* **1** to make a splurge **2** to spend money extravagantly – often + *on* <~ *on a slap-up meal*> to to spend extravagantly or ostentatiously *USE* infml

splutter /ˈsplutə‖ˈsplʌtə/ *vi* **1** to make a noise as if spitting **2** SPUTTER 2 ~*vt* to utter hastily and confusedly – **splutter** *n*, **splutterer** *n*, **spluttery** *adj*

[1]**spoil** /spoyl‖spɔɪl/ *n* **1a** plunder taken from an enemy in war or a victim in robbery; loot – often pl with sing. meaning **b** sthg gained by special effort or skill – usu pl with sing. meaning **2** earth and rock excavated or dredged

[2]**spoil** *vb* **spoilt** /spoylt‖spɔɪlt/, **spoiled** *vt* **1a** to damage seriously; ruin <*heavy rain* ~t *the crops*> **b** to impair the enjoyment of; mar <*a quarrel* ~t *the celebration*> **2a** to impair the character of by overindulgence or excessive praise <~ *an only child*> **b** to treat indulgently; pamper **c** to cause to be unsatisfied with sthg inferior – usu + *for* <*the good meals at this hotel will* ~ *us for canteen food*> ~ *vi* **1** to lose good or useful qualities, usu as a result of decay <*fruit soon* ~s *in warm weather*> **2** to have an eager desire *for* – esp in *spoiling for a fight* – **spoilable** *adj*

spoilage /ˈspoylij‖ˈspɔɪlɪdʒ/ *n* **1** sthg spoiled or wasted **2** loss by being spoiled

ˈ**spoilˌsport** /-ˌspawt‖-ˌspɔːt/ *n* one who spoils the fun of others – infml

[1]**spoke** /spohk‖spəʊk/ *past & archaic past part of* SPEAK

[2]**spoke** *n* **1** any of the small radiating bars inserted in the hub of a wheel to support the rim **2** a rung of a ladder

[3]**spoke** *vt* to provide (as if) with spokes

spoken /ˈspohkən‖ˈspəʊkən/ *adj* **1a** delivered by word of mouth; oral <*a* ~ *request*> **b** used in speaking or conversation; uttered <*the* ~ *word*> **2** characterized by speaking in a specified manner – in combination <*soft*-spoken>

ˈ**spokeˌshave** /-ˌshayv‖-ˌʃeɪv/ *n* a plane having a blade set between 2 handles and used for shaping curved surfaces

spokesman /ˈspohksmən‖ˈspəʊksmən/, *fem* ˈ**spokesˌwoman** *n* one who speaks on behalf of another or others

spoliation /ˌspohliˈaysh(ə)n‖ˌspəʊlɪˈeɪʃ(ə)n/ *n* **1a** the act of plundering **b** the state of being plundered, esp in war **2** the act of damaging or injuring, esp irreparably – **spoliator** *n*

spondee /ˈspondee‖ˈspɒndiː/ *n* a metrical foot consisting of 2 long or stressed syllables – **spondaic** *adj or n*

[1]**sponge** /spunj, spunzh‖spʌndʒ, spʌnʒ/ *n* **1a(1)** an elastic porous mass of interlacing horny fibres that forms the internal skeleton of various marine animals and is able when wetted to absorb water **a(2)** a piece of sponge (e g for cleaning) **a(3)** a porous rubber or cellulose product used similarly to a sponge **b** any of a phylum of aquatic lower invertebrate animals that are essentially double-walled cell colonies and permanently attached as adults **2** a sponger **3a** raised dough (e g for yeast bread) **b** a sponge cake or sweet steamed pudding made from a sponge-cake mixture **c** a metal (e g platinum) in the form of a porous solid composed of fine particles

[2]**sponge** *vt* **1** to cleanse, wipe, or moisten (as if) with a sponge **2** to remove or erase by rubbing (as if) with a sponge **3** to obtain by sponging on another < ~ *the price of a pint*> **4** to soak up (as if) with or in the manner of a sponge ~*vi* to obtain esp financial assistance by exploiting natural generosity or organized welfare facilities – usu + *on*

ˈ**sponge ˌbag** *n, Br* a small waterproof usu plastic bag for holding toilet articles

ˈ**sponge ˌcake** *n* a light sweet cake made with (approximately) equal quantities of sugar, flour, and eggs but no shortening

spongy /ˈspunji‖ˈspʌndʒɪ/ *adj* **1** resembling a sponge, esp in being soft, porous, absorbent, or moist **2** *of a metal* in the form of a sponge – **sponginess** *n*

[1]**sponsor** /ˈsponsə‖ˈspɒnsə/ *n* **1** sby who presents a candidate for baptism or confirmation and undertakes responsibility for his/her religious education or spiritual welfare **2** sby who assumes responsibility for some other person or thing **3** sby who or sthg that pays for a project or activity – **sponsorship** *n*, **sponsorial** *adj*

[2]**sponsor** *vt* to be or stand as sponsor for

spontaneous /sponˈtaynyəs, -ni·əs‖spɒnˈteɪnjəs, -nɪəs/ *adj* **1** proceeding from natural feeling or innate tendency without external constraint <*a* ~ *expression of gratitude*> **2** springing from a sudden impulse <*a* ~ *offer of help*> **3** controlled and directed internally **4** developing without apparent external influence, force, cause, or treatment < ~ *recovery from a severe illness*> **5** not contrived or manipulated; natural – **spontaneously** *adv*, **spontaneousness** *n*, **spontaneity** *n*

[1]**spoof** /spoohf‖spuːf/ *vt* **1** to deceive, hoax **2** to make good-natured fun of; lampoon *USE* infml

[2]**spoof** *n* **1** a hoax, deception **2** a light, humorous, but usu telling parody *USE* infml – **spoof** *adj*

[1]**spook** /spoohk‖spuːk/ *n* a ghost, spectre – chiefly infml – **spookish** *adj*

[2]**spook** *vb, chiefly NAm vt* to make frightened or frantic; *esp* to startle into violent activity (e g stampeding) < ~ed *the herd of horses*> ~*vi* to become frightened

spooky /ˈspoohki‖ˈspuːkɪ/ *adj* causing irrational fear, esp because suggestive of supernatural presences; eerie – chiefly infml

[1]**spool** /spoohl‖spuːl/ *n* **1** a cylindrical device on which wire, yarn, film, etc is wound **2** (the amount of) material wound on a spool **3** *chiefly NAm* [1]REEL c

[2]**spool** *vt* to wind on a spool

[1]**spoon** /spoohn‖spuːn/ *n* **1a** an eating, cooking, or serving implement consisting of a small shallow round or oval bowl with a handle **b** a spoonful **2** sthg curved like the bowl of a spoon (e g a usu metal or shell fishing lure)

[2]**spoon** *vt* **1** to take up and usu transfer (as if) in a spoon < ~ed *soup into his mouth*> **2** to propel (a ball) weakly upwards ~*vi* to indulge in caressing and amorous talk – not now in vogue

spoonerism /ˈspoohnəˌriz(ə)m‖ˈspuːnəˌrɪz-(ə)m/ *n* a transposition of usu initial sounds of 2 or more words (e g in *tons of soil* for *sons of toil*) [William *Spooner* (1844-1930), English clergyman & scholar]

ˈ**spoon-ˌfeed** *vt* **1** to feed by means of a spoon **2a** to present (e g information or entertainment) in an easily assimilable form that precludes independent thought or critical judgment < ~ *political theory to students*> **b** to present information to in this manner

ˈ**spoonful** /-f(ə)l‖-f(ə)l/ *n, pl* **spoonfuls** *also* **spoonsful** as much as a spoon will hold

[1]**spoor** /spooə, spaw‖spʊə, spɔː/ *n* a track, a trail, or droppings, esp of a wild animal

[2]**spoor** *vb* to track (sthg) by a spoor

sporadic /spəˈradik, spaw-‖spəˈrædɪk, spɔː-/ *adj* occurring occasionally or in scattered instances – **sporadically** *adv*

spore /spaw‖spɔː/ *n* a primitive usu single-celled hardy reproductive body produced by plants, protozoans, bacteria, etc and capable of development into a new individual either on its own or after fusion with another spore – **spored** *adj*, **sporiferous** *adj*

sporran /ˈsporən‖ˈspɒrən/ *n* a pouch of animal skin with the hair or fur on that is worn in front of the kilt with traditional Highland dress

[1]**sport** /spawt‖spɔːt/ *vt* **1** to exhibit for all to see; show off < ~ *a new hat*> **2** to put forth as a sport or bud variation ~ *vi* **1** to play about happily; frolic <*lambs* ~ing *in the meadow*> **2** to speak or act in jest; trifle **3** to deviate or vary abruptly from type

[2]**sport** *n* **1a** a source of diversion or recreation; a pastime **b(1)** physical activity engaged in for recreation **b(2)** a particular activity (e g hunting or athletics) so engaged in **2a** pleasantry, jest <*only made the remark in* ~ > **b** mockery, derision **3** sby or sthg manipulated by outside forces <*was made the* ~ *of fate*> **4** sby who is fair, generous, and esp a good loser **5** an individual exhibiting a sudden deviation from type beyond the normal limits of individual variation **6** *chiefly NAm* a playboy **7** *Austr* – used in informal address, chiefly to men

sporting /ˈspawting‖ˈspɔːtɪŋ/ *adj* **1a** concerned with, used for, or suitable for sport **b** marked by or calling for sportsmanship **c** involving such risk as a sports competitor might take or encounter <*a* ~ *chance*> **d** fond of or taking part in sports <~ *nations*> **2** *chiefly NAm* of or for sports that involve betting or gambling – **sportingly** *adv*

sportive /ˈspawtiv‖ˈspɔːtɪv/ *adj* frolicsome, playful – **sportively** *adv*, **sportiveness** *n*

sports /spawts‖spɔːts/, *NAm chiefly* **sport** *adj* of or suitable for sports <~ *equipment*>; *esp* styled in a manner suitable for casual or informal wear <~ *coats*>

ˈ**sports ˌcar** *n* a low fast usu 2-passenger motor car

ˈ**sportsman** /-mən‖-mən/, *fem* ˈ**sportsˌwoman** *n* **1** sby who engages in sports, esp blood sports **2** sby who is fair, a good loser, and a gracious winner – **sportsmanlike** *adj*

ˈ**sportsmanship** /-ship‖-ʃɪp/ *n* conduct becoming to a sportsman

sporty /ˈspawti‖ˈspɔːtɪ/ *adj* **1** fond of sport **2a** notably loose or dissipated; fast <*ran around with a very* ~ *crowd*> **b** flashy, showy <~ *clothes*> **3** suggestive of or capable of giving good sport <*the car had a very* ~ *feel*> *USE* infml – **sportily** *adv*, **sportiness** *n*

[1]**spot** /spot‖spɒt/ *n* **1** a blemish on character or reputation; a stain **2a** a small usu round area different (e g in colour or texture) from the surrounding surface **b(1)** an area marred or marked (e g by dirt) **b(2)** a small surface patch of diseased or decayed tissue <*the* ~s *that appear in measles*> *also* a pimple **c** a conventionalized design used on playing cards to distinguish suits and indicate values **3** a small amount; a bit <*had a* ~ *of bother with the car*> **4** a particular place or area <*a nice* ~ *for a picnic*> **5a** a particular position (e g in an organization or hierarchy) <*a good* ~ *as the director's secretary*> **b** a place on an entertainment programme **6** SPOTLIGHT 1a **7** a usu difficult or embarrassing position; FIX 1 – **on the spot 1** in one place; without travelling away <*running* on the spot> **2** at the place of action; available at the appropriate place and time **3** in an awkward or embarrassing position <*his subordinate's mistake put him* on the spot>

[2]**spot** *vb* **-tt-** *vt* **1** to sully the character or reputation of; disgrace **2** to mark or mar (as if) with spots **3a** to single out; identify **b** to detect, notice <~ *a mistake*> **c** to watch for and record the sighting of <~ *a rare species of duck*> **4** to locate accurately <~ *an enemy position*> **5a** to lie at intervals in or on **b** to fix in or as if in the beam of a spotlight ~ *vi* **1** to become stained or discoloured in spots **2** to cause a spot; leave a stain **3** to act as a spotter; *esp* to locate targets **4** *chiefly Br* to fall lightly in scattered drops <*it's* ~ting *with rain again*> – **spottable** *adj*

[3]**spot** *adj* **1a** being, originating, or done on the spot or in or for a particular spot **b** available for immediate delivery after sale <~ *commodities*> **c(1)** paid out immediately <~ *cash*> **c(2)** involving immediate cash payment <*a* ~ *sale*> **d** broadcast between scheduled programmes <~ *announcements*> **2** given on the spot or restricted to a few random places or instances <*a* ~ *check*> *also* selected at random or as a sample

ˌ**spot-ˈcheck** *vb* to make a quick or random sampling or investigation (of)

ˈ**spotless** /-lis‖-lɪs/ *adj* free from dirt, stains, or blemishes; immaculate – **spotlessly** *adv*, **spotlessness** *n*

[1]ˈ**spotˌlight** /-ˌliet‖-ˌlaɪt/ *n* **1a** a projected spot of light used for brilliant illumination of a person or object on a stage **b** full public attention <*held the political* ~> **2a** a light designed to direct a narrow intense beam on a small area **b** sthg that illuminates brightly or elucidates

[2]**spotlight** *vt* to illuminate (as if) with a spotlight

ˌ**spot-ˈon** *adj, Br* **1** absolutely correct or accurate **2** exactly right <*a shirt that looks* ~ *with jeans*> *USE* infml – **spot-on** *adv*

spotted /ˈspotid‖ˈspɒtɪd/ *adj* **1** marked with spots **2** sullied, tarnished <*inherited a* ~ *name*>

ˌ**spotted ˈdick** /dik‖dɪk/ *n, Br* a steamed or boiled sweet suet pudding containing currants

spotter /ˈspotə‖ˈspɒtə/ *n* **1** sby or sthg that makes or applies a spot (e g for identification) **2** sby or sthg that keeps watch or observes; *esp* a person who watches for and notes down vehicles (e g aircraft or trains)

spotty /ˈspoti‖ˈspɒtɪ/ *adj* **1a** marked with spots **b** having spots, esp on the face <*a* ~ *youth*> **2** lacking evenness or regularity, esp in quality <~ *attendance*> – **spottily** *adv*, **spottiness** *n*

spouse /spows, spowz‖spaʊs, spaʊz/ *n* a married person; a husband or wife

[1]**spout** /spowt‖spaʊt/ *vt* **1** to eject (e g liquid) in a copious stream <*wells* ~ing *oil*> **2** to speak or utter in a strident, pompous, or hackneyed manner; declaim <~ *party slogans*> – infml ~ *vi* **1** to issue with force or in a jet; spurt **2** to eject material, esp liquid, in a jet **3** to declaim – infml – **spouter** *n*

[2]**spout** *n* **1** a projecting tube or lip through which liquid issues from a teapot, roof, kettle, etc **2** a discharge or jet of liquid (as if) from a pipe – **spouted** *adj* – **up the spout 1** beyond hope of improvement; ruined – infml **2** pregnant – slang

[1]**sprain** /sprayn‖spreɪn/ *n* **1** a sudden or violent twist or wrench of a joint with stretching or tearing of ligaments **2** a sprained condition

[2]**sprain** *vt* to subject to sprain

sprang /sprang‖spræŋ/ *past of* SPRING

sprat /sprat‖spræt/ *n* a small or young herring; *also* the young of a similar fish

[1]**sprawl** /sprawl‖sprɔːl/ *vi* **1** to lie or sit with arms and legs spread out carelessly or awkwardly **2** to spread or develop irregularly <*a town that* ~s *across the countryside*> ~ *vt* to cause (e g one's limbs) to spread out

[2]**sprawl** *n* **1** a sprawling position **2** an irregular spreading mass or group <*a* ~ *of buildings*>

[1]**spray** /spray‖spreɪ/ *n* **1** a usu flowering branch or shoot **2** a decorative arrangement of flowers and foliage (e g on a dress) **3** sthg (e g a jewelled pin) resembling a spray

[2]**spray** *n* **1** fine droplets of water blown or falling through the air <*the ~ from the waterfall*> **2a** a jet of vapour or finely divided liquid **b** a device (e g an atomizer or sprayer) by which a spray is dispersed or applied **c(1)** an application of a spray <*give the roses a ~*> **c(2)** a substance (e g paint or insecticide) so applied **3** sthg (e g a number of small flying objects) resembling a spray

[3]**spray** *vt* **1** to discharge, disperse, or apply as a spray **2** to direct a spray on – **sprayer** *n*

'**spray ˌgun** *n* an apparatus resembling a gun for applying a substance (e g paint or insecticide) in the form of a spray

[1]**spread** /spred‖spred/ *vb* **spread** *vt* **1a** to open or extend over a larger area – often + *out* <*~ out the map*> **b** to stretch out; extend <*~ its wings for flight*> **c** to form (the lips) into a long narrow slit (e g when pronouncing the vowel /ee/) **2a** to distribute over an area <*~ manure*> **b** to distribute over a period or among a group <*~ the work over a few weeks*> **c(1)** to apply as a layer or covering **c(2)** to cover or overlay with sthg <*~ bread with butter*> **d** to prepare for dining; set <*~ the table*> **3a** to make widely known <*~ the news*> **b** to extend the range or incidence of <*~ a disease*> **c** to diffuse, emit <*flowers ~ing their fragrance*> **4** to force apart ~ *vi* **1a** to become dispersed, distributed, or scattered <*a race that ~ across the globe*> **b** to become known or disseminated <*panic ~ rapidly*> **2** to cover a greater area; expand **3** to be forced apart (e g from pressure or weight) – **spreadable** *adj*, **spreader** *n*, **spreadability** *n*

[2]**spread** *n* **1** (extent of) spreading **2** sthg spread out: e g **2a** a surface area; an expanse **b(1)** a prominent display in a newspaper or periodical **b(2)** (the matter occupying) 2 facing pages, usu with printed matter running across the fold **c** a wide obstacle for a horse to jump **3** sthg spread on or over a surface: e g **3a** a food product suitable for spreading **b** a sumptuous meal; a feast **c** a cloth cover; *esp* a bedspread

'**spread-ˌeagle** *vb* to (cause to) stand or lie with arms and legs stretched out wide; (cause to) sprawl

'**spreadˌsheet** *n* a software system in which large groups of numerical data can be displayed on a VDU in a set format (e g in rows and columns) and rapid automatic calculations can be made

spree /spree‖spriː/ *n* a bout of unrestrained indulgence in an activity; *esp* a binge [perhaps alteration of Scots *spreath* cattle raid, foray, fr Scottish Gaelic *sprēidh* cattle, fr Latin *praeda* booty]

[1]**sprig** /sprig‖sprɪg/ *n* **1** a small shoot or twig **2** an ornament in the form of a sprig **3** a small headless nail **4** a young offspring; *specif* a youth – chiefly derog; infml

[2]**sprig** *vt* **-gg-** to decorate with a representation of plant sprigs

sprightly /'sprietli‖'spraɪtlɪ/ *adj* marked by vitality and liveliness; spirited – **sprightliness** *n*, **sprightly** *adv*

[1]**spring** /spring‖sprɪŋ/ *vb* **sprang** /sprang‖spræŋ/, **sprung** /sprung‖sprʌŋ/; **sprung** *vi* **1a(1)** to dart, shoot **a(2)** to be resilient or elastic; *also* to move by elastic force <*the lid* sprang *shut*> **b** to become warped **2** to issue suddenly and copiously; pour out <*the tears* sprang *from her eyes*> **3a** to grow as a plant **b** to issue by birth or descent **c** to come into being; arise <*the project ~s from earlier research*> **4a** to make a leap or leaps <sprang *towards the door*> **b** to rise or jump up suddenly <sprang *to his feet when the bell rang*> **5** to extend in height; rise <*the tower ~s to 90 metres*> ~ *vt* **1** to cause to spring **2** to split, crack <*wind* sprang *the mast*> **3a** to cause to operate suddenly <*~ a trap*> **b** to bring into a specified state by pressing or bending <*~ a bar into place*> **4** to leap over **5** to produce or disclose suddenly or unexpectedly <*~ a surprise on them*> <sprang *a leak*> **6** to release from prison – infml

[2]**spring** *n* **1a** a source of supply; *esp* an issue of water from the ground **b** an ultimate source, esp of thought or action <*the inner ~s of being*> **2** a time or season of growth or development; *specif* the season between winter and summer comprising, in the northern hemisphere, the months of March, April, and May **3** a mechanical part that recovers its original shape when released after deformation **4a** the act or an instance of leaping up or forward; a bound **b(1)** capacity for springing; resilience **b(2)** bounce, energy <*a man with ~ in his step*>

'**springˌboard** /-ˌbawd‖-ˌbɔːd/ *n* **1** a flexible board secured at one end that a diver or gymnast jumps off to gain extra height **2** sthg that provides an initial stimulus or impetus

springbok /'springbok‖'sprɪŋbɒk/ *n* **1** a swift and graceful southern African gazelle noted for its habit of springing lightly and suddenly into the air **2** *often cap* a sportsman or sportswoman representing S Africa in an international match or tour abroad [Afrikaans, fr *spring* to jump + *bok* male goat]

ˌ**spring-'clean** *vt* **1** to give a thorough cleaning to (e g a house or furnishings) **2** to put into a proper or more satisfactory order <*~ a government department*> ~*vi* to spring-clean a house – **spring-clean** *n*

springer spaniel /'spring·ə‖'sprɪŋə/ *n* a medium-sized sporting dog of either of 2 breeds that is used chiefly for finding and flushing small game

ˌ**spring 'onion** *n* an onion with a small mild-flavoured thin-skinned bulb and long shoots that is chiefly eaten raw in salads

ˌ**spring 'tide** *n* a tide of maximum height occurring at new and full moon

'**springˌtime** /-ˌtiem‖-ˌtaɪm/ *n* SPRING 2; *also* YOUTH 1

springy /'spring·i‖'sprɪŋɪ/ *adj* having an elastic or bouncy quality; resilient <*walked with a ~ step*> – **springily** *adv*, **springiness** *n*

[1]**sprinkle** /'springkl‖'sprɪŋkl/ *vt* **1** to scatter in fine drops or particles **2a** to distribute (sthg) at intervals (as if) by scattering **b** to occur at (random) intervals on; dot <*meadows ~d with flowers*> **c** to wet lightly ~*vi* to rain lightly in scattered drops

[2]**sprinkle** *n* **1** an instance of sprinkling; *specif* a light fall of rain **2** a sprinkling

sprinkler /ˈspringklə‖ˈsprɪŋklə/ *n* a device for spraying a liquid, esp water: e g **a** a fire extinguishing system that works automatically on detection of smoke or a high temperature **b** an apparatus for watering a lawn – **sprinklered** *adj*

sprinkling /ˈspringkling‖ˈsprɪŋklɪŋ/ *n* a small quantity or number, esp falling in scattered drops or particles or distributed randomly

[1]**sprint** /sprint‖sprɪnt/ *vi* to run or ride a bicycle at top speed, esp for a short distance – **sprinter** *n*

[2]**sprint** *n* **1** (an instance of) sprinting **2a** a short fast running, swimming, or bicycle race **b** a burst of speed

sprite /spriet‖spraɪt/ *n* a (playful graceful) fairy

sprocket /ˈsprokit‖ˈsprɒkɪt/ *n* **1** a tooth or projection on the rim of a wheel, shaped so as to engage the links of a chain **2** *also* **sprocket wheel** a wheel or cylinder having sprockets (e g to engage a bicycle chain)

[1]**sprout** /sprowt‖spraʊt/ *vi* **1** to grow, spring up, or come forth as (if) a shoot **2** to send out shoots or new growth ~*vt* to send forth or up; cause to develop or grow

[2]**sprout** *n* **1** a (young) shoot (e g from a seed or root) **2** BRUSSELS SPROUT

[1]**spruce** /sproohs‖spruːs/ *n* any of a genus of evergreen coniferous trees with a conical head of dense foliage and soft light wood

[2]**spruce** *adj* neat or smart in dress or appearance; trim – **sprucely** *adv*, **spruceness** *n*

[3]**spruce** *vt* to make spruce ~*vi* to make oneself spruce *USE* usu + *up*

sprung /sprung‖sprʌŋ/ *adj*, **1** *past of* SPRING **2** equipped with springs <*a ~ mattress*>

spry /sprie‖spraɪ/ *adj* **sprier, spryer; spriest, spryest** vigorously active; nimble – **spryly** *adv*, **spryness** *n*

[1]**spud** /spud‖spʌd/ *n* **1** a small narrow spade **2** a potato – infml

[2]**spud** *vb* **-dd-** *vt* **1** to dig up or remove with a spud **2** to begin to drill (an oil well) ~*vi* to begin to drill an oil well

spume /spyoohm‖spjuːm/ *vi or n* (to) froth, foam – **spumous, spumy** *adj*

spun /spun‖spʌn/ *past of* SPIN

spunk /spungk‖spʌŋk/ *n* **1** any of various fungi used to make tinder **2** spirit, pluck **3** *Br* semen – vulg – **spunky** *adj*

[1]**spur** /spuh‖spɜː/ *n* **1a** a pointed device secured to a rider's heel and used to urge on a horse **b** *pl* recognition and reward for achievement <*won his academic* ~s> **2** a goad to action; a stimulus **3** sthg projecting like or suggesting a spur: e g **3a(1)** a stiff sharp spine (e g on the wings or legs of a bird or insect); *esp* one on a cock's leg **a(2)** a metal spike fitted to a fighting cock's leg **b** a hollow projection from a plant's petals or sepals (e g in larkspur or columbine) **4** a lateral projection (e g a ridge) of a mountain (range) **5** a short piece of road or railway connecting with a major route (e g a motorway) – **spurred** *adj* – **on the spur of the moment** on impulse; suddenly

[2]**spur** *vb* **-rr-** *vt* **1** to urge (a horse) on with spurs **2** to incite to usu faster action or greater effort; stimulate – usu + *on* ~*vi* to spur a horse on; ride hard

spurge /spuhj‖spɜːdʒ/ *n* any of various mostly shrubby plants with a bitter milky juice

spurious /ˈspyooəri·əs‖ˈspjʊərɪəs/ *adj* **1** of illegitimate birth **2** having a superficial usu deceptive resemblance or correspondence; false **3a** of deliberately falsified or mistakenly attributed origin; forged **b** based on mistaken ideas <*it would be ~ to claim special privileges*> – **spuriously** *adv*, **spuriousness** *n*

spurn /spuhn‖spɜːn/ *vt* to reject with disdain or contempt; scorn – **spurn** *n*

[1]**spurt** /spuht‖spɜːt/ *vi or n* (to make) a sudden brief burst of increased effort, activity, or speed

[2]**spurt** *vb* to (cause to) gush out in a jet

[3]**spurt** *n* a sudden forceful gush; a jet

sputnik /ˈspootnik, ˈsput-‖ˈspʊtnɪk, ˈspʌt-/ *n* a (Soviet) space satellite [Russian, lit., travelling companion, fr *s, so* with + *put'* path]

[1]**sputter** /ˈsputə‖ˈspʌtə/ *vt* **1** to utter hastily or explosively in confusion, anger, or excitement; splutter **2** to dislodge (atoms) from the surface of a material by collision with high energy particles (e g electrons); *also* to deposit (a metallic film) by such a process ~ *vi* **1** to eject particles of food or saliva noisily from the mouth **2** to speak in an explosive or incoherent manner **3** to make explosive popping sounds – **sputterer** *n*

[2]**sputter** *n* **1** confused and excited speech **2** (the sound of) sputtering

sputum /ˈspyoohtəm‖ˈspjuːtəm/ *n, pl* **sputa** /-tə‖-tə/ matter, made up of discharges from the respiratory passages and saliva, that is coughed up

[1]**spy** /spie‖spaɪ/ *vt* **1** to keep under secret surveillance, usu for hostile purposes <~ *out the land*> **2** to catch sight of; see <spied *him lurking in the bushes*> **3** to search or look for intently <~ *out a means of escape*> ~ *vi* **1** to observe or search for sthg; look **2** to watch secretly; act as a spy – often + *on USE* (*vt 1&3*) usu + *out*

[2]**spy** *n* **1** one who keeps secret watch on sby or sthg **2** one who attempts to gain information secretly from a country, company, etc and communicate it to another

ˈ**spy,glass** /-ˌglahs‖-ˌglɑːs/ *n* a small telescope

squab /skwob‖skwɒb/ *n* **1** a fledgling bird, esp a pigeon **2** a thick cushion for a chair, car seat, etc

squabble /ˈskwobl‖ˈskwɒbl/ *vi or n* (to engage in) a noisy or heated quarrel, esp over trifles – **squabbler** *n*

squad /skwod‖skwɒd/ *n sing or pl in constr* a small group of (military) personnel assembled for a purpose

ˈ**squad ˌcar** *n, chiefly NAm* a police car having radio communication with headquarters

squaddy /ˈskwodi‖ˈskwɒdɪ/ *n, chiefly Br informal* a swaddy

squadron /ˈskwodrən‖ˈskwɒdrən/ *n sing or pl in constr* a unit of military organization: **a** a unit of cavalry or of an armoured regiment, usu consisting of 3 or more troops **b** a variable naval unit consisting of a number of warships on a particular operation **c** a unit of an air force consisting usu of between 10 and 18 aircraft

squadron leader *n* an officer in the Royal Air Force ranking below wing commander

squalid /ˈskwolid‖ˈskwɒlɪd/ *adj* **1** filthy and degraded from neglect or poverty **2** SORDID 2 – **squalidly** *adv*, **squalidness** *n*

[1]**squall** /skwawl‖skwɔːl/ *vb* to cry out raucously; scream – **squall** *n*, **squaller** *n*

[2]**squall** *n* **1** a sudden violent wind, often with rain or snow **2** a short-lived commotion – **squally** *adj*

squalor /ˈskwolə‖ˈskwɒlə/ *n* the quality or state of being squalid

squander /ˈskwondə‖ˈskwɒndə/ *vt* to spend extravagantly, foolishly, or wastefully – **squanderer** *n*

[1]**square** /skweə‖skweə/ *n* **1** an instrument (e g a set square or T square) with at least 1 right angle and 2 straight edges, used to draw or test right angles or parallel lines **2** a rectangle with all 4 sides equal **3** sthg shaped like a square: e g **3a** a square scarf **b** an area of ground for a particular purpose (e g military drill) **c** an arrangement of letters, numbers, etc in a square **4** any of the rectangular, square, etc spaces marked out on a board used for playing games **5** the product of a number multiplied by itself **6** an open space in a town, city, etc formed at the meeting of 2 or more streets, and often laid out with grass and trees **7** a solid object or piece approximating to a cube or having a square as its principal face **8** one who is excessively conventional or conservative in tastes or outlook – infml; no longer in vogue – **out of square** not at an exact right angle

[2]**square** *adj* **1a** having 4 equal sides and 4 right angles **b** forming a right angle <*a* ~ *corner*> **2a** approximating to a cube <*a* ~ *cabinet*> **b** of a shape or build suggesting strength and solidity; broad in relation to length or height <~ *shoulders*> **c** square in cross section <*a* ~ *tower*> **3a** *of a unit of length* denoting the area equal to that of a square whose edges are of the specified length <*a* ~ *yard*> **b** being of a specified length in each of 2 equal dimensions meeting at a right angle <*10 metres* ~> **4a** exactly adjusted, arranged, or aligned; neat and orderly **b** fair, honest, or straightforward <~ *in all his dealings*> **c** leaving no balance; settled <*the accounts are all* ~> **d** even, tied **5** of, occupying, or passing through a fielding position near or on a line perpendicular to the line between the wickets and level with the batsman's wicket <~ *leg*> **6** excessively conservative; dully conventional – infml; no longer in vogue – **squarely** *adv*, **squareness** *n*, **squarish** *adj*

[3]**square** *vt* **1a** to make square or rectangular <~ *a building stone*> **b** to test for deviation from a right angle, straight line, or plane surface **2** to set approximately at right angles or so as to present a rectangular outline <~d *his shoulders*> **3a** to multiply (a number) by the same number; to raise to the second power **b** to find a square equal in area to <~ *the circle*> **4a** to balance, settle <~ *an account*> **b** to even the score of (a contest) **5** to mark *off* into squares or rectangles **6a** to bring into agreement; reconcile <~ *theory with practice*> **b** to bribe – infml ~ *vi* **1** to match or agree precisely – usu + *with* **2** to settle matters; *esp* to pay the bill – often + *up* – **square up to 1** to prepare oneself to meet (a challenge) <squared up to *the situation*> **2** to take a fighting stance towards (an opponent)

[4]**square** *adv* **1** in a straightforward or honest manner <*told him* ~> **2a** so as to face or be face to face <*the house stood* ~ *to the road*> **b** at right angles **3** DIRECTLY 1 <*hit the nail* ~ *on the head*>

square away *vt, NAm* to put in order or readiness – infml

ˈ**square-ˌbashing** *n, chiefly Br* military drill, esp marching, on a barrack square

ˌ**square ˈbracket** *n* either of 2 written or printed marks [ ] used to enclose a mathematical expression or other written or printed matter

ˈ**square ˌdance** *n* a dance for 4 couples who form a hollow square – **square dancer** *n*, **square dancing** *n*

square rig *n* a sailing ship rig in which the principal sails are square sails – **square-rigged** *adj*, **square-rigger** *n*

ˌ**square ˈroot** *n* a (positive) number whose square is a usu specified number <*the* ~ *of 9 is* ±*3*>

[1]**squash** /skwosh‖skwɒʃ/ *vt* **1a** to press or beat into a pulp or a flat mass; crush **b** to apply pressure to by pushing or squeezing <*got* ~ed *on the crowded platform*> **2** to reduce to silence or inactivity; PUT DOWN <~ed *her with a cutting remark*> <~ *a revolt*> ~ *vi* **1** to flatten out under pressure or impact **2** to squeeze, press <*we* ~ed *into the front row of spectators*> [Middle French *esquasser*, fr Latin *ex* out + *quassare* to shake violently, shatter] – **squashy** *adj*, **squashily** *adv*, **squashiness** *n*

[2]**squash** *n* **1** the act or soft dull sound of squashing **2** a crushed mass; *esp* a mass of people crowded into a restricted space **3** *also* **squash rackets** a game played in a 4-walled court with long-handled rackets and a rubber ball that can be played off any number of walls **4** *Br* a drink made from sweetened and often concentrated citrus fruit juice

[3]**squash** *n, pl* **squashes, squash** any of various (plants of the cucumber family bearing) fruits widely cultivated as vegetables and for livestock feed [by shortening & alteration fr earlier *isquoutersquash*, fr Natick & Narraganset (American Indian) *askútasquash*]

[1]**squat** /skwot‖skwɒt/ *vi* **-tt- 1** to crouch close to the ground as if to escape detection <*a* ~t*ing hare*> **2** to assume or maintain a position in which the body is supported on the feet and the knees are bent, so that the haunches rest on or near the heels **3** to occupy property as a squatter

[2]**squat** *n* **1a** squatting **b** the posture of sby or sthg that squats **2** an empty building occupied by or available to squatters – infml

[3]**squat** *adj* **-tt- 1** with the heels drawn up under the haunches **2** disproportionately short or low and broad – **squatly** *adv*, **squatness** *n*

squatter /ˈskwotə‖ˈskwɒtə/ *n* **1** one who occupies usu otherwise empty property without rights of ownership or payment of rent **2** *Austr* one who owns large tracks of grazing land

squaw /skwaw‖skwɔː/ *n* a N American Indian (married) woman

squawk /skwawk‖skwɔːk/ *vi or n* **1** (to utter) a harsh abrupt scream **2** (to make) a loud or vehement protest – **squawker** *n*

[1]**squeak** /skweek‖skwiːk/ *vi* **1** to utter or make a squeak **2** SQUEAL 2a – infml ~*vt* to utter in a squeak – **squeaker** *n*

[2]**squeak** *n* **1** a short shrill cry or noise **2** an escape – usu in *a narrow squeak*; infml – **squeaky** *adj*

[1]**squeal** /skweel‖skwiːl/ *vi* **1** to utter or make a squeal **2a** to turn informer <*bribed to ~ on his boss*> **b** to complain, protest ~*vt* to utter with a squeal *USE* (*vi 2*) infml – **squealer** *n*

[2]**squeal** *n* a shrill sharp cry or noise

squeamish /ˈskweemish‖ˈskwiːmɪʃ/ *adj* **1** easily nauseated **2a** excessively fastidious in manners, scruples, or convictions **b** easily shocked or offended – **squeamishly** *adv*, **squeamishness** *n*

squeegee /ˈskweejee‖ˈskwiːdʒiː/ *n* a usu rubber bladed tool used for spreading liquid on or removing it from a surface (e g a window); *also* a roller or other device used similarly in lithography or photography

[1]**squeeze** /skweez‖skwiːz/ *vt* **1a** to apply physical pressure to; compress the (opposite) sides of **b** to extract or discharge under pressure <~ *juice from a lemon*> **c** to force, thrust, or cram (as if) by compression <~ *clothes into a suitcase*> <~d *his way across the room*> **2a** to obtain by force or extortion <*dictators who ~ money from the poor*> **b** to reduce by extortion, oppressive measures, etc <squeezing *the profits*> **c** to cause (economic) hardship to **3** to fit into a limited time span or schedule – usu + *in* or *into* **4** to force (another player) to discard a card to his/her disadvantage, esp in bridge ~ *vi* **1** to force one's way <~ *through a door*> **2** to pass, win, or get by narrowly <*managed to ~ through the month on sick pay*> – **squeezable** *adj*, **squeezer** *n*

[2]**squeeze** *n* **1a** a squeezing or compressing **b** a handshake; *also* an embrace **2a** a quantity squeezed out from sthg <*a ~ of lemon*> **b** a condition of being crowded together; a crush <*it was a tight ~ with 6 in the car*> **3a** a financial pressure caused by narrowing margins or by shortages **b** pressure brought to bear on sby – chiefly in *put the squeeze on*; infml

squelch /skwelch‖skweltʃ/ *vt* **1** to fall or stamp on so as to crush **2** to suppress completely; quell, squash ~ *vi* **1** to emit a sucking sound like that of an object being withdrawn from mud **2** to walk or move, esp through slush, mud, etc, making a squelching noise – **squelch** *n*, **squelchy** *adj*

squib /skwib‖skwɪb/ *n* **1** a small firework that burns with a fizz and finishes with a small explosion **2** a short witty or satirical speech or piece of writing

squid /skwid‖skwɪd/ *n* any of numerous 10-armed cephalopod molluscs, related to the octopus and cuttlefish, that have a long tapered body and a tail fin on each side

squiffy /ˈskwifi‖ˈskwɪfɪ/ *adj* slightly drunk, tipsy – infml

squiggle /ˈskwigl‖ˈskwɪgl/ *vi or n* (to draw) a short wavy twist or line, esp in handwriting or drawing – **squiggly** *adj*

[1]**squint** /skwint‖skwɪnt/ *adj* having a squint; squinting

[2]**squint** *vi* **1** to have or look with a squint **2** to look or peer with eyes partly closed – **squinter** *n*, **squintingly** *adv*

[3]**squint** *n* **1** (a visual disorder marked by) inability to direct both eyes to the same object because of imbalance of the muscles of the eyeball **2** a hagioscope **3** a glance, look – esp in *have/take a squint at*; infml – **squinty** *adj*

[1]**squire** /skwie·ə‖skwaɪə/ *n* **1** a shield-bearer or armour-bearer of a knight **2** an owner of a country estate; *esp* the principal local landowner **3** *Br* PAL 2 – infml

[2]**squire** *vt* to attend on or escort (a woman)

squirearchy, **squirarchy** /ˈskwie·əˌrahki‖ˈskwaɪəˌrɑːkɪ/ *n sing or pl in constr* the gentry or landed-proprietor class – **squirearchical** *adj*

squirm /skwuhm‖skwɜːm/ *vi* **1** to twist about like a worm; wriggle **2** to feel or show acute discomfort at sthg embarrassing, shameful, or unpleasant – **squirm** *n*, **squirmer** *n*

squirrel /ˈskwirəl‖ˈskwɪrəl/ *n* (the usu grey or red fur of) any of various New or Old World small to medium-sized tree-dwelling rodents that have a long bushy tail and strong hind legs [Middle French *esquireul*, deriv of Latin *sciurus*, fr Greek *skiouros*, prob fr *skia* shadow + *oura* tail]

[1]**squirt** /skwuht‖skwɜːt/ *vi* to issue in a sudden forceful stream from a narrow opening ~ *vt* **1** to cause to squirt **2** to direct a jet or stream of liquid at <~ed *his sister with a water pistol*>

[2]**squirt** *n* **1** a small rapid stream of liquid; a jet **2** a small or insignificant (impudent) person – infml

SS /ˌes ˈes‖ˌes ˈes/ *n sing or pl in constr* Hitler's bodyguard and special police force [German, abbr for *Schutzstaffel* elite guard]

[1]**-st** *suffix* (*adj or adv* → *adj or adv*) – used to form the superlative degree of adjectives and adverbs of 1 syllable, and of some adjectives and adverbs of 2 or more syllables, that end in *e* <*sure*st>; compare [1]-EST

[2]**-st** – see [2]-EST

[1]**stab** /stab‖stæb/ *n* **1** a wound produced by a pointed weapon **2a** a thrust (as if) with a pointed weapon **b(1)** a sharp spasm of pain **b(2)** a pang of intense emotion <*felt a ~ of remorse*> **3** an attempt, try – infml

[2]**stab** *vb* **-bb-** *vt* **1** to pierce or wound (as if) with a pointed weapon **2** to thrust, jab <~bed *his finger at the page*> ~*vi* to thrust *at* sby or sthg (as if) with a pointed weapon – **stabber** *n*

stabil·izer, -iser /ˈstayblˌiezə‖ˈsteɪblˌaɪzə/ *n* **1** a chemical substance added to another substance or to a system to prevent or retard an unwanted alteration of physical state **2** a device to keep ships steady in a rough sea **3** *chiefly NAm* the horizontal tailplane of an aircraft

[1]**stable** /ˈstaybl‖ˈsteɪbl/ *n* **1** a building in which domestic animals, esp horses, are sheltered and fed – often pl with sing. meaning **2** *sing or pl in constr* **a** the racehorses or racing cars owned by one person or organization **b** a group of athletes (e g boxers) or performers under one management **c** a group, collection <*a tycoon who owns*

a ~ of newspapers>

[2]**stable** *vt* to put or keep in a stable ~*vi* to dwell (as if) in a stable

[3]**stable** *adj* **1a** securely established; fixed <*a ~ community*> **b** not subject to change or fluctuation; unvarying <*a ~ population*> <*a ~ currency*> **c** permanent, enduring **2** not subject to feelings of mental or emotional insecurity **3a(1)** placed or constructed so as to resist forces tending to cause (change of) motion **a(2)** that develops forces that restore the original condition of equilibrium when disturbed **b(1)** able to resist alteration in chemical, physical, or biological properties **b(2)** not spontaneously radioactive <*a ~ isotope*> – **stably** *adv*, **stabilize** *vb*, **stableness, stabilization** *n*, **stability** *n*

ˈ**stable ˌlad** *n* a groom in a racing stable

stabling /ˈstaybling‖ˈsteɪblɪŋ/ *n* indoor accommodation for animals

staccato /stəˈkahtoh‖stəˈkɑːtəʊ/ *n, adv, or adj, pl* **staccatos** (a manner of speaking or performing, or a piece of music performed) in a sharp, disconnected, or abrupt way [Italian,lit., detached, fr *staccare* to detach]

[1]**stack** /stak‖stæk/ *n* **1** a large usu circular or square pile of hay, straw, etc **2** an (orderly) pile or heap **3a** CHIMNEY STACK **b** a smokestack **4** a pyramid of 3 interlocked rifles **5** a structure of shelves for compact storage of books – usu pl with sing. meaning **6** a stacked group of aircraft **7** a group of loudspeakers for a public address sound system **8** a high pillar of rock rising out of the sea, that was detached from the mainland by the erosive action of waves **9** a large quantity or number – often pl with sing. meaning <~s *of money*>; infml

[2]**stack** *vt* **1** to arrange in a stack; pile **2** to arrange secretly for cheating <*the cards were* ~ed> **3** to assign (an aircraft) to a particular altitude and position within a group of aircraft circling before landing – **stackable** *adj*

stadium /ˈstaydi·əm‖ˈsteɪdɪəm/ *n, pl* **stadiums** *also* **stadia** /-di·ə‖-dɪə/ a sports ground surrounded by a large usu unroofed building with tiers of seats for spectators

[1]**staff** /stahf‖stɑːf/ *n, pl* **staffs, staves** /stayvz‖steɪvz/, (*5*) **staffs** **1a** a long stick carried in the hand for use in walking or as a weapon **b** a supporting rod; *esp* a flagstaff **c** sthg which gives strength or sustains <*bread is the ~ of life*> **2a** a crosier **b** a rod carried as a symbol of office or authority **3** a set of usu 5 parallel horizontal lines on which music is written **4** any of various graduated sticks or rules used for measuring **5** *sing or pl in constr* **5a** the body of people in charge of the internal operations of an institution, business, etc **b** a group of officers appointed to assist a military commander **c** the teachers at a school or university **d** the personnel who assist a superior

[2]**staff** *vt* **1** to supply with a staff or with workers **2** to serve as a staff member of

staff sergeant *n* **1** a high-ranking noncommissioned officer in the British army **2** a middle-ranking noncommissioned officer in the US army, airforce, or marines

[1]**stag** /stag‖stæg/ *n* **1** an adult male red deer; *broadly* the male of any of various deer **2** *Br* a person who buys newly issued shares in the hope of selling them to make a quick profit

[2]**stag** *adj* of or intended for men only <*a ~ party*>

[1]**stage** /stayj‖steɪdʒ/ *n* **1** any of a series of positions or stations one above the other **2a(1)** a raised platform **a(2)** the area of a theatre where the acting takes place, including the wings and storage space **a(3)** *the* acting profession; *also the* theatre as an occupation or activity **b** a centre of attention or scene of action **3a** a scaffold for workmen **b** the small platform of a microscope on which an object is placed for examination **4a** a place of rest formerly provided for those travelling by stagecoach **b** the distance between 2 stopping places on a road **c** a stagecoach **5a** a period or step in a progress, activity, or development **b** any of the distinguishable periods of growth and development of a plant or animal <*the larval ~ of an insect*> **c** any of the divisions (e g 1 day's riding or driving between predetermined points) of a race or rally that is spread over several days **6** a connected group of components in an electrical circuit that performs some well-defined function (e g amplification) and that forms part of a larger electrical circuit **7** a propulsion unit of a rocket with its own fuel and container **8** *chiefly Br* a bus stop from or to which fares are calculated; a fare stage

[2]**stage** *vt* **1** to produce (e g a play) on a stage **2** to produce and organize, esp for public view <~d *the event to get maximum publicity*>

ˈ**stageˌcoach** /-ˌkohch‖-ˌkəʊtʃ/ *n* a horse-drawn passenger and mail coach that in former times ran on a regular schedule between established stops

ˈ**stage diˌrection** *n* a description (e g of a character or setting) or direction (e g to indicate sound effects or the movement or positioning of actors) provided in the text of a play

ˌ**stage ˈdoor** *n* the entrance to a theatre that is used by those who work there

ˈ**stage ˌfright** *n* nervousness felt at appearing before an audience

ˈ**stage-ˌmanage** *vt* to arrange or direct, esp from behind the scenes, so as to achieve a desired result

ˌ**stage ˈmanager** *n* one who is in charge of the stage during a performance and supervises related matters beforehand

stager /ˈstayjə‖ˈsteɪdʒə/ *n* an experienced person; a veteran – chiefly in *old stager*

ˈ**stageˌstruck** /-ˈstruk‖-ˈstrʌk/ *adj* fascinated by the stage; *esp* having an ardent desire to become an actor or actress

stage whisper *n* **1** a loud whisper by an actor, audible to the audience, but supposedly inaudible to others on stage **2** a whisper that is deliberately made audible

stagflation /stagˈflaysh(ə)n‖stægˈfleɪʃ(ə)n/ a condition in which inflation in the economy is accompanied by a level or declining rate of total production [*stag*nation + in*flation*]

[1]**stagger** /ˈstagə‖ˈstægə/ *vi* to reel from side to side (while moving); totter ~ *vt* **1** to dumbfound, astonish **2** to arrange in any of various alternating or overlapping positions or times

<~ *work shifts*> – **staggerer** *n*

[2]**stagger** *n* **1** *pl but sing or pl in constr* an abnormal condition of domestic mammals and birds associated with damage to the brain and spinal cord and marked by lack of muscle coordination and a reeling unsteady gait **2** a reeling or unsteady walk or stance

staggering /'stag(ə)ring‖'stæg(ə)rɪŋ/ *adj* astonishing, overwhelming – **staggeringly** *adv*

staging /'stayjing‖'steɪdʒɪŋ/ *n* **1** a scaffolding or other temporary platform **2** the business of running stagecoaches

stagnant /'stagnənt‖'stægnənt/ *adj* **1a** not flowing in a current or stream; motionless <~ *water*> **b** stale <*long disuse had made the air* ~ *and foul* – Bram Stoker> **2** dull, inactive – **stagnancy** *n*, **stagnantly** *adv*

stagnate /stag'nayt‖stæg'neɪt/ *vi* to become or remain stagnant – **stagnation** *n*

stagy, stagey /'stayji‖'steɪdʒɪ/ *adj* marked by showy pretence or artificiality; theatrical – **stagily** *adv*, **staginess** *n*

staid /stayd‖steɪd/ *adj* sedate and often primly self-restrained; sober – **staidly** *adv*, **staidness** *n*

[1]**stain** /stayn‖steɪn/ *vt* **1** to discolour, soil **2** to suffuse with colour **3** to taint with guilt, vice, corruption, etc; bring dishonour to **4** to colour (e g wood or a biological specimen) by using (chemical) processes or dyes affecting the material itself ~ *vi* **1** to become stained **2** to cause staining – **stainable** *adj*, **stainer** *n*

[2]**stain** *n* **1** a soiled or discoloured spot **2** a moral taint or blemish **3a** a preparation (e g of dye or pigment) used in staining; *esp* one capable of penetrating the pores of wood **b** a dye or mixture of dyes used in microscopy to make minute and transparent structures visible, to differentiate tissue elements, or to produce specific chemical reactions

ˌ**stained** ˈ**glass** /staynd‖steɪnd/ *n* glass coloured or stained for use in windows

ˈ**stainless** /-lis‖-lɪs/ *adj* **1** free from stain or stigma **2** (made from materials) resistant to stain, specif rust – **stainlessly** *adv*

stair /steə‖steə/ *n* **1** a series of (flights of) steps for passing from one level to another – usu pl with sing. meaning **2** any step of a stairway

ˈ**stairˌcase** /-ˌkays‖-ˌkeɪs/ *n* **1** the structure or part of a building containing a stairway **2** a flight of stairs with the supporting framework, casing, and balusters

ˈ**stairˌway** /-ˌway‖-ˌweɪ/ *n* one or more flights of stairs, usu with intermediate landings

ˈ**stairˌwell** /-ˌwel‖-ˌwel/ *n* a vertical shaft in which stairs are located

[1]**stake** /stayk‖steɪk/ *n* **1** a pointed piece of material (e g wood) for driving into the ground as a marker or support **2a** a post to which sby was bound for execution by burning **b** execution by burning at a stake – + *the* **3a** sthg, esp money, staked for gain or loss **b** the prize in a contest, esp a horse race – often pl with sing. meaning **c** an interest or share in an undertaking (e g a commercial venture) **4** *pl but sing or pl in constr, often cap* a horse race in which all the horses are evenly matched (e g in age and amount of weight carried) – chiefly in names of races – **at stake** in jeopardy; AT ISSUE

[2]**stake** *vt* **1** to mark the limits of (as if) by stakes – often + *off* or *out* **2** to tether to a stake **3** to bet, hazard **4** to fasten up or support (e g plants) with stakes **5** *chiefly NAm* to back financially – **stake a/one's claim** to state that sthg is one's by right

stake out *vt, chiefly NAm* to conduct a surveillance of (a suspected area, person, etc) – **stakeout** *n*

stalactite /'staləkˌtiet‖'stæləkˌtaɪt/ *n* an icicle-like deposit of calcium carbonate hanging from the roof or sides of a cavern [deriv of Greek *stalaktos* dripping, fr *stalassein* to let drip] – **stalactitic** *adj*

stalagmite /'staləgmiet‖'stæləgmaɪt/ *n* a deposit of calcium carbonate like an inverted stalactite formed on the floor of a cavern [deriv of Greek *stalagma* drop or *stalagmos* dripping] – **stalagmitic** *adj*

[1]**stale** /stayl‖steɪl/ *adj* **1a** tasteless or unpalatable from age **b** *of air* musty, foul **2** tedious from familiarity <~ *jokes*> **3** impaired in legal force through lack of timely action <*a* ~ *debt*> **4** impaired in vigour or effectiveness, esp from overexertion – **stalely** *adv*, **staleness** *n*

[2]**stale** *vb* to make or become stale

[3]**stale** *vi, esp of horses and cattle* to urinate

stalemate /'staylˌmayt‖'steɪlˌmeɪt/ *vt or n* (to bring into) **a** a drawing position in chess in which only the king can move and although not in check can move only into check **b** a deadlock [*stale* fr Anglo-French *estale*, lit., fixed position, fr Old French *estal* place, position]

[1]**stalk** /stawk‖stɔːk/ *vi* **1** to pursue or approach quarry or prey stealthily **2** to walk stiffly or haughtily ~ *vt* **1** to pursue by stalking <~ *deer*> **2** to go through (an area) in search of prey or quarry <~ *the woods for deer*> – **stalker** *n*

[2]**stalk** *n* **1** the stalking of quarry or prey **2** a stiff or haughty walk

[3]**stalk** *n* **1a** the main stem of a herbaceous plant, often with its attached parts **b** STEM 1b **2** a slender upright supporting or connecting (animal) structure – **stalked** *adj*, **stalkless** *adj*, **stalky** *adj*

[1]**stall** /stawl‖stɔːl/ *n* **1** any of usu several compartments for domestic animals in a stable or barn **2a** a wholly or partly enclosed seat in the chancel of a church **b** a church pew **3a** a booth, stand, or counter at which articles are displayed or offered for sale **b** SIDESHOW 1b **4** a protective sheath for a finger or toe **5** a small compartment <*a shower* ~> **6** *Br* a seat on the main floor of an auditorium (e g in a theatre)

[2]**stall** *vt* **1** to put or keep in a stall **2a** to bring to a standstill; block **b** to cause (e g a car engine) to stop, usu inadvertently **c** to cause (an aircraft or aerofoil) to go into a stall ~ *vi* **1** to come to a standstill; *esp, of an engine* to stop suddenly from failure **2** to experience a stall in flying

[3]**stall** *n* the condition of an aerofoil or aircraft when the airflow is so obstructed (e g from moving forwards too slowly) that lift is lost

[4]**stall** *vi* to play for time; delay ~*vt* to divert or delay, esp by evasion or deception – **stall** *n*

ˈ**stallˌholder** /-ˌhohldə‖-ˌhəʊldə/ *n* one who runs a (market) stall

stallion /ˈstalyən‖ˈstæljən/ *n* an uncastrated male horse; *esp* one kept for breeding

[1]**stalwart** /ˈstawlwət‖ˈstɔːlwət/ *adj* **1** strong in body, mind, or spirit **2** dependable, staunch – **stalwartly** *adv*, **stalwartness** *n*

[2]**stalwart** *n* a stalwart person; *specif* a staunch supporter

stamen /ˈstaymən‖ˈsteɪmən/ *n* the organ of a flower that produces the male gamete in the form of pollen, and consists of an anther and a filament

stamina /ˈstaminə‖ˈstæmɪnə/ *n* (capacity for) endurance

stammer /ˈstamə‖ˈstæmə/ *vb* to speak or utter with involuntary stops and repetitions – **stammer** *n*, **stammerer** *n*

[1]**stamp** /stamp‖stæmp/ *vt* **1** to pound or crush (e g ore) with a pestle or heavy instrument **2a** to strike or beat forcibly with the bottom of the foot **b** to bring down (the foot) forcibly **3a** to impress, imprint <~ *'paid' on the bill*> <*an image* ~ed *on his memory*> **b(1)** to attach a (postage) stamp to **b(2)** to mark with an (official) impression, device, etc **4** to cut out, bend, or form with a stamp or die **5a** to provide with a distinctive character <~ed *with an air of worldly wisdom*> **b** CHARACTERIZE 2 ~ *vi* **1** POUND 2 **2** to strike or thrust the foot forcibly or noisily downwards – **stamper** *n*

[2]**stamp** *n* **1** a device or instrument for stamping **2** the impression or mark made by stamping or imprinting **3a** a distinctive feature, indication, or mark <*the* ~ *of genius*> **b** a lasting imprint <*the* ~ *of time*> **4** the act of stamping **5** a printed or stamped piece of paper that for some restricted purpose is used as a token of credit or occasionally of debit: e g **5a** POSTAGE STAMP **b** a stamp used as evidence that tax has been paid **c** TRADING STAMP

[1]**stampede** /stamˈpeed‖stæmˈpiːd/ *n* **1** a wild headlong rush or flight of frightened animals **2** a sudden mass movement of people [American Spanish *estampida*, fr Spanish, crash, fr *estampar* to stamp]

[2]**stampede** *vb* to (cause to) run away or rush in panic or on impulse

ˈstamping ˌground /ˈstamping‖ˈstæmpɪŋ/ *n* a favourite or habitual haunt

stamp out *vt* to eradicate, destroy

stance /stahns, stans‖stɑːns, stæns/ *n* **1a** a way of standing or being placed **b** intellectual or emotional attitude <*took an anti-union* ~> **2** the position of body or feet from which a sportsman (e g a batsman or golfer) plays

stanch, **staunch** /stawnch, stahnch‖stɔːntʃ, stɑːntʃ/ *vt* to check or stop the flow of <~ed *her tears*>; *also* to stop the flow of blood from (a wound)

stanchion /ˈstahnsh(ə)n‖ˈstɑːnʃ(ə)n/ *vt or n* (to provide with) an upright bar, post, or support (e g for a roof)

[1]**stand** /stand‖stænd/ *vb* **stood** /stood‖stʊd/ *vi* **1a** to support oneself on the feet in an erect position **b** to be a specified height when fully erect <~s *6ft 2*> **c** to rise to or maintain an erect or upright position <*his hair* stood *on end*> **2a** to take up or maintain a specified position or posture <~ *aside*> **b** to maintain one's position <~ *firm*> **3** to be in a specified state or situation <~s *accused*> **4** to sail in a specified direction <~ing *into harbour*> **5a** to have or maintain a relative position (as if) in a graded scale <~s *first in his class*> **b** to be in a position to gain or lose because of an action taken or a commitment made <~s *to make quite a profit*> **6** to occupy a place or location <*the house* ~s *on a hill*> **7** to remain stationary or inactive <*the car* stood *in the garage for a week*> **8** to agree, accord – chiefly in *it stands to reason* **9a** to exist in a definite (written or printed) form <*copy a passage exactly as it* ~s> <*that is how the situation* ~s *at present*> **b** to remain valid or effective <*the order given last week still* ~s> **10** *chiefly Br* to be a candidate in an election ~ *vt* **1a** to endure or undergo <~ *trial*> <*this book will* ~ *the test of time*> **b** to tolerate, bear; PUT UP WITH <*can't* ~ *his boss*> **c** to benefit from; do with <*looks as if he could* ~ *a good sleep*> **2** to remain firm in the face of <~ *a siege*> **3** to perform the duty of <~ *guard*> **4** to cause to stand; set upright **5** to pay the cost of; pay for <*I'll* ~ *you a dinner*> – infml – **stand a chance** to have a chance – **stand by** to remain loyal or faithful to – **stand for** **1** to be a symbol for; represent **2** to permit; PUT UP WITH – **stand on** to insist on <*never* stands *on ceremony*> – **stand one in good stead** to be of advantage or service to one – **stand one's ground** to remain firm and unyielding in the face of opposition – **stand on one's own feet** to think or act independently

[2]**stand** *n* **1** an act, position, or place of standing <*took up a* ~ *near the exit*> **2a** a standstill; *also* a halt for defence or resistance **b** a usu defensive effort of some length or success <*a united* ~ *against the plans for the new motorway*> **c** a stop made by a touring theatrical company, rock group, etc to give a performance **3** a strongly or aggressively held position, esp on a debatable issue **4a** a structure of tiered seats for spectators – often pl with sing. meaning **b** a raised platform serving as a point of vantage or display (e g for a speaker or exhibit) **5** a small usu temporary and open-air stall where goods are sold or displayed <*a hot dog* ~> **6** a place where a passenger vehicle awaits hire <*a taxi* ~> **7** a frame on or in which sthg may be placed for support <*an umbrella* ~> **8** a group of plants or trees growing in a continuous area **9** *NAm the* witness-box

[1]**standard** /ˈstandəd‖ˈstændəd/ *n* **1** a conspicuous flag, object, etc used to mark a rallying point, esp in battle, or to serve as an emblem **2a** a (long narrow tapering) flag **b** the personal flag of a member of a royal family or of the head of a state **3a** sthg established by authority, custom, or general consent as a model or example; a criterion **b** a (prescribed) degree of quality or worth **c** *pl* moral integrity; principles **4** sthg set up and established by authority as a rule for the measure of quantity, weight, value, or quality **5a** the fineness and legally fixed weight of the metal used in coins **b** the basis of value in a money system **6** an upright support **7a** a shrub or herbaceous plant grown with an erect main stem so that it forms or resembles a tree **b** a fruit tree

grafted on a stock that does not induce dwarfing **8** sthg standard: e g **8a** a model of car supplied without optional extras **b** a musical composition, specif a popular song, that has become a part of the established repertoire

[2]**standard** *adj* **1a** being or conforming to a standard, esp as established by law or custom <~ *weight*> **b** sound and usable but not of top quality **2a** regularly and widely used, available, or supplied <*a* ~ *socket*> **b** well established and familiar <*the* ~ *weekend television programmes*> **3** having recognized and permanent value <*a* ~ *reference work*> – **standardize** *vt*, **standardization** *n*

ˈstandard-ˌbearer *n* **1** one who carries a standard or banner **2** the leader of an organization, movement, or party

ˈstandard ˌlamp *n* a lamp with a tall support that stands on the floor

ˌstandard of ˈliving *n* a level of welfare or subsistence maintained by an individual, group, or community and shown esp by the level of consumption of necessities, comforts, and luxuries

ˈstandard ˌtime *n* the officially established time, with reference to Greenwich Mean Time, of a region or country

[1]**standby** /ˈstandˌbie‖ˈstændˌbaɪ/ *n, pl* **standbys** /-ˌbiez‖-ˌbaɪz/ one who or that which is held in reserve and can be relied on, made, or used in case of necessity

[2]**standby** *adj* **1** held near at hand and ready for use <~ *equipment*> **2** relating to the act or condition of standing by <~ *duty*>

stand by *vi* **1** to be present but remain aloof or inactive <*calmly* stood by *and watched those trying to help*> **2** to wait in a state of readiness <stand by *for action*>

stand down *vi* **1** to leave the witness-box **2** *chiefly Br* to relinquish (candidature for) an office or position **3** *chiefly Br, of a soldier* to go off duty ~*vt chiefly Br* to send (soldiers) off duty; *broadly* to dismiss (workers); LAY OFF

ˈstand-ˌin *n* **1** one who is employed to occupy an actor's place while lights and camera are made ready **2** a substitute – **stand in** *vi*

[1]**standing** /ˈstanding‖ˈstændɪŋ/ *adj* **1** used or designed for standing in <~ *places*> **2** not yet cut or harvested <~ *timber*> <~ *grain*> **3** not flowing; stagnant <~ *water*> **4** continuing in existence or use indefinitely <*a* ~ *offer*> **5** established by law or custom <*a* ~ *joke*> **6** done from a standing position <*a* ~ *jump*> <*a* ~ *ovation*>

[2]**standing** *n* **1a** length of service or experience, esp as determining rank, pay, or privilege **b** position, status, or condition, esp in relation to a group or other individuals in a similar field; *esp* good reputation **2** maintenance of position or condition; duration <*a custom of long* ~>

ˌstanding ˈorder *n* **1** a rule governing the procedure of an organization, which remains in force until specifically changed **2** an instruction (e g to a banker or newsagent) in force until specifically changed

ˈstanding ˌroom *n* space for standing; *esp* accommodation available for spectators or passengers after all seats are filled

ˈstandˌoff /-ˌof‖-ˌɒf/ *n, NAm* a tie, deadlock

ˈstand-ˌoff, stand-off half *n* the player in rugby positioned between the scrum-half and the three-quarter backs

standoffish /ˌstandˈofish‖ˌstændˈɒfɪʃ/ *adj* reserved, aloof – **standoffishly** *adv*

stand out *vi* **1a** to appear (as if) in relief; project **b** to be prominent or conspicuous **2** to be stubborn in resolution or resistance

ˈstandˌpipe /-ˌpiep‖-ˌpaɪp/ *n* a pipe fitted with a tap and used for outdoor water supply

ˈstandˌpoint /-ˌpoynt‖-ˌpɔɪnt/ *n* a position from which objects or principles are viewed and according to which they are compared and judged

ˈstandˌstill /-ˌstil‖-ˌstɪl/ *n* a state in which motion or progress is absent; a stop

stand to *vi* to take up a position of readiness (e g for action or inspection) <*ordered the men to* stand to>

ˈstand-ˌup *adj* **1** stiffened to stay upright without folding over <*a* ~ *collar*> **2** performed in or requiring a standing position <*a* ~ *meal*> **3** (having an act) consisting of jokes usu performed solo standing before an audience <*a* ~ *comedian*>

stand up *vi* **1** to rise to or maintain a standing or upright position **2** to remain sound and intact under stress, attack, or close scrutiny ~*vt* to fail to keep an appointment with – **stand up for** to defend against attack or criticism – **stand up to 1** to withstand efficiently or unimpaired <*a car which can* stand up to *rough handling*> **2** to face boldly

stank /stangk‖stæŋk/ *past of* STINK

stanza /ˈstanzə‖ˈstænzə/ *n* a division of a poem consisting of a series of lines arranged together in a usu recurring pattern of metre and rhyme [Italian, stay, abode, room, stanza, deriv of Latin *stare* to stand] – **stanzaic** *adj*

stapes /ˈstaypeez‖ˈsteɪpiːz/ *n, pl* **stapes, stapedes** /ˈstaypiˌdeez‖ˈsteɪpɪˌdiːz/ the innermost of the chain of 3 small bones in the ear of a mammal

[1]**staple** /ˈstaypl‖ˈsteɪpl/ *vt or n* (to provide with or secure by) **a** a U-shaped metal loop both ends of which can be driven into a surface (e g to secure sthg) **b** a small piece of wire with ends bent at right angles which can be driven through thin sheets of material, esp paper, and clinched to secure the items

[2]**staple** *n* **1** a chief commodity or production of a place **2a** a commodity for which the demand is constant **b** sthg having widespread and constant use or appeal **c** the sustaining or principal element; substance **3** RAW MATERIAL **4a** a textile fibre (e g wool or rayon) of relatively short length that when spun and twisted forms a yarn rather than a filament **b** the length of a piece of such textile fibre as a distinguishing characteristic of the raw material

[3]**staple** *adj* **1** used, needed, or enjoyed constantly, usu by many individuals **2** produced regularly or in large quantities <~ *crops such as wheat and rice*> **3** principal, chief

stapler /ˈstayplə‖ˈsteɪplə/ *n* a small usu hand-operated device for inserting wire staples

[1]**star** /stah‖stɑː/ *n* **1** any natural luminous body visible in the sky, esp at night; *specif* any of

many celestial bodies of great mass that give out light and are fuelled by nuclear fusion reactions **2a(1)** a planet or a configuration of the planets that is held in astrology to influence a person's destiny – often pl **a(2)** *pl* an astrological forecast; a horoscope **b** a waxing or waning fortune or fame <*her* ~ *was rising*> **3a** a figure with 5 or more points that represents a star; *esp* an asterisk **b** an often star-shaped ornament or medal worn as a badge of honour, authority, or rank or as the insignia of an order **c** any of a group of stylized stars used to place sthg in a scale of value or quality – often in combination <*a 4*-star *hotel*> **4a** a (highly publicized) performer in the cinema or theatre who plays leading roles **b** an outstandingly talented performer <*a* ~ *of the running track*> – **starless** *adj*, **starlike** *adj*

[2]**star** *vb* **-rr-** *vt* **1** to sprinkle or adorn (as if) with stars **2** to mark with a star or an asterisk **3** to advertise or display prominently; feature <*the film* ~s *a famous stage personality*> ~*vi* to play the most prominent or important role <*now* ~ring *in a West-End musical*>

[3]**star** *adj* of, being, or appropriate to a star <*received* ~ *treatment*>

[1]**starboard** /ˈstahbəd‖ˈstɑːbəd/ *adj or n* (of or at) the right side of a ship or aircraft looking forwards [Old English *stēorbord*, fr *stēor-* steering oar + *bord* ship's side]

[2]**starboard** *vt* to turn or put (a helm or rudder) to the right

[1]**starch** /stahch‖stɑːtʃ/ *vt* to stiffen (as if) with starch

[2]**starch** *n* **1** an odourless tasteless complex carbohydrate that is the chief storage form of carbohydrate in plants, is an important foodstuff, and is used also in adhesives and sizes, in laundering, and in pharmacy and medicine **2** a stiff formal manner; formality

Star Chamber *n* a court in England that was abolished in 1641, had both civil and criminal jurisdiction, and was noted for its arbitrary and oppressive procedures; *broadly, often not cap* any oppressive tribunal

starchy /ˈstahchi‖ˈstɑːtʃɪ/ *adj* **1** of or containing (much) starch **2** marked by formality or stiffness – **starchily** *adv*, **starchiness** *n*

ˈ**star-ˌcrossed** *adj* not favoured by the stars; ill-fated

ˈ**stardom** /-d(ə)m‖-d(ə)m/ *n* the status or position of a celebrity or star <*the actress quickly reached* ~>

ˈ**starˌdust** /-ˌdust‖-ˌdʌst/ *n* a feeling or impression of romance or magic

[1]**stare** /steə‖steə/ *vi* **1** to look fixedly, often with wide-open eyes **2** to stand out conspicuously <*the error* ~d *from the page*> **3** *esp of an animal's coat* to appear rough and lustreless ~*vt* to bring to a specified state by staring <~d *his opponent into submission*>

[2]**stare** *n* a staring look

starfish /ˈstahˌfish‖ˈstɑːˌfɪʃ/ *n* any of a class of sea animals that are echinoderms, have a body consisting of a central disc surrounded by 5 equally spaced arms, and feed largely on molluscs (e g oysters)

ˈ**starˌgaze** /-ˌgayz‖-ˌgeɪz/ *vi* **1** to gaze at stars **2** to gaze raptly, contemplatively, or absent-mindedly; *esp* to daydream

ˈ**starˌgazer** /-ˌgayzə‖-ˌgeɪzə/ *n* **1** an astrologer **2** an astronomer *USE* chiefly humor

[1]**stark** /stahk‖stɑːk/ *adj* **1** sheer, utter <~ *nonsense*> **2a(1)** barren, desolate **a(2)** having few or no ornaments; bare <*a* ~ *white room*> **b** harsh, blunt <*the* ~ *reality of death*> **3** sharply delineated <*a* ~ *outline*> – **starkly** *adv*, **starkness** *n*

[2]**stark** *adv* to an absolute or complete degree; wholly <~ *raving mad*>

starkers /ˈstahkəz‖ˈstɑːkəz/ *adj, Br* completely naked – used predicatively; slang

starlet /ˈstahlit‖ˈstɑːlɪt/ *n* a young film actress being coached and publicized for starring roles

starling /ˈstahling‖ˈstɑːlɪŋ/ *n* any of a family of usu dark social birds; *esp* a dark brown (or in summer, glossy greenish black) European bird that lives in large social groups

starry /ˈstahri‖ˈstɑːrɪ/ *adj* **1a** adorned or studded with stars **b** shining like stars; sparkling **2** (seemingly) as high as the stars <~ *speculations*>

ˌ**starry-ˈeyed** *adj* given to thinking in a dreamy, impractical, or overoptimistic manner

Stars and Stripes *n pl but sing in constr* the flag of the USA, having 13 alternately red and white horizontal stripes and a blue rectangle in the top left-hand corner with white stars representing the states

ˈ**star-ˌstudded** *adj* full of or covered with stars <*a* ~ *cast*> <*a* ~ *uniform*>

[1]**start** /staht‖stɑːt/ *vi* **1a** to move suddenly and violently; spring <~ed *angrily to his feet*> **b** to react with a sudden brief involuntary movement <~ed *when a shot rang out*> **2a** to issue with sudden force <*blood* ~ing *from the wound*> **b** to come into being, activity, or operation <*when does the film* ~?> **3** to (seem to) protrude <*his eyes* ~ing *from their sockets*> **4a** to begin a course or journey <~ed *out at dawn*> **b** to range from a specified initial point <*holiday prices* ~ *from around £80*> **5** to begin an activity or undertaking; *esp* to begin work **6** to be a participant at the start of a sporting contest ~ *vt* **1** to cause to leave a place of concealment; flush <~ *a rabbit*> **2** to bring into being <~ *a rumour*> **3** to begin the use or employment of <~ *a fresh loaf of bread*> **4a** to cause to move, act, operate, or do sthg specified <~ *the motor*> **b** to act as starter of (e g a race) **c** to cause to enter or begin a game, contest, or business activity <*only had £500 to* ~ *him*>; *broadly* to put in a starting position **5** to perform or undergo the first stages or actions of; begin <~ed *studying music at the age of 5*> – **start something** to cause trouble – **to start with 1** at the beginning; initially **2** taking the first point to be considered

[2]**start** *n* **1** a sudden involuntary bodily movement or reaction (e g from surprise or alarm) **2** a beginning of movement, activity, or development **3a** a lead conceded at the start of a race or competition **b** an advantage, lead; HEAD START <*his background gave him a good* ~ *in politics*> **4** a place of beginning

starter /ˈstahtə‖ˈstɑːtə/ *n* **1** one who initiates

or sets going; *esp* one who gives the signal to start a race **2a** one who is in the starting lineup of a race or competition **b** one who begins to engage in an activity or process **3** sby who or sthg that causes sthg to begin operating: e g **3a** a self-starter **b** material containing microorganisms used to induce a desired fermentation **c** a compound used to start a chemical reaction **4a** sthg that is the beginning of a process, activity, or series **b** *chiefly Br* the first course of a meal – often pl with sing. meaning

startle /ˈstahtl‖ˈstɑːtl/ *vb* to (cause to) be suddenly frightened or surprised and usu to (cause to) make a sudden brief movement – **startling** *adj*, **startlingly** *adv*

starve /stahv‖stɑːv/ *vi* **1a** to die from lack of food **b** to suffer or feel extreme hunger **2** to suffer or perish from deprivation <~d *for affection*> **3** *archaic or dial* to suffer or perish from cold ~*vt* to cause to starve – **starvation** *n*

starveling /ˈstahvling‖ˈstɑːvlɪŋ/ *n* a person or animal that is thin (as if) from lack of food

[1]**stash** /stash‖stæʃ/ *vt* to store in a usu secret place for future use – often + *away*

[2]**stash** *n, chiefly NAm* **1** a hiding place; a cache **2** sthg stored or hidden away

[1]**state** /stayt‖steɪt/ *n* **1a** a mode or condition of being (with regard to circumstances, health, temperament, etc) <*a ~ of readiness*> **b** a condition of abnormal tension or excitement <*don't get in a ~ about it*> **2a** a condition or stage in the physical being of sthg <*the gaseous ~ of water*> **b** any of various conditions characterized by definite quantities (e g of energy, angular momentum, or magnetic moment) in which an atomic system may exist **3a** social position; *esp* high rank **b(1)** luxurious style of living **b(2)** formal dignity; pomp – usu + *in* **4** ESTATE 1 **5** a politically organized (sovereign) body, usu occupying a definite territory; *also* its political organization **6** the operations of the government <*matters of ~*> **7** *often cap* a constituent unit of a nation having a federal government – **statehood** *n*

[2]**state** *vt* **1** to set, esp by regulation or authority; specify **2** to express the particulars of, esp in words; *broadly* to express in words – **statable, stateable** *adj*, **stated** *adj*, **statedly** *adv*

ˈ**stateˌcraft** /-ˌkrahft‖-ˌkrɑːft/ *n* the art of conducting state affairs

ˈ**stateless** /-lis‖-lɪs/ *adj* having no nationality <*a ~ person*> – **statelessness** *n*

ˈ**stately** /-li‖-lɪ/ *adj* **1** imposing, dignified <~ *language*> **2** impressive in size or proportions – **stateliness** *n*, **stately** *adv*

ˌ**stately** ˈ**home** *n, Br* a large country residence, usu of historical or architectural interest and open to the public

statement /ˈstaytmənt‖ˈsteɪtmənt/ *n* **1** stating orally or on paper **2** sthg stated: e g **2a** a report of facts or opinions **b** a single declaration or remark; an assertion **3** PROPOSITION 2 **4** the presentation of a theme in a musical composition **5** a summary of a financial account

ˌ**state-of-the-**ˈ**art** *adj* being or using the latest available resources, esp technology

ˈ**stateroom** /-ˌroohm, -room‖-ˌruːm, -rʊm/ *n* **1** a large room in a palace or similar building for use on ceremonial occasions **2** a (large and comfortable) private cabin in a ship

States /stayts‖steɪts/ *n pl but sing or pl in constr* *the* USA

state school *n* a British school that is publicly financed and provides compulsory free education

ˌ**state's** ˈ**evidence** *n, often cap S* (one who gives) evidence for the prosecution in US criminal proceedings

ˈ**stateˌside** /-ˌsied‖-ˌsaɪd/ *adj or adv* of, in, or to the USA

ˈ**statesman** /-mən‖-mən/, *fem* ˈ**statesˌwoman** *n, pl* **statesmen** /-mən‖-mən/, *fem* **stateswomen** **1** one versed in or esp engaged in the business of a government **2** one who exercises political leadership wisely and without narrow partisanship – **statesmanlike, statesmanly** *adj*, **statesmanship** *n*

[1]**static** /ˈstatik‖ˈstætɪk/ *also* **statical** /-kl‖-kl/ *adj* **1** exerting force by reason of weight alone without motion <~ *load*> <~ *pressure*> **2** of or concerned with bodies at rest or forces in equilibrium **3** characterized by a lack of movement, animation, progression, or change <*a ~ population*> **4** of, producing, or being stationary charges of electricity **5** of or caused by radio static – **statically** *adv*

[2]**static** *n* (the electrical disturbances causing) unwanted signals in a radio or television system; atmospherics

statics /ˈstatiks‖ˈstætɪks/ *n pl but sing or pl in constr* a branch of mechanics dealing with the relations of forces that produce equilibrium among solid bodies

[1]**station** /ˈstaysh(ə)n‖ˈsteɪʃ(ə)n/ *n* **1** the place or position in which sthg or sby stands or is assigned to stand or remain **2** a stopping place; *esp* (the buildings at) a regular or major stopping place for trains, buses, etc **3a** a post or sphere of duty or occupation **b** a post or area to which a military or naval force is assigned; *also, sing or pl in constr* the officers or society at a station **c** a stock farm or ranch in Australia or New Zealand **4** standing, rank <*a woman of high ~*> **5** a place for specialized observation and study of scientific phenomena <*a marine biology ~*> **6** a place established to provide a public service; *esp* POLICE STATION **7a** (the equipment in) an establishment equipped for radio or television transmission or reception **b** CHANNEL 1F(2)

[2]**station** *vt* to assign to or set in a station or position; post

stationary /ˈstayshən(ə)ri‖ˈsteɪʃən(ə)rɪ/ *adj* **1a** having a fixed position; immobile **b** geostationary **2** unchanging in condition

stationer /ˈstayshənə‖ˈsteɪʃənə/ *n* one who deals in stationery

stationery /ˈstayshən(ə)ri‖ˈsteɪʃən(ə)rɪ/ *n* materials (e g paper) for writing or typing; *specif* paper and envelopes for letter writing

ˈ**stationˌmaster** /-ˌmahstə‖-ˌmɑːstə/ *n* an official in charge of a railway station

stations of the cross *n pl, often cap S&C* (a devotion involving meditation before) a series of images or pictures, esp in a church, that represent the 14 stages of Christ's sufferings and death

ˈ**station** ˌ**wagon** *n, chiefly NAm* ESTATE CAR

statistic /stə'tistik‖stə'tɪstɪk/ *n* a single term or quantity in or computed from a collection of statistics; *specif* (a function used to obtain) a numerical value (e g the standard deviation or mean) used in describing and analysing statistics

statistics /stə'tistiks‖stə'tɪstɪks/ *n pl but sing or pl in constr* **1** a branch of mathematics dealing with the collection, analysis, interpretation, and presentation of masses of numerical data **2** a collection of quantitative data [German *statistik* study of political facts and figures, fr Modern Latin *statisticus* of politics, fr Latin *status* state] – **statistical** *adj*, **statistically** *adv*, **statistician** *n*

[1]**statuary** /'statyooəri‖'stætjʊərɪ/ *n* statues collectively

[2]**statuary** *adj* of or suitable for statues <~ *marble*>

statue /'statyooh, -chooh‖'stætju:, -tʃu:/ *n* a likeness (e g of a person or animal) sculptured, cast, or modelled in a solid material (e g bronze or stone) – **statuette** *n*

ˌstatu'esque /-'esk‖-'esk/ *adj* resembling a statue, esp in dignity, shapeliness, or formal beauty – **statuesquely** *adv*, **statuesqueness** *n*

stature /'stachə‖'stætʃə/ *n* **1** natural height (e g of a person) in an upright position **2** quality or status gained by growth, development, or achievement

status /'staytəs‖'steɪtəs/ *n* **1** the condition of sby or sthg (in the eyes of the law) **2** (high) position or rank in relation to others or in a hierarchy

ˌstatus 'quo /kwoh‖kwəʊ/ *n* the existing state of affairs <*seeks to preserve the* ~> [Latin, state in which]

statute /'statyooht‖'stætju:t/ *n* **1** a law passed by a legislative body and recorded **2** a rule made by a corporation or its founder, intended as permanent

statute book *n* the whole body of legislation of a given jurisdiction

statute law *n* enacted written law

statutory /'statyoot(ə)ri‖'stætjʊt(ə)rɪ/, **statutable** /-təbl‖-təbl/ *adj* established, regulated, or imposed by or in conformity to statute <*a* ~ *age limit*> – **statutorily, statutably** *adv*

[1]**staunch** /stawnch‖stɔ:ntʃ/ *vt* to stanch

[2]**staunch** *adj* steadfast in loyalty or principle – **staunchly** *adv*, **staunchness** *n*

[1]**stave** /stayv‖steɪv/ *n* **1** STAFF 1a, 2 **2** any of the narrow strips of wood or iron placed edge to edge to form the sides, covering, or lining of a vessel (e g a barrel) or structure **3** a supporting bar; *esp* RUNG 1b **4** a stanza **5** STAFF 3

[2]**stave** *vt* **staved, stove** /stohv‖stəʊv/ **1** to crush or break inwards – usu + *in* **2** to provide with staves

stave off *vt* to ward or fend off, esp temporarily

staves *pl of* STAFF

[1]**stay** /stay‖steɪ/ *n* a strong rope, now usu of wire, used to support a ship's mast or similar tall structure (e g a flagstaff)

[2]**stay** *vt* to support (e g a chimney) (as if) with stays

[3]**stay** *vi* **1** to continue in a place or condition; remain <~ *here*> <~ed *awake*> **2** to take up temporary residence; lodge **3a** to keep even in a contest or rivalry <~ *with the leaders*> **b** *of a racehorse* to run well over long distances **4** *archaic* to stop going forwards; pause **5** *archaic* to stop doing sthg; cease ~ *vt* **1** to last out (e g a race) **2** to stop or delay the proceeding, advance, or course of; halt <~ *an execution*> – **stay put** to be firmly fixed, attached, or established

[4]**stay** *n* **1a** stopping or being stopped **b** a suspension of judicial procedure <*a* ~ *of execution*> **2** a residence or sojourn in a place

[5]**stay** *n* **1** sby who or sthg that serves as a prop; a support **2** a corset stiffened with bones – usu pl with sing. meaning

[6]**stay** *vt* to provide physical or moral support for; sustain

'stay-at-ˌhome *n or adj* (one) preferring to remain in his/her own home, locality, or country

stayer /'stayə‖'steɪə/ *n* a racehorse that habitually stays the course

'staying ˌpower /'staying‖'steɪɪŋ/ *n* stamina

staysail /'stayˌsayl‖'steɪˌseɪl; *tech* -səl‖-səl/ *n* a fore-and-aft sail hoisted on a stay

stead /sted‖sted/ *n* the office, place, or function ordinarily occupied or carried out by sby or sthg else <*acted in his brother's* ~>

steadfast /'stedˌfahst, -fəst‖'stedˌfɑ:st, -fəst/ *adj* **1a** firmly fixed in place or position <*a* ~ *gaze*> **b** not subject to change **2** firm in belief, determination, or adherence; loyal – **steadfastly** *adv*, **steadfastness** *n*

[1]**steady** /'stedi‖'stedɪ/ *adj* **1a** firm in position; not shaking, rocking, etc **b** direct or sure; unfaltering <*a* ~ *hand*> **2** showing or continuing with little variation or fluctuation; stable, uniform <~ *prices*> <*a* ~ *pace*> **3a** not easily moved or upset; calm <~ *nerves*> **b** dependable, constant **c** not given to dissipation; sober – **steadily** *adv*, **steadiness** *n*

[2]**steady** *vb* to make, keep, or become steady – **steadier** *n*

[3]**steady** *adv* **1** in a steady manner; steadily **2** on the course set – used as a direction to the helmsman of a ship

[4]**steady** *n* a boyfriend or girlfriend with whom one is going steady – infml

steady state theory *n* a theory in cosmology: the universe has always existed and has always been expanding with matter being created continuously

steak /stayk‖steɪk/ *n* **1a** a slice of meat cut from a fleshy part (e g the rump) of a (beef) carcass and suitable for grilling or frying **b** a poorer-quality less tender beef cut, usu from the neck and shoulder, suitable for braising or stewing **2** a cross-sectional slice from between the centre and tail of a large fish

steal /steel‖sti:l/ *vb* **stole** /stohl‖stəʊl/; **stolen** /'stohlən‖'stəʊlən/ *vi* **1** to take the property of another **2** to come or go secretly or unobtrusively ~ *vt* **1a** to take without leave, esp secretly or by force and with intent to keep **b** to appropriate entirely to oneself or beyond one's proper share <~ *the show*> **2** to accomplish, obtain, or convey in a secretive, unobserved, or furtive manner <~ *a visit*> <stole *a glance at him*>

3 to seize or gain by trickery or skill <*a footballer adept at* ~ing *the ball*> – **stealer** *n* – **steal a march** to gain an advantage unobserved – usu + *on* – **steal someone's thunder** to appropriate or adapt sthg devised by another in order to take the credit due to him/her

stealth /stelth‖stelθ/ *n* **1** the act or action of proceeding furtively or unobtrusively **2** the state of being furtive or unobtrusive

stealthy /ˈstelthi‖ˈstelθɪ/ *adj* **1** slow, deliberate, and secret in action or character **2** intended to escape observation; furtive – **stealthily** *adv*, **stealthiness** *n*

[1]**steam** /steem‖stiːm/ *n* **1** a vapour given off by a heated substance **2a** the vapour into which water is converted when heated to its boiling point **b** the mist formed by the condensation of water vapour when cooled **3a** energy or power generated (as if) by steam under pressure **b** driving force; power <*got there under his own* ~> – infml – **let/blow off steam** to release pent-up emotions

[2]**steam** *vi* **1** to rise or pass off as vapour **2** to give off steam or vapour **3a** to move or travel (as if) by steam power (e g in a steamship) **b** to proceed quickly **4** to become cooked by steam **5** to be angry; boil <~ing *over the insult he had received*> **6** to become covered *up* or *over* with steam or condensation ~ *vt* **1** to give out as fumes; exhale **2** to apply steam to; *esp* to expose to the action of steam (e g for softening or cooking)

ˈsteamˌboat /-ˌboht‖-ˌbəʊt/ *n* a boat propelled by steam power

steamer /ˈsteemə‖ˈstiːmə/ *n* **1** a device in which articles are steamed; *esp* a vessel in which food is cooked by steam **2a** a ship propelled by steam **b** an engine, machine, or vehicle operated or propelled by steam

ˈsteam ˌiron *n* an electric iron with a compartment holding water that is converted to steam by the iron's heat and emitted through the soleplate onto the fabric being pressed

[1]**ˈsteamˌroller** /-ˌrohlə‖-ˌrəʊlə/ *n* **1** a machine equipped with wide heavy rollers for compacting the surfaces of roads, pavements, etc **2** a crushing force, esp when ruthlessly applied to overcome opposition

[2]**steamroller** *also* **steamroll** *vt* **1** to crush (as if) with a steamroller <~ *the opposition*> **2** to force to a specified state or condition by the use of overwhelming pressure <~ed *the bill through Parliament*> ~*vi* to move or proceed with irresistible force

ˈsteamˌship /-ˌship‖-ʃɪp/ *n* STEAMER 2a

steam up *vt* to make angry or excited; arouse

steed /steed‖stiːd/ *n* a horse; *esp* a spirited horse for state or war – chiefly poetic

[1]**steel** /steel‖stiːl/ *n* **1** commercial iron distinguished from cast iron by its malleability and lower carbon content **2** an instrument or implement (characteristically) of steel: e g **2a** a fluted round steel rod with a handle for sharpening knives **b** a piece of steel for striking sparks from flint **c** a strip of steel used for stiffening **3** a quality (e g of mind or spirit) that suggests steel, esp in strength or hardness <*nerves of* ~>

[2]**steel** *vt* **1** to make unfeeling; harden **2** to fill with resolution or determination

steel band *n* a band that plays tuned percussion instruments cut out of oil drums, developed orig in Trinidad – **steelbandsman** *n*

ˌsteel ˈwool *n* long fine loosely compacted steel fibres used esp for scouring and burnishing

ˈsteelˌworks /-ˌwuhks‖-ˌwɜːks/ *n, pl* **steelworks** an establishment where steel is made – often pl with sing. meaning – **steelworker** *n*

steely /ˈsteeli‖ˈstiːlɪ/ *adj* of or like (the hardness, strength, or colour of) steel – **steeliness** *n*

ˈsteelˌyard /-ˌyahd‖-ˌjɑːd/ *n* a balance in which an object to be weighed is suspended from the shorter arm of a lever and the weight determined by moving a counterbalance along a graduated scale on the longer arm until equilibrium is attained

[1]**steep** /steep‖stiːp/ *adj* **1** making a large angle with the plane of the horizon; almost vertical **2** being or characterized by a rapid and severe decline or increase **3** difficult to accept, comply with, or carry out; excessive – infml – **steepen** *vb*, **steepish** *adj*, **steeply** *adv*, **steepness** *n*

[2]**steep** *vt* **1** to soak in a liquid at a temperature below its boiling point (e g for softening or bleaching) **2** to cover with or plunge into a liquid (e g in bathing, rinsing, or soaking) **3** to imbue with or subject thoroughly to – usu + *in* <~ed *in history*> ~*vi* to undergo soaking in a liquid

[3]**steep** *n* **1** being steeped **2** a liquid in which sthg is steeped

steeple /ˈsteepl‖ˈstiːpl/ *n* (a tower with) a tall spire on a church

ˈsteepleˌchase /-ˌchays‖-ˌtʃeɪs/ *n* **1a** a horse race across country **b** a horse race over jumps; *specif* one over a course longer than 2mi (about 3.2km) containing fences higher than 4ft 6in (about 1.4m) **2** a middle-distance running race over obstacles; *specif* one of 3000m over 28 hurdles and 7 water jumps – **steeplechaser** *n*, **steeplechasing** *n*

ˈsteepleˌjack /-ˌjak‖-ˌdʒæk/ *n* one who climbs chimneys, towers, etc to paint, repair, or demolish them

[1]**steer** /stiə‖stɪə/ *n* a male bovine animal castrated before sexual maturity

[2]**steer** *vt* **1** to direct the course of; *esp* to guide (e g a ship) by mechanical means (e g a rudder) **2** to set and hold to (a course) ~ *vi* **1** to direct the course (e g of a ship or motor vehicle) **2** to pursue a course of action **3** to be subject to guidance or direction <*a car that* ~s *well*> – **steerable** *adj*, **steerer** *n* – **steer clear** to keep entirely away – often + *of*

steerage /ˈstiərij‖ˈstɪərɪdʒ/ *n* **1** the act or practice of steering; *broadly* direction **2** a large section in a passenger ship for passengers paying the lowest fares

ˈsteerage-ˌway *n* a rate of motion sufficient to make a ship or boat respond to movements of the rudder

ˈsteering comˌmittee *n* a committee that determines the order in which business will be taken up (e g in Parliament)

ˈsteering ˌwheel *n* a handwheel by means of which one steers a motor vehicle, ship, etc

steersman /ˈstiəzmən‖ˈstɪəzmən/

n a helmsman

stein /s(h)tien‖staın,ʃt-/ *n* a usu earthenware beer mug often with a hinged lid

stele /ˈsteeli, steel‖ˈsti:lı, sti:l/ *n* **1** a usu carved or inscribed stone slab or pillar used esp as a gravestone **2** the (cylindrical) central vascular portion of the stem of a vascular plant – **stelar** *adj*

stellar /ˈstelə‖ˈstelə/ *adj* of or composed of (the) stars

[1]**stem** /stem‖stem/ *n* **1a** the main trunk of a plant; *specif* a primary plant axis that develops buds and shoots instead of roots **b** a branch, petiole, or other plant part that supports a leaf, fruit, etc **2** the bow or prow of a vessel; *specif* the principal frame member at the bow to which the sides are fixed **3** a line of ancestry; *esp* a fundamental line from which others have arisen **4** that part of a word which has unchanged spelling when the word is inflected **5** sthg that resembles a plant stem: e g **5a** a main (vertical) stroke of a letter or musical note **b** the tubular part of a tobacco pipe from the bowl outwards, through which smoke is drawn **c** the often slender and cylindrical upright support between the base and bowl of a wineglass **d** a shaft of a watch used for winding – **stemless** *adj*, **stemmed** *adj*

[2]**stem** *vt* **-mm-** **1** to make headway against (e g an adverse tide, current, or wind) **2** to check or go counter to (sthg adverse)

[3]**stem** *vb* **-mm-** *vi* to originate – usu + *from* ~ *vt* to remove the stem from

[4]**stem** *vt* **-mm-** to stop or check (as if) by damming <~ *a flow of blood*>

Sten /sten‖sten/, **Sten gun** *n* a lightweight British submachine gun [Major *S*heppard, 20th-c English army officer + Mr *T*urpin, 20th-c English civil servant + *En*gland]

stench /stench‖stentʃ/ *n* a stink

[1]**stencil** /ˈstens(ə)l‖ˈstens(ə)l/ *n* **1** (a printing process using, or a design, pattern, etc produced by means of) an impervious material (e g a sheet of paper or metal) perforated with a design or lettering through which a substance (e g ink or paint) is forced onto the surface below **2** a sheet of strong tissue paper impregnated or coated (e g with paraffin or wax) for use esp in typing a stencil

[2]**stencil** *vt* **-ll-** (*NAm* **-l-**, **-ll-**) **1** to produce by means of a stencil **2** to mark or paint with a stencil – **stenciller** *n*

stenography /steˈnogrəfi‖steˈnɒgrəfı/ *n* the writing and transcription of shorthand [deriv of Greek *stenos* narrow, scanty + *graphein* to write] – **stenographer** *n*, **stenographic** *adj*, **stenographically** *adv*

stentorian /stenˈtawri·ən‖stenˈtɔ:rıən/ *adj* extremely loud [*Stentor*, mythical Greek herald noted for his loud voice]

[1]**step** /step‖step/ *n* **1** a rest for the foot in ascending or descending: e g **1a** a single tread and riser on a stairway; a stair **b** a ladder rung **2a(1)** (the distance or space passed over in) an advance or movement made by raising the foot and bringing it down at another point **a(2)** a combination of foot (and body) movements constituting a unit or a repeated pattern <*a dance* ~> **a(3)** manner of walking; stride **b** FOOTPRINT 1 **c** the sound of a footstep <*heard his* ~s *in the hall*> **3** a short distance <*just a* ~ *from the beach*> **4** *pl* a course, way <*directed his* ~s *towards the river*> **5a** a degree, grade, or rank in a scale **b** a stage in a process <*was guided through every* ~ *of her career*> **6** a block supporting the base of a mast **7** an action, proceeding, or measure often occurring as 1 in a series – often pl with sing. meaning <*is taking* ~s *to improve the situation*> **8** a steplike offset or part, usu occurring in a series **9** *pl* a stepladder – **steplike** *adj*, **stepped** *adj* – **in step 1** with each foot moving to the same time as the corresponding foot of others or in time to music **2** in harmony or agreement – **out of step** not in step

[2]**step** *vb* **-pp-** *vi* **1a** to move by raising the foot and bringing it down at another point or by moving each foot in succession **b** to dance **2a** to go on foot; walk **b** to be on one's way; leave – often + *along* **3** to press down *on* sthg with the foot <~ *on the brake*> ~ *vt* **1** to take by moving the feet in succession <~ *3 paces*> **2** to go through the steps of; perform <~ *a minuet*> **3** to make (e g a mast) erect by fixing the lower end in a step **4** to measure by steps <~ *50 yards*> – usu + *off* or *out* **5** to construct or arrange (as if) in steps <*craggy peaks with terraces* ~ped *up the sides – Time*> – **step into** to attain or adopt (sthg) with ease <stepped into *a fortune*> – **step on it/the gas** to increase one's speed; hurry up – infml

step- *comb form* related by remarriage and not by blood <step*parent*>

ˈ**step,brother** /-ˌbrudhə‖-ˌbrʌðə/ *n* a son of one's stepparent by a former marriage

ˈ**step,child** /-ˌchield‖-ˌtʃaıld/ *n, pl* **stepchildren** /-ˌchildrən‖-ˌtʃıldrən/ a child (**stepdaughter** or **stepson**) of one's wife or husband by a former marriage

step down *vt* to lower (the voltage at which an alternating current is operating) by means of a transformer ~ *vi* to retire, resign <step down *as chairman*> – **step-down** *adj*

ˈ**step-,in** *adj, of clothes* put on by being stepped into

step in *vi* **1** to make a brief informal visit **2** to intervene in an affair or dispute

ˈ**step,ladder** /-ˌladə‖-ˌlædə/ *n* a portable set of steps with a hinged frame

step out *vi* **1** to leave or go outside, usu for a short time <stepped out *for a smoke*> **2** to go or march at a vigorous or increased pace

ˈ**step,parent** /-ˌpeərənt‖-ˌpeərənt/ *n* the husband or wife of one's parent by a subsequent marriage; a **stepfather** or **stepmother**

steppe /step‖step/ *n* a vast usu level and treeless plain, esp in SE Europe or Asia

ˈ**stepping-,stone** *n* **1** a stone on which to step (e g in crossing a stream) **2** a means of progress or advancement

ˈ**step,sister** /-ˌsistə‖-ˌsıstə/ *n* a daughter of one's stepparent by a former marriage

step up *vt* **1** to increase (the voltage at which an alternating current is operating) by means of a transformer **2** to increase, augment, or advance by 1 or more steps <step up *production*> ~ *vi* **1** to come forward <step up *to the front*>

2 to undergo an increase – **step-up** *adj*

-ster /-stə‖-stə/ *comb form* (→ *n*) **1** sby who or sthg that does, handles, or operates <*tap*ster> **2** sby who or sthg that makes or uses <*song*ster> **3** sby who or sthg that is associated with or participates in <*gang*ster> **4** sby who or sthg that is <*young*ster>

stere /stiə‖stɪə/ *n* a metric unit of volume equal to one cubic metre (about 1.3 cubic yd)

stere- /steri-, stiəri-‖sterɪ-, stɪərɪ-/, **stereo-** *comb form* **1** solid (body) <stereo*metry*> **2a** stereoscope <stereo*graphy*> **b** having, involving, or dealing with 3 dimensions of space <stereo*chemistry*>

[1]**stereo** /'sterioh, 'stiərioh‖'sterɪəʊ, 'stɪərɪəʊ/ *n, pl* **stereos** **1** a stereoscopic method, system, or effect **2a** stereophonic reproduction **b** a stereophonic sound system

[2]**stereo** *adj* **1** stereoscopic **2** stereophonic

stereophonic /ˌsteri·ə'fonik, ˌstiəri-, -rioh-‖ˌsterɪə'fɒnɪk, ˌstɪərɪ-, -rɪəʊ-/ *adj* of or being (a system for) sound reproduction in which the sound is split into and reproduced by 2 different channels to give spatial effect [deriv of Greek *stereos* solid + *phōnē* voice, sound] – **stereophonically** *adv*, **stereophony** *n*

stereoscope /'steri·əˌskohp, 'stiəri·ə-‖'sterɪəˌskəʊp, 'stɪərɪə-/ *n* an optical instrument with 2 eyepieces through which the observer views 2 pictures taken from points of view a little way apart to get the effect of a single three-dimensional picture

stereoscopy /ˌsteri'oskəpi, ˌstiəri-‖ˌsterɪ'ɒskəpɪ, ˌstɪərɪ-/ *n* the seeing of objects in 3 dimensions – **stereoscopic** *adj*, **stereoscopically** *adv*

[1]**stereoˌtype** /'steri·əˌtiep, 'stiəri-‖'sterɪəˌtaɪp, 'stɪərɪ-/ *n* **1** a plate made by making a cast, usu in type metal, from a mould of a printing surface **2** sby who or sthg that conforms to a fixed or general pattern; *esp* a standardized, usu oversimplified, mental picture or attitude held in common by members of a group – **stereotypical** *also* **stereotypic** *adj*

[2]**stereotype** *vt* **1** to make a stereotype from **2a** to repeat without variation; make hackneyed **b** to develop a mental stereotype about – **stereotyper** *n*

sterile /'steriel‖'steraɪl/ *adj* **1** failing or not able to produce or bear fruit, crops, or offspring **2a** deficient in ideas or originality **b** free from living organisms, esp microorganisms **3** bringing no rewards or results; not productive <*the* ~ *search for jobs*> – **sterilely** *adv*, **sterilize** *vt*, **sterilizable** *adj*, **sterilizer** *n*, **sterilant** *n*, **sterilization** *n*, **sterility** *n*

[1]**sterling** /'stuhling‖'stɜːlɪŋ/ *n* **1** British money **2** (articles of) sterling silver

[2]**sterling** *adj* **1** of or calculated in terms of British sterling **2a** *of silver* having a fixed standard of purity; *specif* 92.5 per cent pure **b** made of sterling silver **3** conforming to the highest standard <~ *character*>

sterling area *n* a group of countries whose currencies are tied to British sterling

[1]**stern** /stuhn‖stɜːn/ *adj* **1a** hard or severe in nature or manner; austere **b** expressive of severe displeasure; harsh **2** forbidding or gloomy in appearance **3** inexorable, relentless <~ *necessity*> **4** sturdy, firm <*a* ~ *resolve*> – **sternly** *adv*, **sternness** *n*

[2]**stern** *n* **1** the rear end of a ship or boat **2** a back or rear part; the last or latter part – **sternmost** *adj*, **sternwards** *adv*

sternum /'stuhnəm‖'stɜːnəm/ *n, pl* **sternums, sterna** /-nə‖-nə/ a bone or cartilage at the front of the body that connects the ribs, both sides of the shoulder girdle, or both; the breastbone – **sternal** *adj*

steroid /'steroyd, 'stiə-‖'sterɔɪd, 'stɪə-/ *n* any of numerous compounds of similar chemical structure, including the sterols and various hormones (e g testosterone) and glycosides (e g digitalis) – **steroidal** *adj*

sterol /'sterol‖'sterɒl/ *n* any of various solid alcohols (e g cholesterol) widely distributed in animal and plant fats

stertorous /'stuhtərəs‖'stɜːtərəs/ *adj* characterized by a harsh snoring or gasping sound – **stertorously** *adv*

stet /stet‖stet/ *vt* **-tt-** to direct retention of (a word or passage previously ordered to be deleted or omitted) by annotating, usu with the word *stet*

stethoscope /'stethəˌskohp‖'steθəˌskəʊp/ *n* an instrument used to detect and study sounds produced in the body [French *stéthoscope*, fr Greek *stēthos* chest + *skopein* to look at] – **stethoscopic** *adj*, **stethoscopically** *adv*, **stethoscopy** *n*

stetson /'stets(ə)n‖'stets(ə)n/ *n* a broad-brimmed high-crowned felt hat

stevedore /'steevədaw‖'stiːvədɔː/ *n* a docker [Spanish *estibador*, fr *estibar* to pack, fr Latin *stipare* to press together]

[1]**stew** /styooh‖stjuː/ *n* **1a** a savoury dish, usu of meat and vegetables stewed and served in the same liquid **b** a mixture composed of many usu unrelated parts **2** a state of excitement, worry, or confusion – infml

[2]**stew** *vt* to cook (e g meat or fruit) slowly by boiling gently or simmering in liquid ~ *vi* **1** to become cooked by stewing **2** to swelter, esp from confinement in a hot atmosphere **3** to become agitated or worried; fret ***USE*** (*vi 2&3*) infml

[1]**steward** /'styooh·əd‖'stjuːəd/ *n* **1** one employed to look after a large household or estate **2** SHOP STEWARD **3a** one who manages the provisioning of food and attends to the needs of passengers (e g on an airliner, ship, or train) **b** one who supervises the provision and distribution of food and drink in a club, college, etc **4** an official who actively directs affairs (e g at a race meeting) [Old English *stīweard*, fr *stī* hall, sty + *weard* ward] – **stewardship** *n*

[2]**steward** *vb* to act as a steward (for)

stewardess /'styooh·ədis, ˌstyooh·ə'des‖'stjuːədɪs, ˌstjuːə'des/ *n* a woman who performs the duties of a steward; *esp* HOSTESS 2a

stewed /styoohd‖stjuːd/ *adj* **1** *of tea* bitter-tasting because allowed to infuse for too long **2** DRUNK 1 – infml

[1]**stick** /stik‖stɪk/ *n* **1a** a (dry and dead) cut or broken branch or twig **b** a cut or broken branch or piece of wood gathered esp for fuel or

construction material **2a** a long slender piece of wood: e g **2a(1)** a club or staff used as a weapon **a(2)** a walking stick **b** an implement used for striking an object in a game (e g hockey) **c** sthg used to force compliance **d** a baton symbolizing an office or dignity; a rod **3** any of various implements resembling a stick in shape, origin, or use: e g **3a** COMPOSING STICK **b** a joystick **4** sthg prepared (e g by cutting, moulding, or rolling) in a relatively long and slender often cylindrical form <*a ~ of toffee*> **5** a person of a specified type <*a decent old ~* – Robert Graves> **6** a stick-shaped plant stalk (e g of rhubarb or celery) **7** several bombs, parachutists, etc released from an aircraft in quick succession **8** *pl the* wooded or rural and usu backward districts **9** a piece of furniture **10** *Br* hostile comment or activity <*gave the Local Authority plenty of ~*> *USE* (*8, 9, &10*) infml

[2]**stick** *vt* to provide a stick as a support for (e g a plant)

[3]**stick** *vb* **stuck** /stuk‖stʌk/ *vt* **1a** to pierce with sthg pointed; stab **b** to kill by piercing <*~ a pig*> **2a** to push or thrust so as or as if to pierce **b** to fasten in position (as if) by piercing <stuck *a pistol in his belt*> **3** to push, thrust <stuck *his head out of the window*> **4** to cover or adorn (as if) by sticking things on <*a crown* stuck *with rubies*> **5** to attach (as if) by causing to adhere to a surface **6a** to halt the movement or action of **b** to baffle, stump <*got* stuck *doing his maths homework*> **7** to put or set in a specified place or position <*~ your coat over there*> **8** to refrain from granting, giving, or allowing (sthg indignantly rejected by the speaker); stuff <*you can ~ the job for all I care!*> **9** to saddle with sthg disadvantageous or disagreeable <*why do I always get* stuck *with the gardening?*> **10** *chiefly Br* to bear, stand <*can't ~ his voice*> *~ vi* **1a** to become fixed in place by means of a pointed end **b** to become fast (as if) by adhesion <stuck *in the mud*> **2a** to remain in a place, situation, or environment <*don't want to ~ in this job for the rest of my life*> **b** to hold fast or adhere resolutely; cling <*~ to the truth*> **c** to remain effective <*the charge will not ~*> **d** to keep close in a chase or competition <*~*ing *with the leaders*> **3** to become blocked, wedged, or jammed **4a** to hesitate, stop <*would ~ at nothing to get what they wanted*> **b** to be unable to proceed **5** to project, protrude – often + *out* or *up USE* (*vt 7, 8, 9, &10*) infml – **stick by** to continue to support – **stick one's neck out** to take a risk (e g by saying sthg unpopular) and make oneself vulnerable – infml – **stuck on** infatuated with <*he's really* stuck on *her*> – infml

[4]**stick** *n* adhesive quality or substance

stick around *vi* to stay or wait about; linger – infml

sticker /ˈstikə‖ˈstɪkə/ *n* **1** sby who or sthg that pierces with a point **2a** sby who or sthg that sticks or causes sticking **b** a slip of paper with gummed back that, when moistened, sticks to a surface

sticking plaster *n* an adhesive plaster, esp for covering superficial wounds

ˈ**stick-in-the-ˌmud** *n* one who dislikes and avoids change

stickleback /ˈstiklˌbak‖ˈstɪklˌbæk/ *n* any of numerous small scaleless fishes that have 2 or more spines in front of the dorsal fin

stickler /ˈstiklə‖ˈstɪklə/ *n* one who insists on exactness or completeness in the observance of sthg <*a ~ for obedience*>

stick out *vi* **1** to be prominent or conspicuous – often in *stick out a mile, stick out like a sore thumb* **2** to be persistent (e g in a demand or an opinion) – usu + *for ~vt* to endure to the end – often + *it*

stick up *vt* to rob at gunpoint – infml – **stick-up** *n* – **stick up for** to speak or act in defence of; support

sticky /ˈstiki‖ˈstɪkɪ/ *adj* **1a** adhesive <*~ tape*> **b(1)** viscous, gluey **b(2)** coated with a sticky substance <*~ hands*> **2** humid, muggy; *also* clammy **3a** disagreeable, unpleasant <*came to a ~ end*> **b** awkward, stiff <*after a ~ beginning became good friends*> **c** difficult, problematic <*a rather ~ question*> – **stickily** *adv*, **stickiness** *n*

ˌ**sticky** ˈ**wicket** *n* **1** a cricket pitch drying after rain and therefore difficult to bat on **2** a difficult situation – infml; often in *on a sticky wicket*

[1]**stiff** /stif‖stɪf/ *adj* **1a** not easily bent; rigid **b** lacking in suppleness and often painful <*~ muscles*> **c** *of a mechanism* impeded in movement **d** incapable of normal alert response <*scared ~*> **2a** firm, unyielding **b(1)** marked by reserve or decorum; formal **b(2)** lacking in ease or grace; stilted **3** hard fought <*a ~ match*> **4a** exerting great force; forceful <*a ~ wind*> **b** potent <*a ~ drink*> **5** of a dense or glutinous consistency; thick **6a** harsh, severe <*a ~ penalty*> **b** arduous <*a ~ climb*> **7** expensive, steep <*paid a ~ price*> – **stiffen** *vb*, **stiffener** *n*, **stiffening** *n*, **stiffish** *adj*, **stiffly** *adv*, **stiffness** *n*

[2]**stiff** *adv* in a stiff manner; stiffly

[3]**stiff** *n* a corpse – slang

ˌ**stiff-ˈnecked** *adj* haughty, stubborn

stifle *vt* **1a** to overcome or kill by depriving of oxygen; suffocate, smother **b** to muffle <*~ noises*> **2a** to cut off (e g the voice or breath) **b** to prevent the development or expression of; check, suppress <*~*d *his anger*> <*~ a revolt*> *~vi* to become suffocated (as if) by lack of oxygen – **stiflingly** *adv*

stigma /ˈstigmə‖ˈstɪgmə/ *n, pl* **stigmata** /stigˈmahtə, ˈstigmətə‖stɪgˈmɑːtə, ˈstɪgmətə/, **stigmas**, (*2*) **stigmata** **1a** a mark of shame or discredit **b** an identifying mark or characteristic; *specif* a specific diagnostic sign of a disease **2** *pl* marks resembling the wounds of the crucified Christ, believed to be impressed on the bodies of holy or saintly people **3a** a small spot, scar, or opening on a plant or animal **b** the portion of the female part of a flower which receives the pollen grains and on which they germinate – **stigmatic** *adj*, **stigmatically** *adv*

stigmat·ize, -ise /ˈstigmətiez‖ˈstɪgmətaɪz/ *vt* **1** to describe or identify in disparaging terms **2** to mark with the stigmata of Christ – **stigmatization** *n*

[1]**stile** /stiel‖staɪl/ *n* **1** a step or set of steps for passing over a fence or wall **2** a turnstile

[2]**stile** *n* any of the vertical members in a frame or panel into which the secondary members are fitted

stiletto /sti'letoh‖stɪ'letəʊ/ *n, pl* **stilettos, stilettoes 1** a slender rodlike dagger **2** a pointed instrument for piercing holes (e g for eyelets) in leather, cloth, etc **3** *Br* an extremely narrow tapering high heel on a woman's shoe [Italian, diminutive of *stilo* stylus, dagger, fr Latin *stilus* stylus]

[1]**still** /stil‖stɪl/ *adj* **1a** devoid of or abstaining from motion <~ *water*> **b** having no effervescence; not carbonated <~ *orange*> **c** of, being, or designed for taking a static photograph as contrasted with a moving picture **2a** uttering no sound; quiet **b** low in sound; subdued **3a** calm, tranquil **b** free from noise or turbulence – **stillness** *n*

[2]**still** *vt* **1a** to allay, calm **b** to put an end to; settle **2** to arrest the motion or noise of; quiet <~ *the wind*> ~*vi* to become motionless or silent; quiet *USE* chiefly poetic

[3]**still** *adv* **1** as before; even at this or that time <*drink it while it's* ~ *hot*> **2** in spite of that; nevertheless <*very unpleasant;* ~, *we can't help it*> **3a** EVEN 2b <*a* ~ *more difficult problem*> **b** YET 1a

[4]**still** *n* **1** a still photograph; *specif* a photograph of actors or of a scene from a film **2** quiet, silence – chiefly poetic

[5]**still** *n* an apparatus used in distillation, esp of spirits, consisting of either the chamber in which the vaporization is carried out or the entire equipment

'**still,birth** /-,buhth‖-,bɜːθ/ *n* the birth of a dead infant

,**still'born** /-'bawn‖-'bɔːn/ *adj* **1** dead at birth **2** failing from the start; abortive – **stillborn** *n*

,**still 'life** *n, pl* **still lifes** a picture showing an arrangement of inanimate objects (e g fruit or flowers)

[1]**stilly** /'stil·li‖'stɪllɪ/ *adv* in a calm manner

[2]**stilly** /'stili‖'stɪlɪ/ *adj* still, quiet – poetic

stilt /stilt‖stɪlt/ *n* **1a** either of 2 poles each with a rest or strap for the foot, that enable the user to walk along above the ground **b** any of a set of piles, posts, etc that support a building above ground or water level **2** any of various notably long-legged 3-toed wading birds

stilted /'stiltid‖'stɪltɪd/ *adj* stiffly formal and often pompous – **stiltedly** *adv*, **stiltedness** *n*

Stilton /'stilt(ə)n‖'stɪlt(ə)n/ *n* a cream-enriched white cheese that has a wrinkled rind and is often blue-veined [*Stilton*, village in Cambridgeshire, England, where it was originally sold]

stimulant /'stimyoolənt‖'stɪmjʊlənt/ *n* **1** sthg (e g a drug) that produces a temporary increase in the functional activity or efficiency of (a part of) an organism **2** STIMULUS 1 – **stimulant** *adj*

stimulate /'stimyoo,layt‖'stɪmjʊ,leɪt/ *vt* **1** to excite to (greater) activity **2a** to function as a physiological stimulus to **b** to arouse or affect by the action of a stimulant (e g a drug) ~*vi* to act as a stimulant or stimulus – **stimulator** *n*, **stimulative** *adj*, **stimulation** *n*

stimulus /'stimyooləs‖'stɪmjʊləs/ *n, pl* **stimuli** /-li, -lie‖-lɪ, -laɪ/ **1** sthg that rouses or incites to activity; an incentive **2** sthg (e g light) that directly influences the activity of living organisms (e g by exciting a sensory organ or evoking muscular contraction or glandular secretion)

[1]**sting** /sting‖stɪŋ/ *vb* **stung** /stung‖stʌŋ/ *vt* **1a** to give an irritating or poisonous wound to, esp with a sting <stung *by a bee*> **b** to affect with sharp quick pain <*hail* stung *their faces*> **2** to cause to suffer acute mental pain <stung *with remorse*>; *also* to incite or goad thus <stung *into action*> **3** to overcharge, cheat <stung *by a street trader*> – infml ~ *vi* **1** to use a sting; to have stings <*nettles* ~> **2** to feel a sharp burning pain – **stingingly** *adv*

[2]**sting** *n* **1a** a stinging; *specif* the thrust of a sting into the flesh **b** a wound or pain caused (as if) by stinging **2** *also* **stinger** a sharp organ of a bee, scorpion, stingray, etc that is usu connected with a poison gland or otherwise adapted to wound by piercing and injecting a poisonous secretion **3** a stinging element, force, or quality <*a joke with a* ~ *in the tail*> – **stingless** *n*

'**sting,ray** /-,ray‖-,reɪ/ *n* any of numerous rays with a whiplike tail having 1 or more large sharp spines capable of inflicting severe wounds

stingy /'stinji‖'stɪndʒɪ/ *adj* **1** mean or ungenerous in giving or spending **2** meanly scanty or small – **stingily** *adv*, **stinginess** *n*

[1]**stink** /stingk‖stɪŋk/ *vi* **stank** /stangk‖stæŋk/, **stunk** /stungk‖stʌŋk/; **stunk 1** to emit a strong offensive smell **2** to be offensive; *also* to be in bad repute or of bad quality **3** to possess sthg to an offensive degree – usu + *with* <*he* ~s *with money*> *USE* (*except 1*) infml – **stinky** *adj*

[2]**stink** *n* **1** a strong offensive smell; a stench **2** a public outcry against sthg offensive – infml

[1]**stinking** /'stingking‖'stɪŋkɪŋ/ *adj* **1** severe and unpleasant <*a* ~ *cold*> – infml **2** offensively drunk – slang

[2]**stinking** *adv* to an extreme degree <*got* ~ *drunk*> – infml

stink out *vt* **1** to cause to stink or be filled with a stench <*the leaking gas* stank *the house* out> **2** to drive out (as if) by subjecting to an offensive or suffocating smell

[1]**stint** /stint‖stɪnt/ *vt* to restrict to a small share or allowance; be frugal with ~*vi* to be sparing or frugal – **stinter** *n*

[2]**stint** *n* **1** restraint, limitation **2** a definite quantity or period of work assigned

stipend /'stiepend‖'staɪpend/ *n* a fixed sum of money paid periodically (e g to a clergyman) as a salary or to meet expenses [Latin *stipendium*, fr *stip-, stips* gift + *pendere* to weigh, pay]

[1]**stipendiary** /stie'pendyəri, sti-‖staɪ'pendjərɪ, stɪ-/ *adj* of or receiving a stipend

[2]**stipendiary** *n* one who receives a stipend

[1]**stipple** /'stipl‖'stɪpl/ *vt* **1a** to paint, engrave, or draw in stipple **b** to apply (e g paint) in stipple **2** to speckle, fleck – **stippler** *n*

[2]**stipple** *n* (the effect produced by) a method of painting using small points, dots, or strokes to represent degrees of light and shade

stipulate /'stipyoo,layt‖'stɪpjʊ,leɪt/ *vt* **1** to specify as a condition or requirement of an agreement or offer <~ *quality and quantity*> **2**

to give a guarantee of in making an agreement – **stipulator** *n*

stipulation /ˌstipyooˈlaysh(ə)n‖ˌstɪpjʊˈleɪʃ(ə)n/ *n* sthg (e g a condition) stipulated – **stipulatory** *adj*

[1]**stir** /stuh‖stɜː/ *vb* **-rr-** *vt* **1a** to cause a slight movement or change of position of **b** to disturb the quiet of; agitate **2a** to disturb the relative position of the particles or parts of (a fluid or semifluid), esp by a continued circular movement in order to make the composition homogeneous <~ *one's tea*> **b** to mix (as if) by stirring <~ *pigment into paint*> **3** to bestir, exert <*unable to* ~ *himself to wash the car*> **4a** to rouse to activity; produce strong feelings in <*the news* ~red *him to action*> **b** to provoke – often + *up* <~ *up trouble*> ~ *vi* **1a** to make a slight movement **b** to begin to move (e g in waking) **2** to (begin to) be active or busy **3** to pass an implement through a substance with a circular movement – **stirrer** *n*

[2]**stir** *n* **1a** a state of disturbance, agitation, or brisk activity **b** widespread notice and discussion <*caused quite a* ~ *in the neighbourhood*> **2** a slight movement **3** a stirring movement

[3]**stir** *n* prison – slang

stirring /ˈstuhring‖ˈstɜːrɪŋ/ *adj* rousing, inspiring

stirrup /ˈstirəp‖ˈstɪrəp/ *n* **1** STIRRUP IRON **2** the stapes **3** a short rope by which another rope is suspended from the yard of a sailing ship for seamen to walk along

ˈ**stirrup** ˌ**cup** *n* a farewell usu alcoholic drink; *specif* one taken on horseback

ˈ**stirrup** ˌ**iron** *n* either of a pair of D-shaped metal frames that are attached by a strap to a saddle and in which the rider's feet are placed

[1]**stitch** /stich‖stɪtʃ/ *n* **1** a local sharp and sudden pain, esp in the side **2a** a single in-and-out movement of a threaded needle in sewing, embroidering, or suturing **b** a portion of thread left in the material after 1 stitch **3a** a single loop of thread or yarn round a stitching implement **b** such a loop after being worked to form 1 of a series of links in a fabric **4** a series of stitches that are formed in a particular manner or constitute a complete step or design **5** a method of stitching **6** the least scrap of clothing – usu neg <*without a* ~ *on*>; infml – **in stitches** in a state of uncontrollable laughter

[2]**stitch** *vt* **1** to fasten, join, or close (as if) with stitches; sew **2** to work on or decorate (as if) with stitches ~*vi* to sew – **stitcher** *n*

stoat /stoht‖stəʊt/ *n* a European weasel with a long black-tipped tail

[1]**stock** /stok‖stɒk/ *n* **1** a supporting framework or structure: e g **1a** *pl* the frame or timbers holding a ship during construction **b** *pl* a wooden frame with holes for the feet (and hands) in which offenders are held for public punishment **c(1)** the part to which the barrel and firing mechanism of a gun are attached **c(2)** the butt (e g of a whip or fishing rod) **d** the beam of a plough to which handles, cutting blades, and mouldboard are attached **2a** the main stem of a plant or tree **b(1)** a plant (part) consisting of roots and lower trunk onto which a scion is grafted **b(2)** a plant from which cuttings are taken **3** the crosspiece of an anchor **4a** the original (e g a man, race, or language) from which others derive; a source **b(1)** the descendants of an individual; family, lineage **b(2)** a compound organism **c** [3]RACE 2, 3a **d** a group of closely related languages **5a** *sing or pl in constr* livestock **b** a store or supply accumulated (e g of raw materials or finished goods) **6a** a debt or fund due (e g from a government) for money loaned at interest; *also, Br* capital or a debt or fund which continues to bear interest but is not usually redeemable as far as the original sum is concerned **b** (preference) shares – often pl **7** any of a genus of plants of the mustard family with usu sweet-scented flowers **8** a wide band or scarf worn round the neck, esp by some clergymen **9a** the liquid in which meat, fish, or vegetables have been simmered that is used as a basis for soup, gravy, etc **b** raw material from which sthg is made **10a** an estimate or appraisal of sthg <*take* ~ *of the situation*> **b** the estimation in which sby or sthg is held <*his* ~ *with the electorate remains high*> **11** a type of brick – **in stock** in the shop and ready for delivery; ON HAND – **out of stock** having no more on hand; sold out

[2]**stock** *vt* **1** to fit to or with a stock **2** to provide with (a) stock; supply <~ *a stream with trout*> **3** to procure or keep a stock of <*we don't* ~ *that brand*> ~*vi* to take in a stock – often + *up* <~ *up on tinned food*>

[3]**stock** *adj* **1a** kept in stock regularly <*clearance sale of* ~ *goods*> **b** regularly and widely available or supplied <*dresses in all the* ~ *sizes*> **2** used for (breeding and rearing) livestock <*a* ~ *farm*> **3** commonly used or brought forward; standard – chiefly derog <*the* ~ *answer*>

[1]**stockade** /stoˈkayd‖stɒˈkeɪd/ *n* **1** a line of stout posts set vertically to form a defence **2** an enclosure or pen made with posts and stakes

[2]**stockade** *vt* to fortify or surround with a stockade

stockbreeder /ˈstokˌbreedə‖ˈstɒkˌbriːdə/ *n* one who breeds livestock – **stockbreeding** *n*

ˈ**stockˌbroker** /-ˌbrohkə‖-ˌbrəʊkə/ *n* a broker who buys and sells securities – **stockbroking, stockbrokerage** *n*

ˈ**stock** ˌ**car** *n* a racing car having the chassis of a commercially produced assembly-line model

ˈ**stock exˌchange** *n* (a building occupied by) an association of people organized to provide an auction market among themselves for the purchase and sale of securities

ˈ**stockˌfish** /-ˌfish‖-ˌfɪʃ/ *n* cod, haddock, etc dried in the open air without salt

stockinet, stockinette /ˌstokiˈnet‖ˌstɒkɪˈnet/ *n* a soft elastic usu cotton fabric used esp for bandages

stocking /ˈstoking‖ˈstɒkɪŋ/ *n* **1** a usu knitted close-fitting often nylon covering for the foot and leg **2** an area of distinctive colour on the lower part of the leg of an animal – **stockinged** *adj*

ˌ**stock-in-ˈtrade** *n* **1** the equipment necessary to or used in a trade or business **2** sthg like the standard equipment of a tradesman or business <*the tact and charm that are the ~ of a successful society hostess*>

stockist /ˈstokist‖ˈstɒkɪst/ *n, Br* one (e g a retailer) who stocks goods, esp of a particular kind or brand

ˈstock,jobber /-ˌjobə‖-ˌdʒɒbə/ *n* a stock-exchange member who deals only with brokers or other jobbers

ˈstockman /-mən‖-mən/ *n, Austr & NAm* one who owns or takes care of livestock

[1]**ˈstock,pile** /-ˌpiel‖-ˌpaɪl/ *n* an accumulated store; *esp* a reserve supply of sthg essential accumulated for use during a shortage

[2]**stockpile** *vt* **1** to place or store in or on a stockpile **2** to accumulate a stockpile of

ˈstock,pot /-ˌpot‖-ˌpɒt/ *n* a pot in which stock is prepared or kept

ˌstock-ˈstill *adj* completely motionless <*stood ~*>

ˈstock,taking /-ˌtayking‖-ˌteɪkɪŋ/ *n* **1** the checking or taking of an inventory of goods or supplies on hand (e g in a shop) **2** estimating a situation at a given moment (e g by considering past progress and resources)

stocky /ˈstoki‖ˈstɒkɪ/ *adj* short, sturdy, and relatively thick in build – **stockily** *adv*, **stockiness** *n*

ˈstock,yard /-ˌyahd‖-ˌjɑːd/ *n* a yard in which cattle, pigs, horses, etc are kept temporarily for slaughter, market, or shipping

stodge /stoj‖stɒdʒ/ *n* **1** filling (starchy) food **2** turgid and unimaginative writing – infml

stodgy /ˈstoji‖ˈstɒdʒɪ/ *adj* **1** *of food* heavy and filling **2** dull, boring <*a ~ novel*> – infml – **stodgily** *adv*, **stodginess** *n*

[1]**stoic** /ˈstoh·ik‖ˈstəʊɪk/ *n* **1** *cap* a member of an ancient Greek or Roman school of philosophy equating happiness with knowledge and holding that wisdom consists in self-mastery and submission to natural law **2** sby apparently or professedly indifferent to pleasure or pain [Latin *stoicus*, fr Greek *stōikos*, lit., of the portico, fr *Stoa* (*Poikilē*) the Painted Portico, portico at Athens where the philosopher Zeno taught]

[2]**stoic, stoical** /-kl‖-kl/ *adj* **1** *cap* (characteristic) of the Stoics or their doctrines **2** not affected by or showing passion or feeling; *esp* firmly restraining response to pain or distress <*a ~ indifference to cold*> – **stoically** *adv*

stoicism /ˈstoh·iˌsiz(ə)m‖ˈstəʊɪˌsɪz(ə)m/ *n* **1** *cap* the philosophy of the Stoics **2a** indifference to pleasure or pain **b** repression of emotion

stoke /stohk‖stəʊk/ *vt* **1** to poke or stir up (e g a fire); *also* to supply with fuel **2** to feed abundantly ~*vi* to stir up or tend a fire (e g in a furnace); supply a furnace with fuel

ˈstoke,hold /-ˌhohld‖-ˌhəʊld/ *n* a compartment containing a steamship's boilers and furnaces

stoker /ˈstohkə‖ˈstəʊkə/ *n* one employed to tend a furnace, esp on a ship, and supply it with fuel

[1]**stole** /stohl‖stəʊl/ *past of* STEAL

[2]**stole** *n* **1** an ecclesiastical vestment consisting of a long usu silk band worn traditionally over both shoulders and hanging down in front by bishops and priests, and over the left shoulder by deacons **2** a long wide strip of material worn by women usu across the shoulders, esp with evening dress

stolen /ˈstohlən‖ˈstəʊlən/ *past part of* STEAL

stolid /ˈstolid‖ˈstɒlɪd/ *adj* difficult to arouse emotionally or mentally; unemotional – **stolidly** *adv*, **stolidity** *n*

stolon /ˈstohlon‖ˈstəʌlɒn/ *n* a horizontal branch from the base of a plant (e g a strawberry) that produces new plants

[1]**stomach** /ˈstumək‖ˈstʌmək/ *n* **1a** (a cavity in an invertebrate animal analogous to) a saclike organ formed by a widening of the alimentary canal of a vertebrate, that is between the oesophagus at the top and the duodenum at the bottom and in which the first stages of digestion occur **b** the part of the body that contains the stomach; belly, abdomen **2a** desire for food; appetite **b** inclination, desire – usu neg <*had no ~ for an argument*>

[2]**stomach** *vt* **1** to find palatable or digestible <*can't ~ rich food*> **2** to bear without protest or resentment <*couldn't ~ her attitude*> *USE* usu neg

ˈstomach ˌpump *n* a suction pump with a flexible tube for removing liquids from the stomach or injecting liquids into it

[1]**stomp** /stomp‖stɒmp/ *vi* to walk or dance with a heavy step – infml

[2]**stomp** *n* a jazz dance characterized by heavy stamping

[1]**stone** /stohn‖stəʊn/ *n, pl* **stones,** (3) **stone** *also* **stones** **1** a concretion of earthy or mineral matter: **1a(1)** a piece of this, esp one smaller than a boulder **a(2)** rock **b** a piece of rock for a specified function: e g **b(1)** a building or paving block **b(2)** a gem **b(3)** a sharpening stone **b(4)** a smooth flat surface on which a printing forme is made up **c** CALCULUS 1a **2** the hard central portion of a fruit (e g a peach or date) **3** an imperial unit of weight equal to 14lb (about 6.35kg)

[2]**stone** *vt* **1** to hurl stones at; *esp* to kill by pelting with stones **2** to face, pave, or fortify with stones **3** to remove the stones or seeds of (a fruit) **4** to rub, scour, or polish with or on a stone

[3]**stone** *adj* (made) of stone

stone- *comb form* completely <stone-*dead*> <stone-*cold*>

ˈStone ˌAge *n* the first known period of prehistoric human culture characterized by the use of stone tools and weapons

ˈstone,chat /-ˌchat‖-ˌtʃæt/ *n* a common small Eurasian bird, the male of which has a black head and chestnut underparts

stoned *adj* intoxicated by alcohol or a drug (e g marijuana) – infml

ˈstone ˌfruit *n* a fruit with a (large) stone; a drupe

ˈstone's ˌthrow *n* a short distance

ˌstoneˈwall /-ˈwawl‖-ˈwɔːl/ *vi, chiefly Br* **1** to bat excessively defensively and cautiously in cricket; *broadly* to behave obstructively **2** to obstruct or delay parliamentary debate – **stonewaller** *n*

ˌstone ˈwall *n* a wall-like resistance or obstruction (e g in politics or public affairs)

ˈstoneˌware /-ˌweə||-ˌweə/ *n* opaque ceramic ware that is fired at a high temperature and is nonporous

ˈstoneˌwork /-ˌwuhk||-ˌwɜːk/ *n* masonry – **stoneworker** *n*

stony *also* **stoney** /ˈstohni||ˈstəʊnɪ/ *adj* **1** containing many stones or having the nature of stone **2a** insensitive to pity or human feeling **b** showing no movement or reaction; dumb, expressionless <*a* ~ *glance*> **3** stony-broke – infml – **stonily** *adv*, **stoniness** *n*

ˌstony-ˈbroke *adj, Br* completely without funds; broke – infml

stood /stood||stʊd/ *past of* STAND

[1]stooge /stoohj||stuːdʒ/ *n* **1** one who usu speaks the feed lines in a comedy duo **2** one who plays a subordinate or compliant role to another **3** *chiefly NAm* a nark; STOOL PIGEON *USE (2&3)* infml

[2]stooge *vi* **1** to act as a stooge – usu + *for* **2** to move, esp fly, aimlessly to and fro or at leisure – usu + *around* or *about USE* infml

[1]stool /stoohl||stuːl/ *n* **1a** a seat usu without back or arms supported by 3 or 4 legs or a central pedestal **b** a low bench or portable support for the feet or for kneeling on **2** a discharge of faecal matter **3** (a shoot or growth from) a tree stump or plant crown from which shoots grow out

[2]stool *vi* to throw out shoots from a stump or crown

ˈstool ˌpigeon *n, chiefly NAm* sby acting as a decoy; *esp* a police informer

[1]stoop /stoohp||stuːp/ *vi* **1a** to bend the body forwards and downwards, sometimes simultaneously bending the knees **b** to stand or walk with a temporary or habitual forward inclination of the head, body, or shoulders **2a** to condescend <*the gods* ~ *to intervene in the affairs of men*> **b** to lower oneself morally <~ed *to spying*> **3** *of a bird* to fly or dive down swiftly, usu to attack prey ~*vt* to bend (a part of the body) forwards and downwards

[2]stoop *n* **1a** an act of bending the body forwards **b** a temporary or habitual forward bend of the back and shoulders **2** the descent of a bird, esp on its prey

[3]stoop *n, chiefly NAm* a porch, platform, entrance stairway, or small veranda at a house door

[1]stop /stop||stɒp/ *vb* **-pp-** *vt* **1a** to close by filling or obstructing **b** to hinder or prevent the passage of <~ *the flow of blood*> **2a** to close up or block off (an opening) **b** to make impassable; choke, obstruct **c** to cover over or fill in (a hole or crevice) **3a** to restrain, prevent **b** to withhold; CUT OFF <~ped *his wages*> **4a** to cause to cease; check, suppress **b** to discontinue <~ *running*> **5a** to deduct or withhold (a sum due) **b** to instruct one's bank not to honour or pay <~ *a cheque*> **6a** to arrest the progress or motion of; cause to halt <~ped *the car*> **b** to beat in a boxing match by a knockout **7** to change the pitch of **7a** (e g a violin string) by pressing with the finger **b** (a woodwind instrument) by closing 1 or more finger holes **c** (a French horn) by putting the hand into the bell **d** (e g a trumpet) by putting a mute into the bell **8** to get in the way of, esp so as to be wounded or killed <~ped *a bullet*> – infml ~ *vi* **1a** to cease activity or operation **b** to come to an end, esp suddenly; close, finish **2a** to cease to move on; halt **b** to pause, hesitate **3a** to break one's journey – often + *off* <~ped *off at Lisbon*> **b** *chiefly Br* to remain <~ *at home*> **c** *chiefly NAm* to make a brief call; DROP IN – usu + *by* – **stoppable** *adj*

[2]stop *n* **1** a cessation, end <*soon put a* ~ *to that*> **2a** (a switch or handle operating) a graduated set of organ pipes of similar design and tone quality **b** a corresponding set of vibrators or reeds of a reed organ **3a** sthg that impedes, obstructs, or brings to a halt; an impediment, obstacle **b** (any of a series of markings, esp f-numbers, for setting the size of) the circular opening of an optical system (e g a camera lens) **c** STOPPER 2 **4** a device for arresting or limiting motion **5** stopping or being stopped **6a** a halt in a journey <*made a brief* ~ *to refuel*> **b** a stopping place <*a bus* ~> **7** a consonant in the articulation of which there is a stage (e g in the /p/ of *apt* or the /g/ of *tiger*) when the breath passage is completely closed **8** – used in telegrams and cables to indicate a full stop **9** *chiefly Br* any of several punctuation marks; *specif* FULL STOP

ˈstopˌcock /-ˌkok||-ˌkɒk/ *n* a cock for stopping or regulating flow (e g of fluid through a pipe)

stopgap /ˈstopˌgap||ˈstɒpˌgæp/ *n* sthg that serves as a temporary expedient; a makeshift

ˌstop-ˈgo *adj* alternately active and inactive

ˈstop-ˌoff *n* a stopover

ˈstopˌover /-ˌohvə||-ˌəʊvə/ *n* a stop at an intermediate point in a journey

stoppage /ˈstopij||ˈstɒpɪdʒ/ *n* **1** a deduction from pay **2** a concerted cessation of work by a group of employees that is usu more spontaneous and less serious than a strike

[1]stopper /ˈstopə||ˈstɒpə/ *n* **1** sby or sthg that brings to a halt or causes to stop operating or functioning; a check **2** sby or sthg that closes, shuts, or fills up; *specif* sthg (e g a bung or cork) used to plug an opening

[2]stopper *vt* to close or secure (as if) with a stopper

ˌstop ˈpress *n* (space reserved for) late news added to a newspaper after printing has begun

ˈstopˌwatch /-ˌwoch||-ˌwɒtʃ/ *n* a watch that can be started and stopped at will for exact timing

storage /ˈstawrij||ˈstɔːrɪdʒ/ *n* **1a** (a) space for storing **b** MEMORY 4 **2a** storing or being stored (e g in a warehouse) **b** the price charged for keeping goods in storage

ˈstorage ˌcell *n* one or a connected set of secondary cells; an accumulator

[1]store /staw||stɔː/ *vt* **1** to supply; *esp* to provide with a store for the future <~ *a ship with provisions*> **2** to collect as a reserve supply <~ *vegetables for winter use*> – often + *up* or *away* **3** to place or leave in a location (e g a warehouse, library, or computer memory) for preservation or later use or disposal **4** to provide storage room for; hold <*boxes for* storing *the surplus*> – **storable** *adj*

[2]store *n* **1a** sthg stored or kept for future use **b**

pl articles accumulated for some specific object and drawn on as needed <*military* ~s> **c** sthg accumulated **d** a source from which things may be drawn as needed; a reserve fund **2** storage – usu + *in* <*furniture kept in* ~> **3** a large quantity, supply, or number **4** a warehouse **5a** DEPARTMENT STORE **b** *chiefly NAm* SHOP 1 **6** *chiefly Br* MEMORY 4 – **in store** about to happen; imminent <*there's a nasty surprise* in store *for you*>

[3]**store** *adj* of, kept in, or used for a store

ˈstoreˌhouse /-ˌhows‖-ˌhaʊs/ *n* **1** a warehouse **2** an abundant supply or source

ˈstoreˌkeeper /-ˌkeepə‖-ˌkiːpə/ *n* **1** sby who keeps and records stock (e g in a warehouse) **2** *NAm* a shopkeeper

ˈstoreroom /-roohm, -room‖-ruːm, -rʊm/ *n* a place for the storing of goods or supplies

storey, *NAm chiefly* **story** /ˈstawri‖ˈstɔːrɪ/ *n* (a set of rooms occupying) a horizontal division of a building [Medieval Latin *historia* picture, storey of a building, fr Latin, history, tale; prob fr pictures adorning the windows of medieval buildings]

storeyed, *NAm chiefly* **storied** /ˈstawrid‖ˈstɔːrɪd/ *adj* having a specified number of storeys <*a 2-*storeyed *house*>

storied /ˈstawrid‖ˈstɔːrɪd/ *adj* celebrated in story or history

stork /stawk‖stɔːk/ *n* any of various large mostly Old World wading birds that have long stout bills and are related to the ibises and herons

[1]**storm** /stawm‖stɔːm/ *n* **1** a violent disturbance of the weather marked by high winds, thunder and lightning, rain or snow, etc **2** a disturbed or agitated state; a sudden or violent commotion **3** a violent shower of objects (e g missiles) **4** a tumultuous outburst <*a* ~ *of abuse*> **5** a violent assault on a defended position – **by storm** (as if) by using a bold frontal movement to capture quickly

[2]**storm** *vi* **1a** *of wind* to blow with violence **b** to rain, hail, snow, or sleet <*it was* ~ing *in the mountains*> **2** to move in a sudden assault or attack <~ed *ashore at zero hour*> **3** to be in or to exhibit a violent passion; rage <~ing *at the unusual delay*> **4** to rush about or move impetuously, violently, or angrily <*the mob* ~ed *through the streets*> ~*vt* to attack or take (e g a fortified place) by storm

ˈstormˌbound /-ˌbownd‖-ˌbaʊnd/ *adj* confined or delayed by a storm or its effects

ˈstorm ˌlantern *n, chiefly Br* HURRICANE LAMP

ˈstorm ˌpetrel *n* a small sooty black and white petrel frequenting the N Atlantic and Mediterranean

ˈstorm ˌtrooper *n* **1** a member of a Nazi party militia **2** a member of a force of shock troops

stormy /ˈstawmi‖ˈstɔːmɪ/ *adj* marked by turmoil or fury – **stormily** *adv*, **storminess** *n*

stormy petrel *n* **1** STORM PETREL **2** sby fond of strife

[1]**story** /ˈstawri‖ˈstɔːrɪ/ *n* **1a** an account of incidents or events **b** a statement of the facts of a situation in question <*according to their* ~> **c** an anecdote; *esp* an amusing one **2a** a short fictional narrative **b** the plot of a literary work **3** a widely circulated rumour **4** a lie **5** a legend, romance **6** a news article or broadcast [Old French *estorie*, fr Latin *historia* history – see HISTORY]

[2]**story** *n, chiefly NAm* a storey

ˈstoryˌbook /-ˌbook‖-ˌbʊk/ *adj* fairy-tale

ˈstoryˌteller /-ˌtelə‖-ˌtelə/ *n* **1** a relator of tales or anecdotes **2** a liar

stoup /stoohp‖stuːp/ *n* **1** a large drinking mug or glass **2** a basin for holy water at the entrance of a church

[1]**stout** /stowt‖staʊt/ *adj* **1** firm, resolute <~ *resistance*> **2** physically or materially strong: **2a** sturdy, vigorous **b** staunch, enduring **c** solid, substantial **3** forceful <*a* ~ *attack*>; *also* violent <*a* ~ *wind*> **4** corpulent, fat – chiefly euph – **stoutish** *adj*, **stoutly** *adv*, **stoutness** *n*

[2]**stout** *n* a dark sweet heavy-bodied beer

ˌstoutˈhearted /-ˈhahtid‖-ˈhɑːtɪd/ *adj* courageous – **stoutheartedly** *adv*

[1]**stove** /stohv‖stəʊv/ *n* **1a** an enclosed appliance that burns fuel or uses electricity to provide heat chiefly for domestic purposes **b** a cooker **2** *chiefly Br* a hothouse

[2]**stove** *past of* STAVE

ˈstoveˌpipe /-ˌpiep‖-ˌpaɪp/ *n* (metal) piping used as a stove chimney or to connect a stove with a flue

stow /stoh‖stəʊ/ *vt* **1** to put away; store **2a** to pack away in an orderly fashion in an enclosed space **b** to fill (e g a ship's hold) with cargo **3** to cram in (e g food) – usu + *away* <~ed *away a huge dinner*>; infml **4** to stop, desist – slang; esp in *stow it*

stowage /ˈstohij‖ˈstəʊɪdʒ/ *n* **1** goods in storage or to be stowed **2a** storage capacity **b** a place for storage **3** the state of being stored

[1]**stowaway** /ˈstoh·əˌway‖ˈstəʊəˌweɪ/ *n* sby who stows away

[2]**stowaway** *adj* designed to be dismantled or folded for storage <~ *tables and chairs*>

stow away *vi* to hide oneself aboard a vehicle, esp a ship, as a means of travelling without payment or escaping from a place undetected

straddle /ˈstradl‖ˈstrædl/ *vi* to stand or esp sit with the legs wide apart ~ *vt* **1** to stand, sit, or be astride <~ *a horse*> **2** to bracket (a target) with missiles (e g shells or bombs) **3** to be on land on either side of <*the village* ~s *the frontier*> – **straddle** *n*, **straddler** *n*

strafe /strahf, strayf‖strɑːf, streɪf/ *vt* to rake (e g ground troops) with fire at close range, esp with machine-gun fire from low-flying aircraft [German *Gott strafe England* God punish England, slogan of the Germans in WW I] – **strafe** *n*, **strafer** *n*

straggle /ˈstragl‖ˈstrægl/ *vi* **1** to lag behind or stray away from the main body of sthg, esp from a line of march **2** to move or spread untidily away from the main body of sthg <straggling *branches*> – **straggle** *n*, **straggler** *n*

straggly /ˈstragli‖ˈstræglɪ/ *adj* loosely spread out or scattered irregularly <*a* ~ *beard*>

[1]**straight** /strayt‖streɪt/ *adj* **1a** free from curves, bends, angles, or irregularities <~ *hair*> <~ *timber*> **b** generated by a point moving continuously in the same direction <*a* ~ *line*> **c** of, occupying, or passing through a

fielding position in front of the batsman and near the line between the wickets or its extension behind the bowler <*a* ~ *drive*> **2** direct, uninterrupted: e g **2a** holding to a direct or proper course or method <*a* ~ *thinker*> **b** candid, frank <*gave me a* ~ *answer*> **c** coming directly from a trustworthy source <*a* ~ *tip on the horses*> **d** consecutive <*6* ~ *wins*> **e** having the cylinders arranged in a single straight line <*a* ~ *8-cylinder engine*> **f** upright, vertical <*the picture isn't quite* ~> **3a** honest, fair <~ *dealing*> **b** properly ordered or arranged (e g with regard to finance) <*be* ~ *after the end of the month*> **c** correct <*get the facts* ~> **4** unmixed <~ *gin*> **5a** not deviating from the general norm or prescribed pattern <*preferred acting in* ~ *dramas to musicals or comedies*> **b** accepted as usual, normal, or proper **6** *chiefly NAm* marked by no exceptions or deviations in support of a principle or party <*a* ~ *ballot*> **7a** conventional in opinions, habits, appearance etc **b** heterosexual ***USE*** (7) infml – **straightish** *adj*, **straightness** *n*

[2]**straight** *adv* **1** in a straight manner **2** without delay or hesitation; immediately <~ *after breakfast*>

[3]**straight** *n* **1** sthg straight: e g **1a** a straight line or arrangement **b** a straight part of sthg; *esp* HOME STRAIGHT **2** a poker hand containing 5 cards in sequence but not of the same suit **3a** a conventional person **b** a heterosexual ***USE*** (3) infml

ˌ**straight and ˈnarrow** *n the* way of life that is morally and legally irreproachable

ˌ**straightaˈway** /-əˈway‖-əˈweɪ/ *adv* without hesitation or delay; immediately

ˈ**straightˌedge** /-ˌej‖-ˌedʒ/ *n* a piece of wood, metal, etc with an accurate straight edge for testing surfaces and (drawing) straight lines

straighten /ˈstrayt(ə)n‖ˈstreɪt(ə)n/ *vb* to make or become straight – usu + *up* or *out* – **straightener** *n*

straight fight *n* a contest, esp an election contest, between 2 candidates only

ˌ**straightˈforward** /-ˈfaw·wəd‖-ˈfɔːwəd/ *adj* **1** free from evasiveness or ambiguity; direct, candid <*a* ~ *account*> **2** presenting no hidden difficulties <*a perfectly* ~ *problem*> **3** clear-cut, precise – **straightforwardly** *adv*, **straightforwardness** *n*

ˌ**straight-ˈout** *adj, NAm* **1** forthright, blunt <*gave him a* ~ *answer*> **2** outright, thoroughgoing <*a* ~ *Democrat*>

ˌ**straight ˈup** *adv, Br* truly, honestly – infml; used esp in asking or replying to a question <*'This car's worth a good £1500.'* 'Straight up?' 'Straight up.'>

ˌ**straightˈway** /-ˈway‖-ˈweɪ/ *adv, archaic* immediately, forthwith <~ *the clouds began to part*>

[1]**strain** /strayn‖streɪn/ *n* **1a** a lineage, ancestry **b** a group of plants, animals, microorganisms, etc at a level lower than a species <*a high-yielding* ~ *of winter wheat*> **c** a kind, sort <*discussions of a lofty* ~> **2** a trace, streak <*a* ~ *of fanaticism*> **3** a passage of verbal or musical expression – usu pl with sing. meaning **4** the tone or manner of an utterance or of a course of action or conduct <*he continued in the same* ~>

[2]**strain** *vt* **1a** to draw tight <~ *the bandage over the wound*> **b** to stretch to maximum extension and tautness <~ *a canvas over a frame*> **2a** to exert (e g oneself) to the utmost **b** to injure by overuse, misuse, or excessive pressure <~ed *a muscle*> **c** to cause a change of form or size in (a body) by application of external force **3** to squeeze or clasp tightly: e g **3a** to hug **b** to compress painfully; constrict **4a** to cause to pass through a strainer; filter **b** to remove by straining <~ *lumps out of the gravy*> **5** to stretch beyond a proper limit <*that story* ~s *my credulity*> ~ *vi* **1a** to make (violent) efforts <*has to* ~ *to reach the high notes*> **b** to sustain a strain, wrench, or distortion **c** to contract the muscles forcefully in physical exertion **2** to show great resistance; resist strongly **3** to show signs of strain; continue with considerable difficulty or effort <~ing *under the pressure of work*>

[3]**strain** *n* straining or being strained: e g **a** (a force, influence, or factor causing) physical or mental tension **b** excessive or difficult exertion or labour **c** a wrench, twist, or similar bodily injury resulting esp from excessive stretching of muscles or ligaments **d** the deformation of a body subjected to stress

strained *adj* **1** done or produced with excessive effort **2** subjected to considerable tension <~ *relations*>

strainer /ˈstraynə‖ˈstreɪnə/ *n* **1** a device (e g a sieve) to retain solid pieces while a liquid passes through <*tea* ~> **2** any of various devices for stretching or tightening sthg

[1]**strait** /strayt‖streɪt/ *adj, archaic* narrow – **straitly** *adv*, **straitness** *n*

[2]**strait** *n* **1** a narrow passageway connecting 2 large bodies of water – often pl with sing. meaning but sing. or pl in constr **2** a situation of perplexity or distress – usu pl with sing. meaning

straiten /ˈstrayt(ə)n‖ˈstreɪt(ə)n/ *vt* **1** to subject to severely restricting difficulties, esp of a financial kind – often in **straitened circumstances** **2** *archaic* to restrict in range or scope

ˈ**straitˌjacket**, **straightjacket** /-ˌjakit‖-ˌdʒækɪt/ *n* **1** a cover or outer garment of strong material used to bind the body and esp the arms closely, in restraining a violent prisoner or patient **2** sthg that restricts or confines like a straitjacket – **straitjacket** *vt*

ˌ**straitˈlaced**, *NAm also* **straightlaced** /-ˈlayst‖-ˈleɪst/ *adj* excessively strict in manners or morals

[1]**strand** /strand‖strænd/ *n* a shore, beach

[2]**strand** *vt* **1** to run, drive, or cause to drift onto a shore; run aground **2** to leave in a strange or unfavourable place, esp without funds or means to depart

[3]**strand** *n* **1a** any of the threads, strings, or wires twisted or laid parallel to make a cord, rope, or cable **b** sthg (e g a molecular chain) resembling a strand **2** an elongated or twisted and plaited body resembling a rope <*a* ~ *of pearls*> **3** any of the elements interwoven in a complex whole <*follow the* ~s *of the story*> – **stranded** *adj*

strange /straynj‖streɪndʒ/ *adj* **1** not native to or naturally belonging in a place; of external origin, kind, or character **2a** not known, heard, or seen before **b** exciting wonder or surprise **3** lacking experience or acquaintance; unaccustomed *to* – **strangely** *adv*

stranger /ˈstraynjə‖ˈstreɪndʒə/ *n* **1a** a foreigner, alien **b** sby who is unknown or with whom one is unacquainted **2** one ignorant of or unacquainted with sby or sthg <*a ~ to books*>

strangle /strang·gl‖stræŋgl/ *vt* **1** to choke (to death) by compressing the throat; throttle **2** to suppress or hinder the rise, expression, or growth of ~*vi* to die (as if) from being strangled – **strangler** *n*

ˈstrangleˌhold /-ˌhohld‖-ˌhəʊld/ *n* a force or influence that prevents free movement or expression

strangulate /ˈstrang·gyooˌlayt‖ˈstræŋgjʊˌleɪt/ *vt* **1** to strangle **2** to constrict or compress (a blood vessel, loop of intestine, etc) in a way that interrupts the ability to act as a passage <*a ~d hernia*> ~*vi* to become strangulated – **strangulation** *n*

[1]**strap** /strap‖stræp/ *n* **1** a strip of metal or a flexible material, esp leather, for holding objects together or in position **2** (*the* use of, or punishment with) a strip of leather for flogging <*gave him the ~*> – **strapping** *n*

[2]**strap** *vt* **-pp- 1a** to secure with or attach by means of a strap **b** to support (e g a sprained joint) with adhesive plaster **2** to beat with a strap

ˈstrapˌhanger /-ˌhang·ə‖-ˌhæŋə/ *n* a passenger in a train, bus, etc who has to hold a strap or handle for support while standing – **straphanging** *n*

strapping /ˈstraping‖ˈstræpɪŋ/ *adj* big, strong, and sturdy in build

strata /ˈstrahtə‖ˈstrɑːtə/ *pl of* STRATUM

stratagem /ˈstratəjəm‖ˈstrætədʒəm/ *n* **1** an artifice or trick for deceiving and outwitting the enemy **2** a cleverly contrived trick or scheme [Italian *stratagemma*, fr Latin *strategema*, fr Greek *stratēgēma*, fr *stratēgein* to be a general, manoeuvre, fr *stratēgos* general, fr *stratos* army + *agein* to lead]

strategic /strəˈteejik‖strəˈtiːdʒɪk/, **strategical** /-kl‖-kl/ *adj* **1** of, marked by, or important in strategy <*a ~ retreat*> **2a** required for the conduct of war <*~ materials*> **b** of great importance within an integrated whole or to a planned effect **3** designed or trained to strike an enemy at the sources of its power <*a ~ bomber*> – **strategically** *adv*

strategist /ˈstratijist‖ˈstrætɪdʒɪst/ *n* one skilled in strategy

strategy /ˈstratiji‖ˈstrætɪdʒɪ/ *n* **1a(1)** the science and art of employing all the resources of a (group of) nation(s) to carry out agreed policies in peace or war **a(2)** the science and art of military command exercised to meet the enemy in combat under advantageous conditions **b** a variety of or instance of the use of strategy **2a** a clever plan or method **b** the art of employing plans towards achieving a goal

stratify /ˈstratifie‖ˈstrætɪfaɪ/ *vt* **1** to form, deposit, or arrange in strata ~ *vi* **2** to become arranged in strata – **stratification** *n*

stratosphere /ˈstratəˌsfiə‖ˈstrætəˌsfɪə/ *n* the upper part of the atmosphere above about 11km (7mi) in which the temperature changes little and clouds are rare – **stratospheric** *adj*

stratum /ˈstrahtəm, ˈstraytəm‖ˈstrɑːtəm, ˈstreɪtəm/ *n, pl* **strata** /-tə‖-tə/ **1** a horizontal layer or series of layers of any homogeneous material: e g **1a** a sheetlike mass of rock or earth deposited between beds of other rock **b** a layer of the sea or atmosphere **c** a layer of tissue **d** a layer in which archaeological remains are found on excavation **2** a socioeconomic level of society – often pl with sing. meaning <*this* strata *of society*>

[1]**straw** /straw‖strɔː/ *n* **1** (a single stem of) dry stalky plant residue, specif stalks of grain after threshing, used for bedding, thatching, fodder, making hats, etc **2** a dry coarse stem, esp of a cereal grass **3a** sthg of small value or importance <*she doesn't care a ~*> **b** sthg too insubstantial to provide support or help <*clutching at ~s*> **4** a tube of paper, plastic, etc for sucking up a drink **5** pale yellow – **strawy** *adj* – **straw in the wind** a hint or apparently insignificant fact that is an indication of a coming event

[2]**straw** *adj* of or resembling (the colour of) straw

[3]**straw** *vt* to cover (as if) with straw

strawberry /ˈstrawb(ə)ri‖ˈstrɔːb(ə)rɪ/ *n* (the juicy edible usu red fruit of) any of several white-flowered creeping plants of the rose family

strawberry mark *n* a usu red and elevated birthmark composed of small blood vessels

ˈstrawˌboard /-ˌbawd‖-ˌbɔːd/ *n* coarse cardboard made of straw pulp and used usu for boxes and book covers

straw poll *n* an assessment made by an unofficial vote

[1]**stray** /stray‖streɪ/ *vi* **1** to wander from a proper place, course, or line of conduct or argument **2** to roam about without fixed direction or purpose [Middle French *estraier*, deriv of Latin *extra* outside + *vagari* to wander]

[2]**stray** *n* **1** a domestic animal wandering at large or lost **2** a person or animal that strays

[3]**stray** *adj* **1** having strayed; wandering, lost **2** occurring at random or sporadically <*a few ~ hairs*> **3** not serving any useful purpose; unwanted <*~ light*>

[1]**streak** /streek‖striːk/ *n* **1** a line or band of a different colour from the background **2** a sample containing microorganisms (e g bacteria) implanted in a line on a solid culture medium (e g agar jelly) for growth **3a** an inherent quality; *esp* one which is only occasionally manifested <*had a mean ~ in him*> **b** a consecutive series <*on a winning ~*>

[2]**streak** *vt* to make streaks on or in ~ *vi* **1** to move swiftly <*a jet ~ing across the sky*> **2** to run through a public place while naked – infml – **streaker** *n*

streaky /ˈstreeki‖ˈstriːkɪ/ *adj* **1** marked with streaks **2** *of meat, esp bacon* having lines of fat and lean **3** *of a shot in cricket* hit off the edge of the bat – **streakily** *adv*, **streakiness** *n*

[1]stream /streem‖striːm/ *n* **1a** a body of running water, esp one smaller than a river, flowing in a channel on the earth **b** a body of flowing liquid or gas **2a** a steady succession of words, events, etc **b** a continuous moving procession **3** an unbroken flow (e g of gas or particles of matter) **4** a prevailing attitude or direction of opinion – esp in *go against/with the stream* **5** *Br* a group of pupils of the same general academic ability <*the A* ~>

[2]stream *vi* **1** to flow (as if) in a stream **2** to run with a fluid <*her eyes* ~ing *with the cold*> <*walls* ~ing *with condensation*> **3** to trail out at full length <*hair* ~ing *in the wind*> **4** to pour in large numbers in the same direction **5** *Br* to practise the division of pupils into streams ~ *vt* **1** to emit freely or in a stream **2** *Br* to divide (a school or an age-group of pupils) into streams

streamer /ˈstreemə‖ˈstriːmə/ *n* **1a** a pennant **b** a strip of coloured paper used as a party decoration **c** BANNER 2 **2** a long extension of the sun's corona visible only during a total eclipse

[1]ˈstreamˌline /-ˌlien‖-ˌlaɪn/ *n* **1** the path of a fluid (e g air or water) relative to a solid body past which the fluid is moving smoothly without turbulence **2** a contour given to a car, aeroplane, etc so as to minimize resistance to motion through a fluid (e g air)

[2]streamline *vt* **1** to design or construct with a streamline **2** to make simpler, more efficient, or better integrated

streamlined /ˈstreemˌliend‖ˈstriːmˌlaɪnd/ *adj* **1a** having a streamline contour **b** effectively integrated; organized **2** having flowing lines

stream of consciousness *n* (a literary technique used to express) individual conscious experience considered as a continuous flow of reactions and experiences

street /street‖striːt/ *n* **1** a thoroughfare, esp in a town or village, with buildings on either side <*lives in a fashionable* ~> **2** the part of a street reserved for vehicles – **on the street** idle, homeless, or out of a job – **on the streets** earning a living as a prostitute – **up/down one's street** suited to one's abilities or tastes

ˈstreetˌcar /-ˌkah‖-ˌkɑː/ *n, NAm* a tram

ˈstreetˌwalker /-ˌwawkə‖-ˌwɔːkə/ *n* a prostitute who solicits in the streets – **streetwalking** *n*

ˈstreetˌwise *adj* familiar with the (disreputable or criminal) life of city streets; *broadly* resourceful at surviving and prospering in modern urban life

strength /streng(k)th‖streŋ(k)θ/ *n* **1** the quality of being strong; capacity for exertion or endurance **2** solidity, toughness **3a** legal, logical, or moral force **b** a strong quality or inherent asset <*his* ~s *and weaknesses*> **4a** degree of potency of effect or of concentration **b** intensity of light, colour, sound, or smell **5** force as measured in members <*an army at full* ~> **6** firmness of, or a rising tendency in, prices **7** a basis – chiefly in *on the strength of* – **from strength to strength** with continuing success and progress

strengthen /ˈstreng(k)thən‖ˈstreŋ(k)θən/ *vb* to make or become stronger – **strengthener** *n*

strenuous /ˈstrenyoo·əs‖ˈstrenjʊəs/ *adj* **1** vigorously active **2** requiring effort or stamina – **strenuously** *adv*, **strenuousness, strenuosity** *n*

streptococcus /ˌstreptəˈkokəs‖ˌstreptəˈkɒkəs/ *n, pl* **streptococci** /-ˈkok(s)ie‖-ˈkɒk(s)aɪ/ any of a genus of chiefly parasitic bacteria that occur in pairs or chains and include some that cause diseases in human beings and domestic animals [deriv of Greek *streptos* twisted + *kokkos* bacterium] – **streptococcal, streptococcic** *adj*

ˌstreptoˈmycin /-ˈmiesin‖-ˈmaɪsɪn/ *n* an antibiotic obtained from a soil bacterium and used esp in the treatment of tuberculosis

[1]stress /stres‖stres/ *n* **1a** the force per unit area producing or tending to produce deformation of a body; *also* the state of a body under such stress **b** (a physical or emotional factor that causes) bodily or mental tension **c** strain, pressure **2** emphasis, weight **3a** intensity of utterance given to a speech sound, syllable, or word so as to produce relative loudness **b** relative force or prominence given to a syllable in verse **c** ACCENT 2b – **stressful** *adj*, **stressfully** *adv*, **stressless** *adj*

[2]stress *vt* **1** to subject to phonetic stress; accent **2** to subject to physical or mental stress **3** to lay stress on; emphasize – **stressor** *n*

[1]stretch /strech‖stretʃ/ *vt* **1** to extend in a reclining position – often + *out* < ~ed *himself out on the carpet*> **2** to extend to full length **3** to extend (oneself or one's limbs), esp so as to relieve muscular stiffness **4** to pull taut <*canvas was* ~ed *on a frame*> **5a** to enlarge or distend, esp by force **b** to strain < ~ed *his already thin patience*> **6** to cause to reach (e g from one point to another or across a space) **7** to enlarge or extend beyond natural or proper limits < ~ *the rules*> **8** to fell (as if) with a blow – often + *out*; infml ~ *vi* **1a** to extend in space; reach <*broad plains* ~ing *to the sea*> **b** to extend over a period of time **2** to become extended without breaking **3a** to extend one's body or limbs **b** to lie down at full length – **stretchable** *adj*, **stretchy** *adj* – **stretch a point** to go beyond what is strictly warranted in making a claim or concession – **stretch one's legs** to take a walk in order to relieve stiffness caused by prolonged sitting

[2]stretch *n* **1** an exercise of the understanding, imagination, etc beyond ordinary or normal limits **2** the extent to which sthg may be stretched <*at full* ~> **3** stretching or being stretched **4** a continuous expanse of time or space **5** the capacity for being stretched; elasticity **6** a term of imprisonment – infml

stretcher /ˈstrechə‖ˈstretʃə/ *n* **1** a mechanism for stretching or expanding sthg **2a** a brick or stone laid with its length parallel to the face of the wall **b** a timber or rod used, esp when horizontal, as a tie (e g a tie-beam) in a load-bearing frame (e g for a building) **3** a device, consisting of a sheet of canvas or other material stretched between 2 poles, for carrying a sick, injured, or dead person **4** a rod or bar extending between 2 legs of a chair or table

strew /strooh‖struː/ *vt* **strewed, strewn** /stroohn‖struːn/ **1** to spread by scattering **2** to cover (as if) with sthg scattered **3** to become dispersed over

strewth /stroohth‖struːθ/ *interj* struth

stria /'strie·ə‖'straɪə/ *n, pl* **striae** /'strie·i‖'straɪiː/ **1** a minute groove on the surface of a rock, crystal, etc **2** a narrow groove, ridge, line of colours, etc, esp when one of a parallel series – **striate** *vt*, **striate, striated** *adj*

striation /strie'aysh(ə)n‖straɪ'eɪʃ(ə)n/ *n* **1a** being striated **b** an arrangement of striae **2** a stria

stricken /'strikən‖'strɪkən/ *adj* afflicted or overwhelmed (as if) by disease, misfortune, or sorrow

[1]**strickle** /'strikl‖'strɪkl/ *n* **1** an instrument for levelling off measures of grain **2** a tool for sharpening scythes

[2]**strickle** *vt* to smooth or form with a strickle

strict /strikt‖strɪkt/ *adj* **1a** stringent in requirement or control <*under* ~ *orders*> **b** severe in discipline <*a* ~ *teacher*> **2a** inflexibly maintained or kept to; complete <~ *secrecy*> **b** rigorously conforming to rules or standards **3** exact, precise <*in the* ~ *sense of the word*> – **strictly** *adv*, **strictness** *n*

stricture /'strikchə‖'strɪktʃə/ *n* **1** an abnormal narrowing of a bodily passage **2** sthg that closely restrains or limits; a restriction **3** an unfavourable criticism; a censure *USE* (*2&3*) usu pl with sing. meaning

[1]**stride** /stried‖straɪd/ *vb* **strode** /strohd‖strəʊd/; **stridden** /'stridən‖'strɪdən/ *vi* to walk (as if) with long steps to move over or along (as if) with long steps – **strider** *n*

[2]**stride** *n* **1** a long step **2** an advance – often pl with sing. meaning <*technology has made great* ~s> **3a** (the distance covered in) an act of movement completed when the feet regain the initial relative positions **b** a state of maximum competence or capability <*get into one's* ~> **4** a striding gait <*her loose-limbed* ~> – **in one's stride** without becoming upset <*took the dangers* in her stride>

strident /'stried(ə)nt‖'straɪd(ə)nt/ *adj* characterized by harsh and discordant sound; *also* loud and obtrusive – **stridence, stridency** *n*, **stridently** *adv*

stridulate /'stridyoolayt‖'strɪdjʊleɪt/ *vi, esp of crickets, grasshoppers, etc* to make a shrill creaking noise by rubbing together special bodily structures – **stridulatory** *adj*, **stridulation** *n*

strife /strief‖straɪf/ *n* bitter conflict or dissension – **strifeless** *adj*

[1]**strike** /striek‖straɪk/ *vb* **struck** /struk‖strʌk/; **struck** *also* **stricken** /'strikən‖'strɪkən/ *vt* **1a** to strike at; hit **b** to make an attack on **c** to inflict <~ *a blow*> **2a** to haul down <~ *a flag*> **b** to dismantle (e g a stage set) **c** to take down the tents of (a camp) **3** to afflict suddenly <stricken *by a heart attack*> **4** to delete, cancel <~ *a name from a list*> **5a** to send down or out <*trees* struck *roots deep into the soil*> **b** to penetrate painfully <*the news* struck *him to the heart*> **6** to indicate by sounding <*the clock* struck *7*> **7a** *of light* to fall on **b** *of a sound* to become audible to **8** to cause suddenly to become <struck *him dead*> **9** to produce by stamping <~ *a medal*> **10a** to produce (fire) by striking **b** to cause (a match) to ignite **11a** to make a mental impact on <*they were* struck *by its speed*> <*how does that* ~ *you?*> **b** to occur suddenly to **12** to make and ratify (a bargain) **13** to produce (as if) by playing an instrument <~ *a chord*> <~ *a gloomy note*> **14a** to hook (a fish) by a sharp pull on the line **b** *of a fish* to snatch at (bait) **15** to arrive at (a balance) by computation **16** COME ACROSS <~ *gold*> **17** to assume (a pose) **18a** to place (a plant cutting) in a medium for growth and rooting **b** to propagate (a plant) in this manner **19** to cause (an arc) to form (e g between electrodes of an arc lamp) **20** to play or produce on keys or strings **21** *NAm* to engage in a strike against (an employer) ~ *vi* **1** to take a course <struck *off across the field*> **2a** to aim a blow **b** to make an attack **3** to collide forcefully **4a** *of the time* to become indicated by a clock, bell, or chime <*the hour had just* struck> **b** to make known the time by sounding <*the clock* struck> **5** *of a fish* to seize bait or a lure **6** *of a plant cutting* to take root **7** to engage in a strike

[2]**strike** *n* **1** STRICKLE 1 **2** an act of striking **3** a work stoppage by a body of workers, made as a protest or to force an employer to comply with demands **4** the direction of a horizontal line formed at the angle of intersection of an upward-sloping stratum and a horizontal plane **5** a pull on a line by a fish in striking **6** a success in finding or hitting sthg; *esp* a discovery of a valuable mineral deposit <*a lucky oil* ~> **7** a pitched ball in baseball that is either missed by the batter or hit outside the foul lines and that counts against him **8** the knocking down of all 10 pins with the first bowl in a frame in tenpin bowling **9** the opportunity to receive the bowling by virtue of being the batsman at the wicket towards which the bowling is being directed **10** an (air) attack on a target

'strike,bound /-,bownd‖-,baʊnd/ *adj* subjected to a strike

'strike,breaker /-,braykə‖-,breɪkə/ *n* one hired to replace a striking worker

'strike,breaking /-,brayking‖-,breɪkɪŋ/ *n* action designed to break up a strike

strike off *vt* **1** to sever with a stroke **2** to forbid (sby) to continue in professional practice usu because of misconduct or incompetence <struck *the doctor* off *for malpractice*>

strike out *vt* to delete ~*vi* to set out vigorously <struck out *towards the coast*>

'strike ,pay *n* an allowance paid by a trade union to its members on strike

striker /'striekə‖'straɪkə/ *n* **1** a games player who strikes; *esp* a soccer player whose main duty is to score goals **2** a worker on strike

strike up *vi* to begin to sing or play ~ *vt* **1** to cause to begin singing or playing **2** to cause to begin <strike up *a conversation*>

striking /'strieking‖'straɪkɪŋ/ *adj* attracting attention, esp because of unusual or impressive qualities – **strikingly** *adv*

[1]**string** /string‖strɪŋ/ *n* **1** a narrow cord used to bind, fasten, or tie **2** a plant fibre (e g a leaf vein) **3a** the gut or wire cord of a musical instrument **b** a stringed instrument of an orchestra – usu pl **4a** a group of objects threaded on a string <*a* ~ *of beads*> **b** a set of things arranged (as if) in a sequence **c** a group of usu scattered business concerns <*a* ~ *of shops*> **d** the animals,

esp horses, belonging to or used by sby **5** one who is selected (e g for a sports team) for the specified rank; *also, sing or pl in constr* a group of players so selected <*usually plays for the first* ~> **6** a succession, sequence **7a** either of the inclined sides of a stair supporting the treads and risers **b** STRING COURSE **8** *pl* conditions or obligations attached to sthg – **stringed** *adj*, **stringless** *adj*

[2]**string** *vt* **strung** /strung‖strʌŋ/ **1** to equip with strings **2a** to thread (as if) on a string **b** to tie, hang, or fasten with string **3** to remove the strings of <~ *beans*> **4** to extend or stretch like a string

[3]**string** *adj* made with wide meshes and usu of string <~ *vest*> <~ *bag*>

string along *vi* **1** to accompany sby, esp reluctantly **2** to agree; GO ALONG – usu + *with* ~*vt* to deceive, fool <string *him* along *with false promises*> ***USE*** infml

string bean *n* a French bean or runner bean with stringy fibres on the lines of separation of the pods

string course *n* a horizontal ornamental band (e g of bricks) in a building

stringent /ˈstrinj(ə)nt‖ˈstrɪndʒ(ə)nt/ *adj* **1** rigorous or strict, esp with regard to rules or standards **2** marked by money scarcity and credit strictness – **stringency** *n*, **stringently** *adv*

string up *vt* to hang; *specif* to kill by hanging <*they* strung *him* up *from the nearest tree*>

stringy /ˈstring·i‖ˈstrɪŋɪ/ *adj* **1a** containing or resembling fibrous matter or string <~ *hair*> **b** sinewy, wiry **2** capable of being drawn out to form a string – **stringiness** *n*

[1]**strip** /strip‖strɪp/ *vb* **-pp-** *vt* **1a** to remove clothing, covering, or surface or extraneous matter from **b** to deprive of possessions, privileges, or rank **2** to remove furniture, equipment, or accessories from **3** to press the last available milk from the teats of (esp a cow) **4a** to remove cured leaves from the stalks of (tobacco) **b** to remove the midrib from (tobacco leaves) **5** to damage the thread or teeth of (a screw, cog, etc) ~ *vi* **1** to undress **2** to perform a striptease

[2]**strip** *n* **1a** a long narrow piece of material **b** a long narrow area of land or water **2** LANDING STRIP **3** *Br* clothes worn by a rugby or soccer team

strip cartoon *n* a series of drawings (e g in a magazine) in narrative sequence

stripe /striep‖straɪp/ *n* **1** a line or narrow band differing in colour or texture from the adjoining parts **2** a bar, chevron, etc of braid or embroidery worn usu on the sleeve of a uniform to indicate rank or length of service **3** *chiefly NAm* a distinct variety or sort; a type <*men of the same political* ~> – **striped** *adj*

strip lighting *n* lighting provided by 1 or more strip lights

stripling /ˈstripling‖ˈstrɪplɪŋ/ *n* an adolescent boy

stripper /ˈstripə‖ˈstrɪpə/ *n* **1** sby who performs a striptease **2** a tool or solvent for removing sthg, esp paint

ˌstripˈtease /-ˈteez‖-ˈtiːz/ *n* an act or entertainment in which a performer, esp a woman, undresses gradually in view of the audience – **stripteaser** *n*

stripy /ˈstriepi‖ˈstraɪpɪ/ *adj* striped

strive /striev‖straɪv/ *vi* **strove** /strohv‖strəʊv/ *also* **strived; striven** /striv(ə)n‖strɪv(ə)n/, **strived** **1** to struggle in opposition; contend **2** to endeavour; try hard – **striver** *n*

stroboscope /ˈstrohbəˌskohp‖ˈstrəʊbəˌskəʊp/ *n* an instrument for measuring or observing motion, esp rotation or vibration, by allowing successive views of very short duration so that the motion appears slowed or stopped: e g **a** a lamp that flashes intermittently at varying frequencies **b** a disc with marks to be viewed under intermittent light, used to set up the speed of a record player turntable [Greek *strobos* whirling + *skopein* to look at] – **stroboscopic** *adj*, **stroboscopically** *adv*

strode /strohd‖strəʊd/ *past of* STRIDE

[1]**stroke** /strohk‖strəʊk/ *vt* to pass the hand over gently in 1 direction – **stroker** *n*

[2]**stroke** *n* **1** the act of striking; *esp* a blow with a weapon or implement **2** a single unbroken movement; *esp* one that is repeated **3** a striking of the ball in a game (e g cricket or tennis); *specif* an (attempted) striking of the ball that constitutes the scoring unit in golf **4a** an action by which sthg is done, produced, or achieved <*a* ~ *of genius*> **b** an unexpected occurrence <*a* ~ *of luck*> **5** (an attack of) sudden usu complete loss of consciousness, sensation, and voluntary motion caused by rupture, thrombosis, etc of a brain artery **6a** (the technique or mode used for) a propelling beat or movement against a resisting medium <*what* ~ *does she swim?*> <*rowed a fast* ~> **b** an oarsman who sits at the stern of a racing rowing boat and sets the pace for the rest of the crew **7** a vigorous or energetic effort <*never does a* ~> **8** (the distance of) the movement in either direction of a reciprocating mechanical part (e g a piston rod) **9** the sound of a striking clock <*at the* ~ *of 12*> **10** an act of stroking or caressing **11a** a mark or dash made by a single movement of an implement **b** *Br* a solidus – **at a stroke** by a single action – **off one's stroke** in a situation where one performs below a usual standard <*it put him* off his stroke>

[3]**stroke** *vt* **1** to set the stroke for (a rowing crew) or for the crew of (a rowing boat) **2** to hit (a ball) with a controlled swinging blow ~*vi* to row at a specified number of strokes a minute

stroll /strohl‖strəʊl/ *vi* to walk in a leisurely or idle manner – **stroll** *n*

stroller /ˈstrohlə‖ˈstrəʊlə/ *n, NAm* a pushchair

strolling /ˈstrohling‖ˈstrəʊlɪŋ/ *adj* going from place to place, esp in search of work <~ *players*>

strong /strong‖strɒŋ/ *adj* **1** having or marked by great physical power **2** having moral or intellectual power **3** having great resources of wealth, talent, etc <*a film with a* ~ *cast*> **4** of a specified number <*an army ten thousand* ~> **5a** striking or superior of its kind <*a* ~ *resemblance*> **b** effective or efficient, esp in a specified area <~ *on logic*> **6** forceful, cogent <~ *evidence*> **7a** rich in some active agent (e g a flavour or extract) <~ *tea*> **b** *of a colour* intense **c** *of an acid or base* ionizing to a great extent in solution **d** magnifying by refracting greatly <*a* ~ *lens*> **8** moving with vigour or force <*a* ~ *wind*> **9** ardent, zealous <*a* ~ *supporter*> **10** well established; firm <~ *beliefs*> **11** not easily upset or nauseated <*a* ~ *stomach*> **12** having a pungent or offensive smell or flavour **13** tending to steady or higher prices <*a* ~ *market*> **14** of or being a verb that forms inflections by internal vowel change (e g *drink, drank, drunk*) – **strongish** *adj*, **strongly** *adv*

ˈ**strongˌarm** /-ˌahm‖-ˌɑːm/ *adj* using or involving undue force

ˈ**strongˌbox** /-ˌboks‖-ˌbɒks/ *n* a strongly made chest for money or valuables

ˈ**strongˌhold** /-ˌhohld‖-ˌhəʊld/ *n* **1** a fortified place **2a** a place of refuge or safety **b** a place dominated by a specified group

strong language *n* offensive language; *esp* swearing

ˌ**strong-ˈminded** *adj* marked by firmness and independence of judgment – **strong-mindedly** *adv*, **strong-mindedness** *n*

ˈ**strongˌpoint** /-ˌpoynt‖-ˌpɔɪnt/ *n* a small fortified defensive position

ˈ**strong ˌpoint** *n* sthg in which one excels

ˈ**strong ˌroom** *n* a (fireproof and burglarproof) room for money and valuables

strontium /ˈstrontyəm‖ˈstrɒntjəm/ *n* a soft metallic element of the alkaline-earth group chemically similar to calcium [*Strontian*, village in Scotland]

ˌ**strontium ˈ90** /ˈnienti‖ˈnaɪntɪ/ *n* a hazardous radioactive isotope of strontium present in the fallout from nuclear explosions

[1]**strop** /strop‖strɒp/ *n* sthg, esp a leather band, for sharpening a razor

[2]**strop** *vt* **-pp-** to sharpen on a strop

strophe /ˈstrohfi‖ˈstrəʊfɪ/ *n* **1** (the part of a chorale ode sung to accompany) a turning movement made by the classical Greek chorus **2** a rhythmic system composed of 2 or more lines repeated as a unit

stroppy /ˈstropi‖ˈstrɒpɪ/ *adj, Br* quarrelsome, obstreperous – infml

strove /strohv‖strəʊv/ *past of* STRIVE

structural /ˈstrukch(ə)rəl‖ˈstrʌktʃ(ə)rəl/ *adj* **1a** of or affecting structure **b** used in or suitable for building structures <~ *steel*> **c** involved in or caused by structure, esp of the economy <~ *unemployment*> **2** of the physical make-up of a plant or animal body – **structurally** *adv*

[1]**structure** /ˈstrukchə‖ˈstrʌktʃə/ *n* **1a** sthg (e g a building) that is constructed **b** sthg organized in a definite pattern **2** manner of construction **3a** the arrangement of particles or parts in a substance or body <*soil* ~> <*molecular* ~> **b** arrangement or interrelation of elements <*economic* ~> – **structureless** *adj*

[2]**structure** *vt* to form into a structure

strudel /ˈstroohdl‖ˈstruːdl/ *n* a pastry made from a thin sheet of dough rolled up with filling and baked [German, lit., whirlpool]

[1]**struggle** /ˈstrugl‖ˈstrʌgl/ *vi* **1** to make violent or strenuous efforts against opposition **2** to proceed with difficulty or great effort – **struggler** *n*

[2]**struggle** *n* **1** a violent effort; a determined attempt in adverse circumstances **2** a hard-fought contest

strum /strum‖strʌm/ *vb* **-mm-** *vt* **1** to brush the fingers lightly over the strings of (a musical instrument) in playing <~ *a guitar*>; *also* to thrum **2** to play (music) on a guitar <~ *a tune*> ~*vi* to strum a stringed instrument – **strummer** *n*

strumpet /ˈstrumpit‖ˈstrʌmpɪt/ *n* a prostitute

strung /strung‖strʌŋ/ *past of* STRING

[1]**strut** /strut‖strʌt/ *vi* **-tt- 1** to walk with a proud or erect gait **2** to walk with a pompous air; swagger – **strutter** *n*

[2]**strut** *n* **1** a structural piece designed to resist pressure in the direction of its length **2** a pompous step or walk

[3]**strut** *vt* **-tt-** to provide or stiffen with a strut

strychnine /ˈstrikneen‖ˈstrɪkniːn/ *n* a poisonous alkaloid used as a poison (e g for rodents) and medicinally as a stimulant to the central nervous system

[1]**stub** /stub‖stʌb/ *n* **1** [1]STUMP 2 **2** a short blunt part of a pencil, cigarette, etc left after a larger part has been broken off or used up **3a** a small part of a leaf or page (e g of a chequebook) left on the spine as a record of the contents of the part torn away **b** the part of a ticket returned to the user after inspection

[2]**stub** *vt* **-bb- 1a** to grub up by the roots **b** to clear (land) by uprooting stumps **2** to extinguish (e g a cigarette) by crushing – usu + *out* **3** to strike (one's foot or toe) against an object

stubble /ˈstubl‖ˈstʌbl/ *n* **1** the stalky remnants of plants, esp cereal grasses, which remain rooted in the soil after harvest **2** a rough growth (e g of beard) resembling stubble – **stubbly** *adj*

stubborn /ˈstubən‖ˈstʌbən/ *adj* **1** (unreasonably) unyielding or determined **2** refractory, intractable <*a* ~ *cold*> – **stubbornly** *adv*, **stubbornness** *n*

stubby /ˈstubi‖ˈstʌbɪ/ *adj* short and thick like a stub

[1]**stucco** /ˈstukoh‖ˈstʌkəʊ/ *n, pl* **stuccos, stuccoes** a cement or fine plaster used in the covering and decoration of walls

[2]**stucco** *vt* **stuccoes, stuccos; stuccoing; stuccoed** to coat or decorate with stucco

stuck /stuk‖stʌk/ *past of* STICK

ˌ**stuck-ˈup** *adj* superciliously self-important or conceited – infml

[1]**stud** /stud‖stʌd/ *n* **1** *sing or pl in constr* a group of animals, esp horses, kept primarily for breeding **2a** a male animal, esp a stallion, kept for breeding **b** a sexually active man – vulg – **at stud** for breeding as a stud <*retired racehorses standing* at stud>

[2]**stud** *n* **1** any of the smaller upright posts in the walls of a building to which panelling or laths are fastened **2a** a rivet or nail with a large head used for ornament or protection **b** a solid button with a shank or eye on the back inserted through an eyelet in a garment as a fastener or ornament **3a** a piece (e g a rod or pin) projecting from a machine and serving chiefly as a support

or axis **b** a metal cleat inserted in a horseshoe or snow tyre to increase grip **4** *NAm* the height from floor to ceiling

³stud *vt* **-dd-** **1** to provide (e g a building or wall) with studs **2** to decorate, cover, or protect with studs **3** to set thickly with a number of prominent objects <*sky* ~ded *with stars*>

ˈstudˌbook /-ˌbook‖-ˌbʊk/ *n* an official record of the pedigree of purebred horses, dogs, etc

student /ˈstyood(ə)nt‖ˈstjud(ə)nt/ *n* **1** a scholar, learner; *esp* one who attends a college or university **2** an attentive and systematic observer <*a* ~ *of human nature*>

studied /ˈstudid‖ˈstʌdɪd/ *adj* **1** carefully considered or prepared **2** deliberate, premeditated <~ *indifference*> – **studiedly** *adv*

studio /ˈstyoohdi·oh‖ˈstju:dɪəʊ/ *n, pl* **studios** **1a** the workroom of a painter, sculptor, or photographer **b** a place for the study of an art (e g dancing, singing, or acting) **2** a place where films are made; *also, sing or pl in constr* a film production company including its premises and employees **3** a room equipped for the production of radio or television programmes

studio couch *n* an upholstered usu backless couch that can be converted into a double bed by sliding from underneath it the frame of a single bed

studious /ˈstyoohdi·əs‖ˈstju:dɪəs/ *adj* **1** of, concerned with, or given to study **2a** marked by or suggesting serious thoughtfulness or diligence; earnest <*a* ~ *expression on his face*> **b** STUDIED 2 – **studiously** *adv*, **studiousness** *n*

¹study /ˈstudi‖ˈstʌdɪ/ *n* **1** a state of deep thought or contemplation – esp in *a brown study* **2a** the application of the mind to acquiring (specific) knowledge <*the* ~ *of Latin*> **b** a careful examination or analysis of a subject **3** a room devoted to study **4** a branch of learning **5** a literary or artistic work intended as a preliminary or experimental interpretation

²study *vi* to engage in study ~ *vt* **1** to engage in the study of **2** to consider attentively or in detail

¹stuff /stuf‖stʌf/ *n* **1a** materials, supplies, or equipment used in various activities <*the plumber brought his* ~> **b** personal property; possessions **2** a finished textile suitable for clothing; *esp* wool or worsted material **3a** an unspecified material substance <*sold tons of the* ~> **b** a group of miscellaneous objects <*pick that* ~ *up off the floor*> **4** the essence of a usu abstract thing <*the* ~ *of greatness*> **5a** subject matter <*a teacher who knows his* ~> **b** a task involving special knowledge or skill <*the firemen were called on to do their* ~> **6** worthless ideas, opinion, or writing; rubbish *USE* (*5&6*) infml

²stuff *vt* **1a** to fill (as if) by packing things in; cram **b** to gorge (oneself) with food **c** to fill (e g meat or vegetables) with a stuffing **d** to fill with stuffing or padding **e** to fill out the skin of (an animal) for mounting **f** to stop up (a hole); plug **2** to choke or block *up* (the nasal passages) **3** to force into a limited space; thrust **4** *Br, of a male* to have sexual intercourse with – vulg – **stuffer** *n*

ˌstuffed ˈshirt *n* a smug, pompous, and usu reactionary person

stuffing /ˈstufing‖ˈstʌfɪŋ/ *n* material used to stuff sthg; *esp* a seasoned mixture used to stuff meat, eggs, etc

stuffy /ˈstufi‖ˈstʌfɪ/ *adj* **1a** badly ventilated; close **b** stuffed up <*a* ~ *nose*> **2** stodgy, dull **3** prim, straitlaced – **stuffily** *adv*, **stuffiness** *n*

stultify /ˈstultifie‖ˈstʌltɪfaɪ/ *vt* to make futile or absurd – **stultification** *n*

¹stumble /ˈstumbl‖ˈstʌmbl/ *vi* **1** to trip in walking or running **2a** to walk unsteadily or clumsily **b** to speak or act in a hesitant or faltering manner **3** to come unexpectedly or by chance – + *upon, on*, or *across* – **stumbler** *n*, **stumblingly** *adv*

²stumble *n* an act of stumbling

ˈstumbling ˌblock /ˈstumbling‖ˈstʌmblɪŋ/ *n* an obstacle to progress or understanding

¹stump /stump‖stʌmp/ *n* **1a** the part of an arm, leg, etc remaining attached to the trunk after the rest is removed **b** a rudimentary or vestigial bodily part **2** the part of a plant, esp a tree, remaining in the ground attached to the root after the stem is cut **3** a remaining part; a stub **4** any of the 3 upright wooden rods that together with the bails form the wicket in cricket

²stump *vt* **1** *of a wicketkeeper* to dismiss (a batsman who is outside his popping crease but not attempting to run) by breaking the wicket with the ball before it has touched another fieldsman **2** *NAm* to travel over (a region) making political speeches or supporting a cause **3** to baffle, bewilder – infml <*was* ~ed *by her question*> ~ *vi* **1** to walk heavily or noisily **2** *chiefly NAm* to travel about making political speeches

stumper /ˈstumpə‖ˈstʌmpə/ *n* **1** a wicketkeeper **2** a puzzling question; a teaser

stump up *vb, chiefly Br* to pay (what is due), esp unwillingly – infml

stumpy /ˈstumpi‖ˈstʌmpɪ/ *adj* short and thick; stubby

stun /stun‖stʌn/ *vt* **-nn-** **1** to make dazed or dizzy (as if) by a blow **2** to overcome, esp with astonishment or disbelief

stung /stung‖stʌŋ/ *past of* STING

stunk /stungk‖stʌŋk/ *past of* STINK

stunner /ˈstunə‖ˈstʌnə/ *n* an unusually beautiful or attractive person or thing – infml

stunning /ˈstuning‖ˈstʌnɪŋ/ *adj* strikingly beautiful or attractive – infml – **stunningly** *adv*

¹stunt /stunt‖stʌnt/ *vt* to hinder or arrest the growth or development of – **stuntedness** *n*

²stunt *n* an unusual or difficult feat performed to gain publicity

ˈstunt ˌman, *fem* **ˈstunt ˌwoman** *n* sby employed, esp as a substitute for an actor, to perform dangerous feats

stupefy /ˈst(y)oohpifie‖ˈst(j)u:pɪfaɪ/ *vt* **1** to make groggy or insensible **2** to astonish – **stupefaction** *n*

stupendous /styoohˈpendəs‖stju:ˈpendəs/ *adj* of astonishing size or greatness; amazing, astounding – **stupendously** *adv*, **stupendousness** *n*

stupid /ˈstyoohpid‖ˈstju:pɪd/ *adj* **1** slow-witted, obtuse **2** dulled in feeling or perception; torpid **3** annoying, exasperating – infml <*this* ~ *torch won't work*> – **stupidly** *adv*, **stupidness, stupidity** *n*

stupor /ˈstyoohpə‖ˈstju:pə/ *n* a state of extreme apathy, torpor, or reduced sense or feeling (e g resulting from shock or intoxication) – **stuporous** *adj*

sturdy /ˈstuhdi‖ˈstɜːdɪ/ *adj* **1** strongly built or constituted; stout, hardy **2a** having physical strength or vigour; robust **b** firm, resolute – **sturdily** *adv*, **sturdiness** *n*

sturgeon /ˈstuhj(ə)n‖ˈstɜːdʒ(ə)n/ *n* any of various usu large edible fishes whose roe is made into caviar

[1]**stutter** /ˈstutə‖ˈstʌtə/ *vi* to speak with involuntary disruption or blocking of speech (e g by spasmodic repetition or prolongation of vocal sounds) ~*vt* to say, speak, or sound (as if) with a stutter – **stutterer** *n*

[2]**stutter** *n* (a speech disorder involving) stuttering

[1]**sty** /stie‖staɪ/ *n, pl* **sties** *also* **styes** a pigsty

[2]**sty, stye** /~/ *n, pl* **sties, styes** an inflamed swelling of a sebaceous gland at the margin of an eyelid

stygian /ˈstiji·ən‖ˈstɪdʒɪən/ *adj, often cap* extremely dark or gloomy – fml [Latin *stygius*, fr Greek *stygios*, fr *Styg-, Styx* Styx, mythical river of the underworld]

[1]**style** /stiel‖staɪl/ *n* **1a** a stylus **b** a prolongation of a plant ovary bearing a stigma at the top **c** a slender elongated part (e g a bristle) on an animal **2a** a manner of expressing thought in language, esp when characteristic of an individual, period, etc **b** the custom or plan followed in spelling, capitalization, punctuation, and typographic arrangement and display **3** mode of address; a title **4a** a distinctive or characteristic manner of doing sthg **b** a fashionable or elegant life-style <*lived in* ~> **c** excellence or distinction in social behaviour, manners, or appearance – **stylar** *adj*, **styleless** *adj*

[2]**style** *vt* **1** to designate by an identifying term; name **2** to fashion according to a particular mode – **styler** *n*

[3]**style** *n* a stile

[1]**-style** /-stiel‖-staɪl/ *comb form* (→ *adj*) resembling <*leather*-style *briefcase*>

[2]**-style** *comb form* (→ *adv*) in the style or manner of <*seated on the floor Indian*-style>

stylish /ˈstielish‖ˈstaɪlɪʃ/ *adj* fashionably elegant – **stylishly** *adv*, **stylishness** *n*

stylist /ˈstielist‖ˈstaɪlɪst/ *n* **1** a writer who cultivates a fine literary style **2** one who develops, designs, or advises on styles

stylistic /stieˈlistik‖staɪˈlɪstɪk/ *adj* of esp literary or artistic style – **stylistically** *adv*

stylistics /stieˈlistiks‖staɪˈlɪstɪks/ *n pl but sing or pl in constr* the study of style, esp in literature

styl·ize, -ise /ˈstieliez‖ˈstaɪlaɪz/ *vt* to make (e g a work of art) conform to a conventional style rather than to nature – **stylization** *n*

stylus /ˈstieləs‖ˈstaɪləs/ *n, pl* **styli** /-lie‖-laɪ/, **styluses** an instrument for writing, marking, incising, or following a groove: e g **a** an instrument used by the ancients for writing on clay or waxed tablets **b** a tiny piece of material (e g diamond) with a rounded tip used in a gramophone to follow the groove on a record

[1]**stymie** /ˈstiemi‖ˈstaɪmɪ/ *n* a condition on a golf green where a ball nearer the hole lies in the line of play of another ball

[2]**stymie** *vt* to present an obstacle to; thwart

styptic /ˈstiptik‖ˈstɪptɪk/ *adj* tending to contract, bind, or check bleeding; astringent – **styptic** *n*

styrene /ˈstie·əreen‖ˈstaɪəriːn/ *n* a liquid unsaturated hydrocarbon used chiefly in making rubber, plastics, etc

suave /swahv‖swɑːv/ *adj* smoothly though often superficially affable and polite – **suavely** *adv*, **suavity** *n*

[1]**sub** /sub‖sʌb/ *n* a substitute – infml

[2]**sub** *vb* **-bb-** *vi* to act as a substitute ~ *vt* **1** to subedit **2** to subcontract *USE* infml

[3]**sub** *n* a submarine – infml

[4]**sub** *n, Br* **1** a small loan or advance **2** SUBSCRIPTION 2b *USE* infml

[5]**sub** *n* a subeditor – infml

sub- /sub-‖sʌb-/ *prefix* **1** under; beneath; below <sub*soil*> **2a** subordinate; secondary; next in rank below <sub*editor*> **b** subordinate portion of; subdivision of <sub*committee*> **c** repeated or further instance of (a specified action or process) <sub*contract*> **3** bearing an incomplete, partial, or inferior resemblance to; approximately <sub*literature*> **4a** almost; nearly <sub*erect*> **b** adjacent to; bordering on <sub*arctic*>

subaltern /ˈsubəlt(ə)n‖ˈsʌbəlt(ə)n/ *n* sby holding a subordinate position; *specif, Br* a commissioned Army officer ranking below captain

ˌsubaˈtomic /-əˈtomik‖-əˈtɒmɪk/ *adj* of the inside of an atom or of particles smaller than atoms

ˈsubcomˌmittee /-kəˌmiti‖-kəˌmɪtɪ/ *n* a subdivision of a committee usu organized for a specific purpose

[1]**ˌsubˈconscious** /-ˈkonshəs‖-ˈkɒnʃəs/ *adj* **1** existing in the mind but not immediately available to consciousness <*his* ~ *motive*> **2** imperfectly or incompletely conscious <*a* ~ *state*> – **subconsciously** *adv*, **subconsciousness** *n*

[2]**ˌsubˈconscious** *n* the mental activities below the threshold of consciousness

ˌsubˈcontinent /-ˈkontinənt‖-ˈkɒntɪnənt/ *n* **1** a landmass (e g Greenland) of great size but smaller than any of the generally recognized continents **2** a vast subdivision of a continent; *specif, often cap the* Indian subcontinent – **subcontinental** *adj*

[1]**ˌsubconˈtract** /-kənˈtrakt‖-kənˈtrækt/ *vt* **1** to engage a third party to perform under a subcontract all or part of (work included in an original contract) **2** to undertake (work) under a subcontract ~*vi* to let out or undertake work under a subcontract – **subcontractor** *n*

[2]**ˌsubˈcontract** /-ˈkontrakt‖-ˈkɒntrækt/ *n* a contract between a party to an original contract and a third party; *esp* one to provide all or a specified part of the work or materials required in the original contract

ˌsubcuˈtaneous /-kyoohˈtaynyəs, -ni·əs‖-kjuːˈteɪnjəs, -nɪəs/ *adj* being, living, used, or made under the skin – **subcutaneously** *adv*

subdivide /ˌsubdiˈvied, ˈ--ˌ-‖ˌsʌbdɪˈvaɪd, ˈ--ˌ-/ *vt* to divide the parts of into more parts ~*vi* to separate or become separated into subdivisions – **subdivision** *n*

subdue /səbˈdyooh‖səbˈdjuː/ *vt* **1** to conquer

and bring into subjection **2** to bring under control; curb < ~d *her fears*> **3** to bring under cultivation **4** to reduce the intensity or degree of (e g colour) – **subduer** *n*

subˈdued *adj* **1** brought under control (as if) by military conquest **2** reduced or lacking in force, intensity, or strength – **subduedly** *adv*

ˌsubˈeditor /-ˈeditə‖-ˈedɪtə/ *n* **1** an assistant editor **2** *chiefly Br* one who edits sthg (e g newspaper copy) in preparation for printing – **subedit** *vt*, **subeditorial** *adj*

ˈsubˌhead /-ˌhed‖-ˌhed/, **ˈsubˌheading** /-ˌheding‖-ˌhedɪŋ/ *n* a subordinate caption, title, heading, or headline

ˌsubˈhuman /-ˈhyoohmən‖-ˈhjuːmən/ *adj* less than human: e g **a** below the level expected of or suited to normal human beings **b** of animals lower than humans; *esp* anthropoid

¹subject /ˈsubjikt‖ˈsʌbdʒɪkt/ *n* **1a** a vassal **b(1)** sby subject to a ruler and governed by his/her law **b(2)** sby who enjoys the protection of and owes allegiance to a sovereign power or state **2a** that of which a quality, attribute, or relation may be stated **b** the entity (e g the mind or ego) that sustains or assumes the form of thought or consciousness **3a** a department of knowledge or learning **b(1)** an individual whose reactions are studied **b(2)** a dead body for anatomical study and dissection **c(1)** sthg concerning which sthg is said or done <*a* ~ *of dispute*> **c(2)** sby or sthg represented in a work of art **d(1)** the term of a logical proposition denoting that of which sthg is stated, denied, or predicated **d(2)** the word or phrase in a sentence or clause denoting that of which sthg is predicated or asserted **e** the principal melodic phrase on which a musical composition or movement is based – **subjectless** *adj*

²subject *adj* **1** owing obedience or allegiance to another < ~ *to higher authority*> **2a** liable or exposed to **b** having a tendency or inclination; prone to < ~ *to colds*> **3** dependent or conditional on sthg <*the plan is* ~ *to approval*> *USE* usu + *to*

³subject /səbˈjekt‖səbˈdʒekt/ *vt* **1** to bring under control or rule **2** to make liable; expose **3** to cause to undergo sthg *USE* usu + *to* – **subjection** *n*

subjective /səbˈjektiv‖səbˈdʒektɪv/ *adj* **1** of or being a grammatical subject **2a** relating to, determined by, or arising from the mind or self < ~ *reality*> **b** characteristic of or belonging to reality as perceived rather than as independent of mind; phenomenal **3a** peculiar to a particular individual; personal **b** arising from conditions within the brain or sense organs and not directly caused by external stimuli < ~ *sensations*> **c** lacking in reality or substance; illusory – **subjectively** *adv*, **subjectivize** *vt*, **subjectivity** *n*

ˈsubject ˌmatter *n* matter presented for consideration in speech, writing, or artistic form

ˈsubject to *prep* depending on; conditionally upon < ~ *your approval, I will go*>

subjoin /ˌsubˈjoyn‖ˌsʌbˈdʒɔɪn/ *vt* to annex, append – fml

ˌsub ˈjudice /ˈjoohdisi‖ˈdʒuːdɪsɪ/ *adv* before a court; not yet judicially decided

subjugate /ˈsubjoogayt‖ˈsʌbdʒʊgeɪt/ *vt* to conquer and hold in subjection – **subjugator** *n*, **subjugation** *n*

¹subjunctive /səbˈjungktiv‖səbˈdʒʌŋktɪv/ *adj* of or being a grammatical mood that represents the denoted act or state not as fact but as contingent or possible or viewed emotionally (e g with doubt or desire)

²subjunctive *n* (a verb form expressing) the subjunctive mood

¹sublease /ˈsubˌlees‖ˈsʌbˌliːs/ *n* a lease to a subtenant

²ˌsubˈlease *vt* to make or obtain a sublease of

¹ˌsubˈlet /-ˈlet‖-ˈlet/ *vb* **-tt-; sublet** to lease or rent (all or part of a property) to a subtenant

²ˈsubˌlet *n* property for subletting

ˌsublieuˈtenant /-lefˈtenənt‖-lefˈtenənt; *NAm* -loohˈtenənt‖-luːˈtenənt/ *n* an officer in the British navy ranking below lieutenant

sublimate /ˈsublimayt‖ˈsʌblɪmeɪt/ *vt* **1** SUBLIME 1 **2** to divert the expression of (an instinctual desire or impulse) from a primitive form to a socially or culturally acceptable one – **sublimation** *n*

¹sublime /səˈbliem‖səˈblaɪm/ *vt* **1** to cause to pass from the solid to the vapour state (and recondense to the solid form) **2** to make finer or of higher worth ~ *vi* to pass directly from the solid to the vapour state

²sublime *adj* **1** lofty, noble, or exalted in thought, expression, or manner **2** tending to inspire awe, usu because of elevated quality **3** outstanding as such < ~ *indifference*> [Latin *sublimis*, lit., to or in a high position, fr *sub* under, up to + *limen* threshold, lintel] – **sublimely** *adv*, **sublimity** *n*

subliminal /ˌsubˈliminl‖ˌsʌbˈlɪmɪnl/ *adj* **1** *of a stimulus* inadequate to produce a sensation or perception **2** existing, functioning, or having effects below the level of conscious awareness – **subliminally** *adv*

ˌsubmaˈchine ˌgun /ˌsubməˈsheen‖ˌsʌbməˈʃiːn/ *n* an automatic or semiautomatic portable rapid-firing firearm of limited range using pistol-type ammunition

¹ˌsubmaˈrine /-məˈreen‖-məˈriːn/ *adj* being, acting, or growing under water, esp in the sea

²submarine /ˈsubməˌreen, ˌ--ˈ-‖ˈsʌbməˌriːn, ˌ--ˈ-/ *n* a vessel designed for undersea operations; *esp* a submarine warship

submariner /ˈsubməˌreenə, subˈmarinə‖ˈsʌbməˌriːnə, sʌbˈmærɪnə/ *n* a crewman of a submarine

submerge /səbˈmuhj‖səbˈmɜːdʒ/ *vt* **1** to put under water **2** to cover (as if) with water; inundate ~ *vi* to go under water – **submergence** *n*

submersed /səbˈmuhst‖səbˈmɜːst/ *adj* **1** covered with water **2** (adapted for) growing under water < ~ *plants*> – **submersion** *n*

¹submersible /səbˈmuhsəbl‖səbˈmɜːsəbl/ *adj* capable of going under water

²submersible *n* sthg submersible; *esp* a vessel used for undersea exploration and construction work

submission /səbˈmish(ə)n‖səbˈmɪʃ(ə)n/ *n* **1** an act of submitting sthg for consideration, inspection, etc **2** the state of being submissive, humble, or compliant **3** an act of submitting to the authority or control of another

submissive /səb'misiv‖səb'mɪsɪv/ *adj* willing to submit to others – **submissively** *adv*, **submissiveness** *n*

submit /səb'mit‖səb'mɪt/ *vb* **-tt-** *vt* **1a** to yield to the authority or will of another **b** to subject to a process or practice **2a** to send or commit to another for consideration, inspection, etc **b** to put forward as an opinion; suggest <*we ~ that the charge is not proved*> ~ *vi* **1** to yield oneself to the authority or will of another **2** to allow oneself to be subjected to sthg

ˌ**sub'normal** /-'nawməl‖-'nɔːməl/ *adj* **1** lower or smaller than normal **2** having less of sthg, esp intelligence, than is normal – **subnormally** *adj*, **subnormality** *n*

ˌ**sub'orbital** /-'awbitl‖-'ɔːbɪtl/ *adj* **1** situated beneath the orbit of the eye **2** being or involving less than 1 complete orbit <*a spacecraft's ~ flight*>; *also* intended for suborbital flight <*a ~ rocket*>

[1]**subordinate** /sə'bawd(ə)nət‖sə'bɔːd(ə)nət/ *adj* **1** occupying a lower class or rank; inferior **2** subject to or controlled by authority **3** *of a clause* functioning as a noun, adjective, or adverb in a complex sentence (e g the clause 'when he heard' in 'he laughed when he heard') – **subordinate** *n*, **subordinately** *adv*

[2]**subordinate** /sə'bawd(ə)nayt‖sə'bɔːd(ə)neɪt/ *vt* **1** to place in a lower order or class **2** to make subject or subservient; subdue – **subordinative** *adj*, **subordination** *n*

suborn /sə'bawn‖sə'bɔːn/ *vt* to induce to commit perjury or another illegal act – **suborner** *n*

'**subˌplot** /-ˌplot‖-ˌplɒt/ *n* a subordinate plot in fiction or drama

[1]**subpoena** /sə(b)'peenə‖sə(b)'piːnə/ *n* a writ commanding sby to appear in court [Latin *sub poena* under penalty (the first words of the writ)]

[2]**subpoena** *vt* **subpoenaing; subpoenaed** to serve with a subpoena

subscribe /səb'skrieb‖səb'skraɪb/ *vt* **1** to write (one's name) underneath **2a** to sign with one's own hand **b** to give a written pledge to contribute ~ *vi* **1a** to give consent or approval to sthg written by signing **b** to give money (e g to charity) **c** to pay regularly in order to receive a periodical or service **2** to agree to purchase and pay for securities, esp of a new issue <~d *for 1000 shares*> **3** to feel favourably disposed *to* USE (*vi 1*) usu + *to*

subscriber /səb'skriebə‖səb'skraɪbə/ *n* sby who subscribes; *specif* the owner of a telephone who pays rental and call charges

subscription /səb'skripsh(ə)n‖səb'skrɪpʃ(ə)n/ *n* **1** a sum subscribed **2a** a purchase by prepayment for a certain number of issues (e g of a periodical) **b** *Br* membership fees paid regularly **3** a signature – fml

subsequent /'subsikwənt‖'sʌbsɪkwənt/ *adj* following in time or order; succeeding – **subsequently** *adv*

subservience /səb'suhvi·əns‖səb'sɜːvɪəns/ *n* obsequious servility

subservient /səb'suhvi·ənt‖səb'sɜːvɪənt/ *adj* **1** useful in an inferior capacity; subordinate **2** obsequiously submissive – **subserviently** *adv*

subside /səb'sied‖səb'saɪd/ *vi* **1** to sink or fall to the bottom; settle **2a** to descend; *esp* to sink so as to form a depression **b** *of ground* to cave in; collapse **3** to sink down; settle <~d *into a chair*> **4** to become quiet; abate – **subsidence** *n*

[1]**subsidiary** /səb'sidyəri, -'sij(ə)ri‖səb'sɪdjərɪ, -'sɪdʒ(ə)rɪ/ *adj* **1** serving to assist or supplement; auxiliary **2** of secondary importance

[2]**subsidiary** *n* sby or sthg subsidiary; *esp* a company wholly controlled by another

subsid·ize, -ise /'subsiˌdiez‖'sʌbsɪˌdaɪz/ *vt* to provide with a subsidy: e g **a** to purchase the assistance of by payment of a subsidy **b** to aid or promote (e g a private enterprise) with public money – **subsidizer** *n*, **subsidization** *n*

subsidy /'subsidi‖'sʌbsɪdɪ/ *n* a grant or gift of money (e g by a government to a person or organization, to assist an enterprise deemed advantageous to the public) [Latin *subsidium* reserve troops, support, assistance, fr *sub-* near + *sedēre* to sit]

subsist /səb'sist‖səb'sɪst/ *vi* **1** to have or continue in existence **2** to have the bare necessities of life; be kept alive

subsistence /səb'sist(ə)ns‖səb'sɪst(ə)ns/ *n* **1** the state of subsisting **2** the minimum (e g of food and shelter) necessary to support life – **subsistent** *adj*

subsoil /'subˌsoyl‖'sʌbˌsɔɪl/ *n* the layer of weathered material that underlies the surface soil

ˌ**sub'sonic** /-'sonik‖-'sɒnɪk/ *adj* **1** of, being, moving at, or using air currents moving at, a speed less than that of sound in air **2** infrasonic – **subsonically** *adv*

substance /'substəns‖'sʌbstəns/ *n* **1a** a fundamental or essential part or import <*the ~ of his argument*> **b** correspondence with reality <*the allegations were without ~*> **2** ultimate underlying reality **3a** (a) physical material from which sthg is made <*an oily ~*> **b** matter of particular or definite chemical constitution **4** material possessions; property <*a man of ~*> – **in substance** in respect to essentials

ˌ**sub'standard** /-'standəd‖-'stændəd/ *adj* deviating from or falling short of a standard or norm: e g **a** of a quality lower than that prescribed **b** in widespread use but not accepted as linguistically correct by some

substantial /səb'stansh(ə)l‖səb'stænʃ(ə)l/ *adj* **1a** having material existence; real **b** important, essential **2** ample to satisfy and nourish <*a ~ meal*> **3a** well-to-do, prosperous **b** considerable in quantity; significantly large **4** firmly constructed; solid **5** being largely but not wholly the specified thing <*a ~ lie*> – **substantial** *n*, **substantially** *adv*, **substantialize** *vb*, **substantiality** *n*

substantiate /səb'stanshi·ayt‖səb'stænʃɪeɪt/ *vt* to establish (e g a statement or claim) by proof or evidence; verify – **substantiative** *adj*, **substantiation** *n*

[1]**substantive** /'substəntiv‖'sʌbstəntɪv/ *n* a noun; *broadly* a word or phrase functioning syntactically as a noun – **substantivize** *vt*, **substantival** *adj*

[2]**substantive** /'substəntiv, səb'stantiv ‖ 'sʌbstəntɪv, səb'stæntɪv (*usu the latter when applied to position, rank, etc*)/ *adj* **1** being a totally independent entity; not inferred or derived **2a** indicating or expressing existence <*the ~ verb*

to be> **b** not requiring or involving a mordant <*a ~ dyeing process*> **3** relating to or functioning as a noun **4** defining rights and duties <*~ law*> **5** permanent and definite rather than temporary or acting <*~ rank of colonel*> – **substantively** *adv*

substation /ˈsub,staysh(ə)n‖ˈsʌb,steɪʃ(ə)n/ *n* a subsidiary station in which (the voltage of an) electric current is transformed for use

[1]**substitute** /ˈsubstityooht‖ˈsʌbstɪtjuːt/ *n* sby or sthg that takes the place of another – **substitute** *adj*, **substitutive** *adj*

[2]**substitute** *vt* **1** to exchange for another **2** to take the place of; *also* to introduce a substitute for <~d *their centre forward in the second half*> ~*vi* to serve as a substitute – **substitutable** *adj*, **substitution** *n*, **substitutional, substitutionary** *adj*

,subˈstratum /-ˈstrahtəm, -ˈstraytəm‖-ˈstrɑːtəm, -ˈstreɪtəm/ *n, pl* **substrata** /-tə‖-tə/ an underlying support; a foundation: e g **a** matter considered as the enduring basis for all the qualities that can be perceived by the senses (e g colour) **b** a foundation, basis <*his argument has a ~ of truth*> **c** the subsoil

ˈsub,structure /-,strukchə‖-,strʌktʃə/ *n* the foundation or groundwork – **substructural** *adj*

subsume /səbˈsyoohm‖səbˈsjuːm/ *vt* to include as a member of a group or type – **subsumption** *n*

subtenant /ˈsub,tenənt‖ˈsʌb,tenənt/ *n* sby who rents from a tenant

subtend /səbˈtend‖səbˈtend/ *vt* **1a** to define in a given context by extending from one side to the other of <*a hypotenuse* ~s *a right angle*> **b** to fix the angular extent of with respect to a fixed point <*the angle* ~ed *at the eye by an object*> **2** to be lower than, esp so as to embrace or enclose <*a bract that* ~s *a flower*>

subterfuge /ˈsubtə,fyoohj‖ˈsʌbtə,fjuːdʒ/ *n* **1** deception or trickery used as a means of concealment or evasion **2** a trick or ruse [Late Latin *subterfugium*, fr Latin *subterfugere* to escape stealthily, evade, fr *subter* underneath + *fugere* to flee]

,subterˈranean /-təˈraynyən, -ni·ən‖-təˈreɪnjən, -nɪən/, **subterraneous** /-nyəs, -ni·əs‖-njəs, -nɪəs/ *adj* **1** being or operating under the surface of the earth **2** hidden or out of sight [Latin *subterraneus*, fr *sub* under + *terra* earth] – **subterraneanly** *adv*

subtitle /,subˈtietl‖,sʌbˈtaɪtl/ *n* **1** a secondary or explanatory title **2** a printed explanation (e g a fragment of dialogue or a translation) that appears on the screen during a film – **subtitle** *vt*

subtle /ˈsutl‖ˈsʌtl/ *adj* **1a** delicate, elusive <*a ~ fragrance*> **b** difficult to understand or distinguish **2** showing keen insight and perception **3** cleverly contrived; ingenious **4** artful, cunning [Old French *soutil*, fr Latin *subtilis*, lit., finely woven, fr *sub*-near + *tela* web] – **subtleness** *n*, **subtly** *adv*

subtlety /ˈsutl·ti‖ˈsʌtltɪ/ *n* **1** the quality of being subtle **2** sthg subtle; *esp* a fine distinction

subtract /səbˈtrakt‖səbˈtrækt/ *vt* to take away by subtraction <*~ 5 from 9*> ~*vi* to perform a subtraction – **subtracter** *n*

subtraction /səbˈtraksh(ə)n‖səbˈtrækʃ(ə)n/ *n* the operation of finding for 2 given numbers a third number which when added to the first yields the second

subtropical /,subˈtropikl‖,sʌbˈtrɒpɪkl/ *also* **subtropic** *adj* of or being the regions bordering on the tropical zone – **subtropics** *n pl*

suburb /ˈsubuhb‖ˈsʌbɜːb/ *n* **1** an outlying part of a city or large town **2** *pl* the residential area on the outskirts of a city or large town [Latin *suburbium*, fr *sub*- near + *urbs* city] – **suburban** *adj or n*, **suburbanize** *vt*, **suburbanization** *n*, **suburbanite** *n*

suburbia /səˈbuhbyə‖səˈbɜːbjə/ *n* (the inhabitants of) the suburbs of a city

subvention /səbˈvensh(ə)n‖səbˈvenʃ(ə)n/ *n* the provision of assistance or financial support: e g **a** an endowment **b** a subsidy – **subventionary** *adj*

subversion /səbˈvuhsh(ə)n‖səbˈvɜːʃ(ə)n/ *n* a systematic attempt to overthrow or undermine a government by people working secretly within the country – **subversionary** *adj*, **subversive** *adj or n*, **subversively** *adv*, **subversiveness** *n*

subvert /səbˈvuht‖səbˈvɜːt/ *vt* to overthrow or undermine the power of [Middle French *subvertir*, fr Latin *subvertere*, lit., to turn from beneath, fr *sub*- from beneath + *vertere* to turn] – **subverter** *n*

subway /ˈsub,way‖ˈsʌb,weɪ/ *n* an underground way: e g **a** a passage under a street (e g for pedestrians, power cables, or water or gas mains) **b** *chiefly NAm* the underground

succeed /səkˈseed‖səkˈsiːd/ *vi* **1a** to inherit sthg, esp sovereignty, rank, or title **b** to follow after another in order **2a** to have a favourable result; turn out well **b** to achieve a desired object or end ~ *vt* **1** to follow (immediately) in sequence **2** to come after as heir or successor – **succeeder** *n*

success /səkˈses‖səkˈses/ *n* **1** a favourable outcome to an undertaking **2** the attainment of wealth or fame **3** sby or sthg that succeeds <*he was an overnight ~*>

sucˈcessful /-f(ə)l‖-f(ə)l/ *adj* **1** resulting in success <*a ~ experiment*> **2** having gained success <*a ~ banker*> – **successfully** *adv*, **successfulness** *n*

succession /səkˈsesh(ə)n‖səkˈseʃ(ə)n/ *n* **1a** the order or right of succeeding to a property, title, or throne **b** the line having such a right **2a** the act of following in order; a sequence **b** the act or process of becoming entitled to a deceased person's property or title **c** the change in the composition of an ecological system as the competing organisms respond to and modify the environment **3** *sing or pl in constr* a number of people or things that follow each other in sequence – **successional** *adj*, **successionally** *adv*

successive /səkˈsesiv‖səkˈsesɪv/ *adj* following one after the other in succession – **successively** *adv*, **successiveness** *n*

successor /səkˈsesə‖səkˈsesə/ *n* sby or sthg that follows another; *esp* a person who succeeds to throne, title, or office

succinct /səkˈsingkt‖səkˈsɪŋkt/ *adj* clearly expressed in few words; concise – **succinctly** *adv*, **succinctness** *n*

[1]**succour**, *NAm chiefly* **succor** /ˈsukə‖ˈsʌkə/ *n* relief; *also* aid, help

[2]**succour,** *NAm chiefly* **succor** *vt* to go to the aid of (sby in need or distress)

succubus /ˈsukyoobəs‖ˈsʌkjʊbəs/ *n, pl* **succubi** /-ˌbie‖-ˌbaɪ/ a female demon believed to have sexual intercourse with men in their sleep

[1]**succulent** /ˈsukyoolənt‖ˈsʌkjʊlənt/ *adj* **1** full of juice; juicy **2** *of a plant* having juicy fleshy tissues – **succulence** *n*, **succulently** *adv*

[2]**succulent** *n* a succulent plant (e g a cactus)

succumb /səˈkum‖səˈkʌm/ *vi* **1** to yield or give in *to* **2** to die

[1]**such** /such‖sʌtʃ/ *adj or adv* **1a** of the kind, quality, or extent <*his habits are* ~ *that we rarely meet*> – used before *as* to introduce an example or comparison <~ *trees as oak or pine*> **b** of the same sort <*there's no* ~ *place*> **2** of so extreme a degree or extraordinary a nature <*ever* ~ *a lot of people*> <*in* ~ *a hurry*> – used before *as* to suggest that a name is unmerited <*we forced down the soup,* ~ *as it was*>

[2]**such** *pron, pl* **such** **1** *pl* such people; those <~ *as wish to leave may do so*> **2** that thing, fact, or action <~ *was the result*> **3** *pl* similar people or things <*tin and glass and* ~> – **as such** intrinsically considered; in him-/herself, itself, or themselves <as such *the gift was worth little*>

ˈ**such and ˌsuch** *adj* not named or specified – infml

[1]ˈ**suchˌlike** /-ˌliek‖-ˌlaɪk/ *adj* of like kind; similar

[2]**suchlike** *pron, pl* **suchlike** a similar person or thing

[1]**suck** /suk‖sʌk/ *vt* **1a** to draw (e g liquid) into the mouth by the suction of the contracted lips and tongue **b** to eat by means of sucking movements of the lips and tongue **c** to take into the mouth as if sucking out a liquid <~ed *his finger*> **2** to draw in or up (as if) by suction <*plants* ~ing *moisture from the soil*> ~ *vi* **1** to draw sthg in (as if) by suction; *esp* to draw milk from a breast or udder with the mouth **2** to make a sound associated with suction <~ed *at his pipe*> **3** to act in an obsequious manner – infml <~ing *up to his boss*>

[2]**suck** *n* **1** the act of sucking **2** a sucking movement

[1]**sucker** /ˈsukə‖ˈsʌkə/ *n* **1a** a human infant or young animal that sucks, esp at a breast or udder; a suckling **b** a device for creating or regulating suction (e g a piston or valve in a pump) **c** a pipe or tube through which sthg is drawn by suction **d** a mouth (e g of a leech) or other animal organ adapted for sucking or sticking **e** a device, esp of rubber, that can cling to a surface by suction **2** a shoot from the roots or lower part of the stem of a plant **3** any of numerous freshwater fishes closely related to the carps and usu having thick soft lips **4a** a gullible person – infml **b** a person irresistibly attracted by sthg specified <*a* ~ *for chocolate*> – infml

[2]**sucker** *vt* to remove suckers from <~ *tobacco*> ~*vi* to send out suckers

sucking /ˈsuking‖ˈsʌkɪŋ/ *adj* not yet weaned; *broadly* very young

suckle /ˈsukl‖ˈsʌkl/ *vt* **1** to give milk to from the breast or udder <*a mother* suckling *her child*> **2** to draw milk from the breast or udder of <*lambs* suckling *the ewes*>

suckling /ˈsukling‖ˈsʌklɪŋ/ *n* a young unweaned animal

sucrose /ˈs(y)oohkrohs, -krohz‖ˈs(j)uːkrəʊs, -krəʊz/ *n* the disaccharide sugar obtained from sugarcane and sugar beet and occurring in most plants

suction /ˈsuksh(ə)n‖ˈsʌkʃ(ə)n/ *n* **1** the act of sucking **2** the action of exerting a force on a solid, liquid, or gaseous body by means of reduced air pressure over part of its surface – **suctional** *adj*

ˈ**suction ˌpump** *n* a pump in which liquid is raised by suction under a retreating piston

[1]**sudden** /ˈsud(ə)n‖ˈsʌd(ə)n/ *adj* **1a** happening or coming unexpectedly <*a* ~ *shower*> **b** abrupt, steep **2** marked by or showing haste – **suddenly** *adv*, **suddenness** *n*

[2]**sudden** *n* – **all of a sudden** sooner than was expected; suddenly

suds /sudz‖sʌdz/ *n pl but sing or pl in constr* (the lather on) soapy water – **sudsless** *adj*

sue /s(y)ooh‖s(j)uː/ *vt* to bring a legal action against ~ *vi* **1** to make a request or application – usu + *for* or *to* **2** to take legal proceedings in court – **suer** *n*

suede, suède /swayd‖sweɪd/ *n* leather with a napped surface [French *(gants de) Suède* Swedish (gloves)]

suet /ˈs(y)ooh·it‖ˈs(j)uːɪt/ *n* the hard fat round the kidneys and loins in beef and mutton, that yields tallow and is used in cooking

suffer /ˈsufə‖ˈsʌfə/ *vt* **1** to submit to or be forced to endure **2** to undergo, experience **3** to allow, permit <~ *the little children to come unto me*> ~ *vi* **1** to endure pain, distress, or death **2** to sustain loss or damage **3** to be handicapped or at a disadvantage – **sufferable** *adj*, **sufferably** *adv*, **sufferer** *n*

sufferance /ˈsuf(ə)rəns‖ˈsʌf(ə)rəns/ *n* tacit permission; tolerance implied by a lack of interference or objection <*he was only there on* ~>

suffering /ˈsuf(ə)ring‖ˈsʌf(ə)rɪŋ/ *n* the state of one who suffers

suffice /səˈfies‖səˈfaɪs/ *vi* to meet a need; be enough <*a brief note will* ~> ~*vt* to be enough for

sufficiency /səˈfish(ə)nsi‖səˈfɪʃ(ə)nsɪ/ *n* **1** sufficient means to meet one's needs **2** the quality of being sufficient; adequacy

sufficient /səˈfish(ə)nt‖səˈfɪʃ(ə)nt/ *adj* enough to meet the needs of a situation – **sufficiently** *adv*

[1]**suffix** /ˈsufiks‖ˈsʌfɪks/ *n* an affix (e g *-ness* in *happiness*) appearing at the end of a word or phrase or following a root – **suffixal** *adj*

[2]**suffix** *vt* to attach as a suffix – **suffixation** *n*

suffocate /ˈsufəˌkayt‖ˈsʌfəˌkeɪt/ *vt* **1** to stop the breathing of (e g by asphyxiation) **2** to deprive of oxygen **3** to make uncomfortable by want of cool fresh air ~*vi* to become suffocated: **3a** to die from being unable to breathe **b** to be uncomfortable through lack of air – **suffocatingly** *adv*, **suffocative** *adj*, **suffocation** *n*

suffragan /ˈsufrəgən‖ˈsʌfrəgən/ *adj or n* (of or being) **1** a diocesan bishop subordinate to a metropolitan **2** an Anglican bishop assisting a diocesan bishop and having no right of succession

suffrage /ˈsufrij‖ˈsʌfrɪdʒ/ *n* **1** a vote given in favour of a question or in the choice of sby for an office **2** the right of voting

suffragette /ˌsufrəˈjet‖ˌsʌfrəˈdʒet/ *n* a woman who advocates suffrage for her sex

suffuse /səˈfyoohz‖səˈfjuːz/ *vt* to spread over or through, esp with a liquid or colour; permeate – **suffusion** *n*, **suffusive** *adj*

[1]**sugar** /ˈshoogə‖ˈʃʊgə/ *n* **1a** a sweet crystallizable material that consists (essentially) of sucrose, is colourless or white when pure tending to brown when less refined, is obtained commercially esp from sugarcane or sugar beet, and is important as a source of dietary carbohydrate and as a sweetener and preservative of other foods **b** any of a class of water-soluble carbohydrate compounds containing many hydroxyl groups that are of varying sweetness and include glucose, ribose, and sucrose **2** DEAR 1b

[2]**sugar** *vt* **1** to make palatable or attractive **2** to sprinkle or mix with sugar

ˈ**sugar ˌbeet** *n* a white-rooted beet grown for the sugar in its root

ˈ**sugarˌcane** *n* a stout tall grass widely grown in warm regions as a source of sugar

sugar-coated *adj* **1** covered with a hard coat of sugar **2** having its unpleasantness concealed

ˈ**sugar ˌdaddy** *n* a usu elderly man who lavishes gifts and money on a young woman in return for sex or companionship – infml

sugary /ˈshoog(ə)ri‖ˈʃʊg(ə)rɪ/ *adj* **1** containing, resembling, or tasting of sugar **2** exaggeratedly or cloyingly sweet

suggest /səˈjest‖səˈdʒest/ *vt* **1** to put forward as a possibility or for consideration **2a** to call to mind by thought or association; evoke **b** to indicate the presence of <*her look* ~ed *irritation*> [Latin *suggest-*, *suggerere* to put under, furnish, suggest, fr *sub-* under + *gerere* to carry] – **suggester** *n*

suggestible /səˈjestəbl‖səˈdʒestəbl/ *adj* easily influenced by suggestion – **suggestibility** *n*

suggestion /səˈjesch(ə)n‖səˈdʒestʃ(ə)n/ *n* **1a** the act of suggesting **b** sthg suggested; a proposal **2a** indirect means (e g the natural association of ideas) to evoke ideas or feeling **b** the impressing of an idea, attitude, desired action, etc on the mind of another **3** a slight indication; a trace

suggestive /səˈjestiv‖səˈdʒestɪv/ *adj* **1a** conveying a suggestion; indicative **b** conjuring up mental associations; evocative **2** suggesting sthg improper or indecent; risqué – **suggestively** *adv*, **suggestiveness** *n*

suicidal /ˌs(y)ooh·iˈsiedl‖ˌs(j)uːɪˈsaɪdl/ *adj* **1** relating to or of the nature of suicide **2** marked by an impulse to commit suicide **3a** dangerous, esp to life **b** harmful to one's own interests – **suicidally** *adv*

suicide /ˈs(y)ooh·iˌsied‖ˈs(j)uːɪˌsaɪd/ *n* **1a** (an) act of taking one's own life intentionally **b** ruin of one's own interests <*political* ~> **2** one who commits or attempts suicide [Latin *sui* (gen) of oneself + *caedere* to cut, kill]

[1]**suit** /s(y)ooht‖s(j)uːt/ *n* **1** a legal action **2** a petition or appeal; *specif* courtship **3** a group of things forming a unit or constituting a collection – used chiefly with reference to armour, sails, and counters in games **4a** an outer costume of 2 or more matching pieces that are designed to be worn together **b** a costume to be worn for a specified purpose or under particular conditions **5a** all the playing cards in a pack bearing the same symbol (i e hearts, clubs, diamonds, or spades) **b** all the cards in a particular suit held by 1 player <*a 5-card* ~> **c** the suit led <*follow* ~>

[2]**suit** *vi* **1** to be appropriate or satisfactory <*these prices don't* ~> **2** to put on specially required clothing (e g a uniform or protective garb) – usu + *up* ~ *vt* **1** to accommodate, adapt **2a** to be good for the health or well-being of **b** to be becoming to; look right with **3** to satisfy, please <~s *me fine*> – **suit someone down to the ground** to suit sby extremely well

suitable /ˈs(y)oohtəbl‖ˈs(j)uːtəbl/ *adj* appropriate, fitting – **suitableness** *n*, **suitably** *adv*, **suitability** *n*

suitcase /-ˌkays‖-ˌkeɪs/ *n* a rectangular usu rigid case with a hinged lid and a handle, used for carrying articles (e g clothes)

suite /sweet‖swiːt/ *n* **1** *sing or pl in constr* a retinue; *esp* the personal staff accompanying an official or dignitary on business **2a** a group of rooms occupied as a unit **b(1)** a 17th- and 18th-c instrumental musical form consisting of a series of dances **b(2)** a modern instrumental composition in several movements of different character **b(3)** an orchestral concert arrangement in suite form of material drawn from a longer work (e g a ballet) **c** a set of matching furniture (e g a settee and 2 armchairs) for a room <*a 3-piece* ~>

suiting /ˈs(y)oohting‖ˈs(j)uːtɪŋ/ *n* fabric suitable for suits

suitor /ˈs(y)oohtə‖ˈs(j)uːtə/ *n* one who courts a woman with a view to marriage

[1]**sulk** /sulk‖sʌlk/ *vi* to be moodily silent

[2]**sulk** *n* a fit of sulking – usu pl with sing. meaning

[1]**sulky** /ˈsulki‖ˈsʌlkɪ/ *adj* sulking or given to fits of sulking – **sulkily** *adv*, **sulkiness** *n*

[2]**sulky** *n* a light 2-wheeled 1-horse vehicle for 1 person used esp in trotting races

sullen /ˈsulən‖ˈsʌlən/ *adj* **1** silently gloomy or resentful; ill-humoured and unsociable **2** dismal, gloomy – **sullenly** *adv*, **sullenness** *n*

sully /ˈsuli‖ˈsʌlɪ/ *vt* to mar the purity of; tarnish

sulphate /ˈsulfayt‖ˈsʌlfeɪt/ *n* a salt or ester of sulphuric acid

sulphide /ˈsulfied‖ˈsʌlfaɪd/ *n* a binary compound of sulphur, usu with a more electropositive element

[1]**sulphur** /ˈsulfə‖ˈsʌlfə/ *n* **1** a nonmetallic element chemically resembling oxygen that occurs esp as yellow crystals and is used esp in rubber vulcanization and in medicine for treating skin diseases **2** pale greenish yellow

[2]**sulphur** *vt* to treat with (a compound of) sulphur

sulphuret /ˌsulfyooˈret‖ˌsʌlfjʊˈret/ *vt* **-tt-** (*NAm* **-t-**, **-tt-**) to combine or impregnate with sulphur

sulˌphuric ˈacid /sulfyooərik‖sʌlfjʊərɪk/ *n* a

corrosive oily strong acid that is a vigorous oxidizing and dehydrating agent

sulphurous /'sulf(ə)rəs, sul'fyooərəs‖'sʌlf-(ə)rəs, sʌl'fjʊərəs/ *adj* **1** of or containing (low valency) sulphur **2** resembling or coming from (burning) sulphur

sultan /'sult(ə)n‖'sʌlt(ə)n/ *n* a sovereign of a Muslim state – **sultanate** *n*

sultana /səl'tahnə‖səl'tɑːnə/ *n* **1** a female member of a sultan's family; *esp* a sultan's wife **2** (the raisin of) a pale yellow seedless grape

sultry /'sultri‖'sʌltrɪ/ *adj* **1** oppressively hot and humid **2** (capable of) exciting strong sexual desire; sensual – **sultrily** *adv*, **sultriness** *n*

[1]**sum** /sum‖sʌm/ *n* **1** a (specified) amount of money **2** the whole amount; the total **3** *the* gist – esp in *the sum and substance* **4a(1)** the result of adding numbers <~ *of 5 and 7 is 12*> **a(2)** the limit of the sum of the first *n* terms of an infinite series as *n* increases indefinitely **b** numbers to be added; *broadly* a problem in arithmetic **c** UNION 3 – **in sum** briefly

[2]**sum** *vt* **-mm-** to calculate the sum of

sumach, sumac /'s(h)oohmak‖'suːmæk,ʃuː-/ *n* (the dried powdered leaves and flowers, used in tanning and dyeing, of) any of a genus of trees, shrubs, and climbing plants (e g poison ivy) with feathery leaves turning to brilliant colours in the autumn and red or whitish berries

summar·ize, -ise /'sumәriez‖'sʌmәraɪz/ *vt* to express as or reduce to a summary – **summarizer** *n*, **summarization** *n*

[1]**summary** /'sumәri‖'sʌmәrɪ/ *adj* **1** concise but comprehensive **2a** done quickly without delay or formality **b** of or using a summary proceeding; *specif* tried or triable in a magistrates' court <*a* ~ *offence*> – **summarily** *adv*

[2]**summary** *n* a brief account covering the main points of sthg

summat /'sumәt‖'sʌmәt/ *pron, dial N Eng* something

summation /su'maysh(ә)n‖sʌ'meɪʃ(ә)n/ *n* **1** the act or process of forming a sum **2** a total **3** cumulative action or effect **4** (a) summing up of an argument – **summational** *adj*

[1]**summer** /'sumә‖'sʌmә/ *n* **1** the season between spring and autumn comprising in the northern hemisphere the months of June, July, and August **2** a period of maturity **3** a year <*a girl of 17* ~s> – chiefly poetic

[2]**summer** *adj* sown in the spring and harvested in the same year as sown <~ *wheat*>

[3]**summer** *vi* to pass the summer ~*vt* to provide (e g cattle or sheep) with pasture during the summer

[4]**summer** *n* a large horizontal beam or stone used esp in building

'summer,house /-,hows‖-,haʊs/ *n* a small building in a garden designed to provide a shady place in summer

'summer ,school *n* a course of teaching held during the summer vacation, esp on university premises

'summer,time /-,tiem‖-,taɪm/ *n* the summer season

summery /'sum(ә)ri‖'sʌm(ә)rɪ/ *adj* of, suggesting, or suitable for summer

,summing-'up /'suming‖'sʌmɪŋ/ *n* **1** a concluding summary **2** a survey of evidence given by a judge to the jury before it considers its verdict

summit /'sumit‖'sʌmɪt/ *n* **1** a top; *esp* the highest point or peak **2** the topmost level attainable; the pinnacle **3** a conference of highest-level officials

summon /'sumәn‖'sʌmәn/ *vt* **1** to convene, convoke **2** to command by a summons to appear in court **3** to call upon to come; SEND FOR <~ *a doctor*> **4** to call up or muster <~ed *up his courage*> – **summoner** *n*

[1]**summons** /'sumәnz‖'sʌmәnz/ *n, pl* **summonses** **1** a call or order by authority to appear at a particular place or to attend to sthg **2** a written notification warning sby to appear in court

[2]**summons** *vt* SUMMON 2

sump /sump‖sʌmp/ *n* **1** a pit or reservoir serving as a drain or receptacle for esp waste liquids: e g **1a** a cesspool **b** *chiefly Br* the lower section of the crankcase used as a lubricating-oil reservoir in an internal-combustion engine **2** the lowest part of a mine shaft, into which water drains

sumptuary /'sum(p)choo·әri, -tyoo-‖'sʌm(p)tʃʊәrɪ, -tjʊ-/ *adj* designed to regulate personal expenditures and habits <~ *laws*>

sumptuous /'sum(p)choo·әs, -tyoo-‖'sʌm(p)tʃʊәs, -tjʊ-/ *adj* lavishly rich, costly, or luxurious – **sumptuously** *adv*, **sumptuousness** *n*

sum up *vt* **1** to summarize **2** to form or express a rapid appraisal of ~*vi* to present a summary

[1]**sun** /sun‖sʌn/ *n* **1a** the star nearest to the earth, round which the earth and other planets revolve **b** a star or other celestial body that emits its own light **2** the heat or light radiated from the sun – **sunless** *adj* – **under the sun** in the world; ON EARTH <*he was the last person* under the sun *I expected to see*>

[2]**sun** *vb* **-nn-** to expose (e g oneself) to the rays of the sun

'sun,baked /-,baykt‖-,beɪkt/ *adj* baked hard by exposure to sunshine

'sun,bathe /-,baydh‖-,beɪð/ *vi* to expose the body to the rays of the sun or a sunlamp – **sunbathe** *n*

'sun,beam /-,beem‖-,biːm/ *n* a ray of light from the sun

'sun,blind /-,bliend‖-,blaɪnd/ *n, chiefly Br* an awning or a shade on a window (e g a venetian blind) that gives protection from the sun's rays

'sun,bonnet /-,bonit‖-,bɒnɪt/ *n* a bonnet with a wide brim framing the face and usu having a ruffle at the back to protect the neck from the sun

[1]**'sun,burn** /-,buhn‖-,bɜːn/ *vb* **sunburnt** /-,buhnt‖-,bɜːnt/, **sunburned** to burn or tan by exposure to sunlight

[2]**sunburn** *n* inflammation of the skin caused by overexposure to sunlight

sundae /'sunday‖'sʌndeɪ/ *n* an ice cream served with a topping of fruit, nuts, syrup, etc

[1]**Sunday** /'sunday, -di‖'sʌndeɪ, -dɪ/ *n* **1** the day of the week falling between Saturday and Monday, observed by Christians as a day of worship

2 a newspaper published on Sundays [Old English *sunnandæg*, fr *sunne* sun + *dæg* day]

²Sunday *adj* **1** of or associated with Sunday **2** amateur <~ *painters*> – derog

ˌSunday ˈbest *n sing or pl in constr* one's best clothes – infml

ˈSunday ˌschool *n* a class usu of religious instruction held, esp for children, on Sundays

sunder /ˈsundə‖ˈsʌndə/ *vt* to break apart or in two; sever

sundew /ˈsunˌdyooh‖ˈsʌnˌdjuː/ *n* any of a genus of bog plants with long glistening hairs on the leaves that attract and trap insects

ˈsunˌdial /-ˌdie·əl‖-ˌdaɪəl/ *n* an instrument to show the time of day by the shadow of a pointer on a graduated plate or cylindrical surface

ˈsunˌdown /-ˌdown‖-ˌdaʊn/ *n* sunset

ˈsunˌdrenched /-ˌdrencht‖-ˌdrentʃt/ *adj* exposed to much hot sunshine

¹sundry /ˈsundri‖ˈsʌndrɪ/ *adj* miscellaneous, various

²sundry *pron pl in constr* an indeterminate number – chiefly in *all and sundry*

³sundry *n* **1** *pl* miscellaneous small articles or items **2** *Austr* EXTRA C

ˈsunˌfish /-ˌfish‖-ˌfɪʃ/ *n* a large marine bony fish with a nearly oval body, a length of up to 3m (about 10ft), and a weight of 2 tonnes (about 2 tons)

ˈsunˌflower /-ˌflowə‖-ˌflaʊə/ *n* any of a genus of composite plants with large yellow-rayed flower heads bearing edible seeds that are often used as animal feed and yield an edible oil

sung /sung‖sʌŋ/ *past of* SING

ˈsunˌglasses /-ˌglahsiz‖-ˌglɑːsɪz/ *n pl* glasses to protect the eyes from the sun

sunk /sungk‖sʌŋk/ *past of* SINK

sunken /ˈsungkən‖ˈsʌŋkən/ *adj* **1** submerged; *esp* lying at the bottom of a body of water **2a** hollow, recessed **b** lying or constructed below the surrounding or normal level <*a ~ bath*>

sunlamp /ˈsunˌlamp‖ˈsʌnˌlæmp/ *n* an electric lamp that emits esp ultraviolet light and is used esp for tanning the skin

ˈsunˌlight /-ˌliet‖-ˌlaɪt/ *n* sunshine

ˈsunˌlit /-ˌlit‖-ˌlɪt/ *adj* lit (as if) by the sun

ˈsunˌlounge /-ˌlownj‖-ˌlaʊndʒ/ *n, Br* a room having a large glazed area placed to admit much sunlight

sunny /ˈsuni‖ˈsʌnɪ/ *adj* **1** bright with sunshine **2** cheerful, optimistic <*a ~ disposition*> **3** exposed to or warmed by the sun – **sunnily** *adv*, **sunniness** *n*

ˈsunˌrise /-ˌriez‖-ˌraɪz/ *n* (the time of) the rising of the topmost part of the sun above the horizon as a result of the rotation of the earth

ˈsunˌroof /-ˌroohf‖-ˌruːf/ *n* a motor-car roof having an opening or removable panel

sunset /ˈsunsit, -ˌset‖ˈsʌnsɪt, -ˌset/ *n* (the time of) the descent of the topmost part of the sun below the horizon as a result of the rotation of the earth

ˈsunˌshade /-ˌshayd‖-ˌʃeɪd/ *n* sthg used as a protection from the sun's rays: e g **a** a parasol **b** an awning

ˈsunˌshine /-ˌshien‖-ˌʃaɪn/ *n* the sun's light or direct rays – **sunshiny** *adj*

ˈsunˌspot /-ˌspot‖-ˌspɒt/ *n* a transient dark marking on the visible surface of the sun caused by a relatively cooler area

ˈsunˌstroke /-ˌstrohk‖-ˌstrəʊk/ *n* heatstroke caused by direct exposure to the sun

ˈsunˌtan /-ˌtan‖-ˌtæn/ *n* a browning of the skin from exposure to the sun

ˈsunˌtrap /-ˌtrap‖-ˌtræp/ *n* a sheltered place that receives a large amount of sunshine

¹sup /sup‖sʌp/ *vb* **-pp-** *chiefly dial* to drink (liquid) in small mouthfuls

²sup *n, chiefly dial* a mouthful, esp of liquid; a sip

³sup *vi* **-pp- 1** to eat the evening meal **2** to make one's supper – + *on* or *off*

¹super /ˈs(y)oohpə‖ˈs(j)uːpə/ *n* **1** a superfine grade or extra large size **2** a police or other superintendent – infml

²super *adj* – used as a general term of approval; infml <*a ~ time*>

super- /s(y)oohpə-‖s(j)uːpə-/ *prefix* **1a(1)** higher in quantity, quality, or degree than; more than <super*human*> **a(2)** in addition; extra <super*tax*> **b(1)** exceeding or so as to exceed a norm <super*heat*> **b(2)** to an excessive degree <super*subtle*> **c** surpassing all or most others of its kind (e g in size or power) <super*tanker*> **2** situated or placed above, on, or at the top of <super*lunary*> **3** having (the specified atom or radical) present in an unusually large proportion <super*phosphate*> **4** constituting a more inclusive category of <super*family*> **5** superior in status, title, or position <super*power*>

superabundant /ˌsoohpərəˈbund(ə)nt, ˌsyooh-‖ˌsuːpərəˈbʌnd(ə)nt, ˌsjuː-/ *adj* more than ample; excessive – **superabundance** *n*, **superabundantly** *adv*

ˌsuperˈannuate /-ˈanyooayt‖-ˈænjʊeɪt/ *vt* **1** to make or declare obsolete or out-of-date **2** to retire on a pension, esp because of age or infirmity – **superannuation** *n*

ˌsuperˈannuated *adj* incapacitated or disqualified for work, use, or continuance by advanced age: e g **a** obsolete **b** retired on a pension

superb /s(y)oohˈpuhb‖s(j)uːˈpɜːb/ *adj* **1** marked by grandeur or magnificence **2** of excellent quality <*the meal was* ~> – **superbly** *adv*, **superbness** *n*

ˈsuperˌcharge /-ˌchahj‖-ˌtʃɑːdʒ/ *vt* **1** to charge greatly or excessively (e g with energy or tension) <~d *rhetoric*> **2** to supply a charge to (e g an engine) at a pressure higher than that of the surrounding atmosphere – **supercharge** *n*

ˈsuperˌcharger *n* a device supplying fuel or air to an internal-combustion engine at a pressure higher than normal for greater efficiency

ˌsuperˈcilious /-ˈsili·əs‖-ˈsɪlɪəs/ *adj* coolly disdainful [Latin *superciliosus*, fr *supercilium* eyebrow, haughtiness, fr *super* over, above + *cilium* eyelid] – **superciliously** *adv*, **superciliousness** *n*

ˌsuperˌconducˈtivity /-ˌkondukˈtivəti‖-ˌkɒndʌkˈtɪvətɪ/ *n* a complete disappearance of electrical resistance in various metals and alloys at temperatures near absolute zero – **superconducting** *adj*, **superconductive** *adj*, **superconductor** *n*

ˈsuperˌego /-ˌeegoh, -egoh‖-ˌiːgəʊ, ˌegəʊ/ *n*

the one of the 3 divisions of the mind in psychoanalytic theory that is only partly conscious, reflects social rules, and functions as a conscience to reward and punish

ˌsuperˈficial /-ˈfish(ə)l‖-ˈfɪʃ(ə)l/ *adj* **1a** of a surface **b** not penetrating below the surface <~ *wounds*> **2a** not thorough or profound; shallow **b** apparent rather than real <~ *differences*> – **superficially** *adv*, **superficialness** *n*, **superficiality** *n*

ˌsuperˈficies /-ˈfisheez‖-ˈfɪʃi:z/ *n, pl* **superficies 1** a surface **2** the external aspect or appearance of a thing *USE* fml

ˈsuperˌfine /-ˌfien‖-ˌfaɪn/ *adj* **1** of extremely fine size or texture <~ *toothbrush bristles*> **2** *esp of merchandise* of high quality or grade

ˌsuperˈfluity /-ˈflooh·əti‖-ˈflu:ətɪ/ *n* **1** an excess; a supply exceeding what is required **2** sthg unnecessary or superfluous

superfluous /s(y)oohˈpuhfloo·əs‖s(j)u:ˈpɜ:flʊəs/ *adj* exceeding what is sufficient or necessary

ˌsuperˈhuman /-ˈhyoohmən‖-ˈhju:mən/ *adj* **1** being above the human; divine <~ *beings*> **2** exceeding normal human power, size, or capability <*a* ~ *effort*> – **superhumanly** *adv*, **superhumanness, superhumanity** *n*

ˌsuperimˈpose /-imˈpohz‖-ɪmˈpəʊz/ *vt* to place or lay over or above sthg – **superimposable** *adj*, **superimposition** *n*

ˌsuperinˈtend /-inˈtend‖-ɪnˈtend/ *vt* to be in charge of; direct

ˌsuperinˈtendent /-inˈtend(ə)nt‖-ɪnˈtend(ə)nt/ *n* **1** one who supervises or manages sthg **2** a British police officer ranking next above a chief inspector – **superintendent** *adj*

[1]**superior** /s(y)oohˈpiəri·ə‖s(j)u:ˈpɪərɪə/ *adj* **1** situated higher up; upper **2** of higher rank or status **3** indifferent or unyielding to pain, temptation, etc **4a** greater in quality, amount, or worth **b** excellent of its kind **5a** *of an animal or plant part* situated above or at the top of another (corresponding) part **b(1)** *of a calyx* attached to and apparently arising from the ovary **b(2)** *of an ovary* free from and above a floral envelope (e g the calyx) **6** *of a planet* further from the sun than the earth is **7** thinking oneself better than others; supercilious – **superiority** *n*

[2]**superior** *n* **1** a person who is above another in rank or office; *esp* the head of a religious house or order **2** sby or sthg that surpasses another in quality or merit

[1]**superlative** /s(y)oohˈpuhlətiv‖s(j)u:ˈpɜ:lətɪv/ *adj* **1** of or constituting the degree of grammatical comparison expressing an extreme or unsurpassed level or extent **2** surpassing all others; of the highest degree <*he spoke with* ~ *ease*> – **superlatively** *adv*, **superlativeness** *n*

[2]**superlative** *n* **1** the superlative degree or form in a language **2** an exaggerated expression, esp of praise <*talked in* ~s>

ˈsuperman /-man‖-mæn/ *n* a person of extraordinary power or achievements – infml

ˈsuperˌmarket /-ˌmahkit‖-ˌmɑ:kɪt/ *n* a usu large self-service retail shop selling foods and household merchandise

ˌsuperˈnatural /-ˈnach(ə)rəl‖-ˈnætʃ(ə)rəl/ *adj* **1** of an order of existence or an agency (e g a god or spirit) not bound by normal laws of cause and effect **2a** departing from what is usual or normal, esp in nature **b** attributed to an invisible agent (e g a ghost or spirit) – **supernatural** *n*, **supernaturalism** *n*, **supernaturally** *adv*, **supernaturalness** *n*

ˌsuperˈnova /-ˈnohvə‖-ˈnəʊvə/ *n* any of the rarely observed nova outbursts in which the luminosity reaches 100 million times that of the sun

[1]**ˌsuperˈnumerary** /-ˈnyoohmrəri‖-ˈnju:mrərɪ/ *adj* exceeding the usual or stated number <*a* ~ *tooth*>

[2]**supernumerary** *n* **1** a person employed as an extra assistant or substitute **2** an actor employed to play a walk-on

superpower /ˈs(y)oohpəˌpowə‖ˈs(j)u:pəˌpaʊə/ *n* an extremely powerful nation; *specif* one of a very few dominant states in a period when most of the world is divided politically into these states and the states under their influence or control

ˌsuperˈscription /-ˈskripsh(ə)n‖-ˈskrɪpʃ(ə)n/ *n* words written on the surface of, outside, or above sthg else; an inscription

ˌsuperˈsede /-ˈseed‖-ˈsi:d/ *vt* **1** to take the place of (esp sthg inferior or outmoded) <*buses* ~d *trams*> **2** to displace in favour of another; supplant – **superseder** *n*, **supersedure** *n*, **supersession** *n*

ˌsuperˈsonic /-ˈsonik‖-ˈsɒnɪk/ *adj* **1** (using, produced by, or relating to waves or vibrations) having a frequency above the upper threshold of human hearing of about 20,000Hz **2** of, being, or using speeds from 1 to 5 times the speed of sound in air **3** of supersonic aircraft or missiles <*the* ~ *age*> – **supersonically** *adv*

ˌsuperˈstition /-ˈstish(ə)n‖-ˈstɪʃ(ə)n/ *n* **1** a belief or practice resulting from ignorance, fear of the unknown, trust in magic or chance, or a false conception of causation **2** an irrational abject attitude of mind towards the supernatural, nature, or God resulting from superstition – **superstitious** *adj*, **superstitiously** *adv*

ˈsuperˌstructure /-ˌstrukchə‖-ˌstrʌktʃə/ *n* **1a** the part of a building above the ground **b** the structural part of a ship above the main deck **2** an entity or complex based on a more fundamental one – **superstructural** *adj*

ˈsuperˌtax /-ˌtaks‖-ˌtæks/ *n* a tax paid in addition to normal tax by people with high incomes

ˌsuperˈvene /-ˈveen‖-ˈvi:n/ *vi* to happen in a way that interrupts some plan or process – fml – **supervenience** *n*, **supervenient** *adj*, **supervention**

supervise /ˈs(y)oohpəˌviez‖ˈs(j)u:pəˌvaɪz/ *vt* to superintend, oversee – **supervisor** *n*, **supervisory** *adj*, **supervision** *n*

[1]**supine** /ˈs(y)oohˌpien, ˌ-ˈ-‖ˈs(j)u:ˌpaɪn, ˌ-ˈ-/ *adj* **1a** lying on the back or with the face upwards **b** marked by supination **2** mentally or morally lazy; lethargic – **supinely** *adv*, **supineness** *n*

[2]**supine** *n* a Latin verbal noun formed from the stem of the past participle

supper /ˈsupə‖ˈsʌpə/ *n* **1** (the food for) a usu light evening meal or snack **2** a (fund-raising) social affair featuring a supper

supplant /səˈplahnt‖səˈplɑ:nt/ *vt* to take the

place of (another), esp by force or treachery – **supplanter** *n*, **supplantation** *n*

[1]**supple** /'supl‖'sʌpl/ *adj* **1** compliant, often to the point of obsequiousness **2a** capable of easily being bent or folded; pliant **b** able to perform bending or twisting movements with ease and grace; lithe – **suppleness** *n*, **supplely, supply** *adv*

[2]**supple** *vb* to make or become flexible or pliant

[1]**supplement** /'suplimənt‖'sʌplɪmənt/ *n* **1** sthg that completes, adds, or makes good a deficiency, or makes an addition <*dietary* ~s> **2** a part issued to update or extend a book or periodical **3** an angle or arc that when added to a given angle or arc equals 180°

[2]**supplement** /'supliment‖'sʌplɪment/ *vt* to add a supplement to – **supplementer** *n*, **supplementation** *n*

supplementary /,supli'ment(ə)ri‖,sʌplɪ'ment(ə)rɪ/ *adj* **1** additional **2** being or relating to a supplement or an angle that is a supplement

supplementary benefit *n* British social-security benefit paid to those who do not qualify for unemployment benefit

suppliant /'supli·ənt‖'sʌplɪənt/ *adj* humbly imploring or entreating – **suppliant** *n*, **suppliantly** *adv*

supplicant /'suplikənt‖'sʌplɪkənt/ *n or adj* (a) suppliant – **supplicantly** *adv*

supplicate /'suplikayt‖'sʌplɪkeɪt/ *vi* to beg humbly; *esp* to pray to God ~*vt* to ask humbly and earnestly of or for – **supplicatory** *adj*, **supplication** *n*

[1]**supply** /sə'plie‖sə'plaɪ/ *vt* **1** to provide for; satisfy <supplies *a long-felt need*> **2** to provide, furnish – **supplier** *n*

[2]**supply** *n* **1a** the quantity or amount needed or available <*in short* ~ > **b** provisions, stores – usu pl with sing. meaning **2** the act of filling a want or need < ~ *and demand*> **3** the quantities of goods and services offered for sale at a particular time or at one price **4 supply, supply teacher** *Br* a teacher who fills a temporary vacancy

[1]**support** /sə'pawt‖sə'pɔːt/ *vt* **1** to bear, tolerate <*could not* ~ *such behaviour*> **2a(1)** to promote the interests of; encourage **a(2)** to defend as valid or right **a(3)** to argue or vote for < ~s *the Labour Party*> **b(1)** to assist, help **b(2)** to act with (a principal actor or actress) **c** to substantiate, corroborate **3a** to pay the costs of **b** to provide livelihood or subsistence for **4a** to hold up or serve as a foundation or prop for <*steel girders* ~ *the building*> **b** to maintain (a price) at a desired level by purchases or loans; *also* to maintain the price of by purchases or loans – **supportable** *adj*, **supportably** *adv*

[2]**support** *n* **1** supporting or being supported **2** maintenance, sustenance <*without visible means of* ~ > **3** a device that supports sthg **4** *sing or pl in constr* a body of supporters

supporter /sə'pawtə‖sə'pɔːtə/ *n* **1** an adherent or advocate **2** either of 2 figures (e g of men or animals) placed one on each side of a heraldic shield as if holding or guarding it

supporting /sə'pawting‖sə'pɔːtɪŋ/ *adj* **1** that supports <*a* ~ *wall*> **2** of or being a film other than the main feature on a cinema programme

supportive /sə'pawtiv‖sə'pɔːtɪv/ *adj* providing support; *esp* sustaining morale

suppose /sə'pohz‖sə'pəʊz/ *vt* **1a** to lay down tentatively as a hypothesis, assumption, or proposal < ~ *a fire broke out*> < ~ *we wait a bit*> **b(1)** to hold as an opinion; believe **b(2)** to think probable or in keeping with the facts **b(3)** to conjecture, think <*when do you* ~ *he'll arrive?*> **2** to devise for a purpose; intend <*it's* ~d *to cure acne*> **3** to presuppose **4** to allow, permit – used negatively <*you're not* ~d *to go in there*> **5** to expect because of moral, legal, or other obligations <*drivers are* ~d *to wear seat belts*> ***USE*** (*2, 4, & 5*) chiefly in *be supposed to* – **supposable** *adj*

sup'posed *adj* believed or imagined to be such <*her* ~ *wealth*> – **supposedly** *adv*

supposing /sə'pohzing‖sə'pəʊzɪŋ/ *conj* by way of hypothesis

supposition /,supə'zish(ə)n‖,sʌpə'zɪʃ(ə)n/ *n* a hypothesis – **suppositional** *adj*, **suppositionaly** *adv*, **suppositive** *adj*, **suppositively** *adv*

suppository /sə'pozət(ə)ri‖sə'pɒzət(ə)rɪ/ *n* a readily meltable cone or cylinder of medicated material for insertion into a bodily passage or cavity (e g the rectum)

suppress /sə'pres‖sə'pres/ *vt* **1** to put down by authority or force **2** to stop the publication or revelation of **3a** to (deliberately) exclude a thought, feeling, etc from consciousness **b** to hold back, check < ~ed *his impulse to laugh*> **4** to inhibit the growth or development of – **suppressible** *adj*, **suppression** *n*, **suppressive** *adj*, **suppressively** *adv*, **suppressibility** *n*

suppressor /sə'presə‖sə'presə/ *n* an electrical component (e g a capacitor) added to a circuit to suppress oscillations that would otherwise cause radio interference

suppurate /'supyoo,rayt‖'sʌpjʊ,reɪt/ *vi* to form or discharge pus – **suppurative** *adj*, **suppuration** *n*

,supra'national /s(y)oohprə-‖ s(j)uːprə-/ *adj* transcending national boundaries or interests – **supranationalism** *n*, **supranationalist** *n*

su'premacy /s(y)ooh'preməsi‖s(j)uː'preməsɪ/ *n* the state of being supreme; supreme authority, power, or position

supreme /s(y)ooh'preem‖s(j)uː'priːm/ *adj* **1** highest in rank or authority <*the* ~ *commander*> **2** highest in degree or quality – **supremely** *adv*

Supreme Court *n* the highest judicial tribunal in a nation or state

sur- /suh-, sə-‖sɜː-, sə-/ *prefix* above; over; beyond <sur*tax*>

[1]**surcharge** /'suh,chahj‖'sɜː,tʃɑːdʒ/ *vt* **1** to subject to an additional or excessive charge **2** to overprint or mark with a new denomination or surcharge

[2]**surcharge** *n* **1a** an additional tax or cost **b** an extra fare **2** surcharging or being surcharged **3** an overprint; *esp* one on a stamp that alters the denomination

surcoat /'suh,koht‖'sɜː,kəʊt/ *n* an outer coat or cloak; *specif* a loose tunic worn over armour

[1]**surd** /suhd‖sɜːd/ *adj*, *of a speech sound* voiceless

[2]**surd** *n* **1** an irrational root (e g $\sqrt{2}$); *also* an algebraic expression containing irrational roots

<$\sqrt{2} + 5i$ *is a* ~> **2** a surd speech sound

[1]**sure** /shooə, shaw‖ʃʊə, ʃɔː/ *adj* **1** firm, secure **2** reliable, trustworthy **3** assured, confident <*felt* ~ *it was right*> **4** bound, certain <*it's* ~ *to rain*> – **sureness** *n* – **for sure** as a certainty – **to be sure** it must be acknowledged; admittedly

[2]**sure** *adv, chiefly NAm* surely, certainly – infml <*I* ~ *am tired*>

ˌ**sure'fire** /-'fie·ə‖-'faɪə/ *adj* certain to succeed – infml

ˌ**sure'footed** /-'footid‖-'fʊtɪd/ *adj* not liable to stumble or fall – **surefootedly** *adv*, **surefootedness** *n*

'**surely** /-li‖-lɪ/ *adv* **1a** without danger; safely <*slowly but* ~> **b** without doubt; certainly **2** it is to be believed, hoped, or expected that <~ *you like beer*>

surety /'shooəriti‖'ʃʊərɪtɪ/ *n* **1** a guarantee **2** sby who assumes legal liability for the debt, default, or failure in duty (e g appearance in court) of another – **suretyship** *n*

surf /suhf‖sɜːf/ *n* the foam and swell of waves breaking on the shore

[1]**surface** /'suhfis‖'sɜːfɪs/ *n* **1** the external or upper boundary or layer of an object or body **2** (a portion of) the boundary of a three-dimensional object <~ *of a sphere*> **3** the external or superficial aspect of sthg – **on the surface** to all outward appearances; superficially

[2]**surface** *vt* to apply the surface layer to <~ *a road*> ~ *vi* **1** to come to the surface; emerge **2** to wake up; *also* GET UP 1a – infml <*he never* ~s *before 10*> – **surfacer** *n*

[3]**surface** *adj* **1** situated or employed on the surface, esp of the earth or sea **2** lacking depth; superficial

surfboard /'suhfˌbawd‖'sɜːfˌbɔːd/ *n* a usu long narrow buoyant board used in surfing – **surfboard** *vi*, **surfboarder** *n*

'**surfˌboat** /-ˌboht‖-ˌbəʊt/ *n* a boat for use in heavy surf

[1]**surfeit** /'suhfit‖'sɜːfɪt/ *n* **1** an excessive amount **2** excessive indulgence in food, drink, etc

[2]**surfeit** *vt* to fill to excess; satiate – **surfeiter** *n*

surfing /'suhfing‖'sɜːfɪŋ/ *n* the activity or sport of planing on the front part of a wave, esp while standing or lying on a surfboard – **surfer** *n*

[1]**surge** /suhj‖sɜːdʒ/ *vi* **1** to rise and move (as if) in waves or billows <*the crowd* ~d *past her*> <*felt the blood* surging *to her cheeks*> **2** *esp of current or voltage* to rise suddenly to an excessive or abnormal value

[2]**surge** *n* **1** the motion of swelling, rolling, or sweeping forwards like a wave **2** a large rolling wave or succession of waves **3** a short-lived sudden rise of current or voltage in an electrical circuit

surgeon /'suhj(ə)n‖'sɜːdʒ(ə)n/ *n* a medical specialist who practises surgery

surgery /'suhj(ə)ri‖'sɜːdʒ(ə)rɪ/ *n* **1** medicine that deals with diseases and conditions requiring or amenable to operative or manual procedures **2a** the work done by a surgeon **b** OPERATION 3 **3** *Br* (the hours of opening of) a doctor's, dentist's, etc room where patients are advised or treated **4** *Br* a session at which a member of a profession (e g a lawyer) or esp an elected representative (e g an MP) is available for usu informal consultation [Old French *cirurgie, surgerie,* fr Latin *chirurgia,* fr Greek *cheirourgia,* fr *cheirourgos* surgeon, fr *cheir* hand + *ergon* work]

surgical /'suhjikl‖'sɜːdʒɪkl/ *adj* **1a** of surgeons or surgery **b** used in (connection with) surgery <*a* ~ *stocking*> **2** following or resulting from surgery – **surgically** *adv*

surgical spirit *n, Br* a mixture consisting mainly of methylated spirits and used esp as a skin disinfectant

surly /'suhli‖'sɜːlɪ/ *adj* irritably sullen and churlish – **surlily** *adv*, **surliness** *n*

[1]**surmise** /suh'miez‖sɜː'maɪz/ *vt* to infer on scanty evidence; guess – **surmiser** *n*

[2]**surmise** /suh'miez, 'suhmiez‖sɜː'maɪz, 'sɜːmaɪz/ *n* a conjecture or guess – fml

surmount /suh'mownt‖sɜː'maʊnt/ *vt* **1** to overcome, conquer <~ *an obstacle*> **2** to get over or above **3** to stand or lie on the top of – **surmountable** *adj*

surname /'suhnaym‖'sɜːneɪm/ *n* the name shared in common by members of a family – **surname** *vt*

surpass /suh'pahs‖sɜː'pɑːs/ *vt* **1** to go beyond in quality, degree, or performance; exceed **2** to transcend the reach, capacity, or powers of – **surpassable** *adj*

surpassing /suh'pahsing‖sɜː'pɑːsɪŋ/ *adj* greatly exceeding others – **surpassingly** *adv*

surplice /'suhplis‖'sɜːplɪs/ *n* a loose white outer ecclesiastical vestment usu of knee length with large open sleeves

surplus /'suhpləs‖'sɜːpləs/ *n* **1a** the amount in excess of what is used or needed **b** an excess of receipts over disbursements **2** the excess of a company's net worth over the par or stated value of its capital stock – **surplus** *adj*

[1]**surprise** /sə'priez‖sə'praɪz/ *n* **1** an act of taking unawares **2** sthg unexpected or surprising **3** the feeling caused by an unexpected event; astonishment

[2]**surprise** *vt* **1** to attack unexpectedly; *also* to capture by such action **2** to take unawares <*to* ~ *someone in the act*> **3** to fill with wonder or amazement – **surpriser** *n*

surprising /sə'priezing‖sə'praɪzɪŋ/ *adj* causing surprise; unexpected – **surprisingly** *adv*

surreal /sə'riəl‖sə'rɪəl/ *adj* **1** having a dreamlike irrational quality **2** SURREALISTIC 1

surrealism /sə'riəˌliz(ə)m‖sə'rɪəˌlɪz(ə)m/ *n, often cap* a 20th-c movement in art and literature seeking to use the incongruous images formed by the unconscious to transcend reality as perceived by the conscious mind; *also* surrealistic practices or atmosphere – **surrealist** *n or adj*

surrealistic /səˌriə'listik‖səˌrɪə'lɪstɪk/ *adj* **1** of surrealism **2** SURREAL 1 – **surrealistically** *adv*

[1]**surrender** /sə'rendə‖sə'rendə/ *vt* **1a** to hand over to the power, control, or possession of another, esp under compulsion **b** to relinquish; GIVE UP **2** to abandon (oneself) to sthg unrestrainedly ~*vi* to give oneself up into the power of another; yield

[2]**surrender** *n* **1** the act or an instance of surrendering oneself or sthg **2** the voluntary cancellation of an insurance policy by the party insured in return for a payment

surreptitious /ˌsurəpˈtishəs‖ˌsʌrəpˈtɪʃəs/ *adj* done, made, or acquired by stealth; clandestine – **surreptitiously** *adv*, **surreptitiousness** *n*

surrey /ˈsuri‖ˈsʌrɪ/ *n, NAm* a 4-wheeled 2-seat horse-drawn carriage

surrogate /ˈsurəgət‖ˈsʌrəgət/ *n* **1a** a deputy **b** a local judicial officer in the USA who has jurisdiction over probate and the appointment of guardians **2** sthg that serves as a substitute

[1]**surround** /səˈrownd‖səˈraʊnd/ *vt* **1a** to enclose on all sides **b** to be part of the environment of; be present round <~ed *by luxury*> **c** to form a ring round; encircle **2** to cause to be encircled or enclosed by sthg

[2]**surround** *n* a border or edging

surroundings /səˈrowndingz‖səˈraʊndɪŋz/ *n pl* the circumstances, conditions, or objects by which one is surrounded

surtax /ˈsuhtaks‖ˈsɜːtæks/ *n* a graduated income tax formerly imposed in the UK in addition to the normal income tax if one's net income exceeded a specified sum

surveillance /suhˈvayləns, sə-‖sɜːˈveɪləns, sə-/ *n* close watch kept over sby or sthg – **surveillant** *n*

[1]**survey** /suhˈvay, ˈ--‖sɜːˈveɪ, ˈ--/ *vt* **1a** to look over and examine closely **b** to examine the condition of and often give a value for (a building) **2** to determine and portray the form, extent, and position of (e g a tract of land) **3** to view as a whole or from a height <~ed *the panorama below him*>

[2]**survey** /ˈsuhvay‖ˈsɜːveɪ/ *n* a surveying or being surveyed; *also* sthg surveyed

surveyor /səˈvay·ə‖səˈveɪə/ *n* sby whose occupation is surveying land

survival /səˈvievl‖səˈvaɪvl/ *n* **1a** the condition of living or continuing <*the* ~ *of the soul after death*> **b** the continuation of life or existence <*problems of* ~ *in arctic conditions*> **2** sby or sthg that survives, esp after others of its kind have disappeared

survival of the fittest *n* NATURAL SELECTION

survive /səˈviev‖səˈvaɪv/ *vi* to remain alive or in existence; live on <*managed to* ~ *on bread and water*> ~ *vt* **1** to remain alive or in being after the death of <*his son* ~d *him*> **2** to continue to exist or live after <~d *the earthquake*> – **survivable** *adj*, **survivor** *n*, **survivability** *n*

susceptibility /səˌseptəˈbiləti‖səˌseptəˈbɪlətɪ/ *n* **1** being susceptible **2** *pl* feelings, sensibilities **3** the ratio of the magnetization in a substance to the corresponding magnetizing force

susceptible /səˈseptəbl‖səˈseptəbl/ *adj* **1** capable of submitting to an action, process, or operation **2** open, subject, or unresistant to some stimulus, influence, or agency **3** easily moved or emotionally affected; impressionable – **susceptibleness** *n*, **susceptibly** *adv*

[1]**suspect** /ˈsuspekt‖ˈsʌspekt/ *adj* (deserving to be) regarded with suspicion

[2]**suspect** *n* sby who is suspected

[3]**suspect** /səˈspekt‖səˈspekt/ *vt* **1** to be suspicious of; distrust **2** to believe to be guilty without conclusive proof **3** to imagine to be true, likely, or probable

suspend /səˈspend‖səˈspend/ *vt* **1** to debar temporarily from a privilege, office, membership, or employment **2** to make temporarily inoperative <~ *the rules*> **3** to defer till later on certain conditions <*a* ~ed *sentence*> **4** to withhold <~ *judgment*> **5a** to hang, esp so as to be free on all sides **b** to hold immobile in a liquid or air <*dust* ~ed *in the air*>

suspender /səˈspendə‖səˈspendə/ *n* **1** an elasticated band with a fastening device for holding up a sock **2** *Br* any of the fastening devices on a suspender belt **3** *NAm* BRACE 4c – usu pl with sing. meaning

suˈspender ˌbelt *n, Br* a garment consisting of 2 pairs of short straps hanging from a belt or girdle to which are attached fastening devices for holding up a woman's stockings

suspense /səˈspens‖səˈspens/ *n* a state of uncertain expectation as to a decision or outcome – **suspenseful** *adj*

suspension /səˈspensh(ə)n‖səˈspenʃ(ə)n/ *n* **1a** temporary removal from office or privileges **b** temporary withholding or postponement **c** temporary abolishing of a law or rule **d** (the sustaining of) 1 or more notes of a chord held over into the following chord producing a momentary discord **2a** hanging or being hung **b** (the state of or a system consisting of) a solid that is dispersed, but not dissolved, in a solid, liquid, or gas, usu in particles of larger than colloidal size **3** the system of devices supporting the upper part of a vehicle on the axles

suˈspension ˌbridge *n* a type of bridge that has its roadway suspended from 2 or more cables

suspicion /səˈspish(ə)n‖səˈspɪʃ(ə)n/ *n* **1a** suspecting or being suspected <*arrested on* ~ *of spying*> **b** a feeling of doubt or mistrust **2** a slight touch or trace <*just a* ~ *of garlic*>

suspicious /səˈspishəs‖səˈspɪʃəs/ *adj* **1** tending to arouse suspicion; dubious **2** inclined to suspect; distrustful <~ *of strangers*> **3** expressing or indicating suspicion – **suspiciously** *adv*, **suspiciousness** *n*

suss /sus‖sʌs/ *vt, Br* to uncover the truth about – slang

suss out *vt, Br* to investigate, reconnoitre – slang

sustain /səˈstayn‖səˈsteɪn/ *vt* **1** to give support or relief to **2** to provide with sustenance **3** to cause to continue; prolong **4** to support the weight of **5** to buoy up the spirits of **6a** to bear up under; endure **b** to suffer, undergo **7** to allow as valid <*the court* ~ed *the motion*> – **sustainable** *adj*, **sustainer** *n*

sustenance /ˈsustinəns‖ˈsʌstɪnəns/ *n* **1a** means of support, maintenance, or subsistence **b** food, provisions; *also* nourishment **2** sustaining

suttee /ˌsuˈtee, ˈ-ˌ-‖ˌsʌˈtiː, ˈ-ˌ-/ *n* the custom of a Hindu widow willingly being cremated on the funeral pile of her husband; *also* such a widow [Sanskrit *satī* wife who performs suttee, lit., good woman, fr fem of *sat* true, good]

[1]**suture** /ˈsoohchə‖ˈsuːtʃə/ *n* **1a** (a strand or

fibre used in) the sewing together of parts of the living body **b** a stitch made with a suture **2a** the solid join between 2 bones (e g of the skull) **b** a furrow at the junction of animal or plant parts – **sutural** *adj*, **suturally** *adv*

[2]**suture** *vt* to unite, close, or secure with sutures <~ *a wound*>

suzerain /ˈsoohz(ə)rayn‖ˈsuːz(ə)reɪn/ *n* **1** a feudal overlord **2** a dominant state controlling the foreign relations of an internally autonomous vassal state – **suzerainty** *n*

svelte /sfelt, svelt‖sfelt, svelt/ *adj* slender, lithe – **svelteness** *n*

[1]**swab** /swob‖swɒb/ *n* **1** a wad of absorbent material used for applying medication, cleaning wounds, taking bacterial specimens, etc **2** a specimen taken with a swab

[2]**swab** *vt* **-bb- 1** to clean (a wound) with a swab **2** to clean (a surface, esp a deck) by washing (e g with a mop) – often + *down* – **swabber** *n*

swaddle /ˈswodl‖ˈswɒdl/ *vt* **1** to wrap (an infant) in swaddling clothes **2** to swathe, envelop

ˈ**swaddling** ˌ**clothes** /ˈswodling‖ˈswɒdlɪŋ/ *n pl* narrow strips of cloth wrapped round an infant to restrict movement

swaddy /ˈswodi‖ˈswɒdɪ/ *n, chiefly Br informal* a soldier, esp a private

[1]**swag** /swag‖swæg/ *vt* **-gg-** to hang (e g tapestries or curtains) in heavy folds

[2]**swag** *n* **1a** sthg (e g a moulded decoration) hanging in a curve between 2 points **b** a suspended cluster (e g of flowers) **c** an arrangement of fabric hanging in a heavy curve or fold **2** *chiefly Austr* a pack or roll of personal belongings **3** goods acquired, esp by unlawful means; loot – infml

[1]**swagger** /ˈswagə‖ˈswægə/ *vi* to behave in an arrogant or pompous manner; *esp* to walk with an air of overbearing self-confidence or self-satisfaction – **swaggerer** *n*, **swaggeringly** *adv*

[2]**swagger** *n* **1** an act or instance of swaggering **2** arrogant or conceitedly self-assured behaviour

swain /swayn‖sweɪn/ *n* **1** a male admirer or suitor **2** a peasant; *specif* a shepherd – chiefly poetic

[1]**swallow** /ˈswoloh‖ˈswɒləʊ/ *n* any of numerous small long-winged migratory birds noted for their graceful flight, that have a short bill, a forked tail, and feed on insects caught while flying

[2]**swallow** *vt* **1** to take through the mouth and oesophagus into the stomach **2** to envelop, engulf <~ed *up by the shadows*> **3** to accept without question or protest; *also* to believe naively **4** to refrain from expressing or showing **5** to utter indistinctly ~ *vi* **1** to receive sthg into the body through the mouth and oesophagus **2** to perform the action of swallowing sthg, esp under emotional stress – **swallowable** *adj*, **swallower** *n*

[3]**swallow** *n* **1** an act of swallowing **2** an amount that can be swallowed at one time

ˈ**swallow** ˌ**dive** *n, Br* a forward dive executed with the back arched and arms spread sideways

ˈ**swallow**ˌ**tail** /-ˌtayl‖-ˌteɪl/ *n* **1** a deeply forked and tapering tail (e g of a swallow) **2** a tailcoat **3** any of various large butterflies with the hind wing lengthened to resemble a tail – **swallow-tailed** *adj*

swam /swam‖swæm/ *past of* SWIM

swami /ˈswahmi‖ˈswɑːmɪ/ *n* a Hindu ascetic or religious teacher – used as a title

[1]**swamp** /swomp‖swɒmp/ *n* (an area of) wet spongy land sometimes covered with water – **swamp** *adj*, **swampy** *adj*, **swampiness** *n*

[2]**swamp** *vt* **1** to inundate, submerge **2** to overwhelm by an excess of work, difficulties, etc

[1]**swan** /swon‖swɒn/ *n* any of various heavy-bodied long-necked mostly pure white aquatic birds that are larger than geese and are graceful swimmers

[2]**swan** *vi* **-nn-** to wander or travel aimlessly – infml

ˈ**swan** ˌ**dive** *n, NAm* SWALLOW DIVE

[1]**swank** /swangk‖swæŋk/ *vi* to swagger; SHOW OFF – infml

[2]**swank** *n* (one given to) pretentiousness or swagger – infml

swanky /ˈswangki‖ˈswæŋkɪ/ *adj* **1** showy, ostentatious **2** fashionably elegant; smart *USE* infml

swansdown /ˈswonzˌdown‖ˈswɒnzˌdaʊn/ *n* **1** the soft downy feathers of the swan used esp as trimming on articles of dress **2** a heavy cotton flannel that has a thick nap on the face

ˈ**swan** ˌ**song** *n* **1** a song said to be sung by a dying swan **2** a farewell appearance or final work or pronouncement

[1]**swap** /swop‖swɒp/ *vb* **-pp-** *vt* to give in exchange; barter ~*vi* to make an exchange <~ *over to a metric system*> – **swapper** *n*

[2]**swap** *n* **1** the act of exchanging one thing for another **2** sthg exchanged for another

sward /swawd‖swɔːd/ *n* (a piece of ground covered with) a surface of short grass – **swarded** *adj*

swarf /swahf, swawf‖swɑːf, swɔːf/ *n* material (e g metallic particles and abrasive fragments) removed by a cutting or grinding tool

[1]**swarm** /swawm‖swɔːm/ *n* **1a** a colony of honeybees, esp when emigrating from a hive with a queen bee to start a new colony elsewhere **b** a cluster of free-floating or free-swimming single-celled organisms **2** *sing or pl in constr* a group of animate or inanimate things, esp when massing together <~s *of sightseers*>

[2]**swarm** *vi* **1** to collect together and depart from a hive **2** to move or assemble in a crowd **3** to contain a swarm; teem <*streets* ~ing *with cars*> – **swarmer** *n*

[3]**swarm** *vi* to climb, esp with the hands and feet – usu + *up* <~ *up a tree*>

swarthy /ˈswawdhi‖ˈswɔːðɪ/ *adj* of a dark colour, complexion, or cast – **swarthiness** *n*

swashbuckler /ˈswoshˌbuklə‖ˈswɒʃˌbʌklə/ *n* a swaggering adventurer or daredevil

ˈ**swash**ˌ**buckling** /-ˌbukling‖-ˌbʌklɪŋ/ *adj* characteristic of or behaving like a swashbuckler

swastika /ˈswostikə‖ˈswɒstɪkə/ *n* an ancient symbol in the shape of a cross with the ends of the arms extended at right angles in a clockwise or anticlockwise direction [Sanskrit *svastika*, fr *svasti* welfare, fr *su-* well + *asti* he is; fr its being regarded as a good luck symbol]

[1]**swat** /swot‖swɒt/ *vt* **-tt-** to hit with a sharp

slapping blow; *esp* to kill (an insect) with such a blow

²swat *n* **1** a quick crushing blow **2** a swatter

swatch /swoch||swɒtʃ/ *n* a sample piece (e g of fabric)

swath /swawth||swɔːθ/ *n* **1a** a row of cut grain or grass left by a scythe or mowing machine **b** the path cut in 1 passage (e g of a mower) **2** a long broad strip **3** a space cleared as if by a scythe

¹swathe /swaydh||sweɪð/ *vt* **1** to bind or wrap (as if) with a bandage **2** to envelop – **swather** *n*

²swathe *n* a swath

swatter /ˈswotə||ˈswɒtə/ *n* a flyswatter

¹sway /sway||sweɪ/ *vi* **1a(1)** to swing slowly and rhythmically back and forth **a(2)** to walk in a swaying manner **b** to move gently from an upright to a leaning position **2** to fluctuate or alternate between one attitude or position and another ~ *vt* **1** to cause to swing, rock, or oscillate **2a** to exert a controlling influence on **b** to change the opinions of, esp by eloquence or argument **3** to hoist in place <~ *up a mast*> – **swayer** *n*

²sway *n* **1** swaying or being swayed **2a** controlling influence or power **b** rule, dominion

swear /sweə||sweə/ *vb* **swore** /swaw||swɔː/; **sworn** /swawn||swɔːn/ *vt* **1** to utter or take (an oath) solemnly **2a** to assert as true or promise under oath <*a* sworn *affidavit*> **b** to promise emphatically or earnestly <*she* swore *not to be late*> **3a** to administer an oath to **b** to bind by an oath <swore *him to secrecy*> ~ *vi* **1** to take an oath **2** to use profane or obscene language – **swearer** *n* – **swear by** to place great confidence in – **swear to** to have any positive conviction of <*couldn't* swear to *his being the same man*>

swear in *vt* to induct into office by administration of an oath

¹sweat /swet||swet/ *vb* **sweated,** *NAm chiefly* **sweat** *vi* **1** to excrete sweat in visible quantities **2a** to emit or exude moisture <*cheese* ~s *in ripening*> **b** to gather surface moisture as a result of condensation **c** *esp of tobacco* FERMENT 1 **3** to undergo anxiety or tension ~ *vt* **1** to (seem to) emit from pores; exude **2** to get rid of (as if) by sweating <~ *out a fever*> **3a** to cause (e g a patient) to sweat **b** to exact work from under sweatshop conditions **4** to cause to exude or lose moisture: e g **4a** to subject (esp tobacco) to fermentation **b** to cook (e g vegetables) gently in melted fat until the juices run out **5** to heat (e g solder) so as to melt and cause to run, esp between surfaces to unite them; *also* to unite by such means <~ *a pipe joint*> – **sweat blood** to work or worry intensely

²sweat *n* **1** the fluid excreted from the sweat glands of the skin; perspiration **2** moisture gathering in drops on a surface **3a** the state of one sweating <*in a cold* ~> **b** a spell of sweating **4** hard work; drudgery **5** a state of anxiety or impatience *USE* (*4&5*) infml – **no sweat** not a problem or difficulty – infml <*I can do that all right,* no sweat>

ˈsweatˌband /-ˌband||-ˌbænd/ *n* a band of material worn round the head or wrist or inserted in a hat or cap to absorb sweat

ˈsweated *adj* of or produced under a sweatshop system <~ *labour*> <~ *goods*>

sweater /ˈswetə||ˈswetə/ *n* ²JUMPER 1

ˈsweat ˌgland *n* a tubular gland in the skin that secretes sweat through a minute pore on the surface of the skin

sweat out *vt* to endure or wait through the course of

ˈsweat ˌshirt *n* a loose collarless pullover of heavy cotton jersey

ˈsweatˌshop /-ˌshop||-ˌʃɒp/ *n* a place of work in which workers are employed for long hours at low wages and under unhealthy conditions

sweaty /ˈsweti||ˈswetɪ/ *adj* **1** covered with or smelling of sweat **2** causing sweat – **sweatily** *adv*, **sweatiness** *n*

swede /sweed||swiːd/ *n* **1** *cap* a native or inhabitant of Sweden **2** a large type of turnip with edible yellow flesh

Swedish /ˈsweedish||ˈswiːdɪʃ/ *n or adj* (the North Germanic language) of Sweden

¹sweep /sweep||swiːp/ *vb* **swept** /swept||swept/ *vt* **1a** to remove or clean (as if) by brushing **b** to destroy completely; WIPE OUT – usu + *away* **c** to remove or take with a single forceful action <swept *the books off the desk*> **d** to drive or carry along with irresistible force **2** to move through or along with overwhelming speed or violence <*a new craze* ~ing *the country*> **3** to move lightly over with a rapid continuous movement **4** to cover the entire range of <*his eyes* swept *the horizon*> **5** to play a sweep in cricket at ~ *vi* **1a** to clean a surface (as if) by brushing **b** to move swiftly, forcefully, or devastatingly **2** to go with stately or sweeping movements <*she* swept *out of the room*> **3** to move or extend in a wide curve <*the hills* ~ *down to the sea*> **4** to play a sweep in cricket – **sweep someone off his/her feet** to gain immediate and unquestioning support, approval, or acceptance by sby; *esp* to cause sby to fall in love with one – **sweep the board** to win convincingly; win everything (e g in a contest)

²sweep *n* **1a** a long oar **b** a windmill sail **2** a clearing out or away (as if) with a broom **3** a military reconnaissance or attack ranging over a particular area **4a** a curving course or line **b** the compass of a sweeping movement **c** a broad extent <*unbroken* ~ *of woodland*> **5** a sweepstake **6** obliquity with respect to a reference line **7** an attacking stroke in cricket played on one knee with a horizontal bat and designed to send the ball behind the batsman on the leg side

ˈsweepˌback /-ˌbak||-ˌbæk/ *n* the backward slant of an aircraft wing in which the outer portion of the wing is behind the inner portion

sweeper /ˈsweepə||ˈswiːpə/ *n* a defensive player in soccer who plays behind the backs as a last line of defence before the goalkeeper

sweeping /ˈsweeping||ˈswiːpɪŋ/ *adj* **1** extending in a wide curve or over a wide area **2a** extensive, wide-ranging <~ *reforms*> **b** marked by wholesale and indiscriminate inclusion – **sweepingly** *adv*, **sweepingness** *n*

ˈsweepings *n pl* refuse, rubbish, etc collected by sweeping

ˈsweepˌstake /-ˌstayk||-ˌsteɪk/ *n* **1** a race or

contest in which the entire prize is awarded to the winner **2** a lottery ***USE*** often pl with sing. meaning but sing. or pl in constr

[1]**sweet** /sweet||swiːt/ *adj* **1a** being or inducing the one of the 4 basic taste sensations that is typically induced by sucrose **b** *of a beverage* containing a sweetening ingredient; not dry **2a** delightful, charming **b** marked by gentle good humour or kindliness **c** fragrant **d** pleasing to the ear or eye **3** much loved **4a** not sour, rancid, decaying, or stale **b** not salt or salted; fresh <~ *butter*> <~ *water*> **c** free from noxious gases and smells **d** free from excess of acid, sulphur, or corrosive salts <~ *petroleum*> – **sweetish** *adj*, **sweetly** *adv*, **sweetness** *n*

[2]**sweet** *n* **1** a darling or sweetheart **2** *Br* **2a** dessert **b** a toffee, truffle, or other small piece of confectionery prepared with (flavoured or filled) chocolate or sugar; *esp* one made chiefly of (boiled and crystallized) sugar

ˌ**sweet-and-ˈsour** *adj* seasoned with a sauce containing sugar and vinegar or lemon juice <~ *pork*>

ˈ**sweetˌbread** /-ˌbred||-ˌbred/ *n* the pancreas or thymus of a young animal (e g a calf) used for food

ˈ**sweetˌbrier** /-ˌbrie·ə||-ˌbraɪə/ *n* an Old World rose with stout prickles and white to deep rosy pink flowers

ˈ**sweet ˌcorn** *n* (the young kernels of) a maize with kernels that contain a high percentage of sugar and are eaten as a vegetable when young and milky

sweeten /ˈsweet(ə)n||ˈswiːt(ə)n/ *vt* **1** to make (more) sweet **2** to soften the mood or attitude of **3** to make less painful or trying **4** to free from sthg undesirable; *esp* to remove sulphur compounds from <~ *natural gas*> ~*vi* to become sweet – **sweetener** *n*

ˈ**sweetˌheart** /-ˌhaht||-ˌhɑːt/ *n* a darling, lover

sweetie /ˈsweeti||ˈswiːtɪ/ *n* **1** SWEET 1 **2** *Br* SWEET 2b ***USE*** infml

ˈ**sweetˌmeat** /-ˌmeet||-ˌmiːt/ *n* a crystallized fruit, sugar-coated nut, or other sweet or delicacy rich in sugar

sweet pea *n* a leguminous garden plant with slender climbing stems and large fragrant flowers

sweet pepper *n* (a pepper plant bearing) a large mild thick-walled capsicum fruit

sweet potato *n* (the large sweet edible tuberous root of) a tropical climbing plant of the bindweed family with purplish flowers

sweet tooth *n* a craving or fondness for sweet food

sweet william *n, often cap W* a widely cultivated Eurasian pink with small (mottled or striped) white to deep red or purple flowers

[1]**swell** /swel||swel/ *vb* **swollen** /ˈswohlən||ˈswəʊlən/, **swelled** *vi* **1a** to expand gradually beyond a normal or original limit **b** to be distended or puffed up <*her ankle is badly* swollen> **c** to curve outwards or upwards; bulge **2** to become charged with emotion ~ *vt* **1** to affect with a powerful emotion **2** to increase the size, number, or intensity of

[2]**swell** *n* **1** a rounded protuberance or bulge **2** a (massive) surge of water, often continuing beyond or after its cause (e g a gale) **3a** swelling **b(1)** a gradual increase and decrease of the loudness of a musical sound **b(2)** a device used in an organ for governing loudness **b(3)** *also* **swell organ** a division of an organ in which the pipes are enclosed in a box with shutters that open or shut to regulate the volume of sound **4** a person of fashion or high social position – infml

[3]**swell** *adj, chiefly NAm* excellent

swelling /ˈsweling||ˈswelɪŋ/ *n* **1** sthg swollen; *specif* an abnormal bodily protuberance or enlargement **2** being swollen

[1]**swelter** /ˈsweltə||ˈsweltə/ *vi* to suffer, sweat, or be faint from heat

[2]**swelter** *n* a state of oppressive heat

sweltering /ˈswelt(ə)ring||ˈswelt(ə)rɪŋ/ *adj* oppressively hot – **swelteringly** *adv*

ˌ**swept-ˈback** /swept||swept/ *adj* possessing sweepback

swerve /swuhv||swɜːv/ *vb* to (cause to) turn aside abruptly from a straight line or course – **swerve** *n*

[1]**swift** /swift||swɪft/ *adj* **1** (capable of) moving at great speed **2** occurring suddenly or within a very short time **3** quick to respond; ready – **swift** *adv*, **swiftly** *adv*, **swiftness** *n*

[2]**swift** *n* **1** any of several lizards that run swiftly **2** any of numerous dark-coloured birds noted for their fast darting flight in pursuit of insects, that superficially resemble swallows

[1]**swig** /swig||swɪg/ *n* a quantity drunk in 1 draught – infml

[2]**swig** *vb* **-gg-** to drink (sthg) in long draughts – infml – **swigger** *n*

[1]**swill** /swil||swɪl/ *vt* **1** to wash, esp by flushing with water **2** to drink greedily ~*vi* to drink or eat freely or greedily – **swiller** *n*

[2]**swill** *n* **1** a semiliquid food for animals (e g pigs) composed of edible refuse mixed with water or skimmed or sour milk **2** RUBBISH 1

[1]**swim** /swim||swɪm/ *vb* **-mm-; swam** /swam||swæm/; **swum** /swum||swʌm/ *vi* **1** to propel oneself in water by bodily movements (e g of the limbs, fins, or tail) **2** to surmount difficulties; not go under <*sink or* ~> **3** to become immersed (as if) in a liquid <*liver* ~ming *in gravy*> **4** to have a floating or dizzy effect or sensation ~ *vt* **1a** to cross by swimming **b** to use (a stroke) in swimming **2** to cause to swim or float – **swimmer** *n* – **swim against the tide** to move counter to the prevailing or popular trend

[2]**swim** *n* **1** an act or period of swimming **2a** an area frequented by fish **b** the main current of events <*be in the* ~>

swimming /ˈswiming||ˈswɪmɪŋ/ *adj* capable of, adapted to, or used in or for swimming

ˈ**swimming ˌbath** *n, Br* a usu indoor swimming pool – often pl with sing. meaning but sing. or pl in constr

ˈ**swimming ˌcostume** *n, chiefly Br* a close-fitting usu woman's garment for swimming

ˈ**swimmingly** /-li||-lɪ/ *adv* very well; splendidly – infml <*everything went* ~>

ˈ**swimming ˌpool** *n* an artificial pool made for people to swim in

[1]**swindle** /ˈswindl||ˈswɪndl/ *vb* to obtain property or take property from by fraud – **swindler** *n*

[2]**swindle** *n* a fraud, deceit

swine /swien‖swaɪn/ *n, pl* **swine** **1** PIG 1a – used esp technically or in literature **2** a contemptible person **3** sthg unpleasant <*a* ~ *of a job*> *USE* (*2 & 3*) infml – **swinish** *adj*

ˈ**swine,herd** /-ˌhuhd‖-ˌhɜːd/ *n* sby who tends pigs

[1]**swing** /swing‖swɪŋ/ *vb* **swung** /swung‖swʌŋ/ *vt* **1a** to cause to move vigorously through a wide arc or circle **b(1)** to cause to pivot or rotate **b(2)** to cause to face or move in another direction <~ *the car into a side road*> **c** to make (a delivery of a cricket ball) swing **2** to suspend so as to allow to sway <*to* ~ *a hammock*> **3** to play or sing (e g a melody) in the style of swing music **4a** to influence decisively <~ *a lot of votes*> **b** to manage; BRING ABOUT <*wasn't able to* ~ *that trip to Vienna*> ~ *vi* **1a** to move freely to and fro, esp when hanging from an overhead support **b** *of a bowled ball* to deviate from a straight path while travelling through the air before reaching the batsman **2** to die by hanging **3a** to turn (as if) on a hinge or pivot <*she* swung *on her heel*> **b** to convey oneself by grasping a fixed support **4** to play or sing with a lively compelling rhythm; *specif* to play swing music **5** to shift or fluctuate between 2 moods, opinions, etc **6a** to move along rhythmically <~ing *down the street*> **b** to start up in a smooth rapid manner <*ready to* ~ *into action*> **7** to engage freely in sex, specif wife-swapping – slang *USE* (*vt 4; vi 2*) infml – **swingable** *adj*, **swinger** *n*

[2]**swing** *n* **1a(1)** a stroke or blow delivered with a sweeping arm movement **a(2)** a sweeping or rhythmic movement of the body or a bodily part **b** the regular movement of a freely suspended object to and fro along an arc **c** a steady vigorous rhythm or action <*soon got into the* ~ *of it*> **d(1)** a trend towards a high or low point in a fluctuating cycle (e g of business activity) **d(2)** a shift from one condition, form, position, or object of attention or favour to another **2** the progression of an activity; course <*the work is in full* ~> **3** the arc or range through which sthg swings <*a* ~ *of 10% to Labour*> **4** a suspended seat on which one may swing to and fro **5** jazz played usu by a large dance band and characterized by a steady lively rhythm, simple harmony, and a basic melody often submerged in improvisation – **swing** *adj*

swingeing, **swinging** /ˈswinjing‖ˈswɪndʒɪŋ/ *adj, chiefly Br* severe, drastic <~ *cuts in public expenditure*>

swinging /ˈswing·ing‖ˈswɪŋɪŋ/ *adj* lively and up-to-date – no longer in vogue

ˌ**swing-ˈwing** *adj* of or being an aircraft having movable wings giving the best angles of sweepback for both low and high speeds

[1]**swipe** /swiep‖swaɪp/ *n* a strong sweeping blow – infml

[2]**swipe** *vi* to strike or hit out with a sweeping motion ~ *vt* **1** to strike or wipe with a sweeping motion **2** to steal, pilfer *USE* infml

[1]**swirl** /swuhl‖swɜːl/ *n* **1** a whirling mass or motion **2** a twisting shape, mark, or pattern – **swirly** *adj*

[2]**swirl** *vi* to move in eddies or whirls – **swirlingly** *adv*

[1]**swish** /swish‖swɪʃ/ *vb* to move with (the sound of) a swish <*windscreen wipers* ~ing> <*a cow* ~ing *its tail*> – **swisher** *n*, **swishingly** *adv*

[2]**swish** *n* **1a** a sound as of a whip cutting the air **b** a light sweeping or brushing sound **2** a swishing movement – **swishy** *adj*

[3]**swish** *adj* smart, fashionable – infml

[1]**Swiss** /swis‖swɪs/ *n, pl* **Swiss** a native or inhabitant of Switzerland

[2]**Swiss** *adj* (characteristic) of Switzerland

ˌ**Swiss ˈchard** *n* chard

ˌ**Swiss ˈroll** *n* a thin sheet of sponge cake spread with jam and rolled up

[1]**switch** /swich‖swɪtʃ/ *n* **1** a slender flexible twig or rod **2** a shift or change from one to another **3** a tuft of long hairs at the end of the tail of an animal (e g a cow) **4** a device for making, breaking, or changing the connections in an electrical circuit **5** a tress of hair attached to augment a hairstyle **6** *NAm* railway points

[2]**switch** *vt* **1** to strike or beat (as if) with a switch **2** to whisk, lash **3** to shift, change **4a** to shift to another electrical circuit by means of a switch **b** to operate an electrical switch so as to turn *off* or *on* **5** *chiefly NAm* to turn from one railway track to another ~ *vi* **1** to lash from side to side **2** to change, shift – **switchable** *adj*, **switcher** *n*

ˈ**switch,back** /-ˌbak‖-ˌbæk/ *n* **1** a zigzag road or railway in a mountainous region **2** *chiefly Br* any of various amusement rides; *esp* ROLLER COASTER

ˈ**switch,blade** /-ˌblayd‖-ˌbleɪd/ *n, NAm* a flick-knife

ˈ**switch,board** /-ˌbawd‖-ˌbɔːd/ *n* an apparatus consisting of a panel or frame on which switching devices are mounted; *specif* an arrangement for the manual switching of telephone calls

ˌ**switched-ˈon** *adj* alive to experience; *also* swinging – infml

ˈ**switch,gear** /-ˌgiə‖-ˌgɪə/ *n* equipment used for the switching of esp large electrical currents

ˈ**switchman** /-mən‖-mən/ *n* sby who works a switch (e g on a railway)

ˈ**switch,over** /-ˌohvə‖-ˌəʊvə/ *n* a conversion to a different system or method

[1]**swivel** /ˈswivl‖ˈswɪvl/ *n* a device joining 2 parts so that the moving part can pivot freely

[2]**swivel** *vb* **-ll-** (*NAm* **-l-**, **-ll-**) to turn (as if) on a swivel

swiz /swiz‖swɪz/ *n, pl* **-zz-** *Br* sthg that does not live up to one's hopes or expectations – infml

[1]**swizzle** /ˈswizl‖ˈswɪzl/ *n, Br* a swiz – infml

[2]**swizzle** *vt* to mix or stir (as if) with a swizzle stick

ˈ**swizzle ,stick** *n* a thin rod used to stir mixed drinks

swollen /ˈswohlən‖ˈswəʊlən/ *past part of* SWELL

[1]**swoon** /swoohn‖swuːn/ *vi* to faint – **swooningly** *adv*

[2]**swoon** *n* a partial or total loss of consciousness

[1]**swoop** /swoohp‖swuːp/ *vi* to make a sudden attack or downward sweep ~ *vt* to carry off abruptly; snatch

[2]**swoop** *n* an act of swooping <*arrested in a*

drug-squad ~ >
swop /swop‖swɒp/ *vb or n* **-pp-** (to) swap
sword /sawd‖sɔːd/ *n* **1** a cutting or thrusting weapon having a long usu sharp-pointed and sharp-edged blade **2** the use of force < *the pen is mightier than the* ~ – E G Bulwer-Lytton> **3** death caused (as if) by a sword – usu + *the* **4** sthg (e g the beak of a swordfish) that resembles a sword – **swordlike** *adj*
ˈsword ˌdance *n* a dance performed over, round, or brandishing swords; *esp* a Scottish-Highland solo dance usu performed in the angles formed by 2 swords crossed on the ground – **sword dancer** *n*
ˈswordˌfish /-ˌfish‖-ˌfɪʃ/ *n* a very large oceanic food fish that has a long swordlike beak formed by the bones of the upper jaw
ˌsword of ˈDamocles /ˈdaməkleez‖ˈdæməkliːz/ *n, often cap S* an impending disaster [fr the legend of the sword suspended by a single hair over the head of Damocles, a courtier of ancient Syracuse, as a reminder of the insecurity of a tyrant's happiness]
ˈswordˌplay /-ˌplay‖-ˌpleɪ/ *n* the art, skill, or practice of wielding a sword – **swordplayer** *n*
swordsman /ˈsawdzmən‖ˈsɔːdzmən/ *n* one skilled in swordplay
ˈswordsmanˌship /-ship‖-ʃɪp/ *n* swordplay
ˈswordˌstick /-ˌstik‖-ˌstɪk/ *n* a walking stick in which a sword blade is concealed
swore /swaw‖swɔː/ *past of* SWEAR
sworn /swawn‖swɔːn/ *past part of* SWEAR
¹swot /swot‖swɒt/ *n, Br* one who studies hard or excessively – infml
²swot *vb* **-tt-** *Br vi* to study hard ~*vt* to study (a subject) intensively – usu + *up USE* infml
swum /swum‖swʌm/ *past part of* SWIM
swung /swung‖swʌŋ/ *past of* SWING
sybarite /ˈsibəriet‖ˈsɪbəraɪt/ *n, often cap* a voluptuary, sensualist [*Sybaris*, ancient city in Italy whose inhabitants lived in notorious luxury] – **sybaritism** *n*, **sybaritic** *adj*
sycamore /ˈsikəˌmaw‖ˈsɪkəˌmɔː/ *n* **1** a tree of Egypt and Asia Minor that is the sycamore of Scripture and has a sweet edible fruit **2** a Eurasian maple widely planted as a shade tree **3** *NAm* ²PLANE
sycophant /ˈsikəˌfant‖ˈsɪkəˌfænt/ *n* a self-seeking flatterer; a toady – **sycophancy** *n*, **sycophant** *adj*, **sycophantic** *adj*
¹syllabic /siˈlabik‖sɪˈlæbɪk/ *adj* **1** constituting (the nucleus of) a syllable **2** enunciated with separation of syllables **3** of or constituting a type of verse (e g some French poetry) in which the metre is based on a count of syllables – **syllabically** *adv*
²syllabic *n* a syllabic character or sound
syllabify /siˈlabifie‖sɪˈlæbɪfaɪ/ *vt* to form or divide into syllables – **syllabification** *n*
syllable /ˈsiləbl‖ˈsɪləbl/ *n* (a letter or symbol representing) an uninterruptible unit of spoken language that usu consists of 1 vowel sound either alone or with a consonant sound preceding or following [Latin *syllaba*, fr Greek *syllabē*, fr *syllambanein* to gather together, fr *syn* with + *lambanein* to take] – **syllabled** *adj*
syllabub, **sillabub** /ˈsiləbub‖ˈsɪləbʌb/ *n* a cold dessert usu made by curdling sweetened cream or milk with wine, cider, or other acidic liquid
syllabus /ˈsiləbəs‖ˈsɪləbəs/ *n, pl* **syllabi** /-bie‖-baɪ/, **syllabuses** a summary of a course of study or of examination requirements
syllogism /ˈsiləˌjiz(ə)m‖ˈsɪləˌdʒɪz(ə)m/ *n* a pattern of deductive reasoning consisting of 2 premises and a conclusion (e g 'all men are mortal; Socrates is a man; therefore Socrates is mortal') – **syllogistic** *adj*
sylph /silf‖sɪlf/ *n* a slender graceful woman or girl – **sylphlike** *adj*
sylvan, **silvan** /ˈsilvən‖ˈsɪlvən/ *adj* **1** of, located in, or characteristic of the woods or forest **2** full of woods or trees
sym- – see SYN-
symbiosis /ˌsimbiˈohsis, -bie-‖ˌsɪmbɪˈəʊsɪs, -baɪ-/ *n, pl* **symbioses** /-seez‖-siːz/ the living together of 2 dissimilar organisms in intimate association (to their mutual benefit) – **symbiotic** *adj*
symbol /ˈsimbl‖ˈsɪmbl/ *n* **1** sthg that stands for or suggests sthg else by reason of association, convention, etc **2** a sign used in writing or printing to represent operations, quantities, elements, relations, or qualities in a particular field (e g chemistry or music) – **symbology** *n*
symbolic /simˈbolik‖sɪmˈbɒlɪk/, **symbolical** /-kl‖-kl/ *adj* of, using, constituting, or exhibiting a symbol or symbols – **symbolically** *adv*
symbolism /ˈsimbəˌliz(ə)m‖ˈsɪmbəˌlɪz(ə)m/ *n* **1** the literary and artistic mode of expression of the symbolists **2** a system of symbols – **symbolistic** *adj*
symbolist /ˈsimbəlist‖ˈsɪmbəlɪst/ *n* **1** one who employs symbols or symbolism **2** any of a group of esp 19th-c French writers and artists who used symbols to convey a subjective view of reality and esp immaterial or intangible states or truths (e g by exploiting the nonliteral figurative resources of language) – **symbolist** *adj*
symbol·ize, **-ise** /ˈsimbəˌliez‖ˈsɪmbəˌlaɪz/ *vt* **1** to serve as a symbol of **2** to represent, express, or identify by a symbol – **symbolization** *n*
symmetrical /siˈmetrikl‖sɪˈmetrɪkl/, **symmetric** /siˈmetrik‖sɪˈmetrɪk/ *adj* **1a** having the same proportions, design, shape, etc on both sides; *specif* capable of division by a longitudinal plane into similar halves **b** *of a flower* having the same number of members in each whorl of floral leaves **2** *of a chemical compound* having symmetry in the molecular structure – **symmetrically** *adv*
symmetry /ˈsimitri‖ˈsɪmɪtrɪ/ *n* **1** (beauty of form arising from) balanced proportions **2** the property of being symmetrical; *esp* correspondence in size, shape, and relative position of parts on opposite sides of a dividing line or median plane or about a centre or axis SYMMETRY – **symmetrize** *vt*
sympathetic /ˌsimpəˈthetik‖ˌsɪmpəˈθetɪk/ *adj* **1** existing or operating through an affinity, interdependence, or mutual association **2** appropriate to one's mood or temperament; congenial **3** given to or arising from compassion and sensitivity to others' feelings < *a* ~ *gesture*> **4** favourably inclined < *not* ~ *to the idea*> **5** of, being, mediated by, or acting on (the nerves of) the sympathetic nervous system **6** relating to musical sounds produced, or strings sounded, by

sympathetic vibration – **sympathetically** *adv*

sympath·ize, -ise /'simpəthiez‖'sɪmpəθaɪz/ *vi* **1** to react or respond in sympathy **2** to share in distress or suffering; commiserate – **sympathizer** *n*

sympathy /'simpəthi‖'sɪmpəθɪ/ *n* **1a** relationship between people or things in which each is simultaneously affected in a similar way **b** unity or harmony in action or effect **2a** inclination to think or feel alike **b** tendency to favour or support – often pl with sing. meaning <*Tory* sympathies> **3** (the expression of) pity or compassion

symphonic /sim'fonik‖sɪm'fɒnɪk/ *adj* relating to or having the form or character of a symphony <~ *music*> – **symphonically** *adv*

symphonic poem *n* an extended orchestral composition, based on a legend, tale, etc and usu freer in form than a symphony

symphony /'simfəni‖'sɪmfənɪ/ *n* **1a** a usu long and complex sonata for symphony orchestra **b** a composition of similar proportions **2** sthg of great harmonious complexity or variety <*the room was a* ~ *in blue*> **3** *chiefly NAm* SYMPHONY ORCHESTRA

symphony orchestra *n* a large orchestra of wind instruments, strings, and percussion that plays symphonic works

symposium /sim'pohzyəm, -zi·əm‖sɪm'pəʊzjəm, -zɪəm/ *n, pl* **symposia** /-zyə, -zi·ə‖-zjə, -zɪə/, **symposiums** **1** a party (e g after a banquet in ancient Greece) with music and conversation **2a** a formal meeting at which several specialists deliver short addresses on a topic **b** a published collection of opinions on a subject [Latin, fr Greek *symposion*, fr *sympinein* to drink together, fr *syn* with + *pinein* to drink]

symptom /'simptəm‖'sɪmptəm/ *n* **1** sthg giving (subjective) evidence or indication of disease or physical disturbance **2** sthg that indicates the existence of sthg else [Late Latin *symptoma*, fr Greek *symptōma* happening, attribute, symptom, fr *sympiptein* to happen, fr *syn* with + *piptein* to fall] – **symptomless** *adj*, **symptomatology** *n*

symptomatic /ˌsimptə'matik‖ˌsɪmptə'mætɪk/ *adj* **1** being a symptom of a disease **2** concerned with, affecting, or acting on symptoms <~ *treatment for influenza*> **3** characteristic, indicative – **symptomatically** *adv*

syn-, sym- *prefix* with; along with; together; at the same time <sym*pathy*> <syn*thesis*>

synagogue /'sinəgog‖'sɪnəgɒg/ *n* (the house of worship and communal centre of) a Jewish congregation – **synagogal** *adj*

synapse /'sienaps‖'saɪnæps/ *n* the point (between 2 nerves) across which a nervous impulse is transmitted – **synaptic** *adj*

sync *also* **synch** /singk‖sɪŋk/ *n* synchronization, synchronism <*out of* ~> – infml

synchromesh /'singkrəˌmesh‖'sɪŋkrəˌmeʃ/ *adj* designed for effecting synchronized gear changing – **synchromesh** *n*

synchron·ize, -ise /'singkrəˌniez‖'sɪŋkrəˌnaɪz/ *vi* to happen at the same time ~ *vt* **1** to arrange so as to indicate coincidence or coexistence **2** to make synchronous in operation <~ *watches*> **3** to make (sound) exactly simultaneous with the action in a film or a television programme – **synchronizer** *n*, **synchronization** *n*

synchrotron /'singkrətron‖'sɪŋkrətrɒn/ *n* an apparatus that imparts very high speeds to charged particles by combining a high-frequency electric field and a low-frequency magnetic field

syncopate /'singkəˌpayt‖'sɪŋkəˌpeɪt/ *vt* to modify or affect (musical rhythm) by syncopation – **syncopator** *n*

syncopation /ˌsingkə'paysh(ə)n‖ˌsɪŋkə'peɪʃ(ə)n/ *n* (a rhythm or passage characterized by) a temporary displacement of the regular metrical accent in music caused typically by stressing the weak beat – **syncopative** *adj*

syncope /'singkəpi‖'sɪŋkəpɪ/ *n* **1** temporary loss of consciousness; fainting **2** the dropping of 1 or more sounds or letters in a word (e g in *fo'c'sle* for *forecastle*) – **syncopal** *adj*

syndic /'sindik‖'sɪndɪk/ *n* an agent who transacts business for a university or corporation

syndicalism /'sindiklˌiz(ə)m‖'sɪndɪklˌɪz(ə)m/ *n* **1** a revolutionary doctrine according to which workers should seize control of the economy and the government by direct means (e g a general strike) **2** a system of economic organization in which industries are owned and managed by the workers – **syndical** *adj*, **syndicalist** *adj or n*

[1]**syndicate** /'sindikət‖'sɪndɪkət/ *n* **1a** the office of a syndic **b** *sing or pl in constr* a council or body of syndics **2** *sing or pl in constr* a group of people or concerns who combine to carry out a particular transaction (e g buying or renting property) or to promote some common interest **3** a business concern that supplies material for simultaneous publication in many newspapers or periodicals

[2]**syndicate** /'sindiˌkayt‖'sɪndɪˌkeɪt/ *vt* **1** to form into or manage as a syndicate **2** to sell (e g a cartoon) to a syndicate for simultaneous publication in many newspapers or periodicals – **syndicator** *n*, **syndication** *n*

syndrome /'sindrohm‖'sɪndrəʊm/ *n* **1** a group of signs and symptoms that occur together and characterize a particular (medical) abnormality **2** a set of concurrent emotions, actions, etc that usu form an identifiable pattern [Greek *syndromē* combination, syndrome, fr *syn* with + *dramein* to run]

synod /'sinəd, 'sinod‖'sɪnəd, 'sɪnɒd/ *n* **1** a formal meeting to decide ecclesiastical matters **2** a church governing or advisory council **3** the ecclesiastical district governed by a synod – **synodal** *adj*

synonym /'sinənim‖'sɪnənɪm/ *n* any of 2 or more words or expressions in a language that are used with (nearly) the same meaning – **synonymic, synonymical** *adj*, **synonymity** *n*

synonymous /si'nonimǝs‖sɪ'nɒnɪməs/ *adj* alike in meaning – **synonymously** *adv*

synopsis /si'nopsis‖sɪ'nɒpsɪs/ *n, pl* **synopses** /-seez‖-siːz/ a condensed statement or outline (e g of a narrative)

synoptic /si'noptik‖sɪ'nɒptɪk/ *also* **synoptical** /-kl‖-kl/ *adj* **1** affording a comprehensive view of a whole **2** *often cap* of or being the first 3 Gospels of the New Testament **3** relating to or displaying meteorological conditions existing simultaneously over a broad area – **synoptically** *adv*

syntactic /sin'taktik‖sɪn'tæktɪk/, **syntactical**

/-kl‖-kl/ *adj* of or conforming to the rules of syntax or syntactics – **syntactically** *adv*

syntax /'sintaks‖'sɪntæks/ *n* (the part of grammar dealing with) the way in which words are put together to form phrases, clauses, or sentences

synthesis /'sinthəsis‖'sɪnθəsɪs/ *n, pl* **syntheses** /-seez‖-siːz/ **1a** the composition or combination of separate or diverse elements into a coherent whole **b** the artificial production of a substance by chemical reaction **2** the third and final stage of a reasoned argument, based on the thesis and antithesis [Greek, fr *syntithenai* to put together, fr *syn* with + *tithenai* to put, place] – **synthesist** *n*, **synthesize** *vt*

synthes·izer, -iser /'sinthə͵siezə‖'sɪnθə͵saɪzə/ *n* an extremely versatile electronic musical instrument that produces a sound that can be altered in many ways (e g to mimic other instruments) and is usu played by means of a keyboard

[1]**synthetic** /sin'thetik‖sɪn'θetɪk/ *also* **synthetical** /-kl‖-kl/ *adj* produced artificially; man-made < ~ *silk* > – **synthetically** *adv*

[2]**synthetic** *n* a product of (chemical) synthesis

syphilis /'sifəlis‖'sɪfəlɪs/ *n* a contagious usu venereal and often congenital disease caused by a spirochaetal bacterium – **syphilitic** *adj or n*

syphon /'siefən‖'saɪfən/ *vb or n* to siphon

[1]**syringe** /sə'rinj‖sə'rɪndʒ/ *n* a device used to inject fluids into or withdraw them from sthg (e g the body or its cavities); *esp* one that consists of a hollow barrel fitted with a plunger and a hollow needle

[2]**syringe** *vt* to irrigate or spray (as if) with a syringe

syrinx /'siringks‖'sɪrɪŋks/ *n, pl* **syringes** /si'rinjeez‖sɪ'rɪndʒiːz/, **syrinxes** the vocal organ of birds that is a modification of the lower trachea, bronchi, or both

syrup /'sirəp‖'sɪrəp/ *n* **1a** a thick sticky solution of (flavoured, medicated, etc) sugar and water **b** the concentrated juice of a fruit or plant (e g the sugar maple); *esp* the raw sugar juice obtained from crushed sugarcane after evaporation and before crystallization in sugar manufacture **2** cloying sweetness or sentimentality – **syrupy** *adj*

system /'sistəm‖'sɪstəm/ *n* **1a** a group of body organs that together perform 1 or more usu specified functions <*the digestive* ~ > **b** the body considered as a functional unit **c** a group of interrelated and interdependent objects or units **d** a group of devices or an organization that serves a common purpose <*a telephone* ~ > <*a heating* ~ > <*a highway* ~ > <*a data processing* ~ > **e** a major division of rocks including those formed during a period or era **f** a form of social, economic, or political organization <*the capitalist* ~ > **2** an organized set of doctrines or principles usu intended to explain the arrangement or working of a systematic whole <*the Newtonian* ~ *of mechanics*> **3a** an organized or established procedure <*the touch* ~ *of typing*> **b** a manner of classifying, symbolizing, or formalizing <*the decimal* ~ > **4** orderly methods **5** ESTABLISHMENT 2 – + *the* – **systemless** *adj*

systematic /͵sistə'matik‖͵sɪstə'mætɪk/ *also* **systematical** /-kl‖-kl/ *adj* **1** relating to, consisting of, or presented as a system **2** methodical in procedure or plan; thorough < ~ *investigation*> **3** of or concerned with classification; *specif* taxonomic – **systematically** *adv*

systemat·ize, -ise /'sistəmətiez‖'sɪstəmətaɪz/ *vt* to arrange according to a set method; order systematically – **systematizer** *n*, **systematization** *n*

systemic /si'steemik, si'stemik‖sɪ'stiːmɪk, sɪ'stemɪk/ *adj* **1** affecting the body generally **2** *of an insecticide, pesticide, etc* making the organism, esp a plant, toxic to a pest by entering the tissues – **systemically** *adv*

T

t /tee‖tiː/ *n, pl* ***t's, ts often cap*** (a graphic representation of or device for reproducing) the 20th letter of the English alphabet

t' *definite article, NEng dial* the

't *pron* it

ta /tah‖tɑː/ *n, Br* thanks – infml

[1]**tab** /tab‖tæb/ *n* **1a** a flap, loop, etc fixed to or projecting from sthg and used for gripping or suspending or to aid identification **b** a small auxiliary aerofoil hinged to a control surface (e g an aileron) **2** close surveillance; watch – usu pl with sing. meaning <*the police are keeping* ~s *on him*> **3** a tabulator **4** *Br* [1]TAG 2 **5** *chiefly NAm* a statement of money owed; a bill – infml <*the company will pick up the* ~ >

[2]**tab** *vt* **-bb-** to provide or decorate with tabs

tabard /'tabəd‖'tæbəd/ *n* a short loosely fitting sleeveless or short-sleeved coat or cape

Tabasco /tə'baskoh‖tə'bæskəʊ/ *trademark* – used for a pungent condiment sauce made from hot peppers

tabby /'tabi‖'tæbɪ/, '**tabby** ͵**cat** *n* **1** a domestic cat with a usu buff and black striped and mottled coat **2** a female domestic cat

tabernacle /'tabə͵nakl‖'tæbə͵nækl/ *n* **1** *often cap* a tent sanctuary used by the Israelites during the Exodus **2** a receptacle for the consecrated bread and wine used at Communion, often forming part of an altar – **tabernacular** *adj*

[1]**table** /'taybl‖'teɪbl/ *n* **1a** a piece of furniture consisting of a smooth flat slab (e g of wood) fixed on legs **b** the food served at a meal; fare <*keeps a good* ~ > **2** either of the 2 leaves of a backgammon board or either half of a leaf **3** a systematic arrangement of data usu in rows and columns **4** the upper flat surface of a gem **5** sthg having a flat level surface – **on the table** *chiefly Br* under or put forward for discussion <*so far the management have put nothing* on the table> – **under the table 1** into a stupor <*can drink you* under the table> **2** not aboveboard

[2]**table** *vt* **1** to enter in a table **2** *Br* to place on the agenda **3** *NAm* to remove from consideration indefinitely

tableau /'tabloh‖'tæbləʊ/ *n, pl* **tableaux** *also* **tableaus** /'tabloh(z)‖'tæbləʊ(z)/ **1** a graphic representation of a group or scene **2** a depiction of a scene usu presented on a stage by silent and motionless costumed participants

ˈtableˌcloth /-ˌkloth‖-ˌklɒθ/ *n* an often decorative cloth spread over a dining table before the places are set

table d'hôte /ˌtahblə ˈdoht‖ˌtɑːblə ˈdəʊt/ *n* a meal often of several prearranged courses served to all guests at a stated hour and fixed price [French, lit., host's table]

tableland /ˈtaybl̩ˌland‖ˈteɪbl̩ˌlænd/ *n* a broad level area elevated on all sides

table linen *n* linen (e g tablecloths and napkins) for the table

ˈtableˌmat /-ˌmat‖-ˌmæt/ *n* a small often decorative mat placed under a hot dish to protect the surface of a table from heat

ˈtableˌspoon /-ˌspoohn‖-ˌspuːn/ *n* **1** a large spoon used for serving **2** a tablespoonful

ˈtableˌspoonful /-ˌspoohnf(ə)l‖-ˌspuːnf(ə)l/ *n, pl* **tablespoonfuls** *also* **tablespoonsful** as much as a tablespoon can hold

tablet /ˈtablit‖ˈtæblɪt/ *n* **1** a flat slab or plaque suitable for or bearing an inscription **2a** a compressed block of a solid material <*a ~ of soap*> **b** a small solid shaped mass or capsule of medicinal material

table tennis *n* a game resembling lawn tennis that is played on a tabletop with bats and a small hollow plastic ball

ˈtableˌware /-ˌweə‖-ˌweə/ *n* utensils (e g glasses, dishes, plates, and cutlery) for table use

tabloid /ˈtabloyd‖ˈtæblɔɪd/ *n* a newspaper of which 2 pages make up 1 printing plate and which contains much photographic matter

¹taboo *also* **tabu** /təˈbooh‖təˈbuː/ *adj* **1a** too sacred or evil to be touched, named, or used **b** set apart as unclean or accursed **2** forbidden, esp on grounds of morality, tradition, or social usage [Tongan *tabu*]

²taboo *also* **tabu** *n, pl* **taboos** *also* **tabus** **1** a prohibition against touching, saying, or doing sthg for fear of harm from a supernatural force **2** a prohibition imposed by social custom

³taboo *also* **tabu** *vt* **1** to set apart as taboo **2** to avoid or ban as taboo

tabor *also* **tabour** /ˈtaybə‖ˈteɪbə/ *n* a small drum with 1 head of soft calfskin used to accompany a pipe or fife played by the same person

tabular /ˈtabyoolə‖ˈtæbjʊlə/ *adj* **1a** having a broad flat surface **b** laminar **c** *of a crystal* having 2 parallel flat faces **2a** of or arranged in a table **b** computed by means of a table – **tabularly** *adv*

tabulate /ˈtabyoolayt‖ˈtæbjʊleɪt/ *vt* to arrange in tabular form – **tabulation** *n*

tabulator /ˈtabyooˌlaytə‖ˈtæbjʊˌleɪtə/ *n* **1** a business machine that sorts and selects information from marked or perforated cards **2** an attachment to a typewriter that is used for arranging data in columns

tachograph /ˈtakəˌgrahf‖ˈtækəˌgrɑːf/ *n* a device for automatically recording the speed and time of travel of a vehicle [deriv of Greek *tachos* speed + *graphein* to write]

tacit /ˈtakəˌ‖ˈtæsɪt/ *adj* implied or understood but not actually expressed – **tacitly** *adv*

taciturn /ˈtasiˌtuhn‖ˈtæsɪˌtɜːn/ *adj* not communicative or talkative – **taciturnity** *n*

¹tack /tak‖tæk/ *n* **1** a small short sharp-pointed nail, usu with a broad flat head **2** the lower forward corner of a fore-and-aft sail **3a** the direction of a sailing vessel with respect to the direction of the wind <*starboard ~, with the wind to starboard*> **b** the run of a sailing vessel on 1 tack **c** a change of course from one tack to another **d** a course of action <*off on a new ~*> **4** a long loose straight stitch usu used to hold 2 or more layers of fabric together temporarily **5** a sticky or adhesive quality **6** SADDLERY 2

²tack *vt* **1a** to fasten or attach with tacks **b** to sew with long loose stitches in order to join or hold in place temporarily before fine or machine sewing **2** to add as a supplement <*~ a postscript on a letter*> **3** to change the course of (a close-hauled sailing vessel) from one tack to the other by turning the bow to windward ~ *vi* **1a** to tack a sailing vessel **b** *of a sailing vessel* to undergo being tacked **2a** to follow a zigzag course **b** to change one's policy or attitude abruptly – **tacker** *n*

¹tackle /ˈtakl‖ˈtækl/ *n* **1** a set of equipment used in a particular activity <*fishing ~*> **2a** a ship's rigging **b** an assembly of ropes and pulleys arranged to gain mechanical advantage for hoisting and pulling **3** an act of tackling

²tackle *vt* **1** to attach or secure with or as if with tackle – often + *up* **2a** to take hold of or grapple with, esp in an attempt to stop or restrain **b(1)** to (attempt to) take the ball from (an opposing player) in hockey or soccer **b(2)** to seize and pull down or stop (an opposing player with the ball) in rugby or American football **3** to set about dealing with <*~ the problem*> ~*vi* to tackle an opposing player – **tackler** *n*

¹tacky /ˈtaki‖ˈtækɪ/ *adj* slightly sticky to the touch <*~ varnish*> – **tackiness** *n*

²tacky *adj, NAm* shabby, shoddy – slang – **tackily** *adv*, **tackiness** *n*

tact /takt‖tækt/ *n* a keen sense of how to handle people or affairs so as to avoid friction or giving offence – **tactful** *adj*, **tactfully** *adv*, **tactfulness** *n*, **tactless** *adj*, **tactlessly** *adv*, **tactlessness** *n*

tactic /ˈtaktik‖ˈtæktɪk/ *n* **1** a method of employing forces in combat **2** a device for achieving an end

tactical /ˈtaktikl‖ˈtæktɪkl/ *adj* **1a** involving operations of local importance or brief duration **b** of or designed for air attack in close support of friendly ground forces **2a** of small-scale actions serving a wider aim **b** characterized by adroit planning or manoeuvring to accomplish an end – **tactically** *adv*

tactician /takˈtish(ə)n‖tækˈtɪʃ(ə)n/ *n* sby skilled in tactics

tactics /ˈtaktiks‖ˈtæktɪks/ *n pl but sing or pl in constr* **1a** the science and art of disposing and manoeuvring forces in combat **b** the art or skill of employing available means to accomplish an end **2** a system or mode of procedure [Greek *taktika*, fr neuter pl of *taktikos* of order, of tactics, fit for arranging, fr *tassein* to arrange, place in battle formation]

tactile /ˈtaktiel‖ˈtæktaɪl/ *adj* of or perceptible by (the sense of) touch – **tactilely** *adv*, **tactility** *n*

tactual /ˈtakchooəl, -chəl‖ˈtæktʃʊəl, -tʃəl/ *adj* tactile – **tactually** *adv*

tadpole /ˈtad,pohl‖ˈtæd,pəʊl/ *n* the larva of an amphibian; *specif* a frog or toad larva with a rounded body, a long tail, and external gills [Middle English *taddepol*, fr *tode* toad + *polle* head]

taffeta /ˈtafitə‖ˈtæfɪtə/ *n* a crisp plain-woven lustrous fabric of various fibres used esp for women's clothing

taffrail /ˈtaf,rayl, ˈtafrəl‖ˈtæf,reɪl, ˈtæfrəl/ *n* a rail round the stern of a ship

taffy /ˈtafi‖ˈtæfɪ/ *n, NAm* a porous and light-coloured toffee

Taffy *n, Br* a Welshman – chiefly derog

[1]**tag** /tag‖tæg/ *n* **1** a loose hanging piece of torn cloth **2** a rigid binding on an end of a shoelace **3** a piece of hanging or attached material; *specif* a flap on a garment that carries information (e g washing instructions) **4a** a trite quotation used for rhetorical effect **b** a recurrent or characteristic verbal expression **c** a final speech or line (e g in a play) usu serving to clarify a point or create a dramatic effect **5** a marker of plastic, metal, etc used for identification or classification

[2]**tag** *vb* **-gg-** *vt* **1a** to provide with an identifying marker **b** to label, brand <*had him* ~ged *as a chauvinist from the start*> **2** to attach, append **3** LABEL 2 ~*vi* to follow closely <~ging *along behind*>

[3]**tag** *n* a game in which one player chases others and tries to make one of them it by touching him/her

[4]**tag** *vt* **-gg-** to touch (as if) in a game of tag

[1]**tail** /tayl‖teɪl/ *n* **1** (an extension or prolongation of) the rear end of the body of an animal **2** sthg resembling an animal's tail in shape or position <*the* ~ *of a comet*> **3** *pl* a tailcoat; *broadly* formal evening dress for men including a tailcoat and a white bow tie **4** the last, rear, or lower part of sthg **5** the reverse of a coin – usu pl with sing. meaning <~s, *you lose*>; compare HEAD 3 **6** *sing or pl in constr* the group of relatively inexpert batsmen who bat towards the end of a side's innings **7** the stabilizing assembly (e g fin, rudder, and tailplane) at the rear of an aircraft **8** sby who follows or keeps watch on sby – infml **9** the trail of a fugitive <*had the police on her* ~> – infml **10a** women as sexual objects – vulg **b** *NAm* the buttocks – slang – **tailed** *adj*

[2]**tail** *vt* **1** to connect at an end or end to end **2a** to remove the tail of (an animal) **b** to remove the stalk of (e g a gooseberry) **3** to fasten an end of (a tile, brick, or timber) into a wall or other support **4** to follow for purposes of surveillance – infml ~ *vi* **1** to diminish gradually in strength, volume, quantity, etc – usu + *off* or *away* **2** to follow closely

[3]**tail** *adj* entailed

[4]**tail** *n* ENTAIL 1 – often in *in tail*

ˈ**tail,back** /-,bak‖-,bæk/ *n* a long queue of motor vehicles, esp when caused by an obstruction that blocks the road

ˈ**tail,board** /-,bawd‖-,bɔːd/ *n* a hinged or removable board or gate at the rear of a vehicle

ˈ**tail,coat** /-,koht‖-,kəʊt/ *n* a coat with tails; *esp* a man's formal evening coat with 2 long tapering skirts at the back – **tailcoated** *adj*

tail end *n* **1** the back or rear end **2** the concluding period

[1]**tailor** /ˈtaylə‖ˈteɪlə/, *fem* **tailoress** /,tayləˈres, ˈ- -,-‖,teɪləˈres, ˈ--,-/ *n* sby whose occupation is making or altering esp men's garments [Old French *tailleur*, fr *taillier* to cut, fr Late Latin *taliare*, fr Latin *talea* twig, cutting]

[2]**tailor** *vi* to do the work of a tailor ~ *vt* **1a** to make or fashion as the work of a tailor; *specif* to cut and stitch (a garment) so that it will hang and fit well **b** to make or adapt to suit a special need or purpose **2** to style with trim straight lines and finished handwork

,**tailor-ˈmade** *adj* made or fitted for a particular use or purpose

ˈ**tail,piece** /-,pees‖-,piːs/ *n* **1** a piece added at the end; an appendage **2** a triangular piece from which the strings of a stringed instrument are stretched to the pegs **3** an ornament placed below the text on a page (e g at the end of a chapter)

ˈ**tail,spin** /-,spin‖-,spɪn/ *n* SPIN 2

tail wind *n* a wind having the same general direction as the course of an aircraft or ship

[1]**taint** /taynt‖teɪnt/ *vt* **1** to touch or affect slightly with sthg bad <*people* ~ed *with prejudice*> **2** to affect with putrefaction; spoil **3** to contaminate morally; corrupt ~*vi* to become affected with putrefaction; spoil

[2]**taint** *n* a contaminating mark or influence – **taintless** *adj*

[1]**take** /tayk‖teɪk/ *vb* **took** /took‖tʊk/; **taken** /ˈtaykən‖ˈteɪkən/ *Br vt* **1a** to seize or capture physically **b** to get possession of (e g fish or game) by killing or capturing **c(1)** to capture and remove from play <took *my pawn*> **c(2)** to win in a card game <*able to* ~ *12 tricks with that hand*> **2** to grasp, grip <took *his arm*> **3a** to catch or attack through a sudden effect <~n *ill*> **b** to surprise; come upon suddenly <*her death* took *us by surprise*> **c** to attract, delight <*was quite* ~n *with him*> **4a** to receive into one's body, esp through the mouth <~ *medicine*> **b** to eat or drink habitually <*I don't* ~ *milk in my tea*> **5a** to bring or receive into a relationship or connection <took *her as his wife*> **b** to copulate with (a passive partner) **6a** to acquire, borrow, or use without authority or right <took *someone's hat by mistake*> **b(1)** to pay to have (e g by contract or subscription) <~ *a cottage for the summer*> **b(2)** to buy <*the salesman persuaded him to* ~ *the estate car*> **7a** to assume <~ *shape*> **b** to perform or conduct (e g a lesson) as a duty, task, or job **c** to commit oneself to <~ *a decision*> **d** to involve oneself in <~ *the trouble to learn Chinese*> **e** to consider or adopt as a point of view <~ *a more lenient view*> **f** to claim as rightfully one's own <~ *the credit*> **8** to obtain by competition <took *third place*> **9** to pick out; choose <~ *any card*> **10** to adopt or avail oneself of for use <~ *an opportunity*>: e g **10a** to have recourse to as an instrument for doing sthg <~ *a scythe to the weeds*> **b** to use as a means of transport or progression <~ *a plane to Paris*> **c(1)** to turn to for safety or refuge <~ *cover*> **c(2)** to proceed to occupy or hold <~ *a seat*> **d(1)** to need, require <~s *a long time to dry*> **d(2)** to govern <*transitive verbs* ~ *an object*> **11a** to derive,

draw <~s *its title from the name of the hero*> **b(1)** to obtain or ascertain by testing, measuring, etc <~ *his temperature*> **b(2)** to record in writing; WRITE DOWN 1 <~ *notes*> **b(3)** to get or record by photography <~ *some slides*> **b(4)** to get by transference from one surface to another <~ *fingerprints*> **12** to receive or accept either willingly or reluctantly <~ *a bribe*> <~ *a risk*>: e g **12a** to receive when bestowed or tendered <~ *a degree*> **b(1)** to endure, undergo <*can't* ~ *it any longer*> **b(2)** to support, withstand <*won't* ~ *my weight*> **c(1)** to accept as true; believe <took *her word for it*> **c(2)** to follow <~ *my advice*> **c(3)** to respond to in a specified way <~ *things as they come*> **d** to indulge in and enjoy <~ *a holiday*> **e** to accept in payment, compensation, or recompense <*they won't* ~ *dollars*> **13a** to accommodate <*the suitcase wouldn't* ~ *another thing*> **b** to be affected injuriously by (e g a disease) <~ *cold*> **14a** to apprehend, understand <*slow to* ~ *his meaning*> **b** to look upon; consider <~ *it as settled*> **c** to feel, experience <~ *pleasure*> **15a** to lead, carry, or remove with one to another place <~ *her a cup of tea*> **b** to require or cause to go <*her ability will* ~ *her to the top*> **16a** to obtain by removing <~ *eggs from a nest*> **b** to subtract <~ *2 from 4*> **17** to undertake and make, do, or perform <~ *a walk*> <~ *one's revenge*> **18a** to deal with <~ *the comments one at a time*> **b** to consider or view in a specified relation <~n *together, the details were significant*> **c** to apply oneself to the study of or undergo examination in <~ *music lessons*> **d** to succeed in passing or surmounting <*the horse* took *the fence easily*> **19** to cheat, swindle <*was* ~n *for £5000 by a con man*> **20** to remove by death – euph <*was* ~n *in his prime*> ~ *vi* **1a** to receive property in law **b** *of a fish* to receive a lure or bait **2a** to have the natural or intended effect or reaction <*did your vaccination* ~*?*> **b** to begin to grow; strike root <*have the seeds* ~n *yet?*> **3a** to be adversely affected as specified <took *ill*> **b** to be capable of being moved in a specified way <*the table* ~s *apart for packing*> **c** to admit of being photographed **4** *chiefly dial* – used as an intensifier or redundantly with a following verb <took *and ducked her in the pond*> – **taker** *n* – **take account of** TAKE INTO ACCOUNT – **take action 1** to begin to act **2** to begin legal proceedings – **take advantage of 1** to use to advantage; profit by **2** to impose upon; exploit – **take after** to resemble (an older relative) in appearance, character, or aptitudes – **take against** *chiefly Br* to take sides against; come to dislike – **take apart 1** to disassemble, dismantle **2** to analyse, dissect **3** to treat roughly or harshly – infml – **take as read** to accept as axiomatic – **take care** to be careful; exercise caution or prudence; be watchful – **take care of** to attend to or provide for the needs, operation, or treatment of – **take charge** to assume care, custody, command, or control – **take effect 1** to become operative **2** to produce a result – **take exception** to object, demur – **take five** to take a brief intermission – infml – **take for** to suppose, esp mistakenly, to be – **take for a ride** to deceive wilfully; hoodwink – infml – **take for granted 1** to assume as true, real, or certain to occur **2** to value too lightly – **take heart** to gain courage or confidence – **take hold 1** to grasp, grip, seize **2** to become attached or established; TAKE EFFECT – **take in good part** to accept without offence – **take in hand** to embark on the control or reform of – **take into account** to make allowances for – **take into consideration** TAKE INTO ACCOUNT; *specif* to take account of (additional offences admitted by a defendant) so that the sentence to be imposed will preclude any chance of subsequent prosecution – **take into one's head** to conceive as a sudden notion or resolve – **take in vain** to use (a name) profanely or without proper respect – **take it upon oneself** to venture, presume – **take offence** to be offended – **take on board** *Br* to apprehend fully; grasp – infml – **take one's leave** to bid farewell – often + *of* – **take one's time** to be leisurely about doing sthg – **take part** to join, participate, share – **take place** to happen; COME ABOUT – **take root 1** to become rooted **2** to become fixed or established – **take silk** to become a Queen's or King's Counsel – **take someone at his/her word** to believe sby literally – **take someone out of him-/herself** to provide sby with needful diversion – **take someone to task** to rebuke or scold sby – **take stock 1** to make an inventory **2** to make an assessment – **take the biscuit** *Br* to be the most astonishing or preposterous thing heard of or seen – infml – **take the field 1** to go onto the playing field **2** to enter on a military campaign – **take the floor 1** to rise (e g in a meeting) to make a formal address **2** to begin dancing – **take the gilt off the gingerbread** to take away the part that makes the whole attractive – **take the law into one's own hands** to seek redress by force – **take the mickey** to behave disrespectfully; mock – infml – **take the wind out of someone's sails** to frustrate sby by anticipating or forestalling him/her – **take the words out of someone's mouth** to utter the exact words about to be used by sby – **take to 1** to betake oneself to, esp for refuge <take to *the woods*> **2** to apply or devote oneself to (e g a practice, habit or occupation) <take to *begging*> **3** to adapt oneself to; respond to <takes to *water like a duck*> **4** to conceive a liking or affectionate concern for – **take to heart** to be deeply affected by – **take to one's heels** to run away; flee – **take to task** to call to account for a shortcoming – **take to the cleaners 1** to rob, defraud – infml **2** to criticize harshly – infml – **take turns, take it in turns** to act by turns – **what it takes** the qualities or resources needed for success or for attainment of a goal

[2]**take** *n* **1a** the action of killing or catching sthg (e g game or fish) **b** the uninterrupted recording, filming, or televising of sthg (e g a gramophone record or film sequence); *also* the recording or scene produced **2a** proceeds, takings **b** a share, cut <*wanted a bigger* ~> **c** the number or quantity (e g of animals or fish) taken at 1 time

takeaway /ˈtaykə,way‖ˈteɪkə,weɪ/ *n, Br* **1** a cooked meal that is eaten away from the premises from which it was bought **2** a shop or restaurant that sells takeaways

take back *vt* to retract, withdraw

take down *vt* **1** to pull to pieces **2** WRITE DOWN **3** to lower without removing <took down *his trousers*>

take-home pay *n* the part of gross salary or wages remaining after deductions (e g for income tax)

take in *vt* **1a** to furl **b** to make (a garment) smaller (e g by altering the positions of the seams or making tucks) **2** to offer accommodation or shelter to **3** to receive (paid work) into one's house <take in *washing*> **4** to include <*the holiday* took in *Venice*> **5** to perceive, understand **6** to deceive, trick – infml

ˈtakeˌoff /-ˌof‖-ˌɒf/ *n* **1** an imitation; *esp* a caricature **2** an act of leaving or a rise from a surface (e g in making a jump, dive, or flight or in the launching of a rocket) **3** a starting point; a point at which one takes off

take off *vt* **1** to remove <take *your shoes* off> **2a** to release <take *the brake* off> **b** to discontinue, withdraw <took off *the morning train*> **c** to deduct <took *10 per cent* off> **3** to take or spend (a period of time) as a holiday, rest, etc **4** to mimic <*mannerisms that her critics delighted in* taking off> ~ *vi* **1** to start off or away; SET OUT <took off *without delay*> **2** to begin a leap or spring **3** to leave the surface; begin flight

take on *vt* **1a** to agree to undertake <took on *new responsibilities*> **b** to contend with as an opponent <took on *the neighbourhood bully*> **2** to engage, hire **3** to assume or acquire (e g an appearance or quality) <*the city* takes on *a carnival air*> ~*vi* to become emotional or distraught – infml

take out *vt* **1a** to extract <took *the appendix* out> **b** to give vent to – usu + *on* <take out *their frustrations on one another*> **2** to escort or accompany in public **3a** to obtain officially or formally <take out *a warrant*> **b** to acquire (insurance) by making the necessary payment **4** to overcall (a bridge partner) in a different suit – **take it out on** to vent anger, vexation, or frustration on – **take it out of 1** TAKE IT OUT ON **2** to fatigue, exhaust

ˈtakeˌover /-ˌohvə‖-ˌəʊvə/ *n* the action or an act of taking over; *esp* an act of gaining control of a business company by buying a majority of the shares – **take-over** *adj*

take over *vb* to assume control or possession (of) or responsibility (for)

take up *vt* **1** to remove by lifting or pulling up <*the council's* taking *the old tramlines* up> **2** to receive internally or on the surface and hold <*plants* take up *nutrients*> **3a** to begin to engage in or study <took up *Greek*> <*when did he* take up *sailing?*> **b** to raise (a matter) for consideration <took *her case* up *with a lawyer*> **4** to occupy (e g space or time) entirely or exclusively <*outside activities* took up *too much of his time*> **5** to shorten (e g a garment) <*will have to* take *that dress* up> **6** to respond favourably to a bet, challenge, or proposal made by <*I'll* take *you* up *on that*> **7** to begin again or take over from another <*she* took up *the story where she left off*> ~*vi* to begin again; resume – **take up the cudgels** to engage vigorously in a defence – **take up with** to begin to associate with; consort with

taking /ˈtayking‖ˈteɪkɪŋ/ *adj* attractive, captivating

takings /ˈtaykingz‖ˈteɪkɪŋz/ *n pl* receipts, esp of money

talc /talk‖tælk/ *n* **1** a soft usu greenish or greyish mineral consisting of a magnesium silicate **2** TALCUM POWDER – **talcose** *adj*

ˈtalcum ˌpowder /ˈtalkəm‖ˈtælkəm/ *n* a powder for toilet use consisting of perfumed talc

tale /tayl‖teɪl/ *n* **1** a series of events or facts told or presented; an account **2a** a usu fictitious narrative; a story **b** a lie, a falsehood **c** a malicious report or piece of gossip

ˈtaleˌbearer /-ˌbeərə‖-ˌbeərə/ *n* a telltale, gossip – **talebearing** *adj or n*

talent /ˈtalənt‖ˈtælənt/ *n* **1a** any of several ancient units of weight **b** a unit of money equal to the value of a talent of gold or silver **2a** a special often creative or artistic aptitude **b** general ability or intelligence **3** a person or people of talent in a field or activity **4** *sing or pl in constr* sexually attractive members of the opposite sex <*sat eyeing up the local* ~> – slang [Old English *talente*, fr Latin *talentum*, fr Greek *talanton* senses 2-4 fr the parable of the talents in Matthew 25:14–30] – **talented** *adj*, **talentless** *adj*

ˈtalent ˌscout *n* a person engaged in discovering and recruiting people with talent in a specialized field of activity

talisman /ˈtalizmən‖ˈtælɪzmən/ *n, pl* **talismans** **1** an engraved object believed to act as a charm **2** sthg believed to produce magical or miraculous effects [French, fr Arabic *ṭilsam*, fr Greek *telesma* consecration, fr *telein* to consecrate, complete, fr *telos* end] – **talismanic** *adj* **talismanically** *adv*

¹talk /tawk‖tɔːk/ *vt* **1** to express in speech; utter <~ *nonsense*> **2** to make the subject of conversation; discuss <~ *business*> **3** to bring to a specified state by talking; *esp* to persuade by talking <~ed *them into agreeing*> **4** to use (a language) for conversing or communicating <~ *French*> ~ *vi* **1** to express or exchange ideas verbally or by other means <~ed *till daybreak*> <*they* ~ed *by using sign language*> **2** to use speech; speak **3** to imitate human speech <*her budgie can* ~> **4a** to gossip <*you know how people* ~> **b** to reveal secret or confidential information <*we have ways of making you* ~> **5** to give a talk or lecture – **talker** *n* – **talk shop** to talk about one's job, esp outside working hours – **talk through one's hat** to voice irrational, or erroneous ideas, esp in attempting to appear knowledgeable – **talk turkey** *chiefly NAm* to speak frankly or bluntly

²talk *n* **1** a verbal exchange of thoughts or opinions; a conversation **2** meaningless speech; verbiage <*it's all* ~> **3** a formal discussion or exchange of views – often pl with sing. meaning **4** (the topic of) interested comment or gossip <*the* ~ *of the town*> **5** an often informal address or lecture **6** communicative sounds or signs functioning as talk <*baby* ~>

talkative /ˈtawkətiv‖ˈtɔːkətɪv/ *adj* given to talking – **talkatively** *adv*, **talkativeness** *n*

talk down *vt* **1** to defeat or silence by argument or by loud talking **2** to radio instructions to (a pilot) to enable him/her to land when conditions are difficult ~*vi* to speak in a condescending or oversimplified fashion *to*

talkie /ˈtawki‖ˈtɔːkɪ/ *n* a film with a synchronized sound track

talking point *n* a subject of conversation or argument

ˈ**talking-ˌto** *n* a reprimand, scolding

talk out *vt* to clarify or settle by discussion <*tried to* talk out *their differences*>

talk over *vt* to review or consider in conversation

tall /tawl‖tɔːl/ *adj* **1a** of above average height <*a ~ woman*> <*~ trees*> **b** of a specified height <*5 feet ~*> **2** *of a plant* of a higher growing variety or species **3** unreasonably difficult to perform <*a ~ order*> **4** highly exaggerated; incredible <*a ~ story*> – **tall** *adv*, **tallish** *adj*, **tallness** *n*

tallboy /ˈtawlˌboy‖ˈtɔːlˌbɔɪ/ *n* **1** a tall chest of drawers supported on a low legged base **2** a double chest of drawers usu with the upper section slightly smaller than the lower

tallow /ˈtaloh‖ˈtæləʊ/ *n* the solid white rendered fat of cattle and sheep used chiefly in soap, candles, and lubricants – **tallowy** *adj*

[1]**tally** /ˈtali‖ˈtælɪ/ *n* **1** a device for visibly recording or accounting esp business transactions; *specif* a wooden rod notched with marks representing numbers and split lengthways through the notches so that each of 2 parties may have a record of a transaction **2a** a record or account (e g of items or charges) <*keep a daily ~ of accidents*> **b** a record of the score (e g in a game) **3** a part or person that corresponds to an opposite or companion object or member; a counterpart

[2]**tally** *vb* **1a** to mark (as if) on a tally; tabulate **b** to list or check off (e g a cargo) by items **2** to make a count of ~ *vi* **1a** to make a tally (as if) by tabulating **b** to register a point in a contest **2** to correspond, match <*their stories ~*>

tally-ho /ˌtali ˈhoh‖ˌtælɪ ˈhəʊ/ *n* a call of a huntsman at the sight of a fox

tallyman /ˈtalimən‖ˈtælɪmən/ *n* **1** one who checks or keeps an account or record (e g of receipt of goods) **2** *Br* one who sells goods on credit; *also* one who calls to collect hire purchase payments

Talmud /ˈtalmood, ˈtahl-‖ˈtælmʊd, ˈtɑːl-/ *n* the authoritative body of Jewish tradition comprising the Mishnah and Gemara – **talmudic** *also* **talmudical** *adj, often cap*, **talmudism** *n, often cap*

talon /ˈtalən‖ˈtælən/ *n* a claw of an animal, esp a bird of prey – **taloned** *adj*

tamarind /ˈtamərind‖ˈtæmərɪnd/ *n* (a tropical leguminous tree with) a fruit with an acid pulp used for preserves or in a cooling laxative drink

tamarisk /ˈtamərisk‖ˈtæmərɪsk/ *n* any of a genus of chiefly tropical or Mediterranean shrubs and trees having tiny narrow leaves and masses of minute flowers

tambour /ˈtambooə‖ˈtæmbʊə/ *n* **1** [1]DRUM 1 **2** (embroidery made on) a frame consisting of a set of 2 interlocking hoops between which cloth is stretched before stitching

tambourine /ˌtambəˈreen‖ˌtæmbəˈriːn/ *n* a shallow one-headed drum with loose metallic discs at the sides that is held in the hand and played by shaking, striking with the hand, or rubbing with the thumb

[1]**tame** /taym‖teɪm/ *adj* **1** changed from a state of native wildness, esp so as to be trainable and useful to human beings **2** made docile and submissive **3** lacking spirit, zest, or interest – **tamely** *adv*, **tameness** *n*

[2]**tame** *vt* **1a** to make tame; domesticate **b** to subject to cultivation **2** to deprive of spirit; subdue – **tamable**, **tameable** *adj*, **tamer** *n*

Tamil /ˈtamil‖ˈtæmɪl/ *n* (a person speaking) a language of S India and Sri Lanka

tam-o'-shanter /ˌtam ə ˈshantə‖ˌtæm ə ˈʃæntə/ *n* a round flat woollen or cloth cap of Scottish origin, with a tight headband, a full crown, and usu a pom-pom on top [*Tam o' Shanter*, hero of the poem of that name by Robert Burns (1759-96), Scottish poet]

tamp /tamp‖tæmp/ *vt* **1** to fill up (a drill hole above a blasting charge) with material (e g clay) to confine the force of the explosion **2** to drive in or down by a succession of light or medium blows – often + *down* – **tamper** *n*

tamper /ˈtampə‖ˈtæmpə/ *vi* **1** to carry on underhand or improper negotiations (e g by bribery) **2** to interfere or meddle without permission <*the car lock had been* ~ed *with*> *USE* usu + *with* – **tamperer** *n*, **tamperproof** *adj*

tampon /ˈtampon‖ˈtæmpɒn/ *vt or n* (to plug with) an absorbent plug put into a cavity (e g the vagina) to absorb secretions, arrest bleeding, etc

[1]**tan** /tan‖tæn/ *vb* **-nn-** *vt* **1** to convert (hide) into leather, esp by treatment with an infusion of tannin-rich bark **2** to make (skin) tan-coloured, esp by exposure to the sun **3** to thrash, beat – infml ~*vi* to get or become tanned – **tan someone's hide** *or* **tan the hide off someone** to beat sby severely; THRASH 2a –infml

[2]**tan** *n* **1** a brown colour given to the skin by exposure to sun or wind **2** (a) light yellowish brown – **tannish** *adj*

[3]**tan** *adj* of the colour tan

tanbark /ˈtanˌbahk‖ˈtænˌbɑːk/ *n* a bark (e g of an oak) rich in tannin, bruised or cut into small pieces, and used in tanning

[1]**tandem** /ˈtandəm‖ˈtændəm/ *n* **1** (a 2-seat carriage drawn by) horses harnessed one before the other **2** a bicycle or tricycle having 2 or more seats one behind the other [Latin, at last, at length (jokingly taken to mean 'lengthwise'), fr *tam* so] – **in tandem 1** in a tandem arrangement **2** in partnership or conjunction

[2]**tandem** *adv* one behind the other <*ride ~*>

tandoori /tanˈdawri‖tænˈdɔːrɪ/ *n* (food cooked, usu on a long spit by) a N Indian method of cooking in a large clay oven

[1]**tang** /tang‖tæŋ/ *n* **1** a projecting shank or tongue (e g on a knife, file, or sword) that connects with and is enclosed by a handle **2a** a sharp distinctive flavour **b** a pungent or distinctive smell **3** a faint suggestion; a trace – **tanged** *adj*, **tangy** *adj*

[2]**tang** *n* any of various large coarse seaweeds

[1]**tangent** /ˈtanjənt‖ˈtændʒənt/ *adj* **1** touching a curve or surface at only 1 point <*straight line ~ to a curve*> **2** having a common tangent at a

point < ~ *curves*>

[2]**tangent** *n* **1** the trigonometric function that for an acute angle in a right-angled triangle is the ratio between the shorter sides opposite and adjacent to the angle **2** a straight line tangent to a curve **3** an upright flat-ended metal pin at the inner end of a clavichord key that strikes the string to produce the note – **fly/go off at/on a tangent** to change suddenly from one subject, course of action, etc, to another

tangential /tanˈjensh(ə)l‖tænˈdʒenʃ(ə)l/ *adj* **1** of (the nature of) a tangent **2** acting along or lying in a tangent < ~ *forces*> **3a** divergent, digressive **b** incidental, peripheral – **tangentially** *adv*

tangerine /tanjəˈreen‖tændʒəˈriːn/ *n* **1** (a tree that produces) any of various mandarin oranges with deep orange skin and pulp; *broadly* MANDARIN 3 **2** (a) bright reddish orange [French *Tanger* Tangier, city & port in Morocco]

tangible /ˈtanjəbl‖ˈtændʒəbl/ *adj* **1a** capable of being perceived, esp by the sense of touch **b** substantially real; material **2** capable of being appraised at an actual or approximate value < ~ *assets*> – **tangibleness** *n*, **tangibly** *adv*, **tangibility** *n*

[1]**tangle** /ˈtang·gl‖ˈtæŋgl/ *vt* **1** to involve so as to be trapped or hampered **2** to bring together or intertwine in disordered confusion ~ *vi* **1** to become tangled **2** to engage in conflict or argument – usu + *with*; infml

[2]**tangle** *n* **1** a confused twisted mass **2** a complicated or confused state

tango /ˈtang·goh‖ˈtæŋgəʊ/ *n*, *pl* **tangos** (the music for) a ballroom dance of Latin-American origin – **tango** *vi*

[1]**tank** /tangk‖tæŋk/ *n* **1** a large receptacle for holding, transporting, or storing liquids or gas **2** an enclosed heavily armed and armoured combat vehicle that moves on caterpillar tracks – **tankful** *n*

[2]**tank** *vt* to place, store, or treat in a tank

tankard /ˈtangkəd‖ˈtæŋkəd/ *n* a tall one-handled drinking vessel; *esp* a silver or pewter mug with a lid

ˌtanked-ˈup *adj* DRUNK 1 – infml

tanker /ˈtangkə‖ˈtæŋkə/ *n* a ship, aircraft, or road or rail vehicle designed to carry fluid, esp liquid, in bulk (e g an aircraft used for transporting fuel and usu capable of refuelling other aircraft in flight)

tanner /ˈtanə‖ˈtænə/ *n*, *Br* a coin worth 6 old pence – infml

tannery /ˈtanəri‖ˈtænərɪ/ *n* a place where tanning is carried out

tannin /ˈtanin‖ˈtænɪn/ *n* any of various soluble astringent complex phenolic substances of plant origin used esp in tanning, dyeing, and making ink

tanning /ˈtaning‖ˈtænɪŋ/ *n* a beating, thrashing – infml

Tannoy /ˈtanoy‖ˈtænɔɪ/ *trademark* – used for a loudspeaker apparatus that broadcasts to the public, esp throughout a large building

tansy /ˈtanzi‖ˈtænzɪ/ *n* an aromatic plant with yellow flowers and finely divided leaves

tantal·ize, **-ise** /ˈtantəliez‖ˈtæntəlaɪz/ *vt* to tease or frustrate by presenting sthg desirable that is just out of reach [*Tantalus*, mythical King of Phrygia condemned in Hades to stand up to his chin in water that receded whenever he stooped to drink and under branches of fruit that receded whenever he tried to eat] – **tantalizer** *n*, **tantalizing** *adj*

tantalum /ˈtantələm‖ˈtæntələm/ *n* a hard grey-white acid-resisting metallic element

tantamount /ˈtantəˌmownt‖ˈtæntəˌmaʊnt/ *adj* equivalent in value, significance, or effect *to*

tantrum /ˈtantrəm‖ˈtæntrəm/ *n* a fit of childish bad temper

Taoism /ˈtowiz(ə)m‖ˈtaʊɪz(ə)m/ *n* a Chinese philosophy that teaches action in conformity with nature rather than striving against it; *also* a religion developed from this philosophy and concerned with obtaining long life and good fortune often by magical means – **Taoist** *adj or n*, **Taoistic** *adj*

[1]**tap** /tap‖tæp/ *n* **1a** a plug designed to fit an opening, esp in a barrel **b** a device consisting of a spout and valve attached to a pipe, bowl, etc to control the flow of a fluid **2** a removal of fluid from a body cavity **3** a tool for forming an internal screw thread **4** the act or an instance of tapping a telephone, telegraph, etc; *also* an electronic listening device used to do this **5** a small piece of metal attached to the sole or heel of tap-dancing shoes – **on tap 1** *of beer* on draught **2** readily available

[2]**tap** *vt* **-pp- 1** to let out or cause to flow by piercing or by drawing a plug from the containing vessel **2a** to pierce so as to let out or draw off a fluid (e g from a body cavity) **b** to draw from or upon < ~ *new sources of revenue*> **c** to connect an electronic listening device to (e g a telegraph or telephone wire), esp in order to acquire secret information **3** to get money from as a loan or gift – infml – **tapper** *n*

[3]**tap** *vb* **-pp-** *vt* **1a** to strike lightly, esp with a slight sound **b** to produce by striking in this manner – often + *out* < ~ped *out a tune*> **2** to give a light blow with < ~ *a pencil on the table*> ~*vi* to strike a light audible blow; rap – **tapper** *n*

[4]**tap** *n* **1** (the sound of) a light blow **2** any of several usu rapid drumbeats on a snare drum

ˈtap ˌdance *n* a step dance tapped out audibly by means of shoes with hard soles or soles and heels to which taps have been added – **tap-dance** *vi*, **tap dancer** *n*, **tap dancing** *n*

[1]**tape** /tayp‖teɪp/ *n* **1** a narrow band of woven fabric **2** *the* string stretched above the finishing line of a race **3** a narrow flexible strip or band; *esp* MAGNETIC TAPE **4** a tape recording

[2]**tape** *vt* **1** to fasten, tie, or bind with tape **2** to record on tape, esp magnetic tape ~*vi* to record sthg on esp magnetic tape – **have someone/something taped** to have fully understood or learnt how to deal with sby or sthg – infml

ˈtape ˌdeck *n* a mechanism or self-contained unit that causes magnetic tape to move past the heads of a magnetic recording device in order to generate electrical signals or to make a recording

ˈtape ˌmeasure *n* a narrow strip (e g of a limp cloth or steel tape) marked off in units for measuring length

[1]**taper** /ˈtaypə‖ˈteɪpə/ *n* **1a** a slender candle **b** a long waxed wick used esp for lighting candles, fires, etc **2** gradual diminution of thickness, diameter, or width

[2]**taper** *vi* **1** to decrease gradually in thickness, diameter, or width towards one end **2** to diminish gradually <*his voice* ~ed *off*> ~*vt* to cause to taper

tape recorder *n* a device for recording signals, esp sounds, on magnetic tape and for subsequently reproducing them

tapestry /ˈtapəstri‖ˈtæpəstrɪ/ *n* a heavy textile used for hangings, curtains, and upholstery, characterized by complicated pictorial designs – **tapestried** *adj*

tapeworm /ˈtayp,wuhm‖ˈteɪp,wɜːm/ *n* any of numerous flattened worms, which when adult are parasitic in the intestine of human beings or other vertebrates

tapioca /,tapiˈohkə‖,tæpɪˈəʊkə/ *n* (a milk pudding made with) a usu granular preparation of cassava starch used esp in puddings and as a thickening in liquid food

tapir /ˈtaypə‖ˈteɪpə/ *n*, any of several large chiefly nocturnal hoofed mammals with long snouts found in tropical America and Asia

tappet /ˈtapit‖ˈtæpɪt/ *n* a lever or projection moved by or moving some other piece (e g a cam)

taproom /ˈtap,roohm, -room‖ˈtæp,ruːm, -rʊm/ *n* BAR 5a (2)

ˈ**tap,root** /-,rooht‖-,ruːt/ *n* a main root of a plant that grows vertically downwards and gives off small side roots

taps /taps‖tæps/ *n pl but sing or pl in constr, chiefly NAm* the last bugle call at night, blown as a signal that lights are to be put out; *also* a similar call blown at military funerals and memorial services

[1]**tar** /tah‖tɑː/ *n* **1a** a dark bituminous usu strong-smelling viscous liquid obtained by heating and distilling wood, coal, peat, etc **b** a residue present in smoke from burning tobacco that contains resins, acids, phenols, etc **2** a sailor – infml

[2]**tar** *vt* **-rr-** to smear with tar – **tar and feather** to smear (a person) with tar and cover with feathers as a punishment or humiliation – **tarred with the same brush** having the same faults

tarantella /,tarənˈtelə‖,tærənˈtelə/ *n* (music suitable for) a vivacious folk dance of southern Italy [Italian, fr *Taranto*, city & port in Italy]

tarantula /təˈranchoolə‖təˈræntʃʊlə/ *n, pl* **tarantulas** *also* **tarantulae** /-li‖-lɪ/ **1** a European spider formerly held to be the cause of a nervous disease producing dancelike body movements **2** any of various large hairy spiders that can bite sharply but are not significantly poisonous to human beings

tarboosh *also* **tarbush** /tahˈboohsh‖tɑːˈbuːʃ/ *n* a usu red hat similar to the fez, worn esp by Muslim men

tardy /ˈtahdi‖ˈtɑːdɪ/ *adj* **1** moving or progressing slowly; sluggish **2** delayed beyond the expected time; late – **tardily** *adv*, **tardiness** *n*

[1]**tare** /teə‖teə/ *n* **1** any of several vetches **2** *pl* a weed found in cornfields – used in the Bible

[2]**tare** *n* **1a** the weight of the wrapping material or container in which goods are packed **b** a deduction from the gross weight of a substance and its container made in allowance for the weight of the container **2** the weight of an unloaded goods vehicle **3** a container used as a counterweight in calculating the net weight of goods

target /ˈtahgit‖ˈtɑːgɪt/ *n* **1** a small round shield **2a** an object to fire at in practice or competition; *esp* one consisting of a series of concentric circles with a bull's-eye at the centre **b** sthg (e g an aircraft or installation) fired at or attacked **3a** an object of ridicule, criticism, etc **b** a goal, objective

tariff /ˈtarif‖ˈtærɪf/ *n* **1** a duty or schedule of duties imposed by a government on imported or in some countries exported goods **2** a schedule of rates or prices [Italian *tariffa*, fr Arabic *taˈrīf* notification]

[1]**tarmac** /ˈtahmak‖ˈtɑːmæk/ *n* **1** tarmacadam **2** a runway, apron, or road made of tarmac

[2]**tarmac** *vt* to apply tarmac to

tarmacadam /,tahməˈkadəm‖,tɑːməˈkædəm/ *n* a mixture of tar and aggregates used for surfacing roads

tarn /tahn‖tɑːn/ *n* a small mountain lake

[1]**tarnish** /ˈtahnish‖ˈtɑːnɪʃ/ *vt* **1** to dull the lustre of (as if) by dirt, air, etc **2a** to mar, spoil **b** to bring discredit on ~*vi* to become tarnished – **tarnishable** *adj*

[2]**tarnish** *n* a film of chemically altered material on the surface of a metal (e g silver)

tarot /ˈtaroh‖ˈtærəʊ/ *n* any of a set of 78 pictorial playing cards, including 22 trumps, used esp for fortune-telling

tarpaulin /tahˈpawlin‖tɑːˈpɔːlɪn/ *n* (a piece of) heavy waterproof usu tarred canvas material used for protecting objects or ground exposed to the elements

tarragon /ˈtarəgən‖ˈtærəgən/ *n* (a small European wormwood with) pungent aromatic leaves used as a flavouring

tarry /ˈtari‖ˈtærɪ/ *vi* **1** to delay or be slow in acting or doing **2** to stay in or at a place

tarsus /ˈtahsəs‖ˈtɑːsəs/ *n, pl* **tarsi** /-sie‖-saɪ/ **1** (the small bones that support) the back part of the foot of a vertebrate that includes the ankle and heel **2** the part of the limb of an arthropod furthest from the body **3** the plate of dense connective tissue that stiffens the eyelid – **tarsal** *adj or n*

[1]**tart** /taht‖tɑːt/ *adj* **1** agreeably sharp or acid to the taste **2** caustic, cutting <*a* ~ *rejoinder*> – **tartish** *adj*, **tartishly** *adv*, **tartly** *adv*, **tartness** *n*

[2]**tart** *n* **1** a pastry shell or shallow pie containing a usu sweet filling (e g jam or fruit) **2** a prostitute; *broadly* a sexually promiscuous girl or woman – infml – **tarty** *adj*, **tartiness** *n*, **tartlet** *n*

tartan /ˈtaht(ə)n‖ˈtɑːt(ə)n/ *n* (a usu twilled woollen fabric with) a plaid textile design of Scottish origin consisting of checks of varying width and colour usu patterned to designate a distinctive clan

[1]**tartar** /ˈtahtə‖ˈtɑːtə/ *n* **1** a substance consisting essentially of cream of tartar that is derived from the juice of grapes and deposited in wine casks as a reddish crust or sediment **2** an incrustation on the teeth consisting esp of calcium salts

[2]**tartar** *n* **1** *cap, NAm chiefly* **Tatar** a member of a group of people found mainly in the Tartar Republic of the USSR, the north Caucasus, Crimea, and parts of Siberia **2** *cap, NAm chiefly* **Tatar** the language of the Tartars **3** an irritable, formidable, or exacting person – **Tartar** *adj*, **Tartarian** *adj*

tartaric acid /tah'tarik‖tɑː'tærɪk/ *n* a strong carboxylic acid from plants that is usu obtained from tartar, and is used esp in food and medicines

tartar sauce /'tahtə‖'tɑːtə/, **tartare sauce** /~, 'tah,tah‖~, 'tɑː,tɑː/ *n* mayonnaise with chopped pickles, olives, capers, and parsley

tart up *vt, chiefly Br* to dress up, esp cheaply or gaudily – infml

task /tahsk‖tɑːsk/ *n* **1** an assigned piece of work; a duty **2** sthg hard or unpleasant that has to be done; a chore

'**task ,force** *n* a temporary grouping under 1 leader for the purpose of accomplishing a definite objective

'**task,master** /-,mahstə‖-,mɑːstə/ *n* one who assigns tasks <*a hard ~*>

[1]**tassel** /'tasl‖'tæsl/ *n* **1** a dangling ornament (e g for a curtain or bedspread) consisting of a bunch of cords or threads usu of even length fastened at 1 end **2** the tassel-like flower clusters of some plants, esp maize

[2]**tassel** *vb* **-ll-** (*NAm* **-l-**, **-ll-**) *vt* to decorate with tassels ~*vi* to form tassel flower clusters

[1]**taste** /tayst‖teɪst/ *vt* **1** to experience, undergo <*has ~d defeat*> **2** to test the flavour of by taking a little into the mouth **3** to eat or drink, esp in small quantities **4** to perceive or recognize (as if) by the sense of taste ~ *vi* **1** to test the flavour of sthg by taking a little into the mouth **2** to have perception, experience, or enjoyment – usu + *of* **3** to have a specified flavour – often + *of* <*this drink ~s of aniseed*>

[2]**taste** *n* **1a** the act of tasting **b** a small amount tasted **c** a first acquaintance or experience of sthg <*her first ~ of success*> **2** (the quality of a dissolved substance as perceived by) the 1 of the 5 basic physical senses by which the qualities of dissolved substances in contact with taste buds on the tongue are interpreted by the brain as 1 or a combination of the 4 basic taste sensations sweet, bitter, sour, or salt **3** individual preference; inclination **4** (a manner or quality indicative of) critical judgment or discernment esp in aesthetic or social matters <*a remark in bad ~*>

'**taste ,bud** *n* any of the small organs, esp on the surface of the tongue, that receive and transmit the sensation of taste

'**tasteful** /-f(ə)l‖-f(ə)l/ *adj* showing or conforming to good taste – **tastefully** *adv*, **tastefulness** *n*

'**tasteless** /-lis‖-lɪs/ *adj* **1** having no taste; insipid **2** showing poor taste – disapproved of by some speakers – **tastelessly** *adv*, **tastelessness** *n*

taster /'taystə‖'teɪstə/ *n* sby who tests food or drink by tasting, esp in order to assess quality

tasty /'taysti‖'teɪstɪ/ *adj* **1** having an appetizing flavour **2** arousing interest <*a ~ bit of gossip*> – infml – **tastily** *adv*, **tastiness** *n*

[1]**tat** /tat‖tæt/ *vb* **-tt-** *vi* to work at tatting ~*vt* to make by tatting

[2]**tat** *n, Br* low quality material or goods – infml

ta-ta /'tah ,tah‖'tɑː ,tɑː/ *interj, chiefly Br* goodbye – infml

tatter /'tatə‖'tætə/ *n* **1** an irregular torn shred, esp of material **2** *pl* tattered clothing; rags – **in tatters 1** torn in pieces; ragged **2** in disarray; useless

tattered /'tatəd‖'tætəd/ *adj* (dressed in clothes which are) old and torn

tatting /'tating‖'tætɪŋ/ *n* (the act or art of making) a delicate handmade lace formed usu by making loops and knots using a single cotton thread and a small shuttle

[1]**tattle** /'tatl‖'tætl/ *vi* to chatter, gossip ~*vt* to disclose (e g secrets) by gossiping – **tattler** *n*

[2]**tattle** *n* chatter, gossip

[1]**tattoo** /ta'tooh‖tæ'tuː/ *n, pl* **tattoos 1a** an evening drum or bugle call sounded as notice to soldiers to return to quarters **b** an outdoor military display given by troops as a usu evening entertainment **2** a rapid rhythmic beating or rapping [Dutch *taptoe*, fr the phrase *tap toe!* taps shut!]

[2]**tattoo** *n, pl* **tattoos** (an indelible mark made by) tattooing [Tahitian *tatau*]

[3]**tattoo** *vt* **1** to mark (the body) by inserting pigments under the skin **2** to mark (a design) on the body by tattooing – **tattooer** *n*, **tattooist** *n*

tatty /'tati‖'tætɪ/ *adj* shabby, dilapidated – infml

taught /tawt‖tɔːt/ *past & past part of* TEACH

[1]**taunt** /tawnt‖tɔːnt/ *vt* to provoke in a mocking way; jeer at – **taunter** *n*, **tauntingly** *adv*

[2]**taunt** *n* a sarcastic provocation or insult

Taurus /'tawrəs‖'tɔːrəs/ *n* (sby born under) the 2nd sign of the zodiac in astrology which is pictured as a bull – **Taurean** *adj or n*

taut /tawt‖tɔːt/ *adj* **1a** tightly drawn; tensely stretched **b** showing anxiety; tense – **tautly** *adv*, **tautness** *n*

tautology /taw'toləji‖tɔː'tɒlədʒɪ/ *n* **1** (an instance of) needless repetition of an idea, statement, or word **2** a statement that is true by virtue of its logical form; an analytic proposition [Late Latin *tautologia*, fr Greek, fr *tauto* the same + *legein* to say] – **tautological, tautologous** *adj*, **tautologically**, **tautologously** *adv*

tavern /'tavən‖'tævən/ *n* INN 1a, b

tawdry /'tawdri‖'tɔːdrɪ/ *adj* cheap and tastelessly showy in appearance [obs *tawdry lace* cheap necklace, alteration of *St Audrey's Lace*; fr its being originally sold at a fair commemorating St Audrey (died 679), Queen of Northumbria] – **tawdrily** *adv*, **tawdriness** *n*

tawny /'tawni‖'tɔːnɪ/ *adj* of a warm sandy or brownish orange colour like that of well-tanned skin – **tawniness** *n*

tawse /tawz‖tɔːz/ *n, chiefly Scot* a leather strap slit into strips at the end, used for beating children

[1]**tax** /taks‖tæks/ *vt* **1** to assess (legal costs) **2** to levy a tax on **3** to charge, accuse *with* **4** to make strenuous demands on – **taxable** *adj*, **taxingly** *adv*, **taxer** *n*

[2]**tax** *n* **1** a charge, usu of money, imposed by a government on individuals, organizations, or property, esp to raise revenue **2** a heavy demand

or strain – **after tax** net – **before tax** gross

taxation /tak'saysh(ə)n||tæk'seɪʃ(ə)n/ *n* **1** the action of taxing; *esp* the imposition of taxes **2** revenue obtained from taxes **3** the amount assessed as a tax

,tax-'free *adj* exempted from tax

'tax ,haven *n* a country with a relatively low level of taxation, esp on incomes

[1]taxi /'taksi||'tæksɪ/ *n, pl* **taxis** *also* **taxies** a taxicab

[2]taxi *vb* **taxis, taxies; taxiing, taxying; taxied** *vi* **1** to ride in a taxi **2** *of an aircraft* to go at low speed along the surface of the ground or water ~ *vt* **1** to transport by taxi **2** to cause (an aircraft) to taxi

'taxi,cab /-,kab||-,kæb/ *n* a motor car that may be hired, together with its driver, to carry passengers, the fare usu being calculated by a taximeter

taxidermy /'taksi,duhmi||'tæksɪ,dɜːmɪ/ *n* the art of preparing, stuffing, and mounting the skins of animals [deriv of Greek *taxis* arrangement + *derma* skin] – **taxidermist** *n*, **taxidermic** *adj*

taximeter /'taksi,meetə||'tæksɪ,miːtə/ *n* a meter fitted in a taxi to calculate the charge for each journey, usu determined by the distance travelled

taxonomy /tak'sonəmi||tæk'sɒnəmɪ/ *n* (the study of the principles of) classification, specif of plants and animals according to their presumed natural relationships – **taxonomist** *n*, **taxonomic** *adj*, **taxonomically** *adv*

TB *n* tuberculosis

'T-,bone, T-bone steak *n* a thick steak from the thin end of a beef sirloin containing a T-shaped bone

tea /tee||tiː/ *n* **1a** a shrub cultivated esp in China, Japan, and the E Indies **b** the leaves of the tea plant prepared for the market, classed according to method of manufacture (e g green tea or oolong), and graded according to leaf size (e g pekoe) **2** an aromatic beverage prepared from tea leaves by infusion with boiling water **3** any of various plants somewhat resembling tea in appearance or properties; *also* an infusion of their leaves used medicinally or as a beverage **4a** refreshments including tea with sandwiches, cakes, etc served in the late afternoon **b** a late-afternoon or early-evening meal that is usu less substantial than the midday meal [Chinese (Amoy dialect) *t'e*]

'tea ,bag *n* a cloth or filter paper bag holding enough tea for an individual serving when infused

tea cake *n* a round yeast-leavened (sweet) bread bun that often contains currants and is usu eaten toasted with butter

teach /teech||tiːtʃ/ *vb* **taught** /tawt||tɔːt/ *vt* **1** to cause to know (how), esp by showing or instructing <*is* ~ing *me to drive*> **2** to guide the studies of **3** to impart the knowledge of <~ *algebra*> **4** to instruct by precept, example, or experience **5** to cause to suffer the usu disagreeable consequences of sthg – infml <*I'll* ~ *you to come home late*> ~*vi* to provide instruction

teacher /'teechə||'tiːtʃə/ *n* sby whose occupation is teaching

tea chest *n* a large square box used for exporting tea

'teach-,in *n* **1** an informally structured conference on a usu topical issue **2** an extended meeting for lectures, demonstrations, and discussions on a topic

teaching /'teeching||'tiːtʃɪŋ/ *n* **1** the profession of a teacher **2** sthg taught; *esp* a doctrine

teaching hospital *n* a hospital that is affiliated to a medical school and provides medical students with the opportunity of gaining practical experience under supervision

'tea ,cloth *n* **1** a small cloth for a table or trolley on which tea is to be served **2** TEA TOWEL

'tea,house /-,hows||-,haʊs/ *n* a restaurant, esp in China or Japan, where tea and light refreshments are served

teak /teek||tiːk/ *n* (a tall E Indian tree of the vervain family with) hard yellowish brown wood used for furniture and shipbuilding

teal /teel||tiːl/ *n* (any of several ducks related to) a small Old World dabbling duck the male of which has a distinctive green and chestnut head

[1]team /teem||tiːm/ *n* **1a** two or more draught animals harnessed together **b** one or more draught animals together with harness and vehicle **2** *sing or pl in constr* a group formed for work or activity: e g **2a** a group on 1 side (e g in a sporting contest or debate) **b** a crew, gang

[2]team *vt* **1** to yoke or join in a team **2** to combine so as to form a harmonizing arrangement <~ *the shoes with the dress*> ~ *vi* **1** to come together (as if) in a team – often + *up* <*let's* ~ *up with them for a night out*> **2** to form a harmonizing combination

team spirit *n* willingness to subordinate personal aims to group objectives

teamster /'teemstə||'tiːmstə/ *n* **1** sby who drives a team of horses **2** *NAm* a lorry driver

'team,work /-,wuhk||-,wɜːk/ *n* mutual cooperation in a group enterprise

teapot /'tee,pot||'tiː,pɒt/ *n* a pot with a lid, spout, and handle in which tea is brewed and from which it is served

[1]tear /tiə||tɪə/ *n* **1** a drop of clear salty fluid secreted by the lachrymal gland that lubricates the eye and eyelids and is often shed as a result of grief or other emotion **2** a transparent drop of (hardened) fluid (e g resin) – **tearless** *adj* – **in tears** crying, weeping

[2]tear /teə||teə/ *vb* **tore** /taw||tɔː/; **torn** /tawn||tɔːn/ *vt* **1a** to pull apart by force **b** to wound by tearing; lacerate **2** to cause division or distress to <*a mind* torn *with doubts*> **3** to remove by force <tore *the child from him*> **4** to make or effect (as if) by tearing <~ *a hole in the paper*> ~ *vi* **1** to separate on being pulled <*this cloth* ~s *easily*> **2** to move or act with violence, haste, or force <*went* ~ing *down the street*> – **tearer** *n* – **tear a strip off** to rebuke angrily – infml – **tear into** to attack physically or verbally without restraint or caution – **tear one's hair** to experience or express grief, rage, desperation, or anxiety

[3]tear /teə||teə/ *n* **1** damage from being torn – chiefly in *wear and tear* **2** a hole or flaw made by tearing

tearaway /'teərə,way||'teərə,weɪ/ *n, Br* an unruly and reckless young person – infml

tear away *vt* to remove (oneself or another) reluctantly <*she could hardly* tear *herself* away *from the book*>
tear down *vt* to pull down, esp violently; demolish
teardrop /'tiə,drop‖'tɪə,drɒp/ *n* [1]TEAR 1
[1]**tearful** /-f(ə)l‖-f(ə)l/ *adj* **1** flowing with or accompanied by tears **2** causing tears **3** inclined or about to cry – **tearfully** *adv*, **tearfulness** *n*
tear gas /tiə‖tɪə/ *n* a solid, liquid, or gaseous substance that on dispersion in the atmosphere blinds the eyes with tears and is used chiefly in dispelling crowds
tearjerker /'tiə,juhkə‖'tɪə,dʒɜːkə/ *n* an excessively sentimental play, film, etc designed to provoke tears – infml – **tear-jerking** *adj*
tearoom /'tee,roohm‖'tiː,ruːm/ *n* a restaurant where light refreshments are served
tear up /teə‖teə/ *vt* **1** to tear into pieces **2** to cancel or annul, usu unilaterally <tore up *the treaty*>
[1]**tease** /teez‖tiːz/ *vt* **1** to disentangle and straighten by combing or carding <~ *wool*> **2a** to (attempt to) disturb or annoy by persistently irritating or provoking **b** to persuade to acquiesce, esp by persistent small efforts; coax; *also* to obtain by repeated coaxing <~d *the money out of her father*> ~*vi* to tease sby or sthg – **teasingly** *adv*
[2]**tease** *n* sby or sthg that teases
teasel, teazel, teazle /'teezl‖'tiːzl/ *n* **1** (a flower head of) a tall Old World plant with flower heads that are covered with stiff hooked bracts and were formerly used, when dried to raise a nap on woollen cloth **2** a wire substitute for the teasel
teaser /'teezə‖'tiːzə/ *n* **1** a frustratingly difficult problem **2** sby who derives malicious pleasure from teasing
teaspoon /'tee,spoohn‖'tiː,spuːn/ *n* **1** a small spoon used esp for eating soft foods and stirring beverages **2** a teaspoonful
'**tea,spoonful** /-f(ə)l‖-f(ə)l/ *n, pl* **teaspoonfuls** *also* **teaspoonsful** as much as a teaspoon will hold
teat /teet‖tiːt/ *n* **1** NIPPLE 1 **2** a small projection or a nib (e g on a mechanical part); *specif* a rubber mouthpiece with usu 2 or more holes in it, attached to the top of a baby's feeding bottle – **teated** *adj*
teatime /'tee,tiem‖'tiː,taɪm/ *n* the customary time for tea; late afternoon or early evening
'**tea ,towel** *n* a dishcloth
'**tea ,tray** *n* a tray on which a tea service is carried
'**tea ,trolley** *n, chiefly Br* a small trolley used in serving tea or light refreshments
tech /tek‖tek/ *n, Br* a technical school or college – infml
technical /'teknikl‖'teknɪkl/ *adj* **1a** having special and usu practical knowledge, esp of a mechanical or scientific subject **b** marked by or characteristic of specialization **2** of a particular subject; *esp* of a practical subject organized on scientific principles **3** in the strict legal interpretation **4** of technique – **technically** *adv*, **technicalness** *n*
technicality /,tekni'kaləti‖,teknɪ'kælətɪ/ *n* sthg technical; *esp* a detail meaningful only to a specialist
technical knockout /'nok,owt‖'nɒk,aʊt/ *n* the termination of a boxing match when a boxer is declared by the referee to be unable (e g because of injuries) to continue the fight
technician /tek'nish(ə)n‖tek'nɪʃ(ə)n/ *n* **1** a specialist in the technical details of a subject or occupation <*a medical* ~> **2** sby who has acquired the technique of an area of specialization (e g an art)
technique /tek'neek‖tek'niːk/ *n* **1** the manner in which an artist, performer, or athlete displays or manages the formal aspect of his/her skill **2a** a body of technical methods (e g in a craft or in scientific research) **b** a method of accomplishing a desired aim
technocracy /tek'nokrəsi‖tek'nɒkrəsɪ/ *n* (management of society by) a body of technical experts; *also* a society so managed – chiefly derog – **technocrat** *n*, **technocratic** *adj*
technology /tek'noləji‖tek'nɒlədʒɪ/ *n* **1** (the theory and practice of) applied science **2** the totality of the means and knowledge used to provide objects necessary for human sustenance and comfort [Greek *technologia* systematic treatment of an art, fr *technē* art, craft, skill + *logos* speech, reason] – **technologist** *n*, **technological** *adj*, **technologically** *adv*
techy /'techi‖'tetʃɪ/ *adj* tetchy
'**teddy ,bear** /tedi‖tedɪ/ *n* a stuffed toy bear [*Teddy*, nickname of *Theodore* Roosevelt (1858-1919), US president; referring to a cartoon depicting the president sparing the life of a bear cub while hunting]
'**teddy ,boy** *n* any of a cult of (British) youths, esp in the 1950s, adopting the dress of the early 20th c and often having a reputation for unruly behaviour [*Teddy*, nickname for *Edward*, i e King Edward VII (1841-1910)]
Te Deum /,tay 'dayəm, ,tee 'dee-‖,teɪ 'deɪəm, ,tiː 'diː-/ *n, pl* **Te Deums** a liturgical Christian hymn of praise to God
tedious /'teedi·əs‖'tiːdɪəs/ *adj* tiresome because of length or dullness – **tediously** *adv*, **tediousness** *n*
tedium /'teedi·əm‖'tiːdɪəm/ *n* tediousness; *also* boredom
[1]**tee** /tee‖tiː/ *n* **1** sthg shaped like a capital T **2** a mark aimed at in various games (e g curling)
[2]**tee** *n* **1** a peg or a small mound used to raise a golf ball into position for striking at the beginning of play on a hole **2** the area from which a golf ball is struck at the beginning of play on a hole
[3]**tee** *vt* to place (a ball) on a tee – often + *up*
[1]**teem** /teem‖tiːm/ *vi* **1** to abound <*lakes that* ~ *with fish*> **2** to be present in large quantities
[2]**teem** *vi, Br* to rain hard
teenage /'teenayj‖'tiːneɪdʒ/, **teenaged** /'teenayjd‖'tiːneɪdʒd/ *adj* of or being people in their teens – **teenager** *n*
teens /teenz‖tiːnz/ *n pl* the numbers 13 to 19 inclusive; *specif* the years 13 to 19 in a lifetime
teeny /'teeni‖'tiːnɪ/, **teeny-weeny** /,teeni 'weeni‖,tiːnɪ 'wiːnɪ/ *adj* tiny – infml
teenybopper /'teeni ,bopə‖'tiːnɪ ,bɒpə/ *n* a young teenage girl who zealously follows the

latest trends in clothes, pop music, etc

tee off /tee||ti:/ *vi* to drive a golf ball from a tee

'tee ˌshirt *n* a T-shirt

teeter /'teetə||'ti:tə/ *vi* to move unsteadily

teeth /teeth||ti:θ/ *pl of* TOOTH

teethe /teedh||ti:ð/ *vi* to cut one's teeth; grow teeth – **teething** *n*

teetotal /tee'tohtl||ti:'təʊtl/ *adj* practising complete abstinence from alcoholic drinks – **teetotalism** *n*

teetotaller /tee'tohtl·ə||ti:'təʊtlə/, *NAm chiefly* **teetotaler** *n* sby teetotal

Teflon /'teflon||'teflɒn/ *trademark* – used for polytetrafluoroethylene

tele-, tel- *comb form* **1** distant; at a distance; over a distance <tele*gram*> **2a** telegraph <tele*printer*> **b** television <tele*camera*>

telecast /'telikahst||'telɪkɑ:st/ *vb* to televise – **telecast** *n*, **telecaster** *n*

telecommunication /ˌtelikəˌmyoohni'kaysh(ə)n||ˌtelɪkəˌmju:nɪ'keɪʃ(ə)n/ *n* **1** communication at a distance (e g by telegraph) **2** a science that deals with telecommunication – usu pl with sing. meaning

telegram /'teligram||'telɪgræm/ *n* a message sent by telegraph and delivered as a written or typed note

[1]telegraph /'teligrahf, -graf||'telɪgrɑ:f, -græf/ *n* an apparatus or system for communicating at a distance, esp by making and breaking an electric circuit [French *télégraphe*, deriv of Greek *tēle* far off + *graphein* to write]

[2]telegraph *vt* **1** to send or communicate (as if) by telegraph **2** to make known by signs, esp unknowingly and in advance <~ *a punch*> – **telegrapher** *n*, **telegraphist** *n*

telegraphese /ˌteligrah'feez, -gra-||ˌtelɪgrɑ:'fi:z, -græ-/ *n* the terse and abbreviated language characteristic of telegrams

telegraphic /ˌteli'grafik||ˌtelɪ'græfɪk/ *adj* **1** of the telegraph **2** concise, terse – **telegraphically** *adv*

telegraphy /tə'legrəfi||tə'legrəfɪ/ *n* the use or operation of a telegraphic apparatus or system

telemarketing /ˌteli'mahkiting/ *also* **teleselling** *n* the practice of contacting potential customers by telephone to sell goods

telemeter /'teliˌmeetə, tə'lemitə||'telɪˌmi:tə, tə'lemɪtə/ *n* an electrical apparatus for measuring a quantity (e g pressure or temperature) and transmitting the result to a distant point – **telemeter** *n*, **telemetric** *adj*, **telemetry** *n*

teleology /ˌteli'oləji, ˌtee-||ˌtelɪ'ɒlədʒɪ, ˌti:-/ *n* **1** a doctrine explaining phenomena by reference to goals or purposes **2** the character attributed to nature or natural processes of being directed towards an end or designed according to a purpose – **teleologist** *n*, **teleological** *adj*

telepathy /tə'lepəthi||tə'lepəθɪ/ *n* communication directly from one mind to another without use of the known senses – **telepathist** *n*, **telepathic** *adj*

[1]telephone /'telifohn||'telɪfəʊn/ *n* **1** a device for reproducing sounds at a distance; *specif* one for converting sounds into electrical impulses for transmission, usu by wire, to a particular receiver **2** the system of communications that uses telephones <*get in touch by* ~> [deriv of Greek *tēle* far off + *phōnē* voice, sound] – **telephonic** *adj*, **telephony** *n*

[2]telephone *vi* to make a telephone call ~ *vt* **1** to send by telephone <~ *a message*> **2** to (attempt to) speak to by telephone – **telephoner** *n*

'telephone diˌrectory *n* a book giving the telephone numbers of subscribers

telephonist /tə'lefənist||tə'lefənɪst/ *n*, *Br* a telephone switchboard operator

telephoto /'teliˌfohtoh||'telɪˌfəʊtəʊ/ *adj* **1** of telephotography **2** being a camera lens system designed to give a large image of a distant object

telephotography /ˌtelifə'tografi||ˌtelɪfə'tɒgrəfɪ/ *n* the photography of distant objects (e g by a camera provided with a telephoto lens) – **telephotographic** *adj*

teleprinter /'teliˌprintə||'telɪˌprɪntə/ *n* a typewriter keyboard that transmits telegraphic signals, a typewriting device activated by telegraphic signals, or a machine that combines both these functions

TelePrompTer /'teliˌpromptə||'telɪˌprɒmptə/ *trademark* – used for a device for unrolling a magnified script in front of a speaker on television

[1]telescope /'teliskohp||'telɪskəʊp/ *n* **1** a usu tubular optical instrument for viewing distant objects by means of the refraction of light rays through a lens or the reflection of light rays by a concave mirror **2** RADIO TELESCOPE [deriv of Greek *tēleskopos* farseeing, fr *tēle* far off + *skopos* watcher]

[2]telescope *vi* **1** to slide one part within another like the cylindrical sections of a hand telescope **2** to become compressed under impact **3** to become condensed or shortened ~ *vt* **1** to cause to telescope **2** to condense, shorten

telescopic /ˌteli'skopik||ˌtelɪ'skɒpɪk/ *adj* **1a** of or performed with a telescope **b** suitable for seeing or magnifying distant objects **2** able to discern objects at a distance **3** having parts that telescope – **telescopically** *adv*

televise /'teliviez||'telɪvaɪz/ *vt* to broadcast (an event or film) by television

television /'telivizh(ə)n, --'--||'telɪvɪʒ(ə)n, - -'--/ *n* **1** an electronic system of transmitting changing images together with sound along a wire or through space by converting the images and sounds into electrical signals **2** a television receiving set **3a(1)** the television broadcasting industry **a(2)** a television broadcasting organization or station <*Tyne-Tees* Television> **b** the medium of television communication [French *télévision*, fr Greek *tēle* far off + French *vision* vision (fr Latin *vis-*, *vidēre* to see)

televisual /ˌteli'vizhyooəl||ˌtelɪ'vɪʒjʊəl/ *adj*, *chiefly Br* of or suitable for broadcast by television

telex /'teleks||'teleks/ *n* a communications service involving teleprinters connected by wire through automatic exchanges; *also* a message by telex – **telex** *vb*

tell /tel||tel/ *vb* **told** /tohld||təʊld/ *vt* **1** to count, enumerate <*all* told *there were 27 present*> **2a** to relate in detail; narrate <~ *me a story*> **b** to give utterance to; express in words **3** to make known; divulge **4a** to report to; inform **b** to assure emphatically <*he did not do it, I ~ you*> **5** to order <told *her to wait*> **6a** to ascertain by observing <*can never ~ whether he's lying or not*> **b** to distinguish, discriminate <*can't ~ Bach from the Beatles*> ~ *vi* **1** to give an account **2** to make a positive assertion; decide definitely <*you can never ~ for certain*> **3** to act as an informer – often + *on* **4** to take effect <*the worry began to ~ on her nerves*> **5** to serve as evidence or indication <*will ~ against you in court*>

teller /ˈtelə‖ˈtelə/ *n* **1** sby who relates or communicates <*a ~ of stories*> **2** sby who counts: e g **2a** sby appointed to count votes **b** a member of a bank's staff concerned with the direct handling of money received or paid out

telling /ˈteling‖ˈtelɪŋ/ *adj* carrying great weight and producing a marked effect <*the most ~ evidence against him*> – **tellingly** *adv*

tell off *vt* **1** to number and set apart; *esp* to assign to a special duty <told off *a detail and put them to digging a trench*> **2** to give a telling-off to

telltale /ˈtelˌtayl‖ˈtelˌteɪl/ *n* **1** sby who spreads gossip or rumours; *esp* an informer **2** a device for indicating or recording sthg (e g the position of a vessel's rudder) – **telltale** *adj*

telly /ˈteli‖ˈtelɪ/ *n, chiefly Br* (a) television – infml

temerity /təˈmerəti‖təˈmerətɪ/ *n* unreasonable disregard for danger or opposition; *broadly* cheek, nerve

[1]**temp** /temp‖temp/ *n* sby (e g a typist or secretary) employed temporarily – infml

[2]**temp** *vi* to work as a temp – infml

[1]**temper** /ˈtempə‖ˈtempə/ *vt* **1** to moderate (sthg harsh) *with* the addition of sthg less severe <*~ justice with mercy*> **2** to bring to a suitable state, esp by mixing in or adding a liquid ingredient; *esp* to mix (clay) with water or a modifier and knead to a uniform texture **3** to bring (esp steel) to the right degree of hardness by reheating (and quenching) after cooling **4** to strengthen the character of through hardship <*troops* ~ed *in battle*> **5** to adjust the pitch of (a note, chord, or instrument) to a temperament – **temperable** *adj*, **temperer** *n*

[2]**temper** *n* **1** characteristic tone <*the ~ of the times*> **2** the state of a substance with respect to certain desired qualities (e g the degree of hardness or resilience given to steel by tempering) **3a** a characteristic cast of mind or state of feeling **b** composure, equanimity **c** (proneness to displays of) an uncontrolled and often disproportionate rage <*he has/is in a terrible ~*>

tempera /ˈtempərə‖ˈtempərə/ *n* (a work produced by) a method of painting using pigment ground and mixed with an emulsion (e g of egg yolk and water)

temperament /ˈtemprəmənt‖ˈtemprəmənt/ *n* **1a** a person's peculiar or distinguishing mental or physical character (which according to medieval physiology was determined by the relative proportions of the humours) **b** excessive sensitiveness or irritability **2** the modification of the musical intervals of the pure scale to produce a set of 12 fixed notes to the octave which enables a keyboard instrument to play in more than 1 key

temperamental /ˌtemprəˈmentl‖ˌtemprəˈmentl/ *adj* **1** of or arising from individual character or constitution <*~ peculiarities*> **2a** easily upset or irritated; liable to sudden changes of mood **b** unpredictable in behaviour or performance – **temperamentally** *adv*

temperance /ˈtempərəns‖ˈtempərəns/ *n* **1** moderation, self-restraint **2** habitual moderation in the indulgence of the appetites; *specif* moderation in or abstinence from the use of alcoholic drink

temperate /ˈtempərət‖ˈtempərət/ *adj* **1** moderate: e g **1a** not extreme or excessive <*a ~ climate*> <*a ~ speech*> **b** moderate in indulgence of appetite or desire; *esp* abstemious in the consumption of alcohol **2a** having a moderate climate **b** found in or associated with a temperate climate – **temperately** *adv*, **temperateness** *n*

temperature /ˈtemprəchə‖ˈtemprətʃə/ *n* **1a** degree of hotness or coldness as measured on an arbitrary scale (e g in degrees Celsius) **b** the degree of heat natural to the body of a living being **2** an abnormally high body heat

tempered /ˈtempəd‖ˈtempəd/ *adj* **1a** having the elements mixed in satisfying proportions **b** qualified or diluted by the mixture or influence of an additional ingredient **2** having a specified temper – in combination <*short*-tempered>

tempest /ˈtempist‖ˈtempɪst/ *n* **1** a violent storm **2** a tumult, uproar

tempestuous /temˈpeschoo·əs‖temˈpestʃʊəs/ *adj* turbulent, stormy – **tempestuously** *adv*, **tempestuousness** *n*

template /ˈtemplayt‖ˈtempleɪt/, **templet** /ˈtemplit‖ˈtemplɪt/ *n* **1** a short piece or block placed horizontally in a wall under a beam to distribute its weight or pressure (e g over a door) **2a** a gauge, pattern, or mould used as a guide to the form of a piece being made **b** a molecule (e g of RNA) in a biological system that carries the genetic code for protein or other molecules

[1]**temple** /ˈtempl‖ˈtempl/ *n* **1a** a building dedicated to worship among any of various ancient civilizations and present-day non-Christian religions (e g Hinduism and Buddhism) **b** *often cap* any of 3 successive national sanctuaries in ancient Jerusalem **2** a place devoted or dedicated to a specified purpose

[2]**temple** *n* the flattened space on either side of the forehead of some mammals (e g human beings)

[3]**temple** *n* a device in a loom for keeping the cloth stretched

tempo /ˈtempoh‖ˈtempəʊ/ *n, pl* **tempi** /-pi‖-pɪ/, **tempos** **1** the speed of a musical piece or passage **2** rate of motion or activity

temporal /ˈtemp(ə)rəl‖ˈtemp(ə)rəl/ *adj* **1a** of time as opposed to eternity or space; *esp* transitory **b** of earthly life **c** of lay or secular concerns **2** of grammatical tense or a distinction of time <when *is a ~ conjunction*> – **temporally** *adv*

[1]**temporary** /ˈtemp(ə)rəri, ˈtempəˌreri‖ˈtemp(ə)rərɪ, ˈtempəˌrerɪ/ *adj* lasting for a limited time – **temporarily** *adv*, **temporariness** *n*

[2]**temporary** *n* a temp

tempor·ize, -ise /ˈtempəriez‖ˈtempəraɪz/ *vi* **1** to comply temporarily with the demands of the time or occasion **2** to draw out negotiations so as to gain time – **temporizer** *n*, **temporization** *n*

tempt /tempt‖tempt/ *vt* **1** to entice, esp to evil, by promise of pleasure or gain **2** to risk provoking the disfavour of <*shouldn't ~ fate*> **3a** to induce to do sthg **b** to cause to be strongly inclined <*he was ~ed to call it quits*> **c** to appeal to; entice <*the idea ~s me*> – **temptable** *adj*, **tempter, temptress** *n*

temptation /tempˈtaysh(ə)n‖tempˈteɪʃ(ə)n/ *n* **1** tempting or being tempted, esp to evil **2** sthg tempting

ten /ten‖ten/ *n* **1** (the number) 10 **2** the tenth in a set or series <*the ~ of diamonds*> **3** sthg having 10 parts or members or a denomination of 10 **4** the number occupying the position 2 to the left of the decimal point in the Arabic notation; *also, pl* this position – **ten** *adj or pron*, **tenfold** *adj or adv*

tenable /ˈtenəbl‖ˈtenəbl/ *adj* capable of being held, maintained, or defended – **tenableness** *n*, **tenably** *adv*, **tenability** *n*

tenacious /təˈnayshəs‖təˈneɪʃəs/ *adj* **1** tending to stick or cling, esp to another substance **2a** persistent in maintaining or keeping to sthg valued as habitual **b** retentive <*a ~ memory*> – **tenaciously** *adv*, **tenaciousness** *n*, **tenacity** *n*

[1]**tenant** /ˈtenənt‖ˈtenənt/ *n* **1a** a holder of real estate by any kind of right **b** an occupant of lands or property of another; *specif* sby who rents or leases a house or flat from a landlord **2** an occupant, dweller – **tenantless** *adj*, **tenancy** *n*

[2]**tenant** *vt* to hold or inhabit as a tenant – **tenantable** *adj*

ˌ**tenant ˈfarmer** *n* a farmer who works land owned by another and pays rent

tenantry /ˈtenəntri‖ˈtenəntrɪ/ *n sing or pl in constr* tenants collectively

tench /tench‖tentʃ/ *n* a Eurasian freshwater fish related to the dace and noted for its ability to survive outside water

ˌ**Ten Comˈmandments** *n pl* the commandments given by God to Moses on Mt Sinai, recorded in Ex 20:1–17

[1]**tend** /tend‖tend/ *vt* to have charge of; take care of

[2]**tend** *vi* **1** to move, direct, or develop one's course in a specified direction **2** to show an inclination or tendency – + *to, towards*, or *to* and an infinitive

tendency /ˈtendənsi‖ˈtendənsɪ/ *n* **1a** a general trend or movement <*the growing ~ for prices to rise faster than wages*> **b** an inclination or predisposition to some particular end, or towards a particular kind of thought or action **2** the purposeful trend of sthg written or said

tendentious /tenˈdenshəs‖tenˈdenʃəs/ *adj* marked by a tendency in favour of a particular point of view – chiefly derog – **tendentiously** *adv*, **tendentiousness** *n*

[1]**tender** /ˈtendə‖ˈtendə/ *adj* **1a** having a soft or yielding texture; easily broken, cut, or damaged **b** easily chewed **2a** physically weak **b** immature, young <*children of ~ years*> **3** fond, loving <*a ~ lover*> **4a** showing care <*~ regard*> **b** highly susceptible to impressions or emotions <*a ~ conscience*> **5a** gentle, mild <*~ breeding*> <*~ irony*> **b** delicate or soft in quality or tone **6a** sensitive to touch <*~ skin*> **b** sensitive to injury or insult <*~ pride*> **c** demanding careful and sensitive handling <*a ~ situation*> – **tenderly** *adv*, **tenderness** *n*

[2]**tender** *n* **1a** a ship employed to attend other ships (e g to supply provisions) **b** a boat or small steamer for communication between shore and a larger ship **2** a vehicle attached to a locomotive for carrying a supply of fuel and water

[3]**tender** *vt* **1** to make a tender of **2** to present for acceptance <*~ed his resignation*> *~vi* to make a bid <*the company ~s for and builds dams*> – **tenderer** *n*

[4]**tender** *n* **1** an unconditional offer in satisfaction of a debt or obligation, made to avoid a penalty for nonpayment or nonperformance **2** an offer, proposal: e g **2a** a formal esp written offer or bid for a contract **b** a public expression of willingness to buy not less than a specified number of shares at a fixed price from shareholders **3** sthg that may be offered in payment; *specif* money

ˈ**tenderˌfoot** /-ˌfoot‖-ˌfʊt/ *n, pl* **tenderfeet** /-ˌfeet‖-ˌfiːt/ *also* **tenderfoots** an inexperienced beginner

ˌ**tenderˈhearted** /-ˈhahtid‖-ˈhɑːtɪd/ *adj* easily moved to love, pity, or sorrow – **tenderheartedly** *adv*

tender·ize, -ise /ˈtendəriez‖ˈtendəraɪz/ *vt* to make (meat or meat products) tender by beating or adding an enzyme that breaks down fibrous tissue – **tenderizer** *n*, **tenderization** *n*

tenderloin /ˈtendəˌloyn‖ˈtendəˌlɔɪn/ *n* a pork or beef fillet

tendon /ˈtendən‖ˈtendən/ *n* a tough cord or band of dense white fibrous connective tissue that connects a muscle with a bone or other part and transmits the force exerted by the muscle – **tendinous** *adj*

tendril /ˈtendrəl‖ˈtendrəl/ *n* a slender spirally coiling sensitive organ that attaches a plant to its support – **tendriled, tendrilled** *adj*

tenement /ˈtenəmənt‖ˈtenəmənt/ *n* **1** land or other property held by one person from another **2** (a flat in) a large building; *esp* one meeting minimum standards and typically found in the poorer parts of a large city

tenet /ˈtenət‖ˈtenət/ *n* a principle, belief, or doctrine; *esp* one held in common by members of an organization or group

tenner /ˈtenə‖ˈtenə/ *n, Br* a £10 note; *also* the sum of £10 – infml

tennis /ˈtenis‖ˈtenɪs/ *n* **1** REAL TENNIS **2** a singles or doubles game that is played with rackets and a light elastic ball on a flat court divided by a low net [Middle English *tenetz, tenys*, prob fr Anglo-French *tenetz* take, receive, imperative of *tenir* to hold, take (called by server to opponent)]

tennis elbow *n* inflammation and pain of the elbow, usu resulting from excessive twisting movements of the hand

[1]**tenon** /ˈtenən‖ˈtenən/ *n* a projecting part of a piece of material (e g wood) for insertion into a mortise

[2]**tenon** *vt* **1** to unite by a tenon **2** to cut or fit for insertion in a mortise

tenor /'tenə‖'tenə/ *n* **1** the course of thought of sthg spoken or written **2a** the next to the lowest part in 4-part harmony **b** (sby with) the highest natural adult male singing voice **c** a member of a family of instruments having a range next lower than that of the alto **3** a continuance in a course or activity – **tenor** *adj*

tenpin /'ten,pin‖'ten,pɪn/ *n* a bottle-shaped pin used in tenpin bowling

,tenpin 'bowling *n* an indoor bowling game using 10 pins and a large ball in which each player is allowed to bowl 2 balls in each of 10 frames

[1]**tense** /tens‖tens/ *n* (a member of) a set of inflectional forms of a verb that express distinctions of time

[2]**tense** *adj* **1** stretched tight; made taut **2a** feeling or showing nervous tension **b** marked by strain or suspense – **tensely** *adv*, **tenseness** *n*

[3]**tense** *vb* to make or become tense – often + *up*

tensile /'tensiel‖'tensaɪl/ *adj* **1** ductile **2** of or involving tension – **tensility** *n*

[1]**tension** /'tenshən‖'tenʃən/ *n* **1a** stretching or being stretched to stiffness **b** STRESS 1a **2a** either of 2 balancing forces causing or tending to cause extension **b** the stress resulting from the elongation of an elastic body **c** gas pressure **3a** inner striving, unrest, or imbalance, often with physiological indication of emotion **b** latent hostility **c** a balance maintained in an artistic work between opposing forces or elements **4** electrical potential <*high* ~> – **tensional** *adj*, **tensionless** *adj*

[2]**tension** *vt* to tighten to a desired or appropriate degree – **tensioner** *n*

[1]**tent** /tent‖tent/ *n* **1** a collapsible shelter (e g of canvas) stretched and supported by poles **2** a canopy or enclosure placed over the head and shoulders to retain vapours or oxygen during medical treatment – **tented** *adj*, **tentless** *adj*

[2]**tent** *vi* to live in a tent ~*vt* to cover (as if) with a tent

tentacle /'tentəkl‖'tentəkl/ *n* **1** any of various elongated flexible animal parts, chiefly on the head or about the mouth, used for feeling, grasping, etc **2a** sthg like a tentacle (e g in grasping or feeling out) **b** a sensitive hair on a plant (e g the sundew) – **tentacled** *adj*, **tentacular** *adj*

tentative /'tentətiv‖'tentətɪv/ *adj* **1** not fully worked out or developed **2** hesitant, uncertain <*a* ~ *smile*> – **tentative** *n*, **tentatively** *adv*

tenter /'tentə‖'tentə/ *n* an apparatus used for drying and stretching cloth

'tenter,hook /-,hook‖-,hʊk/ *n* a sharp hooked nail used esp for fastening cloth on a tenter – **on tenterhooks** in a state of uneasiness, strain, or suspense

tenth /tenth‖tenθ/ *adj or n* (of or being) number ten in a countable series

tenuous /'tenyoo·əs‖'tenjʊəs/ *adj* **1** not dense in consistency <*a* ~ *fluid*> **2** not thick <*a* ~ *rope*> **3** having little substance or strength <*a* ~ *hold on reality*> – **tenuously** *adv*, **tenuousness** *n*, **tenuity** *n*

tenure /'tenyə‖'tenjə/ *n* **1a** the holding of property, an office, etc **b** *chiefly NAm* freedom from summary dismissal, esp from a teaching post **2** grasp, hold – fml – **tenured** *adj*, **tenurial** *adj*

tepee /'tee,pee‖'ti:,pi:/ *n* a N American Indian conical tent, usu made of skins

tepid /'tepid‖'tepɪd/ *adj* **1** moderately warm <*a* ~ *bath*> **2** not enthusiastic <*a* ~ *interest*> – **tepidly** *adv*, **tepidness** *n*, **tepidity** *n*

tequila /tə'keelə‖tə'ki:lə/ *n* **1** a Mexican agave plant cultivated as a source of mescal **2** a Mexican spirit made by redistilling mescal [*Tequila*, district of Mexico]

tercentenary /,tuhsen'teenəri, -'tenəri‖,tɜ:sen'ti:nərɪ, -'tenərɪ/ *n* a 300th anniversary or its celebration – **tercentenary** *adj*

tercentennial /,tuhsen'teni·əl‖,tɜ:sen'tenɪəl/ *n* a tercentenary – **tercentennial** *adj*

terebinth /'terəbinth‖'terəbɪnθ/ *n* a small European tree of the sumach family yielding turpentine

[1]**term** /tuhm‖tɜ:m/ *n* **1a** an end, termination; *also* a time assigned for sthg (e g payment) **b** the time at which a pregnancy of normal length ends <*had her baby at full* ~> **2a** a limited or definite extent of time; *esp* the time for which sthg lasts <*medium*-term *credit*> **b** an estate or interest held for a term **c** any one of the periods of the year during which the courts are in session **3** any of the usu 3 periods of instruction into which an academic year is divided **4a** a mathematical expression connected to another by a plus or minus sign **b** an expression that forms part of a fraction or proportion or of a series or sequence **5** a concept, word, or phrase appearing as subject or predicate in a logical proposition **6a** a word or expression with a precise meaning; *esp* one peculiar to a restricted field <*legal* ~s> **b** *pl* diction of a specified kind <*spoke in flattering* ~s> **7** *pl* provisions relating to an agreement <~s *of sale*>; *also* agreement on such provisions **8** *pl* mutual relationship <*on good* ~s *with him*> – **in terms** expressly, explicitly – **in terms of** in relation to; concerning

[2]**term** *vt* to apply a term to; call <*wouldn't* ~ *it difficult*>

termagant /'tuhməgənt‖'tɜ:məgənt/ *n* an overbearing or nagging woman

terminable /'tuhminəbl‖'tɜ:mɪnəbl/ *adj* capable of being terminated – **terminableness** *n*

[1]**terminal** /'tuhminl‖'tɜ:mɪnl/ *adj* **1a** of or being an end, extremity, boundary, or terminus **b** growing at the end of a branch or stem <*a* ~ *bud*> **2a** of or occurring in a term or each term **b** occurring at or causing the end of life <~ *cancer*> **3** occurring at or being the end of a period or series – **terminally** *adv*

[2]**terminal** *n* **1** a device attached to the end of a wire or cable or to an electrical apparatus for convenience in making connections **2** the end of a carrier line (e g shipping line or airline) with its associated buildings and facilities <*the West London air* ~> **3** a device (e g a teleprinter) through which a user can communicate with a computer

terminate /'tuhminayt‖'tɜ:mɪneɪt/ *vt* **1a** to bring to an end **b** to form the conclusion of **2** to serve as an ending, limit, or boundary of ~ *vi* **1** to extend only to a limit (e g a point or line); *esp* to reach a terminus <*this train* ~s *at Glasgow*> **2** to come to an end in time – often + *in* or *with* <*the coalition* ~d *with the election*> **3** to form an ending or outcome – often + *in* or *with* <*the match* ~d *with the champion winning*> – **termination** *n*

terminology /ˌtuhmiˈnoləji‖ˌtɜːmɪˈnɒlədʒɪ/ *n* the technical terms used in a particular subject – **terminological** *adj*, **terminologically** *adv*

terminus /ˈtuhminəs‖ˈtɜːmɪnəs/ *n, pl* **termini** /-nie‖-naɪ/, **terminuses** **1** a finishing point; an end **2** a post or stone marking a boundary **3** (the station, town, or city at) the end of a transport line or travel route **4** an extreme point or element

termite /ˈtuhˌmiet‖ˈtɜːˌmaɪt/ *n* any of numerous often destructive pale-coloured soft-bodied insects that live in colonies and feed on wood

ˌterms of ˈreference *n pl* the precise delineation of competence (e g of a committee)

tern /tuhn‖tɜːn/ *n* any of numerous water birds that are smaller than the related gulls and have a black cap, a white body, and often forked tails

terpsichorean /ˌtuhpsikəˈree·ən, ˌtuhpsiˈkawri·ən‖ˌtɜːpsɪkəˈriːən, ˌtɜːpsɪˈkɔːrɪən/ *adj* of dancing [*Terpsichore*, the muse of dancing and choral song]

[1]**terrace** /ˈteris‖ˈterɪs/ *n* **1** a relatively level paved or planted area adjoining a building **2** a raised embankment with a level top **3** a level usu narrow and steep-fronted area bordering a river, sea, etc **4a** a row of houses or flats on raised ground or a sloping site **b** a row of similar houses joined into 1 building by common walls **c** a street

[2]**terrace** *vt* to make into a terrace

terracotta /ˌterəˈkotə‖ˌterəˈkɒtə/ *n* **1** an unglazed brownish red fired clay used esp for statuettes and vases and as a building material **2** brownish orange [Italian *terra cotta*, lit., baked earth]

ˌterra ˈfirma /ˌterə ˈfuhmə‖ˌterə ˈfɜːmə/ *n* dry land; solid ground

terrain /təˈrayn‖təˈreɪn/ *n* **1** (the physical features of) an area of land **2** an environment, milieu

terrapin /ˈterəpin‖ˈterəpɪn/ *n* any of several small edible freshwater reptiles similar to tortoises but adapted for swimming

terrarium /təˈreəri·əm‖təˈreərɪəm/ *n, pl* **terraria** /-riə/, **terrariums** an enclosure or closed container for rearing animals or growing plants

terrestrial /təˈrestri·əl‖təˈrestrɪəl/ *adj* **1a** of the earth or its inhabitants **b** mundane, prosaic **2a** of land as distinct from air or water **b** *of organisms* living on or in land or soil **3** *of a planet* like the earth in density, composition, etc – **terrestrial** *n*, **terrestrially** *adv*

terrible /ˈterəbl‖ˈterəbl/ *adj* **1a** exciting intense fear; terrifying **b** formidable in nature <*a* ~ *responsibility*> **c** requiring great fortitude <*a* ~ *order*>; *also* severe <*a* ~ *winter*> **2** extreme, great <*a* ~ *amount of trouble arranging all this*> **3** of very poor quality; awful <*a* ~ *performance*>; *also* highly unpleasant *USE* (*2&3*) infml – **terribleness** *n*

terribly /ˈterəbli‖ˈterəblɪ/ *adv* very <~ *lucky*> – infml

terrier /ˈteri·ə‖ˈterɪə/ *n* **1** (a member of) any of various breeds of usu small dogs, orig used by hunters to drive out small furred game from underground **2** *usu cap, Br* a territorial [French (*chien*) *terrier*, lit., earth dog, fr *terrier* of earth, fr Medieval Latin *terrarius*, fr Latin *terra* earth]

terrific /təˈrifik‖təˈrɪfɪk/ *adj* **1** exciting fear or awe **2** extraordinarily great or intense **3** unusually fine *USE* (*2&3*) infml – **terrifically** *adv*

terrify /ˈterifie‖ˈterɪfaɪ/ *vt* **1** to fill with terror or apprehension **2** to drive or impel by menacing; scare, deter – **terrifyingly** *adv*

[1]**territorial** /ˌteriˈtawri·əl‖ˌterɪˈtɔːrɪəl/ *adj* **1a** of territory or land **b** of private property <~ *magnates*> **2a** of or restricted to a particular area or district **b** exhibiting territoriality <~ *birds*> – **territorially** *adv*

[2]**territorial** *n* a member of a territorial army, esp the Territorial Army and Volunteer Reserve

ˌterriˌtorial ˈarmy *n* a voluntary force organized by a locality to provide a trained army reserve that can be mobilized in an emergency

ˌterriˌtorial ˈwaters *n pl* the waters under the sovereign jurisdiction of a nation

territory /ˈterit(ə)ri‖ˈterɪt(ə)rɪ/ *n* **1a** a geographical area under the jurisdiction of a government **b** an administrative subdivision of a country **c** a part of the USA not included within any state but with a separate legislature **2a** an indeterminate geographical area **b** a field of knowledge or interest **c** a geographical area having a specified characteristic **3a** an assigned area; *esp* one in which an agent or distributor operates **b** an area, often including a nesting site or den, occupied and defended by an animal or group of animals

terror /ˈterə‖ˈterə/ *n* **1** a state of intense fear **2** sby or sthg that inspires fear **3** REIGN OF TERROR **4** revolutionary violence (e g the planting of bombs) **5** an appalling person or thing; *esp* a brat – infml

terrorism /ˈterəˌriz(ə)m‖ˈterəˌrɪz(ə)m/ *n* the systematic use of terror, esp as a means of coercion – **terrorist** *adj or n*, **terroristic** *adj*

terror·ize, -ise /ˈterəˌriez‖ˈterəˌraɪz/ *vt* **1** to fill with terror or anxiety **2** to coerce by threat or violence – **terrorization** *n*

ˈterror-ˌstricken *adj* overcome with an uncontrollable terror

terry /ˈteri‖ˈterɪ/ *n* an absorbent fabric with uncut loops on both faces – **terry** *adj*

terse /tuhs‖tɜːs/ *adj* concise; *also* brusque, curt – **tersely** *adv*, **terseness** *n*

tertian /ˈtuhsh(ə)n‖ˈtɜːʃ(ə)n/ *adj, of malarial symptoms* recurring at approximately 48-hour intervals

[1]**tertiary** /ˈtuhshəri‖ˈtɜːʃərɪ/ *n* **1** sby belonging to a monastic third order **2** *cap* the Tertiary period or system of rocks

[2]**tertiary** *adj* **1a** of third rank, importance, or value **b** of higher education **c** of or being a service industry **2** *cap* of or being the geological period that extends from about 65 million to 1.8 million years ago **3** occurring in or being a third stage

Terylene /ˈterəleen, -lin‖ˈterəliːn, -lɪn/ *trademark* – used for a synthetic polyester textile fibre

tessellate /ˈtesəlayt‖ˈtesəleɪt/ *vt* to make into or decorate with mosaic – **tesselation** *n*

tessellated /ˈtesəˌlaytid‖ˈtesəˌleɪtɪd/ *adj* chequered

[1]**test** /test‖test/ *n* **1a** a critical examination, observation, or evaluation **b** a basis for evaluation **2** a means or instance of testing: e g **2a** a procedure used to identify a substance <*iodine ~ for the presence of starch*> **b** a series of questions or exercises for measuring the knowledge, intelligence, etc of an individual or group **c** TEST MATCH

[2]**test** *vt* to put to the test; try <~s *my patience*> <*wet roads that ~ a car's tyres*> ~*vi* to apply a test as a means of analysis or diagnosis – often + *for* – **testable** *adj*, **tester** *n*

[3]**test** *n* an external hard or firm covering (e g a shell) of an invertebrate (e g a mollusc)

testament /ˈtestəmənt‖ˈtestəmənt/ *n* **1** *cap* either of the 2 main divisions of the Bible **2** a tangible proof or tribute **3** a will **4** *archaic* a covenant between God and man – **testamentary** *adj*

testate /ˈtestayt‖ˈtesteɪt/ *adj* having made a valid will

testator /teˈstaytə‖teˈsteɪtə/, *fem* **testatrix** /teˈstaytriks‖teˈsteɪtrɪks/ *n* sby who leaves a will

ˈ**test ˌban** *n* a self-imposed ban on the atmospheric testing of nuclear weapons

ˈ**test ˌcase** *n* a representative case whose outcome is likely to serve as a precedent

tester /ˈtestə‖ˈtestə/ *n* the canopy over a bed, pulpit, or altar

testicle /ˈtestikl‖ˈtestɪkl/ *n* a testis, esp of a mammal and usu with its enclosing structures (e g the scrotum) – **testicular** *adj*

testify /ˈtestifie‖ˈtestɪfaɪ/ *vi* **1a** to make a statement based on personal knowledge or belief **b** to serve as evidence or proof **2** to make a solemn declaration under oath ~ *vt* **1a** to bear witness to **b** to serve as evidence of **2** to make known (a personal conviction) **3** to declare under oath – **testifier** *n*

[1]**testimonial** /ˌtestiˈmohnyəl, -ni·əl‖ˌtestɪˈməʊnjəl, -nɪəl/ *adj* **1** of or constituting testimony **2** expressive of appreciation, gratitude, or esteem <*a ~ dinner*>

[2]**testimonial** *n* **1** a letter of recommendation **2** an expression of appreciation or esteem (e g in the form of a gift)

testimony /ˈtestiməni‖ˈtestɪmənɪ/ *n* **1a** firsthand authentication of a fact **b** an outward sign; evidence <*is ~ of his abilities*> **c** a sworn statement by a witness **2** a public declaration of religious experience

testis /ˈtestis‖ˈtestɪs/ *n, pl* **testes** /ˈtesteez‖ˈtestiːz/ a male reproductive gland

ˈ**test ˌmatch** *n* any of a series of international matches, esp cricket matches

ˈ**test ˌpilot** *n* a pilot who specializes in putting new or experimental aircraft through manoeuvres designed to test them by producing strains in excess of normal

ˈ**test-ˌtube** *adj, of a baby* conceived by artificial insemination, esp outside the mother's body

ˈ**test ˌtube** *n* a thin glass tube closed at 1 end and used in chemistry, biology, etc

testy /ˈtesti‖ˈtestɪ/ *adj* impatient, ill-humoured – **testily** *adv*, **testiness** *n*

tetanus /ˈtet(ə)nəs‖ˈtet(ə)nəs/ *n* **1** (the bacterium, usu introduced through a wound, that causes) an infectious disease characterized by spasm of voluntary muscles, esp of the jaw **2** prolonged contraction of a muscle resulting from rapidly repeated motor impulses – **tetanize** *vt*

tetchy /ˈtechi‖ˈtetʃɪ/ *adj* irritably or peevishly sensitive – **tetchily** *adv*, **tetchiness** *n*

[1]**tête-à-tête** /ˌtet ah ˈtet, tayt ah atayt‖ˌtet ɑːˈtet, teɪt ɑː æteɪt/ *adv or adj* (in) private [French, lit., head to head; adj fr adv]

[2]**tête-à-tête** *n* **1** a private conversation between 2 people **2** a seat (e g a sofa) designed for 2 people to sit facing each other

[1]**tether** /ˈtedhə‖ˈteðə/ *n* **1** a rope, chain, etc by which an animal is fastened so that it can move only within a set radius **2** the limit of one's strength or resources – chiefly in *the end of one's tether*

[2]**tether** *vt* to fasten or restrain (as if) by a tether

tetravalent /ˌtetrəˈvaylənt‖ˌtetrəˈveɪlənt/ *adj* having a valency of 4

Teuton /ˈtyoohton‖ˈtjuːtɒn/ *n* **1** a member of an ancient prob Germanic or Celtic people **2** a German – **Teutonic** *adj*

Teutonic /tyoohˈtonik‖tjuːˈtɒnɪk/ *n* Germanic

text /tekst‖tekst/ *n* **1** (a work containing) the original written or printed words and form of a literary composition **2** the main body of printed or written matter, esp on a page or in a book **3a** a passage of Scripture chosen esp for the subject of a sermon or in authoritative support of a doctrine **b** a passage from an authoritative source providing a theme (e g for a speech) **4** a textbook **5** a theme, topic [Middle French *texte*, fr Medieval Latin *textus*, fr Latin, texture, context, fr *text-*, *texere* to weave]

[1]ˈ**textˌbook** /-ˌbook‖-ˌbʊk/ *n* a book used in the study of a subject; *specif* one containing a presentation of the principles of a subject and used by students

[2]**textbook** *adj* conforming to the principles or descriptions in textbooks: e g **a** ideal **b** typical

textile /ˈtekstiel‖ˈtekstaɪl/ *n* **1** CLOTH 1; *esp* a woven or knitted cloth **2** a fibre, filament, or yarn used in making cloth [Latin, fr neuter of *textilis* woven, fr *text-*, *texere* to weave]

textual /ˈtekstyooəl, ˈtekschooəl‖ˈtekstjʊəl, ˈtekstʃʊəl/ *adj* of or based on a text – **textually** *adv*

[1]**texture** /ˈtekschə‖ˈtekstʃə/ *n* **1** the structure formed by the threads of a fabric **2** identifying quality; character <*the ~ of American culture*> **3a** the size or organization of the constituent particles of a body or substance <*a soil that is coarse in ~*> **b** the visual or tactile surface characteristics of sthg, esp fabric <*the roughish ~ of tweed*> **4a** the distinctive or identifying part or quality <*the rich ~ of his prose*> **b** a pattern of musical sound created by notes or lines played or sung together – **textural** *adj*, **textured** *adj*

[2]**texture** *vt* to give a particular texture to

¹-th /-th‖-θ/, **-eth** /-ith‖-ɪθ/ *suffix* (→ *adj*) – used in forming ordinal numbers <*hundred*th>

²-th, -eth *suffix* (→ *n*) – used in forming fractions <*a fort*ieth>

³-th *suffix* (→ *n*) **1** act or process of <*grow*th> **2** state or condition of <*fil*th>

thalidomide /thəˈlidəmied‖θəˈlɪdəmaɪd/ *adj or n* (of or affected by) a sedative and hypnotic drug found to cause malformation of infants born to mothers using it during pregnancy

¹than /dhən‖ðən; *strong* dhan‖ðæn/ *conj* **1a** – used with comparatives to indicate the second member or the member taken as the point of departure in a comparison <*older* ~ *I am*> **b** – used to indicate difference of kind, manner, or degree <*would starve rather* ~ *beg*> **2** rather than – usu only after *prefer, preferable* **3** other than; but <*no alternative* ~ *to sack him*> **4** *chiefly NAm* from – usu only after *different, differently*

²than *prep* in comparison with <*older* ~ *me*> <*less* ~ *£1000*>

thane /thayn‖θeɪn/ *n* **1** a free retainer of an Anglo-Saxon lord; *esp* one holding lands in exchange for military service **2** a Scottish feudal lord – **thaneship** *n*

thank /thangk‖θæŋk/ *vt* **1** to express gratitude to – used in *thank you,* usu without a subject, to express gratitude politely <~ *you for the loan*>; used in such phrases as *thank God, thank heaven,* usu without a subject, to express the speaker's or writer's pleasure or satisfaction in sthg **2** to hold responsible <*had only himself to* ~ *for his loss*> – **thanker** *n*

thankful /ˈthangkf(ə)l‖ˈθæŋkf(ə)l/ *adj* **1** conscious of benefit received; grateful **2** feeling or expressing thanks **3** well pleased; glad <*he was* ~ *that the room was dark*> – **thankfulness** *n*

thankless /ˈthangklis‖ˈθæŋklɪs/ *adj* **1** not expressing or feeling gratitude **2** not likely to obtain thanks; unappreciated; *also* unprofitable, futile <*it's a* ~ *job trying to grow tomatoes in England out of doors*> – **thanklessly** *adv*, **thanklessness** *n*

thanks *n pl* **1** kindly or grateful thoughts; gratitude **2** an expression of gratitude <*received with* ~ *the sum of £50*> – often in an utterance containing no verb and serving as a courteous and somewhat informal expression of gratitude <*many* ~> – **no thanks to** not as a result of any benefit conferred by <*he feels better now,* no thanks to *you*> – **thanks to 1** with the help of <thanks to *modern medicine, man's life span is growing longer*> **2** owing to <*our arrival was delayed,* thanks to *the fog*>

thanksgiving /thangksˈgiving, ˈ---‖θæŋksˈgɪvɪŋ, ˈ---/ *n* **1** an expression of gratefulness, esp to God **2** a prayer of gratitude

ˈthank-ˌyou *n* a polite expression of one's gratitude

¹that /dhat‖ðæt/ *pron, pl* **those** /dhohz‖ðəʊz/ **1a** the thing or idea just mentioned <*after* ~ *he went to bed*> **b** a relatively distant person or thing introduced for observation or discussion <*who is* ~*?*> <those *are chestnuts and these are elms*> **c** the thing or state of affairs there <*look at* ~*!*> – sometimes used disparagingly of a person **d** the kind or thing specified as follows <*the purest water is* ~ *produced by distillation*> **e** what is understood from the context <*take* ~*!*> <*how's* ~*?*> **2** one of such a group; such <~*'s life*> **3** – used to indicate emphatic repetition of an idea previously presented <*is he capable? He is* ~> **4** *pl* the people; such <those *who think the time has come*> THAT IS TO SAY – **that's a** THERE'S A – **that's that** that concludes the matter

²that *adj, pl* **those 1** being the person, thing, or idea specified, mentioned, or understood <~ *cake we bought*> **2** the farther away or less immediately under observation <*this chair or* ~ *one*>

³that /dhət‖ðət; *strong* dhat‖ðæt/ *conj* **1a** – used to introduce a noun clause (1) as subject, object, or complement of a verb <*said* ~ *he was afraid*>, (2) anticipated by *it* <*it is unlikely* ~ *he'll be in*>, or (3) as complement to a noun or adjective <*the fact* ~ *you're here*> **b** – used to introduce a clause modifying an adverb or adverbial expression <*will go anywhere* ~ *he's invited*> **c** – used to introduce an emotional exclamation <~ *it should come to this!*> or express a wish <*oh,* ~ *he would come!*> **2** – used to introduce a subordinate clause expressing (1) purpose <*worked harder* ~ *he might win esteem*>, (2) reason <*glad* ~ *you are free of it*>, or (3) result <*walked so fast* ~ *we couldn't keep up*>

⁴that /dhət‖ðət; *strong* dhat‖ðæt/ *pron* **1** – used to introduce a usu restrictive relative clause in reference to a person, thing, or group as subject <*it was George* ~ *told me*> or as object of a verb or of a following preposition <*the house* ~ *Jack built*> **2a** at, in, on, by, with, for, or to which <*the reason* ~ *he came*> <*the way* ~ *he spoke*> **b** according to what; to the extent of what – used after a negative <*has never been here* ~ *I know of*>

⁵that /dhat‖ðæt/ *adv* **1** to the extent indicated or understood <*a nail about* ~ *long*> **2** very, extremely – usu with the negative <*not really* ~ *expensive*> **3** *dial Br* to such an extreme degree <*I'm* ~ *hungry I could eat a horse*>

¹thatch /thach‖θætʃ/ *vt* to cover (as if) with thatch – **thatcher** *n*

²thatch *n* **1** plant material (e g straw) used as a roof covering **2** the hair of one's head – often humor; *broadly* anything resembling the thatch of a house

¹thaw /thaw‖θɔː/ *vt* to cause to thaw – often + *out* ~ *vi* **1a** to go from a frozen to a liquid state **b** to become free of the effect (e g stiffness, numbness, or hardness) of cold as a result of exposure to warmth – often + *out* **2** to be warm enough to melt ice and snow – + *it*; used in reference to the weather **3** to become less hostile, aloof, cold, or reserved

²thaw *n* **1** the action, fact, or process of thawing <*the* ~ *in relations with Western Europe*> **2** a period of weather warm enough to thaw ice

¹the /*before consonants* dhə‖ðə; *strong and before vowels* dhee‖ðiː/ *definite article* **1a** – used before nouns when the referent has been previously specified by context or circumstance <*put* ~ *cat out*> **b** – indicating that a following noun is unique or universally recognized <~ *Pope*> <~ *south*> <~ *future*> **c** – used before certain proper names and in titles <~*Alps*> <*Peter ~Great*> **d** – designating 1 of a class as the best or most worth singling out <*this is ~ life*> <*you can't be ~ Elvis Presley!*> **2a** which or who is – limiting the application of a modified noun to what is specified <~ *right answer*> **b** – used before a noun to limit its application to that specified by what follows <~ *man on my right*> **3** – used before a singular noun to indicate generic use <~ *dog is a mammal*> **4a** that which is <*nothing but ~ best*> **b** those who are <~ *elite*> **c** he or she who is <~ *accused stands before you*>

[2]the *adv* **1** than before; than otherwise – with comparatives <*so much ~ worse*> **2a** to what extent <~ *sooner the better*> **b** to that extent <*the sooner ~ better*> **3** beyond all others – with superlatives <*likes this ~ best*> <*with ~ greatest difficulty*>

[3]the *prep* PER 2

theatre, *NAm chiefly* **theater** /ˈthiətə‖ˈθɪətə/ *n* **1a** an outdoor structure for dramatic performances or spectacles in ancient Greece and Rome **b** a building for dramatic performances; *also* a cinema **2** a room with rising tiers of seats (e g for lectures) **3** a place of enactment of significant events or action <*the ~ of war*> **4** dramatic literature or performance **5** *the* theatrical world **6** *Br* OPERATING THEATRE [Middle French *theatre*, Latin *theatrum*, fr Greek *theatron*, fr *theasthai* to see, view, fr *thea* act of seeing]

theatrical /thiˈatrikl‖θɪˈætrɪkl/ *adj* **1** of the theatre or the presentation of plays **2** marked by artificiality (e g of emotion) **3** marked by exhibitionism; histrionic <*a ~ gesture*> – **theatrically** *adv*, **theatricalism** *n*, **theatricality** *n*

theˈatricals *n pl* the performance of plays <*amateur ~*>

thee /dhee‖ðiː/ *pron, archaic or dial* **1a** *objective case of* THOU **b** thou – used by Quakers, esp among themselves, in contexts where the subjective form would be expected <*is ~ ready?*> **2** thyself

theft /theft‖θeft/ *n* the act of stealing; *specif* dishonest appropriation of property with the intention of keeping it

their /dhə‖ðə; *strong* dheə‖ðeə/ *adj* **1** of, belonging to, or done by or to them or themselves **2** his or her; his, her, its <*anyone in ~ senses* – W H Auden> *USE* used attributively

theirs /dheəz‖ðeəz/ *pron, pl* **theirs** **1** that which or the one who belongs to them **2** his or hers; his, hers <*I will do my part if everybody else will do ~*>

theism /ˈthee,iz(ə)m‖ˈθiː,ɪz(ə)m/ *n* belief in the existence of a creator god immanent in the universe but transcending it – **theist** *n or adj*, **theistic, theistical** *adj*

-theism /-thi,iz(ə)m‖-θɪ,ɪz(ə)m/ *comb form* (→ *n*) belief in (such) a god or (such or so many) gods <*pan*theism> – **-theist** *comb form* (→ *n*)

[1]them /dhəm‖ðəm; *strong* dhem‖ðem/ *pron, objective case of* THEY

[2]them /dhem‖ðem/ *adj* those <~ *blokes*> – nonstandard

theme /theem‖θiːm/ *n* **1** a subject of artistic representation or a topic of discourse **2** a melodic subject of a musical composition or movement **3** *NAm* a written exercise; a composition

theme park *n* an amusement park in which the structures and settings are all based on a specific theme (e g space travel)

ˈtheme ˌsong *n* **1** a recurring melody in a musical play or in a film that characterizes the production or one of its characters **2** a signature tune

themselves /dhəmˈselvz‖ðəmˈselvz/ *pron pl in constr* **1a** those identical people, creatures, or things that are they – used reflexively <*nations that govern ~*> or for emphasis <*the team ~ were delighted*> **b** himself or herself; himself, herself <*hoped nobody would hurt ~*> **2** their normal selves <*soon be ~ again*>

[1]then /dhen‖ðen/ *adv* **1** at that time **2a** soon after that; next in order (of time) <*walked to the door, ~ turned*> **b** besides; IN ADDITION <~ *there is the interest to be paid*> **3a** in that case <*take it, ~, if you want it so much*> **b** as may be inferred <*your mind is made up, ~?*> **c** accordingly, so – indicating casual connection in speech or writing <*our hero, ~, was greatly relieved*> **d** as a necessary consequence <*if the angles are equal, ~ the complements are equal*> **e** – used after *but* to offset a preceding statement <*he lost the race, but ~ he never expected to win*>

[2]then *n* that time <*since ~, he's been more cautious*>

[3]then *adj* existing or acting at that time <*the ~ secretary of state*>

thence /dhens‖ðens/ *adv* **1** from there <*fly to London and ~ to Paris*> **2** from that preceding fact or premise <*it ~ transpired*> – chiefly fml

ˌthenceˈforth /-ˈfawth‖-ˈfɔːθ/ *adv* from that time or point on – chiefly fml

theocracy /thiˈokrəsi‖θɪˈɒkrəsɪ/ *n* (a state having) government by immediate divine guidance or by officials regarded as divinely guided – **theocrat** *n*, **theocratic** *also* **theocratical** *adj*

theodolite /thiˈod(ə)l,iet‖θɪˈɒd(ə)l,aɪt/ *n* a surveyor's instrument for measuring horizontal and usu also vertical angles – **theodolitic** *adj*

theologian /ˌthee·əˈlohjən‖ˌθiːəˈləʊdʒən/ *n* a specialist in theology

theology /thiˈoləji‖θɪˈɒlədʒɪ/ *n* **1** the study of God, esp by analysis of the origins and teachings of an organized religion **2** a theological theory, system, or body of opinion <*Catholic ~*> – **theological** *adj*

theorem /ˈthiərəm, ˈthee·ərəm‖ˈθɪərəm, ˈθiːərəm/ *n* **1** a proposition in mathematics or logic deducible from other more basic propositions **2** an idea proposed as a demonstrable truth, often as a part of a general theory; a proposition – **theorematic** *adj*

theoretical /thiəˈretikl, ˌthee·ə-‖θɪəˈretɪkl, ˌθiːə-/ *also* **theoretic** /thiəˈretik, ˌthee·ə-‖θɪəˈretɪk, ˌθiːə-/ *adj* **1a** relating to or having the character of theory; abstract **b** confined to theory or speculation; speculative <~ *mechanics*> **2** existing only in theory; hypothetical – **theoretically** *adv*

theoretician /ˌthiərəˈtish(ə)n, ˌthee·ə-‖ˌθɪərəˈtɪʃ(ə)n, θiːə-/ *n* sby who specializes in the theoretical aspects of a subject

theorist /ˈthiərist, ˈthee·ə-‖ˈθɪərɪst, ˈθiːə-/ *n* a theoretician

theor·ize, -ise /ˈthiəˌriez, ˈthee·ə-‖ˈθɪəˌraɪz, ˈθiːə-/ *vi* to form a theory; speculate – **theorizer** *n*

theory /ˈthiəri, ˈthee·ə-‖ˈθɪərɪ, ˈθiːə-/ *n* **1a** a belief, policy, or procedure forming the basis for action <*her method is based on the* ~ *that children want to learn*> **b** an ideal or supposed set of facts, principles, or circumstances – often in *in theory* <*in* ~, *we have always advocated freedom for all, but in practice . . .*> **2** the general or abstract principles of a subject <*music* ~> **3** a scientifically acceptable body of principles offered to explain a phenomenon <*wave* ~ *of light*> **4a** a hypothesis assumed for the sake of argument or investigation **b** an unproved assumption; a conjecture **c** a body of theorems presenting a concise systematic view of a subject <~ *of equations*>

theosophy /thiˈosəfi‖θɪˈɒsəfɪ/ *n* **1** teaching about God and the world stressing the validity of mystical insight **2** *often cap* the teachings of a modern movement originating in the USA in 1875 and following chiefly Buddhist and Brahmanic theories – **theosophist** *n*, **theosophical** *adj*

therapeutic /therəˈpyoohtik‖θerəˈpjuːtɪk/ *adj* of the treatment of disease or disorders by remedial agents or methods [Greek *therapeutikos*, fr *therapeuein* to attend, treat, fr *theraps* attendant] – **therapeutically** *adv*

theraˈpeutics *n pl but sing or pl in constr* medicine dealing with the application of remedies to diseases

therapist /ˈtherəpist‖ˈθerəpɪst/ *n* sby trained in methods of treatment and rehabilitation other than the use of drugs or surgery

therapy /ˈtherəpi‖ˈθerəpɪ/ *n* therapeutic treatment of bodily, mental, or social disorders

[1]**there** /dheə‖ðeə/ *adv* **1** in or at that place <*stand over* ~> – often used to draw attention or to replace a name <~ *goes John*> <*hello* ~*!*> **2** thither <*went* ~ *after church*> **3a** now <~ *goes the hooter*> **b** at or in that point or particular <~ *is where I disagree with you*> **4** – used interjectionally to express satisfaction, approval, encouragement, or defiance <~, *it's finished*> <*won't go, so* ~> – **there and back** for a round trip – **there it is** such is the unfortunate fact – **there's a** – used when urging a course of action <*don't sulk*, there's a *dear!*> – **there you are 1** HERE YOU ARE 1 **2** I told you so

[2]**there** *pron* – used to introduce a sentence or clause expressing the idea of existence <*what is* ~ *to eat?*> <~ *shall come a time*>

[3]**there** *n* that place or point

[4]**there** *adj* **1** – used for emphasis, esp after a demonstrative <*those men* ~ *can tell you*> **2** – used for emphasis between a demonstrative and the following noun <*that* ~ *cow*>; substandard

thereabouts /ˌdheərəˈbowts‖ˌðeərəˈbaʊts/, *NAm also* ˌ**thereaˈbout** *adv* **1** in that vicinity **2** near that time, number, degree, or quantity <*a boy of 18 or* ~>

thereafter /dheəˈrahftə‖ðeəˈrɑːftə/ *adv* after that

thereby /dheəˈbie‖ðeəˈbaɪ/ *adv* **1** by that means; resulting from which **2** in which connection <~ *hangs a tale* – Shak>

therefore /ˈdheəˌfaw‖ˈðeəˌfɔː/ *adv* **1** for that reason; to that end <*We must go. I will* ~ *call a taxi*> **2** by virtue of that; consequently <*was tired and* ~ *irritable*> **3** as this proves <*I think*, ~ *I exist*>

therein /dheəˈrin‖ðeəˈrɪn/ *adv* in that; *esp* in that respect <~ *lies the problem*> – fml

thereof /dheəˈrov‖ðeəˈrɒv/ *adv* **1** of that or it **2** from that or it *USE* fml

thereon /dheəˈron‖ðeəˈrɒn/ *adv* on or onto that or it <*a text with a commentary* ~> – fml

thereto /dheəˈtooh‖ðeəˈtuː/ *adv* to that matter or document <*conditions attaching* ~> – fml

thereunder /dheəˈrundə‖ðeəˈrʌndə/ *adv* under that or it <*the heading and the items listed* ~> – fml

thereupon /ˌdheərəˈpon‖ˌðeərəˈpɒn/ *adv* **1** on that matter <*if all are agreed* ~> **2** immediately after that *USE* fml

therm /thuhm‖θɜːm/ *n* a quantity of heat equal to 100,000Btu (about 105,506MJ) [Greek *thermē* heat]

[1]**thermal** /ˈthuhml‖ˈθɜːml/ *adj* **1 thermal, thermic** of or caused by heat <~ *stress*> <~ *insulation*> **2** designed (e g with insulating air spaces) to prevent the dissipation of body heat <~ *underwear*> – **thermally** *adv*

[2]**thermal** *n* a rising body of warm air

thermion /ˈthuhmˌi·ən, -on‖ˈθɜːmˌɪən, -ɒn/ *n* an electrically charged particle, specif an electron, emitted by an incandescent substance

thermionic /ˌthuhmiˈonik‖ˌθɜːmɪˈɒnɪk/ *adj* of or being (a device, esp a valve using) thermions

thermodynamics /ˌthuhmohdieˈnamiks, -di-‖ˌθɜːməʊdaɪˈnæmɪks, -dɪ-/ *n pl but sing or pl in constr* (physics that deals with) the mechanical action of, or relations between, heat and other forms of energy – **thermodynamic** *adj*, **thermodynamically** *adv*, **thermodynamicist** *n*

thermometer /thəˈmomitə‖θəˈmɒmɪtə/ *n* an instrument for determining temperature; *esp* a glass bulb attached to a fine graduated tube of glass and containing a liquid (e g mercury) that rises and falls with changes of temperature – **thermometry** *n*, **thermometric** *adj*

thermonuclear /ˌthuhmohˈnyoohkli·ə‖ˌθɜːməʊˈnjuːklɪə/ *adj* of, using, or being (weapons using) transformations occurring in the nucleus of low atomic weight atoms (e g hydrogen) at very high temperatures

thermoplastic /ˌthuhməˈplastik‖ˌθɜːməˈplæstɪk/ *adj* capable of softening or melting when heated and of hardening again when cooled <~ *synthetic resins*> – **thermoplastic** *n*

thermos /ˈthuhmos, -məs‖ˈθɜːmɒs, -məs/ *n* THERMOS FLASK

Thermos *trademark* – used for a Thermos flask

thermosetting /ˈthuhmohˌseting‖ˈθɜːməʊˌsetɪŋ/ *adj* capable of becoming permanently rigid when heated <*a* ~ *plastic*>

ˈ**Thermos** ˌ**flask** *n, often not cap T* a cylindrical container with a vacuum between an inner and an outer wall used to keep material, esp liquids, either hot or cold for considerable periods

thermostat /ˈthuhməˌstat‖ˈθɜːməˌstæt/ *n* an automatic device for regulating temperature –

thermostatic *adj*

thesaurus /thi'sawrəs, 'thesərəs‖θɪ'sɔːrəs, 'θesərəs/ *n, pl* **thesauri** /-rie, -ri‖-raɪ, -rɪ/, **thesauruses** a book of words or of information about a particular field or set of concepts; *esp* a book of words and their synonyms [Latin, treasury, treasure, fr Greek *thēsauros*]

these /dheez‖ðiːz/ *pl of* THIS

thesis /'theesis‖'θiːsɪs/ *n, pl* **theses** /-ˌseez‖-ˌsiːz/ **1a** a proposition that a person offers to maintain by argument **b** a proposition to be proved or one advanced without proof; a hypothesis **2** the first stage of a reasoned argument presenting the case **3** a dissertation embodying the results of original research; *specif* one submitted for a doctorate in Britain

1thespian /'thespi·ən‖'θespɪən/ *adj, often cap* relating to the drama [*Thespis* (*fl* 534 BC), Greek poet, reputed founder of Greek drama]

2thespian *n* an actor – chiefly fml or humor

thew /thyooh‖θjuː/ *n* **1** muscle, sinew – usu pl **2a** muscular power or development **b** strength, vitality <*the naked ~ and sinew of the English language* – G M Hopkins>

they /dhay‖ðeɪ/ *pron pl in constr* **1a** those people, creatures, or things <*~ taste better with sugar*>; *also, chiefly Br* that group <*ask the committee whether ~ approve*> **b** HE 2 <*if anyone knows, ~ will tell you*> **2a** PEOPLE 1 <*~ say we'll have a hard winter*> **b** the authorities <*~ took my licence away*>

they'd /dhayd‖ðeɪd/ they had; they would

they'll /dhayl‖ðeɪl/ they will; they shall

they're /dheə‖ðeə/ they are

they've /dhayv‖ðeɪv/ they have

1thick /thik‖θɪk/ *adj* **1a** having or being of relatively great depth or extent between opposite surfaces <*a ~ plank*> **b** of comparatively large diameter in relation to length <*a ~ rod*> **2a** closely-packed; dense <*the air was ~ with snow*> <*a ~ forest*> **b** great in number **c** viscous in consistency <*~ syrup*> **d** foggy or misty <*~ weather*> **e** impenetrable to the eye <*~ darkness*> **3** measuring in thickness <*12 centimetres ~*> **4a** imperfectly articulated <*~ speech*> **b** plainly apparent; marked <*a ~ French accent*> **5a** sluggish, dull <*my head feels ~ after too little sleep*> **b** obtuse, stupid **6** on close terms; intimate <*was quite ~ with his boss*> **7** unreasonable, unfair <*called it a bit ~ to be fired without warning*> *USE* (*5b, 6, & 7*) infml – **thick** *adv*, **thicken** *vb*, **thickener** *n*, **thickish** *adj*, **thickly** *adv*

2thick *n* **1** the most crowded or active part <*in the ~ of the battle*> **2** the part of greatest thickness <*the ~ of the thumb*>

thicket /'thikit‖'θɪkɪt/ *n* **1** a dense growth of shrubbery or small trees **2** sthg like a thicket in density or impenetrability

thickhead /'thikˌhed‖'θɪkˌhed/ *n* a stupid person – infml – **thick-headed** *adj*

thickness /'thiknis‖'θɪknɪs/ *n* **1** the smallest of the 3 dimensions of a solid object **2** the thick part of sthg **3** a layer, ply <*a single ~ of canvas*>

thickset /thik'set‖θɪk'set/ *adj* **1** closely placed; *also* growing thickly **2** heavily built; burly

ˌthick-'skinned *adj* callous, insensitive

thief /theef‖θiːf/ *n, pl* **thieves** /theevz‖θiːvz/ sby who steals, esp secretly and without violence – **thievery** *n*, **thievish** *adj*, **thievishness** *n*

thieve /theev‖θiːv/ *vb* to steal, rob

thigh /thie‖θaɪ/ *n* the segment of the vertebrate hind limb nearest the body that extends from the hip to the knee and is supported by a single large bone – **thighed** *adj*

thimble /'thimbl‖'θɪmbl/ *n* **1** a pitted metal or plastic cap or cover worn to protect the finger and to push the needle in sewing **2a** a thin metal grooved ring used to fit in a spliced loop in a rope as protection from chafing **b** a movable ring, tube, or lining in a hole [Middle English *thymbyl*, prob alter. of Old English *thȳmel* thumbstall, fr *thūma* thumb]

'thimbleful /-f(ə)l‖-f(ə)l/ *n* as much as a thimble will hold; *broadly* a very small quantity

1thin /thin‖θɪn/ *adj* **-nn- 1a** having little depth between opposite surfaces <*a ~ book*> **b** measuring little in cross section <*~ rope*> **2** not dense or closely-packed <*~ hair*> **3** without much flesh; lean **4a** more rarefied than normal <*~ air*> **b** few in number **c** with few bids or offerings <*a ~ market*> **5** lacking substance or strength <*~ broth*> <*a ~ plot*> **6** flimsy, unconvincing <*a ~ disguise*> **7** somewhat feeble and lacking in resonance <*a ~ voice*> **8** lacking in intensity or brilliance <*~ colour*> **9** lacking sufficient photographic contrast **10** disappointingly poor or hard – infml <*had a ~ time of it*> – **thin** *adv*, **thinly** *adv*, **thinness** *n*, **thinnish** *adj* – **thin end of the wedge** sthg apparently insignificant that is the forerunner of a more important development

2thin *vb* **-nn-** *vt* **1** to reduce in thickness or depth; attenuate **2** to reduce in strength or density **3** to reduce in number or bulk ~ *vi* **1** to become thin or thinner **2** to diminish in strength, density, or number

1thine /dhien‖ðaɪn/ *adj, archaic* thy – used esp before a vowel or *h*

2thine *pron, pl* **thine** *archaic or dial* that which belongs to thee – used without a following noun as a pronoun equivalent in meaning to the adjective *thy;* capitalized when addressing God; still surviving in the speech of Quakers, esp among themselves

thing /thing‖θɪŋ/ *n* **1a** a matter, affair, concern <*~s are not improving*> **b** an event, circumstance <*that shooting was a terrible ~*> **2a(1)** a deed, act, achievement <*do great ~s*> **a(2)** an activity, action **b** a product of work or activity <*likes to make ~s*> **c** the aim of effort or activity <*the ~ is to get well*> **d** sthg necessary or desirable <*I've got just the ~ for you*> **3a** a separate and distinct object of thought (e g a quality, fact, idea, etc) **b** the concrete entity as distinguished from its appearances **c** an inanimate object as distinguished from a living being **d** *pl* imaginary objects or entities <*see ~s*> **4a** *pl* possessions, effects <*pack your ~s*> **b** an item of property – used in law **c** an article of clothing <*not a ~ to wear*> **d** *pl* equipment or utensils, esp for a particular purpose <*bring the tea ~s*> **5** an object or entity not (capable of being) precisely designated <*what's that ~*

you're holding?> **6a** a detail, point <*checks every little* ~> **b** a material or substance of a specified kind <*avoid starchy* ~s> **7a** a spoken or written observation or point <*there are some good* ~s *in his essay*> **b** an idea, motion <*says the first* ~ *he thinks of*> <*for one* ~> **c** a piece of news or information <*couldn't get a* ~ *out of him*> **8** an individual, creature <*poor* ~*!*> **9** *the* proper or fashionable way of behaving, talking, or dressing <*it's the latest* ~> **10a** a preoccupation (e g a mild obsession or phobia) of a specified type <*has a* ~ *about driving*> **b** an intimate relationship; *esp* LOVE AFFAIR 1 <*had a* ~ *going with her boss*> **c** sthg (e g an activity) that offers special interest and satisfaction to the individual – infml <*letting people do their own* ~> ***USE*** (*10a, 10b, & 10c*) infml

thingamajig, thingumajig /ˈthing·əməˌjig‖ˈθɪŋəməˌdʒɪg/ *n* sthg or sby that is hard to classify or whose name is unknown or forgotten – infml

[1]think /thingk‖θɪŋk/ *vb* **thought** /thawt‖θɔːt/ *vt* **1** to form or have in the mind **2** to have as an opinion; consider **3a** to reflect on – often + *over* <~ *the matter over*> **b** to determine by reflecting – often + *out* <~ *it out for yourself*> **4** to call to mind; remember <*I didn't* ~ *to ask his name*> **5** to devise by thinking – usu + *up* <thought *up a plan to escape*> **6** to have as an expectation <*we didn't* ~ *we'd have any trouble*> **7** to have one's mind full of <*talks and* ~s *business*> **8** to subject to the processes of logical thought – usu + *out* or *through* <~ *things out*> ~ *vi* **1a** to exercise the powers of judgment, conception, or inference **b** to have in mind or call to mind a thought or idea – usu + *of* **2** to have the mind engaged in reflection – usu + *of* or *about* **3** to hold a view or opinion – usu + *of* <~s *of himself as a poet*> **4** to have consideration – usu + *of* <*a man must* ~ *first of his family*> **5** to expect, suspect <*better than he* ~s *possible*> – **thinkable** *adj*, **thinker** *n* – **think better of** to decide on reflection to abandon (a plan) – **think much of** to have at all a high opinion of <*didn't* think much of *the new car*>

[2]think *n* an act of thinking <*if he thinks he can fool me, he's got another* ~ *coming*> – infml

[1]thinking /ˈthingking‖ˈθɪŋkɪŋ/ *n* **1** the action of using one's mind to produce thoughts **2** opinion that is characteristic (e g of a period, group, or individual) <*the current* ~ *on immigration*> – **put/have on one's thinking cap** to ponder or reflect on sthg

[2]thinking *adj* marked by use of the intellect

think over *vt* to ponder the advantages or disadvantages of; consider <think *it* over>

ˈthink ˌtank *n sing or pl in constr* a group of people formed as a consultative body to evolve new ideas and offer expert advice

thinner /ˈthinə‖ˈθɪnə/ *n* liquid (e g turpentine) used esp to thin paint

ˌthin-ˈskinned *adj* unduly susceptible to criticism or insult

[1]third /thuhd‖θɜːd/ *adj* **1a** next after the second in place or time <*the* ~ *man in line*> **b** ranking next to second in authority or precedence <~ *mate*> **c** being the forward gear or speed 1 higher than second in a motor vehicle **2a** being any of 3 equal parts into which sthg is divisible **b** being the last in each group of 3 in a series <*take out every* ~ *card*> – **third, thirdly** *adv*

[2]third *n* **1a** number three in a countable series **b** sthg or sby that is next after second in rank, position, authority, or precedence <*the* ~ *in line*> **c third, third class** *often cap* the third and usu lowest level of British honours degree **2** any of 3 equal parts of sthg **3a** (the combination of 2 notes at) a musical interval of 3 diatonic degrees **b** a mediant **4** the third forward gear or speed of a motor vehicle

ˌthird deˈgree *n* the subjection of a prisoner to torture to obtain information

ˌthird-deˌgree ˈburn *n* a burn characterized by destruction of the skin and possibly the underlying tissues, loss of fluid, and sometimes shock

ˌthird-ˈparty *adj* of a third party; *specif* of insurance covering loss or damage sustained by sby other than the insured

ˌthird ˈparty *n* **1** sby other than the principals <*a* ~ *to a divorce proceeding*> **2a** a major political party in addition to 2 others in a state normally characterized by a 2-party system **b** a political party whose electoral strength is so small that it can rarely gain control of a government

ˌthird ˈperson *n* a set of linguistic forms (e g verb forms or pronouns) referring neither to the speaker or writer of the utterance in which they occur nor to the one to whom that utterance is addressed

ˌthird ˈrail *n* CONDUCTOR RAIL

ˌthird-ˈrate *adj* third in quality or value; *broadly* of extremely poor quality – **third-rater** *n*

ˌthird ˈworld *n, often cap T&W, sing or pl in constr* **1** a group of nations, esp in Africa and Asia, that are not aligned with either the communist or the capitalist blocs **2** the underdeveloped nations of the world

[1]thirst /thuhst‖θɜːst/ *n* **1** (the sensation of dryness in the mouth and throat associated with) a desire or need to drink **2** an ardent desire; a craving

[2]thirst *vi* **1** to feel thirsty **2** to crave eagerly

thirsty /ˈthuhsti‖ˈθɜːstɪ/ *adj* **1a** feeling thirst **b** deficient in moisture; parched <~ *land*> **2** having a strong desire; avid – **thirstily** *adv*, **thirstiness** *n*

thirteen /thuhˈteen‖θɜːˈtiːn/ *n* (the number) 13 – **thirteen** *adj or pron*, **thirteenth** *adj or n*

thirty /ˈthuhti‖ˈθɜːtɪ/ *n* **1** (the number) 30 **2** *pl* the numbers 30 to 39; *specif* a range of temperatures, ages, or dates in a century characterized by these numbers – **thirtieth** *adj or n*, **thirty** *adj or pron*, **thirtyfold** *adj or adv*

[1]this /dhis‖ðɪs/ *pron, pl* **these** /dheez‖ðiːz/ **1a** the thing or idea that has just been mentioned <*who told you* ~*?*> **b** what is to be shown or stated <*do it like* ~> **c** this time or place <*expected to return before* ~> **2a** a nearby person or thing introduced for observation or discussion <~ *is iron and that is tin*> <*hello!* ~ *is Anne Fry speaking*> **b** the thing or state of affairs here <*please carry* ~> <*what's all* ~*?*>

[2]this *adj, pl* **these** **1a** being the person, thing, or idea that is present or near in time or thought <*early* ~ *morning*> <*who's* ~ *Mrs Fogg anyway?*> **b** the nearer at hand or more immediately under observation <~ *country*> <~ *chair or that one*> **c** constituting the immediate past or future period <*have lived here* these *10 years*> **d** constituting what is to be shown or stated <*have you heard* ~ *one?*> **2** a certain <*there was* ~ *Irishman ...*>

[3]**this** *adv* **1** to this extent <*known her since she was* ~ *high*> **2** to this extreme degree – usu + the negative <*didn't expect to wait* ~ *long*>

thistle /'thisl‖'θɪsl/ *n* any of various prickly composite plants with (showy) heads of mostly tubular flowers – **thistly** *adj*

thistledown /'thisl,down‖'θɪsl,daʊn/ *n* the fluffy hairs from the ripe flower head of a thistle

thither /'dhidhə‖'ðɪðə/ *adv* to or towards that place – chiefly fml

thole /thohl‖θəʊl/, **tholepin** /'thohl,pin‖'θəʊl-,pɪn/ *n* a peg, pin; *esp* either of a pair of wooden pegs serving as rowlocks on a boat

thong /thong‖θɒŋ/ *n* a narrow strip, esp of leather – **thonged** *adj*

thorax /'thaw,raks‖'θɔː,ræks/ *n, pl* **thoraxes, thoraces** /'thawrə,seez‖'θɔːrə,siːz/ (a division of the body of an insect, spider, etc corresponding to) the part of the mammalian body between the neck and the abdomen; *also* its cavity in which the heart and lungs lie – **thoracic** *adj*

thorn /thawn‖θɔːn/ *n* **1** a woody plant (of the rose family) bearing sharp prickles of thorns **2** a short hard sharp-pointed plant part, specif a leafless branch **3** sby or sthg that causes irritation <*he's been a* ~ *in my flesh for years*> – **thorned** *adj*, **thornless** *adj*

thorny /'thawni‖'θɔːnɪ/ *adj* **1** full of or covered in thorns **2** full of difficulties or controversial points <*a* ~ *problem*> – **thorniness** *n*

[1]**thorough** /'thurə‖'θʌrə/ *prep or adv, archaic* through

[2]**thorough** *adj* **1** carried through to completion <*a* ~ *search*> **2a** marked by full detail <*a* ~ *description*> **b** painstaking <*a* ~ *scholar*> **c** complete in all respects <~ *pleasure*> **d** being fully and without qualification as specified <*a* ~ *rogue*> – **thoroughly** *adv*, **thoroughness** *n*

[1]'**thorough,bred** /-,bred‖-,bred/ *adj* **1** bred from the best blood through a long line; purebred **2a** *cap* of or being a Thoroughbred **b** having the characteristics associated with good breeding or pedigree

[2]**thoroughbred** *n* **1** *cap* any of an English breed of horses kept chiefly for racing that originated from crosses between English mares of uncertain ancestry and Arabian stallions **2** a purebred or pedigree animal **3** sby or sthg with the characteristics associated with good breeding

'**thorough,fare** /-,feə‖-,feə/ *n* **1** a public way (e g a road, street, or path); *esp* a main road **2** passage, transit <*no* ~>

'**thorough,going** /-,goh·ing‖-,gəʊɪŋ/ *adj* **1** extremely thorough or zealous **2** absolute, utter <*a* ~ *villain*>

those /dhohz‖ðəʊz/ *pl of* [1, 2]THAT

[1]**thou** /dhow‖ðaʊ/ *pron, archaic or dial* the one being addressed; you – capitalized when addressing God; sometimes used by Quakers as the universal form of address to 1 person

[2]**thou** /thow‖θaʊ/ *n, pl* **thou, thous** **1** a thousand (of sthg, esp money) **2** a unit of length equal to $^{1}/_{1000}$in (about 25.4mm)

[1]**though** *also* **tho** /dhoh‖ðəʊ/ *adv* however, nevertheless

[2]**though** *also* **tho** *conj* **1** in spite of the fact that; while <~ *it's hard work, I enjoy it*> **2** in spite of the possibility that; even if **3** and yet; but <*it works,* ~ *not as well as we hoped*>

[1]**thought** /thawt‖θɔːt/ *past of* THINK

[2]**thought** *n* **1a** thinking <*lost in* ~> **b** serious consideration <*gave no* ~ *to the danger*> **2** reasoning or conceptual power **3a** an idea, opinion, concept, or intention **b** the intellectual product or the organized views of a period, place, group, or individual **c** hope, expectation <*gave up all* ~ *of winning*>

'**thoughtful** /-f(ə)l‖-f(ə)l/ *adj* **1a** having thoughts; absorbed in thought **b** showing careful reasoned thinking <*a* ~ *analysis of the problem*> **2** showing concern for others – **thoughtfully** *adv*, **thoughtfulness** *n*

'**thoughtless** /-lis‖-lɪs/ *adj* **1** lacking forethought; rash **2** lacking concern for others – **thoughtlessly** *adv*, **thoughtlessness** *n*

thousand /'thowz(ə)nd‖'θaʊz(ə)nd/ *n, pl* **thousands, thousand** **1** (the number) 1000 **2** the number occupying the position 4 to the left of the decimal point in the Arabic notation; *also, pl* this position **3** an indefinitely large number <~s *of ants*> – often pl with sing. meaning – **thousand** *adj*, **thousandth** *adj or n*

thrall /thrawl‖θrɔːl/ *n* **1a** a bondman **b** (sby in) a state of (moral) servitude **2** a state of complete absorption or enslavement – **thrall** *adj*, **thraldom,** *NAm chiefly* **thralldom** *n*

[1]**thrash** /thrash‖θræʃ/ *vt* **1** THRESH 1 **2a** to beat soundly (as if) with a stick or whip **b** to defeat heavily or decisively **3** to swing, beat, or strike wildly or violently <~ing *his arms*> ~ *vi* **1** THRESH 1 **2** to deal repeated blows (as if) with a flail or whip **3** to move or stir about violently; toss about – usu + *around* or *about* <~ *around in bed with a fever*> – **thrasher** *n*, **thrashing** *n*

[2]**thrash** *n* **1** an act of thrashing, esp in swimming **2** a wild party – infml

thrash out *vt* to discuss (e g a problem) exhaustively with a view to finding a solution; *also* to arrive at (e g a decision) in this way

[1]**thread** /thred‖θred/ *n* **1** a filament, group of filaments twisted together, or continuous strand formed by spinning and twisting together short textile fibres **2a** any of various natural filaments <*the* ~s *of a spider's web*> **b** sthg (e g a thin stream of liquid) like a thread in length and narrowness **c** a projecting spiral ridge (e g on a bolt or pipe) by which parts can be screwed together **3** sthg continuous or drawn out: e g **3a** a train of thought <*I've lost the* ~ *of this argument*> **b** a pervasive recurring element <*a* ~ *of melancholy marked all his writing*> **4** a precarious or weak support <*to hang by a* ~> – **thready** *adj*

[2]**thread** *vt* **1a** to pass a thread through the eye of (a needle) **b** to arrange a thread, yarn, or

lead-in piece in working position for use in (a machine) **2a(1)** to pass sthg through the entire length of < ~ *a pipe with wire*> **a(2)** to pass (e g a tape or film) into or through sthg < ~ed *elastic into the waistband*> **b** to make one's way cautiously through or between < ~ing *narrow alleys*> **3** to string together (as if) on a thread < ~ *beads*> **4** to intermingle (as if) with threads <*dark hair* ~ed *with silver*> **5** to form a screw thread on or in ~ *vi* **1** to make one's way *through* **2** to form a thread when poured from a spoon – **threader** *n*

threadbare /ˈthred,beə‖ˈθred,beə/ *adj* **1** having the nap worn off so that the threads show; worn, shabby **2** hackneyed < ~ *phrases*> – **threadbareness** *n*

threat /thret‖θret/ *n* **1** an indication of sthg, usu unpleasant, to come **2** an expression of intention to inflict punishment, injury, or damage **3** sthg that is a source of imminent danger or harm; MENACE 2a

threaten /ˈthret(ə)n‖ˈθret(ə)n/ *vt* **1** to utter threats against <*he* ~ed *his employees with the sack*> **2a** to give ominous signs of <*the clouds* ~ *rain*> **b** to be a source of harm or danger to **3** to announce as intended or possible <*the workers* ~ed *a strike*> ~ *vi* **1** to utter threats **2** to appear menacing <*the sky* ~ed> – **threatener** *n*, **threateningly** *adv*

three /three‖θri:/ *n* **1** (the number) 3 **2** the third in a set or series <*the* ~ *of hearts*> **3** sthg having 3 parts or members or a denomination of 3 – **three** *adj or pron*, **threefold** *adj or adv*

,three-ˈD, **3-D** *n* three-dimensional form

,three-ˈdecker /ˈdekə‖ˈdekə/ *n* sthg with 3 tiers, layers, etc; *esp* a sandwich with 3 slices of bread and 2 fillings

,three-diˈmensional *adj* **1** having 3 dimensions **2** giving the illusion of depth – used of an image or pictorial representation, esp when this illusion is enhanced by stereoscopic means **3** describing or being described in great depth; *esp* lifelike <*a story with* ~ *characters*> – **three-dimensionality** *n*

three-legged race *n* a race between pairs in which each contestant has 1 leg tied to 1 of his/her partner's legs

three-line whip *n* an instruction from a party to its Members of Parliament that they must attend a debate and vote in the specified way [fr the triple underlining of words in the written instruction]

,three-ˈquarter *adj* **1** consisting of 3 fourths of the whole **2** *esp of a view of a rectangular object* including 1 side and 1 end <*a* ~ *view of a vehicle*>

,three ˈR's *n pl the* fundamentals taught in primary school; *esp* reading, writing, and arithmetic

threnody /ˈthrenədi, ˈthree-‖ˈθrenədɪ, ˈθri:-/ *n* a song of lamentation, esp for the dead [Greek *thrēnōidia*, fr *thrēnos* dirge + *aeidein* to sing]

thresh /thresh‖θreʃ/ *vt* **1** to separate the seeds from (a harvested plant) by (mechanical) beating **2** to strike repeatedly ~ *vi* **1** to thresh grain **2** THRASH 2, 3

thresher /ˈthreshə‖ˈθreʃə/ *n* a large shark reputed to thresh the water to round up fish on which it feeds using the greatly elongated curved upper lobe of its tail

threshold /ˈthresh,hohld, ˈthresh·ohld‖ˈθreʃ-,həʊld, ˈθreʃəʊld/ *n* **1** the plank, stone, etc that lies under a door **2a** the doorway or entrance to a building **b** the point of entering or beginning <*on the* ~ *of a new career*> **3** a level, point, or value above which sthg is true or will take place

threw /throoh‖θru:/ *past of* THROW

thrice /thries‖θraɪs/ *adv* **1** three times **2a** in a threefold manner or degree **b** to a high degree – usu in combination <thrice-*blessed*>

thrift /thrift‖θrɪft/ *n* careful management, esp of money; frugality – **thriftless** *adj*, **thrifty** *adj*, **thriftily** *adv*, **thriftiness** *n*

thrill /thril‖θrɪl/ *vt* **1a** to cause to experience a sudden feeling of excitement **b** to cause to have a shivering or tingling sensation **2** to cause to vibrate or tremble perceptibly ~ *vi* **1** to experience a sudden tremor of excitement or emotion **2** to tingle, throb – **thrill** *n*, **thrillingly** *adv*

thriller /ˈthrilə‖ˈθrɪlə/ *n* a work of fiction or drama characterized by a high degree of intrigue or suspense

thrive /thriev‖θraɪv/ *vi* **throve** /throhv‖θrəʊv/, **thrived; thriven** /ˈthriv(ə)n‖ˈθrɪv(ə)n/ *also* **thrived** **1** to grow vigorously **2** to gain in wealth or possessions – **thriver** *n*

throat /throht‖θrəʊt/ *n* **1a** the part of the neck in front of the spinal column **b** the passage through the neck to the stomach and lungs **2a** sthg throatlike, esp in being a constricted passageway **b** the opening of a tubular (plant) organ **3** the upper forward corner of a fore-and-aft 4-cornered sail – **throated** *adj*

throaty /ˈthrohti‖ˈθrəʊtɪ/ *adj* uttered or produced low in the throat; hoarse, guttural – **throatily** *adv*, **throatiness** *n*

[1]**throb** /throb‖θrɒb/ *vi* **-bb-** **1** to pulsate with unusual force or rapidity **2** to (come in waves that seem to) beat or vibrate rhythmically <*a* ~bing *pain*> – **throbber** *n*

[2]**throb** *n* a beat, pulse

throe /throh‖θrəʊ/ *n* **1** a pang or spasm – usu pl <*death* ~s> **2** *pl* a hard or painful struggle <*in the* ~s *of revolutionary change*>

thrombosis /thromˈbohsis‖θrɒmˈbəʊsɪs/ *n*, *pl* **thromboses** /-seez‖-si:z/ the formation or presence of a blood clot within a blood vessel during life [Greek *thrombōsis* clotting, deriv of *thrombos* clot] – **thrombotic** *adj*

throne /throhn‖θrəʊn/ *n* **1** the chair of state of a sovereign or bishop **2** sovereignty

[1]**throng** /throng‖θrɒŋ/ *n sing or pl in constr* **1** a multitude of assembled people, esp when crowded together **2** a large number

[2]**throng** *vt* **1** to crowd upon (esp a person) **2** to crowd into <*shoppers* ~ing *the streets*> ~*vi* to crowd together in great numbers

throstle /ˈthrosl‖ˈθrɒsl/ *n* SONG THRUSH

[1]**throttle** /ˈthrotl‖ˈθrɒtl/ *vt* **1a(1)** to compress the throat of; choke **a(2)** to kill by such action **b** to prevent or check expression or activity of; suppress **2a** to control the flow of (e g steam or fuel to an engine) by means of a valve **b** to regulate, esp reduce the speed of (e g an engine), by such means – usu + *back* or *down* – **throttler** *n*

[2]**throttle** *n* **1a** THROAT 1a **b** TRACHEA 1 **2** (the lever or pedal controlling) a valve for regulating the supply of a fluid (e g fuel) to an engine

[1]**through** *also* **thro,** *NAm also* **thru** /throoh‖θruː/ *prep* **1a(1)** into at one side or point and out at the other <*drove a nail ~ the board*> <*a path ~ the woods*> **a(2)** past <*saw ~ the deception*> **b** – used to indicate passage into and out of a treatment, handling, or process <*flashed ~ my mind*> **2** – used to indicate means, agency, or intermediacy: e g **2a** by means of; by the agency of **b** because of <*failed ~ ignorance*> **c** by common descent from or relationship with <*related ~ their grandfather*> **3a** over the whole surface or extent of <*homes scattered ~ the valley*> **b** – used to indicate movement within a large expanse <*flew ~ the air*> **c** among or between the parts or single members of <*search ~ my papers*> **d** – used to indicate exposure to a set of conditions <*put her ~ hell*> **4a** during the entire period of <*all ~ her life*> **b** against and in spite of (a noise) <*heard his voice ~ the howling of the storm*> **5a** – used to indicate completion, exhaustion, or accomplishment <*got ~ the book*> **b** – used to indicate acceptance or approval, esp by an official body <*got the bill ~ Parliament*> **6** *chiefly NAm* up till and including <*Monday ~ Friday*>

[2]**through,** *NAm also* **thru** *adv* **1** from one end or side to the other <*squeezed ~*> **2a** all the way from beginning to end <*read the letter ~*> <*train goes right ~ to London*> **b** to a favourable or successful conclusion <*I failed the exam, but he got ~*> **3** to the core; completely <*wet ~*> **4** into the open; out <*break ~*> **5** *chiefly Br* in or into connection by telephone <*put me ~ to him*>

[3]**through,** *NAm also* **thru** *adj* **1a** extending from one surface to the other <*a ~ beam*> **b** direct <*a ~ road*> **2a** allowing a continuous journey from point of origin to destination without change or further payment <*a ~ train*> **b** starting at and destined for points outside a local zone <*~ traffic*> **3** arrived at completion, cessation, or dismissal; finished <*you're ~: that was your last chance*> <*I'm ~ with women*>

[1]**ˌthroughˈout** /-ˈowt‖-ˈaʊt/ *adv* **1** in or to every part; everywhere <*of 1 colour ~*> **2** during the whole time or action; from beginning to end <*remained loyal ~*>

[2]**throughout** *prep* **1** in or to every part of; THROUGH 3a <*cities ~ Europe*> **2** during the entire period of; THROUGH 4a <*troubled him ~ his life*>

ˈthroughˌput /-ˌpoot‖-ˌpʊt/ *n* the amount of material put through a process <*the ~ of a computer*>

[1]**throw** /throh‖θrəʊ/ *vb* **threw** /throoh‖θruː/; **thrown** /throhn‖θrəʊn/ *vt* **1** to propel through the air in some manner, esp by a forward motion of the hand and arm **2a** to cause to fall <threw *his opponent*> **b** UNSEAT 1 **3a** to fling (oneself) abruptly **b** to hurl violently <*the ship was* ~n *against the rocks*> **4a(1)** to put in a specified position or condition, esp suddenly <*the news* threw *him into confusion*> **a(2)** to put *on* or *off* hastily or carelessly **b** to exert; BRING TO BEAR <threw *all his weight behind the proposal*> **c** to build, construct <threw *a pontoon bridge over the river*> **5** to shape by hand on a potter's wheel **6** to deliver (a punch) **7** to twist 2 or more filaments of (e g silk) into a thread or yarn **8** to make a cast of (dice or a specified number on dice) **9** to send forth; cast, direct <*the setting sun* threw *long shadows*> <*he* threw *me a glance*> **10** to commit (oneself) for help, support, or protection <threw *himself on the mercy of the court*> **11** to bring forth; produce <threw *large litters*> **12** to move (a lever or switch) so as to connect or disconnect parts of a mechanism **13** to project (the voice) **14** to give by way of entertainment <*~ a party*> **15** to disconcert; *also* THROW OFF 4 – infml <*the problem didn't ~ her*> **16** *chiefly NAm* to lose intentionally – infml <*~ a game*> *~vi* to cast, hurl – **thrower** *n* – **throw one's weight about/around** to exercise influence or authority, esp to an excessive degree or in an objectionable manner – infml – **throw together 1** KNOCK TOGETHER <threw together *a delicious curry in no time*> **2** to bring into casual association

[2]**throw** *n* **1a** an act of throwing **b** a method or instance of throwing an opponent in wrestling or judo **2** the distance sthg may be thrown <*lived within a stone's ~ from school*> **3** the amount of vertical displacement produced by a geological fault **4** (the distance of) the extent of movement of a cam, crank, or other pivoted or reciprocating piece

[1]**ˈthrowaˌway** /-əˌway‖-əˌweɪ/ *n* a line of dialogue (e g in a play) made to sound incidental by casual delivery

[2]**throwaway** *adj* **1** designed to be discarded after use; disposable <*~ containers*> **2** written or spoken (e g in a play) with deliberate casualness <*a ~ remark*>

throw away *vt* **1** to get rid of as worthless or unnecessary **2a** to use in a foolish or wasteful manner **b** to fail to take advantage of **3** to make (e g a line in a play) unemphatic by casual delivery

ˈthrowˌback /-ˌbak‖-ˌbæk/ *n* (an individual exhibiting) reversion to an earlier genetic type or phase

throw back *vt* **1** to delay the progress or advance of **2** to cause to rely; make dependent – + *on* or *upon*; usu pass <thrown back *on his own resources*> *~vi* to revert to an earlier genetic type or phase

ˈthrow-ˌin *n* a throw made from the touchline in soccer to put the ball back in play after it has gone over the touchline

throw in *vt* **1** to add as a gratuity or supplement **2** to introduce or interject in the course of sthg <threw in *a casual remark*> **3** to cause (e g gears) to mesh *~vi* to enter into association or partnership *with* – **throw in the sponge/towel** to abandon a struggle or contest; acknowledge defeat

throw off *vt* **1a** to cast off, often in an abrupt or vigorous manner <throw off *the oppressors*> <throw *a cold* off> **b** to divert, distract <*dogs* thrown off *by a false scent*> **2** to emit; GIVE OFF <*stacks* throwing off *plumes of smoke*> **3** to produce or execute in an offhand manner

<*a review* thrown off *in an odd half hour*> **4** to cause to deviate or err ~*vi* to begin hunting with a pack of hounds

throw out *vt* **1a** to remove from a place or from employment, usu in a sudden or unexpected manner **b** THROW AWAY 1 **2** to give expression to <threw out *a remark that utterly foxed them*> **3** to refuse to accept or consider <*the assembly* threw out *the proposed legislation*> **4** to give forth from within <*in spring new shoots will be* thrown out *from the main stem*> **5** to cause to extend from a main body <throw out *a screen of cavalry*> <*rebuilt the house*, throwing out *a new wing to the west*> **6** to confuse, disconcert <*the question quite* threw *him* out>

throw over *vt* to forsake or abandon (esp a lover)

throw up *vt* **1** to raise quickly <threw up *his hands in horror*> **2** GIVE UP 3b <*the urge to* throw up *work and go to Tahiti*> **3** to build hurriedly **4** to bring forth **5** to mention repeatedly by way of reproach **6** to vomit – infml ~*vi* to vomit – infml – **throw up the sponge** THROW IN THE SPONGE/TOWEL

thru /throoh‖θruː/ *prep, adv, or adj, NAm* through

thrum /thrum‖θrʌm/ *vb* **-mm-** *vi* **1** to play or pluck a stringed instrument idly **2** to drum or tap idly **3** to sound with a monotonous hum ~*vt* to play (e g a stringed instrument) in an idle or relaxed manner

[1]**thrush** /thrush‖θrʌʃ/ *n* any of numerous small or medium-sized mostly drab-coloured birds many of which are excellent singers: e g **a** SONG THRUSH **b** MISTLE THRUSH

[2]**thrush** *n* **1** a whitish intensely irritating fungal growth occurring on mucous membranes, esp in the mouth or vagina **2** a suppurative disorder of the feet in various animals, esp horses

[1]**thrust** /thrust‖θrʌst/ *vb* **thrust** *vt* **1** to push or drive with force **2** to push forth <~ *out roots*> **3** to stab, pierce **4** to put (an unwilling person) into a course of action or position <*was* ~ *into power*> **5** to press, force, or impose the acceptance of *on* or *upon* sby ~ *vi* **1** to force an entrance or passage – often + *into* or *through* **2** to make a thrust, stab, or lunge (as if) with a pointed weapon – **thruster, thrustor** *n*

[2]**thrust** *n* **1a** a push or lunge with a pointed weapon **b(1)** a verbal attack **b(2)** a concerted military attack **2a** a strong continued pressure **b** the sideways force of one part of a structure against another **c** the force exerted by a propeller, jet engine, etc to give forward motion **3a** a forward or upward push **b** a movement (e g by a group of people) in a specified direction

[1]**thud** /thud‖θʌd/ *vi* **-dd-** to move or strike with a thud

[2]**thud** *n* **1** [5]BLOW 1 **2** a dull thump

thug /thug‖θʌg/ *n* **1** *often cap* a member of a former religious sect in India given to robbery and murder **2** a violent criminal [Hindi *ṭhag*, lit., thief, fr Sanskrit *sthaga* rogue, fr *sthagati* he covers, conceals] – **thuggish** *adj*, **thuggery** *n*

[1]**thumb** /thum‖θʌm/ *n* **1** the short thick digit of the human hand that is next to the forefinger and is opposable to the other fingers; *also* the corresponding digit in lower animals **2** the part of a glove or mitten that covers the thumb – **all thumbs** extremely awkward or clumsy – **under someone's thumb** under sby's control; in a state of subservience to sby <*her father had her completely* under his thumb>

[2]**thumb** *vt* **1a** to leaf through (pages) with the thumb **b** to soil or wear (as if) by repeated thumbing **2** to request or obtain (a lift) in a passing vehicle ~ *vi* **1** to turn over pages **2** to travel by thumbing lifts; hitchhike

ˈthumbˌnail /-ˌnayl‖-ˌneɪl/ *adj* brief, concise <*a* ~ *sketch*>

ˈthumbˌscrew /-ˌskrooh‖-ˌskruː/ *n* an instrument of torture for squeezing the thumb

ˈthumbˌtack /-ˌtak‖-ˌtæk/ *n, NAm* DRAWING PIN

[1]**thump** /thump‖θʌmp/ *vt* **1** to strike or knock with a thump **2** to thrash; BEAT 1a **3** to produce (music) mechanically or in a mechanical manner <~ed *out a tune on the piano*> ~ *vi* **1** to inflict a thump **2** to produce a thumping sound – **thumper** *n*

[2]**thump** *n* (a sound of) a blow or knock (as if) with sthg blunt or heavy

thumping /ˈthumping‖ˈθʌmpɪŋ/ *adv, Br* VERY 1 – chiefly in *thumping great* and *thumping good*; infml

[1]**thunder** /ˈthundə‖ˈθʌndə/ *n* **1** the low loud sound that follows a flash of lightning and is caused by sudden expansion of the air in the path of the electrical discharge **2** a loud reverberating noise – **thunderous** *adj*, **thunderously** *adv*, **thundery** *adj*

[2]**thunder** *vi* **1a** to give forth thunder – usu impersonally <*it* ~ed> **b** to make a sound like thunder **2** to roar, shout ~*vt* to utter in a loud threatening tone – **thunderer** *n*

ˈthunderˌbolt /-ˌbohlt‖-ˌbəʊlt/ *n* **1a** a single discharge of lightning with the accompanying thunder **b** an imaginary bolt or missile cast to earth in a flash of lightning **2a** sthg like lightning in suddenness, effectiveness, or destructive power **b** a vehement threat or censure

ˈthunderˌclap /-ˌklap‖-ˌklæp/ *n* (sthg loud or sudden like) a clap of thunder

ˈthunderˌcloud /-ˌklowd‖-ˌklaʊd/ *n* a cloud charged with electricity and producing lightning and thunder

thundering /ˈthund(ə)ring‖ˈθʌnd(ə)rɪŋ/ *adv, Br* very, thumping <*a* ~ *great bore*> – infml – **thunderingly** *adv*

ˈthunderˌstorm /-ˌstawm‖-ˌstɔːm/ *n* a storm accompanied by lightning and thunder

ˈthunderˌstruck /-ˌstruk‖-ˌstrʌk/ *adj* dumbfounded, astonished

Thursday /ˈthuhzday, -di‖ˈθɜːzdeɪ, -dɪ/ *n* the day of the week following Wednesday [Old English *thursdæg*, fr Old Norse *thōrsdagr*, lit., day of Thor, fr *Thor*, god of thunder]

thus /dhus‖ðʌs/ *adv* **1** in the manner indicated; in this way **2** to this degree or extent; so <~ *far*> **3** because of this preceding fact or premise; consequently **4** as an example

thwack /thwak‖θwæk/ *vb or n* (to) whack

[1]**thwart** /thwawt‖θwɔːt/ *vt* to defeat the hopes or aspirations of – **thwarter** *n*

[2]**thwart** *n* a seat extending across a boat

thy /dhie‖ðaɪ/ *adj, archaic or dial* of thee or thyself – capitalized when addressing God; used attributively

thyme /tiem‖taɪm/ *n* any of a genus of plants of the mint family with small pungent aromatic leaves

thymus /'thieməs‖'θaɪməs/ *n* a gland in the lower neck region that functions esp in development of the body's immune system

[1]**thyroid** /'thieroyd‖'θaɪrɔɪd/ *also* **thyroidal** /thie'roydl‖θaɪ'rɔɪdl/ *adj* of or being (an artery, nerve, etc associated with) **a** the thyroid gland **b** the chief cartilage of the larynx [Greek *thyreoeidēs* shield-shaped, fr *thyreos* shield shaped like a door, fr *thyra* door]

[2]**thyroid** *n* **1** **thyroid, thyroid gland** a large endocrine gland that lies at the base of the neck and produces hormones (e g thyroxine) that increase the metabolic rate and influence growth and development **2** a preparation of mammalian thyroid gland used in treating conditions such as goitre – **thyroidectomy** *n*

thyself /dhie'self‖ðaɪ'self/ *pron, archaic or dial* yourself

ti /tee‖tiː/ *n* the 7th note of the diatonic scale in tonic sol-fa

tiara /ti'ahrə‖tɪ'ɑːrə/ *n* **1** the 3-tiered crown worn by the pope **2** a decorative usu jewelled band worn on the head by women on formal occasions

tibia /'tibi·ə‖'tɪbɪə/ *n, pl* **tibiae** /'tibi,ee‖'tɪbɪ,iː/ *also* **tibias** **1** the inner and usu larger of the 2 bones of the vertebrate hind limb between the knee and ankle; the shinbone **2** the 4th joint of the leg of an insect between the femur and tarsus – **tibial** *adj*

tic /tik‖tɪk/ *n* **1** (a) local and habitual spasmodic motion of particular muscles, esp of the face; twitching **2** a persistent trait of character or behaviour

[1]**tick** /tik‖tɪk/ *n* **1** any of numerous related bloodsucking arachnids that feed on warm-blooded animals and often transmit infectious diseases **2** any of various usu wingless parasitic insects (e g the sheep ked)

[2]**tick** *n* **1** a light rhythmic audible tap or beat; *also* a series of such sounds **2** a small spot or mark used to mark sthg as correct, to draw attention to sthg, to check an item on a list, or to represent a point on a scale **3** *Br* a moment, second – infml

[3]**tick** *vi* **1** to make the sound of a tick **2** to function or behave characteristically <*I'd like to know what makes him* ~> ~ *vt* **1** to mark with a written tick **2** to mark or count (as if) by ticks

[4]**tick** *n* **1** a strong coarse fabric case of a mattress, pillow, or bolster **2** ticking

[5]**tick** *n* credit, trust <*bought it on* ~> – infml

ticker /'tikə‖'tɪkə/ *n* sthg that produces a ticking sound: e g **a** a watch **b** HEART 1a – infml

'ticker ,tape *n* a paper tape on which a certain type of telegraphic receiving instrument prints out its information

ticket /'tikit‖'tɪkɪt/ *n* **1a** a document that serves as a certificate, licence, or permit; *esp* a mariner's or pilot's certificate **b** a tag, label **2** an official notification issued to sby who has violated a traffic regulation **3** a usu printed card or piece of paper entitling its holder to the use of certain services (e g a library), showing that a fare or admission has been paid, etc **4** *Br* a certificate of discharge from the armed forces **5** *chiefly NAm* a list of candidates for nomination or election; *also* PLATFORM 1 **6** the correct, proper, or desirable thing – infml <*hot tea is just the* ~> [obs French *etiquet* (now *étiquette*) label, fr Middle French *estiquet*, fr *estiquier* to attach, fr Middle Dutch *steken* to stick]

ticking /'tiking‖'tɪkɪŋ/ *n* a strong linen or cotton fabric used esp for a case for a mattress or pillow

[1]**tickle** /'tikl‖'tɪkl/ *vi* to have or cause a tingling or prickling sensation ~ *vt* **1a** to excite or stir up agreeably **b** to provoke to laughter **2** to touch (e g a body part) lightly and repeatedly so as to excite the surface nerves and cause uneasiness, laughter, or spasmodic movements

[2]**tickle** *n* **1** a tickling sensation **2** the act of tickling

ticklish /'tiklish‖'tɪklɪʃ/ *adj* **1** sensitive to tickling **2** easily upset **3** requiring delicate handling – **ticklishly** *adv*, **ticklishness** *n*

tick off *vt* to scold, rebuke

tick over *vi* to operate at a normal or reduced rate of activity

ticktacktoe *also* **tic-tac-toe** /,tik,tak'toh‖,tɪk,tæk'təʊ/ *n, NAm* NOUGHTS AND CROSSES

tidal /'tiedl‖'taɪdl/ *adj* of, caused by, or having tides – **tidally** *adv*

'tidal ,wave *n* **1** an unusually high sea wave that sometimes follows an earthquake **2** an unexpected, intense, and often widespread reaction (e g a sweeping majority vote or an overwhelming impulse)

tidbit /'tid,bit‖'tɪd,bɪt/ *n, chiefly NAm* a titbit

tiddler /'tidlə‖'tɪdlə/ *n, Br* sby or sthg small in comparison to others of the same kind; *esp* a minnow, stickleback, or other small fish

tiddly /'tidli‖'tɪdlɪ/ *adj, Br* **1** very small <*a* ~ *bit of food*> **2** slightly drunk *USE* infml

tiddlywinks /'tidli,wingks‖'tɪdlɪ,wɪŋks/ *n* a game whose object is to flick small discs from a flat surface into a small container

[1]**tide** /tied‖taɪd/ *n* **1a(1)** (a current of water resulting from) the periodic rise and fall of the surface of a body of water, specif the sea, that occurs twice a day and is caused by the gravitational attraction of the sun and moon **a(2)** a periodic movement in the earth's crust caused by the same forces that produce ocean tides **a(3)** a tidal distortion on one celestial body caused by the gravitational attraction of another **b** the level or position of water on a shore with respect to the tide; *also* the water at its highest level **2** sthg that fluctuates like the tides <*the* ~ *of public opinion*> **3** a flowing stream; a current – **tideless** *adj*

[2]**tide** *vi* to drift with the tide, esp in navigating a ship into or out of an anchorage, harbour, or river

'tide,mark /-,mahk‖-,mɑːk/ *n* **1** a mark left by or indicating the (highest) position of the tide **2** a mark left on a bath that shows the level reached by the water; *also* a mark left on the body showing the limit of washing – chiefly infml

tide over *vt* to enable to surmount or withstand a difficulty

ˈtideˌwater /-ˌwawtə‖-ˌwɔːtə/ *n* **1a** water overflowing land at flood tide **b** water affected by the ebb and flow of the tide **2** low-lying coastal land

ˈtideˌway /-ˌway‖-ˌweɪ/ *n* (a current in) a channel in which the tide runs

tiding /ˈtieding‖ˈtaɪdɪŋ/ *n* a piece of news – usu pl with sing. meaning

[1]tidy /ˈtiedi‖ˈtaɪdɪ/ *adj* **1a** neat and orderly in appearance or habits; well ordered and cared for **b** methodical, precise <*a* ~ *mind*> **2** large, substantial – infml <*a* ~ *profit*> – **tidily** *adv*, **tidiness** *n*

[2]tidy *vb* to put (things) in order; make (things) neat or tidy – **tidier** *n*

[3]tidy *n* **1** a receptacle for odds and ends (e g sewing materials) **2** *chiefly NAm* a usu decorative cover used to protect the back, arms, or headrest of a chair or sofa from wear or dirt

[1]tie /tie‖taɪ/ *n* **1a** a line, ribbon, or cord used for fastening or drawing sthg together **b** a structural element (e g a rod or angle iron) holding 2 pieces together **2** sthg that serves as a connecting link: e g **2a** a moral or legal obligation to sby or sthg that restricts freedom of action **b** a bond of kinship or affection **3** a curved line that joins 2 musical notes of the same pitch to denote a single sustained note with the time value of the 2 **4a** a match or game between 2 teams, players, etc <*a cup* ~> **b** (a contest that ends in) a draw or dead heat **5** a narrow length of material designed to be worn round the neck and tied in a knot in the front **6** *NAm* a railway sleeper – **tieless** *adj*

[2]tie *vb* **tying, tieing** *vt* **1a** to fasten, attach, or close by knotting **b** to form a knot or bow in **c** to make by tying constituent elements <~d *a wreath*> **d** to make a bond or connection **2a** to unite in marriage **b** to unite (musical notes) by a tie **3** to restrain from independence or from freedom of action or choice; constrain (as if) by authority or obligation – often + *down* <~d *down by his responsibilities*> **4a** to even (the score) in a game or contest **b** to even the score of (a game) ~ *vi* to make a tie; *esp* to make an equal score <*they* ~d *for first place*>

ˈtie ˌbreak, ˈtie ˌbreaker *n* a contest or game used to select a winner from among contestants with tied scores at the end of a previous (phase of a) contest

tied cottage /tied‖taɪd/ *n, Br* a house owned by an employer (e g a farmer) and reserved for occupancy by an employee

tied house *n* a public house in Britain that is bound to sell only the products of the brewery that owns or rents it out

ˈtie-ˌdye *n* tie-dyeing

ˌtie -ˈdyeing *n* a method of producing patterns in textiles by tying portions of the fabric or yarn so that they will not absorb the dye – **tie-dyed** *adj*

ˈtie-ˌin *n* **1** sthg that ties in, relates, or connects **2** a book published to coincide with a film or television production to which it is related in some way; *also* the act of publishing such a book

tie in *vt* to bring into connection with sthg relevant; *esp* to coordinate so as to produce balance and unity <*the illustrations were cleverly* tied in *with the text*> ~ *vi* to be closely connected; *esp* to correspond <*that* ties in *with what I know already*>

ˈtieˌpin /-ˌpin‖-ˌpɪn/ *n* a decorative pin used to hold a tie in place

[1]tier /tiə‖tɪə/ *n* any of a series of levels (e g in an administration) <*the top* ~ *of local government*>

[2]tier *vb* to place, arrange, or rise in tiers

ˈtie-ˌup *n* a connection, association

tie up *vt* **1** to attach, fasten, or bind securely; *also* to wrap up and fasten **2** to connect closely; link **3** to place or invest in such a manner as to make unavailable for other purposes <*his money was* tied up *in stocks*> **4** to keep busy <*was* tied up *in conference all day*> **5** *NAm* to restrain from operation or progress <*traffic was* tied up *for miles*> ~ *vi* **1** to dock **2** to assume a definite relationship <*this* ties up *with what you were told before*>

tiff /tif‖tɪf/ *vi or n* (to have) a petty quarrel

tiffin /ˈtifin‖ˈtɪfɪn/ *n* a meal or snack taken at midday or in the middle of the morning, esp by the British in India

tiger /tiegə‖taɪgə/, *fem* **tigress** /ˈtiegris‖ˈtaɪgrɪs/ *n* **1** a very large Asiatic cat having a tawny coat transversely striped with black **2** a fierce and often bloodthirsty person – **tigerish** *adj*, **tigerishly** *adv*, **tigerishness** *n*, **tigerlike** *adj*

tiger lily *n* an Asiatic lily commonly grown for its drooping orange-coloured flowers densely spotted with black

[1]tight /tiet‖taɪt/ *adj* **1** so close or solid in structure as to prevent passage (e g of a liquid or gas) <*a* ~ *roof*> – often in combination <*an airtight compartment*> **2a** fixed very firmly in place **b** firmly stretched, drawn, or set **c** fitting (too) closely **3** set close together <*a* ~ *defensive formation in soccer*> **4** difficult to get through or out of <*in a* ~ *situation*> **5** firm in control; *also* characterized by such firmness <*ran a* ~ *ship*> **6** evenly contested <*a* ~ *match*> **7** packed, compressed or condensed to (near) the limit <*a* ~ *bale*> <~ *schedule*> **8** scarce in proportion to demand <~ *money*>; *also* characterized by such a scarcity <*a* ~ *labour market*> **9** playing in unison <*his new band was surprisingly* ~> **10** stingy, miserly **11** intoxicated, drunk *USE* (*10&11*) infml – **tightly** *adv*, **tightness** *n*

[2]tight *adv* **1** fast, tightly <*the door was shut* ~> **2** in a sound manner <*sleep* ~>

tighten /ˈtiet(ə)n‖ˈtaɪt(ə)n/ *vb* to make or become tight or tighter or more firm or severe – often + *up* – **tightener** *n*

tighten up *vi* to enforce regulations more stringently – usu + *on*

ˌtightˈfisted /-ˈfistid‖-ˈfɪstɪd/ *adj* reluctant to part with money

ˌtight-ˈlipped *adj* **1** having the lips compressed (e g in determination) **2** reluctant to speak; taciturn

ˈtightˌrope /-ˌrohp‖-ˌrəʊp/ *n* **1** a rope or wire stretched taut for acrobats to perform on **2** a dangerously precarious situation

tights /tiets‖taɪts/ *n pl* a skintight garment covering each leg (and foot) and reaching to the waist

tigress /ˈtiegris‖ˈtaɪgrɪs/ *n* a female tiger; *also* a tigerish woman

tike /tiek‖taɪk/ *n* a tyke

tilde /ˈtildə‖ˈtɪldə/ *n* a mark ~ placed esp over the letter *n* (e g in Spanish *señor*) to denote the sound /ny/ or over vowels (e g in Portuguese *irmã*) to indicate nasality

[1]**tile** /tiel‖taɪl/ *n* **1** a thin slab of fired clay, stone, or concrete shaped according to use: e g **1a** a flat or curved slab for use on roofs **b** a flat and often ornamented slab for floors, walls, or surrounds **c** a tube-shaped or semicircular and open slab for constructing drains **2** a thin piece of resilient material (e g cork or linoleum) used esp for covering floors or walls – **on the tiles** enjoying oneself socially, esp in an intemperate or wild manner <*looks terrible this morning after a night out* on the tiles>

[2]**tile** *vt* to cover with tiles – **tiler** *n*, **tiling** *n*

[1]**till** /til, tl‖tɪl, tl/ *prep* **1** until **2** *chiefly Scot* to

[2]**till** *conj* until

[3]**till** /til‖tɪl/ *vt* to work (e g land) by ploughing, sowing, and raising crops – **tillable** *adj*, **tillage** *n*, **tiller** *n*

[4]**till** *n* **1a** a receptacle (e g a drawer or tray) in which money is kept in a shop or bank **b** CASH REGISTER **2** the money contained in a till

[1]**tiller** /ˈtilə‖ˈtɪlə/ *n* a lever used to turn the rudder of a boat from side to side

[2]**tiller** *n* a sprout or stalk (from the base of a plant)

[1]**tilt** /tilt‖tɪlt/ *vt* **1** to cause to slope <*don't* ~ *the boat*> **2** to point or thrust (as if) in a joust <~ *a lance*> ~ *vi* **1** to shift so as to lean or incline **2a** to engage in combat with lances **b** to make an impetuous attack <~ *at wrongs*> – **tiltable** *adj*, **tilter** *n*

[2]**tilt** *n* **1** a military exercise in which a mounted person charges at an opponent or mark **2** speed – in *at full tilt* **3** a written or verbal attack – + *at* **4a** tilting or being tilted **b** a sloping surface

[3]**tilt** *n* a canopy for a wagon, boat, lorry, or stall

tiltyard /ˈtiltˌyahd‖ˈtɪltˌjɑːd/ *n* a yard or place for tilting contests

[1]**timber** /ˈtimbə‖ˈtɪmbə/ *n* **1a** growing trees or their wood **b** – used interjectionally to warn of a falling tree **2** wood suitable for carpentry or woodwork **3** material, stuff; *esp* personal character or quality **4** *Br* wood or logs, esp when dressed for use – **timber** *adj*, **timberman** *n*

[2]**timber** *vt* to frame, cover, or support with timbers

timbered /ˈtimbəd‖ˈtɪmbəd/ *adj* having walls framed by exposed timbers

timbre /ˈtambə, ˈtimbə, ˈtahmbə ‖ˈtæmbə, ˈtɪmbə, ˈtɑːmbə (*Fr* tɛ̃ːbr)/ *also* **timber** /ˈtimbə‖ˈtɪmbə/ *n* the quality given to a sound by its overtones: e g **a** the resonance by which the ear recognizes a voiced speech sound **b** the quality of tone distinctive of a particular singing voice or musical instrument [French, fr Middle French, bell struck by a hammer, fr Old French, drum, fr Greek *tympanon*]

timbrel /ˈtimbrəl‖ˈtɪmbrəl/ *n* a small hand drum or tambourine

[1]**time** /tiem‖taɪm/ *n* **1a** the measurable period during which an action, process, or condition exists or continues **b** a continuum in which events succeed one another <*stand the test of* ~> **c** leisure <~ *for reading*> **2a** the point or period when sthg occurs <*at the* ~ *of writing*> **b** the period required for an action <*the winner's* ~ *was under 4 minutes*> **3a** a period set aside or suitable for an activity or event <*a* ~ *for celebration*> **b** an appointed, fixed, or customary moment for sthg to happen, begin, or end; *esp, Br* closing time in a public house as fixed by law <*time, gentlemen, please*> **4a** a historical period – often pl with sing. meaning <*modern* ~s> **b** conditions or circumstances prevalent during a period – usu pl with sing. meaning <~s *are hard*> **c** *the* present time <*issues of the* ~> **d** the expected moment of giving birth or dying <*her* ~ *is near*> **e** the end or course of a future period <*only* ~ *will tell*> <*will happen in* ~> **5a** a period of apprenticeship **b** a term of imprisonment – infml **6** a season <*very hot for this* ~ *of year*> **7a** a tempo **b** the grouping of the beats of music; a rhythm, metre **8a** a moment, hour, day, or year as measured or indicated by a clock or calendar **b** any of various systems (e g sidereal or solar) of reckoning time **9a** any of a series of recurring instances or repeated actions <*you've been told many* ~s> **b** *pl* **b(1)** multiplied instances <*5* ~s *greater*> **b(2)** equal fractional parts of which a specified number equal a comparatively greater quantity <*7* ~s *smaller*> **10** a person's usu specified experience, esp on a particular occasion <*a good* ~> **11a** the hours or days occupied by one's work <*make up* ~> **b** an hourly rate of pay <*on double* ~> **12** the end of the playing time of a (section of a) game – often used as an interjection – **at times** at intervals; occasionally – **behind the times** old-fashioned – **for the time being** for the present – **from time to time** at irregular intervals – **in time 1** sufficiently early **2** eventually **3** in correct tempo <*learn to play* in time> – **on time** at the appointed time – **time and (time) again** frequently, repeatedly

[2]**time** *vt* **1** to arrange or set the time of **2** to regulate the moment, speed, or duration of, esp to achieve the desired effect <*an ill*-timed *remark*> **3** to cause to keep time with sthg **4** to determine or record the time, duration, or speed of <~ *a journey*> ~*vi* to keep or beat time – **timer** *n*

[3]**time** *adj* **1** of or recording time **2** (able to be) set to function at a specific moment <*a* ~ *bomb*> <*a* ~ *switch*>

time exposure *n* (a photograph taken by) exposure of a photographic film for a relatively long time, usu more than 0.5s

ˈ**time-ˌhonoured** *adj* sanctioned by custom or tradition

time immemorial /imiˈmawri·əl‖ɪmɪˈmɔːrɪəl/ *n* time beyond living memory or historical record

ˈ**timeˌkeeper** /-ˌkeepə‖-ˌkiːpə/ *n* sby who records the time worked by employees, elapsed in a race, etc – **timekeeping** *n*

ˈtime ˌlag *n* an interval of time between 2 related phenomena

ˈtimeless /-lis‖-lɪs/ *adj* **1a** unending, eternal **b** not restricted to a particular time or date **2** not affected by time; ageless – **timelessly** *adv*, **timelessness** *n*

ˈtimely /-li‖-lɪ/ *adv or adj* at an appropriate time – **timeliness** *n*

ˈtimeˌpiece /-ˌpees‖-ˌpiːs/ *n* a clock, watch, etc that measures or shows progress of time; *esp* one that does not chime

times /tiemz‖taɪmz/ *prep* multiplied by <*2 ~ 2 is 4*>

ˈtimeˌserver /-ˌsuhvə‖-ˌsɜːvə/ *n* sby who fits behaviour and ideas to prevailing opinions or to his/her superiors' views

ˈtime-ˌsharing *n* **1** simultaneous access to a computer by many users **2** a method of sharing holiday accommodation whereby each of a number of people buys a share of a lease on a property, entitling him/her to spend a proportionate amount of time there each year

time signature *n* a sign placed on a musical staff being usu a fraction whose denominator indicates the kind of note taken as the time unit for the beat (e g 4 for a crotchet or 8 for a quaver) and whose numerator indicates the number of beats per bar

1ˈtimeˌtable /-ˌtaybl‖-ˌteɪbl/ *n* **1** a table of departure and arrival times of public transport **2** a schedule showing a planned order or sequence of events, esp of classes (e g in a school)

2timetable *vt* to arrange or provide for in a timetable

ˈtimeˌworn /-ˌwawn‖-ˌwɔːn/ *adj* **1** worn or impaired by time **2** ancient, age-old

ˈtime ˌzone *n* a geographical region within which the same standard time is used

timid /ˈtimid‖ˈtɪmɪd/ *adj* lacking in courage, boldness, or self-confidence – **timidly** *adv*, **timidness, timidity** *n*

timing /ˈtieming‖ˈtaɪmɪŋ/ *n* selection for maximum effect of the precise moment for doing sthg

timorous /ˈtim(ə)rəs‖ˈtɪm(ə)rəs/ *adj* timid – **timorously** *adv*, **timorousness** *n*

timpani /ˈtimpəni‖ˈtɪmpənɪ/ *n pl but sing or pl in constr* a set of 2 or 3 kettledrums played by 1 performer (e g in an orchestra) – **timpanist** *n*

1tin /tin‖tɪn/ *n* **1** a soft lustrous metallic element that is malleable and ductile at ordinary temperatures and is used as a protective coating, in tinfoil, and in soft solders and alloys **2** a box, can, pan, vessel, or sheet made of tinplate: e g **2a** a hermetically sealed tinplate container for preserving foods **b** any of various usu tinplate or aluminium containers of different shapes and sizes in which food is cooked, esp in an oven <*roasting ~*> <*loaf ~*> **3** a strip of resonant material below the board on the front wall of a squash court – **tinful** *n*

2tin *vt* **-nn-** **1** to cover or plate with tin or a tin alloy **2** *chiefly Br* 3CAN 1a

1tincture /ˈting(k)chə‖ˈtɪŋ(k)tʃə/ *n* **1a** a substance that colours or stains **b** a colour, hue **2** a slight addition; a trace **3** a heraldic metal, colour, or fur **4** a solution of a substance in alcohol for medicinal use <*~ of iodine*>

2tincture *vt* to tint or stain with a colour

tinder /ˈtində‖ˈtɪndə/ *n* any combustible substance suitable for use as kindling – **tindery** *adj*

ˈtinderˌbox /-ˌboks‖-ˌbɒks/ *n* **1a** a metal box for holding tinder and usu a flint and steel for striking a spark **b** a highly inflammable object or place **2** a potentially unstable place, situation, or person

tine /tien‖taɪn/ *n* **1** a prong (e g of a fork) **2** a pointed branch of an antler – **tined** *adj*

tinfoil /ˌtinˈfoyl, ˈ-ˌ-‖ˌtɪnˈfɔɪl, ˈ-ˌ-/ *n* a thin metal sheeting of tin, aluminium, or a tin alloy

1tinge /ˈtinj‖ˈtɪndʒ/ *vt* **tingeing, tinging** **1** to colour with a slight shade **2** to impart a slight smell, taste, or other quality to

2tinge *n* **1** a slight staining or suffusing colour **2** a slight modifying quality; a trace

tingle /ˈting·gl‖ˈtɪŋgl/ *vi or n* (to feel or cause) a stinging, prickling, or thrilling sensation – **tinglingly** *adv*, **tingly** *adj*

tin god *n* **1** a pompous and self-important person **2** sby unjustifiably esteemed or venerated *USE* infml

tin hat *n* a present-day military metal helmet – infml

1tinker /ˈtingkə‖ˈtɪŋkə/ *n* **1** a usu itinerant mender of household utensils **2** *chiefly Scot & Irish* a gipsy

2tinker *vi* to repair, adjust, or work with sthg in an unskilled or experimental manner – usu + *at* or *with* – **tinkerer** *n*

1tinkle /ˈtingkl‖ˈtɪŋkl/ *vi* to make (a sound suggestive of) a tinkle ~ *vt* **1** to sound or make known (the time) by a tinkle **2** to cause to (make a) tinkle – **tinkly** *adj*

2tinkle *n* **1** a series of short light ringing or clinking sounds **2** a jingling effect in verse or prose **3** *Br* a telephone call – infml **4** *Br* an act of urinating – euph

tinny /ˈtini‖ˈtɪnɪ/ *adj* **1** of, containing, or yielding tin **2a** having the taste, smell, or appearance of tin **b** not solid or durable; shoddy <*a ~ car*> **3** having a thin metallic sound – **tinnily** *adv*, **tinniness** *n*

ˌTin Pan ˈAlley *n* a district that is a centre for composers and publishers of popular music; *also, sing or pl in constr* the body of such composers and publishers

ˌtinˈplate /-ˈplayt‖-ˈpleɪt/ *n* thin sheet iron or steel coated with tin – **tin-plate** *vt*

1tinsel /ˈtins(ə)l‖ˈtɪns(ə)l/ *n* **1** a thread, strip, or sheet of metal, plastic, or paper used to produce a glittering and sparkling effect (e g in fabrics or decorations) **2** sthg superficial, showy, or glamorous <*the ~ of stardom*> – **tinselled,** *NAm* **tinseled, tinselled** *adj*

2tinsel *adj* cheaply gaudy; tawdry

1tint /tint‖tɪnt/ *n* **1a** a usu slight or pale coloration; a hue **b** any of various lighter or darker shades of a colour; *esp* one produced by adding white **2** a shaded effect in engraving produced by fine parallel lines close together **3** a panel of light colour serving as background for printing on

2tint *vt* to apply a tint to; colour – **tinter** *n*

tintinnabulation /ˌtintiˌnabyooˈlaysh(ə)n‖ˌtɪntɪˌnæbjʊˈleɪʃ(ə)n/ *n* **1** the ringing of bells **2** a sound as if of bells *USE* fml

tiny /ˈtieni‖ˈtaɪnɪ/ *adj* very small or diminutive

– **tinily** *adv*, **tininess** *n*

[1]**tip** /tip‖tɪp/ *n* **1** the usu pointed end of sthg **2** a small piece or part serving as an end, cap, or point <*a filter*-tip *cigarette*> – **tipped** *adj* – **on the tip of one's tongue** about to be uttered <*it was* on the tip of my tongue *to tell him exactly what I thought*>

[2]**tip** *vt* **-pp- 1a** to supply with a tip **b** to cover or adorn the tip of **2** to attach (an insert) in a book – usu + *in*

[3]**tip** *vb* **-pp-** *vt* **1** to overturn, upset – usu + *over* **2** to cant, tilt **3** *Br* to deposit or transfer by tilting ~ *vi* **1** to topple **2** to lean, slant – **tip the scales 1** to register weight <tips the scales *at 8 stone 4 ounces*> **2** to shift the balance of power or influence <*his greater experience* tipped the scales *in his favour*>

[4]**tip** *n* a place for tipping sthg (e g rubbish or coal); a dump

[5]**tip** *vt* **-pp-** to strike lightly

[6]**tip** *vb or n* **-pp-** (to give or present with) a sum of money in appreciation of a service performed

[7]**tip** *n* **1** a piece of useful or expert information **2** a piece of inside information which, acted upon, may bring financial gain (e g by betting or investment)

[8]**tip** *vt* **-pp-** to mention as a prospective winner, success, or profitable investment

ˈtip-ˌoff *n* a tip given usu as a warning

tip off *vt* to give a tip-off to <*the police were* tipped off *about the raid*>

tippet /ˈtipit‖ˈtɪpɪt/ *n* **1** a shoulder cape of fur or cloth often with hanging ends **2** a long black scarf worn over the surplice by Anglican clergymen during morning and evening prayer

[1]**tipple** /ˈtipl‖ˈtɪpl/ *vt* to drink (esp spirits), esp continuously in small amounts ~*vi* DRINK 2 *USE* infml – **tippler** *n*

[2]**tipple** *n* DRINK 1b – infml

tipstaff /ˈtip,stahf‖ˈtɪp,stɑːf/ *n, pl* **tipstaves** /-ˌstayvz‖-ˌsteɪvz/ an officer in certain lawcourts

tipster /ˈtipstə‖ˈtɪpstə/ *n* one who gives or sells tips, esp for gambling or speculation

tipsy /ˈtipsi‖ˈtɪpsɪ/ *adj* **1** unsteady, staggering, or foolish from the effects of alcoholic drink **2** askew <*a* ~ *angle*> – **tipsily** *adv*, **tipsiness** *n*

[1]**ˈtip,toe** /-ˌtoh‖-ˌtəʊ/ *n* the tip of a toe; *also* the ends of the toes <*walk on* ~>

[2]**tiptoe** *adv* (as if) on tiptoe

[3]**tiptoe** *adj* **1** standing or walking (as if) on tiptoe **2** cautious, stealthy

[4]**tiptoe** *vi* **tiptoeing 1** to stand, walk, or raise oneself on tiptoe **2** to walk silently or stealthily as if on tiptoe

ˌtip-ˈtop *adj* excellent, first-rate <*in* ~ *condition*> – infml – **tip-top** *adv*

tirade /tieˈrayd‖taɪˈreɪd/ *n* a long vehement speech or denunciation

[1]**tire** /tie·ə‖taɪə/ *vi* to become tired ~ *vt* **1** to fatigue **2** to wear out the patience of

[2]**tire** *n* a woman's headband or hair ornament

[3]**tire** *vt* to adorn (the hair) with an ornament

[4]**tire** *n, chiefly NAm* a tyre

tired /tie·əd‖taɪəd/ *adj* **1** weary, fatigued **2** exasperated; FED UP <~ *of listening to your complaints*> **3a** trite, hackneyed <*the same old* ~ *themes*> **b** lacking freshness <*a* ~ *skin*> <~, *overcooked asparagus*> – **tiredly** *adv*, **tiredness** *n*

tireless /ˈtie·əlis‖ˈtaɪəlɪs/ *adj* indefatigable, untiring – **tirelessly** *adv*, **tirelessness** *n*

tiresome /ˈtie·əsəm‖ˈtaɪəsəm/ *adj* wearisome, tedious – **tiresomely** *adv*, **tiresomeness** *n*

tiro /ˈtie,roh‖ˈtaɪ,rəʊ/ *n* a tyro

tissue /ˈtishooh‖ˈtɪʃuː; *also* ˈtisyooh‖ˈtɪsjuː/ *n* **1a** a fine gauzy often sheer fabric **b** a mesh, web <*a* ~ *of lies*> **2** a paper handkerchief **3** a cluster of cells, usu of a particular kind, together with their intercellular substance that form any of the structural materials of a plant or animal – **tissuey** *adj*

[1]**tit** /tit‖tɪt/ *n* **1** a teat or nipple **2** a woman's breast – infml

[2]**tit** *n* any of various small tree-dwelling insect-eating birds (e g a blue tit); *broadly* any of various small plump often long-tailed birds

titan /ˈtiet(ə)n‖ˈtaɪt(ə)n/, *fem* **titaness** /ˌtiet(ə)nˈes, ˈ---‖ˌtaɪt(ə)nˈes, ˈ---/ *n* sby or sthg very large or strong; *also* sby notable for outstanding achievement [Greek, one of a family of mythical giants once ruling the earth]

[1]**titanic** /tieˈtanik‖taɪˈtænɪk/ *adj* colossal, gigantic – **titanically** *adv*

[2]**titanic** /tiˈtanik, tie-‖tɪˈtænɪk, taɪ-/ *adj* of or containing titanium

titanium /tiˈtaynyəm, -ni·əm, tie-‖tɪˈteɪnjəm, -nɪəm, taɪ-/ *n* a light strong metallic element used esp in alloys and combined in refractory materials and in coatings

titbit /ˈtit,bit‖ˈtɪt,bɪt/, *chiefly NAm* **tidbit** /ˈtid-‖ˈtɪd-/ *n* a choice or pleasing piece (e g of food or news)

titfer /ˈtitfə‖ˈtɪtfə/ *n, Br* a hat – infml [rhyming slang *tit for (tat)*]

ˌtit for ˈtat /tat‖tæt/ *n* an equivalent given in retaliation (e g for an injury) [alteration of earlier *tip for tap*, fr *tip* blow + *for* + *tap*]

[1]**tithe** /tiedh‖taɪð/ *vi* to pay a tithe or tithes ~*vt* to levy a tithe on – **tithable** *adj*, **tither** *n*

[2]**tithe** *n* a tax or contribution of a 10th part of sthg (e g income) for the support of a religious establishment; *esp* such a tax formerly due in an English parish to support its church

titillate /ˈtiti,layt‖ˈtɪtɪ,leɪt/ *vt* to excite pleasurably; arouse by stimulation –**titillating** *adj*, **titillatingly** *adv*, **titillation** *n*, **titillative** *adj*

titivate, tittivate /ˈtitivayt‖ˈtɪtɪveɪt/ *vb* to smarten up (oneself or another) – **titivation** *n*

[1]**title** /ˈtietl‖ˈtaɪtl/ *n* **1** (a document giving proof of) legal ownership **2a** sthg that justifies or substantiates a claim **b** an alleged or recognized right **3a** a descriptive or general heading (e g of a chapter in a book) **b** the heading of a legal document or statute **c** a title page and the printed matter on it **d** written material introduced into a film or television programme to represent credits, dialogue, or fragments of narrative – usu pl with sing. meaning **4** the distinguishing name of a work of art (e g a book, picture or musical composition) **5** a descriptive name **6** a division of a legal document; *esp* one larger than a section or article **7** a literary work as distinguished from a particular copy <*published 25* ~s *last year*> **8** designation as champion <*the world heavyweight* ~> **9** a hereditary or acquired appellation given to a person or

family as a mark of rank, office, or attainment

[2]**title** *vt* **1** to provide a title for **2** to designate or call by a title

titled *adj* having a title, esp of nobility

title deed *n* the deed constituting evidence of ownership

title page *n* a page of a book giving the title, author, publisher, and publication details

title role *n* the role in a production (e g a play) that has the same name as the title of the production

titmouse /'titˌmows‖'tɪtˌmaʊs/ *n, pl* **titmice** /-ˌmies‖-ˌmaɪs/ [2]TIT

titter /'titə‖'tɪtə/ *vi* to giggle, snigger – **titter** *n*

tittle /'titl‖'tɪtl/ *n* **1** a point or small sign used as a diacritical mark in writing or printing **2** a very small part

'**tittle-ˌtattle** /'tatl‖'tætl/ *vi or n* (to) gossip, prattle

titty /'titi‖'tɪtɪ/ *n* [1]TIT – infml

titular /'tityoolə‖'tɪtjʊlə/ *adj* **1** in title only; nominal <*the ~ head of a political party*> **2** of or constituting a title <*the ~ hero of the play*> – **titularly** *adv*

tizzy /'tizi‖'tɪzɪ/ *n* a highly excited and confused state of mind – infml

TNT *n* trinitrotoluene

[1]**to** /tooh‖tu:; *unstressed and before vowels* tə‖tə/ *prep* **1** – used to indicate a terminal point or destination: e g **1a** a place where a physical movement or an action or condition suggestive of movement ends <*drive ~ the city*> <*invited them ~ lunch*> **b** a direction <*the road ~ London*> **c** a terminal point in measuring or reckoning or in a statement of extent or limits <*10 miles ~ the nearest town*> <*cost from £5 ~ £10*> **d** a point in time before which a period is reckoned <*5 minutes ~ 5*> **e** a point of contact or proximity <*pinned it ~ my coat*> **f** a purpose, intention, tendency, result, or end <*broken ~ pieces*> <*held them ~ ransom*> <*much ~ my surprise*> **g** the one to or for which sthg exists or is done or directed <*kind ~ animals*> <*my letter ~ John*> **2** – used **2a** to indicate addition, attachment, connection, belonging, or possession <*add 17 ~ 20*> <*the key ~ the door*> **b** to indicate accompaniment or response <*danced ~ live music*> <*rose ~ the occasion*> **3** – used to indicate relationship or conformity: e g **3a** relative position <*next door ~ me*> **b** proportion or composition <*won by 17 points ~ 11*> **c** correspondence to a standard <*second ~ none*> <*compared him ~ a god*> **4a** – used to indicate that the following verb is an infinitive <*wants ~ go*> **b** for the purpose of <*did it ~ annoy them*>

[2]**to** *adv* **1a** – used to indicate direction towards; chiefly in *to and fro* **b** close to the wind <*the ship hove ~*> **2** *of a door or window* into contact, esp with the frame <*the door slammed ~*> **3** – used to indicate application or attention; compare FALL TO, TURN TO **4** back into consciousness or awareness <*brings her ~ with smelling salts*> **5** AT HAND <*saw her close ~*>

toad /tohd‖təʊd/ *n* **1** any of numerous tailless leaping amphibians that differ from the related frogs by living more on land and in having a shorter squatter body with a rough, dry, and warty skin **2** a loathsome and contemptible person or thing

ˌ**toad-in-the-'hole** *n* a dish of sausages baked in a thick Yorkshire-pudding batter

'**toadˌstool** /-ˌstoohl‖-ˌstu:l/ *n* a (poisonous or inedible) umbrella-shaped fungus

toady /'tohdi‖'təʊdɪ/ *vi or n* (to behave as) a sycophant – **toadyism** *n*

ˌ**to-and-'fro** *n or adj* (activity involving alternating movement) forwards and backwards

to and fro *adv* from one place to another; BACK AND FORTH

[1]**toast** /tohst‖təʊst/ *vt* **1** to make (e g bread) crisp, hot, and brown by heat **2** to warm thoroughly (e g at a fire) ~ *vi* to become toasted; *esp* to become thoroughly warm

[2]**toast** *n* **1** sliced bread browned on both sides by heat **2a** sthg in honour of which people drink **b** a highly popular or admired person <*she's the ~ of London*> **3** an act of drinking in honour of sby or sthg

[3]**toast** *vt* to drink to as a toast

toaster /'tohstə‖'təʊstə/ *n* an electrical appliance for toasting esp bread

'**toasting ˌfork** /'tohsting‖'təʊstɪŋ/ *n* a long-handled fork on which bread is held for toasting in front of or over a fire

'**toastˌmaster** /-ˌmahstə‖-ˌmɑ:stə/, *fem* '**toastˌmistress** *n* sby who presides at a banquet, proposes toasts, and introduces after-dinner speakers

tobacco /tə'bakoh‖tə'bækəʊ/ *n, pl* **tobaccos** **1** any of a genus of chiefly American plants of the nightshade family; *esp* a tall erect annual S American herb cultivated for its leaves **2** the leaves of cultivated tobacco prepared for use in smoking or chewing or as snuff; *also* cigars, cigarettes, or other manufactured products of tobacco

tobacconist /tə'bakənist‖tə'bækənɪst/ *n* a seller of tobacco, esp in a shop

toboggan /tə'bogən‖tə'bɒgən/ *vi or n* (to ride on) a long light sledge, usu curved up at the front and used esp for gliding downhill over snow or ice – **tobogganist** *n*

toby /'tohbi‖'təʊbɪ/, **toby jug** *n* a small jug or mug generally used for beer and shaped somewhat like a stout man with a cocked hat for the brim

toccata /tə'kahtə‖tə'kɑ:tə/ *n* a musical composition in a free style and characterized by rapid runs, usu for organ or harpsichord

tocsin /'toksin‖'tɒksɪn/ *n* an alarm bell rung as a warning [Middle French *toquassen*, fr Old Provençal *tocasenh*, fr *tocar* to touch, ring a bell + *senh* sign, bell]

[1]**tod** /tod‖tɒd/ *n, chiefly Scot & NEng* a fox

[2]**tod** *n, Br* – **on one's tod** alone – slang

today /tə'day‖tə'deɪ/ *adv or n* **1** (on) this day **2** (at) the present time or age

toddle /todl‖tɒdl/ *vi* **1** to walk haltingly in the manner of a young child **2a** to take a stroll; saunter **b** *Br* to depart <*I'll just ~ off home*> *USE* (2) infml – **toddle** *n*

toddler /'todlə‖'tɒdlə/ *n* a young child

toddy /'todi‖'tɒdɪ/ *n* a usu hot drink consisting of spirits mixed with water, sugar, and spices

to-ˈdo *n, pl* **to-dos** bustle, fuss – infml

[1]**toe** /toh‖təʊ/ *n* **1a(1)** any of the digits at the end of a vertebrate's foot **a(2)** the fore end of a foot or hoof **b** the front of sthg worn on the foot **2a** a part like a toe in position or form <*the ~ of Italy*> **b** the lowest part (e g of an embankment, dam, or cliff)

[2]**toe** *vt* **toeing** **1** to provide with a toe; *esp* to renew the toe of <*~ a shoe*> **2** to touch, reach, or drive with the toe – **toe the line** to conform rigorously to a rule or standard

ˈ**toe ˌcap** *n* a piece of material (e g steel or leather) attached to the toe of a shoe or boot to reinforce or decorate it

ˈ**toeˌhold** /-ˌhohld‖-ˌhəʊld/ *n* **1a** a hold or place of support for the toes (e g in climbing) **b** a slight footing <*the firm had a ~ in the export market*> **2** a wrestling hold in which the aggressor bends or twists his opponent's foot

toff /tof‖tɒf/ *n, chiefly Br* an upper-class usu well-dressed person – infml

toffee, toffy /ˈtofi‖ˈtɒfɪ/ *n* a sweet with a texture ranging from chewy to brittle, made by boiling sugar, water, and often butter

ˈ**toffee-ˌapple** *n* a toffee-covered apple held on a stick

ˈ**toffee-ˌnosed** *adj, Br* stuck-up – infml

tog /tog‖tɒg/ *vt* **-gg-** to dress, esp in fine clothing – usu + *up* or *out*; infml

toga /ˈtohgə‖ˈtəʊgə/ *n* a loose outer garment worn in public by citizens of ancient Rome – **togaed** *adj*

together /təˈgedhə‖təˈgeðə/ *adv* **1a** in or into 1 place, mass, collection, or group <*the men get ~ every Thursday for poker*> **b** in joint agreement or cooperation; as a group <*students and staff ~ presented the petition*> **2a** in or into contact (e g connection, collision, or union) <*mix these ingredients ~*> <*tie the ends ~*> **b** in or into association, relationship, or harmony <*colours that go well ~*> **3a** at one time; simultaneously <*everything happened ~*> **b** in succession; without intermission <*was depressed for days ~*> **4** *of a single unit* in or into an integrated whole <*pull yourself ~*> **5a** to or with each other <*eyes too close ~*> – used as an intensive after certain verbs <*add ~*> <*confer ~*> **b** considered as a unit; collectively <*these arguments taken ~ make a convincing case*> – **together with** with the addition of

toˈgetherness /-nis‖-nɪs/ *n* the feeling of belonging together

toggle /ˈtog(ə)l‖ˈtɒg(ə)l/ *n* **1** a piece or device for holding or securing; *esp* a crosspiece attached to the end of or to a loop in a chain, rope, line, etc, usu to prevent slipping, to serve as a fastening, or as a grip for tightening **2** (a device having) a toggle joint

togs /togz‖tɒgz/ *n pl* clothes – infml

[1]**toil** /toyl‖tɔɪl/ *n* long strenuous fatiguing labour – **toilful** *adj*, **toilsome** *adj*

[2]**toil** *vi* **1** to work hard and long **2** to proceed with laborious effort <*~ing wearily up the hill*> – **toiler** *n*

[3]**toil** *n* sthg by or with which one is held fast or inextricably involved – usu pl with sing. meaning <*caught in the ~s of the law*>

toilet /ˈtoylit‖ˈtɔɪlɪt/ *n* **1** the act or process of dressing and grooming oneself **2a** a fixture or arrangement for receiving and disposing of faeces and urine **b** a room or compartment containing a toilet and sometimes a washbasin **3** formal or fashionable (style of) dress – fml [Middle French *toilette* cloth put over the shoulders while dressing the hair or shaving, diminutive of *toile* cloth]

ˈ**toilet ˌpaper** *n* a thin usu absorbent paper for sanitary use after defecation or urination

toiletry /ˈtoylitri‖ˈtɔɪlɪtrɪ/ *n* an article or preparation (e g cologne) used in washing, grooming, etc – usu pl

ˈ**toilet ˌwater** *n* (a) liquid containing a high percentage of alcohol used esp as a light perfume

to-ing and fro-ing /ˌtooh·ing ənd ˈfroh·ing‖ˌtuːɪŋ ənd ˈfrəʊɪŋ/ *n, pl* **to-ings and fro-ings** bustling unproductive activity

[1]**token** /ˈtohkən‖ˈtəʊkən/ *n* **1** an outward sign or expression (e g of an emotion) **2a** a characteristic mark or feature <*a white flag is a ~ of surrender*> **b** an instance of a linguistic expression **3a** a souvenir, keepsake **b** sthg given or shown as a guarantee (e g of authority, right, or identity) **4** a coinlike piece issued **4a** as money by anyone other than a government **b** for use in place of money (e g for a bus fare) **5** a certified statement redeemable for a usu specified form of merchandise to the amount stated thereon <*a book ~*> – **by the same token** furthermore and for the same reason

[2]**token** *adj* **1** done or given as a token, esp in partial fulfilment of an obligation or engagement <*a ~ payment*> **2** done or given merely for show <*~ resistance*>

tokenism /ˈtohkəniz(ə)m/ *n* the practice of employing a few people of a certain kind (e g from a minority group) for appearance's sake, while discriminating against others

token money *n* **1** money of regular government issue having a greater face value than intrinsic value **2** a medium of exchange consisting of privately issued tokens

told /tohld‖təʊld/ *past of* TELL

tolerable /ˈtol(ə)rəbl‖ˈtɒl(ə)rəbl/ *adj* **1** capable of being borne or endured **2** moderately good or agreeable – **tolerably** *adv*, **tolerability** *n*

tolerance /ˈtolərəns‖ˈtɒlərəns/ *n* **1** the ability to endure or adapt physiologically to the effects of a drug, virus, radiation, etc **2a** indulgence for beliefs or practices differing from one's own **b** the act of allowing sthg; toleration **3** an allowable variation from a standard dimension

tolerant /ˈtolərənt‖ˈtɒlərənt/ *adj* inclined to tolerate; *esp* marked by forbearance or endurance – **tolerantly** *adv*

tolerate /ˈtolərayt‖ˈtɒləreɪt/ *vt* **1** to endure or resist the action of (e g a drug) without grave or lasting injury **2** to allow to be (done) without prohibition, hindrance, or contradiction – **tolerator** *n*, **tolerative** *adj*

toleration /toləˈraysh(ə)n‖tɒləˈreɪʃ(ə)n/ *n* a government policy of permitting forms of religious belief and worship not officially established

[1]**toll** /tol, tohl‖tol, təʊl/ *n* **1** a fee paid for some

right or privilege (e g of passing over a highway or bridge) or for services rendered **2** a grievous or ruinous price; *esp* cost in life or health

[2]**toll** /tohl‖təʊl/ *vt* **1** to sound (a bell) by pulling the rope **2** to signal, announce, or summon (as if) by means of a tolled bell ~*vi* to sound with slow measured strokes

[3]**toll** /tohl‖təʊl/ *n* the sound of a tolling bell

tollgate /ˈtol,gayt, tohl-‖ˈtɒl,geɪt, təʊl-/ *n* a barrier across a road to prevent passage until a toll is paid

tollhouse /ˈtol-, tohl-‖ˈtɒl-, təʊl-/ *n* a house or booth where tolls are paid

toluene /ˈtolyoo,een‖ˈtɒljʊ,iːn/ *n* a toxic inflammable hydrocarbon that is used esp as a solvent and in organic synthesis

tomahawk /ˈtomə,hawk‖ˈtɒmə,hɔːk/ *n* a light axe used by N American Indians as a throwing or hand weapon

tomato /təˈmahtoh‖təˈmɑːtəʊ/ *n, pl* **tomatoes** **1** any of a genus of S American plants of the nightshade family; *esp* one widely cultivated for its edible fruits **2** the usu large and rounded red, yellow, or green pulpy fruit of a tomato [Spanish *tomate*, fr Nahuatl *tomatl*]

tomb /toohm‖tuːm/ *n* **1a** an excavation in which a corpse is buried **b** a chamber or vault for the dead, built either above or below ground and usu serving as a memorial **2** a tomblike structure; *esp* a large gloomy building – **tombless** *adj*

tombola /tomˈbohlə‖tɒmˈbəʊlə/ *n* a lottery in which people buy tickets which may entitle them to a prize [Italian, fr *tombolare* to tumble, fr *tombare* to fall]

tomboy /ˈtom,boy‖ˈtɒm,bɔɪ/ *n* a girl who behaves in a manner conventionally thought of as typical of a boy – **tomboyish** *adj*, **tomboyishly** *adv*, **tomboyishness** *n*

tombstone /ˈtoohm,stohn‖ˈtuːm,stəʊn/ *n* a gravestone

tomcat /ˈtom,kat‖ˈtɒm,kæt/ *n* a male cat

tome /tohm‖təʊm/ *n* a (large scholarly) book

tomfoolery /,tomˈfoohləri‖,tɒmˈfuːlərɪ/ *n* foolish trifling; nonsense

tommyrot /ˈtomi,rot‖ˈtɒmɪ,rɒt/ *n* utter foolishness or nonsense – infml

tomorrow /təˈmoroh‖təˈmɒrəʊ/ *adv or n* **1** (on) the day after today **2** (in) the future <*the world of* ~>

tomtit /ˈtom,tit‖ˈtɒm,tɪt/ *n* any of various small active birds; *esp* a blue tit

ˈtom-,tom /tom‖tɒm/ *n* a usu long and narrow small-headed drum commonly beaten with the hands

ton /tun‖tʌn/ *n, pl* **tons** *also* **ton** **1a** LONG TON **b** SHORT TON **c** a tonne **2a** REGISTER TON **b** a unit approximately equal to the volume of 1 long ton of seawater, used in reckoning the displacement of ships, and equal to $0.991m^3$ ($35ft^3$) **3a** a great quantity – often pl with sing. meaning <~s *of room on the back seat*> **b** a great weight <*this bag weighs a* ~> **4** a group, score, or speed of 100 ***USE*** (*3&4*) infml

tonal /ˈtohn(ə)l‖ˈtəʊn(ə)l/ *adj* **1** of tone, tonality, or tonicity **2** having tonality – **tonally** *adv*

tonality /tohˈnaləti‖təʊˈnælətɪ/ *n* **1** tonal quality **2a** KEY 7 **b** the organization of all the notes and chords of a piece of music in relation to a tonic

[1]**tone** /tohn‖təʊn/ *n* **1** a vocal or musical sound; *esp* one of a specified quality <*spoke in low* ~s> **2a** a sound of a definite frequency with relatively weak overtones **b** WHOLE TONE **3** an accent or inflection of the voice expressive of a mood or emotion **4** (a change in) the pitch of a word often used to express differences of meaning **5** style or manner of verbal expression <*seemed wise to adopt a conciliatory* ~> **6a** colour quality or value **b** the colour that appreciably modifies a hue or white or black **7** the general effect of light, shade, and colour in a picture **8a** the state of (an organ or part of) a living body in which the functions are healthy and performed with due vigour **b** normal tension or responsiveness to stimuli **9a** prevailing character, quality, or trend (e g of morals) <*lowered the* ~ *of the discussion*> **b** distinction, style; [2]TON **c** FRAME OF MIND **10** *chiefly NAm* NOTE 1a(1)

[2]**tone** *vt* **1** to impart tone to <*medicine to* ~ *up the system*> **2** to soften in colour, appearance, or sound ~ *vi* **1** to assume a pleasing colour quality or tint **2** to blend or harmonize in colour – **toner** *n*

toned *adj* **1** having (a specified) tone; characterized or distinguished by a tone – often in combination <*shrill*-toned> **2** *of paper* having a slight tint

,tone-ˈdeaf *adj* relatively insensitive to differences in musical pitch – **tone deafness** *n*

tone down *vt* to reduce in intensity, violence, or force <*he was told to* tone down *his views*>

ˈtone ,language *n* a language (e g Chinese) in which variations in tone distinguish words of different meaning

toneless /ˈtohnlis‖ˈtəʊnlɪs/ *adj* lacking in expression – **tonelessly** *adv*, **tonelessness** *n*

tone poem *n* SYMPHONIC POEM – **tone poet** *n*

tong /tong‖tɒŋ/ *n* a Chinese secret society or fraternal organization formerly notorious for gang warfare

tongs /tongz‖tɒŋz/ *n pl* any of various grasping devices consisting commonly of 2 pieces joined at 1 end by a pivot or hinged like scissors

[1]**tongue** /tung‖tʌŋ/ *n* **1a** a fleshy muscular movable organ of the floor of the mouth in most vertebrates that bears sensory end organs and small glands and functions esp in tasting and swallowing food and in human beings as a speech organ **b** a part of various invertebrate animals that is analogous to the tongue of vertebrates **2** the tongue of an ox, sheep, etc used as food **3** the power of communication through speech **4a** a (spoken) language **b** manner or quality of utterance <*a sharp* ~> **c** ecstatic usu unintelligible utterance, esp in Christian worship – usu pl with sing. meaning <*the gift of* ~s> **d** the cry (as if) of a hound pursuing or in sight of game – esp in *give tongue* **5** a long narrow strip of land projecting into a body of water **6** sthg like an animal's tongue (e g elongated and fastened at 1 end only):e g **6a** a movable pin in a buckle **b** a piece of metal suspended inside a bell so as to strike against the sides as the

bell is swung **c** the pole of a (horse-drawn) vehicle **d** the flap under the lacing or buckles on the front of a shoe or boot **7** the rib on one edge of a board that fits into a corresponding groove in an edge of another board to make a flush joint **8** a tapering cone – in *tongue of flame/fire* – **tonguelike** *adj*

[2]**tongue** *vt* **1** to touch or lick (as if) with the tongue **2** to articulate (notes) by tonguing ~*vi* to articulate notes on a wind instrument by successively interrupting the stream of wind with the action of the tongue

tongued /tungd‖tʌŋd/ *adj* having a tongue of a specified kind – often in combination <*sharp*-tongued>

ˈ**tongue-ˌtied** *adj* **1** affected with tongue-tie **2** unable to speak freely (e g because of shyness)

ˈ**tongue ˌtwister** *n* a word or phrase difficult to articulate because of several similar consonantal sounds (e g 'she sells seashells on the seashore')

[1]**tonic** /ˈtonik‖ˈtɒnɪk/ *adj* **1** marked by prolonged muscular contraction <~ *convulsions*> **2** increasing or restoring physical or mental tone **3** of or based on the first note of a scale **4** *of a syllable* bearing a principal stress or accent – **tonically** *adv*

[2]**tonic** *n* **1a** sthg (e g a drug) that increases body tone **b** sthg that invigorates, refreshes, or stimulates <*a day in the country was a* ~ *for him*> <*a skin* ~> **c tonic, tonic water** a carbonated drink flavoured with a small amount of quinine, lemon, and lime **2** the first note of a diatonic scale **3** an instance of tonic accent

ˌ**tonic ˈsol-fa** *n* a system of solmization that replaces the normal notation with sol-fa syllables

tonight /təˈniet‖təˈnaɪt/ *adv or n* (on) this night or the night following today

tonnage /ˈtunij‖ˈtʌnɪdʒ/ *n* **1** a duty formerly levied on every cask of wine imported into England **2a** a duty or tax on vessels based on cargo capacity **b** a duty on goods per ton transported **3** ships considered in terms of the total number of tons registered or carried or of their carrying capacity **4** the carrying capacity of a merchant ship in units of $100ft^3$ (about $2.83m^3$) **5** total weight in tons shipped, carried, or produced

tonne /tun‖tʌn/ *n* a metric unit of weight equal to 1000kg

tonsil /ˈtons(ə)l‖ˈtɒns(ə)l/ *n* **1** either of a pair of prominent oval masses of spongy lymphoid tissue that lie 1 on each side of the throat at the back of the mouth **2** any of various masses of lymphoid tissue that are similar to tonsils – **tonsillar** *adj*

tonsillitis /ˌtonsiˈlietəs‖ˌtɒnsɪˈlaɪtəs/ *n* inflammation of the tonsils

tonsorial /tonˈsawri·əl‖tɒnˈsɔːrɪəl/ *adj* of a barber or his work – usu humor

[1]**tonsure** /ˈtonshə‖ˈtɒnʃə/ *n* **1** the Roman Catholic or Eastern rite of admission to the clerical state by the shaving of a portion of the head **2** the shaved patch on a monk's or other cleric's head

[2]**tonsure** *vt* to shave the head of; *esp* to confer the tonsure on

tontine /ˈtonteen, -ˈ-‖ˈtɒntiːn, -ˈ-/ *n* a financial arrangement whereby a group of participants share various advantages on such terms that on the death or default of any member his/her advantages are distributed among the remaining members until 1 member remains or an agreed period has elapsed; *also* the share or right of each individual [French, fr Lorenzo *Tonti* (died 1695), Italian banker]

ˈ**ton-ˌup** *adj, Br* of or being sby who has achieved a score, speed, etc of 100 <*the local motorcycle* ~ *boys*> – infml

too /tooh‖tuː/ *adv* **1** also; IN ADDITION <*sell the house and furniture* ~> **2a** to a regrettable degree; excessively <~ *large a house for us*> **b** to a higher degree than meets a standard <~ *pretty for words*> **3** indeed, so – used to counter a negative charge <*'I didn't do it.' 'You did* ~*.'*>

took /took‖tʊk/ *past of* TAKE

[1]**tool** /toohl‖tuːl/ *n* **1a** an implement that is used, esp by hand, to carry out work of a mechanical nature (e g cutting, levering, or digging) – not usu used with reference to kitchen utensils or cutlery **b** (the cutting or shaping part in) a machine tool **2** sthg (e g an instrument or apparatus) used in performing an operation, or necessary for the practice of a vocation or profession <*books are the* ~s *of a scholar's trade*> **3** sby who is used or manipulated by another **4** a penis – vulg

[2]**tool** *vt* **1** to work, shape, or finish with a tool; *esp* to letter or ornament (e g leather) by means of hand tools **2** to equip (e g a plant or industry) with tools, machines, and instruments for production – often + *up* ~ *vi* **1** to get tooled up for production – usu + *up* **2** to drive, ride <~ed *round the neighbourhood in a small car*> – infml

toot /tooht‖tuːt/ *vi* **1** to produce a short blast or similar sound <*the horn* ~ed> **2** to cause an instrument to toot ~*vt* to cause to produce a short blast <~ *a whistle*> – **toot** *n*, **tooter** *n*

[1]**tooth** /toohth‖tuːθ/ *n, pl* **teeth** /teeth‖tiːθ/ **1a** any of the hard bony structures that are borne esp on the jaws of vertebrates and serve esp for the seizing and chewing of food and as weapons **b** any of various usu hard and sharp projecting parts about the mouth of an invertebrate **2** a taste, liking <*a sweet* ~> **3a** a projection like the tooth of an animal (e g in shape, arrangement, or action) <*a saw* ~> **b** any of the regular projections on the rim of a cogwheel **4** *pl* effective means of enforcement – **toothlike** *adj*, **toothless** *adj* – **in the teeth of** in direct opposition to

[2]**tooth** *vt* to provide with teeth, esp by cutting notches <~ *a saw*> ~*vi, esp of cogwheels* to interlock

ˈ**toothˌache** /-ˌayk‖-ˌeɪk/ *n* pain in or about a tooth

ˈ**toothˌbrush** /-ˌbrush‖-ˌbrʌʃ/ *n* a brush for cleaning the teeth

ˈ**toothˌcomb** /-ˌkohm‖-ˌkəʊm/ *n, Br* a comb with fine teeth

toothed *adj* having teeth, esp of a specified kind or number – often in combination <*sharp*-toothed>

ˈ**toothˌpaste** /-ˌpayst‖-ˌpeɪst/ *n* a paste for cleaning the teeth

ˈtooth̩pick /-ˌpik‖-ˌpɪk/ *n* a pointed instrument for removing food particles lodged between the teeth

ˈtooth ˌpowder *n* a powder for cleaning the teeth

toothsome /ˈtoohths(ə)m‖ˈtu:θs(ə)m/ *adj* **1** delicious **2** (sexually) attractive – **toothsomely** *adv*, **toothsomeness** *n*

toothy /ˈtoohthi‖ˈtu:θɪ/ *adj* having or showing prominent teeth <*a ~ grin*> – **toothily** *adv*

tootle /ˈtoohtl‖ˈtu:tl/ *vi* **1** to toot gently or continuously **2** to drive or move along in a leisurely manner – infml – **tootle** *n*, **tootler** *n*

tootsy *also* **tootsie** /ˈtootsi‖ˈtʊtsɪ/ *n* FOOT 1 – used chiefly to children

1top /top‖tɒp/ *n* **1a(1)** the highest point, level, or part of sthg **a(2)** the (top of the) head – esp in *top to toe* **a(3)** the head of a plant, esp one with edible roots <*beet* ~s> **a(4)** a garment worn on the upper body **b(1)** the highest or uppermost region or part **b(2)** the upper end, edge, or surface **2** a fitted or attached part serving as an upper piece, lid, or covering **3** a platform surrounding the head of a lower mast serving to spread the topmast rigging, or to mount guns **4** the highest degree or pitch conceivable or attained **5** the part nearest in space or time to the source or beginning **6** (sby or sthg in) the highest position (e g in rank or achievement) <~ *of the class*> **7** *Br* the transmission gear of a motor vehicle giving the highest ratio of propeller-shaft to engine-shaft speed and hence the highest speed of travel – **topped** *adj* – **off the top of one's head** in an impromptu manner <*can't give the figures* off the top of my head> – **on top of 1a** in control of <*keep* on top of *my job*> **b** informed about **2** in sudden and unexpected proximity to **3** in addition to <*caught measles on top of flu*> – **on top of the world** in high spirits; in a state of exhilaration and well-being

2top *vt* **-pp- 1a** to cut the top off **b** to shorten or remove the top of (a plant) **2a** to cover with a top or on the top; provide, form, or serve as a top for **b** to supply with a decorative or protective finish or final touch **c** to complete the basic structure of (e g a high-rise building) by putting on a cap or uppermost section – usu + *out* or *off* **3a** to be or become higher than; overtop <~s *the previous record*> **b** to be superior to <~s *everything of its kind in print*> **c** to gain ascendancy over **4a** to rise to, reach, or be at the top of **b** to go over the top of; clear, surmount **5** to strike (a ball) above the centre, thereby imparting top spin

3top *adj* **1** of or at the top **2** foremost, leading <*one of the world's ~ journalists*> **3** of the highest quality, amount, or degree <~ *form*>

4top *n* a child's toy that has a tapering point on which it is made to spin

topaz /ˈtohpaz‖ˈtəʊpæz/ *n* **1** a mineral that is predominantly a silicate of aluminium, usu occurs in variously coloured translucent or transparent crystals, and is used as a gem **2a** a yellow sapphire **b** a yellow quartz (e g cairngorm or citrine)

top boot *n* a high boot often with light-coloured leather bands round the upper part

ˌtop ˈbrass *n sing or pl in constr* BRASS HATS

ˈtopˌcoat /-ˌkoht‖-ˌkəʊt/ *n* **1** a (lightweight) overcoat **2** a final coat of paint

ˌtop ˈdog *n* a person in a position of authority, esp through victory in a hard-fought competition – infml

ˌtop ˈdrawer *n* the highest level, esp of society – esp in *out of the top drawer* – **top-drawer** *adj*

ˈtop-ˌdress *vt* to scatter fertilizer over (land) without working it in – **topdressing** *n*

1tope /tohp‖təʊp/ *vi* to drink alcoholic drink to excess – **toper** *n*

2tope *n* a small shark with a liver very rich in vitamin A

topee, topi /ˈtohpi‖ˈtəʊpɪ/ *n* a lightweight helmet-shaped sunhat made of pith or cork

ˌtop-ˈflight *adj* of the highest grade or quality; best

1topgallant /ˌtopˈgalənt, təˈgalənt‖ˌtɒpˈgælənt, təˈgælənt/ *adj* of or being a part next above the topmast <~ *sails*>

2topgallant *n* a topgallant mast or sail

top hat *n* a man's tall-crowned hat usu of beaver or silk

ˌtop-ˈheavy *adj* **1** having the top part too heavy for or disproportionate to the lower part **2** capitalized beyond what is prudent

topiary /ˈtohpyəri‖ˈtəʊpjərɪ/ *adj or n* (of or being) the practice or art of training, cutting, and trimming trees or shrubs into odd or ornamental shapes; *also* (characterized by) such work

topic /ˈtopik‖ˈtɒpɪk/ *n* **1a** a heading in an outlined argument or exposition **b** the subject of a (section of a) discourse **2** a subject for discussion or consideration

topical /ˈtopikl‖ˈtɒpɪkl/ *adj* **1a** of a place **b** designed for local application <*a ~ remedy*> **2a** of or arranged by topics <*set down in ~ form*> **b** referring to the topics of the day; of current interest – **topically** *adv*, **topicality** *n*

ˈtopˌknot /-ˌnot‖-ˌnɒt/ *n* **1** an ornament (e g of ribbons) worn as a headdress or as part of a hairstyle **2** an arrangement or growth of hair or feathers on top of the head

topless /ˈtoplis‖ˈtɒplɪs/ *adj* **1** nude above the waist; *esp* having the breasts exposed **2** featuring topless waitresses or entertainers

topmast /ˈtopˌmahst‖ˈtɒpˌmɑ:st/ *n* a mast that is next above the lowest mast

topmost /ˈtopmohst‖ˈtɒpməʊst/ *adj* highest of all

ˌtop-ˈnotch *adj* of the highest quality – infml – **topnotcher** *n*

topographical /ˌtopəˈgrafikl‖ˌtɒpəˈgræfɪkl/, **topographic** *adj* **1** of or concerned with topography **2** of or concerned with the artistic representation of a particular locality <*a ~ poem*> <~ *painting*> – **topographically** *adv*

topography /toˈpografi‖tɒˈpɒgræfɪ/ *n* **1** (the mapping or charting of) the configuration of a land surface, including its relief and the position of its natural and man-made features **2** the physical or natural features of an object or entity and their structural relationships [Late Latin *topographia*, fr Greek, fr *topographein* to describe a place, fr *topos* place + *graphein* to write] – **topographer** *n*

topper /ˈtopə‖ˈtɒpə/ *n* **1** TOP HAT **2** sthg (e g a joke) that caps everything preceding – infml

[1]**topping** /'toping||'tɒpɪŋ/ *n* sthg that forms a top; *esp* a garnish or edible decoration on top of a food

[2]**topping** *adj, chiefly Br* excellent – not now in vogue

topple /'topl||'tɒpl/ *vi* **1** to fall (as if) from being top-heavy **2** to be or seem unsteady ~ *vt* **1** to cause to topple **2** to overthrow

topsail /'top,sayl, 'topsl||'tɒp,seɪl, 'tɒpsl/ *also* **tops'l** /'topsl||'tɒpsl/ *n* **1** the sail next above the lowest sail on a mast in a square-rigged ship **2** the sail set above and sometimes on the gaff in a fore-and-aft rigged ship

top secret *adj* **1** demanding the greatest secrecy **2** containing information whose unauthorized disclosure could result in exceptionally grave danger to the nation

[1]**topside** /'top,sied||'tɒp,saɪd/ *n* **1** *pl* the sides of a ship above the waterline **2** a lean boneless cut of beef from the inner part of a round

[2]**topside** *adv or adj* on deck

topsoil /'top,soyl||'tɒp,sɔɪl/ *n* surface soil, usu including the organic layer in which plants form roots and which is turned over in ploughing

top spin *n* a rotary motion imparted to a ball that causes it to rotate forwards in the direction of its travel

topsy-turvy /,topsi 'tuhvi||,tɒpsɪ 'tɜːvɪ/ *adj or adv* **1** UPSIDE DOWN **2** in utter confusion or disorder – **topsy-turvily** *adv*, **topsy-turvydom** *n*

top up *vt* **1** to make up to the full quantity, capacity, or amount **2** to increase (a money sum set aside for a specific purpose)

toque /tohk||təʊk/ *n* a woman's small soft brimless hat

tor /taw||tɔː/ *n* a high rock or rocky mound

Torah /'tawrə||'tɔːrə/ *n* **1** *the* Pentateuch; *broadly* Jewish Scripture and other sacred Jewish literature and oral tradition **2** a leather or parchment scroll of the Pentateuch used in a synagogue

torch /tawch||tɔːtʃ/ *n* **1** a burning stick of resinous wood or twist of tow used to give light **2** sthg (e g wisdom or knowledge) that gives enlightenment or guidance **3** *Br* a small portable electric lamp powered by batteries

tore /taw||tɔː/ *past of* TEAR

toreador /'tori·ə,daw||'tɒrɪə,dɔː/ *n* a bullfighter [Spanish, fr *torear* to fight bulls, fr *toro* bull, fr Latin *taurus*]

[1]**torment** /'tawment||'tɔːment/ *n* **1** extreme pain or anguish of body or mind **2** a source of vexation or pain

[2]**torment** /taw'ment||tɔː'ment/ *vt* to cause severe usu persistent distress of body or mind to – **tormentor** *also* **tormenter** *n*

torn /tawn||tɔːn/ *past part of* TEAR

tornado /taw'naydoh||tɔː'neɪdəʊ/ *n, pl* **tornadoes, tornados** a violent or destructive whirlwind, usu progressing in a narrow path over the land and accompanied by a funnel-shaped cloud [Spanish *tronada* thunderstorm, fr *tronar* to thunder, fr Latin *tonare*] – **tornadic** *adj*

[1]**torpedo** /taw'peedoh||tɔː'piːdəʊ/ *n, pl* **torpedoes** **1** ELECTRIC RAY **2** a self-propelling cigar-shaped submarine explosive projectile used for attacking ships **3** *NAm* a charge of explosive in a container or case [Latin, lit., numbness, fr *torpēre* to be numb; fr the paralysing effect of the electric ray's sting]

[2]**torpedo** *vt* **torpedoing; torpedoed** **1** to hit or destroy by torpedo **2** to destroy or nullify (e g a plan) – infml

torpedo boat *n* a small fast warship armed primarily with torpedoes

torpid /'tawpid||'tɔːpɪd/ *adj* **1a** having temporarily lost the power of movement or feeling (e g in hibernation) **b** sluggish in functioning or acting **2** lacking in energy or vigour – **torpidly** *adv*, **torpidity** *n*

torpor /'tawpə||'tɔːpə/ *n* **1a** a state of mental and motor inactivity with partial or total insensibility **b** extreme sluggishness of action or function **2** apathy

[1]**torque** /tawk||tɔːk/ *n* a twisted metal collar or neck chain worn by the ancient Gauls, Germans, and Britons

[2]**torque** *n* **1** (a measure of the effectiveness of) a force that produces or tends to produce rotation or torsion <*a car engine delivers ~ to the drive shaft*> **2** a turning or twisting force

torrent /'torənt||'tɒrənt/ *n* **1** a violent stream of water, lava, etc **2** a raging tumultuous flow

torrential /tə'rensh(ə)l||tə'renʃ(ə)l/ *adj* **1** resulting from the action of rapid streams **2** of, caused by, or resembling a torrent – **torrentially** *adv*

torrid /'torid||'tɒrɪd/ *adj* **1a** parched with heat, esp of the sun **b** giving off intense heat **2** ardent, passionate <*~ love letters*> – **torridly** *adv*, **torridness** *n*, **torridity** *n*

torsion /'tawsh(ə)n||'tɔːʃ(ə)n/ *n* **1** the act or process of twisting or turning sthg, esp by forces exerted on one end while the other is fixed or twisted in the opposite direction **2** the state of being twisted **3** the twisting of a bodily organ on its own axis – **torsional** *adj*

torso /'tawsoh||'tɔːsəʊ/ *n, pl* **torsos, torsi** /'tawsi||'tɔːsɪ/ **1** (a sculptured representation of) the human trunk **2** sthg (e g a piece of writing) that is mutilated or left unfinished

tort /tawt||tɔːt/ *n* a wrongful act, other than breach of contract, for which a civil action for damages may be brought

tortilla /taw'teeyə||tɔː'tiːjə/ *n* a round thin cake of unleavened maize bread, usu eaten hot with a topping or filling of minced meat or cheese

tortoise /'tawtəs, 'taw,toys||'tɔːtəs, 'tɔː,tɔɪs/ *n* **1** any of an order of land and freshwater (and marine) reptiles with a toothless horny beak and a bony shell which encloses the trunk and into which the head, limbs, and tail may be withdrawn; *esp* a land tortoise commonly kept as a pet **2** sby or sthg slow or laggard

[1]**tortoiseshell** /'tawtəs,shel||'tɔːtəs,ʃel/ *n* **1** the mottled horny substance of the shell of some marine turtles used in inlaying and in making various ornamental articles **2** any of several butterflies with striking orange, yellow, brown, and black coloration

[2]**tortoiseshell** *adj* mottled black, brown, and yellow <*~ cat*>

tortuous /'tawtyoo·əs||'tɔːtjʊəs/ *adj* **1** marked by repeated twists, bends, or turns **2a**

marked by devious or indirect tactics **b** circuitous, involved – **tortuously** *adv*, **tortuousness** *n*, **tortuosity** *n*

[1]**torture** /'tawchə‖'tɔːtʃə/ *n* **1** the infliction of intense physical or mental suffering as a means of punishment, coercion, or sadistic gratification **2** (sthg causing) anguish of body or mind

[2]**torture** *vt* **1** to subject to torture **2** to cause intense suffering to **3** to twist or wrench out of shape; *also* to pervert (e g the meaning of a word) – **torturer** *n*

Tory /'tawri‖'tɔːri/ *n* **1a** a member of a major British political group of the 18th and early 19th c favouring at first the Stuarts and later royal authority and the established church and seeking to preserve the traditional political structure and defeat parliamentary reform **b** CONSERVATIVE 1 **2** an American upholding the cause of the crown during the American Revolution [Irish Gaelic *tōraidhe* pursuer, robber, originally applied to dispossessed Irish Royalists in the 17th c] – **Tory** *adj*, **Toryism** *n*

[1]**toss** /tos‖tɒs/ *vt* **1a** to fling or heave repeatedly about <*a ship* ~ed *by waves*> **b** BANDY 1 **2a** to throw with a quick, light, or careless motion <~ *a ball around*> **b** to throw up in the air <~ed *by a bull*> **c** to flip (a coin) to decide an issue **3** to lift with a sudden jerking motion <~es *her head angrily*> ~ *vi* **1** to move restlessly or turbulently; *esp* to twist and turn repeatedly <~ed *sleeplessly all night*> **2** to decide an issue by flipping a coin – often + *up* – **tosser** *n*

[2]**toss** *n* **1a** being tossed **b** a fall, esp from a horse – chiefly in *take a toss* **2** an act or instance of tossing: e g **2a** an abrupt tilting or upward fling **b** an act or instance of deciding by chance, esp by tossing a coin **c** a throw **3** *Br* DAMN 2 – chiefly in *not give a toss*

toss off *vt* **1** to perform or write quickly and easily **2** to consume quickly; *esp* to drink in a single draught ~*vi*, *Br* to masturbate – infml

'**toss-,up** *n* **1** TOSS 2b **2** an even chance or choice – infml

tot /tot‖tɒt/ *n* **1** a small child; a toddler **2** a small amount or allowance of alcoholic drink <*a* ~ *of rum*>

[1]**total** /'tohtl‖'təʊtl/ *adj* **1** comprising or constituting a whole; entire **2** complete <*a* ~ *success*> **3** concentrating all available personnel and resources on a single objective <~ *war*> – **totally** *adv*

[2]**total** *n* **1** a product of addition **2** an entire quantity

[3]**total** *vt* -**ll**- (*NAm* -**l**-, -**ll**-) **1** to add up **2** to amount to

totalitarian /,tohtali'teəri·ən‖,təʊtæli'teəriən/ *adj* **1** authoritarian, dictatorial **2** of or constituting a political regime based on subordination of the individual to the state and strict control over all aspects of the life and productive capacity of the nation – **totalitarianism** *n*

totality /toh'taləti‖təʊ'tæləti/ *n* **1** an entire amount; a whole **2a** wholeness **b** a period during which one body is completely obscured by another during an eclipse

total·izator, -**isator** /'tohtl·ie,zaytə‖'təʊt(ə)lai,zeitə/ *n* a machine for registering bets and calculating winnings in pari-mutuel betting

[1]**tote** /toht‖təʊt/ *vt* **1** to carry by hand or on the person **2** to transport, convey *USE* infml

[2]**tote** *n* a totalizator

totem /'tohtəm‖'təʊtəm/ *n* **1** a natural object serving as the emblem of a family or clan; *also* a carved or painted representation of this **2** sthg that serves as an emblem or revered symbol – **totemic** *adj*

'**totem ,pole** *n* **1** a pole carved and painted with a series of totemic symbols erected before the houses of some N American Indian tribes **2** an order of rank; a hierarchy

[1]**totter** /'totə‖'tɒtə/ *vi* **1a** to tremble or rock as if about to fall **b** to become unstable; threaten to collapse **2** to move unsteadily; stagger

[2]**totter** *n* an unsteady gait – **tottery** *adj*

tot up *vt* to add together <tot up *the score*> ~*vi* to increase by additions <*the money soon* tots up>

toucan /'tooh,kan‖'tuː,kæn/ *n* any of a family of fruit-eating birds of tropical America with brilliant colouring and a very large but light beak

[1]**touch** /tuch‖tʌtʃ/ *vt* **1** to bring a bodily part into contact with, esp so as to perceive through the sense of feeling; feel **2** to strike or push lightly, esp with the hand or foot or an implement **3** to lay hands on (sby afflicted with scrofula) with intent to heal **4a** to take into the hands or mouth <*never* ~es *alcohol*> **b** to put hands on in any way or degree <*don't* ~ *anything before the police come*>; *esp* to commit violence against <*swears he never* ~ed *the child*> **5** to concern oneself with **6** to cause to be briefly in contact with sthg <~ *a match to the wick*> **7a(1)** to meet without overlapping or penetrating **a(2)** to get to; reach <*the speedometer needle* ~ed *80*> **b** to be tangent to **8** to affect the interest of; concern **9a** to leave a mark or impression on <*few reagents will* ~ *gold*> **b** to harm slightly (as if) by contact; blemish <*fruit* ~ed *by frost*> **c** to give a delicate tint, line, or expression to <*a smile* ~ed *her lips*> **10** to draw or delineate with light strokes **11** to move to esp sympathetic feeling <~ed *by the loyalty of her friends*> **12** to speak or tell of, esp in passing **13** RIVAL 3 **14** to induce to give or lend <~ed *him for 10 quid*> ~ *vi* **1a** to feel sthg with a body part (e g the hand or foot) **b** to lay hands on sby to cure disease (e g scrofula) **2** to be in contact **3** to come close <*his actions* ~ *on treason*> **4** to have a bearing – + *on* or *upon* **5a** to make a brief or incidental stop on shore during a trip by water <~ed *at several ports*> **b** to treat a topic in a brief or casual manner – + *on* or *upon* *USE* (*vt 12*) fml; (*vt 13&14*) infml – **touchable** *adj*, **toucher** *n* – **touch wood 1** with a certain amount of luck <*everything will be all right now*, touch wood> **2** *Br* to touch a wooden surface as a gesture to bring luck

[2]**touch** *n* **1** a light stroke, tap, or push **2** the act or fact of touching **3** the sense of feeling, esp as exercised deliberately with the hands, feet, or lips **4** mental or moral sensitivity, responsiveness, or tact <*has a wonderful* ~ *with children*> **5** a specified sensation conveyed through the sense of touch <*the velvety* ~ *of a fabric*> **6** the testing of gold or silver on a touchstone **7** sthg slight of its kind: e g **7a** a light attack <*a* ~ *of fever*>

b a small amount; a trace <*a ~ of spring in the air*> **c** a bit, little – in the adverbial phrase *a touch* <*aimed a ~ too low and missed*> **8a** a manner or method of touching or striking esp the keys of a keyboard instrument **b** the relative resistance to pressure of the keys of a keyboard (e g of a piano or typewriter) **9** an effective and appropriate detail; *esp* one used in an artistic composition **10** a distinctive or characteristic manner, trait, or quality <*a woman's ~*> **11** the state or fact of being in contact or communication <*out of ~ with modern times*> **12** the area outside the touchlines in soccer or outside and including the touchlines in rugby **13a** an act of soliciting or receiving a gift or loan of money **b** sby who can be easily induced to part with money – chiefly in *a soft/easy touch* ***USE*** (*13*) slang

ˌtouch and ˈgo *n* a highly uncertain or precarious situation

ˈtouchˌdown /-ˌdown‖-ˌdaʊn/ *n* **1** the act of touching down a football **2** (the moment of) touching down (e g of an aeroplane or spacecraft)

touch down *vt* to place (the ball in rugby) by hand on the ground either positioned on or over an opponent's goal line in scoring a try, or behind one's own goal line as a defensive measure ~*vi* to reach the ground

touché /toohˈshay‖tuːˈʃeɪ/ *interj* – used to acknowledge a hit in fencing or the success of an argument, accusation, or witty point [French, fr past participle of *toucher* to touch]

touched /tucht‖tʌtʃt/ *adj* **1** emotionally moved (e g with gratitude) **2** slightly unbalanced mentally – infml

[1]**touching** /ˈtuching‖ˈtʌtʃɪŋ/ *prep* in reference to; concerning – fml

[2]**touching** *adj* capable of arousing tenderness or compassion – **touchingly** *adv*

ˈtouchˌline /-ˌlien‖-ˌlaɪn/ *n* either of the lines that bound the sides of the field of play in rugby and soccer

touch off *vt* **1** to cause to explode (as if) by touching with a naked flame **2** to release with sudden intensity

ˈtouchˌstone /-ˌstohn‖-ˌstəʊn/ *n* **1** a black flintlike siliceous stone that when rubbed by gold or silver showed a streak of colour and was formerly used to test the purity of these metals **2** a test or criterion for determining the genuineness of sthg

ˈtouch-ˌtype *vi* to type without looking at the keyboard, using a system that assigns a particular finger to each key

touch up *vt* **1** to improve or perfect by small alterations; make good the minor defects of **2** to stimulate (as if) by a flick of a whip **3** to make often unwelcome physical advances to; touch with a view to arousing sexually – slang

touchy /ˈtuchi‖ˈtʌtʃɪ/ *adj* **1** ready to take offence on slight provocation **2** calling for tact, care, or caution <*sexism was a ~ subject with his wife*> – **touchily** *adv*, **touchiness** *n*

[1]**tough** /tuf‖tʌf/ *adj* **1a** strong and flexible; not brittle or liable to cut, break, or tear **b** not easily chewed **2** severe or uncompromisingly determined <*a ~ and inflexible foreign policy – New Statesman*> **3** capable of enduring great hardship or exertion **4** very hard to influence **5** extremely difficult or testing <*a ~ question to answer*> **6** aggressive or threatening in behaviour **7** without softness or sentimentality **8** unfortunate, unpleasant – infml <*~ luck*> – **toughly** *adv*, **toughness** *n*

[2]**tough** *n* a tough person; *esp* sby aggressively violent

[3]**tough** *adv* in a tough manner <*talk ~*>

toughen /ˈtuf(ə)n‖ˈtʌf(ə)n/ *vb* to make or become tough

toupee /ˈtoohˌpay‖ˈtuːˌpeɪ/ *n* a wig or hairpiece worn to cover a bald spot

[1]**tour** /tooə‖tʊə/ *n* **1** a period during which an individual or unit is engaged on a specific duty, esp in 1 place <*his regiment did a ~ in N Ireland*> **2a** a journey (e g for business or pleasure) in which one returns to the starting point **b** a visit (e g to a historic site or factory) for pleasure or instruction <*a guided ~ of the castle*> **c** a series of professional engagements involving travel <*a theatrical company on ~*>

[2]**tour** *vi* to make a tour ~ *vt* **1** to make a tour of **2** to present (e g a theatrical production or concert) on a tour

tour de force /ˌtooə də ˈfaws ‖ˌtʊə də ˈfɔːs (*Fr* tuːr də fɔrs)/ *n, pl* **tours de force** /~/ a feat of strength, skill, or ingenuity

tourism /ˈtooəˌriz(ə)m‖ˈtʊəˌrɪz(ə)m/ *n* **1** the practice of travelling for recreation **2** the organizing of tours for commercial purposes **3a** the promotion or encouragement of touring, esp at governmental level **b** the provision of services (e g accommodation) for tourists

tourist /ˈtooərist‖ˈtʊərɪst/ *n* **1** sby who makes a tour for recreation or culture **2** a member of a sports team that is visiting another country to play usu international matches – **tourist** *adj*

tourist class *n* the lowest class of accommodation (e g on a ship)

tournament /ˈtooənəmənt, ˈtaw-‖ˈtʊənəmənt, ˈtɔː-/ *n* **1** a contest between 2 parties of mounted knights armed with usu blunted lances or swords **2** a series of games or contests for a championship

[1]**tourney** /ˈtooəni, ˈtawni‖ˈtʊənɪ, ˈtɔːnɪ/ *vi* to take part in a tournament, esp in the Middle Ages

[2]**tourney** *n* a tournament, esp in the Middle Ages

tourniquet /ˈtooəniˌkay, ˈtaw-‖ˈtʊənɪˌkeɪ, ˈtɔː-/ *n* a bandage or other device for applying pressure to check bleeding or blood flow [French, fr *tourner* to turn]

tousle /ˈtowzl‖ˈtaʊzl/ *vt* to dishevel, rumple

[1]**tout** /towt‖taʊt/ *vi* to solicit for customers ~ *vt* **1a** to solicit or peddle importunately **b** *Br* to sell (tickets in great demand) at exploitative prices **2a** *Br* to spy out information about (e g a racing stable or horse) **b** *NAm* to give a tip or solicit bets on (a racehorse)

[2]**tout** *n* sby who touts: e g **a** sby who solicits custom, usu importunately **b** *Br* sby who offers tickets for a sold-out entertainment (e g a concert or football match) at vastly inflated prices

[3]**tout** *vt* to praise or publicize loudly or extravagantly

[1]**tow** /toh‖təʊ/ *vt* to draw or pull along behind, esp by a rope or chain

[2]**tow** *n* **1** a rope or chain for towing **2** towing or being towed **3** sthg towed (e g a boat or car) – **in tow 1** being towed <*a breakdown lorry with a car* in tow> **2a** under guidance or protection <*taken* in tow *by a friendly neighbour*> **b** in the position of a dependent or devoted follower or admirer <*a young man passed with a good-looking girl* in tow>

[3]**tow** *n* short or broken fibre (e g of flax or hemp) prepared for spinning

towards /tə'wawdz‖tə'wɔːdz/ *prep* **1** moving or situated in the direction of <*driving* ~ *town*> **2a** along a course leading to <*a long stride* ~ *disarmament*> **b** in relation to <*an attitude* ~ *life*> **3** turned in the direction of <*his back was* ~ *me*> **4** not long before <~ *the end of the afternoon*> **5** for the partial financing of <*will put it* ~ *a record*>

[1]**towel** /'towəl‖'taʊəl/ *n* **1** an absorbent cloth or paper for wiping or drying sthg (e g crockery or the body) after washing **2** SANITARY TOWEL

[2]**towel** *vt* **-ll-** (*NAm* **-l-**, **-ll-**) to rub or dry (e g the body) with a towel

towelling, *NAm chiefly* **toweling** /'towəling‖'taʊəlɪŋ/ *n* a cotton or linen fabric often used for making towels

[1]**tower** /'towə‖'taʊə/ *n* **1** a building or structure typically higher than its diameter and high relative to its surroundings that may stand apart or be attached to a larger structure and that may be fully walled in or of skeleton framework **2** a citadel, fortress **3 tower block, tower** a tall multi-storey building, often containing offices – **towered** *adj*, **towerlike** *adj*

[2]**tower** *vi* to reach or rise to a great height

towering /'towəring‖'taʊərɪŋ/ *adj* **1** impressively high or great <~ *pines*> **2** reaching a high point of intensity <*a* ~ *rage*> **3** going beyond proper bounds <~ *ambitions*> – **toweringly** *adv*

towline /'toh,lien‖'təʊ,laɪn/ *n* a towrope

town /town‖taʊn/ *n* **1a** a compactly settled area as distinguished from surrounding rural territory; *esp* one larger than a village but smaller than a city **b** a city **2** a neighbouring city, capital city, or metropolis <*travels into* ~ *daily*> **3** the city or urban life as contrasted with the country or rural life – **town** *adj* – **on the town** in usu carefree pursuit of entertainment or amusement (e g city nightlife)

town clerk *n* the chief official of a British town who until 1974 was appointed to administer municipal affairs and to act as secretary to the town council

town crier /'krie·ə‖'kraɪə/ *n* a town officer who makes public proclamations

town hall *n* the chief administrative building of a town

town house *n* **1** the city residence of sby having a country seat **2** a terrace house typically of 3 storeys

townscape /'town,skayp‖'taʊn,skeɪp/ *n* the overall visual aspect of a town

township /'township‖'taʊnʃɪp/ *n* **1** an ancient unit of administration in England identical in area with or being a division of a parish **2** an urban area inhabited by nonwhite citizens in S Africa

townsman /'townzmən‖'taʊnzmən/, *fem* **'towns,woman** *n* **1** a native or resident of a town or city **2** a fellow citizen of a town

'towns,people /-,peepl‖-,piːpl/ *n pl* the inhabitants of a town or city

towrope /'toh,rohp‖'təʊ,rəʊp/ *n* a line used in towing a boat, car, etc

toxaemia /tok'seemyə, -mi·ə‖tɒk'siːmjə, -mɪə/ *n* an abnormal condition associated with the presence of toxic substances in the blood

toxic /'toksik‖'tɒksɪk/ *adj* **1** of or caused by a poison or toxin **2** poisonous [Late Latin *toxicus*, fr Latin *toxicum* poison, fr Greek *toxikon* arrow poison, fr *toxon* bow, arrow] – **toxicity** *n*

toxicology /,toksi'koləji‖,tɒksɪ'kɒlədʒɪ/ *n* a branch of biology that deals with poisons and their effects and with medical, industrial, legal, or other problems arising from them – **toxicologist** *n*

toxin /'toksin‖'tɒksɪn/ *n* an often extremely poisonous protein produced by a living organism (e g a bacterium), esp in the body of a host

[1]**toy** /toy‖tɔɪ/ *n* **1** a trinket, bauble **2a** sthg for a child to play with **b** sthg designed for amusement or diversion rather than practical use **3** sthg tiny; *esp* an animal of a breed or variety of exceptionally small size – **toylike** *adj*

[2]**toy** *vi* **1** to act or deal *with* sthg without purpose or conviction **2** to amuse oneself as if with a toy – **toyer** *n*

[3]**toy** *adj* **1** designed or made for use as a toy <*a* ~ *stove*> **2** toylike, esp in being small

[1]**trace** /trays‖treɪs/ *n* **1** a mark or line left by sthg that has passed; *also* a footprint **2** a vestige of some past thing; *specif* an engram **3** sthg traced or drawn (e g the graphic record made by a seismograph) **4** (the path taken by) the spot that moves across the screen of a cathode-ray tube **5** a minute and often barely detectable amount or indication, esp of a chemical <*a* ~ *of a smile*>

[2]**trace** *vt* **1a** to delineate, sketch **b** to write (e g letters or figures) painstakingly **c** to copy (e g a drawing) by following the lines or letters as seen through a semitransparent superimposed sheet **2a** to follow the trail of **b** to follow back or study in detail or step by step <~ *the history of the labour movement*> **c** to discover signs, evidence, or remains of ~ *vi* to be traceable historically – **traceable** *adj*

[3]**trace** *n* either of 2 straps, chains, or lines of a harness for attaching a vehicle to a horse

trace element *n* a chemical element present in minute quantities; *esp* one essential to a living organism for proper growth and development

tracer /'traysə‖'treɪsə/ *n* **1** ammunition containing a chemical composition to mark the flight of projectiles by a trail of smoke or fire **2** a substance, esp a labelled element or atom, used to trace the course of a chemical or biological process

tracery /'traysəri‖'treɪsərɪ/ *n* ornamental stone openwork in architecture, esp in the head of a Gothic window – **traceried** *adj*

trachea /trə'kee·ə‖trə'kiːə/ *n, pl* **tracheae** *also* **tracheas 1** the main trunk of the system of tubes by which air passes to and from the lungs in vertebrates; the windpipe **2** VESSEL 3b **3** any of the small tubes carrying air in most insects and many other arthropods – **tracheal** *adj*, **tracheate** *adj*

trachoma /trə'kohmə‖trə'kəʊmə/ *n* a chronic contagious eye disease that is caused by a rickettsia and commonly causes blindness if left untreated – **trachomatous** *adj*

tracing /'traysing‖'treɪsɪŋ/ *n* sthg traced: e g **a** a copy (e g of a design or map) made on a superimposed semitransparent sheet **b** (a map of) the ground plan of a military installation

tracing paper *n* a semitransparent paper for tracing drawings

[1]**track** /trak‖træk/ *n* **1a** detectable evidence (e g a line of footprints or a wheel rut) that sthg has passed **b** a path beaten (as if) by feet **c** a specially laid-out course, esp for racing **d(1)** the parallel rails of a railway **d(2)** a rail or length of railing along which sthg, esp a curtain, moves or is pulled **e(1)** any of a series of parallel elongated regions on a magnetic tape on which a recording is made **e(2)** a more or less independent sequence of recording (e g a single song) visible as a distinct band on a gramophone record **2** a recent or fossil footprint <*the huge* ~ *of a dinosaur*> **3a** the course along which sthg moves **b** the projection on the earth's surface of the path along which sthg (e g a missile) has flown **4** the condition of being aware of a fact or development <*keep* ~ *of the costs*> **5a** the width of a wheeled vehicle from wheel to wheel, usu from the outside of the rims **b** either of 2 endless usu metal belts on which a tracklaying vehicle travels – **trackless** *adj* – **in one's tracks** where one stands or is at the moment <*was stopped* in his tracks>

[2]**track** *vt* **1** to follow the tracks or traces of **2** to observe or plot the course of (e g a spacecraft) instrumentally **3a** to make tracks on **b** *NAm* to carry on the feet and deposit <~ *mud into the house*> ~ *vi* **1a** *of a gramophone needle* to follow the groove of a record **b** *of a rear wheel of a vehicle* to follow accurately the corresponding fore wheel on a straight track **2** to move a film or television camera towards, beside, or away from a subject while shooting a scene **3** *NAm* to leave tracks (e g on a floor) – **tracker** *n*

track down *vt* to search for until found

track suit *n* a warm loose-fitting suit worn by athletes when training

[1]**tract** /trakt‖trækt/ *n* a short practical treatise; *esp* a pamphlet of religious propaganda

[2]**tract** *n* **1** a region or area of land of indefinite extent **2** a system of body parts or organs that collectively serve some often specified purpose <*the digestive* ~>

tractable /'traktəbl‖'træktəbl/ *adj* **1** easily taught or controlled <*a* ~ *horse*> **2** easily handled or wrought – **tractableness** *n*, **tractably** *adv*, **tractability** *n*

traction /'traksh(ə)n‖'trækʃ(ə)n/ *n* **1** pulling or being pulled; *also* the force exerted in pulling **2** the drawing of a vehicle by motive power; *also* the motive power employed **3a** the adhesive friction of a body on a surface on which it moves <*the* ~ *of a wheel on a rail*> **b** a pulling force exerted on a skeletal structure (e g in treating a fracture) by means of a special device – **tractional** *adj*, **tractive** *adj*

traction engine *n* a large steam- or diesel-powered vehicle used to draw other vehicles or equipment over roads or fields and sometimes to provide power (e g for sawing or ploughing)

tractor /'traktə‖'træktə/ *n* **1** TRACTION ENGINE **2a** a 4-wheeled or tracklaying vehicle used esp for pulling or using farm machinery **b** a truck with a short chassis and no body except a driver's cab, used to haul a large trailer or trailers

[1]**trad** /trad‖træd/ *adj, chiefly Br* traditional – infml

[2]**trad** *n* traditional jazz

[1]**trade** /trayd‖treɪd/ *n* **1a** the business or work in which one engages regularly **b** an occupation requiring manual or mechanical skill; a craft **c** the people engaged in an occupation, business, or industry **d** (the social group deriving its income from) commerce as opposed to the professions or landed property **2a** the business of buying and selling or bartering commodities **b** business, market <*when* ~ *was brisk*> <*novelties for the tourist* ~> **3** *sing or pl in constr the* people or group of firms engaged in a particular business or industry **4** TRADE WIND – usu pl **5** *chiefly NAm* a transaction; *also* an exchange of property usu without use of money

[2]**trade** *vt* to give in exchange for another commodity; *also* to make an exchange of <~d *secrets*> ~ *vi* **1** to engage in the exchange, purchase, or sale of goods **2** to give one thing in exchange for another – **tradable** *also* **tradeable** *adj* – **trade on** to take often unscrupulous advantage of <*they* traded on *her good nature*>

[3]**trade** *adj* **1** of or used in trade <*a* ~ *agreement*> **2** intended for or limited to people in a business or industry <*a* ~ *publication*> <~ *discount*>

trade gap *n* the value by which a country's imports exceed its exports

'trade-,in *n* an item of merchandise (e g a car or refrigerator) that is traded in

trade in *vt* to give as payment or part payment for a purchase or bill

'trade,mark /-,mahk‖-,mɑːk/ *n* **1** a name or distinctive symbol or device attached to goods produced by a particular firm or individual and legally reserved to the exclusive use of the owner of the mark as maker or seller **2** a distinguishing feature firmly associated with sby or sthg

trade name *n* **1a** the name used for an article by the trade **b** a name given by a manufacturer or seller to an article or service to distinguish it as his/hers **2** the name under which a concern does business

trader /'traydə‖'treɪdə/ *n* **1** a retail or wholesale dealer **2** a ship engaged in trade

tradesman /'traydzmən‖'treɪdzmən/ *n* **1a** a shopkeeper **b** one who delivers goods to private houses **2** a workman in a skilled trade

trade union *also* **trades union** *n* an organization of workers formed for the purpose of advancing its members' interests – **trade unionism** *n*, **trade unionist** *n*

trade wind, **trade** *n* a wind blowing almost

continually towards the equator from the NE in the belt between the N horse latitudes and the doldrums and from the SE in the belt between the S horse latitudes and the doldrums

trading estate /'trayding‖'treɪdɪŋ/ *n* INDUSTRIAL ESTATE

trading stamp *n* a printed stamp of a certain value given by a retailer to a customer, to be accumulated and redeemed in merchandise or cash

tradition /trə'dish(ə)n‖trə'dɪʃ(ə)n/ *n* **1** the handing down of information, beliefs, and customs by word of mouth or by example from one generation to another **2a** an inherited practice or opinion **b** conventions associated with a group or period <*the title poem represents a complete break with 19th-c* ~ – F R Leavis> **3** cultural continuity in attitudes and institutions – **traditionless** *adj*

traditional /trə'dish(ə)nl‖trə'dɪʃ(ə)nl/ *adj* **1** of or handed down by tradition **2** of or being a style of jazz orig played in New Orleans in the early 1900s – **traditionally** *adv*

tra'ditionalism /-iz(ə)m‖-ɪz(ə)m/ *n* respect for tradition as opposed to modernism or liberalism – **traditionalist** *n or adj*, **traditionalistic** *adj*

traduce /trə'dyoohs‖trə'dju:s/ *vt* to (attempt to) damage the reputation or standing of, esp by misrepresentation – fml – **traducement** *n*, **traducer** *n*

[1]**traffic** /'trafik‖'træfɪk/ *n* **1a** import and export trade **b** the business of bartering or buying and selling **c** illegal or disreputable trade <*drug* ~> **2** exchange <*a lively* ~ *in new ideas*> **3a** the movement (e g of vehicles or pedestrians) through an area or along a route **b** the vehicles, pedestrians, ships, or aircraft moving along a route **c** the information or signals transmitted over a communications system **4a** the passengers or cargo carried by a transport system **b** the business of transporting passengers or freight **5** dealings between individuals or groups – fml

[2]**traffic** *vb* **-ck-** *vi* to carry on traffic ~*vt* to trade, barter – **trafficker** *n*

trafficator /'trafi,kaytə‖'træfɪ,keɪtə/ *n, Br* INDICATOR 1c; *esp* a hinged retractable illuminated arm on the side of an old motor car

traffic circle *n, NAm* a roundabout

traffic island *n* a paved or planted island in a road designed to guide the flow of traffic and provide refuge for pedestrians

traffic light *n* an automatically operated signal of coloured lights for controlling traffic – usu pl

tragedian /trə'jeedi·ən‖trə'dʒi:dɪən/ *n* **1** a writer of tragedies **2** *fem* **tragedienne** an actor who plays tragic roles

tragedy /'trajədi‖'trædʒədɪ/ *n* **1** (a) serious drama in which destructive circumstances result in adversity for and usu the deaths of the main characters **2** a disastrous event; a calamity **3** tragic quality or element [Middle French *tragedie*, fr Latin *tragoedia*, fr Greek *tragōidia*, prob fr *tragos* goat + *aeidein* to sing]

tragic /'trajik‖'trædʒɪk/ *also* **tragical** /-kl‖-kl/ *adj* **1** (expressive) of tragedy <*the* ~ *significance of the atomic bomb* – H S Truman> **2** of, appropriate to, dealing with, or treated in tragedy **3a** deplorable, lamentable <*the* ~ *disparity between the actual and the ideal*> **b** marked by a sense of tragedy – **tragically** *adv*

tragicomedy /,traji'komədi‖,trædʒɪ'kɒmədɪ/ *n* a literary work in which tragic and comic elements are mixed in a usu ironic way; *also* a situation or event of such a character – **tragicomic** *also* **tragicomical** *adj*

[1]**trail** /trayl‖treɪl/ *vi* **1a** to hang down so as to sweep the ground **b** *of a plant, branch, etc* to grow to such length as to droop over towards the ground **2a** to walk or proceed draggingly or wearily – usu + *along* **b** to lag behind; do poorly in relation to others **3** to move or extend slowly in thin streams <*smoke* ~ing *from chimneys*> **4a** to extend in an erratic course or line **b** to dwindle <*voice* ~ing *off*> **5** to follow a trail; track game ~ *vt* **1a** to drag loosely along a surface; allow to sweep the ground **b** to haul, tow **2a** to drag (e g a limb or the body) heavily or wearily **b** to carry or bring along as an addition **c** to draw along in one's wake <~ing *clouds of glory* – William Wordsworth> **3a** TRACK 1a **b** to follow behind, esp in the footsteps of **c** to lag behind (e g a competitor)

[2]**trail** *n* **1** the part of a gun carriage that rests on the ground when the piece is unlimbered **2a** sthg that follows as if being drawn behind **b** the streak of light produced by a meteor **3a** a trace or mark left by sby or sthg that has passed or is being followed <*a* ~ *of blood*> **b(1)** a track made by passage, esp through a wilderness **b(2)** a marked path through a forest or mountainous region – **trailless** *adj*

trailer /'traylə‖'treɪlə/ *n* **1** a trailing plant **2** a wheeled vehicle designed to be towed (e g by a lorry or car); *specif, NAm* CARAVAN 2 **3** a set of short excerpts from a film shown in advance for publicity purposes

[1]**train** /trayn‖treɪn/ *n* **1** a part of a gown that trails behind the wearer **2a** a retinue, suite **b** a moving file of people, vehicles, or animals **3** the vehicles, men, and sometimes animals that accompany an army with baggage, supplies, ammunition, or siege artillery **4** a connected series of ideas, actions, or events **5** a line of gunpowder laid to lead fire to a charge **6** a series of connected moving mechanical parts (e g gears) **7** a connected line of railway carriages or wagons with or without a locomotive – **trainful** *n*

[2]**train** *vt* **1** to direct the growth of (a plant), usu by bending, pruning, etc **2a** to form by instruction, discipline, or drill **b** to teach so as to make fit or proficient **3** to prepare (e g by exercise) for a test of skill **4** to aim at an object or objective <~ed *his rifle on the target*> ~ *vi* **1** to undergo training **2** to go by train – **trainable** *adj*

'train,bearer /-,beərə‖-,beərə/ *n* an attendant who holds the train of a robe or gown (e g on a ceremonial occasion)

trainee /,tray'nee‖,treɪ'ni:/ *n* one who is being trained for a job

trainer /'traynə‖'treɪnə/ *n* **1** sby who or sthg which trains (e g a person who trains the members of a sport team) **2** a sports shoe used esp for running, jogging, or casual wear

training /'trayning‖'treɪnɪŋ/ *n* **1** the bringing of a person or animal to a desired degree of proficiency in some activity or skill **2** the condition of being trained, esp for a contest <*an athlete out of* ~>

training college *n, Br* a school offering specialized instruction <*a* ~ *for traffic wardens*>

traipse /trayps‖treɪps/ *vi* to walk or trudge about, often to little purpose – **traipse** *n*

trait /trayt, tray‖treɪt, treɪ/ *n* a distinguishing (personal) quality or characteristic

traitor /ˈtraytə‖ˈtreɪtə/, *fem* **traitress** /ˈtraytris‖ˈtreɪtrɪs/ *n* **1** sby who betrays another's trust **2** sby who commits treason – **traitorous** *adj*, **traitorously** *adv*

trajectory /trəˈjektəri‖trəˈdʒektərɪ/ *n* **1** the curve that a planet, projectile, etc follows **2** a path, progression, or line of development like a physical trajectory

tram /tram‖træm/ *n* any of various vehicles: e g **a** a boxlike wagon running on rails (e g in a mine) **b** *chiefly Br* a passenger vehicle running on rails and typically operating on urban streets

ˈtramˌline /-ˌlien‖-ˌlaɪn/ *n, Br* **1** a track on which trams run **2** *pl* (the area between) either of the 2 pairs of sidelines on a tennis court that mark off the area used in doubles play

¹trammel /ˈtraml‖ˈtræml/ *n* **1** a net for catching birds or fish; *esp* one having 3 layers with the middle one finer-meshed and slack so that fish passing through carry some of the centre net through the coarser opposite net and are trapped **2** sthg that impedes freedom of action – usu pl with sing. meaning <*the* ~s *of convention*>

²trammel *vt* **-ll-** (*NAm* **-l-**, **-ll-**) **1** to enmesh **2** to impede the free play of

¹tramp /tramp‖træmp/ *vi* **1** to walk or tread, esp heavily **2a** to travel about on foot **b** to journey as a tramp ~ *vt* **1** to trample **2** to travel or wander through on foot – **tramper** *n*

²tramp *n* **1** a wandering vagrant who survives by taking the occasional job or by begging or stealing money and food **2** a usu long and tiring walk **3** the heavy rhythmic tread of feet **4** an iron plate to protect the sole of a shoe **5** a merchant vessel that does not work a regular route but carries general cargo to any port as required **6** *chiefly NAm* a promiscuous woman

trample /ˈtrampl‖ˈtræmpl/ *vi* **1** to tread heavily so as to bruise, crush, or injure **2** to treat destructively with ruthlessness or contempt – usu + *on, over*, or *upon* <trampling *on the rights of others*> ~*vt* to press down, crush, or injure (as if) by treading – **trample** *n*, **trampler** *n*

trampoline /ˌtrampəˈleen‖ˌtræmpəˈliːn/ *n* a resilient sheet or web supported by springs in a frame and used as a springboard in tumbling – **trampoliner** *n*, **trampolining** *n*

trance /trahns‖trɑːns/ *n* **1** a state of semiconsciousness or unconsciousness with reduced or absent sensitivity to external stimulation **2** a usu self-induced state of altered consciousness or ecstasy in which religious or mystical visions may be experienced **3** a state of profound abstraction or absorption – **trancelike** *adj*

tranny /ˈtrani‖ˈtrænɪ/ *n, chiefly Br* TRANSISTOR RADIO – infml

tranquil /ˈtrangkwil‖ˈtræŋkwɪl/ *adj* free from mental agitation or from disturbance or commotion – **tranquilly** *adv*, **tranquillity** *n*

tranquill·ize, **-ise**, *NAm chiefly* **tranquilize** /ˈtrangkwiliez‖ˈtræŋkwɪlaɪz/ *vt* to make tranquil or calm; *esp* to relieve of mental tension and anxiety by drugs ~*vi* to become tranquil

tranquill·izer, **-iser**, *NAm chiefly* **tranquilizer** /ˈtrangkwiˌliezə‖ˈtræŋkwɪˌlaɪzə/ *n* a drug (e g diazepam) used to tranquillize

trans- /tranz, trahnz‖trænz, trɑːnz/ *prefix* **1** on or to the other side of; across; beyond <trans*atlantic*> **2** beyond (a specified chemical element) in the periodic table <trans*uranic*> **3** through <trans*cutaneous*> **4** so or such as to change or transfer <trans*ship*>

transact /tranˈzakt‖trænˈzækt/ *vt* to perform; CARRY OUT 1; *esp* to conduct <*business to be* ~ed *by experts*> – **transactor** *n*

transaction /tranˈzaksh(ə)n, trahn-‖trænˈzækʃ(ə)n, trɑːn-/ *n* **1** transacting **2a** sthg transacted; *esp* a business deal **b** *pl* the (published) record of the meeting of a society or association – **transactional** *adj*

transatlantic /ˌtranzətˈlantik, ˌtrahn-‖ˌtrænzətˈlæntɪk, ˌtrɑːn-/ *adj* **1** crossing or extending across the Atlantic ocean <*a* ~ *cable*> **2** situated beyond the Atlantic ocean **3** (characteristic) of people or places situated beyond the Atlantic ocean; *specif, chiefly Br* American <*a* ~ *accent*>

transcend /tranˈsend, trahn-‖trænˈsend, trɑːn-/ *vt* **1a** to go beyond the limits of **b** to be or extend beyond and above (the universe or material existence) **2** to surpass, excel ~*vi* to rise above or extend notably beyond ordinary limits

transcendent /tranˈsend(ə)nt‖trænˈsend(ə)nt; *also* trahn-‖trɑːn-/ *adj* **1a** exceeding usual limits; surpassing **b** beyond the limits of ordinary experience **c** beyond the limits of possible experience and knowledge – used in Kantianism **2** transcending the universe or material existence – **transcendence, transcendency** *n*, **transcendently** *adv*

transcendental /ˌtransenˈdentl‖ˌtrænsenˈdentl; *also* trahn-‖trɑːn-/ *adj* **1** of or employing the basic categories (e g space and time) presupposed by knowledge and experience <*a* ~ *proof*> **2** TRANSCENDENT 1a **3a** TRANSCENDENT 1b **b** supernatural **c** abstruse, abstract **d** of transcendentalism – **transcendentally** *adv*

ˌtranscenˈdentalism /-ˌiz(ə)m‖-ˌɪz(ə)m/ *n* **1** a philosophy that emphasizes the basic categories of knowledge and experience, or asserts fundamental reality to be transcendent **2** a philosophy that asserts the primacy of the spiritual over the material – **transcendentalist** *adj or n*

transcontinental /ˌtranzˌkontiˈnentl, trahnz-‖ˌtrænzˌkɒntɪˈnentl, trɑːnz-/ *adj* crossing or extending across a continent

transcribe /tranˈskrieb‖trænˈskraɪb; *also* trahn-‖trɑːn-/ *vt* **1a** to make a written copy or version of (e g sthg written or printed) **b** to write in a different medium; transliterate <~ *shorthand*> **c** to write down, record **2** to transfer (data) from one recording form to another **3** to make a musical transcription of – **transcriber** *n*

transcript /ˈtranskript, ˈtrahn-‖ˈtrænskrɪpt, ˈtrɑːn-/ *n* **1** a written, printed, or typed copy, esp of dictated or recorded material **2** an official written copy <*a court reporter's* ~>

transcription /tran'skripsh(ə)n, trahn-‖træn-'skrɪpʃ(ə)n, trɑːn-/ *n* **1** transcribing **2** a copy, transcript: e g **2a** an often free arrangement of a musical composition for some instrument or voice other than the original **b** a sound recording suitable for broadcasting and thus usu of high quality **3** the naturally occurring process of constructing a molecule of nucleic acid (e g messenger RNA) using a DNA molecule as a template, with resulting transfer of genetic information to the newly formed molecule – **transcriptional** *adj*

transept /'transept‖'trænsept/ *n* (either of the projecting arms of) the part of a cross-shaped church that crosses the E end of the nave at right angles – **transeptal** *adj*

[1]**transfer** /trans'fuh, trahns-‖træns'fɜː, trɑːns-/ *vb* **-rr-** *vt* **1a** to convey or cause to pass from one person, place, or situation to another **b** to move or send to another location <~red *her business to the capital*>; *specif* to move (a professional soccer player) to another football club **2** to make over the possession or control of **3** to copy (e g a design) from one surface to another by contact ~ *vi* **1** to move to a different place, region, or situation **2** to change from one vehicle or transport system to another – **transferable, transferrable** *adj*, **transferral** *n*, **transferor, transferrer** *n*, **transferee** *n*

[2]**transfer** /'transfuh, 'trahns-‖'trænsfɜː, 'trɑːns-/ *n* **1** conveyance of right, title, or interest in property **2a** transferring **b** transference **3** sthg or sby that transfers or is transferred; *esp* a design or picture transferred by contact from one surface (e g specially prepared paper) to another **4** *NAm* a ticket entitling a passenger on a public conveyance to continue a journey on another route

transference /'transf(ə)rəns, trans'fuhrəns, trahns-‖'trænsf(ə)rəns, træns'fɜːrəns, trɑːns-/ *n* the redirection of feelings and desires, esp those unconsciously retained from childhood, towards a new object (e g towards a psychoanalyst conducting therapy) – **transferential** *adj*

transfiguration /ˌtransˌfigə'raysh(ə)n, ˌtrahns-‖ˌtrænsˌfɪgə'reɪʃ(ə)n, ˌtrɑːns-/ *n* **1a** a change in form or appearance; a metamorphosis **b** an exalting, glorifying, or spiritual change **2** *cap* August 6 observed as a Christian festival in commemoration of the transfiguration of Christ as described in Matthew 17:2 and Mark 9:2–3

transfigure /trans'figə, trahns-‖træns'fɪgə, trɑːns-/ *vt* to give a new appearance to; transform outwardly and usu for the better

transfix /trans'fiks, trahns-‖træns'fɪks, trɑːns-/ *vt* **1** to pierce through (as if) with a pointed weapon **2** to hold motionless (as if) by piercing <~ed *by horror*> – **transfixion** *n*

transform /trans'fawm, trahns-‖træns'fɔːm, trɑːns-/ *vt* **1** to change radically (e g in structure, appearance, or character) **2** to change (a current) in potential (e g from high voltage to low) or in type (e g from alternating to direct) – **transformable** *adj*, **transformation** *n*, **transformational** *adj*

transformer /trans'fawmə, trahns-‖træns-'fɔːmə, trɑːns-/ *n* an electrical device making use of the principle of mutual induction to convert variations of current in a primary circuit into variations of voltage and current in a secondary circuit

transfuse /trans'fyoohz, trahns-‖træns'fjuːz, trɑːns-/ *vt* **1** to diffuse into or through; *broadly* to spread across **2** to transfer (e g blood) into a vein – **transfusible, transfusable** *adj*, **transfusion** *n*

transgress /trans'gres, trahns-‖træns'gres, trɑːns-/ *vt* **1** to go beyond limits set or prescribed by <~ *the divine law*> **2** to pass beyond or go over (a boundary) ~*vi* to violate a command or law – **transgressive** *adj*, **transgressor** *n*

tranship /tranz'ship, trahnz-‖trænz'ʃɪp, trɑːnz-/ *vb* to transship

[1]**transient** /'tranzi·ənt‖'trænzɪənt/ *adj* **1** passing quickly away; transitory **2** making only a brief stay <*a ~ summer migrant*> – **transience, transiency** *n*, **transiently** *adv*

[2]**transient** *n* **1** a transient guest or worker **2a** a temporary oscillation that occurs in a circuit because of a sudden change of voltage or load **b** a transient current or voltage

transistor /tran'zistə, trahn-‖træn'zɪstə, trɑːn-/ *n* **1** any of several semiconductor devices that have usu 3 electrodes and make use of a small current to control a larger one **2** TRANSISTOR RADIO [[1]*trans*fer + re*sistor*; fr its transferring an electrical signal across a resistor]

tran'sistor·ize, -ise /-riez‖-raɪz/ *vt* to construct (a device) using transistors – **transistorization** *n*

transistor radio *n* a radio using transistorized circuitry

[1]**transit** /'transit, -zit‖'trænsɪt, -zɪt/ *n* **1a** passing or conveying through or over **b** a change, transition **2** passage of a smaller celestial body **2a** across the disc of a larger one **b** over a meridian or through the field of a telescope **3** *NAm* conveyance of people or things from one place to another – **in transit** in passage <*goods lost* in transit>

[2]**transit** *vi* to make a transit ~*vt* to traverse

transition /tran'zish(ə)n, trahn-‖træn'zɪʃ(ə)n, trɑːn-/ *n* **1a** passage from one state or stage to another **b** a movement, development, or evolution from one form, stage, or style to another **2a** a musical modulation **b** a musical passage leading from one section of a piece to another **3** an abrupt change in energy state or level (e g of an atomic nucleus or a molecule), usu accompanied by loss or gain of a single quantum of energy – **transitional** *adj*, **transitionally** *adv*

transitive /'transitiv, 'trahn-, -zitiv‖'trænsɪtɪv, 'trɑːn-, -zɪtɪv/ *adj* **1** having or containing a direct object <*a ~ verb*> **2** of or being a relation such that if the relation holds between a first element and a second and between the second element and a third, it holds between the first and third elements **3** of or characterized by transition – **transitive** *n*, **transitively** *adv*, **transitiveness, transitivity** *n*

transitory /'transit(ə)ri, 'trahn-, -zi-‖'trænsɪt-(ə)rɪ, 'trɑːn-, -zɪ-/ *adj* **1** tending to pass away **2** of brief duration – **transitorily** *adv*, **transitoriness** *n*

translate /trans'layt, trahns-‖træns'leɪt, trɑːns-/ *vt* **1a** to bear, remove, or change from one place, state, form, or appearance to another

<*a country boy* ~d *to the city*> <~ *ideas into action*> **b** to convey to heaven or to a nontemporal condition without death **c** to transfer (a bishop) from one see to another **2a** to turn into another language **b** to turn from one set of symbols into another **c** to express in different or more comprehensible terms **3** to subject (genetic information, esp messenger RNA) to translation ~ *vi* **1** to practise or make (a) translation **2** to undergo (a) translation – **translatable** *adj*, **translator** *n*

translation /trans'laysh(ə)n, trahns-‖træns'leɪʃ(ə)n, trɑːns-/ *n* **1a** (a version produced by) a rendering from one language into another **b** a change to a different substance or form **c** uniform motion of a body in a straight line **2** the process of forming a protein synthesis from information contained usu in messenger RNA – **translational** *adj*

transliterate /tranz'litərayt, trahnz-, trans-, trahns-‖trænz'lɪtəreɪt, trɑːnz-, træns-, trɑːns-/ *vt* to represent or spell in the characters of another alphabet – **transliteration** *n*

translucent /tranz'loohs(ə)nt, trahnz-‖trænz'luːs(ə)nt, trɑːnz-/ *adj* permitting the passage of light: e g **a** transparent **b** transmitting and diffusing light so that objects beyond cannot be seen clearly <~ *porcelain*> – **translucence, translucency** *n*, **translucently** *adv*

transmigrate /ˌtranzmie'grayt, ˌtrahnz-‖ˌtrænzmaɪ'greɪt, ˌtrɑːnz-/ *vi* **1** *of a soul* to pass at death from one body or being to another **2** to migrate – **transmigrator** *n*, **transmigration** *n*, **transmigratory** *adj*

transmission /trans'mish(ə)n, trahns-, tranz-, trahnz-‖træns'mɪʃ(ə)n, trɑːns-, trænz-, trɑːnz-/ *n* **1** transmitting <~ *of a nerve impulse across a synapse*>; *esp* transmitting by radio waves or over a wire **2** the assembly by which the power is transmitted from a motor vehicle engine to the axle **3** sthg transmitted – **transmissive** *adj*

transmit /trans'mit, trahns-, tranz-, trahnz-‖træns'mɪt, trɑːns-, trænz-, trɑːnz-/ *vb* **-tt-** *vt* **1a** to send or transfer from one person or place to another **b(1)** to convey (as if) by inheritance or heredity **b(2)** to convey (infection) abroad or to another **2a(1)** to cause (e g light or force) to pass or be conveyed through a medium **a(2)** to allow the passage of <*glass* ~s *light*> **b** to send out (a signal) either by radio waves or over a wire ~*vi* to send out a signal by radio waves or over a wire – **transmissible** *adj*, **transmittable** *adj*, **transmittal** *n*

trans'mitter /-tə‖-tə/ *n* **1** the portion of a telegraphic or telephonic instrument that sends the signals **2** a radio or television transmitting station or set **3** a neurotransmitter

transmogrify /tranz'mogrifie‖trænz'mɒgrɪfaɪ/ *vt* to transform, often with grotesque or humorous effect – **transmogrification** *n*

transmutation /ˌtranzmyooh'taysh(ə)n, ˌtrahnz-‖ˌtrænzmjuː'teɪʃ(ə)n, ˌtrɑːnz-/ *n* **1** the conversion of base metals into gold or silver **2** the natural or artificial conversion of one element or nuclide into another – **transmutative** *adj*

transmute /tranz'myooht, trahnz-‖trænz'mjuːt, trɑːnz-/ *vt* **1** to change in form, substance, or characteristics **2** to subject (e g an element) to transmutation – **transmutable** *adj*

transom /'transəm‖'trænsəm/ *n* a transverse piece in a structure: e g **a** a lintel **b** a horizontal crossbar in a window, over a door, or between a door and a window or fanlight above it **c** any of several transverse timbers or beams secured to the sternpost of a boat

transparency /tran'sparənsi, trahn-‖træn'spærənsɪ, trɑːn-/ *n* **1** being transparent **2a** a picture or design on glass, film, etc viewed by a light shining through it from behind; *esp* SLIDE 5b **b** a framework covered with thin cloth or paper bearing a device for public display (e g for advertisement) and lit from within

transparent /tran'sparənt, trahn-‖træn'spærənt, trɑːn-/ *adj* **1a(1)** transmitting light without appreciable scattering so that bodies lying beyond are entirely visible **a(2)** penetrable by a specified form of radiation (e g X rays or ultraviolet) **b** fine or sheer enough to be seen through **2a** free from pretence or deceit <~ *sincerity*> **b** easily detected or seen through <*a* ~ *lie*> **c** readily understood <*the meaning of this word is* ~> – **transparence** *n*, **transparently** *adv*, **transparentness** *n*

transpire /tran'spie·ə, trahn-‖træn'spaɪə, trɑːn-/ *vt* to pass off or give passage to (a gas or liquid) through pores or interstices; *esp* to excrete (e g water vapour) through a skin or other living membrane ~ *vi* **1** to give off a vapour; *specif* to give off or exude water vapour, esp from the surfaces of leaves **2** to pass in the form of a vapour, esp from a living body **3** to become known; come to light **4** to occur; TAKE PLACE – disapproved of by some speakers

[1]**transplant** /trans'plahnt, trahns-‖træns'plɑːnt, trɑːns-/ *vt* **1** to lift and reset (a plant) in another soil or place **2** to remove from one place and settle or introduce elsewhere **3** to transfer (an organ or tissue) from one part or individual to another – **transplantable** *adj*, **transplanter** *n*, **transplantation** *n*

[2]**transplant** /'transˌplahnt, 'trahns-‖'trænsˌplɑːnt, 'trɑːns-/ *n* **1** transplanting **2** sthg transplanted

[1]**transport** /tran'spawt, trahn-‖træn'spɔːt, trɑːn-/ *vt* **1** to transfer or convey from one place to another <*mechanisms of* ~ing *ions across a living membrane*> **2** to carry away with strong and often pleasurable emotion **3** to send to a penal colony overseas – **transportable** *adj*

[2]**transport** /'transpawt, 'trahn-‖'trænspɔːt, 'trɑːn-/ *n* **1** the conveying of goods or people from one place to another **2** strong and often pleasurable emotion – often pl with sing. meaning <~s *of joy*> **3a** a ship or aircraft for carrying soldiers or military equipment **b** a lorry, aeroplane, etc used to transport people or goods **4** a mechanism for moving a tape, esp a magnetic tape, or disk past a sensing or recording head

transportation /ˌtranspaw'taysh(ə)n, trahn-‖ˌtrænspɔː'teɪʃ(ə)n, trɑːn-/ *n* **1** the act of transporting **2** banishment to a penal colony **3** *NAm* means of conveyance or travel from one place to another

transport café *n, Br* an inexpensive roadside cafeteria catering mainly for long-distance lorry drivers

transporter /tran'spawtə, trahn-‖træn-'spɔːtə, trɑːn-/ *n* a vehicle for transporting large or heavy loads

transpose /tran'spohz, trahn-‖træn'spəʊz, trɑːn-/ *vt* **1** to transfer from one place or period to another **2** to change the relative position of; alter the sequence of <~ *letters to change the spelling*> **3** to write or perform (music) in a different key **4** to bring (a term) from one side of an algebraic equation to the other with change of sign ~*vi* to transpose music – **transposable** *adj*

transship, tranship /tranz'ship, trahnz-‖trænz-'ʃɪp, trɑːnz-/ *vb* to transfer from one ship or conveyance to another for further transportation – **transshipment** *n*

transubstantiate /ˌtranz·səb'stanshiayt, ˌtrahnz-, -'stahn-‖ˌtrænzsəb'stænʃɪeɪt, ˌtrɑːnz-, -'stɑːn-/ *vb* to change into another substance

ˌtransubˌstantiˈation /-shi'aysh(ə)n‖-ʃɪ-'eɪʃ(ə)n/ *n* the miraculous change by which, according to Roman Catholic and Eastern Orthodox dogma, bread and wine used at communion become the body and blood of Christ when they are consecrated, although their appearance remains unchanged

transverse /tranz'vuhs, trahnz-, '--‖trænz-'vɜːs, trɑːnz-, '--/ *adj* lying or being across; set or made crosswise – **transversely** *adv*

transvestism /tranz'vestiz(ə)m, trahnz-‖trænz'vestɪz(ə)m, trɑːnz-/ *n* the adoption of the dress and often the behaviour of the opposite sex [Latin *trans* across + *vestire* to clothe, fr *vestis* clothing] – **transvestite** *adj or n*

[1]**trap** /trap‖træp/ *n* **1** a device for taking animals; *esp* one that holds by springing shut suddenly **2a** sthg designed to catch sby unawares; *also* PITFALL 1 **b** a situation from which it is impossible to escape <*caught in a poverty* ~>; *also* a plan to trick a person into such a situation <*police laid a* ~ *for the criminal*> **3a** a trapdoor **b** a device from which a greyhound is released at the start of a race **4a** a device for hurling clay pigeons into the air **b** BUNKER 2b **5** a light usu 1-horse carriage with springs **6** any of various devices for preventing passage of sthg often while allowing other matter to proceed; *esp* a device for drains or sewers consisting of a bend or partitioned chamber in which the liquid forms a seal to prevent the passage of sewer gas **7** *pl* a group of percussion instruments used esp in a dance or jazz band **8** the mouth – slang

[2]**trap** *vb* **-pp-** *vt* **1** to catch or take (as if) in a trap **2** to provide or set (a place) with traps **3** to stop, retain <*these mountains* ~ *the rain*> **4** to stop and control (the ball) in soccer, hockey, etc ~*vi* to engage in trapping animals – **trapper** *n*

[3]**trap, 'trapˌrock** *n* any of various dark-coloured fine-grained igneous rocks (e g basalt) used esp in road making

ˌtrap'door /-'daw‖-'dɔː/ *n* a lifting or sliding door covering an opening in a floor, ceiling, etc

trapeze /trə'peez‖trə'piːz/ *n* a gymnastic or acrobatic apparatus consisting of a short horizontal bar suspended by 2 parallel ropes

trapezium /trə'peezi·əm‖trə'piːzɪəm/ *n, pl* **trapeziums, trapezia** /-zi·ə‖-zɪə/ *Br* a quadrilateral having only 2 sides parallel [Greek *trapezion*, lit., small table, fr *trapeza* table, fr *tra-* four + *peza* foot]

trapezoid /'trapiˌzoyd, trə'peezoyd‖'træpɪ-ˌzɔɪd, trə'piːzɔɪd/ *n, chiefly NAm* a trapezium – **trapezoidal** *adj*

trappings /'trapingz‖'træpɪŋz/ *n pl* outward decoration or dress; *also* outward signs and accessories <*all the* ~ *of power with none of the substance*>

Trappist /'trapist‖'træpɪst/ *n* a member of a reformed branch of the Roman Catholic Cistercian Order noted for its vow of silence – **Trappist** *adj*

trapshooting /'trapˌshoohting‖'træpˌʃuːtɪŋ/ *n* shooting at clay pigeons sprung into the air from a trap so as to simulate the angles of flight of birds – **trapshooter** *n*

trash /trash‖træʃ/ *n* **1** sthg of little or no value: e g **1a** junk, rubbish **b(1)** empty talk **b(2)** inferior literary or artistic work **2** sthg in a crumbled or broken condition or mass **3** a worthless person; *also, sing or pl in constr* such people as a group – infml

'trash ˌcan *n, NAm* a dustbin

trashy /'trashi‖'træʃɪ/ *adj* of inferior quality or worth – **trashiness** *n*

trauma /'trawmə‖'trɔːmə; *also* 'trowmə‖'traʊmə/ *n, pl* **traumata** /-mətə‖-mətə/, **traumas** **1a** an injury (e g a wound) to living tissue caused by an outside agent **b** a disordered mental or behavioural state resulting from mental or emotional stress or shock **2** an agent, force, or mechanism that causes trauma [Greek *traumat-, trauma* wound] – **traumatic** *adj*

[1]**travail** /'travayl, trə'vayl‖'træveɪl, trə'veɪl/ *n* **1** physical or mental exertion, esp of a painful or laborious nature **2** *archaic* labour pains

[2]**travail** *vi* **1** to labour hard – fml **2** *archaic* to suffer labour pains

[1]**travel** /'travl‖'trævl/ *vb* **-ll-** (*NAm* **-l-, -ll-**) *vi* **1a** to go (as if) on a tour **b** to go as if by travelling <*my mind* ~led *back to our last meeting*> **c** to go from place to place as a sales representative <~s *in cosmetics*> **2a** to move or be transmitted from one place to another <*wine* ~s *badly*> **b** *esp of machinery* to move along a specified direction or path <*the stylus* ~s *in a groove*> **c** to move at high speed – infml <*a car that can really* ~> ~ *vt* **1a** to journey through or over <~ *the world*> **b** to follow (a course or path) as if by travelling **2** to traverse (a specified distance) **3** to cover (a place or region) as a sales representative – **travel light** to travel with a minimum of equipment or baggage

[2]**travel** *n* **1** a journey, esp to a distant or unfamiliar place – often pl <*set off on her* ~s> **2a** movement, progression <*the* ~ *of satellites round the earth*> **b** the motion of a piece of machinery

'travel ˌagent *n* sby engaged in selling and arranging personal transport, tours, or trips for travellers – **travel agency** *n*

'travelled, *NAm chiefly* **traveled** *adj* **1** experienced in travel <*a widely* ~ *journalist*> **2** used by travellers <*a well-*travelled *route*>

traveller, *NAm chiefly* **traveler** /ˈtravlə, ˈtravl·ə‖ˈtrævlə, ˈtrævələ/ *n* **1** SALES REPRESENTATIVE **2** any of various devices for handling sthg that is being moved laterally **3** *dial Br* a gipsy

ˈtraveller's ˌcheque, *NAm* **traveler's check** *n* a cheque that is purchased from a bank, travel agency, etc, and that may be exchanged abroad for foreign currency

travelogue, *NAm also* **travelog** /ˈtravəˌlog‖ˈtrævəˌlɒg/ *n* **1** a film or illustrated talk or lecture on some usu exotic or remote place **2** a narrated documentary film about travel

[1]**traverse** /ˈtravuhs, -ˈ-‖ˈtrævɜːs, -ˈ-/ *n* **1** sthg that crosses or lies across **2** a transverse gallery in a large building (e g a church) **3** a route or way across or over: e g **3a** a curving or zigzag way up a steep slope **b** the course followed in traversing **4** (a) traversing **5a** a lateral movement (e g of the saddle of a lathe carriage) **b** the lateral movement of a gun to change direction of fire **6** a survey consisting of a series of measured lines whose bearings are known

[2]**traverse** /trəˈvuhs, ˈtravuhs‖trəˈvɜːs, ˈtrævɜːs/ *vt* **1** to pass or travel across, over, or through <~ *a terrain*> <*light rays* traversing *a crystal*> **2** to lie or extend across <*the bridge* ~s *a brook*> **3a** to move to and fro over or along **b** to ascend, descend, or cross (a slope or gap) at an angle **c** to move (a gun) to right or left ~ *vi* **1** to move back and forth or from side to side **2** to climb or ski across rather than straight up or down a hill – **traversable** *adj*, **traversal** *n*, **traverser** *n*

[3]**traverse** /ˈtravuhs, -ˈ-‖ˈtrævɜːs, -ˈ-/ *adj* lying across

[1]**travesty** /ˈtravəsti‖ˈtrævəstɪ/ *n* **1** a crude or grotesque literary or artistic parody **2** a debased, distorted, or grossly inferior imitation <*a* ~ *of justice*>

[2]**travesty** *vt* to make a travesty of

[1]**trawl** /trawl‖trɔːl/ *vb* to fish (for or in) with a trawl

[2]**trawl** *n* **1** a large conical net dragged along the sea bottom to catch fish **2** *NAm* a setline

trawler /ˈtrawlə‖ˈtrɔːlə/ *n* a boat used in trawling

tray /tray‖treɪ/ *n* an open receptacle with a flat bottom and a low rim for holding, carrying, or exhibiting articles – **trayful** *n*

treacherous /ˈtrech(ə)rəs‖ˈtretʃ(ə)rəs/ *adj* **1** characterized by treachery; perfidious **2a** of uncertain reliability **b** providing insecure footing or support <*a* ~ *surface of black ice*> **c** marked by hidden dangers or hazards <*the* ~ *waters round the coast*> – **treacherously** *adv*, **treacherousness** *n*

treachery /ˈtrech(ə)ri‖ˈtretʃ(ə)rɪ/ *n* (an act of) violation of allegiance; (a) betrayal of trust

treacle /ˈtreekl‖ˈtriːkl/ *n, chiefly Br* **1** any of the edible grades of molasses that are obtained in the early stages of sugar refining **2** GOLDEN SYRUP [Middle French *triacle* medicinal compound used as antidote to poison, fr Latin *theriaca*, fr Greek *thēriakē* antidote against a poisonous bite, fr *thēriakos* of a wild animal, fr *thērion* wild animal, diminutive of *thēr* wild animal]

[1]**tread** /tred‖tred/ *vb* **trod** /trod‖trɒd/ *also* **treaded; trodden** /ˈtrod(ə)n‖ˈtrɒd(ə)n/, **trod** *vt* **1a** to step or walk on or over **b** to walk along **2a** to beat or press with the feet **b** to subdue or repress as if by trampling **3** *of a male bird* to copulate with **4a** to form by treading <~ *a path*> **b** to execute by stepping or dancing <~ *a measure*> ~ *vi* **1** to move on foot **2a** to set foot **b** to put one's foot <trod *on a stone*> – **treader** *n* – **tread on someone's toes/corns** to give offence or hurt sby's feelings, esp by encroaching on his/her rights – **tread water** to keep the body nearly upright in the water and the head above water by a treading motion of the feet, usu aided by the hands

[2]**tread** *n* **1** an imprint made (as if) by treading **2a** the action or an act of treading **b** the sound or manner of treading <*the heavy* ~ *of feet*> **3a** the part of a wheel or tyre that makes contact with a road or rail **b** the pattern of ridges or grooves made or cut in the face of a tyre **4** (the width of) the upper horizontal part of a step – **treadless** *adj*

[1]**treadle** /ˈtredl‖ˈtredl/ *n* a lever pressed by the foot to drive a machine (e g a sewing machine)

[2]**treadle** *vi* to operate a treadle

treadmill /ˈtredˌmil‖ˈtredˌmɪl/ *n* **1a** a mill used formerly in prison punishment that was worked by people treading on steps inside a wide wheel with a horizontal axis **b** a mill worked by an animal treading an endless belt **2** a wearisome or monotonous routine

treason /ˈtreez(ə)n‖ˈtriːz(ə)n/ *n* **1** the betrayal of a trust **2** the offence of violating the duty of allegiance owed to one's crown or government – **treasonous** *adj*

treasonable /ˈtreez(ə)nəbl‖ˈtriːz(ə)nəbl/ *adj* of or being treason – **treasonably** *adv*

[1]**treasure** /ˈtrezhə‖ˈtreʒə/ *n* **1** wealth, esp in a form which can be accumulated or hoarded <*buried* ~> **2** sthg of great worth or value; *also* sby highly valued or prized

[2]**treasure** *vt* to hold or preserve as precious <~d *those memories*>

treasurer /ˈtrezh(ə)rə‖ˈtreʒ(ə)rə/ *n* the financial officer of an organization (e g a society) – **treasurership** *n*

ˈtreasure ˌtrove /trohv‖trəʊv/ *n* treasure that anyone finds; *specif* gold or silver money, plate, or bullion which is found hidden and whose ownership is not known [Anglo-French *tresor trové*, lit., found treasure]

treasury /ˈtrezh(ə)ri‖ˈtreʒ(ə)rɪ/ *n* **1a** a place in which stores of wealth are kept **b** the place where esp public funds that have been collected are deposited and disbursed **2** *often cap* (the building which houses) a government department in charge of finances, esp the collection, management, and expenditure of public revenues **3** a source or collection of treasures <*a* ~ *of poems*>

ˈtreasury ˌbill *n* a bill issued by the treasury in return for money lent to the government

[1]**treat** /treet‖triːt/ *vi* **1** to discuss terms of accommodation or settlement **2** to deal with a matter, esp in writing – usu + *of*; fml <*a book* ~ing *of conservation*> ~ *vt* **1** to deal with <*food is plentiful and* ~ed *with imagination* – Cecil Beaton> **2a** to behave oneself towards <~ *a horse cruelly*> **b** to regard and deal

with in a specified manner – usu + *as* <~ed *it as a serious matter*> **3a** to provide with free food, drink, or entertainment – usu + *to* **b** to provide with enjoyment – usu + *to* **4** to care for or deal with medically or surgically <~ *a disease*> **5** to act on with some agent, esp so as to improve or alter **6** to deal with in speech or writing – fml – **treatable** *adj*, **treater** *n*

[2]**treat** *n* **1** an entertainment given free of charge to those invited **2** a source of pleasure or amusement; *esp* an unexpected one – **a treat** very well or successfully <*the speech went down* a treat> – infml

treatise /ˈtreetiz‖ˈtriːtɪz/ *n* a formal written exposition on a subject

treatment /ˈtreetmənt‖ˈtriːtmənt/ *n* **1a** treating sby or sthg **b** the actions customarily applied in a particular situation <*the author got the standard* ~ *of cocktail parties and interviews*> **2** a substance or technique used in treating

treaty /ˈtreeti‖ˈtriːtɪ/ *n* **1** the action of treating, esp of negotiating – chiefly in *in treaty* **2** (a document setting down) an agreement or contract made by negotiation (e g between states)

[1]**treble** /ˈtrebl‖ˈtrebl/ *n* **1a** the highest voice part in harmonic music; *also* sby, esp a boy, who performs this part **b** a member of a family of instruments having the highest range **c** a high-pitched voice or sound **d** the upper half of the whole vocal or instrumental tonal range **e** the higher part of the audio frequency range considered esp in relation to its electronic reproduction **2** sthg treble in construction, uses, amount, number, or value: e g **2a** a type of bet in which the winnings and stake from a previous race are bet on the next of 3 races **b** (a throw landing on) the middle narrow ring on a dart board counting treble the stated score

[2]**treble** *adj* **1a** having 3 parts or uses **b** TRIPLE 2 **2a** relating to or having the range or part of a treble **b** high-pitched, shrill – **trebly** *adv*

[3]**treble** *vb* to increase to 3 times the size, amount, or number

treble chance *n* a method of competing in football pools in which the chances of winning are based on the numbers of home wins, away wins, and draws

treble clef *n* a clef that places the note G above middle C on the second line of the staff

[1]**tree** /tree‖triː/ *n* **1a** a tall woody perennial plant having a single usu long and erect main stem, generally with few or no branches on its lower part **b** a shrub or herbaceous plant having the form of a tree <*rose* ~s> <*a banana* ~> **2** a device for inserting in a boot or shoe to preserve its shape when not being worn **3a** a diagram or graph that branches, usu from a single stem <*genealogical* ~> **b** a much-branched system of channels, esp in an animal or plant body <*the vascular* ~> **4** *archaic* **4a** *the* cross on which Jesus was crucified **b** *the* gallows – **treeless** *adj*, **treelike** *adj*

[2]**tree** *vt* to drive to or up a tree <~d *by a bull*>

tree fern *n* a treelike fern with a woody stem

trefoil /ˈtrefoyl, ˈtree-‖ˈtrefɔɪl, ˈtriː-/ *n* **1a** (a) clover; *broadly* any of several leguminous plants having leaves of 3 leaflets **b** a leaf consisting of 3 leaflets **2** a stylized figure or ornament in the form of a 3-lobed leaf or flower

trek /trek‖trek/ *vi or n* **-kk-** (to make) **1** a journey; *esp* an arduous one **2** *chiefly SAfr* a journey by ox wagon [Afrikaans, fr Middle Dutch *treck* pull, haul, fr *trecken* to pull, haul, migrate]

trellis /ˈtrelis‖ˈtrelɪs/ *n* a frame of latticework used as a screen or as a support for climbing plants – **trellised** *adj*

[1]**tremble** /ˈtrembl‖ˈtrembl/ *vi* **1** to shake involuntarily (e g with fear or cold) **2** to be affected (as if) by a quivering motion <*the building* ~d *from the blast*> <*his voice* ~d *with emotion*> **3** to be affected with fear or apprehension – **trembler** *n*

[2]**tremble** *n* **1a** a fit or spell of involuntary shaking or quivering **b** a tremor or series of tremors **2** *pl but sing in constr* a severe disorder of livestock, esp cattle, characterized by muscular tremors, weakness, and constipation – **trembly** *adj*

tremendous /trəˈmendəs‖trəˈmendəs/ *adj* **1** such as to arouse awe or fear **2** of extraordinary size, degree, or excellence – **tremendously** *adv*, **tremendousness** *n*

tremolo /ˈtreməloh‖ˈtreməlǝʊ/ *n, pl* **tremolos** **1a** the rapid reiteration of a musical note or of alternating notes to produce a tremulous effect **b** a perceptible rapid variation of pitch in the (singing) voice; vibrato **2** a mechanical device in an organ for causing a tremulous effect

tremor /ˈtremə‖ˈtremə/ *n* **1** a trembling or shaking, usu from physical weakness, emotional stress, or disease **2** a (slight) quivering or vibratory motion, esp of the earth **3** a thrill, quiver <*experienced a sudden* ~ *of fear*>

tremulous /ˈtremyooləs‖ˈtremjʊləs/ *adj* **1** characterized by or affected with trembling or tremors **2** uncertain, wavering – **tremulously** *adv*, **tremulousness** *n*

[1]**trench** /trench‖trentʃ/ *n* **1** a deep narrow excavation (e g for the laying of underground pipes); *esp* one used for military defence **2** a long narrow usu steep-sided depression in the ocean floor

[2]**trench** *vb* to dig a trench (in) – **trencher** *n*

trenchant /ˈtrenchənt‖ˈtrentʃənt/ *adj* **1** keen, sharp **2** vigorously effective and articulate **3a** incisive, penetrating **b** clear-cut, distinct – **trenchancy** *n*, **trenchantly** *adv*

ˈ**trench ˌcoat** *n* **1** a waterproof overcoat with a removable lining, designed for wear in trenches **2** a double-breasted raincoat with deep pockets, a belt, and epaulettes

trencher /ˈtrenchə‖ˈtrentʃə/ *n* a wooden platter for serving food

trencherman /ˈtrenchəmən‖ˈtrentʃəmən/ *n* a hearty eater

[1]**trend** /trend‖trend/ *vi* **1** to show a general tendency to move or extend in a specified direction **2** to deviate, shift <*opinions* ~ing *towards conservatism*>

[2]**trend** *n* **1** a line of general direction **2a** a prevailing tendency or inclination **b** a general movement, esp in taste or fashion

ˈ**trendˌsetter** /-ˌsetə‖-ˌsetə/ *n* sby who starts new trends, esp in fashion – **trendsetting** *n or adj*

[1]**trendy** /ˈtrendi‖ˈtrendɪ/ *adj, chiefly Br* very

fashionable; *also* characterized by uncritical adherence to the latest fashions or progressive ideas – infml

[2]**trendy** *n, chiefly Br* sby trendy – chiefly derog <*educational* trendies>

[1]**trepan** /tri'pan‖trɪ'pæn/ *n* **1** a primitive trephine **2** a heavy tool used in boring mine shafts

[2]**trepan** *vt* **-nn-** to use a trephine on (the skull)

trephine /tri'feen‖trɪ'fiːn/ *vt or n* (to operate on with, or extract by means of) a surgical instrument for cutting out circular sections, esp of bone or the cornea of the eye

trepidation /ˌtrepi'daysh(ə)n‖ˌtrepɪ'deɪʃ(ə)n/ *n* nervous agitation or apprehension

[1]**trespass** /'trespəs‖'trespəs/ *n* **1a** a violation of moral or social ethics; *esp* a sin **b** an unwarranted infringement **2** any unlawful act that causes harm to the person, property, or rights of another; *esp* wrongful entry on another's land

[2]**trespass** *vi* **1a** to err, sin **b** to make an unwarranted or uninvited intrusion *on* **2** to commit a trespass; *esp* to enter sby's property unlawfully [Middle French *trespasser*, fr Old French, lit., to go across, fr *tres* across + *passer* to pass] – **trespasser** *n*

tress /tres‖tres/ *n* **1** a plait of hair **2** a long lock of hair – usu pl

trestle /'tresl‖'tresl/ *n* **1** a (braced) frame serving as a support (e g for a table top) **2** a braced framework of timbers, piles, or girders for carrying a road or railway over a depression

trestle table *n* a table consisting of a board or boards supported on trestles

trews /troohz‖truːz/ *n pl in constr, pl* **trews** trousers; *specif* tartan trousers

tri- /trie-‖traɪ-/ *comb form* **1** three <tri*partite*>; having 3 elements or parts <tri*graph*> **2** into 3 <tri*sect*> **3a** thrice <tri*weekly*> **b** every third <tri*monthly*>

triad /'trieˌad‖'traɪˌæd/ *n* **1** a union or group of 3 (closely) related or associated persons, beings, or things **2** a chord of 3 notes consisting of a root with its third and fifth and constituting the harmonic basis of tonal music **3** *often cap* any of various Chinese secret societies, esp engaging in drug trafficking – **triadic** *adj*

[1]**trial** /trie·əl‖traɪəl/ *n* **1a** trying or testing **b** a preliminary contest or match (e g to evaluate players' skills) **2** the formal examination and determination by a competent tribunal of the matter at issue in a civil or criminal cause **3** a test of faith, patience, or stamina by suffering or temptation; *broadly* a source of vexation or annoyance **4** an experiment to test quality, value, or usefulness **5** an attempt, effort **6a** a competition of vehicle-handling skills, usu over rough ground **b** a competition in which a working animal's skills are tested <*a sheepdog* ~>

[2]**trial** *adj* **1** of a trial **2** made or done as, or used or tried out in, a test or experiment

trial run *n* an exercise to test the performance of sthg (e g a vehicle or vessel); *also* EXPERIMENT 1

triangle /'trieˌang·gl‖'traɪˌæŋgl/ *n* **1** a polygon of 3 sides and 3 angles **2** a percussion instrument consisting of a steel rod bent into the form of a triangle open at 1 angle and sounded by striking with a small metal rod **3** TRIAD 1 **4** *NAm* SET SQUARE

triangular /trie'ang·gyoolə‖traɪ'æŋgjʊlə/ *adj* **1a** (having the form) of a triangle <*a* ~ *plot of land*> **b** having a triangular base or principal surface <*a* ~ *pyramid*> **2** between or involving 3 elements, things, or people <*a* ~ *love affair*> – **triangularly** *adv*, **triangularity** *n*

Triassic /trie'asik‖traɪ'æsɪk/ *adj or n* (of or being) the earliest period of the Mesozoic era

triathlon /'trieˌathlon‖'traɪˌæθlɒn/ an athletic contest in which all contestants compete in 3 events; *specif* one involving running, swimming, and cycling – **triathlete** *n*

tribal /'triebl‖'traɪbl/ *adj* (characteristic) of a tribe – **tribally** *adv*

tribalism /'triebl̩ˌiz(ə)m‖'traɪblˌɪz(ə)m/ *n* **1** tribal consciousness and loyalty **2** strong loyalty or attachment to a group

tribe /trieb‖traɪb/ *n sing or pl in constr* **1a** a social group comprising numerous families, clans, or generations together with slaves, dependants, or adopted strangers **b** any of orig 3 political divisions of the ancient Roman people **2** a group of people having a common character or interest **3** a category in the classification of living things ranking above a genus and below a family; *also* a natural group irrespective of taxonomic rank <*the cat* ~>

tribesman /'triebzmən‖'traɪbzmən/, *fem* **tribeswoman** /-ˌwoomən‖-ˌwʊmən/ *n* a member of a tribe

tribulation /tribyoo'laysh(ə)n‖trɪbjʊ'leɪʃ(ə)n/ *n* distress or suffering resulting from oppression

tribunal /trie'byoohnl‖traɪ'bjuːnl/ *n* **1** a court of justice; *specif* a board appointed to decide disputes of a specified kind <*rent* ~> **2** sthg that arbitrates or determines <*the* ~ *of public opinion*>

tribune /'tribyoohn‖'trɪbjuːn/ *n* **1** an official of ancient Rome with the function of protecting the plebeian citizens from arbitrary action by the patrician magistrates **2** an unofficial defender of the rights of the individual – **tribuneship** *n*, **tribunate** *n*

[1]**tributary** /'tribyoot(ə)ri‖'trɪbjʊt(ə)rɪ/ *adj* **1** paying tribute to another; subject **2** paid or owed as tribute **3** providing with material or supplies

[2]**tributary** *n* **1** a tributary ruler or state **2** a stream feeding a larger stream or a lake

tribute /'tribyooht‖'trɪbjuːt/ *n* **1** a payment by one ruler or nation to another in acknowledgment of submission or as the price of protection **2a** sthg (e g a gift or formal declaration) given or spoken as a testimonial of respect, gratitude, or affection **b** evidence of the worth or effectiveness of sthg specified – chiefly in *a tribute to* <*the vote was a* ~ *to their good sense*>

[1]**trice** /tries‖traɪs/ *vt* to haul up or in and lash or secure – usu + *up*

[2]**trice** *n* a brief space of time – chiefly in *in a trice*

triceps /'trieˌseps‖'traɪˌseps/ *n, pl* **tricepses** /-seez‖-siːz/ *also* **triceps** a muscle with 3 points of attachment; *specif* the large muscle along the back of the upper arm that acts to straighten the arm at the elbow

trichina /tri'kienə‖trɪ'kaɪnə/ *n, pl* **trichinae**

/-ni‖-nı/ *also* **trichinas** a small slender nematode worm that in the larval state is parasitic in the muscles of flesh-eating mammals (e g human beings and pigs) – **trichinal** *adj*

trichinosis /ˌtrikə'nohsis‖ˌtrıkə'nəʊsıs/ *n* infestation with or disease caused by trichinae and marked esp by muscular pain, fever, and oedema

1**trick** /trik‖trık/ *n* **1a** a crafty practice or stratagem meant to deceive or defraud **b** a mischievous act <*played a harmless* ~ *on me*> **c** a deceptive, dexterous, or ingenious feat designed to puzzle or amuse <*a conjurer's* ~s> **2a** a habitual peculiarity of behaviour or manner <*had a* ~ *of stammering slightly*> **b** a deceptive appearance, esp when caused by art or sleight of hand <*a mere* ~ *of the light*> **3a** a quick or effective way of getting a result **b** a technical device or contrivance (e g of an art or craft) <~s *of the trade*> **4** the cards played in 1 round of a card game, often used as a scoring unit **5** a turn of duty at the helm

2**trick** *adj* **1** of or involving tricks or trickery <*a* ~ *question*> **2** skilled in or used for tricks <*a* ~ *horse*>

3**trick** *vt* **1** to deceive by cunning or artifice – often + *into, out of* **2** to dress or embellish showily – usu + *out* or *up* <~ed *out in a gaudy uniform*>

trickery /'trikəri‖'trıkərı/ *n* the use of crafty underhand ingenuity to deceive

1**trickle** /'trikl‖'trıkl/ *vi* **1** to flow in drops or a thin slow stream **2a** to move or go gradually or one by one <*the audience* ~d *out of the hall*> **b** to dissipate slowly <*time* ~s *away*>

2**trickle** *n* a thin slow stream or movement

trickster /'trikstə‖'trıkstə/ *n* one who tricks: e g **a** a person who defrauds others by trickery **b** a person (e g a stage magician) skilled in the performance of tricks

tricky /'triki‖'trıkı/ *adj* **1** inclined to or marked by trickery **2** containing concealed difficulties or hazards <*a* ~ *path through the swamp*> **3** requiring skill, adroitness, or caution (e g in doing or handling) <~ *gadgets*> – **trickily** *adv*, **trickiness** *n*

1**tricolour**, *NAm* **tricolor** /'trieˌkulə‖'traıˌkʌlə/ *n* a flag of 3 colours

2**tricolour, tricoloured,** *NAm* **tricolor, tricolored** *adj* having or using 3 colours

tricycle /'triesikl‖'traısıkl/ *vi or n* (to ride or drive) a 3-wheeled pedal-driven vehicle – **tricyclist** *n*

1**trident** /'tried(ə)nt‖'traıd(ə)nt/ *n* a 3-pronged (fish) spear **a** serving as the attribute of a sea god **b** used by ancient Roman gladiators

2**trident** *adj* having 3 prongs or points

tried /tried‖traıd/ *adj* **1** found to be good or trustworthy through experience or testing <*a* ~ *recipe*> **2** subjected to trials or severe provocation – often in combination <*a sorely*-tried *father*>

triennial /trie'enyəl, -ni·əl‖traı'enjəl, -nıəl/ *adj* **1** consisting of or lasting for 3 years **2** occurring every 3 years – **triennial** *n*, **triennially** *adv*

trier /'trie·ə‖'traıə/ *n* **1** sby who makes an effort or perseveres **2** an implement (e g a tapered hollow tube) used in obtaining samples of bulk material, esp foodstuffs, for examination and testing

1**trifle** /'triefl‖'traıfl/ *n* **1** sthg of little value or importance; *esp* an insignificant amount (e g of money) **2** *chiefly Br* a dessert typically consisting of sponge cake soaked in wine (e g sherry), spread with jam or jelly, and topped with custard and whipped cream – **a trifle** to some small degree <a trifle *annoyed at the delay*>

2**trifle** *vi* **1** to act heedlessly or frivolously – often + *with* <*not a woman to be* ~d *with*> **2** to handle sthg idly ~*vt* to spend or waste in trifling or on trifles <trifling *his time away*> – **trifler** *n*

trifling /'triefling‖'traıflıŋ/ *adj* lacking in significance or solid worth: e g **a** frivolous **b** trivial, insignificant

1**trigger** /'trigə‖'trıgə/ *n* **1** a device (e g a lever) connected with a catch as a means of release; *esp* the tongue of metal in a firearm which when pressed allows the gun to fire **2** a stimulus that initiates a reaction or signal in an electronic apparatus – **trigger** *adj*, **triggered** *adj*

2**trigger** *vt* **1a** to release, activate, or fire by means of a trigger **b** to cause the explosion of <~ *a missile with a proximity fuse*> **2** to initiate or set off as if by pulling a trigger <*an indiscreet remark that* ~ed *a fight*> – often + *off* ~*vi* to release a mechanical trigger

'**trigger-ˌhappy** *adj* **1** irresponsible in the use of firearms **2a** aggressively belligerent **b** too prompt in one's response

trigonometric function /ˌtrigənə'metrik‖ˌtrıgənə'metrık/ *n* **1** a function (specif the sine, cosine, tangent, cotangent, secant, or cosecant) of an arc or angle most simply expressed in terms of the ratios of pairs of sides of a right-angled triangle **2** the inverse (e g the arc sine) of a trigonometric function

trigonometry /ˌtrigə'nomətri‖ˌtrıgə'nɒmətrı/ *n* the study of the properties of triangles and trigonometric functions and of their applications [deriv of Greek *trigōnon* triangle (fr *tri-* three + *gōnia* angle) + *metrein* to measure (fr *metron* measure)] – **trigonometric** *also* **trigonometrical** *adj*

trilateral /ˌtrie'lat(ə)rəl‖ˌtraı'læt(ə)rəl/ *adj* having 3 sides <*a triangle is* ~> – **trilaterally** *adv*

trilby /'trilbi‖'trılbı/ *n, chiefly Br* a soft felt hat with an indented crown [fr such a hat having been worn in the London stage version of *Trilby*, novel by George Du Maurier (1834-96), English artist & writer]

trilingual /ˌtrie'ling·gwəl‖ˌtraı'lıŋgwəl/ *adj* **1** of, containing, or expressed in 3 languages **2** using or able to use 3 languages, esp with the fluency of a native – **trilingually** *adv*

1**trill** /tril‖trıl/ *n* **1** the alternation of 2 musical notes 2 semitones apart **2** a sound resembling a musical trill **3** (a speech sound made by) the rapid vibration of the tip of the tongue against the ridge of flesh behind the front teeth, or of the uvula against the back of the tongue

2**trill** *vt* to utter as or with a trill ~*vi* to play or sing with a trill – **triller** *n*

trillion /'trilyən‖'trıljən/ *n* **1a** *Br* a million million millions (10^{18}) **b** *chiefly NAm* a million millions (10^{12}) **2** an indefinitely large number; a zillion – often pl with sing. meaning – **trillion**

adj, **trillionth** *adj or n*

trilobite /'trielə,biet‖'traɪlə,baɪt/ *n* any of numerous extinct Palaeozoic marine arthropods that had a 3-lobed body

trilogy /'triləji‖'trɪlədʒɪ/ *n* a group of 3 closely related works (e g novels)

[1]**trim** /trim‖trɪm/ *vb* **-mm-** *vt* **1** to decorate (e g clothes) with ribbons, lace, or ornaments; adorn **2** to make trim and neat, esp by cutting or clipping **3** to remove (as if) by cutting <*~med thousands from the running costs of the department*> **4a** to cause (e g a ship, aircraft, or submarine) to assume a desired position by arrangement of ballast, cargo, passengers, etc **b** to adjust (e g a sail) to a desired position *~vi* to maintain a neutral attitude towards opposing parties or favour each equally

[2]**trim** *adj* **-mm-** appearing neat or in good order; compact or clean-cut in outline or structure <*~ houses*> <*a ~ figure*> – **trimly** *adv*, **trimness** *n*

[3]**trim** *n* **1** the readiness or fitness of a person or thing for action or use; *esp* physical fitness **2a** one's clothing or appearance **b** material used for decoration or trimming **c** the decorative accessories of a motor vehicle **3a** the position of a ship or boat, esp with reference to the horizontal **b** the inclination of an aircraft or spacecraft in flight with reference to a fixed point (e g the horizon), esp with the controls in some neutral position **4** (sthg removed by) trimming

trimaran /'triemə,ran‖'traɪmə,ræn/ *n* a sailing vessel used for cruising or racing that has 3 hulls side by side

trimmer /'trimə‖'trɪmə/ *n* **1** a short beam or rafter fitted at 1 side of an opening to support the free ends of floor joists, studs, or rafters **2** a person who modifies his/her policy, position, or opinions out of expediency

trimming /'triming‖'trɪmɪŋ/ *n* **1** *pl* pieces cut off in trimming sthg; scraps **2a** a decorative accessory or additional item (e g on the border of a garment) that serves to finish or complete **b** an additional garnish or accompaniment to a main item – usu pl

trinitrotoluene /,trie,nietroh'tolyoo,een‖,traɪ,naɪtrəʊ'tɒljʊ,iːn/ *n* an inflammable derivative of toluene used as a high explosive and in chemical synthesis

Trinity /'trinəti‖'trɪnətɪ/ *n* **1** the unity of Father, Son, and Holy Spirit as 3 persons in 1 Godhead according to Christian theology **2** *not cap* TRIAD 1 **3** the Sunday after Whitsunday observed as a festival in honour of the Trinity [Old French *trinité*, fr Late Latin *trinitas* state of being threefold, fr Latin *trinus* triple, fr *trini* three each]

trinket /'tringkit‖'trɪŋkɪt/ *n* a small (trifling) article; *esp* an ornament or piece of (cheap) jewellery – **trinketry** *n*

trio /'tree·oh‖'triːəʊ/ *n, pl* **trios** **1a** (a musical composition for) 3 instruments, voices, or performers **b** the secondary or episodic division of a minuet, scherzo, etc **2** *sing or pl in constr* a group or set of 3

[1]**trip** /trip‖trɪp/ *vb* **-pp-** *vi* **1a** to dance, skip, or walk with light quick steps **b** to proceed smoothly, lightly, and easily; flow <*words that ~ off the tongue*> **2** to catch the foot against sthg so as to stumble **3** to make a mistake or false step (e g in morality or accuracy) **4** to stumble in articulation when speaking **5** to make a journey **6** to become operative or activated <*the circuit breaker ~s when the voltage gets too high*> **7** to get high on a psychedelic drug (e g LSD); TURN ON 2a – slang *~ vt* **1a** to cause to stumble **b** to cause to fail **2** to detect in a fault or blunder; CATCH OUT – usu + *up* **3** to raise (an anchor) from the bottom so as to hang free **4** to release or operate (a device or mechanism), esp by releasing a catch or producing an electrical signal **5** to perform (e g a dance) lightly or nimbly – archaic except in *trip the light fantastic* ***USE*** (*vi 2, 3, & 4; vt 1*) often + *up*

[2]**trip** *n* **1a** a voyage, journey, or excursion **b** a single round or tour (e g on a business errand) **2** an error, mistake **3** a quick light step **4** a faltering step caused by stumbling **5** a device (e g a catch) for tripping a mechanism **6a** an intense, often visionary experience undergone by sby who has taken a psychedelic drug (e g LSD) **b** a highly charged emotional experience <*his divorce was a really bad ~*> **7** a self-indulgent or absorbing course of action, way of behaving, or frame of mind <*on a nostalgia ~*> <*gave up the whole super-star ~*> ***USE*** (*6&7*) infml

tripartite /trie'pahtiet‖traɪ'pɑːtaɪt/ *adj* **1** divided into or composed of 3 (corresponding) parts **2** made between or involving 3 parties <*a ~ treaty*> – **tripartitely** *adv*, **tripartition** *n*

tripe /triep‖traɪp/ *n* **1** the stomach tissue of an ox, cow, etc for use as food **2** sthg inferior, worthless, or offensive – infml

[1]**triple** /'tripl‖'trɪpl/ *vb* to make or become 3 times as great or as many

[2]**triple** *n* **1** a triple sum, quantity, or number **2** a combination, group, or series of 3

[3]**triple** *adj* **1** having 3 units or members **2** being 3 times as great or as many **3** marked by 3 beats per bar of music <*~ metre*> **4** having units of 3 components – **triply** *adv*

triple jump *n* an athletic field event consisting of a jump for distance combining a hop, a step, and a jump in succession

triplet /'triplit‖'trɪplɪt/ *n* **1** a unit of 3 lines of verse **2** a combination, set, or group of 3 **3** any of 3 children or animals born at 1 birth **4** a group of 3 musical notes performed in the time of 2 of the same value

triplex /'tripleks, 'trie-‖'trɪpleks, 'traɪ-/ *adj* threefold, triple

[1]**triplicate** /'triplikət‖'trɪplɪkət/ *adj* **1** consisting of or existing in 3 corresponding or identical parts or examples <*~ invoices*> **2** being the third of 3 things exactly alike <*file the ~ copy*>

[2]**triplicate** /'triplikayt‖'trɪplɪkeɪt/ *vt* **1** to make triple **2** to prepare in triplicate – **triplication** *n*

[3]**triplicate** /'triplikət‖'trɪplɪkət/ *n* **1** any of 3 things exactly alike; *specif* any of 3 identical copies **2** three copies all alike – + *in* <*typed in ~*>

tripod /'trie,pod‖'traɪ,pɒd/ *n* **1** a stool, table, or vessel (e g a cauldron) with 3 legs **2** a 3-legged stand (e g for a camera) – **tripodal** *adj*

tripos /'triepos‖'traɪpɒs/ *n* either part of the

honours examination for the Cambridge BA degree

tripper /'tripə‖'trɪpə/ *n, chiefly Br* one who goes on an outing or pleasure trip, esp one lasting only 1 day – often used disparagingly

trippingly /'tripingli‖'trɪpɪŋlɪ/ *adv* nimbly; *also* fluently

triptych /'trip,tik‖'trɪp,tɪk/ *n* a picture or carving on 3 panels side by side; *esp* an altarpiece consisting of a central panel hinged to 2 flanking panels that fold over it [Greek *triptychos* having 3 folds, fr *tri-* three + *ptychē* fold]

'trip ,wire *n* a concealed wire placed near the ground that is used to trip up an intruder or to actuate an explosive or warning device when pulled

trireme /'trie,reem‖'traɪ,ri:m/ *n* a galley with 3 banks of oars

trisect /trie'sekt, '--‖traɪ'sekt, '--/ *vt* to divide into 3 (equal) parts – **trisection** *n*, **trisector** *n*

trite /triet‖traɪt/ *adj* hackneyed from much use – **tritely** *adv*, **triteness** *n*

¹triumph /'trie,um(p)f‖'traɪ,ʌm(p)f/ *n* **1** a ceremony attending the entering of ancient Rome by a general who had won a decisive victory over a foreign enemy **2** the joy or exultation of victory or success **3** (a) notable success, victory, or achievement – **triumphal** *adj*

²triumph *vi* **1** to celebrate victory or success boastfully or exultantly **2** to obtain victory – often + *over*

triumphant /trie'um(p)fənt‖traɪ'ʌm(p)fənt/ *adj* **1** victorious, conquering **2** rejoicing in or celebrating victory – **triumphantly** *adv*

triumvir /trie'umvə, -viə‖traɪ'ʌmvə, -vɪə/ *n, pl* **triumvirs** *also* **triumviri** /-vərie‖-vəraɪ/ a member of a commission or ruling body of 3 – **triumviral** *adj*

triumvirate /trie'umvirət‖traɪ'ʌmvɪrət/ *n* **1** the office of triumvirs **2** *sing or pl in constr* **2a** a body of triumvirs **b** a group of 3

trivalent /trie'vaylənt‖traɪ'veɪlənt/ *adj* having a valency of 3

trivet /'trivit‖'trɪvɪt/ *n* **1** a three-legged (iron) stand for holding cooking vessels over or by a fire; *also* a bracket that hooks onto a grate for this purpose **2** a (metal) stand with 3 feet for holding a hot dish at table

trivia /'trivi·ə‖'trɪvɪə/ *n pl but sing or pl in constr* unimportant matters or details

trivial /'trivi·əl‖'trɪvɪəl/ *adj* **1** commonplace, ordinary **2a** of little worth or importance; insignificant **b** of or being the mathematically simplest case <*a ~ solution to an equation*> [Latin *trivialis* commonplace, vulgar, fr *trivium* road junction, fr *tri-* three + *via* way] – **trivialness** *n*, **trivially** *adv*, **trivialize** *vt*, **trivialization** *n*, **triviality** *n*

trochee /'troh,kee‖'trəʊ,ki:/ *n* a metrical foot consisting of 1 long or stressed syllable followed by 1 short or unstressed syllable (e g in *apple*) – **trochaic** *adj or n*

trod /trod‖trɒd/ *past of* TREAD

trodden /'trod(ə)n‖'trɒd(ə)n/ *past part of* TREAD

troglodyte /'trogladiet‖'trɒglədaɪt/ *n* **1** one who lives in a cave **2** a person resembling a troglodyte, esp in being solitary or unsocial or in having primitive or outmoded ideas **3** APE 1 [Latin *troglodytae* (pl), fr Greek *trōglodytai*, fr *trōglē* hole, cave + *dyein* to enter] – **troglodytic** *adj*

troika /'troykə‖'trɔɪkə/ *n* **1** (a Russian vehicle drawn by) a team of 3 horses abreast **2** TRIAD 1; *esp* an administrative or ruling body of 3 people

Trojan /'trohj(ə)n‖'trəʊdʒ(ə)n/ *n* **1** a native of Troy **2** one who shows qualities (e g pluck or endurance) attributed to the defenders of ancient Troy – chiefly in *work like a Trojan* – **Trojan** *adj*

¹troll /trohl, trol‖trəʊl, trɒl/ *vt* **1** to sing loudly **2** to fish for or in with a hook and line drawn through the water behind a moving boat ~ *vi* **1** to sing or play an instrument in a jovial manner **2** to fish, esp by drawing a hook through the water **3** to move about; stroll, saunter – **troller** *n*

²troll *n* (a line with) a lure used in trolling

³troll *n* a dwarf or giant of Germanic folklore inhabiting caves or hills

trolley *also* **trolly** /'troli‖'trɒlɪ/ *n* **1** a device (e g a grooved wheel or skid) attached to a pole that collects current from an overhead electric wire for powering an electric vehicle **2** *chiefly Br* **2a** a shelved stand mounted on castors used for conveying sthg (e g food or books) **b** a basket on wheels that is pushed or pulled by hand and used for carrying goods (e g purchases in a supermarket) **3** *Br* a small 4-wheeled wagon that runs on rails **4** *NAm* TRAM b

'trolley,bus /-,bus‖-,bʌs/ *n* an electrically propelled bus running on a road and drawing power from 2 overhead wires via a trolley

trollop /'troləp‖'trɒləp/ *n* a slovenly or immoral woman – **trollopy** *adj*

trombone /trom'bohn‖trɒm'bəʊn/ *n* a brass instrument consisting of a long cylindrical metal tube with a movable slide for varying the pitch and a usual range 1 octave lower than that of the trumpet – **trombonist** *n*

¹troop /troohp‖tru:p/ *n* **1** *sing or pl in constr* **1a** a military subunit (e g of cavalry) corresponding to an infantry platoon **b** a collection of people or things **c** a unit of scouts under a leader **2** *pl* the armed forces

²troop *vi* to move in a group, esp in a way that suggests regimentation <*everyone* ~ed *into the meeting*>

trooper /'troohpə‖'tru:pə/ *n* **1a** a cavalry soldier; *esp* a private soldier in a cavalry or armoured regiment **b** the horse of a cavalry soldier **2** *chiefly NAm & Austr* a mounted policeman

trope /trohp‖trəʊp/ *n* a figurative use of a word or expression

trophy /'trohfi‖'trəʊfɪ/ *n* **1a** a memorial of an ancient Greek or Roman victory raised on or near the field of battle **b** a representation of such a memorial (e g on a medal); *also* an architectural ornament representing a group of military weapons **2** sthg gained or awarded in victory or conquest, esp when preserved as a memorial

tropic /'tropik‖'trɒpɪk/ *n* **1** either of the 2 small circles of the celestial sphere on each side of and parallel to the equator at a distance of $23^1/_2$ degrees, which the sun reaches at its greatest declination N or S **2a(1)** TROPIC OF CANCER **a(2)** TROPIC OF CAPRICORN **b** *pl, often cap* the region between the 2 terrestrial tropics

tropical /ˈtropikl‖ˈtrɒpɪkl/ *adj* **1** *also* **tropic** of, occurring in, or characteristic of the tropics **2** *of a sign of the zodiac* beginning at either of the tropics – **tropically** *adv*

tropic of Cancer /ˌtropik əv ˈkansə‖ˌtrɒpɪk əv ˈkænsə/ *n* the parallel of latitude that is $23^1/_2$ degrees N of the equator

tropic of Capricorn /ˌtropik əv ˈkapri-ˌkawn‖ˌtrɒpɪk əv ˈkæprɪˌkɔːn/ *n* the parallel of latitude that is $23^1/_2$ degrees S of the equator

¹trot /trot‖trɒt/ *n* **1** a moderately fast gait of a horse or other quadruped in which the legs move in diagonal pairs **2** an instance or the pace of trotting or proceeding briskly **3** *pl but sing or pl in constr* diarrhoea – usu + *the*; humor – **on the trot** in succession – infml

²trot *vb* **-tt-** *vi* **1** to ride, drive, or proceed at a trot **2** to proceed briskly ~ *vt* **1** to cause to go at a trot **2** to traverse at a trot

Trot *n* a Trotskyite; *broadly* any adherent of the extreme left – chiefly derog

troth /trohth‖trəʊθ/ *n, archaic* one's pledged word; *also* betrothal – chiefly in *plight one's troth*

trot out *vt* **1** to produce or bring forward (as if) for display or scrutiny **2** to produce or utter in a trite or predictable manner <trotted out *all the old clichés*>

Trotskyism /ˈtrotskiˌiz(ə)m‖ˈtrɒtskɪˌɪz(ə)m/ *n* the political, economic, and social principles advocated by Trotsky; *esp* adherence to the concept of permanent worldwide revolution [Leon *Trotsky* (1879-1940), Russian Communist leader] – **Trotskyist, Trotskyite** *n or adj*

trotter /ˈtrotə‖ˈtrɒtə/ *n* **1** a horse trained for trotting races **2** the foot of an animal, esp a pig, used as food

troubadour /ˈtroohbədaw, -dooə‖ˈtruːbədɔː, -dʊə/ *n* any of a class of lyric poets and poet-musicians, chiefly in France in the 11th to 13th c, whose major theme was courtly love

¹trouble /ˈtrubl‖ˈtrʌbl/ *vt* **1a** to agitate mentally or spiritually; worry **b** to produce physical disorder or discomfort in <~d *with deafness*> **c** to put to exertion or inconvenience <*could I ~ you to close the door?*> **2** to make (e g the surface of water) turbulent ~ *vi* **1** to become mentally agitated <*refused to ~ over trifles*> **2** to make an effort; be at pains <*don't ~ to come*>

²trouble *n* **1a** being troubled **b** an instance of distress, annoyance, or disturbance **2** a cause of disturbance, annoyance, or distress: e g **2a** public unrest or demonstrations of dissatisfaction – often pl with sing. meaning **b** effort made; exertion **c(1)** a disease, ailment, or condition of physical distress <*heart ~*> **c(2)** a malfunction <*engine ~*> **d** pregnancy out of wedlock – chiefly in *in/into trouble* **3** a problem, snag <*that's the ~ with these newfangled ideas*> – **troublous** *adj, archaic or poetic*

ˈtroubleˌmaker /-ˌmaykə‖-ˌmeɪkə/ *n* one who causes trouble

ˈtroubleˌshooter /-ˌshoohtə‖-ˌʃuːtə/ *n* **1** a skilled workman employed to locate faults and make repairs in machinery and technical equipment **2** one who specializes or is expert in resolving disputes – **troubleshooting** *n*

ˈtroublesome /-s(ə)m‖-s(ə)m/ *adj* giving trouble or anxiety; annoying or burdensome <*a ~ cough*> <*a ~ neighbour*> – **troublesomely** *adv*, **troublesomeness** *n*

trough /trof‖trɒf/ *n* **1a** a long shallow receptacle for the drinking water or feed of farm animals **b** a long narrow container used for domestic or industrial purposes **2a** a conduit, drain, or channel for water **b** a long narrow or shallow trench between waves, ridges, etc **3a** the (region round the) lowest point of a regularly recurring cycle of a varying quantity (e g a sine wave) **b** an elongated area of low atmospheric pressure **c** a low point (in a trade cycle)

trounce /trowns‖traʊns/ *vt* **1** to thrash or punish severely **2** to defeat decisively

troupe /troohp‖truːp/ *n* a company or troop (of theatrical performers)

trouper /ˈtroohpə‖ˈtruːpə/ *n* **1** a member of a troupe **2** a loyal or dependable person

trousers /ˈtrowzəz‖ˈtraʊzəz/ *n pl* a 2-legged outer garment extending from the waist to the ankle or sometimes only to the knee [alteration of earlier *trouse*, fr Scottish Gaelic *triubhas*] – **trouser** *adj*

trousseau /ˈtroohsoh‖ˈtruːsəʊ/ *n, pl* **trousseaux, trousseaus** /-sohz‖-səʊz/ the personal outfit of a bride including clothes, accessories, etc [French, diminutive of *trousse* bundle, fr *trousser* to truss]

trout /trowt‖traʊt/ *n* **1** any of various food and sport fishes of the salmon family restricted to cool clear fresh waters; *esp* any of various Old World or New World fishes some of which ascend rivers from the sea to breed **2** an ugly unpleasant old woman – slang

trove /trohv‖trəʊv/ *n* TREASURE TROVE

¹trowel /ˈtrowəl‖ˈtraʊəl/ *n* any of various smooth-bladed hand tools used to apply, spread, shape, or smooth loose or soft material; *also* a scoop-shaped or flat-bladed garden tool for taking up and setting small plants

²trowel *vt* **-ll-** (*NAm* **-l-, -ll-**) to smooth, mix, or apply (as if) with a trowel

ˈtroy ˌweight /troy‖trɔɪ/ *n* the series of units of weight based on the pound of 12oz and the ounce of 20 pennyweights or 480 grains

truant /ˈtrooh·ənt‖ˈtruːənt/ *n* one who shirks duty; *esp* one who stays away from school without permission – **truant** *adj*, **truanting** *n*, **truancy** *n*

truce /troohs‖truːs/ *n* a (temporary) suspension of fighting by agreement of opposing forces

¹truck /truk‖trʌk/ *vt* to give in exchange; barter ~ *vi* **1** to trade, barter **2** to negotiate or traffic, esp in an underhand way

²truck *n* **1** (commodities suitable for) barter or small trade **2** close association; dealings – chiefly in *have no truck with* **3** payment of wages in goods instead of cash **4** miscellaneous small articles; *also* rubbish – infml

³truck *n* **1** a small strong wheel **2** a small wooden cap at the top of a flagstaff or masthead, usu having holes for flag or signal halyards **3a** a usu 4- or 6-wheeled vehicle for moving heavy loads; a lorry **b** a usu 2- or 4-wheeled cart for carrying heavy articles (e g luggage at railway stations) **4** *Br* an open railway goods wagon

[4]**truck** *vt* to load or transport on a truck ~*vi, NAm* to be employed as a lorry driver – **truckage** *n*

truckle /ˈtrukl‖ˈtrʌkl/ *vi* to act in a subservient or obsequious manner – usu + *to* – **truckler** *n*

ˈ**truckle ˌbed** *n* a low bed, usu on castors, that can be slid under a higher bed

truculent /ˈtrukyoolənt‖ˈtrʌkjʊlənt/ *adj* aggressively self-assertive; belligerent – **truculence, truculency** *n*, **truculently** *adv*

[1]**trudge** /truj‖trʌdʒ/ *vb* to walk steadily and laboriously (along or over) – **trudger** *n*

[2]**trudge** *n* a long tiring walk

[1]**true** /trooh‖truː/ *adj* **1** steadfast, loyal <*a ~ friend*> **2a** in accordance with fact or reality <*a ~ story*> **b** essential <*the ~ nature of socialist economics*> **c** being that which is the case rather than what is claimed or assumed <*the ~ dimensions of the problem*> **d** consistent, conforming <*~ to expectations*> <*~ to type*> **3a(1)** properly so called <*the ~ faith*> **a(2)** genuine, real <*~ love*> **b(1)** possessing the basic characters of and belonging to the same natural group as <*a whale is a ~ but not a typical mammal*> **b(2)** typical <*the ~ cats*> **4a** accurately fitted, adjusted, balanced, or formed **b** exact, accurate <*a ~ voice*> <*a ~ copy*> **5** determined with reference to the earth's axis rather than the magnetic poles <*~ north*>

[2]**true** *n* the state of being accurate (e g in alignment or adjustment) – chiefly in *in/out of true*

[3]**true** *vt* to bring or restore to a desired mechanical accuracy or form – **truer** *n*

[4]**true** *adv* **1** TRULY 1 **2a** without deviation; straight **b** without variation from type <*breed ~*>

ˌ**true-ˈblue** *adj* staunchly loyal; *specif, Br* being a staunch supporter of the Conservative party – **true-blue** *n*

ˈ**trueˌlove** /-ˌluv‖-ˌlʌv/ *n* a sweetheart – poetic

truffle /ˈtrufl‖ˈtrʌfl/ *n* **1** (any of several European fungi with) a usu dark and wrinkled edible fruiting body that grows under the ground and is eaten as a delicacy **2** a rich soft creamy sweet made with chocolate – **truffled** *adj*

trug /trug‖trʌg/ *n, Br* a shallow rectangular wooden basket for carrying garden produce

truism /ˈtroohˌiz(ə)m‖ˈtruːˌɪz(ə)m/ *n* an undoubted or self-evident truth – **truistic** *adj*

truly /ˈtroohli‖ˈtruːlɪ/ *adv* **1** in accordance with fact or reality; truthfully **2** accurately, exactly **3a** indeed **b** genuinely, sincerely <*he was ~ sorry*> **4** properly, duly <*well and ~ beaten*>

[1]**trump** /trump‖trʌmp/ *n* a trumpet (call) – chiefly poetic

[2]**trump** *n* **1a** a card of a suit any of whose cards will win over a card that is not of this suit **b** *pl* the suit whose cards are trumps for a particular hand **2** a worthy and dependable person – infml [alteration of *triumph*] – **come/turn up trumps** to prove unexpectedly helpful or generous

[3]**trump** *vb* to play a trump on (a card or trick) when another suit was led

ˈ**trump ˌcard** *n* **1** [2]TRUMP 1a **2** a telling or decisive factor; a clincher – esp in *play one's trump card*

trumpery /ˈtrumpəri‖ˈtrʌmpərɪ/ *adj* **1** worthless, useless **2** cheap, tawdry – **trumpery** *n*

[1]**trumpet** /ˈtrumpit‖ˈtrʌmpɪt/ *n* **1** a wind instrument consisting of a usu metal tube, a cup-shaped mouthpiece, and a flared bell **2** sthg that resembles (the flared bell or loud penetrating sound of) a trumpet: e g **2a** a megaphone **b** the loud cry of an elephant – **trumpeter** *n*, **trumpetlike** *adj*

[2]**trumpet** *vi* **1** to blow a trumpet **2** to make a sound as of a trumpet ~*vt* to sound or proclaim loudly (as if) on a trumpet

trump up *vt* to concoct, fabricate <*charges trumped up by the police*>

[1]**truncate** /ˈtrungkayt, -ˈ-‖ˈtrʌŋkeɪt, -ˈ-/ *vt* to shorten (as if) by cutting off a part – **truncation** *n*

[2]ˈ**truncate** *adj* having the end square or even <*the ~ leaves of the tulip tree*>

truncheon /ˈtrunchən‖ˈtrʌntʃən/ *n* **1** a staff of office or authority **2** a short club carried esp by policemen

[1]**trundle** /ˈtrundl‖ˈtrʌndl/ *n* a small wheel or roller

[2]**trundle** *vb* to move heavily or pull along (as if) on wheels

ˈ**trundle ˌbed** *n* TRUCKLE BED

trunk /trungk‖trʌŋk/ *n* **1a** the main stem of a tree as distinguished from branches and roots **b** the human or animal body apart from the head and limbs **c** the main or central part of sthg (e g an artery, nerve, or column) **2** a large rigid box used usu for transporting clothing and personal articles **3** a proboscis; *esp* the long muscular proboscis of the elephant **4** *pl* men's usu close-fitting shorts worn chiefly for swimming or sports **5** a chute, shaft, or similar (major) supply channel **6** TRUNK LINE **7** *NAm* [3]BOOT 4

ˈ**trunk ˌcall** *n* a telephone call made on a trunk line

ˈ**trunk ˌline** *n* a major route of communication: e g **a** a main line of a railway system **b** a telephone line between towns

ˈ**trunk ˌroad** *n* a road of primary importance, esp for long distance travel

[1]**truss** /trus‖trʌs/ *vt* **1a** to secure tightly; bind – often + *up* **b** to bind the wings or legs of (a fowl) closely in preparation for cooking **2** to support or stiffen (e g a bridge) with a truss

[2]**truss** *n* **1a** a corbel; BRACKET 1 **b** a usu triangular assemblage of members (e g beams) forming a rigid framework (e g in a roof or bridge) **2** a device worn to reduce a hernia by pressure **3** a compact flower or fruit cluster (e g of tomatoes) – **trussing** *n*

[1]**trust** /trust‖trʌst/ *n* **1** confident belief in or reliance on (the ability, character, honesty, etc of) sby or sthg <*take it on ~*> **2** financial credit **3a** a property interest held by one person for the benefit of another **b** a combination of companies formed by a legal agreement **4a** a charge or duty imposed in faith or as a condition of some relationship **b** responsible charge or office <*in a position of ~*> **c** care, custody <*child committed to his ~*> – **trustful** *adj*, **trustfully** *adv* – **in trust** in the care or possession of a trustee

[2]**trust** *vi* **1** to place confidence; depend <*~ in God*> **2** to be confident; hope <*we'll see you soon, I ~*> ~ *vt* **1a** to place in sby's care or

keeping **b** to permit to do or be without fear or misgiving <*won't ~ it out of his sight*> **2a** to place confidence in; rely on – also used ironically <*~ him to arrive late!*> **b** to expect or hope, esp confidently <*I ~ you are well?*> **3** to extend credit to – **trustable** *adj*, **trusting** *adj*, **trustingly** *adv*

trustee /tru'stee‖trʌ'sti:/ *n* **1** a country charged with the supervision of a trust territory **2a** a natural or legal person appointed to administer property in trust for a beneficiary **b** any of a body of people administering the affairs of a company or institution and occupying a position of trust – **trusteeship** *n*

'trust,worthy /-,wuhdhi‖-,wɜ:ðɪ/ *adj* dependable, reliable – **trustworthily** *adv*, **trustworthiness** *n*

¹trusty /'trusti‖'trʌstɪ/ *adj* trustworthy – **trustily** *adv*, **trustiness** *n*

²trusty *n* a trusted person; *specif* a convict considered trustworthy and allowed special privileges

truth /troohth‖tru:θ/ *n, pl* **truths** /troohdhz, troohths‖tru:ðz, tru:θs/ **1** sincerity, honesty **2a(1)** the state or quality of being true or factual <*there's ~ in what she says*> **a(2)** reality, actuality <*~ is stranger than fiction*> **a(3)** *often cap* a transcendent (e g spiritual) reality **b** a judgment, proposition, idea, or body of statements that is (accepted as) true <*scientific ~s*> **3** conformity to an original or to a standard – **truthful** *adj*, **truthfully** *adv*, **truthfulness** *n*

¹try /trie‖traɪ/ *vt* **1a** to investigate judicially **b** to conduct the trial of **2a(1)** to test by experiment or trial – often + *out* **a(2)** to investigate the state, capabilities, or potential of, esp for a particular purpose <*~ the shop next door*> **b** to subject to sthg that tests the patience or endurance **3** to melt down and obtain in a pure state – usu + *out* <*~ out whale oil from blubber*> **4** to make an attempt at *~vi* to make an attempt – **try for size** to test for appropriateness or fittingness – **try one's hand** to make an attempt for the first time

²try *n* **1** an experimental trial; an attempt **2** a score in rugby that is made by touching down the ball behind the opponent's goal line and that entitles the scoring side to attempt a kick at the goal for additional points

try on *vt* **1** to put on (a garment) in order to examine the fit or appearance **2** *Br* to attempt to impose on sby <*don't go* trying *anything* on *with me, mate*> – infml – **try-on** *n*

tryout /'trie,owt‖'traɪ,aʊt/ *n* an experimental performance or demonstration; *specif* a test of the ability of sby (e g an actor or athlete) or sthg to meet requirements

¹tryst /trist, triest‖trɪst, traɪst/ *n* **1** an agreement, esp by lovers, to meet **2** an appointed meeting or meeting place *USE* poetic

²tryst *vi, chiefly Scot* to make a tryst – poetic

tsar, czar, tzar /zah‖zɑ:/ *n* **1** a male ruler of Russia before 1917 **2** one having great power or authority [Russian *tsar'*, fr Gothic *kaisar*, fr Latin *Caesar*, title of Roman emperors, fr Gaius Julius Caesar (100-44 BC), Roman statesman] – **tsarism** *n*, **tsarist** *n or adj*

tsarina /zah'reenə‖zɑ:'ri:nə/ *n* the wife of a tsar

tsetse /'tetsi, 'tsetsi‖'tetsɪ, 'tsetsɪ/, **'tsetse ,fly** *n, pl* **tsetse, tsetses** any of several two-winged flies that occur in Africa south of the Sahara desert and transmit diseases, esp sleeping sickness, by bites

'T-,shirt /tee‖ti:/ *n* a collarless upper garment of light stretchy fabric for casual wear

'T ,square *n* a ruler with a crosspiece or head at 1 end used in making parallel lines

tub /tub‖tʌb/ *n* **1a** any of various wide low often round vessels typically made of wood, metal, or plastic, and used industrially or domestically (e g for washing clothes) **b** a small round (plastic) container in which cream, ice cream, etc may be bought **2** BATH 2b **3** an old or slow boat – infml – **tubful** *n*

tuba /'tyoohbə‖'tju:bə/ *n* a large brass instrument having valves, a conical tube, a cup-shaped mouthpiece, and a usual range an octave lower than that of the euphonium

tubby /'tubi‖'tʌbɪ/ *adj* podgy, fat – **tubbiness** *n*

tube /tyoohb‖tju:b/ *n* **1a** a hollow elongated cylinder; *esp* one to convey fluids **b** a slender channel within a plant or animal body **2** any of various usu cylindrical structures or devices: e g **2a** a small cylindrical container of soft metal or plastic sealed at one end, and fitted with a cap at the other, from which a paste is dispensed by squeezing **b** TEST TUBE **c** the basically cylindrical section between the mouthpiece and bell of a wind instrument **3** ELECTRON TUBE; *specif, chiefly NAm* a thermionic valve **4** *Br* (a train running in) an underground railway running through deep bored tunnels **5** *chiefly Austr* a can of beer – infml

'tubeless /-lis‖-lɪs/ *adj* being a pneumatic tyre that does not depend on an inner tube to be airtight

tuber /'tyoohbə‖'tju:bə/ *n* (a root resembling) a short fleshy usu underground stem (e g a potato) that is potentially able to produce a new plant – **tuberous** *adj*

tubercle /'tyoohb·ə,kl‖'tju:bə,kl/ *n* **1** a small knobby prominence, esp on a plant or animal **2** a bacterium al lump in an organ or in the skin; *esp* one characteristic of tuberculosis – **tubercled** *adj*, **tuberculate** *also* **tuberculated** *adj*

tubercular /tyoo'buhkyoolə‖tjʊ'bɜ:kjʊlə/ *adj* **1** of, resembling, or being a tubercle **2** of or affected with tuberculosis

tuberculosis /tyoo,buhkyoo'lohsis, tə-‖tjʊ-,bɜ:kjʊ'ləʊsɪs, tə-/ *n* a serious infectious disease of human beings and other vertebrates caused by a bacterium and characterized by fever and the formation of abnormal lumps in the body – **tuberculoid** *adj*

tubing /'tyoohbing‖'tju:bɪŋ/ *n* **1** (a length of) material in the form of a tube **2** a series or system of tubes

tub-thumper /'tub ,thumpə‖'tʌb ,θʌmpə/ *n* an impassioned or ranting public speaker – **tub-thumping** *n or adj*

tubular /'tyoohbyoolə‖'tju:bjʊlə/ *also* **tubulous** /-ləs‖-ləs/ *adj* **1** having the form of or consisting of a tube **2** made of or fitted with tubes or tube-shaped pieces

¹tuck /tuk‖tʌk/ *vt* **1a** to draw into a fold or

folded position **b** to make a tuck or series of tucks in **2** to place in a snug often concealed or isolated spot <*cottage* ~ed *away in the hills*> **3a** to push in the loose end or ends of so as to make secure or tidy **b** to cover snugly by tucking in bedclothes <~ed *up in bed*> **4** to eat – usu + *away* ~*vi* to eat heartily – usu + *in* or *into USE* (*vt 4; vi*) infml

²tuck *n* **1** a (narrow) fold stitched into cloth to shorten, decorate, or reduce fullness **2** *Br* food, esp chocolate, pastries, etc, as eaten by schoolchildren – infml

¹tucker /'tukə‖'tʌkə/ *n, Austr & NZ* food <*a* ~ *bag*> – infml

²tucker *vt, chiefly NAm* to exhaust – often + *out*

'tuck-,in *n, chiefly Br* a hearty meal – infml

Tuesday /'tyoohzday, -di‖'tju:zdeɪ, -dɪ/ *n* the day of the week following Monday [Old English *tīwesdæg*, fr *Tīw*, god of war + *dæg* day]

tuft /tuft‖tʌft/ *n* **1a** a small cluster of long flexible hairs, feathers, grasses, etc attached or close together at the base **b** a bunch of soft fluffy threads cut off short and used for ornament **2** a clump, cluster – **tufted** *adj*, **tufty** *adj*

¹tug /tug‖tʌg/ *vb* **-gg-** to pull hard (at)

²tug *n* **1a** a hard pull or jerk **b** a strong pulling force <*felt the* ~ *of the past*> **2** a struggle between 2 people or opposite forces **3a tug, tugboat** a strongly built powerful boat used for towing or pushing large ships (e g in and out of dock) **b** an aircraft that tows a glider

,tug-of-'war *n, pl* **tugs-of-war** **1** a struggle for supremacy **2** a contest in which teams pulling at opposite ends of a rope attempt to pull each other across a line marked between them

tuition /tyooh'ish(ə)n‖tju:'ɪʃ(ə)n/ *n* teaching, instruction – **tuitional** *adj*

tulip /'tyoohlip‖'tju:lɪp/ *n* (the flower of) any of a genus of Eurasian bulbous plants of the lily family widely grown for their showy flowers [deriv of Turkish *tülbend* turban – see TURBAN]

'tulip ,tree *n* a tall N American tree of the magnolia family with large tulip-shaped flowers and soft white wood

tulle /t(y)oohl‖t(j)u:l/ *n* a sheer, often silk, net used chiefly for veils and dresses [*Tulle*, city in France]

¹tumble /'tumbl‖'tʌmbl/ *vi* **1a** to perform gymnastic feats without the use of apparatus **b** to turn end over end in falling or flight **2a** to fall or decline suddenly and helplessly **b** to suffer a sudden overthrow or defeat **3** to roll over and over, to and fro, or around **4** to move hurriedly and confusedly <~d *into his clothes*> **5** to realize suddenly – often + *to*; infml ~ *vt* **1** to cause to tumble (e g by pushing) **2** to rumple, disorder **3** to whirl in a tumbler (e g in drying clothes)

²tumble *n* **1** a confused heap **2** an act of tumbling; *specif* a fall

'tumble,down /-,down‖-,daʊn/ *adj* dilapidated, ramshackle

,tumble-'drier /-'drie·ə‖-'draɪə/ *n* a machine consisting of a rotating heated drum in which wet laundry is dried – **tumble-dry** *vb*

tumbler /'tumblə‖'tʌmblə/ *n* **1a** an acrobat **b** any of various domestic pigeons that tumble or somersault backwards in flight or on the ground **2** a relatively large drinking glass without a foot, stem, or handle **3a** a movable obstruction (e g a lever, wheel, or pin) in a lock that must be adjusted to a particular position (e g by a key) before the bolt can be moved **b** a lever that when released by the trigger forces the hammer of a firearm forwards **4a** a tumble-drier **b** a revolving drum, often lined with abrasive material, in which gemstones, castings, etc are polished by friction – **tumblerful** *n*

tumbleweed /'tumbl,weed‖'tʌmbl,wi:d/ *n* a plant that breaks away from its roots in the autumn and is blown about by the wind

tumbrel, tumbril /'tumbrəl‖'tʌmbrəl/ *n* **1** a farm cart that can be tipped to empty the contents **2** a vehicle used to carry condemned people to a place of execution during the French Revolution

tumescent /tyooh'mes(ə)nt‖tju:'mes(ə)nt/ *adj* somewhat swollen; *esp, of the penis or clitoris* engorged with blood in response to sexual stimulation – **tumescence** *n*

tumid /'tyoohmid‖'tju:mɪd/ *adj* **1** *esp of body parts* swollen, protuberant, or distended **2** bombastic, turgid – **tumidly** *adv*, **tumidity** *n*

tummy /'tumi‖'tʌmɪ/ *n* STOMACH 1b – infml

tumour, *NAm chiefly* **tumor** /'tyoohmə‖'tju:mə/ *n* an abnormal mass of tissue that arises without obvious cause from cells of existing tissue – **tumorous** *adj*

tumult /'tyooh,mult‖'tju:mʌlt/ *n* **1a** commotion, uproar (e g of a crowd) **b** a turbulent uprising; a riot **2** violent mental or emotional agitation – **tumultuous** *adj*, **tumultuously** *adv*, **tumultuousness** *n*

tumulus /'tyoohmyooləs‖'tju:mjʊləs/ *n, pl* **tumuli** /-lie‖-laɪ/ an ancient grave; a barrow

tun /tun‖tʌn/ *n* **1** a large cask, esp for wine **2** any of various units of liquid capacity of about 954l

¹tuna /'tyoohnə‖'tju:nə/ *n* (the edible fruit of) any of various prickly pears

²tuna *n* **1** any of numerous large vigorous food and sport fishes related to the mackerels **2** the flesh of a tuna, often canned for use as food

tundra /'tundrə‖'tʌndrə/ *n* a plain with a permanently frozen subsoil that is characteristic of arctic and subarctic regions

¹tune /tyoohn‖tju:n/ *n* **1a** a pleasing succession of musical notes; a melody **b** *the* dominant tune in a musical composition **2** correct musical pitch (with another instrument, voice, etc) **3a** accord, harmony <*in* ~ *with the times*> **b** general attitude; approach <*soon changed his* ~> **4** amount, extent – chiefly in *to the tune of*

²tune *vi* **1** to bring a musical instrument or instruments into tune, esp with a standard pitch – usu + *up* **2** to become attuned **3** to adjust a receiver for the reception of a particular broadcast or station – + *in* or *to* <~ *in again next week*> ~ *vt* **1** to adjust the musical pitch of; *esp* to cause to be in tune **2a** to bring into harmony; attune **b** to adjust for optimum performance – often + *up* <~d *up the engine*> **3** to adjust (a radio or television receiver) to respond to signals of a particular frequency – often + *in* – **tunable, tuneable** *adj*, **tuner** *n*

tuneful /'tyoohnf(ə)l‖'tju:nf(ə)l/ *adj* melodious, musical – **tunefully** *adv*, **tunefulness** *n*

'tuneless /-lis‖-lɪs/ *adj* without an intended or recognizable melody; not tuneful – **tunelessly** *adv*, **tunelessness** *n*

tungsten /'tungstən‖'tʌŋstən/ *n* a hard metallic element with a high melting point that is used esp for electrical purposes and in hard alloys (e g steel) [Swedish, fr *tung* heavy + *sten* stone]

tunic /'tyoohnik‖'tju:nɪk/ *n* **1** a simple (hip- or knee-length) slip-on garment usu belted or gathered at the waist **2** an enclosing or covering membrane or tissue <*the* ~ *of a seed*> **3** a close-fitting jacket with a high collar worn esp as part of a uniform

'tuning ,fork /'tyoohning‖'tju:nɪŋ/ *n* a 2-pronged metal implement that gives a fixed tone when struck and is useful for tuning musical instruments and setting pitches for singing

¹tunnel /'tunl‖'tʌnl/ *n* **1** a hollow conduit or recess (e g for a propeller shaft) **2a** a man-made horizontal passageway through or under an obstruction **b** a subterranean passage (e g in a mine)

²tunnel *vb* **-ll-** (*NAm* **-l-**, **-ll-**) *vt* **1** to make a passage through or under **2** to make (e g one's way) by excavating a tunnel ~ *vi* to make or pass through a tunnel

tunny /'tuni‖'tʌnɪ/ *n* ²TUNA

¹tup /tup‖tʌp/ *n* **1** the heavy metal head of a steam hammer, pile driver, etc **2** *chiefly Br* RAM 1

²tup *vt* **-pp-** *chiefly Br, of a ram* to copulate with (a ewe)

tuppence /'tup(ə)ns‖'tʌp(ə)ns/ *n* (a) twopence – **tuppenny** *adj*

turban /'tuhbən‖'tɜ:bən/ *n* (a headdress, esp for a lady, resembling) a headdress worn esp by Muslims and Sikhs and made of a long cloth wound round a cap or directly round the head [Middle French *turbant*, fr Italian *turbante*, fr Turkish *tülbend*, fr Persian *dulband*] – **turbaned, turbanned** *adj*

turbid /'tuhbid‖'tɜ:bɪd/ *adj* **1a** opaque (as if) with disturbed sediment; cloudy **b** thick with smoke or mist **2** (mentally or emotionally) confused – **turbidly** *adv*, **turbidness, turbidity** *n*

turbine /'tuhbien‖'tɜ:baɪn/ *n* a rotary engine whose central driving shaft is fitted with vanes whirled round by the pressure of water, steam, exhaust gases, etc

turbocharger /'tuhboh,chahjə‖'tɜ:bəʊ-,tʃɑ:dʒə/ *n* a compressor device that is used to supercharge an internal-combustion engine and is usu driven by an exhaust-gas turbine – **turbocharge** *vt*

'turbo,jet /-,jet‖-,dʒet/ *n* (an aircraft powered by) a turbojet engine

turbojet engine *adj* a jet engine in which a compressor driven by power from a turbine supplies compressed air to the combustion chamber and in which thrust is derived from the rearward expulsion of hot gases

'turbo,prop /-,prop‖-,prɒp/ *n* (an aircraft powered by) an engine that has a turbine-driven propeller for providing the main thrust

turbot /'tuhbət‖'tɜ:bət/ *n* a large European flatfish that is a highly valued food fish

turbulence /'tuhbyooləns‖'tɜ:bjʊləns/ *n* **1** wild commotion or agitation **2** irregular atmospheric motion, esp when characterized by strong currents of rising and falling air **3** the formation of disturbances that interfere with the smooth flow of a liquid or gas

turbulent /'tuhbyoolənt‖'tɜ:bjʊlənt/ *adj* **1** causing unrest, violence, or disturbance <*a* ~ *crowd*> **2** agitated, stormy, or tempestuous <~ *water*> <*a* ~ *childhood*> **3** exhibiting physical turbulence – **turbulently** *adv*

turd /tuhd‖tɜ:d/ *n* **1** a piece of excrement **2** a despicable person *USE* vulg

tureen /tyoo'reen, tə-‖tjʊ'ri:n, tə-/ *n* a deep (covered) dish from which a food, esp soup, is served at table

¹turf /tuhf‖tɜ:f/ *n, pl* **turfs, turves** /tuhvz‖tɜ:vz/ **1** (a piece of or an artificial substitute for) the upper layer of soil bound by grass and plant roots into a thick mat **2** (a piece of dried) peat **3** *the* sport or business of horse racing or the course on which horse races are run – **turfy** *adj*

²turf *vt* to cover with turf

'turf ac,countant *n, Br* a bookmaker

turf out *vt, chiefly Br* to dismiss or throw out forcibly – infml

turgid /'tuhjid‖'tɜ:dʒɪd/ *adj* **1** distended, swollen; *esp* exhibiting excessive turgor **2** in a pompous inflated style; laboured – **turgidly** *adv*, **turgidness** *n*, **turgescence** *n*, **turgescent** *adj*, **turgidity** *n*

turkey /'tuhki‖'tɜ:kɪ/ *n* (the flesh of) a large orig American bird that is farmed for its meat in most parts of the world [*Turkey*, country in W Asia and SE Europe; so called fr confusion with the guinea fowl, supposed to be imported from Turkish territory]

Turkic /'tuhkik‖'tɜ:kɪk/ *adj* **1** of a branch of the Altaic language family including Turkish **2** of the peoples who speak Turkic languages – **Turkic** *n*

¹Turkish /'tuhkish‖'tɜ:kɪʃ/ *adj* **1** (characteristic) of Turkey or the Turks **2** TURKIC 1

²Turkish *n* **1** the Turkic language of the Republic of Turkey **2 Turkish, Turkish tobacco** an aromatic tobacco grown chiefly in Turkey and Greece

,Turkish 'bath *n* a steam bath followed by a rubdown, massage, and cold shower

,Turkish de'light *n* a jellylike confection, usu cut in cubes and dusted with sugar

turmeric /'tuhmərik‖'tɜ:mərɪk/ *n* **1** an E Indian plant of the ginger family **2** the dried and usu powdered underground stem of the turmeric plant used as a colouring agent or condiment

turmoil /'tuhmoyl‖'tɜ:mɔɪl/ *n* an extremely confused or agitated state

¹turn /tuhn‖tɜ:n/ *vt* **1a** to make rotate or revolve <~ *a wheel*> **b(1)** to cause to move through an arc of a circle <~ *a key*> **b(2)** to alter the functioning of (as if) by turning a knob <~ *the oven to a higher temperature*> **c** to perform by rotating or revolving <~ *cartwheels*> **2a** to reverse the sides or surfaces of so as to expose another side <~ *the page*>: e g **2a(1)** to dig or plough so as to bring the lower soil to the surface **a(2)** to renew (e g a garment) by reversing the material and resewing <~ *a collar*> **b** to throw into disorder or confusion <*everything*

~ed *topsy-turvy*> **c** to disturb the mental balance of; unsettle <*a mind* ~ed *by grief*> **d** to cause to change or reverse direction <~ed *his car in the street*> **3a** to bend or change the course or outcome of <~ *the tide of history*> **b** to go round or about <~ed *the corner at full speed*> **c** to reach or go beyond (e g an age or time) <*he's just* ~ed *21*> **4a** to direct, present, or point (e g the face) in a specified direction **b** to aim, train <*cannon were* ~ed *on the troops*> **c** to direct, induce, or influence in a specified direction, esp towards or away from sby or sthg <~ed *his thoughts inwards*> **d** to apply, devote <~ed *his hand to plumbing*> **e(1)** to drive, send <~ed *them out of their home*> **e(2)** to direct into or out of a receptacle (as if) by inverting <~ *the meat into a pot*> **5a** to make acid or sour **b** to cause to become by change; transform, convert <*illness* ~ed *his hair white*> **6a** to give a rounded form to <~ing *wood on a lathe*> **b** to fashion elegantly or neatly <*well* ~ed *ankles*> **7** to fold, bend <~ *his collar up*> **8** to gain in the course of business – esp in *turn an honest penny* ~ *vi* **1a** to (appear to) move round (as if) on an axis or through an arc of a circle <*I tossed and* ~ed *all night*> **b(1)** to become giddy or dizzy **b(2)** *of the stomach* to feel nauseated **c** to centre or hinge on sthg <*the argument* ~s *on this point*> **2a** to direct one's course <*didn't know which way to* ~> **b(1)** to change or reverse direction <*the main road* ~s *sharply to the right*> **b(2)** to become reversed or inverted **3a** to change position so as to face another way <*they* ~ed *to stare at him*> **b** to change one's attitude to one of hostility <~ed *against his parents*> **c** to make a sudden violent physical or verbal assault – usu + *on* or *upon* <*she* ~ed *on him with ferocity*> **4a** to direct one's attention, efforts, or interests to or away from sby or sthg <~ed *to studying law*> **b** to have recourse; resort <~ed *to a friend for help*> **5a** to become changed, altered, or transformed: e g **5a(1)** to change colour <*the leaves have* ~ed> **a(2)** to become acid or sour <*the milk had* ~ed> **b** to become by change <*water had* ~ed *to ice*> <~ *traitor*> **6** to become folded or bent – **turnable** *adj* – **turn a blind eye** to refuse to see; be oblivious – **turn a deaf ear** to refuse to listen – **turn back the clock** to revert to an earlier or past state or condition – **turn in one's grave** to be disturbed at goings-on that would have shocked one when alive – said of a dead person – **turn King's/Queen's evidence** *Br, of an accomplice* to testify for the prosecution in court – **turn one's back on** to reject, deny <turned his back on *the past*> – **turn one's hand** to apply oneself; SET TO WORK – **turn someone's head** to cause sby to become infatuated or to harbour extravagant notions of conceit – **turn someone's stomach 1** to disgust sby completely **2** to sicken, nauseate – **turn tail** to run away; flee – **turn the other cheek** to respond to injury or unkindness with patience; forgo retaliation – **turn the scale/scales 1** to register a usu specified weight **2** to prove decisive <*air support might just* turn the scale> – **turn the tables** to bring about a reversal of the relative conditions or fortunes of 2 contending parties – **turn turtle** to capsize, overturn

[2]**turn** *n* **1a** a turning about a centre or axis; (a) rotation **b** any of various rotating or pivoting movements (in dancing) **2a** a change or reversal of direction, stance, position, or course <*illegal left* ~s> <*an about* ~> **b** a deflection, deviation <*the twists and* ~s *of the story*> **c** the place of a change in direction; a turning **3** a short trip out and back or round about <*took a* ~ *through the park*> **4** an act or deed of a specified kind <*one good* ~ *deserves another*> **5a** a place, time, or opportunity granted in succession or rotation <*waiting his* ~ *in the queue*> **b** a period of duty, action, or activity **c** (the performer who gives) a short act or performance (e g in a variety show) **6** a musical ornament played on the principal note and the notes next above and below **7a** an alteration, change <*an unusual* ~ *of events*> <*a* ~ *for the better*> **b** a point of change in time <*the* ~ *of the century*> **8** a style of expression <*an odd* ~ *of phrase*> **9a** the state or manner of being coiled or twisted **b** a single coil (e g of rope wound round an object) **10** a bent, inclination <*an optimistic* ~ *of mind*> **11a** a spell or attack of illness, faintness, etc **b** a nervous start or shock <*gave me quite a* ~> – **at every turn** on every occasion; constantly, continually – **by turns** one after another in regular succession – **in turn** in due order of succession; alternately – **on the turn** at the point of turning <*tide is* on the turn> <*milk is* on the turn> – **out of turn 1** not in due order of succession <*play* out of turn> **2** at a wrong time or place <*spoke* out of turn> – **to a turn** to perfection <*roasted* to a turn> – **turn and turn about** BY TURNS

turnabout /ˈtuhnə,bowt‖ˈtɜːnə,baʊt/ *n* a change or reversal of direction, trend, etc

turn away *vt* to refuse admittance or acceptance to

ˈ**turn,coat** /-,koht‖-,kəʊt/ *n* one who switches to an opposing side or party; a traitor

turn down *vt* **1** to reduce the intensity, volume, etc of (as if) by turning a control <turn *the radio* down> **2** to decline to accept; reject

turner /ˈtuhnə‖ˈtɜːnə/ *n* one who forms articles on a lathe – **turnery** *n*

turn in *vt* **1** to deliver, hand over; *esp* to deliver up to an authority **2** to give, execute <turned in *a good performance*> ~*vi* to go to bed – infml

turning /ˈtuhning‖ˈtɜːnɪŋ/ *n* **1** a place of turning, turning off, or turning back, esp on a road <*take the third* ~ *on the right*> **2a** a forming or being formed by use of a lathe **b** *pl* waste produced in turning sthg on a lathe **3** the width of cloth that is folded under for a seam or hem

ˈ**turning ,point** *n* a point at which a significant change occurs

turnip /ˈtuhnip‖ˈtɜːnɪp/ *n* (a plant of the mustard family with) a thick white-fleshed root eaten as a vegetable or fed to stock

turnkey /ˈtuhn,kee‖ˈtɜːn,kiː/ *n* a prison warden

ˈ**turn,off** /-,of‖-,ɒf/ *n* **1** a turning off **2** a place where one turns off; *esp* a motorway junction

turn off *vt* **1** to stop the flow or operation of (as if) by turning a control <turn *the radio* off>

2 to cause to lose (sexual) interest – infml ~*vi* to deviate from a straight course or from a main road <turned off *into a side road*>

turn on *vt* **1** to cause to flow or operate (as if) by turning a control <turn *the water* on *full*> <turned on *the charm*> **2a** to cause to undergo an intense often visionary experience by taking a drug; *broadly* to cause to get high **b** to excite or interest pleasurably and esp sexually ~*vi* to become turned on ***USE*** (*vt 2*) infml – **turn-on** *n*

[1]**ˈturnˌout** /-ˌowt‖-ˌaʊt/ *n* **1** a turning out **2** people in attendance (e g at a meeting) <*a good* ~ *tonight*> **3** manner of dress; getup **4** quantity of produce yielded

turn out *vt* **1** to put (e g a horse) to pasture **2a** to turn inside out **b** to empty the contents of, esp for cleaning **3** to produce often rapidly or regularly (as if) by machine **4** to equip or dress in a specified way <*he was nicely* turned out> **5** to put out (esp a light) by turning a switch **6** to call (e g a guard) out from rest or shelter and into formation ~ *vi* **1** to leave one's home for a meeting, public event, etc <*voters* turned out *in droves*> **2** to prove to be ultimately <*the play* turned out *to be a flop*> **3** to get out of bed – infml

ˈturnˌover /-ˌohvə‖-ˌəʊvə/ *n* **1** a small semicircular filled pastry made by folding half of the crust over the other half **2a** the total sales revenue of a business **b** the ratio of sales to average stock for a stated period **3** (the rate of) movement (e g of goods or people) into, through, and out of a place

turn over *vt* **1** to cause (an internal-combustion engine) to revolve and usu to fire **2** to think over; meditate on **3** to deliver, surrender **4a** to receive and dispose of (a stock of merchandise) **b** to do business to the amount of <turning over *£1000 a week*> ~ *vi* **1** *of an internal combustion engine* to revolve at low speed **2** *of merchandise* to be stocked and disposed of – **turn over a new leaf** to make a change for the better, esp in one's way of living

ˈturnˌpike /-ˌpiek‖-ˌpaɪk/ *n* **1** *chiefly NAm* a road on which a toll is payable **2** *archaic* a tollgate

ˈturnˌstile /-ˌstiel‖-ˌstaɪl/ *n* a gate with arms pivoted on the top that turns to admit 1 person at a time

ˈturnˌtable /-ˌtaybl‖-ˌteɪbl/ *n* **1** a circular platform for turning wheeled vehicles, esp railway engines **2** the platform on which a gramophone record is rotated while being played

turn to *vi* to apply oneself to work

ˈturn-ˌup *n* **1** *chiefly Br* a turned-up hem, esp on a pair of trousers **2** an unexpected or surprising event – esp in *turn-up for the book*; infml

turn up *vt* **1** to find, discover **2** to increase the intensity, volume, etc of (as if) by turning a control <turn *the sound* up> ~ *vi* **1** to come to light unexpectedly **2** to appear, arrive **3** to happen or occur unexpectedly **4** *of a sailing vessel* TACK 1b – **turn up one's nose** to show scorn or disdain

[1]**turpentine** /ˈtuhpənˌtien‖ˈtɜːpənˌtaɪn/ *n* **1a** a yellow to brown semifluid oleoresin exuded from the terebinth tree **b** an oleoresin obtained from various conifers **2a** an essential oil obtained from turpentines by distillation and used esp as a solvent and paint thinner **b** WHITE SPIRIT

[2]**turpentine** *vt* to apply turpentine to

turpitude /ˈtuhpityoohd‖ˈtɜːpɪtjuːd/ *n* baseness, depravity <*moral* ~>

turquoise /ˈtuhkwoys, -kwoyz‖ˈtɜːkwɔɪs, -kwɔɪz/ *n* **1** a sky blue to greenish mineral consisting of a hydrated copper aluminium phosphate and used as a gem **2** light greenish blue [French *(pierre) turquoise*, lit., Turkish (stone)]

turret /ˈturit‖ˈtʌrɪt/ *n* **1** a little tower, often at the corner of a larger building **2** a rotatable holder (e g for a tool or die) in a lathe, milling machine, etc **3** a usu revolving armoured structure on warships, forts, tanks, aircraft, etc in which guns are mounted – **turreted** *adj*

turtle /ˈtuhtl‖ˈtɜːtl/ *n* any of several marine reptiles of the same order as and similar to tortoises but adapted for swimming; *broadly, NAm* any of the land, freshwater, and sea reptiles of this order

ˈturtleˌdove /-ˌduv‖-ˌdʌv/ *n* any of several small wild pigeons noted for plaintive cooing

ˈturtleˌneck /-ˌnek‖-ˌnek/ *n* a high close-fitting neckline, esp of a sweater

tush /tush‖tʌʃ/ *interj* – used to express disdain or reproach

tusk /tusk‖tʌsk/ *vt or n* (to dig up or gash with) a long greatly enlarged tooth of an elephant, boar, walrus, etc, that projects when the mouth is closed and serves for digging food or as a weapon – **tusked** *adj*, **tusklike** *adj*

tusker /ˈtuskə‖ˈtʌskə/ *n* an animal with tusks; *esp* a male elephant with 2 large tusks

[1]**tussle** /ˈtusl‖ˈtʌsl/ *vi* to struggle roughly; scuffle

[2]**tussle** *n* a (physical) contest or struggle

tussock /ˈtusək‖ˈtʌsək/ *n* a compact tuft of grass, sedge, etc – **tussocky** *adj*

[1]**tut** /tut‖tʌt; *or clicked* t/, **tut-tut** *interj* – used to express disapproval or impatience

[2]**tut**, **ˌtut-ˈtut** *vi* **-tt-** to express disapproval or impatience by uttering 'tut' or 'tut-tut'

tutelage /ˈtyoohtilij‖ˈtjuːtɪlɪdʒ/ *n* **1** guardianship **2** the state or period of being under a guardian or tutor **3** instruction, esp of an individual

tutelary /ˈtyoohtiləri‖ˈtjuːtɪlərɪ/ *also* **tutelar** /-lə‖-lə/ *adj* **1** having the guardianship of sby or sthg <*a* ~ *deity*> **2** of a guardian

[1]**tutor** /ˈtyoohtə‖ˈtjuːtə/ *n* **1** a private teacher **2** a British university teacher who **2a** gives instruction to students, esp individually **b** is in charge of the social and moral welfare of a group of students **3** *Br* an instruction book – **tutorship** *n*

[2]**tutor** *vt* to teach or guide usu individually; coach ~*vi* to do the work of a tutor

[1]**tutorial** /tyoohˈtawri·əl‖tjuːˈtɔːrɪəl/ *adj* of or involving (individual tuition by) a tutor – **tutorially** *adv*

[2]**tutorial** *n* a class conducted by a tutor for 1 student or a small number of students

tutti-frutti /ˌtoohti ˈfroohti‖ˌtuːtɪ ˈfruːtɪ/ *n* (a

confection, esp an ice cream, containing) a mixture of chopped, dried, or candied fruits [Italian *tutti frutti*, lit., all fruits]

tutu /ˈtoohˌtooh‖ˈtuːˌtuː/ *n* a very short projecting stiff skirt worn by a ballerina

tu-whit tu-whoo /tə ˌwit tə ˈwooh‖tə ˌwɪt tə ˈwuː/ *n* the cry of a (tawny) owl

tuxedo /tukˈseedoh‖tʌkˈsiːdəʊ/ *n, pl* **tuxedos, tuxedoes** *NAm* DINNER JACKET [*Tuxedo* Park, resort in New York]

TV /ˌtee ˈvee‖ˌtiː ˈviː/ *n* television

twaddle /ˈtwodl‖ˈtwɒdl/ *vi or n* (to speak or write) rubbish or drivel – **twaddler** *n*

twain /twayn‖tweɪn/ *n, adj, or pron, archaic* two

[1]twang /twang‖twæŋ/ *n* **1** a harsh quick ringing sound like that of a plucked bowstring **2** nasal speech or resonance – **twangy** *adj*

[2]twang *vi* to speak or sound with a twang ~ *vt* **1** to utter or cause to sound with a twang **2** to pluck the string of

twat /twot‖twɒt/ *n* **1** the female genitals **2** *Br* an unpleasant or despicable person *USE* vulg

tweak /tweek‖twiːk/ *vb* to pinch and pull with a sudden jerk and twist – **tweak** *n*

twee /twee‖twiː/ *adj* excessively sentimental, pretty, or coy – **tweeness** *n*

tweed /tweed‖twiːd/ *n* **1** a rough woollen fabric made usu in twill weaves and used esp for suits and coats **2** *pl* tweed clothing; *specif* a tweed suit

tweedy /ˈtweedi‖ˈtwiːdɪ/ *adj* **1** of or resembling tweed **2a** given to or associated with wearing tweeds **b** suggesting the outdoors in taste or habits; *esp* brisk and healthy in manner – **tweediness** *n*

tween /tween‖twiːn/ *prep* between – chiefly poetic

tweet /tweet‖twiːt/ *vi or n* (to) chirp

tweeter /ˈtweetə‖ˈtwiːtə/ *n* a small loudspeaker that responds mainly to the higher frequencies

tweezers /ˈtweezəz‖ˈtwiːzəz/ *n pl, pl* **tweezers** a small metal instrument that is usu held between thumb and forefinger, is used for plucking, holding, or manipulating, and consists of 2 prongs joined at 1 end

twelfth /twel(f)th‖twel(f)θ/ *n* **1** number twelve in a countable series **2** *often cap, Br the* twelfth of August on which the grouse-shooting season begins – **twelfth** *adj or adv*, **twelfthly** *adj*

twelve /twelv‖twelv/ *n* **1** (the number) 12 **2** the twelfth in a set or series **3** sthg having 12 parts or members or a denomination of 12 – **twelve** *adj or pron*, **twelvefold** *adj or adv*

ˈtwelveˌmonth /-ˌmunth‖-ˌmʌnθ/ *n* a year – archaic or poetic

twenty /ˈtwenti‖ˈtwentɪ/ *n* **1** (the number) 20 **2** *pl the* numbers 20 to 29; *specif* a range of temperature, ages, or dates in a century characterized by those numbers **3** sthg (e g a bank note) having a denomination of 20 – **twentieth** *adj or n*, **twenty** *adj or pron*, **twentyfold** *adj or adv*

twerp *also* **twirp** /twuhp‖twɜːp/ *n* a silly, insignificant, or contemptible person – infml

twice /twies‖twaɪs/ *adv* **1** on 2 occasions < ~ *a week*> **2** two times;in doubled quantity or degree < ~ *2 is 4*> < ~ *as much*>

ˌtwice-ˈtold *adj* familiar, well-known – chiefly in *a twice-told tale*

[1]twiddle /ˈtwidl‖ˈtwɪdl/ *vi* to play negligently with sthg ~*vt* to rotate lightly or idly < ~d *the knob on the radio*>

[2]twiddle *n* a turn, twist

[1]twig /twig‖twɪg/ *n* a small woody shoot or branch, usu without its leaves – **twigged** *adj*, **twiggy** *adj*

[2]twig *vb* **-gg-** to catch on (to); understand – infml

twilight /ˈtwieˌliet‖ˈtwaɪˌlaɪt/ *n* **1a** the light from the sky between full night and sunrise or esp between sunset and full night **b** the period between sunset and full night **2a** a shadowy indeterminate state **b** a period or state of decline <*elderly ladies in their* ~ *years*>

twill /twil‖twɪl/ *n* (a fabric with) a textile weave in which the weft threads pass over 1 and under 2 or more warp threads to give an appearance of diagonal lines – **twilled** *adj*

[1]twin /twin‖twɪn/ *adj* **1** born with one other or as a pair at 1 birth < ~ *brother*> < ~ *girls*> **2a** having or made up of 2 similar, related, or identical units or parts **b** being one of a pair, esp of officially associated towns

[2]twin *n* **1** either of 2 offspring produced at 1 birth **2** either of 2 people or things closely related to or resembling each other **3 twin, twin crystal** a compound crystal composed of 2 or more (parts of) related crystals grown together in an oriented manner – **twinship** *n*

[3]twin *vb* **-nn-** *vt* **1** to bring together in close association **2** to form into a twin crystal ~ *vi* **1** to become paired or closely associated **2** to give birth to twins **3** to grow as a twin crystal

ˌtwin ˈbed *n* either of 2 matching single beds

[1]twine /twien‖twaɪn/ *n* **1** a strong string of 2 or more strands twisted together **2** a coil, twist **3** an act of twining or interlacing

[2]twine *vt* **1a** to twist together **b** to form by twisting; weave **2** to twist or coil round sthg ~*vi* to coil round a support – **twiner** *n*

twinge /twinj‖twɪndʒ/ *vi or n* **twinging, twingeing** (to feel) **1** a sudden sharp stab of pain **2** an emotional pang <*a* ~ *of conscience*>

[1]twinkle /ˈtwingkl‖ˈtwɪŋkl/ *vi* **1** to shine with a flickering or sparkling light **2** to appear bright with gaiety or amusement <*his eyes* ~d> ~*vt* to cause to shine (as if) with a flickering light – **twinkler** *n*

[2]twinkle *n* **1** an instant, twinkling **2** an (intermittent) sparkle or gleam – **twinkly** *adj*

twinkling /ˈtwingkling‖ˈtwɪŋklɪŋ/ *n* a very short time; a moment

ˈtwin ˌset *n* a jumper and cardigan designed to be worn together, usu by a woman

[1]twirl /twuhl‖twɜːl/ *vi* to revolve rapidly ~ *vt* **1** to cause to rotate rapidly; spin **2** TWINE 2

[2]twirl *n* **1** an act of twirling **2** a coil, whorl – **twirly** *adj*

twirp /twuhp‖twɜːp/ *n* a twerp

[1]twist /twist‖twɪst/ *vt* **1a** to join together by winding; *also* to mingle by interlacing **b** to make by twisting strands together **2** to wind or coil round sthg **3a** to wring or wrench so as to dislocate or distort < ~ed *my ankle*> **b** to distort the meaning of; pervert **c** to contort < ~ed *his* *face into a grin>* **d** to pull off, turn, or break by a turning force **e** to cause to move with a rotating motion **f** to form into a spiral **g** WARP 1b <*a* ~ed *mind*> ~ *vi* **1** to follow a winding course; snake **2a** to turn or change shape by a turning force **b** to take on a spiral shape **c** to dance the twist **3** *of a ball* to rotate while following a curving path **4** TURN 3a <~ed *round to see behind him*> – **twist someone's arm** to bring strong pressure to bear on sby <*he decided to come with us, but we had to* twist his arm *a bit first*>

[2]**twist** *n* **1** sthg formed by twisting: e g **1a** a thread, yarn, or cord formed by twisting 2 or more strands together **b** tobacco twisted into a thick roll **c** a screw of paper used as a container **d** a curled strip of citrus peel used to flavour a drink <*... gin, ice, bitters and a* ~ *of lemon*> **2a** a twisting or being twisted **b** a dance popular esp in the 1960s and performed with gyrations, esp of the hips **c** a spiral turn or curve **3a** torsional strain **b** the angle through or amount by which a thing is twisted **4a** a turning off a straight course; a bend **b** a (personal) eccentricity or idiosyncrasy **c** a distortion of meaning or sense **5** an unexpected turn or development <*a strange* ~ *of fate*> **6** a dive in which the diver twists the body sideways for 1 or more half or full turns before entering the water – **twisty** *adj*

twister /ˈtwistə‖ˈtwɪstə/ *n* **1** *NAm* a tornado, waterspout, etc in which the rotatory ascending movement of a column of air is very apparent **2** a dishonest person; a swindler – infml

[1]**twit** /twit‖twɪt/ *vt* **-tt-** to tease, taunt

[2]**twit** *n, Br* an absurd or silly person

[1]**twitch** /twich‖twɪtʃ/ *vt* to move or pull with a sudden motion ~ *vi* **1** to pull, pluck <~ed *at my sleeve*> **2** to move jerkily or involuntarily – **twitcher** *n*

[2]**twitch** *n* **1** a short sudden pull or jerk **2** a physical or mental pang **3** a loop of rope or a strap that is tightened over a horse's upper lip as a restraining device **4** (the recurrence of) a short spasmodic contraction or jerk; a tic – **twitchily** *adv*, **twitchy** *adj*

[3]**twitch** *n* COUCH GRASS

twitcher /ˈtwichə‖ˈtwɪtʃə/ *n* a keen bird-watcher – infml

[1]**twitter** /ˈtwitə‖ˈtwɪtə/ *vi* **1** to utter twitters **2** to talk in a nervous chattering fashion **3** to tremble with agitation; flutter ~*vt* to utter (as if) in twitters

[2]**twitter** *n* **1** a nervous agitation – esp in *all of a twitter* **2** a small tremulous intermittent sound characteristic of birds – **twittery** *adj*

twixt /twikst‖twɪkst/ *prep* between – chiefly poetic

twizzle /ˈtwizl‖ˈtwɪzl/ *vt, Br* to twirl

[1]**two** /tooh‖tuː/ *pron, pl in constr* **1** two unspecified countable individuals <*only* ~ *were found*> **2** a small approximate number of indicated things <*only a shot or* ~ *were fired*>

[2]**two** *n, pl* **twos** **1** (the number) 2 **2** the second in a set or series <*the* ~ *of spades*> **3** sthg having 2 parts or members or a denomination of 2 – **two** *adj*, **twofold** *adj or adv*

ˌ**two-ˈbit** *adj, NAm* petty, small-time

ˌ**two-ˈedged** *adj* double-edged

ˌ**two-ˈfaced** *adj* double-dealing, hypocritical – **two-facedness** *n*

ˌ**two-ˈhanded** *adj* **1** used with both hands <*a* ~ *sword*> **2** requiring 2 people <*a* ~ *saw*> **3** ambidextrous

twopence *also* **tuppence** /ˈtup(ə)ns‖ˈtʌp(ə)ns/ *n* (a coin worth) 2 pence

twopenny *also* **tuppenny** /ˈtup(ə)ni‖ˈtʌp(ə)nɪ/ *adj* costing or worth twopence

ˈ**two-ˌpiece** *n or adj* (a suit of clothes, swimming costume, etc) consisting of 2 matching pieces

two-ply /ˌ-ˈ-, ˈ-ˌ-/ *adj* consisting of 2 strands, layers, or thicknesses <~ *wool*>

twosome /ˈtoohs(ə)m‖ˈtuːs(ə)m/ *n* **1** a group of 2 people or things **2** a golf single

ˈ**two-ˌstep** *n* (a piece of music for) a ballroom dance in either $^2_4$ or $^4_4$ time

ˌ**two-ˈtime** *vb* to be unfaithful to (a spouse or lover) by having a secret relationship with another – **two-timer** *n*

ˈ**two-ˌtone** *adj* **1** *also* **two-toned** having 2 colours or shades **2** of or being popular music played by groups consisting of black, esp W Indian, and white musicians and including elements of reggae and new wave – **two-tone** *n*

ˌ**two-ˈway** *adj* **1** moving or allowing movement or use in 2 (opposite) directions <*a* ~ *road*> **2a** *of a radio, telephone, etc* designed for both sending and receiving messages **b** involving mutual responsibility or a reciprocal relationship **3** involving 2 participants **4** usable in either of 2 ways

ˌ**two-winged ˈfly** *n* any of a large order of insects including the housefly, mosquito, and gnat with functional front wings and greatly reduced rear wings used to control balance

tycoon /tieˈkoohn‖taɪˈkuːn/ *n* a businessman of exceptional wealth and power [Japanese *taikun* shogun, fr Chinese (Peking dialect) *ta*[4] great + *chün*[1] ruler] – **tycoonery** *n*

tying /ˈtie·ing‖ˈtaɪɪŋ/ *pres part of* TIE

tyke, tike /tiek‖taɪk/ *n* **1** a (mongrel) dog **2** *chiefly Br* a boorish churlish person **3** a small child **4** a native of Yorkshire *USE* (*3&4*) infml

tympanic membrane /timˈpanik‖tɪmˈpænɪk/ *n* a thin membrane separating the outer ear from the middle ear that functions in the mechanical reception of sound waves and in their transmission to the site of sensory reception; the eardrum

tympanum /ˈtimpənəm‖ˈtɪmpənəm/ *n, pl* **tympana** /-nə‖-nə/, **tympanums** **1a(1)** TYMPANIC MEMBRANE **a(2)** MIDDLE EAR **b** a thin tense membrane covering the hearing-organ of an insect **2a** the recessed triangular face of a pediment **b** the space within an arch and above a lintel (e g in a medieval doorway) – **tympanic** *adj*

[1]**type** /tiep‖taɪp/ *n* **1a** a person or thing (e g in the Old Testament) regarded as foreshadowing another (e g in the New Testament) **b** a model, exemplar, or characteristic specimen (possessing the distinguishable or essential qualities of a class) **c** a lower taxonomic category selected as reference for a higher category <*a* ~ *genus*> **2a** (any of) a collection of usu rectangular blocks or characters bearing a relief from which an inked print can be made **b** a typeface <*italic*

~> **c** printed letters **3a** a set of qualities common to a number of individuals that distinguish them as an identifiable class (e g the form common to all instances of a linguistic expression **b(1)** a member of a specified class or variety of people <*sporting* ~s> **b(2)** a person of a specified nature <*he's a peculiar* ~> **c** a particular kind, class, or group with distinct characteristics **d** sthg distinguishable as a variety; a sort – **typal** *adj*

[2]**type** *vt* **1** to represent beforehand as a type; prefigure **2** to represent in terms of typical characteristics; typify **3** to write with a typewriter; *also* to keyboard **4a** to identify as belonging to a type **b** to determine the natural type of (e g a blood sample) ~*vi* to use a typewriter

-type *comb form* (*n* → *adj*) of (such) a type; resembling <*Cheddar*-type *cheese*>

'type,cast /-ˌkahst‖-ˌkɑːst/ *vt* **typecast** to cast (an actor) repeatedly in the same type of role; *broadly* to stereotype

'type,face /-ˌfays‖-ˌfeɪs/ *n* (the appearance of) a single design of printing type

'type,script /-ˌskript‖-ˌskrɪpt/ *n* a typewritten manuscript

'type,set /-ˌset‖-ˌset/ *vt* **-tt-; typeset** to set in type; compose – **typesetter** *n*, **typesetting** *n*

'type,write /-ˌriet‖-ˌraɪt/ *vb* **typewrote** /-ˌroht‖-ˌrəʊt/; **typewritten** /-ˌritn‖-ˌrɪtn/ to write with a typewriter

'type,writer /-ˌrietə‖-ˌraɪtə/ *n* a machine with a keyboard for writing in characters resembling type

[1]**typhoid** /'tiefoyd‖'taɪfɔɪd/ *adj* **1** (suggestive) of typhus **2** of or being typhoid

[2]**typhoid, typhoid fever** *n* a serious communicable human disease caused by a bacterium and marked esp by fever, diarrhoea, headache, and intestinal inflammation

typhoon /tie'foohn‖taɪ'fuːn/ *n* a tropical cyclone occurring in the Philippines or the China sea

typhus /'tiefəs‖'taɪfəs/ *n* a serious human disease marked by high fever, stupor alternating with delirium, intense headache, and a dark red rash, caused by a rickettsia, and transmitted esp by body lice

typical /'tipikl‖'tɪpɪkl/ *adj* **1** *also* **typic** being or having the nature of a type; symbolic, representative **2a** having or showing the essential characteristics of a type <~ *suburban houses*> **b** showing or according with the usual or expected (unfavourable) traits <*just* ~ *of him to get so annoyed*> – **typically** *adv*, **typicalness, typicality** *n*

typify /'tipifie‖'tɪpɪfaɪ/ *vt* **1a** to represent in symbolic fashion (e g by an image or model) **b** to constitute a typical instance of **2** to embody the essential characteristics of – **typification** *n*

typist /'tiepist‖'taɪpɪst/ *n* one who uses a typewriter, esp as an occupation

typographer /tie'pogrəfə‖taɪ'pɒgrəfə/ *n* **1** a compositor **2** a specialist in the design, choice, and arrangement of typographical matter

typography /tie'pogrəfi‖taɪ'pɒgrəfɪ/ *n* the style, arrangement, or appearance of typeset matter – **typographic, typographical** *adj*, **typographically** *adv*

tyrannical /ti'ranikl‖tɪ'rænɪkl/ *also* **tyrannic** *adj* characteristic of a tyrant or tyranny; oppressive, despotic – **tyrannically** *adv*

tyrann·ize, -ise /'tirəniez‖'tɪrənaɪz/ *vb* to exercise power (over) with unjust and oppressive cruelty

tyrannosaur /ti'ranəˌsaw‖tɪ'rænəˌsɔː/, **tyrannosaurus** /tiˌranə'sawrəs‖tɪˌrænə'sɔːrəs/ *n* a very large flesh-eating dinosaur having small forelegs and walking on its hind legs [deriv of Greek *tyrannos* tyrant + *sauros* lizard]

tyranny /'tirəni‖'tɪrənɪ/ *n* **1** a government in which absolute power is vested in a single ruler **2** oppressive power (exerted by a tyrant) **3** sthg severe, oppressive, or inexorable in effect – **tyrannous** *adj*

tyrant /'tie(ə)rənt‖'taɪ(ə)rənt/ *n* **1** a ruler who exercises absolute power, esp oppressively or brutally **2** one who exercises authority harshly or unjustly

tyre, *NAm chiefly* **tire** /tie·ə‖taɪə/ *n* a continuous solid or inflated hollow rubber cushion set round a wheel to absorb shock

tyro, tiro /'tie·əroh‖'taɪərəʊ/ *n, pl* **tyros, tiros** a beginner, novice

tzar /zah‖zɑː/ *n* a tsar

u /yooh‖juː/ *n, pl* **u's, us** *often cap* (a graphic representation of or device for reproducing) the 21st letter of the English alphabet

[1]**U** *adj, chiefly Br* upper-class

[2]**U** *n or adj* (a film that is) certified in Britain as suitable for all age groups

ubiquitous /yooh'bikwitəs‖juː'bɪkwɪtəs/ *adj* existing or being everywhere at the same time [Latin *ubique* everywhere] – **ubiquitousness, ubiquity** *n*

'U-,boat *n* a German submarine [German *u-boat*, short for *unterseeboot*, fr *unter* under + *see* sea + *boot* boat]

udder /'udə‖'ʌdə/ *n* a large pendulous organ consisting of 2 or more mammary glands enclosed in a common envelope and each having a single nipple

UFO /'yoohfoh, ˌyooh ef 'oh‖'juːfəʊ, ˌjuː ef 'əʊ/ *n, pl* **UFO's, UFOs** an unidentified flying object; *esp* FLYING SAUCER

ugh /ookh, uh‖ʊx, ɜː/ *interj* – used to express disgust or horror

ugly /'ugli‖'ʌglɪ/ *adj* **1** frightful, horrible <*an* ~ *wound*> **2** offensive or displeasing to any of the senses, esp to the sight **3** morally offensive or objectionable **4a** ominous, threatening <~ *weather*> **b** surly, quarrelsome <*an* ~ *disposition*> – **uglily** *adv*, **ugliness** *n*, **uglify** *vt*

ˌugly 'duckling *n* sby who or sthg that appears unpromising but turns out successful [*The Ugly Duckling*, story by Hans Christian Andersen (1805-75), Danish writer, in which an ugly 'duckling' grows into a beautiful swan]

ukase /yooh'kayz‖juː'keɪz/ *n* **1** a proclamation by a Russian emperor or government having

the force of law **2** an edict
ukulele /ˌyoohkəˈlayli‖ˌjuːkəˈleɪlɪ/ *n* a small usu 4-stringed guitar of Portuguese origin [Hawaiian *ʼukulele*, fr *ʼuku* small person, flea + *lele* jumping]
ulcer /ˈulsə‖ˈʌlsə/ *n* **1** a persistent open sore in skin or mucous membrane that often discharges pus **2** sthg that festers and corrupts – **ulcerous** *adj*
ulcerate /ˈulsəˌrayt‖ˈʌlsəˌreɪt/ *vb* to (cause to) become affected (as if) with an ulcer – **ulcerative** *adj*, **ulceration** *n*
ullage /ˈulij‖ˈʌlɪdʒ/ *n* the amount by which a container (e g a tank or bottle) is less than full
ulna /ˈulnə‖ˈʌlnə/ *n* the bone of the human forearm on the little-finger side; *also* a corresponding part of the forelimb of vertebrates above fishes – **ulnar** *adj*
ulterior /ulˈtiəri·ə‖ʌlˈtɪərɪə/ *adj* going beyond what is openly said or shown
[1]**ultimate** /ˈultimət‖ˈʌltɪmət/ *adj* **1a** last in a progression or series **b** eventual **2a** fundamental, basic <~ *reality*> **b** incapable of further analysis, division, or separation **3** maximum
[2]**ultimate** *n* sthg ultimate; *the* highest point
ˈ**ultimately** /-li‖-lɪ/ *adv* finally; AT LAST
ultimatum /ˌultiˈmaytəm‖ˌʌltɪˈmeɪtəm/ *n, pl* **ultimatums, ultimata** /-tə‖-tə/ a final proposition or demand; *esp* one whose rejection will end negotiations and cause a resort to direct action
ultimo /ˈultimoh‖ˈʌltɪməʊ/ *adj* of or occurring in the previous month
ultra- /ˌultrə-‖ˌʌltrə-/ *prefix* **1** beyond in space; on the other side of; trans- <ultra*planetary*> **2** beyond the range or limits of; super- <ultra*microscopic*> **3** excessively; extremely <ultra*modern*>
ultrahigh frequency /ˌultrəˈhie‖ˌʌltrəˈhaɪ/ *n* a radio frequency in the range between 300 megahertz and 3000 megahertz
ultramarine /ˌultrəməˈreen‖ˌʌltrəməˈriːn/ *n* **1** a deep blue pigment **2** vivid deep blue
[1]ˌ**ultraˈsonic** /-ˈsonik‖-ˈsɒnɪk/ *adj* supersonic: **a** *of waves and vibrations* having a frequency above about 20,000Hz **b** using, produced by, or relating to ultrasonic waves or vibrations – **ultrasonically** *adv*
[2]**ultrasonic** *n* an ultrasonic wave or frequency
ultrasound /ˈultrəsownd/ *n* vibrations like sound waves but with a frequency above those registered by human hearing
ˌ**ultraˈviolet** /-ˈvie·ələt‖-ˈvaɪələt/ *n* electromagnetic radiation having a wavelength between the violet end of the visible spectrum and X rays – **ultraviolet** *adj*
[1]**umber** /ˈumbə‖ˈʌmbə/ *n* **1** a brown earth used as a pigment **2** dark or yellowish brown
[2]**umber** *adj* of the colour of umber
umbilical cord /umˈbilikl‖ʌmˈbɪlɪkl/ *n* **1** a cord arising from the navel that connects the foetus with the placenta **2** a cable conveying power to a rocket or spacecraft before takeoff; *also* a tethering or supply line (e g for an astronaut outside a spacecraft or a diver underwater)
umbrage /ˈumbrij‖ˈʌmbrɪdʒ/ *n* a feeling of pique or resentment <*took* ~ *at the chairman's comment*> [Middle French, shade, shadow, deriv of Latin *umbra*
umbrella /umˈbrelə‖ʌmˈbrelə/ *n* **1** a collapsible shade for protection against weather, consisting of fabric stretched over hinged ribs radiating from a central pole **2** the bell-shaped or saucer-shaped largely gelatinous structure that forms the chief part of the body of most jellyfishes **3** sthg which provides protection <*the American nuclear* ~> **4** sthg that embraces a broad range of elements or factors [Italian *ombrella*, fr Latin *umbella*, diminutive of *umbra* shade]
umlaut /ˈoomlowt‖ˈʊmlaʊt/ *n* (a mark¨ placed over a letter in some Germanic languages to indicate) the change of a vowel caused by the influence of a following vowel or semivowel
[1]**umpire** /ˈumpie·ə‖ˈʌmpaɪə/ *n* **1** one having authority to settle a controversy or question between parties **2** a referee in any of several sports (e g cricket, table tennis, badminton, and hockey) [Middke English *oumpere*, alteration (by incorrect division of *a noumpere*) of *noumpere*, fr Middle French *nomper* not equal, not paired, fr *non-* not + *per* equal]
[2]**umpire** *vb* to act as or supervise (e g a match) as umpire
umpteen /ˌumpˈteen‖ˌʌmpˈtiːn/ *adj* very many; indefinitely numerous – infml – **umpteen** *n*, **umpteenth** *adj*
[1]**un-** /un-‖ʌn-/ *prefix* **1** not; in-, non- <un*skilled*> <un*belief*> **2** opposite of; contrary to <un*grateful*>
[2]**un-** *prefix* **1** do the opposite of; reverse (a specified action); DE- 1a, DIS- 1a <un*fold*> **2a** deprive of; remove (sthg specified) from; remove <un*frock*> **b** release from; free from <un*tie*> **c(1)** remove from; extract from; take out of <un*earth*> **c(2)** dislodge from <un*horse*> **d** cause to cease to be <un*man*> **3** completely <un*loose*>
unabashed *adj*
unabated *adj*
unable /unˈayb(ə)l‖ʌnˈeɪb(ə)l/ *adj* not able; incapable: **a** unqualified, incompetent **b** impotent, helpless
unabridged *adj*
unaccompanied *adj*
unaccountable /ˌunəˈkowntəbl‖ˌʌnəˈkaʊntəbl/ *adj* **1** inexplicable, strange **2** not to be called to account; not responsible – **unaccountably** *adv*, **unaccountability** *n*
unaccustomed /ˌunəˈkustəmd‖ˌʌnəˈkʌstəmd/ *adj* **1** not customary; not usual or common **2** not used *to* – **unaccustomedly** *adv*
unadopted /ˌunəˈdoptid‖ˌʌnəˈdɒptɪd/ *adj, Br* not looked after by local authority <*an* ~ *road*>
unadulterated /ˌunəˈdultəraytid‖ˌʌnəˈdʌltəreɪtɪd/ *adj* unmixed, esp with anything inferior; pure – **unadulteratedly** *adv*
unadvised /ˌunədˈviezd‖ˌʌnədˈvaɪzd/ *adj* not prudent; indiscreet, rash – **unadvisedly** *adv*
unaffected /ˌunəˈfektid‖ˌʌnəˈfektɪd/ *adj* **1** not influenced or changed mentally, physically, or chemically **2** free from affectation; genuine – **unaffectedly** *adv*, **unaffectedness** *n*
ˌ**un-Aˈmerican** *adj* not consistent with US customs, principles, or traditions

unanimous /yoo'nanimǝs‖jʊ'nænɪmǝs/ *adj* **1** being of one mind; agreeing **2** characterized by the agreement and consent of all [Latin *unanimus*, fr *unus* one + *animus* mind] – **unanimously** *adv*, **unanimity** *n*
unannounced *adj*
unanswerable /un'ahns(ǝ)rǝbl‖ʌn'ɑːns(ǝ)rǝbl/ *adj* not answerable; *esp* irrefutable – **unanswerably** *adv*, **unanswerabillty** *n*
unapproachable /ˌunǝ'prohchǝbl‖ˌʌnǝ'prǝʊtʃǝbl/ *adj* **1** physically inaccessible **2** reserved, unfriendly – **unapproachably** *adv*, **unapproachability** *n*
unarmed /ˌun'ahmd‖ˌʌn'ɑːmd/ *adj* **1** not armed or armoured **2** having no spines, spurs, claws, etc
unasked /ˌun'ahskt‖ˌʌn'ɑːskt/ *adj* **1** not asked or invited **2** not sought or asked for < ~ *advice*>
unassuming /ˌunǝ'syoohming‖ˌʌnǝ'sjuːmɪŋ/ *adj* not arrogant or presuming; modest – **unassumingness** *n*
unattached /ˌunǝ'tacht‖ˌʌnǝ'tætʃt/ *adj* **1** not assigned or committed; *esp* not married or engaged **2** not joined or united
unavailing /ˌunǝ'vayling‖ˌʌnǝ'veɪlɪŋ/ *adj* futile, useless – **unavailingly** *adv*, **unavailingness** *n*
unawares /ˌunǝ'weǝz‖ˌʌnǝ'weǝz/ *adv* **1** without noticing or intending **2** suddenly, unexpectedly
unbalance /un'balǝns‖ʌn'bælǝns/ *vt* to put out of balance; *esp* to derange mentally
unbar /ˌun'bah‖ˌʌn'bɑː/ *vt* **-rr-** to remove a bar from; unlock, open
unbearable /un'beǝrǝbl‖ʌn'beǝrǝbl/ *adj* not endurable; intolerable – **unbearably** *adv*
unbeknown /ˌunbi'nohn‖ˌʌnbɪ'nǝʊn/ *adj* happening without one's knowledge – usu + *to*
unbelief /ˌunbi'leef‖ˌʌnbɪ'liːf/ *n* incredulity or scepticism, esp in matters of religious faith
unbelievable /ˌunbi'leevǝbl‖ˌʌnbɪ'liːvǝbl/ *adj* too improbable for belief; incredible – **unbelievably** *adv*
unbeliever /ˌunbi'leevǝ‖ˌʌnbɪ'liːvǝ/ *n* one who does not believe, esp in a particular religion
unbelieving /ˌunbi'leeving‖ˌʌnbɪ'liːvɪŋ/ *adj* marked by unbelief; sceptical – **unbelievingly** *adv*
unbend /ˌun'bend‖ˌʌn'bend/ *vb* **unbent** /ˌun'bent‖ˌʌn'bent/ *vt* **1** to put into or allow to return to a straight position **2a** to unfasten (e g a sail) from a spar or stay **b** to cast loose or untie (e g a rope) ~ *vi* **1** to become more relaxed, informal, or outgoing in manner **2** to become straight
unbending /un'bending‖ʌn'bendɪŋ/ *adj* **1** unyielding, inflexible **2** aloof or unsociable in manner
unbidden /un'bidn‖ʌn'bɪdn/ *adj* unasked, uninvited
unbind /un'biend‖ʌn'baɪnd/ *vt* **unbound** /un'bownd‖ʌn'baʊnd/ **1** to untie, unfasten **2** to set free; release
unblushing /ˌun'blushing‖ˌʌn'blʌʃɪŋ/ *adj* shameless, unabashed – **unblushingly** *adv*
unborn /ˌun'bawn‖ˌʌn'bɔːn/ *adj* **1** not yet born **2** still to appear; future < ~ *ages*>
unbosom /un'boozǝm‖ʌn'bʊzǝm/ *vt* to disclose the thoughts or feelings of (oneself)
unbounded /un'bowndid‖ʌn'baʊndɪd/ *adj* having no limits or constraints – **unboundedness** *n*
unbowed /un'bowd‖ʌn'baʊd/ *adj* not bowed down; *esp* not subdued
un'bridled *adj* **1** not confined by a bridle **2** unrestrained, ungoverned
unbuckle /un'bukl‖ʌn'bʌkl/ *vt* to loose the buckle of; unfasten
unburden /un'buhd(ǝ)n‖ʌn'bɜːd(ǝ)n/ *vt* to free or relieve from anxiety, cares, etc
uncalled-for /un'kawld faw‖ʌn'kɔːld fɔː/ *adj* **1** unnecessary **2** offered without provocation or justification; gratuitous
uncanny /un'kani‖ʌn'kænɪ/ *adj* **1** eerie, mysterious **2** beyond what is normal or expected – **uncannily** *adv*, **uncanniness** *n*
unceremonious /ˌunserǝ'mohnyǝs, -ni·ǝs‖ˌʌnserǝ'mǝʊnjǝs, -nɪǝs/ *adj* **1** not ceremonious; informal **2** abrupt, rude – **unceremoniously** *adv*, **unceremoniousness** *n*
uncertain /un'suhtn‖ʌn'sɜːtn/ *adj* **1** not reliable or trustworthy **2a** not definitely known; undecided, unpredictable **b** not confident or sure; doubtful – **uncertainly** *adv*, **uncertainness** *n*
uncertainty /un'suht(ǝ)nti‖ʌn'sɜːt(ǝ)ntɪ/ *n* the state of being uncertain; doubt
uncharitable /un'charitǝbl‖ʌn'tʃærɪtǝbl/ *adj* severe in judging others; harsh – **uncharitableness** *n*, **uncharitably** *adv*
unchecked *adj*
unchristian /un'kristi·ǝn‖ʌn'krɪstɪǝn/ *adj* **1** contrary to the Christian spirit or character **2** barbarous, uncivilized
uncle /'ungkl‖'ʌŋkl/ *n* **1a** the brother of one's father or mother **b** the husband of one's aunt **2** a man who is a very close friend of a young child or its parents
unclean /un'kleen‖ʌn'kliːn/ *adj* **1** morally or spiritually impure **2a** ritually prohibited as food **b** ceremonially unfit or defiled **3** dirty, filthy – **uncleanness** *n*
ˌUncle 'Sam /sam‖sæm/ *n* the American nation, people, or government [prob jocular expansion of *US*, abbr of *United States*]
ˌUncle 'Tom /tom‖tɒm/ *n* a black American eager to win the approval of white people and willing to cooperate with them – chiefly derog [*Uncle Tom*, faithful black slave in the novel *Uncle Tom's Cabin* by Harriet Beecher Stowe (1811-96), US author]
uncomfortable /un'kumftǝbl‖ʌn'kʌmftǝbl/ *adj* **1** causing discomfort **2** feeling discomfort; ill at ease – **uncomfortably** *adv*
uncommitted /ˌunkǝ'mitid‖ˌʌnkǝ'mɪtɪd/ *adj* not pledged to a particular belief, allegiance, or course of action
uncommon /un'komǝn‖ʌn'kɒmǝn/ *adj* **1** not normally encountered; unusual **2** remarkable, exceptional – **uncommonly** *adv*, **uncommonness** *n*
uncompromising /un'komprǝmiezing‖ʌn'kɒmprǝmaɪzɪŋ/ *adj* not making or accepting a compromise; unyielding – **uncompromisingly** *adv*
unconcerned /ˌunkǝn'suhnd‖ˌʌnkǝn'sɜːnd/ *adj* **1** not involved or interested **2** not anxious or worried – **unconcernedly** *adv*, **unconcernedness** *n*
unconditional /ˌunkǝn'dish(ǝ)nl‖ˌʌnkǝn'dɪʃ(ǝ)nl / *adj* absolute, unqualified –

unconditionally *adv*

unconscionable /un'konsh(ə)nəbl‖ʌn'kɒnʃ(ə)nəbl/ *adj* **1** unscrupulous, unprincipled **2** excessive, unreasonable – **unconscionably** *adv*

[1]**unconscious** /un'konshəs‖ʌn'kɒnʃəs/ *adj* **1** not knowing or perceiving **2a** not possessing mind or having lost consciousness **b** not marked by or resulting from conscious thought, sensation, or feeling **3** not intentional or deliberate – **unconsciously** *adv*, **unconsciousness** *n*

[2]**unconscious** *n* the part of the mind that does not ordinarily enter a person's awareness but nevertheless influences behaviour and may be manifested in dreams or slips of the tongue

unconsidered /ˌunkən'sidəd‖ˌʌnkən'sɪdəd/ *adj* **1** disregarded, unnoticed **2** not carefully thought out

uncork /ˌun'kawk‖ˌʌn'kɔːk/ *vt* **1** to draw a cork from **2** to release from a pent-up state; unleash

uncouple /ˌun'kupl‖ˌʌn'kʌpl/ *vt* **1** to release (dogs) from a couple **2** to detach, disconnect – **uncoupler** *n*

uncouth /un'koohth‖ʌn'kuːθ/ *adj* awkward and uncultivated in speech or manner; boorish [Old English *uncūth*, fr *un-* + *cūth* familiar, known] – **uncouthly** *adv*, **uncouthness** *n*

uncover /un'kuvə‖ʌn'kʌvə/ *vt* **1** to disclose, reveal **2a** to remove the cover from **b** to remove the hat from (one's head)

uncritical /un'kritikl‖ʌn'krɪtɪkl/ *adj* lacking in discrimination or critical analysis – **uncritically** *adv*

uncrowned /un'krownd‖ʌn'kraʊnd/ *adj* **1** not having yet been crowned **2** having a specified status in fact but not in name <*the ~ champion*>

unction /'ungksh(ə)n‖'ʌŋkʃ(ə)n/ *n* the act of anointing as a rite of consecration or healing

unctuous /'ungktyoo·əs‖'ʌŋktjʊəs/ *adj* **1** fatty, oily, or greasy in texture or appearance **2** marked by ingratiating smoothness and false sincerity – **unctuously** *adv*, **unctuousness** *n*

uncut /un'kut‖ʌn'kʌt/ *adj* **1** not cut down or into **2** not shaped by cutting <*an ~ diamond*> **3** *of a book* not having the folds of the leaves trimmed off **4** not abridged or curtailed

undaunted /un'dawntid‖ʌn'dɔːntɪd/ *adj* not discouraged by danger or difficulty – **undauntedly** *adv*

undeceive /ˌundi'seev‖ˌʌndɪ'siːv/ *vt* to free from deception, illusion, or error

undecided /ˌundi'siedid‖ˌʌndɪ'saɪdɪd/ *adj* **1** in doubt **2** without a result <*the match was left ~*> – **undecidedly** *adv*, **undecidedness** *n*

undeniable /ˌundi'nie·əbl‖ˌʌndɪ'naɪəbl/ *adj* **1** plainly true; incontestable **2** unquestionably excellent or genuine – **undeniably** *adv*

[1]**under** /'undə‖'ʌndə/ *adv* **1** in or to a position below or beneath sthg **2a** in or to a lower rank or number <*£10 or ~*> **b** to a subnormal degree; deficiently – often in combination <under-*staffed*> **3** in or into a condition of subjection, subordination, or unconsciousness **4** so as to be covered, buried, or sheltered **5** BELOW 3

[2]**under** *prep* **1a** below or beneath so as to be overhung, surmounted, covered, protected, or hidden <*~ cover of darkness*> **b** using as a pseudonym or alias <*wrote ~ the name 'George Eliot'*> **2a(1)** subject to the authority, control, guidance, or instruction of <*served ~ the general*> **a(2)** during the rule or control of <*India ~ the Raj*> **b** receiving or undergoing the action or effect of <*courage ~ fire*> <*~ discussion*> **3** within the group or designation of <*~ this heading*> **4** less than or inferior to <*~ an hour*>; *esp* falling short of (a standard or required degree)

[3]**under** *adj* **1a** lying or placed below, beneath, or on the lower side **b** facing or pointing downwards **2** lower in rank or authority; subordinate **3** lower than usual, proper, or desired in amount or degree ***USE*** often in combination

ˌunder'act /-'akt‖-'ækt/ *vt* **1** to perform (a dramatic part) without adequate force or skill **2** to perform with restraint for greater dramatic impact or personal force ~*vi* to perform feebly or with restraint

[1]**'underˌarm** /-ˌahm‖-ˌɑːm/ *adj* **1** under or on the underside of the arm <*~ seams*> **2** made with the hand brought forwards and up from below shoulder level

[2]**underarm** *vt or adv* (to throw) with an underarm motion <*bowl ~*>

[3]**underarm** *n* the part of a garment that covers the underside of the arm

'underˌbelly /-ˌbeli‖-ˌbelɪ/ *n* **1** the underside of an animal, object, etc **2** a vulnerable area <*the soft ~ of capitalism*>

'underˌbrush /-ˌbrush‖-ˌbrʌʃ/ *n, NAm* undergrowth in a wood or forest

'underˌcarriage /-ˌkarij‖-ˌkærɪdʒ/ *n* **1** a supporting framework (e g of a motor vehicle) **2** the part of an aircraft's structure that supports its weight, when in contact with the land or water

ˌunder'charge /-'chahj‖-'tʃɑːdʒ/ *vb* to charge (e g a person) too little – **undercharge** *n*

'underˌclothes /-ˌklohdhz‖-ˌkləʊðz/ *n pl* underwear

'underˌcoat /-ˌkoht‖-ˌkəʊt/ *n* **1** a growth of short hair or fur partly concealed by a longer growth <*a dog's ~*> **2** a coat (e g of paint) applied as a base for another coat

'underˌcover /-ˌkuvə‖-ˌkʌvə/ *adj* acting or done in secret; *specif* engaged in spying

'underˌcurrent /-ˌkurənt‖-ˌkʌrənt/ *n* **1** a current below the upper currents or surface **2** a hidden opinion, feeling, or tendency

[1]**ˌunder'cut** /-'kut‖-'kʌt/ *vt* **-tt-; undercut** **1** to cut away the underpart of <*~ a vein of ore*> **2** to cut away material from the underside of so as to leave a portion overhanging **3** to offer sthg at lower prices than or work for lower wages than (a competitor)

[2]**'underˌcut** *n* **1** the action or result of undercutting **2** *Br* the underside of sirloin; a beef tenderloin **3** *NAm* a notch cut in a tree to determine the direction of falling during felling

ˌunderde'veloped /-di'veləpt‖-dɪ'veləpt/ *adj* **1** not normally or adequately developed <*~ muscles*> <*an ~ film*> **2** failing to realize a potential economic level – **underdevelopment** *n*

'underˌdog /-ˌdog‖-ˌdɒg/ *n* **1** an (expected) loser in a contest **2** a victim of

injustice or persecution

ˌunderˈdone /-ˈdun‖-ˈdʌn/ *adj* not thoroughly cooked

ˌunderˈestimate /-ˈestimayt‖-ˈestɪmeɪt/ *vt* **1** to estimate as being less than the actual size, quantity, etc **2** to place too low a value on; underrate – **underestimate** *n*, **underestimation** *n*

ˈunderˌfelt /-ˌfelt‖-ˌfelt/ *n* a thick felt underlay placed under a carpet

ˌunderˈfoot /-ˈfoot‖-ˈfʊt/ *adv* **1** under the feet, esp against the ground <*trampled* ~> **2** in the way <*children always getting* ~>

ˈunderˌgarment /-ˌgahmənt‖-ˌgɑːmənt/ *n* a garment to be worn under another

ˌunderˈgo /-ˈgoh‖-ˈgəʊ/ *vt* **underwent** /-ˈwent‖-ˈwent/; **undergone** /-ˈgon‖-ˈgɒn/ to be subjected to; experience

ˈunderˌgraduate /-ˌgradyoo·ət‖-ˌgrædjʊət/ *n* a college or university student who has not taken a first degree

¹ˌunderˈground /-ˈgrownd‖-ˈgraʊnd/ *adv* **1** beneath the surface of the earth **2** in or into hiding or secret operation

²underground *adj* **1** growing, operating, or situated below the surface of the ground **2a** conducted in hiding or in secret **b** existing or operated outside the establishment, esp by the avant-garde

³ˈunderˌground *n* **1** *sing or pl in constr* **1a** a secret movement or group esp in an occupied country, for concerted resistive action **b** a conspiratorial organization set up for disruption of a civil order **c** a usu avant-garde group or movement that functions outside the establishment **2** *Br* a usu electric underground urban railway; *also* a train running in an underground

ˈunderˌgrowth /-ˌgrohth‖-ˌgrəʊθ/ *n* shrub, bushes, saplings, etc growing under larger trees in a wood or forest

¹underhand /ˌundəˈhand‖ˌʌndəˈhænd; *sense 2* ˈ--ˌ-/ *adv* **1** in an underhand manner; secretly **2** underarm

²underhand *adj* **1** not honest and aboveboard; sly **2** UNDERARM 2

ˌunderˈhung /-ˈhung‖-ˈhʌŋ/ *adj* **1** *of a lower jaw* projecting beyond the upper jaw **2** having an underhung jaw

¹ˌunderˈlay /-ˈlay‖-ˈleɪ/ *vt* **ˌunderˈlaid** /-ˈlayd‖-ˈleɪd/ **1** to cover or line the bottom of; give support to on the underside or below **2** to raise by sthg laid under

²ˈunderˌlay *n* sthg that is (designed to be) laid under sthg else <*a carpet with foam* ~>

ˌunderˈlie /-ˈlie‖-ˈlaɪ/ *vt* **underlying** /-ˈlie·ing‖-ˈlaɪɪŋ/; **underlay** /-ˈlay‖-ˈleɪ/; **underlain** /-ˈlayn‖-ˈleɪn/ **1** to lie or be situated under **2** to form the basis or foundation of **3** to be concealed beneath the exterior of <underlying *hostility*>

ˌunderˈline /-ˈlien‖-ˈlaɪn/ *vt* **1** to mark (a word or passage) with a line underneath **2** to emphasize, stress – **underline** *n*

ˈunderling /-ling‖-lɪŋ/ *n* a subordinate or inferior

ˌunderˈmanned /-ˈmand‖-ˈmænd/ *adj* inadequately staffed

ˈunderˌmentioned /-ˌmensh(ə)nd‖-ˌmenʃ(ə)nd/ *adj*, *Br* referred to at a later point in a text

ˌunderˈmine /-ˈmien‖-ˈmaɪn/ *vt* **1** to form a mine under; sap **2** to weaken or destroy gradually or insidiously

¹underneath /ˌundəˈneeth‖ˌʌndəˈniːθ/ *prep* directly below; close under

²underneath *adv* **1** under or below an object or a surface; beneath **2** on the lower side

³underneath *n* the bottom part or surface <*the* ~ *of the bowl*>

ˌunderˈnourished /-ˈnurisht‖-ˈnʌrɪʃt/ *adj* supplied with less than the minimum amount of the foods essential for sound health and growth – **undernourishment** *n*

ˈunderˌpants /-ˌpants‖-ˌpænts/ *n pl* men's pants

ˈunderˌpass /-ˌpahs‖-ˌpɑːs/ *n* a tunnel or passage taking a road and pavement under another road or a railway

ˈunderˌpin /-ˌpin‖-ˌpɪn/ *vt* **-nn-** to form part of, strengthen, or replace the foundation of <~ *a sagging building*>

ˌunderˈplay /-ˈplay‖-ˈpleɪ/ *vt* **1** to underact (a role) **2** to play down the importance of

ˌunderˈprivileged /-ˈpriv(i)lijd‖-ˈprɪv(ɪ)lɪdʒd/ *adj* deprived of some of the fundamental social or economic rights of a civilized society <~ *children*>

ˌunderˈproof /-ˈproohf‖-ˈpruːf/ *adj* containing less alcohol than proof spirit

ˌunderˈquote /-ˈkwoht‖-ˈkwəʊt/ *vt* **1** to quote a lower price than (another person) **2** to quote a price for (e g goods or services) that is lower than another's offer or the market price

ˌunderˈrate /-ˈrayt‖-ˈreɪt/ *vt* to rate too low; undervalue

ˌunderˈscore /-ˈskaw‖-ˈskɔː/ *vt* to underline – **underscore** *n*

ˈunderˌsecretary /-ˌsekrətri, -ˌteri‖-ˌsekrətrɪ, -ˌterɪ/ *n* a secretary immediately subordinate to a principal secretary

ˌunderˈsell /-ˈsel‖-ˈsel/ *vt* **ˌunderˈsold** /-ˈsohld‖-ˈsəʊld/ **1** to be sold cheaper than <*imported cars that* ~ *domestic ones*> **2** to make little of the merits of <*he* undersold *himself*>; *esp* to promote or publicize in a (deliberately) low-key manner

ˌunderˈsexed /-ˈsekst‖-ˈsekst/ *adj* deficient in sexual drive or interest

ˈunderˌside /-ˌsied‖-ˌsaɪd/ *n* the side or surface lying underneath

ˈunderˌsigned /-ˌsiend‖-ˌsaɪnd/ *n*, *pl* **undersigned** *the* one who signs his/her name at the end of a document

ˌunderˈsized /-ˈsiezd‖-ˈsaɪzd/ *also* **ˈunderˌsize** *adj* of less than average size

ˌunderˈstaffed /-ˈstahft‖-ˈstɑːft/ *adj* undermanned

understand /ˌundəˈstand‖ˌʌndəˈstænd/ *vb* **understood** /-ˈstood‖-ˈstʊd/ *vt* **1a** to grasp the meaning of; comprehend **b** to have a thorough knowledge of or expertise in <~ *finance*> **2** to assume, suppose <*we* ~ *that he is abroad*> **3** to interpret in one of a number of possible ways <*as I* ~ *it*> **4** to supply mentally (sthg implied though not expressed) ~ *vi* **1** to have a grasp or understanding of sthg **2** to believe or infer sthg to be the case **3** to show a sympathetic or tolerant attitude <*if he loves her he'll* ~> – **understandable** *adj*, **understandably** *adv*, **understandability** *n*

[1]**ˌunder'standing** /-'standing‖-'stændɪŋ/ *n* **1** a mental grasp; comprehension **2** the power of comprehending; intelligence; *esp* the power to make experience intelligible by applying concepts **3a** a friendly or harmonious relationship **b** an informal mutual agreement

[2]**understanding** *adj* tolerant, sympathetic – **understandingly** *adv*

ˌunder'state /-'stayt‖-'steɪt/ *vt* **1** to state as being less than is the case **2** to present with restraint, esp for greater effect – **understatement** *n*

[1]**understudy** /ˌundə'studi, '--ˌ--‖ˌʌndə'stʌdɪ, '--ˌ--/ *vi* to study another actor's part in order to take it over in an emergency ~*vt* to prepare (e g a part) as understudy; *also* to prepare a part as understudy to

[2]**'underˌstudy** *n* one who is prepared to act another's part or take over another's duties

ˌunder'take /-'tayk‖-'teɪk/ *vt* **ˌunder'took** /-'took‖-'tʊk/; **ˌunder'taken** /-'taykən‖-'teɪkən/ **1** to take upon oneself as a task **2** to put oneself under obligation to do; contract **3** to guarantee, promise

'underˌtaker /-ˌtaykə‖-ˌteɪkə/ *n* sby whose business is preparing the dead for burial and arranging and managing funerals

'underˌtaking /-ˌtayking‖-ˌteɪkɪŋ/ *n* **1** the business of an undertaker **2** an enterprise **3** a pledge, guarantee

ˌunder-the-'counter *adj* surreptitious and usu illicit – infml

'underˌtone /-ˌtohn‖-ˌtəʊn/ *n* **1** a subdued utterance **2** an underlying quality (e g of emotion) **3** a subdued colour; *specif* one seen through and modifying another colour

'underˌtow /-ˌtoh‖-ˌtəʊ/ *n* **1** an undercurrent that flows in a different direction from the surface current, esp out to sea **2** a hidden tendency often contrary to the one that is publicly apparent

ˌunder'water /-'wawtə‖-'wɔːtə/ *adj* **1** situated, used, or designed to operate below the surface of the water **2** being below the waterline of a ship – **underwater** *adv*

'underˌwear /-ˌweə‖-ˌweə/ *n* clothing worn next to the skin and under other clothing

underweight /ˌundə'wayt‖ˌʌndə'weɪt; *noun* '--ˌ-/ *adj or n* (of a) weight below average or normal

'underˌworld /-ˌwuhld‖-ˌwɜːld/ *n* **1** the place of departed souls; Hades **2** the world of organized crime

ˌunder'write /-'riet‖-'raɪt/ *vb* **underwrote** /-'roht‖-'rəʊt/; **underwritten** /-'ritn‖-'rɪtn/ *vt* **1**to write under or at the end of sthg else **2** to set one's signature to (an insurance policy) thereby assuming liability in case of specified loss or damage; *also* to assume (a sum or risk) by way of insurance **3** to subscribe to; agree to **4a** to agree to purchase (a security issue) usu on a fixed date at a fixed price with a view to public distribution **b** to guarantee financial support of ~*vi* to carry on the business of an underwriter

'underˌwriter /-ˌrietə‖-ˌraɪtə/ *n* **1** one who underwrites sthg, esp an insurance policy **2** one who selects risks to be solicited or rates the acceptability of risks solicited

undesirable /ˌundi'zie·ərəbl‖ˌʌndɪ'zaɪərəbl/ *n or adj* (sby or sthg) unwanted or objectionable <~ *elements in society*> – **undesirably** *adv*, **undesirability** *n*

undeveloped *adj*

undies /'undiz‖'ʌndɪz/ *n pl* underwear; *esp* women's underwear – infml

undistinguished *adj*

undivided *adj*

undo /un'dooh‖ʌn'duː/ *vb* **undid** /un'did‖ʌn'dɪd/; **undone** /un'dun‖ʌn'dʌn/ *vt* **1** to open or loosen by releasing a fastening **2** to reverse or cancel out the effects of **3** to destroy the standing, reputation, hopes, etc of ~*vi* to come open or apart – **undoer** *n*

undoing /un'dooh·ing‖ʌn'duːɪŋ/ *n* (a cause of) ruin or downfall

[1]**undone** /un'dun‖ʌn'dʌn/ *past part of* UNDO

[2]**undone** *adj* not performed or finished

undoubted /un'dowtid‖ʌn'daʊtɪd/ *adj* not disputed; genuine – **undoubtedly** *adv*

undreamed /un'dreemd, un'dremt‖ʌn'driːmd, ʌn'dremt/ *also* **undreamt** /un'dremt‖ʌn'dremt/ *adj* not conceived of; unimagined – usu + *of*

[1]**undress** /un'dres‖ʌn'dres/ *vt* to remove the clothes or covering of ~*vi* to take off one's clothes

[2]**undress** *n* **1** ordinary dress **2** a state of having little or no clothing on

un'dressed *adj* **1** partially or completely unclothed **2** not fully processed or finished <~ *hides*> **3** not cared for or tended <*an* ~ *wound*>

undue /un'dyooh‖ʌn'djuː/ *adj* **1** not yet due **2** excessive, immoderate

[1]**undulate** /'undyooˌlayt‖'ʌndjʊˌleɪt/, **undulated** /-ˌlaytid‖-ˌleɪtɪd/ *adj* having a wavy surface, edge, or markings [Latin *undulatus*, fr *unda* wave; akin to Old English *wæter* water – see WATER]

[2]**undulate** *vi* **1** to rise and fall in waves; fluctuate **2** to have a wavy form or appearance

undulation /ˌundyoo'laysh(ə)n‖ˌʌndjʊ'leɪʃ(ə)n/ *n* **1a** a gentle rising and falling (as if) in waves **b** a wavelike motion; *also* a single wave or gentle rise **2** a wavy appearance, outline, or form

unduly /un'dyoohli‖ʌn'djuːlɪ/ *adv* excessively

undying /un'die·ing‖ʌn'daɪɪŋ/ *adj* eternal, perpetual

unearth /un'uhth‖ʌn'ɜːθ/ *vt* **1** to dig up out of the ground **2** to make known or public

unearthly /un'uhthli‖ʌn'ɜːθlɪ/ *adj* **1** not terrestrial <~ *radio sources*> **2** exceeding what is normal or natural; supernatural **3** weird, eerie **4** unreasonable, outrageous <*getting up at an* ~ *hour*> – **unearthliness** *n*

unease /un'eez‖ʌn'iːz/ *n* a feeling of disquiet or awkwardness

uneasy /un'eezi‖ʌn'iːzɪ/ *adj* **1** uncomfortable, awkward **2** apprehensive, worried **3** precarious, unstable – **uneasily** *adv*, **uneasiness** *n*

uneconomic /ˌunekə'nomik, -eekə-‖ˌʌnekə'nɒmɪk, -iːkə-/ *also* **uneconomical** /-kl‖-kl/ *adj* not

economically practicable
uneducated *adj*
unemployed /ˌunim'ployd‖ˌʌnɪm'plɔɪd/ *adj* **1** not engaged in a job **2** not invested – **unemployed** *n pl in constr*
unemployment /ˌunim'ploymənt‖ˌʌnɪm'plɔɪmənt/ *n* the state of being unemployed; lack of available employment
unenviable *adj*
unequal /un'eekwəl‖ʌn'iːkwəl/ *adj* **1a** not of the same measurement, quantity, or number as another **b** not like in quality, nature, or status **c** not the same for every member of a group, class, or society **2** badly balanced or matched **3** not uniform **4** incapable of meeting the requirements of sthg – + *to* – **unequally** *adv*
un'equalled *adj* not equalled; unparalleled
unequivocal /ˌuni'kwivəkl‖ˌʌnɪ'kwɪvəkl/ *adj* clear, unambiguous – **unequivocally** *adv*
unerring /un'uhring‖ʌn'ɜːrɪŋ/ *adj* faultless, unfailing – **unerringly** *adv*
uneven /un'eev(ə)n‖ʌn'iːv(ə)n/ *adj* **1a** not level, smooth, or uniform **b** varying from the straight or parallel **c** irregular, inconsistent **d** varying in quality **2** UNEQUAL 2 – **unevenly** *adv*, **unevenness** *n*
uneventful /ˌuni'ventf(ə)l‖ˌʌnɪ'ventf(ə)l/ *adj* without any noteworthy or untoward incidents – **uneventfully** *adv*
unexceptionable /ˌunik'sepsh(ə)nəbl‖ˌʌnɪk'sepʃ(ə)nəbl/ *adj* beyond reproach or criticism – **unexceptionableness** *n*, **unexceptionably** *adv*
unexpected /ˌunik'spektid‖ˌʌnɪk'spektɪd/ *adj* not expected or foreseen – **unexpectedly** *adv*, **unexpectedness** *n*
unfailing /un'fayling‖ʌn'feɪlɪŋ/ *adj* that can be relied on; constant <*a subject of* ~ *interest*> – **unfailingly** *adv*, **unfailingness** *n*
unfaithful /un'faythf(ə)l‖ʌn'feɪθf(ə)l/ *adj* **1** disloyal, faithless **2** not faithful to a marriage partner, lover, etc, esp in having sexual relations with another person – **unfaithfully** *adv*, **unfaithfulness** *n*
unfaltering /un'fawltəring‖ʌn'fɔːltərɪŋ/ *adj* not wavering or hesitating; firm – **unfalteringly** *adv*
unfavourable /un'fayv(ə)rəbl‖ʌn'feɪv(ə)rəbl/ *adj* **1** expressing disapproval; negative **2** disadvantageous, adverse – **unfavourably** *adv*
unfeeling /un'feeling‖ʌn'fiːlɪŋ/ *adj* not kind or sympathetic; hardhearted – **unfeelingly** *adv*, **unfeelingness** *n*
unfetter /un'fetə‖ʌn'fetə/ *vt* **1** to release from fetters **2** to free from restraint; liberate
[1]**unfit** /un'fit‖ʌn'fɪt/ *adj* **1** unsuitable, inappropriate **2** incapable, incompetent **3** physically or mentally unsound – **unfitness** *n*
[2]**unfit** *vt* **-tt-** to make unfit; disqualify
unflagging /un'flaging‖ʌn'flægɪŋ/ *adj* never flagging; tireless – **unflaggingly** *adv*
unflappable /un'flapəbl‖ʌn'flæpəbl/ *adj* remaining calm and composed; imperturbable – **unflappability** *n*
unflinching /un'flinching‖ʌn'flɪntʃɪŋ/ *adj* not flinching or shrinking; steadfast – **unflinchingly** *adv*
unfold /un'fohld‖ʌn'fəʊld/ *vt* **1** to open the folds of; spread or straighten out **2** to disclose gradually ~ *vi* **1** to open from a folded state **2** to open out gradually to the mind or eye
unforeseen *adj*
unforgettable /ˌunfə'getəbl‖ˌʌnfə'getəbl/ *adj* incapable of being forgotten; memorable – **unforgettably** *adv*
[1]**unfortunate** /un'fawch(ə)nət‖ʌn'fɔːtʃ(ə)nət/ *adj* **1a** unsuccessful, unlucky **b** accompanied by or resulting in misfortune **2** unsuitable, inappropriate
[2]**unfortunate** *n* an unfortunate person
un'fortunately /-li‖-lɪ/ *adv* **1** in an unfortunate manner **2** as is unfortunate
unfounded /un'fowndid‖ʌn'faʊndɪd/ *adj* lacking a sound basis; groundless
unfrequented /ˌunfri'kwentid, -'freekwəntid‖ˌʌnfrɪ'kwentɪd, -'friːkwəntɪd/ *adj* not often visited or travelled over
unfrock /un'frok‖ʌn'frɒk/ *vt* to deprive (esp a priest) of the right to exercise the functions of office
unfurl /un'fuhl‖ʌn'fɜːl/ *vb* to (cause to) open out from a furled state; unroll
ungainly /un'gaynli‖ʌn'geɪnlɪ/ *adj* lacking in grace or dexterity; clumsy – **ungainliness** *n*
ungenerous /un'jen(ə)rəs‖ʌn'dʒen(ə)rəs/ *adj* **1** petty, uncharitable **2** stingy, mean – **ungenerously** *adv*
ungodly /un'godli‖ʌn'gɒdlɪ/ *adj* **1a** denying God or disobedient to him; heathen **b** sinful, wicked **2** UNEARTHLY 4 – **ungodliness** *n*
ungovernable /un'guv(ə)nəbl‖ʌn'gʌv(ə)nəbl/ *adj* not capable of being controlled or restrained
ungracious /un'grayshəs‖ʌn'greɪʃəs/ *adj* rude, impolite – **ungraciously** *adv*, **ungraciousness** *n*
ungrateful /un'graytf(ə)l‖ʌn'greɪtf(ə)l/ *adj* **1** showing no gratitude **2** disagreeable, unpleasant – **ungratefully** *adv*, **ungratefulness** *n*
ungrudging /un'grujing‖ʌn'grʌdʒɪŋ/ *adj* generous, wholehearted – **ungrudgingly** *adv*
unguarded /un'gahdid‖ʌn'gɑːdɪd/ *adj* **1** vulnerable to attack **2** showing lack of forethought or calculation; imprudent – **unguardedly** *adv*, **unguardedness** *n*
unguent /'ung·gwənt‖'ʌŋgwənt/ *n* a soothing or healing salve; ointment
unhand /un'hand‖ʌn'hænd/ *vt* to remove the hands from; let go
unhappily /un'hapəli‖ʌn'hæpəlɪ/ *adv* **1** in an unhappy manner **2** UNFORTUNATELY 2
unhappy /un'hapi‖ʌn'hæpɪ/ *adj* **1** not fortunate; unlucky **2** sad, miserable **3** unsuitable, inappropriate <*an* ~ *remark*> – **unhappiness** *n*
unhealthy /un'helthi‖ʌn'helθɪ/ *adj* **1** not in or conducive to good health **2** unnatural; *esp* morbid <*an* ~ *interest in death*> – **unhealthily** *adv*, **unhealthiness** *n*
unheard /un'huhd‖ʌn'hɜːd/ *adj* **1** not perceived by the ear **2** not given a hearing
un'heard-of *adj* previously unknown; unprecedented
unhinge /un'hinj‖ʌn'hɪndʒ/ *vt* **1** to remove (e g a door) from hinges **2** to make unstable; unsettle <*her mind was* ~d *by grief*>
unholy /un'hohli‖ʌn'həʊlɪ/ *adj* **1** wicked, reprehensible <*an* ~ *alliance*> **2** terrible, awful –

infml <*making an* ~ *racket*> – **unholiness** *n*

unhook /un'hook‖ʌn'hʊk/ *vt* **1** to remove from a hook **2** to unfasten the hooks of

unhorse /un'haws‖ʌn'hɔːs/ *vt* to dislodge (as if) from a horse

uni- /yoohni-‖juːnɪ-/ *prefix* one; single <uni*cellular*>

unicorn /'yoohni,kawn‖'juːnɪ,kɔːn/ *n* a mythical animal usu depicted as a white horse with a single horn in the middle of the forehead

unidentified *adj*

[1]**uniform** /'yoohni,fawm‖'juːnɪ,fɔːm/ *adj* **1** not varying in character, appearance, quantity, etc <*a* ~ *speed*> **2** conforming to a rule, pattern, or practice; consonant – **uniformly** *adv*, **uniformness** *n*, **uniformity** *n*

[2]**uniform** *vt* to clothe in a uniform <*a* ~ed *officer*>

[3]**uniform** *n* dress of a distinctive design or fashion worn by members of a particular group and serving as a means of identification

unify /'yoohni,fie‖'juːnɪ,faɪ/ *vt* to make into a unit or a coherent whole; unite – **unifier** *n*, **unifiable** *adj*, **unification** *n*

,uni'lateral /-'lat(ə)rəl‖-'læt(ə)rəl/ *adj* **1a** done or undertaken by 1 person or party <~ *disarmament*> **b** of or affecting 1 side **2** produced or arranged on or directed towards 1 side <*a stem bearing* ~ *flowers*> **3** having only 1 side – **unilaterally** *adv*

unimpeachable /,unim'peechəbl‖,ʌnɪm'piːtʃəbl/ *adj* **1** not to be doubted; beyond question **2** irreproachable, blameless – **unimpeachably** *adv*

uninhibited /,unin'hibitid‖,ʌnɪn'hɪbɪtɪd/ *adj* acting spontaneously without constraint or regard for what others might think – **uninhibitedly** *adv*, **uninhibitedness** *n*

uninterested *adj*

uninterrupted *adj*

[1]**union** /'yoohnyən‖'juːnjən/ *n* **1a(1)** the formation of a single political unit from 2 or more separate and independent units **a(2)** a uniting in marriage; *also* SEXUAL INTERCOURSE **b** combination, junction **2a(1)** an association of independent individuals (e g nations) for some common purpose **a(2)** a political unit made up from previously independent units **b** TRADE UNION **3** a coupling for pipes (and fittings)

[2]**union** *adj* of, dealing with, or constituting a union

unionism /'yoohnyə,niz(ə)m‖'juːnjə,nɪz(ə)m/ *n* **1** adherence to the principles of trade unions **2** *cap* adherence to the policy of union between the states of the USA, esp during the Civil War **3** *cap* the principles and policies of the Unionist party

unionist /'yoohnyənist‖'juːnjənɪst/ *n* an advocate or supporter of union or unionism

Unionist *adj* of or constituting a political party of N Ireland that supports the union with Britain and draws support generally from the Protestant community

union·ize, -ise /'yoohnyə,niez‖'juːnjə,naɪz/ *vt* to cause to become a member of or subject to the rules of a trade union; form into a trade union – **unionization**

,Union 'Jack /jak‖dʒæk/ *n* the national flag of the UK combining crosses representing England, Scotland, and N Ireland

unique /yooh'neek, yoo-‖juː'niːk, jʊ-/ *adj* **1a** sole, only <*his* ~ *concern*> **b** producing only 1 result <*the* ~ *factorization of a number into prime factors*> **2** without a like or equal; unequalled **3** very rare or unusual – disapproved of by some speakers [French, fr Latin *unicus*, fr *unus* one] – **uniquely** *adv*, **uniqueness** *n*

unisex /'yoohni,seks‖'juːnɪ,seks/ *adj* **1** able to be worn by both sexes <*a* ~ *hair style*> **2** dealing in unisex products or styles <*a* ~ *barber's*>

unison /'yoohnis(ə)n, -z(ə)n‖'juːnɪs(ə)n, -z(ə)n/ *n* **1a** (the state of) identity in musical pitch; the interval between 2 notes of the same pitch **b** the writing, playing, or singing of parts in a musical passage at the same pitch or in octaves **2** harmonious agreement or union – **unison** *adj*

unit /'yoohnit‖'juːnɪt/ *n* **1a(1)** the first and lowest natural number; one **a(2)** a single quantity regarded as a whole in calculation **b** the number occupying the position immediately to the left of the decimal point in the Arabic notation; *also, pl* this position **2** a determinate quantity (e g of length, time, heat, value, or housing) adopted as a standard of measurement **3a** a single thing, person, or group that is a constituent of a whole **b** a part of a military establishment that has a prescribed organization (e g of personnel and supplies) **c** a piece of apparatus serving to perform 1 particular function – **unit** *adj*, **unitive** *adj*, **unitize** *vt*

unitarian /,yoohni'teəri·ən‖,juːnɪ'teərɪən/ *n* **1** *often cap* a person who rejects the doctrine of the Trinity and believes in one god who is a single being **2** *cap* a member of a Christian denomination that stresses individual freedom of belief, the free use of reason in religion, a united world community, and liberal social action – **unitarian** *adj, often cap*, **unitarianism** *n, often cap*

unite /yoo'niet, yooh-‖jʊ'naɪt, juː-/ *vt* **1** to join together to form a single unit **2** to link by a legal or moral bond <~d *by marriage*> ~ *vi* **1** to become (as if) 1 unit **2** to act in concert – **uniter** *n*

u'nited *adj* **1** combined, joined **2** relating to or produced by joint action <*a* ~ *effort*> **3** in agreement; harmonious – **unitedly** *adv*

unit trust *n* an investment company that minimizes the risk to investors by collective purchase of shares in many different enterprises

unity /'yoohnəti‖'juːnətɪ/ *n* **1a** the state of being 1 or united <*strength lies in* ~> **b(1)** a definite amount taken as 1 or for which 1 is made to stand in calculation <*in a table of natural sines the radius of the circle is regarded as* ~> **b(2)** a number by which any element of an arithmetical or mathematical system can be multiplied without change in the resultant value **2a** concord, harmony **b** continuity and agreement in aims and interests <~ *of purpose*> **3** singleness of effect or symmetry in a literary or artistic work **4** a whole made up of related parts

univalent /,yoohni'vaylənt‖,juːnɪ'veɪlənt/ *adj* **1** having a valency of 1 **2** *of a chromosome* not pairing with another chromosome at meiotic cell division

[1]**universal** /ˌyoohniˈvuhs(ə)l‖ˌjuːnɪˈvɜːs(ə)l/ *adj* **1** including or covering all or a whole without limit or exception **2** present or occurring everywhere or under all conditions **3** including a major part or the greatest portion (e g of mankind) < ~ *practices*> – **universalize** *vt*, **universally** *adv*, **universalness** *n*, **universality** *n*

[2]**universal** *n* **1** a universal proposition in logic **2** a general concept or term

universal joint *n* a shaft coupling capable of transmitting rotation from one shaft to another at an angle

universe /ˈyoohniˌvuhs‖ˈjuːnɪˌvɜːs/ *n* **1a(1)** all things that exist; the cosmos **a(2)** a galaxy **b** the whole world; everyone **2** POPULATION 5 [Latin *universum*, fr neuter of *universus* entire, whole, fr *unus* one + *versus* turned towards, fr past participle of *vertere* to turn]

university /ˌyoohniˈvuhsəti‖ˌjuːnɪˈvɜːsətɪ/ *n* (the premises of) an institution of higher learning that provides facilities for full-time teaching and research, is authorized to grant academic degrees, and in Britain receives a Treasury grant

unkempt /unˈkempt‖ʌnˈkempt/ *adj* **1** not combed; dishevelled < ~ *hair*> **2** not neat or tidy

unkind /unˈkiend‖ʌnˈkaɪnd/ *adj* **1** not pleasing or mild <*an* ~ *climate*> **2** lacking in kindness or sympathy; harsh – **unkindly** *adv*, **unkindness** *n*

unknowing /unˈnoh·ing‖ʌnˈnəʊɪŋ/ *adj* not knowing – **unknowingly** *adv*

[1]**unknown** /unˈnohn‖ʌnˈnəʊn/ *adj* not known; *also* having an unknown value <*an* ~ *quantity*>

[2]**unknown** *n* **1** a person who is little known (e g to the public) **2** a symbol in a mathematical equation representing an unknown quantity

unlawful /unˈlawf(ə)l‖ʌnˈlɔːf(ə)l/ *adj* **1** illegal **2** not morally right or conventional – **unlawfully** *adv*, **unlawfulness** *n*

unlearn /unˈluhn‖ʌnˈlɜːn/ *vt* to put out of one's knowledge or memory

unleash /unˈleesh‖ʌnˈliːʃ/ *vt* to free (as if) from a leash; loose from restraint or control

unleavened *adj*

unless /ənˈles‖ənˈles/ *conj* **1** except on the condition that <*won't work* ~ *you put in some money*> **2** without the necessary accompaniment that; except when <*we swim* ~ *it's very cold*>

unlettered /unˈletəd‖ʌnˈletəd/ *adj* illiterate

[1]**unlike** /ˌunˈliek‖ˌʌnˈlaɪk/ *prep* **1** different from **2** not characteristic of < ~ *him to be late*> **3** in a different manner from

[2]**unlike** *adj* **1** marked by dissimilarity; different **2** unequal – **unlikeness** *n*

unˈlikely /-li‖-lɪ/ *adj* **1** having a low probability of being or occurring <*an* ~ *possibility*> **2** not believable; improbable <*an* ~ *story*> **3** likely to fail; unpromising **4** not foreseen <*the* ~ *result*> – **unlikelihood** *n*, **unlikeliness** *n*

unload /unˈlohd‖ʌnˈləʊd/ *vt* **1a(1)** to take off or out **a(2)** to take the cargo from **b** to give vent to; pour forth **2** to relieve of sthg burdensome **3** to draw the charge from **4** DUMP 2 ~*vi* to perform the act of unloading – **unloader** *n*

unlock /unˈlok‖ʌnˈlɒk/ *vt* **1** to unfasten the lock of **2** to open, release **3** to provide a key to; disclose < ~ *the secrets of nature*> ~*vi* to become unlocked

unlooked-for /unˈlookt faw‖ʌnˈlʊkt fɔː/ *adj* not foreseen or expected

unloose /unˈloohs‖ʌnˈluːs/ *vt* **1** to relax the strain of < ~ *a grip*> **2** to release (as if) from restraints; set free **3** to loosen the ties of

unloosen /unˈloohs(ə)n‖ʌnˈluːs(ə)n/ *vt* to unloose

unmade /ˌunˈmayd‖ˌʌnˈmeɪd/ *adj, of a bed* not put in order ready for sleeping

unmannerly /unˈmanəli‖ʌnˈmænəlɪ/ *adj* discourteous, rude – **unmannerliness** *n*

unmarried *adj*

unmask /unˈmahsk‖ʌnˈmɑːsk/ *vt* **1** to remove a mask from **2** to reveal the true nature of; expose

unmentionable /unˈmensh(ə)nəbl‖ʌnˈmenʃ(ə)nəbl/ *adj* not fit to be mentioned; unspeakable

unˈmentionables *n pl* underwear – euph or humor

unmindful /unˈmiendf(ə)l‖ʌnˈmaɪndf(ə)l/ *adj* not taking into account; forgetful *of*

unmistakable /ˌunmiˈstaykəbl‖ˌʌnmɪˈsteɪkəbl/ *adj* clear, obvious – **unmistakably** *adv*

unmitigated /unˈmitigaytid‖ʌnˈmɪtɪgeɪtɪd/ *adj* **1** not diminished in severity, intensity, etc **2** out-and-out, downright <*an* ~ *evil*> – **unmitigatedly** *adv*

unnatural /unˈnachərəl‖ʌnˈnætʃərəl/ *adj* **1** not in accordance with nature or a normal course of events **2a** not in accordance with normal feelings or behaviour; perverse **b** artificial or contrived in manner – **unnaturally** *adv*, **unnaturalness** *n*

unnecessary /unˈnesəs(ə)ri, -ˌseri‖ʌnˈnesəs(ə)rɪ, -ˌserɪ/ *adj* not necessary – **unnecessarily** *adv*

unnerve /unˈnuhv‖ʌnˈnɜːv/ *vt* to deprive of nerve, courage, or the power to act – **unnervingly** *adv*

unnumbered /ˌunˈnumbəd‖ˌʌnˈnʌmbəd/ *adj* **1** innumerable **2** without an identifying number < ~ *pages*>

unobtrusive /ˌunəbˈtroohsiv, -ziv‖ˌʌnəbˈtruːsɪv, -zɪv/ *adj* not too easily seen or noticed; inconspicuous – **unobtrusively** *adv*, **unobtrusiveness** *n*

unofficial *adj*

unorthodox /unˈawthədoks‖ʌnˈɔːθədɒks/ *adj* not conventional in behaviour, beliefs, doctrine, etc – **unorthodoxly** *adv*, **unorthodoxy** *n*

unpack /unˈpak‖ʌnˈpæk/ *vt* **1** to remove the contents of **2** to remove or undo from packing or a container ~*vi* to set about unpacking sthg – **unpacker** *n*

unparalleled /unˈparəleld‖ʌnˈpærəleld/ *adj* having no equal or match; unique

unparliamentary /ˌunpahləˈmentəri‖ˌʌnpɑːləˈmentərɪ; *also* -lyə-‖-ljə-/ *adj* not in accordance with parliamentary practice

unperson /unˈpuhs(ə)n‖ʌnˈpɜːs(ə)n/ *n, pl* **unpersons** a person who, usu for political or ideological reasons, is officially unrecognized

unpick /unˈpik‖ʌnˈpɪk/ *vt* to undo (e g sewing) by taking out stitches

unplaced /un'playst‖ʌn'pleɪst/ *adj, chiefly Br* having failed to finish in a leading place in a competition, esp a horse race
unplayable *adj*
unpleasant /un'plez(ə)nt‖ʌn'plez(ə)nt/ *adj* not pleasant or agreeable; displeasing – **unpleasantly** *adv*
unplumbed /un'plumd‖ʌn'plʌmd/ *adj* not thoroughly explored
unprecedented /un'presidentid‖ʌn'presɪdentɪd/ *adj* having no precedent; novel – **unprecedentedly** *adv*
unprejudiced /un'prejoodist, -jə-‖ʌn'predʒʊdɪst, -dʒə-/ *adj* impartial, fair
unpretentious /,unpri'tenshəs‖,ʌnprɪ'tenʃəs/ *adj* not seeking to impress others by means of wealth, standing, etc; not affected or ostentatious – **unpretentiously** *adv*, **unpretentiousness** *n*
unprincipled /un'prinsip(ə)ld‖ʌn'prɪnsɪp(ə)ld/ *adj* without moral principles; unscrupulous – **unprincipledness** *n*
unprintable /un'printəbl‖ʌn'prɪntəbl/ *adj* unfit to be printed
unprovoked *adj*
unqualified /un'kwolified‖ʌn'kwɒlɪfaɪd/ *adj* **1** not having the necessary qualifications **2** not modified or restricted by reservations – **unqualifiedly** *adv*
unquestionable /un'kwesch(ə)nəbl‖ʌn'kwestʃ(ə)nəbl/ *adj* not able to be called in question; indisputable – **unquestionably** *adv*
unquestioning /un'kwesch(ə)ning‖ʌn'kwestʃ(ə)nɪŋ/ *adj* not expressing doubt or hesitation – **unquestioningly** *adv*
unquiet /un'kwie·ət‖ʌn'kwaɪət/ *adj* **1** agitated, turbulent **2** physically or mentally restless; uneasy – **unquietly** *adv*, **unquietness** *n*
unquote /,un'kwoht‖,ʌn'kwəʊt/ *n* – used orally to indicate the end of a direct quotation
unravel /un'ravl‖ʌn'rævl/ *vb* **-ll-** (*NAm* **-l-**, **-ll-**) *vt* **1** to disentangle **2** to clear up or solve (sthg intricate or obscure) ~*vi* to become unravelled
unreal *adj*
unreasonable /un'reez(ə)nəbl‖ʌn'ri:z(ə)nəbl/ *adj* **1** not governed by or acting according to reason **2** excessive, immoderate – **unreasonableness** *n*, **unreasonably** *adv*
unreasoning /un'reezəning‖ʌn'ri:zənɪŋ/ *adj* not moderated or controlled by reason – **unreasoningly** *adv*
unrelenting /,unri'lenting‖,ʌnrɪ'lentɪŋ/ *adj* **1** not weakening in determination; stern **2** not letting up in vigour, pace, etc – **unrelentingly** *adv*
unrelieved *adj*
unremitting /,unri'miting‖,ʌnrɪ'mɪtɪŋ/ *adj* constant, incessant – **unremittingly** *adv*
unrequited *adj*
unreserved /,unri'zuhvd‖,ʌnrɪ'zɜ:vd/ *adj* **1** entire, unqualified **2** frank and open in manner – **unreservedly** *adv*, **unreservedness** *n*
unrest /un'rest‖ʌn'rest/ *n* agitation, turmoil
unrestrained /unri'straynd‖ʌnrɪ'streɪnd/ *adj* not held in check; uncontrolled – **unrestrainedly** *adv*, **unrestrainedness** *n*
unrivalled, *NAm chiefly* **unrivaled** /un'rievld‖ʌn'raɪvld/ *adj* unequalled, unparalleled
unroll /un'rohl‖ʌn'rəʊl/ *vt* to open out; uncoil ~*vi* to be unrolled; unwind
unruffled /un'rufld‖ʌn'rʌfld/ *adj* **1** poised, serene **2** smooth, calm <~ *water*>
unruly /un'roohli‖ʌn'ru:lɪ/ *adj* difficult to discipline or manage – **unruliness** *n*
unsaddle /un'sadl‖ʌn'sædl/ *vt* **1** to take the saddle from **2** to throw from the saddle ~*vi* to remove the saddle from a horse
unsaid /un'sed‖ʌn'sed/ *adj* not said or spoken
unsavoury /un'sayvəri‖ʌn'seɪvərɪ/ *adj* disagreeable, distasteful; *esp* morally offensive
unscathed /un'skaydhd‖ʌn'skeɪðd/ *adj* entirely unharmed or uninjured
unschooled /un'skoohld‖ʌn'sku:ld/ *adj* untaught, untrained
unscramble /,un'skrambl‖,ʌn'skræmbl/ *vt* **1** to separate into original components **2** to restore (scrambled communication) to intelligible form – **unscrambler** *n*
unscrew /un'skrooh‖ʌn'skru:/ *vt* **1** to remove the screws from **2** to loosen or withdraw by turning ~*vi* to become unscrewed
unscrupulous /un'skroohpyooləs‖ʌn'skru:pjʊləs/ *adj* unprincipled – **unscrupulously** *adv*, **unscrupulousness** *n*
unseat /,un'seet‖,ʌn'si:t/ *vt* **1** to dislodge from one's seat, esp on horseback **2** to remove from a (political) position
unseeing *adj*
unseemly /un'seemli‖ʌn'si:mlɪ/ *adj* not conforming to established standards of good behaviour or taste
[1]**unseen** /,un'seen‖,ʌn'si:n/ *adj* done without previous preparation <*an* ~ *translation*>
[2]**unseen** *n, chiefly Br* a passage of unprepared translation
unserviceable *adj*
unsettle /un'setl‖ʌn'setl/ *vt* **1** to move from a settled state or condition **2** to perturb or agitate ~*vi* to become unsettled – **unsettlingly** *adv*
unsettled /un'setld‖ʌn'setld/ *adj* **1a** not calm or tranquil; disturbed **b** variable, changeable <~ *weather*> **2** not resolved or worked out; undecided **3** not inhabited or populated **4** not paid or discharged <~ *debts*> – **unsettledness** *n*
unsex /,un'seks‖,ʌn'seks/ *vt* to deprive of sexual power or the typical qualities of one's sex
unshakable *adj*
unsightly /un'sietli‖ʌn'saɪtlɪ/ *adj* not pleasing to the eye; ugly
unskilled /,un'skild‖,ʌn'skɪld/ *adj* **1** of, being, or requiring workers who are not skilled in any particular branch of work **2** showing a lack of skill
unsociable /un'sohsh(i)əbl‖ʌn'səʊʃ(ɪ)əbl/ *adj* not liking social activity; reserved, solitary – **unsociableness** *n*, **unsociably** *adv*, **unsociability** *n*
unsocial /un'sohsh(ə)l‖ʌn'səʊʃ(ə)l/ *adj* **1** unsociable **2** *Br* worked at a time that falls outside the normal working day and precludes participation in normal social activities <~ *hours*> – **unsocially** *adv*
unsophisticated /,unsə'fisti,kaytid‖,ʌnsə'fɪstɪ,keɪtɪd/ *adj* **1** pure, unadulterated **2** not socially or culturally sophisticated **3** simple, straightforward – **unsophistication** *n*

unsound /ˌun'sownd‖ˌʌn'saʊnd/ *adj* **1** not healthy or whole **2** mentally abnormal <*of ~ mind*> **3** not firmly made, placed, or fixed **4** not valid or true; specious – **unsoundly** *adv*, **unsoundness** *n*

unsparing /ˌun'speəring‖ˌʌn'speərɪŋ/ *adj* **1** not merciful; hard, ruthless **2** liberal, generous – **unsparingly** *adv*

unspeakable /un'speekəbl‖ʌn'spiːkəbl/ *adj* **1** incapable of being expressed in words **2** too terrible or shocking to be expressed – **unspeakably** *adv*

unspotted /ˌun'spotid‖ˌʌn'spɒtɪd/ *adj* morally blameless

unstop /ˌun'stop‖ˌʌn'stɒp/ *vt* **-pp- 1** to free from an obstruction **2** to remove a stopper from

unstressed /un'strest‖ʌn'strest/ *adj* **1** not bearing a stress or accent <*~ syllables*> **2** not subjected to stress <*~ wires*>

unstring /un'string‖ʌn'strɪŋ/ *vt* **unstrung** /ˌ-'strung‖-'strʌŋ/ **1** to loosen or remove the strings of **2** to make mentally disordered or unstable <*was* unstrung *by the news*>

unstuck /un'stuk‖ʌn'stʌk/ *adj* – **come unstuck** to go wrong; be unsuccessful

unstudied /un'studid‖ʌn'stʌdɪd/ *adj* **1** not acquired by study **2** not done or planned for effect

unsung /ˌun'sung‖ˌʌn'sʌŋ/ *adj* not celebrated or praised (e g in song or verse)

unswerving /un'swuhving‖ʌn'swɜːvɪŋ/ *adj* not deviating; constant <*~ loyalty*>

untangle /un'tang·gl‖ʌn'tæŋgl/ *vt* to loose from tangles or entanglement; unravel

untapped /un'tapt‖ʌn'tæpt/ *adj* **1** not yet tapped <*an ~ keg*> **2** not drawn on or exploited <*as yet ~ markets*>

untenable /un'tenəbl‖ʌn'tenəbl/ *adj* not able to be defended <*an ~ opinion*> – **untenability** *n*

unthinkable /un'thingkəbl‖ʌn'θɪŋkəbl/ *adj* contrary to what is acceptable or probable; out of the question – **unthinkably** *adv*, **unthinkability** *n*

unthinking /un'thingking‖ʌn'θɪŋkɪŋ/ *adj* not taking thought; heedless, unmindful – **unthinkingly** *adv*

unthought /ˌun'thawt‖ˌʌn'θɔːt/ *adj* not anticipated; unexpected – often + *of* or *on*

untie /un'tie‖ʌn'taɪ/ *vt* **1** to free from sthg that fastens or restrains **2a** to separate out the knotted parts of **b** to disentangle, resolve ~*vi* to become untied

[1]**until** /un'til, ən-‖ʌn'tɪl, ən-/ *prep* **1** up to as late as <*not available ~ tomorrow*> **2** up to as far as <*stay on the train ~ Birmingham*>

[2]**until** *conj* up to the time that; until such time as

untimely /un'tiemli‖ʌn'taɪmlɪ/ *adj* **1** occurring before the natural or proper time; premature <*~ death*> **2** inopportune, unseasonable <*an ~ joke*> – **untimeliness** *n*

unto /'untoo, -tə‖'ʌntʊ, -tə/ *prep, archaic* TO 1, 2, 3

untold /un'tohld‖ʌn'təʊld/ *adj* **1** incalculable, vast **2** not told or related

[1]**untouchable** /un'tuchəbl‖ʌn'tʌtʃəbl/ *adj* **1** that may not be touched **2** lying beyond reach <*~ mineral resources buried deep within the earth*> – **untouchability** *n*

[2]**untouchable** *n* sby or sthg untouchable; *specif, often cap* a member of a large formerly segregated hereditary group in India who in traditional Hindu belief can defile a member of a higher caste by contact or proximity

untoward /ˌuntə'wawd‖ˌʌntə'wɔːd/ *adj* not favourable; adverse, unfortunate – **untowardly** *adv*, **untowardness** *n*

untrue /un'trooh‖ʌn'truː/ *adj* **1** not faithful; disloyal **2** not level or exact <*~ doors and windows*> **3** inaccurate, false – **untruly** *adv*

untruth /ˌun'troohth‖ˌʌn'truːθ/ *n* **1** lack of truthfulness **2** sthg untrue; a falsehood

untruthful /un'troohthf(ə)l‖ʌn'truːθf(ə)l/ *adj* not telling the truth; false, lying – **untruthfully** *adv*, **untruthfulness** *n*

untutored /un'tyoohtəd‖ʌn'tjuːtəd/ *adj* **1** having no formal learning or education **2** not produced by instruction; native <*his ~ shrewdness*>

unused /un'yoohst‖ʌn'juːst; *senses 2a and 2b* -'yoohzd‖-'juːzd/ *adj* **1** unaccustomed – usu + *to* **2a** fresh, new **b** not used up <*~ sick leave*>

unusual /un'yoohzhooəl, -zhəl‖ʌn'juːʒʊəl, -ʒəl/ *adj* **1** uncommon, rare **2** different, unique <*an ~ painting*> – **unusually** *adv*, **unusualness** *n*

unutterable /un'ut(ə)rəbl‖ʌn'ʌt(ə)rəbl/ *adj* **1** beyond the powers of description; inexpressible **2** out-and-out, downright <*an ~ fool*> – **unutterably** *adv*

unvarnished /ˌun'vahnisht‖ˌʌn'vɑːnɪʃt/ *adj* not adorned or glossed; plain <*told the ~ truth*>

unveil /un'vayl‖ʌn'veɪl/ *vt* **1** to remove a veil or covering from **2** to make public; divulge ~*vi* to remove a veil or protective cloak

unvoiced /un'voyst‖ʌn'vɔɪst/ *adj* **1** not expressed in words **2** voiceless

unwaged /un'wayjd‖ʌn'weɪdʒd/ *adj, Br* out of work – chiefly euph

unwarranted /un'worəntid‖ʌn'wɒrəntɪd/ *adj* not justified; (done) without good reason

unwell /un'wel‖ʌn'wel/ *adj* in poor health

unwieldy /un'weeldi‖ʌn'wiːldɪ/ *adj* difficult to move or handle; cumbersome – **unwieldily** *adv*, **unwieldiness** *n*

unwind /un'wiend‖ʌn'waɪnd/ *vb* **unwound** /-'wownd‖-'waʊnd/ *vt* to cause to uncoil; unroll ~ *vi* **1** to become unwound **2** to become less tense; relax

unwitting /un'witing‖ʌn'wɪtɪŋ/ *adj* **1** not intended; inadvertent <*an ~ mistake*> **2** ignorant, unaware <*an ~ accomplice*> – **unwittingly** *adv*

unwonted /un'wohntid, -'won-‖ʌn'wəʊntɪd, -'wɒn-/ *adj* out of the ordinary; unusual – **unwontedly** *adv*, **unwontedness** *n*

unwritten /un'ritn‖ʌn'rɪtn/ *adj* **1** not (formally) written down **2** containing no writing; blank

unyielding /un'yeelding‖ʌn'jiːldɪŋ/ *adj* **1** lacking in softness or flexibility **2** firm, obdurate – **unyieldingly** *adv*

unzip /un'zip‖ʌn'zɪp/ *vb* **-pp-** to open (as if) by means of a zip

[1]**up** /up‖ʌp/ *adv* **1a** at or towards a relatively

high level <*live ~ in the mountains*> **b** from beneath the ground or water to the surface **c** above the horizon **d** upstream **e** in or to a raised or upright position <*hands ~!*>; *specif* out of bed <*soon be ~ and about*> **f** off or out of the ground or a surface <*pull ~ a daisy*> **g** UPWARDS 1b **h** to the top; *esp* so as to be full <*top ~ the radiator*> **2a** into a state of, or with, greater intensity or activity <*speak ~*> **b** into a faster pace or higher gear **3a** in or into a relatively high condition or status <*family went ~ in the world*> – sometimes used interjectionally as an expression of approval <*~ Liverpool!*> **b** above a normal or former level <*sales are ~*>: e g **b(1)** UPWARDS 2b **b(2)** higher in price **c** ahead of an opponent <*we're 3 points ~*> **4a(1)** in or into existence, evidence, prominence, or prevalence <*new houses haven't been ~ long*> **a(2)** in or into operation or full power <*get ~ steam*> **b** under consideration or attention; *esp* before a court <*~ for robbery*> **5** so as to be together <*add ~ the figures*> **6a** entirely, completely <*eat ~ your spinach*> **b** so as to be firmly closed, joined, or fastened **c** so as to be fully inflated **7** in or into storage **8** in a direction conventionally the opposite of down: **8a(1)** to windward **a(2)** with rudder to leeward – used with reference to a ship's helm **b** in or towards the north **c** so as to arrive or approach <*walked ~ to her*> **d** to or at the rear of a theatrical stage **e** *chiefly Br* to or in the capital of a country or a university city <*~ in London*> **9** in or into parts <*chop ~*> **10** to a stop – usu + *draw, bring, fetch,* or *pull*

[2]**up** *adj* **1** moving, inclining, bound, or directed upwards or up **2** ready, prepared <*dinner's ~!*> **3** going on, taking place; *esp* being the matter <*what's ~?*> **4** at an end <*time's ~*>; *esp* hopeless <*it's all ~ with him now*> **5a** well informed **b** ABREAST 2 <*~ on her homework*> **6** *of a road* being repaired; having a broken surface **7** ahead of an opponent <*2 strokes ~ after 9 holes*> **8** *of a ball in court games* having bounced only once on the ground or floor after being hit by one's opponent and therefore playable <*not ~*> **9** *Br, of a train* travelling towards a large town; *specif* travelling towards London – **up against** faced with; confronting – **up against it** in great difficulties

[3]**up** *vb* **-pp-** *vi* – used with *and* and another verb to indicate that the action of the following verb is either surprisingly or abruptly initiated <*he ~ped and married*> ~ *vt* **1** to increase <*they ~ped the price of milk*> **2** RAISE 8c

[4]**up** *prep* **1a** up along, round, through, towards, in, into, or on <*walk ~ the hill*> **b** at the top of <*the office is ~ those stairs*> **2** *Br* (up) to <*going ~ the West End*> – nonstandard

[5]**up** *n* **1** (sthg in) a high position or an upward incline **2** a period or state of prosperity or success <*has had some ~s and downs*> **3** the part of a ball's trajectory in which it is still rising after having bounced <*hit the ball on the ~*>

ˌup-and-ˈcoming *adj* likely to advance or succeed

ˌup-and-ˈup *n, chiefly Br* a potentially or increasingly successful course – chiefly in *on the up-and-up*

[1]**upbeat** /ˈupˌbeet‖ˈʌpˌbiːt/ *n* an unaccented (e g the last) beat in a musical bar

[2]**upbeat** *adj, chiefly NAm* optimistic, cheerful – infml

upbraid /upˈbrayd‖ʌpˈbreɪd/ *vt* to scold or reproach severely – **upbraider** *n*

upbringing /ˈupˌbring·ing‖ˈʌpˌbrɪŋɪŋ/ *n* a particular way of bringing up a child <*had a strict Calvinist ~*>

upcoming /ˈupˌkuming‖ˈʌpˌkʌmɪŋ/ *adj, NAm* about to happen; forthcoming

ˌup-ˈcountry *adj* **1** (characteristic) of an inland, upland, or outlying region **2** not socially or culturally sophisticated – **up-country** *n*, **up-country** *adv*

[1]**update** /ˌupˈdayt‖ˌʌpˈdeɪt/ *vt* to bring up to date

[2]**ˈupˌdate** *n* an act of updating <*a computer file ~*>

upend /ˌupˈend‖ˌʌpˈend/ *vt* **1** to cause to stand on end **2** to knock down

upfront /ˌupˈfrunt/ *adj* direct and open

upgrade /ˌupˈgrayd‖ˌʌpˈgreɪd/ *vt* to raise or improve the grade of; *esp* to advance to a job requiring a higher level of skill

upheaval /upˈheevl‖ʌpˈhiːvl/ *n* **1** an upheaving, esp of part of the earth's crust **2** (an instance of) extreme agitation or radical change

[1]**uphill** /ˈupˌhil‖ˈʌpˌhɪl/ *n* rising ground

[2]**ˌupˈhill** *adv* upwards on a hill or incline

[3]**ˌupˈhill** *adj* **1** situated on elevated ground **2** going up; ascending **3** difficult, laborious <*an ~ struggle*>

uphold /upˈhohld‖ʌpˈhəʊld/ *vt* **upheld** /-ˈheld‖-ˈheld/ **1** to give support to; maintain **2** to support against an opponent or challenge

upholster /upˈhohlstə, -ˈhol-‖ʌpˈhəʊlstə, -ˈhɒl-/ *vt* to provide with upholstery – **upholsterer** *n*

upˈholstery /-ri‖-rɪ/ *n* materials (e g fabric, padding, and springs) used to make a soft covering, esp for a seat

upkeep /ˈupˌkeep‖ˈʌpˌkiːp/ *n* (the cost of) maintaining or being maintained in good condition

upland /ˈuplənd‖ˈʌplənd/ *n* (an area of) high (inland) land – often pl with sing. meaning – **upland** *adj*, **uplander** *n*

[1]**uplift** /upˈlift‖ʌpˈlɪft/ *vt* **1** to raise, elevate **2** to improve the spiritual, social, or intellectual condition of – **uplifter** *n*

[2]**ˈupˌlift** *n* **1** a moral or social improvement **2** influences intended to uplift

upload /ˈupˌlohd‖ˈʌpˌləʊd/ *vb* to transfer (programs or data) from a smaller to a larger or more central computer

upon /əˈpon‖əˈpɒn/ *prep* on – chiefly fml

[1]**upper** /ˈupə‖ˈʌpə/ *adj* **1a** higher in physical position, rank, or order **b** farther inland <*the ~ Thames*> **2** being the branch of a legislature consisting of 2 houses that is usu more restricted in membership, is in many cases less powerful, and possesses greater traditional prestige than the lower house

[2]**upper** *n* the parts of a shoe or boot above the sole – **on one's uppers** at the end of one's means

[3]**upper** *n* a stimulant drug; *esp*

amphetamine – infml

ˌupper-ˈcase *adj* CAPITAL 2 [fr the compositor's practice of keeping capital letters in the upper of a pair of type cases]

upper case *n* **1** a type case containing capitals and usu small capitals, fractions, symbols, and accents **2** capital letters

ˌupper ˈclass *n* the class occupying the highest position in a society; *esp* the wealthy or the aristocracy – **upper-class** *adj*

ˌupper ˈcrust *n sing or pl in constr* the highest social class – infml

uppercut /ˈupəˌkut‖ˈʌpəˌkʌt/ *n* a swinging blow directed upwards with a bent arm – **uppercut** *vb*

ˌupper ˈhand *n* mastery, advantage – + *the*

uppermost /ˈupəˌmohst‖ˈʌpəˌməʊst/ *adv* in or into the highest or most prominent position – **uppermost** *adj*

uppish /ˈupish‖ˈʌpɪʃ/ *adj* **1** hit up and travelling far in the air **2** uppity – infml – **uppishly** *adv*, **uppishness** *n*

uppity /ˈupəti‖ˈʌpətɪ/ *adj* putting on airs of superiority; supercilious – infml – **uppityness** *n*

[1]**upright** /ˈupˌriet‖ˈʌpˌraɪt/ *adj* **1a** perpendicular, vertical **b** erect in carriage or posture **c** having the main part perpendicular <*an ~ freezer*> **2** marked by strong moral rectitude – **uprightly** *adv*, **uprightness** *n*

[2]**upright** *adv* in an upright or vertical position

[3]**upright** *n* **1** sthg that stands upright **2 upright, upright piano** a piano with vertical frame and strings

uprising /ˈupˌriezing‖ˈʌpˌraɪzɪŋ/ *n* a usu localized rebellion

uproar /ˈupˌraw‖ˈʌpˌrɔː/ *n* a state of commotion or violent disturbance [by folk etymology fr Dutch *oproer*, fr *op* up + *roer* motion]

uproarious /ˌupˈrawri·əs‖ˌʌpˈrɔːrɪəs/ *adj* **1** marked by noise and disorder **2** extremely funny <*an ~ comedy*> – **uproariously** *adv*, **uproariousness** *n*

uproot /ˌupˈrooht‖ˌʌpˈruːt/ *vt* **1** to remove by pulling up by the roots **2** to displace from a country or traditional habitat or environment – **uprooter** *n*

ˌups and ˈdowns *n pl* alternating rises and falls, esp in fortune

[1]**upset** /upˈset‖ʌpˈset/ *vb* **-tt-; upset** *vt* **1** to thicken and shorten (e g a heated iron bar) by hammering on the end **2** to overturn, knock over **3a** to trouble mentally or emotionally **b** to throw into disorder **4** to make somewhat ill ~ *vi* to become overturned – **upsetter** *n*

[2]**ˈupˌset** *n* **1** a minor physical disorder <*a stomach ~*> **2** an emotional disturbance **3** an unexpected defeat (e g in politics)

upshot /ˈupˌshot‖ˈʌpˌʃɒt/ *n* the final result; the outcome – infml

ˌupside ˈdown /ˈupˌsied‖ˈʌpˌsaɪd/ *adv* **1** with the upper and the lower parts reversed **2** in or into great disorder or confusion – **upside-down** *adj*

[1]**upstage** /ˌupˈstayj‖ˌʌpˈsteɪdʒ/ *adv* at the rear of a theatrical stage; *also* away from the audience or film or television camera

[2]**upstage** *adj* **1** of or at the rear of a stage **2** haughty, aloof

[3]**ˈupˌstage** *n* the part of a stage that is farthest from the audience or camera

[4]**upstage** *vt* **1** to force (an actor) to face away from the audience by holding a dialogue with him/her from an upstage position **2** to steal attention from

[1]**upstairs** /ˌupˈsteəz‖ˌʌpˈsteəz/ *adv* **1** up the stairs; to or on a higher floor **2** to or at a higher position

[2]**upstairs** *adj* situated above the stairs, esp on an upper floor

[3]**upstairs** /ˈ-ˌ-, ˌ-ˈ-/ *n pl but sing or pl in constr* the part of a building above the ground floor

upstanding /upˈstanding‖ʌpˈstændɪŋ/ *adj* **1** erect, upright **2** marked by integrity; honest – **upstandingness** *n*

upstart /ˈupˌstaht‖ˈʌpˌstɑːt/ *n* one who has risen suddenly (e g from a low position to wealth or power); *esp* one who claims more personal importance than he/she warrants – **upstart** *adj*

upstream /ˌupˈstreem‖ˌʌpˈstriːm/ *adv or adj* in the direction opposite to the flow of a stream

upsurge /ˈupˌsuhj‖ˈʌpˌsɜːdʒ/ *n* a rapid or sudden rise

upswing /ˈupˌswing‖ˈʌpˌswɪŋ/ *n* **1** an upward swing **2** a marked increase or rise

uptake /ˈupˌtayk‖ˈʌpˌteɪk/ *n* **1** an absorbing and incorporating, esp into a living organism **2** understanding, comprehension <*quick on the ~*> – infml

uptight /ˌupˈtiet‖ˌʌpˈtaɪt/ *adj* **1** tense, nervous, or uneasy **2** angry, indignant *USE* infml – **uptightness** *n*

ˈup to *prep* **1** – used to indicate an upward limit or boundary <*sank ~ his knees in mud*> **2** as far as; until **3a** equal to <*didn't feel ~ par*> **b** good enough for <*my German isn't ~ reading this book*> **4** engaged in (a suspect activity) <*what's he ~?*> **5** being the responsibility of <*it's ~ me*>

ˌup-to-ˈdate *adj* **1** including the latest information **2** abreast of the times; modern – **up-to-dateness** *n*

ˌup-to-the-ˈminute *adj* **1** including the very latest information **2** completely up-to-date

ˌupˈtown *adv, adj, or n, chiefly NAm* (to, towards, or in) the upper part or residential district of a town or city

[1]**upturn** /ˌupˈtuhn‖ˌʌpˈtɜːn/ *vt* **1** to turn up or over **2** to direct upwards ~ *vi* to turn upwards

[2]**ˈupˌturn** *n* an upward turn, esp towards better conditions or higher prices

upward /ˈupwood‖ˈʌpwʊd/ *adj* moving or extending upwards; ascending <*an ~ movement*> – **upwardly** *adv*

upwards *adv* **1a** from a lower to a higher place, condition, or level; in the opposite direction from down **b** so as to expose a particular surface <*held out his hand, palm ~*> **2a** to an indefinitely greater amount, price, figure, age, or rank <*from £5 ~*> **b** towards a higher number, degree, or rate <*attendance figures have risen ~*>

ˈupwards of *adv* more than; IN EXCESS OF <*they cost ~ £25*>

uranium /yoo(ə)ˈraynyəm, -ni·əm‖jʊ(ə)ˈreɪnjəm, -nɪəm/ *n* a heavy radioactive metallic element found in pitchblende

Uranus /yoo(ə)'raynəs, 'yooərənəs‖jʊ(ə)'reɪnəs, 'jʊərənəs/ *n* the planet 7th in order from the sun

urban /'uhbən‖'ɜːbən/ *adj* (characteristic) of or constituting a city or town

urbane /uh'bayn‖ɜː'beɪn/ *adj* notably polite or smooth in manner; suave – **urbanely** *adv*, **urbanity** *n*

urban·ize, **-ise** /'uhbə,niez‖'ɜːbə,naɪz/ *vt* **1** to cause to take on urban characteristics **2** to impart an urban way of life to – **urbanization** *n*

urchin /'uhchin‖'ɜːtʃɪn/ *n* **1** a hedgehog **2** a mischievous and impudent young boy, esp one who is scruffy **3** SEA URCHIN

Urdu /'ooədooh, 'uhdooh‖'ʊədu:, 'ɜːdu:/ *n* an Indo-European language, similar to Hindi but written in a different script, which is an official language of Pakistan and is widely used in India

-ure *suffix* (*vb* → *n*) **1** act or process of <*exposure*> **2** body performing (a specified function) <*legislature*>

[1]**urge** /uhj‖ɜːdʒ/ *vt* **1** to advocate or demand earnestly or pressingly **2** to undertake the accomplishment of with energy or enthusiasm **3a** to try to persuade **b** to serve as a motive or reason for **4** to force or impel in a specified direction or to greater speed ~*vi* to urge an argument, claim, etc – **urger** *n*

[2]**urge** *n* a force or impulse that urges

urgent /'uhjənt‖'ɜːdʒənt/ *adj* **1** calling for immediate attention; pressing <~ *appeals*> **2** conveying a sense of urgency – **urgency** *n*, **urgently** *adv*

uric /'yooərik‖'jʊərɪk/ *adj* of or found in urine

urinal /yoo(ə)'rienl‖jʊ(ə)'raɪnl/ *n* a fixture used for urinating into, esp by men; *also* a room, building, etc containing a urinal

urinary /'yooərin(ə)ri‖'jʊərɪn(ə)rɪ/ *adj* **1** relating to (or occurring in or constituting the organs concerned with the formation and discharge of) urine **2** excreted as or in urine

urinate /'yooəri,nayt‖'jʊərɪ,neɪt/ *vi* to discharge urine – **urination** *n*

urine /'yooərin‖'jʊərɪn/ *n* waste material that is secreted by the kidney in vertebrates and forms a clear amber and usu slightly acid fluid in mammals but is semisolid in birds and reptiles [Middle French, fr Latin *urina*; akin to Old English *wæter* water – see WATER] – **urinous** *adj*

urn /uhn‖ɜːn/ *n* **1** an ornamental vase on a pedestal used esp for preserving the ashes of the dead after cremation **2** a large closed container, usu with a tap at its base, in which large quantities of tea, coffee, etc may be heated or served

,**Ursa** '**Major** /'uhsə‖'ɜːsə/ *n* the most conspicuous of the N constellations that is situated near the N pole of the heavens and contains 7 stars pictured as a plough, 2 of which are in a line indicating the direction of the Pole Star

,**Ursa** '**Minor** *n* a constellation that includes the N pole of the heavens and 7 stars which resemble Ursa Major with the Pole Star at the tip of the handle

urticaria /uhti'keəri·ə‖ɜːtɪ'keərɪə/ *n* an allergic disorder marked by raised itching patches of skin and caused by contact with a specific factor (e g a food or drug) – **urticarial** *adj*

us /əs‖əs; *strong* us‖ʌs/ *pron* **1** *objective case of* WE <*please let* ~ *go*> **2** *chiefly Br* me <*give* ~ *a kiss*> – nonstandard

usage /'yoohsij, -zij‖'juːsɪdʒ, -zɪdʒ/ *n* **1a** (an instance of) established and generally accepted practice or procedure **b** (an instance of) the way in which words and phrases are actually used in a language **2** the action, amount, or manner of using

[1]**use** /yoohs‖juːs/ *n* **1a** using or being used <*in daily* ~> <*made good* ~ *of his time*> **b** a way of using sthg <*a machine with many different* ~s> **2a** habitual or customary usage **b** a liturgical form or observance; *esp* a liturgy having modifications peculiar to a local church or religious order **3a** the right or benefit of using sthg <*gave him the* ~ *of her car*> **b** the ability or power to use sthg (e g a limb) **c** the legal enjoyment of property **4a** a purpose or end <*put learning to practical* ~> **b** practical worth or application <*saving things that might be of* ~> **5** a favourable attitude; a liking <*had no* ~ *for modern art*>

[2]**use** /yoohz‖juːz/ *vb* **used** / *vt* yoohzd‖juːzd; *vi* yoohst‖juːst/ *vt* **1** to put into action or service **2** to consume or take (e g drugs) regularly **3** to carry out sthg by means of <~ *tact*> **4** to expend or consume **5** to treat in a specified manner <~d *the prisoners cruelly*> ~*vi* – used in the past with *to* to indicate a former fact or state <~d *to dislike fish*> <*didn't* ~d *to be so pernickety*> – **user** *n*, **usable** *adj*, **usably** *adv*

used /*senses 1 and 2* yoohzd‖juːzd; *sense 3* yoohst‖juːst/ *adj* **1** employed in accomplishing sthg **2** that has endured use; *specif* secondhand **3** accustomed

useful /'yoohsf(ə)l‖'juːsf(ə)l/ *adj* **1** having utility, esp practical worth or applicability; *also* helpful **2** of highly satisfactory quality – **usefully** *adv*, **usefulness** *n*

useless /'yoohslis‖'juːslɪs/ *adj* **1** having or being of no use **2** inept – infml – **uselessly** *adv*, **uselessness** *n*

user-friendly *adj* **1** *of a computer system* designed for easy operation by guiding users along a series of simple steps **2** easy to operate or understand – **user-friendliness** *n*

use up /yoohz‖juːz/ *vt* **1** to consume completely **2** to deprive wholly of strength or useful properties; exhaust

[1]**usher** /'ushə‖'ʌʃə/ *n* **1** an officer or servant who acts as a doorkeeper (e g in a court of law) **2** an officer who walks before a person of rank **3** *fem* **usherette** one who shows people to their seats (e g in a theatre)

[2]**usher** *vt* **1** to conduct to a place **2** to precede as an usher **3** to inaugurate, introduce <~ *in a new era*>

usual /'yoohzhooəl, -zhəl‖'juːʒʊəl, -ʒəl/ *adj* **1** in accordance with usage, custom, or habit; normal **2** commonly or ordinarily used <*followed his* ~ *route*> – **usually** *adv*, **usualness** *n* – **as usual** in the accustomed or habitual way <as usual *he was late*>

usurer /'yoohzhərə‖'juːʒərə/ *n* one who lends money, esp at an exorbitant rate

usurp /yooh'suhp, -'zuhp‖juː'sɜːp, -'zɜːp/ *vt* to seize and possess by force or without right <~ *a throne*> ~*vi* to seize possession wrongfully –

usurper *n*, **usurpation** *n*
usury /'yoohzyəri, -zhəri‖'ju:zjərɪ, -ʒərɪ/ *n* **1** the lending of money at (exorbitant) interest **2** an exorbitant or illegal rate or amount of interest – **usurious** *adj*, **usuriously** *adv*
utensil /yooh'tens(i)l‖ju:'tens(ɪ)l/ *n* **1** an implement, vessel, or device used in the household, esp the kitchen **2** a useful tool or implement
uterine /'yoohtərin, -rien‖'ju:tərɪn, -raɪn/ *adj* **1a** born of the same mother but by a different father **b** matrilineal **2** of or affecting the uterus
uterus /'yoohtərəs‖'ju:tərəs/ *n, pl* **uteri** /-ˌrie, -ri‖-ˌraɪ, -rɪ/ *also* **uteruses** **1** an organ of the female mammal for containing and usu for nourishing the young during development before birth **2** a structure in some lower animals analogous to the uterus in which eggs or young develop
[1]**utilitarian** /yoohˌtili'teəri·ən‖ju:ˌtɪlɪ'teərɪən/ *n* an advocate of utilitarianism
[2]**utilitarian** *adj* **1** marked by utilitarian views or practices **2a** of or aiming at utility **b** made for or aiming at practical use rather than beautiful appearance
uˌtili'tarianism /-niz(ə)m‖-nɪz(ə)m/ *n* **1** a doctrine that the criterion for correct conduct should be the usefulness of its consequences; *specif* a theory that the aim of action should be the greatest happiness of the greatest number **2** utilitarian character, spirit, or quality
[1]**utility** /yooh'tiləti‖ju:'tɪlətɪ/ *n* **1** fitness for some purpose; usefulness **2** sthg useful or designed for use **3** a business organization performing a public service
[2]**utility** *adj* **1** capable of serving as a substitute in various roles or positions <*a ~ player*> **2** serving primarily for utility rather than beauty; utilitarian <*~ furniture*> **3** designed or adapted for general use
util·ize, -ise /'yoohtiliez‖'ju:tɪlaɪz/ *vt* to make use of; turn to practical use or account – **utilizable** *adj*, **utilizer** *n*, **utilization** *n*
[1]**utmost** /'utˌmohst‖'ʌtˌməʊst/ *adj* **1** situated at the farthest or most distant point; extreme **2** of the greatest or highest degree <*a matter of ~ concern*>
[2]**utmost** *n* **1** the highest point or degree **2** the best of one's abilities, powers, etc
utopia /yooh'tohpi·ə‖ju:'təʊpɪə/ *n* **1** *often cap* a place or state of ideal (political and social) perfection **2** an impractical scheme for social or political improvement [*Utopia*, imaginary ideal country in *Utopia* by Sir Thomas More (1478-1535), English statesman & writer, fr Greek *ou* not, no + *topos* place]
utopian /yooh'tohpi·ən‖ju:'təʊpɪən/ *adj, often cap* **1** impossibly ideal, esp in social and political organization **2** proposing impractically ideal social and political schemes – **utopianism** *n*
[1]**utter** /'utə‖'ʌtə/ *adj* absolute, total – **utterly** *adv*
[2]**utter** *vt* **1a** to emit as a sound **b** to give (verbal) expression to **2** to put (e g currency) into circulation; *specif* to circulate (e g a counterfeit note) as if legal or genuine – used technically – **utterer** *n*, **utterable** *adj*
utterance /'ut(ə)rəns‖'ʌt(ə)rəns/ *n* **1** an oral or written statement **2** vocal expression; speech – esp in *give utterance to*
uttermost /'utəˌmohst‖'ʌtəˌməʊst/ *adj* utmost
'U-ˌturn /yooh‖ju:/ *n* **1** a turn executed by a motor vehicle without reversing that takes it back along the direction from which it has come **2** a total reversal of policy
uvula /'yoohvyoolə‖'ju:vjʊlə/ *n, pl* **uvulas, uvulae** /-li‖-lɪ/ the fleshy lobe hanging in the middle of the back of the soft palate – **uvular** *adj*
uxorious /uk'sawri·əs, ug'zaw-‖ʌk'sɔ:rɪəs, ʌg'zɔ:-/ *adj* (excessively) fond of or submissive to one's wife – fml [Latin *uxorius*, fr *uxor* wife] – **uxoriously** *adv*, **uxoriousness** *n*

v /vee‖vi:/ *n, pl* **v's** *or* **vs** *often cap* **1** (a graphic representation of or device for reproducing) the 22nd letter of the English alphabet **2** five
vac /vak‖væk/ *n, Br* a vacation, esp from college or university – infml
vacancy /'vaykənsi‖'veɪkənsɪ/ *n* **1** physical or mental inactivity; idleness **2** a vacant office, post, or room **3** an empty space **4** the state of being vacant
vacant /'vaykənt‖'veɪkənt/ *adj* **1** not occupied by an incumbent or officer <*a ~ office*> **2** without an occupant <*a ~ room*> **3** free from activity or work <*~ hours*> **4a** stupid, foolish <*a ~ mind*> **b** expressionless <*a ~ look*> **5** not lived in <*~ houses*> – **vacantly** *adv*, **vacantness** *n*
vacant possession *n* availability (e g of a house) for immediate occupation
vacate /vay'kayt‖veɪ'keɪt/ *vt* **1** to annul legally **2** to give up the possession or occupancy of **3** to make vacant; leave empty
[1]**vacation** /vay'kaysh(ə)n, və-‖veɪ'keɪʃ(ə)n, və-/ *n* **1** a scheduled period during which activity (e g of a university) is suspended **2** an act of vacating **3** *chiefly NAm* a holiday
[2]**vacation** *vi, chiefly NAm* to take or spend a holiday – **vacationer** *n*
vaccinate /'vaksinayt‖'væksɪneɪt/ *vt* **1** to inoculate with cowpox virus in order to produce immunity to smallpox **2** to administer a vaccine to, usu by injection *~vi* to perform or practise the administration of vaccine – **vaccinator** *n*, **vaccination** *n*
vaccine *n* material (e g a preparation of killed or modified virus or bacteria) used in vaccinating [Latin *vaccinus* of or from cows, fr *vacca* cow] – **vaccinal** *adj*
vacillate /'vasəˌlayt‖'væsəˌleɪt/ *vi* **1a** to sway through imperfect balance **b** to fluctuate, oscillate **2** to hesitate or waver in choosing between opinions or courses of action – **vacillatingly** *adv*, **vacillator** *n*, **vacillation** *n*
vacuity /və'kyooh·əti‖və'kju:ətɪ/ *n* **1** an empty space **2** meaninglessness **3** sthg (e g an idea) that is stupid or inane
vacuous /'vakyoo·əs‖'vækjʊəs/ *adj* **1** empty **2** stupid, inane <*a ~ expression*> **3** idle, aimless – **vacuously** *adv*, **vacuousness** *n*

[1]**vacuum** /'vakyoohm, 'vakyooəm, 'vakyoom‖'vækjuːm, 'vækjʊəm, 'vækjʊm/ *n, pl* **vacuums, vacua** /'vakyooh·ə‖'vækjuːə/ **1a** a space absolutely devoid of matter **b** a space from which as much air or other substance as possible has been removed (e g by an air pump) **c** an air pressure below atmospheric pressure **2a** a vacant space; a void **b** a state of isolation from outside influences **3** VACUUM CLEANER

[2]**vacuum** /'vakyoohm, 'vakyoom‖'vækjuːm, 'vækjʊm/ *vb* to clean using a vacuum cleaner

'**vacuum ˌcleaner** *n* an (electrical) appliance for removing dust and dirt (e g from carpets or upholstery) by suction – **vacuum-clean** *vb*

'**vacuum ˌflask** *n, chiefly Br* THERMOS FLASK

'**vacuum-ˌpacked** *adj* packed in a wrapping from which most of the air has been removed

'**vacuum ˌpump** *n* a pump for producing a vacuum

[1]**vagabond** /'vagəˌbond‖'vægəˌbɒnd/ *adj* **1** (characteristic) of a wanderer **2** leading an unsettled, irresponsible, or disreputable life [Middle French fr Latin *vagabundus*, fr *vagari* to wander, fr *vagus* wandering] – **vagabondish** *adj*

[2]**vagabond** *n* a wanderer; *esp* a tramp – **vagabondage** *n*, **vagabondism** *n*

vagary /'vaygəri‖'veɪgərɪ/ *n* an erratic, unpredictable, or extravagant notion, action, etc – **vagarious** *adj*

vagina /və'jienə‖və'dʒaɪnə/ *n, pl* **vaginae** /-ni‖-nɪ/, **vaginas** a canal in a female mammal that leads from the uterus to the external orifice of the genital canal – **vaginal** *adj*

[1]**vagrant** /'vaygrənt‖'veɪgrənt/ *n* **1** one who has no established residence or lawful means of support **2** a wanderer, vagabond

[2]**vagrant** *adj* **1** wandering about from place to place, usu with no means of support **2** having no fixed course; random – **vagrancy** *n*, **vagrantly** *adv*

vague /vayg‖veɪg/ *adj* **1a** not clearly defined, expressed, or understood; indistinct **b** not clearly felt or sensed **2** not thinking or expressing one's thoughts clearly – **vaguely** *adv*, **vagueness** *n*

vain /vayn‖veɪn/ *adj* **1** idle, worthless **2** unsuccessful, ineffectual **3** having or showing excessive pride in one's appearance, ability, etc; conceited – **vainly** *adv*, **vainness** *n* – **in vain** to no end; without success or result

vainglorious /ˌvayn'glawri·əs‖ˌveɪn'glɔːrɪəs/ *adj* boastful – **vaingloriously** *adv*, **vaingloriousness** *n*

vainglory /ˌvayn'glawri‖ˌveɪn'glɔːrɪ/ *n* **1** excessive or ostentatious pride **2** vanity

valance /'vayləns, 'va-‖'veɪləns, 'væ-/ *n* **1** a piece of drapery hung as a border, esp along the edge of a bed, canopy, or shelf **2** a pelmet

vale /vayl‖veɪl/ *n* VALLEY 1a – poetic or in place-names

valediction /ˌvalə'diksh(ə)n‖ˌvælə'dɪkʃ(ə)n/ *n* **1** an act of bidding farewell **2** an address or statement of farewell or leave-taking *USE* fml

[1]**valedictory** /ˌvalə'dikt(ə)ri‖ˌvælə'dɪkt(ə)rɪ/ *adj* expressing or containing a farewell – fml

[2]**valedictory** *n* VALEDICTION 2 – fml

valency /'vaylənsi‖'veɪlənsɪ/, *NAm chiefly* **valence** /'vayləns‖'veɪləns/ *n* **1** the degree of combining power of an element or radical as shown by the number of atomic weights of a univalent element (e g hydrogen) with which the atomic weight of the element will combine or for which it can be substituted or with which it can be compared **2** a unit of valency <*the 4* valencies *of carbon*>

valentine /'valəntien‖'væləntaɪn/ *n* **1** a sweetheart chosen on St Valentine's Day **2** a gift or greeting card sent or given, esp to a sweetheart, on St Valentine's Day

valerian /və'liəri·ən‖və'lɪərɪən/ *n* any of several usu perennial plants, many of which possess medicinal properties

valet /'valay‖'væleɪ/ *n* a gentleman's male servant who performs personal services (e g taking care of clothing); *also* an employee (e g of a hotel) who performs similar services for patrons

valetudinarian /ˌvaliˌtyoohdi'neəri·ən‖ˌvælɪˌtjuːdɪ'neərɪən/ *n* a person of a weak or sickly constitution; *esp* a hypochondriac – fml – **valetudinarian** *adj*, **valetudinarianism** *n*

valiant /'vali·ənt‖'vælɪənt/ *adj* characterized by or showing valour; courageous – **valiance** *n*, **valiant** *n*, **valiantly** *adv*, **valiantness** *n*

valid /'valid‖'vælɪd/ *adj* **1** having legal efficacy; *esp* executed according to the proper formalities <*a* ~ *contract*> **2a** well-grounded or justifiable; relevant and meaningful **b** logically sound – **validly** *adv*, **validness** *n*, **validity** *n*

validate /'validayt‖'vælɪdeɪt/ *vt* **1** to make legally valid **2** to corroborate, authenticate – **validation** *n*

valley /'vali‖'vælɪ/ *n* **1a** an elongated depression of the earth's surface, usu between hills or mountains **b** an area drained by a river and its tributaries **2a** a hollow, depression **b** the internal angle formed at the meeting of 2 roof surfaces

valour, *NAm chiefly* **valor** /'valə‖'vælə/ *n* strength of mind or spirit that enables sby to encounter danger with firmness; personal bravery – **valorous** *adj*, **valorously** *adv*

[1]**valuable** /'valyoo(ə)bl‖'vælju(ə)bl/ *adj* **1** having (high) money value **2** of great use or worth – **valuableness** *n*, **valuably** *adv*

[2]**valuable** *n* a usu personal possession of relatively great money value – usu pl

valuation /ˌvalyoo'aysh(ə)n‖ˌvælju'eɪʃ(ə)n/ *n* **1** the act of valuing sthg, esp property **2** the estimated or determined value, esp market value, of a thing **3** judgment or appraisal of worth or character – **valuational** *adj*, **valuationally** *adv*

valuator /'valyooˌaytə‖'væljuˌeɪtə/ *n* sby who judges the (money) value of sthg

[1]**value** /'valyooh‖'væljuː/ *n* **1** a fair return or equivalent for sthg exchanged **2** the worth in money or commodities of sthg **3** relative worth, utility, or importance <*had nothing of* ~ *to say*> **4a** a numerical quantity assigned or computed **b** the magnitude of a physical quantity **5** the relative duration of a musical note **6a** relative lightness or darkness of a colour **b** the relation of one part in a picture to another with respect to lightness and darkness **7** sthg (e g a

principle or quality) intrinsically valuable or desirable **8** DENOMINATION 3

[2]**value** *vt* **1a** to estimate the worth of in terms of money **b** to rate in terms of usefulness, importance, etc **2** to consider or rate highly; esteem – **valuer** *n*

ˌvalue-ˈadded ˌtax *n, often cap V, A, & T* a tax levied at each stage of the production and distribution of a commodity and passed on to the consumer as a form of purchase tax

valve /valv‖vælv/ *n* **1** a structure, esp in the heart or a vein, that closes temporarily to obstruct passage of material or permits movement of fluid in 1 direction only **2a** any of numerous mechanical devices by which the flow of liquid, gas, or loose material in bulk may be controlled, usu to allow movement in 1 direction only **b** a device in a brass musical instrument for quickly varying the tube length in order to change the fundamental tone by a definite interval **3** any of the separate joined pieces that make up the shell of an (invertebrate) animal; *specif* either of the 2 halves of the shell of a bivalve mollusc **4** any of the segments or pieces into which a ripe seed capsule or pod separates **5** *chiefly Br* a vacuum- or gas-filled device for the regulation of electric current by the control of free electrons or ions – **valved** *adj*, **valveless** *adj*

valvular /ˈvalvyoolə‖ˈvælvjʊlə/ *adj* **1** resembling or functioning as a valve; *also* opening by valves **2** of a valve, esp of the heart

vamoose /vaˈmoohs‖væˈmuːs/ *vi, chiefly NAm* to depart quickly – slang [Spanish *vamos* let us go, fr Latin *vadere* to]

[1]**vamp** /vamp‖væmp/ *n* **1** the part of a shoe or boot covering the front of the foot **2** a simple improvised musical accompaniment [Middle English *vampe* sock, fr Old French *avantpié*, fr *avant-* fore- + *pié* foot]

[2]**vamp** *vt* **1** to provide (a shoe) with a new vamp **2** to patch (sthg old) with a new part <~ *up old sermons*> ~*vi* to play a musical vamp – **vamper** *n*

[3]**vamp** *n* a woman who uses her charm to seduce and exploit men [short for *vampire*]

vampire /ˈvampie·ə‖ˈvæmpaɪə/ *n* **1** a dead person believed to come from the grave at night and suck the blood of sleeping people **2** any of various S American bats that feed on blood and are dangerous to human beings and domestic animals, esp as transmitters of disease (e g rabies); *also* any of several other bats that do not feed on blood but are sometimes reputed to do so

[1]**van** /van‖væn/ *n, dial Eng* a winnowing device (e g a fan)

[2]**van** *n* the vanguard

[3]**van** *n* **1** an enclosed motor vehicle used for transport of goods, animals, furniture, etc **2** *chiefly Br* an enclosed railway goods wagon

vanadium /vəˈnaydi·əm‖vəˈneɪdɪəm/ *n* a malleable metallic element found combined in minerals and used esp to form alloys

vandal /ˈvandl‖ˈvændl/ *n* **1** *cap* a member of a Germanic people who overran Gaul, Spain, and N Africa in the 4th and 5th c AD and in 455 sacked Rome **2** one who wilfully or ignorantly destroys or defaces (public) property – **vandal** *adj, often cap*, **Vandalic** *adj*

ˈvandalˌism /-ˌiz(ə)m‖-ˌɪz(ə)m/ *n* wilful destruction or defacement of property – **vandalize** *vt*, **vandalistic** *adj*

vane /vayn‖veɪn/ *n* **1** WEATHER VANE **2** a thin flat or curved object that is rotated about an axis by wind or water <*the* ~s *of a windmill*>; *also* a device revolving in a similar manner and moving in water or air <*the* ~s *of a propeller*> **3** the flat expanded part of a feather **4a** the target of a levelling staff **b** any of the sights of a compass or quadrant – **vaned** *adj*

vanguard /ˈvan·gahd‖ˈvængɑːd/ *n* **1** *sing or pl in constr* the troops moving at the head of an army **2** the forefront of an action or movement

vanilla /vəˈnilə‖vəˈnɪlə/ *n* **1** any of a genus of tropical American climbing orchids whose long capsular fruits yield an important flavouring; *also* the fruit of the vanilla **2** a commercially important extract of the vanilla pod that is used esp as a flavouring

vanish /ˈvanish‖ˈvænɪʃ/ *vi* **1a** to pass quickly from sight; disappear **b** to cease to exist **2** to assume the value zero ~*vt* to cause to disappear – **vanisher** *n*

ˈvanishing ˌcream /ˈvanishing‖ˈvænɪʃɪŋ/ *n* a light cosmetic cream used chiefly as a foundation for face powder

vanishing point *n* **1** a point at which receding parallel lines seem to meet when represented in linear perspective **2** a point at which sthg disappears or ceases to exist

vanity /ˈvanəti‖ˈvænətɪ/ *n* **1** sthg vain, empty, or worthless **2** the quality of being vain or futile; worthlessness **3** excessive pride in oneself; conceit

ˈvanity ˌcase *n* a small bag used by women for carrying toilet articles and cosmetics

vanquish /ˈvangkwish, ˈvan-‖ˈvæŋkwɪʃ, ˈvæn-/ *vt* **1** to overcome, conquer <*the* ~ed *foe*> **2** to gain mastery over (an emotion, passion, etc) – **vanquishable** *adj*, **vanquisher** *n*

vantage /ˈvahntij‖ˈvɑːntɪdʒ/ *n* **1** a position giving a strategic advantage or commanding perspective **2** *Br* ADVANTAGE 3

vapid /ˈvapid‖ˈvæpɪd/ *adj* lacking liveliness, interest, or force; insipid – **vapidly** *adv*, **vapidness** *n*, **vapidity** *n*

vapor·ize, -ise /ˈvaypəˌriez‖ˈveɪpəˌraɪz/ *vt* **1** to convert (e g by the application of heat) into vapour **2** to destroy by conversion into vapour ~*vi* to become vaporized – **vaporizable** *adj*, **vaporizer** *n*, **vaporization** *n*

vaporous /ˈvayp(ə)rəs‖ˈveɪp(ə)rəs/ *adj* **1** resembling, consisting of, or characteristic of vapour **2** producing vapours; volatile **3** containing or obscured by vapours; misty – **vaporously** *adv*, **vaporousness** *n*

[1]**vapour**, *NAm chiefly* **vapor** /ˈvaypə‖ˈveɪpə/ *n* **1** smoke, fog, etc suspended floating in the air and impairing its transparency **2** a substance in the gaseous state; *esp* such a substance that is liquid under normal conditions **3** *pl, archaic* a depressed or hysterical condition

[2]**vapour**, *NAm chiefly* **vapor** *vi* **1** to rise or pass off in vapour **2** to emit vapour

ˈvapour ˌtrail *n* a contrail

[1]**variable** /ˈveəri·əbl‖ˈveərɪəbl/ *adj* **1** subject to

variation or changes <~ *winds*> **2** having the characteristics of a variable <*a ~ number*> – **variableness** *n*, **variably** *adv*, **variability** *n*

[2]**variable** *n* **1** sthg (e g a variable star) that is variable **2** (a symbol representing) a quantity that may assume any of a set of values

variance /ˈveəri·əns‖ˈveərɪəns/ *n* **1** a discrepancy **2** dissension, dispute – esp in *at variance* **3** the square of the standard deviation – **at variance** not in harmony or agreement

[1]**variant** /ˈveəri·ənt‖ˈveərɪənt/ *adj* varying (slightly) from the standard form <~ *readings*>

[2]**variant** *n* any of 2 or more people or things displaying usu slight differences: e g **a** sthg that shows variation from a type or norm **b** any of 2 or more different spellings, pronunciations, or forms of the same word

variation /ˌveəriˈaysh(ə)n‖ˌveərɪˈeɪʃ(ə)n/ *n* **1a** varying or being varied **b** an instance of varying **c** the extent to which or the range in which a thing varies **2** DECLINATION 3 **3** a change in the mean motion or orbit of a celestial body **4** the repetition of a musical theme with modifications in rhythm, tune, harmony, or key **5a** divergence in characteristics of an organism or genotype from those typical or usual of its group **b** an individual or group exhibiting variation **6** a solo dance in ballet – **variational** *adj*, **variationally** *adv*

varicoloured /ˈveəriˌkuləd‖ˈveərɪˌkʌləd/ *adj* having various colours

varicose /ˈvarikəs, -kohs‖ˈværɪkəs, -kəʊs/ *also* **varicosed** *adj* abnormally swollen or dilated <~ *veins*> – **varicosity** *n*

varied /ˈveərid‖ˈveərɪd/ *adj* **1** having numerous forms or types; diverse **2** variegated – **variedly** *adv*

variegate /ˈveəri·əˌgayt, -riˌgayt‖ˈveərɪəˌgeɪt, -rɪˌgeɪt/ *vt* to diversify in appearance, esp with patches of different colours; dapple – **variegator** *n*, **variegation** *n*

variety /vəˈrie·əti‖vəˈraɪətɪ/ *n* **1** the state of having different forms or types; diversity **2** an assortment of different things, esp of a particular class **3a** sthg differing from others of the same general kind; a sort **b** any of various groups of plants or animals ranking below a species **4** theatrical entertainment consisting of separate performances (e g of songs, skits, acrobatics, etc)

variform /ˈveəriˌfawm‖ˈveərɪˌfɔːm/ *adj* varied in form

variorum /ˌveəriˈawrəm, ˌva-‖ˌveərɪˈɔːrəm, ˌvæ-/ *n* an edition or text with notes by different people [Latin *variorum* of various persons (in the phrase *cum notis variorum* with the notes of various persons)]

various /ˈveəri·əs‖ˈveərɪəs/ *adj* **1a** of differing kinds; diverse <~ *remedies*> **b** dissimilar in nature or form; unlike **2** more than one; several <*stop at ~ towns*> – **variousness** *n*

ˈ**variously** /-li‖-lɪ/ *adv* in various ways; at various times

varlet /ˈvahlit‖ˈvɑːlɪt/ *n, archaic* a base unprincipled person

[1]**varnish** /ˈvahnish‖ˈvɑːnɪʃ/ *n* **1** a liquid preparation that forms a hard shiny transparent coating on drying **2** outside show; VENEER 3 – **varnishy** *adj*

[2]**varnish** *vt* **1** to apply varnish to **2** to cover (sthg unpleasant) with a fair appearance; gloss *over* – **varnisher** *n*

varsity /ˈvahsiti‖ˈvɑːsɪtɪ/ *n, Br* university – now chiefly humor

vary /ˈveəri‖ˈveərɪ/ *vt* **1** to make a (partial) change in **2** to ensure variety in; diversify ~ *vi* **1** to exhibit or undergo change **2** to deviate **3** to exhibit biological variation – **varyingly** *adv*

vascular /ˈvaskyoolə‖ˈvæskjʊlə/ *adj* of or being a channel or system of channels conducting blood, sap, etc in a plant or animal – **vascularity** *n*

vas deferens /ˌvaz ˈdefərenz, vas‖ˌvæz ˈdefərenz, væs/ *n, pl* **vasa deferentia** /ˌvaysə defəˈrenshi·ə, -si·ə, -shə, ˌvayzə‖ˌveɪsə defəˈrenʃɪə, -sɪə, -ʃə, ˌveɪzə/ a duct, esp of a higher vertebrate animal, that carries sperm from the testis towards the penis

vase /vahz‖vɑːz/ *n* an ornamental vessel used esp for holding flowers

vasectomy /vəˈsektəmi, va-‖vəˈsektəmɪ, væ-/ *n* surgical cutting out of a section of the vas deferens, usu to induce permanent sterility – **vasectomize** *vt*

Vaseline /ˌvas(ə)lˈeen‖ˌvæs(ə)lˈiːn/ *trademark* – used for petroleum jelly

vassal /ˈvas(ə)l‖ˈvæs(ə)l/ *n* **1** sby under the protection of another who is his/her feudal lord **2** sby in a subservient or subordinate position – **vassal** *adj*

vast /vahst‖vɑːst/ *adj* very great in amount, degree, intensity, or esp in extent or range – **vastly** *adv*, **vastness** *n*

[1]**vat** /vat‖væt/ *n* **1** a tub, barrel, or other large vessel, esp for holding liquids undergoing chemical change or preparations for dyeing or tanning **2** a liquid containing a dye in a soluble form, that, on textile material being steeped in the liquor and then exposed to the air, is converted to the original insoluble dye by oxidation and is precipitated in the fibre

[2]**vat** *n, often cap, Br* VALUE-ADDED TAX

Vatican /ˈvatikən‖ˈvætɪkən/ *n* the official residence of the Pope and the administrative centre of Roman Catholicism – **Vatican** *adj*

vaudeville /ˈvawdəˌvil‖ˈvɔːdəˌvɪl/ *n* **1** a light often comic theatrical piece frequently combining pantomime, dialogue, dancing, and song **2** *NAm* VARIETY 4 [French, fr Middle French, popular satirical song, alteration of *vaudevire*, fr *vau-de-Vire* valley of Vire, fr *Vire*, town in NW France where such songs were composed]

[1]**vault** /vawlt, volt‖vɔːlt, vɒlt/ *n* **1a** an arched structure of masonry, usu forming a ceiling or roof **b** sthg (e g the sky) resembling a vault **2a** an underground passage, room, or storage compartment **b** a room or compartment for the safekeeping of valuables **3a** a burial chamber, esp beneath a church or in a cemetery **b** a prefabricated container, usu of metal or concrete, into which a coffin is placed at burial – **vaulted** *adj*, **vaulty** *adj*

[2]**vault** *vt* to form or cover (as if) with a vault

[3]**vault** *vb* to bound vigorously (over); *esp* to execute a leap (over) using the hands or a pole – **vaulter** *n*

[4]**vault** *n* an act of vaulting

[1]**vaulting** /ˈvawlting, ˈvolting‖ˈvɔːltɪŋ, ˈvɒltɪŋ/

n vaulted construction

[2]**vaulting** *adj* **1** reaching for the heights <~ *ambition*> **2** designed for use in vaulting

ˈ**vaulting ˌhorse** *n* an apparatus like a pommel horse without pommels that is used for vaulting in gymnastics

vaunt /vawnt‖vɔːnt/ *vt* to call attention to, proudly and often boastfully – **vaunter** *n*, **vauntingly** *adv*

VD /ˌvee ˈdee‖ˌviː ˈdiː/ *n* VENEREAL DISEASE

've /v‖v/ *vb* have <*we've been there*>

veal /veel‖viːl/ *n* the flesh of a young calf used as food [Middle French *veel*, fr Latin *vitellus* small calf, fr *vitulus* calf] – **vealy** *adj*

[1]**vector** /ˈvektə‖ˈvektə/ *n* **1a** a quantity (e g velocity or force) that has magnitude and direction and that is commonly represented by a directed line segment whose length represents the magnitude and whose orientation in space represents the direction **b** a course or compass direction, esp of an aircraft **2** an organism (e g an insect) that transmits a disease-causing agent – **vectorial** *adj*

[2]**vector** *vt* to change the direction of (the thrust of a jet engine) for steering

[1]**veer** /viə‖vɪə/ *vt* to let or pay out (e g a rope)

[2]**veer** /viə‖vɪə/ *vi* **1** to change direction, position, or inclination **2** *of the wind* to shift in a clockwise direction **3** to wear ship ~*vt* to direct to a different course; *specif* WEAR 7 – **veeringly** *adv*

[3]**veer** *n* a change in direction, position, or inclination

veg /vej‖vedʒ/ *n, pl* **veg** *Br* a vegetable – infml

vegan /ˈveegən, vaygən‖ˈviːgən, veɪgən/ *n* a strict vegetarian who avoids food or other products derived from animals – **vegan** *adj*, **veganism** *n*

[1]**vegetable** /ˈvej(i)təbl‖ˈvedʒ(ɪ)təbl/ *adj* **1a** of, constituting, or growing like plants **b** consisting of plants **2** made or obtained from plants or plant products – **vegetably** *adv*

[2]**vegetable** *n* **1** PLANT 1b **2** a usu herbaceous plant (e g the cabbage, bean, or potato) grown for an edible part which is usu eaten with the principal course of a meal; *also* this part of the plant **3a** a person with a dull undemanding existence **b** a person whose physical and esp mental capacities are severely impaired by illness or injury

ˌ**vegetable ˈmarrow** *n* (any of various large smooth-skinned elongated fruits, used as a vegetable, of) a cultivated variety of a climbing plant of the cucumber family

[1]**vegetarian** /ˌvejiˈteəri·ən‖ˌvedʒɪˈteərɪən/ *n* one who practises vegetarianism

[2]**vegetarian** *adj* **1** of vegetarians or vegetarianism **2** consisting wholly of vegetables <*a* ~ *diet*>

ˌ**vegeˈtariaˌnism** /-ˌniz(ə)m‖-ˌnɪz(ə)m/ *n* the theory or practice of living on a diet that excludes the flesh of animals and often other animal products and that is made up of vegetables, fruits, cereals, and nuts

vegetate /ˈvejiˌtayt‖ˈvedʒɪˌteɪt/ *vi* **1a** to grow in the manner of a plant **b** to produce vegetation **2** to lead a passive monotonous existence

vegetation /ˌvejiˈtaysh(ə)n‖ˌvedʒɪˈteɪʃ(ə)n/ *n* **1** plant life or total plant cover (e g of an area) **2** an abnormal outgrowth on a body part (e g a heart valve) – **vegetational** *adj*, **vegetationally** *adv*

vehement /ˈvee·əmənt‖ˈviːəmənt/ *adj* **1** intensely felt; impassioned **2** forcibly expressed – **vehemently** *adv*, **vehemence** *n*

vehicle /ˈvee·ək(ə)l‖ˈviːək(ə)l/ *n* **1** any of various usu liquid media acting esp as solvents, carriers, or binders for active ingredients (e g drugs) or pigments **2** a means of transmission; a carrier **3** a medium through which sthg is expressed or communicated **4** MOTOR VEHICLE **5** a work created to display the talents of a particular performer

vehicular /veeˈikyoolə‖viːˈɪkjʊlə/ *adj* of or designed for vehicles, esp motor vehicles

[1]**veil** /vayl‖veɪl/ *n* **1a** a length of cloth worn by women as a covering for the head and shoulders and often, esp in eastern countries, the face; *specif* the outer covering of a nun's headdress **b** a piece of sheer fabric attached for protection or ornament to a hat or headdress **c** any of various liturgical cloths; *esp* one used to cover the chalice **2** *the* cloistered life of a nun **3** a concealing curtain or cover of cloth **4a** sthg that hides or obscures like a veil **b** a disguise, pretext <*under the* ~ *of national defence preparations for war began*> **5** a velum

[2]**veil** *vt* to cover, provide, or conceal (as if) with a veil ~*vi* to put on or wear a veil

veiled /vayld‖veɪld/ *adj* **1** indistinct, muffled **2** disguised <~ *threats*>

[1]**vein** /vayn‖veɪn/ *n* **1** a deposit of ore, coal, etc, esp in a rock fissure **2a** BLOOD VESSEL – not used technically **b** any of the tubular converging vessels that carry blood from the capillaries towards the heart **3a** any of the vascular bundles forming the framework of a leaf **b** any of the thickened cuticular ribs that serve to stiffen the wings of an insect **4** a streak or marking suggesting a vein (e g in marble) **5** a distinctive element or quality; a strain **6** a frame of mind; a mood – **veinal** *adj*, **veinlet** *n*, **veiny** *adj*

[2]**vein** *vt* to pattern (as if) with veins

veining /ˈvayning‖ˈveɪnɪŋ/ *n* a pattern of veins

velar /ˈveelə‖ˈviːlə/ *adj* of or forming a velum, esp the soft palate – **velar** *n*, **velarize** *vt*

veld, veldt /velt, felt‖velt, felt/ *n* a (shrubby or thinly forested) grassland, esp in southern Africa

velleity /vəˈlee·əti‖vəˈliːətɪ/ *n* a slight wish or tendency; an inclination – fml

vellum /ˈveləm‖ˈveləm/ *n* **1** a fine-grained skin (e g calf) prepared esp for writing on or binding books **2** a strong cream-coloured paper [Middle French *veelin*, fr *veelin* of a calf, fr *veel* calf – see VEAL]

velocipede /vəˈlosipeed‖vəˈlɒsɪpiːd/ *n* **1** an early type of bicycle propelled by the rider's feet in contact with the ground **2** *NAm* a child's tricycle

velocity /vəˈlosəti‖vəˈlɒsətɪ/ *n* **1** speed, esp of inanimate things **2** speed in a given direction

velour, velours /vəˈlooə‖vəˈlʊə/ *n, pl* **velours** /-z‖-z/ **1** any of various fabrics with a pile or napped surface resembling velvet **2** a fur felt finished with a long velvety nap, used esp for hats

velum /ˈveeləm‖ˈviːləm/ *n, pl* **vela** /-lə‖-lə/ a curtainlike membrane or anatomical partition;

esp SOFT PALATE

velvet /'velvit||'velvɪt/ *n* **1** a fabric (e g of silk, rayon, or cotton) characterized by a short soft dense pile **2** sthg suggesting velvet in softness, smoothness, etc **3** the soft skin that envelops and nourishes the developing antlers of deer

velveteen /'velvi,teen||'velvɪ,tiːn/ *n* a fabric made with a short close weft pile in imitation of velvet

velvety /'velviti||'velvɪtɪ/ *adj* soft and smooth like velvet

venal /'veenl||'viːnl/ *adj* open to corrupt influence, esp bribery – **venally** *adv*, **venality** *n*

vend /vend||vend/ *vi* to sell ~ *vt* **1** to sell, esp in a small way **2** to sell by means of a vending machine – **vendable** *adj*, **vendee** *n*, **vendible** *adj*

vendetta /ven'detə||ven'detə/ *n* **1** a blood feud arising from the murder or injury of a member of one family by a member of another **2** a prolonged bitter feud [Italian, lit., revenge, fr L *vindicta*, fr *vindicare* to lay claim to, avenge, fr *vindic-*, *vindex* claimant, avenger]

'vending ma,chine /'vending||'vendɪŋ/ *n* a coin-operated machine for selling merchandise

vendor, vender /'vendə||'vendə/ *n* **1** a seller; *specif, Br* the seller of a house **2** VENDING MACHINE

[1]**veneer** /və'niə||və'nɪə/ *n* **1** a thin layer of wood of superior appearance or hardness used esp to give a decorative finish (e g to joinery) **2** a protective or ornamental facing (e g of brick or stone) **3** a superficial or deceptively attractive appearance

[2]**veneer** *vt* **1** to overlay (e g a common wood) with veneer; *broadly* to face with a material giving a superior surface **2** to conceal under a superficial and deceptive attractiveness – **veneerer** *n*

venerable /'ven(ə)rəbl||'ven(ə)rəbl/ *adj* **1** – used as a title for an Anglican archdeacon, or for a Roman Catholic who has been accorded the lowest of 3 degrees of recognition for sanctity **2** made sacred, esp by religious or historical association **3a** commanding respect through age, character, and attainments **b** impressive by reason of age <*under ~ pines*> – **venerableness** *n*, **venerably** *adv*, **venerability** *n*

venerate /'venərayt||'venəreɪt/ *vt* to regard with reverence or admiring deference – **venerator** *n*, **veneration** *n*

venereal /və'niəri·əl||və'nɪərɪəl/ *adj* **1** of sexual desire or sexual intercourse **2a** resulting from or contracted during sexual intercourse <~ *infections*> **b** of or affected with venereal disease <*a high ~ rate*> [Latin *venereus*, fr *vener-*, *venus* love, sexual desire]

ve'nereal di,sease *n* a contagious disease (e g gonorrhoea or syphilis) that is typically acquired during sexual intercourse

ve,netian 'blind /və'neesh(ə)n||və'niːʃ(ə)n/ *n* a blind (e g for a window) made of horizontal slats that may be adjusted so as to vary the amount of light admitted

vengeance /'venj(ə)ns||'vendʒ(ə)ns/ *n* punishment inflicted in retaliation for injury or offence – **with a vengeance 1** with great force or vehemence **2** to an extreme or excessive degree

vengeful /'venjf(ə)l||'vendʒf(ə)l/ *adj* revengeful, vindictive – **vengefully** *adv*, **vengefulness** *n*

venial /'veenyəl, -ni·əl||'viːnjəl, -nɪəl/ *adj* forgivable, pardonable – **venially** *adv*, **venialness** *n*

venison /'venis(ə)n||'venɪs(ə)n/ *n* the flesh of a deer as food

venom /'venəm||'venəm/ *n* **1** poisonous matter normally secreted by snakes, scorpions, bees, etc and transmitted chiefly by biting or stinging **2** ill will, malevolence

venomous /'venəməs||'venəməs/ *adj* **1a** poisonous **b** spiteful, malevolent <~ *criticism*> **2** able to inflict a poisoned wound – **venomously** *adv*, **venomousness** *n*

venous /'veenəs||'viːnəs/ *adj* **1** having or consisting of veins <*a ~ system*> **2** *of blood* containing carbon dioxide rather than oxygen – **venously** *adv*, **venosity** *n*

[1]**vent** /vent||vent/ *vt* **1** to provide with a vent **2** to give (vigorous) expression to

[2]**vent** *n* **1** a means of escape or release; an outlet – chiefly in *give vent to* **2a** the anus, esp of the cloaca of a bird or reptile **b** an outlet of a volcano **c** a hole at the breech of a gun through which the powder is ignited – **ventless** *adj*

[3]**vent** *n* a slit in a garment; *specif* an opening in the lower part of a seam (e g of a jacket or skirt)

ventilate /'ventilayt||'ventɪleɪt/ *vt* **1** to examine freely and openly; expose publicly **2** to expose to (a current of fresh) air; oxygenate **3a** *of a current of air* to pass or circulate through so as to freshen **b** to cause fresh air to circulate through – **ventilative** *adj*

ventilation /,venti'laysh(ə)n||,ventɪ'leɪʃ(ə)n/ *n* **1** the act or process of ventilating **2** a system or means of providing fresh air

ventilator /'venti,laytə||'ventɪ,leɪtə/ *n* an apparatus or aperture for introducing fresh air or expelling stagnant air

ventral /'ventrəl||'ventrəl/ *adj* **1a** abdominal **b** relating to or situated near or on the front or lower surface of an animal or aircraft opposite the back **2** being or located on the lower or inner surface of a plant structure – **ventrally** *adv*

ventricle /'ventrikl||'ventrɪkl/ *n* a cavity of a bodily part or organ: e g **a** a chamber of the heart which receives blood from a corresponding atrium and from which blood is pumped into the arteries **b** any of the system of communicating cavities in the brain that are continuous with the central canal of the spinal cord – **ventricular** *adj*

ventriloquism /ven'trilə,kwiz(ə)m||ven'trɪlə,kwɪz(ə)m/ *n* the production of the voice in such a manner that the sound appears to come from a source other than the vocal organs of the speaker and esp from a dummy manipulated by the producer of the sound [Late Latin *ventriloquus* ventriloquist, fr Latin *venter* belly + *loqui* to speak] – **ventriloquist** *n*, **ventriloquial** *adj*

[1]**venture** /'venchə||'ventʃə/ *vt* **1** to expose to hazard; risk, gamble **2** to face the risks and dangers of; brave **3** to offer at the risk of opposition or censure <~ *an opinion*> ~*vi* to proceed despite danger; dare to go or do

[2]**venture** *n* **1** an undertaking involving chance, risk, or danger, esp in business **2** sthg (e g money or property) at risk in a speculative venture

'venturesome /-s(ə)m||-s(ə)m/ *adj* **1** daring **2** involving risk; hazardous

venue /'venyooh‖'venju:/ *n* **1** the place in which a legal case is to be tried and from which the jury is drawn **2** the place where a gathering takes place

Venus /'veenəs‖'vi:nəs/ *n* the planet second in order from the sun

veracious /və'rayshəs‖və'reɪʃəs/ *adj* **1** reliable in testimony; truthful **2** true, accurate – **veraciously** *adv*, **veraciousness** *n*, **veracity** *n*

veranda, verandah /və'randə‖və'rændə/ *n* a usu roofed open gallery or portico attached to the outside of a building

verb /vuhb‖vɜ:b/ *n* any of a class of words that characteristically are the grammatical centre of a predicate and express an act, occurrence, or mode of being

[1]**verbal** /'vuhbl‖'vɜ:bl/ *adj* **1** of, involving, or expressed in words **2** of or formed from a verb **3** spoken rather than written; oral **4** verbatim, word-for-word – **verbally** *adv*

[2]**verbal** *n* **1** a word that combines characteristics of a verb with those of a noun or adjective **2** *Br* a spoken statement; *esp* one made to the police admitting or implying guilt and used in evidence

verbal·ize, -ise /'vuhbl,iez‖'vɜ:bl,aɪz/ *vi* **1** to speak or write verbosely **2** to express sthg in words ~ *vt* **1** to convert into a verb **2** to name or describe in words – **verbalizer** *n*, **verbalization** *n*

,verbal 'noun *n* a noun derived from, and having some of the constructions of, a verb; *esp* a gerund

verbatim /vuh'baytim‖vɜ:'beɪtɪm/ *adv or adj* in the exact words

verbiage /'vuhbi·ij‖'vɜ:bɪɪdʒ/ *n* wordiness, verbosity

verbose /vuh'bohs‖vɜ:'bəʊs/ *adj* **1** containing more words than necessary **2** given to wordiness – **verbosely** *adv*, **verboseness** *n*, **verbosity** *n*

verdant /'vuhd(ə)nt‖'vɜ:d(ə)nt/ *adj* **1a** green in tint or colour **b** green with growing plants **2** immature, unsophisticated – **verdancy** *n*, **verdantly** *adv*

verdict /'vuhdikt‖'vɜ:dɪkt/ *n* **1** the decision of a jury on the matter submitted to them **2** an opinion, judgment [Anglo-French *verdit*, fr Old French *ver* true + *dit* saying, pronouncement]

verdigris /'vuhdigris‖'vɜ:dɪgrɪs; *also* -,gree‖-,gri:/ *n* a green or bluish deposit formed on copper, brass, or bronze surfaces [Old French *vert de Grice*, lit., green of Greece]

verdure /'vuhdyə, -jə‖'vɜ:djə, -dʒə/ *n* **1** (the greenness of) growing vegetation **2** a condition of health, freshness, and vigour – **verdurous** *adj*, **verdurousness** *n*

[1]**verge** /vuhj‖vɜ:dʒ/ *n* **1** a rod or staff carried as an emblem of authority or symbol of office **2** sthg that borders, limits, or bounds: e g **2a** an outer margin of an object or structural part **b** the edge of a roof projecting over the gable **3** the brink, threshold **4** *Br* a surfaced or planted strip of land at the side of a road

[2]**verge** *vi* – **verge on** to be near to; border on

[3]**verge** *vi* **1** *of the sun* to incline towards the horizon; sink **2** to move or extend *towards* a specified condition

verger /'vuhjə‖'vɜ:dʒə/ *n* **1** a church official who keeps order during services or serves as an usher or sacristan **2** *chiefly Br* an attendant who carries a verge (e g before a bishop or justice)

verify /'verifie‖'verɪfaɪ/ *vt* **1** to substantiate in law, esp formally or on oath **2** to ascertain the truth, accuracy, or reality of **3** to bear out, fulfil <*my fears were* verified> – **verifier** *n*, **verifiable** *adj*, **verification** *n*

verily /'verəli‖'verəlɪ/ *adv, archaic* **1** indeed, certainly **2** truly, confidently

verisimilitude /,verisi'milityoohd‖,verɪsɪ'mɪlɪtju:d/ *n* **1** the quality or state of appearing to be true **2** a statement that has the appearance of truth *USE* fml – **verisimilitudinous** *adj*

veritable /'veritəbl‖'verɪtəbl/ *adj* being truly the thing named <*a* ~ *mountain of references*> – **veritableness** *n*, **veritably** *adv*

verity /'veriti‖'verɪtɪ/ *n* **1** the quality or state of being true or real **2** sthg (e g a statement) that is true; *esp* a permanently true value or principle

vermicelli /,vuhmi'cheli‖,vɜ:mɪ'tʃelɪ/ *n* **1** pasta in the form of long thin solid threads smaller in diameter than spaghetti **2** small thin sugar strands that are used as a decoration (e g on iced cakes) [Italian, lit., little worms, fr *verme* worm, fr Latin *vermis*]

vermiform /'vuhmi,fawm‖'vɜ:mɪ,fɔ:m/ *adj* resembling a worm in shape

,vermiform ap'pendix *n* a narrow short blind tube that extends from the caecum in the lower right-hand part of the abdomen

vermilion, vermillion /və'milyən‖və'mɪljən/ *adj or n* (of the brilliant red colour of) mercuric sulphide used as a pigment

vermin /'vuhmin‖'vɜ:mɪn/ *n, pl* **vermin** **1** *pl* **1a** lice, rats, or other common harmful or objectionable animals **b** birds and mammals that prey on game **2** an offensive person – **verminous** *adj*, **verminously** *adv*

vermouth /'vuhməth‖'vɜ:məθ/ *n* a dry or sweet alcoholic drink that has a white wine base and is flavoured with aromatic herbs

[1]**vernacular** /və'nakyoolə‖və'nækjʊlə/ *adj* **1a** expressed or written in a language or dialect native to a region or country rather than a literary, learned, or foreign language **b** of or being the normal spoken form of a language **2** of or being the common building style of a period or place – **vernacularly** *adv*

[2]**vernacular** *n* **1** the local vernacular language **2** the mode of expression of a group or class – **vernacularism** *n*

vernal /'vuhnl‖'vɜ:nl/ *adj* **1** of or occurring in the spring **2** fresh, youthful – **vernally** *adv*

veronica /və'ronikə‖və'rɒnɪkə/ *n* speedwell

verruca /və'roohkə‖və'ru:kə/ *n, pl* **verrucas** also **verruccae** /-ki‖-kɪ/ **1** a wart or warty skin growth **2** a warty prominence on a plant or animal – **verrucose** *adj*

versatile /'vuhsətiel‖'vɜ:sətaɪl/ *adj* **1** embracing a variety of subjects, fields, or skills; *also* turning with ease from one thing to another **2** capable of moving easily forwards or backwards, or esp up and down <~ *antennae*> <~ *anther*> **3** having many uses or applications

<~ *building material*> – **versatilely** *adv*, **versatileness** *n*, **versatility** *n*

verse /vuhs‖vɜːs/ *n* **1** a line of metrical writing **2a** (an example of) metrical language or writing, distinguished from poetry esp by its lower level of intensity **b** POETRY 2 **c** a body of metrical writing (e g of a period or country) <*Elizabethan* ~> **3** a stanza **4** any of the short divisions into which a chapter of the Bible is traditionally divided [Old French *vers*, fr Latin *versus*, lit., turning, fr *vers-*, *vertere* to turn]

versed *adj* possessing a thorough knowledge (of) or skill *in* – chiefly in *well versed in*

versify /ˈvuhsifie‖ˈvɜːsɪfaɪ/ *vi* to compose verses ~ *vt* to turn into verse – **versifier** *n*, **versification** *n*

version /ˈvuhsh(ə)n, -zh(ə)n‖ˈvɜːʃ(ə)n, -ʒ(ə)n/ *n* **1** a translation from another language; *esp, often cap* a translation of (part of) the Bible **2a** an account or description from a particular point of view, esp as contrasted with another account **b** an adaptation of a work of art into another medium <*the film* ~ *of the novel*> **c** an arrangement of a musical composition **3** a form or variant of a type or original <*an experimental* ~ *of the plane*> **4** manual turning of a foetus in the uterus to aid delivery – **versional** *adj*

verso /ˈvuhsoh‖ˈvɜːsəʊ/ *n, pl* **versos** a left-hand page

versus /ˈvuhsəs‖ˈvɜːsəs/ *prep* **1** against **2** in contrast to or as the alternative of <*free trade* ~ *protection*>

vertebra /ˈvuhtibrə‖ˈvɜːtɪbrə/ *n, pl* **vertebrae** /-bri‖-brɪ/, **vertebras** any of the bony or cartilaginous segments composing the spinal column – **vertebral** *adj*

[1]**vertebrate** /ˈvuhtibrət, -brayt‖ˈvɜːtɪbrət, -breɪt/ *adj* **1** having a spinal column **2** of the vertebrates

[2]**vertebrate** *n* any of a large group of animals (e g mammals, birds, reptiles, amphibians, and fishes) with a segmented backbone, together with a few primitive forms in which the backbone is represented by a notochord

vertex /ˈvuhteks‖ˈvɜːteks/ *n, pl* **vertices** /ˈvuhtiseez‖ˈvɜːtɪsiːz/ *also* **vertexes** **1a(1)** the point opposite to and farthest from the base in a figure **a(2)** the termination or intersection of lines or curves <*the* ~ *of an angle*> **a(3)** a point where an axis of an ellipse, parabola, or hyperbola intersects the curve **b** ZENITH 1 **2** the top of the head **3** the highest point; the summit

vertical /ˈvuhtikl‖ˈvɜːtɪkl/ *adj* **1** situated at the highest point; directly overhead or in the zenith **2** perpendicular to the plane of the horizon or to a primary axis **3** of, involving, or integrating discrete elements (e g from lowest to highest) <*the* ~ *arrangement of society*> **4** of or concerning the relationships between people of different rank in a hierarchy – **vertical** *n*, **vertically** *adv*, **verticalness** *n*, **verticality** *n*

vertiginous /vuhˈtijinəs‖vɜːˈtɪdʒɪnəs/ *adj* **1** characterized by or suffering from vertigo **2** inclined to frequent and often pointless change; inconstant **3** causing or tending to cause dizziness <*the* ~ *heights*> **4** marked by turning; rotary – **vertiginously** *adv*

vertigo /ˈvuhtigoh‖ˈvɜːtɪgəʊ/ *n* a disordered state in which the individual loses balance and the surroundings seem to whirl dizzily

verve /vuhv‖vɜːv/ *n* **1** the spirit and enthusiasm animating artistic work **2** energy, vitality

[1]**very** /ˈveri‖ˈverɪ/ *adj* **1** properly so called; actual, genuine <*the* ~ *man you met*> **2** absolute <*the* ~ *thing for the purpose*> **3** being no more than; mere <*the* ~ *thought terrified me*> *USE* used attributively

[2]**very** *adv* **1** to a high degree; exceedingly **2** – used as an intensive to emphasize *same, own*, or the superlative degree <*the* ~ *best shop in town*>

ˌvery ˌhigh ˈfrequency *n* a radio frequency in the range between 30MHz and 300MHz

Very light /ˈviəri, ˈveri‖ˈvɪərɪ, ˈverɪ/ *n* a white or coloured ball of fire that is projected from a special pistol and that is used as a signal flare [Edward W *Very* (died 1910), US naval officer]

vesicle /ˈvesikl‖ˈvesɪkl/ *n* **1a** a membranous usu fluid-filled pouch (e g a cyst or cell) in a plant or animal **b** a blister **c** a pocket of embryonic tissue that is the beginning of an organ **2** a small cavity in a mineral or rock – **vesicular** *adj*, **vesiculate** *adj*, **vesicularity** *n*

[1]**vesper** /ˈvespə‖ˈvespə/ *n* **1** *cap* EVENING STAR **2** *archaic* evening, eventide

[2]**vesper** *adj* of vespers or the evening

vespers /ˈvespəz‖ˈvespəz/ *n pl but sing or pl in constr, often cap* **1** the sixth of the canonical hours that is said or sung in the late afternoon **2** a service of evening worship

vessel /ˈvesl‖ˈvesl/ *n* **1a** a hollow utensil (e g a jug, cup, or bowl) for holding esp liquid **b** sby into whom some quality (e g grace) is infused **2** a large hollow structure designed to float on and move through water carrying a crew, passengers, or cargo **3a** a tube or canal (e g an artery) in which a body fluid is contained and conveyed or circulated **b** a conducting tube in a plant

[1]**vest** /vest‖vest/ *vt* **1a** to give (e g property or power) into the possession or discretion of another **b** to clothe with a particular authority, right, or property **2** to clothe (as if) with a garment; *esp* to robe in ecclesiastical vestments ~ *vi* to become legally vested

[2]**vest** *n* **1** *chiefly Br* a usu sleeveless undergarment for the upper body **2** *chiefly NAm* a waistcoat – **vested** *adj*, **vestlike** *adj*

[1]**vestal** /ˈvestl‖ˈvestl/ *adj* **1** of a vestal virgin **2** chaste; *esp* virgin – **vestally** *adv*

[2]**vestal**, **ˌvestal ˈvirgin** *n* a priestess of the Roman goddess Vesta, responsible for tending the sacred fire perpetually kept burning on her altar

ˌvested ˈinterest /ˈvestid‖ˈvestɪd/ *n* **1a** an interest carrying a legal right **b** an interest (e g in an existing political or social arrangement) in which the holder has a strong personal commitment **2** sby or sthg having a vested interest in sthg; *specif* a group enjoying benefits from an existing privilege

vestibule /ˈvestibyoohl‖ˈvestɪbjuːl/ *n* **1** a lobby or chamber between the outer door and the interior of a building **2** any of various bodily cavities, esp when serving as or resembling an entrance to some other cavity or space: e g **2a** the central cavity of the bony labyrinth of the ear **b** the part of the mouth cavity outside the teeth and gums – **vestibuled** *adj*, **vestibular** *adj*

vestige /ˈvestij‖ˈvestɪdʒ/ *n* **1a** a trace or visible sign left by sthg vanished or lost **b** a minute remaining amount **2** a small or imperfectly formed body part or organ that remains from one more fully developed in an earlier stage of the individual, in a past generation, or in closely related forms – **vestigial** *adj*, **vestigially** *adv*

vestment /ˈvestmənt‖ˈvestmənt/ *n* **1** an outer garment; *esp* a robe of ceremony or office **2** any of the ceremonial garments and insignia worn by ecclesiastical officiants and assistants as appropriate to their rank and to the rite being celebrated – **vestmental** *adj*

vestry /ˈvestri‖ˈvestrɪ/ *n* **1a** a sacristy **b** a room used for church meetings and classes **2a** the business meeting of an English parish **b** an elective administrative body in an Episcopal parish in the USA

vesture /ˈveschə‖ˈvestʃə/ *n* clothing, apparel – fml

[1]vet /vet‖vet/ *n* sby qualified and authorized to treat diseases and injuries of animals

[2]vet *vt* **-tt-** **1** to subject (a person or animal) to a physical examination or checkup **2** *chiefly Br* to subject to careful and thorough appraisal <~ *your application*>

[3]vet *adj or n*, *NAm* (a) veteran

vetch /vech‖vetʃ/ *n* any of a genus of climbing or twining leguminous plants including valuable fodder and soil-improving plants

veteran /ˈvet(ə)rən‖ˈvet(ə)rən/ *n* **1** sby who has had long experience of an occupation, skill, or (military) service **2 veteran, veteran car** *Br* an old motor car; *specif* one built before 1916 **3** *NAm* a former serviceman – **veteran** *adj*

[1]veterinary /ˈvet(ə)rinəri‖ˈvet(ə)rɪnərɪ/ *adj* of or being the medical care of animals, esp domestic animals

[2]veterinary, *Br chiefly* ˈ**veterinary** ˌ**surgeon** *n* [1]VET

[1]veto /ˈveetoh‖ˈviːtəʊ/ *n*, *pl* **vetoes** **1** an authoritative prohibition **2** a right to declare inoperative decisions made by others; *esp* a power vested in a chief executive to prevent permanently or temporarily the enactment of measures passed by a legislature [Latin, I forbid, fr *vetare* to forbid]

[2]veto *vt* **vetoing; vetoed** to subject to a veto – **vetoer** *n*

vex /veks‖veks/ *vt* **vexed** *also* **vext** **1a** to bring distress, discomfort, or agitation to **b** to irritate or annoy by petty provocations; harass **2** to puzzle, baffle

vexation /vekˈsaysh(ə)n‖vekˈseɪʃ(ə)n/ *n* a cause of trouble; an affliction

vexatious /vekˈsayshəs‖vekˈseɪʃəs/ *adj* **1** causing vexation; distressing **2** intended to harass – **vexatiously** *adv*, **vexatiousness** *n*

ˌ**vexed** ˈ**question** /vekst‖vekst/ *n* a question that has been discussed at length, usu without a satisfactory solution being reached

via /ˈvie·ə‖ˈvaɪə/ *prep* **1** passing through or calling at (a place) on the way **2** through the medium of; *also* by means of

viable /ˈvie·əbl‖ˈvaɪəbl/ *adj* **1** (born alive and developed enough to be) capable of living **2** capable of growing or developing <~ *seeds*> **3** capable of working; practicable <~ *alternatives*> – **viably** *adv*, **viability** *n*

viaduct /ˈvie·əˌdukt‖ˈvaɪəˌdʌkt/ *n* a usu long bridge, esp on a series of arches, that carries a road, railway, canal, etc over a deep valley

vial /ˈvie·əl, viel‖ˈvaɪəl, vaɪl/ *n* a phial

viand /ˈvie·ənd‖ˈvaɪənd/ *n* **1** a (choice or tasty) item of food **2** *pl* provisions, food *USE* fml

vibes /viebz‖vaɪbz/ *n pl* **1** *sing or pl in constr* a vibraphone **2** VIBRATIONS 3 *USE* infml – **vibist** *n*

vibrant /ˈviebrənt‖ˈvaɪbrənt/ *adj* **1a** oscillating or pulsating rapidly **b** pulsating with life, vigour, or activity <*a* ~ *personality*> **2** sounding as a result of vibration; resonant <*a* ~ *voice*> – **vibrantly** *adv*

vibraphone /ˈviebrəˌfohn‖ˈvaɪbrəˌfəʊn/ *n* a percussion instrument resembling the xylophone but having metal bars and motor-driven resonators for sustaining its sound and producing a vibrato – **vibraphonist** *n*

vibrate /vieˈbrayt‖vaɪˈbreɪt/ *vt* **1** to cause to swing or move to and fro; cause to oscillate **2** to emit (e g sound) (as if) with a vibratory motion **3** to mark or measure by oscillation <*a pendulum* vibrating *seconds*> **4** to set in vibration ~ *vi* **1** to move to and fro; oscillate **2** to have an effect as of vibration; throb <*music* vibrating *in the memory*> **3** to be in a state of vibration; quiver – **vibrative** *adj*, **vibratory** *adj*

vibration /vieˈbraysh(ə)n‖vaɪˈbreɪʃ(ə)n/ *n* **1a** a periodic motion of the particles of an elastic body or medium in alternately opposite directions from a position of equilibrium **b** an oscillation or quivering **2** an instance of vibrating **3a** a characteristic aura or spirit felt to emanate from sby or sthg and instinctively sensed or experienced **b** a distinctive usu emotional atmosphere capable of being sensed – usu pl with sing. meaning – **vibrational** *adj*, **vibrationless** *adj*

vibrato /viˈbrahtoh‖vɪˈbrɑːtəʊ/ *n*, *pl* **vibratos** a slightly tremulous effect imparted to musical tone to add expressiveness, by slight and rapid variations in pitch

vibrator /vieˈbraytə‖vaɪˈbreɪtə/ *n* a vibrating electrical apparatus used in massage, esp to provide sexual stimulation

vicar /ˈvikə‖ˈvɪkə/ *n* **1** a Church of England incumbent receiving a stipend but formerly not the tithes of a parish **2** a clergyman exercising a broad pastoral responsibility as the representative of a prelate [Latin *vicarius* substitute, deputy, fr *vicis* change, succession] – **vicarship** *n*

vicarage /ˈvikərij‖ˈvɪkərɪdʒ/ *n* the benefice or house of a vicar

vicarious /vieˈkeəri·əs, vi-‖vaɪˈkeərɪəs, vɪ-/ *adj* **1a** serving instead of another **b** delegated <~ *authority*> **2** performed or suffered by one person as a substitute for, or to the benefit of, another <*a* ~ *sacrifice*> **3** experienced through imaginative participation in the experience of another <~ *pleasure*> – **vicariously** *adv*, **vicariousness** *n*

[1]vice /vies‖vaɪs/ *n* **1a** moral depravity or corruption; wickedness **b** a grave moral fault **c** a habitual and usu minor fault or shortcoming **2** habitual abnormal behaviour in a domestic animal detrimental to its health or usefulness **3** sexual immorality; *esp* prostitution [Old French, fr Latin *vitium* fault, vice]

[2]**vice,** *NAm chiefly* **vise** /vies‖vaɪs/ *n* any of various tools, usu attached to a workbench, that have 2 jaws that close for holding work by operation of a screw, lever, or cam [Middle French *vis, viz* something winding, fr Latin *vitis* vine] – **vicelike** *adj*

[3]**vice,** *NAm chiefly* **vise** *vt* to hold, force, or squeeze (as if) with a vice

vice- /vies-‖vaɪs-/ *prefix* **1** person next in rank below or qualified to act in place of; deputy <vice-*president*> **2** office next in rank below <vice-*admiralty*>

vice admiral *n* an officer in the navy ranking below admiral

ˌvice-ˈchancellor *n* an officer ranking next below a chancellor; *esp* the administrative head of a British university

viceregal /ˌviesˈreegl‖ˌvaɪsˈri:gl/ *adj* of a viceroy – **viceregally** *adv*

vicereine /ˈviesˌrayn‖ˈvaɪsˌreɪn/ *n* **1** the wife of a viceroy **2** a woman viceroy

viceroy /ˈviesroy‖ˈvaɪsrɔɪ/ *n* the governor of a country or province who rules as the representative of his sovereign – **viceroyalty** *n*, **viceroyship** *n*

ˈvice ˌsquad *n sing or pl in constr* a police department enforcing laws concerning gambling, pornography, and prostitution

vice versa /ˌviesi ˈvuhsə, ˌviesə, ˌvies‖ˌvaɪsɪ ˈvɜ:sə, ˌvaɪsə, ˌvaɪs/ *adv* with the order changed and relations reversed; conversely <*Ann hates Jane and* ~>

vicinity /viˈsinəti‖vɪˈsɪnətɪ/ *n* **1** a surrounding area or district **2** NEIGHBOURHOOD 3b **3** being near; proximity – fml

vicious /ˈvishəs‖ˈvɪʃəs/ *adj* **1** having the nature or quality of vice; depraved <~ *habits*> **2** *esp of language or reasoning* defective, faulty **3a** dangerous, refractory <*a* ~ *horse*> **b** unpleasantly fierce, malignant, or severe <*a* ~ *form of flu*> **4** malicious, spiteful <~ *gossip*> **5** worsened by internal causes that reciprocally augment each other <*a* ~ *wage-price spiral*> – **viciously** *adv*, **viciousness** *n*

ˌvicious ˈcircle *n* **1** a chain of events in which the apparent solution of 1 difficulty creates a new problem that makes the original difficulty worse **2** the logical fallacy of using 1 argument or definition to prove or define a second on which the first depends

vicissitude /viˈsisityoohd‖vɪˈsɪsɪtju:d/ *n* **1** a change or alteration (e g in nature or human affairs) **2** an accident of fortune – usu pl <*the* ~s *of daily life*> **3** the quality of being changeable; mutability – fml – **vicissitudinous** *adj*

victim /ˈviktim‖ˈvɪktɪm/ *n* **1** a living animal offered as a sacrifice in a religious rite **2** sby or sthg that is adversely affected by a force or agent: e g **2a** one who or that which is injured, destroyed, or subjected to oppression or mistreatment **b** a dupe, prey

victim·ize, -ise /ˈviktimiez‖ˈvɪktɪmaɪz/ *vt* **1** to make a victim of **2** to punish selectively (e g by unfair dismissal) – **victimizer** *n*, **victimization** *n*

victor /ˈviktə‖ˈvɪktə/ *n* a person, country, etc that defeats an enemy or opponent; a winner – **victor** *adj*

victoria /vikˈtawri·ə‖vɪkˈtɔ:rɪə/ *n* **1** a low 4-wheeled carriage for 2 with a folding hood **2** any of a genus of S American water lilies with large spreading leaves and immense bright white flowers **3** a large red sweet type of plum

Vicˌtoria ˈCross *n* a bronze Maltese cross that is the highest British military decoration

[1]**Victorian** /vikˈtawri·ən‖vɪkˈtɔ:rɪən/ *adj* **1** (characteristic) of the reign of Queen Victoria or the art, letters, or taste of her time **2** typical of the moral standards or conduct of the age of Queen Victoria, esp prudish or hypocritical

[2]**Victorian** *n* sby living during Queen Victoria's reign

victorious /vikˈtawri·əs‖vɪkˈtɔ:rɪəs/ *adj* **1a** having won a victory **b** (characteristic) of victory **2** successful, triumphant – **victoriously** *adv*, **victoriousness** *n*

victory /ˈvikt(ə)ri‖ˈvɪkt(ə)rɪ/ *n* **1** the overcoming of an enemy or antagonist **2** achievement of mastery or success in a struggle or endeavour

[1]**victual** /ˈvitl‖ˈvɪtl/ *n* **1** food usable by human beings **2** *pl* supplies of food; provisions

[2]**victual** *vb* **-ll-** (*NAm* **-l-, -ll-**) *vb* to supply with or lay in food

victualler, *NAm also* **victualer** /ˈvitl·ə‖ˈvɪtlə/ *n* **1** PUBLICAN 2 **2** sby who or sthg that provisions an army, a navy, or a ship with food **3** a provisioning ship

vicuña, vicuna /viˈkyoohnə‖vɪˈkju:nə/ *n* (the wool from the fine undercoat of) a wild ruminant mammal of the Andes related to the domesticated llama and alpaca

vide /ˈviedi‖ˈvaɪdɪ/ *vb imper* see – used to direct a reader to another item

videlicet /viˈdeliˌset‖vɪˈdelɪˌset/ *adv* that is to say; namely – used to introduce 1 or more examples [Latin, fr *vidēre* to see + *licet* it is permitted, fr *licēre* to be permitted]

[1]**video** /ˈvidioh‖ˈvɪdɪəʊ/ *adj* **1** of television; *specif* of reproduction of a television image or used in its transmission or reception <*a* ~ *signal*> **2** of a form of magnetic recording for reproduction on a television screen [Latin *vidēre* to see]

[2]**video** *n* **1 video, videorecorder, videocassette recorder** a machine for videotaping **2** *chiefly NAm* television

ˌvideo ˈnasty *n* a sensational video film, usu including scenes of explicit sex, violence, and horror

videotape /ˈvidiohˌtayp‖ˈvɪdɪəʊˌteɪp/ *vt* to make a recording of (e g sthg that is televised) on magnetic tape – **videotape** *n*

vie /vie‖vaɪ/ *vi* **vying; vied** to strive for superiority; contend – **vier** *n*

[1]**view** /vyooh‖vju:/ *n* **1** the act of seeing or examining; inspection; *also* a survey <*a* ~ *of English literature*> **2** a way of regarding sthg; an opinion <*in my* ~ *the conference has no chance of success*> **3** a scene, prospect <*the lovely* ~ *from the balcony*>; *also* an aspect <*the rear* ~ *of the house*> **4** extent or range of vision; sight <*tried to keep the ship in* ~> **5** an intention, object <*bought a gun with a* ~ *to murdering his mother*> **6** the foreseeable future <*no hope in* ~> **7** a pictorial representation – **in view of 1** taking the specified feature into consideration <in view of *his age, the police have decided not to*

prosecute> **2** able to be seen by or from <in *full* view of *interested spectators*> – **on view** open to public inspection

[2]**view** *vt* **1a** to see, watch **b** to look on in a specified way; regard <*doesn't ~ himself as a rebel*> **2** to look at attentively; inspect <~ed *the house but decided not to buy it*> **3** to survey or examine mentally; consider <~ *all sides of a question*> **4** to see (a hunted animal) break cover ~*vi* to watch television – **viewable** *adj*

viewer /'vyooh·ə‖'vju:ə/ *n* **1** an optical device used in viewing **2** sby who watches television

viewfinder /'vyooh,fiendə‖'vju:,faındə/ *n* a device on a camera for showing what will be included in the picture

'**viewless** /-lis‖-lıs/ *adj* **1** affording no view **2** holding no opinions – **viewlessly** *adv*

'**view,point** /-,poynt‖-,pɔınt/ *n* a standpoint; POINT OF VIEW

vigesimal /vie'jesiməl‖vaı'dʒesıməl/ *adj* based on the number 20

vigil /'vijil‖'vıdʒıl/ *n* **1a** a devotional watch formerly kept on the night before a religious festival **b** the day before a religious festival, observed as a day of spiritual preparation **2** the act of keeping awake at times when sleep is customary; *also* a period of wakefulness **3** an act or period of watching or surveillance; a watch

vigilant /'vijilənt‖'vıdʒılənt/ *adj* alert and watchful, esp to avoid danger – **vigilance** *n*, **vigilantly** *adv*

vigilante /,viji'lanti‖,vıdʒı'læntı/ *n* sby who seeks to keep order and punish crime without recourse to the established processes of law – **vigilantism** *n*

vignette /vi'nyet, vee-‖vı'njet, vi:-/ *n* **1** a decorative design (e g of vine leaves, tendrils, and grapes) on a title page or at the beginning or end of a chapter **2** a picture (e g an engraving or photograph) that shades off gradually into the surrounding background **3a** a short descriptive literary sketch **b** a brief incident or scene (e g in a play or film) – **vignettist** *n*

vigorous /'vigərəs‖'vıgərəs/ *adj* **1** possessing or showing vigour; full of active strength **2** done with vigour; carried out forcefully and energetically <~ *exercises*> – **vigorously** *adv*, **vigorousness** *n*

vigour, *NAm* **vigor** /'vigə‖'vıgə/ *n* **1** active physical or mental strength or force **2** active healthy well-balanced growth, esp of plants **3** intensity of action or effect; force

Viking /'vieking‖'vaıkıŋ/ *n* **1** a Norse trader and warrior of the 8th to 10th c **2** a Scandinavian

vile /viel‖vaıl/ *adj* **1a** morally despicable or abhorrent **b** physically repulsive; foul **2** tending to degrade <~ *employments*> **3** disgustingly or utterly bad; contemptible <*in a ~ temper*> – **vilely** *adv*, **vileness** *n*

vilify /'vilifie‖'vılıfaı/ *vt* to utter slanderous and abusive statements against; defame – **vilifier** *n*, **vilification** *n*

villa /'vilə‖'vılə/ *n* **1** a country mansion **2** an ancient Roman mansion and the surrounding agricultural estate **3** *Br* a detached or semidetached suburban house, usu having a garden and built before WW I

village /'vilij‖'vılıdʒ/ *n* **1** a group of dwellings in the country, larger than a hamlet and smaller than a town **2** *sing or pl in constr* the residents of a village **3** sthg (e g a group of burrows or nests) suggesting a village

villager /'vilijə‖'vılıdʒə/ *n* **1** an inhabitant of a village **2** a rustic

villain /'vilən‖'vılən/ *n* **1** a scoundrel, rascal; *also* a criminal **2** a character in a story or play whose evil actions affect the plot

villainous /'vilənəs‖'vılənəs/ *adj* **1** being, befitting, or characteristic of a villain; evil <*a ~ attack*> **2** highly objectionable <~ *weather*> – **villainously** *adv*, **villainousness** *n*

villainy /'viləni‖'vılənı/ *n* **1** villainous conduct; *also* a villainous act **2** depravity

-ville /-,vil‖-,vıl/ *suffix* (*adj, n → n*) place or thing of (such) a nature <*dulls*ville> – infml

villein /'vilən‖'vılən/ *n* **1** a free village peasant **2** an unfree peasant standing as the slave of his feudal lord

villeinage, villenage /'vilənij‖'vılənıdʒ/ *n* the tenure or status of a villein

vim /vim‖vım/ *n* robust energy and enthusiasm – infml

vinaigrette /,vinə'gret‖,vınə'gret/ *n* **1** a small ornamental box or bottle with a perforated top used for holding an aromatic preparation (e g smelling salts) **2** (a dish made with) a sharp sauce of oil and vinegar flavoured with salt, pepper, mustard, herbs, etc and used esp on green salads

vindicate /'vindikayt‖'vındıkeıt/ *vt* **1a** to exonerate, absolve **b** to provide justification for; justify **2** to maintain the existence of; uphold <~ *his honour*> – **vindicator** *n*

vindication /,vindi'kaysh(ə)n‖,vındı'keıʃ(ə)n/ *n* justification against denial or censure; defence

vindictive /vin'diktiv‖vın'dıktıv/ *adj* **1a** disposed to seek revenge; vengeful **b** intended as revenge <~ *punishments*> **2** intended to cause anguish; spiteful – **vindictively** *adv*, **vindictiveness** *n*

vine /vien‖vaın/ *n* **1** the climbing plant that bears grapes **2** (a plant with) a stem that requires support and that climbs by tendrils or twining – **viny** *adj*

vinegar /'vinigə‖'vınıgə/ *n* a sour liquid obtained esp by acetic fermentation of wine, cider, etc and used as a condiment or preservative [Old French *vinaigre*, fr *vin* wine + *aigre* keen, sour]

vinegary /'vinig(ə)ri‖'vınıg(ə)rı/ *adj* **1** containing or resembling vinegar; sour **2** bitter or irascible in character or manner

vinery /'vienəri‖'vaınərı/ *n* an area or building in which vines are grown

vineyard /'vinyahd, -yəd‖'vınja:d, -jəd/ *n* a plantation of grapevines

vino /'veenoh‖'vi:nəʊ/ *n* wine – infml

vinous /'vienəs‖'vaınəs/ *adj* **1** of or made with wine **2** (showing the effects of being) addicted to wine – **vinously** *adv*, **vinosity** *n*

[1]**vintage** /'vintij‖'vıntıdʒ/ *n* **1a(1)** a season's yield of grapes or wine from a vineyard **a(2)** wine, specif one of a particular type, region, and year and usu of superior quality that is dated and allowed to mature **b** *sing or pl in constr* a

collection of contemporaneous and similar people or things; a crop **2** the act or time of harvesting grapes or making wine **3** a period of origin or manufacture <*a piano of 1845* ~>

[2]**vintage** *adj* **1** of a vintage; *esp* being a product of 1 particular year rather than a blend of wines from different years **2** of enduring interest or quality; classic **3** of the best and most characteristic – with a proper noun <~ *Shaw: a wise and winning comedy – Time*> **4** *Br, of a motor vehicle* built between 1917 and 1930 <*a* ~ *Rolls*>

vintner /ˈvintnə‖ˈvɪntnə/ *n* WINE MERCHANT

vinyl /ˈvienl‖ˈvaɪnl/ *n* (a plastic that is a polymer of a derivative of) a radical CH_2=CH derived from ethylene by removal of 1 hydrogen atom – **vinylic** *adj*

viol /ˈvie·əl‖ˈvaɪəl/ *n* any of a family of bowed stringed instruments chiefly of the 16th and 17th c with usu 6 strings and a fretted fingerboard, played resting on or between the player's knees

[1]**viola** /viˈohlə‖vɪˈəʊlə/ *n* a musical instrument of the violin family that is intermediate in size and range between the violin and cello and is tuned a 5th below the violin – **violist** *n*

[2]**viola** /ˈvie·ələ, vieˈohlə‖ˈvaɪələ, vaɪˈəʊlə/ *n* VIOLET 1; *esp* any of various cultivated violets with (variegated) flowers resembling but smaller than those of pansies

violate /ˈvie·əlayt‖ˈvaɪəleɪt/ *vt* **1** to fail to comply with; infringe <~ *the law*> **2** to do harm to; *specif* to rape **3** to fail to respect; desecrate <~ *a shrine*> **4** to interrupt, disturb <~ *your privacy*> – **violator** *n*, **violable** *adj*, **violative** *adj*, **violation** *n*

violence /ˈvie·ələns‖ˈvaɪələns/ *n* **1** (an instance of) exertion of physical force so as to injure or abuse **2** unjust or unwarranted distortion; outrage <*did* ~ *to her feelings*> **3a** intense or turbulent action or force <*the* ~ *of the storm*> **b** (an instance of) vehement feeling or expression; fervour **4** distortion or misinterpretation of meaning <*editor did* ~ *to the text*>

violent /ˈvie·ələnt‖ˈvaɪələnt/ *adj* **1** marked by extreme force or sudden intense activity <*a* ~ *attack*> **2a** notably furious or vehement <*a* ~ *denunciation*>; *also* excited or mentally disordered to the point of loss of self-control <*the patient became* ~ *and had to be restrained*> **b** extreme, intense <~ *pain*> **3** caused by force; not natural <*a* ~ *death*> – **violently** *adv*

violet /ˈvie·ələt‖ˈvaɪələt/ *n* **1** any of a genus of plants with often sweet-scented flowers, usu of all 1 colour, esp as distinguished from the usu larger-flowered violas and pansies **2** bluish purple

violin /ˌvie·əˈlin‖ˌvaɪəˈlɪn/ *n* a bowed stringed instrument having a fingerboard with no frets, 4 strings, and a usual range from G below middle C upwards for more than $4^1/_2$ octaves – **violinist** *n*

violoncello /ˌvie·ələnˈcheloh‖ˌvaɪələnˈtʃeləʊ/ *n* a cello – **violoncellist** *n*

VIP *n, pl* **VIPs** a person of great influence or prestige <*a* ~ *lounge*> [*v*ery *i*mportant *p*erson]

viper /ˈviepə‖ˈvaɪpə/ *n* **1** (any of various Old World snakes related to) the adder **2** a malignant or treacherous person

virago /viˈrahgoh‖vɪˈrɑːgəʊ/ *n, pl* **viragoes, viragos 1** a loud overbearing woman; a termagant **2** *archaic* a woman of great stature, strength, and courage

[1]**virgin** /ˈvuhjin‖ˈvɜːdʒɪn/ *n* **1** an unmarried girl or woman **2** *often cap* (a statue or picture of) *the* Virgin Mary **3** a person, esp a girl, who has not had sexual intercourse **4** a female animal that has never copulated – **virginity** *n*, **virginal** *adj*

[2]**virgin** *adj* **1** free of impurity or stain; unsullied **2** being a virgin **3** characteristic of or befitting a virgin; modest **4** untouched, unexploited; *specif* not altered by human activity <*a* ~ *forest*> **5** *of metal* produced directly from ore; not scrap

virginal *n* a small rectangular harpsichord popular in the 16th and 17th c – often pl with sing. meaning

ˌ**virgin ˈbirth** *n* **1** birth from a virgin **2** *often cap V&B* the doctrine that Jesus was born of a virgin mother

Virginia /vəˈjinyə, -ni·ə‖vəˈdʒɪnjə, -nɪə/ *n* a usu mild-flavoured flue-cured tobacco grown orig in N America and used esp in cigarettes

Virˌginia ˈcreeper *n* a climbing plant of the grape family with reddish leaves and bluish-black berries

ˌ**Virgin ˈMary** /ˈmeəri‖ˈmeərɪ/ *n* *the* mother of Jesus

Virgo /ˈvuhgoh‖ˈvɜːgəʊ/ *n* (sby born under) the 6th sign of the zodiac in astrology, which is pictured as a woman holding an ear of corn – **Virgoan** *adj or n*

virile /ˈviriel‖ˈvɪraɪl/ *adj* **1** having the nature, properties, or qualities of a man; *specif* capable of functioning as a male in copulation **2** vigorous, forceful **3** characteristic of or associated with adult males; masculine

virility /vəˈriləti‖vəˈrɪlətɪ/ *n* **1** power to procreate **2** manly vigour; masculinity

virology /vie·əˈroləji‖vaɪəˈrɒlədʒɪ/ *n* a branch of science that deals with viruses – **virologic, virological** *adj*, **virologically** *adv*, **virologist** *n*

virtual /ˈvuhchooəl‖ˈvɜːtʃʊəl/ *adj* that is such in essence or effect though not formally recognized or admitted

virtually /ˈvuhchəli, -chooəli‖ˈvɜːtʃəlɪ, -tʃʊəlɪ/ *adv* almost entirely; for all practical purposes

virtue /ˈvuhtyooh, -chooh‖ˈvɜːtjuː, -tʃuː/ *n* **1a** conformity to a standard of right; morality **b** a particular moral excellence **2** a beneficial or commendable quality **3** a capacity to act; potency **4** chastity, esp in a woman – **virtueless** *adj* – **by virtue of 1** through the force of; having as a right **2** as a result of; because of

virtuosity /ˌvuhtyoohˈosəti‖ˌvɜːtjuːˈɒsətɪ/ *n* great technical skill, esp in the practice of a fine art

[1]**virtuoso** /ˌvuhtyoohˈohsoh, -zoh‖ˌvɜːtjuːˈəʊsəʊ, -zəʊ/ *n, pl* **virtuosos, virtuosi** /-si, -zi‖-sɪ, -zɪ/ **1** one skilled in or having a taste for the fine arts **2** one who excels in the technique of an art, esp in musical performance – **virtuosic** *adj*

[2]**virtuoso** *adj* (characteristic) of a virtuoso

virtuous /ˈvuhchoo·əs‖ˈvɜːtʃʊəs/ *adj* **1** having or exhibiting virtue; *esp* morally excellent; righteous **2** chaste – **virtuously** *adv*, **virtuousness** *n*

virulence /'viryooləns, -rə-‖'vɪrjʊləns, -rə-/, **virulency** /-si‖-sɪ/ *n* **1** extreme bitterness or malignity of temper; rancour **2** malignancy, venomousness **3** the relative capacity of a pathogen to overcome body defences

virulent /'viryoolənt, -rə-‖'vɪrjʊlənt, -rə-/ *adj* **1a** *of a disease* severe and developing rapidly **b** able to overcome bodily defensive mechanisms **2** extremely poisonous or venomous **3** full of malice; malignant – **virulently** *adv*

virus /'vie·ərəs‖'vaɪərəs/ *n* **1a** the causative agent of any infectious disease – not now used technically **b** (a disease caused by) any of a large group of submicroscopic often disease-causing agents that multiply only in living cells **2** sthg that poisons the mind or soul – **viral** *adj*

[1]**visa** /'veezə‖'vi:zə/ *n* an endorsement made on a passport by the proper authorities (e g of a country at entrance or exit) denoting that the bearer may proceed

[2]**visa** *vt* **visaing; visaed** to provide (a passport) with a visa

visage /'vizij‖'vɪzɪdʒ/ *n* **1** a face, countenance **2** an aspect, appearance <*grimy* ~ *of a mining town*> *USE* fml or poetic – **visaged** *adj*

vis-à-vis /ˌvee zah 'vee‖ˌvi: zɑ: 'vi:/ *prep* **1** face to face with; opposite **2** in relation to [French, lit., face to face]

viscera /'visərə‖'vɪsərə/ *n pl* the internal body organs collectively

visceral /'visərəl‖'vɪsərəl/ *adj* **1** deeply or intensely felt < ~ *sensation*> **2** of or located on or among the viscera **3** instinctive, unreasoning <*a* ~ *conviction*> – fml – **viscerally** *adv*

viscid /'visid‖'vɪsɪd/ *adj* **1a** adhesive, sticky **b** glutinous, viscous **2** covered with a sticky layer – **viscidly** *adv*, **viscidity** *n*

viscosity /vis'kosəti‖vɪs'kɒsətɪ/ *n* **1** being viscous **2** (a measure of the force needed to overcome) the property of a liquid, gas, or semifluid that enables it to offer resistance to flow

viscount /'viekownt‖'vaɪkaʊnt/ *n* a member of the peerage in Britain ranking below an earl and above a baron – **viscountcy** *n*, **viscounty** *n*

viscountess /ˌviekown'tes, 'viekowntis‖ˌvaɪkaʊn'tes, 'vaɪkaʊntɪs/ *n* **1** the wife or widow of a viscount **2** a woman having the rank of a viscount

viscous /'viskəs‖'vɪskəs/ *adj* **1** viscid **2** having or characterized by (high) viscosity – **viscously** *adv*, **viscousness** *n*

vise /vies‖vaɪs/ *vt or n, chiefly NAm* (to hold with) a mechanical vice

visibility /ˌvizə'biləti‖ˌvɪzə'bɪlətɪ/ *n* **1** being visible **2** the clearness of the atmosphere as revealed by the greatest distance at which prominent objects can be identified visually with the naked eye

visible /'vizəbl‖'vɪzəbl/ *adj* **1** capable of being seen <*stars* ~ *to the naked eye*> < ~ *light*> **2a** exposed to view <*the* ~ *horizon*> **b** in the public eye; prominent <*a panel of highly* ~ *people*> **3** capable of being perceived; noticeable <*her* ~ *impatience*> **4** tangibly or implicitly present **5** of or being trade in goods rather than services < ~ *exports*> – **visibleness** *n*, **visibly** *adv*

vision /'vizh(ə)n‖'vɪʒ(ə)n/ *n* **1a** sthg (revelatory) seen in a dream, trance, or ecstasy **b** a mental image of sthg immaterial <*had* ~s *of missing the train*> **2a** the power of imagination; *also* the manner of perceiving mental images <*an artist's* ~> **b** discernment, foresight <*a man of* ~> **c** a supernatural apparition **3a** the act or power of seeing; SIGHT 3a **b** the sense by which the qualities of an object (e g colour, luminosity, shape, and size) constituting its appearance are perceived and which acts through the eye **4a** sthg seen **b** a lovely or charming sight – **visional** *adj*, **visionally** *adv*, **visionless** *adj*

[1]**visionary** /'vizh(ə)nri, -əri‖'vɪʒ(ə)nrɪ, -ərɪ/ *adj* **1a** able or likely to see visions **b** disposed to daydreaming or imagining; dreamy **2a** of the nature of a vision; illusory **b** impracticable, utopian <*a* ~ *scheme*> **3** of or characterized by visions or the power of vision – **visionariness** *n*

[2]**visionary** *n* **1** one who sees visions; a seer **2** one whose ideas or projects are impractical; a dreamer

[1]**visit** /'vizit‖'vɪzɪt/ *vt* **1a** *archaic, of God* to comfort < ~ *us with Thy salvation* – Charles Wesley> **b** to afflict <*a city frequently* ~ed *by the plague*> **c** to inflict punishment for < ~ed *the sins of the fathers upon the children*> **2a** to pay a call on for reasons of kindness, friendship, ceremony, or business < ~ing *the sick*> **b** to reside with temporarily as a guest **c** to go or come to look at or stay at (e g for business or sightseeing) **d** to go or come officially to inspect or oversee <*a bishop* ~ing *the parish*> ~ *vi* to make a visit or visits – **visitable** *adj*

[2]**visit** *n* **1a** an act of visiting; a call **b** a temporary residence as a guest **c** an extended but temporary stay <*his annual* ~s *abroad*> **2** an official or professional call; a visitation

visitant /'vizit(ə)nt‖'vɪzɪt(ə)nt/ *n* **1** a (supernatural) visitor **2** VISITOR 2 – **visitant** *adj*

visitation /ˌvizi'taysh(ə)n‖ˌvɪzɪ'teɪʃ(ə)n/ *n* **1** the act or an instance of visiting; *esp* an official visit (e g for inspection) **2a** a special dispensation of divine favour or wrath **b** a severe trial; an affliction **3** *cap the* visit of the Virgin Mary to Elizabeth recounted in Luke 1:39–56 and celebrated on July 2 by a Christian festival – **visitational** *adj*

'visiting ˌcard /'viziting‖'vɪzɪtɪŋ/ *n* a small card of introduction bearing the name and sometimes the address and profession of the owner

visitor /'vizitə‖'vɪzɪtə/ *n* **1** sby who or sthg that makes (formal) visits **2** a migratory bird that visits a locality for a short time at regular intervals

'visitors' ˌbook *n* a book in which visitors (e g to a place of interest or hotel) write their names and addresses and sometimes comments

visor, vizor /'viezə‖'vaɪzə/ *n* **1** the (movable) part of a helmet that covers the face **2** a usu movable flat sunshade attached at the top of a vehicle windscreen **3** *chiefly NAm* a peak on a cap – **visored** *adj*, **visorless** *adj*

vista /'vistə‖'vɪstə/ *n* **1** a distant view esp through or along an avenue or opening; a prospect **2** an extensive mental view (e g over a stretch of time or a series of events) – **vistaless** *adj*

visual /'viz(h)yooəl‖'vɪzjʊəl, 'vɪʒjʊəl/ *adj* **1** of, used in, or produced by vision <~ *organs*> <~ *impressions*> **2** visible <*a ~ equivalent for his feelings*> **3** producing mental images; vivid **4** done or executed by sight only <~ *navigation*> – **visually** *adv*

ˌvisual ˈaid *n* an instructional device (e g a chart or film) that appeals chiefly to vision

visual·ize, -ise /ˈvizhooəˌliez‖ˈvɪʒʊəˌlaɪz/ *vt* **1** to make visible **2** to see or form a mental image of – **visualization** *n*

vital /ˈvietl‖ˈvaɪtl/ *adj* **1** concerned with or necessary to the maintenance of life <~ *organs*> **2** full of life and vigour; animated **3** concerned with, affecting, or being a manifestation of life or living beings **4a** tending to renew or refresh the living; invigorating **b** of the utmost importance; essential to continued worth or well-being – **vitally** *adv*

vitality /vieˈtaləti‖vaɪˈtæləti/ *n* **1a** the quality which distinguishes the living from the dead or inanimate **b** capacity to live and develop; *also* physical or mental liveliness **2** power of enduring <*the ~ of an idiom*>

vital·ize, -ise /ˈvietlˌiez‖ˈvaɪtlˌaɪz/ *vt* to endow with vitality; animate – **vitalization** *n*

vitals /ˈvietlz‖ˈvaɪtlz/ *n pl* **1** the vital organs (e g the heart, liver, or brain) **2** essential parts

ˌvital staˈtistics *n pl* **1** statistics relating to births, deaths, health, etc **2** facts considered to be interesting or important; *specif* a woman's bust, waist, and hip measurements

vitamin /ˈvitəmin, ˈvie-‖ˈvɪtəmɪn, ˈvaɪ-/ *n* any of various organic compounds that are essential in minute quantities to the nutrition of most animals and act esp as (precursors of) coenzymes in the regulation of metabolic processes [Latin *vita* life + English *amine*]

vitiate /ˈvishiayt‖ˈvɪʃɪeɪt/ *vt* **1** to make faulty or defective; debase <*a spirit* ~d *by luxury*> **2** to invalidate – **vitiator** *n*

viticulture /ˈvitiˌkulchə‖ˈvɪtɪˌkʌltʃə/ *n* (the science of) the cultivation of grapevines – **viticultural** *adj*, **viticulturist** *n*

vitreous /ˈvitri·əs‖ˈvɪtrɪəs/ *adj* **1a** resembling glass in colour, composition, brittleness, etc <~ *rocks*> **b** characterized by low porosity and usu translucence <~ *china*> **2** of or being the vitreous humour – **vitreously** *adv*, **vitreousness** *n*

ˌvitreous ˈhumour *n* the colourless transparent jelly that fills the eyeball behind the lens

vitrify /ˈvitrifie‖ˈvɪtrɪfaɪ/ *vb* to convert into or become glass or a glassy substance (by heat and fusion) – **vitrifiable** *adj* **vitrification** *n*

vitriol /ˈvitri·əl‖ˈvɪtrɪəl/ *n* **1a** a (hydrated) sulphate of iron, copper, zinc, etc **b** concentrated sulphuric acid **2** virulent speech, expression, feeling, etc – **vitriolic** *adj*

vituperate /viˈtyoohpərayt‖vɪˈtjuːpəreɪt/ *vt* to subject to severe or abusive censure; berate ~*vi* to use harsh condemnatory language – **vituperator** *n*, **vituperative** *adj*, **vituperation** *n*

vivacious /viˈvayshəs‖vɪˈveɪʃəs/ *adj* lively in temper or conduct; sprightly – **vivaciously** *adv*, **vivaciousness** *n*, **vivacity** *n*

vivarium /vieˈveəri·əm‖vaɪˈveərɪəm/ *n, pl* **vivaria** /-ri·ə‖-rɪə/, **vivariums** an enclosure for keeping and observing plants or esp terrestrial animals indoors

viva voce /ˌvievə ˈvohsi, ˌveevə, ˈvohchi‖ˌvaɪvə ˈvəʊsɪ, ˌviːvə, ˈvəʊtʃɪ/ *n, adj, or adv* (an examination conducted) by word of mouth [Latin, with the living voice]

vivid /ˈvivid‖ˈvɪvɪd/ *adj* **1** full of vigorous life or freshness; lively <~ *personality*> **2** *of a colour* very intense **3** producing a strong or clear impression on the senses; *specif* producing distinct mental images <*a ~ description*> – **vividly** *adv*, **vividness** *n*

viviparous /viˈvipərəs‖vɪˈvɪpərəs/ *adj* **1** producing living young, instead of eggs, from within the body in the manner of nearly all mammals, many reptiles, and a few fishes **2** germinating while still attached to the parent plant <*the ~ seed of the mangrove*> – **viviparously** *adv*, **viviparousness** *n*, **viviparity** *n*

vivisect /ˈvivisekt, --ˈ-‖ˈvɪvɪsekt, --ˈ-/ *vb* to perform vivisection (on) – **vivisector** *n*

vivisection /viviˈseksh(ə)n‖vɪvɪˈsekʃ(ə)n/ *n* operation or (distressful) experimentation on a living animal, usu in the course of medical or physiological research – **vivisectional** *adj*, **vivisectionally** *adv*, **vivisectionist** *n*

vixen /ˈviks(ə)n‖ˈvɪks(ə)n/ *n* **1** a female fox **2** a scolding ill-tempered woman – **vixenish** *adj*, **vixenishly** *adv*

vizier /viˈziə‖vɪˈzɪə/ *n* a high executive officer of various Muslim countries, esp of the former Ottoman Empire – **vizierate** *n*, **vizierial** *adj*, **viziership** *n*

V neck /vee‖viː/ *n* (a garment with) a V-shaped neck

vocabulary /vohˈkabyooləri, və-‖vəʊˈkæbjʊlərɪ, və-/ *n* **1** a list of words, and sometimes phrases, usu arranged alphabetically and defined or translated <*a ~ at the back of the book*> **2a** the words employed by a language, group, or individual or in a field of work or knowledge <*her limited ~*> **b** a list or collection of terms or codes available for use (e g in an indexing system) **3** a supply of expressive techniques or devices (e g of an art form)

¹vocal /ˈvohkl‖ˈvəʊkl/ *adj* **1** uttered by the voice; oral **2** of, composed or arranged for, or sung by the human voice **3a** having or exercising the power of producing voice, speech, or sound **b** given to strident or insistent expression; outspoken – **vocally** *adv*, **vocality** *n*

²vocal *n* **1** a vocal sound **2** a usu accompanied musical composition or passage for the voice

vocal cords *n pl* either of 2 pairs of mucous membrane folds in the cavity of the larynx whose free edges vibrate to produce sound

vocalist /ˈvohk(ə)list‖ˈvəʊk(ə)lɪst/ *n* a singer

vocal·ize, -ise /ˈvohklˌiez‖ˈvəʊklˌaɪz/ *vt* to give voice to; utter; *specif* to sing ~ *vi* **1** to utter vocal sounds **2** to sing (without words) – **vocalizer** *n*, **vocalization** *n*

vocation /vohˈkaysh(ə)n, və-‖vəʊˈkeɪʃ(ə)n, və-/ *n* **1a** a summons or strong inclination to a particular state or course of action; *esp* a divine call to the religious life **b** an entry into the priesthood or a religious order **2** the work in which a person is regularly employed; a career **3** the special function of an individual or group

vocational /voh'kaysh(ə)nl, və-‖vəʊ'keɪʃ(ə)nl, və-/ *adj* of or being training in a skill or trade to be pursued as a career < ~ *courses*> – **vocationally** *adv*

vocative /'vokətiv‖'vɒkətɪv/ *n* (a form in) a grammatical case expressing the one addressed – **vocative** *adj*, **vocatively** *adv*

vociferate /voh'sifərayt, və-‖vəʊ'sɪfəreɪt, və-/ *vb* to cry out or utter loudly; clamour, shout – **vociferant** *n*, **vociferator** *n*, **vociferation** *n*

vociferous /voh'sif(ə)rəs, və-‖vəʊ'sɪf(ə)rəs, və-/ *adj* marked by or given to vehement insistent outcry – **vociferously** *adv*, **vociferousness** *n*

vodka /'vodkə‖'vɒdkə/ *n* a colourless and unaged neutral spirit distilled from a mash (e g of rye or wheat) [Russian, fr *voda* water; akin to OE *wæter* water – see WATER]

vogue /vohg‖vəʊg/ *n* **1** the prevailing, esp temporary, fashion **2** popular acceptance or favour; popularity – **vogue** *adj*

[1]**voice** /voys‖vɔɪs/ *n* **1a** sound produced by humans, birds, etc by forcing air from the lungs through the larynx in mammals or syrinx in birds **b(1)** (the use, esp in singing or acting, of) musical sound produced by the vocal cords and resonated by the cavities of the head, throat, lungs, etc **b(2)** the power or ability to sing **b(3)** any of the melodic parts in a vocal or instrumental composition **b(4)** condition of the vocal organs with respect to singing <*be in good* ~ > **c** expiration of air with the vocal cords drawn close so as to vibrate audibly (e g in uttering vowels or consonant sounds such as /v/ or /z/) **d** the faculty of utterance; speech **2** a sound suggesting vocal utterance <*the* ~ *of a foghorn*> **3** an instrument or medium of expression <*the party became the* ~ *of the workers*> **4a** the expressed wish or opinion <*claimed to follow the* ~ *of the people*> **b** right of expression; say <*I have no* ~ *in this matter*> **c** expression – chiefly in *give voice to* **5** distinction of form or a particular system of inflections of a verb to indicate whether it is the subject of the verb that acts <*the passive* ~>

[2]**voice** *vt* **1** to express (a feeling or opinion) in words; utter **2** to adjust (e g an organ pipe) in manufacture, for producing the proper musical sounds **3** to pronounce with voice

'**voice ˌbox** *n* the larynx

voiced *adj* **1** having a usu specified type of voice <*soft*-voiced> **2** uttered with vocal cord vibration (e g in /b/) – **voicedness** *n*

'**voiceless** /-lis‖-lɪs/ *adj* not voiced (e g in /p/) – **voicelessly** *adv*, **voicelessness** *n*

'**voice-ˌover** *n* the voice of an unseen narrator in a film or television programme; *also* the voice of a visible character indicating his thoughts

[1]**void** /voyd‖vɔɪd/ *adj* **1** containing nothing; unoccupied **2a** devoid <*a nature* ~ *of all malice*> **b** having no members or examples; *specif, of a suit* having no cards represented in a particular hand **3** vain, useless **4** of no legal effect **5** having no holder or occupant; vacant <*a* ~ *bishopric*> – fml – **voidness** *n*

[2]**void** *n* **1a** empty space; vacuum **b** an opening, gap **2** a feeling of lack, want, or emptiness

[3]**void** *vt* **1** to make empty or vacant; clear **2** to discharge or emit < ~ *excrement*> **3** to nullify, annul < ~ *a contract*> – **voidable** *adj*, **voider** *n*

voile /voyl‖vɔɪl/ *n* a fine soft sheer fabric used esp for women's summer clothing or curtains

[1]**volatile** /'voləˌtiel‖'vɒləˌtaɪl/ *n* a volatile substance

[2]**volatile** *adj* **1** capable of being readily vaporized at a relatively low temperature <*alcohol is a* ~ *liquid*> **2a** lighthearted, lively **b** dangerously unstable; explosive <*a* ~ *social situation*> **3a** frivolously changeable; fickle **b** characterized by rapid change **4** evanescent, transitory – **volatility** *n*

vol-au-vent /ˌvol oh 'vonh, '- - ˌ-‖ˌvɒl əʊ 'vɑ̃, '- - ˌ-/ *n* a round case of puff pastry filled with a mixture of meat, poultry, or fish in a thick sauce

volcanic /vol'kanik‖vɒl'kænɪk/ *adj* **1a** of or produced by a volcano **b** characterized by volcanoes **2** explosively violent; volatile < ~ *emotions*> – **volcanically** *adv*

volcano /vol'kaynoh‖vɒl'keɪnəʊ/ *n, pl* **volcanoes, volcanos** **1** (a hill or mountain surrounding) an outlet in a planet's crust from which molten or hot rock and steam issue **2** a dynamic or violently creative person; *also* a situation liable to become violent [Italian *vulcano*, fr *Vulcan*, Roman god of fire & metalworking] – **volcanology** *n*, **volcanologist** *n*

vole /vohl‖vəʊl/ *n* any of various small plant-eating rodents usu with a stout body, blunt nose, and short ears

volition /və'lish(ə)n‖və'lɪʃ(ə)n/ *n* **1** (an act of making) a free choice or decision **2** the power of choosing or determining; will – **volitional** *adj*

[1]**volley** /'voli‖'vɒlɪ/ *n* **1a** a flight of arrows, bullets, or other missiles **b** simultaneous discharge of a number of missile weapons **c(1)** (the course of) the flight of the ball, shuttle, etc before striking the ground; *also* a return or succession of returns made by hitting the ball, shuttle, etc before it touches the ground **c(2)** a kick of the ball in soccer before it touches the ground **2** a burst or emission of many things at once or in rapid succession <*a* ~ *of oaths*>

[2]**volley** *vb* **volleying; volleyed** *vt* **1** to discharge (as if) in a volley **2** to propel (an object that has not yet hit the ground), esp with an implement or the hand or foot ~ *vi* **1** to be discharged (as if) in a volley **2** to make a volley – **volleyer** *n*

'**volleyˌball** /-ˌbawl‖-ˌbɔːl/ *n* a game between 2 teams of usu 6 players who volley a ball over a high net in the centre of a court

volt /vohlt, volt‖vəʊlt, vɒlt/ *n* the derived SI unit of electrical potential difference and electromotive force equal to the difference of potential between 2 points in a conducting wire carrying a constant current of 1 ampere when the power dissipated between these 2 points is equal to 1 watt [Alessandro *Volta* (1745-1827), Italian physicist]

voltage /'vohltij, 'voltij‖'vəʊltɪdʒ, 'vɒltɪdʒ/ *n* an electric potential difference; electromotive force

volte-face /ˌvolt 'fahs, fas‖ˌvɒlt 'fɑːs, fæs/ *n* a sudden reversal of attitude or policy;

an about-face

voluble /ˈvolyoobl‖ˈvɒljʊbl/ *adj* characterized by ready or rapid speech; talkative – **volubleness** *n*, **volubly** *adv*, **volubility** *n*

volume /ˈvolyoohm, ˈvolyoom‖ˈvɒljuːm, ˈvɒljʊm/ *n* **1a** a series of printed sheets bound typically in book form; a book **b** a series of issues of a periodical **2** space occupied as measured in cubic units (e g litres); cubic capacity **3a** an amount; *also* a bulk, mass **b** the amount of a substance occupying a particular volume **c** (the representation of) mass in art or architecture **d** a considerable quantity; a great deal – often pl with sing. meaning; esp in *speak volumes for* **4** the degree of loudness or the intensity of a sound [Middle French, fr Latin *volumen* roll, scroll, fr *volvere* to roll] – **volumed** *adj*

voluminous /vəˈlyoohminəs‖vəˈljuːmɪnəs/ *adj* **1** having or containing a large volume; *specif, of a garment* very full **2a** consisting of or (capable of) filling a large volume or several volumes <*a ~ correspondence*> **b** writing much or at great length – **voluminously** *adv*, **voluminousness** *n*, **voluminosity** *n*

[1]**voluntary** /ˈvolənt(ə)ri‖ˈvɒlənt(ə)rɪ/ *adj* **1** proceeding from free choice or consent **2** acting without compulsion and without payment <~ *workers*> **3** intentional <~ *manslaughter*> **4** of, subject to, or regulated by the will <~ *behaviour*> **5** having power of free choice <*man is a ~ agent*> **6** provided or supported by voluntary action <*a ~ hospital*> – **voluntarily** *adv*, **voluntariness** *n*

[2]**voluntary** *n* an organ piece played before or after a religious service

[1]**volunteer** /ˌvolənˈtiə‖ˌvɒlənˈtɪə/ *n* one who undertakes a service of his/her own free will; *esp* sby who enters into military service voluntarily

[2]**volunteer** *adj* being, consisting of, or engaged in by volunteers <*a ~ army*>

[3]**volunteer** *vt* **1** to offer or bestow voluntarily <~ *one's services*> **2** to communicate voluntarily; say ~*vi* to offer oneself as a volunteer

voluptuary /vəˈluptyoo(ə)ri‖vəˈlʌptjʊ(ə)rɪ/ *n* one whose chief interest is luxury and sensual pleasure – **voluptuary** *adj*

voluptuous /vəˈluptyoo·əs‖vəˈlʌptjʊəs/ *adj* **1** causing delight or pleasure to the senses; conducive to, occupied with, or arising from sensual gratification <*a ~ dance*> **2** suggestive of sensual pleasure <*a ~ mouth*>; *broadly* sexually attractive, esp owing to shapeliness – **voluptuously** *adv*, **voluptuousness** *n*

volute /vəˈlyooht‖vəˈljuːt/ *n* **1** a form that is shaped like a spiral or curled over on itself like a scroll **2** an ornament characteristic of classical architecture that is shaped like a roll of material or a scroll **3** (the short-spined thick shell of) any of numerous marine gastropod molluscs – **volute, voluted** *adj*

[1]**vomit** /ˈvomit‖ˈvɒmɪt/ *n* **1** a vomiting; *also* the vomited matter **2** an emetic

[2]**vomit** *vb* **1** to disgorge (the contents of the stomach) through the mouth **2** to eject (sthg) violently or abundantly; spew – **vomiter** *n*

[1]**voodoo** /ˈvoohdooh‖ˈvuːduː/ *n, pl* **voodoos** **1** a set of magical beliefs and practices, mainly of W African origin, practised chiefly in Haiti and characterized by communication by trance with deities **2a** one skilled in (voodoo) spells and necromancy **b** a voodoo spell – **voodoo** *adj*, **voodooism** *n*

[2]**voodoo** *vt* to bewitch (as if) by means of voodoo

voracious /vəˈrayshəs‖vəˈreɪʃəs/ *adj* **1** having a huge appetite; ravenous **2** excessively eager; insatiable <*a ~ reader*> – **voraciously** *adv*, **voraciousness** *n*, **voracity** *n*

vortex /ˈvawteks‖ˈvɔːteks/ *n, pl* **vortices** /ˈvawtiseez‖ˈvɔːtɪsiːz/ *also* **vortexes** **1a** a mass of whirling water, air, etc that tends to form a cavity or vacuum in the centre of the circle into which material is drawn; *esp* a whirlpool or whirlwind **b** a region within a body of fluid in which the fluid is rotating **2** sthg that resembles a whirlpool in violent activity or in engulfing or overwhelming – **vortical** *adj*, **vorticity** *n*

votary /ˈvohtəri‖ˈvəʊtərɪ/, **votarist** /-rist‖-rɪst/ *n* a staunch admirer, worshipper, or advocate; a devotee

[1]**vote** /voht‖vəʊt/ *n* **1a** a (formal) expression of opinion or will in response to a proposed decision **b** BALLOT 1 **2** the collective verdict of a body of people expressed by voting **3** *the* franchise **4** a definable group of voters <*getting the Labour ~ to the polls*> **5** a sum of money voted for a special use

[2]**vote** *vi* **1** to cast one's vote; *esp* to exercise a political franchise **2** to express an opinion ~ *vt* **1** to choose, decide, or authorize by vote **2a** to judge by general agreement; declare <*concert was ~*d *a flop*> **b** to offer as a suggestion; propose <*I ~ we all go home*> – infml – **voter** *n*

votive /ˈvohtiv‖ˈvəʊtɪv/ *adj* **1** offered or performed in fulfilment of a vow and often in gratitude or devotion **2** consisting of or expressing a religious vow, wish, or desire – **votively** *adv*, **votiveness** *n*

vouch /vowch‖vaʊtʃ/ *vi* **1** to give or act as a guarantee *for* **2** to supply supporting evidence or personal assurance *for*

voucher /ˈvowchə‖ˈvaʊtʃə/ *n* **1a** a documentary record of a business transaction **b** a written certificate or authorization **2** *Br* a ticket that can be exchanged for specific goods or services

vouchsafe /vowchˈsayf‖vaʊtʃˈseɪf/ *vt* **1** to grant as a special privilege or in a gracious or condescending manner **2** to condescend, deign *to* do sthg – **vouchsafement** *n*

[1]**vow** /vow‖vaʊ/ *n* a solemn and often religiously binding promise or assertion; *specif* one by which a person binds him-/herself to an act, service, or condition

[2]**vow** *vt* **1** to promise solemnly; swear **2** to dedicate or consecrate by a vow **3** to resolve to bring about <~ *revenge*> ~*vi* to make a vow – **vower** *n*

[3]**vow** *vt* to avow, declare

vowel /vowl‖vaʊl/ *n* (a letter, in English usu *a, e, i, o, u*, and sometimes *y*, representing) any of a class of speech sounds characterized by lack of closure in the breath channel or lack of audible friction

vox populi /ˌvoks ˈpopyoolie, -li‖ˌvɒks ˈpɒpjʊlaɪ, -lɪ/ *n* the opinion of the general public [Latin, voice of the people]

[1]**voyage** /ˈvoyij‖ˈvɔɪɪdʒ/ *n* a considerable course or period of travelling by other than land routes; *broadly* a journey

[2]**voyage** *vb* to make a voyage (across) – **voyager** *n*

voyeur /vwahˈyuh‖vwɑːˈjɜː/ *n* **1** one who obtains sexual gratification by visual means, specif by looking at sexual organs and sexual acts **2** a prying observer who is usu seeking the sordid or the scandalous [French, lit., one who sees, fr *voir* to see, fr Latin *vidēre*] – **voyeurism** *n*, **voyeuristic** *adj*, **voyeuristically** *adv*

ˈ**V** ˌ**sign** /vee‖viː/ *n* a gesture made by raising the index and middle fingers in a V **a** with the palm outwards signifying victory **b** with the palm inwards signifying insult or contempt

vulcan·ization, -isation /ˌvulkənieˈzaysh(ə)n‖ˌvʌlkənaɪˈzeɪʃ(ə)n/ *n* the process of chemically treating rubber or similar material to give it elasticity, strength, stability, etc – **vulcanize** *vb*

vulgar /ˈvulgə‖ˈvʌlgə/ *adj* **1** generally used, applied, or accepted **2a** of or being the common people; plebeian **b** generally current; public <~ *opinion*> **3a** lacking in cultivation, breeding, or taste; coarse **b** ostentatious or excessive in expenditure or display; pretentious **4** lewdly or profanely indecent; obscene – **vulgarly** *adv*, **vulgarity** *n*

ˌ**vulgar** ˈ**fraction** *n* a fraction in which both the denominator and numerator are explicitly present and are separated by a horizontal or slanted line

vulgarian /vulˈgeəri·ən‖vʌlˈgeərɪən/ *n* a vulgar and esp rich person

vulgarism /ˈvulgəˌriz(ə)m‖ˈvʌlgəˌrɪz(ə)m/ *n* **1** a word or expression originated or used chiefly by illiterate people **2** vulgarity

vulgar·ize, -ise /ˈvulgəriez‖ˈvʌlgəraɪz/ *vt* **1** to diffuse generally; popularize **2** to make vulgar; coarsen – **vulgarizer** *n*, **vulgarization** *n*

ˌ**Vulgar** ˈ**Latin** *n* the informal Latin of ancient Rome, established as the chief source of the Romance languages

vulgate /ˈvulgayt, -gət‖ˈvʌlgeɪt, -gət/ *n* **1** *cap the* Latin version of the Bible authorized and used by the Roman Catholic church **2** a commonly accepted text or reading

vulnerable /ˈvuln(ə)rəbl‖ˈvʌln(ə)rəbl/ *adj* **1** capable of being physically or mentally wounded **2** open to attack or damage; assailable – **vulnerableness** *n*, **vulnerably** *adv*, **vulnerability** *n*

vulpine /ˈvulpien‖ˈvʌlpaɪn/ *adj* **1** of or resembling a fox **2** foxy, crafty

vulture /ˈvulchə‖ˈvʌltʃə/ *n* **1** any of various large usu bald-headed birds of prey that feed on carrion **2** a rapacious or predatory person – **vulturous** *adj*, **vulturine** *adj*

vulva /ˈvulvə‖ˈvʌlvə/ *n, pl* **vulvas, vulvae** /-vi‖-vɪ/ the (opening between the projecting) external parts of the female genital organs – **vulval, vulvar** *adj*

vying /ˈvie·ing‖ˈvaɪɪŋ/ *pres part of* VIE

W

w /ˈdublˌyooh‖ˈdʌblˌjuː/ *n, pl* **w's, ws** *often cap* (a graphic representation of, or device for reproducing,) the 23rd letter of the English alphabet

wack /wak‖wæk/ *n, N Eng* – used as a familiar form of address

wacky /ˈwaki‖ˈwækɪ/ *adj, chiefly NAm* absurdly or amusingly eccentric or irrational; crazy – infml – **wackily** *adv*, **wackiness** *n*

[1]**wad** /wod‖wɒd/ *n* **1a** a soft mass, esp of a loose fibrous material, variously used (e g to stop an aperture or pad a garment) **b(1)** a soft plug used to retain a powder charge, esp in a muzzle-loading cannon or gun **b(2)** a felt or paper disc that separates the components of a shotgun cartridge **2** a roll of paper money **3** *chiefly NAm* a considerable amount – infml; often pl with sing. meaning

[2]**wad** *vt* **-dd- 1** to form into a wad or wadding **2a** to insert a wad into <~ *a gun*> **b** to hold in by a wad <~ *a bullet in a gun*> **3** to stuff, pad, or line with some soft substance **4** *chiefly NAm* to roll or crush tightly <~ *his shirt up into a ball*> – **wadder** *n*

wadding /ˈwoding‖ˈwɒdɪŋ/ *n* stuffing or padding in the form of a soft mass or sheet of short loose fibres

[1]**waddle** /ˈwodl‖ˈwɒdl/ *vi* **1** to walk with short steps swinging the forepart of the body from side to side **2** to move clumsily in a manner suggesting a waddle – **waddler** *n*

[2]**waddle** *n* an awkward clumsy swaying gait

[1]**wade** /wayd‖weɪd/ *vi* **1** to walk through a medium (e g water) offering more resistance than air **2** to proceed with difficulty or effort <~ *through a dull book*> **3** to attack with determination or vigour – + *in* or *into* ~*vt* to cross by wading

[2]**wade** *n* an act of wading

wader /ˈwaydə‖ˈweɪdə/ *n* **1** *pl* high waterproof boots used for wading **2** any of many long-legged birds (e g sandpipers and snipes) that wade in water in search of food

wadge /woj‖wɒdʒ/ *n, Br* a thick bundle; a wad – infml

wadi /ˈwodi‖ˈwɒdɪ/ *n* the bed of a stream in regions of SW Asia and N Africa that is dry except during the rainy season

ˈ**wading** ˌ**bird** /ˈwayding‖ˈweɪdɪŋ/ *n* WADER 2

wafer /ˈwayfə‖ˈweɪfə/ *n* **1a** a thin crisp biscuit; *also* a biscuit consisting of layers of wafer sometimes sandwiched with a filling **b** a round piece of thin unleavened bread used in the celebration of the Eucharist **2** an adhesive disc of dried paste used, esp formerly, as a seal

[1]**waffle** /ˈwofl‖ˈwɒfl/ *n* a cake of batter that is baked in a waffle iron and has a crisp dimpled surface

[2]**waffle** *vi, chiefly Br* to talk or write foolishly, inconsequentially, and usu at length; blather – infml – **waffler** *n*

[3]**waffle** *n, chiefly Br* empty or pretentious words – infml – **waffly** *adj*

ˈwaffle ˌiron *n* a cooking utensil with 2 hinged metal parts that shut on each other and impress surface projections on the waffle being cooked

[1]**waft** /woft‖wɒft/ *vb* to convey or be conveyed lightly (as if) by the impulse of wind or waves – **wafter** *n*

[2]**waft** *n* **1** sthg (e g a smell) that is wafted; a whiff **2** a slight breeze; a puff

[1]**wag** /wag‖wæg/ *vb* **-gg-** *vi* **1** to move to and fro, esp with quick jerky motions **2** to move in chatter or gossip <*tongues* ~ged> ~ *vt* **1** to cause to swing to and fro, esp with quick jerky motions; *esp* to nod (the head) or shake (a finger) in assent or mild reproof – often + *at* **2** to move (e g the tongue) animatedly in conversation – **wagger** *n*

[2]**wag** *n* an act of wagging; a shake

[3]**wag** *n* a wit, joker

[1]**wage** /wayj‖weɪdʒ/ *vt* to engage in or carry on (a war, conflict, etc)

[2]**wage** *n* **1a** a payment for services, esp of a manual kind, usu according to contract and on an hourly, daily, weekly, or piecework basis – usu pl with sing. meaning **b** *pl* the share of the national product attributable to labour as a factor in production **2** a recompense, reward – usu pl with sing. meaning but sing. or pl in constr – **wageless** *adj*

[1]**wager** /ˈwayjə‖ˈweɪdʒə/ *n* **1** sthg (e g a sum of money) risked on an uncertain event **2** sthg on which bets are laid

[2]**wager** *vb* to lay as or make a bet – **wagerer** *n*

ˈwage ˌslave *n* a person dependent on wages or a salary for his/her livelihood

waggery /ˈwagəri‖ˈwægərɪ/ *n* **1** mischievous merriment **2** a jest; *esp* PRACTICAL JOKE

waggish /ˈwagish‖ˈwægɪʃ/ *adj* befitting or characteristic of a wag; humorous – **waggishly** *adv*, **waggishness** *n*

waggle /ˈwagl‖ˈwægl/ *vb* to (cause to) sway or move repeatedly from side to side; wag – **waggle** *n*, **waggly** *adj*

wagon, *chiefly Br* **waggon** /ˈwagən‖ˈwægən/ *n* **1** a usu 4-wheeled vehicle for transporting bulky or heavy loads, drawn originaly by animals **2** TROLLEY 2a; *esp* one used in a dining room or for serving light refreshments (e g afternoon tea) **3** *Br* a railway goods vehicle – **on/off the wagon** abstaining/no longer abstaining from alcoholic drinks – infml

wagonette /wagəˈnet‖wægəˈnet/ *n* a light horse-drawn wagon with 2 inward-facing seats along the sides behind a forward-facing front seat

wagon-lit /ˌvagonh ˈlee‖ˌvægɑ̃ ˈliː/ *n, pl* **wagons-lits, wagon-lits** /lee(z)‖liː(z)/ a sleeping car on a continental train [French, fr *wagon* railway car + *lit* bed]

wagtail /ˈwagˌtayl‖ˈwægˌteɪl/ *n* any of numerous chiefly Old World birds with trim slender bodies and very long tails that they habitually jerk up and down

waif /wayf‖weɪf/ *n* **1** a piece of property found but unclaimed **2** a stray helpless person or animal; *esp* a homeless child

[1]**wail** /wayl‖weɪl/ *vi* **1** to express sorrow by uttering mournful cries; lament **2** to make a sound suggestive of a mournful cry **3** to express dissatisfaction plaintively; complain – **wailer** *n*

[2]**wail** *n* **1** a usu loud prolonged high-pitched cry expressing grief or pain **2** a sound suggestive of wailing

wain /wayn‖weɪn/ *n* **1** a usu large and heavy wagon for farm use **2** *cap* URSA MAJOR

[1]**wainscot** /ˈwaynskət‖ˈweɪnskət/ *n* **1a** a usu panelled wooden lining of an interior wall **b** the lower part of an interior wall when finished differently from the remainder of the wall **2** *Br* a fine grade of oak imported for woodwork

[2]**wainscot** *vt* **-t-, -tt-** to line (as if) with boards or panelling

waist /wayst‖weɪst/ *n* **1a** the (narrow) part of the body between the chest and hips **b** the greatly constricted part of the abdomen of a wasp, fly, etc **2** the part of sthg corresponding to or resembling the human waist: e g **2a(1)** the part of a ship's deck between the poop and forecastle **a(2)** the middle part of a sailing ship between foremast and mainmast **b** the middle section of the fuselage of an aircraft **3** the part of a garment covering the body at the waist or waistline

ˈwaistˌband /-ˌband‖-ˌbænd/ *n* a band (e g on trousers or a skirt) fitting round the waist

ˈwaistˌcoat /-ˌkoht‖-ˌkəʊt/ *n, chiefly Br* a sleeveless upper garment that fastens down the centre front and usu has a V-neck; *esp* such a garment worn under a jacket as part of a man's suit – **waistcoated** *adj*

ˈwaistˌline /-ˌlien‖-ˌlaɪn/ *n* **1** an imaginary line encircling the narrowest part of the waist; *also* the part of a garment corresponding to this line or to the place where fashion dictates this should be **2** body circumference at the waist

[1]**wait** /wayt‖weɪt/ *vt* **1a** to stay in place in expectation of; await <~ *your turn*> **b** to delay in hope of a favourable change in <~ *out a storm*> **2** to delay serving (a meal), esp in expectation of further arrivals – infml ~ *vi* **1a** to remain stationary in readiness or expectation <~ *for a train*> **b** to pause for another to catch up **2a** to look forward expectantly <*just* ~ing *to see his rival lose*> **b** to hold back expectantly <*have to* ~ *till Thursday*> **3** to serve at meals – usu in *wait at table* or NAm *wait on table* **4** to be ready and available <*slippers* ~ing *by the bed*> – **wait on/upon 1** to act as an attendant to; serve **2** to await **3** *archaic* to make a formal call on

[2]**wait** *n* **1** any of a group who serenade for gratuities, esp at the Christmas season **2** an act or period of waiting <*a long* ~ *for the bus*>

waiter /ˈwaytə‖ˈweɪtə/ *n, fem* **waitress** one who waits at table (e g in a restaurant), esp as a regular job

ˈwaiting ˌlist *n* a list of those waiting (e g for a vacancy or for sthg to become available), arranged usu in order of application

ˈwaiting ˌroom *n* a room for the use of people who are waiting (e g for a train or to see a doctor)

waive /wayv‖weɪv/ *vt* **1** to refrain from demanding or enforcing; relinquish, forgo **2** to put off from immediate consideration; postpone

waiver /ˈwayvə‖ˈweɪvə/ *n* (a document giving

proof of) the relinquishing of a right

[1]**wake** /wayk‖weɪk/ *vb* **waked, woke** /wohk‖wəʊk/; **waked, woken** /ˈwohkən‖ˈwəʊkən/, **woke** *vi* **1** to be or remain awake **2** to awake – often + *up* ~ *vt* **1** to rouse (as if) from sleep; awake – often + *up* **2** to arouse, evoke < ~ *memories*> **3** to arouse conscious interest in; alert – usu + *to* < ~ *him to the fact of her existence*> – **waker** *n*

[2]**wake** *n* **1a** an annual English parish festival formerly held in commemoration of the church's patron saint **b** VIGIL 1a **2** a watch held over the body of a dead person prior to burial and sometimes accompanied by festivity; *broadly* any festive leavetaking **3** *Br* an annual holiday in northern England – usu pl but sing. or pl in constr

[3]**wake** *n* the track left by a moving body (e g a ship) in a fluid (e g water)

ˈ**wakeful** /-f(ə)l‖-f(ə)l/ *adj* **1** not sleeping or able to sleep **2** spent without sleep <*a* ~ *night*> – **wakefully** *adv*, **wakefulness** *n*

waken /ˈwaykən‖ˈweɪkən/ *vi* to awake – often + *up* ~*vt* to rouse out of sleep; wake – **wakener** *n*

[1]**walk** /wawk‖wɔːk/ *vi* **1** *of a spirit* to move about in visible form; appear **2a** to move along on foot; advance by steps, in such a way that at least 1 foot is always in contact with the ground **b** to go on foot for exercise or pleasure **c** to go at a walk **3** *of an inanimate object* to move in a manner suggestive of walking ~ *vt* **1** to pass on foot through, along, over, or on < ~ *the streets*> **2a** to cause (an animal) to go at a walk < ~ *a horse*> **b** to take (an animal) for a walk < ~ing *a dog*> **c** to cause (an inanimate object) to move in a manner suggestive of walking **3** to accompany on foot; walk with < ~ed *her home*> **4** to bring to a specified condition by walking < ~ed *us off our feet*> **5** to follow on foot for the purposes of examining, measuring, etc < ~ed *the horse before the jump-off*> – **walk off with 1a** to steal and take away **b** to take away unintentionally **2** to win or gain, esp by outdoing one's competitors without difficulty <walked off with *first prize*> – **walk over** to treat contemptuously – **walk tall** to bear oneself proudly – **walk the plank** to be forced to walk, esp blindfold, along a board laid over the side of a ship until one falls into the sea

[2]**walk** *n* **1a** an act or instance of going on foot, esp for exercise or pleasure **b** SPACE WALK **2** a route for walking <*many delightful* ~s *in the neighbourhood*> **3** a place designed for walking: e g **3a** a footpath **b** a railed or colonnaded platform **c** a promenade **4** a place where animals (e g sheep) are kept with minimal restraint **5** distance to be walked <*a quarter of a mile's* ~ *from here*> **6a** the gait of a 2-legged animal in which the feet are lifted alternately with 1 foot always (partially) on the ground **b** the slow 4-beat gait of a quadruped, specif a horse, in which there are always at least 2 feet on the ground **c** a low rate of speed **7** a route regularly traversed by a person (e g a postman or policeman) in the performance of a particular activity **8** a manner of walking <*his* ~ *is just like his father's*> **9** an occupation, calling – chiefly in *walk of life*

walkabout /ˈwawkəˌbowt‖ˈwɔːkəˌbaʊt/ *n* **1** a short period of wandering bush life engaged in occasionally by an Australian aborigine for ceremonial reasons **2** an informal walk among the crowds by a public figure

walker /ˈwawkə‖ˈwɔːkə/ *n* sthg used in walking; *specif* a framework designed to support a baby learning to walk or a cripple who cannot walk unaided

walkie-talkie /ˌwawki ˈtawki‖ˌwɔːkɪ ˈtɔːkɪ/ *n* a compact battery-operated radio transmitter and receiver

walking *adj* **1a** animate; *esp* human <*a* ~ *encyclopedia*> **b** able to walk **c** that moves in a manner suggestive of walking <*a* ~ *toy*> **d** guided or operated by a walker <*a* ~ *plough*> **2a** used for or in walking < ~ *shoes*> **b** characterized by or consisting of walking <*a* ~ *tour*>

ˈ**walking ˌpapers** *n pl, chiefly NAm* MARCHING ORDERS – infml

ˈ**walk-ˌon** *n* (sby who has) a small usu nonspeaking part in a dramatic production

ˈ**walkˌout** /-ˌowt‖-ˌaʊt/ *n* **1** STRIKE 3 **2** the action of leaving a meeting or organization as an expression of protest

walk out *vi* **1** to go on strike **2** to depart suddenly, often as an expression of protest **3** *chiefly Br* COURT 1 – often + *with*; no longer in vogue – **walk out on** to leave in the lurch; abandon

ˈ**walkˌover** /-ˌohvə‖-ˌəʊvə/ *n* an easily won contest; *also* an advance from one round of a competition to the next without contest, due to the withdrawal or absence of other entrants

[1]**wall** /wawl‖wɔːl/ *n* **1** a usu upright and solid structure, esp of masonry or concrete, having considerable height and length in relation to width and serving esp to divide, enclose, retain, or support: e g **1a** a structure bounding a garden, park, or estate **b** any of the upright enclosing structures of a room or house **c** RETAINING WALL **d** the surface of a wall <*the* ~ *is painted cream*> **2** a material layer enclosing space <*the* ~ *of a container*> **3** sthg resembling a wall: e g **3a** an almost vertical rock surface **b** sthg that acts as a barrier or defence <*tariff* ~ > – **walled** *adj* – **to the wall** into a hopeless position <*small businesses being driven* to the wall *by government policy*> – **up the wall** *Br* into a state of exasperation – infml

[2]**wall** *vt* **1a** to protect or surround (as if) with a wall <*a lake* ~ed *in by mountains*> **b** to separate or shut out (as if) by a wall < ~ed *off half the house*> **2a** to immure **b** to close (an opening) (as if) with a wall *USE* (2) usu + *up* – **waller** *n*, **walling** *n*

wallaby /ˈwoləbi‖ˈwɒləbɪ/ *n*, any of various small or medium-sized and usu less dull-coloured kangaroos

wallah /ˈwolə‖ˈwɒlə/ *n* a person who does a specified type of work or performs a specified duty – usu in combination; infml <*the book* ~ *was an itinerant peddler* – George Orwell> [Hindi *-wālā* man, one in charge, fr Sanskrit *pāla* protector]

wallet /ˈwolit‖ˈwɒlɪt/ *n* **1** a holder for paper money, usu with compartments for other items (e g credit cards and stamps) **2** a flat case or folder <*a ~ of maps*>

walleye /ˈwawl,ie‖ˈwɔːl,aɪ/ *n* **1** an eye with a whitish iris or opaque white (area in the) cornea **2** (a squint marked by) an eye that turns outwards – **walleyed** *adj*

ˈ**wall,flower** /-,flowə‖-,flaʊə/ *n* **1** any of several Old World perennial plants of the mustard family; *esp* a hardy erect plant with showy fragrant flowers **2** sby who from shyness or unpopularity remains on the sidelines of a social activity; *esp* a woman who fails to get partners at a dance – infml

[1]**wallop** /ˈwoləp‖ˈwɒləp/ *n* **1** a powerful body blow; [2]PUNCH 2; infml **2** emotional or psychological force; impact – infml **3** *Br* beer – slang

[2]**wallop** *vt* **1** to hit with force; thrash **2** to beat by a wide margin; trounce *USE* infml – **walloper** *n*, **walloping** *n*

walloping /ˈwoləping‖ˈwɒləpɪŋ/ *adj* large, whopping – infml

[1]**wallow** /ˈwoloh‖ˈwɒləʊ/ *vi* **1** to roll or lie around lazily or luxuriously <*pigs* ~ing *in mud*> **2** to indulge oneself immoderately; revel *in* <~ing *in sentiment*> **3** *of a ship* to struggle laboriously in or through rough water; *broadly* to pitch – **wallower** *n*

[2]**wallow** *n* **1** an act or instance of wallowing **2a** a muddy or dusty area used by animals for wallowing **b** a depression formed (as if) by the wallowing of animals

[1]ˈ**wall,paper** /-,paypə‖-,peɪpə/ *n* decorative paper for the walls of a room

[2]**wallpaper** *vb* to apply wallpaper to (the walls of a room)

,**wall-to-ˈwall** *adj*, *of carpeting* covering the whole floor of a room

wally /ˈwoli‖ˈwɒlɪ/ *n*, *Br* a feeble or foolish person – slang

walnut /ˈwawl,nut‖ˈwɔːl,nʌt/ *n* (an edible nut or the wood of) any of a genus of trees with richly grained wood used for cabinetmaking and veneers [Old English *wealhhnutu*, lit., foreign nut, fr *Wealh* Welshman, foreigner + *hnutu* nut]

walrus /ˈwawlrəs‖ˈwɔːlrəs/ *n* either of 2 large tusked sea mammals of northern seas, related to the seals

[1]**waltz** /wawlts‖wɔːlts/ *n* (music for or in the tempo of) a ballroom dance in $^3_4$ time with strong accent on the first beat

[2]**waltz** *vi* **1** to dance a waltz **2** to move *along* in a lively or confident manner **3** to proceed easily or boldly; breeze ~ *vt* **1** to dance a waltz with <~ed *her round the room*> **2** to grab and lead (e g a person) unceremoniously; march – usu + *off USE* (*vi 2&3; vt* 2) infml – **waltzer** *n*

wampum /ˈwompəm‖ˈwɒmpəm/ *n* beads of polished shells strung together and used by N American Indians as money and ornaments [short for *wampumpeag*, fr Narraganset (an American Indian language) *wampompeag*, fr *wampan* white + *api* string + *-ag*, pl suffix]

wan /won‖wɒn/ *adj* **-nn- 1a** suggestive of poor health; pallid **b** lacking vitality; feeble **2** *of light* dim, faint – **wanly** *adv*, **wanness** *n*

wand /wond‖wɒnd/ *n* a slender rod **a** carried as a sign of office **b** used by conjurers and magicians

wander /ˈwondə‖ˈwɒndə/ *vi* **1** to go or travel idly or aimlessly <~ *across the room*> **2** to meander **3a** to deviate (as if) from a course; stray <*eyes* ~ed *from the page*> **b** to lose concentration; stray in thought ~*vt* to roam over <~ed *the hillside in search of shelter*> – **wander** *n*, **wanderer** *n*

[1]**wandering** /ˈwondəring‖ˈwɒndərɪŋ/ *n* **1** a going about from place to place **2** movement away from the proper or usual course or place *USE* often pl with sing. meaning

[2]**wandering** *adj* **1** winding, meandering <*a ~ course*> **2** not keeping a rational or sensible course <~ *thoughts*> **3** nomadic <~ *tribes*>

wanderlust /ˈwondə,lust‖ˈwɒndə,lʌst/ *n* eager longing for or impulse towards travelling [German, fr *wandern* to wander + *lust* desire, pleasure]

[1]**wane** /wayn‖weɪn/ *vi* **1** to decrease in size or extent; dwindle: e g **1a** *of the moon, satellites, etc* to diminish in phase or intensity **b** *of light or colour* to become less brilliant; dim **2** to fall gradually from power, prosperity, or influence; decline

[2]**wane** *n* **1** the act or process of waning **2** a time of waning; *specif* the period from full phase of the moon to the new moon – **on the wane** in a state of decline; waning

wangle /ˈwang·gl‖ˈwæŋgl/ *vt* **1** to adjust or manipulate for personal or fraudulent ends **2** to bring about or get by devious means *USE* infml – **wangler** *n*

wank /wangk‖wæŋk/ *vi*, *Br* to masturbate – vulg – **wank** *n*

wanker /ˈwangkə‖ˈwæŋkə/ *n* **1** one who masturbates – vulg **2** a foolish or superficial fellow – slang

[1]**want** /wont‖wɒnt/ *vt* **1** to fail to possess, esp in customary or required amount; lack <*his answer* ~s *courtesy*> **2a** to have a desire for <*he* ~s *to go*> **b** to have an inclination to; like <*say what you* ~, *he is efficient*> **3a** to have need of; require <*the room* ~s *decorating*> **b** to suffer from the lack of; need <*thousands still ~ food and shelter*> **4** to wish or demand the presence of <*the boss* ~s *you*> **5** ought – + *to* and infinitive <*you ~ to see a doctor about that cold*> ~ *vi* **1** to be deficient or short by a specified amount <*it* ~s *3 minutes to 12*> **2** to be needy or destitute **3** to have need; be lacking in the specified respect <*never* ~s *for friends*> **4** *chiefly NAm* to desire to come or go <~s *out of the syndicate*>

[2]**want** *n* **1a** the quality or state of lacking sthg required or usual **b** extreme poverty **2** sthg wanted; a need

wanting /ˈwonting‖ˈwɒntɪŋ/ *adj* **1** not present or in evidence; absent **2a** not up to the required standard or expectation **b** lacking in the specified ability or capacity; deficient

[1]**wanton** /ˈwont(ə)n‖ˈwɒnt(ə)n/ *adj* **1** mischievous **2** sexually unbridled; promiscuous **3** having no just foundation or provocation; malicious **4** uncontrolled, unbridled <~ *inflation*> **5** luxuriant, lavish – now chiefly poetic – **wantonly** *adv*, **wantonness** *n*

[2]**wanton** *n* a wanton person; *esp* a lewd or lascivious woman

wapiti /'wopiti||'wɒpɪtɪ/ *n*, an American deer similar to the European red deer but larger

[1]**war** /waw||wɔː/ *n* **1** a state or period of usu open and declared armed hostile conflict between states or nations **2** a struggle between opposing forces or for a particular end <*a ~ against disease*>

[2]**war** *vi* **-rr-** **1** to engage in warfare **2a** to be in active or vigorous conflict **b** to be opposed or inconsistent <~ring *principles*>

[1]**warble** /'wawbl||'wɔːbl/ *vb* to sing or sound in a trilling manner or with many turns and variations – **warble** *n*

[2]**warble** *n* (a swelling under the hide of cattle, horses, etc caused by) the maggot of a fly

warbler /'wawblə||'wɔːblə/ *n* any of numerous small Old World birds (e g a whitethroat) which are related to the thrushes and many of which are noted songsters

'**war ˌbride** *n* a woman who marries a (foreign) serviceman met during a time of war

'**war ˌcrime** *n* a crime (e g genocide or maltreatment of prisoners) committed during or in connection with war – **war criminal** *n*

'**war ˌcry** *n* **1** a cry used during charging or rallying by a body of fighters in war **2** a slogan used esp to rally people to a cause

ward /wawd||wɔːd/ *n* **1** the inner court of a castle or fortress **2** a division of a prison or hospital **3** a division of a city or town for electoral or administrative purposes **4** a projecting ridge of metal in a lock casing or keyhole allowing only a key with a corresponding notch to operate; *also* a corresponding notch on a key **5** a person under guard, protection, or surveillance; *esp* one under the care or control of a legal guardian

[1]**-ward** /-wood||-wʊd/ *also* **-wards** /-woodz||-wʊdz/ *suffix* (→ *adj*) **1** facing or tending in (such) a direction <*home*ward> **2** occurring or situated in (such) a direction <*left*ward>

[2]**-ward** *suffix* (→ *adv*), *chiefly NAm* -wards

'**war ˌdance** *n* a dance performed esp by primitive peoples as preparation for battle or in celebration of victory

warden /'wawd(ə)n||'wɔːd(ə)n/ *n* **1** one having care or charge of sthg; a guardian **2** the governor of a town, district, or fortress **3** an official charged with special supervisory duties or with the enforcement of specified laws or regulations **4** any of various British college officials **5** *NAm* a prison governor – **wardenship** *n*

warder /'wawdə||'wɔːdə/, *fem* **wardress** /'wawdris||'wɔːdrɪs/ *n* **1** *Br* a prison guard **2** *archaic* a watchman, guard – **wardership** *n*

ward off *vt* to deflect, avert

wardrobe /'waw,drohb||'wɔː,drəʊb/ *n* **1** a room or (movable) cupboard, esp fitted with shelves and a rail or pegs, where clothes are kept **2a** a collection of clothes (e g belonging to 1 person) **b** a collection of stage costumes and accessories **3** the department of a royal or noble household entrusted with the care of clothes, jewels, and personal articles [Old North French *warderobe*, fr *warder* to guard + *robe* robe]

wardroom /'wawdroohm, -room||'wɔːdruːm, -rʊm/ *n* the space in a warship allotted to the commissioned officers excepting the captain

-wards /-woodz||-wʊdz/ *suffix* (→ *adv*) **1** in (such) a spatial or temporal direction <*up*wards> **2** towards (such) a point, position, or place <*earth*wards>

ware *n* **1a** manufactured articles or products of art or craft; goods – often in combination <*tin*ware> **b** *pl* goods for sale **2** articles of fired clay; *esp* a specified make of pottery or china <*Parian ~*>

warehouse /'weə,hows||'weə,haʊs/ *vt or n* (to deposit, store, or stock in) a structure or room for the storage of merchandise or commodities – **warehouser** *n*

warfare /'waw,feə||'wɔː,feə/ *n* **1** hostilities, war **2** struggle, conflict

warhead /'waw,hed||'wɔː,hed/ *n* the section of a missile containing the explosive, chemical, or incendiary charge

'**war-ˌhorse** *n* **1** a powerful horse used in war **2** a veteran soldier or public figure **3** a work of art (e g a musical composition) that has become hackneyed from repetition in the standard repertoire

'**war,like** /-,liek||-,laɪk/ *adj* **1** fond of war **2** of or useful in war **3** hostile

warlock /'wawlok||'wɔːlɒk/ *n* a man practising black magic; a sorcerer [Old English *wǣrloga* one who breaks faith, the Devil, fr *wǣr* faith, troth + *lēogan* to lie]

warlord /'waw,lawd||'wɔː,lɔːd/ *n* a supreme military leader

[1]**warm** /wawm||wɔːm/ *adj* **1a** having or giving out heat to a moderate or adequate degree <*a ~ bath*>; *also* experiencing heat to this degree <*are you ~ enough?*> **b** serving to maintain or preserve heat, esp to a satisfactory degree <*a ~ sweater*> **c** feeling or causing sensations of heat brought about by strenuous exertion <*a ~ climb*> **2a** cordial <*a ~ welcome*> **b** marked by excitement, disagreement, or anger <*a ~ debate*> **3** affectionate and outgoing in temperament <*a ~ personality*> **4** dangerous, hostile **5** *of a trail, scent, etc* newly made; fresh **6** *of a colour* producing an impression of being warm; *specif* in the range yellow to red **7** near to a goal, object, or solution sought – chiefly in children's games – **warmish** *adj*, **warmness** *n*, **warmly** *adv*

[2]**warm** *vt* **1** to make warm **2** to infuse with a feeling of love, friendship, well-being, or pleasure **3** to reheat (cooked food) for eating – often + *up* in Br or *over* in NAm ~ *vi* **1** to become warm **2** to become filled with interest, enthusiasm, or affection – + *to* or *towards* <*did not ~ to the newcomer*> – **warm the cockles of one's heart** to make one happy; cheer, encourage

ˌ**warm-'blooded** *adj* **1** having a relatively high and constant body temperature more or less independent of the environment **2** fervent or ardent in spirit – **warm-bloodedness** *n*

ˌ**warm'hearted** /-'hahtid||-'hɑːtɪd/ *adj* marked by ready affection, cordiality, generosity, or sympathy – **warmheartedly** *adv*, **warmheartedness** *n*

'**warming ˌpan** /'wawming||'wɔːmɪŋ/ *n* a usu long-handled flat covered pan (e g of brass) filled with hot coals, formerly used to warm a bed

warmonger /'waw,mung·gə||'wɔː,mʌŋgə/ *n*

one who attempts to stir up war – **warmongering** *n*

warmth /wawmth‖wɔːmθ/ *n* the quality or state of being warm **a** in temperature **b** in feeling <*a child needing human* ~ >

ˈwarm-ˌup *n* the act or an instance of warming up; *also* a procedure (e g a set of exercises) used in warming up

warm up *vi* **1** to engage in exercise or practice, esp before entering a game or contest; *broadly* to get ready **2** HOT UP ~*vt* HOT UP; *esp* to put (an audience) into a receptive mood (e g before a show), esp by telling jokes, singing, etc

warn /wawn‖wɔːn/ *vt* **1a** to give notice to beforehand, esp of danger or evil < ~ *them of the floods*> **b** to give admonishing advice to; counsel < ~ *them not to open the door*> **c** to notify, inform **2** to order to go or stay away – often + *off* or *away* ~*vi* to give a warning – **warner** *n*

warning /ˈwawning‖ˈwɔːnɪŋ/ *n* sthg that warns; *also* NOTICE 1b – **warning** *adj*, **warningly** *adv*

ˌwar of ˈnerves *n* (a conflict characterized by) the use of psychological tactics (e g bluff, threats, or intimidation) designed to destroy the enemy's morale

[1]warp /wawp‖wɔːp/ *n* **1a** a series of yarns extended lengthways in a loom and crossed by the weft **b** the cords forming the carcass of a pneumatic tyre **2** a rope for warping a ship or boat **3** sediment deposited by (standing) water **4a** a twist or curve that has developed in sthg formerly flat or straight **b** a mental twist or aberration – **warpage** *n*

[2]warp *vt* **1a** to turn or twist (e g planks) out of shape, esp out of a plane **b** to cause to think or act wrongly; pervert **2** to arrange (yarns) so as to form a warp **3** to manoeuvre (e g a ship) by hauling on a line attached to a fixed object ~ *vi* **1** to become warped **2** to move a ship by warping – **warper** *n*

ˈwar ˌpaint *n* **1** paint put on the body by N American Indians as a sign of going to war **2** ceremonial dress; regalia **3** cosmetics *USE* (*2&3*) infml

warpath /ˈwawˌpahth‖ˈwɔːˌpɑːθ/ *n* the route taken by a war party of N American Indians – **on the warpath** pursuing an angry or hostile course

[1]warrant /ˈworənt‖ˈwɒrənt/ *n* **1a** a sanction, authorization; *also* evidence for or token of authorization **b** a guarantee, security **c** a ground, justification; *also* proof <*his assertion was totally without* ~> **2** a commission or document giving authority: e g **2a** a document authorizing sby to receive money or other consideration <*travel* ~> **b** a document authorizing an officer to make an arrest, a search, etc **c** an official certificate of appointment issued to a noncommissioned officer **d(1)** a short-term obligation of a governmental body (e g a municipality) issued in anticipation of revenue **d(2)** a document issued by a company giving to the holder the right to purchase the capital stock of the company at a stated price either prior to a stipulated date or at any future time

[2]warrant *vt* **1** to declare or maintain with certainty **2** to guarantee to be as represented **3** to give sanction to <*the law* ~s *this procedure*> **4a** to prove or declare the authenticity or truth of **b** to give assurance of the nature of or for the undertaking of; guarantee **5** to serve as or give adequate ground or reason for <*the situation* ~s *dramatic action*> – **warrantable** *adj*, **warrantor, warranter** *n*

warrantee /ˌworənˈtee‖ˌwɒrənˈtiː/ *n* sby to whom a warranty is made

ˈwarrant ˌofficer *n* an officer in the army, airforce, marines, or US navy, ranking between noncommissioned officer and commissioned officer

warranty /ˈworənti‖ˈwɒrəntɪ/ *n* **1** a collateral undertaking that a fact regarding the subject of a contract is or will be as declared **2** sthg that authorizes, supports, or justifies; a warrant **3** a usu written guarantee of the soundness of a product and of the maker's responsibility for repair or replacement

warren /ˈworən‖ˈwɒrən/ *n* **1** an area of ground (or a structure) where rabbits breed **2a** a crowded tenement or district **b** a maze of narrow passageways or cubbies; *broadly* anything intricate or confused

warrior /ˈwori·ə‖ˈwɒrɪə/ *n* a man engaged or experienced in warfare

warship /ˈwawˌship‖ˈwɔːˌʃɪp/ *n* an (armed) ship for use in warfare

wart /wawt‖wɔːt/ *n* **1** a horny projection on the skin, usu of the hands or feet, caused by a virus; *also* a protuberance, esp on a plant, resembling this **2** an ugly or objectionable man or boy – chiefly Br schoolboy slang **3** a blemish – often in *warts and all* – **warty** *adj*

warthog /ˈwawtˌhog‖ˈwɔːtˌhɒg/ *n* any of a genus of African wild pigs with 2 pairs of rough warty lumps on the face and large protruding tusks

wartime /ˈwawˌtiem‖ˈwɔːˌtaɪm/ *n* a period during which a war is in progress

wary /ˈweəri‖ˈweərɪ/ *adj* marked by caution and watchful prudence in detecting and escaping danger – **warily** *adv*, **wariness** *n*

was /wəz‖wəz; *strong* woz‖wɒz/ *past 1 & 3 sing of* BE

[1]wash /wosh‖wɒʃ/ *vt* **1a** to cleanse (as if) by the action of liquid (e g water) **b** to remove (e g dirt) by applying liquid **2** *of an animal* to cleanse (fur or a furry part) by licking or by rubbing with a paw moistened with saliva **3a** to flush or moisten (a body part or injury) with liquid **b** to suffuse with light **c** to pass water over or through, esp so as to carry off material from the surface or interior **4** to flow along, over, or against <*waves* ~ing *the shore*> **5** to move, carry, or deposit (as if) by the force of water in motion <*houses* ~ed *away by the flood*> **6a** to agitate (e g crushed ore) in water to separate valuable material; *also* to separate (particles) thus **b** to pass (e g a gas) through or over a liquid to carry off impurities or soluble components **7** to cover or daub lightly with a thin coating (e g of paint or varnish) ~ *vi* **1a** to wash oneself or a part of one's body **b** to wash articles; do the washing **2** to bear washing without damage <*does this dress* ~?> **3** to drift along on water **4** to pour or flow in a stream or current **5** to gain acceptance; inspire belief <*an interesting theory, but it just won't* ~> – infml [Old English *wascan*; akin to Old English *wæter* water – see WATER] – **wash one's hands of** to disclaim interest in, responsibility for, or further connection with

[2]**wash** *n* **1a** (an instance of) washing or being washed **b** articles for washing **c** an area or structure equipped with facilities for washing a vehicle <*a car* ~> **2** the surging action of waves **3a** a piece of ground washed by the sea or river **b** a shallow body of water **4a** worthless esp liquid waste; *also* swill **b** vapid writing or speech **5a** a thin coat of paint (e g watercolour) **b** a thin liquid used for coating a surface (e g a wall) **6** a lotion **7** loose or eroded surface soil, rock debris, etc transported and deposited by running water **8a** BACKWASH 1 **b** a disturbance in the air produced by the passage of an aircraft

washable /ˈwoshəbl‖ˈwɒʃəbl/ *adj* capable of being washed without damage – **washability** *n*

ˈwashˌbasin /-ˌbays(ə)n‖-ˌbeɪs(ə)n/ *n* a basin or sink usu connected to a water supply for washing the hands and face

ˈwashˌboard /-ˌbawd‖-ˌbɔːd/ *n* a corrugated board for scrubbing clothes on when washing

washbowl /-ˌbohl‖-ˌbəʊl/ *n* a washbasin

ˈwashˌcloth /-ˌkloth‖-ˌklɒθ/ *n, NAm* FLANNEL 3

wash down *vt* **1** to send downwards by action of a liquid; *esp* to facilitate the swallowing of (food) by taking gulps of liquid **2** to wash the whole surface of <washed down *and scrubbed the front step*>

ˈwash ˌdrawing *n* (a) watercolour painting done (mainly) in washes, esp in black, white, and grey tones only

ˌwashed-ˈout *adj* **1** faded in colour **2** listless, exhausted – infml

ˌwashed-ˈup *adj* no longer successful or useful; finished – infml

washer /ˈwoshə‖ˈwɒʃə/ *n* **1** WASHING MACHINE **2** a thin flat ring (e g of metal or leather) used to ensure tightness or prevent friction in joints and assemblies

ˈwasherwoman /-woomən‖-wʊmən/, *masc* **ˈwasherman** /-mən‖-mən/ *n* a woman who takes in washing

ˈwashˌhouse /-ˌhows‖-ˌhaʊs/ *n* a building used or equipped for washing clothes

washing /ˈwoshing‖ˈwɒʃɪŋ/ *n* articles, esp clothes, that have been or are to be washed

ˈwashing maˌchine *n* a machine for washing esp clothes and household linen

ˈwashing ˌsoda *n* a transparent crystalline hydrated sodium carbonate

ˌwashing-ˈup *n, chiefly Br* the act or process of washing dishes and kitchen utensils; *also* the dishes and utensils to be washed

ˈwash-ˌleather *n* a soft leather similar to chamois

ˈwashˌout /-ˌowt‖-ˌaʊt/ *n* **1** the washing out or away of a road, railway line, etc by a large amount of water; *also* a place where this has occurred **2** a failure, fiasco

wash out *vt* **1a** to wash free of a usu unwanted substance (e g dirt) <washed *the milk bottles* out> **b** to remove (e g a stain) by washing <washed *the tea stain* out *of the tablecloth*> **2a** to cause to fade by laundering **b** to deplete the strength or vitality of <*feeling very* washed out> ~ *vi* to become depleted of colour or vitality; fade

ˈwashroom /-ˌroohm, -room‖-ˌruːm, -rʊm/ *n, NAm* TOILET 2b – euph

ˈwashˌstand /-ˌstand‖-ˌstænd/ *n* a piece of furniture used, esp formerly, to hold a basin, jug, etc needed for washing one's face and hands

wash up *vi* **1** *Br* to wash used dishes and kitchen utensils, esp after a meal **2** *NAm* to wash one's face and hands ~ *vt* **1** to bring into the shore <*a dead whale was* washed up *on the sand*> **2** *Br* to wash (the dishes and utensils) after a meal

ˈwashˌwoman /-ˌwoomən‖-ˌwʊmən/ *n, NAm* a washerwoman

washy /ˈwoshi‖ˈwɒʃɪ/ *adj* **1** weak, watery <~ *tea*> **2** deficient in colour; pallid **3** lacking in vigour, individuality, or definite form – **washiness** *n*

wasn't /ˈwoznt‖ˈwɒznt/ was not

wasp /wosp‖wɒsp/ *n* any of numerous largely flesh-eating slender narrow-waisted insects many of which have an extremely painful sting; *esp* a very common social wasp with black and yellow stripes – **wasplike** *adj*

WASP, Wasp /wosp‖wɒsp/ *n* an American of N European, esp British, stock and of Protestant background; *esp* one in North America considered to be a member of the dominant and most privileged class [*w*hite *A*nglo-*S*axon *P*rotestant] – **Waspish** *adj*, **Waspy** *adj*

waspish /ˈwospish‖ˈwɒspɪʃ/ *adj* resembling a wasp in behaviour; *esp* snappish – **waspishly** *adv*, **waspishness** *n*

wasp waist *n* a very slender waist – **wasp-waisted** *adj*

[1]**wassail** /ˈwosayl‖ˈwɒseɪl/ *n* **1** a toast to sby's health made in England in former times **2 wassail, wassail bowl, wassail cup** a liquor made of spiced ale or wine and often baked apples, and served in a large bowl, esp formerly, at Christmas and other festive occasions **3** *archaic* revelry, carousing [Old Norse *ves heill* be well]

[2]**wassail** *vi* **1** to carouse **2** *dial Eng* to sing carols from house to house at Christmas – **wassailer** *n*

wast /wəst, wost‖wəst, wɒst/ *archaic past 2 sing of* BE

wastage /ˈwaystij‖ˈweɪstɪdʒ/ *n* **1a** loss, decrease, or destruction of sthg (e g by use, decay, or leakage); *esp* wasteful or avoidable loss of sthg valuable **b** waste, refuse **2** reduction or loss in numbers (e g of employees or students), usu caused by individuals leaving or retiring voluntarily – esp in *natural wastage*

[1]**waste** /wayst‖weɪst/ *n* **1a** a sparsely settled, barren, or devastated region; a desert **b** uncultivated land **c** a broad and empty expanse (e g of water) **2** wasting or being wasted **3** gradual loss or decrease by use, wear, or decay **4** damaged, defective, or superfluous material produced by a manufacturing process: e g **4a** material rejected during a textile manufacturing process and used usu for wiping away dirt and oil **b** fluid (e g

steam) allowed to escape without being used **5** human or animal refuse

[2]**waste** *vt* **1** to lay waste; devastate **2** to cause to be reduced in physical bulk or strength; enfeeble **3** to wear away gradually; consume **4** to spend or use carelessly or inefficiently; squander ~ *vi* **1** to lose weight, strength, or vitality – often + *away* **2** to become consumed gradually and esp wastefully – **waste one's breath** to accomplish nothing by speaking

[3]**waste** *adj* **1a** uninhabited, desolate **b** not cultivated or used; not productive <~ *land*> **2** ruined, devastated **3** discarded as refuse <~ *material*> **4** serving to conduct or hold refuse material; *specif* carrying off superfluous fluid <~ *pipe*>

ˈwasteful /-f(ə)l‖-f(ə)l/ *adj* given to or marked by waste; prodigal – **wastefully** *adv*, **wastefulness** *n*

ˌwasteˈpaper /-ˈpaypə‖-ˈpeɪpə/ *n* paper discarded as used or unwanted

ˌwasteˈpaper ˌbasket *n* a receptacle for refuse, esp wastepaper

waste product *n* **1** debris resulting from a process (e g of manufacture) that is of no further use to the system producing it **2** material (e g faeces) discharged from, or stored in an inert form in, a living body as a by-product of metabolic processes

waster /ˈwaystə‖ˈweɪstə/ *n* **1** one who spends or consumes extravagantly without thought for the future **2** a good-for-nothing, idler

wastrel /ˈwaystrəl‖ˈweɪstrəl/ *n* **1** a vagabond, waif **2** a waster

[1]**watch** /woch‖wɒtʃ/ *vi* **1** to remain awake during the night, esp in order to keep vigil **2a** to be attentive or vigilant; wait *for* <~ed *for a chance to get her revenge*> **b** to keep guard <~ *over their flocks*> **3** to be closely observant of an event or action ~ *vt* **1** to keep under protective guard **2a** to observe closely, esp in order to check on action or change <*being* ~ed *by the police*> **b** to look at (an event or moving scene) <~ *television*> **3a** to take care of; tend <~ *the baby*> **b** to be careful of <~es *his diet*> **c** to take care that <~ *you don't spill it*> **4** to be on the alert for; bide <~ed *his opportunity*> – **watcher** *n* – **watch it** to be careful; LOOK OUT – **watch one's step** to proceed with extreme care; act or talk warily – **watch over** to have charge of; superintend

[2]**watch** *n* **1a** the act of keeping awake or alert to guard, protect, or attend <*kept a close* ~ *on his movements*> **b** a state of alert and continuous attention; lookout **2** a wakeful interval during the night – usu pl **3** a watchman; *also, sing or pl in constr* a body of watchmen, specif those formerly assigned to patrol the streets of a town at night **4a** a period of keeping guard **b(1)** a period of time during which a part of a ship's company is on duty while another part rests **b(2)** *sing or pl in constr* the part of a ship's company on duty during a particular watch **5** a small portable timepiece powered esp by a spring or battery and usu worn on a wrist – **on the watch** on the alert

ˈwatchˌdog /-ˌdog‖-ˌdɒg/ *n* **1** a dog kept to guard property **2** a person or group (e g a committee) that guards against inefficiency, undesirable practices, etc

ˈwatchful /-f(ə)l‖-f(ə)l/ *adj* carefully observant or attentive; ON THE WATCH – **watchfully** *adv*, **watchfulness** *n*

ˈwatchˌmaking /-ˌmayking‖-ˌmeɪkɪŋ/ *n* the making or repairing of watches or clocks – **watchmaker** *n*

ˈwatchman /-mən‖-mən/ *n*, *pl* **watchmen** sby who keeps watch; a guard

watch out *vi* **1** to be on the lookout *for* **2** to be careful; take care – often imper

ˈwatchˌtower /-ˌtowə‖-ˌtaʊə/ *n* a tower from which a lookout can keep watch

ˈwatchˌword /-ˌwuhd‖-ˌwɜːd/ *n* **1** a word or phrase used as a sign of recognition among members of the same group **2** a motto that embodies a guiding principle

[1]**water** /ˈwawtə‖ˈwɔːtə/ *n* **1a** the colourless odourless liquid that descends from the clouds as rain, forms streams, lakes, and seas, is a major constituent of all living matter, and is an oxide of hydrogen which freezes at 0°C and boils at 100°C **b** a natural mineral water – usu pl with sing. meaning **2a(1)** *pl* the water occupying or flowing in a particular bed <*the* ~s *of the Nile*> **a(2)** *chiefly Br* a body of water (e g a river or lake) <*Derwent* ~> **b(1)** *pl* a stretch of sea surrounding and controlled by a country <*territorial* ~s> **b(2)** the sea of a specified part of the earth – often pl with sing. meaning <*in tropical* ~s> **3** travel or transport by water <*we went by* ~> **4a** the level of water at a specified state of the tide **b** the surface of the water <*swam under* ~> **5** liquid containing or resembling water: e g **5a** a pharmaceutical or cosmetic preparation (e g a toilet water) made with water **b** a watery solution of a gaseous or readily volatile substance <*ammonia* ~> **c** a watery fluid (e g tears, urine, or sap) formed or circulating in a living body **6** degree of excellence <*a scholar of the first* ~> **7** a wavy lustrous pattern (e g of a textile) [Old English *wæter*; fr a hypothetical Indo-European root from which come also such words as OTTER, URINE, WASH, WET, as well as Greek *hydōr* water (hence HYDR-), Latin *unda* wave (hence UNDULATE), Russian *voda* water (hence VODKA)] – **water under the bridge** past events which it is futile to attempt to alter

[2]**water** *vt* **1** to moisten, sprinkle, or soak with water <~ *the garden*> **2a** to supply with water for drink <~ *the horses*> **b** to supply water to <~ *a ship*> **3** to be a source of water for <*land* ~ed *by the Thames*> **4** to impart a lustrous appearance and wavy pattern to (cloth) by calendering <~ed *silk*> **5** to dilute (as if) by the addition of water – often + *down* ~ *vi* **1** to form or secrete water or watery matter (e g tears or saliva) **2a** to take on a supply of water **b** *of an animal* to drink water – **waterer** *n*

ˈwater ˌbiscuit *n* an unsweetened biscuit made with flour and water

ˈwater ˌblister *n* a blister with a clear watery content that does not contain pus or blood

ˈwaterˌborne /-ˌbawn‖-ˌbɔːn/ *adj* supported or carried by water

ˈ**water ˌbuffalo** *n* an often domesticated Asiatic buffalo

ˈ**water ˌcannon** *n* a device for shooting out a jet of water with great force (e g to disperse a crowd)

ˈ**water ˌcloset** *n* (a room or structure containing) a toilet with a bowl that can be flushed with water

ˈ**waterˌcolour** /-ˌkulə‖-ˌkʌlə/ *n* **1** a paint made from pigment mixed with water rather than oil **2** (a work produced by) the art of painting with watercolours

ˈ**waterˌcourse** /-ˌkaws‖-ˌkɔːs/ *n* (a natural or man-made channel for) a stream of water

ˈ**waterˌcress** /-ˌkres‖-ˌkres/ *n* any of several cresses of wet places widely grown for use in salads

ˈ**waterˌfall** /-ˌfawl‖-ˌfɔːl/ *n* a vertical or steep descent of the water of a river or stream

ˈ**waterˌfowl** /-ˌfowl‖-ˌfaʊl/ *n*, **1** a bird, esp a duck, that frequents water **2** *pl* swimming game birds (e g duck) as distinguished from upland game birds (e g grouse)

ˈ**waterˌfront** /-ˌfrunt‖-ˌfrʌnt/ *n* land or a section of a town fronting or bordering on a body of water

ˈ**water ˌhen** *n* any of various birds (e g a coot or moorhen) related to the rails

ˈ**water ˌhole** *n* a natural hollow in which water collects, used esp by animals as a drinking place

ˈ**water ˌice** *n* a frozen dessert of water, sugar, and flavouring

ˈ**watering ˌcan** /ˈwawt(ə)ring‖ˈwɔːt(ə)rɪŋ/ *n* a vessel having a handle and a long spout often fitted with a rose, used for watering plants

ˈ**watering ˌplace** *n* **1** a place where water may be obtained; *esp* one where animals, esp livestock, come to drink **2** a health or recreational resort featuring mineral springs or bathing; *esp* a spa

ˈ**water ˌjacket** *n* an outer casing which holds water or through which water circulates, esp for cooling

ˈ**water ˌjump** *n* an obstacle (e g in a steeplechase) consisting of a pool or ditch of water

ˈ**water ˌlevel** *n* **1** the level reached by the surface of a body of water **2** WATER TABLE

ˈ**water ˌlily** *n* any of a family of aquatic plants with floating leaves and usu showy colourful flowers

ˈ**waterˌline** /-ˌlien‖-ˌlaɪn/ *n* the level on the hull of a vessel to which the surface of the water comes when it is afloat; *also* any of several lines marked on the hull to correspond with this level

ˈ**waterˌlogged** /-ˌlogd‖-ˌlɒgd/ *adj* filled or soaked with water; *specif, of a vessel* so filled with water as to be (almost) unable to float – **waterlog** *vt*

waterloo /ˌwawtəˈlooh‖ˌwɔːtəˈluː/ *n, often cap* a decisive defeat [*Waterloo*, village in Belgium, site of Napoleon's decisive defeat by British and Prussian forces in 1815]

ˈ**water ˌmain** *n* a major pipe for conveying water

ˈ**waterman** /-mən‖-mən/ *n* a man who works on or near water or who engages in water recreations; *esp* a boatman whose boat and services are available for hire

[1]ˈ**waterˌmark** /-ˌmahk‖-ˌmɑːk/ *n* **1** a mark indicating the height to which water has risen **2** (the design or the metal pattern producing) a marking in paper visible when the paper is held up to the light

[2]**watermark** *vt* to mark (paper) with a watermark

ˈ**water ˌmeadow** *n* a meadow kept fertile by a regular influx of water (e g from the flooding of a bordering river)

ˈ**waterˌmelon** /-ˌmelən‖-ˌmelən/ *n* (an African climbing plant of the cucumber family that bears) a large oblong or roundish fruit with a hard green often striped or variegated rind, a sweet watery pink pulp, and many seeds

ˈ**water ˌmill** *n* a mill whose machinery is moved by water

ˈ**water ˌpipe** *n* **1** a pipe for conveying water **2** a large chiefly oriental smoking apparatus consisting of a bowl containing tobacco or other smoking material mounted on a vessel of water through which smoke is drawn and cooled before reaching the mouth

ˈ**water ˌpolo** *n* a game played in water by teams of 7 swimmers using a ball that is thrown or dribbled with the object of putting it into a goal

ˈ**waterˌpower** /-ˌpowə‖-ˌpaʊə/ *n* the power derived from movement of a body of water; *also* a fall of water suitable for such use

[1]ˈ**waterˌproof** /-ˌproohf‖-ˌpruːf/ *adj* impervious to water; *esp* covered or treated with a material to prevent passage of water – **waterproofness** *n*

[2]**waterproof** *n* (a garment made of) waterproof fabric

[3]**waterproof** *vt* to make waterproof – **waterproofer** *n*, **waterproofing** *n*

ˈ**water ˌrate** *n* the charge made to a British householder for the use of the public water supply

ˈ**waterˌshed** /-ˌshed‖-ˌʃed/ *n* **1** a dividing ridge between 2 drainage areas **2** a crucial turning point

ˈ**waterˌside** /-ˌsied‖-ˌsaɪd/ *n* the margin of a body of water

ˈ**water ˌski** *n* a board used singly or in pairs for standing on and planing over water while being towed at speed – **water-ski** *vi*, **water-skier** *n*

ˈ**water-ˌskiing** *n* the sport of planing and jumping on water skis

ˈ**water-ˌsoftener** *n* a substance or device for softening hard water

ˈ**water ˌspaniel** *n* a rather large spaniel with a heavy curly coat, used esp for retrieving waterfowl

ˈ**waterˌspout** /-ˌspowt‖-ˌspaʊt/ *n* a funnel-shaped column of rotating wind usu extending from the underside of a cumulus or cumulonimbus cloud down to a cloud of spray torn up from the surface of a sea, lake, etc

ˈ**water supˌply** *n* the source, means, or process of supplying water (e g to a town or house), usu including reservoirs, tunnels, and pipelines

ˈ**water ˌtable** *n* the level below which the ground is wholly saturated with water

ˈ**waterˌtight** /-ˌtiet‖-ˌtaɪt/ *adj* **1** of such tight

construction or fit as to be impermeable to water **2** *esp of an argument* impossible to disprove; without loopholes **3** isolated from other ideas, influences, etc; discrete <*experiences cannot be divided into ~ compartments*> – **watertightness** *n*

ˈwater ˌtower *n* **1** a tower supporting a raised water tank to provide the necessary steady pressure to distribute water **2** a fire fighting apparatus that can supply water at various heights and at great pressure

ˈwater ˌvapour *n* water in a vaporous form, esp when below boiling temperature and diffused (e g in the atmosphere)

ˈwater ˌvole *n* a common large vole of W Europe that inhabits river banks and often digs extensive tunnels

ˈwaterˌway /-ˌway‖-ˌweɪ/ *n* **1** a navigable route or body of water **2** a groove at the edge of a ship's deck for draining the deck

ˈwaterˌwheel /-ˌweel‖-ˌwiːl/ *n* **1** a wheel made to rotate by direct action of water, and used esp to drive machinery. **2** a wheel for raising water

ˈwater ˌwings *n pl* a pair of usu air-filled floats worn to give support to the body of sby learning to swim

ˈwaterˌworks /-ˌwuhks‖-ˌwɜːks/ *n, pl* **waterworks** **1** the reservoirs, mains, building, and pumping and purifying equipment by which a water supply is obtained and distributed (e g to a city) – often pl with sing. meaning **2** *chiefly Br* the urinary system – euph or humor **3** (the shedding of) tears – infml

watery /ˈwawt(ə)ri‖ˈwɔːt(ə)rɪ/ *adj* **1a** consisting of or filled with water **b** containing, sodden with, or yielding water or a thin liquid <*a ~ solution*> **c** containing too much water <*~ soup*> **d** secreting water, esp tears <*~ eyes*> **2a** pale, faint <*~ sun*> **b** vapid, wishy-washy <*a ~ writing style*> – **waterily** *adv*, **wateriness** *n*

watt /wot‖wɒt/ *n* the SI unit of power equal to the power that in 1s gives rise to an energy of 1 joule [James *Watt* (1736-1819), Scottish engineer]

wattage /ˈwotij‖ˈwɒtɪdʒ/ *n* amount of power expressed in watts

[1]wattle /ˈwotl‖ˈwɒtl/ *n* **1** (material for) a framework of poles interwoven with slender branches or reeds and used, esp formerly, in building **2a** a fleshy protuberance usu near or on the head or neck, esp of a bird **b** [2]BARBEL **3** *Austr* ACACIA 1 – **wattled** *adj*

[2]wattle *vt* **1** to form or build of or with wattle **2a** to interlace to form wattle **b** to unite or make solid by interweaving light flexible material

[1]wave /wayv‖weɪv/ *vi* **1** to flutter or sway to and fro <*flags* waving *in the breeze*> **2** to give a signal or salute by moving (sthg held in) the hand <~d *cheerily to them*> **3** to be flourished to and fro <*his sword* ~d *and flashed*> **4** to follow a curving line or form; undulate ~ *vt* **1** to cause to swing to and fro **2** to direct by waving; signal <*~ the car to a halt*> **3a** to move (the hand or an object) to and fro in greeting, farewell, or homage **b** to convey by waving <~d *farewell*> **4** to brandish, flourish <~d *a pistol menacingly*> **5** to give a curving or undulating shape to <~d *her hair*> – **wave aside** to dismiss or put out of mind; disregard

[2]wave *n* **1a** a moving ridge or swell on the surface of a liquid (e g the sea) **b** open water – usu pl with sing. meaning; chiefly poetic **2a** a shape or outline having successive curves **b** a waviness of the hair **c** an undulating line or streak **3** sthg that swells and dies away: e g **3a** a surge of sensation or emotion **b** a movement involving large numbers of people in a common activity <~s *of protest*> **c** a sudden increase or wide occurrence of a specified activity <*a ~ of house-buying*> **4** a sweep of the hand or arm or of some object held in the hand, used as a signal or greeting **5** a rolling or undulatory movement or any of a series of such movements passing along a surface or through the air **6** a movement like that of an ocean wave: e g **6a** a surging movement; an influx <*a sudden ~ of new arrivals*> **b** *sing or pl in constr* a line of attacking or advancing troops, aircraft, etc **7** (a complete cycle of) a periodic variation of pressure, electrical or magnetic intensity, electric potential, etc by which energy is transferred progressively from point to point without a corresponding transfer of a medium <*light ~*> <*radio ~*> <*sound ~*> **8** an undulating or jagged line constituting a graphic representation of an action <*a sine ~*> **9** a marked change in temperature; a period of hot or cold weather

ˈwave ˌband *n* a band of radio frequency waves

ˈwaveˌlength /-ˌleng(k)th‖-ˌleŋ(k)θ/ *n* the distance in the line of advance of a wave from any 1 point to the next point of corresponding phase (e g from 1 peak to the next) – **be on somebody's/the same wavelength** to have the same outlook, views, etc as sby else

waver /ˈwayvə‖ˈweɪvə/ *vi* **1** to vacillate between choices; fluctuate **2a** to sway unsteadily to and fro; reel **b** to quiver, flicker <~ing *flames*> **c** to hesitate as if about to give way; falter – **waverer** *n*, **waveringly** *adv*

wavy /ˈwayvi‖ˈweɪvɪ/ *adj* **1** having waves <*~ hair*> **2** having a wavelike form or outline <*~ line*> – **wavily** *adv*, **waviness** *n*

[1]wax /waks‖wæks/ *n* **1** beeswax **2a** any of numerous plant or animal substances that are harder, more brittle, and less greasy than fats **b** a solid substance (e g paraffin wax) of mineral origin consisting usu of higher hydrocarbons **c** a pliable or liquid composition used esp for sealing, taking impressions, or polishing **d** a resinous preparation used by shoemakers for rubbing thread **3** a waxy secretion; *esp* cerumen

[2]wax *vt* to treat or rub with wax

[3]wax *vi* **1** to increase in size and strength; *esp, of the moon, satellites, etc* to increase in phase or intensity **2** *archaic* to assume a specified quality or state; become <~ed *lyrical*>

[4]wax *n* a fit of temper – infml

ˌwaxed ˈpaper, wax paper *n* paper coated or impregnated with wax to make it resistant to water and grease, used esp as a wrapping for food

waxen /ˈwaks(ə)n‖ˈwæks(ə)n/ *adj* **1** made of or covered with wax **2** resembling wax, esp in being pliable, smooth, or pallid

ˈwaxˌwork /-ˌwuhk‖-ˌwɜːk/ *n* **1** an effigy in wax, usu of a person **2** *pl but sing or pl in constr* an exhibition of wax effigies

waxy /ˈwaksi‖ˈwæksɪ/ *adj* **1** made of, full of, or covered with wax **2** resembling wax, esp in smooth whiteness or pliability – **waxiness** *n*

[1]**way** /way‖weɪ/ *n* **1a** a thoroughfare for travel or transport from place to place **b** an opening for passage <*this door is the only* ~ *out*> **c** space or room, esp for forward movement <*get out of the* ~*!*> **2** the course to be travelled from one place to another;a route <*ask one's* ~ *to the station*> **3a** a course leading in a direction or towards an objective <*took the easy* ~ *out*> **b** the course of one's life <*puts opportunities in her* ~> **c** what one desires, or wants to do <*always manages to get her own* ~> **4a** the manner in which sthg is done or happens <*the British* ~ *of life*> **b** a method of doing or accomplishing; a means <*the best* ~ *to make coffee*> **c** a characteristic, regular, or habitual manner or mode of being, behaving, or happening <~s *of the world*> **d** a feature, respect <*useful in more* ~s *than one*> **5** a category, kind <*porridge is all right in its* ~> **6** the distance to be travelled in order to reach a place or point <*a long* ~ *from home*> **7** an advance accompanied by or achieved through a specific action <*hacked his* ~ *through the jungle*> **8a** a direction – often in combination <*come this* ~> <*a one*-way *street*> **b** (the direction of) the area in which one lives <*do drop in if you're ever down our* ~> **9** a state of affairs; a condition <*my finances are in a bad* ~> **10** *pl but sometimes sing in constr* an inclined structure on which a ship is built or supported in launching **11** motion or speed of a ship or boat through the water – **by the way** incidentally – usu used to introduce or to comment on the introduction of a new subject – **by way of 1** to be considered as; as a sort of <by way of *light relief*> **2** by the route through; via **3** in the form of <*money recovered* by way of *grants*> – **in a way** from one point of view; to some extent – **in the way of** in the form of <*what have we* in the way *of food?*> – **no way** under no circumstances – infml – **on one's way** ON THE WAY 1 – **on the way 1** while moving along a course; in the course of travelling **2** coming, approaching; *specif* conceived but not yet born – **on the way out** about to disappear or die – **out of the way 1** unusual, remarkable <*didn't know he'd said anything* out of the way> **2** in or to a secluded or remote place **3** done, completed <*got his homework* out of the way> – **under way** in progress; started

[2]**way** *adv* **1** AWAY 7 <*is* ~ *ahead of the class*> **2** *chiefly NAm* all the way <*pull the switch* ~ *back*> – **way back** long ago <*friends from* way back>

ˈwayˌbill /-ˌbil‖-ˌbɪl/ *n* a document showing the number of passengers or parcels carried and the fares charged

ˈwayˌfarer /-ˌfeərə‖-ˌfeərə/ *n* a traveller, esp on foot

waylay /wayˈlay‖weɪˈleɪ/ *vt* **waylaid** /way-ˈlayd‖weɪˈleɪd/ **1** to attack from ambush **2** to accost

ˌway-ˈout *adj* far-out – infml

ways /wayz‖weɪz/ *n pl but sing in constr, NAm* WAY 6 <*a long* ~ *from home*>

-ways /-wayz‖-weɪz/ *suffix* (→ *adv*) in (such) a way, direction, or manner <*side*ways> <*length*ways>

ˌways and ˈmeans *n pl* **1** methods and resources for accomplishing sthg, esp for paying expenses **2** *often cap W&M* methods and resources for raising revenue for the use of government

ˈwayˌside /-ˌsied‖-ˌsaɪd/ *n* the side of or land adjacent to a road – **wayside** *adj*

ˈwayward /-wood‖-wʊd/ *adj* **1** following one's own capricious or wanton inclinations; ungovernable **2** following no clear principle or law; unpredictable – **waywardly** *adv*, **waywardness** *n*

we /wi‖wɪ; *strong* wee‖wiː/ *pron pl in constr* **1** I and the rest of a group; you and I; you and I and another or others; I and another or others not including you **2** I – used, esp formerly, by sovereigns; used by writers to maintain an impersonal character **3** YOU 1 – used esp to children and the sick <*how are* ~ *feeling today, Mr Jones?*>

weak /week‖wiːk/ *adj* **1a** deficient in physical vigour; feeble **b** not able to sustain or exert much weight, pressure, or strain **c** not able to resist external force or withstand attack **2a** lacking determination or decisiveness; ineffectual **b** unable to withstand temptation or persuasion **3** not factually grounded or logically presented <*a* ~ *argument*> **4a** unable to function properly <~ *eyes*> **b** lacking skill or proficiency **c** wanting in vigour or strength **5a** deficient in a specified quality or ingredient <~ *in trumps*> **b** lacking normal intensity or potency <~ *strain of virus*> **c** mentally or intellectually deficient **d** deficient in strength or flavour; dilute <~ *coffee*> **6** not having or exerting authority or political power <~ *government*> **7** of or constituting a verb (conjugation) that in English forms inflections by adding the suffix *-ed* or *-d* or *-t* **8** UNSTRESSED 1 **9** characterized by falling prices <*a* ~ *market*> **10** ionizing only slightly in solution <~ *acids and bases*> – **weaken** *vb*, **weakish** *adj*, **weakly** *adv*

ˌweak-ˈkneed *adj* lacking in resolution; easily intimidated

weakling /ˈweekling‖ˈwiːklɪŋ/ *n* a person or animal weak in body, character, or mind

weakness /ˈweeknis‖ˈwiːknɪs/ *n* **1** a fault, defect **2** (an object of) a special desire or fondness

weal, wheal /weel‖wiːl/ *n* WELT 3, [2]SCAR 1

wealth /welth‖welθ/ *n* **1** the state of being rich **2** abundance of money and valuable material possessions **3** abundant supply; a profusion <*a* ~ *of detail*> – **wealthy** *adj*, **wealthily** *adv*, **wealthiness** *n*

wean /ween‖wiːn/ *vt* **1** to accustom (a child or other young mammal) to take food other than mother's milk **2** to cause to abandon a state of usu unwholesome dependence or preoccupation **3** to cause to become acquainted with an idea, writer, etc at an early age; bring up *on*

weapon /ˈwepən‖ˈwepən/ *n* **1** an instrument

of offensive or defensive combat **2** a means used to further one's cause in conflict <*his caustic wit was his best* ~>

ˈ**weaponry** /-ri‖-rɪ/ *n* (the science of designing and making) weapons

[1]**wear** /weə‖weə/ *vb* **wore** /waw‖wɔː/; **worn** /wawn‖wɔːn/ *vt* **1a** to have or carry on the body as clothing or adornment <wore *a coat*> **b** to dress in (a particular manner, colour, or garment), esp habitually <~ *green*> **c** to have (hair) in a specified style **2** to hold the rank, dignity, or position signified by (an ornament) <~ *the royal crown*> **3a** to have or show on the face <wore *a happy smile*> **b** to show or fly (a flag or colours) on a ship **4** to impair, damage, or diminish by use or friction <*letters on the stone* worn *away by weathering*> **5** to produce gradually by friction or attrition <~ *a hole in the rug*> **6** to exhaust or lessen the strength of; weary **7** to cause (a ship, esp a square-rigged vessel) to go about with the stern presented to the wind **8** *chiefly Br* to find (a claim, proposal etc) acceptable; STAND FOR – infml <*just won't* ~ *that feeble excuse*> ~ *vi* **1a** to endure use, esp to a specified degree; last <*this material* ~s *well*> **b** to retain vitality or young appearance to a specified degree <*you've* worn *well*> **2a** to diminish or decay through use **b** to go by slowly or tediously <*the day* ~s *on*> **c** to grow or become by attrition, use, or the passage of time <*hair* ~ing *thin*> **3** *of a ship, esp a square-rigged vessel* to change to an opposite tack by turning the stern to the wind – **wearable** *adj*, **wearer** *n* – **wear the trousers** to have the controlling authority in a household – **wear thin 1** to become weak or ready to give way <*his patience was* wearing thin> **2** to become trite, unconvincing, or out-of-date <*that argument's* wearing *a bit* thin>

[2]**wear** *n* **1** wearing or being worn **2** clothing, usu of a specified kind <*men's* ~>; *esp* clothing worn for a specified occasion – often in combination <*swim*wear> **3** capacity to withstand use; durability <*plenty of* ~ *left in it*> **4** minor damage or deterioration through use

ˌ**wear and** ˈ**tear** *n* the normal deterioration or depreciation which sthg suffers in the course of use

wear down *vt* to weary and overcome by persistent resistance or pressure

wearing /ˈweəring‖ˈweərɪŋ/ *adj* causing fatigue; tiring – **wearingly** *adv*

wearisome /ˈwiəris(ə)m‖ˈwɪərɪs(ə)m/ *adj* causing weariness; tiresome – **wearisomely** *adv*, **wearisomeness** *n*

wear off *vi* to decrease gradually and finally end <*the effect of the drug* wore off>

wear out *vt* **1** to make useless by long or excessive wear or use **2** to tire, exhaust ~*vi* to become useless from long or excessive wear or use

[1]**weary** /ˈwiəri‖ˈwɪərɪ/ *adj* **1** exhausted, tired **2** expressing or characteristic of weariness <*a* ~ *smile*> **3** having one's patience, tolerance, or pleasure exhausted – + *of* **4** wearisome – **wearily** *adv*, **weariness** *n*

[2]**weary** *vb* to make or become weary

weasel /ˈweezl‖ˈwiːzl/ *n*, any of various small slender flesh-eating mammals with reddish-brown fur which, in northern forms, turns white in winter

[1]**weather** /ˈwedhə‖ˈweðə/ *n* the prevailing (bad) atmospheric conditions, esp with regard to heat or cold, wetness or dryness, calm or storm, and clearness or cloudiness – **under the weather** mildly ill or depressed; not fully well – infml

[2]**weather** *adj* windward

[3]**weather** *vt* **1** to expose or subject to atmospheric conditions **2** to sail or pass to the windward of **3** to bear up against and come safely through <~ *a storm*> ~*vi* to undergo or be resistant to change by weathering

ˈ**weather-**ˌ**beaten** *adj* **1** worn or damaged by exposure to weather **2** toughened or tanned by the weather

ˈ**weather**ˌ**board** /-ˌbawd‖-ˌbɔːd/ *n* **1** a board fixed horizontally and usu overlapping the board below to form a protective outdoor wall covering that will throw off water **2** a sloping board fixed to the bottom of a door for excluding rain, snow, etc

ˈ**weather-**ˌ**bound** *adj* unable to proceed or take place because of bad weather

ˈ**weather**ˌ**cock** /-ˌkok‖-ˌkɒk/ *n* WEATHER VANE; *esp* one in the figure of a cockerel

ˈ**weather**ˌ**glass** /-ˌglahs‖-ˌglɑːs/ *n* a barometer

ˈ**weather**ˌ**man** /-ˌman‖-ˌmæn/ *n* sby, esp a meteorologist, who reports and forecasts the weather, usu on the radio or television

ˈ**weather**ˌ**proof** /-ˌproohf‖-ˌpruːf/ *adj* able to withstand exposure to weather without damage or loss of function – **weatherproof** *vt*, **weatherproofness** *n*

ˈ**weather** ˌ**ship** *n* a ship that makes observations on weather conditions for use by meteorologists

ˈ**weather** ˌ**station** *n* a station for taking, recording, and reporting meteorological observations

ˈ**weather** ˌ**vane** *n* a movable device attached to an elevated structure (e g a spire) in order to show the direction of the wind

[1]**weave** /weev‖wiːv/ *vb* **wove** /wove‖wɒve/, **weaved; woven** /ˈwohv(ə)n‖ˈwəʊv(ə)n/, **weaved** *vt* **1a** to form (cloth) by interlacing strands (e g of yarn), esp on a loom **b** to interlace (e g threads) into a fabric, design, etc **c** to make (e g a basket) by intertwining **2** *of spiders and insects* SPIN 2 **3a** to produce by elaborately combining elements into a coherent whole **b** to introduce; work in – usu + *in* or *into* ~*vi* to work at weaving; make cloth

[2]**weave** *n* a pattern or method for interlacing the threads of woven fabrics

[3]**weave** *vb* **weaved** *vt* to direct (e g the body or one's way) in a winding or zigzag course, esp to avoid obstacles ~*vi* to move by weaving

weaver /ˈweevə‖ˈwiːvə/ *n* **1** sby who weaves, esp as an occupation **2 weaver, weaverbird** any of numerous Old World birds that resemble finches and usu construct elaborate nests of interlaced vegetation

[1]**web** /web‖web/ *n* **1** a woven fabric; *esp* a length of fabric still on the loom **2** SPIDER'S WEB; *also* a similar network spun by various insects **3**

a tissue or membrane; *esp* that uniting fingers or toes either at their bases (e g in human beings) or for most of their length (e g in many water birds) **4** a thin metal sheet, plate, or strip (e g joining the upper and lower flanges of a girder or rail) **5** an intricate structure suggestive of sthg woven; a network **6** a continuous sheet of paper for use in a printing press – **webbed** *adj*, **webby** *adj*, **weblike** *adj*

[2]**web** *vb* **-bb-** *vt* **1** to cover with a web or network **2** to entangle, ensnare ~ *vi* to construct or form a web

webbing /ˈwebing‖ˈwebɪŋ/ *n* a strong narrow closely woven tape used esp for straps, upholstery, or harnesses

ˈweb͵foot /-͵foot‖-͵fʊt/ *n* a foot with webbed toes – **web-footed** *adj*

͵web ˈoffset *n* offset printing by web press

web press *n* a press that prints a continuous roll of paper

wed /wed‖wed/ *vb* **-dd-; wedded** *also* **wed** *vt* **1** to marry **2** to unite as if by marriage ~ *vi* to enter into matrimony

we'd /wid‖wɪd; *strong* weed‖wi:d/ we had; we would; we should

wedded /ˈwedid‖ˈwedɪd/ *adj* **1** joined in marriage **2** conjugal, connubial <~ *bliss*> **3** strongly emotionally attached; committed *to*

wedding /ˈweding‖ˈwedɪŋ/ *n* **1** a marriage ceremony, usu with its accompanying festivities; nuptials **2** a joining in close association **3** a wedding anniversary or its celebration – usu in combination <*golden* ~>

wedding breakfast *n* a celebratory meal that follows a marriage ceremony

ˈwedding ͵ring *n* a ring usu of plain metal (e g gold) given by 1 marriage partner to the other during the wedding ceremony and worn thereafter to signify marital status

[1]**wedge** /wej‖wedʒ/ *n* **1** a piece of wood, metal, etc tapered to a thin edge and used esp for splitting wood or raising heavy objects **2a** sthg wedge-shaped <*a* ~ *of pie*> **b** (a shoe with) a wedge-shaped sole raised at the heel and tapering towards the toe **c** an iron golf club with a broad face angled for maximum loft **3** sthg causing a breach or separation

[2]**wedge** *vt* **1** to fasten or tighten by driving in a wedge **2** to force or press into a narrow space; cram – usu + *in* or *into* **3** to split or force apart (as if) with a wedge

Wedgwood /ˈwejwood‖ˈwedʒwʊd/ *trademark* – used for pottery (e g earthenware, stoneware, or bone china) made by Josiah Wedgwood and his successors and typically decorated with a classical cameo-like design in white relief

wedlock /ˈwedlok‖ˈwedlɒk/ *n* the state of being married; marriage – **out of wedlock** with the natural parents not legally married to each other

Wednesday /ˈwenzday, -di, ˈwednz-‖ˈwenzdeɪ, -dɪ, ˈwednz-/ *n* the day of the week following Tuesday [Old English *wōdnesdæg*, fr *Wōden* Odin, the chief god in Germanic mythology + *dæg* day]

[1]**wee** /wee‖wi:/ *adj* very small; diminutive – often used to or by children or to convey an impression of Scottishness

[2]**wee** *n* (an act of passing) urine – used esp by or to children – **wee** *vi*

[1]**weed** /weed‖wi:d/ *n* **1** an unwanted wild plant which often overgrows or chokes out more desirable plants **2a** an obnoxious growth or thing **b** an animal, esp a horse, unfit to breed from **3** *Br* a weedy person – infml **4a** TOBACCO 2 – chiefly humor; usu + *the* **b** MARIJUANA 2 – slang; usu + *the*

[2]**weed** *vi* to remove weeds or sthg harmful ~ *vt* **1** to clear of weeds <~ *a garden*> **2** to remove the undesirable parts of <~ *the files*> – **weeder** *n*

weed out *vt* to get rid of (sby or sthg harmful or unwanted); remove

weeds /weedz‖wi:dz/ *n pl* MOURNING 2a

weedy /ˈweedi‖ˈwi:dɪ/ *adj* **1** covered with or consisting of weeds **2** noticeably weak, thin, and ineffectual – infml – **weediness** *n*

week /week‖wi:k/ *n* **1a** any of several 7-day cycles used in various calendars **b** a week beginning with a specified day or containing a specified event **2a** a period of 7 consecutive days **b** the working days during each 7-day period **c** a weekly period of work <*works a 40-hour* ~> **3** a time 7 days before or after a specified day <*next Sunday* ~> – **week in, week out** for an indefinite or seemingly endless number of weeks

ˈweekday /-day‖-deɪ/ *n* any day of the week except (Saturday and) Sunday

weekend /͵weekˈend, ˈ-͵-‖͵wi:kˈend, ˈ-͵-/ *n* the end of the week; *specif* the period from Friday night to Sunday night

[1]**weekly** /ˈweekli‖ˈwi:klɪ/ *adv* every week; once a week; by the week

[2]**weekly** *adj* **1** occurring, appearing, or done weekly **2** calculated by the week

[3]**weekly** *n* a weekly newspaper or periodical

ˈweek͵night /-͵niet‖-͵naɪt/ *n* a night of any day of the week except Saturday and Sunday

weeny /ˈweeni‖ˈwi:nɪ/ *also* **weensy** /ˈweenzi‖ˈwi:nzɪ/ *adj* exceptionally small; tiny – infml

[1]**weep** /weep‖wi:p/ *vb* **wept** /wept‖wept/ *vt* **1** to express deep sorrow for, usu by shedding tears; bewail **2** to pour forth (tears) from the eyes **3** to exude (a fluid) slowly; ooze ~ *vi* **1a** to express passion (e g grief) by shedding tears **b** to mourn *for* sby or sthg **2** to give off or leak fluid slowly; ooze

[2]**weep** *n* a fit of weeping

weeping /ˈweeping‖ˈwi:pɪŋ/ *adj, of a tree* (being a variety) having slender drooping branches

weepy /ˈweepi‖ˈwi:pɪ/ *adj* inclined to weep; tearful

weevil /ˈweevl‖ˈwi:vl/ *n* any of numerous usu small beetles with a long snout bearing jaws at the tip, many of which are injurious, esp as larvae, to grain, fruit, etc – **weevily, weevilly** *adj*

weft /weft‖weft/ *n* the thread or yarn that interlaces the warp in a fabric; the crosswise yarn in weaving

weigh /way‖weɪ/ *vt* **1** to ascertain the weight of (as if) on a scale **2** to consider carefully; evaluate – often + *up* **3** to measure (a definite quantity) (as if) on a scale – often + *out* ~ *vi* **1a** to have weight or a specified weight **b** to register a weight (e g on a scale) – + *in* or *out*; compare WEIGH IN 1, WEIGH OUT **2** to merit consideration as important; count <*evidence will* ~

heavily against him> **3** to be a burden or cause of anxiety to – often + *on* or *upon* <*her responsibilities* ~ed *upon her*> – **weighable** *adj*, **weigher** *n* – **weigh anchor** to pull up an anchor preparatory to sailing

ˈweighˌbridge /-ˌbrij‖-ˌbrɪdʒ/ *n* a large scale used for weighing vehicles which usu consists of a plate level with the surface of a road onto which the vehicles are driven

weigh down *vt* **1** to make heavy; weight **2** to oppress, burden

weigh in *vi* **1** to have oneself or one's possessions (e g luggage) weighed; *esp* to be weighed after a horse race or before a boxing or wrestling match **2** to make a contribution; join in <*a bystander* weighed in *to stop the fight*> – **weigh-in** *n*

weigh out *vi* to be weighed after a boxing or wrestling match

[1]**weight** /wayt‖weɪt/ *n* **1a** the amount that a quantity or body weighs, esp as measured on a particular scale **b(1)** any of the classes into which contestants in certain sports (e g boxing and wrestling) are divided according to body weight **b(2)** a horse carrying a usu specified weight in a handicap race <*the top* ~ *won the race*> **b(3)** poundage required to be carried by a horse in a handicap race **2a** a quantity weighing a certain amount <*equal* ~s *of flour and sugar*> **b** a heavy object thrown or lifted as an athletic exercise or contest **3a** a system of units of weight <*troy* ~> **b** any of the units of weight used in such a system **c** a piece of material (e g metal) of known weight for use in weighing articles **4a** sthg heavy; a load **b** a heavy object to hold or press sthg down or to counterbalance <*the* ~s *of the clock*> **5a** a burden, pressure <*took a* ~ *off my mind*> **b** corpulence **6a** relative heaviness <~ *is a quality of material substances*> **b** the force with which a body is attracted towards a celestial body (e g the earth) by gravitation and which is equal to the product of the mass of the body and the local gravitational acceleration **7a** relative importance, authority, or influence <*his views don't carry much* ~> **b** *the* main force or strength <*the* ~ *of the argument*> **8** a numerical value assigned to an item to express its relative importance in a frequency distribution

[2]**weight** *vt* **1** to load or make heavy (as if) with a weight **2** to oppress with a burden <~ed *down with cares*> **3** to assign a statistical weight to **4** to arrange in such a way as to create a bias <*a wage structure* ~ed *heavily in favour of employees with long service*>

weighting /ˈwayting‖ˈweɪtɪŋ/ *n*, *Br* an additional sum paid on top of wages; *esp* one paid to offset the higher cost of living in a particular area <*a London* ~ *of £500*>

ˈweightless /-lis‖-lɪs/ *adj* having little weight; lacking apparent gravitational pull – **weightlessly** *adv*, **weightlessness** *n*

ˈweight-ˌlifter *n* one who lifts heavy weights, esp barbells, in competition or as an exercise – **weight-lifting** *n*

weighty /ˈwayti‖ˈweɪtɪ/ *adj* **1** of much importance, influence, or consequence; momentous **2** heavy, esp in proportion to bulk **3** burdensome, onerous – **weightily** *adv*, **weightiness** *n*

weir /wiə‖wɪə/ *n* **1** a fence or enclosure set in a waterway for trapping fish **2** a dam in a stream to raise the water level or control its flow

weird /wiəd‖wɪəd/ *adj* **1** of or caused by witchcraft or the supernatural **2** of a strange or extraordinary character; odd – infml – **weirdly** *adv*, **weirdness** *n*

weirdie, **weirdy** /ˈwiədi‖ˈwɪədɪ/ *n* sby who is very strange or eccentric – infml

weirdo /ˈwiədoh‖ˈwɪədəʊ/ *n*, *pl* **weirdos** a weirdie – infml

welch /welch‖weltʃ/ *vi* to welsh – **welcher** *n*

[1]**welcome** /ˈwelkəm‖ˈwelkəm/ *interj* – used to express a greeting to a guest or newcomer on his/her arrival

[2]**welcome** *vt* **1** to greet hospitably and with courtesy **2** to greet or receive in the specified, esp unpleasant, way <*they* ~d *the intruder with a hail of bullets*> **3** to receive or accept with pleasure – **welcomer** *n* – **welcome with open arms** to greet or accept with great cordiality or pleasure

[3]**welcome** *adj* **1** received gladly into one's presence or companionship <*was always* ~ *in their home*> **2** giving pleasure; received with gladness, esp because fulfilling a need <*a* ~ *relief*> **3** willingly permitted or given the right <*you're* ~ *to read it*> **4** – used in the phrase 'You're welcome' as a reply to an expression of thanks – **welcomely** *adv*, **welcomeness** *n*

[4]**welcome** *n* **1** a greeting or reception on arrival or first appearance **2** the hospitable treatment that a guest may expect <*outstayed their* ~>

[1]**weld** /weld‖weld/ *vi* to become or be capable of being welded ~ *vt* **1a** to fuse (metallic parts) together by heating and allowing the metals to flow together or by hammering or compressing with or without previous heating **b** to unite (plastics) in a similar manner by heating or by using a chemical solvent **c** to repair, produce, or create (as if) by such a process **2** to unite closely or inseparably – **weldable** *adj*, **welder** *n*, **weldability** *n*

[2]**weld** *n* a welded joint

welfare /ˈwelfeə‖ˈwelfeə/ *n* **1** well-being <*concerned for her child's* ~> **2** WELFARE WORK **3** aid in the form of money or necessities for those not well able to provide for themselves (e g through poverty, age, or handicap)

ˌwelfare ˈstate *n* (a country operating) a social system based on the assumption by the state of responsibility for the individual and social welfare of its citizens

ˈwelfare ˌwork *n* organized efforts to improve the living conditions of the poor, elderly, etc – **welfare worker** *n*

welkin /ˈwelkin‖ˈwelkɪn/ *n* **1a** *the* sky, firmament **b** heaven **2** the upper atmosphere *USE* poetic

[1]**well** /wel‖wel/ *n* **1** (a pool fed by) a spring of water **2** a pit or hole sunk into the earth to reach a supply of water **3** an enclosure round the pumps of a ship **4** a shaft or hole sunk in the earth to reach a natural deposit (e g oil or gas) **5** an open space extending vertically through floors of a structure <*a stair* ~> **6** a vessel, space, or hole having a construction or shape

suggesting a well for water **7** a source from which sthg springs; a fountainhead **8** *Br* the open space in front of the judge in a law court

[2]**well** *vi* **1** to rise to the surface and usu flow forth <*tears* ~ed *from her eyes*> **2** to rise to the surface like a flood of liquid <*longing* ~ed *up in his breast*>

[3]**well** *adv* **better** /ˈbetə‖ˈbetə/; **best** /best‖best/ **1** in a good or proper manner; rightly **2** in a way appropriate to the circumstances: e g **2a** satisfactorily, advantageously **b** with good appearance or effect <*carried himself* ~> **c** with skill or aptitude <~ *caught!*> **d** with prudence; sensibly <*would do* ~ *to ask*> **3** in a kind or friendly manner; favourably <*spoke* ~ *of your idea*> **4** in a prosperous manner <*he lives* ~> **5a** to an extent approaching completeness; thoroughly <*after being* ~ *dried with a towel*> **b** on a close personal level; intimately <*knew her* ~> **6a** easily, fully <~ *worth the price*> **b** much, considerably <~ *over a million*> **c** in all likelihood; indeed <*may* ~ *be true*> – **as well 1** also; IN ADDITION **2** to the same extent or degree <*open* as well *to the poor as to the rich*> **3** with equivalent or preferable effect <*you may* as well *tell him*> **4** [5]WELL 2, 4 – **as well as** [2]BESIDES 2 <*skilful* as well as *strong*> – **well and truly** totally, completely – **well away 1** making good progress **2** (almost) DRUNK 1 – infml – **well out of** lucky to be free from

[4]**well** *interj* **1** – used to express surprise, indignation, or resignation **2** – used to indicate a pause in talking or to introduce a remark

[5]**well** *adj* **1** satisfactory, pleasing <*all's* ~ *that ends* ~> **2** advisable, desirable <*it's* ~ *to ask*> **3** prosperous, well-off **4** HEALTHY 1 **5** being a cause for thankfulness; fortunate <*it is* ~ *that this has happened*> – **wellness** *n*

we'll /weel‖wiːl/ we will; we shall

ˌwell-adˈvised *adj* **1** acting with wisdom; prudent **2** resulting from or showing wisdom <~ *plans*>

ˌwell-apˈpointed *adj* having good and complete facilities, furniture, etc <*a* ~ *house*>

ˌwell-ˈbeing *n* the state of being happy, healthy, or prosperous

ˌwellˈborn /-ˈbawn‖-ˈbɔːn/ *adj* born of a respected and esp noble family

ˌwell-ˈbred *adj* **1** having or indicating good breeding; refined **2** of good pedigree

ˌwell-conˈnected *adj* having useful social or family contacts

ˌwell-diˈsposed *adj* having a favourable or sympathetic disposition

ˌwell-ˈdone *adj*, *of food* cooked thoroughly

ˌwell-ˈfounded *adj* based on good grounds or reasoning

ˌwell-ˈgroomed *adj* well dressed and scrupulously neat

ˌwell-ˈgrounded *adj* **1** having a good basic knowledge <~ *in Latin and Greek*> **2** well-founded

ˌwell-ˈheeled *adj* having a great deal of money; wealthy – infml

ˌwell-ˈhung *adj* **1** having large breasts **2** having a large penis *USE* vulg

ˌwell-inˈformed *adj* **1** having a good knowledge of a wide variety of subjects **2** having reliable information on a usu specified topic, event, etc

ˌwellington ˈboot, **wellington** /ˈweling-t(ə)n‖ˈwelɪŋt(ə)n/ *n, chiefly Br* a waterproof rubber boot that usu reaches the knee [Arthur Wellesley, 1st Duke of *Wellington* (1769-1852), British general & statesman]

ˌwell-inˈtentioned *adj* well-meaning

ˌwell-ˈknit *adj* well constructed; *esp* having a compact usu muscular physique <*a* ~ *athlete*>

ˌwell-ˈknown *adj* fully or widely known; *specif* famous

ˌwell-ˈlined *adj* full of money – infml <~ *pockets*>

ˌwell-ˈmeaning *adj* having or based on good intentions though often failing

ˌwell-ˈmeant *adj* based on good intentions

ˌwell-ˈnigh *adv* almost, nearly

ˌwell-ˈoff *adj* **1** well-to-do, rich **2** in a favourable or fortunate situation **3** well provided <*not very* ~ *for sheets*>

ˌwell-ˈoiled *adj, chiefly Br* DRUNK 1 – infml

ˌwell-preˈserved *adj* retaining a youthful appearance

ˌwell-ˈread /red‖red/ *adj* well-informed through much and varied reading

ˌwell-ˈrounded *adj* **1** having a pleasantly curved or rounded shape <*a* ~ *figure*> **2** having or consisting of a background of broad experience or education <*a* ~ *person*> **3** agreeably complete and well-constructed

ˌwell-ˈspoken *adj* **1** speaking clearly, courteously, and usu with a refined accent **2** spoken in a pleasing or fitting manner <~ *words*>

ˈwellˌspring /-ˌspring‖-ˌsprɪŋ/ *n* **1** a source of continual supply **2** FOUNTAINHEAD 1

ˌwell-ˈthought-of *adj* of good repute

ˌwell-ˈtimed *adj* said or done at an opportune moment; timely

ˌwell-to-ˈdo *adj* moderately rich; prosperous

ˌwell-ˈtried *adj* thoroughly tested and found reliable

ˌwell-ˈturned *adj* **1** pleasingly formed; shapely <*a* ~ *ankle*> **2** concisely and appropriately expressed <*a* ~ *compliment*>

ˈwell-ˌwisher *n* one who feels goodwill towards a person, cause, etc – **well-wishing** *adj or n*

ˌwell-ˈworn *adj* **1** having been much used or worn **2** made trite by overuse; hackneyed

welly /ˈweli‖ˈwelɪ/ *n* WELLINGTON BOOT – infml

welsh /welsh‖welʃ/ *vi* **1** to evade an obligation, esp payment of a debt **2** to break one's word *USE* usu + *on* – **welsher** *n*

Welsh *n* **1** *pl in constr* the people of Wales **2** the Celtic language of the Welsh – **Welsh** *adj*, **Welshman** *n*

ˌWelsh ˈrabbit *n* WELSH RAREBIT

ˌWelsh ˈrarebit /ˈreəbit‖ˈreəbɪt/ *n* a snack of melted cheese (and ale) on toast

[1]**welt** /welt‖welt/ *n* **1** a strip, usu of leather, between a shoe sole and upper through which they are fastened together **2** a doubled edge, strip, insert, or seam (e g on a garment) for ornament or reinforcement **3** (a ridge or lump raised on the body usu by) a heavy blow

[2]**welt** *vt* **1** to provide with a welt **2a** to raise a welt on the body of **b** to hit hard

weltanschauung /ˈveltahn͵showəng‖ ˈveltɑːn͵ʃaʊəŋ/ *n, pl* **weltanschauungs, weltanschauungen** /-əng·ən‖-əŋən/ *often cap* a philosophy of life [German, fr *welt* world + *anschauung* view]

[1]**welter** /ˈweltə‖ˈweltə/ *vi* **1** to writhe, toss; *also* to wallow **2** to become soaked, sunk, or involved *in* sthg

[2]**welter** *n* **1** a state of wild disorder; a turmoil **2** a chaotic mass or jumble

ˈ**welter͵weight** /-͵wayt‖-͵weɪt/ *n* a boxer who weighs not more than 10st 7lb (66.7kg) if professional or above 63.5kg (about 10st) but not more than 67kg (about 10st 8lb) if amateur

wen /wen‖wen/ *n* a cyst formed by obstruction of a sebaceous gland and filled with fatty material

wench /wench‖wentʃ/ *n* **1** a female servant or rustic working girl **2** a young woman; a girl – now chiefly humor or dial

wend /wend‖wend/ *vt* to proceed on (one's way)

ˈ**wendy** ͵**house** /ˈwendi‖ˈwendɪ/ *n, often cap W, chiefly Br* a small toy house for children to play in [*Wendy*, character in *Peter Pan*, children's book by J M Barrie (1860-1937), Scottish writer]

Wensleydale /ˈwenzli͵dayl‖ˈwenzlɪ͵deɪl/ *n* a crumbly mild-flavoured English cheese [*Wensleydale*, district in Yorkshire]

went /went‖went/ *past of* GO

were /wə‖wə; *strong* wuh‖wɜː/ *past 2 sing, past pl, substandard past 1 & 3 sing, or past subjunctive of* BE

we're /wiə‖wɪə/ we are

werewolf /ˈweə͵woolf, ˈwiə-‖ˈweə͵wʊlf, ˈwɪə-/ *n, pl* **werewolves** /-woolvz‖-wʊlvz/ a person transformed into a wolf or capable of assuming a wolf's form [Old English *werwulf*, fr *wer* man + *wulf* wolf]

wert /wuht‖wɜːt/ *archaic past 2 sing of* BE

Wesleyanism /ˈwezli·ə͵niz(ə)m‖ˈwezlɪə͵nɪz(ə)m/ *n* Methodism [John *Wesley* (1703-91), English preacher] – **Wesleyan** *adj or n*

[1]**west** /west‖west/ *adj or adv* towards, at, belonging to, or coming from the west

[2]**west** *n* **1** (the compass point corresponding to) the direction 90° to the left of north that is the general direction of sunset **2** *often cap* regions or countries lying to the west of a specified or implied point of orientation: e g **2a** the part of the USA to the west of the Mississippi **b** the non-Communist countries of Europe and America **3** European civilization in contrast with that of the Orient – **westward** *adv, adj, or n*, **westwards** *adv*

͵**West** ˈ**End** *n the* western part of central London where the main shopping centres, theatres, etc are located – **West-End** *adj*

[1]**westerly** /ˈwestəli‖ˈwestəlɪ/ *adj or adv* west

[2]**westerly** *n* a wind from the west

[1]**western** /ˈwestən‖ˈwestən/ *adj* **1** *often cap* (characteristic) of a region conventionally designated West: e g **1a** of or stemming from European traditions in contrast with those of the Orient **b** of the non-Communist countries of Europe and America **c** of the American West **2** west **3** *cap* of the Roman Catholic or Protestant segment of Christianity – **westernmost** *adj*

[2]**western** *n, often cap* a novel, film, etc dealing with cowboys, frontier life, etc in the W USA, esp during the latter half of the 19th c

Westerner /ˈwestənə‖ˈwestənə/ *n, chiefly NAm* a native or inhabitant of the West, esp the W USA

western·ize, -ise /ˈwestəniez‖ˈwestənaɪz/ *vb* to imbue or be imbued with qualities associated with the West – **westernization** *n*

͵**West** ˈ**Indian** *n* **1** a native or inhabitant of the W Indies **2** a descendant of W Indians – **West Indian** *adj*

[1]**wet** /wet‖wet/ *adj* **-tt- 1** consisting of, containing, or covered or soaked with liquid (e g water) **2** rainy **3** still moist enough to smudge or smear <~ *paint*> **4** involving the use or presence of liquid <~ *processes*> **5** *of an aircraft wing* containing fuel tanks **6** *chiefly Br* feebly ineffectual or dull; *also, of a politician* moderate – infml **7** *chiefly NAm* permitting the sale or consumption of alcoholic drink <*a* ~ *State*> [Old English *wǣt*; akin to Old English *wæter* water – see WATER] – **wetly** *adv*, **wetness** *n*, **wettish** *adj* – **wet behind the ears** immature, inexperienced – infml

[2]**wet** *n* **1** moisture, wetness **2** rainy weather; rain **3** *chiefly Br* a wet person; a drip; *also* a moderate (Conservative) politician – infml

[3]**wet** *vt* **-tt-**; (2) **wet 1** to make wet **2** to urinate in or on – **wettable** *adj*, **wettability** *n* – **wet one's whistle** to take an esp alcoholic drink – infml

͵**wet** ˈ**blanket** *n* one who quenches or dampens enthusiasm or pleasure

͵**wet** ˈ**dream** *n* an erotic dream culminating in orgasm

wether /ˈwedhə‖ˈweðə/ *n* a male sheep castrated before sexual maturity

wet-nurse /ˈ-͵-, ͵-ˈ-/ *vt* **1** to act as wet nurse to **2** to give constant and often excessive care to

ˈ**wet** ͵**nurse** *n* a woman who cares for and suckles another's children

ˈ**wet** ͵**suit** *n* a close-fitting suit made of material, usu rubber, that admits water but retains body heat so as to insulate its wearer (e g a skin diver), esp in cold water

ˈ**wetting** ͵**agent** /ˈweting‖ˈwetɪŋ/ *n* a substance that prevents a surface from being repellent to a wetting liquid

we've /wiv‖wɪv; *strong* weev‖wiːv/ we have

[1]**whack** /wak‖wæk/ *vt* **1** to strike with a smart or resounding blow **2** *chiefly Br* to get the better of; defeat *USE* infml – **whacker** *n*

[2]**whack** *n* **1** (the sound of) a smart resounding blow **2** a portion, share **3** an attempt, go <*have a* ~ *at it*> *USE* infml

whacked /wakt‖wækt/ *adj, chiefly Br* completely exhausted; DONE IN – infml

[1]**whacking** /ˈwaking‖ˈwækɪŋ/ *adj* extremely big; whopping – infml

[2]**whacking** *adv* very, extremely – infml <*a* ~ *great oil tanker*>

[1]**whale** /wayl‖weɪl/ *n*, any of an order of often enormous aquatic mammals that superficially resemble large fish, have tails modified as paddles, and are frequently hunted for oil, flesh, or whalebone – **whale of a time** an exceptionally enjoyable time

[2]**whale** *vi* to engage in whale fishing and processing

[3]**whale** *vt, NAm* to hit or defeat soundly – infml

ˈ**whaleˌbone** /-ˌbohn‖-ˌbəʊn/ *n* a horny substance found in 2 rows of plates up to 4m (about 12ft) long attached along the upper jaw of whalebone whales and used for stiffening things

whaler /ˈwaylə‖ˈweɪlə/ *n* a person or ship engaged in whaling

whaling /ˈwayling‖ˈweɪlɪŋ/ *n* the occupation of catching and processing whales for oil, food, etc

[1]**wham** /wam‖wæm/ *n* (the sound made by) a forceful blow – infml

[2]**wham** *interj* – used to express the noise of a forceful blow or impact; infml

[3]**wham** *vb* **-mm-** *vt* to throw or strike with a loud impact ~*vi* to crash or explode with a loud impact *USE* infml

wharf /wawf‖wɔːf/ *n, pl* **wharves** /wawvz‖wɔːvz/ *also* **wharfs** a structure built along or out from the shore of navigable water so that ships may load and unload

[1]**what** /wot‖wɒt/ *pron, pl* **what** **1a** – used as an interrogative expressing inquiry about the identity, nature, purpose, or value of sthg or the character, nature, occupation, position, or role of sby < ~ *is this?*> **b** – used as an exclamation expressing surprise or excitement and frequently introducing a question < ~, *no breakfast?*> **c** – used to direct attention to a statement that the speaker is about to make <*guess* ~ > **d** *chiefly Br* – used in demanding assent <*a clever play,* ~*?*>; not now in vogue **2** [4]THAT 1, WHICH 3, WHO 2 – substandard **3** that which; the one that <*no income but* ~ *he gets from his writing*> **4a** WHATEVER 1a <*say* ~ *you will*> **b** how much – used in exclamations < ~ *it must cost!*> – **or what** – used at the end of a question to express inquiry about additional possibilities <*is it raining, or snowing,* or what*?*> – **what about 1** what news or plans have you concerning **2** *also* **what do you say to, what's wrong with** let's; HOW ABOUT – **what for 1** for what purpose or reason; why **2** punishment, esp by blows or by a sharp reprimand <*gave him* what for> – **what have you** any of various other things that might also be mentioned <*paper clips, pins, and* what have you> – **what if 1** what will or would be the result if **2** what does it matter if – **what it takes** the qualities or resources needed for success or for attainment of a usu specified goal – **what not** WHAT HAVE YOU – **what of 1** what is the situation with respect to **2** what importance can be assigned to – **what of it** what does it matter – **what's what** the true state of things <*knows* what's what *when it comes to fashion*>

[2]**what** *adv* in what respect?; how much? < ~ *does he care?*>

[3]**what** *adj* **1a** – used with a following noun as an adjective equivalent in meaning to the interrogative pronoun *what* < ~ *minerals do we export?*> **b** WHICH 1 < ~ *size do you take?*> **c** how remarkable or striking – used esp in exclamatory utterances and dependent clauses < ~ *a suggestion!*> **2** the . . . that; as much or as many . . . as <*told him* ~ *little I knew*>

[1]**whatever** /wotˈevə‖wɒtˈevə/ *pron* **1a** anything or everything that <*take* ~ *you want*> **b** no matter what **2** what in the world? – infml < ~ *do you mean?*> – **or whatever** or anything else at all – infml <*buffalo or rhinoceros* or whatever – Alan Moorehead>

[2]**whatever** *adj* **1a** any . . . that; all . . . that <*buy peace on* ~ *terms could be obtained* – C S Forester> **b** no matter what **2** of any kind at all – used after a noun with *any* or with a negative <*of any shape* ~ >

whatnot /ˈwotˌnot‖ˈwɒtˌnɒt/ *n* **1** a lightweight open set of shelves for bric-a-brac **2** other usu related goods, objects, etc <*carrying all his bags and* ~ > **3** a whatsit *USE* (*2&3*) infml

whatsit /ˈwotsit‖ˈwɒtsɪt/ *n* sby or sthg that is of unspecified, nondescript, or unknown character, or whose name has been forgotten – infml

ˈ**what with** *prep* having as a contributory circumstance or circumstances <*very busy* what with *all these guests to feed*>

wheat /weet‖wiːt/ *n* (any of various grasses cultivated in most temperate areas for) a cereal grain that yields a fine white flour and is used for making bread and pasta, and in animal feeds

wheaten /ˈweet(ə)n‖ˈwiːt(ə)n/ *adj* made of (the grain, meal, or flour of) wheat

ˈ**wheat ˌgerm** *n* the embryo of the wheat kernel separated in milling and used esp as a source of vitamins

wheedle /ˈweedl‖ˈwiːdl/ *vb* **1** to influence or entice by soft words or flattery **2** to cause to part with sthg by wheedling – + *out of* < ~ *her out of her last £5*> ~*vi* to use soft words of flattery

[1]**wheel** /weel‖wiːl/ *n* **1** a circular frame of hard material that may be (partly) solid or spoked and that is capable of turning on an axle **2** a contrivance or apparatus having as its principal part a wheel: e g **2a** a chiefly medieval instrument of torture to which the victim was tied while his/her limbs were broken by a metal bar **b** any of various revolving discs or drums that produce an arbitrary value on which to gamble, usu by stopping at a particular number <*roulette* ~ > **3** sthg resembling a wheel in shape or motion; *esp* CATHERINE WHEEL **4a** a curving or circular movement **b** a rotation or turn, usu about an axis or centre; *specif* a turning movement of troops or ships in line in which the units preserve alignment and relative positions **5a** *pl* the workings or controlling forces of sthg <*the* ~s *of government*> **b** *chiefly NAm* a person of importance, esp in an organization <*a big* ~ > **6** *pl* a motor vehicle, esp a motor car *USE* (*5b&6*) infml

[2]**wheel** *vi* **1** to turn (as if) on an axis; revolve **2** to change direction as if revolving on a pivot < ~ed *round and walked away*> **3** to move or extend in a circle or curve <*birds in* ~ing *flight*> **4** to alter or reverse one's opinion – often + *about* or *round* ~ *vt* **1** to cause to turn (as if) on an axis; rotate **2** to convey or move (as if) on wheels; *esp* to push (a wheeled vehicle or its occupant) < ~ *the baby into the shade*> **3** to cause to change direction as if revolving on a pivot **4** to make or perform in a circle or curve – **wheel and deal** to pursue one's own usu commercial interests, esp in a shrewd or unscrupulous manner

ˈ**wheelˌbarrow** /-ˌbaroh‖-ˌbærəʊ/ *n* a

load-carrying device that consists of a shallow box supported at 1 end by usu 1 wheel and at the other by a stand when at rest or by handles when being pushed

'wheelˌbase /-ˌbays‖-ˌbeɪs/ *n* the distance between the front and rear axles of a vehicle

'wheelˌchair /-ˌcheə‖-ˌtʃeə/ *n* an invalid's chair mounted on wheels

'wheelˌhouse /-ˌhows‖-ˌhaʊs/ *n* a deckhouse for a vessel's helmsman

'wheelˌwright /-ˌriet‖-ˌraɪt/ *n* sby who makes or repairs wheels, esp wooden ones for carts

[1]**wheeze** /weez‖wiːz/ *vi* **1** to breathe with difficulty, usu with a whistling sound **2** to make a sound like that of wheezing ~*vt* to utter wheezily

[2]**wheeze** *n* **1** a sound of wheezing **2** a cunning trick or expedient – infml – **wheezy** *adj*, **wheezily** *adv*, **wheeziness** *n*

[1]**whelk** /welk‖welk/ *n* any of numerous large marine snails; *esp* one much used as food in Europe

[2]**whelk** *n* a pustule, pimple

[1]**whelp** /welp‖welp/ *n* **1** any of the young of various flesh-eating mammals, esp a dog **2** a disagreeable or impudent child or youth

[2]**whelp** *vt* to give birth to (esp a puppy) ~*vi*, *esp of a bitch* to bring forth young

[1]**when** /wen‖wen/ *adv* **1** at what time? **2a** at or during which time <*the day ~ we met*> **b** and then; WHEREUPON 1

[2]**when** *conj* **1a** at or during the time that <*went fishing ~ he was a boy*> **b** as soon as <*will look nice ~ finished*> **c** whenever <*~ he listens to music, he falls asleep*> **2** in the event that; if **3a** considering that <*why smoke ~ you know it's bad for you?*> **b** in spite of the fact that; although <*gave up politics ~ he might have done well*>

[3]**when** *pron* what or which time <*since ~ have you known that?*>

whence /wens‖wens/ *adv or conj* **1a** from where?; from which place, source, or cause? **b** from which place, source, or cause **2** to the place from which <*returned ~ they came*> *USE* chiefly fml

[1]**whenever** /wen'evə‖wen'evə/ *conj* **1** at every or whatever time <*roof leaks ~ it rains*> **2** in any circumstance <*~ possible, he tries to help*> – **or whenever** or at any similar time – infml <*in 1922* or whenever>

[2]**whenever** *adv* when in the world? – infml <*~ did you find the time?*>

[1]**where** /weə‖weə/ *adv* **1a** at, in, or to what place? <*~ is the house?*> **b** at, in, or to what situation, direction, circumstances, or respect? <*~ does this plan lead?*> **2** at, in, or to which (place) <*the town ~ she lives*>

[2]**where** *conj* **1a** at, in, or to the place at which <*stay ~ you are*> **b** [2]WHEREVER <*goes ~ he likes*> **c** in a case, situation, or respect in which <*outstanding ~ endurance is called for*> **2** whereas, while <*he wants a house, ~ I would prefer a flat*> – **where it's at** the real scene of the action – slang

[3]**where** *n* **1** what place or point? <*~ are you from?*> **2** a place, point <*bought from any old ~*> – infml

[1]**whereabouts** /ˌweərə'bowts‖ˌweərə'baʊts/ *also* **whereabout** *adv or conj* in what vicinity <*do you know ~ he lives?*>

[2]**whereabouts** /'weərəˌbowts‖'weərəˌbaʊts/ *n pl but sing or pl in constr* the place or general locality where a person or thing is <*his present ~ are a secret*>

whereas /weə'raz‖weə'ræz/ *conj* **1** in view of the fact that; since – used, esp formally, to introduce a preamble **2** while on the contrary; although

whereat /weə'rat‖weə'ræt/ *conj, archaic* **1** at or towards which **2** in consequence of which; whereupon

whereby /weə'bie‖weə'baɪ/ *conj* **1** in accordance with which <*a law ~ children receive cheap milk*> **2** by which means – chiefly fml

[1]**wherefore** /'weəfaw, ˌ-'-‖'weəfɔː, ˌ-'-/ *adv* **1** for what reason; why **2** for that reason; therefore *USE* chiefly fml

[2]**'whereˌfore** *n* a reason, cause – chiefly in *the whys and wherefores*

[1]**wherein** /weə'rin‖weə'rɪn/ *adv* in what; how <*showed him ~ he was wrong*> – chiefly fml

[2]**wherein** *conj* in which; where <*the city ~ he lived*> – chiefly fml

whereof /weə'rov‖weə'rɒv/ *conj, pron, or adv, archaic* of what, which, or whom

whereon /weə'ron‖weə'rɒn/ *adv or conj, archaic* on which or what <*the base ~ it rests*>

whereto /weə'tooh‖weə'tuː/ *adv or conj* to which or what; whither – chiefly fml

whereupon /ˌweərə'pon‖ˌweərə'pɒn/ *adv or conj* **1** closely following and in consequence of which <*he saw me coming, ~ he offered me his seat*> **2** on which; whereon – chiefly fml

[1]**wherever** /weə'revə‖weə'revə/ *adv* where in the world? – chiefly infml – **or wherever** or anywhere else at all – chiefly infml <*go to China* or wherever>

[2]**wherever** *conj* at, in, or to every or whatever place <*he can sleep ~ he likes*>

wherewithal /'weəwiˌdhawl‖'weəwɪˌðɔːl/ *n* means, resources; *specif* money <*didn't have the ~ for an expensive dinner*>

wherry /'weri‖'werɪ/ *n* **1** a long light rowing boat used to transport passengers on rivers and about harbours **2** a large light barge, lighter, or fishing boat used in Britain

[1]**whet** /wet‖wet/ *vt* **-tt-** **1** to sharpen by rubbing on or with sthg (e g a stone) **2** to make keen or more acute; stimulate <*~ the appetite*> – **whetter** *n*

[2]**whet** *n* **1** a goad, incitement **2** an appetizer

whether /'wedhə‖'weðə/ *conj* – used usu with correlative *or* or with *or whether* to indicate **a** an indirect question involving alternatives <*decide ~ he should agree or protest*> or a choice between 2 alternatives <*I wonder ~ he heard*> **b** indifference between alternatives <*seated him next to her ~ by accident or design*>

whetstone /'wetˌstohn‖'wetˌstəʊn/ *n* **1** a stone for sharpening an edge (e g of a chisel) **2** sthg that stimulates or makes keen

whew /fyooh‖fjuː/ *n* a half-formed whistle uttered as an exclamation expressing amazement, discomfort, or relief

whey /way‖weɪ/ *n* the watery part of milk separated from the curd, esp in cheese-making, and rich in lactose, minerals, and vitamins – **wheyey** *adj*

[1]**which** /wich‖wɪtʃ/ *adj* **1** being what one or ones out of a known or limited group? <*~ tie should I wear?*> **2** whichever <*it will not fit, turn it ~ way you like*> **3** – used to introduce a nonrestrictive relative clause by modifying the noun which refers either to a preceding word or phrase or to a whole previous clause <*he may come, in ~ case I'll ask him*>

[2]**which** *pron, pl* **which** **1** what one out of a known or specified group? <*~ of those houses do you live in?*> **2** whichever <*take ~ you like*> **3** – used to introduce a relative or esp a nonrestrictive relative clause; used in any grammatical relation except that of a possessive; used esp in reference to an animal, thing, or idea <*the office in ~ I work*> <*a large dog, ~ bit me*>

[1]**whichever** /wi'chevə‖wɪ'tʃevə/ *pron, pl* **whichever** **1** whatever one out of a group <*take 2 of the 4 optional papers, ~ you prefer*> **2** no matter which **3** which in the world? – chiefly infml

[2]**whichever** *adj* being whatever one or ones out of a group; no matter which

[1]**whiff** /wif‖wɪf/ *n* **1** a quick puff, slight gust, or inhalation, esp of air, a smell, smoke, or gas **2** a slight trace <*a ~ of scandal*>

[2]**whiff** *vi* **1** to emit whiffs; puff **2** to inhale an odour; sniff **3** to smell unpleasant

Whig /wig‖wɪg/ *n or adj* (a member) of a major British political group of the 18th and early 19th c seeking to limit royal authority and increase parliamentary power [short for *Whiggamore*, member of a Scottish group that marched to Edinburgh in 1648 to oppose the court party, prob fr Scots *whig* to drive + *more* horse, mare] – **Whiggery, Whiggism** *n*, **Whiggish** *adj*

[1]**while** /wiel‖waɪl/ *n* **1** a period of time, esp when short and marked by the occurrence of an action or condition; a time **2** the time and effort used; trouble <*it's worth your ~*>

[2]**while** *conj* **1a** during the time that **b** providing that; as long as <*~ there's life there's hope*> **2a** when on the other hand; whereas **b** in spite of the fact that; although <*~ respected, he is not liked*>

[3]**while** *prep, archaic or dial* until

while away *vt* to pass (time) in a leisurely, often pleasant, manner <while away *the afternoon*>

whilst /wielst‖waɪlst/ *conj, chiefly Br* while

whim /wim‖wɪm/ *n* a sudden, capricious, or eccentric idea or impulse; a fancy

whimper /'wimpə‖'wɪmpə/ *vi or n* **1** (to make) a low plaintive whining sound **2** (to make) a petulant complaint or protest

whimsical /'wimzikl‖'wɪmzɪkl/ *adj* **1** full of whims; capricious **2** resulting from or suggesting whimsy; *esp* quizzical, playful – **whimsically** *adv*, **whimsicalness, whimsicality** *n*

whimsy, whimsey /'wimzi‖'wɪmzɪ/ *n* **1** a whim, caprice **2** an affected or fanciful device, creation, or style, esp in writing or art

whin /win‖wɪn/ *n* furze

whinchat *n* a small brown and buff Old World bird

[1]**whine** /wien‖waɪn/ *vi* to utter or make a whine ~*vt* to utter or express (as if) with a whine – **whiner** *n*, **whiningly** *adv*

[2]**whine** *n* **1** (a sound like) a prolonged high-pitched cry, usu expressive of distress or pain **2** a querulous or peevish complaint – **whiny, whiney** *adj*

whinny /'wini‖'wɪnɪ/ *vb or n* (to make or utter with or as if with) a low gentle neigh or similar sound

[1]**whip** /wip‖wɪp/ *vb* **-pp-** *vt* **1** to take, pull, jerk, or move very quickly <~ped *out a gun*> **2a** to strike with a whip or similar slender flexible implement, esp as a punishment; *also* to spank **b** to drive or urge on (as if) by using a whip **c** to strike as a whip does <*rain* ~ping *the pavement*> **3a** to bind or wrap (e g a rope or rod) with cord for protection and strength **b** to wind or wrap (e g cord) round sthg **4** to oversew (an edge, hem, or seam) using a very small stitch; *also* to hem or join (e g ribbon or lace) by whipping **5** to beat (e g eggs or cream) into a froth with a whisk, fork, etc **6** to overcome decisively; defeat – infml **7** to snatch suddenly; *esp* STEAL 1 – slang ~*vi* to move, go, or come quickly or violently <~ped *out of the turning at top speed*> – **whipper** *n*

[2]**whip** *n* **1** an instrument consisting usu of a lash attached to a handle, used for driving and controlling animals and for punishment **2** a dessert made by whipping some of the ingredients **3** a light hoisting apparatus consisting of a single pulley, a block, and a rope **4** one who handles a whip: e g **4a** a driver of horses; a coachman **b** a whipper-in **5a** a member of Parliament or other legislative body appointed by a political party to enforce discipline and to secure the attendance and votes of party members **b** *often cap* an instruction (e g a three-line whip or a two-line whip) to each member of a political party in Parliament to be in attendance for voting **c** (the privileges and duties of) membership of the official parliamentary representation of a political party <*was deprived of the Labour ~*> **6** a whipping or thrashing motion **7** the quality of resembling a whip, esp in being flexible – **whiplike** *adj*

'**whip,cord** /-,kawd‖-,kɔːd/ *n* **1** a thin tough cord made of tightly braided or twisted hemp or catgut **2** a usu cotton or worsted cloth with fine diagonal cords or ribs

,**whip 'hand** *n* a controlling position; *the* advantage

whip in *vt* to keep (hounds in a pack) from scattering by use of a whip

'**whip,lash** /-,lash‖-,læʃ/ *n* **1** the lash of a whip **2** **whiplash, whiplash injury** injury to the neck resulting from a sudden sharp whipping movement of the neck and head (e g in a car collision)

whippersnapper /'wipə,snapə‖'wɪpə,snæpə/ *n* an insignificant but impudent person, esp a child

whippet /'wipit‖'wɪpɪt/ *n* (any of) a breed of small swift slender dogs related to greyhounds

whipping /ˈwiping‖ˈwɪpɪŋ/ *n* **1** a severe beating or chastisement **2** material used to whip or bind

ˈ**whipping ˌboy** *n* **1** a boy formerly educated with a prince and punished in his stead **2** a scapegoat

whippoorwill /ˈwipəˌwil‖ˈwɪpəˌwɪl/ *n* a N American nightjar

whippy /ˈwipi‖ˈwɪpɪ/ *adj* unusually resilient; springy <*a* ~ *fishing rod*>

ˈ**whip-ˌround** *n, chiefly Br* a collection of money made usu for a benevolent purpose – infml

whip up *vt* **1** to stir up; stimulate <whipped up *the emotions of the crowd*> **2** to produce in a hurry <*I'll* whip *a meal* up *in no time*>

[1]**whirl** /wuhl‖wɜːl/ *vi* **1** to move along a curving or circling course, esp with force or speed <*planets* ~ing *in their orbits*> **2** to turn abruptly or rapidly round (and round) on an axis; rotate, wheel <*he* ~ed *round to face me*> **3** to pass, move, or go quickly <*she* ~ed *down the hallway*> **4** to become giddy or dizzy; reel <*my head's* ~ing> ~ *vt* **1** to convey rapidly; whisk <*the ambulance* ~ed *him away*> **2** to cause to turn usu rapidly round (and round) on an axis; rotate – **whirler** *n*, **whirly** *adj*

[2]**whirl** *n* **1** (sthg undergoing or having a form suggestive of) a rapid rotating or circling movement **2a** a confused tumult; a bustle <*the social* ~> **b** a confused or disturbed mental state; a turmoil **3** an experimental or brief attempt; a try – infml <*I'll give it a* ~>

whirligig /ˈwuhliˌgig‖ˈwɜːlɪˌgɪg/ *n* **1** a child's toy (e g a top) that whirls **2a** sthg that continuously whirls, moves, or changes **b** a whirling or circling course (e g of events)

whirlpool /ˈwuhlˌpoohl‖ˈwɜːlˌpuːl/ *n* **1** (sthg resembling, esp in attracting or engulfing power) a circular eddy of rapidly moving water with a central depression into which floating objects may be drawn **2** WHIRL 2a

ˈ**whirlˌwind** /-ˌwind‖-ˌwɪnd/ *n* **1** a small rapidly rotating windstorm of limited extent marked by an inward and upward spiral motion of the lower air round a core of low pressure **2** a confused rush; a whirl

whirlybird /ˈwuhliˌbuhd‖ˈwɜːlɪˌbɜːd/ *n* a helicopter – infml; not now in vogue

whirr, whir /wuh‖wɜː/ *vi or n* **-rr-** (to make or revolve or move with) a continuous buzzing or vibrating sound made by sthg in rapid motion

[1]**whisk** /wisk‖wɪsk/ *n* **1** a quick light brushing or whipping motion **2a** any of various small usu hand-held kitchen utensils used for whisking food **b** a small bunch of flexible strands (e g twigs, feathers, or straw) attached to a handle for use as a brush

[2]**whisk** *vi* to move lightly and swiftly ~ *vt* **1** to convey briskly <~ed *the children off to bed*> **2** to mix or fluff up (as if) by beating with a whisk **3** to brush or wipe off (e g crumbs) lightly **4** to brandish lightly; flick <~ed *its tail*>

whisker /ˈwiskə‖ˈwɪskə/ *n* **1a** a hair of the beard or sideboards **b** a hair's breadth <*lost the race by a* ~> **2** any of the long projecting hairs or bristles growing near the mouth of an animal (e g a cat) – **whiskered** *adj*, **whiskery** *adj*, **whiskeriness** *n*

whiskey /ˈwiski‖ˈwɪskɪ/ *n* whisky produced in Ireland or the USA

whisky /ˈwiski‖ˈwɪskɪ/ *n* a spirit distilled from fermented mash of rye, corn, wheat, or esp barley [Irish Gaelic *uisce beathadh* & Scottish gaelic *uisge beatha*, lit., water of life]

[1]**whisper** /ˈwispə‖ˈwɪspə/ *vi* **1** to speak softly with little or no vibration of the vocal cords **2** to make a hissing or rustling sound like whispered speech ~ *vt* **1** to address or order in a whisper **2** to utter in a whisper **3** to report or suggest confidentially <*it is* ~ed *that he will soon resign*> – **whisperer** *n*

[2]**whisper** *n* **1a** whispering; *esp* speech without vibration of the vocal cords **b** a hissing or rustling sound like whispered speech **2** sthg communicated (as if) by whispering: e g **2a** a rumour **b** a hint, trace

[1]**whist** /wist‖wɪst/ *vi, dial Br* to be silent; hush – often used as an interjection to call for silence

[2]**whist** *n* (any of various card games similar to) a card game for 4 players in 2 partnerships in which each trick made in excess of 6 tricks scores 1 point

ˈ**whist ˌdrive** *n, Br* an evening of whist playing with a periodic change of partners, usu with prizes at the finish

[1]**whistle** /ˈwisl‖ˈwɪsl/ *n* **1** a device (e g a small wind instrument) in which the forcible passage of air, steam, the breath, etc through a slit or against a thin edge in a short tube produces a loud sound **2** (a sound like) a shrill clear sound produced by whistling or by a whistle <*the* ~ *of the wind*>

[2]**whistle** *vi* **1** to utter a (sound like a) whistle (by blowing or drawing air through the puckered lips) **2** to make a whistle by rapid movement; *also* to move rapidly (as if) with such a sound <*the train* ~d *by*> **3** to blow or sound a whistle ~ *vt* **1** to send, bring, call, or signal to (as if) by whistling **2** to produce, utter, or express by whistling <~ *a tune*> – **whistleable** *adj*, **whistler** *n* – **whistle for** to demand or request in vain

ˈ**whistleˈ-blower** *n* sby who reveals something secret or informs against another person – **whistle-blowing** *n*

ˈ**whistle-ˌstop** *n* **1** *NAm* **1a** a small station at which trains stop only on signal **b** a small community **2** *chiefly NAm* a brief personal appearance (to give an election speech) by a politician during a tour – **whistle-stop** *adj*

whit /wit‖wɪt/ *n* the smallest part imaginable; a bit

Whit *n* Whitsuntide

[1]**white** /wiet‖waɪt/ *adj* **1a** free from colour **b** of the colour white **c** light or pallid in colour <*lips* ~ *with fear*> **d** *of wine* light yellow or amber in colour **e** *Br, of coffee* served with milk or cream **2a** of a group or race characterized by reduced pigmentation **b** of or for white people <~ *schools*> **3** free from spot or blemish: e g **3a(1)** free from moral impurity; innocent **a(2)** *of a wedding* in which the woman wears white clothes as a symbol of purity **b** not intended to cause harm <*a* ~ *lie*> **4a** dressed in white **b**

accompanied by snow <*a ~ Christmas*> **5** notably ardent; passionate <*in a ~ rage*> **6** reactionary, counterrevolutionary **7** *of light, sound, electromagnetic radiation, etc* consisting of a wide range of frequencies simultaneously <*~ noise*> – **whitely** *adv*, **whitish** *adj*, **whiteness** *n*

[2]**white** *n* **1** the achromatic and lightest colour that belongs to objects that reflect diffusely nearly all incident light **2** a white or light-coloured part of sthg: e g **2a** the mass of albumin-containing material surrounding the yolk of an egg **b** the white part of the ball of the eye **c** (the player playing) the light-coloured pieces in a two-handed board game **3** sby or sthg that is or approaches the colour white: e g **3a** *pl* white (sports) clothing <*tennis ~s*> **b** a white animal (e g a butterfly or pig) **4** *pl* leucorrhoea **5** sby belonging to a light-skinned race

,white 'ant *n* a termite

whitebait /'wiet,bayt||'waɪt,beɪt/ *n* (any of various small food fishes similar to) the young of any of several European herrings (e g the common herring or the sprat) eaten whole

white blood cell, white cell *n* any of the white or colourless blood cells that have nuclei, do not contain haemoglobin, and are primarily concerned with body defence mechanisms and repair

,white-'collar *adj* of or being the class of nonmanual employees whose duties do not call for the wearing of work clothes or protective clothing

,whited 'sepulchre *n* a hypocrite [fr the simile applied by Jesus to the scribes & Pharisees, Matthew 23:27]

,white 'dwarf *n* a small whitish star of high surface temperature, low brightness, and high density

,white 'elephant *n* **1** a property requiring much care and expense and yielding little profit **2** sthg that is no longer of value (to its owner)

,white 'feather *n* a mark or symbol of cowardice

,white 'flag *n* **1** a flag of plain white used as a flag of truce or as a token of surrender **2** a token of weakness or yielding

,white 'heat *n* **1** a temperature higher than red heat, at which a body emits white light **2** a state of intense mental or physical activity or strain

,white 'hope *n* a person expected to bring fame and glory to his/her group, country, etc

,white 'horse *n* **1** a usu prehistoric figure of a horse made by cutting away the turf from a chalk hillside **2** a wave with a crest breaking into white foam – usu pl

,white 'lead /led||led/ *n* any of several white lead-containing pigments; *esp* a heavy poisonous carbonate of lead used formerly in exterior paints

,white-'livered *adj* lily-livered

,white 'magic *n* magic used for good purposes (e g to cure disease)

white meat *n* light-coloured meat (e g poultry breast or veal)

white metal *n* any of several alloys based on tin or sometimes lead used esp for bearings, type metal, and domestic utensils

whiten /'wiet(ə)n||'waɪt(ə)n/ *vb* to make or become white or whiter; bleach – **whitener** *n*, **whitening** *n*

,white 'paper *n, often cap W&P* a (British) government report usu less extensive than a blue book

,white 'pepper *n* a condiment prepared from the husked dried berries of an E Indian plant used either whole or ground

,white 'pudding *n* a sausage made from minced pork meat and fat

,white 'sauce *n* a sauce made with milk, cream, or a chicken, veal, or fish stock

,white 'slave *n* a woman or girl held unwillingly, esp abroad, and forced to be a prostitute – **white slavery** *n*

,white 'spirit *n* an inflammable liquid distilled from petroleum and used esp as a solvent and thinner for paints

'white,throat /-,throht||-,θrəʊt/ *n* an Old World warbler with a white throat, reddish-brown wings, and buff underparts tinged with pink

,white-'tie *adj* characterized by or requiring the wearing of formal evening dress by men <*a ~ dinner*>

[1]**'white,wash** /-,wosh||-,wɒʃ/ *vt* **1** to apply whitewash to **2a** to gloss over or cover up (e g vices or crimes) **b** to exonerate by concealment or through biased presentation of data **3** to defeat overwhelmingly in a contest or game – infml – **whitewasher** *n*

[2]**whitewash** *n* **1** a liquid mixture (e g of lime and water or whiting, size, and water) for whitening outside walls or similar surfaces **2** a whitewashing

whither /'widhə||'wɪðə/ *adv or conj* **1** to or towards what place? – also used in rhetorical questions without a verb <*~ democracy?*> **2** to the place at, in, or to which <*go ~ you wish*> **3** to which place *USE* chiefly fml

[1]**whiting** /'wieting||'waɪtɪŋ/ *n* any of various marine food fishes; *esp* one related to the cod

[2]**whiting** *n* washed and ground chalk used esp as a pigment and in paper coating

whitlow /'witloh||'wɪtləʊ/ *n* a deep usu pus-producing inflammation of the finger or toe, esp round the nail

Whitsun /'wits(ə)n||'wɪts(ə)n/ *adj or n* (of, being, or observed on or at) Whitsunday or Whitsuntide

Whitsunday /wit'sunday, -di||wɪt'sʌndeɪ, -dɪ/ *n* a Christian feast on the 7th Sunday after Easter commemorating the descent of the Holy Spirit at Pentecost [Old English *hwīta sunnandæg*, lit., white Sunday; prob fr the custom of wearing white robes by the newly baptized, who were numerous at this season]

Whitsuntide /'wits(ə)n,tied||'wɪts(ə)n,taɪd/ *n* Whitsunday and Whitmonday and/or the days of public holiday celebrated together with or in place of these days

whittle /'witl||'wɪtl/ *vb* **1a** to pare or cut off chips from the surface of (wood) with a knife **b** to shape or form by so paring or cutting **2** to reduce, remove, or destroy gradually as if by cutting off bits with a knife; pare – usu + *down* or *away* <*~ down expenses*> *~vi* to cut or shape sthg, esp wood, (as if) by paring it with a knife – **whittler** *n*

[1]**whiz, whizz** /wiz‖wɪz/ *vi* **-zz-** **1** to (move with a) buzz, whirr, or hiss like an arrow or ball passing through air **2** to move swiftly – infml – **whiz** *n*, **whizzer** *n*

[2]**whiz** *n* WIZARD 2 – infml

ˈ**whiz** ˌ**kid, whizz kid** *n* sby who is unusually intelligent, clever, or successful, esp at an early age

who /hoo‖hʊ; *strong* hooh‖huː/ *pron, pl* **who** **1** what or which person or people? **2** – used to introduce a restrictive or nonrestrictive relative clause in reference to a person or animal <*my father, ~ was a lawyer*>, or to a human group **3** *archaic* the person or people that; whoever

whoa /ˈwoh·ə, woh‖ˈwəʊə, wəʊ/ *interj* – used as a command (e g to a draught animal) to stand still

whodunit *also* **whodunnit** /ˌhoohˈdunit‖ˌhuː-ˈdʌnɪt/ *n* a play, film, or story dealing with the detection of crime or criminals

whoever /hoohˈevə‖huːˈevə/ *pron* **1** whatever person **2** no matter who **3** who in the world? – chiefly infml ***USE*** (*1&2*) used in any grammatical relation except that of a possessive

[1]**whole** /hohl‖həʊl/ *adj* **1a** free of wound, injury, defect, or impairment; intact, unhurt, or healthy **b** restored **2** having all its proper constituents; unmodified <~ *milk*> **3** each or all of; entire <*made the ~ class stay in*> **4a** constituting an undivided unit; unbroken <*the snake swallowed the rabbit ~*> **b** directed to (the accomplishment of) 1 end or aim <*we have concentrated our ~ efforts on it*> **5** very great – in *a whole lot* <*feels a ~ lot better now*> **6** having the same parents as another <*a ~ brother*> – **wholeness** *n*

[2]**whole** *n* **1** a complete amount or sum; sthg lacking no part, member, or element <*the ~ of society*> **2** sthg constituting a complex unity; a coherent system or organization of parts – **as a whole** considered all together as a body rather than as individuals – **on the whole 1** in view of all the circumstances **2** in most instances; typically

wholefood /ˈhohlˌfoohd‖ˈhəʊlˌfuːd/ *n* food (e g wholemeal flour and unrefined sugar) that has undergone little processing and refining and thus has a high nutritional and roughage content

ˌ**wholeˈhearted** /-ˈhahtid‖-ˈhɑːtɪd/ *adj* earnestly committed or devoted; free from all reserve or hesitation – **wholeheartedly** *adv*

ˈ**wholeˌmeal** /-ˌmeel‖-ˌmiːl/ *adj* made with (flour from) ground entire wheat kernels

ˈ**whole** ˌ**note** *n, NAm* a semibreve

whole ˈ**number** *n* an integer

[1]ˈ**wholeˌsale** /-ˌsayl‖-ˌseɪl/ *n* the sale of commodities in large quantities usu for resale (by a retailer)

[2]**wholesale** *adj or adv* **1** (sold or selling) at wholesale **2** (performed) on a large scale, esp without discrimination <~ *slaughter*>

ˈ**wholeˌsaler** /-ˌsaylə‖-ˌseɪlə/ *n* one who sells chiefly to retailers, merchants, or industrial, institutional, and commercial users mainly for resale or business use – **wholesale** *vb*

ˈ**wholesome** /-s(ə)m‖-s(ə)m/ *adj* **1** promoting health or well-being of mind or spirit **2** promoting health of body; *also* healthy **3** based on well-grounded fear; prudent <*a ~ respect for the law*> – **wholesomely** *adv*, **wholesomeness** *n*

ˈ**whole** ˌ**tone** *n* a musical interval (e g C-D or G-A) comprising 2 semitones

wholly /ˈhohl·li‖ˈhəʊllɪ/ *adv* **1** to the full or entire extent; completely **2** to the exclusion of other things; solely <*a book dealing ~ with herbs*>

whom /hoohm‖huːm/ *pron, objective case of* WHO – used as an interrogative or relative; used as object of a preceding preposition <*to know for ~ the bell tolls* – John Donne>; or less frequently as object of a verb or of a following preposition <*the man ~ you wrote to*>

[1]**whoop** /woohp‖wuːp/ *vi* to utter or make a whoop ~ *vt* **1** to utter or express with a whoop **2** to urge or cheer on with a whoop – **whoop it up** to celebrate riotously; carouse – infml

[2]**whoop** *n* **1** a loud yell expressive of eagerness, exuberance, or jubilation **2** the hoot of an owl, crane, etc **3** the crowing intake of breath following a paroxysm in whooping cough

[1]**whoopee** /wooˈpee‖wʊˈpiː/ *interj* – used to express exuberance

[2]**whoopee** /ˈwoopi‖ˈwʊpɪ/ *n* boisterous convivial fun – in *make whoopee*; infml

ˈ**whooping** ˌ**cough** /ˈhoohping‖ˈhuːpɪŋ/ *n* an infectious bacterial disease, esp of children, marked by a convulsive spasmodic cough sometimes followed by a crowing intake of breath

whoosh /woosh, woohsh‖wʊʃ, wuːʃ/ *vi or n* (to move quickly with) a swift or explosive rushing sound <*cars ~ing along the motorway*>

whop /wop‖wɒp/ *vt* **-pp-** **1** to beat, strike **2** to defeat totally ***USE*** infml

whopper /ˈwopə‖ˈwɒpə/ *n* **1** sthg unusually large or otherwise extreme of its kind **2** an extravagant or monstrous lie ***USE*** infml

[1]**whopping** /ˈwoping‖ˈwɒpɪŋ/ *adj* extremely big – infml <*won by a ~ majority*>

[2]**whopping** *adv* very, extremely – infml <*a ~ great oil tanker*>

whore /haw‖hɔː/ *n* a prostitute

ˈ**whoreˌhouse** /-ˌhows‖-ˌhaʊs/ *n* a brothel

ˈ**whoreˌmonger** /-ˌmung·gə‖-ˌmʌŋgə/ *n* a man who consorts with prostitutes or is given to lechery

whorl /wuhl, wawl‖wɜːl, wɔːl/ *n* **1** an arrangement of similar anatomical parts (e g leaves) in a circle round a point on an axis (e g a stem) **2** sthg spiral in form or movement; a swirl <~*s of smoke*> **3** a single turn of a spiral (shape) **4** a fingerprint in which the central ridges turn through at least 1 complete circle – **whorled** *adj*

whortleberry /ˈwuhtlb(ə)ri, -ˌberi‖ˈwɜːtl-b(ə)rɪ, -ˌberɪ/ *n* a bilberry

[1]**whose** /hoohz‖huːz/ *adj* of whom or which, esp as possessor or possessors <~ *hat is this?*>, agent or agents <*the courts, ~ decisions I uphold*>, or object or objects of an action <*the factory in ~ construction they were involved*>

[2]**whose** *pron, pl* **whose** that which belongs to whom – used without a following noun as a pronoun equivalent in meaning to the adjective *whose*

whosoever /ˌhoohsohˈevə‖ˌhuːsəʊˈevə/ *pron, archaic* whoever

[1]**why** /wie‖waɪ/ *adv* for what cause, reason, or purpose? – **why not** – used in making a suggestion <why not *boil them?*>

[2]**why** *conj* **1** the cause, reason, or purpose for which <*that's* ~ *I'm so tired*> **2** on which grounds <*the reason* ~ *I left*>

[3]**why** *interj* – used to express mild surprise, hesitation, approval, disapproval, or impatience <~*, here's what I was looking for*>

wick /wik‖wɪk/ *n* a cord, strip, or cylinder of loosely woven material through which a liquid (e g paraffin, oil, or melted wax) is drawn by capillary action to the top in a candle, lamp, oil stove, etc for burning

wicked /ˈwikid‖ˈwɪkɪd/ *adj* **1** morally bad; evil **2** disposed to mischief; roguish <*a* ~ *grin*> **3** very unpleasant, vicious, or dangerous <*a* ~ *waste*> – infml – **wickedly** *adv*, **wickedness** *n*

wicker /ˈwikə‖ˈwɪkə/ *adj or n* (made of) interlaced osiers, twigs, canes, or rods

ˈwickerˌwork /-ˌwuhk‖-ˌwɜːk/ *n* (work consisting of) wicker

wicket /ˈwikit‖ˈwɪkɪt/ *n* **1** a small gate or door; *esp* one forming part of or placed near a larger one **2** an opening like a window; *esp* a grilled or grated window through which business is transacted (e g at a bank) **3** a small gate for emptying the chamber of a canal lock or regulating the amount of water passing through a channel **4a** either of the 2 sets of stumps set 22yd (20.12m) apart, at which the ball is bowled and which the batsman defends in cricket **b** the area 12ft (3.66m) wide bounded by these wickets **c** a terminated innings of a batsman; *also* a partnership between 2 batsmen who are in at the same time **d** an innings of a batsman that is not completed or never begun <*won by 5* ~s> **5** situation or set of circumstances – in *on a good/bad wicket, on a sticky wicket*; infml

ˈwicketˌkeeper /-ˌkeepə‖-ˌkiːpə/ *n* the fieldsman in cricket who is stationed directly behind the batsman's wicket – **wicketkeeping** *n*

[1]**wide** /wied‖waɪd/ *adj* **1a** having great horizontal extent; vast <*a* ~ *area*> **b** embracing much; COMPREHENSIVE 1 <*reaches a* ~ *public*> **2a** having a specified width <*3ft* ~> **b** having much extent between the sides; broad <*a* ~ *doorway*> **c** fully opened <wide-*eyed*> **3a** extending or fluctuating over a considerable range <*a* ~ *variation*> **b** distant or deviating from sthg specified <*his remark was* ~ *of the truth*> **4** *Br* shrewd, astute – slang <*the* ~ *boys*> – **widely** *adv*, **widen** *vb*, **wideness** *n*, **widish** *adj*

[2]**wide** *adv* **1** over a great distance or extent; widely <*searched far and* ~> **2a** so as to leave much space or distance between <*legs* ~ *apart*> **b** so as to miss or clear a point by a considerable distance <*the bullet went* ~> **3** to the fullest extent; completely – often as an intensive + *open*

[3]**wide** *n* a ball bowled in cricket that is out of reach of the batsman in his normal position and counts as 1 run to his side

-wide *comb form* (*n* → *adj*) over (a specified distance, area, or extent); throughout (a specified area or scope) <*a nation*wide *business*>

ˌwide-ˈangle *adj* (having or using a camera with a lens) that has an angle of view wider than the ordinary

ˌwide-aˈwake *adj* **1** fully awake **2** alertly watchful, esp for advantages or opportunities

ˌwide-ˈeyed *adj* **1** amazed, astonished **2** marked by uncritical acceptance or admiration; naive <~ *innocence*>

ˈwideˌspread /-ˌspred‖-ˌspred/ *adj* **1** widely extended or spread out **2** widely diffused or prevalent <~ *public interest*>

widgeon *also* **wigeon** /ˈwijin‖ˈwɪdʒɪn/ *n*, (a duck related to) an Old World freshwater dabbling duck the male of which has a chestnut head

[1]**widow** /ˈwidoh‖ˈwɪdəʊ/ *n* **1a** a woman whose husband has died (and who has not remarried) **b** a woman whose husband spends much time away from her pursuing a specified (sporting) activity <*a golf* ~> **2** a single usu short last line (e g of a paragraph) at the top of a printed page or column

[2]**widow** *vt* **1** to cause to become a widow **2** to deprive of sthg greatly valued or needed

widower /ˈwidoh·ə‖ˈwɪdəʊə/ *n* a man whose wife has died (and who has not remarried)

ˈwidowhood /-hood‖-hʊd/ *n* (the period during which a woman remains in) the state of being a widow

width /wit·th, width‖wɪtθ, wɪdθ/ *n* **1** the measurement taken at right angles to the length **2** largeness of extent or scope **3** a measured and cut piece of material <*a* ~ *of calico*>

wield /weeld‖wiːld/ *vt* **1** to handle (e g a tool) effectively <~ *a broom*> **2** to exert, exercise <~ *influence*> – **wielder** *n*

wife /wief‖waɪf/ *n, pl* **wives** /wievz‖waɪvz/ **1** a woman acting in a specified capacity – in combination <*fish*wife> **2** a married woman, esp in relation to her husband **3** *dial* a woman – **wifehood** *n*, **wifeless** *adj*

ˈwifely /-li‖-lɪ/ *adj* of or befitting a good wife – **wifeliness** *n*

wig /wig‖wɪg/ *n* a manufactured covering of natural or synthetic hair for the (bald part of a) head – **wigged** *adj*, **wigless** *adj*

wigging /ˈwiging‖ˈwɪgɪŋ/ *n* a severe scolding – infml

[1]**wiggle** /ˈwigl‖ˈwɪgl/ *vb* to (cause to) move with quick jerky or turning motions or smoothly from side to side – **wiggler** *n*

[2]**wiggle** *n* **1** a wiggling movement **2** a wavy line; a squiggle – **wiggly** *adj*

wigwam /ˈwigˌwam‖ˈwɪgˌwæm/ *n* a N American Indian hut having a framework of poles covered with bark, rush mats, or hides

wilco /ˈwilkoh‖ˈwɪlkəʊ/ *interj* – used esp in radio and signalling to indicate that a message received will be complied with [*will comply*]

[1]**wild** /wield‖waɪld/ *adj* **1a** (of organisms) living in a natural state and not (ordinarily) tame, domesticated, or cultivated **b(1)** growing or produced without the aid and care of humans <~ *honey*> **b(2)** related to or resembling a corresponding cultivated or domesticated organism <~ *strawberries*> **2** not (amenable to being)

inhabited or cultivated **3a(1)** free from restraint or regulation; uncontrolled **a(2)** emotionally overcome <~ *with grief*>; *also* passionately eager or enthusiastic <*was* ~ *about jazz*> **a(3)** very angry; infuriated **b** marked by great agitation <~ *frenzy*>; *also* stormy <*a* ~ *night*> **c** going beyond reasonable or conventional bounds; fantastic <*beyond my* ~est *dreams*> **d** indicative of strong passion or emotion <*a* ~ *gleam in his eyes*> **4** uncivilized, barbaric **5a** deviating from the intended or regular course <*the throw was* ~> **b** having no logical basis; random <*a* ~ *guess*> **6** *of a playing card* able to represent any card designated by the holder – **wildish** *adj*, **wildly** *adv*, **wildness** *n*

[2]**wild** *n* **1** WILDERNESS 1a **2** a wild, free, or natural state or existence

[3]**wild** *adv* in a wild manner: e g **a** without regulation or control <*rhododendrons growing* ~> **b** off an intended or expected course

ˌwild ˈboar *n* an Old World wild pig from which most domestic pigs have derived

[1]**ˈwildˌcat** /-ˌkat‖-ˌkæt/ *n*, **1a** either of 2 cats that resemble but are heavier in build than the domestic cat and are usu held to be among its ancestors **b** any of various small or medium-sized cats (e g the lynx or ocelot) **2** a savage quick-tempered person **3** a wildcat oil or gas well

[2]**wildcat** *adj* **1** operating, produced, or carried on outside the bounds of standard or legitimate business practices **2** of or being an oil or gas well drilled in territory not known to be productive **3** initiated by a group of workers without formal union approval or in violation of a contract <*a* ~ *strike*>

[3]**wildcat** *vi* **-tt-** to prospect and drill an experimental oil or gas well – **wildcatter** *n*

wildebeest /ˈwildəˌbeest, ˈvil-‖ˈwɪldəˌbiːst, ˈvɪl-/ *n*, a gnu

wilderness /ˈwildənis‖ˈwɪldənɪs/ *n* **1a** a (barren) region or area that is (essentially) uncultivated and uninhabited by human beings **b** an empty or pathless area or region <*the remote* ~es *of space*> **c** a part of a garden or nature reserve devoted to wild growth **2** a confusing multitude or mass **3** *the* state of exclusion from office or power

ˈwildˌfire /-ˌfie·ə‖-ˌfaɪə/ *n* **1** sthg that spreads very rapidly – usu in *like wildfire* **2** a phosphorescent glow (e g will-o'-the-wisp)

ˈwildˌfowl /-ˌfowl‖-ˌfaʊl/ *n* a wild duck, goose, or other game bird, esp a waterfowl – **wildfowler** *n*, **wildfowling** *n*

ˌwild-ˈgoose ˌchase *n* a hopeless pursuit after sthg unattainable

ˈwildˌlife /-ˌlief‖-ˌlaɪf/ *n* wild animals

ˌwild ˈoat *n* **1** a wild grass common as a weed in meadows **2** *pl* offences and indiscretions of youth; *esp* premarital promiscuity – usu in *sow one's wild oats*

[1]**wile** /wiel‖waɪl/ *n* a deceitful or beguiling trick or stratagem – usu pl

[2]**wile** *vt* **1** to lure; entice **2** to while

wilful, *NAm chiefly* **willful** /ˈwilf(ə)l‖ˈwɪlf(ə)l/ *adj* **1** obstinately and often perversely self-willed **2** done deliberately; intentional – **wilfully** *adv*, **wilfulness** *n*

[1]**will** /wil‖wɪl/ *vb, pres sing & pl* **will**; *pres neg* **won't** /wohnt‖wəʊnt/; *past* **would** /wəd‖wəd; *strong* **wood/** *va* **1** – used to express choice, willingness, or consent or in negative constructions refusal <*can find no one who* ~ *take the job*> <*if we* ~ *all do our best*>; used in the question form with the force of a request <~ *you please stop talking*> or of an offer or suggestion <~ *you have some tea?*> **2** – used to express custom or inevitable tendency <*accidents* ~ *happen*> **3** – used to express futurity <*tomorrow I* ~ *wake up at home*> **4** can <*the back seat* ~ *hold 3 passengers*> **5** – used to express logical probability <*that* ~ *be the milkman*> **6** – used to express determination or to command or urge <*I have to go, and go I* ~> <*you* ~ *do as I say, at once*> ~ *vi* to wish, desire <*whether we* ~ *or no*>

[2]**will** *n* **1** a desire, wish: e g **1a** a resolute intention <*where there's a* ~ *there's a way*> **b** an inclination <*I did it against my* ~> **c** a choice, wish <*the* ~ *of the people*> **2** what is wished or ordained by the specified agent <*God's* ~ *be done*> **3a** a mental power by which one (apparently) controls one's wishes, intentions, etc <*has a* ~ *of her own*> **b** an inclination to act according to principles or ends <*the* ~ *to believe*> **c** a specified attitude towards others <*bear him no ill* ~> **4** willpower, self-control <*a man of iron* ~> **5** a (written) legal declaration of the manner in which sby would have his/her property disposed of after his/her death – **will-less** *adj* – **at will** as one wishes; as or when it pleases or suits oneself

[3]**will** *vt* **1** to bequeath **2a** to determine deliberately; purpose **b** to decree, ordain <*Providence* ~s *it*> **c** to (attempt to) cause by exercise of the will <~ed *her to go away*> ~*vi* to exercise the will – **willer** *n*

willies /ˈwiliz‖ˈwɪlɪz/ *n pl* nervousness, jitters – + *the*; infml

[1]**willing** /ˈwiling‖ˈwɪlɪŋ/ *adj* **1** inclined or favourably disposed in mind; ready <~ *to work*> **2** prompt to act or respond <*a* ~ *horse*> **3** done, borne, or given without reluctance <~ *help*> – **willingly** *adv*, **willingness** *n*

[2]**willing** *n* cheerful alacrity – in *show willing*

will-o'-the-wisp /ˌwil ə dhə ˈwisp‖ˌwɪl ə ðə ˈwɪsp/ *n* **1** a phosphorescent light sometimes seen over marshy ground and often caused by the combustion of gas from decomposed organic matter **2** an enticing but elusive goal **3** an unreliable or elusive person

willow /ˈwiloh‖ˈwɪləʊ/ *n* **1** any of a genus of trees and shrubs bearing catkins of petal-less flowers **2** an object made of willow wood; *esp* a cricket bat – infml – **willowlike** *adj*

ˈwillow ˌpattern *n* china tableware decorated with a usu blue-and-white story-telling design of oriental style

willowy /ˈwiloh·i‖ˈwɪləʊɪ/ *adj* **1** full of willows **2a** supple, pliant **b** gracefully tall and slender

ˈwillˌpower /-ˌpowə‖-ˌpaʊə/ *n* self-control, resoluteness

willy-nilly /ˌwili ˈnili‖ˌwɪlɪ ˈnɪlɪ/ *adv or adj* **1** by compulsion; without choice **2** (carried out or occurring) in a haphazard or random manner

[1]**wilt** /wilt‖wɪlt/ *archaic pres 2 sing of* [1]WILL

[2]**wilt** *vi* **1** *of a plant* to lose freshness and become flaccid; droop **2** to grow weak or faint; languish ~*vt* to cause to wilt

[3]**wilt** *n* a disease of plants marked by wilting

wily /ˈwieli‖ˈwaɪlɪ/ *adj* full of wiles; crafty – **wilily** *adv*, **wiliness** *n*

wimple /ˈwimpl‖ˈwɪmpl/ *vt or n* (to cover with or as if with) a cloth covering worn over the head and round the neck and chin, esp by women in the late medieval period and by some nuns

[1]**win** /win‖wɪn/ *vb* **-nn-; won** /wun‖wʌn/ *vi* **1a** to gain the victory in a contest; succeed <*always* ~s *at chess*> **b** to be right in an argument, dispute, etc; *also* to have one's way <*OK, you* ~*, we'll go to the theatre*> **2** to succeed in arriving at a place or a state – esp in *to win free* ~ *vt* **1a** to get possession of by qualities or fortune <~ *their approval*> <won *£10*> **b** to obtain by effort; earn <*striving to* ~ *a living from the soil*> **2a** to gain (as if) in battle or contest <~ *the victory*> **b** to be the victor in <won *the war*> **3a** to solicit and gain the favour of; *also* to persuade – usu + *over* or *round* **b** to induce (a woman) to accept oneself in marriage **4** to obtain (e g ore, coal, or clay) by mining **5** to reach by expenditure of effort <~ *the summit*> – **winnable** *adj*

[2]**win** *n* **1** a victory or success, esp in a game or sporting contest **2** first place at the finish, esp of a horse race

wince /wins‖wɪns/ *vi* to shrink back involuntarily (e g from pain); flinch – **wince** *n*

winceyette /ˌwinsiˈet‖ˌwɪnsɪˈet/ *n* a lightweight usu cotton fabric napped on 1 or both sides

[1]**winch** /winch‖wɪntʃ/ *n* **1** any of various machines or instruments for hoisting or pulling; a windlass **2** a crank or handle for giving motion to a machine (e g a grindstone)

[2]**winch** *vt* to hoist (as if) with a winch – often + *up* – **wincher** *n*

[1]**wind** /wind‖wɪnd/ *n* **1** a (natural) movement of air, esp horizontally **2** a force or agency that carries along or influences; a trend <*the* ~s *of change*> **3a** BREATH 4 <*the fall knocked the* ~ *out of him*> **b** BREATH 2a <*soon recovered his* ~> **c** the pit of the stomach **4** gas generated in the stomach or the intestines **5** mere talk; idle words **6** air carrying a scent (e g of a hunter or game) **7a** musical wind instruments collectively **b** *sing or pl in constr* the group of players of such instruments **8** (a compass point corresponding to) a direction from which the wind may blow – **windless** *adj*, **windlessly** *adv*, **windlessness** *n* – **close to the wind 1** as nearly as possible against the main force of the wind **2** close to a point of danger; near the permissible limit – **have the wind up** to be scared or frightened – **in the wind** about to happen; astir, afoot – **put the wind up** to scare, frighten

[2]**wind** /wind‖wɪnd/ *vt* **1** to detect or follow by scent **2** to make short of breath **3** to rest (e g a horse) in order to allow the breath to be recovered

[3]**wind** /wiend‖waɪnd/ *vt* **winded, wound** /wownd‖waʊnd/ to sound (e g a call or note) on a horn

[4]**wind** /wiend‖waɪnd/ *vb* **wound** /wownd‖waʊnd/ *also* **winded** *vi* **1** to bend or warp **2** to have a curving course; extend or proceed in curves **3** to coil, twine ~ *vt* **1a** to surround or wrap with sthg pliable <~ *the baby in a shawl*> **b** to turn completely or repeatedly, esp about an object; coil <~ *wool into a ball*> **c(1)** to hoist or haul by means of a rope or chain and a windlass **c(2)** to move (a ship) by hauling on a capstan **d(1)** to tighten the spring of <~ *the clock*> **d(2)** to put into the specified state or position by winding <~ *the speedometer back*> **e** to raise to a high level (e g of excitement or tension) – usu + *up* <wound *himself up into a frenzy*> **2** to make (one's way or course) (as if) by a curving route – **winder** *n*

[5]**wind** /wiend‖waɪnd/ *n* a coil, turn

windbag /ˈwindˌbag‖ˈwɪndˌbæg/ *n* an excessively talkative person – infml

windbreak /ˈwindˌbrayk‖ˈwɪndˌbreɪk/ *n* sthg (e g a growth of trees or a fence) that breaks the force of the wind

ˈ**windˌcheater** /-ˌcheetə‖-ˌtʃiːtə/ *n, chiefly Br* a weatherproof or windproof coat or jacket; an anorak

wind down /wiend‖waɪnd/ *vi* to become gradually more relaxed; unwind ~*vt* to bring to an end gradually; cause to cease <*are* winding down *their operations in France*>

windfall /ˈwindˌfawl‖ˈwɪndˌfɔːl/ *n* **1** sthg, esp a fruit, blown down by the wind **2** an unexpected gain or advantage; *esp* a legacy

winding /ˈwiending‖ˈwaɪndɪŋ/ *n* **1** material (e g wire) wound or coiled about an object (e g an armature); *also* a single turn of the wound material **2** the manner of winding sthg **3** a curved course, line, or progress <*the* ~s *of the path*> – **windingly** *adv*

ˈ**winding-ˌsheet** /ˈwiending‖ˈwaɪndɪŋ/ *n* a sheet in which a corpse is wrapped for burial

ˈ**wind ˌinstrument** /wind‖wɪnd/ *n* a musical instrument (e g a trumpet, clarinet, or organ) sounded by wind; *esp* a musical instrument sounded by the player's breath

windjammer /ˈwindˌjamə‖ˈwɪndˌdʒæmə/ *n* a large fast square-rigged sailing vessel

windlass /ˈwindləs‖ˈwɪndləs/ *n* any of various machines for hoisting or hauling: e g **a** a horizontal drum supported on vertical posts and turned by a crank so that the hoisting rope is wound round the drum **b** a steam, electric, etc winch with a horizontal or vertical shaft and 2 drums, used to raise a ship's anchor [Old Norse *vindāss*, fr *vinda* to wind + *āss* pole]

[1]**windmill** /ˈwindˌmil‖ˈwɪndˌmɪl/ *n* **1** a mill operated by vanes that are turned by the wind **2** a toy consisting of lightweight vanes that revolve at the end of a stick

[2]**windmill** *vb* to (cause to) move like a windmill

window /ˈwindoh‖ˈwɪndəʊ/ *n* **1** an opening, esp in the wall of a building, for admission of light and air that is usu fitted with a frame containing glass **2** a pane (e g of glass) in a window **3** sthg (e g a shutter, opening, or valve) suggestive of or functioning like a window **4** a transparent panel in an envelope, through which the address on the enclosure is visible **5** a range of wavelengths in the electromagnetic spectrum that can pass through a planet's atmosphere **6** an interval of time within which a rocket or spacecraft must be launched to accomplish a particular mission **7** an area at the limits of the earth's atmosphere through which a spacecraft must pass for successful reentry [Old Norse *vindauga*, fr *vindr* wind + *auga* eye]

'window ˌbox *n* a box for growing plants on the (outside) sill of a window

'window ˌdressing *n* **1** the display of merchandise in a shop window **2** the means by which sthg is made superficially more attractive or favourable – **window dresser** *n*

'window-ˌshop *vi* to look at the displays in shop windows for amusement or to assess goods, prices, etc – **window-shopper** *n*

windpipe /'windˌpiep‖'wɪndˌpaɪp/ *n* the trachea – not used technically

windscreen /'windˌskreen‖'wɪndˌskriːn/ *n, Br* a transparent screen, esp of glass, at the front of a (motor) vehicle

windshield /'windˌsheeld‖'wɪndˌʃiːld/ *n, NAm* a windscreen

'wind-ˌsock /wind‖wɪnd/ *n* a truncated cloth cone that is open at both ends and mounted on a pole and is used to indicate the direction of the wind, esp at airfields

'wind-ˌsurfing /wind‖wɪnd/ *n* the sport of sailing with sailboards

windswept /'windˌswept‖'wɪndˌswept/ *adj* **1** swept by wind **2** dishevelled (as if) from being exposed to the wind

'wind ˌtunnel /wind‖wɪnd/ *n* a tunnel-like apparatus through which air is blown at a known velocity to determine the effects of wind pressure on an object

wind up /wiend‖waɪnd/ *vt* **1** to bring to a conclusion; *specif* to bring (a business) to an end by liquidation **2** to put in order; settle **3** WIND 1d(1) **4** *Br* to deceive playfully; pull (someone's) leg – slang ~ *vi* **1a** to come to a conclusion **b** to arrive in a place, situation, or condition at the end of or because of a course of action <wound up *a millionaire*> **2** to give a preliminary swing to the arms (e g before bowling)

windward /'windwood‖'wɪndwʊd/ *adj, adv, or n* (in or facing) the direction from which the wind is blowing

windy /'windi‖'wɪndɪ/ *adj* **1a** windswept **b** marked by strong or stormy wind **2** FLATULENT 1 **3** verbose, bombastic **4** *chiefly Br* frightened, nervous – infml – **windily** *adv*, **windiness** *n*

[1]**wine** /wien‖waɪn/ *n* **1** fermented grape juice containing varying percentages of alcohol together with ethers and esters that give it bouquet and flavour **2** the usu fermented juice of a plant or fruit used as a drink <*rice* ~> **3** sthg that invigorates or intoxicates **4** the colour of red wine

[2]**wine** *vb* to entertain with or drink wine – usu in *wine and dine*

'wineˌglass /-ˌglahs‖-ˌglɑːs/ *n* any of several variously shaped and sized drinking glasses for wine, that usu have a rounded bowl and are mounted on a stem and foot

'wine ˌmerchant *n, Br* a usu wholesale dealer in alcoholic drinks, esp wine

[1]**wing** /wing‖wɪŋ/ *n* **1a** (a part of a nonflying bird or insect corresponding to) any of the movable feathered or membranous paired appendages by means of which a bird, bat, or insect flies **b** any of various body parts (e g of a flying fish or flying lemur) providing means of limited flight **2** an appendage or part resembling a wing in shape, appearance, or position: e g **2a** any of various projecting anatomical parts **b** a sidepiece at the top of a high-backed armchair **c** a membranous, leaflike, or woody expansion of a plant, esp along a stem or on a seed pod **d** any of the aerofoils that develop a major part of the lift which supports a heavier-than-air aircraft **e** *Br* a mudguard, esp when forming an integral part of the body of a motor vehicle **3** a means of flight – usu pl with sing. meaning <*fear lent me* ~*s*> **4** a part of a building projecting from the main or central part **5a** any of the pieces of scenery at the side of a stage **b** *pl* the area at the side of the stage out of sight of the audience **6a** a left or right flank of an army or fleet **b(1)** any of the attacking positions or players on either side of a centre position in certain team sports **b(2)** the left or right section of a playing field that is near the sidelines **7** *sing or pl in constr* a group or faction holding distinct opinions or policies within an organized body (e g a political party) **8** *pl* a pilot's badge, esp in the British armed forces **9** an operational and administrative unit of an air force; *specif* a unit of the Royal Air Force higher than a squadron and lower than a group – **in the wings** in the background; in readiness to act – **on the wing** in flight; flying – **under one's wing** under one's protection; in one's care

[2]**wing** *vt* **1a** to fit with wings **b** to enable to fly or move swiftly **2a** to wound in the wing **b** to wound (e g with a bullet) without killing **3a** to traverse (as if) with wings **b** to make (one's way) by flying ~*vi* to go (as if) with wings; fly

wing commander *n* an officer in the Royal Air Force ranking below group captain

winger /'wing·ə‖'wɪŋə/ *n, chiefly Br* a player (e g in soccer) in a wing position

'wing ˌnut *n* a nut that has projecting wings or flanges so that it may be turned by finger and thumb

'wingˌspan /-ˌspan‖-ˌspæn/ *n* the distance from the tip of one of a pair of wings to that of the other

[1]**wink** /wingk‖wɪŋk/ *vi* **1** to shut 1 eye briefly as a signal or in teasing; *also, of an eye* to shut briefly **2** to avoid seeing or noting sthg – usu + *at* <~ *at his absence*> **3** to gleam or flash intermittently; twinkle ~*vt* to cause (one's eye) to wink

[2]**wink** *n* **1** a brief period of sleep; a nap **2** an act of winking **3** the time of a wink; an instant <*quick as a* ~> **4** a hint or sign given by winking – infml

winkle /'wingkl‖'wɪŋkl/ *n* [2]PERIWINKLE

winkle out *vt chiefly Br* to displace or extract from a position; *also* to discover or identify with difficulty

winner /'winə‖'wɪnə/ *n* sthg (expected to be) successful <*this new scheme is a real* ~> – infml

[1]**winning** /'wining‖'wɪnɪŋ/ *n* **1a** the act of sby

or sthg that wins; victory **b** acquisition, gaining **2** *pl* money won by success in a game or competition

[2]**winning** *adj* tending to please or delight – **winningly** *adv*

winnow /ˈwinoh‖ˈwɪnəʊ/ *vt* **1a** to get rid of (sthg undesirable or unwanted); remove – often + *out* **b** to separate, sift <~ *a mass of evidence*> **2** to remove waste matter from (e g grain) by exposure to a current of air ~ *vi* **1** to separate chaff from grain by exposure to a current of air **2** to separate desirable and undesirable elements – **winnower** *n*

winsome /ˈwins(ə)m‖ˈwɪns(ə)m/ *adj* pleasing and engaging, often because of a childlike charm and innocence – **winsomely** *adv*, **winsomeness** *n*

[1]**winter** /ˈwintə‖ˈwɪntə/ *n* **1** the season between autumn and spring comprising in the N hemisphere the months December, January, and February **2** the colder part of the year **3** a year – usu pl <*happened many* ~s *ago*> **4** a period of inactivity or decay

[2]**winter** *adj* **1** of, during, or suitable for winter <*a* ~ *holiday*> **2** sown in autumn and harvested the following spring or summer <~ *wheat*>

[3]**winter** *vi* to pass or survive the winter ~*vt* to keep or feed (e g livestock) during the winter

ˈ**winter**ˌ**green** /-ˌgreen‖-ˌgriːn/ *n* **1** any of several perennial evergreen plants related to the heaths **2** (the flavour of) an essential oil from a wintergreen

ˌ**winter** ˈ**sport** *n* a usu open-air sport on snow or ice (e g skiing or tobogganing)

win through *vi* to reach a desired or satisfactory end, esp after overcoming difficulties

wintry, **wintery** /ˈwint(ə)ri‖ˈwɪnt(ə)rɪ/ *adj* **1** characteristic of winter; cold, stormy **2a** weathered (as if) by winter; aged, hoary **b** chilling, cheerless <*a bitter* ~ *smile*> – **wintrily** *adv*, **wintriness** *n*

[1]**wipe** /wiep‖waɪp/ *vt* **1a** to clean or dry by rubbing, esp with or on sthg soft **b** to draw or pass for rubbing or cleaning <~d *a cloth over the table*> **2a** to remove (as if) by rubbing <~ *that smile off your face*> **b** to erase completely; obliterate <~ *the scene from his memory*> – **wipe the floor with** to defeat decisively

[2]**wipe** *n* **1** an act or instance of wiping **2** power or capacity to wipe

ˈ**wipe**ˌ**out** /-ˌowt‖-ˌaʊt/ *n* a fall from a surfboard caused usu by loss of control

wipe out *vt* **1** to clean the inside of (sthg hollow) by wiping **2** to destroy completely; annihilate **3** to obliterate, cancel

wiper /ˈwiepə‖ˈwaɪpə/ *n* **1a** sthg (e g a towel or sponge) used for wiping **b** a mechanically operated rubber strip for cleaning windscreens **2** a cam; *also* a tappet

[1]**wire** /wie·ə‖waɪə/ *n* **1** metal in the form of a usu very flexible thread or slender rod **2a** a line of wire for conducting electrical current **b** a telephone or telegraph wire or system **c** a telegram, cablegram **3** a barrier or fence of usu barbed wire **4** *pl, chiefly NAm* strings <*that woman behind the president pulling the* ~s> – **wirelike** *adj*

[2]**wire** *vt* **1** to provide or connect with wire or wiring **2** to send or send word to by telegraph ~*vi* to send a telegraphic message – **wirable** *adj*, **wirer** *n*

ˌ**wire**ˈ**haired** /-ˈheəd‖-ˈheəd/ *adj, esp of a dog* having a stiff wiry coat of hair

[1]**wireless** /ˈwie·əlis‖ˈwaɪəlɪs/ *adj, chiefly Br* of radiotelegraphy, radiotelephony, or radio

[2]**wireless** *n* **1** WIRELESS TELEGRAPHY **2** *chiefly Br* RADIO 1, 2, 3d

[3]**wireless** *vt, chiefly Br* to radio

ˌ**wireless te**ˈ**legraphy** *n* the wireless transmission and reception of signals, usu voice communications, by means of electromagnetic waves

ˌ**wire** ˈ**netting** *n* a network of coarse woven wire

ˈ**wire**ˌ**tap** /-ˌtap‖-ˌtæp/ *n* an electrical connection for wiretapping

ˈ**wire**ˌ**tapping** /-ˌtaping‖-ˌtæpɪŋ/ *n* the act or an instance of tapping a telephone or telegraph wire

ˌ**wire** ˈ**wool** *n* an abrasive material consisting of fine wire strands woven into a mass and used for scouring esp kitchen utensils

ˈ**wire**ˌ**worm** /-ˌwuhm‖-ˌwɜːm/ *n* the slender hard-coated larva of various beetles, destructive esp to plant roots

wiring /ˈwie·əring‖ˈwaɪərɪŋ/ *n* a system of wires; *esp* an arrangement of wires that carries electric currents

wiry /ˈwie·əri‖ˈwaɪərɪ/ *adj* **1** resembling wire, esp in form and flexibility **2** lean and vigorous; sinewy – **wirily** *adv*, **wiriness** *n*

wisdom /ˈwizd(ə)m‖ˈwɪzd(ə)m/ *n* **1** accumulated learning; knowledge **2** the thoughtful application of learning; insight **3** good sense; judgment

ˈ**wisdom** ˌ**tooth** *n* any of the 4 molar teeth in humans which are the last to erupt on each side at the back of each jaw

[1]**wise** /wiez‖waɪz/ *n* manner, way <*in any* ~>

[2]**wise** *adj* **1a** characterized by or showing wisdom; marked by understanding, discernment, and a capacity for sound judgment **b** judicious, prudent <*not* ~ *to eat oysters*> **2** well-informed <*I'm none the* ~r> **3** possessing inside knowledge; shrewdly cognizant – often + *to* <*was* ~ *to what was happening*> **4** *archaic* skilled in magic or divination – **wisely** *adv*, **wiseness** *n*

-wise /-ˌwiez‖-ˌwaɪz/ *comb form* (*n* → *adv*) **1a** in the manner of <*entered the room crab*wise> **b** in the position or direction of <*a clock*wise *movement*> **2** with regard to; in respect of <*career*wise *it's a good idea*>

wisecrack /ˈwiezˌkrak‖ˈwaɪzˌkræk/ *vi or n* (to make) a sophisticated or knowing witticism – infml – **wisecracker** *n*

ˈ**wise** ˌ**guy** *n* a conceited and self-assertive person; *esp* a know-it-all – infml

wise up *vb* to (cause to) become informed or aware – infml

[1]**wish** /wish‖wɪʃ/ *vt* **1** to express the hope that sby will have or attain (sthg) <*I* ~ *them success*>; *esp* to bid <~ *him good night*> **2a** to give form to (a wish) **b** to feel or express a wish for; want <*I* ~ *to be alone*> **c** to request in

the form of a wish; order <*he* ~es *us to leave*> ~ *vi* **1** to have a desire – usu + *for* **2** to make a wish <~ *on a star*> – **wisher** *n* – **wish on/upon 1** to hope or will that (sby else) should have to suffer (a difficult person or situation) **2** to confer or foist (sthg unwanted) on (sby)

[2]**wish** *n* **1a** an act or instance of wishing or desire; a want <*his* ~ *to become a doctor*> **b** an object of desire; a goal <*you got your* ~> **2a** an expressed will or desire <*obeyed their* ~es> **b** an expressed greeting – usu pl <*send my best* ~es> **3** a ritual act of wishing <*made a* ~>

ˈ**wishˌbone** /-ˌbohn‖-ˌbəʊn/ *n* a forked bone in front of the breastbone of a bird consisting chiefly of the 2 clavicles fused at their lower ends

ˈ**wishful** /-f(ə)l‖-f(ə)l/ *adj* **1a** expressive of a wish **b** having a wish; desirous **2** according with wishes rather than reality <~ *thinking*> – **wishfully** *adv*, **wishfulness** *n*

wishy-washy /ˈwishi ˌwoshi‖ˈwɪʃɪ ˌwɒʃɪ/ *adj* **1** lacking in strength or flavour **2** lacking in character or determination; ineffectual ***USE*** infml

wisp /wisp‖wɪsp/ *n* **1** a small handful; *esp, chiefly Br* a pad of hay or straw for grooming an animal **2a** a thin separate streak or piece <*a* ~ *of smoke*> **b** sthg frail, slight, or fleeting <*a* ~ *of a girl*> **3** a flock of birds (e g snipe) – **wispish** *adj*, **wispily** *adv*, **wisplike** *adj*, **wispy** *adj*

wisteria /wiˈstiəri·ə, -ˈsteə-‖wɪˈstɪərɪə, -ˈsteə-/, **wistaria** /wiˈsteəri·ə‖wɪˈsteərɪə/ *n* any of a genus of chiefly Asiatic climbing plants with showy blue, white, purple, or rose flowers like those of the pea [Caspar *Wistar* (1761-1818), US physician]

wistful /ˈwistf(ə)l‖ˈwɪstf(ə)l/ *adj* **1** full of unfulfilled desire; yearning **2** musingly sad; pensive – **wistfully** *adv*, **wistfulness** *n*

wit /wit‖wɪt/ *n* **1** reasoning power; intelligence – often pl. with sing. meaning **2a** the ability to relate seemingly disparate things so as to illuminate or amuse **b(1)** a talent for banter or raillery **b(2)** repartee, satire **3** a witty individual

witch /wich‖wɪtʃ/ *n* **1** one who is credited with supernatural powers; *esp* a woman practising witchcraft **2** an ugly old woman; a hag **3** a charming or alluring woman – no longer in vogue

ˈ**witchˌcraft** /-ˌkrahft‖-ˌkrɑːft/ *n* (the use of) sorcery or magic

ˈ**witch ˌdoctor** *n* a professional sorcerer, esp in a primitive tribal society

witchery /ˈwichəri‖ˈwɪtʃərɪ/ *n* witchcraft

ˈ**witch ˌhazel** *n* (a soothing mildly astringent lotion made from the bark of) any of a genus of shrubs with slender-petalled yellow flowers

ˈ**witch-ˌhunt** *n* the searching out and harassment of those with unpopular views – **witch-hunter** *n*, **witch-hunting** *n or adj*

with /widh‖wɪð/ *prep* **1a** in opposition to; against <*had a fight* ~ *his brother*> **b** so as to be separated or detached from <*I disagree* ~ *you*> **2a** in relation to <*the Italian frontier* ~ *Yugoslavia*> **b** – used to indicate the object of attention, behaviour, or feeling <*in love* ~ *her*> **c** in respect to; so far as concerns <*the trouble* ~ *this machine*> **d** – used to indicate the object of an adverbial expression of imperative force <*off* ~ *his head*> **3a** – used to indicate accompaniment or association <*live* ~ *the gipsies*> **b** – used to indicate one to whom a usu reciprocal communication is made <*talking* ~ *a friend*> **c** – used to express agreement or sympathy <*must conclude,* ~ *him, that the painting is a forgery*> **d** able to follow the reasoning of <*are you* ~ *me?*> **4a** on the side of; for <*vote* ~ *the government*> **b** employed by <*he's a salesman* ~ *ICI*> **5a** – used to indicate the object of a statement of comparison, equality, or harmony <*level* ~ *the street*> **b** as well as <*can ride* ~ *the best of them*> **c** in addition to – used to indicate combination <*his money,* ~ *his wife's, comes to a million*> **d** inclusive of <*costs £5* ~ *tax*> **6a** by means of; using **b** through the effect of <*pale* ~ *anger*> **7a** – used to indicate manner of action <*ran* ~ *effort*> **b** – used to indicate an attendant or contributory circumstance <*stood there* ~ *his hat on*> **c** in possession of; having, bearing <*came* ~ *good news*> **d** in the possession or care of <*the decision rests* ~ *you*> **e** so as to have or receive <*got off* ~ *a light sentence*> **8a** – used to indicate a close association in time <~ *the outbreak of war they went home*> **b** in proportion to <*the pressure varies* ~ *the depth*> **9a** notwithstanding; IN SPITE OF <*love her* ~ *all her faults*> **b** EXCEPT FOR 2 <*very similar,* ~ *1 important difference*> **10** in the direction of <~ *the wind*>

withal /wiˈdhawl‖wɪˈðɔːl/ *adv* **1** together with this; besides **2** on the other hand; nevertheless

withdraw /widhˈdraw‖wɪðˈdrɔː/ *vb* **withdrew** /-ˈdrooh‖-ˈdruː/; **withdrawn** /-ˈdrawn‖-ˈdrɔːn/ *vt* **1a** to draw back, away, or aside; remove <~ *one's hand*> **b** to remove (money) from a place of deposit **2** to take back; retract <~ *my offer*> ~ *vi* **1a** to go back or away; retire from participation **b** to retreat **2** to become socially or emotionally detached <*had* ~n *into himself*> **3** to retract a statement – **withdrawable** *adj*

withdrawal /widhˈdrawəl‖wɪðˈdrɔːəl/ *n* **1a** the act or an instance of withdrawing **b(1)** social or emotional detachment **b(2)** a pathological retreat from objective reality (e g in some schizophrenic states) **2a** removal of money or other assets from a place of deposit or investment **b** the discontinuance of use of a drug, often accompanied by unpleasant side effects

withdrawn /widhˈdrawn‖wɪðˈdrɔːn/ *adj* **1** secluded, isolated **2** socially detached and unresponsive; *also* shy – **withdrawnness** *n*

withe /with‖wɪθ/ *n* a slender flexible branch or twig used esp for binding things together

wither /ˈwidhə‖ˈwɪðə/ *vi* **1** to become dry and shrivel (as if) from loss of bodily moisture **2** to lose vitality, force, or freshness ~ *vt* **1** to cause to wither **2** to make speechless or incapable of action; stun – **withering** *adj*, **witheringly** *adv*

withers /ˈwidhəz‖ˈwɪðəz/ *n pl* the ridge between the shoulder bones of a horse or other quadruped

withhold /widhˈhohld‖wɪðˈhəʊld/ *vt* **withheld** /-ˈheld‖-ˈheld/ **1** to hold back from action; check **2** to refrain from granting or giving <~ *permission*> – **withholder** *n*

[1]**within** /wi'dhin||wɪ'ðɪn/ *adv* **1** in or into the interior; inside **2** in one's inner thought, mood, or character

[2]**within** *prep* **1** inside – used to indicate enclosure or containment, esp in sthg large < ~ *the castle walls*> **2** – used to indicate situation or circumstance in the limits or compass of: e g **2a(1)** before the end of <*gone ~ a week*> **a(2)** since the beginning of <*been there ~ the last week*> **b(1)** not beyond the quantity, degree, or limitations of <*lives ~ his income*> **b(2)** in or into the scope or sphere of < ~ *his rights*> **b(3)** in or into the range of < ~ *reach*> **b(4)** – used to indicate a specific difference or margin < ~ *a mile of the town*> **3** to the inside of; into

[3]**within** *n* an inner place or area <*revolt from ~*>

[1]**without** /wi'dhowt||wɪ'ðaʊt/ *prep* **1** – used to indicate the absence or lack of or freedom from sthg <*go ~ sleep*> **2** outside – now chiefly poetic

[2]**without** *adv* **1** with sthg lacking or absent <*has learned to do ~*> **2** on or to the exterior; outside – now chiefly poetic

[3]**without** *n* an outer place or area <*seen from ~*>

withstand /widh'stand||wɪð'stænd/ *vt* **withstood** /-'stood||-'stʊd/ **1** to resist with determination; *esp* to stand up against successfully **2** to be proof against <*boots won't ~ the wet*>

withy /'widhi||'wɪðɪ/ *n* **1** OSIER 1 **2** a withe of osier

witless /'witlis||'wɪtlɪs/ *adj* **1** lacking wit or understanding; foolish **2** CRAZY 1

[1]**witness** /'witnis||'wɪtnɪs/ *n* **1** testimony **2** sby who gives evidence, specif before a tribunal **3** sby asked to be present at a transaction so as to be able to testify to its having taken place **4** sby who personally sees or hears an event take place **5a** sthg serving as evidence; a sign **b** public affirmation by word or example of usu religious faith or conviction **6** *cap* a member of the Jehovah's Witnesses

[2]**witness** *vt* **1** to testify to **2** to act as legal witness of (e g by signing one's name) **3** to give proof of; betoken <*his appearance* ~es *what he has suffered*> **4** to observe personally or directly; see for oneself ~ *vi* **1** to bear witness **2** to bear witness to one's religious convictions

'**witness-,box** *n, chiefly Br* an enclosure in which a witness testifies in court

-witted /-'witid||-'wɪtɪd/ *comb form* (*adj → adj*) having wit or understanding of the specified kind <*dull*-witted>

witticism /'witi,siz(ə)m||'wɪtɪ,sɪz(ə)m/ *n* a witty and often ironic remark

witty /'witi||'wɪtɪ/ *adj* **1** amusingly or ingeniously clever in conception or execution <*a ~ musical theme*> **2** having or showing wit <*a ~ speaker*> **3** quick to see or express illuminating or amusing relationships or insights – **wittily** *adv*, **wittiness** *n*

wives /wievz||waɪvz/ *pl of* WIFE

[1]**wizard** /'wizəd||'wɪzəd/ *n* **1** a man skilled in magic **2** one who is very clever or skilful, esp in a specified field <*a ~ at maths*> – infml

[2]**wizard** *adj, chiefly Br* great, excellent – infml

wizardry /'wizədri||'wɪzədrɪ/ *n* the art or practices of a wizard; sorcery

wizen /'wiz(ə)n||'wɪz(ə)n/ *vb* to (cause to) become dry, shrunken, and wrinkled, often as a result of aging – usu in past participle

woad /wohd||wəʊd/ *n* (a European plant of the mustard family formerly grown for) the blue dyestuff yielded by its leaves

[1]**wobble** /'wobl||'wɒbl/ *vb* **1a** to proceed with an irregular swerving or staggering motion **b** to rock unsteadily from side to side **c** to tremble, quaver **2** to waver, vacillate ~*vt* to cause to wobble – **wobbler** *n*, **wobbliness** *n*, **wobbly** *adj*

[2]**wobble** *n* **1** an unequal rocking motion **2** an act or instance of vacillating or fluctuating

[1]**woe** /woh||wəʊ/ *interj* – used to express grief, regret, or distress

[2]**woe** *n* **1** great sorrow or suffering caused by misfortune, grief, etc **2** a calamity, affliction – usu pl <*economic* ~s>

woebegone /'wohbi,gon||'wəʊbɪ,gɒn/ *adj* expressive of great sorrow or misery

woeful *also* **woful** /'wohf(ə)l||'wəʊf(ə)l/ *adj* **1** feeling or expressing woe **2** inspiring woe; grievous – **woefully** *adv*, **woefulness** *n*

wog /wog||wɒg/ *n, chiefly Br* a nonwhite person; *broadly* any dark-skinned foreigner – derog [prob short for *golliwog*]

wok /wok||wɒk/ *n* a round-bottomed frying pan used esp in Chinese cookery

woke /wohk||wəʊk/ *past of* WAKE

woken /'wohkən||'wəʊkən/ *past part of* WAKE

wold /wohld||wəʊld/ *n* **1** an upland area of open country **2** *pl, cap* a hilly or rolling region – in names of various English geographical areas

[1]**wolf** /woolf||wʊlf/ *n, pl* **wolves** /woolvz||wʊlvz/ **1** (the fur of) any of various large predatory flesh-eating mammals that resemble the related dogs, prey on livestock, and usu hunt in packs **2** a fiercely rapacious person **3a** dissonance in some chords produced on instruments with fixed notes tuned by unequal temperament (e g organs and pianos) **b** a harshness due to faulty vibration in various notes in a bowed instrument **4** a man who pursues women in an aggressive way – infml – **keep the wolf from the door** to avoid or prevent starvation or want – **wolf in sheep's clothing** one who cloaks a hostile intention with a friendly manner

[2]**wolf** *vt* to eat greedily; devour – often + *down*

'**wolf,hound** /-,hownd||-,haʊnd/ *n* any of several large dogs used, esp formerly, in hunting large animals (e g wolves)

wolfram /'woolfrəm||'wʊlfrəm/ *n* **1** tungsten **2** wolframite

wolframite /'woolfrə,miet||'wʊlfrə,maɪt/ *n* a brownish-black mineral containing tungsten, iron, and manganese

wolfsbane /'woolfs,bayn||'wʊlfs,beɪn/ *n* a (yellow-flowered Eurasian) aconite

'**wolf ,whistle** *n* a distinctive whistle sounded by a man to express sexual admiration for a woman – **wolf-whistle** *vi*

woman /'woomən||'wʊmən/ *n, pl* **women** /'wimin||'wɪmɪn/ **1a** an adult female human as distinguished from a man or child **b** a woman belonging to a particular category (e g by birth, residence, membership, or occupation) – usu in combination <*council*woman> **2** womankind **3** distinctively feminine nature; womanliness <*there's something of the ~ in him*> **4a** a charwoman <*the daily ~*> **b** a personal maid, esp in former times **5a** a female sexual partner; *esp* a mistress **b** GIRLFRIEND 1 – chiefly derog [Old English *wīfman*, fr *wīf* woman, wife + *man* human being]

ˈ**womanhood** /-hood‖-hʊd/ *n* **1a** the condition of being an adult female as distinguished from a child or male **b** the distinguishing character or qualities of a woman or of womankind **2** women, womankind

womanish /ˈwoomənish‖ˈwʊmənɪʃ/ *adj* unsuitable to a man or to a strong character of either sex; effeminate – **womanishly** *adv*, **womanishness** *n*

woman·ize, -ise /ˈwoomәniez‖ˈwʊmənaɪz/ *vi* to associate with many women habitually, esp for sexual relations – **womanizer** *n*

ˌ**womanˈkind** /-ˈkiend‖-ˈkaɪnd/ *n sing or pl in constr* female human beings; women as a whole, esp as distinguished from men

ˈ**womanly** /-li‖-lɪ/ *adj* having or exhibiting the good qualities befitting a woman – **womanliness** *n*

womb /woohm‖wuːm/ *n* **1** the uterus **2a** a hollow enveloping cavity or space **b** a place where sthg is generated – **wombed** *adj*

wombat /ˈwombat‖ˈwɒmbæt/ *n* any of several stocky Australian marsupial mammals resembling small bears

womenfolk /ˈwiminˌfohk‖ˈwɪmɪnˌfəʊk/ *also* **womenfolks** *n pl* **1** women in general **2** the women of a family or community

won /wun‖wʌn/ *past of* WIN

1**wonder** /ˈwundə‖ˈwʌndə/ *n* **1a** a cause of astonishment or admiration; a marvel **b** a miracle **2** rapt attention or astonishment at sthg unexpected, strange, new to one's experience, etc

2**wonder** *adj* noted for outstanding success or achievement <*~ drugs*>

3**wonder** *vi* **1a** to be in a state of wonder; marvel *at* **b** to feel surprise <*I shouldn't ~ if he's late*> **2** to feel curiosity or doubt; speculate <*~ about his motives*> *~vt* to be curious or in doubt about – with a clause <*~ who she is*> – **wonderer** *n*

ˈ**wonderful** /-f(ə)l‖-f(ə)l/ *adj* **1** exciting wonder; astonishing **2** unusually good; admirable – **wonderfully** *adv*, **wonderfulness** *n*

ˈ**wonderˌland** /-ˌland‖-ˌlænd/ *n* **1** a fairylike imaginary place **2** a place that excites admiration or wonder

ˈ**wonderment** /-mənt‖-mənt/ *n* **1** astonishment, marvelling **2** a cause of or occasion for wonder **3** curiosity

wondrous /ˈwundrəs‖ˈwʌndrəs/ *adj* wonderful – poetic – **wondrous** *adv, archaic*, **wondrously** *adv*, **wondrousness** *n*

wonky /ˈwongki‖ˈwɒŋkɪ/ *adj, Br* awry, crooked; *also* shaky, unsteady <*he's still a bit ~ after the flu*> – infml

1**wont** /wohnt‖wəʊnt/ *adj* **1** accustomed, used <*places where people are ~ to meet*> **2** inclined, apt <*her letters are ~ to be tedious*> *USE* + *to* and infin; fml

2**wont** *n* customary practice – fml <*according to my ~*>

won't /wohnt‖wəʊnt/ will not

wonted /ˈwohntid‖ˈwəʊntɪd/ *adj* customary, habitual – used attributively; fml <*spoke with his ~ slowness*> – **wontedly** *adv*, **wontedness** *n*

woo /wooh‖wuː/ *vt* **1** to try to win the affection of and a commitment of marriage from (a woman); court **2** to solicit or entreat, esp with importunity *~vi* to court a woman – **wooer** *n*

1**wood** /wood‖wʊd/ *n* **1** a dense growth of trees, usu greater in extent than a copse and smaller than a forest – often pl with sing. meaning **2a** a hard fibrous plant tissue that is basically xylem and makes up the greater part of the stems and branches of trees or shrubs beneath the bark **b** wood suitable or prepared for some use (e g burning or building) **3** sthg typically made of wood: e g **3a** a golf club with a wooden head **b** a wooden cask **c** 2BOWL 1 – **not see the wood for the trees** to be unable to see broad outlines because of a mass of detail – **out of the wood** *Br* escaped from peril or difficulty

2**wood** *adj* **1** WOODEN 1 **2** suitable for cutting, storing, or carrying wood <*a ~ saw*>

wood alcohol *n* methanol

woodbine /ˈwoodˌbien‖ˈwʊdˌbaɪn/ *n* **1** honeysuckle **2** VIRGINIA CREEPER [Old English *wudubinde*, fr *wudu* wood + *bindan* to tie, bind; so called fr its winding round trees]

1ˈ**woodˌblock** /-ˌblok‖-ˌblɒk/ *n* a woodcut – **wood-block** *adj*

2**woodblock** *adj, of a floor* made of parquet

ˈ**woodˌcock** /-ˌkok‖-ˌkɒk/ *n*, an Old World long-billed wading bird of wooded regions that is shot as game

ˈ**woodˌcraft** /-ˌkrahft‖-ˌkrɑːft/ *n* **1** skill and practice in anything relating to woods or forests, esp in surviving, travelling, and hunting **2** skill in shaping or making things from wood

ˈ**woodˌcut** /-ˌkut‖-ˌkʌt/ *n* (a print taken from) a relief-printing surface consisting of a wooden block with a design cut esp in the direction of the grain

ˈ**woodˌcutter** /-ˌkutə‖-ˌkʌtə/ *n* one who chops down trees

wooded /ˈwoodid‖ˈwʊdɪd/ *adj* covered with growing trees

wooden /ˈwood(ə)n‖ˈwʊd(ə)n/ *adj* **1** made or consisting of or derived from wood **2** lacking ease or flexibility; awkwardly stiff – **woodenly** *adv*, **woodenness** *n*

ˌ**woodenˈheaded** /-ˈhedid/ *adj* dense, stupid

ˌ**wooden ˈspoon** *n* a consolation or booby prize

ˈ**woodland** /-lənd‖-lənd/ *n* land covered with trees, scrub, etc – often pl with sing. meaning – **woodland** *adj*, **woodlander** *n*

ˈ**woodˌlouse** /-ˌlows‖-ˌlaʊs/ *n, pl* **woodlice** /-ˌlies‖-ˌlaɪs/ a small ground-living crustacean with a flattened elliptical body often capable of rolling into a ball in defence

ˈ**woodˌpecker** /-ˌpekə‖-ˌpekə/ *n* any of numerous usu multicoloured birds with very hard bills used to drill holes in the bark or wood of trees to find insect food or to dig out nesting cavities

ˈ**woodˌpile** /-ˌpiel‖-ˌpaɪl/ *n* a pile of wood

(e g firewood)

ˈwood ˌpulp *n* pulp from wood used in making cellulose derivatives (e g paper or rayon)

ˈwoodˌshed /-ˌshed‖-ˌʃed/ *n* a shed for storing wood, esp firewood

woodsman /ˈwoodzmən‖ˈwʊdzmən/ *n* one who lives in, frequents, or works in the woods

wood sorrel *n* any of a genus of plants with acid sap; *esp* a stemless plant of shady places with leaves made up of 3 leaflets that is sometimes held to be the original shamrock

ˈwoodˌwind /-ˌwind‖-ˌwɪnd/ *n* **1** any of a group of wind instruments (e g a clarinet, flute, or saxophone) that is characterized by a cylindrical or conical tube of wood or metal, usu with finger holes or keys, that produces notes by the vibration of a single or double reed or by the passing of air over a mouth hole **2** *sing or pl in constr* the woodwind section of a band or orchestra – often pl with sing. meaning

ˈwoodˌwork /-ˌwuhk‖-ˌwɜːk/ *n* **1** work made of wood; *esp* wooden interior fittings (e g mouldings or stairways) **2** the craft of constructing things from wood – **woodworker** *n*, **woodworking** *adj*

ˈwoodˌworm /-ˌwuhm‖-ˌwɜːm/ *n* an insect larva, esp that of the furniture beetle, that bores in dead wood; *also* an infestation of woodworm

woody /ˈwoodi‖ˈwʊdɪ/ *adj* **1** overgrown with or having many woods **2a** of or containing (much) wood, wood fibres, or xylem <~ *plants*> **b** *of a plant stem* tough and fibrous **3** characteristic of or suggestive of wood <*wine with a* ~ *flavour*> – **woodiness** *n*

[1]woof /woohf‖wuːf/ *n* **1** the weft **2** a basic or essential element or material

[2]woof /woof‖wʊf/ *vi or n* (to make) the low gruff sound characteristic of a dog

woofer /ˈwoohfə‖ˈwuːfə/ *n* a loudspeaker that responds mainly to low frequencies

wool /wool‖wʊl/ *n* **1** the soft wavy coat of various hairy mammals, esp the sheep, that is made up of keratin fibres covered with minute scales **2** sthg, esp a garment or fabric, made of wool **3a** a dense felted hairy covering, esp on a plant **b** a wiry or fibrous mass (e g of steel or glass) – usu in combination – **woolled, wooled** *adj*

ˈwoolˌgathering /-ˌgadh(ə)ring‖-ˌgæð(ə)rɪŋ/ *n* indulging in idle daydreaming – **woolgather** *vi*, **woolgatherer** *n*

[1]woollen, *NAm chiefly* **woolen** /ˈwoolən‖ˈwʊlən/ *adj* **1** made of wool **2** of or for the manufacture or sale of woollen products <~ *mills*>

[2]woollen, *NAm chiefly* **woolen** *n* **1** a fabric made of wool **2** *pl* garments of woollen fabric

[1]woolly, *NAm also* **wooly** /ˈwooli‖ˈwʊlɪ/ *adj* **1** (made) of or resembling wool; *also* bearing (sthg like) wool **2a** lacking in clearness or sharpness of outline <*a* ~ *TV picture*> **b** marked by mental vagueness or confusion <~ *thinking*> **3** boisterously rough – chiefly in *wild and woolly* – **woollily** *adv*, **woolliness** *n*

[2]woolly, woolie, *NAm also* **wooly** *n, chiefly Br* a woollen jumper or cardigan

ˈwoolˌsack /-ˌsak‖-ˌsæk/ *n* *the* official seat of the Lord Chancellor in the House of Lords

woozy /ˈwoohzi‖ˈwuːzɪ/ *adj* **1** mentally unclear or hazy **2** dizzy or slightly nauseous *USE* infml – **woozily** *adv*, **wooziness** *n*

wop /wop‖wɒp/ *n, often cap* an Italian – chiefly derog

ˌWorcester ˈsauce /ˈwoostə‖ˈwʊstə/ *n* a pungent sauce containing soy sauce, vinegar, and spices [*Worcester, Worcestershire*, former county of England (now *Hereford and Worcester*) where it was originally made]

[1]word /wuhd‖wɜːd/ *n* **1a** sthg that is said **b** *pl* **b(1)** talk, discourse <*putting one's feelings into* ~*s*> **b(2)** the text of a vocal musical composition **c** a short remark, statement, or conversation <*would like to have a* ~ *with you*> **2a** a meaningful unit of spoken language that can stand alone as an utterance; *also* a written or printed representation of a spoken word **b** a string of adjacent binary digits that is typically longer than a byte and is processed by a computer as a unit <*a 16-bit* ~> **3** an order, command <*don't move till I give the* ~> **4** *often cap* **4a** *the* divine wisdom manifest in the creation and redemption of the world, and identified in Christian thought with the second person of the Trinity **b** GOSPEL 1 **c** the expressed or manifested mind and will of God **5a** news, information <*sent* ~ *that he would be late*> **b** rumour <~ *has it that they're leaving*> **6** the act of speaking or of making verbal communication <*in* ~ *and deed*> **7** a promise <*kept her* ~> **8** *pl* a quarrelsome utterance or conversation <*been having* ~*s with my wife*> **9** a verbal signal; a password **10** *the* most appropriate description <*'hot' wasn't the* ~ *for it*> – **from the word go** from the beginning – **in a word** IN SHORT – **in so many words** in exactly those terms – **my word** – used to express surprise or astonishment – **of one's word** that can be relied on to keep a promise – used only after *man* or *woman* <*a man* of his word>

[2]word *vt* to express in words; phrase

ˈword-ˌblindness *n* a condition (e g dyslexia) that impairs the ability to read

ˌword-for-ˈword *adj, of a report or translation* in or following the exact words; verbatim – **word for word** *adv*

wording /ˈwuhding‖ˈwɜːdɪŋ/ *n* the act or manner of expressing in words <*the exact* ~ *of the will*>

ˌword of ˈmouth *n* oral communication

ˌword-ˈperfect *adj* having memorized sthg perfectly

ˈwordˌplay /-ˌplay‖-ˌpleɪ/ *n* verbal wit

word processor *n* a computer that stores text which can then be manipulated (e g by adding corrections or new text) and that performs routine or repetitive typing tasks

wordy /ˈwuhdi‖ˈwɜːdɪ/ *adj* using or containing (too) many words – **wordily** *adv*, **wordiness** *n*

wore /waw‖wɔː/ *past of* WEAR

[1]work /wuhk‖wɜːk/ *n* **1** activity in which one exerts strength or faculties to do or produce sthg: **1a** sustained physical or mental effort to achieve a result **b** the activities that afford one's accustomed means of livelihood **c** a specific task, duty, function, or assignment **2a** the (result of) expenditure of energy by natural phenomena

b the transference of energy that is produced by the motion of the point of application of a force and is measured by the product of the force and the distance moved along the line of action **3a** (the result of) a specified method of working <*the* ~ *of many hands*> – often in combination <*needle*work> **b** sthg made from a specified material – often in combination <*iron*work> **4a** a fortified structure (e g a fort, earthen barricade, or trench) **b** *pl* structures in engineering (e g docks, bridges, or embankments) or mining (e g shafts or tunnels) **5** *pl but sing or pl in constr* a place where industrial activity is carried out; a factory – often in combination <*a water*works> **6** *pl* the working or moving parts of a mechanism **7** an artistic production or creation **8** *pl* performance of moral or religious acts <*salvation by* ~s> **9a** effective operation; an effect, result <*wait for time to do its healing* ~> **b** activity, behaviour, or experience of the specified kind <*dancing reels is thirsty* ~> **11** *pl* **11a** everything possessed, available, or belonging – infml; + *the* **b** subjection to all possible abuse – infml <*gave him the* ~s> – **workless** *adj* – **at work 1** engaged in working; busy; *esp* engaged in one's regular occupation **2** at one's place of work – **in the works** in process of preparation, development, or completion – **one's work cut out** as much as one can do – **out of work** without regular employment; unemployed

[2]**work** *adj* **1** suitable for wear while working <~ *clothes*> **2** used for work <~ *elephant*>

[3]**work** *vb* **worked, wrought** /rawt‖rɔːt/ *vt* **1** to bring to pass; effect <~ *miracles*> **2a** to fashion or create sthg by expending labour on; forge, shape <~ *flint into tools*> **b** to make or decorate with needlework; embroider <~ *a sampler*> **3** to prepare or form into a desired state for use by kneading, hammering, etc **4** to operate <*a pump* ~ed *by hand*> **5** to solve (a problem) by reasoning or calculation – usu + *out* **6** to cause to labour <~ed *his horses nearly to death*> **7** to carry on an operation in (a place or area) <*the salesman* ~ed *both sides of the street*> **8** to finance by working <~ed *his way through college*> **9a** to manoeuvre (oneself or an object) gradually or with difficulty into or out of a specified condition or position <*the screw* ~ed *itself loose*> **b** to contrive, arrange <*we can* ~ *it so that you can take your holiday early*> **10** to excite, provoke <~ed *himself into a rage*> ~ *vi* **1a** to exert oneself, esp in sustained, purposeful, or necessary effort <~ed *all day over a hot stove*> **b** to perform work or fulfil duties regularly for wages or a salary **2** to operate, function <*the lifts don't* ~ *at night*> **3** to exert an influence or have a tendency <*events have* ~ed *in our favour*> **4** to produce a desired effect; succeed <*hope your plan will* ~> **5a** to make one's way slowly and with difficulty; move or progress laboriously **b** to sail to windward **6** to produce artefacts by shaping or fashioning a specified material <*she* ~s *in copper*> **7a** to be in agitation or restless motion <*her mouth* ~ed *nervously*> **b** FERMENT 1 **c** to move slightly in relation to another part **d** to get into a specified condition by slow or imperceptible movements <*the knot* ~ed *loose*> – **work on** to strive to influence or persuade; affect – **work to rule** to obey the rules of one's work precisely and so reduce efficiency, esp as a form of industrial action

workable /ˈwuhkəbl‖ˈwɜːkəbl/ *adj* **1** capable of being worked <~ *vein of coal*> **2** practicable, feasible – **workableness** *n*, **workability** *n*

workaday /ˈwuhkəday‖ˈwɜːkədeɪ/ *adj* **1** of or suited for working days **2** prosaic, ordinary

workbag /ˈwuhkˌbag‖ˈwɜːkˌbæg/ *n* a bag for implements or materials for work, esp needlework

ˈ**workˌbasket** /-ˌbahskit‖-ˌbɑːskɪt/ *n* a basket for needlework implements and materials

ˈ**workˌbench** /-ˌbench‖-ˌbentʃ/ *n* a bench on which work, esp of mechanics or carpenters, is performed

ˈ**workˌbook** /-ˌbook‖-ˌbʊk/ *n* an exercise book of problems to be solved directly on the pages

ˌ**worked** ˈ**up** *adj* emotionally aroused; excited

worker /ˈwuhkə‖ˈwɜːkə/ *n* **1a** one who works, esp at manual or industrial work or with a particular material – often in combination **b** a member of the working class **2** any of the sexually underdeveloped usu sterile members of a colony of ants, bees, etc that perform most of the labour and protective duties of the colony

workforce /ˈwuhkˌfaws‖ˈwɜːkˌfɔːs/ *n sing or pl in constr* the workers engaged in a specific activity or potentially available

ˈ**workˌhouse** /-ˌhows‖-ˌhaʊs/ *n* **1** *Br* an institution formerly maintained at public expense to house paupers **2** *NAm* a house of correction for minor offenders

ˈ**work-ˌin** *n* a continuous occupation of a place of employment by employees continuing to work normally as a protest, usu against the threat of factory closure

work in *vt* **1** to cause to penetrate by persistent effort <work *the ointment thoroughly* in> **2** to insinuate unobtrusively <worked in *a few topical jokes*>; *also* to find room for

[1]**working** /ˈwuhking‖ˈwɜːkɪŋ/ *adj* **1a** that functions or performs labour <*a* ~ *model*> **b** *of a domestic animal* trained or bred for useful work <*a* ~ *dog*> **2** adequate to permit effective work to be done <*a* ~ *majority*> **3** serving as a basis for further work <~ *draft*> **4** during which one works <~ *hours*>; *also* during which one discusses business or policy <*a* ~ *lunch*>

[2]**working** *n* **1** (a part of) a mine, quarry, or similar excavation **2** the fact or manner of functioning or operating – usu pl with sing. meaning <*the* ~s *of his mind*>

ˌ**working** ˈ**class** *n sing or pl in constr* the class of people who work (manually) for wages – often pl with sing. meaning; – **working-class** *adj*

ˌ**working** ˈ**day** *n* **1** a day on which work is done as distinguished from Sunday or a holiday **2** the period of time in a day during which work is performed

ˈ**working** ˌ**party** *n, chiefly Br* a committee set up (e g by a government) to investigate and report on a particular problem

ˈ**workman** /-mən‖-mən/, *fem* ˈ**workˌwoman** *n* an artisan

ˈworkmanˌlike /-ˌliek‖-ˌlaɪk/ *also* **workmanly** /-li‖-lɪ/ *adj* worthy of a good workman: **a** skilful **b** efficient in appearance

ˈworkmanˌship /-ˌship‖-ˌʃɪp/ *n* the relative art or skill of a workman; craftsmanship; *also* the quality or finish exhibited by a thing

work off *vt* to dispose of or get rid of by work or activity <work off *one's anger*>

ˈworkˌout /-ˌowt‖-ˌaʊt/ *n* a practice or exercise to test or improve fitness, ability, or performance, esp for sporting competition

work out *vt* **1a** to find out by calculation **b** to devise by resolving difficulties <work out *an agreement*> **c** to elaborate in detail <work out *a scheme*> **2** to discharge (e g a debt) by labour **3** to exhaust (e g a mine) by working ~ *vi* **1a** to prove effective, practicable, or suitable <*their marriage didn't* work out> **b** to amount to a total or calculated figure – often + *at* or *to* <works out *at £17.50*> <*gas heating might* work out *expensive*> **c** *of a sum* to yield a result **2** to engage in a workout

work over *vt* **1** to subject to thorough examination, study, or treatment **2** to beat up thoroughly; manhandle – infml

ˈworkˌpeople /-ˌpeepl‖-ˌpiːpl/ *n pl, chiefly Br* workers, employees

ˈworkroom /-roohm, -room‖-ruːm, -rʊm/ *n* a room used for esp manual work

works /wuhks‖wɜːks/ *adj* of a place of industrial labour <~ *council*>

ˈworkˌshop /-ˌshop‖-ʃɒp/ *n* **1** a room or place (e g in a factory) in which manufacture or repair work is carried out **2** a brief intensive educational programme for a relatively small group of people in a given field that emphasizes participation

ˈworkˌshy /-ˌshie‖-ˌʃaɪ/ *adj* disliking work; lazy

ˈworkˌtop /-ˌtop‖-ˌtɒp/ *n* a flat surface (e g of Formica) on a piece of esp kitchen furniture (e g a cupboard or dresser) suitable for working on

ˌwork-to-ˈrule *n* an instance of industrial action designed to reduce output by deliberately keeping very rigidly to rules and regulations

work up *vt* **1** to stir up; rouse <*can't* work up *much interest*> **2** to produce by mental or physical work <worked up *a sweat in the gymnasium*> **3** to improve, esp by mental work <work up *your French*> ~*vi* to rise gradually in intensity or emotional tone <work up *to a climax*>

[1]**world** /wuhld‖wɜːld/ *n* **1** the earth with its inhabitants and all things on it **2** the course of human affairs <*knowledge of the* ~> **3** the human race **4** the concerns of earthly existence or secular affairs as distinguished from heaven and the life to come or religious and ecclesiastical matters **5** the system of created things; the universe **6a** a division, section, or generation of the inhabitants of the earth distinguished by living together at the same place or at the same time <*the medieval* ~> **b** a distinctive class of people or their sphere of interest <*the academic* ~> **7a** human society as a whole <*all the* ~ *knows*>; *also* the public <*announced his discovery to the* ~> **b** fashionable or respectable people; public opinion **8** a part or section of the earth that is a separate independent unit <*the third* ~> **9a** one's personal environment in the sphere of one's life or work <*the external* ~> **b** a particular aspect of one's life <*the* ~ *of dreams*> **10** an indefinite multitude or a great quantity or amount <*makes a* ~ *of difference*> **11** KINGDOM 4 <*the animal* ~> **12** a planet; *esp* one that is inhabited ***USE*** (*except 10 & 12*) + *the* – **best of both worlds** the benefit of the advantages of 2 alternatives, esp without their disadvantages – **for all the world** in every way; exactly –**for the world** in any circumstances; for anything <*wouldn't hurt her feelings* for the world> – **in the world** among innumerable possibilities; ever <*what* in the world *is it?*> – **out of this world** of extraordinary excellence; superb

[2]**world** *adj* **1** of the whole world <*a* ~ *championship*> **2** extending or found throughout the world; worldwide <*a* ~ *state*>

ˌworld-ˈclass *adj* of the highest quality in the world, esp in playing a sport or game

worldly /ˈwuhldli‖ˈwɜːldlɪ/ *adj* of or devoted to this world and its pursuits rather than to religion or spiritual affairs – **worldliness** *n*

ˌworldly-ˈwise *adj* possessing a practical and often shrewd and materialistic understanding of human affairs; sophisticated

ˈworld-ˌshaking *adj* earthshaking

ˌworld ˈwar *n* a war engaged in by (most of) the principal nations of the world; *esp, cap both Ws* either of 2 such wars of the first half of the 20th c

ˌworld-ˈweary *adj* bored with the life of the world and its material pleasures – **world-weariness** *n*

ˌworldˈwide /-ˈwied‖-ˈwaɪd/ *adj* extended throughout or involving the entire world – **worldwide** *adv*

[1]**worm** /wuhm‖wɜːm/ *n* **1a** any of numerous relatively small elongated invertebrate animals, typically with a soft limbless body; *esp* an earthworm **b** any of various invertebrate animals resembling worms e g **b(1)** a (destructive) caterpillar, maggot, or other insect larva **b(2)** a shipworm **b(3)** a blindworm **2** a human being who is an object of contempt, loathing, or pity; a wretch **3** infestation with or disease caused by parasitic worms – usu pl with sing. meaning but sing. or pl in constr **4a** the thread of a screw **b** a short revolving screw whose threads engage with a worm wheel or a rack **c** a spiral condensing tube used in distilling

[2]**worm** *vi* to proceed windingly or insidiously ~ *vt* **1** to free (e g a dog) from worms **2a** to cause to move or proceed (as if) in the manner of a worm **b** to insinuate or introduce (oneself) by devious or subtle means **c** to make (one's way) insidiously or deviously <*tried to* ~ *her way out of the situation*> **3** to obtain or extract by artful or insidious questioning or by pleading, asking, or persuading – usu + *out of* <~ed *the secret out of her*> – **wormer** *n*

ˈwormˌcast /-ˌkahst‖-ˌkɑːst/ *n* a small heap of earth excreted by an earthworm on the soil surface

ˈworm-ˌeaten *adj* **1** eaten or burrowed into (as if) by worms **2** worn-out, antiquated

'worm ,gear *n* **1** WORM WHEEL **2** a gear consisting of a worm and a worm wheel working together

'worm,hole /-,hohl‖-,həʊl/ *n* a hole or passage burrowed by a worm

'worm ,wheel *n* a toothed wheel gearing with the thread of a worm

'wormwood /-wood‖-wʊd/ *n* **1** a European composite plant yielding a bitter slightly aromatic dark green oil used in absinthe **2** sthg bitter or mortifying; bitterness

wormy /'wuhmi‖'wɜːmɪ/ *adj* containing, infested with, having, or damaged by (many) worms

worn /wawn‖wɔːn/ *past part of* WEAR

,worn-'out *adj* exhausted or used up (as if) by wear

worrisome /'wuris(ə)m‖'wʌrɪs(ə)m/ *adj* **1** causing distress or worry **2** inclined to worry or fret – **worrisomely** *adv*, **worrisomeness** *n*

[1]**worry** /'wuri‖'wʌrɪ/ *vt* **1a** to harass by tearing, biting, etc, esp at the throat <*a dog* ~ing *sheep*> **b** to shake or pull at with the teeth <*a terrier* ~ing *a rat*> **c** to touch or disturb repeatedly **2** to subject to persistent or nagging attention or effort **3** to afflict with mental distress or agitation; make anxious ~ *vi* **1** to work at sthg difficult <*he* worried *away at the problem*> **2** to feel or experience concern or anxiety; fret – **worriedly** *adv*, **worrier** *n* – **not to worry** *Br* do not worry; do not feel anxious, dispirited, or troubled – infml

[2]**worry** *n* **1** mental distress or agitation resulting from concern, usu for sthg impending or anticipated; anxiety **2** a cause of worry; a trouble, difficulty

[1]**worse** /wuhs‖wɜːs/ *adj, comparative of* BAD *or* ILL **1** of lower quality **2** in poorer health – **worsen** *vb* – **the worse for** harmed by <*none* the worse for *his fall*>

[2]**worse** *n, pl* **worse** sthg worse

[3]**worse** *adv, comparative of* BAD, BADLY, *or* ILL in a worse manner; to a worse extent or degree

[1]**worship** /'wuhship‖'wɜːʃɪp/ *n* **1** (an act of) reverence offered to a divine being or supernatural power **2** a form of religious practice with its creed and ritual **3** extravagant admiration for or devotion to an object of esteem **4** *chiefly Br* a person of importance – used as a title for various officials (e g magistrates and some mayors)

[2]**worship** *vb* **-pp-** (*NAm* **-p-**, **-pp-**) *vt* **1** to honour or reverence as a divine being or supernatural power **2** to regard with great, even extravagant respect, honour, or devotion ~*vi* to perform or take part in (an act of) worship – **worshipper** *n*

'worshipful /-f(ə)l‖-f(ə)l/ *adj* **1** rendering worship or veneration **2** *chiefly Br* – used as a title for various people or groups of rank or distinction – **worshipfully** *adv*, **worshipfulness** *n*

[1]**worst** /wuhst‖wɜːst/ *adj, superlative of* BAD *or* ILL **1** most productive of evil **2** most wanting in quality

[2]**worst** *n, pl* **worst** **1** the worst state or part <*always at my* ~ *before breakfast*> **2** sby or sthg that is worst **3** the utmost harm of which one is capable <*do your* ~> – **at worst, at the worst** under the worst circumstances; seen in the worst light – **if the worst comes to the worst** if the very worst thing happens

[3]**worst** *adv, superlative of* BAD, BADLY, *or* ILL in the worst manner; to the worst extent or degree

[4]**worst** *vt* to get the better of; defeat

worsted /'woostid‖'wʊstɪd/ *n* **1** a smooth compact yarn from long wool fibres used esp for firm napless fabrics, carpeting, or knitting **2** a fabric made from worsted yarns [*Worsted* (now *Worstead*), village in Norfolk, England] – **worsted** *adj*

[1]**wort** /wuht‖wɜːt/ *n* a (herbaceous) plant – now used only in combination <*stink*wort>

[2]**wort** *n* a dilute solution containing sugars obtained typically from malt by infusion and fermented to form beer

[1]**worth** /wuhth‖wɜːθ/ *prep* **1a** equal in value to **b** having property equal to <*he's* ~ *£1,000,000*> **2** deserving of <*well* ~ *the effort*> – **worth it** worthwhile

[2]**worth** *n* **1a** (money) value **b** the equivalent of a specified amount or figure <*3 quids*worth *of petrol*> **2** moral or personal merit, esp high merit <*proved his* ~>

'worthless /-lis‖-lɪs/ *adj* **1a** lacking worth; valueless <~ *currency*> **b** useless <~ *to continue searching*> **2** contemptible, despicable – **worthlessly** *adv*, **worthlessness** *n*

,worth'while /-'wiel‖-'waɪl/ *adj* worth the time or effort spent

[1]**worthy** /'wuhdhi‖'wɜːðɪ/ *adj* **1a** having moral worth or value <*a* ~ *cause*> **b** honourable, meritorious <*they were all honoured and* ~ *men*> **2** important enough; deserving <*a deed* ~ *to be remembered*> – **worthily** *adv*, **worthiness** *n*

[2]**worthy** *n* a worthy or prominent person – often humor

-worthy /-,wuhdhi‖-,wɜːðɪ/ *comb form* (*n* → *adj*) **1** fit or safe for <*a sea*worthy *vessel*> **2** deserving of <*praise*worthy>

wotcher /'wochə‖'wɒtʃə/ *interj, Br* – used as a greeting; slang

would /wəd‖wəd; *strong* wood‖wʊd/ *past of* WILL **1a** to desire, wish **b** – used in auxiliary function with *rather* or *soon, sooner* to express preference <~ *sooner die than face them*> **2a** – used in auxiliary function to express wish, desire, or intent <*those who* ~ *forbid gambling*> or, in negative constructions, reluctance <~ *not hurt a fly*>; used in the question form with the force of a polite request <~ *you please help me?*> or of an offer or suggestion <~ *you like some tea?*> **b** – used in auxiliary function in reported speech or writing to represent *shall* or *will* <*said he* ~ *come*> **3a** used to <*we* ~ *meet often for lunch*> – used with emphatic stress to express exasperation <*she* ~ *keep complaining*> **b** – used in auxiliary function with emphatic stress as a comment on the annoyingly typical <*you* ~ *say that*> **4** – used in auxiliary function to introduce a contingent fact, possibility, or presumption (1) in the main clause of a conditional sentence <*it* ~ *break if you dropped it*> (2) after a verb expressing desire, request, or advice <*wish he* ~ *go*> **5** could <*door* would*n't open*> **6** – used in auxiliary function to soften direct statement <~ *be glad to know*>

'**would-be** *adj* desiring or intended to be <*a ~ tycoon*>

wouldn't /'woodnt‖'wʊdnt/ would not

wouldst /woodst‖wʊdst/, **wouldest** /'woodist‖'wʊdɪst/ *archaic past 2 sing of* WILL

[1]**wound** /woohnd‖wu:nd/ *n* **1** an injury to the body or to a plant (e g from violence or accident) that involves tearing or breaking of a membrane (e g the skin) and usu damage to underlying tissues **2** a mental or emotional hurt or blow

[2]**wound** *vt* to cause a wound to or in ~*vi* to inflict a wound

[3]**wound** /wownd‖waʊnd/ *past of* WIND

[1]**wove** /wohv‖wəʊv/ *past of* WEAVE

[2]**wove** *n* paper made in such a way that no fine lines run across the grain

woven /'wohv(ə)n‖'wəʊv(ə)n/ *past part of* WEAVE

[1]**wow** /wow‖waʊ/ *interj* – used to express strong feeling (e g pleasure or surprise); slang

[2]**wow** *n* a striking success; a hit – slang

[3]**wow** *vt* to excite to enthusiastic admiration or approval – slang

[4]**wow** *n* a distortion in reproduced sound that is heard as a slow rise and fall in the pitch of the sound and is caused by variations in the speed of the reproducing system

[1]**wrack** /rak‖ræk/ *n* **1** destruction <~ *and ruin*> **2** (a remnant of) sthg destroyed

[2]**wrack** *n* (dried) marine vegetation; *esp* kelp

[3]**wrack** *vt* [4]RACK

[4]**wrack** *n* [1]RACK

wraith /rayth‖reɪθ/ *n*, an apparition of a living person in his/her exact likeness seen before or after death

[1]**wrangle** /'rang·gl‖'ræŋgl/ *vi* to dispute angrily or peevishly; bicker ~*vt*, *NAm* to herd and care for (livestock, esp horses) on the range

[2]**wrangle** *n* an angry, noisy, or prolonged dispute or quarrel

wrangler /'rang·glə‖'ræŋglə/ *n* **1** a bickering disputant **2** the holder of a Cambridge first in mathematics – **wranglership** *n*

[1]**wrap** /rap‖ræp/ *vb* **-pp-** *vt* **1a** to envelop, pack, or enfold in sthg flexible **b** to fold round sthg specified <~ *a blanket round her*> **2a** to obscure or surround with the specified covering <~ped *in mist*> **b** to involve completely; engross – usu + *up* <~ped *up in his daughter*> ~*vi* to curl round sthg <*skirt that* ~s *over*>

[2]**wrap** *n* **1** a wrapping; *specif* a waterproof wrapping placed round food to be frozen, esp in a domestic freezer **2** an article of clothing that may be wrapped round a person; *esp* an outer garment (e g a shawl) – **under wraps** secret

wrapper /'rapə‖'ræpə/ *n* that in which sthg is wrapped: e g **a** a fine quality tobacco leaf used for the covering of a cigar **b** DUST JACKET

wrapping /'raping‖'ræpɪŋ/ *n* material used to wrap an object

wrap up *vt* to bring to a usu successful conclusion; end – infml ~ *vi* **1** to protect oneself with outer garments <wrap up *warm*> **2** *Br* to stop talking; SHUT UP – slang

wrath /roth‖rɒθ/ *n* **1** strong vengeful anger or indignation **2** retributory, esp divine, chastisement – **wrathful** *adj*

wreak /reek‖ri:k/ *vt* **1** to give free play to (malevolent feeling); inflict <~ed *her revenge*> **2** to cause or create (havoc or destruction)

wreath /reeth‖ri:θ/ *n, pl* **wreaths** /reedhz‖ri:ðz/ **1** sthg intertwined into a circular shape; *esp* a garland **2** a representation of a wreath (e g in heraldry) **3** a drifting and coiling whorl <~s *of smoke*>

wreathe /reedh‖ri:ð/ *vt* **1** to cause (the face) to take on a happy joyful expression – usu pass <*face* ~d *in smiles*> **2a** to shape (e g flowers) into a wreath **b** to coil about sthg **3** to encircle (as if) with a wreath <*bust* ~d *with laurel*> ~ *vi* to twist or move in coils; writhe <*smoke* ~d *from the chimney*>

[1]**wreck** /rek‖rek/ *n* **1** sthg cast up on the land by the sea, esp after a shipwreck **2a** (a) shipwreck **b** wrecking or being wrecked; destruction <*after the* ~ *of our hopes*> **3a** the broken remains of sthg (e g a building or vehicle) wrecked or ruined **b** a person or animal of broken constitution, health, or spirits

[2]**wreck** *vt* **1** to cast ashore **2a** to reduce to a ruinous state by violence <~ *a train*> **b** to cause (a vessel) to be shipwrecked **c** to involve in disaster or ruin <~ *one's marriage*> ~ *vi* to become wrecked

wreckage /'rekij‖'rekɪdʒ/ *n* **1** wrecking or being wrecked **2** broken and disordered parts or material from a wrecked structure

wrecker /'rekə‖'rekə/ *n* **1a** sby who wrecks ships (e g by false lights) for plunder **b** sby whose work is the demolition of buildings **2a** sby who searches for or works on the wrecks of ships (e g for rescue or plunder) **b** *NAm* a breakdown lorry **c** *NAm* a dealer in scrap, esp scrapped motor vehicles

wren /ren‖ren/ *n* a very small European bird that has a short erect tail and is noted for its loud song

Wren *n* a woman serving in the Women's Royal Naval Service

[1]**wrench** /rench‖rentʃ/ *vi* to pull or strain at sthg with violent twisting ~ *vt* **1** to pull or twist violently <~ *the door open*> **2** to injure or disable by a violent twisting or straining **3** to distort, pervert <~ *language*> **4** to snatch forcibly; wrest <~ *the knife from her hand*>

[2]**wrench** *n* **1a** a violent twisting or a sideways pull **b** (a sharp twist or sudden jerk causing) a strain to a muscle, ligament, etc (e g of a joint) **c** (sthg causing) acute emotional distress or violent mental change **2a** a spanner with jaws adjustable for holding nuts of different sizes **b** *NAm* a spanner

wrest /rest‖rest/ *vt* **1** to obtain or take away by violent wringing or twisting **2** to obtain with difficulty by force or determined labour <~ *a living from the stony soil*> **3** WRENCH 3

[1]**wrestle** /'resl‖'resl/ *vi* **1** to contend with an opponent in wrestling **2** to engage in a violent or determined struggle; grapple <~ *with a problem*> ~ *vt* **1** to wrestle with **2** to push, pull, or manhandle by force – **wrestler** *n*

[2]**wrestle** *n* the action or an instance of wrestling; *esp* a wrestling bout

wrestling /'resling‖'reslɪŋ/ *n* a sport or contest in which 2 unarmed individuals struggle hand to hand, with each trying to subdue or unbalance the other

wretch /rech‖retʃ/ *n* **1** a profoundly unhappy or unfortunate person **2** a base, despicable, or vile person or animal

wretched /ˈrechid‖ˈretʃɪd/ *adj* **1** deeply afflicted, dejected, or unfortunate **2** deplorably bad <*was in ~ health*> **3** (appearing) mean, squalid, or contemptible <*dressed in ~ old clothes*> **4** causing annoyance; damned – used as a general expression of annoyance <*lost my ~ socks*> – **wretchedly** *adv*, **wretchedness** *n*

[1]**wriggle** /ˈrigl‖ˈrɪgl/ *vi* **1** to move the body or a bodily part to and fro with short writhing motions; squirm **2** to move or advance by twisting and turning **3** to extricate or insinuate oneself by manoeuvring, equivocation, evasion, or ingratiation <*managed to ~ out of a difficult question*> ~ *vt* **1** to cause to move in short quick contortions <*she* ~d *her hips*> **2** to manoeuvre into a state or place by wriggling **3** to make (one's way) by wriggling – **wriggler** *n*, **wriggly** *adj*

[2]**wriggle** *n* a short or quick writhing motion or contortion

wright /riet‖raɪt/ *n* a craftsman – usu in combination <*ship*wright> <*play*wright>

wring /ring‖rɪŋ/ *vt* **wrung** /rung‖rʌŋ/ **1** to twist or compress, esp so as to extract liquid <*~ the towel dry*> **2a** to expel or obtain (as if) by twisting and compressing <*~ the water from the towel*> **b** to exact or extort by coercion or with difficulty <*~ a confession from the suspect*> **3a** to twist so as to strain, sprain, or break <*~ a chicken's neck*> **b** to twist together (one's clasped hands) as a sign of anguish **4** to distress, torment <*a tragedy that* ~s *the heart*> **5** to shake (sby's hand) vigorously in greeting – **wring** *n*

wringer /ˈring·ə‖ˈrɪŋə/ *n* a mangle

[1]**wrinkle** /ˈringkl‖ˈrɪŋkl/ *n* **1** a small ridge, crease, or furrow formed esp in the skin due to aging or stress or on a previously smooth surface (e g by shrinkage or contraction) **2** a valuable trick or dodge for effecting a result – infml – **wrinkly** *adj*

[2]**wrinkle** *vt* to contract into wrinkles ~ *vi* to become marked with or contracted into wrinkles

wrist /rist‖rɪst/ *n* **1** (a part of a lower animal corresponding to) the (region of the) joint between the human hand and the arm **2** the part of a garment or glove covering the wrist

ˈ**wrist**ˌ**band** /-ˌband‖-ˌbænd/ *n* a band (e g on the sleeve of a garment) encircling the wrist

ˈ**wrist**ˌ**watch** /-ˌwoch‖-ˌwɒtʃ/ *n* a small watch attached to a bracelet or strap and worn round the wrist

wristy /ˈristi‖ˈrɪstɪ/ *adj* characterized by or tending to use a lot of wrist movement (e g in hitting a ball with a bat or club) – **wristily** *adv*

writ /rit‖rɪt/ *n* **1a** an order in writing issued under seal in the name of the sovereign or of a court or judicial officer commanding or forbidding an act specified in it **b** a written order constituting a symbol of the power and authority of the issuer **2** *archaic* sthg written; writing – esp in *holy writ, sacred writ*

write /riet‖raɪt/ *vb* **wrote** /roht‖rəʊt/; **written** /ˈritn‖ˈrɪtn/ *also* **writ** /rit‖rɪt/ *vt* **1a** to form (legible characters, symbols, or words) on a surface, esp with an instrument **b** to spell in writing **c** to cover, fill, or fill in by writing <*~ a cheque*> **2** to set down in writing: e g **2a** to be the author of; compose **b** to use (a specific script or language) in writing <*~ shorthand*> **3** to express, record, or reveal (as if) in writing <written *on my heart*> **4** to make (a quality or condition) evident – usu pass <*guilt was* written *all over his face*> **5** to introduce or remove by writing <*~ a clause into a contract*> **6** to introduce or transfer (information) into or from a computer memory **7** *chiefly NAm* to communicate with in writing <wrote *them on his arrival*> ~ *vi* **1** to make significant written characters, inscriptions, words, or sentences <*learning to ~*>; *also* to be adapted to writing <*pen* ~s *badly*> **2** to compose, communicate by, or send a letter **3** to produce or compose a written work, esp professionally, for publication or performance – **writable** *adj*

ˈ**write-**ˌ**down** *n* a deliberate reduction in the book value of an asset (e g to reflect the effect of obsolescence or deflation)

write down *vt* **1** to record in written form **2** to disparage, injure, or minimize by writing ~ *vi* to write so as to appeal to a lower level of taste, comprehension, or intelligence – usu + *to*

ˈ**write-**ˌ**off** *n* sthg written off as a total loss

write off *vt* **1** to cancel <write off *a bad debt*> **2** to concede to be irreparably lost, useless, or dead ~ *vi* to write and send a letter

write out *vt* to put in writing; *esp* to put into a full and complete written form

writer /ˈrietə‖ˈraɪtə/ *n* **1** one who writes as an occupation; an author **2** *Scot* WRITER TO THE SIGNET

ˌ**writer's** ˈ**cramp** *n* a painful spasmodic cramp of the hand or finger muscles brought on by excessive writing

ˌ**Writer to the** ˈ**Signet** *n* a Scottish solicitor

ˈ**write-**ˌ**up** *n* a written, esp flattering, account

write up *vt* **1a** to write an account of; describe <wrote up *the fire*> **b** to put into finished written form <write up *my notes*> **2** to bring up to date the writing of (e g a diary) **3** to praise or maximize in writing

writhe /riedh‖raɪð/ *vt* to twist (the body or a bodily part) in pain ~ *vi* **1** to proceed with twists and turns **2** to twist (as if) from pain or struggling **3** to suffer keenly <*~ under an insult*> – **writhe** *n*

writing /ˈrieting‖ˈraɪtɪŋ/ *n* **1** the act, practice, or occupation of literary composition **2a** written letters or words; *esp* handwriting <*put it in ~*> **b** a written composition <*the* ~s *of Marx*> **c** a written or printed letter, notice, document, or inscription – **writing on the wall** an omen of one's unpleasant fate

ˈ**writing** ˌ**desk** *n* a desk often with a sloping top for writing on

ˈ**writing** ˌ**paper** *n* a sized paper that can be written on with ink; *esp* notepaper

[1]**wrong** /rong‖rɒŋ/ *n* **1** an injurious, unfair, or unjust act; action or conduct inflicting harm without due provocation or just cause **2** what is

wrong, immoral, or unethical **3a** the state of being mistaken or incorrect <*my guess was hopelessly in the* ~> **b** the state of being or appearing to be the offender <*put me in the* ~>

[2]**wrong** *adj* **1** against moral standards; evil **2** not right or proper according to a code, standard, or convention; improper **3** not according to truth or facts; incorrect; *also* in error; mistaken **4** not satisfactory (e g in condition, results, health, or temper) **5** not in accordance with one's needs, intent, or expectations **6** of or being the side of sthg not meant to be used or exposed or thought the less desirable – **wrongly** *adv*, **wrongness** *n*

[3]**wrong** *adv* **1** without accuracy; incorrectly **2** without regard for what is proper **3** on a mistaken course; astray **4** out of proper working order

[4]**wrong** *vt* **1** to do wrong to; injure, harm **2** to mistakenly impute a base motive to; misrepresent – **wronger** *n*

wrongdoer /ˌrongˈdooh·ə, ˈ-ˌ--‖ˌrɒŋˈduːə, ˈ-ˌ--/ *n* one who transgresses (moral) laws – **wrongdoing** *n*

ˈ**wrongful** /-f(ə)l‖-f(ə)l/ *adj* **1** wrong, unjust **2** unlawful – **wrongfully** *adv*, **wrongfulness** *n*

ˌ**wrongˈheaded** /-ˈhedid‖-ˈhedɪd/ *adj* stubborn in adherence to wrong opinion or principles; perverse – **wrongheadedly** *adv*, **wrongheadedness** *n*

wrote /roht‖rəʊt/ *past of* WRITE

wroth /roth‖rɒθ/ *adj* wrathful – poetic or humor

wrought /rawt‖rɔːt/ *adj* **1** worked into shape by artistry or effort **2** processed for use; manufactured **3** *of metals* beaten into shape by tools **4** deeply stirred; excited – usu + *up*

ˌ**wrought ˈiron** *n* a tough malleable iron containing very little carbon and 1 or 2 per cent slag

wrung /rung‖rʌŋ/ *past of* WRING

wry /rie‖raɪ/ *adj* **1** bent or twisted, esp to one side **2** ironically or grimly humorous – **wryly** *adv*, **wryness** *n*

x /eks‖eks/ *n, pl* **x's, xs** *often cap* **1** (a graphic representation of or device for reproducing) the 24th letter of the English alphabet **2** ten **3** one designated *x*, esp as the 24th in order or class or the 1st in a series that includes *x*, *y*, and sometimes *z* **4** sby or sthg whose identity is unknown or withheld

X *n or adj* (a film that is) certified in Britain as suitable only for people over 18 – no longer used technically

ˈ**X ˌchromosome** *n* a sex chromosome that in humans occurs paired in each female cell and single in each male cell

xenon /ˈzeenon, ˈzenon‖ˈziːnɒn, ˈzenɒn/ *n* a heavy noble gaseous element used esp in specialized flashtubes

xenophobia /ˈzenəfohbi·ə, -byə‖ˈzenəfəʊbɪə, -bjə/ *n* hatred or fear of strangers or foreigners [deriv of Greek *xenos* stranger + *phobos* fear] – **xenophobe** *n*, **xenophobic** *adj*

xerography /zeˈrogrəfi, ziə-‖zeˈrɒgrəfɪ, zɪə-/ *n* a process for copying graphic matter by the action of light on an electrically charged surface in which the latent image is developed with a resinous powder [deriv of Greek *xēros* dry + *graphein* to write] – **xerographic** *adj*

xerox /ˈzeroks, ˈziəroks‖ˈzerɒks, ˈzɪərɒks/ *vt, often cap* to copy on a Xerox machine

Xerox *trademark* – used for a xerographic copier

Xmas /ˈeksməs‖ˈeksməs/ *n* Christmas

x-ray /ˈeksray‖ˈeksreɪ/ *vt, often cap* to examine, treat, or photograph with X rays

X ray /ˈeks ray‖ˈeks reɪ/ *n* **1** an electromagnetic radiation of extremely short wavelength that has the properties of ionizing a gas when passing through it and of penetrating various thicknesses of all solids **2** an examination or photograph made by means of X rays

xylem /ˈzieləm, ˈzielem‖ˈzaɪləm, ˈzaɪlem/ *n* a complex vascular tissue of higher plants that functions chiefly in the conduction of water, gives support, and forms the woody part of many plants

xylophone /ˈzieləˌfohn‖ˈzaɪləˌfəʊn/ *n* a percussion instrument that has a series of wooden bars graduated in length and sounded by striking with 2 small wooden hammers [deriv of Greek *xylon* wood + *phōnē* voice, sound] – **xylophonist** *n*

y /wie‖waɪ/ *n, pl* **y's, ys** *often cap* **1** (a graphic representation of or device for reproducing) the 25th letter of the English alphabet **2** one designated *y*, esp as the 2nd in a series that includes *x*, *y*, and sometimes *z*

[1]**-y** *also* **-ey** /-i‖-ɪ/ *suffix* (*n, vb* → *adj*) **1a** covered with; full of <*dirty*> **b** having the quality of <*waxy*> **c** addicted to; enthusiastic about <*horsy*> **d** like; like that of <*wintry*> – often derog <*stagy*> **2** tending or inclined to <*sleepy*> **3** slightly; rather; -ish <*chilly*>

[2]**-y** *suffix* (→ *n*) **1** state, condition, or quality of <*beggary*> **2** whole body or group sharing (a specified class or state) <*soldiery*>

[3]**-y** *suffix* (*n* → *n*) instance of (a specified action) <*entreaty*>

[4]**-y** *suffix* (→ *n*) little; dear <*doggy*> – used esp in pet names by or to children

[1]**yacht** /yot‖jɒt/ *n* any of various relatively small sailing or powered vessels that characteristically have a sharp prow and graceful lines and are used for pleasure cruising or racing [obs Dutch *jaght*, fr Middle Low German *jacht*, short for *jachtschiff*, lit., hunting ship]

[2]**yacht** *vi* to race or cruise in a yacht – **yachting** *n*

yachtsman /ˈyotsmən‖ˈjɒtsmən/ *n* sby who owns or sails a yacht

yahoo /'yah·hooh, 'yay-‖'jɑːhuː, 'jeɪ-/ *n, pl* **yahoos** an uncouth, rowdy, or degraded person [*Yahoo*, a member of a race of human brutes in *Gulliver's Travels* by Jonathan Swift (1667-1745), Irish satirist]

[1]**yak** /yak‖jæk/ *n*, a large long-haired wild or domesticated ox of Tibet and nearby mountainous regions

[2]**yak, yack** /yak‖jæk/ *n* persistent or voluble talk – slang

[3]**yak, yack** *vi* **-kk-** to talk persistently; chatter – slang

yam /yam‖jæm/ *n* **1** (any of various related plants with) an edible starchy tuberous root used as a staple food in tropical areas **2** *NAm* a moist-fleshed usu orange sweet potato

yammer /'yamə‖'jæmə/ *vt* to say in voluble complaint ~ *vi* **1** to wail, whimper **2** to complain, grumble **3** to talk volubly; clamour ***USE*** infml – **yammer** *n*

yang /yang‖jæŋ/ *n* the masculine active principle in nature that in Chinese thought eternally interacts with its opposite and complementary principle, yin

yank /yangk‖jæŋk/ *vb* to pull or extract (sthg) with a quick vigorous movement – infml – **yank** *n*

Yank *n, chiefly Br slang* a Yankee

Yankee /'yangki‖'jæŋkɪ/ *n* a native or inhabitant of **a** *chiefly Br* the USA **b** *chiefly NAm* the N USA **c** *NAm* New England [perhaps fr the Dutch names *Jantje* (diminutive of *Jan* John) or *Jan Kees* (John Cornelius), allegedly used as nicknames by early Dutch settlers in America] – **Yankee** *adj*

[1]**yap** /yap‖jæp/ *vi* **-pp-** **1** to bark snappishly; yelp **2** to talk in a shrill insistent querulous way; scold – infml – **yapper** *n*

[2]**yap** *n* **1** a quick sharp bark; a yelp **2** (foolish) chatter – infml

[1]**yard** /yahd‖jɑːd/ *n* **1a** a unit of length equal to 3ft (about 0.914m) **b** a unit of volume equal to $1yd^3$ (about $0.765m^3$) **2** a long spar tapered towards the ends to support and spread a sail

[2]**yard** *n* **1a** a small usu walled and often paved area open to the sky and adjacent to a building; a courtyard **b** the grounds of a specified building or group of buildings – in combination <*a farm*yard> **2a** an area set aside for a specified business or activity – often in combination <*a brick*yard> **b** a system of tracks for the storage and maintenance of railway carriages and wagons and the making up of trains **3** *cap, Br* SCOTLAND YARD – + *the* **4** *NAm* a garden of a house

yardage /'yahdij‖'jɑːdɪdʒ/ *n* the length, extent, or volume of sthg as measured in yards

yardarm /'yahd,ahm‖'jɑːd,ɑːm/ *n* either end of the yard of a square-rigged ship

'yard,stick /-,stik‖-,stɪk/ *n* **1** a graduated measuring stick 1yd long **2** a standard basis of calculation or judgment; a criterion

[1]**yarn** /yahn‖jɑːn/ *n* **1a** THREAD 1; *esp* a spun thread (e g of wool, cotton, or hemp) as prepared and used for weaving, knitting, and rope-making **b** a similar strand of metal, glass, asbestos, paper, or plastic **2a** a narrative of adventures; *esp* a tall tale **b** a conversation, chat ***USE*** (2) infml

[2]**yarn** *vi* to tell a yarn; *also* to chat garrulously – infml

yarrow /'yaroh‖'jærəʊ/ *n* a strong-scented Eurasian composite plant with dense heads of small usu white flowers

yashmak /'yashmak‖'jæʃmæk/ *also* **yasmak** /~, 'yas-‖~, 'jæs-/ *n* a veil worn over the face by Muslim women, so that only the eyes remain exposed

[1]**yaw** /yaw‖jɔː/ *n* the action of yawing; *esp* a side-to-side movement

[2]**yaw** *vi* **1** to deviate erratically from a course **2** *of an aircraft, spacecraft, or projectile* to deviate from a straight course by esp side-to-side movement

yawl /yawl‖jɔːl/ *n* **1** a small boat carried on a ship **2** a fore-and-aft rigged sailing vessel with sails set from a mainmast and a mizzenmast that is situated aft of the rudder

[1]**yawn** /yawn‖jɔːn/ *vt* to utter with a yawn ~ *vi* **1** to open wide; gape <*a* ~*ing chasm*> **2** to open the mouth wide and inhale, usu in reaction to fatigue or boredom – **yawner** *n*, **yawningly** *adv*

[2]**yawn** *n* **1** a deep usu involuntary intake of breath through the wide open mouth **2** a boring thing or person – slang

yaws /yawz‖jɔːz/ *n pl but sing or pl in constr* an infectious tropical disease caused by a spirochaetal bacterium and marked by ulcerating sores

'Y ,chromosome *n* a sex chromosome that in humans occurs paired with an X chromosome in each male cell and does not occur in female cells

[1]**ye** /yee‖jiː/ *pron, archaic or dial* the ones being addressed; you – used orig only as a nominative pl pron

[2]**ye** /dhee, yee‖ðiː, jiː/ *definite article, archaic* the

[1]**yea** /yay‖jeɪ/ *adv* **1** more than this; indeed <*boys,* ~ *and girls too*> **2** *archaic* yes

[2]**yea** *n* **1** affirmation, assent **2** *chiefly NAm* (a person casting) an affirmative vote

yeah /yeə‖jeə/ *adv* yes – used in writing to represent a casual pronunciation

year /yiə‖jɪə/ *n* **1** the period of about $365^1/_4$ solar days required for 1 revolution of the earth round the sun **2a** a cycle in the Gregorian calendar of 365 or 366 days divided into 12 months beginning with January and ending with December **b** a period of time equal to 1 year of the Gregorian calendar but beginning at a different time **3** a calendar year specified usu by a number **4** *pl* age <*a man in* ~*s but a child in understanding*>; *also* old age <*beginning to show his* ~*s*> **5** a period of time (e g that in which a school is in session) other than a calendar year – **year in, year out** for an indefinite or seemingly endless number of successive years

'year,book /-,book‖-,bʊk/ *n* a book published yearly as a report or summary of statistics or facts

yearling /'yiəling‖'jɪəlɪŋ/ *n* sby or sthg 1 year old: e g **a** an animal 1 year old or in its second year **b** a racehorse between January 1st of the year following its birth and the next January 1st – **yearling** *adj*

yearly /'yiəli‖'jɪəlɪ/ *adj* **1** reckoned by the year **2** done or occurring once every year;

annual – **yearly** *adv*

yearn /yuhn‖jɜːn/ *vi* **1** to long persistently, wistfully, or sadly **2** to feel tenderness or compassion – **yearner** *n*, **yearningly** *adv*

yeast /yeest‖jiːst/ *n* **1** a (commercial preparation of) yellowish surface froth or sediment that consists largely of fungal cells, occurs esp in sweet liquids in which it promotes alcoholic fermentation, and is used esp in making alcoholic drinks and as a leaven in baking **2** a minute fungus that is present and functionally active in yeast, usu has little or no mycelium, and reproduces by budding

yeasty /ˈyeesti‖ˈjiːstɪ/ *adj* **1** of or resembling yeast **2a** churning with growth and change; turbulent **b** trivial, frivolous – **yeastily** *adv*, **yeastiness** *n*

[1]**yell** /yel‖jel/ *vt* to utter or declare (as if) with a scream; shout ~ *vi* to utter a sharp loud cry, scream, or shout – **yeller** *n*

[2]**yell** *n* a scream, shout

[1]**yellow** /ˈyeloh‖ˈjeləʊ/ *adj* **1a** of the colour yellow **b** yellowish through age, disease, or discoloration; sallow **c** having a yellow or light brown complexion or skin **2a** featuring sensational or scandalous items or ordinary news sensationally distorted <~ *journalism*> **b** dishonourable, cowardly – infml – **yellowish** *adj*, **yellowy** *adj*

[2]**yellow** *vb* to make or become yellow

[3]**yellow** *n* **1** a colour whose hue resembles that of ripe lemons or dandelions and lies between green and orange in the spectrum **2** sthg yellow: e g **2a** sby with yellow or light brown skin **b** the yolk of an egg **c** a yellow ball (e g in snooker) **3** *pl but sing in constr* any of several plant diseases caused esp by viruses and marked by yellowing of the foliage and stunting

ˌ**yellow** ˈ**fever** *n* an often fatal infectious disease of warm regions caused by a mosquito-transmitted virus and marked by fever, jaundice, and often bleeding

ˌ**yellow** ˈ**peril** *n, often cap Y&P* a danger to Western civilization held to arise from expansion of the power and influence of Oriental peoples

ˌ**yellow** ˈ**pimpernel** *n* a common European pimpernel with nearly prostrate stems and bright yellow flowers

yelp /yelp‖jelp/ *vi or n* (to utter) a sharp quick shrill cry <*dogs* ~> – **yelper** *n*

[1]**yen** /yen‖jen/ *n, pl* **yen** the standard unit of money in Japan

[2]**yen** *n* a strong desire or propensity; a longing – infml [obs slang *yen-yen* (craving for opium), fr Chinese (Cantonese dialect) *in-yăn*, fr *in* opium + *yăn* craving]

[3]**yen** *vi* **-nn-** to yearn

yeoman /ˈyohmən‖ˈjəʊmən/ *n, pl* **yeomen** **1** a petty officer who **1a** carries out visual signalling in the British navy **b** carries out clerical duties in the US navy **2** a small farmer who cultivates his own land

ˌ**yeoman of the** ˈ**guard** *n* a member of a military corps attached to the British Royal Household who serve as ceremonial attendants of the sovereign and as warders of the Tower of London

ˈ**yeomanry** /-ri‖-rɪ/ *n sing or pl in constr* **1** the body of small landed proprietors **2** a British volunteer cavalry force created from yeomen in 1761 as a home defence force and reorganized in 1907 as part of the territorial force

[1]**yes** /yes‖jes/ *adv* **1** – used in answers expressing affirmation, agreement, or willingness; contrasted with *no* <*are you ready?* Yes, *I am*> **2** – used in answers correcting or contradicting a negative assertion or direction <*don't say that!* Yes, *I will*> **3** YEA 1 **4** – indicating uncertainty or polite interest or attentiveness <Yes? *What do you want?*>

[2]**yes** *n* an affirmative reply or vote; an aye

ˈ**yes-**ˌ**man** *n* one who endorses or supports everything said to him, esp by a superior; a sycophant – infml

[1]**yesterday** /ˈyestəday, -di‖ˈjestədeɪ, -dɪ/ *adv* on the day before today

[2]**yesterday** *n* **1** the day before today **2** recent time; time not long past

[1]**yet** /yet‖jet/ *adv* **1a** again; IN ADDITION <*gives* ~ *another reason*> **b** EVEN 2b <*a* ~ *higher speed*> **2a** up to this or that time; so far – not in affirmative statements <*hasn't had breakfast* ~> **b** STILL 1, 2 <*have* ~ *to learn the truth*> **c** at some future time and despite present appearances <*we may win* ~> **3** nevertheless <*strange and* ~ *true*> – **yet again** still one more time

[2]**yet** *conj* but nevertheless

yeti /ˈyeti‖ˈjetɪ/ *n* ABOMINABLE SNOWMAN

yew /yooh‖juː/ *n* (the wood of) any of a genus of evergreen coniferous trees and shrubs with stiff straight leaves and red fruits

Y-fronts *n* men's underpants in which the stitching at the front forms an inverted Y

Yiddish /ˈyidish‖ˈjɪdɪʃ/ *n* a High German language containing elements of Hebrew and Slavonic that is usu written in Hebrew characters and is spoken by Jews chiefly in or from E Europe – **Yiddish** *adj*

[1]**yield** /yeeld‖jiːld/ *vt* **1** to give or render as fitting, rightfully owed, or required **2** to give up possession of on claim or demand: e g **2a** to surrender or submit (oneself) to another **b** to give (oneself) up to an inclination, temptation, or habit **c** to relinquish (e g a position of advantage or point of superiority) <~ *precedence*> **3a** to bear or bring forth as a natural product <*the tree* ~s *good fruit*> **b** to give as a return or in result of expended effort <*properly handled this soil should* ~ *good crops*> **c** to produce as revenue <*the tax is expected to* ~ *millions*> ~ *vi* **1** to be fruitful or productive **2** to give up and cease resistance or contention; submit, succumb **3** to give way to pressure or influence; submit to urging, persuasion, or entreaty **4** to give way under physical force (e g bending, stretching, or breaking) **5** to give place or precedence; acknowledge the superiority of another – **yielder** *n*

[2]**yield** *n* (the amount of) sthg yielded or produced

yielding /ˈyeelding‖ˈjiːldɪŋ/ *adj* lacking rigidity or stiffness; flexible

yin /yin‖jɪn/ *n* the feminine passive principle in

nature that in Chinese thought eternally interacts with its opposite and complementary principle, yang

yippee /yi'pee‖jɪ'pi:/ *interj* – used to express exuberant delight or triumph

yob /yob‖jɒb/ *n, Br* a loutish youth; *esp* a hooligan – slang [back slang for *boy*]

yobbo /'yoboh‖'jɒbəʊ/ *n, Br* a yob – slang

[1]**yodel** /'yohdl‖'jəʊdl/ *vb* **-ll-** (*NAm* **-l-**, **-ll-**) to sing, shout, or call (a tune) by suddenly changing from a natural voice to a falsetto and back – **yodeller** *n*

[2]**yodel** *n* a yodelled song, shout, or cry

yoga /'yohgə‖'jəʊgə/ *n* **1** *cap* a Hindu philosophy teaching the suppression of all activity of body, mind, and will so that the self may attain liberation from them **2** a system of exercises for attaining bodily or mental control and well-being [Sanskrit, lit., yoking, fr *yunakti* he yokes] – **yogic** *adj, often cap*

yoghourt, yoghurt, yogurt /'yogət‖'jɒgət/ *n* a slightly acid semisolid food made of milk fermented by bacteria

yogi /'yohgi‖'jəʊgɪ/ *n* **1** sby who practises or is a master of yoga **2** *cap* an adherent of Yoga philosophy

[1]**yoke** /yohk‖jəʊk/ *n* **1a** a bar or frame by which 2 draught animals (e g oxen) are joined at the heads or necks for working together **b** an arched device formerly laid on the neck of a defeated person **c** a frame fitted to sby's shoulders to carry a load in 2 equal portions **d** a crosspiece on a rudder to which steering lines are attached **2** *sing or pl in constr* 2 animals yoked or worked together **3a** an oppressive agency **b** a tie, link; *esp* marriage **4** a fitted or shaped piece at the top of a garment from which the rest hangs

[2]**yoke** *vt* **1** to attach (a draught animal) to (sthg) **2** to join (as if) by a yoke

yokel /'yohkl‖'jəʊkl/ *n* a naive or gullible rustic; a country bumpkin

yolk *also* **yoke** /yohk‖jəʊk/ *n* **1** the usu yellow spheroidal mass of stored food that forms the inner portion of the egg of a bird or reptile and is surrounded by the white **2** a mass of protein, lecithin, cholesterol, etc that is stored in an ovum as food for the developing embryo – **yolked** *adj*, **yolky** *adj*

yomp /yomp‖jɒmp/ *vi, Br* to march laboriously, esp while carrying heavy baggage – slang

yonder /'yondə‖'jɒndə/ *adj or adv* over there

yonks /yongks‖jɒŋks/ *n, Br* a long time; ages – infml

yore /yaw‖jɔ:/ *n* time (long) past – usu in *of yore*

yorker /'yawkə‖'jɔ:kə/ *n* a ball bowled in cricket that is aimed to bounce on the popping crease and so pass under the bat

,Yorkshire 'pudding *n* a savoury baked pudding made from a batter and usu eaten before or with roast beef

,Yorkshire 'terrier *n* a compact toy terrier with long straight silky hair mostly bluish grey but tan on the head and chest

you /yoo‖jʊ; *strong* yooh‖ju:/ *pron, pl* **you** **1** the one being addressed **2** a person; one <*funny, when* ~ *come to think of it*>

you'd /yoohd‖ju:d/ you had; you would

you'll /yoohl‖ju:l/ you will; you shall

[1]**young** /yung‖jʌŋ/ *adj* **1** in the first or an early stage of life, growth, or development **2** recently come into being; new **3** of or having the characteristics (e g vigour or gaiety) of young people – **youngish** *adj*, **youngness** *n*

[2]**young** *n pl* **1** young people; youth **2** immature offspring, esp of an animal – **with young** *of a female animal* pregnant

youngster /'yungstə‖'jʌŋstə/ *n* **1** a young person or creature **2** a child, baby

your /yə‖jə; *strong* yaw‖jɔ:/ *adj* **1** of, belonging to, or done by or to you or yourself or yourselves **2** of one or oneself **3** – used for indicating sthg well-known and characteristic; infml < ~ *typical commuter*> *USE* used attributively

you're /yaw, yooə‖jɔ:, ʹjʊə/ you are

yours /yawz‖jɔ:z/ *pron, pl* **yours** that which or the one who belongs to you – **yours truly 1** I, me, myself <*I can take care of* yours truly> **2** your letter <yours truly *of the 19th*>

yourself /yə'self, yaw'self‖jə'self, jɔ:'self/ *pron, pl* **yourselves** /-'selvz‖-'selvz/ **1a** that identical person or creature that is you – used reflexively <*enjoy* yourselves, *everyone*>, for emphasis <*carry it* ~>, or in absolute constructions **b** your normal self <*soon be* ~ *again*> **2** oneself

youth /yoohth‖ju:θ/ *n, pl* **youths** /yoohdhz‖ju:ðz/ **1** the time of life when one is young; *esp* adolescence **2a** a young male adolescent **b** young people – often pl in constr <*modern* ~> **3** the quality of being youthful

'youthful /-f(ə)l‖-f(ə)l/ *adj* **1** (characteristic) of youth **2** young – **youthfully** *adv*, **youthfulness** *n*

'youth ,hostel *n* a lodging typically providing inexpensive bed and breakfast accommodation for young travellers or hikers – **youth-hosteller** *n*, **youth-hostelling** *n*

you've /yoohv‖ju:v/ you have

yowl /yowl‖jaʊl/ *vi or n* (to utter) the loud long wail of a cat or dog in pain or distress

Yo-yo /'yoh ,yoh‖'jəʊ ,jəʊ/ *trademark* – used for a toy that consists of 2 discs separated by a deep groove in which a string is attached and wound and that is made to fall and rise when held by the string

yucca /'yukə‖'jʌkə/ *n* any of a genus of sometimes treelike plants of the lily family with long often rigid leaves and a large cluster of white flowers

Yugoslavian, Jugoslavian /,yoohgoh'slahvi·ən‖,ju:gəʊ'slɑ:vɪən/ (a native or inhabitant) of Yugoslavia

yule /yoohl‖ju:l/ *n, often cap, archaic* Christmas

'Yule ,log *n* a large log formerly put on the hearth on Christmas Eve as the foundation of the fire

yuppy, yuppie /'yupi‖'yʌpɪ/ *n, chiefly NAm* a trendy and relatively affluent young person living in a city and engaged in a professional career

Z

z /zed‖zed/ *n, pl* **z's, zs** *often cap* **1** (a graphic representation of or device for reproducing) the 26th letter of the English alphabet **2** one designated *z*, esp as the 3rd in a series that includes *x*, *y*, and *z*

[1]zany /ˈzayni‖ˈzeɪnɪ/ *n* one who acts the buffoon

[2]zany *adj* fantastically or absurdly ludicrous – **zanily** *adv*, **zaniness** *n*

zeal /zeel‖ziːl/ *n* eagerness and ardent interest in pursuit of sthg; keenness

zealot /ˈzelət‖ˈzelət/ *n* a zealous person; *esp* a fanatical partisan – **zealot** *adj*, **zealotry** *n*

zealous /ˈzeləs‖ˈzeləs/ *adj* filled with or characterized by zeal – **zealously** *adv*, **zealousness** *n*

zebra /ˈzebrə, ˈzeebrə‖ˈzebrə, ˈziːbrə/ *n*, any of several black and white striped fast-running African mammals related to the horse – **zebrine** *adj*, **zebroid** *adj*

ˌzebra ˈcrossing *n* a road crossing in Britain marked by a series of broad white stripes to indicate that pedestrians have the right of way

zebu /ˈzeeb(y)ooh‖ˈziːb(j)uː/ *n* an ox of any of several breeds of domesticated Asiatic oxen with a large fleshy hump over the shoulders

Zen /zen‖zen/ *n* a Japanese Buddhist sect that aims at enlightenment by direct intuition through meditation (e g on paradoxes)

zenith /ˈzenith‖ˈzenɪθ/ *n* **1** the point of the celestial sphere that is directly opposite the nadir and vertically above the observer **2** the highest point reached in the heavens by a celestial body **3** the culminating point or stage <*at the* ~ *of his powers* – John Buchan>

zephyr /ˈzefə‖ˈzefə/ *n* **1** a gentle breeze, esp from the west **2** any of various lightweight fabrics or articles of clothing

zeppelin /ˈzep(ə)lin‖ˈzep(ə)lɪn/ *n, often cap* a large rigid cigar-shaped airship of a type built in Germany in the early 20th c; *broadly* an airship [Count Ferdinand von *Zeppelin* (1838-1917), German general & aeronaut]

[1]zero /ˈziəroh‖ˈzɪərəʊ/ *n, pl* **zeros** *also* **zeroes** **1** the arithmetical symbol 0 or /0 denoting the absence of all magnitude or quantity **2** (the number) 0 **3** the point of departure in reckoning; *specif* the point from which the graduation of a scale begins **4a** nothing <*slow down to* ~ *in the traffic*> **b** the lowest point <*his spirits fell to* ~> [Italian fr Medieval Latin *zephirum*, fr Arabic *ṣifr*]

[2]zero *adj* **1** having no magnitude or quantity <~ *growth*> **2a** *of a cloud ceiling* limiting vision to 15m (about 50ft) or less **b** *of horizontal visibility* limited to 50m (about 165ft) or less

[3]zero *vt* to adjust the sights of (e g a rifle) ~ *vi* **1** to concentrate firepower on a specified target **2** to move near to or focus attention as if on a target; close *USE* (*vi*) usu + *in on*

ˈzero ˌhour *n* the time at which an event is scheduled to take place

zest /zest‖zest/ *n* **1** the outer peel of a citrus fruit used as flavouring **2** piquancy, spice **3** keen enjoyment; gusto – **zestful** *adj*, **zesty** *adj*

ziggurat /ˈzigərat‖ˈzɪgəræt/ *n* a temple tower of ancient Mesopotamia in the form of a stepped pyramid

[1]zigzag /ˈzigˌzag‖ˈzɪgˌzæg/ *n* a line, course, or pattern consisting of a series of sharp alternate turns or angles <*a blue shirt with red* ~s>

[2]zigzag *adj* forming or going in a zigzag; consisting of zigzags – **zigzag** *adv*

[3]zigzag *vb* **-gg-** *vt* to form into a zigzag ~ *vi* to proceed along or consist of a zigzag course

[1]zinc /zingk‖zɪŋk/ *n* a bluish-white metallic element that is used esp as a protective coating for iron and steel

[2]zinc *vt* **-c-, -ck-** to treat or coat with zinc

zinnia /ˈzinyə, ˈzini·ə‖ˈzɪnjə, ˈzɪnɪə/ *n* any of a small genus of tropical American composite plants with showy flower heads and long-lasting ray flowers [Johann *Zinn* (1727-59), German botanist]

Zionism /ˈzie·əˌniz(ə)m‖ˈzaɪəˌnɪz(ə)m/ *n* a movement for setting up a Jewish homeland in Palestine – **Zionist** *adj or n*

[1]zip /zip‖zɪp/ *vb* **-pp-** *vi* **1** to move with speed and vigour **2** to become open, closed, or attached by means of a zip **3** to travel with a sharp hissing or humming sound ~ *vt* **1** to close or open (as if) with a zip **2** to add zest or life to – often + *up*

[2]zip *n* **1** a light sharp hissing sound **2** energy, liveliness **3** *chiefly Br* a fastener that joins 2 edges of fabric by means of 2 flexible spirals or rows of teeth brought together by a sliding clip – **zippy** *adj*, **zippily** *adv*

[3]zip *adj* zip-up

ˈzip ˌcode *n, often cap Z&I&P* a 5-digit number that is used in the postal address of a place in the USA to assist sorting [*z*one *i*mprovement *p*lan]

zipper /ˈzipə‖ˈzɪpə/ *n, chiefly NAm* ZIP 3

ˈzip-ˌup *adj* fastened by means of a zip

zither /ˈzidhə‖ˈzɪðə/ *n* a stringed instrument having usu 30 to 40 strings over a shallow horizontal soundboard and played with plectrum and fingers – **zitherist** *n*

zizz /ziz‖zɪz/ *vi or n, Br* (to) nap, doze – infml

zodiac /ˈzohdiak‖ˈzəʊdɪæk/ *n* an imaginary belt in the heavens that encompasses the apparent paths of all the principal planets except Pluto, has the ecliptic as its central line, and is divided into 12 constellations or signs each taken for astrological purposes to extend 30 degrees of longitude [Middle French *zodiaque*, fr Latin *zodiacus*, fr Greek *zōidiakos*, fr *zōidion* carved figure, sign of the zodiac, fr diminutive of *zōion* living being, figure] – **zodiacal** *adj*

zombie, *NAm also* **zombi** /ˈzombi‖ˈzɒmbɪ/ *n* **1** a human in the W Indies capable only of automatic movement who is held, esp in Haitian voodooism, to have died and been reanimated **2** a person resembling the walking dead; *esp* a shambling automaton – **zombielike** *adj*

[1]zone /zohn‖zəʊn/ *n* **1a** any of 5 great divisions of the earth's surface with respect to latitude and temperature **b** a portion of the surface of a sphere included between 2 parallel planes **2** an area distinct from adjoining parts **3** any of the sections into which an area is divided for a particular purpose – **zonal** *adj*, **zonate, zonated** *adj*

[2]zone *vt* **1** to arrange in, mark off, or partition into zones **2** to assign to a zone

<*neighbourhood has been* ~d *as residential*> – **zoner** *n*

zonked /zongkt‖zɒŋkt/ *adj* **1** highly intoxicated by alcohol, LSD, etc – often + *out* **2** completely exhausted *USE* slang

zoo /zooh‖zuː/ *n, pl* **zoos** a zoological garden or collection of living animals usu open to the public

zoo- – see ZO-

ˌzooˌlogical ˈgarden /ˌzooh·əˈlojikl, ˌzoh·ə-‖ˌzuːəˈlɒdʒɪkl, ˌzəʊə-/ *n* a garden or park where wild animals are kept for exhibition – often pl with sing. meaning

zoology /zoohˈoləji, zoh-‖zuːˈɒlədʒɪ, zəʊ-/ *n* (biology that deals with) animals and animal life, usu excluding human beings [deriv of Greek *zōion* living being, animal + *logos* speech, reason] – **zoologist** *n*, **zoological** *also* **zoologic** *adj*, **zoologically** *adv*

[1]**zoom** /zoohm‖zuːm/ *vt* to operate the zoom lens of (e g a camera) ~ *vi* **1** to move with a loud low hum or buzz **2** to rise sharply <*retail sales* ~ed>

[2]**zoom** *n* **1** an act or process of zooming **2** ZOOM LENS

zoom lens *n* a lens (e g in a camera) in which the image size can be varied continuously so that the image remains in focus at all times

zoophyte /ˈzoh·əˌfiet‖ˈzəʊəˌfaɪt/ *n* a coral, sponge, or other (branching or treelike) invertebrate animal resembling a plant [Greek *zōophyton*, fr *zōion* living being, animal + *phyton* plant] – **zoophytic** *adj*

zucchini /zoohˈkeeni, tsooh-‖zuːˈkiːnɪ, tsuː-/ *n, pl* **zucchini, zucchinis** *chiefly NAm* a courgette

Zulu /ˈzoohlooh‖ˈzuːluː/ *n* **1** a member of a Bantu-speaking people of Natal **2** a Bantu language of the Zulus – **Zulu** *adj*

zygote /ˈziegoht, ˈzigoht‖ˈzaɪgəʊt, ˈzɪgəʊt/ *n* (the developing individual produced from) a cell formed by the union of 2 gametes – **zygotic** *adj*

zymurgy /ˈziemuhji‖ˈzaɪmɜːdʒɪ/ the science of fermentation processes, esp in brewing [deriv of Greek *zymē* leaven + *ergon* work]

Abbreviations in common use

For abbreviations relating to office procedures see pages 1–13 of the **A–Z Office Guide.**

A **1** ampere **2** Associate
AA **1** Alcoholics Anonymous **2** antiaircraft **3** Automobile Association
AAA Amateur Athletic Association
A and M ancient and modern – used of hymns
AB **1** able seaman; able-bodied seaman **2** *NAm* Bachelor of Arts
ABA **1** Amateur Boxing Association
ABC **1** American Broadcasting Company **2** Australian Broadcasting Commission
ABM antiballistic missile
AC **1** alternating current **2** appellation contrôlée **3** athletic club
a/c account
ACAS Advisory Conciliation and Arbitration Service
AD anno domini
ADC **1** aide-de-camp **2** amateur dramatic club
AEA Atomic Energy Authority
AERE Atomic Energy Research Establishment
AEU Amalgamated Engineering Union
AEW airborne early warning
AF audio frequency
AFM Air Force Medal
AGM *chiefly Br* annual general meeting
AGR advanced gas-cooled reactor
AI **1** artificial insemination **2** artificial intelligence
AIA Associate of the Institute of Actuaries
AID artificial insemination by donor
AIH artificial insemination by husband
AKA also known as
ALA Associate of the Library Association
am ante meridiem
AM **1** Albert Medal **2** amplitude modulation **3** associate member **4** *NAm* Master of Arts
AMDG to the greater glory of God
A/O account of
aob any other business
AOC Air Officer Commanding
AP Associated Press
APEX Association of Professional, Executive, Clerical, and Computer Staff
ARA Associate of the Royal Academy
ARC Agricultural Research Council
ARCA Associate of the Royal College of Art
ARCM Associate of the Royal College of Music
ARCS Associate of the Royal College of Science
ARIBA Associate of the Royal Institute of British Architects
ARP air-raid precautions
asap as soon as possible
ASLEF Associated Society of Locomotive Engineers and Firemen
ASSR Autonomous Soviet Socialist Republic
ASTMS Association of Scientific, Technical, and Managerial Staffs
ATC **1** air traffic control **2** Air Training Corps
ATV Associated Television
AUEW Amalgamated Union of Engineering Workers
AUT Association of University Teachers
AV **1** ad valorem **2** audiovisual **3** Authorized Version (of the Bible)
AVM Air Vice Marshal

b **1** born **2** bowled by **3** bye – used in cricket
B **1** bachelor **2** bishop – used in chess **3** black – used esp on lead pencils
BA **1** Bachelor of Arts **2** British Academy **3** British Airways **4** British Association
b and b, *often cap B & B, Br* bed and breakfast
BAOR British Army of the Rhine
Bart baronet
BB **1** Boys' Brigade **2** double black – used on lead pencils
BBBC British Boxing Board of Control
BBC British Broadcasting Corporation
BC **1** before Christ **2** British Columbia **3** British Council
BCh Bachelor of Surgery
BCom Bachelor of Commerce
BD Bachelor of Divinity
BDA British Dental Association
BDS Bachelor of Dental Surgery
BEd Bachelor of Education
BEF British Expeditionary Force
BEM British Empire Medal
BEng Bachelor of Engineering
BeV billion electron volts
BFPO British Forces Post Office
BL **1** Bachelor of Law **2** bill of lading **3** British Legion **4** British Leyland **5** British Library
BLitt Bachelor of Letters
BM **1** Bachelor of Medicine **2** bench mark **3** British Medal **4** British Museum
BMA British Medical Association
BMJ British Medical Journal
BMus Bachelor of Music
BMX Bicycle Motorcross
BO body odour – euph
BOSS Bureau of State Security (SAfr)
Bp bishop
BP **1** boiling point **2** British Petroleum **3** British Pharmacopoeia
BPC British Pharmaceutical Codex
BPhil Bachelor of Philosophy
BR British Rail
BRS British Road Services
BS **1** Bachelor of Surgery **2** British Standard

BSA Building Societies Association
BSc Bachelor of Science
BSC 1 British Steel Corporation 2 British Sugar Corporation
BSI 1 British Standards Institution 2 Building Societies Institute
BST British Standard Time; British Summer Time
Bt Baronet
BTh Bachelor of Theology
Btu British thermal unit
BUPA British United Provident Association
BV Blessed Virgin
BVM Blessed Virgin Mary

c 1 canine 2 carat 3 caught by 4 centi- 5 century 6 chapter 7 circa 8 copyright
C 1 calorie 2 castle – used in chess 3 Catholic 4 Celsius 5 centigrade 6 *Br* Conservative 7 corps
ca circa
CA 1 California 2 chartered accountant 3 chief accountant 4 Consumers' Association
CAA Civil Aviation Authority
CAB Citizens' Advice Bureau
Cal 1 California 2 (large) calorie
c and b caught and bowled by – used in cricket
C and G City and Guilds
C and W country and western
Cantab of Cambridge
Cantuar of Canterbury
CAP Common Agricultural Policy
CAT 1 College of Advanced Technology 2 computerized axial tomography
CB 1 Citizens' Band 2 Companion of the (Order of the) Bath
CBC Canadian Broadcasting Corporation
CBE Commander of the (Order of the) British Empire
CBI Confederation of British Industry
CBS Columbia Broadcasting System
cc 1 carbon copy 2 chapters 3 cubic centimetre
CC 1 Chamber of Commerce 2 County Council 3 Cricket Club
CD 1 civil defence 2 diplomatic corps
CE 1 Church of England 2 civil engineer 3 Council of Europe
CEGB Central Electricity Generating Board
CENTO Central Treaty Organization
cf compare
CFE College of Further Education
cgs centimetre-gram-second (system)
ch 1 chain – a unit of length 2 central heating 3 chapter 4 check – used in chess 5 church
CH Companion of Honour
ChB Bachelor of Surgery
ChM Master of Surgery
CI Channel Islands
CIA Central Intelligence Agency
CID Criminal Investigation Department
C in C Commander in Chief
cl centilitre
cm centimetre
CMG Companion of (the Order of) St Michael and St George
CND Campaign for Nuclear Disarmament
CO 1 commanding officer 2 conscientious objector
c/o 1 care of 2 carried over
COD cash on delivery
C of E 1 Church of England 2 Council of Europe
C of S Church of Scotland
COHSE Confederation of Health Service Employees
COI Central Office of Information
Col 1 Colonel 2 Colorado
Corp 1 Corporal 2 corporation
cp 1 candlepower 2 compare
CP Communist Party
Cpl Corporal
CPR Canadian Pacific Railway
CPRE Council for the Protection of Rural England
cresc, cres crescendo
CRO 1 cathode ray oscilloscope 2 Criminal Records Office
CRT cathode-ray tube
CS 1 chartered surveyor 2 Civil Service 3 Court of Session – the supreme civil court of Scotland
CSE Certificate of Secondary Education
CSM Company Sergeant Major
CSO 1 Central Statistical Office 2 Community Service Order
CV curriculum vitae
CVO Commander of the (Royal) Victorian Order
CWS Cooperative Wholesale Society
cwt hundredweight

d 1 date 2 daughter 3 day 4 deca- 5 deci- 6 delete 7 penny; pence – used before introduction of decimal currency 8 died
DA district attorney
D & C dilatation and curettage
dB decibel
DBE Dame Commander of the (Order of the) British Empire
DC 1 from the beginning 2 Detective Constable 3 direct current 4 District of Columbia 5 District Commissioner 6 District Council
DCB Dame Commander of the (Order of the) Bath
DCh Doctor of Surgery
DCL Doctor of Civil Law
DCM Distinguished Conduct Medal
DCMG Dame Commander of (the Order of) St Michael and St George
DCVO Dame Commander of the (Royal) Victorian Order
DD Doctor of Divinity
DDS Doctor of Dental Surgery
dec 1 deceased 2 declared – used esp in cricket
DES Department of Education and Science
DF Defender of the Faith
DFC Distinguished Flying Cross
DFM Distinguished Flying Medal
DG 1 by the grace of God 2 director general
DHSS Department of Health and Social Security
DI Detective Inspector
Dip Ed Diploma in Education
Dip HE Diploma in Higher Education
DIY do-it-yourself
DLitt Doctor of Letters

DM Doctor of Medicine
DMus Doctor of Music
do ditto
DOE Department of the Environment
DoT Department of Trade
DP **1** data processing **2** displaced person
dpc damp proof course
DPhil Doctor of Philosophy
DPP Director of Public Prosecutions
dr **1** debtor **2** drachm **3** dram
Dr **1** doctor **2** Drive – used in street names
DS **1** from the sign **2** Detective Sergeant
DSc Doctor of Science
DSC Distinguished Service Cross
DSM Distinguished Service Medal
DSO Distinguished Service Order
DTh, DTheol Doctor of Theology
DV God willing
DVLC Driver and Vehicle Licensing Centre
dz dozen

E **1** Earl **2** earth – used esp on electrical plugs **3** East; Easterly; Eastern **4** energy **5** English
E and OE errors and omissions excepted
ECG electrocardiogram; electrocardiograph
ECT electroconvulsive therapy
EEC European Economic Community
EEG electroencephalogram; electroencephalograph
EFL English as a foreign language
EFTA European Free Trade Association
eg for example
EHF extremely high frequency
EHT extremely high tension
ELF extremely low frequency
ELT English language teaching
EMI Electrical and Musical Industries
EMS European Monetary System
ENEA European Nuclear Energy Agency
ENSA Entertainments National Service Association
ENT ear, nose, and throat
EO Executive Officer
EOC Equal Opportunities Commission
ep en passant
EPNS electroplated nickel silver
ER **1** Eastern Region **2** King Edward **3** Queen Elizabeth
ESA European Space Agency
ESL English as a second language
ESN educationally subnormal
Esq *also* **Esqr** esquire
EST **1** Eastern Standard Time **2** electro-shock treatment
ETA estimated time of arrival
ETD estimated time of departure
et seq and the following one(s)
ETU Electrical Trades Union
EVA extravehicular activity

f **1** fathom **2** female **3** forte **4** focal length **5** folio **6** following (e g page) **7** foot
F **1** Fahrenheit **2** false **3** Fellow **4** filial generation **5** fine – used esp on lead pencils
FA Football Association
FBI Federal Bureau of Investigation
FBR fast breeder reactor
FC **1** Football Club **2** Forestry Commission
FCA Fellow of the (Institute of) Chartered Accountants
FCIS Fellow of the Chartered Institute of Secretaries
FCO Foreign and Commonwealth Office
FCS Fellow of the Chemical Society
FD Defender of the Faith
ff **1** folios **2** following (e g pages) **3** fortissimo
FIFA International Football Federation
fl **1** flourished **2** fluid
FL **1** Florida **2** local length
fl oz fluid ounce
FM Field Marshal
fn footnote
fo, fol folio
FO **1** Field Officer **2** Flying Officer **3** Foreign Office
FOC Father of the Chapel (in a Trade Union)
FOE Friends of the Earth
fpm feet per minute
fps **1** feet per second **2** foot-pound-second
Fr **1** Father **2** French **3** Friar
FRCM Fellow of the Royal College of Music
FRCOG Fellow of the Royal College of Obstetricians and Gynaecologists
FRCP Fellow of the Royal College of Physicians
FRCS Fellow of the Royal College of Surgeons
FRCVS Fellow of the Royal College of Veterinary Surgeons
FRIBA Fellow of the Royal Institute of British Architects
FRIC Fellow of the Royal Institute of Chemistry
FRICS Fellow of the Royal Institution of Chartered Surveyors
FRS Fellow of the Royal Society
FSA Fellow of the Society of Actuaries
ft **1** feet; foot **2** fort

g **1** gauge **2** good **3** gram
G acceleration due to gravity
GB Great Britain
GBE Knight/Dame Grand Cross of the (Order of the) British Empire
GBH *Br* grievous bodily harm
GC George Cross
GCB Knight/Dame Grand Cross of the (Order of the) Bath
GCE General Certificate of Education
GCHQ Government Communications Headquarters
GCMG Knight/Dame Grand Cross of (the Order of) St Michael and St George
GCVO Knight/Dame Grand Cross of the (Royal) Victorian Order
GDP gross domestic product
GDR German Democratic Republic
GHQ general headquarters
GLC Greater London Council
gm gram
GM **1** general manager **2** George Medal **3** guided missile
GMC **1** General Medical Council **2** general management committee
GMT Greenwich Mean Time
GMWU General and Municipal Workers Union
GNP gross national product

GOC General Officer Commanding
GP 1 general practitioner 2 Grand Prix
GPI general paralysis of the insane
GPO general post office
GR King George
GT grand tourer

h 1 hot 2 hour
H 1 harbour 2 hard – used esp on lead pencils
ha hectare
h and c hot and cold (water)
HB hard black – used on lead pencils
HBM His/Her Britannic Majesty
HCF highest common factor
HE 1 high explosive 2 His Eminence 3 His/Her Excellency
HEO Higher Executive Officer
HG 1 His/Her Grace 2 Home Guard
HGV *Br* heavy goods vehicle
HH 1 double hard – used on lead pencils 2 His/Her Highness 3 His Holiness
HIH His/Her Imperial Highness
HIM His/Her Imperial Majesty
HM 1 headmaster 2 headmistress 3His/Her Majesty
HMF His/Her Majesty's Forces
HMG His/Her Majesty's Government
HMI His/Her Majesty's Inspector (of Schools)
HMS His/Her Majesty's Ship
HMSO His/Her Majesty's Stationery Office
HMV His Master's Voice
HNC Higher National Certificate
HND Higher National Diploma
HO Home Office
HP 1 high pressure 2 hire purchase 3 horsepower 4 Houses of Parliament
HQ headquarters
HRH His/Her Royal Highness
HT high-tension
HV 1 high velocity 2 high-voltage
HW 1 high water 2 hot water
Hz hertz

IAEA International Atomic Energy Agency
IATA International Air Transport Association
IBA Independent Broadcasting Authority
ibid ibidem
IBM International Business Machines
i/c in charge
IC integrated circuit
ICBM intercontinental ballistic missile
ICC International Cricket Conference
ICE 1 Institute of Civil Engineers 2 internal-combustion engine
ICI Imperial Chemical Industries
ICL International Computers Limited
id idem
ID 1 Idaho 2 (proof of) identification
IDA International Development Association
i e that is
IHS Jesus
ILEA Inner London Education Authority
ILO International Labour Organization
ILP Independent Labour Party
IMF International Monetary Fund
inc 1 increase 2 *chiefly NAm* incorporated
INRI Jesus of Nazareth, King of the Jews
I/O input/output
IOC International Olympic Committee
IOM Isle of Man
IOW Isle of Wight
IPA International Phonetic Alphabet
IPC International Publishing Corporation
IPM 1 inches per minute 2 Institute of Personnel Management
IPS inches per second
IR 1 information retrieval 2 infrared 3 Inland Revenue
IRA Irish Republican Army
IRBM intermediate range ballistic missile
ISBN International Standard Book Number
ISD international subscriber dialling
ITA Independent Television Authority – now IBA
ITN Independent Television News
ITT International Telephone and Telegraph (Corporation)
ITU International Telecommunications Union
ITV Independent Television
IUD intrauterine device
IVR International Vehicle Registration
IWW Industrial Workers of the World

J 1 joule 2 Judge 3 Justice
JC 1 Jesus Christ 2 Julius Caesar
JCD 1 Doctor of Canon Law 2 Doctor of Civil Law
JCR Junior Common Room
jnr junior
JP Justice of the Peace
Jr junior

k 1 carat 2 kilo- 3 knot
K 1 kelvin 2 king – used in chess 3 knit
KB 1 King's Bench 2 Knight Bachelor
KBE Knight (Commander of the Order of the) British Empire
KC 1 Kennel Club 2 King's Counsel
KCB Knight Commander of the (Order of the) Bath
KCMG Knight Commander of (the Order of) St Michael and St George
KCVO Knight Commander of the (Royal) Victorian Order
kg kilogram
KG Knight of the (Order of the) Garter
KGB (Soviet) State Security Committee
kHz kilohertz
KKK Ku Klux Klan
kl kilolitre
km kilometre
kph kilometres per hour
kt karat
KT 1 knight – used in chess 2 Knight Templar 3 Knight of the (Order of the) Thistle
kV kilovolt
kW kilowatt
kWh, kwh kilowatt-hour

l 1 Lady 2 lake 3 large 4 left 5 length 6 Liberal 7 pound 8 line 9 litre
L 1 live 2 *Br* learner (driver)
La 1 lane – used esp in street names 2 Louisiana
LA 1 Library Association 2 *Br* local authority 3

Los Angeles **4** Louisiana
Lab **1** Labour **2** Labrador
lb **1** pound **2** leg bye
LBC London Broadcasting Company
lbw leg before wicket
lc **1** letter of credit **2** in the place cited **3** lowercase
LCC London County Council
lcd **1** liquid crystal display **2** lowest (*or* least) common denominator
LCM lowest (*or* least) common multiple
LCpl lance corporal
Ld Lord
LDS Licentiate in Dental Surgery
LEA Local Education Authority
led light emitting diode
leg legato
LEM lunar excursion module
LF low frequency
lh left hand
LHA Local Health Authority
LHD Doctor of Letters; Doctor of Humanities
Litt D doctor of letters; doctor of literature
ll lines
LLB Bachelor of Laws
LLD Doctor of Laws
LLM Master of Laws
LOB Location of Offices Bureau
loc cit in the place cited
LPG liquefied petroleum gas
LPO London Philharmonic Orchestra
LRAM Licentiate of the Royal Academy of Music
LSE London School of Economics
LSO London Symphony Orchestra
LT **1** lieutenant **2** low-tension
LTA Lawn Tennis Association
Ltd limited
LV **1** low velocity **2** low voltage **3** *Br* luncheon voucher
LVT **1** landing vehicle, tracked **2** landing vehicle (tank)
LW **1** long wave **2** low water
LWR light water reactor
LWT London Weekend Television

m **1** maiden (over) – used in cricket **2** male **3** married **4** masculine **5** mass **6** metre **7** mile **8** milli- **9** million **10** minute **11** month
M **1** Mach **2** Master **3** mega- **4** Member **5** Monsieur **6** motorway
MA **1** Massachusetts **2** Master of Arts
MAFF Ministry of Agriculture, Fisheries, and Food
MASH *NAm* mobile army surgical hospital
MB Bachelor of Medicine
MBE Member of the (Order of the) British Empire
MC **1** Master of Ceremonies **2** Member of Congress **3** Military Cross
MCC Marylebone Cricket Club
mcg microgram
MCh, MChir Master of Surgery
MD **1** Managing Director **2** Doctor of Medicine **3** right hand – used in music
MDS Master of Dental Surgery
MEP Member of the European Parliament
mf **1** medium frequency **2** mezzo forte
MFH Master of Foxhounds
mg milligram
Mgr **1** Monseigneur **2** Monsignor
MHz megahertz
MI **1** Michigan **2** military intelligence
MIRAS Mortgage Interest Relief at Source
ml **1** mile **2** millilitre
MLitt Master of Letters
Mlle mademoiselle
MLR minimum lending rate
mm millimetre
MM **1** Maelzel's metronome **2** messieurs **3** Military Medal
Mme madame
Mmes mesdames
MN **1** Merchant Navy **2** Minnesota
MO **1** Medical Officer **2** Missouri **3** money order
MoD Ministry of Defence
MOH Medical Officer of Health
MP **1** Member of Parliament **2** Metropolitan Police **3** Military Police; Military Policeman
mpg miles per gallon
mph miles per hour
MPhil Master of Philosophy
MRCP Member of the Royal College of Physicians
MRCS Member of the Royal College of Surgeons
MRCVS Member of the Royal College of Veterinary Surgeons
MS **1** left hand – used in music **2** manuscript **3** Mississippi **4** multiple sclerosis
MSc Master of Science
MSS manuscripts
Mt **1** Matthew **2** Mount
MW **1** medium wave **2** megawatt
mW milliwatt

N **1** name **2** net **3** new **4** neuter **5** note
N **1** knight – used in chess **2** newton **3** North; Northerly; Northern **4** neutral
NA **1** North America **2** not applicable
NAAFI Navy, Army, and Air Force Institutes
NACODS National Association of Colliery Overmen, Deputies and Shotfirers
NALGO National and Local Government Officers Association
NASA National Aeronautics and Space Administration – a US government organization
NATO North Atlantic Treaty Organization
NATSOPA National Society of Operative Printers, Graphical and Media Personnel
nb no ball – used in cricket
NB **1** Nebraska **2** New Brunswick **3** note well
NCB National Coal Board
NCC Nature Conservancy Council
NCO non-commissioned officer
NCP National Car Parks
NCR National Cash Register (Company)
nd no date
NE Northeast; Northeastern
NEB **1** National Enterprise Board **2** New English Bible
NEC National Executive Committee
NEDC National Economic Development Council

NERC Natural Environment Research Council
NF 1 National Front 2 Newfoundland
NFU National Farmers' Union
NFWI National Federation of Women's Institutes
NGA National Graphical Association
NHS National Health Service
NI 1 National Insurance 2 Northern Ireland
NLF National Liberation Front
no 1 not out 2 number 3 *NAm* north
NSB National Savings Bank
NSPCC National Society for the Prevention of Cruelty to Children
NSW New South Wales
NT 1 National Trust 2 New Testament 3 no trumps
NUJ National Union of Journalists
NUM National Union of Mineworkers
NUPE National Union of Public Employees
NUR National Union of Railwaymen
NUS 1 National Union of Seamen 2 National Union of Students
NUT National Union of Teachers
NW Northwest; Northwestern
NY New York
NYC New York City
NZ New Zealand

o ohm
O & M organization and methods
OAP *Br* old-age pensioner
OB outside broadcast
OBE Officer of the (Order of the) British Empire
OC *Br* Officer Commanding
OCTU Officer Cadets Training Unit
OECD Organization for Economic Cooperation and Development
OHMS On His/Her Majesty's Service
OM Order of Merit
ONC Ordinary National Certificate
OND Ordinary National Diploma
ono or near offer
op opus
op cit in the work cited
OPEC Organization of Petroleum Exporting Countries
OS 1 ordinary seaman 2 Ordnance Survey 3 out of stock 4 outsize
OT 1 occupational therapy; Occupational Therapist 2 Old Testament 3 overtime
OTC Officers' Training Corps
OU Open University
OXFAM Oxford Committee for Famine Relief
Oxon 1 Oxfordshire 2 of Oxford
oz ounce; ounces

p 1 page 2 pence; penny 3 per 4 piano – used as an instruction in music 5 pint 6 pressure
P pawn – used in chess
pa per annum
Pa 1 Pennsylvania 2 pascal
PA 1 Pennsylvania 2 personal assistant 3 press agent 4 public addresss (system)
PABX *Br* private automatic branch (telephone) exchange
P & O Peninsular and Oriental (Steamship Company)
p & p *Br* postage and packing
PAX *Br* private automatic (telephone) exchange
PAYE pay as you earn
PBX private branch (telephone) exchange
pc 1 per cent 2 postcard
PC 1 police constable 2 Privy Councillor
PDSA People's Dispensary for Sick Animals
PE physical education
PER Professional Employment Register
per pro by the agency (of)
PGA Professional Golfers' Association
PhB Bachelor of Philosophy
PhD Doctor of Philosophy
plc public limited company
PLO Palestine Liberation Organization
PLP Parliamentary Labour Party
PLR Public Lending Right
pm post meridiem
PM 1 postmortem 2 Prime Minister 3 Provost Marshal
PO 1 Petty Officer 2 Pilot Officer 3 postal order 4 Post Office
POB Post Office Box
POP *Br* Post Office Preferred
POW prisoner of war
pp 1 pages 2 by proxy 3 pianissimo
PPE Philosophy, Politics, and Economics
PPL Private Pilot's Licence
PPS 1 Parliamentary Private Secretary 2 further postscript
PR 1 proportional representation 2 public relations 3 Puerto Rico
PRO 1 Public Records Office 2 public relations officer
PROM programmable read-only memory
PS 1 Police Sergeant 2 postscript 3 Private Secretary
psf pounds per square foot
psi pounds per square inch
PSV *Br* public service vehicle
pt 1 part 2 pint 3 point 4 port
PT 1 Pacific time 2 physical training
PTA Parent-Teacher Association
PTO please turn over
Pty *chiefly Austr, NZ, & SAfr* Proprietary
PVC polyvinyl chloride
pw per week
PW *Br* policewoman
PX post exchange

Q queen – used in chess
QB Queen's Bench
QC Queen's Counsel
QED which was to be demonstrated
QM quartermaster
qqv which (*pl*) see
QSO quasi-stellar object
qt quart
qv which see

R 1 radius 2 railway 3 recto 4 resistance 5 right
R 1 Réaumur 2 queen 3 registered (as a trademark) 4 king 5 river 6 röntgen 7 rook – used in chess 8 Royal

RA 1 Rear Admiral 2 Royal Academician; Royal Academy 3 Royal Artillery
RAAF Royal Australian Air Force
RAC 1 Royal Armoured Corps 2 Royal Automobile Club
RADA Royal Academy of Dramatic Art
RAF Royal Air Force
RAM 1 random access memory 2 Royal Academy of Music
RAMC Royal Army Medical Corps
R & B rhythm and blues
R and D research and development
RAOC Royal Army Ordnance Corps
RC 1 Red Cross 2 reinforced concrete 3 Roman Catholic
RCAF Royal Canadian Air Force
RCM Royal College of Music
RCMP Royal Canadian Mounted Police
RCN 1 Royal Canadian Navy 2 Royal College of Nursing
RE 1 religious education 2 Royal Engineers
Rev, Revd Reverend
RFC 1 Royal Flying Corps 2 Rugby Football Club
RFU Rugby Football Union
rh right hand
RH Royal Highness
RHS 1 Royal Historical Society 2 Royal Horticultural Society 3 Royal Humane Society
RI 1 refractive index 2 religious instruction 3 Rhode Island
RIBA Royal Institute of British Architects
RIC Royal Institute of Chemistry
RICS Royal Institution of Chartered Surveyors
RIP may he/she/they rest in peace
RK religious knowledge
RM 1 Royal Mail 2 Royal Marines
RMA Royal Military Academy (Sandhurst)
RN Royal Navy
RNAS Royal Naval Air Service
RNIB Royal National Institute for the Blind
RNLI Royal National Lifeboat Institution
RNR Royal Naval Reserve
RNVR Royal Naval Volunteer Reserve
ROC Royal Observer Corps
ROM read-only memory
RoSPA Royal Society for the Prevention of Accidents
RPI *Br* retail price index
rpm 1 *Br, often cap* retail price maintenance 2 revolutions per minute
rps revolutions per second
RS 1 right side 2 Royal Society
RSM 1 Regimental Sergeant Major 2 Royal Society of Medicine
RSPB Royal Society for the Protection of Birds
RSPCA Royal Society for the Prevention of Cruelty to Animals
RSV Revised Standard Version (of the Bible)
RSVP please answer
RU Rugby Union
RUC Royal Ulster Constabulary
RV Revised Version (of the Bible)

S 1 second 2 shilling 3 son
S 1 saint 2 South; Southerly; Southern
SA 1 Salvation Army 2 limited liability company 3 Society of Actuaries 4 South Africa 5 South America
sae stamped addressed envelope
SALT Strategic Arms Limitation Talks
SAM surface-to-air missile
SAS Special Air Service
SAYE save-as-you-earn
ScD Doctor of Science
SCE Scottish Certificate of Education
SDI Strategic Defence Initiative
SDLP Social Democratic and Labour Party
SDP Social Democratic Party
SE southeast; southeastern
SEATO Southeast Asia Treaty Organization
SEN State Enrolled Nurse
seq, seqq the following
SERPS State Earnings-Related Pension Scheme
SF science fiction
SG 1 Solicitor General 2 *often not cap* specific gravity
SHAPE Supreme Headquarters Allied Powers Europe
SI International System of Units
SIS Secret Intelligence Service
SJ Society of Jesus
SLADE Society of Lithographic Artists, Designers and Etchers
SLP Scottish Labour Party
SM Sergeant Major
SNP Scottish National Party
SOGAT Society of Graphical and Allied Trades
SP 1 without issue 2 starting price
SPCK Society for Promoting Christian Knowledge
SPQR the Senate and the people of Rome
Sr 1 senior 2 Senor 3 Sir 4 Sister
SRC Science Research Council
SRN State Registered Nurse
SS 1 saints 2 steamship
SSE south-southeast
SSM surface-to-surface missile
SSR Soviet Socialist Republic
SSRC Social Science Research Council
SSW south-southwest
st 1 stánza 2 stitch 3 stone 4 stumped by
St 1 Saint 2 street
STD 1 doctor of sacred theology 2 subscriber trunk dialling
STOL short takeoff and landing
STP standard temperature and pressure
STUC Scottish Trades Union Congress
SW 1 shortwave 2 southwest; southwestern
SWAPO South-West Africa People's Organization

T ton; tonne
TA 1 Territorial Army 2 Transactional Analysis
T & AVR Territorial and Army Volunteer Reserve
TASS the official news agency of the Soviet Union
TB tubercle bacillus
TCCB Test and County Cricket Board
TGWU Transport and General Workers' Union
TIR International Road Transport
TM 1 trademark 2 transcendental meditation

TOPS Training Opportunities Scheme
TSB Trustee Savings Bank
TT **1** teetotal; teetotaller **2** Tourist Trophy **3** tuberculin tested
TU trade union
TUC Trades Union Congress
TV television
TVP textured vegetable protein
TWA Trans-World Airlines

UAE United Arab Emirates
UAR United Arab Republic
UAU Universities Athletic Union
uc upper case
UCCA Universities Central Council on Admissions
UDA Ulster Defence Association
UDI unilateral declaration of independence
UDM Union of Democratic Mineworkers
UDR Ulster Defence Regiment
UEFA Union of European Football Associations
UFO Unidentified Flying Object
UHF ultrahigh frequency
UHT ultrahigh temperature
UK United Kingdom
UKAEA United Kingdom Atomic Energy Authority
UN United Nations
UNA United Nations Association
UNESCO United Nations Educational, Scientific, and Cultural Organization
UNICEF United Nations Children's Fund
UNO United Nations Organization
UPI United Press International
US United States
USA **1** United States Army **2** United States of America
USAF United States Air Force
USN United States Navy
USS United States Ship
USSR Union of Soviet Socialist Republics
UV ultraviolet
UVF Ulster Volunteer Force

v **1** vector **2** verb **3** verse **4** versus **5** very **6** verso **7** vide
V **1** velocity **2** volt; voltage **3** volume
V & A Victoria and Albert Museum
VAT value-added tax
VC **1** Vice Chairman **2** Vice Chancellor **3** Vice Consul **4** Victoria Cross
VCR video cassette recorder
VD venereal disease
VDT visual display terminal
VDU visual display unit
VE Victory in Europe
Vet MB Bachelor of Veterinary Medicine
VHF very high frequency
viz videlicet
VLF very low frequency
VR **1** Queen Victoria **2** Volunteer Reserve
VSO Voluntary Service Overseas
VSOP Very Special Old Pale – a type of brandy
VTOL vertical takeoff and landing
VTR video tape recorder
VV **1** verses **2** vice versa **3** volumes

W **1** Watt **2** West; Westerly; Western
WAAC Women's Army Auxiliary Corps
WAAF Women's Auxiliary Air Force
WAC Women's Army Corps
WAF Women in the Air Force
WBA World Boxing Association
WBC **1** white blood cells; white blood count **2** World Boxing Council
WC water closet
WEA Workers' Education Association
WHO World Health Organization
WI **1** West Indies **2** Wisconsin **3** Women's Institute
WNP Welsh National Party
WO Warrant Officer
WOW War on Want
wpb wastepaper basket
WPC Woman Police Constable
wpm words per minute
WPS Woman Police Sergeant
WR Western Region
WRAC Women's Royal Army Corps
WRAF Women's Royal Air Force
WRNS Women's Royal Naval Service
WRVS Women's Royal Voluntary Service
WW World War

x **1** ex **2** extra
X Christ
XL extra large
XT Christ

yd yard
YHA Youth Hostels Association
YMCA Young Men's Christian Association
YMHA Young Men's Hebrew Association
YTS Youth Training Scheme
YWCA Young Women's Christian Association
YWHA Young Women's Hebrew Association

ZANU Zimbabwe African National Union
ZAPU Zimbabwe African People's Union

A-Z Office Guide

Contents

Preface

The role of the secretary has been transformed in recent years as a result of the new technologies which have been introduced into offices, especially for processing text and distributing information. Although the normal practices and procedures for secretarial duties have taken on a new form, the objectives have remained very similar, with the secretary continuing to provide an efficient communication and administrative service. Throughout this period of transformation the demand from industry and commerce for well-qualified secretaries has remained unabated and there is every indication that secretaries will continue to occupy key positions in the future electronic office.

The A-Z Office Guide has been compiled with these objectives in mind by supplying the key factors to practices and procedures and a 'signpost' pointing the way to the acquisition of more detailed and up-to-date data. For example, the various references to office machinery and equipment include a representative list of suppliers' names and addresses to enable the secretary to send for details of their latest products. Indeed, the aim throughout the book has been to create an awareness of the procedures and sources for finding any information that may be required.

The contents of the book include practical advice, check-lists and hints on a wide range of relevant topics which include: caring for floppy disks and what to do if the word processor fails to work; choosing a new typewriter; using copiers; writing letters and press releases; interview technique; tips for surviving stress, etc. Together, these provide ideal support material for those returning to office work after a period away from it or for college leavers about to enter business for the first time.

The A-Z Office Guide is a practical office guide – an indispensable 'tool' which should be readily available for reference in the desk drawer of the discerning and competent secretary.

JH

Acknowledgements

I should like to express my appreciation to the following people and organisations who have contributed in many different ways to the preparation of this book:

Mrs V Bell, Miss M Leishman and Mrs J Wyeth of the Eastleigh College of Further Education
Mr C Golding, Manager of the Chandler's Ford branch of the Midland Bank
Staff at the Chandler's Ford Library and Winchester Reference Library
The Business Equipment and Information Technology Association and their members who supplied information

Abbreviations and phrases in common use

(for abbreviations of decorations and honours see page 46)

AA	Automobile Association Alcoholics Anonymous
ab initio	from the beginning
ABTA	Association of British Travel Agents
A/c	accounts
AC	alternating current
ACA	Associate, Institute of Chartered Accountants (FCA – Fellow)
ACAS	Advisory, Conciliation and Arbitration Service
ACBSI	Associate, Chartered Building Societies Institute (FCBSI – Fellow)
ACCA	Associate, Association of Certified Accountants (FCCA – Fellow)
ACCS	Associate, Corporation of Certified Secretaries (FCCS – Fellow)
ACII	Associate, Chartered Insurance Institute (FCII – Fellow)
ACIMA	Associate, Chartered Institute of Management Accountants (FCIMA – Fellow)
ACIPFA	Associate, Chartered Institute of Public Finance and Accountancy (FCIPFA – Fellow)
ACIS	Associate, Chartered Institute of Secretaries and Administrators (FCIS – Fellow)
ACIT	Associate, Chartered Institute of Transport (FCIT – Fellow)
AD	Anno Domini – in the year of the Lord
ADC	Advice of duration and charge
ad hoc	for this purpose
ad infinitum	to infinity
ad lib/ *ad libitum*	at pleasure
ad val/ *ad valorem*	in proportion to the value
AEA	Atomic Energy Authority
AEC	Atomic Energy Commission
AEU	Amalgamated Engineering Union
AFRAeS	Associate Fellow, Royal Aeronautical Society
AFTCom	Associate, Faculty of Teachers in Commerce (FFTCom – Fellow)
AGM	annual general meeting

AIA	Associate, Institute of Actuaries (FIA – Fellow)
AIB	Associate, Institute of Bankers (FIB – Fellow)
AIL	Associate, Institute of Linguists (FIL – Fellow)
AIMechE	Associate, Institute of Mechanical Engineers (FIMechE – Fellow; MIMechE – Member)
AInstAM	Associate, Institute of Administrative Management (FInstAM – Fellow; MInstAM – Member)
AInstM	Associate, Institute of Marketing (FInstM – Fellow)
AIOB	Associate, Institute of Builders (FIOB – Fellow)
AIQS	Associate, Institute of Quantity Surveyors (FIQS – Fellow)
ALA	Associate, Library Association (FLA – Fellow)
à la mode	fashionable
AMBIM	Associate Member, British Institute of Management (FMBIM – Fellow)
AMICE	Associate Member, Institute of Civil Engineers (FMICE – Fellow)
AMIEE	Associate Member, Institute of Electrical Engineers (FMIEE – Fellow)
AMIMechE	Associate Member, Institute of Mechanical Engineers (FIMechE – Fellow)
AMIMunE	Associate Member, Institute of Municipal Engineers (FIMunE – Fellow)
AMIPE	Associate Member, Institute of Production Engineers (FIPE – Fellow)
amp	ampere
AN	advice note
anon	anonymous
AOB	any other business
AP	Associated Press
APEX	Association of Professional, Executive, Clerical and Computer Staff
appro	approval
appx	appendix
AR	all risks (marine insurance)
ARIBA	Associate, Royal Institute of British Architects (FRIBA – Fellow)
ARIC	Associate, Royal Institute of Chemistry (FRIC – Fellow)
ARICS	Associate, Royal Institute of Chartered Surveyors (FRICS – Fellow)
asap	as soon as possible
ASBT	Associate, Society of Teachers in Business Education (FSBT – Fellow)
ASF	Associate of the Institute of Shipping and Forwarding Agents (FSF – Fellow)

ASLEF	Associated Society of Locomotive Engineers and Firemen
ASLIB	Association of Special Libraries and Information Bureaux
ASTMS	Association of Scientific, Technical and Management Staff
AUEW	Amalgamated Union of Engineering Workers
au fait	(to be) well informed
au revoir	goodbye until we meet again
AUT	Association of University Teachers
av	average
BA	Bachelor of Arts (MA – Master)
	British Airways
BAA	British Airports Authority
BACIE	British Association for Commercial and Industrial Education
BACS	Bankers' Automated Clearing Service
BBC	British Broadcasting Corporation
BC	before Christ
BCh or ChB	Bachelor of Surgery (MCh – Master)
BCL	Bachelor of Civil Law (DCL – Doctor)
BCom	Bachelor of Commerce (MCom – Master)
BCS	British Computer Society
BD	Bachelor of Divinity (DD – Doctor)
b/d	brought down
B/D	bank draft
BDA	British Dental Association
B/E	bill of exchange
BEd	Bachelor of Education (MEd – Master)
BEITA	Business Equipment and Information Technology Association
B Eng	Bachelor of Engineering (M Eng – Master)
b/f	brought forward
BIFU	Banking, Insurance and Finance Union
BIM	British Institute of Management
BIR	Board of Inland Revenue
BIS	Bank for International Settlements
B/L	bill of lading
BLitt	Bachelor of Letters (MLitt – Master)
BM or MB	Bachelor of Medicine (MD – Doctor)
BMA	British Medical Association
BMTA	British Motor Trades Association
BMus/MusB	Bachelor of Music
BNEC	British National Export Council
bona fide	of good faith
bon voyage	an expression wishing a traveller a good journey
BOT	Board of Trade
BP	bill payable

BPhil	Bachelor of Philosophy (MPhil – Master)
BR	British Rail
	bill receivable
B/S	balance sheet
	bill of sale
BSA	Building Societies Association
BSc	Bachelor of Science (MSc – Master)
BSI	British Standards Institute
	Building Societies Institute
BSS	British Standards Specification
BST	British summer time
BT	British Telecom
BTEC	Business and Technician Education Council
Btu	British thermal unit
BUPA	British United Provident Association
c	circa (approx)
C	centigrade
¢	cent
©	copyright
C/A	chartered accountant
	current account
CAA	Civil Aviation Authority
CAD	cash against documents
	computer aided design
CAL	computer assisted learning
CAP	common agricultural policy (EEC)
CAR	computer assisted retrieval
carte blanche	full discretionary power
CBI	Confederation of British Industry
cc	copies
CC	County Council
	County Councillor
c/d	carried down
CE	Civil Engineer
CEGB	Central Electricity Generating Board
CEng	Chartered Engineer
CET	Central European Time
cf	compare
c/f	carried forward
cg	centigram
CGT	capital gains tax
chq	cheque
CID	Criminal Investigation Department
	Council of Industrial Design
CIF	cost, insurance and freight
CIR	Commission on Industrial Relations
cl	centilitre
cm	centimetre

C/N	credit note
CNAA	Council for National Academic Awards
c/o	care of
COBOL	common business orientated language (computing)
COD	cash on delivery
C of E	Church of England
	Council of Europe
COHSE	Confederation of Health Service Employees
COI	Central Office of Information
COM	computer output microfilm
cordon bleu	first-class cook
COSIRA	Council for Small Industries in Rural Areas
cp	compare
CPI	consumer price index
CPU	central processing unit
Cr	credit/creditor
CR	company's risk (insurance)
CRAC	Careers Research and Advisory Centre
CRE	Commission for Racial Equality
CRO	Criminal Records Office
CSC	Civil Service Commission
CSU	Civil Service Union
C/T	credit transfer
CTT	capital transfer tax
cum pref	cumulative preference
cv	curriculum vitae
CWO	cash with order
D/A	deposit account
dag	decagram
dal	decalitre
dam	decametre
DC	district council
	direct current
d/d	days after date
DD	Doctor of Divinity
	direct debit
DE	Department of Employment
deb	debenture
de facto	in fact
DES	Department of Education and Science
dft	draft
dg	decigram
div	dividend
dl	decilitre
DL	Deputy Lieutenant
DLit	Doctor of Literature
DLitt	Doctor of Letters

dm	decimetre
DM	Deutschmark
D/N	debit note
do.	ditto – the same
DO	delivery order
dob	date of birth
DOE	Department of the Environment
DOH	Department of Health
DP	data processing
D/P	deferred payment
DPhil	Doctor of Philosophy
DPP	Director of Public Prosecutions
Dr	debit/debtor doctor
DSc	Doctor of Science
DSS	Department of Social Security
DTh	Doctor of Theology
DTI	Department of Trade and Industry
DTP	desk top publishing
DW	dock warrant
E & OE	errors and omissions excepted
EAPS	European Association of Professional Secretaries
EC	European Community
ECGD	Export Credits Guarantee Department
EDP	electronic data processing
EFTA	European Free Trade Association
EFTPOS	electronic funds transfer at point of sale
eg	*exempli gratia* – for example
EMA	European Monetary Agreement
EMF	European Monetary Fund
enc	enclosure
en masse	all together
en route	on the way
entente cordiale	friendly understanding
EOC	Equal Opportunities Commission
ERNIE	electronic randon number indicator equipment
esc	escudo – Portuguese currency
ETA	estimated time of arrival
et al.	*et alia* – and others
etc	*et cetera* – and other things
et seq.	*et sequentia* – and the following
ETU	Electrical Trades Union
ETUC	European Trade Union Confederation
EURATOM	European Atomic Energy Community
ex div	exclusive of dividend
ex gratia	as a favour but implying no right
ex officio	by virtue of office

ext	extension
F	fahrenheit
FAI	Fellow, Chartered Auctioneers and Estate Agents Institute
fait accompli	task already completed
FAO	Food and Agriculture Organisation
faux pas	an error or indiscreet action
fax	facsimile telegraphy
FBI	Federation of British Industries Federal Bureau of Investigation
FIFO	first in, first out
fo	folio
FOB	free on board
FOQ	free on quay
FOR	free on rail
force majeure	an act of God; excuse for failure to fulfil a contract
Fortran	formula translation (computing)
fr	franc
FRCS	Fellow of the Royal College of Surgeons
FRIBA	Fellow of the Royal Institute of British Architects
FRSA	Fellow of the Royal Society of Arts
FTI	Financial Times index
F/U	follow up
g	gram
GATT	general agreement on tariffs and trade
GCSE	general certificate of secondary education
GDP	gross domestic product
GLC	Greater London Council
GMBATU	General, Municipal, Boilermakers and Allied Trades Union
GMC	General Medical Council
GMT	Greenwich mean time
GNP	gross national product
GP	general practitioner
GRN	goods received note
gr wt	gross weight
ha	hectare
hg	hectogram
hl	hectolitre
hm	hectometre
HMSO	Her Majesty's Stationery Office
Hon	Honorary/Honourable
HP	hire purchase horse-power

Hr	Herr
HRH	Her/His Royal Highness
hrs	hours
HSE	Health and Safety Executive
IA	Institute of Actuaries
IAEA	International Atomic Energy Agency
IATA	International Air Transport Association
IBA	Independent Broadcasting Authority
ib/ibid.	in the same place
IBRD	International Bank for Reconstruction and Development
ICAO	International Civil Aviation Organisation
ICFTU	International Confederation of Free Trade Unions
id/idem	the same
ID	identification
IDD	International direct dialling
ie/id est	that is
IF	insufficient funds (cheques)
IFAD	International Fund for Agricultural Development
II	indorsement irregular (cheques)
ILO	International Labour Organisation
IMF	International Monetary Fund
IMO	International Maritime Organisation
Inc	incorporated
in extenso	at full length
infra dig	beneath one's dignity
in loc/in loco	in its place
in loco parentis	in the place of a parent
inter alia	among other things
Interpol	International Criminal Police Commission
in toto	wholly
intra vires	within the power
inv	invoice
IPS	International paper size
ipso facto	by the very fact
IQPS	Institute of Qualified Private Secretaries
IRO	International Refugee Organisation
ISBN	International Standard Book Number
ISO	International Standards Organisation
IT	information technology
ITB	Industrial Training Board
ITU	International Telecommunications Union
J/A	joint account
JP	Justice of the Peace

kg	kilogram
kl	kilolitre
km	kilometre
kw	kilowatt
l	litre
LAN	local area network
L/C	letter of credit
	lower case
LCC	London Chamber of Commerce
LEA	Local Education Authority
LIFO	last in, first out
LILO	last in, last out
LLB	Bachelor of Laws (LLM – Master)
LLD	Doctor of Laws
lm	lumen
LOB	Location of Offices Bureau
locum tenens	a deputy
LS	*locus sigilli* – the place of the seal
Ltd	Limited
LV	luncheon voucher
m	metre
M	Monsieur
MA	Master of Arts
MAAT	Member, Association of Accounting Technicians
MB	Bachelor of Medicine
MD	Doctor of Medicine
MEP	Member of European Parliament
mg	milligram
Mgr	Monsignor/Monsiegneur
MIAE	Member, Institution of Automobile Engineers
MICE	Member, Institution of Civil Engineers
MIChemE	Member, Institute of Chemical Engineers
MICR	magnetic ink character recognition
MIEE	Member, Institution of Electrical Engineers
MIMechE	Member, Institution of Mechanical Engineers
MInstPS	Member, Institute of Purchasing and Supply
MIPM	Member, Institute of Personnel Management (FIPM – Fellow)
MIQPS	Member, Institute of Qualified Private Secretaries
MIS	Management information systems
ml	millilitre
MLA	Member, Legislative Assembly
MLC	Member, Legislative Council
Mlle	Mademoiselle
MLR	minimum lending rate

mm	millimetre
MOD	Ministry of Defence
modus operandi	method of working
Monsig	Monsignor
MOT	Ministry of Transport
MP	Member of Parliament
mpg	miles per gallon
MRCP	Member of the Royal College of Physicians (FRCP – Fellow)
MS	manuscript
MSS	manuscripts
MTh	Master of Theology

N/A	not applicable
NALGO	National Association of Local Government Officers
NAS	National Association of School Masters
NATFHE	National Association of Teachers in Further and Higher Education
NATO	North Atlantic Treaty Organisation
NB	*nota bene* – note thoroughly
NCB	National Coal Board
NCCL	National Council for Civil Liberties
NCR	no carbon required
NEB	National Enterprise Board
NEDC	National Economic Development Council
nem con	*nemine contradicente* – no one contradicting
N/F	no funds (banking)
NFU	National Farmers Union
NGA	National Graphical Association
NHS	National Health Service
NI	National insurance
No	number
NOP	National opinion poll
NP	Notary Public
N/P	net proceeds
	new paragraph
NR	No risk (insurance)
NRDC	National Research Development Corporation
NTDA	National Trade Development Association
NUGMW	National Union of General and Municipal Workers
NUJ	National Union of Journalists
NUM	National Union of Mineworkers
NUPE	National Union of Public Employees
NUR	National Union of Railwaymen
NUS	National Union of Students
NUT	National Union of Teachers

O & M	Organisation and Methods
OCR	optical character recognition/reader
O/D	overdraft/overdrawn
OECD	Organisation for Economic Co-operation and Development
OFT	Office of Fair Trading
OHMS	On Her Majesty's Service
OMR	optical mark recognition
OPEC	Organisation of Petroleum Exporting Countries
OR	owner's risk (insurance)
OS	Ordnance Survey
O/S	outstanding
p	page
pa	per annum
PA	Press Association
PABX	private automatic branch exchange
P & P	postage and packing
PAYE	pay as you earn
PC	Privy Counsellor
	Police Constable
	petty cash
PEI	Pitman Examinations Institute
per capita	each per unit
per cent	*per centum* – for every hundred
per se	by itself
PhD	Doctor of Philosophy
PIN	personal identity number
P/L	profit and loss
PLA	Port of London Authority
PLC	Public limited company
PM	Prime Minister
PN	promissory note
PO	Post Office
	postal order
POP	post office preferred (envelope)
post mortem	after death
pp	pages
	per pro (on behalf of)
prima facie	on the face of it
PRO	Public Relations Officer
pro forma	as a matter of form
pro rata	in proportion
pro tem	*pro tempore* – for the time being
QC	Queen's Counsel
quasi	similar to
quid pro quo	something for something
qv	*quod vide* – which see

RAC	Royal Automobile Club
R/D	refer to drawer (cheques)
Re	with reference to
RIBA	Royal Institute of British Architects
RICS	Royal Institute of Chartered Surveyors
rm	ream
ROM	read only memory
RP	reply paid
RPI	retail price index
RRP	recommended retail price
RSA	Royal Society of Arts
RSVP	*répondez s'il vous plait* – please reply
SAE	stamped, addressed envelope
SALT	Strategic Arms Limitation Talks
SAV	stock at valuation
SAYE	save as you earn
SCOTVEC	Scottish Vocational Education Council
SE	Stock Exchange
SEATO	South-East Asia Treaty Organisation
seq	*sequentes* – the following
Sfr	Swiss franc
SHAPE	Supreme Headquarters of the Allied Powers in Europe
sine die	without an appointed day
S/N	shipping note
SO	standing order
Soc	Society
SOGAT	Society of Graphical and Allied Trades
SOR	sale or return
SSP	statutory sick pay
status quo	no change
STD	subscriber trunk dialling
stet	let it stand
stg.	sterling
sub judice	under judicial (legal) consideration
SWIFT	Society for Worldwide Interbank Financial Communications
t	tonne
TA	Training Agency
TB	trial balance
TGWU	Transport and General Workers Union
TM	trade mark
TUC	Trades Union Congress
TWI	Training within industry
UC	upper case (capital letters)
UDI	Unilateral Declaration of Independence

ultra vires	beyond legal authority
UNESCO	United Nations Educational, Scientific and Cultural Organisation
UNO	United Nations Organisation
UPU	Universal Postal Union
UPW	Union of Post Office Workers
USDAW	Union of Shop, Distributive and Allied Workers
VAT	value added tax
VDU	visual display unit
verbatim	word for word
VHF	very high frequency
vice versa	the other way round
VIP	very important person
viva voce	by word of mouth
viz	*videlicet* – namely
VN	voucher number
VTR	video tape recorder
w	watt
WASH	Women Against Sexual Harassment
WCC	World Council of Churches
w/e	week ending
WEA	Workers Educational Association
wef	with effect from
WEU	Western European Union
WHO	World Health Organisation
WIPO	World Intellectual Property Organisation
WMO	World Meteorological Organisation
wp	word processing without prejudice
wpm	words per minute

Addressing envelopes

The Post Office advise their customers that high-speed postal deliveries depend on correct addressing and, in order to comply with good practice, the address should normally comprise:

1 name of addressee
2 house number (or name) and street
3 locality name, where necessary
4 post town (in block capitals)

5 county name where required
6 postcode

```
For the attention of Mr P Stringer

Cable Communications (UK) Ltd
208 Milton Road
Stockley Park
UXBRIDGE
Middlesex
UB18 2RG
```

Example of an addressed envelope

Guidelines

- Begin each item of the address on a separate line.
- Allow sufficient space at the top of the envelope for the postage stamps/franking impression and postmarks.
- Use block capitals for the post town.
- Normally include the name of the county. A list of post towns not requiring county names is given in the *Post Office Guide*.
- Type the postcode at the bottom of the address in block capitals with a space between the two parts.
- Place any special directions, such as 'Private', 'Confidential' or 'For the attention of…', clear of the address – usually two spaces above the addressee's name.
- Use titles as follows:
  Mrs or Ms – for a married lady
    Examples: Mrs J R Barnes, Ms W Harris
  Miss or Ms – for a single lady
    Examples: Miss R A Smart, Ms P Finch
    Ms is used when a lady indicates that she prefers to use this title in preference to a title indicating her marital status.
  The Misses – for unmarried sisters
    Example: The Misses P & L Spencer
  Mr – for a man
    Esq is rarely used today
    Example: Mr J Partridge
  Mr & Mrs – for husband and wife using the husband's christian name or initials
    Example: Mr & Mrs Graham Stone

Reference sources

Post Office Guide – for advice on addressing envelopes
Postcode Directories – for postcodes
Types and sizes of envelopes: *see* Stationery p 148
Addressing machines: *see* Office Equipment p 118

Advertising

1 Selecting the newspaper or journal:
  - refer to an appropriate reference book such as Willing's *Press Guide* or Benn's *Media Directory* for details of names, addresses and telephone numbers of newspapers and journals and their publication days
  - choose publications which will be read by the people the advertisement aims to reach
  - before placing an advertisement, compare costs of various publications and find out the time required for booking space and delivering the copy
  - decide whether to advertise with the journal direct or use the services of an advertising agency

2 When drafting the advertisement:
  - use words sparingly, selecting only those which give the salient facts and attract the attention of readers
  - create interest by including information which encourages readers to respond to the advertisement, eg aspects of the work which give job satisfaction, salary offered, etc
  - state clearly any basic requirements, eg competence in word processing, so that only those qualified will apply

PRIVATE SECRETARY TO MANAGING DIRECTOR

required by international manufacturing organisation. Interesting and varied work in a post which calls for initiative, organising ability, above average secretarial skills and competence in word processing.

Salary: £0000

Applicants must have experience in a responsible secretarial position.

Please apply in writing giving details of previous experience and qualifications to the Personnel Manager, DBA Limited, 29 George Street, Maidenhead, Berks SL9 2AP

Example of an advertisement

- display the draft in a suitable style and in the manner required for publication, emboldening and enlarging text to give prominence to any eye-catching information
- ensure that the advertisement sets out clearly the contact name and address or telephone number for replies

3 When submitting the advertisement to the newspaper or journal state:
- the type of advertisement required, ie
  classified (the cheapest form of advertising as it is grouped with other advertisements under headings without any form of display)
  semi-displayed (more expensive but set apart from other advertisements and usually displayed in a box)
  displayed (the most expensive form, in which the advertisement will be fully displayed with different typefaces and may be illustrated)
- the amount of space required
- the date(s) of publication
- the number of entries required

Appointments

When making appointments for your employer:
- Be conscious of the routine office matters with which the employer prefers to deal at specific times of the day.
- Enter appointments in both your employer's diary and your own. Provisional appointments should be entered in pencil first and inked in when they are confirmed.
- Confirm by letter any appointment made by telephone.
- Allow sufficient travelling time between appointments arranged outside the office on the same day.
- Meetings can extend beyond their estimated finishing time and care should be taken when arranging appointments which follow them.
- If a caller requests an appointment and a date and time are agreed, make a note of the caller's name, address and telephone number in case you need to contact them to amend the date or time.
- If you are in doubt about an appointment, possibly because it is requested at a time which is after hours or involves the employer's partner, make it a provisional one and consult your employer as soon as possible. When it is agreed with the

employer, write a letter of confirmation to the person concerned.

- Provide sufficient time for discussion with your employer and for dealing with the mail.
- Avoid making appointments to be attended immediately on the employer's return after being away from the office.
- If an appointment has to be cancelled because of illness or other unforeseen circumstances, telephone an apology and arrange another appointment.

Bank services

Current account – where cheques and cheque cards are used to make payments

Interest bearing accounts – interest is given on money invested, some banks providing autobank withdrawal facilities

Personal budget 'flexiloan'-type accounts – where the outlay on expenditure is spread over a fixed period

Lending to approved borrowers – customers are provided with bank loans and overdrafts

Standing orders and direct debits – where regular payments are made by the bank on behalf of customers

Credit cards – provide facilities for purchasing goods on credit

Credit transfer – the transfer of credit from one account to another

Cash cards – enable cash to be withdrawn from autobanks

EFTPOS – electronic funds transfer at point of sale; a facility for paying for goods without the need to use cash or write cheques

Drafts – a facility for the payment of large sums where cheques are not acceptable

Bills of exchange
Letters of credit
Mail and telegraphic transfer
Computer message switching system (SWIFT)
Foreign currency
Travellers cheques
} – methods of making payments abroad

Night safe – a place to deposit money after bank hours

Safe keeping – a means of depositing securities, jewellery, etc

Mortgages – a loan made for the conveyance of property with endowment, pension or capital repayment options

Business/professional services – executor, trustee, investment management, insurance advice, finance of exports/imports and pensions

Current account

Advice for bank current account holders:

1 Keep your cheque book in a safe place. If it is lost or stolen, advise the bank and the police immediately. It is advisable to keep a separate record of your account number.
2 When making out a cheque:
   - always use a pen
   - write the payee's name exactly as described in the invoice or notice to pay, eg J R Brooks & Sons
   - write the amount of pounds in words as well as in figures
   - begin writing as far to the left as possible and do not leave spaces for other words or figures to be added; draw a line to close up all blank spaces
   - the date must contain the day, month and year
   - sign the cheque with your normal signature as supplied to the bank
   - keep a record of the date, payee's name and amount on the counterfoil
3 If you have a cheque card, keep it separately from your cheque book for security reasons.
4 Never keep your personal identification number (PIN) with your cheque card.
5 When transferring amounts from your account to another bank account you will need to quote your bank, branch and account numbers. On other occasions you may need to refer to the cheque serial number. These numbers are located on cheques, as follows:
   a Bank and branch number, eg 40–09–18
   b Account number, eg 12345678
   c Cheque serial number, eg 460423
6 When paying money into a bank account, check the following points:
   - cheques bear current dates
   - amounts in words and figures are the same
   - payees' names are correct
   - cheques are signed
   - any alterations on cheques are clear and have been signed
   - cross any open cheques
7 Complete a paying-in slip with the following details:
   Date
   Bank code no, name and branch
   Name* and account no of payee
   Cash (notes and coins)*

   * Also entered on the counterfoil.

Cheques (listed separately)*; state total number
Signature of person paying-in

8 Bank statements, issued by the bank, should be kept safely in a wallet. A statement is a copy of the customer's account with the bank and it shows:
   - the balance of the account at the end of the previous statement
   - credits for money paid into the account
   - debits for money paid out by cheques and other means
   - debits for bank charges
   - the balance of the account at the end of this statement

   The entries should be checked and any new items, such as charges, should be recorded.

Bank cards

Cheque card

This is a card of authority which makes the cheque more acceptable as a method of payment when goods or services are supplied. A cheque up to the value of £50/£100 accompanied by a cheque card will normally be accepted by a trader as he is assured that such a cheque will be honoured by the bank on which it is drawn. Cheque card holders are also entitled to cash cheques up to £50/£100 at any branch of the bank without prior arrangements or any additional charge being incurred.

Credit card

A credit card enables a person to purchase goods on credit at shops or other establishments which have agreed to participate in the scheme. It may also be used for withdrawing cash up to the card holder's credit limit, without prior notice, from any branch of the bank. The individual is notified of his credit limit, which is the maximum amount that he can owe to the bank at any time. The Credit Card Centre issues each card holder with a monthly statement of the amount owing and, provided the card holder makes the payment not later than 25 days after the date on the statement, no charge is incurred.

Charge card

On payment of an annual membership subscription, a charge card, such as American Express or Diners Card, may be used to borrow money for the payment of goods and services. With these cards a credit limit is not usually placed on the holder and no interest is charged. Accounts are paid monthly by cheque or direct debit.

Cash/autobank card

Bank customers can use a cash/autobank card to withdraw cash from autobanks at any time of the day. On application for an autobank card, the bank advises the customer of their personal identity number (PIN). This must then be remembered as it is not recorded on the autobank card or on any document for security reasons. If the card is lost or stolen it cannot be used for withdrawing cash unless the personal number is known. To obtain cash the card has to be inserted into the autobank equipment, the personal number keyed in and buttons pressed to select the service and amount required. Step-by-step directions are displayed on a screen to guide the user in operating the machine. The customer is allocated a daily cash withdrawal limit by the bank which remains the same from week to week.

With some machines, the customer can check their current account balance from the display on the autobank screen. It is also possible to request a more detailed statement to be sent to the customer's address. The most recent machines provide for customers to see details of their last 10 debits or credits and to have a printout of their statement showing the last 30 transactions.

Advice from the banks for autobank card holders:

- keep your cheque book and card separately
- never leave your card in public places or in your car
- keep your card away from any magnetic card used for opening security doors
- do not tell your PIN to anyone
- do not record your PIN in a way that allows another person to discover it
- do not keep a record of your PIN with your card
- never quote your PIN in correspondence or over the telephone
- if you think that someone has discovered your PIN, inform your bank immediately
- if your card is lost or stolen, inform your bank immediately

Overseas travel facilities

Services for people travelling abroad:

Travellers cheques

It is advisable to use travellers cheques for most of the money to be taken abroad as they can be cashed in most banks and are normally accepted in hotels, restaurants, airports and shops in place of cash. They can be supplied in a wide range of currencies, such as sterling; French and Swiss francs; US, Canadian, Australian and Hong Kong dollars; Japanese yen, etc, and are acceptable as cash to the local trades people if they are made out in the currency of the country being visited. Because they can be used as cash, it is wise to order a mixture of small and large denominations to cater for different amounts. A bank will usually require several days' notice to supply travellers cheques, although sterling and US dollar travellers cheques are normally held in the branch and can be obtained on demand. Before the cheques can be released they must be signed at the bank by the person travelling.

Foreign currency

While most money taken abroad should be in travellers cheques, it is useful to have some foreign currency for use on immediate arrival for such things as taxi fares, postage stamps, refreshments, etc. The bank normally requires several days' notice to supply foreign currency. There are restrictions on the amount of currency that can be taken in or out of some countries, but the bank will advise on this. When returning from abroad it is advisable to change as many coins as possible into notes as the banks do not usually exchange coins of low value.

Eurocheque cards

With these cards it is possible for ordinary cheques to be cashed (up to the value of £50/£100 each) at banks abroad (mostly in European and Mediterranean countries) which display the Eurocheque symbol. They can also be used for payment of goods and services up to a specified sum, usually the equivalent of £100, and made out in the currency of the country concerned.

Credit/charge cards

Cards, such as Access, Barclaycard and American Express may also be used abroad to pay for goods and services on credit from traders participating in the schemes. These cards can also be used for obtaining cash from certain banks abroad.

See also Travel Arrangements p 171.

British Standards Specifications

British Standards Specifications are obtainable from the British Standards Institute, Linford Wood, Milton Keynes MK14 6LE, or they may be referred to in principal public libraries. The following is a selection of the specifications which are of interest to secretaries:

Computer – operating procedures	6650:	1985
Dictation equipment	3738:	1980
Duplicators and copiers	5479:	1977
Envelopes – terms and sizes	4264:	1976
Filing cabinets	4438:	1981
Filing – dimensions of folders and files	1467:	1972/1983
Forms – letterheads and business forms	1808:	1985
Office furniture – desks and chairs	5940:	1980
Printers' correction signs	5261:	1975/1976
Typewriters	2481:	1982

Business documents

Document	*Prepared by*	*Distribution*
Stores requisition	Person in department requesting goods from stock – countersigned by head of department	Storekeeper
Purchases requisition	Person in department requesting goods to be purchased – countersigned by head of department	Storekeeper/ buyer
Price list	Sales department	Customers
Quotation	Sales department	Customers
Order	Buyer	Supplier Stores Accounts Buyer
Advice note	Despatch	Customer
Delivery note	Despatch	Driver Customer
Goods received note	Stores	Accounts Buyer
Invoice	Sales	Customer Accounts Despatch Sales Stores
Credit note	Sales	Customer Accounts Despatch Sales Stores
Statement	Accounts	Customer Accounts

Suppliers of office forms and stationery

Kalamazoo Ltd, Northfield, Birmingham B31 2RW

Kardex Systems (UK) Ltd, 2 Dyers Buildings, Holborn, London EC1N 2JT

Kenrick & Jefferson Ltd, High Street, West Bromwich, W Midlands B70 8NB

Purpose
A request to the storekeeper to issue stock
A request to the storekeeper/buyer to order goods
To provide customers with a brief description and current prices of goods offered for sale
To provide customers with full particulars of goods or services offered for sale and the conditions of sale Similar information may be supplied in an estimate
A request to the seller to supply goods
Informs customer that the order has been despatched or is ready for despatch
Serves as an advice of goods delivered (for customer) and a receipt for goods delivered (for supplier)
Internal document notifying accounts, stores and buyer of the arrival of goods and their condition
Informs customer of goods purchased and the amounts charged
Notifies customer of a reduction in the amount charged on an invoice
A record of transactions for a given period, informing the customer of the total amount owing and requesting payment

Mandergraph Ltd, Chapel House, High Street, Deanshanger, Milton Keynes MK19 6HD

Snows Business Forms Ltd, Manor House Avenue, Millbrook, Southampton

Unisys Ltd, Stonebridge Park, London NW10 8LS

Business expansion/ enterprise schemes

The following sources of information and financial incentive schemes are available for the development and expansion of small firms, as well as providing assistance to people who wish to become self-employed and start their own business:

Source of information	*Details available from*
Government Schemes:	
Regional Development Grants Regional Selective Assistance Loan Guarantee Scheme EEC Assistance Grants	Department of Trade and Industry
Enterprise Allowance Scheme: to assist unemployed people to set up their own business Business Enterprise Programme: free training courses	Local Job Centres Training Agency
Export Market Research Market Entry Guarantee Scheme	British Overseas Trade Board
Small Firms Service The Government-funded Small Firms Service is an information and business counselling service to help owners and managers of small businesses employing less than 200 people with their plans and problems. It also acts as an advisory service to those thinking of starting their own business. The service, which operates through a nationwide network of Small Firms Centres, is designed to encourage business efficiency.	Freefone ENTERPRISE
Council for Small Industries in Rural Areas (COSIRA) The Council is represented in most counties and provides advice and counselling for small businesses in the English rural areas, as well as loans, help with premises and training in skills and crafts.	Head Office: 141 Castle Street Salisbury, Wilts SP1 3TP who will advise you on your nearest local organiser
Business Expansion Scheme (for tax relief)	Inland Revenue

Bank Schemes:	Your Local Bank Manager
National Federation of Self-Employed and Small Businesses	Head Office: 32 St Anne's Road West Lytham St Annes Lancs FY8 1NY
Local Government business development schemes	County and District Council Offices

Publications

Running your own business, R Edwards, Longman
The Small Business Guide: Sources of Information for a new and small business, C Barow, BBC
Starting your own business, Consumers Association
Business Enterprise Book: How to set up and run your own business, Daily Telegraph
The small business handbook, B Wilson, Blackwell
Small Business Guide, S Williams, Lloyds Bank

Circulation of documents

Different methods of circulating documents within an organisation:

- Type **carbon copies** with the names of the recipients included in a list at the bottom of the first page. A tick is placed against the name to whom each individual copy is sent, eg:
  cc
  Sales Manager
  Chief Buyer
  Chief Acountant ✓
  Personnel Manager
  Works Manager
- As above, but instead of typing carbon copies, they are **reproduced** on an office copier or word processor. It is, however, necessary to write or type the distribution list on the original before it is copied.
- Distribute the original document(s) with a **circulation or action slip** (*see* p 26). Each recipient would be requested to take the necessary action, delete their name from the list and pass on the document(s) to the next person on the list.
- Use a **computer linked by VDUs**.

ACTION SLIP	
To JK, RT, PB	URGENT ☐
Please:	
☐ Draft a reply for my signature	
☐ Give me your comments	
☑ Circulate and return to me	
☐ Note and return to me	
☐ Take appropriate action	
☐ Note for your information	
REMARKS	
From: KR	Date: 1/3/–

Example of an action slip

- Use **facsimile telegraphy** for distribution of documents between branches of a firm.
- Distribute the original document(s) in an **internal mail envelope**.

Communication

1 The most commonly mis-spelt words:

accessible	catalogue	developed
accommodation	committee	disappointed
acknowledge	compatible	discrepancy
acquaintance	competent	dissatisfied
address	conscious	eliminated
advertisement	consistent	embarrassment
aggravate	correspondence	independent
apparently	corroborate	equipped
approximately	courteous	exaggerated
argument	criticism	expenses
believe	decision	feasible
benefited	definitely	financial
business	deterrent	grievance

guarantee
harassed
immediately
indispensable
influential
irresistible
liaison
lose
manœuvre
manufacturer
miscellaneous
necessary
negotiate
noticeable
occasional
occurred
omitted
omission
opportunity
parallel
permissible
possession
potential
precede
predecessor
preference
preferred
privilege
procedure
professional
professor
pronunciation
psychology
receipt
recommend
reference
referred
relieved
seize
separate
stationery
supersede
temporary
transferred
woollen

2 The most commonly mis-used words:

	Examples of correct usage
WHO and WHOM	To *whom* do you wish the letters to be sent? *Whom* did you select? *Who* is the most suitable person to ask?
AS and LIKE	Type the letters *as* you were instructed by the Supervisor. Type them *like* the specimen you were given.
ME and MY	He has asked *me* to attend the meeting. I hope the Chairman will not mind *my* leaving early to catch the train.
SHALL and WILL	I *shall* be grateful if you *will* work late tonight.
SHOULD and WOULD	I *should* be glad if you *would* participate in the discussion.
I and ME	My wife and *I* will be pleased to attend. The invitation is addressed to my wife and *me*.
EITHER and NEITHER	We will be happy to use *either* of the machines for the task. I regret that *neither* of the machines is suitable for the task.
OR and NOR	We can use *either* telex *or* fax for this communication. *Neither* the Chairman *nor* the Secretary could attend the next meeting.
ONE and YOU	When *one* appreciates the state of the market, *one* is not surprised at the response. If *you* attend an interview, *you* should be punctual.

ACCEPT and EXCEPT	I am pleased to *accept* your invitation to attend. All of the candidates *except* one were invited to attend the interview.
PRACTICE and PRACTISE	You will need to *practise* regularly if you wish to be successful. She was taught office *practice* on her training course.
PRINCIPAL and PRINCIPLE	The *Principal* of the College is a member of the committee. Offset litho duplicating is based on the *principle* that water and grease do not mix.
STATIONARY and STATIONERY	The vehicle was *stationary* at the time of the accident. Envelopes, ribbons and labels were included on the *stationery* requisition.

3 Listening skills:

- Prepare to listen – 'tune in' and focus on what the speaker is saying.
- Be natural and relaxed but try not to be distracted by others who may be present in the room.
- Make sure you listen selectively to assimilate the essentials of the message conveyed.
- As you listen, concentrate on key words/phrases that will help you to grasp the message.
- Show interest in the speaker by your expression and by looking at them.
- Be a patient listener and do not interrupt before the speaker has finished speaking.
- Concentrate on what is being said so that you keep pace with the speaker and do not lag behind. This allows you to consider the implications of what is being said.
- If it is essential to remember detailed information such as telephone numbers, names and addresses, reference numbers, etc, write them down in note form as they are given to you.
- Ask the speaker to explain anything that is unclear or difficult for you to understand.
- Be prepared to give the speaker a reaction verbally or non-verbally, if appropriate. A nod or a smile can be used very effectively to satisfy the speaker that you are following what has been said.

4 Speaking skills:

- Organise your thoughts before you speak – for important matters prepare a plan of what you wish to say.
- Present your ideas logically and clearly.
- Use simple, concise sentences and avoid unnecessary jargon.

- Speak clearly with the right volume, tone and pace.
- Be polite and considerate in what you say.
- Avoid repeating what you have already said and be sure to keep to the point of the subject under discussion.
- Try to maintain the listener's attention by your own enthusiasm and interest in what you have to say.
- Develop a rapport with the listener so that they are receptive to your message.
- Obtain feedback by checking that the recipient has understood you.
- Say what you mean and mean what you say!

5 Writing skills:

- Plan what you are going to write – jot down the points you wish to make and arrange them in logical order.
- Make sure that what you write is clear and can be understood by the recipient.
- Use the correct style and tone of writing to suit the circumstances of the communication.
- Write your communication in the appropriate format and layout, eg message form, memo, letter or report.
- Use correct syntax and grammar.
- Spell and punctuate accurately.
- Use words which convey the correct meaning and avoid unnecessary jargon.
- Take care to avoid emotive or provocative language.
- Use sentences which are simple and concise.
- Group your points into paragraphs and grade them so that they follow in their correct sequence with each paragraph leading systematically to the next. If appropriate, use paragraph headings.
- Always try to be courteous and helpful in your writing.

Books for communication studies

Communication at Work, D W Evans, Pitman
English for Business (3rd edition), Mavor, Pitman
Improving English Skills, D W Evans, Pitman
People, Communication and Organisations, D W Evans, Pitman
Spotlight on Communication, D Robinson and R Power, Pitman

Communications in business

The different forms of business communication are listed below. For fuller information, turn to the pages indicated.

	Page Ref
Audio-conferencing/Confertel – a British Telecom service for conferences	40
Ceefax – the BBC televised information service	162
Computer terminal/Datel – a means of transmitting and receiving computer data/text	161
Confravision – a British Telecom service for closed circuit television of conferences	40
Dictating machine – for communicating to typist	168
Face-to-face conversation – the ideal form for personal/confidential matters	28
Facsimile telegraphy/Telecopiers – a means of sending replicas of documents any distance with complete accuracy, combining the speed of the telephone with the reproduction facility of the office copier	160
Intercom – internal oral communication	
Letter – written communication of any length	41
Loudspeaker/public address system – a means of conveying information to a large number of people	
Memo – written communication within an organisation	44
Meeting – a useful means of collecting the views of several people, the information being conveyed by minutes or reports	107
Mobile telephones – for communicating with people on the move	156
Notice board – a means of displaying information for a large number of people	
Oracle – the ITV/4-tel televised information services	162
Paging – a system by which staff can be located as they move around a building	157
Prestel – the British Telecom television information service	162
Report – written information for several sources	140
Telegram/Telemessage – a means of sending urgent written information, both nationally and internationally	159
Telephone – a system for oral communication, both internally and externally	154
Telephone answering machine – a device for recording telephone messages	158
Teleprinter/Telex – a system which combines the speed of the telephone with the authority of the written word	159

Television: closed circuit – a means of communicating data within an organisation

Voice Mail – a computerised 'mailbox' for recording messages 158

Word processor/Electronic mail – a means of communicating information, after processing, by electronic mail direct to a correspondent 161

Factors to be considered when choosing a method of communication

	Examples:
• Speed of delivery	– for telephoning an urgent message
• Reliability	– written communication, such as letters or fax, ensure accuracy
• Security	– registered letter for valuables
• Destination – internal	– memo or intercom
external: in this country	– letter or fax
external: abroad	– airmail letter or telex
• Length of communication	– short: memo or telephone – long: letter or report
• Written or oral	– written communication, such as telex, if a permanent record is required, otherwise a telephone message will do
• Cost of transmitting the message	– telephone is cheap for local calls, but not for an overseas correspondent
• Influence	– face-to-face conversation is usually more effective than a written message
• Equipment at the disposal of the recipient	– telex or facsimile telegraphy NB requires equipment
• Number of people to receive the communication	– notice board or meeting for a large number
• Appearance of the message	– greetings telemessage for a special occasion

Computing and word processing glossary of terms

Abort A procedure for terminating the operation of a routine or program.
Access time The time taken to find and read data from a memory device.
Acoustic coupler *See* 'Modem'.
Address The reference number or name which identifies a particular area of computer storage.
ADP Automatic data processing.
ALGOL Algorithmic language – a high-level programming language used for scientific applications.
Alphanumeric A combination of alphabetical letters, numerical digits and sometimes special characters which can be processed by computer.
Applications program package A computer program with instructions for operating a specific task, such as wages or word processing.
Assembler A program for translating an assembly code into a machine code.
Backing store Computer storage, such as disks and tapes, used to supplement the main store.
Back up A duplicate copy of a working disk, kept as a safeguard in the event of loss or damage of the original disk.
BASIC An acronym for 'Beginner's All-purpose Symbolic Instruction Code' – a programming language used mainly with microcomputers and time-sharing systems.
Batch A quantity of records or data which form a unit of work for processing by computer.
Batch processing A process of coding and collating items into groups before processing.
Binary code The arithmetical process of counting using only two digits.
Bit A contracted binary digit representing a zero or one in binary arithmetic.
Block move A word processing term for moving a block of text, eg a paragraph, from one position of a document to another. Also referred to as 'cut and paste'.
Boiler plating Using a selected group of standard paragraphs and merging them to form one document.
Booting The process of setting up the system by switching on the computer and loading the software into it.
Buffer A temporary storage area to hold data before it is processed or printed.

Bug An error in a program or computer system.
Byte 8 bits = 1 byte – a byte representing one alphabetical or numerical symbol.
Central processing unit (or CPU) The central part of a computer system containing the control unit, main store and arithmetic/logic unit; controls the operations of the computer, interpreting and executing instructions.
Character string A group of identical alphabetic/numeric characters, eg words, date, etc, appearing within a text; a search can be made by comparing a character string with the characters contained in a document.
Chip An integrated electronic circuit created on a silicon wafer to perform complex automated operations.
COBOL 'Common business orientated language' – a high-level programming language used for data processing.
COM An acronym for 'computer output microfilm' or 'computer originated microfilm'; a process used for preparing microfilm directly from a computer.
Command key The key used in a word processing system to activate an operator command.
Communicating word processors Word processors linked via a network either internally or externally to provide an electronic mail service.
Compiler A program which converts high-level language to low-level machine language.
Configuration The way in which the hardware is organised within a system, eg stand-alone, shared resource, shared logic, distributed logic and local area network.
Constant Data which remains unchanged during a complete process.
Control key The key operated simultaneously with another key to provide access to editing or formating for setting margins, inserting spaces, etc.
Cursor Device on a video screen for positioning the next entry.
Cut and paste *See* Block move.
Daisy wheel Printing element used in conjunction with a printer in a word processor.
Data Information which has been coded for processing.
Database A set of related files providing a data processing base which can be used by several programs.
Data capture The method of recording information before processing.
Data preparation The conversion of data into a form which can be read automatically by machine.
Data processing The ordering and sorting of data to produce the desired results.
Data transmission The movement of data from one device (computer, word processor, etc) to another by means of a communication network.

Debug To eradicate bugs, ie to correct errors in a computer system or program.

Dedicated Equipment specially designed, ie dedicated, for one type of application such as word processing.

Direct (or random) access Access of data in any order; data does not have to be sorted since access is made directly to the master record and only those records which need changing have to be accessed.

Disk/disc A flat metal disk coated with a magnetic material for storing text or programs.

Disk drive The device which reads and writes the data to and from the disks.

Diskette *See* floppy disk.

Document assembly A means of creating and storing names or numbered paragraphs for recall when required.

Dongle A device which is plugged into a computer to prevent the unauthorised copying of programs.

DOS Disk operating system – software which controls the use of disks for the storage and retrieval of information.

Dot matrix printer An output device on a computer or word processor which uses a matrix of tiny dots for printing.

EDP Electronic data processing.

Emboldening Overprinting to reproduce bolder type.

Erase To remove data from storage without replacing it.

Field A subdivision of an item of information, eg a customer's account number from a customer record.

File A single unit of related records used in a computer system.

Floppy disk (or diskette) Flexible magnetic disk for storage and rapid access of data used mainly in mini-computers, micro-computers and word processors.

Flowchart A diagram using special symbols to depict the various stages in a system or computer program.

Footers Page numbers and other information automatically generated at the bottom of specified pages in a document.

Format The layout and design of a document.

Fortran An acronym for 'formula translator' – a high-level programming language used for mathematical and scientific computations.

Function key A key used to activate an operation or format command.

Global search and replace Searching for a character string and replacing it with a different one, eg changing all references to 1989 to 1990.

Hard copy The machine output in readable printed form.

Hardware The physical parts of a computer system, including the computer itself and peripherals such as printers and terminals.

Headers Headings and other information which can be automatically generated at the top of specified pages in a document.

Help menu A menu providing assistance to the operator in using the various commands.

High-level language A programming language designed to simplify the writing of complex programs without having to use machine language.

Housekeeping The routine tasks that are required for the day-to-day upkeep and security of a computer system such as duplicating disks, removing redundant files, etc.

IDP Integrated data processing, in which the same files are used by different programs.

Immediate access (or core) store A short-term memory of the central processing unit used for holding data to be processed.

Information retrieval The process of accessing information from a database.

Input The process of feeding data into a computer.

Input device The device that converts information into a form which can be stored in a computer memory.

Intelligent terminal A terminal which is independent of a connected computer for carrying out certain processing and computing facilities.

Interface A link between a word processor and a peripheral such as a disk drive.

Justification A means of producing text with aligned left- and right-hand margins.

Kilobyte 1000 bytes or characters.

Laser printer A high-speed printer which uses laser beams to charge ink on to paper to produce a top-quality image.

Log on/off The terms used for on-line interaction on a terminal for entering in or exiting from a computer program.

Machine code/language A low-level basic language used in computer programming.

Mail merge An automatic process for merging a document file (eg a standard letter) with a mailing list containing names, addresses, dates, amounts, etc, to produce personalised letters.

Mainframe Another term for a central processing unit.

Mark sense reading The automatic reading of marks recorded on documents for input to a computer.

Megabyte 1 000 000 bytes or characters.

Memory The computer device which stores information.

Menu The method of making a word processing system 'user friendly': sets of commands are displayed on the screen so that the operator does not have to constantly refer to a manual.

Merge Combining text from two separate files.

MICR 'Magnetic ink character recognition': printing magnetic ink numbers on the bottom of cheques for automatic reading and sorting, eg

⑈000651⑈ 00⑉0000⑆ 10476375⑈ 11

Microprocessor A small processor which controls the operation of a computer or word processor.
Mode An operating function such as insert, delete or merge on a word processor.
Modem An acronym for 'modulator–demodulator'; used to convert computer input/output into a form which can be sent by telephone.
Mouse A portable instrument consisting of a hand-held box containing a rolling ball, which, when rolled across the desk moves a pointer on the computer screen. When the mouse button is depressed, the computer activates the item in the position occupied by the mouse.
Multi-access A system in which several users have access to one processor at the same time.
OCR Optical character recognition, an input process in which lines are printed within a pre-determined area to be read by a scanning device, as in the following example:

On-line A terminal interacting directly with a computer.
Operating system The software which co-ordinates the operation of a computer by interpreting the commands and providing the communication between the computer and the operator.
Output The information transferred from the computer's memory unit to a storage or output device.
Pagination The means of specifying the number of lines to be allocated to each page.
Peripheral Any part of a computer system which is linked to the central processor, eg disk drive, printer, etc.
Program A sequence of instructions to a computer to perform particular tasks.
PROM Programmable read-only memory.
Prompt The instructions which help the operator of a word processor to carry out the correct procedure or identify faults.
RAM Random access memory – temporary storage where each item can be read or updated at the same time, irrespective of its location.
Random access *See* Direct access.
Real time The processing of data where each transaction is fully processed at the time of operation, as in an airline seat reservation system.

Retrieval The extraction of information from a computer file.
ROM Read only memory, ie the permanent storage which cannot be updated.
Save A method of transferring a file from the screen of a word processor to a disk.
Scrolling The movement of text vertically or horizontally on a screen.
Search and replace Searching for characters and replacing them with different ones.
Serial (or sequential) access Locating information by searching for it in the order or sequence in which it is stored.
Shared logic system A computer or word processing system in which several terminals have access to the same central processor, storage devices and printer.
Silicon chip *See* Chip.
Software The non-physical, or intangible, parts of a computer system, ie the programs and operating manuals.
Speech generation A program which provides the input for a computer to create speech.
Spelling check A means of checking a passage for spelling errors against a program containing a dictionary of standard words. Users can add their own words to meet their individual needs.
Spreadsheet An applications program which provides a means of making rapid calculations to aid decision making. Data is entered and manipulated on a matrix which allows the operator to see at a glance the effect when one of the values is changed.
Stand-alone system A single computer or word processor which is not connected to any other terminals.
Status line The line which appears at the top or bottom of a word processor screen giving information about the work situation under review, eg name of file, page no., column no., line no., etc.
Store *See* Memory.
System disk A disk containing the program which operates the computer or word processing system.
Terminal A peripheral (usually a keyboard with a printer and/or visual display unit) for feeding information into a computer (input) and extracting information from a computer (output).
Time sharing The system by which several users have simultaneous access to computer facilities.
Update The changes made to a master file brought about by the insertion of current data.
VDU Visual display unit – a peripheral device which displays data on a screen.
Winchester disk A compact high-capacity hard disk unit for holding a large volume of data on a microcomputer.
Word processor The electronic equipment used for preparing text, including editing, storage, retrieval and transmission of information – *see also* p 164.

Work station A stand-alone microcomputer or a terminal linked to a computer with the ability to handle various computing and/or word processing applications.

Wraparound A means of automatically transferring the last word(s) on a line to the next line if it does not fit within the line length.

Write protect tag A tag which prevents data from being added to a disk.

Conference planning

1 Before any arrangements can be made, decisions must be taken by the employer or conference organising committee concerning:
a theme or purpose of the conference
b date
c place
A new file should be opened for each conference and all documents relevant to the conference should be kept in it.

2 Select the conference venue and hotels suitable for accommodating the delegates. You will need to consider the rooms and conference facilities available and the cost and accessibility by road and rail.

3 Arrange a meeting with the employer or conference organising committee to discuss the title and content of the conference. Include suggestions for chairpersons, speakers, social activities, mayor's or company directors' reception (if appropriate).

4 Draft the programme for approval by the employer or chairperson.

5 Write to the chairpersons and speakers for each session, inviting them to take part. Make arrangements for the social activities and reception.

6 A preliminary notice of the conference should be circulated to delegates, and possibly a notice in a professional journal.

7 Discuss the programme with the conference hotel/centre and make the arrangements for rooms, catering, etc.

8 Make arrangements for the printing and despatch of the conference programme, booking form (giving details of recommended hotels) and invitation cards for the social events. At this stage the charges for delegates can be calculated and included in the programme. Determine the minimum number of delegates required for financial

viability. If it is a company conference, charges will be met by the company.

9 If there is to be a conference dinner, the following arrangements may be necessary:
  a invite special guests and arrange for the after-dinner speeches
  b arrange entertainment
  c arrange for cocktails in an ante-room for guests
  d discuss the menu, wines and floral decorations with the hotel
  e book a photographer
  f arrange for the printing of the menu card
  g draw up a table plan with place names

10 Book a room at the conference centre to serve as a conference office to deal with the registration of delegates, preparation and issue of conference papers and to supply information to delegates. Arrange a rota of staff to work in the conference office for the duration of the conference.

11 Arrange for the recording of the conference proceedings and, if appropriate, for the press to be invited to the public sessions.

12 Arrange for visual aids to be available for speakers and check on the provision of amplifying equipment.

13 Arrange for the secure transportation and insurance against the loss or theft, etc, of any items of value to be used at the conference and make a record of the serial numbers of all items of equipment transported.

14 Arrange with the AA or RAC for direction signs to be installed in the town.

15 When the booking forms and cheques arrive, make arrangements with the bank to open a special conference account and pay the cheques into it. Acknowledge the booking forms and cheques. Keep a careful check on the number of bookings received so that you do not accept more people than can be accommodated.

16 At a date to be agreed, confirm the number of bookings with the conference centre and hotels concerned.

17 Prepare conference folders with lists of delegates, handouts, publicity material, badges, etc.

18 On the day of the conference:
  a supervise the conference office – signing-in procedure, issuing conference folders and dealing with delegates' queries
  b check that the directional notices are in place, rooms are prepared and ready, refreshments are available and equipment is in position and working
  c introduce visiting speakers to the leading delegates
  d arrange for the reproduction of conference papers, as requested by speakers

e if the press are in attendance, ensure that they have access to the required information

19 After the conference:

a write letters of thanks to the delegates, speakers and all who contributed to the conference

b arrange for the payment of speakers, entertainments, florist, hotel, etc

c prepare a report of the conference for issue to delegates and possibly for the press

d despatch conference photographs and reports to delegates

e prepare a receipts and payments account for the accountant or for submission to the next meeting of the conference organising committee

f any problems encountered at the conference should be noted in the conference file so that these can be avoided when planning future conferences

Teleconferencing

Audioconferencing

Audioconferencing is a telecommunication service which enables two or more groups of people located anywhere in the UK and in some countries abroad to be linked simultaneously by telephone. It is an economic and flexible way to run a conference, update staff or hold training courses without the expense and disruption of face-to-face meetings. Organisations can either install their own equipment or use the Confertel Bureau operated by British Telecom.

Videoconferencing

Videoconferencing is the linking of groups of people in different locations by sound and vision. Although it is an expensive method, it provides the advantages of a face-to-face meeting while avoiding the travelling and accommodation costs, and makes better use of people's time. Any documents, models or technical drawings being discussed can be shown in close-up on the TV monitors installed at each location. The two main services currently available from British Telecom are:

1 **Confravision** which provides closed-circuit television studios in several major cities in the UK for videoconferences. Participants simply travel to their nearest studio, where they are linked to whichever other studios have been hired for the conference. Groups of up to five people can participate at each location.

2 **Videostream** – a service which can be used by organisations with their own camera and monitoring equipment. New digital technology enables colour video signals to be transmitted over telephone lines, making this a useful conference service for large organisations.

Correspondence: key factors in composition and construction

1 **Date** It is essential to date all correspondence – state the day, month and year, eg 14 January 19—.

2 **Reference** To provide a means of identification to a letter, state your reference and that of the addressee if one is provided.

3 **Telephone extension** When letters are sent from large organisations, it is helpful if the writer's telephone extension number is inserted in the heading.

4 **Inside name and address** This is the name and address of the addressee and should be accommodated in three or four lines, if possible. When the letter is being despatched in a window envelope, the postal town should be in capitals followed by the post code.

5 **Security notations** If these are required, they are shown above the inside name and address for the following reasons:

Personal or Private	– to indicate that the letter should be opened and read only by the addressee
Confidential	– to indicate that the letter should be opened and read only by the addressee or by those he has authorised to do so
Personal & Confidential *or* Private & Confidential.	– as in Personal or Private above

6 **Attention line** If the letter has to be addressed to an organisation but you know the name of the person who will deal with it, it is helpful to include an attention line above the inside name and address, eg For the attention of Mrs J Hicks.

7 **Heading** Use a heading line if possible as it is a quick reference to the content of the document. A letter in reply to one with a heading should be given the same subject heading.

8 **Salutation and complimentary close** These are normally either:

formal – Dear Sir
Yours faithfully

informal – Dear Mr Smith or Dear John
Yours sincerely

9 **Paragraphing** Divide the letter into paragraphs, each dealing with one point only and arranged as follows:

a introductory paragraph
b body of the letter (further subdivided into paragraphs)
c concluding paragraph

The message in a long letter is easier to follow and understand when the different points are made in small paragraphs, arranged in a logical order with each point leading logically to the next.

10 **Introductory paragraph** This should follow on from the heading and introduce the subject matter by referring to any previous letter, telephone conversation or, if there has not been any previous correspondence, directly to the subject matter.

11 **Concluding paragraph** This will normally indicate to the addressee the next stage in the communication as the writer sees it.

12 **Signature block** This should contain the name of the writer and their title/description, eg:

a when employer dictates a letter and signs it	–	Yours faithfully BETA DYNAMICS PLC (*signature*) John Smith Marketing Manager
b when a letter is signed on the employer's behalf in their absence	–	Yours faithfully BETA DYNAMICS PLC (*signature*) for John Smith Marketing Manager OR Dictated by John Smith and signed in his absence (*signature*) Anna Jones Secretary to Marketing Manager
c when secretary composes a letter and signs it	–	Yours faithfully BETA DYNAMICS PLC (*signature*) Anna Jones Secretary to Mr John Smith Marketing Manager

13 **Enclosures** If enclosures accompany the letter, indicate this by typing 'enc' at the bottom of the letter.

14 **Composition** Choose your words carefully and avoid business jargon and unnecessarily long phrases. The following are some examples of phrases to be avoided, together with suggested alternatives:

- I am in receipt of your favour
- I acknowledge receipt of your letter

} – Thank you for your letter, or With reference to your letter

- Please be advised that – a formal preliminary which is unnecessary

Beta Dynamics plc
81 Winterside Road, Weston-Super-Mare, Avon BS24 8AR

Company no: 2464815 England
Telex: 248193 BETACS
Fax: 0934–62313
Telephone: 0934 27624 Ext 124 (3)

(2) Our Ref: 189/82
Your Ref:

(1) 1 March 19--

(4) The Manager
Queen's Hotel
20 Bloomsbury Square
LONDON WC1A 4PR

(8) Dear Sir

(7) RESERVATION OF ACCOMMODATION

(10) In confirmation of my telephone conversation today with your receptionist, Miss P Jarrett, I shall be grateful if you will reserve a single room with bath for the evenings of 15-18 March 19-- inclusive for Mr J Smith of this company. He would appreciate a room on the quiet side of the hotel.

I wish to confirm, also, that Mr Smith will be entertaining ten business associates for dinner at 2000 hrs on 16 March 19--. He would like you to arrange this in a private room and to serve cocktails there at 1930 hrs. The meal will be selected by Mr Smith's guests from the 'â la carte' menu.

All expenses incurred by Mr Smith during his stay at your hotel will be paid by this company and I shall be glad if you will forward the account to the above address for my attention.

(11) Will you please confirm that these arrangements are in order.

(8) Yours faithfully
BETA DYNAMICS plc

(12) Anna Jones
Secretary to Mr John Smith
Marketing Manager

A specimen letter

- Referring to the matter – state the matter
- This is to inform you – give the information without these preliminary words
- I have enclosed
- Attached please find
- I enclose herewith

} – I enclose

- In view of the fact that – since
- At this time – now

Select and use words which express your ideas adequately and with the right amount of emphasis; if a word is used too often it loses its emphasis.

15 **Tone** The tone or language used in a letter will need to be varied according to the nature of the message and the relationship between the correspondents. If you are writing on behalf of your employer, you must adopt the tone which is intended to be used. It must, above all, be courteous without failing to express the message clearly. A letter reflects the writer's personality so every opportunity should be taken to give a human and personal impression, even though the letter itself may be typed automatically from a word processor!

16 **Layout** Use the organisation's standard practice for the layout of correspondence. The fully blocked style is now commonly used but other forms of layout are equally acceptable as long as consistency is maintained throughout. In the fully blocked layout all lines begin flush at the left-hand margin, as in the example.

17 **Punctuation** This is as important as correct facts. The omission of punctuation marks or their incorrect use can give misleading or wrong impressions. Open punctuation is now common practice for the information above and below the body of the letter, as illustrated in the example, because the punctuation marks do not serve any useful purpose and do not contribute anything to the appearance. An added advantage of open punctuation is the saving of typists' time.

18 **Internal communications** Memos are normally used internally and for communications to branches, agents or representatives in other parts of the country or the world. Salutations and complimentary closes are not used and the inside name and address is usually condensed to the person's name or title, as in the following example:

MEMO

To: Training Manager Date: 8 January 19--

From: Office Manager Ref: P1436

FACSIMILE TELEGRAPHY

The new facsimile system will be installed on 21 January and the manufacturers have agreed to provide an instructor to train the staff in using it. The instructor will attend all day on Wednesday 22 January 19-- and I would like at least one representative from each department to attend the training course.

Can you please make the necessary arrangements with the departmental heads for members of their staff to attend.

Another method of internal communication is an *action slip*, as illustrated on p 26.

Decorations, honours and qualifications

The decorations, honours and qualifications which follow a person's name should be arranged in the following order:

1 Decorations and Honours – in the order of precedence given on pp 46–7.

2 Royal appointments, including some made on behalf of the Queen, consisting of the following:

PC	Privy Counsellor
ADC	Aide-de-camp
QHP	Queen's Honorary Physician
QHS	Queen's Honorary Surgeon
QHDS	Queen's Honorary Dental Surgeon
QHNS	Queen's Honorary Nursing Sister
QHC	Queen's Honorary Chaplain
QC	Queen's Counsel
JP	Justice of the Peace
DL	Deputy Lieutenant

3 University degrees – *see* p 84.

4 Professional qualifications

5 Titles relating to membership of learned societies, academies and professional institutions

} abbreviations for a selection of these are given on pp 1–13.

6 Appointments or offices held, eg MP (Member of Parliament), MEP (Member of the European Parliament), CC (County Councillor), etc.

Examples:

Air Vice Marshal S C Canning, CB, JP, BSc, FRSA
Miss P Walker, OBE, FCA, MP.

Decorations and honours

A selection of decorations and honours in the correct order of precedence:

VC	Victoria Cross
GC	George Cross
KG	Knight of the Order of the Garter
KT	Knight of the Order of the Thistle
KP	Knight of the Order of St Patrick
GCB	Knight or Dame Grand Cross of the Order of the Bath
OM	Order of Merit
GCSI	Grand Commander of the Order of the Star of India
GCMG	Knight or Dame Grand Cross of the Order of St Michael and St George
GCIE	Knight Grand Commander of the Order of the Indian Empire
CI	Imperial Order of the Crown of India
GCVO	Knight or Dame Grand Cross of the Royal Victorian Order
GBE	Knight or Dame Grand Cross of the Order of the British Empire
CH	Companion of Honour
KCB	Knight Commander, Order of the Bath
KCSI	Knight Commander, the Order of the Star of India
KCMG	Knight Commander, Order of St Michael and St George
KCIE	Knight Commander, Order of the Indian Empire
KCVO	Knight Commander of the Royal Victorian Order
KBE	Knight Commander of the Order of the British Empire
CB	Companion of the Order of the Bath
CSI	Companion of the Order of the Star of India
CMG	Companion of the Order of St Michael and St George
CIE	Companion of the Order of the Indian Empire
CVO	Commander of the Royal Victorian Order
CBE	Commander of the Order of the British Empire
DSO	Companion of the Distinguished Service Order

MVO (4th class)	Member, Royal Victorian Order
OBE	Officer, Order of the British Empire
ISO	Imperial Service Order
MVO (5th class)	Member, Royal Victorian Order
MBE	Member, Order of the British Empire
RRC	Member, Royal Red Cross (1st class)
DSC	Distinguished Service Cross
MC	Military Cross
DFC	Distinguished Flying Cross
AFC	Air Force Cross
ARRC	Associate, Royal Red Cross
AM	Albert Medal
DCM	Distinguished Conduct Medal
CGM	Conspicuous Gallantry Medal
GM	George Medal
DSM	Distinguished Service Medal
MM	Military Medal
DFM	Distinguished Flying Medal
AFM	Air Force Medal
QGM	Queen's Gallantry Medal
BEM	British Empire Medal
QPM	Queen's Police Medal
SGM	Sea Gallantry Medal
VD	Volunteer Officer's Decoration
ERD	Emergency Reserve Decoration (Army)
TD	Territorial Efficiency Decoration
ED	Efficiency Decoration
RD	Royal Navy Reserve Decoration
VRD	Royal Naval Volunteer Reserve Officer's Decoration
AE	Air Efficiency Award

Desk diaries and other memory aids

Key factors in using desk diaries:

- Be systematic. At the beginning of the day take the necessary action on all entries, eg prepare the papers and files for meetings and appointments. During the course of the day keep in mind and prepare for the various appointments and engagements – make amendments, additions and deletions as required. At the end of the day, ensure that all items have been dealt with or, if necessary, transferred to a future date.

Secretary's Diary

May **19--**

17 Monday

Time	Entry	Place
1000	Executives Meeting	Boardroom
1130	Appointment (TJM) Mr R W Parker, Conway Engineering Ltd – File 739/82	
1300	TJM ~ Lunch: Institute of Marketing	Tyrol Restaurant
1500	Interviews for Sales Rep for Wales	Room 100
1900	Squash with Betty and Paul	Staff club
2000	TJM – Dinner (with Mrs Mason) at Major Wilson's house	29 Grange Rd
NOTES:	Joan Perkins attending Secretarial Development Course	
	Agenda for Sales Meeting (26 May)	
	Follow up: Files 812/81, 389/82, 467/82	

Meetings

Appointments

Luncheon engagements

Social engagements

Key staff absences

Anniversary reminders

Work planning

Files to be followed up

Employer's Diary
(Mr T J Mason – Marketing Manager)

May **19--**

17 Monday

Time	Entry	Place
1000	Executives Meeting	Boardroom
1130	Mr R W Parker, Conway Engineering Ltd	
1300	Lunch ~ Institute of Marketing	Tyrol Restaurant
1500	Interviews for Sales Rep for Wales	Room 100
2000	Dinner (with Mrs Mason) at Major Wilson's house	29 Grange Rd
NOTES:	Chief Accountant on holiday (until 24 May)	
	Paul Pringle ~ 25 yrs with firm on 19 May	

- Write entries clearly with a pen. Enter provisional appointments in pencil and ink them in when they are confirmed.
- Appointments for each day should be entered in the correct time sequence.
- Enter essential details such as full descriptions of appointments, time and place.
- All entries affecting the employer should be entered in his diary as well as in the secretary's diary (*see* specimen diaries on p 48).

Memory aids

The office diary This is the simplest of the aids and one of the most effective methods, provided that it is systematically maintained and referred to daily.

Indexed memory aids Index cards or memos are used to record matters which require attention in the future. The system has folders for each day of the month and each month of the year which are stored in a filing cabinet. When a matter requiring attention on a future date arises or when appointments are made, an entry is made on a card or memo and placed in the appropriate folder. The folders are then referred to every day, and after a day's entries have been dealt with, that file is placed at the back of the month's files.

Signalling devices Used in association with visible record cards (*see* p 61) to highlight the date when the item on a card requires attention.

Plastic year planners Large plastic calendars with spaces for every day of the year can be used for planning appointments, meetings and other business activities. With these you can see at a glance a year's activities and so plan engagements methodically on one single sheet.

Appointments cards An alternative to the office diary for the employer who is away from his office for a whole day, attending various functions and appointments. The card lists the appointments, including time and venue, and is an extract from the diary.

Computerised desk diary planner A desk diary can be kept on a computer so that the entries can be seen on a VDU and a printout made when required. An entry is made by keying in the date, time and brief details of the item, and if an appointment is cancelled or changed to another time or date it can be removed from the 'memory' and re-entered on another date, if necessary. The computer can be programmed to reject any entries at certain times of the day or even whole days when the employer does not wish to have appointments. An appointment which occurs several times during the year at regular intervals can be entered once with the relevant dates and is automatically entered on each of the dates. Also annual events, such as anniversaries, can be automatically entered in the diary for subsequent years. Each day's entries can be viewed at the beginning of the day and, for planning purposes, it is possible to view a month's entries. All forthcoming events, reminders and 'unavailable' days can be displayed up to a maximum of 30 days.

A computerised system, such as this, is particularly good for following up correspondence and for reminders of work to be done on particular dates, such as the preparation of an agenda for a meeting.

Computerised diary programs can be used to co-ordinate dates for meetings if all the executives of a company keep their diaries on computer. When it is necessary to call a meeting of the executives, the secretary can call up the program on the work-station and enter the likely duration of the meeting. The computer searches the diaries of each of the executives and gives a choice of times and dates when all are free to attend. The secretary can then select one of the options and the diaries are automatically updated with the selected meeting date and time.

Electronic office

The diagram on p 51 illustrates the main features of an electronic, 'paperless' office with:

- word processing and data processing systems linked in an integrated network
- computers, word processors, copiers and telex terminals linked to each other and to a central database to provide rapid exchange of information without the need for paperwork
- office workers using terminals to communicate with the terminals of other employees within the organisation
- terminals linked to the national and international public telecommunications networks to provide instant communication with customers, suppliers, banks, etc, in other organisations
- data held in a memory bank for the storage and retrieval of records and correspondence

Data protection

The Data Protection Act 1984 establishes rights for individuals to have access to their own personal data held on computer files. The Act contains the following principles which govern the processing of personal data:

1 Data must be obtained fairly and lawfully, ie people must not

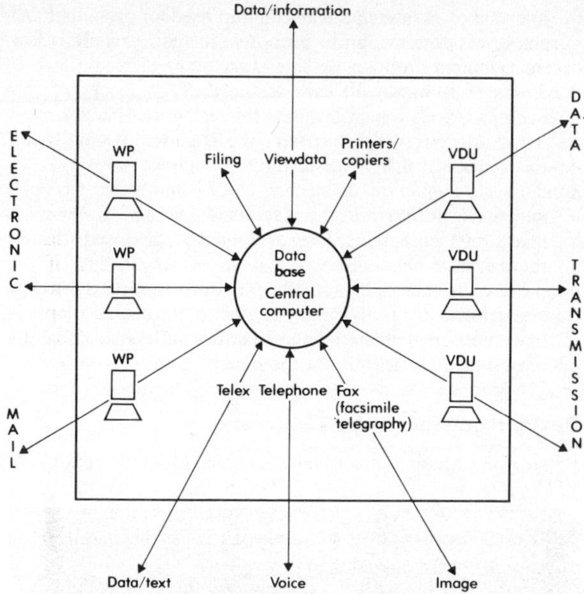

be misled as to the use to which information they supply about themselves will be put.

2 Data must only be held for registered and lawful purposes. Data users are required to register the personal data they hold with the Data Protection Registrar.

3 Data must only be used and disclosed for the purposes registered.

4 Data must be adequate, relevant and not excessive for its purpose.

5 Data must be accurate and, where necessary, kept up to date.

6 Data must be held for no longer than is necessary.

7 Individuals must be allowed access to data about themselves at reasonable intervals and without undue expense and they must be provided with a copy of it in an intelligible form. Where appropriate, the data must be corrected or erased.

8 Data users must take appropriate security measures to prevent unauthorised access, disclosure, alteration or destruction of personal data and against its accidental loss or destruction.

The Act gives an individual, ie data subject, the following rights:

1 To be informed whether or not a data user has personal information about him/her, eg an application form for employment should contain a signed statement by the applicant saying: 'I understand that if I am appointed, personal

information about me will be computerised for personnel and employee administrative purposes including analysis for management purposes and statutory returns.'

2 To receive, within 40 days of the request, a copy of this information expressed in terms intelligible to him/her.
3 To seek a court order to enforce the data user to comply with this request if the data user refuses to do so.
4 To seek compensation for any damage and distress he/she may have suffered if the data held by the data user is inaccurate, misleading, lost, destroyed or disclosed without the data user's authority.
5 To have inaccurate data rectified, erased or supplemented by a statement of the true facts if a court is satisfied that it is inaccurate or that the data subject has suffered damage by reason of the disclosure of the data.

Health requirements for VDU operators

Potential health problems which may arise from the operation of VDUs include:

	Possible remedies
1 Eyestrain caused by glare from the screen	• sustained keyboarding may lead to a build-up of fatigue and regular short breaks throughout the day should prevent this from happening • avoid siting the VDU in a brightly lit area where the lights are reflected in the screen; but the light must be adequate for reading the copy and the screen image • do not look directly at windows or bright lights • use task lighting specially designed for VDU operation – avoid unshielded fluorescent lights • use the brightness controls to suit the lighting conditions in the office • keep the screen clean, removing dirt and 'grease' finger marks from it • operators wearing glasses or contact lenses may have to have them corrected to the range of focus required
2 Stress caused by boredom and slow computer response time	• job variation and rotation will help to relieve this

3 Posture fatigue	• use adjustable chairs to provide the correct seat height and back-rest positions – *see* p 21 for British Standards Institute specifications
4 Screen flicker	• as a VDU ages it is inclined to develop more faults such as drift and jitter of the images and it is possible that the brilliance control will need to be adjusted to a higher level • screen flicker may affect epileptics but it should be possible to avoid excessive flicker by adjusting the VDU controls • regular servicing is essential to correct deterioration of the visual image
5 Heat and humidity	• as computing and word processing equipment generates heat, effective methods of ventilation are essential to control the temperature in the office. A humidifier may also be necessary to avoid a dry atmosphere

Radiation

Current research suggests that no health hazards result from radiation and that you do not need any protective devices. Some reports have suggested that there could be a possible danger for pregnant women, but the National Radiological Protection Board has made it clear that radiation emissions from a VDU will put neither the woman nor her unborn child at any risk at all.

Maintenance and care of equipment

Guidelines for the day-to-day care and maintenance of electronic equipment

- Keep a copy of the operating manual with the machine and follow the instructions given for regular cleaning.
- Do not smoke, drink or eat when operating the equipment.
- If the machine has to be moved, be sure to disconnect it from the electrical supply.
- Keep a log record of any intermittent faults which occur and the dates and times when maintenance engineers call to attend to the equipment.
- Have access to a maintenance service for remedying faults, but before calling in a mechanic for a breakdown CHECK:
  - that the power supply is on
  - that fuses in the equipment are working

– that there are no faults in the connecting cables and plugs
– the operating manual 'trouble shooting' for useful tips on tracing the fault

If, after taking these steps, there is still a fault with the equipment, call for the services of a maintenance engineer.

Care of floppy disks

Do	*Do not*
• Keep floppy disks in their wallets, when not in use, to protect them from dust	• bend, fold or scratch disks
• Return disks to their wallets after use and store them upright in the disk box supplied	• Touch the exposed portion of a disk
• Label each disk with a description of its contents	• Write directly on to the disk wallet
• Insert disks carefully into the disk drive, without forcing them, to avoid damage	• Store disks near a hot radiator, fire or heat of the sun
	• Remove disks when the drive light is on
• As a safeguard against damage or loss, keep a back-up (duplicate) of any disk containing important data, eg all master program disks should be copied and the masters stored in a secure place	• Leave disks around on the top of a screen, printer, telephone and other electronic equipment (sources of magnetism) which could corrupt them
• Use a write protect tag on a system disk to prevent data from being added to it	

Entertaining in business

The secretary may be involved in the following tasks:

1 Arranging with the firm's catering manager to serve lunch for the employer and their visitors. The catering manager will normally need several days' notice if a special meal is required. After discussing with the catering manager the meal and wine requested by the employer, confirm these in writing together with the date and time.

2 Reserving a table for lunch or dinner at a hotel or restaurant. With some knowledge of the area, the employer will probably suggest the place, or otherwise could be invited to suggest one from a guide such as *Hotel Guide*, the *Good Food Guide* or the *AA Members Handbook*. Telephone in the first place to make sure that a table is available and state the requirements, ie date, time, number of places, and then write a letter to confirm the details.

3 Organising a buffet lunch in the employer's office or in the board room. This may be arranged by the firm's catering manager or by an outside caterer. Confirmation in writing of the date, time, venue, number of guests and content of meal and wine is required in either case.

4 When arranging a dinner party, the major tasks include:

- discussing the function in detail with your employer
- telephoning and writing a letter booking accommodation and arranging the necessary catering facilities – stating the approximate number of people expected to attend; estimates from several places may have to be obtained before a decision is made
- printing (or typing) and despatching invitation cards to guests (*see* specimen invitation card below)
- printing or typing the menu cards or arranging for the caterers to do this for you (*see* specimen menu card on p 57)
- when replies have been received, confirming with the caterer the number expected; on the actual day, telephoning the caterer with any last-minute adjustment to the number expected and checking that all arrangements are in hand

The Directors and Staff of Computer Accessories PLC
request the pleasure of the company of

....

at a dinner party
to be held at The Country House Hotel, Warwick
on Friday 27 July 19—
1930 for 2000 hrs

RSVP Mrs P Barber, PA to Managing Director, Computer Accessories PLC, Barford, Warwickshire, by 20 July 19—

A specimen invitation card

A selection of common menu terms in French with English translations

French term	*English translation*
Avocat	Avocado pear
Beignets de langoustines	Scampi
Bœuf bourgignon	Braised beef prepared in red wine with mushrooms and onions
Café	Coffee
Caneton à l'orange	Braised duckling served with orange slices
Cassade	Ice cream with fruit
Choux de Bruxelles	Brussel sprouts served in butter
Consommé	A clear soup
Coq au vin	Chicken prepared in red wine with onions and bacon
Crème anglaise	Egg custard
Entrecôte Bercy	Grilled steak served with Bercy butter
Entrecôte maître d'hôtel	Grilled steak served with a butter containing chopped parsley and lemon juice
Filet de bœuf	Fillet of beef
Filet de sole meunière	Fillet of sole fried in butter
Fromages	Cheeses
Fruits rafraichis	Fresh fruit salad
Glace	Ice cream
Homard à la nage	Lobster boiled in white wine
Hors d'œuvres	A starter which may include fish, salads, pâtés, sea foods and snails
Jambon	Ham
Meringue glacée	Ice cream with meringue
Oeuf dur mayonnaise	Hard-boiled egg with mayonnaise
Pâtisserie	A cake or pastry-based sweet
Plat du jour	Special dish of the day
Pointes d'asperges	Asparagus tips
Poire belle Hélène	Ice cream and pears served with a chocolate sauce
Pommes à l'anglaise	Boiled potatoes
Pommes au four	Baked potatoes
Pommes frites	French fried potatoes
Pommes sautées	Sliced potatoes fried in butter
Potage	Soup
Potage aux légumes	Vegetable soup
Poularde rôtie	Roast chicken

Profiteroles	Pastry balls filled with cream
Quiche Lorraine	Savoury flan containing bacon, eggs and cream
Ratatouille	Courgettes, aubergines, tomatoes, green peppers and onions cooked in oil with garlic
Rumsteack grillé	Grilled rump steak
Salade	Salad
Saumon grillé	Grilled salmon
Sorbet	Water ice
Soupe à l'oignon	Onion soup
Tournedos	Small pieces of beef fillet fried in butter or grilled

COMPUTER ACCESSORIES PLC

DINNER PARTY

27 July 19––

MENU

Hors d'oeuvres
or
Fruit juice

Filet de sole meunière

Boeuf bourgignon
Courgettes
Cauliflower
New potatoes

Poire belle Hélène

Cheese and Biscuits

Coffee

A specimen menu card

Selecting wine to complement food

Food	Suggested wine					
	Dry white	*Sweet white*	*Rosé*	*Red*	*Port/Madeira*	*Dry sherry*
Soup	x					x
Sea food	x		x			
Fish	x		x			
Chicken	x		x			
Eggs	x		x			
Meat				x		
Casserole dishes				x		
Duck				x		
Pheasant				x		
Guinea fowl				x		
Rabbit				x		
Cheese	x			x	x	
Desserts and fruit		x				

NB: Champagne is the only wine that can be served throughout a meal, complementing all courses.

Aperitif

It is usual to offer guests:
Sherry.
Champagne (dry).
Martini, Cinzano (dry vermouth).

Wine temperatures

Champagne – served very cold.
Dry sherry and white wines – served cold.
Red wines (with the exception of Beaujolais Nouveau, which should be served cold) – at room temperature.

Filing and indexing: glossary of terms

Absent folders/cards Method of controlling and recording files removed from a filing system.
Alphabetical filing Method of classifying files alphabetically by name of correspondent – suitable for correspondence with customers, clients, etc in a small/medium-sized organisation.
Box-file Used for storing a limited amount of correspondence when it needs to be kept in a separate container.
Centralised filing All files held in one central office.
Chronological filing Numerical method of filing documents according to their dates.
Computer-assisted retrieval Linking of computer and microfilming systems for rapid retrieval of data. Stages in this process:

a documents for filing are filmed and coded
b key information is entered into the computer as a record which can be accessed on-line or held on a floppy disk for use on a stand-alone computer
c information is retrieved by keying in search details on a terminal keyboard
d information from the computer index is displayed on a VDU screen which indicates to the operator the appropriate film required
e when the necessary code is keyed in, the required document image is automatically displayed on the screen
f the operator arranges for a 'hard' copy to be printed

Concertina or expanding file Contains a series of pockets which can be opened up like a concertina and papers placed in them for sorting prior to filing.
Cross-referencing Reference in a filing system to the position of a file or card when it is known by more than one name. The cross-reference is placed in the position where the folder or card is not held.
Data storage and retrieval Use of computers (floppy disks and hard disks) for the storage and retrieval of large quantities of data.
Dead file File which is no longer required for current use.
Decimal filing Numerical classification method used for subject divisions, especially in the arrangement of library books.
Departmental filing Each department holds its own files.
Electronic filing An automatic filing system in which files are retrieved by operating a push-button panel.
Follow-up system System for bringing forward files to check whether replies have been received to letters sent out.

Geographical filing Files classified alphabetically by geographical location of correspondents – suitable for correspondence with agents or representatives relating to the same area.
Guide cards Used in filing cabinets or index drawers to separate different sections, letters of the alphabet etc, to help find files/cards.
Index cards Used for recording and locating information, especially in a numerical method to supply the file numbers.
Lateral filing Files suspended laterally from rails in cabinets, cupboards, racks or shelves (like books on a shelf).
Lever arch file Loose-leaf file where papers are secured by two arch-shaped metal fasteners which are opened and closed by raising or lowering a lever.
Loose-leaf post/prong binders Used for holding stationery with holes punched in it which fit over the posts/prongs. Used especially for filing computer printouts.
Microfilming *See* p 115.
Miscellaneous file Contains correspondence relating to several subjects/customers which do not have separate files in the system.
Numerical filing Files are allocated numbers and arranged in numerical order – suitable for correspondence with customers, clients etc when a large number of files are involved.
Pending file Used to hold daily correspondence and routine papers until acted on.
Plan filing Horizontal or vertical cabinets for filing plans, drawings and large photographs.
Punches Used for punching holes in papers for filing in prong or ring files and binders.
Retention policy Used by an organisation to determine the date when files can be removed from current filing systems and/or destroyed. In deciding this policy, the following factors should be considered:

- volume of correspondence
- frequency of reference required
- access to the information from alternative sources
- audit requirements
- legal requirements

Rotary indexing equipment Indexing unit holding a large number of index cards or line reference strips on a rotating wheel for quick location of information.
Rotary suspended filing Files suspended and linked on rotating platforms for holding large numbers of files.
Safety first Avoid opening a heavy top drawer of a vertical filing cabinet because the whole cabinet is liable to topple over. It is advisable to open the bottom drawer before the top one so that it serves as a prop and lessens the risk. If possible, load all of the drawers evenly. Do not allow the drawers of filing cabinets and cupboards to protrude into gangways.

Strip indexing Reference data, such as commodity prices, telephone numbers, addresses etc, are recorded on cardboard strips which are built up one above the other in suitable carrying devices so that they are all clearly visible.
Subject filing Files classified alphabetically by subject – suitable for correspondence relating to projects or events where it is important to bring together all papers which relate to the same subject.
Transfer file File or box for holding documents which have to be kept but are no longer in current use.
Vertical filing Files arranged vertically (upright) in cabinets.
Visible card records Cards held in flat trays overlapping each other but with their edges visible. The visible edges contain 'key' information which can be extracted quickly without handling individual cards, eg file numbers, customer numbers, stock numbers, etc.

Suppliers of filing cabinets and accessories

Flexiform Ltd, 16 Duncan Terrace, London N1 8BZ

Leabank Office Equipment Ltd, Halesfield 1, Telford, Shropshire TF7 4QQ

Rotadex Systems Ltd, 3–5 Fortnum Close, Kitts Green, Birmingham B33 0JL

Sheer Pride Ltd, Weybridge Trading Estate, Addlestone, Weybridge, Surrey KT15 2RL

Vickers plc, PO Box 10, Hawley Road, Dartford, Kent DA1 1NY

Pointers to efficient filing

- Ensure that all correspondence has been passed for filing.
- Sort and group correspondence before filing. A concertina file is useful for this purpose.
- Remove paper clips before filing correspondence.
- Check that you are placing correspondence in the correct file.
- Place papers squarely on the files so that the edges are straight and neat.
- Arrange the correspondence in chronological order with the most recent on top.
- Always keep a record if:
  a a document has to be removed from a file
  b a file has to be removed from a cabinet
- Keep your files up to date by filing daily.
- If a file title is known by more than one name, use cross-references in places where the file is not held.
- Thin out files regularly in accordance with a file retention policy.
- Always close filing cabinet drawers after use.
- Lock filing cabinets before leaving the office at night or for any length of time.

Rules for indexing

	Examples
• The surname is placed before the Christian names and, if the surnames are the same, the first Christian name determines the position.	Atkins, James Atkins, John
• If the Christian name and surname are contained in the name of a firm, the surname is written first, followed by the Christian name and finally by the remainder of the name.	Brown, Peter PLC
• If a firm includes several names, the first is taken as the surname for indexing purposes.	Clarke, Rogers & Arnold
• The first name is taken in hyphenated names.	Davis, R Ewing-Davis R
• For impersonal names, such as county councils, use the name that distinguishes it from the others, for indexing purposes.	Hampshire County Council
• Names beginning with Mac, Mc or M' are treated as if they were spelt 'Mac'.	M'Bride G R McBride P T MacBride W G
• Names beginning with St are treated as if they were spelt 'Saint'.	St John Courtney Salon Sellers R T
• Names which begin with a number should either be listed before the alphabetical names or converted to words and placed in the appropriate alphabetical position, depending on the rules of the organisation.	3M United Kingdom plc file as 'Three M'
• Nothing comes before something, ie a name without an initial precedes a name with one.	Thomas Thomason Thomason P Thomason P P
• Names which consist of initials separated by spaces or full stops are placed before full names. Those which are not separated are treated as words and are placed in the usual alphabetical position.	W.E.A. Watson E A

First aid in the office

The law states that all business premises must provide an acceptable first aid box or first aid cupboard. Where the number of persons employed in the premises exceeds 150 at any one time, an additional box or cupboard must be provided for each unit of 150 persons (or fraction of a unit). Each box or cupboard must:

- contain first aid requisites and appliances, as specified in the Health and Safety (First Aid) Regulations 1981
- contain no articles other than first aid requisites and appliances
- be in the charge of a responsible person (no person can be in charge of more than one box or cupboard).

Where the number of persons exceeds 150, at least one must be trained in first aid treatment and always available during working hours. Notices must be displayed at such posts so that they can be easily seen and read by the employees working in the premises. They must state the names of those who are in charge of the boxes/cupboards and that these persons are always available during working hours. Certain exemptions may, however, be granted where a first aid room is provided.

When an accident causes loss of life or serious injury or prevents a person from doing his usual work for more than three days, you must notify the Health and Safety Executive, in accordance with the Notification of Accidents and Dangerous Occurrences Regulations 1980.

The importance of first aid in the office cannot be emphasised too strongly and it is as important in small offices as it is in large ones. Accidents and illnesses occur in offices of every size, even when elaborate safety precautions are observed. Speedy and proper treatment of injuries and illnesses is essential to protect employees from unnecessary suffering and to help them to recover as quickly as possible.

An organisation's first aid service can only be fully effective when all of its employees:

a are conscious of the need for safety at all times
b know where the nearest first aid box and facilities are
c know how to contact the named first aider when an accident or illness occurs
d know how to send quickly for a doctor or an ambulance in major accidents or illnesses
e know how to help an injured person by:
   - making the casualty as comfortable as possible (but do not attempt to move the casualty until you know what is wrong)

- ensuring that the casualty can breathe freely – allow plenty of fresh air to enter the room
- disconnecting the electric power as quickly as possible in the case of an electric shock
- keeping the casualty warm by wrapping them in blankets or coats – for treatment of shock

f know that first aid treatment, apart from simple procedures such as the above, should only be applied by qualified first aiders

g complete a detailed report on the incident in accordance with the organisation's policy

First aid measures

First aid is emergency treatment given immediately to:

- restore breathing
- stop choking
- prevent bleeding
- prevent an injury becoming worse when medical or surgical care is not immediately available

In circumstances other than the most minor, call in a doctor or ambulance as well as giving first aid.

Look at the sick or injured person. Do not move them unless they are in danger of being hurt further. Treat them very gently, and keep them warm.

Breathing

If the person does not appear to be breathing:

- Loosen clothing and remove any obstruction from nose, mouth or throat.
- Give artificial respiration if you have been taught the correct procedure; if not, send for a qualified first aider.
- In the meantime, lay the casualty on their side and make sure there is a clear airway to the mouth and nose.

Shock

- Keep the casualty warm and give reassurance.
- *Do not* give the casualty alcohol; only weak warm drinks.
- Do not leave the casualty.

Choking

- Immediately bend casualty over so that the head is lower than the lungs if possible.
- Strike them three or four sharp blows between the shoulder blades.
- If the casualty loses consciousness open their mouth and, with your crooked forefinger, try to find any obstruction and remove it; then give artificial respiration.

Fainting

- Lay the casualty down and raise feet higher than head.
- Loosen clothing at the neck, chest and waist.
- Make sure the casualty has fresh air.

Electric shock

- Switch off current.
- Apply artificial respiration if necessary.
- Cover any burns with clean, dry dressings.

Epilepsy

- Do not try to stop any convulsions but move furniture, etc, out of the way to prevent the person from being injured.
- If unconsciousness results (breathing will be slow, skin colour pale and pupils will not react to light), lay the person on their side and make sure there is a clear airway to the mouth. Watch for vomiting.

Bleeding

- Stop bleeding by direct pressure on and elevation of the injured part.
- If bleeding is heavy, press firmly with the fingers over the wound, preferably with a *clean* pad. Secure with a firm but not overtight bandage.
- Raise and support the injured limb if movement is not painful, using a sling where appropriate. If pain is severe this could mean a fracture as well, so support the limb but do not move it.

Broken limbs

- *Do not move* the casualty unless essential for safety.
- Immobilise the limb.
- Cover all open fractures. Build up dressings around the wound so that no pressure is applied on the broken ends of the bone. *Do not* attempt to replace ends of bones.

Arm If upper arm and elbow, *do not* attempt to bend the arm; instead strap the arm to the body. If lower arm and hand, protect the soft tissues of the hand with padding then place the whole arm in a sling.

Leg Bring sound limb to injured one and, placing soft padding between natural hollows and bony joints, tie the limbs together. Put a figure of eight bandage around the feet (leave shoes on), and tie the knees together. Make a splint only when both legs are broken or long or rough transportation is necessary.

Ankle Rest the limb on a pillow in a raised position.

Scalds and burns

- Cool the area with cold water for at least 10 minutes, dry the area, then cover with clean, soft dressings.

- *Do not* remove clothing; *do not* apply lotions, etc. Remove constricting items like rings, belts, bracelets, etc.
- Treat for shock.

If clothing is on fire:

- Wrap the casualty in a rug, blanket or coat to smother the flames. *Do not* use nylon or other synthetic material.
- Lay the casualty on the floor and cover burns with clean, dry dressings.

Poisoning

- Rush the person to hospital. Take containers to indicate the poison taken.
- *Do not* induce vomiting. (Strong acid or alkali, if vomited, can cause more harm to the already damaged throat and stomach.)

Bee and wasp stings

- Extract the sting (with a sterile needle if necessary) and apply anti-histamine cream.

(Extract from *Pitman's Secretary's Diary*)

A thorough knowledge of first aid requires a course of lectures. Details are available from the HQ, St John Ambulance, 1 Grosvenor Crescent, London SW1X 7EF or from the local Centre of the Association or Unit of the Brigade. Further information on first aid is supplied in *The First Aid Manual*, obtainable from the Supplies Department, Order of St John, Priory House, St John's Gate, Clerkenwell, London EC1 M4DA.

Flexitime

Flexitime is a method of controlling staff working hours and allowing them to use more flexible starting and leaving times.

In a flexible system there are certain times of the day when all staff are required to be at work. These are known as 'core' times and are usually 1000 to 1200 hours and 1400 to 1600 hours. In addition to these times, staff are required to work a certain number of hours per week or month. These are the flexible hours and can be worked to suit either the convenience of staff or the employer, especially in meeting 'deadlines' for urgent jobs. With people arriving and leaving at different times it is clearly necessary to have some means of recording their individual working hours. Such records can be kept manually by staff signing a book or filling in time sheets or by time-recording systems. Modern time-recording systems not only record the time staff arrive and leave work but with the aid of a computer automatically calculate their wages. Each employee uses a personalised plastic key card to register attendance in a terminal and this is fed directly into a central computer to provide such information as hours worked, staff attendance, lateness, overtime, etc. The system provides management and staff with a visual display of hours worked, together with a printout of staff time data.

Features of the flexitime system:

- Staff plan their times of arrival and departure to fit in with their domestic circumstances and, as a result, are able to concentrate better on their work. This is particularly beneficial for married people with young children to take and collect from school.
- There is less traffic congestion as staff arrive and leave at different times.
- The occasional day or half-day's leave can be earned by working longer hours for a previous period.
- Staff are aware of the need to plan their time effectively throughout the day.
- Time-keeping is more effectively controlled and fewer lateness and absence problems occur.
- Staff are more willing to work overtime to alleviate peaks of work and to meet 'deadlines'.
- A disadvantage is that internal communication is less effective outside 'core' times when staff may not be in their offices.

Foreign countries

Country	*Capital*	*Nationality*	*Official language*
Afghanistan	Kabul	Afghan	Persian, Pushtu
Albania	Tirana	Albanian	Albanian
Algeria	Algiers	Algerian	Arabic, French
Andorra	Andorre, La Vieille	Andorran	Catalan
Angola	Luanda	Angolan	Portuguese
Argentina	Buenos Aires	Argentine	Spanish
Australia	Canberra	Australian	English
Austria	Vienna	Austrian	German
Bahamas	Nassau	Bahamian	English
Bahrain	Manama	Bahraini	Arabic
Bangladesh	Dhaka	Bengali	Bengali
Barbados	Bridgetown	Barbadian	English
Belgium	Brussels	Belgian	Flemish, French
Belize	Belmopan	Belizean	English, Spanish
Bermuda	Hamilton	Bermudian	English
Bolivia	Sucre	Bolivian	Spanish
Botswana	Gaborone	Botswanan	English
Brazil	Brasilia	Brazilian	Portuguese
Brunei	Banda Seri Begawan	Bruneian	English, Malay
Bulgaria	Sofia	Bulgarian	Bulgarian
Burma	Rangoon	Burmese	Burmese
Burundi	Bujumbura	Burundian	French, Rundi
Cameroon	Yaoundé	Cameroonian	English, French
Canada	Ottawa	Canadian	English, French
Chile	Santiago	Chilean	Spanish
China	Peking/Beijing	Chinese	Chinese
Colombia	Bogotà	Colombian	Spanish
Congo	Brazzaville	Congolese	French
Costa Rica	San José	Costa Rican	Spanish
Côte D'Ivoire	Abidjan	Ivorian	French
Cuba	Havana	Cuban	Spanish
Cyprus	Nicosia	Cypriot	Greek, Turkish
Czechoslovakia	Prague	Czechoslovak	Czech, Slovak

Currency unit	*Currency symbol*	*High Commission/ Embassy address in London*	*Country*
Afghani	Af	31 Princes Gate, SW7 1QQ	**Afghanistan**
Lek	L	—	**Albania**
Dinar	AD	54 Holland Park, W11 3RS	**Algeria**
{ Fr Franc	Fr	—	**Andorra**
{ Sp Peseta	Pa	—	
Kwanza	Kz	87 Jermyn Street, SW1	**Angola**
Austral	Arg$	—	**Argentina**
Dollar	A$	Australia House, Strand, WC2B 4LA	**Australia**
Schilling	Sch	18 Belgrave Mews West, SW1X 8HU	**Austria**
Dollar	BA$	10 Chesterfield Street, W1X 8AH	**Bahamas**
Dinar	BD	98 Gloucester Road, SW7 4AU	**Bahrain**
Taka	Tk	28 Queen's Gate, SW7 5JA	**Bangladesh**
Dollar	Bds$	1 Great Russell Street, WC1B 3NH	**Barbados**
Franc	BFr	103 Eaton Square, SW1W 9AB	**Belgium**
Dollar	Bz$	15 Thayer Street, W1M 5DL	**Belize**
Dollar	Ba$	—	**Bermuda**
Peso	B$	106 Eaton Square, SW1W 9AD	**Bolivia**
Pula	Pu	6 Stratford Place, W1N 9AE	**Botswana**
Cruzeiro	Cr	32 Green Street, W1Y 4AT	**Brazil**
Dollar	Br$	49 Cromwell Road, SW7 2ED	**Brunei**
Lev	Lv	186 Queen's Gate Gardens, SW7 5HL	**Bulgaria**
Kyat	K	19A Charles Street, Berkeley Square, W1X 8ER	**Burma**
Franc	BuFr	—	**Burundi**
Franc	CFA Fr	84 Holland Park, W11 3SB	**Cameroon**
Dollar	C$	Macdonald House, 1 Grosvenor Square, W1X 0AB	**Canada**
Peso	Ch$	12 Devonshire Street, W1N 2FS	**Chile**
Yuan	Y	49 Portland Place, W1N 3AH	**China**
Peso	Col$	3 Hans Crescent, SW1X 0LR	**Colombia**
Franc	CFA Fr	—	**Congo**
Colon	₡	93 Star Street, W2	**Costa Rica**
Franc	CFA Fr	2 Upper Belgrave Street, SW1X 8BJ	**Côte D'Ivoire**
Peso	Cub$	167 High Holborn, WC1 8AB	**Cuba**
Pound	C£	93 Park Street, W1Y 4ET	**Cyprus**
Koruna	Kčs	25 Kensington Palace Gardens, W8 4QY	**Czechoslovakia**

Country	*Capital*	*Nationality*	*Official language*
Denmark	Copenhagen	Danish	Danish
Dominican Republic	Santo Domingo	Dominican	Spanish
Ecuador	Quito	Ecuadorean	Spanish
Egypt	Cairo	Egyptian	Arabic
El Salvador	San Salvador	Salvadoran	Spanish
Ethiopia	Addis Ababa	Ethiopian	Amharic
Fiji	Suva	Fijian	English
Finland	Helsinki	Finnish	Finnish
France	Paris	French	French
Gabon	Libreville	Gabonese	French
Gambia	Banjul	Gambian	English
Germany, Democratic Republic	East Berlin	East German	German
Germany, Federal Republic	Bonn	West German	German
Ghana	Accra	Ghanaian	English
Greece	Athens	Greek	Greek
Grenada	St Georges	Grenadian	English
Guatemala	Guatemala City	Guatemalan	Spanish
Guinea	Conakry	Guinean	French
Guyana	Georgetown	Guyanese	English
Haiti	Port-au-Prince	Haitian	French
Hondurus	Tegucigalpa	Honduran	Spanish
Hong Kong	Victoria/Kowloon	Hong Kong	English, Cantonese
Hungary	Budapest	Hungarian	Hungarian
Iceland	Reykjavik	Icelandic	Icelandic
India	New Delhi	Indian	English, Hindi
Indonesia	Jakarta	Indonesian	Indonesian
Iran	Tehran	Iranian	Persian
Iraq	Baghdad	Iraqi	Arabic
Ireland (Eire)	Dublin	Irish	Irish, English
Israel	Jerusalem	Israeli	Hebrew, Arabic
Italy	Rome	Italian	Italian

Currency unit	*Currency symbol*	*High Commission/ Embassy address in London*	*Country*
Krone	DKr	55 Sloane Street, SW1X 9SR	**Denmark**
Peso	DR$	—	**Dominican Republic**
Sucre	Su	3 Hans Crescent, SW1X 0LS	**Ecuador**
Pound	E£	26 South Street, W1Y 8EL	**Egypt**
Colon	₡	62 Welbeck Street, W1	**El Salvador**
Birr	Br	17 Prince's Gate, SW7 1PZ	**Ethiopia**
Dollar	F$	34 Hyde Park Gate, SW7 5DN	**Fiji**
Markka	FMk	38 Chesham Place, SW1X 8HW	**Finland**
Franc	Fr	58 Knightsbridge, SW1X 7JT	**France**
Franc	CFP Fr	48 Kensington Court, W8 5DB	**Gabon**
Dalasi	Di	57 Kensington Court, W8 5DG	**Gambia**
Ostmark	OM	34 Belgrave Square, SW1X 8QB	**Germany, Democratic Republic**
Deutschemark	DM	23 Belgrave Square, SW1X 8PZ	**Germany, Federal Republic**
Cedi	₡	13 Belgrave Square, SW1X 8PR	**Ghana**
Drachma	Dr	1a Holland Park, W11 3TP	**Greece**
Dollar	EC$	1 Collingham Gardens, SW5	**Grenada**
Quetzal	Q	13 Fawcett Street, SW10 9HN	**Guatemala**
Syli	Sy	—	**Guinea**
Dollar	G$	3 Palace Court, Bayswater Road, W2 4LP	**Guyana**
Gourde	Gde	—	**Haiti**
Lempira	La	47 Manchester Street, W1M 5PB	**Honduras**
Dollar	HK$	—	**Hong Kong**
Forint	Ft	35 Eaton Place, SW1X 8BY	**Hungary**
Krona	IKr	1 Eaton Terrace, SW1W 8EY	**Iceland**
Rupee	Re	India House, Aldwych, WC2B 4NA	**India**
Rupiah	Rp	157 Edgware Road, W2 2HR	**Indonesia**
Rial	RI	27 Prince's Gate, SW7 1PX	**Iran**
Dinar	ID	21 Queen's Gate, SW7 5JG	**Iraq**
Pound	IR£	17 Grosvenor Place, SW1X 7HR	**Ireland (Eire)**
Shekel	IS	2 Palace Green, Kensington, W8 4QB	**Israel**
Lira	L	14 Three Kings Yard, Davies Street, W1Y 2EH	**Italy**

Country	*Capital*	*Nationality*	*Official language*
Jamaica	Kingston	Jamaican	English
Japan	Tokyo	Japanese	Japanese
Jordan	Amman	Jordanian	Arabic
Kampuchea (Cambodia)	Phnom Penh	Kampuchean	Kampuchean
Kenya	Nairobi	Kenyan	English, Swahili
Korea (North)	Pyongyang	North Korean	Korean
Korea (South)	Seoul	South Korean	Korean
Kuwait	Kuwait City	Kuwaiti	Arabic
Laos	Vientiane	Laotian	Lao
Lebanon	Beirut	Lebanese	Arabic
Lesotho	Maseru	Basotho	English
Liberia	Monrovia	Liberian	English
Libya	Tripoli	Libyan	Arabic
Liechtenstein	Vaduz	Liechtensteiner	German
Luxembourg	Luxembourg City	Luxembourger	French, German
Madagascar	Antananarivo	Malagasy	French, Malagasy
Malawi	Lilongwe	Malawian	English, Nyanja
Malaysia	Kuala Lumpur	Malaysian	Malay
Maldive Islands	Male	Maldivian	Maldivian
Mali	Bamako	Malian	French
Malta	Valletta	Maltese	English, Maltese
Mauritania	Nouakchott	Mauritanian	Arabic, French
Mauritius	Port Louis	Mauritian	English
Mexico	Mexico City	Mexican	Spanish
Monaco	Monaco	Monegasque/ Monacan	French
Mongolia	Ulan Bator	Mongol	Mongolian
Morocco	Rabat	Moroccan	Arabic
Mozambique	Maputo	Mozambican	Portuguese
Nepal	Katmandu	Nepalese	Nepali
Netherlands (Holland)	Amsterdam	Dutch	Dutch
New Zealand	Wellington	New Zealander	English
Nicaragua	Managua	Nicaraguan	Spanish

Currency unit	*Currency symbol*	*High Commission/ Embassy address in London*	*Country*
Dollar	J$	63 St James's Street, SW1A 1LS	**Jamaica**
Yen	Y	43 Grosvenor Street, W1X 0BA	**Japan**
Dinar	JD	6 Upper Phillimore Gardens, W8 7HB	**Jordan**
Riel	CRI	—	**Kampuchea (Cambodia)**
Shilling	KSh	24 New Bond Street, W1Y 9HD	**Kenya**
Won	NK W	—	**Korea (North)**
Won	W	4 Palace Gate, W8 5NF	**Korea (South)**
Dinar	KD	45 Queen's Gate, SW7 5JA	**Kuwait**
Kip	Kp	—	**Laos**
Pound	Leb£	21 Kensington Palace Gardens, W8 4QM	**Lebanon**
Maloti	LSM	10 Collingham Road, SW5 0NR	**Lesotho**
Dollar	L$	2 Pembridge Place, W2	**Liberia**
Dinar	LD	—	**Libya**
Sw. Franc	SFr	—	**Liechten-stein**
Franc	LFr	27 Wilton Crescent, SW1X 8SD	**Luxembourg**
Franc	Mg Fr	—	**Madagascar**
Kwacha	MK	33 Grosvenor Street, W1X 0DE	**Malawi**
Dollar	M$	45 Belgrave Square, SW1X 8QT	**Malaysia**
Rufiyaa	MRf	—	**Maldive Islands**
Franc	CFA Fr	—	**Mali**
Lira	LM	16 Kensington Square, W8 5HH	**Malta**
Ouguiya	O	—	**Mauritania**
Rupee	MR	32 Elvaston Place, SW7 5HL	**Mauritius**
Peso	Mex$	8 Halkin Street, SW1X 7DW	**Mexico**
Franc	Mon Fr	—	**Monaco**
Tugrik	Tug	7 Kensington Court, W8 5DL	**Mongolia**
Dirham	DH	49 Queen's Gate Gardens, SW7 5NE	**Morocco**
Metzal	MzM	—	**Mozambique**
Rupee	NRp	12A Kensington Palace Gardens, W8 4QU	**Nepal**
Guilder	Gld	38 Hyde Park Gate, SW7 5DP	**Netherlands (Holland)**
Dollar	NZ$	New Zealand House, Haymarket, SW1Y 4TQ	**New Zealand**
Cordoba	C$	8 Gloucester Road, SW7 4PP	**Nicaragua**

Country	*Capital*	*Nationality*	*Official language*
Niger	Niamey	Nigerois	French
Nigeria	Lagos	Nigerian	English
Norway	Oslo	Norwegian	Norwegian
Oman	Muscat	Omani	Arabic
Pakistan	Islamabad	Pakistani	Bengali, English, Urdu
Panama	Panama City	Panamanian	Spanish
Papua New Guinea	Port Moresby	Papua New Guinean	English
Paraguay	Asuncion	Paraguayan	Spanish
Peru	Lima	Peruvian	Spanish
Philippines	Manila	Filipino	English, Filipino
Poland	Warsaw	Polish	Polish
Portugal	Lisbon	Portuguese	Portuguese
Qatar	Doha	Qatari	Arabic
Romania	Bucharest	Romanian	Romanian
Rwanda	Kigali	Rwandan	French, Ruada
San Marino	San Marino	San Marinese	Italian
Sao Tome & Principe	Sao Tome	Sao Tomean	Portuguese
Saudi Arabia	Riyadh	Saudi Arabian	Arabic
Senegal	Dakar	Senegalese	French
Seychelles	Victoria	Seychellois	English
Sierra Leone	Freetown	Sierra Leonean	English
Singapore	Singapore	Singaporean	Chinese, English, Malay, Tamil
Somalia	Mogadishu	Somali	Somali
South Africa	Pretoria	South African	Afrikaans, English
Spain	Madrid	Spanish	Spanish
Sri Lanka	Colombo	Sri Lankan	Sinhalese
Sudan	Khartoum	Sudanese	Arabic
Suriname	Paramaribo	Surinamese	Dutch
Swaziland	Mbabane	Swazi	English
Sweden	Stockholm	Swedish	Swedish
Switzerland	Berne	Swiss	French, German, Italian, Romansh
Syria	Damascus	Syrian	Arabic
Tanzania	Dodoma	Tanzanian	English, Swahili
Thailand	Bangkog	Thai	Thai
Togo	Lomé	Togolese	French

Currency unit	*Currency symbol*	*High Commission/ Embassy address in London*	*Country*
Franc	CFA Fr	—	**Niger**
Naira	N	Nigeria House, 9 Northumberland Avenue, WC2 5BX	**Nigeria**
Krone	NKr	25 Belgrave Square, SW1X 8QD	**Norway**
Rial Omani	RO	44A Montpelier Square, SW7 1JJ	**Oman**
Rupee	Rp	35 Lowndes Square, SW1X 9JN	**Pakistan**
Balbao	Ba	119 Crawford Street, W1	**Panama**
Kina	K	14 Waterloo Place, SW1R 4AR	**Papua New Guinea**
Guarani	G	51 Cornwall Gardens, SW7 4AQ	**Paraguay**
Sol	S	52 Sloane Street, SWQX 9SP	**Peru**
Peso	PP	9a Palace Green, W8 4QE	**Philippines**
Zloty	Zl	47 Portland Place, W1N 3AG	**Poland**
Escudo	Esc	11 Belgrave Square, SW1X 8PP	**Portugal**
Riyal	QR	27 Chesham Place, SW1X 8HG	**Qatar**
Leu	L	4 Palace Green, W8 4QD	**Romania**
Franc	RW Fr	—	**Rwanda**
Lira	SM L	—	**San Marino**
Dobra	D	—	**Sao Tome & Principe**
Rial	SAR	30 Belgrave Square, SW1X 8QB	**Saudi Arabia**
Franc	CFA Fr	11 Phillimore Gardens, W8 7QG	**Senegal**
Rupee	SR	50 Conduit Street, W1A 4PE	**Seychelles**
Leone	Le	33 Portland Place, W1N 3AG	**Sierra Leone**
Dollar	S$	2 Wilton Crescent, SW1X 8RW	**Singapore**
Shilling	So Sh	60 Portland Place, W1N 3DG	**Somalia**
Rand	R	South Africa House, Trafalgar Square, WC2N 5DP	**South Africa**
Peseta	Pa	24 Belgrave Square, SW1X 8QA	**Spain**
Rupee	SLR	13 Hyde Park Gardens, W2 2LU	**Sri Lanka**
Pound	S£	3 Cleveland Row, SW1A 1DD	**Sudan**
Guilder	SGld	—	**Suriname**
Emalangeni	E	58 Pont Street, SW1X 0AE	**Swaziland**
Krona	SKR	11 Montagu Place, W1H 2AL	**Sweden**
Franc	SFr	16 Montagu Place, W1H 2BQ	**Switzerland**
Pound	Syr£	—	**Syria**
Shilling	TSh	43 Hertford Street, W1Y 7TF	**Tanzania**
Baht	Bt	30 Queen's Gate, SW7 5JB	**Thailand**
Franc	CFA Fr	30 Sloane Street, SW1	**Togo**

Country	*Capital*	*Nationality*	*Official language*
Tonga	Nukualofa	Tongan	English, Tongan
Trinidad & Tobago	Port of Spain	Trinidadian and Tobagonian	English
Tunisia	Tunis	Tunisian	Arabic
Turkey	Ankara	Turkish	Turkish
Uganda	Kampala	Ugandan	English
United Arab Emirates	Abu Dhabi	Arabic	Arabic
United States of America (USA)	Washington DC	American	English
Union of Soviet Socialist Republics (USSR)	Moscow	Russian	Russian
Uruguay	Montevideo	Uruguayan	Spanish
Venezuela	Caracas	Venezuelan	Spanish
Vietnam	Hanoi	Vietnamese	Vietnamese
Western Samoa	Apia	Western Samoan	English, Samoan
Yemen (South)	Aden	Yemeni	Arabic, English
Yemen (Arab Republic)	Sana	Yemeni	Arabic
Yugoslavia	Belgrade	Yugoslav	Macedonian, Serbo-Croatian, Slovenian
Zaire	Kinshasa	Zairian	French
Zambia	Lusaka	Zambian	English
Zimbabwe	Harare	Zimbabwean	English

Currency unit	*Currency symbol*	*High Commission/ Embassy address in London*	*Country*
Pa'anga	T$	New Zealand House, Haymarket, SW1Y 4TE	**Tonga**
Dollar	TT$	42 Belgrave Square, SW1X 8NT	**Trinidad & Tobago**
Dinar	TD	29 Prince's Gate, SW7 1QG	**Tunisia**
Lira	TL	43 Belgrave Square, SW1X 8PA	**Turkey**
Shilling	USh	Uganda House, Trafalgar Square, WC2N 5DX	**Uganda**
Dirham	DH	30 Prince's Gate, SW7 1PT	**United Arab Emirates**
Dollar	$	Grosvenor Square, W1A 1AE	**United States of America (USA)**
Ruble	Rub	13 Kensington Palace Gardens, W8 4QX	**Union of Soviet Socialist Republics (USSR)**
Peso	Urug$	48 Lennox Gardens, SW1X 0DL	**Uruguay**
Bolivar	B	1 Cromwell Road, SW7 2ED	**Venezuela**
Dong	D	12 Victoria Road, W8 5JU	**Vietnam**
Tala	WS$	—	**Western Samoa**
Dinar	YD	57 Cromwell Road, SW7 2ED	**Yemen (South)**
Riyal	YR	41 South Street, W1Y 5PD	**Yemen (Arab Republic)**
Dinar	Din	5 Lexham Gardens, W8 5JU	**Yugoslavia**
Zaire	Z	26 Chesham Place, SW1X 8HH	**Zaire**
Kwacha	K	7 Cavendish Place, W1N 0HB	**Zambia**
Dollar	$	Zimbabwe House, Strand, WC2R 0SA	**Zimbabwe**

Forms of address

The table of forms of address which follows is a selection of those in common use. A more comprehensive collection can be found in *Black's Titles and Forms of Address* or, if you want further informa-

Title	*Form of address*
Royalty	
The Queen	Her Majesty the Queen
Prince: Duke	His Royal Highness the Duke of —
Non-Duke Child of the Sovereign	His Royal Highness the Prince —
Other Dukes	His Royal Highness Prince — of —
The peerage	
Duke	His Grace the Duke of —
Duchess	Her Grace the Duchess of —
Marquess	The Most Hon. the Marquess of —
Marchioness	The Most Hon. the Marchioness of —
Earl	The Right Hon. the Earl of —
Countess	The Right Hon. the Countess of —
Viscount	The Right Hon. the Viscount —
Viscountess	The Right Hon. the Viscountess —
Baron	The Right Hon. Lord —
Baroness	The Right Hon. Lady —
Knights	
Knight	Sir — KG (or appropriate title)

tion concerning protocol and the correct methods of addressing public dignitaries, you can apply to the Protocol Office at the Foreign and Commonwealth Office, King Charles Street, Whitehall, London SW1A 2AH (telephone: 01 233 3000).

The forms of address given are appropriate for formal correspondence, but less formal expressions may be used, depending on the relationship of the writers. A secretary should have a clear understanding with the boss concerning any departure from formal practice.

Salutation	*Complimentary close*
Madam or May it please your Majesty	I have the honour to be, Madam, Your Majesty's most humble and obedient servant
Sir	I have the honour to be, Sir, Your Royal Highness's most humble and obedient servant
My Lord Duke	My Lord Duke, I remain, Your Grace's most obedient servant
Madam	Madam, I remain, Your Grace's most obedient servant
My Lord Marquess	I have the honour to remain, Your Lordship's obedient servant
Madam	I have the honour to remain, Your Ladyship's obedient servant
My Lord	I have the honour to remain, Your Lordship's obedient servant
Madam	I have the honour to remain, Your Ladyship's obedient servant
My Lord	I have the honour to remain, Your Lordship's obedient servant
Madam	I have the honour to remain, Your Ladyship's obedient servant
My Lord	I have the honour to remain, Your Lordship's obedient servant
Madam	I have the honour to remain, Your Ladyship's obedient servant
Sir	I am, Sir, Your obedient servant

Title	*Form of address*
Knight's wife	Lady —
Dame	Dame — DCB (or appropriate title)
Church	
Anglican	
Archbishop	The Most Revd. and Right Hon. the Lord Archbishop of —
Bishop	The Right Revd. the Lord Bishop of —
Dean	The Very Revd. the Dean of —
Provost	The Very Revd. the Provost of —
Canon	The Revd. Canon —
Archdeacon	The Venerable the Archdeacon of —
Clergyman (Vicar/Rector)	The Revd. —
Roman Catholic	
Pope	His Holiness, the Pope
Archbishop	The Most Revd. —, Archbishop of —
Cardinal	His Eminence Cardinal —
Bishop	The Right Revd. —, Bishop of —
Priest	The Revd. Father —
Free churches	
Minister	The Revd. —
The armed forces	
Officers	(1) Rank (2) Title (if any) (3) Name, eg Air Marshal Sir Robert Price, KBE, DFC

Salutation	*Complimentary close*
Madam	I am, Madam, Your obedient servant
Madam	I am, Madam, Your obedient servant
My Lord Archbishop	I have the honour to remain, My Lord Archbishop, Your Grace's devoted and obedient servant
My Lord Bishop	I have the honour to remain, Your Lordship's obedient servant
Very Reverend Sir	I have the honour to remain, Very Reverend Sir, Your obedient servant
Very Reverend Sir	I have the honour to remain, Very Reverend Sir, Your obedient servant
Reverend Sir	I have the honour to remain, Reverend Sir, Your obedient servant
Venerable Sir	I have the honour to remain, Venerable Sir, Your obedient servant
Dear Sir/Mr —	Yours faithfully/sincerely
Your Holiness or Most Holy Father	I have the honour to be, Your Holiness's most devoted and obedient child (servant)
My Lord Archbishop	I have the honour to be, My Lord Archbishop, Your Grace's devoted and obedient child (servant)
My Lord Cardinal	I have the honour to be, Your Eminence's devoted and obedient child (servant)
My Lord Bishop	I have the honour to be, Your Lordship's devoted and obedient child (servant)
Dear Reverend Father	Your devoted and obedient child (servant)
Dear Minister	Yours faithfully/sincerely
Sir or Dear (rank)	Yours faithfully or as appropriate to rank

Title	*Form of address*
Diplomatic service	
Ambassador – British	His Excellency Mr — Her Majesty's Ambassador
Ambassador – Foreign	His Excellency, The Ambassador of —
Consul	Mr — British Consul/ Consul-General/ Vice Consul
Law	
High Court Judge	The Hon. Mr Justice —
Circuit Judge	His Honour Judge —
Queen's Counsel	Mr — QC
Justice of the Peace	Mr/Mrs — JP
Government	
Prime Minister	The Right Hon. — PC, MP
Secretary of State (in cabinet)	The Right Hon. — PC, MP
Minister	Mr/Mrs —, MP Minister of —
Member of Parliament	Mr/Mrs —, MP
Lord Mayor (for London, Belfast, Cardiff, Dublin and York)	The Right Hon. the Lord Mayor of —
Lord Mayor (other than those listed above)	The Right Worshipful the Lord Mayor of —
Lady Mayoress	The Lady Mayoress of —
Lord Provost: Edinburgh and Glasgow	The Right Hon. the Lord Provost of —
Aberdeen and Dundee	The Lord Provost of —
Lady Provost	The Lady Provost of —
Mayor: City	The Right Worshipful the Mayor of —
Non-city	The Worshipful Mayor of —
Mayoress	The Mayoress of —

Salutation	*Complimentary close*
Sir	Your Excellency's obedient servant
Your Grace/My Lord (appropriate to title)	
Your Excellency	Your Excellency's obedient servant
Sir	I am, Sir, Your obedient servant
Sir	I am, Sir, Your obedient servant
Dear Sir	Yours faithfully
Dear Sir	Yours faithfully
Dear Sir/Madam	Yours faithfully
Madam/Sir	I have the honour to be, Madam/Sir, Your obedient servant
Madam/Sir	I have the honour to be, Madam/Sir, Your obedient servant
Dear Madam/Sir	Yours faithfully
Dear Madam/Sir	Yours faithfully
My Lord Mayor	I am, My Lord Mayor, Your obedient servant
My Lord Mayor	I am, My Lord Mayor, Your obedient servant
My Lady Mayoress	I am, My Lady Mayoress, Your obedient servant
My Lord Provost	I am, My Lord Provost, Your obedient servant
My Lord Provost	I am, My Lord Provost, Your obedient servant
My Lady Provost	I am, My Lady Provost, Your obedient servant
Sir or Mr Mayor	I am, Sir, Your obedient servant
Sir or Mr Mayor	I am, Sir, Your obedient servant
Madam or Madam Mayoress	I am, Madam, Your obedient servant

Academic

Academic qualifications are not normally shown in business and social correspon John Brown *or* Mr John Brown Ph.D (never both). Academic qualifications may, if a person has two degrees in the same faculty, only the higher one should be

Forms of address for letters to Europe

Country	*Form of address*
France: men	M –
married women	Mme –
unmarried women	Mlle –
Germany: men	Herr –
married women	Frau –
unmarried women	Fräulein –
Italy: men	Gentilissimo Signore –, or Egregio Signore
married women	Distinta Signora –
unmarried women	Esimia Signorina –
Spain: men	Señor –
married women	Señora –
unmarried women	Señorita –

Government departments

Department	*Address*	*Telephone no*
Advisory, Conciliation and Arbitration Service	11–12 St James's Square, London SW1Y 4LA	01 210 3600
Ministry of Agriculture, Fisheries and Food	Whitehall Place, London SW1A 2HH	01 270 3000
British Broadcasting Corporation	Broadcasting House, London W1A 1AA	01 580 4468
The British Council	10 Spring Gardens, London SW1A 2BN	01 930 8466
British Overseas Trade Board	1 Victoria Street, London SW1H 0ET	01 215 4858
British Railways Board	Euston Square, PO Box 100, London NW1 1DZ	01 262 3232
British Tourist Authority	Thames Tower, Black's Road, London W6 9EL	01 846 9000

dence with the exception of doctors who should be addressed: Dr however, be used in circumstances where they are appropriate, but given.

Salutation	*Complimentary close*
Monsieur Madame Mademoiselle or Madame	Avec mes meilleurs sentiments
Sehr geehrter Herr Sehr geehrte Frau Sehr geehrtes Fräulein	Mit Freundlichem Gruss
Gentilissimo Signore, or Egregio Signore Distinta Signora Esimia Signorina	Cordiali saluti
Muy Señor Mio Muy Estimada Señora Muy Distinguida Señorita	le saluda atentamente

Department	*Address*	*Telephone no*
British Waterways Board	Melbury House, Melbury Terrace, London NW1 6JX	01 262 6711
Civil Aviation Authority	CAA House, 45–59 Kingsway, London WC2B 6TE	01 379 7311
Commonwealth Development Corporation	33 Hill Street, London W1A 3AR	01 629 8484
The Commonwealth Institute	Kensington High Street, London W8 6NQ	01 603 4535
Companies Registration Office	Companies House, Crown Way, Maindy, Cardiff CF4 3UT	0222 388588
Board of Customs and Excise	King's Beam House, Mark Lane, London EC3R 7HE	01 626 1515
Data Protection Registrar	Springfield House, Water Lane, Wilmslow, Cheshire SK9 5AX	0625 535777
Department of Education and Science	Elizabeth House, York Road, London SE1 7PH	01 934 9000

Department	*Address*	*Telephone no*
The Electricity Council	30 Millbank, London SW1P 4RD	01 834 2333
Department of Employment	Caxton House, Tothill Street, London SW1H 9NF	01 213 3000
Department of Energy	Thames House South, Millbank, London SW1P 4QJ	01 211 3000
Department of the Environment	2 Marsham Street, London SW1P 3EB	01 212 3434
Equal Opportunities Commission	Overseas House, Quay Street, Manchester M3 3HN	061 833 9244
Export Credits Guarantee Department	PO Box 272, Export House, 50 Ludgate Hill, London EC4M 7AJ	01 606 6699
Office of Fair Trading	Field House, Bream's Buildings, London EC4A 1PR	01 242 2858
Foreign and Commonwealth Office	Downing Street, London SW1A 2AL	01 270 3000
Department of Health	Alexander Fleming House, Elephant and Castle, London SE1 6BY	01 407 5522
Health and Safety Commission	Regina House, Old Marylebone Road, London NW1	01 723 1262
Home Office	50 Queen Anne's Gate, London SW1H 9AT	01 213 3000
Independent Broadcasting Authority	70 Brompton Road, London SW3 1HA	01 584 7011
Industrial Injuries Advisory Council	Friars House, 157–168 Blackfriars Road, London SE1 8EU	01 703 6380
Central Office of Information	Hercules Road, London SE1 7DU	01 928 2345
Board of Inland Revenue	Somerset House, London WC2R 1LB	01 438 6622
Monopolies and Mergers Commission	48 Carey Street, London WC2A 2JT	01 831 6111
National Consumer Council	20 Grosvenor Gardens, London SW1W 0DH	01 730 3469
National Economic Development Office	Millbank Tower, Millbank, London SW1P 4QX	01 211 6998
Northern Ireland Office	Whitehall, London, SW1A 2AZ	01 210 3000
	Stormont House, Belfast BT4 3ST	0232 63255
Ordnance Survey	Romsey Road, Maybush, Southampton SO9 4DH	0703 775555
Overseas Development Administration	Eland House, Stag Place, London SW1E 5DH	01 213 3000
Office of the Parliamentary Commissioner and Health Service Commissioner	Church House, Great Smith Street, London SW1P 3BW	01 212 7676
Patent Office	State House, 66–71 High Holborn, London WC1R 4TP	01 831 2525
The Post Office	33 Grosvenor Place, London SW1X 1PX	01 235 8000
Racial Equality Commission	Elliott House, 10/12 Allington Street, London SW1E 5EH	01 828 7022

Department	*Address*	*Telephone no*
Scottish Office	Dover House, Whitehall, London SW1A 2AU	01 270 3000
	New St Andrew's House, St James Centre, Edinburgh EH1 3SX	031 556 8400
Department of Social Security	Alexander Fleming House, Elephant and Castle, London SE1 6BY	01 407 5522
Her Majesty's Stationery Office	St Crispins, Duke Street, Norwich NR3 1PD	0603 622211
Department of Trade and Industry	1 Victoria Street, London SW1H 0ET	01 215 7877
Training Agency	Moorfoot, Sheffield S1 4PQ	0742 753275
Department of Transport	2 Marsham Street, London SW1P 3EB	01 212 3434
Welsh Office	Gwydyr House, Whitehall, London SW1A 2ER	01 270 3000
	Cathays Park, Cardiff CF1 3NQ	0222 825111

Holiday rota

Important factors to consider when organising a staff holiday rota:

- Start planning in the autumn preceding the year in question to give staff the opportunity to book their holidays in good time and to allow time for discussion and consultation.
- Give staff as much choice as possible for their holiday dates but have regard to the following constraints:
  - *a* continuity of office services throughout the year; it is essential to have adequate cover at different staff levels, eg supervisory, senior secretarial, typing and reception
  - *b* if there are set dates for the factory employees to take their holidays, the majority of office staff should be encouraged to choose the same dates, retaining a 'skeleton' staff only
  - *c* the fluctuating work cycle, ie fewer staff should be away when there is known to be a peak load of work
- Managers/supervisors should be asked to approve holiday dates for staff in their departments.
- Use a chart, such as the one on p 88, to plot the dates when staff are on holiday.
- If holidays are taken for periods of less than a week, a different type of aid should be used, such as a plastic year planner. This provides spaces for every day of the year and different coloured plastic markers can be used for various staff categories.

Holiday rota 19—

Name	*Position*	*Weeks commencing*																	
		June					*July*				*August*					*September*			
		1	8	15	22	29*	6	13	20*	27	3	10	17	24	31*	7	14	21	28*
J Brown	Supervisor						x			x	x						x		
R Williams	Asst Supervisor				x								x	x					
R Platt	Senior secretary	x	x							x									
T Davies	Senior secretary										x					x	x		
R Fox	Secretary			x	x					x									
T Grant	Secretary										x	x						x	
M Neal	Word processing operator						x			x	x								
C May	Receptionist/telephonist		x	x												x			
J Gould	Receptionist/telephonist							x	x				x						
T Clark	Reprographics operator									x	x				x				
	Total staff absent	1	2	2	2	0	2	1	1	5	5	1	2	1	1	2	2	1	0

Notes: 50 per cent of staff are taking holidays during the works holiday, ie 27 July and 3 August.
* Peak work loads occur in these weeks – staff absences reduced to a minimum.
Assistant Supervisor deputises for Supervisor.
Secretary covers for word processing operator.
Receptionist/telephonist covers for reprographics operator.

Information sources

	Information	Source of reference
1	**Business magazines, journals and newspapers**	
	British Business	– Millbank Tower, Millbank, London SW1P 4QU
	Business	– 234 King's Road, London SW3 5VA
	Business Education Today	– Pitman Publishing, Periodicals, 128 Long Acre, London WC2E 9AN
	Business Equipment Digest	– BED Business Journals Ltd, 44 Wallington Square, Wallington, Surrey SM6 8RG
	Business Systems and Equipment	– Maclean Hunter Ltd, 76 Oxford Street, London W1N 9FD
	COMLON	– LCC Examinations Board, Marlowe House, Station Road, Sidcup, Kent DA15 7BJ
	The Economist	– 25 James's Street, London SW1A 1HG
	The Financial Times	– 10 Cannon Street, London EC4P 4BY
	Focus on Business Education	– The Society of Teachers in Business Education, Saffron Hill, Uplands Road, Totland Bay, Isle of Wight PO39 0DY
	Management Today	– 30 Lancaster Gate, London W2 3LP
	Mind Your Own Business	– 106 Church Road, London SE19 2UB
	Office and Information Management	– The Institute of Administrative Management, 40 Chatsworth Parade, Petts Wood, Orpington, Kent BR5 1RW
	Office Equipment Index	– Maclaren Publishers Ltd, PO Box 109, Maclaren House, 19 Scarbrook Road, Croydon CR9 1QH
	Office Equipment News	– AGB Business Publications, Audit House, Field End Road, Eastcote, Ruislip, Middx HA4 9LT
	Office Magazine	– Patey Doyle (Publishing) Ltd, Wilmington House, Church Hill, Wilmington, Dartford, Kent DA2 7EF

Information	*Source of reference*
RSA News	– RSA Publications, Murray Road, Orpington, Kent BR5 3RB
Small Business	– Small Business Bureau, 32 Smith Square, London SW1P 3HH

2 Governmental

Governments for countries throughout the world and international organisations	– *Statesman's Year Book*
Local government authorities	– *Municipal Year Book and Public Services Directory*
Members of Parliament	– *The Times Guide to the House of Commons*
Members of the European Parliament	– *The Times Guide to the European Parliament*
News reference service	– *Keesing's Record of World Events*
Parliamentary reports	– *Hansard*
Statistics for government departments	– *Monthly* (and *Annual) Digest of Statistics* – HMSO
World affairs, British and foreign embassies, Royal family, peerage, cabinet ministers, members of parliament, Bank of England, law courts, European Community, United Nations	– *Whitaker's Almanack*

3 Office services

Employment legislation	– *Croner's Reference Book for Employers, see also* other sources of reference on p 102
Postal services (inland and overseas), postal order services, savings	– *Post Office Guide*
Printing terms and procedures	– *Authors' and Printers' Dictionary*
Safety	– *See* pp 141–3
Sources of information	– *Walford's Guide to Reference Material, Whitaker's British Books in Print* (microfiche), *Lists of HMSO Publications* (daily, weekly, monthly and annually), *Catalogue of British Official Publications* (not published by HMSO) (Chadwyck-Healey)
Telex subscribers	– *UK Telex Directory*
Training and personnel management	– *Personnel and Training Management Year Book and Directory*

Information	*Source of reference*
4 Organisations	
Banks	– *Banker's Almanac and Year Book*
Building societies	– *Building Societies' Year Book*
Engineering	– *Kempe's Engineer's Year Book*
Insurance companies	– *Insurance Directory and Year Book*
Names, addresses and telephone numbers	– Telephone directories
Newspapers, trade journals	– *Benn's Media Directory, Willing's Press Guide*
Trade and professional associations, chambers of trade and commerce, trade unions	– *Directory of British Associations and Associations in Ireland*
5 People	
Barristers, solicitors, judges and legal officers	– *The Solicitors' and Barristers' Directory and Diary*
Biographies of living eminent people	– *Who's Who*
Biographies of people of international importance	– *International Year Book* and *Statesmen's Who's Who*
Civil servants	– *Civil Service Year Book*
Clergymen of the Church of England	– *Crockford's Clerical Directory* (similar clerical directories are published for the other religious denominations)
Dentists	– *Dentists Register*
Directors and their joint stock companies	– *Directory of Directors*
Forms of address	– *Black's Titles and Forms of Address*
Medical practitioners	– *Medical Directory*
Names, addresses and telephone numbers	– Telephone directories
Nurses	– *Royal College of Nursing*
Peerage and baronetage	– *Debrett's Peerage and Baronetage* and *Burke's Peerage, Baronetage and Knightage*
Qualifications and addresses of professional bodies	– *British Qualifications*
Services personnel	– *Army List, Air Force List, Navy List*
6 Secretarial services	
Abbreviations and initials	– *Acronyms, Initialisms and Abbreviations Dictionary*
Business equipment	– *See* p 118
Forms of address	– *Black's Titles and Forms of Address*
French, German, Spanish and Italian phrases	– Hamlyn pocket dictionaries and phrase books
Shortland outlines and meaning of words	– *Pitman's English and Shorthand Dictionary*

Information		*Source of reference*
Synonyms and antonyms	–	*Roget's Thesaurus of English Words and Phrases*
Typewriting terms and procedures	–	*Pitman's Typewriting Dictionary*
7 Trade		
Company data (industry and commerce)	–	*UK Kompass* *Who Owns Whom*
Companies (financial data, directors)	–	*International Stock Exchange Official Year Book*
Manufacturers	–	*Kelly's Directory of Manufacturers and Merchants*
Names, addresses and telephone numbers	–	*Yellow Pages* (telephone directories)
Prominent firms in the United Kingdom	–	*Key British Enterprises*
Prominent international firms	–	*Principal International Business*
8 Travel		
Advice to businessmen travelling abroad	–	*Hints to Exporters* (British Overseas Trade Board)
Air services	–	*ABC World Airways Guide*
Coach and bus services	–	*ABC Coach and Bus Guide*
Hotels and restaurants	–	*ABC Worldwide Hotel Guide, AA Members Handbook, Good Food Guide, Hotels and Restaurants in Great Britain, Financial Times World Hotel Directory, Michelin Guides*
Location of places, names of towns, etc	–	*Ordnance Survey Gazetteer of Great Britain*
Motoring information (road maps, hotels, garages, distances between towns)	–	*Automobile Association Members Handbook, Royal Automobile Club Guide and Handbook, AA and RAC Guides for motoring in Europe*
Shipping services	–	*ABC Passenger Shipping Guide, Lloyd's International List*
Train times	–	*ABC Rail Guide, British Rail timetables*
Travel information (general)	–	*Travel Trade Directory* and other sources of reference on pp 171–83, *ABC Guide to International Travel*

International organisations

Organisation	*Headquarters*
The Commonwealth	Marlborough House, Pall Mall, London SW1 5HX
Council of Europe	Palais de l'Europe, 67006, Strasbourg, Cedex, France
European Community	200 rue de la Loi, 1049, Brussels, Belgium
European Free Trade Association	9–11 rue de Varembe, 1211 Geneva 20, Switzerland
European Trade Union Confederation	Rue Montagne aux Herbes Potagères 37, 1000 Brussels
Food and Agriculture Organisation of the United Nations	Via della Terme di Caracalla, Rome, Italy
General Agreement on Tariffs and Trade	Centre William Rappard, 154 rue de Lausanne, 1211 Geneva 21, Switzerland
International Atomic Energy Agency	Vienna International Centre, PO Box 100, A-1400 Vienna, Austria
International Bank for Reconstruction and Development	1818 H St, NW, Washington DC, 20433, USA London office: New Zealand House, Haymarket, SW1Y 4TE
International Civil Aviation Organisation	1000 Sherbrooke Street West, Montreal, Quebec, Canada H3A 2R2
International Confederation of Free Trade Unions	37–41 rue Montague aux Herbes Potagères, Brussels 1000, Belgium
International Fund for Agricultural Development	107 Via del Serafico, Rome, Italy
International Labour Organisation	CH-1211, Geneva 22, Switzerland London office: Vincent House, Vincent Square, SW1P 2NB
International Maritime Organisation	4 Albert Embankment, London SE1 7SR
International Monetary Fund	700 19th St, NW, Washington DC, 20431, USA
International Telecommunication Union	Place des Nations, 1211, Geneva 10, Switzerland
North Atlantic Treaty Organisation	1110 Brussels, Belgium
Organisation for Economic Co-operation and Development	2 Rue André Pascal, 75775 Paris, Cedex 16, France

Organisation	*Headquarters*
United Nations	Palais des Nations, 1211, Geneva 10, Switzerland London office: 36 Westminster Palace Gardens, SW1P 1RR
United Nations Educational, Scientific and Cultural Organisation	UNESCO House, 7 Place de Fontenoy, Paris
Universal Postal Union	Weltpoststrasse 4, 3000, Berne 15, Switzerland
Western European Union	9 Grosvenor Place, London SW1X 7HL
World Council of Churches	PO Box 66, 150 route de Ferney, 1211 Geneva 20, Switzerland
World Health Organisation	Headquarters: 1211 Geneva 27, Switzerland
World Intellectual Property Organisation	Headquarters: 34 Chemin des Colombettes, 1211 Geneva 20, Switzerland
World Meteorological Organisation	Case postale 5, CH-1211, Geneva 20, Switzerland

Interviewing

Senior secretaries are often asked to help interview staff for junior secretarial positions. The following is intended to help you in this and bring to your notice some of the more salient points in selecting staff.

An interview is a conversation between two or more people, face to face, to exchange information and views and assess attitudes, etc, to achieve a defined objective, eg in the case of a job interview, to select the most suitable candidate.

To accomplish this with as much precision and reliability as possible it will be necessary to bring about free and uninhibited flow of conversation between the parties concerned.

Factors involved in creating these conditions:

- Define the objectives of the interview by:
  - *a* describing the job to be performed (job description – *see* p 95)
  - *b* specifying the requirements of the job (job specification – *see* p 95)

- Supply the candidates with all relevant information about the organisation, the job description and clear directions for locating the premises, preferably a location plan.
- Prepare for the interviewer(s) full details of the candidates – obtained from the application forms and the results of any tests which have been set prior to the interview.
- Arrange suitable accommodation for the interview which provides a quiet, private and relaxed atmosphere.
- Allocate a comfortable waiting room for the candidates with cloakroom and refreshment facilities.
- Arrange for the candidates to be shown round the premises to meet the staff and see the office where the successful candidate will work.
- Allow sufficient time for each interview so that an accurate assessment can be made.

A **job description** should contain the following:

- job title
- job grading/salary scale
- purpose of the job and how it fits into the overall organisation, ie the name of the department, the immediate superior to whom the person reports, any staff who report to the person and those with whom the person liaises
- a detailed description of the duties and responsibilities involved in the job

A **job specification** describes the sort of person required to do the job, including:

- physical attributes, eg age, voice, sight, etc
- attainments, eg qualifications and previous experience
- general intelligence
- special aptitudes, eg secretarial skills
- interests
- disposition
- special circumstances

Techniques of interviewing

A successful interviewer:

- Studies the candidates' papers; knows the qualities and skills needed to fill the vacancy (from a job description/specification); and plans the approach to be used at the interview in order to achieve the objectives.
- Welcomes the candidates, arranges introductions and explains the interview procedure.
- Is pleasant and has the ability to establish an early rapport and put the candidates at ease so that they communicate freely.
- Asks questions clearly and concisely, allowing the candidate to do most of the talking; listens carefully to what is said and notes what is not said.
- Asks questions which encourage the candidate to demonstrate

not only their knowledge and experience, but their attitude, manner and motivation. Questions which can be answered simply by 'yes' or 'no' rarely contribute much to the interview.

- Asks extra questions to discover the depth of knowledge and information which might otherwise be withheld if not questioned.
- Does not make a judgment until a candidate has had a full hearing and all relevant facts have been established.
- Avoids excessive note-taking during the interview. Brief, unobtrusive notes can normally be made without it being obvious to the candidate that everything spoken is being recorded. More detailed note-taking should follow immediately after the candidate has left the room and, at this stage, an interview merit grading form can be completed to provide a score of the candidate's performance.
- Gives the candidate the chance to ask questions about the organisation or the vacancy.
- Knows when sufficient information has been obtained for the interview to be ended.

An interview merit grading form, designed to place the candidates in the order of acceptability, may include some or all of the following:

- results from a pre-interview test
- qualifications – general education
- qualifications – business and secretarial
- relevant business experience
- general appearance
- health record
- ability to communicate
- integrity/reliability/adaptability
- initiative
- personality, including the ability to relate to others
- energy/stability
- attitude/motivation
- organising ability
- quality of interests, hobbies, etc

Each item is graded on a five-point scale

Legislation relating to office practice and employment

This section contains references to some of the major Acts of Parliament which have been passed in recent years with important provisions for employees and for those who are responsible for the employment of staff and the administration of offices.

Equal Pay Act 1970

The aim of this Act is to prevent discrimination between men and women concerning their terms and conditions of employment. Employers are required to give equal pay where men and women are employed on the same or broadly similar work. Any disputes arising under the Act can be referred to an industrial tribunal.

Health and Safety at Work Act 1974

The health and safety of office employees is protected by this Act. It is additional to other health and safety at work legislation, such as the Offices, Shops and Railway Premises Act of 1963. The greater part of that Act and subsidiary regulations remain current, but revision and updating will be made as necessary in the future.

The aim of the Health and Safety at Work Act is to:

- secure the health, safety and welfare of people at work
- protect people other than those at work against risks to health or safety arising out of or in connection with the activities of persons at work
- control the keeping and use of explosive or highly flammable or otherwise dangerous substances, and generally preventing the unlawful acquisition, possession and use of such substances
- control the emission into the atmosphere of noxious or offensive substances from premises

One of the principal objectives of the Act is to involve everybody at the workplace – both management and employees – and to create an awareness of the importance of achieving high standards of health and safety.

Duties of the employer

The employer must provide his employees with:

1 A safe place of work with safe access and exit.
2 Safe equipment (including efficient maintenance).
3 Safe systems of work.

4 A safe working environment and adequate facilities and arrangements for their welfare.
5 Safe methods for handling, storing and transporting goods.
6 Instruction, training and supervision of safe practices.
7 Consultation with a view to making and maintaining effective arrangements for promoting health and safety.
8 Where appropriate, a written statement on health and safety and the means of carrying out that policy.

It is also the employer's duty to protect persons not in his employment, eg the public, customers, visiting workers, delivery men, etc, when they are on the premises.

Duties of employees

It is the duty of every employee while at work to:

1 Take reasonable care for the health and safety of himself and of other persons who may be affected by his acts or omissions at work.
2 Co-operate with his employer, supervisor or any other persons to enable them to fulfil their obligations.
3 Refrain from misusing or interfering with anything provided for the health and safety of themselves or others.

Safety precautions extend beyond the office as office employees are sometimes required to visit other parts of the organisation, such as warehouses, workshops and stores, and are then subject to the dangers entailed in the operation of, for instance, fork-lift trucks and cranes and the movement of heavy goods. The fact that office staff are infrequent visitors to these workplaces can easily add to the risks of injury unless they are especially careful and conscious of the dangers.

Offices, Shops and Railway Premises Act 1963

The performance of clerical work suffers if the physical conditions are below standard. The provisions contained in this Act are, therefore, very important for efficient office administration.

After providing that all premises must be kept clean, with floors cleaned at least once weekly, the Act deals with overcrowding. There must be not less than 3.715 sq m (40 sq ft) of floor space for each worker – inclusive of furniture and equipment. A reasonable temperature must be provided and maintained in all rooms in which employees work otherwise than for short periods. A temperature will not be regarded as reasonable if it falls below 16°C (60.8°F) after the first hour of work.

Suitable and sufficient lighting must be provided. No specific standard is stated regarding the intensity of the light, but later regulations may do this (20–30 lumens are normally regarded as satisfactory). Adequate supplies of either fresh air or artificially purified air must be circulated to secure the ventilation of offices.

Premises must have suitable conveniences and washing facilities at places conveniently accessible to all employees. Running hot and cold water must be supplied, together with soap and clean towels. Drinking water must be available and also suitable places to hang up clothing and facilities for drying them. First aid boxes must be provided in all premises so as to be readily accessible. Safety measures and fire precautions are also included in the Act. Seats provided for workers who normally perform their work sitting must be suitable in design, construction and dimensions for the worker and for the kind of work to be carried out.

Trade Union and Labour Relations Act 1974 (as amended by the Employment Acts 1980, 1982 and 1988 and the Trade Union Act 1984)

This Act provides codes of practice for industrial relations and provisions for 'no strike' clauses in trade disputes; rights to take part in trade union activities; picketing; collection of union dues; employee involvement in company affairs for firms with over 250 employees; payment for ballots by the government, etc.

Sex Discrimination Act 1975 (as amended by the Sex Discrimination Act 1986)

This Act aims to make sex discrimination unlawful in employment (including opportunities for promotion); training and education; the provision of goods, facilities and services and in the disposal and management of premises. The Equal Opportunities Commission enforces the Act and seeks to promote equality of opportunity between the sexes.

Race Relations Act 1976

This Act makes it unlawful to discriminate by race, colour, etc, in the employment of staff (including recruitment, terms of employment, promotion and dismissal); education, public services and housing; membership of trade unions and professional bodies and in advertisements. The Commission for Racial Equality enforces the Act and seeks to promote good race relations.

Employment Protection (Consolidation) Act 1978 (as amended by the Employment Acts 1980, 1982 and 1988)

This Act deals with various individual rights of people at work. The major provisions are as follows:

Minimum periods of notice to terminate employment The employee must give at least one week's notice if he has been with his employer continuously for one month or more, but this does not increase with length of service.

The employer must give at least one week's notice after one

month's continuous service, at least two weeks' notice after two years' continuous service, and thereafter one week for each completed year of service up to twelve weeks after twelve years.

Written contracts of employment Employers must give their employees written particulars of their main terms of employment not later than thirteen weeks after commencement of employment. These should include: job title; date when employment began and whether any previous employment is to be counted; rate of remuneration; intervals at which remuneration is paid; hours of work; holidays; sick pay entitlement; pension schemes; length of notice by both parties; grievance procedure and any disciplinary rules applicable.

Medical suspension An employee who has been employed continuously for one month or more and who would normally be able and willing to work but who has been suspended from work on medical grounds, eg under certain specific health regulations, will be entitled to receive a normal week's pay from his employer while he is suspended, for a maximum of twenty-six weeks.

Written statement of reasons for dismissal Any employee with at least twenty-six weeks' service who is dismissed by his employer is entitled to ask his employer for a written statement of the reasons for the dismissal, and if he does so request, the employer must give him one within fourteen days of the request being made.

Itemised pay statements Employees have the right to be given itemised pay statements by their employers. The pay statements must specify the following:

- gross amount of pay
- amounts of any fixed deductions and the purposes for which they are made
- amounts of any variable deductions and the purposes for which they are made
- net amount of pay, and where different amounts of the net amount are paid in different ways, the amount and method of payment of each part-payment

Unfair dismissal The Act gives employees the right not to be unfairly dismissed.

Redundancy Employees who have been given notice of dismissal because of redundancy can be given time off work for job hunting or training for new employment.

Union membership rights and the closed shop Employees are given rights to belong to a trade union or not to belong to one, as they wish. There are also certain rights and safeguards for those who work in a closed shop situation.

Time off for public duties Employers are required, under certain circumstances, to permit employees who hold public positions reasonable time off to perform their duties. These include justices of the peace, members of local authorities, school governors, etc.

Maternity provisions An employee who is expecting a baby may acquire the following rights:

- not to be unreasonably refused time off for antenatal care and to be paid when permitted that time off
- to complain of unfair dismissal because of pregnancy
- to return to work with her employer after a period of absence on account of pregnancy or confinement
- to receive statutory maternity pay for up to eighteen weeks

These rights are generally available to all women employees, married or unmarried, but they are subject to conditions and limitations (contained in the Department of Employment's leaflet *Employment rights for the expectant mother* and the Department of Social Security's leaflet *A guide to maternity benefits*). For example, one of the conditions for the right to return to work is that the employee must give the following information to her employer, in writing, at least twenty-one days before she begins her maternity absence:

- that she will be (or is) absent from work to have a baby
- that she intends to return to work for her employer after her absence
- the expected week of confinement (or if the confinement has occurred, the date of confinement). If requested by her employer, she must produce for inspection a certificate of the expected week of confinement signed by a doctor or midwife

After maternity absence has begun the employee must inform her employer of the date she proposes to return, in writing, at least twenty-one days before that date.

Social Security and Housing Benefits Act 1982

This Act introduced the statutory sick pay scheme (SSP) in which employers are required to pay sick pay to their employees for up to twenty-eight weeks of sickness absence. All employees are covered by the scheme if they are sick for four or more consecutive days and are not disqualified for payment, due to being over minimum state pension age; having a contract of employment which is for a period of less than three months; earning less than the lower weekly earnings limit for National Insurance contribution liability. Employees can normally claim the state sickness benefit if they are not eligible for SSP. The employee may be required to produce evidence in support of his entitlement, eg a self-certificate for four to seven days or a doctor's statement for an absence in excess of seven days.

Data Protection Act 1984

This Act protects individuals from misuse of personal information held about them on computer files and lays down codes of practice for those who use or process data relating to personnel (*see also* p 50).

Financial Services Act 1986

This Act aims to protect investors by regulating the conduct of investment business involving shares, debentures, gilts, local authority securities, unit trusts, most life assurance policies, etc. Investment businesses are regulated by a Securities and Investment Board to ensure that they deal honestly and fairly and aspire to best market practice in all their dealings. It is the Board's responsibility to oversee firms to ensure that they have adequate financial resources to carry on their businesses. The investors' financial outlay is also protected by the Act in the event of the insolvency of an investment business. Written agreements with investors are required to cover the basis for charging commissions or fees and explanations of the risks in the type of transaction undertaken. The Act defines the relationship to be established with investors and lays down codes of practice for promoting, selling and managing investment business.

Further information on legislation

		Telephone:
HMSO Books	*Enquiries:*	01 211 5656
PO Box 276	*Orders:*	01 622 3316
London SW8 5DT		
Commission for Racial Equality		01 828 7022
Elliott House		
10/12 Allington Street		
London SW1E 5EH		
Equal Opportunities Commission		061 833 9244
Overseas House		
Quay Street		
Manchester M3 3HN		
Health and Safety Commission		01 723 1262
Regina House		
Old Marylebone Road		
London NW1		
(and local offices of the Health and Safety Executive)		
The Data Protection Registrar		0625 535711
Springfield House		
Water Lane		
Wilmslow		
Cheshire SK9 5AX		
Local Offices of the Departments of Employment and Social Security.		

In addition, a useful source of reference on all aspects of

employment law is *Croner's Reference Book for Employers.* A monthly amendment service is provided in order to keep the information up-to-date.

Licences

Applying for, or renewing, licences is frequently a task which the secretary is expected to do. The renewal dates can be remembered by entering them in your diary or in a follow-up system (*see* pp 47–50).

Licence	*Address for renewal*
Broadcast receiving Black and white Colour	– Post offices or National Television Licence Records Office, Bristol BS98 1TL
Business reply postal packets Franking machine Freepost Postage Forward parcel	– The Head Postmaster of your district
Game	– Post offices
Motor vehicles Driving licences	– Driver and Vehicle Licensing Centre, Swansea SA99 1AN (application forms obtainable from post offices)
Heavy goods vehicle driving licences	– Traffic Area Offices of Department of Transport
Taxation	– Post offices

Mail – incoming and outgoing

Check list for incoming mail

- When signing for recorded delivery and registered mail, check that you receive the correct packages and that they are not damaged in any way.

- **Open:** business mail addressed to the firm *but*
  Do not open: private, personal and confidential letters and mail not addressed to the firm.
- Check that the correct enclosures accompany letters, and that they are pinned together.
- Check that any enclosed remittances are correct and recorded.
- Stamp all mail with the date of receipt.
- Sort and distribute the mail as soon as possible after receipt.
- Check all envelopes to make sure that nothing has been left in them.
- Take special precautions with suspicious packages – *see* p 144.

Check list for outgoing mail

- Check that letters are signed and, where necessary, have the correct enclosures attached.
- Check that addresses on the envelopes agree with those in the letters.
- Avoid folding letters more than is necessary to fit them into their envelopes.
- Seal envelopes securely.
- Ensure that the correct postage is used for each item in accordance with current postage rates and, if a franking machine is used, check that the date is correct.
- Separate first-class mail from second-class mail.
- Package the envelopes ready for posting with all the addresses facing one direction.
- If a franking machine is used, complete the day's entries on the control card and lock the machine.
- Complete any special Post Office forms required and, when delivering the post, collect and retain any receipts supplied.

Post office services for mailroom procedures

Collection of mail by the Post Office The Post Office will collect mail from an office provided the following quantities are being despatched:

- first- and second-class letters, when there are at least 1000 or the total postage is £140 or more
- special collections of parcels where the number at any one time is at least 100
- a regular collection of parcels if there are at least 20 at a time

Private box A box, rented at the Post Office, for the collection of mail.

Franking machines *See* p 105.

Franking of mail by the Post Office Mail can be franked 'paid' by the Post Office when there are at least 120 packets (or 20 parcels).

Parcel service A parcel contract can be arranged with the Post Office for regular large postings of parcels (over 1000 per annum). The contract provides for the weighing, stamping and delivery of parcels to the Post Office, thus relieving the mailroom staff of these time-consuming operations.

Full details of all services: *Post Office Guide*.

Mailing equipment

Equipment	*Purpose*
Addressing machine	– addressing envelopes, etc; *see also* p 118
Collating machine	– sorting and collating of documents
Date and time stamp	– stamping the date and time on incoming mail
Folding machine	– automatic folding of documents
Franking machine	– printing postal impressions on mail. Machines must be leased or purchased from the supplying companies authorised by the Post Office: Envopak Ltd, Powerscroft Road, Sidcup, Kent DA14 5EF; Pitney Bowes Plc, The Pinnacles, Harlow, Essex CM19 5BD; Roneo Alcatel Ltd, Mailroom Division, PO Box 66, South Street, Romford RM1 2AR; Scriptomatic Ltd, Scriptomatic House, Torrington Park, London N12 9SU
Inserting and mailing machine	– mechanises the following procedures: collating; opening envelope flap; sealing envelope; franking postage impression; counting number of items and stacking envelopes
Jogger	– Vibrating papers into alignment ready for stapling or binding

Equipment		*Purpose*
Letter opening machine	–	slitting envelopes received in the mail
Package tying machine	–	tying string/tape round parcels
Post scales	–	weighing packets for calculation of postage (electronic post scales have postal rates programmed into its memory with touch selection for different categories of mail)
Rolling and wrapping machine	–	preparing newspapers, magazines, etc, for posting
Sealing machine	–	moistening and sealing flaps of envelopes
Shredder	–	shredding documents
Sponge/roller moistener	–	moistening stamps and envelopes
Stapler	–	fixing wire staples into documents
Tucking and folding machine	–	preparing documents for posting without envelopes
Weighing machine	–	weighing packets for calculation of postage

Mailing equipment suppliers

Bell & Howell Ltd, 33–35 Woodthorpe Road, Ashford, Middx TW15 2RZ

Envopak Group Ltd, Powerscroft Road, Sidcup, Kent DA14 5EF

Hasler (Great Britain) Ltd, Commerce Way, Croydon, Surrey CR0 4XA

Pitney Bowes plc, The Pinnacles, Elizabeth Way, Harlow, Essex CM19 5BD

Roneo Alcatel Ltd, PO Box 66, South Street, Romford, Essex RM1 2AR

Scriptomatic Ltd, Scriptomatic House, Torrington Park, London N12 9SU

Meetings

Documents

Agenda A programme of business to be discussed at a meeting, usually incorporating the notice convening the meeting. Sources for the agenda:

- previous agenda (recurring items)
- previous minutes (continuing items)

STAFF WELFARE COMMITTEE

A meeting of the Staff Welfare Committee will be held in the Boardroom on Friday 14 October 19-- at 1530 hrs.

AGENDA

1 Apologies for absence.

2 Minutes of the last meeting.

3 Matters arising from the minutes.

4 Staff canteen: To receive a report from the Canteen Manager concerning proposed increases in prices. — Paper 1 attached

5 Car park: To consider the working party report on a new layout for the car park. — Paper 2 to follow

6 To receive proposals for the staff Christmas Dinner.

7 Any other business.

8 Date of next meeting.

K ABRAHAM

Secretary

A specimen agenda

- constitution (constitutional items)
- chairman and members may request items to be included

An agenda is sent out seven to fourteen days before the meeting so that the participants can consider the matters to be discussed.

Attendance sheet Record of people present at a meeting. Usually members sign the attendance sheet as they enter the room.

Chairman's agenda This contains more information than the ordinary agenda, and spaces are left on the right-hand side of the paper for the chairman to make his own notes. The additional information provides the chairman with details necessary for the efficient conduct of the meeting.

Minutes A record of the proceedings of a meeting. The key factors concerning the taking of minutes:

1 Record the exact wording of resolutions passed or decisions reached with the names of the proposers and seconders.
2 Note the main arguments for and against the decisions.
3 Write the minutes as soon as possible after the meeting while the discussions are fresh in the mind.
4 Write minutes wholly in the third person and in the past tense.
5 Be as brief as possible as a summary is required – not a verbatim record.
6 Write clearly so that there is no possible doubt about the decisions reached.
7 Arrange the items in the same order as on the agenda.
8 Prepare a draft for approval by the chairman before typing the final copy.

Reports of meeting

See p 140.

Glossary of meeting terms

Ad hoc 'Arranged for this purpose'. An *ad hoc* sub-committee is appointed to carry out one particular piece of work, such as the arrangements for the visit of a very important person (VIP). These committees are sometimes called special or special-purpose committees.

Addendum An amendment which adds words to a motion.

Addressing the chair A member wishing to speak on a point must rise and address the chair in the following way:

Mr Chairman – for a gentleman.

Madam Chairman – for a lady.

All remarks must be addressed to the chair, and members must not discuss matters between themselves at a meeting.

Adjournment Subject to the articles, rules or constitution of an organisation, the chairman, with the consent of the members of the meeting, may adjourn it in order to postpone further discus-

MINUTES OF MEETING	A meeting of the Staff Welfare Committee was held in the Boardroom on Friday 14 October 19-- at 1530 hrs.
	<u>Present</u>:
	Miss C Parsons (in the Chair) Mr P L Brown Mrs J Clarke Miss C H Ellis Mr T R Moon Mr G Strong Miss K Abraham (Secretary) Mr F Morris (Canteen Manager)
Apologies	Apologies were received on behalf of Miss J Tucker and Mr V Williams.
Minutes	The minutes of the last meeting, which had been circulated, were taken as read and approved and were signed by the Chairman.
Matters arising	There were no matters arising out of the minutes.
Staff canteen	The Canteen Manager submitted a report outlining the current financial position of the canteen. Since October of last year, when the price of meals was last increased, food costs had risen by 20% and he proposed a similar increase in the price of meals in order to meet the extra costs. It was generally felt that, at a time when salary increases were less than 10%, an increase of 20% for canteen meals would be unacceptable. Miss Ellis suggested offering a smaller choice of meals as a possible means of reducing costs. Mr Strong was of the opinion that the firm's subsidy should be increased to meet the higher costs. After much discussion it was agreed to defer increasing prices until the Chairman and the Canteen Manager have had a meeting with the Personnel Manager to seek an increase in the meals subsidy, and the Canteen Manager has considered other means of saving expenditure such as reducing the choice of meals offered.
Any other business	Miss Parsons stated that the London office had adopted flexitime and she considered that the majority of staff at this branch would like to change over to it. Members agreed to seek the views of staff and to report back their findings to the next meeting.
Date of next meeting	It was decided to hold the next meeting of the Committee on Tuesday 7 November 19--.
	Chairman
	7 November 19--

An example of minutes

sion, or because of the shortage of time. Adequate notice of an adjourned meeting must be given.

Amendment A proposal to alter a motion by adding or deleting words. It must be proposed, seconded and put to the meeting in the customary way.

Casting vote A second vote usually allowed to the chairman, except in the case of a company meeting. A casting vote is used only when there is an equal number of votes 'for' and 'against' a motion.

Closure A motion submitted with the object of ending the discussion on a matter before the meeting.

Disturbance A person causing a disturbance at a meeting may be ejected with or without the aid of the police, provided that the meeting has not been announced as 'public'.

Dropped motion A motion that has to be dropped either because there is no seconder or because attendants want it to be abandoned.

En bloc The voting of, say, a committee *en bloc*, that is, electing or re-electing all members of a committee by the passing of one resolution.

Going into committee A motion 'that the meeting go into committee' is moved if less restricted discussion is thought necessary. A motion 'that the meeting be resumed' gives the meeting authority to proceed at the point where it left off.

In camera A meeting which is not open to the public.

Intra vires Within the power of the person or body concerned.

Kangaroo closure The chair of a committee can jump from one amendment to another omitting those considered to be less important or repetitive.

Lie on the table A letter or document is said to 'lie on the table' when it is decided at a meeting to take no action upon the business in it.

Majority The articles and rules of the organisation will state the majority of votes needed to carry a motion.

Memorandum and articles of association Regulations drawn up by a company setting out the objects for which the company is formed and defining the manner in which its business shall be conducted.

Motion A motion must normally be written and handed to the chairman or secretary before the meeting. The mover of the motion speaks on it and has the right to reply at the close of the discussion. The seconder may then speak to the motion only once. If there is no seconder, a motion is dropped and cannot be introduced again. When put to a meeting, the motion becomes 'the question' or 'the proposal', and when it is passed, it is called 'the resolution'. A motion on something which has not been included on the agenda can be moved only if 'leave of urgency' has been agreed by the meeting or it has been included under the customary item 'any other business'.

Nem Con 'No one contradicting', ie there are no votes against the motion, but some members have not voted at all.

Next business A motion 'that the meeting proceed with next business' is a method of delaying the decision on any matter brought before the meeting.

No confidence When the members of a meeting disagree with the chair they pass a vote of 'no confidence' in the chair. When this happens the chair must be vacated in favour of a deputy or some other person nominated by the meeting. There must be a substantial majority of members in favour of this decision.

Point of order This is a question regarding the procedure at a meeting or a query relating to the standing orders or constitution raised by a member during the course of the meeting, eg. absence of quorum.

Poll Term for the method of voting at an election, usually a secret vote by ballot paper. The way in which a poll is to be conducted is generally laid down in the standing orders or constitution of the organisation.

Postponement The action taken to defer a meeting to a later date.

Putting the question To conclude the discussion on a motion it is customary for the chair to 'put the question' by announcing 'The question before the meeting is...'

Question be now put When members feel that sufficient discussion has taken place on a motion, it may be moved 'that the question be now put'. If this is carried, only the proposer of the motion may speak and then a vote is taken. If the motion 'question be now put' is defeated, discussion may be continued.

Quorum The minimum number of persons who must be in attendance to constitute a meeting. This is stated in the constitution or rules of the organisation.

Reference back An amendment referring a report or other item of business back for further consideration to the body or person submitting it. If the motion 'reference back' is defeated, the discussion is continued.

Resolution A formal decision carried at a meeting. It must be proposed, seconded and put to the meeting in the customary way. A resolution cannot be rescinded at the meeting at which it is adopted.

Rider An additional clause or sentence added to a resolution after it has been passed. It differs from an amendment in that it adds to a resolution instead of altering it. A rider has to be proposed, seconded and put to the meeting in the same way as a motion.

Right of reply The proposer of a resolution has the right of reply when the resolution has been fully discussed. He is allowed to reply only once, and afterwards the motion is put to the meeting.

Sine die Without an appointed day, or indefinitely.

Standing orders Rules compiled by the organisation regulating the manner in which its business is to be conducted. It may also have the title 'Constitution'.

Status quo Used to refer to a matter in which there is to be no change.

Sub-committee A sub-committee may be appointed by a committee to deal with some specific branch of its work. It must carry out such functions as are delegated to it by the committee and must report to the committee periodically.

Ultra vires Beyond the legal power or authority of a company or organisation.

Unanimous When all members of a meeting have voted in favour of a resolution it is said to be carried 'unanimously'.

Personnel involved in meetings

Chair	(Note the title 'chairperson' is sometimes used.) The chairman is appointed by a meeting to: • manage the proceedings of a meeting and keep order • approve the items to be discussed on the agenda • conduct the business according to the agenda and standing orders or constitution; keep the discussion within prescribed limits and allow all points of view to be expressed • deal with points of order • guide the discussion and assist the meeting to make decisions by passing resolutions, amendments, etc • take a vote or poll and declare the result • sign the minutes and ensure that action is taken, as approved • close, adjourn or postpone meetings
Secretary	Responsible for the meeting arrangements as given on p 113
Treasurer	A treasurer is involved when a meeting is responsible for the receipt and payment of money. Duties include: • presentation of financial reports • advice to the meeting on financial matters • submission of audited accounts when required
Convenor	A person authorised to call a meeting
Ex-officio member	A person who is a member of a committee by virtue of office, eg the Canteen Manager may be an ex-officio member of the Staff Welfare Committee
Co-opted member	A person who serves on a committee as a result of the committee's power of co-option, ie the committee approves of the appointment by a majority vote in order to engage the services of a person who can assist them in their work
In attendance	Those who attend a meeting to provide a

Meetings – the secretary's role

Before the meeting	*On the day of the meeting*	*After the meeting*
1 Book a suitable room 2 Prepare the agenda in consultation with the chairman and distribute it to members 3 Prepare a chairman's agenda 4 Obtain any necessary statements or documents from members who cannot be present but who are known to have strong views on items to be discussed 5 Collect together the following items required for the meeting: • stationery, including writing paper and shorthand note book • spare copies of the agenda • minutes of the previous meeting • all relevant papers and files of the correspondence, including letters of apology received from members unable to attend • attendance register or sheet • any books of reference, standing orders, etc	1 Attend early, bringing with you the items referred to in **5** of the previous column 2 Arrange for direction signs to the committee room to be displayed 3 Ensure that the seating arrangements are in order 4 See that each member has a supply of writing paper 5 Check that members sign the attendance register 6 Read the minutes of the last meeting, if these have not been circulated, letters of apology and any other correspondence 7 Assist the chairman in supplying information from files as required during the meeting 8 Record the details of the decisions reached, noting who proposed and who seconded motions as well as the results of the voting	1 Clear the room of all papers 2 Ensure that all documents are returned to the office 3 Prepare draft minutes for approval by the chairman 4 When approved, type the minutes in final form for distribution to members 5 Type any correspondence resulting from the meeting 6 File any papers used at the meeting, as well as copies of correspondence typed in **5** (before the meeting) 7 If the chairman is also your employer, ensure that the date of the next meeting is entered in their diary and yours

	service such as secretarial, legal, financial, etc, but do not have voting powers
Proxy	A person appointed to attend a meeting and vote on behalf of a member who is unable to attend
Teller	A person who counts the votes at a meeting

Methods of payment

Name	*Issued by*	*Description*
Bill of exchange	Bank	A document mainly used as payment for exports, accompanied by shipping documents giving title to goods.
Cash	—	A means of making payment 'on the spot', eg petty cash transactions. When sent through the post, cash must be registered in a special registered envelope supplied by the Post Office.
Cash on delivery	Post Office	Invoices up to £350 can be sent by parcel, compensation fee parcel, registered letter or inland datapost package for collection, and remitted to the sender by Girobank cheque. Sums in excess of £50 have to be collected on Post Office premises.
Charge card	American Express, Diners Club, etc	A means of borrowing money for the payment of goods or services.
Cheque	Bank/ Girobank	*See* p 18 for advice to bank account holders.
Credit card	Bank	A means of purchasing goods or services on credit, eg by the use of Access or Barclaycards.
Credit transfer (bank giro)	Bank	A means of making payments through a bank without having to send cheques by post, credit being transferred from the drawer's bank to the payee's bank.
	Girobank	A means of using a transfer slip for making payments through the Girobank Centre.
Direct debit	Bank/ Girobank	A system for arranging periodic payments, the payee requesting the bank to collect them from the drawer's account.
Documentary Letter of Credit	Bank	A written undertaking by a bank to an exporter to pay within a specified period of time for goods or services on presentation of documentary evidence.

Name	Issued by	Description
Draft	Bank/ Girobank	A draft drawn up by a bank in favour of a creditor in settlement of an amount owing, normally payable on demand. This is used for paying large sums where an ordinary cheque may not be acceptable, eg when paying a deposit on the purchase of a house.
EFTPOS	Bank	Electronic funds transfer at point of sale for paying for goods without using cash or cheques.
International money transfer	Bank	A method by which an importer's bank instructs an overseas bank by airmail to pay an exporter.
International payments	Girobank	Payments may be made overseas by: International Giro Transfer; International Bank Transfer; Foreign Bank Cheques.
Postal Orders	Post Office	A form of payment that can be issued in various amounts up to £20, and can be crossed to ensure that payment is made only through a bank.
Standing order	Bank/ Girobank	An order to a bank to pay a person or business a specified sum periodically from a customer's account.
SWIFT	Bank	The Society for Worldwide Interbank Financial Communications providing a computerised international service for the transfer of funds for export/ import transactions, letters of credit and transmitting messages.
Transcash	Girobank	A credit transfer system where the remitter deposits the cash for payment at a post office.

Microfilming

Microfilming is a method of filming documents in a reduced size for storage and integration with the computer and word processor for information handling. The main advantage of microfilming is space-saving, eg 25 000 documents can be stored in one film cartridge measuring only 4 × 4 × 1 in.

Recent developments in microfilm technology make it possible for microfilm images, both text and graphic, to be scanned into digital form so that it can be transmitted by telephone line. The images can also be edited, if required, and integrated into a computer-generated file, allowing for them to be stored on an optical disk for immediate access from computer terminals.

Glossary of terms

Acetate jacket A 'loose-leaf' system for holding strips of microfilm in horizontal grooves – useful for periodic updating.
Aperture card An 80-column punched card with a microfilm mounted on it. The punched holes denote the contents. Reference numbers are used for quick sorting and retrieval of the card when it is required for viewing or for reproducing paper copies.
Camera Equipment for filming documents.
CAR Computer-assisted retrieval (or automatic retrieval units), a system which has a built-in microprocessor which interrogates the computer and retrieves the required microfilm. A reference number is keyed into a terminal and relevant information from the computer index is displayed on a VDU indicating the film magazine where the microfilm is stored. The desired documents are then automatically displayed on the reader/printer and a hard copy made, if required.
Cartridge A container which holds microfilm and makes it easier to handle because there is no lacing of the film, no rewinding and the film is protected.
CIM Computer input microfilm, a system which uses a camera to film documents for subsequent optical character recognition input into a computer.
COM Computer output microfilm or computer-originated microfilm. Data from a computer is recorded directly on to roll film or microfiche. When documents are required for reference they are either viewed on a reader or a hard copy is produced using a reader/printer.
COM recorder Equipment for microfilming computer output.
Duplicator Equipment for reproducing copies of microfiche.
Micro-comparator Equipment for viewing and comparing two microfiches.
Microfiche A sheet of microfilm containing rows of images. Appropriate for quick reference to a large number of related documents which do not require periodic updating.
Microplotter Equipment for producing microfilm from CAD (computer-aided design) output.
Processor Equipment for developing and processing film.
Reader/printer Equipment for viewing film and printing copies.
Roll film Continuous roll of film used for sequentially filed documents where no insertions are required.

Microfilm applications

- Cheap transportation of documents, especially when sent by airmail.
- Security of valuable documents, eg legal documents can be stored in more than one place.
- Engineering drawings.
- Systems such as sales invoicing, copy orders, cheque payments.
- Parts manuals.
- Journals and newspapers for reference in libraries.

Key factors when considering the use of microfilm:

- The volume and nature of records which must be kept for reference and the office space available for storing them.
- The frequency of reference to the records and the need for speedy retrieval.
- The importance of security and durability of records.
- The need for standardising the storage and retrieval of documents.
- The cost of the necessary microfilming equipment set against savings in filing cabinets, copy papers, files and office space.
- The need for microfilming equipment to be compatible with existing equipment and procedures.
- The type of microfilm to be used, eg jacket, cartridge, roll film, aperture card and microfiche and the equipment to operate it, eg camera, COM recorder, microplotter, printer reader, etc.

Suppliers of microfilm equipment and accessories

Agfa Gavaert Ltd, 27 Great West Road, Brentford, Middx TW8 9AX

Bell & Howell Ltd, 33–35 Woodthorpe Road, Ashford, Middx TW15 2BR

Canon (UK) Ltd, Canon House, Manor Road, Wallington, Surrey SM6 0AJ

Imtec Group plc, 170 Honeypot Lane, Stanmore, Middx HA7 1LB

Kodak Ltd, PO Box 66, Kodak House, Station Road, Hemel Hempstead, Herts HP1 1JU

3M United Kingdom plc, 3M House, PO Box 1, Bracknell, Berks RG12 1JU

Office equipment

When selecting a new item of equipment, consider the following questions:

- Is it necessary? Will it produce better quality work and what are its advantages over existing methods?
- Will the equipment serve its purpose for future needs, say four or five years?
- Is it appropriate for your use? Would it be suitable for other uses and what size do you need?
- Would it be compatible with equipment already in use?
- What is the price of the equipment, installation, maintenance, software and stationery?
- What is the cheapest method of purchase: outright purchase, hire purchase, leasing or renting? How soon will it become obsolete?
- Consider the manufacturer's reputation: Is the firm reliable and is there a good after-sales service? Have other local firms bought it?
- What is involved in training existing staff to operate the equipment? Will new staff have to be employed and, if so, are they available locally?
- Are there any special requirements to house the equipment and store materials?
- Will there be a noise/ventilation problem?
- What will the effect be on staff morale? Have staff/unions been consulted?
- What will its effects be on customers?

Addressing machines

Equipment used to reproduce information from stencil cards, plates, foils, etc, on to envelopes, labels and forms.

Computers, word processors and copiers can also be used to print out names and addresses and other repetitive data on sheets, with adhesive backing if required, thus providing a rapid and efficient means of supplying address labels for envelopes and other addressing machine applications. An electronic addressing system can be used which is controlled by a microprocessor and data held on mini-diskettes. New addresses, deletions and amendments are displayed on a VDU and entered using a typewriter-style keyboard. Labels can be addressed by this process at a speed of up to 9000 per hour. The programs provide:

- alphabetic sorting by name, post town or postcode

- selection by categories or addresses, as required
- listing of data for reports

Applications

Addressing envelopes/labels/cards
Entering descriptions on stock cards
Imprinting clock cards, pay envelopes and fixed data on pay record sheets
Addressing advertising literature
Entering details of customers on ledger sheets, index cards and files
Addressing monthly statements and invoices

Suppliers of addressing machines

Addressing Systems International Ltd, Rosedale Works, Rosedale Road, Richmond, Surrey TW9 2SZ
Data Card UK Ltd, New Lane, Havant, Hants PO9 2NR
Macrodata Ltd, Enterprise House, Central Way, Feltham, Middx TW14 0RX
Mandergraph Ltd, Chapel House, High Street, Deanshanger, Milton Keynes, MK19 6HD
Scriptomatic Ltd, Scriptomatic House, Torrington Park, North Finchley, London N12 9SU
Target Addressing & Business Systems, 40 Sterling Way, London N18 2XZ

Calculators

Electronic calculators with printing facilities are commonly used in offices for tasks which involve calculations. The tally roll is useful for providing printed proof of the accuracy of calculations and also for attaching to documents for future reference and checking. Calculators can be used for addition, subtraction, multiplication, division, percentages and square roots. Functions include:

- a decimal point selector (including a floating decimal point)
- sub-total key
- rounding switch which rounds up or down when the fixed decimal point is chosen in multiplication and division
- item counter switch providing the total number of items added or subtracted
- non-add key for printing reference numbers which are not to be included in the calculation
- automatic constant feature which enables you to add, subtract, multiply or divide by the same number repeatedly without having to re-enter the number for each new calculation
- memory to provide for the storage of products or quotients during the course of a calculation

Applications
Calculating and checking time cards and pay roll totals
Invoice extensions
Stock valuations
Foreign exchange rates
Bills of quantities
Sales analysis

Suppliers of calculators
Brother Office Equipment, Shepley Street, Guide Bridge, Audenshaw, Manchester M34 5JD
Canon (UK) Ltd, Canon House, Manor Road, Wallington, Surrey SM6 0AJ
Facit Ltd, Maidstone Road, Rochester, Kent ME1 3QN
Olympia Business Machines Co Ltd, Olympia House, 199–205 Old Marylebone Road, London NW1 5QS
Sharp Electronics (UK) Ltd, Sharp House, Thorp Road, Newton Heath, Manchester M10 9BE
Peter Williams (Business Machines & Systems) Ltd, Williams House, 821 Woolwich Road, London SE7 8LS

Computers

See pp 32–8 and 50–4.

Copiers

There are over 250 different models of copiers currently on the market, ranging from small desk-top copiers for personal use to high-capacity heavy duty copiers for large-scale print operations, with prices ranging from £1000 to £50 000. When selecting a copier you will need to take into consideration the following:

- price – as referred to above for outright purchase, although they can also be leased or rented
- size – the quantity and nature of copying must be considered when determining the size
- speed – this ranges from 20 copies per minute to 135 per minute, although full colour copiers are much slower
- document feed – this can be manual, semi-automatic or fully automatic, feeding (20–50 originals); a recirculating document feeder allows for copying double-sided originals
- paper feed – uses magazines, trays or cassettes with paper quantities ranging from 250 to 4000

Some machines hold different sizes of paper and make automatic selection of the size of paper required

Facilities are also provided to allow for copying on both sides of the paper

- paper size – most copiers handle originals and copies of A3–A5 international paper size but the range can extend to A2–A6
- image editing – this includes: mask and trim facilities for cutting out unwanted material; image shift for relocating parts of an original from one position to another; reversing out graphics or text, ie white on black instead of black on white
- reduction and enlargement of original – different ratios of reduction and enlargement may be provided
- collation – if collating is a major requirement, consider how many bin sorters you require – these range from 10 to 40
- finishing functions – these can include on-line sorting (as above); jogging; folding; stitching/adhesive binding; auto-stapling
- memory – the storage of sets of programmed instructions in a memory so that they can be recalled at a later date by operating a pre-set key or for storing images of originals. Consider how many copying routines and/or images are required in the memory
- integration with other equipment – using, eg, a computer to merge an original with database information
- colour reproduction – there are several different processes, eg dual colour copying using colour toners designated with a pressure pen on an editor board; a dry photographic process on thermal paper; xerographic, ie using a photoconductive drum; laser electrostatic plain paper output with digital input. The user must consider whether colour is advantageous and, if so,

whether to choose full or dual colour reproduction

- other features – the ability to prepare overhead transparencies
  – billing and access control, eg use of credit cards (for controlling the use made of the copier)
  – modular design, allowing the user to extend the configuration if required in the future

Laser 'intelligent' copiers

These are advanced copiers capable of volume copying and accepting information directly from computers and word processors. The image of the original is converted into a digital electrical signal as the intermediate process instead of using a drum. This signal turns the laser on and off to reproduce the image which can be processed, transmitted to other locations or stored for later recall. The machine is in two parts: a reader and a print unit which work separately from one another, allowing one reader to be interfaced with up to three printers to produce 135 copies a minute. The printer units can be remote from the reader unit to meet the departmental copying needs of a company. Long-life toner is used which produces up to 20 000 copies at one filling.

Guidelines for copying

What you should know about your copier:

- the warm-up procedure at the beginning of the day
- how to insert/replenish copy paper
- how to insert the originals and set the machine up for copying
- how to top-up the toner
- techniques of image editing
- copyright restrictions
- the methods used for sorting, collating and binding copies
- how to prepare overhead projector transparencies
- the method used to control the use of the copier
- ways of ensuring economic use of the copier
- safety procedures
- the procedure for clearing paper jammed in the machine
- the procedure for reporting faults and arranging for a mechanic to attend
- day-to-day maintenance in accordance with the operating manual
- the closing-down procedure at the end of the day

Suppliers of copiers

Canon (UK) Ltd, Canon House, Manor Road, Wallington, Surrey SM6 0AJ

Kodak Ltd, PO Box 66, Kodak House, Station Road, Hemel Hempstead, Herts HP1 1JU

Konica Business Machines (UK) Ltd, 6 Miles Gray Road, Basildon, Essex SS14 3AR

Rank Xerox (UK) Ltd, Bridge House, Oxford Road, Uxbridge, Middx UB8 1HS

Roneo Alcatel Ltd, PO Box 3, South Street, Romford, Essex RM1 2AR

Toshiba Information Systems (UK) Ltd, Toshiba House, Brooklands Close, Sunbury on Thames, Middx TW16 7DX

Desk-top publishing

Desk-top publishing, or electronic publishing as it is sometimes called, is a means of producing artwork 'in-house' with integrated text and graphics in preparation for copying or printing. It consists of a computer, specially designed software combining text creation and editing and an output device (in most cases a laser printer). The design and layout of the page can be manipulated by a mouse and a light pen or graphics pad used to draw the image. A scanner can also be used to incorporate existing graphics on to a page.

Desk-top publishing is ideal for producing forms, letter headings, advertising copy, brochures, in-house journals, technical manuals, reports, 35mm slides and overhead projector transparencies.

It can be used to advantage by:

- storing and retrieving documents for use at a later date to avoid holding large stocks
- reducing the expenditure incurred in overruns
- updating documents and publications
- allowing users to create their own 'in-house' styles of text and graphic presentation
- providing a quicker turnaround of printed material without having to rely on external printers
- providing a cheaper means of producing artwork, compared with typesetting
- enhancing a company's reputation by the quality and professionalism of its paperwork. This, however, depends on the training and ability of the staff employed on the work.

Suppliers of desk-top publishing equipment and systems

Agfa Gevaert Ltd, 27 Great West Road, Brentford, Middx TW8 9AX

Ericsson Information Systems Ltd, Swan Office Centre, 1508 Coventry Road, Yardley, Birmingham B25 8BN

Hewlett Packard Ltd, Nine Mile Road, Wokingham, Berks RG11 3LL

IBM United Kingdom Ltd, PO Box 41, North Harbour, Portsmouth, Hants PO6 3AU
Kodak Ltd, PO Box 66, Kodak House, Station Road, Hemel Hempstead, Herts HP1 1JU
Rank Xerox (UK) Ltd, Bridge House, Oxford Road, Uxbridge, Middx UB8 1HS

Dictating machines

See p 168.

Duplicators

Although there are still a few spirit and stencil duplicators in use today, most organisations use an offset-litho duplicator or a copier capable of reproducing large quantities.

The duplicating medium in the stencil process is ink which is fed through indentations made into a stencil and on to semi-absorbent paper.

The spirit process reproduces copies using an aniline dye which is transferred from the master to the copy paper by spirit.

In the offset-litho process, copies are reproduced in ink from a plate containing a 'greasy' litho image. The master, fitted round a plate cylinder, is dampened with water, which the greasy material refuses to accept, but which is retained by the non-greasy areas. The master also comes into contact with an inking roller, the ink being accepted by the greasy image and repelled by the moistened areas. The image on the master, which has attracted the ink, is offset in negative form on to a rubber blanket which in turn is offset on to the copy paper in positive form. The principle involved in this process is illustrated below.

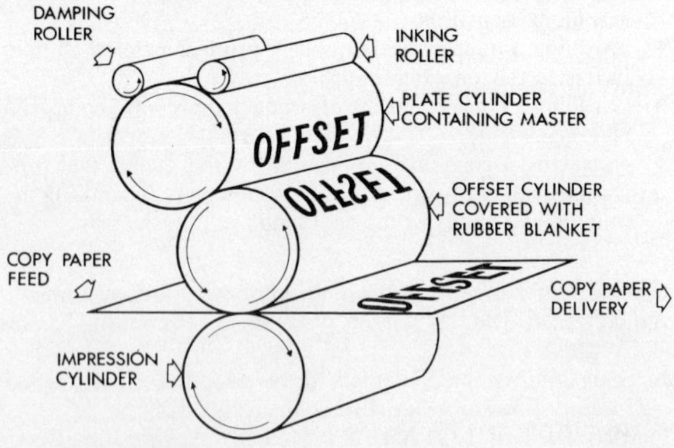

The principle of offset

Almost any type and weight of copy paper can be used for this process of duplicating. Copies of a high quality can be obtained and it is particularly good for producing large quantities of circular letters, leaflets, price lists, parts lists, letter headings and forms.

Suppliers of duplicators and accessories

Electromet Reprographic Ltd, Gladiator House, Gladiator Street, London SE23 1NA

Gestetner Ltd, PO Box 23, Gestetner House, 210 Euston Road, London NW1 2DA

Itek Graphix Ltd, Westlink House, 981 Great West Road, Brentford, Middx TW8 9DN

Office and Electronic Machines plc, 140–154 Borough High Street, London SE1 1LH

Roneo Alcatel Ltd, PO Box 3, South Street, Romford, Essex RM1 2AR

Skycopy Ltd, 412–420 The Highway, London E14 8ED

Filing equipment

See p 59.

Laminating equipment

Machines are available for laminating papers or cards for protection against moisture, dirt, grease and tampering. The document is placed in a machine with a heat process which seals it between layers of transparent film. Lamination is used for notice board notices, valuable documents, identity cards, sales literature, book or record dust jackets, menus and any papers or cards which require protection against wear and tear.

Supplier of laminating equipment

Data Card UK Ltd, New Lane, Havant, Hants PO9 2NR

Mailing equipment

See p 105.

Microfilm equipment

See p 115.

Telecommunications equipment

See p 154.

Typewriters and word processors

See p 163.

Office furniture and layout

Office furniture should be carefully chosen as it contributes to the health, welfare and safety of employees as well as increasing efficiency and making the most effective use of space. Furniture for the modern electronic office should be of the purpose-built type, to cater for the needs of people operating such equipment as VDUs, word processors, computers, etc. Several finishes are available but the choice is usually between wood, plastic or metal.

Provision must also be made for cabling which should be as unobtrusive as possible. Wiring channels can be incorporated in desks so that telephones and lighting can be positioned in convenient places without the need for trailing cables.

Modern designs also provide for the needs of staff working in groups and sharing inter-related equipment. Such multiple workstation configurations facilitate the collaboration of staff in joint projects and the furniture easily interfaces with computing equipment. Terminal desks can include keyboard extensions for efficient and comfortable operation and the printer table can incorporate a paper feed slot with a paper storage shelf below.

The secretary's office will usually be located in one of the following situations:

- a separate 'cellular' office adjoining the employer's office
- a work area in the employer's own office
- a work area in an open-plan office

Whichever of these positions you occupy, the working environment, furniture requirements and layout are much the same and in planning your office bear in mind the following:

Work flow Occupy a position as near as possible to your boss's office to reduce the amount of walking between the two offices.

Space Allow enough space for working. The Health and Safety at Work Act specifies a minimum 3.715 sq m per person.

Desk situation For security reasons, position your desk so that visitors will not be able to read confidential documents in your typewriter. If you are in an office with others it is not a good idea to be face-to-face with another person.

Lighting Correct lighting is important in creating the right conditions. Position lamps carefully to spread the light evenly across work surfaces. Also remember that a VDU emits light as well as reflecting it, so it should be positioned where reflections will not shine into your eyes.

Layout This should be balanced and pleasing, boosting morale and prestige.

Noise If possible, isolate noisy machines in a separate office or screen them off with soundproof panels.

Equipment Filing cabinets, telephones, etc, should be positioned within easy reach. However, do not place cabinets so that extended drawers obstruct a passageway.
Display Use pinboards, visual control boards, display areas, etc, for displaying information which you use frequently. These provide good memory aids and are easily accessible.
Decor Create a pleasing environment which reflects your own personality by displaying a favourite picture, photograph, pot plant, etc, but if you have some form of greenery remember to water it!
Furniture The size and design of desks should take account of office technological equipment, including telephones, wp keyboard and dictation machine. Ergonomically designed chairs are essential to ensure that office workers enjoy a comfortable and healthy environment. Chairs for secretaries should have automatic height adjustment, swivel seat for ease of movement and a pivoted adjustable back rest. Measurements for office desks and chairs are recommended in the British Standards Institute specification BS 5940: 1980.

Suppliers of office furniture

Abbott Bros (Southall) Ltd, Abbess House, 39–47 High Street, Southall, Middx UB1 3HE
Carson Office Furniture Ltd, Desk House, Cranes Farm Road, Basildon, Essex SS14 3JE
Martela plc, Rooksley, Milton Keynes MK13 8PD
Herman Miller Ltd, Lower Bristol Road, Bath, Avon BA2 3ER
Sheer Pride Ltd, Weybridge Trading Estate, Addlestone, Weybridge, Surrey KT15 2RL
Tansad Ltd, Lodge Causeway, Fishponds, Bristol BS16 3JU

Petty cash

Key factors in recording petty cash:

- The imprest (or float), £100 in the example on p 128, should always be the value of the petty cash vouchers plus cash in hand.
- At the beginning of the period, the imprest is the balance of cash brought forward from the previous period plus any cash received.
- To calculate the amount needed to restore the imprest at the end of the period, subtract the balance of cash in hand from the imprest. This amount should equal the total payments.

PETTY CASH BOOK

Dr. Received	Date	Folio	Details	V'ch'r no	Total paid out	Stationery	Cleaning	Postage	Office sundries	VAT Cr.
	19 —									
5 60	Jan 1		Balance b/f							
94 40	" 1	CB1	Cash received							
	" 2		Adhesive tape	119	1 61	1 40				– 21
	" 8		Newspapers	120	8 65				8 65	
	" 9		Cleaning materials	121	2 78		2 42			– 36
	" 10		Aerogrammes	122	3 00			3 00		
	" 15		Registered envelopes	123	17 50			17 50		
	" 22		Pot plant	124	10 00				10 00	
	" 23		Laundry	125	16 25		16 25			
	" 25		Typewriter ribbons	126	14 49	12 60				1 89
					74 28	14 00	18 67	20 50	18 65	2 46
	" 31		Balance c/f		25 72	L1	L2	L3	L4	L5
100 00					100 00					
25 72	Feb 1		Balance b/f							
74 28	" 1	CB2	Cash received							

A page from a petty cash book

- Every item of expenditure should be entered twice in the petty cash account; once in the total column and once in the appropriate analysis column.
- When totalling the columns at the end of a period, the total of all analysis columns should be equal to the total payments column.
- Whenever cash is paid out, a receipt or voucher should be obtained.
- Petty cash vouchers are signed twice; once by the person who spends the money and once by a person who is authorised to approve the expenditure.
- The vouchers should be numbered as they are received and filed numerically for audit purposes; the voucher numbers being entered in the petty cash account to facilitate reference to the documents.
- The analysis columns are not always the same and can be varied to suit individual requirements.
- The cash box should be locked when not in use.

Postal mail services

Aerogrammes Specially designed forms for sending letters abroad by airmail at a cheap postage rate, but not suitable for enclosures.

Airmail letters/cards/parcels A means of sending letters, cards and parcels abroad by airmail to most destinations. A blue airmail label must accompany each of these.

All-up Letters and cards for Europe go by air or surface mail, whichever is the quicker.

Bulk rebate service A service in which rebates are given for bulk mailing of second-class letters in excess of 4250.

Business reply A method which allows a person to receive first- and second-class cards or letters from correspondents without putting them to the expense of paying postage.

Cash on delivery The method for collecting cash from the addressee on delivery of a package.

Compensation fee parcel A parcel service which provides compensation if lost or damaged.

Datapost inland A service guaranteeing next-day delivery of a package by courier.

Datapost international A service for the speedy delivery by courier of parcels and letters abroad.
First-class letter contracts An agreement which allows discounts when posting 5000 or more first-class letters at any one time, presorted by post towns.
First-class letters/cards For urgent mail. It will normally be delivered on the first working day after collection.
Freepost Enables a person to receive replies by first- or second-class post from correspondents without putting them to the expense of paying postage. They are required to quote a special Freepost address.
Household delivery service A service for the delivery of unaddressed material on a door-to-door basis.
Intelpost A method of sending documents by facsimile telegraphy between post offices.
Late posting facility A facility providing posting boxes on mail trains for the acceptance of late mail.
Newspapers A special service which enables publications registered as newspapers to be given first-class service at cheaper rates of postage.
Overseas printed papers A means of sending printed papers abroad by airmail or surface mail at reduced rates of postage.
Overseas small packets A means of transmitting goods, including trade samples, whether dutiable or not, in the same mail as printed papers, which normally travel quicker than parcel mails.
Parcels A means of transmitting articles up to a maximum weight of 25 kg.
Postage forward parcels A means by which a person can receive parcels from correspondents without being put to the expense of paying postage.
Poste restante A facility allowing letters and parcels addressed to a post office to be collected by a person without a fixed address.
Private boxes Private boxes which may be rented at a normal delivery post office for the reception of postal packets to be collected by the users as an alternative to delivery by postmen.
Recorded delivery A service for the correspondent who requires not only proof of posting but, if necessary, proof of delivery.
Registered letters A means of sending articles of value and providing for compensation if lost.
Reply coupons A method used internationally for prepaying replies from correspondents. Reply coupons are exchangeable for postage stamps at post offices abroad.
Second-class discount service A service which allows a discount when posting 5000 or more second-class letters at any one time, presorted by post towns.
Second-class letters/cards A cheaper service for letters/cards which will normally be delivered up to the third working day after collection.

Selectapost A service in which the post office arranges to sort mail into specified categories before it is delivered.
Special delivery A service for special priority next-day delivery of letters.
Super service A 48-hour guaranteed parcel delivery service for business users.
Swiftair A special high-speed overseas letter post which delivers airmail letters earlier than those sent by ordinary airmail or the all-up service.

Reference sources

Post Office Guide and *Supplements*
A Comprehensive Guide: International Letter Rates
A Comprehensive Guide: UK Letter Rates
Royal Mail International Parcels: Compendium of prices

Press relations

In many organisations it is normal for a public relations manager to be responsible for dealing with the press but there are occasions, particularly when the senior executive is away from the office, when a secretary will be called upon to deal with telephone calls or callers from the press, radio or television. Unless the secretary is authorised to speak to reporters on behalf of the organisation, a tactful and discreet approach must be adopted for explaining the absence of the executive without making any observations on the subject of the enquiry. If there is no public relations manager to whom the enquiry could be directed, the secretary should:

- be friendly and co-operative
- be careful to avoid divulging any information which is secret or confidential
- note the enquirer's name, telephone number, name of newspaper, radio or television studio and details of the subject of the enquiry
- if appropriate, arrange an interview with the executive allowing time for them to prepare a response.

Effective press relations can help to promote good public relations and it is normally in the best interests of a business organisation to supply the press with news, pictures and background information in a form which is acceptable to them and while it is still news.

A press release is the normal channel for encouraging the

media to publicise the activities of a business. When preparing press releases, particular care should be taken that:

- the heading is clear and indicates what the story is about
- the subject is conveyed within the first three words and preferably in the first
- the opening paragraph summarises the main points of the whole story
- facts are accurate and presented logically
- style, content, vocabulary and length are appropriate for the publication chosen
- supporting photographs, diagrams, etc, are included with the press release
- the final paragraph gives the name and address of the organisation
- the deadline set for receipt of copy is met
- the press release has the name and telephone number of the author and is dated

A press release may be sent by post to the media or it may be given to visiting reporters at a press conference which might be organised at the firm's premises or at a local hotel.

Printing

Preparation and correction of printed matter

Key factors when typing matter to be printed:

- Type on one side of the paper only, with double spacing and with a two-inch margin at the left-hand side of each sheet.
- Number the pages consecutively.
- Type footnotes immediately following the line containing the reference.
- Use headings within chapters to break up the text into convenient sections. Where more than one type of heading is used, their relative importance should be clearly indicated, eg section heading, subheading, sub-subheading, etc, so that these variations may be interpreted typographically with the correct emphasis.
- Any photographs or drawings should be kept separate from the text but their position clearly indicated in the text.
- When sending 'copy' for printing, state your requirements, such as type sizes, quality of paper, colour, size and the quantity required, etc.
- The printer supplies a set of proofs before he carries out the

No	Correction	Sign in margin	Sign in text
1	Insert full stop	⊙	⋏
2	Insert colon	(:)	⋏
3	Insert comma	,/	⋏
4	Insert semi-colon	;/	⋏
5	Insert question mark	?/	⋏
6	Insert exclamation mark	!/	⋏
7	Insert apostrophe	' 7	⋏
8	Insert quotation marks	" 7 " 7	⋏ ⋏
9	Insert hyphen	|-|	⋏
10	Insert dash	/-/	⋏
11	Insert brackets	(/)/	⋏ ⋏
12	Insert square brackets	[/]/	⋏ ⋏
13	Use capital letters	Caps	≡
14	Use small capital letters	SC	=
15	Underline word(s)	Underline	—
16	Insert word(s)	Words to be inserted /	⋏
17	Use italics	ital	—
18	Use Roman type	Rom	encircle word(s)
19	Use bold type	Bold	~~~
20	Use lower case letters	l c	encircle letter(s)
21	Transpose words or letters	trs	⌴⌐
22	Delete	ꝺ	Word(s) or Letter (s) crossed out
23	To remain as it was before correction	Stet	--------- under word(s) to remain
24	Space required	#	⋏
25	Equalise the spacing	eq #	⋏
26	Close up the space	⁐	⁐
27	Start a new paragraph	NP	[
28	Continue without a new paragraph	Run on	⟵⟶
29	Improve damaged character	×	encircle character
30	Wrong fount	W.f.	encircle character
31	Letter upside down	9	encircle character
32	Move to the left	⊐	⊐
33	Move to the right	⊏	⊏
34	Place in the centre	Centre	⌐¬ indicating position
35	Raise line	Raise	⊥
36	Lower line	Lower	⊤
37	Straighten margin	‖	▌
38	Passage omitted	Out see copy	⋏
39	Remove printer's space	⊥	encircle space
40	Abbreviation or figure to be printed in full	Spell out	encircle words or figures

Printers' correction signs

actual printing. No major alterations should be carried out on the proof. This will involve the printer in a considerable amount of work and, of course, the cost will be increased.

Key factors when checking proofs:

- Check the proof very carefully with the 'copy'.
- Mark the proof clearly with the correct signs – a table giving the usual printers' correction signs is given above.
- Mark every error in the margin and in the text itself.
- On a second copy, repeat all the correction marks made on the first. This copy should be retained for reference purposes.
- If a second proof is required, mark the corrected proof 'Revise'. If the first proof is quite satisfactory and no further

proofs are required, mark it 'Press' or 'Press after correction' (where minor corrections have been made).

The following is a printer's proof with a selection of the correction signs given in the previous table. The numbers refer to the signs given in the table. A full list of printers' correction signs is given in *Printers' Correction Signs* (BS 5261: 1975/1976).

Fulbridge Manufacturing Company Limited

The 10th Ord. Gen. Meeting of Fulbridge Manufacturing Company Limited was held recently in Bristol. Mr. Hugh Watkins the Chairman presided and, in the course of his speech, said It is pleasing for the Directors to be able once again to report record trading profits these, I may say have been achieved under the most difficult circumstances when prices of raw materials have shown marked changes from time to time, and when the prices of some metals which we have to buy in very largequantities have increased considerably. This striving after the highest possible production has been the companys regular policy. At the present time we are proud to say we have not passed on any increases to our customers since the last general increase took place nearly four years ago.

I am sorry to say that the prices of ~~all our~~ new commodities are still rising, the demands of all branches of labour for higher wages are increasing, and if these movements continue we shall, of course, sooner or later be compelled to pass on some part of these increased costs.

The financial position of the company is I think you will agree very strong. Adequate stocks of materials are available and we are making steady progress towards improving the position of our deliveries.

Perhaps our greatest difficulty has been to obtain sufficient labour for our requirements, and to meet this position we have spent large sums on the provision of mechanized new equipment and also on the improved ~~production~~ methods in each of our factories, and we are now benefiting from these changes.

You will also be pleased to know that your New Zealand Branch has shown remarkable progress during this year.

A printer's proof with corrections marked

Desk-top publishing

See p 123.

Professional associations for secretaries

Association of Legal Secretaries
Address: 46 Orchard Way, Woodhatch, Reigate, Surrey
Publication: *Legal Secretary*

Association of Medical Secretaries, Practice Administrators and Receptionists Limited
Address: Tavistock House North, Tavistock Square, London WC1H 9LN
Publication: *AMSPAR Magazine*

Association of Personal Assistants and Secretaries Ltd
Address: 14 Victoria Terrace, Leamington Spa, Warwickshire
Publication: *Secretary*

European Association of Professional Secretaries
Address: 43 Upper Grosvenor Street, London W1X 9PG
Publication: *EAPS Brief*

Institute of Agricultural Secretaries
Address: NAC, Stoneleigh, Kenilworth, Warwickshire CV8 2LZ
Publication: *Newsletter and Bulletin*

Institute of Qualified Private Secretaries Ltd
Address: 126 Farnham Road, Slough, Bucks SL1 4XA
Publication: *Career Secretary*

Public relations

Although only large organisations will normally employ a public relations officer or use the services of a public relations agency, no organisation can ignore the need to establish good relationships with the public, as well as with those associated with the organisation.

A secretary can influence public relations in the following ways:

- receiving visitors in a friendly and efficient manner (*see* p 139)
- being courteous and helpful with telephone callers (*see* p 154)
- paying attention to neatness, style and tone in the preparation of correspondence and replying promptly to letters received
- taking a pride in personal appearance
- keeping a tidy and well-organised office
- maintaining good communications both within and outside the organisation through house magazines, press reports, broadcasts, etc

- being punctual for appointments and meetings, and efficient in making arrangements for them
- establishing good relationships with employees and organising social events for them
- cultivating and maintaining friendly contacts with local organisations involving traders and the community in general.

Qualifications for secretaries

The chief examining bodies offering private secretarial examinations, ie the Business and Technician Education Council, the London Chamber of Commerce, Pitman Examinations Institute and the Royal Society of Arts, all recognise the need for private secretaries not only to be highly skilled in shorthand-typewriting and information processing, but to have a sound knowledge and understanding of business and secretarial subjects. A brief description follows of each of the examinations suitable for secretaries. Students who wish to progress to senior positions should seek to qualify at the highest level.

Business and Technician Education Council

The Business and Technician Education Council (BTEC), which administers business education in England and Wales (and SCOTVEC for Scotland), recognises the need for a national system of awards which reflect levels of attainment of secretarial skills within the context of a broad business education. Those gaining BTEC awards should be potentially employable in positions involving a greater degree of initiative and responsibility than the mere exercise of typing and shorthand skills.

At national level, ie for those with at least four GCSE qualifications or equivalent, the two-year course for secretarial students may contain the following units:

Year 1	*Year 2*
People in organisations	People in organisations
Finance	Accounting
Organisation in its environment	Organisation in its environment
Secretarial skills (double unit)	Secretarial skills (double unit)
Optional business study, eg information processing	Optional business study, eg business law

By means of the BTEC national-level course, secretarial students should acquire the necessary educational base for a range of careers in business, providing the student not only with the necessary secretarial skills but, if desired, a means to branch out into other business careers. Similar courses are offered at the higher national levels for students with the national qualification or GCE 'A' levels.

For further details write to: The Business and Technician Education Council, Central House, Upper Woburn Place, London WC1H 0HH.

The London Chamber of Commerce

The London Chamber of Commerce offers three levels of grouped secretarial examinations, as follows:

Secretarial Studies Certificate This examination is intended for those who wish to seek employment as junior secretaries and shorthand-typists. The examinations consist of: Communication; Background to business; Office procedures; Shorthand and/or Audio transcription (a recording).

Private Secretary's Certificate This examination is intended for those who wish to seek employment as private secretaries to middle management. The examinations consist of: Communication; Office organisation and secretarial procedures; Structure of business; Shorthand and/or Audio transcription (a recording); and an Interview.

Private and Executive Secretary's Diploma This examination is set at a higher level than the certificate examination and it is intended for senior private secretaries wishing to be employed by top-level management and capable of holding a senior appointment in connection with the secretarial or information-based aspects of management. The examination consists of six sections: Communication; Secretarial administration; Management appreciation; Meetings (a video recording); Shorthand transcription or Audio transcription (a recording); and an Interview. The examiners set out to assess high-level secretarial skill, common sense, tact, poise, experience and efficiency – all indispensable for success as a private secretary.

Information processing is an optional component in all grouped awards.

For further details write to: The London Chamber of Commerce Examinations Board, Marlowe House, Station Road, Sidcup, Kent DA15 7BJ.

Pitman Examinations Institute

Pitman Examinations Institute offers a range of examinations which are appropriate for shorthand-typists and secretaries, including the following:

Secretarial Practice Examinations These are single-subject examinations which, at the intermediate level, assess candidates for higher secretarial positions and, at the advanced level, assess their knowledge and aptitude for secretarial posts that carry an executive responsibility.
Secretarial Group Certificates These are awards recognising all-round secretarial efficiency and, at the higher level, supervisory potential. Five secretarial-related subjects are examined, including the secretarial practice subjects referred to above.

For further details write to: Pitman Examinations Institute, Godalming, Surrey GU7 1UU.

Royal Society of Arts

The Royal Society of Arts offers a series of single-subject examinations as well as a grouped certificate, as follows:
Diploma for Personal Assistants This is a senior secretarial qualification for personal assistants with the following aim: to provide a suitable background of knowledge and skills, and to encourage the development of self-confidence and initiative, to enable the student, in due course, to play a responsible role in an administrative environment.

The examinations are arranged under two main headings:

Administration	*Communication*
Economic and financial aspects	Written
Legal aspects	Office skills applied (a recording)
Personnel and functional aspects	Oral

Secretarial Duties Stage II This is a single-subject examination with the aim of assessing knowledge of secretarial duties and the ability to apply this knowledge at the level of a potential secretary.

For further details write to: Royal Society of Arts (Publications), Murray Road, Orpington, Kent BR5 3RB.

Books for secretarial and business studies students

By the same author:

Office Procedures and *Practical Office Procedures*	elementary clerical studies
Secretarial Duties	intermediate secretarial studies
Secretarial Case Studies	advanced secretarial studies
People in Organisations	BTEC national administrative studies

Available in all good bookshops and from
Pitman Publishing, 128 Long Acre, London WC2E 9AN.

Reception

Visitors gain their first impressions of an organisation when they are received by the receptionist or secretary. It is important to create a favourable first impression and this can be done when:

- The reception office is tastefully furnished and tidy. Decorative plants enhance the appearance of an office.
- The receptionist or secretary is pleasant, polite, helpful, smart and well spoken.
- The visitor is made welcome and well looked after, eg:
  1 invite them to sit in an easy chair while waiting
  2 supply them with an appropriate newspaper/journal to read
  3 if there is a delay, apologise and offer a cup of coffee or tea and keep them fully informed of the situation
- A record is kept of callers expected and callers received (a register of callers or visitors' book will normally be compiled – *see* below).
- The visitor is introduced correctly to the firm's representative by announcing their name, title and company clearly. Give the visitor's name before the name of your firm's representative, but when introducing a man and a woman, it is courteous to announce the woman's name first.
- The receptionist uses the visitor's name during conversation with them. The efficient receptionist or secretary will know by name the visitors who call regularly.
- The receptionist is tactful and helpful when a visitor (without

Date	*Name of caller*	*Organisation*	*Time of arrival*	*Referred to*
19--				
Feb 1	P R Francis	Barker Bros	0930	J Smith
" 1	K Clarke	Cannock College of FE	0945	R Payne
" 1	Dr T Berner	Werner & Wildt	1015	G R Docherty

A register of callers

an appointment) cannot see the person requested. In such cases, arrangements are made for the visitor to see someone else or another appointment is arranged on a mutually agreed date.

- The receptionist has a thorough knowledge of the organisation, its activities and personnel, and can supply information to visitors without having to consult others.
- Full information is immediately available concerning the organisation, as well as local hotels, train/air services, telephone numbers, etc.

Reports

Always aim to present facts accurately, clearly, concisely and in a logical order. If the report is a personal one between two persons, ie from the secretary to the personnel manager, it should be written in the first person. If it is of a meeting, it should be written wholly in the third person. A report of an event or a meeting should always be written in the past tense.

Before writing a report, prepare a plan and group the facts or ideas in a logical sequence, as follows:

1 The heading or title containing:
   - the subject of the report, eg the type of meeting
   - the date of the meeting or event
   - the place
   - if a meeting, those present – identifying the chairman and officers
   - a file reference number for future identification
   - the name of the person to whom the report is sent
   - any security classification, eg confidential or secret

2 The opening paragraph, which should state the terms of reference or the circumstances which called for the report, eg the personnel manager's memo, or changing circumstances which called for the discussion of future policy.

3 The body of the report containing the facts of the case or the major points discussed at a meeting. Use subheadings to divide the main topics.

4 Recommendations or conclusions.

5 State the action necessary to carry out the recommendations, including:
   - the names of the persons who should take the action
   - the date by which the action should be taken
   - the date of the next meeting to review the situation

6 The name and description of the signatory (unless this is incorporated in the heading).

Safety and accident prevention in the office

Safety and accident prevention is the concern and responsibility of us all. *See* the duties of employees required by the Health and Safety at Work Act 1974 on p 98.

Office layout and organisation

- Plan your office layout to reduce the danger of accidents caused by poorly sited furniture and equipment or obstructions in gangways or corridors.
- Avoid opening a heavy top drawer of a vertical filing cabinet because the whole cabinet is liable to topple over. It is advisable to open the bottom drawer before the top drawer to serve as a prop and lessen the risk. Load all the drawers evenly and, if possible, avoid placing heavy files in the top one. This danger is not present in modern cabinets as only one drawer can be opened at any one time.
- Do not stand on a swivel chair to reach a file or other object placed in a high position: use a secure step-ladder.
- Avoid putting portable heaters where they might cause an obstruction or a fire.

Use of equipment

- Handle equipment as instructed and switch off machines and remove plugs when not in use.
- Avoid having a trailing flex from a socket to a machine which can be a hazard for the operator and passers-by.
- Regular care and maintenance of equipment is necessary. If a machine does not work properly, do not tamper with electrical parts but call a mechanic.
- Report to your supervisor, without delay, any faults in equipment or frayed flexes.
- Check that dangerous parts of machinery are fitted with guards, especially paper-cutting machines, and that the correct operating procedures are used.
- Make sure that equipment is placed securely on desks and tables.

Fire precautions

- Make sure that you and your colleagues know what to do should a fire break out, eg how to raise the fire alarm; how to use fire-fighting equipment if required to do so; and which escape route and assembly point to use.
- Keep fire doors closed when not in use.
- Do not smoke in any part of the building where there is a risk of fire. When in the office, make sure that smokers use ash-trays and not the waste-paper bin or floor.
- Many of the correcting and cleaning fluids give off a highly inflammable vapour. After use, immediately replace the stopper. Make sure that inflammable materials are locked away in a well-ventilated store room when not in use.
- Insist that combustible materials such as papers and envelopes are placed in waste bins and that they are removed regularly for disposal.

First aid

Make sure that you know who the first aider is in your organisation and the position of the first aid cabinet or sick room (*see also* pp 63–66).

BE CONSCIOUS OF SAFETY AT ALL TIMES!

Publications on safety

Is my Office Safe? A handbook for supervisors, HMSO.

Health and Safety at Work etc Act 1974. Advice to Employees, Health and Safety Commission.

Various publications from The British Safety Council, National Safety Centre, Chancellor's Road, London W6 9RS, and The Fire Protection Association, Aldermary House, Queen Street, London EC4N 1TJ.

AIDS

AIDS (Acquired Immune Deficiency Syndrome) is a new and serious public health hazard throughout the world. At present it is important to prevent any further spread of infection by ensuring that people know how it is transmitted. Information on this is given in the booklet, *AIDS and Employment*, prepared by the Department of Employment and the Health and Safety Executive and obtainable from: AIDS and Employment, The Mailing House, Leeland Road, London W13 9HL. The booklet sets out the facts and explains the employment implications; general guidance on the legal obligations and responsibilities of employers; employees' rights and sources of further information on the subject.

Harassment in the office

In the event of mental or sexual harassment in the office, staff are advised to discuss the problem in a confidential interview with a member of their personnel department, but further help and information can be sought from:

The Equal Opportunities Commission, Overseas House, Quay Street, Manchester M3 3HN (Telephone: 061 833 9244)

Rights of Women, 52–54 Featherstone Street, London EC1Y 8R (Telephone: 01 251 6575)

Women Against Sexual Harassment, 242 Pentonville Road, London N1 (Telephone: 01 833 0222)

Security

The following are the key factors involved in safeguarding confidential information, cash, property and people's lives.

Confidentiality of information

- Make sure that records containing confidential information are housed in locked filing cabinets or cupboards when not in use.
- Precautions must be taken to safeguard computerised data against loss or corruption. This may be done by keeping 'back-up' duplicate copies of disks. Also, the staff authorised to use the computer can use personal passwords (changed at regular intervals) to access it and codes, only known to the users, can be used for document files. (*See* Data Protection Act 1984 on p 50.)
- Confidential information recorded on tapes and disks for use on dictating machines, word processors and computers should receive the same security treatment as documents.
- Take special care of the carbon paper and carbon ribbons used when typing confidential documents as it is possible to detect information from them.
- Mark confidential documents and envelopes clearly to indicate their security category.
- Burn or destroy with a shredder any secret or confidential documents that are no longer required.
- If you are asked for confidential information by an unauthorised person, tactfully evade the question and suggest that enquiries should be made elsewhere.

- If you have to reproduce confidential documents on a duplicator or copier, supervise the work yourself so that the contents are not seen by others.

Cash handling

- Keep cash and other valuables locked in a safe.
- Arrange for money to be paid into a bank as soon as possible after receipt to avoid holding large sums of money in the office.
- Large sums of money should be transported to and from the bank by a security agency. However, if this is undertaken by your staff, two people should go using specially designed cash-carrying cases.
- Spot checks should be made regularly on any transactions involving the transfer of money.

Access to buildings

The following is a list of the common methods used to control access to buildings by staff and visitors:

- Locking doors to offices with central control of keys.
- Visitors' book.
- Identity passes. Magnetic or infra-red coded cards are used by staff in some organisations to gain entry to buildings where security is essential.
- Coded electronic cards incorporating pre-programmed number combinations or computerised cards can be used to operate door locks, allowing only authorised personnel to enter premises.
- Large firms employ security officers to control the admission of visitors and maintenance staff.
- Closed-circuit television for observation of buildings.
- A broadcasting system used for staff announcements and personnel location during the day can be reversed at night to perform a sound-detection system.

Bomb scares

Postal packages

If you receive a suspicious package in the post, eg of an unusual shape or size, with wires attached to it, or with grease marks on the cover,

Do not:

- attempt to open it or allow anyone else to handle it
- put it in sand or water or in a container
- press or prod it in any way

But do:

- handle the package gently, placing it on a flat surface above floor level and away from a corner of the office

- leave the office as soon as possible, lock the door and hold on to the key for use by the police when they arrive
- inform your security or safety officer and the police (dial 999) immediately
- keep the entrance to the office clear of people

Telephone calls

If you receive a telephone call stating that a bomb has been planted on the premises, you should try to get as much information as possible from the caller, such as:
- location of the bomb
- time it is expected to go off
- any circumstances concerning the motive for the bomb
- identity of the caller

Make as many notes as possible of the conversation and try to detect the nationality and any accent of the informer. Immediately after the call:

a inform your security or safety officer and the police (dial 999)

b assist the security or safety officer to take the necessary precautions until the police arrive to take charge of the situation.

Manufacturers of security equipment and devices

Alpha Industries Ltd, 234–262 Maybank Road, South Woodford, London E18 1ET

C W Cave & Tab Ltd, 5 Tenter Road, Moulton Park, Northampton NN3 1PZ

Chubb Security Installations Ltd, Ronald Close, Kempston, Bedford MK42 7SH

Envopak Group Ltd, Planmail House, Sidcup, Kent DA14 5EF

Mailtronic Ltd, 19 Peerglow Industrial Estate, Olds Approach, Watford, Herts WD1 8SR

Unisys Ltd, Stonebridge Park, London NW10 8LS.

Seeking and starting a new job

Sources

To find out information about job vacancies, consult:

Careers offices

Job centres

Staffing agencies

Newspapers
Firm's notice board or staff bulletin for internal vacancies

Applying for a vacancy

Great care should be taken in preparing the letter of application for a post so that the prospective employer will be favourably impressed. When writing your letter, bear in mind the following points:

- Write the letter in your best handwriting, unless a typed letter has been specially requested.
- The letter should be neat, free from grammatical or punctuation errors, and businesslike (*see* Correspondence, p 41).
- The source of the advertisement should be referred to, eg if it appeared in the *Southern Evening Echo*, write 'In reply to your advertisement in yesterday's Southern Evening Echo . . .'
- Plan the letter carefully, covering all the essential points asked for and explain why the job appeals to you in the further particulars.
- The salutation should normally be 'Dear Sir' or 'Dear Madam' and the complimentary close 'Yours faithfully'.
- It is usual to attach a curriculum vitae supplying the following details:
- *a* full name, address and telephone number
  b date of birth
  c education
  d examination successes (include grades with GCSE results)
  e additional training and qualifications for the post
  f present employment and previous experience of office work
  g hobbies and interests
  h names and addresses of persons to whom reference may be made
- If you receive a letter inviting you to attend for interview, reply by return of post confirming that you will be pleased to attend at the stated time.

The interview

When attending an interview:

Do	*Do not*
• Be prepared by finding out as much as possible about the organisation and the vacancy you hope to fill, ie read the job description carefully, if one has been supplied.	• Waste the interviewer's time by attending when you have no intention of accepting.

- Pay particular attention to your appearance, ie clothes, hair etc are smart and tidy.
- Be punctual, demonstrating your ability to be well organised.
- Bring with you any documents, writing materials, etc, which were requested in the letter.
- Be perfectly natural and speak clearly and deliberately.
- Be pleasant – a smile always creates a favourable impression.
- Make the most of the subjects which you have experience or knowledge of.
- Be perfectly honest about your capabilities and achievements, drawing attention to any which support your application.
- Show that you are interested and enthusiastic by your attitude to the questions asked.
- If you are given a typing test concentrate on accuracy rather than speed.
- Listen carefully to the questions you are asked, think before you speak and try not to lose your concentration.

- Wear clothes which are not usually worn in an office.
- Rush the journey so that you arrive agitated and ill-prepared to answer questions calmly.
- Bring your raincoat, umbrella, etc, into the interview room – leave them outside in the waiting room.
- Sit down in the interview room until you are invited to do so.
- Be afraid to look at the interviewer.
- Discuss irrelevancies, departing from the point of a question.
- Question the interviewer, but be prepared to ask questions if you are invited to do so. You may wish to have more information about job prospects, salary, terms of employment, etc.
- Fiddle with your handkerchief, handbag, etc, while you are being interviewed – it can distract and annoy the interviewer.
- Be defensive and negative.
- Irritate the interviewer with nervous laughter.

Accepting an offer of employment

If you receive a letter offering you a job, it is important to reply as soon as possible informing the employer of your acceptance or rejection. If you are accepting the offer, confirm that you will begin on the date suggested.

Starting the new job

Adequate and thorough preparation for a new post is essential if you are to get off to a good start, eg:

- Be punctual – plan the necessary travel arrangements so that you are familiar with the route to your new employment.
- Make sure that you have your income tax form P45 and any other documents requested, such as birth certificate or medical certificate.
- When you start, enquire about the firm's style of display for correspondence and your boss's personal preferences.
- Be pleasant, helpful and cheerful – no one wants to work with a misery!
- If you require additional skills or updating in new technology, agree to attend training courses.
- Get to know as quickly as possible people's names and their positions in the firm; the location and function of offices/departments and the special requirements of your job. Most firms organise an induction course for new staff and this will help you to acquire essential information about the firm and your place in it.
- Note the duties placed upon you by the Health and Safety at Work Act (*see* p 98).
- Within 13 weeks of beginning your job you should be given a written contract of employment (*see* p 100).
- Now that you've got the job, do everything possible to make it a success.

Stationery

The following are examples of some common uses for the different sizes of paper:

A3 – legal documents
balance sheets and financial statements

A4 – business letters, reports, minutes, agenda, specifications, bills of quantities, estimates, quotations, invoices

A5 – short letters, memos, invoices (small), credit notes, statements

A6 – post cards, index cards, requisitions, petty cash vouchers, compliment slips

A7 – business visiting cards, labels

Paper quantities

Quire = 25 sheets (formerly 24)
Ream = 500 sheets (formerly 480)

International paper sizes

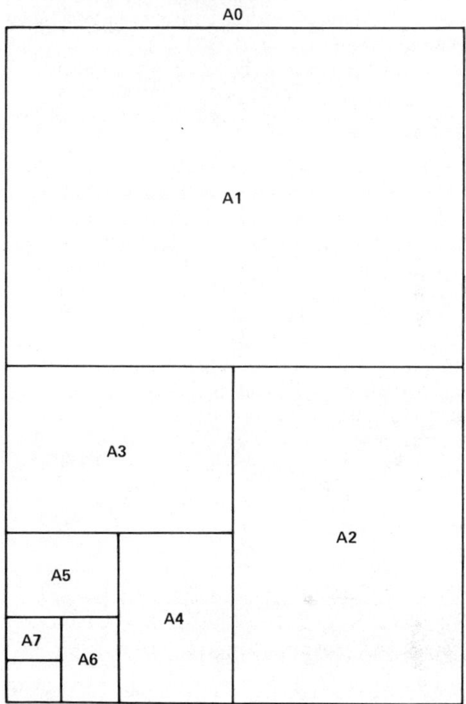

Sizes

A0 = 841 mm × 1189 mm	A4 = 210 mm × 297 mm
A1 = 594 mm × 841 mm	A5 = 148 mm × 210 mm
A2 = 420 mm × 594 mm	A6 = 105 mm × 148 mm
A3 = 297 mm × 420 mm	A7 = 74 mm × 105 mm

Types of paper

Bond – a good quality paper used for headed paper and 'top-copy' work

Bank (flimsy) – a cheaper and lighter grade used for carbon copies and sets of forms

Airmail	– very thin (lightweight) paper for correspondence sent by airmail
Duplicating	– semi-absorbent paper used for stencil duplicating or non-absorbent paper used for offset-litho duplicating
NCR (no carbon required) Carbon-free	– copying paper used for sets of forms such as invoices, delivery notes, etc (*see also* p 151)

International envelope sizes

C3	324 mm × 458 mm		
C4	229 mm × 324 mm	B4	250 mm × 353 mm
C5	162 mm × 229 mm	B5	176 mm × 250 mm
C6*	114 mm × 162 mm	B6/C4	125 mm × 324 mm
C5/6 (DL)*	110 mm × 220 mm	B6	125 mm × 176 mm
C7/6	81 mm × 162 mm		
C7	81 mm × 114 mm		

* Within the POP range (see below).

Examples of common uses for the different sizes of envelope:

Envelope	*Paper unfolded*	*Paper folded once*	*Paper folded twice*
C3	A3	A2	A1
C4 or B4	A4	A3	A2
C5 or B5	A5	A4	A3
C6 or B6 or C5/6	A6	A5	A4
C7/6			A5

Post Office Preferred (POP) envelopes

The Post Office has the power to state that, in future, only the Post Office Preferred range of envelopes and cards will be accepted for the lowest postage rates. To fall within the preferred range, envelopes and cards should be at least 90 mm × 140 mm and not larger than 120 mm × 235 mm.

Types of envelopes

Banker – the opening is on the longer side.

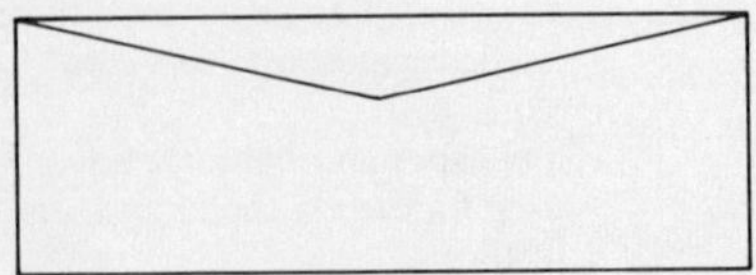

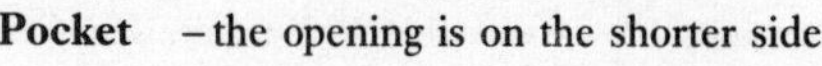

Pocket – the opening is on the shorter side

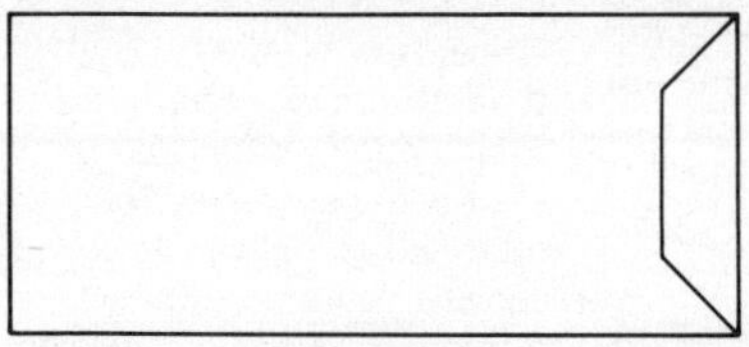

Window – contains a transparent 'window' opening, so the name and address do not need to be typed on the envelope

Aperture – as above, but with an uncovered address panel

Carbon paper

Several copies can be made of one document with the aid of carbon paper. Typewriter carbon papers are manufactured in a number of grades, colours and sizes.

Sets of forms such as those used for invoices or orders may be interleaved with sheets of 'one-time' carbon paper. This carbon paper is inexpensive and is intended for use once only. It is supplied and fixed in position by the manufacturer and is quick and easy to use.

Forms are sometimes supplied with a carbon backing which takes the place of separate carbon paper. When the top copy of the form is completed, one or two copies are automatically produced below it.

NCR (no carbon required) paper may also be used for forms as an alternative to using carbon paper or carbon-backed paper. The reverse side of the top copy and the top sides of the sheets below are specially treated with chemical to allow copies to be made without carbon paper. When an impression is made on the top copy it causes the chemically treated surfaces of the paper to reproduce the impressions on the copies beneath.

Carbon-free copying paper may also be used for letters and memos. In a two-part set of carbon-free copying paper the top copy has an emulsion coating of dye on the back and the top of the second sheet is coated with a clay material. When pressure is applied by writing or typing on the top sheet, the coating of dye penetrates the clay surface of the second sheet and a blue copy is formed. When more than one copy is required, intermediate sheets are inserted which have the clay coating on top and the dye coating at the back. More copies can be obtained with this type of paper than with normal carbon paper as fewer sheets are required. The copies produced are permanent, even under exposure to direct sunlight.

Suppliers of stationery

For further details about office forms and stationery refer to the *Yellow Pages* and the firms listed on p 22.

Stress and how to avoid it

Stress is a major problem in business today, largely resulting from the changing nature of the business world with its pressures on staff at all levels to cut costs and achieve higher productivity with smaller workforces. The pressures which bring about stress are, however, counter-productive and costly to an organisation as they generate high absenteeism as a result of illness, high labour turnover, poor quality of work, accidents, unsatisfactory industrial relations and apathy.

Stress in secretaries can be caused by:

- too much or too little work
- too much direction or a lack of direction by management
- too many or too few decisions to make
- a fear of making mistakes or wrong decisions
- time pressures and the fear of not being able to meet deadlines
- an inability to cope with change, eg new technology
- competition from other secretaries and a lack of job security
- the relationship with subordinates (assistant secretaries) and an inability to delegate work to them
- frustration at having reached one's career ceiling causing mid-career apathy
- personal problems involving health, family and financial matters

Tips for surviving stress

Work routine

- Prioritise your work: at the beginning of each day decide which tasks must be done and make them your top priority. Leave the less important non-urgent tasks for another day.
- Use your time wisely: eg read the instructions for a job carefully so that you do it correctly first time, thereby avoiding repeats.
- Prevent the frustration of searching endlessly for a missing document/file by carefully monitoring the movement of papers and files.
- Write important information down at the time it is given to

you: it is fatal to rely on your memory when you have to handle so much information.

- Keep the telephone numbers and addresses you use regularly up to date and easily accessible, making the fullest use of computerised systems.

Personal relationships

- Establish a good working relationship with your boss so that you are able to discuss with him/her your work and any problems or frustrations associated with it.
- Secure the fullest co-operation and interest of your subordinates in the secretarial service you provide, involving them in some of the decisions you have to make and delegating work to them appropriately.
- Communicate effectively with other secretaries in your organisation to create a happy and trouble-free environment.
- A flexitime working day will help to ease the pressures so that you can plan your time of arrival and departure to fit in with your home commitments and family relationships.

Attitudes

- Be prepared for new challenges throughout your career: be receptive to new ideas, new technology and new career opportunities.
- Keep in view the overall objectives for your job and do not be put off course by the detail of day-to-day routine business.
- Think positively and act with confidence.
- Be your own O & M Investigator in your job – regularly question:

  WHAT is done
  WHERE is it done
  WHEN is it done
  WHO does it
  HOW is it done.
- Whenever you require additional skills or updating in new technology, agree to attend training courses.

Counselling

- Do not hesitate to seek clarification and advice from others when you are uncertain about any aspect of your job.
- If health, financial or family problems occur, do not put off talking to advisers, to prevent the matters getting out of hand.
- In turn, do your part by listening patiently to the problems of your juniors, and if requested, offer them your opinions and advice.

Telecommunications

Telephone

When answering the telephone:

- Answer promptly when the telephone rings and state your name or your firm's name.
- Do not say 'Hello' as this wastes time and does not help the caller.
- Try not to keep a caller waiting. If there is likely to be a long delay in connecting the caller, it may be better to ring him back and save his time on the telephone. This is particularly important if the call is made from a call-box telephone where the caller may not have the additional coins.
- Have a message pad and pencil at hand so that you can write down a message.
- You may have to leave the telephone for a while to make an enquiry or collect some information. If so, let the caller know how long you expect to be and ask if he would prefer you to call him back. Arrange for calls to be answered for you.
- When an incoming call has to be transferred from one extension to another, convey the caller's name and request to the new extension so that he does not have to repeat his message.
- If there is a delay before a caller can be connected, keep him informed of the action you are taking.
- If an incoming call is disconnected, replace the telephone receiver so that the person making the call can re-establish the connection as soon as possible.
- If you receive a call which is a wrong number, remember that the intrusion is not intentional and that it is probably just as irritating to the caller as it is to you. You need not apologise, but an apology made by the caller should be accepted politely.
- Always try to greet people cheerfully, even at the end of the day. If you know a caller's name, do not hesitate to use it when speaking to him.
- A caller who wishes to speak to someone who is absent should not be kept waiting but asked whether he would like to:
  a speak to someone else
  b be rung back when the person returns
  c ring again later
  d leave a message

  Whatever the answer, the caller's name, firm's name and telephone number should be noted.

When making a telephone call:

- Check the correct code and number before dialling. If you are in doubt, look it up in the telephone directory and write it down.
- After dialling the number, allow sufficient time for the call to be connected.
- If you make a mistake while dialling, replace the receiver for a short while and then start dialling again.
- When the person answers, say who you are and to whom you wish to speak and their extension number, if you know it.
- If you are connected to a wrong number, remember to apologise.
- If a number cannot be dialled, dial 100 and ask the operator to connect the call for you, stating the number required and your own telephone number.
- A telephone call should be planned in exactly the same way as a business letter. Even before dialling the number, you should have any necessary papers at hand. It is also advisable to prepare beforehand a short list of points to be discussed.

When making a telephone call abroad

- Check the correct codes and number and write them down. If you do not know these numbers you can obtain them from the appropriate international operator by dialling the number given in the international dialling section of your telephone directory.
- With International Direct Dialling (IDD) you can dial the call yourself. Dial the four groups of digits in the following order:
  a international code (010)
  b country code
  c area code
  d subscriber's number
  If you are not able to dial direct the call must be placed with the international operator (dial the number given in your telephone directory).
- Be prepared to wait up to a minute before you are connected because of the long distance involved.
- Bear in mind the time differences for each country. Note that between March and October, British Summer Time is one hour later than GMT (Greenwich Mean Time).

British Telecom telephone services

Advice of duration and charge (ADC)	– a means of finding out the cost and length of a call
Alarm calls	– a service requesting the exchange to ring you at a specified time
Credit cards	– a service allowing calls to be made from any telephone, the cost being charged to the user's account at a later date

Directory enquiries – a service for enquiring about telephone numbers

Fixed-time calls – calls booked in advance to be connected at a specified time

Freefone – a means by which customers or agents in the UK can make calls to a firm without payment by using a special Freefone name

International 8000 – a telephone service for overseas customers which enables them to dial direct to a company in the UK via a number specially allocated to the company in their own country. Calls are free of charge to the caller from most countries and cost no more than a local call from others.

Linkline 0345 – a call-forwarding service in which customers are able to make direct calls to a firm's headquarters from any part of the country for the price of a local telephone call

Linkline 0800 – a special code followed by a six-digit number allows a company to offer its callers free direct connection of telephone calls nationwide

Personal calls – a system allowing for a call to be connected only when a specified person is on the line

– a means of arranging for a call to be charged to

Timeline – a 'speaking clock' which gives the correct time throughout the day

Transferred charge calls – a means of arranging for a call to be charged to the called subscriber's account

Weatherline – a service providing local weather conditions and forecasts

Telephone equipment and facilities

Callmakers – a facility for the automatic dialling of previously selected and stored numbers

Cordless telephone – a telephone which can be operated by the user, anywhere within a prescribed distance from the base unit, eg 100 m. It works by radio transmission between the cordless handset and the base unit and the power for the handset is provided by batteries which are recharged every time you replace the handset on the base unit

Loudspeaking telephone – a facility allowing the user to make and receive calls without holding the handset. Also useful for small conferences as the people present can all hear what is said by the incoming caller and anyone at the conference can reply

Mobile telephones – a means of speedy communication with colleagues and clients when they are on the move. Two-way battery-operated radio telephones can be used to keep in touch with other people operating within a closed circuit, but the advent of cellular phones has extended the area of coverage with the setting up of 'cells', each with their own transmitter in different parts of the country.

A cellular telephone enables the user to call an ordinary telephone number or another cellular phone user. Calls can also be received from either source providing that you are in an area served by your operating network, Cellnet or Vodaphone.

There are three different types of cellular phone:

- mobile – one which is permanently installed in a motor vehicle
- portable – one which can be used in any situation and is powered by battery
- transportable – one which can be used in or out of a motor vehicle powered by a rechargeable battery

The use of a car telephone must never be allowed to distract your attention from driving. The *Highway Code* states:

1 Do not use a hand-held microphone or telephone handset while your vehicle is moving, except in an emergency.
2 You should only speak into a fixed, neck-slung or clipped-on microphone when it would not distract your attention from the road.
3 Do not stop on the hard shoulder of a motorway to answer or make a call, however urgent.

Pager – a paging device for contacting people when they are away from their offices using bleeps to alert them of a telephone call or using a two-way speech system. Message Master is a battery-operated alpha-numeric radio pager with the ability to display written messages of up to seventy characters in length. When a message is received a tone and flashing light alerts the user that a message is being conveyed. The system operates throughout most of the UK but the user can select and pay for the area required.

Switchboards – a system allowing for incoming calls to be received at a switchboard and routed through an operator to the various extensions. External calls may also be made from the switchboard although it is normal for such calls to be made from the extensions. Modern private telephone exchange switchboards, or call-connect systems as they are sometimes called, incorporate microprocessor technology and are operated electronically to provide fast and efficient communication links both within the organisation and externally. The facilities provided by digital exchanges may include:

- Internal and external calling from all terminals – internal and external calls are distinguished by different ringing signals and calls can be made with press-button speed.
- A memory stores the last number called and will reconnect the caller at the press of a button – tedious redialling of engaged numbers is eliminated.
- Repertory dialling – automatic dialling from a directory of stored 'frequently used' numbers.
- Ring back when free – an engaged extension rings the caller back when the current call is finished.
- A call can be held 'on line' while the user makes an enquiry by ringing another number or transferring the call to another extension.
- Group hunting – a call can be diverted to another extension or a group of extensions in order to leave the user undisturbed. It is still possible to make outgoing calls and any urgent calls can be returned if required.
- Telephone conferences can be arranged with several extension users.
- Selected terminals can be allowed to interrupt calls to convey urgent messages.
- Incoming calls are automatically placed in a queuing system so that the operator can answer them in order.
- When connected to recording equipment, all calls can be logged providing a printed record of numbers dialled and the extensions making the calls.
- Music on hold – music is played to callers while they wait to be connected to the required extension.
- Appointment reminders – the exchange calls when it is time to leave for an appointment.
- Call forwarding – incoming calls transferred to another venue.
- Liquid crystal display on the switchboard giving time, date, number dialled, extension called or a message from an extension.

Telephone answering machine – a device used for answering the telephone, giving callers a pre-recorded announcement and recording their message

Videophone – a device which connects the telephone to a TV monitor to enable the callers to see each other

Voice mail – a development of the telephone answering

machine using a computerised 'mail box' for recording spoken messages when staff are not available to receive calls in person. It is linked to an existing telephone system and a caller's message can be played back by dialling the voice mail number and keying in a personal code. Each extension user is allocated a box number which is usually the same as their extension number. Messages can be reviewed, deleted and, if necessary, re-recorded before being transmitted and users can be informed when a message has been cleared by the recipient. Urgent messages can receive top priority treatment by automatically being placed at the front of all other messages in the mail box. If a message is exceptionally important, the system can be requested to ring the telephone of the recipient at repeated intervals. If a person is away from his office, any messages received can be diverted to another box number. Voice mail ensures that messages are delivered quickly and accurately without the harassment of making repeated telephone calls when people are not available to receive them.

Telephone services

Emergency calls – For the FIRE, POLICE, AMBULANCE, COASTGUARD, CAVE or MOUNTAIN Rescue Services, dial 999 unless the dial label on your telephone states otherwise. It is important to remember that you are connected first to an operator, who will then put you through to the required emergency service.

When the operator answers give:

a details of the emergency service required
b your telephone number

When the emergency service answers give:

a the address where help is needed
b all other information for which you are asked.

Telemessage service – messages transmitted by telephone, public pay-phones or telex, but not delivered to post office counters. When telephoning a telemessage you are required to dial 100 (190 in London, Birmingham or Glasgow) and ask for the Telemessage Service. A 'telegram-style' typed message is then delivered by first-class post next morning. Special telemessages printed on attractively designed greetings forms may be used for special occasions.

Telex – the main teleprinter communication service in Britain, maintained by British Telecom. It provides a quick means of communication in printed form among subscribers, combining the speed of the telephone with the authority of the printed word. The printed copy of the message is produced on teleprinters at both the sending and receiving subscribers' installations. Calls may be made to any telex subscriber in the UK and to subscribers in certain countries overseas, including the USA. The service is available day and night and messages may be transmitted to a subscriber even though his teleprinter is unattended, provided it is switched on. The message is then available for attention when the operator returns to the machine.

There is a standard rental charge for the provision of the necessary equipment and for hiring the line to the telex exchange. Charges are based on the distance between the calling and called subscribers' telex centres and the duration of the calls.

Modern electronic teleprinters use microprocessors which have 'memories' so that telex messages can be stored and sent automatically at fast speeds when required. If the number called is engaged, the electronic teleprinter will make further attempts, and the same message can be sent to more than one destination. Other facilities include message editing (similar to a word processor) by which operators can insert, correct or delete parts of a message and the text can be rearranged.

The teleprinter has a visual display screen. Outgoing messages are typed into the electronic store and presented to the operator on the screen, while the teleprinter continues to receive incoming messages or transmit other outgoing messages. Copies of the messages transmitted are produced on the teleprinter's printer.

With the use of a 'mailbox' facility, telex messages can be operated directly from an electronic typewriter, word processor or computer, giving many more people access to telex communications. The messages received can be read on a VDU screen or printed out on an electronic typewriter or printer.

Fax (Facsimile telegraphy) – equipment which uses the telephone network to transmit, within a few minutes, any form of printed, typed or hand-written matter, drawings, diagrams and photographs from one location to another in this country or abroad. Replicas of documents can be sent any distance with complete accuracy by combining

	the speed of the telephone with the reproduction facility of the office copier.
Teletex	– a means of transmitting text or data directly from its source – a word processor or computer – providing a system for electronic mail without using the postal service. It is an international electronic communications network specifically designed for use with automated text-processing machines, thus eliminating the need to convert digital signals into punched-tape form. Teletex is over fifty times faster than telex, can reproduce upper- and lower-case characters and all the symbols on a standard typewriter keyboard and its printouts are identical to a 'top copy' word-processed letter. Copies can be stored electronically on disks or printed as 'hard copy' for normal filing.
Data communications (Datel)	– a British Telecom service for the transmission of digital data using the telephone network to link up terminals with a computer. Modems (which translate digital language into analogue signals for transmission by telephone and back to digital codes at the other end) and multiplexers (which monitor and adjust the communications flow to avoid bottlenecks) are used in this service to manage the flow of data.
Teleconferencing	– *see* p 40

Sources of information on telecommunications services

Telephone directories	– these list, in alphabetical order, all the telephone subscribers in a locality, together with local, national and international codes and charge rates/bands. There are about seventy telephone directories covering the whole country
Yellow Pages	– these list all business subscribers under their respective trade or profession, eg office equipment dealers, solicitors, etc
British Telecom booklets and literature	– these are obtainable from your British Telecom Area Office
British Telecom fax book	– this contains fax numbers for British Telecom fax subscribers
Telex directory	– this contains telex numbers and answerback codes for all telex subscribers

Suppliers of communications equipment

British Telecommunications plc, 81 Newgate Street, London EC1A 7AJ

Ericsson Information Systems Ltd, Swan Office Centre, 1508 Coventry Road, Yardley, Birmingham B25 8BN

Ferranti Computer Systems Ltd, Wythenshawe Division, Simonsway, Wythenshawe, Manchester M22 5LA
Mitel Telecom Ltd, Severnbridge Industrial Estate, Portskewett, Newport NP6 4YR
Panasonic Industrial UK Ltd, 280–290 Bath Road, Slough, Berks SL1 6JG
Plessey Communication Systems Ltd, Technology Drive, Beeston, Nottingham NG9 1LA

Televised information services

Videotex

Videotex is the name given to the services which provide quick access to a wide range of information through the medium of a television receiver or communicating data/word processing equipment. It is available using the television companies' teletext services or British Telecom's Viewdata service.

- Teletext: Ceefax (BBC), Oracle (ITV) and 4-TEL (C4) are computer-based information retrieval systems transmitting pages of data to television sets specially adapted for the purpose – a one-way source of information.
- Viewdata: The British Telecom Prestel Service uses the telephone network to connect the user's television receiver with the computer supplying pages of data. This is an interactive two-way service in which users can receive and send data from their homes or offices, eg placing orders for goods, making payments through a bank, reserving hotel accommodation. The *Prestel Users Guide and Directory* provides full details of the information providers and the services available.

  Private viewdata systems are used by organisations requiring specialised or restricted information. It is operated within a closed circuit for such needs as police, investments and travel. Access may be via Prestel or directly through the public telephone network.

In all systems, the page of information required is selected by means of a remote-controlled push-button handset connected to a television receiver. Information is provided on such topics as foreign and London stock market reports; share prices; foreign exchange rates; commodity prices; weather maps; train and air services; road conditions; news headlines; entertainment and sport; guides to manufacturing and service industries; marketing news; interest rates, etc.

Text processing

The main processes involved in producing and manipulating words and text are:

- Typewriting
- Word processing
- Shorthand and audio transcription

Typewriting

While many manual and electric typewriters are still in use, most secretaries and typists now use electronic typewriters. These vary according to their size of memory and the facilities provided for text editing. An important feature of the electronic typewriter is that it allows work to be viewed before it is reproduced on paper which makes correction easier. The top end of the market includes electronic typewriters with screens incorporating many of the features that are found on microcomputers. All models have the facility to make corrections and have a memory which can range from a single line of text to as many as 64 000 characters, ie approximately thirty pages of A4 typescript. The larger machines have a visual display screen to aid the typist in editing and processing text and, when a piece of work has been typed in its final form, it can either be automatically printed on paper and cleared from the memory or transferred to a floppy disk for permanent storage. These machines, with their extended memory capacities and visual displays, are sometimes referred to as word processors as they carry out similar functions.

Other features include formatting storage, ie retaining tabulation settings in the memory; automatic centring; margin justification and additional print and pitch selection, including emboldening for printing characters in bold type.

Key factors to be considered when choosing a new typewriter:

- Why does your present typewriter fail to satisfy your needs?
- What sort of work will be typed?
- What size are the documents?
- How many copies do you normally make?
- What type pitch and style are most effective for your requirements and do you need to vary these at all?
- Do you require any special characters or symbols?

- What correction facilities do you require?
- Do you type much repetitive work and use standard paragraphs?
- What type of ribbon/ribbon cartridge do you currently use in your organisation?
- Does your typewriter need to be compatible with equipment already in use?
- Do you require an interface for:
  - electronic mail;
  - telex;
  - printing?

Suppliers of typewriters and supplies

Brother Office Equipment, Shepley Street, Guide Bridge, Audenshaw, Manchester M34 5JD
Canon (UK) Ltd, Canon House, Manor Road, Wallington, Surrey SM6 0AJ
Facit Ltd, Maidstone Road, Rochester, Kent ME1 3QN
IBM United Kingdom Ltd, PO Box 41, North Harbour, Portsmouth, Hants PO6 3AU
Olympia Business Machines Co Ltd, Olympia House, 199–205 Old Marylebone Road, London NW1 5QS
Sharp Electronics (UK) Ltd, Sharp House, Thorp Road, Newton Heath, Manchester M10 9BE

Word processing

Word processors have been developed from typewriters using computer technology to automate many of the procedures involved in the production of letters, reports, forms, lists, etc, and, as a result, have freed the typist from time-consuming and repetitive tasks.

Word processing systems normally consist of five components:

- Keyboard
- VDU screen
- Central processing unit (CPU) and disk storage (internal memory)
- Printer
- Backing storage (floppy disks)

These components can be arranged or configured in a variety of ways depending on whether the system is a single unit (stand-alone word processor) or part of a shared resource or shared logic system involving several workstations. Word processors are screen-based systems, ie the operator's keyboard actions are displayed on a screen. The text can be stored on hard disks or floppy disks for subsequent amendment or printing.

Word processors are normally capable of:

- editing text on the screen by inserting new material and deleting unwanted material

- adding or deleting paragraphs
- moving words, sentences, paragraphs and columns to other parts of the page
- numbering pages automatically
- justifying margins, ie providing equal and perfectly straight left- and right-hand margins
- aligning decimals atuomatically for typing columns and tabulations
- scrolling text vertically and horizontally on the screen, ie moving the cursor through text from one position to another
- holding data in a buffer store for later use
- allowing documents to be merged or a mailing list to be merged with a circular letter
- printing one page of a document while the operator is typing the next page
- allowing a number of documents to queue for printing in turn
- underscoring, centring and indexing automatically
- verifying the spelling of words. A program with a built-in electronic dictionary of commonly-used words. It highlights any words which do not comply with the dictionary spellings and enables the typist to make any necessary corrections before printing the document

Key factors when considering the purchase of a word processing system

- Analyse the work to be undertaken and estimate the memory capacity required, bearing in mind both current and future needs. This will normally be incorporated in a feasibility study.
- Decide which configuration is required, such as:
  a stand-alone (a single self-contained word processor)
  b shared resource (two or more workstations sharing the same printer and possibly storage devices)
  c shared logic (several workstations having access to the same processor, storage devices and printer)
  d local area network (for connecting word processors, computers and telecommunications in one network)
- Decide whether to have a dedicated word processor or a microcomputer with a word processing package. A dedicated word processor is one which has been specially designed solely for word processing.
- Consider the need for compatibility with equipment already in use.
- Bear in mind the costs involved in:
  a hardware (the physical parts of the word processor)
  b software (the programs and operating manuals)
  c furniture
  d accommodation
  e materials (stationery, disks, ribbons, etc)

f training of users and authors and redeployment of staff
g maintenance of equipment and software packages

- Arrange for demonstrations of various makes and seek advice from other users of the equipment.
- Consider the changes in office procedures which must be made.
- Consult and keep staff informed of your proposals.
- Consider the advantages and disadvantages of purchasing equipment outright, leasing and rental schemes – bearing in mind obsolescence and the rapid changes in technology.

Common applications for word processors include:

a automatic typing of standard or form letters merged with a mailing list to provide top copies of letters to selected names and addresses
b updating price lists, telephone directories, mailing lists, parts lists where amendments can be inserted without retyping all of the matter
c typing the drafts of reports, minutes, articles, etc. Once the draft has been typed, the typist can make amendments and the machine automatically reformats the pages without any further retyping and checking

Correction of errors

Procedures for the correction of errors vary with the different word processing systems, but the following methods are commonly used:

- To amend a character or word discovered whilst typing the line – back-space to the error (this automatically erases all characters up to that point) and re-type the correct material
- To amend a single character after completion of a paragraph or page – position cursor under the incorrect character and key in the correct one
- To delete character(s), words or paragraphs – position cursor under the unwanted character(s) and press the delete key: the text is automatically adjusted to correct the spacing
- To add character(s) – position cursor under the character following the omission, press the insert key and key in the new character: the text is automatically adjusted in length to accommodate the new material
- To amend a group of identical characters in a text, ie a character string – carry out the procedure for global search and replace

Care of the word processor
See p 53.

Care of floppy disks
See p 54.

Trouble shooting
If the word processor does not work check that:

- the power is on
- there are no faults in the connecting cables and plugs
- the fuses are working
- you have keyed in the correct filename/command code
- you have loaded the program correctly
- the disks are inserted properly
- you have inserted the right disks
- the disks are not damaged or corrupted in any way
- the disk rotates freely in its wallet – if not, free it manually, but be careful not to touch the disk itself
- the printer is on-line and the print element is fixed securely in its position
- the paper feed mechanism is working properly, making sure that the bail and platen release levers are in their correct positions and there is no paper jammed in the machine
- you have not used up the printer ribbon
- you have sufficient memory space on a disk for your needs
- the brightness of the screen has not reduced too low so that nothing appears on the screen
- you have looked up your operating manual 'trouble shooting' section for useful tips in tracing a fault

Suppliers of word processing equipment
Amstrad plc, PO Box 462, Brentwood, Essex CM14 4EF
Dictaphone Company Ltd, Regent Square House, The Parade, Leamington Spa, Warwickshire CV32 4NL
Digital Equipment Co Ltd, Digital Park, Worton Grange, Imperial Way, Reading RG2 0TE
IBM United Kingdom Ltd, PO Box 41, North Harbour, Portsmouth, Hants PO6 3AU
Philips Business Systems, Elektra House, Bergholt Road, Colchester, Essex, CO4 5BE
Rank Xerox (UK) Ltd, Bridge House, Oxford Road, Uxbridge, Middx UB8 1HS

Shorthand

Shorthand continues to be a popular method for receiving dictation, especially at the senior executive level. Although it is accepted that this is a relatively time-consuming method, its advantage is that it allows discussion to take place and any queries and doubtful points to be settled on the spot. As a result, time can be saved which is crucial in the management of the executive's administrative duties. The secretary's notebook also provides a valuable record of the correspondence dictated and reference can easily be made to previously dictated matters.

Receiving dictation

The secretary must possess an adequate shorthand speed in order to be capable of taking down bursts of dictation at high speeds.

If the employer deletes a passage which has been dictated, the secretary must be certain to cross it out completely in the dictated notes. If a corrected passage is to be inserted, it is advisable to put a mark or number in the place where it is to go, and then, in the margin of the corrected passage, repeat the mark or number.

The secretary is justified in interrupting an employer during the dictation if a point has not been fully understood or heard; it is not advisable to guess a word or phrase, nor to be afraid to ask questions when in doubt.

The employer should not, however, be interrupted immediately the query arises, as this may cause the train of thought to be lost; instead, the secretary should wait for a suitable opportunity such as a brief pause. It is difficult to generalise on questions of relationship between employer and secretary, but in all matters the secretary must be the person to adapt to the methods preferred by the employer.

The secretary must be certain about all the correspondence dictated; eg, when in doubt about the type of salutation or complimentary close to use in a particular case, it is advisable to ask the employer before leaving the office.

Audio dictation and transcription

There are three main categories of dictation equipment:

- Central dictation network systems used by large organisations which are either connected to a telephone system or to a separately wired circuit.
- Desk-top machines.
- Portable hand-held (pocket-size) recorders.

Recording dictation

The following is a guide for the recording of dictation.

At the beginning of the dictation:

- Announce your name and department.
- Indicate any special reference to be used for your correspondence.
- Say if you wish any item to be given priority.

At the beginning of each passage:

- Assemble your facts before you start dictating.
- Indicate the document required and whether it is for internal or external use.
- Mark the index or scale to show the starting point of each passage.
- Say how many copies you require with any instructions concerning distribution.
- Quote the reference number/file number.
- Dictate the names and addresses of correspondents or refer to their names in the correspondence which will accompany the recording.
- Say if you require a variation from the normal layout of correspondence.
- Dictate the salutation.

During the course of dictation:

- Indicate paragraphing and capital letters *before* the text to which the instruction refers.
- It is advisable to dictate the full stops, question marks, colons, semi-colons, dashes, exclamation marks, brackets and quotation marks. You are not expected to dictate every comma, but you can assist the typist by the inflexions of your voice. It is also helpful if you can give special instructions, ie 'open brackets ... close brackets', in a slightly different tone from your normal voice, so that they can be recognised as instructions and not typed by mistake.
- Spell out foreign and unusual words, using the phonetic alphabet (if necessary) and pronounce difficult words slowly and clearly.
- Keep the volume of your voice as low as practicable.
- Hold the microphone fairly close to the mouth and speak directly into it.
- Do not speak too quickly or in jerks, but speak into the microphone at the speed which is used for dictating to a shorthand-typist.
- Avoid clipping words using the 'on–off' switch.

At the conclusion of each passage:

- Dictate the complimentary close.
- If there are enclosures, state the size of envelope required.
- If a correction has to be made, refer to it on the index slip.
- Mark the index or slip to show the end of the passage.

At the conclusion of the whole dictation:

- Indicate that you are signing off.

Transcribing recorded dictation

The following is a guide for transcribing recorded dictation.

- Pay attention to any special instructions and corrections accompanying the record.
- Letters required urgently by the dictators should be typed, checked and returned to them first of all.
- The size of each letter must be assessed before typing, to enable the correct size of paper to be used.
- Any doubtful points in the dictation should be checked with the dictator or another responsible member of staff.
- Consult a dictionary whenever there is any doubt about the spelling of a word.
- Insert the proper punctuation marks and allow adequate paragraphs.
- Every transcription must be accurately typed and the utmost care must be taken in checking letters, etc, before they are removed from the typewriter.
- Take great care of the transcribing machine and always cover it when not in use.

Recording medium

Tapes are normally supplied in cassettes in the following sizes:
Universal (standard) cassette – 90 min each side
Micro-cassette – 60 min each side
Mini-cassette (for use on portable machines) – 20 min each side

Suppliers of dictation and recording equipment

Dictaphone Company Ltd, Regent Square House, The Parade, Leamington Spa, Warwickshire CV32 4NL
Grundig Business Systems Ltd, Premier House, 10 Greycoat Place, Westminster, London SW1P 1SB
Olympia Business Machines Co Ltd, Olympia House, 199–205 Old Marylebone Road, London NW1 5QS
Philips Business Systems, Elektra House, Bergholt Road, Colchester, Essex CO4 5BE
Sanyo Marubeni (UK) Ltd, Sanyo House, Otterspool Way, Watford, Herts WD2 8JX
Sony (UK) Ltd, Sony House, South Street, Staines, Middx TW18 4PF

Translation and interpreter services

Facilities for translations and the hiring of interpreters may be arranged through the following:

Public libraries	– many of the larger libraries maintain registers of translators who reside in their areas and can usually supply the language and specialist subjects offered
Chambers of Commerce	
Language schools and colleges	
The Embassy or High Commission of the country concerned	– (*see* pp 68–77)
Travel agents	
Department of Trade (Export Services and Promotions Division)	– Export House, 50 Ludgate Hill, London EC4M 7HO
Institute of Linguists	– 24A Highbury Grove, London N5 2EA
Translators Association	– 84 Drayton Gardens, London SW10 9SB

Publications

Register of Translators and Translating Agencies in the UK, Merton Press

The Translators' Handbook, ASLIB

Travel arrangements

Road

Reference books and sources of information

AA or *RAC Handbook*

AA and RAC guides for motoring in Europe

ABC Coach and Bus Guide

National Express Service Guide

Telephone numbers of the employer's garage, mechanic and nearest AA and RAC office

Road maps

Final preparations

- Arrange for the appropriate road maps and route plans to be available.
- Verify the weather conditions in the area in which the employer is travelling.
- Confirm the booking of hotels.
- Prepare the itinerary (*see* example on p 175) and include telephone numbers of hotels, appointments, meetings, etc, and have a clear understanding of the times and places where the employer may be contacted.
- Collect and hand to the employer all the documents required.
- Prepare a supply of office stationery so that the employer can write letters, reports, etc, during his travels.
- Discuss outstanding matters.

Rail

Reference books and sources of information

British Rail Guides, plus a regular supply of the supplementary issues concerning train times

Telephone numbers of the local British Rail Enquiry Bureaux

Final preparations

- Confirm the time, station, platform of departure of train and the time of arrival at destination.
- Obtain the ticket for the journey plus one for a reserved seat and/or sleeping berth if applicable.
- Make arrangements for the employer to be met at the destination.
- Other salient points under 'Road'.

Air

Reference books and sources of information

ABC World Airways Guide

Current visa, passport, baggage, export licence, health and insurance regulations

Telephone numbers of the nearest airline booking office and private charter office

Telephone number of the local travel agency office

Telephone number of the employer's bank for arranging currency, travellers' cheques, etc

Final preparations

- Confirm the air terminus from which the employer is leaving, details of the check-in time and the actual take-off time.
- Obtain the employer's tickets.
- Ensure that the employer has a passport, visa, health certifi-

cates and any other documents required and that they are all valid for the duration of the trip.

- Obtain foreign currency and travellers' cheques.
- Make arrangements for the employer to be met at the airport or book a hire car.
- Other salient points under 'Road'.

Key factors in planning business visits abroad

Information

Useful information for preparing a business trip abroad can be obtained from the Department of Trade and Industry, Sanctuary Buildings, 16–20 Great Smith Street, London SW1P 3DB. They publish a series of booklets for different countries entitled 'Hints to Exporters' containing general information about the country, such as areas, population, principal cities and towns, climate, clothing, hours of business; travel information relating to passport, visa and health regulations, currency, customs, travel routes, etc; hotels and restaurants; postal, telephone and telegraphic facilities; economic factors; import and exchange control regulations; government and commercial organisations and methods of doing business.

Passport

A current passport is essential for visitors entering a foreign country. Standard British passports are issued for a ten-year period although temporary one-year passports can be obtained directly at principal post offices on production of a birth certificate and two identical passport-size photographs. An application form for a new passport or an extension of an existing one can be obtained from a post office and on completion should be sent to the regional passport office named on the form. Application must be made at least twenty-eight days before departure. The form has to be countersigned and a photograph certified by a British person in authority, such as a bank manager, justice of the peace or head teacher who has known the applicant personally for at least two years.

Visa

A visa is also required for entry to many overseas countries. Travel agents can give you advice on visas and can make arrangements for them to be obtained. Application can also be made direct to the consulate of the country to be visited.

Health regulations

Establish, well in advance of the visit, the inoculations and vaccinations required for entering the country concerned and obtain the relevant certificates. The local office of the Department of Health will supply a leaflet giving details concerning health protection when travelling abroad.

Money

See 'Overseas Travel Facilities' on p 20.

Insurance

Insurance cover for personal accident, medical treatment and loss of baggage can be arranged directly with an insurance company or by an agent such as a bank or travel agent.

Tickets

The airline tickets should normally be obtained before the day of departure from a travel agent or direct from an airline booking office, with the exception of the Shuttle Service which operates on a 'walk on/walk off' basis and advance booking is not required. The Shuttle Service operates at regular daily times between the major UK airports.

Most airlines offer three classes of seats:

- First class
- Executive class (Business/Club)
- Economy class (Tourist)

If there is any doubt about the date for the return journey, it is advisable to book an open ticket in which the return journey is not fixed.

Business visiting cards

A business executive doing business abroad will normally require a supply of business visiting cards, with the information printed on the back in the language of the country visited.

Use of car

A car can be hired from one of the car hire firms direct or through a travel agent and the car collected at an airport. Most car hire firms expect drivers to have held a full licence for at least one year. An International Driving Permit, issued by the AA or RAC, is required by some countries. Also, if a car is to be taken to the continent and the car insurance policy does not include comprehensive cover for foreign travel, a green card should be obtained from the insurance company which insures the car.

Itinerary

See the specimen itinerary on p 175.

The following is a checklist for preparing itineraries for foreign travel:

ITINERARY	
Friday 1 January 19--	
Depart London (Heathrow) Terminal 2 Flight BA191	1015 hrs
Arrive Paris (Charles de Gaulle)	1105 hrs
Luncheon engagement with Monsieur Jacques Thievenot (French Agent) at Hotel Sofitel, Porte de Versailles (Telephone: 1 272 52 05)	1230 hrs
Depart Paris (Charles de Gaulle)	1645 hrs
Arrive London (Heathrow) (A company car will meet you at Terminal 2)	1735 hrs
Meeting with Sir Ronald Briggs at 140 Langham Place, London W1	1845 hrs
Dinner at Cumberland Hotel, Marble Arch with Mrs Jones and Sir Ronald Briggs	2000 hrs
Room reserved at Cumberland Hotel	

A specimen travel itinerary

- An itinerary should contain:
  a departure and arrival times of aircraft and trains
  b flight numbers
  c airport names and terminal names/numbers
  d businsss addresses, telephone numbers and names of contacts
  e hotel addresses and telephone numbers
- Use paper/card of a convenient size so that it can be handled easily.
- Keep a copy for your use and for any others who require information about the employer's movements.
- Use the 24-hour clock system, eg 1400 hours for 2.00 pm to save any confusion which may arise between am and pm. The 24-hour clock sequence begins at midnight and continues throughout the day and night for 24 hours, as shown in the illustration on p 176.

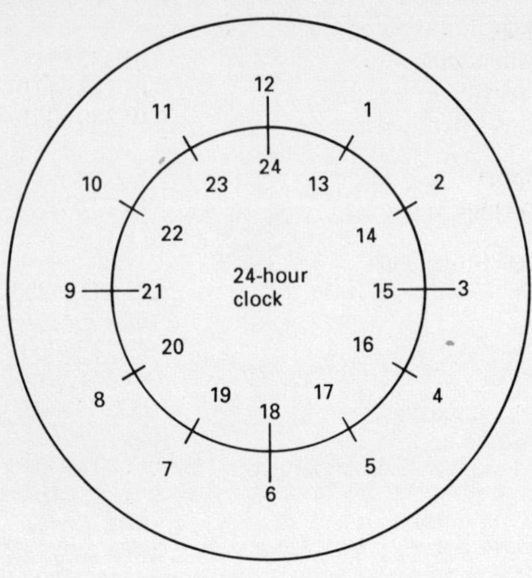

Travel information

Passenger train service information

London Area **For train services to:**	*General enquiries*
East Anglia and Essex	01 283 7171
West Yorkshire, North East, East Coast to Scotland	01 278 2477
Midlands, North Wales, North West, West Coast to Scotland	01 387 7070
West of England, West Midlands, South Wales	01 262 6767
South East and South	01 928 5100
Continental Reservations/Enquiries	01 834 2345

Sleeper Services
London Reservation Offices:

Euston	01 388 6061
King's Cross	01 278 2411
Paddington	01 723 7681

Motorail Services

London Reservation Office	01 387 8541
Credit Card Bookings	01 278 9431
	01 388 6061

London Transport

Passenger Information	01 222 1234
Services from:	
Birmingham (New Street and International)	021 643 2711
Bristol	0272 294255
Cardiff	0222 28000
Glasgow	041 204 2844
Leeds	0532 448133
Liverpool	051 709 9696
Manchester	061 832 8353
Newcastle	091 232 6262
Sheffield	0742 726411
York	0904 642155

Air travel information

UK airlines

Air UK Limited

Cross Keys House, Haslett Avenue, Crawley RH10 1HS	0293 517654
Norwich Airport, Norfolk NR6 6ER	
Ticket Office	0603 44248
Flight Enquiries/Information/ Fares	0603 44244 01 249 7073

British Air Ferries Ltd

Southend Airport, Viscount House, Southend-on-Sea, Essex SS2 6YL	0702 354435
Reservations and holiday bookings	0702 335900

British Airways

Speedbird House, PO Box 10, Heathrow Airport, Hounslow, Middx TW6 2JA	01 897 4000
Flight Enquiries	01 759 2525

British Caledonian Airways

Caledonian House, Crawley RH10 2XA	0293 27890

Reservations	0293 518888
	01 668 4222
	Freefone 6071
London Central Air Terminal, Victoria Station, SW1V 1JT	01 834 9411

British Midland Airways Ltd

East Midlands Airport, Castle Donington, nr Derby DE7 2SB	0332 810741
Reservations	0332 810552

Dan-Air Services Ltd

New City Court, 20 St Thomas Street, SE1 9RJ	01 378 6464
Reservations	0345 100200
	01 680 1011

Loganair Limited

St Andrew's Drive, Glasgow Airport, Abbotsinch, Paisley PA3 2TG	041 889 1311
Reservations	041 889 3181

Airport information – Heathrow

Terminal 1 Information Desk	01 745 7702/3/4
Terminal 2 Information Desk	01 745 7115/6/7
Terminal 3 Information Desk	01 745 7412/3/4
Terminal 4 Information Desk	01 745 4540
Private Car Parking	01 745 7160

Airport Information – Gatwick

Information Desk	0293 503600

Air commuter services

British Airways Super Shuttle London Heathrow to Belfast/ Edinburgh/Glasgow/Manchester	01 897 4000
British Caledonian London Gatwick to Aberdeen/ Glasgow/Edinburgh/Manchester	01 668 4222
British Midland Diamond Service London Heathrow to Edinburgh/ Glasgow	01 581 0864

Airport telephone numbers

Aberdeen	0224 722331
Alderney	048 182 2886
Belfast	0232 229271
Birmingham	021 767 5511

Blackpool	0253 43061
Bournemouth	0202 570266
Bristol	027 587 4441
Cardiff	0446 711211
Carlisle	0228 73641
Cork, Eire (ask first for Irish Republic)	021 965388
Coventry	0203 301717
Dublin, Eire	0001 379900
East Midlands (Derby)	0332 810621
Edinburgh	031 333 1000
Exeter	0392 67433
Glasgow	041 887 1111
Guernsey	0481 37766
Humberside (Ulceby)	0652 688456
Inverness	0463 232471
Islay (Port Ellen)	0496 2361
Isle of Man (Castletown)	062 482 3311
Jersey	0534 46111
Kirkwall, Orkney	0856 2421
Leeds, Bradford	0532 509696
Liverpool	051 486 8877
London, Gatwick	0293 28822
London, Heathrow	01 759 4321
Luton	0582 36061
Lydd	0679 20401
Manchester	061 489 3000
Newcastle	091 286 0966
Newquay (St Mawgan)	0637 860551
Norwich	0603 411923
Plymouth	0752 705151
Prestwick	0292 79822
Shannon, Eire (ask first for Irish Republic)	0006 61 61444
Southampton	0703 612341
Southend-on-Sea	0702 340201
Stansted (Bishop's Stortford)	0279 502380
Stornoway	0851 2256
Sumburgh, Shetland	0950 60654
Teesside (Dinsdale)	0325 332811
Wick	0955 2215

Airline addresses (London)

Air Lingus

2–4 Maddox Street, W1

Transatlantic Reservations	01 437 8000
Ireland/Departures, Reservations	01 734 1212

Aeroflot Soviet Airlines	
69–72 Piccadilly, W1V 9HH	01 491 1756
Bookings and Information	01 493 7436
Air Canada	
140–144 Regent Street,	
W1R 6AT	01 439 7941
Reservations	01 759 2636
Air France	
158 New Bond Street, W1Y 0AY	01 499 8611
Reservations	01 499 9511
Air New Zealand	
New Zealand House, SW1Y 4TE	01 930 1088
Reservations/Ticket Office	01 930 3434
Alitalia Italian Airlines	
27–28 Piccadilly, W1V 9PF	01 745 8200
Reservations	01 745 8286
El Al Israel Airlines	
185 Regent Street, W1R 9BS	01 439 2496
Reservations	01 734 9255
Iberia Air Lines of Spain	
130 Regent Street, W1R 5RG	01 437 9822
Reservations	01 437 5622
Icelandair	
73 Grosvenor Street, W1X 9DD	01 493 6382
Reservations	01 499 9971
Japan Air Lines	
Hanover Court, 5 Hanover	
Square, W1R 0DR	01 629 9244
Reservations	01 408 1000
KLM Royal Dutch Airlines	
Time & Life Buildings, New Bond	
Street, W1Y 0AD	01 750 9200
Reservations	01 568 9144
Lufthansa German Airlines	
23–26 Piccadilly, W1V 0EJ	01 408 0322
Reservations	01 408 0442
Olympic Airways	
164–166 Piccadilly, W1V 9DE	01 846 9966
Reservations	01 846 9080

Pakistan International Airlines

45–46 Piccadilly, W1V 0LD	01 734 5544
Ticket Office, Heathrow, Terminal 3	01 759 2544

Pan American World Airways Inc

193 Piccadilly, W1V 0LD	01 409 0688
Reservations	01 409 3377

Quantas Airways Ltd

395–405 King Street, London, W6 9NJ	01 748 3131
Reservations	0800 747767

Sabena Belgian World Airlines

36–37 Piccadilly, W1V 0BU	01 437 6960
Reservations	01 437 6950

Scandinavian Airlines System – SAS

52–53 Conduit Street, W1R 0AY	01 734 6777
Reservations	01 734 4020

South African Airways

251–259 Regent Street, W1R 7AD	01 437 9621
Reservations	01 734 9841

Swissair

Swiss Centre, 3 New Coventry Street, W1V 4BJ	01 734 6737
Reservations	01 439 4144

Trans World Airlines Inc

200 Piccadilly, W1	01 636 4090

Passport offices

Belfast

Hampton House, 47–53 High Street, Belfast BT1 2AB	0232 232371

Glasgow

Empire House, 131 West Nile Street, Glasgow G1 2RY	041 332 0271

Liverpool

5th Floor, India Building, Water Street, Liverpool L2 0QZ	051 237 3010

London

Clive House, 70–78 Petty France,
London SW1H 9HD — 01 213 3000
(A–D) — 01 213 3261
(E–K) — 01 213 7272
(L–Q) — 01 213 6098
(R–Z) — 01 213 6915

Newport

Olympia House, Upper Dock Street, Newport NPT 1XA — 0633 56292

Peterborough

55 Westfield Road, Westwood, PE3 6TG — 0733 895555

Time differences

The following map gives a general idea of the time differences throughout the world in relation to Greenwich Mean Time. Note that between March and October British Summer Time is one hour later than GMT.

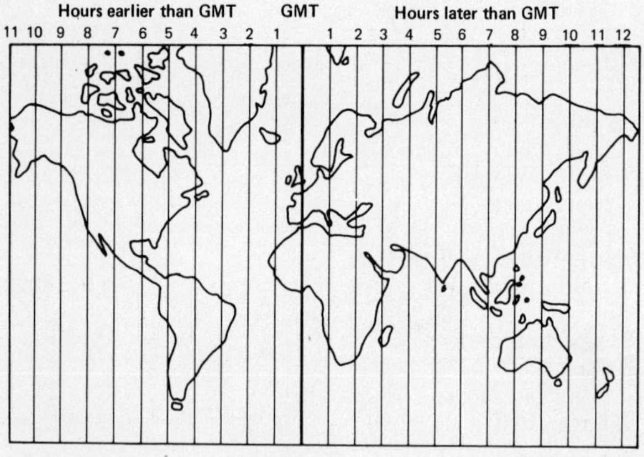

Underground travel in London

See map opposite.

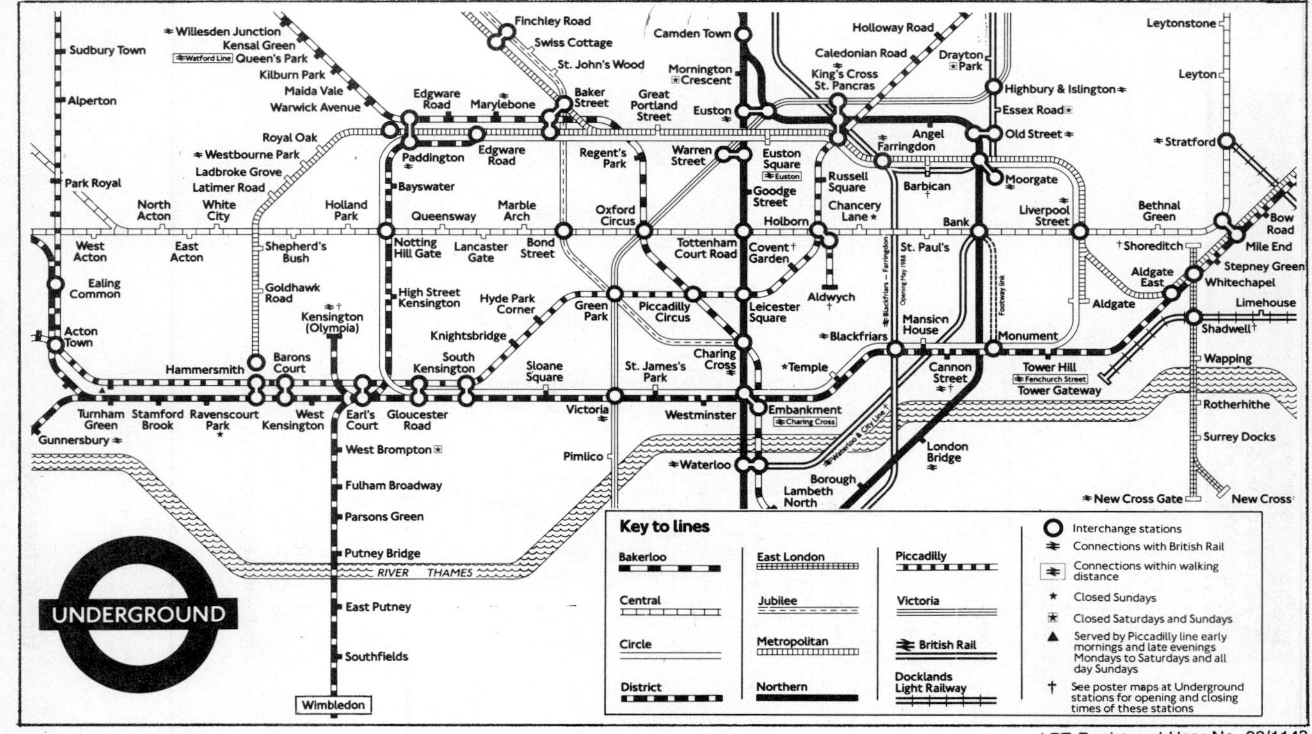

LRT Registered User No. 90/1143

Visual data

The following are some of the methods of presenting information visually.

Bar graph

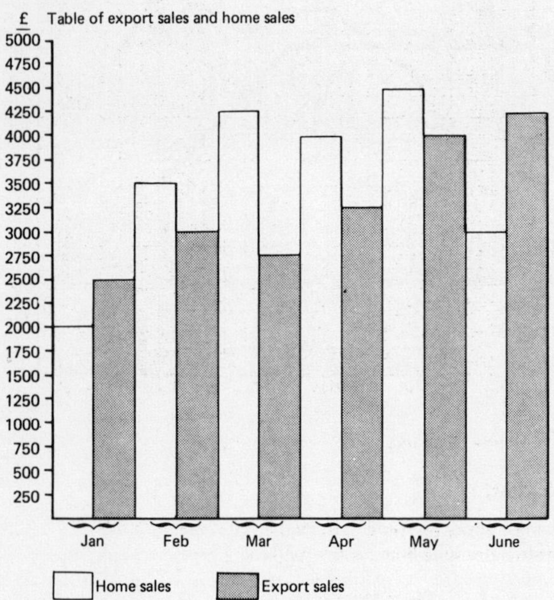

Overhead projector

An overhead projector (OHP) can give a presentation greater impact and focus attention on the major issues. Transparencies for the OHP can either be prepared by pen on a clear acetate sheet, using fibre-tipped pens or the image can be reproduced on an office copier. When preparing an OHP transparency the image should:

- be clear, ie sufficiently large characters used for ease of reading in any part of the room
- be well displayed, bright and attractive to the eye
- focus attention on the salient points

- contain variety of presentation, ie variable character sizes, different colours, etc

Line graph

(Showing same data as in the bar graph)

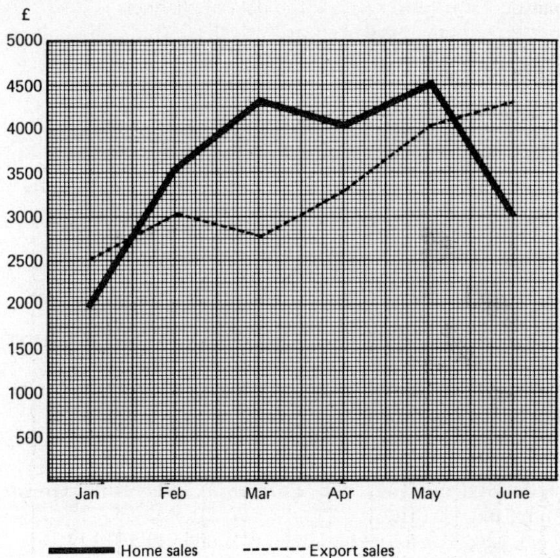

Pie chart

(Using figures for June extracted from above graph)
Export sales and home sales for June 19—.

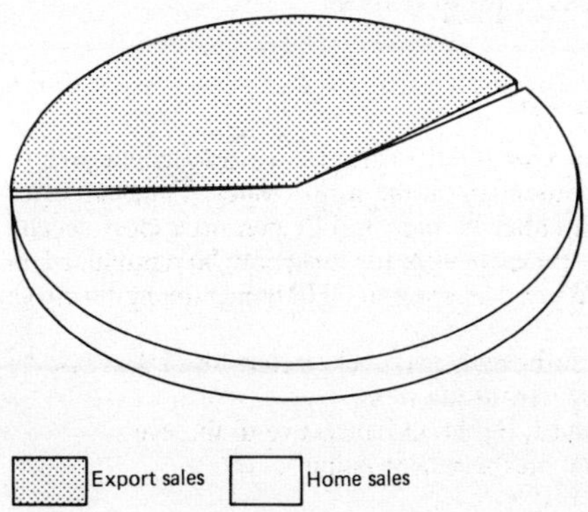

Visual control equipment

Equipment for displaying and controlling data includes:

- computers which display graphics on VDUs and provide printouts, if required – a light pen can be used as a drafting aid for plotting images on the screen
- channel planboards which use cards, work tickets, job cards or plastic strips for displaying the data in channels
- perforated panels and pegboards which use studs, clips, plugs, pegs or discs to depict trends
- magnetic boards which use individual name strips to display the data
- plastic self-adhesive boards containing a smooth transparent skin of plastic. Plastic markers are pressed on to the board to display the data or entries are made on to the board using a pen, as in the case of a year planner.

Suppliers of visual aids equipment

Agfa Gevaert Ltd, 27 Great West Road, Brentford, Middx TW8 9AX

3M United Kingdom plc, 3M House, PO Box 1, Bracknell, Berks RG12 1JU

Matthews Office Furniture Ltd, PO Box 81, 61–63 Dale Street, Liverpool L69 2DN

Nobo Visual Aids Ltd, Alder Close, Eastbourne, E Sussex BN23 6QB

Rotadex Systems Ltd, 3–5 Fortnum Close, Kitts Green, Birmingham B33 0JL

Skycopy Ltd, 412–420 The Highway, London E14 8ED

Weights and measures

Imperial measures and equivalents			*Metric measures and equivalents*		
Length					
1 inch		= 2.54 cm	1 centimetre (cm)	= 10 millimetres	= 0.3937 in
1 foot	= 12 inches	= 30.48 cm	1 metre (m)	= 100 cm	= 1.0936 yd
1 yard	= 3 feet	= 0.9144 m	1 kilometre (km)	= 1000 m	= 0.6214 mile
1 mile	= 1760 yards	= 1.6093 km			
1 nautical mile	= 6080 feet	= 1.8532 km			
Area					
1 sq in		= 6.4516 cm^2	1 sq cm (cm^2)	= 100 mm^2	= 0.1550 sq in
1 sq ft	= 144 sq inches	= 929.0304 cm^2	1 sq metre (m^2)	= 10 000 cm^2	= 1.1960 sq yd
1 sq yd	= 9 sq feet	= 0.8361 m^2	1 hectare (ha)	= 100 ares	= 2.4711 acres
1 acre	= 4840 sq yards	= 4046.86 m^2	1 sq km (km^2)	= 100 hectares	= 0.3861 sq miles
1 sq mile	= 640 acres	= 2.58999 km^2			

Note:

10 millimetres (mm)	= 1 centimetre (cm)	1 m = 10 dm = 100 cm = 1000 mm
10 centimetres	= 1 decimetre (dm)	
10 decimetres	= 1 metre (m)	
10 metres	= 1 decametre (dam)	
10 decametres	= 1 hectometre (hm)	
10 hectometres	= 1 kilometre (km)	

Imperial measures and equivalents			*Metric measures and equivalents*		
Capacity					
1 cu inch		= 16.387 cm^3	1 cu cm (cm^3)		= 0.0610 cu in
1 cu foot	= 1728 cu inches	= 0.0283 m^3	1 cu metre (m^3)		= 1.3080 cu yd
1 cu yard	= 27 cu feet	= 0.7646 m^3	1 litre (l)		= 1.7598 pints
1 pint		= 0.5683 litres	1 hectolitre (hl)	= 100 litres	= 21.9976 gallons
1 quart	= 2 pints	= 1.1365 litres			
1 gallon	= 8 pints	= 4.5461 litres			
Weight					
1 ounce (oz)	= 437½ grains	= 28.3495 g	1 milligram (mg)		= 0.0154 grain
1 pound (lb)	= 16 ounces	= 0.4536 kg	1 gram (g)	= 1000 mg	= 0.0353 oz
1 hundredweight (cwt)	= 112 pounds	= 50.802 kg	1 kilogram (kg)	= 1000 g	= 2.2046 lb
			1 tonne (t)	= 1000 kg	= 0.9842 ton
1 ton	= 20 cwt	= 1.0161 tonnes			

Note:

10 millilitres (ml)	= 1 centilitre (cl)	10 milligrams (mg)	= 1 centigram (cg)
10 centilitres	= 1 decilitre (dl)	10 centigrams	= 1 decigram (dg)
10 decilitres	= 1 litre (l)	10 decigrams	= 1 gram (g)
10 litres	= 1 decalitre (dal)	10 grams	= 1 decagram (dag)
10 decalitres	= 1 hectolitre (hl)	10 decagrams	= 1 hectogram (hg)
10 hectolitres	= 1 kilolitre (kl)	10 hectograms	= 1 tonne (t) (metric)

Telephone index of numbers used frequently

Name	Organisation	Telephone	
		Code	Number

Personal reminders

Name			
Address			
Post code			
Telephone			
Business address			
Telephone no.		*Telex no.*	*Fax no.*
Car registration no.			
Car insurance policy no.			*Renewal date:*

Car key nos	
Car tax due	
Driving licence no.	
AA/RAC membership no.	*Renewal date:*
Credit card no.	
Passport no.	*Renewal date:*
TV licence due	
Blood group	
National Insurance no.	
Notes:	

Index

Notes